Short forms and labels

Short forms

adj	adjective
adv	adverb
n	noun
phr v	phrasal verb
prep	preposition
pron	pronoun
v	verb
sb	someone
sth	something

Labels

1 Words which are used only or mainly in one region or country are marked:

BrE	British English
AmE	American English
AusE	Australian English

2 Words which are used in a particular situation, or show a particular attitude:

formal	a word that is suitable for formal speech or writing, but would not normally be used in ordinary conversation
informal	a word or phrase that is used in normal conversation, but may not be suitable for use in more formal contexts, for example in writing essays or business letters
humorous	a word that is normally used in a joking way

3 Words which are used in a particular context or type of language:

biblical	a word that is used in the language of the Bible, and would sound old-fashioned to a modern speaker
law	a word with a technical meaning used by lawyers, in legal documents etc
literary	a word used mainly in English literature, and not in normal speech or writing
medical	a word or phrase that is more likely to be used by doctors than by ordinary people, and that often has a more common equivalent
not polite	a word or phrase that is considered rude, and that might offend some people
old-fashioned	a word that was commonly used in the past, but would sound old-fashioned today
old use	a word used in earlier centuries
spoken	a word or phrase used only, or nearly always, in conversation
taboo	a word that should not be used because it is very rude or offensive
technical	a word used by doctors, scientists and other specialists
trademark	a word that is the official name of a particular product
written	a word or phrase that is used only, or nearly always, in written English

Grammar codes and patterns

Grammar codes

[C] countable: a noun that has both a singular and a plural form: *He lent me a* **book** *about photography.* | *Some of the* **books** *were very old.*

[U] uncountable: a noun that has no plural form and refers to something that cannot be counted: *the* **importance** *of education* | *a bucket of* **water**

[I] intransitive: a verb that has no object: *Jack* **sneezed**. | *House prices* **are rising**.

[T] transitive: a verb that is followed by an object, which can be either a noun phrase or a clause: *I* **love** *chocolate.* | *She* **said** *she was too busy.* | *I* **remember** *going on holiday there.*

[singular] a noun that is used only in the singular, and has no plural form: *The room has a modern* **feel**. | *a* **sprinkling** *of snow*

[plural] a noun that is used only in the plural, and has no singular form: *His* **clothes** *were soaking wet.* | *Those are my* **scissors**.

[linking verb] a verb that is followed by a noun or adjective complement that describes the subject of the verb: *I* **felt** *very tired.* | *Her father* **is** *a doctor.* | *Your dinner's* **getting** *cold.*

[always + adv/prep] shows that a verb must be followed by an adverb or a preposition: *She* **went** *upstairs.* | *Robert* **put** *the letter in his briefcase.*

[not in progressive] shows that a verb is not used in the progressive form, that is, the -ing form after 'be': *I* **admire** *his work. (not I am admiring his work)* | *I don't* **know** *where it is.*

[no comparative] shows that an adjective is not used in the comparative or superlative form, that is, not with -er and -est, or 'more' and 'most': *He played a* **key** *role in the negotiations.*

[only before noun] shows that an adjective can be used only before a noun: *the* **main** *reason for her visit* | *You* **poor** *thing!*

[not before noun] shows that an adjective cannot be used before a noun: *I don't even know if he's still* **alive**. | *I'm* **glad** *you're here.*

[only after noun] shows that an adjective is used only immediately after a noun: *some matters to be discussed before the meeting* **proper**

[sentence adverb] shows that an adverb modifies a whole sentence: **Fortunately** *no one was hurt.*

[+adj/adv] shows that an adverb of degree is used before adjectives and adverbs: *The room was* **very** *dark.* | *We've got to act* **fairly** *quickly.*

[also + plural verb *BrE*] shows that a group noun can take a plural verb in British English: *The* **team** *are feeling confident.*

Patterns

[+about] [+along] shows that a word can be followed immediately by a particular preposition or adverb: *I'm* **worried** *about Rachel.* | *The children* **skipped** *along.*

throw sth at sb/sth shows that a verb can be followed by an object and a particular preposition: *Tom* **threw** *a cushion at her.*

request that shows that a word can be followed by a clause beginning with 'that': *He* **requested** *that his name be removed from the list of candidates.*

surprised (that) or tell sb (that) shows that a word can be followed by a clause beginning with 'that', or the word 'that' can be left out: *I'm* **surprised** *you didn't know that.* | *Bill* **told** *me you were here.*

decide who/what/whether etc or ask (sb) who/what/where etc shows that a word can be followed by a clause beginning with a word such as 'who', 'what', 'whether' or 'where': *I can't* **decide** *what to do.* | *I* **asked** *her what she meant.* | *I'm not* **sure** *where James is.*

try to do sth or order sb to do sth shows that a word can be followed by an infinitive: **Try** *to forget about it.* | *He* **ordered** *them to leave.* | *He's* **sure** *to win.*

help do sth or see sb/sth do sth shows that a verb can be followed by an infinitive without 'to': *This can* **help** *prevent infection.* | *Did anyone* **see** *them leave?*

enjoy doing sth or hear sb doing sth shows that a verb can be followed by a present participle: *I* **enjoy** *meeting new people.* | *Peter could* **hear** *them laughing.*

bring sb sth shows that a verb can be followed by an indirect object and then a direct object: *Could you* **bring** *us the bill?* | *Let me* **buy** *you a drink.*

LONGMAN
Dictionary of Contemporary English

Acknowledgements

Director
Della Summers

Managing Editor
Stephen Bullon

Editors
Chris Fox
Elizabeth Manning
Michael Murphy
Ruth Urbom
Karen Cleveland Marwick

Lexicographers
Evadne Adrian-Vallance
Daniel Barron
Lisa Beizai
Jane Bradbury
Rosalind Combley
Sheila Dignen
Gill Francis
Alex Henderson
Lucy Hollingworth
Ted Jackson
Jo Leigh
Dan Malt
Julie Moore
Carole Murphy
Stella O'Shea
Liz Potter
Valerie Smith
Martin Stark
Miranda Steel
Penny Stock
Laura Wedgeworth
Deborah Yuill

Pronunciation Editor
Dinah Jackson

Proofreaders
Barbara Burge
Lynda Carey
Isabel Griffiths
Wendy Lee
Sue Lightfoot
Joy Marshall
Carole Murphy
Ruth Noble
Stella O'Shea

Editorial Director
Adam Gadsby

Project Management
Sheila Dallas
Alan Savill

Corpus and CD-ROM Development
Steve Crowdy

Computational Linguist and
CD-ROM Project Management
Allan Ørsnes

Language Notes
Laurence Delacroix
Chris Fox

Production Editors
Michael Brooks
Jennifer Sagala
Matthew Allen

Technical Support Manager
Trevor Satchell

Production
Clive McKeough

Design
Paul Price-Smith
Mick Harris

Project and Databases Administrator
Denise McKeough

Network Administrator
Kim Larkin

Keyboarders
Pauline Savill
Janine Trainor

CD-ROM Development
Software developed by IDM, Paris

Illustrations
Kevin Jones Associates
IFA Design
Maltings Partnership
Oxford Designers and Illustrators
Dave Bowyer Illustration

The Publishers and editorial team would like to thank the many people who
have contributed advice to the making of this dictionary, in particular the
Linglex Dictionary and Corpus Advisory Committee:

Lord Quirk (Chair)
Professor Douglas Biber, Professor Gillian Brown, Professor David Crystal,
Professor Geoffrey Leech, Philip Scholfield, Professor Katie Wales,
Professor John Wells

LONGMAN

Dictionary of Contemporary English

NEW EDITION

Pearson Education Limited
Edinburgh Gate
Harlow
Essex CM20 2JE
England
and associated Companies throughout the world

www. longman.com.ldoce

First published 1978
Second edition 1987
Third edition 1995
This edition published 2003
Fourth impression 2003

ISBN 0 582 50666 2 (Cased edition)
    0 582 77649 X (Cased edition + CD-ROM)
    0 582 50668 9 (Flexicover edition)
    0 582 77648 1 (Flexicover edition + CD-ROM)
    0 582 50664 6 (Paper edition)
    0 582 77646 5 (Paper edition + CD-ROM)
    0 582 50670 0 (Special edition)*
    0 582 77647 3 (Special edition + CD-ROM)*
    3 526 50820 8 (German cased edition)
    3 526 50822 4 (German cased edition + CD-ROM)
    3 526 50821 6 (German paper edition)
    3 526 50823 2 (German paper edition + CD-ROM)

    *available in certain markets only

Library of Congress Cataloging-in-Publication Data
Longman dictionary of contemporary English / [director, Della Summers].– New ed.
    p. cm.
    ISBN 0-582-50664-6 (pbk)
    1. English language-Dictionaries. 2. English language--Terms snd phrases. I. Title:
Dictionary of contemporary English. II. Summers, Della.

PE1628.L58 2003
423--dc21

British Library Cataloguing-in-Publication Data
A catalogue record for this book is available from the
British Library.

Set in Nimrod
by Letterpart, UK

Printed in China
GCC/04

Photographs and Maps
Hemera Technologies Inc
"Copyright © 2003 (Pearson Education) and its licensors. All rights reserved"
© 2002 Philip's for maps on pages 1925–28
Corbis Images for page 253

Contents

Remarkably, in only a few recent years, the computer has become a powerful and increasingly indispensable tool in every conceivable aspect of our daily lives. That most certainly includes the daily lives of lexicographers! They can now not only conveniently store many millions of sentences from authentic spoken and written language, but also manipulate, display, and study the components of these sentences – the words and word partnerships (collocations) along with contextual factors that come into play as different meanings are expressed.

But if the computer is indispensable, so too is the sensitive, highly trained professional skill of the lexicographers. Indeed, their subtle judgment is all the more needed as the speed, power, and vast capacity of the computer reveal as never before the lexical complexity of a living language.

And there is a third indispensable factor: the pedagogical experience and expertise that guide the Pearson Education team to present language learners with the information on current world English that is most necessary for them. The information is presented in a way that anticipates the learners' needs to understand meanings and to express those meanings idiomatically in their own speech and writing.

The new *LDOCE* is a magnificent culmination of innovative energetic research along with computational techniques that are married to well-honed educational and lexicographical skills. It builds on the vital experience of earlier editions and incorporates a host of new features – such as the full-colour printing, the extra wealth of information on collocations (just glance for a moment at the entry for the word **pace** and its 'collocation box'). And everything in the printed dictionary can be extensively followed up in the accompanying CD-ROM where you will find a further eighty thousand example sentences, plus more than a million sentences direct from the Corpus. Not to mention the enormous bonus of having the *Longman Language Activator*® included as well.

What better way for learners to immerse themselves in today's English at its most vivid and lively!

RANDOLPH QUIRK
(Professor the Lord Quirk, FBA)
University College, London

Each time we produce a new edition of the *Longman Dictionary of Contemporary English*, our aim is always the same: what can we do to make the dictionary more helpful for advanced level students of English? As a result of our continuous research with students and detailed discussions with teachers, we decided to focus on two areas for this, the fourth edition of the *Longman Dictionary of Contemporary English*. Those two areas were: **examples** and **collocation**.

EXAMPLES

Students tell us that examples help them to remember the word they have looked up because it is easier both to remember and to understand the word within a context. It also shows that words are often used in many different contexts. For these reasons, we have included 40 per cent more examples in this new edition of the book. (See the entry for **drama**, for example, where there are now 14 examples of the various meanings of the word.)

All the examples are based on the Longman Corpus Network, an increasingly large database (now standing at 300 million words) covering books, newspapers, magazines and spoken English. We also scan the Internet for examples of new words.

Natural English

The examples that appear in the book are usually slightly edited versions of real sentences from the Corpus. Our editors and lexicographers edit them to remove difficult words and to ensure they are comprehensible examples of that meaning of the word within a single sentence or phrase. This means that Longman dictionary examples are more realistic than in some other dictionaries, and they prepare students for the way that words are really used. As one student in our research said: 'A dictionary should describe how people actually use the language.'

80,000 additional examples on the CD-ROM

This edition uses the space available on the CD-ROM to include a vastly greater number of examples than ever before, so if you are using the CD-ROM edition of the dictionary, you can access not just the examples in the printed dictionary, but also a further 80,000 dictionary examples on the CD-ROM in the Longman Examples Bank. These examples are also corpus-based, and come from other Longman dictionaries.

Over a million corpus sentences

For very advanced learners and teachers of English we have also included over one million sentences direct from the Longman Corpus Network in the Longman Examples Bank on the CD-ROM. These sentences have been automatically selected from the Corpus, and, although various linguistic filters have been applied, they have not been edited. Therefore, users can not only see even more sentences that include the word they have looked up in all its various meanings, but they can also see sentences for many words that would not normally have any examples at all in the paper dictionary. Having one million sentences also means that phrases and collocations on the CD-ROM, of which there are a vast number (see below), have far more examples than is possible in the printed paper dictionary. Of course, those who prefer to buy the book dictionary without the CD-ROM still have a huge number of examples to show them how words are used.

COLLOCATION
(words that are typically used together)

As another student so neatly put it: 'When you speak or write you can't just use word, word, word – you need to know how to join them together.' It is in the area of collocation and English phraseology that our extensive use of the Longman Corpus Network bears most fruit. In the book, a very large percentage of entries have phrases highlighted in bold, often within the examples themselves. We have also introduced new Collocation boxes in colour with the collocations being illustrated by many examples drawn directly from or based on the corpus.

Collocations on the CD-ROM

In addition to everything that is in the dictionary, the CD-ROM has a Phrase Bank. Here you can click to see collocations that are entered in other parts of the dictionary (for example, **powers of observation** is entered under **powers**, but on the CD-ROM all you need do if you are at **observation** is click to go to that phrase). Also on the CD-ROM, we have included 150,000 extra words (collocates) that are used with the headword, so at **observation** the information is given that **based** and **confirm** are other verbs that are often used with **observation**. You can then click on either of those words and see up to eight corpus sentences of **based** and **confirm** with the word **observation**. Again, this information comes direct from statistical analysis of the Corpus.

MUCH MORE PRODUCTION INFORMATION

Examples and collocations are both used to help the student use words, and so are important aids to producing correct natural English. Some 7000 synonyms and antonyms have also been added as well as Word Focus, Word Choice, and Grammar boxes, which again are new and in addition to the Usage Notes of previous editions (see **airport** and **angry** for examples). All these provide help with vocabulary building.

On the CD-ROM, the new edition of the *Longman Language Activator®* is integrated into the entries of the *Longman Dictionary of Contemporary English* as an even greater aid towards writing better and more natural English.

Frequency and frequency ordering

The top 3000 most frequent words are indicated in red in this, the first full-colour Longman ELT dictionary. This is a very popular feature with students and teachers alike, and of special significance is the fact that the *Longman Dictionary of Contemporary English* distinguishes between spoken and written frequency.

The meanings in the entries are as far as possible ordered in accordance with their frequency in the language as shown by the Corpus, which means that the most frequent meanings are placed first. If the most common use of the word is a phrase, that phrase will be shown first, as is the case for **lookout**, where **be on the lookout** is the first meaning listed. This principle gives users a good indication of which meanings they need to learn first. There are also Frequency Graphs at some entries, for example at **remain** where a graph shows just how much more frequent the word **stay** is in spoken English than in written English, where the preferred word is **remain**.

Spoken English

Thanks to our extensive corpora of British and American spontaneous speech, coverage of the spoken language is second to none, and the Spoken Phrase boxes such as the one at **story** show the importance of phrases such as **end of story**.

EASY, FAST EXPLANATIONS

Although students want as much information as possible in order to use English words (encoding), the primary use of any dictionary remains to explain the meaning of unknown words (decoding). The Longman Defining Vocabulary of only 2000 common words is used to define all words and meanings in this dictionary, resulting in clear accurate definitions that cause students no problems of understanding. On the CD-ROM, you can click on any word – in definitions, examples, or collocations – to be taken instantly to the definition of that word. Some words in the corpus sentences, however, are not entered in the dictionary.

Signposts

Due to the revolutionary Signpost system introduced in the previous edition, it is not necessary to read all the definitions in a long entry. For this edition, the Signposts have been highlighted in blue to make it even easier and quicker to scan down the entry and find the meaning you want. (See **fire** for an example.)

Full colour

This is our first ELT dictionary in full colour on every page. This makes the dictionary easier and more interesting to use, and the colour photographs and drawings make studying English more lively.

CD-ROM

You do not have to use the CD-ROM edition to profit from all the other improvements in the dictionary, but as explained above, there are more examples and collocations and extra corpus sentences as well as the full text of the book. (Word Focus boxes, Collocation boxes, etc are accessed by clicking on the Usage Notes tab.)

In addition, the CD-ROM has pronunciations in British and American English. You can record your own pronunciation, practise for exams with thousands of exercises, and do many other things. There are also 7000 encyclopedic entries for people, places, and things, taken from the *Longman Dictionary of English Language and Culture* and 15,000 word origins or etymologies (see **gazette** for an example on the CD-ROM).

As always in Longman dictionaries we treat American English in as much detail as British English in the same volume, and, of course, there are many interesting new words such as **drop dead date**, **wasabi**, and **prebuttal**. We very much hope this new edition is useful for you, and we welcome all comments on our work. Please email us at any of the following addresses:

Della.Summers@pearsoned-ema.com
Adam.Gadsby@pearsoned-ema.com
Stephen.Bullon@pearsoned-ema.com

Stephen Bullon
Managing Editor – *Longman Dictionary of Contemporary English*

How to use the dictionary

→ See inside front cover for a list of
symbols and sounds.

PRONUNCIATION

Pronunciation is shown using the
International Phonetic Alphabet.
If the British and American
pronunciations are different, the
British pronunciation is shown first
and the American pronunciation
has a dollar sign $ in front of it.

For compound words the primary
stress (') and the secondary stress
(ˌ) are shown.

→ See inside front cover for a list of
symbols and sounds.

---

cat S1 W3 /kæt/ n [C]
1 a) a small animal with four legs that people often
keep as a pet. Cats sometimes kill small animals and
birds

---

cot·ton[1] /ˈkɒtən $ ˈkɑːtn/ n [U] *BrE* **1** cloth or thread
made from the white hair of the cotton plant: *a white
cotton shirt* | *Made from 100% cotton.* → see picture at
MATERIAL **2** a plant with white hairs on its seeds that
are used for making cotton cloth and thread **3** *BrE*
thread used for sewing: *a needle and cotton* | *a cotton
reel* (=small round tube which cotton thread is wound
around) **4** *AmE* COTTON WOOL

ˌcotton 'wool n [U] *BrE* **1** a soft mass of cotton that
you use especially for cleaning and protecting wounds:
*She put some disinfectant on a piece of cotton wool and
dabbed it on her cheek.* **2** wrap sb (up) in cotton wool
to protect someone completely from the dangers, difficulties etc of life: *You can't wrap those kids in cotton
wool all their lives.*

HELP WITH MEANING

Definitions explain the meaning of
the word in clear simple language,
using the 2000-word Longman
Defining Vocabulary.

→ See back of the book for the full
list of these words.

If a word used in a definition is
outside the Longman Defining
Vocabulary, it is shown in SMALL
CAPITAL LETTERS.

Signposts help to guide you to the
meaning you want, if a word has a
lot of different meanings.

---

couch[1] /kaʊtʃ/ n plural **couches** [C] **1** a comfortable piece of furniture big enough for two or three
people to sit on; ☐ sofa, settee: *Tom offered to sleep on
the couch.* → see picture at SOFA **2** a long narrow bed for
a doctor's or PSYCHIATRIST'S patients to lie on

---

cry[1] S2 W2 /kraɪ/ v past tense and past participle **cried**,
present participle **crying**, third person singular **cries**
1 PRODUCE TEARS [I] to produce tears from your
eyes, usually because you are unhappy or hurt: *Don't
cry, Laura. It'll be OK.* | *Upstairs, a baby began to cry.* |
Jamie looked like he'd been crying. | *I just couldn't stop
crying.* | *That film always makes me cry.* | [+over/
about] *I am too old to be crying over some young guy.* |
[+with/in] *She felt like crying with frustration.* | [+for]
She could hear him crying for his mother. | cry your
eyes/heart out (=be extremely sad and cry a lot) |
Oliver, alone, began to cry bitterly (=cry a lot). | cry
yourself to sleep (=cry until you fall asleep)
2 SAY LOUDLY [T] written to shout or say something
loudly; ☐ cry out: *'Stop!' she cried.* | *It was painful, and
made me cry aloud.* | [+to] *'Goodbye then!' he cried to
her.* | [+for] *I could hear voices crying for help.*
3 cry over spilt milk to waste time feeling sorry about
an earlier mistake or problem that cannot be changed:
It's no use crying over spilt milk.
4 for crying out loud spoken used when you feel
annoyed or impatient with someone: *For crying out
loud, stop nagging!*
5 cry foul to protest because you think something is
wrong or not fair: *When the ads appeared, it was the
Democrats' turn to cry foul.*
6 ANIMALS/BIRDS [I] if animals or birds cry, they
make a loud sound: *I could hear gulls crying and the
soft whisper of the sea.*

EXAMPLES

There are thousands of useful
natural examples, based on
information from the Longman
Corpus Network and the Longman
Web Corpus.

The Longman Corpus Network is
a database of 300 million words
of written and spoken British and
American English from books,
newspapers, conversations,
advertisements, and many other
sources.

In addition to the Corpus, we also
use the World Wide Web to
discover new words and new
meanings of existing words.

---

cul·ture[1] S2 W1 /ˈkʌltʃə $ -ər/ n
1 IN A SOCIETY [C,U] the beliefs, way of life, art, and
customs that are shared and accepted by people in a
particular society: *We speak Danish at home so that the
boys don't lose touch with their language and culture.* |
*In our culture, it is rude to ask someone how much they
earn.* | *I love working abroad and meeting people from
different cultures.* | **Western/American/Japanese etc
culture** *A brief history of Western culture.* | **modern/
contemporary culture** *Business is one of the major
forces in modern culture.*

dog¹ S1 W1 /dɒg $ dɔːg/ n [C]
  1 ANIMAL a common animal with four legs, fur, and a tail. Dogs are kept as pets or trained to guard places, find drugs etc
dog² v **dogged, dogging** [T] **1** if a problem or bad luck dogs you, it causes trouble for a long time

doubt² S2 v [T not in progressive]
  1 to think that something may not be true or that it is unlikely: *Kim never doubted his story.* | **doubt (that)** *I doubt we'll ever see him again.* | **doubt if/whether** *You can complain, but I doubt if it'll make any difference.*

duck² v **1** also **duck down** [I,T] to lower your head or body very quickly, especially to avoid being seen or hit: *If she hadn't ducked, the ball would have hit her.* | [+behind/under etc] *Jamie saw his father coming and ducked quickly behind the wall.* | *Tim ducked down to comb his hair in the mirror.* | *She ducked her head to look more closely at the inscription.* **2** [I always + adv/prep] to move somewhere very quickly, especially to avoid being seen or to get away from someone: [+into] *The two men ducked into a block of flats and disappeared.*

eat S1 W1 /iːt/ v past tense **ate** /et, eɪt $ eɪt/ past participle **eaten** /'iːtn/
  1 FOOD [I,T] to put food in your mouth and chew and swallow it

ed·u·ca·tion S1 W1 /ˌedjʊ'keɪʃən $ ˌedʒə-/ n
  1 [singular, U] the process of teaching and learning, usually at school, college, or university: *the education system* | **get/receive an education** *She also hopes her children will get a good education.* | **university/college education** *I'm sure he has a college education.* | *efforts to increase access to* **higher education** (=education at college or university)

ef·fect¹ S1 W1 /ɪ'fekt/ n
  1 CHANGE/RESULT [C,U] the way in which an event, action, or person changes someone or something

> **have an effect (on sb/sth)**
> **big/major/profound/significant/dramatic effect**
> **bad/harmful/negative/damaging/detrimental/adverse effect**
> **beneficial/positive effect**
> **long-term effect**
> **feel the effect (of sth)**
> **knock-on-effect** *BrE* (=an effect caused by the thing that happened before)
> **cumulative effect** (=the effect of many things happening one after another)
> **the desired effect** (=the effect you wanted)
> **cause and effect** (=one thing directly causing the other)

[+on] *My parents' divorce* **had** *a big* **effect** *on me.* | [+of] *the* **harmful effects** *of modern farming practices* | *the* **long-term effects** *of the drug* | *I could* **feel the effects** *of the thin mountain air.* | *This ingredient also* **has the effect of** *making your skin look younger.* | *A system failure has a* **knock-on effect** *throughout the whole hotel.* | *the* **cumulative effect** *of human activities on the global environment* | *A much lower dose of the painkiller can still produce* **the desired effect.** | *In mental illness, there is a complex relationship between* **cause and effect.** → GREENHOUSE EFFECT, SIDE EFFECT

GRAMMAR

Part of speech is shown first, then information about whether a word is countable, uncountable, transitive, intransitive etc.

Common grammar patterns are shown before the examples, so that you can see clearly how the word operates in a sentence.

Common prepositions are also shown before the examples.

Information about irregular forms of verbs, nouns, and adjectives is shown at the beginning of the entry.

→ See front of book for lists of parts of speech and grammar codes.

COLLOCATION

Collocations are words that are often used with a particular word. Collocations are shown before the examples, or highlighted in bold in the examples.

If a word has a lot of collocations, these are listed in a special box before the word.

After the box there are lots of examples which show how the collocations are used. The collocations are highlighted in bold type, so that they are easy to find.

IDIOMS & PHRASES

Idioms and phrases are shown at the first important word of the phrase or idiom. For example **have egg on your face** is shown at **egg** and **have a nice day** is shown at **nice**.

Idioms and phrases are listed together with the other senses of the word in frequency order.

PHRASAL VERBS

Phrasal verbs are listed in alphabetical order after the main verb.

If the phrasal verb has an object, this is shown as **sb** (=someone) or **sth** (=something). The symbol ⇔ means that the object can come before or after the particle.

→ See Language Notes section for more information on phrasal verbs.

FREQUENCY

The meanings of each word are listed in order of frequency. The most common meaning is shown first.

The 3000 most common words in English are printed in red letters. This shows you which are the most important words to know. **S2** means that the word is one of the 2000 most common words in spoken English. **W2** means that the word is one of the 2000 most common words in written English.

There are also graphs that show you extra information about which are the most common words to use in a particular context in written and spoken English, or which structures are most commonly used with a word. The graphs are based on research from the Longman Corpus Network, a database of over 300 million words of written and spoken English.

egg¹ S1 W2 /eg/ n
1 BIRD [C] a round object with a hard surface, that contains a baby bird, snake, insect etc and which is produced by a female bird, snake, insect etc: *Blackbirds lay their eggs in March.* | *an ostrich egg* | *The eggs hatch* (=break open to allow the baby out) *in 26 days.*
2 FOOD [C,U] an egg, especially one from a chicken, that is used for food: **fried/poached/boiled etc eggs** | *Joe always has* **bacon and egg** *for breakfast.* | *Whisk the* **egg white** (=the white part) *until stiff.* | *Beat in two of the* **egg yolks** (=the yellow part). → SCRAMBLED EGG
3 EGG SHAPE [C] something the same shape as an egg: *a chocolate Easter egg* → EASTER EGG
4 ANIMALS/PEOPLE [C] a cell produced by a woman or female animal that combines with SPERM (=male cell) to make a baby; ▯ **ovum**
5 (have) egg on your face if someone, especially someone in authority, has egg on their face, they have been made to look stupid by something embarrassing: *The Pentagon's been left with egg on its face.*
6 put all your eggs in one basket to depend completely on one thing or one course of action in order to get success, so that you have no other plans if this fails: *When planning your investments, it's unwise to put all your eggs in one basket.*

egg² v
egg sb ⇔ **on** phr v to encourage someone to do something, especially something that they do not want to do or should not do: *Bob didn't want to jump, but his friends kept egging him on.*

eke /iːk/ v
eke sth ⇔ **out** phr v **1 eke out a living/existence** to manage to live with very little money or food: *They eke out a miserable existence in cardboard shacks.* **2** to make a small supply of something such as food or money last longer by carefully using small amounts of it: *How did Mum manage to eke out the food when we were kids?*

er·ror S2 W2 /'erə $ 'erər/ n
1 [C,U] a mistake: [**+in**] *There must be an error in our calculations.* | **make/commit an error** *The government has committed a serious error.*

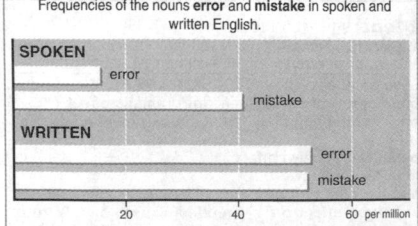

Frequencies of the nouns **error** and **mistake** in spoken and written English.

This graph shows that the word **mistake** is more common in spoken English than the word **error**. This is because error is not used in a very general way. It is used when describing particular types of mistake, for example in the expressions **computer error** or **error of judgement**, and sounds formal when used on its own. It is therefore more common in written English.

el·e·va·tor [S3] [W3] /'elɪveɪtə $ -ər/ n [C]
1 AmE a machine that takes people and goods from one level to another in a building; **≠ lift** BrE: We'll have to take the elevator. → see picture at STAY

es'tate ,agent n [C] BrE someone whose business is to buy and sell houses or land for people; **≠ real estate agent, realtor** AmE —**estate agency** n [C]

es·teemed /ɪ'stiːmd/ adj [usually before noun] formal respected and admired: the esteemed French critic Olivier Boissiere | **highly esteemed** scholars

fab /fæb/ adj BrE informal extremely good: a fab new car

fact [S1] [W1] /fækt/ n
4 the fact (of the matter) is spoken used when you are telling someone what is actually true in a particular situation, especially when this may be difficult to accept, or different from what people believe: The fact of the matter is that he's just not up to the job.

fair¹ [S1] [W2] /feə $ fer/ adj

SPOKEN PHRASES
14 fair enough especially BrE used to say that you agree with someone's suggestion or that something seems reasonable; **≠ OK**: 'I think we should split the bill.' 'Fair enough.'
15 to be fair used when adding something after someone has been criticized, which helps to explain or excuse what they did; **≠ in fairness**: She should have phoned to tell us what her plans were although, to be fair, she's been very busy.
16 be fair! especially BrE used to tell someone not to be unreasonable or criticize someone too much: Now Pat, be fair, the poor girl's trying her hardest!
17 fair's fair used when you think it is fair that someone should do something, especially because of something that has happened earlier: Come on, fair's fair – I paid last time so it's your turn.
18 fair comment BrE used to say that a remark or criticism seems reasonable
19 you can't say fairer than that BrE used to say that an offer you are making to someone is the best and fairest offer they can possibly get: I'll give you £25 for it – you can't say fairer than that, can you?

fault¹ [S2] [W3] /fɔːlt $ fɒːlt/ n [C]

WORD CHOICE: fault, blame, mistake
If someone causes something bad, you can say that it is **their fault** or that they are **to blame**: The accident was my fault. | Nobody is to blame for what happened.
⚠ Do not say that someone 'has the/a etc fault': We didn't think that it was our fault OR that we were to blame (NOT that we had any fault).
⚠ Do not say that something is 'someone's blame'.
Use **fault** to mean something that is wrong with a machine or system, or something that you could criticize about a person or thing: The car engine had developed a fault. | The book's only fault is that it is too long.
Use **mistake** to mean something that is wrong in someone's grammar, spelling, calculations, decisions etc: Please correct any mistakes (NOT faults) in my letter.

AMERICAN & BRITISH ENGLISH

This dictionary has full coverage of both American and British English.

If a word is only used in American English, it is marked AmE.

If a word is only used in British English, it is marked BrE.

If there is another word with the same meaning in British or American English, it is shown after the definition.

REGISTER

Labels before the definition show you if a word is used in informal, formal, literary, legal, or technical English.

→ See inside front cover for a full list of the labels used.

SPOKEN ENGLISH

If a word is used mainly in spoken English, it is labelled spoken.

If a word is used in a large number of phrases in spoken English, these phrases are shown together in a box, so that you can see them all together in a single group.

HELP WITH USAGE

Word choice notes explain the differences between closely related words and give examples that show how they are used differently.

Warning notes tell you about common mistakes that people make when using a word, based on research from the Longman Learners' Corpus (a database of over 10 million words of English written by students from around the world).

WORDS THAT HAVE MORE THAN ONE SPELLING

If a word is spelled differently in British and American English, the definition and examples are shown at the British spelling, and there is a cross reference from the American spelling.

If a word has more than one spelling, the different spellings are shown together at the beginning of the entry.

WORDS THAT HAVE MORE THAN ONE PART OF SPEECH

Words that have the same spelling, but have different parts of speech, are listed separately and given different numbers.

SYNONYMS, OPPOSITES, & RELATED WORDS

Synonyms (=words with the same meaning), opposites, and related words are shown after the definition.

COMPOUND WORDS

Compound words are treated like ordinary words and listed in alphabetical order as if there were no space or hyphen in them.

---

fa·vor·a·ble /ˈfeɪvərəbəl/ *adj* the American spelling of FAVOURABLE

fa·vour·a·ble *BrE*; **favorable** *AmE* /ˈfeɪvərəbəl/ *adj* **1** a favourable report, opinion, or reaction shows that you think that someone or something is good or that you agree with them: *favourable film reviews*

fax¹ /fæks/ *n* **1** [C] a letter or message that is sent in electronic form down a telephone line and then printed using a special machine: *Did you get my fax?* **2** [C] also **fax machine** a machine used for sending and receiving faxes: *What's your fax number?* **3** [U] the system of sending letters and messages using a fax machine: **by fax** *You can book tickets by fax or on-line.*

fax² *v* [T] to send someone a letter or message using a fax machine: **fax sb sth** *She asked me to fax her the details.*

fear·ful /ˈfɪəfəl $ ˈfɪr-/ *adj* **1** *formal* frightened that something might happen: *a shy and fearful child* | [+of] *People are fearful of rising crime in the area.* | **fearful that** *Officials are fearful that the demonstrations will cause new violence.* **2** *BrE* extremely bad; ▣ **awful**, **terrible**: *The room was in a fearful mess.* **3** [only before noun] *written* very frightening; ▣ **terrifying**: *a fearful creature* —**fearfulness** *n* [U]

fec·und /ˈfekənd, ˈfiːkənd/ *adj formal* able to produce many children, young animals, or crops; ➤ **fertile** —**fecundity** /fɪˈkʌndɨti/ *n* [U]

fe·male¹ |S3| |W2| /ˈfiːmeɪl/ *adj* **1** relating to women or girls, ▣ **male**; → **feminine**: *female voters* | *Over half of the staff is female.* **2** belonging to the sex that can have babies or produce eggs; ▣ **male**: *a female spider* **3** a female plant or flower produces fruit; ▣ **male**

fend·er /ˈfendə $ -ər/ *n* [C] **1** *AmE* the side part of a car that covers the wheels; ▣ **wing** *BrE*; → see picture at **CAR 2** a low metal wall around a FIREPLACE that prevents burning wood or coal from falling out

fender-ˌbender *n* [C] *AmE informal* a car accident in which little damage is done

feng shui¹ /ˌfʌŋ ˈʃweɪ/ *n* [U] a Chinese system of organizing the furniture and other things in a house or building in a way that people believe will bring good luck and happiness

feng shui² *v* [T] **feng shui a room/house etc** to place the furniture and other things in a room or house in a particular position so that it is arranged according to the feng shui system

fen·land /ˈfenlənd, -lænd/ *n* [C,U] a FEN

fen·nel /ˈfenl/ *n* [U] a pale green plant whose seeds are used to give a special taste to food and which is also used as a vegetable

fer·vent /ˈfɜːvənt $ ˈfɜːr-/ *adj* believing or feeling something very strongly and sincerely: *a fervent appeal for peace* | **fervent admirer/believer etc** *a fervent supporter of human rights* —**fervently** *adv*

fiend·ish /ˈfiːndɪʃ/ *adj* **1** cruel and unpleasant: *a particularly fiendish practical joke* **2** very clever in an unpleasant way: *a fiendish plan* **3** extremely difficult or complicated: *several fiendish exam questions* —**fiendishly** *adv*

air·port S2 W3 /ˈeəpɔːt $ ˈerpɔːrt/ *n* [C] a place where planes take off and land, with buildings for passengers to wait in; → **airfield**: *The plane landed at Heathrow Airport.* | *Her family went to see her off at the airport.*

> **WORD FOCUS: AIRPORT**
> *what you do at the airport*: When you arrive at the airport, you go into the **terminal** building. You **check in** for your flight at the **check-in desk**. You show your passport at **passport control** and then go through **security**, where they check that you are not carrying any weapons. If you have time you can wait for your flight in the **departure lounge**. When your flight is called, you go through the **departure gate** in order to get onto the plane. The plane then takes off from the **runway**. After your plane has landed, you go to the **baggage reclaim** to collect your bags, then go through **customs** and **immigration**, where they check your passport and your bags. You then go out into the **arrivals** area of the airport.

meal S2 W2 /miːl/ *n*
1 [C] an occasion when you eat food, for example breakfast or dinner, or the food that you eat on that occasion

> **WORD FOCUS: MEAL**
> *meals at different times of day*: **breakfast**, **brunch**, **lunch**, **tea** *BrE*, **dinner**, **supper**
> *a meal outside*: **picnic**, **barbecue** *also* **barbie** *informal*, **cookout** *AmE*
> *when you quickly eat a little food*: **snack**, **a bite to eat**
> *a very big meal for a lot of people*: **banquet**, **feast**
> *parts of a meal*: **starter** *BrE*, **appetizer** *AmE* (the first course) | **main course/entree** *especially AmE*, **side dish** (eaten with the main course) | **dessert** *also* **pudding**, **sweet** *BrE* (sweet food eaten at the end of the meal)

wet¹ S2 W3 /wet/ *comparative* **wetter**, *superlative* **wettest** *adj*
1 WATER/LIQUID covered in or full of water or another liquid; ◳ **dry**: *I've washed your shirt but it's still wet.* | *wet grass* | **get (sth) wet** *Take an umbrella or you'll get wet.* | [+with] *His face was wet with sweat.* | *The man in the boat was* **wet through** (=completely wet). | **soaking/dripping/sopping wet** (=very wet) *The towel was soaking wet.*

> **WORD FOCUS: WET**
> *very wet*: **soaked**, **drenched**
> *a little wet*: **damp**, **moist**
> *wet and soft*: **soggy**
> *when the air feels wet*: **humid**, **damp**, **muggy**

DERIVED WORDS

Derived words are shown at the end of the entry. These are words that can easily be understood if you know the meaning of the main word. Many of them end in '~ly' or '~ness'.

WORD FOCUS BOXES

These are a completely new feature. The Word Focus boxes show you groups of words that are related to the word you have looked up in the dictionary. Here are some examples of Word Focus boxes:

At **airport** the box takes you through all the things that you have to do when catching a plane at an airport

At **meal** the box tells you about different types of meals, and different parts of a meal.

At **wet** there is a list of different ways of saying that something is 'wet'.

This is a very useful tool for vocabulary-building, and it can also remind you of a word that you may have forgotten.

A, a

A¹, **a** /eɪ/ *n plural* **A's, a's** **1** [C,U] the first letter of the English alphabet **2** [C,U] the sixth note in the musical SCALE of C MAJOR or the musical KEY based on this note **3** [C] the highest mark that a student can get in an examination or for a piece of work: *I got an A in French.* | *Julia got straight As* (=all A's) *in high school.* **4** **an A student** *AmE* someone who regularly gets the best marks possible for their work in school or college **5** [U] used to refer in a short way to one of two different things or people. You can call the second one B: *A demands £500, B offers £100.* → **plan A** at PLAN¹ (5) **6** **from A to B** from one place to another: **get/go from A to B** *Hiring a car was the best way to get from A to B.* **7** **from A to Z** describing, including, or knowing everything about a subject: *the history of 20th century art from A to Z* **8** **A34, A40 etc** the name of a road in Britain that is smaller than a MOTORWAY, but larger than a B-ROAD → **A-ROAD** **9** [U] a common type of blood → **A LEVEL**

A² the written abbreviation of *amp* or amps

a [S1] [W1] /ə; *strong* eɪ/ also **an** *indefinite article, determiner* **1** used to show that you are talking about someone or something that has not been mentioned before, or that your listener does not know about: *We have a problem.* | *There was a hole in the fence.* | *Suddenly they heard a loud bang.* → **THE¹** **2** used to show that you are referring to a general type of person or thing and not a specific person or thing: *Would you like a sandwich?* | *I want to train to be an engineer.* | *He's a really nice man.* | *Take a look at this.* | *It needs a good clean.* **3** used before someone's family name to show that they belong to that family: *One of his daughters had married a Rothschild.* **4** one: *a thousand pounds* | *a dozen eggs* | *You'll have to wait an hour or two.* **5** used in some phrases that say how much of something there is: *There were* **a lot** *of people at the party.* | *A few weeks from now I'll be in Venice.* | *You have caused* **a great deal** *of trouble.* **6** used to mean 'each' when stating prices, rates, or speeds: *I get paid once a month.* | *The eggs cost $2 a dozen.* **7** used before singular nouns to mean all things of a particular type: *A square has four sides* (=all squares have four sides). | *A child needs love and affection.* **8** used once before two nouns that are mentioned together very often: *I'll fetch you a cup and saucer.* | *Does everyone have a knife and fork?* **9** used before the -ing forms of verbs when they are used as nouns referring to an action, event, or sound: *There was a beating of wings overhead.* | *Bernice became aware of a humming that seemed to come from all around her.* **10** used before nouns that are usually UNCOUNTABLE when other information about the quality, feeling etc is added by an adjective, phrase, or CLAUSE: *Candidates must have a good knowledge of chemistry.* **11** used before the name of a substance, food etc to refer to a particular type of it: *Use a good cheese to make the sauce.* | *plants that grow well in a rich moist soil* **12** used before the name of a drink to refer to a cup or glass of that drink: *Can I get you a coffee?* | *Renwick went to the bar and ordered a beer.* **13** used before the name of a famous artist to refer to a painting by that artist: *an early Rembrandt* **14** used before a name to mean someone or something that has the same qualities as that person or thing: *She was hailed as a new Marilyn Monroe.* **15** used before someone's name when you do not know who they are: *There is a Mr Tom Wilkins on the phone.* **16** used before the names of days, months, seasons, and events in the year to refer to a particular one: *We arrived in England on a cold wet Sunday in 1963.* | *I can't remember a Christmas like it.*

> **WORD CHOICE: a, an**
> Before a word beginning with a vowel sound, use **an**: *an elephant* | *an umbrella* | *an obvious mistake*
> ⚠ Use **an** before an 'h' that is not pronounced: *an hour later* | *an honest explanation*
> ⚠ Use **a** before a 'u' that is pronounced like 'you': *a university* | *a unique opportunity*
> ⚠ Use **an** before an abbreviation that is pronounced with a vowel sound at the start: *an SOS call* | *an MP3 file*

A & E /ˌeɪ ənd ˈiː/ *n* [U] *BrE* **Accident and Emergency** the part of a hospital where people who are injured or who need urgent treatment are brought

a-¹ /ə/ *prefix* **1** in a particular condition or way: *aloud* | *alive* (=living) | *with nerves all a-tingle* (=tingling) **2** *old use* in, to, at, or on something: *abed* (=in bed) | *afar* (=far away)

a-² /eɪ, æ, ə/ *prefix* not or without: *amoral* (=not moral) | *atypically* (=not typically)

A-1 /ˌeɪ ˈwʌn/ *adj old-fashioned* very good or completely healthy: *Everything about the resort was A-1.*

A3 /ˌeɪ ˈθriː/ *n* [U] a standard size of paper, used in Europe and Japan. A3 paper measures 297 x 420 MILLIMETRES; → **A4, A5**

A4 /ˌeɪ ˈfɔː $ -ˈfɔːr/ *n* [U] a standard size of paper, used in Europe and Japan. A4 paper measures 210 x 297 MILLIMETRES; → **A3, A5**

A5 /ˌeɪ ˈfaɪv/ *n* [U] a standard size of paper, used in Europe and Japan. A5 paper measures 148 x 210 MILLIMETRES; → **A3, A4**

AA /ˌeɪ ˈeɪ/ *n* **1** **Alcoholics Anonymous** an organization for ALCOHOLICS who want to stop drinking alcohol **2** **the AA** **Automobile Association** a British organization which provides services for people who own cars **3** [C] **Associate of Arts** a two-year college degree in the US

AAA /ˌtrɪpəl ˈeɪ/ *n* **American Automobile Association** an American organization which provides services to people who own cars

aard·vark /ˈɑːdvɑːk $ ˈɑːrdvɑːrk/ *n* [C] a large animal from southern Africa that has a very long nose and eats small insects

aargh /ɑːx, ɑː $ ɑːrg, ər/ *interjection* used to show you are disappointed, hurt, or annoyed: *Aargh, the lid won't close.*

AB /ˌeɪ ˈbiː/ *n* [U] a common type of blood

a·back /əˈbæk/ *adv* **be taken aback (by sth)** to be very surprised or shocked by something: *For a moment, I was completely taken aback by her request.*

ab·a·cus /ˈæbəkəs/ *n* [C] a frame with small balls that can be slid along on thick wires, used for counting and calculating

ab·a·lo·ne /ˌæbəˈləʊni $ -ˈloʊ-/ *n* [C,U] a kind of SHELLFISH which is used as food and whose shell contains MOTHER-OF-PEARL

a·ban·don¹ [W3] /əˈbændən/ *v* [T] **1** to leave someone, especially someone you are responsible for: *How could she abandon her own child?* **2** to go away from a place, vehicle etc permanently, especially because the situation makes it impossible for you to stay: ▪ **leave:** *We had to abandon the car and walk the rest of the way.* | *Fearing further attacks, m... of the population had abandoned the city.* **3** to stop doing something because there are too m... problems and it is impossible to continue: *The... had to be abandoned due to bad weather.* | *The... doned their attempt to recapture the castle.* | *B... the fog they abandoned their idea of driving...*

4 to stop having a particular idea, belief, or attitude: *They were accused of abandoning their socialist principles.* | *Rescuers had* **abandoned** *all* **hope** *of finding any more survivors.*
5 abandon yourself to sth *literary* to feel an emotion so strongly that you let it control you completely: *She abandoned herself to grief.*
6 abandon ship to leave a ship because it is sinking
—**abandonment** *n* [U]

abandon² *n* [U] if someone does something with abandon, they behave in a careless or uncontrolled way, without thinking or caring about what they are doing: **with reckless/wild abandon** *They drank and smoked with reckless abandon.*

a·ban·doned /ə'bændənd/ *adj* **1** an abandoned building, car, boat etc has been left by the people who owned or used it: *The car was found abandoned in Bristol.* | *the demolition of abandoned buildings* **2** [only before noun] an abandoned person or animal has been left completely alone by the person that was looking after them **3** *literary* behaving in a wild and uncontrolled way

a·base /ə'beɪs/ *v* **abase yourself** to behave in a way that shows you accept that someone has complete power over you —**abasement** *n* [U]

a·bashed /ə'bæʃt/ *adj* [not before noun] *written* embarrassed or ashamed because you have done something wrong or stupid: *She looked rather abashed.*

a·bate /ə'beɪt/ *v* [I] *formal* to become less strong or decrease: *We waited for the storm to abate.*

ab·at·toir /'æbətwɑː $ -ɑːr/ *n* [C] *BrE* a place where animals are killed for their meat; ⬛ **slaughterhouse**

a·ba·ya /ə'beɪə/ *n* [C] a long black piece of clothing worn by Muslim women in some countries, which covers the body and is usually worn with a separate head covering; → **burqa, chador**

ab·bess /'æbɪs, 'æbes/ *n* [C] a woman who is in charge of a CONVENT (=place where a group of NUNS live)

ab·bey /'æbi/ *n* [C] a large church with buildings next to it where MONKS and NUNS live or used to live

ab·bot /'æbət/ *n* [C] a man who is in charge of a MONASTERY (=a place where a group of MONKS live)

abbr. also **abbrev.** the written abbreviation of *abbreviation*

ab·bre·vi·ate /ə'briːvieɪt/ *v* [T] to make a word or expression shorter by not including letters or using only the first letter of each word; ⬛ **shorten: be abbreviated to sth** *'Information technology' is usually abbreviated to 'IT'.*

ab·bre·vi·at·ed /ə'briːvieɪt̬d/ *adj* made shorter: *Orders were passed to the commander at the front in an abbreviated form.*

ab·bre·vi·a·tion /ə,briːvi'eɪʃən/ *n* **1** [C] a short form of a word or expression: [+of/for] *'Dr' is the written abbreviation of 'Doctor'.* **2** [U] the act of abbreviating something

ABC /,eɪ biː 'siː/ *n* **1** [singular] *BrE*, **ABCs** [plural] *AmE* the letters of the English alphabet as taught to children **2 the ABC of sth** *BrE*, **the ABCs of sth** *AmE* the basic facts about a particular subject: *the ABCs of your computer* **3 American Broadcasting Corporation** one of the national television companies in the US

ab·di·cate /'æbdɪkeɪt/ *v* [I,T] **1** to give up the position of being king or queen: *King Alfonso XIII abdicated in favour of his eldest son.* | *The king was forced to abdicate the throne.* **2 abdicate (your) responsibility** ... *rmal* to refuse to be responsible for something, when ... should be or were before: *The government has ...ely abdicated its responsibility in dealing with hous...eeds.* —**abdication** /,æbdɪ'keɪʃən/ *n* [C,U]

·men /'æbdəmən, æb'dəʊ- $ -'doʊ-/ *n* ...the part of your body between your chest and ...ch contains your stomach, BOWELS etc **2** the ... of an insect's body, joined to the THORAX

—abdominal /æb'dɒmɪn̩əl $ -'dɑː-/ *adj: acute abdo... nal pains;* → see picture at INSECT

ab·duct /əb'dʌkt, æb-/ *v* [T] to take someone away by force; ⬛ **kidnap:** *She was abducted late last night.* —**abductor** *n* [C] —**abduction** /əb'dʌkʃən, æb-/ *n* [C,U]: *child abduction* —**abductee** /,æbdʌk'tiː/ *n* [C]

a·bed /ə'bed/ *adj* [not before noun] in bed

a·ber·rant /'æbərənt, ə'berənt/ *adj formal* not usual or normal; ⬛ **abnormal:** *aberrant behaviour*

ab·er·ra·tion /,æbə'reɪʃən/ *n* [C] *formal* an action or event that is different from what usually happens or what someone usually does: *a temporary aberration in US foreign policy* | *a mental aberration*

a·bet /ə'bet/ *v* **abetted, abetting** [T] to help someone do something wrong or illegal → **aid and abet** at AID² (3)

a·bey·ance /ə'beɪəns/ *n* **in abeyance** something such as a custom, rule, or system that is in abeyance is not being used at the present time: **fall into abeyance** (=no longer be used)

ab·hor /əb'hɔː $ əb'hɔːr, æb-/ *v* **abhorred, abhorring** [T not in progressive] *formal* to hate a kind of behaviour or way of thinking, especially because you think it is morally wrong: *I abhor discrimination of any kind.*

ab·hor·rence /əb'hɒrəns $ -'hɔːr-/ *n* [U] *formal* a deep feeling of hatred towards something

ab·hor·rent /əb'hɒrənt $ -'hɔːr-/ *adj* something that is abhorrent is completely unacceptable because it seems morally wrong; ⬛ **repugnant:** [+to] *The practice of killing animals for food is utterly abhorrent to me.*

a·bide /ə'baɪd/ *v* **1 sb can't abide sb/sth** used to say that someone dislikes something or someone very much: *I can't abide that man – he's so self-satisfied.* **2** *past tense* **abode** /ə'bəʊd $ ə'boʊd/ [I always + adv/prep] *old use* to live somewhere
abide by sth *phr v* to accept and obey a decision, rule, agreement etc, even though you may not agree with it: *You have to abide by the referee's decision.*

a·bid·ing /ə'baɪdɪŋ/ *adj* [only before noun] *written* an abiding feeling or belief continues for a long time and is not likely to change; ⬛ **lasting:** *Phil has a deep and abiding love for his family.*

a·bil·i·ty **S1** **W1** /ə'bɪl̩ti/ *n plural* **abilities** **1** [C] the state of being able to do something: **ability to do sth** *the ability to walk* | *The health center serves all patients, regardless of their ability to pay.* | *I don't have the ability to say 'no'.* **2** [C,U] someone's level of skill at doing something: **athletic/musical/artistic etc ability** *The test measures verbal and mathematical ability.* | *leadership ability* | *It takes hard work and* **natural ability** *to make it as a professional athlete.* | *There are musicians of all abilities in the orchestra.* | **of great/exceptional etc ability** *He's a writer of remarkable ability.* | **of high/low/average ability** *students of average ability* | **mixed ability** *classes* (=classes that include students who are at different levels) **3 to the best of your ability** as well as you can: *He completed the job to the best of his ability.*

-ability /əbɪl̩ti/ also **-ibility** *suffix* makes nouns from adjectives ending in -ABLE and -IBLE: *manageability* | *suitability*

ab·ject /'æbdʒekt/ *adj* **1 abject poverty/misery/failure etc** the state of being extremely poor, unhappy, unsuccessful etc **2** an abject action or expression shows that you feel very ashamed: *an abject apology* —**abjectly** *adv*

ab·jure /əb'dʒʊə, æb- $ -'dʒʊr/ *v* [T] *formal* to state publicly that you will give up a particular belief or way of behaving; ⬛ **renounce**

a·blaze /ə'bleɪz/ *adj* [not before noun] *written* **1** burning strongly with a lot of flames; → **blaze:** *Within minutes the whole house was ablaze.* | *The factory had been set ablaze* (=made to burn). **2** very bright and colourful: *a passing pleasure-boat, with all its lights ablaze* | [+with] *Her yard was ablaze with summer* *lowers.* **3** feeling or showing strong emotion, especially anger: [+**with**] *His eyes were ablaze with fury.*

a·ble S1 W1 /'eɪbəl/ *adj*
1 be able to do sth a) to have the skill, strength, knowledge etc needed to do something: *I've always wanted to be able to speak Japanese.* → see box at CAN¹ **b)** to be in a situation in which it is possible for you to do something: *I'd like to do more gardening, but I never seem able to find the time.* | *I haven't been able to read that report yet.*
2 clever or good at doing something: *one of my more able students*

-able /əbəl/ also **-ible** *suffix* [in adjectives] **1** that you can do something to: *washable* (=it can be washed) | *unbreakable* (=it cannot be broken) | *loveable* (=easy to love) **2** having a particular quality or condition: *knowledgeable* (=knowing a lot) | *comfortable* —**-ably** /əbli/, **-ibly** *suffix* [in adverbs]: *unbelievably*

‚able-'bodied *adj* **1** physically strong and healthy, especially when compared with someone who is DIS-ABLED: *Every able-bodied man had to fight for his country.* **2 the able-bodied** [plural] people who are able-bodied

‚able 'seaman *n* [C] a low rank in the navy, or someone who has this rank

a·blu·tions /ə'bluːʃənz/ *n* [plural] *formal* if you perform your ablutions, you wash yourself – sometimes used humorously

a·bly /'eɪbli/ *adv* cleverly, skilfully, or well: *She was ably assisted by her team of researchers.*

ab·ne·ga·tion /‚æbnɪ'geɪʃən/ *n* [U] *formal* when you do not allow yourself to have or do something that you want

ab·norm·al /æb'nɔːməl $ -'nɔːr-/ *adj* very different from usual in a way that seems strange, worrying, wrong, or dangerous; ☒ **normal**: *abnormal behaviour* | *an abnormal level of cholesterol* | *My parents thought it was abnormal for a boy to be interested in ballet.* —**abnormally** *adv*: *an abnormally high pulse rate*

ab·nor·mal·i·ty /‚æbnɔː'mælti $ -nər-/ *n plural* **abnormalities** [C,U] an abnormal feature, especially something that is wrong with part of someone's body: *tests that can detect genetic abnormalities in the foetus*

abo, Abo /'æbəʊ $ -boʊ/ *n plural* **abos** [C] *taboo* a very offensive word for an Australian ABORIGINE. Do not use this word.

a·board¹ /ə'bɔːd $ ə'bɔːrd/ *prep* on or onto a ship, plane, or train: *They finally went aboard the plane.*

aboard² *adv* **1** on or onto a ship, plane, or train: *The plane crashed, killing all 200 people aboard.* | *The boat swayed as he stepped aboard.* **2 All aboard!** *spoken* used to tell passengers of a ship, bus, or train that they must get on because it will leave soon

a·bode¹ /ə'bəʊd $ ə'boʊd/ *n* [C] **1** *formal* someone's home – sometimes used humorously: *Welcome to my humble abode.* | *a homeless person with no fixed abode* (=no permanent home) **2 right of abode** *law* the right to live in a country

abode² the past tense of ABIDE

a·bol·ish /ə'bɒlɪʃ $ ə'bɑː-/ *v* [T] to officially end a law, system etc, especially one that has existed for a long time: *Slavery was abolished in the US in the 19th century.*

ab·o·li·tion /‚æbə'lɪʃən/ *n* [U] when a law or a system is officially ended: [+**of**] *the abolition of the death penalty*

ab·o·li·tion·ist /‚æbə'lɪʃən‚ɪst/ *n* [C] someone who wants to end a system or law

A-bomb /'eɪ bɒm $ -bɑːm/ *n* [C] *old-fashioned* an ATOMIC BOMB

a·bom·i·na·ble /ə'bɒmɪnəbəl, -mənə- $ ə'bɑː-/ *adj* extremely unpleasant or of very bad quality; ☒ **terrible**: *abominable cruelty* —**abominably** *adv*: *Mavis behaved abominably.*

a‚bominable 'snowman *n* [C] a YETI

a·bom·i·nate /ə'bɒmɪ‚neɪt $ ə'bɑː-/ *v* [T not in progressive] *formal* to hate something very much

a·bom·i·na·tion /ə‚bɒmɪ'neɪʃən $ ə‚bɑː-/ *n* [C] someone or something that is extremely offensive or unacceptable: *He preached that slavery was an abomination.*

ab·o·rig·i·nal¹ /‚æbə'rɪdʒnəl./ *adj* **1** also **Aboriginal** relating to the Australian aborigines **2** *formal* relating to the people or animals that have existed in a place or country from the earliest times; ☒ **indigenous**

aboriginal², Aboriginal *n* [C] an aborigine

ab·o·rig·i·ne, Aborigine /‚æbə'rɪdʒni/ *n* [C] someone who belongs to the race of people who have lived in Australia from the earliest times

a·bort /ə'bɔːt $ -ɔːrt/ *v* **1** [T] to stop an activity because it would be difficult or dangerous to continue it: *The rescue mission had to be aborted.* **2** [T] to deliberately end a PREGNANCY when the baby is still too young to live **3** [I] if a PREGNANT woman or animal aborts, the baby is born too early and is dead when it is born: *The disease causes pregnant animals to abort.*

a·bor·tion /ə'bɔːʃən $ ə'bɔːr-/ *n* [C,U] a medical operation to end a PREGNANCY so that the baby is not born alive; ☒ **termination**: *She decided to have an abortion.* | *anti-abortion campaigners*

a·bor·tion·ist /ə'bɔːʃən‚ɪst $ ə'bɔːr-/ *n* [C] someone who performs abortions, especially illegally

a·bor·tive /ə'bɔːtɪv $ ə'bɔːr-/ *adj* an abortive action is not successful: *an abortive military coup* | **abortive attempt/effort** *an abortive attempt to reform local government*

a·bound /ə'baʊnd/ *v* [I] to exist in very large numbers: *Rumours abound as to the reasons for his resignation.* | *Examples of this abound in her book.*

abound with/in sth *phr v* if a place, situation etc abounds with things of a particular type, it contains a very large number of them: *The forests abound with deer, birds and squirrels.*

a·bout¹ S1 W1 /ə'baʊt/ *prep*
1 concerning or relating to a particular subject: *a book about politics* | *She said something about leaving town.* | *He lied about his age.* | *About that car of yours. How much are you selling it for?* | *What's he on about* (=talking about)? | *It's about Tommy, doctor. He's been sick again.* | *Naturally, my mother wanted to know all about it* (=all the details relating to it).
2 used to show why someone is angry, happy, upset etc: *I'm really worried about Jack.* | *She's upset about missing the party.*
3 in many different directions within a particular place, or in different parts of a place; ☒ **around, round**: *We spent the whole afternoon walking about town.* | *Books were scattered about the room.*
4 in the nature or character of a person or thing: *There's something really strange about Liza.* | *What I like about the job is that it's never boring.*
5 what/how about sb/sth *spoken* **a)** used to ask a question that directs attention to another person or thing: *What about Jack? We can't just leave him here.* | *I'm feeling hungry. How about you?* **b)** used to make a suggestion: *How about a salad for lunch?*
6 do something about sth to do something to solve ⦂ problem or stop a bad situation: *If we don't do som⦂ thing about it, the problem is going to get worse.* | *W⦂ can be done about the rising levels of pollution?*
7 if an organization, a job, an activity etc is ⦂ something, that is its basic purpose: *Leadershi⦂ about getting your team to co-operate.*
8 while you're about it *spoken* used to tell som⦂ something while they are doing somet⦂ because it would be easier to do both things ⦂ time: *Go and see what's the matter, and ⦂ about it you can fetch me my sweater.*
9 what was all that about? *spoken* u⦂

reason for something that has just happened, especially someone's angry behaviour
10 *literary* surrounding a person or thing: *Jo sensed fear and jealousy all about her.* → **be quick about it** at QUICK[1] (5); → **go about your business** at BUSINESS (12)

about[2] S1 W1 *adv*
1 also **round about** *spoken* a little more or less than a particular number, amount, or size; ▣ **roughly**: *I live about 10 miles away.* | *a tiny computer about as big as a postcard* | *We left the restaurant at round about 10.30.*
2 *BrE* in many different directions within a place or in different parts of a place; ▣ **around**: *People were rushing about, trying to find the driver.* | *Cushions were scattered about on the chairs.*
3 near to you or in the same place as you: *Is Derrick about? There's a phone call for him.* | *Quick! Let's go while there's no-one about.*
4 *BrE spoken* existing or available now: *I hope she hasn't caught flu.* **There's a lot of it about.** | *She might get temporary work, but there's not much about.*
5 *informal* almost or probably: *I was about ready to leave when somebody rang the doorbell.* | *'Have you finished?' 'Just about.'* | *It's* **just about** *the worst mistake anyone could make.*
6 that's about it/all *spoken* **a)** used to tell someone that you have told them everything you know: *He was a quiet chap, married with kids. That's about it, really.* **b)** used to say that there is nothing else available: *There's some cheese in the fridge and that's about it.*
7 so as to face in the opposite direction: *He quickly turned about and walked away.*

about[3] *adj* **1 be about to do sth** if someone is about to do something, or if something is about to happen, they will do it or it will happen very soon: *We were just about to leave when Jerry arrived.* | *Work was about to start on a new factory building.* **2 not be about to do sth** *informal* used to emphasize that you have no intention of doing something: *I've never smoked in my life and I'm not about to start now.* → **out and about** at OUT[1] (3); → **be up and about** at UP[1] (11)

a,bout-'face also **a,bout-'turn** *BrE n* [C usually singular] a complete change in the way someone thinks or behaves: *The administration seems to have done a complete about-face on gun-control.*

a·bove[1] S2 W1 /ə'bʌv/ *adv, prep*
1 in a higher position than something else; ▣ **over**; ▣ **below**: *Our office is above the hairdresser's.* | *He had a bruise just above his left eye.* | *I heard a strange noise coming from the room above.* | *The great bird hovered* **high above** *our heads.*
2 more than a particular number, amount, or level; ▣ **below**: *50 metres above sea level* | **above freezing/zero** (=higher than the temperature at which water freezes) *Tonight, temperatures should be just above freezing.* | **and/or above** *free medical care for pensioners aged 65 and above* | *Prize winners must have gained marks of 80% or above.* | *The salaries we offer are* **well above** (=much higher than) *average.*
3 to a greater degree than something else: *Many employers value personality* **above** *experience or qualifications.* | **above all (else)** (=used to say that something is more important than anything else) *Max is hardworking, cheerful, and above all honest.* | *medals awarded for bravery* **above and beyond** *the call of duty* (=greater than it is your duty to show)
louder or clearer than other sounds: *You can always* ⌐ar *her voice above everybody else's.*
*i*gher in rank, power, or importance; ▣ **below**: *He* ⌐ *rose above the rank of corporal.* | **and/or above** ⌐s *of the rank of Major and above* | **from above** ⌐ople *in higher authority) We just obey orders* ⌐ve.
⌐efore, in the same piece of writing; ▣ **below**: ⌐*ed above, there is a service charge.* | *Write to* ⌐*above for further information.*
⌐*e* **(doing) sth** to not be too good or honest

to do something: *Eileen's not above flirting with the bos⌐ when it suits her.*
8 be above suspicion/reproach/criticism etc to be so good that no one can doubt or criticize you: *Even the king's closest advisers were not above suspicion.*
9 get above yourself to think you are better or more important than you really are → **over and above** at OVER[1] (14); → **be above the law** at LAW (13)

above[2] W3 *adj* [only before noun] **a)** used in a piece of writing to refer to something mentioned in an earlier part of the same piece of writing: *For the above reasons, the management has no choice but to close the factory.* **b) the above** *formal* something mentioned before in the same piece of writing: *If none of the above applies to you, then you may be able to reclaim tax.*

a,bove 'board / $.'. ./ *adj* [not before noun] honest and legal: *His plans for opening a coffee shop are completely above board.*

a,bove-'mentioned *adj* [only before noun] *formal* mentioned on a previous page or higher up on the same page

ab·ra·ca·dab·ra /ˌæbrəkə'dæbrə/ *interjection* a word you say when you do a magic trick, which is supposed to make it successful

a·brade /ə'breɪd/ *v* [I,T] *technical* to rub something so hard that the surface becomes damaged

a·bra·sion /ə'breɪʒən/ *n* **1** [C] an area on the surface of your skin that has been injured by being rubbed against something hard: *She was treated for cuts and abrasions.* **2** [U] the process of rubbing a surface very hard so that it becomes damaged or disappears: *extra protection against abrasion*

a·bra·sive[1] /ə'breɪsɪv/ *adj* **1** rude or unkind: *She was a tough girl with rather an abrasive manner.* **2** having a rough surface, especially one that can be used to clean something or make it smooth: *Smooth down with a fine abrasive paper.* —**abrasively** *adv*

abrasive[2] *n* [C] a rough powder or substance that you use for cleaning something or making it smooth

a·breast /ə'brest/ *adv* **1 keep/stay abreast of sth** to make sure that you know all the most recent facts or information about a particular subject or situation: *It's important to keep abreast of the latest developments in computers.* **2 walk/ride etc abreast** to walk, ride etc next to each other, all facing the same way: **two/three/four etc abreast** (=with two, three, four etc people or vehicles next to each other) *The planes were flying four abreast.* **3** level with someone or something or in line with them: *As the car* **drew abreast** *of him, Jack suddenly recognised the driver.*

a·bridged /ə'brɪdʒd/ *adj* [usually before noun] an abridged book, play etc has been made shorter but keeps its basic structure and meaning: *The abridged edition was published in 1988.* —**abridge** *v* [T] —**abridgement** also **abridgment** *n* [C,U]

a·broad S2 W3 /ə'brɔːd $ ə'brɒːd/ *adv*
1 in or to a foreign country: *I've never lived abroad before.* | *She often goes abroad on business.* | *We never travelled abroad when we were kids.* | *goods imported from abroad* | *The books about Harry Potter are very popular now, both at home and abroad.*
2 *formal* if a feeling, piece of news etc is abroad, a lot of people feel it or know about it: *commercial secrets which we did not want to be spread abroad*

ab·ro·gate /'æbrəgeɪt/ *v* [T] *formal* to officially end a legal agreement, practice etc: *Both governments voted to abrogate the treaty.* —**abrogation** /ˌæbrə'geɪʃən/ *n* [C,U]

a·brupt /ə'brʌpt/ *adj* **1** sudden and unexpected: *an abrupt change of plan* | **come to an abrupt end/halt etc** *The bus came to an abrupt halt.* **2** seeming rude and unfriendly, especially because you do not waste time in friendly conversation: *Sorry, I didn't mean to be so abrupt.* —**abruptly** *adv* —**abruptness** *n* [U]

abs /æbz/ *n* [plural] *informal* the muscles on your ABDO-MEN (=stomach): *exercises that improve your butt, legs, and abs*

ABS /ˌeɪ biː 'es/ *n* [U] the abbreviation of *anti-lock braking system*

ab·scess /'æbses/ *n* [C] a painful swollen part of your skin or inside your body that has become infected and is full of a yellowish liquid

ab·scond /əb'skɒnd, æb- $ æb'skɑːnd/ *v* [I] *formal* **1** to escape from a place where you are being kept: [+**from**] *The boy absconded from a children's home.* **2** to secretly leave somewhere, taking with you something that does not belong to you: [+**with**] *He has to convince a judge that he wasn't going to abscond with the money.*

ab·seil /'æbseɪl/ *v* [I + down] *BrE* to go down a cliff or a rock by sliding down a rope and pushing against the rock with your feet; **ᗺ rappel** *AmE*; → see picture at OUTDOOR

ab·sence S3 W2 /'æbsəns/ *n*
1 [C,U] when you are not in the place where people expect you to be, or the time that you are away: **in/during sb's absence** *Ms Leighton will be in charge during my absence* (=while I am away). | [+**from**] *Her work involved repeated absences from home.*
2 [singular] the lack of something or the fact that it does not exist; ᗺ **presence**: [+**of**] *a complete absence of any kind of planning* | **In the absence** *of any evidence, the police had to let Myers go.*
3 absence makes the heart grow fonder used to say that being away from someone makes you like them more → **leave of absence** at LEAVE² (3); → **conspicuous by your absence** at CONSPICUOUS (3)

ab·sent¹ /'æbsənt/ *adj* **1** not at work, school, a meeting etc, because you are sick or decide not to go; ᗺ **present**: [+**from**] *students who are regularly absent from school* **2** if someone or something is absent, they are missing or not in the place where they are expected to be: **absent parent/father** *plans to force absent fathers to pay child maintenance* | [+**from**] *Local women were conspicuously absent* (=obviously not there) *from the meeting.* **3** [only before noun] a look etc that shows you are not paying attention to or thinking about what is happening; → **absently**: *The dull, absent look on her face implied boredom.*

ab·sent² /əb'sent, æb- $ æb-/ *v* [T] *formal* **absent yourself (from sth)** to not go to a place or take part in an event where people expect you to be

ab·sen·tee /ˌæbsən'tiː‹ / *n* [C] someone who should be in a place or at an event but is not there

absentee 'ballot *n* [C] a process by which people in the United States can vote before an election because they will be away during the election

ab·sen·tee·is·m /ˌæbsən'tiːɪzəm/ *n* [U] regular absence from work or school without a good reason

absentee 'landlord *n* [C] someone who lives a long way away from a house or apartment which they rent to other people, and who rarely or never visits it

absentee 'vote *n* [C] *AmE* a vote which you send by post in an election because you cannot be in the place where you usually vote; ᗺ **postal vote** *BrE*

ab·sen·ti·a /æb'sentiə/ *n formal* **in absentia** when you are not at a court or an official meeting where a decision is made about you

ab·sent·ly /'æbsəntli/ *adv* in a way that shows that you are not paying attention to or thinking about what is happening: *Laura gazed absently out of the window.*

absent-'minded *adj* likely to forget things, especially because you are thinking about something else; ᗺ **forgetful**: *Grandad's been getting rather absent-minded lately.* —**absent-mindedly** *adv* —**absent-mindedness** *n* [U]

ab·sinth, absinthe /'æbsɪnθ/ *n* [U] a bitter green very strong alcoholic drink

ab·so·lute¹ S2 W3 /'æbsəluːt/ *adj*
1 complete or total: *I have absolute confidence in her.* |

We don't know with absolute certainty that the project will succeed.
2 [only before noun] *especially BrE informal* used to emphasize your opinion about something or someone: *Some of the stuff on TV is absolute rubbish.* | *How did you do that? You're an absolute genius.* | *That meal last night cost an absolute fortune.*
3 definite and not likely to change: *We need absolute proof that he took the money.*
4 not restricted or limited: *an absolute monarch* | *Parents used to have absolute power over their children.*
5 true, correct, and not changing in any situation: *You have an absolute right to refuse medical treatment.*
6 in absolute terms measured by itself, not in comparison with other things: *In absolute terms wages have risen, but not in comparison with the cost of living.*

absolute² *n* [C] something that is considered to be true or right in all situations: *She believed in the importance of moral absolutes.*

ab·so·lute·ly S1 W3 /'æbsəluːtli, ˌæbsə'luːtli/ *adv*
1 completely and in every way: *He made his reasons for resigning absolutely clear.* | *Are you absolutely sure?* | *This cake is absolutely delicious.*
2 used to emphasize something: *The burglars took absolutely everything.* | *Jim knew absolutely nothing about the business when he joined the firm.* | *He has absolutely no experience of marketing.*
3 absolutely not! *spoken* used when you strongly disagree with someone or when you do not want someone to do something: *'Do you let your kids travel alone at night?' 'Absolutely not!'*
4 absolutely! *spoken* used to say that you completely agree with someone

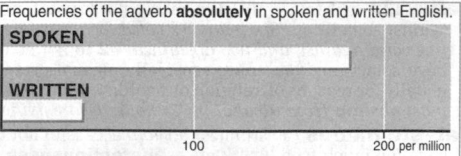

Frequencies of the adverb **absolutely** in spoken and written English.

SPOKEN	
WRITTEN	

100   200 per million

This graph shows that the adverb **absolutely** is much more common in spoken English than in written English. This is because it is used to emphasize adjectives like **brilliant**, **stupid**, **fantastic** etc in spoken English.

absolute ma'jority *n* [singular] when a party or person wins more than half of the total votes in an election

absolute 'zero *n* [U] the lowest temperature that is believed to be possible

ab·so·lu·tion /ˌæbsə'luːʃən/ *n* [U] when someone is formally forgiven by the Christian Church or a priest for the things they have done wrong: *Pope Leo gave him absolution.*

ab·so·lut·is·m /'æbsəluːtɪzəm/ *n* [U] a political system in which a ruler has complete power and authority

ab·solve /əb'zɒlv $ -ɑːlv/ *v* [T] **1** to say publicly that someone is not guilty or responsible for something: **absolve sb from/of sth** *He cannot be absolved of all responsibility for the accident.* **2** [often passive] if someone is absolved by the Christian Church or a priest for something they have done wrong, they are formally forgiven

ab·sorb W3 /əb'sɔːb, əb'zɔːb $ -ɔːrb/ *v* [T]
1 LIQUID/GAS to take in liquid, gas, or another substance from the surface or space around something: *Plants absorb nutrients from the soil.* | **absorb sth into sth** *Water and salts are absorbed into our blood stream.*
2 INFORMATION to read or hear a large amount of new information and understand it: *Her capacity to absorb information is amazing.*
3 INTEREST to interest someone so much that they do not pay attention to other things: *The movement and noise of the machines absorbed him completely.* | **be**

1 000, 2 000, 3 000, most frequent words in Spoken and Written English

A

absorbed in sth *Judith lay on the settee, absorbed in her book.*
4 BECOME PART OF STH to become part of something larger: *California absorbs many of the legal immigrants to the US.* | **be absorbed into sth** *We were soon absorbed into local village life.*
5 LIGHT/HEAT/ENERGY/NOISE if something absorbs light, heat, energy, or noise, it takes it in: *Darker surfaces absorb heat.*
6 DEAL WITH CHANGE/COSTS if something absorbs changes or costs, it accepts them and deals with them successfully: *The beer industry had absorbed a doubling of federal tax in 1991.*
7 MONEY/TIME if something absorbs money, time etc it uses a lot of it: *Defence spending absorbs almost 20% of the country's wealth.*
8 FORCE to reduce the effect of a sudden violent movement: *A well-designed sports shoe should absorb the impact on your feet.*

ab·sor·bent /əbˈsɔːbənt, -ˈzɔː- $ -ɔːr-/ *adj* material that is absorbent is able to take in liquids easily: *absorbent kitchen paper*

ab·sorb·ing /əbˈsɔːbɪŋ, -ˈzɔː- $ -ɔːr-/ *adj* enjoyable and interesting, and keeping your attention for a long time: *an absorbing hobby*

ab·sorp·tion /əbˈsɔːpʃən, -ˈzɔːp- $ -ɔːr-/ *n* [U] **1** a process in which something takes in liquid, gas, or heat: [+of] *the body's absorption of iron* **2** a process in which people or things become part of something larger: [+of] *the absorption of Soviet immigrants into Israel* **3** when you are very interested in something: [+with/in] *I don't understand James' absorption with military history.*

ab·stain /əbˈsteɪn/ *v* [I] **1** to choose not to vote for or against something: *Six countries voted for the change, five voted against, and two abstained.* **2** to not do or have something you enjoy, especially alcohol or sex, usually for reasons of religion or health: [+from] *Pilots must abstain from alcohol for 24 hours before flying.*

ab·ste·mi·ous /əbˈstiːmiəs/ *adj formal* careful not to have too much food, drink etc —**abstemiousness** *n* [U]

ab·sten·tion /əbˈstenʃən/ *n* **1** [C,U] an act of not voting for or against something: *The draft law was passed by 134 votes to 19, with 5 abstentions.* **2** [U] *formal* when you do not do something you enjoy doing: [+from] *fasting and abstention from intoxicating drinks*

ab·sti·nence /ˈæbstɪnəns/ *n* [U] the practice of not having something you enjoy, especially alcohol or sex, usually for reasons of religion or health —**abstinent** *adj*

ab·stract¹ /ˈæbstrækt/ *adj* **1** based on general ideas or principles rather than specific examples or real events; **■** theoretical: *abstract idea/concept the ability to translate abstract ideas into words* | *By the age of seven, children are capable of thinking in abstract terms.* | *Human beings are the only creatures capable of abstract thought* (=thinking about ideas). **2** existing only as an idea or quality rather than as something real that you can see or touch; **■** concrete: *the abstract nature of beauty* **3** abstract paintings, designs etc consist of shapes and patterns that do not look like real people or things → ABSTRACT NOUN

abstract² *n* [C] **1** a painting, design etc which contains shapes or images that do not look like real things or people → see picture at PAINTING **2** a short written statement containing only the most important ideas in a speech, article etc **3 in the abstract** considered in a general way rather than being based on specific details and examples: *Talking about crime in the abstract just isn't enough.*

ab·stract³ /əbˈstrækt, æb-/ *v* [T] **1** to write a document containing the most important ideas or points from a speech, article etc **2** *formal* to remove something from somewhere

ab·stract·ed /əbˈstræktɪd, æb-/ *adj* not noticing anything around you because you are thinking carefully about something else —**abstractedly** *adv*

ab·strac·tion /əbˈstrækʃən, æb-/ *n* **1** [C] a general idea about a type of situation, thing, or person rather than a specific example from real life: *He's always talking in abstractions.* **2** [U] when you do not notice what is happening around you because you are thinking carefully about something else: *She rocked the baby gently, gazing in abstraction at the flickering fire.* **3** [U] the use of shapes and patterns that do not look like real things

abstract ˈnoun *n* [C] a noun that names a feeling, quality, or state rather than an object, animal, or person. For example, 'hunger' and 'beauty' are abstract nouns.

ab·struse /əbˈstruːs, æb-/ *adj formal* unnecessarily complicated and difficult to understand: *Maths is a mix of abstruse theory and detailed calculations.*

ab·surd /əbˈsɜːd, -ˈzɜːd $ -ɜːrd/ *adj* **1** completely stupid or unreasonable; **■** ridiculous: *quite/slightly/completely etc absurd It seems quite absurd to expect anyone to drive for 3 hours just for a 20 minute meeting.* | *It seems an absurd idea.* **2 the absurd** something that is completely stupid and unreasonable: *Some of the stories he tells verge on the absurd.* —**absurdity** *n* [C,U]: *Duncan laughed at the absurdity of the situation.*

ab·surd·ly /əbˈsɜːdli, -ˈzɜːd- $ -ɜːr-/ *adv* surprisingly or unreasonably; **■** ridiculously: *absurdly low/high Prices on the island seem absurdly low to Western tourists.*

a·bun·dance /əˈbʌndəns/ *n* [singular, U] a large quantity of something: [+of] *an abundance of wavy red hair* | *in abundance One quality the team possessed in abundance was fighting spirit.*

a·bun·dant /əˈbʌndənt/ *adj* something that is abundant exists or is available in large quantities so that there is more than enough; **⬛** scarce: *an abundant supply of fresh water* | *abundant opportunities for well qualified staff*

a·bun·dant·ly /əˈbʌndəntli/ *adv* **1 abundantly clear** very easy to understand: *She'd made her feelings towards him abundantly clear.* **2** in large quantities: *Melons grow abundantly in this region.*

a·buse¹ [S2] [W3] /əˈbjuːs/ *n* **1** [plural, U] cruel or violent treatment of someone: *several cases of child abuse* | *physical/sexual/racial abuse Many children suffer racial abuse at school.* | *An independent committee will look into alleged human rights abuses.* **2** [C,U] the use of something in a way that it should not be used; **■** misuse: [+of] *government officials' abuse of power* | *A self-monitoring tax system is clearly open to abuse* (=able to be used wrongly). | *alcohol/drug abuse* (=the practice of drinking too much or taking illegal drugs) → SOLVENT ABUSE **3** [U] rude or offensive things that someone says when they are angry: *vandalism and verbal abuse directed at old people* | *a torrent/stream of abuse* (=a series of rude or angry words) | *shout/hurl/scream abuse at sb The other driver started hurling abuse at me.*; → **a term of abuse** at TERM¹ (3)

a·buse² /əˈbjuːz/ *v* [T] **1** to treat someone in a cruel and violent way, often sexually: *sexually/physically abused She was sexually abused as a child.* **2** to deliberately use something for the wrong purpose or for your own advantage: *Williams abused his position as Mayor to give jobs to his friends.* | *Morris abused the trust the firm had shown in him.* | *people who abuse the system* | *abuse alcohol/drugs The proportion of drinkers who abuse alcohol is actually quite small.* **3** to say rude or offensive things to someone; **■** insult: *Many soldiers in Belfast are verbally abused.* | *He came to the help of another driver who was being racially abused by three white passengers.* **4** to treat something so badly that you start to destroy it: *James abused his body for years with heroin and cocaine.* —**abuser** *n* [C]

a·bu·sive /əˈbjuːsɪv/ *adj* using cruel words or physical violence: *Smith denies using abusive language to the referee.* | *He became abusive and his wife was injured in the struggle.* —**abusively** *adv* —**abusiveness** *n* [U]

a·but /əˈbʌt/ also **abut on** *v* abutted, abutting [T] *formal* if one piece of land or a building abuts another, it is next to it or touches one side of it

a·bys·mal /əˈbɪzməl/ *adj* very bad or of bad quality; ■ **terrible**: *The reunion was an abysmal failure.* —**abysmally** *adv*

a·byss /əˈbɪs/ *n* [C] **1** a very dangerous or frightening situation: [+of] *The country might plunge into the abyss of economic ruin.* | *At that time Bosnia was standing on the edge of an abyss.* **2** a deep empty hole in the ground **3** a very big difference that separates two people or groups: *the gaping abyss between these grand buildings and my own miserable home*

AC /ˌeɪ ˈsiː/ **1** the abbreviation of *alternating current*; → **DC 2** the written abbreviation of *air-conditioning* → AC/DC

a/c the written abbreviation of ACCOUNT¹ (2)

a·ca·cia /əˈkeɪʃə/ *n* [C] a tree with small yellow or white flowers that grows in warm countries

ac·a·deme /ˈækəˌdiːm, ˌækəˈdiːm/ *n* [U] the work that university teachers and students do – often used humorously

ac·a·de·mi·a /ˌækəˈdiːmiə/ *n* [U] the activities and work done at universities and colleges, or the teachers and students involved in it

ac·a·dem·ic¹ W2 /ˌækəˈdemɪk◂/ *adj*
1 [usually before noun] relating to education, especially at college or university level: *He possessed no academic qualifications.* | *a program designed to raise academic standards*
2 [usually before noun] concerned with studying from books, as opposed to practical work: *the study of art as an academic discipline*
3 good at studying: *He's a popular child, but not very academic.*
4 if a discussion about something is academic, it is a waste of time because the speakers cannot change the existing situation: *The question of where we go on holiday is purely academic since we don't have any money.* —**academically** /-kli/ *adv*

academic² *n* [C] a teacher in a college or university

a·cad·e·mi·cian /əˌkædəˈmɪʃən $ ˌækədə-/ *n* [C] a member of an official organization which encourages the development of literature, art, science etc

academic ˈyear *n* [C] the period of the year during which there are school or university classes

a·cad·e·my /əˈkædəmi/ *n plural* **academies** [C] **1** an official organization which encourages the development of literature, art, science etc: *the American Academy of Arts and Letters* **2** a college where students are taught a particular subject or skill: *a military academy* | *the Royal Academy of Music* **3** a school in Scotland for children between 11 and 16 **4** a private school in the US

a cap·pel·la /ˌæ kæˈpelə $ ˌɑː kə-/ *adj, adv* sung without any musical instruments

ac·cede /əkˈsiːd, æk-/ *v*
accede to sth *phr v formal* **1** to agree to a demand, proposal etc, especially after first disagreeing with it: *the doctor's refusal to accede to his patient's request* **2** if someone accedes to the THRONE, they become king or queen

ac·cel·e·ran·do /æk,seləˈrændəʊ $ -ˈrɑːndoʊ/ *adj, adv* getting gradually faster

ac·cel·e·rate /əkˈseləreɪt/ *v* **1** [I,T] if a process accelerates or if something accelerates it, it happens faster than usual or sooner than you expect: *measures to accelerate the rate of economic growth* **2** [I] if a vehicle or someone who is driving it accelerates, it starts to go faster; ■ **decelerate**: *The car accelerated smoothly away.*

ac·cel·e·ra·tion /ək,seləˈreɪʃən/ *n* **1** [singular, U] a process in which something happens more and more quickly: [+in] *an acceleration in the rate of inflation* | [+of] *the rapid acceleration of economic progress in South East Asia* **2** [U] the rate at which a car or other vehicle can go faster: *The latest model has excellent acceleration.* **3** [U] *technical* the rate at which the speed of an object increases

ac·cel·e·ra·tor /əkˈseləreɪtə $ -ər/ *n* [C] **1** the part of a car or other vehicle that you press with your foot to make it go faster; ■ **gas pedal** *AmE*; → see picture at CAR **2** *technical* a large machine used to make extremely small pieces of MATTER¹ (3) move at extremely high speeds

ac·cent¹ /ˈæksənt $ ˈæksent/ *n* [C] **1** the way someone pronounces the words of a language, showing which country or which part of a country they come from; → **dialect**: *He noticed that I spoke Polish with an accent.* | **English/American/Indian etc accent** *a slight American accent* | **a broad/strong/slight/faint etc accent** *a broad Irish accent* **2** the accent is on sth if the accent is on a particular quality, feeling etc, special importance is given to it: *accommodation with the accent on comfort* **3** the part of a word that you should emphasize when you say it; ■ **stress**: [+on] *In the word 'dinner' the accent is on the first syllable.* **4** a written mark used above or below particular letters in some languages to show how to pronounce that letter

ac·cent² /əkˈsent $ ˈæksent/ *v* [T] **1** to make something more noticeable so that people will pay attention to it; ■ **highlight**: *Use make-up to accent your cheekbones and eyes.* **2** *technical* to emphasize a part of a word in speech

ac·cen·ted /əkˈsentɪd $ ˈæksen-/ *adj* **1** spoken with a foreign accent: *He spoke heavily accented English.* **2** emphasized or given special importance: *accented lighting*

ac·cen·tu·ate /əkˈsentʃueɪt/ *v* [T] to make something more noticeable: *The photograph seemed to accentuate his large nose.* —**accentuation** /ək,sentʃuˈeɪʃən/ *n* [C,U]

ac·cept S1 W1 /əkˈsept/ *v*
1 GIFT/OFFER/INVITATION [I,T] to take something that someone offers you, or to agree to do something that someone asks you to do; ■ **refuse**: *Rick accepted her offer of coffee.* | *He accepted the invitation to stay with us.* | *His school reports said that he is always ready to accept a challenge* (=agree to do something difficult). | *Please accept this small gift.* | *They offered me a job and I accepted.* | **accept sth from sb** *He accepted a glass of water from Helen.* | *He readily accepted her invitation* (=accepted it quickly).
2 SITUATION/PROBLEM ETC [T] to decide that there is nothing you can do to change a difficult and unpleasant situation or fact and continue with your normal life: *He's not going to change, and you just have to accept it.* | **accept that** *We have to accept that this is not an ideal world.* | *You need to accept the fact that most of your problems are caused by jealousy.*
3 THINK SB/STH IS GOOD ENOUGH [T] to decide that someone has the necessary skill or intelligence for a particular job, course etc or that a piece of work is good enough; ■ **reject**: *Students accepted by Stanford Law School had very high scores on the LSAT.* | **accept sb/sth as sth** *They have accepted him as the repre[sen]tative of the company.* | **accept sb/sth for sth** *Ra[ndom] House accepted the book for publication.*
4 BECOME PART OF A GROUP [T] to allow sor[neone to] become part of a group, society, or organizati[on and] treat them in the same way as the other[s]; ■ **reject**: **accept sb as sth** *The childre[n] began to accept her as one of the family.* | **[accept] sth** *It often takes years for immigrants [to settle] into the host community.*
5 AGREE TO TAKE/DEAL WITH STH take or deal with something that sor

to say that it is suitable or good enough: *The govern-ment has accepted the resignation of a senior army commander.* | *Please accept my sincere apologies.* | *Sorry, we don't accept travellers' cheques.*
6 SUGGESTION/ADVICE [T] to decide to do what some-one advises or suggests you should do: *Be prepared to accept the advice of members of staff.*
7 BELIEVE AN EXPLANATION/STATEMENT [T] to agree that what someone says is right or true; **⊠ reject**: *She has accepted your explanation as to why you didn't attend the meeting.*
8 accept responsibility/blame for sth to admit that you were responsible for something bad that happened: *The University will not accept responsibility for items lost or stolen.*

ac·cept·a·ble S3 W3 /ək'septəbəl/ adj
1 good enough to be used for a particular purpose or to be considered satisfactory: [+to] *an agreement which is acceptable to all sides* | *Students who achieve an accept-able standard will progress to degree studies.* | *How do we reach an acceptable level of data security?*
2 acceptable behaviour is considered to be morally or socially good enough: *Alcohol is not an acceptable way out of your problems.* | *Here, the students set the stan-dards for acceptable behaviour.* | **acceptable (for sb) to do sth** *It is not socially acceptable for parents to leave children unattended at that age.* | *It is perfectly acceptable to sample the food before you buy.*
—**acceptably** adv —**acceptability** /ək,septə'bɪlɪti/ n [U]

ac·cept·ance W3 /ək'septəns/ n
1 [U] when you officially agree to take something that you have been offered: [+of] *the formal acceptance of an invitation* | *He wrote a letter of acceptance* (=a letter in which you agree to accept a job, university place etc) *to the university.*
2 [singular, U] when people agree that an idea, state-ment, explanation etc is right or true: [+of] *the accep-tance of Einstein's theory* | **acceptance that** *There is still not widespread acceptance that fathers can care for children as well as mothers do.* | **gain/find acceptance** *This type of management style gained acceptance in the 1980s.*
3 [U] the ability to accept an unpleasant situation which cannot be changed, without getting angry or upset about it: [+of] *By the end of the trial, Nicolas moved towards acceptance of his fate.*
4 [U] the process of allowing someone to become part of a group or a society and of treating them in the same way as the other members: *Acceptance by their peer group is important to most youngsters.*

ac·cept·ed /ək'septɪd/ adj considered right or suit-able by most people: *Having more than one wife is a normal and accepted practice in some countries.* | **generally/widely/universally etc accepted** *generally accepted principles of fairness and justice*

ac·cess¹ S3 W1 /'ækses/ n [U]
1 the right to enter a place, use something, see someone etc: [+to] *Access to the papers is restricted to senior management.* | *Cats should always have access to fresh, clean water.*
2 how easy or difficult it is for people to enter a public building, to reach a place, or talk to someone: [+for] *We're trying to improve access for disabled visitors.* | *[+to] a villa with easy access to the sea*
the way you use to enter a building or reach a place: is by means of a small door on the right. | [+to] *to the restrooms is through the foyer.*
access to a car/a computer etc to have a car, *etc that you can use*
legal right to see and spend time with your prisoner, an official etc: My ex-husband has children once a week.
ess (to sth) to succeed in entering a place *meone or something: The police man-ss through an upstairs window.*

access² v [T] to find information, especially on a computer: *Users can access their voice mail remotely.*
'access ,course n [C] *BrE* an educational course for adults which prepares them for study at a university or college

ac·ces·si·ble /ək'sesɪbəl/ adj **1** a place, building, or object that is accessible is easy to reach or get into; **⊠ inaccessible**: *The island is only accessible by boat.* | *There is a church which is easily accessible from my home.* **2** easy to obtain or use: [+to] *the need for an efficient health service that is accessible to all* | **easily/ readily accessible** *Computers should be made readily accessible to teachers and pupils.* **3** someone who is accessible is easy to meet and talk to, even if they are very important or powerful: *I think that you'll find she's very accessible.* **4** a book, poem, painting etc that is accessible is easy to understand and enjoy: [+to] *He wants his music to be accessible to everyone.*
—**accessibly** adv —**accessibility** /ək,sesə'bɪlɪti/ n [U]

ac·ces·sion /ək'seʃən/ n **1** [U] an official process in which someone becomes king, queen, president etc; **→ succession**: [+of] *the accession of James I* | **acces-sion to power/to the throne** (=the act of becoming king, queen, president etc) **2** [U] *formal* the act of agreeing to a demand **3** [C] *technical* an object or work of art that is added to a collection of objects or paintings

ac·ces·so·rize also **-ise** *BrE* /ək'sesəraɪz/ v [T usu-ally passive] to add accessories to clothes, a room etc

ac·ces·so·ry /ək'sesəri/ n plural **accessories** [C] **1** [usually plural] something such as a piece of equipment or a decoration that is not necessary, but that makes a machine, car, room etc more useful or more attractive: *bathroom accessories such as mirrors and towel-rails* **2** [usually plural] something such as a bag, belt, or jewellery that you wear or carry because it is attractive: *fashion accessories* | *a set of fully match-ing clothes and accessories* **3** someone who helps a criminal, especially by helping them hide from the police: [+to] *an accessory to murder* | **an accessory before/after the fact** (=someone who helps a criminal before or after the crime)

'access pro,vider n [C] a company that provides the technical services that allow people to use the Internet, usually in exchange for a monthly payment; **⊟ Inter-net Service Provider**

'access ,road n [C] a road which allows traffic to reach a particular place: *the access road to the farm*

'access ,time n [C,U] *technical* the time taken by a computer to find and use a piece of information in its memory

ac·ci·dent S1 W2 /'æksɪdənt/ n

accident

1 by accident in a way that is not planned or intended; **⊠ on purpose, deliberately**: *I met her quite by accident.* (=com-pletely by accident) | *The discovery was made almost by accident.* | *The pilot, whether by acci-dent or design* (=whether it was planned or not planned), *made the plane do a sharp turn.*
2 [C] a crash involving cars, trains, planes etc: **road/ car/traffic etc accident** *Over 70,000 people are killed or seriously injured every year in road accidents.* | **fatal/ serious/tragic etc accident** *a fatal accident on the freeway* | *The accident happened at the junction of Forest Road and Pine Walk.*
3 [C] a situation in which someone is injured or something is damaged without anyone intending them to be: *Ken had an accident at work and had to go to hospital.* | *I'm sorry about breaking the vase – it was an accident* (=I did not intend to do it).
4 [C,U] something that happens without anyone plan-

ning or intending it: *My third baby was an accident.* | *It is no accident that men fill most of the top jobs in nursing, while women remain on the lower grades.* | **an accident of birth/geography/history etc** (=an event or situation caused by chance)

5 accidents (will) happen *spoken* used to tell someone who has broken something that they should not worry that it has happened

6 an accident waiting to happen used about a situation in which an accident is likely to happen because no one is trying to prevent it: *The boats are being left to drift; it's an accident waiting to happen.*

> **WORD FOCUS: ACCIDENT**
> *similar words:* **crash, wreck** *AmE*, **pile-up, collision, disaster, catastrophe**

ac·ci·den·tal /ˌæksɪ'dentl◂/ *adj* happening without being planned or intended; ⊟ **deliberate**: *an accidental discharge of toxic waste* | *Buy an insurance policy that covers accidental damage.* —**accidentally** *adv*: *I accidentally locked myself out of the house.*

‚accidental 'death *n* [U] *law especially BrE* an expression used by a court when it has decided that someone's death was caused by an accident

‚accident and e'mergency *n* [C] *BrE* the room or department in a hospital where people go if they have an accident or suddenly become ill; ⊟ **A & E**; ⊟ **emergency room** *AmE*

'accident prone *adj* more likely to have accidents than other people

ac·claim¹ /ə'kleɪm/ *v* [T] to praise someone or something publicly: *His work was acclaimed by art critics.*

acclaim² *n* [U] praise for a person or their achievements: *The young singer is enjoying massive **critical acclaim** (=praise by people who are paid to give their opinion on art, music etc).* | **international/great/popular/public etc acclaim** *Their recordings have **won** great acclaim.*

ac·claimed /ə'kleɪmd/ *adj* publicly praised by a lot of people: **highly/widely/universally acclaimed** *The book has been widely acclaimed by teachers and pupils.* | *His work was **critically acclaimed** (=praised by people who are paid to give their opinion on art, music etc).*

ac·cla·ma·tion /ˌæklə'meɪʃən/ *n* **1** [C,U] *formal* a loud expression of approval or welcome **2** [singular, U] *formal* the act of electing someone, using a spoken rather than written vote

ac·cli·ma·tize also **-ise** *BrE* /ə'klaɪmətaɪz/ also **ac·cli·mate** /ə'klaɪmət $ 'ækləmeɪt, ə'klaɪmət/ *AmE v* [I,T] to become used to a new place, situation, or type of weather, or to make someone become used to it: [+to] *Runners had to acclimatize to the humid tropical conditions.* | **acclimatize yourself (to sth)** *I found it hard to acclimatize myself to working at weekends.* —**acclimatization** /ə,klaɪmətaɪ'zeɪʃən $ -tə-/ *n* [U]

ac·co·lade /'ækəleɪd/ *n* [C] praise for someone who is greatly admired, or a prize given to them for their work: **ultimate/highest/supreme etc accolade** *She received a Grammy Award, the highest accolade in the music business.*

ac·com·mo·date /ə'kɒmədeɪt $ ə'kɑː-/ *v* **1** [T] if a room, building etc can accommodate a particular number of people or things, it has enough space for them: *He bought a huge house to accommodate his library.* | *The ballroom can accommodate 400 people.* **2** [T] to provide someone with a place to stay, live, or work: *The island was used to accommodate child refugees.* **3** [T] to accept someone's opinions and try to do what they want, especially when their opinions or needs are different from yours: *We've made every effort to accommodate your point of view.* **4** [I] to get used to a new situation or to make yourself do this: [+to] *Her eyes took a while to accommodate to the darkness.*

ac·com·mo·dat·ing /ə'kɒmədeɪtɪŋ $ ə'kɑː-/ *adj* helpful and willing to do what someone else wants: *an accommodating child*

ac·com·mo·da·tion   S2   W2   /ə,kɒmə'deɪʃən $ ə,kɑː-/ *n*

1 [U] also **accommodations** *AmE* a place for someone to stay, live, or work: *The price for the holiday includes flights and accommodation.* | *living accommodations for the crews* | *travel and hotel accommodations* | **rented accommodation** | **secure accommodation** *for young offenders* | *Universities have to provide **student accommodation** for first-year students.*

2 [singular, U] *formal* an agreement between people or groups who have different views or opinions, that satisfies everyone: *We **reached an accommodation** between both parties.*

ac·com·pa·ni·ment /ə'kʌmpənimənt/ *n* **1** [C,U] music that is played in the background at the same time as another instrument or singer that plays or sings the main tune: **piano/orchestral/organ/guitar etc accompaniment** *He plays folk music with guitar accompaniment.* | **to the accompaniment of sth** *An elderly man puffed on a trumpet to the accompaniment of drums and piano.* **2** [C] something that is provided or used with something else: *White wine makes an excellent accompaniment to fish.* **3 to the accompaniment of sth** while something else is happening or while another sound can be heard: *They were exercising to the accompaniment of cheerful music.* **4** [C] something that happens at the same time as another thing

ac·com·pa·nist /ə'kʌmpənɪst/ *n* [C] someone who plays a musical instrument while another person sings or plays the main tune

ac·com·pa·ny   W2   /ə'kʌmpəni/ *v* **accompanied, accompanying, accompanies** [T]

1 to go somewhere with someone: *Children under 14 must be accompanied by an adult.* | *Wherever her husband went, she would accompany him.* ⚠ In spoken English, it is more usual to use **go/come with** *He came with me to the airport.*

2 to play a musical instrument while someone sings a song or plays the main tune: *Daniel wanted Liz to accompany him on violin.*

3 [usually passive] to happen or exist at the same time as something else: *The disease is accompanied by sneezing and fever.*

4 if a book, document etc accompanies something, it comes with it: *Please see accompanying booklet for instructions.* | *Your passport application form should be accompanied by two recent photographs.*

ac·com·plice /ə'kʌmplɪs $ ə'kɑːm-, ə'kʌm-/ *n* [C] a person who helps someone such as a criminal to do something wrong

ac·com·plish /ə'kʌmplɪʃ $ ə'kɑːm-, ə'kʌm-/ *v* [T] to succeed in doing something, especially after trying very hard; ⊟ **achieve**: *We have accomplished all we set out to do.* | **Mission accomplished** (=we have done what we intended to do).

ac·com·plished /ə'kʌmplɪʃt $ ə'kɑːm-, ə'kʌm-/ *adj* **1** an accomplished writer, painter, singer etc is very skilful: **highly/very accomplished** *a highly accomplished designer* **2 an accomplished fact** *BrE* something that is known to be true and cannot be doubted

ac·com·plish·ment /ə'kʌmplɪʃmənt $ ə'kɑːm-, ə'kʌm-/ *n* **1** [C] something successful or impressive that is achieved after a lot of effort and hard work; ⊟ **achievement**: **impressive/significant/great etc accomplishment** *Cutting the budget was an impressive accomplishment.* | *It was a **major accomplishment** for a player who had been injured so recently.* **2** [U] the act of finishing or achieving something good: [+of] *the accomplishment of policy goals* **3** [C,U] an ability to do something well, or the skill involved in doing something well: *Playing the piano is one of her many accomplishments.*

ac·cord¹ /ə'kɔːd $ -ɔːrd/ *n* **1 of sb's/sth's o** **accord** without being asked or forced to do someth

He decided to go of his own accord. | *The door seemed to move of its own accord.* **2** [U] *formal* a situation in which two people, ideas, or statements agree with each other: **be in accord with sth** *These results are in accord with earlier research.* | **in perfect/complete accord** *It is important to the success of any firm that its partners should be in complete accord.* **3** [C] a formal agreement between countries or groups: *the Helsinki accord on human rights* **4 with one accord** *formal* if two or more people do something with one accord, they do it together or at the same time: *There was a silence as the women turned with one accord to stare at Doreen.*

accord² v *formal* **1** [T] to give someone or something special attention or a particular type of treatment: *You will not be accorded any special treatment.* | **accord sth to sth/sb** *Every school accords high priority to the quality of teaching.* **2 accord with sth** to match or agree with something: *The punishments accorded with the current code of discipline.*

ac·cord·ance /ə'kɔːdəns $ ə'kɔːr-/ n **in accordance with sth** *formal* according to a rule, system etc: *Article 47 may only be used in accordance with international law.* | *Use this product only in accordance with the manufacturer's instructions.*

ac·cord·ing·ly /ə'kɔːdɪŋli $ ə'kɔːr-/ adv **1** in a way that is suitable for a particular situation or that is based on what someone has done or said: *Katherine still considered him a child and treated him accordingly.* **2** [sentence adverb] as a result of something; ◨ **therefore**: *Some of the laws were contradictory. Accordingly, measures were taken to clarify them.*

according to [S2] [W1] prep
1 as shown by something or stated by someone: *According to the police, his attackers beat him with a blunt instrument.* | *There is now widespread support for these proposals, according to a recent public opinion poll.* ⚠ Do not say 'according to me' or 'according to my opinion/point of view'. Say **in my opinion** *In my opinion his first book is much better.*
2 in a way that depends on differences in situations or amounts: *You will be paid according to the amount of work you do.*
3 in a way that agrees with a system or plan, or obeys a set of rules: *The game will be played according to rules laid down for the 1992 Cup.* | *Everything went according to plan, and we arrived on time.*

ac·cor·di·on /ə'kɔːdiən $ ə'kɔːr-/ also **piano accordion** *BrE* n [C] a musical instrument like a large box that you hold in both hands. You play it by pressing the sides together and pulling them out again, while you push buttons and KEYS.
—**accordionist** n [C]

accordion

ac·cost /ə'kɒst $ ə'kɔːst, ə'kɑːst/ v [T] *written* to go towards someone you do not know and speak to them in an unpleasant or threatening way: *He was accosted by four youths and forced to give them all his money.*

ac·count¹ [S2] [W1] /ə'kaʊnt/ n [C]
1 DESCRIPTION a written or spoken description that says what happens in an event or process: [+of] *He was too shocked to give an account of what had happened.* | **blow-by-blow account** (=a description of all the details of an event in the order that they happened) *a blow-by-blow account of how England lost to Portugal* | *Chomsky's account of how children learn their first language* | **eye-witness/first-hand account** (=description of events by someone who saw them) *Eye-witness*

accounts told of the unprovoked shooting of civilians. This gives a first-hand account of the war.
2 AT A BANK written abbreviation **a/c** or **acct.** an arrangement in which a bank keeps your money safe so that you can pay more in or take money out: *My salary is paid directly into my bank account.* | *I've opened an account with Barclay's Bank.* | *My husband and I have a joint account* (=one that is shared between two people). → BANK ACCOUNT, CHECKING ACCOUNT, CURRENT ACCOUNT, DEPOSIT ACCOUNT, PROFIT AND LOSS ACCOUNT, SAVINGS ACCOUNT
3 take account of sth also **take sth into account** to consider or include particular facts or details when making a decision or judgment about something: *These figures do not take account of changes in the rate of inflation.*
4 on account of sth because of something else, especially a problem or difficulty: *She was told to wear flat shoes, on account of her back problem.*
5 accounts a) [plural] an exact record of the money that a company has received and the money it has spent: *The accounts for last year showed a profit of $2 million.* **b)** [U] a department in a company that is responsible for keeping records of the amount of money spent and received: *Eileen works in accounts.*
6 on account if you buy goods on account, you take them away with you and pay for them later
7 WITH A SHOP/COMPANY an arrangement that you have with a shop or company, which allows you to buy goods or use a service now and pay for them later; ◨ **credit account**: *Can you charge this to my account please?* | *an unlimited-use Internet account*
8 BILL a statement that shows how much money you owe for things you have bought from a shop; ◨ **bill**: **pay/settle your account** (=pay what you owe) *James left the restaurant, settling his account by credit card.*
9 ARRANGEMENT TO SELL GOODS an arrangement to sell goods and services to another company over a period of time: *Our sales manager has secured several big accounts recently.*
10 by/from all accounts according to what a lot of people say: *It has, from all accounts, been a successful marriage.*
11 on sb's account if you do something on someone's account, you do it because you think they want you to: *Please don't change your plans on my account.*
12 on your own account by yourself or for yourself: *Carrie decided to do a little research on her own account.*
13 on no account/not on any account used when saying that someone must not, for any reason, do something: *On no account must you disturb me when I'm working.*
14 by sb's own account according to what you have said, especially when you have admitted doing something wrong: *Bentley was, by his own account, oversensitive to criticism.*
15 on that account/on this account concerning a particular situation: *There needn't be any more worries on that account.*
16 give a good/poor account of yourself to do something or perform very well or very badly: *Kevin gave a good account of himself in today's game.*
17 bring/call sb to account *formal* to force someone who is responsible for a mistake or a crime to explain publicly why they did it and punish them for it if necessary: *The people responsible for the accident have never been brought to account.*
18 put/turn sth to good account *formal* to use something for a good purpose: *Perhaps she could put some of her talents to good account by helping us.*
19 of no/little account *formal* not important: *As she grew up, her father was of no account to her.*

account² [W2] v
account for sth *phr v*
1 to form a particular amount or part of something: *Afro-Americans account for 12% of the US population.*
2 to be the reason why something happens; ◨ **explain**: *Recent pressure at work may account for his behavior.*

3 to give a satisfactory explanation of why something has happened or why you did something; ⊟ **explain**: *Can you account for your movements on that night?*
4 to say where all the members of a group of people or things are, especially because you are worried that some of them may be lost: *Three days after the earthquake, more than 150 people had still to be accounted for.*

ac·count·a·ble /əˈkaʊntəbəl/ *adj* [not before noun] responsible for the effects of your actions and willing to explain or be criticized for them: [+to] *The government should be accountable to all the people of the country.* | [+for] *Managers must be accountable for their decisions.* | *The hospital should be **held accountable** for the quality of care it gives.* —**accountability** /əˌkaʊntəˈbɪləti/ *n* [U]

ac·coun·tan·cy /əˈkaʊntənsi/ *n* [U] *BrE* the profession or work of keeping or checking financial accounts, calculating taxes etc

ac·coun·tant [S3] /əˈkaʊntənt/ *n* [C] someone whose job is to keep and check financial accounts, calculate taxes etc

ac·coun·ting /əˈkaʊntɪŋ/ *n* [U] accountancy

ac·cou·tre·ments /əˈkuːtrəmənts/ also **ac·cou·ter·ments** /əˈkuːtəmənts $ -tər-/ *AmE n* [plural] *formal* the equipment needed for a particular activity or way of life: *the stylish accoutrements of an English country gentleman*

ac·cred·it·ed /əˈkredɪtɪd/ *adj* **1** having official approval to do something, especially because of having reached an acceptable standard: *an accredited counsellor* | *an accredited language school* **2** if a government official is accredited to another country, they are sent to that country to officially represent their government there: *the UK accredited representative* —**accredit** *v* [T] —**accreditation** /əˌkredɪˈteɪʃən/ *n* [U]

ac·cre·tion /əˈkriːʃən/ *n* [C,U] *formal* **1** a layer of a substance which slowly forms on something **2** a gradual process by which new things are added and something gradually changes or gets bigger

ac·crue /əˈkruː/ *v* [I,T] **1** if advantages accrue to you, you get those advantages over a period of time: [+to] *benefits that accrue to students* | [+from] *advantages accruing from the introduction of new technology* **2** if money accrues or is accrued, it gradually increases over a period of time: *Interest will accrue until payment is made.* —**accrual** *n* [C usually singular]

acct. the written abbreviation of *account*

ac·cu·mu·late /əˈkjuːmjʊleɪt/ *v* **1** [T] to gradually get more and more money, possessions, knowledge etc over a period of time: *It is unjust that a privileged few should continue to accumulate wealth.* **2** [I] to gradually increase in numbers or amount until there is a large quantity in one place: *Fat tends to accumulate around the hips and thighs.* —**accumulation** /əˌkjuːmjʊˈleɪʃən/ *n* [C,U]: *the accumulation of data*

ac·cu·mu·la·tive /əˈkjuːmjʊlətɪv $ -leɪ-, -lə-/ *adj* gradually increasing in amount or degree over a period of time; ⊟ **cumulative** —**accumulatively** *adv*

ac·cu·mu·la·tor /əˈkjuːmjʊleɪtə $ -ər/ *n* [C] **1** *technical* a part of a computer that stores numbers **2** *especially BrE* a kind of BETTING on the results of a series of horse races, by which any money you win from a race is bet on the next race

ac·cu·ra·cy /ˈækjʊrəsi/ *n* [U] **1** the ability to do something in an exact way without making a mistake: *He passes the ball with unerring accuracy.* **2** the quality of being correct or true; ⊟ **inaccuracy**: [+of] *worries about the accuracy of government statistics*

ac·cu·rate [S2] [W3] /ˈækjʊrət/ *adj* **1** INFORMATION correct and true in every detail; ⊟ **inaccurate**: *The brochure tries to give a fair and accurate description of each hotel.* | *fairly/reasonably accurate Police believe Derek gave a reasonably accurate account of what happened.* | *not strictly/entirely/completely accurate The evidence she gave to the court*

was not strictly accurate (=not exactly accurate).
2 MEASUREMENT measured or calculated correctly; ⊟ **inaccurate**: *It is difficult to get accurate figures on population numbers.*
3 MACHINE a machine that is accurate is able to do something in an exact way without making a mistake: *The cutter is accurate to within ½ a millimetre.*
4 WELL-AIMED an accurate shot, throw etc succeeds in hitting or reaching the thing that it is intended to hit: *an accurate shot* | *accurate bowling* —**accurately** *adv*: *It's impossible to predict the weather accurately.*

ac·curs·ed /əˈkɜːsɪd, əˈkɜːst $ -ɜːr-/ *adj* **1** [only before noun] *formal* used to show that something makes you very angry **2** *old use* someone who is accursed has had a CURSE put on them

ac·cu·sa·tion /ˌækjʊˈzeɪʃən/ *n* [C] a statement saying that someone is guilty of a crime or of doing something wrong

make an accusation (against sb)
bring/level an accusation (against sb) (=make an accusation)
face an accusation (=have an accusation made against you)
deny an accusation
serious accusation
false accusation
wild accusations
amid accusations of/that (=when people are making accusations)

[+**against**] *A number of **serious accusations** have been **made** against her.* | *The main **accusation levelled against** him was that he tried to avoid military service.* | [+of] *His administration now **faces accusations** of corruption.* | + **that** *The organizers of the march strongly **denied** government **accusations** that they intended to cause trouble.* | *Burton's enemies had made **false accusations** against him.* | *She's made all sorts of **wild accusations** against me in the past.* | *They fled the country, **amid accusations of** corruption.*

ac·cu·sa·tive /əˈkjuːzətɪv/ *n* [C] *technical* a form of a noun in languages such as Latin or German, which shows that the noun is the DIRECT OBJECT of a verb or a PREPOSITION —**accusative** *adj*

ac·cu·sa·to·ry /əˈkjuːzətəri $ -tɔːri/ *adj* an accusatory remark or look from someone shows that they think you have done something wrong

ac·cuse [W3] /əˈkjuːz/ *v* [T] to say that you believe someone is guilty of a crime or of doing something bad: *accuse sb of (doing) sth He was accused of murder.* | *Smith accused her of lying.* | *The professor stands accused of* (=has been accused of) *stealing his student's ideas and publishing them.* —**accuser** *n* [C]

ac·cused /əˈkjuːzd/ *n* **the accused** [singular or plural] the person or group of people who have been officially accused of a crime or offence in a court of law

ac·cus·ing /əˈkjuːzɪŋ/ *adj* an accusing look from someone shows that they think that you have done something wrong —**accusingly** *adv*

ac·cus·tom /əˈkʌstəm/ *v* [T] to make yourself o another person become used to a situation or pla **accustom yourself to sth** *It took a while for m accustom myself to all the new rules and regulat'*

ac·cus·tomed /əˈkʌstəmd/ *adj* **1 be accu to (doing) sth** to be familiar with something a it as normal: *We were accustomed to workin become accustomed to sth Her became accustomed to the dark.* ⚠ In spo more usual to say **be/get used to (doin get used to the hot climate.* **2** [only b usual: *The pans were in their accus*

AC/DC /ˌeɪ siː ˈdiː siː/ *adj informal* both men and women

ace¹ /eɪs/ *n* [C]
1 PLAYING CARD a playing

A

it, which usually has the highest value in a game: *the ace of hearts* | *I've got a pair of aces.*
2 SKILFUL PERSON someone who is extremely skilful at doing something: *a soccer ace* | *cycling ace Chris Boardman*
3 TENNIS SHOT a first shot in tennis or VOLLEYBALL which is hit so well that your opponent cannot reach the ball and you win the point: *She has already hit 13 aces in the match.*
4 hold the aces to have the advantages in a situation so that you are sure to win: *The Americans hold most of the aces in this technology.*
5 within an ace of (doing) sth very close to doing or achieving something: *The team came within an ace of winning the championship.*
6 have an ace up your sleeve to have a secret advantage which could help you to win or be successful
7 ace in the hole *AmE informal* something that you keep secretly to use when you need it: *That fifty dollars is my ace in the hole.*

ace² *adj* **1** ace pilot/player/skier etc someone who is a very skilful pilot, player etc: *an ace marksman* **2** *BrE spoken* very good: *The party was ace.*

ace³ *v* [T] **1** *AmE informal* to do very well in an examination, a piece of written work etc: *I think I aced the History test.* **2** to hit your first shot in tennis or VOLLEYBALL so well that your opponent cannot reach the ball

a·cer·bic /əˈsɜːbɪk $ -ɜːr-/ *adj* criticizing someone or something in a clever but cruel way: *acerbic wit* —**acerbity** *n* [U]

ac·e·tate /ˈæsɪ̩teɪt/ *n* **1** [U] a chemical made from acetic acid **2** [U] a smooth artificial cloth used to make clothes **3** [C] a transparent sheet that you write or print something on, and that is used with an OVERHEAD PROJECTOR

a·ce·tic ac·id /əˌsiːtɪk ˈæsɪ̩d/ *n* [U] the acid in VINEGAR

ac·e·tone /ˈæsɪ̩təʊn $ -toʊn/ *n* [U] a clear liquid with a strong smell, used for cleaning surfaces, making paint more liquid, or for making other chemical substances

a·cet·y·lene /əˈsetɪ̩liːn $ -tl-ən, -iːn/ *n* [U] a gas which burns with a bright flame and is used in equipment for cutting and joining pieces of metal; → oxyacetylene

ache¹ /eɪk/ *v* [I] **1** if part of your body aches, you feel a continuous, but not very sharp pain there; ▤ hurt: *His feet were aching from standing so long.* **2** to want to do or have something very much: [+for] *I'm aching for sleep.* | **ache to do sth** *He ached to reach out and hold her close.* **3** to have a strong unhappy feeling: [+with] *Sarah ached with sadness that her brother was so ill.* | *Tim's heart was aching for her.*

ache² *n* [C] **1** a continuous pain that is not sharp or very strong: *a stomach ache* | *A dull ache throbbed at the back of David's head.* | **aches and pains** (=slight feelings of pain that are not considered to be serious) *Apart from the usual aches and pains, she felt all right.* **2** a strong, mostly unhappy, feeling: *the ache of his loneliness* —**achy** *adj*: *I'm feeling tired and achy.*

·chieve S1 W1 /əˈtʃiːv/ *v*
T] to successfully complete something or get a good
't, especially by working hard: *Frances achieved
ʼood exam results.* | *Wilson has achieved consider-
ʼess as an artist.* | *She eventually achieved her
ʼecoming a professor.*
successful in a particular kind of job or
want all our students to achieve within
ʼrofession.*

·t S3 W2 /əˈtʃiːvmənt/ *n*
ʼmportant that you succeed in doing
· [+of] *We try to celebrate the achieve-
ʼts.* | *His great achievement is to
ʼto a united team.* | **sb's achieve-
ʼt measures children's achieve-

ments in reading, spelling and maths.
2 [U] when you achieve something or when people achieve something: *Roberts is researching the effect of social class on educational achievement.* | *As we climbed the final few metres, we felt a sense of achievement.*

a·chiev·er /əˈtʃiːvə $ -ər/ *n* [C] someone who is successful because they are determined and work hard; → underachiever, overachiever

A·chil·les' heel /əˌkɪliːz ˈhiːl/ *n* [C] a weak part of someone's character, which could cause them to fail at something: *I think Frank's vanity is his Achilles' heel.*

Achilles ten·don /əˌkɪliːz ˈtendən/ *n* [C] the part of your body that connects the muscles in the back of your foot with the muscles of your lower leg

a·choo /əˈtʃuː/ *n* [C] used to represent the sound you make when you SNEEZE

ac·id¹ W2 /ˈæsɪ̩d/ *n*
1 [C,U] a chemical substance that has a PH of less than 7. Strong acids can burn holes in material or damage your skin: *sulphuric acid*
2 [U] *informal* the drug LSD

acid² *adj* **1** having a sharp sour taste; ▤ bitter: *a juicy apple with a slightly acid flavour* **2** acid remark/comment/tone etc an acid remark uses humour in an unkind way to criticize someone: *I was expecting another of his acid remarks, but he remained silent.* **3** the acid test a way of finding out whether something is as good as people say it is, whether it works, or whether it is true: *People ask if the team is good enough. This match will be the acid test.* **4** *technical* an acid soil does not contain much LIME¹ (3): *Blueberry bushes need a very acid soil.* —**acidly** *adv* —**acidity** /əˈsɪdɪ̩ti/ *n* [U]

'acid house *n* [U] a kind of dance music that is played loudly using electronic instruments

a·cid·ic /əˈsɪdɪk/ *adj* **1** very sour: *Some fruit juices taste a bit acidic.* **2** containing acid

a·cid·i·fy /əˈsɪdɪ̩faɪ/ *v* acidified, acidifying, acidifies [I,T] *technical* to become an acid or make something become an acid

'acid jazz *n* [U] a type of popular music that combines features of many other kinds of music, especially JAZZ, HIP-HOP, and SOUL

ac·id·ly /ˈæsɪ̩dli/ *adv* if you say something acidly, you say it in a cruel or unkind way: *'I'm sure you're right,' he said acidly.*

,acid 'rain *n* [U] rain that contains harmful acid which can damage the environment and is caused by chemicals in the air, for example from cars or factories → see picture at ENVIRONMENT

ac·knowl·edge S3 W3 /əkˈnɒlɪdʒ $ -ˈnɑː-/ *v* [T]
1 ADMIT to admit or accept that something is true or that a situation exists: *The family acknowledge the need for change.* | **acknowledge that** *He acknowledges that when he's tired he gets bad-tempered.* | *Claire acknowledged that she was guilty.* | *The government must acknowledge what is happening and do something about it.* | *'Maybe you are right,' she acknowledged.* | *This is a fact that most smokers readily acknowledge.*
2 RECOGNIZE STH'S IMPORTANCE [usually passive] if people acknowledge something, they recognize how good or important it is: **acknowledge sth as sth** *The film festival is acknowledged as an event of international importance.* | **be widely/generally acknowledged to be sth** *The mill produces what is widely acknowledged to be the finest wool in the world.*
3 ACCEPT SB'S AUTHORITY to accept that someone or something has authority over people: *Both defendants refused to acknowledge the authority of the court.* | **acknowledge sb as sth** *Many of the poor acknowledged him as their spiritual leader.*
4 THANK to publicly announce that you are grateful for the help that someone has given you: *We wish to acknowledge the support of the university.*
5 SHOW YOU NOTICE SB to show someone that you have noticed them or heard what they have said: *Tom acknowledged her presence by a brief glance.*

SAY YOU HAVE RECEIVED STH to let someone know that you have received something from them: *I would be grateful if you would acknowledge receipt of this letter.*

ac·knowl·edge·ment, **acknowledgment** /ək'nɒlɪdʒmənt $ -'nɑː-/ n **1** [C,U] the act of admitting or accepting that something is true: [+of] *We want an acknowledgement of the existence of the problem.* | **acknowledgement that** *The reduction in their grant is an acknowledgement that they have been paid too much.* **2** [singular] a movement of your body that shows that you have noticed someone or heard what they have said: *Basil nodded an acknowledgement as he entered the room.* | *He gave her a faint smile of acknowledgement.* **3** [C,U] the act of publicly thanking someone for something they have done: **in acknowledgement of sth** *She received a special award in acknowledgement of all her hard work.* **4** [C,U] a letter written to tell someone that you have received their letter, message etc: *Do you want a written acknowledgement?* **5** **acknowledgements** [plural] a short piece of writing at the beginning or end of a book in which the writer thanks all the people who have helped him or her

ac·me /'ækmi/ n **the acme of sth** *formal* the best and highest level of something: *the acme of perfection*

ac·ne /'ækni/ n [U] a medical problem which causes a lot of red spots on your face and neck and mainly affects young people

ac·o·lyte /'ækəlaɪt/ n [C] **1** *formal* someone who serves a leader or believes in their ideas **2** someone who helps a priest at a religious ceremony

a·corn /'eɪkɔːn $ -ɔːrn, -ərn/ n [C] the nut of the OAK tree

a·cous·tic /ə'kuːstɪk/ adj **1** relating to sound and the way people hear things **2** an acoustic GUI-TAR or other musical instrument does not have its sound made louder electronically; → **electric** —**acoustically** /-kli/ adv

acoustic guitar

acoustic guitar

electric guitar

a·cous·tics /ə'kuːstɪks/ n [plural] **1** the shape and size of a room, which affect the way sound is heard in it: *The hall has excellent acoustics.* **2** the scientific study of sound

ac·quaint /ə'kweɪnt/ v [T] **1** **acquaint yourself with sth** *formal* to deliberately find out about something: *I need to acquaint myself with the new regulations.* **2** **acquaint sb with sth** *formal* to give someone information about something: *You need to acquaint the police with the facts.*

ac·quaint·ance /ə'kweɪntəns/ n **1** SB YOU KNOW [C] someone you know, but who is not a close friend: *She was a casual acquaintance of my family in Vienna.* | *He heard about the job through a mutual acquaintance* (=someone you and another person both know). **2** RELATIONSHIP [singular, U] a relationship with someone you know, but who is not a close friend: *They developed an acquaintance over the Internet.* | *You can't judge her on such short acquaintance* (=when you have not known her long). | *My uncle did not improve on further acquaintance* (=when you knew him better). **3** **make sb's acquaintance** *formal* to meet someone for the first time: *I should be delighted to make Mrs McGough's acquaintance.* | *At the hotel, I made the acquaintance of a young American actor.* **4** KNOWLEDGE [U] *formal* knowledge or experience of a particular subject: [+with] *The practice of a lawyer requires acquaintance with court procedures.* | **have a passing/nodding acquaintance with sth** (=have only

slight knowledge or experience of something) *He has a passing acquaintance with a lot of different subjects.* **5** **of your acquaintance** *formal* a person of your acquaintance is someone that you know: *The poems were written by various women of her acquaintance.* **6** **on first acquaintance** *formal* when you meet someone for the first time: *Most people are nicer than you think on first acquaintance.*

ac·quaintance ,rape n [C,U] a crime in which a person forces someone they know to have sex with them; ☐ **date rape**

ac·quaint·ance·ship /ə'kweɪntənsʃɪp/ n [U] **1** your experience or knowledge of a subject **2** a slight friendship with someone: *Sheridan had struck up an acquaintanceship with Giles* (=had met him and became friendly with him).

ac·quaint·ed /ə'kweɪntᵻd/ adj [not before noun] **1** if you are acquainted with someone, you have met them a few times but do not know them very well: [+with] *Were you acquainted with a friend of mine, Daniel Green?* | *We would like to get better acquainted.* **2** *formal* **be acquainted with sth** to know about something, because you have seen it, read it, used it etc: *She was well acquainted with classical literature.*

ac·qui·esce /,ækwi'es/ v [I] *formal* to do what someone else wants, or allow something to happen, even though you do not really agree with it: [+in/to] *Oil companies have been accused of acquiescing in the pollution of the ocean.*

ac·qui·es·cent /,ækwi'esənt◂/ adj too ready to agree with someone or do what they want, without complaining or saying what you want to do —**acquiescence** n [U]

ac·quire W2 /ə'kwaɪə $ ə'kwaɪr/ v [T] **1** *formal* to obtain something by buying it or being given it: *Manning hoped to acquire valuable works of art as cheaply as possible.* | *She has acquired an email address and a site on the WorldWide Web.* **2** to get or gain something: *The college acquired a reputation for very high standards.* **3** to gain knowledge or learn a skill: *He spent years acquiring his skills as a surgeon.* | *Elsie acquired a good knowledge of Chinese.* **4** **acquire a taste for sth** to begin to like something: *She had acquired a taste for European beer.* **5** **an acquired taste** something that people only begin to like after they have tried it a few times

ac·qui·si·tion W3 /,ækwᵻ'zɪʃən/ n **1** [U] the process by which you gain knowledge or learn a skill: *the acquisition of language* **2** [U] the act of getting land, power, money etc: [+of] *the acquisition of new sites for development* **3** [C] *formal* something that you have obtained by buying it or being given it: *The Art Society is holding an exhibition of recent acquisitions.*

ac·quis·i·tive /ə'kwɪzᵻtɪv/ adj wanting to have and keep a lot of possessions —**acquisitiveness** n [U]

ac·quit /ə'kwɪt/ v **acquitted, acquitting 1** [T usually passive] to give a decision in a court of law that someone is not guilty of a crime: *All the defendants were acquitted.* | **acquit sb of sth** *The judge directed the jury to acquit Phillips of the murder.* **2** **acquit yourself well/honourably** to do something well, especially something difficult that you do for the first time in front of other people

ac·quit·tal /ə'kwɪtl/ n [C,U] an official statement in a court of law that someone is not guilty

a·cre /'eɪkə $ -ər/ n [C] **1** a unit for measuring area, equal to 4840 square yards or 4047 square metres: *They own 200 acres of farmland.* | *a 200-acre wood* **2 acres of space/room** *BrE informal* a large amount of space

a·cre·age /'eɪkərɪdʒ/ n [U] the area of a piece of land measured in acres .

ac·rid /ˈækrɪ̯d/ adj **1** an acrid smell or taste is strong and unpleasant and stings your nose or throat: *a cloud of acrid smoke* **2** formal an acrid remark expresses anger and criticizes someone strongly

ac·ri·mo·ni·ous /ˌækrɪ̯ˈməʊniəs◂ $ -ˈmoʊ-/ adj an acrimonious meeting or discussion is one in which people argue a lot and get very angry: *The meeting ended in an acrimonious dispute.* —**acrimoniously** adv —**acrimoniousness** n [U]

ac·ri·mo·ny /ˈækrɪ̯məni $ -moʊni/ n [U] formal feelings of anger between people who disagree strongly and do not like each other

ac·ro·bat /ˈækrəbæt/ n [C] someone who entertains people by doing difficult physical actions such as walking on their hands or balancing on a high rope, especially at a CIRCUS

ac·ro·bat·ic /ˌækrəˈbætɪk◂/ adj acrobatic movements involve moving your body in a very skilful way, for example by jumping through the air or balancing on a rope: *They performed some amazing acrobatic feats.* —**acrobatically** /-kli/ adv

ac·ro·bat·ics /ˌækrəˈbætɪks/ n [plural] skilful movements of your body, for example jumping through the air or balancing on a rope

ac·ro·nym /ˈækrənɪm/ n [C] a word made up from the first letters of the name of something such as an organization. For example NATO is an acronym for the North Atlantic Treaty Organization.

a·cross S1 W1 /əˈkrɒs $ əˈkrɔːs/ adv, prep
1 from one side of something to the other: *the first flight across the Atlantic* | *They ran straight across the road* (=without stopping). | *There isn't a bridge. We'll have to swim across.* | *We'd got halfway across before Philip realized he'd left his money at home.* | *We gazed across the valley.*
2 towards someone or something on the other side of an area: *There's Brendan. Why don't you go across and say hello?* | [+to/at] *The referee looked across at his linesman before awarding the penalty.* | *He walked across to where I was sitting.*
3 used to say that something exists or reaches from one side of an area to the other: *a deep crack across the ceiling* | *the only bridge across the river* | *Do you think this shirt is too tight across the shoulders?* | *Someone's parked right across the entrance to the driveway.*
4 on the opposite side of something: *My best friend lives across the road.* | *He knew that just across the border lay freedom.* | **across (sth) from sb/sth** *Across the street from where we're standing, you can see the old churchyard.* | *the woman sitting across from me* (=opposite me) *on the train*
5 in every part of a country, organization etc: *a TV series that became popular across five continents* | *Teachers are expected to teach a range of subjects right across the curriculum.*
6 used to show how wide something is: **10 feet/five metres etc across** *At its widest point the river is 2 km across.*

a·cross-the-board also **across the board** adj, adv affecting everyone or everything in a situation or organization: *an across-the-board pay increase* | *In July everything we sell is reduced right across the board.*

a·cros·tic /əˈkrɒstɪk $ əˈkrɔː-/ n [C] a poem or piece of writing in which the first or last letter of each line spells a word

a·cryl·ic /əˈkrɪlɪk/ adj acrylic paints or cloth are made from chemical substances, not natural substances

a·cryl·ics /əˈkrɪlɪks/ n [plural] acrylic paints

act¹ S1 W1 /ækt/ n
1 ACTION [C] one thing that you do: *The new president's first act should be to end the war.* | *a thoughtless act* | **act of (doing) sth** *an act of violence* | *Her many acts of kindness have given me great comfort.* | *The act of writing a list can help to calm you down.* | **in the act of doing sth** (=at the moment that you are doing some-

thing) *Lindsay paused in the act of putting down t... phone.*
2 LAW also **Act** [C] a law that has been officially accepted by Parliament or Congress: *the Housing and Community Development Act of 1977* | *an act of Parliament*
3 PRETENDING [singular] insincere behaviour in which you pretend to have a particular kind of feeling or to be a particular kind of person: *Mike played the loving husband in front of the children but it was all an act.* | *Be natural. Don't feel you have to put on an act.*
4 get your act together informal to become more organized and behave in a more effective way, especially in order to achieve something: *You need to get your act together if you're going to find the right house to buy.*
5 PLAY [C] one of the main parts into which a stage play, OPERA etc is divided: *I arrived at the theatre late and missed the first act.* | *the beginning of Act 3*
6 PERFORMANCE [C] a short performance on stage or television by someone who plays music or tells jokes: *The argument was just part of their act.*
7 PERFORMER [C] a performer or a group of performers who perform together: *The band is one of many acts that have been booked for the concert.*
8 a hard/tough etc act to follow someone who does such an excellent job that it would be difficult for someone doing the same job after them to be as good: *He has been a very successful captain and will be a hard act to follow.*
9 get in on the act informal to take part in an activity that someone else has started, especially in order to get a share of the advantages for yourself
10 act of God an event that is caused by natural forces, such as a storm, flood, or fire, which you cannot prevent or control
11 act of worship an occasion when people pray together and show their respect for God
12 balancing/juggling act a situation in which you are trying to do several different types of work at the same time → **catch sb in the act** at CATCH¹ (3); → **clean up your act** at CLEAN UP (3)

act² S2 W1 v
1 DO SOMETHING [I] to do something in a particular way or for a particular reason: *The company acted correctly in sacking him.* | *The jury decided that Walker had acted in self-defence.* | **act to do sth** *The UN must act now to restore democracy.* | *Politicians will only act when enough people demand that they do something.*
2 BEHAVE [I always + adv/prep] to behave in a particular way: *They acted unreasonably when they turned down Jill's application.* | *He's been acting strangely ever since his Mom died.* | [+as if] *Pip acted as if he was better than everyone else.* | [+like] *Stop acting like a baby.* | [+with] *She acted with dignity.* | **act your age** (=used to tell someone to behave in a more adult way, suitable for someone of their age)
3 PRETEND [I,T] to pretend to have feelings, qualities etc that are different from your true ones: *When he's angry, he acts the fool.* | *That guy is acting crazy.* | **a part/role** *Stella felt unnatural in their company, as if she was acting a part.* | [+as if/like] *Why does he act as if he was stupid?*
4 PLAY/FILM [I,T] to perform in a play or film: *I first started acting when I was 12 years old.* | **act a part/role** *She is acting the role of Lady Macbeth six evenings a week.* | *The movie is very well acted.*
5 HAVE AN EFFECT [I] to have an effect or use: [+as] *The padding acts as a cushion if the player falls or is hit by the ball.* | [+on] *Disinfectants act on bacteria in two main ways.*
6 act for sb/act on sb's behalf to represent someone, especially in a court of law or by doing business for them: *Makin, a solicitor, is acting for the young people in their case against the county council.* | *I am acting on behalf of the bank.* → ACTING¹
  act as sth phr v
to do a particular job for a short time, for example while the usual person is absent: *My brother speaks French – he can act as interpreter.*

act on/upon sth *phr v*
to do something because of another person's advice or
order, or because you have received information or had
an idea: *She is **acting on** the **advice** of her lawyers.* |
*Police say they **acted on** information received.*

act sth ⇔ **out** *phr v*
1 if a group of people act out an event, they show how
it happened by pretending to be the people who were
involved in it: *The children were acting out the story of
the birth of Jesus.*
2 to express your feelings about something through
your behaviour or actions, especially when you have
been feeling angry or nervous: *These teenagers are
likely to act out their distress by running away.*

act up *phr v*
1 if children act up, they behave badly: *He's a tough kid
and he acts up a lot.*
2 if a machine or part of your body acts up, it does not
work properly: *The computer is acting up again.*

act·ing¹ /'æktɪŋ/ *adj* **acting manager/head teacher/
director etc** someone who does an important job while
the usual person is not there, or until a new person is
chosen for the job

acting² *n* [U] the job or skill of performing in plays
and films

ac·tion¹ S1 W1 /'ækʃən/ *n*
1 DOING STH [U] the process of doing something,
especially in order to achieve a particular thing

> **take action** (=do something to deal with a problem)
> **course/plan of action** (=something that you plan to do
>   in order to achieve something)
> **tough/firm/decisive action**
> **drastic action** (=action that has a very severe effect)
> **demand/call for action**
> **put your ideas/plans etc into action** (=do what you had
>   planned to do)
> **spring/swing into action** (=start doing something
>   immediately)
> **military action** (=a military attack)
> **industrial action** (=a strike or other protest at work)
> **no further action is needed/required/called for** (=it is
>   not necessary to do anything else)

> *The government must **take action** now to stop the rise
> in violent crime.* | *What do you think is our best **course
> of action**?* | *They met to discuss a **plan of action**.* |
> [+on] *Environmental groups want **tougher action** on
> pollution from cars.* | ***Firm action** is needed to keep the
> situation from getting out of control.* | *Business leaders
> **demanded** immediate and **decisive action** to end the
> dispute.* | *The situation called for **drastic action**.* | *She
> was looking forward to **putting** her ideas **into action**.* |
> *Ambulance crews are ready to **spring into action** if
> anything goes wrong during the race.* | *The United
> States threatened **military action** against Iraq.* |
> *Teachers have voted in favour of **industrial action**.* |
> *The doctor says that if the results are negative, **no
> further action is required**.*

2 STH DONE [C] something that someone does: **quick/
swift/prompt action** *Her **prompt actions** probably
saved my life.* | *The child could not be **held responsible
for** his actions* (=he was too young to be blamed for
them). | **defend/justify your action(s)** *The chief of police
tried to justify his actions.*
3 in action someone or something that is in action is
doing the job or activity that they are trained or designed to
do: *photos of ski jumpers in action* | **see/watch sth/sb in
action** *I'd like see the new computer system in action.*
4 out of action a) broken and not working: *The photocopier **is out of action** again.* **b)** injured and unable to
do anything: **put/keep sth out of action** *The injury will
keep him out of action for a month.*
5 FIGHTING [U] fighting during a war: *There have been
reports of widespread enemy action in the area.* |
killed/wounded in action (=killed or wounded while
fighting) *His father was killed in action in Vietnam.* |
*530 servicemen were reported **missing in action** (=they
had disappeared).* | *The men were **sent into action** with*

little or no training. | *He had **seen action** (=been
involved in fighting) in Korea.*
6 LEGAL [C,U] a legal or formal process to decide
whether someone has done something wrong: *They are
threatening to **take legal action** against the hospital*
(=start a court case against them). | *The director faces
disciplinary action (=official action to punish him).* |
*The matter is now the subject of a **court action** (=a court
case).* | *The students agreed to **drop** their **action**
(=decide not to continue with a court case or an official
complaint).* | *The sisters **brought a libel action** against
the newspaper* (=started a court case).
7 EXCITEMENT [U] exciting things that are
happening: *There hasn't been much action around here
for months.* | *New York is **where all the action is**.* **b)** an
action film has a lot of exciting scenes in it, in which
people fight, chase, and kill each other: *Gibson became
famous in action movies, but he has also played some
more serious roles.* | *a TV action hero*
8 THE EVENTS IN A STORY/FILM ETC the action the
events in a story, film, play etc: *Most of the action takes
place in San Francisco.* | *The action opens* (=starts) *in
a barber shop.*
9 MOVEMENT [C,U] the way something moves or
works: [+of] *the action of the heart* | *a smooth braking
action*
10 EFFECT [U] the effect that a substance, especially a
chemical, has on something: [+of] *The drug blocks the
action of the cancer gene.* | [+on/upon] *the action of
alcohol on the liver*
11 action group/committee etc a group formed to
change a social or political situation – often used in
names: *the Child Poverty Action Group*
12 a piece/slice of the action *informal* an opportunity to
be involved in an event or activity, especially one that
will be enjoyable or will make money: *If you want a
slice of the action, tickets may still be available.*
13 actions speak louder than words used to say that
you are judged by what you do, and not by what you say
14 action! used by film DIRECTORS to give the instruction
to begin filming: *Lights, camera, action!* ➔ AFFIRMATIVE
ACTION

action² *v* [T] *formal* to do a specific thing that needs to
be done, especially after discussing it: *How are we
actually going to action these objectives?*

ac·tion·a·ble /'ækʃənəbəl/ *adj law* if something you
say or do is actionable, it is so bad or damaging that a
claim could be made against you in a court of law: *His
remarks are actionable in my view.*

action-'packed *adj* an action-packed film, book etc
contains a lot of exciting events

'action point *n* [C] something that must be done, as a
result of a meeting

action 'replay *n* [C] *BrE* **1** an important or exciting
moment in a sports game that is shown again on
television immediately after it happens, sometimes at a
slower speed; ▤ **instant replay** *AmE* **2** [usually singu-
lar] an event in your life that is very similar to one that
you have experienced before: [+of] *an action replay of
the week we spent in Jamaica*

'action ,stations *noun* [plural] *BrE* the positions that
people such as soldiers or the police take when they are
getting ready to fight or deal with a difficult situation –
often used to tell people to go to these positions: *Crew,
return to action stations!*

ac·tiv·ate /'æktɪveɪt/ *v* [T] *technical* to make an electrical system or chemical process start working;
▤ **deactivate**: *Cooking fumes may activate the alarm.* |
The yeast's growth is activated by sugar and warmth.
—**activation** /,æktɪ'veɪʃən/ *n* [U]

ac·tive¹ S2 W2 /'æktɪv/ *adj*
1 BUSY always busy doing things, especially physical
activities; ▤ **inactive**: *games for active youngsters* |
She's over 80, but is still very active. | **active life/lifestyle**
My father always led a very active life. | **active mind/**

imagination *a child with a very active imagination*
2 INVOLVED involved in an organization or activity and doing lots of practical things to achieve your aims: *He became politically active at college.* | **be active in (doing) sth** *The Bureau is active in promoting overseas investment.* | **take/play an active part/role in sth** *Encourage students to take an active part in discussions.* | *She took an active interest in local charities.* | **active participation/involvement** *the importance of active participation by elderly people in the life of the community* | *We're taking active steps* (=doing practical things) *to deal with the problem.* | *We maintain active links with other European universities.* | **active member/supporter**
3 FUNCTIONING operating in a way that is normal or expected; ◆ **inactive**: *The virus is active even at low temperatures.*
4 DOING STH doing something regularly: *sexually active teenagers*
5 VOLCANO an active VOLCANO is likely to explode at any time: *The volcano became active last year with a series of eruptions.*
6 GRAMMAR an active verb or sentence has the person or thing doing the action as its SUBJECT. In 'The boy kicked the ball', the verb 'kick' is active → **PASSIVE**[1] (2)
7 CHEMICAL producing a chemical reaction: *nicotine, the active ingredient in tobacco* —**actively** *adv: Carol was actively involved in the local sports club.*

active[2] *n* **the active** the active form of a verb, for example 'destroyed' in the sentence 'Enemy planes destroyed the village.' → **PASSIVE**[2]

active 'service also **active 'duty** *n* [U] the work that soldiers do in a war: *Powell was declared unfit for active service.* | **on active service/duty** *More than 20,000 women are on active duty.*

ac·tiv·ist S3 /'æktɪvɪst/ *n* [C] someone who works hard doing practical things to achieve social or political change: **political/gay/animal rights etc activist** —**activist** *adj* [only before noun]: *activist groups*

ac·tiv·i·ty S1 W1 /æk'tɪvɪti/ *n plural* **activities**
1 [C usually plural] something that you do because you enjoy it: **leisure/recreation/outdoor/cultural etc activities** *outdoor activities such as hiking or climbing*
2 [C,U] things that people do in order to achieve a particular aim: **political/economic/business etc activity** *Everyone is free to engage in peaceful political activity.* | **criminal/terrorist/illegal etc activity** | **fundraising activities**
3 [U] a situation in which a lot of things are happening or a lot of things are being done: *the noise and activity of the city* | *There's an amazing level of activity in the town centre currently.* | **physical/mental activity** *Regular physical activity helps to control your weight.*

ac·tor W3 /'æktə $ -ər/ *n* [C] someone who performs in a play or film: **leading/principal actor** *She has starred with many leading actors.* | **character actor** (=an actor who takes unusual or interesting roles)

ac·tress /'æktrɪs/ *n* [C] a woman who performs in a play or film

ac·tu·al S1 W2 /'æktʃuəl/ *adj* [only before noun]
1 used to emphasize that something is real or exact: *I'm not joking. Those were his actual words.* | *I know Germany won, but I can't tell you the actual score.* | *Interest is only charged on the actual amount borrowed.* | **In actual fact** (=really), *there is little evidence to support the allegations.* ⚠ Do not use **actual** to mean 'at the present time'. Use **current** or **present** *the current (NOT actual) economic policy.*
2 the actual sth used to introduce the most important part of an event or activity: *The programme starts at 8.00 but the actual film doesn't start until 8.30.*

ac·tu·al·i·ty /ˌæktʃu'ælɪti/ *n plural* **actualities** *formal* **1** [C usually plural] facts, rather than things that people believe or imagine; ◆ **realities**: *the grim actualities of prison life* **2** [U] the state of being real or

really existing: **In actuality**, *it's much more complex than that* (=used when talking about what a situation is really like).

ac·tu·a·lize also **-ise** *BrE* /'æktʃuəlaɪz/ *v* [T] to make a plan or wish become true; ◆ **realize**: *Mistakes are a necessary part of actualizing your vision.* —**actualization** /ˌæktʃuəlaɪ'zeɪʃən $ -lə-/ *n* [U]

ac·tu·al·ly S1 W1 /'æktʃuəli, -tʃəli/ *adv*
1 [sentence adverb] *spoken* used to add new information to what you have just said, to give your opinion, or to start a new conversation: *I've known Barbara for years. Since we were babies, actually.* | *Actually, on second thoughts, I don't think I want to go out tonight.*
2 used to emphasize the real or exact truth of a situation, rather than what people may think: *What time are you actually leaving?* | *Labor costs have actually fallen.* | *Disappointed? No, actually I'm rather glad.*

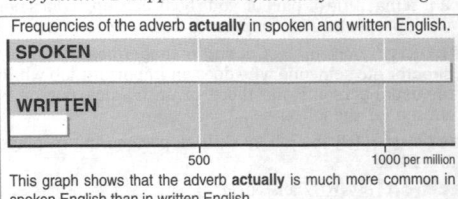

Frequencies of the adverb **actually** in spoken and written English.

| SPOKEN | |
| WRITTEN | |

500   1000 per million

This graph shows that the adverb **actually** is much more common in spoken English than in written English.

ac·tu·als /'æktʃuəlz/ *n* [plural] numbers that relate to something that has actually happened, rather than what was expected to happen: *Mobile phone operators had expected monthly usage of up to 250 minutes. Actuals are very different, at 100 minutes.*

ac·tu·a·ry /'æktʃuəri $ -tʃueri/ *n plural* **actuaries** [C] someone whose job is to advise insurance companies on how much to charge for insurance, after calculating the risks —**actuarial** /ˌæktʃu'eəriəl $ -'er-/ *adj*

ac·tu·ate /'æktʃueɪt/ *v* [T] *formal* **1** be actuated by sth to behave in a particular way because of something: *He was actuated by violent jealousy.* **2** to make a piece of machinery start to operate

a·cu·i·ty /ə'kjuːɪti/ *n* [U] *formal* the ability to think, see, or hear clearly: *A motorist needs good visual acuity.*

ac·u·men /'ækjʊmən, ə'kjuːmən/ *n* [U] the ability to think quickly and make good judgments: **business/political/financial etc acumen** *The firm's success is largely due to Brannon's commercial acumen.*

ac·u·pres·sure /'ækjʊˌpreʃə $ -ər/ *n* [U] a treatment for pain and disease that involves pressing your hands on particular parts of the body

ac·u·punc·ture /'ækjʊˌpʌŋktʃə $ -ər/ *n* [U] a treatment for pain and disease that involves pushing special needles into parts of the body: *the four main acupuncture points* —**acupuncturist** *n* [C]: *a qualified acupuncturist*

a·cute /ə'kjuːt/ *adj*
1 PROBLEM an acute problem is very serious: *The housing shortage is more acute than first thought.*
2 FEELING an acute feeling is very strong: *acute pain* | *acute embarrassment* | *acute anxiety*
3 ILLNESS *technical* an acute illness or disease quickly becomes very serious; ◆ **chronic**: *acute arthritis*
4 SENSES acute senses such as hearing, taste, touch etc are very good and sensitive: *Young children have a particularly acute sense of smell.*
5 INTELLIGENT quick to notice and understand things; ◆ **sharp**: *Simon's vague manner concealed an acute mind.* | *an acute analysis of Middle Eastern politics*
6 MATHEMATICS *technical* an acute angle is less than 90°; → **obtuse**
7 PUNCTUATION an acute ACCENT (=a mark used to show pronunciation) is a small mark written above a vowel. In 'café', the letter 'e' has an acute accent; → **grave**, **circumflex** —**acuteness** *n* [U]

a·cute·ly /əˈkjuːtli/ adv feeling or noticing something very strongly: **acutely aware/conscious (of/that)** Students are becoming acutely aware that they need more than just paper qualifications. | acutely embarrassed

ad S3 W3 /æd/ n [C] informal an advertisement; → **classified ad**

AD BrE; **A.D.** AmE /ˌeɪ ˈdiː/ Anno Domini used to show that a date is a particular number of years after the birth of Christ; ◨ **CE**; → **BC**: the first century AD | 54 AD

ad·age /ˈædɪdʒ/ n [C] a well-known phrase that says something wise about human experience; ◨ **proverb**: the old adage that a picture is worth a thousand words

a·da·gi·o /əˈdɑːdʒiəʊ $ -dʒoʊ/ n plural adagios [C] technical a piece of music that should be played or sung slowly —**adagio** adj, adv

Ad·am /ˈædəm/ n **not know someone from Adam** informal to not know someone at all

ad·a·mant /ˈædəmənt/ adj determined not to change your opinion or a decision that you have made: She begged me to change my mind, but I remained adamant. | [+that] Michael Jackson is adamant that he will not tour this year. —**adamantly** adv: Britain is adamantly opposed to the new directive.

Adam's apple / $ ˈ.. ˌ../ n [C] the lump at the front of your neck that moves when you talk or swallow

a·dapt W3 /əˈdæpt/ v
1 [I,T] to gradually change your behaviour and attitudes in order to be successful in a new situation: [+to] The children are finding it hard to adapt to the new school. | flowers which are well adapted to harsh winters | The ability to adapt is a definite asset in this job. | **adapt yourself/itself etc (to sth)** How do these insects adapt themselves to new environments?
2 [T] to change something to make it suitable for a different purpose: **adapt sth to do sth** The car has been adapted to take unleaded gas. | **adapt sth for sb** These teaching materials can be adapted for older children.
3 [T usually passive] if a book or play is adapted for film, television etc, it is changed so that it can be made into a film, television programme etc: **be adapted for sth** Many children buy books after they have been adapted for television. —**adapted** adj: She lives in a specially adapted flat.

a·dapt·a·ble /əˈdæptəbəl/ adj [usually after noun] able to change in order to be successful in new and different situations: The American Constitution has proved adaptable in changing political conditions. | [+to] The catfish is adaptable to a wide range of water conditions. —**adaptability** /əˌdæptəˈbɪlɪti/ n [U]

ad·ap·ta·tion /ˌædæpˈteɪʃən/ also **a·dap·tion** /əˈdæpʃən/ n **1** [C] a film or television programme that is based on a book or play: [+of] the BBC adaptation of the bestselling book | **television/film/stage etc adaptation** He's working on a screen adaptation of his latest novel. **2** [U] formal the process of changing something to make it suitable for a new situation: [+to] adaptation to the environment

a·dapt·er, adaptor /əˈdæptə $ -ər/ n [C] an object that you use to connect two different pieces of electrical equipment, or to connect two pieces of equipment to the same power supply

add S1 W1 /æd/ v
1 PUT WITH STH ELSE [T] to put something with something else or with a group of other things: If the mixture seems dry, add water. | **add sth to sth** Do you want to add your name to the list? | Suzuki has added extra doors to its sports off-roader. | Material about recent research has been added to this new edition.
2 COUNT [I,T] if you add numbers or amounts together, you calculate their total; → **subtract: add sth and sth (together)** Add 7 and 5 to make 12. | For tax purposes, your pension and earnings are added together. | **add sth to sth** Add £2.20 to the cost for postage.
3 INCREASE [I,T] to increase the amount or cost of something: **add (sth) to sth** Spell-checking your docu-

ment adds time to the process. | Sales tax adds to the price.
4 SAY MORE [T] to say more about something that has just been said: 'And I don't care what you think,' she added defiantly. | That's all I have to say. Is there anything you'd like to add, David? | [+that] Everyone will be invited to vote, he said, adding that voting is likely to be via the web. | I was refused accommodation — not, **I hasten to add**, on account of my appearance (=used to explain more about what you have just said). | She was trying to entertain us — unsuccessfully, **I might add** (=used to comment on what you have just said).
5 GIVE A QUALITY [T] to give a particular quality to something: **add sth to sth** We've **added value** to the information by organizing it. | **add a touch of glamour/ class (to sth)** Champagne always adds a touch of glamour to the occasion. | Coloured glass can be added for effect.
6 **add(ed) to that/this** used to introduce another fact that supports your opinion: Our hospitals are short of cash. Add to that the long hours doctors work, and you have a recipe for disaster.
7 **add weight to sth** if something adds weight to an argument, idea etc, it makes it stronger: **add weight to the suggestion/idea etc** Recent research adds weight to the theory that the climate is changing.
8 **to add insult to injury** to make a bad situation worse for someone who has already been treated badly: She not only deceived him but, to add insult to injury, allowed him to pay for her meal.
9 **add fuel to the fire/flames** to make an argument or disagreement worse: Rather than providing a solution, their statements merely added fuel to the fire.
add sth ⇔ **in** phr v
to include something with something else: Don't forget to add in the cost of your time.
add sth ⇔ **on** also **add sth on sth** phr v
to include or put on something extra: proposals to add a penny on income tax | [+to] The private chapel was added on to the church much later.
add to sth phr v
to make a feeling or quality stronger and more noticeable: This show will no doubt add to his growing reputation.
add up phr v
1 to calculate the total of several numbers: I can add up in my head quite easily. | **add sth** ⇔ **up** Specialized software adds up the statistics.
2 **not add up a)** if a set of facts does not add up, it does not provide a reasonable explanation for a situation: He was troubled by a feeling that things just didn't add up. **b)** if sums, numbers etc do not add up, there is a mistake in them: These figures don't add up.
3 **it all adds up** informal used to say that lots of small amounts gradually make a large total: There are five of us using the phone so it all adds up.
add up to sth phr v
to produce a particular total or result: Rising prison population and overcrowding add up to a real crisis.

ADD /ˌeɪ diː ˈdiː/ n [U] medical the abbreviation of **attention deficit disorder**

ad·ded /ˈædɪd/ adj in addition to what is usual or expected; ◨ **extra**: cereal with added vitamins | no added sugar | **added advantage/bonus/benefit etc** The system has the added advantage of recordable DVD drives. | Include people in your picture for **added interest**. | added **difficulty/problem etc** Our yard is only small, and has the added disadvantage of facing north. | It may not be necessary to go to the **added expense** of updating your virus software.

ad·den·dum /əˈdendəm/ n plural addenda /-də/ or **addendums** [C] something you add to the end of a speech or book to change it or give more information: [+to] an addendum to section 4

A

ad·der /'ædə $ -ər/ n [C] a type of poisonous snake

ad·dict /'ædɪkt/ n [C] **1** someone who is unable to stop taking drugs: **drug/heroin/morphine etc addict** *a recovering heroin addict* **2** someone who is very interested in something and spends a lot of time doing it: **TV/sports etc addict** *My nephew is a complete video game addict.*

ad·dic·ted /ə'dɪktɪ̥d/ adj **1** unable to stop taking a harmful substance, especially a drug: [+to] *50 million Americans are thought to be addicted to nicotine.* **2** liking something so much that you do not want to stop doing it or having it: [+to] *kids addicted to surfing the Net*

ad·dic·tion /ə'dɪkʃən/ n [C,U] **1** the need to take a harmful drug regularly, without being able to stop: **drug/heroin/alcohol etc addiction** | [+to] *addiction to alcohol* **2** a strong desire to do or have something regularly

ad·dic·tive /ə'dɪktɪv/ adj **1** if a substance, especially a drug, is addictive, your body starts to need it regularly and you are unable to stop taking it: *Tobacco is **highly addictive**.* **2** an activity that is addictive is so enjoyable that you do not want to stop: *It started as a hobby, but it got so addictive I had to keep on doing it.* | *addictive arcade games*

ad·di·tion S3 W1 /ə'dɪʃən/ n
1 in addition used to add another piece of information to what you have just said: *The company provides cheap Internet access. In addition, it makes shareware freely available.* | **in addition to sth** *In addition to his movie work, Redford is known as a champion of environmental causes.*
2 [U] the act of adding something to something else: **the addition of sth** *The addition of networking facilities will greatly enhance the system.* | **with the addition of sth** *Turn sparkling wine into Buck's Fizz with the addition of chilled orange juice.*
3 [C] something that is added to something else, often in order to improve it: [+to] *This excellent book will be a **welcome addition** to the library of any student.* | **latest/new/recent addition** *the latest addition to our designer range*
4 [U] the process of adding numbers or amounts to make a total; → **subtraction**
5 [C] AmE an extra room that is added to a building: *They built a big addition onto the back of the house.*

ad·di·tion·al S2 W2 /ə'dɪʃənəl/ adj more than what was agreed or expected; ⊟ **extra**: *Additional information can be obtained from the centre.* | **additional costs/expenditure etc** *An additional charge is made on baggage exceeding the weight allowance.*

ad·di·tion·al·ly /ə'dɪʃənəli/ adv [sentence adverb] in addition; ⊟ **also**: *A new contract is in place. Additionally, staff will be offered a bonus scheme.*

ad·di·tive /'ædɪ̥tɪv/ n [C usually plural] a substance that is added to food to improve its taste, appearance etc: *permitted food additives* | *Our products are free from **artificial additives**.*

ad·dle /'ædl/ v [T] old-fashioned to confuse someone so they cannot think properly: **addle sb's brains/wits** *All that drink has addled his brains!*

'add-on n [C] **1** something extra that is added to an existing plan, agreement, law etc: [+to] *We bought legal protection as an add-on to our home insurance policy.* **2** a piece of equipment that you connect to a computer to improve its performance: *an add-on circuit board* **3** a product that is designed to be used with another product

ad·dress¹ S2 W2 /ə'dres $ ə'dres, 'ædres/ n
1 [C] the details of the place where someone lives or works, that you use to send them letters, emails etc: *Please write your **name and address** on a postcard.* | *What's your new address?* | *I can give you the address of a good attorney.* | **home/private/website etc address** *My email address is on my business card.* | *Please notify*

us of any **change of address**. | *I can't find my address book* (=a book or place on a computer where you keep a list of people's addresses). | *a 25-year-old man of no fixed address* (=no permanent home)
2 [C] a formal speech that someone makes to a group of people: [+to] *an address to the European parliament* | **presidential/inaugural etc address** *The new President delivered his inaugural address in Creole.*
3 form/mode/style of address the correct title or name that you should use when speaking or writing to someone

ad·dress² S3 W2 /ə'dres/ v [T]
1 if you address an envelope, package etc, you write on it the name and address of the person you are sending it to: **address sth to sb** *That letter was addressed to me.* | *Send a **stamped, self-addressed envelope** (=with your address on it so it can be sent back to you).*
2 formal if you address a problem, you start trying to solve it: **address a problem/question/issue etc** *Our products address the needs of real users.* | **address yourself to sth** *Marlowe now addressed himself to the task of searching the room.*
3 formal to speak to someone directly: *She turned to address the man on her left.*
4 formal if you address remarks, complaints etc to someone, you say or write them directly to that person: *You will have to address your comments to our Head Office.*
5 to make a formal speech to a large group of people: **address a meeting/conference etc** *He addressed an audience of 10,000 supporters.*
6 to use a particular title or name when speaking or writing to someone: **address sb as sth** *The president should be addressed as 'Mr. President'.*

ad·dress·ee /ˌædre'siː, ˌədres'iː/ n [C] the person a letter, package etc is addressed to

ad·duce /ə'djuːs $ ə'duːs/ v [T] formal to give facts or reasons in order to prove that something is true

ad·e·noid·al /ˌædɪ̥'nɔɪdl◂, ˌædən'ɔɪdl◂/ adj an adenoidal voice is unpleasant and sounds as if it comes mainly through someone's nose; ⊟ **nasal**: *her adenoidal singing voice*

ad·e·noids /'ædɪnɔɪdz, 'ædən-/ n [plural] the small soft pieces of flesh at the top of your throat, behind your nose, that sometimes become swollen

ad·ept /'ædept, ə'dept $ ə'dept/ adj good at something that needs care and skill; ⊟ **skilful**: [+at] *Melissa quickly became adept at predicting his moods.* | [+in] *Silas proved adept in the art of avoiding potholes in the road.* | *I'm afraid she's also an adept liar.* —**adept** /'ædept/ n [C]: *a form of kung fu practiced by only a handful of adepts* —**adeptly** adv

ad·e·quate S3 W3 /'ædɪkwə̥t/ adj
1 enough in quantity or of a good enough quality for a particular purpose; ⊟ **sufficient**; ⊟ **inadequate**: *Farmers have been slow to make **adequate provision** for their retirement.* | *Some creams we tested failed to give adequate protection against UV light.* | *The standard of his work is **barely adequate**.* | *The company has yet to provide an adequate explanation for its actions.* | [+for] *Are the parking facilities adequate for 50 cars?* | **adequate to do sth** *The lunchtime menu is **more than adequate** to satisfy the biggest appetite.*
2 fairly good but not excellent: *Her performance was adequate but lacked originality.* —**adequately** adv: *She wasn't adequately insured.* —**adequacy** n [U]

ad·here /əd'hɪə $ -'hɪr/ v [I] formal to stick firmly to something: [+to] *The eggs of these fish adhere to plant leaves.*
 adhere to sth phr v formal to continue to behave according to a particular rule, agreement, or belief: *We **adhere to the principles** of equal rights and freedom of expression for all.* | *I have **adhered** strictly to the **rules**.*

ad·her·ence /əd'hɪərəns $ -'hɪr-/ n [U] when someone behaves according to a particular rule, belief, principle etc: [+to] *adherence to democratic principles* | strict/rigid/slavish adherence *strict adherence to Judaic law*

ad·her·ent /əd'hɪərənt $ -'hɪr-/ *n* [C] someone who supports a particular belief, plan, political party etc: [+of] *adherents of the Greek Orthodox church* | [+to] *The anti-globalization movement is attracting new adherents to its principles.*

ad·he·sion /əd'hiːʒən/ *n* **1** [U] when something sticks to something else **2** [C] *medical* a piece of TISSUE (=skin) that grows around a cut or diseased area

ad·he·sive /əd'hiːsɪv/ *n* [C,U] a substance such as glue that you use to stick two things together: *waterproof adhesive* —**adhesive** *adj*: *adhesive tape*

ad hoc /æd 'hɒk‹ $ -'hɑːk‹ ,-'hoʊk‹ / *adj, adv formal* not planned, but arranged or done only when necessary: **ad hoc committee/group etc** | *decisions made on an ad hoc basis*

a·dieu /ə'djuː/ *n plural* **adieus** *or* **adieux** /ə'djuːz/ [C, interjection] *literary* goodbye: *He bid her adieu.*

ad in·fi·ni·tum /ˌæd ɪnfⁱ'naɪtəm/ *adv formal* continuing without ever ending – often used humorously: *I have to explain A, then B, and C, and so on ad infinitum.*

ad·i·os /ˌædi'ɒs $ -'oʊs/ *interjection* goodbye

adj. also **adj** *BrE* the written abbreviation of *adjective*

ad·ja·cent /ə'dʒeɪsənt/ *adj* a room, building, piece of land etc that is adjacent to something is next to it: *We stayed in adjacent rooms.* | [+to] *the building adjacent to the library*

ad·jec·tive /'ædʒ³ⁱktɪv/ *n* [C] a word that describes a noun or PRONOUN. In the phrase 'black hat', 'black' is an adjective and in the sentence 'It makes her happy', 'happy' is an adjective. —**adjectival** /ˌædʒ³ⁱk'taɪvəl‹ / *adj: an adjectival phrase*

ad·join /ə'dʒɔɪn/ *v* [T] a room, building, or piece of land that adjoins something is next to it and connected to it: *A vacant plot of land adjoins his house.* —**adjoining** *adj* [usually before noun]: *adjoining rooms*

ad·journ /ə'dʒɜːn $ -ɜːrn/ *v* **1** [I,T] if a meeting, parliament, law court etc adjourns, or if the person in charge adjourns it, it stops for a short time: *It was almost noon when the meeting adjourned.* | [+for/until] *Congress has adjourned for the November elections.* | *His **trial** was **adjourned** until May.* **2 adjourn to sth** to finish an activity and go somewhere – often used humorously: *The rest of us adjourned to a nearby pub for some refreshments.* —**adjournment** *n* [C,U]: *We sought an adjournment of the proceedings.*

ad·judge /ə'dʒʌdʒ/ *v* [T usually passive] *formal* to make a judgment about something or someone: *The reforms of 1979 were generally adjudged to have failed.*

ad·ju·di·cate /ə'dʒuːdɪkeɪt/ *v* **1** [I,T] to officially decide who is right in a disagreement and decide what should be done: *The Dean adjudicates any faculty disputes.* | [+on/upon/in/between] *The owner can appeal to the court to adjudicate on the matter.* | **adjudicate that** *The judge adjudicated that he should be released.* **2** [I] to be the judge in a competition: *He adjudicated at all the regional music competitions.* —**adjudicator** *n* [C]: *an impartial adjudicator* —**adjudication** /əˌdʒuːdɪ'keɪʃən/ *n* [U]

ad·junct /'ædʒʌŋkt/ *n* [C] **1** something that is added or joined to something that is bigger or more important: [+to] *On-line instruction is a useful adjunct to the real thing.* **2** *technical* an ADVERBIAL word or phrase that adds information to another part of a sentence: 'They arrived on Sunday', 'on Sunday' is an adjunct.

ad·jure /ə'dʒʊə $ ə'dʒʊr/ *v* [T] *formal* to order or try to persuade someone to do something: **adjure sb to do sth** *Gwen adjured him to be truthful.*

ad·just W3 /ə'dʒʌst/ *v* **1** [I,T] to gradually become familiar with a new situation – often used with *to*: *They'll soon settle in – kids are very good at adjusting.* | [+to] *It took a few seconds for her eyes to adjust to the darkness.* | **adjust to doing sth** *My parents had trouble adjusting to living in an apartment.* |

adjust yourself to sth *It took time to adjust myself to motherhood.* **2** [T] to change or move something slightly to improve it or make it more suitable for a particular purpose: *Check and adjust the brakes regularly.* | *Taste the soup and adjust the seasoning.* | *If your employment status changes, your tax code will be adjusted accordingly.* **3** [T] if you adjust something you are wearing, you move it slightly so that it is neater, more comfortable etc: *He paused to adjust his spectacles.* → **WELL-ADJUSTED**

ad·just·a·ble /ə'dʒʌstəbəl/ *adj* something that is adjustable can be changed or moved slightly to make it suitable for different purposes: *an adjustable spanner*

ad·just·ment /ə'dʒʌstmənt/ *n* [C,U] **1** a small change made to a machine, system, or calculation: [+for] *Once we **make** the **adjustments** for inflation, the fall in interest rates is quite small.* | [+to] *a slight adjustment to the mechanism* | **minor/slight adjustment** *It just needs a few minor adjustments.* **2** a change in the way that someone behaves or thinks: *a **period of adjustment*** | [+to] *her adjustment to her new role*

ad·ju·tant /'ædʒᵘtənt/ *n* [C] an army officer responsible for office work

ad·land /'ædlænd/ *n* [U] the activity or business of advertising, considered as a whole: *Anything that grabs your attention is good in adland.*

ad-lib /ˌæd 'lɪb/ *v* **ad-libbed, ad-libbing** [I,T] to say things that you have not prepared or planned when you are performing or giving a speech: *I never use a script; I just ad lib the whole programme.* —**ad-lib** *n* [C]

ad·man /'ædmæn/ *n plural* **admen** /-men/ [C] *informal* someone who works in advertising

ad·min /'ædmɪn/ *n* [U] *informal* ADMINISTRATION: *an admin assistant* | *She works in admin.*

ad·min·is·ter /əd'mɪnⁱstə $ -ər/ *v* **1** [T usually passive] to manage the work or money of a company or organization: *The money will be administered by local charities.* | *Our office **administers the affairs** of the Society.* **2** [I,T] to provide or organize something officially as part of your job: **administer justice/punishment etc** *It is not the job of the police to administer justice; that falls to the courts.* | [+to] *Pillai had responsibility for administering to the needs of half a million people.* | **administer sth to sb** *The test was administered to all 11-year-olds.* | **administer an oath** (=be the official person who listens to it) **3** [T] *formal* to give someone a medicine or medical treatment: **administer sth to sb** *Painkillers were administered to the boy.* | *This unit teaches students how to **administer First Aid**.*

ad·min·is·tra·tion S2 W2 /ədˌmɪnⁱ'streɪʃən/ *n* **1** [U] the activities that are involved in managing the work of a company or organization: *We're looking for someone with experience in administration.* | *The health service spends too much on administration.* | **the administration** (=the people who do this work) *the college administration*

2 [C] the government of a country at a particular time: *the Kennedy Administration* | *The problem has been ignored by successive administrations.* **3** [U] the act of administering something, especially a law, test, or medicine: [+of] *the administration of justice* | *the administration of sedatives*

ad·min·is·tra·tive W3 /əd'mɪnⁱstrətɪv $ -streɪt•/ *adj* relating to the work of managing a compan• organization: *The job is mainly administrati* **administrative staff/duties/job etc** *the adminis• costs of health care systems* | *an admini• assistant* | *staff who provide technical and • trative support to the college* —**administra•**

ad·min·is·tra·tor /əd'mɪnⁱstreɪtə $ -ər• one whose job involves managing the w• pany or organization

ad·mi·ra·ble /'ædmərəbəl/ *adj* forr good qualities that you respect and • rable achievement* —**admirably** *a•*

ad·mi·ral /ˈædmərəl/ n [C] a high rank in the British or US navy, or someone with this rank

Ad·mi·ral·ty /ˈædmərəlti/ n **the Admiralty** the government department that controls the British navy

ad·mi·ra·tion /ˌædməˈreɪʃən/ n [U] a feeling of great respect and liking for something or someone: **in admiration** Daniel gazed at her in admiration. | [+for] I'm full of admiration for the crew who handled this crisis. | [+of] Her riding soon drew the admiration of the older girls. | **grudging/sneaking admiration** (=that you do not really want to feel or express) Despite her annoyance, she couldn't help feeling a grudging admiration for him.

ad·mire S3 /ədˈmaɪə $ -ˈmaɪr/ v [T not in progressive]
1 to respect and like someone because they have done something that you think is good: I really **admire the way** she brings up those kids all on her own. | **admire sb for (doing) sth** Lewis was much admired for his work on medieval literature.
2 to look at something and think how beautiful or impressive it is: We stopped halfway to **admire the view**. | Sal stood back to admire her work.
3 admire sb from afar literary to be attracted to someone, without letting them know —**admired** adj: the widely admired boss of Channel 4

ad·mir·er /ədˈmaɪərə $ -ˈmaɪrər/ n [C] **1** literary someone who likes a person and thinks that they are attractive: a beautiful woman with many admirers | a **secret admirer 2** someone who respects a famous person, especially because they like their work; ◧ **fan**: a crowd of fervent admirers | [+of] 'I'm a great admirer of yours,' she managed to stammer.

ad·mir·ing /ədˈmaɪərɪŋ $ -ˈmaɪr-/ adj [usually before noun] showing that you think someone or something is very impressive or attractive: admiring glances —**admiringly** adv

ad·mis·si·ble /ədˈmɪsɪbəl/ adj admissible reasons, facts etc are acceptable or allowed, especially in a court of law; ⬧ **inadmissible**: **admissible evidence** —**admissibility** /ədˌmɪsɪˈbɪlɪti/ n [U]

ad·mis·sion W3 /ədˈmɪʃən/ n
1 [C] a statement in which you admit that something is true or that you have done something wrong; ⬛ **confession**: **admission that** The Senator's admission that he had lied to Congress shocked many Americans. | **admission of guilt/defeat/failure etc** Silence is often interpreted as an admission of guilt. | Reese, **by his own admission**, lacks the necessary experience.
2 [U] permission given to someone to enter a building or place, or to become a member of a school, club etc: No admission after 10 pm. | The young men tried to enter a nightclub but were **refused admission**. | Women **gained admission** to the club only recently. | [+to] those applying for admission to university
3 admissions [plural] the process of allowing people to enter a university, institution etc, or the number of people who can enter: **university/college/school admissions** | **admissions policy/procedures etc** The college has a very selective admissions policy. | the **admissions officer**
4 [C,U] the process of taking someone into a hospital for treatment, tests, or care: There are 13,000 **hospital ·dmissions** annually due to playground accidents.
·U] the cost of entrance to a concert, sports event, ·ma etc; ◧ **admittance**: Admission: $10 for adults, ·children. | The cost includes **free admission** to the ·. | The Museum has no **admission charge**.

S2 W1 /ədˈmɪt/ v **admitted, admitting**
·TRUTH [I,T] to agree unwillingly that some-·e or that someone else is right: 'Okay, so ·n little bit scared,' Jenny admitted. | **admit** ·not like her, but you **have to admit** that ·r job. | **admit to sb (that)** Paul admitted ·netimes feels jealous of my friendship · **must admit**, I didn't actually do

anything to help her. | **Admit it!** I'm right, aren't I? | **admit (to) doing sth** Dana admitted feeling hurt by what I had said. | **freely/openly/frankly etc admit** (=admit without being ashamed) Phillips openly admits to having an alcohol problem.
2 ACCEPT BLAME [I,T] to say that you have done something wrong, especially something criminal; ⬛ **confess**; ⬧ **deny**: **admit doing sth** Greene admitted causing death by reckless driving. | **admit to (doing) sth** A quarter of all workers admit to taking time off when they are not ill. | After questioning, he admitted to the murder. | No organization has **admitted responsibility** for the bombing.
3 ALLOW TO ENTER [T] to allow someone to enter a public place to watch a game, performance etc; → **admittance, admission**: **admit sb to/into sth** Only ticket-holders will be admitted into the stadium.
4 ALLOW TO JOIN [T] to allow someone to join an organization, club etc: **admit sb to/into sth** Drake was admitted into the club in 1997.
5 HOSPITAL [T] if people at a hospital admit someone, that person is taken in to be given treatment, tests, or care: What time was she admitted? | **be admitted to hospital** BrE/**be admitted to the hospital** AmE
6 admit defeat to stop trying to do something because you realize you cannot succeed: For Haskill, selling the restaurant would be admitting defeat.
7 admit evidence to allow a particular piece of EVIDENCE to be used in a court of law: Courts can refuse to admit evidence obtained illegally by police.
admit of sth phr v formal
if a situation admits of a particular explanation, that explanation can be accepted as possible: The facts admit of no other explanation.

ad·mit·tance /ədˈmɪtəns/ n [U] formal permission to enter a place; → **admission (5)**: Gaining admittance to the club was no easy matter.

ad·mit·ted·ly /ədˈmɪtədli/ adv [sentence adverb] used when you are admitting that something is true: The technique is painful, admittedly, but it benefits the patient greatly. | This has led to financial losses, though admittedly on a fairly small scale.

ad·mix·ture /ədˈmɪkstʃə, æd- $ ædˈmɪkstʃər/ n [C] technical a substance that is added to another substance in a mixture

ad·mon·ish /ədˈmɒnɪʃ $ -ˈmɑː-/ v [T] formal to tell someone severely that they have done something wrong: **admonish sb for (doing) sth** The witness was admonished for failing to answer the question. —**admonishment** n [C]

ad·mo·ni·tion /ˌædməˈnɪʃən/ n [C,U] formal a warning or expression of disapproval about someone's behaviour —**admonitory** /ədˈmɒnɪtəri $ -ˈmɑːnɪtɔːri/ adj: an admonitory glance

ad nau·se·am /ˌæd ˈnɔːziəm, -iæm $ -ˈnɒː-/ adv if you say or do something ad nauseam, you say or do it so often that it becomes annoying for other people: Look, we've been over this ad nauseam. I think we should move on to the next item.

a·do /əˈduː/ n **without more/further ado** without delaying or wasting any time: So without further ado, I'll now ask Mr Davis to open the debate.

a·do·be /əˈdəʊbi $ əˈdoʊ-/ n [U] earth and STRAW that are made into bricks for building houses

ad·o·les·cence /ˌædəˈlesəns/ n [U] the time, usually between the ages of 12 and 18, when a young person is developing into an adult

ad·o·les·cent /ˌædəˈlesənt◂/ n [C] a young person, usually between the ages of 12 and 18, who is developing into an adult —**adolescent** adj: adolescent girls → **CHILD**

A·do·nis /əˈdəʊnɪs $ əˈdɑː-/ n [C usually singular] an extremely attractive young man

a·dopt S2 W2 /əˈdɒpt $ əˈdɑːpt/ v
1 CHILD [I,T] to take someone else's child into your home and legally become its parent; → **foster (11)**: Sally was adopted when she was four. | The couple are

unable to have children of their own, but hope to adopt.
2 adopt an approach/policy/attitude etc [T] to start to deal with or think about something in a particular way: *The courts were asked to adopt a more flexible approach to young offenders.* | *The store recently adopted a drug testing policy for all new employees.* | *California has adopted a tough stance on the issue.*
3 STYLE/MANNER [T] to use a particular style of speaking, writing, or behaving, especially one that you do not usually use: *Kim adopts a southern accent when speaking to family back home.*
4 LAW/RULE [T] to formally approve a proposal, AMENDMENT etc, especially by voting: *Congress finally adopted the law after a two-year debate.*
5 NAME/COUNTRY ETC [T] to choose a new name, country, custom etc, especially to replace a previous one: *Stevens became a Muslim and adopted the name Yusuf Islam.* | *Becoming a member of a society means adopting its values.*
6 ELECTION *BrE* [T] to officially choose someone to represent a political party in an election —**adopter** *n* [C] —**adoptee** /ə,dɒp'tiː $ ə,dɑːp-/ *n* [C]

a·dopt·ed /ə'dɒptᵻd $ ə'dɑːp-/ *adj* **1** an adopted child has been legally made part of a family that he or she was not born into: *his adopted son* **2** your adopted country is one that you have chosen to live in permanently

a·dop·tion /ə'dɒpʃən $ ə'dɑːp-/ *n* **1** [C,U] the act or process of adopting a child: *She decided to put the baby up for adoption.* **2** [U] the act of starting to use a particular plan, method, way of speaking etc **3** [U] *BrE* the choice of a particular person to represent a political party in an election

a·dop·tive /ə'dɒptɪv $ ə'dɑːp-/ *adj* [only before noun] an adoptive parent is one who has adopted a child

a·dor·a·ble /ə'dɔːrəbəl/ *adj* someone or something that is adorable is so attractive that they fill you with feelings of love: *Oh what an adorable little baby!*

ad·o·ra·tion /,ædə'reɪʃən/ *n* **1** great love and admiration: *the look of adoration in his eyes* **2** *literary* the showing of great love and respect for God

a·dore /ə'dɔː $ ə'dɔːr/ *v* [T not in progressive] **1** to love someone very much and feel very proud of them: *Betty adores her grandchildren.* **2** *informal* to like something very much: *I simply adore chocolate.*

a·dor·ing /ə'dɔːrɪŋ/ *adj* [only before noun] liking and admiring someone very much: *his adoring fans* —**adoringly** *adv*

a·dorn /ə'dɔːn $ -ɔːrn/ *v* [T] *formal* to decorate something: **adorn sth with sth** *church walls adorned with religious paintings*

a·dorn·ment /ə'dɔːnmənt $ -ɔːr-/ *n formal* **1** [C] something that you use to decorate something **2** [U] the act of decorating something

a·dren·a·lin, **adrenaline** /ə'drenəl-ᵻn/ *n* [U] a chemical produced by your body when you are afraid, angry, or excited, which makes your heart beat faster: *There's nothing like a good horror film to get the adrenalin going* (=make you feel nervously excited).

a·drift /ə'drɪft/ *adj, adv* **1** a boat that is adrift is not fastened to anything or controlled by anyone: *Several of the lifeboats were still afloat a month after being cast adrift.* **2** someone who is adrift is confused about what to do in their life: *a young woman adrift in London* **3 come adrift** *BrE* if something comes adrift, it is no longer fastened or attached to something: *Her hair was forever coming adrift from the pins she used to keep it in place.* **4 two points/five seconds etc adrift (of sb)** two points, five seconds etc behind someone in a competition, race etc

a·droit /ə'drɔɪt/ *adj* clever and skilful, especially in the way you use words and arguments: *an adroit negotiator* —**adroitly** *adv* —**adroitness** *n* [U]

ADSL /,eɪ diː es 'el/ *n* [U] *asymmetric digital subscriber line* a system that makes it possible for information, such as video images, to be sent to computers through telephone wires at a very high speed

ad·u·la·tion /,ædʒʊ'leɪʃən/ *n* [U] *formal* praise and admiration for someone that is more than they really deserve —**adulatory** /,ædʒʊ'leɪtəri, 'ædʒʊleɪtəri $ 'ædʒələtɔːri/ *adj*

ad·ult¹ S2 W2 /'ædʌlt, ə'dʌlt/ *n* [C] **1** a fully-grown person, or one who is considered to be legally responsible for their actions: *Some children find it difficult to talk to adults.* **2** a fully-grown animal: *The adults have white bodies and grey backs.*

adult² W3 *adj* **1** [only before noun] fully grown or developed: *an adult lion* | *the adult population* | *He lived most of his adult life in Scotland.* **2** typical of an adult's behaviour or of the things adults do: *dealing with problems in an adult way* | *That wasn't very adult of you.* **3** [only before noun] adult films, magazines, etc are about sex or related to sex: *The film is rated R for language and adult themes.*

adult edu·ca·tion *n* [U] education provided for adults outside schools and universities, usually by means of classes that are held in the evening

a·dul·ter·ate /ə'dʌltəreɪt/ *v* [T] to make food or drink less pure by adding another substance of lower quality to it; → **unadulterated** —**adulteration** /ə,dʌltə'reɪʃən/ *n* [U]

a·dul·ter·er /ə'dʌltərə $ -ər/ *n* [C] someone who is married and has sex with someone who is not their wife or husband

a·dul·ter·ess /ə'dʌltərᵻs/ *n* [C] a married woman who has sex with a man who is not her husband

a·dul·ter·y /ə'dʌltəri/ *n* [U] sex between someone who is married and someone who is not their wife or husband: *She had committed adultery on several occasions.* —**adulterous** *adj*

ad·ult·hood /'ædʌlthʊd, ə'dʌlt-/ *n* [U] the time when you are an adult; **⊞** childhood

ad·um·brate /'ædʌmbreɪt/ *v* [T] *formal* to suggest or describe something in an incomplete way

adv. also **adv** *BrE* the written abbreviation of *adverb*

ad·vance¹ S3 W2 /əd'vɑːns $ əd'væns/ *n*
1 **in advance (of sth)** before something happens or is expected to happen: *I should warn you in advance that I'm not a very good dancer.* | *Many thanks, in advance, for your help.* | **six months/a year etc in advance** *The airline suggests booking tickets 21 days in advance.* | *Could you distribute copies well in advance of the meeting?*
2 **be in advance of sb/sth** to be more developed or modern than someone or something else: *Their aircraft were in advance of those used by the US.*
3 DEVELOPMENT/IMPROVEMENT [C] a change, discovery, or INVENTION that brings progress: **technological/scientific/medical etc advance** *one of the great technological advances of the 20th century* | **a major advance** | [+in] *Recent advances in genetics have raised moral questions.* | [+on] *an advance on previous treatments* | the **advances made** in the understanding of mental handicap
4 FORWARD MOVEMENT [C] forward movement or progress of a group of people – used especially to talk about soldiers: [+on] *the enemy's advance on St. Petersburg.*
5 MONEY [C usually singular] money paid to someone before the usual time, especially someone's salary: *$500 advance* | [+on] *Krebs decided to ask for an advance on his salary.*
6 advances [plural] *formal* an attempt to start a sexual relationship with someone: *She accused her boss of making advances to her.* | *The witness said that he 'went berserk' when she rejected his sexual advances.*

7 INCREASE [C] an increase in the price or value of something – used especially to talk about the STOCK EXCHANGE

advance² W3 v

1 MOVE FORWARD [I] to move towards someone or something, especially in a slow and determined way – used especially to talk about soldiers: *A line of US tanks slowly advanced.* | [+on] *Troops advanced on the rebel stronghold* (=moved towards it in order to attack it). | [+across/through/towards] *The army advanced across the plain.*
2 DEVELOP [I,T] if scientific or technical knowledge advances, or if something advances it, it develops and improves: *Our understanding of human genetics has advanced considerably.* | *The group's research has done much to advance our knowledge of the HIV virus.*
3 MONEY [T] to give someone money before they have earned it: **advance sb sth** *Will they advance you some money until your get your first paycheck?* | **advance sth to sb** *I advanced $1,500 to Kramer last Thursday.*
4 advance your career/a cause/your interests etc to do something that will help you achieve an advantage or success for yourself or someone else: *Jameson agreed to the deal in an effort to advance his political career.*
5 PRICE [I] if the price or value of something advances, it increases – used especially when talking about the STOCK EXCHANGE
6 TIME/DATE [T] *formal* to change the time or date when an event should happen to an earlier time or date: *The meeting has been advanced to ten o'clock.*
7 MACHINE [I,T] *formal* if you advance a film, clock, musical recording etc, or if it advances, it goes forward → ADVANCING

advance³ *adj* **1 advance planning/warning/booking etc** planning etc that is done before an event: *We received no advance warning of the storm.* **2 advance party/team** a group of people who go first to a place where something will happen to prepare for it **3 advance copy** a copy of a book, record etc that has not yet been made available to the public

ad·vanced W3 /əd'vɑːnst $ əd'vænst/ *adj*
1 very modern: *advanced weapon systems* | *advanced technology* | *high levels of unemployment in the advanced industrial societies*
2 studying or dealing with a school subject at a difficult level: *advanced learners of English* | *advanced physics*
3 having reached a late point in time or development: *By this time, the disease was too far advanced to be treated.*
4 advanced age/years used to talk about the age of someone who is old: *Despite his advanced age, he often travelled abroad.*

Ad'vanced ,level *n* [C,U] A LEVEL

ad·vance·ment /əd'vɑːnsmənt $ əd'væn-/ *n* [C,U] *formal* progress or development in your job, level of knowledge etc: *career advancement* | *advancements in science*

ad·vanc·ing /əd'vɑːnsɪŋ $ əd'væn-/ *adj* **advancing years/age** the fact of growing older: *Blake had grown much quieter – another sign of his advancing years.*

ad·van·tage S1 W1 /əd'vɑːntɪdʒ $ əd'væn-/ *n*
1 [C,U] something that helps you to be more successful than others, or the state of having this; E **disadvantage**

have an advantage
give sb an advantage
big/great/major/distinct advantage
unfair advantage
joy an advantage (=have an advantage)
at an advantage (=have an advantage)
o your advantage/work to your advantage (=some-
g gives you an advantage)

] *Her experience meant that she had a big 'age over her opponent.* | *His height gives him*

an advantage over the other players. | *Companies that receive government subsidies have an unfair advantage.* | *Western countries enjoyed considerable advantages in terms of technology.* | *Younger workers tend to be at an advantage when applying for jobs.* | *It might be to your advantage to take a computer course of some kind.*
2 [C,U] a good or useful quality or condition that something has: [+of] *One of the many advantages of living in New York is that you can eat out at almost any time of day.* | *The hotel is not very modern, but it does have the advantage of being close to the city centre.* | [+over] *The printer has several advantages over conventional printers.* | **big/great/considerable advantage** *The big advantage of this system is that it is fast.*
3 take advantage of sb to treat someone unfairly in order to get what you want, especially someone who is generous or easily persuaded: *Don't lend them the car – they're taking advantage of you!*
4 take advantage of sth (to do sth) to use a particular situation to do or get what you want: *I took advantage of the good weather to paint the shed.* | *You'll want to take full advantage of the beachfront clubs.*
5 use/turn sth to your/good advantage to use something that you have or that happens in order to achieve something: *How could he turn the situation to his advantage?* | *Burns used his family connections to good advantage.*
6 show sth to (good/great) advantage to make the best features of someone or something very noticeable: *Her dress showed her tanned skin to great advantage.*
7 advantage sb used in tennis to show that the person named has won the next point after the score was 40–40

ad·van·taged /əd'vɑːntɪdʒd $ əd'væn-/ *adj formal* having more money, a higher social position etc than someone else; E **disadvantaged**: *Some of the boys come from less advantaged backgrounds.* | **socially/geographically/economically etc advantaged**

ad·van·ta·geous /,ædvən'teɪdʒəs, ,ædvæn-/ *adj* helpful and likely to make you successful; E **disadvantageous**: *He was now in a more advantageous position.* | [+to] *terms advantageous to foreign companies* —**advantageously** *adv*

ad·vent /'ædvent/ *n written* **the advent of sth** the time when something first begins to be widely used: *the advent of the computer*

Advent *n* [U] the period of four weeks before Christmas in the Christian religion

'Advent ,calendar *n* [C] a picture on thick paper which has parts like doors with smaller pictures behind them. You open one door each day in December until Christmas.

ad·ven·ti·tious /,ædvən'tɪʃəs‹, ,ædven-/ *adj formal* happening by chance; E **unexpected** —**adventitiously** *adv*

ad·ven·ture /əd'ventʃə $ -ər/ *n* [C,U] **1** an exciting experience in which dangerous or unusual things happen: *a great adventure* | *Ahab's adventures at sea* | *an adventure story* **2 sense/spirit of adventure** willingness to try new things, take risks etc: *Come on – where's your sense of adventure?*

ad,venture 'playground *n* [C] *BrE* an area of ground for children to play on, with equipment and structures for climbing on

ad·ven·tur·er /əd'ventʃərə $ -ər/ *n* [C] **1** someone who enjoys adventure: *an adventurer travelling the world* **2** *old-fashioned* someone who tries to become rich or socially important by using dishonest or immoral methods – used to show disapproval

ad·ven·tur·is·m /əd'ventʃərɪzəm/ *n* [U] when someone who is in charge of a government, business, army etc takes dangerous risks

ad·ven·tur·ous /əd'ventʃərəs/ *adj* **1** not afraid of taking risks or trying new things: *Andy isn't a very adventurous cook.* **2** also **adventuresome** *AmE* eager to go to new places and do exciting or dangerous things

ad·verb /ˈædvɜːb $ -vɜːrb/ *n* [C] a word that adds to the meaning of a verb, an adjective, another adverb, or a whole sentence, such as 'slowly' in 'He ran slowly', 'very' in 'It's very hot', or 'naturally' in 'Naturally, we want you to come.' → **ADJECTIVE**

ad·ver·bi·al /ədˈvɜːbiəl $ -ɜːr-/ *adj technical* used as an adverb: *an adverbial phrase* —**adverbial** *n* [C]

ad·ver·sa·ri·al /ˌædvɜːˈseəriəl $ -vərˈser-/ *adj* an adversarial system, especially in politics and the law, is one in which two sides oppose and attack each other: *the adversarial nature of two-party politics*

ad·ver·sa·ry /ˈædvəsəri $ ˈædvərseri/ *n plural* **adversaries** [C] *formal* a country or person you are fighting or competing against; ▯ **opponent**: *his old adversary*

ad·verse /ˈædvɜːs $ -ɜːrs/ *adj* **1** not good or favourable: *They fear it could have an **adverse effect** on global financial markets.* | *Miller's campaign has received a good deal of **adverse publicity**.* **2 adverse conditions** conditions that make it difficult for something to happen or exist: *The expedition was abandoned because of adverse weather conditions.* —**adversely** *adv*: *developments which had **adversely affected** their business*

ad·ver·si·ty /ədˈvɜːsˌti $ -ɜːr-/ *n* [U] a situation in which you have a lot of problems that seem to be caused by bad luck: *his courage **in the face of adversity***

ad·vert¹ /ˈædvɜːt $ -ɜːrt/ *n* [C] *BrE* an advertisement

ad·vert² /ədˈvɜːt $ -ɜːrt/ *v*
advert to sth *phr v formal* to mention something

ad·ver·tise /ˈædvətaɪz $ -ər-/ *v* [I,T] **1** to tell the public about a product or service in order to persuade them to buy it: *They no longer advertise alcohol or cigarettes at sporting events.* | **advertise (sth) on television/in a newspaper etc** *Many companies will only advertise in the Sunday paper.* | **be advertised as sth** *The inn is advertised as being from the early 16th century.* | *Colleges and universities have found that **it pays to advertise** (=advertising brings good results).* **2** to make an announcement, for example in a newspaper or on a POSTER, that a job is available, an event is going to happen etc: *a poster advertising the concert* | [+**for**] *I see they're advertising for a new Sales Director.* **3** advertise the fact (that) to let people know something about yourself: *Don't advertise the fact that you're looking for another job.*

ad·ver·tise·ment 〔S3〕 /ədˈvɜːtˌsmənt $ ˌædvərˈtaɪz-/ *n* [C]
1 also **ad** *informal*; **advert** *BrE* a picture, set of words, or a short film, which is intended to persuade people to buy a product or use a service, or that gives information about a job that is available, an event that is going to happen etc

put/place an advertisement in a newspaper
take out an advertisement (=ask for an advertisement to be printed or shown)
a newspaper/television/radio advertisement
a full-page/half-page/two-page advertisement
a job advertisement
answer/reply to an advertisement
run a series of advertisements (=print or broadcast a series of them)

[+**for**] *The Sunday papers are full of advertisements for cars.* | *She saw an advertisement for a ski vacation in Vermont.* | *They **put an advertisement in** The Morning News, offering a high salary for the right person.* | *The organizers of the concert had **taken out** a **full page advertisement** in The New York Times.* | *Only a handful of people **answered the advertisement**.*

2 be an advertisement for sth to be a good example of something or show how effective it can be: *He's a very good advertisement for the benefits of regular exercise.*

WORD FOCUS: ADVERTISEMENT
types of advertisement: **commercial** on TV or radio | **poster** on a wall, often with a picture on it | **junk mail** unwanted letters in the post, advertising things | **flyer** a sheet of paper with an advertisement on it, given to you in the street or pushed through your door | **the blurb** a piece of writing on the back of a book, which talks about the good things in it | **the classified ads** *also* **the small ads** *BrE* short advertisements in a newspaper, in which people offer things for sale | **the personal ads/ the lonely hearts (ads)** newspaper advertisements in which people say they want to meet someone for romance
→ slogan, jingle² (1), plug² (2)

ad·ver·tis·er /ˈædvətaɪzə $ -vərtaɪzər/ *n* [C] **1** a person or company that advertises something **2 Advertiser** used in the names of newspapers: *the Stockport Advertiser*

ad·ver·tis·ing 〔W3〕 /ˈædvətaɪzɪŋ $ -ər-/ *n* [U] the activity or business of advertising things on television, in newspapers etc: *advertising aimed at 18–25 year olds* | *a career in advertising* | **television/radio/newspaper advertising** *Both candidates are spending millions on television advertising.* | **advertising campaign/strategy** *the **advertising slogan** 'Come alive with Pepsi'*

'advertising ˌagency *n* [C] a company that designs and makes advertisements for other companies

ad·ver·to·ri·al /ˌædvɜːˈtɔːriəl $ -vər-/ *n* [C] an advertisement in a newspaper or magazine that is made to look like a normal article

ad·vice 〔S1〕 〔W1〕 /ədˈvaɪs/ *n* [U] an opinion you give someone about what they should do: [+**on/about**] *There's lots of advice in the book on baby care.* | *Could you **give** me some **advice** about buying a home?* | **legal/medical/financial etc advice** *If I were you, I'd get some legal advice.* | **professional/expert advice** (=advice from someone who knows a lot about a subject) *I want to **ask** your **advice** about where to stay in Taipei.* | **follow/take sb's advice** (=do what they advise you) *I followed my father's advice and sold the car.* | *Take my advice and study something practical.* | **a piece/word of advice** *Let me give you a piece of advice.* | **on sb's advice** *Wear a blue or grey suit to the interview.* | **on sb's advice** *On her doctor's advice* (=because her doctor advised her) *Smith decided to take early retirement.* ⚠ Do not confuse the noun **advice** /ədˈvaɪs/ with the verb **advise** /ədˈvaɪz/ *He gave me some useful advice. Can you advise me on college courses?*

ad'vice ˌcolumn *n* [C] part of a newspaper or magazine in which someone gives advice to readers who have written to them about their personal problems; ▯ **agony column** *BrE* —**advice columnist** *n* [C]

ad·vi·sa·ble /ədˈvaɪzəbəl/ *adj* [not before noun] *formal* something that is advisable should be done in order to avoid problems or risks; ▯ **inadvisable**: *Regular medical check-ups are advisable.* | *It is advisable to write a career objective at the start of your resume.* —**advisability** /ədˌvaɪzəˈbɪlˌti/ *n* [U]

ad·vise 〔S2〕 〔W2〕 /ədˈvaɪz/ *v*
1 [I,T] to tell someone what you think they should do, especially when you know more than they do about something: *She needed someone to advise her.* | *'Make sure that you keep the documents in a safe place,' Otley advised him.* | **advise sb to do sth** *Evans advised him ▮ leave London.* | *You are **strongly advised** to take medical insurance when visiting China.* | **advis▮ against (doing) sth** *I'd advise you against sayir▮ thing to the press.* | **advise that** *Experts ad▮ sunscreen be reapplied every one to two hour▮* | **caution/patience/restraint etc** (=advise p▮ careful, patient etc) *The makers advise e▮ when handling this material.*
2 [I,T] to be employed to give advice o▮ which you have special knowledge ▮ been asked to advise on training ▮ **advise sb on sth** *He advises us o▮*
3 [T] *formal* to tell someone abo▮ **of sth** *We'll advise you of a▮ dates.* | *Keep us **advised of** ▮ any new developments.* |

him that the tour would proceed.
4 you would be well/ill advised to do sth used to tell someone that it is wise or unwise to do something: *You would be well advised to stay in bed and rest.*

ad·vis·ed·ly /əd'vaɪzɪdli/ *adv formal* after careful thought; ⬛ **deliberately**: *He behaved like a dictator, and I use the term advisedly.*

ad·vis·er S3 W3 , **advisor** /əd'vaɪzə $ -ər/ *n* [C] someone whose job is to give advice because they know a lot about a subject, especially in business, law, or politics: *a financial adviser*

ad·vi·so·ry /əd'vaɪzəri/ *adj* having the purpose of giving advice: **advisory committee/body** *the Environmental Protection Advisory Committee* | **advisory role/capacity** *He was employed in a purely advisory role.*

ad·vo·ca·cy /'ædvəkəsi/ *n* [U] public support for a course of action or way of doing things

ad·vo·cate¹ /'ædvəkeɪt/ *v* [T] to publicly say that something should be done: *Extremists were openly advocating violence.* | [+for] *AmE: Those who advocate doctor-assisted suicide say the terminally ill should not have to suffer.*

ad·vo·cate² /'ædvəkɪt, -keɪt/ *n* [C] **1** someone who publicly supports someone or something: [+of] *She's a passionate advocate of natural childbirth.* | [+for] *an advocate for the disabled* **2** a lawyer who speaks in a court of law, especially in Scotland → **DEVIL'S ADVOCATE**

adze, **adz** /ædz/ *n* [C] a sharp tool with the blade at a right angle to the handle, used to shape wood

ae·gis /'iːdʒɪs/ *n formal* **under the aegis of sb/sth** with the protection or support of a person or organization: *a refugee camp operating under the aegis of the UN*

ae·on, **eon** /'iːən/ *n* [C] an extremely long period of time

aer·ate /'eəreɪt $ 'er-/ *v* [T] *technical* to put a gas or air into a liquid or into soil

aer·i·al¹ /'eəriəl $ 'er-/ *adj* [only before noun] **1** from a plane: *an aerial view* | *aerial photographs* | *an aerial view of the Three Gorges Dam project* **2** in or moving through the air

aerial sports

hang-gliding

microlighting

parachuting

piece of equipment for receiving or
evision signals, usually consisting
r wire; ⬛ **antenna** *AmE*; → see
s a sport in which someone goes
s and performs complicated

aer·i·al·ist /'eəriəlɪst $ 'er-/ *n* [C] someone who goes down a mountain on SKIS and performs complicated jumps and turns in the air

aero- /eərəʊ, eərə $ erəʊ, -rə/ *prefix* concerning the air or aircraft: *aerodynamics* (=science of movement through air) | *an aeroengine*

aer·o·bat·ics /ˌeərə'bætɪks, ˌeərəʊ- $ ˌerə-/ *n* [plural] tricks done in a plane that involve making difficult or dangerous movements in the air

ae·ro·bic /eə'rəʊbɪk $ e'rəʊ-/ *adj* **1** *technical* using oxygen; ⬛ **anaerobic** **2** **aerobic exercise** a type of exercise intended to strengthen the heart and lungs: *running, swimming, and other forms of aerobic exercise*

aer·o·bics /eə'rəʊbɪks $ e'rəʊ-/ *n* [U] a very active type of physical exercise done to music, usually in a class → see picture at SPORTS CENTRE

aer·o·drome /'eərədrəʊm $ 'erədrəʊm/ *n* [C] *BrE old-fashioned* a place that small planes fly from

aer·o·dy·nam·ic /ˌeərəʊdaɪ'næmɪk◂ $ ˌerəʊ-/ *adj* **1** an aerodynamic car, design etc uses the principles of aerodynamics to achieve high speed or low use of petrol **2** *technical* related to or involving aerodynamics: *aerodynamic efficiency* —**aerodynamically** /-kli/ *adv*

aer·o·dy·nam·ics /ˌeərəʊdaɪ'næmɪks $ ˌerəʊ-/ *n* [U] **1** the scientific study of how objects move through the air **2** the qualities needed for something to move smoothly through the air

aer·o·gramme also **aerogram** *AmE* /'eərəɡræm $ 'erə-/ *n* [C] a very light letter you send by AIRMAIL

aer·o·nau·tics /ˌeərə'nɔːtɪks $ ˌerə'nɒː-/ *n* [U] the science of designing and flying planes —**aeronautical** *adj*

aer·o·plane /'eərəpleɪn $ 'erə-/ *BrE*; **airplane** *AmE n* [C] a flying vehicle with wings and at least one engine; ⬛ **plane** → AIRCRAFT

aer·o·sol /'eərəsɒl $ 'erəsɑːl/ *n* [C] a small metal container with liquid inside. You press a button on the container to make the liquid come out in very small drops.; → **spray**

aer·o·space¹ /'eərəʊspeɪs $ 'erəʊ-/ *adj* involving the designing and building of aircraft and space vehicles: *the aerospace industry*

aerospace² *n* [U] the industry that designs and builds aircraft and space vehicles: **aerospace company/worker etc** *employment in the aerospace industry*

aes·thete, **esthete** /'iːsθiːt $ 'es-/ *n* [C] *formal* someone who loves and understands beautiful things, such as art and music

aes·thet·ic¹, **esthetic** /iːs'θetɪk, es- $ es-/ *adj* connected with beauty and the study of beauty: *From an esthetic point of view, it's a nice design.* | *a work of great aesthetic appeal* —**aesthetically** /-kli/ *adj*: *aesthetically pleasing*

aesthetic² *n formal* **1** **aesthetics** [U] the study of beauty, especially beauty in art **2** [C] a set of principles about beauty or art: *A new aesthetic had been evolved.*

ae·ther /'iːθə $ -ər/ *n* [U] an old spelling of ETHER (=the air or sky)

ae·ti·ol·o·gy, **etiology** /ˌiːti'ɒlədʒi $ -'ɑːl-/ *n* [U] *medical* the study of what causes disease

a·far /ə'faː $ ə'faːr/ *adv literary* **from afar** from a long distance away: *I saw him from afar.*

af·fa·ble /'æfəbəl/ *adj* friendly and easy to talk to; ⬛ **pleasant**: *an affable guy* —**affably** *adv* —**affability** /ˌæfə'bɪləti/ *n* [U]

af·fair S2 W1 /ə'feə $ ə'fer/ *n* [C]
1 PUBLIC/POLITICAL ACTIVITIES affairs [plural] **a)** public or political events and activities: *world affairs* | *They were accused of interfering in China's internal affairs.* | *the exclusion of women from public affairs* | *a foreign affairs respondent for CNN* **b)** things connected with your personal life, your financial situation etc: *I am not prepared to discuss my financial*

2 [EVENT] **a)** an event or set of related events, especially one that is impressive or shocking: *the Watergate affair* | *The whole affair was a disaster.* **b)** used when describing an event: *The party was a very grand affair.*
3 [RELATIONSHIP] a secret sexual relationship between two people, when at least one of them is married to someone else; ▪ **love affair**: [+with] *He had an affair with his boss that lasted six years.*
4 [OBJECT] *informal old-fashioned* used when describing an object, machine etc: *The computer was one of those little portable affairs.*
5 be sb's affair if something is your affair, it only concerns you and you do not want anyone else to get involved in it: *What I do in my free time is my affair.*

af·fect [S1] [W1] /ə'fekt/ *v* [T]
1 to do something that produces an effect or change in something or in someone's situation: *the areas affected by the hurricane* | *a disease that affects the central nervous system* | *decisions which affect our lives* | *Trading has been adversely affected by the downturn in consumer spending.*
2 [usually passive] to make someone feel strong emotions: *We were all deeply affected by her death.*
3 *formal* to pretend to have a particular feeling, way of speaking etc: *As usual, Simon affected complete boredom.* | *He used to affect a foreign accent.*

af·fec·ta·tion /ˌæfek'teɪʃən/ *n* [C,U] a way of behaving, speaking etc that is not sincere or natural: *Calling everyone 'darling' is just an affectation.*

af·fect·ed /ə'fektɪd/ *adj* not sincere or natural: *an affected laugh*

af·fect·ing /ə'fektɪŋ/ *adj formal* producing strong emotions of sadness, pity etc; ▪ **upsetting**: *a deeply affecting story*

af·fec·tion /ə'fekʃən/ *n* [singular, U] **1** a feeling of liking or love and caring; ▪ **fondness**: [+for] *Bart had a deep affection for the old man.* | *She looked back on those days with affection.* | *Their father never showed them much affection.* | *The church was held in great affection* (=loved and cared about a lot) *by the local residents.* **2** sb's affections the feelings of love and caring that someone has: *Africa has always had a special place in my affections.*

af·fec·tion·ate /ə'fekʃənət/ *adj* showing in a gentle way that you love someone and care about them; ▪ **loving**: [+towards] *Jo is very affectionate towards her.* | *an affectionate hug* —**affectionately** *adv*

af·fec·tive /ə'fektɪv/ *adj medical* or *technical* relating to or having an effect on the emotions: *affective disorders*

af·fi·anced /ə'faɪənst/ *adj old use* ENGAGED (1)

af·fi·da·vit /ˌæfɪ'deɪvɪt/ *n* [C] *law* a written statement that you swear is true, for use as proof in a court of law

af·fil·i·ate¹ /ə'fɪlieɪt/ *v* **1** [I,T usually passive] if a group or organization affiliates to or with another larger one, it forms a close connection with it: [+with] *The Society is not affiliated with any political party.* | [+to] *the church's right to affiliate to Rome* **2** affiliate yourself to/with sb/sth to join or become connected with a larger group or organization: *She affiliated herself with the Impressionist school of painting.*

af·fil·i·ate² /ə'fɪliət/ *n* [C] a company, organization etc that is connected with or controlled by a larger one: *Volvo's Japanese affiliate, Mitsubishi*

af·fil·i·at·ed /ə'fɪlieɪtɪd/ *adj* [only before noun] an affiliated organization/club/member etc an organization, club etc that is a member of a larger group or organization, or is closely connected with it: *The Association provides information on affiliated clubs.*

af·fil·i·a·tion /ə,fɪli'eɪʃən/ *n* **1** [C,U] the connection or involvement that someone or something has with a political, religious etc organization: sb's (political/religious etc) affiliation *the newspaper's political affiliations* **2** [U] when a smaller group or organization joins a larger one

af·fin·i·ty /ə'fɪnɪti/ *plural* **affinities** *n* **1** [singular] a strong feeling that you like and understand someone or something: [+with/for/between] *his remarkable affinity with animals* **2** [C,U] a close relationship between two things because of qualities or features that they share: [+with/between] *the affinity between Christian and Chinese concepts of the spirit*

af'finity ˌcard *n* [C] a type of CREDIT CARD, where an amount of money is given by the credit card company to a CHARITY every time the card is used

af·firm /ə'fɜːm $ -ɜːrm/ *v* [T] *formal* **1** to state publicly that something is true; ▪ **confirm**: *The general affirmed rumors of an attack.* | affirm that *A spokesman for the company affirmed that a merger was likely.* **2** to strengthen a feeling, belief, or idea: *He claims that modern physics affirms his Christian beliefs.* —**affirmation** /ˌæfə'meɪʃən $ ˌæfər-/ *n* [C,U]

af·fir·ma·tive¹ /ə'fɜːmətɪv $ -ɜːr-/ *adj formal* an affirmative answer or action means 'yes' or shows agreement; ▪ **negative**: *an affirmative nod* —**affirmatively** *adv*

affirmative² *n* answer/reply in the affirmative *formal* to say 'yes' → answer/reply in the negative at NEGATIVE² (2)

af,firmative 'action *n* [U] *especially AmE* the practice of choosing people for a job, college etc who are usually treated unfairly because of their race, sex etc; ▪ **positive discrimination** *BrE*

af·fix¹ /ə'fɪks/ *v* [T often passive] *formal* to fasten or stick something to something else: affix sth to sth *A label must be affixed to all parcels.*

af·fix² /'æfɪks/ *n* [C] a group of letters added to the beginning or end of a word to change its meaning or use, such as 'un-', 'mis-', '-ness', or '-ly' → PREFIX¹ (1), SUFFIX

af·flict /ə'flɪkt/ *v* [T often passive] *formal* to affect someone or something in an unpleasant way, and make them suffer: [+with/by] *a country afflicted by famine*

af·flic·tion /ə'flɪkʃən/ *n* [C,U] *formal* something that causes pain or suffering, especially a medical condition: *the afflictions of old age*

af·flu·ent /'æfluənt/ *adj formal* having plenty of money, nice houses, expensive things etc; ▪ **wealthy**: *affluent families* | an affluent society/country/area etc *the affluent Côte d'Azur* —**affluence** *n* [U]; → see box at RICH

af·ford [S1] [W3] /ə'fɔːd $ -ɔːrd/ *v* [T]
1 can/could afford [usually negative] **a)** to have enough money to buy or pay for something: afford [to do] sth *We can't afford to go on vacation this year.* | *I couldn't afford the rent on my own.* | *How can she afford to eat out every night?* **b)** to have enough time to do something: *Dad can't afford any more time off work.* **c)** if you cannot afford to do something, you must not do it because it could cause serious problems for you: afford to do sth *We can't afford to wait any longer or we'll miss the plane.* ⚠ Afford can be followed by an infinitive with 'to', but not an -ing form: *I can't afford to buy* (NOT *can't afford buying/can't afford buy*) *a car.*
2 *formal* to provide something or allow something to happen: *The room affords a beautiful view over the city.* | afford (sb) an opportunity/chance *It afforded her the opportunity to improve her tennis skills.* | *The new law will afford protection to employees.* —**affordable** *adj*: *affordable housing*

af·for·es·ta·tion /ə,fɒrɪ'steɪʃən $ ə,fɔː-, ə,fɑː-/ *n* [U] *technical* the act of planting trees in order to make a forest; ▪ **deforestation**

af·fray /ə'freɪ/ *n* [C,U] *law* a noisy fight in a public place, or when someone is involved in such a fight

af·fri·cate /'æfrɪkət/ *n* [C] *technical* a PLOSIVE so such as /t/ or /d/ that is immediately followe

A

A

a FRICATIVE sound made in the same part of the mouth, such as /s/ or /ʒ/. The word 'church', for example, contains the affricate /tʃ/.

af·front¹ /ə'frʌnt/ v [T usually passive] *formal* to offend or insult someone, especially by not showing respect: *He stepped back, affronted by the question.*

affront² n [C usually singular] a remark or action that offends or insults someone: [+to] *The comments were an affront to his pride.*

Af·ghan¹ /'æfgæn/ adj relating to Afghanistan or its people

Afghan² n [C] **1** someone from Afghanistan **2** also **Afghan hound** a tall thin dog with a pointed nose and very long silky hair

a·fi·cio·na·do /ə,fɪʃə'nɑːdəʊ $ -doʊ/ n plural aficionados [C] someone who is very interested in a particular activity or subject and knows a lot about it: [+of] *an aficionado of fine food*

a·field /ə'fiːld/ adv **far/further/farthest afield** far away, especially from home: *They were exporting as far afield as Alexandria.* | *students who come from further afield.*

a·fire /ə'faɪə $ ə'faɪr/ adj, adv [not before noun] *literary* burning; ■ **ablaze**: *One of the boats had been set afire.*

a·flame /ə'fleɪm/ adj [not before noun] **1** burning; ■ **ablaze**: *Most of the city was aflame.* **2** very bright with colour or light; ■ **ablaze**: [+with] *trees aflame with autumn leaves* **3** filled with strong emotions or excitement —**aflame** adv

AFL-CIO /,eɪ ef ,el ,siː aɪ 'əʊ $ -'oʊ/ n **the AFL-CIO** *the American Federation of Labor and Congress of Industrial Organizations* an organization of American TRADE UNIONS

a·float /ə'fləʊt $ ə'floʊt/ adj [not before noun] **1** having enough money to operate or stay out of debt: **keep (sb/sth) afloat/stay afloat** *The Treasury borrowed £40 billion, just to stay afloat.* **2** floating on water: **keep (sb/sth) afloat/stay afloat** *Somehow we kept the ship afloat.* —**afloat** adv

a·foot /ə'fʊt/ adj [not before noun] being planned or happening: **moves/plans/changes afoot** *There were plans afoot for a second attack.* —**afoot** adv

a·fore·men·tioned /ə'fɔːmenʃənd $ 'æfər,menʃənd, ə'fɔːr-/ also **a·fore·said** /ə'fɔːsed $ ə'fɔːr-/ adj [only before noun] *law* **the aforementioned** mentioned before in an earlier part of a document, article, book etc: *The property belongs to the aforementioned Mr Jones.* —**aforementioned** n [singular or plural]

a·fore·thought /ə'fɔːθɔːt $ ə'fɔːrθɒːt/ adj → **with malice aforethought** at MALICE (2)

a·foul /ə'faʊl/ adv **run afoul of sb/sth** *formal* to do something that is not allowed or legal, or that is against people's beliefs

a·fraid S1 W2 /ə'freɪd/ adj [not before noun]
1 frightened because you think that you may get hurt or that something bad may happen; ■ **scared**: *There's no need to be afraid.* | **afraid of (doing) sth** *kids who are afraid of the dark* | *He was afraid of being caught by the police.* | **afraid to do sth** *Zoe was half afraid* (=a little afraid) *to go back in the house.*; → see box at FEAR¹
2 worried about what might happen, or that something bad will happen: **afraid (that)** *He was afraid that the other kids would laugh at him.* | **afraid of (doing) sth** *I didn't tell her because I was afraid of upsetting her.* | *The government was afraid of a public outcry.* | **afraid to do sth** *Don't be afraid to ask for help.*
3 **afraid for sb/sth** worried that something bad may happen to a particular person or thing: *Her father looked ill and she was suddenly afraid for him.* | *Many of us were afraid for our jobs.*
4 **I'm afraid** *spoken* used to politely tell someone something that may annoy, upset, or disappoint them: *That's the most we can offer you, I'm afraid.* | [+(that)] *I'm afraid you've come to the wrong address.* | *'Is she very ill?' 'I'm afraid so* (=yes).' | *'Did you see him?' 'I'm afraid not* (=no).'

a·fresh /ə'freʃ/ adv if you do something afresh, you do it again from the beginning: *He moved to America to start afresh.*

Af·ri·can¹ /'æfrɪkən/ adj relating to Africa or its people

African² n [C] someone from Africa

African A·merican n [C] an American with dark skin, whose family originally came from the part of Africa south of the Sahara Desert

Af·ri·kaans /,æfrɪ'kɑːns/ n [U] a language of South Africa that is similar to Dutch

Af·ri·ka·ner /,æfrɪ'kɑːnə $ -ər/ n [C] a white South African whose first language is Afrikaans and who is usually related to the Dutch people who settled in South Africa in the 1600s; → **Boer**

Af·ro /'æfrəʊ $ -roʊ/ n [C] a hair style popular with black people in the 1970s in which the hair is cut into a large round shape

Afro- /æfrəʊ $ -roʊ/ prefix [in nouns and adjectives] African and something else: *an Afro-American* | *Afro-Caribbean children*

aft /ɑːft $ æft/ adj, adv *technical* in or towards the back part of a boat or aircraft; ▣ **fore (2)**

af·ter¹ S1 W1 /'ɑːftə $ 'æftər/ prep, conjunction, adv
1 when a particular event or time has happened, or when someone has done something; ▣ **before**: *After the war many soldiers stayed in France.* | *I go swimming every day after work.* | *Do you believe in life after death?* | *The first attack started just after midnight.* | *David went to bed straight after* (=immediately after) *supper.* | *After you'd called the police, what did you do?* | *Zimmerman changed his name after he left Germany.* | *People still remember the 1958 revolution and what came after* (=happened after it). | **after doing sth** *After leaving school, Mackay worked in a restaurant for a year.* | **2 days/3 weeks etc after (sth)** *Ten years after he bought the painting, Carswell discovered that it was a fake.* | **the day/week/year etc after (sth)** (=the next day, week etc) *His car was outside your house the morning after Bob's engagement party.* | *I'll see you again tomorrow or the day after.* | *She retired from politics the year after she received the Nobel Prize.* | **soon/not long/shortly after (sth)** *Not long after the wedding, his wife became ill.* | *The family moved to Hardingham in June 1983, and Sarah's first child was born soon after.*
2 when a particular amount of time has passed; ▣ **before**: *After 10 minutes remove the cake from the oven.* | *It's a hard life, but you'll get used to it after a while.* | *After months of negotiation, an agreement was finally reached.*
3 following someone or something else in a list or a piece of writing, or in order of importance: *Whose name is after yours on the list?* | *The date should be written after the address.* | *After football, tennis is my favourite sport.* | *The UK is the world's third largest arms producer, after the USA and Russia.*
4 *AmE* used when telling the time to say how many minutes have passed since a particular hour; ▣ **past** *BrE*: *The movie starts at a quarter* (=fifteen minutes) *after seven.*
5 **day after day/year after year etc** continuously for a very long time: *He's worked in that same office week after week, year after year, since he was 18.*
6 a) following someone in order to stop or speak to them: *Go after him and apologize.* | *I heard someone running after me, and a voice called my name.* **b)** in the direction of someone who has just left: *'Good luck,' she called after me as I left.* | *Harry stood in the doorway gazing after her.*
7 when someone has left a place or has finished doing something: *Remember to close the door after you.* | *I spend all day cleaning up after the kids.*
8 because of something that happened earlier: *I'm not surprised he walked out, after the way she treated him.* |

After your letter, I didn't think I'd ever see you again.
9 in spite of something that was done in the past: *How can you treat me like this after all I've done for you?*
10 when you have passed a particular place or travelled a certain distance along a road: *Turn left after the Crown Hotel.* | *After half a mile you will come to a crossroads.*
11 be after sb/sth a) to be looking for someone or something: *That boy's always in trouble – the police are after him again.* | *'Were you after anything in particular?' 'No, we're just looking.'* **b)** *informal* to want to have something that belongs to someone else: *I think Chris is after my job.*
12 one after another/one after the other if a series of events or actions happen one after another, each one happens soon after the previous one: *Ever since we moved here it's been one problem after another.*
13 after all a) in spite of what you thought was true or expected to happen: *He wrote to say they couldn't give me a job after all.* | *Union leaders announced that they would, after all, take part in the national conference.* **b)** used to say that something should be remembered or considered, because it helps to explain what you have just said: *Prisoners should be treated with respect – they are human beings after all.* | *I don't know why you're so concerned – it isn't your problem after all.*
14 *especially BrE* used to say who or what first had the name that someone or something has been given: *His name is Alessandro, after his grandfather.* | *It was named Waterloo Bridge, after the famous battle.*
15 *formal* in the same style as a particular painter, musician etc: *a painting after Rembrandt*
16 a) after you *spoken* used to say politely that someone else can use or do something before you do: *'Do you need the copier?' 'After you.'* **b) after you with sth** used to ask someone if you can have or use something after they have finished: *After you with that knife, please.* → **a man/woman after my own heart** at HEART (21); → **take after** at TAKE[1]

WORD CHOICE: after, in, afterwards
after is usually used as a preposition (followed by a noun): *I'll do it after lunch.* | *Please call after 9.30.*
after followed by a time period is more often used to talk about past events: *After a few minutes he stopped.*
in followed by a time period is more often used to talk about future events: *He'll be here in a few minutes.*
after can be used as an adverb, but only following another time adverb such as **soon**, **not long**, or **shortly**: *Tim came in at midnight, and Lucy not long after.*
afterwards can be used instead, and can also be used as an adverb on its own: *His parents came shortly afterwards.* | *You can meet the actors afterwards (NOT after).*

---

after[2] *adj* [only before noun] **1 in after years** *literary* in the years after the time that has been mentioned **2** *technical* in the back part of a boat or an aircraft

after- /ˈɑːftə $ ˈæftər/ *prefix* coming or happening afterwards: *an after-dinner speech* | *after-school activities*

af·ter·birth /ˈɑːftəbɜːθ $ ˈæftərbɜːrθ/ *n* [U] the substance that comes out of female humans or animals just after they have had a baby; → **placenta**

af·ter·care /ˈɑːftəkeə $ ˈæftərker/ *n* [U] *BrE* care or treatment given to someone after they leave hospital, prison etc: *the aftercare of ex-offenders*

after-ef·fect *BrE*, **af·ter·ef·fect** *AmE* /ˈɑːftərɪfekt $ ˈæf-/ *n* [C usually plural] a bad effect that continues for a long time after the thing that caused it: **the after-effects (of sth)** *the after-effects of his illness*

af·ter·glow /ˈɑːftəgləʊ $ ˈæftərgloʊ/ *n* [C usually singular] **1** a pleasant feeling that remains after a good experience: [+of] *the afterglow of victory* **2** the light that remains in the sky after the sun goes down

af·ter·life /ˈɑːftəlaɪf $ ˈæftər-/ *n* [singular] the life that some people believe people have after death

af·ter·math /ˈɑːftəmæθ $ ˈæftər-/ *n* [singular] the period of time after something such as a war, storm, or accident when people are still dealing with the results: [+of] *the danger of disease in the aftermath of the earthquake*

af·ter·noon[1] S1 W2 /ˌɑːftəˈnuːn◂ $ ˌæftər-/ *n* [C,U]
1 the part of the day after the morning and before the evening; → **morning, evening**

on Monday/Friday/Saturday etc afternoon
in the afternoon
tomorrow afternoon
yesterday afternoon
this afternoon (=today in the afternoon)
early/late afternoon
afternoon nap/snack/session/meeting etc

---

*There's a meeting **on Thursday afternoon**.* | *It was very hot **in the afternoon**.* | *See you **tomorrow afternoon**.* | *Are you going into town **this afternoon**?* | *We met in the **early afternoon**, Micky had changed his mind.* | *By **late afternoon**, he was having his **afternoon nap**.*

2 afternoons during the afternoon every day: *She only works afternoons.*

afternoon[2] *interjection BrE informal* used to greet someone when you meet them in the afternoon

af·ters /ˈɑːftəz $ ˈæftərz/ *n* [plural] *BrE informal* the part of a meal that comes after the main dish; **dessert**

af·ter·shave /ˈɑːftəʃeɪv $ ˈæftər-/ *n* [C,U] a liquid with a nice smell that a man puts on his face after he has shaved

af·ter·shock /ˈɑːftəʃɒk $ ˈæftərʃɑːk/ *n* [C] **1** a small EARTHQUAKE that happens after a larger one **2** the effects of a shocking event: *the war and its aftershocks*

af·ter·taste /ˈɑːftəteɪst $ ˈæftər-/ *n* [C usually singular] a taste that stays in your mouth after you have eaten or drunk something: *The wine leaves a strong aftertaste.*

af·ter·thought /ˈɑːftəθɔːt $ ˈæftərθɒːt/ *n* [C] something that you mention or add later because you did not think of it or plan it before: *He added as an afterthought, 'Bring Melanie too'.*

af·ter·wards S2 W3 /ˈɑːftəwədz $ ˈæftərwərdz/ *adv*
also **afterward** after an event or time that has already been mentioned: *Charles arrived **shortly afterwards**.* | **days/weeks etc afterwards** *The experience haunted me **for years afterward**.* | *She died **not long afterwards**.* | *Afterwards, I was asked to write a book.*; → see box at AFTER[1]

a·gain S1 W1 /əˈgen, əˈgeɪn $ əˈgen/ *adv*
1 one more time – used when something has happened or been done before: *Can you say that again? I didn't hear.* | *I'll never go there again.* | *Mr Khan's busy. Can you try again later?* | **once again/yet again** (=used to emphasize that something has happened several or many times before) *In 1997, the family moved house yet again.* | *Once again, Drew was under arrest.*
2 back to the same state or situation that you were in before: *She stayed and nursed him back to health again.* | *It's great to have you home again.*
3 all over again if you do something all over again, you repeat it from the beginning: *I had to write the essay all over again.*
4 as much/as many/the same again the same amount or number as you have just had, said etc: *What a fantastic lunch. I could eat the same again.* | *Nearly as many again died from pneumonia.* | *The amount of crime is about **half as much again** (=the same in addition to half that amount) as it was in 1973.* | *'Another drink?' 'Yes, **same again** (=the same drink again), please.'*
5 *spoken* used to give a fact or opinion that explains or adds to something you have just said: *And again, these workshops will benefit the community widely.*

6 then/there again *spoken* used to introduce an idea or fact that is different from something you have just said, or makes it seem less likely to be true: *She says she's thirty-five.* **But then again** *she might be lying.*

7 again and again/time and (time) again/over and over again – used in order to show disapproval: *I've told you again and again, don't do that!*

8 *spoken* used when you want someone to repeat information that they have already given you: *What did you say your name was again?* → **now and again** at NOW[1] (5)

a·gainst [S1] [W1] /ə'genst, ə'geɪnst $ ə'genst/ *prep*
1 a) used to say that someone opposes or disagrees with something: *Every council member voted against the proposal.* | *those who are campaigning against the new road* | *He advised me against travelling.* | *Mr Howard has declared that he is against all forms of racism.* | *the fight against terrorism* **b)** used to say that an action is not wanted or approved of by someone: *They got married against her parents' wishes* (=although they knew her parents did not want them to). | *She has been kept in the house against her will* (=she does not want to stay in the house). | *The use of certain drugs is against the law* (=illegal). | *It's against my principles to borrow money* (=I do not believe it is right). **c)** used to say that something is not allowed by a law or rule: *There ought to be a law against it.*

2 used to say who someone is competing with or trying to defeat in a game, battle etc: *Gambotti was injured in last Saturday's game against the Lions.* | *We'll be competing against some of the best companies in Europe.*

3 used to say who is harmed, threatened, or given a disadvantage: *violence against elderly people* | *crimes against humanity* | *discrimination against women* | *There had been death threats against prison staff.* | *Your lack of experience could count against you.* | *The regulations tend to work against smaller companies.*

4 used to say that something touches, hits, or rubs a surface: *the sound of the rain drumming against my window* | *The car skidded and we could hear the crunch of metal against metal.*

5 next to and touching an upright surface, especially for support: *There was a ladder propped up against the wall.* | *The younger policeman was leaning against the bureau with his arms folded.*

6 in the opposite direction to the movement or flow of something; ◪ **with**: *sailing against the wind* | *She dived down and swam out strongly against the current.*

7 seen with something else behind or as a background: *He could see a line of figures silhouetted against the sky.* | *It is important to know what colours look good against your skin.*

8 used to show that you are considering particular events in relation to other events that are happening at the same time: *The reforms were introduced against a background of social unrest.*

9 used to say what you are comparing something with: *The pound has fallen 10% against the dollar.* | *She checked the contents of the box against the list.* | *The cost of the proposed research needs to be balanced against its benefits.*

10 used to say who or what you are trying to protect someone or something from: *insurance against accident and sickness* | *a cream to protect against sunburn* | *a vaccine which is effective against pneumonia*

11 used to say who is said or shown to have done something wrong: *He has always emphatically denied the allegations against him.* | *The evidence against you is overwhelming.*

12 be/come up against sb/sth to have to deal with a difficult opponent or problem: *You see, this is what we're up against – the suppliers just aren't reliable.*

13 have sth against sb/sth to dislike or disapprove of someone or something: *I don't have anything against babies. I just don't feel very comfortable with them.*

a·gape /ə'geɪp/ *adj* [not before noun] with your mouth wide open, especially because you are surprised or shocked: *Vince watched, his mouth agape in horror.*

ag·ate /'ægət/ *n* [C] a hard stone with bands of different colours, used in jewellery

age[1] [S1] [W1] /eɪdʒ/ *n*
1 HOW OLD [C,U] the number of years someone has lived or something has existed: *Francis is the same age as me.* | *Experts disagree over the age of the drawings.* | *Dad retired at the age of 56.* | **at age 5/18 etc** *In Britain, schooling starts at age 5.* | **4/15 etc years of age** (=4, 15 etc years old) *She was just over 16 years of age.* | **at my/your etc age** (=when you are as old as me etc) *At my age, it's quite difficult getting up stairs.* | **at/from an early age** (=at or from the time when someone is very young) *girls who become mothers at an early age* | **over/under the age of 5/18 etc** *people over the age of 65* | **of his/her own age** (=of the same age as him, her etc) *Kids need friends of their own age to play with.* | **for his/her etc age** (=compared with other people of the same age) *She's tall for her age, isn't she?* | **act your age** (=behave in a way that is suitable for how old you are) *It's time you started acting your age, Jeff.* | *My mother* **reached the age of** *90* (=lived until she was 90). | *children* **ranging in age** *from 6 to 17*
2 LEGAL AGE [U] the age when you are legally old enough to do something: *What's* **the minimum age** *for getting a driver's license?* | *You're not allowed to buy alcohol. You're* **under age** (=too young by law). | **retirement/pension age** (=when you are old enough to stop working or receive a pension) *the normal retirement age of 65*
3 PERIOD OF LIFE [C,U] one of the particular periods of someone's life; → **old age**, **middle age**, **teenage**: *women of childbearing age* | **a difficult/awkward age** *The early teens are often a difficult age.*
4 BEING OLD [U] the state of being old: **with age** | *High blood pressure increases with age.* | *Some of the furniture was* **showing** *signs of* **age.**
5 PERIOD OF HISTORY [C usually singular] a particular period of history: *We are living in the age of technology.* | *Molecular biology is pushing medicine into* **a new age.** | **the computer/industrial/nuclear etc age**; → **in this day and age** at DAY (6); → **BRONZE AGE, IRON AGE, MIDDLE AGES, STONE AGE**
6 ages [plural] also **an age** *informal especially BrE* a long time: *Simon! I haven't seen you* **for ages.** | *That recipe* **takes ages.** | **it's ages since/before/until etc sth** *It's ages since we've played that game.*
7 come of age a) to reach the age when you are legally considered to be a responsible adult **b)** if something comes of age, it reaches a stage of development at which people accept it as being important, valuable etc: *During this period the movies really came of age as an art form.* → **NEW AGE[1], NEW AGE[2]**

age[2] *v present participle* **aging or ageing** **1** [I,T] to start looking older or to make someone or something look older: *He was worried to see how much she'd aged.* | *The experience had aged him in advance of his years.* **2** [I] to become older: *The buildings are ageing, and some are unsafe.* **3** [I,T] to improve and develop in taste over a period of time, or to allow food or alcohol to do this: *Cheddar cheese ages well.* | *The whisky is aged for at least ten years.*

'age ,bracket *n* [C] the people between two particular ages, considered as a group; ◪ **age group**: **in the ... age bracket** *single people in the 40–50 age bracket*

aged[1] [W3] /eɪdʒd/ *adj* **aged 5/25 etc** 5 etc years old: [+between] *Police are looking for a man aged between 30 and 35.* | *The course is open to children aged 12 and over.*

a·ged[2] /'eɪdʒɪd/ *adj* **1** very old: *my aged parents* **2 the aged** [plural] old people: *the care of children and the aged*

'age discrimi,nation *n* [U] unfair treatment of people because they are old; ◪ **ageism** *BrE*

'age group n [C] the people between two particular ages, considered as a group: **in the ... age group** a book for children in the 12–14 age group

age·ing /'eɪdʒɪŋ/ a British spelling of AGING

age·is·m, agism /'eɪdʒɪzəm/ n [U] BrE unfair treatment of people because they are old; ▤ **age discrimination** —**ageist** adj BrE: negative ageist attitudes

age·ist /'eɪdʒ‿ɪst/ adj treating older people unfairly because of a belief that they are less important than younger people: The article seemed somewhat insensitive and ageist to me. —**ageist** n [C]

age·less /'eɪdʒləs/ adj **1** never looking old or old-fashioned: Her face seemed to be ageless. **2** having existed for a very long time and continuing forever: the ageless charm of a country kitchen —**agelessness** n [U]

'age ˌlimit n [C] the oldest or youngest age at which you are allowed to do something: [+for] The **upper age limit** for entrants was set at 25.

a·gen·cy S2 W1 /'eɪdʒənsi/ n plural **agencies** [C] **1** a business that provides a particular service for people or organizations: **an advertising/employment/ travel etc agency** a local housing agency ➔ DATING AGENCY, NEWS AGENCY

2 an organization or department, especially within a government, that does a specific job: a UN agency responsible for helping refugees | the Environmental Protection Agency

3 by/through the agency of sb formal being done as the result of someone's help

a·gen·da S3 /ə'dʒendə/ n [C] **1** a list of problems or subjects that a government, organization etc is planning to deal with: **be high on the agenda/be top of the agenda** (=be one of the most important problems to deal with) Measures to combat terrorism will be high on the agenda. | The government **set an agenda** for constitutional reform. | **political/ economic/legislative/domestic etc agenda** Our Centre has limited its research agenda to four areas.

2 the ideas that a political party thinks are important and the things that party aims to achieve: The Republicans have stuck to their conservative agenda.

3 a list of the subjects to be discussed at a meeting: the next **item** (=subject) **on the agenda** ➔ hidden agenda at HIDDEN² (3)

a·gent S3 W2 /'eɪdʒənt/ n [C] **1** a person or company that represents another person or company, especially in business: Our agent in Rio deals with all our Brazilian business. | [+for] We're acting as agents for Mr Watson. ➔ ESTATE AGENT, REAL ESTATE AGENT, LAND AGENT, TRAVEL AGENT

2 someone who finds work for actors, musicians etc, or who finds someone to PUBLISH a writer's work: My agent has a new script for me to look at. | a **literary agent**

3 someone who works for a government or police department, especially in order to get secret information about another country or organization: an **intelligence agent** | an FBI agent | an **undercover** (=secret) agent ➔ SECRET AGENT, DOUBLE AGENT

4 technical a chemical or substance that is used for a particular purpose or that has a particular effect: Soap is a cleansing agent.

5 someone or something that affects or changes a situation: **agent for/of change** Technological advances are the chief agents of change. ➔ FREE AGENT

a·gent pro·voc·a·teur /ˌæʒɒn prɒvɒkəˈtɜː $ ˌɑːʒɑːn pruːvɑːkəˈtɜːr/ n plural **agents provocateurs** (same pronunciation) [C] someone who is employed to encourage people who are working against a government to do something illegal so that they are caught

ˌage of conˈsent n **the age of consent** the age when someone can legally get married or have a sexual relationship

ˌage-ˈold adj having existed for a very long time: **an age-old tradition/practice/custom etc** BrE: age-old customs | the **age-old problem** of sexual discrimination

'age range n [C] the people between two particular ages, considered as a group; ▤ **age group: in the ... age range** young people in the 15–18 age range | This affects people across a wide age range.

ag·glom·er·ate /ə'glɒmərₐt $ ə'glɑː-/ n [singular, U] technical a type of rock formed from pieces of material from a VOLCANO that have melted together

ag·glom·e·ra·tion /əˌglɒmə'reɪʃən $ əˌglɑː-/ n [C,U] a large collection of things that do not seem to belong together: [+of] buildings in an agglomeration of styles

ag·glu·ti·na·tion /əˌgluːtₐ'neɪʃən $ əˌgluːtn'eɪ-/ n [U] **1** the state of being stuck together **2** the process of making new words by combining two or more words, such as combining 'ship' and 'yard' to make 'shipyard'

ag·gran·dize·ment also **-isement** BrE /ə'grændₐzmənt/ n [U] when a person or country tries to increase their power or importance – used to show disapproval: the misuse of authority for **personal aggrandizement**

ag·gra·vate /'ægrəveɪt/ v [T] **1** to make a bad situation, an illness, or an injury worse; ▤ **improve**: Their money problems were **further aggravated** by a rise in interest rates. | Building the new road will only **aggravate the situation**. **2** to make someone angry or annoyed; ▤ **irritate**: What really aggravates me is the way she won't listen. —**aggravating** adj —**aggravatingly** adv —**aggravation** /ˌægrə'veɪʃən/ n [C,U]

ag·gra·va·ted /'ægrəveɪtₐd/ adj [only before noun] law an aggravated offence is one in which a criminal does something that makes their original crime more serious: He was charged with **aggravated assault**.

ag·gre·gate¹ /'ægrɪgₐt/ n formal **1** [C] the total after a lot of different figures or points have been added together: [+of] The smaller minorities got an aggregate of 1,327 votes. | **In the aggregate** (=as a group or in total), women outlive men by 7 or more years. | **on aggregate** BrE (=when the points from two football games are added together) Manchester United won 2–1 on aggregate. **2** [singular, U] technical sand or small stones that are used in making CONCRETE

aggregate² adj [only before noun] technical being the total amount of something after all the figures or points have been added together: an increase in the aggregate production

ag·gre·gate³ /'ægrɪgeɪt/ v formal **1** [linking verb] to be a particular amount when added together: Sheila's earnings from all sources aggregated £100,000. **2** [I,T usually passive] to put different amounts, pieces of information etc together to form a group or a total: [+with] A wife's income is no longer aggregated with that of her husband. —**aggregation** /ˌægrɪ'geɪʃən/ n [U]

ag·gres·sion /ə'greʃən/ n [U] **1** angry or threatening behaviour or feelings that often result in fighting: Television violence can encourage aggression in children. | [+towards] Our dogs have never shown aggression towards other dogs. **2** the act of attacking a country, especially when that country has not attacked first: an unprovoked **act of aggression** | [+against] Athenian aggression against Persia

ag·gres·sive S3 /ə'gresɪv/ adj **1** behaving in an angry, threatening way, as if you want to fight or attack someone: Jim's voice became aggressive. | Teachers apparently expect a certain amount of aggressive behaviour from boys. **2** very determined to succeed or get what you want: A successful businessman has to be aggressive. | an aggressive marketing campaign —**aggressively** adv —**aggressiveness** n [U]

A

[1] 000, [2] 000, [3] 000, most frequent words in [S]poken and [W]ritten English

A

ag·gres·sor /əˈgresə $ -ər/ n [C] a person or country that begins a fight or war with another person or country: *measures taken to deter potential aggressors*

ag·grieved /əˈgriːvd/ adj **1** angry and sad because you think you have been unfairly treated: *an aggrieved tone of voice* **2** *law* having suffered as a result of the illegal actions of someone else: *the aggrieved party* (=person who has suffered)

ag·gro /ˈægrəʊ $ -roʊ/ n [U] *BrE informal* **1** angry behaviour or fighting: *I hope he doesn't cause any aggro.* **2** problems or difficulties that annoy you: *I can't cope with all this aggro.*

a·ghast /əˈɡɑːst $ əˈɡæst/ adj [not before noun] *written* feeling or looking shocked by something you have seen or just found out: [+at] *Everyone was aghast at the verdict.* | *Hank looked at her aghast.*

a·gile /ˈædʒaɪl $ ˈædʒəl/ adj **1** able to move quickly and easily: *Dogs are surprisingly agile.* **2** someone who has an agile mind is able to think very quickly and intelligently: *He was physically strong and mentally agile.* —**agility** /əˈdʒɪləti/ n [U]: *With surprising agility, Karl darted across the road.*

ag·ing[1] also **ageing** *BrE* /ˈeɪdʒɪŋ/ adj [only before noun] becoming old: *aging movie stars* | *Europe's ageing population* (=with more old people than before)

aging[2] also **ageing** *BrE* /ˈeɪdʒɪŋ/ n [U] the process of getting old: *Memory loss is often a part of ageing.*

ag·is·m /ˈeɪdʒɪzəm/ n an American spelling of AGEISM

a·gi·tate /ˈædʒəteɪt/ v **1** [I] to argue strongly in public for something you want, especially a political or social change: [+for/against] *unions agitating for higher pay* | **agitate to do sth** *His family are agitating to get him freed.* **2** [T] *formal* to make someone feel anxious, upset, and nervous: *I must warn you that any mention of Clare agitates your grandmother.* **3** [T] *technical* to shake or mix a liquid quickly

a·gi·ta·ted /ˈædʒəteɪtəd/ adj so nervous or upset that you are unable to keep still or think calmly: *Amanda was getting visibly agitated.*

a·gi·ta·tion /ˌædʒəˈteɪʃən/ n **1** [U] when you are so anxious, nervous, or upset that you cannot think calmly: *She was in a state of considerable agitation.* **2** [C,U] public argument or action for social or political change: [+for/against] *mass agitation for political reform* **3** [U] *technical* the act of shaking or mixing a liquid

a·gi·ta·tor /ˈædʒəteɪtə $ -ər/ n [C] someone who encourages people to work towards changing something in society – used to show disapproval: *a political agitator*

a·git·prop /ˌædʒəɪtˈprɒp $ -ˈprɑːp/ n [U] music, literature, or art that tries to persuade people to follow a particular set of political ideas

a·glow /əˈgləʊ $ əˈgloʊ/ adj [not before noun] *literary* **1** having a soft light, or a strong, warm colour: *The evening sky was still aglow.* **2** if someone's face is aglow, they seem happy and excited: [+with] *Linda's face was aglow with happiness.*

AGM /ˌeɪ dʒiː ˈem/ n [C] *BrE* **annual general meeting** a meeting held once a year by a club, business, or organization for the members to discuss the previous year's business, elect officials etc; ◼ **annual meeting** *AmE*

ag·nos·tic /æɡˈnɒstɪk, əɡ- $ -ˈnɑː-/ n [C] someone who believes that people cannot know whether God exists or not; → **atheist** —**agnostic** adj —**agnosticism** /-tˈsɪzəm/ n [U]

a·go /əˈɡəʊ $ əˈɡoʊ/ adv used to show how far back in the past something happened: **5 minutes/an hour/20 years etc ago** *Her husband died 14 years ago.* | **long ago/a long time ago** *He should have finished at university long ago, but he kept taking extra courses.* | **minute/moment ago** *The little girl you saw a moment ago was my niece.* | **a little/short while ago** *Tom got a*

letter from him just a little while ago. | *They moved to a new house some time ago* (=a fairly long time ago). | *We had our bicentenary celebrations not that long ago.*

WORD CHOICE: **ago, before, previously**
Use **ago** to say how much time has passed from the time something happened to now, the time of speaking: *I saw her a few minutes ago.* | *We went to Madrid two years ago.*
Use **before** to say how much time passed from the time something happened to a time in the past: *We went back to the same hotel where we had stayed two years before.*
Previously is used in the same way, but is more formal: *The meeting was a follow-up to one that had been held four days previously.*
⚠ Do not use a preposition ('at', 'in', 'on' etc) before a phrase with **ago**: *They first met fifteen years ago (NOT at/in fifteen years ago).*
⚠ Do not use 'since' or 'before' with **ago**: *I came to the USA two months ago (NOT since/before two months ago).*
⚠ Use the past tense, not the present perfect, with **ago**: *I started (NOT I've started) a new job a few weeks ago.*

a·gog /əˈgɒg $ əˈɡɑːg/ adj [not before noun] very excited about something and wanting to find out more: *I've been agog all afternoon, waiting for the next part of your story.* | *Paul was agog with curiosity.*

ag·o·nize also **-ise** *BrE* /ˈægənaɪz/ v [I] to think about a difficult decision very carefully and with a lot of effort: [+over/about] *All the way home she agonized about what she should do.* —**agonizing** n [U]

ag·o·nized also **-ised** *BrE* /ˈægənaɪzd/ adj [only before noun] expressing very severe pain: *an agonized scream* | *From some place close by she heard agonized sobbing.*

ag·o·niz·ing also **-ising** *BrE* /ˈægənaɪzɪŋ/ adj **1** extremely painful: *The pain was agonizing.* **2** very unpleasant to experience, especially because of involving a difficult choice or a long wait: *an agonizing decision* —**agonizingly** adv: *at an agonizingly slow pace*

ag·o·ny /ˈægəni/ n plural **agonies** [C,U] **1** very severe pain: *the agony of arthritis* | **in agony** *I was in agony.* | *He groaned in agony.* **2** a very sad, difficult, or unpleasant experience: *It was agony not knowing if she would live.* | [+of] *He was in agonies of remorse.* → **pile on the pressure/agony** at PILE ON (2); → **prolong the agony** at PROLONG (2)

'agony ˌaunt n [C] *BrE* someone who writes an agony column

'agony ˌcolumn n [C] *BrE* a part of a newspaper or magazine in which someone gives advice to readers about their personal problems; ◼ **advice column**

ag·o·ra·pho·bi·a /ˌægərəˈfəʊbiə $ -ˈfoʊ-/ n [U] fear of crowds and open spaces; → **claustrophobia**

ag·o·ra·pho·bic /ˌægərəˈfəʊbɪk◂ $ -ˈfoʊ-/ n [C] someone who suffers from agoraphobia —**agoraphobic** adj

a·grar·i·an /əˈgreəriən $ əˈgrer-/ adj [usually before noun] relating to farming or farmers: *an agrarian economy* (=based on farming)

a·gree S1 W1 /əˈgriː/ v
1 SAME OPINION [I,T not in progressive] to have or express the same opinion about something as someone else; ◼ **disagree**: *Teenagers and their parents rarely agree.* | [+with] *If she felt he was right, she would agree with him.* | **agree that** *Most people nowadays would agree that a good pub is one of our best traditions.* | [+on/about] *We don't agree on everything, of course.* | **quite agree/I couldn't agree more** (=I agree completely) *'We have to talk.' 'Absolutely,' Meredith replied. 'I couldn't agree more.'*
2 SAY YES [I,T not in progressive] to say yes to an idea, plan, suggestion etc; ◼ **refuse**: *I suggested we go somewhere for the weekend and she agreed at once.* |

agree to do sth *No one really knows why he agreed to do the film.* | [+to] *My sister won't agree to our mother going into a nursing home.*
3 BE THE SAME [I,T not in progressive] to make a decision with someone after a discussion with them: **agree to do sth** *We agreed to meet again the following Monday.* | [+on] *They managed to agree on a date for the wedding.* | **agree that** *It was agreed that elections would be held in May.* | **agree a price/plan/strategy etc** *We agreed a new four-year contract.*
4 BE THE SAME [I not in progressive] if two pieces of information agree with each other, they match or are the same: [+with] *Your story doesn't agree with what the police have told us.*
5 agree to differ/disagree if two people agree to differ, they accept that they have different opinions about something and stop arguing about it
     agree with sth *phr v*
1 to believe that a decision, action, or suggestion is correct or right: *I don't agree with hitting children.*
2 not agree with sb if a type of food does not agree with you, it makes you feel ill: *Green peppers don't agree with me.*
3 if an adjective, verb etc agrees with a word, it matches that word by being plural if the word is plural etc

a·gree·a·ble /ə'griːəbəl/ *adj* **1** *written* or *old-fashioned* pleasant; ☒ **disagreeable**: *We spent a most agreeable couple of hours.* | *an agreeable young man* **2 be agreeable to sth** *formal* to be willing to do something or willing to allow something to be done: *My parents are quite agreeable to my studying abroad.* **3** acceptable: [+to] *The main objective is to find a solution that is agreeable to the company in terms of cost.* —**agreeably** *adv*: *I think you'll be agreeably surprised by what I'm going to say.*

a·greed /ə'griːd/ *adj* [only before noun] **1** an agreed plan, price, arrangement etc is one that people have discussed and accepted: *The important thing is to have agreed objectives.* **2 be agreed** if people are agreed, they have discussed something and agree about what to do: [+on] *All parties are now agreed on the plan.* | **be agreed that** *We're all agreed that we cannot spend what we have not earned.* **3 Agreed** used to check if someone agrees, or to show that you agree: *'Let's just forget it ever happened. Agreed?' 'Agreed.'*

a·gree·ment S1 W1 /ə'griːmənt/ *n*
1 [C] an arrangement or promise to do something, made by two or more people, companies, organizations etc: *a trade agreement* | [+with] *Does your employer have an agreement with a union?* | [+on] *an agreement on arms reduction* | **come to/reach an agreement** *Failure to reach an agreement will result in a strike.* | *Haydon came to an agreement with his creditors.* | **under an agreement** *Under the agreement, most agricultural prices would be frozen or cut.* | *They* **had an agreement that** *she would give them any leftover food from her shop.* | *They claimed the company had broken* **the terms of the agreement.**
2 [U] when people have the same opinion as each other; ☒ **disagreement**: **agreement that** *There is general agreement that copyright is a good idea.* | [+on] *There is widespread agreement on the need for prison reform.* | **be in agreement** *A decision will not be made until everyone is in agreement.* | *It is easier for two parties to* **reach agreement** *than for three.*
3 [U] when someone says yes to an idea, plan, suggestion etc: **agreement to do sth** *Would their discussion result in his agreement to visit his stepmother?* | [+of] *Such arrangements cannot be altered without the agreement of the bank.*
4 [C] an official document that people sign to show that they have agreed to something: *Please read the agreement and sign it.* | *a hire purchase agreement*

ag·ri·busi·ness /'ægrɪ,bɪznᵻs/ *n* [C,U] the production and sale of farm products, or a company involved in this

ag·ri·cul·ture W2 /'ægrɪ,kʌltʃə $ -ər/ *n* [U] the practice or science of farming: *More than 75% of the land is used for agriculture.* —**agricultural** /,ægrɪ'kʌltʃərəl◂/ *adj*: *agricultural land* | *agricultural labourers* —**agriculturalist** *n* [C] → HORTICULTURE

agro- /ægrəʊ $ -roʊ/ *prefix* also **agri-** /ægrɪ/ relating to farming: *agrobiology*

a·gron·o·my /ə'grɒnəmi $ ə'grɑː-/ *n* [U] the study of the growing of crops —**agronomist** *n* [C]

a·ground /ə'graʊnd/ *adv* **run/go aground** if a ship runs aground, it becomes stuck in a place where the water is not deep enough

a·gue /'eɪgjuː/ *n* [C,U] *old-fashioned* a fever that makes you shake and feel cold

ah /ɑː/ *interjection* used to show surprise, happiness, agreement etc: *Ah! There you are!*

a·ha /ɑː'hɑː/ *interjection* used to show that you understand or realize something: *Aha! So you planned all this, did you?* → HA

a·head S2 W2 /ə'hed/ *adv*
1 IN FRONT a short distance in front of someone or something; ☒ **behind**: *He kept his gaze fixed on the car ahead.* | [+of] *A hill loomed ahead of them.* | *We could see the lights of Las Vegas* **up ahead**. | **some/a little/a long way ahead** *The clinic was now in sight, some way ahead.* | **straight/dead ahead** (=straight in front) *The river is eight miles away dead ahead.* | *Henry hurried on ahead* (=went in front of the others).
2 FORWARD if someone or something looks or moves ahead, they look or move forward: *He stared* **straight ahead**. | *The ship forged ahead through the thin ice.*
3 BEFORE SB ELSE before someone else: [+of] *There were four people ahead of me at the doctor's.*
4 FUTURE in the future: [+of] *You* **have** *a long trip* **ahead** *of you.* | *Considerable problems may* **lie ahead**. | **the years/days/months etc ahead** *We do not foresee any major changes in our way of life in the years ahead.* | *Unless we* **plan ahead** (=plan for the future) *we are going to be in a mess.*
5 BEFORE AN EVENT before an event happens; ☒ **advance**: *I cook rice two or three hours ahead.* | *Can you tell me* **ahead of time** *if you're coming?* | [+of] *He's giving a series of concerts in London ahead of his international tour.*
6 ahead of schedule earlier than planned or arranged: *I arrived at Jack's suite half an hour ahead of schedule.*
7 PROGRESS/SUCCESS making progress and being successful in your job, education etc: **get/keep/stay ahead** *Getting ahead at work is the most important thing to her at the moment.*
8 ADVANCED ideas, achievements etc that are ahead of others have made more progress or are more developed: *This design is* **light years ahead** (=much more advanced) *in performance and comfort.* | **ahead of your/its time** (=very advanced or new, and not understood or accepted) *Coleridge was in many ways far ahead of his time.*
9 WINNING winning in a competition or election: *Two shots from Gardner* **put** *the Giants 80–75* **ahead**. | *We are 10 points ahead in the polls.* | [+of] *At this stage, Smith appeared to be ahead of his rivals.*
10 go ahead **a)** *spoken* used to tell someone they can do something: *'Can I have the sports section?' 'Yeah, go ahead, I've read it.'* **b)** to do something that was planned, especially in spite of a problem: [+with] *Frank'll be late but we'll go ahead with the meeting anyway.* **c)** to take place: *Tests of anti-cancer drugs are to go ahead this year.* → GO-AHEAD¹
11 ahead of the game/curve *AmE informal* in a position where you are in control of something, and more successful than your competitors: *Belmont city leaders have never been ahead of the curve in environmental matters.*

A

A

a·hem /m'hm; *spelling pronunciation* ə'hem/ *interjection* a sound like a cough that you make to attract someone's attention, or when you are saying something embarrassing

-aholic /əhɒlɪk $ əhɒː-, əhɑː-/ *suffix* [in nouns and adjectives] someone who cannot stop doing something or using something: **a workaholic** (=someone who never stops working) | **a chocaholic** (=someone who loves chocolate)

a·hoy /ə'hɔɪ/ *interjection old-fashioned* used by sailors to get someone's attention or greet them

AI /ˌeɪ 'aɪ/ *n* [U] the abbreviation of *artificial intelligence*

aid¹ [S2] [W2] /eɪd/ *n*
1 [U] help, such as money or food, given by an organization or government to a country or to people who are in a difficult situation: *Foreign aid* from many countries poured into the famine area. | *convoys delivering humanitarian aid* | *a substantial aid programme* | *He has been granted legal aid* (=free legal services).
2 [U] help that you need to do a particular thing: **with/without the aid of sth** *Father Poole walked painfully, with the aid of a stick.*
3 in aid of sth in order to help a CHARITY: *We're collecting money in aid of cancer research.*
4 [U] help or advice that is given to someone who needs it: **come/go to sb's aid** (=help someone) *I didn't speak any French, but a nice man came to my aid and told me where to go.*
5 [C] something such as a machine or tool that helps someone do something: *A video is a useful aid in the classroom.* | *a hearing aid*
6 what's this in aid of? *BrE spoken* used to ask what something is used for or why someone is doing something: *What's this meeting tomorrow in aid of, then?*
7 an American spelling of aide → FIRST AID

aid² *v* [T] **1** to help someone do something: *an index to aid the reader* | **aid sb in/with (doing) sth** *Mrs Coxen was aided in looking after the children by her niece.* **2** to make something happen more quickly or easily: *Welfare spending aids economic development in three ways.* **3 aid and abet** *law* to help someone do something illegal

aide /eɪd/ *n* [C] someone whose job is to help someone who has an important job, especially a politician: *a presidential aide*

aide-de-camp /ˌeɪd də 'kɑːmp/ *n plural* **aides-de-camp** (*same pronunciation*) [C] a military officer whose job is to help an officer of a higher rank

AIDS also **Aids** *BrE* /eɪdz/ *n* [U] *Acquired Immune Deficiency Syndrome* a very serious disease that stops your body from defending itself against infections, and usually causes death: *the AIDS virus* | *Aids sufferers* | *full-blown AIDS* (=AIDS at its most advanced stage)

'aid ˌworker *n* [C] someone who works for an organization that brings food and other supplies to people in danger from wars, floods etc: *UN aid workers*

ail /eɪl/ *v* **1 what ails sth** *formal* the thing or things that are causing difficulties for something: *This initiative is not the answer to what ails our educational system.* **2** [I,T] *old-fashioned* to be ill, or to make someone feel ill or unhappy

ail·ing /'eɪlɪŋ/ *adj* [usually before noun] **1** an ailing company, organization, or ECONOMY is having a lot of problems and is not successful: *the ailing car industry* **2** *formal* ill and not likely to get better

ail·ment /'eɪlmənt/ *n* [C] an illness that is not very serious: *minor ailments*

aim¹ [S2] [W2] /eɪm/ *n*
1 [C] something you hope to achieve by doing something: [+of] *The aim of the research is to find new food sources.* | *The main aim of the course is to improve your writing.* | **with the aim of doing sth** *a campaign with the aim of helping victims of crime* | *Teamwork is required in order to achieve these aims.* | *a policy which sets out the school's aims and objectives*
2 take aim to point a gun or weapon at someone or something you want to shoot: [+at] *Alan took aim at the target.*
3 take aim at sb/sth *AmE* to criticize someone or something: *Critics took aim at both the Senator and the President.*
4 [U] someone's ability to hit what they are aiming at when they throw or shoot something: *Val's aim was very good.*

aim² [S2] [W2] *v*
1 [I] to try or intend to achieve something: **aim to do sth** *We aim to finish by Friday.* | **(be) aimed at doing sth** *an initiative aimed at reducing road accidents* | [+for] *We're aiming for a big improvement.*
2 aim sth at sb to say or do something that is intended for a particular person or group of people: *a program that's aimed at teenagers* | *The criticism wasn't aimed at you.*
3 [I,T] to choose the place, person etc that you want to hit or reach and point a weapon or another object towards them: *Denver aimed his gun but did not shoot.* | [+at/for] *The pilot was aiming for the runway but came down in a nearby field.*

aim·less /'eɪmləs/ *adj* not having a clear purpose or reason: *a young man drifting through life in an aimless way* —**aimlessly** *adv* —**aimlessness** *n* [U]

ain't /eɪnt/ a short form of 'am not', 'is not', 'are not', 'has not', or 'have not', that many people think is incorrect

air¹ [S1] [W1] /eə $ er/ *n*
1 [GAS] [U] the mixture of gases around the Earth, that we breathe: *You need to put some air in the tyres.* | **in the air** *There was a strong smell of burning in the air.* | *Let's go outside and get some fresh air:* | *public opposition to air pollution* → **a breath of fresh air** at BREATH (2)
2 [SPACE ABOVE THE GROUND] **the air** the space above the ground or around things: **into the air** *Flames leapt into the air.* | **through the air** *He fell 2000 metres through the air without a parachute.*
3 [PLANES] **a)** **by air** travelling by, or using a plane: *I'd prefer to travel by air.* **b)** relating to or involving planes: *the victims of Britain's worst air disaster* | *Air travel was growing rapidly.* | *air traffic congestion* | *His brother died in an air crash.*
4 be in the air a) if a feeling is in the air, a lot of people feel it at the same time: *There was a sense of excitement in the air.* **b)** to be going to happen very soon: *Change is in the air.*
5 [APPEARANCE] [singular] if something or someone has an air of confidence, mystery etc, they seem confident, mysterious etc: [+of] *She had an air of quiet confidence.* | *She looked at him with a determined air.*
6 be up in the air if something is up in the air, no decision has been made about it yet: *Our trip is still very much up in the air.*
7 be on/off (the) air to be broadcasting on the radio or television at the present moment, or to stop broadcasting: *We'll be on air in three minutes.*
8 [MUSIC] [C] a simple tune, often used in the title of a piece of CLASSICAL music
9 airs [plural] a way of behaving that shows someone thinks they are more important than they really are: **put on airs/give yourself airs** *Trudy is always putting on airs.* | *an actor with no airs and graces*
10 be walking/floating on air to feel very happy → HOT AIR, ON-AIR; → **clear the air** at CLEAR² (15); → **disappear/vanish into thin air** at THIN¹ (15); → **out of thin air** at THIN¹ (16)

air² *v*
1 [OPINION] [T] to express your opinions publicly: **air your views/grievances/complaints etc** *Staff will get a chance to ask questions and air their views.*
2 [TV/RADIO] [I,T] to broadcast a programme on television or radio: *KPBS airs such popular children's programs as 'Barney' and 'Sesame Street'.* | *The program is due to air next month.*
3 [ROOM] [T] *especially BrE*; **air sth out** *AmE* to let fresh

air into a room, especially one that has been closed for a long time

4 CLOTHES [I,T] *especially BrE*; **air (sth) out** *AmE* to put a piece of clothing in a place that is warm or has a lot of air, so that it smells clean: *I've left my sweater outside to air.* → AIRING; → **air your dirty laundry** at DIRTY¹ (7)

'**air ,ambulance** n [C] a special aircraft used for taking people to hospital

air·bag /'eəbæg $ 'er-/ n [C] a bag in a car that fills with air to protect the driver or passenger in an accident

air·base /'eəbeɪs $ 'er-/ n [C] a place where military aircraft begin and end their flights, and where members of an air force live

air·bed /'eəbed $ 'er-/ n [C] something that you fill with air and use as a bed → see picture at BED¹

air·borne /'eəbɔːn $ 'erbɔːrn/ adj **1** a plane that is airborne is in the air **2** airborne soldiers are trained to fight in areas that they get to by jumping out of a plane **3** carried through the air: *airborne pollutants*

'**air brakes** n [plural] BRAKES that work using air pressure

air·brush¹ /'eəbrʌʃ $ 'er-/ n [C] a piece of equipment that uses air to put paint onto a surface

airbrush² v [T] to use an airbrush to make a picture or photograph look better

    airbrush sb/sth ⇔ **out** phr v to remove someone or something from a picture or photograph using an airbrush

Air·bus /'eəbʌs $ 'er-/ n [C] trademark a large plane that carries a lot of people for short distances

,**air chief 'marshal** n [C] a high rank in the British air force, or someone who has this rank

,**air 'commodore** n [C] a high rank in the British air force, or someone who has this rank

'**air con,ditioner** n [C] a machine that makes the air in a room or building cooler and drier

'**air con,ditioning** n [U] a system that makes the air in a room or building cooler and drier —**air-conditioned** adj

air·craft S2 W2 /'eəkrɑːft $ 'erkræft/ n [C] plural **aircraft** a plane or other vehicle that can fly → LIGHT AIRCRAFT

'**aircraft ,carrier** n [C] a type of ship that planes can fly from and land on

air·craft·man /'eəkrɑːftmən $ 'erkræft-/ n plural **aircraftmen** /-mən/ [C] a low rank in the British air force, or someone who has this rank

air·crew /'eəkruː $ 'er-/ n [C] the pilot and the people who are responsible for flying a plane

air·drop /'eədrɒp $ 'erdrɑːp/ n [C] the action of delivering supplies to people by dropping them from a plane —**airdrop** v [T]

air·fare /'eəfeə $ 'erfer/ n [C] the price of a journey by plane

air·field /'eəfiːld $ 'er-/ n [C] a place where planes can fly from, especially one used by military planes

air·flow /'eəfləʊ $ 'erfloʊ/ n [U] the movement of air through or around something

'**air force** n [C] the part of a country's military organization that uses planes to fight; → army, navy

'**air ,freshener** n [C,U] a substance or object used to make a room smell pleasant

air·gun /'eəgʌn $ 'er-/ n [C] a gun that uses air pressure to fire a small round bullet

air·head /'eəhed $ 'er-/ n [C] informal someone who behaves in a stupid way

'**air ,hostess** n [C] BrE old-fashioned a woman who serves food and drink to passengers on a plane

air·i·ly /'eərɪli $ 'er-/ adv in a way that shows you are not worried about something or do not think it is serious: *'I don't really care,' he replied airily.*

air·ing /'eərɪŋ $ 'er-/ n **1** [singular] an occasion when an opinion, idea etc is discussed: **get/be given an airing**

A

an issue that wasn't given an airing during the campaign **2** [C] an occasion when a programme is broadcast on television or radio: *the program's first airing in 2000* **3** [C] an occasion when something is shown to people: *a car which had its first airing at the Paris Motor Show* **4** [singular] an occasion when you let fresh air move around something: *Put your houseplants outside to **give** them **an airing**.*

'**airing ,cupboard** n [C] BrE a warm cupboard in a house where you keep sheets

'**air kiss** n [C] a way of greeting someone with a kiss that is near the side of their face, but that does not touch them —**air-kiss** v [I,T]

air·less /'eələs $ 'er-/ adj airless places or conditions are unpleasant because there is not enough fresh air: *an airless room*

air·lift /'eə,lɪft $ 'er-/ n [C] an occasion when people or supplies are taken to a place by plane, especially during a war or dangerous situation —**airlift** v [T]

air·line S2 W3 /'eəlaɪn $ 'er-/ n [C] a company that takes passengers and goods to different places by plane: *an airline pilot*

air·lin·er /'eə,laɪnə $ 'er,laɪnər/ n [C] a large plane for passengers

'**air lock** n [C] **1** a small room used for moving between two places that do not have the same air pressure, for example in a spacecraft **2** a small amount of air in a pipe that stops liquid flowing through it

air·mail /'eəmeɪl $ 'er-/ n [U] letters and packages that are sent somewhere using a plane, or the system of doing this: *Send the letter by airmail.*

air·man /'eəmən $ 'er-/ n plural **airmen** /-mən/ [C] someone who is a member of their country's air force

air·plane /'eəpleɪn $ 'er-/ n [C] AmE a vehicle that flies through the air and has one or more engines; ⊟ aeroplane BrE; ⊟ plane

air·play /'eəpleɪ $ 'er-/ n [U] the number of times that a particular song is played on the radio: *The new single is already **getting airplay**.*

'**air ,pocket** n [C] **1** a current of air that makes a plane suddenly move down **2** a small area that becomes filled with air

air·port S2 W3 /'eəpɔːt $ 'erpɔːrt/ n [C] a place where planes take off and land, with buildings for passengers to wait in; → airfield: *The plane landed at Heathrow Airport.* | *Her family went to see her off at the airport.*

WORD FOCUS: AIRPORT
what you do at the airport: When you arrive at the airport, you go into the **terminal** building. You check in for your flight at the **check-in desk**. You show your passport at **passport control** and then go through **security**, where they check that you are not carrying any weapons. If you have time you can wait for your flight in the **departure lounge**. When your flight is called, you go through the **departure gate** in order to get onto the plane. The plane then takes off from the **runway**. After your plane has landed, you go to the **baggage reclaim** to collect your bags, then go through **customs** and **immigration**, where they check your passport and your bags. You then go out into the **arrivals** area of the airport.

'**airport fiction** n [U] books that are not very serious, and that people buy at airports to read when they are on a plane journey

'**air pump** n [C] a piece of equipment used to put air into something

'**air quote** n [C usually plural] a movement that someone makes in the air with their fingers to show that what they are saying should be in QUOTATION MARKS, and that it should not be taken as their real opinion or their usual way of speaking

1 000, 2 000, 3 000, most frequent words in S poken and W ritten English

'air rage n [U] violence and angry behaviour by a passenger on a plane towards other passengers or the people who work on it

'air raid n [C] an attack in which bombs are dropped on a place by planes

'air ,rifle n [C] a gun that uses air pressure to fire a small bullet

air·ship /'eə,ʃɪp $ 'er-/ n [C] a large aircraft with no wings, that has an engine and is filled with gas to make it float

air·show /'eəʃəʊ $ 'erʃoʊ/ n [C] an event at which people watch planes fly and do very complicated movements in the sky

air·sick /'eə,sɪk $ 'er-/ adj feeling sick because of the movement of a plane —**airsickness** n [U]

air·space /'eəspeɪs $ 'er-/ n [U] the sky above a particular country, that is legally controlled by that country: Canadian airspace

air·speed /'eəspiːd $ 'er-/ n [singular, U] the speed at which a plane travels

'air strike n [C] an attack in which military aircraft drop bombs

air·strip /'eə,strɪp $ 'er-/ n [C] a long narrow piece of land that planes can fly from or land on

'air ,terminal n [C] a large building at an airport where passengers wait to get on planes

air·tight /'eətaɪt $ 'er-/ adj **1** not allowing air to get in or out: airtight containers **2** planned or done so carefully that there is no chance of any problems or mistakes: an airtight alibi

air·time /'eətaɪm $ 'er-/ n [U] **1** the amount of time that a radio or television station gives to a particular subject, advertisement etc: Advertisers have bought airtime on all the major TV networks. **2** the amount of time that has been paid for when using a MOBILE PHONE

'airtime pro,vider n [C] a company that provides the service that allows you to make and receive calls on a MOBILE PHONE

,air-to-'air adj shot from one plane to another while both planes are flying: an air-to-air missile

,air 'traffic con,trol n [U] **1** the process or job of giving instructions to pilots by radio **2** the people whose job is to do this

,air 'traffic con,troller n [C] someone at an airport whose job is to give instructions to pilots by radio

,air vice-'marshal n [C] a high rank in the British air force, or someone who has this rank

air·waves /'eəweɪvz $ 'er-/ n **the airwaves** informal radio and television broadcasts: **on/over the airwaves** a subject that's been debated on the airwaves

air·way /'eəweɪ $ 'er-/ n [C] **1** the passage in your throat that you breathe through **2** an area of the sky that is regularly used by planes

air·wor·thy /'eə,wɜːði $ 'er,wɜːrði/ adj a plane that is airworthy is safe enough to fly —**airworthiness** n [U]

air·y /'eəri $ 'eri/ adj **1** an airy room or building has plenty of fresh air because it is large or has a lot of windows: All the hotel's bedrooms are **light and airy**. **2** done in a happy and confident way, even when you should be serious or worried: He dismissed her concerns with an airy wave of the hand.

,airy 'fairy adj BrE informal not sensible or practical: airy fairy ideas

aisle /aɪl/ n [C] **1** a long passage between rows of seats in a church, plane, theatre etc, or between rows of shelves in a shop **2 go/walk down the aisle** informal to get married → **be rolling in the aisles** at ROLL¹ (20)

aitch /eɪtʃ/ n plural **aitches** [C,U] the letter H when written as a word not a letter: **drop your aitches** (=not pronounce the letter H at the beginning of words) People with Cockney accents tend to drop their aitches.

a·jar /ə'dʒɑː $ ə'dʒɑːr/ adj [not before noun] a door that is ajar is slightly open

ak·a, aka /,eɪ keɪ 'eɪ, 'ækə/ also known as used when giving someone or something's real name together with a different name they are known by: John Phillips, aka The Mississippi Mauler

a·kim·bo /ə'kɪmbəʊ $ -boʊ/ adj **1 (with)** arms akimbo with your hands on your HIPS so that your elbows point away from your body **2 (with)** legs akimbo with your legs wide apart

a·kin /ə'kɪn/ adj formal **akin to sth** very similar to something: Something akin to panic overwhelmed him.

à la /'æ lə, 'ɑː lɑː/ prep in the same style as someone or something else: detective stories à la Agatha Christie

al·a·bas·ter¹ /'æləbɑːstə $ -bæstər/ n [U] a white stone, used for making STATUES or other objects for decoration

alabaster² adj **1** made of alabaster **2** white and smooth

à la carte /,æ lə 'kɑːt, ,ɑː lɑː- $ -'kɑːrt/ adj, adv if food in a restaurant is à la carte, each dish has a separate price

a·lac·ri·ty /ə'lækrɨti/ n [U] formal quickness and eagerness: **with alacrity** I She accepted with alacrity.

à la mode /,æ lə 'məʊd, ,ɑː lɑː- $ -'moʊd/ adj, adv **1** old-fashioned fashionable **2** AmE served with ICE CREAM: apple pie à la mode

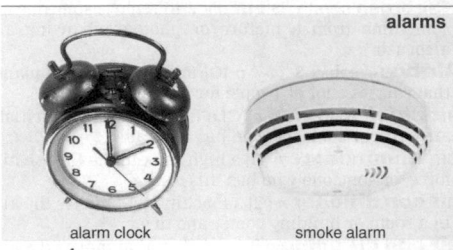
alarms

alarm clock   smoke alarm

a·larm¹ S2 /ə'lɑːm $ ə'lɑːrm/ n
1 [C] a piece of equipment that makes a loud noise to warn you of danger: **a burglar/fire/smoke alarm** I forgot to set the burglar alarm. I He **set off the alarm** (=made it start ringing) by accident. I The fire **alarm's going off** (=it is ringing). I a sophisticated alarm system → see picture at STAY
2 [U] a feeling of fear or worry because something bad or dangerous might happen: [+at] There is growing alarm at the increase in crime. I **in alarm** She looked up in alarm. I Scientists have said **there is no cause for alarm**.
3 [C] an alarm clock: I've **set the alarm** for 7 o'clock. I I was still asleep when the **alarm went off**.
4 raise/sound the alarm especially BrE to warn people that something bad is happening: Neighbours raised the alarm when they smelled smoke.
5 alarm bells ring if alarm bells ring, you feel worried that something bad may be happening: Alarm bells started to ring when he failed to return home. → FALSE ALARM

alarm² v [T] to make someone feel worried or frightened: I don't want to alarm you, but I can't find the key.

a'larm clock n [C] a clock that makes a noise at a particular time to wake you up → see picture at ALARM¹

a·larmed /ə'lɑːmd $ -ɑːr-/ adj **1** worried or frightened: [+by/at] Environmentalists are alarmed by the dramatic increase in pollution. I **alarmed to see/hear etc** He was alarmed to discover that his car was gone. **2** protected by an alarm: The whole building is alarmed.

a·larm·ing /ə'lɑːmɪŋ $ -ɑːr-/ adj making you feel worried or frightened: an alarming increase in violent crime I The rainforest is disappearing **at an alarming rate**. —**alarmingly** adv

a·larm·ist /ə'lɑːmɨst $ -ɑːr-/ adj making people feel worried about dangers that do not really exist: alarmist reports of health risks

a·las¹ /əˈlæs/ adv [sentence adverb] formal used when mentioning a fact that you wish was not true: *Donald, alas, died last year.*

alas² interjection literary used to express sadness, shame, or fear

al·ba·tross /ˈælbətrɒs $ -trɒːs, -trɑːs/ n [C] **1** a very large white sea bird **2 an albatross (around your neck)** something that causes problems for you and prevents you from succeeding: *The issue has become a political albatross for the government.*

al·be·it /ɔːlˈbiːɪt $ ɒːl-/ conjunction formal used to add information that reduces the force or importance of what you have just said; ◫ **although**: *He accepted the job, albeit with some hesitation.* | *Chris went with her, albeit reluctantly.*

al·bi·no /ælˈbiːnəʊ $ ælˈbaɪnoʊ/ n plural **albinos** [C] a person or animal with a GENETIC condition that makes their skin and hair very white and their eyes pink

al·bum W3 /ˈælbəm/ n [C]
1 a group of songs or pieces of music on a CD, tape etc: *The band plan to release their new album next week.*
2 a book that you put photographs, stamps etc in: *a photograph album*

al·bu·men /ˈælbjʊmᵻn $ ælˈbjuː-/ n [U] technical the colourless part inside an egg; ◫ **white**

al·che·my /ˈælkəmi/ n [U] **1** a science studied in the Middle Ages, that involved trying to change ordinary metals into gold **2** literary magic —**alchemist** n [C]

al·co·hol W3 /ˈælkəhɒl $ -hɒːl/ n
1 [U] drinks such as beer or wine that contain a substance which can make you drunk: *I don't drink alcohol anymore.* | **alcohol abuse** (=when someone drinks too much) | *people with alcohol problems* (=people who drink too much)
2 [C,U] the chemical substance in alcoholic drinks that can make you drunk, which is also used in other types of products: *low alcohol drinks*

al·co·hol·ic¹ /ˌælkəˈhɒlɪk◂ $ -ˈhɒː-/ adj **1** relating to alcohol or containing alcohol; ◫ **nonalcoholic**: *alcoholic drinks* **2** caused by drinking alcohol: *an alcoholic stupor*

alcoholic² n [C] someone who regularly drinks too much alcohol and has difficulty stopping

al·co·hol·is·m /ˈælkəhɒlɪzəm $ -hɒː-/ n [U] the medical condition of being an alcoholic

al·co·pop /ˈælkəʊpɒp $ -koʊpɑːp/ n [C] BrE a sweet FIZZY drink that contains alcohol

al·cove /ˈælkəʊv $ -koʊv/ n [C] a place in the wall of a room that is built further back than the rest of the wall

al den·te /æl ˈdenti, -teɪ/ adj food, especially PASTA, that is al dente is still pleasantly firm after it has been cooked

al·der·man /ˈɔːldəmən $ ˈɒːldər-/ plural **aldermen** /-mən/ n [C] **1** an elected member of a town or city council in the US **2** an important member of a town council in Britain in the past

ale /eɪl/ n [U] **1** a type of beer made from MALT (1) **2** old-fashioned beer → **LIGHT ALE**

al·eck /ˈælᵻk/ n → **SMART ALEC**

ale·house /ˈeɪlhaʊs/ n [C] old-fashioned a place where people drank beer in the past

a·lert¹ /əˈlɜːt $ -ɜːrt/ adj **1** giving all your attention to what is happening, being said etc: *The animal raised its head, suddenly alert.* | *Taking notes is one of the best ways to stay alert in lectures.* **2** able to think quickly and clearly: *Jack was as mentally alert as a man half his age.* **3** be alert to sth to know about or understand something, especially a possible danger or problem: *The authorities should have been alert to the possibility of invasion.* —**alertness** n [U]

alert² v [T] **1** to officially warn someone about a problem or danger so that they are ready to deal with it: *The school immediately alerted the police.* **2** to make someone realize something important or dangerous: **alert sb to sth** *campaigns to alert the public to the dangers of HIV*

alert³ n **1** [C] a warning to be ready for possible danger: **a bomb/fire/terrorist etc alert** *a full-scale flood alert* | *The bomb alert was raised soon after midnight.* → **RED ALERT 2 on (the) alert (for sth/sb)** ready to notice and deal with a situation or problem: *Be on the alert for anyone acting suspiciously.* | *Troops in the vicinity were put on alert.* | **on full alert** also **on high alert** (=completely ready to deal with a dangerous situation) *All our border points are on full alert.*

A lev·el /ˈeɪ ˌlevəl/ n [C,U] **Advanced level** an examination that students in England and Wales take, usually when they are 18; → **A/S level, GCSE, GNVQ, O level**: **do/take (your) A levels** *She decided to stay on at school and do her A levels.* | **at A level** *I took maths, physics and chemistry at A level.*

al·fal·fa /ælˈfælfə/ n [U] a plant grown especially in the US to feed farm animals

al·fres·co /ælˈfreskəʊ $ -koʊ/ adj, adv if you eat alfresco, you eat in the open air: *We dined alfresco, on a balcony overlooking the sea.* | **alfresco lunch/supper etc**

al·gae /ˈældʒiː, -giː/ n [U] a very simple plant without stems or leaves that grows in or near water

al·ge·bra /ˈældʒᵻbrə/ n [U] a type of mathematics that uses letters and other signs to represent numbers and values —**algebraic** /ˌældʒᵻˈbreɪ-ɪk◂/ adj —**algebraically** /-kli/ adv

al·go·rith·m /ˈælgərɪðəm/ n [C] technical a set of instructions that are followed in a fixed order and used for solving a mathematical problem, making a computer program etc

a·li·as¹ /ˈeɪliəs/ prep used when giving someone's real name, especially an actor's or a criminal's name, together with another name they use: *'Friends' star Jennifer Aniston, alias Rachel Green*

alias² n [C] a false name, usually used by a criminal: *a spy operating under the alias Barsad*

al·i·bi /ˈælᵻbaɪ/ n [C] **1** something that proves that someone was not where a crime happened and therefore could not have done it: **a perfect/cast-iron/unshakeable etc alibi** *He had a perfect alibi and the police let him go.* **2** an excuse for something you have failed to do or have done wrong

a·li·en¹ /ˈeɪliən/ adj **1** very different from what you are used to, especially in a way that is difficult to understand or accept; ◫ **strange**: *the alien environment of the city* | **be alien to sb** *a way of life that is totally alien to us* **2** belonging to another country or race; ◫ **foreign**: *alien cultures* | *an alien multiracial society* **3** [only before noun] relating to creatures from another world: *alien beings from another planet*

alien² n [C] **1** someone who is not a legal citizen of the country they are living or working in: *illegal aliens entering the country.* **2** in stories, a creature from another world

a·li·en·ate /ˈeɪliəneɪt/ v [T] **1** to do something that makes someone unfriendly or unwilling to support you: *The latest tax proposals will alienate many voters.* **2** to make it difficult for someone to belong to a particular group or to feel comfortable with a particular person: **alienate sb from sth** *He felt that his experiences had alienated him from society.* —**alienated** adj: *Gina had become increasingly alienated from her family.*

a·li·en·a·tion /ˌeɪliəˈneɪʃən/ n [U] **1** the feeling of not being part of a society or a group: [+from] *Unemployment may provoke a sense of alienation from society.* **2** when someone becomes less friendly, understanding, or willing to give support as the result of something that happens or is done: [+of] *the alienation of voters*

a·light¹ /əˈlaɪt/ adj [not before noun] **1** burning: *The car was set alight and pushed over a hill.* **2** literary someone whose face or eyes are alight looks excited, happy, etc: **alight with excitement/pleasure/laughter etc** *Jed's face was alight with excitement.* **3** *literary* bright with light or colour

alight² *v* [I] *formal* **1** if a bird or insect alights on something, it stops flying and stands on it; ▣ **land** **2** to step out of a vehicle after a journey: [+from] *She alighted from the train at 74th Street.*

alight on/upon sth *phr v formal* to suddenly think of or notice something or someone: *His mind alighted on several possible answers.*

a·lign /əˈlaɪn/ *v* **1** [T] to publicly support a political group, country, or person that you agree with: **align yourself with sb/sth** *Church leaders have aligned themselves with the opposition.* | *a country closely aligned with the West* **2** [I,T] to arrange things so that they form a line or are parallel to each other, or to be in a position that forms a line etc: *The desks were neatly aligned in rows.* | *Make sure that all the holes align.* **3** [T usually passive] to organize or change something so that it has the right relationship to something else: [+with] *This policy is closely aligned with the goals of the organization.*

a·lign·ment /əˈlaɪnmənt/ *n* **1** [U] the state of being arranged in a line with something or parallel to something: [+of] *the geometrical alignment of the Sun, Moon and Earth at the eclipse* | **out of/into alignment** *The wheels were out of alignment.* **2** [C,U] support given by one country or group to another in politics, defence etc: [+with] *their military alignment with the US*

a·like¹ /əˈlaɪk/ *adj* [not before noun] very similar: *My mother and I are alike in many ways.*

alike² *adv* **1** in a similar way: *The twins were dressed alike.* → **great minds think alike** at GREAT¹ (15) **2** used to emphasize that you mean both the people, groups, or things that you have just mentioned: *I learned a lot from teachers and students alike.*

al·i·men·ta·ry ca·nal /ˌæləˌmentəri kəˈnæl/ *n* [C] the tube in your body that takes food through your body from your mouth to your ANUS

al·i·mo·ny /ˈæləˌməni $ -mouni/ *n* [U] money that a court orders someone to pay regularly to their former wife or husband after their marriage has ended; → **maintenance**

A-list /ˈeɪ lɪst/ *n* **the A-list** all the most popular or famous film stars, musicians etc; → **B-list**: *the Hollywood A-list* | *A-list celebrities*

a·lit /əˈlɪt/ the past tense and past participle of ALIGHT

a·live S2 W3 /əˈlaɪv/ *adj* [not before noun]
1 NOT DEAD still living and not dead: *It was a really bad accident – they're lucky to be alive.* | *My grandparents are still alive.* | *We stayed alive by eating berries and roots.* | *He was kept alive on a life-support machine.* | *Apparently he's alive and well and living in Brazil.*
2 STILL EXISTING continuing to exist: *Ancient traditions are very much alive in rural areas.* | *Christianity is alive and well in Asia.* | *The sport is still very much alive and kicking in this country.*
3 CHEERFUL full of energy, happiness, activity etc: *It was the kind of morning when you wake up and feel really alive.* | [+with] *Her face was alive with excitement.* | *The whole house was alive with activity.*
4 come alive a) if a subject or event comes alive, it becomes interesting and seems real: *Hopefully, we can make history come alive for the children.* **b)** if someone comes alive, they suddenly become happy and interested in what is happening: *She only came alive when she sat down at the piano.* **c)** if a town, city etc comes alive, it becomes busy: *seaside resorts that come alive in the summer*
5 be alive to a fact/possibility/danger etc to know that a particular fact etc exists and that it is important: *The company is alive to the threat posed by foreign imports.*
6 be alive with sth to be full of living things that are moving: *The pond was alive with fish.*

7 bring sth alive to make something interesting and real: *The way he describes his characters really brings them alive.* → **skin sb alive** at SKIN² (3)

al·ka·li /ˈælkəlaɪ/ *n* [C,U] a substance that forms a chemical salt when combined with an acid

al·ka·line /ˈælkəlaɪn/ $ -ˈælkəlaɪn/ *adj* containing an alkali

all¹ S1 W1 /ɔːl $ ɒːl/ *determiner, predeterminer, pron*
1 the whole of an amount, thing, or type of thing: *Have you done all your homework?* | **all your life/all day/all year etc** (=during the whole of your life, a day, a year etc) *He had worked all his life in the mine.* | *The boys played video games all day.* | *They were quarrelling all the time* (=very often or continuously). | *Hannah didn't say a single word all the way back home* (=during the whole of the journey). | [+of] *Almost all of the music was from Italian operas.* | *I've heard it all before.* | *She'd given up all hope of having a child.*
2 every one of a number of people or things, or every thing or person of a particular type: *Someone's taken all my books!* | *Will all the girls please stand over here.* | *All children should be taught to swim.* | *16 per cent of all new cars sold in Western Europe these days are diesel-engined.* | *They all speak excellent English.* | [+of] *important changes that will affect all of us*
3 the only thing or things: *All you need is a hammer and some nails.* | *All I'm asking for is a little respect.*
4 *formal* everything: *I'm doing all I can to help her.* | *I hope all is well with you.* | *All was dark and silent down by the harbour wall.*
5 used to emphasize that you mean the greatest possible amount of the quality you are mentioning: *Can any of us say in all honesty that we did everything we could?*
6 at all used in negative statements and questions to emphasize what you are saying: *They've done nothing at all to try and put the problem right.* | *He's not looking at all well.* | *'Do you mind if I stay a little longer?' 'No, not at all.'* | *Has the situation improved at all?*
7 all sorts/kinds/types of sth many different kinds of something: *Social workers have to deal with all kinds of problems.*
8 of all people/things/places etc used to emphasize that your statement is true of one particular person, thing, or place more than any other: *Of course, you shouldn't have done it. You of all people should know that.* | *She did not want to quarrel with Maria today, of all days.*
9 all in all used to show that you are considering every part of a situation: *All in all, it had been one of the most miserable days of Henry's life.*
10 for all sth in spite of a particular fact: *For all his faults, he's a kind-hearted old soul.* | *For all my love of landscape, nothing could persuade me to spend another day in the Highlands.*
11 in all including every thing or person: *In all, there were 215 candidates.* | *We received £1550 in cash and promises of another £650, making £2200 in all.*
12 and all a) including the thing or things just mentioned: *They ate the whole fish – head, bones, tail, and all.* **b)** *spoken informal* used to emphasize a remark that you have added: *And you can take that smelly old coat out of here, and all!*
13 all of 50p/20 minutes etc *spoken* used to emphasize how large or small an amount actually is: *The game lasted all of 58 seconds.* | *The repairs are going to cost all of £15,000.*
14 it's all or nothing used to say that unless something is done completely, it is not acceptable: *Half-heartedness won't do – it's got to be all or nothing.*
15 give your all to make the greatest possible effort in order to achieve something: *The coach expects every player to give their all in every game.*
16 it was all I could do to do sth used to say that you only just succeeded in doing something: *It was all I could do to stop them hitting each other.*
17 when all's said and done *spoken* used to remind someone about an important point that needs to be considered: *When all's said and done, he's only a kid.* →

for all sb cares at CARE² (8); → for all sb knows at KNOW¹ (33); → all and sundry at SUNDRY (1); → after all at AFTER¹ (13)

all² S1 W1 *adv*
1 [always + adj/adv/prep] completely: *You shouldn't be sitting here by yourself, all alone.* | *a strange woman, dressed all in black* | *If people want more freedom of choice, then I'm **all for** it* (=I strongly support it). | *'It was a dreadful experience.' 'Never mind, it's **all over*** (=completely finished) *now.'*
2 all over (sth) a) everywhere on an object or surface: *There were bits of paper all over the floor.* | *He has cuts all over his legs.* | *She ached all over* (=her whole body ached). **b)** everywhere in a place: *Antique clocks from all over the world are on display.* | *People came from all over the country.* | *They're putting up new offices all over the place.*
3 all the better/easier/more etc used to emphasize how much better, easier etc something is than it would be in a different situation: *Clayton's achievement is all the more remarkable when you consider his poor performance last season.* | *The job was made all the easier by having the proper tools.*
4 all but almost completely: *Britain's coal industry has all but disappeared.* | *His left arm was all but useless.*
5 all too used to mean 'very' when talking about a bad situation: *All too often it's the mother who gets blamed for her children's behaviour.* | *In these conditions it was all too easy to make mistakes.*
6 all along *informal* all the time from the beginning while something was happening: *Chapman had known all along that the plan wouldn't work.* | *We had to admit that Dad had been right all along.*
7 one all/two all etc used when giving the score of a game in which both players or teams have scored the same number of points: *The game ended one-all.*
8 all told including everything or everyone: *a project costing £10,000, all told*
9 it's all up (with sb) *informal BrE* used to say that someone's success or happiness has ended: *If someone tells the police, then it'll be all up with me.*
10 be not all there *informal* someone who is not all there seems stupid or slightly crazy
11 be all smiles/innocence/sweetness etc to be showing a lot of a particular quality or type of behaviour: *The mayor and mayoress were all smiles and kisses during the grand ceremony.*
12 be all over sb *informal* to be trying to kiss someone and touch them, especially in a sexual way: *Before I could speak, he was all over me.*

SPOKEN PHRASES
13 very: *You're getting me all confused.*
14 that's sb all over used to say that a particular way of behaving is typical of someone: *He was late of course, but that's Tim all over!*
15 be all in *BrE* to be very tired
16 sb was all ... *AmE* used to report what someone said or did, when telling them a story: *He drove me home, and he was all, 'I love this car ... it's like a rocket.'*
17 not all that not very: *It doesn't sound all that good, does it?* | *I don't think it matters all that much.*
18 sb/sth is not all that used to say that someone or something is not very attractive or desirable: *I don't know why you keep chasing her around. She's not all that.*

---

all- /ɔːl $ ɒːl/ *prefix* **1** consisting of or made of only one kind of thing: *an all-male club* | *an all-wool coat* **2 all-day/all-night** continuing for the whole day or night: *an all-day seminar* | *an all-night café*

Al·lah /ˈælə/ *n* the Muslim name for God

all-A'merican *adj* [usually before noun] **1** having qualities that are considered to be typically American and that American people admire, such as being healthy and working hard: *an all-American family* **2** belonging to a group of players who have been chosen as the best in their sport at American universities: *an all-American football player*

all-a'round *adj* [only before noun] *AmE* good at doing many different things, especially sports; ⊟ **all-round** *BrE*: *an all-around athlete*

al·lay /əˈleɪ/ *v* [T] **allay (sb's)** fear/concern/suspicion etc to make someone feel less afraid, worried etc: *The president made a statement to allay public anxiety.*

all 'clear, all-clear *n* **the all clear a)** official permission to begin doing something: **give (sb)/get the all clear** *We've got the all clear for the new project.* **b)** a signal such as a loud whistle that tells you that a dangerous situation has ended

all 'comers, all-comers *n* [plural] everyone who wants to take part in something, especially a competition: *The marathon is open to all comers.*

al·le·ga·tion /ˌælɪˈɡeɪʃən/ *n* [C usually plural] a statement that someone has done something wrong or illegal, but that has not been proved: **allegations of corruption/fraud/misconduct etc** *Mr Singh has strongly denied the allegations of sexual harassment.* | **allegation that** *an allegation that senior government figures were involved* | [+against] *The teacher made serious allegations against a colleague.* | [+of] *A committee will investigate allegations of racial discrimination.*

al·lege /əˈledʒ/ *v* [T often passive] *formal* to say that something is true or that someone has done something wrong, although it has not been proved: **it is alleged (that)** *It was alleged that the policeman had accepted bribes.* | **allege that** *The prosecution alleged that the man had been responsible for an act of terrorism.* | **be alleged to be/do something** *The water is alleged to be polluted with mercury.*

al·leged /əˈledʒd/ *adj* [only before noun] *formal* an alleged crime, fact etc is one that someone says has happened or is true, although it has not been proved: **alleged offence/crime/incident etc** | *their alleged involvement in international terrorism* | *The alleged victim made the complaint at a police station in York.*

al·leg·ed·ly /əˈledʒɪdli/ *adv* [sentence adverb] *formal* used when reporting something that people say is true, although it has not been proved: *a sports car, allegedly stolen in Manchester*

al·le·giance /əˈliːdʒəns/ *n* [C,U] loyalty to a leader, country, belief etc: [+to] *You owe allegiance* (=have a duty to give allegiance) *to your king.* | **swear/pledge allegiance** *I pledge allegiance to the flag of the United States of America.* | *an oath of allegiance* | **switch/transfer allegiance** (=start to support a different person, group etc) | *The people here have strong political allegiances.*

al·le·go·ry /ˈælɪɡəri $ -ɡɔːri/ *n plural* **allegories** [C,U] a story, painting etc in which the events and characters represent ideas or teach a moral lesson —**allegorical** /ˌælɪˈɡɒrɪkəl $ -ˈɡɔːr-/ *adj* —**allegorically** /-kli/ *adv*

al·le·gro /əˈleɡrəʊ, əˈleɪ- $ -groʊ/ *n plural* **allegros** [C] a piece of music played or sung quickly —**allegro** *adj, adv*

al·le·lu·ia /ˌælɪˈluːjə/ *interjection* another spelling of HALLELUJAH

all-em'bracing *adj* including everyone or everything: *an all-embracing vision of society*

Al·len key /ˈælən kiː/ *n* [C] *BrE* a tool used to turn an Allen screw; ⊟ **Allen wrench** *AmE*

Allen screw /ˈælən skruː/ *n* [C] a type of screw with a hole that has six sides

Allen wrench /ˈælən rentʃ/ *n* [C] *AmE* a tool used to turn an Allen screw; ⊟ **Allen key** *BrE*

al·ler·gen /ˈælədʒən $ -lər-/ *n* [C] a substance that causes an allergy

al·ler·gic /əˈlɜːdʒɪk $ -ɜːr-/ *adj* **1** having an allergy: [+to] *I'm allergic to penicillin.* **2** caused by an allergy: *an allergic reaction to nuts* | *an allergic rash* **3 be**

---

1 000, 2 000, 3 000, most frequent words in S poken and W ritten English

allergic to sth *informal* if you are allergic to something, you do not like it and try to avoid it – used humorously: *Most men are allergic to housework!*

al·ler·gy /'ælədʒi $ -ər-/ *n plural* **allergies** [C,U] a medical condition in which you become ill or in which your skin becomes red and painful because you have eaten or touched a particular substance: [+**to**] *I have an allergy to cats.* | *a food allergy*

al·le·vi·ate /ə'li:vieit/ *v* [T] to make something less painful or difficult to deal with: **alleviate the problem/ situation/suffering etc** *a new medicine to alleviate the symptoms of flu* | *measures to alleviate poverty* —**alleviation** /ə,li:vi'eiʃən/ *n* [U]

al·ley /'æli/ *also* **alleyway** *n* [C] **1** a narrow street between or behind buildings, not usually used by cars: *The alley led to the railway bridge.* | *She found the side alley where the stage door was located.* **2** **right up/down sb's alley** very suitable for someone: *The job sounds right up your alley.* → **BLIND ALLEY, BOWLING ALLEY**

alley cat *n* [C] a cat that lives on the streets and does not belong to anyone

al·ley·way /'æliwei/ *n* [C] an ALLEY

all-'fired *adv AmE* completely – used when describing a quality that you think is extreme: *If he weren't so all-fired sure of himself, I'd like him better.*

all fours → **on all fours** at **FOUR** (2)

all 'go *adj BrE* **it's all go** *spoken* used to say that a situation is very busy and full of activity: *It was all go from 8.00 until we finished at 5.00.*

al·li·ance W3 /ə'laiəns/ *n* [C]
1 an arrangement in which two or more countries, groups etc agree to work together to try to change or achieve something: [+**with**] *Britain's military alliance with her NATO partners* | [+**between**] *the possibility of a political alliance between the two parties* | **make/ enter into/form/forge an alliance** (=agree to work together) *The companies have formed an alliance to market the product.*
2 a group of two or more countries, groups etc who work together to achieve something: *independent organizations and alliances*
3 **in alliance (with sb/sth)** if two groups, countries etc are in alliance, they work together to achieve something or protect each another: *Relief workers in alliance with local charities are trying to help the famine victims.*
4 *formal* a close relationship, especially a marriage, between people → **unholy alliance** at **UNHOLY** (1)

al·lied /'ælaid, ə'laid/ *adj* **1** usually **Allied** [only before noun] belonging or relating to the countries that fought with Britain, the US etc in the First or Second World War: *an Allied bombing raid* | *Allied forces* **2** **(be) allied to/with sth** *formal* to be related to something or to be very similar: *Anthropology is closely allied to the field of psychology.* **3** *allied industries/organizations/ trades etc* connected with each other because of being similar to or dependent on each other: *agriculture and allied industries* **4** joined by the same political, military, or economic aims: *loosely allied guerilla groups*

Al·lies /'ælaiz/ *n* **the Allies** [plural] the countries that fought together against Germany during the First and Second World War

al·li·ga·tor /'æligeitə $ -ər/ *n* **1** [C] a large animal with a long mouth and tail and sharp teeth that lives in the hot wet parts of the US and China → see picture at **REPTILE** **2** [U] the skin of this animal used as leather: *alligator shoes*

all-im'portant *adj* extremely important: *the all-important question in everyone's minds*

all 'in, all-in *adj, adv BrE* used to describe the total cost of something, or the total amount of money charged for something: ◙ **inclusive: all-in price/package/deal etc** *all-in deals to Australia and New Zealand* | *The hourly rate is £20 all in.*

all-'in *adj* extremely tired: *You look all-in. Are you OK?*

all-in'clusive *adj* including the cost of everything in the price charged; ◙ **all in: an all-inclusive price/ package/holiday etc** *an all-inclusive vacation cruise*

all-in-'one *adj* [only before noun] *BrE* combining two or more things that are usually separate into one thing: *an all-in-one TV and video*

al·lit·er·a·tion /ə,litə'reiʃən/ *n* [U] the use of several words together that begin with the same sound or letter in order to make a special effect, especially in poetry

all-'nighter *n* [C] *informal* an occasion when you spend the whole night studying or doing written work in university

al·lo·cate /'æləkeit/ *v* [T] to use something for a particular purpose, give something to a particular person etc, especially after an official decision has been made: **allocate sth to sb/sth** *the importance of allocating resources to local communities* | *You should allocate the same amount of time to each question.* | **allocate sth for sth** *One million dollars was allocated for disaster relief.* | **allocate sb/sth sth** *Several patients were waiting to be allocated a bed.*

al·lo·ca·tion /,ælə'keiʃən/ *n* **1** [C] the amount or share of something that has been allocated for a particular purpose: *Twelve hours a week seemed a generous allocation of your time.* **2** [U] the decision to allocate something, or the act of allocating it: [+**of**] *the allocation of funds to universities*

al·lot /ə'lɒt $ ə'lɑ:t/ **allotted, allotting** *v* [T] to use a particular amount of time for something, or give a particular share of money, space etc to someone or something: **allot sth to sth/sb** *Try and allot 2 or 3 hours a day to revision.* | *Each school will be allotted twenty seats.* | **allot sb sth** *Everyone who works for the company has been allotted 10 shares.* —**allotted** *adj* [only before noun]: *The department has already spent more than its allotted budget.*

al·lot·ment /ə'lɒtmənt $ ə'lɑ:t-/ *n* **1** [C,U] an amount or share of something such as money or time that is given to someone or something, or the process of doing this: *The budget allotment for each county is below what is needed.* | [+**of**] *the allotment of shares in the company* **2** [C] *BrE* a small area of land that people can rent for growing vegetables

all-'out *adj* [only before noun] done in a very determined way, and involving a lot of energy or anger: **all-out war/attack/offensive etc** | *an all-out effort to win* —**all out** *adv*: *Canada will have to* **go all out** *on the ice if they want to win.*

al·low S1 W1 /ə'lau/ *v* [T]
1 CAN DO STH to let someone do or have something, or let something happen; ◙ **permit: allow sb/sth to do sth** *My parents wouldn't allow me to go to the party.* | *Women are not allowed to enter the mosque.* | *Don't allow your problems to dominate your life.* | **allow sb sth** *Passengers are allowed one item of hand luggage each.* | *How much time are we allowed?* | **allow sb in/out/up etc** *I don't allow the cat in the bedroom.* | *The audience is not allowed backstage.* | **sth is (not) allowed** (=something is or is not officially permitted) *Are dictionaries allowed in the exam?* | *We don't allow diving in the pool.*
2 MAKE STH POSSIBLE to make it possible for something to happen or for someone to do something, especially something helpful or useful; ◙ **permit:** *This adjustment of the figures allows a fairer comparison.* | [+**for**] *Our new system will allow for more efficient use of resources.* | **allow sb to do sth** *A 24-hour ceasefire allowed the two armies to reach an agreement.* | **allow sb sth** *a seatbelt that allows the driver greater freedom of movement*
3 HAVE ENOUGH OF STH to be sure that you have enough time, money, food etc available for a particular purpose: **allow sb sth** *Allow yourselves plenty of time to get to the airport.* | **allow sth for sb/sth** *I've allowed half a bottle of wine for each person.*
4 CORRECT/PERMITTED *formal* to accept that some-

thing is correct or true, or that something is acceptable according to the rules or law: **allow that** *I allow that there may have been a mistake.* | *The judge allowed the evidence.*
5 allow me *formal* used as a polite way of offering to help someone do something: *'Allow me,' the waiter said, opening the door.* → LET¹ → FORBID (1)
allow for sb/sth *phr v*
to consider the possible problems, costs etc involved in something when making a plan, calculation, or judgment: *Allowing for inflation, the cost of the project will be $2 million.* | *You should always allow for the possibility that it might rain.*
allow of sth *phr v formal*
to make it possible for something to happen or be accepted: *The facts allow of only one interpretation.*

al·low·a·ble /ə'lauəbəl/ *adj* **1** acceptable according to the rules; ■ **permissible**: *The maximum allowable dosage is two tablets a day.* **2** allowable costs are costs that you do not pay tax on: *allowable deductions such as alimony and business expenses*

al·low·ance S2 W3 /ə'lauəns/ *n*
1 [C usually singular] an amount of money that you are given regularly or for a special purpose: **a monthly/ annual etc allowance** *His father gives him a monthly allowance of £200.* | [+**for**] *Do you get an allowance for clothes?* | *Sales staff get a generous mileage allowance or a company car.* | *If you are entitled to sickness allowance, you must claim it from your employer.*
2 [C usually singular] an amount of something that is acceptable or safe: *the recommended daily allowance of Vitamin C* | *Passengers' baggage allowance is 75 pounds per person.*
3 [C] *BrE* an amount of money that you can earn without paying tax on it: *a new tax allowance from the government*
4 [C usually singular] *especially AmE* a small amount of money that a parent regularly gives to a child; ■ **pocket money** *BrE*
5 [C,U] something that you consider when deciding what is likely to happen, what you should expect etc: [+**for**] *There is always an allowance in insurance premiums for whether someone smokes or not.* | **make (an) allowance/make allowances (for sth)** *The budget makes allowances for extra staff when needed.*
6 make allowance/allowances (for sb) to let someone behave in a way you do not normally approve of, because you know there are special reasons for their behaviour: *Dad's under pressure – you have to make allowances.*

al·loy¹ /'ælɔɪ $ 'ælɔɪ, ə'lɔɪ/ *n* [C,U] a metal that consists of two or more metals mixed together: *Brass is an alloy of copper and zinc.*

al·loy² /ə'lɔɪ $ ə'lɔɪ, 'ælɔɪ/ *v* [T + with] *technical* to mix one metal with another

,all-'powerful *adj* having complete power or control: *an all-powerful dictator*

,all-'purpose *adj* [only before noun] able to be used in any situation: *an all-purpose cleaner*

all 'right S1 W2 *adj* [not before noun] *adv, interjection*
1 GOOD satisfactory, but not excellent; ■ **okay**: *'What's the food like?' 'It's all right, but the place on campus is better.'* | *'How's school going, Steve?' 'Oh, all right, I guess.'*
2 NO PROBLEMS not ill, hurt, or upset or not having any problems; ■ **okay**: *Kate looks really unhappy – I'd better make sure she's all right.* | *Are you feeling all right?* | *The kids seem to be getting on all right at school.* | *Tony was worried about the meeting but it went all right* (=happened with no problems). | *Don't worry, it'll turn out all right.*
3 do all right (for yourself/herself etc) to be successful in your job, life etc: *She's doing all right – she's got a job with Microsoft.*
4 SUITABLE used to say whether something is suitable or convenient; ■ **okay**: [+**with/by/for**] *Is Thursday*

morning all right with you? | *We'll eat at eight. Does that sound all right to you?*
5 it's all right used to make someone feel less afraid or worried: *It's all right, Mommy's here.*
6 it's/that's all right used to reply to someone who thanks you or says they are sorry about something: *'Thanks for all your help!' 'That's quite all right.'*
7 PERMISSION used to ask or give permission for something; ■ **okay**: *Would it be all right if I left early today?* | **be all right to do sth** *Is it all right to bring my dog?*
8 AGREEMENT used to agree with someone's suggestion, although you may be slightly unwilling; ■ **okay**: *'Why not come along?' 'Oh, all right.'*
9 UNDERSTANDING [sentence adverb] used to check that someone understands what you have said, or to show that you understand; ■ **okay**: *I'll leave a key with the neighbours, all right?* | *'The train leaves at 5.30.' 'All right, I'm coming!'*
10 THREATEN used when asking in a threatening or angry way what someone's intentions are; ■ **okay**: *All right, you two. What are you doing in my room?*
11 CHANGE/END SUBJECT used to introduce a new subject or to end a conversation; ■ **okay**: *All right, now I'd like to introduce our first speaker.*
12 it's all right for sb *BrE informal* used to say that someone else does not have the problems that you have, or that you are jealous because someone else is luckier than you: *'I get eight weeks' holiday a year.' 'Well, it's all right for some.'*
13 EMPHASIZE *informal* used to emphasize that you are certain about something: *'Are you sure it was Bill?' 'Oh, yes, it was him all right.'*
14 HAPPY *AmE informal* used to say you are happy about something you have just been told: *You passed? All right!*
15 LIKE *BrE* used to describe someone you like or approve of: *'The new boss isn't too bad, is she?' 'No, she's all right.'*
16 GREETING *informal especially BrE* used as a greeting when you meet someone you know well, or reply to a greeting: *'How are you, John?' 'Oh, all right – can't complain.'*
17 I'm all right Jack *BrE informal* used to describe someone's attitude when they do not care about other people as long as they themselves are happy, comfortable etc
18 it'll be all right on the night *BrE informal* used to say that something will be successful, even though there have been lots of problems: *Workmen have yet to finish the new complex, but the organisers are confident it will be all right on the night.* → **a bit of all right** at BIT¹ (12)

all 'round *BrE*; **all a'round** *AmE adv* used to say that you are describing the total quality or effect of something, rather than the details: *All round it's not a bad car.* | *It was a nasty business all round.*

,all-'round *BrE*; **all-a'round** *AmE adj* [only before noun] good at doing many different things: *an all-round athlete*

all-'rounder *n* [C] *BrE* someone with many different skills: *a good all-rounder*

,all-'seater *adj BrE* an all-seater football ground, STADIUM etc is one where everyone has a seat

,all-,singing, all-'dancing *adj* [only before noun] *BrE* an all-singing, all-dancing machine or system can do many things because it is so technically advanced – used humorously

all·spice /'ɔːlspaɪs $ 'ɒːl-/ *n* [U] the dried fruit of a tropical American tree, crushed and used in cooking

'all-star *adj* [only before noun] including many famous actors, sports players etc: *an all-star cast*

,all-'ter·rain *adj* [only before noun] all-terrain vehicles are very strong with thick tyres and are suitable for use in many different conditions: *an all-terrain bike*

'all-time adj used when you compare things to say that one of them is the best, worst etc that there has ever been: **an all-time high/low** The price of wheat had reached an all-time low. | They reached an **all-time record** score.

al·lude /əˈluːd/ v
allude to sb/sth phr v formal to mention something or someone indirectly: Rick didn't want to discuss his past, though he alluded darkly to 'some bad things that happened.'

al·lure /əˈljʊə $ əˈlʊr/ n [singular, U] a mysterious, exciting, or desirable quality: [+of] the allure of foreign travel | At 50, she had lost none of her sexual allure. —**allure** v [T]: harmonies that never fail to allure the listener —**alluring** adj: the alluring magic of Hong Kong —**allurement** n [C,U]

al·lu·sion /əˈluːʒən/ n [C,U] something said or written that mentions a subject, person etc indirectly: [+to] The committee **made** no **allusion** to the former President in its report. | **literary/classical/cultural** etc allusions Eliot's poetry is full of biblical allusions. | In his poetry we find many allusions to the human body. —**allusive** /-sɪv/ adj [only before noun]

al·lu·vi·al /əˈluːviəl/ adj [usually before noun] technical made of soil left by rivers, lakes, floods etc: alluvial flood plains

al·lu·vi·um /əˈluːviəm/ n [U] soil left by rivers, lakes, floods etc

al·ly¹ [W3] /ˈælaɪ $ ˈælaɪ, əˈlaɪ/ n plural allies [C]
1 a country that agrees to help or support another country in a war: a meeting of the European allies
2 the Allies the group of countries including Britain and the US that fought together in the First and Second World Wars
3 someone who helps and supports you when other people are trying to oppose you: Ridley was one of the Queen's **closest allies**. | a **staunch ally** (=very close ally) of President Soares | a network of **political allies** | She knew she had found an ally in Ted.
4 something that helps you succeed in a difficult situation: Exercise is an important ally in your campaign to lose weight.

al·ly² /əˈlaɪ $ əˈlaɪ, ˈælaɪ/ v allied, allying, allies [T always +adv/prep] to help and support other people or countries, especially in a war or disagreement: **ally yourself to/with** sb Some of the northern cities allied themselves with the emperor. → ALLIED

al·ma ma·ter /ˌælmə ˈmɑːtə, -ˈmeɪ- $ -ˈmɑːtər/ n [singular] **1** sb's alma mater the school, college etc that someone used to attend **2** AmE the song of a particular school, college etc

al·ma·nac, almanack old-fashioned /ˈɔːlmənæk $ ˈɒːl-, ˈæl-/ n [C] a book produced each year containing information about a particular subject, especially a sport, or important dates, times etc: a football almanac | a nautical almanac

al·might·y /ɔːlˈmaɪti $ ɒːl-/ adj **1 the Almighty/Almighty God/Almighty Father** expressions used to talk about God that emphasize His power **2 God/Christ Almighty** an expression used when you are angry or upset. Some people consider this use offensive. **3 almighty din/crash/row** BrE old-fashioned informal a very loud noise, argument etc: There was an almighty bang and the car came to a halt.

al·mond /ˈɑːmənd $ ˈɑː-, ˈæ-, ˈæl-/ n [C] a flat pale nut with brown skin that tastes sweet, or the tree that produces these nuts: Stir in the ground almonds and egg. → see picture at NUT¹

al·most [S1] [W1] /ˈɔːlməʊst $ ˈɒːlmoʊst, ɒːlˈmoʊst/ adv nearly, but not completely or not quite: Have you almost finished? | Supper's almost ready. | It was almost midnight. | Almost nothing was done to improve the situation. | The story is **almost certainly** true. | He's **almost as** old as I am. | **almost all/every/everything** Marsha visits her son almost every day.

alms /ɑːmz $ ɑːmz, ɑːlmz/ n [plural] literary money, food etc given to poor people in the past

alms·house /ˈɑːmzhaʊs/ n [C] in Britain in the past, a house where a poor person was allowed to live without paying rent

a·loe ve·ra /ˌæləʊ ˈvɪərə $ ˌæloʊ ˈverə/ n [U] a tropical plant with thick leaves that are filled with a liquid which is used to make medicine, COSMETICS etc

a·loft /əˈlɒft $ əˈlɒːft/ adv formal high up in the air: **hold/bear sth aloft** He emerged, triumphantly holding a baby aloft.

a·lone [S2] [W1] /əˈləʊn $ əˈloʊn/ adj [not before noun] adv
1 if you are alone in a place, there is no one with you; ▣ **by yourself**: She lives alone. | You shouldn't **leave** a child alone in the house. | My wife and I like to spend time **alone together** away from the kids.
2 without any friends or people you know: It was scary being **all alone** in a strange city. | She was **all alone in the world** (=she had no family or friends to help her or look after her).
3 feeling unhappy and lonely: I cried like a child because I **felt so alone**.
4 without any help from other people: He was left to raise their two children alone.
5 without including anything else: The case will cost thousands of pounds in legal fees alone.
6 you/he etc alone used to emphasize that there is only one person who knows, can do something etc: Julie alone knew the truth.
7 go it alone to start working or living on your own, especially after working or living with other people: After years of working for a big company I decided to go it alone.
8 leave sb alone, let sb alone old-fashioned to stop annoying or interrupting someone: 'Leave me alone!' she screamed.
9 leave sth alone also **let sth alone** old-fashioned to stop touching an object or changing something: Leave those cakes alone. They're for the guests. | **leave well (enough) alone** (=not change something that is satisfactory) In economic matters, they should leave well alone.
10 be yours/hers/his etc alone used to emphasize that something belongs to someone: The responsibility is yours and yours alone.
11 not be alone in (doing) sth to not be the only person to do something: You're not alone in feeling upset, believe me.
12 stand alone a) to be strong and independent: the courage to stand alone **b)** to be at a distance from other objects or buildings: The house stood alone at the end of the road.

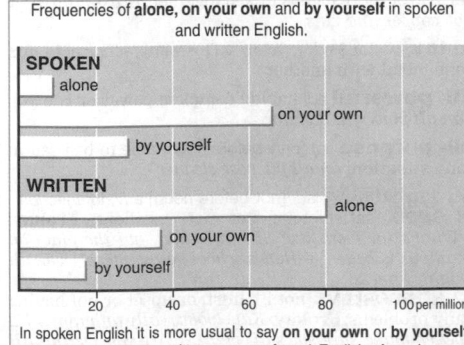

Frequencies of **alone, on your own** and **by yourself** in spoken and written English.

	20	40	60	80	100 per million
SPOKEN					
alone					
on your own					
by yourself					
WRITTEN					
alone					
on your own					
by yourself					

In spoken English it is more usual to say **on your own** or **by yourself** rather than **alone**. In written or more formal English **alone** is more common.

a·long¹ [S1] [W1] /əˈlɒŋ $ əˈlɒːŋ/ adv
1 going forward: I was driving along, thinking about Chris. | a group of children walking along in a line
2 go/come along to go or come to a place where something is happening: You're welcome to come along if you like. | I think I'll go along and watch the game.
3 take/bring sb/sth along to take someone or some-

thing with you to a place: *Mandy brought some of her friends along.* | *Why don't you take your guitar along?*
4 be/come along to arrive: *Another bus should be along in a minute.* | *Every so often, a band comes along that changes music history.*
5 come/go/get along to improve, develop, or make progress: *After a five-hour operation, Wendy is coming along just fine.*
6 along with sb/sth together with someone or something else: *Dunne was murdered, along with three guards.*
7 all along all the time from the beginning, while something was happening: *They should have known all along that she was lying.*

a·long² [S1] [W1] *prep*
1 from one place on something such as a line, road, or edge towards the other end of it: *We were driving along Follyfoot Road.* | *She glanced anxiously along the line of faces.* | *He slid his hand along her arm.*
2 forming a line beside something long: *The palm trees along the shore swayed in the wind.* | *the toolbar along the top of your screen* | *There were cheering crowds all along Pennsylvania Avenue.*
3 a particular distance away, on or beside something long such as a line, road, edge etc: *Hugo's house was about two hundred yards away along the main street.* | *The bathroom is just along* (=a short distance along) *the corridor.*
4 along the way/line during a process or experience, or during someone's life: *I've been lucky, but I've had my share of heartbreak along the way.*

a·long·side [W3] /ə,lɒŋ'saɪd $ ə,lɔːŋ-/ *adv, prep*
1 next to the side of something: *A car drew up alongside.* | *Children's prices are shown alongside adult prices.*
2 used to say that people or things do something or exist together at the same time: *Charles spent a week working alongside the miners.* | *Organized crime continued to flourish alongside the mainstream economy.*
3 in comparison with something: *His achievement may seem small alongside the great triumphs of 20th century technology.* | *Athletics should* **rank alongside** (=be equal to) *soccer and cricket as a major sport.*

a·loof /ə'luːf/ *adj, adv* **1** unfriendly and deliberately not talking to other people: **remain/stay aloof (from sb)** *They worked hard, but tended to stay aloof from the local inhabitants.* | **keep/hold yourself aloof (from sb)** *She had always kept herself aloof from the boys in class.* | *Beneath that aloof exterior, Gayle is a warm, sympathetic person.* **2** deliberately not becoming involved in something: **remain/stand aloof (from sth)** *Initially, the President remained aloof from the campaign.* | **hold/keep (yourself) aloof from sth** *The doctor held himself somewhat aloof from the rest of the ship's crew.* —**aloofness** *n* [U]

a·loud /ə'laʊd/ *adv* if you read, laugh, say something etc aloud, you read etc so that people can hear you; ▤ **out loud: read/say sth aloud** *Joanne, would you read the poem aloud?* | **laugh/groan/cry etc aloud** *The pain made him cry aloud.* | *She could have laughed aloud.* | **think aloud** (=say the things you are thinking) *'What did you say?' ' Sorry, I was just thinking aloud.'* ⚠ Do not use **aloud** to mean 'in a loud voice'. Use **loudly** *You need to speak quite loudly for the people at the back.*

al·pac·a /æl'pækə/ *n* **1** [C] an animal from South America with long hair that looks like a LLAMA **2** [U] cloth made from the wool of an alpaca

al·pha /'ælfə/ *n* [C usually singular] **1** the first letter of the Greek alphabet **2 the alpha and omega** *formal* the start and finish of something, and therefore the whole of it: *Collective bargaining was viewed as the alpha and omega of trade unionism.*

al·pha·bet /'ælfəbet/ *n* [C] a set of letters, arranged in a particular order, and used in writing: **the Greek/Roman etc alphabet** *the international phonetic alphabet*

al·pha·bet·i·cal /,ælfə'betɪkəl◂ / also
al·pha·bet·ic /,ælfə'betɪk◂ / *adj* relating to the alpha-

bet: *The files are arranged* **in alphabetical order**. —**alphabetically** /-kli/ *adv*: *Are the records* **filed alphabetically?**

al·pha·bet·ize also **-ise** *BrE* /'ælfəbetaɪz/ *v* [T] to arrange things in order according to the letters of the alphabet

,alpha 'male *n* [C usually singular] **1** the male with the highest rank in a group of animals such as CHIMPANZEES **2** the man who has the most power and influence and the highest social position in a particular group – used humorously

al·pha·nu·mer·ic /,ælfənjuː'merɪk◂ $ -nuː-/ also
al·pha·nu·mer·i·cal /-'merɪkəl/ *adj* using letters and numbers: *alphanumeric codes*

'alpha ,test *n* [C] a test of software to see if it works properly, done by the company that is writing the software; → **beta test**

'alpha ,version *n* [C] software that is being tested by the company that is writing it, to see if it works properly; → **beta version**

al·pine /'ælpaɪn/ *adj* [only before noun] relating to the Alps (=a mountain range in central Europe) or to mountains in general: *breathtaking alpine scenery* | *alpine flowers* | *alpine skiing*

al·read·y [S1] [W1] /ɔːl'redi $ ɒːl-/ *adv*
1 before now, or before a particular time: *The design of the new house is similar to those that have already been built.* | *The performance had already started when we arrived.*
2 used to say that something has been done before and does not need doing again: *You already told me that.* | *'Fancy a coffee?' 'No thanks, I already have one.'*
3 used to say that something has happened too soon or before the expected time: *Have you eaten all that food already?* | *Is it 5 o'clock already?*
4 used to say that a situation exists and it might get worse, greater, etc: *Hurry up, we're already late.* ⚠ **already** or **yet?** → see box at YET¹

al·right /,ɔːl'raɪt $,ɒːl-/ *adj, adv* another spelling of ALL RIGHT that some people think is incorrect

Al·sa·tian /æl'seɪʃən/ *n* [C] *BrE* a large dog, often used by the police or to guard places; ▤ **German Shepherd**

al·so [S1] [W1] /'ɔːlsəʊ $ 'ɒːlsoʊ/ *adv*
1 in addition to something else that you have mentioned: *Information is also available on women's health care.* | *She sings beautifully and also plays the flute and piano.* | *The system is* **not only** *complicated* **but also** *ineffective.*
2 used to say that the same thing is true about another person or thing: *My girlfriend was also called Helen.*

WORD CHOICE: also, too, as well, either
also, too and **as well** can be used in many of the same contexts: *She's a valued colleague, and a great friend too* OR *and a great friend as well* OR *and also a great friend.*
also is the most formal and the most likely to be used in formal writing such as reports.
as well is the most informal and the most likely to be used in speech.
⚠ **too** is never used at the beginning of a clause. **Also** is not usually used at the end of a clause: *Smoking makes you ill. It costs a lot too/as well* OR *It's also expensive* OR *Also, it's expensive.*
Use **either** when you are adding another negative fact: *Our first attempt didn't work, and our second didn't either* (NOT *also didn't*).

'also-ran *n* [C] someone who fails to win a competition, election etc: *Ten months ago he was just an also-ran for the Democratic nomination.*

al·tar /'ɔːltə $ 'ɒːltər/ *n* [C] **1** a holy table or surface used in religious ceremonies: *a crucifix above the* **high altar** (=the main altar in a church) | *The victim was* *tied to a sacrificial altar.* **2** the area furthest from the entrance of a church, where the priest or minister stands

altar boy n [C] a boy who helps a Catholic priest during a church service

al·tar·piece /'ɔːltəpiːs $ 'ɒːltər-/ n [C] a painting or SCULPTURE behind an altar

al·ter S3 W3 /'ɔːltə $ 'ɒːltər/ v
1 [I,T] to change, or to make someone or something change: *Her face hadn't altered much over the years.* | *The city centre has altered beyond recognition* (=changed very much). | *Nothing can alter the fact that the refugees are our responsibility.*
2 [T] to make a piece of clothing longer, wider etc so that it fits: **have/get sth altered** *She had the dress altered for the wedding.*

al·ter·a·tion /,ɔːltə'reɪʃən $,ɒːl-/ n [C,U] a small change that makes someone or something slightly different, or the process of this change: [+to] *If you* **make alterations to** *the Windows setup, save the new settings before closing.* | [+in] *Have you noticed any alteration in the patient's behaviour?* | **minor/major etc alterations** *The King's Arms pub is to undergo extensive alterations.*

al·ter·ca·tion /,ɔːltə'keɪʃən $,ɒːltər-/ n [C] *formal* a short noisy argument: *They became involved in an altercation.*

al·ter e·go /,æltər 'iːɡəʊ, ,ɔːl- $,æltər 'iːɡoʊ, ,ɒːl-/ n [C] **1 sb's alter ego** an invented person that you use to represent part of your character that is very different from your usual one: *Gissing used his fictional alter ego to attack Victorian morals.* **2** someone you trust and who has similar opinions, attitudes etc: *Mrs Reagan was widely regarded as the President's alter ego.*

al·ter·nate¹ /ɔːl'tɜːnət $ 'ɒːltər-, 'æl-/ adj [usually before noun] **1** if something happens on alternate days, weeks etc, it happens on one day etc and not the next, and continues in this pattern: **alternate Mondays/weekends etc** *The service runs on alternate days.* **2** two alternate things are placed one after the other in a regular pattern: *alternate blue and red stripes* | *Arrange the leeks and noodles in alternate layers.* **3** used to replace another thing of the same type; ◆ **alternative**: *the appointment of an alternate director*

al·ter·nate² /'ɔːltəneɪt $ 'ɒːltər-, 'æl-/ v [I,T] if two things alternate, or if you alternate them, they happen one after the other in a repeated pattern: [+between] *She alternated between outrage and sympathy.* | [+with] *Periods of depression alternate with excited behavior.* | **alternate sth and/with sth** *Twist your body, alternating right and left stretches.* —**alternation** /,ɔːltə'neɪʃən $,ɒːltər , ,æl / n [C,U]

alternating current n [U] *AC* a flow of electricity that changes direction regularly and quickly; → **direct current**

al·ter·na·tive¹ S2 W2 /ɔːl'tɜːnətɪv $ ɒːl'tɜːr-, æl-/ adj **1** [only before noun] an alternative idea, plan etc is different from the one you have and can be used instead: **alternative ways/approach/methods etc** *alternative approaches to learning* | *Have you any alternative suggestions?* | *An alternative route is along the Via Unione.* **2** deliberately different from what is usual, expected, or traditional: **alternative music/theatre etc** *Tucson's alternative radio station* | **sources of alternative energy** (=energy produced by the sun, wind etc rather than by gas, coal etc) | **tolerance of alternative lifestyles** | **alternative medicine/therapies** (=medical treatment that is not based on the usual western methods) *Acupuncture is widely used by practitioners of alternative medicine.* —**alternatively** adv: *You can relax on the beach* **or alternatively** *try the bustling town centre.*

alternative² S2 W3 n [C] something you can choose to do or use instead of something else: [+to] *Is there a*

viable alternative to the present system? | *If payment is not received within five days, legal action will be our* **only alternative.** | *I* **had no alternative** *but to report him to the police.* | *He quickly assessed what alternatives were open to him.*

alternative lifestyle n [C] the way that someone lives their life, when this is not the usual way that other people live: *Some people say schools need to teach tolerance of alternative lifestyles.*

al·ter·na·tor /'ɔːltəneɪtə $ 'ɒːltərneɪtər, 'æl-/ n [C] an object that produces an ALTERNATING CURRENT, especially in a car

al·though S1 W1 /ɔːl'ðəʊ $ ɒːl'ðoʊ/ conjunction
1 used to introduce a statement that makes your main statement seem surprising or unlikely; ◆ **though**: *Although in poor health, she continued to carry out her duties.* | *We decided to take rooms in Longwood House, although we knew we could not really afford the rent.* | *Although I can't help admiring the man's courage, I do not approve of his methods.*
2 used to add a statement that balances or reduces the effect of what you have just said; ◆ **but**: *You can copy down my answers, although I'm not sure they're right.* | *No, this is my responsibility, although I appreciate your offer.*

al·ti·me·ter /'æltɪ,miːtə $ æl'tɪmᵻtər/ n [C] an instrument in an aircraft that tells you how high you are

al·ti·tude /'æltᵻtjuːd $ -tuːd/ n [C] the height of an object or place above the sea: [+of] *We're flying at an* **altitude** *of 40,000 feet.* | **high/low altitudes** *At high altitudes it is difficult to get enough oxygen.*

al·to¹ /'æltəʊ $ -toʊ/ adj an alto instrument or voice produces notes at the second highest level, below a SOPRANO: *an alto sax*

alto² n plural **altos 1** [C] a singing voice that is lower than a SOPRANO, or a singer with a voice like this **2** [singular] the part of a musical work that is written for an alto voice or instrument → BARITONE¹ (2), BASS¹ (2), SOPRANO¹ (2), TENOR¹ (2)

al·to·geth·er¹ S2 W3 /,ɔːltə'geðə◂ $,ɒːltə'geðər◂/ adv
1 used to emphasize that something has been done completely or has finished completely: *an old custom that has vanished altogether* | *Congress could ban the procession altogether.*
2 [+adj/adv] used to emphasize that the way you describe something is completely true: *In Canada, the situation is altogether different.* | *This latest problem is* **altogether more** *serious.* | **not altogether** (=not completely) *I wasn't altogether happy about Mike staying over.* | *The results were not altogether surprising.*
3 used to show that you are referring to the total amount: *There were five people altogether.* | *How much do I owe you altogether?*
4 used to make a final statement about several things you have just mentioned; ◆ **all in all**: *Lots of sunshine, wonderful food, and amazing nightlife – altogether a great vacation!*

altogether² n **in the altogether** not wearing any clothes – used humorously: *Several of the men were parading around in the altogether.*

al·tru·is·m /'æltru-ɪzəm/ n [U] when you care about or help other people, even though this brings no advantage to yourself: *Many choose to work in developing countries out of altruism.* —**altruist** n [C]

al·tru·is·tic /,æltru'ɪstɪk◂/ adj altruistic behaviour shows that you care about and will help other people, even though this brings no advantage for yourself; ◆ **selfish**: *Were his motives entirely altruistic?* —**altruistically** /-kli/ adv

al·um /'æləm/ n [C] *AmE informal* a former student of a school, college etc: *a Crawford High alum*

al·u·min·i·um /,ælə'mɪniəm/ *BrE*; **a·lu·mi·num** /ə'luːmᵻnəm/ *AmE* n [U] a silver-white metal that is very light and is used to make cans, cooking pans, window frames etc. It is a chemical ELEMENT: symbol Al: *recycled aluminium cans*

a·lum·na /ə'lʌmnə/ n plural **alumnae** /-niː/ [C] formal a woman who is a former student of a school, college, etc

a·lum·ni /ə'lʌmnaɪ/ n [plural] the former students of a school, college etc: *the University alumni association*

a·lum·nus /ə'lʌmnəs/ n plural **alumni** /-naɪ/ [C] formal a former student of a school, college etc

al·ve·o·lar /ˌælvi'əʊlə◂, æl'viːələ $ æl'viːələr/ n [C] technical a CONSONANT sound such as /t/ or /d/ that you make by putting the end of your tongue behind your upper front teeth

al·ways S1 W1 /'ɔːlwɪ̆z, -weɪz $ 'ɒːl-/ adv
1 all the time, at all times, or every time: *Always lock your bicycle to something secure.* | *She'd always assumed that Gabriel was a girl's name.* | *He hadn't always been a butler.*
2 for a very long time: *I've always wanted to go to Paris.* | *John's always been keen on music.*
3 for ever: *I'll always remember that day.*
4 if someone or something is always doing something, they do it often, especially in an annoying way: *That woman next door's always complaining.*
5 always assuming/supposing (that) sth BrE used to say that one important fact has to be accepted as true for something else to happen, be true etc: *We'll leave on Tuesday — always assuming the car's repaired by then.*
6 as always as is usual or expected: *The truth, as always, is more complicated.* | *As always, Deborah was the last to arrive.*
7 can/could always do sth, there's always sth spoken used to make a polite suggestion: *You could always try ringing again.* | *If you can't get it locally, there's always the Internet.*
8 sb always was lucky/untidy etc used to say you are not surprised by what someone has done because it is typical of them: *You always were a stubborn creature.* | *He's a troublemaker! Always was and always will be!*; → see box at STILL[1]

Alz·heim·er's dis·ease /'æltshaɪməz dɪˌziːz $ -ərz-/ also **Alzheimer's** n [U] a disease that affects the brain, especially of old people, and that gradually makes it difficult to move, talk, or remember things; 🖅 **dementia**

am /m, əm; strong æm/ v the first person singular of the present tense of the verb BE

a.m. also **am** BrE /ˌeɪ 'em/ ante meridiem used to talk about times that are after MIDNIGHT but before MIDDAY; → PM: *Work starts at 9 am.*

AM /ˌeɪ 'em/ n [U] **amplitude modulation** a system used for broadcasting radio programmes; → FM

a·mal·gam /ə'mælgəm/ n [C] formal a mixture of different things: [+of] *an amalgam of different styles*

a·mal·ga·mate /ə'mælgəmeɪt/ v formal **1** [I,T] if two organizations amalgamate, or if one amalgamates with another, they join and make one big organization; 🖅 **merge**: amalgamate sth with/into/under sth *The agency is expected to amalgamate with the National Rivers Authority.* **2** [T] to combine two or more things together to make one thing: *Stir until the ingredients are amalgamated.* | amalgamate sth with/into sth *The editors will amalgamate all the information into one article.* —**amalgamation** /əˌmælgə'meɪʃən/ n [C,U]: *an amalgamation between two companies*

a·man·u·en·sis /əˌmænju'ensɪ̆s/ n [C] formal someone whose job is to write down what someone else says

a·mass /ə'mæs/ v [T] if you amass money, knowledge, information etc, you gradually collect a large amount of it: *For 25 years, Darwin amassed evidence to support his theories.* | *He amassed a fortune after the war.*

am·a·teur /'amətə, -tʃʊə, -tʃə, ˌæmə'tɜː $ 'æmətʃʊr, -tər/ n [C] **1** someone who does an activity just for pleasure, not as their job; 🖅 **professional**: *a gifted amateur* | *Mickelson won his first major golf tournament while still an amateur.* **2** informal someone who you think is not very skilled at something: *You English are a bunch of amateurs when it comes to romance.* —**amateur** adj: *an amateur orchestra* | *amateur dra-*

matics BrE (=producing or acting in plays as an interest) —**amateurism** n [U]: *well-meaning amateurism*

am·a·teur·ish /'æmətərɪʃ, -tʃʊə-,-tʃə- ˌæmə'tɜːrɪʃ $ ˌæmə'tʊr-, -'tɜːr-/ adj not skilfully done or made; 🖅 **professional**: *His paintings are rather amateurish.* —**amateurishly** adv —**amateurishness** n [U]

am·a·to·ry /'æmətəri $ -tɔːri/ adj formal expressing sexual or romantic love

a·maze /ə'meɪz/ v [T] to surprise someone very much; 🖅 **astonish**: *Dave amazed his friends by suddenly getting married.* | **it amazes sb how/what etc** *It still amazes me how much she has improved.* | [+that] *It never ceased to amaze him that women were attracted to Sam.*

a·mazed /ə'meɪzd/ adj very surprised; 🖅 **astonished**: **amazed (that)/how** *I'm amazed you've never heard of the Rolling Stones.* | *You'd be amazed how much money you can save.* | [+at/by] *We were absolutely amazed at his rapid recovery.* | **amazed to see/find/discover sth** *Visitors are often amazed to discover how little the town has changed.*

a·maze·ment /ə'meɪzmənt/ n [U] a feeling of great surprise; 🖅 **astonishment**: **do sth in amazement** *Ralph gasped in amazement.* | **to sb's amazement** *To everyone's amazement, the goal was disallowed.*

a·maz·ing S2 /ə'meɪzɪŋ/ adj
1 very good, especially in an unexpected way: *He's an amazing player to watch.* | *an amazing bargain*
2 so surprising you can hardly believe it: *It's amazing how often you see drivers using mobile phones.* —**amazingly** adv: *These shoes were amazingly cheap.*

Am·a·zon /'æməzən $ -zɑːn -zən/ n [C] literary a strong, tall woman —**amazonian** /ˌæmə'zəʊniən◂ $ -'zoʊ-/ adj

am·bas·sa·dor /æm'bæsədə $ -ər/ n [C] **1** an important official who represents his or her government in a foreign country: [+to] *the US ambassador to Spain* **2** someone who represents a particular sport, business etc because they behave in a way that people admire: [+for] *He has made some good films and he is a good ambassador for the industry.* —**ambassadorial** /æmˌbæsə'dɔːriəl/ adj: *relations at ambassadorial level*

am·ber /'æmbə $ -ər/ n [U] **1** a yellowish brown colour **2** a hard yellowish brown substance used to make jewellery: *an amber necklace* —**amber** adj

am·bi·ance /'æmbiəns/ n [singular] another spelling of ambience

am·bi·dex·trous /ˌæmbi'dekstrəs◂/ adj able to use either hand equally well; → left-handed, right-handed

am·bi·ence, ambiance /'æmbiəns/ n [singular] the qualities and character of a particular place and the way these make you feel; 🖅 **atmosphere**: pleasant/relaxing/friendly etc ambience *The restaurant's new owners have created a welcoming ambience.*

am·bi·ent /'æmbiənt/ adj **1** ambient temperature/light etc technical the temperature etc of the surrounding area **2** ambient music/sounds a type of modern music or sound that is slow, peaceful, and does not have a formal structure

am·bi·gu·i·ty /ˌæmbɪ'gjuːɪ̆ti/ n plural ambiguities [C,U] the state of being unclear, confusing, or not certain, or things that produce this effect: [+in] *There was an element of ambiguity in the president's reply.* | *legal ambiguities*

am·big·u·ous /æm'bɪgjuəs/ adj something that is ambiguous is unclear, confusing, or not certain, especially because it can be understood in more than one way; 🖅 **unambiguous**: *The language in the Minister's statement is highly ambiguous.* | *His role in the affair is ambiguous.* —**ambiguously** adv: *The legislation had been ambiguously worded.*

am·bit /'æmbɪt/ *n* [singular] *formal* the range or limit of someone's authority, influence etc: **fall within the ambit of sth** *areas falling within the ambit of our research*

am·bi·tion /æm'bɪʃən/ *n* **1** [C] a strong desire to achieve something: **achieve/fulfil/realize an ambition** *She fulfilled her ambition to become the first woman to run the 10,000 metres in under 30 minutes.* | **lifelong ambition** *He always had this* **burning ambition** (=very strong desire) *to start his own business.* | *the* **political ambitions** *of the working class* | **an ambition to do sth/of doing sth** *His ambition to become a pilot was thwarted by poor eyesight.* | **cherish/nurse/harbour an ambition** (=have it secretly for a long time) *He harboured ambitions of becoming leader.* **2** [U] determination to be successful, rich, powerful etc: *a* **lack of ambition**

am·bi·tious /æm'bɪʃəs/ *adj* **1** determined to be successful, rich, powerful etc: *Alfred was intensely ambitious, obsessed with the idea of becoming rich.* | [+for] *mothers who are* **highly ambitious** *for their children* (=who want their children to be successful) **2** an ambitious plan, idea etc shows a desire to do something good but difficult: *an ambitious engineering project* | *an* **over-ambitious** *health reform program* —**ambitiously** *adv* —**ambitiousness** *n* [U]

am·biv·a·lent /æm'bɪvələnt/ *adj* not sure whether you want or like something or not: [+about] *We are both somewhat ambivalent about having a child.* | **ambivalent attitude/feelings etc** —**ambivalence** *n* [singular, U]: *O'Neill had a genuine* **ambivalence toward** *US involvement in the war.* —**ambivalently** *adv*

am·ble /'æmbəl/ *v* [I always + adv/prep] to walk slowly in a relaxed way; **≙ saunter**: *An old man came out and ambled over for a chat.* —**amble** *n* [singular]: *a pleasant amble by the river*

am·bro·si·a /æm'brəʊziə $ -'broʊʒə/ *n* [U] *literary* food or drink that tastes very good

am·bu·lance [S3] /'æmbjʊləns/ *n* [C] a special vehicle that is used to take people who are ill or injured to hospital: *the ambulance service* | **ambulance staff/crew/worker** *The ambulance crew removed him from the wreckage.* | *the* **ambulance service** | **by ambulance** *Mike had to be taken by ambulance to hospital.* | *Do you think we need to* **call an ambulance** (=phone to ask an ambulance to come)?

'ambulance ,chaser *n* [C] a lawyer who uses a lot of pressure to persuade someone who has been hurt in an accident to SUE other people or companies in court, so that the lawyer will get part of the money if they win – used to show disapproval

am·bush /'æmbʊʃ/ *n* [C,U] a sudden attack on someone by people who have been hiding and waiting for them, or the place where this happens: *The soldiers were killed in an ambush.* | *In winter the danger of ambush is much reduced.* | **lie/wait in ambush** *Armed police lay in ambush behind the hedge.* —**ambush** *v* [T]: *Everybody thought our train would be ambushed, but we got out safely.*

a·me·ba /ə'miːbə/ *n* [C] an American spelling of AMOEBA

a·me·li·o·rate /ə'miːliəreɪt/ *v* [T] *formal* to make a bad situation better or less harmful; **≙ improve**: *It is not clear what can be done to ameliorate the situation.* —**amelioration** /ə,miːliə'reɪʃən/ *n* [U]

a·men /ɑː'men, eɪ-/ *interjection, n* [C] **1** a word used to end a prayer: *Blessed be the Lord, Amen!* | *McAllister murmured a fervent amen.* **2** **amen to that** *informal* used to show that you agree with a suggestion or remark: *'I think we can close the meeting now.' 'Amen to that.'*

a·me·na·ble /ə'miːnəbəl $ ə'miːn- ə'men-/ *adj* **1** willing to accept what someone says or does without arguing: *She was always a very amenable child.* | [+to] *Young people are more amenable than*

older citizens to the idea of immigration. **2** suitable for a particular type of treatment: [+for/to] *Such conditions may be amenable to medical intervention.*

a·mend [S3] /ə'mend/ *v* [T] *formal* to correct or make small changes to something that is written or spoken: *The law was amended to include women.* | *The defendant later amended his evidence.* | *'Steve stole it – or rather borrowed it,' he amended.* —**amended** *adj*: *an amended version*

a·mend·ment /ə'mendmənt/ *n* [C,U] a small change, improvement, or addition that is made to a law or document, or the process of doing this: *constitutional amendments* | [+to] *an amendment to the resolution*

a·mends /ə'mendz/ *n* **make amends (to sb/for sth)** to do something to show you are sorry for hurting or upsetting someone, especially something that makes it better for them: *He seized the chance to make amends for his behavior.*

a·me·ni·ty /ə'miːnəti $ ə'me-/ *n plural* **amenities** [C usually plural] something that makes a place comfortable or easy to live in: *The hotel is in the city centre, close to shops and local amenities.* | *houses that lack* **basic amenities** (=basic things that people need, such as heat and running water)

Am·er·a·sian /,æmə'reɪʒən , -ʃən/ *n* [C] someone who has one American parent and one Asian parent; → **Asian-American**

A·mer·i·can¹ /ə'merɪkən/ *adj* **1** relating to the US or its people: *Her mother is American.* | *a famous American writer* **2 sth is as American as apple pie** used to say that something is very typically American → LATIN AMERICAN

American² *n* [C] someone from the US

A·mer·i·ca·na /ə,merɪ'kɑːnə $ -'kɑːnə, -'kænə/ *n* [U] objects that are considered to be typical of the US, especially when they are in a COLLECTION: *1940s Americana*

A,merican 'football *n* [U] *BrE* a game played in the US by two teams of eleven players, who carry, throw, or kick an OVAL ball; **≙ football** *AmE*

A,merican 'Indian *n* [C] another name for a NATIVE AMERICAN (=someone who belongs to one of the races that lived in North America before Europeans arrived)

A·mer·i·can·is·m /ə'merɪkənɪzəm/ *n* [C] a word or phrase that is typically used in American English

A·mer·i·can·ize also **-ise** *BrE* /ə'merɪkənaɪz/ *v* [T] to change a society, language, system etc so that it becomes more American in character —**Americanization** /ə,merɪkənaɪ'zeɪʃən $ -nə-/ *n* [U]: *the Americanization of youth culture*

am·e·thyst /'æmɪθɪst/ *n* **1** [C] a valuable purple stone used in jewellery **2** [U] a light purple colour —**amethyst** *adj*

a·mi·a·ble /'eɪmiəbəl/ *adj* friendly and easy to like: *The driver was an amiable young man.* | *She was in an amiable mood.* —**amiably** *adv* —**amiability** /,eɪmiə'bɪləti/ *n* [U]

am·i·ca·ble /'æmɪkəbəl/ *adj* an amicable agreement, relationship etc is one in which people feel friendly towards each other and do not want to quarrel: *Their relationship hasn't always been amicable.* | **amicable settlement/agreement** *The two parties have reached an amicable settlement.* —**amicably** *adv*: *In the end, the matter was resolved amicably.*

a·mid /ə'mɪd/ *prep* **1** while noisy, busy, or confused events are happening – used in writing or news reports: *The dollar has fallen in value amid rumors of weakness in the US economy.* | *Demonstrators ripped up the national flag amid shouts of 'Death to the tyrants!'* **2** *literary* among or surrounded by things: *He sat amid the trees.*

a·mid·ships /ə'mɪd,ʃɪps/ *adv technical* in the middle part of a ship

a·midst /ə'mɪdst/ *prep literary* amid: *a light that shines amidst the darkness*

a·mi·no ac·id /ə,miːnəʊ ˈæsˌɪd, ə,maɪ- $ -noʊ-/ n [C] one of the substances that combine to form PROTEINS

a·miss¹ /əˈmɪs/ adj [not before noun] if something is amiss, there is a problem; **✪ wrong**: Elsa continued as if nothing was amiss. | [+with/in] There's something amiss in their relationship.

amiss² adv BrE **1 sth would not come/go amiss** informal used to say that something would be suitable or useful in a situation: A cup of tea wouldn't go amiss. **2 take sth amiss** to feel upset or offended about something that someone has said or done: Don't take it amiss – I was just teasing.

am·i·ty /ˈæmⱼti/ n [U] formal friendship, especially between countries; **✪ hostility**: a spirit of perfect amity

am·me·ter /ˈæmɪtə, ˈæm,miːtə $ -ər/ n [C] a piece of equipment used to measure the strength of an electric current

am·mo /ˈæməʊ $ -moʊ/ n [U] informal ammunition

am·mo·ni·a /əˈməʊniə $ -ˈmoʊ-/ n [U] **1** a clear liquid with a strong bad smell that is used for cleaning or in cleaning products **2** a poisonous gas with a strong bad smell that is used in making many chemicals, FERTILIZERS etc

am·mu·ni·tion /,æmjʊˈnɪʃən/ n [U] **1** bullets, shells SHELL¹ (2) etc that are fired from guns **2** information that you can use to criticize someone or win an argument against them: **give sb ammunition/provide sb with ammunition** His mistakes provided political opponents with even more ammunition.

am·ne·si·a /æmˈniːziə $ -ʒə/ n [U] the medical condition of not being able to remember anything —**amnesiac** /-ziæk $ -ʒiæk, -ziæk/ n [C]

am·nes·ty /ˈæmnəsti/ n plural **amnesties** [C] **1** an official order by a government that allows a particular group of prisoners to go free: [+for] The government granted an amnesty for all former terrorists. **2** a period of time when you can admit to doing something illegal without being punished: [+on] an amnesty on illegal handguns —**amnesty** v [T]

am·ni·o·cen·te·sis /,æmniəʊsenˈtiːsⱼs $ -nioʊ-/ n [U] a test to see if an unborn baby has a disease or other problem, done by taking liquid from the mother's WOMB

a·moe·ba, also **ameba** AmE /əˈmiːbə/ n or [C] a very small creature that has only one cell —**amoebic** adj

a·mok /əˈmɒk $ əˈmɑːk/ also **amuck** adv **run amok a)** to suddenly behave in a very violent and uncontrolled way: Drunken troops ran amok in the town. **b)** to get out of control and cause a lot of problems: an age in which global capitalism has run amok

a·mong S1 W1 /əˈmʌŋ/ also **a·mongst** /əˈmʌŋst/ prep **1** in or through the middle of a group of people or things: The girl quickly disappeared among the crowd. | I could hear voices coming from somewhere among the bushes. | We walked among the chestnut woods on the mountain slopes. | She began rummaging among the books on her desk. → BETWEEN
2 with a particular group of people: Jim relaxed, knowing he was **among friends**.
3 used to say that many people in a group have the same feeling or opinion, or that something affects many people in a group: The problem is causing widespread concern among scientists. | The general opinion among police officers was that the law should be tightened. | The changes will mean 7,000 job losses among railway workers.
4 used to talk about a particular person, thing, or group as belonging to a larger group: She was the eldest among them. | Innocent civilians were among the casualties. | My grandfather had among his possessions a portrait by Matisse. | Representatives were chosen by the students from among themselves.
5 among other things/places/factors etc used to say that you are only mentioning one or two people or things out of a much larger group: At the meeting they

discussed, among other things, recent events in Japan.
6 if something is divided or shared among a group of people, each person is given a part of it: A father's property was divided among his heirs.
7 among yourselves/ourselves/themselves with each other: The allies found it hard to agree among themselves.

a·mor·al /eɪˈmɒrəl, æ- $ eɪˈmɔː-, -ˈmɑː-/ adj having no moral standards at all; **✪ moral**: a completely amoral person —**amorality** /,eɪmɒˈrælⱼti, ,æ- $,eɪmə-/ n [U]

am·o·rous /ˈæmərəs/ adj formal showing or concerning sexual love: She resisted his **amorous advances**. | He was always boasting about his **amorous adventures**. —**amorously** adv

a·mor·phous /əˈmɔːfəs $ -ɔːr-/ adj formal having no definite shape or features: an **amorphous mass** of twisted metal

a·mor·tize also **-ise** BrE /əˈmɔːtaɪz $ ˈæmərtaɪz/ v [T] technical to pay a debt by making regular payments —**amortization** /æ,mɔːtaɪˈzeɪʃən $,æmərtə-/ n [C,U]

a·mount¹ S1 W1 /əˈmaʊnt/ n [C,U]
1 a quantity of something such as time, money, or a substance: [+of] They spend equal amounts of time in California and New York. | a considerable/large/enormous etc amount a considerable amount of money | a small/tiny etc amount a tiny amount of dirt | Please pay **the full amount** (=of money) by the end of the month.
2 used to talk about how much there is of a feeling or quality: a large/considerable etc amount of sth Her case has attracted an enormous amount of public sympathy. | a certain/fair amount of sth Dina encountered a fair amount of envy among her colleagues.
3 no amount of sth can/will etc do sth used to say that something has no effect: No amount of persuasion could make her change her mind.
4 any amount of sth used to say that there is plenty of something, and no more is needed: The school has any amount of resources and equipment.

amount² v
amount to sth phr v **1** if figures, sums etc amount to a particular total, they equal that total when they are added together: Time lost through illness amounted to 1,357 working days. **2** if an attitude, remark, situation etc amounts to something, it has the same effect: The court's decision amounts to a not guilty verdict. | Ultimately, their ideas **amount to the same thing**. **3 not amount to much/anything/a great deal etc** to not be important, valuable, or successful: Her academic achievements don't amount to much. | Jim's never going to amount to much.

a·mour /əˈmʊə $ əˈmʊr/ n [C] literary a sexual relationship, especially a secret one

amp /æmp/ n [C] **1** also **am·pere** /ˈæmpeə $ -pɪr/ a unit for measuring electric current: a 3 amp fuse **2** informal an AMPLIFIER

am·per·sand /ˈæmpəsænd $ -ər-/ n [C] the sign '&' that means 'and': Mills & Boon

am·phet·a·mine /æmˈfetəmiːn, -mⱼn/ n [C,U] a drug that gives you a feeling of excitement and a lot of energy

am·phib·i·an /æmˈfɪbiən/ n [C] animals such as FROGS that can live both on land and in water

am·phib·i·ous /æmˈfɪbiəs/ adj **1** able to live on both land and water: amphibious creatures **2 amphibious vehicle** a vehicle that is able to move on both land and water **3 amphibious operation/force/assault** an amphibious operation etc involves both sea and land vehicles

am·phi·thea·tre BrE; **amphitheater** AmE /ˈæmfⱼ,θɪətə $ -ər/ n [C] a large circular building without a roof and with many rows of seats

---

1 000, 2 000, 3 000, most frequent words in S poken and W ritten English

am·pho·ra /'æmfərə/ *n* [C] a tall clay container for oil or wine, used in ancient times

am·ple /'æmpəl/ *adj* **1** more than enough; ◨ **sufficient**; ◨ **insufficient: ample time/evidence/opportunity** *You'll have ample time for questions later.* | *There is ample evidence that climate patterns are changing.* | **ample room/space etc** *She found ample room for her things in the wardrobe.* **2** *literary* large in a way that is attractive or pleasant: *an ample bosom* —**amply** *adv*: *Recent US history has amply demonstrated the risks of foreign intervention.*

am·pli·fi·er /'æmpl₃far/ $ -faɪər/ *n* [C] a piece of electrical equipment that makes sound louder; ◨ **amp**

am·pli·fy /'æmpl₃faɪ/ *v* **amplified, amplifying, amplifies** [T] **1** to make sound louder, especially musical sound: *an amplified guitar* **2** *formal* to increase the effects or strength of something: *These stories only amplified her fears.* **3** *formal* to explain something that you have said by giving more information about it: *Would you care to amplify that remark?* —**amplification** /ˌæmpl₃fɪˈkeɪʃən/ *n* [U]

am·pli·tude /'æmpl₃tjuːd $ -tuːd/ *n* [U] *technical* the distance between the middle and the top or bottom of a WAVE such as a SOUND WAVE

am·poule, ampule /'æmpuːl $ -pjuːl/ *n* [C] a small container for medicine that will be put into someone with a special needle

am·pu·tate /'æmpjʊteɪt/ *v* [I,T] to cut off someone's arm, leg, finger etc during a medical operation: *Two of her toes were amputated because of frostbite.* —**amputation** /ˌæmpjʊˈteɪʃən/ *n* [C,U]

am·pu·tee /ˌæmpjʊˈtiː/ *n* [C] someone who has had an arm or a leg amputated

a·muck /əˈmʌk/ *adv* AMOK

am·u·let /'æmjʊlət, -let $ -lət/ *n* [C] a small piece of jewellery worn to protect against bad luck, disease etc

a·muse /əˈmjuːz/ *v* [T] **1** to make someone laugh or smile: *He made funny faces to amuse the children.* | *The question seemed to amuse him in some way.* | **it amuses sb to do sth** | *It amused me to think back to my life in London.* **2** to make time pass in an enjoyable way, so that you do not get bored; ◨ **entertain**: *Doing jigsaws would amuse Amy for hours on end.* | *The kids amused themselves playing hide-and-seek.*

a·mused /əˈmjuːzd/ *adj* **1** if you are amused by something, you think it is funny and you smile or laugh: [+at/by] *Ellen seemed amused by the whole situation.* | *I could see she was highly amused* (=very amused). | *The man looked a little amused.* | *He won't be very amused* (=he will be annoyed) *when he finds out what's happened to his garden.* | **an amused smile/look/expression etc** **2** **keep sb amused** to entertain or interest someone for a long time so that they do not get bored: *There were puzzles and games to keep the children amused.*

a·muse·ment /əˈmjuːzmənt/ *n* **1** [U] the feeling you have when you think something is funny: **with/in amusement** *Her eyes sparkled with amusement.* | *She looked at him in amusement.* | *Steve couldn't hide his amusement.* | **to sb's amusement** (=in a way that makes someone laugh or smile) *They were dancing and singing in the car, **much to the amusement** of passers-by.* | *The cats are a constant **source of amusement** to us.* **2 amusements** [plural] **a)** things that entertain you and make time pass in an enjoyable way: *childhood amusements* **b)** *BrE* special machines or games that are intended to entertain people, for example at a FAIR: *The kids can ride on the amusements.* **3** [U] the process of getting or providing pleasure and enjoyment: *What do you do for amusement in this town?*

a·musement ar·cade *n* [C] *BrE* a place where you play games on machines by putting coins into them; ◨ **video arcade** *AmE*

big wheel
big dipper

a·muse·ment ˌpark *n* [C] a large park with many special machines that you can ride on, such as ROLLER COASTERS and MERRY-GO-ROUNDS

a·mus·ing /əˈmjuːzɪŋ/ *adj* funny and entertaining: *I don't find his jokes at all **amusing**.* | *a **highly amusing** (=very amusing) film* | *an amusing story/anecdote/incident etc The book is full of amusing stories about his childhood.* | **mildly/vaguely amusing** (=a little amusing, but not very) *a mildly amusing spectacle* —**amusingly** *adv*

an S1 W1 /ən; *strong* æn/ *indefinite article, determiner* used when the following word begins with a vowel sound; ➔ **a**: *an orange* | *an X-ray*; ➔ see box at A

an- /ən, æn/ *prefix* **1** the form used for A before a vowel sound **2** not; ◨ **without**: *anarchy* (=without government) | *anoxia* (=condition caused by lack of oxygen)

-an /ən/ *suffix* also **-ean, -ian** **1** [in adjectives and nouns] someone or something of, from, or connected with a particular thing, place, or person: *suburban* | *Jamesian* **2** [in nouns] someone skilled in or studying a particular subject: *a historian* (=someone who studies history)

-ana /ɑːnə $ ɑːnə, ænə/ *suffix* [in nouns] another form of the suffix -IANA: *Americana*

an·a·bol·ic ste·roid /ˌænəbɒlɪk ˈstɪərɔɪd, -ˈster- $ -bɑːlɪk ˈstɪrɔɪd, -ˈster-/ *n* [C] a drug that makes muscles grow quickly, sometimes used illegally by people in sport

a·nach·ro·nis·m /əˈnækrənɪzəm/ *n* [C] **1** someone or something that seems to belong to the past, not the present: *The monarchy is something of an anachronism these days.* **2** something in a play, film etc that seems wrong because it did not exist in the period of history in which the play etc is set: *The film is full of anachronisms.* —**anachronistic** /əˌnækrəˈnɪstɪk◂/ *adj*: *His painting style was seen as outdated and anachronistic.*

an·a·con·da /ˌænəˈkɒndə $ -ˈkɑːn-/ *n* [C] a very large South American snake

a·nae·mi·a, also **anemia** *AmE* /əˈniːmiə/ *n* [U] a medical condition in which there are too few red cells in your blood

a·nae·mic, also **anemic** *AmE* /əˈniːmɪk/ *adj* **1** suffering from anaemia: *his anaemic-looking face* **2** *written* seeming weak and uninteresting: *an anaemic first novel*

an·ae·ro·bic /ˌænəˈrəʊbɪk◂ $ -ˈroʊ-/ *adj* not needing oxygen in order to live; ◨ **aerobic**

an·aes·the·si·a, also **anesthesia** *AmE* /ˌænəsˈθiːziə $ -ʒə/ *n* [U] **1** the use of anaesthetics in medicine **2** the state of being unable to feel pain

an·aes·thet·ic, also **anesthetic** *AmE* /ˌænəsˈθetɪk◂/ *n* [C,U] a drug that stops you feeling pain: **under anaesthetic** *The operation will have to be done under anaesthetic* (=using anaesthetic). | *Eye surgery is often performed using a **local anaesthetic** (=one that only affects a particular area of your body).* | *You will need to have a **general anaesthetic** (=one that makes you completely unconscious).* —**anaesthetic** *adj* [only before noun]: *anaesthetic drugs*

a·naes·the·tist, also **anesthetist** *AmE* /ə'niːsθ₂̣tɪst $ ə'nes-/ *n* [C] a doctor or nurse who has been specially trained to give people anaesthetics

a·naes·the·tize also **-ise** *BrE* /ə'niːsθ₂̣taɪz $ ə'nes-/ *v* [T] to give someone an anaesthetic so that they do not feel pain

an·a·gram /'ænəgræm/ *n* [C] a word or phrase that is made by changing the order of the letters in another word or phrase: *'Silent' is an anagram of 'listen'*.

a·nal /'eɪnl/ *adj* **1** connected with the ANUS **2** also **anal retentive** showing too much concern with small details, especially in a way that annoys other people – used to show disapproval: *Don't be so anal.*

an·al·ge·si·a /ˌænəl'dʒiːziə $ -ʒə/ *n* [U] *technical* the condition of being unable to feel pain while conscious

an·al·ge·sic /ˌænəl'dʒiːzɪk◂/ *n* [C] *technical* a drug that reduces pain; **◨ painkiller**: *Aspirin is a popular analgesic.* —**analgesic** *adj* [only before noun]: *drugs that have an analgesic effect on ulcers*

a·nal·o·gous /ə'næləgəs/ *adj formal* similar to another situation or thing so that a comparison can be made: [+to/with] *The report's findings are analogous with our own.*

an·a·logue also **analog** *AmE* /'ænəlɒg $ -lɔːg, -lɑːg/ *adj* **1 analogue clock/watch** a clock or watch that uses POINTERS, not changing numbers; ➔ **digital 2** *technical* analogue technology uses changing physical quantities such as VOLTAGE to store data; ➔ **digital: analogue computer/circuit/technology**

a·nal·o·gy /ə'nælədʒi/ *n plural* **analogies** [C,U] something that seems similar between two situations, processes etc: [+with/to/between] *analogies between human and animal behaviour* | **draw/make an analogy** (=make a comparison) *She drew an analogy between childbirth and the creative process.* | **by analogy with** | *Dr Wood explained the movement of light by analogy with* (=using the analogy of) *the movement of water.*

an·a·lyse W3 , **analyze** /'ænəl-aɪz/ *v* [T] **1** to examine or think about something carefully, in order to understand it: *She still needs to analyse the data.* | *You need to sit down and analyse why you feel so upset.* | *Joe had never tried to analyze their relationship.* **2** to examine a substance to see what it is made of: *The cell samples are analyzed by a lab.* **3** to examine someone's mental or emotional problems by using PSYCHOANALYSIS

a·nal·y·sis S3 W1 /ə'næl₂s₂s/ *n plural* **analyses** /-siːz/ **1** [C,U] **a)** a careful examination of something in order to understand it better: [+of] *a detailed analysis of the week's news* | *Further analysis of the data is needed.* | **do/carry out/conduct an analysis** *They were doing some type of statistical analysis.* **b)** the way in which someone describes a situation or problem, and says what causes it to happen: [+of] *Do you agree with Marx's analysis of the failure of free-market capitalism?* **2** [C,U] a careful examination of a substance to see what it is made of: [+of] *analysis of genetic material* | **for analysis** *Blood samples were sent to the laboratory for analysis.* | *You'll get the results when the analysis is complete.* **3** [U] a process in which a doctor makes someone talk about their past experiences, relationships etc in order to help them with mental or emotional problems; **◨ psychoanalysis**; ➔ **therapy**: *She's been in analysis for three years.* **4 in the final/last analysis** used when giving the most basic or important facts about a situation: *In the final analysis, profit is the motive.*

an·a·lyst /'ænəl-₁st/ *n* [C] **1** someone whose job is to think about something carefully in order to understand it, and often to advise other people about it: *Political analysts expect the Conservatives to win.* | **investment/financial/business analyst** | *Cleary has been working as a computer analyst in Winchester.* **2** a doctor who helps people who have mental or emotional

problems by making them talk about their experiences and relationships ➔ SYSTEMS ANALYST

an·a·lyt·i·cal /ˌænəl'ɪtɪkəl/ also **an·a·lyt·ic** /ˌænəl'ɪtɪk◂/ *adj* **1** thinking about things in a detailed and intelligent way, so that you can examine and understand things: *She's got an analytical mind.* | **analytical method/techniques/approach/skills** *During the course, students will develop their analytical skills.* **2** using scientific analysis to examine something: *analytical chemistry* —**analytically** /-kli/ *adv*

an·a·lyze /'ænəl-aɪz/ *v* [T] the American spelling of ANALYSE

an·a·phy·lac·tic shock /ˌænəf₂ˈlæktɪk 'ʃɒk $ -'ʃɑːk/ *n* [U] *medical* a very sudden serious physical reaction that is caused by an ALLERGY to something such as nuts, eggs, or the STING of some insects. The reaction causes shock, breathing difficulties, and sometimes death.

an·ar·chic /æ'nɑːkɪk $ -ɑːr-/ *adj* lacking any rules or order, or not following the moral rules of society: *a lawless, anarchic city* | *an anarchic sense of humour*

an·ar·chis·m /'ænəkɪzəm $ -ər-/ *n* [U] the political belief that there should be no government and ordinary people should work together to improve society

an·ar·chist /'ænək₁st $ -ər-/ *n* [C] someone who believes that governments, laws etc are not necessary —**anarchistic** /ˌænə'kɪstɪk◂ $ -ər-/ *adj*

an·ar·chy /'ænəki $ -ər-/ *n* [U] a situation in which there is no effective government in a country or no order in an organization or situation: *The prison is close to anarchy.* | *The classroom was in a constant state of anarchy.* | **slide/fall/descend into anarchy** *The nation is in danger of falling into anarchy.*

a·nath·e·ma /ə'næθ₂mə/ *n* [singular, U] *formal* something that is completely the opposite of what you believe in: [+to] *His political views were anathema to me.*

an·a·tom·i·cal /ˌænə'tɒmɪkəl◂ $ -'tɑː-/ *adj* relating to the structure of human or animal bodies: *an anatomical examination* —**anatomically** /-kli/ *adv*

a·nat·o·mist /ə'nætəmɪst/ *n* [C] a scientist who studies anatomy

a·nat·o·my /ə'nætəmi/ *n plural* **anatomies 1** [U] the scientific study of the structure of human or animal bodies: *a professor of anatomy* | **human/animal anatomy** *Knowledge of human anatomy is essential to figure drawing.* **2** [C usually singular] the structure of a body, or of a part of a body: [+of] *the anatomy of the nervous system* **3** [C] your body – often used in a humorous way: *You could see a part of his anatomy that I'd rather not mention.* **4 the/an anatomy of sth a)** study or examination of an organization, process etc in order to understand and explain how it works: *Elkind's book is an anatomy of one man's discussion with his son about life.* **b)** the structure of an organization, process etc or the way it works: *For the first time, we have the chance to examine the anatomy of a secret government operation.*

-ance /əns/, **-ence** *suffix* [in nouns] the action, state, or quality of doing something or of being something: *his sudden appearance* (=he appeared suddenly) | *her brilliance* (=she is BRILLIANT)

an·ces·tor /'ænsəstə, -ses- $ -sestər/ *n* [C] **1** a member of your family who lived a long time ago; ➔ **descendant**: *My ancestors were French.* **2** an animal that lived in the past, that modern animals have developed from: *Lions and house cats evolved from a common ancestor* (=the same ancestor). **3** the form in which a modern machine, vehicle etc first existed: [+of] *Babbage's invention was the ancestor of the modern computer.* —**ancestral** /æn'sestrəl/ *adj*: *the family's ancestral home*

an·ces·try /'ænsəstri, -ses- $ -ses-/ *n plural* **ancestries** [C usually singular, U] *formal* the members of your family who lived a long time ago: **of ... ancestry** | *Her* mother is of German ancestry (=has German ancestors). | Helen's family can trace their ancestry back to the 1700s.

an·chor¹ /'æŋkə $ -ər/ n [C] **1** a piece of heavy metal that is lowered to the bottom of the sea, lake etc to prevent a ship or boat moving: **at anchor** The ship was at anchor. | We **dropped anchor** a few yards offshore. | The next morning, they **weighed anchor** (=lifted the anchor) and began to move south again. → see picture at WRECK¹ **2** especially AmE someone who reads the news on TV and introduces news reports; 🔲 **newsreader** BrE: Dan Rather, anchor of the CBC Evening News **3** someone or something that provides a feeling of support and safety: Dad was the anchor of the family.

anchor² v **1** [I,T] to lower the anchor on a ship or boat to hold it in one place; 🔲 **moor**: Three tankers were anchored in the harbor. **2** [T usually passive] to fasten something firmly so that it cannot move: The shelves should be securely anchored to the wall. **3 be anchored in sth** to be strongly connected with a particular system, way of life etc: John's outlook has always been anchored in the political mainstream. **4** [T] to provide a feeling of support, safety or help for someone or an organization: Steve anchors the team's defense. | Her life was anchored by her religion. **5** [T] AmE to be the person who reads the news and introduces reports on television: Collins anchors the 6 o'clock news.

an·chor·age /'æŋkərɪdʒ/ n **1** [C] a place where ships can anchor **2** [C,U] a place where something can be firmly fastened

an·chor·per·son /'æŋkə,pɜːsən $ -kər,pɜːr-/ **an·chor·man** /-mæn/, **an·chor·wom·an** /-,wʊmən/ n [C] someone who reads the news on TV and introduces reports

an·cho·vy /'æntʃəvi $ 'æntʃoʊvi/ n plural **anchovies** [C,U] a very small fish that tastes strongly of salt

an·cient¹ W2 /'eɪnʃənt/ adj **1** belonging to a time long ago in history, especially thousands of years ago; 🔲 **modern**: the ancient civilizations of Asia | Kyoto, the ancient capital of Japan | **ancient Greece/Egypt/Rome** the religion of ancient Egypt **2** having existed for a very long time; 🔲 **new**: an ancient walled city | an ancient forest | the ancient art of calligraphy **3** very old – used humorously: That photo makes me look ancient! **4 ancient history a)** the history of ancient societies, such as Greece or Rome: a professor of ancient history **b)** informal if you say that something is ancient history, you mean that it happened a long time ago and is not important now: It's all ancient history and I'm not upset any more.

ancient² n **the ancients** people who lived long ago, especially the Greeks and Romans: The ancients believed that the sun and moon were planets.

an·cil·la·ry /æn'sɪləri $ 'æns̩leri/ adj **1 ancillary workers/staff etc** workers who provide additional help and services for the people who do the main work in hospitals, schools etc **2** formal connected with or supporting something else, but less important than it: Agreement was reached on several ancillary matters.

-ancy /ənsi/, **-ency** suffix [in nouns] the state or quality of doing something or of being something: expectancy (=state of expecting) | hesitancy | complacency (=being complacent)

and S1 W1 /ənd, ən; strong ænd/ conjunction **1** used to join two words, phrases etc referring to things that are related in some way: He's gone to get some fish and chips. | The film starred Jack Lemmon and Shirley Maclaine. | We've dealt with items one, two, and eleven. | He was tall, dark and handsome. | He plays the guitar and sings folk songs. | She didn't speak to anyone and nobody spoke to her.

2 used to say that one action or event follows another: Sit down and tell me all about it. | She picked up the kitten and put it in the box. | He knocked on the door and went in. | You'll have to wait and see what happens. **3** used to say that something is caused by something else: I missed supper and I'm starving! | She fell downstairs and broke her leg. **4** used when adding numbers: Six and four is ten. **5** especially BrE used after verbs such as 'go', 'come', and 'try' to show what your intention is: Shall we go and have a cup of coffee? | I'll see if I can try and persuade her to come. **6** spoken used to introduce a statement, remark, question etc: And now I'd like to introduce our next speaker, Mrs Thompson. | 'She's getting married in June.' 'And who's the lucky man?' **7** used between repeated words to emphasize what you are saying: More and more people are losing their jobs. | We waited for hours and hours! | That was years and years ago. | We ran and ran. **8 a)** used before saying the part of a large number which is less than 100: a hundred and four | five hundred and seventy-six | by the year two thousand and ten **b)** used when saying a number which consists of a whole number followed by a FRACTION: three and three-quarters | in about two and a half hours' time | five and a quarter per cent **9** used between repeated plural nouns to say that some things of a particular kind are much better than others: 'They said this guy was an expert.' 'Yes, but there are experts and experts.' **10 and?** spoken used when you want someone to add something to what they have just said: 'I'm sorry.' 'And?' 'And I promise it won't happen again.'

an·dan·te /æn'dænti,-teɪ $ ɑːn'dɑːn-/ adj played or sung at a speed that is neither very fast or very slow **—andante** adv

Andante n [C] a piece of music played or sung at a speed that is neither very fast or very slow

an·drog·y·nous /æn'drɒdʒɪnəs $ -'drɑː-/ adj **1** having both male and female parts **2** someone who is androgynous looks both female and male: Bowie had a kind of androgynous sex appeal.

an·droid /'ændrɔɪd/ n [C] a ROBOT that looks completely human

an·ec·dot·al /,ænɪk'dəʊtl◂ $ -'doʊ-/ adj consisting of short stories based on someone's personal experience: His findings are based on **anecdotal evidence** rather than serious research.

an·ec·dote /'ænɪkdəʊt $ -doʊt/ n [C] a short story based on your personal experience: The book is full of amusing anecdotes about his life in Japan.

a·ne·mi·a /ə'niːmiə/ n [U] the usual American spelling of ANAEMIA

a·ne·mic /ə'niːmɪk/ adj the usual American spelling of ANAEMIC

a·nem·o·ne /ə'neməni/ n [C] a plant with red, white, or blue flowers → SEA ANEMONE

an·es·the·si·a /,ænəs'θiːziə $ -ʒə/ n [U] the usual American spelling of ANAESTHESIA

an·es·the·si·ol·o·gist /,ænəsθiːzi'ɒlədʒ̩ɪst $ -'ɑːl-/ n [C] AmE a doctor who gives ANAESTHETICS to a patient

an·es·thet·ic /,ænəs'θetɪk◂/ n [C,U] the usual American spelling of ANAESTHETIC

a·nes·the·tist /ə'niːsθət̩ɪst $ ə'nes-/ n [C] the usual American spelling of ANAESTHETIST

a·nes·the·tize /ə'niːsθət̩aɪz $ ə'nes-/ v [T] the usual American spelling of ANAESTHETIZE

a·new /ə'njuː $ ə'nuː/ adv written **1 start/begin anew** to begin something new, start to live in a different place etc, especially after a difficult period in your life: I was ready to leave everything behind and start anew in California. **2** if you do something anew, you start doing it again: The committee is going to examine the whole situation anew.

an·gel /'eɪndʒəl/ n [C] **1** a SPIRIT who is God's servant in heaven, and who is often shown as a person dressed in white with wings: *the angel Gabriel* **2** someone who is very kind, very good, or very beautiful: *That little girl of theirs is an angel.* | *Sam is no angel* (=often behaves badly). **3** *old-fashioned spoken* used when asking someone to help you or when thanking someone for helping you: *Thanks for mailing those letters, you're an angel.* | *Be an angel and get me my glasses, will you?* → GUARDIAN ANGEL

an·gel·ic /æn'dʒelɪk/ adj **1** looking good, kind, and gentle or behaving in this way: *She had an angelic smile, but a dreadful temper.* **2** connected with angels: *the angelic hosts* —**angelically** /-kli/ adv

an·gel·i·ca /æn'dʒelɪkə/ n [U] a plant that smells sweet and is used in cooking

an·ger¹ W3 /'æŋgə $ -ər/ n [U]
1 a strong feeling of wanting to hurt or criticize someone because they have done something bad to you or been unkind to you: *Paul's face was filled with anger.* | **in anger** *'It's a lie!' he shouted in anger.* | **[+at]** *She struggled to control her anger at her son's disobedience.* | *There is growing anger among the people against the government.*
2 do/use sth in anger to do or use something for the first time, or in a real situation: *He joined the club last month, but has yet to kick a ball in anger.*

anger² v [T] to make someone angry; 🔁 **annoy**: *What angered me most was his total lack of remorse.* | **be angered by/at sth** *Environmental groups were disappointed and angered by the president's decision.*

an·gi·na /æn'dʒaɪnə/ n [U] a medical condition in which you have bad pains in your chest because your heart is weak

an·gle¹ S3 W3 /'æŋgəl/ n [C]
1 the space between two straight lines or surfaces that join each other, measured in degrees: **an angle of sth** *an angle of 45°* | **[+of]** *the angles of a triangle* | *You didn't measure the angle accurately.* | **[+between]** *the angle between walls and ceiling* → RIGHT ANGLE
2 a way of considering a problem or situation: *We're approaching the issue from many different angles.* | *Look at every angle of the situation.* | **[+to]** *There's another angle to this question.*
3 a position from which you look at something or photograph it: **from a ... angle** | *This drawing of the monastery was done from an unusual angle.* | *Some of the pictures have strange camera angles.*
4 at an angle leaning to one side and not straight or upright: *The portrait was hanging at an angle.* | **at a slight/steep angle** *The sign leaned over at a slight angle.*
5 the shape formed when two lines or surfaces join: **[+of]** *My head struck the angle of the shelf.*

angle² v [T] **1** to move or place something so that it is not straight or upright: *a mirror angled to reflect light from a window* | *Philip angled his chair towards the door.* **2** to present information from a particular point of view or for a specific group of people: *The book is angled towards a business audience.*
   angle for sth phr v to try to get something you want without asking directly for it: *She was obviously angling for an invitation.* | *I didn't want him to think I was just angling for sympathy.*

'angle ,brackets n [plural] *BrE* a pair of BRACKETS ( ) used for enclosing information

an·gle·poise lamp /'æŋgəlpɔɪz 'læmp/ n [C] *BrE trademark* a type of lamp that can be moved into different positions

an·gler /'æŋglə $ -ər/ n [C] someone who catches fish as a sport; → **fisherman**

An·gli·can /'æŋglɪkən/ n [C] a Christian who is a member of the Church of England or related churches —**Anglican** adj: *members of the Anglican church* —**Anglicanism** n [U]

an·gli·cize also **-ise** *BrE* /'æŋglɪsaɪz/ v [T] to make something or someone more English: *Leszek anglicized his name to 'Lester.'*

an·gling /'æŋglɪŋ/ n [U] the sport of catching fish with a fishing rod; 🔁 **fishing**

Anglo- /ˈæŋgləʊ $ -gloʊ/ *prefix* [in nouns and adjectives] **1** relating to England or Britain: *an anglophile* (=someone who loves Britain) **2** English or British and something else: *an Anglo-Scottish family* | *an improvement in Anglo-American relations*

Anglo-'Catholic n [C] a Christian who is a member of the part of the Church of England that is similar to the Roman Catholic church —**Anglo-Catholic** adj —**Anglo-Ca'tholicism** n [U]

Anglo-'Indian n [C] someone whose family is partly British and partly Indian —**Anglo-Indian** adj

an·glo·phile /'æŋgləʊfaɪl, -glə- $ -gloʊ-, -glə-/ n [C] someone who is not English but likes England and anything English

an·glo·phobe /'æŋgləʊfəʊb, -glə- $ -gloʊfoʊb, -glə-/ n [C] someone who dislikes anything English —**anglophobia** /ˌæŋgləʊ'fəʊbiə, -glə- $ -gloʊ'fou-, -glə-/ n [U]

an·glo·phone /'æŋgləʊfəʊn, -glə- $ -gloʊfoʊn, -glə-/ n [C] someone who speaks English as their first language —**anglophone** adj: *the US and other anglophone countries*

Anglo-'Saxon n **1** [C] someone who belonged to the race of people who lived in England from about 600 AD **2** [U] the language used by the Anglo-Saxons **3** [C] a white person, especially someone whose family originally came from England —**Anglo-Saxon** adj

an·go·ra /æŋ'gɔːrə/ n **1** [C] a type of goat, rabbit, or cat with very long soft hair or fur **2** [U] wool or thread made from the fur of an angora goat or rabbit: *soft pink angora sweaters*

an·gry S3 W3 /'æŋgri/ adj comparative **angrier**, superlative **angriest**
1 feeling strong emotions which make you want to shout at someone or hurt them because they have behaved in an unfair, cruel, offensive etc way, or because you think that a situation is unfair, unacceptable etc; → **annoyed**: *I was angry because he hadn't told me his plans.* | *He was beginning to get angry.* | **[+with]** *His comments brought an angry response from opposition politicians.* | *'Calm down,' she said, looking at his angry face.* | *'Please don't be angry with me,' she said. Jesse laughed, which made me even angrier.* | **[+about/at/over]** *Kate's still so angry about the whole thing.* | **angry (that)** *The workers are angry that they haven't been paid for the week.*
2 angry with/at yourself feeling strongly that you wish you had done something or had not done something: *David was angry with himself for letting the others see his true feelings.*
3 *literary* an angry sky or cloud looks dark and stormy
4 *literary* an angry wound etc is painful and red and looks infected —**angrily** adv: *Joey reacted angrily to the news.*

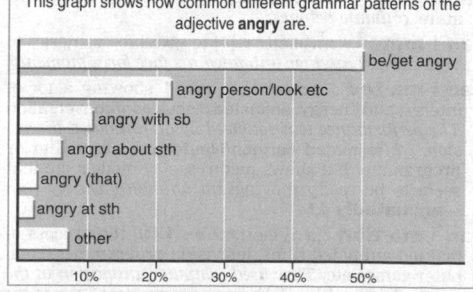
This graph shows how common different grammar patterns of the adjective **angry** are.

be/get angry	
angry person/look etc	
angry with sb	
angry about sth	
angry (that)	
angry at sth	
other	

10% 20% 30% 40% 50%

WORD FOCUS: ANGRY

a little angry: **miffed** *informal*, **peeved** *informal*
rather angry: **annoyed, irritated, cross, in a bad/foul mood**
very angry: **furious, livid, outraged, incensed, incandescent with rage** *formal*
to become angry: **lose your temper, go mad** *BrE*, **go berserk** *informal*, **go ballistic** *informal*, **hit the roof** *informal*
words for describing someone who often gets angry: **bad-tempered, grouchy, cantankerous, crabby, stroppy** *BrE informal*

angst /æŋst/ *n* [U] strong feelings of anxiety and unhappiness because you are worried about your life, your future, or what you should do in a particular situation: *love letters full of angst*

an·guish /'æŋgwɪʃ/ *n* [U] *written* mental or physical suffering caused by extreme pain or worry: *the anguish of not knowing what had happened to her* —**anguished** *adj: an anguished cry for help*

an·gu·lar /'æŋgjʊlə $ -ər/ *adj* **1** thin and not having much flesh on your bones: *a tall, angular young man* **2** having sharp and definite corners: *a cubist painting with angular shapes*

an·i·mal¹ S1 W1 /'ænɨməl/ *n* [C]
1 a living creature such as a dog or cat, that is not an insect, plant, bird, fish, or person: *furry little animals* | **wild/domestic/farm animals** *cattle, sheep, and other domestic animals* | *The cosmetics have not been tested on animals.* | *Beth is an **animal lover** (=someone who likes animals).*
2 any living creature that is not a plant or a person: *He can't stand **cruelty to animals** of any sort.* | *the animal welfare movement in Britain* | *the enormous diversity of **the animal kingdom***
3 any living creature, including people: *Man is a highly intelligent animal.*
4 *informal* someone who behaves in a cruel, violent, or very rude way: *Football hooligans are just animals.*
5 a **(very/completely/entirely) different animal** *informal* something that is very different from the thing you have mentioned: *Writing e-mail is a very different animal from all other forms of writing.*
6 a **political/social animal etc** *informal* someone who is interested in politics, in meeting other people etc: *He is simply not a social animal.*

animal² *adj* **1** **animal urges/instincts etc** human feelings, desires etc that are connected with sex, food, and other basic needs **2** **animal products/fats/protein etc** things that are made or come from animals: *a diet rich in red meat and animal fats.*

animal 'husbandry *n* [U] farming that involves keeping animals and producing milk, meat etc

animal 'rights *n* [U] the idea that people should treat animals well, and especially not use them in tests to develop medicines or other products: **animal rights activists/campaigners/groups** etc *Bill has been involved in the animal rights movement for years.*

an·i·mate¹ /'ænɨmɨt/ *adj formal* living; **⊟** inanimate: *animate beings*

an·i·mate² /'ænɨmeɪt/ *v* [T] to give life or energy to something: *Laughter animated his face for a moment.*

an·i·ma·ted /'ænɨmeɪtɨd/ *adj* **1** showing a lot of interest and energy: **animated discussion/conversation** *The performance was followed by an animated discussion.* **2** **animated cartoon/film/feature etc** a film or programme that shows pictures, clay models etc that seem to be really moving: *an animated Disney film* —**animatedly** *adv*

an·i·ma·tion /ˌænɨ'meɪʃən/ *n* **1** [U] the process of making animated films, television programmes, computer games etc: *They used computer animation in the film.* **2** [C] a film, television programme, computer game etc that has pictures, clay models etc that seem to

be really moving: *3-D animations* **3** [U] liveliness and excitement: **with animation** | *They were talking with animation.*

an·i·ma·tor /'ænɨmeɪtə $ -ər/ *n* [C] someone who makes animated films

an·i·ma·tron·ics /ˌænɨmə'trɒnɪks $ -'trɑː-/ *n* [U] the method or process of making or using moving models that look like real animals or people in films

an·i·mis·m /'ænɨmɪzəm/ *n* [U] a religion in which animals and plants are believed to have spirits

an·i·mos·i·ty /ˌænɨ'mɒsɨti $ -'mɑː-/ *n plural* **animosities** [C,U] strong dislike or hatred; **⊟** hostility: [+**between**] *There is no personal animosity between the party leaders.* | [+**towards/against**] *She felt a certain amount of animosity towards him.*

an·i·mus /'ænɨməs/ *n* [singular, U] *formal* a feeling of strong dislike or hatred; **⊟** animosity, hostility: [+**against/towards**] *I have no animus towards Robert.*

an·ise /'ænɨs/ *n* [U] a plant with seeds that have a strong taste

an·i·seed /'ænɨsiːd/ *n* [U] the seeds of an anise plant, which are used in alcoholic drinks and in sweets

an·kle /'æŋkəl/ *n* [C] **1** the joint between your foot and your leg: **break/twist/sprain your ankle** *Janet slipped on the stairs and twisted her ankle.* | **slender ankles** **2** **ankle socks/boots** socks or boots that only come up to your ankle

an·klet /'æŋklɨt/ *n* [C] a ring or BRACELET worn around your ankle

an·nals /'ænlz/ *n* [plural] **1** **in the annals of sth** in the whole history of something: *one of the most unusual cases in the annals of crime* **2** used in the titles of official records of events or activities: *the Annals of the Zoological Society*

an·neal /ə'niːl/ *v* [T] *technical* to make metal or glass hard by heating it and then slowly letting it get cold

an·nex /ə'neks $ ə'neks, 'æneks/ *v* [T] to take control of a country or area next to your own, especially by using force: *The Baltic republics were annexed by the Soviet Union in 1940.* —**annexation** /ˌænek'seɪʃən/ *n* [C,U]

an·nexe, annex /'æneks/ *n* [C] **1** a separate building that has been added to a larger one: *Some of us will be sleeping in the annexe.* **2** *formal* a part that has been added to the end of a document, report etc

an·ni·hi·late /ə'naɪəleɪt/ *v* [T] **1** to destroy something or someone completely: *Just one of these bombs could annihilate a city the size of New York.* **2** to defeat someone easily and completely in a game or competition: *Tyson annihilated his opponent in the first round.* —**annihilation** /ə,naɪə'leɪʃən/ *n* [U]

an·ni·ver·sa·ry /ˌænɨ'vɜːsəri $ -ɜːr-/ *n plural* **anniversaries** [C] a date on which something special or important happened in a previous year: *Jack and Kim celebrated their twentieth **wedding anniversary** in January.* | [+**of**] *A huge parade was held on the anniversary of the 1959 revolution.*

An·no Dom·i·ni /ˌænəʊ 'dɒmɨnaɪ $ ˌænoʊ 'dɑː-/ AD

an·no·tate /'ænəteɪt/ *v* [T usually passive] to add short notes to a book or piece of writing to explain parts of it: *an annotated edition of 'Othello'* —**annotation** /ˌænə'teɪʃən/ *n* [C,U]

an·nounce S2 W1 /ə'naʊns/ *v* [T]
1 to officially tell people about something, especially about a plan or a decision: *They announced their engagement in 'The Times'.* | **announce a decision/intention/plan** *The government has announced plans to create 10,000 new jobs.* | **announce that** *A government spokesman announced that the hostages had been released.* | *At the end of their meeting, it was announced that an agreement had been reached.* | **announce sth to sb** *Cordon announced his resignation to staff members on Wednesday.*
2 to say something, especially something that other people will not like, in a loud and confident way; **⊟** state: *'I'm not going to their party,' Maggie announced.* | **announce (that)** *He stood up and*

announced that he was ready to go.
3 to give information to people using a LOUDSPEAKER or MICROPHONE, especially at an airport or railway station: *We arrived just as they were announcing the arrival of Flight 207 from Minneapolis.*
4 announce sb/yourself to officially tell people that someone has arrived at a particular place: *All visitors to the apartment building must be announced.* | *After announcing himself at the reception desk, James was led upstairs.*
5 to introduce a programme on television or radio

an·nounce·ment S3 W3 /əˈnaʊnsmənt/ n
1 [C] an important or official statement: *Dillon made the announcement at a news conference.* | [+about] *an important announcement about tax increases* | *announcement that We were shocked by the announcement that the mayor was resigning.* | *The announcement came as no great surprise.*
2 [singular] the act of telling people that something important is going to happen: [+of] *the announcement of the company's annual results*
3 [C] a small advertisement or statement in a newspaper: *a wedding announcement in the local paper*

an·nounc·er /əˈnaʊnsə $ -ər/ n [C] **1** someone who reads news or information on the television or radio **2** someone who gives information to people using a LOUDSPEAKER or MICROPHONE, especially at an airport or railway station

an·noy S3 /əˈnɔɪ/ v [T] to make someone feel slightly angry and unhappy about something; ◨ **irritate**: *What annoyed him most was that he had received no apology.* | *It really annoys me when I see people drop ping litter.* | *She annoyed him with her stupid questions.*

an·noy·ance /əˈnɔɪəns/ n **1** [U] a feeling of slight anger; ◨ **irritation**: *A look of annoyance crossed her face.* | **to sb's annoyance** *To his annoyance, he discovered they hadn't waited.* | **in annoyance** *Kelly shook her head in annoyance.* **2** [C] something that makes you slightly angry: *Alan found the constant noise of the traffic an annoyance.*

an·noyed /əˈnɔɪd/ adj slightly angry; ◨ **irritated**; → **angry**: *I'll be annoyed if we don't finish by eight.* | **be annoyed at/with sb** *She was annoyed with Duncan for forgetting to phone.* | **be annoyed about/by sth** *He was annoyed by her apparent indifference.* | **annoyed that** *Mr Davies was annoyed that the books were missing.*; → see box at NERVOUS

an·noy·ing /əˈnɔɪ-ɪŋ/ adj making you feel slightly angry; ◨ **irritating**: *an annoying habit of interrupting* | *The annoying thing is he's usually right.* | *It's annoying that we didn't know about this before.* —**annoyingly** adv

an·nu·al¹ S2 W2 /ˈænjuəl/ adj
1 happening once a year: *The school trip has become an annual event.* | **annual report/meeting/conference**
2 based on or calculated over a period of one year: **annual budget/income/cost etc** *a household with an annual income of $60,000* —**annually** adv: *The jazz festival is held annually in July.*

annual² n [C] **1** a plant that lives for one year or season; → **biennial (2)**, **perennial 2** a book, especially for children, that is produced once a year with the same title but different stories, pictures etc

an·nu·a·lized also **-ised** BrE /ˈænjuəlaɪzd/ adj [only before noun] technical if money or an amount is annualized, it is calculated for one year, based on amounts for shorter periods of time: *an annualized inflation rate of 15%*

an·nu·i·ty /əˈnjuːɪti $ əˈnuː-/ n plural **annuities** [C] a fixed amount of money that is paid each year to someone, usually until they die

an·nul /əˈnʌl/ v **annulled, annulling** [T often passive] to officially state that a marriage or legal agreement no longer exists: *Their marriage was annulled last year.* —**annulment** n [C,U]

an·ode /ˈænəʊd $ ˈænoʊd/ n [C] technical the part of a BATTERY that collects ELECTRONS, often a wire or piece of metal with the sign (+); → **cathode**

an·o·dyne¹ /ˈænədaɪn/ adj formal expressed in a way that is unlikely to offend anyone; ◨ **bland**: *anodyne topics of conversation*

anodyne² n [C] **1** technical a medicine that reduces pain; ◨ **painkiller 2** formal an activity or thing that comforts people

a·noint /əˈnɔɪnt/ v [T] to put oil or water on someone's head or body, usually as part of a religious ceremony: *the anointed king* | **anoint sb with sth** *He was anointed with sacred oil.* —**anointment** n [C,U]

a·nom·a·lous /əˈnɒmələs $ əˈnɑː-/ adj formal different from what you expected to find: *a highly anomalous situation* | *anomalous results* —**anomalously** adv

a·nom·a·ly /əˈnɒməli $ əˈnɑː-/ n plural **anomalies** [C,U] formal something that is noticeable because it is different from what is usual: *In those days, a woman professor was still an anomaly.* | [+in] *various anomalies in the tax system*

a·non /əˈnɒn $ əˈnɑːn/ adv literary soon: *See you anon.*

anon. also **anon** BrE the written abbreviation of *anonymous*

an·o·nym·i·ty /ˌænəˈnɪmɪti/ n [U] when other people do not know who you are or what your name is: *Every step will be taken to preserve your anonymity.* | *One official, who spoke on condition of anonymity* (=he would only speak if his name was not told), *said the White House took the threat very seriously.* | *the anonymity of city streets* (=you do not know anyone, and no one knows you)

a·non·y·mous /əˈnɒnɪməs $ əˈnɑː-/ adj **1** unknown by name: *the anonymous author of a collection of poems* | **anonymous donor/benefactor** *the anonymous donor of a large sum of money* | *According to one employee, who wishes to remain anonymous, the company engaged in illegal activities.* **2** done, sent, or given by someone who does not want their name to be known: *an anonymous donation of $5,000* | **anonymous phone call/letter etc** (=one that is often unpleasant or contains threats) **3** written uninteresting in features or qualities – used to show disapproval: *grey, anonymous housing estates* —**anonymously** adv

an·o·rak /ˈænəræk/ n [C] **1** especially BrE a short coat with a HOOD that keeps out the wind and rain **2** BrE informal a boring person who is interested in the unimportant details of a particular subject and does not know how to behave properly in social situations; ◨ **nerd**

an·o·rex·i·a /ˌænəˈreksiə/ also **anorexia ner·vo·sa** /-nɜːˈvəʊsə $ -nɜːˈvoʊ-/ n [U] a mental illness that makes someone stop eating

an·o·rex·ic /ˌænəˈreksɪk/ adj suffering from or relating to anorexia —**anorexic** n [C]

an·oth·er S1 W1 /əˈnʌðə $ -ər/ determiner, pron
1 ADDITIONAL one more person or thing of the same type: *I'm going to have another cup of coffee.* | *There'll be another bus along in a few minutes.* | *Buy two CDs and get another completely free.* | [+of] *Is this another of your schemes to make money?* | *Not another word was spoken.* | *Oh look, there's another one of those birds.* | *This misunderstanding is yet another example of bad communication* (=there have already been several). | **another two/10/100 etc** (=an additional amount or number) *We'll have to wait another three weeks for the results.* | *There's still another £100 to pay.*
2 A DIFFERENT ONE not the same thing, person etc, but a different one: *They must have returned by another route.* | *We finally moved to another apartment.* | *I'm busy right now. Could you come back another time?* | *Helen resigned from her last job and has yet to find another.* | [+of] *The gold watch was a present from another of his girlfriends.* | **from one ... to another** *She spends the day rushing from one meeting to another.*

A

3 one another used to say that two or more people or things do the same thing to each other or share a relationship: *They seem to love one another very much.* | *The streets are all at right angles to one another.*
4 one ... or another used to say that there are many different types of something, or many possibilities, rather than being specific: *All the kids in this class have learning difficulties of one sort or another.* | *people who, for one reason or another, can't have children*
5 one after another used to talk about a series of similar things or events: *Small businesses have been collapsing one after another.*
6 not another ... ! *spoken* used when a series of bad or annoying things have happened and something of the same type seems to have just happened again: *Oh no! Not another accident!*
7 be another thing/matter used to suggest that something may not be true, possible, easy etc, after mentioning something that is: *It is true that his programme is original, though whether it is funny is quite another matter.* | *It is one thing to talk about 'involving the students'; it is quite another thing to actually do this.*
8 and another thing *spoken* used to introduce something additional that you want to say to someone about a different subject: *And another thing. You were late for work again this morning.*
9 SIMILAR PERSON/THING used with the name of a well-known person, thing, event etc to mean someone or something else that is similar because they have the same good or bad qualities: *warnings that not enough has been done to prevent another Chernobyl* | *There'll never be another Elvis Presley.*

an·swer¹ S1 W1 /ˈɑːnsə $ ˈænsər/ n
1 REPLY [C,U] something you say when you reply to a question that someone has asked you; ⯀ response

give (sb) an answer
get/receive an answer
wait for an answer
an honest/straight answer
a definite answer (=when you say definitely yes or no)
the short/simple answer is ... *spoken*
in answer to sb's question
the answer is yes/no *spoken*

You don't have to give them an answer now. | *Every time I ask him about it, I get a different answer.* | *[+to] These are important questions, and we want answers to them.* | *She's still waiting for an answer from the school.* | *The honest answer was that I didn't know.* | *He was never able to get a straight answer about why it happened.* | *It's impossible for me to give you a definite answer at this time.* | *The short answer is that it can't be done.* | *In answer to your question, yes, you can go.* | *If it's money you want, the answer is no!*

2 TEST/COMPETITION ETC [C] something that you write or say in reply to a question in a test or competition: *[+to] What was the answer to question 4?* | *the right/wrong/correct/incorrect answer Score two points for each correct answer.*
3 INVITATION/LETTER ETC [C] a written reply to a letter, invitation, advertisement etc: *[+to] Did you ever get an answer to your letter?*
4 PROBLEM [C] a way of dealing with a problem; ⯀ solution: *simple/easy/obvious answer There is no simple answer.* | *[+to] The police do not have an answer to rising crime.* | *Some people think cars should be banned from the city, but I don't think that's the answer.* | *be the answer to sb's problems/worries etc If he could get a job it'd be the answer to all his worries.*
5 ON THE PHONE [singular, U usually in negative] if you get an answer when you call someone on the phone, they pick up the phone and talk to you: *I tried calling him all day but couldn't get an answer.*
6 AT THE DOOR [singular, U usually in negative] if you get an answer when you knock on a door, someone opens it and talks to you: *I tried knocking on her door, but there was no answer.*

7 have/know all the answers *informal* to be very sure that you know everything about a situation, especially when you do not: *He acts like he has all the answers.*
8 sb's answer to sth *written* someone or something that is considered to be just as good as a more famous person or thing: *The Space Needle is Seattle's answer to the Eiffel Tower.*

answer² S1 W2 v
1 REPLY [I,T] to say something to someone as a reply when they have asked you a question, made a suggestion etc: *She thought for a moment before answering.* | *He still hadn't answered my question.* | *'Why don't you just leave?' 'I'd like to,' she answered, 'but I have nowhere else to go.'* | *answer (that) When questioned, Hughes answered that he knew nothing about the robbery.* | *How much was it? Come on, answer me.*
2 TEST [I,T] to write or say the answer to a question in a test or competition: *Answer as many questions as possible in the time provided.*
3 answer the phone/a call/the door to pick up the telephone and speak when it rings or open the door when someone knocks or rings the bell
4 LETTER [T] if you answer a letter or advertisement, you write a letter to the person who has written it: *Simon got the job by answering an advert in the paper.*
5 answer criticism/charges/accusations etc to explain why you did something when people are criticizing you – used in news reports: *How do you answer the criticism that your government has done nothing to help the homeless?*
6 REACT TO STH [I,T] to do something as a reaction to criticism or an attack; ⯀ respond: *The army answered by firing into the crowd.*
7 DEAL WITH A PROBLEM [T] to be a way of dealing with or solving a problem: *'You can borrow my car if you like.' 'Well, that answers one problem.'*
8 answer a need to provide something that is needed: *Our transportation system is designed to answer the needs of the city's commuters.*
9 answer a description if someone answers a description, they match that description: *A man answering the police's description was seen entering the building.*
answer back *phr v*
to reply in a rude way to someone that you are supposed to obey: *answer sb back Don't answer me back young man!*
answer for sb/sth *phr v*
1 to explain to people in authority why you did something wrong or why something happened, and be punished if necessary: *Their coach must answer for the team's poor performance.*
2 have a lot to answer for *informal* to be responsible for causing a lot of trouble
3 can't answer for sb *spoken* used to say that you cannot make a decision for someone who is not there, or give their opinion: *I'm sure John will help us – I can't really answer for the others.*
answer to sb/sth *phr v*
1 to give an explanation to someone, especially about something that you have done wrong: *Phipps answers to me and me alone.*
2 answer to the name of sth to be called a particular name – used humorously: *a well-dressed young woman answering to the name of Suzanne*

an·swer·a·ble /ˈɑːnsərəbəl $ ˈæn-/ adj **1** answerable to sb (for sth) to have to explain your actions to someone in authority: *The agency is answerable to the governor.* **2** a question that is answerable can be answered

ˈanswering maˌchine also **ˈanswerˌphone** BrE /ˈɑːnsəfəʊn $ ˈænsərfoʊn/ n [C] a machine that records your telephone calls when you cannot answer them

ant /ænt/ n [C] **1** a small insect that lives in large groups → see picture at INSECT **2** have ants in your pants *spoken* to be so excited or full of energy that you are unable to sit or stand still – used humorously

-ant /ənt/, **-ent** *suffix* [in nouns and adjectives] someone or something that does something: *a servant (=some-*

one who serves others) | *disinfectant* (=substance for killing germs) | *expectant* (=expecting) | *pleasant* (=pleasing)

ant·a·cid /ænt'æsɪ̯d/ *n* [C] a substance that gets rid of the burning feeling in your stomach when you have eaten too much, drunk too much alcohol etc

an·tag·o·nis·m /æn'tægənɪzəm/ *n* [U] **1** hatred between people or groups of people; ◧ **hostility**: [+between] *the antagonism between the army and other military groups* **2** opposition to an idea, plan etc: [+to/towards] *his obvious antagonism towards the press*

an·tag·o·nist /æn'tægənɪ̯st/ *n* [C] your opponent in a competition, battle, quarrel etc → PROTAGONIST

an·tag·o·nis·tic /ən͵tægə'nɪstɪk◂/ *adj* **1** unfriendly; wanting to argue or disagree; ◧ **hostile**: *an antagonistic attitude* **2** opposed to an idea or group: [+to/towards] *antagonistic to new ideas* —**antagonistically** /-kli/ *adv*

an·tag·o·nize also **-ise** *BrE* /æn'tægənaɪz/ *v* [T] to annoy someone very much by doing something that they do not like: *Do not antagonize your customers.*

An·tarc·tic /æn'tɑːktɪk $ -ɑːr-/ *n* **the Antarctic** the very cold most southern part of the world

An͵tarctic 'Circle *n* **the Antarctic Circle** an imaginary line drawn around the world at a certain distance from the most southern point (the South Pole)

an·te¹ /'ænti/ *n* **up/raise the ante** to increase your demands or try to get more things from a situation, even though this involves more risks: *They've upped the ante by making a $120 million bid to buy the company.* → PENNY ANTE

ante² *v past tense and past participle* **anted** or **anteed**, *present participle* **anteing**
  ante up (sth) *phr v* to pay an amount of money in order to be able to do or be involved in something: *Small firms that want to expand must ante up large legal fees.*

ante- /ænti/ *prefix* before; → anti-, post-, pre-: *antedate* (=earlier than something) | *antenatal* (=before birth)

ant·eat·er /'ænt͵iːtə $ -ər/ *n* [C] an animal that has a very long nose and eats small insects

an·te·ced·ent /͵æntɪ̯'siːdənt/ *n* [C] **1** *formal* an event, organization, or thing that is similar to the one you have mentioned but existed earlier: *historical antecedents* **2** **antecedents** [plural] *formal* the people in your family who lived a long time ago; ◧ **ancestors** **3** *technical* a word, phrase, or sentence that is represented by another word, for example a PRONOUN —**antecedent** *adj*

an·te·cham·ber /'ænti͵tʃeɪmbə $ -ər/ *n* [C] ANTEROOM

an·te·date /'æntɪdeɪt, ͵ænti'deɪt/ *v* [T] *formal* to come from an earlier time in history than something else; ◧ **predate**: *The economic troubles antedate the current administration.*

an·te·di·lu·vi·an /͵æntɪdɪ̯'luːviən◂/ *adj formal* very old-fashioned: *antediluvian ideas about women*

an·te·lope /'æntɪ̯ləʊp $ 'æntəl-oʊp/ *n* [C] an animal with long horns that can run very fast and is very graceful

an·te·na·tal /͵æntɪ'neɪtl◂/ *adj* [only before noun] *BrE* relating to the medical care given to women who are going to have a baby; ◧ **prenatal**; → **postnatal**: *an antenatal clinic* | *regular antenatal care* | *Many young mothers do not attend antenatal classes.*

an·ten·na /æn'tenə/ *n* [C] **1** *plural* **antennae** /-niː/ one of two long thin parts on an insect's head, that it uses to feel things → see picture at INSECT **2** *plural* **antennas** or **antennae** a wire ROD etc used for receiving radio and television signals; ◧ **aerial**: *television antennas* → see picture at CAR

an·ter·i·or /æn'tɪəriə $ -'tɪriər/ *adj* [no comparative] **1** *technical* at or towards the front; → **posterior**: *anterior vertebrae* **2** *formal* happening or existing before something else

an·te·room /'æntɪrʊm, -ruːm/ *n* [C] a small room that is connected to a larger room, especially where people wait to go into the larger room; ◧ **antechamber**

an·them /'ænθəm/ *n* [C] **1** a formal or religious song → NATIONAL ANTHEM **2** a song that a particular group of people consider to be very important: *The Rolling Stones' 'Satisfaction' was an anthem for a generation.*

an·the·mic /æn'θemɪk, -'θiː-/ *adj* having the qualities of an anthem: *anthemic rock music*

an·ther /'ænθə $ -ər/ *n* [C] *technical* the part of a male flower which contains POLLEN

ant·hill /'ænt͵hɪl/ *n* [C] a place where ANTS live

an·thol·o·gy /æn'θɒlədʒi $ æn'θɑː-/ *n plural* **anthologies** [C] a set of stories, poems, songs etc by different people collected together in one book; ◧ **collection**: *an anthology of American literature* —**anthologist** *n* [C]

an·thra·cite /'ænθrəsaɪt/ *n* [U] a very hard type of coal that burns slowly and produces a lot of heat

an·thrax /'ænθræks/ *n* [U] a serious disease affecting cattle and sheep, which can affect humans

anthropo- /ænθrəpə, -pəʊ $ -pə, -poʊ/ *prefix* like or concerning HUMAN BEINGS: *anthropomorphic* (=having human form or qualities)

an·thro·poid /'ænθrəpɔɪd/ *adj* an anthropoid animal, such as an APE, looks like a human —**anthropoid** *n* [C]

an·thro·pol·o·gy /͵ænθrə'pɒlədʒi $ -'pɑː-/ *n* [U] the scientific study of people, their societies, CULTURES etc; → **ethnology**, **sociology** —**anthropologist** *n* [U] —**anthropological** /͵ænθrəpə'lɒdʒɪkəl◂ $ -'lɑː-/ *adj*

an·thro·po·mor·phis·m /͵ænθrəpə'mɔːfɪzəm $ -ɔːr-/ *n* [U] **1** the belief that animals or objects have the same feelings and qualities as humans **2** *technical* the belief that God can appear in a human or animal form —**anthropomorphic** *adj*

anti- /ænti $ ænti, æntaɪ/ *prefix* **1** opposed to; ◧ **pro-**: *antinuclear* (=opposing the use of NUCLEAR weapons and power) | *anti-American* **2** the opposite of something: *anticlimax* (=an unexciting ending instead of the expected exciting ending) | *antimatter* (=material completely opposite in kind to the ordinary material in the universe) **3** acting to prevent something: *antifreeze* (=a liquid added to a car's engine to prevent freezing) | *antiseptic* (=a liquid that kills harmful bacteria)

͵anti-'aircraft *adj* [only before noun] anti-aircraft weapons are used against enemy aircraft: *anti-aircraft missiles*

an·ti·bi·ot·ic /͵æntibaɪ'ɒtɪk◂ $ -'ɑː-/ *n* [C usually plural] a drug that is used to kill BACTERIA and cure infections

an·ti·bod·y /'ænti͵bɒdi $ -͵bɑː-/ *n plural* **antibodies** [C] a substance produced by your body to fight disease

͵anti-'choice *adj* against women having the right to have an ABORTION; ◧ **pro-choice**

an·tic·i·pate [S3] /æn'tɪsɪ̯peɪt/ *v* [T]
1 to expect that something will happen and be ready for it: *Sales are better than anticipated.* | **anticipate changes/developments** *The schedule isn't final, but we don't anticipate many changes.* | **anticipate problems/difficulties** *We don't anticipate any problems.* | *A good speaker is able to anticipate an audience's needs and concerns.* | **anticipate (that)** *This year, we anticipate that our expenses will be 15% greater.* | **It is anticipated that** *the research will have many different practical applications.* | **anticipate doing sth** *I didn't anticipate having to do the cooking myself!*
2 to think about something that is going to happen, especially something pleasant: *Daniel was eagerly*

[1] 000, [2] 000, [3] 000, most frequent words in [S]poken and [W]ritten English

anticipating her arrival.
3 to do something before someone else: *Copernicus anticipated in part the discoveries of the 17th and 18th centuries.* —**anticipatory** /æn,tɪsə'peɪtəri $ æn'tɪsəpətɔːri/ *formal adj*: *the anticipatory atmosphere of a big college football game*

an·tic·i·pa·tion /æn,tɪsɪ'peɪʃən/ *n* [U] **1** when you are expecting something to happen: *She waited in eager anticipation for Robert to arrive.* | *Taylor was excited and full of anticipation at the prospect of the trip.* **2 do sth in anticipation of sth** to do something because you expect something to happen: *The workers have called off their strike in anticipation of a pay offer.*

an·ti·cler·i·cal /,ænti'klerɪkəl◂/ *adj* being opposed to priests having any political power or influence —**anticlericalism** *n* [U]

an·ti·cli·max /,ænti'klaɪmæks/ *n* [C,U] a situation or event that does not seem exciting because it happens after something that was much better: *Going back to work after a month travelling in China was bound to be an anticlimax.*

an·ti·clock·wise /,ænti'klɒkwaɪz◂ $ -'klɑːk-/ *adv, adj BrE* moving in the opposite direction to the hands of a clock; **□ counterclockwise** *AmE*; **▣ clockwise**: *Turn the lid anticlockwise.*

an·tics /'æntɪks/ *n* [plural] behaviour that seems strange, funny, silly, or annoying: *We're all growing tired of his childish antics.*

an·ti·cy·clone /,ænti'saɪkləʊn $ -kloʊn/ *n* [C] an area of high air pressure that causes calm weather in the place it is moving over; → **cyclone**

an·ti·de·pres·sant /,æntidɪ'presənt/ *n* [C,U] a drug used to treat DEPRESSION (=a mental illness that makes people very unhappy)

an·ti·dote /'æntidəʊt $ -doʊt/ *n* [C] **1** a substance that stops the effects of a poison: [+to] *There is no known antidote to a bite from this snake.* **2** something that makes an unpleasant situation better: *laughter, the antidote to stress*

an·ti·freeze /'æntifriːz/ *n* [U] a liquid that is put in the water in car engines to stop it from freezing

an·ti·gen /'æntɪdʒən/ *n* [C] *technical* a substance that makes the body produce ANTIBODIES

an·ti·her·o /'ænti,hɪərəʊ $ -,hɪroʊ/ *n plural* **antiheroes** [C] a main character in a book, play, or film who is an ordinary or unpleasant person and lacks the qualities that you expect a hero to have

an·ti·his·ta·mine /,ænti'hɪstəmiːn, -mɪn/ *n* [C,U] a drug that is used to treat an ALLERGY (=an unpleasant reaction to particular foods, substances etc)

anti-lock 'braking ,system *n* [U] *ABS* a piece of equipment that makes a vehicle easier to control when you have to stop very suddenly

an·ti·mat·ter /'ænti,mætə $ -ər/ *n* [U] a form of MATTER (30) (=substance which the things in the universe are made of) consisting of antiparticles

an·tim·o·ny /æn'tɪməni $ 'æntɪˌmoʊni/ *n* [U] a silver-white metal that breaks easily and is often combined with other metals. It is a chemical ELEMENT: symbol Sb

an·ti·ox·i·dant /,ænti'ɒksɪdənt $ -'ɑːk-/ *n* [C] a substance in some foods that cleans the body and protects it from CANCER

an·ti·par·ti·cle /'ænti,pɑːtɪkəl $ -,pɑːr-/ *n* [C] a very small part of an atom that has the opposite electrical charge to the one usually found in atoms

an·ti·pas·to /'æntipæstəʊ $,ænti'pɑːstoʊ/ *n* [U] an Italian dish consisting of cold meat or vegetables that you eat before the main part of a meal

an·ti·pa·thet·ic /,æntipə'θetɪk◂/ *adj formal* having a very strong feeling of disliking or opposing someone or something; **□ hostile**: [+to] *It's human nature to be antipathetic to change.*

an·tip·a·thy /æn'tɪpəθi/ *n* [U] *formal* a feeling of strong dislike towards someone or something: [+to/

towards] *a growing antipathy towards the government* | [+between] *There's always been a certain amount of antipathy between the two doctors.*

,anti-person'nel *adj* [only before noun] an anti-personnel weapon is designed to hurt people rather than to damage buildings, vehicles etc

,anti-'perspirant *n* [U] a substance that prevents you SWEATING

An·tip·o·des /æn'tɪpədiːz/ *n* **the Antipodes** Australia and New Zealand —**Antipodean** /æn,tɪpə'diːən◂ / *adj*: *antipodean culture*

an·ti·quar·i·an /,ænti'kweəriən◂ $ -'kwer-/ *adj* [only before noun] an antiquarian bookshop sells old books

an·ti·quat·ed /'æntiˌkweɪtɪd/ *adj* old-fashioned and not suitable for modern needs or conditions – used to show disapproval; **□ outdated**: *antiquated laws*

an·tique¹ /æn'tiːk◂ / *adj* [usually before noun] antique furniture, jewellery etc is old and often valuable: *an antique rosewood desk*

antique² *n* [C] a piece of furniture, jewellery etc that was made a very long time ago and is therefore valuable: *The palace is full of priceless antiques.* | *They bought the clock at an antique shop in Bath.* | *antique dealer* (=someone who buys and sells antiques)

an·tiq·ui·ty /æn'tɪkwəti/ *n plural* **antiquities** **1** [U] ancient times: **in antiquity** *The common household fork was nearly unknown in antiquity.* **2** [U] the state of being very old: *a building of great antiquity* **3** [C usually plural] a building or object made in ancient times: *a collection of Roman antiquities*

anti-Se·mite /,ænti 'siːmaɪt $ -'sem-/ *n* [C] someone who hates Jewish people —**anti-Semitic** /,æntisɪ'mɪtɪk◂ / *adj*: *He made a few anti-Semitic remarks.*

anti-Sem·i·tis·m /,ænti 'semɪˌtɪzəm/ *n* [U] hatred of Jewish people: *the struggle against fascism and anti-Semitism*

an·ti·sep·tic¹ /,ænti'septɪk◂ / *n* [C,U] a medicine that you put onto a wound to stop it from becoming infected: *He dabbed the cut with antiseptic.* | *Mint is a mild antiseptic.*

antiseptic² *adj* helping to prevent infection: *an antiseptic cream* | *Some herbs have antiseptic qualities.*

an·ti·so·cial /,ænti'səʊʃəl◂ $ -'soʊ-/ *adj* **1** antisocial behaviour is violent or harmful to other people, or shows that you do not care about other people: *She was finding it hard to cope with her son's increasingly antisocial behaviour.* | *Smoking is an antisocial habit.* **2** someone who is antisocial does not enjoy meeting or being with other people; **▣ sociable**: *If I don't go tonight, everyone will accuse me of being antisocial.* **3** an activity or job that is antisocial does not give you the chance to meet other people: *I got fed up with the low pay and antisocial hours.*

,anti-'tank *adj* an anti-tank weapon is designed to destroy enemy TANKS

an·tith·e·sis /æn'tɪθəsɪs/ *n plural* **antitheses** /-siːz/ [C] *formal* the complete opposite of something: [+of] *This is not democratic. It is the antithesis of democracy.*

an·ti·thet·i·cal /,ænti'θetɪkəl/ also **an·ti·thet·ic** /-'θetɪk◂ / *adj formal* exactly opposite to something: [+to] *This violence is completely antithetical to the teaching of the church.*

an·ti·tox·in /,ænti'tɒksɪn $ -'tɑːk-/ *n* [C] a medicine or substance produced by your body which stops the effects of a poison

,anti 'trust *adj* [only before noun] intended to prevent companies from unfairly controlling prices: *new, tougher anti trust laws* | *an anti trust investigation*

,anti-'virus ,software also **anti-'virus ,program** *n* [U] a type of SOFTWARE that looks for and removes VIRUSES in programs and documents on your computer: *You need to update your anti-virus software regularly.*

ant·ler /'æntlə $ -ər/ *n* [C] one of the two horns of a male DEER

an·to·nym /'æntənɪm/ *n* [C] a word that means the opposite of another word; → **synonym**: *a dictionary of synonyms and antonyms*

ant·sy /'æntsi/ *adj informal* nervous and unable to keep still because you are waiting for something to happen

a·nus /'eɪnəs/ *n* [C] the hole in your bottom through which solid waste leaves your body

an·vil /'ænvᵻl/ *n* [C] a heavy iron block on which pieces of hot metal are shaped using a hammer

anx·i·e·ty S3 W3 /æŋ'zaɪəti/ *n plural* **anxieties**
1 [C,U] the feeling of being very worried about something; ◨ **concern**: [+about/over] *There is considerable anxiety among staff about job losses.* | *There is growing public anxiety over levels of air pollution in our cities.* | **deep/acute/great anxiety** *The fear of unemployment can be a source of deep anxiety to people.* | *his feelings of anxiety* | *A high level of anxiety was created by the introduction of cameras into the factory.* | *It can help if you discuss your anxieties with someone.*
2 [U] a feeling of wanting to do something very much: **anxiety to do sth** *I nearly fell in my anxiety to get downstairs quickly.*

anx·ious S3 W3 /'æŋkʃəs/ *adj*
1 worried about something: [+about] *He was a bit anxious about the safety of the machinery.* | [+for] *We were anxious for you.* | *She gave me an anxious look.* | **anxious (that)** *She was anxious that it might be cancer.*; → see box at NERVOUS
2 an anxious time or situation is one in which you feel nervous or worried; ◨ **worrying**: *We had an anxious couple of weeks waiting for the test results.* | *There was an anxious moment when the plane suddenly dropped.*
3 feeling strongly that you want to do something or want something to happen; ◨ **keen**: **anxious to do sth** *The company is anxious to improve its image.* | *He seemed most anxious to speak to me alone.* | *The president is anxious not to have another crisis.* | **anxious for sb to do sth** *Why was she so anxious for me to stay?* | [+for] *We were all anxious for news.* | **anxious (that)** *Both sides were anxious that the agreement should be signed as quickly as possible.* —**anxiously** *adv*: *She waited anxiously by the phone*

an·y¹ S1 W1 /'eni/ *determiner, pron*
1 [usually in questions and negatives] some or even the smallest amount or number: *Have you got any money?* | *Do you need any further information?* | [+of] *Are any of the paintings for sale?* | *They didn't invite any of us.* | *Are there any other questions?* | *They haven't shown any interest at all in my research.* | *The universities have shown few if any signs of a willingness to change.*
2 used to refer to a person or thing of a particular type when what you are saying is true of all people or things of that type: *Any child who breaks the rules will be punished.* | *Always check the details carefully before you sign any written agreement.* | *I can see you any time on Monday.* | *If I can help in any way, let me know.* | [+of] *You can choose any of the books on the list.* | *This excuse was as good as any other.*
3 as much as possible: *They're going to need any help they can get.*
4 **not just any (old) man/woman/job etc** used to say that someone or something is special: *She's not just any actress, she's one of the best.* → **any old thing** at OLD (10); → **any old how** at OLD (11); → **not in any way** at WAY¹ (40)

any² S2 *adv* [usually in questions and negatives]
1 used before the comparative form of an adjective to mean 'even a small amount': *I can't run any faster.* | *Are you feeling any better?*
2 **not any more/longer** if something does not happen any more or any longer, it used to happen but does not happen now: *Sarah doesn't live here any more.* | *He was told he wasn't wanted any longer.*
3 *AmE spoken* used with a verb to mean 'at all': *We tried talking to him but that didn't help any.*

an·y·bod·y S1 W3 /'eni,bɒdi, 'enibədi $ -,bɑːdi/ *pron*
ANYONE

an·y·how S3 /'enihaʊ/ *adv*
1 [sentence adverb] *informal* ANYWAY: *The scandal could damage her reputation but the press reported it anyhow.* | *I've never been to a circus, not recently anyhow.*
2 in a careless or untidy way: *The cupboard would hardly close, with all the shoes thrown in anyhow.*

an·y·more /,eni'mɔː $ -'mɔːr/ *adv* **not anymore** not any longer: *Nick doesn't live here anymore.* | *She told me not to phone her anymore.*

an·y·one S1 W1 /'eniwʌn/ *pron*
1 used to refer to any person, when it is not important to say exactly who: *Anyone could win tonight.* | *They offer help and advice to anyone interested in becoming a teacher.* | *If anyone sees Lisa, ask her to call me.* | **Anyone else** *who is interested in going on the trip should see me at the end of this lesson.*
2 used in questions to mean 'someone': *Does anyone want a drink?* | *Is there anyone new coming to tonight's meeting?* | *Do you know anyone else who wants a ticket?*
3 used in negative sentences to mean no person: *I went to the bar but there wasn't anyone there.* | *I haven't spoken to anyone all day.*

an·y·place /'enipleɪs/ *adv AmE* ANYWHERE: *I can't imagine living anyplace else now.*

an·y·thing S1 W1 /'eniθɪŋ/ *pron*
1 any thing, event, situation etc, when it is not important to say exactly which: *You can buy anything you want.* | *He was prepared to do anything to make a bit of money.* | *Anything would be better than staying at home!* | *You can write about swimming, skiing, or anything else you enjoy doing.*
2 used in questions to mean 'something': *Is there anything I can do to help?* | *Do you want anything from the shops?* | *Would you like anything else to eat?*
3 used in negative sentences to mean no thing, event, etc: *We didn't have anything to eat for three days.* | *Don't do anything until we get there.*
4 **anything but** used to emphasize that someone or something does not have a particular quality: *Maria is anything but stupid!*
5 **anything like sb/sth** similar in any way to something or someone else: *You don't look anything like your mother.* | *If you're anything like me, you'll want to be where the action is.*
6 **not anything like/near** *spoken* used to emphasize a negative sentence: *We don't have anything like enough money to buy a new car.*
7 **as important/clear/big etc as anything** *informal* extremely important/clear etc: *He was as nice as anything to me.*
8 **or anything** *spoken* or something that is similar: *Would you like a drink or anything?*
9 **anything goes** *informal* used to say that anything someone says or does is acceptable: *From what other people were wearing, it looked like anything goes.*
10 **for anything** *informal* if you will not do something for anything, you will definitely not do it: *I wouldn't go back there for anything.*
11 **like anything** *informal* if you do something like anything, you do it a lot: *We all encouraged him like anything.*
12 **if anything** *spoken* used when you are adding something to emphasize what you have just said: *Sam didn't seem too disappointed at losing. If anything, he seemed relieved that it was all over.*
13 **anything you say** *spoken* used to tell someone you agree with what they suggest: *Yes, of course, anything you say.*

an·y·time /'enitaɪm/ *adv* at any time: *Call me anytime. I'm always home.* | *They should arrive anytime between noon and 3 p.m.*

an·y·way S1 W2 /'eniweɪ/ also **anyhow** *adv* [sentence adverb]
1 in spite of the fact that you have just mentioned: *Catherine wasn't sure the book was the right one, but*

she bought it anyway. | *This idea probably won't work, but let's try it anyway.*
2 used when adding a remark which shows that the fact just mentioned is not important: *They didn't have any trainers in my size, and anyway I'd already decided I'd rather save the money.* | *'I hope you haven't told anyone.' 'No. Who would believe me anyway?'*
3 used when adding something that corrects or slightly changes what you have just said: *Let's think about it for a while, for a few days anyway.* | *There seems to have been a technical problem – anyway, that's what they told me.*
4 spoken used when you are ignoring details so that you can talk immediately about the most important thing: *He got lost and spent hours looking for the station, and anyway it was past midnight by the time he got home.* | *Anyway, why didn't you call the police?*
5 spoken used when you are changing the subject of a conversation or returning to a previous subject: *Anyway, let's leave that for the moment and look at this month's profit figures.* | *Anyway, how are things with you?*
6 spoken used when you want to end a conversation or leave a place: *Anyway, I must be going now.*

an·y·ways /'eniweɪz/ *adv* [sentence adverb] ANYWAY Many teachers think this is not correct English

an·y·where S1 W3 /'eniweə $ -wer/ also **anyplace** *AmE adv*
1 in or to any place: *Sit anywhere you like.* | *You can buy clothes like these anywhere.* | *I don't want to live in London, but I'd be happy living anywhere else.*
2 used in questions to mean 'somewhere': *Do you need anywhere to stay for the night?* | *Did you go anywhere exotic on vacation this year?* | *Have you been anywhere else in Spain?*
3 used in negative sentences to mean no place: *I can't find my passport anywhere.*
4 not anywhere near a) not at all near: *I wasn't anywhere near him when he fell.* **b)** not at all: *I don't think these figures are anywhere near accurate.*
5 anywhere between one and ten/anywhere from one to ten etc used to mean any age, number, amount etc between the ones that you say: *She could have been anywhere between 45 and 60 years of age.* | *We can accommodate anywhere between 60 and 300 people.*
6 not get anywhere informal to not be successful at all: *You won't get anywhere without qualifications.*
7 not get sb anywhere informal if something does not get you anywhere, it does not change a situation or help you to achieve something: *You can try writing to complain, but I don't think it will get you anywhere.*
8 not be going anywhere informal to not be achieving success in your life: *He's a nice enough lad, but he's not going anywhere.*

AOB /ˌeɪ əʊ 'biː $ -oʊ-/ BrE **any other business** things which are not written on the list of subjects to discuss at a meeting, but which people want to talk about after all the other subjects have been discussed

A-OK /ˌeɪ əʊ'keɪ $ -oʊ-/ *adj AmE spoken informal* in good condition; ▯ **satisfactory**: *We took the car in for a check, and it was A-OK.* —**A-OK** *adv*: *Everything's been going A-OK since Jack got home.*

a·or·ta /eɪ'ɔːtə $ -'ɔːr-/ *n* [C] the largest ARTERY that takes blood away from your heart

a·pace /ə'peɪs/ *adv* happening quickly: *Expansion of the company has continued apace.*

a·part S3 W1 /ə'pɑːt $ -ɑːrt/ *adv, adj*
1 NOT CLOSE/TOUCHING if things are apart, they are not close to each other or touching each other: **two miles/six feet etc apart** *Place the two posts 6 metres apart.* | *They have offices in countries as **far apart** as India and Peru.* | *The police try to **keep** rival supporters **apart** at all matches.* | *A couple of men started fighting and we had to **pull** them **apart**.* | *Joel stood apart from the group, frowning.*

2 IN DIFFERENT PIECES if something comes apart, or you take it apart, it is separated into different pieces: *The whole thing **comes apart** so that you can clean it.* | *They **took** the engine **apart** to see what was wrong.*
3 SEPARATE if you keep things apart, you keep them separate from each other: *I try to keep my work and private life as far apart as possible.*
4 NOT AT SAME TIME if things are a particular time apart, they do not happen at the same time but have that much time between them: **two days/three weeks/five years etc apart** *Our birthdays are exactly a month apart.*
5 PEOPLE if people are apart, they are not together in the same place, or not having a relationship with each other: *The children have never been apart before.* | *My wife and I are living apart at the moment.* | [+**from**] *He's never been apart from his mother.*
6 fall apart a) if something falls apart, it breaks into different pieces: *It just fell apart in my hands!* **b)** if something is falling apart, it is in very bad condition: *He drives around in an old car that's falling apart.* **c)** if something falls apart, it fails completely: *He lost his job and his marriage fell apart.* | *The country's economy is in danger of falling apart.*
7 be torn apart if a marriage, family etc is torn apart, it can no longer continue because of serious difficulties: *The play portrays a good marriage torn apart by external forces.*
8 be worlds/poles apart if people, beliefs, or ideas are worlds or poles apart, they are completely different from each other: *I realized we were still worlds apart.*
9 grow/drift apart if people drift or grow apart, their relationship slowly becomes less close: *Lewis and his father drifted apart after he moved to New York.*
10 joking apart used to say that you want to say something seriously: *Joking apart, they did do quite a good job for us.*
11 sb/sth apart except for someone or something: *The car industry apart, most industries are now seeing an improvement in their economic performance.*
12 set sb/sth apart to make someone or something different from other people or things: *Her unusual lifestyle set her apart as a child.*

a·part from also **a·side from** *AmE prep* **1** except for: *We didn't see anyone all day, apart from a couple of kids on the beach.* | *Apart from the ending, it's a really good film.* → see box at EXCEPT¹ **2** as well as: *Apart from his earnings as a football coach, he also owns and runs a chain of sports shops.* | *Quite apart from the cost, we need to think about how much time the job will take.*

a·part·heid /ə'pɑːtaɪt, -teɪt, -taɪd $ -aɪr-/ *n* [U] the former political and social system in South Africa, in which only white people had full political rights and people of other races, especially black people, were forced to go to separate schools, live in separate areas etc

a·part·ment S2 W3 /ə'pɑːtmənt $ -ɑːr-/ *n* [C]
1 especially AmE a set of rooms on one floor of a large building, where someone lives; ▯ **flat** BrE: *She lives in a small apartment.* | *a holiday apartment*
2 [usually plural] a room or set of rooms used by an important person such as a president: *I had never been in the prince's private apartments before.* | *the presidential apartments*

a·partment ˌblock BrE, **a·partment ˌbuilding**, **a·partment ˌhouse** *AmE n* [C] a large building containing many apartments

ap·a·thet·ic /ˌæpə'θetɪk◂/ *adj* not interested in something, and not willing to make any effort to change or improve things: *She felt too apathetic even to move.* | [+**about**] *How can you be so apathetic about the world and its problems?* —**apathetically** /-kli/ *adv*

ap·a·thy /'æpəθi/ *n* [U] the feeling of not being interested in something, and not willing to make any effort to change or improve things: *The campaign failed because of public apathy.*

ape¹ /eɪp/ n [C] **1** an animal that is similar to a monkey but has no tail or only a very short tail **2 go ape** informal to suddenly become very angry

ape² v [T] **1** to copy the way someone speaks or behaves in order to make fun of them; ☐ **mimic**: *He could ape his teachers perfectly.* **2** to copy someone's way of doing something, so that what you do or produce is not good or original; ☐ **mimic**: *cheap clothes which ape the high fashions of the day*

a·per·i·tif /ə,perə'tiːf/ n [C] an alcoholic drink that people drink before a meal

ap·er·ture /'æpətʃə $ 'æpərtʃʊr/ n [C] **1** formal a small hole or space in something **2** the small hole at the front of a camera, which can be made larger or smaller to let more or less light in when you take a photograph

ape·shit /'eɪpʃɪt/ adj **go apeshit** informal to suddenly become very angry

a·pex /'eɪpeks/ n [C] **1** technical the top or highest part of something pointed or curved: *the apex of the roof* | *the apex of a pyramid* **2** formal the most important position in an organization or society: *The king was at the apex of society.* **3** formal the most successful part of something: *He was at the apex of his career.*

APEX /'eɪpeks/ adj APEX tickets for planes or trains are cheaper than normal ones, and have to be bought several days before you travel: *The APEX fare is £222 return.* —**APEX** n [C]: *I managed to get an APEX for less than £100.*

a·phid /'eɪfd, 'æfd/ n [C] a type of small insect that feeds on the juices of plants

aph·o·ris·m /'æfərɪzəm/ n [C] formal a short phrase that contains a wise idea —**aphoristic** /,æfə'rɪstɪk◂/ adj

aph·ro·dis·i·ac /,æfrə'dɪziæk◂/ n [C] a food, drink, or drug that makes you want to have sex —**aphrodisiac** adj: *a fruit that is believed to have aphrodisiac properties*

a·piece /ə'piːs/ adv [only after number or noun] costing or having a particular amount each: *The pictures are worth about £10,000 apiece.* | *The two top teams have ten points apiece.*

a·plen·ty /ə'plenti/ adj [only after noun] literary in large amounts, especially more than you need: *There was food aplenty.*

a·plomb /ə'plɒm $ ə'plɑːm/ n [U] formal **with aplomb** in a confident and skilful way, especially when you have to deal with difficult problems or a difficult situation: *Ms Sharpe handled their questions with great aplomb.*

a·poc·a·lypse /ə'pɒkəlɪps $ ə'pɑː-/ n [C] **1 the apocalypse** the destruction and end of the world: *anti-nuclear protestors who fear the apocalypse* **2** a situation in which a lot of people die or suffer, and a lot of damage is done: *A lot of investors now fear a stock market apocalypse.*

a·poc·a·lyp·tic /ə,pɒkə'lɪptɪk◂ $ ə,pɑː-/ adj **1** warning people about terrible events that will happen in the future: *The novel presents us with an apocalyptic vision of the future* **2** connected with the final destruction and end of the world, or with any great destruction: *Before them was an apocalyptic landscape of burnt villages and bomb craters.*

a·poc·ry·phal /ə'pɒkrɪfəl $ ə'pɑː-/ adj an apocryphal story is well-known but probably not true

ap·o·gee /'æpədʒiː/ n [C] formal the most successful part of something; ☐ **apex**: *His political career reached its apogee in the 1960s.*

a·po·lit·i·cal /,eɪpə'lɪtɪkəl◂/ adj not interested in politics, or not connected with any political party: *a group of apolitical young professional people* | *an apolitical organization*

a·pol·o·get·ic /ə,pɒlə'dʒetɪk◂ $ ə,pɑː-/ adj showing or saying that you are sorry that something has happened, especially because you feel guilty or embarrassed about it: [+**about**] *The manager was very* apologetic about everything.* | *She gave me an apologetic smile.* | **look/sound apologetic** *Dan came in looking very apologetic.* —**apologetically** /-kli/ adv: *'I know,' she said apologetically.*

ap·o·lo·gi·a /,æpə'ləʊdʒiə, -dʒə $ -'loʊ-/ n [C] formal a statement in which you defend an idea or organization that you believe in: [+**for**] *an apologia for the Christian church*

a·pol·o·gist /ə'pɒlədʒɪst $ ə'pɑː-/ n [C] someone who tries to explain and defend an idea, person, or political system: [+**for**] *an apologist for socialism*

a·pol·o·gize [S2] also **-ise** BrE /ə'pɒlədʒaɪz $ ə'pɑː-/ v [I] to tell someone that you are sorry that you have done something wrong: *I'm so sorry, I do apologize.* | [+**to**] *I think you should apologize to your brother.* | **apologize for (doing) sth** *He later apologized for his behaviour.* | *I apologize for losing my temper.*

a·pol·o·gy [S3] /ə'pɒlədʒi $ ə'pɑː-/ n plural **apologies** **1** [C,U] something that you say or write to show that you are sorry for doing something wrong

---

receive an apology
owe sb an apology
demand an apology
accept an apology
make an apology (for sth)
issue an apology (=make an official apology – used about governments, companies etc)
I make no apology (for sth) (=used when saying you are not sorry about something)
letter of apology
written apology
formal apology
public apology
by way of apology (=in order to show you are sorry)

[+**from**] *She finally received an apology from the company.* | *I feel I owe you an apology.* | *He wrote to the editor of the newspaper demanding an immediate apology.* | [+**for**] *Please accept my sincere apologies for my behaviour yesterday.* | *She had to make a formal public apology for her remarks.* | *I make no apology for repeating the question.* | *Those affected have been sent letters of apology.* | *'He always does this,' said Isabelle, by way of apology.*

---

2 apologies [plural] a message that you send to a meeting to say that you will not be able to come to the meeting: *Edward can't be here today, but he sends his apologies.*
3 make your apologies to say that you are sorry but you have to leave: *I quickly made my apologies and left.*
4 [C] literary a statement in which you defend something you believe in after it has been criticized by other people: [+**for**] *an apology for Christianity*
5 an apology for sth a very bad example of something: *They served us up an apology for a meal.*

ap·o·plec·tic /,æpə'plektɪk◂/ adj **1** informal so angry that your face becomes red: *The colonel was apoplectic with rage.* **2** old-fashioned relating to apoplexy

ap·o·plex·y /'æpəpleksi/ n [U] old-fashioned an illness in your brain which causes you to suddenly lose your ability to move or think; ☐ **stroke**

a·pos·ta·sy /ə'pɒstəsi/ n [U] formal when someone suddenly stops believing in a religion or supporting a political party

a·pos·tate /ə'pɒsteɪt, -stət $ ə'pɑː-/ n [C] formal someone who has stopped believing in a religion or supporting a political party

a pos·te·ri·o·ri /,eɪ pɒsteri'ɔːraɪ, ,ɑː pɒsteri'ɔːri $,ɑː poʊstɪri'ɔːri, ,eɪ pɑː-/ adj formal using facts that you know now to form a judgment about what must have happened before → A PRIORI

a·pos·tle /ə'pɒsəl $ ə'pɑː-/ n [C] **1** one of the 12 people chosen by Jesus Christ to teach and spread the

Christian religion **2** *formal* someone who believes strongly in an idea and tries to persuade other people: [+of] *a great apostle of non-violence*

ap·o·stol·ic /ˌæpəˈstɒlɪk◂ $ -ˈstɑː-/ *adj technical* **1** connected with the Pope (=leader of the Catholic church) **2** connected with one of Christ's 12 apostles

a·pos·tro·phe /əˈpɒstrəfi $ əˈpɑː-/ *n* [C] **a)** the sign (') that is used in writing to show that numbers or letters have been left out, as in 'don't' (=do not) and '86 (=1986) **b)** the same sign used before 's' to show that something belongs to someone or something, or is connected with them, as in 'John's book', or 'Charles' mother', or 'Henry's first year as a teacher' **c)** the same sign used before 's' to show the plural of letters and numbers as in 'Your r's look like v's.'

a·poth·e·ca·ry /əˈpɒθɪ̯kəri $ əˈpɑːˌkeri/ *n plural* **apothecaries** [C] someone who mixed and sold medicines in the past

a·poth·e·o·sis /əˌpɒθiˈəʊsɪ̯s $ əˌpɑːθiˈoʊsɪ̯s, ˌæpəˈθiːəsɪ̯s/ *n* [singular] *formal* **1** the best and most perfect example of something: [+of] *the apotheosis of romantic art* **2** the best or highest point in someone's life or job; ☐ **apex**: [+of] *the apotheosis of his career*

ap·pal *BrE*, **appall** *AmE* /əˈpɔːl $ əˈpɒːl/ *v* [T] to make someone feel very shocked and upset: *The way we kill animals appals a lot of people.* | *The decision to execute the two men has appalled many politicians.*

ap·palled /əˈpɔːld $ əˈpɒːld/ *adj* very shocked and upset by something very bad or unpleasant: [+by] *I was appalled by what I saw.* | [+at] *He was appalled at how dirty the place was.* | *When I heard what had happened I was **absolutely appalled**.*

ap·pal·ling /əˈpɔːlɪŋ $ əˈpɒː-/ *adj* **1** very unpleasant and shocking; ☐ **terrible**: *She suffered appalling injuries.* | *He was kept in appalling conditions in prison.* | *an appalling famine* **2** very bad; ☐ **atrocious**: *The weather was **absolutely appalling**.* —**appallingly** *adv*: *He behaved appallingly.* | *an appallingly difficult job*

ap·pa·loo·sa /ˌæpəˈluːsə/ *n* [C] *AmE* a type of horse that is pale in colour, with dark spots

ap·par·at·chik /ˌɑːpəˈrɑːtʃɪk/ *n* [C] an official who works for a government or other organization and who obeys orders without thinking: *a Communist party apparatchik*

ap·pa·ra·tus /ˌæpəˈreɪtəs $ -ˈræ-/ *n* **1** [U] the set of tools and machines that you use for a particular scientific, medical, or technical purpose; ☐ **equipment**: *Astronauts have special breathing apparatus.* **2** [C] the way in which a lot of people are organized to work together to do a job or control a company or country; ☐ **machinery**: *The tax will require a massive administrative apparatus.* | *The state apparatus has become corrupt.* | *the apparatus of government*

ap·par·el /əˈpærəl/ *n* [U] *formal* clothes: *She looked lovely, despite her strange apparel.* | *men wearing protective apparel* | *We sell a full range of sports apparel.*

ap·par·ent W2 /əˈpærənt/ *adj* **1** easy to notice; ☐ **obvious**: **it is apparent (that)** *It soon became apparent that we had a major problem.* | **it is apparent from sth that** *It is apparent from scientific studies that the drug has some fairly nasty side effects.* | **it is apparent to sb that** *It was apparent to everyone that he was seriously ill.* | *The difference in quality was **immediately apparent**.* | *He left suddenly, **for no apparent reason**.* **2** seeming to have a particular feeling or attitude, although this may not be true: *He did well in his exams, despite his apparent lack of interest in his work.*

ap·par·ent·ly S1 W2 /əˈpærəntli/ *adv* **1** [sentence adverb] used to say that you have heard that something is true, although you are not completely sure about it: *Apparently the company is losing a lot of money.* | *I wasn't there, but apparently it went well.* **2** according to the way someone looks or a situation

appears, although you cannot be sure: *She turned to face him, her anger apparently gone.*

ap·pa·ri·tion /ˌæpəˈrɪʃən/ *n* [C] something that you imagine you can see, especially the spirit of a dead person: *He stared at the strange apparition before him.* | *a ghostly apparition of a man*

ap·peal¹ S2 W1 /əˈpiːl/ *n* **1** REQUEST [C] an urgent request for something important: [+for] *The police have issued a new appeal for information.* | [+to] *All the organizations involved have sent urgent appeals to the government, asking for extra funding.* | *The girl's family have **made** a public appeal for help to try and catch her killer.* | **appeal to sb to do sth** *an appeal to the army to not use too much force* **2** REQUEST FOR MONEY [C] an attempt to persuade people to give money in order to help people who need something: *The appeal has nearly reached its target of £100,000.* | *The hospital has **launched** an appeal to raise money for new equipment.* **3** REQUEST TO CHANGE DECISION [C,U] a formal request to a court or to someone in authority asking for a decision to be changed: [+to] *an appeal to the European Court of Human Rights* | **on appeal** *The sentence was reduced to three years on appeal.* | *All prisoners have a **right of appeal**.* | *He has **lodged** an appeal against the size of the fine.* **4** BEING ATTRACTIVE [U] a quality that makes people like something or someone: *What is the particular appeal of this island?* | *The programme has a very **wide appeal**.* | [+for] *The film has great appeal for young audiences.* | *She's definitely got **sex appeal** (=she is sexually attractive).* → COURT OF APPEAL

appeal² S3 W3 *v* **1** ASK [I] to make a serious public request for help, money, information etc: [+for] *Church and community leaders have appealed for calm.* | [+to] *Farmers have appealed to the government for help.* | **appeal to sb to do sth** *The police have appealed to anyone with information to come forward and talk to them.* **2** ASK TO CHANGE DECISION [I,T] to make a formal request to a court or someone in authority asking for a decision to be changed: *She is not happy with the decision and plans to appeal.* | [+against] *Both men intend to appeal against their convictions.* | [+to] *Appealing to the referee does not often result in a decision being changed.* **3** BE ATTRACTIVE [I] if someone or something appeals to you, they seem attractive and interesting: [+to] *The programme appeals especially to young children.* | *The idea of working abroad **really appeals** to me.* **4 appeal to sb's better nature/sense of justice etc** to try to persuade someone to do something by reminding them that it is a good or fair thing to do: *You could always try appealing to his better nature.*

Ap'peal ˌCourt *n* [singular] the COURT OF APPEAL

ap·peal·ing /əˈpiːlɪŋ/ *adj* **1** attractive or interesting; ☒ **unappealing**: *The city offers an appealing combination of sporting and cultural events.* | *It creates an atmosphere which visitors **find** so appealing.* **2** appealing look/expression/voice etc a look etc that shows that someone wants help or sympathy: *'Are you sure it's okay?' she said with an appealing smile.* —**appealingly** *adv*: *She looked appealingly at Ben.*

ap'peals ˌcourt *n* [C] a court of law in some countries which deals with cases when people are not satisfied with the judgement given by a lower court; ☐ **Court of Appeals**: *a ruling by a US federal appeals court*

ap·pear S1 W1 /əˈpɪə $ əˈpɪr/ *v* **1** SEEM [linking verb, not in progressive] used to say how something seems, especially from what you know about it or from what you can see: **appear to be sth** *Police say there appear to be signs of a break-in.* | **appear to do sth** *The survey appears to contradict motor industry claims.* | **it appears (that)** *It appears that all the files have been deleted.* | *Police have found **what appear***

to be human remains. | *He tried to* **make it appear that** *she had committed suicide.* | *It may be less useful than it appears at first.* | **so it would appear** (=used to say that something seems likely to be true, although you are not completely sure)

2 GIVE IMPRESSION [linking verb, not in progressive] used to say that someone or something seems to have a particular quality or feeling: *He tried hard to* **appear** *calm.* | *I don't want to appear rude.* | *The right colours can* **make** *a small room* **appear** *much bigger.*

3 START TO BE SEEN [I always + adv/prep] to start to be seen, to arrive, or to exist in a place, especially suddenly: *Two faces appeared at our window.* | *A man suddenly appeared from behind a tree.* | *Small cracks appeared in the wall.* | *It was nearly an hour before Sweeney appeared in the pub.* | **appear from nowhere/ out of nowhere** (=appear suddenly and unexpectedly) *The car seemed to appear from nowhere.*

4 FILM/TV PROGRAMME ETC [I always + adv/prep] to take part in a film, play, concert, television programme etc: **appear in a film/play** *She has already appeared in a number of films.* | **appear on television/stage** *He appeared on national television to deny the claims.* | **appear at a theatre etc**

5 BOOK/NEWSPAPER ETC [I always + adv/prep] to be written or shown on a list, in a book or newspaper, in a document etc: *The story appeared in all the national newspapers.* | *Some of the material used has* **appeared** *in print before* (=has been published).

6 AVAILABLE/KNOWN [I always + adv/prep] to become widely available or known about: *The new range will be appearing in shops in the autumn.* | *New courses are appearing every year.*

7 LAW COURT/MEETING [I always + adv/prep] to go to a law court or other official meeting to give information, answer questions etc: *The three men are due to* **appear in court** *tomorrow.* | **appear before a court/ judge/committee etc** *She appeared before Colchester magistrates charged with attempted murder.* | **appear for sb/on behalf of sb** (=to be the legal representative for someone) *Sir Nicholas Gammon QC appeared on behalf of the defendant.*; → see box at SEEM

ap·pear·ance W2 /əˈpɪərəns $ əˈpɪr-/ *n*

1 WAY SB/STH LOOKS [C,U] the way someone or something looks to other people

---

sb's appearance
physical appearance
personal appearance
outward/external appearance
spoil the appearance of sb/sth
improve/enhance the appearance of sb/sth
take pride in your appearance (=think that it is important to look good)
judge by appearances (=make judgements based on the way someone or something looks)
give the appearance of sth/give every appearance of sth (=seem to be something)
have all the appearances of sth (=seem exactly like something)
appearances can be deceptive (=people or things are not always the way they look)
to all appearances (=based on the way someone or something seems to most people)

He was always criticising his wife's appearance. | [+of] *They've changed the appearance of the whole building.* | *We are often attracted to somebody first by their* **physical appearance***.* | *Women, in general, tend to be more concerned than men about their* **personal appearance***.* | *She had an* **outward appearance** *of calm, but deep down she was really worried.* | *The metal posts* **spoiled the appearance** *of the garden.* | *A garnish helps to* **enhance the appearance** *of any dish.* | *She's the kind of woman who* **takes pride in her appearance***.* | *You shouldn't* **judge by appearances***.* | *They work hard at school without* **giving the appearance** *of being particularly hard-working.* | *The case* **had all the appearances** *of a straightforward*

murder. | *The pupils looked angelic – but* **appearances** **can be deceptive***.* | *He was,* **to all appearances***, a respectable, successful businessman.*

2 SB TAKES PART IN A PUBLIC EVENT [C] when a famous person takes part in a film, concert or other public event: *It was his first* **public appearance** *since the election.* | *He* **made** *his last* **appearance** *for the club in the Cup Final.* | **appearance money/fee** (=money paid to a famous person to attend an event)

3 STH NEW STARTS TO EXIST [singular] when something new begins to exist or starts being used: [+of] *The industry has changed greatly with the appearance of new technologies.* | *the appearance of buds on the trees*

4 ARRIVAL [C usually singular] the unexpected or sudden arrival of someone or something: [+of] *Eileen was deep in concentration, and the sudden appearance of her daughter startled her.*

5 keep up appearances to dress and behave in the way in which people expect you to, especially to hide your true situation: *She just wanted to keep up appearances for the kids.*

6 for appearances' sake/for the sake of appearances if you do something for appearances' sake, you are trying to behave how people expect you to, especially to hide your true situation or feelings

7 put in an appearance/make an appearance to go to an event for a short time, because you think you should rather than because you want to: *At least Marc managed to put in an appearance at the party.*

8 AT A LAW COURT/MEETING [C] an occasion when someone goes to a court of law or official meeting to give information, answer questions etc: *He is due to make another court appearance on Monday.*

ap·pease /əˈpiːz/ *v* [T] *formal* to make someone less angry or stop them from attacking you by giving them what they want: *They attempted to appease international opposition by promising to hold talks.* —**appeasement** *n* [C,U]: *Chamberlain's policy of appeasement towards Hitler in the 30s*

ap·pel·lant /əˈpelənt/ *n* [C] *law* a person who APPEALS against the decision in a court of law

ap·pel·late court /əˌpelət ˈkɔːt $ -ˈkɔːrt/ *n* [C] a court in which people APPEAL against decisions made in other courts of law

ap·pel·la·tion /ˌæpəˈleɪʃən/ *n* [C] *literary* a name or title

ap·pend /əˈpend/ *v* [T] *formal* to add something to a piece of writing; → **appendix**: [+to] *The results of the client survey are appended to this report.*

ap·pend·age /əˈpendɪdʒ/ *n* [C] **1** something that is connected to a larger or more important thing **2** *formal* an arm, leg or other body part

ap·pen·dec·to·my /ˌæpɪnˈdektəmi/ *n plural* **appendectomies** [C,U] a medical operation in which your APPENDIX is removed

ap·pen·di·ci·tis /əˌpendɪˈsaɪtɪs/ *n* [U] an illness in which your APPENDIX swells and causes pain

ap·pen·dix /əˈpendɪks/ *n or* [C] **1** *plural* **appendixes** a small organ near your BOWEL, which has little or no use: *Christine had to go into hospital to have her appendix out* (=have it removed). **2** *plural* **appendices** /-dɪsiːz/ a part at the end of a book containing additional information: *See Appendix 2.6*

ap·per·tain /ˌæpəˈteɪn $ -ər-/ *v*
appertain to sth *phr v* [not in passive] *formal* to belong to or concern something: *A monthly forum was set up to deal with all issues appertaining to Everton Park.*

ap·pe·tite /ˈæpɪtaɪt/ *n* **1** [C usually singular, U] a desire for food: *All that walking has given me* **an appetite** *for dinner.* | *I seem to have* **lost my appetite** *lately.* | *Symptoms include headaches, tiredness and* **loss of appetite** | *Let's just say he's* **got a healthy appetite***.* | **spoil/ruin your appetite** *Don't eat that cake now; you'll spoil your appetite.* **2** [C] a desire or liking for a particular activity: [+for] *She has an amazing appetite for knowledge.* | *People seem to have an insatiable appetite* (=always wanting more of something) *for news of any kind.* | *a loss of sexual appetite* → whet sb's appetite at WHET (1)

ap·pe·tiz·er also **-iser** *BrE* /'æpᵻtaɪzə $ -ər/ *n* [C] a small dish that you eat at the beginning of a meal

ap·pe·tiz·ing also **-ising** *BrE* /'æpᵻtaɪzɪŋ/ *adj* food that is appetizing smells or looks very good, making you want to eat it; ⟐ **unappetizing**: *an appetizing aroma* | *The food wasn't particularly appetizing.*

ap·plaud /ə'plɔːd $ ə'plɒːd/ *v* 1 [I,T] to hit your open hands together to show that you have enjoyed a play, concert, speaker etc; ⟐ **clap**: *The audience applauded loudly.* | *A crowd of 300 supporters warmly applauded her speech.* 2 [T] *formal* to express strong approval of an idea, plan etc: *I applaud the decision to install more security cameras.* | **applaud sb for sth** *She should be applauded for her honesty.*

ap·plause /ə'plɔːz $ ə'plɒːz/ *n* [U] the sound of many people hitting their hands together and shouting, to show that they have enjoyed something: *She got a round of applause* (=a short period of applause) *when she finished.* | **rapturous/enthusiastic applause** *He left the stage to rapturous applause.* | **loud/thunderous applause**

ap·ple S2 W3 /'æpəl/ *n*
1 [C,U] a hard round fruit that has red, light green, or yellow skin and is white inside: *apple pie* | *an apple tree* | *roast pork and apple sauce* (=a thick sauce made from cooked apples) → COOKING APPLE, EATING APPLE; → see picture at FRUIT[1]
2 **be the apple of sb's eye** to be loved very much by someone: *Ben was always the apple of his father's eye.*
3 **bob/dunk/dip for apples** to play a game in which you must use your teeth to pick up apples floating in water
4 **be as American as apple pie** used to describe something that is typically American
5 **the apple doesn't fall far from the tree** *AmE* used to say that children are usually similar to their parents, especially in a bad way → **upset the apple cart** at UPSET[2] (5); → **a rotten apple** at ROTTEN[1] (7); → ADAM'S APPLE, BIG APPLE

'apple ˌpolisher *n* [C] *AmE spoken* someone who tries to gain something, become popular etc by praising or helping someone else without being sincere

ap·plet /'æplᵻt/ *n* [C] *technical* a computer program that is part of a larger program, and which performs a particular job, such as finding documents on the Internet

ap·pli·ance /ə'plaɪəns/ *n* [C] a piece of equipment, especially electrical equipment, such as a COOKER or WASHING MACHINE, used in people's homes: **domestic/ household etc appliance** *There's plenty of space for all the usual kitchen appliances.* | **electrical/gas appliance** → see box at MACHINE[1]

ap·plic·a·ble /ə'plɪkəbəl, 'æplɪkəbəl/ *adj* if something is applicable to a particular person, group, or situation, it affects them or is related to them: [+to] *The offer is only applicable to bookings for double rooms.* | **where/if/as applicable** *Ms/Miss/Mrs/Mr Please delete as applicable.* —**applicability** /ə,plɪkə'bɪlᵻti/ *n* [U]

ap·pli·cant /'æplɪkənt/ *n* [C] someone who has formally asked, usually in writing, for a job, university place etc: [+for] *He was one of 30 applicants for the manager's job.* | **successful/unsuccessful applicant** (=someone who is accepted or not accepted for a job etc) *Successful applicants will be expected to travel extensively.*

ap·pli·ca·tion S1 W1 /ˌæplɪ'keɪʃən/ *n*
1 WRITTEN REQUEST [C,U] a formal, usually written, request for something such as a job, place at university, or permission to do something

job application
fill in/out an application
application form
make/put in/submit an application
accept sb's application
reject sb's application
process an application (=deal with it)
planning application (=a request for permission to build something)
letter of application

[+for] *an application for a grant* | [+from] *The university welcomes applications from overseas students.* | *We receive hundreds of job applications each year.* | *I filled in the application form and sent it off.* | *You have to submit your application before the end of the month.* | *I've put in an application for a transfer.* | *He received a letter saying that his application had been rejected.* | *It can take a long time for your visa application to be processed.* | *The Council is currently reviewing the way it deals with planning applications.* | *Thank you for your letter of application, which we received yesterday.*

2 PRACTICAL USE [C,U] practical purpose for which a machine, idea etc can be used, or a situation when this is used: [+of/to/in] *the applications of genetic engineering in agriculture* | *The research has many practical applications.*
3 COMPUTERS [C] a piece of computer software which does a particular job: *We received training on a number of spreadsheet and database applications.*
4 PAINT/LIQUID [C,U] when you put something such as paint, liquid, medicine etc onto a surface: [+of] *The application of fertilizer increased the size of the plants.*
5 EFFORT [U] attention or effort over a long period of time: *Making your new business successful requires luck, patience, and application.*

ˌapplication 'service proˌvider *n* [C] an ASP
ˌapplication 'software *n* [U] *technical* computer software that is designed for a particular use or user: *We need to ensure that the application software on both the PC and the Macintosh produces compatible files.*

ap·pli·ca·tor /'æplɪkeɪtə $ -ər/ *n* [C] a special brush or tool used to spread a cream, liquid, medicine etc onto a surface

ap·plied /ə'plaɪd/ *adj* applied science/physics/linguistics etc science etc that has a practical use; → **pure** (10), **theoretical** (1)

ap·pli·qué /ə'pliːkeɪ $ ˌæplᵻ'keɪ/ *n* [C,U] the process of sewing pieces of material onto a piece of clothing for decoration, or the pieces themselves —**appliqué** *v* [T]

ap·ply S1 W1 /ə'plaɪ/ *v* applied, applying, applies
1 REQUEST [I] to make a formal request, usually written, for something such as a job, a place in a university, or permission to do something: [+for] *She applied for a job with the local newspaper.* | *We need to apply for planning permission to build a garage.* | [+to] *I applied to four universities and was accepted by all of them.*
2 AFFECT [I,T not in progressive] to have an effect on or to concern a particular person, group, or situation: [+to] *Do the same rules apply to part-time workers?* | *The offer only applies to flights from London and Manchester.*
3 USE [T] to use something such as a method, idea, or law in a particular situation, activity, or process: **apply sth to sth** *New technology is being applied to almost every industrial process.* | *These ideas are often difficult to apply in practice.*
4 **apply yourself** to work hard at something, especially with a lot of attention for a long time: *Stephen would do well if only he applied himself.* | [+to] *Over the next months, he applied himself to improving the technique.*
5 MAKE STH WORK [T] to make something such as a piece of equipment operate, usually by pushing or pressing something: *apply the brakes*
6 SPREAD PAINT/LIQUID ETC [T] to put or spread something such as paint, liquid, or medicine onto a

surface: *Apply the cream evenly over the skin.* | **apply make-up/lipstick etc**

7 apply force/pressure to push on something

8 USE A WORD [T] to use a particular word or name to describe something or someone: *The term 'mat' can be applied to any small rug.*

ap·point S2 W2 /ə'pɔɪnt/ v [T]

1 to choose someone for a position or a job: *officials appointed by the government* | **appoint sb to sth** *He's been appointed to the State Supreme Court.* | **appoint sb to do sth** *A committee was appointed to consider the plans.* | **appoint (sb) as sth** *O'Connell was appointed as chairman.*

2 *formal* to arrange or decide a time or place for something to happen: *The committee appointed a day in June for celebrations.* | *Everyone assembled in the hall* **at the appointed time** (=at the time that had been arranged). —**appointee** /ə,pɔɪn'tiː, ,æpɔɪn-/ n [C]: *a presidential appointee* → SELF-APPOINTED, WELL-APPOINTED

ap·point·ment S1 W2 /ə'pɔɪntmənt/ n

1 [C] an arrangement for a meeting at an agreed time and place, for a particular purpose

> **have an appointment**
> **make an appointment**
> **an appointment to do sth**
> **book an appointment** *BrE*
> **schedule an appointment** *AmE* (=make an appointment)
> **cancel an appointment**
> **miss an appointment**
> **keep an appointment** (=go to an appointment you have arranged)
> **doctor's/dentist's/dental appointment**
> **by appointment (only)** (=only if you make an appointment in advance)

> [+with] *She* **has an appointment** *with a client at 10.30.* | *You should phone his secretary if you want to* **make an appointment.** | *I* **have an appointment to** *see the doctor.* | *Please give us plenty of notice if you have to* **cancel an appointment.** | *For the third time in a row, she had failed to* **keep her appointment.** | *I was already forty-five minutes late for a* **dental appointment.** | *All consultations are* **by appointment only.**

2 [C,U] when someone is chosen for a position or job: [+of] *Other changes included the appointment of a new Foreign Minister.* | [+as] *They congratulated him on his appointment as chairman.*

3 [C] a job or position, usually involving some responsibility: [+as] *He has taken up an appointment as Professor of Chemistry.*

4 by appointment to the Queen *BrE* a phrase that can be used by a business that sells goods or services to the Queen

ap'pointment book n [C] **1** *AmE* a DIARY **2** a large book divided into days and times containing the names of people you have appointments with, for example a doctor or a HAIRDRESSER etc

ap·por·tion /ə'pɔːʃən $ -ɔːr-/ v [T] *formal* to decide how something should be shared between various people: *It's not easy to* **apportion blame** (=say who deserves to be blamed) *when a marriage breaks up.* | [+among/between] *Court costs were equally apportioned between them.* —**apportionment** n [C,U]

ap·po·site /'æpəzɪt/ adj *formal* suitable to what is happening or being discussed; **appropriate**; **inapposite**: [+to] *His observations are, indeed, apposite to the present discussion.* —**appositely** adv —**appositeness** n [U]

ap·po·si·tion /,æpə'zɪʃən/ n [U] *technical* in grammar, an occasion when a simple sentence contains two or more noun phrases that describe the same thing or person, appearing one after the other without a word such as 'and' or 'or' between them. For example, in the sentence 'The defendant, a woman of thirty, denies kicking the policeman' the two phrases 'the defendant' and 'a woman of thirty' are in apposition.

ap·prais·al /ə'preɪzəl/ n **1** [C,U] a statement or opinion judging the worth, value, or condition of something: [+of] *It needed a calmer appraisal of her situation.* | *a critical appraisal of the existing facilities* **2** [C] a meeting between a manager and a worker to discuss the quality of the worker's work and how well they do their job

ap·praise /ə'preɪz/ v [T] **1** *formal* to officially judge how successful, effective, or valuable something is; **evaluate**: *Greenpeace has been invited to appraise the environmental costs of such an operation.* **2** *literary* to look carefully at someone or something to make an opinion about them: *His eyes appraised her face.*

ap·pre·cia·ble /ə'priːʃəbəl/ adj large enough to be noticed or considered important; **significant**: *There's no appreciable change in the patient's condition.* —**appreciably** adv: *The two plans are not appreciably different.*

ap·pre·ci·ate S2 W3 /ə'priːʃieɪt/ v

1 [T not in progressive] to understand how serious or important a situation or problem is or what someone's feelings are; **realize**: **appreciate the significance/importance/value of sth** *He did not fully appreciate the significance of signing the contract.* | **appreciate that** *We appreciate that caring for children is an important job.* | **appreciate what/how/why** *It is difficult to appreciate how bad the situation had become.*

2 [T] used to thank someone in a polite way or to say that you are grateful for something they have done: *Thanks ever so much for your help, I really appreciate it.* | *I* **appreciate** *your* **concern,** *but honestly, I'm fine.* | *I'd* **appreciate it** *if you let me get on with my job.*

3 [T] to understand how good or useful someone or something is: *Her abilities are not fully appreciated by her employer.* | *I'm not an expert, but I appreciate fine works of art.*

4 [I] *technical* to gradually become more valuable over a period of time; **depreciate**: *Most investments are expected to appreciate at a steady rate.*

ap·pre·ci·a·tion /ə,priːʃi'eɪʃən/ n **1** [U] pleasure you feel when you realize something is good, useful, or well done: [+of] *It helps children to develop an appreciation of poetry and literature.* **2** [U] a feeling of being grateful for something someone has done: **show/express your appreciation** *The chairman asked me to express our appreciation of all your hard work.* | *He was presented with a watch* **in appreciation of** *his long service.* **3** [C,U] an understanding of the importance or meaning of something: [+of] *a realistic appreciation of the situation* **4** [singular, U] a rise in value, especially of land or possessions; **depreciation**: *an appreciation of 50% in property values.*

ap·pre·cia·tive /ə'priːʃətɪv/ adj **1** feeling or showing that you enjoy something or are pleased about it: **appreciative audience/crowd** | **appreciative laughter/applause** **2** [not before noun] grateful for something: [+of] *She was appreciative of Greg's concern for her health.* —**appreciatively** adv

ap·pre·hend /,æprɪ'hend/ v [T] **1** *formal* if the police apprehend a criminal, they catch him or her; **arrest**: *The police have failed to apprehend the culprits.* **2** *old-fashioned* to understand something: *They were slow to apprehend the danger.*

ap·pre·hen·sion /,æprɪ'henʃən/ n **1** [C,U] anxiety about the future, especially about dealing with something unpleasant or difficult; **anxiety**: *a feeling of apprehension* | *I woke before the alarm, filled with apprehension.* **2** [U] *formal* the act of apprehending a criminal; **arrest** **3** [U] *old-fashioned* understanding

ap·pre·hen·sive /,æprɪ'hensɪv‹/ adj worried or nervous about something that you are going to do, or about the future: [+about/of] *We'd been a little apprehensive about their visit.* | **apprehensive that** *I was apprehen-*

sive that something would go wrong. | *Some had apprehensive looks on their faces.* —**apprehensively** *adv*: *'What's wrong?' I asked apprehensively.*

ap·pren·tice /ə'prentɪ̯s/ *n* [C] someone who works for an employer for a fixed period of time in order to learn a particular skill or job: *She works in the hairdresser's as an apprentice.* | *an apprentice electrician* —**apprentice** *v* [T usually passive]: *He was apprenticed to a local architect.*

ap·pren·tice·ship /ə'prentɪ̯sʃɪp/ *n* [C,U] the job of being an apprentice, or the period of time in which you are an apprentice: *He's serving an apprenticeship as a printer.* | *a five-year apprenticeship*

ap·prise /ə'praɪz/ *v* [T] *formal* to tell or give someone information about something: **apprise sb of sth** *The district chairman was fully apprised of all the details.*

ap·proach¹ S3 W2 /ə'prəʊtʃ $ ə'proʊtʃ/ *v*
1 MOVE TOWARDS [I,T] to move towards or nearer to someone or something: *As I approached the house, I noticed a light on upstairs.* | *She heard footsteps approaching.*
2 ASK [T] to ask someone for something, or ask them to do something, especially when you are asking them for the first time or when you are not sure if they will do it: **approach sb for sth** *Students should be able to approach teachers for advice.* | **approach sb/sth about (doing) sth** *The charity approached several stores about giving food aid.* | *I have already been approached by several other companies* (=offered a job, work etc). →
APPROACHABLE
3 FUTURE EVENT [I,T] if an event or a particular time approaches, or you approach it, it is coming nearer and will happen soon: *She was then approaching the end of her career.* | *The time is fast approaching when we will have to make a decision.* | *With winter approaching, many animals are storing food.*
4 DEAL WITH [T] to begin to deal with a situation or problem in a particular way or with a particular attitude: **approach a problem/task/matter etc** *It might be possible to approach the problem in a different way.*
5 ALMOST [I,T] to be almost equal to something: *temperatures approaching 35°C* | *He's never had anything approaching a normal life.*

approach² S3 W1 *n*
1 METHOD [C] a method of doing something or dealing with a problem: [+to] *a new approach to teaching languages* | *He decided to adopt a different approach and teach the Bible through story-telling.* | *This book takes an unorthodox approach to art criticism.* | *organizations which take a positive approach to creative thinking*
2 ASK [C] a request from someone, asking you to do something for them: *They made a direct approach to the minister of education.*
3 the approach of sth the approach of a particular time or event is the fact that it is getting closer: *the approach of autumn* | *It's a sign of the approach of middle age.*
4 MOVEMENT TOWARDS [U] movement towards or near to something: *Our approach frightened the birds.*
5 PATH/ROAD [C] a road, path etc that leads to a place, and is the main way of reaching it: *Soldiers were guarding the approaches to the city.* | *an approach road*
6 AIRCRAFT [C] the final part of a plane's flight, before it lands at an airport: *It was clear to land so we made our approach.*

ap·proach·a·ble /ə'prəʊtʃəbəl $ ə'proʊtʃ-/ *adj* friendly and easy to talk to; ◪ **unapproachable**: *The head teacher is very approachable.*

ap·pro·ba·tion /ˌæprə'beɪʃən/ *n* [U] *formal* official praise or approval

ap·pro·pri·ate¹ S1 W1 /ə'prəʊpri-ɪ̯t $ ə'proʊ-/ *adj* correct or suitable for a particular time, situation, or purpose; ◪ **inappropriate**: [+for] *clothes appropriate for a job interview* | [+to] *an education system which is*

more appropriate to the needs of the students | **it is appropriate (for sb) to do sth** *It would not be appropriate for me to discuss that now.* | **it is appropriate (that)** *It seemed somehow appropriate that we should begin our journey here.* | **appropriate time/place etc** *I didn't feel that this was an appropriate time to mention the subject of money.* | **highly/entirely/wholly appropriate** *I thought his remark was highly appropriate, given the circumstances.* | *The timing of the announcement was particularly appropriate.* | **Where appropriate**, *I delegate as much work as possible.* | *Mark box 1 or 2, as appropriate.* | *I can assure you that appropriate action will be taken.* —**appropriately** *adv*: *The painters met, appropriately enough, in an art gallery* (=used to emphasize that something is very appropriate). | *appropriately dressed* —**appropriateness** *n* [U]

ap·pro·pri·ate² /ə'prəʊprieɪt $ ə'proʊ-/ *v* [T] *formal* **1** to take something for yourself when you do not have the right to do this; ◪ **steal**: *He is suspected of appropriating government funds.* **2** to take something, especially money, to use for a particular purpose: **appropriate sth for sth** *Congress appropriated $5 million for International Woman's Year.*; → misappropriate

ap·pro·pri·a·tion /ə,prəʊpri'eɪʃən $ ə,proʊ-/ *n* [C,U] *formal* **1** the process of saving money for a special purpose, or the money that is saved, especially by a business or government: [+of] *the appropriation of $2 million for the new hospital* **2** the act of taking control of something without asking permission: [+of] *the appropriation of company property*

ap·prov·al S2 W3 /ə'pruːvəl/ *n*
1 [C,U] when a plan, decision, or person is officially accepted

give/grant your approval
receive/obtain approval
with/without sb's approval
submit/send sth for approval
subject to sb's approval (=if it is accepted by someone)
pending sb's approval (=waiting to be accepted by someone)
sb gives their seal of approval (=an important person, organization etc says officially that they agree with something and will allow it)
formal/official approval
Congressional/parliamentary etc approval

The president has already given his approval to the plan. | *It is just three months since we received official approval to go ahead with the project.* | *A company cannot be sold without the approval of the shareholders.* | *The bill will be submitted for approval by Congress.* | *The President would appoint the Council of Ministers, subject to the approval of the National Assembly.* | *The IMF has given its seal of approval to the government's economic strategy.* | *appointments requiring parliamentary approval*

2 [U] *formal* when someone likes something or someone and thinks that they are good; ◪ **disapproval**: *A murmur of approval passed through the crowd.* | **nod/smile/clap etc in approval** *They clapped their hands in approval.* | *His ideas have won widespread public approval* (=many people agree with them and think they are good). | *Does the design meet with your approval* (=do you like it?)? | *Children are always seeking approval from their parents.* | *She looked to Greg for approval.*
3 on approval if you buy something on approval, you have the right to return it to the shop if you decide you do not want it

ap·prove S2 W2 /ə'pruːv/ *v*
1 [T] to officially accept a plan, proposal etc: *The conference approved a proposal for a referendum.*
2 [I] to think that someone or something is good, right, or suitable; ◪ **disapprove**: [+of] *Catherine's parents now approve of her marriage.* | *I don't approve of cosmetic surgery.*

ap·proved /ə'pruːvd/ *adj* [only before noun] officially recognized as being of a particular level or standard: *Funding is available for approved courses.*

ap'proved ,school *n* [C] *BrE* a special school in Britain in the past, where children who had done something illegal were sent if they were under 18

ap·prov·ing /ə'pruːvɪŋ/ *adj* showing support or agreement for something; ⊟ **disapproving**: **an approving nod/glance/smile etc** —**approvingly** *adv*: *She smiled approvingly at the child.*

approx. also **approx** *BrE* /ə'prɒks $ ə'prɑːks/ the written abbreviation of *approximately*

ap·prox·i·mate[1] S3 W3 /ə'prɒksɪmət $ ə'prɑːk-/ *adj* an approximate number, amount, or time is close to the exact number, amount etc, but could be a little bit more or less than it; ⊟ **rough**; ⊟ **exact**: *What is the approximate number of students in each class?* | *These percentages are only approximate.* —**approximately** *adv*: *The plane will be landing in approximately 20 minutes.* | *How much do think it will cost, approximately?*

ap·prox·i·mate[2] /ə'prɒksɪmeɪt $ ə'prɑːk-/ *v* [I, linking verb] *formal* **1** to be close to a particular number: [+to] *This figure approximates to a quarter of the UK's annual consumption.* **2** to be similar to but not exactly the same as something: [+to] *Your story only approximates to the real facts.*

ap·prox·i·ma·tion /ə,prɒksɪ'meɪʃən $ ə,prɑːk-/ *n* [C,U] **1** a number, amount etc that is not exact, but is almost correct; ⊟ **estimate**: [+of] *an approximation of the total number* | **a rough/crude approximation** (=one that is not very exact) *Could you give us a rough approximation of the likely cost?* | **a good/close/reasonable approximation** **2** something that is similar to another thing, but not exactly the same: [+of/to] *It was the nearest approximation to a crisis she'd ever experienced.*

ap·pur·te·nance /ə'pɜːtɪnəns, -tən- $ ə'pɜːrtənəns/ *n* [C usually plural] *formal* a part of something more important

Apr. also **Apr** *BrE* the written abbreviation of *April*

APR /,eɪ piː 'ɑː $ -'ɑːr/ *n* [C usually singular] *annual percentage rate* the rate of INTEREST that you must pay when you borrow money

ap·rès-ski /,æpreɪ 'skiː◂ $,ɑː-/ *n* [U] activities such as eating and drinking that you do after SKIING —**après-ski** *adj*

a·pri·cot /'eɪprɪkɒt $ 'æprɪkɑːt/ *n* **1** [C] a small round fruit that is orange or yellow and has a single large seed **2** [U] the orange-yellow colour of an apricot —**apricot** *adj*

A·pril /'eɪprəl/ *n* [C,U] written abbreviation **Apr.** the fourth month of the year, between March and May: *next/last April I'm going to Cuba next April.* | *in April Our new office opened in April 2001.* | **on April 6th** *The meeting will be on April 6th.* | **on 6th April** *BrE: I arrived on 6th April.* | **April 6** *AmE: Jim's birthday's April 6.*

April 'fool *n* [C] someone who is tricked on April Fools' Day, or the trick that is played on them

April 'Fools' Day also **All 'Fools' Day** *n* April 1st, a day when people play tricks on each other

a pri·o·ri /,eɪ praɪ'ɔːraɪ, ,ɑː priː'ɔːriː/ *adj, adv formal* using previous experiences or facts to decide what the likely result or effect of something will be; → **a posteriori**: *a ruling made on a priori grounds*

a·pron /'eɪprən/ *n* [C] **1** a piece of clothing that covers the front part of your clothes and is tied around your waist, worn to keep your clothes clean, especially while cooking **2 apron strings** *informal* the relationship between a child and its mother, especially if the mother controls an adult son or daughter too much: *You're 25 years old, and you still haven't cut the apron strings.* | *Jeff is still tied to his mother's apron strings.* **3** *technical* the hard surface in an airport on which planes are turned around, loaded, unloaded etc **4** *technical* also **apron stage** the part of the stage in a theatre that is in front of the curtain

ap·ro·pos /,æprə'pəʊ, 'æprəpəʊ $ -poʊ/ *adv formal* **apropos of sth** used to introduce a new subject that is related to something just mentioned: *He had nothing to say apropos of the latest developments.* | **apropos of nothing** (=not relating to anything previously mentioned) *Apropos of nothing, he suddenly asked me if I liked cats!*

apse /æps/ *n* [C] *technical* the curved inside end of a building, especially the east end of a church

apt /æpt/ *adj* **1 be apt to do sth** to have a natural tendency to do something: *Some of the staff are apt to arrive late on Mondays.* **2** exactly right for a particular situation or purpose; ⊟ **appropriate**: *'Love at first sight' is a very apt description of how he felt when he saw her.* | [+for] *The punishment should be apt for the crime.* **3 an apt pupil/student** *formal* a student who is quick to learn and understand —**aptness** *n* [U]

ap·ti·tude /'æptɪtjuːd $ -tuːd/ *n* [C,U] **1** natural ability or skill, especially in learning: [+for] *He has a natural aptitude for teaching.* **2 aptitude test** a test that measures your natural skills or abilities

apt·ly /'æptli/ *adv* **aptly named/described/called etc** named, described etc in a way that seems very suitable: *The aptly named Skyline Restaurant provides spectacular views of the city below.*

Aq·ua·lung /'ækwəlʌŋ/ *n* [C] *trademark BrE* a piece of equipment that provides a DIVER (=someone who swims underwater) with air, and which they wear on their backs

aq·ua·ma·rine /,ækwəmə'riːn◂ $,æ-, ,ɑː-/ *n* **1** [C,U] a greenish blue jewel, or the type of stone it comes from **2** [U] a greenish blue colour —**aquamarine** *adj*

aq·ua·plane[1] /'ækwəpleɪn/ *v* [I] *BrE* **1** if a car aquaplanes, it slides over a wet road in an uncontrolled way; ⊟ **hydroplane** *AmE* **2** to be pulled over the water on an aquaplane

aquaplane[2] *n* [C] *BrE* a thin board that you stand on while you are pulled over the water by a fast boat

a·quar·i·um /ə'kweəriəm $ ə'kwer-/ *n plural* **aquariums** or **aquaria** /-riə/ [C] **1** a clear glass or plastic container for fish and other water animals **2** a building where people go to look at fish and other water animals

A·quar·i·us /ə'kweəriəs $ ə'kwer-/ *n* **1** [U] the 11th sign of the ZODIAC, represented by a person pouring water, which some people believe affects the character and life of people born between January 21 and February 19 **2** also **Aquarian** [C] someone who was born between January 21 and February 19 —**Aquarian** *adj*

a·quat·ic /ə'kwætɪk, ə'kwɒ- $ ə'kwæ-, ə'kwɑː-/ *adj* **1** living or growing in water: *an aquatic plant* **2** involving or happening in water: *aquatic sports*

aq·ua·tint /'ækwətɪnt/ *n* [C,U] a method of producing a picture using acid on a sheet of metal, or a picture printed using this method

aq·ue·duct /'ækwɪdʌkt/ *n* [C] a structure like a bridge, that carries water across a river or valley → see picture at ARCH[1]

a·que·ous /'eɪkwiəs, 'ækwiəs/ *adj technical* containing water or similar to water

aq·ui·line /'ækwɪlaɪn $ -laɪn, -lən/ *adj* **aquiline nose** a nose with a curved shape like the beak of an EAGLE

-ar /ə, ɑː $ ər, ɑːr/ *suffix* **1** [in adjectives] relating to something: *stellar* (=relating to stars) | *polar* (=relating to the North or South Pole) **2** [in nouns] someone who does something: *a liar* (=someone who lies)

Ar·ab /'ærəb/ *n* [C] someone whose language is Arabic and whose family comes from, or originally came from the Middle East or North Africa

ar·a·besque /ˌærəˈbesk/ n [C] **1** a position in BAL-
LET, in which you stand on one foot with the other leg
stretched out straight behind you **2** a decorative pattern of flowing lines

A·ra·bi·an /əˈreɪbiən/ adj relating to Arabia or its
people

Ar·a·bic /ˈærəbɪk/ n [U] the language or writing of the
Arabs, which is the main language of North Africa and
the Middle East —**Arabic** adj

Arabic ˈnumeral n [C] the sign 1,2,3,4,5,6,7,8,9, or 0,
or a combination of these signs, used as a number; →
Roman numeral

ar·a·ble /ˈærəbəl/ adj relating to growing crops:
arable farming | *arable land* (=land that is suitable for
growing crops)

a·rach·nid /əˈræknɪd/ n [C] a small creature such as a
SPIDER, that has eight legs and a body with two parts

ar·bi·ter /ˈɑːbɪtə $ ˈɑːrbɪtər/ n [C] **1** someone who
influences society's opinions about what is STYLISH,
socially acceptable etc: *The designer has received rave
reviews from such **arbiters** of taste as Elle magazine.* **2** someone or something that settles an argument between two opposing sides; ▣ **judge**: *The
European Court of Justice will be **the final arbiter***
(=make the final decision) *in the dispute.*

ar·bi·trage /ˈɑːbɪtrɑːʒ $ ˈɑːr-/ n [U] technical the
process of buying something such as raw materials or
CURRENCY in one place and selling them immediately in
another place in order to make a profit from the
difference in prices —**arbitrageur** /ˌɑːbɪtrɑːˈʒɜː
$ ˌɑːrbɪtrɑːˈʒɜːr/ also **arbitrager** BrE /ˈɑːbɪtrɑːʒə
$ ˈɑːrbɪtrɑːʒər/ n [C]

ar·bi·tra·ry /ˈɑːbɪtrəri, -tri $ ˈɑːrbɪtreri/ adj decided
or arranged without any reason or plan, often unfairly:
*an **arbitrary** decision* | *the **arbitrary** arrests of
political opponents* —**arbitrariness** n [U]
—**arbitrarily** /ˈɑːbɪtrərˌli $ ˌɑːrbɪˈtrerˌli/ adv: *an arbi-
trarily chosen number*

ar·bi·trate /ˈɑːbɪtreɪt $ ˈɑːr-/ v [I,T] to officially judge
how an argument between two opposing sides should
be settled: [+**between**] *A committee will arbitrate
between management and unions.* | [+**in**] *The tribunal
has the power to arbitrate in disputes.* —**arbitrator** n
[C]

ar·bi·tra·tion /ˌɑːbɪˈtreɪʃən $ ˌɑːr-/ n [U] the process
of judging officially how an argument should be
settled: *The dispute is **going to arbitration*** (=someone
is being asked to arbitrate). | *Both sides in the dispute
have agreed to **binding arbitration**.*

ar·bo·re·al /ɑːˈbɔːriəl $ ɑːr-/ adj technical or literary
relating to trees, or living in trees

ar·bo·re·tum /ˌɑːbəˈriːtəm $ ˌɑːr-/ n plural **arbore-
tums** or **arboreta** /-tə/ [C] a place where trees are
grown for scientific study

ar·bour BrE; **arbor** AmE /ˈɑːbə $ ˈɑːrbər/ n [C] a
shelter in a garden made by making plants grow
together on a frame shaped like an ARCH

arc /ɑːk $ ɑːrk/ n [C] **1** a curved shape or line: *the arc
of a rainbow* **2** part of a curved line or a circle: *The
sun moves across the sky in an arc.* **3** a flash of light
formed by the flow of electricity between two points
—**arc** v [T]

ar·cade /ɑːˈkeɪd $ ɑːr-/ n [C] **1** a covered passage at
the side of a row of buildings with PILLARS and ARCHES
supporting it on one side **2** a covered passage
between two streets with shops on each side of
it **3** BrE also **shopping arcade** a large building or part
of a building where there are many shops **4** an
AMUSEMENT ARCADE: *arcade games*

arˈcade ˌgame n [C] a type of electronic game that
was first popular in AMUSEMENT ARCADES (=a place where
you play games by putting coins in machines) in the
early 1980s, but is now usually played on a computer

ar·cane /ɑːˈkeɪn $ ɑːr-/ adj secret and known or
understood by only a few people: *the arcane language of
the law*

arch

arches of an aqueduct

arch¹ ▣ /ɑːtʃ $ ɑːrtʃ/ n [C]
1 a structure with a curved top and straight sides that
supports the weight of a bridge or building
2 a curved structure above a door, window etc
3 a curved structure of bones in the middle of your foot
4 something with a curved top and straight sides

arch² v [I,T] to form or make something form a curved
shape: *Two rows of trees arched over the driveway.* | *The
dog **arched** its back.*

arch³ adj amused because you think you understand
something better than other people: *'I think he's in for
a surprise,' Ian said, in a somewhat arch tone.* —**archly**
adv

arch- /ɑːtʃ, ɑːk $ ɑːrtʃ, ɑːrk/ prefix belonging to the
highest class or rank: *an archbishop* (=an important
BISHOP) | *our archenemy* (=our worst enemy) | *the
company's arch-rivals* (=main competitors)

ar·chae·ol·o·gy also **archeology** AmE /ˌɑːkiˈɒlədʒi
$ ˌɑːrkiˈɑː-/ n [U] the study of ancient societies by
examining what remains of their buildings, GRAVES,
tools etc —**archaeologist** n —**archaeological**
/ˌɑːkiəˈlɒdʒɪkəl◂ $ ˌɑːrkiəˈlɑː-/ adj: *an archaeological
site* —**archaeologically** /-kli/ adv

ar·cha·ic /ɑːˈkeɪ-ɪk $ ɑːr-/ adj **1** old and no longer
used; ▣ **outdated**; ▨ **modern**: *archaic words* **2** old-
fashioned and needing to be replaced: *Many smaller
radio stations broadcast on archaic equipment.* **3** from or relating to ancient times: *archaic
civilizations*

ar·cha·is·m /ˈɑːkeɪ-ɪzəm, ɑːˈkeɪ- $ ˈɑːrki-/ n [C] an
old word or phrase that is no longer used

arch·an·gel /ˈɑːkeɪndʒəl $ ˈɑːrk-/ n [C] one of the
most important ANGELS in the Jewish, Christian, and
Muslim religions

arch·bish·op /ˌɑːtʃˈbɪʃəp◂ $ ˌɑːrtʃ-/ n [C] a priest of
the highest rank, who is in charge of all the churches
in a particular area

arch·bish·op·ric /ˌɑːtʃˈbɪʃəprɪk $ ˌɑːrtʃ-/ n
[C] **1** the area governed by an archbishop **2** the
rank of archbishop

arch·dea·con /ˌɑːtʃˈdiːkən◂ $ ˌɑːrtʃ-/ n [C] a priest
of a high rank in the Anglican church who works under
a BISHOP

arch·di·o·cese /ˌɑːtʃˈdaɪəsˌs, -siːs $ ˌɑːrtʃ-/ n [C]
the area that is governed by an archbishop

arch·duke /ˌɑːtʃˈdjuːk◂ $ ˌɑːrtʃˈduːk◂ / n [C] a prince
who belonged to the royal family of Austria

arch·en·e·my /ˌɑːtʃˈenˌmi $ ˌɑːrtʃ-/ n plural **arch-
enemies** [C] the main enemy

ar·che·ol·o·gy /ˌɑːkiˈɒlədʒi $ ˌɑːrkiˈɑː-/ n [U] an
American spelling of ARCHAEOLOGY

ar·cher /ˈɑːtʃə $ ˈɑːrtʃər/ n [C] someone who shoots
ARROWS from a BOW

ar·cher·y /ˈɑːtʃəri $ ˈɑːr-/ n [U] the sport of shooting
ARROWS from a BOW → see picture at OUTDOOR

ar·che·type /ˈɑːkɪtaɪp $ ˈɑːr-/ n [C usually singular] a
perfect example of something, because it has all the

most important qualities of things that belong to that type: [+of] *France is the archetype of the centralized nation-state.* —**archetypal** /ˌɑːkɪˈtaɪpəl◂ $ ˌɑːr-/ *adj: Byron was the archetypal Romantic hero.*

ar·chi·pel·a·go /ˌɑːkɪˈpeləɡəʊ $ ˌɑːrkɪˈpeləɡoʊ/ *n plural* **archipelagos** [C] a group of small islands

ar·chi·tect W3 /ˈɑːkɪtekt $ ˈɑːr-/ *n* [C]
1 someone whose job is to design buildings
2 the architect of sth the person who originally thought of an important and successful idea: *Tinoco was one of the architects of the government's economic reforms.*

ar·chi·tec·ture S3 W3 /ˈɑːkɪtektʃə $ ˈɑːrkɪtektʃər/ *n*
1 [U] the style and design of a building or buildings: [+of] *the architecture of Venice* | **modern/classical/medieval etc architecture**
2 [U] the art and practice of planning and designing buildings: *He studied architecture at university.*
3 [U] the structure of something: *the architecture of DNA*
4 [C,U] *technical* the structure of a computer system and the way it works —**architectural** /ˌɑːkɪˈtektʃərəl◂ $ ˌɑːr-/ *adj: architectural features* —**architecturally** *adv: Architecturally, Chengdu is quite different from most of China.*

ar·chive[1] /ˈɑːkaɪv $ ˈɑːr-/ *n* [C] **1** a place where a large number of historical records are stored, or the records that are stored: *an archive of the writer's unpublished work* **2** *technical* copies of a computer's FILES that are stored on a DISK or in the computer's memory in a way that uses less space than usual, so that the computer can keep them for a long time —**archive** *adj: interesting archive material* —**archival** /ɑːˈkaɪvəl $ ɑːr-/ *adj: archival footage of the President's visit in 1969*

archive[2] *v* [T] **1** to put documents, books, information etc in an archive **2** to save a computer FILE in a way that uses less space than usual, because you do not use that file often but may need it in the future —**archiving** *n* [U]: *electronic archiving systems*

ar·chi·vist /ˈɑːkɪvɪst $ ˈɑːr-/ *n* [C] someone who works in an archive

arch·way /ˈɑːtʃweɪ $ ˈɑːrtʃ-/ *n* [C] a passage or entrance under an ARCH or arches: *He was standing in the archway outside the club.*

-archy /əki, ɑːki $ ərki, ɑːrki/ *suffix* [in nouns] used to talk about a particular type of government: *anarchy* (=no government) | *monarchy* (=having a king or queen)

Arc·tic, **arctic** /ˈɑːktɪk $ ˈɑːrk-/ *adj* [only before noun] **1** relating to the most northern part of the world; → **Antarctic**: *the Arctic island of Novaya Zemlya* **2** extremely cold: *arctic conditions*

arc 'welding *n* [U] a method of joining two pieces of metal together by heating them with a special tool

-ard /əd $ ərd/ *suffix* [in nouns] someone who is usually or always in a particular state: *a drunkard*

ar·dent /ˈɑːdənt $ ˈɑːr-/ *adj* [usually before noun] **1** showing strong positive feelings about an activity and determination to succeed at it: *an ardent supporter of free trade* **2** *literary* showing strong feelings of love: *an ardent lover* —**ardently** *adv*

ar·dour *BrE*; **ardor** *AmE* /ˈɑːdə $ ˈɑːrdər/ *n* [U] **1** very strong admiration or excitement: *with ardour They sang with real ardour.* **2** *literary* strong feelings of love

ar·du·ous /ˈɑːdjuəs $ ˈɑːrdʒuəs/ *adj* involving a lot of strength and effort: **arduous task/work** *the arduous task of loading all the boxes into the van* | **arduous journey/voyage** *an arduous journey through the mountains* —**arduously** *adv*

are /ə; *strong* ɑː $ ər; *strong* ɑːr/ *v* the present tense and plural of 'be'

ar·e·a S1 W1 /ˈeəriə $ ˈeriə/ *n* [C]
1 a particular part of a country, town etc: **in an area** *Only cheeses made in this area may be labelled*

'Roquefort.' | *There were over 2 inches of rain in **coastal** **areas**.* | [+of] *a **working-class area** of Birmingham* | *Many areas of Africa have suffered severe drought this year.* | *a **rural area** (=countryside) of woodlands and fields* | *Crime rates are significantly higher in **urban areas** (=towns, cities etc).* | *The police have searched the farm and the **surrounding area** (=the area around it).* | *children from the **local area*** | *a **residential area** of the town*
2 a part of a house, office, garden etc that is used for a particular purpose: *a **no-smoking area*** | *Their apartment has a large **kitchen area**.* | *Come through into the **dining area**.* | *the **reception area** of the hotel* | *a **storage area** on the ground floor*
3 a particular subject, range of activities, or group of related subjects: *The course covers three main **subject areas**.* | *This study has clearly identified a major **problem area** for the National Health Service.* | *We're funding research into new areas such as law enforcement technology.* | [+of] *reforms in the **key areas** of health and education*
4 the amount of space that a flat surface or shape covers: [+of] *an area of 2,000 square miles* | *a formula to calculate the area of a circle* → **grey area** at GREY[1] (7)

'area ˌcode *n* [C] numbers you use before a phone number when you phone someone in a different area of the country

a·re·na /əˈriːnə/ *n* [C] **1** a building with a large flat central area surrounded by seats, where sports or entertainments take place: *a **sports arena*** | *an **indoor arena*** **2** the political/international/public etc arena all the activities and people connected with politics, public life etc: *Women are entering the political arena in larger numbers.* | *American economic activity in the international arena*

aren't /ɑːnt $ ɑːrənt/ *v* **a)** the short form of 'are not': *They aren't here.* **b)** the short form of 'am not', used in questions: *I'm in big trouble, aren't I?*

Ar·gen·tin·i·an[1] /ˌɑːdʒənˈtɪniən◂ $ ˌɑːr-/ *also* **Ar·gen·tine** /ˈɑːdʒəntaɪn, -tiːn $ ˈɑːr-/ *adj* relating to Argentina or its people

Argentinian[2] *also* **Argentine** *n* [C] someone from Argentina

ar·gon /ˈɑːɡɒn $ ˈɑːrɡɑːn/ *n* [U] a colourless gas that is found in very small quantities in the air and is sometimes used in electric light BULBS. It is a chemical ELEMENT: symbol Ar

ar·got /ˈɑːɡəʊ $ ˈɑːrɡət/ *n* [C,U] *written* expressions used by a particular group of people; ⊟ **jargon**: *teenage argot*

ar·gu·a·ble /ˈɑːɡjuəbəl $ ˈɑːr-/ *adj* **1** not certain, or not definitely true or correct, and therefore easy to doubt; ⊟ **debatable**: *Whether or not Webb is the best person for the job is arguable.* **2 it is arguable that** used in order to give good reasons why something might be true: *It's arguable that the legislation has had little effect on young people's behaviour.*

ar·gu·a·bly /ˈɑːɡjuəbli $ ˈɑːr-/ *adv* [sentence adverb] used when giving your opinion to say that there are good reasons why something might be true: *Senna was arguably the greatest racing driver of all time.*

ar·gue S1 W1 /ˈɑːɡjuː $ ˈɑːr-/ *v*
1 [I] to disagree with someone in words, often in an angry way: *We could hear the neighbours arguing.* | [+with] *Gallacher continued to argue with the referee throughout the game.* | [+about] *They were arguing about how to spend the money.* | [+over] *The children were arguing over which TV programme to watch.*
2 [I,T] to state, giving clear reasons, that something is true, should be done etc: **argue that** *Croft argued that a date should be set for the withdrawal of troops.* | *It could be argued that a dam might actually increase the risk of flooding.* | **argue for/against (doing) sth** *Baker argued against cutting the military budget.* | *She*

A

argued the case for changing the law. | *The researchers put forward a well-argued case for banning the drug.* | They **argued the point** (=discussed it) *for hours without reaching a conclusion.*
3 argue sb into/out of doing sth *BrE* to persuade someone to do or not do something: *Joyce argued me into buying a new jacket.*
4 [T] *formal* to show that something clearly exists or is true: *The statement argues a change of attitude by the management.*
5 argue the toss *BrE informal* to continue to argue about a decision that has been made and cannot be changed: *There was no point arguing the toss after the goal had been disallowed.*

WORD FOCUS: ARGUE
synonyms: **fight, quarrel, have a row** *BrE*
to argue about unimportant things: **squabble, bicker, quibble**
to stop arguing: **bury the hatchet, settle your differences, make your peace with sb, make it up** (used about friends or lovers)

ar·gu·ment S1 W1 /'ɑːgjᵿmənt $ 'ɑːr-/ n
1 [C] a situation in which two or more people disagree, often angrily; ▤ **disagreement**: [+with] *I broke the vase during an argument with my husband.* | [+about/ over] *an argument about who was responsible for the accident* | *Henning told the police that she and her husband had an argument before he left.* | *I got into an argument with the other driver.* | *Shelton and the woman had a heated argument* (=very angry one). | *a fierce argument between the two politicians* | **win/lose an argument** *The party hopes to win the argument about how to reform the health system.*
2 [C] a set of reasons that show that something is true or untrue, right or wrong etc: *We need to provide a convincing argument as to why the system should be changed.* | [+for/against] *a powerful argument against smoking* | *A good argument can be made for comparing the IT revolution with the invention of writing itself.* | *the arguments in favour of banning tobacco advertising* | *argument that the familiar argument that the costs outweigh the benefits*
3 [U] when you disagree with something or question whether it is right: **do sth without (further) argument** *Ian accepted the suggestion without argument.* | **for the sake of argument** (=in order to discuss all the possibilities) *If, for the sake of argument, you aren't offered the job, what will you do?*

ar·gu·men·ta·tive /ˌɑːgjᵿ'mentətɪv◂ $ ˌɑːr-/ adj someone who is argumentative often argues or likes arguing: *He quickly becomes argumentative after a few drinks.*

ar·gy-bar·gy /ˌɑːdʒi 'bɑːdʒi $ ˌɑːrdʒi 'bɑːr-/ n [U] *BrE informal* noisy arguments or quarrelling: *Jones was sent off after a bit of argy-bargy with other players.*

a·ri·a /'ɑːriə/ n [C] a song that is sung by only one person in an OPERA or ORATORIO

-arian /eəriən $ eriən/ suffix **1** [in nouns] someone who believes in or does a particular thing: *a vegetarian* (=someone who does not eat meat) | *a librarian* (=someone who works in a library) **2** [in adjectives] for people of this type, or relating to them: *a vegetarian restaurant*

ar·id /'ærᵻd/ adj **1** arid land or an arid CLIMATE is very dry because it has very little rain: *Water from the Great Lakes is pumped to arid regions.* **2** not having any new, interesting, or exciting features or qualities: *My mind was arid, all inspiration gone.* —**aridity** /ə'rɪdᵻti/ n [U]

Ar·ies /'eəriːz, 'eəri-iːz $ 'eriːz/ n **1** [U] the first sign of the ZODIAC, represented by a RAM (=male sheep), which some people believe affects the character and life of people born between March 21 and April 20 **2** [C] someone who was born between March 21 and April 20

a·right /ə'raɪt/ adv *BrE old use* **1** correctly: *I was not certain I had heard aright.* **2 set things aright** to deal with problems or difficulties

a·rise S3 W2 /ə'raɪz/ v *past tense* **arose** /ə'rəʊz $ ə'roʊz/ *past participle* **arisen** /ə'rɪzən/ [I]
1 if a problem or difficult situation arises, it begins to happen: *A crisis has arisen in the Foreign Office.* | *More problems like those at the nuclear power plant are certain to arise.*
2 if something arises from or out of a situation, event etc, it is caused or started by that situation etc: *Several important legal questions arose in the contract negotiations.* | [+from/out of] *Can we begin by discussing matters arising from the last meeting?*
3 when/if the need arises also **should the need arise** *formal* when or if it is necessary: *Should the need arise for extra staff, we will contact you.*
4 *literary* to get out of bed, or stand up
5 *literary* if a group of people arise, they fight for or demand something they want
6 *literary* if something arises when you are moving towards it, you are gradually able to see it as you move closer

ar·is·toc·ra·cy /ˌærᵻ'stɒkrəsi $ -'stɑː-/ n *plural* **aristocracies** [C usually singular] the people in the highest social class, who traditionally have a lot of land, money, and power: *dukes, earls, and other members of the aristocracy* | *the landed aristocracy* (=who own a lot of land) → **UPPER CLASS**

ar·is·to·crat /'ærᵻstəkræt, ə'rɪs- $ ə'rɪs-/ n [C] someone who belongs to the highest social class

ar·is·to·crat·ic /ˌærᵻstə'krætɪk◂, ə,rɪs- $ ə,rɪs-/ adj belonging to or typical of the aristocracy; ▤ **noble**: **aristocratic society** | *an aristocratic family*

a·rith·me·tic¹ /ə'rɪθmətɪk/ n [U] the science of numbers involving adding, multiplying etc; → **mathematics**

ar·ith·met·ic² /ˌærɪθ'metɪk◂/ also **ar·ith·met·i·cal** /-tɪkəl/ adj *technical* involving or related to arithmetic: *the arithmetic mean* (=average) —**arithmetically** /-kli/ adv

arithmetic pro'gression n [C] a set of numbers in order of value in which a particular number is added to each to produce the next (as in 2, 4, 6, 8, ...); → **geometric progression**

ark /ɑːk $ ɑːrk/ n [C] **1** a large ship **2 the Ark** in the Bible, the large boat built by Noah to save his family and the animals from a flood that covered the earth

arm¹ S1 W1 /ɑːm $ ɑːrm/ n [C]
1 BODY one of the two long parts of your body between your shoulders and your hands: *Dave has a broken arm.* | **left/right arm** *He had a tattoo on his left arm.* | *Tim's mother put her arms around him.* | *Pat was carrying a box under his arm.* | *He had a pile of books in his arms.* | *They walked along the beach arm in arm* (=with their arms bent around each other's). | **take sb by the arm** (=lead someone somewhere by holding their arm) *She took him by the arm and pushed him out of the door.* | **take sb in your arms** (=gently hold someone with your arms) *Gerry took Fiona in his arms and kissed her.* | **cross/fold your arms** (=bend your arms so that they are resting on top of each other against your body) *He folded his arms and leaned back in his chair.* | *The old lady rushed to greet him, arms outstretched.*
2 WEAPONS **arms** [plural] weapons used for fighting wars: *Sales of arms to the Middle East have dramatically increased.* | **nuclear arms** | **the arms trade** | **an arms dealer** | *The government is cutting arms expenditure.* | *The United Nations will lift its arms embargo against the country.* | **take up arms** (=get weapons and fight) *Boys as young as 13 are taking up arms to defend the city.* | *He appealed for the rebels to lay down their arms* (=stop fighting). | **under arms** (=with weapons and ready to fight) *All available forces are under arms.* → **small arms** at SMALL¹ (15)

3 FURNITURE the part of a chair, SOFA etc that you rest your arms on

4 CLOTHING the part of a piece of clothing that covers your arm; **≡** sleeve

5 be up in arms to be very angry and ready to argue or fight: *Residents are up in arms about plans for a new road along the beach.*

6 with open arms if you do something with open arms, you show that you are happy to see someone or eager to accept an idea, plan etc: *We welcomed Henry's offer with open arms.* | *My new in-laws accepted me with open arms.*

7 sb would give their right arm to do sth used to say that someone would be willing to do anything to get or do something because they want it very much: *I'd give my right arm to be 21 again.*

8 hold sth at arm's length to hold something away from your body

9 keep/hold sb at arm's length to avoid developing a relationship with someone: *Petra keeps all men at arm's length to avoid getting hurt.*

10 as long as your arm *informal* a list or written document that is as long as your arm is very long: *I've got a list of things to do as long as your arm.*

11 PART OF GROUP a part of a large group that is responsible for a particular type of activity: *the political arm of a terrorist organization* | *Epson America is the US marketing arm of a Japanese company.*

12 OBJECT/MACHINE a long part of an object or piece of equipment: *the arm of a record player* | *There is a 15-foot arm supporting the antenna.*

13 on sb's arm *old-fashioned* if a man has a woman on his arm, she is standing beside him holding his arm

14 DESIGN arms [plural] a set of pictures or patterns, usually painted on a SHIELD, that is used as the special sign of a family, town, university etc; **≡** coat of arms → arms akimbo at AKIMBO (1); → babe in arms at BABE (1); → brothers in arms at BROTHER¹ (6); → cost an arm and a leg at COST² (1); → fold sb/sth in your arms at FOLD¹ (7); → twist sb's arm at TWIST¹ (9)

arm² *v* [T] **1** to provide weapons for yourself, an army, a country etc in order to prepare for a fight or a war: **arm sb with sth** *The local farmers have armed themselves with rifles and pistols.* | *The rebels armed a group of 2000 men to attack the city.* → ARMED, UNARMED **2** to provide all the information, skills, or equipment you need to do something; **≡** equip: **arm sb with sth** *Arm yourself with all the facts you need to argue your case.* | *The guidebook arms the reader with a mass of useful information.*

ar·ma·da /ɑːˈmɑːdə $ ɑːr-/ *n* [C] a large group of things, especially ships or boats: *an armada of US naval vessels*

ar·ma·dil·lo /ˌɑːməˈdɪləʊ $ ˌɑːrməˈdɪloʊ/ *n plural* **armadillos** [C] a small animal that has a shell made of hard material, and lives in parts of North and South America

Ar·ma·ged·don /ˌɑːməˈɡedn $ ˌɑːr-/ *n* [singular, U] a terrible battle that will destroy the world: *a nuclear Armageddon*

ar·ma·ment /ˈɑːməmənt $ ˈɑːr-/ *n* **1** [C usually plural] the weapons and military equipment used by an army: *nuclear armaments* **2** [U] the process of preparing an army or country for war by giving it weapons; → disarmament

ar·ma·ture /ˈɑːmətʃə $ ˈɑːrmətʃər/ *n* [C] *technical* **1** the part of a GENERATOR, motor etc that turns around to produce electricity, movement etc **2** a frame that you cover with clay or other soft material to make a model

arm·band /ˈɑːmbænd $ ˈɑːrm-/ *n* [C] **1** a band of material that you wear around your arm to show that you have an official position, or as a sign of MOURNING **2** [usually plural] *BrE* one of two bands of plastic filled with air that you wear around your arms when you are learning to swim

arm·chair¹ /ˈɑːmtʃeə, ˌɑːmˈtʃeə $ ˈɑːrmtʃer, ˌɑːrmˈtʃer/ *n* [C] a comfortable chair with sides that you can rest your arms on → see picture at CHAIR¹

arm·chair² /ˈɑːmtʃeə $ ˈɑːrmtʃer/ *adj* **armchair traveller/fan etc** someone who talks or reads about being a traveller, or watches sport on television but does not have any real experience of doing it: *Her books about her adventures give enjoyment and inspiration to armchair travellers.* | *Armchair fans will have to pay extra to watch the best games live.*

armed S3 W3 /ɑːmd $ ɑːrmd/ *adj*
1 carrying weapons, especially a gun; **⬛** unarmed: **armed police** | *The Minister was kidnapped by armed men* on his way to the airport. | *The prisoners were kept under armed guard.* | [+with] *The suspect is armed with a shotgun.* | *She got ten years in prison for armed robbery* (=stealing using a gun). | *The President fears that armed conflict* (=a war) *is possible.* | *There is very little support for an armed struggle* (=fighting with weapons) *against the government.* | *a heavily armed battleship* | *Many of the gangs are armed to the teeth* (=carrying a lot of weapons).
2 having the knowledge, skills, or equipment you need to do something: [+with] *She came to the meeting armed with all the facts and figures to prove us wrong.* | *I went out, armed with my binoculars, to see what I could find in the fields.*

armed 'forces *n* the armed forces [plural] a country's military organizations, including the army, navy, and AIR FORCE

arm·ful /ˈɑːmfʊl $ ˈɑːrm-/ *n* [C] the amount of something that you can hold in one or both arms: [+of] *an armful of books*

arm·hole /ˈɑːmhəʊl $ ˈɑːrmhoʊl/ *n* [C] a hole in a shirt, dress, jacket etc that you put your arm through

ar·mi·stice /ˈɑːmɪstɪs $ ˈɑːrm-/ *n* [C] an agreement to stop fighting; → ceasefire, truce

arm·lock /ˈɑːmlɒk $ ˈɑːrmlɑːk/ *n* [C] a way in which a WRESTLER holds an opponent's arm so that he or she cannot move

ar·moire /ɑːmˈwɑː $ ɑːrmˈwɑːr/ *n* [C] *AmE* a large piece of furniture with doors, and sometimes shelves, that you hang clothes in; **≡** wardrobe *BrE*

ar·mour *BrE*; **armor** *AmE* /ˈɑːmə $ ˈɑːrmər/ *n* [U] **1** metal or leather clothing that protects your body, worn by soldiers in battles in past times: *a knight wearing a suit of armour* **2** a strong metal layer that protects military vehicles: *armour-clad warships* **3** a strong layer or shell that protects some plants and animals → **a chink in sb's armour** at CHINK (3); → **a knight in shining armour** at KNIGHT¹ (4)

ar·moured *BrE*; **armored** *AmE* /ˈɑːməd $ ˈɑːrmərd/ *adj* **1** armoured vehicles have an outside layer of metal to protect them from attack: *armored personnel carriers* **2** an armoured army uses armoured vehicles: *an armoured division*

armoured 'car *BrE*; **armored car** *AmE* *n* [C] **1** a military vehicle with a strong metal cover and usually a powerful gun **2** a car that has special protection from bullets etc, used especially by important people

ar·mour·er *BrE*; **armorer** *AmE* /ˈɑːmərə $ ˈɑːrmərər/ *n* [C] someone who makes or repairs weapons and ARMOUR

armour-'plated *BrE*; **armor-plated** *AmE* *adj* something, especially a vehicle, that is armour-plated has an outer metal layer to protect it —**armour plating** *n* [U] —**armour plate** *n* [U]

ar·mour·y *BrE*; **armory** *AmE* /ˈɑːməri $ ˈɑːr-/ *n plural* **armouries** [C] **1** a place where weapons are stored **2** all the skills, information etc someone has available to achieve something: *Interest rates have become powerful weapons in the government's armoury.*

arm·pit /ˈɑːmˌpɪt $ ˈɑːrm-/ *n* [C] **1** the hollow place under your arm where it joins your body **2** the armpit

of sth *AmE informal* the ugliest or worst place in a particular city or area: *Dale says Butte is the armpit of Montana.*

'arms con,trol *n* [U] the attempts by powerful countries to limit the number and types of war weapons that exist

'arms race *n* [C usually singular] the competition between different countries to have a larger number of powerful weapons: *the nuclear arms race*

ar·my [S1] [W1] /'ɑːmi $ 'ɑːr-/ *n plural* **armies**
1 the army [also + plural verb *BrE*] the part of a country's military force that is trained to fight on land in a war: *The army are helping to clear up after the floods.* | *an army officer.* | *Army units launched attacks on bases near Jounieh port.* | *He joined the army when he was 17.* | **in the army** *Both my sons are in the army.*
2 [C] a large organized group of people trained to fight on land in a war: *Rebel armies have taken control of the radio station.* | **raise an army** (=collect together and organize an army to fight a battle) *The Slovenians say they can raise an army of 20,000 men.*
3 [C] a large number of people involved in the same activity: [+of] *The village hall is maintained by an army of volunteers.*

> **WORD FOCUS: ARMY**
> *similar words:* **armed forces, the military, the services**
> *people in the army:* **soldier, troops, infantry, G.I.** *AmE old-fashioned,* **squaddy** *BrE*
> *to join the army:* **join up/enlist**
> *to leave the army:* **be discharged, desert** (without permission) | **go A.W.O.L.** (without permission)
> *to make people serve in the armed forces:* **call up** *BrE*/ **draft** *AmE*
> *the system of making people serve in the armed forces:* **conscription, military service, the draft** *AmE,* **national service** *BrE*
> *relating to the armed forces:* **military**
> → navy, air force, marine corps, court-martial

A-road /'eɪ rəʊd $ -roʊd/ *n* [C] a type of road in Britain that is smaller than a MOTORWAY, but larger than a B-ROAD
a·ro·ma /ə'rəʊmə $ ə'roʊ-/ *n* [C] a strong pleasant smell: *the aroma of fresh coffee*
a·ro·ma·ther·a·py /ə,rəʊmə'θerəpi $ ə,roʊ-/ *n* [U] a treatment that uses MASSAGE (=rubbing the body) with pleasant smelling natural oils to reduce pain and make you feel well —**aromatherapist** *n* [C]
ar·o·mat·ic /,ærə'mætɪk◂/ *adj* having a strong pleasant smell; ☐ **fragrant:** *aromatic oils* | *aromatic herbs*
a·rose /ə'rəʊz $ ə'roʊz/ the past tense of ARISE
a·round [S1] [W1] /ə'raʊnd/ *adv, prep*
1 surrounding or on all sides of something or someone; ☐ **round** *BrE: The whole family was sitting around the dinner table.* | *The Romans built a defensive wall around the city.* | *She wore a beautiful silk shawl around her shoulders.* | *People crowded around to see what was happening.* | *We would hear the birds singing all around us.*
2 moving in a circle; ☐ **round** *BrE: A helicopter was circling around, looking for somewhere to land.* | *They danced around the bonfire.*
3 in or to many places or parts of an area; ☐ **about** *BrE: He wandered around the streets, looking in shop windows.* | *There are over 40 radio stations dotted around the country.* | *When I finished college, I travelled around for a while before I got my first job.* | *Since it's your first day here, would you like me to show you around?* | *We started looking around for somewhere to live.*
4 a) *BrE* in an area near a place or person, **round:** *Is there a bank around here?* | *When you've been around a person long enough, you start to know how they'll react.* | *the new housing areas in and around Dublin* | *Catherine was the most beautiful girl for miles around.*
b) if someone or something is around, they are somewhere in the place where you are: *Why is there never a policeman around when you need one?* | *Jake went down*

to the bar, but there was no-one around that he knew. | *Is your dad around?* | *The list is somewhere around.*
5 *BrE* on the other side of something, or to the other side of it without going through it or over it; ☐ **round** *BrE: If the gate's locked, you'll have to go around the side of the house.* | *There's a door around the back.* | *She ran around the corner and straight into the arms of John Delaney.*
6 used to say that someone or something turns so that they face in the opposite direction; ☐ **round** *BrE: Rex spun around and kicked the gun from her hand.* | *Slowly he turned the boat around towards the open sea.*
7 also **around about** used when guessing a number, amount, time etc, without being exact: *There must have been around 40,000 people in the stadium.* | *The whole project will probably cost around $3 million.* | *Most guests started to make their way home around about ten o'clock.*
8 existing; ☐ **about** *BrE: That joke's been around for years.* | *Manson has a reputation as one of the most stylish designers around.*
9 if something is organized around a particular person or thing, it is organized according to their needs, wishes, ideas etc: *Why does everything have to be arranged around what Callum wants to do?* | *Their whole society was built around their religious beliefs.*
10 used to show that someone spends time in a place without doing anything useful; ☐ **about** *BrE: I've been waiting around all morning.* | *They could be seen hanging around street corners, watching the girls go by.*
11 a way around a difficult situation or problem is a way to solve it or avoid it; ☐ **round** *BrE: We must find a way around these difficulties.* | *The company is expected to get around this problem by borrowing from the banks.*
12 to other people or positions; ☐ **round** *BrE: Write your name on this list and pass it around.* | *Someone's been moving the furniture around.*
13 have been around *informal* **a)** to have had experience of many different situations so that you can deal with new situations confidently: *You could tell this guy had been around a bit by the knowing way he talked.* **b)** to have had many sexual experiences – used humorously
14 *AmE* used to show the length of a line surrounding something: *Redwood trees can measure 30 or 40 feet around.* → ROUND[1]; → **get around (sth)** at GET AROUND (1); → **go around in circles** at CIRCLE[1] (5)

,around-the-'clock *adj* [only before noun] ROUND-THE-CLOCK
a·rous·al /ə'raʊzəl/ *n* [U] excitement, especially sexual excitement
a·rouse /ə'raʊz/ *v* [T] **1 arouse interest/expectations etc** to make you become interested, expect something etc: *Matt's behavior was arousing the interest of the neighbors.* **2 arouse hostility/suspicion/resentment/anger etc** to make someone feel very unfriendly and angry, or SUSPICIOUS: *A great deal of anger was aroused by Campbell's decision.* **3** to make someone feel sexually excited; ☐ **excite:** *She felt aroused by the pressure of his body so close to hers.* **4** *literary* to wake someone: [+from] *Anne had to be aroused from a deep sleep.*
ar·peg·gi·o /ɑː'pedʒiəʊ $ ɑːr'pedʒioʊ/ *n plural* **arpeggios** [C] the notes of a musical CHORD played separately but quickly one after the other
arr. also **arr** *BrE* **1** the written abbreviation of **arranged by:** *music by Mozart, arr. Britten* **2** the written abbreviation of **arrives** or **arrival**
ar·raign /ə'reɪn/ *v* [T] *law* to make someone come to court to hear what their crime is: **arraign sb on sth** *Thompson was arraigned on a charge of murder.* —**arraignment** *n* [C,U]
ar·range [S2] [W2] /ə'reɪndʒ/ *v*
1 [I,T] to organize or make plans for something such as a meeting, party, or trip: *Contact your local branch to arrange an appointment.* | *I'd like to arrange a business loan.* | **arrange to do sth** *Have you arranged to meet Mark this weekend?* | **arrange sth with sb** *Beth arranged a meeting with the marketing director.* | **arrange when/**

where/how etc *We still have to arrange how to get home.* | **arrange that** *We had arranged that I would go for the weekend.* | *Matthew arrived at 2 o'clock as arranged.*
2 [I,T] to make it possible for someone to have or do something: **arrange for sth** *The company will arrange for a taxi to meet you at the airport.* | **arrange for sb to do sth** *Dave arranged for someone to drive him home.*
3 [T] to put a group of things or people in a particular order or position: *Ben arranged the flowers in a vase.* | *The list is arranged alphabetically.* | **arrange sth in pairs/groups etc** *The children were arranged in lines according to height.*
4 [T] to write or change a piece of music so that it is suitable for a particular instrument: **arrange sth for sth** *a symphony arranged for the piano*

ar‚ranged ˈmarriage *n* [C,U] a marriage in which your parents choose a husband or wife for you

ar·range·ment S2 W2 /əˈreɪndʒmənt/ *n*
1 PLAN [C usually plural] plans and preparations that you must make so that something can happen: [+for] *I've agreed to help with arrangements for the party.* | *The family are making arrangements for his funeral.* | *Special arrangements can be made for guests with disabilities.* | *The hotel was full so we had to make alternative arrangements.* | *travel arrangements*
2 AGREEMENT [C,U] something that has been organized or agreed on; **■ agreement**: [+between] *An arrangement between the two couples ensured there was always someone to look after the children.* | [+with] *The school has an arrangement with local businesses.* | **an arrangement to do sth** *Maxine cancelled our arrangement to meet.* | **come to an/some arrangement (with sb)** (=make an agreement that is acceptable to everyone) *It would usually cost $500, but I'm sure we can come to some kind of arrangement.* | *Pets are permitted at the resort by prior arrangement.*
3 WAY STH IS ORGANIZED [C usually plural] the way in which something is organized: *The airport is currently reviewing its security arrangements.* | *domestic arrangements*
4 POSITION [C,U] a group of things that are put in a particular position, or the process of doing this: [+of] *the traditional arrangement of desks in rows* | *a beautiful flower arrangement*
5 MUSIC [C] a piece of music that has been written or changed for a particular instrument: *a piano arrangement of an old folk song*

ar·rang·er /əˈreɪndʒə $ -ər/ *n* [C] **1** someone who changes music that has been written by someone else so that it is suitable for a particular instrument or performance **2** someone who arranges things for other people

ar·rant /ˈærənt/ *adj formal* used to emphasize how bad something is: *What arrant nonsense!*

ar·ray¹ /əˈreɪ/ *n* [C] **1** [usually singular] a group of people or things, especially one that is large or impressive: [+of] *a dazzling array of flowers* | *a bewildering array of options* | **a vast/impressive/wide array** *There was a vast array of colours to choose from.* **2** *technical* a set of numbers or signs, or of computer memory units, arranged in lines across or down

array² *v* [T usually passive] **1** *literary* to wear particular clothes, especially clothes of good quality: **arrayed in sth** | *She came in arrayed in all her finery.* **2** *literary* to arrange something in an attractive way: **arrayed on sth** *make-up arrayed on the bathroom counter* **3** *formal* to put soldiers in position ready to fight

ar·rears /əˈrɪəz $ əˈrɪrz/ *n* [plural] **1 be in arrears** if someone is in arrears, or if their payments are in arrears, they are late in paying something that they should pay regularly, such as rent: *Many people are in arrears with their rent.* | **be four weeks/three months etc in arrears** *The rent money is two months in arrears.* | **fall/get into arrears** (=become late with payments) **2** money that you owe someone because you have not made regular payments at the correct time:

We've got 3 months arrears to pay. | **rent/mortgage/tax arrears** *He was ordered to pay rent arrears of £550.* **3 paid in arrears** *BrE* if your salary is paid in arrears, it is paid at the end of the period you have worked: *a salary paid monthly in arrears*

ar·rest¹ W3 /əˈrest/ *v* [T]
1 if the police arrest someone, the person is taken to a POLICE STATION because the police think they have done something illegal: *He was arrested and charged with murder.* | **arrest sb for sth** *Her father was arrested for fraud.* | *I got arrested for careless driving.* | **arrest sb in connection with sth** *Five youths were arrested in connection with the attack.* | **arrest sb on charges/suspicion of (doing) sth** *He was arrested on suspicion of supplying drugs.*
2 *formal* to stop something happening or to make it happen more slowly: *drugs used to arrest the spread of the disease*
3 *literary* if something arrests you or arrests your attention, you notice it because it is interesting or unusual: *The mountains are the most arresting feature of the glen.*

arrest² *n* [C,U] when the police take someone away and guard them because they may have done something illegal: *The police made several arrests.* | *A man is under arrest* (=the police are guarding him) *following the suspicious death of his wife.* | **place/ put sb under arrest** (=arrest someone) | *He sued the police for wrongful arrest* (=when someone who is not guilty is arrested). → HOUSE ARREST; → cardiac arrest at CARDIAC

arrest

making an arrest

ar·riv·al W3 /əˈraɪvəl/ *n*
1 [C,U] when someone or something arrives somewhere; **■ departure**: *Only the timely arrival of the police prevented the situation from becoming worse.* | *Traffic problems account for one third of late arrivals.* | [+at/in] *Shortly after our arrival in London, Lisa was attacked.* | **on arrival** *A deposit is payable on arrival* (=when you arrive).
2 the arrival of sth a) the time when a new idea, product etc is first used or discovered: *The demand for phone numbers has increased since the arrival of mobile phones.* **b)** the time when an event or period of time starts to happen: *The arrival of winter can make many people feel depressed.*
3 [C] someone who has just arrived in a place: *New arrivals were greeted with suspicion.* | *Late arrivals will not be admitted to the theatre.*
4 arrivals the place at an airport where people arrive when they get off a plane: *the arrivals lounge*
5 new arrival a baby who has just been born

ar·rive S2 W1 /əˈraɪv/ *v* [I]
1 GET SOMEWHERE to get to the place you are going to: *Give me a call to let me know you've arrived safely.* | [+in/at] *What time does the plane arrive in New York?* | **arrive late/early** *He arrived late as usual.* | *By the time the police arrived on the scene, the burglars had fled.*
2 BE DELIVERED if something arrives, it is brought or delivered to you; **■ come**: *The card arrived on my birthday.*
3 HAPPEN if an event or particular period of time arrives, it happens; **■ come**: *When her wedding day arrived, she was really nervous.*
4 STH NEW if a new idea, method, product etc arrives, it begins to exist or starts being used: *Since computers arrived, my job has become much easier.*
5 BE BORN to be born: *Sharon's baby arrived just after midnight.*

6 arrive at a decision/solution/compromise etc to reach a decision, solution etc after a lot of effort: *After much consideration, we have arrived at a decision.*

7 SUCCESS sb has arrived used to say that someone has become successful or famous: *When he saw his name painted on the door he knew he'd arrived!*

ar·ro·gance /'ærəgəns/ *n* [U] when someone behaves in a rude way because they think they are very important: *I couldn't believe the arrogance of the man!*

ar·ro·gant /'ærəgənt/ *adj* behaving in an unpleasant or rude way because you think you are more important than other people: *He was unbearably arrogant.* | *an arrogant attitude* —**arrogantly** *adv*; → see box at PROUD

ar·ro·gate /'ærəgeɪt/ *v* **arrogate (to yourself) sth** *formal* to claim that you have a particular right, position etc, without having the legal right to it

ar·row /'ærəʊ $ 'æroʊ/ *n* [C] **1** a weapon usually made from a thin straight piece of wood with a sharp point at one end, that you shoot with a BOW **2** a sign in the shape of an arrow, used to show direction: *Follow the arrows to the X-ray department.* → STRAIGHT ARROW

ar·row·head /'ærəʊhed $ 'æroʊ-/ *n* [C] the sharp pointed end of an arrow

ar·row·root /'ærəʊruːt, 'ærəruːt $ 'æroʊ-, 'ærə-/ *n* [U] a type of flour made from the root of a tropical American plant, used in cooking to make sauces thicker

arse¹ /ɑːs $ ɑːrs/ *n* [C] *BrE spoken not polite* **1** the part of your body that you sit on; **≡ ass** *AmE* **2** a stupid and annoying person **3 my arse!** used to say that you do not believe something **4 get off your arse** used to tell someone to stop being lazy and start doing something **5 shift/move your arse** or **get your arse into gear** used to tell someone to hurry up **6 not know your arse from your elbow** to be stupid and confused about simple things → ASS; → **be a pain in the arse** at PAIN¹ (3); → SMART ARSE; → **work your arse off** at WORK¹ (30)

arse² *v BrE spoken not polite* **can't/couldn't be arsed (to do sth)** to not do something because you are feeling too lazy

arse about/around *phr v spoken not polite* to waste time behaving in a silly way instead of doing the things you should do

arse·hole /'ɑːshəʊl $ 'ɑːrshoʊl/ *n* [C] *BrE spoken not polite* **1** a stupid and annoying person. Do not use this word. **2** someone's ANUS

'arse-ˌlicker *n* [C] *BrE spoken not polite* someone who is always very nice to people in authority because he or she wants to be liked by them – used to show disapproval —**arse-licking** *n* [U]

ar·se·nal /'ɑːsənəl $ 'ɑːr-/ *n* [C] **1** a large group of weapons that someone has: *Britain's nuclear arsenal* | [+of] *an arsenal of guns* **2** a building where weapons are stored **3** the equipment, methods etc that someone can use to help them achieve something: *a software package that's now part of our arsenal* | [+of] *He has a whole arsenal of cameras.*

ar·se·nic /'ɑːsənɪk $ 'ɑːr-/ *n* [U] a very poisonous chemical substance that is sometimes used to kill rats, insects, and WEEDS. It is a chemical ELEMENT: symbol As

ar·son /'ɑːsən $ 'ɑːr-/ *n* [U] the crime of deliberately making something burn, especially a building: *The school was destroyed in an arson attack.*

ar·son·ist /'ɑːsənɪst $ 'ɑːr-/ *n* [C] someone who commits the crime of arson

art¹ ‖S1‖ ‖W1‖ /ɑːt $ ɑːrt/ *n*
1 [U] the use of painting, drawing, SCULPTURE etc to represent things or express ideas: *an example of Indian art* | *contemporary/modern art the Museum of Modern Art* → ART FORM, FINE ART, PERFORMANCE ART
2 [plural, U] objects that are produced by art, such as paintings, drawings etc: *an art exhibition* | *an art critic* | *an arts and crafts fair* | *The exhibition features 175 works of art.*

3 [U] the skill of drawing or painting: *He's very good at art.* | *an art teacher*
4 the arts [plural] art, music, theatre, film, literature etc all considered together: *Government funding for the arts has been reduced.*
5 arts also **the arts** [plural] subjects you can study that are not scientific, for example history, languages etc; → **humanities**
6 [C,U] the ability or skill involved in doing or making something: *Television is ruining the art of conversation.* | *Writing advertisements is quite an art* (=it is difficult to do). | **have/get sth down to a fine art** (=do something very well) *I've got the early morning routine down to a fine art.*

art² *v old-fashioned* or *biblical* **thou art** a phrase meaning 'you are'

Art Dec·o /ˌɑːt 'dekəʊ $ ˌɑːrt 'dekoʊ/ *n* [U] a style of art and decoration that uses simple shapes and was popular in Europe and America in the 1920s and 1930s

'art diˌrector *n* [C] someone whose job is to decide on how pictures, photographs etc will look in a magazine, film, advertisement etc

ar·te·fact *especially BrE* also **artifact** *especially AmE* /'ɑːtɪfækt $ 'ɑːr-/ *n* [C] an object such as a tool, weapon etc that was made in the past and is historically important: *ancient Egyptian artefacts*

ar·te·ri·al /ɑːˈtɪəriəl $ ɑːrˈtɪr-/ *adj* **1** involving the arteries: *arterial blood* **2** [only before noun] an arterial road is one of the main roads in a city, country etc

ar·te·ri·o·scle·ro·sis /ɑːˌtɪəriəʊsklɪˈrəʊsɪs, $ ɑːrˌtɪrioʊsklɪˈroʊ-/ *n* [U] a disease in which your arteries become hard, which makes it difficult for the blood to flow through

ar·te·ry /'ɑːtəri $ 'ɑːr-/ *n plural* **arteries** [C] **1** one of the tubes that carries blood from your heart to the rest of your body; → **vein** (1); → see picture at HUMAN¹ **2** a main road, railway line, river etc

ar·te·si·an well /ɑːˌtiːziən 'wel $ ɑːrˌtiːʒən-/ *n* [C] a WELL from which the water is forced up out of the ground by natural pressure

'art form *noun* [C] **1** a way of expressing ideas, for example in a painting, dance, piece of writing etc: *Music is quite unlike any other art form.* **2 make/turn sth into an art form** to do something so often that you become very good at it: *a company that's in danger of turning mismanagement into an art form*

art·ful /'ɑːtfəl $ 'ɑːrt-/ *adj* **1** clever at deceiving people; **≡ cunning**: *artful tricks* **2** designed or done in a clever and attractive way: *artful photographs* —**artfully** *adj*: *artfully concealed pockets* —**artfulness** *n* [U]

'art ˌgallery *n* [C] a building where paintings are shown to the public

'art house *n* [C] a cinema that shows mainly foreign films, or films made by small film companies: *art house films*

ar·thri·tis /ɑːˈθraɪtɪs $ ɑːr-/ *n* [U] a disease that causes the joints of your body to become swollen and very painful —**arthritic** /-ˈθrɪtɪk/ *adj*: *arthritic fingers*

ar·ti·choke /'ɑːtɪtʃəʊk $ 'ɑːrtɪtʃoʊk/ *n* [C] **1** also **globe artichoke** a type of round green vegetable, which has BUDS with leaves that you eat, which are like the PETALS of a flower **2** also **Jerusalem artichoke** a plant that has a root like a potato that you can eat

ar·ti·cle ‖S2‖ ‖W1‖ /'ɑːtɪkəl $ 'ɑːr-/ *n* [C]
1 NEWSPAPER/MAGAZINE a piece of writing about a particular subject in a newspaper or magazine: [+on/about] *an article on environmental issues* | *The paper's leading article* (=the main article) *described the government as weak.* | *newspaper articles*
2 OBJECT *formal* a thing, especially one of a group of things; **≡ item**: *household articles* | *She only took a few articles of clothing with her.*
3 LAW a part of a law or legal agreement that deals with a particular point: *Article 1 of the constitution guarantees freedom of religion.*

A

4 GRAMMAR *technical* a word used before a noun to show whether the noun refers to a particular example of something or to a general example of something. In English, 'the' is called the definite article and 'a' and 'an' are called the indefinite article.
5 articles *BrE* an agreement by which someone finishes their training, especially as a lawyer, by working for a company
6 an article of faith something that you feel very strongly about so that it affects how you think or behave

ar·ti·cled /'ɑːtɪkəld $ 'ɑːr-/ *adj BrE* someone who is articled to a company of lawyers, ACCOUNTANTS etc, is employed by that company while they are training to become a lawyer etc: *an articled clerk* | [+**to**] *He was articled to a firm of architects.*

ar·tic·u·late¹ /ɑːˈtɪkjɕleɪt $ ɑːr-/ *v* **1** [T] *formal* to express your ideas or feelings in words: *Many people are unable to articulate the unhappiness they feel.* **2** [I,T] to pronounce what you are saying in a clear and careful way: *He was so drunk that he could barely articulate his words.* **3** [I,T] *technical* if something such as a bone in your body is articulated to another thing, it is joined to it in a way that allows movement **4 articulate sth with sth** *formal* if one idea, system etc articulates with another idea, system etc, the two things are related and exist together: *a new course that is designed to articulate with the current degree course*

ar·tic·u·late² /ɑːˈtɪkjɕlɪt $ ɑːr-/ *adj* **1** able to talk easily and effectively about things, especially difficult subjects; **F** **inarticulate**: *bright, articulate 17-year-olds* | *a highly articulate speaker* **2** writing or speech that is articulate is very clear and easy to understand even if the subject is difficult —**articulately** *adv*

ar·tic·u·la·ted /ɑːˈtɪkjɕleɪtɪd $ ɑːr-/ *adj* an articulated vehicle has two parts joined together to make it easier to turn

ar·tic·u·la·tion /ɑːˌtɪkjɕˈleɪʃən $ ɑːr-/ *n* **1** [U] the act of making a sound or of speaking words **2** [U] the expression of thoughts or feelings in words: [+**of**] *the articulation of ideas* **3** [C,U] *technical* a joint that allows movement

ar·ti·fact /'ɑːtɕfækt $ 'ɑːr-/ *n* [C] *especially AmE* another spelling of ARTEFACT

ar·ti·fice /'ɑːtɕfɕs $ 'ɑːr-/ *n* *formal* **1** [U] the use of clever tricks to deceive someone; **E cunning** **2** [C] a trick used to deceive someone

ar·ti·fi·cial S3 /ˌɑːtɕˈfɪʃəl◄ $ ˌɑːr-/ *adj* [usually before noun]
1 not real or not made of natural things but made to be like something that is real or natural; **F natural**; **E false**: *artificial flowers* | *artificial light* | *artificial fertilizers* → see picture at NATURAL¹
2 an artificial situation or quality exists because someone has made it exist, and not because it is really necessary: *artificial distinctions* | *artificial barriers of gender and race*
3 artificial behaviour is not sincere – used to show disapproval; **F genuine**: *an artificial smile* —**artificially** *adv*: *Food prices are being kept artificially low.* —**artificiality** /ˌɑːtɕfɪʃiˈælɕti $ ˌɑːr-/ *n* [U]

,**artificial insemi'nation** *n* [U] the medical process of making a woman or female animal PREGNANT by using a piece of equipment, rather than by having sex

,**artificial in'telligence** *n* [U] *AI* the study of how to make computers do intelligent things that people can do, such as think and make decisions

,**artificial respi'ration** *n* [U] a way of making someone breathe again when they have stopped, by blowing air into their mouth

ar·til·le·ry /ɑːˈtɪləri $ ɑːr-/ *n* **1** [U] large guns, either on wheels or fixed in one place **2 the artillery** the part of the army that uses these weapons

ar·ti·san /ˌɑːtɕˈzæn $ 'ɑːrtɕzən/ *n* [C] someone who does skilled work, making things with their hands; **E craftsman**

art·ist S3 W2 /'ɑːtɕst $ 'ɑːr-/ *n* [C]
1 someone who produces art, especially paintings or drawings: *an exhibition of paintings by local artists* → **make-up artist** at MAKE-UP (1)
2 a professional performer, especially a singer, dancer, or actor: *Many of the artists in the show donated their fee to charity.*
3 *informal* someone who is extremely good at something: *He's an artist in the kitchen.* → CON ARTIST

ar·tiste /ɑːˈtiːst $ ɑːr-/ *n* [C] a professional singer, dancer, actor etc who performs in a show

ar·tis·tic /ɑːˈtɪstɪk $ ɑːr-/ *adj* **1** relating to art or culture: *artistic work* | *Opinion about the artistic merit of his paintings has been mixed.* **2** good at painting, drawing, or producing beautiful things: *John is very artistic.* **3** an artistic arrangement, design etc looks attractive and has been done with skill and imagination: *food presented in an artistic way* —**artistically** /-kli/ *adv*

art·ist·ry /'ɑːtɕstri $ 'ɑːr-/ *n* [U] skill in a particular artistic activity: *the artistry of dance*

art·less /'ɑːtləs $ 'ɑːrt-/ *adj* **1** *literary* natural, honest, and sincere: *artless sincerity* **2** *formal* made or done without any skill: *an artless copy of European art* —**artlessly** *adj* —**artlessness** *n* [U]

Art Nou·veau /ˌɑːt nuːˈvəʊ $ ˌɑːrt nuːˈvoʊ/ *n* [U] a style of art that used plants and flowers in paintings and in the design of objects and buildings, popular in Europe and America at the end of the 19th century

'**arts ,cinema** *n* [C] *BrE* a cinema that shows mainly foreign films or films made by small film companies

art·work /'ɑːtwɜːk $ 'ɑːrtwɜːrk/ *n* **1** [U] drawings and photographs that are specially prepared to be in a book, magazine, or advertisement **2** [C,U] paintings and other objects produced by artists

art·y /'ɑːti $ 'ɑːrti/ *BrE*; **art·sy** /'ɑːtsi $ 'ɑːrt-/ *AmE adj* **1** someone who is arty knows a lot about art, film, theatre etc – often used to show disapproval: *He was one of those arty types.* **2** intended for, or used by people who are interested in art, film, theatre etc: *an arty film* | *Paris's arty Marais district*

art·y-fart·y /ˌɑːti ˈfɑːti◄ $ ˌɑːrti ˈfɑːr-/ *BrE*; **art·sy-fart·sy** /ˌɑːtsi ˈfɑːtsi $ ˌɑːrtsi ˈfɑːr-/ *AmE adj informal* trying too hard to show that you are interested in art – used to show disapproval

Ar·y·an /'eəriən $ 'er-/ *n* [C] someone from Northern Europe, especially someone with BLOND hair and blue eyes —**Aryan** *adj*

a·ru·gu·la /əˈruːɡjɕlə $ -ɡələ/ *n* [U] ROCKET¹ (4)

as¹ S1 W1 /əz; *strong* æz/ *prep, adv*
1 used when you are comparing two people, things, situations etc: **as ... as** *Tom's not as old as you, is he?* | *an old woman with hair as white as snow* | *Some of the doctors are paid almost twice as much as the nurses.* | *We work as hard as any other team in England.* | *Please let me know your decision **as soon as possible*** (=as soon as you can). | *His last album sold half a million copies and we hope this one will be **just as** (=equally) popular.*
2 used to say what job, duty, use, or appearance someone or something has: *As a parent, I feel that more should be done to protect our children.* | *A large flat stone was used as a table.* | *Dad dressed up as Santa Claus.*
3 used to say what someone thinks or says a person or thing is: *The problem is regarded as serious.* | *The result of last week's election will be seen as a victory for the right-wing government.* | *He's described as being in his late teens, tall, and of slim build.*
4 when someone was in a particular age group: *As a young man, Eliot had studied art in Paris.* | *I'll take you to all the places I loved as a girl.* → **such as** at SUCH (2); → **as one** at ONE² (16)

WORD CHOICE: as, like, as if
Use **as** in comparisons in the expression **as ... as**, with an adjective or adverb in between: *Basketball is as popular as football here.* | *He can't read as well as his classmates.*
as is also used in the expressions **not so ... as** and **the same (...) as**: *I wouldn't go so far as that.* | *He is the same age as me.*
Use **like** in comparisons followed by a noun: *A movie is not like a book (NOT not as a book).* | *Like other people (NOT as other people), he values his privacy.*
Use **as if** followed by a clause to compare a real situation with an imaginary situation: *He talked to them as if they were children.*
⚠ Some people use **like** in this sort of comparison: *They act like they own the place.* It is better not to do this as many people think it is incorrect.
⚠ **as if** cannot be followed directly by a noun: *You treat them as if they were your parents (NOT as if your parents).*

as² [S1] [W1] *conjunction*
1 used in comparisons: **as ... as** *They want peace as much as we do.* | *Helen comes to visit me as often as she can.* | *I can't run as fast as I used to.*
2 in the way that someone says or that something happens, or in the condition something is in: *Do as I say!* | *We'd better leave things as they are until the police arrive.* | *The money was repaid, as promised.* | *He did not need to keep moving house, as his father had.* | *Roberta was late as usual* (=in the way that she usually was).
3 used to say that what you are saying is already known or has been stated before: *David, as you know, has not been well lately.* | *As I explained on the phone, your request will be considered at the next meeting.* | *As Napoleon once said, attack is the best method of defence.*
4 while or when: *I saw Peter as I was getting off the bus.* | *As time passed, things seemed to get worse.* | *Just as the two men were leaving, a message arrived.*
5 used to state why a particular situation exists or why someone does something: *As it was getting late, I turned around to start for home.* | *We asked Philip to come with us, as he knew the road.*
6 though: *Unlikely as it might seem, I'm tired too.* | *Try as she might, Sue couldn't get the door open.* | *As popular as he is, the President hasn't always managed to have his own way.*
7 as for sb/sth used when you are starting to talk about someone or something new that is connected with what you were talking about before: *Kitty's got so thin. And as for Carl, he always seems to be ill.* | *You can ask the others, but as for myself, I'll be busy in the office.*
8 as yet [used in negatives] until and including the present time – used to say that something has not happened although it may happen in the future: *We've had no word from Colin as yet.*
9 as if.../as though... **a)** in a way that makes it seem that something is true or that something is happening: *It sounds as though she's been really ill.* | *Gary was behaving as though nothing had happened.* | *Mrs Crump looked as if she was going to explode.* | *Beckworth shook his head as if to say 'Don't trust her'.* **b)** used to emphasize that something is not true or will not happen: *She said she'd never speak to me again. As if I cared* (=I do not care at all). | *'Don't try any funny business, now.' 'As if I would.'* | **As if!** *spoken informal*: *He asked if I'd go out with him. As if!* (=it is extremely unlikely that I would go out with him); → see box at AS¹
10 it's not as if used to say that something cannot be the explanation for a situation or someone's behaviour because it is not true: *Why do they never go on holiday? I mean it's not as if they're poor is it? I don't know why you're so frightened of her, it's not as if she's got any power over you.*
11 as it is a) because of the situation that actually exists – used when that situation is different from what

you expected or need: *They hoped to finish the kitchen by Friday, but as it is they'll probably have to come back next week.* **b)** already: *Just keep quiet – you're in enough trouble as it is.*
12 as from/of sth starting from a particular time or date and continuing: *As from today, you are in charge of the office.* | *As of now, there will be no more paid overtime.*
13 as against sth in comparison with something: *Profits this year are $2.5 million as against $4 million last year.*
14 as to sth a) concerning: *Frank was very uncertain as to whether it was the right job for him.* | *advice as to which suppliers to approach* | *He kept his rivals guessing as to his real intentions.* **b)** *formal* used when you are starting to talk about something new that is connected with what you were talking about before: *As to our future plans, I think I need only say that the company intends to expand at a steady rate.*
15 as it were used when describing someone or something in a way that is not quite exact: *Jim Radcliffe became our idol, as it were, the man we all wanted to be.*
16 as is/was/does etc *formal* used to add that what you have said is also true of someone or something else: *Eve's very tall, as was her mother.* | *I voted Labour, as did my wife.* → **not as such** at SUCH (8); → **as well** at WELL¹ (5); → **as well as** at WELL¹ (5); → **might (just) as well** at MIGHT¹ (9); → **so as to do sth** at SO² (5)

asap, ASAP /ˌeɪ es eɪˈpiː, ˈeɪsæp/ the abbreviation of *as soon as possible*

as·bes·tos /æsˈbestəs/ *n* [U] a grey mineral that does not burn easily, that was used in the past as a building material or in protective clothing

as·cend /əˈsend/ *v* **1** [I] *formal* to move up through the air; 🔁 **descend**: *The plane ascended rapidly.* **2** [T] *written* to climb something or move to a higher position; 🔁 **descend**: *Without a word, he began to ascend the stairs.* **3** [I] *written* to lead up to a higher position; 🔁 **descend**: *The road ascends steeply from the harbour.* **4** [I,T] *formal* to move to a more important or powerful job.: *The number of women decreases as you ascend the professional hierarchy.* **5 ascend the throne** to become king or queen **6 in ascending order** if a group of things are arranged in ascending order, each thing is higher, or greater in amount, than the one before it

as·cen·dan·cy, ascendency /əˈsendənsi/ *n* [U] *formal* a position of power, influence, or control; → **ascendant**: *moral ascendancy* | [+of] *the ascendancy of nationalist forces* | [+over] *Butler established ascendancy over his critics.* | He slowly **gained ascendancy** *in the group.* | **in the ascendancy** *a teaching method that is currently in the ascendancy*

as·cen·dant¹, ascendent /əˈsendənt/ *n* **be in the ascendant** *formal* to be or become powerful or popular: *a political party that's in the ascendant*

ascendant², ascendent *adj formal* becoming more powerful or popular: *a politically ascendant country*

as·cen·sion /əˈsenʃən/ *n* **1 the Ascension** in the Christian religion, when Jesus Christ left the earth and went to heaven **2** [U] *formal* when someone moves to a more important or higher position or job: *his ascension to the ranks of senior management*

as·cent /əˈsent/ *n* **1** [C usually singular] the act of climbing something or moving upwards; 🔁 **descent**: *the first ascent of Everest* **2** [C usually singular] a path or way up to the top of something, for example a mountain; 🔁 **descent**: *a rugged and steep ascent* **3** [U] the process of becoming more important, powerful, or successful than before; 🔁 **rise**; 🔁 **fall**: [+to] *the President's ascent to power*

as·cer·tain /ˌæsəˈteɪn $ ˌæsər-/ *v* [I,T] *formal* to find out something: *A postmortem was ordered to try to ascertain the cause of death.* | **ascertain whether/what/how etc** *Tests were conducted to ascertain whether pollution levels have dropped.* | **ascertain that** *Police had ascertained that the dead man knew his killer.* |

ascertain sth from sb/sth *You should ascertain the level of insurance cover from the car rental company.* —**ascertainable** *adv*

as·cet·ic /ə'setɪk/ *adj* living without any physical pleasures or comforts, especially for religious reasons: *an ascetic life* —**ascetic** *n* [C] —**asceticism** /-tɪ-sɪzəm/ *n* [U]

ASCII /'æski/ *n* [U] *technical* **American Standard Code for Information Interchange** a system used for exchanging information between computers by allowing them to recognize letters, numbers etc in the same way

as·cot /'æskɒt $ -kət/ *n* [C] *AmE* a wide piece of material that a man wears loosely folded around his neck and inside his collar; ▣ **cravat**

as·cribe /ə'skraɪb/ *v*
 ascribe sth to sb/sth *phr v written* **1** to claim that something is caused by a particular person, situation etc: *The report ascribes the rise in childhood asthma to the increase in pollution.* **2** to claim that something has been written, said, made etc by a particular person: *a quotation that's often been ascribed to Marilyn Monroe* **3** to believe that something or someone has a particular quality: *Local people ascribe healing properties to this fruit.* —**ascribable** *adj*: *Most of the accidents were ascribable to the bad weather.*

a·sep·tic /eɪ'septɪk, ə-/ *adj* *technical* a wound that is aseptic is completely clean without any harmful BACTERIA

a·sex·u·al /eɪ'sekʃuəl/ *adj* **1** *technical* not having sexual organs or not involving sex: *asexual reproduction* **2 a)** not having any sexual qualities **b)** not interested in sex —**asexually** *adv*

ash /æʃ/ *n* **1** [C,U] the soft grey powder that remains after something has been burned: *cigarette ash* | *The house burnt to ashes.* → see picture at VOLCANO **2 ashes** [plural] **a)** the ash that remains when a dead person's body is burned: *His ashes were scattered at sea.* **b)** a situation in which something is completely destroyed: *The organization has risen from the ashes to become very successful.* | *All her hopes and dreams had turned to ashes.* **3** [C,U] a tree that is common in Britain and North America, or the wood from this tree

Ash Wednesday *n* [C,U] the first day of Lent

a·shamed S3 /ə'ʃeɪmd/ *adj* [not before noun]
1 feeling embarrassed and guilty because of something you have done: [+of/at] *I felt ashamed of the things I'd said to him.* | **be ashamed to do sth** *I'm ashamed to admit that I've never read any of his books.* | *ashamed that I'm ashamed that I haven't replied to your letter yet.* | **bitterly/deeply/thoroughly ashamed** *Anna felt thoroughly ashamed when she realized what she'd said.* | *Everyone cries sometimes – it's* **nothing to be ashamed of.** | **be/feel ashamed of yourself** *You should be ashamed of yourself.*
2 feeling uncomfortable because someone does something that embarrasses you: [+of] *Many children feel ashamed of their parents.* | **be ashamed to be/do sth** *Their behaviour makes me ashamed to be British.*

ash·can /'æʃkæn/ *n* [C] *AmE old-fashioned* a GARBAGE CAN

ash·en /'æʃən/ *adj* **1** looking very pale because you are ill, shocked, or frightened; ▣ **white**: *His face was ashen.* **2** *literary* pale grey in colour: *ashen hills*

a·shore /ə'ʃɔː $ ə'ʃɔːr/ *adv* on or towards the shore of a lake, river, sea etc; ▣ **onshore**: **come/go ashore** *Seals come ashore to breed.* | *Several dead birds had been washed ashore.*

ash·ram /'æʃrəm/ *n* [C] a place where Hindus live together, away from other people

ash·tray S3 /'æʃtreɪ/ *n* [C] a small dish where you put used cigarettes → see picture at TRAY

A·sian¹ /'eɪʃən, 'eɪʒən $ 'eɪʒən, 'eɪʃən/ *n* [C] **1** *BrE* someone from Asia, or whose family originally came from Asia, especially India or Pakistan **2** *AmE* some-one from Asia, or whose family originally came from Asia, especially from Japan, China, Korea etc

Asian² *adj* **1** *BrE* from or relating to Asia, especially India or Pakistan **2** *AmE* from or relating to Asia, especially Japan, China, Korea etc

Asian-A'merican *n* [C] an American citizen whose family originally came from Asia

a·side¹ S3 W3 /ə'saɪd/ *adv*
1 kept to be used later: *I've been setting aside a few pounds each week.* | *One of the rooms was set aside for a yoga class.* | *Try to set aside a few hours a week for exercise.* | *Could you put this cake aside for me?*
2 moved to one side or away from you: *He pushed his half-eaten salad aside and left.* | *He stepped aside to let Katherine go in first.* | *Mark drew me aside and explained the problem.* | *She swept her thick hair aside.*
3 left to be considered or dealt with later, or not considered and dealt with at all: *He brushed aside criticisms of his performance.* | *Leaving aside the heat, we really enjoyed our holiday.* | *You must put aside your pride and call her.*
4 [only after noun] used to show that something you have just said is not as important as what you are going to say next: *These problems aside, we think the plan should go ahead.*
5 aside from sb/sth *especially AmE* **a)** except for: *Aside from Durang's performance, the actors are ordinary.* **b)** in addition to: *In the poetry competition, aside from Hass, are four other entrants.*

aside² *n* [C] **1** words spoken by an actor to the people watching a play, that the other characters in the play do not hear **2** a remark made in a low voice that you only intend particular people to hear **3** a remark or story that is not part of the main subject of a speech: *I should add, as an aside, that the younger the child, the faster they learn.*

as·i·nine /'æsɪnaɪn/ *adj* extremely stupid or silly; ▣ **ridiculous**: *What an asinine remark!*

ask¹ S1 W1 /ɑːsk $ æsk/ *v*
1 QUESTION [I,T] to speak or write to someone in order to get an answer, information, or a solution: *'What's your name?' she asked.* | *Don't ask him – he won't know anything about it.* | *That kid's always asking awkward questions.* | **ask sb who/what/where etc** *I just asked him where he lived.* | **ask sb sth** *We'll have to ask someone the way to the station.* | **ask sb if/whether** *Go and ask Tom whether he's coming tonight.* | **ask (sb) about sth** *Visitors usually ask about the history of the castle.* | **ask around** (=ask in a lot of places or ask a lot of people) *I'll ask around, see if I can find you a place to stay.*
2 FOR HELP/ADVICE ETC [I,T] to make a request for help, advice, information etc: *If you need anything, you only have to ask.* | **ask sb to do sth** *Ask John to mail those letters tomorrow.* | **ask to do sth** *Karen asked to see the doctor.* | [+for] *Some people find it difficult to ask for help.* | **ask (sb) if/whether you can do sth** *Ask your mom if you can come with us.* | **ask that** *Was it too much to ask that he be allowed some privacy?*
3 PRICE [T] to want a particular amount of money for something you are selling: *How much is he asking?* | **ask $50/$1,000 etc for sth** *He's asking £2,000 for his car.* | *They're asking a fortune for that house.*
4 INVITE [T usually + adv/prep] to invite someone to your home, to go out with you etc: **ask sb to do sth** *Let's ask them to have dinner with us some time.* | **ask sb out** (=ask someone, especially someone of the opposite sex, to go to a film, a restaurant etc with you) *Jerry's too scared to ask her out.* | **ask sb in** (=invite someone into your house, office etc) *Don't leave them standing on the doorstep – ask them in!* | **ask sb over/round** (=invite someone to come to your home) *We must ask our new neighbours over for a drink.*

A

5 DEMAND [T] if you ask something of someone, you want them to do it for you: *It would be better if he cooperated, but perhaps I'm asking too much.* | **ask sth of sb** *You have no right to ask anything of me.* | *Expecting the children to do an hour's homework after school is asking a lot of them.*
6 be asking for trouble to do something that is very likely to have a bad effect or result: *Saying that to a feminist is just asking for trouble.*
7 ask yourself sth to think carefully and honestly about something: *You have to ask yourself where your responsibilities really lie.*

SPOKEN PHRASES
8 if you ask me used to emphasize your own opinion: *He's just plain crazy, if you ask me.*
9 don't ask me used to say you do not know the answer to something: *'Where's she gone then?' 'Don't ask me!'*
10 don't ask used to say that something is too embarrassing or strange to explain: *'What was that woman selling?' 'Don't ask.'*
11 be asking for it used to say that someone deserves something bad that happens to them: *It's his own fault he got hit – he was asking for it.*

12 be sb's for the asking *informal* if something is yours for the asking, you can have it if you want it: *The job was hers for the asking.*

WORD FOCUS: words meaning ASK
request to officially ask for something | **consult** to ask someone for advice | **demand** to ask for something very forcefully | **nag/pester** to keep asking for something many times, in an annoying way | **beg/plead** to ask for something in an anxious or urgent way, because you want it very much | **question/interrogate** to ask someone questions – used especially about the police or the army | **grill** *informal* to ask someone a lot of difficult questions | **cross-examine** to ask someone questions in court – used about lawyers | **poll** to ask a lot of people for their opinion about something

ask after sb *phr v BrE*
if you ask after someone, you want to know whether they are well, what they are doing etc: *I spoke to James today. He was asking after you.*
ask for sb *phr v*
if you ask for someone, you want to speak to them: *There's someone at the door asking for Dad.*

ask² *n* **a big ask** a situation in a sports competition when someone needs to get a lot of points or do something very difficult in order to win: *We need to win the next three games. It's a big ask, but I'm confident we can do it.*

a·skance /ə'skæns, ə'skɑːns $ ə'skæns/ *adv* **look askance (at sb/sth)** if you look askance at something, you do not approve of it or think it is good: *A waiter looked askance at Ellis's jeans.*

a·skew /ə'skjuː/ *adv* [not before noun] not quite straight or in the right position: *Matilda ran towards us with her hat askew.*

'asking ,price *n* [usually singular] the price that someone wants to sell something for; → **selling price**

a·slant /ə'slɑːnt $ ə'slænt/ *adj, adv* [not before noun] *formal* not straight up or down, but across at an angle

a·sleep S2 /ə'sliːp/ *adj* [not before noun]
1 sleeping; E **awake**: *Quiet! The baby's asleep.* | **fast/sound asleep** (=sleeping deeply)
2 fall asleep a) to begin to sleep: *Grandad fell asleep watching TV.* | *One in seven road accidents is caused by drivers falling asleep at the wheel* (=fall asleep while driving). **b)** *literary* used to mean that someone dies, when you want to avoid saying this directly
3 half asleep very tired or not completely awake: *Still half asleep, Jenny began to make the kids' breakfast.*
4 an arm or leg that is asleep has been in one position for too long, so you cannot feel it properly
5 asleep at the wheel/switch not paying attention to a

situation, so that something bad happens: *Several publishers were asleep at the switch, and missed the book's potential.* → **go to sleep** at SLEEP² (3); → see box at SLEEP¹

A/S level /ˌeɪ 'es ˌlevəl/ *n* [C,U] *Advanced Supplementary level* an examination that is taken by students in schools in England and Wales the year after they finish their GCSES. Students usually continue with three or four of the same subjects after A/S level, in order to complete their A LEVELS: **do/take A/S levels** | [+in] *I'm taking A/S levels in French, Spanish, English, and Maths.*

ASP /ˌeɪ es 'piː/ *n* [C] *technical* **application service provider** a company that supplies organized sets of computer software to other companies so that they can do business on the Internet

asp /æsp/ *n* [C] a small poisonous snake from North Africa

as·par·a·gus /ə'spærəgəs/ *n* [U] a long thin green vegetable with a point at one end → see picture at VEGETABLE¹

as·pect S3 W1 /'æspekt/ *n*
1 [C] one part of a situation, idea, plan etc that has many parts: [+of] *Dealing with people is the most important aspect of my work.* | *Alcoholism affects all aspects of family life.*
2 [C] the direction in which a window, room, front of a building etc faces: *a south-facing aspect*
3 [singular, U] *literary* the appearance of someone or something: *The storm outside gave the room a sinister aspect.*
4 [C,U] *technical* the form of a verb in grammar that shows whether an action is continuing, or happens always, again and again, or once: *'He sings' differs from 'He is singing' in aspect.*

as·pen /'æspən/ *n* [C] a type of tree from western North America with leaves that shake a lot in the wind

as·per·i·ty /æ'sperᵻti, ə-/ *n* [U] *formal* if you speak with asperity, you say something in a way that is rough or severe, showing that you are feeling impatient

as·per·sion /ə'spɜːʃən, ʒən $ ə'spɜːrʒən/ *n* [C] *formal* an unkind remark or an unfair judgment: *No one is casting aspersions on you or your men, Major.*

as·phalt /'æsfælt $ 'æsfɒːlt/ *n* [U] a black sticky substance that becomes hard when it dries, used for making the surface of roads —**asphalt** *v* [T]

as·phyx·i·a /æs'fɪksiə, əs-/ *n* [U] *formal* death caused by not being able to breathe; E **suffocation**

as·phyx·i·ate /æs'fɪksieɪt, əs-/ *v* [I,T] *formal* to prevent someone from breathing normally, usually so that they die; E **suffocate** —**asphyxiation** /æs,fɪksi'eɪʃən, əs-/ *n* [U]

as·pic /'æspɪk/ *n* [U] **1** a clear brownish JELLY in which cold meat is sometimes served **2 preserve/set/remain in aspic** *BrE* if something is preserved in aspic, it has not changed for a very long time: *a part of town preserved in aspic for tourists*

as·pi·dis·tra /ˌæspᵻ'dɪstrə/ *n* [C] an indoor plant with broad green pointed leaves

as·pi·rant /ə'spaɪərənt, 'æspᵻrənt $ ə'spaɪr-,'æsp-/ *n* [C] *formal* someone who hopes to get a position of importance or honour

as·pi·rate¹ /'æspᵻreɪt/ *v* [T] *technical* to make the sound of an 'H' when speaking, or to blow out air when pronouncing some CONSONANTS

as·pi·rate² /'æspᵻrᵻt/ *n* [C] *technical* the sound of the letter 'H', or the letter itself

as·pi·ra·tion /ˌæspᵻ'reɪʃən/ *n* **1** [C usually plural, U] a strong desire to have or achieve something; E **ambition**: *a high level of political aspiration* | [+of] *the aspirations of the working classes* | [+for] *their hopes and aspirations for the future* **2** [U] *technical* the sound of air blowing out that happens when some CONSONANTS are pronounced, such as the /p/ in pin —**aspirational** *adj*

as·pire /əˈspaɪə $ əˈspaɪr/ v [I] to desire and work towards achieving something important: [+to] *college graduates aspiring to careers in finance* | **aspire to do sth** *At that time, all serious artists aspired to go to Rome.*

As·pirin® /ˈæsprɪ̩n/ n plural **aspirin** or **aspirins** [C,U] a medicine that reduces pain, INFLAMMATION, and fever

as·pir·ing /əˈspaɪərɪŋ $ əˈspaɪr-/ adj [only before noun] hoping to be successful in a particular job, activity, or way of life: *aspiring young writers* | *the aspiring middle classes*

ass [S2] /æs/ n [C]
1 *not polite* a stupid, annoying person; ◫ **fool**: *He's a pompous ass.* | **make an ass of yourself** (=do something stupid or embarrassing)
2 *AmE not polite* the part of your body that you sit on
3 *old use* a DONKEY → ARSE[1]; → **get your butt/ass in gear** at GEAR[1] (8); → **haul ass** at HAUL[1] (5); → **kick ass** at KICK[1] (8); → **kick sb's ass** at KICK[1] (7); → **kiss sb's ass** at KISS[1] (6); → **be a pain in the ass** at PAIN[1] (3); → **piece of ass** at PIECE[1] (22); → SMART ARSE; → **work your ass off** at WORK[1] (30)

as·sail /əˈseɪl/ v [T] *formal* **1** [usually passive] if you are assailed by unpleasant thoughts or feelings, they worry or upset you: *Carla was suddenly assailed by doubts.* **2** if a strong smell or loud sound assails you, you suddenly experience it: *The smell of rotten meat assailed her nostrils.* **3** to attack someone or something violently **4** to criticize someone or something severely: **assail sb for sth** *He was assailed for gross misconduct.*

as·sai·lant /əˈseɪlənt/ n [C] *formal* someone who attacks another person; ◫ **attacker**

as·sas·sin /əˈsæsɪ̩n/ n [C] someone who murders an important person: *Kennedy's assassin is assumed to have been Lee Harvey Oswald.*

as·sas·sin·ate /əˈsæsɪ̩neɪt $ -səneɪt/ v [T] to murder an important person: *a plot to assassinate the President*; → see box at KILL[1]

as·sas·sin·a·tion /ə,sæsɪ̩ˈneɪʃən $ ə,sæsənˈeɪ-/ n [C,U] the act of murdering an important person: [+of] *the assassination of Anwar Sadat* | *He narrowly escaped an **assassination attempt** (=when someone tries but fails to kill someone else).* → **character assassination** at CHARACTER (6)

as·sault¹ [W3] /əˈsɔːlt $ əˈsɒːlt/ n
1 [C,U] the crime of physically attacking someone: *a case of robbery and assault* | **for assault** *He was jailed for assault.* | **sexual/indecent assault** *victims of indecent assault* | [+on/against] *sexual assaults on women* | *Several soldiers have been **charged with assault**.*
2 [C,U] a military attack to take control of a place controlled by the enemy: [+on] *an unsuccessful assault on the enemy lines* | *The refugee camp **came under assault** again last night.* | *a powerful assault rifle*
3 [C,U] a strong spoken or written criticism of someone else's ideas, plans etc; ◫ **attack**: [+on] *an assault on the capitalist system* | **under assault** *Traditional family values are increasingly under assault.*
4 [C] an attempt to achieve something difficult, especially using physical force: [+on] *an assault on Mt Everest* (=an attempt to climb it)

assault² v [T] **1** to attack someone in a violent way: *Two men assaulted him after he left the bar.* | **sexually/indecently assault** *He was found guilty of indecently assaulting a student.* **2** *literary* if a feeling, sound, smell etc assaults you, it affects you in a way that makes you uncomfortable or upset: *The noises and smells of the market assaulted her senses.* **3** to strongly criticize someone's ideas, plans etc **4** to try to do something very difficult: *a task force to assault the problems*

as,sault and 'battery n [U] *law* the crime of threatening to attack someone physically and then attacking them

as'sault ,course n [C] *BrE* an area of land with special equipment to climb, jump over, run through etc

that is used for developing physical strength, especially by soldiers; ◫ **obstacle course** *AmE*

as·say /əˈseɪ/ v [T] to test a substance, especially a metal, to see how pure it is or what it is made of —**assay** /əˈseɪ, ˈæseɪ $ ˈæseɪ, æˈseɪ/ n [C]

as·sem·blage /əˈsemblɪdʒ/ n *formal* **1** [C] a group of things collected together: [+of] *a unique assemblage of wildlife* **2** [U+of] when parts are put together in order to make something

A

assemble

assemble   construct

build   make

as·sem·ble /əˈsembəl/ v **1** [I,T] if you assemble a large number of people or things, or if they assemble, they are gathered together in one place, often for a particular purpose: *A large crowd had assembled outside the American embassy.* | *He looked around at the **assembled company** (=all the people who had come there).* | *She had assembled a collection of her favourite songs.* **2** [T] to put all the parts of something together: *The aircraft will continue to be assembled in France.*

as·sem·bly [S3] [W2] /əˈsembli/ n plural **assemblies**
1 [C] a group of people who are elected to make decisions or laws for a particular country, area, or organization: *the General Assembly of the Church of Scotland* | *the speaker of the California state assembly* **2** [C,U] the meeting together of a group of people for a particular purpose: [+of] *an assembly of reporters* | *Police have imposed conditions on **public assemblies**.* | *Restrictions on **freedom of assembly** have gradually been relaxed.* | *an **assembly point** (=a place where people go in a particular situation)* **3** [C,U] a regular meeting of all the teachers and students of a school **4** [U] the process of putting the parts of something together: *instructions for assembly*

as'sembly ,language n [C,U] *technical* a computer language used in programs that are written to work with a specific kind of PROCESSOR

as'sembly ,line n [C] a system for making things in a factory in which the products move past a line of workers who each make or check one part

as·sem·bly·man /əˈsemblimən/ n plural **assemblymen** /-mən/ [C] *AmE* a male member of an assembly

as·sem·bly·wom·an /əˈsembli,wʊmən/ n plural **assemblywomen** /-,wɪmɪn/ [C] *AmE* a female member of an assembly

as·sent¹ /əˈsent/ n [U] *formal* approval or agreement from someone who has authority: *a nod of assent* | [+of] *the assent of the Board of Governors* | [+to] *Parliament **gave** its **assent** to war.*

assent² v [I] formal to agree to a suggestion, idea etc after considering it carefully: [+to] *They assented to his request to work from home.*

as·sert /əˈsɜːt $ -ɜːrt/ v [T] **1** to state firmly that something is true: *French cooking, she asserted, is the best in the world.* | **assert that** *He asserted that nuclear power was a safe and non-polluting energy source.* **2 assert your rights/independence/superiority** etc to state very strongly your right to something: *Native Americans asserting their rights to ancestral land* **3 assert yourself** to behave in a determined way and say clearly what you think: *Women began to assert themselves politically.* **4 assert itself** if an idea or belief asserts itself, it begins to influence something: *National pride began to assert itself.*

as·ser·tion /əˈsɜːʃən $ -ɜːr-/ n [C] something that you say or write that you strongly believe: **assertion that** *the assertion that house prices are falling* | [+of] *her assertion of independence* | [+about] *her assertions about the murder of her father* | *She makes very general assertions about marriage in the poem.*

as·ser·tive /əˈsɜːtɪv $ -ɜːr-/ adj behaving in a confident way, so that people notice you —**assertively** adv —**assertiveness** n [U]: *assertiveness training*

as·sess S2 W2 /əˈses/ v [T]
1 to make a judgment about a person or situation after thinking carefully about it; ◻ **judge**: **assess the impact/extent/effectiveness etc of sth** *a report to assess the impact of advertising on children* | **assess what/how etc** *The technique is being tried in classrooms to assess what effects it may have.* | **be assessed as sth** *Many of the adults were assessed as having learning difficulties.*
2 to calculate the value or cost of something: **be assessed at sth** *The value of the business was assessed at £1.25 million.*

as·sess·ment S2 W2 /əˈsesmənt/ n [C,U]
1 a process in which you make a judgment about a person or situation, or the judgment you make: [+of] *What's Michael's assessment of the situation?* | *a reading assessment test*
2 a calculation about the cost or value of something: *a tax assessment* → **continuous assessment** at CONTINUOUS (3)

as·ses·sor /əˈsesə $ -ər/ n [C] **1** someone whose job is to calculate the value of something or the amount of tax someone should pay **2** BrE someone who decides how well someone has done in an examination; ◻ **examiner** **3** someone who knows a lot about a subject or activity and who advises a judge or an official committee

as·set S2 W2 /ˈæset/ n [C]
1 [usually plural] the things that a company owns, that can be sold to pay debts: **in assets** *a corporation with $9 billion in assets* | *the value of a company's assets*
2 [usually singular] something or someone that is useful because they help you succeed or deal with problems; ◻ **liability**: *A sense of humor is a great asset in this business.* | **be an asset to sb/sth** *I think Rachel would be an asset to the department.* → FIXED ASSETS, LIQUID ASSETS

ˈasset ˌstripping n [U] the practice of buying a company cheaply and then selling all the things it owns to make a quick profit – used to show disapproval

ass·hole /ˈæʃəʊl $ -hoʊl/ n [C] AmE spoken not polite **1** someone who you think is stupid and annoying; ◻ **arsehole** BrE **2** the ANUS

as·sid·u·ous /əˈsɪdjuəs $ -dʒuəs/ adj formal very careful to make sure that something is done properly or completely; ◻ **meticulous**: [+in] *He was assiduous in his attendance at church.* —**assiduously** adv: *Even young children worked assiduously for a reward.* —**assiduity** /ˌæsɪˈdjuːɪti $ -ˈduː-/ n [U]

as·sign /əˈsaɪn/ v [T] **1** to give someone a particular job or make them responsible for a particular person or thing: **assign sb a task/role** *I've been assigned the task*

of looking after the new students. | **assign sb to sth** *Jan's been assigned to the Asian Affairs Bureau.* | **assign sb to do sth** *Madison was assigned to investigate a balloon accident.* | **assign sb sth** *Assign each student a partner.* **2** to give a particular time, value, place etc to something: *How much time have you assigned for the meeting?* | **assign sth to sth** *A code was assigned to each batch of work.* **3** to give money, equipment etc to someone to use: **assign sth to sb** *A personal bodyguard had been assigned to her.* | **assign sb sth** *They assigned me a small room.*

as·sig·na·tion /ˌæsɪɡˈneɪʃən/ n [C] formal a secret meeting, especially with someone you are having a romantic relationship with – often used humorously

as·sign·ment S2 /əˈsaɪnmənt/ n
1 [C,U] a piece of work that is given to someone as part of their job: **on an assignment** *She's gone to Italy on a special assignment.* | **on assignment** *He was killed while on assignment abroad.*
2 [C] a piece of work that a student is asked to do: *a history assignment*
3 [U] when people are given particular jobs to do
4 [C] something such as a place to sit, piece of equipment etc that you are given to use for a particular purpose: *an aeroplane seat assignment*

as·sim·i·late /əˈsɪmɪleɪt/ v **1** [T] to completely understand and begin to use new ideas, information etc; ◻ **absorb**: *It will take time to assimilate all these facts.* **2** [I,T] if people assimilate or are assimilated into a country or group, they become part of that group and are accepted by the people in that group: [+into] *Refugees find it difficult to become assimilated into the community.*

as·sim·i·la·tion /əˌsɪmɪˈleɪʃən/ n **1** [U + of] the process of understanding and using new ideas **2** [U + into] the process of becoming an accepted part of a country or group

as·sist¹ S3 W3 /əˈsɪst/ v formal
1 [I,T] to help someone to do something: **assist (sb) with/in sth** *You will be employed to assist in the development of new equipment.*; → see box at HELP¹
2 [T] to make it easier for someone to do something: *They had no maps to assist them.*

assist² n [C] an action that helps another player on your sports team to make a point

as·sist·ance S3 W2 /əˈsɪstəns/ n [U] help or support: **offer/provide/give assistance (to sb)** *We offer financial assistance to students.* | **financial/technical/legal/military assistance** *Technical assistance for the product is free of charge.* | *Can I be of any assistance* (=can I help you)*?* | **with the assistance of sb/sth** *We've only been able to rebuild the theatre with the assistance of the National Lottery.* | *One of her fellow passengers came to her assistance* (=helped her).

as·sis·tant¹ /əˈsɪstənt/ adj **assistant manager/director/cook etc** someone whose job is just below the level of manager, etc

assistant² S3 n [C]
1 someone who helps someone else in their work, especially by doing the less important jobs: *a clerical assistant*
2 BrE a SHOP ASSISTANT → PERSONAL ASSISTANT

asˌsistant proˈfessor n [C] the lowest rank of PROFESSOR at an American university

asˌsisted reproˈduction n [U] medical methods that are used to help a woman have a baby

asˌsisted ˈsuicide n [C,U] when a doctor or someone else helps a person who is very ill to kill themselves in order to end their suffering; → euthanasia

as·siz·es /əˈsaɪzɪz/ n [plural] old use a meeting of a court in which a judge who travelled to different towns in Britain dealt with cases

assn. also **assn** BrE a written abbreviation of *association*

assoc. also **assoc** BrE a written abbreviation of *association*

1 [T] to make a connection in your mind between one thing or person and another: **associate sb/sth with sth** *I don't associate him with energetic sports.*
2 be associated (with sb/sth) a) to be related to a particular subject, activity etc: *problems associated with cancer treatment* **b)** also **associate yourself with sb/sth** to show that you support someone or something: *He did not associate himself with the pro-democracy movement.*
3 associate with sb to spend time with someone, especially someone that other people disapprove of: *I don't like these layabouts you're associating with.*

as·so·ci·ate² /ə'səʊʃi̱t, ə'səʊsi- $ ə'soʊ-/ n [C] someone who you work or do business with; **■ colleague**: *one of his business associates*

associate³ *adj* **associate member/director/head etc** someone who is a member etc of something, but who is at a lower level and has fewer rights

as,sociated 'company n [C] a company of which 20 to 50 per cent of the SHARES are owned by another company

As,sociate of 'Arts, **as'sociate de,gree** n [C] *AmE* a degree given after two years of study at a COMMUNITY COLLEGE in the US

as,sociate pro'fessor n [C] a PROFESSOR at an American university whose job is above the level of ASSISTANT PROFESSOR and below the level of PROFESSOR

as·so·ci·a·tion [S3] [W1] /ə,səʊsi'eɪʃən, ə,səʊʃi- $ ə,soʊ-/ n
1 [C] an organization that consists of a group of people who have the same aims, do the same kind of work etc: *the Association of Master Builders* → HOUSING ASSOCIATION
2 [C,U] a relationship with a particular person, organization, group etc: [+with] *his close association with the Green Party*
3 in association with sb/sth made or done with another person, organization etc: *concerts sponsored by the Arts Council in association with local businesses*
4 [C] a connection or relationship between two events, ideas, situations etc: [+between] *the strong association between the disease and middle-aged women*
5 [C] a feeling or memory that is related to a particular place, event, word etc: *Scotland has all kinds of happy associations for me.*

As,sociation 'football n [U] *BrE* FOOTBALL

as·so·cia·tive /ə'səʊʃətɪv, ə'səʊsiə- $ ə'soʊ-/ *adj* technical reminding you of something else: *the brain's ability to form associative links between different things*

as·so·nance /'æsənəns/ n [U] technical similarity in the vowel sounds of words that are close together in a poem, for example between 'born' and 'warm'

as·sort·ed /ə'sɔːt̪d $ -ɔːr-/ adj of various different types: *paintbrushes in assorted sizes* | *assorted vegetables* → ILL-ASSORTED

as·sort·ment /ə'sɔːtmənt $ -ɔːr-/ n [C] a mixture of different things or of various kinds of the same thing: [+of] *a wide assortment of friends* | *an odd assortment of knives and forks*

asst. also **asst** *BrE* the written abbreviation of *assistant*

as·suage /ə'sweɪdʒ/ v [T] literary to make an unpleasant feeling less painful or severe; **■ relieve**: *Nothing could assuage his guilt.*

as·sume [S1] [W1] /ə'sjuːm $ ə'suːm/ v [T]
1 to think that something is true, although you do not have definite proof; **■ presume**: **assume (that)** *I didn't see your car, so I assumed you'd gone out.* | **it is/seems reasonable to assume (that)** *It seems reasonable to assume that the book was written around 70 AD.* | *I think we can safely assume* (=it is almost certain) *that interest rates will go up again soon.* | **let us/let's assume (that)** (=used when thinking about a possible event or situation and its possible results) *Let us assume for a moment that we could indeed fire her. Should we?* | *When it got to midnight and Paul was still not back, I began to*

assume the worst (=think that the worst possible thing had happened).
2 assume control/responsibility etc formal to start to have control, responsibility etc or to start in a particular position or job: *Whoever they appoint will* **assume responsibility for** *all financial matters.* | *He* **assumed power** *in a bloody coup in 1990.* | *Jim Paton will* **assume the role of** *managing director.*
3 assume a manner/air/expression etc formal to behave in a way that does not show how you really feel, especially in order to seem more confident, happy etc than you are; **■ put on**: *Andy assumed an air of indifference whenever her name was mentioned.*
4 to start to have a particular quality or appearance; **■ take on**: *These relationships* **assume** *great importance in times of crisis.* | *The problem is beginning to* **assume massive proportions**.
5 to be based on the idea that something else is correct; **■ presuppose**: **assume (that)** *The theory assumes that both labour and capital are mobile.* | *Coen's economic forecast assumes a 3.5% growth rate.* → ASSUMING

as,sumed 'name n [C] if you do something under an assumed name, you do it using a name that is not your real name; **■ pseudonym**: *He's been living in Peru under an assumed name.*

as·sum·ing /ə'sjuːmɪŋ $ ə'suː-/ also **as'suming that** conjunction used when talking about an event or situation that might happen, and what you will do if it happens: *Assuming that you get a place at university, how are you going to finance your studies?*

as·sump·tion [S2] [W2] /ə'sʌmpʃən/ n
1 [C] something that you think is true although you have no definite proof: **assumption that** *A lot of people* **make the assumption** *that poverty only exists in the Third World.* | *My calculations were* **based on the assumption** *that house prices would remain steady.* | *We are* **working on the assumption** *that the conference will take place as planned.* | [+about] *People make a lot of assumptions about me.* | **underlying assumption** (=a belief that is used as the basis for an idea, but which may not be correct)
2 [U] formal when someone starts to have control or power: [+of] *the assumption of responsibility*

as·sur·ance /ə'ʃʊərəns $ ə'ʃʊr-/ n   **1** [C] a promise that something will definitely happen or is definitely true, made especially to make someone less worried: *Despite my repeated assurances, Rob still looked very nervous.* | **give/seek/receive an assurance (that)** *He gave an assurance that the work would be completed by Wednesday.*   **2** [U] a feeling of calm confidence about your own abilities, or that you are right about something: *the calm assurance with which she handled the horse* | *'Jack will never agree to that,' he said with assurance.*   **3** [U] *BrE* technical insurance, especially to provide money when someone dies; **■ insurance** *AmE* → LIFE ASSURANCE

as·sure [S2] [W3] /ə'ʃʊə $ ə'ʃʊr/ v [T]
1 to tell someone that something will definitely happen or is definitely true so that they are less worried; **■ reassure**: **assure sb that** *Her doctor has assured us that she'll be fine.* | *The document is genuine, I can assure you.* | **assure sb of sth** *The dealer had assured me of its quality.* → **rest assured** at REST² (5)
2 to make something certain to happen or to be achieved; **■ ensure**: *Excellent reviews have assured the film's success.* | **assure sb (of) sth** *A win on Saturday will assure them of promotion to Division One.*
3 assure yourself formal to check that something is correct or true: **assure yourself that** *Tim waited a moment to assure himself that he was not being followed.* | [+of] *I took steps to assure myself of her guilt.*
4 the sum assured formal the amount of insurance money to be paid out when someone dies

[1] 000, [2] 000, [3] 000, most frequent words in [S]poken and [W]ritten English

as·sured /ə'ʃʊəd $ ə'ʃʊrd/ adj **1** confident about your own abilities; ☰ **self-assured**: *an assured manner* **2 be assured of sth** if you are assured of something, you will definitely get it or achieve it: *His victory means that he is now assured of a place in the final.* **3** certain to happen or to be achieved: *Her political future looks assured.* **4 the assured** BrE technical someone whose life has been insured

as·sur·ed·ly /ə'ʃʊərᵻdli $ ə'ʃʊr-/ adv formal definitely or certainly: *I am most assuredly in favour.*

as·te·risk /'æstərɪsk/ n [C] a mark like a star (*), used especially to show something interesting or important —**asterisk** v [T]

a·stern /ə'stɜːn $ -ɜːrn/ adv in or at the back of a ship

as·te·roid /'æstərɔɪd/ n [C] one of the many small PLANETS that move around the sun, especially between Mars and Jupiter

asth·ma /'æsmə $ 'æzmə/ n [U] a medical condition that causes difficulties in breathing

asth·mat·ic /æs'mætɪk $ æz-/ n [C] someone who suffers from asthma —**asthmatic** adj: *My son's asthmatic.* | *an asthmatic attack*

as·tig·ma·tis·m /ə'stɪgmətɪzəm/ n [U] difficulty in seeing clearly that is caused by a change in the inner shape of the eye

as·ton·ish /ə'stɒnɪʃ $ ə'staː-/ v [T] to surprise someone very much; ☰ **amaze**: *Her reply astonished me.* | *It astonished him that she had changed so little.* | *What astonishes me most is his complete lack of fear.*

as·ton·ished /ə'stɒnɪʃt $ ə'staː-/ adj very surprised about something; ☰ **amazed**: **astonished to see/find/hear/learn etc** *We were astonished to find the temple still in its original condition.* | **[+by/at]** *I was astonished by the result.* | **astonished (that)** *I'm astonished that you should even think such a thing!*

as·ton·ish·ing /ə'stɒnɪʃɪŋ $ ə'staː-/ adj so surprising that it is difficult to believe; ☰ **amazing**: *an astonishing decision* | *their astonishing success* —**astonishingly** adv: *an astonishingly good voice*

as·ton·ish·ment /ə'stɒnɪʃmənt $ ə'staː-/ n [U] complete surprise; ☰ **amazement**: **in astonishment** *She stared at him in astonishment.* | **to sb's astonishment** *To my astonishment, the car was gone.*

as·tound /ə'staʊnd/ v [T] to make someone very surprised or shocked; ☰ **astonish**: *The judge's decision astounded everyone.*

as·tound·ed /ə'staʊndᵻd/ adj very surprised or shocked; ☰ **astonished**: **[+by/at]** *She was astounded by his arrogance.*

as·tound·ing /ə'staʊndɪŋ/ adj so surprising that it is almost impossible to believe; ☰ **astonishing**: *The concert was an astounding success.* —**astoundingly** adv: *astoundingly beautiful scenery.*

as·tra·khan /ˌæstrə'kæn◂ $ 'æstrəkən/ n [U] curly black or grey fur used for making coats and hats

as·tral /'æstrəl/ adj **1** relating to ideas and experiences connected with the mind and SPIRIT rather than the body: *out-of-body experiences and astral travel* **2** relating to the stars

a·stray /ə'streɪ/ adv **1 go astray a)** to be lost or stolen: *The letter had gone astray in the post.* **b)** if a plan or action goes astray, it goes wrong: *The best-laid plans can go astray.* **2 lead sb astray a)** to encourage someone to do bad or illegal things that they would not normally do: *The older boys led him astray.* **b)** to make someone believe something that is not true: *It's easy to be led astray by the reports in the papers.*

a·stride /ə'straɪd/ adv, prep **1** with one leg on each side of something: *a photograph of my mother sitting astride a horse* **2** on both sides of a river, road etc: *The ancient town of Bridgwater, astride the River Parrett, is an ideal touring centre.*

as·trin·gent¹ /ə'strɪndʒənt/ adj **1** an astringent liquid is able to make your skin less oily or stop a

wound from bleeding **2** criticizing someone very severely: *astringent remarks* **3** having a sharp acid taste —**astringency** n [U]

astringent² n [C,U] technical a liquid used to make your skin less oily or to stop a wound from bleeding

astro- /'æstrəʊ, -trə $ -troʊ, -trə/ prefix relating to the stars, the PLANETS, or space: *an astronaut* (=someone who travels in space) | *astronomy* (=scientific study of the stars)

as·trol·o·ger /ə'strɒlədʒə $ ə'straːlədʒər/ n [C] someone who uses astrology to tell people about their character, life, or future

as·trol·o·gy /ə'strɒlədʒi $ ə'straː-/ n [U] the study of the positions and movements of the stars and how they might influence people and events; → **astronomy** —**astrological** /ˌæstrə'lɒdʒɪkəl◂ $ -'laː-/ adj

as·tro·naut /'æstrənɔːt $ -nɒːt, -naːt/ n [C] someone who travels and works in a spacecraft

as·tron·o·mer /ə'strɒnəmə $ ə'straːnəmər/ n [C] a scientist who studies the stars and PLANETS

as·tro·nom·i·cal /ˌæstrə'nɒmɪkəl◂ $ -'naː-/ adj **1** informal astronomical prices, costs etc are extremely high **2** [only before noun] relating to the scientific study of the stars —**astronomically** /-kli/ adv: *astronomically high rents*

as·tron·o·my /ə'strɒnəmi $ ə'straː-/ n [U] the scientific study of the stars and PLANETS; → **astrology**

as·tro·phys·ics /ˌæstrəʊ'fɪzɪks $ ˌæstrə-, -troʊ-/ n [U] the scientific study of the chemical structure of the stars and the forces that influence them —**astrophysicist** /-'fɪzᵻsᵻst/ n [C]

As·tro·Turf /'æstrəʊtɜːf $ -troʊtɜːrf/ n [U] trademark an artificial surface like grass that sports are played on

as·tute /ə'stjuːt $ ə'stuːt/ adj able to understand situations or behaviour very well and very quickly, especially so that you can get an advantage for yourself; ☰ **clever**: *an astute politician* | *astute investments* —**astutely** adv —**astuteness** n [U]

a·sun·der /ə'sʌndə $ -ər/ adv literary **be torn/split/rent etc asunder** to be torn violently apart or destroyed: *a nation torn asunder by internal conflicts*

a·sy·lum /ə'saɪləm/ n **1** [U] protection given to someone by a government because they have escaped from fighting or political trouble in their own country: **apply for/seek/be granted asylum** *He has been granted asylum in France.* → POLITICAL ASYLUM **2** [C] old use a MENTAL HOSPITAL

a'sylum ˌseeker n [C] someone who leaves their own country because they are in danger, especially for political reasons, and who asks the government of another country to allow them to live there; → **refugee**: *The government halted its policy of returning Zimbabwean asylum seekers to their homeland.*

a·sym·met·ri·cal /ˌeɪsᵻ'metrɪkəl/ also **a·sym·met·ric** /-'metrɪk◂/ adj **1** having two sides that are different in shape; ☒ **symmetrical**: *asymmetrical patterns* **2** formal not equal; ☒ **symmetrical** —**asymmetrically** /-kli/ adv —**asymmetry** /eɪ'sɪmᵻtri/ n [U]

a·symp·to·mat·ic /ˌeɪˌsɪmptəmætɪk, eɪ- $ eɪ-/ adj medical if someone or the illness that they have is asymptomatic, the illness has no physical signs

at S1 W1 /ət; strong æt/ prep **1** used to say exactly where something or someone is, or where something happens: *They live at 18 Victoria Street.* | *Does this train stop at Preston?* | *I was waiting at the bus stop.* | *Liz and her friend sat down at a corner table.* | *Turn left at the church.* | *We'll meet at Harry's* (=at Harry's house). | *I spent an unpleasant hour at the dentist's.* | *Dad's at work* (=in the place where he works). | **at the top/bottom/end etc (of sth)** *At the top of the stairs, she paused.* **2** used to say what event or activity someone is taking part in: *I met my wife at a disco.* | *The matter was discussed at a meeting of the finance committee.* | *I'm sorry, Pam's at lunch just now.*

3 used to say that someone is studying somewhere regularly: *Is Jessica still at school?* | *Hulme was a student at Oxford in the 1960s.*
4 used to say exactly when something happens: *The film starts at 8 o'clock.*
5 during a particular period of time: *My husband often works at night.* | *We go to Midnight Mass at Christmas.*
6 used to say which thing or person an action is directed towards or intended for: *He gazed up at the sky.* | *You don't have to shout at me.* | *The older girls used to throw stones at me.* | *The course is aimed at those aged 16 or over.*
7 used to say what or who causes an action or feeling: *The children all laughed at his jokes.* | *I'm surprised at you!* | *Dad got really mad at me for scratching the car.* | *her distress at having to leave*
8 used to say which subject or activity you are talking about when you say whether someone is skilful, successful etc or not: *Barbara's getting on really well at her new job.* | **good/bad etc at (doing) sth** *I've always been good at maths.* | *Matt's bad at handling people.* | *He's an expert at making things out of junk.*
9 used to say that someone or something is in a particular state: *two nations at war* | *Many children are still at risk from neglect or abuse.*
10 used to show a price, rate, level, age, speed etc: *old books selling at 10 cents each* | *You should have more sense at your age.* | *The Renault was travelling at about 50 mph.* | *Amanda rode off at a gallop.*
11 at your best/worst/most effective etc used to say that, at a particular time, someone or something is as good, bad etc as they can be: *The garden is at its best in June.* | *This was Sampras at his most powerful.*
12 used to say what someone tries to touch, or keeps touching: *I clutched at the rope but missed.* | *George was just picking at his food.* | *Sarah took another sip at her wine.*
13 used to say what someone tries to do: *the student's first attempt at a piece of research* | *They were so beautiful that I decided to have a go at growing them.*
14 because of what someone has said: *Chapman visited Austria at the invitation of his friend, Hugo Meisl.* | *At my suggestion, Bernard went to see his former teacher.*
15 while I'm/you're etc at it *spoken* used to suggest that someone should do something while they are doing something else: *I'm just going for a cup of coffee. Shall I bring you one while I'm at it?*
16 be at it again *informal* if you say that someone is at it again, you mean that they are doing something you disapprove of, which they have done before: *She's at it again. Interfering in other people's business.*
17 at that a) also or besides: *It's a new idea, and a good one, at that.* **b)** after something is said: *Tess called him a liar and at that he stormed out of the room.*
18 be where it's at *old-fashioned informal* used to say that a place or activity is very popular, exciting, and fashionable → **at all** at ALL¹ (6)

A

at·a·vis·tic /ˌætəˈvɪstɪk◂/ *adj formal* atavistic feelings are very basic human feelings that people have felt since humans have existed
ate /et, eɪt $ eɪt/ the past tense of EAT
-ate /ʒt, eɪt/ *suffix* **1** [in adjectives] full of or showing a particular quality: *affectionate* (=showing love)   **2** [in verbs] to make something have a particular quality: *activate* (=make something start working) | *regulate* (=control something or make it regular)   **3** [in nouns] a group of people with particular duties: *the electorate* (=voters)   **4** [in nouns] the job, rank, or degree of a particular type of person: *She was awarded her doctorate* (– PhD).   **5** [in nouns] a chemical salt formed from a particular acid: *phosphate* —**ately** /ʒtli/ [in adverbs]: *fortunately*
a·tel·i·er /əˈteliei $ ˌætʒlˈjeɪ/ *n* [C] a room or building where an artist works; **□ studio**
a·the·is·m /ˈeɪθi-ɪzəm/ *n* [U] the belief that God does not exist; → **agnosticism (agnostic)** —**atheist** *n* [C] —**atheistic** /ˌeɪθiˈɪstɪk◂/ *adj*
ath·lete /ˈæθliːt/ *n* [C]   **1** someone who competes in sports competitions, especially running, jumping, and throwing: *a professional athlete*   **2** someone who is good at sports and who often does sports: *I was a natural athlete as a kid.*
athlete's 'foot *n* [U] a medical condition in which the skin between your toes cracks
ath·let·ic /æθˈletɪk, əθ-/ *adj*   **1** physically strong and good at sport: *a tall athletic man*   **2** [only before noun] relating to athletics: *athletic ability*
ath·let·i·cis·m /æθˈletᵻsɪzəm, əθ-/ *n* [U] the ability to play sports or do physical activities well
ath·let·ics /æθˈletɪks, əθ-/ *n* [U]   **1** *BrE* sports such as running and jumping; **□ track and field** *AmE*   **2** *AmE* physical activities such as sports and exercise
-athon /əθɒn $ əθɑːn/ *suffix* [in nouns] an event in which a particular thing is done for a very long time, especially to collect money: *a swimathon*
-ation /eɪʃən/ *suffix* [in nouns] the act, state, or result of doing something: *an examination of the contents* (=examining them) | *the combination of several factors*
a·tish·oo *BrE* /əˈtɪʃuː/ also **achoo** a word used to represent the sound you make when you SNEEZE
-ative /ətɪv $ ətɪv, eɪtɪv/ *suffix* [in adjectives] liking something or tending to do something or show a par-

ticular quality: *talkative* (=liking to talk a lot) | *argumentative* (=enjoying arguments) | *imaginative* (=showing imagination)

at·las /'ætləs/ n [C] a book containing maps, especially of the whole world → ROAD ATLAS

ATM /,eɪ ti: 'em/ n [C] *automated teller machine* a machine outside a bank that you use to get money from your account; ⊟ **cashpoint**; → see picture at CASH MACHINE

at·mo·sphere W2 /'ætməsfɪə $ -fɪr/ n
1 [C,U] the feeling that an event or place gives you: *The hotel had a lovely relaxed atmosphere.* | *The atmosphere at home was rather tense.* | [+of] *An atmosphere of optimism dominated the conference.*
2 [U] if a place or event has atmosphere, it is interesting: *The castle was centuries old and full of atmosphere.* | *The match was lacking in atmosphere.*
3 the atmosphere the mixture of gases that surrounds the Earth → see picture at GREENHOUSE EFFECT
4 [C] the mixture of gases that surround a PLANET
5 [C usually singular] the air inside a room: *a smoky atmosphere*

at·mo·spher·ic /,ætməs'ferɪk◂/ adj **1** [only before noun] relating to the Earth's atmosphere: *atmospheric pressure* **2** if a place, event, sound etc is atmospheric, it gives you a particular feeling, especially a pleasant or mysterious one: *the atmospheric decor in the restaurant* | *atmospheric music*

at·mo·spher·ics /,ætməs'ferɪks/ n [plural] **1** features or qualities in something, especially a piece of music or a book, that give you a particular feeling **2** continuous cracking noises that sometimes interrupt radio broadcasts

at·oll /'ætɒl $ 'ætɔːl, 'ætɑːl/ n [C] a CORAL island in the shape of a ring

at·om /'ætəm/ n [C] **1** the smallest part of an ELEMENT that can exist alone or can combine with other substances to form a MOLECULE: *carbon atoms* | [+of] *two atoms of hydrogen* **2** a very small amount of something – used for emphasis: [+of] *There isn't an atom of truth in it.*

a·tom·ic /ə'tɒmɪk $ ə'tɑː-/ adj **1** relating to the energy produced by splitting atoms or the weapons that use this energy: *atomic power* | *an atomic submarine* **2** relating to the atoms in a substance: *atomic weight*

a,tomic 'bomb also **'atom ,bomb** n [C] a NUCLEAR bomb that splits atoms to cause an extremely large explosion

a,tomic 'energy n [U] NUCLEAR energy

at·om·ize also **-ise** BrE /'ætəmaɪz/ v [T] **1** to make a substance change into ATOMS **2** especially AmE to divide something so that it is no longer whole or united: *a society that has become atomized*

at·om·izer /'ætəmaɪzə $ -ər/ n [C] a container from which you can make a liquid such as PERFUME come out in very small drops like mist

a·ton·al /eɪ'təʊnəl, æ- $ -'toʊ-/ adj a piece of music that is atonal is not based on a particular KEY² (4) —**atonality** /,eɪtəʊ'nælᵻti, ,æ- $ -toʊ-/ n [U]

a·tone /ə'təʊn $ ə'toʊn/ v [I] formal to do something to show that you are sorry for having done something wrong: [+for] *Richard was anxious to atone for his thoughtlessness.*

a·tone·ment /ə'təʊnmənt $ ə'toʊn-/ n [singular, U] formal something you do to show that you are sorry for having done something wrong: [+for] | *The priest is a representative of his people, making atonement for their sin.*

a·top /ə'tɒp $ ə'tɑːp/ prep literary on top of something

-ator /eɪtə $ -ər/ suffix [in nouns] someone or something that does something: *a narrator* (=someone who tells a story) | *a generator* (=machine that produces electricity)

A to Z /,eɪ tə 'zed $ -'ziː/ n [C] trademark a book with maps that show every street in a British city

at-'risk adj at-risk children/patients/groups etc people who need special care because they are likely to be in danger from violent parents, to become ill etc: at-risk register (=an official list of people in this situation)

at·ri·um /'eɪtriəm/ n [C] **1** a large high open space in a tall building **2** one of the two spaces in the top of your heart that push blood into the VENTRICLES

a·tro·cious /ə'trəʊʃəs $ ə'troʊ-/ adj extremely bad; ⊟ **awful**: *atrocious weather* | *Her singing was atrocious.* —**atrociously** adv

a·troc·i·ty /ə'trɒsᵻti $ ə'trɑː-/ n plural atrocities [C usually plural, U] an extremely cruel and violent action, especially during a war

at·ro·phy /'ætrəfi/ v atrophied, atrophying, atrophies [I,T] if a part of the body atrophies or is atrophied, it becomes weak because of lack of use or lack of blood: *therapy to prevent the leg muscles from atrophying* —**atrophy** n [U]

at·tach S2 W2 /ə'tætʃ/ v
1 [T] to fasten or connect one object to another; ⊟ **fix**: attach sth to sth *Attach a recent photograph to your application form.* | *a small battery attached to a little loudspeaker* | the attached form/cheque/leaflet etc *Please fill in and return the attached reply slip.*
2 be attached to sb/sth to like someone or something very much, because you have known them or had them for a long time: *It's easy to become attached to the children you work with.*
3 attach importance/significance etc to sth to believe that something is important: *People attach too much importance to economic forecasts.*
4 [I,T] if blame attaches or is attached to someone, they are responsible for something bad that happens: *No blame can be attached to Roy for the incident.*
5 [I,T] if a quality, feeling, idea etc attaches or is attached to a person, thing, or event, it is connected with them: [+to] *It's easy to let the emotions attached to one situation spill over into others.*
6 be attached to sth a)** to work for part of a particular organization, especially for a short period of time: *He was attached to the foreign affairs department of a Japanese newspaper.* **b)** to be part of a bigger organization: *The Food Ministry is attached to the Ministry of Agriculture.*
7 [T] to connect a document or FILE to an email so that you can send them together
8 attach yourself to sb to join someone and spend a lot of time with them, often without being invited or welcome: *A young man from Canada had attached himself to Sam.*
9 attach a condition (to sth) to allow something to happen, but only if someone agrees to do a particular thing or accept a particular idea: *When approving a merger, the commission can attach conditions.*
10 attach a label to sb/sth to think of or describe someone or something as being a particular thing, especially in a very general way: *You can't really attach a label to this type of art.*

at·ta·ché /ə'tæʃeɪ $,ætə'ʃeɪ/ n [C] someone who works in an EMBASSY, and deals with a particular subject: *a cultural attaché*

at'taché ,case /,..'. ,./ n [C] a thin case used for carrying business documents

at·tach·ment /ə'tætʃmənt/ n **1** [C,U] a feeling that you like or love someone or something and that you would be unhappy without them: [+to/for] *a child's attachment to its mother* **2** [C] a part that you can put onto a machine to make it do a particular job: *The vacuum cleaner has various attachments.* **3** [U] belief in and loyalty towards a particular idea, organization etc: [+to/for] *old people's attachment to traditional customs* **4** [C] a document or FILE that is sent with an email message: *I'll send the spreadsheet as an attachment.* **5** [C,U] when you fasten or connect one thing to another, or the thing that you use to do this: *Hooks were* *fixed to the wall for the attachment of the ropes.* | *the attachments that secure your boots firmly to the skis* **6 on attachment** working for a particular organization, especially for a short period of time: *He was sent on attachment to their offices in Hong Kong.* **7** [C,U] *law* a situation in which part of the money someone earns or money that is owed to them is taken by a court of law and used to pay their debts **8** [C] *technical* a piece of paper fastened to a document such as an insurance agreement, which shows a special condition of the agreement

at·tack¹ S2 W1 /ə'tæk/ *n*
1 VIOLENCE AGAINST SB/STH [C] an act of violence that is intended to hurt a person or damage a place: [+on] *There have been several attacks on foreigners recently.* | *a bomb attack* | *a knife attack* | *an arson attack* (=an attempt to destroy a building using fire) | *victims of racial attacks*
2 IN A WAR [C,U] the act of using weapons against an enemy in a war: *The attack began at dawn.* | [+on] *the attack on Pearl Harbor* | **be/come under attack** *Once again we came under attack from enemy fighter planes.* | *Rebel forces launched an attack late Sunday night.* | **air/missile/nuclear etc attack** *the threat of nuclear attack*
3 CRITICISM [C,U] a strong and direct criticism of someone or something: [+on] *The magazine recently published a vicious personal attack on the novelist.* | **be/come under attack** (=be strongly criticized) *The company has come under fierce attack for its decision to close the factory.* | **go on the attack** (=start to criticize someone severely)
4 ILLNESS [C] a sudden short period of suffering from an illness, especially an illness that you have often: [+of] *I had a bad attack of flu at Christmas.* | *He died after suffering a severe asthma attack.* → HEART ATTACK
5 EMOTION [C] a short period of time when you suddenly feel extremely frightened or worried and cannot think normally or deal with the situation: **panic/anxiety attack** *Her heart began to pound frantically, as if she were having a panic attack.* | [+of] *a sudden attack of nerves*
6 ATTEMPT TO STOP STH [C,U] actions that are intended to get rid of or stop something such as a system, a set of laws etc: [+on] *The new measures were seen by many as an attack on the Scottish way of life.*
7 SPORT a) [C,U] an attempt by a player or group of players to score GOALS or win points **b)** *BrE* [singular] the players in a team that are responsible for trying to score GOALS or win points; **目 offense** *AmE*; → **defence: in attack** *Heath will play alongside Smith in attack.*
8 DAMAGE [C,U] when something such as a disease, insect, or chemical damages something: *Unfortunately, the carved ceilings have suffered woodworm attack over the years.*

attack² S2 W2 *v*
1 USE VIOLENCE [I,T] to deliberately use violence to hurt a person or damage a place: *She was attacked while walking home late at night.* | *His shop was attacked by a gang of youths.* | *Snakes will only attack if you disturb them.* | **attack sb/sth with sth** *He needed 200 stitches after being attacked with a broken bottle.*
2 IN A WAR [I,T] to start using guns, bombs etc against an enemy in a war: *Army tanks attacked a village near the capital on Sunday.*
3 CRITICIZE [T] to criticize someone or something very strongly: *Last year Dr Travis publicly attacked the idea that abortion should be available on demand.* | **attack sb for (doing) sth** *Newspapers attacked the government for failing to cut taxes.* | **strongly/bitterly/ savagely etc attack sb/sth**
4 DAMAGE [T] if something such as a disease, insect, or chemical attacks something, it damages it: *a cruel disease that attacks the brain and nervous system*
5 BEGIN DOING [T] to begin to do something in a determined and eager way: *She immediately set about attacking the problem.* | *Martin attacked his meal* (=started eating) *with vigour.*

6 SPORT [I,T] to move forward and try to score GOALS or win points; → **defend**: *Brazil began to attack more in the second half of the match.*

at·tack·er /ə'tækə $ -ər/ *n* [C] **1** a person who deliberately uses violence to hurt someone: *Her attacker then dragged her into bushes.* | *a sex attacker* **2** a member of a sports team whose job is to move forward and try to score GOALS or win points; → **defender**

at·tain /ə'teɪn/ *v* [T] *formal* **1** to succeed in achieving something after trying for a long time: *More women are attaining positions of power in public life.* **2** to reach a particular level, age, size etc: *Share prices attained a high of $3.27.* | *After a year she had attained her ideal weight.* —**attainable** *adj*: *This target should be attainable.*

at·tain·ment /ə'teɪnmənt/ *n formal* **1** [U] success in achieving something or reaching a particular level; **目 achievement**: *a low level of educational attainment* **2** [C] something that you have succeeded in achieving or learning, such as a skill; **目 achievement**: *a society remarkable for its cultural attainments*

at·tempt¹ S2 W1 /ə'tempt/ *n* [C]
1 an act of trying to do something, especially something difficult: **attempt to do sth** *All attempts to control inflation have failed.* | *The protesters made no attempt to resist arrest.* | *his first unsuccessful attempt to become an MP* | **In an attempt to** *diffuse the tension I suggested that we break off for lunch.* | **attempt at (doing) sth** *her feeble attempt at humour* | **at the first/ second etc attempt** *She passed her driving test at the first attempt.* | **assassination/suicide/murder attempt**
2 an attempt on sb's life an act of trying to kill someone, especially someone famous or important

attempt² S2 W2 *v* [T]
1 to try to do something, especially something difficult: **attempt to do sth** *In this chapter I will attempt to explain what led up to the revolution.* | *Weather conditions prevented them from attempting the jump.*
2 attempted murder/suicide/rape etc an act of trying to kill or harm someone, kill yourself etc: *He pleaded guilty to attempted murder.*

at·tend S2 W2 /ə'tend/ *v formal*
1 [I,T] to go to an event such as a meeting or a class: *Only 12 people attended the meeting.* | *Please let us know if you are unable to attend.*
2 [I,T] to go regularly to a school, church etc: *I am the first child in my family to attend college.*
3 [T] *formal* to happen or exist at the same time as something: *the peculiar atmosphere which attends such an event*
4 [T usually passive] to look after someone, especially because they are ill: *On his deathbed the General was attended by several doctors.*
   attend to sb/sth *phr v*
1 to deal with business or personal matters: *I may be late – I have got one or two things to attend to.*
2 to help a customer in a shop or a restaurant; **目 serve**

at·tend·ance /ə'tendəns/ *n* **1** [C,U] the number of people who attend a game, concert, meeting etc: *We have an average attendance of 4000 fans per game.* | *Last year's fair saw attendance figures of 32,000.* **2** [C,U] when someone goes to a meeting, class etc, or an occasion when they go: [+at] *Most courses involve an average of eight hours attendance at college each week.* | *The doctor will have a record of her attendances.* **3 be in attendance (at sth)** *formal* to be at a special or important event: *Over 2000 people were in attendance at yesterday's demonstration.* **4 be in attendance on sb** *formal* to look after someone or serve them → **dance attendance on sb** at DANCE² (5)

at·tend·ant¹ /ə'tendənt/ *n* [C] **1** someone whose job is to look after or help customers in a public place: *a carpark attendant* **2** someone who looks after a very important person, for example a king or queen

A

A

attendant² *adj formal* relating to or caused by something: **attendant problems/difficulties/dangers** etc *nuclear power, with all its attendant risks* | [+**on**] *Drugs are one of the issues attendant on running a school.*

at·ten·dee /ə,ten'diː, ˌæten-/ *n* [C] someone who is at an event such as a meeting or a course

at·tend·er /ə'tendə $ -ər/ *n* [C] someone who regularly goes to an event such as a meeting or a class: *Daniel was a **regular attender** at the Baptist Church.*

at·ten·tion S1 W1 /ə'tenʃən/ *n*
1 LISTEN/LOOK/THINK CAREFULLY [U] when you carefully listen to, look at, or think about someone or something

> **sb's attention is on sb/sth**
> **pay attention (to sb/sth)**
> **turn your attention to sb/sth** (=start listening to, looking at, or thinking about something)
> **give (your) attention to sb/sth** (=listen to, look at, or think about something, so that you can deal with a problem)
> **sb's full/complete/undivided attention**
> **keep sb's attention**
> **close/careful attention**
> **attention to detail**
> **sb's attention wanders**
> **may/could I have your attention?** (=used when asking a group of people to listen carefully to you)

*My **attention** wasn't really **on** the game.* | *She tried to **pay attention to** what he was saying.* | *If you **paid** more **attention** in class, you might actually learn something!* | *Scott sat down at his desk and **turned** his **attention** to the file he had in front of him.* | *As a society we need to **give** more **attention to** the needs of older people.* | *Now he's gone, I can **give you my undivided attention**.* | *This game is fun and is sure to **keep the attention of** any young student.* | *They listened to the speech with **close attention**.* | ***Attention to detail** is essential in this job.* | *During the lecture Sarah's **attention** began to **wander**.*

2 INTEREST [plural,U] the interest that people show in someone or something: *She was flattered by all the **attention** he was **giving** her.* | **attract/receive/enjoy attention** *a player who quickly attracted the attention of several clubs* | *The exhibition received little attention in the press.* | **public/media/press attention** *Her case attracted a great deal of media attention.* | **hold/keep sb's attention** (=make someone stay interested and keep reading, listening, watching etc) *The book holds the reader's attention right to the very end.* | *Rob loves being **the centre of attention** (=the person who everyone is interested in, listens to etc).* | *She spent a lot of time trying to avoid the **attentions** (=romantic interest) of her boss.* | *The man then **turned his attentions to** (=became romantically interested in) her sister.*

3 NOTICE **a)** **attract/catch/get sb's attention** to make someone notice you, especially because you want to speak to them or you need their help: *She waved to attract the attention of the waitress.* **b)** **get attention** to make someone notice you and be interested in what you are doing: *Children often misbehave in order to get attention.* **c)** **draw/call attention to sth** also **focus attention on sth** to make people notice and be concerned or think about something: *The purpose of the article was to draw attention to the problems faced by single parents.* | *We wanted to focus public attention on this matter.* | *He left quietly to avoid drawing attention to himself.* **d)** **divert/distract/draw attention from sth** to make people stop being concerned about something such as a social problem: *All this talk of war is just an attempt to draw attention away from the serious economic problems that face our country.* **e)** **bring sth to sb's attention** to tell someone, especially someone in authority, about something such as a problem: *The matter was first brought to my attention earlier this year.* **f)** **come to sb's attention** if something such as a

problem comes to the attention of someone in authority, they find out about it: *It came to my attention that Jenny was claiming overtime pay for hours she had not worked.* **g)** **escape your attention** if something escaped your attention, you did not notice it: *This fact had not escaped the attention of the authorities.*

4 REPAIR/CLEANING [U] something you do to repair or clean something: *The bike's in fairly good condition, but the gears **need** a bit of **attention**.*

5 CARE [U] things that you do to help or to take care of someone or something: *Pets need a lot of **care and attention**.* | *Anyone who comes into contact with these chemicals should seek urgent **medical attention**.* | *Your plants look like they **could do with a bit of attention**.*

6 **stand to/at attention** if soldiers stand to attention, they stand up straight in neat lines

7 **attention! a)** used to ask people to listen to important information that is being announced, especially on a LOUDSPEAKER (=piece of equipment used to make sounds louder): *Attention, please! Could Passenger Marie Thomas please proceed to Gate 25 immediately.* **b)** used when ordering a group of soldiers to stand up straight in neat lines

8 **for the attention of sb** used on the front of an official letter when you want a particular person to read it or deal with it: *Letters should be marked 'for the attention of Joe Benson'.*

at,tention 'deficit dis,order *n* [U] ADD a medical condition that especially affects children. It causes them to be too active and to be unable to pay attention or be quiet for very long.

at'tention ,span *n* [C usually singular] the period of time during which you continue to be interested in something: *Children often have a **short attention span**.*

at·ten·tive /ə'tentɪv/ *adj* **1** listening to or watching someone carefully because you are interested; ⚡ **inattentive**: *an attentive audience* **2** making sure someone has everything they need: [+**to**] *Customers want companies that are attentive to their needs.* —**attentively** *adv* —**attentiveness** *n* [U]

at·ten·u·ate /ə'tenjueɪt/ *v* [T] *formal* to make something weaker or less: *an attenuated form of the polio virus*

at·test /ə'test/ *v formal* **1** [I,T] to show or prove that something is true: [+**to**] *Luxurious furnishings attested to the wealth of the owner.* **2** [T] to officially state that you believe something is true, especially in a court of law

at·tes·ta·tion /ˌæte'steɪʃən/ *n* [C,U] *formal* a legal statement made by someone in which they say that something is definitely true

at·tic /'ætɪk/ *n* [C] a space or room just below the roof of a house, often used for storing things: *a small **attic room***

at·tire /ə'taɪə $ ə'taɪr/ *n* [U] *formal* clothes: *business attire*

at·tired /ə'taɪəd $ ə'taɪrd/ *adj* [not before noun] *formal* dressed in a particular way: *He arrived **suitably attired** in a dark dinner suit.*

at·ti·tude S1 W1 /'ætᵻtjuːd $ -tuːd/ *n*
1 [C,U] the opinions and feelings that you usually have about something: [+**to/towards**] *Pete's attitude towards women really scares me.* | **positive/negative attitude** *people with a positive attitude to life* | *the country's **attitude of mind** (=way of thinking) during the crisis*
2 [C,U] the way that you behave towards someone or in a particular situation, especially when this shows how you feel: *an aggressive attitude* | *As soon as they found out I was a doctor their whole attitude changed.* | *Ben has a real **attitude problem** (=is not helpful or pleasant to be with).*
3 [U] *informal* a style of dressing, behaving etc that shows you have the confidence to do unusual and exciting things without caring what other people think: **with attitude** *a coat with attitude* —**attitudinal** /ˌætᵻ'tjuːdənəl $ -'tuː-/ *adj*

attn. *attention* used to say that a letter or package is for a particular person

at·tor·ney S2 W2 /ə'tɜːni $ -ɜːr-/ *n* [C] *AmE* a lawyer; → see box at LAWYER

at,torney 'general *n* [C] the lawyer with the highest rank in some countries or in the US government

at·tract S2 W2 /ə'trækt/ *v* [T]
1 to make someone interested in something, or make them want to take part in something: **attract sb to sth** *What attracted me most to the job was the chance to travel.* | **attract attention/interest etc** *The story has attracted a lot of interest from the media.*
2 be attracted to sb to feel that you like someone and want to have a sexual relationship with them: *I'm not usually attracted to blondes.*
3 to make someone like or admire something or feel romantically interested in someone: *I guess it was his eyes that attracted me first.*
4 to make someone or something move towards another thing: *Leftover food attracts flies.* | *low rents designed to attract new businesses to the area*

at·trac·tion W3 /ə'trækʃən/ *n*
1 [C,U] a feeling of liking someone, especially in a sexual way: *The attraction between them was almost immediate.*
2 [C] something interesting or enjoyable to see or do: *The beautiful beaches are the island's main attraction* (=most popular place, activity etc). | **tourist attraction** (=a place that many tourists visit)
3 [C,U] a feature or quality that makes something seem interesting or enjoyable: [+of] *Being your own boss is one of the attractions of owning your own business.*
4 [C,U] *technical* a force which makes things move together or stay together: *gravitational attraction*

at·trac·tive S2 W2 /ə'træktɪv/ *adj*
1 someone who is attractive is good looking, especially in a way that makes you sexually interested in them: *an attractive young woman* | *Women seem to find him attractive.* → see box at BEAUTIFUL
2 pleasant to look at: *Kitchen utensils should be attractive as well as functional.*
3 having qualities that make you want to accept something or be involved in it: [+to] *a political movement that is attractive to young people* | **attractive offer/proposition/package etc** *I must say, it's a very attractive offer.* —**attractively** *adv* —**attractiveness** *n* [U]

at·trib·u·ta·ble /ə'trɪbjˈtəbəl/ *adj* [not before noun] likely to have been caused by something: [+to] *Death was attributable to gunshot wounds.*

at·tri·bute¹ /ə'trɪbjuːt $ -bjət/ *v*
attribute sth **to** sb/sth *phr v* **1** to believe or say that a situation or event is caused by something: *The fall in the number of deaths from heart disease is generally attributed to improvements in diet.* **2** if people in general attribute a particular statement, painting, piece of music etc to someone, they believe that person said it, painted it etc: *a saying usually attributed to Confucius* **3** to believe or say that someone or something has a particular quality: *One should not attribute human motives to animals.* —**attribution** /,ætrˈbjuːʃən/ *n* [U]

at·tri·bute² /'ætrˌbjuːt/ *n* [C] a quality or feature, especially one that is considered to be good or useful: *What attributes should a good manager possess?*

at·trib·u·tive /ə'trɪbjˈtɪv/ *adj* describing and coming before a noun. For example, in the phrase 'big city', 'big' is an attributive adjective, and in the phrase 'school bus', 'school' is a noun in an attributive position.; → **predicative** —**attributively** *adv*

at·tri·tion /ə'trɪʃən/ *n* [U] *formal* **1** the process of gradually destroying your enemy or making them weak by attacking them continuously: *a war of attrition* **2** *especially AmE* when people leave a company or course of study and are not replaced: *Staff reductions could be achieved through attrition and early retirements.*

at·tuned /ə'tjuːnd $ ə'tuːnd/ *adj* **be/become attuned to sth** to be or become familiar with the way someone thinks or behaves so that you can react to them in a suitable way: *British companies still aren't really attuned to the needs of the Japanese market.*

atty. *n AmE* the written abbreviation of *attorney*

ATV /,eɪ tiː 'viː/ *n* [C] **all terrain vehicle** a vehicle which is designed to be ridden on rough ground where there are no roads. ATVs have one seat, no roof, and three or four large wheels.

a·typ·i·cal /eɪ'tɪpɪkəl/ *adj* not typical or usual

au·ber·gine /'əʊbəʒiːn $ 'oʊbər-/ *n* [C,U] *BrE* a large dark purple vegetable; ⊟ **eggplant** *AmE*; → see picture at VEGETABLE¹

au·burn /'ɔːbən $ 'ɒːbərn/ *adj* auburn hair is a reddish brown colour —**auburn** *n* [U]

auc·tion¹ /'ɔːkʃən $ 'ɒːk-/ *n* [C,U] a public meeting where land, buildings, paintings etc are sold to the person who offers the most money for them: **at auction** *The house was sold at auction.* | **put sth up for auction** (=try to sell something at an auction) *This week 14 of his paintings were put up for auction.* | **auction house** (=a company that arranges auctions)

auction² *v* [T + off] to sell something at an auction

auc·tio·neer /,ɔːkʃə'nɪə $,ɒːkʃə'nɪr/ *n* [C] someone who is in charge of selling the things at an auction and who calls out how much money has already been offered for something

au·da·cious /ɔː'deɪʃəs $ ɒː-/ *adj* showing great courage or confidence in a way that is impressive or slightly shocking: *the risks involved in such an audacious operation* —**audaciously** *adv*

au·dac·i·ty /ɔː'dæsˌti $ ɒː-/ *n* [U] the quality of having enough courage to take risks or say impolite things: **have the audacity to do sth** | *I can't believe he had the audacity to ask me for more money!*

au·di·ble /'ɔːdˌbəl $ 'ɒː-/ *adj* a sound that is audible is loud enough for you to hear it; ⊟ **inaudible**: *His voice was barely audible* (=could only just be heard) *above the roar of the crowd.* —**audibly** *adv* —**audibility** /,ɔːdˌ'bɪlˌti $,ɒː-/ *n* [U]

audience

crowd

audience

au·di·ence S2 W2 /'ɔːdiəns $ 'ɒː-, 'ɑː-/ *n*
1 [C also + plural verb] *BrE* a group of people who come to watch and listen to someone speaking or performing in public: *The audience began clapping and cheering.* | [+of] *an audience of 250 business people* | *One member of the audience described the opera as 'boring'.*
2 [C also + plural verb] *BrE* the people who watch or listen to a particular programme, or who see or hear a particular artist's, writer's etc work: *The show attracts a regular audience of about 20 million.* | **target audience** (=the type of people that a programme, advertisement etc is supposed to attract) | *Goya was one of the first painters to look for a wider audience for his work.* | *The book is not intended for a purely academic audience.*
3 [C] a formal meeting with a very important person: [+with] *He was granted an audience with the Pope.*

au·di·o[1] /'ɔːdiəʊ $ 'ɒːdioʊ/ adj [only before noun] relating to sound that is recorded or broadcast: *audio and video equipment*

audio[2] n [U] the part of a recording that contains sounds and music but not pictures: *You can save the audio for editing later.*

audio- prefix [in nouns and adjectives] relating to hearing or sound: *an audio-cassette*

au·di·o·tape /'ɔːdiəʊteɪp $ 'ɒːdioʊ-/ n [C,U] technical a long thin band of MAGNETIC material used to record sound

au·di·o·ty·pist /'ɔːdiəʊˌtaɪpɪ̣st $ 'ɒːdioʊ-/ n [C] BrE someone whose job is to type letters that have been recorded

au·di·o·vis·u·al /ˌɔːdiəʊ'vɪʒuəl◂ $ ˌɒːdioʊ-/ adj [only before noun] involving the use of recorded pictures and sound: *the use of audiovisual materials in the classroom*

au·dit[1] /'ɔːdɪ̣t $ 'ɒː-/ n [C,U] **1** an official examination of a company's financial records in order to check that they are correct: *the annual audit* | **internal audit** (=an audit carried out by a company's own staff) **2** formal a detailed examination of something in order to check if it is good enough: *Start with an audit of existing services within the community.*

audit[2] v [T] **1** to officially examine a company's financial records in order to check that they are correct **2** AmE to attend a course at university without intending to take examinations in it or get a CREDIT for it

au·di·tion[1] /ɔː'dɪʃən $ ɒː-/ n [C] a short performance by an actor, singer etc that someone watches to judge if they are good enough to act in a play, sing in a concert etc: [+for] *I've got an audition for the Bournemouth Symphony Orchestra on Friday.*

audition[2] v **1** [I] to take part in an audition: [+for] *She's auditioning for Ophelia in 'Hamlet'.* **2** [T] to watch and judge someone's performance in an audition: *We auditioned more than 200 dancers before deciding on Carole Ann.*

au·di·tor /'ɔːdɪ̣tə $ 'ɒːdɪ̣tər/ n [C] someone whose job is to officially examine a company's financial records

au·di·to·ri·um /ˌɔːdɪ'tɔːriəm $ ˌɒː-/ n plural **auditoriums** or **auditoria** /-riə/ [C] **1** the part of a theatre where people sit when watching a play, concert etc **2** AmE a large building used for concerts or public meetings

au·di·to·ry /'ɔːdɪ̣təri $ 'ɒːdɪ̣tɔːri/ adj [only before noun] technical relating to the ability to hear

au fait /əʊ 'feɪ $ oʊ-/ adj **be au fait with sth** to be familiar with a system or way of doing something: *I'm not really au fait with the computer system yet.*

Aug. also **Aug** BrE the written abbreviation of *August*

au·ger /'ɔːgə $ 'ɒːgər/ n [C] a tool used for making a hole in wood or in the ground

aught /ɔːt $ ɒːt, ɑːt/ pron old use anything

aug·ment /ɔːg'ment $ ɒːg-/ v [T] formal to increase the value, amount, effectiveness etc of something: *Any surplus was sold to augment their income.* —**augmentation** /ˌɔːgmen'teɪʃən, -mən- $ ˌɒːg-/ n [C,U]

au·gur /'ɔːgə $ 'ɒːgər/ v **augur well/badly/ill** formal to be a sign that something will be successful or unsuccessful; **bode**: *Today's announcement of 300 redundancies does not augur well for the local economy.*

au·gu·ry /'ɔːgjˌ̊ri $ 'ɒː-/ n plural **auguries** [C] literary a sign of what will happen in the future

au·gust /ɔː'gʌst $ ɒː-/ adj impressive and respected: *an august institution*

Au·gust /'ɔːgəst $ 'ɒː-/ n [C,U] written abbreviation **Aug.** the eighth month of the year, between July and September: **next/last August** *I was there last August.* | **in August** *My birthday's in August.* | **on August 6th** *The new store opened on August 6th.* | **on 6th August** BrE: *He arrived at Berwick on 6th August 1823.* | **August 6** AmE: *We'll expect you to call August 6.*

auk /ɔːk $ ɒːk/ n [C] a black and white seabird with short wings

Auld Lang Syne /ˌɔːld læŋ 'zaɪn, ˌəʊld-, -'saɪn $ ˌoʊld-/ n a Scottish song that people sing when they celebrate the beginning of the new year at 12 o'clock MIDNIGHT on December 31st

au na·tu·rel /əʊ ˌnætjʊ'rel $ oʊ ˌnætʃə'rel/ adv wearing any clothes, or not wearing MAKE-UP, hair products etc that change the way you would naturally look

aunt /ɑːnt $ ænt/ n [C] the sister of your father or mother, or the wife of your father's or mother's brother: *Aunt Mary* → AGONY AUNT

aunt·ie, **aunty** /'ɑːnti $ 'æn-/ n [C] informal **1** an aunt: *Auntie Lou* **2** used by children to address a woman who is a friend of their parents

au pair /əʊ 'peə $ oʊ 'per/ n [C] a young person, usually a woman, who stays with a family in a foreign country to learn the language, and looks after their children for a small wage

au·ra /'ɔːrə/ [C] a quality or feeling that seems to surround or come from a person or a place: [+of] *The building retains an aura of mystery.*

au·ral /'ɔːrəl/ adj relating to the sense of hearing, or someone's ability to understand sounds: *an aural stimulus* —**aurally** adj

au·re·ole /'ɔːriəʊl $ -oʊl/ n [C] literary a bright circle of light; **halo**

au re·voir /ˌəʊ rə'vwɑː, ˌɒ- $ ˌoʊ rə'vwɑːr/ interjection goodbye

au·ro·ra bo·re·a·lis /əˌrɔːrə bɔːri'eɪlɪ̣s, ɔː- $ -'æl-/ n [singular] the NORTHERN LIGHTS

aus·pic·es /'ɔːspɪ̣sˌ̊z $ 'ɒː-/ n **under the auspices of sb/sth** formal with the help and support of a particular organization or person: *negotiations held under the auspices of the United Nations*

aus·pi·cious /ɔː'spɪʃəs $ ɒː-/ adj formal showing that something is likely to be successful; **inauspicious**: **auspicious start/beginning** *Saccani's excellent recording is an auspicious start to what promises to be a distinguished musical career.* —**auspiciously** adv

Aus·sie /'ɒzi $ 'ɒːzi, 'ɑːzi/ n [C] informal someone from Australia —**Aussie** adj

aus·tere /ɔː'stɪə, ɒ- $ ɒː'stɪr/ adj **1** plain and simple and without any decoration: *the church's austere simplicity* **2** someone who is austere is very strict and serious – used to show disapproval: *Her father is a very austere man.* **3** an austere way of life is very simple and has few things to make it comfortable or enjoyable: *Cuthbert led an austere life of prayer and solitude.* —**austerely** adv

aus·ter·i·ty /ɔː'sterˌ̊ti, ɒ- $ ɒː-/ n plural **austerities** **1** [C usually plural, U] bad economic conditions in which people do not have much money to spend: *a time of great austerity after the war* | *the austerities of post-communist Eastern Europe* **2** [U] when a government has a deliberate policy of trying to reduce the amount of money it spends: **austerity programme/plan/package** *a tough new austerity programme* | *IMF-backed austerity measures* (=reductions in government spending) **3** [U] the quality of being austere: *a life of austerity*

Aus·tra·la·sian /ˌɒstrə'leɪʒən◂, -ʃən $ ˌɒː-, ˌɑː-/ adj relating to Australasia (=Australia and the islands that are near to it) or its people

Aus·tra·li·an[1] /ɒ'streɪliən $ ɒː-, ɑː-/ adj relating to Australia or its people

Australian[2] n [C] someone from Australia

Aus·tri·an[1] /'ɒstriən $ 'ɒː-, 'ɑː-/ adj relating to Austria or its people

Austrian[2] n [C] someone from Austria

Austro- /ɒstrəʊ $ ɒːstroʊ, -trə, ɑːs-/ prefix [in nouns and adjectives] Austrian and something else: *Austro-Hungarian*

au·tar·chy *especially BrE*; **autarky** *AmE* /'ɔːtɑːki $ 'ɒːtɑːr-/ *n plural* **autarchies** [C,U] *formal* a policy in which a country or area does not want or need goods, food etc from any other country or area, or a country which has this policy

au·teur /əʊ'tɜː $ oʊ'tɜːr/ *n* [C] a film DIRECTOR who has a strong influence on the style of the films that he or she makes

au·then·tic /ɔː'θentɪk $ ɒː-/ *adj* **1** done or made in the traditional or original way; ☐ **genuine**: *authentic French food* **2** a painting, document, book etc that is authentic has been proved to be by a particular person; ☐ **genuine**: *an authentic work by Picasso* **3** based on facts: *an authentic account* **4** used to describe a copy that is the same as, or as good as, the original: *Actors dressed in authentic costumes re-enact the battle.* —**authentically** /-kli/ *adv*

au·then·tic·ate /ɔː'θentɪkeɪt $ ɒː-/ *v* [T] to prove that something is true or real: *The painting has been authenticated by experts.* | *passwords which can authenticate electronic documents* —**authentication** /ɔːˌθentɪ'keɪʃən $ ɒː-/ *n* [U]

au·then·tic·i·ty /ˌɔːθen'tɪsəti, -θən- $ ˌɒː-/ *n* [U] the quality of being real or true: [+of] *Archaeological evidence may help to establish the authenticity of the statue.*

au·thor¹ W2 /'ɔːθə $ 'ɒːθər/ *n* [C] **1** someone who has written a book; ☐ **writer**: *Nothomb is a Belgian author.* | [+of] *He was the author of two books on China.* | *It's clear that the author is a woman.* **2** *formal* the person who starts a plan or idea: [+of] *the author of the state reforms* —**authorial** /ɔː'θɔːriəl $ ɒː-/ *adj* [only before noun]

author² *v* [T] to be the writer of a book, report etc

au·thor·ess /'ɔːθərəs $ 'ɒː-/ *n* [C] *old-fashioned* a woman who writes books; ☐ **writer**

au·thor·ing /'ɔːθərɪŋ $ 'ɒː-/ *n* [U] the activity of writing and designing WEBSITES: *Here are a few tips on authoring and site design.*

au·thor·i·tar·i·an /ɔːˌθɒrɪ'teəriən◂ $ ɒːˌɑːrɪ'ter-, əˌθɒː-/ *adj* strictly forcing people to obey a set of rules or laws, especially ones that are wrong or unfair: *an authoritarian government* | *Critics claim his management has become too authoritarian.* —**authoritarian** *n* [C] —**authoritarianism** *n* [U]

au·thor·i·ta·tive /ɔː'θɒrɪtətɪv, ə- $ ə'θɑːrəteɪtɪv, ə'θɒː-/ *adj* **1** an authoritative book, account etc is respected because the person who wrote it knows a lot about the subject: *the most authoritative work on English surnames* **2** behaving or speaking in a confident, determined way that makes people respect and obey you: *He has a commanding presence and an authoritative voice.* —**authoritatively** *adv*

au·thor·i·ty W1 /ɔː'θɒrɪti, ə- $ ə'θɑː-, ə'θɒː-/ *n plural* **authorities**
1 POWER [U] the power you have because of your official position: *people in positions of authority* | *in authority Could I speak to someone in authority (=who has a position of power) please?* | [+over] *Several countries claim authority over the islands.* | *authority to do sth The court held that school officials have the authority to dismiss teachers.*
2 the authorities the people or organizations that are in charge of a particular country or area: *an agreement between the US and Columbian authorities*
3 ORGANIZATION [C] an official organization or a government department that has the power to make decisions, and has particular responsibilities: *the local authority* | *East Sussex Education Authority* | *the San Diego Water Authority* | *Welsh health authorities face a £13m deficit this year.*
4 EXPERT [C] someone who knows a lot about a subject and whose knowledge and opinions are greatly respected: [+on] *Mr Li is a leading authority on Chinese food.*
5 PERMISSION [C,U] official permission to do something: *under the authority of sb The attack took place*

under the authority of the UN security council. | **without sb's authority** *No one may enter without my authority.*
6 authority figure someone who has a position of power, especially because of their job: *teenage rebellion against authority figures*
7 PERSONAL QUALITY [U] a quality in the way you speak or behave which makes people obey you: *Jack's air of quiet authority*
8 I have it on good authority used to say that you are sure that something is true because you trust the person who told you about it
9 speak with authority to be sure of what you are saying, because of your knowledge or experience

au·thor·i·za·tion also **-isation** *BrE* /ˌɔːθəraɪ'zeɪʃən $ ˌɒːθərə-/ *n* [C,U] official permission to do something, or the document giving this permission; ☐ **authority**: *You need special authorization to park here.* | *Children may not leave the building without the authorization of the principal.*

au·thor·ize also **-ise** *BrE* /'ɔːθəraɪz $ 'ɒː-/ *v* [T] to give official permission for something: *an authorized biography* | **authorize sb to do sth** *Napoleon III authorized Haussmann to rebuild Paris.*

au·thor·ship /'ɔːθəʃɪp $ 'ɒːθər-/ *n* [U] **1** the fact that you have written a particular book, document etc: *There's no evidence to dispute his claim to authorship.* | [+of] *an investigation into the authorship of the Bible* **2** *formal* the profession of writing books

au·tis·m /'ɔːtɪzəm $ 'ɒː-/ *n* [U] a mental DISORDER (=problem) that makes people unable to communicate properly, or to form relationships —**autistic** /ɔː'tɪstɪk $ ɒː-/ *adj*: *an autistic child*

au·to /'ɔːtəʊ $ 'ɒːtoʊ/ *plural* **autos** *n* [C] a car: *imported autos* | *the auto industry* | *auto insurance*

auto- /ɔːtəʊ, -tə $ ɒːtoʊ, -tə/ *prefix* **1** of or by yourself: *an autobiography* **2** working by itself: *a camera with an auto-focus lens*

au·to·bi·og·ra·phy /ˌɔːtəbaɪ'ɒɡrəfi $ ˌɒːtəbaɪ'ɑː-/ *n plural* **autobiographies** [C,U] a book in which someone writes about their own life, or books of this type; → **biography** —**autobiographical** /ˌɔːtəbaɪə'ɡræfɪkəl $ ˌɒː-/ *adj*: *an autobiographical novel* (=one based on the author's own experiences)

au·toc·ra·cy /ɔː'tɒkrəsi $ ɒː'tɑː-/ *n plural* **autocracies** **1** [U] a system of government in which one person or group has unlimited power **2** [C] a country or organization that is completely controlled by one powerful person or group

au·to·crat /'ɔːtəkræt $ 'ɒː-/ *n* [C] **1** someone who makes decisions and gives orders to people without asking them for their opinion **2** a ruler who has complete power over a country —**autocratic** /ˌɔːtə'krætɪk◂ $ ˌɒː-/ *adj*: *an autocratic leadership style* —**autocratically** /-kli/ *adv*

Au·to·cue /'ɔːtəʊkjuː $ 'ɒːtoʊ-/ *n* [C] *trademark* a machine that shows the words that someone must say while they are speaking in public, especially on television

au·to·graph¹ /'ɔːtəɡrɑːf $ 'ɒːtəɡræf/ *n* [C] a famous person's signature that they give to someone who admires them: *Can I have your autograph?* | *a player who would always sign autographs and chat with fans*

autograph² *v* [T] if a famous person autographs a book, photograph etc, they sign it: *a shirt autographed by the whole team*

auto-immune dis'ease *n* [U] a condition in which substances that normally prevent illness in the body attack and harm parts of it instead

au·to·mak·er /'ɔːtəʊˌmeɪkə $ 'ɒːtoʊˌmeɪkər/ *n* [C] *AmE* a company that makes cars – used especially in newspapers: *US automakers*

au·to·mate /'ɔːtəmeɪt $ 'ɒː-/ *v* [T] to start using computers and machines to do a job, rather than

1 000, 2 000, 3 000, most frequent words in S poken and W ritten English

people: *Cash machines automate two basic functions of a bank – deposits and withdrawals.*

au·to·ma·ted /ˈɔːtəmeɪtᵻd $ ˈɒː-/ *adj* using computers and machines to do a job, rather than people: *a highly automated factory* | *The production process is now fully automated.*

au·to·mat·ic¹ S3 /ˌɔːtəˈmætɪk◂ $ ˌɒː-/ *adj*
1 an automatic machine is designed to work without needing someone to operate it for each part of a process: *an automatic weapon* | *an automatic gearbox* | *My camera is fully automatic.*
2 something that is automatic always happens as a result of something you have done, especially because of a rule or law: *Littering results in an automatic fine.*
3 done without thinking, especially because you have done the same thing many times before: *Practise the breathing techniques until they become automatic.*

automatic² *n* [C] **1** a weapon that can fire bullets continuously **2** a car with a system of GEARS that operate themselves without the driver needing to change them

au·to·mat·i·cally S3 W3 /ˌɔːtəˈmætɪkli $ ˌɒː-/ *adv*
1 as the result of a situation or action, and without you having to do anything more: *Join now and you will automatically receive 50% off your first purchase.*
2 without thinking about what you are doing: *Of course I automatically said yes.*
3 by the action of a machine, without a person making it work: *The doors opened automatically as we approached.*

automatic ˈpilot *n* [C,U] **1** a machine that flies a plane by itself without the need for a pilot **2** be on automatic pilot to do something without thinking about it, especially because you have done it many times before: *Moving on automatic pilot, she tidied the room.*

automatic transˈmission *n* [C,U] a system that operates the GEARS of a car without the driver needing to change them

au·to·ma·tion /ˌɔːtəˈmeɪʃən $ ˌɒː-/ *n* [U] the use of computers and machines instead of people to do a job; → **automated**

au·tom·a·ton /ɔːˈtɒmətən $ ɒːˈtɑː-/ *plural* **automata** /-tə/ *or* **automatons** *n* [C] **1** a machine, especially one in the shape of a human, that moves without anyone controlling it; ◻ **robot 2** someone who seems unable to feel emotions or to think about what they are doing

au·to·mo·bile /ˈɔːtəməbiːl $ ˈɒːtəmoʊ-/ *n* [C] *AmE* a car: *the automobile industry*

au·to·mo·tive /ˌɔːtəˈməʊtɪv◂ $ ˌɒːtəˈmoʊ-/ *adj* [only before noun] relating to cars: *automotive technology*

au·ton·o·mous /ɔːˈtɒnəməs $ ɒːˈtɑː-/ *adj* **1** an autonomous place or organization is free to govern or control itself; ◻ **independent: an autonomous region/state/republic etc** *Galicia is an autonomous region of Spain.* **2** *formal* having the ability to work and make decisions by yourself without any help from anyone else; ◻ **independent** —**autonomously** *adv*

au·ton·o·my /ɔːˈtɒnəmi $ ɒːˈtɑː-/ *n* [U] **1** freedom that a place or an organization has to govern or control itself; ◻ **independence:** *campaigners who want greater autonomy for Corsica* **2** the ability or opportunity to make your own decisions without being controlled by anyone else; ◻ **independence:** *Teachers are given considerable individual autonomy.*

au·to·pi·lot /ˈɔːtəʊˌpaɪlət $ ˈɒːtoʊ-/ *n* [C,U] AUTOMATIC PILOT

au·top·sy /ˈɔːtɒpsi $ ˈɒːtɑːp-/ *n plural* **autopsies** [C] *especially AmE* an examination of a dead body to discover the cause of death; ◻ **post mortem** *BrE: an autopsy report*

au·tumn /ˈɔːtəm $ ˈɒː-/ also **fall** *AmE n* [C,U] the season between summer and winter, when leaves change colour and the weather becomes cooler: *autumn mists*

au·tum·nal /ɔːˈtʌmnəl $ ɒː-/ *adj* relating to or typical of autumn: *autumnal colours*

aux.; aux *BrE* /ɔːks $ ɒːks/ the written abbreviation of **auxiliary** or **auxiliary verb**

aux·il·ia·ry¹ /ɔːɡˈzɪljəri, ɔːk- $ ɒːɡˈzɪljəri, -ˈzɪləri/ *adj* **1** auxiliary workers provide additional help for another group of workers: *an auxiliary nurse* | *auxiliary staff* **2** an auxiliary motor, piece of equipment etc is kept ready to be used if the main one stops working properly: *an auxiliary power supply* | *auxiliary equipment*

auxiliary² *n plural* **auxiliaries** [C] **1** a worker who provides additional help for another group of workers: *a nursing auxiliary* **2** an auxiliary verb: *a modal auxiliary*

auxˈiliary ˈverb *n* [C] a verb that is used with another verb to show its tense, PERSON, MOOD etc. In English the auxiliary verbs are 'be', 'do', and 'have' (as in 'I am running', 'I didn't go', 'they have gone') and all the MODALS

AV, A.V. /ˌeɪ ˈviː/ the abbreviation of **audiovisual**

a·vail¹ /əˈveɪl/ *n* **be to/of no avail** if something you do is to no avail or of no avail, you do not succeed in getting what you want: *We searched the whole area but all to no avail. Robbie had disappeared.*

avail² *v* **avail yourself of sth** *formal* to accept an offer or use an opportunity to do something: *How many schools avail themselves of this opportunity each year?*

a·vail·a·ble S1 W1 /əˈveɪləbəl/ *adj*
1 something that is available is able to be used or can easily be bought or found: *Tickets are available from the box office.* | **[+to]** *Not enough data is available to scientists.* | **available to do sth** *Funds are available to assist teachers who want to attend the conference.* | **[+for]** *No figures are available for the number of goods sold.* | **[+in]** *There are plenty of jobs available in the area.* | **readily/widely available** (=very easy to obtain) *Parking is readily available near the station entrance.* | *Meetings were held to update employees as soon as new information became available.* | *Further building can continue when money is made available.* | *Every available space on the wall was covered in pictures.*
2 [not before noun] someone who is available is not busy and has enough time to talk to you: *Collins was not available for comment on Thursday night.*
3 someone who is available does not have a wife, BOYFRIEND etc, and therefore may want to start a new romantic relationship with someone else —**availability** /əˌveɪləˈbɪləti/ *n* [U]: *the availability of affordable housing* | *Rooms are offered subject to availability.*

av·a·lanche /ˈævəlɑːntʃ $ -læntʃ/ *n* [C] **1** a large mass of snow, ice, and rocks that falls down the side of a mountain: *Two skiers were killed in the avalanche.* **2** an avalanche of sth a very large number of things such as letters, messages etc that arrive suddenly at the same time: *The school received an avalanche of applications.*

av·ant-garde /ˌævɒŋ ˈɡɑːd◂ $ ˌævɑːŋ ˈɡɑːrd◂/ *adj* **1** avant-garde music, literature etc is extremely modern and often seems strange or slightly shocking: *an avant-garde play* **2** **the avant-garde** the group of artists, writers etc who produce avant-garde books, paintings etc: *a member of the avant-garde*

av·a·rice /ˈævərᵻs/ *n* [U] *formal* a desire to have a lot of money that is considered to be too strong; ◻ **greed** —**avaricious** /ˌævəˈrɪʃəs/ *adj* —**avariciously** *adv*

av·a·tar /ˈævətɑː $ -tɑːr/ *n* [C] **1** *literary* a person or animal who is really a god in human or animal form **2** *formal* a person who represents an idea or quality **3** a picture of a person or animal that represents you on a computer screen, for example in some CHAT ROOMS or when you are playing games over the Internet

Ave. also **Ave** *BrE* the written abbreviation of *Avenue*, used in addresses: *36, Rokesly Ave*

a·venge /ə'vendʒ/ *v* [T] *literary* to do something to hurt or punish someone because they have harmed or offended you: *He wanted to avenge his brother's death.* —**avenger** *n* [C]

av·e·nue S3 /'ævɪˌnjuː $ -nuː/ *n* [C]
1 Avenue used in the names of streets in a town or city: *Fifth Avenue | Shaftesbury Avenue*
2 a possible way of achieving something: *The president wants to explore every avenue towards peace in the region. | There are many avenues open to researchers.*
3 *BrE* a road or broad path between two rows of trees, especially one leading to a big house: *a tree-lined avenue*

a·ver /ə'vɜː $ ə'vɜːr/ *v* **averred, averring** [T] *formal* to say something firmly and strongly because you are sure that it is true; **☐ declare**

av·e·rage¹ S2 W2 /'ævərɪdʒ/ *adj*
1 the average amount is the amount you get when you add together several quantities and divide this by the total number of quantities: *The age of the candidates ranged from 29 to 49 with an average age of 37. | The average cost of making a movie has risen by 15%. | Last winter was colder than average. | The cars were being sold at an average price of $11000.*
2 an average amount or quantity is not unusually big or small: *They have an average-size front garden and a large rear garden. | of average height/build/intelligence etc He was in his late twenties and of average height.*
3 having qualities that are typical of most people or things: *The average American has not even thought about next year's election. | In an average week I drive about 250 miles.*
4 neither very good nor very bad

average² S2 *n*
1 [C] the amount calculated by adding together several quantities, and then dividing this amount by the total number of quantities: [+of] *The average of 3, 8 and 10 is 7. | Each person raised an average of £60 to plant an acre of trees. | The December figures brought the annual average for 2001 up to 10.6 per cent.*
2 on average based on a calculation about how many times something usually happens, how much money someone usually gets, how often people usually do something etc: *On average, men still earn more than women. | Nearly 80% of Swiss citizens on average turn out to vote.*
3 [C,U] the usual level or amount for most people or things: *Streets in the town centre are wider than the average. | above/below average The school's eighth-graders are above average in science. | The murder rate in the city has risen to four times the national average.*
→ law of averages at LAW (9)

average³ *v* [linking verb] **1** to usually do something or usually happen a particular number of times, or to usually be a particular size or amount: *The water in the lake is not particularly deep, averaging about 12 metres. | The airport averages about a thousand flights a month. | Inflation averaged just under 2.8% per year.* **2** to calculate the average of figures: *The rate of growth was averaged over a period of three years.*
average out *phr v* **1** if something averages out at a particular figure, it has that figure as an average over a period of time: [+at] *Training costs for last year averaged out at £5,100 per trainee. | The government's share of the cost was intended to average out at 25%.* **2 average sth ⇔ out** to calculate the average of something: *I averaged out the total increase at about 10%.*

a·verse /ə'vɜːs $ -ɜːrs/ *adj* **1 not be averse to sth** to quite enjoy something, especially something that is slightly wrong or bad for you: *I was not averse to fighting with any boy who challenged me.* **2** *formal*

unwilling to do something or not liking something: *be averse to (doing) sth Jim is averse to using chemicals in the garden | Some banks are risk averse (=do not like taking a risk).*

a·ver·sion /ə'vɜːʃən $ ə'vɜːrʒən/ *n* [singular, U] a strong dislike of something or someone; **☐ hatred**: [+to] *Despite his aversion to publicity, Arnold was persuaded to talk to the press.* | **have an aversion to sth** *I have an aversion to housework.*

a·vert /ə'vɜːt $ -ɜːrt/ *v* [T] **1** to prevent something unpleasant from happening: *The tragedy could have been averted if the crew had followed safety procedures.* **2 avert your eyes/gaze etc** to look away from something so that you do not see it: *Henry averted his eyes as she undressed.*

a·vi·a·ry /'eɪviəri $ 'eɪvieri/ *n plural* **aviaries** [C] a large CAGE where birds are kept

a·vi·a·tion /ˌeɪvi'eɪʃən $ ˌeɪ-, ˌæ-/ *n* [U] **1** the science or practice of flying in aircraft **2** the industry that makes aircraft

a·vi·a·tor /'eɪvieɪtə $ 'eɪvieɪtər, 'æ-/ *n* [C] *old-fashioned* a pilot

av·id /'ævɪd/ *adj* [only before noun] doing something as much as possible; **☐ keen**: *an avid collector of old jazz records | an avid reader*

a·vi·on·ics /ˌeɪvi'ɒnɪks $ -'ɑːn-/ *n* [U] *technical* the electronic equipment used in aircraft and the science of developing it

av·o·ca·do /ˌævə'kɑːdəʊ $ -doʊ/ also **ˌavocado 'pear** *n plural* **avocados** [C] a fruit with a thick green or dark purple skin that is green inside and has a large seed in the middle **→ see picture at** FRUIT¹

a·void S2 W1 /ə'vɔɪd/ *v* [T]
1 to prevent something bad from happening: *Road safety is taught to young children to avoid road accidents. | It is important to take measures to avoid the risk of fire.* | **avoid doing sth** *The refugees left to avoid getting bombed.* | *Alan narrowly avoided an accident.*
2 to stay away from someone or something, or not use something: *Everyone seemed to be avoiding Nick. | She carefully avoided his eyes (=did not look directly at his face). | Pregnant women should avoid certain foods such as raw eggs. | Why did you speak to him? You usually avoid him like the plague (=try hard to avoid him).*
3 to deliberately not do something, especially something wrong, dangerous, or harmful: *There are ways of legally avoiding taxes.* | **avoid doing sth** *You should avoid over-spending in the first half of the year.*

a·void·a·ble /ə'vɔɪdəbəl/ *adj* something bad that is avoidable can be avoided or prevented: *an almost entirely avoidable cause of death | Nearly 1,000 children die each year from accidents in the home which are avoidable.*

a·void·ance /ə'vɔɪdəns/ *n* [U] the act of avoiding someone or something: [+of] *the avoidance of issues such as domestic violence* | **a tax avoidance** *scheme* (=legal way of not paying tax)

av·oir·du·pois /ˌævwɑːdjuː'pwɑː, ˌævədə'pɔɪz $ ˌævərdə'pɔɪz/ *n* [U] the system of weighing things that uses the standard measures of the OUNCE, POUND, and TON **→** METRIC SYSTEM

a·vow /ə'vaʊ/ *v* [T] *formal* to make a public statement about something you believe in: *He avowed his commitment to Marxist ideals.* —**avowal** *n* [C,U]

a·vowed /ə'vaʊd/ *adj* [only before noun] admitted or said publicly: *an avowed atheist*

a·vun·cu·lar /ə'vʌŋkjˈlə $ -ər/ *adj* behaving in a kind and nice way to someone who is younger, rather like an uncle: *an avuncular pat on the shoulder*

a·wait /ə'weɪt/ *v* [T] **1** to wait for something: *Several men are awaiting trial for robbery.* **→ see box at** WAIT¹ **2** if a situation, event etc awaits you, it is going to happen in the future: *A terrible surprise awaited them at Mr Tumnus' house.*

a·wake¹ [S3] /əˈweɪk/ *adj* [not before noun]
1 not sleeping: *I hope he's awake now.* | *She was still only half awake when I brought her a cup of coffee.* | *How do you stay awake during boring lectures?* | *Emma lay awake half the night, worrying.* | *The noise brought him wide awake* (=completely awake). | *To keep themselves awake* (=stop themselves from going to sleep) *they sat on the floor and told each other stories.*
2 be awake to sth to understand a situation and its possible effects: *Too few people are awake to the dangers of noise pollution.*

awake² *v past tense* **awoke** /əˈwəʊk $ əˈwoʊk/ *past participle* **awoken** /əˈwəʊkən $ əˈwoʊ-/ [I,T] **1** *formal* to wake up, or to make someone wake up: *It was midday when she awoke.* | *We awoke to a day of brilliant sunshine.* **2** *literary* if something awakes an emotion, or if an emotion awakes, you suddenly begin to feel that emotion: *The gesture awoke an unexpected flood of tenderness towards her.*

awake to sth *phr v* to begin to realize the possible effects of a situation: *Artists finally awoke to the aesthetic possibilities of photography.*

a·wak·en /əˈweɪkən/ *v formal* **1** [I,T] to wake up or to make someone wake up: *She was awakened by a noise at two in the morning.* | *Bill slept a little until he was awakened to take his turn on guard.* **2** [T] if something awakens an emotion, interest, memory etc it makes you suddenly begin to feel that emotion etc: *Early involvement in music can awaken an interest that will last a lifetime.*

awaken sb ⇔ **to** sth *phr v* to make someone understand a situation and its possible effects: *We must awaken people to the dangers for the environment.*

a·wak·en·ing /əˈweɪkənɪŋ/ *n* [C] **1** an occasion when you suddenly realize that you understand something or feel something: *It was during the period of 1943–1945 that his political awakening took place.* | *Confident that he would win, he had a rude awakening* (=very unpleasant surprise) *on election day.* **2** the act of waking from sleep

a·ward¹ [S2] [W1] /əˈwɔːd $ -ɔːrd/ *n* [C]
1 something such as a prize or money given to someone to reward them for something they have done: [+for] *the Presidential Award for Excellence in Science and Mathematics Teaching* | **win/receive an award** *Rosie was in London to receive her award as Mum of the Year.* | *The hotel's award-winning restaurant specializes in traditional food.* | *Magnusson presented the £1000 award to the group's chairman.*
2 something, especially money, that is officially given to someone as a payment or after a legal decision: *the teachers' pay award* | *an award for unfair dismissal*

award² [W3] *v* [T]
1 to officially give someone something such as a prize or money to reward them for something they have done: *Moodie has been awarded a golf scholarship at the University of Hawaii.* | **award sb sth** *The judge awarded me first prize.* | **award sth to sb** *A Nobel Prize was awarded to Waksman in 1952.*
2 to officially decide that someone should receive a payment or a formal agreement: **award sb sth** *The government awarded a German company the contract.* | **award sth to sb** *£45,000 was awarded to a typist with an injured hand.*

a·ware [S1] [W1] /əˈweə $ əˈwer/ *adj* [not before noun]
1 if you are aware that a situation exists, you realize or know that it exists: [+of] *The children are aware of the danger of taking drugs.* | *Mr Braley has been made aware of the need for absolute secrecy.* | **aware that** *Were you aware that Joe had this problem with his knee?* | **well/fully/acutely aware** *They were well aware that the company was losing money.* | *As you are aware, a fee will be charged annually.*

2 if you are aware of something, you notice it, especially because you can see, hear, feel or smell it: [+of] *She was aware of a tall dark figure watching her.* | *He was aware of the wind in his face.* | **aware that** *Bill became aware that he was still holding his glass.*
3 understanding a lot about what is happening around you and paying attention to it, especially because you realize possible dangers and problems: **politically/socially/environmentally etc aware** *the socially aware novels of Dickens* | *We should promote environmentally aware and responsible science.*
4 so/as far as I am aware *spoken* used when you are saying something that you think is true, although you might be wrong because you do not know all the facts: *As far as I am aware, they are a happily married couple.*

a·ware·ness [W3] /əˈweənɨs $ əˈwer-/ *n* [U]
1 knowledge or understanding of a particular subject or situation: **environmental/political/social awareness** | *Health officials have tried to raise awareness* (=improve people's knowledge) *about AIDS.*
2 the ability to notice something using your senses: [+of] *an artist's awareness of light and color*

a·wash /əˈwɒʃ $ əˈwɔːʃ, əˈwɑːʃ/ *adj* [not before noun] **1** covered with water or another liquid **2** containing too many things or people of a particular kind: [+with] *All the pavements were awash with rubbish.*

a·way¹ [S1] [W1] /əˈweɪ/ *adv*
1 used to say that someone leaves a place or person, or stays some distance from a place or person: *Go away!* | *Dinah was crying as she drove slowly away.* | [+from] *Stay away from the fire.*
2 towards a different direction: *She turned away and stared out of the window.* | *Charley blushed and looked away, embarrassed.*
3 if someone is away from school, work, or home, they are not there; ▪ **absent**: *Simon is away with flu.* | *Kate is away on holiday.* | [+from] *You must bring a note from your parents if you've been away from school.*
4 used to say how far it is to a place or thing: **five miles/10 feet etc away** *Geneva is about 20 miles away.* | *There's another hotel not far away.* | [+from] *She was sitting ten feet away from the microphone.* | **five minutes/two hours etc away** *The beach is only five minutes away* (=it only takes five minutes to get there).
5 if an event is two days, three weeks etc away, it will happen after that period of time has passed: *Christmas is only a month away.*
6 used to say how close someone is to achieving something or experiencing something: [+from] *At one stage, they were just two points away from victory.*
7 into or in a safe or enclosed place: *Put your money away, I'm paying.* | *Thousands of archaeological treasures are being kept hidden away.*
8 used to show that something disappears or is removed: *The music died away.* | *Ruben gave all his money away to charity.* | *Support for the Democrats has dropped away.* | *Cut away all the dead wood.*
9 used to emphasize that an action continues: *Sue was singing away to herself in the bath.* | *They've been hammering away all day.*
10 used to say that someone spends the whole of a period of time doing something: *You can dance the night away in one of Benidorm's many discos.*
11 if a team is playing away, it is playing a game at its opponent's field or sports hall; ▪ **at home**: *Liverpool are playing away at Everton on Saturday.* → **far and away** at FAR¹ (12); → **right away** at RIGHT³ (2); → **straight away** at STRAIGHT¹ (7)

away² *adj* [only before noun] an away game or match is played at your opponent's field or sports hall; ▪ **home**

awe¹ /ɔː $ ɒː/ *n* [U] **1** a feeling of great respect and liking for someone or something: *He felt great awe for the landscape.* | **with/in awe** *Kate gazed at the statue with awe.* **2 be/stand in awe of sb** also **hold sb in awe** to admire someone and have great respect for them and sometimes a slight fear of them: *All of the neighbours were a little in awe of my mother.* | *The villagers hold them in awe and think of them as gods.*

awe² v [T usually passive] *formal* if you are awed by someone or something, you feel great respect and liking for them, and are often slightly afraid of them: *The girls were awed by the splendour of the cathedral.* —**awed** adj: *an awed silence*

'awe-in,spiring adj extremely impressive in a way that makes you feel great respect: *a truly awe-inspiring achievement*

awe·some /'ɔːsəm $ 'ɒː-/ adj **1** extremely impressive, serious, or difficult so that you feel great respect, worry, or fear: *an awesome responsibility* | *the awesome sweep of the scenery* **2** *especially AmE informal* very good: *Their last concert was really awesome.* —**awesomely** adv

'awe-,stricken adj AWESTRUCK

awe·struck /'ɔːstrʌk $ 'ɒː-/ adj feeling great respect for the importance, difficulty, or seriousness of someone or something: *She gazed awestruck at the jewels.*

aw·ful¹ [S1] /'ɔːfəl $ 'ɒː-/ adj
1 very bad or unpleasant; ⊟ **terrible**: *The weather was awful.* | *He is a pretty awful driver.* | *That fridge smells awful.* | *The last six months have been awful for her.* | *I've stopped believing most of what he says. Isn't that awful?* | *I'm sure Suzy is dead but the awful thing is not knowing how it happened.*
2 [only before noun] *spoken* used to emphasize how much or how good, bad etc something is: *An awful lot of people* (=a large number of people) *died in the war.* | *He made me feel an awful fool.*
3 look/feel awful to look or feel ill: *She's lost a lot of weight and she looks awful.*
4 *literary* making you feel great respect or fear
—**awfulness** n [U]

awful² adv [+ adj/adv] *AmE spoken* very: *That kid's awful cute, with her red curls.*

aw·ful·ly /'ɔːfəli $ 'ɒː-/ adv very: *It's awfully cold in here. Is the heater on?*

a·while /ə'waɪl/ adv for a short time

awk·ward [S2] /'ɔːkwəd $ 'ɒːkwərd/ adj
1 making you feel embarrassed so that you are not sure what to do or say; ⊟ **difficult**: *I hoped he would stop asking awkward questions.* | *There was an awkward moment when she didn't know whether to shake his hand or kiss his cheek.* | *an awkward silence* | *A laugh can help people over an awkward situation.* | *Philip's remarks put her in an awkward position* (=made it difficult for her to know what to do).
2 not relaxed or comfortable: *She liked to dance but felt awkward if someone was watching her.* | *Geoff looked uneasy and awkward.* | *Make sure that the baby is not sleeping in an awkward position.*
3 difficult to do, use, or deal with: *It'll be awkward getting cars in and out.* | *The new financial arrangements were awkward to manage.* | *A good carpenter can make a cupboard to fit the most awkward space.* | *She was afraid he was going to ask an awkward question.*
4 not convenient: *I'm sorry to call at such an awkward time but I won't keep you a minute.*
5 an awkward person is deliberately unhelpful; ⊟ **difficult**: [+**about**] *The staff wanted to go home and they were getting awkward about a meeting starting so late.* | *an awkward customer* (=person who is difficult and unhelpful) —**awkwardly** adv: *'I'm very sorry about your sister,' he said awkwardly.* | *Vera smiled awkwardly.* —**awkwardness** n [U]: *He tried to smooth over the awkwardness of the situation.*

awl /ɔːl $ ɒːl/ n [C] a pointed tool for making holes in leather

aw·ning /'ɔːnɪŋ $ 'ɒː-/ n [C] a sheet of material outside a shop, tent etc to keep off the sun or the rain

a·woke /ə'wəʊk $ ə'woʊk/ the past tense of AWAKE

a·wok·en /ə'wəʊkən $ ə'woʊ-/ the past participle of AWAKE

AWOL /,eɪ ,dʌbəljuː əʊ 'el, 'eɪwɒl $ -oʊ-, 'eɪwɒːl/ adj **absent without leave** absent from somewhere without permission, especially from the army: *Two soldiers had gone AWOL the night before.*

a·wry /ə'raɪ/ adj **1** go awry if something goes awry, it does not happen in the way that was planned: *My carefully laid plans had already gone awry.* **2** not in the correct position: *He rushed out, hat awry.*

aw shucks /,ɔː 'ʃʌks $,ɒː-/ *AmE interjection* used in a joking way to show that you feel embarrassed or sad

axe¹ also **ax** *AmE* /æks/ n [C] **1** a tool with a heavy metal blade on the end of a long handle, used to cut down trees or split pieces of wood → PICKAXE **2 the axe** *informal* if someone gets the axe, they are dismissed from their job: *100 workers are facing the axe in a cost-cutting exercise.* **3 the axe** *informal* if a plan, system, or service gets the axe, someone gets rid of it: *MPs know there will be cuts in public spending but do not know on which department the axe will fall.* **4 have an axe to grind** to have a strong personal opinion about something which is the reason why you do something: *I need objective advice from someone with no axe to grind.*

axe² also **ax** *AmE* v [T] **1** to suddenly dismiss someone from their job: *There are plans to axe 2600 staff.* **2** to get rid of a plan, system, or service, especially in order to save money: *TV's longest running show is to be axed.*

ax·i·om /'æksiəm/ n [C] *formal* a rule or principle that is generally considered to be true

ax·i·o·mat·ic /,æksiə'mætɪk◂/ adj something that is axiomatic does not need to be proved because you can easily see that it is true; ⊟ **self-evident** —**axiomatically** /-kli/ adv

ax·is /'æksɪs/ n plural **axes** /-siːz/ [C] **1** the imaginary line around which a large round object, such as the Earth, turns: *The Earth rotates on an axis between the north and south poles.* → see picture at GLOBE **2** a line drawn across the middle of a regular shape that divides it into two equal parts **3** either of the two lines of a GRAPH, by which the positions of points are measured

ax·le /'æksəl/ n [C] the bar connecting two wheels on a car or other vehicle

a·ya·tol·lah /,aɪə'tɒlə $ -'toʊ-/ n [C] a religious leader of the Shiite Muslims, especially a very powerful one

aye [S3] /aɪ/ adv
1 used to say yes when voting; ⊟ **nay**: **the ayes have it** (=used to say that most people in a meeting have voted in favour of something)
2 a word meaning yes, used especially in Scotland

a·za·le·a /ə'zeɪliə $ -jə/ n [C] a small bush that has large flowers

AZT /,eɪ zed 'tiː $ -ziː-/ *trademark* azidothymidine – a drug used to treat AIDS

az·ure /'æʒə, 'æʒjʊə, 'æzjʊə $ 'æʒər/ adj having a bright blue colour like the sky —**azure** n [U]

deposit and no interest: that can't be bad, can it?
31 *comparative* **badder**, *superlative* **baddest** *especially AmE spoken informal* **a)** used when you think something is very good: *Now that's a bad car!* **b)** someone who is bad is very determined and does not always obey rules – used to show approval —**badness** *n* [U]

WORD FOCUS: BAD
very bad: **awful, terrible, horrible, lousy** *informal,* **appalling, ghastly, atrocious, horrendous**
bad, but not very bad: **not very good, mediocre, second-rate, so-so, lacklustre**
of bad quality: **shoddy, inferior, poor quality, cheap, crummy** *informal*
bad at doing something: **be no good at sth**
very bad at doing something: **hopeless, terrible, useless, lousy** *informal,* **incompetent**
morally bad: **evil, wicked, immoral, corrupt, sick, perverted, degenerate**

bad² *n* **1 to the bad** *BrE informal* if you are a particular amount to the bad, you are that much poorer or you owe that much: *Thanks to your mistake, I'm £500 to the bad!* **2 my bad!** *AmE spoken informal* used to say that you have made a mistake or that something is your fault **3 go to the bad** *BrE old-fashioned* to begin living in a wrong or immoral way

bad³ *adv spoken* a word used to mean 'badly' which many people think is incorrect: *I need that money bad.*

bad-ass *adj* [only before noun] *AmE informal* **1** very good or impressive: *This site is the best online magazine for bad-ass biker gear.* **2** a bad-ass person is very determined and does not always obey rules – used to show approval: *Johnson plays this bad-ass cop named O'Riley.* —**bad-ass, badass** *n* [C]

bad 'debt *n* [C] a debt that is unlikely to be paid

bad·die, baddy /'bædi/ *n* [C] *BrE informal* someone who is bad, especially in a book or film; ➡ **bad guy** *AmE*

bade /bæd, beɪd/ the past tense and past participle of BID

badge /bædʒ/ *n* [C] **1** *BrE* a small piece of metal, cloth, or plastic with a picture or words on it, worn to show rank, membership of a group, support for a political idea etc; ➡ **button** *AmE,* **pin** *AmE: We were each handed a badge with our name on it.* **2** a small piece of metal or plastic that you carry to show people that you work for a particular organization, for example that you are a police officer **3 a badge of honour/courage etc** something that shows that you have a particular quality: *He now sees his wartime injuries as a badge of honor.* **4** also **merit badge** *AmE* a small piece of cloth with a picture on it, given to SCOUTS, GUIDES etc to show what skills they have learned: *Steve won a photography badge in the Boy Scouts.* **5 badge of office** *BrE* an object which shows that you have an official position: *Mayors wear chains around their necks as badges of office.*

bad·ger¹ /'bædʒə $ -ər/ *n* [C] an animal which has black and white fur, lives in holes in the ground, and is active at night

badger² *v* [T] to try to persuade someone by asking them something several times; ➡ **pester:** *She badgered me for weeks until I finally gave in.* | **badger sb to do sth** *My friends keep badgering me to get a cell phone.* | **badger sb into doing sth** *I had to badger the kids into doing their homework.*

bad guy *n* [C] *AmE informal* a man in a film, book etc who is evil or dangerous; ➡ **baddie** *BrE: In the film, he plays a bad guy trying to find his brother's killer.*

bad 'hair day *n* [C] *informal* a day when you are unhappy and easily upset, especially because your hair does not look the way you want it to look

bad·i·nage /'bædɪnɑːʒ $ ˌbædən'ɑːʒ/ *n* [U] *literary* conversation that involves a lot of jokes or humour

bad·lands /'bædlændz/ *n* [plural] an area of land in North America that is not useful for growing crops, with rocks and hills that have been worn into strange shapes by the weather

bad·ly S2 W3 /'bædli/ *adv comparative* **worse** /wɜːs $ wɜːrs/ *superlative* **worst** /wɜːst $ wɜːrst/
1 in an unsatisfactory or unsuccessful way; ➡ **well:** *The company has been very badly managed.* | *The novel was translated badly into English.* | *badly made furniture* | *Rob did very badly in the History exam.*
2 to a great or serious degree: *He's been limping badly ever since the skiing accident.* | *We badly wanted to help, but there was nothing we could do.* | *He was beaten so badly that his brother didn't recognize him.* | *The school is badly in need of* (=very much needs) *some new computers.* | *Things started to go badly wrong* (=go wrong in a serious way) *for Eric after he lost his job.*
3 think badly of sb/sth to have a bad opinion of someone or something: *I'm sure they won't think badly of you if you tell them you need some help.*

badly 'off *adj comparative* **worse-off,** *superlative* **worst-off** [not before noun] *especially BrE* **1** also **bad-off** *AmE* not having much money; ➡ **poor; 1** well-off **2 badly off for sth** *BrE* not having enough of something that you need; ➡ **well-off:** *The school is rather badly off for equipment.*

bad·min·ton /'bædmɪntən/ *n* [U] a game that is similar to tennis but played with a SHUTTLECOCK (=small feathered object) instead of a ball ➡ see picture at SPORTS CENTRE

bad-mouth *v* [T] *informal especially AmE* to criticize someone or something: *Her former colleagues accused her of bad-mouthing them in public.*

bad-'tempered *adj BrE* someone who is bad-tempered becomes easily annoyed and talks in an angry way to people; ➡ **irritable:** *Why are you so bad-tempered today?*

baf·fle¹ /'bæfəl/ *v* [T] if something baffles you, you cannot understand or explain it at all: *The question baffled me completely.* —**bafflement** *n* [U] —**baffling** *adj: a baffling mystery*

baffle² *n* [C] *technical* a board, sheet of metal etc that controls the flow of air, water, or sound into or out of something

bag¹ S1 W2 /bæg/ *n* [C]
1 CONTAINER a) a container made of paper, cloth, or thin plastic which usually opens at the top: *a paper bag* | *a plastic bag* | *a carrier bag* | *a garbage bag* **b)** a HANDBAG: *Don't leave your bag in the office when you go for lunch.* **c)** a large bag that you use to carry your clothes etc when you are travelling: *Just throw your bags in the back of the car.* | *a garment bag* ➡ see picture at CONTAINER
2 AMOUNT the amount that a bag will hold: [+of] *a bag of popcorn*
3 *old/stupid bag spoken* an insulting word for an old woman: *You silly old bag!*
4 A LOT OF STH bags of sth *spoken especially BrE* a lot of something; ➡ **plenty:** *She's got bags of money.* | *No need to rush, we've got bags of time.*
5 pack your bags *informal* to leave a place where you have been living, usually after an argument: *We told her to pack her bags at once.*
6 EYES bags [plural] dark circles or loose skin under your eyes, usually because of old age or being tired
7 a bag of bones *informal* a person or animal who is too thin
8 in the bag *informal* certain to be won or achieved: *The governor's closest advisors quietly believe the election is in the bag.*
9 TROUSERS bags [plural] *BrE old-fashioned* loose-fitting trousers: *Oxford bags*
10 not sb's bag *old-fashioned informal* something that someone is not very interested in or not very good at: *Thanks but dancing is not really my bag.*
11 bag and baggage *BrE* with all your possessions: *They threw her out of the house, bag and baggage.*

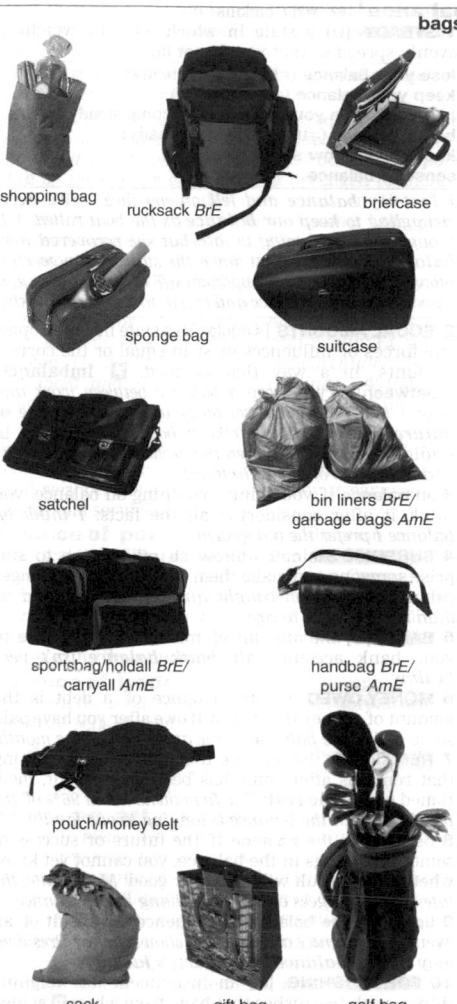

shopping bag

rucksack *BrE*

briefcase

sponge bag

suitcase

satchel

bin liners *BrE/*
garbage bags *AmE*

sportsbag/holdall *BrE/*
carryall *AmE*

handbag *BrE/*
purse *AmE*

pouch/money belt

sack

gift bag

golf bag

12 HUNTING [usually singular] *BrE* the number of birds or animals that someone kills when they go hunting: *We had a good bag that day.* → SLEEPING BAG, AIRBAG, DUFFEL BAG, TOTE BAG, BEANBAG, PUNCHBAG, SANDBAG[1], TEABAG; → **let the cat out of the bag** at CAT (2); → **be left holding the bag** at HOLD[1] (26); → **a mixed bag** at MIXED (6)

bag[2] *v* **bagged, bagging** [T] **1** to put things into bags: *He got a job bagging groceries.* **2** *informal* to manage to get something that a lot of people want: *Try to bag a couple of seats at the front.* **3** *BrE informal* to score a GOAL or a point in sport: *Larsson bagged his thirtieth goal of the season in Celtic's win.* **4** *informal especially BrE* to kill or catch an animal or bird: *We bagged a rabbit.*

bag sth ⇔ **up** *phr v especially BrE* to put things into bags: *We bagged up the money before we closed the shop.*

ba·gel /'beɪɡəl/ *n* [C] a small ring-shaped type of bread → see picture at BREAD

bag·ful /'bæɡfʊl/ *n* [C] the amount a bag can hold

bag·gage /'bæɡɪdʒ/ *n* **1** [U] *especially AmE* the cases, bags, boxes etc carried by someone who is travelling; ▣ **luggage**: *Check your baggage in at the desk.* → see picture at STAY **2** [U] *informal* the beliefs, opinions, and experiences that someone has, which make them think in a particular way, especially in a way that makes it difficult to form good relationships: *Each employee brings his or her own psychological baggage to the workplace.*

baggage ,car *n* [C] *AmE* the part of a train where boxes, bags etc are carried

baggage ,reclaim *especially BrE* also **baggage ,claim** *AmE n* [U] the place at an airport where you collect your cases and bags after a flight

baggage room *n* [C] *AmE* a place, usually in a train station, where you can leave your bags and collect them later

bag·gy /'bæɡi/ *adj* baggy clothes are big and do not fit tightly on your body; ▣ **tight**: *She was wearing jeans and a baggy T-shirt.* → see picture at LOOSE[1]

bag ,lady *n* [C] *informal* an impolite word for a homeless woman who lives on the streets and carries all her possessions with her

bag·pipes /'bæɡpaɪps/ *n* [plural] a musical instrument played especially in Scotland in which air blown into a bag is forced out through pipes to produce the sound —**bagpipe** *adj*

ba·guette /bæ'ɡet/ *n* [C] a long thin LOAF of bread, made especially in France → see picture at BREAD

bah /bɑː/ *interjection old-fashioned* used to show disapproval of something: *Bah! That's stupid.*

bail[1] /beɪl/ *n*

1 [U] money left with a court of law to make sure that a prisoner will return when their TRIAL starts

(out) on bail
release sb on bail
grant sb bail
refuse sb bail
post bail
hold sb without bail (=make someone stay in prison until their trial)
stand bail/put up bail *BrE* (=pay someone's bail)
jump bail also **skip bail** *BrE* (=not return to trial as you promised)
set sb's bail at sth (=say how much bail they must pay)
conditional bail *BrE* (=bail given if someone agrees to do something)
unconditional bail *BrE* (=bail given without having to agree to do something)

Carpenter is free on bail while he appeals his conviction. | *She was murdered by a man who was out on bail for rape.* | *The three men were released on bail pending an appeal.* | *He is not likely to be granted bail.* | *Carter has been refused bail and will remain in custody.* | *The judge ordered that Jones be held without bail.* | *Why can't you ask your father to put up bail for you?* | *Two of the defendants jumped bail and fled to New York.* | *Bail was set at $30,000.*

2 [C usually plural] one of the two small pieces of wood laid on top of the STUMPS in a game of CRICKET

bail[2] *v* **1** also **bail out** *AmE*; **bale out** *BrE* [I] *informal* to escape from a situation that you do not want to be in any more: *After ten years in the business, McArthur is baling out.* | *I don't know anybody at this party – let's bail.* **2** [T usually passive] *BrE* if someone is bailed, they are let out of prison to wait for their TRIAL after they have left a sum of money with the court: *Dakers was bailed to appear at Durham Crown Court.*

bail out *phr v* **1** bail sb/sth ⇔ **out** also **bale sb/sth** ⇔ **out** *BrE* to do something to help someone out of trouble, especially financial problems: *Some local businesses have offered to bail out the museum.* | *Sutton bailed his team out with a goal in the last minute.* **2** bail sth ⇔ **out** to leave a large sum of money with a court so that someone can be let out of prison while waiting for their TRIAL: *Clarke's family paid £500 to bail him out.* **3** *AmE* also **bale out** to escape from a plane, using a PARACHUTE **4** bail sth ⇔ **out** also **bale sth** ⇔ **out** *BrE* to remove water that has come into a boat

bai·ley /'beɪli/ *n* [C] an open area inside the outer wall of a castle

your knee, elbow etc by falling or knocking against something; ⊟ **graze**: *I barked my shin against the step.*

bark² *n* **1** [C] the sharp loud sound made by a dog **2** [U] the outer covering of a tree **3** [C] a loud sound or voice: *Amy's voice was a hoarse bark.* **4 sb's bark is worse than their bite** used to say that someone who seems unpleasant or difficult to deal with, is not really too bad

bar·keep·er /ˈbɑːkiːpə $ ˈbɑːrkiːpər/ also **bar·keep** /ˈbɑːkiːp $ ˈbɑːr-/ *AmE n* [C] someone who serves drinks in a bar; ⊟ **bartender**

bark·er /ˈbɑːkə $ ˈbɑːrkər/ *n* [C] in the past, someone who stood outside a place where there was a CIRCUS or FAIR shouting to people to come in

barking 'mad also **bark·ing** /ˈbɑːkɪŋ $ ˈbɑːr-/ *adj* [not before noun] *BrE* completely crazy or acting very strangely – used humorously

bar·ley /ˈbɑːli $ ˈbɑːrli/ *n* [U] a plant that produces a grain used for making food or alcohol

barley ˌsugar *n* [C,U] *BrE* a hard sweet made of boiled sugar

barley ˌwater *n* [U] *BrE* a drink made from barley boiled with water, with the flavour of lemon or orange

barley 'wine *n* [U] *BrE* a type of very strong beer

bar·maid /ˈbɑːmeɪd $ ˈbɑːr-/ *n* [C] *BrE* a woman who serves drinks in a bar; ⊟ **bartender**

bar·man /ˈbɑːmən $ -mən/ *n plural* **barmen** /-mən/ [C] *especially BrE* a man who serves drinks in a bar; ⊟ **bartender**

bar mitz·vah /ˌbɑː ˈmɪtsvə $ ˌbɑːr-/ *n* [C] **1** the religious ceremony held when a Jewish boy reaches the age of 13 and is considered an adult in his religion; → **bat mitzvah 2** a boy for whom this ceremony is held

barm·y /ˈbɑːmi $ ˈbɑːrmi/ *adj BrE informal* slightly crazy: *That's a barmy idea.*

barn /bɑːn $ bɑːrn/ *n* [C] **1** a large farm building for storing crops, or for keeping animals in → see picture at COUNTRY; → see picture at HOME **2** *informal* a large plain building: *a huge barn of a house*

bar·na·cle /ˈbɑːnəkəl $ ˈbɑːr-/ *n* [C] a small sea animal with a hard shell that sticks firmly to rocks and the bottom of boats

barn dance *n* [C] *BrE* a social event at which there is COUNTRY DANCING; → **square dance**

bar·net /ˈbɑːnɪt $ ˈbɑːr-/ *n* [C] *BrE informal old-fashioned* hair or a way of wearing your hair

bar·ney /ˈbɑːni $ ˈbɑːrni/ *n* [C usually singular] *BrE informal* a noisy argument

barn·storm /ˈbɑːnstɔːm $ ˈbɑːrnstɔːrm/ *v* [I] *AmE* to travel from place to place making short stops to give political speeches, theatre performances, or aircraft flying shows —**barnstormer** *n* [C]

barn·storm·ing /ˈbɑːnˌstɔːmɪŋ $ ˈbɑːrnˌstɔːr-/ *adj* [only before noun] done with a lot of energy and very exciting to watch: *a barnstorming speech*

barn·yard /ˈbɑːnjɑːd $ ˈbɑːrnjɑːrd/ *n* [C] an area on a farm surrounded by farm buildings; ⊟ **farmyard**

ba·rom·e·ter /bəˈrɒmɪtə $ -ˈrɑːmɪtər/ *n* [C] **1** an instrument that measures changes in the air pressure and the weather, or that calculates height above sea level **2** something that shows any changes that are happening in a particular situation: *The skin is an accurate barometer of emotional and physical health.* —**barometric** /ˌbærəˈmetrɪk / *adj* [only before noun] —**barometrically** /-kli/ *adv*

bar·on /ˈbærən/ *n* [C] **1** a man who is a member of a low rank of the British NOBILITY or of a rank of European NOBILITY **2** a businessman with a lot of power or influence: *drug barons | conservative press barons like Beaverbrook* → ROBBER BARON

bar·on·ess /ˈbærənɪs/ *n* [C] **1** a woman who is a member of a low rank of the British NOBILITY **2** the wife of a baron

bar·on·et /ˈbærənɪt, -net/ *n* [C] a member of the British NOBILITY, lower in rank than a baron, whose title passes to his son when he dies

bar·on·et·cy /ˈbærənɪtsi/ *n plural* **baronetcies** [C] the rank of a baronet

ba·ro·ni·al /bəˈrəʊniəl $ -ˈroʊ-/ *adj* **1** very large and richly decorated: *a splendid baronial house* **2** belonging to or involving BARONS

bar·on·y /ˈbærəni/ *n plural* **baronies** [C] the rank of a BARON

ba·roque¹ /bəˈrɒk, bəˈrəʊk $ bəˈroʊk, -ˈrɑːk/ *adj* relating to the very decorated style of art, music, buildings etc, that was common in Europe in the 17th and early 18th centuries: *furnished in a baroque style | elaborate baroque façades | baroque music/architecture/paintings etc*

baroque² *n* **the baroque** used to describe baroque art, music, buildings etc

barque /bɑːk $ bɑːrk/ *n* [C] a sailing ship with three, four, or five MASTS (=poles that the sails are fixed to)

bar·rack /ˈbærək/ *v* [I,T] **1** *BrE* to interrupt someone, especially a performer or a player, by shouting criticism at them: *At the 1965 Newport Folk Festival Bob Dylan was barracked for using electric instruments.* **2** *AusE* to shout to show that you support someone or something

bar·racks /ˈbærəks/ *n* [plural] a building or group of buildings in which soldiers live

bar·ra·cu·da /ˌbærəˈkjuːdə $ -ˈkuːdə/ *n* [C] a large tropical fish that eats flesh

bar·rage¹ /ˈbærɑːʒ $ bəˈrɑːʒ/ *n* **1** [C usually singular] the continuous firing of guns, dropping of bombs etc, especially to protect soldiers as they move towards an enemy: [+of] *a barrage of anti-aircraft fire* **2** [singular] a lot of criticism, questions, complaints etc that are said at the same time, or very quickly one after another: [+of] *a barrage of questions*

bar·rage² /ˈbærɑːʒ $ ˈbærɪdʒ/ *n* [C] a wall of earth, stones etc built across a river to provide water for farming or to prevent flooding

barrage balˌloon / $.ˈ. .ˌ./ *n* [C] a large bag that floats in the air to prevent enemy planes from flying near the ground

barred /bɑːd $ bɑːrd/ *adj* **1** a barred window, gate etc has bars across it; → **bar 2** *formal* having bands of different colour; → **bar**: *red barred tail feathers*

bar·rel¹ S3 /ˈbærəl/ *n* [C]
1 a large curved container with a flat top and bottom, made of wood or metal, and used for storing beer, wine etc: *The wine is aged in oak barrels.* | [+of] *barrels of beer*; → see picture at CONTAINER
2 a unit of measurement for oil, equal to 159 litres: [+of] *two million barrels of oil*
3 the part of a gun that the bullets are fired through
4 have sb over a barrel to put someone in a situation in which they are forced to accept or do what you want: *The manager had us over a barrel – either we work on a Saturday or we lose our jobs.*
5 be a barrel of laughs [often in negatives] to be very enjoyable: *Life is not exactly a barrel of laughs at the moment.* → PORK BARREL; → scrape (the bottom of) the barrel at SCRAPE¹ (5); → lock, stock, and barrel at LOCK² (3)

barrel² *v* [I] *AmE informal* to move very fast, especially in an uncontrolled way: *A vehicle barreled out of a shopping center and crashed into the side of my car.*

barrel-'chested *adj* a man who is barrel-chested has a round chest that sticks out

barrel ˌorgan *n* [C] a musical instrument that you play by turning a handle, often used on the streets in order to get money, especially in the past

bar·ren /ˈbærən/ *adj* **1** land or soil that is barren has no plants growing on it: *Thousands of years ago the surface was barren desert.* **2** *old-fashioned* unable to produce children or baby animals – used of a woman or of female animals; ◨ **infertile**; ◪ **fertile** **3** a tree or plant that is barren does not produce fruit or seeds **4** used to describe something that does not look interesting or attractive: *The sports hall was a rather barren concrete building.* **5** used to describe a period of time during which you do not achieve anything or get any useful results: *I scored five in the first seven games, but I've had a bit of a barren patch since then.*

bar·rette /bæˈret/ *n* [C] *AmE* a small metal or plastic object used to keep a woman's hair in place; ◨ **hairslide** *BrE*

bar·ri·cade[1] /ˈbærɪkeɪd, ˌbærɪˈkeɪd/ *n* [C] a temporary wall or fence across a road, door etc that prevents people from going through: *The fans were kept back behind barricades.* → see picture at BARRIER

barricade[2] *v* [T] to build a barricade to prevent someone or something from getting in: *During the riots, some of the prisoners barricaded their cells.* | **barricade sb/yourself in/into sth** *Shopkeepers had to barricade themselves in.*

barrier

barrier

obstruction

barricade   ramp

bar·ri·er W3 /ˈbæriə $ -ər/ *n* [C]
1 a rule, problem etc that prevents people from doing something, or limits what they can do: *the removal of trade barriers* (=something such as a tax that makes trade between countries difficult) | [+to] *Problems with childcare remain the biggest barrier to women succeeding at work.* | [+between] *We want to break down barriers between doctors and patients.* | *The language barrier* (=the inability to communicate with someone because you speak a different language) *makes debate impossible.*
2 a type of fence or gate that prevents people from moving in a particular direction: *Crowds burst through the barriers and ran onto the pitch.*
3 a physical object that keeps two areas, people etc apart: [+between] *The mountains form a natural barrier between the two countries.*
4 the 10-second/40% etc barrier a level or amount of 10 seconds, 40% etc, that is seen as a limit which it is difficult to get beyond: *I'm hoping to crash the 20-second barrier in the final and get a bronze.* → SOUND BARRIER

barrier ˌmethod *n* [C] barrier methods of CONTRACEPTION involve the use of CONDOMS etc, which physically prevent the SPERM from reaching the egg

barrier ˈreef *n* [C] a line of CORAL (=pink stone-like substance) separated from the shore by water

bar·ring /ˈbɑːrɪŋ/ *prep* unless something happens: *His back is broken and, barring a miracle, he won't walk again.*

bar·ri·o /ˈbæriəʊ $ ˈbɑːriou/ *n plural* **barrios** [C] *AmE* a part of an American town or city where many poor Spanish-speaking people live

bar·ris·ter /ˈbærɪstə $ -ər/ *n* [C] a lawyer in Britain who can argue cases in the higher law courts; → **solicitor**; → see box at LAWYER

ˈbar-room also **ˈbar room** *n* [C] a bar

bar·row /ˈbærəʊ $ -rou/ *n* [C] **1** a small vehicle like a box on wheels, from which fruits, vegetables etc used to be sold **2** a large pile of earth like a small hill that was put over a GRAVE in ancient times **3** a WHEELBARROW

bar·row·boy /ˈbærəʊbɔɪ $ -rou-/ *n* [C] *BrE* a man or boy who sells fruit, vegetables etc from a barrow

bar·tend·er /ˈbɑːˌtendə $ ˈbɑːrˌtendər/ *n* [C] *AmE* someone who makes, pours, and serves drinks in a bar or restaurant; ◨ **barman, barmaid** *BrE*

bar·ter[1] /ˈbɑːtə $ ˈbɑːrtər/ *v* [I,T] to exchange goods, work, or services for other goods or services rather than for money: **barter (with sb) for sth** *I had to barter with the locals for food.* | **barter sth for sth** *They bartered their grain for salt.*

barter[2] *n* [U] **1** a system of exchanging goods and services for other goods and services rather than using money: *Trading was carried out under a barter system.* **2** goods or services that are exchanged by bartering: *We used cigarettes for barter.*

bas·alt /ˈbæsɔːlt, bəˈsɔːlt $ ˈbæsɒːlt, ˈbeɪ-/ *n* [U] a type of dark green-black rock

base[1] S1 W1 /beɪs/ *v*
[T usually passive] to have your main place of work, business etc in a particular place: *The paper had intended to base itself in London.* | **be based in sth** *The new organization will be based in Dallas.* → BASED
  base sth on/upon sth *phr v*
to use something as the thing from which something else is developed: *Their relationship was based upon mutual respect.* | *an economy based on farming* | *On what do you base your theory?*

base[2] S2 W2 *n*
1 LOWEST PART [C usually singular] **a)** the lowest part or surface of something; ◨ **bottom**: [+of] *There is a door at the base of the tower.* | *the base of a triangle* | *a frozen dessert with a biscuit base* | *a wine glass with a heavy base* | *The leather of his left trainer was coming away from its rubber base.* **b)** the lowest point on a plant or part of your body, where it joins another part; ◨ **bottom**: [+of] *a hole in the base of the tree* | *He was killed by an axe blow to the base of his skull.*
2 KNOWLEDGE/IDEAS [C] the most important part of something, from which new ideas develop; ◨ **foundation**: *India has a good scientific research base.* | [+for] *They were laying the base for a new economic recovery.* | *Changes in working practices will provide a base for improved performance.*
3 MILITARY [C] a place where people in a military organization live and work: **military/naval/air base**
4 COMPANY/ORGANIZATION [C,U] the main place from which a person, company, or organization controls their activities: [+for] *He used the house as a base for his printing business.*
5 PEOPLE/GROUPS [C usually singular] the people, money, groups etc that form the main part of something: *The company has built up a loyal customer base.* | *By broadening the tax base* (=all the people who pay taxes), *he could raise more revenues.* | *an attempt to strengthen the city's economic base* (=things that produce jobs and money) | *The country's manufacturing base* (=all the factories, companies etc that produce goods in a country) *has shrunk by 20%.* → POWER BASE
6 SUBSTANCE/MIXTURE [singular, U] the main part of a substance, meal etc to which other things are added: *paint with an oil base* | [+for] *Jacket potatoes form the base for a healthy meal.* | *Vodka is the base for many cocktails.*
7 SPORT [C] one of the four places that a player must

touch in order to get a point in games such as BASEBALL
8 be off base *AmE informal* to be completely wrong: *His estimate for painting the kitchen seems way off base.*
9 CHEMICAL [C] *technical* a chemical substance that combines with an acid to form a SALT
10 NUMBERS [C usually singular] *technical* the number in relation to which a number system or mathematical table is built up, for example 10 in the DECIMAL system
11 touch base (with sb) to talk to someone to find out what is happening about something —**basal** *adj* → cover (all) the bases at COVER¹ (12)

base³ *adj* not having good moral principles: *base attitudes and desires* → BASE METAL

base·ball S3 W2 /'beɪsbɔːl $ -bɒːl/ *n*
1 [U] an outdoor game between two teams of nine players, in which players try to get points by hitting a ball and running around four BASES
2 [C] the ball used in baseball

baseball cap *n* [C] a hat that fits closely around your head with a round part that sticks out at the front → see picture at HAT

base·board /'beɪsbɔːd $ -bɔːrd/ *n* [C] *AmE* a narrow board fixed to the bottom of indoor walls where they meet the floor; ▤ skirting board *BrE*

based /beɪst/ *adj* **1** [not before noun] if you are based somewhere, that is the place where you work or where your main business is: *It is a professional service based at our offices in Oxford.* | **London-based/New York-based etc** *a London-based firm of accountants* **2** oil-based/carbon-based/computer-based etc used to describe the basic feature or part of something: *computer-based teaching* | *community-based services* | *carbon-based fuels* **3** broadly-based based on many kinds of things or people: *a broadly-based government of national reconciliation*

BASE jumping, base jumping /'beɪs ˌdʒʌmpɪŋ/ *n* [U] *Building, Antenna, Span, Earth* a sport in which people jump off tall objects such as buildings, bridges, or cliffs, using a PARACHUTE

base·less /'beɪsləs/ *adj* not based on facts or good reasons – used to show disapproval; ▤ unfounded: *baseless rumours/charges/accusations*

base·line /'beɪslaɪn/ *n* [C usually singular] **1** *technical* a standard measurement or fact against which other measurements or facts are compared, especially in medicine or science: *The company's waste emissions were 14% lower than in 1998, the baseline year.* **2** the line at the back of the court in games such as tennis or VOLLEYBALL **3** the area that a player must run within, on a BASEBALL field

base·ment /'beɪsmənt/ *n* [C] a room or area in a building that is under the level of the ground

base metal *n* [C,U] a metal that is not very valuable, such as iron or lead

base rate *n* [C] *BrE* in Britain, the standard rate of INTEREST¹ (4), set by the Bank of England, on which all British banks base their charges; → prime rate

bas·es /'beɪsiːz/ the plural of BASIS

bash¹ /bæʃ/ *v* **1** [I always + adv/prep, T] to hit someone or something hard, in a way that causes pain or damage: *Someone bashed him on the back of his head.* | *Police bashed down the door to get in.* | **bash sth on/against sth** *He bashed his head on the back of the seat.* | [+into] *I accidentally bashed into a woman pushing a pram.* **2** [T] to criticize someone or something very strongly: *He was always bashing the trade unions.* —**basher** *n* [C]: *union-bashers*
bash on *phr v informal* to continue working in order to finish something: *Well, I'd better bash on.*
bash sth ⇔ out *phr v informal* to produce something quickly or in great quantities but without much care

baskets

bicycle basket

dog basket

fruit basket

picnic hamper

laundry basket *BrE*/
hamper *AmE*

wicker basket

wastepaper basket *BrE*/
wastebasket *AmE*

bread basket

shopping basket

sewing basket

or thought: *I bashed out replies as fast as I could.*

bash sb ⇔ **up** *phr v* to seriously hurt someone by attacking them violently

bash² *n* [C] **1** *informal* a hard strong hit; ⊟ **bang**: [+on] *a bash on the head* **2** *informal* a party or an event to celebrate something: *a birthday bash* **3** **have a bash (at sth)** *BrE spoken* to try to do something, especially when you are not sure that you will succeed: *Why not have a bash at windsurfing?*

bash·ful /'bæʃfəl/ *adj* easily embarrassed in social situations; ⊟ **shy**: *a bashful grin* | *Don't be bashful about telling people how you feel.* —**bashfully** *adv* —**bashfulness** *n* [U]

bash·ing /'bæʃɪŋ/ *n* [singular,U] **1** the action of attacking someone and hitting them: *Gay-bashing* (=attacks on gay people) *is on the increase.* | **give sb a bashing** *They gave him a real bashing.* **2** strong and usually unfair public criticism of a particular group or person: *union-bashing in the right-wing press*

ba·sic S1 W1 /'beɪsɪk/ *adj* **1** forming the most important or most necessary part of something; → **basics**: *the basic principles of chemistry* | *The basic idea is simple.* | *basic research* | *basic information* | [+to] *medical techniques basic to the control of infection* **2** at the simplest or least developed level; → **basics**: *the basic skills of programming* | *Their knowledge is very basic.* | *The farm lacks even basic equipment.* **3** **basic salary/pay/pension etc** the amount of money that you are paid before any special payments are added: *On top of the basic salary there are numerous other benefits.* **4** [only before noun] basic rights, needs etc are ones that everyone needs or should have: *basic human rights* | *poor families unable to meet their basic needs*

ba·sic·ally S1 /'beɪsɪkli/ *adv* **1** [sentence adverb] *spoken* used to emphasize the most important reason or fact about something, or a simple explanation of something: *Basically, I'm just lazy.* | *Well, basically, it's a matter of filling in a few forms.* | *I used to see him every night, basically.* **2** in the main or most important ways, without considering additional details or differences; ⊟ **fundamentally**: *All cheeses are made in basically the same way.* | *I believe that human beings are basically good.* | *Basically, he hadn't changed at all.*

ba·sics /'beɪsɪks/ *n* [plural] **1** the most important and necessary facts about something, from which other possibilities and ideas may develop: [+of] *the basics of French grammar* | *Here are some of the basics you will need to know.* **2** things which everyone needs in order to live or to deal with a particular situation: *basics like food and education* **3** **back to basics** used to describe a return to teaching or doing the most important or simplest things: *A lot of parents want schools to get back to basics.*

basic 'training *n* [U] the period when a new soldier learns military rules and does a lot of exercise

bas·il /'bæzəl $ 'beɪ-/ *n* [U] a strong-smelling and strong-tasting HERB used in cooking

ba·sil·i·ca /bə'sɪlɪkə, -'zɪl-/ *n* [C] a church in the shape of a long room with a round end: *the basilica of St Peter's in Rome*

bas·i·lisk /'bæzɪlɪsk, 'bæz-/ *n* [C] an imaginary animal like a snake in ancient stories, supposed to be able to kill people by looking at them

ba·sin /'beɪsən/ *n* [C] **1** *BrE* a round container attached to the wall in a bathroom, where you wash your hands and face; ⊟ **sink**: *The room has a wash basin.* **2** a large bowl-shaped container for liquids or food: *Fill the basin with the cake mixture.* **3** also **basinful** /'beɪsənfʊl/ the amount of liquid that a basin can contain: *a basin of hot water* **4** an area of land that is lower at the centre than at the edges, especially one from which water runs down into a river: *the Amazon basin* **5** a place where the Earth's surface is lower than in other areas: *the Pacific Basin* → PUDDING BASIN

ba·sis S3 W1 /'beɪsɪs/ *n plural* **bases** /-siːz/ [C] **1** the facts, ideas, or things from which something can be developed: *Their claim had no basis in fact* (=it was not true). | [+of] *Bread forms the basis of their daily diet.* | [+for] *The video will provide a basis for class discussion.* **2** **on the basis of sth** because of a particular fact or situation: *discrimination on the basis of sex* **3** **on a regular/daily/weekly etc basis** every day, week etc: *I'm saving money on a regular basis.* **4** **on a voluntary/part-time/temporary etc basis** a system or agreement by which someone or something is VOLUNTARY etc: *Wherever possible redundancies should be on a voluntary basis.* | *Nurses are employed on a full-time basis.*

bask /bɑːsk $ bæsk/ *v* [I] **1** to enjoy sitting or lying in the heat of the sun or a fire: [+in] *Lizards were basking in the morning sun.* **2** if a place basks in the sun, it is sunny and warm: [+in] *Tenerife was basking in afternoon sunshine as they arrived.* **3** to enjoy the approval or attention that you are getting from other people: [+in] *She basked in the admiration of the media.* → **bask/bathe in sb's reflected glory** at GLORY¹ (4)

bas·ket S3 /'bɑːskɪt $ 'bæs-/ *n* [C] **1** a container made of thin pieces of plastic, wire, or wood woven together, used to carry things or put things in: *a shopping basket* | *a basket full of vegetables* | *a picnic basket* | **clothes/laundry basket** (=for dirty clothes) **2** a net with a hole at the bottom attached to a metal ring, through which the ball is thrown in BASKETBALL: **make/shoot a basket** (=to throw the ball through the basket) **3** *technical* the average or total value of a number of different goods or CURRENCIES → **put all your eggs in one basket** at EGG¹ (6); → WASTEPAPER BASKET

bas·ket·ball S3 W2 /'bɑːskɪtbɔːl $ 'bæskɪtbɒːl/ *n* **1** [U] a game played indoors between two teams of five players, in which each team tries to win points by throwing a ball through a net **2** [C] the ball used in this game

'basket case *n* [C] **1** *informal* someone who you think is crazy; ⊟ **nut case** **2** a country with many severe economic and social problems that are likely to continue for a long time

bas·ket·ry /'bɑːskɪtri $ 'bæs-/ also **bas·ket·work** /'bɑːskɪtwɜːk $ 'bæskɪtwɜːrk/ *n* [U] **1** baskets or other objects made by weaving together thin dried branches **2** the skill of making baskets

basque /bæsk/ *n* [C] a piece of underwear for a woman that covers her body from under her arms to the top of her legs

bas-re·lief /,bɑː rɪ'liːf, ,bæs-/ *n* [C,U] *technical* a style of art in which stone or wood is cut so that shapes are raised above the surrounding surface; → **high relief**

bass¹ /beɪs/ *n* **1** [C] a very low male singing voice, or a man with a voice like this **2** [singular] the part of a musical work that is written for a singer with a bass voice → ALTO² (2), BARITONE¹ (2), SOPRANO¹ (2), TENOR¹ (2) **3** [U] the lower half of the whole range of musical notes; → **treble** **4** [C] a BASS GUITAR: *The band features Johnson on bass* (=playing the bass guitar). **5** [C] a DOUBLE BASS → see picture at DRUM¹ ⚠ Do not confuse **bass** and **base**, although they have the same pronunciation.

bass² *adj* [only before noun] a bass instrument or voice produces low notes: *a bass drum*

bass³ /bæs/ *n plural* **bass** [C] a fish that can be eaten and lives in both rivers and the sea

bass clef /,beɪs 'klef/ *n* [C] a sign (𝄢) at the beginning of a line of written music that shows that the top line of the STAVE is the A below MIDDLE C

bas·set /'bæsɪt/ also **'basset ,hound** *n* [C] a dog with short legs and long ears, used for hunting

---

B

bass gui·tar /ˌbeɪs gɪˈtɑː/ $ -ˈtɑːr/ also **bass** *n* [C] an electric GUITAR with four strings, that plays low notes → BASSIST

bas·sist /ˈbeɪsɪst/ *n* [C] someone who plays a BASS GUITAR or a DOUBLE BASS

bas·soon /bəˈsuːn/ *n* [C] a musical instrument like a very long wooden tube, that produces a low sound. You hold it upright and play it by blowing into a thin curved metal pipe. —**bassoonist** *n* [C]

bas·tard S3 /ˈbɑːstəd, ˈbæ- $ ˈbæstərd/ *n* [C]
1 *taboo* a very offensive word for someone, especially a man, who you think is unpleasant. Do not use this word.: *You lying bastard!*
2 *spoken informal not polite* a man who you think is very lucky or very unlucky – often used humorously: *He's gone straight to the top, the lucky bastard.* | *The poor bastard fell off his horse.*
3 *BrE spoken informal* something that causes difficulties or problems: *Life's a bastard sometimes.*
4 *old-fashioned* someone who was born to parents who were not married

bas·tard·ize also **-ise** *BrE* /ˈbɑːstədaɪz, ˈbæ- $ ˈbæstər-/ *v* [T] to spoil something by changing its good parts: *a bastardized version of the play*

baste /beɪst/ *v* [I,T] **1** to pour liquid or melted fat over food that is cooking: *Baste the potatoes occasionally.* **2** to fasten cloth with long loose stitches, in order to hold it together so that you can SEW it properly later; ⊟ **tack**

bas·ti·on /ˈbæstiən $ -tʃən/ *n* [C] **1** something that protects a way of life, principle etc that seems likely to change or end completely: [+of] *These clubs are the last bastions of male privilege.* **2** a place where a country or army has strong military defences: *Pearl Harbor was the principal American bastion in the Pacific.* **3** *technical* a part of a castle wall that sticks out from the rest

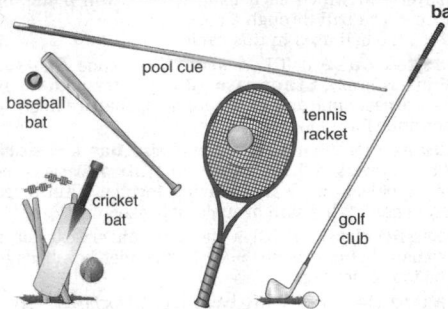

bat

baseball bat

pool cue

tennis racket

cricket bat

golf club

bat¹ S3 /bæt/ *n* [C]
1 a small animal like a mouse with wings that flies around at night → FRUIT BAT
2 a) a long wooden stick with a special shape that is used in some sports and games: *a baseball bat* | *a cricket bat* **b)** *BrE* a round flat piece of wood with a handle, used to hit a ball in TABLE TENNIS; ⊟ **paddle** *AmE*
3 be at bat to be the person who is trying to hit the ball in a game of BASEBALL
4 do sth off your own bat *BrE informal* to do something without being told to do it: *She went to see a solicitor off her own bat.*
5 do sth right off the bat *AmE informal* to do something immediately: *He said yes right off the bat.*
6 like a bat out of hell *informal* very fast: *I drove like a bat out of hell to the hospital.*
7 old bat *spoken* an unpleasant old woman → **as blind as a bat** at BLIND¹ (1c)

bat² *v* **batted, batting** **1** [I,T] to hit the ball with a bat in CRICKET or BASEBALL **2 not bat an eye/eyelid** *informal* to not seem to be shocked, surprised, or embarrassed: *They started talking about sex, but she didn't bat an*

eyelid. **3 bat your eyes/eyelashes** if a woman bats her eyes, she opens and closes them several times quickly in order to look attractive to men **4 go to bat for sb** *AmE informal* to help and support someone **5 be batting a thousand** *AmE informal* to be very successful: *She's been batting a thousand ever since she got that new job.*

bat sth ⇔ **around** *phr v informal* to discuss various ideas or suggestions

bat·boy /ˈbætbɔɪ/ *n* [C] a boy whose job is to look after the equipment of a BASEBALL team

batch /bætʃ/ *n* [C] **1** a group of people or things that arrive or are dealt with together: [+of] *Every day another batch of papers reaches the manager demanding his attention.* **2** a quantity of food, medicine etc that is produced or prepared at the same time: [+of] *She was in the kitchen taking a batch of bread out of the oven.* **3** a set of jobs that are dealt with together on a computer: *an overnight **batch file*** | *a **batch job***

batch 'processing *n* [U] *technical* a type of computer system in which the computer does several jobs one after the other, without needing instructions between each job

bat·ed /ˈbeɪtɪd/ *adj* **with bated breath** feeling very anxious or excited: *He **waited** for a reply to his offer **with bated breath**.*

bath¹ S2 W3 /bɑːθ $ bæθ/ *n plural* **baths** /bɑːðz, bɑːθs $ bæðz, bæθs/ [C]
1 if you take a bath, you wash your body in a bath: *After a week of camping, I really needed a bath.* | **take/have a bath** *I'll have a bath and go to bed.* | *How often do you take a bath?* | *I'll **give** the children their **bath*** (=wash them in a bath).
2 *BrE* a large long container that you fill with water and sit or lie in to wash yourself; ⊟ **bathtub** *AmE*
3 water that you sit or lie in to wash yourself: *a hot bath* | *She **ran a bath*** (=put water into a bath) *for herself.*
4 a bathroom, used especially in advertising: *All our luxury bedrooms have a private bath.*
5 a container full of liquid in which something is placed for a particular purpose: [+of] *Plunge the fabric into a bath of black dye.*
6 baths a) *BrE old-fashioned* a public building in which there is a swimming pool **b)** a public building where people could go in the past to wash themselves: *the Roman baths at Cirencester*
7 take a bath *AmE informal* to lose money, especially in a business deal: *We took a bath in the market over that stock.* → BIRDBATH, BUBBLE BATH; → **throw the baby out with the bath water** at THROW¹ (37)

bath² *v BrE* **1** [T] to wash someone in a bath; ⊟ **bathe** *AmE*: *I'll bath the children.* **2** [I] *old-fashioned* to wash yourself in a bath; ⊟ **bathe** *AmE* ⚠ It is more usual to say **have a bath** *BrE* or **take a bath** *AmE*.

'bath chair *n* [C] *BrE* a special chair with wheels and a cover, used in the past for moving someone old or sick around; → **wheelchair**

bathe¹ /beɪð/ *v* **1** [I,T] *especially AmE* to wash yourself or someone else in a bath; ⊟ **bath** *BrE*: *I bathed, washed my hair, and got dressed.* | *He bathed the children and put them to bed.* ⚠ It is more usual to say **have a bath** *BrE* or **take a bath** *AmE*. **2** [I] *BrE old-fashioned* to swim in the sea, a river, or a lake: *They bathed in the lake in the moonlight.* ⚠ It is more usual to say **go for/have a swim.** **3** [T] to wash or cover part of your body with a liquid, especially as a medical treatment: *She brought a bowl of water and began to bathe the injured arm.* **4 be bathed in light/sunshine etc** *written* an area or building that is bathed in light has light shining onto it in a way that makes it look pleasant or attractive: *The top of Pea Hill was bathed in brilliant sunshine.* **5 be bathed in sweat** *written* to be covered in SWEAT: *I was tired and bathed in sweat.*

bathe² *n* a **bathe** *BrE old-fashioned* when you swim in the sea, a river, or a lake: *They went for a bathe before lunch.*

bath·er /'beɪðə $ -ər/ n **1** [C] BrE someone who is swimming in the sea, a river, or a lake **2 bathers** [plural] AusE a SWIMSUIT

bath·ing /'beɪðɪŋ/ n [U] BrE the activity of swimming in the sea, a river, or a lake: Is the beach safe for bathing?

bathing cap /'beɪðɪŋ kæp/ n [C] old-fashioned a special hat that you wear for swimming

bathing cos·tume /'beɪðɪŋ ˌkɒstjuːm $ -ˌkɑːstuːm/ n [C] BrE old-fashioned a SWIMSUIT

bathing suit /'beɪðɪŋ suːt, -sjuːt $ -suːt/ n [C] old-fashioned a SWIMSUIT

bathing trunks /'beɪðɪŋ trʌŋks/ n [C] BrE old-fashioned a piece of clothing worn by men for swimming; ▤ **swimming trunks**

bath mat n [C] **1** a piece of thick cloth that you put on the floor next to the bath **2** a piece of rubber that you put in the bath to prevent yourself from slipping

ba·thos /'beɪθɒs $ -θɑːs/ n [U] formal in writing, a play etc, a sudden change from a subject that is beautiful, moral, or serious to something that is ordinary, silly, or not important

bath·robe /'bɑːθrəʊb $ 'bæθroʊb/ n [C] a long loose piece of clothing shaped like a coat, that you wear especially before or after having a bath or SHOWER; → **dressing gown**

bath·room S2 W3 /'bɑːθrʊm, -ruːm $ 'bæθ-/ n [C]
1 a room where there is a bath or SHOWER, a BASIN, and sometimes a toilet
2 AmE a room where there is a toilet: Can you tell me where the bathroom is? | I really need to **go to the bathroom** (=use a toilet).

bath towel n [C] a large TOWEL (=piece of material for drying yourself)

bath·tub /'bɑːθtʌb $ 'bæθ-/ n [C] especially AmE a long large container that you fill with water and sit or lie in to wash yourself; ▤ **bath** BrE

ba·tik /bə'tiːk, 'bætɪk/ n **1** [U] a way of printing coloured patterns on cloth that involves putting WAX over some parts of the cloth **2** [C,U] cloth that has been coloured in this way

bat·man /'bætmən/ n plural **batmen** /-mən/ [C] an officer's personal servant in the British army

bat mitzvah /ˌbɑːt 'mɪtsvə/ n [C] **1** a religious ceremony held when a Jewish girl reaches the age of 13 and is considered an adult in her religion; → **bar mitzvah 2** a girl for whom this ceremony is held

bat·on /'bætɒn, -tn $ bæ'tɑːn, bə-/ n [C] **1** a short thin stick used by a CONDUCTOR (=the leader of a group of musicians) to direct the music **2** a short light stick that is passed from one person to another during a race **3** a short thick stick used as a weapon by a police officer; ▤ **truncheon 4** a short stick that is carried as a sign of a special office or rank **5** a light metal stick that is spun and thrown into the air by a MAJORETTE

bats·man /'bætsmən/ n plural **batsmen** /-mən/ [C] the person who is trying to hit the ball in CRICKET

bat·tal·ion /bə'tæljən/ n [C] **1** a large group of soldiers consisting of several companies (COMPANY) **2** a large group of people who are doing something with a particular purpose: [+of] a battalion of supporters

bat·ten¹ /'bætn/ v **1 batten down the hatches a)** to prepare yourself for a period of difficulty or trouble **b)** to firmly fasten the entrances to the lower part of a ship **2 batten on sb** BrE formal to live well by using someone else's money, possessions etc – used to show disapproval

batten² n [C] a long narrow piece of wood that is attached to other pieces of wood or another building material to strengthen them and keep them in place

bat·ter¹ /'bætə $ -ər/ v [I always + adv/prep, T] to hit someone or something again and again, in a way that hurts someone or causes damage: He was **battered to death.** | As a child she was battered by her father. | [+at/on/against etc] People were battering at the door. | **batter sb with sth** | He was battered on the head with a

cricket bat. | [+away] She battered away at his chest with her fists. | **batter sth down** Armed police battered his door down. —**battering** n [C,U]

batter² n **1** [C,U] a mixture of flour, eggs, milk etc, used in cooking and for making bread, cakes etc: Fry the fish in batter. | pancake batter **2** [C] the person who is trying to hit the ball in BASEBALL

bat·tered /'bætəd $ -ərd/ adj **1** old and in bad condition: a battered old suitcase **2 battered woman/wife/ husband/baby etc** someone who has been violently attacked by their husband, wife, father etc

battering ram n [C] a long heavy piece of wood used in wars in the past to break through walls or doors

bat·ter·y S2 /'bætəri/ n plural **batteries**
1 ELECTRICITY [C] an object that provides a supply of electricity for something such as a radio, car, or toy

> **change the batteries (in sth)** (=put new batteries in something)
> **charge/recharge a battery** (=fill it with electricity again after it has been used)
> **flat battery** BrE
> **dead battery** AmE (=one that has no more electricity in it)
> **rechargeable battery** (=one that can be recharged and used again)
> **car battery**
> **battery powered/operated**
> **battery compartment** (=the place where the batteries go)
> **battery charger** (=a piece of equipment for charging batteries)

> You have to take the top off to **change the batteries.** | When the red light comes on, you should **recharge the battery** so it is ready for the next time. | The car's got a **flat battery.** | a **battery-operated** hair dryer → see picture at ELECTRICITY

2 a battery of sth a group of many things of the same type: a battery of medical tests
3 FARM [C] BrE a row of small CAGES in which chickens are kept, so that the farm can produce large numbers of eggs: battery hens → FREE-RANGE
4 GUNS [C] several large guns used together: an anti-aircraft battery
5 CRIME [U] law the crime of hitting someone: He was charged with assault and battery. → ASSAULT AND BATTERY
6 recharge your batteries informal to rest or relax in order to get back your energy: A week in the mountains should recharge my batteries.

bat·tle¹ W2 /'bætl/ n [C]
1 FIGHT a fight between opposing armies, groups of ships, groups of people etc, especially one that is part of a larger war: the Battle of Trafalgar | **in battle** Her son was killed in battle. | **into battle** a knight riding into battle | [+between] battles between government forces and the rebels | a **pitched battle** (=a long and serious battle) between police and drug gangs
2 COMPETITION/ARGUMENT a situation in which opposing groups or people compete or argue with each other when trying to achieve success or control: a long-running legal battle | [+for] a battle for custody of their children | [+between] a fierce ratings battle between rival TV stations | [+with] an on-going battle with my mother about eating properly
3 CHANGE BAD SITUATION an attempt to solve a difficult problem or change an unpleasant situation

> **fight a battle**
> **win a battle**
> **lose a battle**
> **a losing battle** (=something you cannot achieve)
> **an uphill battle** (=something that is very difficult to do)

> [+against] a battle against the racism of the school system | [+with] a long battle with lung cancer | [+for] Scientology has fought long battles for acceptance as a religion. | Learning to read as an adult is tough work, but you can **win this battle** if you try. | We've tried to

*mend the fence several times, but we're **fighting a losing battle**. | Keeping the house tidy is **an uphill battle** when the kids are all at home.*

4 be half the battle to be a difficult or important part of what you have to do: *Just getting an interview is half the battle.*

5 a battle of wits a situation in which opposing sides try to win by using their intelligence: *A good mystery story is a battle of wits between author and reader.*

6 battle of wills a situation in which opposing sides refuse to change what they want, in the hope that the other side will decide to change first: *a battle of wills between teacher and student*

7 do battle (with sb) to argue with someone or fight against someone: *She walked into the room with her eyes blazing, ready to do battle.*

8 fight your own battles to argue with someone or compete in a difficult situation without having help from other people – used to show approval: *It's all right, Mum. I can fight my own battles.*

9 the battle of the sexes the relationship between men and women when it is considered as a fight for power

10 the battle of the bulge the act of trying to lose weight – used humorously

battle² v **1** [I,T] to try very hard to achieve something that is difficult or dangerous: *Firefighters battled the flames for four hours last night.* | [+**against/with**] *She had battled bravely against cancer.* | [+**for**] *a pressure group battling for better schools* | **battle to do sth** *Doctors battled to save his life.* **2 battle it out** to keep fighting or opposing each other until one person or team wins: *32 teams will battle it out in the finals.* **3** [I] *literary* to take part in a fight or war

bat·tle·axe also **battleax** *AmE* /'bætl-æks/ n [C] **1** *informal* a very unpleasant woman who tries to control other people **2** a large AXE used as a weapon in the past

battle ˌcruiser n [C] a large fast ship used in war

battle cry n [C usually singular] **1** a phrase used to encourage people, especially members of a political organization: *'Socialism Now!' was their battle cry.* **2** a loud shout used in war to encourage your side and frighten the enemy

bat·tle·dress /'bætldres/ n [U] also **battle ˌfatigues** *BrE* [plural] clothes worn by soldiers when they are fighting

battle faˌtigue n [U] *old-fashioned* a type of mental illness caused by the frightening experiences of war, in which someone feels very anxious and upset

bat·tle·field /'bætlfiːld/ also **bat·tle·ground** /'bætlgraʊnd/ n [C] **1** a place where a battle is being fought or has been fought **2** a subject that people disagree or argue a lot about: *Education has become a political battleground.* **3** a place where an argument or disagreement happens, or where people are competing against each other: *a battleground state during the election* | *His battlefield experience in Congress will help him in the election.*

bat·tle·ments /'bætlmənts/ n [plural] a low wall around the top of a castle, that has spaces to shoot guns or ARROWS through

bat·tle·ship /'bætl,ʃɪp/ n [C] the largest type of ship used in war, with very big guns and heavy ARMOUR

battleship 'grey; **battleship gray** *AmE* n [U] a medium grey colour —**battleship grey** *adj*

bat·ty /'bæti/ *adj* slightly crazy, but not in an unpleasant or frightening way; ▤ **nutty**

bau·ble /'bɔːbəl $ 'bɒː-/ n [C] **1** a cheap piece of jewellery **2** *BrE* a brightly coloured decoration that looks like a ball and is used to decorate a CHRISTMAS TREE

baud rate /'bɔːd reɪt $ 'bɒːd-/ n [C] *technical* a measurement of how fast information is sent to or from a computer, for example through a telephone line

baulk /bɔːk, bɔːlk $ bɒːk, bɒːlk/ a British spelling of BALK

baux·ite /'bɔːksaɪt $ 'bɒːk-/ n [U] a soft substance that ALUMINIUM is obtained from

bawd·y /'bɔːdi $ 'bɒːdi/ *adj* bawdy songs, jokes, stories etc are about sex and are funny, enjoyable, and often noisy: *a bawdy new play* —**bawdiness** n [U]

'bawdy house n [C] *old use* a place where women have sex with men for money

bawl /bɔːl $ bɒːl/ v **1** [I,T] also **bawl out** to shout in a loud voice; ▤ **yell**: *'Tickets please!' bawled the conductor.* **2** [I] to cry loudly; ▤ **scream**: *They could hear a baby bawling somewhere.*

bawl sb ⇔ out *phr v* to speak angrily to someone because they have done something wrong: *He was afraid Vic would bawl him out for being late.*

bay¹ /beɪ/ n [C]

1 SEA a part of the sea that is partly enclosed by a curve in the land: *a house with a view across the bay* | *Montego Bay*

2 keep/hold sth at bay to prevent something dangerous or unpleasant from happening or from coming too close: *A thick wall keeps the noise at bay.*

3 AREA an area within a large room or just outside a building that is used for a particular purpose: *a storage bay* | *loading bay*

4 FOR CARGO the part of a ship or plane where things are stored: *the cargo bay*

5 TREE also **bay tree** a tree that has leaves which smell sweet and are often used in cooking

6 HORSE a horse that is a reddish brown colour

bay² v [I] **1** if a dog bays, it makes a long high noise, especially when it is chasing something; ▤ **howl**: *dogs baying at the moon* **2** to make strong demands to get answers to questions or force someone to give you something: [+**for**] *Reporters began baying for the president's blood* (=demanding that he be punished).

bay³ *adj* a bay horse is reddish brown in colour

'bay leaf n [C] a sweet-smelling leaf from the bay tree, used in cooking

bay·o·net¹ /'beɪənɪt, -net/ n [C] a long knife that is fixed to the end of a RIFLE (=long gun)

bayonet² v [T] to push the point of a bayonet into someone

bay·ou /'baɪu $ 'baɪu, -oʊ/ n [C] a large area of water in the southeast US that moves very slowly and has many water plants

ˌbay 'window n [C] a window that sticks out from the wall of a house, usually with glass on three sides → see picture at WINDOW

ba·zaar /bə'zɑː $ -'zɑːr/ n [C] **1** a market or area where there are a lot of small shops, especially in India or the Middle East **2** an occasion when a lot of people sell different things to collect money for a good purpose: *a church bazaar*

ba·zoo·ka /bə'zuːkə/ n [C] a long light gun that rests on your shoulder and is used for shooting at TANKS

BBC /ˌbiː biː 'siːˌ/ n *British Broadcasting Corporation* the British radio and television company that is paid for by the public

BB gun /'biː biː ɡʌn/ n [C] *AmE* a gun that uses air pressure to shoot small round metal balls; ▤ **airgun**

BBQ n [C] the abbreviation for *barbecue*

BC *BrE*; **B.C.** *AmE* /ˌbiː 'siːˌ/ *before Christ* used after a date to show that it was before the birth of Christ; → AD: *The Great Pyramid dates from around 2600 BC.*

bcc *blind carbon copy* used in an EMAIL to show that you are sending someone a copy of a message that you have also sent to someone else, and that this person does not know that other people will also receive the message

BCE *BrE*; **B.C.E.** *AmE* /ˌbiː siː 'iːˌ/ *before common era* used after a date to show that it is before the birth of Christ

be¹ S1 W1 /bi; *strong* biː/ *past tense* **was, were,** *past participle* **been,** *present participle* **being,** *first person singular* **am,** *second person singular and plural* **are,** *third person singular* **is** *auxiliary verb*
1 used with a present participle to form the CONTINUOUS (4) tenses of verbs: *Don't disturb me while I'm working.* | *Gemma was reading when her son called.* | *They've been asking a lot of questions.* | *That guy's always causing trouble.* | *We'll be starting in about half an hour.* | *He isn't leaving, is he?*
2 used with past participles to form the PASSIVE: *Smoking is not permitted.* | *I was told about it yesterday.* | *The house is being painted.* | *She's been invited to a party.* | *The flames could be seen several miles away.* | *The police should have been informed about this.*
3 be to do sth *formal* **a)** used to talk about arrangements for the future: *Audrey and Jimmy are to be married in June.* | *Two men are to appear in court on charges of armed robbery.* | *We were to have gone away last week, but I was ill.* **b)** used to give an order or to tell someone about a rule: *You are to wait here in this room until I return.* | *All staff are to wear uniforms.* **c)** used to say or ask what someone should do or what should happen: *What am I to tell her?* | *He is not to be blamed.* **d)** used to ask how something can be done: *How are we to get out of the present mess?*
4 be to be seen/found/heard etc used to say that something can be seen, found, or heard somewhere: *A large range of species are to be seen in the aquarium.* | *We searched everywhere but the ring was nowhere to be found* (=could not be found). | *The only sound to be heard was the twittering of the birds above us.*
5 was/were to do sth used when talking about a time in the past to say what happened later: *This discovery was to have a major effect on the treatment of heart disease.*
6 a) used in CONDITIONAL¹ (2) sentences about an imagined situation: **were sb to do sth/if sb were to do sth** *Even if England were to win the next two matches, Germany would still be three points ahead.* | *Were we to offer you the job, would you take it?* **b)** used in CONDITIONAL sentences to introduce an aim when you are saying what must be done in order to achieve it: **if sb/sth is to do sth** *If we are to succeed in this enterprise, we shall need to plan everything very carefully.*
7 *old use* used instead of 'have' to form the PERFECT³ tense of some verbs: *The hour is come.*

be² S1 W1 *v*
1 [linking verb] used to say that someone or something is the same as the subject of the sentence: *My name is Susan.* | *These are my favourite pictures.* | *He's my brother.* | *The problem is finding the time to get things done.* | *Our aim was to reduce the number of accidents.*
2 [I always + adv/prep] used to say where something or someone is: *Jane's upstairs.* | *Are my keys in the drawer?* | *The principal's in his office.* | *How long has she been here?*
3 [I always + adv/prep] used to say when something happens: *The concert was last night.* | *The party is on Saturday.*
4 [linking verb] used to describe someone or something, or say what group or type they belong to: *The sky was grey.* | *Spiders are not really insects.* | *Mr Cardew was a tall thin man.* | *She wants to be a doctor when she leaves school.* | *Her dress was pure silk.* | *I'm not ready yet.*
5 there is/are used to say that something exists or happens: *There's a hole in your trousers.* | *There was a loud explosion.* | *'I thought there was going to be a party.' 'No, there isn't.' | Is there a problem?*
6 [linking verb] to behave in a particular way: *He was just being rude.* | *Don't be silly.* | *You'd better be careful.*
7 [linking verb] used to say how old someone is: *His mother died when he was twenty.* | *Rachel will be three in November.*
8 [linking verb] used to say who something belongs to: *Whose is this bag? It isn't mine and it isn't Sarah's.*
9 [linking verb] used to talk about the price of something: *'How much are the melons?' 'The big ones are £2 each.'*

10 [linking verb] to be equal to a particular number or amount: *32 divided by 8 is 4.*
11 be that as it may *formal* used to say that even though you accept that something is true, it does not change a situation: *'He was only joking.' 'Be that as it may, silly remarks like that can do a lot of harm.'*
12 [I] *formal* to exist: *What was once a great and powerful empire has effectively ceased to be.*
13 be yourself to behave in a natural way, rather than trying to pretend to be different: *Don't try too hard – just be yourself.*
14 not be yourself to be behaving in a way that is unusual for you, especially because you are ill or upset: *Sorry – I'm not myself this morning.*
15 the be-all and end-all the most important part of a situation or of someone's life: [+of] *For Jim, making money was the be-all and end-all of his job.*

be- /bɪ/ *prefix* **1** [in verbs] used to mean that someone or something is treated in a particular way: *Don't belittle him* (=say he is unimportant). | *He befriended me* (=became my friend) **2** *literary* [in adjectives] wearing or covered by a particular thing: *a bespectacled boy* (=wearing glasses)

beach¹ S3 W2 /biːtʃ/ *n* [C] an area of sand or small stones at the edge of the sea or a lake: *a sandy beach* | *tourists walking along the beach* → see picture at COUNTRY

beach² *v* [T] **1** to pull a boat onto the shore away from the water **2** if a WHALE beaches itself or is beached, it swims onto the shore and cannot get back in the water

beach ball *n* [C] a large coloured plastic ball that you blow air into and use for playing games on the beach

beach chair *n* [C] *AmE* a folding chair with a seat and back made of cloth or plastic, which is used outdoors, especially at the beach; ⊟ **deckchair** *BrE*

beach·comb·er /'biːtʃ,kəʊmə $ -,koʊmər/ *n* [C] someone who searches beaches for interesting or useful things

beach·head /'biːtʃhed/ *n* [C] an area of shore that has been taken from an enemy by force, and from which the army can prepare to attack a country

beach·wear /'biːtʃweə $ -wer/ *n* [U] clothes that you wear for swimming, lying on the beach etc

bea·con /'biːkən/ *n* [C] **1** a light that is put somewhere to warn or guide people, ships, vehicles, or aircraft **2** a radio or RADAR signal used by aircraft or boats to help them find their position and direction **3** *especially literary* a person, idea etc that guides or encourages you: [+of] *The education program offers a beacon of hope to these children.* **4** a fire on top of a hill used in the past as a signal → BELISHA BEACON

bead /biːd/ *n* [C] **1** one of a set of small, usually round, pieces of glass, wood, plastic etc, that you can put on a string and wear as jewellery: *She wore a string of green glass beads around her neck.* **2** a small drop of liquid such as water or blood: *Beads of sweat trickled down his face.* **3 draw a bead on sb/sth** to aim carefully before shooting a weapon → WORRY BEADS

bead·ed /'biːdɪd/ *adj* **1** decorated with beads: *a beaded dress* **2 beaded with sweat/perspiration** having drops of SWEAT (=liquid produced by your body when you are hot) on your skin

bead·ing /'biːdɪŋ/ *n* [U] **1** long thin pieces of wood or stone that are used as a decoration on the edges of walls, furniture etc **2** a lot of beads sewn close together on clothes, leather etc as decoration

bea·dle /'biːdl/ *n* [C] an officer in British churches in the past, who helped the priest in various ways, especially by keeping order

bead·y /'biːdi/ *adj* **1** beady eyes are small, round, and shiny – used especially about someone who you think looks dishonest or strange **2 have/keep your**

B

beast·ly /'biːstli/ *adj BrE* very unpleasant; ■ **nasty**: *What beastly weather!* —**beastly** *adv* —**beastliness** *n* [U]

beast of 'burden *n* [C] *old use* an animal that does heavy work

beat¹ S2 W2 /biːt/ *v past tense* **beat**, *past participle* **beaten** /'biːtn/

1 COMPETITION/ELECTION [T] to get the most points, votes etc in a game, race, or competition; ■ **defeat**: *Brazil were beaten, 2–1.* | *Labour easily beat the Conservatives in the last election.* | **beat sb at/in sth** *I beat him more often at pool than he beats me.* | **beat sb hollow** *BrE*/**beat the pants off sb** *AmE* (=defeat them easily)

2 HIT [T] to hit someone or something many times with your hand, a stick etc: *photographs of rioters beating a policeman* | *He was questioned and beaten.* | *The woman had been **beaten to death** by her husband.* | *Two prisoners were **beaten unconscious**.* | **beat sb black and blue** (=hit someone until it makes marks on their body) | **beat the living daylights out of sb** (=beat someone very hard)

3 HIT AGAINST [I always + adv/prep] to hit against something many times or continuously: [+on/against/at etc] *Waves beat against the cliffs.* | *rain beating on the windows* | *Sid beat on the door with his hand.*

4 DO BETTER [T] to do something better, faster etc than what was best before: **beat a record/score etc** *The record set by Kierson in '84 has yet to be beaten.* | *The company's profits are unlikely to beat last year's £10 million.* | *See how many times you can do it in a minute, and then try to beat that amount.*

5 BE BETTER [T not in progressive] *especially spoken* to be much better and more enjoyable than something else: *Fresh milk beats powdered milk any time.* | **beat doing sth** *'Well,' said Culley, 'it beats going to the office.'* | *You can't beat swimming as a good all-body exercise.* | *Nothing beats homemade cake.* | **you can't beat sth (for sth)** *For excitement, you just can't beat college basketball.*

6 FOOD [I,T] to mix things together quickly with a fork or special kitchen machine: *Beat the eggs, then add the milk.* | **beat sth in** *Gradually beat in the sugar.* | **beat sth together** *Beat the butter and sugar together until fluffy.*

7 CONTROL/DEAL WITH [T] to successfully deal with a problem that you have been struggling with; ■ **conquer**: *advice on how to beat depression* | *the government's long fight to beat inflation*

8 HEART [I] when your heart beats, it moves in a regular RHYTHM as it pumps your blood: *The average person's heart beats 70 times a minute.* | *Jennifer's heart was beating fast.*

9 DRUMS [I,T] if you beat drums, or if drums beat, they make a regular continuous sound

10 WINGS [I,T] if a bird beats its wings, or if its wings beat, they move up and down quickly and regularly; ■ **flap**

11 take some beating if something or someone will take some beating, it will be difficult for anyone or anything to be or do better: *Schumacher has 42 points, which will take some beating.* | *For ease of use, this program will take some beating.* | *Florida takes some beating as a vacation destination.*

12 AVOID [T] to avoid situations in which a lot of people are trying to do something, usually by doing something early: *We left at four a.m. to beat the traffic.* | *Shopping by mail order lets you beat the queues.* | *Shop now and beat the Christmas rush!*

13 DO BEFORE SB ELSE [T] *informal* to get or do something before someone else, especially if you are both trying to do it first: **beat sb to sth** *John had beaten me to the breakfast table.* | *I wanted the last piece of pie, but somebody beat me to it.* | *They wanted to beat it into a film, but another studio beat them to the punch.*

14 beat about/around the bush to avoid or delay talking about something embarrassing or unpleasant: *Don't beat around the bush. Ask for your account to be paid, and paid quickly.*

15 beat the system to find ways of avoiding or breaking the rules of an organization, system etc, in order to achieve what you want: *Accountants know a few ways to beat the system.*

16 beat a path (to sb's door) also beat down sb's door if people beat a path to your door, they are interested in something you are selling, a service you are providing etc: *The new design was supposed to have consumers beating a path to their door.*

17 beat a (hasty) retreat to leave somewhere or stop doing something very quickly, in order to avoid a bad situation: *Spicer beat a hasty retreat when he saw me.*

18 beat the clock to finish something very quickly, especially before a particular time: *The company managed to beat the clock on delivering its new system.*

19 (it) beats me used to say that you do not know something or cannot understand or explain it: *Beats me why he wants such a big car.* | *'What's he saying?' 'Beats me.'*

20 beat it! used to tell someone to leave at once, because they are annoying you or should not be there

21 can you beat that/it? used to show that you are surprised or annoyed by something: *They've got eight children! Can you beat that?*

22 beat your brains out to think about something very hard and for a long time: *I've been beating my brains out all week trying to finish this essay.*

23 if you can't beat 'em, join 'em used when you decide to take part in something even though you disapprove of it, because everyone else is doing it and you cannot stop them

24 beat the rap *AmE informal* to avoid being punished for something you have done

25 beat time to make regular movements or sounds to show the speed at which music should be played: *a conductor beating time with his baton*

26 beat a path/track to make a path by walking over an area of land

27 to beat the band *AmE informal* in large amounts or with great force: *It's raining to beat the band.*

28 beat the heat *AmE informal* to make yourself cooler: *Fresh lemonade is a great way to beat the heat.*

29 METAL also beat out [T] to hit metal with a hammer in order to shape it or make it thinner

30 HUNTING [I,T] to force wild birds and animals out of bushes, long grass etc so that they can be shot for sport

31 beat your breast *literary* to show clearly that you are very upset or sorry about something → BEATEN, BEATING

beat down *phr v*
1 if the sun beats down, it shines very brightly and the weather is hot
2 if the rain beats down, it is raining very hard
3 beat the door down to hit a door so hard that it falls down
4 beat sb down *BrE* to persuade someone to reduce a price: [+to] *He wanted £4500 for the car but I beat him down to £3850.*
5 beat sb ⇔ down to make someone feel defeated, so they no longer respect themselves: *The women seemed beaten down.*

beat off *phr v*
1 beat sb/sth ⇔ off to succeed in defeating someone who is attacking, opposing, or competing with you: *McConnell beat off a challenge for his Senate seat.*
2 *AmE informal not polite* if a man beats off, he MASTURBATES

beat sb/sth ⇔ out *phr v*
1 if a drum or something else beats out a RHYTHM, or if you beat out a rhythm on a drum, it makes a continuous regular sound
2 *especially AmE* to defeat someone in a competition: *Lockheed beat out a rival company to win the contract.* | [+for] *Roberts beat out Tony Gwynn for the Most Valuable Player Award.*

3 to put out a fire by hitting it many times with something such as a cloth

beat up *phr v*

1 beat sb ⇔ up to hurt someone badly by hitting them: *Her boyfriend got drunk and beat her up.*

2 beat up on sb *AmE* to hit someone and harm them, especially someone younger or weaker than yourself

3 beat yourself up also **beat up on yourself** *AmE informal* to blame yourself too much for something: *If you do your best and you lose, you can't beat yourself up about it.*

beat² S3 *n*

1 [C] one of a series of regular movements or hitting actions: *a heart rate of 80 beats a minute* | *the steady beat of the drum*

2 [singular] a regular repeated noise; ◨ **rhythm**: [+of] *the beat of marching feet*

3 [C] the main RHYTHM that a piece of music or a poem has: *a song with a beat you can dance to* | *a poem with a very regular beat*

4 [singular] a subject or area of a city that someone is responsible for as their job: *journalists covering the Washington beat* | **on the beat** *People like to see police officers on the beat.*

5 [C] one of the notes in a piece of music that sounds stronger than the other notes

beat³ *adj* [not before noun] *informal* very tired; ◨ **exhausted**: *I'm beat.* | *Come and sit down, you must be dead beat.*

beat·box /'bi:tbɒks $ -ba:ks/ *n* **1** also **beat·box·er** /-bɒksə $ -ba:ksər/ [C] someone who provides the words or other spoken sounds that go with HIP HOP **2** [U] a computer program that is used to mix the sounds of popular electronic music with a strong beat, or the type of music produced by this —**beatboxing** *n* [U]

beat·en /'bi:tn/ *adj* [only before noun] **1** **off the beaten track/path** a place that is off the beaten track is not well known and is far away from the places that people usually visit **2** a beaten path, track etc has been made by many people walking the same way: *a well-beaten path through the forest* **3** a beaten person feels defeated and not respected: *a beaten man who had lost his job* **4** beaten metal has been shaped with a hammer to make it thinner

beat·er /'bi:tə $ -ər/ *n* [C] **1** an object that is designed to beat something: *an egg beater* | *a carpet beater* **2** **wife/child beater** someone who hits his wife or child, especially someone who does this often **3** someone who forces wild birds or animals out of bushes, long grass etc so that they can be shot for sport **4** *AmE informal* an old car in bad condition → **WORLD-BEATER**

bea·tif·ic /ˌbiːəˈtɪfɪk◂/ *adj* a beatific look, smile etc shows great peace and happiness —**beatifically** /-kli/ *adv*

be·at·i·fy /biˈætɪfaɪ/ *v* **beatified, beatifying, beatifies** [T] if the Roman Catholic church beatifies someone who has died, it says officially that they are a holy or special person —**beatification** /biˌætɪfɪˈkeɪʃən/ *n* [U]

beat·ing /'bi:tɪŋ/ *n* [C] **1** an act of hitting someone many times as a punishment or in a fight: *a brutal beating* **2** **take a beating** to lose very badly in a game or competition: *The Dodgers took a real beating on Saturday.* → **take some beating** at BEAT¹ (11)

beat·nik /'bi:tnɪk/ *n* [C] one of a group of young people in the late 1950s and early 1960s, who did not accept the values of society and showed this by their clothes and the way they lived

beat-up *adj* a beat-up car, bicycle etc is old and in bad condition; ◨ **battered**: *a beat-up old Ford Escort*

beau /bəʊ $ boʊ/ *n plural* **beaux** /bəʊz $ boʊz/ *or* **beaus** [C] *old-fashioned* **1** a woman's close friend or lover **2** a fashionable well-dressed man

beaut /bju:t/ *n* [singular] *AmE, AusE spoken* used to say that something is either very good, attractive, or impressive: *That last catch was a beaut.*

beau·te·ous /'bju:tiəs/ *adj literary* beautiful: *the beauteous Helen of Troy* —**beauteously** *adv*

beau·ti·cian /bju:'tɪʃən/ *n* [C] someone whose job is to give beauty treatments to your skin, hair etc

beau·ti·ful S1 W2 /'bju:tɪfəl/ *adj*

1 someone or something that is beautiful is extremely attractive to look at: *She was even more beautiful than I had remembered.* | *a beautiful bunch of flowers*

2 very good or giving you great pleasure; ◨ **lovely**: *beautiful music* | *What a beautiful shot!* | *The weather was beautiful.* —**beautifully** *adv*

beau·ti·fy /'bju:tɪfaɪ/ *v* **beautified, beautifying, beautifies** [T] *formal* to make someone or something beautiful: *plants to beautify the garden*

beau·ty S3 W2 /'bju:ti/ *n plural* **beauties**

1 **APPEARANCE** [U] a quality that people, places, or things have that makes them very attractive to look at: *her beauty and grace* | *an area of outstanding **natural beauty*** | *Millions of dollars are spent each year on beauty products.*

2 **WOMAN** [C] a woman who is very beautiful: *She was considered a great beauty in her youth.*

3 **POEM/MUSIC/EMOTION ETC** [U] a quality that something such as a poem, song, emotion etc has, which gives you pleasure or joy: [+of] *the beauty of Shakespeare's verse*

4 **ADVANTAGE** the beauty of sth a particularly good quality that makes something especially suitable or useful: *The beauty of e-mail is its speed and ease of use.*

5 [C] *spoken* a very good, large etc example of something: *You should have seen the boat – a real beauty.*

6 **beauty is in the eye of the beholder** used to say that different people have different opinions about what is beautiful

7 **beauty is only skin-deep** used to say that how someone looks is not as important as a good character

'beauty ˌcontest *n* [C] a competition in which women are judged on how attractive they look

'beauty mark *n* [C] *AmE* a small dark mark on a woman's face – used when you think it is attractive; ◨ **beauty spot** *BrE*

'beauty ˌparlor *n* [C] *AmE* a beauty salon

'beauty queen *n* [C] the winner of a beauty contest

'beauty ˌsalon / $ ˈ.. ˌ./ also **'beauty ˌshop** *AmE n* [C] a place where you can receive treatments for your skin, hair, nails etc to make you look more attractive

'beauty sleep *n* [U] enough sleep to keep you healthy and looking good – used humorously

'beauty spot *n* [C] *BrE* **1** a place in the countryside which is famous because it is very pretty: *Guests will be able to visit some of the local beauty spots.* **2** a small

B

dark mark on a woman's face – used when you think it is attractive; ▣ **beauty mark** *AmE*

bea·ver¹ /'biːvə $ -ər/ *n* [C] a North American animal that has thick fur and a wide flat tail, and cuts down trees with its teeth → **eager beaver** at EAGER (2)

beaver² *v*

beaver away *phr v informal* to work very hard, especially at writing or calculating something: [+at] *He's been beavering away at his homework for hours.*

be·bop /'biːbɒp $ -bɑːp/ *n* [U] a type of JAZZ music

be·calmed /bɪ'kɑːmd $ -'kɑːmd, -'kɑːlmd/ *adj formal* **1** a sailing boat that is becalmed cannot move because there is no wind **2** if something such as a company, the economy, or a discussion about something is becalmed, no progress is being made: *The Stock Market was becalmed yesterday as dealers waited for company results.*

be·came /bɪ'keɪm/ the past tense of BECOME

be·cause¹ S1 W1 /bɪ'kɒz, bɪ'kəz $ bɪ'kɒːz, bɪ'kəz/ *conjunction*
1 used when you are giving the reason for something: *We didn't enjoy the day because the weather was so awful.* | *Because he had been in prison, employers were unwilling to offer him a job.* | *'Why can't I go?' 'Because you're not old enough.'* | *Hubert never experienced any fear, and this was **partly because** he was not particularly intelligent.* | *Many exam candidates lose marks **simply because** they do not read the questions properly.* | *I decided to go with them, **mainly because** I had nothing better to do.*
2 just because ... *spoken* used to say that although one thing is true, it does not mean that something else is true: *Just because you're my brother doesn't mean I have to like you!*

because² *prep* **because of sb/sth** used to say who or what causes something to happen or is the reason for something: *He had to retire because of ill health.* | *We spent three hours waiting in the rain because of you!*; → see box at OWING TO

beck /bek/ *n* [C] **1 be at sb's beck and call** to always be ready to do what someone wants: *I was tired of being at her beck and call all day long.* **2** *BrE* a small stream

beck·on /'bekən/ *v* **1** [I,T] to make a signal to someone with your hand, to show that you want them to come towards you or to follow you: *I could see my husband beckoning me.* | **beckon (to) sb to do sth** *She beckoned to the waitress to bring more wine.* | **beckon sb forward/over etc** *He beckoned us over and introduced us to his wife.* **2** [I,T] if something such as a place or opportunity beckons, it appears so attractive that you want to have it: *A career in the film industry beckoned.* **3** [I] if something beckons for someone, it will probably happen to them: [+for] *Early retirement beckoned for George.*

be·come S1 W1 /bɪ'kʌm/ *v past tense* **became** /-'keɪm/ *past participle* **become**
1 [linking verb] to begin to be something, or to develop in a particular way: *George became King at the age of 54.* | *Pollution from cars has become a major problem.* | *The weather became warmer.* | *Slowly my eyes became accustomed to the darkness.* | *Helen became increasingly anxious about her husband's strange behaviour.* | *It soon became clear that Wilson lacked the ability to carry out his duties.*
2 [T not in progressive] *formal* to be suitable for someone or to look attractive on them; ▣ **suit**: *Blue really becomes her.* | *Don't try to be clever – it doesn't become you.*
3 what became of ...?/whatever will become of ...? used to ask what has happened to someone or something, especially when you have not seen them for a long time, or what will happen to someone that you are worried about: *What became of those Chinese vases that Mum used to have?* | *Whatever will become of Sam when his wife dies?*

WORD CHOICE: become, get, go, turn, grow, come
become can be followed by an adjective or noun, not a verb: *Her husband became jealous.* | *We soon became friends.*
get is very often used instead of **become**, and is more usual in spoken English: *I was getting hungry.* | *Things got worse and worse.*
go is used
to say that something changes colour: *The sky went pink.*
to say that someone feels a change in their body: *My fingers have gone numb.*
with **blind** and **deaf**: *He went blind.*
with **mad, insane, crazy** etc: *The crowd went wild.*
turn is used especially to say that something changes colour: *The liquid turned green.* | *His face turned pale.*
grow can be used in fairly literary written English
to say that something changes gradually: *It grew dark as we walked.*
with a to-infinitive, to say that someone gradually starts doing something: *We grew to love each other.*
come is used
with adjectives like **apart, undone,** and **unstuck**: *Your shoelace has come undone.* | *A few pages came loose.*
with **true**: *Her prediction came true.*
with a to-infinitive to say that someone starts doing something: *I eventually came to realize (NOT became to realize) I was wrong.*

be·com·ing /bɪ'kʌmɪŋ/ *adj formal* **1** a piece of clothing, a hairstyle, etc that is becoming makes you look attractive: *Her short hairstyle is very becoming.* **2** words or actions that are becoming are suitable for you or for the situation you are in: *She received the praise with becoming modesty.* —**becomingly** *adv*

bec·que·rel /ˌbekə'rel/ *n* [C] a unit for measuring RADIOACTIVITY

bed¹ S1 W1 /bed/ *n*
1 SLEEP [C,U] a piece of furniture that you sleep on

in bed
single/double bed (=a bed for one person/two people)
get into bed/get out of bed
go to bed
make your bed (=tidy the covers after you have slept in your bed)
put sb to bed (=put a child in their bed)
get sb out of bed (=make someone get out of bed)
time for bed (=time to go to sleep)
climb/crawl into bed
jump out of bed
before bed (=before going to bed)
take to your bed (=go to bed because you feel ill)
spare bed (=a bed for visitors to your home)

*Simon lay **in bed** thinking about the meeting next day.* | *She **got into bed** and turned out the light.* | *I was too tired to **get out of bed**.* | *You should **go to bed** early tonight.* | *Have you **made** your **bed**, Penny?* | *I'll just **put** the children **to bed**.* | *Sorry for calling so early – I hope I didn't **get** you **out of bed**.* | *Come on kids, it's **time for bed**.* | *Dad always has a whisky **before bed**.* | *He felt so ill that he **took to** his **bed**.* | *We'd love you to come and stay. The **spare bed's** available for you.* → CAMP BED, DOUBLE BED, FOUR-POSTER BED, SOFA BED, TWIN BED

2 SEX [U] *informal* used to refer to having sex: *I came home early and found him **in bed with** (=having sex with) my best friend.* | *He wanted me to **go to bed with** him.* | *He's been trying to **get** his secretary **into bed** for ages.* | *She told me he was actually very **good in bed** (=a skilful lover).*
3 RIVER/LAKE/SEA [C] the flat ground at the bottom of a river, lake, or sea: *the sea bed*
4 GARDEN [C] an area of a garden, park etc that has been prepared for plants to grow in: *rose beds*
5 ROCK [C] a layer of rock → BEDROCK (2)
6 LOWEST LAYER [singular] a layer of something that forms a base that other things are put on top of: [+of] *prawns on a bed of lettuce*

pillows

sheet

duvet/quilt

camp bed

bunk beds

futon

hammock

cot *BrE*/
crib *AmE*

single bed

air bed

twin beds

four-poster bed

7 IN RIVER/WATER [C] an area at the edge of a river or in deeper water where things grow: *an oyster bed* | *The birds build their nests in reed beds along the river bank.*
8 get out of bed on the wrong side *BrE*, **get up on the wrong side of the bed** *AmE* to feel slightly angry or annoyed for no particular reason
9 not a bed of roses not a happy, comfortable, or easy situation: *Life isn't always a bed of roses, you know.*
10 you've made your bed and you must lie on it *spoken* used to say that you must accept the results of your actions, even if they are bad

bed² v bedded, bedding [T] **1** to fix something firmly and deeply into something else: **bed sth in sth** *The foundations were bedded in cement.* **2** *old-fashioned* to have sex with someone
bed down *phr v* **1** to sleep somewhere which is not your bed and where you do not usually sleep: *Can I bed down on your sofa?* **2 bed sb/sth ⇔ down** to make a person or animal comfortable in a place where they do not usually sleep
bed sth ⇔ out *phr v* to put plants into the ground so that they can grow

BEd *BrE*; **B.Ed.** *AmE* /ˌbiː ˈed/ *n* [C] *Bachelor of Education* a first university DEGREE in education

bed and board *n* [U] *BrE* food and a place to sleep

bed and breakfast *n B & B* **1** [U] the providing of a room for a night and breakfast in the morning, for example in a hotel: *Is there anyone who does bed and breakfast round here?* | *bed and breakfast accommodation* **2** [C] a private house or small hotel where you can sleep and have breakfast: *There's a bed and breakfast in the next village.* → see picture at STAY

be·daz·zled /bɪˈdæzəld/ *adj literary* if you are bedazzled by something, you find it so impressive that it surprises and confuses you; ◘ **dazzled**

bed bath *n* [C] a thorough body wash given to someone who cannot leave their bed

bed-blocking *n* [U] *BrE* a situation in which someone stays in hospital because there is no other suitable place where they can go to be looked after. This means that other people cannot go into hospital when they need to, because there is no bed for them.

bed·bug /ˈbedbʌg/ *n* [C] an insect that sucks blood and lives in dirty houses, especially in beds

bed·cham·ber /ˈbedˌtʃeɪmbə $ -ər/ *n* [C] *old use* a bedroom

bed·clothes /ˈbedkləʊðz, -kləʊz $ -kloʊðz, -kloʊz/ *n* [plural] the sheets, covers etc that you put on a bed

bed·ding /ˈbedɪŋ/ *n* [U] **1** sheets, covers etc that you put on a bed **2** something soft for animals to sleep on, such as dried grass or STRAW **3** garden plants that will look good for one season and then be removed: *bedding plants*

be·deck /bɪˈdek/ *v* [T usually passive] *literary* to decorate something such as a building or street by hanging things all over it: **be bedecked with sth** *a balcony bedecked with hanging baskets*

be·dev·il /bɪˈdevəl/ *v* **bedevilled, bedevilling** *BrE*, **bedeviled, bedeviling** *AmE* [T usually passive] to cause a lot of problems and difficulties for someone or something over a period of time; ◘ **plague**: *a society bedevilled by racial tensions*

bed·fel·low /ˈbedˌfeləʊ $ -loʊ/ *n* **strange bedfellows** two or more people, ideas etc that are related or working together in an unexpected way: *Rugby and art seem strange bedfellows.*

bed·head /ˈbedhed/ *n* [C] *BrE* the part of a bed that is behind your head when you are sleeping

bed·lam /ˈbedləm/ *n* [U] a situation where there is a lot of noise and confusion; ◘ **chaos**: *When the bomb exploded, there was bedlam.*

bed linen *n* [U] the sheets and PILLOWCASES for a bed

Bed·ou·in /ˈbeduɪn/ also **Bedu** *n plural* **Bedouin** or **Bedouins** [C] **1** someone who belongs to an Arab tribe that traditionally lives in tents in the desert **2 the Bedouin** the people who belong to this tribe —**Bedouin** *adj*

bed·pan /ˈbedpæn/ *n* [C] a low wide container used as a toilet by someone who is too ill to get out of bed

bed·post /ˈbedpəʊst $ -poʊst/ *n* [C] one of the four main supports at the corners of an old-fashioned bed

be·drag·gled /bɪˈdrægəld/ *adj* looking untidy, wet, and dirty, especially because you have been out in the rain: *Exhausted soldiers crawled into camp, frozen and bedraggled.*

bed·rid·den /ˈbedˌrɪdn/ *adj* unable to leave your bed, especially because you are old or ill

bed·rock /ˈbedrɒk $ -rɑːk/ *n* **1** [singular] the basic ideas, features, or facts on which something is based: *Marriage and children are the bedrock of family life.* **2** [U] solid rock in the ground below soil or sand

bed·roll /ˈbedrəʊl $ -roʊl/ *n* [C] *AmE* a number of BLANKETS rolled together and used for sleeping outdoors

bed·room S1 W2 /ˈbedrum, -ruːm/ *n* [C]
1 a room for sleeping in: *a hotel with 50 bedrooms* | **three-bedroomed/five-bedroomed** etc *They've just bought a new four-bedroomed house in Edinburgh.*; → see picture at STAY

B

B

2 bedroom eyes a look in your eyes that shows that you are sexually attracted to someone

bedroom com·munity also **bedroom ·suburb** n [C] *AmE* a place where people live but that does not have many businesses, so that people have to go to another town or city to work; ⊟ **dormitory town** *BrE*

bed·side /'bedsaɪd/ n [C usually singular] the area beside your bed – used especially when talking about someone who is ill in bed: **at sb's bedside** *Relatives have been at his bedside all week.* | **bedside lamp/table/ cabinet etc** *The clock on her bedside table said half past four.*; → see picture at TABLE[1]

bedside 'manner n [singular] the way that a doctor talks to the people that he or she is treating

bed·sit /ˌbed'sɪt/ also **bed·sit·ter** /-'sɪtə $ -ər/, **bed-sitting room** /bed'sɪtɪŋ rʊm, -ru:m/ n [C] *BrE* a rented room used for both living and sleeping in

bed·sore /'bedsɔ: $ -sɔːr/ n [C] a sore place on your skin caused by lying in bed for a long time

bed·spread /'bedspred/ n [C] an attractive cover for a bed that goes on top of all the other covers

bed·stead /'bedsted/ n [C] the wooden or metal frame of a bed

bed·time /'bedtaɪm/ n [C,U] the time when you usually go to bed: *It's way past your bedtime!* | *a bedtime story*

Bed·u /'bedu:/ n plural **Bedu** another word for a BEDOUIN

bed-·wetting n [U] the problem that some children have of passing URINE (=liquid from the body) while they are asleep

bee /bi:/ n [C] **1** a black and yellow flying insect that makes HONEY and can sting you: *a swarm of bees* | *a bee sting* → BUMBLEBEE; → see picture at INSECT **2 have a bee in your bonnet (about sth)** *informal* to think something is so important, so necessary etc that you keep mentioning it or thinking about it: *Dad's got a bee in his bonnet about saving electricity.* **3 sewing/quilting etc bee** *AmE informal* an occasion when people, usually women, meet in order to do a particular type of work **4 a busy bee** *spoken* someone who enjoys being busy or active **5 be the bee's knees** *spoken* old-fashioned to be very good: *She thought the party was just the bee's knees.* → SPELLING BEE; → **the birds and the bees** at BIRD (3)

beech /bi:tʃ/ n [C,U] a large tree with smooth grey BARK (=outer covering), or the wood from this tree

beef[1] S3 /bi:f/ n
1 [U] the meat from a cow: *roast beef* | *We have both dairy and beef cattle on the farm.*
2 [C] *informal* a complaint: *OK, so what's the beef this time?*
3 where's the beef? *AmE spoken* used when you think someone's words and promises sound good, but you want to know what they actually plan to do → CORNED BEEF

beef[2] v [I] *informal* to complain a lot: [+about] *They're always beefing about something.*
beef sth ⇔ **up** *phr v informal* to improve something or make it more interesting, more important etc: *a beefed-up news story* | *We need to beef the campaign up.*

beef·bur·ger /'bi:fbɜ:gə $ -bɜːrgər/ n [C] *BrE* a HAMBURGER

beef·cake /'bi:fkeɪk/ n [U] *informal* strong attractive men with large muscles

Beef·eat·er /'bi:fˌi:tə $ -ər/ n [C] *BrE* a traditional guard at the Tower of London

beef·steak /'bi:fsteɪk/ n [C,U] STEAK

beef 'tea n [U] a hot drink made from BEEF that used to be given to people when they were ill

beef·y /'bi:fi/ comparative **beefier**, superlative **beefiest** adj someone who is beefy is big, strong, and often quite fat

bee·hive /'bi:haɪv/ n [C] **1** a structure where BEES are kept for producing HONEY **2** a way of arranging a woman's hair in a high pile on the top of her head, which was popular in the 1960s

bee·keep·er /'bi:ki:pə $ -ər/ n [C] someone who owns or takes care of BEES —**beekeeping** n [U]

bee·line /'bi:laɪn/ n **make a beeline for sb/sth** *informal* to go quickly and directly towards someone or something: *Rob always makes a beeline for beautiful women at parties.*

been /bi:n, bɪn $ bɪn/ **1** the past participle of BE **2 a)** used to say that someone has gone to a place and come back: [+to] *I've never been to Japan.* | **have been to do sth** *Have you been to see the Van Gogh exhibition yet?* **b)** *BrE* used to say that someone has come to a place and left again: *The postman hasn't been yet.* **3 been there, seen that, done that** *spoken* used to say that you are no longer interested in doing something, because you already have a lot of experience of it

> **WORD CHOICE: been in, been to, went to**
> Use **been in** when you are living or staying in a place: *How long have you been in London?* | *He had been in hospital for several days.*
> Use **been to** when you have visited a place and come back again: *Have you ever been to Kyoto?* | *She's been to the hospital for a check-up.*
> Use **went to** (the simple past) to talk about a specific trip you made in the past: *Last May I went to a conference in Montreal.*

beep /bi:p/ v **1** [I] if a machine beeps, it makes a short high sound; ⊟ **bleep**: *Why does the computer keep beeping?* **2** [I,T] if a car horn beeps or if you beep your car horn, it makes a loud noise —**beep** n [C]: *Leave your message after the beep.*

beep·er /'bi:pə $ -ər/ n [C] a small machine that you carry with you which makes short high electronic sounds to tell you that you must telephone someone; ⊟ **bleeper, pager**

beer S2 W3 /bɪə $ bɪr/ n
1 [U] an alcoholic drink made from MALT and HOPS: *a pint of beer* | *We sell traditional **draught beer** (=beer served from a large container, not a bottle).* → see picture at GLASS[1]
2 [C] a glass, bottle, or can of beer: *Do you fancy a beer?* —**beery** adj: *his beery breath* → GINGER BEER, ROOT BEER; **small beer** at SMALL[1] (16)

beer ·belly also **beer gut** n [C] an unattractive fat stomach caused by drinking too much beer

beer mat n [C] *BrE* a small circle of card that you put under a glass, especially in a bar

beer ·money n [U] *BrE informal* a little extra money to buy a drink or have fun with: *The job was never going to make me rich, but it kept me in beer money for a while.*

bees·wax /'bi:zwæks/ n [U] **1** a substance produced by BEES, used especially for making furniture POLISH and CANDLES **2 none of your beeswax** *AmE spoken* used to tell someone that what they have asked you is private or personal

beet /bi:t/ n [C,U] **1** also **sugar beet** a vegetable that sugar is made from **2** *AmE* a plant with a round dark red root that you cook and eat as a vegetable; ⊟ **beetroot** *BrE* **3 red as a beet** *AmE informal* having a red face, especially because you are embarrassed

bee·tle[1] /'bi:tl/ n [C] an insect with a round hard back which is usually black → see picture at INSECT

beetle[2] v [I always + adv/prep] *BrE informal* to go somewhere quickly and leaning forward; ⊟ **scurry**: *He went beetling off down the corridor.*

beet·root /'bi:tru:t/ n [C,U] **1** *BrE* a plant with a round dark red root that you cook and eat as a vegetable; ⊟ **beet** *AmE* **2 go beetroot** *BrE informal* to become red in the face, especially because you are embarrassed

be·fall /bɪ'fɔ:l $ -'fɔ:l/ v past tense **befell** /-'fel/ past participle **befallen** /-'fɔ:lən $ -'fɔ:-/ [T] *literary* if

light shade

bookshelf

lampshade

poster

stereo

alarm clock

mirror

scanner

computer

TV
DVD player

printer

cable

camcorder

mobile phone *BrE*/
cellular phone *AmE*

digital camera

remote control

video recorder

disk

chest of drawers

games console

something unpleasant or dangerous befalls you, it happens to you: *We prayed that no harm should befall them.*

be·fit /bɪˈfɪt/ v **befitted, befitting** [T] *formal* to be proper or suitable for someone or something: *As befits a castle of such national importance, there are many stories connected with its history.*

be·fore[1] [S1] [W1] /bɪˈfɔː $ -ˈfɔːr/ *conjunction*
1 earlier than a particular event or action; ⚡ **after**: *Say goodbye before you go.* | *I saw her a few days before she died.* → see box at AGO
2 so that something does not or cannot happen: *Put that money somewhere safe before it gets stolen.* | *That dog ought to be destroyed before it attacks any more children.* | *Before I could say anything more, Holmes had rushed off towards the station.*
3 used to say that something happens after a period of time: *It was several minutes before we realised what was happening.* | *It will be a while before we know the results.*
4 used to say that something must happen in order for something else to be possible: *You have to pass a test before you can get a licence.*
5 *spoken* used to warn someone that something bad will happen to them if they do not do something: *Get out before I call the police!*
6 used to emphasize that someone does not want to do something: *She would die before she would admit she was wrong.*

before[2] [S1] [W1] *prep*
1 earlier than something or someone; ⚡ **after**: *The new road should be completed before the end of the year.* | *Let's meet at our house before the show.* | *Larry arrived home before me.* | **five minutes/two hours etc before sth** *Hugh arrived just five minutes before the ceremony.* | **before doing sth** *I usually take a shower before having my breakfast.* | *We only got back from Scotland* **the day before yesterday** (=two days ago). | *Other students joined in the protest, and* **before long** (=soon) *there was a crowd of 200 or so.* → see box at AGO
2 ahead of someone or something else in a list or order; ⚡ **after**: *I think you were before me in the queue.* | *The files are arranged in alphabetical order, so B1 comes before C1.*
3 used to say that something happens where it can be watched by people: *Italy will face Brazil this afternoon before a crowd of 100,000 spectators.* | *an actor who had performed before the Queen*
4 used to say that someone or something comes to be judged or considered by a person or group of people: *The proposal was put before the planning committee.* | *The men are due to appear before the court tomorrow.*
5 used to say that one thing or person is considered more important than another: *I put my wife and kids before anyone else.* | *In the air transport business, safety must always come before profit.*
6 *formal* in front of something or someone: *The priest stood before the altar.* | *The sea stretched out before them.*
7 if one place is before another place on a road or journey, the first place is nearer to you than the second, so you will reach it first; ⚡ **after**: *The pub is 100m before the church on the right.* | *the last station before the Simplon Tunnel*
8 *formal* if there is a job or situation before you, you will have to do the job or face the situation: *The task of emptying the house lay before us.*
9 *formal* if a period of time is before you, it is about to start and you can do what you want during it: *We had a glorious summer afternoon before us to do as we pleased.* | *You have your whole life before you.*

before[3] [S1] [W2] *adv*
1 at an earlier time: *Haven't I met you before somewhere?* | *Never before had he seen so many people starving.* | *She looked just the same as before.*
2 the day/week/month etc before the previous day,

week, month etc: *She was in Paris last week and in Rome the week before.*
3 *old use* ahead of someone or something else: *The king's herald walked before.*

be·fore·hand [S3] /bɪˈfɔːhænd $ -ˈfɔːr-/ *adv* before something else happens or is done: *The police need to be briefed beforehand on how to deal with this sort of situation.* | *When you give a speech, it's natural to feel nervous beforehand.*

be·friend /bɪˈfrend/ v [T] to behave in a friendly way towards someone, especially someone who is younger or needs help: *They befriended me when I first arrived in London as a student.*

be·fud·dled /bɪˈfʌdəld/ *adj* completely confused: *Even in my befuddled state I could find my key.*

beg /beg/ v **begged, begging**
1 ASK [I,T] to ask for something in an anxious or urgent way, because you want it very much: *She begged and pleaded with them until they finally agreed.* | *She fought back the sudden urge to run to him and* **beg** his **forgiveness.** | **beg to do sth** *The children begged to come with us.* | **beg sb to do sth** *I begged Helen to stay, but she wouldn't listen.* | **beg (sb) for sth** *She ran to the nearest house and* **begged for help.** | *We could hear the prisoners* **begging** for mercy. | **I beg of you** *formal* (=please) *Listen to me, I beg of you.* | **beg leave to do sth** *formal* (=ask permission to do something)
2 MONEY/FOOD [I,T] to ask people to give you food, money etc, usually because you are very poor: **beg (sth) from sb** *a ragged child begging from passing shoppers* | [+for] *The old man went from door to door begging for food.* | *a* **begging letter** (=a letter asking for money)
3 ANIMAL [I] if a dog begs, it sits up with its front legs off the ground
4 I beg your pardon *spoken* **a)** used to ask someone to repeat what they have just said: *'The meeting's on Wednesday.' 'I beg your pardon?' 'I said the meeting's on Wednesday.'* **b)** used to say sorry when you have made a mistake, or said something wrong or embarrassing: *Oh, I beg your pardon. I thought you said 15 pence, not 50.* → see box at EXCUSE[1] **c)** used to show that you strongly disagree with something that someone has said, or think it is unacceptable: *'Chicago's an awful place.' 'I beg your pardon, that's where I'm from!'*
5 I beg to differ *spoken formal* used to say firmly that you do not agree with something that has been said: *I must beg to differ on this point.*
6 beg the question a) to make you want to ask a question that has not yet been answered: [+of] *This proposal begs the question of who is going to pay for the new building.* **b)** to treat an idea as though it were true or had been proved, when this may not be the case
7 be going begging *BrE spoken* if something is going begging, it is available for anyone who wants it: *There's a beer going begging if anyone's interested.*
8 beg, borrow, or steal to do whatever you must in order to get what you want – often used humorously: *She'd beg, borrow, or steal the money for those shoes.*

be·gan /bɪˈgæn/ the past tense of BEGIN

be·get /bɪˈget/ v *past tense* **begot** /-ˈgɒt $-ˈgɑːt/ *past participle* **begotten** /-ˈgɒtn $ -ˈgɑːtn/ *present participle* **begetting** [T] **1** *old use* to become the father of a child **2** to cause something or make it happen: *Hunger begets crime.* —**begetter** n [C]

beg·gar[1] /ˈbegə $ -ər/ n [C] **1** someone who lives by asking people for food and money: *the beggars on the streets* **2 lucky/lazy/cheeky etc beggar** *BrE spoken* used when speaking to or about someone you like: *'How's Dave?' 'The lucky beggar's in the south of France!'* **3 beggars can't be choosers** used to say that when you have no money or no power to choose, you have to accept whatever you are given

beggar[2] v [T] **1 beggar description/belief** if something beggars description or belief, it is impossible to describe or believe it: *They showed a lack of common sense that beggars belief.* **2** *literary* to make someone very poor: *Why should he beggar himself for you?*

beg·gar·ly /ˈbegəli $ -ərli/ adj literary poor

beg·gar·y /ˈbegəri/ n [U] formal the state of being very poor

begging ‚bowl n [C] **1** used to talk about a request for money made by an organization or country: Arts and theatre groups are constantly thrusting the begging bowl at the government. **2** a container which a beggar holds out to people for money

be·gin S1 W1 /bɪˈgɪn/ v past tense **began** /-ˈgæn/ past participle **begun** /-ˈgʌn/ present participle **beginning**
1 START DOING STH [I,T] to start doing something: As everybody's here, let's begin. | In the third year students begin the study of classical Chinese. | The President begins talks with the Prime Minister tonight. | **begin to do sth** She began to feel a sense of panic. | I began to wonder if I'd ever be able to afford my own apartment. | **begin doing sth** I began teaching in 1984.
2 START HAPPENING [I,T] if something begins, or you begin something, it starts to happen or exist from a particular time: It was the coldest winter since records began. | They began a system of blood tests for employees. | [+at] The meeting begins at 10.30 am.
3 DO FIRST [I] if you begin with something or begin by doing something, this is the first thing you do: [+with] Shall we begin with a prayer? | **begin by doing sth** I'll begin by thanking you all for being here tonight.
4 BOOK/WORD ETC [I] if a book, film, or word begins with something, it starts with a particular event or letter: [+with] 'Psychosis' begins with a P.
5 SPEECH [I,T] to start speaking: 'Ladies and gentlemen,' he began. ' I am delighted to be here.'
6 to begin with a) spoken used to introduce the first and most important point you want to make: Well, to begin with, he shouldn't even have been driving my car. b) used to say that something was already in a particular condition before something else happened: I didn't break it! It was like that to begin with. c) during the first part of a process or activity: The kids helped me to begin with, but they soon got bored.
7 can't begin to understand/imagine etc spoken used to emphasize how difficult something is to understand etc: I can't begin to imagine how awful it must have been.
begin (sth) as sth phr v
to be a particular thing at the start of your existence, working life etc: Roger began his career as an office boy.

be·gin·ner /bɪˈgɪnə $ -ər/ n [C] **1** someone who has just started to do or learn something: an **absolute beginner 2 beginner's luck** unusual success that you have when you start something new

be·gin·ning S1 W2 /bɪˈgɪnɪŋ/ n [C usually singular]
1 the start or first part of an event, story, period of time etc

since the beginning (of sth)
at the beginning (of sth)
from the beginning
in the beginning
mark the beginning of sth
herald/signal the beginning of sth (=show that something is starting)
be just/only the beginning (=used to emphasize that something will continue or develop)
right at the beginning
right from the beginning
the very beginning
from beginning to end
a new beginning
start at the beginning (=start an activity or story at the point where it is meant to start)

[+of] She's been here **since the beginning** of the year. | There's a short poem **at the beginning** of every chapter. | **From the beginning** of my career as a journalist, I've been writing about gender issues. | I thought he loved me; perhaps he did **in the beginning**. | That chance meeting **marked the beginning** of a long and happy relationship. | This is **just the beginning** of a new and different life for you. | I said he would cause

trouble, **right from the beginning**. | I opposed it from **the very beginning**. | The whole trip was a disaster **from beginning to end**. | I feel like I've been offered **a new beginning**. | Could we **start at the beginning?** Tell me where you first met him.
2 beginnings [plural] the early signs or stages of something that later develops into something bigger or more important: [+of] I think I **have the beginnings** of a cold. | **from humble/small beginnings** He rose from humble beginnings to great wealth.
3 the beginning of the end the time when something good starts to end

be·gone /bɪˈgɒn $ bɪˈgɔːn/ interjection old use used to tell someone to go away

be·go·ni·a /bɪˈgəʊniə $ -ˈgoʊ-/ n [C] a plant with yellow, pink, red, or white flowers

be·got /bɪˈgɒt $ bɪˈgaːt/ the past tense of BEGET

be·got·ten /bɪˈgɒtn $ bɪˈgaːtn/ the past participle of BEGET

be·grudge /bɪˈgrʌdʒ/ v [T usually in negatives] **1** to feel angry or upset with someone because they have something which you think they do not deserve: **begrudge sb sth** We shouldn't begrudge her this success. **2** to feel annoyed or unhappy that you have to pay something, give someone something etc: **begrudge sb sth** The farmer's wife never begrudged him a meal at the end of the day. | **begrudge doing sth** I begrudge spending so much money on train fares.

be·guile /bɪˈgaɪl/ v [T] **1** to interest and attract someone: She was beguiled by his smooth talk. **2** to persuade or trick someone into doing something: **beguile sb into doing sth** He was beguiled into buying another copy of her book. **3** literary to do something that makes the time pass in an enjoyable way

be·guil·ing /bɪˈgaɪlɪŋ/ adj attractive and interesting: a beguiling smile —**beguilingly** adv

be·gum /ˈbeɪgəm, ˈbiː-/ n [C] a title of respect, used for married Muslim women, especially of high rank

be·gun /bɪˈgʌn/ the past participle of BEGIN

be·half /bɪˈhɑːf $ bɪˈhæf/ n **on behalf of sb** also **in behalf of sb** AmE a) instead of someone, or as their representative: She asked the doctor to speak to her parents on her behalf. | On behalf of everyone here, may I wish you a very happy retirement. b) because of or for someone: Oh, don't go to any trouble on my behalf.

be·have S3 W3 /bɪˈheɪv/ v [I]
1 [always + adv/prep] to do things that are good, bad, sensible etc; ◯ **act**: She **behaved in a** very responsible **way**. | [+towards] I think he behaved disgracefully towards you. | [+like] grown men behaving like schoolboys | **behave as if/though** He was a little boy, but he behaved as if he was an adult.
2 also **behave yourself** to not do things that annoy or offend people; ◯ **misbehave**: Will you children please behave! | I hope Nicholas behaved himself at the party. | **well-behaved/badly-behaved** a badly-behaved class
3 [always + adv/prep] if something behaves in a particular way, it does those things: Quantum mechanics is the study of the way atoms behave.

be·hav·iour S2 W1 BrE; **behavior** AmE /bɪˈheɪvjə $ -ər/ n [U]
1 the things that a person or animal does

good/bad behaviour
violent/aggressive/criminal etc behaviour
human/social behaviour
pattern of behaviour/behaviour pattern
behaviour problem (=when someone often behaves badly)
change/modify your behaviour
influence sb's behaviour

It is important to reward **good behaviour**. | The headmaster will not tolerate **bad behaviour**. | [+towards] She complained of her boss's inappropriate behavior towards her. | Can TV violence cause **aggres-**

B

sive behavior? | *We are trying to understand the causes of* **criminal behaviour.** | *the effects of alcohol on* **human behaviour** | *the boundaries of acceptable* **social behavior** | *common animal* **behavior patterns** | *It's hard to* **change your behaviour,** *even harder to keep it changed.* | *They argued that the presence of TV cameras at the trial* **influenced the behavior of** *attorneys, witnesses, and jurors.*

2 **be on your best behaviour** to behave as well and politely as you can in order to please someone: *I want you both to be on your best behaviour at Grandad's.*
3 the things that something in science normally does: [+of] *the behaviour of human chromosomes* —**behavioural** *adj:* *behavioural science* —**behaviourally** *adv*

be·hav·iour·is·m *BrE;* **behaviorism** *AmE* /bɪˈheɪvjərɪzəm/ *n* [U] the belief that the scientific study of the mind should be based only on people's behaviour, not on what they say about their thoughts and feelings —**behaviourist** *n* [C]

be·head /bɪˈhed/ *v* [T] to cut off someone's head as a punishment: *Charles I was beheaded in 1649.*

be·held /bɪˈheld/ the past tense and past participle of BEHOLD

be·he·moth /bɪˈhiːmɒθ $ -maːθ/ *n* [C] *formal* something that is very large: *a trade behemoth that shipped abroad $800 billion worth of goods*

be·hest /bɪˈhest/ *n* **at the behest of sb** *formal* because someone has asked for something or ordered something to happen: *The committee was set up at the behest of the president.*

be·hind¹ [S1] [W1] /bɪˈhaɪnd/ *prep, adv*
1 at or towards the back of a thing or person: *I turned to speak to the person standing behind me.* | *Someone could easily creep up behind us.* | *The car behind was hooting impatiently.* | *A figure in a brown suit stepped out from behind the bushes.* | *Jane shut the door behind her.* | *The manager was sitting behind a large desk.* | **close behind/not far behind** *He set off down the road with the rest of us following close behind.* ⚠ Do not say 'behind of': *He hid behind a chair (NOT behind of a chair).*
2 not as successful or not having made as much progress as someone or something else: *Mark's always behind the rest of his class in mathematics.* | *This victory lifts Ferguson's team into fifth place, nine points behind leaders Norwich.* | *Compared with the United States, Europe was falling behind in the important field of computer technology.*
3 used to say that someone is late in doing what they have to do: *This work should have been finished yesterday. I'm getting terribly behind.* | *Victor had fallen behind with his mortgage payments after losing his job.* | *an important research project that is already two years* **behind schedule** (=not ready at the time planned)
4 used for talking about the hidden reason for something: *I wonder what's behind this change of plan.* | *Perhaps a bitter experience lay behind her anger.*
5 supporting a person, idea etc: *The workers are very much behind these proposals.* | *I suppose I'm lucky because my parents were behind me all the way.*
6 responsible for a plan, idea etc or for organizing something: *It was alleged that foreign agents were behind the recent violence.* | *The Rotary Club is behind the fund-raising for the new hospital.*
7 if an unpleasant experience or situation is behind you, it no longer upsets you or affects your life: *Now you can put all these worries behind you.* | *a chance to start a new life and leave all your troubles behind*
8 if you have experience behind you, you have gained valuable skills or important qualities that can be used: *Marjorie is one of the top designers in the business, with years of experience behind her.*
9 used when the real facts about a situation or someone's character are hidden by the way things seem or

by the way a person behaves: *We were determined to find the truth behind this mystery.* | *You could see the burning hatred behind Graham's calm manner.*
10 if a student stays behind after school or after a lesson, they stay after it has finished → **behind sb's back** at BACK² (9); → **behind bars** at BAR¹ (7); → **behind the times** at TIME¹ (38)

behind² *n* [C] *informal* the part of your body that you sit on; ▤ **bottom**

be·hold /bɪˈhəʊld $ -ˈhoʊld/ *v* [T] *past tense and past participle* **beheld** *literary* to see or to look at something – sometimes used humorously: **be a sight/joy/pleasure etc to behold** *The beauty of the garden was a pleasure to behold.* —**beholder** *n* [C] → **lo and behold** at LO (2)

be·hold·en /bɪˈhəʊldn $ -ˈhoʊl-/ *adj* **feel/be beholden to sb** to feel that you have a duty to someone because they have done something for you: *I hate feeling beholden to anyone.*

be·hove /bɪˈhəʊv $ bɪˈhoʊv/ *BrE;* **be·hoove** /bɪˈhuːv/ *AmE v* **it behoves sb to do sth** *formal* used to say that someone should do something because it is right or necessary, or it will help them

beige /beɪʒ/ *n* [U] a pale brown colour —**beige** *adj*

be·ing¹ /ˈbiːɪŋ/ *v* [linking verb] **1** the present participle of BE **2** used to give the reason for something: *Being a quiet sort of person, I didn't want to get involved.* | *You can't expect them to sit still for that long, children being what they are.* **3** **being as** *BrE spoken* because; ▤ **as:** *You might as well drink it, being as you've paid for it.*

being² [S2] [W3] *n*
1 **come into being/be brought into being** to start to exist: *a law that first came into being in 1912*
2 [C] a living thing, especially a person: **a human being** | **intelligent/conscious/rational etc being** *a story about alien beings who invade Earth*
3 [U] *literary* the most important quality or nature of something, especially of a person: **the core/roots/whole of sb's being** *The whole of her being had been taken over by a desire to return to her homeland.*

be·jew·elled *BrE;* **bejeweled** *AmE* /bɪˈdʒuːəld/ *adj* *literary* wearing jewels or decorated with jewels: *bejewelled hands*

be·la·bour *BrE;* **belabor** *AmE* /bɪˈleɪbə $ -ər/ *v* [T] **1** **belabour the point** *formal* to keep emphasizing a fact or idea in a way that is annoying **2** *old-fashioned* to hit someone or something hard

be·lat·ed /bɪˈleɪtɪd/ *adj* happening or arriving late: *a belated attempt to increase support* | **belated recognition/realization/acknowledgement** *The statement was a belated acknowledgement that the project had not been a success.* | *a belated birthday present* —**belatedly** *adv*

be·lay /bɪˈleɪ/ *v* [I,T] *technical* to make someone who is climbing a mountain etc safe by attaching a rope to them and to a rock

belch /beltʃ/ *v* **1** [I] to let air from your stomach come out loudly through your mouth; ▤ **burp** **2** also **belch out** [I,T] to send out a large amount of smoke, flames etc, or to come out of something in large amounts: *a line of chimneys belching out smoke* | *Flames belched from the wreckage.* —**belch** *n* [C]

be·lea·guered /bɪˈliːgəd $ -ərd/ *adj* [usually before noun] *formal* **1** experiencing a lot of problems or criticism: *the country's beleaguered steel industry* **2** surrounded by an army: *Supplies are being brought into the beleaguered city.*

bel·fry /ˈbelfri/ *n plural* **belfries** [C] a tower for a bell, especially on a church

Bel·gian¹ /ˈbeldʒən/ *adj* from or relating to Belgium or its people

Belgian² *n* [C] someone from Belgium

be·lie /bɪˈlaɪ/ *v* **belied, belying** [T] **1** to give someone a false idea about something: *Her pleasant manner belied her true character.* **2** to show that something cannot be true or real: *His cheerful smile belied his words.*

be·lief S3 W2 /bɪˈliːf/ n
1 [singular, U] the feeling that something is definitely true or definitely exists

a **strong/firm belief**
a **sincere/passionate belief**
it is sb's belief that
a **mistaken/false belief**
a **widespread/common/widely held belief** (=something that many people think)
a **deeply held/strongly held belief** (=something you believe very much)
a **growing belief**
popular belief (=what most people think)
contrary to popular belief (=despite what most people think)

[+in] *a strong belief in God* | [+that] *his passionate belief that technology is a tool to be used with imagination* | *It is my belief that we will find a cure for cancer in the next ten years.* | *Thieves broke into the building in the mistaken belief that there was expensive computer equipment inside.* | *It is a widely held belief that violent crime is increasing.* | *a strongly held belief that stealing is wrong* | *a growing belief that war was inevitable* | *Contrary to popular belief, eating carrots does not improve your eyesight.*

2 [singular] the feeling that something is good and can be trusted: [+in] *If you're selling, you have to have genuine belief in the product.* | *When you get something wrong, it can shake your belief in yourself.*
3 [C] an idea that you believe to be true, especially one that forms part of a system of ideas: *religious beliefs* | *Several members hold very right-wing beliefs.*
4 beyond belief used to emphasize that something is so extreme that it is difficult to believe: *What she did was stupid beyond belief.* → **it beggars belief** at BEGGAR² (1); → **to the best of your belief** at BEST³ (4); → DISBELIEF, UNBELIEF

be·liev·a·ble /bɪˈliːvəbəl/ adj something that is believable can be believed because it seems possible, likely, or real: *a story with believable characters in it* | *That scenario is entirely believable.*

be·lieve S1 W1 /bɪˈliːv/ v
1 [T not in progressive] to be sure that something is true or that someone is telling the truth: *You shouldn't believe everything you read.* | *I believed him, even though his story sounded unlikely.* | **believe (that)** *I don't believe he's only 25.* | *I don't believe a word of it* (=I think it is completely untrue).
2 [T not in progressive] to think that something is true or possible, although you are not completely sure: **believe (that)** *Detectives believe that the victim knew his killer.* | **it is believed (that)** | *It is believed that the house was built in 1735.* | **believe so** (=think that something is true) *'Have they arrived yet?' 'Yes, I believe so.'* | **be believed to be sth** *At 115, Mrs Jackson is believed to be the oldest person in the country.* | *The four men are widely believed* (=believed by a lot of people) *to have been killed by their captors.* | *Did you honestly believe that I'd be stupid enough to do that?* | *I firmly believe that the business will be a success.*
3 it's difficult/hard to believe (that) used when you are surprised that something is true: *Sometimes, it's hard to believe we've been married for 50 years.*

SPOKEN PHRASES
4 can't/don't believe sth used when you are very surprised or shocked by something: *I can't believe he's expecting us to work on Sunday as well!* | *I couldn't believe it when he told me what had happened.* | **can hardly/scarcely believe sth** *I could scarcely believe my luck.*
5 believe it or not used when you are saying something that is true but surprising: *He enjoys school, believe it or not.*
6 would you believe it! or **I don't believe it!** used when you are surprised or angry about something: *And then he just walked out. Would you believe it!*
7 believe (you) me used to emphasize that something is definitely true: *There'll be trouble when they find out*

about this, believe you me!
8 you'd better believe it! used to emphasize that something is true
9 don't you believe it! used to emphasize that something is definitely not true
10 can't believe your eyes/ears used to say that someone is very surprised by something they see or hear
11 if you believe that, you'll believe anything used to say that something is definitely not true, and that anyone who believes it must be stupid
12 seeing is believing or **I'll believe it when I see it** used to say that you will only believe that something happens or exists when you actually see it

13 [I] to have a religious faith: *She says those who believe will go to heaven.* → **make believe** at MAKE¹ (19)
believe in sb/sth phr v
1 to be sure that someone or something exists: *Do you believe in God?*
2 to think that something is effective or right: *I don't believe in all these silly diets.* | **believe in doing sth** *The school believes in letting children learn at their own pace.*
3 to trust someone and be confident that they will be successful: *The people want a President they can believe in.* | *You've got to believe in yourself, or you'll never succeed.*

WORD CHOICE: **believe, believe in**
If you **believe** something, you think it is true. If you **believe** someone, you think they are telling the truth: *Nobody believed what I said.* | *I didn't do it – you've got to believe me!*
Use **believe in** to mean:
that you think something exists: *Do you believe in God?*
that you think that something is good: *He doesn't believe in private education.*
that you think someone is good and will achieve good things: *My mother always believed in me.*

be·liev·er /bɪˈliːvə $ -ər/ n [C] **1 be a (great/firm) believer in sth** to believe strongly that something is good and effective: *I'm a great believer in regular exercise.* **2** someone who believes in a particular god, religion, or system of beliefs

Be·li·sha bea·con /bəˌliːʃə ˈbiːkən/ n [C] in Britain, one of two posts with a round flashing orange light on the top, marking a place that cars must stop at to allow people to cross a road

be·lit·tle /bɪˈlɪtl/ v [T] formal to make someone or something seem small or unimportant: *He tends to belittle her efforts.*

bells

bell

cowbell

bell S2 W3 /bel/ n [C]
1 a piece of electrical equipment that makes a ringing sound, used as a signal or to get someone's attention: **ring/press the bell** *He rang the bell and waited for someone to answer the door.* | *She walked up the path and rang the door bell.* | **a bell rings/goes** *The bell went and everyone rushed out of the classroom.*
2 a hollow metal object like a cup with a piece of metal hanging inside it, which makes a ringing noise when it moves or you shake it: *church bells*

1 000, **2** 000, **3** 000, most frequent words in S poken and W ritten English

3 give sb a bell *BrE spoken* to telephone someone: *I must give Vicky a bell later.*
4 something that is shaped like a bell: *the bell of a flower* → **alarm bells ring** at **ALARM**[1] (5); → **as clear as a bell** at **CLEAR**[1] (10); → **DIVING BELL**; → **ring a bell** at **RING**[2] (4)

bel·la·don·na /ˌbeləˈdɒnə $ -ˈdɑːnə/ *n* [U] **1** a poisonous plant; ☐ **deadly nightshade** **2** a substance from this plant, used as a drug

'bell-ˌbottoms *n* [plural] trousers with legs that get wider from the knee to the bottom; ☐ **flares**

bell·boy /ˈbelbɔɪ/ *n* [C] *especially BrE* a young man who carries bags, takes messages etc in a hotel

belle /bel/ *n* [C] *old-fashioned* a beautiful girl or woman: **the belle of the ball** (=the most beautiful girl at a dance or party)

bell·hop /ˈbelhɒp $ -hɑːp/ *n* [C] *especially AmE* a young man who carries bags, takes messages etc in a hotel

bel·li·cose /ˈbelɪkəʊs $ -koʊs/ *adj formal* behaving in a way that is likely to start an argument or fight; ☐ **aggressive**: *bellicose criticism* —**bellicosity** /ˌbelɪˈkɒsᵻti $ -ˈkɑː-/ *n* [U]

bel·lig·er·ent /bᵻˈlɪdʒərənt/ *adj* **1** very unfriendly and wanting to argue or fight; ☐ **aggressive**: *a belligerent attitude* **2** [only before noun] *formal* a belligerent country is fighting a war against another country —**belligerence, belligerency** *n* [U]

bel·low[1] /ˈbeləʊ $ -loʊ/ *v* **1** [I,T] to shout loudly in a deep voice; ☐ **yell**: *'That's your problem!' bellowed Hurley.* | *Tony was bellowing orders from upstairs.* **2** [I] to make the deep sound that a BULL makes

bellow[2] *n* [C] **1** a loud deep shout: *His voice rose to a bellow.* | *a bellow of rage/laughter etc Alex gave another bellow of laughter.* **2** the deep sound that a BULL makes **3 bellows** [plural] **a)** an object used for blowing air into a fire to make it burn better **b)** part of a musical instrument that pushes air through pipes to produce a sound, for example in an ORGAN

'bell ˌpepper *n* [C] *AmE* a hollow red, green, or yellow vegetable; ☐ **pepper** *BrE*; → see picture at **VEGETABLE**

'bell-ˌringer *n* [C] someone who rings church bells —**bell-ringing** *n* [U]

bel·ly[1] **S3** /ˈbeli/ *n plural* **bellies** [C]
1 a) your stomach: *a full belly* **b)** *BrE* the front part of your body between your chest and your legs; ☐ **abdomen**: *She was lying on her belly.*
2 the middle part of an animal's body, near its stomach
3 *literary* a curved or rounded part of an object: *the belly of a plane*
4 black-bellied/fat-bellied/big-bellied etc having a black, fat, big etc stomach
5 go belly up *informal* if a business or company goes belly up, it stops operating because it cannot pay its debts → **BEER BELLY, POTBELLY**

belly[2] also **belly out** *v* **bellied, bellying, bellies** [I] *literary* to fill with air and become rounder in shape: *The curtains bellied in the breeze.*

bel·ly·ache[1] /ˈbeli-eɪk/ *n* [C,U] *informal* a pain in your stomach; ☐ **stomachache**

bellyache[2] *v* [I] *informal* to complain a lot, especially about something unimportant; ☐ **whinge**: [+about] *She never stops bellyaching about money.*

'belly ˌbutton *n* [C] *informal* the small round mark in the middle of your stomach; ☐ **navel**

'belly dance *n* [C] a dance from the Middle East in which a woman moves her stomach and HIPS around —**belly dancer** *n* [C] —**belly dancing** *n* [U]

'belly flop *n* [C] a way of jumping into water, in which the front of your body falls flat against the surface of the water —**bellyflop** *v* [I]

bel·ly·ful /ˈbelɪfʊl/ *n* **have had a bellyful of sb/sth** *informal* to be annoyed by someone or something

because you have had to deal with them for too long: *I had a bellyful of his family by the end of the weekend.*

'belly laugh *n* [C] *informal* a deep loud laugh

be·long **S2** **W2** /bɪˈlɒŋ $ bɪˈlɔːŋ/ *v* [I not in progressive]
1 [always + adv/prep] if something belongs somewhere, that is the right place or situation for it: *Put the chair back where it belongs.* | [+in] *an attitude that doesn't belong in modern society*
2 if you feel you belong in a place or situation, you feel happy and comfortable in it, because you have the same interests and ideas as other people: *I worked there for five years but never really felt I belonged.* —**belonging** *n* [U]: *It's important to have a* **sense of belonging** (=a feeling that you are happy and comfortable somewhere).

belong to sb/sth *phr v*
1 if something belongs to someone, they own it: *The house belonged to my grandfather.* | *Who does this scarf belong to?*
2 to be a member of a group or organization: *He belongs to the golf club.*
3 to be related to something or form part of: *cars that belong to a different era*
4 to be related to or produced by a particular person: *She recognized the voice as belonging to the man who had attacked her.*
5 if a competition or period of time belongs to someone, they are the most important or successful person in it: *All the acts were good, but the evening belonged to a dance group from Moscow.*

be·long·ings /bɪˈlɒŋɪŋz $ bɪˈlɔːŋ-/ *n* [plural] the things you own, especially things that you can carry with you; ☐ **possessions**: *an insurance policy that covers your* **personal belongings**

be·lov·ed /bɪˈlʌvᵻd/ *adj* **1** *literary* or *humorous* loved very much by someone: *He never recovered from the death of his beloved daughter.* | *He's always talking about his beloved computer!* | [+of/by] *a book beloved of children everywhere* **2 my/her etc beloved** *literary* the person that you love most → **dearly beloved** at **DEARLY** (3)

be·low **S2** **W2** /bɪˈləʊ $ -ˈloʊ/ *adv, prep*
1 in a lower place or position, or on a lower level; ⊞ **above**: *an animal that lives* **below ground** | *Water was dripping onto the floor below.* | *I could hear voices in the courtyard below my window.* | *They camped a few hundred feet below the summit.* | *There was an ugly scar below his left eye.* | **Down below***, people were talking and laughing.* | *Somewhere* **far below***, a door slammed.* | *The kitchen is* **directly below** *her bedroom.* | *Captain Parker* **went below** (=to the lower level of the ship), *leaving Clooney in charge.*
2 of a lower rank or having a less important job than someone else; ⊞ **above**: *A captain is below a general.* | *No one below the level of senior manager was present.* | **and/or below** *officers of the rank of captain and below*
3 less than a particular number, amount, level etc; ⊞ **above**: *Test scores below 50 were classed as 'unsatisfactory'.* | *In June the rate of inflation fell below 3%.* | *Tom's spelling is* **well below** *average* (=much worse than the normal standard). | **below freezing/zero** (=lower than the temperature at which water freezes) *In winter, temperatures dip to 40 degrees below freezing.* | **and/or below** *free travel for children four years old and below*
4 lower on the same page, or on a later page; ⊞ **above**: *Details of courses are listed below.* | *For more information, see below.* → **below par** at **PAR** (2); → **below the belt** at **BELT**[1] (4) ⚠ **below or under?** → see box at **UNDER**

belt[1] **S2** **W3** /belt/ *n* [C]
1 a band of leather, cloth etc that you wear around your waist to hold up your clothes or for decoration: *He unbuckled his leather belt.* → see picture at **MATERIAL**[1]
2 a large area of land that has particular features or where particular people live: *America's farming belt* | *the green* (=countryside) *belt BrE* → **GREEN BELT**
3 a circular band of something such as rubber that connects or moves parts of a machine → **CONVEYOR BELT, FAN BELT**

4 below the belt *informal* unfair or cruel: *That was a bit below the belt, Paul.* | *The comments* **hit below the belt** (=they were unfair or cruel).

5 have/get sth under your belt to have achieved something useful or important: *a secretary with several years' experience under her belt*

6 belt and braces *BrE informal* a belt and braces way of doing something is one in which you do more than necessary in order to make sure that it succeeds → BLACK BELT, GARTER BELT, SEAT BELT, SAFETY BELT, SUSPENDER BELT; → **tighten your belt** at TIGHTEN (6)

belt² *v*
1 HIT [T] *informal* to hit someone or something hard: *Dan belted the ball towards the goal.*
2 GO QUICKLY [I always + adv/prep] *BrE spoken* to go somewhere very fast; ■ **charge:** [+**down/along etc**] *We were belting down the motorway at 95 miles per hour.*
3 FASTEN [T] to fasten something with a belt: *Maria belted her raincoat firmly.* | *a dress belted loosely at the waist*

belt sth ⇔ **out** *phr v*
to sing a song or play an instrument loudly: *She was belting out old Broadway favourites.*

belt up *phr v BrE*
1 *spoken* used to tell someone rudely to be quiet
2 *informal* to fasten your SEAT BELT in a vehicle

belt·ed /ˈbeltʒd/ *adj* fastened with a belt: *a belted jacket*

belt·way /ˈbeltweɪ/ *n* [C] *AmE* a fast main road that goes around a city, not through the centre; ■ **ring road** *BrE*

be·moan /bɪˈməʊn $ -ˈmoʊn/ *v* [T] *formal* to complain or say that you are disappointed about something: *He was **bemoaning the fact that** lawyers charge so much.* | **bemoan the lack/absence/loss of sth** *an article bemoaning the lack of sports facilities in the area*

be·mused /bɪˈmjuːzd/ *adj* looking as if you are confused; ■ **bewildered:** *a bemused expression* | [+**by**] *He looked slightly bemused by all the questions.* —**bemusedly** /bɪˈmjuːzɪdli/ *adv* —**bemusement** *n* [U]: *a look of bemusement* —**bemuse** *v* [T]

bench¹ S2 W3 /bentʃ/ *n*
1 OUTDOOR SEAT [C] a long seat for two or more people, especially outdoors: *We sat on a park bench and talked.*
2 IN A LAW COURT **the bench a)** the seat where a judge or MAGISTRATE sits in a court of law: *Would the prisoner please approach the bench?* **b)** the position of being a judge or MAGISTRATE in a court of law: *He was appointed to the bench last year.* | **sit/serve on the bench** (=work as a judge or MAGISTRATE)
3 SPORTS **the bench** the seat where members of a sports team sit when they are not playing in the game: *Batts and Dorigo are* **on the bench** *tonight.* | *Simpson* **came off the bench** *to play in midfield.*
4 PARLIAMENT **benches** [plural] *BrE* the seats in the British parliament where members of a particular party sit: *There was cheering from the Conservative benches.* → BACKBENCH, BACKBENCHES, FRONT BENCH
5 TABLE [C] a long heavy table used for working on with tools or equipment: *a carpenter's bench*

bench² *v* [T] *AmE* to not allow a sports player to play in a game, or to remove them from a game: *Anderson has been benched until his injury has healed.*

bench·mark¹ /ˈbentʃmaːk $ -maːrk/ *n* [C] something that is used as a standard by which other things can be judged or measured: *benchmark data* | *The valuation becomes a benchmark against which to judge other prices.* | [+**for**] *figures that are a useful benchmark for measuring the company's performance* | [+**of**] *results that are used as a benchmark of success*

benchmark² *v* [T] to use a company's good performance as a standard by which to judge the performance of other companies of the same type: **benchmark sb/sth against sth** *British Steel is benchmarked against the best operations anywhere in the world.* —**benchmarking** *n* [U]

bend¹ S3 W3 /bend/ *v past tense and past participle* **bent** /bent/
1 [I,T] to move part of your body so that it is not straight or so that you are not upright: *Lee bent and kissed her.* | *She bent her head.* | *Bend your knees, but keep your back straight.* | [+**over**] *Emma bent over to pick up the coins.* | [+**down**] *I bent down to lift the box off the floor.* | [+**towards/across etc**] *He bent towards me and whispered in my ear.*
2 [T] to push or press something so that it is no longer flat or straight: *You need a special tool to bend the steel.*
3 [I] to become curved and no longer flat or straight: *Several branches started bending towards the ground.*
4 [I] when a road bends, it changes direction to form a curve: *The road bends sharply to the left.*
5 bend the truth to say something that is not completely true
6 bend over backwards (to do sth) to try very hard to be helpful: *We bent over backwards to get it finished on time.*
7 bend sb's ear *spoken* to talk to someone, especially for a long time about something that is worrying you
8 on bended knee a) trying very hard to persuade someone to do something: *He begged on bended knee for another chance.* **b)** in a kneeling position: *He went down on bended knee and asked her to marry him.*
9 bend your mind/efforts to sth *formal* to give all your energy or attention to one activity, plan etc
10 bend to sb's will *formal* to do what someone else wants, especially when you do not want to → **bend the rules** at RULE¹ (1)

bend² *n* [C] **1** a curved part of something, especially a road or river: *The car came round the bend at a terrifying speed.* | [+**in**] *a sharp bend in the road* **2** an action in which you bend a part of your body: *We started the session with a few knee bends to warm up.* **3 drive sb round the bend** *BrE spoken* to annoy someone: *His attitude drives me round the bend.* **4 be/go round the bend** *BrE spoken* to be or become crazy: *I sometimes feel I'm going round the bend looking after young children all day.* **5 the bends** a painful and serious condition that DIVERS get if they come up from deep water too quickly

bend·er /ˈbendə $ -ər/ *n* [C] *informal* **1** a time when people drink a lot of alcohol or take a lot of drugs: *The whole team* **went on a bender** *and were arrested.* **2** *BrE taboo* a very offensive word for a man who is attracted to other men. Do not use this word.; ■ **homosexual**

bend·y /ˈbendi/ *adj* **1** easy to bend: *a bendy rubber doll* **2** with many curves or angles: *a bendy road*

be·neath W2 /bɪˈniːθ/ *adv, prep formal*
1 in or to a lower position than something, or directly under something; ■ **underneath:** *The dolphins disappeared beneath the waves.* | *Jo enjoyed feeling the warm sand beneath her feet.* | *He was standing on the bridge looking at the river beneath.* | *Some roofs collapsed* **beneath the weight of** (=unable to support the weight of) *so much snow.* → see box at UNDER
2 covered by something: *Shiona shivered beneath the bedclothes.* | *Suddenly Cranston pulled out a large handgun from beneath his robes.*
3 used to say that someone's real character or feelings are not shown because their appearance or behaviour is different; ■ **underneath:** *Dave sensed that something more sinister lay beneath the woman's cheerful exterior.* | *She tried to keep calm but* **beneath the surface** *she was angry.*
4 not good enough or suitable for someone: *She acts as if even speaking to us is beneath her.* | *He felt it would be* **beneath his dignity** *to comment.* | *His mother felt he was* **marrying beneath** *him* (=marrying someone who was not good enough). | *I consider such behaviour to be*

beneath contempt (=so bad you have no respect for the person involved).
5 in a lower, less important rank or job than someone else; ⊟ **below**

ben·e·dic·tine /ˌbenɪˈdɪktiːn/ n [C,U] a strong alcoholic drink that is a type of LIQUEUR

Ben·e·dic·tine /ˌbenɪˈdɪktɪn◂/ n [C] a member of a Christian religious order of MONKS —**Benedictine** adj

ben·e·dic·tion /ˌbenɪˈdɪkʃən/ n [C,U] a Christian prayer that asks God to protect and help someone

ben·e·fac·tion /ˌbenɪˈfækʃən/ n formal [C,U] something, especially money, that someone gives a person or organization in order to help them do something good or when someone gives money in this way

ben·e·fac·tor /ˈbenɪˌfæktə $ -ər/ n [C] someone who gives money for a good purpose: *An anonymous benefactor donated $2 million.* | [+of/to] *a generous benefactor of the university*

ben·e·fice /ˈbenɪfɪs/ n [C] the pay and position of a Christian priest who is in charge of a PARISH

be·nef·i·cent /bɪˈnefɪsənt/ adj formal helping people, or resulting in something good: *the beneficent properties of natural remedies* —**beneficence** n [U] —**beneficently** adv

ben·e·fi·cial /ˌbenɪˈfɪʃəl◂/ adj having a good effect; ⊟ **detrimental**: *a drug that has a beneficial effect on the immune system* | [+to/for] *Cycling is highly beneficial to health and the environment.* | *an arrangement that is mutually beneficial* (=it has advantages for everyone who is involved) —**beneficially** adv

ben·e·fi·cia·ry /ˌbenɪˈfɪʃəri $ -ˈfɪʃieri/ n plural **beneficiaries** [C] **1** someone who gets advantages from an action or change: [+of] *The rich were the main beneficiaries of the tax cuts.* **2** someone who receives money or property from someone else who has died: [+of] *He was the chief beneficiary of his father's will.*

ben·e·fit¹ S3 W1 /ˈbenɪfɪt/ n
1 ADVANTAGE [C,U] an advantage, improvement, or help that you get from something

> be of benefit (to sb) (=be useful to someone)
> have the benefit of sth
> get/gain/derive benefit (from sth)
> reap the benefits (of sth) (=enjoy the advantages of something)
> the full benefit (of sth)
> for sb's benefit
> be to the benefit of sb
> mutual benefit (=useful to two or more people)
> with/without the benefit (of sth) (=using/not using something)
> economic/financial/social benefits
> health benefits
> sth outweighs the benefits of sth (=something is more important than the benefits)

[+of] *the benefits of contact lenses* | *The new credit cards will be of great benefit to our customers.* | *I never had the benefit of a university education.* | *We want him to get maximum benefit from the course.* | *We're just beginning to reap the benefits of all our hard work.* | *You need to spend at least a week there to get the full benefit.* | *Could you just explain again for Mark's benefit?* | *I hope that the decision taken today will be to the benefit of the whole nation.* | *My proposition, I assure you, would be to our mutual benefit.* | *Most motorists manage without the benefit of four-wheel drive.* | *the airport's economic benefit to the region* | *the health benefits of moderate wine consumption* | *How does one decide whether the economic costs of regulation will outweigh the economic benefits?*

2 MONEY FROM GOVERNMENT [C,U] BrE money provided by the government to people who are sick, unemployed, or have little money; ⊟ **welfare** AmE: **unemployment/housing/child etc benefit** *You might be entitled to housing benefit.* | **on benefit** *families on*

benefit | *those people eligible to claim benefit*
3 EXTRA THINGS [C usually plural] extra money or other advantages that you get as part of your job or from insurance that you have: *We offer an excellent salary and benefits package.* | *medical benefits* → FRINGE BENEFIT
4 give sb the benefit of the doubt to accept what someone tells you even though you think they may be wrong or lying, but you cannot be sure: *The referee gave him the benefit of the doubt.*
5 with the benefit of hindsight/experience used to say it is easier to know the right thing to do after something has happened or if you have a lot of experience: *He admitted that with the benefit of hindsight the original launch had not been large enough.*
6 benefit concert/performance/match a concert, performance etc arranged to make money for CHARITY: *a benefit concert for famine relief*

benefit² S2 W3 v **benefited, benefiting** [I,T] if you benefit from something or it benefits you, it gives you an advantage, improves your life, or helps you in some way: *They are working together to benefit the whole community.* | [+from/by] *Many thousands have benefited from the new treatment.* | *They would benefit by reducing their labour costs.* | **benefit greatly/enormously/considerably etc** *I'm sure you'll benefit greatly from the visit.*

Ben·e·lux /ˈbenɪlʌks/ n [singular] the countries of Belgium, the Netherlands, and Luxembourg considered as a group

be·nev·o·lent /bɪˈnevələnt/ adj kind and generous: *A benevolent uncle paid for her to have music lessons.* | *a benevolent smile* —**benevolence** n [U] —**benevolently** adv

BEng BrE; **B.Eng.** AmE /ˌbiː ˈeŋ/ n [C] a first university DEGREE in ENGINEERING

Ben·ga·li /benˈɡɔːli $ -ˈɡɑːli/ n **1** [U] the language used in Bangladesh and West Bengal **2** [C] someone from Bengal —**Bengali** adj

be·night·ed /bɪˈnaɪtɪd/ adj literary having no knowledge or understanding —**benightedly** adv

be·nign /bɪˈnaɪn/ adj **1** kind and gentle: *He shook his head in benign amusement.* **2** a benign TUMOUR (=unnatural growth in the body) is not caused by CANCER; ⊟ **malignant**

bent¹ /bent/ the past tense and past participle of BEND

bent² adj **1** something that is bent is no longer flat or straight: *a bent nail* | *Stand with your knees slightly bent.* | *He breathed in deeply, bent double in pain* (=with the top part of your body leaning forward towards your legs). | *a bent old man* (=not standing straight) → see picture at BROKEN² **2** bent on sth completely determined to do something, especially something bad: *a crowd of hooligans bent on violence* | be **bent on doing sth** *They seemed bent on destroying his career.* → HELL-BENT **3** BrE informal financially dishonest and willing to use your official position unfairly; ⊟ **honest**: *a bent policeman* **4** BrE informal not polite an insulting word meaning HOMOSEXUAL **5** bent out of shape AmE spoken very angry or upset

bent³ n [singular] formal special natural skill or interest in a particular area: **musical/artistic/literary etc bent** *readers of a more literary bent*

ben·zene /ˈbenziːn, benˈziːn/ n [U] a liquid obtained from coal, used for making plastics

ben·zine /ˈbenziːn, benˈziːn/ n [U] a liquid obtained from PETROLEUM, used to clean clothes

be·queath /bɪˈkwiːð, bɪˈkwiːθ/ v [T] **1** to officially arrange for someone to have something that you own after your death; ⊟ **leave**: **bequeath sth to sb** *She bequeathed her collection of paintings to the National Gallery.* | **bequeath sb sth** *His father bequeathed him a fortune.* **2** to pass knowledge, customs etc to people who come after you or live after you

be·quest /bɪˈkwest/ n [C] formal money or property which you arrange to give to someone after your death: a bequest of $5000

be·rate /bɪˈreɪt/ v [T + for] formal to speak angrily to someone because they have done something wrong

be·reaved /bɪˈriːvd/ adj **1** having lost a close friend or relative because they have recently died: a bereaved mother **2** **the bereaved** the person or people whose close friend or relative has just died: Our sympathies go to the bereaved.

be·reave·ment /bɪˈriːvmənt/ n [C,U] formal when someone loses a close friend or relative because they have died: depression caused by bereavement or divorce

be·reft /bɪˈreft/ adj **1** **bereft of hope/meaning/life etc** completely without any hope etc: The team now seems bereft of inspiration. **2** feeling very sad and lonely: His death in 1990 left her completely bereft.

be·ret /ˈbereɪ $ bəˈreɪ/ n [C] a round cap with a tight band around the head and a soft loose top part → see picture at HAT

ber·i·ber·i /ˌberiˈberi/ n [U] a disease of the nerves caused by lack of VITAMINS

berk /bɜːk $ bɜːrk/ n [C] BrE informal a stupid person: No, you berk, they only do that in films!

Ber·mu·da shorts /bəˌmjuːdə ˈʃɔːts $ bərˌmjuːdə ˈʃɔːrts/ also **Bermudas** n [plural] short trousers that end at the knee

ber·ry /ˈberi/ n plural **berries** [C] a small soft fruit with small seeds

ber·serk /bɜːˈsɜːk, bə- $ bəˈrsɜːrk, ˈbɜːrsɜːrk/ adj **go berserk** informal to become very angry and violent: Dad went berserk when he found out.

berth¹ /bɜːθ $ bɜːrθ/ n [C] **1** a place where a ship can stop and be tied up **2** a place for someone to sleep in a ship or on a train; ➡ **bunk** ➔ **give sb/sth a wide berth** at WIDE¹ (7)

berth² v [I,T] to bring a ship into a berth or arrive at a berth

ber·yl /ˈberɪl/ n [C] a valuable stone that is usually green or yellow

be·seech /bɪˈsiːtʃ/ v past tense and past participle **besought** /-ˈsɔːt $ -ˈsɔːt/ or **beseeched** [T] literary to eagerly and anxiously ask someone for something; ➡ **beg**

be·set /bɪˈset/ v past tense and past participle **beset**, present participle **besetting** [T] formal **1** [usually passive] to make someone experience serious problems or dangers: **beset sb with/by sth** The business has been beset with financial problems. | the injuries which have beset the team all season **2** **besetting sin** a particular bad feature or habit – often used humorously

be·side S3 W2 /bɪˈsaɪd/ prep **1** next to or very close to the side of someone or something: Wendy came up and sat beside me. | the table beside the bed | I was standing right beside her at the time. ⚠ Do not confuse beside (=next to) and besides (=in addition to): He sat down beside Mary. | Who was there besides you? **2** in comparison with someone or someone: This year's sales figures don't look very good beside last year's results. | The children seemed tiny beside him. **3** **be beside yourself** to be feeling so angry, excited etc that you find it difficult to control yourself: The poor girl was almost beside herself. | **be beside yourself with anger/excitement/rage etc** Mom and Dad will be beside themselves with worry. **4** **be beside the point** to not be directly connected with the main subject or problem that you are talking about: Yes, he's a very charming young man, but that's beside the point.

be·sides /bɪˈsaɪdz/ adv, prep informal **1** spoken used when adding another reason: I need the money. And besides, when I agree to do something, I do it. **2** in addition to someone or something else that you are mentioning: The area has stunning scenery, beautiful beaches, and much more besides. | People choose jobs for

other reasons besides money. | Besides myself, the only English people there were Keith and Doreen. | **besides doing sth** Besides being heartbroken, she felt foolish.; ➔ see box at EXCEPT¹

be·siege /bɪˈsiːdʒ/ v [T] **1** to surround a city or castle with military force until the people inside let you take control: In April 655, Osman's palace was besieged by rebels. **2** [usually passive] if people, worries, thoughts etc, besiege you, you are surrounded by them: Miller was besieged by press photographers. **3** **be besieged with letters/demands/requests etc** to receive a very large number of letters, requests etc

be·smirch /bɪˈsmɜːtʃ $ -ɜːrtʃ/ v [T] literary besmirch sb's honour/reputation to spoil the good opinion that people have of someone

be·sot·ted /bɪˈsɒtɪd $ bɪˈsɑː-/ adj **be besotted (with sb/sth)** to love or want someone or something so much that you cannot think or behave sensibly: He's completely besotted with her.

be·sought /bɪˈsɔːt $ -ˈsɔːt/ the past tense and past participle of BESEECH

be·speak /bɪˈspiːk/ v [T] past tense **bespoke** /-ˈspəʊk $ -ˈspoʊk/, past participle **bespoken** /-ˈspəʊkən $ -ˈspoʊ-/ literary to be a sign of something

be·spec·ta·cled /bɪˈspektəkəld/ adj formal wearing glasses

be·spoke /bɪˈspəʊk $ -ˈspoʊk/ adj BrE a bespoke product, especially clothing or a piece of computer software, has been specially made for a particular customer: the cost of development of a bespoke system | bespoke tailoring

best¹ S1 W1 /best/ adj [superlative of good] **1** better than anything else or anyone else in quality, skill, how effective it is etc: He won the best actor award. | What's the **best way** to cook this fish? | The **best thing** to do is to stop worrying. | **it's best to do sth** It's best to go later in the season. | **easily the best/by far the best** (=much better than anything else) John's idea is by far the best option. | Our pilots are given **the best possible** training. | We use only **the very best** ingredients. **2** **best friend** the friend that you know and like better than anyone else: She was my best friend in college. **3** **best dress/shoes/clothes etc** clothing that you keep for special occasions: I put on my best suit especially. **4** **the next best thing** something that is not exactly what you want but is as similar to it as possible: If sterile equipment isn't available, the next best thing is to clean equipment with disinfectant. **5** **best of all** used to introduce the fact about a situation that is even better than the other good things: It's clean and well-located, but best of all, it's affordable. **6** **best before** BrE written on food packets with the date before which the food should be eaten: Best before 13 July. | a best-before date ➔ **be on your best behaviour** at BEHAVIOUR (2); ➔ **your best bet** at BET² (2); ➔ **the best/better part of** at PART¹ (6)

best² S1 W2 adv [superlative of well] **1** in a way that is better than any other: It works best if you let it warm up first. | This can best be described as a series of steps. | the best-dressed man in Paris **2** to the greatest degree; ➡ **most**: You know him best – you should ask him. | The part I like best is the meal afterwards. | He's perhaps **best known** for his role in 'Midnight Cowboy.' **3** **as best you can** spoken as well as you can, even if this is not very good: I'll try and fix it as best I can. **4** **had best** spoken ought to: We'd best be getting back. ➔ **had better** at BETTER² (3)

best³ n **1** **the best a)** the most helpful, most successful etc situation or results that you can achieve: We all want the best for our children. | It's the best we can do in the circumstances. **b)** the person or thing that is better than any other: She's the best of the new young writers. **2 do your best** to try as hard as you can to do something: *As long as you do your best, we'll be happy.* | **do your best to do sth** *She did her best to make him comfortable.* **3 at best** used to emphasize that something is not very good, pleasant, honest etc even if you consider it in the best possible way: *The campaign was at best only partially successful.* | *The technique is at best ineffective and at worst dangerous.* **4 to the best of your ability/knowledge/belief etc** used to say that something is as much as you know, believe, or are able to do: *I'm sure he'll do the work to the best of his ability.* **5 not the best of sth** used to say that something is not very good or could be better: *He hasn't been in the best of health lately.* | *They didn't part on the best of terms.* **6 with the best of intentions/for the best of reasons** used to mean that someone does something with good intentions or for good reasons, even if the result is not always good: *I'm sure he went there with the best of intentions.* **7 the best of both worlds** a situation in which you have the advantages of two different things without any of the disadvantages: *They live in a village but it's only an hour from London so they have the best of both worlds.* **8 at your best** performing as well or effectively as you are able to: *At her best, she's a really stylish player.* | *He was never at his best early in the morning.* **9 make the best of sth** to accept a situation which is not very good, and do whatever you can to make it better: *We are stuck here so we might as well make the best of it.* | **make the best of a bad job/situation etc** *BrE* **10 all the best** used to express good wishes to someone for the future: *We'd just like to wish him all the best in his new job.* | [+for] *All the best for the New Year!* **11 at the best of times** if something is not very good, pleasant etc at the best of times, it is usually even worse than this: *It's crowded at the best of times but today it was unbearable.* **12 the best of a bad lot/bunch** *BrE* the least bad person or thing in a group of not very good people or things **13 be for the best** *especially spoken* used to say that a particular event may seem bad now, but might have a good result later: *I still don't want him to go but maybe it's for the best.* **14 your Sunday best** *old-fashioned* your best clothes, which you only wear on special occasions

best⁴ *v* [T] *old-fashioned* to defeat someone

bes·ti·al /'bestiəl $ 'bestʃəl/ *adj literary* behaving like an animal, especially in a cruel way: *bestial and barbaric acts* —**bestially** *adv*

bes·ti·al·i·ty /ˌbestiˈælɨti $ ˌbestʃi-/ *n* [U] **1** sexual relations between a person and an animal **2** *formal* very cruel behaviour

bes·ti·ar·y /'bestiəri $ 'bestʃieri/ *n plural* **bestiaries** [C] an old book about strange animals, written in the Middle Ages

ˌbest 'man *n* [singular] the man who helps the BRIDEGROOM at a wedding ceremony

be·stow /bɪˈstəʊ $ -ˈstoʊ/ *v* [T] *formal* to give someone something of great value or importance: **bestow sth on/upon sb** *honours bestowed on him by the Queen*

ˌbest 'practice *n* [C,U] a description of the best way of performing a particular activity, especially in business, that can be used by other people or companies as a set of rules to follow: *We are currently developing a number of best practices to enhance network security.*

ˌbest-'sel·ler, best·sell·er /ˌbestˈselə $ -ər/ *n* [C] a popular product, especially a book, which many people buy: *His new book went straight to number one on the best-seller list.* | *The game is already a bestseller in Japan.* —**best-selling** *adj* [only before noun]: *a best-selling author* | *the UK's best-selling album*

bet¹ [S1] /bet/ *v past tense and past participle* **bet**, *present participle* **betting**
1 [I,T] to risk money on the result of a race, game, competition, or other future event; → **gamble**: *How much do you want to bet?* | **bet (sb) that** *He bet me £10*

that I wouldn't do it.* | **bet (sth) on sth** *She bet all her money on a horse that came last.* | [+against] *I wouldn't bet against him winning the championship this year.*
2 I bet, I'll bet *spoken* **a)** used to say that you are fairly sure that something is true, something is happening etc, although you cannot prove this: *I bet Nigel's sitting at home now laughing his head off.* | *Bet you wish you'd arrived earlier.* | *I bet you she won't come.* **b)** used to show that you understand or can imagine the situation that someone has just told you about: *'God, I was so angry.' 'I bet you were.'* | *'It makes things much easier.' 'Yeah, I'll bet it does.'* **c)** used to show that you do not believe what someone has just told you: *'I'm definitely going to give up smoking this time.' 'Yeah, I bet!'*
3 you bet! *spoken* used to emphasize that you agree with someone or are keen to do what they suggest: *'Going to the party on Saturday?' ' You bet!'*
4 you (can) bet your life/your bottom dollar *spoken* used when you are sure that you know what someone will do or what will happen: *You can bet your bottom dollar he won't be back.*
5 (do you) want to bet?/wanna bet? *spoken* used to say that you think something that someone has just said is not true or not likely to happen: *'I'm sure Tom'll be here soon.' 'Wanna bet?'*
6 don't bet on it, I wouldn't bet on it *spoken* used to say that you do not think something is likely to happen: *He said he'd finish by tomorrow, but I wouldn't bet on it.*

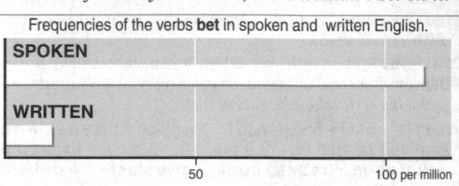

Frequencies of the verbs **bet** in spoken and written English.

SPOKEN		
WRITTEN		
	50	100 per million

This graph shows that the verb **bet** is much more common in spoken English than in written English. This is because it is used in some common spoken phrases.

bet² *n* [C] **1** an agreement to risk money on the result of a race, game etc or on something happening, or the money that you risk: *a £50 bet* | [+on] *A few of us had a bet on who'd get married first.* | **place/put/lay a bet** *We placed bets on three horses.* | *Bookmakers are already taking bets on the outcome.* | **win/lose a bet** *If he scores now, I'll win my bet.* **2 your best bet** *spoken* used when advising someone what to do: *Your best bet is to put an advert in the local newspaper.* | *The train might be a better bet.* **3 a good/safe bet** an action or situation that is likely to be successful or does not involve much risk: *If you're looking for long-term growth, the government's own saving certificates are a pretty good bet.* → **hedge your bets** at HEDGE² (2) **4 it's a safe/sure/fair bet (that)** *spoken* used to say that something seems almost certain: *I think it's a pretty safe bet that he'll get the job.* **5 my bet** *spoken* used when saying what you expect to happen in the future: *My bet is he'll be back this time next week.* **6 do sth for a bet** to do something stupid, dangerous etc to win money from someone or to prove that you can do it: *He climbed the tree for a bet.*

be·ta /'bi:tə $ 'beɪtə/ *n* [singular] the second letter of the Greek alphabet, β or B

'beta-ˌblock·er *n* [C] a drug used to help prevent HEART ATTACKS

'beta ˌtest *n* [C] *technical* a test of software in which it is given to customers to use, so that any problems will be found; → **alpha test**

'beta ˌversion *n* [C] *technical* software that is being tested by people who will use it, to see if it works properly; → **alpha version**

be·tel /'bi:tl/ *n* [U] a plant whose leaves have a fresh taste, and which some people chew, especially in Asia

'betel nut *n* [C,U] small pieces of red nut with a bitter taste, that are wrapped in a betel leaf and chewed

bête noire /ˌbet ˈnwɑː $ -ˈnwɑːr/ *n* [singular] **sb's bête noire** the person or thing that someone dislikes most

be·tide /bɪˈtaɪd/ v **woe betide sb** used to say that someone will be in trouble if they do something – often humorous: *Woe betide anyone who wakes the baby!*

be·to·ken /bɪˈtəʊkən $ -ˈtoʊ-/ v [T] *literary* to be a sign of something

be·tray /bɪˈtreɪ/ v [T]
1 FRIENDS to be disloyal to someone who trusts you so that they are harmed or upset: *He felt that she had betrayed him.* | **betray sb to sb** *What kind of man would betray his own sister to the police?* | *She had betrayed her parents' trust.* | *I would never betray a confidence* (=tell a secret which someone has trusted me with).
2 COUNTRY to be disloyal to your country, company etc, for example by giving secret information to its enemies: *people who betray their country for money*
3 EMOTIONS [not in progressive or passive] to show feelings that you are trying to hide; **◘ give away**: *His voice betrayed his nervousness.* | *His face betrayed nothing* (=showed no emotion).
4 TRUTH to show that something is true or exists, especially when it is not easily noticed; **◘ give away**: *The slightest sound might betray his presence.* | *The crumpled sheets betrayed the fact that someone had been sleeping there.*
5 betray your beliefs/principles/ideals etc to stop supporting your old beliefs and principles, especially in order to get power or avoid trouble —**betrayer** *n* [C]

be·tray·al /bɪˈtreɪəl/ *n* [C,U] when you betray your country, friends, or someone who trusts you: [+of] *a ruthless betrayal of their election pledges* | *She felt a great sense of betrayal.*

be·troth·al /bɪˈtrəʊðəl $ -ˈtroʊ-/ *n* [C] *old-fashioned* an agreement that two people will be married; **◘ engagement**

be·trothed /bɪˈtrəʊðd $ -ˈtroʊðd/ *adj old-fashioned* **1 be betrothed to sb** to have promised to marry someone **2 sb's betrothed** the person that someone has agreed to marry —**betroth** *v* [T]

bet·ter¹ S1 W1 /ˈbetə $ -ər/ *adj*
1 [comparative of **good**] more useful, interesting, satisfactory, effective, suitable etc; **◘ worse**: *Your stereo is better than mine.* | *a better job with a better salary* | *There must be a better way to do this.* | *a better-quality car* | **much/a lot/far better** *We now have a much better understanding of the disease.* | **better still/even better** *It was even better than last year.* ⚠ **Better** is a comparative form. Do not say 'more better'.
2 [comparative of **well**] **a)** more healthy or less ill or painful than before; **◘ worse**: *She is a little better today, the doctor says.* | *I'm feeling much better, thank you.* **b)** completely well again after an illness: *When you're better we can see about planning a trip.* | *I hope he gets better* (=recovers from an illness) *soon.*
3 it is better/it would be better used to give your opinion or make a suggestion about what you think should be done or happen: **it is better to do sth** *It's much better to get a proper written agreement.* | [+if] *It might be better if you stayed here.*
4 get better to improve: *Her English isn't really getting any better.* | *Things can only get better.*
5 no better a) not better than something else or something before: *The following day the weather was no better.* | *John's no better; he never does any washing up either.* **b)** used to say that something is the best: **there is no better way/example/place etc** *There's no better way of exploring the region.*
6 nothing better a) used to say that you really like something or think that something is very good: **like/love/enjoy nothing better (than)** *She likes nothing better than a nice long walk along the beach.* | *There's nothing better than beating someone who's playing well.* **b)** used to say that a thing or situation is not very good, but is the only thing possible or available: **have nothing better to do** *Have you got nothing better to do than sit there playing that silly game?* | *I only picked it up because there was nothing better to read.*
7 that's better *spoken* used to say that something has improved, that you are happier or more comfortable,

or to encourage someone: *Ah, that's better. I needed to sit down.* | *Move it just a bit. Yes, that's better.* | *'Can you turn it down a bit?' 'Is that better?'*
8 better late than never *spoken* used to say that even if something happens late or someone arrives late, this is better than it not happening or them not arriving at all → **your better half/other half** at HALF² (8); → **the best/better part of sth** at PART¹ (9); → **against your better judgment** at JUDGMENT (1); → **sb's better nature** at NATURE (2); → **better luck next time** at LUCK¹ (14); → **better the devil you know** at DEVIL (11); → **have seen better days** at SEE¹ (30)

better² S1 W1 *adv* [comparative of **well**]
1 to a higher standard or quality; **◘ worse**: *He can speak French a lot better than I can.* | *Your bike will run better if you oil it.* → **fare better** at FARE²
2 to a higher degree; **◘ more**: *She knows this town better than you do.* | *I think I like the red one better.* | *Potter is better known for his TV work.*
3 had better a) used to give advice about what someone should do or to say what you should do or need to do: *I'd better go and get ready.* | *I think you'd better ask Jo first.* | *Better just check she's okay.* | *You had better not tell Oliver* (=it is not a good idea). **b)** used to threaten someone: *You'd better keep your mouth shut about this.* ⚠ In speech, people usually shorten **had** to **'d**, and may not pronounce it at all. But do not leave out **had** or **'d** in writing: *You'd better come here* (NOT *You better!*)
4 do better to perform better or reach a higher standard: *We did better than all the other schools.* | *You can do better than that!*
5 the sooner the better/the bigger the better etc used to emphasize that you would prefer something to happen as soon as possible, want something to be as big as possible etc: *School finishes at the end of the week, and the sooner the better as far as I'm concerned.* | *The younger you start learning a language, the better you'll speak it.*
6 go one better (than sb) *informal* to do something more successfully than someone else: *The following year Lewis went one better by winning the gold medal.* | *Of course, they had to go one better and have the whole garden redesigned.* → BETTER OFF

better³ *n* **1 the better** the one that is higher in quality, more suitable etc when you are comparing two similar people or things: *It's hard to decide which one's the better.* **2 get the better of sb a)** if your feelings or wishes get the better of you, they make you behave in a way you would not normally behave: *My curiosity finally got the better of me and I opened the letter.* | *I think her nerves got the better of her.* **b)** to defeat someone or deal successfully with a problem **3 for the better** in a way that improves the situation: *a definite change for the better* | *The President's fortunes seem, at last, to have taken a turn for the better* (=started to improve). **4 so much the better** used to say that something would be even better or bring even more advantages: *If they can do them both at the same time, then so much the better.* **5 be all the better for sth** to be improved by a particular action, change etc: *I think it's all the better for that extra ten minutes' cooking.* **6 for better or (for) worse** used to say that something must be accepted, whether it is good or bad, because it cannot be changed: *Work is, for better or worse, becoming more flexible nowadays.* **7 your betters** *old-fashioned* people who are more important than you or deserve more respect → WORSE²; → **elders and betters** at ELDER² (2)

better⁴ *v* [T] **1** to be higher in quality, amount etc than someone or something else: *His total of five gold medals is unlikely to be bettered.* **2 better yourself** to improve your position in society by getting a better education or earning more money **3** *formal* to improve something: *bettering the lot of the working classes*

bet·ter·ment /'betəmənt $ -tər-/ n [singular] formal improvement, especially in someone's social and economic position: **for the betterment of sb/sth** social change for the betterment of society as a whole

,**better 'off** adj [no comparative] **1** having more money than someone else or than you had before; → **worse off:** She'll be about £50 a week better off. → **WELL-OFF (1) 2** happier, improved, more successful etc; → **worse off:** [+with/without] I think she's better off without him. | **be better off doing sth** (=used to give advice or an opinion) He'd be better off starting with something simpler.

bet·ting /'betɪŋ/ n **1** [U] when people risk money on the results of games, competitions etc or other future events; → **gambling 2 what's the betting, the betting is** BrE used to say that something seems very likely to happen or to be true: What's the betting Dan's involved in this somewhere?

,**betting ,shop** n [C] a place in Britain where people go to place BETS on the results of races, competitions etc; ▣ **bookmaker's**

be·tween ▣ W1 /bɪ'twiːn/ adv, prep
1 also **in between** in or through the space that separates two things, people, or places: I sat down between Sue and Jane. | a house and stables with a yard in between | The ball rolled between his feet. | a small town halfway between Salt Lake City and Denver
2 also **in between** in the time that separates two times or events: Are there any public holidays between Christmas and Easter? | You shouldn't eat between meals. | The team have a lot of work to do between now and Sunday. | A lot of students spend a year abroad in between school and university. | I've had a few jobs with long periods of unemployment in between.
3 within a range of amounts, numbers, distances etc: The project will cost between eight and ten million dollars. | Most of the victims were young men between the ages of 16 and 21.
4 used to say which two places are joined or connected by something: They're building a new road between Manchester and Sheffield. | a regular air service between London and Paris
5 used to say which people or things are involved in something together or are connected: the long-standing friendship between Bob and Bryan | co-operation between the two countries | She had overheard a private conversation between two MPs. | the link between serious sunburn and deadly skin cancer
6 used to say which people or things get, have, or are involved in something that is shared: Tom divided his money between his children. | Between the four of them they managed to lift her into the ambulance. | We collected £17 between us.
7 used to say which two things or people you are comparing: the contrast between town and country life | In her book she makes a comparison between Russian and British ballet. | the difference between good music and really great music
8 between you and me also **between ourselves** spoken used before telling someone something that you do not want them to tell anyone else: Between you and me, I think Schmidt's about to resign.
9 come between sb if something comes between two people, it causes an argument or problems between them: I let my stupid pride come between us.
10 used when it is difficult to give an exact description of something and you therefore have to compare it to two things that are similar to it: He uttered a sound that was something between a sigh and a groan.

be·twixt /bɪ'twɪkst/ prep **1** literary between **2 betwixt and between** old-fashioned not quite belonging to one group or to another

bev·el /'bevəl/ n [C] **1** a sloping edge or surface, usually along the edge of a piece of wood or glass **2** a tool for making this kind of edge or surface —**bevelled** adj: bevelled glass

bev·er·age /'bevərɪdʒ/ n [C] formal a hot or cold drink: alcoholic beverages | the Food and Beverage Manager

bev·vied up /,bevid 'ʌp/ adj [not before noun] BrE informal drunk: We're all going out to get bevvied up.

bev·vy /'bevi/ n [C] plural bevvies BrE informal a drink, especially an alcoholic drink: Maybe she'd had a few bevvies.

bev·y /'bevi/ n [singular] a large group of people of the same kind, especially girls or young women: [+of] a bevy of beauties

be·wail /bɪ'weɪl/ v [T] literary to express deep sadness or disappointment about something

be·ware /bɪ'weə $ -'wer/ v [I,T only in imperative and infinitive] used to warn someone to be careful because something is dangerous: [+of] Beware of the dog! | **beware of doing sth** They should beware of making hasty decisions. | Police warned drivers to beware.

be·wil·der /bɪ'wɪldə $ -ər/ v [T usually passive] to confuse someone: He was bewildered by his daughter's reaction.

be·wil·dered /bɪ'wɪldəd $ -ərd/ adj totally confused: a bewildered expression on his face

be·wil·der·ing /bɪ'wɪldərɪŋ/ adj confusing, especially because there are too many choices or things happening at the same time: **a bewildering variety/array/range** a bewildering variety of choices —**bewilderingly** adv: The details are bewilderingly complex.

be·wil·der·ment /bɪ'wɪldəmənt $ -dər-/ n [U] a feeling of being very confused; ▣ **confusion: in bewilderment** She looked at him in bewilderment.

be·witch /bɪ'wɪtʃ/ v [T usually passive] **1** to make someone feel so interested or attracted that they cannot think clearly: Tim's utterly bewitched by her. **2** to get control over someone by putting a magic SPELL on them —**bewitching** adj: a bewitching smile

be·yond¹ ▣ W1 /bɪ'jɒnd $ -'jɑːnd/ prep, adv
1 on or to the further side of something: They crossed the mountains and headed for the valleys beyond. | Beyond the river, cattle were grazing. | She drove through Westport, and stopped a few miles beyond at a wayside inn.
2 later than a particular time, date etc; ▣ **after:** What changes await us in the coming year and beyond? | The ban has been extended beyond 2003. | The disco went on until beyond midnight.
3 more or greater than a particular amount, level, or limit: More people are choosing to work beyond retirement age. | Inflation has risen beyond the 5% level.
4 outside the range or limits of something or someone: Such tasks are **far beyond** the scope of the average schoolkid. | expensive luxuries that are beyond the reach of ordinary people
5 used to say that something is impossible to do: **beyond repair/control/belief etc** (=impossible to repair, control, believe etc) Scott's equipment was damaged beyond repair. | The town centre had changed beyond all recognition. | Due to circumstances beyond our control the performance has had to be cancelled.
6 be beyond sb to be too difficult for someone to understand: The whole problem was quite beyond him. | Why Joan ever married such an idiot in the first place is beyond me.
7 used to mean 'except' in negative sentences: Fred owns nothing beyond the clothes on his back. | I can't tell you anything beyond what you know already.

beyond² n **the beyond** literary whatever comes after this life

bha·ji, bhajee /'bɑːdʒiː/ n [C] a hot-tasting Indian vegetable cake cooked in BATTER (=a liquid mixture of flour, egg, and milk or water): onion bhajis

bi- /baɪ/ prefix two, twice, or double; → **semi-, di-, tri-:** bilingual (=speaking two languages) | to bisect (=cut in two)

bi·an·nu·al /baɪˈænjuəl/ adj happening twice each year: a biannual report; → annual, biennial

bi·as¹ /ˈbaɪəs/ n **1** [singular, U] an opinion about whether a person, group, or idea is good or bad which influences how you deal with it: **political/gender/racial etc bias** a discussion about political bias in the press | Students were evaluated without bias or favoritism. | [+against/towards/in favour of] It's clear that the company has a bias against women and minorities. **2** [singular] a natural skill or interest in one type of thing: Lydia has a strong artistic bias. **3 on the bias** in a DIAGONAL direction

bias² v [T] to unfairly influence attitudes, choices, or decisions: Several factors could have biased the results of the study.

bi·ased, **biassed** /ˈbaɪəst/ adj **1** unfairly preferring one person or group over another: Of course I'm biased, but I thought my daughter's paintings were the best. | racially biased attitudes | [+against/towards/in favour of] news reporting that was **heavily biased** towards the government **2** more interested in a particular thing than in another: [+towards] The majority of infants are biased towards being social rather than being antisocial.

bi·ath·lon /baɪˈæθlɒn $ -lɑːn, -lən/ n [C] a sports competition in which competitors SKI across fields and then shoot a RIFLE; → decathlon, pentathlon

bib /bɪb/ n [C] **1** a piece of cloth or plastic tied under a baby's chin to protect its clothes when it is eating **2** the part of an APRON, DUNGAREES, or OVERALLS that covers your chest **3 your best bib and tucker** your best clothes – used humorously

bi·ble, **Bible** /ˈbaɪbəl/ n **1 the Bible** the holy book of the Christian religion, consisting of the OLD TESTAMENT and the NEW TESTAMENT **2** [C] a copy of the Bible **3** [singular] informal the most useful and important book on a particular subject: It's the anatomy student's bible!

bib·li·cal /ˈbɪblɪkəl/ adj [usually before noun] relating to or written in the Bible: The disease dates back to **biblical times**. | **biblical story/text/reference** the biblical story of Noah

bib·li·og·ra·phy /ˌbɪbliˈɒɡrəfi $ -ˈɑːɡ-/ n plural **bibliographies** [C] **1** a list of all the books and articles used in preparing a piece of writing **2** a list of books and articles that are all about a particular subject —**bibliographer** n [C]

bib·li·o·phile /ˈbɪbliəfaɪl/ n [C] formal someone who likes books

bib·u·lous /ˈbɪbjʊləs/ adj formal liking to drink too much alcohol – sometimes used humorously

bi·cam·er·al /baɪˈkæmərəl/ adj [only before noun] technical a bicameral LEGISLATURE (=part of the government that makes laws) consists of two parts, such as the Senate and the House of Representatives in the US Congress; → unicameral

bi·car·bon·ate of so·da /baɪˌkɑːbənət əv ˈsəʊdə, -bəneɪt- $ -ˌkɑːr-, -ˈsoʊdə/ also **bicarbonate** also **bi·carb** /ˈbaɪkɑːb $ -kɑːrb/ n [U] technical a chemical substance used especially in baking, and sometimes taken with water as a medicine; → baking soda

bi·cen·te·na·ry /ˌbaɪsenˈtiːnəri $ -ˈtenəri, -ˈsentəneri/ n plural **bicentenaries** [C] especially BrE the day or year exactly 200 years after an important event; → centenary: [+of] the bicentenary of Mozart's death —**bicentenary** adj [only before noun]: the bicentenary year

bi·cen·ten·ni·al /ˌbaɪsenˈteniəl/ n [C] AmE the day or year exactly 200 years after an important event: the bicentennial of the Declaration of Independence —**bicentennial** adj: bicentennial celebrations

bi·cep /ˈbaɪsep/ n [C usually plural] the large muscle on the front of your upper arm: He had an eagle tattoo on one of his biceps.

bick·er /ˈbɪkə $ -ər/ v [I] to argue, especially about something very unimportant: I wish you two would stop

bickering. | [+about/over] They kept bickering over who should answer the phone. —**bickering** n [U]

bi·cy·cle¹ W3 /ˈbaɪsɪkəl/ n [C] a vehicle with two wheels that you ride by pushing its PEDALS with your feet; ▣ **bike**: Can James **ride a bicycle** yet? → EXERCISE BIKE

bicycle² v [I always + adv/prep] formal to go somewhere by bicycle; ▣ **bike**, **cycle** —**bicyclist** n [C]

bicycle ˌshorts n [plural] especially AmE CYCLING SHORTS

bid¹ W3 /bɪd/ n [C]
1 an offer to pay a particular price for something, especially at an AUCTION: [+for] They put in a bid for the house. | the person who places the highest bid | We've **made a bid** of nearly £400m for the company. | A takeover bid for the airline was launched today.
2 an offer to do work or provide services for a specific price: [+for] rival bids for the cleaning contract
3 an attempt to achieve or obtain something: [+for] a bid for power | **bid to do sth** a desperate bid to free herself from a loveless marriage
4 a statement of how many points you hope to win in a card game

bid² v past tense and past participle **bid**, present participle **bidding**
1 [I,T] to offer to pay a particular price for goods, especially in an AUCTION: **bid (sb) sth for sth** She bid £100 for a Victorian chair. | What am I bid for lot 227? Shall we start at $500? | [+against] The two men ended up bidding against each other at the auction.
2 [I] to offer to do work or provide services for a specific price, in competition with other offers: [+for] Three firms bid for the contract on the new buildings.
3 [I,T] to say how many points you think you will win in a game of cards

bid³ v past tense **bade** /bæd, beɪd/ or **bid**, past participle **bid** or **bidden** /ˈbɪdn/, present participle **bidding** literary **1 bid sb good afternoon/good morning etc** to greet someone **2** [T] to order or tell someone what to do: **bid sb (to) do sth** The queen bade us enter.

bid·da·ble /ˈbɪdəbəl/ adj willing to do what you are told without arguing

bid·der /ˈbɪdə $ -ər/ n [C] **1** someone who offers to pay a particular amount of money for something that is being sold: The antiques will be sold to the **highest bidder** (=the person who offers to pay the most). **2** someone who offers to do work or provide services for a particular amount of money, in competition with others: one of 13 bidders for the contract

bid·ding /ˈbɪdɪŋ/ n [U] **1** when you BID for goods, especially in an AUCTION: The bidding was brisk and sales went well. **2 at sb's bidding** formal because someone has told you to **3 do sb's bidding** formal to obey someone's requests or orders

bid·dy /ˈbɪdi/ n plural **biddies old biddy** informal an old woman, especially one who is unpleasant or annoying

bide /baɪd/ v **1 bide your time** to wait until the right moment to do something: They are stronger than us and can afford to bide their time. **2** [I] old use to wait or stay somewhere, often for a long time; ▣ **abide**

bi·det /ˈbiːdeɪ $ bɪˈdeɪ/ n [C] a small low bath that you sit on to wash your bottom

bi·en·ni·al /baɪˈeniəl/ adj **1** a biennial event happens once every two years; → annual **2** a biennial plant stays alive for two years; → annual, perennial —**biennially** adv

bier /bɪə $ bɪr/ n [C] a frame like a table on which a dead body or COFFIN is placed

biff¹ /bɪf/ v **1** [T] old-fashioned informal to hit someone hard with your FIST; ▣ **thump**: He biffed me on the nose. **2** [I] informal to fall or hit something when riding a bicycle, SNOWBOARD etc: I was skiing too fast and biffed at the bottom of the hill. —**biff** n [C]

biff² n [C] informal an embarrassing mistake

1 000, 2 000, 3 000, most frequent words in S poken and W ritten English

bi·fo·cals /baɪˈfəʊkəlz $ ˈbaɪfoʊ-/ n [plural] special glasses with an upper part made for seeing things that are far away, and a lower part made for reading —**bifocal** adj

bi·fur·cate /ˈbaɪfəkeɪt $ -ər-/ v [I] formal if a road, river etc bifurcates, it divides into two separate parts —**bifurcation** /ˌbaɪfəˈkeɪʃən $ -fər-/ n [C,U]

big[1] [S1] [W1] /bɪg/ adj comparative **bigger**, superlative **biggest**

1 SIZE of more than average size or amount: a big house | I need a bigger desk. | She had a big grin on her face. | a big increase in crime | Los Angeles is the biggest city in California. | The garage isn't big enough for two cars. | When they lose, they lose **in a big way** (=to a large degree). | There was this **great big** (=extremely big) spider in the sink. → see box at FAT[1]

2 IMPORTANT important and serious: a big decision | Buying your own house is a big commitment. | The big game is on Friday. | There's a **big difference** between understanding something and being able to explain it to others. | Everyone was getting ready for the **big day** (=a day when an important event will happen).

3 POPULAR/SUCCESSFUL successful or popular, especially in business or entertainment: Julia Roberts became a big star after 'Pretty Woman'. | She's very big in Australia. | After years as a small-time actor, he suddenly **made it big** (=became very successful) in Hollywood. | **the big boys** (=the most powerful people or companies) → BIG CHEESE, BIG NOISE; → **big shot** at SHOT[1] (14); → BIG TIME[1]

4 OLDER a) **big sister/brother** your older sister or brother **b)** older or more like an adult – used especially by children or when you are talking to children: Come on, don't cry. You're a big girl now.

5 LARGE DEGREE [only before noun] informal **a)** doing something to a large degree: a **big eater/drinker/**

spender etc Des is a big gambler, you know. | **be a big fan/admirer of sb/sth b)** done to a large degree or with great energy: **give sb a big hug/kiss** Mama gave me a big hug. | **give sb a big hand** (=clap loudly)

6 BAD [only before noun] informal used to emphasize how bad something is: AIDS remains a **big problem** in many parts of the world. | Buying that house was a **big mistake**. | I never said that, you big liar!

7 have big ideas/plans to have impressive plans for the future: I've got big plans for this place.

8 be big on sth spoken **a)** to like something very much: I'm not big on kids. **b)** to have a lot of a quality or feature: The new BMW is big on safety features.

9 what's the big idea? spoken used when someone has done something annoying, especially when you want them to explain why they did it: Hey, what's the big idea? Who said you could use my computer?

10 GENEROUS **it is big of sb to do sth** spoken **a)** used to say that someone is very kind or generous to do something **b)** used when you really think that someone is not kind or helpful at all: A whole £5! That was very big of her, I must say!

11 big mouth spoken someone who has a big mouth cannot be trusted to keep things secret: I'm sorry. I shouldn't have opened my big mouth. | **me and my big mouth** (=said when you wish you had not told someone a secret) → BIGMOUTH

12 LETTERS informal big letters are CAPITALS, for example G, R, A etc

13 WORDS informal big words are long or unusual and are difficult to read or understand

14 be/get too big for your boots informal to be too proud of yourself

15 use/wield the big stick informal to threaten to use your power to get what you want → **think big** at THINK[1] (39)

bicycle

saddle · handlebar · gear lever · crossbar · brake · rear light · front light · mudguard BrE/fender AmE · pump · tyre BrE/tire AmE · fork · valve · hub · spokes · reflector · chain · pedal

big and **large** have the same meaning, but **large** is
slightly more formal and more likely to be used in written
than spoken English: *a big lunch* | *a large house*
large is used with quantity words such as 'number' and
'amount': *large amounts of money* | *a large proportion of
the students*
great is not usually used to talk about size but it can be
used in literary writing to describe very large and impressive things: *Before them stood a great palace.*
great is used with **length**, **height**, and **age**, and in the
expression **a great deal** (=a lot): *The grass had reached
a great height.* | *a great deal of money*
WORD CHOICE: big, tall, high
big is not used just to describe a person's height. It is
used to describe a child who is growing, or a person
who is heavy, with a lot of fat or muscle on their body.
tall is used to describe a person's height. It can also be
used to describe trees, buildings, or other things that are
narrow and measure a long distance from bottom to top:
She is tall and thin. | *the tallest building in London*
high is used to describe things or places that are a long
way from the ground: *a high shelf* | *the highest mountain
in the world*

big² *v* **bigged, bigging big it up** *BrE spoken informal* to
spend a lot of money and enjoy yourself in a social
situation, in a way that other people will notice
big·a·my /ˈbɪgəmi/ *n* [U] the crime of being married
to two people at the same time; → **monogamy,
polygamy** —**bigamist** *n* [C] —**bigamous** *adj*
Big 'Apple *n* **the Big Apple** New York City
'big band *n* [C] a large musical band, especially
popular in the 1940s and 1950s, that plays JAZZ or dance
music and has a leader who plays SOLOS: *Tommy
Dorsey's big band* —**big-band** *adj*
big 'bang ,theory *n* **the big bang theory** the idea that
the universe began with a single large explosion (the
'big bang'), and that the pieces are still flying apart; →
steady state theory
big-'boned *adj* a big-boned person is large without
being fat
big 'brother, Big Brother *n* [U] any person, organization, or system that seems to want to control
people's lives and restrict their freedom: *Increasingly,
the state is taking a big brother role in this area.*
big 'bucks *n* [plural] *informal especially AmE* a lot of
money: *Her parents spent big bucks on her wedding.*
big 'business *n* [U] **1** very large companies, considered as a powerful group with a lot of influence **2** a
product or type of activity that people spend a lot of
money on: *Dieting has become big business.*
big 'cat *n* [C] a large animal of the cat family, such as
a lion or tiger
big 'cheese *n* [C] *informal* an important and powerful
person in an organization – used humorously
big 'deal *n* [singular] *spoken* **1** used to say that you do
not think something is as important as someone else
thinks it is: *It's just a game. If you lose, big deal.* |
What's the big deal? *It's only a birthday, not the end of
the world.* | **It's no big deal.** *Everybody forgets things
sometimes.* **2** an important or exciting event or situation: *This audition is a big deal for Joey.* **3 make a big
deal of/out of/about sth** to get too excited or upset
about something, or make something seem more
important than it is: *I know I'm probably making a big
deal out of nothing, but I'm worried about you.*
big 'dipper *n* [C] **1** *BrE* old-fashioned a small railway
in a FUNFAIR, with steep slopes and sharp curves to give
an exciting ride → see picture at AMUSEMENT PARK **2 the
Big Dipper** *AmE* a group of seven bright stars seen only
from northern parts of the world; ⊟ **the Plough** *BrE*
big 'game *n* [U] large wild animals hunted for sport,
such as lions and ELEPHANTS: *a big game hunter*
big·gie /ˈbɪgi/ *n* [C] **1** *informal* something very large,
important, or successful: *I think their new CD is going*

big cats

whiskers
jaguar
cheetah
tiger
tail
claw
panther
lynx *BrE*/bobcat *AmE*
mane
lion
leopard
haunch
puma/cougar

to be a biggie. **2 no biggie** *AmE spoken* said when
something is not important or when you are not upset
or angry about something: *'Oh, I'm sorry.' 'That's okay,
no biggie.'*
big 'government *n* [U] *AmE* government – used
when people think it is controlling their lives too
much: *big government welfare policies*
big 'gun *n* [C] *informal* a person or company that has a
lot of power and influence: *one of the party's big guns*
big-head·ed /ˌbɪgˈhedɪd◂/ *adj informal* someone who
is big-headed thinks they are very important, clever etc
– used to show disapproval —**big-head** *n* [C]; → see
box at PROUD
big-heart·ed /ˌbɪg ˈhɑːtɪd◂ $ -ɑːr-/ *adj* very kind and
generous
big 'hitter *n* [C] someone who is very important and
successful and who has a lot of influence: *one of the big
hitters of the Conservative Party*
big·horn sheep /ˌbɪghɔːn ˈʃiːp $ -hɔːrn-/ *n* [C] a wild
sheep with long curved horns that lives in the mountains of western North America
bight /baɪt/ *n* [C] a slight bend or curve in a coast
Big Man on 'Campus *n* [C] *AmE informal* an
important and popular male student at a college or
university, especially someone who is good at sports
big 'money *n* [U] *informal* a large amount of money:
Carter won big money in Vegas last year.
big·mouth /ˈbɪgmaʊθ/ *n* [C] *informal* someone who
cannot be trusted to keep secrets
big 'name *n* [C] a famous person or group, especially
a musician, actor etc: *Poor attendance at the concert
was put down to the lack of big names.*
big 'noise *n* [C] *informal* an important and powerful
person in an organization
big·ot /ˈbɪgət/ *n* [C] someone who is bigoted: *racist
bigots*
big·ot·ed /ˈbɪgətɪd/ *adj* having such strong opinions
about a group of people that you are unwilling to listen
to anyone else's opinions: *The decision not to allow
disabled athletes to take part was seen as petty and
bigoted.*

big·ot·ry /'bɪgətri/ *n* [U] bigoted behaviour or beliefs: *sensational news stories that just encourage bigotry and intolerance*

big 'screen *n* **the big screen** the cinema, rather than the television or theatre: *on the big screen She was last seen on the big screen in the comedy 'Jawbreaker'.*

'big shot *n* [C] *informal* someone who has a lot of power or influence in a company or an area of business: *His father's a big shot and he thinks he is, too.*

'big ticket *adj* [only before noun] *AmE informal* expensive: *big ticket items such as cars or jewelry*

'big time¹ *n* **the big time** *informal* the position of being very famous or important, for example in the entertainment business or in politics: *The 46-year-old author has finally hit the big time.* —**big-time** *adj* [only before noun]: *big-time cocaine dealers*

big time² *adv spoken especially AmE* to a very large degree: *Morris messed up big time.*

big 'toe *n* [C] the largest toe on your foot

big 'top *n* [C] the very large tent in which a CIRCUS performance takes place

big 'wheel *n* [C] *BrE* a machine used in AMUSEMENT PARKS, consisting of a very large upright wheel with seats hanging from it, which turns round slowly; ▪ **fer-ris wheel**; → see picture at AMUSEMENT PARK

big·wig /'bɪgwɪg/ *n* [C] *informal* an important person: *A few of the company bigwigs have their own jets.*

bi·jou /'biːʒuː/ *adj* [only before noun] *BrE* a bijou house or apartment is small and fashionable – often used humorously: *a bijou residence in Mayfair*

bike¹ /baɪk/ *n* [C]
1 a bicycle: *Let's go for a bike ride.* | **by bike** *They'll be coming by bike.*
2 *informal* a MOTORCYCLE
3 on your bike! *BrE spoken* used to tell someone rudely to go away

bike² *v* **1** [I always + adv/prep] *informal* to ride a bicycle: *She bikes to work every day.* **2** [T] to take something to someone by MOTORCYCLE in order to get it there quickly: **bike sth over/round** *We're late for our deadline. Can you bike the photos over to us?*

bik·er /'baɪkə $ -ər/ *n* [C] **1** someone who rides a MOTORCYCLE, especially as part of a group: *Most of the bikers rode Harley-Davidsons.* **2** someone who rides a bicycle: *trails for bikers and hikers*

bi·ki·ni /bə'kiːni/ *n* [C] a piece of clothing in two separate parts that women wear for swimming

bi'kini line *n* [C] the place on a woman's legs where the hair around her sexual organs stops growing

bi·la·bi·al /baɪ'leɪbiəl/ *n* [C] *technical* a CONSONANT sound such as /p/ or /b/ that is made using both lips —**bilabial** *adj* → LABIAL

bi·lat·er·al /baɪ'lætərəl/ *adj* involving two groups or nations: **bilateral relations/trade/agreements/negotiations etc** *bilateral negotiations between Israel and Syria* —**bilaterally** *adv* → MULTILATERAL, UNILATERAL

bil·ber·ry /'bɪlbəri $ -beri/ *n plural* **bilberries** [C] a blue-black fruit that grows in Northern Europe, or the bush it grows on

bile /baɪl/ *n* [U] **1** a bitter green-brown liquid formed in the LIVER, which helps you to DIGEST fats **2** *literary* anger and hatred

bilge /bɪldʒ/ *n* **1** [C usually plural] the broad bottom part of a ship **2** [U] *old-fashioned informal* nonsense

bi·lin·gual /baɪ'lɪŋgwəl/ *adj* **1** written or spoken in two languages: *a bilingual dictionary* | *The report proposed bilingual education in schools.* **2** able to speak two languages equally well: *Their kids are completely bilingual.* | [+in] *Louis is virtually bilingual in Dutch and German.* —**bilingual** *n* [C]; → monolingual, multilingual

bil·i·ous /'bɪliəs/ *adj* **1** feeling as if you might VOMIT: *I got up feeling bilious and with a terrible headache.* |

She felt a bilious attack coming on. **2** very unpleasant: *bilious green walls* **3** *literary* bad-tempered —**biliousness** *n* [U]

bilk /bɪlk/ *v* [T] *informal* to cheat someone, especially by taking their money; ▪ **swindle**: **bilk sb out of sth** *Consumers were bilked out of more than $15,000.*

bill¹ [S1] [W1] /bɪl/ *n* [C]
1 REQUEST FOR PAYMENT a written list showing how much you have to pay for services you have received, work that has been done etc: [+for] *The bill for the repairs came to $650.* | **phone/electricity/gas/water etc bill** *Have you paid the phone bill?*
2 RESTAURANT *especially BrE* a list showing how much you have to pay for food you have eaten in a restaurant; ▪ **check** *AmE*: *Could we have the bill, please?*
3 LAW a written proposal for a new law, which is brought to a parliament so that it can be discussed: **approve/pass/veto a bill** *The House of Representatives passed a new gun-control bill.* | *The senator introduced a bill that would increase the minimum wage.*
4 MONEY *AmE* a piece of paper money; ▪ **note** *BrE*; → **coin**: *a five-dollar bill*
5 fit/fill the bill to be exactly what you need: *This car fits the bill perfectly. It's cheap and gets good mileage.*
6 CONCERT/SHOW ETC a programme of entertainment at a theatre, concert, cinema etc, with details of who is performing, what is being shown etc: *Tricia topped the bill* (=was the most important performer) *at the Children's Variety Show.*
7 give sb/sth a clean bill of health to officially state that someone is in good health or that something is working correctly: *Maddox was given a clean bill of health.*
8 BIRD a bird's beak → see picture at BIRD OF PREY
9 ADVERTISEMENT a printed notice advertising an event
10 PART OF A HAT *AmE* the front part that sticks out on a hat such as a BASEBALL CAP
11 the (old) bill *BrE spoken* the police

bill² *v* [T] **1** to send someone a bill: *Clients will be billed monthly.* | **bill sb for sth** *I was billed for equipment that I didn't order.* **2 be billed to do sth** if someone is billed to appear, perform etc somewhere, it has been planned and advertised that they will do this: *Johnson was billed to speak at two conferences.* **3 bill and coo** *old-fashioned* if two lovers are billing and cooing, they are kissing and talking softly
bill sth as sth *phr v* to advertise or describe something in a particular way: *The castle bills itself as the oldest in England.*

bill·board /'bɪlbɔːd $ -bɔːrd/ *n* [C] a large sign used for advertising; ▪ **hoarding** *BrE*; → see picture at TOWN

bil·let¹ /'bɪlɪt/ *n* [C] a private house where soldiers are living temporarily

billet² *v* [T] to put soldiers in a private house to live there temporarily

bill·fold /'bɪlfəʊld $ -foʊld/ *n* [C] *AmE* a small flat leather case, used for carrying paper money, CREDIT CARDS etc in your pocket; ▪ **wallet**

bill·hook /'bɪlhʊk/ *n* [C] a tool which has a curved blade with a hooked point, used for cutting off tree branches etc

bil·liards /'bɪljədz $ -ərdz/ *n* [U] a game played on a cloth-covered table in which balls are hit with a CUE (=a long stick) against each other and into pockets at the edge of the table; → **pool, snooker** —**billiard** *adj* [only before noun]: *a billiard table*

bill·ing /'bɪlɪŋ/ *n* **give sb top/star billing** to name a particular performer, actor etc as being the most important person in a show, play etc

bil·lion /'bɪljən/ *number plural* **billion** or **billions** **1** the number 1,000,000,000: *The final cost could be as much as one billion dollars.* | **two/three/four etc billion** *3.5 billion years ago* | *Overseas debt is a staggering £16 billion.* | **billions of pounds/dollars etc** *Many airlines have lost billions of dollars.* **2** an extremely large number of things or people: **a billion** *A billion* stars shone in the night sky. | **billions of sth** *There are billions of things I want to say.* **3** *BrE old use* the number 1,000,000,000,000 —**billionth** *adj* —**billionth** *n* [C]

bil·lion·aire /ˌbɪljəˈneə◂ $ -ˈner◂ / *n* [C] someone who has more than a billion dollars or pounds

bill of ex·change *n plural* **bills of exchange** [C] *technical* a signed document ordering someone to pay someone else a particular amount of money

bill of 'fare *n plural* **bills of fare** [C] *old-fashioned* a list of the food that is served in a restaurant; ⊟ **menu**

bill of 'lading *n plural* **bills of lading** [C] *technical* a list of the goods being carried, especially on a ship

bill of 'rights *n plural* **bills of rights** [C] a written statement of the most important rights of the citizens of a country

bill of 'sale *n plural* **bills of sale** [C] *technical* a written document showing that someone has bought something

bil·low¹ /ˈbɪləʊ $ -loʊ/ *v* [I] **1** also **billow out** if something made of cloth billows, it moves in the wind: *Her long skirt billowed in the breeze.* **2** if a cloud or smoke billows, it rises in a round mass: [+out of/up etc] *There was smoke billowing out of the windows.*

billow² *n* [C usually plural] **1** a moving cloud or mass of something such as smoke or cloth **2** *literary* a wave, especially a very large one

bil·ly /ˈbɪli/ also **bil·ly·can** /ˈbɪlikæn/ *n plural* **billies** [C] *BrE* a pot for cooking or boiling water when you are camping

billy goat *n* [C] a male goat – used especially by or to children; → **nanny goat**

bim·bo /ˈbɪmbəʊ $ -boʊ/ *n plural* **bimbos** [C] *informal* an insulting word for an attractive but unintelligent young woman: *He picked up some bimbo at the club.*

bi·month·ly /baɪˈmʌnθli/ *adj* appearing or happening every two months or twice each month; → **monthly**, **quarterly**: *a bimonthly magazine* —**bimonthly** *adv*

bins

recycling bin

bread bin

wheelie bin *BrE*

kitchen bin *BrE*/
trash can *AmE*

wastepaper basket *BrE*/
wastebasket *AmE*

litter bin *BrE*

dustbin *BrE*/
garbage can *AmE*

bin¹ S2 /bɪn/ *n* [C]
1 *BrE* a container for putting waste in; → **trash can**, **waste paper basket**: *Throw it in the bin.* → DUSTBIN, LITTER BIN

2 a large container for storing things, such as goods in a shop or substances in a factory

bin² *v* **binned**, **binning** [T] *BrE informal* to throw something away: *'What should I do with this letter?' 'Just bin it!'*

bi·na·ry /ˈbaɪnəri/ *adj* **1** **the binary system** a system of counting, used in computers, in which only the numbers 0 and 1 are used **2** consisting of two parts; ⊟ **double**: *a binary star system*

bind¹ /baɪnd/ *v past tense and past participle* **bound** /baʊnd/
1 **TIE/FASTEN** [T] *written* **a)** to tie someone so that they cannot move or escape: *They bound my arms and legs with rope.* | **bound and gagged** (=tied up, and with cloth tied around your mouth so you cannot speak) **b)** also **bind up** to tie things firmly together with cloth or string: *The pile of newspapers was bound with string.*
2 **FORM A CONNECTION** [T] to form a strong emotional or economic connection between two people, countries etc; ⊟ **unite**: **bind sb/sth together** *Their shared experiences in war helped to bind the two communities together.*
3 **MAKE SB DO STH** [T usually passive] if you are bound by an agreement, promise etc, you must do what you have agreed to do or promised to do: *The monks are bound by vows of silence.* | **bind sb to do sth** *Employees are not bound to give their reasons for leaving.*
4 **STICK TOGETHER** [I,T] *technical* to stick together in a mass, or to make small pieces of something stick together: *The flour mixture isn't wet enough to bind properly.* | [+with] *The hydrogen molecule binds with the oxygen molecule.*
5 **BOOK** [T] to fasten the pages of a book together and put them in a cover → BOUND² (9)
6 **STITCH** [T] to sew cloth over the edge of a piece of material, or stitch over it, to strengthen it: *The edges of the blanket were bound with ribbon.*
  bind sb **over** *phr v* [usually passive] *law*
  a) *BrE* if someone is bound over by a court of law, they are warned that if they cause more trouble, they will be legally punished: *The demonstrators were bound over to keep the peace.* **b)** *AmE* if someone is bound over for TRIAL, they are forced by law to appear in a court of law

bind² *n* [singular] *informal* an annoying or difficult situation: *It's a real bind having to look after the children.* | **in a bind** *Caroline was really in a bind.*

bind·er /ˈbaɪndə $ -ər/ *n* **1** [C] a removable cover for holding loose sheets of paper, magazines etc → RING BINDER; → see picture at OFFICE **2** [C] a person or machine that fastens the parts of a book together **3** [C,U] a substance that makes things stick together **4** [C] *AmE* an agreement in which you pay something to show that you intend to buy some property

bind·ing¹ /ˈbaɪndɪŋ/ *adj* **a binding contract/promise/agreement etc** a promise, agreement etc that must be obeyed

binding² *n* **1** [C] a book cover **2** [U] material sewn or stuck along the edge of a piece of cloth for strength or decoration

bind·weed /ˈbaɪndwiːd/ *n* [U] a wild plant that winds itself around other plants

binge¹ /bɪndʒ/ *n* [C] *informal* a short period when you do too much of something, such as eating or drinking: *a drinking binge* | *a week-long binge of shopping* | **on a binge** *Ken's gone on a binge with his mates.*

binge² *v* [I] *informal* to do too much of something, such as eating or drinking, in a short period of time: [+on] *Whenever she's depressed she binges on chocolates.*

bin·go¹ /ˈbɪŋgəʊ $ -goʊ/ *n* [U] a game played for money or prizes in which numbers are chosen by

B

chance and called out, and if you have the right numbers on your card you win: *Vera won £20 at bingo.*

bingo[2] *interjection* used when you have just done something successfully and are pleased: *Bingo! That's the one I've been looking for.*

bin liner *n* [C] *BrE* a plastic bag used inside a BIN for holding waste

bin·man /ˈbɪnmæn/ *n plural* **binmen** /-men/ [C] *BrE* someone who comes to people's houses to collect their waste; ⊟ **garbage collector**

bi·noc·u·lars /bɪˈnɒkjᵿləz, baɪ- $ -ˈnɑːkjᵿlərz/ *n* [plural] a pair of special glasses, that you hold up to your eyes to look at objects that are a long distance away; ⊟ **field glasses**; → see picture at OPTICAL

bi nocular vision *n* [U] *technical* the ability to FOCUS both eyes on one object, which humans, monkeys, and some birds and other animals have

bi·no·mi·al /baɪˈnəʊmiəl $ -ˈnoʊ-/ *n* [C] *technical* a mathematical expression that has two parts connected by the sign + or the sign -, for example $3x + 4y$ or $x - 7$ —**binomial** *adj*

bio- /baɪəʊ, baɪə $ baɪoʊ, baɪə/ *prefix* relating to or using living things: *bio-genetics* | *biophysics*

bi·o·chem·ist /ˌbaɪəʊˈkemɪst $ ˌbaɪoʊ-/ *n* [C] someone who studies or works in biochemistry

bi·o·chem·is·try /ˌbaɪəʊˈkemɪstri $ ˌbaɪoʊ-/ *n* [U] the scientific study of the chemistry of living things —**biochemical** *adj*

bi·o·de·gra·da·ble /ˌbaɪəʊdɪˈɡreɪdəbəl $ ˌbaɪoʊ-/ *adj* materials, chemicals etc that are biodegradable are changed naturally by BACTERIA into substances that do not harm the environment; ⊟ **non biodegradable**: *This carton is made of biodegradable plastic.*

bi·o·di·ver·si·ty /ˌbaɪəʊdaɪˈvɜːsᵻti, -dᵻ- $ ˌbaɪoʊ daɪˈvɜːr-, -dᵻ-/ *n* [U] *technical* the variety of plants and animals in a particular place: *the biodiversity of the rainforest*

bi·o·feed·back /ˌbaɪəʊˈfiːdbæk $ ˌbaɪoʊ-/ *n* [U] a method of helping people to relax by teaching them to control their heart rate, breathing etc, using an instrument attached to the body

bi·og·ra·pher /baɪˈɒɡrəfə $ -ˈɑːɡrəfər/ *n* [C] someone who writes a biography of someone else

bi·og·ra·phy /baɪˈɒɡrəfi $ -ˈɑːɡ-/ *plural* **biographies** *n* **1** [C] a book that tells what has happened in someone's life, written by someone else: [+of] *Boswell's biography of Dr. Johnson* **2** [U] literature that consists of biographies; → **autobiography** —**biographical** /ˌbaɪəˈɡræfᵻkəl◂/ *adj*: *biographical information*

bi·o·log·i·cal /ˌbaɪəˈlɒdʒɪkəl◂ $ -ˈlɑː-/ *adj* **1** relating to the natural processes performed by living things: *the biological functions of the body* | *Depression is both biological and psychological.* **2** **biological weapons/warfare/attack etc** weapons, attacks etc that involve the use of living things, including BACTERIA, to harm other living things: *a ban on chemical and biological weapons* **3** [only before noun] relating to biology: *the biological sciences* **4** **biological parent/father/mother etc** a child's parent through birth, rather than through ADOPTION —**biologically** /-kli/ *adv*

biological clock *n* [singular] **1** *technical* the system in plants and animals that controls when they sleep, eat, produce babies etc; ⊟ **body clock** **2** the idea that when a woman reaches a certain age, she will soon be too old to have a baby: *career women who hear the biological clock ticking*

bi·ol·o·gist /baɪˈɒlədʒᵻst $ -ˈɑːl-/ *n* [C] someone who studies or works in biology

bi·ol·o·gy /baɪˈɒlədʒi $ -ˈɑːl-/ *n* [U] **1** the scientific study of living things: *a degree in biology* | *molecular*

biology **2** the scientific laws that control the life of a particular type of animal, plant etc: *the biology of bacteria*

bi·o·mass /ˈbaɪəʊmæs $ ˈbaɪoʊ-/ *n* [U] *technical* plant and animal matter used to provide power or energy

bi·ome /ˈbaɪəʊm $ -oʊm/ *n* [C] *technical* a type of environment that is described according to the typical weather conditions and plants that exist there

bi·on·ic /baɪˈɒnɪk $ -ˈɑːn-/ *adj* bionic arms, legs etc are electronic and therefore stronger or faster than normal arms etc – often used humorously: *I swear Mom has bionic ears.*

bi·o·phys·ics /ˌbaɪəʊˈfɪzɪks $ ˌbaɪoʊ-/ *n* [U] the scientific study of how PHYSICS relates to biological processes

bi·o·pic /ˈbaɪəʊˌpɪk $ ˈbaɪoʊ-/ *n* [C] *informal* a film that tells the story of someone's life

bi·op·sy /ˈbaɪɒpsi $ -ɑːp-/ *n plural* **biopsies** [C] the removal of cells, TISSUE etc from someone's body in order to find out more about a disease they may have: *a breast biopsy*

bi·o·rhythms /ˈbaɪəʊˌrɪðəmz $ ˈbaɪoʊ-/ *n* [plural] regular changes in the speed at which physical processes happen in your body, which some people believe can affect the way you feel

bi·o·sphere /ˈbaɪəsfɪə $ -sfɪr/ *n* [singular] *technical* the part of the world in which animals, plants etc can live

bi·o·tech·nol·o·gy /ˌbaɪəʊtekˈnɒlədʒi $ ˌbaɪoʊ tekˈnɑː-/ also **bi·o·tech** /ˈbaɪəʊtek $ ˈbaɪoʊ-/ *informal* *n* [U] the use of living things such as cells, BACTERIA etc to make drugs, destroy waste matter etc: *the biotech industries* —**biotechnological** /ˌbaɪəʊteknəˈlɒdʒɪkəl $ ˌbaɪoʊteknəˈlɑː-/ *adj*

bi·par·ti·san /ˌbaɪpɑːtᵻˈzæn $ baɪˈpɑːrtᵻzən/ *adj* involving two political parties, especially parties with opposing views: *a bipartisan committee* | *bipartisan cooperation*

bi·par·tite /baɪˈpɑːtaɪt $ -ˈpɑːr-/ *adj* *formal* involving two different parts or groups: *a bipartite treaty* | *bipartite DNA structures*

bi·ped /ˈbaɪped/ *n* [C] *technical* an animal with two legs, such as a human

bi·plane /ˈbaɪpleɪn/ *n* [C] a type of aircraft with two sets of wings, especially one built in the early 20th century

bi·po·lar /baɪˈpəʊlə $ -ˈpoʊlər/ *adj* [usually before noun] **1** involving two opposing countries, groups etc: *the bipolar view of the world during the Cold War* **2** **bipolar disorder** *technical* MANIC DEPRESSION

bi·ra·cial /ˌbaɪˈreɪʃəl / *adj* *AmE* representing or including people from two different races; ⊟ **mixed race** *BrE*: *biracial families*

birch[1] /bɜːtʃ $ bɜːrtʃ/ *n* **1** [C,U] a tree with smooth BARK (=outer covering) and thin branches, or the wood from this tree **2** **the birch** *BrE* the practice of hitting people with birch sticks as an official punishment → SILVER BIRCH

birch[2] *v* [T] to hit someone with a birch sticks as an official punishment

bird [S2] [W2] /bɜːd $ bɜːrd/ *n* [C] **1** a creature with wings and feathers that can usually fly. Many birds sing and build nests, and female birds lay eggs.: *wild birds* | *The dawn was filled with the sound of birds.* | *a flock of birds* (=a group of birds flying together) | *a wooden bird cage* **2** *BrE informal* a word meaning a young woman, which some people think is offensive **3** **the birds and the bees** the facts about sex – used humorously or to children **4** **a little bird told me (sth)** *informal* used to say that you know something, but you will not say how you found out: *A little bird told me that you've got engaged.* **5** **birds of a feather (flock together)** *informal* used to say that two or more people have similar attitudes, beliefs etc

6 give sb the bird a) *AmE informal* to make a very rude sign at someone by holding your middle finger up **b)** *BrE* to show strong disapproval of someone who is performing or speaking in public by shouting, making rude noises etc
7 a bird in the hand (is worth two in the bush) used to say that it is better to keep what you have than to risk losing it by trying to get more
8 the bird has flown *informal* used to say that the person you are looking for has already left or escaped
9 be (strictly) for the birds *old-fashioned informal* to be silly, useless, or not practical
10 wise/wily/funny/weird etc old bird *old-fashioned informal* a person who seems wise, funny etc
11 do bird *BrE old-fashioned informal* to serve a prison sentence; ▤ **do time** → **early bird** at EARLY¹ (9); → **kill two birds with one stone** at KILL¹ (13)

bird·bath /'bɜːdbɑːθ $ 'bɜːrdbæθ/ n [C] a bowl in a garden that is filled with water for birds to wash in

'bird-brain n [C] *AmE informal* someone who is silly or stupid —**bird-brain** or **birdbrained** adj

'bird dog n [C] *AmE* a dog that is trained to find and return with birds that have been shot for sport; ▤ **gun dog** *BrE*

bird·ie¹ /'bɜːdi $ 'bɜːrdi/ n [C]　**1** *spoken* a word meaning a little bird, used especially by or to children　**2** in golf, a score that is one less than PAR　**3** *AmE* a small object with feathers that you hit across the net in a game of BADMINTON; ▤ **shuttlecock** *BrE*

birdie² v [T] in golf, to get the ball into the hole in one hit less than PAR: *Woods birdied the last two holes to take a 10-stroke lead.*

,bird of 'paradise n plural **birds of paradise** [C]　**1** a brightly coloured bird from New Guinea　**2** a tall orange flower

,bird of 'passage n plural **birds of passage** [C]　**1** *technical* a bird that flies from one area or country to another, according to the seasons　**2** *literary* someone who never stays in the same place for long

birds of prey

beak/bill
eagle
wing
owl
falcon
talon
vulture

,bird of 'prey n plural **birds of prey** [C] a bird that kills other birds or small animals for food

bird·seed /'bɜːdsiːd $ 'bɜːrd-/ n [U] a mixture of seeds for feeding birds

,bird's-eye 'view n [singular]　**1** a view of something from high above it: *Visitors can enjoy a bird's-eye view of the area from the castle turrets.*　**2** a general report or account of something, without many details: *a bird's-eye view of recent research*

bird·shot /'bɜːdʃɒt $ 'bɜːrdʃɑːt/ n [U] a type of very small bullet that is fired in large numbers: *The crowd was dispersed by police using tear gas and birdshot.*

bird·song /'bɜːdsɒŋ $ 'bɜːrdsɒːŋ/ n [U] the musical noises made by birds

'bird ,table n [C] *BrE* a high wooden structure in a garden that you put food on for birds

'bird-,watcher n [C] someone who watches wild birds and tries to recognize different types —**bird-watching** n [U]

bi·ret·ta /bɪ'retə/ n [C] a square cap worn by Roman Catholic priests

bi·ro /'baɪərəʊ $ 'baɪroʊ/ n plural **biros** [C] *trademark BrE* a pen with a small ball at the end that puts ink onto paper; ▤ **ball point**: *a red biro* → PEN¹

birth S2 W2 /bɜːθ $ bɜːrθ/ n
1 give birth **(to sb)** if a woman gives birth, she produces a baby from her body: *Patsy was celebrating last night after giving birth to twins.*
2 [C,U] the time when a baby comes out of its mother's body

at birth
from/since birth
date of birth especially *BrE*
birth date especially *AmE*
place of birth
time of birth
home birth (=when a mother gives birth at home instead of in a hospital)
hospital birth (=when a mother gives birth in hospital)
premature birth (=when a baby is born earlier than it should be)
stillbirth (=when a baby is born dead)
multiple birth (=when a mother gives birth to two babies or more at the same time)
birth weight
birth defect (=something wrong with a baby when it is born)

Congratulations on the birth of your daughter! | *He only weighed 2 kilos at birth.* | *Henry has been blind from birth.* | *What's your date of birth?* | *The exact place of birth is not recorded.* | *They believe that the position of the planets at the time of birth determines the fate of the individual.* | *More and more women are choosing to have home births.* | *Smoking in pregnancy has been linked to premature birth.* | *the association between birth weight and blood pressure* | *The drug was found to cause serious birth defects.*

3 [singular] the time when something new starts to exist: [+of] *the birth of a nation* | *The film gave birth to a TV show of the same name.*
4 [U] the character, language, social position etc that you have because of the family or country you come from: *a woman of noble birth* | **French/German etc by birth**

'birth cer,tificate n [C] an official document showing when and where you were born, and your parents' names

'birth con,trol n [U] the practice of controlling the number of children you have; ▤ **contraception**: *a safe method of birth control*

birth·day S2 W3 /'bɜːθdeɪ $ 'bɜːr-/ n [C]
1 your birthday is a day that is an exact number of years after the day you were born: *He was in Kansas to celebrate his 74th birthday.* | **happy birthday!** (=what you say on someone's birthday) | **birthday card/gift/party etc** *Are you going to Anne's birthday party?* | **the birthday girl/boy** *informal* (=the person whose birthday it is)
2 a day that is an exact number of years since an organization was established or an event first happened; → **anniversary**: *The City of Cleveland Orchestra is celebrating its 200th birthday.*
3 in your birthday suit *informal* not wearing any clothes – used humorously

'birth ,father n [C] a child's natural father, rather than a man who has become the child's legal father through ADOPTION

birth·ing /'bɜːθɪŋ $ 'bɜːrθ-/ n [U] the process of giving birth to a baby: *a birthing class*

birth·mark /'bɜːθmɑːk $ 'bɜːrθmɑːrk/ n [C] a permanent mark on your skin that you have had since you were born: *Paul had a birthmark on his left cheek.*

'birth ˌmother n [C] a child's natural mother, rather than a woman who has become the child's legal mother through ADOPTION

'birth ˌparent n [C] a child's natural mother or father, rather than someone who has become the child's legal mother or father through ADOPTION

birth·place /'bɜːθpleɪs $ 'bɜːrθ-/ n [C usually singular] **1** the place where someone was born, used especially when talking about someone famous: *Stratford-upon-Avon was Shakespeare's birthplace.* **2** the place where something first started to happen or exist: *New Orleans is the birthplace of jazz.*

birth·rate /'bɜːθreɪt $ 'bɜːrθ-/ n [C] the number of births for every 100 or every 1000 people in a particular year in a particular place: *the rising birthrate*

birth·right /'bɜːθraɪt $ 'bɜːrθ-/ n [C usually singular] something such as a right, property, money etc that you believe you should have because of the family or country you belong to: *Freedom of speech is every American's birthright.* | *Charles felt cheated of his birthright.*

bis·cuit S3 /'bɪskət/ n
1 [C] *BrE* a small thin dry cake that is usually sweet and made for one person to eat; ☰ **cookie** *AmE*: *a packet of chocolate biscuits* | *cheese and biscuits*
2 [C] *AmE* a type of soft bread baked in small round pieces
3 [U] a light brown colour
4 take the biscuit *BrE informal* to be the most surprising, annoying etc thing you have ever heard: *I've heard some excuses, but this really takes the biscuit!*

bi·sect /baɪ'sekt $ 'baɪsekt/ v [T] *formal* to divide something into two equal parts: *A long cobbled street bisects the town from east to west.*

bi·sex·u·al /baɪ'sekʃuəl/ adj **1** sexually attracted to both men and women **2** *technical* having features of both males and females: *a bisexual plant* —**bisexual** n [C] —**bisexuality** /ˌbaɪsekʃu'æləti/ n [U]

bish·op W3 /'bɪʃəp/ n [C]
1 a priest with a high rank in some Christian religions, who is the head of all the churches and priests in a large area: *the Bishop of Durham*
2 a piece in the game of CHESS that can be moved sideways over any number of squares of the same colour → see picture at CHESS

bish·op·ric /'bɪʃəprɪk/ n [C] **1** the area that a bishop is in charge of; ☰ **diocese** **2** the position of being a bishop

bis·muth /'bɪzməθ/ n [U] a grey-white metal that is often used in medicines. It is a chemical ELEMENT: symbol Bi.

bi·son /'baɪsən/ n plural **bison** or **bisons** [C] an animal like a large cow with hair on its head and shoulders; → **buffalo**

bisque /bɪsk/ n [U] a thick creamy soup made from SHELLFISH: *lobster bisque*

bis·tro /'biːstrəʊ $ -troʊ/ n plural **bistros** [C] a small restaurant or bar: *a French bistro*

bit¹ S1 W1 /bɪt/ adv, pron
1 ONLY SLIGHTLY a bit especially *BrE* **a)** slightly or to a small degree; ☰ **a little**: *Could you turn the TV up a bit?* | *Try to relax a bit.* | *That's a bit odd.* | *'Are you sorry to be leaving?' 'Yes, I am a bit.'* | *Aren't you being a little bit unfair?* | *I think you're a bit too young to be watching this.* | *She looks a bit like my sister.* | *a bit better/older/easier etc I feel a bit better now.* **b)** sometimes, but not very often: *I used to act a bit when I was younger.*
2 AMOUNT a bit especially *BrE informal* a small amount

of a substance or of something that is not a physical object; ☰ **a little**: [+of] *I may need a bit of help.* | *He still likes to do a bit of gardening.* | *I want to spend a bit of time with him before he goes.* | *With a bit of luck we should have finished by five o'clock.* | *Everyone needs a little bit of encouragement.* | *'Would you like cream in your coffee?' 'Yes please, just a bit.'* | *a bit more/less Can we have a bit less noise please?;* → see box at FEW
3 QUITE A LOT quite a bit also a good bit *BrE* a fairly large amount or to a fairly large degree: *She's quite a bit older than you, isn't she?* | *He knows quite a bit about painting.* | [+of] *I expect you do quite a bit of travelling?* | *quite a bit more/less They're worth quite a bit more than I thought.*
4 TIME/DISTANCE a bit especially *BrE* a short period of time or a short distance; ☰ **a while**: *You'll have to wait a bit.* | **in a bit** *I'll see you in a bit.* | **for a bit** *We sat around for a bit chatting.* | *I walked on a bit and then turned back.*
5 a bit of a sth especially *BrE* used to show that the way you describe something is only true to a limited degree: *The news came as a bit of a shock.* | *I felt a bit of a fool.* | *It looks like they left in a bit of a hurry.*
6 not a bit/not one bit especially *BrE* not at all: *You're not a bit like your brother.* | *Am I cross? No, not a bit of it.* | *I'm not in the least bit interested in whose fault it is.* | *Well, you haven't surprised me, not one bit.*
7 every bit as important/bad/good etc especially *BrE* used to emphasize that something is equally important, bad etc as something else: *Jodi plays every bit as well as the men.*
8 bit by bit especially *BrE* gradually: *Bit by bit, I was starting to change my mind.*
9 a/one bit at a time especially *BrE* in several small parts or stages: *Try to improve your lifestyle a bit at a time.*
10 take a bit of doing/explaining etc *BrE* to be difficult to do, explain etc: *The new system took a bit of getting used to.*
11 be a bit much *BrE* to be unacceptable, impolite, or unfair: *It's a bit much when he criticizes us for doing something that he does himself.*
12 be a bit of all right *BrE informal* used to say that someone is sexually attractive
13 bit on the side *BrE informal* someone's bit on the side is a person they are having a sexual relationship with, even though they already have a wife, husband, or partner – used humorously or to show disapproval: *She stayed in the hope that he'd tire of his bit on the side.*
14 a bit of stuff/fluff/skirt *BrE informal not polite* offensive expressions meaning a young woman, especially one who is sexually attractive
15 a bit of rough *BrE informal* someone of a lower social class that someone has a sexual relationship with – used humorously

---

WORD CHOICE: a bit, a bit of
Use **a bit** before an adjective, not before a noun, nor before an adjective+noun: *He's a bit shy (NOT a bit shy man).*
Before a noun or adjective+noun, use **a bit of**: *Let's listen to a bit of music (NOT a bit music).* | *It was a bit of a strange decision (NOT a bit strange decision).*
You can also use **a bit** after the main verb: *I cried a bit (NOT a bit cried).*

---

bit² S1 W1 n [C]
1 PIECE a small piece of something: [+of] *bits of broken glass* | *He wedged the door open with a bit of wood.* | **break/rip/shake etc sth to bits** *The aircraft was blown to bits.* | *He's taken the engine to bits.* | **fall/come to bits** *The old house was falling to bits.*
2 PART *BrE informal* a part of something larger: *This is the boring bit.* | [+of] *We did the last bit of the journey on foot.* | [+about] *Did you like the bit about the monkey?*
3 to bits *BrE informal* very much or extremely: *Mark's a darling, I love him to bits.* | **thrilled/chuffed/pleased to bits** *I've always wanted a car, so I'm thrilled to bits.*

4 COMPUTER the smallest unit of information that a computer uses: *a 32-bit processor*
5 TOOL the sharp part of a tool for cutting or making holes: *a drill bit*
6 HORSE the metal bar attached to a horse's BRIDLE that is put into its mouth and used to control it → **be champing at the bit** at CHAMP¹ (2)
7 bits and pieces also **bits and bobs** *BrE informal* any small things of various kinds: *Let me get all my bits and pieces together.*
8 do your bit *informal* to do a fair share of the work, effort etc that is needed to achieve something good or important: *Everyone should do their bit for the environment.*
9 get the bit between your teeth *BrE*; **take the bit between your teeth** *AmE* to do something or deal with something in a very determined way, so that you are not likely to stop until it is done
10 MONEY a) **two bits/four bits** *AmE informal* 25 cents or 50 cents **b)** *BrE old-fashioned* a small coin: *a three-penny bit*
11 pull sth to bits *BrE informal* to criticize something strongly: *The critics pulled his new play to bits.*
12 TYPICAL BEHAVIOUR/EXPERIENCE *informal* used to mean a kind of behaviour or experience that is typical of someone or something: **the (whole) student/movie star/travelling etc bit** *Then she gave us the concerned mother bit.*

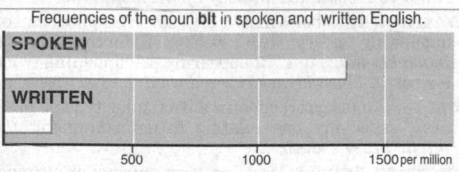

Frequencies of the noun **blt** in spoken and written English.

SPOKEN			
WRITTEN			
500	1000	1500 per million	

This graph shows that the noun **bit** is much more common in spoken English than in written English. This is because **a bit** is more common than **a little** in spoken English, and **bit** is used in a lot of common spoken phrases.

bit³ the past tense of BITE

bitch¹ /bɪtʃ/ *n* [C] **1** *especially BrE* a female dog **2** *informal* an insulting word for a woman that you dislike or think is unpleasant – also used humorously between friends: *The silly bitch went and told the police.* | *Ooh, you're such a bitch!* **3** *informal* something that causes problems or difficulties: *I love that silk dress, but it's a bitch to wash.* → SON OF A BITCH; → **life's a bitch** at LIFE (20)

bitch² *v* [I] *informal* **1** to make unpleasant remarks about someone: [+about] *He never bitches about other members of the team.* **2** *AmE* to complain continuously: *Stop bitching!* | [+at] *He's always bitching at me.*

bitch·in, **bitching** /ˈbɪtʃən/ *adj AmE spoken informal* very good: *That guy has one bitchin truck.*

bitch·y /ˈbɪtʃi/ *adj* unkind and unpleasant about other people; ▣ **catty**: *a bitchy remark* | *She can be really bitchy sometimes.* —**bitchily** *adv* —**bitchiness** *n* [U]

bite¹ S2 /baɪt/ *v past tense* **bit** /bɪt/ *past participle* **bitten** /ˈbɪtn/ *present participle* **biting**
1 TEETH [I,T] to use your teeth to cut, crush, or chew something: *The dog bit him and made his hand bleed.* | [+into/through/at/down] *She bit into a croissant and took a sip of coffee.* | *An adult conger eel can easily bite through a man's leg.* | *Nina pushed her fist into her mouth and bit down hard.* | **bite sth off** *a man whose arm was bitten off by an alligator* | **bite your nails** (=bite the nails on your fingers, especially because you are nervous) *I wish I could stop biting my nails.* | **bite your lip** (=because you are upset or not sure what to say) *She paused uncertainly, biting her lip.*
2 INSECT/SNAKE [I,T] to injure someone by making a hole in their skin; → **sting**: *I think I've been bitten.* | *The dog's been badly bitten by fleas.* | *Spiders generally bite only in self-defence.*
3 PRESS HARD [I] if an object bites into a surface, it presses firmly into it and does not move or slip: [+into]

bite

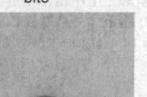

bite   chew

peck   nibble

The hooves of the galloping horses had bitten deep into the soft earth. | *He wore boots that bit into the ice.*
4 EFFECT [I] to start to have an unpleasant effect: *The new tobacco taxes have begun to bite.* | [+into] *The recession is biting into the music industry.*
5 ACCEPT [I] to believe what someone tells you or to buy something they are selling, especially when they have persuaded you to do this: *The new camcorders were withdrawn after consumers failed to bite.*
6 FISH [I] if a fish bites, it takes food from a hook and so gets caught: *The fish just aren't biting today.*
7 bite your tongue to stop yourself from saying what you really think, even though this is difficult: *She should have bitten her tongue.*
8 bite the dust *informal* to die, fail, or be defeated: *Italy's championship hopes eventually bit the dust.*
9 bite the bullet *informal* to start dealing with an unpleasant or dangerous situation because you cannot avoid it any longer: *I finally bit the bullet and left.*
10 bite off more than you can chew to try to do more than you are able to do
11 he/she won't bite *spoken* used to say that there is no need to be afraid of someone, especially someone in authority: *Well go and ask him – he won't bite!*
12 what's biting you/her etc? *spoken* used to ask why someone is annoyed or upset
13 sth/sb bites *spoken not polite* used to say that you dislike someone or something very much or think that something is very bad
14 once bitten, twice shy used to say that if you have failed or been hurt once, you will be more careful next time
15 bite the hand that feeds you to harm someone who has helped or supported you
16 be bitten by the showbiz/travel/flying etc bug to develop a very strong interest in something → **bite sb's head off** at HEAD¹ (33) → NAIL-BITING
  bite back *phr v*
1 bite sth ⇔ back to stop yourself from saying or showing what you really think: *Tamar bit back the retort which sprang to her lips.*
2 to react strongly and angrily to something: [+at] *Determined to bite back at car thieves, he wired his car to an electric fence.*

bite² S3 *n*
1 USING TEETH [C] the act of cutting or crushing something with your teeth: *Antonio devoured half his burger in one bite.* | **take/have a bite (of sth/out of sth)**

1 000, 2 000, 3 000, most frequent words in S poken and W ritten English

She picked up the sandwich and took a bite. | *Can I have a bite of your apple?* | **give sb a bite** *Some fish can give you a nasty bite.* | *Her body was covered in* **bite marks**.
2 WOUND [C] a small hole made where an animal or insect has bitten you: **snake/mosquito/ant etc bites** | [+of] *The infection is transmitted by the bite of a mosquito.*
3 a bite (to eat) *informal* a small meal: *We had a bite to eat and a couple of drinks before the flight.*
4 TASTE [U] a pleasantly sharp taste: *Goat's cheese adds extra bite to any pasta dish.*
5 COLD [singular] a feeling of coldness: *There was no mistaking the approach of winter; he could feel its bite.*
6 STRONG EFFECT [U] a special quality in a performance, piece of writing etc that makes its arguments very effective and likely to persuade people: *The film gains incisive bite from Sellers' performance as the union chief.*
7 FISH [C] when a fish takes the food from a hook: *Sometimes I sit for hours and never get a bite.*
8 another/a second bite at the cherry *BrE* a second chance to do something
9 JAW [C usually singular] *technical* the way that a person or animal's top and bottom teeth touch when their mouth is closed: *Our dentist said that Emmy should wear a brace to improve her bite.* → LOVE BITE, SOUND BITE; → sb's bark is worse than their bite at BARK² (4)

bite-sized also **bite-size** *adj* [only before noun] small enough to put into your mouth to eat: *sushi served in convenient* **bite-size pieces**

bit·ing /ˈbaɪtɪŋ/ *adj* **1** a biting wind is unpleasantly cold; ◨ icy: *A biting wind blew down from the hills.* **2** a biting criticism, remark etc is cruel or unkind: *a biting satire on corruption* —**bitingly** *adv*

bit·map /ˈbɪtmæp/ *n* [C] written abbreviation **BMP** *technical* a computer image that is stored or printed as an arrangement of BITS: *bitmap fonts* —**bitmapped** *adj*: *bitmapped graphics*

bit part *n* [C] a small and unimportant acting job in a play or film: *He's had bit parts in a couple of soaps.*

bit player *n* [C] someone who is not important and who has little influence in a particular situation: *Although he was NRC chairman, Hervey was strictly a bit player in government.*

bit·ten /ˈbɪtn/ the past participle of BITE

bit·ter¹ S3 W3 /ˈbɪtə $ -ər/ *adj*
1 feeling angry, jealous, and upset because you think you have been treated unfairly; → bitterly: [+about] *I feel very* **bitter** *about what has happened.* | *a bitter and vindictive old man*
2 [only before noun] making you feel very unhappy and upset; → bitterly: **a bitter disappointment/blow** *If he failed, it would be a* **bitter disappointment** *to his parents.* | *His photo stirred up bitter memories.* | **from bitter experience** (=because of your own very unpleasant experiences) *She* **knew from bitter experience** *that it would be impossible to talk it over with Julian.*
3 a bitter argument, battle etc is one in which people oppose or criticize each other with strong feelings of hate and anger: **bitter dispute/battle/struggle etc** *The couple are locked in a* **bitter battle** *for custody of the children.* | *The government faces* **bitter opposition** *to these policies.* | *The countries are still* **bitter enemies**.
4 having a sharp strong taste like black coffee without sugar; → sour; sweet: *Enjoy the beer's* **bitter taste** *as you slowly drink it.* | *bitter chocolate*
5 unpleasantly cold; → bitterly: *a bitter wind* | *the* **bitter cold** *of the Midwestern winters*
6 to the bitter end continuing until the end, even though this is difficult: *Employees have vowed to* **fight** *the closure* **to the bitter end**.
7 a bitter pill (to swallow) something very unpleasant that you must accept: *The knowledge that his friends no longer trusted him was a* **bitter pill** *to swallow.* —**bitterness** *n* [U]

bitter² *n* **1** [C,U] *BrE* a type of dark beer that is popular in Britain, or a glass of this: *A pint of bitter, please.* **2 bitters** [U] a strong bitter liquid made from plants that is added to alcoholic drinks

bit·ter·ly /ˈbɪtəli $ -ər-/ *adv* **1** in a way that produces or shows feelings of great sadness or anger: *He complained bitterly about his exam grades.* | *I was bitterly disappointed.* | *The march was bitterly opposed by local residents.* **2 bitterly cold** very cold

bit·ter·sweet /ˌbɪtəˈswiːt◂ $ -tər-/ *adj* **1** feelings, memories, or experiences that are bittersweet are happy and sad at the same time: *bittersweet memories of childhood* **2** a taste or smell that is bittersweet is both sweet and bitter at the same time

bit·ty /ˈbɪti/ *adj BrE* having too many small parts that do not seem to be related or connected to each other: *I thought the film was rather bitty.* —**bittiness** *n* [U]

bi·tu·men /ˈbɪtʃʊmən $ bə̀ˈtuː-/ *n* [U] a dark sticky substance that is used for making the surface of roads —**bituminous** /bə̀ˈtjuːmə̀nəs $ -ˈtuː-/ *adj*

bi·valve /ˈbaɪvælv/ *n* [C] *technical* any sea animal that has two shells joined together: *bivalve molluscs*

biv·ou·ac¹ /ˈbɪvuːæk/ *n* [C] a temporary camp built outside without any tents

bivouac² *v* **bivouacked, bivouacking** [I] to spend the night outside without tents in a temporary camp: *The climbers bivouacked halfway up the mountain.*

bi·week·ly /ˌbaɪˈwiːkliː◂ / *adj, adv* **1** appearing or happening every two weeks; ◨ **fortnightly**: *a bi-weekly magazine* **2** appearing or happening twice a week: *a bi-weekly television drama*

biz /bɪz/ *n* [singular] *informal* a particular type of business, especially one relating to entertainment: *the music biz* → SHOWBIZ

bi·zarre /bə̀ˈzɑː $ -ˈzɑːr/ *adj* very unusual or strange: *a bizarre coincidence* | *dancers in rather bizarre costumes* —**bizarrely** *adv*; → see box at UNUSUAL

blab /blæb/ *v* **blabbed, blabbing** [I] *informal* to tell someone something that should be kept secret: [+to] *This is not something you go blabbing to your friends about.*

blab·ber /ˈblæbə $ -ər/ *v* [I] *informal* to talk in a silly or annoying way for a long time: [+on] *I wish she'd stop blabbering on about her boyfriends.*

blab·ber·mouth /ˈblæbəmaʊθ $ -ər-/ *n* [C] *informal* someone who tells secrets because they always talk too much

black¹ S1 W1 /blæk/ *adj* **comparative blacker**, *superlative* **blackest**
1 COLOUR having the darkest colour, like coal or night: *a black evening dress* | **jet/inky black** (=very dark) *jet black hair*
2 NO LIGHT very dark because there is no light: *It was still* **pitch black** (=very dark) *at that time of the morning.*
3 PEOPLE also **Black a)** belonging to the race of people who originally came from Africa and who have dark brown skin; → white: *Over half the students are black.* **b)** [only before noun] relating to black people: *politics from a black perspective* | *Black and Asian music*
4 DRINK [only before noun] black coffee or tea does not have milk in it; ◨ white: *Black coffee, no sugar, please.*
5 DIRTY *informal* very dirty: **be black with soot/dirt/age etc**
6 WITHOUT HOPE sad and without hope for the future: *the blackest period of European history* | *a mood of black despair* | *It's been another* **black day** *for the car industry with more job losses announced.*
7 HUMOUR making jokes about serious subjects, especially death: *a very black joke*
8 ANGRY [only before noun] full of feelings of anger or hate; → blackly: *Denise gave me a black look.*
9 a black mark (against sb) if there is a black mark against you, someone has a bad opinion of you because of something you have done

10 not be as black as you are painted not to be as bad as people say you are

11 **BAD** *literary* very bad: *black deeds* —**blackness** *n* [C]

black² *n* **1** [C,U] the dark colour of coal or night: *You look good wearing black.* | *thick fur patterned in blacks and browns* → COAL-BLACK **2** [C] also **Black** someone who belongs to the race of people who originally came from Africa and who have dark brown skin; → white: *laws that discriminated against blacks* **3 be in the black** to have money in your bank account; ■ **be in the red**

black³ *v* [T] **1** *BrE* if a TRADE UNION blacks goods or a company, it refuses to work with them: *The union has blacked all non-urgent work.* **2** *old-fashioned* to make something black

black out *phr v* **1** to become UNCONSCIOUS; ■ **faint**, **pass out**: *For a few seconds, he thought he was going to black out.* **2 black sth ⇔ out** to put a dark mark over something so that it cannot be seen: *The censors had blacked out several words.* **3 black sth ⇔ out** to hide or turn off all the lights in a town or city, especially during war; → **blackout**

black and 'blue *adj* skin that is black and blue has BRUISES (=dark marks) on it as a result of being hit: *If you do that again, I'll beat you back and blue.*

black and 'white *adj* **1** showing pictures or images only in black, white, and grey; → colour: *black and white photos* | *an old black and white TV* **2 black and white** considering things in a way that is too simple and as if things are either completely good or completely bad: *There's still a tendency to see the issues in black and white.* **3 in black and white** in written form, and therefore definite: *Once it's down in black and white, you can't forget it.*

black 'art *n* [C] also **the black arts** [plural] BLACK MAGIC

black·ball /'blækbɔːl $ -bɔːl/ *v* [T] to vote against someone, especially so that they cannot join a club or social group

black belt *n* [C] **1** a high rank in sports such as JUDO and KARATE **2** someone who has this rank: [+in] *Sandy's a black belt in judo.*

black·ber·ry /'blækbəri $ -beri/ *n plural* **blackberries** [C] a small black or purple BERRY from a bush that has THORNS (=sharp points)

black·bird /'blækbɜːd $ -bɜːrd/ *n* [C] a common European and American bird, the male of which is completely black

black·board /'blækbɔːd $ -bɔːrd/ *n* [C] a board with a dark smooth surface, used in schools for writing on with CHALK; → **whiteboard**

black 'box *n* [C] *informal* a piece of equipment on an aircraft that records what happens on a flight and can be used to discover the cause of accidents; ■ **flight recorder**

black 'comedy *n* [C,U] a play, story etc that is funny, but also shows the unpleasant side of human life

black·cur·rant /ˌblæk'kʌrənt◂ $ -'kɜːr-/ *n* [C] a small blue-black BERRY that grows in bunches on a bush

Black 'Death *n* **the Black Death** the illness that killed large numbers of people in Europe and Asia in the 14th century → BUBONIC PLAGUE, PLAGUE¹ (2)

black e'conomy *n* [singular] business activity that takes place secretly, especially in order to avoid tax; → **black market**

black·en /'blækən/ *v* **1** [I,T] to become black, or make something black: *The thunder became louder and the sky blackened.* **2 blacken sb's name/character/reputation** to say unpleasant things about someone in order to make other people have a bad opinion of them

Black 'English *n* [U] the variety of English spoken by some black people in the US

black 'eye *n* [C] if you have a black eye, you have a dark area around your eye because you have been hit: *Jack looked like someone had given him a black eye.*

black-eyed 'bean, **black-eyed 'pea** *n* [C] a small white bean with a black spot on it

black 'gold *n* [U] *informal* oil

black·guard /'blægɑːd, -əd $ -ərd, -ɑːrd/ *n* [C] *old use* a man who treats other people very badly

black·head /'blækhed/ *n* [C] a small dark spot on the skin, with a black centre

black 'hole *n* [C] **1** an area in outer space into which everything near it, including light, is pulled **2** *informal* something that uses up a lot of money: *I'm worried that the project could become a financial black hole.*

black 'humour *n* [U] jokes or funny stories that deal with the unpleasant parts of human life

black 'ice *n* [U] an area of ice that is very difficult to see: *Driving conditions are dangerous, with black ice in many areas.*

black·jack /'blækdʒæk/ *n* **1** [U] a card game, usually played for money, in which you try to get as close to 21 points as possible **2** [C] a weapon like a stick covered with leather, used to hit people

black·leg /'blækleg/ *n* [C] *BrE* someone who continues to work when other workers are on STRIKE - used to show disapproval

black·list¹ /'blæklɪst/ *v* [T] to put a person, country, product etc on a blacklist: *Many people in the industry were blacklisted for their alleged communist sympathies.*

blacklist² *n* [C] a list of people, countries, products etc that are disapproved of, and should therefore be avoided or punished: *Friends of the Earth have produced a blacklist of environmentally damaging products.*

black 'magic *n* [U] magic that is believed to use the power of the Devil for evil purposes; → white magic

black·mail¹ /'blækmeɪl/ *n* [U] **1** when someone tries to get money from you or make you do what they want by threatening to tell other people your secrets **2** when someone tries to make you do what they want by making threats or by making you feel guilty if you do not do it: *She had already tried emotional blackmail* (=tried to make him feel guilty) *to stop him leaving.*

blackmail² *v* [T] to use blackmail against someone: *He was jailed for four years for blackmailing gay businessmen.* | **blackmail sb into (doing) sth** *I refuse to be blackmailed into making a quick decision.* —**blackmailer** *n* [C]

black Ma·ri·a /ˌblæk mə'raɪə/ *n* [C] *BrE* a vehicle used by police in the past to transport prisoners

black 'market *n* [C] the system by which people illegally buy and sell foreign money, goods that are difficult to obtain etc: [+in] *There was a thriving black market in foreign currency.* | *Many foods were only available on the black market.* | *black market cigarettes*; → black economy

black market'eer *n* [C] someone who sells things on the black market

Black 'Muslim *n* [C] a member of a group of black people who believe in the religion of Islam and want a separate black society

black·out /'blækaʊt/ *n* [C] **1** a period of darkness caused by a failure of the electricity supply; ■ **power cut** **2** a situation in which particular pieces of news or information are not allowed to be reported: *As the crisis worsened, the authorities imposed a news blackout.* **3** a period during a war when all the lights in a town or city must be turned off **4** if someone has a blackout, they suddenly become unconscious

black 'pepper *n* [U] pepper made from crushed seeds from which the dark outer covering has not been removed; → white pepper

black 'pudding *n* [C,U] *BrE* a kind of thick dark SAUSAGE made from animal blood and fat

black 'sheep n [C usually singular] someone who is regarded by other members of their family or group as a failure or embarrassment: *Amy's always been the black sheep of the family*.

black·smith /'blæk,smιθ/ n [C] someone who makes and repairs things made of iron, especially HORSESHOES

black·spot /'blækspɒt $ -spɑːt/ n [C] BrE a place or area where there are more problems than usual: *Arbroath is now the unemployment blackspot of north-east Scotland.* | *an accident blackspot* (=where there are a lot of road accidents)

black·thorn /'blækθɔːn $ -θɔːrn/ n [C] a European bush that has small white flowers

black-'tie adj a black-tie event is one at which people wear special formal clothes, such as TUXEDOS for men; → **white tie**

black·top /'blæktɒp $ -tɑːp/ n AmE **1** [U] a thick black sticky substance that becomes hard as it dries, used to cover roads; ☐ **tarmac** BrE **2 the blacktop** the surface of a road covered by this substance: *We left the blacktop and drove along a forest road.*

black 'widow n [C] a very poisonous type of SPIDER that is black with red marks

blad·der /'blædə $ -ər/ n [C] **1** the organ in your body that holds URINE (=waste liquid) until it is passed out of your body **2** a bag of skin, leather, or rubber, for example inside a football, that can be filled with air or liquid → GALL BLADDER

blad·dered /'blædəd $ -ərd/ adj [not before noun] BrE informal very drunk: *Geoff got completely bladdered last night.*

blade [S3] /bleɪd/ n [C]

1 the flat cutting part of a tool or weapon; → **edge**: [+of] *The blade of the knife flashed in the moonlight.* | *a razor blade*

2 the flat wide part of an object that pushes against air or water: *the blade of an oar*

3 blade of grass a single thin flat piece of grass

4 the metal part on the bottom of an ICE-SKATE → SHOULDER BLADE

blad·er /'bleɪdə $ -ər/ n [C] informal someone who SKATES or ROLLERBLADES

blag /blæg/ v **blagged, blagging** [I,T] BrE informal to obtain something you want by talking in a clever way: *He blagged his way in by saying he was a friend of the owner.*

blag·ger /'blægə $ -ər/ n [C] BrE informal someone who gets something they want by lying to people in a clever way

blah¹ [S2] /blɑː/ n

1 blah, blah, blah spoken used when you do not need to complete what you are saying because it is boring or because the person you are talking to already knows it: *You know how Michelle talks: 'Tommy did this, and Jesse did that, blah, blah, blah.'*

2 [U] BrE spoken remarks or statements that are boring and do not mean much: *the usual blah about everyone working harder*

3 the blahs [plural] AmE informal a feeling of being sad and bored: *a case of the winter blahs*

blah² adj AmE spoken informal **1** not having an interesting taste, appearance, character etc: *The chili was kind of blah.* **2** slightly ill or unhappy: *I feel really blah today.*

blame¹ [S2] [W3] /bleɪm/ v [T]

1 to say or think that someone or something is responsible for something bad: *Don't blame me – it's not my fault.* | *I blame his mother. She does everything for him.* | **blame sb/sth for sth** *Marie still blames herself for Patrick's death.* | *The report blames poor safety standards for the accident.* | *The decision to increase interest rates was **widely blamed** (=blamed by many people) for the crisis.* | **blame sth on sb/sth** *One of the computers is broken and she's blaming it on me.* | *The*

crash was blamed on pilot error.

2 sb/sth is to blame (for sth) used to say that someone or something is responsible for something bad: *Officials believe that more than one person may be to blame for the fire.* | **partly/largely/entirely etc to blame** *Television is partly to blame.*

3 I don't blame sb/you you can hardly blame him etc spoken used to say that you think it was right or reasonable for someone to do what they did: *'She's left her husband.' 'I don't blame her, after the way he treated her.'* | *You can hardly blame him for not waiting. You were in there for an hour.*

4 don't blame me spoken used when you are advising someone not to do something but you think that they will do it in spite of your advice: *Buy it then, but don't blame me when it breaks down.*

5 sb only has himself/herself to blame spoken used to say that someone's problems are their own fault: *If he fails his exams, he'll only have himself to blame.*

blame² n [U] responsibility for a mistake or for something bad

> **take/accept the blame** (=say that something is your fault)
> **get the blame** (=be blamed)
> **put/lay/pin/place the blame (for sth) on sb** (=blame someone, especially for something that is not their fault)
> **share the blame**
> **apportion/assign blame** formal (=blame someone)
> **shift the blame (onto sb)** (=blame someone else for something you did)
> **the blame lies with sb** (=used to say that someone did something)

[+for] *Do you **accept** any **blame** for what happened?* | *You can't expect Terry to **take** all **the blame**.* | *I always **get the blame** for his mistakes!* | *She stole the money but she's trying to **put the blame on** me.* | *There was no safety barrier, but the court ruled that the child's parents must **share the blame** for the accident.* | *We are not here to **apportion blame**.* | *It's no use trying to **shift the blame** onto other people.* | *In my opinion, **the blame lies with** the police.*; → see box at FAULT¹

blame·less /'bleɪmləs/ adj not guilty of anything bad; ☐ **innocent**: *The police are **not** always **entirely blameless** (=are guilty of doing something bad) in these matters.* | *She had led a **blameless life**.* —**blamelessly** adv

blame·wor·thy /'bleɪm,wɜːði $ -ɜːr-/ adj deserving blame or disapproval: *blameworthy conduct*

blanch /blɑːntʃ $ blæntʃ/ v **1** [T] to put vegetables, fruit, or nuts into boiling water for a short time: *Blanch the peaches and remove the skins.* **2** [I] literary to become pale because you are frightened or shocked: *Patrick visibly blanched.*

blanc·mange /blə'mɒnʒ, -'mɒndʒ $ -'mɑː-/ n [C,U] BrE a cold sweet food made from CORNFLOUR, milk, and sugar; ☐ **pudding** AmE

bland /blænd/ adj **1** without any excitement, strong opinions, or special character; ☐ **dull**: *a few bland comments* **2** food that is bland has very little taste: *a bland diet* —**blandly** adv —**blandness** n [U]

blan·dish·ments /'blændɪʃmənts/ n [plural] formal pleasant things that you say in order to persuade or influence someone: *How sensible she had been to resist his blandishments.*

blank¹ [S3] /blæŋk/ adj

1 without any writing, print, or recorded sound: *Leave the last page blank.* | *a blank cassette*

2 a blank face or look shows no emotion, understanding, or interest; → **blankly**: **blank face/look/expression/eyes** *Zoe looked at me with a blank expression.* | *She gazed at him in blank astonishment.*

3 go blank a) if your mind goes blank, or if you go blank, you are suddenly unable to remember something: *My heart began to race and my mind went blank.* **b)** to stop showing any images, writing etc: *Suddenly the screen went blank.* —**blankness** n [U] → BLANK VERSE

blank² n [C] **1** an empty space on a piece of paper, where you are supposed to write a word or letter: *When you've **filled in the blanks**, hand the form back to me.* **2** **my mind's a blank** *spoken* used to say that you cannot remember something: *I'm trying to think of his name, but my mind's a complete blank.* **3** a CARTRIDGE (=container for a bullet in a gun) that contains an explosive but no bullet: *Soldiers **fired blanks** into the crowd.* → **draw a blank** at DRAW¹ (32)

blank³ v **1** also **blank out** [I] *informal* if you blank, or if your mind blanks, you are suddenly unable to remember something: *I just blanked in the oral exam.* **2** [T] *BrE informal* to ignore someone who you would usually greet or speak to: *Last time I saw Mike Adams he completely blanked me.*

blank sth ⇔ **out** *phr v* **1** to cover something so that it cannot be seen: *The actual names had been blanked out.* **2** to completely forget something, especially deliberately: *I tried to blank out everything he had said.*

blank 'cheque *BrE*; **blank 'check** *AmE* n [C] **1** a cheque that has been signed, but has not had the amount written on it **2** **give sb a blank cheque** *BrE* /check *AmE* to give someone permission to do whatever they think is necessary in a particular situation

blan·ket¹ /'blæŋkɨt/ n **1** [C] a cover for a bed, usually made of wool **2** [singular] a thick covering or area of something: [+of] *The hills were covered with a **thick blanket of snow**.* | *blanket of fog/cloud* **3** [singular] something that makes it hard for you to find information or the truth about something: [+of] *The inquiry was conducted under **a blanket of secrecy**.* → **electric blanket** at ELECTRIC (1); → WET BLANKET, SECURITY BLANKET

blanket² v [T usually passive] to cover something with a thick layer: **be blanketed in/with sth** *The rooftops were blanketed in snow.*

blanket³ adj [only before noun] **blanket statement/rule/ban etc** a statement, rule etc that affects everyone or includes all possible cases: *the proposed **blanket ban** on tobacco advertising* | *a **blanket strategy***

blank·e·ty-blank /ˌblæŋkɨti 'blæŋk/ adj [only before noun] *AmE spoken* used to show annoyance when you want to avoid swearing: *The blankety-blank key is stuck!*

blank·ly /'blæŋkli/ adv in a way that shows no emotion, understanding, or interest: *Anna stared blankly at the wall.*

blank 'verse n [U] poetry that has a fixed RHYTHM but does not RHYME → FREE VERSE

blare /bleə $ bler/ also **blare out** v [I,T] to make a very loud unpleasant noise: *Horns blared in the street outside.* | *The radio was blaring out the latest pop songs.* —**blare** n [singular]

blar·ney /'blɑːni $ -ɑːr-/ n [U] *informal* pleasant but untrue things that you say to someone in order to trick or persuade them

bla·sé /'blɑːzeɪ $ blɑː'zeɪ/ adj not worried or excited about things that most people think are important, impressive etc: [+about] *He's very blasé about money now that he's got that job.*

blas·pheme /blæs'fiːm/ v [I] to speak in a way that insults God or people's religious beliefs, or to use the names of God and holy things when swearing —**blasphemer** n [C]

blas·phe·my /'blæsfɨmi/ n plural **blasphemies** [C,U] something you say or do that is insulting to God or people's religious beliefs —**blasphemous** adj: *The book has been widely condemned as blasphemous.* —**blasphemously** adv

blast¹ /blɑːst $ blæst/ n [C]
1 AIR/WIND a sudden strong movement of wind or air: [+of] *A **blast of cold air** swept through the hut.*
2 EXPLOSION an explosion, or the very strong movement of air that it causes: **in the blast** | *Thirty-six people died in the blast.* | **bomb/shotgun/nuclear etc blast** *A bomb blast completely destroyed the building.*

3 LOUD NOISE a sudden very loud noise, especially one made by a whistle or horn: [+on] *The station master **gave** a **blast** on his whistle and we were off.* | **long/short blast** *a long trumpet blast*
4 **(at) full blast** as powerfully or loudly as possible: *I had the gas fire **going full blast**.* | *The radio was **on at full blast**.*
5 FUN a blast *informal* an enjoyable and exciting experience: *The concert **was a blast**.* | *We **had a blast** at the fair.*
6 EMOTION a sudden strong expression of a powerful emotion: [+of] *She was totally unprepared for the **blast** of criticism she received.*
7 **a blast from the past** *informal* something from the past that you remember, see, or hear again, and that reminds you of that time in your life: *That's **a blast from the past**. No one has called me that for years.*

blast² v
1 GUN/BOMB [T] to damage or destroy something, or to injure or kill someone, using a gun or a bomb: **blast sb with sth** *She blasted her husband with a shotgun because he was having an affair.* | *The first shot missed and **blasted** a **hole** in the far wall.* | *The plane was blasted out of the sky by a terrorist bomb.*
2 BREAK STH INTO PIECES [I,T] to break something into pieces using explosives, especially in order to build something such as a road: **blast sth through sth** *A 1.5 km tunnel was blasted through the mountain.* | **blast sth out of sth** *The road will have to be blasted out of solid rock.* | [+through] *Railway workers had blasted through the mountains 90 years before.*
3 LOUD NOISE also **blast out** [I,T] to produce a lot of loud noise, especially music: *He was woken by the radio alarm clock blasting out rock music.* | [+from] *Dance music blasted from the stereo.*
4 CRITICIZE [T] to criticize someone or something very strongly – used especially in news reports: **blast sb for (doing) sth** *Union leaders blasted the Government for failing to tackle the jobs crisis.*
5 KICK/HIT A BALL [T] to hit or kick a ball very hard: *With six minutes remaining, he **blasted** the **ball** through the Coleraine defences for his 19th goal of the season.*
6 AIR/WATER [I,T] if air or water is blasted somewhere, or if it blasts somewhere, it moves there with great force: *The wind ripped through the trees and blasted a curtain of rain up the meadow.* | *Icy winds and driving snow blasted through the pine trees.*
7 SPORTS [T] *AmE informal* to beat another team very easily: *The Seahawks were blasted 35–14 by the Broncos.*

blast off *phr v* if a spacecraft blasts off, it leaves the ground → BLAST-OFF

blast³ interjection also **'blast her/it etc** used when you are very annoyed about something: *Oh blast! I've forgotten my key.*

blas·ted /'blɑːstɨd $ 'blæs-/ adj [only before noun] *spoken informal* used to express annoyance: *I wish that blasted baby would stop crying!*

blast furnace n [C] a large industrial structure in which iron is separated from the rock that surrounds it

blast-off n [U] the moment when a SPACECRAFT leaves the ground: *10 seconds to blast-off* → **blast off** at BLAST²

bla·tant /'bleɪtənt/ adj something being bad that is blatant is very clear and easy to see, but the person responsible for it does not seem embarrassed or ashamed: *a blatant abuse of power* | *blatant discrimination* —**blatantly** adv

blath·er /'blæðə $ -ər/ v [I] to talk for a long time about unimportant things —**blather** n [C,U]

blaze¹ /bleɪz/ n
1 FIRE **a)** [C usually singular] a big dangerous fire – used especially in news reports; → **ablaze**: *It took almost 100 firemen to bring the blaze under control.* | **fight/tackle/control a blaze** *Helicopters were used to help fight the*

B

blaze. | **house/factory/barn etc blaze** *a huge chemical factory blaze* **b)** [singular] a fire burning with strong bright flames: *I lit the fire and soon had a **cheerful blaze** going.*
2 LIGHT/COLOUR [singular] very bright light or colour; **→ ablaze**: [+of] *the blaze of light from the security lamps* | *The garden is a **blaze of colour** at this time of year.*
3 blaze of publicity/glory a lot of public attention or success and praise: *As soon as the trial was over, the blaze of publicity surrounding him vanished.* | *She played the Canada tournament then retired, **going out in a blaze of glory** (=ending her career with a lot of success and praise).*
4 [singular] a sudden show of very strong emotion: *A **blaze of anger** flashed across his face.*
5 what the blazes/who the blazes etc *old-fashioned spoken* used to emphasize a question when you are annoyed: *What the blazes is going on here?*
6 like blazes *old-fashioned spoken* as fast, as much, or as strongly as possible: *We had to run like blazes.*
7 [C usually singular] a white mark, especially one down the front of a horse's face

blaze² *v* [I]
1 FIRE to burn very brightly and strongly; **→ blazing**: *The room was warm and cosy, with a **fire blazing** in the hearth.*
2 LIGHT to shine with a very bright light: *A huge truck was advancing towards us, its headlights blazing.* | *The sun **blazed down** as we walked along the valley.*
3 EYES [usually in progressive] *literary* if someone's eyes are blazing, their eyes are shining brightly because they are feeling a very strong emotion, usually anger: [+with] *Linda leapt to her feet, her dark eyes blazing with anger.*
4 GUN also **blaze away** if guns blaze, they fire bullets quickly and continuously: *An enemy plane roared overhead, its guns blazing.*
5 blaze a trail to develop or do something new and important, or to do something important that no one has done before: *an innovative young company that has blazed a trail for others to follow*
6 be blazed across/all over sth if something is blazed across a newspaper etc, it is written in a way that everyone will notice: *News of their divorce was blazed across all the tabloids.*

blaz·er /ˈbleɪzə $ -ər/ *n* [C] a jacket, sometimes with the special sign of a school, club etc on it

blaz·ing /ˈbleɪzɪŋ/ *adj* [only before noun] **1** extremely hot: *a blazing August afternoon* **2** full of strong emotions, especially anger: *He jumped to his feet in a blazing fury.* | **blazing row** (=very angry argument)

bla·zon /ˈbleɪzən/ *v* [T] **be blazoned across/on/over sth** to be written or shown on something in a very noticeable way

bleach¹ /bliːtʃ/ *n* [U] a chemical used to make things pale or white, or to kill GERMS

bleach² *v* [T] to make something pale or white, especially by using chemicals or the sun: *She **bleached** her **hair** blond.* | *The wood had been **bleached by the sun.***

bleach·ers /ˈbliːtʃəz $ -ərz/ *n* [plural] *especially AmE* long wooden BENCHES arranged in rows, where you sit to watch sport

bleak /bliːk/ *adj* **1** without anything to make you feel happy or hopeful: **a bleak future/prospect** *The company still hopes to find a buyer, but the future **looks bleak.*** **2** cold and without any pleasant or comfortable features: *a bleak January afternoon* | *The landscape was bleak and bare.* —**bleakly** *adv* —**bleakness** *n* [U]

blear·y /ˈblɪəri $ ˈblɪri/ also ˌbleary-ˈeyed *adj* unable to see very clearly, because you are tired or have been crying: *Steve emerged from his room, unshaven and bleary-eyed.* —**blearily** *adv* —**bleariness** *n* [U]

bleat /bliːt/ *v* [I] **1** to make the sound that a sheep or goat makes **2** *informal* to complain in a silly or annoying way: *'But I've only just got here,' bleated Simon.* —**bleat** *n* [C]

bleed /bliːd/ *v past tense and past participle* **bled** /bled/
1 BLOOD **a)** [I] to lose blood, especially because of an injury: *Your nose is bleeding.* | *Tragically, she **bled to death.*** | **bleed profusely/heavily** (=bleed a lot) *Mrs Burke was found unconscious and bleeding profusely.* **b)** [T] to take some blood from someone's body, done in the past in order to treat a disease: *When he fell sick several days later, he had a doctor bleed him.*
2 MONEY [T] to force someone to pay an unreasonable amount of money over a period of time: *His ex-wife clearly intends to bleed him for every last penny.* | **bleed sb dry/white** (=take all their money, possessions etc) *The ten-year war has bled the country dry.*
3 AIR/LIQUID [T] to remove air or liquid from a system in order to make it work properly, for example from a heating system: *We need to bleed the radiators.*
4 COLOUR [I] to spread from one area of cloth or paper to another; ☰ **run**: *Wash it in cold water so the colours don't bleed.*
5 bleed red ink *informal* if a company or business bleeds red ink, it loses a lot of money rather than making money: *Analysts predict the retailer will continue to bleed red ink, with losses topping $180 million.* **→ my heart bleeds (for sb)** at HEART (37)

bleed·er /ˈbliːdə $ -ər/ *n* [C] *BrE spoken not polite* a very offensive word for a person, especially a man that you dislike

bleed·ing¹ /ˈbliːdɪŋ/ *n* [U] the condition of losing blood from your body: *Use pressure to **control** the bleeding.* | *The **bleeding** had almost **stopped**.* | *He died of **internal bleeding.*** | **severe/heavy bleeding** (=when someone is losing a lot of blood)

bleeding² *adj* [only before noun] *BrE spoken not polite* an offensive way of emphasizing something when you are angry: *Get your bleeding hands off my car!*

ˌbleeding ˈheart also ˌbleeding heart ˈliberal *n* [C] *informal* someone who feels sympathy for poor people or criminals, in a way that you think is not practical or helpful

bleep¹ /bliːp/ *n* [C] **1** a short high sound made by a piece of electronic equipment **2** a bleeper

bleep² *v* **1** [I] to make a high electronic sound: *The timer on the cooker started to bleep.* **2** [T] *BrE* to let someone know, through their bleeper, that you want them to telephone you; ☰ **beep** *AmE* **3** [T] also **bleep out** to prevent an offensive word being heard on television or the radio by making a high electronic sound: *All the swear words had been bleeped out.*

bleep·er /ˈbliːpə $ -ər/ *n* [C] *BrE* a small machine that you carry with you, that makes short high electronic sounds to tell you that you must telephone someone; ☰ **pager**; ☰ **beeper** *AmE*

blem·ish¹ /ˈblemɪʃ/ *n* [C] a small mark, especially a mark on someone's skin or on the surface of an object, that spoils its appearance

blemish² *v* [T often passive] to spoil the beauty or appearance of something, so that it is not perfect; **→ unblemished** —**blemished** *adj*

blend¹ /blend/ *v* **1** [I,T] to combine different things in a way that produces an effective or pleasant result or to become combined in this way: *a story that blends fact and legend* | [+with/together] *Leave the sauce for at least one hour to allow the flavours to blend together.* **2** [T] to thoroughly mix together soft or liquid substances to form a single smooth substance: *Blend the sugar, eggs, and flour.* **3** [T usually passive] to produce tea, tobacco, WHISKY etc by mixing several different types together

blend in *phr v* if someone or something blends in with people or objects, they match them or are similar and you do not notice them: [+with] *The old house blends in perfectly with the countryside.*

blend² n [C] **1** a product such as tea, tobacco, or WHISKY that is a mixture of several different types **2** a mixture of different things that combine together well: *an excellent team, with a nice blend of experience and youthful enthusiasm*

blended 'family n [C] a family in which one or both parents have children from previous marriages living with the family

blend·er /'blendə $ -ər/ n [C] an electric machine that you use to mix liquids and soft foods together; ▣ **liquidizer** BrE; → see picture at EAT

bless ▣S3 /bles/ v [T]
1 bless you! *spoken* **a)** what you say when someone SNEEZES **b)** used to thank someone for doing something for you
2 bless (him/her etc) *spoken* used to show that you are fond of someone, amused by them, or pleased by something they have done: *He's always willing to help. Bless him!* | *'Jess made this card for me.' 'Bless!'*
3 be blessed with sth to have a special ability, good quality etc: *Fortunately we're both blessed with good health.*
4 if God blesses someone or something, He helps and protects them: *May God bless you.*
5 to ask God to protect someone or something: *The couple later had their marriage blessed in their local parish church.*
6 to make something holy: *Then the priest blesses the bread and wine.*
7 bless my soul/I'll be blessed! *old-fashioned spoken* used to express surprise

bless·ed /'blesɪd/ adj **1** [only before noun] *spoken* used to express annoyance: *Now where have I put that blessed book?* **2** [only before noun] very enjoyable or desirable: *a few moments of blessed silence* **3** holy: *the Blessed Virgin* —**blessedly** adv —**blessedness** n [U]

bless·ing /'blesɪŋ/ n **1** [C] something that you have or something that happens which is good because it improves your life, helps you in some way, or makes you happy: *The dishwasher has been a real blessing!* | **it is a blessing (that)** *It's a blessing no-one was badly hurt.* **2** [U] someone's approval or encouragement for a plan, activity, idea etc: **with sb's blessing** *They were determined to marry, with or without their parents' blessing.* | *The Defense Department has given its blessing to the scheme.* **3 a mixed blessing** a situation that has both good and bad parts: *Having children so early in their marriage was a mixed blessing.* **4 a blessing in disguise** something that seems to be bad or unlucky at first, but which you later realize is good or lucky **5 count your blessings** used to tell someone to remember how lucky they are, especially when they are complaining about something **6** [C,U] protection and help from God, or words spoken to ask for this: *The priest gave the blessing.*

bleth·er /'bleðə $ -ər/ v [I] to talk about things that are not important – used especially in Scotland —**blether** n [C,U]

blew /bluː/ the past tense of BLOW

blight¹ /blaɪt/ n **1** [singular,U] an unhealthy condition of plants in which parts of them dry up and die **2** [singular] something that makes people unhappy or that spoils their lives or the environment they live in: [+on] *Her guilty secret was a blight on her happiness.* | *the blight of poverty*

blight² v [T] to spoil or damage something, especially by preventing people from doing what they want to do: *a disease which, though not fatal, can blight the lives of its victims* | *a country blighted by poverty* —**blight·ed** adj: *blighted hopes*

blight·er /'blaɪtə $ -ər/ n [C] BrE old-fashioned informal **1** used to talk about someone that you feel sorry for or JEALOUS of: *Poor old blighter.* | *You lucky blighter!* **2** a bad or unpleasant person

bli·mey /'blaɪmi/ interjection BrE spoken informal used to express surprise: *Blimey, look at that!*

blimp /blɪmp/ n [C] **1** a small AIRSHIP (=type of aircraft without wings) **2** AmE spoken not polite an offensive word for a very fat person

Blimp also **,Colonel 'Blimp** n [C] BrE someone, especially an old man, with old-fashioned political ideas – used to show disapproval —**Blimpish** adj

blind¹ ▣S2 ▣W3 /blaɪnd/ adj
1 UNABLE TO SEE a) unable to see; → **colour-blind, visually impaired, handicapped**: *a school for blind children* | *the needs of blind and partially-sighted people* | *totally/completely/almost/partially blind She's almost blind in her right eye.* | *He was slowly going blind* (=becoming blind). | *Beverley was born blind and deaf.* **b)** **the blind** [plural] people who are unable to see: *talking books for the blind* **c)** **as blind as a bat** unable to see well – used humorously: *I'm as blind as a bat without my glasses.* **d)** **blind with tears/rage/pain etc** unable to see because of tears, pain, or a strong emotion; → **blindly**: *She screamed at him, her eyes blind with tears.*
2 be blind to sth to completely fail to notice or realize something; → **blindly**: *International companies are all too often blind to local needs.* | *He was totally blind to the faults of his children.*
3 turn a blind eye (to sth) to deliberately ignore something that you know should not be happening: *Teachers were turning a blind eye to smoking in school.*
4 not take/pay a blind bit of notice BrE informal to completely ignore what someone does or says, especially in a way that is annoying: *He never pays a blind bit of notice to what his staff tell him.*
5 not make a blind bit of difference BrE informal used to emphasize that whatever someone says or does will not change the situation at all: *Try and talk to her if you want. But I don't think it'll make a blind bit of difference.*
6 FEELINGS a) blind faith/prejudice/obedience etc strong feelings that someone has without thinking about why they have them – used to show disapproval: *Blind faith sent thousands of people to a pointless war.* | *a story about blind loyalty* **b) blind panic/rage** strong feelings of fear or anger that you cannot control: *In a moment of blind panic she had pulled the trigger and shot the man dead.* | *Blind rage took hold of him.*
7 ROAD blind bend/corner a corner in a road that you cannot see beyond when you are driving
8 the blind leading the blind used to say that people who do not know much about what they are doing are guiding or advising others who know nothing at all
9 AIRCRAFT blind flying is when you use only instruments to fly an aircraft because you cannot see through cloud, mist etc
10 blind drunk BrE informal extremely drunk —**blindness** n [U] → **rob sb blind** at ROB (3); → **swear blind** at SWEAR (3)

blind² v [T] **1** to make it difficult for someone to see for a short time: *For a moment I was blinded by the glare of headlights coming towards me.* | *The dust choked and blinded him.* | *Blinded by tears, I walked towards the door.* **2** to make someone lose their good sense or judgment and be unable to see the truth about something: *He should have known better. But he was blinded by his own self-centredness.* | **blind sb to sth** *Children's bad behaviour should not blind us to their need for love.* | *His single-minded determination to win the war is blinding him to other dangers.* **3** to permanently destroy someone's ability to see: *He had been blinded in an explosion.* **4 blind sb with science** to confuse or trick someone by using complicated language → **effing and blinding** at EFF (1)

blind³ n [C] **1** also **(window) shade** AmE a covering, especially one made of cloth, that can be rolled up and down to cover a window inside a building: *The blinds were drawn* (=pulled down) *to protect the new furniture from the sun.* | **open/pull down/draw the blinds** → ROLLER BLIND, VENETIAN BLIND **2** AmE a small shelter where you can watch birds or animals without being seen by them; ◼ **hide** *BrE* **3** [singular] a trick or excuse to stop someone from discovering the truth

blind alley n [C] **1** a small narrow street with no way out at one end **2** a way of doing something that seems as if it will have a successful result, but which in fact does not: *False information has led the police up a series of blind alleys.*

blind date n [C] an arranged meeting between a man and woman who have not met each other before: *Would you ever go on a blind date?*

blind·er /ˈblaɪndə $ -ər/ n **1** [singular] *BrE informal* an excellent performance, especially in sport: *He played an absolute blinder!* **2** **blinders** [plural] *AmE* pieces of leather that are put beside a horse's eyes to stop it from seeing objects on either side; ◼ **blinkers** *BrE*

blind·fold¹ /ˈblaɪndfəʊld $ -foʊld/ n [C] a piece of cloth that covers someone's eyes to prevent them from seeing anything

blindfold² v [T] to cover someone's eyes with a piece of cloth: *Blindfold the prisoner!*

blindfold³ *BrE* also **blind·fold·ed** /ˈblaɪndfəʊldɪd $ -foʊld-/ adv **1** with your eyes covered by a piece of cloth **2** **can do sth blindfold** *informal* used to say that it is very easy for you to do something because you have done it so often

blind·ing /ˈblaɪndɪŋ/ adj **1** [usually before noun] so bright or strong that you cannot see properly: **blinding flash/light/glare etc** *the desert with its strange twisted plants and its blinding light* | **blinding rain/snow/heat etc** *I struggled back to the hut through blinding rain.* **2** **blinding headache** a very bad HEAD-ACHE **3 blinding realization/clarity/revelation etc** a sudden realization, clear understanding, or new idea about something: *It was then that she realised, with blinding clarity, that she loved him.* | *Suddenly I had a **blinding flash** of inspiration.* **4** *BrE spoken informal* very good and enjoyable: *It's a blinding album.*

blind·ing·ly /ˈblaɪndɪŋli/ adv very or extremely: *It was **blindingly obvious** that Max wasn't really interested.*

blind·ly /ˈblaɪndli/ adv **1** not thinking about something or trying to understand it: *Don't just blindly accept what you are told.* **2** not seeing or noticing what is around you, especially because you are upset: *'I don't know,' she repeated as she **stared blindly** down into her glass.* | *I ran blindly upstairs.*

blind man's buff n [U] a children's game in which one player whose eyes are covered tries to catch the others

blind·side /ˈblaɪndsaɪd/ v [T] *AmE informal* **1** to hit the side of a vehicle with your vehicle in an accident: *Their car was blindsided by a bus at the intersection.* **2** to give someone an unpleasant surprise: *I was blindsided by his suggestion.*

blind spot n [C] **1** something that you are unable or unwilling to understand: *I have a blind spot where computers are concerned.* **2** the part of the road that you cannot see when you are driving a car **3** the point in your eye where the nerve enters, which is not sensitive to light

bling bling /blɪŋ ˈblɪŋ/ n [U] *informal* expensive objects such as JEWELLERY that are worn in a way that is very easy to notice

blink¹ /blɪŋk/ v **1** [I,T] to shut and open your eyes quickly: *I blinked as I came out into the sunlight.* **2** [I] if lights blink, they shine unsteadily or go on and off quickly: *The light on your answering machine is blinking.* **3** **not (even) blink** to not seem at all surprised: *When I told her how much it would cost, she didn't even blink.* **4 before you could blink** *spoken* extremely quickly **5 blink back/away tears** to shut and open your eyes in order to get rid of tears: *Lynn laughed, blinking back unexpected tears.*

blink² n **1 on the blink** *spoken* not working properly: *My computer's on the blink again.* **2 in the blink of an eye** very quickly **3** [C] the action of quickly shutting and opening your eyes

blink·ered /ˈblɪŋkəd $ -ərd/ adj **1** having a limited view of a subject, or refusing to accept or consider different ideas; ◼ **narrow-minded: a blinkered attitude/approach** *a blinkered attitude to other cultures* **2** a horse that is blinkered is wearing blinkers

blink·ers /ˈblɪŋkəz $ -ərz/ n [plural] **1** *BrE* pieces of leather that are put beside a horse's eyes to stop it from seeing objects on either side; ◼ **blinders** *AmE* **2** *AmE informal* the small lights on a car that you flash on and off to show which way you are turning

blink·ing /ˈblɪŋkɪŋ/ adj [only before noun] *BrE informal* used to show that you are annoyed: *Turn that blinking music down!*

blip /blɪp/ n [C] **1** a short high electronic sound, or a flashing light on the screen of a piece of electronic equipment: *blips on a radar screen* **2** a short pause or change in a process or activity, especially when the situation gets worse for a while before it improves again: *A government spokesman described the rise in inflation as a **temporary blip**.*

bliss /blɪs/ n [U] perfect happiness or enjoyment: **domestic/wedded/marital bliss** *Mr Lowe has just celebrated six months of wedded bliss to his sweetheart Ellen.* | *I didn't have to get up till 11 – it was sheer bliss.*

blissed out /ˌblɪst ˈaʊt/ adj *BrE informal* extremely happy and relaxed, especially as a result of using illegal drugs: *blissed-out partygoers* —**bliss out** v [I]

bliss·ful /ˈblɪsfəl/ adj **1** extremely happy or enjoyable: *blissful sunny days* **2 blissful ignorance** a situation in which you do not yet know about something unpleasant —**blissfully** adv: *Jean seems blissfully happy.* | *blissfully unaware of the impending danger*

B-list /ˈbiː lɪst/ adj [only before noun] among the group of film stars, musicians etc who are fairly famous or popular, but are not the most popular or famous; → **A-list:** *B-list celebrities*

blis·ter¹ /ˈblɪstə $ -ər/ n [C] **1** a swelling on your skin containing clear liquid, caused for example by a burn or continuous rubbing: *New shoes always give me blisters.* **2** a swelling on the surface of metal, rubber, painted wood etc

blister² v [I,T] to develop blisters or make blisters form: *The paint will blister in the heat.* —**blistered** adj: *My hands were blistered from all the digging.*

blis·ter·ing /ˈblɪstərɪŋ/ adj **1** extremely hot; ◼ **blazing:** *the blistering heat of the desert* **2 blistering attack/criticism etc** very critical remarks expressing anger and disapproval: *She launched into a blistering attack on her boss.* **3** used to describe actions in sport which are very fast or forceful: *Schumacher set a blistering pace from the start.* —**blisteringly** adv: *a blisteringly hot day*

blithe /blaɪð $ blaɪθ, blaɪð/ adj **1** seeming not to care or worry about the effects of what you do: *a blithe disregard for the facts* **2** *literary* happy and having no worries —**blithely** adv: *He seems blithely unaware of how much anger he's caused.* | *'Don't worry. I'll pay,' she said blithely.*

blith·er·ing /ˈblɪðərɪŋ/ adj **blithering idiot** *spoken* someone who has done something very stupid

blitz /blɪts/ n [C usually singular] **1** a sudden military attack, especially from the air: **the Blitz** (=the bombing of British cities by German aircraft in 1940 and 1941) **2** *informal* a period of great effort in order to deal with something quickly and completely: [+on] *We'll have to have a blitz on the house before your parents arrive.* **3** a big effort to make people notice something or buy something: **a media/marketing/advertising etc blitz** *The campaign was launched with a nationwide publicity blitz.* —**blitz** v [T]: *News came that Rotterdam had been blitzed.*

bliz·zard /'blɪzəd $ -ərd/ *n* [C] **1** a severe snow storm: *We got stuck in a blizzard.* **2** a sudden large amount of something unpleasant or annoying that you must deal with: [+of] *a blizzard of emails*

bloat·ed /'bləʊtɪd $ 'bloʊ-/ *adj* **1** full of liquid, gas, food etc, so that you look or feel much larger than normal: *a red bloated face* | *I feel really bloated after that meal.* **2** if you describe an organization as bloated, you mean that it is too big and does not work effectively: *the bloated state bureaucracy*

bloa·ter /'bləʊtə $ 'bloʊtər/ *n* [C] a smoked fish

blob /blɒb $ blɑːb/ *n* [C] **1** a very small round mass of a liquid or sticky substance: [+of] *a blob of honey* **2** something that cannot be clearly seen, especially because it is far away: *Without a telescope, the comet will look like a fuzzy blob.*

bloc /blɒk $ blɑːk/ *n* [C usually singular] a large group of people or countries with the same political aims, working together: *the former Soviet bloc* → EN BLOC

block

knife block

block of ice

breeze-block *BrE*/
cinder block *AmE*

block¹ ⒮₂ ⒲₂ /blɒk $ blɑːk/ *n* [C]
1 SOLID MATERIAL a piece of hard material such as wood or stone with straight sides → BREEZE-BLOCK, BUILDING BLOCK, CINDER BLOCK: [+of] *a block of ice* | *a wall made of concrete blocks* → see picture at ICE¹
2 STREETS/AREA a) *AmE* the distance along a city street from where one street crosses it to the next: *Head for 44th Street, a few blocks east of Sixth Avenue.* | *The church is down the block.* **b)** the four city streets that form a square around an area of buildings: *Let's walk round the block.* | *She grew up playing with the other kids on the block.* **c)** *AusE* a large piece of land: *a ten acre block near the city*
3 LARGE BUILDING a large building divided into separate parts: [+of] *a block of flats* | *an office block* | *an apartment block* | *the school science block*
4 QUANTITY OF THINGS a quantity of things of the same kind, considered as a single unit: [+of] *New employees receive a block of shares in the firm.* | *a system for storing large blocks of data* | *Set aside blocks of time for doing your homework.*
5 block booking/voting an arrangement that is made for a whole group to buy something or to vote together
6 INABILITY TO THINK [usually singular] the temporary loss of your normal ability to think, learn, write etc: *I have a **mental block** whenever I try to remember my password.* | *After his second novel Garland had **writer's block** (=he could not write anything).*
7 STOPPING MOVEMENT [usually singular] something that prevents movement or progress: [+to] *a major block to progress* → ROADBLOCK, STUMBLING BLOCK
8 PUNISHMENT the block in the past, a solid block of wood on which someone's head was cut off as a punishment
9 put your head/neck on the block to risk destroying other people's opinion of you or losing your job by doing or saying something: *I'm not prepared to put my head on the block for him.*
10 SPORT a movement in sport that stops an opponent going forward or playing the ball forward
11 SELL go on the block to be sold, especially at an AUCTION: *$500 million worth of art will go on the block.* →

BLOCK CAPITALS, TOWER BLOCK; → be a chip off the old block at CHIP¹ (7); → I'll knock your block off at KNOCK¹ (24)

block² ⒮₃ *v* [T]
1 also **block up** to prevent anything moving through a space by being or placing something across it or in it: *A fallen tree is blocking the road.* | *The sink's blocked up.*
2 block sb's way/path/exit/escape etc to stand in front of someone, so that they cannot go past: *I tried to get through, but there were too many people blocking my way.*
3 to stop something happening, developing, or succeeding: *The Senate blocked publication of the report.* | *laws designed to block imports of cheap tobacco*
4 block sb's view to be in front of someone so that they cannot see something: *The huge building across the street blocked our view of the sea.*
5 also **block out** to stop light reaching a place: *Can you move? You're blocking my light.*
6 to stop a ball, a blow etc from getting to where your opponent wants it to: *a shot blocked by the goalkeeper*
block sb/sth ⇔ **in** *phr v*
1 to park your car too close to another car, so that the other one cannot drive away
2 to paint or draw simple shapes or areas of colour: *I'll just block in the main buildings.*
block sth ⇔ **off** *phr v*
to completely close something such as a road or an opening: *Police blocked off the city centre streets.* | *The fireplace had been blocked off.*
block sth ⇔ **out**
1 to stop light reaching a place: *There was a heavy curtain blocking out the light.*
2 to stop yourself thinking about something or remembering it: *a memory so terrible that she tried to block it out*

block·ade¹ /blɒ'keɪd $ blɑː-/ *n* [C] **1** [usually singular] the surrounding of an area by soldiers or ships to stop people or supplies leaving or entering: *a naval blockade* | *They've **imposed** an economic **blockade** on the country.* | *an agreement to **lift the blockade** (=end it)* **2** something that is used to stop vehicles or people entering or leaving a place: *Angry farmers used tractors as blockades on the streets.*

blockade² *v* [T] to put a place under a blockade: *The ships blockaded the port.*

block·age /'blɒkɪdʒ $ 'blɑː-/ *n* **1** [C] something that is stopping movement in a narrow place: *a blockage in the pipe* **2** [U] the state of being blocked or prevented

block and 'tackle *n* [C usually singular] a piece of equipment with wheels and ropes, used for lifting heavy things

block·bust·er /'blɒk,bʌstə $ 'blɑːk,bʌstər/ *n* [C] *informal* a book or film that is very good or successful: *the latest Hollywood blockbuster* —**blockbusting** *adj*: *a blockbusting movie*

block 'capitals *n* [plural] letters in their large form such as A, B, C, rather than a, b, c: *Complete the form in block capitals.*

block·head /'blɒkhed $ 'blɑːk-/ *n* [C] *old-fashioned informal* a very stupid person

block·house /'blɒkhaʊs $ 'blɑːk-/ *n* [C] a small strong building used as a shelter from enemy guns

block 'letters *n* [plural] block capitals

block ,party *n* [C] *AmE* a party held in the street for all the people living in the area

blog /blɒg $ blɑːg/ *n* [C] a web page that is made up of information about a particular subject, in which the newest information is always at the top of the page; ⊟ web log —**blogger** *n* [C]

bloke ⒮₃ /bləʊk $ bloʊk/ *n* [C] *BrE informal* a man: *He's a nice bloke.*

B

blok·ish, blokeish /ˈbləʊkɪʃ $ ˈbloʊ-/ *adj BrE informal*
if you do blokish things, you behave in a traditionally male way: *playing football, fixing the car, and other blokish activities*

blond /blɒnd $ blɑːnd/ *adj* **1** another spelling of
BLONDE **2** a man who is blond has pale or yellow hair

blonde¹ S3 /blɒnd $ blɑːnd/ *adj*
1 blonde hair is pale or yellow in colour
2 a woman who is blonde has pale or yellow hair

blonde² S3 *n* [C] *informal* a woman with pale or
yellow-coloured hair: *a beautiful blonde*

blood¹ S1 W1 /blʌd/ *n* [U]
1 the red liquid that your heart pumps around your body

---
lose blood
draw blood (=make someone bleed)
give/donate blood (=have blood taken from you for the medical treatment of other people)
blood clots (=blood that forms a mass and stops flowing)
dried blood
be caked with blood (=covered in dry blood)
pool of blood
drop of blood
trickle of blood
blood flows/oozes/gushes
blood test
blood cell
blood sample

She lost a lot of blood in the accident. | *The dog bit her but didn't draw blood.* | *I'm going to give blood this afternoon.* | *Cooked garlic helps to prevent blood clotting, and so reduces the risk of heart attack.* | *Dried blood matted his hair on each side of his head.* | *My trousers were caked with blood.* | *Her body was found in a pool of blood.* | *A single drop of blood can transport the virus.* | *the steady trickle of blood from the corner of his mouth* | *Blood oozed from a cut on his forehead.* | *Blood tests proved he was not the father.*

---

2 (have) sb's blood on your hands to have caused someone's death: *dictators with blood on their hands*
3 in cold blood in a cruel and deliberate way: *Evans had been murdered in cold blood.*
4 make sb's blood boil to make someone extremely angry: *The way they treat people makes my blood boil.*
5 make sb's blood run cold to make someone feel extremely frightened
6 like getting blood out of a stone almost impossible: *Getting the truth out of her is like getting blood out of a stone.*
7 blood is thicker than water used to say that family relationships are more important than any other kind
8 be after sb's blood to be angry enough to want to hurt someone
9 sb's blood is up *BrE* someone is extremely angry about something and determined to do something about it: *They tried to stop me, but my blood was up.*
10 the family to which you belong from the time that you are born: *There's Irish blood on his mother's side.*
11 be/run in sb's blood if an ability or tendency is in, or runs in, someone's blood, it is natural to them and others in their family
12 sweat blood to work extremely hard to achieve something: *Beth sweated blood over that article.*
13 blood, sweat, and tears extremely hard work
14 new/fresh blood new members in a group or organization who bring new ideas and energy: *We need to bring in some new blood and fresh ideas.*
15 blood on the carpet a situation where people have a very strong disagreement, with the result that something serious happens, such as someone losing his or her job
16 young blood *old-fashioned* a fashionable young man

→ **bad blood** at BAD¹ (27); → BLUE-BLOODED, RED BLOOD CELL, WHITE BLOOD CELL; → **your own flesh and blood** at FLESH¹ (6); → **shed blood** at SHED² (5)

blood² *v* [T] *BrE* to give someone their first experience of an activity, especially a difficult or unpleasant one

blood-and-ˈguts *adj* full of action or violence: *a blood-and-guts struggle between the two teams*

blood-and-ˈthunder *adj* [only before noun] *BrE* full of exciting and violent action or emotion

blood bank *n* [C] a store of human blood to be used in hospital treatment

blood·bath /ˈblʌdbɑːθ $ -bæθ/ *n* [singular] the violent killing of many people at one time; ◉ **massacre**

blood ˈbrother *n* [C] a man who promises loyalty to another, often in a ceremony in which the men's blood is mixed together

blood count *n* [C] **1** a medical examination of someone's blood to see if it contains the right substances in the right amounts **2** the number of cells in someone's blood: *Her blood count is very low.*

blood·cur·dling /ˈblʌd,kɜːdlɪŋ $ -ɜːr-/ *adj* extremely frightening: *a bloodcurdling scream*

blood ˌdonor *n* [C] someone who gives their blood to be used in the medical treatment of other people

blood feud *n* [C] a quarrel between people or families that lasts for many years, in which each side murders or injures members of the other side

blood group *n* [C] *especially BrE* one of the classes into which human blood can be separated, including A, B, AB and O; ◉ **blood type** *AmE*

blood heat *n* [U] the normal temperature of the human body

blood·hound /ˈblʌdhaʊnd/ *n* [C] a large dog with a very good sense of smell, often used for hunting

blood·less /ˈblʌdləs/ *adj* **1** without killing or violence: *a bloodless coup* **2** a bloodless part of your body is very pale: *His lips were thin and bloodless.* **3** lacking in human feeling —**bloodlessly** *adv*

blood·let·ting /ˈblʌd,letɪŋ/ *n* [U] **1** killing people; ◉ **bloodshed**: *The movie contains scenes of violence and bloodletting.* **2** a medical treatment used in the past which involved removing some of a person's blood **3** a reduction in the number of people working for an organization, industry etc: *Many jobs have been lost, and the bloodletting isn't over yet.*

blood·line /ˈblʌdlaɪn/ *n* [C] all the members of a family of people or animals over a period of time; → **pedigree**: *a royal bloodline* | *Hereford cattle with bloodlines going back 200 years*

blood lust *n* [U] a strong desire to be violent

blood ˌmoney *n* [U] **1** money paid for murdering someone **2** money paid to the family of someone who has been murdered

blood ˌorange *n* [C] an orange with red juice

blood ˌpoisoning *n* [U] a serious illness in which an infection spreads through your blood

blood ˌpressure *n* [U] the force with which blood travels through your body: *high blood pressure* | *check/ take sb's blood pressure* (=measure it) *The nurse will take your blood pressure.*

blood-red *adj* dark red, like blood —**blood-red** *n* [U]

blood reˌlation also **blood ˌrelative** *n* [C] someone related to you by birth rather than by marriage

blood·shed /ˈblʌdʃed/ *n* [U] the killing of people, usually in fighting or war: *diplomacy aimed at stopping further bloodshed*

blood·shot /ˈblʌdʃɒt $ -ʃɑːt/ *adj* if your eyes are bloodshot, the parts that are normally white are red or pink

blood sport *n* [C] a sport that involves the killing of animals: *a demonstration against blood sports*

blood·stain /ˈblʌdsteɪn/ *n* [C] a mark or spot of blood —**bloodstained** *adj*: *a bloodstained handkerchief*

blood·stock /'blʌdstɒk $ -staːk/ n [U] horses that have been bred for racing: *a bloodstock auction*

blood·stream /'blʌdstriːm/ n [C usually singular] the blood flowing in your body: *The drug is injected directly into the bloodstream.*

blood·suck·er /'blʌd,sʌkə $ -ər/ n [C] **1** a creature that sucks blood from the bodies of other animals **2** *informal* someone who always uses other people's money or help – used in order to show disapproval

blood·thirst·y /'blʌd,θɜːsti $ -ɜːr-/ adj **1** eager to kill and wound, or enjoying killing and violence: *a bloodthirsty crowd* **2** describing or showing violence: *The film was too bloodthirsty for me.*

blood trans,fusion n [C,U] the process of putting blood into someone's body as a medical treatment

blood type n [C] *especially AmE* one of the classes into which human blood can be separated, including A, B, AB, and O; **ᵇ blood group** *BrE*

blood ,vessel n [C] one of the tubes through which blood flows in your body; → artery, vein

blood·y¹ [S3] [W3] /'blʌdi/ adj, adv *spoken especially BrE* **1** used to emphasize what you are saying in a slightly rude way: *It's bloody cold out there! | That's a bloody good idea. | Bloody hell! | 'Are you going to go with him?' 'Not bloody likely* (=definitely not).' **2 bloody well** used to emphasize an angry statement or order: *It serves you bloody well right.*

bloody² adj **1** covered in blood, or bleeding **2** with a lot of killing and injuries: *a bloody battle* **3 scream/ yell bloody murder** *AmE informal* to protest in a loud very angry way: *She was furious – screaming bloody murder at the manager!* **4 bloody/bloodied but unbowed** harmed by events but not defeated by them: *He emerged from the discussions bloody but unbowed.*

bloody³ v **bloodied, bloodying, bloodies** [T] to injure someone so that blood comes, or to cover something with blood

Bloody 'Mary n [C] an alcoholic drink made from VODKA, tomato juice, and spices

bloody-'minded adj deliberately making things difficult for other people; → awkward: *Stop being so bloody-minded!* —**bloody-mindedness** n [U]

bloom¹ /bluːm/ n **1** [C,U] a flower or flowers: *beautiful red blooms | a mass of bloom on the apple trees* **2 in (full) bloom** with the flowers fully open **3** [singular,U] the healthy happy appearance that someone has, especially when they are young: *The rosy bloom of her cheeks had faded.*

bloom² v [I] **1** if a plant or a flower blooms, its flowers appear or open **2** to become happier, healthier, or more successful in a way that is very noticeable: *She was positively blooming the last time I saw her.*

bloom·er /'bluːmə $ -ər/ n **1 bloomers** [plural] underwear that women wore in the past, like loose trousers that end at the knees **2** [C] *BrE old-fashioned* an embarrassing mistake that you make in front of other people – used humorously; **ᵇ blooper** *AmE*

bloom·ing /'bluːmɪŋ, 'blʊmᵊn/ adj [only before noun] adv *BrE spoken old-fashioned* used for emphasizing a remark, especially when you are angry or surprised: *It's blooming ridiculous!*

bloop·er /'bluːpə $ -ər/ n [C] *AmE* **1** an embarrassing mistake that you make in front of other people; **ᵇ bloomer** *BrE* **2** a ball in baseball that is high and slow and easy to catch or hit

blos·som¹ /'blɒsəm $ 'blaː-/ n [C,U] **1** a flower or the flowers on a tree or bush: *pale pink blossoms | The cherry tree was covered in blossom.* **2 in (full) blossom** with the flowers fully open

blossom² v [I] **1** if trees blossom, they produce flowers: *The apple trees are just beginning to blossom.* **2** also **blossom out** to become happier, more beautiful, more successful etc: *Pete's blossomed out in his new school. | [+into] The idea blossomed into a successful mail order business.*

---

blot¹ /blɒt $ blaːt/ **blotted, blotting** v [T] **1** to make a wet surface become dry by pressing soft paper or cloth on it **2 blot your copybook** *BrE informal* to do something that spoils the idea that people have of you

blot sth ⇔ **out** phr v **1** to cover or hide something completely: *Thick white smoke blotted out the sun.* **2** if you blot out an unpleasant memory, a thought etc, you deliberately try to forget it: *She said she took drugs to blot out her problems.*

blot sth ⇔ **up** phr v to remove liquid from a surface by pressing soft paper or cloth onto it

blot² n [C] **1** a mark or dirty spot on something, especially made by ink: *ink blots* **2** a building, structure etc that is ugly and spoils the appearance of a place: *The new power station is a blot on the landscape.* **3** something that spoils the good opinion that people have of someone or something: [+on] *The increase in juvenile crime is a blot on our time.*

blotch /blɒtʃ $ blaːtʃ/ n [C] a pink or red mark on the skin, or a coloured mark on something —**blotchy** adj —**blotched** adj

blot·ter /'blɒtə $ 'blaːtər/ n [C] **1** a large piece of blotting paper kept on top of a desk **2** *AmE* a book in which an official daily record is kept: *the police blotter* **3** *AmE informal* the drug LSD

blotting ,paper n [U] soft thick paper used for drying wet ink on a page after writing

blot·to /'blɒtəʊ $ 'blaːtoʊ/ adj *BrE informal* drunk

blouse /blaʊz $ blaʊs/ n [C] a shirt for women: *a silk blouse* → see picture at MATERIAL¹

blow¹ [S2] [W3] /bləʊ $ bloʊ/ v *past tense* **blew** /bluː/ *past participle* **blown** /bləʊn $ bloʊn/

1 WIND MOVING [I,T] if the wind or a current of air blows, it moves: *A cold breeze was blowing hard. | It was blowing from an easterly direction. | Outside, the weather was blowing a gale.*

2 WIND MOVING STH [I,T usually + adv/prep] to move or to move something by the force of the wind or a current of air: *Her hair was blowing in the breeze. | The wind blew the rain into our faces. | My ticket blew away. | blow (sth) open/shut A sudden draught blew the door shut.*

3 AIR FROM YOUR MOUTH [I,T always + adv/prep] to send air out from your mouth: **blow (sth) into/onto/out** etc *She blew onto her coffee to cool it down. | He blew the smoke right in my face. | You'll have to blow harder than that!*

4 MAKE A NOISE [I,T] to make a sound by passing air through a whistle, horn etc: *The whistle blew for halftime. | A truck went by and blew its horn at her.*

5 VIOLENCE [T always + adv/prep] to damage or destroy something violently with an explosion or by shooting: **blow sth away/out/off sth** *Part of his leg had been blown off. | blow sth/sb to pieces/bits/smithereens A bomb like that could blow you to bits.*

6 LOSE AN OPPORTUNITY [T] *informal* to lose a good opportunity by making a mistake or by being careless: *We've blown our chances of getting that contract. | You've got a great future ahead of you. Don't blow it.*

7 WASTE MONEY [T] *informal* to spend a lot of money in a careless way, especially on one thing: *I blew all the money I won on a trip to Hawaii.*

8 blow your nose to clean your nose by forcing air through it into a cloth or a piece of soft paper

9 blow sb a kiss to kiss your hand and then pretend to blow the kiss towards someone: *She leant out of the window and blew him a kiss.*

10 ELECTRICITY STOPS [I,T] if an electrical FUSE blows, or a piece of electrical equipment blows a fuse, the electricity suddenly stops working because a thin wire has melted: *The floodlights blew a fuse.*

11 TYRE [I,T] if a tyre blows or if a car blows a tyre, it bursts

12 MAKE A SHAPE [T] to make or shape something by sending air out from your mouth: *The kids were blowing bubbles in the backyard. | blow glass* (=shape glass by blowing into it when it is very hot and soft)

13 SURPRISE/ANNOYANCE blow/blow me/blow it etc *BrE spoken* said to show annoyance or surprise: *Blow it! I forgot to phone Jane.* | *Blow me down if she didn't just run off!* | *Well, I'm blowed!*

14 TELL A SECRET [T] to make known something that was meant to be a secret: *Your coming here has blown the whole operation.* | **blow sb's cover** (=make known what someone's real job or name is) *It would only take one phone call to blow his cover.*

15 blow sb's mind *spoken* to make you feel very surprised and excited by something: *Seeing her again really blew my mind.* → MIND-BLOWING

16 blow your top/stack/cool also blow a fuse/gasket *informal* to become extremely angry quickly or suddenly: *One day, I just blew my top and hit him.*

17 blow the whistle on sb *informal* to tell someone in authority about something wrong that someone is doing: *He blew the whistle on his colleagues.* → WHISTLE-BLOWER

18 blow sth (up) out of (all) proportion to make something seem much more serious or important than it is: *The issue was blown up out of all proportion.*

19 blow your own trumpet *especially BrE* also blow your own horn *AmE informal* to talk a lot about your own achievements – used to show disapproval: *Dave spent the whole evening blowing his own trumpet.*

20 blow sb/sth out of the water to defeat someone or something that you are competing with, or to achieve much more than they do: *Motown had blown all the other record companies out of the water.*

21 blow hot and cold *BrE informal* to keep changing your attitude towards someone or something

22 blow sth sky-high *BrE* to destroy an idea, plan etc by showing that it cannot be true or effective: *This new information blows his theory sky-high.*

blow sb ⇔ away *phr v informal especially AmE*
1 to make someone feel very surprised, especially about something they like or admire: *It just blows me away, the way everyone's so friendly round here.*
2 to kill someone by shooting them with a gun: *One move and I'll blow you away!*
3 to defeat someone completely, especially in a game: *Nancy blew away the rest of the skaters.*

blow down *phr v*
if the wind blows something down, or if something blows down, the wind makes it fall: *The garden gate has blown down.* | **blow sth ⇔ down** *Several trees were blown down in the night.*

blow in *phr v*
1 also **blow into sth** *informal* to arrive in a place, especially suddenly: *Jim blew in about an hour ago.* | *Guess who's just blown into town?*
2 if a storm or bad weather blows in, it arrives and begins to affect a particular area: *The first snowstorm blew in from the north.*

blow sb/sth ⇔ off *phr v AmE informal*
1 to treat someone or something as unimportant, for example by not meeting someone or not going to an event: *Tanya just blew me off – she said she didn't want to see me any more.* | *Bud got into trouble for blowing off the meeting.*
2 blow the lid off sth to make known something that was secret, especially something involving important or famous people: *Her book blew the lid off the Reagan years.*
3 blow sb's head off to kill someone by shooting them in the head
4 blow off steam *AmE* to get rid of anger or energy by doing something; ■ let off steam *BrE*: *I went jogging to blow off some steam.*

blow out *phr v*
1 if you blow a flame or a fire out, or if it blows out, it stops burning: *The match blew out in the wind.* | **blow sth ⇔ out** *Blow out all the candles.*
2 if a tyre blows out, it bursts
3 blow itself out if a storm blows itself out, it ends

4 blow your/sb's brains out to kill yourself or someone else with a shot to the head
5 blow sb ⇔ out *AmE spoken* to easily defeat someone: *We blew them out 28 – 0.*
6 *AmE* if you blow out your knee or another joint in your body, or if it blows out, you injure it badly
7 if an oil or gas WELL blows out, oil or gas suddenly escapes from it
8 blow sb out to stop having a friendship or relationship with someone

blow over *phr v*
1 if the wind blows something over, or if something blows over, the wind makes it fall: *Our fence blew over in the storm.* | **blow sth ⇔ over** *The hurricane blew some palm trees over.*
2 if an argument or unpleasant situation blows over, it ends or is forgotten: *They weren't speaking to each other, but I think it's blown over now.*
3 if a storm blows over, it goes away

blow up *phr v*
1 to destroy something, or to be destroyed, by an explosion: *The plane blew up in mid-air.* | **blow sth ⇔ up** *Rebels attempted to blow up the bridge.* → see picture at EXPLOSION
2 blow sth ⇔ up to fill something with air or gas: *Can you blow up this balloon?* | *We'll blow the tyres up.*
3 if a situation, argument etc blows up, it suddenly becomes important or dangerous: *A crisis had blown up over the peace talks.*
4 blow sth ⇔ up if you blow up a photograph, you make it larger; ■ enlarge: *How much would it cost to have this photo blown up?*
5 *informal* to become very angry with someone: *Jenny's father blew up when she didn't come home last night.* | [+at] *I was surprised at the way he blew up at Hardy.*
6 if bad weather blows up, it suddenly arrives: *It looks as if there's a storm blowing up.*
7 blow up in sb's face if something you have done or planned to do blows up in your face, it suddenly goes wrong: *One of his deals had just blown up in his face.*

blow² W3 *n* [C]
1 BAD EFFECT an action or event that causes difficulty or sadness for someone

serious/severe/major blow
shattering/devastating/bitter blow (=something that makes you extremely disappointed and upset)
cruel/heavy/grievous blow
deal a blow (to sb/sth)/deal (sb/sth) a blow
strike a blow
suffer/receive a blow
come as a blow (to sb)
fatal/final/mortal blow (=one that ends something)

Joe resigned, which was a severe blow because we needed him desperately. | *His mother's death was a shattering blow.* | *The election result dealt a further blow to the party.* | *The factory closures came as a blow to the local economy.* | *The final blow for many firms was the government's abolition of import duties.*

2 HARD HIT a hard hit with someone's hand, a tool, or a weapon: *She died from a heavy blow to the head.* | *He struck a blow which threw her to the floor.* | *Martin received a blow on the nose.* | *He had been struck a glancing blow* (=a blow that did not hit him directly) *by the car.* | [+to] *He gave her a violent blow to the head.*
3 BLOWING an action of blowing: *One big blow and the candles were out.*
4 come to blows (with sb) if two people come to blows, they start arguing or hitting each other because they disagree about something: [+over] *They almost came to blows over the money.*
5 soften/cushion the blow to make something unpleasant easier for someone to accept: *A reduction in interest rates would soften the blow of tax increases.*
6 low blow *AmE informal* something unkind you say to deliberately embarrass or upset someone → strike a blow for sb/sth at STRIKE¹ (13)

blow-by-blow *adj* a blow-by-blow account/description etc an account that includes all the details of an event exactly as they happened: *Jenny bored us with a blow-by-blow account of her holiday.*

'blow-dry blow-dried, blow-drying, blow-dries *v* [T] to dry hair and give it shape by using an electric HAIRDRYER —**blow-dry** *n* [C]: *a cut and blow-dry*

'blow-,dryer *n* [C] a small electric machine that blows hot air onto your hair in order to dry it; ▣ **hair dryer**

blow·er /'bləʊə $ 'bloʊər/ *n* [C] **1** a machine that blows out air, for example inside a car **2 on the blower** *BrE old-fashioned* on the telephone in order to talk to someone

'blow-fly *n* [C] a fly that lays its eggs on meat or wounds

blow·hard /'bləʊhɑːd $ 'bloʊhɑːrd/ *n* [C] *AmE informal* someone who talks too much and has very strong opinions

'blow-hole *n* [C] **1** a hole in the surface of ice where water animals such as SEALS come to breathe **2** a hole in the top of the head of a WHALE, DOLPHIN etc through which they breathe

'blow job *n* [C] *informal* the practice of touching a man's sexual organs with your lips and tongue to give him sexual pleasure

blow·lamp /'bləʊlæmp $ 'bloʊ-/ *n* [C] *BrE* a piece of equipment that produces a very hot flame, used especially for removing paint; ▣ **blowtorch** *AmE*

blown /bləʊn $ bloʊn/ the past participle of BLOW

'blow-out also **blow·out** *especially AmE* /'bləʊaʊt $ 'bloʊ-/ *n* [C] **1** a sudden bursting of a tyre; → **puncture**: *I had a blow-out on the driver's side.* **2** [usually singular] *informal* a big expensive meal or large social occasion: *We went for a real blow out to celebrate.* **3** *AmE informal* an easy victory over someone in a game **4** a sudden uncontrolled escape of oil or gas from a WELL

blow·pipe /'bləʊpaɪp $ 'bloʊ-/ *n* [C] a tube through which you can blow a small stone, ARROW etc, used as a weapon

blowsy, blowzy /'blaʊzi/ *adj* a blowsy woman is fat and looks untidy

blow·torch /'bləʊtɔːtʃ $ 'bloʊtɔːrtʃ/ *n* [C] a piece of equipment that produces a small very hot flame, used especially for removing paint; ▣ **blowlamp** *BrE*

'blow-up *n* [C] **1** a photograph or part of a photograph that has been made larger **2** [C usually singular] *AmE* a sudden big argument or disagreement → **blow up** at BLOW[1]

blow·y /'bləʊi $ 'bloʊi/ *adj* windy

blow·zy /'blaʊzi/ *adj* another spelling of blowsy

BLT /ˌbiː el 'tiː/ *n* [C] *bacon, lettuce, and tomato* the name of a sandwich that contains these foods

blub·ber[1] /'blʌbə $ -ər/ also **blub** /blʌb/ *v* [I] to cry noisily, especially in a way that annoys people

blubber[2] *n* [U] the fat of sea animals, especially WHALES

blud·geon[1] /'blʌdʒən/ *v* [T] **1** to hit someone several times with something heavy: *He was **bludgeoned to death** with a hammer.* **2** to force someone to do something by making threats or arguing with them: [+into] *I won't let myself be bludgeoned into marriage.* **3 bludgeon your way through/to/past etc sb/sth** to get somewhere or achieve something by pushing past other people, or not caring about them: *He bludgeoned his way through the crowd.*

bludgeon[2] *n* [C] a heavy stick with a thick end, used as a weapon

blue[1] S1 W2 /bluː/ *adj*
1 having the colour of the sky or the sea on a fine day; → **navy, navy blue**: *the blue waters of the lake* | *dark/light/pale/bright blue a dark blue raincoat*
2 [not before noun] *informal* sad and without hope; ▣ **depressed**: *I've been feeling kind of blue.*
3 *informal* blue jokes, stories etc are about sex, in a way that might offend some people → BLUE MOVIE
4 argue/talk etc till you're blue in the face *informal* to argue, talk etc about something a lot, but without

achieving what you want: *You can tell them till you're blue in the face, but they'll still do what they want.*
5 blue with cold *especially BrE* someone who is blue with cold looks extremely cold
6 go blue *BrE* if someone goes blue, their skin becomes blue because they are cold or cannot breathe properly
7 talk a blue streak *AmE informal* to talk very quickly without stopping —**blueness** *n* [U] → BLACK AND BLUE; → **once in a blue moon** at ONCE[1] (15); → **scream blue murder** at SCREAM[1] (1)

blue[2] *n* **1** [C,U] the colour of the sky or the sea on a fine day: *She nearly always dresses in blue.* | *the rich greens and blues of the tapestry* **2 blues** [U] also **the blues** a slow sad style of music that came from the southern US: *a blues singer* → RHYTHM AND BLUES **3 the blues** [plural] *informal* feelings of sadness: *A lot of women **get the blues** after the baby is born.* **4 out of the blue** *informal* if something happens out of the blue, it is very unexpected → **a bolt from/out of the blue** at BOLT[1] (3) **5** [C] **Blue** *BrE* someone who has represented Oxford or Cambridge University at a sport, or the title given to such a person **6 the blue** *literary* the sea or the sky → **boys in blue** at BOY[1] (9)

'blue ,baby *n* [C] a baby whose skin is slightly blue when it is born because it has a heart problem

blue·bell /'bluːbel/ *n* [C] a small plant with blue flowers that grows in woods

blue·ber·ry /'bluːbəri $ -beri/ *n plural* blueberries [C,U] a small blue fruit, or the plant it grows on: *blueberry pie*

blue·bird /'bluːbɜːd $ -bɜːrd/ *n* [C] a small blue bird that lives in North America

,blue-'blooded *adj* a blue-blooded person belongs to a royal or NOBLE family —**blue-blood** *n* [U]

'blue book *n* [C] *AmE* **1** a book with a list of prices that you can expect to pay for any used car **2** a book with a blue cover that is used in American colleges for writing answers to examination questions

blue·bot·tle /'bluː,bɒtl $ -,bɑːtl/ *n* [C] *BrE* a large blue fly

,blue 'cheese *n* [C,U] a type of cheese with blue lines in it and a strong taste

'blue chip *adj* blue-chip companies/shares etc companies or SHARES that make a profit and are considered safe —**blue chip** *n* [C]

,blue-'collar *adj* [only before noun] blue-collar workers do physical work, rather than working in offices; → **white-collar, pink-collar**

,blue-eyed 'boy *n* [C usually singular] *BrE informal* the man or boy in a group who is most liked and approved of by someone in authority: *John was always the blue-eyed boy at school.*

blue·grass /'bluːgrɑːs $ -græs/ *n* [U] a type of music from the southern and western US, played on instruments such as the GUITAR and VIOLIN

blue·jay /'bluː,dʒeɪ/ *n* [C] a common large North American bird with blue feathers

'blue jeans *n* [plural] *AmE* blue trousers made in a heavy material; ▣ **jeans**

'blue law *n* [C] *AmE* a law used in the past in the US to control activities that were considered immoral, such as drinking alcohol and working on Sundays

,blue 'movie *n* [C] a film that shows a lot of sexual activity

blue·print /'bluː,prɪnt/ *n* [C] **1** a plan for achieving something: [+for] *a blueprint for health-care reform* **2** a photographic print of a plan for a building, machine etc on special blue paper: [+for] *a blueprint for the new shopping mall* **3** *technical* a pattern that all living cells contain, which decides how a person, animal, or plant develops and what it looks

1 000, 2 000, 3 000, most frequent words in S poken and W ritten English

like: *By changing the tomato's **genetic blueprint**, scientists can alter the rate at which it ripens.*

blue 'ribbon also **blue rib·and** *BrE* /ˌbluː ˈrɪbənd/ *n* [C] the first prize in a competition, sometimes consisting of a small piece of blue material —**blue ribbon** also **blue riband** *BrE adj* [only before noun]: *the club's prized blue riband award*

'blue-sky *adj* [only before noun] *AmE* blue-sky tests etc are done to test ideas and not for any practical purpose

blue·stock·ing /ˈbluːˌstɒkɪŋ $ -ˌstɑː-/ *n* [C] *BrE* a woman who is more interested in ideas and studying than in parties, men etc – sometimes used to show disapproval

blue·sy /ˈbluːzi/ *adj* bluesy music is slow and sad, like BLUES

blue·tooth /ˈbluːtuːθ/ *n* [U] *trademark* bluetooth technology allows electronic equipment to communicate by using radio, so that, for example, a computer and printer can work together without having a wire connecting them

bluff¹ /blʌf/ *v* [I,T] to pretend something, especially in order to achieve what you want in a difficult or dangerous situation: *You wouldn't really tell her. You're bluffing!* | **bluff your way out of/through/past etc sb/sth** (=go somewhere or succeed in doing something by deceiving someone) *I hope we'll be able to bluff our way past the guard.* | *'I was with Don,' she said, deciding to **bluff** it out* (=continue to pretend something). | **bluff sb into (doing) sth** (=make someone do something by deceiving them)

bluff² *n* **1** [C,U] an attempt to deceive someone by making them think you will do something when you do not intend to do it: *The threat was only a bluff.* | *Whatever you say, you must do it. This isn't a **game of bluff**.* → DOUBLE BLUFF **2 call sb's bluff** to tell someone to do what they have threatened because you do not believe that they will really do it **3** [C] a very steep cliff or slope

bluff³ *adj* a bluff person, usually a man, is pleasant but very direct and does not always consider other people: *He was a bluff no-nonsense administrator.*

blu·ish /ˈbluːɪʃ/ *adj* slightly blue: *Her skin had **a bluish tinge**.*

blun·der¹ /ˈblʌndə $ -ər/ *n* [C] a careless or stupid mistake: *A last-minute blunder cost them the match.*

blunder² *v* **1** [I always + adv/prep] to move in an unsteady way, as if you cannot see properly: [+about/around] *Someone was blundering about in the kitchen.* | **blunder into/past/through etc sth** *Phil came blundering down the stairs.* **2** [I] to make a big mistake, especially because you have been careless or stupid: *They blundered badly when they gave him the job.* **3** [I always + adv/prep] to enter a place or become involved in a difficult situation by mistake: [+into] *Somehow we blundered into the war.* | [+in] *He would have agreed if you hadn't blundered in.*

blun·der·buss /ˈblʌndəbʌs $ -ər-/ *n* [C] a type of gun used in the past

blun·der·ing /ˈblʌndərɪŋ/ *adj* [only before noun] careless or stupid: *You blundering idiot!*

blunt¹ /blʌnt/ *adj* **1** not sharp or pointed; ◪ sharp: *Sharpen all your blunt knives.* | *a blunt pencil* **2** speaking in an honest way even if this upsets people; → **bluntly**: *To be blunt, many of the candidates cannot read or write.* | *Julian's blunt words hurt her.* **3 blunt instrument a)** a heavy object that is used to hit someone: *The victim suffered a blow to the head from a blunt instrument.* **b)** a method of doing something that does not work very well because it has a lot of other effects which you do not want: *The mini-exams in English, science, and maths are a blunt instrument which will reveal little about children's abilities.* —**bluntness** *n* [U]

blunt² *v* [T] **1** to make a feeling less strong: *The bad weather blunted their enthusiasm for camping.* **2** to make the point of a pencil or the edge of a knife less sharp

blunt·ly /ˈblʌntli/ *adv* speaking in a direct honest way that sometimes upsets people: *'You're drunk,' she said bluntly.* | **To put it bluntly**, *she's not up to the job.*

blur¹ /blɜː $ blɜːr/ *n* [C usually singular] **1** a shape that you cannot see clearly: [+of] *I just saw the blur of the car as it passed in front of me.* | *The island was a faint blur through misty rain.* **2** something that you cannot remember clearly: *The days before the accident were a blur.*

blur² *v* **blurred, blurring** [I,T] **1** to become difficult to see or to make something difficult to see, because the edges are not clear: *The street lights were blurred by the fog.* | *Many of the details in the picture are blurred.* **2** to be unable to see clearly: *Tears blurred her eyes.* | *His vision was blurred.* **3** to make the difference between two ideas, subjects etc less clear: *His films blur the boundaries between fact and fiction.* | *The design of the conservatory is meant to blur the distinction between the house and the garden.* —**blurry** *adj*: *a few blurry photos of their holiday together* → BLURRED

blurb /blɜːb $ blɜːrb/ *n* [C] a short description giving information about a book, new product etc

blurred /blɜːd $ blɜːrd/ *adj* **1** unclear in shape, or making it difficult to see shapes: *a blurred photo* **2** difficult to remember or understand clearly: *blurred memories*

blurt /blɜːt $ blɜːrt/ *v*
 blurt sth ⇔ out *phr v* to say something suddenly and without thinking, usually because you are nervous or excited: *Peter blurted the news out before we could stop him.*

blush¹ /blʌʃ/ *v* [I] **1** to become red in the face, usually because you are embarrassed: *Wilson saw she was watching him and blushed.* | *Joan blushed at the unexpected compliment.* | *Kate blushed scarlet.* **2** to feel ashamed or embarrassed about something: **blush to do sth** *I blush to admit that I haven't read it.* **3 sth that would make sb blush** something so shocking that it would shock someone who is not normally easily shocked: *language that would make a sailor blush* **4 the blushing bride** a young woman on her wedding day – used humorously —**blushingly** *adv*

blush² *n* **1** [C] the red colour on your face that appears when you are embarrassed: *Donald felt a blush warm his cheeks.* | *She bent her head to hide her blushes.* **2 at first blush** *literary* when first thought of or considered: *At first blush, this sounds like good news.* → **spare sb's blushes** at SPARE² (10)

blush·er /ˈblʌʃə $ -ər/ also **blush** *AmE n* [U] cream or powder used for making your cheeks look red or pink

blus·ter /ˈblʌstə $ -ər/ *v* **1** [I,T] to speak in a loud angry way that is not really very impressive: *'That's hardly the point,' he blustered.* **2** [I] if the wind blusters, it blows violently —**bluster** *n* [U] —**blustering** *adj*: *blustering wintry weather*

blus·ter·y /ˈblʌstəri/ *adj* blustery weather is very windy: *a cold and blustery day*

Blu-Tack /ˈbluːtæk/ *n* [U] *trademark* a blue sticky material used to fix paper to a wall

blvd. also **blvd** *BrE* the written abbreviation of *boulevard*

B-mov·ie /ˈbiː ˌmuːvi/ *n* [C] a film that is made cheaply and is of low quality

BMP /ˌbiː em ˈpiː/ *n* [C,U] *technical* **bitmap** a type of computer FILE that contains images

BO /ˌbiː ˈəʊ $ -ˈoʊ/ *n* [U] *body odour* an unpleasant smell from someone's body caused by SWEAT

bo·a /ˈbəʊə $ ˈboʊə/ *n* [C] **1** also **'boa con·strictor** a large snake that is not poisonous, but kills animals by crushing them **2** a FEATHER BOA

boar /bɔː $ bɔːr/ *n* [C] **1** a wild pig **2** a male pig

board[1] S1 W1 /bɔːd $ bɔːrd/ n

1 [C] INFORMATION a flat wide piece of wood, plastic etc that you can use to show information: **on a board** *The plan of the new building is displayed on a board at the back of the room.* | *I've put a list of names up on the board.* | *I'll check the departure board for train times.* → BILLBOARD, BLACKBOARD, NOTICEBOARD, SCOREBOARD

2 FOR PUTTING THINGS ON [C] a flat piece of wood, plastic, card etc that you use for a particular purpose such as cutting things on, or for playing indoor games: *Martha was chopping vegetables on a wooden board.* | *a chess board* → BREADBOARD, CHEESEBOARD, CHOPPING BOARD

3 also **Board** GROUP OF PEOPLE [C also + plural verb] *BrE* a group of people in a company or other organization who make the rules and important decisions: *a board meeting* | *a **board member*** | [+of] *The Board of Directors met yesterday.* | *There was disagreement among the agency's board of governors.* | *The decision was discussed and agreed at board level.* | **sit on a board/have a seat on a board** (=be a member of a board) *He gave up his seat on the board after 40 years.*

4 IN NAMES **Board** used in the name of some organizations: *the New York State Board of Elections* | *the British Boxing Board of Control*

5 IN BUILDING [C] a long thin flat piece of wood used for making floors, walls, fences etc: *We'll have to take the boards up to check the wiring.* → FLOORBOARD

6 **on board a)** on a ship, plane, or spacecraft; ⊟ **aboard**: *There are 12 children on board the ship.* **b)** involved with something or working for an organization: *Supporters of the treaty say that it will be necessary to have the United States on board.* | *He **came on board** in the late Sixties and spent two decades with the agency.*

7 MEALS [U] the meals that are provided for you when you pay to stay somewhere: *In the nursing home she will have to pay for **room and board**.* | *The landlord provides **board and lodging** (=meals and a place to stay).* → FULL BOARD, HALF BOARD

8 **go by the board** if an idea, way of behaving, or plan goes by the board, it fails to happen, ends, or is no longer possible: *It seems that loyalty has gone by the board.*

9 IN WATER SPORTS [C] a SURFBOARD or SAILBOARD

10 **across the board** if something happens or is done across the board, it affects everyone in a particular group, place etc: *The changes will affect local authorities across the board.* | *We find jobs for people **right across the board** from chief executives to cleaners.*

11 **take sth on board** to listen to and accept a suggestion, idea etc: *The school refused to take any of the parents' criticisms on board.*

12 ELECTRICITY [C] a CIRCUIT BOARD

13 THEATRE **the boards** [plural] the stage in a theatre → **tread the boards** at TREAD[1] (7)

14 SPORTS AREA **boards** [plural] *AmE* the low wooden wall around the area in which you play ICE HOCKEY

15 **college/medical boards** *AmE* examinations that you take in the US when you formally ask to be accepted as a student at a college or medical school → ABOVE BOARD, DIVING BOARD, DRAWING BOARD, IRONING BOARD, SOUNDING BOARD; → **sweep the board** at SWEEP[1] (11)

board[2] v **1** [I,T] *formal* to get on a bus, plane, train etc in order to travel somewhere: *The couple boarded the train for New York.* | *Passengers were standing on the dock, waiting to board.* **2** **be boarding** if a plane or ship is boarding, passengers are getting onto it: *Olympic Airways Flight 172 to Istanbul is now boarding at Gate No. 37.* **3** [I always + adv/prep] to stay in a room in someone's house that you pay for: *Several students boarded with Mrs. Smith.* **4** [I] to stay at a school at night as well as during the day: *Dickie was sent away to school as soon as he was old enough to board.*

board sth ⇔ **out** *phr v* to pay money and arrange for an animal to stay somewhere: *We'll have to board the cat out while we're away.*

board sth ⇔ **up** *phr v* to cover a window or door, or all the windows and doors of a building, with wooden boards: *The shop was boarded up.*

board·er /ˈbɔːdə $ ˈbɔːrdər/ n [C] **1** a student who stays at a school during the night, as well as during the day; → **day pupil** **2** someone who pays to live in another person's house with some or all of their meals provided; ⊟ **lodger**

board games

chess

draughts *BrE*/ checkers *AmE*

snakes and ladders *BrE*/ chutes and ladders *AmE*

chinese checkers

B

ˈ**board game** n [C] an indoor game played on a specially designed board made of thick card or wood

board·ing /ˈbɔːdɪŋ $ ˈbɔːr-/ n [U] **1** the act of getting on a ship, plane etc in order to travel somewhere: *Boarding is now taking place at Gate 38.* **2** narrow pieces of wood that are fixed side by side, usually to cover a broken door or window

ˈ**boarding card** n a British word for BOARDING PASS

ˈ**boarding house** n [C] a private house where you pay to sleep and eat; ⊟ **guesthouse**

ˈ**boarding pass** also **boarding card** *BrE* n [C] an official card that you have to show before you get onto a plane

ˈ**boarding school** n [C] a school where students live as well as study → DAY SCHOOL

board·room /ˈbɔːdruːm, -rʊm $ ˈbɔːrd-/ n [C] a room where the DIRECTORS of a company have meetings

board·walk /ˈbɔːdwɔːk $ ˈbɔːrdwɒːk/ n [C] *AmE* a raised path made of wood, usually built next to the sea

boast[1] /bəʊst $ boʊst/ v **1** [I,T] to talk too proudly about your abilities, achievements, or possessions: *'I wouldn't be afraid,' she boasted.* | **boast that** *Amy boasted that her son was a genius.* | [+about] *He's boasting about how much money he has made.* | [+of] *The company is inclined to boast of its success.* **2** [T not in progressive] if a place, object, or organization boasts something, it has something that is very good: *The city boasts two excellent museums.* | *The Society boasts 3000 members worldwide.* —**boaster** n [C]

boast[2] n [C] something that you like telling people because you are proud of it: *It is the company's **proud boast** that it can deal with all a customer's needs in one phone call.* | *Philip's boast is that he started out without any outside financial backing.* | **an empty/idle/vain boast** (=a false statement that something is good or possible) *She claimed that she could beat anyone, but it was an empty boast.* | *'Making knowledge work' is the university's phrase, and it is **no idle boast** (=not a boast, but true).*

boast·ful /ˈbəʊstfəl $ ˈboʊst-/ adj talking too proudly about yourself —**boastfully** adv —**boastfulness** n [U]

boat S1 W2 /bəʊt $ boʊt/ n [C]

1 a vehicle that travels across water: *If we had a boat, we could row across to the island.* | *a fishing boat* | **on/in a boat** *MacKay said he would sleep on his boat.* | **by boat** *Some of the beaches can only be reached by boat.* | *The tour includes boat trips up the river.* → LIFEBOAT, MOTORBOAT, POWERBOAT, ROWING BOAT, SPEEDBOAT, STEAMBOAT

2 *informal* a ship, especially one that carries passen-

gers: *We're taking the night boat to St. Malo.*
3 be in the same boat (as sb) to be in the same unpleasant situation as someone else: *Everyone has lost their job. We're all in the same boat.* → GRAVY BOAT, SAUCE BOAT; → **burn your bridges/boats** at BURN[1] (18); → **miss the boat** at MISS[1] (14); → **push the boat out** at PUSH[1] (15); → **rock the boat** at ROCK[2] (3)

boat·er /ˈbəʊtə $ ˈboʊtər/ n [C] a hard STRAW hat with a flat top

boat hook n [C] a long pole with an iron hook at the end, used to pull or push a small boat

boat·house /ˈbəʊthaʊs $ ˈboʊt-/ n [C] a building beside a lake or river where boats are kept

boat·ing /ˈbəʊtɪŋ $ ˈboʊt-/ n [U] the activity of travelling in a small boat for pleasure: *Let's go boating on the lake.*

boat·man /ˈbəʊtmən $ ˈboʊt-/ n plural **boatmen** /-mən/ [C] a man who you pay to take you out in a boat or for the use of a boat

boat people n [plural] people who escape from bad conditions in their country in small boats; → **refugees**

boat·swain /ˈbəʊsən $ ˈboʊ-/ n another spelling of BOSUN

boat train n [C] a train that takes people to or from ships in a port

boat·yard /ˈbəʊtjɑːd $ ˈboʊtjɑːrd/ n [C] an area where boats are built and repaired

bob[1] /bɒb $ bɑːb/ v **bobbed, bobbing**
1 MOVE ON WATER [I] to move up and down when floating on the surface of water: *The boat bobbed gently up and down on the water.*
2 MOVE SOMEWHERE [I always + adv/prep] to move quickly in a particular direction: *Mrs Foster bobbed about, gathering up her things.*
3 bob your head to move your head down quickly as a way of showing respect, greeting someone, or agreeing with them: *He spoke rapidly to the girl, who bobbed her head.*
4 CUT HAIR [T] to cut someone's, especially a woman's, hair in a bob: *her neatly bobbed hair*

bob[2] n [C] **1** a way of cutting hair so that it hangs to the level of your chin and is the same length all the way round your head → see picture at HAIRSTYLE **2** a quick up and down movement of your head or body, to show respect, agreement, greeting etc: *The maid gave a little bob and left the room.* **3** [plural] informal a SHILLING (=coin used in the past in Britain): *At last I'm making a few bob* (=a reasonable amount of money). → **bits and bobs** at BIT[2] (7)

Bob n **Bob's your uncle!** BrE spoken used to say that something will be easy to do: *Just copy the disk, and Bob's your uncle!*

bob·bin /ˈbɒbɪn $ ˈbɑː-/ n [C] a small round object that you wind thread onto, especially for a SEWING MACHINE; → **spool, reel**

bob·ble[1] /ˈbɒbəl $ ˈbɑː-/ n [C] BrE a small soft ball, usually made of wool, that is used especially for decorating clothes: *Her pullover had bobbles on the front.* —**bobbly** adj

bobble[2] v **1** [T] AmE to drop or hold a ball in an uncontrolled way; ≡ **fumble 2** [I] BrE if a piece of clothing bobbles, especially a sweater, it forms little balls on the surface of the cloth after it has been worn or washed; ≡ **pill** AmE

bobble hat n [C] a WOOLLEN hat with a bobble on the top → see picture at HAT

bob·by /ˈbɒbi $ ˈbɑːbi/ n plural **bobbies** [C] BrE informal old-fashioned a policeman

bobby pin n [C] AmE a thin piece of metal bent into a narrow U shape that you use to hold your hair in place; ≡ **hairgrip** BrE

bobby socks, **bobby sox** n [plural] AmE girls' short socks that have the tops turned over

bob·cat /ˈbɒbkæt $ ˈbɑːb-/ n [C] a large North American wild cat that has no tail; ≡ **lynx**

bobs /bɒbz $ bɑːbz/ n [plural] → **bits and bobs** at BIT[2] (7)

bob·sleigh /ˈbɒbsleɪ $ ˈbɑːb-/ also **bob·sled** /ˈbɒbsled $ ˈbɑːb-/ n **1** [C] a small vehicle with two long thin metal blades instead of wheels, that is used for racing down a special ice track **2** [U] a sports event in which people race against each other in bobsleighs: *Sixteen teams took part in the 400m bobsleigh.* —**bobsleigh** v [I]; → see picture at WINTER SPORTS

bob·tail /ˈbɒbteɪl $ ˈbɑːb-/ n [C] → **ragtag and bobtail** at RAGTAG

bob·white /bɒbwaɪt $ ˈbɑːb-/ n [C] a bird from North America, often shot for sport; ≡ **quail**

bod /bɒd $ bɑːd/ n [C] **1** BrE spoken a person: *He's a clever bod.* **2** informal someone's body: *She's got a lovely bod.* **3 odd bod** informal a strange person: *He's a bit of an odd bod but very pleasant.*

bode /bəʊd $ boʊd/ v **1** the past tense of BIDE **2 bode well/ill (for sb/sth)** to be a good or bad sign for the future: *The opinion polls do not bode well for the Democrats.*

bodge /bɒdʒ $ bɑːdʒ/ also **bodge up** n [singular] spoken a mistake or something that is not as good as it should be; → **botch**: *The builders have made a complete bodge of the kitchen.* —**bodge** v [T]

bod·ice /ˈbɒdɪs $ ˈbɑː-/ n [C] **1** the part of a woman's dress above her waist **2** a tight-fitting woman's WAISTCOAT worn over a BLOUSE in former times **3** old use a piece of woman's underwear that covers the upper part of her body; ≡ **corset**

bod·i·ly[1] /ˈbɒdɪli $ ˈbɑː-/ adj [only before noun] related to the human body: *Many bodily changes occur during adolescence.* | *bodily sensations*

bodily[2] adv **1** by moving the whole of your or someone else's body: *He lifted the child bodily aboard.* **2** by moving a large object in one piece: *The column was transferred bodily to a new site by the bank of the river.*

bod·kin /ˈbɒdkɪn $ ˈbɑːd-/ n [C] a long thick needle without a point

bod·y S1 W1 /ˈbɒdi $ ˈbɑːdi/ n plural **bodies**
1 PEOPLE/ANIMALS [C] the physical structure of a person or animal: *the human body* | *My fingers were numb and my whole body ached.* | **body weight/temperature/size** *Your body temperature is higher in the daytime than at night.* | *For their body size, these birds lay very small eggs.* | *He needs to overcome a negative body image* (=what you think about your own body).
2 DEAD PERSON [C] the dead body of a person: *A dog found the body of a girl in the woods.* | *Laura had never seen a dead body before.*
3 GROUP [C] a group of people who work together to do a particular job or who are together for a particular purpose: *The British Medical Association is the doctors' professional body.* | [+of] *There were reports of a large body of armed men near the border.* | *Kaplan served on the governing body of the museum* (=the group who control the museum). | *The student body* (=all the students in a school or college) *numbers 5000.* | *The research will be used by government departments and other public bodies* (=groups whose work is connected to the government). | **in a body** (=as a group, together) *The women moved towards the building in a body.*
4 body of sth a) a large amount or mass of something, especially something that has been collected: **body of knowledge/evidence/opinion etc** *There is now a considerable body of knowledge of the different stages of childhood.* | *There is a growing body of evidence that charges are too high.* **b)** the main, central, or most important part of something: *The arguments are explained in the body of the text.* | *Leave three blank lines between the date and the body of the letter.*
5 body of water a large area of water such as a lake: *The city was built near a large body of water.*
6 MIDDLE PART [C] the central part of a person or animal's body, not including the head, arms, legs or wings: *Nick had bruises on his face and body.* | *The bird*

has a small body and long wings.
7 VEHICLE [C] the main structure of a vehicle not including the engine, wheels etc: *Workers at the factory are making steel bodies for cars.*
8 OBJECT [C] *technical* an object that is separate from other objects: *Keep the caps on the bottles to prevent foreign bodies entering them* (=objects that should not be there). → **heavenly body** at HEAVENLY (3)
9 HAIR [U] if your hair has body, it is thick and healthy: *This shampoo will give more body to your hair.*
10 TASTE [U] if food or an alcoholic drink has body, it has a strong FLAVOUR (=taste): *A small amount of tomato paste will give extra colour and body to the sauce.*
11 full/medium/light bodied used to describe how much taste an alcoholic drink has, with a full bodied drink having the strongest taste: *a full bodied wine*
12 long/thick etc bodied etc having a long, thick etc body: *a slim bodied orange-gold fish* → ABLE-BODIED
13 keep body and soul together to continue to exist with only just enough food, money etc: *He's working at the shop to keep body and soul together*
14 body and soul a) completely: *She threw herself body and soul into her work.* **b)** the whole of a person: *They think they own the employees, body and soul.*
15 INSTRUMENT [C] the wide part of a musical instrument such as a VIOLIN or GUITAR, or of a sports RACKET (=bat): *The guitar is 16 inches wide across the body.*
16 CLOTHING [C] *BrE*; **body suit** *AmE* a type of tight fitting shirt worn by women that fastens between their legs → see picture at UNDERWEAR → **over my dead body** at DEAD[1] (11)

body ,armour *n* [U] clothing worn by the police that protects them against bullets
body bag *n* [C] a large bag in which a dead body is removed: *No pictures of dead soldiers, body bags, or coffins were allowed.*
body blow *n* [C] **1** a serious loss, disappointment, or defeat; → **blow**: *Hopes of economic recovery were dealt a body blow by this latest announcement.* **2** a hard hit between your neck and waist during a fight
body ,building *n* [U] an activity in which you do hard physical exercise in order to develop big muscles —**body builder** *n* [C]
body clock *n* [C] the system in your body that controls types of behaviour which happen at regular times, such as sleeping or eating; ▣ **biological clock**
body ,count *n* [C] the number of dead soldiers after a period of fighting, or the process of counting their bodies
body ,double *n* [C] someone whose body appears instead of an actor's or actress's in a film, especially in scenes where they are not wearing any clothes; → **double**
bod·y·guard /'bɒdigɑːd $ 'bɑːdigɑːrd/ *n* [C] **1** someone whose job is to protect an important person: *The Senator arrived, surrounded by personal bodyguards.* **2** a group of people who work together to protect an important person
body ,language *n* [U] changes in your body position and movements that show what you are feeling or thinking: *It was obvious from Luke's body language that he was nervous.*
body ,odour *n* [U] the natural smell of someone's body, especially when this is unpleasant; ▣ **BO**
body ,piercing *n* [U] making a hole in a part of the body in order to fix a ring or other piece of jewellery to the body
body ,politic *n* [singular] *formal* all the people in a nation forming a state under the control of a single government
body search *n* [C] a thorough search for drugs, weapons etc, that might be hidden on someone's body: *Everyone entering the building had a body search.* —**body-search** *v* [T]
body shop *n* [C] a building where the main structure of a car is repaired

body spray *n* [U] a chemical substance that you put onto your body to make it smell nice; → **deodorant**
body ,stocking *n* [C] a close-fitting piece of clothing that covers the whole of your body
body suit *n* [C] *AmE* a type of tight fitting shirt worn by women that fastens between their legs; ▣ **body** *BrE*
body ,warmer *n* [C] *BrE* a piece of warm clothing without arms that you wear over a SWEATER or a shirt, especially when you are outside: *a fleece body warmer*
bod·y·work /'bɒdiwɜːk $ 'bɑːdiwɜːrk/ *n* [U] the metal frame of a vehicle, not including the engine, wheels etc: *The bodywork's beginning to rust.*
Boer /bɔː, bʊə $ bɔːr, bʊr/ *n* [C] a white South African whose family is related to the Dutch people who settled in South Africa in the 1600s; → **Afrikaner**
bof·fin /'bɒfɪn $ 'bɑː-/ *n* [C] *BrE informal* **1** a scientist **2** someone who is very clever: *He was always a bit of a boffin, even at school.* | *computer boffins*
bog[1] /bɒg $ bɑːg, bɔːg/ *n* **1** [C,U] an area of low wet muddy ground, sometimes containing bushes or grasses; → **marsh, swamp** **2** [C] *BrE informal* a toilet
bog[2] *v* **bogged, bogging**
bog sb/sth ⇔ **down** *phr v* [usually passive] **1** if a process or plan becomes bogged down, it is delayed so that no progress is made: *Talks to settle the pay dispute have become bogged down.* | [+in] *Don't let yourself get bogged down in minor details.* **2** if something gets bogged down, it becomes stuck in soft ground and is unable to move: *The car got bogged down in the mud.*
bog off *phr v BrE spoken informal* used to tell someone rudely to go away: *Just bog off and leave me alone!*
bo·gey, bogie /'bəʊgi $ 'boʊgi/ *n* [C] **1** *technical* when you take one more shot than PAR (=the usual number of shots) to get the ball into the hole in GOLF; → **birdie, eagle** **2** a problem or difficult situation that makes you feel anxious: [+of] *the bogey of recession* **3** *BrE informal* a piece of MUCUS from inside your nose **4** a bogeyman
bo·gey·man /'bəʊgimæn $ 'boʊ-/ *n plural* **bogeymen** /-men/ [C] **1** an evil spirit, especially in children's imagination or stories **2** someone who people think is evil or unpleasant: *Manson was and remains America's number one bogeyman.*
bog·gle /'bɒgəl $ 'bɑː-/ *v* **the/your mind boggles** also **sth makes the/your mind boggle** also **sth boggles the/your mind** *informal* if your mind boggles when you think of something, it is difficult for you to imagine or accept it: *The sheer amount of data makes the mind boggle.* | [+at] *My mind boggles at the amount of work still to do.*
bog·gy /'bɒgi $ 'bɑː-/ *adj* boggy ground is wet and muddy; → **bog**: *a boggy patch at the edge of the field*
bo·gie[1] /'bəʊgi $ 'boʊ-/ *n* [C] a BOGEY
bogie[2] *v* [T] to use one more than PAR (=the usual number of strokes) to get the ball into the hole in GOLF
bog roll *n* [C,U] *BrE informal* TOILET PAPER
bog-'standard *adj* [only before noun] *BrE informal* not special or interesting in any way; ▣ **average**
bo·gus /'bəʊgəs $ 'boʊ-/ *adj* not true or real, although someone is trying to make you think it is; ▣ **false**: *bogus insurance claims* | *bogus applications for asylum*
bo·he·mi·an /bəʊ'hiːmiən, bə- $ boʊ-, bə-/ *adj* living in a very informal or relaxed way and not accepting society's rules of behaviour: *bohemian cafes frequented by artists, musicians, and actors* —**bohemian** *n* [C]
boil[1] ▣ S3 /bɔɪl/ *v*
1 [I,T] when a liquid boils, or when you boil it, it becomes hot enough to turn into gas: [+at] *The solution boiled at 57.4°C.* | *Put the spaghetti into plenty of boiling salted water.* | *We were advised to boil the water before drinking it.*

[1] 000, [2] 000, [3] 000, most frequent words in [S]poken and [W]ritten English

2 [I,T] to cook something in boiling water: *a boiled egg* | *Boil the rice for 15 minutes.* | *She fried the chicken and put the vegetables on to boil.* → see picture at EGG[1]
3 [I,T] if something containing liquid boils, the liquid inside it is boiling: *The kettle's boiling – shall I turn it off?* | *The saucepan boiled dry on the stove.*
4 [T] to wash something, using boiling water: *I always boil the cotton sheets.*
5 [I] if you are boiling with anger, you are extremely angry: [+with] *Lewis was boiling with rage and misery.* → BOILING POINT (2); → make sb's blood boil at BLOOD[1] (4)

boil away *phr v*
if a liquid boils away, it disappears because it has been heated too much: *The soup's almost boiled away.*

boil down *phr v*
1 boil down to sth *informal* if a long statement, argument etc boils down to a single statement, that statement is the main point or cause: *Think of the money you can make – that's what it all boils down to.* | *It boils down to a question of priorities.*
2 boil sth ⇔ down to make a list or piece of writing shorter by not including anything that is not necessary: *You can boil this down so that there are just two main categories.*
3 if a food or liquid boils down, or if you boil it down, it becomes less after it is cooked: *Spinach tends to boil down a lot.* | *boil sth ⇔ down glue made from boiling down old sheepskins*

boil over *phr v*
1 if a liquid boils over when it is heated, it rises and flows over the side of the container: *The milk was boiling over on the stove behind her.*
2 if a situation or an emotion boils over, the people involved stop being calm: *All the bitterness of the last two years seemed to boil over.* | [+into] *Anger eventually boils over into words and actions that are later regretted.*

boil up *phr v*
1 if a situation or emotion boils up, bad feelings grow until they reach a dangerous level: *She could sense that trouble was boiling up at work.* | *He could feel the anger boiling up inside him.*
2 boil sth ⇔ up to heat food or a liquid until it begins to boil: *Boil the fruit up with sugar.*

boil² *n* **1 the boil** *BrE*; **a boil** *AmE* the act or state of boiling: *Add the seasoning and bring the sauce to the boil.* | *She waited for the water to come to the boil* (=begin to boil). **2** [C] a painful infected swelling under someone's skin: *The boy's body is covered in boils.* **3 go off the boil** *BrE* to become less good at something that you are usually very good at: *He's gone off the boil after a tournament win in Dubai.*

boiled sweet *n* [C] *BrE* a hard SWEET that often tastes of fruit; ➡ **hard candy** *AmE*

boil·er [S3] /'bɔɪlə $ -ər/ *n* [C] a container for boiling water that is part of a steam engine, or is used to provide heating in a house

boil·er·plate /'bɔɪləpleɪt $ -ər-/ *n* [C,U] *AmE* a standard piece of writing or a design for something that can be easily used each time you need it, for example in business or legal documents; → **template**: *a boilerplate for a fax message* | *lawyers selling boilerplate wills*

boiler room *n* [C] **1** a room in a large building where the building's boiler is **2** *AmE informal* a room or office where people sell SHARES or services on the telephone, using unfair and sometimes dishonest methods

boiler suit *n* [C] *BrE* a piece of loose clothing like trousers and a shirt joined together, that you wear over your clothes to protect them when you are working; → **overalls**

boil·ing [S3] /'bɔɪlɪŋ/ *adj spoken* very hot; ➡ **freezing**: *Can I open a window? It's boiling in here.* | *It was a boiling hot morning.*

boiling point *n* [C usually singular] **1** the temperature at which a liquid boils **2** a point where people can no longer deal calmly with a problem; → **flashpoint**: *Relations between the two countries have almost reached boiling point.*

bois·ter·ous /'bɔɪstərəs/ *adj* someone, especially a child, who is boisterous makes a lot of noise and has a lot of energy: *a class of boisterous five year olds*

bok choy /ˌbɒk 'tʃɔɪ $ ˌbɑːk-/ *n* another spelling of PAK CHOI

bold /bəʊld $ boʊld/ *adj comparative* **bolder**, *superlative* **boldest**
1 PERSON/ACTION not afraid of taking risks and making difficult decisions: *In a surprisingly bold move, he is threatening court action against the company.* | *My aunt Flo was a bold determined woman.* | *He had the ability to take bold imaginative decisions.*
2 MANNER/APPEARANCE so confident or determined that you sometimes offend people: *You should be feeling confident and bold when you meet your bank manager.* | *She marched into his office as bold as brass* (=very confident and not showing enough respect).
3 COLOURS/SHAPES very strong or bright so that you notice them: *bold geometric shapes* | *Stripes are bold, bright, and fun to wear.* | *bold colours*
4 LINES/WRITING written or drawn in a very clear way: *an envelope addressed to her in a bold black hand* | *The graphics are bold and colourful.* | *The print should be bold and easy to read.*
5 PRINTED LETTERS printed in letters that are darker and thicker than ordinary printed letters: *All the headings are in bold type.*
6 make/be so bold (as to do sth) *formal* to do something that other people feel is rude or not acceptable: *I see that you have been so bold as to ask for food at this late hour.*
7 if I may be so bold *BrE spoken formal* used when asking someone a question, to show that you are slightly annoyed with them: *Tell me, if I may be so bold as to ask, precisely what you are talking about.* —**boldly** *adv* —**boldness** *n* [U]

bold·face /'bəʊldfeɪs $ 'boʊld-/ *n* [U] *technical* a way of printing letters that makes them thicker and darker than normal —**boldfaced** *adj* —**boldface** *adj*

bole /bəʊl $ boʊl/ *n* [C] *literary* the main part of a tree; ➡ **trunk**

bo·le·ro¹ /bə'leərəʊ $ -'leroʊ/ *n plural* **boleros** [C] a type of Spanish dance, or the music for this dance

bol·e·ro² /'bɒlərəʊ $ bə'leroʊ/ *n plural* **boleros** [C] a short jacket for a woman

boll /bəʊl $ boʊl/ *n* [C] the part of a cotton plant that contains the seeds

bol·lard /'bɒləd, -lɑːd $ 'bɑːlərd/ *n* [C] **1** *BrE* a short thick post in the street that is used to stop traffic entering an area or to show a JUNCTION more clearly → see picture at TOWN **2** a thick stone or metal post used for tying ships to when they are in port

bol·lock /'bɒlək $ 'bɑː-/ *v* [T] *BrE spoken informal* to tell someone angrily that you do not like what they have done: *I'll bollock him for sticking his rubbish in my cupboard.*

bol·lock·ing /'bɒləkɪŋ $ 'bɑː-/ *n* [C] *BrE spoken informal* when someone tells you that they are very angry with you: *I expect I'll get a right bollocking from my boss when she finds out.*

bol·locks /'bɒləks $ 'bɑː-/ *n* [plural] *BrE spoken informal* **1** used to say rudely that you think something is wrong or stupid; ➡ **rubbish**: *Your lyrics are complete bollocks; they don't actually mean anything, do they?* | *She's just talking a load of old bollocks.* **2** a word used to emphasize that you are annoyed or angry: *Oh bollocks! We've missed it.* **3 bollocks to you/that/it etc** used when you refuse to accept or obey something: *Yeah well bollocks to you too mate!* **4** the two round male organs that produce SPERM; ➡ **testicle**

boll 'weevil n [C] an insect that eats and destroys cotton plants

bo·lo·gna /bə'ləʊni, -njə $ -'loʊ-/ n [U] a type of cooked meat often eaten in sandwiches

bo·lo·ney /bə'ləʊni $ -'loʊ-/ n [U] another spelling of BALONEY

bo·lo tie /'bəʊləʊ taɪ $ 'boʊloʊ-/ n [C] AmE a string worn around your neck that you fasten with a decoration

Bol·she·vik /'bɒlʃəvɪk $ 'boʊl-/ n [C] **1** someone who supported the COMMUNIST party at the time of the Russian Revolution in 1917 **2** old-fashioned an insulting way of talking about a communist or someone who has strong LEFT-WING opinions —**bolshevik** adj

bol·shie, bolshy /'bəʊlʃi $ 'boʊl-/ adj BrE informal tending to be angry or annoyed and not to obey people: There's no need to be so bolshie. —**bolshiness** n [U]

bol·ster¹ /'bəʊlstə $ 'boʊlstər/ v also **bolster up** [T] **1** to help someone to feel better and more positive: He is making a bold attempt to bolster the territory's confidence. **2** to improve something: his efforts to bolster his career

bolster² n [C] a long firm PILLOW, usually shaped like a tube

bolt¹ /bəʊlt $ boʊlt/ n [C]
1 LOCK a metal bar that you slide across a door or window to fasten it → see picture at LOCK²
2 SCREW a screw with a flat head and no point, for fastening things together
3 a bolt from (out of) the blue news that is sudden and unexpected: Was this money a bolt from the blue or did you know you were going to get it?
4 bolt of lightning lightning that appears as a white line in the sky: There's not much left of his house after it was struck by a bolt of lightning. → THUNDERBOLT
5 make a bolt for it BrE to suddenly try to escape from somewhere: They attacked the driver and he straightaway made a bolt for it.
6 WEAPON a short heavy ARROW that is fired from a CROSSBOW
7 CLOTH a large long roll of cloth → have shot your bolt at SHOOT¹ (24); → the nuts and bolts of sth at NUT¹ (6)

bolt² v **1** [I] to suddenly run somewhere very quickly, especially in order to escape or because you are frightened: The horse reared up and bolted. | Kevin had bolted through the open window. **2** [T] also **bolt down** to eat very quickly; ☐ gobble: He bolted down his breakfast. **3** [T] to fasten two things together using a bolt: **bolt sth to sth** The cell contained an iron bedframe bolted to the floor. | **bolt sth together** The boxes were made of heavy panels of metal bolted together. **4** [T] to lock a door or window by sliding a bolt across

bolt³ adv sit/stand bolt upright to sit or stand with your back straight, often because something has frightened you: She sat bolt upright in the back seat during the whole journey.

bolt·hole /'bəʊlthəʊl $ 'boʊlthoʊl/ n [C] BrE a place where you can escape to and hide: a bolthole in the country

bolt-on adj especially BrE **bolt-on part/component/extra** something that is connected to the outside of a machine after it has been made, and is then part of the machine

bomb¹ S2 W3 /bɒm $ bɑːm/ n [C]
1 WEAPON a weapon made of material that will explode

| a bomb explodes/goes off |
| drop a bomb |
| plant a bomb (=leave a bomb somewhere) |
| detonate a bomb (=make a bomb explode) |
| unexploded bomb |
| bomb attack |
| bomb threat |
| bomb blast |

Fortunately the house was empty when the **bomb exploded**. | The **bomb went off** at 9.30 in the

---

morning. | Enemy planes **dropped** over 200 **bombs** during the raid. | Terrorists had **planted a bomb** somewhere in the station. | One theory is that the **bomb was detonated** by remote control. | Unexploded **bombs** were found there as late as the 1960s. | a **bomb attack** on a crowded bus in the city centre | The station was closed for six hours following a **bomb threat**. | the **bomb blast** that killed more than one and injured more than 100 people → ATOMIC BOMB, CAR BOMB, CLUSTER BOMB, HYDROGEN BOMB, LETTER BOMB, NEUTRON BOMB, NUCLEAR BOMB, PARCEL BOMB, PETROL BOMB, SMART BOMB, SMOKE BOMB, STINK BOMB, TIME BOMB

2 BAD PERFORMANCE/EVENT AmE informal a play, film, event etc that is not successful: This is just another one of Hollywood's bland and boring bombs.
3 be the bomb informal to be very good or exciting: That new P Diddy CD is the bomb.
4 the bomb used to describe NUCLEAR weapons, and especially the HYDROGEN BOMB: Voices of dissent began to rise against the bomb.
5 cost a bomb BrE informal to cost a lot of money
6 make a bomb BrE informal to get a lot of money by doing something

bomb² v **1** [T] to attack a place by leaving a bomb there, or by dropping bombs on it from a plane: The town was heavily bombed in World War II. | Government aircraft have been bombing civilian areas. → CARPET-BOMB, DIVE-BOMB **2** [I always + adv/prep] BrE informal to move or drive very quickly: Suddenly a police car came bombing down the high street. **3** [I,T] AmE informal to fail a test very badly: I bombed my midterm. **4** [I] AmE if a play, film, event etc bombs, it is not successful: His latest play bombed on Broadway.

be bombed out phr v if a building or the people in it are bombed out, the building is completely destroyed: My family were bombed out in 1941.

bom·bard /bɒm'bɑːd $ bɑːm'bɑːrd/ v [T] **1** to attack a place for a long time using large weapons, bombs etc: I had been in action bombarding the Normandy coast. **2** to do something too often or too much, for example criticizing or questioning someone, or giving too much information: The office was bombarded by telephone calls. | **bombard sb with sth** They bombarded him with questions. | Today we are bombarded with advice on what to eat and what to avoid.

bom·bar·dier /ˌbɒmbə'dɪə◂ $ ˌbɑːmbər'dɪr/ n [C] **1** the person on a military aircraft responsible for dropping bombs **2** a low rank in the British army

bom·bard·ment /bɒm'bɑːdmənt $ bɑːm'bɑːrd-/ n [C,U] a continuous attack on a place by big guns and bombs: The bombardment continued for a terrible nine hours. | **aerial/artillery/naval bombardment** (=attack from the air, land, or sea) The effects of the artillery bombardment were devastating.

bom·bas·tic /bɒm'bæstɪk $ bɑːm-/ adj bombastic language contains long words that sound important but have no real meaning: He is best known for three rather bombastic poems. —**bombast** /'bɒmbæst $ 'bɑːm-/ n [U]

'bomb dis·pos·al n [U] the job of dealing with bombs that have not exploded, and making them safe: **bomb disposal experts/team/squad/unit** The device, which contained 400lbs of explosive, was made safe by army bomb disposal experts.

bombed /bɒmd $ bɑːmd/ adj [not before noun] informal very drunk or affected by illegal drugs; ☐ stoned: I feel like going out and getting completely bombed.

bomb·er /'bɒmə $ 'bɑːmər/ n [C] **1** a plane that carries and drops bombs **2** someone who hides a bomb somewhere in order to destroy something

'bomber jacket n [C] a short jacket which fits tightly around your waist

bomb·ing /'bɒmɪŋ $ 'bɑːm-/ n [C,U] the use of bombs to attack a place: The south-west of the country suffered an intensive **bombing campaign**. | They were planning *bombing raids in some of America's major cities.* | *terrorist network responsible for a **wave of bombings** in Paris* | [+of] *the bombing of Hiroshima*

'**bomb scare** n [C] when people have to be moved out of a building because there may be a bomb there: *a bomb scare in Central London*

bomb·shell /'bɒmʃel $ 'ba:m-/ n [C] **1** an unexpected and very shocking piece of news: *Then came the bombshell: the factory was to close down.* | *Finally she **dropped the bombshell**. She was pregnant, she said.* **2 blonde bombshell** *humorous* a sexually attractive woman with light-coloured hair

'**bomb ,shelter** n [C] a room or building that is built to protect people from bomb attacks

'**bomb site** n [C] a place where a bomb has destroyed several buildings in a town: *They've pulled down so many buildings around here it looks like a bomb site.*

bo·na fi·de /ˌbəʊnə 'faɪdi $ 'bəʊnə faɪd/ adj real, true, and not intended to deceive anyone: *Only bona fide members are allowed to use the club pool.*

bona fi·des /ˌbəʊnə 'faɪdiːz $ ˌbəʊnə-, 'bəʊnə faɪdz/ n [plural] *BrE* if you check someone's bona fides, you check that they are who they say they are, and that their intentions are good and honest: *The firm required a reference to establish the bona fides of the client.*

bo·nan·za /bə'nænzə, bəʊ- $ bə-, bəʊ-/ n [C] a lucky or successful situation where people can make a lot of money: *2002 will be a bonanza year for the computer industry.* | *an amazing cash bonanza*

bon ap·pe·tit /ˌbɒn æpə'tiː $ ˌbəʊn æpeɪ-/ interjection said to someone before they start eating a meal, to tell them you hope they enjoy their food

bonce /bɒns $ ba:ns/ n [C] *BrE informal* your head

bond[1] W3 /bɒnd $ ba:nd/ n [C]
1 MONEY an official document promising that a government or company will pay back money that it has borrowed, often with INTEREST: *My father put all his money into stock market bonds.* | *furious trading on the bond market*
2 RELATIONSHIP something that unites two or more people or groups, such as love, or a shared interest or idea; → **tie**: [+between] *the emotional bond between mother and child* | [+with] *the United States' special bond with Britain* | [+of] *lifelong bonds of family and friendship*
3 bonds [plural] *literary* something that limits your freedom and prevents you from doing what you want: [+of] *the bonds of fear and guilt*
4 WITH GLUE the way in which two surfaces become attached to each other using glue: *Use a glue gun to form a strong bond on wood or china.*
5 CHEMISTRY *technical* the chemical force that holds atoms together in a MOLECULE: *In each methane molecule there are four CH bonds.*
6 WRITTEN AGREEMENT a written agreement to do something, that makes you legally responsible for doing it; → **contract**
7 my word is my bond *formal* used to say that you will definitely do what you have promised
8 in/out of bond *technical* in or out of a BONDED WAREHOUSE

bond[2] v **1** [I] if two things bond with each other, they become firmly fixed together, especially after they have been joined with glue: *It takes less than 10 minutes for the two surfaces to bond.* **2** [I] to develop a special relationship with someone: [+with] *Time must be given for the mother to bond with her baby.* **3** [T] *technical* to keep goods in a bonded warehouse

bond·age /'bɒndɪdʒ $ 'ba:n-/ n [U] **1** the state of having your freedom limited, or being prevented from doing what you want: *young women lost to the bondage of early motherhood* **2** *literary* the state of being a slave: **in bondage** *Since the age of 13 he had been in bondage.* **3** the practice of being tied up for sexual pleasure

bonded 'warehouse n [C] *technical* an official place for storing goods that have been brought into a country before tax has been paid on them

bond·hold·er /'bɒnd,həʊldə $ 'ba:nd,hoʊldər/ n [C] *technical* someone who owns government or industrial BONDS

bond·ing /'bɒndɪŋ $ 'ba:n-/ n [U] **1** a process in which a special relationship develops between two or more people: [+between] *the bonding between mare and foal* **2 male/female bonding** *informal* the activity of doing things with other people of the same sex, so that you feel good about being a man or a woman: *They're in the bar again doing some male bonding!* **3** *technical* the connection of atoms or of two surfaces that are glued together: *chemical bonding*

bone[1] S2 W2 /bəʊn $ boʊn/ n
1 [C] one of the hard parts that together form the frame of a human, animal, or fish body: *The X-ray showed that the bone was broken in two places.* | **hip/leg/cheek etc bone** (=the bone in your hip etc) *He broke his collar bone.* | **big-boned/fine-boned/small-boned etc** (=with big etc bones) *She was tall and big-boned.* | *Amelia had inherited her mother's good **bone structure**.*
2 [U] a substance made of bones: *the bone handle of his dagger*
3 the bare bones the simplest and most important details of something: *I can't tell you more than the bare bones of what happened.*
4 make no bones about (doing) sth to not feel nervous or ashamed about doing or saying something: *Mary made no bones about enjoying a drink.*
5 bone of contention something that causes arguments between people: *The examination system has long been a serious bone of contention in this country.*
6 be chilled/frozen to the bone to be extremely cold
7 skin and bone very thin: *She was all skin and bone.*
8 a bag of bones someone who is much too thin
9 feel/know sth in your bones to be certain that something is true, even though you have no proof and cannot explain why you are certain: *She knew that something good was sure to happen; she could feel it in her bones.*
10 have a bone to pick with sb *spoken* used to tell someone that you are annoyed with them and want to talk about it
11 close to the bone a remark, statement etc that is close to the bone is close to the truth in a way that may offend someone: *His jokes were a bit close to the bone.*
12 cut sth to the bone to reduce costs, services etc as much as possible: *Shops cut prices to the bone in the January sales.*
13 on the bone meat that is served on the bone is still joined to the bone: *a boiled ham on the bone*
14 off the bone meat that is served off the bone has been cut away from the bone: *roasted duck, off the bone*
→ **dry as a bone** at DRY[1] (1); → **work your fingers to the bone** at WORK[1] (29)

bone[2] v [T] to remove the bones from fish or meat: *boned breast and thigh meat*
bone up on sth *phr v* to learn as much as you can about a subject, because you need the knowledge, for example for an examination: *I have to bone up on criminal law for a test next week.*

bone 'china n [U] delicate and expensive cups, plates etc that are made partly with crushed bone

bone 'dry adj completely dry: *There had been no rain for months and the land was bone dry.*

bone·head /'bəʊnhed $ 'boʊn-/ n [C] *informal* a stupid person

bone 'idle adj *BrE* extremely lazy: *He's just bone idle.*

bone·less /'bəʊnləs $ 'boʊn-/ adj boneless meat or fish has had the bones taken out: *boneless chicken breasts*

'**bone ,marrow** n [U] the soft substance in the hollow centre of bones; ◪ **marrow**: *a bone marrow transplant*

bone·meal also **bone meal** /ˈbəʊnmiːl $ ˈboʊn-/ n [U] a substance used to feed plants that is made of crushed bones

bon·er /ˈbəʊnə $ ˈboʊnər/ n [singular] informal not polite an ERECTION

bon·fire /ˈbɒnfaɪə $ ˈbɑːnfaɪr/ n [C] a large outdoor fire, either for burning waste or for a party: Someone had lit a bonfire and we sat round it chatting.

bonfire ˌnight, Bonfire Night n [U] November 5th, when people in Britain light FIREWORKS and burn a GUY on a large outdoor fire; ◲ **Guy Fawkes' night**

bong /bɒŋ $ bɑːŋ/ n [C] **1** a deep sound made by a large bell **2** informal an object used for smoking CAN-NABIS, in which the smoke goes through water to make it cool

bon·gos /ˈbɒŋɡəʊz $ ˈbɑːŋɡoʊz/ also **ˈbongo drums** n [plural] a pair of small drums that you play with your hands → see picture at DRUM[1]

bon·ho·mie /ˈbɒnəmi $ ˌbɑːnəˈmiː/ n [U] formal a friendly feeling among a group of people: They were relaxed and full of bonhomie.

bonk[1] /bɒŋk $ bɑːŋk/ v [I,T] **1** BrE informal to have sex with someone – used humorously **2** informal to hit someone lightly on the head or to hit your head on something: He fell, bonking his head against a tree.

bonk[2] n **1** [singular] BrE informal the action of having sex – used humorously: a quick bonk **2** [C] informal the action of hitting someone lightly on the head, or hitting your head against something **3** [C] informal a sudden short deep sound, for example when something hits the ground

bon·kers /ˈbɒŋkəz $ ˈbɑːŋkərz/ adj [not before noun] **1** slightly crazy **2** **drive sb bonkers** to make someone feel crazy or very annoyed: Thinking about the whole problem has driven me nearly bonkers.

bon mot /ˌbɒn ˈməʊ $ ˌboʊn ˈmoʊ/ n [C] written a clever remark

bon·net /ˈbɒnɪt $ ˈbɑː-/ n [C] **1** BrE the metal lid over the front of a car; ◲ **hood** AmE: I'll need to check under the bonnet. → see picture at CAR **2 a)** a warm hat that a baby wears which ties under its chin **b)** a type of hat that women wore in the past which tied under their chin and often had a wide BRIM → see picture at HAT → **have a bee in your bonnet** at BEE (2)

bon·ny /ˈbɒni $ ˈbɑːni/ adj BrE pretty and healthy: a bonny baby

bon·sai /ˈbɒnsaɪ, ˈbəʊn- $ bɒnˈsaɪ, ˈbɑːnsaɪ/ n [C,U] a tree that is grown so that it always stays very small, or the art of growing trees in this way —**bonsai** adj

bonsai tree

bo·nus S2 /ˈbəʊnəs $ ˈboʊ-/ n [C] **1** money added to someone's wages, especially as a reward for good work: Long-term savers qualify for a cash bonus. | Further additions to your pay may take the form of bonus payments. | a Christmas bonus | Each worker receives an annual bonus. | a £20,000 bonus **2** something good that you did not expect in a situation: [+for] Britain's possession of North Sea oil has proved a bonus for British technology. | He promised to take me to the match with the **added bonus** of an afternoon off school. **3** **no-claims bonus** BrE a reduction in the cost of your car insurance when you do not make a CLAIM in a particular year

bon vi·vant /ˌbɒn viːˈvɒnt $ ˌboʊn viːˈvɑːnt/ also **bon viveur** /-viːˈvɜː $ -viːˈvɜːr/ n [C] formal someone who enjoys good food and wine, and being with people

bon voy·age /ˌbɒn vɔɪˈɑːʒ $ ˌboʊn-/ interjection used to wish someone a good journey

bon·y /ˈbəʊni $ ˈboʊ-/ adj **1** someone or part of their body that is bony is very thin: She had a bony intelligent face. | He was tall and bony. **2** bony meat or fish contains a lot of small bones **3** a part of an animal that is bony consists mostly of bone

boo[1] /buː/ v [I,T] to shout 'boo' to show that you do not like a person, performance, idea etc: Some of the audience started booing. | She was **booed off stage** (=they shouted 'boo' until she left the stage).

boo[2] interjection **1** a noise made by people who do not like a person, performance, idea etc **2** a word you shout suddenly to someone as a joke in order to frighten them **3** **wouldn't say boo to a goose** an expression used to describe a shy quiet person

boob[1] /buːb/ n [C] **1** [usually plural] informal a woman's breast **2** BrE informal a silly mistake **3** AmE old-fashioned a stupid or silly person

boob[2] v [I] BrE informal to make a stupid mistake; ◲ **goof** AmE: I think Jean's boobed again.

ˈboo-boo n [C] informal a silly mistake: I **made** a bit of a boo-boo asking her about David!

ˈboob tube n [C] **1** BrE a piece of women's clothing made of material that stretches, that covers her chest; ◲ **tube top** AmE **2** **the boob tube** AmE informal the television

boo·by /ˈbuːbi/ n plural **boobies** [C] informal a silly or stupid person

ˈbooby hatch n [singular] AmE old-fashioned informal a mental hospital

ˈbooby prize n [C] informal a prize given as a joke to the person who is last in a competition

ˈbooby trap, booby-trap n [C] **1** a hidden bomb that explodes when you touch something else that is connected to it: He lost both legs in a booby trap bomb blast. **2** a HARMLESS trap that you arrange for someone as a joke —**booby-trapped** adj —**booby trap** v

boog·er /ˈbʊɡə, ˈbuː- $ -ər/ n [C] AmE informal a thick piece of MUCUS from your nose

boo·gey·man /ˈbuːɡimæn/ n [C] a BOGEYMAN

boo·gie[1] /ˈbuːɡi $ ˈbʊɡi/ v [I] informal to dance, especially to fast popular music

boogie[2] also **boogie woo·gie** /ˌbuːɡi ˈwuːɡi $ ˌbʊɡi ˈwʊɡi/ n [U] **1** a type of music played on the piano with a strong fast RHYTHM: boogie rock at its finest **2** a boogie informal a dance, or an occasion when you dance, especially to fast popular music: You work hard all week – you deserve a boogie now and then.

boo·hoo /ˌbuː ˈhuː/ interjection written used in stories to show that someone is crying

book[1] S1 W1 /bʊk/ n
1 PRINTED PAGES [C] a set of printed pages that are held together in a cover so that you can read them: I've just started reading a book by Graham Greene. | a cookery book | a special exhibition of children's books | [+about/on] a book about cats | a cheap paperback book | I can't afford to buy hardback books.
2 TO WRITE IN [C] a set of sheets of paper held together in a cover so that you can write on them: a black address book | a notebook
3 SET OF THINGS [C] a set of things such as stamps, matches, or tickets, held together inside a paper cover: a cheque book
4 books [plural] **a) ACCOUNTS** written records of the financial accounts of a business: An accountant will examine the company's books. | A small firm that is having problems **balancing** the books (=keeping its profits and spending equal) | **on the books** They have £50 billion worth of orders on the books. → **cook the books** at COOK[1] (3) **b) JOBS** the names of people who use a company's services, or who are sent by a company to work for other people: **on sb's books** an agent

with a lot of popular actors on his books
5 by the book exactly according to rules or instructions: *She feels she has to go by the book and can't use her creativity.* | **do/play sth by the book** *The police were careful to do everything by the book.*
6 a **closed book** a subject that you do not understand or know anything about: *Chemistry is a closed book to me.*
7 be in sb's good/bad books *informal* used to say that someone is pleased or annoyed with you
8 LAW be on the books if a law is on the books, it is part of the set of laws in a country, town, area etc
9 PART OF A BOOK [C] one of the parts that a very large book such as the Bible is divided into: [+of] *the Book of Isaiah*
10 in my book *spoken* said when giving your opinion: *In my book, nothing is more important than football.*
11 bring sb to book to punish someone for breaking laws or rules, especially when you have been trying to punish them for a long time: *War criminals must be brought to book.* → STATUTE BOOK; → take a leaf out of sb's book at LEAF[1] (2); → read sb like a book at READ[1] (16); → suit sb's book at SUIT[2] (5); → a turn-up for the book at TURN-UP (2); → throw the book at sb at THROW[1] (26)

WORD FOCUS: BOOK
a book about imaginary events: **novel, thriller, mystery, horror story, love story, detective story, whodunit**
books about imaginary events in general: **fiction, science fiction, romantic fiction, crime fiction, chick lit** *informal*
famous or important novels, poems etc: **literature**
books about real events: **non-fiction**
a book that gives information: **reference book, encyclopedia, textbook**
a book about someone's life: **biography, autobiography, journal, diary**
someone who writes books: **writer, author, novelist**
a book with a hard cover: **hardback** *BrE/* **hardcover** *AmE*
a book with a cover made of paper or card: **paperback**

book[2] [S2] *v*
1 [I,T] to make arrangements to stay in a place, eat in a restaurant, go to a theatre etc at a particular time in the future; → **reserve**: *Have you booked a holiday this year?* | *You need to book well in advance for Christmas.* | *The flight was already fully booked* (=no more seats were available). | *To get tickets, you have to book in advance.* | *The show's booked solid* (=all the tickets have been sold) *until February.*
2 [T] to arrange for someone such as a singer to perform on a particular date: *The band was booked for a benefit show in Los Angeles.*
3 be booked up a) if a hotel, restaurant etc is booked up, there are no more rooms, places, seats etc still available: *The courses quickly get booked up.* **b)** if someone is booked up, they are extremely busy and have arranged a lot of things they must do: *I'm all booked up this week – can we get together next Friday?*
4 [T] to arrange for someone to go to a hotel, fly on a plane etc: *I've booked you a flight on Saturday.* | **book sb on/in etc** *I'll book you in at the Hilton.*
5 [T] to put someone's name officially in police records, along with the charge made against them: *Smith was booked on suspicion of attempted murder.*
6 [T] *BrE* when a REFEREE in a sports game books a player who has broken the rules, he or she officially writes down the player's name in a book as a punishment
book in also **book into sth** *phr v*
BrE to arrive at a hotel and say who you are etc; → **check in**: *Several tourists were booking in.*

book·a·ble /'bʊkəbəl/ *adj* **1** *BrE* tickets for a concert, performance etc that are bookable can be ordered before it happens **2 bookable offence** an offence for which a sports player can be punished by having his or her name written into the REFEREE's book

book·bind·ing /'bʊk,baɪndɪŋ/ *n* [U] the process of fastening the pages of books inside a cover —**bookbinder** *n* [C]
book·case /'bʊk-keɪs/ *n* [C] a piece of furniture with shelves to hold books
'book club *n* [C] **1** a club that offers books cheaply to its members **2** a group of people who meet regularly to discuss a particular book they have all read
book·end /'bʊkend/ *n* [C usually plural] one of a pair of objects that you put at the end of a row of books to prevent them from falling over
book·ie /'bʊki/ *n* [C] *informal* a BOOKMAKER
book·ing [S3] /'bʊkɪŋ/ *n* [C]
1 an arrangement to travel by train, use a hotel room etc at a particular time in the future; → **reservation**: *bookings on cruise ships* | *I made a booking for two double rooms.* | *I'm calling to confirm my booking* (=say definitely that I want to travel etc). | *If you cancel your booking, there will be a small charge.* | *Places on the course are limited and advance booking is essential.* | *block booking* (=a booking for a large number of dates, seats, rooms etc)
2 an arrangement made by a performer to perform at a particular time in the future
3 *BrE* the act of writing a football player's name in a book as a punishment for breaking the rules
'booking ,office *n* [C] *BrE* a place where you can buy train or bus tickets; ▣ **ticket office** → BOX OFFICE
book·ish /'bʊkɪʃ/ *adj* someone who is bookish is more interested in reading and studying than in sports or other activities: *a shy bookish man*
book·keep·ing /'bʊk,kiːpɪŋ/ *n* [U] the job or activity of recording the financial accounts of an organization; → **accountancy**
book·let [S2] /'bʊklɪt/ *n* [C] a very short book that usually contains information on one particular subject; → **leaflet**: *a free booklet on drug abuse*
book·mak·er /'bʊk,meɪkə $ -ər/ also **bookie** *informal n* [C] someone whose job is to collect money that people want to risk on the result of a race, competition etc, and who pays them if they guess correctly
book·mark[1] /'bʊkmɑːk $ -mɑːrk/ *n* [C] **1** a piece of paper, leather etc that you put in a book to show you the last page you have read **2** a way of saving the address of a page on the Internet so that you can find it again easily
bookmark[2] *v* [T] to save the address of a page on the Internet so that you can find it again easily
book·mo·bile /'bʊkməbiːl/ *n* [C] *AmE* a vehicle that contains a library and travels to different places so that people can use it; ▣ **mobile library** *BrE*
book·plate /'bʊkpleɪt/ *n* [C] a decorated piece of paper with your name on it, that you stick in the front of your books
book·rest /'bʊk-rest/ *n* [C] a metal or wood frame that holds a book upright so that you can read it without holding it in your hands
book·sell·er /'bʊk,selə $ -ər/ *n* [C] a person or company that sells books
book·shelf /'bʊkʃelf/ *n plural* **bookshelves** /-ʃelvz/ [C] a shelf that you keep books on, or a piece of furniture used for holding books; → **bookcase**; → see picture at BEDROOM
book·shop /'bʊkʃɒp $ -ʃɑːp/ *n* [C] *especially BrE* a shop that sells books; ▣ **bookstore** *AmE*
book·stall /'bʊkstɔːl $ -stɒːl/ *n* [C] *BrE* a small shop that has an open front and sells books and magazines, often at a railway station; ▣ **newsstand** *AmE*
book·store /'bʊkstɔː $ -stɔːr/ *n* [C] *AmE* a shop that sells books; ▣ **bookshop**
'book ,token *n* [C] *BrE* a card that you can exchange for books: *She gave me a book token for Christmas.*
'book ,value *n* [C] **1** how much a car of a particular age, style etc should be worth if you sold it **2** *technical* **a)** the value of a business after you sell all of its ASSETS

and pay all of its debts **b)** the value of something that a company owns, which it lists in its accounts

book·worm /'bʊkwɜːm $ -wɜːrm/ *n* [C] **1** someone who likes reading very much **2** an insect that eats books

boom¹ S3 /buːm/ *n*
1 INCREASE IN BUSINESS [singular] a quick increase of business activity; ◪ **slump**: *The boom has created job opportunities.* | [+in] *a sudden boom in the housing market* | **consumer/investment/property etc boom** *the post-war property boom* | **boom years/times** *In boom times, airlines do well.* | *the economic boom of the 1950s* | *The economy went from boom to bust* (=from increasing to decreasing) *very quickly.* → BOOM TOWN
2 WHEN STH IS POPULAR [singular] an increase in how popular or successful something is, or in how often it happens: *the disco boom of the 1970s* | [+in] *the boom in youth soccer in the U.S.* → BABY BOOM
3 SOUND [C] a deep loud sound that you can hear for several seconds after it begins, especially the sound of an explosion or a large gun: *the dull boom of the cannons* → SONIC BOOM
4 BOAT [C] a long pole on a boat that is attached to the bottom of a sail, and that you move to change the position of the sail
5 LONG POLE [C] **a)** a long pole used as part of a piece of equipment that loads and unloads things **b)** a long pole that has a camera or MICROPHONE on the end
6 ON A RIVER/HARBOUR [C] something that is stretched across a river or a BAY to prevent things floating down or across it

boom² *v* **1** [I usually in progressive] if business, trade, or a particular area is booming, it is increasing and being very successful: *Business was booming, and money wasn't a problem.* | *Tourism on the island has boomed.* **2** also **boom (sth ⇔) out** [T] to say something in a loud deep voice: *'Ladies and gentlemen,' his voice boomed out.* **3** also **boom out** [I] to make a loud deep sound: *Guns boomed in the distance.* —**booming** *adj*: *a booming economy*

boom box *n* [C] *AmE informal* a GHETTO BLASTER

boo·me·rang¹ /'buːməræŋ/ *n* [C] a curved stick that flies in a circle and comes back to you when you throw it, first used in Australia

boomerang² *v* [I] if a plan or action boomerangs on someone, it affects them badly instead of the person who it was intended to affect

boom town *n* [C] a town or city that suddenly becomes very successful because there is a lot of new industry

boon /buːn/ *n* [C usually singular] something that is very useful and makes your life a lot easier or better: *The bus service is a real boon to people in the village.*

boon com·pan·ion *n* [C] *literary* a very close friend

boon·docks /'buːndɒks $ -dɑːks/ *n* [plural] *AmE informal* **the boondocks** a place that is a long way from the nearest town

boon·dog·gle /'buːn ˌdɒgl $ -ˌdɑːgl/ *n* [singular] *AmE informal* an officially organized plan or activity that is very complicated and wastes a lot of time, money, and effort: *a bureaucratic boondoggle*

boo·nies /'buːniz/ *n* [plural] *AmE informal* the boondocks

boor /bʊə $ bʊr/ *n* [C] a man who behaves in a very rude way —**boorish** *adj* —**boorishly** *adv*

boost¹ /buːst/ *v* [T] **1** to increase or improve something and make it more successful: *The new resort area has boosted tourism.* | **boost sb's confidence/morale/ego** *The win boosted the team's confidence.* **2** also **boost up** to help someone reach a higher place by lifting or pushing them: *She put her foot on his hands, and he boosted her up.* **3** if a ROCKET or motor boosts a SPACECRAFT, it makes it go up into space or go in a particular direction **4** *AmE informal* to steal something

boost² *n* **1** [singular] something that gives someone more confidence, or that helps something increase, improve, or become successful: [+to] *a major boost to the economy* | [+for] *a multi-million pound boost for the British film industry* | *Add a little more vanilla, to give the flavor a boost.* | **get/receive a boost** *The community will get a boost from a new library and recreation center.* | **morale/ego boost** *The poll provided a morale boost for the Conservatives.* **2** **give sb a boost (up)** to lift someone so that they can reach a higher place: *If I give you a boost, could you reach the window?* **3** [U] an increase in the amount of power available to a ROCKET, piece of electrical equipment etc

boost·er /'buːstə $ -ər/ *n* [C] **1** a small quantity of a drug that increases the effect of one that was given before, so that someone continues to be protected against a disease: *a booster shot* **2** something that helps someone or something to increase or improve, or to be more successful or confident: *a booster pump* | *a profit booster for the company* | **morale/confidence booster** *Mail from home is a big morale booster for far-away troops.* **3** a rocket that is used to provide extra power for a SPACECRAFT to leave the Earth: *a giant booster rocket* **4** *AmE* someone who gives a lot of support to a person, organization, or an idea: *a dance organized by the school's booster club*

booster ˌseat also **booster ˌchair**; **booster ˌcushion** *BrE n* [C] a special seat for a small child that lets them sit in a higher position in a car or at a table

boot¹ S2 W3 /buːt/ *n* [C]
1 a type of shoe that covers your whole foot and the lower part of your leg; → **Wellington**: *hiking boots* | *a pair of walking boots* → RUBBER BOOT; → see picture at FOOTWEAR
2 *BrE* an enclosed space at the back of a car, used for carrying bags etc; ◪ **trunk** *AmE*: *The new model has a bigger boot.*
3 **the boot** *informal* when someone is forced to leave their job; ◪ **the sack**; → **dismiss**: *The chairman denied that he had been given the boot.* | *He should have got the boot years ago.*
4 **to boot** in addition to everything else you have mentioned: *She was a great sportswoman, and beautiful to boot.*
5 **put the boot in** *BrE informal* **a)** to criticize or be cruel to someone who is already in a bad situation **b)** to attack someone by kicking them repeatedly, especially when they are on the ground
6 **the boot is on the other foot** *BrE* used to say someone who has caused problems for other people in the past is now in a situation in which people are causing problems for them
7 *AmE* a metal object that the police attach to one of the wheels of an illegally parked car so that it cannot be moved; ◪ **wheel clamp** *BrE* → **be/get too big for your boots** at BIG¹ (14); → **lick sb's boots** at LICK¹ (7); → **tough as old boots** at TOUGH¹ (2)

boot² *v* **1** also **boot up** [I,T] to start the program that makes a computer ready to be used; → **load** **2** [T] *informal* to kick someone or something hard: **boot sth in/round/down etc** *The goalkeeper booted the ball upfield.* **3** [T] *AmE* to stop someone from moving their illegally parked vehicle by fixing a piece of equipment to one of the wheels; ◪ **clamp** *BrE*

boot sb ⇔ **out** *phr v informal* to force someone to leave a place, job, or organization, especially because they have done something wrong; ◪ **throw out**: *His fellow students booted him out of the class.*

boot camp *n* [C] a training place for people who have just joined the US Army, Navy, or Marine Corps

boot·ee, bootie /'buːtiː, buːˈtiː/ *n* [C] a short thick sock that a baby wears instead of a shoe

booth /buːð $ buːθ/ *n* [C] **1** a small partly enclosed place where one person can do something privately, such as use the telephone or vote: *a voting booth* **2** a small partly enclosed structure or tent where you can buy things, play games, or get information, usually at a market or a FAIR: *a crafts booth*   **3** a partly enclosed place in a restaurant with a table between two long seats

boot·lace /'buːtleɪs/ *n* [C usually plural] a long piece of string that you use to fasten a boot

boot·leg¹ /'buːtleg/ *adj* [only before noun] bootleg alcohol, software, or RECORDINGS are made and sold illegally: *bootleg tapes*

bootleg² *n* [C] an illegal recording of a music performance

bootleg³ *v* **bootlegged, bootlegging** [I,T] to illegally make or sell alcohol, or to illegally make or sell copies of software or RECORDINGS —**bootlegger** *n* [C] —**bootlegging** *n* [U]

boot sale *n* [C] *BrE* a CAR BOOT SALE

boot·straps /'buːtstræps/ *n* [plural] **pull/haul yourself up by your bootstraps** to improve your position and get out of a difficult situation by your own efforts, without help from other people

boot·y /'buːti/ *n* [U] *especially literary* valuable things that a group of people, especially an army that has just won a victory, take away or steal from somewhere; ▤ **loot**

boo·ty·li·cious /ˌbuːtɪˈlɪʃəs/ *adj informal* extremely nice, enjoyable, or attractive: *bootylicious babes*

booze /buːz/ *n* [singular, U] *informal* alcoholic drink: *a bottle of booze* | **on the booze** *He's been on the booze* (=drinking too much alcohol) *for five days.* | **off the booze** *My husband is now off the booze* (=no longer drinking too much alcohol) *and he is a different person.*

booz·er /'buːzə $ -ər/ *n* [C]   **1** *BrE* a PUB   **2** someone who often drinks a lot of alcohol

booze-up *n* [C] *BrE old-fashioned informal* a party where people drink a lot of alcohol

booz·ing /'buːzɪŋ/ *n* [U] *informal* when someone drinks alcohol, especially a lot of it: *You've been out boozing, haven't you?* —**booze** *v* [I]

booz·y /'buːzi/ *adj* showing that someone has drunk too much alcohol: *boozy laughter*

bop¹ /bɒp $ baːp/ *v* **bopped, bopping** *informal*   **1** [T] to hit someone, especially gently: *Tom bopped him on the nose.*   **2** [I] to dance to popular music: *kids happily bopping on the dance floor*   **3** *informal* [I always + adv/prep] to go somewhere or to several different places, especially to enjoy yourself: *We spent the afternoon just bopping around town.*

bop² *n*   **1** another word for BEBOP   **2** [C] a gentle hit: *a bop on the head*   **3** [singular] *BrE informal* a dance

bop·per /'bɒpə $ 'baːpər/ *n* → TEENYBOPPER

bo·rax /'bɔːræks/ *n* [U] a mineral used for cleaning

bor·del·lo /bɔːˈdeləʊ $ bɔːrˈdeloʊ/ *n plural* **bordellos** [C] *especially literary* a house where men can pay to have sex; ▤ **brothel**

bor·der¹ S3 W2 /'bɔːdə $ 'bɔːrdər/ *n* [C]
1 the official line that separates two countries, states, or areas, or the area close to this line

on the border
across/over the border
cross the border
a common/shared border
border town
border region/area
border controls
border guard
border crossing
border dispute (=a disagreement about where the border should be)
north/south/east/west of the border

the German-Polish border | [+**between**] *The river lies on the border between the US and Mexico.* | [+**with**] *regular patrols along the border with France* | *a market town* **on the border** *of England and Wales* | *He*

fled **across the border** *to freedom.* | *To* **cross the border**, *you will need a valid passport.* | *The two governments have settled their differences over their* **common border**. | *the* **border town** *of El Paso, Texas* | *The coach took us* **south of the border** *to Tia Juana.*

2 a band along or around the edge of something such as a picture or piece of material: *writing paper with a black border*

3 an area of soil where you plant flowers or bushes, along the edge of an area of grass: *a flower and shrub border* → see picture at LIMIT¹

4 something that separates one situation, state etc from another: *new scientific discoveries that are stretching the borders of knowledge*

border² *v* [T]   **1** if one country, state, or area borders another, it is next to it and shares a border with it: *countries that border the Mediterranean* | [+**on**] *The area borders on the Yorkshire Dales.*   **2** to form a border along the edge of something: *a path bordered by a high brick wall*

border on sth *phr v* to be very close to being something extreme: *His confidence bordered on arrogance.*

bor·der·land /'bɔːdəlænd $ 'bɔːrdər-/ *n* [C]   **1** the land near the border between two countries   **2** the borderland between two qualities is an unclear area that contains features of both of them

bor·der·line¹ /'bɔːdəlaɪn $ 'bɔːrdər-/ *adj*   **1** very close to not being acceptable: *In borderline cases, the student's coursework is considered, as well as exam grades.* | *The referee's decision was borderline.*   **2** [usually before noun] having qualities of both one situation, state etc and another more extreme situation or state: *a borderline schizophrenic* (=someone who has some signs of being mentally ill)

borderline² *n*   **1** [singular] the point at which one quality, situation, emotion etc ends and another begins: *She slipped over the borderline into sleep.* | **on the borderline** *I was on the borderline between a first- and a second-class degree.*   **2** [C] a border between two countries

bore¹ /bɔː $ bɔːr/ *v* the past tense of BEAR

bore² *v*   **1** [T] to make someone feel bored, especially by talking too much about something they are not interested in: *He's the sort of person who bores you at parties.* | *a film that will bore its young audience* | **bore sb with sth** *I won't bore you with all the technical details.* | **bore sb to death/tears** (=make them very bored)   **2** [I,T] to make a deep round hole in a hard surface: **bore sth through/into/in sth** *The machine bores a hole through the cards.* | [+**through/into**] *To build the tunnel they had to bore through solid rock.*   **3** [I + into] if someone's eyes bore into you, they look at you in a way that makes you feel uncomfortable

bore³ *n*   **1** [singular] something that is not interesting to you or that annoys you: *Waiting is a bore.* | *You'll find it's a terrible bore.*   **2** [C] someone who is boring, especially because they talk too much about themselves or about things that do not interest you: *He turned out to be a crashing bore* (=used to emphasize that someone is very boring).   **3** [singular] the measurement of the width of the inside of a long hollow object such as a pipe or the BARREL of a gun: *Take a length of piping with a bore of about 15mm.* | **12-/16-/20- etc bore** *a 12-bore shotgun* | **wide/narrow/fine bore** *a fine bore tube*   **4** [singular] a wave of water that moves quickly along a river from the sea at particular times of the year: *the Severn bore*   **5** [C] a BOREHOLE

bored S3 /bɔːd $ bɔːrd/ *adj* tired and impatient because you do not think something is interesting, or because you have nothing to do: *He was easily bored.* | *After a while I got bored and left.* | [+**with**] *Are you bored with your present job?* | **bored stiff/to tears/death/out of your mind** (=extremely bored) ⚠ Do not confuse **bored**, which describes a feeling, and **boring**, which describes something that makes you feel bored: *bored students* | *a boring job*

bore·dom /ˈbɔːdəm $ ˈbɔːr-/ n [U] the feeling you have when you are bored, or the quality of being boring: *a game to* **relieve the boredom** *of a long journey* | *the* **sheer boredom** *of being in jail* | [+with] *his boredom with life in a small town*

bore·hole /ˈbɔːhəul $ ˈbɔːrhoul/ n [C] a deep hole made using special equipment, especially in order to get water or oil out of the ground

bor·ing S2 /ˈbɔːrɪŋ/ adj not interesting in any way: *Her husband is about the most boring person I've ever met.* | *The job was dull and boring.* | **dead/incredibly/ terribly etc boring** (=very boring)

WORD FOCUS: BORING
similar words: **not very interesting, dull, dreary, drab**
very boring: **tedious, mind-numbing, soul-destroying**

born[1] /bɔːn $ bɔːrn/ a past participle of BEAR

born[2] S1 W2 v
1 be born when a person or animal is born, they come out of their mother's body or out of an egg: *Forty lambs were born this spring.* | [+in] *Swift was born in 1667.* | *She was born in India, where her father was a British official.* | [+at] *Then, most babies were born at home.* | [+on] *I was born on December 15th, 1973.* | **be born into/to/of sth** (=be born in a particular situation, type of family etc) *One-third of all children are born into single-parent families.* | **be born with sth** (=have a particular disease, type of character etc since birth) *Jenny was born with a small hole in her heart.* | *I was* **born and raised** (=born and grew up) *in Alabama.* | **be born blind/deaf etc** (=be blind, deaf etc when born) | *a* **newly-born baby** | *the queen's* **firstborn** *son* | **be born lucky/unlucky etc** (=always be lucky, unlucky etc) | **Australian/French etc born** (=born in or as a citizen of Australia etc) △ Do not say 'I born', 'I have been born', or 'I am born'. Say **I was born**: *He was born in Pakistan.*
2 START EXISTING be born something that is born starts to exist: *the country where the sport of cricket was born* | [+(out) of] (=existing as a result of a particular situation) *The alliance was born of necessity in 1941.* | *Bill spoke with a cynicism born of bitter experience.*
3 born and bred born and having grown up in a particular place and having the typical qualities of someone from that place: *I was born and bred in Liverpool.*
4 be born to do/be sth to be very suitable for a particular job, activity etc: *He was born to be a politician.*
5 I wasn't born yesterday *spoken* used to tell someone you think is lying to you that you are not stupid enough to believe them
6 there's one born every minute *spoken* used to say that someone has been very stupid or easily deceived
7 be born under a lucky/unlucky star to always have good or bad luck in your life
8 be born with a silver spoon in your mouth to be born into a rich family → NATURAL-BORN

born[3] adj [only before noun] **1** born leader/musician/ teacher etc someone who has a strong natural ability to lead, play music etc: *the skill of a born actor* **2** born loser someone who always seems to have bad things happen to them **3** in all your born days *old-fashioned* used to express surprise or annoyance at something that you have never heard about before: *In all her born days she had never heard anything like it.*

born-again adj **1** born-again Christian someone who has become an EVANGELICAL Christian **2** born-again non-smoker/vegetarian etc *informal* someone who has recently stopped smoking, eating meat etc, and who is always talking about it and suggesting that other people do the same

borne[1] /bɔːn $ bɔːrn/ the past participle of BEAR

borne[2] adj **1** water-borne/sea-borne/air-borne etc carried by water, the sea, air etc: *waterborne diseases* **2** be borne in on/upon sb if a fact is borne in on someone, they realize that it is true

bo·rough S2 /ˈbʌrə $ -rou/ n [C] a town, or part of a large city, that is responsible for managing its own

---

schools, hospitals, roads etc: *the borough of Queens in New York City* | *Lambeth Borough Council*

borough council n [C] *especially BrE* the organization that controls a borough

bor·row S2 W3 /ˈbɒrəu $ ˈbɑːrou, ˈbɔː-/ v [I,T]
1 to use something that belongs to someone else and that you must give back to them later; → **lend, loan**: *Can I borrow your pen for a minute?* | **borrow sth from sb** *You are allowed to borrow six books from the library at a time.* | *They* **borrowed heavily** (=borrowed a lot of money) *from the bank to start their new business.* △ Do not confuse **borrow** and **lend** (=give someone permission to use something of yours): *I borrowed his bike.* | *Can you lend me your pen?*
2 to take or copy someone's ideas, words etc and use them in your own work, language etc: **borrow sth from sb/sth** *I borrowed my ideas from Eliot's famous poem 'The Waste Land'.* | *To* **borrow a phrase** (=use what someone else has said), *if you can't stand the heat get out of the kitchen.* | [+from] *English has borrowed words from many languages.*
3 borrow trouble *AmE informal* to worry about something when it is not necessary → **be living on borrowed time** at LIVE[1] (17); → **beg, borrow, or steal** at BEG (8)

bor·row·er /ˈbɒrəuə $ ˈbɑːrouər, ˈbɔː-/ n [C] someone who has borrowed money and has not yet paid it all back: *Most borrowers pay 7% interest.*

bor·row·ing /ˈbɒrəuɪŋ $ ˈbɑːrou-, ˈbɔː-/ n **1** [C,U] when a person, government, company etc borrows money, or the money that they borrow: *Public borrowing has to be increased.* **2** [C] something such as a word, phrase, or idea that has been copied from another language, book etc: *words that are French borrowings* | [+from] *His music is full of borrowings from other composers.* **3** borrowings [plural] the total amount of money that a company or organization owes

borrowing powers n [plural] the amount of money that a company is allowed to borrow, according to its own rules

bor·stal /ˈbɔːstl $ ˈbɔːr-/ n [C,U] *BrE old-fashioned* a special prison for criminals who are not old enough to be in an ordinary prison

bosh /bɒʃ $ bɑːʃ/ n [U] *especially BrE old-fashioned* something that you think is silly, not good, or not true: *He thinks modern art is bosh.* —**bosh** *interjection*

bos·om /ˈbuzəm/ n **1** [C usually singular] *written* the front part of a woman's chest: *She cradled the child to her bosom.* **2** [C usually plural] a woman's breast **3** the bosom of the family/the Church etc the situation where you feel safe because you are with people who love and protect you **4** [singular] *literary* a word meaning someone's feelings and emotions, used especially when these are bad or unpleasant: *Drury harboured bitterness in his bosom.* **5** bosom friend/ buddy/pal *literary* a very close friend

bos·om·y /ˈbuzəmi/ adj having large breasts

boss[1] S2 W3 /bɒs $ bɔːs/ n [C]
1 the person who employs you or who is in charge of you at work; → **employer, manager, supervisor**: *I'll have to ask my boss for a day off.* | *Since I'm* **my own boss** (=I work for myself, rather than for an employer), *my hours are flexible.*
2 *informal* someone with an important position in a company or other organization: *the new boss at Paramount Pictures* | *union bosses* | *An alleged Mafia boss was acquitted last night.*
3 the person who is the strongest in a relationship, who controls a situation etc: *Remember, you're the parent. You're the boss.* | *When you first start training a dog, it's important to let him see that you're the boss.* | *You've got to* **show the kids who's boss.**
4 a round decoration on the surface of something, for example on the ceiling of an old building

[1] 000, [2] 000, [3] 000, most frequent words in [S] poken and [W] ritten English

boss² v [T] to tell people to do things, give them orders etc, especially when you have no authority to do it: **boss sb about** BrE/**around** *Five-year-old girls love to boss people around.*

boss³ adj informal very good, attractive, or fashionable: *a boss car*

bos·sa·no·va /ˌbɒsəˈnəʊvə $ ˌbɑːsəˈnoʊ-/ n [C] a dance that comes from Brazil, or the music for this dance

boss·y /ˈbɒsi $ ˈbɔːsi/ comparative **bossier**, superlative **bossiest** adj **1** always telling other people what to do, in a way that is annoying: *her loud bossy sister* **2 bossy-boots** BrE informal someone who you think tells other people what to do too often —**bossily** adv —**bossiness** n [U]

bo·sun /ˈbəʊsən $ ˈboʊ-/ n [C] an officer on a ship whose job is to organize the work and look after the equipment; ⊟ **boatswain**

bot /bɒt $ bɑːt/ n [C] technical a computer PROGRAM that performs the same operation many times in a row, for example one that searches for information on the Internet as part of a SEARCH ENGINE

bo·tan·i·cal /bəˈtænɪkəl/ adj [only before noun] relating to plants or the scientific study of plants —**botanically** /-kli/ adv

bo,tanical 'garden n [C] a large public garden where many different types of flowers and plants are grown for scientific study

bot·a·nist /ˈbɒtənɪst $ ˈbɑː-/ n [C] someone whose job is to make scientific studies of wild plants

bot·a·ny /ˈbɒtəni $ ˈbɑː-/ n [U] the scientific study of plants

botch¹ /bɒtʃ $ bɑːtʃ/ also **botch up** v [T] informal to do something badly, because you have been careless or because you do not have the skill to do it properly: *The builders really botched up our patio.* | *a botched investigation*

botch² also '**botch-up** BrE n [C] informal especially BrE a piece of work, a job etc that has been badly or carelessly done: *I've just made an awful botch of my translation.* | *The whole thing was a botch job.*

both¹ S1 W1 /bəʊθ $ boʊθ/ determiner, predeterminer, pron

1 used to talk about two people, things etc together, and emphasize that each is included; → **either**: *Both Helen's parents are doctors.* | *Hold it in both hands.* | *You can both swim, can't you?* | *They both started speaking together.* | *Oxford is not far from Stratford, so you can easily visit both in a day.* | [+of] *Both of my grandfathers are farmers.*

2 sb can't have it both ways used to say that someone cannot have the advantages that come from two separate situations because they cannot exist together: *It's either me or her. You can't have it both ways.*

both² conjunction **both...and...** used to emphasize that something is true not just of one person, thing, or situation but also of another: *He's lived in both Britain and America.* | *She can both speak and write Japanese.* | *Both he and his wife enjoy tennis.*

both·er¹ S1 W3 /ˈbɒðə $ ˈbɑːðər/ v

1 MAKE AN EFFORT [I,T usually in questions and negatives] to make the effort to do something: (not) **bother to do sth** *He didn't bother to answer the question.* | **not bother about/with** *He didn't bother with a reply.* | (not) **bother doing sth** *Many young people didn't bother voting.* | **don't/didn't/won't etc bother** *'Do you want me to wait for you?' 'No, don't bother.'* | *Why bother to go abroad, when there are so many nice places here at home?*

2 WORRY [I,T] to make someone feel slightly worried, upset, or concerned: *Being in a crowd really bothers me.* | *It was very noisy, but that didn't bother me.* | [+about] especially BrE *I try not to bother about what other people think.* | **bother sb that** *It really bothered me*

that he'd forgotten my birthday.

3 ANNOY [I,T] to annoy someone, especially by interrupting them when they are trying to do something: *Danny, don't bother Ellen while she's reading.* | *Would it bother you if I put on some music?* | **bother sb about/with sth** *It didn't seem worth bothering the doctor about.*

4 sb can't/couldn't be bothered (to do sth) especially BrE used to say that you do not want to make the effort to do something, or that you are not interested in doing something: *It was so hot I couldn't be bothered to cook.* | *I should be revising, but I just can't be bothered.*

5 CAUSE PAIN [T] if a part of your body bothers you, it is slightly painful or uncomfortable: *My back's been bothering me.*

6 sorry to bother you spoken used as a very polite way of interrupting someone when you want their attention: *Sorry to bother you, but Mr. Grey is on the line.*

7 FRIGHTEN [T] to upset or frighten someone by talking to them when they do not want to talk to you, trying to hurt them, touch them sexually etc: *Don't worry, my dog won't bother you.* | *If he starts bothering you, let me know.*

8 not bother yourself/not bother your head to not spend time or effort on something, either because it is not important or because it is too difficult: [+with/about] *Cliff didn't want to bother himself with masses of detail.*

9 bother it/them etc BrE spoken old-fashioned used to express a sudden feeling of annoyance about something: *Oh bother it! The thread's broken again!*

both·er² n **1** [U] especially BrE trouble or difficulty that has been caused by small problems and that usually only continues for a short time; ⊟ **trouble**: *It's an old car, but it's never caused me any bother.* | [+with] *Joe's been having a bit of bother with his back again.* | *'Thanks for your help.' ' It was no bother* (=used to emphasize that you were happy to help someone) *at all.'* | *My mother hardly ever went to* **the bother of** (=the effort of) *making cakes.* | *Are you sure the station is on your way? I don't want to* **give** *you any extra* **bother.** | *I should have phoned the shop first and* **saved** *myself the* **bother of** *going there.* | **sth is more bother than it's worth** (=it is too difficult to be worth doing) **2 a bother** especially BrE a person or job that slightly annoys you by causing trouble or problems: *I hate to be a bother, but could you show me how the photocopier works?*

both·er³ interjection BrE informal used when you are slightly annoyed: *Oh bother! I forgot to phone Jean.*

both·er·a·tion /ˌbɒðəˈreɪʃən $ ˌbɑː-/ interjection used when you are slightly annoyed: *Botheration. I forgot my glasses.*

both·ered /ˈbɒðəd $ ˈbɑːðərd/ adj [not before noun] **1** worried or upset: [+about] *He doesn't seem too bothered about the things that are written about him in the papers.* | **bothered that** *No one else seemed bothered that Grandfather wasn't there.* **2 not bothered** especially BrE if you are not bothered about something, it is not important to you: *'What film do you want to see?' 'I'm not bothered.'* | [+about] *He's not really bothered about getting the facts right.* → **hot and bothered** at HOT¹ (12)

both·er·some /ˈbɒðəsəm $ ˈbɑːðər-/ adj slightly annoying

bot·tle¹ S1 W2 /ˈbɒtl $ ˈbɑːtl/ n

1 [C] a container with a narrow top for keeping liquids in, usually made of plastic or glass: *an empty bottle* | **a wine/milk/beer etc bottle** | [+of] *a bottle of champagne*

2 [C] also **bottleful** the amount of liquid that a bottle contains: *Between us, we drank three bottles of wine.*

3 [C] a container for babies to drink from, with a rubber part on top that they suck, or the milk contained in this bottle: *My first baby just wouldn't take a bottle at all.*

4 the bottle alcoholic drink – used when talking about the problems drinking can cause: *Peter let the bottle ruin his life.* | **hit the bottle** (=regularly drink too much)

She was under a lot of stress, and started hitting the bottle. | **be on the bottle** *BrE* (=be drinking lot of alcohol regularly)

5 [U] *BrE informal* courage to do something that is dangerous or unpleasant; ◨ **nerve**: *I never thought she'd have the bottle to do it!*

6 bring a bottle *BrE*; **bring your own bottle** *AmE* used when you invite someone to an informal party to tell them that they should bring their own bottle of alcoholic drink → HOT-WATER BOTTLE

bottle² *v* [T] **1** to put a liquid, especially wine or beer, into a bottle after you have made it: *The whisky is bottled here before being sent abroad.* **2** *BrE* to put vegetables or fruit into special glass containers in order to preserve them; ◨ **can** *AmE*

bottle out *phr v BrE informal* also **bottle it** to suddenly decide not to do something because you are frightened; ◨ **cop out**: *'Did you tell him?' 'No, I bottled out at the last minute.'*

bottle sth ⇔ **up** *phr v* **1** to deliberately not allow yourself to show a strong feeling or emotion: *It is far better to cry than to bottle up your feelings.* **2** to cause problems by delaying something: *The bill was bottled up in Congress.*

bottle bank *n* [C] *BrE* a container in the street that you put empty bottles into, so that the glass can be used again → see picture at ENVIRONMENT

bot·tled /ˈbɒtld $ ˈbɑː-/ *adj* **bottled water/beer etc** water, beer etc that is sold in a bottle

bottle-feed *v past tense and past participle* **bottle-fed** [T] to feed a baby or young animal with milk from a bottle rather than from their mother's breast —**bottle-feeding** *n* [U] —**bottle-fed** *adj*

bottle green *n* [U] a very dark green colour —**bottle green** *adj*

bot·tle·neck /ˈbɒtlnek $ ˈbɑː-/ *n* [C] **1** a place in a road where the traffic cannot pass easily, so that there are a lot of delays **2** a delay in one stage of a process that makes the whole process take longer: *Understaffing has caused a real bottleneck.*

bottle opener *n* [C] a small tool used for removing the metal lids from bottles → see picture at MULTIPURPOSE

bot·tom¹ [S1] [W3] /ˈbɒtəm $ ˈbɑː-/ *n*
1 LOWEST PART the bottom the lowest part of something; ◨ **top**: [+of] *Can you hold the bottom of the ladder for me?* | **at the bottom (of sth)** *Grandma was standing at the bottom of the stairs.* | *at the bottom of the page* | *Go downstairs and wait for me at the bottom.* | **the bottom of the page/screen** *There should be a menu bar at the bottom of your screen.*
2 LOWEST SIDE [C usually singular] the flat surface on

the lowest side of an object: **the bottom of sth** *Something's hanging from the bottom of your car.* | *What's that on the bottom of your shoe?*
3 LOWEST INNER PART [C usually singular] the lowest inner surface of something such as a container: **at/in the bottom of sth** *I found the keys – they were at the bottom of my handbag.* | *The drugs had been hidden in a suitcase with a false bottom.*
4 LOWEST SOCIAL POSITION/RANK the bottom the lowest position in an organization or company; ◨ **top**: [+of] *The Giants are at the bottom of the league.* | **the bottom of the ladder/pile/heap** (=the lowest position in society, an organization etc) *Immigrants were at the bottom of the pile.* | *Higgins had* **started at the bottom** (=in a low position in a company) *and worked his way up to become managing director.* | **second/third etc from bottom** *United currently lie second from bottom of the Premier League.*
5 OCEAN/RIVER the bottom the ground under a sea, river etc, or the flat land in a valley: [+of] *The bottom of the pool is very slippery.* | **at/on the bottom (of sth)** *A body was found at the bottom of the canal.* | **the sea/river bottom** *fish living on the sea bottom*
6 BODY [C] the part of your body that you sit on; ◨ **backside**: *I just sat on my bottom and slid down.*
7 CLOTHES [C usually plural] the part of a set of clothes that you wear on the lower part of your body: *pyjama bottoms* | *a blue bikini bottom*
8 FURTHEST PART the bottom the part of a road/garden etc *especially BrE* the part of a road, area of land etc that is furthest from where you are: *There's a shop at the bottom of the street.*
9 get to the bottom of sth to find out the cause of a problem or situation: *I never got to the bottom of this!*
10 be/lie at the bottom of sth to be the basic cause of a problem or situation: *Lack of money is at the bottom of many family problems.*
11 be at/hit/reach rock bottom a) to be in a very bad situation that could not be any worse: *I was at rock bottom, and knew I had to try and stop drinking.* **b)** to be at a very low level: *We bought the house when prices were at rock bottom.*
12 from the bottom of your heart in a very sincere way: *Thank you from the bottom of my heart.*
13 the bottom drops/falls out of the market when people stop buying a particular product, so that the people who sell it can no longer make any money
14 bottoms up! *spoken* used to tell someone to enjoy or finish their alcoholic drink
15 big-bottomed/round-bottomed etc having a bottom or base that is big, round etc

bottles

bottle of beer

hot-water bottle

bottle of pills

hip flask

bottle of wine

baby's bottle

magnum of champagne

water bottle

perfume bottle

carafe

vinaigrette bottle

boun·ty /'baʊnti/ n plural **bounties** **1** [C] an amount of money that is given to someone by the government as a reward for doing something, especially catching or killing a criminal: [+on] a notorious cattle rustler with **a bounty on his head** **2** [U] literary food or wealth that is provided in large amounts: People came from all over the world to enjoy America's bounty. **3** [U] literary the quality of being generous

'bounty ˌhunter n [C] someone who catches criminals and brings them to the police for a reward

bou·quet /bəʊ'keɪ, buː- $ boʊ-, buː-/ n **1** [C] an arrangement of flowers, especially one that you give to someone **2** [C,U] the smell of a wine

bouquet

bouquet of flowers

bouquet ˌgar·ni /ˌbuːkeɪ 'gɑːni $ -gɑːr'niː/ n plural **bouquets garnis** [C] a small bag full of herbs that you put into food that you are cooking to give it a special taste

bour·bon /'bʊəbən $ 'bɜːr-/ n [U] a type of American WHISKY

bour·geois /'bʊəʒwɑː $ bʊr'ʒwɑː/ adj **1** belonging to the MIDDLE CLASS: She came from a respectable bourgeois family. | bourgeois morality **2** too interested in having a lot of possessions and a high position in society: the Sixties backlash against bourgeois materialism **3** belonging to or typical of the part of society that is rich, educated, owns land etc, according to Marxism; → **proletarian** —**bourgeois** n [C] → PETTY BOURGEOIS

bour·geoi·sie /ˌbʊəʒwɑː'zi: $ ˌbʊr-/ n **the bourgeoisie** the people in a society who are rich, educated, own land etc, according to Marxism; → **the proletariat**

'bout /baʊt/ adv, prep spoken informal about: What are you talking 'bout?

bout /baʊt/ n [C] **1 a bout of depression/flu/sickness etc** a short period of time during which you suffer from an illness **2** a short period of time during which you do something a lot, especially something that is bad for you: a drinking bout | [+of] a bout of unemployment **3** a BOXING or WRESTLING match

bou·tique /buː'tiːk/ n [C] a small shop that sells fashionable clothes or other objects

bou·ton·ni·ere /buːˌtɒni'eə $ ˌbuːtn'ɪr/ n [C] AmE a flower that a man wears fastened to his jacket, at a wedding; ⊟ **buttonhole** BrE

bou·zou·ki /bʊ'zuːki/ n [C] a Greek musical instrument similar to a GUITAR

bo·vine /'bəʊvaɪn $ 'boʊ-/ adj **1** technical relating to cows: bovine diseases **2** written slow and slightly stupid, like a cow – used to show disapproval: a bovine expression of contentment

bov·ver /'bɒvə $ 'bɑːvər/ n [U] BrE informal old-fashioned violent behaviour, especially by a group of young men: **bovver boy** (=someone who behaves in a violent way)

bow¹ /baʊ/ v **1** [I] to bend the top part of your body forward in order to show respect for someone important, or as a way of thanking an AUDIENCE: She bowed and left the stage. | Corbett entered the room, bowing respectfully. | The servant **bowed low** and handed his master the sealed note. | [+before/to] He bowed before the king. **2 bow your head** to bend your neck so that you are looking at the ground, especially because you want to show respect for God, or because you are embarrassed or upset: She bowed her head and prayed. | Phil stood there, his head bowed in shame. **3** [I,T] to bend your body over something, especially in order to see it more closely: [+over] Teague sat at his desk, bowed over a book. **4** [I,T] to

bend or to make something bend: The trees bowed in the wind. | He made his way up the steep stairs, his back bowed under the weight of the heavy bag. **5 bow and scrape** to show too much respect to someone in authority – used to show disapproval

bow down phr v **1** to bend your body forward, especially when you are already kneeling, in order to show respect: [+before/to etc] Maria entered the room and bowed down before the statue. | Come, let us **bow down in worship**. **2 bow down to sb** literary to let someone give you orders or tell you what to do – used to show disapproval

bow out phr v **1** to stop taking part in an activity, job etc, especially one that you have been doing for a long time: [+of] Reeves thinks it is time for him to bow out of politics. **2** to not do something that you have promised or agreed to do; ⊟ **get out of**: [+of] You're not trying to bow out of this, are you?

bow to sb/sth phr v to finally agree to do something that people want you to do, even though you do not want to do it: Congress may **bow to public pressure** and lift the arms embargo. | Myers finally **bowed to the inevitable** (=accepted something he could not change) and withdrew from the campaign.

bow² /baʊ/ n **1** [C] the act of bending the top part of your body forward to show respect for someone when you meet them, or as a way of thanking an AUDIENCE: **take/give a bow** (=bow to the audience at the end of a performance) The music ended and the girl took a bow. | He gave a final bow just as the curtains came down. | This is done with a **formal bow** to the king or queen. **2** [C] also **bows** [plural] the front part of a ship; → **stern, yacht**

bow³ /bəʊ/ n [C] **1** a weapon used for shooting ARROWS, made of a long thin piece of wood held in a curve by a tight string: a **bow and arrow** **2** a knot of cloth or string with a curved part on either side, and two loose ends, worn in the hair as decoration or for tying SHOELACES: Ella wore a bow in her hair. | **in a bow** long chestnut hair tied back in a bow **3** a long thin piece of wood with a tight string fastened along it, used to play musical instruments such as the VIOLIN or CELLO → **have more than one string to your bow** at STRING¹ (8)

bow⁴ /bəʊ/ v [I,T] to play a piece of music on a musical instrument with a bow

bowd·ler·ize also **-ise** BrE /'baʊdləraɪz/ v [T] to remove all the parts of a book, play etc that you think might offend someone – used to show disapproval: a bowdlerized version of 'Antony and Cleopatra'

bow·el /'baʊəl/ n **1 bowels** [plural] the system of tubes inside your body where food is made into solid waste material and through which it passes out of your body; → **intestine**: **move/empty/open your bowels** (=get rid of solid waste from your body) **2** [singular] one part of this system of tubes: cancer of the bowel **3 a bowel movement** formal the act of getting rid of solid waste from your body **4 the bowels of sth** literary the lowest or deepest part of something: the **bowels of the earth** (=deep under the ground)

bow·er /'baʊə $ -ər/ n [C] literary a pleasant place in the shade under a tree: a rose-scented bower

bowl¹ [S2] [W3] /bəʊl $ boʊl/ n

1 CONTAINER [C] a wide round container that is open at the top, used to hold liquids, food, flowers etc; → **dish**: Mix all the ingredients thoroughly in a large bowl. | Fill the bowl with water. | **a mixing/serving bowl** (=a bowl used for mixing foods or serving them) Beat the butter in a mixing bowl until creamy and soft. | **a soup/salad/cereal etc bowl** (=a bowl to eat or serve soup, salad etc from)

2 AMOUNT [C] also **bowlful** the amount of something contained in a bowl: [+of] a bowl of rice | a bowl of fruit

3 GAME a) bowls BrE [plural] an outdoor game played on grass in which you try to roll big balls as near as possible to a small ball; ⊟ **lawn bowling** AmE **b)** [C] usually singular] a special game in American football played by the best teams after the normal playing season: the Rose Bowl

4 BALL [C] *BrE* a ball that you use in the game of bowls
5 SHAPE [C] the part of an object such as a spoon, pipe, toilet etc that is shaped like a bowl: *the bowl of a pipe* | **a toilet/lavatory bowl**
6 STADIUM [C usually singular] *AmE* a large STADIUM shaped like a bowl, where people go to watch special events, such as sports games or music CONCERTS: *the Hollywood Bowl*

bowl² *v* **1** [I,T] to roll a ball along a surface when you are playing the game of bowls **2** [I,T] **a)** to throw a ball at the BATSMAN (=the person who hits the ball) in CRICKET; → **bat b)** [T] to make a batsman have to leave the field by throwing a ball so that it hits the WICKET behind him → see picture at THROW¹ **3** [I always + adv/prep] to travel along very quickly and smoothly: [+along/down] *We were bowling along at about 90 miles per hour.*

bowl sb ⇔ out *phr v* in CRICKET, when a team is bowled out, each member of the team has had to leave the field and there is no one left to BAT

bowl sb ⇔ over *phr v* **1** to accidentally hit someone and knock them down because you are running in a place that is full of people or things; ◼ **knock over** **2** to surprise, please, or excite someone very much; ◼ **knock out**: *He was bowled over by her beauty.*

bow legs /ˌbəʊ ˈlegz $ ˌboʊ-/ *n* [plural] legs that curve outwards at the knees —**bow-legged** /-ˈlegd◂, -ˈlegɪd◂/ *adj*

bowl·er /ˈbəʊlə $ ˈboʊlər/ *n* [C] **1** a player in CRICKET who throws the ball at a BATSMAN **2** also **bowler hat** *BrE* a hard round black hat that businessmen sometimes wear; ◼ **derby** *AmE*; → see picture at HAT

bowl·ing /ˈbəʊlɪŋ $ ˈboʊ-/ *n* [U] **1** an indoor game in which you roll a large heavy ball along a wooden track in order to knock down a group of PINS (=wooden objects shaped like bottles): *Do you want to go bowling with us Friday?* → see picture at FOOTWEAR **2** the act of throwing a ball at the BATSMAN in CRICKET

bowling ˌalley *n* [C] a building where you go bowling
bowling ball *n* [C] the heavy ball you use in the game of bowling
bowling green *n* [C] an area of short grass where you play the game of bowls

bow·man /ˈbəʊmən $ ˈboʊ-/ *n plural* **bowmen** /-mən/ [C] a soldier in the past whose weapon was a BOW

bow tie /ˌbəʊ ˈtaɪ $ ˈboʊ taɪ/ *n* [C] a short piece of cloth tied in the shape of a bow that men sometimes wear around their neck

bow win·dow /ˌbəʊ ˈwɪndəʊ $ ˌboʊ ˈwɪndoʊ/ *n* [C] a window that curves out from a wall

bow-wow /ˈbaʊ waʊ/ *n* [C] a word meaning a dog, used by and to small children

bow·wow /ˌbaʊˈwaʊ/ *interjection* a word used to make the sound a dog makes, used by and to small children

box¹ [S1] [W1] /bɒks $ bɑːks/ *n*
1 CONTAINER [C] a container for putting things in, especially one with four stiff straight sides: **cardboard/ wooden/plastic etc box** *a strong cardboard box* | **tool-box/shoebox/matchbox etc** (=a box used for keeping tools etc in)
2 AMOUNT also **boxful** [C] the amount of something contained in a box: [+of] *a box of chocolates*
3 SHAPE [C] **a)** a small square on a page for people to write information in: *Put an 'X' in the box if you would like to join our mailing list.* **b)** a SQUARE or RECTANGLE on a page where information is given or where an answer can be written: *The box on the left gives a short history of the battle.*
4 IN A COURT/THEATRE ETC [C] a small area of a theatre or court that is separate from where other people are sitting: *the jury box* | *a box at the Palace Theatre*
5 SMALL BUILDING [C] a small building or structure used for a particular purpose; ◼ **booth**: *a sentry box* | **telephone box** *BrE*
6 AT A POST OFFICE **box 25/450 etc** a box with a number in a POST OFFICE, where you can have letters etc sent instead of to your own address; ◼ **PO Box**

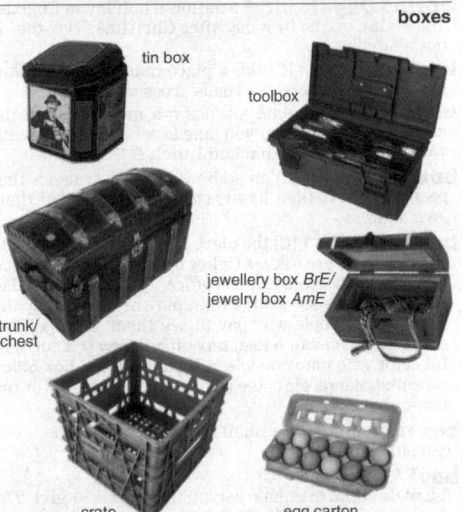

boxes

tin box

toolbox

jewellery box *BrE*/
jewelry box *AmE*

trunk/
chest

crate

egg carton

7 SPORTS FIELD [C usually singular] a special area of a sports field that is marked by lines and used for a particular purpose: *the penalty box*
8 PROTECTION [C] *BrE* a piece of plastic that a man wears over his sex organs to protect them when he is playing a sport, especially CRICKET
9 TREE [C,U] a small tree that keeps its leaves in winter and is often planted around the edge of a garden or field: *a box hedge*
10 TELEVISION **the box** *informal* the television: *What's on the box tonight?*
11 be out of your box *BrE informal* to be very drunk or have taken an illegal drug → BLACK BOX

box² *v* **1** [I,T] to fight someone as a sport by hitting them with your closed hands inside big leather GLOVES **2** also **box up** [T] to put things in boxes: *Want to help me box up the Christmas tree lights?* → BOXED **3** [T] to draw a box around something on a page **4 box sb's ears** *old-fashioned* to hit someone on the side of their head

box sb/sth ⇔ in *phr v* **1** to surround someone or something so that they are unable to move freely: *Someone had parked right behind them, boxing them in.* **2 feel boxed in a)** to feel that you cannot do what you want to do because a person or situation is limiting you: *Married for only a year, Connie already felt boxed in.* **b)** to feel that you cannot move freely, because you are in a small space

box sth ⇔ off *phr v* to separate a particular area from a larger one by putting walls around it: *We're going to box off that corner to get extra storage space.*

box ˌcanyon *n* [C] *AmE* a deep narrow valley with very straight sides and no way out; ◼ **gorge**

box·car /ˈbɒkskɑː $ ˈbɑːkskɑːr/ *n* [C] *AmE* a railway carriage with high sides and a roof, used for carrying goods

boxed /bɒkst $ bɑːkst/ *adj* [usually before noun] sold in a box or boxes: *a boxed set of CDs*

box end ˈwrench *n* [C] *AmE* a type of WRENCH with a hollow end that fits over a NUT that is being screwed or unscrewed; ◼ **ring spanner** *BrE*

box·er /ˈbɒksə $ ˈbɑːksər/ *n* [C] **1** someone who BOXES, especially as a job **2** a large dog with short light brown hair and a flat nose

boxer ˌshorts *n* [plural] loose cotton underwear for men; → see picture at UNDERWEAR

box·ing /ˈbɒksɪŋ $ ˈbɑːk-/ *n* [U] the sport of fighting while wearing big leather GLOVES

B

Boxing Day n [C,U] BrE a national holiday in England and Wales, on the first day after Christmas Day that is not a Sunday

box junction n [C] BrE a place marked with yellow painted lines where two roads cross each other

box lunch n [C] AmE a LUNCH (=a meal eaten in the middle of the day) that you take to school or work with you in a LUNCHBOX; ⊟ **packed lunch** BrE

box number n [C] an address at the POST OFFICE that people can have their letters etc sent to instead of their own address

box office n **1** [C] the place in a theatre, cinema etc where tickets are sold; → **ticket office: at the box office** Collect your tickets at the box office. **2** [singular] used to describe how successful a film, play, or actor is, by the number of people who pay to see them: **a (huge) box office hit/success** | **a (big) box office draw** (=a successful actor who many people will pay to see) | **box office receipts/takings etc** (=the number of tickets sold or the money received)

box room n [C] BrE a small room in a house where you can store things

boy¹ [S1] [W1] /bɔɪ/ n [C]
1 a male child, or a male person in general; → **girl**: The boys wanted to play football. | The school has over 1,200 boys and girls aged 11 – 18. | **a teenage/adolescent boy** A group of teenage boys stood talking in a group outside. | **bad/naughty boy** 'You naughty boy!' she said in a harsh voice. | What a polite **little boy** (=young male child) you are. | Come on, Timmy, act like a **big boy** (=an older boy) now.
2 a son: I love my boys, but I'd like to have a girl too. | How old is your **little boy** (=young son)?
3 office/paper/delivery etc boy a young man who does a particular job
4 city/local/country boy informal a man of any age who is typical of people from a particular place, or who feels a strong connection with the place he grew up in: The classic story of a local boy who's made good (=who has succeeded). | I'm just a country boy.
5 the boys [plural] informal a group of men who are friends and often go out together: Friday is his **night out with the boys**. | He considers himself just **one of the boys** (=not anyone special, but liked by other men).
6 a way of talking to a male horse or dog: Good boy!
7 boys [plural] informal **a)** a group of men who do the same job: Oh no! Wait until the press boys get hold of this story. **b)** men in the army, navy etc, especially those who are fighting in a war: our boys on the front lines
8 boys will be boys used to say that you should not be surprised when boys or men behave badly, are noisy etc
9 the boys in blue informal the police
10 old boy/my dear boy BrE old-fashioned a friendly way for one man to speak to another man
11 AmE not polite an offensive way of talking to a black man → BLUE-EYED BOY; → **jobs for the boys** at JOB (15); → MAMA'S BOY, MUMMY'S BOY, OLD BOY, WIDE BOY

boy² interjection AmE informal **1** used when you are excited or pleased about something: Boy, that was a great meal! **2** oh boy! used when you are slightly annoyed or disappointed about something: Oh boy! Bethany's sick again.

boy band n [C] a group of attractive young men who perform by singing and dancing, and who are especially popular with teenage girls: Christy's favorite boy band is Boyzone.

boy·cott¹ /'bɔɪkɒt $ -kɑːt/ v [T] to refuse to buy something, use something, or take part in something as a way of protesting: We boycott all products tested on animals.

boycott² n [C] an act of boycotting something, or the period of time when it is boycotted: They are now trying to **organize a boycott**. | [+of/on/against] a boycott on GM crops | He **called for a boycott** of the elections.

boy·friend /'bɔɪfrend/ n [C] a man that you are having a romantic relationship with; → **girlfriend**: Have you met Jilly's new boyfriend yet?

boy·hood /'bɔɪhʊd/ n [U] the time of a man's life when he is a boy; → **girlhood**: boyhood memories

boy·ish /'bɔɪ-ɪʃ/ adj someone who is boyish looks or behaves like a boy in a way that is attractive; → **girlish**: boyish good looks | At 45, she still had a trim boyish figure. —**boyishly** adv: boyishly handsome —**boyishness** n [U]

boy scout / $ '../ n [C] a member of the SCOUTS; → **girl scout, guide**

boy toy n [C] an attractive young man who an older, usually rich or successful woman has a sexual relationship with

boy wonder n [C] a young man who is very successful: Robson, the boy wonder of the department

bo·zo /'bəʊzəʊ $ 'bouzou/ n plural **bozos** [C] informal someone who you think is silly or stupid: Who's the bozo in the pyjamas?

bps, BPS /ˌbiː piː 'es/ technical **bits per second** a measurement of how fast a computer or MODEM can send or receive information: a 28,800 bps modem

Br. also **Br** BrE **1** the written abbreviation of **brother 2** the written abbreviation of **British**

bra /brɑː/ n [C] a piece of underwear that a woman wears to support her breasts → see picture at UNDERWEAR

brace¹ /breɪs/ v **1** [T] to mentally or physically prepare yourself or someone else for something unpleasant that is going to happen: **brace yourself (for sth)** Nancy braced herself for the inevitable arguments. | You had better brace yourself – I have some bad news. | The military needs to brace itself for further spending cuts, says McCoy. | **brace yourself to do sth** Cathy braced herself to see Matthew, who she expected to arrive at any minute. | **be braced for sth** The base was braced for an attack. **2** [T] to push part of your body against something solid in order to make yourself more steady: **brace sth against sth** Gina braced her back against the wall and pushed as hard as she could. | **brace yourself (for sth)** Before he could brace himself she'd shoved him out of the door. | The pilot told passengers and crew to brace themselves for a rough landing. **3** [T] to make something stronger by supporting it: Wait until we've braced the ladder. | Workers used steel beams to brace the roof. **4** [I,T] to make your body or part of your body stiff in order to prepare to do something difficult

brace² n **1** [C] something that is used to strengthen or support something, or to make it stiff: The miners used special braces to keep the walls from collapsing. | **neck/back/knee brace** (=a brace which supports the neck etc) He was being fitted for a back brace. | She had to **wear a brace** after the accident. **2** [C] also **braces** AmE a system of metal wires that people, usually children, wear on their teeth to make them grow straight **3** [C usually plural] AmE a metal support that someone with weak legs wears to help them walk; ⊟ **callipers** BrE **4 braces** [plural] BrE two long pieces of material that stretch over someone's shoulders and fasten to their trousers at the front and the back to stop them falling down; ⊟ **suspenders** AmE **5** [C] one of a pair of signs { } used to show that information written between them should be considered together; → **bracket 6 a brace of sth** especially BrE two things of the same type, especially two birds or animals that have been killed for food or sport: a brace of partridge

brace·let /'breɪslɪt/ n [C] a band or chain that you wear around your wrist or arm as a decoration; → **bangle**: a gold bracelet → see picture at JEWELLERY

brac·ing /'breɪsɪŋ/ adj bracing air or weather is cold and makes you feel very awake and healthy: a bracing sea breeze

brack·en /'brækən/ n [U] a plant that often grows in forests and becomes reddish brown in the autumn

B

brack·et¹ /'bræk‍ᵻt/ n [C]   **1** [usually plural] also **round bracket** BrE one of the pair of signs ( ) put around words to show extra information; ▤ **parenthesis** AmE: **in brackets** Last year's sales figures are given in brackets. → ANGLE BRACKETS → SQUARE BRACKET → PUNCTUATION MARK   **2** income/tax/age etc **bracket** a particular income, tax etc range: Peter's salary puts him in the highest tax bracket. | families in lower income brackets   **3** a piece of metal, wood, or plastic, often in the shape of the letter L, fixed to a wall to support something such as a shelf

bracket² v [T usually passive]   **1** to consider two or more people or things as being similar or the same: **bracket sb together** Women and minors were bracketed together for the legislation. | **bracket sb with sb** Arizona has been bracketed with Iowa in the tournament.   **2** to put brackets around a written word, piece of information etc: Debit amounts are bracketed.

brack·ish /'brækɪʃ/ adj brackish water is not pure because it is slightly salty

brad /bræd/ n [C] AmE   **1** a small metal object like a button with two metal sticks that are put through several pieces of paper and folded down to hold the papers together   **2** a small thin wire nail with either a small head or a part that sticks out to the side instead of a head

brad·awl /'brædɔːl $ -ɔːl/ n [C] especially BrE a small tool with a sharp point for making holes; ▤ **awl**

brag /bræg/ v **bragged**, **bragging** [I,T] to talk too proudly about what you have done, what you own etc – used to show disapproval; ▤ **boast**: 'I came out top in the test,' he bragged. | [+about] Ben's always bragging about his success with women. | **brag that** Julia used to brag that her family had a villa in Spain.

brag·ga·do·ci·o /ˌbrægə'dəʊʃiəʊ $ -'dəʊʃioʊ/ n [U] especially literary proud talk about something that you claim to own, to have done etc

brag·gart /'brægət $ -ərt/ n [C] old-fashioned someone who is always talking too proudly about what they own or have done

Brah·man /'brɑːmən/ also **Brah·min** /'brɑːmᵻn/ n [C] someone of the highest rank in the Hindu faith

braid¹ /breɪd/ n   **1** [U] a narrow band of material formed by twisting threads together, used to decorate the edges of clothes: a jacket **trimmed with red braid**   **2** [C] a length of hair that has been separated into three parts and then woven together; ▤ **plait** BrE: **in braids** Suzy always wears her hair in braids. —**braided** adj; → see picture at HAIRSTYLE

braid² v [T] to weave or twist together three pieces of hair or cloth to form one length; ▤ **plait** BrE

braille /breɪl/ n [U] a form of printing for blind people, with raised parts that they can read by touching the paper with their fingers

brain¹ S2 W2 /breɪn/ n
1 ORGAN [C] the organ inside your head that controls how you think, feel, and move: Messages from the brain are carried by the central nervous system. | the chemistry of the brain | the human brain | the **right/left hemisphere of the brain** (=the right or left side of brain) Emotional responses are a function of the right hemisphere of the brain. | She died of a brain tumour. | **brain tissue/cell**; → see picture at HUMAN¹
2 INTELLIGENCE [C usually plural,U] the ability to think clearly and learn quickly: If you had any brains, you'd know what I meant. | The job requires brains. | Something's **addled your brains** (=made you confused). | Come on, **use your brain**, John.
3 PERSON [C usually plural] informal someone who is intelligent, with good ideas and useful skills: Some of our best brains are leaving the country to work in the US. → BRAIN DRAIN
4 FOOD [U] also **brains** [plural] the brain of an animal, used as food
5 have sth on the brain informal to be always thinking about something: I've got that song on the brain today.
6 be the brains behind/of sth to be the person who

thought of and developed a particular plan, system, or organization, especially a successful one: Danny's definitely the brains of the project.
7 brain dead **a)** in a state where your brain has stopped working properly even though your heart may still be beating **b)** informal in a state in which you seem stupid or uninteresting, especially because you live a boring life or are very tired
8 brain box BrE informal a very intelligent person → BIRD-BRAIN, HARE-BRAINED; → beat your brains out at BEAT¹ (22); → pick sb's brains at PICK¹ (7); → rack your brain(s) at RACK² (2)

brain² v [T] informal to hit someone very hard on the head – used humorously: I wanted to brain him.

brain·child /'breɪnʃaɪld/ n [singular] an idea, plan, organization etc that someone has thought of without any help from anyone else: [+of] The festival was the brainchild of Reeves.

brain ˌdamage n [U] damage to someone's brain caused by an accident or illness: Potts **suffered** severe **brain damage** in the crash. —**brain-damaged** adj

brain drain n the brain drain a movement of highly skilled or professional people from their own country to a country where they can earn more money

brain·less /'breɪnləs/ adj completely stupid: What a brainless thing to do! —**brainlessly** adv

brain·pow·er also **ˈbrain power** /'breɪnpaʊə $ -paʊr/ n [U]   **1** intelligence, or the ability to think: A lot of brainpower went into solving the problem.   **2** educated intelligent people who have special skills, especially in science, considered as a group: the country's shortage of scientific brainpower

brain scan n [C] a process in which detailed photographs of the inside of your brain are taken and examined by a doctor

brain·storm /'breɪnstɔːm $ -stɔːrm/ n   **1** [C usually singular] a sudden clever idea; ▤ **brainwave** BrE: Kirby **had a sudden brainstorm**.   **2** [C] BrE informal if you have a brainstorm, you are suddenly unable to think clearly or sensibly: I must have **had a brainstorm** that afternoon.

brain·storm·ing /'breɪnstɔːmɪŋ $ -ɔːr-/ n [U] when a group of people meet in order to try to develop ideas and think of ways of solving problems: a **brainstorming session** to come up with slogans for new products —**brainstorm** v [I,T]: Employees get together and brainstorm ideas.

brain ˌteaser n [C] a difficult problem that is fun trying to solve

brain·wash /'breɪnwɒʃ $ -wɒːʃ, -wɑːʃ/ v [T] to make someone believe something that is not true, by using force, confusing them, or continuously repeating it over a long period of time: Young people are being brainwashed by this religious group. | **brainwash sb into doing sth** Commercials brainwash consumers into buying things they don't need. —**brainwashing** n [U]

brain·wave /'breɪnweɪv/ n [C]   **1** BrE a sudden clever idea; ▤ **brainstorm** AmE: I've had a brainwave! Let's go this weekend instead.   **2** an electrical force that is produced by the brain and that can be measured

brain·y /'breɪni/ adj comparative **brainier**, superlative **brainiest** able to learn easily and think quickly; ▤ **clever**; ▤ **smart** AmE: He always was the brainy one, except at maths.

braise /breɪz/ v [T] to cook meat or vegetables slowly in a small amount of liquid in a closed container; → **stew** —**braised** adj

brake¹ /breɪk/ n [C]   **1** a piece of equipment that makes a vehicle go more slowly or stop: Test your brakes after driving through water. | Moira **slammed on the brakes** (=use them suddenly and with a lot of force) and skidded to a halt. | I managed to **put on the brakes** just in time. | the rear/front brakes | a car

B

equipped with **anti-lock brakes** | the **screech of brakes** (=the loud unpleasant noise they can make) | **apply the brakes** formal: Williams testified that he tried to apply the brakes but couldn't stop the vehicle in time. → EMERGENCY BRAKE, HANDBRAKE; → see picture at BICYCLE[1]; → see picture at CAR **2 act as a brake on sth** to make something develop more slowly, be more difficult to do, or happen less: Rises in interest rates usually act as a brake on expenditure. **3 put the brakes on sth** to stop something that is happening

brake² v [I] to make a vehicle or bicycle go more slowly or stop by using its brake: **brake sharply/hard** (=brake quickly) He braked sharply to avoid the dog.

'brake ,fluid n [U] liquid used in certain kinds of brakes so that the different parts move smoothly

'brake light n [C] a light on the back of a vehicle that comes on when you use the brake

'brake ,shoe n [C] one of the two curved parts that press against the wheel of a vehicle in order to make it go more slowly or stop

bram·ble /'bræmbəl/ n [C] a wild BLACKBERRY bush

bran /bræn/ n [U] the crushed outer skin of wheat or a similar grain that is separated from the rest of the grain when making white flour

branch¹ S1 W2 /brɑːntʃ $ bræntʃ/ n [C]
1 OF A TREE a part of a tree that grows out from the TRUNK (=main stem) and that has leaves, fruit, or smaller branches growing from it; → **limb**: After the storm, the ground was littered with twigs and branches. | The **topmost branches** were full of birds. → see picture at TREE
2 OF A BUSINESS/SHOP/COMPANY ETC a local business, shop etc that is part of a larger business etc: The bank has branches all over the country. | a **branch office** in Boston | She now works in our Denver branch. | Where's their nearest branch? | They're planning to **open a branch** in St. Louis next year. | Have you met our **branch manager**, Mr. Carlson?
3 OF GOVERNMENT a part of a government or other organization that deals with one particular part of its work; → **department**: All branches of government are having to cut costs. | the **executive/judicial/legislative branch** (=the three main parts of the US government)
4 OF A SUBJECT one part of a large subject of study or knowledge; → **field**: **a branch of mathematics/ physics/biology etc**
5 OF A FAMILY a group of members of a family who all have the same ANCESTORS; → **side**: the wealthy South American branch of the family
6 OF A RIVER/ROAD ETC a smaller less important part of a river, road, or railway that leads away from the larger more important part of it: The rail company may have to close the **branch line** to Uckfield.

branch² v [I] to divide into two or more smaller, narrower, or less important parts; → **fork**: Another road branched northward. | When you reach the village green, the street **branches into two**.
branch off phr v **1** if a road, passage, railway etc branches off from another road etc, it separates from it and goes in a different direction; ☐ **fork off**: [+from] a passage branching off from the main tunnel **2** BrE to leave a main road; ☐ **fork off**: [+from/into] We branched off from the main road and turned down a country lane. **3** to start talking about something different from what you were talking about before: [+into] Then the conversation branched off into a discussion about movies.
branch out phr v to start doing something different from the work or activities that you normally do: Don't be afraid to branch out and try something new. | **branch out into (doing) sth** Profits were falling until the bookstore branched out into selling CDs.

brand¹ /brænd/ n [C] **1** a type of product made by a particular company, that has a particular name or design; → **make**: [+of] What brand of detergent do you

use? | **brand leader/leading brand** (=the brand that sells the most) | products which lack a strong **brand image** | **brand loyalty** (=the tendency to always buy a particular brand) | **own brand** BrE; **store brand** AmE (=a product made and sold by a particular store) **2 brand of humour/politics/religion etc** a particular type of humour, religion, politics etc: a strange macabre brand of humour **3** a mark made or burned on a farm animal's skin that shows who it belongs to

brand² v [T] **1** to describe someone or something as a very bad type of person or thing, often unfairly: **brand sb (as) sth** You can't brand all football supporters as hooligans. | Stealing that money has **branded** Jim **for life** - no-one will trust him again. **2** to burn a mark onto something, especially a farm animal, in order to show who it belongs to: **brand sth with sth** Each cow was branded with the ranch's logo. **3** technical to give a name to a product or group of products so that they can be easily recognized by their name or design

brand·ed /'brændɪd/ adj [only before noun] a branded product is made by a well-known company and has the company's name on it

brand·ing /'brændɪŋ/ n [U] a practice which involves a company giving a group of their products the same brand name, helping this name to become well-known

'branding ,iron n [C] a piece of metal that is heated and used for burning marks on cattle or sheep, to show who they belong to

bran·dish /'brændɪʃ/ v [T] written to wave something around in a dangerous or threatening way, especially a weapon: A man leapt out brandishing a kitchen knife.

'brand ,name n [C] the name given to a product by the company that makes it; ☐ **trade name**

,brand-'new adj new and not yet used: a brand-new car | His clothes looked brand-new.

bran·dy /'brændi/ n plural **brandies** [C,U] a strong alcoholic drink made from wine, or a glass of this drink → see picture at GLASS¹

'brandy ,butter n [U] a mixture of butter, sugar, and brandy, usually eaten with CHRISTMAS PUDDING

brash /bræʃ/ adj **1** behaving too confidently and speaking too loudly - used to show disapproval: Brash noisy journalists were crowding around the ambassador. **2** a brash building, place, or object attracts attention by being very colourful, large, exciting etc: The painting was bold, brash, and modern. —**brashly** adv —**brashness** n [U]

brass /brɑːs $ bræs/ n
1 METAL [U] a very hard bright yellow metal that is a mixture of COPPER and ZINC: an old brass bedstead
2 MUSIC a) [U] musical instruments that are made of metal, such as the TRUMPET and the TROMBONE: brass instruments → PERCUSSION, STRINGED INSTRUMENT, WIND INSTRUMENT, WOODWIND **b)** the brass (section) the people in an ORCHESTRA or band who play musical instruments that are made of metal
3 DECORATIONS [C usually plural] an object made of brass, usually with a design cut into it, or several brass objects
4 get down to brass tacks informal to start talking about the most important facts or details of something
5 PEOPLE WITH TOP JOBS the brass AmE informal people who hold the most important positions; ☐ **top brass** BrE
6 it's brass monkeys/brass monkey weather BrE spoken informal used to say that it is very cold
7 MONEY [U] BrE old-fashioned informal money → **as bold as brass** at BOLD (2)

,brass 'band n [C] a band consisting mostly of brass musical instruments such as TRUMPETS, horns etc

brassed off /,brɑːst 'ɒf $,bræst 'ɔːf/ adj BrE informal annoyed; ☐ **fed up**

bras·se·rie /'bræsəri $,bræsə'riː/ n [C] a cheap informal restaurant, usually serving French food

bras·si·ere /'bræziə $ brə'zɪr/ n [C] formal a BRA

,brass 'knuckles n [plural] AmE a set of connected metal rings worn over a person's fingers, used as a weapon; ⊟ **knuckleduster** BrE

brass·y /'brɑːsi $ 'bræsi/ adj **1** a woman who is brassy is too loud, confident, or brightly dressed: a drunken brassy nightclub singer **2** sounding hard and loud like the sound made by a BRASS musical instrument **3** having a bright gold-yellow colour like BRASS

brat /bræt/ n [C] informal **1** a badly behaved child: a spoiled brat **2** Army/Navy/military etc brat AmE a child whose family moves often because one or both parents works for the army, navy etc —**bratty** adj

bra·va·do /brə'vɑːdəʊ $ -doʊ/ n [U] behaviour that is deliberately intended to make other people believe you are brave and confident: youthful bravado

brave¹ S3 /breɪv/ adj comparative **braver**, superlative **bravest**
1 a) dealing with danger, pain, or difficult situations with courage and confidence; ⊟ **courageous**: brave soldiers | her brave fight against cancer | it is brave of sb (to do sth) | It was brave of you to speak in front of all those people. **b) the brave** [plural] brave people: Today we remember the brave who died in the last war. **2** very good: Despite their captain's brave performance, Arsenal lost 2–1. | **brave effort/attempt** the brave efforts of the medical staff to save his life **3 put on a brave face/front** to pretend that you are happy when you are really very upset **4 brave new world** a situation or a way of doing something that is new and exciting and meant to improve people's lives: the brave new world of digital television —**bravely** adv: She smiled bravely.

brave² v [T] **1** to deal with a difficult, dangerous, or unpleasant situation: I decided to take the train to work rather than brave the traffic. | **brave the elements/weather etc** (=go out in bad weather) More than 100 people braved the elements and attended the rally. **2 brave it out** to deal bravely with something that is frightening or difficult

brave³ n [C] a young fighting man from a Native American tribe

brav·e·ry /'breɪvəri/ n [U] actions, behaviour, or an attitude that shows courage and confidence; ⊟ **courage**: an act of great bravery

bra·vo /'brɑːvəʊ, brɑː'vəʊ $ -voʊ/ interjection used to show your approval when someone, especially a performer, has done something very well: Bravo! Encore!

bra·vu·ra /brə'vjʊərə $ -'vjʊrə/ n [U] great skill shown in the way you perform, write, paint etc, especially when you do something very difficult: a bravura performance

brawl¹ /brɔːl $ brɒːl/ n [C] a noisy quarrel or fight among a group of people, especially in a public place: a drunken brawl in the street

brawl² v [I] to quarrel or fight in a noisy way, especially in a public place: Fans brawled outside the stadium. —**brawler** n [C]

brawn /brɔːn $ brɒːn/ n [U] **1** physical strength, especially when compared with intelligence: Mina has the brains, I have the brawn. **2** BrE meat from a pig's head that has been boiled and pressed in a container and is often served in thin flat pieces; ⊟ **headcheese** AmE

brawn·y /'brɔːni $ 'brɒː-/ adj very large and strong: His brawny arms glistened with sweat.

bray /breɪ/ v [I] **1** if a DONKEY brays, it makes a loud sound **2** if someone brays, they laugh or talk in a loud, slightly annoying way —**bray** n [C]

bra·zen¹ /'breɪzən/ adj **1** used to describe a person or the actions of a person who is not embarrassed about behaving in a wrong or immoral way: At first I was scared, but as I went on, I became more brazen. | her brazen admission that she was cheating on him **2** literary having a shiny yellow colour

brazen² v
brazen sth **out** phr v to deal with a situation that is

difficult or embarrassing for you by appearing to be confident rather than ashamed: She knew she could either admit the truth or brazen it out.

bra·zen·ly /'breɪzənli/ adv doing something openly, without showing or feeling any shame: She smiled at him brazenly.

bra·zi·er /'breɪziə $ -zər/ n [C] a metal container that holds a fire and is used to keep people warm outside

bra·zil /brə'zɪl/ also **bra'zil nut** n [C] a type of curved nut that has a hard shell

Bra·zil·i·an¹ /brə'zɪliən/ adj relating to Brazil or its people

Brazilian² n [C] someone from Brazil

breach¹ W3 /briːtʃ/ n
1 [C,U] an action that breaks a law, rule, or agreement: [+of] This was a clear breach of the 1994 Trade Agreement. | They sued the company for **breach of contract**. | a breach of professional duty | be in breach of sth He was clearly in breach of the law.
2 [C] a serious disagreement between people, groups, or countries: [+with] Britain did not want to risk a breach with the US over sanctions. | [+between] What had caused the sudden breach between Henry and his son? | She wanted to help **heal the breach** between them.
3 breach of confidence/trust an action in which someone does something that people have trusted them not to do: We regard the publication of this information as a serious breach of trust.
4 breach of security an action in which someone manages to learn secret information or manages to get into a place that is guarded: There had been a major breach of security at the air base.
5 breach of the peace BrE the crime of making too much noise or fighting in a public place: He was arrested and charged with breach of the peace.
6 [C] a hole made in a wall that is intended to protect a place: [+in] a breach in the castle wall | a breach in the flood defence barrier
7 step into the breach to help by doing someone else's job or work when they are unable to do it; ⊟ **step in**: Thanks for stepping into the breach last week.

breach² v [T] **1** to break a law, rule, or agreement; ⊟ **break**: The company accused him of breaching his contract. | Traders who breach the rules could face a fine of up to £10,000. **2** to break a hole in a wall that is intended to protect a place: The storm had breached the sea wall in two places.

bread S2 W3 /bred/ n [U]
1 a type of food made from flour and water that is mixed together and then baked: Would you like some bread with your soup? | the smell of **fresh bread** | a **loaf of bread** | Could you cut me a **slice of bread** please? | a piece of **bread and butter** | white/brown/rye etc bread a brown bread sandwich
2 your/sb's bread and butter informal the work that provides you with most of the money that you need in order to live: Writing is my bread and butter.
3 know which side your bread is buttered on informal to know which people to be nice to in order to get advantages for yourself
4 old-fashioned informal money

,bread-and-'butter adj [only before noun] **1** BrE bread-and-butter questions are very important basic ones: bread-and-butter political issues such as jobs and housing **2** bread-and-butter work is work that is not very exciting but provides you with most of the money that you need in order to live

bread·bas·ket /'bred,bɑːskɪt $ -,bæ-/ n **1** [C] a basket in which you keep or serve bread **2** [singular] the part of a country or area that provides most of its food: Zambia could be the breadbasket of Africa.

bread bin n [C] BrE a container that you keep bread in so that it stays fresh; ⊟ **bread box**

bread·board /'bredbɔːd $ -bɔːrd/ n [C] a wooden board on which you cut bread

B

Let your breath out slowly. | *He's got **bad breath*** (=breath that smells unpleasant). **b)** [U] air that you take into your lungs: *Eric came running into the room, **out of breath*** (=having difficulty breathing because he had just been running). | *She was fat and **short of breath*** (=unable to breathe easily, especially because of ill health). | **gasp/fight etc for breath** (=breathe quickly because you are having difficulty breathing) *When he reached the top of the stairs, his heart was pounding and he was gasping for breath.* **c)** [C] an amount of air that you take into your lungs: **take a (deep/long/big etc) breath** (=breathe in a lot of air at one time) *Shaun took a deep breath and dived in.* ⚠ Do not confuse the noun **breath** /breθ/with the verb **breathe** /briːð/.*She took a breath and continued.* | *I can't breathe in here!*

2 a breath of fresh air a) something that is new and different in a way you think is exciting and good: *Osborne's play brought a breath of fresh air to the British theatre.* **b)** clean air outside, which you feel you need after being inside for a long time: *I'm going outside for a breath of fresh air.*

3 don't hold your breath *informal* used to say that something is not going to happen soon: *The system's due for an update, but don't hold your breath.*

4 catch your breath also **get your breath back** to start breathing normally again after running or making a lot of effort: *Slow down, I need a minute to catch my breath.*

5 don't waste your breath also **save your breath** *spoken* used to say that someone will not be able to persuade someone else, so there is no point in trying: *Save your breath. She's already made up her mind.* | *Will he listen to me or will I just be wasting my breath?*

6 take sb's breath away to be extremely beautiful or exciting: *The view from the top will take your breath away.*

7 under your breath in a quiet voice so that no one can hear you: *'Son of a bitch,' he muttered under his breath.*

8 in the same breath a) also **in the next breath** used to say that someone has said two things at once that are so different from each other they cannot both be true: *He criticized the film, then predicted in the same breath that it would be a great success.* **b)** if you mention two people or things in the same breath, you show that you think they are alike or are related: *I became nervous when the doctor mentioned my mother's name and 'cancer' in the same breath.* | [+as/with] *a young poet mentioned in the same breath as T.S. Eliot*

9 with your last/dying breath at the moment when you are dying: *With his last breath he cursed his captors.*

10 [singular] *written* a very small amount or a sign of something: [+of] *They did everything they could to avoid the slightest breath of scandal.*

11 a breath of air/wind *literary* a slight movement of air: *Scarcely a breath of air disturbed the stillness of the day.* → **with bated breath** at BATED; → **draw breath** at DRAW[1] (24); → **hold your breath** at HOLD[1] (17)

breath·a·ble /ˈbriːðəbəl/ *adj* clothing that is breathable allows air to pass through it easily

breath·a·lyze also **-lyse** *BrE* /ˈbreθəl-aɪz/ *v* [T] to make someone breathe into a special piece of equipment in order to see if they have drunk too much alcohol to be allowed to drive

breath·a·lyz·er also **Breathalyser** *BrE trademark* /ˈbreθəl-aɪzə $ -ər/ *n* [C] a piece of equipment used by the police to see if a driver of a car has drunk too much alcohol

breathe S3 W3 /briːð/ *v*

1 AIR [I,T] to take air into your lungs and send it out again: *The room filled with smoke, and it was becoming difficult to breathe.* | *People are concerned about the quality of the air they breathe.* | *Relax and **breathe deeply*** (=take in a lot of air).

2 BLOW [I,T] to blow air or smoke out of your mouth: [+on] *Roy breathed on his hands and rubbed them together vigorously.* | **breathe sth over sb** *The fat man*

opposite was breathing garlic all over me.

3 sb can breathe easy/easily used when saying that someone can relax because a worrying or dangerous situation has ended: *With stocks going up, investors can breathe easily.*

4 breathe a sigh of relief to stop being worried or frightened about something: *Once the deadline passed, everyone breathed a sigh of relief.*

5 be breathing down sb's neck *informal* to pay very close attention to what someone is doing in a way that makes them feel nervous or annoyed: *How can I concentrate with you breathing down my neck all the time?*

6 not breathe a word to not tell anyone anything at all about something, because it is a secret: *Don't breathe a word; it's supposed to be a surprise.*

7 breathe life into sth to change a situation so that people feel more excited or interested: *Critics are hoping the young director can breathe new life into the French film industry.*

8 SKIN [I] if your skin can breathe, air can reach it

9 CLOTHES/FABRIC [I] if cloth or clothing breathes, air can pass through it so that your body feels pleasantly cool and dry

10 WINE [I] if you let wine breathe, you open the bottle to let the air get to it before you drink it

11 SAY STH QUIETLY [T] *written* to say something very quietly, almost in a whisper: *'Wait,' he breathed.*

12 breathe your last (breath) *literary* to die

13 breathe fire to talk and behave in a very angry way → **live and breathe sth** at LIVE[1] (19)

breathe in *phr v* to take air into your lungs: *The doctor made me breathe in while he listened to my chest.* | **breathe sth ⇔ in** *Wyatt breathed in the cool ocean air.*

breathe out *phr v* to send air out from your lungs: *Jim breathed out deeply.* | **breathe sth ⇔ out** *Lauren lit up a cigarette, then breathed out a puff of smoke.*

breath·er /ˈbriːðə $ -ər/ *n* **have/take a breather** *informal* to stop what you are doing for a short time in order to rest, especially when you are exercising → HEAVY BREATHER

breath·ing /ˈbriːðɪŋ/ *n* [U] the process of breathing air in and out: *His breathing was deep and regular.* | *When I picked up the phone all I heard was **heavy breathing*** (=loud breathing).

breathing space also **breathing room** *n* [C,U] **1** a short time when you have a rest from doing something before starting again: *This deal should give the company some extra breathing room before its loans are due.* **2** enough room to move or breathe easily and comfortably in

breath·less /ˈbreθləs/ *adj* **1** having difficulty breathing, especially because you are very tired, excited, or frightened: *The long climb left Jan feeling breathless.* | [+with] *They waited, breathless with anticipation.* **2** *written* excited: *His first novel drew breathless superlatives from critics.* **3 at (a) breathless pace/speed** extremely fast **4** *literary* unpleasantly hot, with no fresh air or wind: *the breathless heat of a midsummer night in Rome* —**breathlessly** *adv* —**breathlessness** *n* [U]

breath·tak·ing /ˈbreθˌteɪkɪŋ/ *adj* very impressive, exciting, or surprising: *The view from my bedroom window was absolutely breathtaking.* | *an act of breathtaking arrogance* —**breathtakingly** *adv*

'breath ˌtest n [C] BrE a test in which the police make a car driver breathe into a special bag to see if he or she has drunk too much alcohol; → **breathalyze**

breath·y /'breθi/ adj if someone's voice is breathy, you can hear their breath when they speak

bred /bred/ the past tense and past participle of BREED

breech /briːtʃ/ n [C] the part of a gun into which you put the bullets

'breech birth also **'breech deˌlivery** n [C] a birth in which the lower part of a baby's body comes out of its mother first

breech·es /'brɪtʃəz/ n [plural] short trousers that fasten just below the knees: riding breeches

breed[1] [S3] /briːd/ v past tense and past participle **bred** /bred/
1 [I] if animals breed, they MATE in order to have babies: Eagles breed during the cooler months of the year.
2 [T] to keep animals or plants in order to produce babies or new plants, especially ones with particular qualities: These dogs were originally bred in Scotland to round up sheep. → CROSSBREED[1], PUREBRED, THOROUGHBRED
3 [T] to cause a particular feeling or condition: Poor living conditions breed violence and despair.
4 [T] if a place, situation, or thing breeds a particular type of person, it produces that type: Society's obsession with sex has bred a generation of unhappy children. → WELL-BRED; → **born and bred** at BORN[2] (3)

breed[2] n [C] **1** a type of animal that is kept as a pet or on a farm: [+of] Spaniels are my favourite breed of dog. **2** a particular kind of person or type of thing: Real cowboys are **a dying breed** (=not many exist anymore). | Dodd was one of that **rare breed** (=there are not many of them) who could make the game of football look simple. | [+of] **a new breed** of international criminal

breed·er /'briːdə $ -ər/ n [C] someone who breeds animals or plants as a job: a dog breeder

breed·ing /'briːdɪŋ/ n [U] **1** when animals produce babies: Open-sea fish lay several million eggs each **breeding season**. **2** the activity of keeping animals or plants in order to produce animals or plants that have particular qualities: the breeding of pedigree dogs | Benson took great care in selecting **breeding stock** (=animals you keep to breed from). **3** the fact of coming from a family of high rank and having polite social behaviour: The young lieutenant had an air of wealth and **good breeding**.

'breeding ˌground n [C] **1** a place or situation where something bad or harmful develops: [+for] Overcrowded slums are breeding grounds for crime. **2** a place where animals go in order to breed

breeze[1] /briːz/ n [C] **1** a gentle wind: flowers waving in the breeze **2** **be a breeze** informal to be very easy: Don't think that learning Dutch will be a breeze. → **shoot the breeze** at SHOOT[1] (13)

breeze[2] v **1** [I always + adv/prep] to walk somewhere in a calm confident way: [+in/into/out etc] She just breezed into my office and said she wanted a job. **2** [T] to do very well in a test, a piece of written work etc, with very little effort: Don't bother studying for the English exam – you'll breeze it.
breeze through sth phr v to achieve something very easily: He breezed through the exam.

'breeze-block n [C] BrE a light brick used in building, made of CEMENT and CINDERS; ▣ **cinder block** AmE

breez·y /'briːzi/ adj **1** a breezy person is happy, confident, and relaxed: a breezy and relaxed air of confidence **2** if the weather is breezy, the wind blows quite strongly —**breezily** adv

breth·ren /'breðrən/ n [plural] old use used to address or talk about the members of an organization or group, especially a religious group

breve /briːv/ n [C] BrE a musical note which continues for twice as long as a SEMIBREVE

brev·i·ty /'brevɪti/ n [U] formal **1** the quality of expressing something in very few words; → **brief**:

Letters published in the newspaper are edited for brevity and clarity. **2** the quality of continuing for only a short time; → **brief**: the brevity of her visit

brew[1] /bruː/ v **1** [T] to make beer: Every beer on the menu was brewed locally. **2** [I] if a drink of tea or coffee is brewing, the taste is getting into the hot water: He read the paper while the tea brewed. **3** [T] to make a drink of tea or coffee: freshly brewed coffee **4** **be brewing a)** if something unpleasant is brewing, it will happen soon: There's **trouble brewing** in the office. **b)** if a storm is brewing, it will happen soon
brew up phr v BrE informal to make a drink of tea

brew[2] n **1** [C] especially BrE a drink that is brewed, especially tea **2** [C,U] AmE beer, or a can or glass of beer: a cold brew in a frosty glass | We grabbed a six-pack of brew and headed for the porch. **3** [C usually singular] a combination of different things: [+of] The band played a strange brew of rock, jazz, and country music. → HOME BREW

brew·er /'bruːə $ -ər/ n [C] a person or company that makes beer

brew·er·y /'bruːəri/ n plural **breweries** [C] a place where beer is made, or a company that makes beer

bri·ar, brier /'braɪə $ -ər/ n **1** [C,U] a wild bush with branches that have small sharp points **2** [C] a tobacco pipe made from briar

bribe[1] /braɪb/ v [T] **1** to illegally give someone, especially a public official, money or a gift in order to persuade them to do something for you: The only way we could get into the country was by bribing the border officials. | **bribe sb to do sth** He bribed one of the prison guards to smuggle out a note. **2** to offer someone, especially a child, something special in order to persuade them to do something: **bribe sb with sth** Samantha wouldn't do her homework until I bribed her with ice cream.

bribe[2] n [C] **1** money or a gift that you illegally give someone to persuade them to do something for you: The officials said that they had been **offered bribes** before an important game. | **accept/take a bribe** A Supreme Court judge was charged with taking bribes. **2** something special offered to someone, especially a child, in order to persuade them to do something

brib·er·y /'braɪbəri/ n [U] the act of giving bribes: We tried everything – persuasion, bribery, threats. | He was found guilty of **bribery and corruption** (=bribery and dishonest behaviour).

bric-a-brac /'brɪk ə ˌbræk/ n [U] BrE small objects that are not worth very much money but are interesting or attractive

brick[1] [S2] [W3] /brɪk/ n
1 [C,U] a hard block of baked clay used for building walls, houses etc: a brick wall | a house made of brick | Protesters attacked the police with stones and bricks.
2 **bricks and mortar** houses – used especially when talking about them as an INVESTMENT
3 [C] BrE a small square block of wood, plastic etc used as a toy
4 [C] old-fashioned a good person who you can depend on when you are in trouble → **be (like) banging/bashing etc your head against a brick wall** at HEAD[1] (31); → **drop a brick** at DROP[1] (27)

brick[2] v
brick sth ⇔ **off** phr v to separate an area from a larger area by building a wall of bricks: Some of the rooms had been bricked off.
brick sth ⇔ **up/in** phr v to fill or close a space by building a wall of bricks in it: The windows were bricked up.

brick·bat /'brɪkbæt/ n [C] written a criticism of something: The plan has drawn both brickbats and praise.

[1] 000, [2] 000, [3] 000, most frequent words in [S]poken and [W]ritten English

brick·lay·er /'brɪk,leɪə $ -ər/ also **brick·ie** /'brɪki/ *informal BrE n* [C] someone whose job is to build walls, buildings etc with bricks —**bricklaying** *n* [U]

,**brick 'red** *n* [U] a brownish red colour —**brick red** *adj*

brick·work /'brɪkwɜːk $ -wɜːrk/ *n* [U] **1** the bricks that have been used to build something: *The brickwork was cracked and in need of repair.* **2** the work of building something with bricks

brid·al /'braɪdl/ *adj* [only before noun] relating to a wedding or a woman who is getting married: *a bridal gown*

'**bridal ,party** *n* [C] the group of people who arrive at the church with the bride

'**bridal ,suite** *n* [C] a special set of rooms in a hotel for two people who have just got married

bride /braɪd/ *n* [C] a woman at the time she gets married or just after she is married; → **groom**: *You may kiss the bride.*

bride·groom /'braɪdgruːm, -grʊm/ also **groom** *n* [C] a man at the time he gets married, or just after he is married

brides·maid /'braɪdzmeɪd/ *n* [C] a girl or woman, usually unmarried, who helps a bride on her wedding day and is with her at the wedding → **BEST MAN**

,**bride-to-'be** *n plural* **brides-to-be** [C] a woman who is going to be married soon: *Jonathan's bride-to-be*

bridges

road bridge

viaduct

drawbridge

footbridge

hump-backed bridge

suspension bridge

flyover *BrE*/overpass *AmE*

bridge¹ [S2] [W2] /brɪdʒ/ *n*
1 OVER A RIVER/ROAD ETC [C] a structure built over a river, road etc that allows people or vehicles to cross from one side to the other → **SUSPENSION BRIDGE, SWING BRIDGE**; → see picture at **TOWN**
2 CONNECTION [C] something that provides a connection between two things; ▤ **link**: [+between/to] *The training programme is seen as a bridge between school and work.* | *a scheme to* **build bridges** (=make a better relationship) *between the police and the community*
3 SHIP [C usually singular] the raised part of a ship from which the officers control it
4 CARD GAME [U] a card game for four players who play in pairs
5 the bridge of your nose the upper part of your nose

between your eyes
6 PAIR OF GLASSES [C usually singular] the part of a pair of glasses that rests on your nose
7 MUSICAL INSTRUMENT [C usually singular] a small piece of wood under the strings of a VIOLIN or GUITAR, used to keep them in position
8 FOR TEETH [C] a small piece of metal that keeps false teeth in place by attaching them to your real teeth → **burn your bridges** at BURN¹ (18); → **cross that bridge when you come to it** at CROSS¹ (10); → **be (all) water under the bridge** at WATER¹ (6)

bridge² *v* [T] **1** to reduce or get rid of the difference between two things: *The differences between our two cultures can be bridged if we continue to communicate.* | *Alvin managed to* **bridge the gap between** *ballet and modern dance.* **2** *written* to build or form a bridge over something: *a fallen tree bridging the stream*

bridge·head /'brɪdʒhed/ *n* [C] a strong position far forward in enemy land from which an army can go forward or attack

'**bridging ,loan** *BrE*, '**bridge loan** *AmE n* [C] an amount of money that a bank lends you for a short period of time until you receive money from somewhere else

bri·dle¹ /'braɪdl/ *n* [C] a set of leather bands put around a horse's head and used to control its movements

bridle² *v* **1** [I] *written* to become angry and offended about something: [+at] *The senator bridled at the reporter's question.* **2** [T] to put a bridle on a horse

'**bridle path** also **bri·dle·way** /'braɪdlweɪ/ *n* [C] a path that you ride a horse on

Brie /briː/ *n* [U] a soft French cheese

brief¹ [S2] [W2] /briːf/ *adj*
1 continuing for a short time: *We stopped by Alice's house for a brief visit.* | *Let's keep this conversation brief; I have a plane to catch.* | **a brief period/moment/spell etc** *Greene spent a brief time at Cambridge.*
2 using very few words or including few details: *The President read a brief statement to reporters before boarding his plane.* | *a brief description of the film*
3 be brief to say or write something using only a few words, especially because there is little time: *I'll be brief; a lot of changes are going to happen.*
4 clothes which are brief are short and cover only a small area of your body: *a very brief bikini*

brief² *n* [C] **1** [usually singular] official instructions that explain what someone's job is, what their duties are etc: *The architect's brief is to design an extension that is modern but blends with the rest of the building.* **2** *law* a short spoken or written statement giving facts about a law case: *The ACLU filed a brief* (=gave one to the court) *opposing the decision.* **3** *BrE law* a law case that a lawyer will argue in a court **4** a short report about something **5 in brief a)** in as few words as possible: *We should, in brief, invest heavily in digital systems.* **b)** without any details: *Here again are today's headlines in brief.* **6 briefs** [plural] men's or women's underwear worn on the lower part of the body

brief³ *v* [T] to give someone all the information about a situation that they will need: **brief sb on sth** *The president has been fully briefed on the current situation in Haiti.* → **DEBRIEF**

brief·case /'briːfkeɪs/ *n* [C] a flat case used especially by business people for carrying papers or documents → see picture at **OFFICE**; → see picture at **CASE¹**

brief·ing /'briːfɪŋ/ *n* [C,U] information or instructions that you get before you have to do something

brief·ly [S2] [W3] /'briːfli/ *adv*
1 for a short time: *We stopped off briefly in London on our way to Geneva.*
2 in as few words as possible: *Sonia explained briefly what we had to do.* | [sentence adverb]: *Briefly, I think we should accept their offer.*

bri·er /'braɪə $ -ər/ *n* [C] a BRIAR

brig /brɪg/ *n* [C]   **1** a ship with two MASTS (=poles) and large square sails   **2** *AmE* a military prison, especially on a ship

bri·gade S3 /brɪ'geɪd/ *n* [C]
1 a large group of soldiers forming part of an army
2 an insulting word for a group of people who have the same beliefs: *the anti-nuclear brigade*
3 a group of people who are organized to do something: *Snowmobile brigades delivered food and medicine.* →
FIRE BRIGADE

brig·a·dier /ˌbrɪgə'dɪə◂ $ -'dɪr◂/ *n* [C] a high military rank in the British Army, or the person who has this rank

brigadier-'general *n* [C] a high army rank or someone holding this rank

brig·and /'brɪgənd/ *n* [C] *literary* a thief, especially one of a group that attacks people in mountains or forests

bright S2 W2 /braɪt/ *adj comparative* **brighter**, *superlative* **brightest**
1 LIGHT shining strongly, or with plenty of light: *Her eyes were hurting from the bright lights.* | *The buildings looked lovely in the bright sunshine.* | *a large bright room*
2 SUNNY if the weather is bright, the sun is shining and there is a lot of light; ▣ **dull**: *The weather was bright and sunny.* | *a bright autumn day*
3 INTELLIGENT intelligent and able to learn things quickly: *He was an exceptionally bright child.* | *a bright ambitious young man* | *He is constantly coming up with **bright ideas** for making money.*
4 COLOURS bright colours are strong and easy to see: *a bright red jumper* | *I never wear bright colours.*
5 CHEERFUL happy and full of energy: *Her voice was bright and cheerful.* | *She gave him a bright smile.* | *He looked up at me with bright eyes.*
6 SUCCESSFUL if the future looks bright, you think that something will be successful; ▣ **promising**: *The school's future now looks very bright.* | *I'm sure the company **has a bright future** now.*
7 as bright as a button very intelligent and full of energy
8 look on the bright side to see the good points in a situation that seems to be bad: *Come on, try to look on the bright side.*
9 bright and early very early in the morning: *He was up bright and early, keen to get started.*
10 bright spark *informal* someone who says or does something that they think is intelligent but is really wrong or stupid: *Some bright spark thought the building was on fire and called the fire brigade.*
11 bright and breezy happy and confident
12 bright-eyed and bushy-tailed happy and full of energy
13 the bright lights the interesting exciting life in a big city: *She missed the bright lights of London.*
14 bright spot an event or a period of time that is more pleasant when everything else is unpleasant: *The only bright spot of the weekend was our trip to the theatre.*
—**brightly** *adv*: *The sun shone brightly.* | *brightly-coloured clothes* | *She smiled brightly.* —**brightness** *n* [U]

bright·en /'braɪtn/ *v*
1 MAKE LIGHTER [T] also **brighten sth** ⇔ **up** to make something lighter or brighter: *Use blonde highlights to brighten your hair.* | *The morning sunshine brightened up the room.*
2 MAKE MORE ATTRACTIVE [T] also **brighten sth** ⇔ **up** to make something more colourful or attractive: *She bought some flowers to brighten the room.* | *I want to brighten the place up a bit.*
3 MAKE MORE ENJOYABLE [T] also **brighten sth** ⇔ **up** to make something more enjoyable, exciting or interesting: *His letter brightened my day.* | *I felt I needed something to brighten up my life.*
4 BECOME LIGHTER/BRIGHTER [I] to shine more strongly, or become brighter in colour: *The stage lights brightened to reveal a street scene.*
5 BECOME SUNNY [I] also **brighten up** if the weather

brightens, the sun begins to shine and it becomes lighter: *The sky brightened after lunch.* | *Let's hope the weather brightens up later.* | *It brightened up a bit in the afternoon.*
6 BECOME HAPPY [I] also **brighten up** to become happier or more excited: *His eyes brightened when we started talking about money.* | *She brightened up a bit when she saw us.*

brights /braɪts/ *n* [plural] *AmE* car HEADLIGHTS when they are shining as brightly as possible: *driving with brights on*

brill /brɪl/ *adj BrE informal* very good: *It sounds really brill!*

bril·liance /'brɪljəns/ *n* [U]   **1** a very high level of intelligence or skill: *He is also respected for his brilliance as an artist.*   **2** very great brightness: *The stars glittered with the brilliance of jewels.*

bril·liant S3 W3 /'brɪljənt/ *adj*
1 BRIGHT brilliant light or colour is very bright and strong: *She closed her eyes against the **brilliant light**.* | *We sat outside in the **brilliant sunshine**.* | *She was dressed in brilliant white.*
2 CLEVER extremely clever or skilful: *I think that's a **brilliant idea**.* | *a brilliant performance* | *a brilliant young musician*
3 EXCELLENT *BrE* excellent: *The film was absolutely brilliant.*
4 SUCCESSFUL very successful: *He had a long and **brilliant career**.* | *The project was a **brilliant success**.*
—**brilliantly** *adv*: *The sun was shining brilliantly.* | *The goalkeeper played brilliantly.*

bril·lian·tine /'brɪljəntiːn/ *n* [U] an oily substance that was used in the past on men's hair

Bril·lo pad /'brɪləʊ pæd $ -loʊ-/ *n* [C] *trademark* a ball of wire filled with soap, which is used for cleaning pans

brim¹ /brɪm/ *n* [C]   **1** the bottom part of a hat that sticks out to protect you from sun and rain: *an old straw hat with a broad brim*   **2** the top edge of a container: *She filled each glass to the brim.* | **filled/full to the brim** (=completely full) *The cup was filled to the brim with coffee.*

brim² *v* **brimmed, brimming** [I]   **1** if your eyes brim with tears, or if tears brim from your eyes, you start to cry: [+with] *Her eyes brimmed with tears.* | *Her tears brimmed over again as she started to speak.*   **2** **be brimming (over) with sth** to have a lot of a particular thing, quality, or emotion: *The flowerbeds were brimming over with flowers* | *He seemed to be **brimming with confidence**.* | *Rob was just brimming with enthusiasm.*

brim·ful /'brɪmfʊl/ *adj* [not before noun] very full of something: [+of] *The team is brimful of confidence after their win last week.* | *a glass brimful of red wine*

brin·dled /'brɪndld/ also **brin·dle** /'brɪndl/ *adj* a brindled animal is brown and has marks or bands of another colour —**brindle** *n* [C,U]

brine /braɪn/ *n* [U]   **1** water which contains a lot of salt and is used for preserving food: *fish pickled in brine*   **2** sea water

bring S1 W1 /brɪŋ/ *v past tense and past participle* **brought** /brɔːt $ brɒːt/ [T]
1 a) to take something or someone with you to the place where you are now, or to the place you are talking about; → **take**: *Did you bring an umbrella?* | *It was the first time Joey had ever **brought** a girl **home**.* | *They **brought news** of further fighting along the border.* | **bring sth/sb to sth/sb** *Is it OK if I bring some friends to the party?* | **bring sb/sth with you** *For some reason, Jesse had brought a tape recorder with him.* **b)** to get something for someone and take it to them: **bring sb sth** *Can you bring me another beer?* | *Robert asked the waiter to bring him the check.* | *While she was in prison, friends used to bring her books and writing materials.* | **bring sth/sb to sth/sb** *He expects me to bring everything to him in bed.*

B

2 a) to make a particular situation exist or cause a particular feeling: *efforts to **bring peace** to the region* | *The strikes are expected to bring chaos.* | *The senator's speech brought an angry response from Civil Rights groups.* **b)** to cause someone or something to reach a particular state or condition: **bring sth to an end/a close/a halt/a conclusion** (=make something stop) *The trial was swiftly brought to an end.* | *It was the war that first **brought** him **to power*** (=make someone have power over a country). | *So far the US has been unable to **bring** him **to justice*** (=make him be punished for his actions).* | ***Bring** the sauce **to the boil*** (=heat it until it boils).* | *The country had been **brought to its knees*** (=caused to be in such a bad condition that it is almost impossible to continue).*

3 [always + adv/prep] to make something move in a particular direction: **bring sth up/down/round etc** *Bring your arm up slowly until it's level with your shoulder.* | *He lifted the axe above his head, then brought it down with a thud on the tree trunk.* | *The storm brought the old oak tree crashing down.*

4 [always + adv/prep] if something brings people to a place, it makes them go there: *The discovery of gold brought thousands of people to the Transvaal.* | **what brings you here?** (=used to ask why someone is in a particular place) *What brings you here on a night like this?*

5 to make something available for people to use, have, enjoy etc: *The expansion of state education brought new and wider opportunities for working class children.* | **bring sth to sb/sth** *The government is launching a new initiative to bring jobs to deprived areas.* | **bring sb sth** *It's a good sign – let's hope it will bring us some luck.*

6 if a period of time brings a particular event or situation, the event or situation happens during that time: *The 1930s brought unemployment and economic recession.* | *Who knows what the future will bring?*

7 bring charges/a lawsuit/a court case/a prosecution/a claim (against sb) to begin a court case in order to try to prove that someone has done something wrong or is legally responsible for something wrong: *Survivors of the fire later brought a billion dollar lawsuit against the company.* | *The police say they are planning to bring charges against him.*

8 bring a smile to sb's lips/face to make someone smile: *Her words brought a sudden smile to his lips.*

9 bring tears to sb's eyes to make someone start to cry: *The pain brought tears to his eyes.*

10 bring the total/number/score etc to sth used when saying what the new total etc is: *This brings the total to 46.*

11 cannot/could not bring yourself to do sth to feel unable to do something because it would upset you or someone else too much: *She still can't bring herself to talk about it.*

12 *spoken* used when saying that something is the next thing that you want to talk about: **that/this/which brings me to ...** *This brings me to the main point of today's meeting.*

13 if a programme is brought to you by a particular television or radio company, they broadcast it or make it: **sth is brought to you by sb** *This programme is brought to you by the BBC.*

14 bring sth to bear (on/upon sth) *formal* to use something, for example your power, authority, or your knowledge, in a way that will have a big effect on something or someone: *The full force of the law was brought to bear on anyone who criticized the government.*

15 bring home the bacon *informal* to earn the money that your family needs to live

bring sth ⇔ **about** *phr v*
to make something happen; ▪ **cause**: *How can we bring about a change in attitudes?* | *A huge amount of environmental damage has been brought about by the destruction of the rainforests.*

bring sb/sth ⇔ **along** *phr v*
to take someone or something with you when you go somewhere: *You're welcome to bring along a friend.* | *I've brought some pictures along to show you.*

bring sb/sth **around/round** *phr v*
1 bring the conversation around/round to sth to deliberately and gradually introduce a new subject into a conversation: *I'll try to bring the conversation around to the subject of money.*
2 to make someone become conscious again: *I slapped his face a couple of times to try to bring him round.*
3 to manage to persuade someone to do something or to agree with you: *She won't listen to me. Let's see if Sue can bring her round.* | [+to] *I'm sure I can bring him around to our point of view.*
4 to bring someone or something to someone's house: *I'll bring the books around tomorrow.*

bring back *phr v*
1 bring sth ⇔ back to start to use something again that was used in the past; ▪ **reintroduce**: *The city council has decided to bring back the old electric trams.* | *Bringing back the death penalty has done absolutely nothing to reduce crime.*
2 bring sth ⇔ back to make you remember something: *The trip **brought back** a lot of happy **memories**.* | *Seeing those pictures on TV **brought it all back** to me.*
3 bring sth ⇔ back to take something or someone with you when you come back from somewhere: **bring sth back for sb** *Don't forget to bring something back for the kids.* | **bring sb back sth** *If you're going to the store, could you bring me back a six-pack?*
4 bring sb ⇔ back to return someone to their previous job or position of authority; ▪ **reinstate**: *Following their latest defeat, soccer fans are urging the club to bring back the former manager.*
5 bring sb back to sth if something that is said brings you back to a particular subject, it is connected with that subject, so you will start talking about it again: *This brings us back to the question of funding.*

bring sb/sth ⇔ **down** *phr v*
1 to reduce something to a lower level: *The government hopes these measures will help to bring down inflation.*
2 to fly a plane down to the ground; ▪ **land**: *The pilot managed to bring the plane down safely.*
3 to make a plane, bird, or animal fall to the ground by shooting at it: *A bomber had been brought down by anti-aircraft fire.*
4 to force a government or ruler to stop ruling a country: *a crisis that could bring down the government*
5 to make someone fall over: *He was brought down by the goalkeeper and awarded a penalty.*

bring sth ⇔ **down on/upon** sb *phr v*
to make something bad happen to someone, especially to yourself or to people connected with you: *His recklessness brought down disaster on the whole family.*

bring sth ⇔ **forth** *phr v literary*
to produce something or make it appear: *a tragic love affair that brought forth only pain*

bring sth ⇔ **forward** *phr v*
1 to change an arrangement so that something happens sooner: [+to] *The meeting's been brought forward to Thursday.*
2 bring forward legislation/plans/policies etc to officially introduce plans etc for people to discuss: *The government has brought forward new proposals to tackle the problem of increasing crime.*
3 to record the result of a calculation so that it can be used in a further calculation: *The balance brought forward is £21,765.*

bring sb/sth ⇔ **in** *phr v*
1 to introduce a new law: *Harsh anti-Trade Union laws were brought in in the early 1980s.*
2 to ask someone to become involved in a discussion or situation: *I'd like to bring in Doctor Hall here and ask him his views.* | **bring sb in to do sth** *The police were brought in to investigate the matter.*
3 to earn a particular amount or produce a particular amount of profit: *The sale of the house only brought in about £45,000.*

4 to attract customers to a shop or business: *We've got to bring in more business if we want the restaurant to survive.*
5 bring in a verdict to say officially in a law court whether someone is guilty or not guilty of a crime; ▤ **return a verdict**: *The jury brought in a verdict of not guilty.*

bring sb/sth **into** sth *phr v*
1 to cause someone or something to be in a particular situation: *Most of the land has now been brought into cultivation.* | *The work brought me into contact with a lot of very interesting people.*
2 to make someone become involved in a discussion or situation: *The government is trying to bring teachers into the debate on education.* | *There is a danger that this could bring other countries into the war.*

bring sth ⇔ **off** *phr v*
to succeed in doing something difficult; ▤ **pull off**: *They managed to bring off the most daring jewellery robbery in history.*

bring sth ⇔ **on** *phr v*
1 to make something bad or unpleasant happen; ▤ **cause**: *Stress can bring on an asthma attack.* | *What's brought this on? Have I upset you somehow?*
2 to help someone to improve or make progress: *Teachers have to bring on the bright children and at the same time give extra help to those who need it.*
3 to make plants or crops grow faster: *Keeping the young plants in a greenhouse will help bring them on.*

bring sth **on/upon** sb *phr v*
to make something unpleasant happen to someone: *You have brought disaster on the whole village!* | **bring sth on/upon yourself** *I've got no sympathy for him – he's brought this all on himself!*

bring sb **onto** sth *phr v*
if something brings you onto a particular subject, it is a good time for you to start talking about it: *This brings me onto the question of pay rises.*

bring sth ⇔ **out** *phr v*
1 to make something easier to see, taste, notice etc: *The spices really bring out the flavour of the meat.* | *Fatherhood seems to have brought out the caring side of him.*
2 to produce something that will be sold to the public: *He's bringing out a new album next month.* | *They've brought out a new perfume called 'Desire'.*
3 to take something out of a place: *Jenny opened the cupboard and brought out a couple of bottles.*
4 bring out the best/worst in sb to make someone behave in the best or worst way that they can: *Alcohol just brings out the worst in her.*
5 bring sb out of himself/herself to make someone feel more confident and able to talk to people: *Changing schools has really brought her out of herself.*

bring sb **out in** sth *phr v*
if something brings you out in spots, it makes them appear on your skin: *Any foods containing wheat bring him out in a rash.*

bring sb/sth **round** → BRING AROUND

bring sb **through** (sth) *phr v*
to help someone to successfully deal with a very difficult event or period of time: *Both my children have brought me through extremely difficult times since my husband died.*

bring sb ⇔ **together** *phr v*
1 to arrange for people to meet and do something together: *We brought together researchers from three different universities to work on the project.*
2 to make people have a better relationship or feel closer to each other: *Any attack by a foreign power will inevitably bring the people of a country together.*

bring sb/sth ⇔ **up** *phr v*
1 to mention a subject or start to talk about it; ▤ **raise**: *Why did you have to bring up the subject of money?*
2 to look after and influence a child until he or she is grown up; ▤ **raise**: *He was brought up by his grandparents.* | **bring sb up to do sth** *In my day, children were brought up to respect the law.* | **be brought up (as) a Catholic/Muslim etc** *I was brought up a Catholic.* → UPBRINGING

3 to make something appear on a computer screen: *Can you bring up the list of candidates again?*
4 *BrE* if you bring food up, it comes back up from your stomach and out of your mouth: *I had a sandwich for lunch and promptly brought it up again.*
5 to charge someone with a particular crime and make them go to a court to be judged: [+before] *He was brought up before a magistrate, charged with dangerous driving.*
6 bring sb up short/with a start to surprise someone and make them suddenly stop talking or doing something: *Her question brought me up short.*

> **WORD CHOICE: bring, take, get, fetch**
> **bring** means to carry something or come with someone to the place where you are or to the place where you are talking about: *Would you like me to bring anything to the party?* | *She brought her Spanish friend into class.*
> **take** means to carry something or go with someone to another place, away from where you are or where you are talking about: *Don't forget to take your umbrella.* | *I'll take you home.*
> **get** means to go to another place and come back with something or someone: *I went upstairs to get my jacket.* In British English, you can also use **fetch**: *Will you fetch Susan from the airport?*
> In American English, you only use **fetch** to talk about a dog getting something.

brink /brɪŋk/ *n* **1 the brink (of sth)** a situation when you are almost in a new situation, usually a bad one: **on the brink of death/disaster/war etc** *In October 1962 the world seemed on the brink of nuclear war.* | *The company had huge debts and was on the brink of collapse.* | **to the brink (of sth)** *managers who have taken their companies to the brink of disaster* | **back from the brink (of sth)** *He will go down in history as the leader who pulled us back from the brink* (=saved us from disaster). **2 push/tip sb over the brink** to make someone start doing crazy or extreme things **3 the brink of sth** *literary* the edge of a very high place such as a cliff

brink·man·ship /ˈbrɪŋkmənʃɪp/ also **brinks·man·ship** /ˈbrɪŋksmən-/ *AmE n* [U] a method of gaining political advantage by pretending that you are willing to do something very dangerous

brin·y¹ /ˈbraɪni/ *adj* briny water is water that contains a lot of salt

briny² *n* **the briny** *old-fashioned* the sea

bri·o /ˈbriːəʊ $ -oʊ *n* [U] *literary* energy and confidence

bri·oche /ˈbriːɒʃ, briːˈəʊʃ $ briːˈoʊʃ, -ˈɔːʃ/ *n* [C,U] a type of sweet bread made with flour, eggs, and butter

bri·quette /brɪˈket/ *n* [C] a block of pressed coal dust, to burn in a fire or BARBECUE

brisk /brɪsk/ *adj* **1** quick and full of energy: *a brisk walk* | *They set off at a brisk pace.* **2** quick, practical and showing that you want to get things done quickly: *Her tone of voice is brisk.* **3** trade or business that is brisk is very busy, with a lot of products being sold: *The public bar was already doing a brisk trade.* **4** weather that is brisk is cold and clear —**briskly** *adv*: *They walked briskly.* —**briskness** *n* [U]

bris·ket /ˈbrɪsk‚ɪt/ *n* [U] meat from the chest of an animal, especially a cow

bris·tle¹ /ˈbrɪsəl/ *n* **1** [C,U] a short stiff hair that feels rough: *His chin was covered with bristles.* **2** [C] a short stiff hair, wire etc that forms part of a brush

bristle² *v* [I] **1** to behave in a way that shows you are very angry or annoyed: **bristle with rage/indignation etc** *John pushed back his chair, bristling with rage.* | [+at] *He bristled at her rudeness.* **2** if an animal's hair bristles, it stands up stiffly because the animal is afraid or angry

bristle with sth *phr v* to have a lot of something or be full of something: *a battleship bristling with guns*

B

B

bris·tly /ˈbrɪsli/ *adj* **1** bristly hair is short and stiff **2** a bristly part of your body has short stiff hairs on it: *a bristly chin*

Brit /brɪt/ *n* [C] *informal* someone from Britain

britch·es /ˈbrɪtʃ₁z/ *n* [plural] *old-fashioned* trousers

Brit·ish[1] /ˈbrɪtɪʃ/ *adj* relating to Britain or its people: *the British government* | *a British-born scientist* —**Britishness** *n* [U]

British[2] *n* **the British** [plural] people from Britain

Brit·ish·er /ˈbrɪtɪʃə $ -ər/ *n* [C] *AmE old-fashioned* someone from Britain

,British 'Isles *n* the group of islands that includes Great Britain, Ireland, and the smaller islands around them

,British 'Summer Time *n* [U] *BST* the time one hour ahead of Greenwich Mean Time that is used in Britain from late March to late October; → **daylight saving time**

Brit·on /ˈbrɪtn/ *n* [C] *formal* someone from Britain: *the ancient Britons* | *the first Briton to win the championship for twenty years*

brit·tle /ˈbrɪtl/ *adj* **1** hard but easily broken: *The branches were dry and brittle.* | *Joanna was diagnosed as having brittle bones.* **2** a situation, relationship, or feeling that is brittle is easily damaged or destroyed: *He spoke with the brittle confidence of someone who, underneath, was very worried.* **3** showing no warm feelings: *a brittle laugh*

bro /brəʊ $ broʊ/ *n plural* **bros** [C] *spoken* **1** your brother **2** *AmE* a way of greeting a friend

broach /brəʊtʃ $ broʊtʃ/ *v* [T] **1 broach the subject/question/matter etc** to mention a subject that may be embarrassing or unpleasant or cause an argument: *I broached the subject of his past.* **2** to open a bottle or BARREL containing wine, beer etc

broad[1] **S2** **W2** /brɔːd $ brɒːd/ *adj*
1 WIDE a road, river, or part of someone's body etc that is broad is wide; ☒ **narrow**; → **breadth**: *We went along a broad passage.* | *He was six feet tall, with broad shoulders.* | **six feet/three metres etc broad** *The room is three metres long and two metres broad.*; → see box at **WIDE**[1]
2 INCLUDING A LOT including many different kinds of things or people; ☒ **narrow**; → **breadth**: *The show aims to reach the broadest possible audience.* | **broad range/spectrum** *Students here study a broad range of subjects.* | **broad category/field/area etc** *Private pension schemes fall into two broad categories.* | *a party which lacks a broad base of political support* | *The play is a comedy,* **in the broadest sense of the word.**
3 GENERAL concerning the main ideas or parts of something rather than all the details: *The client should understand,* **in broad terms**, *the likely cost of the case.* | **broad consensus/agreement etc** *The members were in broad agreement.* | **broad outline/framework** *I'll give you a broad outline of the plan.*
4 LARGE AREA covering a large area: *a broad expanse of water*
5 WAY OF SPEAKING a broad ACCENT clearly shows where you come from; ☒ **strong**: *a broad Scottish accent*
6 broad smile/grin a big smile: *Abby came in with a broad smile on her face.*
7 in broad daylight if something, especially a crime, happens in broad daylight, it happens in the daytime and in public: *The attack happened in broad daylight, in one of the busiest parts of town.*
8 broad hint a HINT (=suggestion) that is very clear and easy to understand: *In June he gave a broad hint that he might retire.*
9 a **broad church** *BrE* an organization that contains a wide range of opinions: *The Labour Party has to be a broad church.*

10 HUMOUR broad humour is rather rude or concerned with sex
11 broad in the beam *informal* having large or fat HIPS

broad[2] *n* [C] *AmE spoken not polite* an offensive word for a woman

B-road /ˈbiː rəʊd $ -roʊd/ *n* [C] a type of road in Britain that is smaller than an A-ROAD

broad·band /ˈbrɔːdbænd $ ˈbrɒːd-/ *n* [U] **1** *technical* a system of sending radio signals which allows several messages to be sent at the same time **2** a system of connecting computers to the Internet and moving information, such as messages or pictures, at a very high speed —**broadband** *adj* [only before noun]: *broadband communications*

,broad 'bean /$ ˈ. ./ *n* [C] *BrE* a round pale green bean

broad·brush /ˈbrɔːdbrʌʃ $ ˈbrɒːd-/ *adj* [only before noun] dealing only with the main parts of something, and not with the details; ☒ **general**: *a broadbrush strategy*

broad·cast[1] /ˈbrɔːdkɑːst $ ˈbrɒːdkæst/ *n* [C] a programme on the radio or on television: *a news broadcast* | *CNN's* **live broadcast** *of the trial* (=sent out at the same time as the events are happening)

broadcast[2] *v past tense and past participle* **broadcast 1** [I,T] to send out radio or television programmes: *The interview was* **broadcast live** *across Europe.* **2** [T] to tell something to a lot of people: *There was no need to broadcast the fact that he lost his job.*

broad·cast·er /ˈbrɔːdkɑːstə $ ˈbrɒːdkæstər/ *n* [C] **1** someone who speaks on radio or television programmes: *a well-known journalist and broadcaster* **2** a company which sends out television or radio programmes: *the British broadcaster Channel Four*

broad·cast·ing /ˈbrɔːdkɑːstɪŋ $ ˈbrɒːdkæstɪŋ/ *n* [U] the business of making television and radio programmes: *a career in broadcasting*

broad·en /ˈbrɔːdn $ ˈbrɒːdn/ *v* **1** [T] to increase something such as your knowledge, experience, or range of activities: *The course helps school-leavers broaden their knowledge of the world of work.* | *I'd like to work abroad to* **broaden** *my* **horizons** (=learn, experience, or attempt new things). | *Travel* **broadens the mind** (=helps you to understand and accept other people's beliefs, customs etc). **2** [I,T] to affect or include more people or things, or to make something affect or include more people or things; ☒ **widen**, **expand**: *Mr Mates said the party must broaden its appeal to younger voters.* | *Flynn's appeal broadened as the campaign continued into the summer months.* | *I want to broaden the discussion to other aspects of the problem.* **3** [I,T] to make something wider or to become wider; ☒ **widen**: *Mark's smile broadened.* | *The council decided to broaden the pavement.*
broaden out *phr v* if something, especially a river or road, broadens out, it becomes wider; ☒ **widen out**: *The river broadens out at this point.*

'broad jump *n AmE* **the broad jump** the LONG JUMP

broad·loom /ˈbrɔːdluːm $ ˈbrɒːd-/ *n* [U] CARPET that is woven in a single wide piece

broad·ly /ˈbrɔːdli $ ˈbrɒːd-/ *adv* **1** in a general way, relating to the main facts rather than details: *She knows broadly what to expect.* | **broadly similar/comparable/equivalent etc** *We reached broadly similar conclusions.* | **Broadly speaking**, *there are four types of champagne.* | *Independent films are,* **broadly defined**, *movies that appeal to sophisticated audiences.* **2 smile/grin broadly** to have a big smile on your face which clearly shows that you are happy or amused **3** including a range of different things or subjects: *a broadly based school curriculum* | *We invest broadly to lessen the risk.*

broad·mind·ed, broad-minded /ˌbrɔːdˈmaɪndₐd $ ˌbrɒːd-/ *adj* willing to respect opinions or behaviour that are very different from your own; ☒ **narrow-**

minded: *Her parents were broadminded, tolerant, and liberal.* —**broad-mindedness** *n* [U] → SMALL-MINDED

broad·sheet /'brɔːdʃiːt $ 'brɒːd-/ *n* [C] a newspaper printed on large sheets of paper, especially a serious newspaper; → tabloid

broad·side[1] /'brɔːdsaɪd $ 'brɒːd-/ *n* [C] **1** a strong criticism of someone or something: *Can the government survive this latest broadside from its own supporters?* **2** an attack in which all the guns on one side of a ship are fired at the same time

broadside[2] *adv* with the longest side facing something; ▤ **sideways**: [+to] *I brought the boat in broadside to the beach.*

broadside[3] *v* [T] *especially AmE* to crash into the side of another vehicle

broad·sword /'brɔːdsɔːd $ 'brɒːdsɔːrd/ *n* [C] a heavy sword with a broad flat blade

bro·cade /brə'keɪd $ brou-/ *n* [C,U] thick heavy decorative cloth which has a pattern of gold and silver threads: *brocade curtains | deluxe brocades and satins* —**brocaded** *adj*

broc·co·li /'brɒkəli $ 'brɑː-/ *n* [U] a green vegetable that has short branch-like stems → see picture at VEGETABLE[1]

bro·chure /'brəʊʃə, -ʃʊə $ brou'ʃʊr/ *n* [C] a thin book giving information or advertising something: *a holiday brochure*

brogue /brəʊg $ broʊg/ *n* [C] **1** [usually plural] a thick strong leather shoe with a pattern in the leather: *a new pair of brogues* **2** [usually singular] an ACCENT, especially an Irish or Scottish accent

broil /brɔɪl/ *v* **1** [T] *AmE* to cook something under direct heat, or over a flame on a BARBECUE; ▤ **grill** *BrE*: *broiled chicken* **2** [I,T] *AmE* to become very hot: *We lay broiling in the sun.*

broil·er /'brɔɪlə $ -ər/ *n* [C] **1** *AmE* a special area of a STOVE used for cooking food under direct heat; ▤ **grill** *BrE* **2** a broiler chicken

broiler ,chicken *n* [C] a chicken that is suitable to be cooked by broiling

broil·ing /'brɔɪlɪŋ/ *adj AmE* broiling weather, sun etc makes you feel extremely hot; ▤ **boiling**: *a broiling day*

broke[1] /brəʊk $ broʊk/ the past tense of BREAK

broke[2] *adj* [not before noun] **1** having no money: *I'm fed up with being broke all the time.* | **flat/stony broke** (=completely broke) **2** **go broke** if a company or business goes broke, it can no longer operate because it has no money: *A lot of small businesses went broke in the recession.* **3** **go for broke** *informal* to take big risks when you try to achieve something: *At 2–0 down with ten minutes left, you have to go for broke.*

bro·ken[1] /'brəʊkən $ 'broʊ-/ *v* the past participle of BREAK

---

broken

a bent disk

a broken tile

a broken calculator

broken[2] ⬛S3⬛ ⬛W3⬛ *adj*
1 PIECE OF EQUIPMENT not working properly: *The CD player's broken again.* | *Do you know how the phone got broken* (=became broken)?
2 OBJECT in small pieces because it has been hit, dropped etc: *Mind the broken glass.* | *Wrap it up well so*

it doesn't get broken (=become broken) *in the mail.*
3 BONE cracked because you have had an accident: *a badly broken leg* | *Gibbs had an X-ray which revealed no broken bones.*
4 NOT CONTINUOUS interrupted and not continuous: *a broken white line* | *a long noisy night of broken sleep*
5 PERSON extremely weak mentally or physically because you have suffered a lot: *He returned from the war a broken man.*
6 **broken English/French etc** if you speak in broken English, French etc, you speak slowly and make a lot of mistakes because you only know a little of the language
7 **broken home** a family that no longer lives together because the parents have DIVORCED: *The majority of offenders do not come from broken homes.*
8 **broken marriage** a marriage that has ended because the husband and wife do not live together any more
9 **a broken heart** a feeling of extreme sadness, especially because someone you love has died or left you: *I reckon she died of a broken heart.*

broken-'down *adj* not working or in very bad condition: *a broken-down truck*

broken-'hearted *adj* extremely sad, especially because someone you love has died or left you; → **heartbroken**: *He was broken-hearted when she left.*

bro·ken·ly /'brəʊkənli $ 'broʊ-/ *adv written* if you say something brokenly, you speak in short phrases with a lot of pauses, because you are feeling a strong emotion

bro·ker[1] /'brəʊkə $ 'broʊkər/ *n* [C] **1** someone who buys and sells things such as SHARES in companies or foreign money for other people → STOCKBROKER **2** someone who arranges sales or business agreements for other people: *a real estate broker*

broker[2] *v* [T] **broker a deal/settlement/treaty etc** to arrange the details of a deal etc so that everyone can agree to it: *a ceasefire agreement brokered by the UN*

bro·ker·age /'brəʊkərɪdʒ $ 'broʊ-/ *n* [U] **1** the business of being a broker **2** the amount of money a broker charges **3** **brokerage house/firm** a company of brokers, or the place where they work

brol·ly /'brɒli $ 'brɑːli/ *n plural* **brollies** [C] *BrE informal* an UMBRELLA

bro·mide /'brəʊmaɪd $ 'broʊ-/ *n* **1** [C,U] a chemical which is sometimes used in medicine to make people feel calm **2** [C] *formal* a statement which is intended to make someone less angry but which is not effective

bronc /brɒŋk $ brɑːŋk/ *n* [C] *AmE informal* a BRONCO

bron·chi·al /'brɒŋkiəl $ 'brɑːŋ-/ *adj medical* affecting the bronchial tubes: *a bronchial infection*

bronchial ,tube *n* [C] *medical* one of the tubes that take air into your lungs

bron·chi·tis /brɒŋ'kaɪtɪs $ brɑːŋ-/ *n* [U] an illness which affects your bronchial tubes and makes you cough —**bronchitic** /-'kɪtɪk/ *adj*

bron·co /'brɒŋkəʊ $ 'brɑːŋkoʊ/ *n plural* **broncos** [C] a wild horse from the western US: *a bucking bronco*

bron·to·sau·rus /,brɒntə'sɔːrəs $,brɑːn-/ *n* [C] a large DINOSAUR with a small head and a long neck

Bronx cheer /,brɒŋks 'tʃɪə $,brɑːŋks 'tʃɪr/ *n* [C] *AmE* a sound that you make by sticking out your tongue and blowing, often considered rude; ▤ **raspberry** *BrE*

bronze[1] /brɒnz $ brɑːnz/ *n* **1** [U] a hard metal that is a mixture of COPPER and TIN: *a bell cast in bronze* **2** [U] the dark reddish brown colour of bronze **3** [C] a work of art such as a STATUE (=model of a person), made of bronze: *three bronzes by Giacometti* **4** [C,U] a BRONZE MEDAL: *King won a bronze in the 100 metres.*

bronze[2] *adj* **1** made of bronze: *a bronze statuette by Degas* **2** having the dark reddish brown colour of bronze

Bronze Age *n* **the Bronze Age** the time, between about 6000 and 4000 years ago, when bronze was used for making tools, weapons etc → IRON AGE, STONE AGE

B

bronzed /brɒnzd $ brɑːnzd/ *adj* having skin that is attractively brown because you have been in the sun; ▯ **tanned**

bronze 'medal *n* [C] a MEDAL made of bronze given to the person who comes third in a race or competition: *The bronze medal went to Nool of Estonia.* —**bronze medallist** *BrE*; **bronze medalist** *AmE n* [C]: *an Olympic bronze medallist* → GOLD MEDAL, SILVER MEDAL

brooch /brəʊtʃ $ brəʊtʃ/ *n* [C] a piece of jewellery that you fasten to your clothes, usually worn by women; ▯ **pin** *AmE*; → see picture at JEWELLERY

brood¹ /bruːd/ *v* [I] **1** to keep thinking about something that you are worried or upset about: *Don't sit at home brooding all day.* | [+over/about/on] *There's no point brooding over it – she's gone.* **2** if a bird broods, it sits on its eggs to make the young birds break out

brood² *n* [C] **1** a family of young birds all born at the same time **2** a family with a lot of children – used humorously: [+of] *Mary has a whole brood of grandchildren.*

brood·ing /ˈbruːdɪŋ/ *adj literary* **1** mysterious and threatening: *the brooding silence of the forest* **2** looking thoughtful and sad: *brooding eyes* —**broodingly** *adv*

'brood mare *n* [C] a MARE (=female horse) that is kept for breeding

brood·y /ˈbruːdi/ *adj* **1** *BrE informal* wishing that you had a baby: *I get broody when I see baby clothes in shop windows.* **2** silent because you are thinking or worrying about something: *Damian's been really broody lately.* **3** if a female bird is broody, it wants to lay eggs or to sit on them to make the young birds break out —**broodiness** *n* [U]

brook¹ /brʊk/ *n* [C] a small stream: *a babbling brook*

brook² *v* **not brook sth/brook no sth** *formal* to not allow or accept something: *He would brook no criticism, even from his beloved daughter.*

broom /bruːm, brʊm/ *n* **1** [C] a large brush with a long handle, used for sweeping floors → see picture at BRUSH¹ **2** [U] a large bush with small yellow flowers

broom·stick /ˈbruːmˌstɪk, ˈbrʊm-/ *n* [C] a broom with a long handle and thin sticks tied at one end that a WITCH is supposed to fly on in stories

Bros. also **Bros** *BrE* /brɒs $ brɒːs/ the written abbreviation of *Brothers*, used in the names of companies: *Warner Bros.*

broth /brɒθ $ brɒːθ/ *n* [C,U] soup with meat, rice, or vegetables: *chicken broth* → SCOTCH BROTH

broth·el /ˈbrɒθəl $ ˈbrɑːθ-, ˈbrɔː-/ *n* [C] a house where men pay to have sex with PROSTITUTES

broth·er¹ [S1] [W1] /ˈbrʌðə $ -ər/ *n* [C]
1 a male who has the same parents as you; → **sister**: *I have two brothers, William and Mark.* | **elder/older/younger etc brother** *My younger brother is a doctor.* | **little/kid brother** (=younger brother) *I have to take my little brother to school.* | *My* **big brother** (=older brother) *has always looked after me.* | *my twin brother*
2 *spoken informal* a word meaning a black man, used especially by other black men
3 a male member of a group with the same interests, religion, profession etc as you
4 *plural* **brothers** or **brethren** a male member of a religious group, especially a MONK: *Brother Justin*
5 *AmE* a member of a FRATERNITY (=a club of male university students)
6 **brothers in arms** *literary* soldiers who have fought together in a war → BIG BROTHER, BLOOD BROTHER, HALF BROTHER, STEPBROTHER

brother² *interjection especially AmE* used to show you are annoyed or surprised: *Oh, brother – I really don't want to deal with this now.*

broth·er·hood /ˈbrʌðəhʊd $ -ər-/ *n* **1** [U] a feeling of friendship between people: *the spirit of brotherhood* **2** [C] an organization formed for a particular

purpose, especially a religious one: *the Franciscan brotherhood* **3** [C] *old-fashioned* a union of workers in a particular trade **4** [U] the relationship between brothers

'brother-in-law *n* [C] *plural* **brothers-in-law**
1 the brother of your husband or wife **2** the husband of your sister **3** the husband of your husband or wife's sister; → **sister-in-law**

broth·er·ly /ˈbrʌðəli $ -ər-/ *adj* showing feelings of kindness, loyalty etc that you would expect a brother to show; → **sisterly**: *brotherly love* | *brotherly advice*

brough·am /ˈbruːəm/ *n* [C] a carriage used in the past, which had four wheels and a roof and was pulled by a horse

brought /brɔːt $ brɒːt/ the past tense and past participle of BRING

brou·ha·ha /ˈbruːhɑːhɑː $ bruːˈhɑːhɑː/ *n* [singular, U] unnecessary excitement, criticism, or activity – used especially in news reports to show disapproval: *the pre-election brouhaha*

brow /braʊ/ *n* [C] **1** *literary* the part of your face above your eyes and below your hair; ▯ **forehead**: **mop/wipe your brow** (=dry your brow with your hand or a cloth because you are hot or nervous) | **your brow furrows/creases/wrinkles** (=lines appear on your brow because you are thinking or are worried) *His brow furrowed. 'I don't understand,' he said.* **2** an EYEBROW **3** **the brow of a hill** the top part of a slope or hill

brow·beat /ˈbraʊbiːt/ *v past tense* **browbeat**, *past participle* **browbeaten** /-biːtn/ [T] to try to make someone do something, especially in a threatening way: **browbeat sb into doing sth** *She was determined to browbeat everyone into believing her.*

brown¹ [S2] [W2] /braʊn/ *adj*
1 having the colour of earth, wood, or coffee: *dark brown hair*
2 having skin that has been turned brown by the sun: *He'd been on vacation and looked very brown.* | *He was as* **brown as a berry** *after two weeks in the sun.*

brown² *n* [C,U] the colour of earth, wood, or coffee: *This particular model is available in brown, white, or grey.* | *the browns and greens of the landscape*

brown³ *v* [I,T] **1** to heat food so that it turns brown, or to become brown by being heated: *First brown the meat in a frying pan.* **2** to become brown because of the sun's heat, or to make something brown in this way: *The children's faces were browned by the sun.* **3** **browned off** *BrE informal* annoyed or bored; ▯ **fed up**: *They are getting browned off by the situation.*

brown·field site /ˈbraʊnfiːld ˌsaɪt/ *n* [C] *BrE* a place, especially in a city, that is used for building homes, offices etc, where in the past there have already been buildings, industries etc; → **greenfield site**

'brown goods *n* [plural] *BrE* electrical goods that provide entertainment at home, such as televisions and computers → WHITE GOODS

brown·ie /ˈbraʊni/ *n* [C] a thick flat chocolate cake: *chocolate brownies*

Brownie *n* **1** **the Brownies** the part of the Girl Guides Association that is for younger girls **2** [C] also **'Brownie ˌGuide** a member of this organization

'brownie ˌpoint *n* **win/earn/score etc brownie points** *informal* to get praise for something you have done after trying to make someone have a good opinion of you: *I'm not doing it just to get brownie points.*

'brown-nose *v* [I,T] *informal* to try to make someone in authority like you by being very nice to them – used in order to show disapproval —**brown-noser** *n* [C] —**brown-nosing** *n* [U]

brown·out /ˈbraʊnaʊt/ *n* [C] *AmE* a time when the amount of electrical power supplied to an area is reduced

ˌbrown 'rice *n* [U] rice that still has its outer layer

brown·stone /'braʊnstəʊn $ -stoʊn/ *n* [C] a house in the US with a front made of reddish-brown stone, common in New York City

brown 'sugar *n* [U] a type of sugar that is brown in colour and contains MOLASSES

browse /braʊz/ *v* **1** [I] to look through the pages of a book, magazine etc without a particular purpose, just looking at the most interesting parts: [+**through**] *Jon was browsing through the photographs.* **2** [I,T] to look at the goods in a shop without wanting to buy any particular thing: [+**around**] *The trip allows you plenty of time for browsing around the shops.* | *tourists browsing the boutiques and souvenir stalls* **3** [I,T] to search for information on a computer or on the Internet: *a feature that allows you to browse your hard drive and choose the graphic you want to display* **4** [I] if a goat, DEER etc browses, it eats plants —**browse** *n* [singular]: *We had a quick browse around the shops.*

brows·er /'braʊzə $ -ər/ *n* [C] a computer program that finds information on the Internet and shows it on your computer screen: *a Web browser*

bruise[1] /bruːz/ *n* [C] **1** a purple or brown mark on your skin that you get because you have fallen, been hit etc: *minor cuts and bruises* **2** a mark on a piece of fruit that spoils its appearance

bruise[2] *v* **1** [I,T] if part of your body bruises or if you bruise part of your body, it gets hit or hurt and a bruise appears: *She fell off her bike and bruised her knee.* **2** [T] to affect someone badly and make them feel less confident: **bruise sb's pride/ego** *The incident had bruised his pride.* **3** [I,T] if a piece of fruit bruises or is bruised, it gets a bruise by being hit, dropped etc —**bruised** *adj: a badly bruised knee* | *a bruised ego*

bruis·er /'bruːzə $ -ər/ *n* [C] *informal* a big strong man who likes fighting or arguing

bruis·ing[1] /'bruːzɪŋ/ *n* [U] purple or brown marks that you get on your skin where you have fallen, been hit etc: [+**to/on**] *She suffered severe bruising to her arms and legs.*

bruising[2] *adj* difficult and unpleasant, and leaving you feeling tired or emotionally harmed: *a bruising contest*

Brum·mie /'brʌmi/ *n* [C] *BrE informal* someone from the city of Birmingham in England —**Brummie** *adj*

brunch /brʌntʃ/ *n* [C,U] a meal eaten in the late morning, as a combination of breakfast and LUNCH

bru·nette /bruː'net/ *n* [C] a woman with dark brown hair

brunt /brʌnt/ *n* **bear/take/suffer etc the brunt of sth** to receive the worst part of an attack, criticism, bad situation etc: *an industry that bore the brunt of the recession* | *The car took the full brunt of the explosion.*

brush[1] [S3] /brʌʃ/ *n*
1 OBJECT FOR CLEANING/PAINTING [C] an object that you use for cleaning, painting, making your hair tidy etc, made with a lot of hairs, BRISTLES, or thin pieces of plastic fastened to a handle; → **broom**: *a scrubbing brush* → HAIRBRUSH, NAILBRUSH, PAINTBRUSH, TOOTHBRUSH
2 TREES [U] **a)** small bushes and trees that cover an area of land **b)** branches that have broken off bushes and trees
3 MOVEMENT [singular] a movement in which you brush something to remove dirt, make something smooth, tidy etc: *I'll just give my hair a quick brush.*
4 TOUCH [singular] a quick light touch, made by chance when two things or people pass each other: *the brush of her silk dress as she walked past*
5 [C] a time when you only just avoid an unpleasant situation or argument: [+**with**] *His first brush with the law came when he was arrested for disorderly behaviour.* | *A brush with death can make you appreciate life more.*
6 TAIL [C] the tail of a FOX → BROADBRUSH; → **daft as a brush** at DAFT (1)

brush[2] *v*
1 CLEAN/MAKE TIDY [T] to clean something or make

B

brushes

toothpaste

broom

toothbrush

hairbrush

dustpan and brush

shaving brush

paintbrushes

shoe brush

scrubbing brush *BrE/* scrub brush *AmE*

nail brush

something smooth and tidy using a brush; → **sweep**: *Don't forget to brush your teeth.*
2 REMOVE [T always + adv/prep] to remove something with a brush or with your hand: **brush sth off/from etc sth** *Ella brushed the crumbs off her jacket.* | *He brushed the tears from his eyes.*
3 TOUCH LIGHTLY [I always + adv/prep,T] to touch someone or something lightly when passing them: *Something brushed her shoulders.* | [+**past**] *I felt her hair brush against my arm.* | [+**past**] *Nell brushed past him in the doorway.*
4 PUT STH ON STH [T always + adv/prep] to put a liquid onto something using a brush: **brush sth with sth** *Brush the pastry with milk.* | **brush sth over/onto sth** *Brush a little oil over the top of the pizza.* → **brush sth under the carpet** at SWEEP[1] (15)

brush sb/sth ⇔ **aside** *phr v*
to refuse to listen to someone, or refuse to consider something; ☐ **dismiss**: *He simply brushed all my objections aside.*

brush sb/sth ⇔ **down** *phr v*
1 to clean something using a brush: *He was brushing the pony down.*
2 **brush yourself down** to use your hands to remove dirt from your clothes, especially after you have fallen

brush sb/sth ⇔ **off** *phr v*
to refuse to listen to someone or their ideas, especially by ignoring them or saying something rude: *Corman brushed off accusations that he had acted dishonestly.* → BRUSH-OFF

brush up (on) sth *phr v*
to practise and improve your skills or your knowledge of something that you learned in the past: *I must brush up on my French before I go to Paris.*

brushed /brʌʃt/ *adj* [only before noun] brushed cloth has been made so it is soft: *brushed cotton*

brush-off *n* [singular] rude or unfriendly behaviour that shows you are not interested in someone: *She gave him the brush-off.* | *I tried to be friendly but I just got the brush-off.* → **brush off** at BRUSH[2]

[1] 000, [2] 000, [3] 000, most frequent words in [S]poken and [W]ritten English

B

brush·wood /'brʌʃwʊd/ n [U] small dead branches broken from trees or bushes

brush·work /'brʌʃwɜːk $ -wɜːrk/ n [U] the way in which an artist puts paint on a picture using a brush

brusque /bruːsk, brʊsk $ brʌsk/ adj using very few words in a way that seems rude; ◧ **abrupt**: *a brusque manner* —**brusquely** adv —**brusqueness** n [U]

Brus·sels sprout /ˌbrʌsəlz 'spraʊt/ n [C] a small round green vegetable that looks like a very small CABBAGE

bru·tal /'bruːtl/ adj **1** very cruel and violent: *brutal murder/attack/assault a brutal attack on a defenceless old man* | *a brutal man* **2** not pleasant and not sensitive to people's feelings: *He replied with brutal honesty.* —**brutally** adv: *He was brutally murdered.* | *If I'm brutally honest, I don't like her dress.*

bru·tal·i·ty /bruː'tælɪ̯ti/ n plural **brutalities** [C,U] cruel and violent behaviour, or an event involving cruel and violent treatment: *allegations of police brutality* | [+of] *the brutalities of war*

bru·tal·ize also **-ise** BrE /'bruːtəl-aɪz/ v [T usually passive] **1** to affect someone so badly that they lose their normal human feelings: *He was brutalized by his experiences in jail.* **2** to treat someone in a cruel or violent way: *Demonstrators claimed they had been brutalized by police officers.* —**brutalization** /ˌbruːtl-aɪˈzeɪʃən $ -tl-ə-/ n [U]

brute¹ /bruːt/ n [C] a man who is cruel, violent, and not sensitive

brute² adj **1** brute force/strength physical strength rather than intelligence and careful thinking: *Discussion can be more effective than the use of brute force.* **2** [only before noun] simple and not involving any other facts or qualities: *The brute fact is that the situation will not improve.* | *brute stupidity*

brut·ish /'bruːtɪʃ/ adj cruel and not sensitive to people's feelings —**brutishness** n [U]

Bryl·creem /'brɪlkriːm/ n [U] trademark a type of oil used on men's hair to make it shiny and smooth

B.S. /ˌbiː 'es/ n AmE **1** [C] *Bachelor of Science* a first university DEGREE in a science subject; ◧ **BSc** BrE: ; → **B.A.** [+in] *a B.S. in Biology* **2** [U] not polite the abbreviation of *bullshit*

BSc, B.Sc. /ˌbiː es 'siː/ n [C] BrE *Bachelor of Science* a first university DEGREE in a science subject; ◧ **B.S.** AmE: [+in] *He's going to Birmingham to do a BSc in Biochemistry.* | *Catherine McBride, BSc*

BSE /ˌbiː es 'iː/ n [U] *bovine spongiform encephalopathy* a serious brain disease that affects cows; ◧ **mad cow disease**

B-side /'biː saɪd/ n [C] **1** the side of a record that has the less well-known song on it **2** the song on this side of the record

BST /ˌbiː es 'tiː/ n [U] the abbreviation of *British Summer Time*

BTEC /'biːtek/ n [C,U] *Business and Technical Education Council* a range of examinations that are done by students in England and Wales at different levels in a variety of subjects relating to work. BTEC courses are usually done after the age of 17.; → GNVQ: *a BTEC Diploma in Art and Design*

BTW, btw the written abbreviation of *by the way*, often used in email or TEXT MESSAGES on MOBILE PHONES

B2B /ˌbiː tə 'biː/ adj *business to business* used to refer to business activities between companies, especially using the Internet

bub /bʌb/ n [C] AmE old-fashioned used to speak to a man, especially when you are angry: *Hey, what do you think you're doing, bub?*

bub·ble¹ /'bʌbəl/ n [C] **1** a ball of air or gas in liquid: *When water boils, bubbles rise to the surface.* | *soap bubbles* | *She was blowing bubbles in her milk with a straw.* **2** a small amount of air trapped in a solid substance: *Examine the glass carefully for*

bubbles. **3** a bubble of sth literary a small amount of a feeling: *A bubble of anger rose in Pol's throat.* **4** also **speech bubble** a circle around the words said by someone in a CARTOON **5** the bubble bursts used for saying that a very successful or happy period of time suddenly ends: *The bubble has finally burst in the mobile phone industry.* **6** burst/prick sb's bubble to make someone suddenly realize that something is not as good as they thought it was

bubble² v [I] **1** to produce bubbles: *Heat the cheese until it bubbles.* | [+up] *The cola bubbled up when I unscrewed the lid.* **2** to make the sound that water makes when it boils: [+away] *The water was bubbling away on the stove.* **3** also **bubble over** to be excited: [+with] *Mary was bubbling over with excitement.* **4** also **bubble away/up** if a feeling or activity bubbles, it continues to exist: *Resentment was still bubbling inside her.* | *Speculation has been bubbling away for months that he plans to resign.*

bubble and 'squeak n [U] a British dish of potatoes and CABBAGE mixed together and cooked in fat

'bubble bath n **1** [U] a liquid soap that smells pleasant and makes bubbles in your bath water **2** [C] a bath with this in the water

'bubble gum n [U] a type of CHEWING GUM that you can blow into a bubble

'bubble jet ˌprinter n [C] a type of machine for printing from a computer, that SPRAYS ink onto the paper

'bubble wrap also **'bubble pack** n [U] a sheet of plastic covered with bubbles of air, used for wrapping and protecting things

bub·bly¹ /'bʌbli/ adj **1** always happy, friendly, and eager to do things: *She has a very bubbly personality.* **2** full of bubbles → see picture at STILL²

bubbly² n [U] informal CHAMPAGNE: *a glass of bubbly*

bu·bon·ic plague /bjuːˌbɒnɪk 'pleɪg $ buːˌbɑː-/ n [U] a very serious disease spread by rats, that killed a lot of people in the Middle Ages; → **Black Death**

buc·ca·neer /ˌbʌkə'nɪə $ -'nɪr/ n [C] **1** someone who attacks ships at sea and steals from them; ◧ **pirate** **2** someone who is very successful, especially in business, but may not be honest

buck¹ [S1] /bʌk/ n [C]

1 DOLLAR informal a US, Canadian, or Australian dollar: *He owes me ten bucks.* | *The movie is about a group of men trying to make a buck* (=earn some money) *as male strippers.* | **big/mega bucks** (=a lot of money) *Using celebrities in advertising is guaranteed to pull in big bucks.* | **make a fast/quick buck** (=make some money quickly, often dishonestly)

2 the buck stops here also **the buck stops with sb** used to say that a particular person is responsible for something: *The buck stops firmly with the boss.*

3 pass the buck to make someone else responsible for something that you should deal with

4 ANIMAL plural **buck** or **bucks** a male rabbit, DEER, and some other male animals; → **doe**

5 feel/look like a million bucks informal especially AmE to feel or look very healthy, happy, and beautiful

6 MAN old-fashioned a young man → (get) a bigger/better etc bang for your buck at BANG¹ (5)

buck² v

1 HORSE [I] if a horse bucks, it kicks its back feet into the air, or jumps with all four feet off the ground

2 MOVE SUDDENLY [I] to suddenly move up and down or backwards and forwards in an uncontrolled way: *The plane bucked sharply.*

3 OPPOSE [T] to oppose something in a direct way: *He was a rebel who continually bucked the system* (=opposed rules or authority). | *Unemployment in the area has bucked the national trend by falling over the last month.* | [+against] *Initially he had bucked against her restraints.*

4 MAKE SB HAPPIER [T] to make someone feel more happy, confident, or healthy: *He was bucked by the success he'd had.* | *She gave me a tonic which bucked me a little.*

buck for sth *phr v*
to try very hard to get something, especially a good position at work: *He's bucking for promotion.*

buck up *phr v*
1 to become happier or to make someone happier: *Come on, buck up, things aren't that bad!* | **buck sb** ⇔ **up** *You need something to buck you up.*
2 buck up! *BrE old-fashioned* used to tell someone to hurry up: *Buck up, John! We'll be late.*
3 *informal* to improve, or to make something improve: *It'll be a long time before the situation starts to buck up.* | **buck sth** ⇔ **up** *a company that is looking to buck up its networking capabilities*
4 buck your ideas up *BrE informal* used to tell someone to improve their behaviour or attitude

buck³ *adv AmE* **buck naked** not wearing any clothes

buck·a·roo /ˌbʌkəˈruː/ *n* [C] *AmE informal* a COWBOY - used especially when talking to children

buck·board /ˈbʌkbɔːd $ -bɔːrd/ *n* [C] a light vehicle with four wheels that is pulled by a horse, and was used in the US in the 19th century

buck·et¹ S2 /ˈbʌkɪt/ *n* [C]
1 an open container with a handle, used for carrying and holding things, especially liquids; ☐ **pail**
2 also **bucketful** the quantity of liquid that a bucket can hold: [+of] *a bucket of water*
3 a part of a machine shaped like a large bucket and used for moving earth, water etc
4 *informal* a large amount of something: *They were drinking beer by the bucket.* | [+of] *They made buckets of cash on the deal.*
5 weep buckets *informal* to cry a lot
6 in buckets *informal* if rain comes down in buckets, it is raining very hard → **kick the bucket** at KICK¹ (20); → **a drop in the bucket** at DROP² (8)

bucket² *v*
bucket down *phr v BrE informal* to rain very hard; ☐ **pour**: *It's been bucketing down all day.*

bucket seat *n* [C] a car seat with a high curved back, for one person

bucket shop *n* [C] *BrE informal* a place that sells cheap plane tickets

buck·le¹ /ˈbʌkəl/ *v*
1 BEND [I,T] to become bent or curved because of heat or pressure, or to make something bend or curve in this way: *The steel pillars began to buckle.* | [+under] *The rails buckled under the intense heat of the fire.*
2 KNEES/LEGS [I] if your knees or legs buckle, they become weak and bend; ☐ **give way**: *John felt his knees start to buckle.*
3 DO STH YOU DO NOT WANT [I] to do something that you do not want to do because a difficult situation forces you to do it; ☐ **give in**: *To his credit, he refused to buckle.* | **buckle under the pressure/strain/weight** *A weaker person would have buckled under the weight of criticism.*
4 FASTEN [I,T] to fasten a buckle or be fastened with a buckle: *Amy buckled the belt around her waist.* | **buckle sth on/up/together** *Lou was buckling on his revolver.*

buckle down *phr v*
to start working very hard: [+to] *You'd better buckle down to some revision now.*

buckle up *phr v*
to fasten your SEAT BELT in a car, aircraft etc

buckle² *n* [C] a piece of metal used for fastening the two ends of a belt, for fastening a shoe, bag etc, or for decoration → see picture at WATCH²

buck·ram /ˈbʌkrəm/ *n* [U] stiff cloth, used in the past for covering books and making the stiff parts of clothes

Buck's Fizz /ˌbʌks ˈfɪz/ *n* [C,U] *BrE* a mixture of CHAMPAGNE and orange juice, or a glass of this

buck·shot /ˈbʌkʃɒt $ -ʃɑːt/ *n* [U] a lot of small metal balls that are fired together from a gun

buck·skin /ˈbʌkˌskɪn/ *n* [U] strong soft leather made from the skin of a DEER or goat

buck 'teeth *n* [plural] teeth that stick forward out of your mouth —**buck-toothed** /ˌbʌk ˈtuːθt◂ / *adj*

buck·wheat /ˈbʌkwiːt/ *n* [U] a type of small grain used as food for chickens, and for making flour

bu·col·ic /bjuːˈkɒlɪk $ -ˈkɑː-/ *adj literary* relating to the countryside

bud¹ /bʌd/ *n* [C]
1 a young tightly rolled up flower or leaf before it opens: *rose buds* | **in bud** (=having buds but no flowers yet) | **come into bud** (=start to produce buds)
2 *spoken especially AmE* BUDDY: *Hey, bud, how's it going?* → COTTON BUD, TASTE BUD; → **nip sth in the bud** at NIP¹ (3)

bud² *v* **budded, budding** [I] to produce buds

Bud·dhis·m /ˈbʊdɪzəm $ ˈbuː-, ˈbʊ-/ *n* [U] a religion of east and central Asia, based on the teaching of Gautama Buddha —**Buddhist** *n* [C] —**Buddhist** *adj*

bud·ding /ˈbʌdɪŋ/ *adj* **1** budding artist/actor/writer etc someone who is just starting to paint, act etc and will probably be successful at it **2** [only before noun] beginning to develop: *a budding romance*

bud·dy /ˈbʌdi/ *n plural* **buddies** [C] **1** *informal* a friend: *We're good buddies.* **2** *AmE spoken* used to talk to a man or boy, especially one you do not know: *Hey, buddy! This your car?*

buddy-buddy *adj informal especially AmE* be buddy-buddy (with sb) to be very friendly with someone

buddy list *n* [C] a place on a computer where you keep a list of the names of people that you regularly send INSTANT MESSAGES to

buddy ˌsystem *n* [C] *AmE* a system in which two people in a group are put together to help each other or keep each other safe

budge /bʌdʒ/ *v* [I,T usually in negatives] **1** to move, or to make someone or something move: *She leaned on the door, but it wouldn't budge.* | [+from] *Will hasn't budged from his room all day.* | *The horse refused to budge an inch.* **2** to change your opinion, or to make someone change their opinion: *The government has refused to budge.* | [+on] *He won't budge on the issue.* | [+from] *Treacy refuses to budge from his principles.*

bud·ge·ri·gar /ˈbʌdʒərɪɡɑː $ -ɡɑːr/ *n* [C] *BrE formal* a BUDGIE

bud·get¹ S1 W2 /ˈbʌdʒɪt/ *n* [C]
1 the money that is available to an organization or person, or a plan of how it will be spent

defence/education/advertising etc budget (=the amount of money available for a particular activity) **budget deficit** (=when more money has been spent than is available) **budget cut** (=when less money becomes available) **on/within budget** (=not costing more money than planned) **under budget** (=costing less money than planned) **over budget** (=costing more money than planned) **a tight budget** (=when there is not much money available) **balance the budget** (=make sure only the money available is spent)

[+of] *a welfare program with a budget of $2 million* | [+for] *The budget for photography has been cut.* | *The defence budget was still growing.* | *80% of the annual education budget was spent on teachers' salaries.* | *a package of fiscal policies designed to cut the budget deficit* | *the problems posed by budget cuts and staff shortages* | *The project was completed within budget.* | *If you come in under budget, everyone will be very impressed.* | *Feature movies always run over budget.* | *We have to keep within a tight budget.* | *They need to save £8 million this year to balance the budget.*

2 on a budget if you are on a budget, you do not have much money to spend: *Travellers on a budget might prefer to camp.* | *a book which offers great ideas for decorating on a budget* | *families on a tight budget*
3 also **Budget** *BrE* an official statement that a govern-

ment makes about how much it intends to spend and what taxes will be necessary

budget² v [I,T] **1** to carefully plan and control how much money you spend and what you will buy with it: *We'll have to budget more carefully in the future.* | *This scheme enables you to budget the cost through fixed monthly payments.* | [+**for**] *We've budgeted for a new car next year.* **2** if you budget something such as time, you decide how much of it you will need —**budgeting** n [U]

budget³ adj [only before noun] **1** very low in price – often used in advertisements; 🔲**cheap**: *budget flights* **2 low-budget/big-budget** used for saying how much money has been spent on doing something, especially making a film: *low-budget movies*

bud·get·a·ry /ˈbʌdʒətəri $ -teri/ adj relating to the way money is spent in a budget

bud·gie /ˈbʌdʒi/ n [C] BrE a small brightly coloured bird that people keep as a pet

buff¹ /bʌf/ n **1 wine/film/opera etc buff** someone who is interested in wine, films etc and knows a lot about them **2** [U] a pale yellow-brown colour; 🔲 **beige**: *buff envelopes* **3 in the buff** old-fashioned not wearing any clothes; 🔲 **naked** —**buff** adj

buff² also **buff up** v [T] to polish something with a cloth: *Sandra was buffing her nails.*
   buff up phr v informal to exercise in order to make your muscles bigger: *Smith buffed up for his role as Muhammad Ali.*

buf·fa·lo /ˈbʌfələʊ $ -loʊ/ n [C] plural **buffaloes** or **buffalo** **1** an African animal similar to a large cow with long curved horns → WATER BUFFALO **2** a BISON

buff·er¹ /ˈbʌfə $ -ər/ n [C]
1 PROTECTION someone or something that protects one thing or person from being harmed by another: [+**against**] *Eastern Europe was important to Russia as a buffer against the West.* | [+**between**] *She often had to act as a buffer between father and son.*
2 RAILWAY one of the two special metal springs on the front or back of a train or at the end of a railway track to take the shock if the train hits something
3 buffer zone an area between two armies, which is intended to separate them so that they do not fight
4 buffer state a smaller country between two larger countries, which makes war between them less likely
5 COMPUTER a place in a computer's memory for storing information temporarily
6 PERSON BrE old-fashioned an old man who is not good at managing things: *He's a nice old buffer.*
7 FOR POLISHING something used to polish a surface
8 run into/hit the buffers informal an activity or plan that hits the buffers is stopped and does not succeed

buffer² v [T] **1** to reduce the bad effects of something: *Consumer spending is buffering the effects of the recession.* **2** if a computer buffers information, it holds it for a short while before using it

buf·fet¹ /ˈbʊfeɪ $ bəˈfeɪ/ n [C] **1** a meal at a party or other occasion, in which people serve themselves at a table and then move away to eat: *a cold buffet* | **buffet breakfast/lunch/supper** *The price includes morning coffee, buffet lunch, and afternoon tea.* **2** a place in a railway station, bus station etc where you can buy and eat food or drink **3** AmE a piece of furniture in which you keep the things you use to serve and eat a meal; 🔲 **sideboard** BrE

buf·fet² /ˈbʌfɪt/ v [T usually passive] **1** if something, especially wind, rain, or the sea, buffets something, it hits it with a lot of force: *London was buffeted by storms last night.* **2** literary to treat someone unkindly: *I was weary of being buffeted by life.* —**buffeting** n [C,U]
   buffet sth **about** phr v to move something in one direction and then another, again and again, with force: *The body was buffeted about in the waves.*

buffet car /ˈbʊfeɪ kɑː $ bəˈfeɪ kɑːr/ also **buffet** n [C] BrE a part of a train where you can buy food and drink

buf·foon /bəˈfuːn/ n [C] old-fashioned someone who does silly things that make you laugh —**buffoonery** n [U]

bug¹ /bʌg/ n [C] **1** informal an illness that people catch very easily from each other but is not very serious: **catch/pick up/get a bug** *I picked up a bug last weekend.* | *There's a nasty bug going round* (=which a lot of people have caught). | **tummy/stomach bug** (=illness affecting your stomach) *He's off work with a stomach bug.* | *a 24-hour flu bug* **2** especially AmE a small insect **3** a fault in the system of instructions that operates a computer: *a bug in the software* → DEBUG **4** a small piece of electronic equipment for listening secretly to other people's conversations **5** informal a sudden strong interest in doing something: **the travel/sailing etc bug** *She's got the travel bug.* | *I had one flying lesson and immediately caught the bug* (=became very interested in flying).

bug² v **bugged, bugging** [T] **1** informal to annoy someone: *It just bugs me that I have to work so many extra hours for no extra money.* | *The baby's crying is really bugging him.* **2** to put a BUG (=small piece of electronic equipment) somewhere secretly in order to listen to conversations: *Do you think the room is bugged?*

bug·a·boo /ˈbʌgəbuː/ n [C] AmE something that makes people anxious or afraid

bug·bear /ˈbʌgbeə $ -ber/ n [C] something that makes people feel annoyed or worried: *Paperwork is our worst bugbear.*

bug·eyed /ˌbʌgˈaɪd◂/ adj having eyes that stick out

bug·ger¹ [S2] /ˈbʌgə $ -ər/ n [C]
1 BrE not polite an offensive word for someone who is very annoying or unpleasant
2 not polite someone that you pretend to be annoyed with, although you actually like or love them: *The poor little bugger got an awful shock.*
3 BrE not polite a job or activity that is very difficult: *The exam was a bit of a bugger.*
4 bugger all BrE not polite nothing: *There's bugger all wrong with this machine.*

bugger² v [T] BrE **1** spoken not polite said when you are annoyed or angry: *Bugger it! I don't see why I should pay for everything.* **2 I'm buggered/bugger me!** spoken not polite said when you are surprised about something: *Well I'm buggered! I never thought you'd do that.* **3 bugger the ...** spoken not polite used to say that you do not care about the person or thing you are talking about: *Bugger the expense, I'm going to buy it!* **4** taboo or law to have ANAL sex with someone
   bugger about also **bugger around** phr v spoken not polite **1** to behave in a stupid way or waste time; 🔲 **mess about/around**: *Let's stop buggering about and go.* **2 bugger sb about** to cause unnecessary problems for someone; 🔲 **mess sb about/around**: *Don't let Peter bugger you about.*
   bugger off phr v spoken not polite to go away or leave a place: *Tim buggered off to Australia years ago.* | *'Bugger off!' she screamed.*
   bugger sth ⇔ **up** phr v spoken not polite to ruin something or do something very badly; 🔲 **cock up**, **mess up**: *It really buggered up our plans when the train was cancelled.*

bug·gered /ˈbʌgəd $ -ərd/ adj [not before noun] BrE spoken not polite **1** extremely tired **2** completely ruined or broken: *The washing machine's buggered.* **3 I'm buggered if ...** used to say that you do not know something, will not do something, or are not able to do something: *I'm buggered if I can remember.*

bug·ger·y /ˈbʌgəri/ n [U] BrE law ANAL sex

bug·gy /ˈbʌgi/ n plural **buggies** [C] **1** BrE a light folding chair on wheels that you push small children in; 🔲 **pushchair**; 🔲 **stroller** AmE **2** a light carriage pulled by a horse **3** AmE a small bed on wheels, that a baby lies in; 🔲 **baby carriage**; 🔲 **pram** BrE

bu·gle /ˈbjuːɡəl/ n [C] a musical instrument like a TRUMPET, which is used in the army to call soldiers —**bugler** n [C]

build¹ [S1] [W1] /bɪld/ v past tense and past participle **built** /bɪlt/
1 MAKE STH [I,T] to make something, especially a building or something large: *The purpose is to build new houses for local people.* | *The road took many years to build.* | *They needed $3m to build the bridge.* | *It is the female birds that build the nests.* | *Developers want to build on the site of the old gas works.* | *a row of recently built houses* | **build sb sth** *He's going to build the children a doll's house.*; → see picture at ASSEMBLE
2 MAKE STH DEVELOP also **build up** [T] to make something develop or form: *She had built a reputation as a criminal lawyer.* | *She's been busy building her career.* | *Ross took twenty years to build up his business.* | **build (up) a picture of sb/sth** (=form a clear idea about someone or something) *We're trying to build up a picture of what happened.*
3 **be built of sth** to be made using particular materials: *The church was built of brick.*
4 FEELING also **build up** [I,T] if a feeling builds or if you build it, it increases gradually over a period of time: *Tension began to build as they argued more frequently.* | *In order to build your self esteem, set yourself targets you can reach.*
5 **build bridges** to try to establish a better relationship between people who do not like each other: *Peter needs to try and build bridges with Lizzie.*
build sth around sth phr v
to base something on an idea or thing and develop it from there: *Successful businesses are built around good personal relationships.*
build sth ⇔ in phr v
to make something so that it is a permanent part of a wall, room etc: *You could build in a wardrobe with mirrored doors.* → BUILT-IN
build sth into sth phr v
1 to make something so that it is a permanent part of a wall, room etc: *There are three cash machines built into the wall.*
2 to make something a permanent part of a system, agreement etc: *Opportunities for reviewing the timings should be built into the plan.*
build on phr v
1 build on sth to base something on an idea or thing: *Our relationship is built on trust.*
2 build on sth to use your achievements as a base for further development: *The new plan will build on the success of the previous programme.*
3 to add another room to a building in order to have more space: **build sth ⇔ on** *We're planning to build on a conservatory.*
build up phr v
1 INCREASE GRADUALLY if something builds up somewhere or if you build it up, it gradually becomes bigger or greater: **build sth ⇔ up** *The museum has built up a fine art collection.* | *the rate at which the pension builds up* → BUILD-UP
2 DEVELOP build sth ⇔ up to make something develop or form: [+into] *He's built up the family firm into a multinational company.*
3 FEELING if a feeling builds up or if you build it up, it increases gradually over a period of time: *If you don't express your feelings, frustration and anger can build up.* | **build up sth** *You have to build up trust.*
4 MAKE HEALTHY build sb/sth ⇔ up to make someone well and strong again, especially after an illness: *Taking exercise will build up your strength.*
5 PRAISE build sb/sth ⇔ up to praise someone or something so that other people think they are really good or so that they have more confidence: *The coach has been building his men up before the match.*
6 build up sb's hopes/build sb's hopes up to unfairly encourage someone to think that they will get what they hope for: *Don't build your hopes up too much.*

build up to sth phr v
to prepare for a particular moment or event: *I could tell she was building up to some kind of announcement.*
build² n [singular,U] the shape and size of someone's body

> slim/slender build
> **slight build** (=a body shape that looks thin)
> **stocky/sturdy build** (=a body shape that looks broad and heavy)
> muscular build
> medium/average build
> strong build
> athletic build

*a woman of **slim build** | You're a surprisingly strong swimmer for one of such a **slight build**. | I wanted a more **athletic** and **muscular build**.*

build·er [S3] /ˈbɪldə $ -ər/ n [C] especially BrE a person or a company that builds or repairs buildings
build·ing [S1] [W1] /ˈbɪldɪŋ/ n
1 [C] a structure such as a house, church, or factory, that has a roof and walls: *They need money to pay for new buildings.* | *The offices are on the top two floors of the building.* | *a farmhouse and other farm buildings*
2 [U] the process or business of building things: *There is a limited supply of land for building.* | *stone, timber, and other building materials* | [+of] *The enquiry recommended the building of a tunnel.*
ˈbuilding ˌblock n [C] **1** a block of wood or plastic for young children to build things with **2** building blocks [plural] the pieces or parts which together make it possible for something big or important to exist: *Amino acids are the building blocks of protein.*
ˈbuilding con,tractor / $ .. ,.../ n [C] someone whose job is to organize the building of a house, office, factory etc
ˈbuilding ,site n [C] a place where a house, factory etc is being built
ˈbuilding so,ciety n [C] BrE a type of bank that you pay money into in order to save it and earn interest and that will lend you money to buy a house or apartment; ⊟ savings and loan association AmE
ˈbuild-up n [C usually singular] **1** an increase over a period of time: [+of] *a heavy build-up of traffic on the motorway* **2** a description of someone or something before an event in which you say they are very special or important: *The presenter gave her a big build-up.* **3** the length of time spent preparing an event: *I was running 20 miles a week in my build-up for the race.* → build up at BUILD¹
built¹ /bɪlt/ the past tense and past participle of BUILD
built² adj used to describe someone's size or shape: *She is built like a dancer.* | *a heavily-built man*
,built en'vironment n [singular] especially BrE places where there are buildings and roads, and not the countryside: *The overall strategy involves a major improvement to the built environment.*
,built-'in adj forming a part of something that cannot be separated from it; → inbuilt: *a built-in microphone*
,built-'up adj a built-up area has a lot of buildings and not many open spaces: *He was fined for speeding in a built-up area.*
bulb /bʌlb/ n [C] **1** the glass part of an electric light, that the light shines from; ⊟ light bulb: *a 100 watt bulb* → see picture at ELECTRICITY **2** a root shaped like a ball that grows into a flower or plant: *tulip bulbs*
bul·bous /ˈbʌlbəs/ adj fat, round, and unattractive: *a bulbous nose*
bulge¹ /bʌldʒ/ n [C] **1** a curved mass on the surface of something, usually caused by something under or inside it: *The gun made a bulge under his jacket.* **2** a sudden temporary increase in the amount or level of something: *a bulge in the birthrate* —**bulgy** adj

[1] 000, [2] 000, [3] 000, most frequent words in [S]poken and [W]ritten English

bulge[2] *v* [I] also **bulge out** to stick out in a rounded shape, especially because something is very full or too tight: [+**with**] *His pockets were bulging with candy.* | *He fell heavily to the floor, his **eyes bulging** wide with fear.*

bu·lim·i·a /bjuːˈlɪmiə, bʊ-, -ˈliː-/ *n* [U] an illness in which a person cannot stop themselves from eating too much, and then vomits in order to control their weight —**bulimic** *adj*

bulk[1] /bʌlk/ *n* **1 the bulk (of sth)** the main or largest part of something: *The bulk of consumers are based in towns.* **2** [C usually singular] a large mass or shape of something: *the great bulk of a building* **3** [U] the size of something or someone: *The dough will rise until it is double in bulk.* **4 in bulk** if you buy goods in bulk, you buy large amounts each time you buy them

bulk[2] *adj* **1 bulk buying/orders etc** the buying etc of goods in large quantities at one time **2** [only before noun] bulk goods are sold or moved in large quantities: *bulk flour for commercial bakeries* **3 bulk mail** if you send something bulk mail, you send large amounts of it for a smaller cost than normal

bulk[3] *v*, **bulk large** to be the main or most important part of something
  bulk sth ⇔ **out** *phr v* to make something bigger or thicker by adding something else: *We can bulk out the report with lots of diagrams.*

bulk·head /ˈbʌlkhed/ *n* [C] a wall which divides the structure of a ship or aircraft into separate parts

bulk·y /ˈbʌlki/ *adj* **1** something that is bulky is bigger than other things of its type and is difficult to carry or store: *a bulky parcel* **2** someone who is bulky is big and heavy: *Andrew is a bulky man.* —**bulkiness** *n* [U]

bull[1] /bʊl/ *n*
1 MALE COW [C] an adult male animal of the cattle family: *a herd of cows with one bull*
2 MALE ANIMAL [C] the male of some other large animals such as the ELEPHANT or WHALE
3 take the bull by the horns to bravely or confidently deal with a difficult, dangerous, or unpleasant problem: *Nora decided to take the bull by the horns and organize things for herself.*
4 NONSENSE [U] *informal* nonsense or something that is completely untrue; ☰ **rubbish**: *What a load of bull!*
5 like a bull in a china shop if you are like a bull in a china shop, you keep knocking things over, dropping things, breaking things etc
6 like a bull at a gate if you move somewhere like a bull at a gate, you move there very fast, ignoring everything in your way
7 RELIGION [C] an official statement from the Pope
8 CENTRE [C] also **bullseye** the centre of a TARGET that you are shooting at
9 BUSINESS [C] *technical* someone who buys SHARES because they expect prices to rise; → **bear** → BULL MARKET → **cock and bull story** at COCK[1] (4); → **like a red rag to a bull** at RED[1] (5); → **shoot the bull** at SHOOT[1] (13)

bull[2] *interjection* used to say that you do not believe or agree with what someone has said: *Bull! Where did you get that idea?*

bull bars *n* [plural] *BrE* a set of metal bars fixed to the front of a large vehicle such as a Jeep or Land Rover in order to protect it from damage —**bullbarred** /ˈbʊlbɑːd $ -bɑːrd/ *adj*: *bullbarred vehicles*

bull·dog /ˈbʊldɒg $ -dɔːg/ *n* [C] a powerful dog with a large head, a short neck, and short thick legs

Bulldog clip *n* [C] *trademark BrE* a small metal object that shuts tightly to hold papers together

bull·doze /ˈbʊldəʊz $ -doʊz/ *v* [T] **1** to destroy buildings etc with a bulldozer **2** to push objects such as earth and rocks out of the way with a bulldozer **3 bulldoze sb into (doing) sth** to force someone to do something that they do not really want to do

bull·doz·er /ˈbʊldəʊzə $ -doʊzər/ *n* [C] a powerful vehicle with a broad metal blade, used for moving earth and rocks, destroying buildings etc

bul·let /ˈbʊlɪt/ *n* [C] a small piece of metal that you fire from a gun; → **shell**, **shot**: *He was killed by a single bullet.* | *a bullet wound in the shoulder* | *Several bullet holes could be seen beside a window.* → PLASTIC BULLET; → **bite the bullet** at BITE[1] (9)

bul·le·tin /ˈbʊlətɪn/ *n* [C] **1** a news report on radio or television **2** an official statement that tells people about something important **3** a letter or printed statement that a group or organization produces to tell people its news

bulletin board *n* [C] **1** *AmE* a board on the wall that you put information or pictures on; ☰ **notice-board** *BrE* **2** a place in a computer information system where you can read or leave messages

bullet point *n* [C] a thing in a list that consists of a word or short phrase, with a small printed symbol in front of it

bullet-proof *adj* something that is bullet-proof is designed to stop bullets from going through it: *an inch-thick wall of bullet-proof glass*

bull·fight /ˈbʊlfaɪt/ *n* [C] a type of entertainment popular in Spain, in which a person fights and kills a BULL —**bullfighter** *n* [C] —**bullfighting** *n* [U]

bull·finch /ˈbʊlfɪntʃ/ *n* [C] a small grey and red European bird

bull·frog /ˈbʊlfrɒg $ -frɑːg, -frɔːg/ *n* [C] a kind of large FROG that makes a loud noise

bull-headed *adj* determined to get what you want without really thinking enough about it —**bullheadedly** *adv*

bull·horn /ˈbʊlhɔːn $ -hɔːrn/ *n* [C] *AmE old-fashioned* a piece of equipment that you hold up to your mouth to make your voice louder; ☰ **megaphone** *BrE*

bul·lion /ˈbʊljən/ *n* [U] bars of gold or silver: *gold bullion*

bul·lish /ˈbʊlɪʃ/ *adj* **1** [not before noun] feeling confident about the future: *He's very bullish about the company's prospects.* **2** *technical* in a business market that is bullish, the prices of SHARES are rising or seem likely to rise; → **bearish** —**bullishly** *adv* —**bullishness** *n* [U]

bull market *n* [C] *technical* a STOCK MARKET in which the price of SHARES is going up and people are buying them

bull-necked /ˌbʊlˈnekt◂/ *adj* having a short and very thick neck

bul·lock /ˈbʊlək/ *n* [C] a young male cow that cannot breed

bull pen *n* [C] **1** the area in a baseball field in which PITCHERS practise throwing **2** the PITCHERS of a baseball team

bull·ring /ˈbʊlˌrɪŋ/ *n* [C] the place where a BULLFIGHT is held

bull session *n* [C] *AmE informal* an occasion when a group of people meet to talk in a relaxed and friendly way: *an all-night bull session*

bulls-eye, bull's-eye /ˈbʊlzaɪ/ *n* [C] **1** the centre of a TARGET that you try to hit when shooting or in games like DARTS; ☰ **bull 2** *BrE* a large hard round sweet

bull·shit[1] /ˈbʊlˌʃɪt/ *n* [U] *spoken not polite* something that is stupid and completely untrue; ☰ **rubbish**: *For get all that bullshit and listen to me!* | *What he told me was a load of bullshit.*

bullshit[2] *v* **bullshitted, bullshitting** [I,T] to say something stupid or completely untrue, especially in order to deceive someone or make them think you are important: *Don't believe him, he's probably bullshitting.* —**bullshitter** *n* [C]

bull terrier *n* [C] a strong short-haired dog → PIT BULL TERRIER

bul·ly[1] /ˈbʊli/ *n plural* **bullies** [C] someone who uses their strength or power to frighten or hurt someone who is weaker: *Bullies are often cowards.*

bully[2] *v* **bullied, bullying, bullies** [T] **1** to threaten to hurt someone or frighten them, especially someone smaller or weaker   **2** to put pressure on someone in order to make them do what you want: **bully sb into (doing) sth** *Don't let them bully you into working on Saturdays.* —**bullying** *n* [U]: *an attempt to tackle the problem of bullying in schools*

    bully off *phr v BrE* to start a game of HOCKEY —**bully-off** *n* [C]

bully³ *adj* **bully for you/him etc** *spoken* used when you do not think that someone has done anything special but they want you to praise them: *Yes, I know you've done all the dishes. Bully for you!*

bully boy *n* [C] *BrE informal* someone who behaves in a violent and threatening way

bul·rush /'bʊlrʌʃ/ *n* [C] a tall plant that looks like grass and grows by water

bul·wark /'bʊlwək $ -wərk/ *n* [C]   **1** something that protects you from an unpleasant situation: [+against] *a bulwark against dictatorship*   **2 bulwarks** [plural] the sides of a boat or ship above the DECK   **3** a strong structure like a wall, built for defence

bum¹ [S3] /bʌm/ *n* [C] *informal*
  1 *BrE* the part of your body that you sit on; ➡ **bottom**
  2 *AmE* someone, especially a man, who has no home or job, and who asks people for money
  3 beach/ski etc bum someone who spends all their time on the beach SKIING etc without having a job
  4 someone who is very lazy
  5 get/put bums on seats *BrE informal* to make a large number of people go to see a film, play, sports match etc: *She's the kind of star who will put bums on seats.*

bum² *v* **bummed, bumming** [T] *BrE informal* to ask someone for something such as money, food, or cigarettes; ➡ **cadge**: *She bummed a little cash off me.*

    bum around *phr v informal*   **1** also **bum about** to spend time lazily doing nothing   **2 bum around sth** to travel around, living very cheaply, without having any plans: *He spent a year bumming around Australia.*

bum³ *adj* [only before noun] *informal*   **1** bad and useless: *The orchestra was excellent. No one played a bum note.* | *I thought Jim got **a bum deal** (=unfair treatment).*   **2 a bum ankle/leg etc** *AmE* an injured ANKLE, leg etc

bum bag *n* [C] *BrE* a small bag that you wear around your waist to hold money, keys etc

bum·ble /'bʌmbəl/ *v* [I]   **1** also **bumble on** to speak in a confused way so that no one can understand you: *What was Karl bumbling on about?*   **2** also **bumble around** to move in an unsteady way

bum·ble·bee /'bʌmbəl,biː/ *n* [C] a large hairy BEE

bum·bling /'bʌmblɪŋ/ *adj* [only before noun] behaving in a careless way and making a lot of mistakes: *a kind bumbling man with a gentle smile*

bumf, bumph /bʌmf/ *n* [U] *BrE informal* boring written information that you have to read: *I got loads of bumf about the introduction of the Euro.*

bum·mer /'bʌmə $ -ər/ *n* **a bummer** *informal* a situation that is disappointing or annoying: *It was a real bummer being ill on holiday.*

bump¹ [S3] /bʌmp/ *v*
  1 [I always + adv/prep,T] to hit or knock against something: [+against] *I ran after him, bumping against people in my hurry.* | [+into] *Tim was a clumsy boy, always bumping into the furniture.* | **bump sth on sth** *She bumped her arm on the table.* | *The roof was so low he **bumped** his **head** (=his head hit the roof).*
  2 [I always + adv/prep] to move up and down as you move forward, especially in a vehicle: *A police car bumped down the track.* | [+along] *The plane was bumping along the runway.*
  3 [T always + adv/prep] to push or pull something somewhere in an irregular or unsteady way: *Flora was bumping her bags down the steps.*
  4 [T] *informal* to move someone or something into a different class or group, or to remove them from a class or group altogether: *The flight was overbooked, and Dad was the first one to be bumped.* | **bump sb up to/out**

of/from etc sth *The reforms bumped many families off the state-provided healthcare list.*
  5 [T] to move a radio or television programme to a different time: *'Married with Children' will be bumped from Sundays to Saturdays.*

    bump into sb *phr v*
to meet someone who you know when you were not expecting to; ▣ **run into**: *I bumped into Jean in town this morning.*

    bump sb ⇔ **off** *phr v informal*
to kill someone

    bump sth ⇔ **up** *phr v*
to suddenly increase something by a large amount: *Prices were bumped up by 10 percent last week.*

bump² *n* [C]   **1** an area of skin that is raised because you have hit it on something; ➡ **lump**: *She has a bump on the back of her head.* | *He had a few injuries, mostly bumps and bruises.*   **2** a small raised area on a surface: *The car hit a bump on the road.* ➡ SPEED BUMP   **3** the sound or sudden movement of something hitting a hard surface: *We heard a bump in the next room.* | **fall/sit down etc with a bump** *Rose fell, landing with a bump.*   **4** *informal* a small accident in which your car hits something but you are not hurt

bump·er¹ /'bʌmpə $ -ər/ *n* [C]   **1** *BrE* a bar fixed on the front and back of a car to protect it if it hits anything; ▣ **fender** *AmE*; ➡ see picture at CAR   **2 bumper-to-bumper** bumper-to-bumper traffic is very close together and moving slowly

bumper² *adj* [only before noun] unusually large: **bumper crop/harvest** | *We hope readers will enjoy this bumper issue of 'Homes and Gardens'.*

bumper car *n* [C] a small electric car that you drive in a special area at a FUNFAIR and deliberately try to hit other cars; ➡ **dodgems**

bumper ,sticker *n* [C] a small sign on the bumper of a car, with a humorous, political, or religious message

bumph /bʌmf/ *n* another spelling of BUMF

bump·kin /'bʌmpkɪn/ *n* [C] *informal* someone from the countryside who is considered to be stupid

bump·tious /'bʌmpʃəs/ *adj* too proud of your abilities in a way that annoys other people; ▣ **arrogant** —**bumptiously** *adv* —**bumptiousness** *n* [U]

bump·y /'bʌmpi/ *adj* *comparative* **bumpier,** *superlative* **bumpiest**   **1** a bumpy surface is flat but has a lot of raised parts so it is difficult to walk or drive on it; ▣ **uneven**; ▣ **smooth**: *a bumpy road* | *The ground is bumpy in places.* ➡ see picture at SURFACE   **2** a bumpy journey by car or plane is uncomfortable with movements up and down because of bad road or weather conditions; ▣ **smooth**: *The plane made a bumpy landing.*   **3 a bumpy ride/time** having a lot of problems for a long time: *Shareholders have had a bumpy ride.*

bun /bʌn/ *n* [C]   **1** *BrE* a small round sweet cake: *a sticky bun*   **2** a small round type of bread: *a hamburger bun*   **3** if a woman has her hair in a bun, it fastens it in a small round shape at the back of her head ➡ see picture at HAIRSTYLE   **4 buns** [plural] *AmE informal* the two round parts of a person's bottom; ▣ **buttocks**   **5 have a bun in the oven** *BrE informal* to be PREGNANT - used humorously

bunch¹ [S2] /bʌntʃ/ *n*
  1 GROUP OF THINGS [C] a group of things that are fastened, held, or growing together: [+of] *I'll send her a **bunch of flowers**.* | *He had a **bunch of keys** on his belt.* | *a **bunch of grapes*** ➡ see picture at BUNDLE¹
  2 GROUP OF PEOPLE [singular] *informal* a group of people: *The ancient Egyptians were a clever bunch.* | [+of] *a friendly bunch of people*
  3 the best/pick of the bunch the best among a group of people or things
  4 LARGE AMOUNT [singular] *AmE* a large number of people or things, or a large amount of something: [+of] *There's a **whole bunch** of places I want to visit.*
  5 bunches [plural] *BrE* if a girl wears her hair in

bunches, she ties it together at each side of her head → **thanks a bunch** at THANKS¹ (5)

bunch² also **bunch together, bunch up** *v* **1** [I,T] to stay close together in a group, or to make people do this: *The children bunched together in small groups.* | *John stopped, forcing the rest of the group to bunch up behind him.* **2** [I,T] to make part of your body tight or to become tight like this: *Sean bunched his fists.* **3** [I,T] to pull material together tightly in folds: *She bunched the cloth up and threw it away.* **4** [T] to hold or tie things together in a bunch

bundle

a bundle of washing

a heap of letters

a bunch of flowers

a stack of CDs

a pile of books

a wad of bank notes

bun·dle¹ /ˈbʌndl/ *n* [C] **1** a group of things such as papers, clothes, or sticks that are fastened or tied together: [+of] *bundles of newspapers* | *a small bundle containing mostly clothing* **2** a number of things that belong or are dealt with together: [+of] *bundles of data* **3** computer software and sometimes other equipment or services that are included with a new computer at no extra cost **4** a bundle *informal* a lot of money: *College evening classes cost a bundle.* | *A company can* **make a bundle** *by selling unwanted property.* **5 be a bundle of nerves** *informal* to be very nervous **6 be a bundle of laughs/fun** *BrE informal* an expression meaning a person or situation that is fun or makes you laugh, often used jokingly when they are not fun at all: *Being a teenager isn't a bundle of laughs.* **7 not go a bundle on sth/sb** *BrE informal* to not like something or someone very much: *Jim never drank, and certainly didn't go a bundle on gambling.*

bundle² *v* **1** [T always + adv/prep] to quickly push someone or something somewhere because you are in a hurry or you want to hide them: **bundle sb into/through etc sth** *They bundled Perez into the car and drove off.* **2** [I always + adv/prep] *BrE* to move somewhere quickly in a group: [+into/through etc] *Six of us bundled into a taxi.* **3** [T] to include computer software or other services with a new computer at no extra cost: **bundle sth with/into sth** *Microsoft can bundle Windows NT at discounted prices with its popular desktop application programs.* | **bundle sth together** *The company offered customers a single computer solution, bundling together hardware and software.*

bundle sb ⇔ **off** *phr v* to send someone somewhere quickly without asking them if they want to go

bundle sb/sth ⇔ **up** *phr v* **1** also **bundle sth** ⇔ **together** to make a bundle by tying things together: *Bundle up the newspapers and take them to the skip.* **2** also **bundle sth** ⇔ **together** to put different things together so that they are dealt with at the same time: *The lawsuit bundles together the claims of many*

individuals into one big case. **3** to put warm clothes on someone or yourself because it is cold: *People sat bundled up in scarves, coats, and boots.* | [+against] *spectators bundled up against the cold*

bung¹ /bʌŋ/ *n* [C] **1** a round piece of rubber, wood etc used to close the top of a container **2** *BrE informal* money given to someone secretly, and usually illegally, to make them do something

bung² *v* [T always + adv/prep] *BrE informal* to put something somewhere quickly and carelessly: **bung sth in/into etc sth** *Can you bung these clothes in the washing machine?*

bung sth ⇔ **up** *phr v BrE* **1** to block something, especially a hole **2 be bunged up** to find it difficult to breathe because you have a cold

bun·ga·low S2 /ˈbʌŋɡələu $ -lou/ *n* [C] **1** *BrE* a house which is all on ground level → see picture at HOUSE¹ **2** *AmE* a small house which is often on one level

bun·gee jump·ing /ˈbʌndʒi ˌdʒʌmpɪŋ/ *n* [U] a sport in which you jump off something very high with a long length of special rope that stretches tied to your legs, so that you go up again without touching the ground —**bungee jump** *n* [C] —**bungee jumper** *n* [C]

bun·gle /ˈbʌŋɡəl/ *v* [T] to fail to do something properly, because you have made stupid mistakes – used especially in news reports: *The whole police operation was bungled.* —**bungled** *adj*: *a bungled rescue attempt* —**bungle** *n* [C] —**bungler** *n* [C]

bun·ion /ˈbʌnjən/ *n* [C] a painful lump on the first joint of your big toe

bunk¹ /bʌŋk/ *n* **1** [C] a narrow bed that is attached to the wall, for example on a train or ship **2** also **bunk bed** [often plural] one of two beds that are attached together, one on top of the other → see picture at BED¹ **3 do a bunk** *BrE informal* to suddenly leave a place without telling anyone **4** [U] *informal* nonsense; ▪ **bunkum**: *What a load of bunk!*

bunk² also **bunk down** *v* [I] *informal* to sleep somewhere, especially in someone else's house: *You can bunk down on the sofa for tonight.*

bunk off (sth) *phr v informal* to stay away from somewhere such as school or to leave somewhere early without permission; ▪ **skive**: *John and I used to bunk off school.*

bun·ker¹ /ˈbʌŋkə $ -ər/ *n* [C] **1** a strongly built shelter for soldiers, usually underground **2** *BrE* a large hole on a golf course filled with sand; ▪ **sand trap** *AmE*; → see picture at GOLF **3** a place where you store coal, especially on a ship or outside a house

bunker² *v* [T] *BrE* to hit a golf ball into a bunker

bunk·house /ˈbʌŋkhaus/ *n* [C] a building where workers sleep

bun·kum /ˈbʌŋkəm/ *n* [U] BUNK

bun·ny S3 /ˈbʌni/ also **'bunny ˌrabbit** *n plural* **bunnies** [C] a word for a rabbit, used especially by or to children

'bunny ˌslope *n* [C] *AmE* the area of a mountain where people learn to SKI; ▪ **nursery slope** *BrE*

Bun·sen bur·ner /ˌbʌnsən ˈbɜːnə $ -ˈbɜːrnər/ *n* [C] a piece of equipment that produces a hot gas flame, for scientific EXPERIMENTS

bunt /bʌnt/ *v* [I] *AmE* to deliberately hit the ball a short distance in a game of baseball —**bunt** *n* [C]

bun·ting /ˈbʌntɪŋ/ *n* [U] small flags on strings, used to decorate buildings and streets on special occasions

buoy¹ /bɔɪ $ ˈbuːi, bɔɪ/ *n* [C] an object that floats on the sea, a lake etc to mark a safe or dangerous area

buoy² also **buoy up** *v* [T] **1** to make someone feel happier or more confident: *The party is buoyed up by the latest opinion poll results.* **2** to keep profits, prices etc at a high level: *Increased demand for computers buoyed their profits.* **3** to keep something floating

buoy·an·cy /ˈbɔɪənsi $ ˈbɔɪənsi, ˈbuːjənsi/ *n* [U] **1** the ability of an object to float **2** the power of a liquid to make an object float: *Salt water has more* *buoyancy than fresh water.* **3** a feeling of happiness and a belief that you can deal with problems easily **4** the ability of prices, a business etc to quickly get back to a high level after a difficult period

buoy·ant /'bɔɪənt $ 'bɔɪənt, 'buːjənt/ *adj* **1** happy and confident: *Phil was in buoyant mood.* **2** buoyant prices etc tend to rise: *a buoyant economy* **3** able to float or keep things floating: *Cork is very buoyant.* —**buoyantly** *adv*

bur·ble /'bɜːbəl $ 'bɜːr-/ *v* **1** [I,T] to talk about something in a confused way that is difficult to understand: [+on/away] *I had to listen for an hour while she burbled away.* **2** [I] to make a sound like a stream flowing over stones —**burble** *n* [singular]

burbs /bɜːbz $ bɜːrbz/ *n* **the burbs** [plural] *AmE informal* the SUBURBS (=areas around a city where people live)

bur·den¹ S3 W3 /'bɜːdn $ 'bɜːrdn/ *n*
1 [C] something difficult or worrying that you are responsible for: [+of] *The burden of taxation has risen considerably.* | [+on] *I don't like being a burden on other people.* | *Nothing can lift the burden from my shoulders.* | **the tax/financial/debt burden**
2 the burden of proof *law* the duty to prove that something is true
3 [C] something that is carried; ⟹ **load** → BEAST OF BURDEN

burden² *v* **1 be burdened with/by sth** to have a lot of problems because of a particular thing: *a company burdened with debt* → UNBURDEN **2 be burdened with sth** to be carrying something heavy

bur·den·some /'bɜːdnsəm $ 'bɜːr-/ *adj formal* causing problems or additional work: *These charges are particularly burdensome for poor parents.*

bu·reau /'bjʊərəʊ $ 'bjʊroʊ/ *n plural* **bureaus** *or* **bureaux** /-rəʊz $ -roʊz/ [C] **1** an office or organization that collects or provides information: *an employment bureau* | *the Citizens Advice Bureau* **2** a government department or a part of a government department in the US: *the Federal Bureau of Investigation* **3** an office of a company or organization that has its main office somewhere else: *the London bureau of the Washington Post* **4** *BrE* a large desk or writing table **5** *AmE* a piece of furniture with several drawers, used to keep clothes in; ⟹ **chest of drawers** *BrE*

bu·reauc·ra·cy /bjʊəˈrɒkrəsi $ bjʊˈrɑː-/ *n plural* **bureaucracies 1** [U] a complicated official system which is annoying or confusing because it has a lot of rules, processes etc; → **red tape**: *the reduction of unnecessary bureaucracy* **2** [C,U] the officials who are employed rather than elected to do the work of a government, business etc

bu·reau·crat /'bjʊərəkræt $ 'bjʊr-/ *n* [C] someone who works in a bureaucracy and uses official rules very strictly

bu·reau·crat·ic /ˌbjʊərəˈkrætɪk◂ $ ˌbjʊr-/ *adj* involving a lot of complicated official rules and processes —**bureaucratically** /-kli/ *adv*

bureau de change /ˌbjʊərəʊ də ˈʃɒndʒ $ ˌbjʊroʊ də ˈʃɑːndʒ/ *n plural* **bureaux de change** /-rəʊ- $ -roʊ-/ [C] *BrE* a shop where you can change foreign money; → **exchange**

bu·rette also **buret** *AmE* /bjʊˈret/ *n* [C] a glass tube with measurements on it, used in scientific EXPERIMENTS

bur·geon /'bɜːdʒən $ 'bɜːr-/ *v* [I] *formal* to grow or develop quickly: *the burgeoning market for digital cameras*

burg·er /'bɜːgə $ 'bɜːrgər/ *n* [C] a flat round piece of finely cut BEEF, which is cooked and eaten, or one of these served in a bread BUN; ⟹ **hamburger** → CHEESEBURGER, VEGEBURGER

burgh /'bʌrə $ bɜːrg, 'bʌroʊ/ *n* [C] a BOROUGH - used in Scotland

bur·gher /'bɜːgə $ 'bɜːrgər/ *n* [C] *old use* someone who lives in a particular town

bur·glar /'bɜːglə $ 'bɜːrglər/ *n* [C] someone who goes into houses, shops etc to steal things; → **robber, thief**
→ CAT BURGLAR

burglar a,larm *n* [C] a piece of equipment that makes a loud noise when someone tries to get into a building illegally

bur·gla·rize /'bɜːgləraɪz $ 'bɜːr-/ *v* [T] *AmE* to go into a building and steal things; ⟹ **burgle** *BrE*

bur·gla·ry /'bɜːgləri $ 'bɜːr-/ *n plural* **burglaries** [C,U] the crime of getting into a building to steal things: *Burglaries in the area have risen by 5%.* | *He was charged with burglary.* | *Most burglaries happen at night.*

bur·gle /'bɜːgəl $ 'bɜːr-/ *v* [T] *BrE* to go into a building and steal things; ⟹ **burglarize** *AmE*: *We've been burgled three times.*

bur·gun·dy /'bɜːgəndi $ 'bɜːr-/ *n plural* **burgundies 1** [C,U] red or white wine from the Burgundy area of France **2** [U] a dark red colour —**burgundy** *adj*: *a burgundy skirt*

bur·i·al /'beriəl/ *n* [C,U] **1** the act or ceremony of putting a dead body into a GRAVE **2** the act of burying something in the ground: [+of] *the burial of solid wastes*

bur·ka /'bɜːkə $ 'bɜːr-/ *n* another spelling of BURQA

bur·lap /'bɜːlæp $ 'bɜːr-/ *n* [U] *AmE* a type of thick rough cloth; ⟹ **hessian** *BrE*

bur·lesque /bɜːˈlesk $ bɜːr-/ *n* [C,U] **1** speech, acting, or writing in which a serious subject is made to seem silly or an unimportant subject is treated in a serious way **2** *AmE* a performance involving a mixture of COMEDY and STRIPTEASE, popular in America in the past

bur·ly /'bɜːli $ 'bɜːrli/ *adj* a burly man is big and strong: *a burly policeman*

burn¹ S2 W3 /bɜːn $ bɜːrn/ *v past tense and past participle* **burnt** /bɜːnt $ bɜːrnt/ *or* **burned**
1 PRODUCE FLAMES AND HEAT [I] **a)** if a fire burns, it produces heat and flames: *There was a fire burning in the fireplace.* | *An average household candle will burn for about six hours.* **b)** if something is burning, it is producing flames and being damaged or destroyed by fire: *Parts of the building are still burning.*
2 DESTROY STH WITH FIRE [T] to destroy or damage something with fire: *I burnt all his old letters.* | *Cars were burned and shops were looted during the rioting.* | *The Grand Hotel had burnt to the ground.* | *Make sure the iron isn't too hot or you'll burn the cloth.* | *He dropped his cigarette and burnt a hole in the carpet.*
3 INJURE/KILL SB WITH FIRE [T] to hurt yourself or someone else with fire or something hot: *I burned my hand on the oven door.* | *She was badly burned in a road accident.* | *16 passengers were burned to death* (=died in a fire). | *A family of five were burned alive in their home last night* (=died in a fire). | *Heretics were burnt at the stake* (=burnt in a fire as a punishment).
4 SUN [I,T] if the sun burns your skin, or if your skin burns, it becomes red and painful from the heat of the sun; → **sunburn**: *I burn quite easily.* | *Don't forget you can still get burnt when you're swimming or when it's cloudy.* | *Her face and neck were quite badly burned.*
5 FOOD [I,T] to spoil food by cooking it for too long, or to become spoiled in this way: *I'm afraid I've burnt the pizza.* | **burn sth to a crisp/cinder** *The meat was burned to a crisp.*
6 CHEMICALS [T] to damage or destroy something by a chemical action: *Quite a lot of household chemicals can burn your skin.*
7 FUEL [I,T] if you burn a FUEL, or if it burns, it is used to produce power, heat, light etc: *The boiler burns oil to produce heat.* | *greenhouse gases caused by the burning of fossil fuels*
8 FAT/ENERGY [T] if you burn fat or CALORIES, you use up energy stored in your body by being physically active: *Taking a brisk walk every morning is a great way to burn calories.* | *a fat-burning exercise*

1 000, 2 000, 3 000, most frequent words in S poken and W ritten English

several burnt out cars.
3 burn sth ⇔ out to remove something by burning it: *The cancer cells are burnt out using a laser beam.*
4 to work so hard over a period of time that you become unable to continue working because you are tired, ill, or unable to think of any new ideas: *It's a high-pressure job and you could burn out young.* | **be/get burnt out** *He was almost burnt out by the time he was 21.* | **burn yourself out** *She's in danger of burning herself out.* → BURNOUT (1)
5 if an engine or electric wire burns out or is burnt out, it stops working because it has been damaged by getting too hot: *The plugs are wired so that if one burns out, the others will still start the engine.* | **burn sth ⇔ out** *I think you've burnt out one of the gaskets.*
6 if a ROCKET or JET burns out, it stops working because all its FUEL has been used → BURNOUT (2)

burn up *phr v*
1 if something burns up or is burnt up, it is completely destroyed by fire or heat: *The satellite will burn up as it re-enters the earth's atmosphere.* | **burn sth ⇔ up** *Most of the woodland has now been burnt up.*
2 burn sth ⇔ up *informal* to use a lot of something in a careless way: *Most household appliances burn up loads of electricity.* | *He just burns up money!*
3 be burning up *spoken* if someone is burning up, they are very hot, usually because they are ill: *Feel his forehead – he's burning up.*
4 burn sb up *AmE informal* to make someone very angry: *The way he treats her really burns me up.*
5 burn sth ⇔ up to use energy that is stored in your body, by being physically active: *As we get older, our body becomes less efficient at burning up calories.*

burn² S3 *n* [C]
1 an injury caused by fire, heat, the light of the sun, or acid: *His body was covered in bruises and cigarette burns.* | **severe/serious burns** *She was taken to the hospital with serious burns.* | *Several of the survivors* suffered *severe* **burns**. | *She is being treated for* **minor burns**.
2 a mark on something caused by fire or heat: *The desk was covered with graffiti and* **burn marks**.
3 a painful mark on the skin caused by it rubbing hard against something rough
4 the burn *informal* a painful hot feeling in your muscles when you exercise a lot: *Go for the burn.*
5 *BrE* a small stream

burn·er /ˈbɜːnə $ ˈbɜːrnər/ *n* [C] **1** *BrE* the part of an OVEN or heater that produces heat or a flame: *a gas burner* **2** *AmE* one of the round parts on the top of a COOKER that produce heat **3 put/leave sth on the back burner** *informal* to delay doing something until a later time: *The government quietly put the scheme on the back burner.* → BUNSEN BURNER

burn·ing¹ /ˈbɜːnɪŋ $ ˈbɜːr-/ *adj* [only before noun] **1** on fire: *She was rescued from a burning building.* **2** feeling very hot: *Claudia put her hands to her burning face.* **3 burning ambition/desire/need etc** a burning AMBITION, desire, need etc is very strong: *My burning ambition is to be world champion.* **4 burning issue/question** a burning ISSUE or question is very important and urgent: *Education has become a burning issue in this election.* **5** *written* burning eyes look at you very hard or show very strong feeling

burning² *adv* **burning hot** very hot

bur·nish /ˈbɜːnɪʃ $ ˈbɜːr-/ *v* [T] *formal* **1** to polish metal or another substance until it shines **2** to work hard in order to improve something: *He missed no opportunity to burnish his image.* —**burnished** *adj*

burn·out /ˈbɜːnaʊt $ ˈbɜːrn-/ *n* **1** [U] the feeling of always being tired because you have been working too hard: *Many of the teachers are suffering from burn-out.* **2** [C,U] the time when a ROCKET or JET has finished all of its FUEL and stops operating

burnt¹ /bɜːnt $ bɜːrnt/ *v* especially *BrE* the past tense and past participle of BURN

---

9 LIGHT [I] if a light or lamp burns, it shines or produces light: *A lamp was burning in the kitchen window.* | *The hall light was still burning.*
10 FEEL HOT AND PAINFUL [I,T] if a part of your body burns, or if something burns it, it feels unpleasantly hot: *The whisky burned my throat as it went down.* | *My eyes were burning from the smoke.*
11 FACE/CHEEKS [I] if your face or cheeks are burning, they feel hot because you are embarrassed or upset: *I could feel my cheeks burning as I spoke.*
12 CD [T] if you burn a CD or DVD, you record music, images, or other information onto it
13 be burning with rage/desire etc to feel a particular emotion very strongly: *She was burning with curiosity.*
14 be burning to do sth to want to do or find out something very much: *I was burning to know how he had got on in New York.*
15 be/get burned *informal* **a)** to be emotionally hurt by someone or something: *Take things slowly – you don't want to get burned again.* **b)** to lose a lot of money: *The company got badly burned in the dot.com collapse.*
16 burn your fingers/get your fingers burned *informal* to suffer the unpleasant results of something that you have done: *I tried a dating agency once, but got my fingers badly burnt – I'll never do it again.*
17 burn a hole in your pocket if money burns a hole in your pocket, you want to spend it as soon as you can
18 burn your bridges/boats *informal* to do something with the result that you will not be able to return to a previous situation again, even if you want to: *I'm really tempted to take up that job offer in Washington, but I don't want to burn my boats with this company.*
19 burn the candle at both ends *informal* to get very tired by doing things until very late at night and getting up early in the mornings
20 burn the midnight oil *informal* to work or study until late at night
21 it burns sb that/how etc *AmE* used to say that something makes someone feel angry or jealous: *It really burns me the way they treat us.*
22 burn rubber to drive a car very fast
23 GO FAST [I always + adv/prep] *informal* to travel very fast: [+along/up etc] *a sports car burning up the motorway*

> **WORD FOCUS: BURN**
> *to be burning*: **be on fire, be ablaze, be alight**
> *to start burning*: **catch fire, burst into flames, ignite**
> *to make something start burning*: **light, set fire to sth**
> *to make something stop burning*: **put out, extinguish**
> *to hurt or damage your skin with hot liquid or steam*: **scald**
> *the crime of deliberately setting fire to buildings*: **arson**

burn away *phr v*
if something burns away or is burned away, it is destroyed by fire: **burn sth ⇔ away** *All her hair had been burnt away.*

burn down *phr v*
1 if a building burns down or is burned down, it is destroyed by fire: *She was worried that the house might burn down while they were away.* | **burn sth ⇔ down** *The old town hall was burnt down in the 1970s.*
2 if a fire burns down, the flames become weaker and it produces less heat

burn sth ⇔ off *phr v*
1 to remove something by burning it: *You can use a blowlamp to burn off the old paint.*
2 to use energy that is stored in your body by doing physical exercise: *I decided to go for a run to try and burn off a few calories.*

burn out *phr v*
1 if a fire burns out or burns itself out, it stops burning because there is no coal, wood etc left: *He left the fire to* **burn itself out**.
2 be burnt out if a building or vehicle is burnt out, the inside of it is destroyed by fire: *The hotel was completely burnt out. Only the walls remained.* | *We passed*

burnt² S3 *adj*

1 damaged or hurt by burning: *burnt toast*
2 burnt offering a) something that is offered as a gift to a god by being burnt on an ALTAR **b)** *BrE humorous* food that you accidentally burnt while you were cooking it

burp /bɜːp $ bɜːrp/ *v* **1** [I] to pass gas loudly from your stomach out through your mouth; ☐ **belch** **2** [T] to help a baby to do this, especially by rubbing or gently hitting its back —**burp** *n* [C]

bur·qa, **burka** /ˈbɜːkə $ ˈbɜːr-/ *n* [C] a long piece of clothing worn by Muslim women in some countries, which covers the head, face, and body, with only a small square to see through; → **abaya**, **chador**

burr /bɜː $ bɜːr/ *n* [C] **1** also **bur** the seed container of some plants, covered with sharp points that make it stick to things **2** *BrE* a way of pronouncing English with a strong 'r' sound **3** a fairly quiet regular sound like something turning quickly; ☐ **whirr**: *the burr of a motor* **4** a rough spot on a piece of metal

bur·ri·to /bəˈriːtəʊ $ -toʊ/ *n plural* **burritos** [C] a Mexican dish made with a TORTILLA (=flat thin bread) folded around meat or beans with cheese

bur·ro /ˈbʊrəʊ $ ˈbɜːroʊ/ *n plural* **burros** [C] *AmE* a small DONKEY

bur·row¹ /ˈbʌrəʊ $ ˈbɜːroʊ/ *v* **1** [I always + adv/prep, T] to make a hole or passage in the ground; ☐ **dig down**: [+into/under/through etc] *Mother turtles burrow into the sand to lay their eggs.*; → see picture at DIG¹ **2** [I,T always + adv/prep] to press your body close to someone or under something because you want to get warm or feel safe; ☐ **nestle**: [+into/under/down etc] *The child stirred and burrowed deeper into the bed.* | **burrow sth into/against etc sth** *She burrowed her head into his shoulder.* **3** [I always + adv/prep] to search for something that is hidden in a container or under other things; ☐ **rummage**: [+in/into/through etc] *Helen burrowed in her bag for a handkerchief.*

burrow² *n* [C] a passage in the ground made by an animal such as a rabbit or FOX as a place to live

bur·sar /ˈbɜːsə $ ˈbɜːrsər/ *n* [C] someone at a school or college who deals with the accounts and office work

bur·sa·ry /ˈbɜːsəri $ ˈbɜːr-/ *n plural* **bursaries** [C] *BrE* an amount of money given to someone so that they can study at a university or college; ☐ **grant**

burst¹ /bɜːst $ bɜːrst/ *v past tense and past participle* **burst**

1 BREAK OPEN [I,T] if something bursts or if you burst it, it breaks open or apart suddenly and violently so that its contents come out: *The pipes had burst and the house was under two feet of water.* → see picture at EXPLOSION
2 be bursting with sth to have a lot of something or be filled with something: *John was bursting with ideas and good humour.* | *The shops are bursting with food.* | **be bursting with pride/energy/excitement etc** *Your mum's bursting with pride for you.*
3 MOVE SUDDENLY [I always + adv/prep] to move somewhere suddenly or quickly, especially into or out of a place: [+into/through/in etc] *Jo burst into the room.*
4 burst open to open suddenly: *The door burst open and Tom ran into the room.*
5 be bursting to do sth *informal* to want to do something very much: *Zach was bursting to tell them something.*
6 be bursting a) *BrE informal* to need to go to the toilet very soon **b)** also **be bursting at the seams** to be so full that nothing else can fit inside
7 burst sb's bubble *informal* to destroy someone's beliefs or hopes about something: *Steve was so happy I couldn't bear to burst his bubble.*
8 burst its banks if a river bursts its banks, water from it goes on to the land → **full (up) to bursting** at FULL¹ (1); → **burst the bubble** at BUBBLE¹ (6); → **the bubble bursts** at BUBBLE¹ (5)

burst in on/upon sb/sth *phr v*
to interrupt something by entering a room, in a way that embarrasses you or other people: *I'm sorry to burst in on you like this.*

burst into sth *phr v*
1 to suddenly begin to make a sound, especially to start singing, crying, or laughing: *Claire looked as if she were about to burst into tears.* | *Suddenly, the group burst into laughter.* | *Lydia burst into song.*
2 burst into flames/flame to suddenly start to burn very strongly: *Their car crashed and burst into flames.*
burst onto/upon/on sth *phr v*
to suddenly appear and become very successful: *The band burst onto the music scene in 1997.*
burst out *phr v*
1 burst out laughing/crying/singing etc to suddenly start to laugh, cry etc: *Everyone in the room burst out laughing.*
2 to suddenly say something in a forceful way: *'I don't believe it!' she burst out angrily.* → OUTBURST (1)

burst² *n* [C] **1** the act of something bursting or the place where it has burst: *a burst in the water pipe* **2 a)** a short sudden effort or increase in activity: [+of] *The van gave a sudden burst of speed.* **b)** a short sudden and usually loud sound: [+of] *sharp bursts of machine gun fire* **c)** a sudden strong feeling or emotion: **burst of anger/enthusiasm/temper etc**

bur·then /ˈbɜːðən $ ˈbɜːr-/ *n* [C] *literary* a BURDEN

bur·ton /ˈbɜːtn $ ˈbɜːrtn/ *n* **gone for a burton** *BrE old-fashioned informal* lost, broken, or dead

bur·y W3 /ˈberi/ *v* **buried**, **burying**, **buries** [T]

1 DEAD PERSON to put someone who has died in a GRAVE: **bury sb in/at etc sth** *He was buried in the churchyard of St Mary's.*
2 OBJECT to put something under the ground, often in order to hide it: *Electric cables are buried beneath the streets.*
3 FALL ON STH [usually in passive] to fall on top of someone or something, usually harming or destroying them: **be buried under/beneath etc sth** *The skiers were buried under the snow.* | *57 miners were buried alive.*
4 HIDDEN [usually in passive] to cover something so that it cannot be found: *His glasses were buried under a pile of papers.*
5 FEELING/MEMORY to ignore a feeling or memory and pretend that it does not exist: *a deeply buried memory*
6 bury your face/head etc (in sth) to press your face etc into something soft: *Noel buried his face in the pillow.*
7 bury your face/head in your hands to cover your face with your hands because you are very upset
8 bury your head in the sand to ignore an unpleasant situation and hope it will stop if you do not think about it
9 bury the hatchet/bury your differences to agree to stop arguing about something and become friends
10 IN A SURFACE to push something, especially something sharp, into something else with a lot of force: **bury sth in sth** *The dog buried its teeth in my leg.* | *The bullet buried itself in the wall.*
11 bury yourself in your work/studies etc to give all your attention to something: *After the divorce, she buried herself in her work.*
12 INFORMATION to put a fact or information somewhere in a larger document so that it is unlikely to be found or read: *The story was buried at the back of the paper.*
13 LOVED ONE *literary* to have someone you love die: *She had buried her husband, two sons, and a daughter.* → **be dead and buried** at DEAD¹ (14)

bus¹ S1 W2 /bʌs/ *n plural* **buses** also **busses** *especially AmE* [C]

1 a large vehicle that people pay to travel on

get on a bus
get off a bus
wait for a bus
catch a bus
take a bus
ride a bus *AmE*
miss a bus (=be too late to get on a bus)
bus fare (=money you pay for a bus journey)
bus pass (=a card you buy that allows you to make
several bus journeys)
bus ride/trip/journey
bus route (=the way a bus goes)
school bus

There were a lot of people on the bus this morning. |
She got on the bus at Clark Street. | *I'll tell you when
to get off the bus.* | *a line of people waiting for a bus* |
Sally had to run to catch the bus. | *I took the bus to the
university.* | *Too tired to walk? Try riding the bus for
a peso or two.* | *Hurry up or we'll miss the bus!* | *by bus
The best way to get there is by bus.* | *Unable to afford
bus fares, she walked to interviews.* | *I lost my glasses
on the school bus.*

2 a CIRCUIT that connects the main parts of a computer
so that signals can be sent from one part of the
computer to another

bus² *v* **bused** *or* **bussed** *present participle* **busing** *or*
bussing **1** [T usually passive] to take a person or a
group of people somewhere in a bus: **bus sb to/in/into
sth** *Casey was bussed to the school.* **2** [T] *AmE* to take
away dirty dishes from the tables in a restaurant:
Shelley had a job bussing tables.

bus·boy /'bʌsbɔɪ/ *n* [C] *AmE* a young man whose job is
to take away dirty dishes from the tables in a restaurant

bus·by /'bʌzbi/ *n* [C] a tall fur hat worn by some
British soldiers

bush /bʊʃ/ *n* [C] **1** a plant with many thin branches
growing up from the ground; → **tree, shrub:** *a rose
bush* | *The child was hiding in the bushes.* → see picture
at COUNTRY **2 the bush** wild country that has not been
cleared, especially in Australia or Africa **3** a bush of
hair is a lot of thick untidy hair → **beat about the bush**
at BEAT¹ (14)

bushed /bʊʃt/ *adj* [not before noun] *informal* very tired

bush·el /'bʊʃəl/ *n* **hide your light under a bushel** to not
tell anyone that you are good at something

bush league *adj AmE informal* badly done or of such
bad quality that it is not acceptable: *bush league reporting*

Bush·man /'bʊʃmən/ *n plural* **Bushmen** /-mən/ [C]
someone who belongs to a southern African tribe who
live in the BUSH (=wild country)

bush·whack /'bʊʃwæk/ *v* [I,T] to push or cut your
way through thick trees or bushes

bush·y /'bʊʃi/ *adj comparative* **bushier**, *superlative*
bushiest **1** bushy hair or fur grows thickly: *a bushy
tail* **2** bushy plants grow thickly, with a lot of
branches and leaves —**bushiness** *n* [U]

bus·i·ly /'bɪzɪli/ *adv* in a busy way: *Students were
busily writing notes.*

busi·ness S1 W1 /'bɪznɪs/ *n*
1 BUYING OR SELLING GOODS OR SERVICES [U] the
activity of making money by producing or buying and
selling goods, or providing services; → **commerce**,
trade: *Students on the course learn about all aspects of
business.* | *We do business with a number of Italian
companies.* | *Vanessa decided to go into business as an
art-dealer.* | *set up/start up in business The scheme
offers free advice to people wanting to set up in
business.* | *In order to stay in business, you must do
better than your competitors.* | *the advertising/music/
fashion etc business Carl began in the music business
by running a recording studio.* | *business activities/
interests etc He has a wide range of business interests.*

2 COMPANY [C] an organization such as a company,
shop, or factory that produces or sells goods or provides a service: *She now has her own $25 million
home-shopping business.* | *They don't know how to run
a business.* | *The company began as a small family
business* (=owned and controlled by one family). |
Owners of small businesses (=that employ only a few
people) *will be hit hardest by these tax changes.* | **big
business** (=large and powerful companies in general)
*Does big business have more control over our everyday
lives than our elected governments?* | **the business
community** (=people who work in business generally)
the international business community
3 HOW MUCH WORK A COMPANY HAS [U] the
amount of work a company does or the amount of
money it makes: *We're now doing twice as much busi-
ness as we did last year.* | *Exports account for 72% of
overall business.* | **business is good/bad/slow etc** *Busi-
ness is slow during the summer.* | **drum up business**
(=try to get more work for you or your company) *Perot
was in Europe, drumming up business for his new
investment company.*
4 FOR YOUR JOB [U] work that you do as part of your
job: *She's in New York this week on business* (=for her
work). | *Hi Maggie! Is this phone call business or
pleasure?* | **business trip/meeting etc** *We discussed the
idea over a business lunch.* | *useful business contacts*
5 WHAT SOMEONE SHOULD BE INVOLVED IN [U] **a)** if
something is not your business or none of your business, you should not be involved in it or ask about it: *It
was not her business, she decided, to ask where the
money came from.* | *It's none of your business how
much I weigh.* | *'Who's that girl you were with?' 'Mind
your own business* (=Don't ask questions about some-
thing that does not concern you)!' | *Are you going out
with Kate tonight?' 'That's my business'* (=it doesn't
concern you, so don't ask me questions about it). **b)** if
it is someone's business to do something, it is their
duty or responsibility to do it: **it is the business of sb to
do sth** *It is the business of government to listen to the
various groups within society.*
6 THINGS TO BE DEALT WITH [U] things that need to
be done or discussed: *Okay, let's get down to business*
(=start doing or discussing something). | *'Is there any
other business?' the chairman asked.*
7 MATTER [singular] a situation or activity, especially
one that you have a particular opinion about or attitude towards: **a serious/strange/funny etc business**
Leon regards keeping fit as a serious business. | *Tanya
found the whole business ridiculous.*
8 be in business a) to be involved in business activities:
The company has been in business for over thirty years.
b) *spoken* to have all that you need to start doing
something: *I've just got to buy the paint and then we're
in business.*
9 (go) out of business if a company goes out of
business, or something puts it out of business, it stops
operating, especially because of financial problems:
*Higher interest rates will drive small firms out of
business.*
10 be back in business to be working or operating in a
normal way again: *The band are back in business after
a long break.*
11 sb was (just) minding their own business *spoken*
used to say that someone was not doing anything
unusual or wrong at the time when something unfair
or bad happened to them: *I was driving along, minding
my own business, when the police stopped my car.*
12 go about your business to do the things that you
normally do: *The street was full of ordinary people
going about their business.*
13 make it your business to do sth to make a special
effort to do something: *Ruth made it her business to get
to know the customers.*
14 mean business *informal* to be serious about doing
something even if it involves harming someone: *The
border is guarded by troops who mean business.*
15 unfinished business something you need to discuss
further with someone or a situation that has not yet

reached a satisfactory solution: *The sudden death of a loved one can often leave the bereaved with an agonising sense of unfinished business.*

16 business is business *spoken* used to say that profit is the most important thing to consider: *We can't afford to employ someone who isn't good at the job – business is business.*

17 business as usual when someone or something is still working or operating normally when you think they might not be: *Despite last night's scare, it was business as usual in the White House today.*

18 have no business doing sth/have no business to do sth to do something you should not be doing: *He was drunk and had no business driving.*

19 not be in the business of doing sth to not be intending to do something because you think it is a bad idea: *I'm not in the business of selling my best players.*

20 and all that business *spoken informal* and other things of the same general kind: *She handles the publicity and all that business.*

21 (it's) the business *BrE informal* used to say that something is very good or works well: *Have you seen David's new car? It's the business!*

22 do the business *BrE informal* **a)** to do what you are expected to do or what people want you to do: *Come on, then, and do the business.* **b)** to have sex → BIG BUSINESS; → funny business at FUNNY (3); → like nobody's business at NOBODY[1] (2); → monkey business at MONKEY[1] (3); → SHOW BUSINESS

'business ,card *n* [C] a card that shows a business person's name, position, company, address etc

'business ,class *n* [U] travelling conditions on an aircraft that are more expensive than TOURIST CLASS, but not as expensive as FIRST CLASS → ECONOMY CLASS

'business end *n* the business end (of sth) *informal* the end of a tool or weapon that does the work or causes the damage: *the business end of a gun*

'business ,hours *n* [plural] the normal hours that shops and offices are open

busi·ness·like /ˈbɪznɪ̩s-laɪk/ *adj* effective and practical in the way that you do things: *a businesslike manner*

busi·ness·man /ˈbɪznɪ̩smən/ *n plural* **business-men** /-mən/ [C] a man who works in business

'business ,park *n* [C] an area where many companies and businesses have buildings and offices

'business ,person *n plural* **business people** [C] a person who works in business

'business ,plan *n* [C] a document which explains what a company wants to do in the future, and how it plans to do it

'business ,studies *n* [U] a course of study on economic and financial subjects and managing a business

'business ,suit *n* [C] *AmE* a suit that someone wears during the day at work

busi·ness·wom·an /ˈbɪznɪ̩s,wʊmən/ *n plural* **businesswomen** /-,wɪmɪn/ [C] a woman who works in business

bus·ing /ˈbʌsɪŋ/ *n* [U] a system in the US in which students ride buses to schools that are far from where they live, so that a school has students of different races

busk /bʌsk/ *v* [I] *BrE* to play music in a public place in order to earn money —**busker** *n* [C]

'bus lane *n* [C] a part of a wide road that only buses are allowed to use → see picture at TOWN

bus·load /ˈbʌsləʊd $ -loʊd/ *n* [C] *AmE* an amount of people on a bus that is full

bus·man's hol·i·day /,bʌsmənz ˈhɒlɪ̩di $ -ˈhɑːlɪ̩-deɪ/ *n* [singular] *BrE* a holiday spent doing the same work as you do in your job – often used humorously

'bus pass *n* [C] a special ticket giving cheap or free bus travel

buss /bʌs/ *v* [T] *AmE old-fashioned* to kiss someone in a friendly rather than sexual way: *politicians bussing babies*

busses /ˈbʌsɪ̩z/ *n* a plural of bus

'bus ,shelter *n* [C] *especially BrE* a small structure with a roof that keeps people dry while they are waiting for a bus → see picture at TOWN

'bus ,station also **'bus ,terminal** *n* [C] a place where buses start and finish their journeys → see picture at TOWN

'bus stop *n* [C] a place at the side of a road, marked with a sign, where buses stop for passengers

bust[1] /bʌst/ *v past tense and past participle* **bust** *BrE* also **busted** *especially AmE* [T]

1 BREAK *informal* to break something: *I bust my watch this morning.* | *Tony busted the door down.*

2 POLICE a) if the police bust someone, they charge them with a crime: *He was busted by U.S. inspectors at the border.* | **bust sb for sth** *Davis got busted for drugs.* **b)** *informal* if the police bust a place, they go into it to look for something illegal: *Federal agents busted several money-exchange businesses.*

3 TRY HARD bust a gut *informal* also bust your butt/ass *AmE spoken* to try extremely hard to do something: *I bust a gut trying to finish that work on time.*

4 MONEY *AmE informal* to use too much money, so that a business etc must stop operating: *The trip to Spain will probably bust our budget.*

5 crime-busting/union-busting/budget-busting etc *informal* used with nouns to show that a situation is being ended or an activity is being stopped: *crime-busting laws*

6 ... or bust! *informal* used to say that you will try very hard to go somewhere or do something: *Idaho or bust!*

7 MILITARY *especially AmE* to give someone a lower military rank as a punishment; ⊟ demote

bust out *phr v informal*
to escape from a place, especially prison

bust up *phr v informal*
1 *BrE* if people bust up, they end their relationship or friendship; ⊟ **break up**: *They bust up after six years of marriage.* → BUST-UP (1)

2 bust sth ⇔ up to prevent an illegal activity or bad situation from continuing; ⊟ **break up**: *A couple of teachers stepped in to bust up the fight.*

3 bust sth ⇔ up *AmE* to damage or break something: *A bunch of bikers busted up the bar.*

4 *AmE* to start laughing a lot; ⊟ **crack up**: *Elaine busted up laughing at the sight of him.*

bust[2] *n* [C] **1** a model of someone's head, shoulders, and upper chest, usually made of stone or metal: [+of] *a bust of Beethoven* **2** a woman's breasts, or the part of her clothes that covers her breasts **3** a measurement around a woman's breast and back: *a 36-inch bust* **4** *informal* a situation in which the police go into a place in order to catch people doing something illegal: *a drug bust* → boom to bust at BOOM[1] (1)

bust[3] *adj* [not before noun] **1** go bust *informal* a business that goes bust cannot continue operating **2** *BrE informal* broken: *The television's bust again.*

bust·ed /ˈbʌstɪ̩d/ *adj AmE spoken informal* **1** broken: *a busted arm* **2** [not before noun] caught doing something wrong and likely to be punished: *You guys are so busted!*

bus·ter /ˈbʌstə $ -ɚ/ *n* **1** *AmE spoken* used to speak to a man who is annoying you or who you do not respect: *You're under arrest, buster!* **2** crime-buster/budget-buster/sanctions-buster etc *informal* used with nouns to mean someone or something that ends a situation or stops an activity

bus·ti·er /ˈbʌstɪeɪ, ˈbuːs- buːsˈtjeɪ, bʌs-/ *n* [C] a tight piece of clothing that women wear on the top half of the body, which does not cover their shoulders or arms

bus·tle[1] /'bʌsəl/ v [I always + adv/prep] to move around quickly, looking very busy: [+about/round etc] *Madge bustled round the room, putting things away.*

bustle[2] n **1** [singular] busy and usually noisy activity: [+of] *a continual bustle of people coming and going* → **hustle and bustle** at HUSTLE[2] (1) **2** [C] a frame held out by women in the past to hold out the back of their skirts

bus·tling /'bʌsəlɪŋ/ adj a bustling place is very busy: **bustling with sb/sth** *The flower market was bustling with shoppers.*

'bust-up n [C] informal **1** the end of a relationship: [+of] *the bust-up of their marriage* → **bust up** at BUST[1] **2** BrE a very bad quarrel or fight: *Cathy and I had a real bust-up yesterday.*

bust·y /'bʌsti/ adj informal a woman who is busty has large breasts

bus·y[1] S1 W2 /'bɪzi/ adj comparative **busier**, superlative **busiest**
1 PERSON if you are busy, you are working hard and have a lot of things to do: *She's busy now – can you phone later?* | *a busy mother of four* | [+with] *Mr Haynes is busy with a customer at the moment.* | **busy doing sth** *Rachel's busy studying for her exams.* | *There were lots of activities to* **keep** the kids **busy**.
2 TIME a busy period of time is full of work or other activities: *December is the busiest time of year for shops.* | *a busy day* | *He took time out of his busy schedule to visit us.*
3 PLACE a busy place is very full of people or vehicles and movement: *We live on a very busy road.*
4 TELEPHONE especially AmE if a telephone you are calling is busy, it makes a repeated sound to tell you that the person you are calling is talking on their telephone; **engaged** BrE: *I called Sonya, but her line was busy.* | *I keep getting a busy signal.*
5 PATTERN a pattern or design that is busy is too full of small details – used to show disapproval

busy[2] v **busied, busying, busies** [T] **busy yourself with sth** to use your time dealing with something: *He busied himself with answering letters.*

bus·y·bod·y /'bɪzi,bɒdi $ -,bɑːdi/ n plural **busybodies** [C] someone who is too interested in other people's private activities – used to show disapproval

busy Liz·zie /,bɪzi 'lɪzi/ n [C] a small plant with bright flowers

bus·y·work /'bɪziwɜːk $ -wɜːrk/ n [U] AmE work that gives someone something to do, but that is not really necessary

but[1] S1 W1 /bət; strong bʌt/ conjunction
1 used to connect two statements or phrases when the second one adds something different or seems surprising after the first one: *It's an old car, but it's very reliable.* | *They rushed to the hospital, but they were too late.* | *We've invited the boss, but she may decide not to come.* | *an expensive but extremely useful book* | 'Has he got any experience?' 'No, but he's keen to learn.'
2 used to introduce a statement that explains why the thing you have mentioned did not happen or is not possible: *I'd like to go but I'm too busy.* | *They would have married sooner, but they had to wait for her divorce.*
3 used after a negative to emphasize that it is the second part of the sentence that is true: *He lied to the court not just once, but on several occasions.* | *The purpose of the scheme is not to help the employers but to provide work for young people.*
4 except: *What can we do but sit and wait?* | *I had no choice but to accept the challenge.* | *Not a day goes by but I think of dear old Larry* (=I think of him every day).
5 but for a) used when you are saying that something would have happened if something or someone else had not prevented it: *But for these interruptions, the meeting would have finished earlier.* | *The score could have been higher but for some excellent goalkeeping by*

Simon. | *I might never have got to university but for you.* **b)** except for something or someone: *All was silent but for the sound of the wind in the trees.*
6 but then (again) spoken **a)** used when you are adding a statement that says almost the opposite of what you have just said: *John might be ready to help us, but then again, he might not.* | *You feel really sorry for him. But then again, it's hard to like him.* **b)** used when you are adding a statement that makes what you have just said seem less surprising: *Dinah missed the last rehearsal, but then she always was unreliable, wasn't she?*
7 spoken used when you are replying to someone and expressing strong feelings such as anger, surprise etc: *But that's marvellous news!* | 'They won't even discuss the problem.' 'But how stupid!'
8 sb cannot but do sth formal used to say that someone has to do something or cannot stop themselves from doing it: *I could not but admire her.*
9 spoken used when disagreeing with someone: 'It was a good idea.' 'But it didn't work.'
10 spoken used to emphasize a word or statement: *It'll be a great party – everyone, but everyone, is coming.* | *They're rich, but I mean rich.*
11 spoken used to change the subject of a conversation: *But now to the main question.* | *But tell me, are you really planning to retire?*
12 spoken used after expressions such as 'excuse me' and 'I'm sorry': *Excuse me, but I'm afraid this is a no-smoking area.*

but[2] S2 W3 prep
1 apart from; **except**: *I could come any day but Thursday.* | *There's no one here but me.* | *I could still see nothing but the spirals of desert dust.* | *He was unable to swallow anything but liquids.*
2 the last but one/the next but two etc especially BrE the last or next thing or person except for one, two etc: *Pauline and Derek live in the next house but one* (=they live two houses away from us).

but[3] S2 W3 adv only: *This is but one example of what can happen when things go badly wrong.* | *It's going to be difficult. Anyway, we can but try.* | *We have relationships of many different sorts — with our children, our parents, our boss and our friends, to name but a few.*

but[4] /bʌt/ n **buts** [plural] spoken reasons that someone gives for not doing something or agreeing with something: *'I don't want to hear any buts,' Jo snapped.* | *He is the best player – no ifs, ands, or buts about that.*

bu·tane /'bjuːteɪn/ n [U] a gas stored in liquid form, used for cooking and heating

butch /bʊtʃ/ adj informal **1** a woman who is butch looks, behaves, or dresses like a man **2** a man who is butch seems big and strong, and typically male

butch·er[1] S3 /'bʊtʃə $ -ər/ n [C]
1 someone who owns or works in a shop that sells meat
2 the butcher's a shop where you can buy meat
3 someone who has killed someone else cruelly and unnecessarily, especially someone who has killed a lot of people
4 have/take a butcher's BrE spoken informal to have a look at something

butcher[2] v [T] **1** to kill animals and prepare them to be used as meat **2** to kill someone cruelly or unnecessarily, especially to kill a lot of people **3** informal to spoil something by working carelessly: *That hairdresser really butchered my hair!*

butch·er·y /'bʊtʃəri/ n [U] **1** cruel and unnecessary killing: *the butchery of battle* **2** the preparation of meat for sale

but·ler /'bʌtlə $ -ər/ n [C] the main male servant of a house

butt[1] /bʌt/ n [C]
1 PART OF YOUR BODY AmE informal the part of your body that you sit on; **buttocks**: *a baby's soft little butt* → **be a pain in the butt** at PAIN[1] (3)
2 CIGARETTE the end of a cigarette after most of it has been smoked
3 be the butt of sth to be the person or thing that other

people often make jokes about: *Paul quickly became the butt of everyone's jokes.*
4 GUN the thick end of the handle of a gun: *a rifle butt*
5 get your butt in/out/over etc *AmE spoken* used to rudely tell someone to go somewhere or do something: *Kevin, get your butt over here!*
6 *AmE spoken* **work/play etc your butt off** to work, play etc very hard: *I worked my butt off in college.*
7 CONTAINER *BrE* a large round container for collecting or storing liquids: *a rainwater butt*
8 HITTING WITH YOUR HEAD the act of hitting someone with your head

butt² *v* [I,T] **1** to hit or push against something or someone with your head **2** if an animal butts someone, it hits them with its horns
butt in *phr v* **1** to interrupt a conversation rudely: *Stop butting in!* **2** to become involved in a private situation that does not concern you: [+on] *They don't want outsiders butting in on their decision-making.*
butt out *phr v especially AmE spoken* used to tell someone rudely that you do not want them to be involved in a conversation or situation: *This has nothing to do with you, so just butt out!*

butte /bjuːt/ *n* [C] a hill with steep sides and a flat top in the western US

but·ter¹ S2 /'bʌtə $ -ər/ *n* [U]
1 a solid yellow food made from milk or cream that you spread on bread or use in cooking → BREAD-AND-BUTTER
2 butter wouldn't melt in sb's mouth used to say that someone seems to be very kind and sincere but is not really —**buttery** *adj*

butter² *v* [T] to spread butter on something: *buttered toast*
butter sb ⇔ up *phr v informal* to say nice things to someone so that they will do what you want: *Don't think you can butter me up that easily.*

butter bean *n* [C] a large pale yellow bean

but·ter·cream /'bʌtəkriːm $ -ər-/ *n* [U] a soft mixture of butter and sugar used inside or on top of cakes

but·ter·cup /'bʌtəkʌp $ -ər-/ *n* [C] a small shiny yellow wild flower

but·ter·fat /'bʌtəfæt $ -ər-/ *n* [U] the natural fat in milk

but·ter·fin·gers /'bʌtə,fɪŋɡəz $ 'bʌtər,fɪŋɡərz/ *n* [singular] *informal* someone who often drops things they are carrying or trying to catch

but·ter·fly /'bʌtəflaɪ $ -ər-/ *n plural* **butterflies** [C] **1** a type of insect that has large wings, often with beautiful colours → see picture at INSECT **2 have/get butterflies (in your stomach)** *informal* to feel very nervous before doing something: *I always get butterflies before an exam.* **3 the butterfly** a way of swimming by lying on your front and moving your arms together over your head while your legs move up and down: → see picture at SWIMMING **4** someone who usually moves on quickly from one activity or person to the next: *Gwen's a real social butterfly.*

but·ter·milk /'bʌtə,mɪlk $ -ər-/ *n* [U] the liquid that remains after butter has been made

but·ter·scotch /'bʌtəskɒtʃ $ -ərskɑːtʃ/ *n* [U] a type of sweet or sauce made from butter and sugar boiled together, or the taste this has: *butterscotch pudding*

butt·hole /'bʌthəʊl $ -hoʊl/ *n* [C] *AmE spoken not polite* **1** someone's ANUS **2** used to insult someone: *You butthole!*

but·tock /'bʌtək/ *n* [C usually plural] one of the fleshy parts of your body that you sit on

but·ton¹ S2 /'bʌtn/ *n* [C]
1 a small round flat object on your shirt, coat etc which you pass through a hole to fasten it: *small pearl buttons* | *A button was missing from his shirt.* | *She* **undid** (=unfastened) *the buttons of her blouse.* | **do up a button** *BrE* (=fasten a button); → see picture at SEWING **2** a small part or area of a machine that you press to make it do something: *Press the pause button.* | *Click*

on the icon with the right mouse button. → PUSH-BUTTON; → see picture at WATCH²
3 a small area on a computer screen, especially on a website, that you CLICK on in order to perform an action
4 *AmE* a small metal or plastic pin with a message or picture on it; ▣ **badge** *BrE*: *presidential campaign buttons*
5 button nose/eyes a nose or eyes that are small and round
6 on the button *especially AmE informal* exactly right, or at exactly the right time: *She got to our house at two, on the button.*
7 press/push (all) the right buttons to get what you want by behaving in a clever way: *She seemed to push all the right buttons.*
8 press/push sb's buttons to make someone angry by doing or saying something that annoys them: *He really knows how to push Dad's buttons.*
9 at/with the push/touch of a button used to emphasize how easy a machine is to use because it is controlled by pushing a button: *The instrument can gauge a distance with the push of a button.* → **as bright as a button** at BRIGHT (7)

button² *v* [I,T] **1** also **button up** to fasten clothes with buttons or to be fastened with buttons: *Sam, make sure Nina buttons up her jacket.* **2 button it!** *BrE*; **button your lip/mouth** *AmE spoken* used to tell someone in a rude way to stop talking

button-down *adj* [only before noun] **1** a button-down shirt or collar has the ends of the collar fastened to the shirt with buttons **2** a button-down company or style is formal and traditional: *He didn't fit in with the button-down culture of his new boss.*

buttoned-'up *adj informal* someone who is buttoned-up is not able to express their feelings, especially sexual feelings

but·ton·hole /'bʌtnhəʊl $ -hoʊl/ *n* [C] **1** a hole for a button to be put through to fasten a shirt, coat etc **2** *BrE* a flower you fasten to your clothes; ▣ **boutonniere** *AmE*

but·tress¹ /'bʌtrəs/ *n* [C] a brick or stone structure built to support a wall

buttress² *v* [T] *formal* to support a system, idea, argument etc, especially by providing money: *The evidence seemed to buttress their argument.*

but·ty /'bʌti/ *n plural* **butties** [C] *BrE informal* a SANDWICH

bux·om /'bʌksəm/ *adj* a woman who is buxom is attractively large and healthy and has big breasts

buy¹ S1 W1 /baɪ/ *v past tense and past participle* **bought** /bɔːt $ bɒːt/
1 a) [I,T] to get something by paying money for it; ▣ **sell**: *Where did you buy that dress?* | *Ricky showed her the painting he'd bought that morning.* | **buy sb sth** *Let me buy you a drink.* | **buy sth for sb/sth** *The money will be used to buy equipment for the school.* | **buy (sth) from sb** *It's cheaper to buy direct from the manufacturer.* | **buy sth for $10/£200 etc** *Dan bought the car for $2000.* | *It's much cheaper to buy in bulk* (=buy large quantities of something). **b)** [T] if a sum of money buys something, it is enough to pay for it: *$50 doesn't buy much these days.* | **buy sb sth** *$15 should buy us a pizza and a drink.*
2 buy (sb) time to deliberately make more time for yourself to do something, for example by delaying a decision: *'Can we talk about it later?' he said, trying to buy a little more time.*
3 [T] *informal* to believe something that someone tells you, especially when it is not likely to be true: *'Let's just say it was an accident.' 'He'll never buy that.'*
4 [T] *informal* to pay money to someone, especially someone in a position of authority, in order to persuade them to do something dishonest; ▣ **bribe**: *People say the judge had been bought by the Mafia.*
5 buy sth at the cost/expense/price of sth to get

something that you want, but only by losing something else: *The town has been careful not to buy prosperity at the expense of its character.*
6 sb bought it *old-fashioned informal* someone was killed

buy sth ⇔ **in** *phr v*
to buy something in large quantities: *Companies are buying in supplies of paper, in case the price goes up.*
buy into sth *phr v*
1 *informal* to accept that an idea is right and allow it to influence you: *I never bought into this idea that you have to be thin to be attractive.*
2 to buy part of a business or organization, especially because you want to control it: *Investors were invited to buy into state-owned enterprises.*
buy sb ⇔ **off** *phr v*
to pay someone money to stop them causing trouble or threatening you; ▣ **bribe**
buy out *phr v*
1 buy sb/sth ⇔ **out** to buy someone's share of a business or property that you previously owned together, so that you have complete control → BUYOUT
2 buy sb out of sth to pay money so that someone can leave an organization such as the army before their contract has ended
buy sth ⇔ **up** *phr v*
to quickly buy as much of something as possible, for example land, tickets, or goods: *Much of the land was bought up by property developers.*

buy² *n* [C, usually singular] **1** something that is worth buying, because it is cheap, good quality, or likely to gain in value: **a good/excellent etc buy** *The wine is a good buy at $6.50.* | *It's worth shopping around for* **the best buy** (=what you want at the lowest price). **2** *informal* an act of buying something, especially something illegal; ▣ **deal**

buy·er [S3] [W3] /'baɪə $ -ər/ *n* [C]
1 someone who buys something expensive such as a house or car; ▣ **seller, vendor**: *There were several potential buyers.* | *discounts for* **first-time buyers**
2 someone whose job is to choose and buy the goods for a shop or company: *a buyer for a chain store*

buyer's 'market *n* [singular] a situation in which there is plenty of something available, so that buyers have a lot of choice and prices tend to be low; ▣ **seller's market**

buy·out /'baɪaʊt/ *n* [C] a situation in which someone gains control of a company by buying all or most of its SHARES: *a management buyout* → **buy out** at BUY¹

buzz¹ /bʌz/ *v*
1 MAKE A SOUND [I] to make a continuous noise, like the sound of a BEE: *a loud buzzing noise*
2 MOVING AROUND [I always + adv/prep] **a)** to move around in the air making a continuous sound like a BEE: *Bees were buzzing around the picnic tables.* **b)** to move quickly around a place: *Pamela buzzed around checking that everything was ready.* | *There were all sorts of rumours buzzing through the office.*
3 EXCITEMENT [I] if a group of people or a place is buzzing, there is a lot of activity or excitement: [+with] *a classroom* **buzzing with activity**
4 CALL [I,T] **a)** to call someone by pressing a BUZZER: *Kramer buzzed at the security door, and I let him in.* | [+for] *Tina buzzed for her secretary.* **b)** to make something happen, for example make a door or gate open or close, by pressing a buzzer: **buzz sb in/out** *She buzzed them in and greeted them warmly.* | **buzz sb through sth** *The guard buzzed me through the gate.*
5 THOUGHTS [I] if your head or mind is buzzing with thoughts, ideas etc, you cannot stop thinking about them: [+with] *My mind was buzzing with new ideas.* | *Questions started buzzing round in my head.*
6 EARS [I] if your ears or head are buzzing, you can hear a continuous low unpleasant sound
7 AIRCRAFT [T] *informal* to fly an aircraft low and fast over buildings, people etc: *Military jets buzzed the city.*

buzz off *phr v spoken*
1 buzz off! used to tell someone in a rude way to go away
2 *BrE* to go away: *I've finished everything, so I'll buzz off now.*

buzz² *n* **1** [C] a continuous noise like the sound of a BEE: [+of] *the buzz of mosquitoes* **2** [singular] a lot of activity, noise, and excitement: [+of] *the buzz of conversation and laughter* **3** [singular] *informal* a strong feeling of excitement, pleasure, or success, or a similar feeling from drinking alcohol or taking drugs: *Playing well* **gives me a buzz.** | *Neil* **gets a buzz** *from drinking one beer.* **4 give sb a buzz** *informal* to telephone someone: *I'll give you a buzz on Monday.* **5 the buzz** *informal* unofficial news or information that is spread by people telling each other; → **gossip, rumour**

buz·zard /'bʌzəd $ -ərd/ *n* [C] **1** *BrE* a type of large HAWK (=hunting bird) **2** *AmE* a type of large bird that eats dead animals

buzz·cut /'bʌzkʌt/ *n* [C] *AmE* a hair style that is very short, usually worn by men

buzz·er /'bʌzə $ -ər/ *n* [C] a small thing, usually shaped like a button, that BUZZES when you press it: *Press the buzzer if you know the answer.*

'buzz saw *n* [C] *AmE* a SAW with a round blade that is spun around by a motor; ▣ **circular saw**

buzz·word /'bʌzwɜːd $ -wɜːrd/ *n* [C] a word or phrase from one special area of knowledge that people suddenly think is very important: *'Multimedia' has been a buzzword in the computer industry for years.*

by¹ [S1] [W1] /baɪ/ *prep*
1 WHO/WHAT DOES STH used especially with a PASSIVE verb to say who or what does something or makes something happen: *I was attacked by a dog.* | *a church designed by the famous architect, Sir Christopher Wren* | *We are all alarmed by the rise in violent crime.* | *interference by the state in the affairs of the Church* | *his appointment by the BBC as a producer*
2 MEANS/METHOD used to say what means or method someone uses to do something: *You can reserve the tickets by phone.* | *Send it by airmail.* | *Some customers prefer to pay by cheque.* | **by car/train/bus/taxi etc** *They travelled to Chicago by train.* | **by air/sea/land/road/rail etc** *All supplies are transported by air.* | **by doing sth** *She earns her living by selling insurance.* | *He was taken from his home by force.*
3 ROAD/DOOR used to say which road, entrance, door etc someone uses to get to a place: *They came in by the back door.* | *It's quicker to go by the country route.*
4 TAKING HOLD used to say which part of an object or of a person's body someone takes hold of: *He took Elaine by the arm and led her across the road.* | *She grabbed the hammer by the handle.*
5 WRITER/COMPOSER ETC used to give the name of someone who wrote a book, produced a film, wrote a piece of music etc: *the 'New World Symphony' by Dvorak* | *a short story by Charles Dickens* | *Who's it by?*
6 BESIDE beside or near something: *She stood by the window.* | *Jane went and sat by Patrick.*
7 PAST past someone or something without stopping: *He walked right by me without even saying hello.* | *I pass by the farm every day on my way to work.*
8 BEFORE before or not later than a particular time: *The documents need to be ready by next Friday.* | *I reckon the film should be over by 9.30.* | *By the end of the day we had sold over 2000 tickets.* | *By the time we got home we were tired and hungry.*
9 ACCORDING TO according to a particular rule, method, or way of doing things: *You've got to play by the rules.* | *Profits were £6 million, but by our standards this is low.*
10 CHANGE/DIFFERENCE used to say how great a change or difference is: *The price of oil fell by a further $2 a barrel.* | *I was overcharged by £3.* | *Godard's first film was better* **by far** (=by a large amount or degree).
11 MEASUREMENTS used to give the measurements of a room, container etc: *a room 15 metres by 23 metres*

12 QUANTITY used to show what unit of measurement or quantity is involved in selling, paying for, producing etc something: *Eggs are sold by the dozen.* | *We're paid by the hour.* | *She wanted to tear his hair out by the handful.*
13 GRADUAL CHANGE used to say that something happens gradually: *Day by day he grew weaker.* | *Little by little I was beginning to discover the truth about Garfield.* | *One by one, the men stepped forward.*
14 QUICK CHANGE used to say that something or someone is quickly becoming worse, better etc: *The financial crisis was growing more serious by the hour.*
15 LIGHT used to say that something happens in a particular kind of light: *We walked through the palace gardens by moonlight.*
16 by day/night during the day or the night: *a tour of Paris by night*
17 JOB/NATURE ETC used when you are giving information about someone's character, job, origin etc: *George I and George II were Germans by birth.* | *Cautious by nature, Simpkin was reluctant to interfere.* | *Robert Key was a teacher by profession.*
18 VISITING in order to visit a person or place for a short time: *On the way, I stopped by the post office.*
19 (all) by yourself **a)** completely alone: *Dave spent Christmas all by himself.* **b)** without help from anyone: *You can't move the furniture all by yourself.*
20 MULTIPLYING/DIVIDING used between two numbers when talking about multiplying or dividing: *What's 48 divided by 4?*
21 EMPHASIS used when expressing strong feelings or making serious promises: *By God, I'll kill that boy when I see him!*
22 FATHER if a woman has children by a particular man, that man is the children's father: *She's got two children by her previous husband.*
23 by the by *spoken* used when mentioning something that may be interesting but is not particularly important: *By the by, Ian said he might call round tonight.* → **by the way** at WAY¹ (46)

> **WORD CHOICE: by, with, in**
> **by** is used especially in passives, to say who or what does or causes something: *She was hit by a truck.* | *a book written by Peter Carey*
> Use **with** or **in** after verbs which describe a state rather than an action: *The room was lit with candles.* | *Her house is always filled with music.* | *The books were covered in dust.*
> Use **with** to say what tool you use to do something: *I got the stain out with this brush (NOT by this brush).*

by² S1 W1 *adv*
1 past someone or something: *As I was standing on the platform, the Liverpool train went whizzing by.* | *James walked by without even looking in my direction.*
2 used to say that time passes: *As the summer days slipped by, it was easy to forget about the war.* | *Ten years had gone by since I had last seen Marilyn.*
3 beside or near someone or something: *A crowd of people were standing by, waiting for an announcement.*
4 in order to visit a person or place for a short time: *Why don't you stop by for a drink after work?*
5 by and large used when making a general statement: *By and large, the new arrangements have worked well.*
6 by and by *old use* soon: *She will be better by and by.*

by-, bye- /baɪ/ *prefix* less important: *a by-product* (=something made in addition to the main product) | *a by-election* (=one held between regular elections)

bye¹ S1 /baɪ/ *interjection informal* goodbye: *Bye, Dave.* | **bye for now** (=used to say that you will see or speak to someone again soon)

bye² S3 *n* [C] a situation in a sports competition in which a player or a team does not have an opponent to play against and continues to the next part of the competition

bye- /baɪ/ *prefix* another spelling of BY-

bye-'bye *interjection informal* goodbye – used especially when speaking to children, friends, or members of your family: *Say bye-bye to Daddy, Tommy.*

'bye-byes *n* go (to) bye-byes *BrE* an expression meaning go to sleep, used by or to children

by-e,lection, 'bye-e,lection *n* [C] *especially BrE* a special election to replace a politician who has left parliament or died; → **general election**

by·gone /'baɪgɒn $ -gɒːn/ *adj* bygone age/era/days etc a period of time in the past: *The buildings reflect the elegance of a bygone era.*

by·gones /'baɪgɒnz $ -gɒːnz/ *n* let bygones be bygones to forget something bad that someone has done to you and forgive them

by·law /'baɪlɔː $ -lɒː/ *n* [C] **1** a law made by a local government that people in that area must obey **2** *AmE* a rule made by an organization to control the people who belong to it

by-line *n* [C] a line at the beginning of an article in a newspaper or magazine that gives the writer's name

by·pass¹ /'baɪpɑːs $ -pæs/ *n* [C] **1 (heart) bypass operation/ surgery** an operation to direct blood through new VEINS (=blood tubes) outside the heart because the veins in the heart are blocked or diseased: *a triple heart bypass operation* **2** a road that goes around a town or other busy area rather than through it; → **ring road 3** *technical* a tube that allows gas or liquid to flow around something rather than through it

bypass² *v* [T] **1** to go around a town or other busy place rather than through it: *Interstate 8 bypasses the town to the north.* **2** to avoid obeying a rule, system, or someone in an official position: *Francis bypassed his manager and wrote straight to the director.*

by-,product also **by·prod·uct** /'baɪ,prɒdʌkt $ -,prɑː-/ *n* [C] **1** something additional that is produced during a natural or industrial process: [+of] *a by-product of oil refining* **2** an unplanned additional result of something that you do: [+of] *Job losses are an unfortunate byproduct of the recession.* → END PRODUCT

byre /baɪə $ baɪr/ *n* [C] *BrE old-fashioned* a farm building in which cattle are kept; ▣ **cowshed**

by·stand·er /'baɪ,stændə $ -ər/ *n* [C] someone who watches what is happening without taking part; ▣ **onlooker**: *Several innocent bystanders were killed by the blast.*

byte /baɪt/ *n* [C] a unit for measuring computer information, equal to eight BITS (=the smallest unit on which information is stored on a computer): *Each character requires one byte of storage space.* → GIGABYTE, KILOBYTE, MEGABYTE, TERABYTE

by·way /'baɪweɪ/ *n* [C] **1** a small road or path which is not used very much **2 byways** [plural] the less important parts of an activity or subject: *a scholar exploring the highways and byways of Russian music* (=the important and less important parts)

by·word /'baɪwɜːd $ -wɜːrd/ *n* **1 be a byword for sth** to be so well known for a particular quality that your name is used to represent that quality: *His name has become a byword for honesty in the community.* **2** [singular] a word, phrase, or saying that is very well known: *Caution should be a byword for investors.*

By·zan·tine /baɪ'zæntaɪn, -tiːn, bɪ- $ 'bɪzəntiːn, -taɪn / *adj* **1** also **byzantine** complicated and difficult to understand: *the byzantine complexity of our tax laws* **2** relating to the Byzantines or the Byzantine empire: *a 5th century Byzantine church*

B

C, c

C **1** the written abbreviation of *Celsius* or *Centigrade*: *Water boils at 100°C.* **2** *written informal* a way of writing "see", used especially in emails and TEXT MESSAGES: *CU (=see you) in class!*

C, c /siː/ *plural* **C's, c's** n [C,U] **1** the third letter of the English alphabet **2** the first note in the musical SCALE of C MAJOR, or the musical KEY based on this note **3** a mark given to a student's work to show that it is of average quality **4** the number 100 in the system of ROMAN NUMERALS

c also *c.* **1** also **C** the written abbreviation of *century*: *the economic changes of the C20th* **2** a written abbreviation of *circa* (=about), used especially before dates: *c. 1830* **3** © the written abbreviation of *copyright* **4** *AmE* the written abbreviation of *cup*, used in cooking

C & W the written abbreviation of *country and western*

ca. also **ca** *BrE* a written abbreviation of *circa* (=about): *dating from ca. 1900*

cab /kæb/ n [C] **1** a taxi: *New York's yellow cabs* | **take/get a cab** *I took a cab to the airport.* | **call (sb) a cab** (=telephone for a taxi) | *Ralph tried to **hail a cab*** (=wave to get a cab to stop for you). **2** the part of a bus, train, or truck in which the driver sits **3** a carriage pulled by horses that was used like a taxi in the past

ca·bal /kəˈbæl/ n [C] *formal* a small group of people who make secret plans, especially in order to have political power

ca·ba·na /kəˈbɑːnə $ -ˈbæ-/ n [C] a tent or small wooden structure used for changing clothes at a beach or pool

cab·a·ret /ˈkæbəreɪ $ ˌkæbəˈreɪ/ n **1** [C,U] entertainment, usually with music, songs, and dancing, performed in a restaurant or club while the customers eat and drink: *a cabaret singer* **2** [C] a restaurant or club where this is performed: *the most famous Parisian cabaret, the Moulin Rouge*

cab·bage /ˈkæbɪdʒ/ n **1** [C,U] a large round vegetable with thick green or purple leaves **2** [C] *BrE informal* someone who cannot think, move, speak etc as a result of brain injury; ◪ **vegetable**; → see picture at VEGETABLE

cab·bie, cabby /ˈkæbi/ n [C] *informal* a taxi driver

ca·ber /ˈkeɪbə $ -ər/ n [C] a long heavy wooden pole that is thrown into the air as a test of strength in sports competitions in Scotland

cab·in /ˈkæbən/ n [C] **1** a small house, especially one built of wood in an area of forest or mountains: *a log cabin* **2** a small room on a ship in which you live or sleep **3** an area inside a plane where the passengers sit or where the pilot works: *the First Class cabin*

cabin boy n [C] a young man who works as a servant on a ship

cabin class n [U] travelling conditions on a ship that are better than TOURIST CLASS but not as good as FIRST CLASS

cabin crew n [U] the group of people whose job is to take care of the passengers on a plane; → **flight attendant, stewardess**

cabin cruiser n [C] a large motor boat with one or more cabins for people to sleep in

cab·i·net S2 W2 /ˈkæbənət/ n [C]
1 also **Cabinet** [also + plural verb] *BrE* the politicians with important positions in a government who meet to make decisions or advise the leader of the government: *a cabinet meeting* | *a member of the Cabinet*

2 a piece of furniture with doors and shelves or drawers, used for storing or showing things; ◪ **cupboard**: *The aspirin's in the medicine cabinet.* → FILING CABINET; → **Shadow Cabinet** at SHADOW³ (2); → see picture at OFFICE

cabinet-maker n [C] someone whose job is to make good quality wooden furniture

cabin fever n [U] *informal* when you feel upset and impatient because you have not been outside for a long time

ca·ble¹ W3 /ˈkeɪbəl/ n
1 [C] a plastic or rubber tube containing wires that carry telephone messages, electronic signals, television pictures etc: *cables and switches for computers* | **overhead/underground/undersea cable** *overhead power cables*; → see picture at BEDROOM
2 [C,U] a thick strong metal rope used on ships, to support bridges etc
3 [U] a system of broadcasting television by using cables, paid for by the person watching it: **on cable** *I'll wait for the movie to come out on cable.* | **cable network/channel/programme** *HBO, CNN and other cable networks*
4 [C] a TELEGRAM

cable² v [I,T] to send someone a TELEGRAM: **cable sb sth** *I cabled Mary the good news.*

cable car n [C] **1** a vehicle that hangs from a moving cable, and is used to take people up and down mountains **2** a vehicle similar to a train that is pulled along by a moving cable

ca·ble·cast /ˈkeɪbəlkɑːst $ -kæst/ n [C] *AmE* a show, sports event etc that is broadcast on a CABLE TELEVISION station; → **broadcast**: *the MTV Video Awards cablecast* —**cablecast** v [T]

cable-knit adj a cable-knit SWEATER has a raised pattern of crossing lines on it

cable modem n [C] a MODEM (=piece of equipment that allows information from one computer to be sent to another) that uses CABLE connections instead of telephone wires, and allows you to search the Internet very quickly

cable railway n [C] a railway on which vehicles are pulled up steep slopes by a moving CABLE

cable-ready adj a television that is cable-ready is able to receive cable television signals directly without needing any special equipment

cable television, cable TV n a system of broadcasting television programmes by CABLE → SATELLITE TELEVISION

ca·bling /ˈkeɪblɪŋ/ n [U] all the wires that are used for electrical equipment or an electrical system: *new cabling to handle 30 Internet terminals*

ca·boo·dle /kəˈbuːdl/ n **the whole (kit and) caboodle** *informal* everything: *I think it's time to replace the whole caboodle: computer, printer, and monitor.*

ca·boose /kəˈbuːs/ n [C] *AmE* a small railway carriage at the back of a train, usually where the person in charge of it travels; ◪ **guard's van** *BrE*

cab rank n [C] *BrE* a place where taxis wait for customers; ◪ **cabstand** *AmE*

cab·ri·o·let /ˈkæbriəleɪ $ ˌkæbriəˈleɪ/ n [C] *BrE* a car with a roof that can be folded back; ◪ **convertible**

cab·stand /ˈkæbstænd/ n [C] *AmE* a place where taxis wait for customers; ◪ **taxi rank** *BrE*

ca·cao /kəˈkaʊ/ n [U] the seed from which chocolate and COCOA are made

cache¹ /kæʃ/ n [C] **1** a number of things that have been hidden, especially weapons, or the place where they have been hidden: [+of] *a cache of explosives* | *a large arms cache* **2** *technical* a special part of a computer's memory that helps it work faster by storing information for a short time: *cache memory*

cache² v [T] **1** to hide something in a secret place, especially weapons **2** *technical* to store information in a computer's memory for a short time

cach·et /'kæʃeɪ $ kæ'ʃeɪ/ n [singular, U] *formal* if something has cachet, people think it is very good or special: *It's a good college, but lacks the cachet of Harvard.*

cack-hand·ed /ˌkæk ˈhændɪd/ *adj BrE informal* careless and tending to drop things, or badly done; ⊟ **clumsy**

cack·le¹ /'kækəl/ v [I] **1** to laugh in a loud unpleasant way, making short high sounds **2** when a chicken cackles, it makes a loud high sound

cackle² n [C] **1** a loud high sound that a chicken makes; → **cluck 2** a short high unpleasant laugh

ca·coph·o·ny /kəˈkɒfəni $ ˌkəˈkɑː-/ n [singular] a loud unpleasant mixture of sounds: [+of] *a cacophony of car horns* —**cacophonous** adj

cac·tus /'kæktəs/ n plural **cacti** /-taɪ/ or **cactuses** [C] a desert plant with sharp points instead of leaves

cad /kæd/ n [C] *old-fashioned* a man who cannot be trusted, especially one who treats women badly

CAD /kæd, ˌsiː eɪ 'diː/ n [U] *computer-aided design* the use of computers to design industrial products

ca·dav·er /kəˈdævə, kəˈdeɪ- $ kəˈdævər/ n [C] *technical* a dead human body, especially one used for study; ⊟ **corpse**

ca·dav·er·ous /kəˈdævərəs/ adj *literary* looking extremely thin, pale, and unhealthy: *cadaverous cheeks*

cad·dy¹ /'kædi/ n plural **caddies** [C] **1** also **caddie** someone who carries the GOLF CLUBS for someone who is playing golf **2** a small box for storing tea

caddy², **caddle** v **caddied, caddying, caddies** [I + for] to carry GOLF CLUBS for someone who is playing golf

ca·dence /'keɪdəns/ n [C] **1** the way someone's voice rises and falls, especially when reading out loud: *the cadence of my mother's voice* **2** a regular repeated pattern of sounds or movements: *the Brazilian cadences of the music* **3** *technical* a set of CHORDS

ca·den·za /kəˈdenzə/ n [C] *technical* a difficult part of a long piece of music, which a performer plays alone in order to show his or her skill

ca·det /kəˈdet/ n [C] someone who is training to be an officer in the army, navy, AIR FORCE, or police

cadge /kædʒ/ v [I,T] *BrE informal* to ask someone you know for something such as food, money, or cigarettes, because you do not have any or do not want to pay: *cadge sth from/off sb I cadged a lift from Joanna.*

Cad·il·lac /'kædɪlæk, -dəl-/ n **1** *trademark* a very expensive and comfortable car **2** *AmE informal* something that is regarded as an example of the highest quality of a particular type of product: [+of] *the Cadillac of stereo systems*

cad·mi·um /'kædmiəm/ n [U] a soft poisonous metal that is used in BATTERIES and in the protective SHIELDS in NUCLEAR REACTORS. It is a chemical ELEMENT: symbol Cd

ca·dre /'kɑːdə, -drə, 'keɪdə $ 'kædri, 'kɑːdrə/ n [C also + plural verb] *BrE* a small group of specially trained people in a profession, political party, or military force: [+of] *a cadre of highly trained scientists*

cae·sar·e·an /sɪˈzeəriən $ -'zer-/ also **cae,sarean 'section** n [C] an operation in which a woman's body is cut open to take a baby out: **born/delivered etc by caesarean** *Both her children were born by caesarean section.* | *She had to have a caesarean.*

cae·si·um *BrE*; **cesium** *AmE* /'siːziəm/ n [U] a soft silver-white metal that is used in PHOTOELECTRIC CELLS. It is a chemical ELEMENT: symbol Cs

cae·su·ra /sɪˈzjʊərə $ sɪˈʒʊrə, sɪˈzʊrə/ n [C] *technical* a pause in the middle of a line of poetry

café /'kæfeɪ $ kæ'feɪ, kə-/ n [C] **1** a small restaurant where you can buy drinks and simple meals → see picture at TOWN **2** a public place that is connected to a computer network, where people with similar interests discuss things by sending and receiving messages: *an Internet café*

caf·e·te·ri·a /ˌkæfɪˈtɪəriə $ -'tɪr-/ n [C] a restaurant, often in a factory, college etc, where you choose from

207 **cake pan**

foods that have already been cooked and carry your own food to a table; ⊟ **canteen** *BrE: the school cafeteria*

caf·e·tière /ˌkæfəˈtjeə $ -'tjer/ n [C] *BrE* a special pot for making coffee, with a metal FILTER that you push down

caff /kæf/ n [C] *BrE informal* a café

caf·feine /'kæfiːn $ kæˈfiːn/ n [U] a substance in tea, coffee, and some other drinks that makes you feel more active; → **decaffeinated**: *Avoid caffeine* (=drinks with caffeine) *before bedtime.* | *a caffeine-free cola* —**caffeinated** /'kæfɪneɪtɪd/ adj

caf·fé lat·te /ˌkæfeɪ ˈlæteɪ $ ˌkɑːfeɪ ˈlɑːteɪ, ˌkæf-/ n [C,U] a drink made with coffee and hot milk

caf·tan, kaftan /'kæftæn $ kæf'tæn/ n [C] a long loose piece of clothing, usually made of silk or cotton, and worn in the Middle East

cage¹ /keɪdʒ/ n [C] a structure of wires or bars in which birds or animals can be kept → see picture at NET

cage² v [T] to put or keep an animal or bird in a cage: *caged birds*

cag·ey /'keɪdʒi/ adj unwilling to tell people about your plans, intentions, or opinions: [+about] *He was very cagey about the deal.* —**cagily** adv —**caginess** n

ca·goule /kəˈguːl/ n [C] *BrE* a thin coat with a HOOD that stops you from getting wet

ca·hoots /kəˈhuːts/ n **be in cahoots (with sb)** to be working secretly with another person or group, especially in order to do something dishonest: *The Forest Service and the timber industry were in cahoots.*

cairn /keən $ kern/ n [C] a pile of stones that marks a particular place, especially at the top of a mountain

cais·son /'keɪsən, kəˈsuːn $ 'keɪsɑːn, -sən/ n [C] **1** a large box filled with air, that people go into to work under water, for example when building bridges **2** a large box for carrying AMMUNITION

ca·jole /kəˈdʒəʊl $ -'dʒoʊl/ v [I,T] to gradually persuade someone to do something by being nice to them, or making promises to them: **cajole sb into doing sth** *Aid workers do their best to cajole rich countries into helping.*

Ca·jun /'keɪdʒən/ n **1** [C] someone from Louisiana in the US who has French-Canadian ANCESTORS **2** [U] a type of music played by Cajun people —**Cajun** adj: *Cajun cooking*

cake¹ S2 W3 /keɪk/ n

1 [C,U] a soft sweet food made by baking a mixture of flour, butter, sugar, and eggs: *cake and ice cream* | *chocolate cake* | **birthday/wedding/Christmas cake** *Do you want some birthday cake?* | **slice/piece of cake** *Would you like a slice of cake?* | **make/bake a cake** *Sally decided to bake him a cake.*

2 fish/rice/potato etc cake fish, rice etc that has been formed into a flat round shape and then cooked

3 [C] a small block of something: [+of] *a cake of soap*

4 be a piece of cake *spoken* to be very easy: *'How do you do that?' 'It's a piece of cake! Watch!'*

5 take the cake also **take the biscuit** *BrE informal* to be worse than anything else you can imagine: *I've heard some pretty dumb ideas, but that takes the cake!*

6 have your cake and eat it *BrE*; **have your cake and eat it too** *AmE spoken* to have all the advantages of something without its disadvantages

7 a slice of the cake *BrE* a share of the profit, help etc that is available: *Both companies expect to get a big slice of the cake.* → **sell like hot cakes** at HOT CAKE (1)

cake² v **1** be caked with/in sth to be covered with a layer of something soft or wet that becomes thick and hard when it dries: *Our boots were caked with mud.* **2** [I] if a substance cakes, it forms a thick hard layer when it dries

cake·hole /'keɪkhəʊl $ -hoʊl/ n [C] *BrE spoken* someone's mouth

'cake pan n [C] *AmE* a cake TIN¹ (4)

'cake slice n [C] a piece of kitchen equipment with a handle and a wide flat end that you use for cutting and serving cakes, TARTS etc

'cake tin n [C] **1** BrE a metal container in which you bake a cake; ▤ **cake pan** AmE **2** a metal container with a lid, that you keep a cake in

cake·walk /ˈkeɪkwɔːk $ -wɔːk/ n [singular] AmE informal a very easy thing to do, or a very easy victory; ▤ **piece of cake**: The game was a cakewalk.

cal·a·mine lo·tion /ˈkæləmaɪn ˌləʊʃən $ -ˌloʊ-/ n [U] a pink liquid that you put on sore, ITCHY or SUNBURNED skin to make it less painful

ca·lam·i·ty /kəˈlæməti/ n plural **calamities** [C] a terrible and unexpected event that causes a lot of damage or suffering; ▤ **disaster**: It would be a calamity for the farmers if the crops failed again. —**calamitous** adj

cal·ci·fy /ˈkælsɪfaɪ/ v **calcified, calcifying, calcifies** [I,T] technical to become hard, or make something hard, by adding LIME

cal·ci·um S3 /ˈkælsiəm/ n [U] a silver-white metal that helps to form teeth, bones, and CHALK. It is a chemical ELEMENT: symbol Ca

cal·cu·la·ble /ˈkælkjʊləbəl/ adj [no comparative] something that is calculable can be measured by using numbers, or studying the facts available; ▤ **incalculable**: clear and calculable benefits

cal·cu·late S2 W3 /ˈkælkjʊleɪt/ v [T]
1 to find out how much something will cost, how long something will take etc, by using numbers: These instruments calculate distances precisely. | **calculate how much/how many etc** I'm trying to calculate how much paint we need. | **calculate (that)** Sally calculated that she'd have about £100 left. | **calculate sth on sth** Rates are calculated on an hourly basis.
2 to guess something using as many facts as you can find: **calculate (that)** Researchers calculated that this group was at a higher risk of heart disease. | **calculate how/what/whether etc** It's difficult to calculate what effect all these changes will have on the company.
3 be calculated to do sth to be intended to have a particular effect: a question calculated to embarrass him
calculate on sth phr v
if you calculate on something, you are depending on it for your plans to succeed: We're calculating on an early start. | **calculate on sb/sth doing sth** Ken hadn't calculated on Polson refusing his offer.

cal·cu·lat·ed /ˈkælkjʊleɪtɪd/ adj **1** a calculated crime or dishonest action is deliberately and carefully planned – used to show disapproval: a **calculated attempt** to deceive the American public **2** a **calculated risk/gamble** something risky that you do after thinking carefully about what might happen: The police took a calculated risk in releasing him. —**calculatedly** adv

cal·cu·lat·ing /ˈkælkjʊleɪtɪŋ/ adj thinking carefully about how to get exactly what you want, often without caring about anyone else – used to show disapproval: He gave her a calculating look.

cal·cu·la·tion S2 /ˌkælkjʊˈleɪʃən/ n
1 [C usually plural, U] when you use numbers in order to find out an amount, price, or value: **make/do a calculation** Dee looked at the bill and made some rapid calculations. | **by sb's/some/many calculations** By some calculations, the population will reach 8 million soon.
2 [C,U] careful planning in order to get what you want, especially without caring about the effects on other people; → **miscalculation**: political calculation
3 [U] when you think carefully about what the probable results will be if you do something; → **miscalculation**

cal·cu·la·tor S3 /ˈkælkjʊleɪtə $ -ər/ n [C] a small electronic machine that can add, multiply etc → see picture at MATHEMATICS; → see picture at ICE

cal·cu·lus /ˈkælkjʊləs/ n [U] the part of mathematics that deals with changing quantities, such as the speed of a falling stone or the slope of a curved line

cal·dron /ˈkɔːldrən $ ˈkɒl-/ n the American spelling of CAULDRON

cal·en·dar /ˈkæləndə $ -ər/ n [C] **1** a set of pages that show the days, weeks, and months of a particular year, that you usually hang on a wall **2** AmE **a)** a book with separate spaces or pages for each day of the year, on which you write down the things you have to do; ▤ **diary** BrE: a desk calendar **b)** all the things you plan to do in the next days, months etc: an event that deserves a place on your calendar **3** a system that divides and measures time in a particular way, usually starting from a particular event: **the Roman/Islamic/Gregorian etc calendar** The Islamic calendar has fewer days than the Gregorian calendar. **4** all the events in a year that are important for a particular organization or activity: **golfing/sporting/racing etc calendar** The Derby is a major event in the racing calendar.

calendar 'month n [C] **1** one of the 12 months of the year: Salaries will be paid at the end of the calendar month. **2** a period of time from a specific date in one month to the same date in the next month

calendar 'year n [C] the period of time from January 1st to December 31st of the same year

calf /kɑːf $ kæf/ n plural **calves** /kɑːvz $ kævz/ [C] **1** the part of the back of your leg between your knee and your ANKLE **2** the baby of a cow, or of some other large animals, such as an ELEPHANT **3 be in/with calf** if a cow is in or with calf, it is going to have a baby → **kill the fatted calf** at KILL¹ (15)

calf·skin /ˈkɑːfskɪn $ ˈkæf-/ n [U] the skin of a calf, used for making shoes, bags etc

cal·i·ber /ˈkæləbə $ -ər/ n the American spelling of CALIBRE

cal·i·brate /ˈkæləbreɪt/ v [T] technical **1** to check or slightly change an instrument or tool, so that it does something correctly **2** to mark an instrument or tool so that you can use it for measuring

cal·i·bra·tion /ˌkæləˈbreɪʃən/ n [U] technical **1** the process of checking or slightly changing an instrument or tool so that it does something correctly: the calibration of flight instruments **2** a set of marks on an instrument or tool used for measuring, or the act of making these marks correct

cal·i·bre BrE; **caliber** AmE /ˈkæləbə $ -ər/ n **1** [U] the level of quality or ability that someone or something has achieved: **of sb's calibre** Where will we find another man of his calibre? | The school has always attracted a **high calibre** of student. | **of high/the right etc calibre** The paintings were of the highest calibre. | **of this/that calibre** The city needs a hotel of this calibre (=of this high standard). **2** [C] **a)** the width of the inside of a gun or tube: a .22 caliber weapon **b)** the width of a bullet

cal·i·co /ˈkælɪkəʊ $ -koʊ/ n [U] **1** BrE heavy cotton cloth that is usually white **2** AmE light cotton cloth with a small printed pattern **3 calico cat** AmE a cat that has black, white, and brown fur; ▤ **tortoiseshell** BrE

cal·i·pers /ˈkæləpəz $ -ərz/ n the American spelling of CALLIPERS

ca·liph /ˈkeɪlɪf/ n [C] a Muslim ruler, especially in the past

ca·li·phate /ˈkeɪlɪfeɪt/ n [C] the country a caliph rules, or the period of time when they rule it

cal·is·then·ics /ˌkæləsˈθenɪks/ n the American spelling of CALLISTHENICS

calk /kɔːk $ kɒːk/ v an American spelling of CAULK

call¹ S1 W1 /kɔːl $ kɒːl/ v
1 TELEPHONE [I,T] to telephone someone: She calls her father every couple of days. | I'll call you soon. | What time did Tony call? | **call a doctor/the police/a cab etc** (=telephone someone and ask them to come to you) I think we should call a doctor. | I'm gonna call the cops

2 **DESCRIBE** [T] to use a word or name to describe someone or something in a particular way: **call sb sth** *Are you calling me a liar?* | *You may call it harmless fun, but I call it pornography.* | **call sb names** (=use insulting names for someone) *The other kids used to call me names, but I tried to ignore them.*

3 **HAVE A NAME** [T] to have a particular name or title, or use a particular name or title for someone or something: **be called sth** *Their eldest son is called Matthew.* | *The arrow that appears on the screen is called a cursor.* | **call sb sth** *My name's Virginia, but my friends call me Ginny.* | *Do you want to be called Miss or Ms?* | **call sb by sth** *I prefer to be called by my middle name.*

4 **GIVE SB/STH A NAME** [T] *especially BrE* to give someone or something the name they will be known by in the future; ▣ **name** *AmE*: *What are you going to call the new puppy?* | **call sb sth** *They've decided to call the baby Louise.*

5 **ASK/ORDER BY SPEAKING** [T] to ask or order someone to come to you: **call sb into/over/across etc** *Peter called the waitress over and ordered a large brandy.* | *Marcie was called up to the principal's office.*

6 **ARRANGE** [T] to arrange for something to happen at a particular time: **call a meeting/strike/election etc** *The Security Council has called an emergency session to discuss the crisis.* | *According to the law, the election must be called within the next two months.*

7 **SAY/SHOUT** [I,T] to say or shout something loudly so that someone can hear you: *I heard someone calling in the distance.* | *'I'm coming!' she called down the stairs.* | *Sheila was just sneaking out when her mother called her.* | *She heard him* **call** *her* **name.**

8 **call yourself sth** to say that you are a particular type of person, although you do nothing to show this is true: *How could Julian call himself a friend and then let me down so badly?*

9 **call the shots/tune** *informal* to be in a position of authority so that you can give orders and make decisions: *It was a job in which she was able to call the shots.*

10 **call it a day** *informal* to decide to stop working, especially because you have done enough or you are tired: *Come on, let's call it a day and go home.*

11 **call collect** *AmE* to make a telephone call that is paid for by the person who receives it; ▣ **reverse the charges** *BrE*

12 **READ NAMES** [T] also **call out** to read names or numbers in a loud voice in order to get someone's attention: *When I call your name, go and stand in line.*

13 **COURT** [T usually passive] to tell someone that they must come to a law court or official committee: **call sb to do sth** *They were called to give evidence at the trial.*

14 **call (sth) into question** to make people uncertain about whether something is right, good, or true: *I feel that my competence is being called into question here.*

15 **be/feel called to do sth** to feel strongly that you should do something: *He felt called to write to all his fellow investors, warning them of the impending crisis.*

16 **call sb/sth to order** *formal* to tell people to obey the rules of a formal meeting

17 **VISIT** [I] also **call round** *BrE* to stop at a house or other place for a short time to see someone or do something: *She called round for a chat.* | **call on sb** *We thought we'd call on James on the way home.* | **call (in) at sth** *I regularly called in at his office for news.* | **call into sth** *People often call into the library while they're out shopping.*

18 **call it £10/2 hours etc** *spoken* used to suggest a general figure rather than a more specific one, especially in order to make things simpler: *'I owe you £10.20.' 'Oh, call it £10!'*

19 **call it a draw** if two opponents in a game call it a draw, they agree that neither of them has won → **call it quits** at QUITS (2)

20 **call it/things even** *spoken* use this to say that someone who owes you something does not have to give you anything more than they have already given you

21 **call (sb's) attention to a)** to ask people to pay attention to a particular subject or problem: *May I call*

your attention to item seven on the agenda. **b)** to make someone notice someone or something: *I wanted to shout out to Ken, but I didn't want to call attention to myself.*

22 **call sth to mind a)** to remind you of something: *Don't those two call to mind the days when we were courting?* **b)** to remember something: *I couldn't call to mind where I'd seen him before.*

23 **call a huddle** *AmE informal* to make people come together to talk about something

24 **call time (on sb/sth)** to say that it is time for something to finish or stop

25 **TRAINS/SHIPS** [I] if a train, ship, bus etc calls at a place, it stops there for a short time; ▣ **stop**: *This train calls at all stations to Broxbourne.*

26 **COIN** [I,T] to guess which side of a coin will land upwards when it is thrown in the air, in order to decide who will play first in a game: *It's your turn to call.*

27 **CARD GAME** [I,T] to risk the same amount of money as the player who plays before you in a POKER game → **so-called**; → **call sb's bluff** at **BLUFF²** (2); → **too close to call** at **CLOSE²** (8)

call back *phr v*
1 **call (sb) back** to telephone someone again, for example because they were not at home when you telephoned last time: *I'll call back later.* | *Can you ask John to call me back when he gets in?*
2 *BrE* to return to a place you went to earlier: *You could call back to collect her at noon.*

call by *phr v*
to stop and visit someone when you are near the place where they live or work: *I thought I'd call by and see how you were.*

call down sth *phr v*
formal to ask for someone, especially a god, to make something unpleasant happen to someone or something: [+**on/upon**] *He called down vengeance on them.*

call for sb/sth *phr v*
1 if a group of people calls for something, they ask publicly for something to be done: *Human Rights groups are calling for the release of political prisoners.*
2 to need or deserve a particular type of behaviour or treatment: *Dealing with children who are so damaged calls for immense tact and sensitivity.* | *That kind of abuse is really* **not called for** (=it is unnecessary and unwelcome). → **UNCALLED FOR**
3 *BrE* to meet someone at their home in order to take them somewhere: *I'll call for you at 8 o'clock.*
4 *AmE* to say that a particular kind of weather is likely to happen; ▣ **predict**: *The forecast calls for more rain.*

call sth ⇔ **forth** *phr v*
formal to produce a particular reaction: *Great works of classical music can often call forth a mixture of responses from the listener.*

call in *phr v*
1 **call sb/sth ⇔ in** to ask someone to come and help you with a difficult situation: *The government then called in troops to deal with the disturbances.*
2 to telephone somewhere, especially the place where you work, to tell them where you are, what you are doing etc: *Rachael* **called in sick** (=telephoned to say she was too ill to come to work).
3 to telephone a radio or television show to give your opinion or to ask a question: *Over 2000 viewers called in with complaints about the bad language used in the programme.*
4 **call in a loan/debt** to officially tell someone to pay back money you lent them: *The economy slid further into bankruptcy when several foreign banks called in unpaid loans.*
5 *BrE* to visit a person or place while you are on your way to somewhere else: [+**on/at**] *Could you call in on Mum on your way home?*

▢ 1 000, ▢ 2 000, ▢ 3 000, most frequent words in S poken and W ritten English

C

call sb/sth ⇔ **off** phr v
1 to decide that a planned event will not take place; ⊟ **cancel**: *The trip to Italy might be called off.*
2 to officially decide that something should be stopped after it has already started: *Rescuers had to call off the search because of worsening weather conditions.*
3 to order an animal or person to stop attacking or threatening someone: *Call your dog off.*

call on/upon sb/sth phr v
1 to formally ask someone to do something: **call on sb to do sth** *The UN has called on both sides to observe the ceasefire.*
2 to visit someone for a short time: *Why don't you call on my sister when you're in Brighton?*

call out phr v
1 to say something loudly: **call sth ⇔ out** *'Hi there!' I called out.* | [+to] *The firemen called out to him.*
2 call sb ⇔ out to ask or order a person or an organization to help, especially in a difficult or dangerous situation: *The army was called out to help fight fires.*
3 call sb/sth ⇔ out BrE to order workers to go on STRIKE: *The transport workers were called out.*

call up phr v
1 informal especially AmE to telephone someone: **call sb ⇔ up** *He called me up to tell me about it.* | *I'm going to call up and cancel my subscription.*
2 call sth ⇔ up if you call up information on a computer, you make the computer show it to you: *I called up their website, but it didn't have the information I was looking for.*
3 call sb ⇔ up BrE to officially order someone to join the army, navy, or air force; ⊟ **draft** AmE: *I was called up three months after war broke out.*
4 call sb ⇔ up to choose someone for a national sports team; → **call-up**: *Hurst was called up for the game against Mexico.*
5 call sth ⇔ up to produce something or make it appear: *Local people believe she can call up the spirits of the dead.*

WORD CHOICE: **call, phone, telephone, ring**
In spoken English, it is usual to say that you **call** or **phone** someone: *He calls me almost every day.* | *Phone me when you get there.*
In spoken British English, it is also very usual to say that you **ring** someone: *Have you rung Kim yet?*
It is fairly formal and not very usual in spoken English to say that you **telephone** someone.
⚠ Do not say that you 'call to' someone: *I called him* (NOT *called to him*) *to let him know.*
⚠ There is no verb 'phone call': *I need to call* (NOT *to phone call*) *Monica.*
You can also say that you **give** someone **a (phone) call** or, in British English, **give** them **a ring**: *Give me a call sometime.* | *I think I'll give Mum a ring.*
⚠ Do not say 'give someone a phone'.

---

call² S1 W1 n
1 TELEPHONE [C] when you speak to someone on the telephone

---

phone call
make a call
give sb a call
get/receive a call
take a call (=speak to someone on the phone when someone else has answered)
return a call (=telephone someone who tried to telephone you earlier)
local call
long-distance call
incoming call (=a call someone makes to you)
hoax/crank call (=a call intended to trick someone)
anonymous call (=from an unknown person)

[+for] *Were there any phone calls for me while I was out?* | [+from] *There was a call from Ann for you.* | *It's cheaper to make calls after 6pm.* | *I'll give you a call*

at the weekend. | *I got a call from Jane last week.* | *I'll take the call in my office.* | *Why haven't you returned any of my calls?* | *You can make a local call for under 2p a minute.* | *I don't make many long-distance calls, so my phone bill's usually quite low.* | *This telephone only accepts incoming calls.* | *Detectives are investigating a hoax call which led to the evacuation of an office block.* | *an anonymous call to a Sunday newspaper*

2 be on call if someone such as a doctor or engineer is on call, they are ready to go and help whenever they are needed as part of their job: *Don't worry, there's a doctor on call 24 hours a day.*
3 SHOUT/CRY [C] **a)** a loud sound that a particular bird or animal makes; ⊟ **cry**: [+of] *I again heard the call of an owl.* **b)** a shout that you make to get someone's attention
4 VISIT [C] a visit, especially for a particular reason: *Sorry, Doctor Pugh is out on a call at the moment.* | **pay/make a call (on sb)** (=visit someone)
5 REQUEST/ORDER [C] a request or order for something or for someone to do something: *Members obediently answered the calls for funds.* | **call for sb to do sth** *There have been calls for the secretary to resign.* | **a call to arms** (=an order for people to fight against an enemy)
6 DECISION **a)** [C] the decision made by a REFEREE in a sports game: **make a good/bad call** *There may have been a few bad calls, but they're making them for a reason.* **b)** [singular] especially AmE informal: *Don't just say what you think I would like. It's your call.* | **make a call** (=decide something) | **an easy/hard call** (=an easy or difficult decision) | **judgement call** (=a decision based on your personal judgement of a situation)
7 there isn't much call for sth used for saying that not many people want a particular thing: *There isn't much call for black and white televisions these days.*
8 there is no call for sth spoken used to tell someone that their behaviour is wrong and unnecessary: *There's no call for that kind of language! I'm doing my best!*
9 AT AN AIRPORT [C] a message announced at an airport that a particular plane will soon leave: *This is the last call for flight BA872 to Moscow.*
10 have first call on sth **a)** to have the right to be the first person to use something **b)** to be the first person that you will help because they are important to you: *Her children had first call on her time.*
11 the call of sth literary the power that a place or way of life has to attract someone: *the call of the sea*
12 the call of nature a need to URINATE (=pass liquid from your body) - used especially humorously → **be at sb's beck and call** at BECK (1); → PORT OF CALL, ROLL-CALL, WAKE-UP CALL

CALL /kɔːl $ kɒːl/ n [U] *computer-assisted language learning* the use of computers to help people learn foreign languages

'**call box** n [C] **1** BrE a PHONE BOX **2** AmE a public telephone beside a road or FREEWAY used to telephone for help

'**call ,centre** BrE; **call center** AmE n [C] an office where people answer customers' questions, make sales etc by using the telephone rather than by meeting people

call·er /'kɔːlə $ 'kɒːlər/ n [C] **1** someone making a telephone call: *'Could you hold for one moment?' he asked the caller.* **2** old-fashioned someone who visits your house

,**caller di'splay** BrE; ,**caller I'D** AmE n [C,U] a special service on your telephone that lets you know who is calling before you answer the telephone

'**call girl** n [C] a PROSTITUTE who arranges by telephone to meet men

cal·lig·ra·phy /kə'lɪgrəfi/ n [U] the art of producing beautiful writing using special pens or brushes, or the writing produced this way —**calligrapher** n [C]

came

call-in n [C] AmE a radio or television programme in which people telephone to give their opinions; ▣ **phone-in** BrE: a call-in talk show

call·ing /'kɔːlɪŋ $ 'kɒ:-/ n [C] **1** a strong desire or feeling of duty to do a particular kind of work, especially religious work; ▣ **vocation**: It wasn't until Durant was in her thirties that she found her calling. **2** formal someone's profession or trade

calling card n [C] AmE a small card with a name and often an address printed on it, that people in the past gave to people they visited; ▣ **visiting card** BrE

cal·li·pers BrE; **calipers** AmE /'kælɪpəz $ -ərz/ n [plural] **1** a tool used for measuring thickness, or the distance between two surfaces, or the DIAMETER (=inside width) of something **2** BrE metal bars that someone wears on their legs to help them walk; ▣ **brace** AmE

cal·lis·then·ics BrE; **calisthenics** AmE /,kæl₁s'θenɪks/ n [U] a set of physical exercises that are intended to make you strong and healthy

call ,letters n [plural] especially AmE a CALL SIGN

call ,option n [C] technical the right to buy a particular number of SHARES at a special price within a particular period of time

cal·lous /'kæləs/ adj not caring about other people are suffering: We were shocked at the callous disregard for human life. | a callous attitude | the callous slaughter of seals —**callously** adv —**callousness** n [U]

cal·loused /'kæləst/ adj calloused skin is rough and covered in CALLUSES: rough, **calloused hands**

call-out n [C] BrE a situation in which someone is called to another person's house or place of business to do repairs, help them etc: The lifeboat has had ten call-outs in the past year. | call-out charges

cal·low /'kæləʊ $ -loʊ/ adj young and without experience – used to show disapproval; ▣ **immature**: a callow youth

call ,screening n [U] **1** a special service that you can buy from your telephone company which prevents particular people from calling you **2** when you let an answering machine answer your telephone calls, and you then only talk to callers that you want to speak to

call sign n [C usually singular] also **call letters** especially AmE a name made up of letters and numbers, used by people operating communication radios to prove who they are

call·time /'kɔːltaɪm $ 'kɒ:l-/ n [U] the amount of time that is available for the user of a MOBILE PHONE to make calls

call-up n [C] BrE **1** an order to join the army, navy etc; ▣ **draft** AmE: He got his call-up papers in July. **2** an opportunity or invitation to play for a professional sports team, especially a national one: [+to] Stewart's recent call-up to the Wales squad

cal·lus /'kæləs/ n [C] an area of thick hard skin: the calluses on his hands

call 'waiting n [U] a telephone service that allows you to receive another call when you are already talking on the telephone, without ending the first call

calm¹ ⑤³ /kɑːm $ kɑːm, kɑːlm/ adj comparative **calmer**, superlative **calmest**
1 relaxed and quiet, not angry, nervous, or upset: Glen was calm and composed at the funeral. | **remain/stay/keep calm** I tried to stay calm and just ignore him.
2 if a place, period of time, or situation is calm, there is less activity, trouble etc than there sometimes is, or than there has been recently: The financial markets are calm at the moment. | The streets are calm again after last night's disturbances.
3 a sea, lake etc that is calm is smooth or has only gentle waves: The seas were **dead calm**. —**calmly** adv —**calmness** n [U]

calm² n [singular, U] **1** a situation or time that is quiet and peaceful: [+of] They remained on the terrace after dinner, enjoying the calm of the evening. | **morning/afternoon/evening calm** A scream shattered the late afternoon calm. | Hindu leaders **appealed for calm**

(=asked that the public stay calm) after a temple was burnt to the ground. | The presence of soldiers helped restore calm. | The last five years have seen a period of relative calm. **2 the calm before the storm** a calm peaceful situation that will not continue because a big argument, problem etc is coming

calm³ also **calm down** v [I,T] **1** to become quiet and relaxed after you have been angry, excited, nervous, or upset, or to make someone become quiet and relaxed: He tried to calm the frightened children. | Calm down and tell me what happened. | We have tried to **calm people's fears**. | **calm yourself (down)** She lit a cigarette to calm herself down. **2** if a situation calms down, it becomes easier to deal with because there are fewer problems and it is not as busy as it was before: It took about six months for **things** to **calm down** after we had the baby.

Cal·or gas /'kælə gæs $ -lər-/ n [U] BrE trademark a type of gas that is sold in metal containers and used for heating and cooking where there is no gas supply

cal·o·rie /'kæləri/ n [C] **1** a unit for measuring the amount of ENERGY that food will produce: An average potato has about 90 calories. | a calorie-controlled diet | **low-calorie/high-calorie** a low-calorie snack | Do you need to **burn off** a few calories (=lose some weight by exercising)? | My wife convinced me to finally start **counting calories** (=control my weight by being careful about what I eat). **2** technical the amount of heat that is needed to raise the temperature of one gram of water by one degree Celsius. It is used as a unit for measuring energy. —**caloric** /kə'lɒrɪk, 'kælərɪk $ kə'lɔːrɪk/ adj

cal·o·rif·ic /,kælə'rɪfɪk◂ / adj **1** food that is calorific tends to make you fat **2** technical producing heat

cal·um·ny /'kæləmni/ n plural **calumnies 1** [C] an untrue and unfair statement about someone that is intended to give people a bad opinion of them **2** [U] when someone says things like this

calve /kɑːv $ kæv/ v [I] to give birth to a CALF

calves /kɑːvz $ kævz/ the plural of CALF

Cal·vin·is·m /'kælv₁nɪzəm/ n [U] the Christian religious teachings of John Calvin, based on the idea that events on Earth are controlled by God and cannot be changed by humans

Cal·vin·ist /'kælv₁n₁st/ adj **1** following the teachings of Calvinism **2** also **Calvinistic** /,kælv₁'nɪstɪk◂ / having strict moral standards and tending to disapprove of pleasure; ▣ **puritanical** —**Calvinist** n [C]

ca·lyp·so /kə'lɪpsəʊ $ -soʊ/ n plural **calypsos** [C] a type of Caribbean song based on subjects of interest in the news

ca·lyx /'keɪlɪks, 'kæ- $ 'keɪ-/ n plural **calyxes** or **calyces** /-l₁siːz/ [C] the green outer part of a flower that protects it before it opens

cam /kæm/ n [C] a wheel or part of a wheel that is shaped to change circular movement into backwards and forwards movement

CAM /kæm/ n [U] computer-aided manufacturing the use of computers to make industrial products

cam·a·ra·de·rie /,kæmə'rɑːdəri $ -'ræ-, -'rɑː-/ n [U] a feeling of friendship that a group of people have, especially when they work together: the camaraderie of the women's basketball team

cam·ber /'kæmbə $ -ər/ n [C,U] technical a slight curve from the centre of a road or other surface to the side, which makes water flow to the side

cam·bric /'keɪmbrɪk/ n [U] thin white cloth made of LINEN or cotton

cam·cor·der /'kæm,kɔːdə $ -,kɔːrdər/ n [C] a type of camera that records pictures and sound on VIDEOTAPE → see picture at BEDROOM

came /keɪm/ the past tense of COME

C

cam·el /'kæməl/ n [C] a large desert animal with a long neck and either one or two HUMPS (=large raised parts) on its back

cam·el·hair /'kæməlheə $ -her/ n [U] a thick yellowish brown cloth, usually used for making coats

ca·mel·li·a /kə'miːliə/ n [C] a plant with dark green leaves and red, pink, or white flowers, or the flowers of this plant

cam·em·bert /'kæməmbeə $ -ber/ n [C,U] a soft French cheese that is white outside and yellow inside

cam·e·o /'kæmi-əʊ $ -oʊ/ n plural **cameos** [C] **1** a short appearance in a film or play by a well-known actor: **cameo role/appearance** Denholm Eliot put in a cameo appearance as a butler. **2** a small piece of jewellery with a raised shape, usually a person's face, on a flat background of a different colour: a cameo brooch **3** a short piece of writing that gives a clear idea of a person, place, or event

cam·e·ra [S2] [W3] /'kæmərə/ n [C]

camera — shutter button, viewfinder, film rewind, lens, zoom lens

1 a piece of equipment used to take photographs or make films or television programmes; → **camcorder**, **video camera**: **on/off camera** (=while a camera is recording or not recording) The crime was **caught on camera** by police. **2 in camera** law a law case that is held in camera takes place secretly or privately

cam·e·ra·man /'kæmərəmən/ n plural **cameramen** /-mən/ [C] someone who operates a camera for films or television ⚠ Do not confuse with **photographer** (=person who takes still photographs).

camera-shy adj not liking to have your photograph taken

cam·i·knick·ers /'kæmi,nɪkəz $ -ərz/ n [plural] BrE a piece of women's underwear that combines a CAMISOLE and KNICKERS

cam·i·sole /'kæmɪˌsəʊl $ -soʊl/ n [C] a light piece of women's underwear that covers the chest down to the waist and has narrow bands over the shoulders → see picture at UNDERWEAR

cam·o·mile, **chamomile** /'kæməmaɪl/ n [C,U] a plant with small white and yellow flowers that are sometimes used to make tea

cam·ou·flage[1] /'kæməflɑːʒ/ n **1** [U] a way of hiding something, especially soldiers and military equipment, by using paint, leaves etc to make it look like the things around it: soldiers learning camouflage technique | the camouflage netting over the tanks **2** [U] the type of green and brown clothes, paint etc that soldiers wear to make themselves more difficult to see: The men were dressed **in camouflage** and carrying automatic weapons. | camouflage trousers **3** [singular, U] the way that the colour or shape of an animal protects it by making it difficult to see in the area in which it lives: The whiteness of the arctic fox **acts as camouflage**, hiding it from its enemies. **4** [singular, U] behaviour that is designed to hide something: [+for] Aggression is often a camouflage for insecurity.

camouflage[2] v [T] to hide something, especially by making it look the same as the things around it, or by making it seem like something else: **camouflage sth with sth** I saw a truck, heavily camouflaged with netting and branches. | The strain she was under was **well camouflaged** by skilful make-up.

camp[1] [S3] [W3] /kæmp/ n
1 IN THE MOUNTAINS/FOREST ETC [C,U] a place where people stay in tents, shelters etc for a short time, usually in the mountains, a forest etc: Let's go back to

camp – it's getting dark. | a camp near Lake Ellen Wilson | The soldiers **broke camp** (=took down their tents etc) and left before dawn. | **pitch/make camp** (=set up a tent or shelter) It was dark by the time we pitched camp. | We **set up camp** (=made the camping place ready) at nearby Icicle Lake. | The expedition's **base camp** (=main camp) was 6,000 feet below the summit. | **mining/logging etc camp** (=a camp where people stay when they are doing these kinds of jobs)
2 prison/labour/detention etc camp a place where people are kept for a particular reason, when they do not want to be there: a **refugee camp** just across the border → CONCENTRATION CAMP
3 FOR CHILDREN [C,U] a place where young people go to take part in activities, and where they usually stay for several days or weeks: The camp offers hiking, fishing, canoeing, and boating. | scout camp | Two years ago, she started a **summer camp** for girls aged 8 and older. | **tennis/football etc camp** (=a camp where you can do one particular activity) → DAY CAMP, HOLIDAY CAMP
4 GROUP OF PEOPLE [C] a group of people or organizations who have the same ideas or principles, especially in politics: the extreme right-wing camp of the party | At least you know that Lynne is definitely **in your camp** (=supports you rather than someone else, and agrees with your ideas). → **have a foot in both camps** at FOOT[1] (21)
5 MILITARY [C] a permanent place where soldiers live or train: Donny is stationed at Camp Pendleton.

camp[2] v [I] **1** to set up a tent or shelter and stay there for a short time: We'll camp by the river for the night, and move on tomorrow. | **camping gear/equipment** camping gear such as a sleeping bag, tent, and backpack **2 go camping** to visit an area, especially the mountains or a forest, and stay in a tent: We went camping in the San Bernardino Mountains.

camp out phr v **1** to sleep outdoors, usually in a tent: What he liked best about scouting was camping out. **2** to stay somewhere where you do not have all the usual things that a house has: We'll just have to camp out until our furniture arrives.

camp sth up phr v informal **camp it up** to deliberately use unnatural body or face movements, in a way that some people think is typical of a HOMOSEXUAL man

camp[3] adj **1** a man who is camp moves or speaks in the way that people used to think was typical of HOMOSEXUALS **2** also **campy** AmE clothes, decorations etc that are camp are very strange, bright, or unusual

cam·paign[1] [S3] [W1] /kæm'peɪn/ n [C]
1 a series of actions intended to achieve a particular result relating to politics or business, or a social improvement: Florida was a key state in his campaign for re-election. | an anti-bullying campaign | an advertising campaign | [+for/against] a campaign for equal rights | Jones **ran** a good **campaign**. | **campaign funds/money/financing** He raised nearly $30 million in campaign funds. | **launch/mount a campaign** (=plan, organize, and begin a campaign) Police have launched a campaign to crack down on drug dealers.
2 a series of battles, attacks etc intended to achieve a particular result in a war

campaign[2] v [I] to lead or take part in a series of actions intended to achieve a particular social or political result: [+for/against] a group campaigning against the destruction of the rainforests —**campaigner** n [C]

cam·pa·ni·le /ˌkæmpə'niːli/ n [C] a high bell tower that is usually separate from any other building

cam·pa·nol·o·gy /ˌkæmpə'nɒlədʒi $ -'nɑː-/ n [U] formal the skill of ringing bells, and the study of bells

camp bed n [$ '. ,./ [C] BrE a light narrow bed that folds flat and is easy to carry; ▣ **cot** AmE; → see picture at BED

camp·er /'kæmpə $ -ər/ n [C] **1** someone who is staying in a tent or shelter **2** also **camper van** BrE a vehicle that has cooking equipment and beds in it **3** AmE a special type of tent on wheels that has cooking equipment and beds in it **4** *AmE* a child who is taking part in a camp **5 happy camper** *spoken* someone who seems to be happy with their situation

camp·fire /ˈkæmpfaɪə $ -faɪr/ *n* [C] a fire made outdoors by people who are camping

ˈcamp ˌfollower *n* [C] *especially BrE* someone who supports an organization or a political party, but who is not actually a member of it

camp·ground /ˈkæmpɡraʊnd/ *n* [C] *AmE* an area where people can camp, often with a water supply and toilets; ⊟ **campsite** *BrE*

cam·phor /ˈkæmfə $ -ər/ *n* [U] a white substance with a strong smell, used especially to keep insects away

camp·site /ˈkæmpsaɪt/ *n* [C] **1** *BrE* an area where people can camp, often with a water supply and toilets; ⊟ **campground** *AmE*; → see picture at **STAY** **2** *AmE* a place, usually within a campground, where one person or group can camp

camp·stool /ˈkæmpstuːl/ *n* [C] *BrE* a small folding seat with no back

cam·pus /ˈkæmpəs/ *n* [C,U] **1** the land and buildings of a university or college, including the buildings where students live: *a beautiful campus in New England* | **on/off campus** *Most first-year students live on campus.* **2** the land and buildings belonging to a large company: *the Microsoft campus outside Seattle*

cam·shaft /ˈkæmʃɑːft $ -ʃæft/ *n* [C] a metal bar that a CAM is fastened to in an engine

can¹ S1 W1 /kən; *strong* kæn/ *modal verb negative short form* **can't**
1 ABILITY to be able to do something or to know how to do something: *You can swim, can't you?* | *Even a small personal computer can store vast amounts of information.* | *Gabriella can speak French fluently.* | *I'm afraid Mr Harding can't see you now – he's busy.* | *The police are doing all they can to find her.*
2 REQUESTING *spoken* used to ask someone to do something or give you something: *Can I have a cigarette, please?* | *Can you help me lift this box?*
3 ALLOWED to be allowed to do something or to have the right or power to do something: *You can't park here – it's a no parking zone.* | *'Can we go home now, please?' 'No you can't.'* | *Any police officer can insist on seeing a driver's license.*
4 POSSIBILITY used to say that something is possible: *I am confident that a solution can be found.* | *There can be no doubt that he is guilty.* | *Some packaging cartons can be stored flat.* | *Can he still be alive after all this time?*
5 SEEING/HEARING ETC used with the verbs 'see', 'hear', 'feel', 'taste', and 'smell', and with verbs connected with thinking, to mean that someone sees something, hears something etc: *Here they are – I can see their car.* | *Can you smell something burning?* | *I can't understand why you're so upset.* | *He can't remember where he put the tickets.*
6 NOT TRUE [in negatives] used to say that you do not believe that something is true: *This can't be the right road.* | *It can't be easy caring for a man and a child who are not your own.*
7 SHOULD NOT [in questions and negatives] used to say that someone should not or must not do something: *You can't expect the world to change overnight.* | *We can't go on like this.* | *Jill's left her husband, but can you blame her after the way he treated her?*
8 SURPRISE/ANGER [usually in questions and negatives] *spoken* used when you are surprised or angry: *You can't be serious!* | *They can't have arrived already, surely!* | *How can you be so stupid!*
9 SOMETIMES used to say what sometimes happens or how someone sometimes behaves: *It can be quite cold here at night.* | *Peter can be really annoying.*
10 GIVING ORDERS *spoken* used to tell someone in an angry way to do something: *And you can stop that quarrelling, the pair of you.* | *If you won't keep quiet, you can get out.*

C

WORD CHOICE: can, could, be able to
Use **can** and **be able to** to say that someone has the ability to do something. **Be able to** is more formal: *Can you swim?* | *Young children are not able to open the bottle.*
Use **could** to say that someone has the ability to do something, but does not do it: *He could do a lot better.* **Could** is also the past form of **can**. Use **could** or a past form of **be able to** to say that someone had the ability to do something in the past: *She could ride a bike when she was three.* | *He was able to walk with a stick.*
⚠ In the following cases, you cannot use **can**. You must use **be able to**:
with **used to**, to say that someone had the ability to do something in the past but no longer does: *I used to be able to play the violin.*
to talk about future ability. Use **will be able to**: *After only a few lessons, you will be able to understand basic Spanish.*
after other verbs, for example **might**, **may**, **would**, **want**, or **hope**: *He might be able to fix your car.* | *You should be able to taste the difference.* | *I want her to be able to use a computer.*

cans

tin can
oil can
spray can
can of tuna
watering can

can² S2 /kæn/ *n* [C]
1 a metal container in which food or drink is preserved without air: *a Coke can* | [+of] *All we've got is a couple of cans of soup.*; → see picture at **CONTAINER**
2 a special metal container that keeps the liquid inside it under pressure. The liquid is released as a SPRAY when you press the button: [+of] *a can of hairspray*
3 *especially AmE* a metal container with a lid that can be removed, used for holding liquid: *Two large cans of paint ought to be enough.*
4 can of worms a very complicated situation that causes a lot of problems when you start to deal with it: *I just don't know what to do – every solution I can think of would just open up a whole new can of worms.*
5 in the can *informal* a film that is in the can is complete and ready to be shown
6 the can *informal* **a)** a prison **b)** *AmE* a toilet → **carry the can** at **CARRY¹** (26)

can³ *v* **canned, canning** [T] *AmE* **1** to preserve food by putting it into a metal container from which all the air is removed; ⊟ **tin** *BrE*; → **canned** **2** *informal* to dismiss someone from a job; ⊟ **sack** **3 can it!** *spoken* used to tell someone to stop talking or making a noise

Ca·na·di·an¹ /kəˈneɪdiən/ *adj* relating to Canada or its people

Canadian² *n* [C] someone from Canada

Ca,nadian ˈbacon *n* [U] *AmE* meat from the back or sides of a pig, served in thin narrow pieces

ca·nal /kəˈnæl/ *n* [C] a long passage dug into the ground and filled with water, either for boats to travel along, or to take water to a place: *We walked along by the side of the canal.* | *the Panama Canal* | **by canal** *The goods were transported by canal to London.*

ca·nal boat *n* [C] a long narrow boat that is used for travelling on a canal

can·a·lize also **-ise** *BrE* /'kænəl-aɪz/ *v* [T] **1** *technical* to make a river deeper or straighter, especially in order to prevent flooding **2** *formal* to direct people's energy or feelings towards one particular thing

can·a·pé /'kænəpeɪ $ -pi, -peɪ/ *n* [C] a small piece of bread with cheese, meat etc on top, which is served with drinks at a party

ca·nard /kæ'nɑːd $ kə'nɑːrd/ *n* [C] *written* a piece of news that is false and is told to people deliberately in order to harm someone

ca·nar·y /kə'neəri $ -'neri/ *n plural* **canaries** [C] a small yellow bird that people often keep as a pet

ca·nas·ta /kə'næstə/ *n* [U] a card game

can·can /'kænkæn/ *n* [C] a fast dance in which a line of women kick their legs high into the air

can·cel S2 /'kænsəl/ *v* **cancelled, cancelling** *BrE*, **canceled, canceling** *AmE* **1** [I,T] to say that an event that was planned will not happen: *Our flight was cancelled.* | *I'm afraid I'll have to cancel our meeting tomorrow.* | *You'll just have to ring John and cancel.* **2** [I,T] to end an agreement or arrangement that you have with someone: *I phoned the hotel to cancel my reservation.* | *The bank agreed to cancel all the company's debts.* **3** [T] to say officially that a document can no longer be used or no longer has any legal effect: *I phoned the bank to cancel the cheque.*
cancel sth ⇔ **out** *phr v*
if two things cancel each other out, they are equally important and have an opposite effect to each other, so that neither one has any effect: *The losses in our overseas division have cancelled out the profits made in the home market.*

can·cel·la·tion /,kænsə'leɪʃən/ *n* [C,U] **1** a decision that an event that was planned will not happen: *Rail passengers are fed up with cancellations and delays.* | *Bad weather led to the cancellation of the game.* **2** a decision to end an agreement or arrangement that you have with someone: *There is a cancellation fee of £20.* | *The restaurant is fully booked this evening, but we will let you know if there are any cancellations.*

can·cer S2 W2 /'kænsə $ -ər/ *n* **1** a very serious disease in which cells in one part of the body start to grow in a way that is not normal; → **tumour**: *A lot of cancers can now be treated successfully.* | **lung/breast/stomach etc cancer** *Smoking causes lung cancer.* | *She was told last year that she* **had cancer**. | *He* **died of cancer** *last month.* | [+of] *cancer of the womb* | *a new treatment which effectively kills* **cancer cells** **2** [C] an evil influence that affects a lot of people and is difficult to stop: *Drug abuse is the cancer of our society.* —**cancerous** *adj*: *a cancerous growth* | *cancerous cells*

Cancer *n* **1** [U] the fourth sign of the ZODIAC, represented by a CRAB, which some people believe affects the character and life of people born between June 22 and July 23 **2** also **Cancerian** /kæn'sɪəriən $ -'sɪr-/ [C] someone who was born between June 22 and July 23 —**Cancerian** *adj*

can·de·la·bra /,kændə'lɑːbrə/ also **can·de·la·brum** /-'lɑːbrəm/ *n plural* **candelabra** [C] a decorative object which holds several CANDLES or lamps

can·did /'kændɪd/ *adj* telling the truth, even when the truth may be unpleasant or embarrassing; ▤ **frank**: [+about] *She was quite candid about the difficulties the government is having.* | [+with] *He was remarkably candid with me.* | *It struck me as an unusually candid confession for a politician.* —**candidly** *adv* → CANDOUR

can·di·da /'kændɪdə/ *n* [U] an infection in the mouth and throat of children or in a woman's VAGINA

can·di·da·cy /'kændɪdəsi/ *plural* **candidacies** also **can·di·da·ture** /'kændɪdətʃə $ -ər/ *n* [C,U] the position of being one of the people who are competing in an election; → **candidate**: [+for] *The local party supported her candidacy for the post of chairman.* | **announce/declare your candidacy** *He has not yet officially announced his candidacy for the presidential election.* | *She later* **withdrew** *her* **candidacy**.

can·di·date W2 /'kændɪdət $ -deɪt, -dɪt/ *n* [C] **1** someone who is being considered for a job or is competing in an election: *a presidential candidate* | [+for] *There are only three candidates for the job.* **2** *BrE* someone who is taking an examination: *Candidates are not allowed to use a calculator in this exam.* **3** someone or something that is likely to experience or get something: [+for] *The school is an obvious candidate for extra funding.* | *The novel must be a* **prime candidate** *for the award.*

can·died /'kændid/ *adj* [only before noun] candied fruit has been cooked in sugar as a way of preserving it

can·dle S3 /'kændl/ *n* [C] **1** a stick of WAX with a string through the middle, which you burn to give light **2 can't hold a candle to sb/sth** *informal* if something or someone cannot hold a candle to something or someone else, they are not as good as the other thing or person: *No other singer can hold a candle to her.* → **burn the candle at both ends** at BURN[1] (19)

can·dle·light /'kændl-laɪt/ *n* [U] the gentle light produced when a candle burns: *The jewels sparkled in the candlelight.* | **by candlelight** *We ate by candlelight.*

candle-lit *adj* lit by the gentle light of candles: *a candle-lit dinner for two*

can·dle·stick /'kændl,stɪk/ *n* [C] a specially shaped metal or wooden stick that you put a candle into

can·dle·wick /'kændl,wɪk/ *n* [U] cloth decorated with patterns of raised threads

can-'do *adj* [only before noun] *informal* willing to try anything and expect that it will work: *He has a wonderful can-do attitude towards work.*

can·dour *BrE*; **candor** *AmE* /'kændə $ -ər/ *n* [U] the quality of being honest and telling the truth, even when the truth may be unpleasant or embarrassing; → **candid**: *She spoke with remarkable candour about her experiences.*

can·dy S3 /'kændi/ *n plural* **candies** [C,U] **1** *AmE* a sweet food made from sugar or chocolate: *a box of candies* | *a candy bar* | *Do you want a piece of candy?* **2 mind/brain candy** *informal* something that is entertaining or pleasant to look at, but which you do not approve of because you think it is not serious: *Most video games are just brain candy.*

candy apple *n* [C] *AmE* an apple covered with a sweet sticky mixture

candy cane *n* [C] *AmE* a stick of hard red and white sugar with a curved end

can·dy·floss /'kændiflɒs $ -flɑːs, -flɔːs/ *n* [U] *BrE* a type of sweet food made from sticky threads of pink sugar wound around a stick

candy-striped *adj* candy-striped cloth has narrow coloured lines on a white background

cane¹ /keɪn/ *n* **1** [U] thin pieces of the stems of plants, used for making furniture and baskets: *a cane chair* | *cane furniture* **2** [C] a long, thin stick made from the stem of a plant, used for supporting other plants in a garden **3** [C] a long thin stick with a curved handle that you can use to help you walk **4** [C] a stick that was used in the past by teachers to hit children with as a punishment: *Children knew that if they misbehaved they would* **get the cane** (=be punished with a cane).

cane² *v* [T] to punish someone, especially a child, by hitting them with a stick

ca·nine¹ /'keɪnaɪn, 'kæ- $ 'keɪ-/ *adj* relating to dogs: *canine diseases* | *her loyal canine friend*

canine² *n* [C] **1** also **canine tooth** one of the four sharp pointed teeth in the front of your mouth **2** *formal* a dog

can·is·ter /'kænɪstə $ -ər/ *n* [C] **1** a round metal case that contains gas and bursts when it is thrown or fired from a gun: *Police fired tear gas canisters into the crowd.* **2** a metal container for keeping something in: *a tea canister* | *a petrol canister*

can·ker /'kæŋkə $ -ər/ *n* [C,U] **1** an evil influence that spreads quickly among people and is difficult to destroy: *the canker of violence in modern society* **2** a disease that affects trees or plants

can·na·bis /'kænəbɪs/ *n* [U] *especially BrE* an illegal drug that is usually smoked in cigarettes; ◲ **marijuana** *AmE*

canned /kænd/ *adj* **1** canned food is preserved in a round metal container; ◲ **tinned** *BrE*: *canned tomatoes* | *canned fruit* **2** canned music/laughter music or laughter that has been recorded and is used on television or in radio programmes

can·nel·lo·ni /ˌkænəˈləʊni $ -ˈloʊ-/ *n* [U] small tubes of PASTA filled with meat and sometimes cheese, and covered in a sauce

can·ne·ry /'kænəri/ *n plural* **canneries** [C] a factory where food is put into cans

can·ni·bal /'kænɪbəl/ *n* [C] **1** a person who eats human flesh **2** an animal that eats the flesh of other animals of the same kind —**cannibalism** *n* [U] —**cannibalistic** /ˌkænɪbəˈlɪstɪk/ *adj*

can·ni·bal·ize also **-ise** *BrE* /'kænɪbəlaɪz/ *v* [T] **1** to take parts of one machine to use in another, for example to repair it: *The truck was cannibalized for parts.* **2** *technical* if one of a company's products cannibalizes another, it takes sales away from it

can·non¹ /'kænən/ *n* [C] a large heavy powerful gun that was used in the past to fire heavy metal balls

cannon² *v* [I always + adv/prep] to hit someone or something while moving fast: [+into] *She came hurtling round the corner and cannoned straight into me.* | [+off] *The ball cannoned off the far post.*

can·non·ade /ˌkænəˈneɪd/ *n* [C] a continuous heavy attack by large guns

can·non·ball /'kænənbɔːl $ -bɒːl/ *n* [C] a heavy iron ball fired from a cannon

cannon ˌfodder *n* [U] ordinary soldiers whose lives are not considered to be very important, and who are sent to fight where they are likely to get killed

can·not /'kænət, -nɒt $ -nɑːt/ *modal verb* **1** a negative form of 'can': *Mrs Armstrong regrets that she cannot accept your kind invitation.* **2** cannot but *formal* used to say that you feel you have to do something: *One cannot but admire her determination.*

can·ny /'kæni/ *adj* **1** clever, careful, and not easily deceived, especially in business or politics: *a canny political advisor* **2** nice, good – used in Scotland: *a canny lass* —**cannily** *adv*

ca·noe¹ /kəˈnuː/ *n* [C] a long light boat that is pointed at both ends and which you move along using a PADDLE → **paddle your own canoe** at PADDLE² (5)

canoe² *v* [I] to travel by canoe —**canoeist** *n* [C]

can·oe·ing /kəˈnuːɪŋ/ *n* [U] the sport of travelling in a canoe; → see picture at OUTDOOR

can·on /'kænən/ *n* [C] **1** a Christian priest who has special duties in a CATHEDRAL **2** *formal* a standard, rule, or principle, or set of these, that are believed by a group of people to be right and good: [+of] *Mapplethorpe's pictures offended the canons of American good taste.* **3** *formal* **a)** a list of books or pieces of music that are officially recognized as being the work of a certain writer: *the Shakespearean canon* **b)** all the books that are recognized as being the most important pieces of literature: *the literary canon* **4** a piece of music in which a tune is started by one singer or

---

instrument and is copied by each of the others **5** an established law of the Christian church

ca·non·i·cal /kəˈnɒnɪkəl $ kəˈnɑː-/ *adj* **1** according to CANON LAW **2** *technical* in the simplest mathematical form

can·on·ize also **-ise** *BrE* /'kænənaɪz/ *v* [T] to officially state that a dead person is a SAINT —**canonization** /ˌkænənaɪˈzeɪʃən $ -nənə-/ *n* [C,U]

ˌcanon ˈlaw *n* [U] the laws of the Christian Church

ca·noo·dle /kəˈnuːdl/ *v* [I] *BrE old-fashioned* if two people canoodle, they kiss and hold each other in a sexual way

ˈcan ˌopener *n* [C] a tool for opening a can of food

can·o·py /'kænəpi/ *n plural* **canopies** [C] **1** a cover made of cloth that is fixed above a bed, seat etc as a decoration or as a shelter **2** the leaves and branches of trees, that make a kind of roof in a forest: *the forest canopy* **3** *literary* something that spreads above you like a roof: *a canopy of twinkling stars* —**canopied** *adj*

canst /kənst; *strong* kænst/ *v* **thou canst** *old use* used to mean 'you can' when talking to one person

can't /kɑːnt $ kænt/ **1** the short form of cannot: *Sorry, I can't help you.* | *You can swim, can't you?* **2** used to say that something is impossible or unlikely: *You can't miss it – it's a huge building.*

cant¹ /kænt/ *n* **1** [U] insincere talk about moral or religious principles by someone who is pretending to be better than they really are **2** [U] *formal* special words used by a particular group of people, especially in order to keep things secret; ◲ *slang*: *thieves' cant*

cant² *v* [I,T] to lean, or make something lean

Can·tab /'kæntæb/ used after the title of a degree from Cambridge University: *Jane Smith MA (Cantab)*

can·ta·loup, cantaloupe /'kæntəluːp $ -loup/ *n* [C,U] a type of MELON with a hard green skin and sweet orange flesh

can·tan·ker·ous /kænˈtæŋkərəs/ *adj* bad-tempered and complaining a lot: *a cantankerous old man*

can·ta·ta /kænˈtɑːtə, kən- $ kən-/ *n* [C] a piece of religious music for singers and instruments

can·teen /kænˈtiːn/ *n* [C] **1** *BrE* a place in a factory, school etc where meals are provided, usually quite cheaply **2** a small container in which water or other drink is carried by soldiers, travellers etc **3** a canteen of cutlery *BrE* a set of knives, forks, and spoons in a box

can·ter /'kæntə $ -ər/ *v* [I,T] to ride or make a horse run quite fast, but not as fast as possible; → **gallop** —**canter** *n* [C]: *She rode off at a canter.*

can·ti·cle /'kæntɪkəl/ *n* [C] a short religious song usually sung with words from the Bible

can·ti·le·ver /'kæntɪˌliːvə $ -tl-iːvər/ *n* [C] a long piece of metal or wood that sticks out from an upright post or wall and supports a shelf, the end of a bridge etc —**cantilevered** *adj*: *a cantilevered staircase*

can·to /'kæntəʊ $ -toʊ/ *n plural* **cantos** [C] one of the parts into which a very long poem is divided; → **stanza**

can·ton /'kæntɒn, kænˈtɒn $ 'kæntən, -tɑːn/ *n* [C] one of the areas that a country such as Switzerland is divided up into, that has limited political powers

Can·to·nese /ˌkæntəˈniːz/ *n* [U] a Chinese language spoken in Southern China and Hong Kong

can·ton·ment /kænˈtuːnmənt $ -ˈtɑːn-/ *n* [C] *technical* a camp where soldiers live

can·tor /'kæntə, -tɔː $ -ər, -ɔːr/ *n* [C] **1** a man who leads the prayers and songs in a Jewish religious service **2** the leader of a group of singers in a church

Ca·nuck /kəˈnʌk/ *n* [C] *AmE informal* someone from Canada

can·vas /'kænvəs/ *n* **1** [U] strong cloth used to make bags, tents, shoes etc: *a canvas bag* **2** [C] a painting done with oil paints, or the piece of cloth it is painted on: *The gallery has a canvas by Paul Cézanne.* | *'Four*

Women on a Bench', oil on canvas, 1991 **3 a broader/ wider/larger canvas** the whole of a situation, and not just a part of it: *These questions must be considered on a broader canvas.* **4 under canvas** BrE in a tent

can·vass /'kænvəs/ *v* **1** [I,T] to try to persuade people to support a political party, politician, plan etc by going to see them and talking to them, especially when you want them to vote for you in an election: *Candidates from all three parties were out canvassing in Darlington today.* | [+**for**] *Chapman spent the rest of May canvassing for votes.* | *The US has been* **canvassing support** *from other Asian states.* **2** [I,T] to ask people about something in order to get their opinion or to get information: *Police canvassed the neighborhood, but didn't find any witnesses.* **3** [T] to talk about a problem, suggestion etc in detail: *A committee was set up to* **canvass** *the city's educational* **options.** —**canvasser** *n* [C] —**canvass** *n* [C]

can·yon /'kænjən/ *n* [C] a deep valley with very steep sides of rock that usually has a river running through it → see picture at HOLE

can·yon·ing /'kænjəniŋ/ also **can·yon·eer·ing** /ˌkænjə'nɪərɪŋ $ -'nɪr-/ AmE *n* [U] a sport in which you walk and swim along a fast-moving river at the bottom of a canyon

cap¹ S3 /kæp/ *n* [C]
1 HAT a) a type of flat hat that has a curved part sticking out at the front, and is often worn as part of a uniform: *a baseball cap* | *old men in flat caps* | *a chauffeur's peaked cap* **b)** a covering that fits very closely to your head: *a swimming cap* | *a shower cap* **c)** a type of simple hat that fits very closely to your head, worn especially by women in the past: *a white lace cap*
2 COVERING a protective covering that you put on the end or top of an object; ▣ **top**: *Make sure you put the cap back on the pen.* | *a bottle cap* → see picture at LID
3 LIMIT an upper limit that is put on the amount of money that someone can earn, spend, or borrow: *a cap on local council spending*
4 SPORT BrE **a)** if a sports person wins a cap or is given a cap, he or she is chosen to play for their country: *He won his first England cap against Wales in 1994.* **b)** a sports person who has played for his or her country: *Mason is one of two new caps in the team.*
5 SMALL EXPLOSIVE a small paper container with explosive inside it, used especially in toy guns
6 SEX a CONTRACEPTIVE made of a round piece of rubber that a woman puts inside her VAGINA; ▣ **diaphragm**
7 go cap in hand (to sb) BrE; **go hat in hand** AmE to ask for money or help in a very respectful way, from someone who has a lot more power than you: *Elderly people should receive a heating allowance every winter, instead of having to go cap in hand to the government.*
→ **FLAT CAP, ICE CAP, KNEECAP, MOB CAP, SKULL CAP, TOECAP;** → **a feather in your cap** at FEATHER¹ (2); → **if the cap fits (, wear it)** at FIT¹ (8); → **put your thinking cap on** at THINKING¹ (3)

cap² *v* **capped, capping** [T]
1 COVER be capped with sth to have a particular substance on top: *a graceful tower capped with a golden dome* | *magnificent cliffs capped by lovely wild flowers*
2 LIMIT [often passive] to limit the amount of something, especially money, that can be used, allowed, or spent: *the only county to have its spending capped by the government*
3 GOOD/BAD to say, do, or be something that is better, worse, or more extreme than something that has just happened or been said: *Well, we went three nights with no sleep at all. I bet you can't cap that!*
4 be capped by sth to have something very good or very bad at the end of an event: *a fabulous weekend, capped by dinner in the Times Square Hotel*
5 SPORT [usually passive] BrE to choose someone for a national sports team: *He's been capped three times for England.*
6 to cap it all (off) BrE spoken used before a statement

to say that something is the last in a series of annoying, unpleasant, or funny events: *To cap it all, the phones didn't work, and there was no hot water.*
7 snow-capped, white-capped etc with snow on top, with white on top etc: *snow-capped mountains*
8 TOOTH to cover a tooth with a special hard white substance: *He's had his teeth capped.*

cap. also **caps.** the abbreviation of *capital letter*

ca·pa·bil·i·ty S3 /ˌkeɪpə'bɪlₑti/ *n plural* **capabilities** [C]
1 the natural ability, skill, or power that makes a machine, person, or organization able to do something, especially something difficult: *the country's manufacturing capability* | **capability to do sth** *Does the company have the capability to change to meet market needs?* | *I can speak French, but simultaneous translation is* **beyond** *my* **capabilities** (=too difficult).
2 the ability that a country has to take a particular kind of military action: **military/nuclear etc capability** *America's nuclear capability*

ca·pa·ble S2 W2 /'keɪpəbəl/ *adj*
1 capable of (doing) sth having the qualities or ability needed to do something: *I don't think he's capable of murder.* | *The company isn't capable of handling an order that large.* | *I'm perfectly capable of looking after myself, thank you!*
2 able to do things well: *a strong, capable woman*
3 capable hands someone who is able to do something well: *Helen was put in the capable hands of hair stylist Daniel Herson.* —**capably** *adv*

ca·pa·cious /kə'peɪʃəs/ *adj formal* able to contain a lot: *a capacious suitcase* —**capaciousness** *n* [U]

ca·pac·i·tor /kə'pæsₑtə $ -ər/ *n* [C] a piece of equipment that collects and stores electricity

ca·pac·i·ty S3 W2 /kə'pæsₑti/ *n plural* **capacities**
1 [singular] the amount of space a container, room etc has to hold things or people: [+**of**] *The fuel tank has a capacity of 40 litres.* | *The room had seating capacity for about 80.* | *The orchestra played to a* **capacity crowd** (=the largest number of people who can fit into a hall, theatre etc). | *All the hotels were* **filled to capacity** (=completely full).
2 [C,U] someone's ability to do something: [+**for**] *a child's capacity for learning* | *an infinite capacity for love* | **capacity to do sth** *a capacity to think in an original way*
3 [singular] *formal* someone's job, position, or duty: ▣ **role**: **in a professional/official etc capacity** *Rollins will be working in an advisory capacity on this project.* | **(do sth) in your capacity as sth** *I attended the meeting in my capacity as chairman of the safety committee.*
4 [singular, U] the amount of something that a factory, company, machine etc can produce or deal with: *The company has the capacity to build 1500 trucks a year.* | *The factory has been working* **at full capacity** (=making the most amount of things that it can)
5 [singular, U] the size or power of something such as an engine: *The tax on cars is still based on engine capacity.*

cape /keɪp/ *n* [C] **1** a long loose piece of clothing without SLEEVES that fastens around your neck and hangs from your shoulders **2** a large piece of land surrounded on three sides by water: *Cape Cod*

ca·per¹ /'keɪpə $ -ər/ *v* [I always + adv/prep] to jump around and play in a happy excited way

caper² *n* [C] **1** a small dark green part of a flower used in cooking to give a sour taste to food **2** *informal* a planned activity, especially an illegal or dangerous one: *I'm too old for this sort of caper.* **3** behaviour or an activity that is amusing or silly and not serious: *the comic capers of a cartoon cat and mouse* **4** a short jumping or dancing movement

ca·pil·la·ry /kə'pɪləri $ 'kæpəleri/ *n plural* **capillaries** [C] the smallest type of BLOOD VESSEL (=tube carrying blood) in the body

ca·pillary 'action / $,.... '../ *n* [U] *technical* the force that makes a liquid rise up a narrow tube

cap·i·tal¹ S3 W1 /'kæpɪtl/ n
1 CITY [C] an important city where the main government of a country, state etc is: *Washington, D.C., the capital of the United States*
2 MONEY [singular, U] money or property, especially when it is used to start a business or to produce more wealth: *The government is eager to attract foreign capital.* → WORKING CAPITAL, VENTURE CAPITAL
3 LETTER [C] a letter of the alphabet written in its large form as it is, for example, at the beginning of someone's name; → lower case, upper case
4 CENTRE OF ACTIVITY [C] a place that is a centre for an industry, business, or other activity: *Hollywood is the capital of the movie industry.*
5 make capital from/out of sth to use a situation or event to help you get an advantage
6 BUILDING [C] *technical* the top part of a COLUMN (=a long stone post used in some buildings)

capital² S3 W3 adj
1 a capital letter is one that is written or printed in its large form; → lower case, upper case: *capital 'B'*
2 relating to money that you use to start a business or to make more money: *capital investments*
3 capital offence/crime an offence that is punished by death
4 trouble with a capital T, fast with a capital F etc *informal* used with any word in order to emphasize that you are talking about an extreme type of something
5 *old-fashioned* excellent

capital 'assets n [plural] *technical* machines, buildings, and other property belonging to a company

capital 'gains n [plural] profits you make by selling your possessions

capital 'gains tax n [U] a tax that you pay on profits that you make when you sell your possessions

capital 'goods n [plural] goods such as machines or buildings that are made for the purpose of producing other goods; → consumer goods

capital-in'tensive adj a capital-intensive business, industry etc needs a lot of money in order to operate properly; → labour-intensive

cap·i·tal·is·m /'kæpɪtl-ɪzəm/ n [U] an economic and political system in which businesses belong mostly to private owners, not to the government; → communism, socialism

cap·i·tal·ist¹ /'kæpɪtl-ɪst/ n [C] **1** someone who supports capitalism; → communist, socialist **2** someone who owns or controls a lot of money and lends it to businesses, banks etc to produce more wealth → venture capitalist at VENTURE CAPITAL

capitalist² also **cap·i·ta·lis·tic** /ˌkæpɪtl'ɪstɪk◂/ adj using or supporting capitalism; → communist, socialist: *the capitalist system*

cap·i·tal·ize also **-ise** BrE /'kæpɪtl-aɪz/ v [T] **1** to write a letter of the alphabet using a CAPITAL letter **2** to supply a business with money so that it can operate **3** *technical* to calculate the value of a business based on the value of its SHARES or on the amount of money it makes —**capitalization** /ˌkæpɪtl-aɪ'zeɪʃən $ -tl-ə-/ n [U]
   capitalize on sth phr v to use a situation or something good that you have, in order to get an advantage for yourself: *Ecuador has capitalized on its natural beauty to attract tourism.*

capital 'levy n [C] *technical* a tax on private or industrial wealth that is paid to the government

capital 'punishment n [U] punishment which involves killing someone who has committed a crime; → death penalty

cap·i·ta·tion /ˌkæpɪ'teɪʃən/ n [C] a tax or payment of the same amount from each person

Cap·i·tol /'kæpɪtl/ n **1 the Capitol** the building in Washington D.C. where the US Congress meets **2** [C] the building in each US state where the people who make the laws for that state meet

Capitol 'Hill n **1** the US Congress **2** the hill in Washington D.C. where the Capitol building stands

ca·pit·u·late /kə'pɪtʃəleɪt/ v [I] **1** *formal* to accept or agree to something that you have been opposing for a long time; ▤ give in: *Helen finally capitulated and let her son have a car.* **2** *formal* to accept defeat by your enemies in a war; ▤ surrender —**capitulation** /kəˌpɪtʃʊ'leɪʃən/ n [C,U]

cap·let /'kæplɪt/ n [C] a small smooth PILL (=solid piece of medicine) with a shape that is slightly longer and narrower than a TABLET (=a small round pill)

cap·o·ei·ra /ˌkæpəʊ'eərə $ ˌkaːpoʊ'erə/ n [U] an Afro-Brazilian mixture of dance, song, and fighting that is similar to the MARTIAL ARTS

ca·pon /'keɪpən $ -paːn, -pən/ n [C] a male chicken that has had its sex organs removed to make it grow big and fat

cap·puc·ci·no /ˌkæpʊ'tʃiːnəʊ $ -noʊ/ n plural **cappuccinos** [C,U] Italian coffee made with hot milk and with chocolate powder on top

ca·price /kə'priːs/ n **1** [C,U] a sudden and unreasonable change of mind or behaviour: *the caprices of a spoilt child* **2** [U] the tendency to change your mind suddenly or behave in an unexpected way

ca·pri·cious /kə'prɪʃəs/ adj **1** likely to change your mind suddenly or behave in an unexpected way: *She was as capricious as her mother had been.* **2** *literary* changing quickly and suddenly: *a capricious wind* —**capriciously** adv

Cap·ri·corn /'kæprɪkɔːn $ -kɔːrn/ n **1** [U] the tenth sign of the ZODIAC, represented by a goat, which some people believe affects the character and life of people born between December 22 and January 20 **2** [C] someone who was born between December 22 and January 20

cap·si·cum /'kæpsɪkəm/ n [C,U] *technical* a kind of PEPPER (=a green, red, or yellow vegetable)

capsize

cap·size /kæp'saɪz $ 'kæpsaɪz/ v [I,T] if a boat capsizes, or if you capsize it, it turns over in the water

caps lock n [singular, U] the button that you press on a computer when you want to use capital letters

cap·stan /'kæpstən/ n [C] a round machine shaped like a drum, used to wind up a rope that pulls or lifts heavy objects

cap·sule /'kæpsjuːl $ -səl/ n [C] **1** a plastic container shaped like a very small tube with medicine inside that you swallow whole; → tablet **2** a small plastic container with a substance or liquid inside **3** the part of a spacecraft in which people live and work: *a space capsule orbiting the Earth* → TIME CAPSULE

C

cap·tain¹ W3 /ˈkæptˌn/ *n* [C]
1 the sailor in charge of a ship, or the pilot in charge of an aircraft: *The Captain and crew welcome you aboard.*
2 a military officer with a fairly high rank → GROUP CAPTAIN
3 someone who leads a team or other group of people: [+of] *Julie's captain of the quiz team.* | *The Black-hawk's **team captain** was the first to score.*
4 captain of industry someone who owns or has an important job in a big company

captain² *v* [T] **1** to lead a group or team of people and be their captain: *The U.S. team, captained by Arthur Ashe, won the Davis Cup in 1981 and 1982.* **2** to be in charge of a ship, aircraft etc

cap·tain·cy /ˈkæptˌnsi/ *n plural* **captaincies** [C,U] the position of being captain of a team, or the period during which someone is captain

cap·tion /ˈkæpʃən/ *n* [C] words printed above or below a picture in a book or newspaper or on a television screen to explain what the picture is showing; → **subtitle** —**caption** *v* [T usually passive]: *a photograph of the couple captioned 'rebuilding their romance'*

cap·ti·vate /ˈkæptˌveɪt/ *v* [T] to attract someone very much, and hold their attention: **be captivated by sb/sth** *He was captivated by her beauty.*

cap·ti·vat·ing /ˈkæptˌveɪtɪŋ/ *adj* very attractive and interesting, in a way that holds your attention: *a captivating smile* | *a captivating account of her child-hood in Beijing*

cap·tive¹ /ˈkæptɪv/ *adj* **1** kept in prison or in a place that you are not allowed to leave: *captive soldiers* | *captive animals* | *His son had been **taken captive** (=became a prisoner) during the raid.* | *a pilot who was **held captive** (=kept as a prisoner) for six years* **2 captive audience** people who listen or watch someone or something because they have to, not because they are interested **3 captive market** the people who must buy a particular product or service, because they need it and there is only one company selling it **4 be captive to sth** to be unable to think or speak freely, because of being influenced too much by something: *Our commu-nities should not be captive to the mistakes of the past.*

captive² *n* [C] someone who is kept as a prisoner, especially in a war

cap·tiv·i·ty /kæpˈtɪvˌti/ *n* [U] when a person or ani-mal is kept in a prison, CAGE etc and not allowed to go where they want: *The hostages were released from captivity.* | **in captivity** *animals bred in captivity*

cap·tor /ˈkæptə $ -ər/ *n* [C] someone who is keeping another person prisoner; → **captive**: *He managed to escape from his captors.*

cap·ture¹ W3 /ˈkæptʃə $ -ər/ *v* [T]
1 PERSON to catch a person and keep them as a prisoner: *Government troops have succeeded in captur-ing the rebel leader.* | *40 captured French soldiers*
2 PLACE/THING to get control of a place or object that previously belonged to an enemy, during a war: *The town was captured after a siege lasting ten days.* | *The Dutch fleet captured two English ships.*
3 ANIMAL to catch an animal after chasing or follow-ing it: *The tiger was finally captured two miles outside the village.*
4 FILM/RECORD/ART to succeed in recording, show-ing, or describing a situation or feeling, using words or pictures: *These photographs capture the essence of working-class life at the turn of the century.* | *The robbery was captured on police video cameras.*
5 capture sb's imagination/attention etc to make some-one feel very interested in something: *His stories of foreign adventure captured my imagination.*
6 capture sb's heart to make someone love you
7 BUSINESS/POLITICS to get something that previ-ously belonged to one of your competitors: *We aim to capture eight percent of the UK wine market.* | *Repub-*

licans captured three Senate seats that had been held by Democrats.
8 capture the headlines to be talked or written about a lot in the newspapers or on television: *Irvine Welsh first captured the headlines with his novel 'Trainspotting'.*
9 COMPUTER *technical* to put something in a form that a computer can use: *The data is captured by an optical scanner.*
10 CHESS to remove one of your opponent's pieces from the board in CHESS

capture² *n* [U] **1** when you catch someone in order to make them a prisoner: *The two soldiers somehow managed to avoid capture.* **2** when soldiers get con-trol of a place that previously belonged to an enemy: [+of] *the capture of Jerusalem in 1099* **3** when you get control of something that previously belonged to one of your competitors **4** when you put information into a form a computer can use

car S1 W1 /kɑː $ kɑːr/ *n* [C]
1 a vehicle with four wheels and an engine, that can carry a small number of passengers

> **by car**
> **get in/into a car**
> **get out of a car**
> **drive a car**
> **park a car**
> **parked car**
> **take the car** (=drive it somewhere)
> **car crash/accident**
> **car chase**
> **car crime**
> **police car**
> **company car** (=a car you are given to use by your company)

> *I've left my bag in the car.* | *I always go to work **by car**.* | *Dan **got out of the car** and locked the door.* | *He wasn't even old enough to **drive a car**.* | *Cars were **parked** on both sides of the road.* | *A line of **parked cars** ran parallel to the pavements.* | *You really ought to walk a bit more, rather than **taking the car** everywhere.* | *Coughlan was killed in a **car accident**.* | *a high-speed **car chase** through the streets of London* | ***Car crime** is the fastest-growing crime.* | ***Police cars** occasionally circled the building.*

⚠ Do not use **go in/out** with 'car'. Use **get in/out**: *She got into her car (NOT went into her car) and drove off.* | *'Stop the car. I want to get out!' (NOT go out)*
2 sleeping/dining/buffet car a train carriage used for sleeping, eating etc
3 *AmE* a train carriage
4 the part of a lift, BALLOON, or AIRSHIP in which people or goods are carried

WORD FOCUS: CAR
big cars: **limousine**, **people carrier** *BrE*, **gas-guzzler** *AmE informal*, **estate car** *BrE*
small cars: **compact** *AmE*, **hatchback** *BrE*
other types of car: **pickup**, **van**, **saloon** *BrE*/**sedan** *AmE*, **sports car**, **convertible**, **SUV** *AmE*, **off-roader**, **four-wheel drive/4X4**
where you park your car: **garage**, **car park** *BrE*/**parking lot** *AmE*, **multi-storey car park** *BrE*, **parking space**, **carport**
someone who drives a car: **driver**, **motorist**, **learner driver**
someone who drives a rich or important person's car for them: **chauffeur**, **driver**

ca·rafe /kəˈræf, kəˈrɑːf/ *n* [C] a glass container with a wide neck, used for serving wine or water at meals → see picture at BOTTLE

ˈcar aˌlarm *n* [C] special equipment in a car that makes a loud noise if anyone tries to steal or damage the car

car·a·mel /ˈkærəməl, -mel/ *n* **1** [C,U] a sticky brown sweet made of boiled sugar, butter, and milk **2** [U]

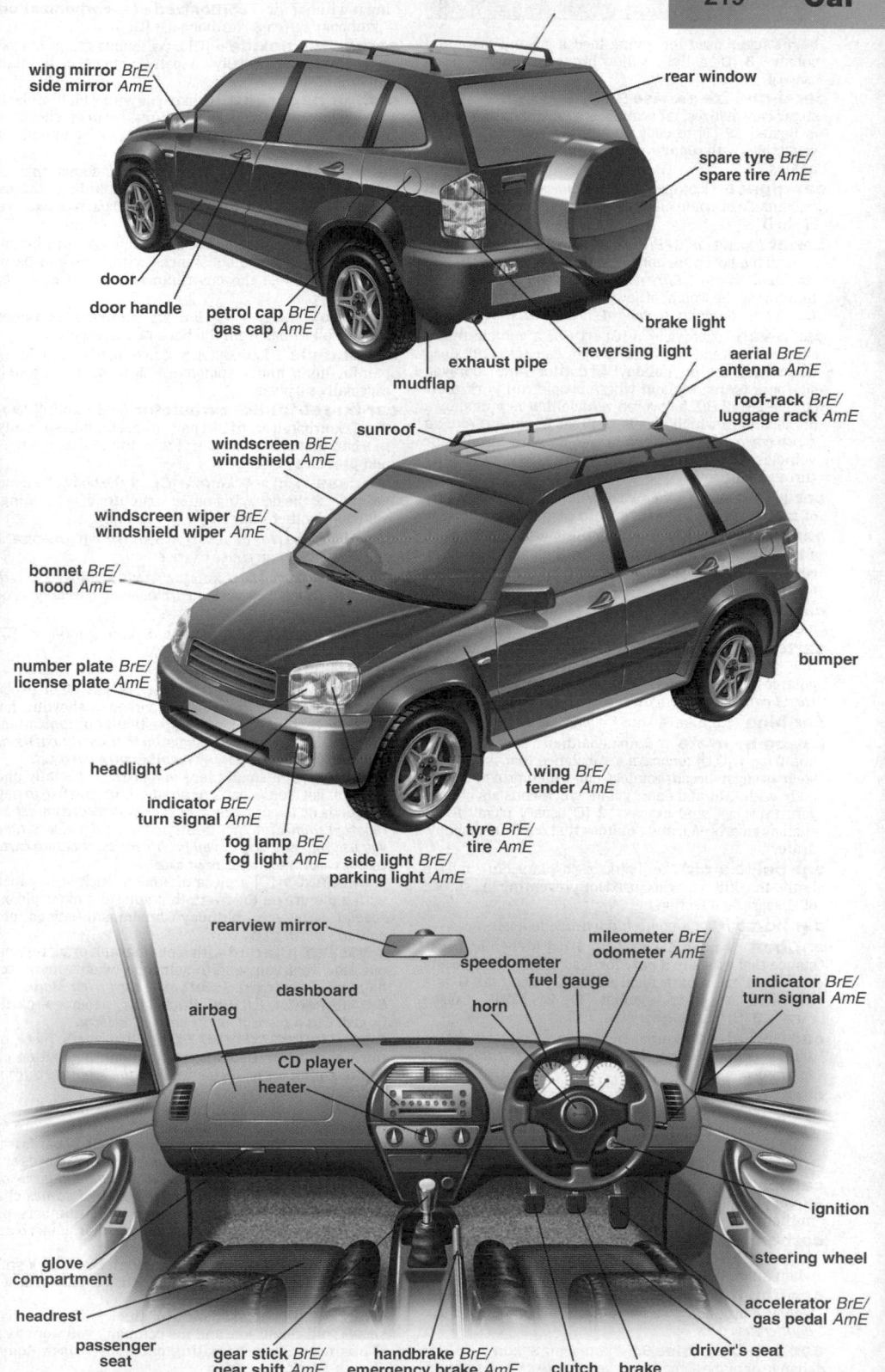

wing mirror *BrE*/
side mirror *AmE*

rear window

spare tyre *BrE*/
spare tire *AmE*

door

door handle

petrol cap *BrE*/
gas cap *AmE*

exhaust pipe

mudflap

brake light

reversing light

aerial *BrE*/
antenna *AmE*

roof-rack *BrE*/
luggage rack *AmE*

sunroof

windscreen *BrE*/
windshield *AmE*

windscreen wiper *BrE*/
windshield wiper *AmE*

bonnet *BrE*/
hood *AmE*

number plate *BrE*/
license plate *AmE*

bumper

headlight

indicator *BrE*/
turn signal *AmE*

fog lamp *BrE*/
fog light *AmE*

side light *BrE*/
parking light *AmE*

wing *BrE*/
fender *AmE*

tyre *BrE*/
tire *AmE*

rearview mirror

speedometer

mileometer *BrE*/
odometer *AmE*

fuel gauge

dashboard

horn

indicator *BrE*/
turn signal *AmE*

airbag

CD player

heater

ignition

glove
compartment

headrest

passenger
seat

gear stick *BrE*/
gear shift *AmE*

handbrake *BrE*/
emergency brake *AmE*

clutch

brake

driver's seat

steering wheel

accelerator *BrE*/
gas pedal *AmE*

burnt sugar used for giving food a special taste and colour   **3** [U] a light yellow-brown colour → **CRÈME CARAMEL**

car·a·mel·ize also **-ise** BrE /'kærəməlaɪz/ v   **1** [I] if sugar caramelizes, it becomes brown and hard when it is heated   **2** [T] to cook something such as fruit or vegetables with sugar —**caramelized** adj: caramelized onions

car·a·pace /'kærəpeɪs/ n [C] technical a hard shell on the outside of some animals such as a CRAB or TORTOISE; ☐ **shell**

car·at /'kærət/ n [C] BrE   **1** also **karat** AmE a unit for measuring how pure gold is: **9/18/22/24 carat gold** a 22 carat gold chain | Pure gold is 24 carats.   **2** a unit for measuring the weight of jewels, equal to 200 MILLIGRAMS: the Orloff diamond, a stone of 194.5 carats

car·a·van /'kærəvæn/ n [C]   **1** BrE a vehicle that a car can pull and in which people can live and sleep when they are on holiday; ☐ **trailer** AmE: **caravan site/park** (=area of land where people can park their caravans)   **2** BrE a covered vehicle that is pulled by a horse, and in which people can live; ☐ **wagon** AmE: a gipsy caravan   **3** a group of people with animals or vehicles who travel together for safety, especially through a desert

car·a·van·ning /'kærəvænɪŋ/ n [U] BrE the activity of taking holidays in a caravan: a caravanning holiday

car·a·van·se·rai /ˌkærə'vænsəraɪ/ n [C] a hotel with a large open central area, used in the past in Eastern countries by groups of people and animals travelling together

car·a·way /'kærəweɪ/ n [C,U] a plant whose seeds are used in cooking

carb /kɑːb $ kɑːrb/ n [C] informal   **1** BrE a CARBURETTOR   **2** [usually plural] especially AmE a food such as rice, potatoes, or bread that contains CARBOHYDRATE: Before a race I eat plenty of carbs.

car·bine /'kɑːbaɪn $ 'kɑːr-/ n [C] a short light RIFLE

car·bo·hy·drate /ˌkɑːbəʊ'haɪdreɪt, -drət $ ˌkɑːrboʊ-/ n   **1** [C,U] technical a substance that is in foods such as sugar, bread, potatoes etc, which provides your body with heat and energy and which consists of oxygen, HYDROGEN, and CARBON   **2** [C usually plural] foods such as rice, bread, and potatoes that contain carbohydrates

car·bol·ic a·cid /kɑːˌbɒlɪk 'æsɪd $ kɑːr,bɑː-/ n [U] a liquid that kills BACTERIA, used for preventing the spread of disease or infection

'car bomb n [C] a bomb hidden inside a car

car·bon /'kɑːbən $ 'kɑːr-/ n   **1** [U] a chemical substance that exists in a pure form as diamonds, GRAPHITE etc, or in an impure form as coal, petrol etc. It is a chemical ELEMENT: symbol C   **2** [C,U] CARBON PAPER   **3** [C] a CARBON COPY (1)

car·bon·at·ed /'kɑːbəneɪtɪd $ 'kɑːr-/ adj carbonated drinks contain small bubbles; → **fizzy**: carbonated spring water

ˌcarbon 'copy n [C]   **1** a copy, especially of something that has been TYPED using CARBON PAPER; → **cc**   **2** someone or something that is very similar to another person or thing: [+of] The robbery is a carbon copy of one that took place last year.

ˌcarbon 'dating n [U] a method of finding out the age of very old objects by measuring the amount of carbon in them

ˌcarbon di'oxide n [U] the gas produced when animals breathe out, when carbon is burned in air, or when animal or vegetable substances decay

car·bon·if·er·ous /ˌkɑːbə'nɪfərəs‹ $ ˌkɑːr-/ adj technical producing or containing carbon or coal: carboniferous rocks

car·bon·ize also **ise** BrE /'kɑːbənaɪz $ 'kɑːr-/ v [I,T] to change or make something change into CARBON by burn-

ing it without air —**carbonized** adj —**carbonization** /ˌkɑːbənaɪ'zeɪʃən $ ˌkɑːrbənə-/ n [U]

ˌcarbon mo'noxide n [U] a poisonous gas produced when CARBON, especially in petrol, burns in a small amount of air

'carbon ˌpaper n [C,U] thin paper with a blue or black substance on one side, that you put between sheets of paper when TYPING on a typewriter in order to make a copy onto the second sheet of paper

'carbon sink n [C] a large area of forest that is believed to help the environment by taking in CARBON from the air so that the effects of GLOBAL WARMING are reduced

'carbon ˌtax n [C,U] a tax on businesses and industries which produce substances with a carbon base, that can damage the environment: carbon taxes on fossil fuels

ˌcar 'boot ˌsale n [C] BrE an outdoor sale where people sell things from the back of their cars

car·bun·cle /'kɑːbʌŋkəl $ 'kɑːr-/ n [C]   **1** a large painful lump under someone's skin   **2** a red jewel, especially a GARNET

car·bu·ret·tor BrE; **carburetor** AmE /ˌkɑːbjʊ'retə, -bə- $ 'kɑːrbəreɪtər/ n [C] a part of an engine, especially in a car, that mixes the petrol with air so that it burns and provides power

car·cass /'kɑːkəs $ 'kɑːr-/ n [C]   **1** the body of a dead animal   **2** the decaying outer structure of a building, vehicle, or other object

car·cin·o·gen /kɑː'sɪnədʒən $ kɑːr-/ n [C] medical a substance that can cause CANCER

car·cin·o·gen·ic /ˌkɑːsɪnə'dʒenɪk‹ $ ˌkɑːr-/ adj likely to cause CANCER: the carcinogenic effects of coal dust

car·ci·no·ma /ˌkɑːsɪ'nəʊmə $ ˌkɑːrsɪ'noʊ-/ n [C] medical a CANCER

card¹ [S1] [W2] /kɑːd $ kɑːrd/ n

1 INFORMATION [C] a small piece of plastic or paper containing information about a person or showing, for example, that they belong to a particular organization, club etc: Employees must show their **identity cards** at the gate. | I haven't got my **membership card** yet.

2 MONEY [C] a small piece of plastic, especially one that you get from a bank or shop, which you use to pay for goods or to get money: Lost or stolen cards must be reported immediately. | a £10 phone card | Every time you use your store card, you get air miles. → **CHARGE CARD, CHEQUE CARD, CREDIT CARD, DEBIT CARD**

3 GREETINGS [C] a piece of folded thick stiff paper with a picture on the front, that you send to people on special occasions: **birthday/Christmas/greetings etc card** a Mother's Day card

4 HOLIDAY [C] a card with a photograph or picture on one side, that you send to someone when you are on holiday; ☐ **postcard**: I sent you a card from Madrid.

5 STIFF PAPER [U] BrE thick stiff paper; → **cardboard**: Cut a piece of white card 12 × 10cm.

6 FOR WRITING INFORMATION [C] a small piece of thick stiff paper that information can be written or printed on: a set of recipe cards | the score card from their golf game

7 GAMES [C] **a)** a small piece of thick stiff paper with numbers and signs or pictures one side. There are 52 cards in a set; ☐ **playing card: pack/deck of cards** (=a complete set of cards) **b)** game in which these cards are used: I'm no good at cards. | We were having **a game of cards**. | Let's **play cards**. | a book of **card games c)** a small piece of thick stiff paper with numbers or pictures on them, used to play a particular game: a set of cards for playing Snap

8 football/baseball etc card a small piece of thick stiff paper with a picture on one side, that is part of a set which people collect

9 BUSINESS [C] a small piece of thick stiff paper that shows your name, job, and the company you work for;; ☐ **business card;** → **visiting card**: My name's Adam Carver. Here's my card.

10 COMPUTER [C] the thing inside a computer that the CHIPS are attached to, that allows the computer to do specific things: *a graphics card*
11 be on the cards *BrE*, **be in the cards** *AmE* to seem likely to happen: *At 3–1 down, another defeat seemed to be on the cards.*
12 play your cards right to deal with a situation in the right way, so that you are successful in getting what you want: *If he plays his cards right, Tony might get a promotion.*
13 put/lay your cards on the table to tell people what your plans and intentions are in a clear, honest way: *What I'd like us to do is put our cards on the table and discuss the situation in a rational manner.*
14 play/keep your cards close to your chest to keep your plans, thoughts, or feelings secret
15 get/be given your cards *BrE informal* to have your job taken away from you
16 have another card up your sleeve to have another advantage that you can use to be successful in a particular situation
17 trump/best/strongest card something that gives you a big advantage in a particular situation: *The promise of tax cuts proved, as always, to be the Republican Party's trump card.*
18 sb's card is marked *BrE* if someone's card is marked, they have done something that makes people in authority disapprove of them
19 PERSON [C usually singular] *old-fashioned informal* an amusing or unusual person: *Old Fred's a real card, isn't he!*
20 SPORT [C] a small piece of stiff red or yellow paper, shown to a player who has done something wrong in a game such as football
21 LIST AT SPORTS EVENT [C] a list of races or matches at a sports event, especially a horse race: *a full card of 120 riders for the Veterans race*
22 TAROT [C] a small piece of thick stiff paper with a special picture on one side, that is put down in a pattern in order to tell someone what will happen in their future
23 TOOL [C] *technical* a tool that is similar to a comb and is used for combing, cleaning, and preparing wool or cotton for SPINNING → **hold all the cards** at HOLD[1] (30); → **play the race/nationalist/environmentalist etc card** at PLAY[1] (14); → **stack the cards** at STACK[2] (4)

card[2] v [T] **1** *especially AmE* to ask someone to show a card proving that they are old enough to do something, especially to buy alcohol **2** to show a red or yellow card to someone playing a sport such as football, to show that they have done something wrong **3** to comb, clean, and prepare wool or cotton, before making cloth

car·da·mom /ˈkɑːdəməm $ ˈkɑːr-/ n [C,U] the seeds of an Asian fruit, used to give a special taste to Indian and Middle Eastern food

card·board[1] /ˈkɑːdbɔːd $ ˈkɑːrdbɔːrd/ n [U] a stiff brown material like very thick paper, used especially for making boxes: *We covered the hole with a sheet of cardboard.* → see picture at MATERIAL

cardboard[2] adj **1** made from cardboard: *a cardboard box* **2** [only before noun] seeming silly and not real: *a romantic novel full of cardboard characters*

cardboard 'city n [C] an area in a large town or city where people who have no home sleep outside using cardboard boxes to try to keep warm

cardboard 'cut-out n [C] **1** a picture drawn on cardboard so that it can stand up on a surface **2** a person or character in a book, film etc who does not seem natural or real: *the sort of movie in which the characters are just cardboard cut-outs*

card-,carrying adj [only before noun] **1** card-carrying member someone who has paid money to a political organization and is an official and active member of it: *a card-carrying member of the Labour Party* **2** believing very strongly in something – used to show disapproval: *One of them is a card-carrying ecology freak.*

'card ,catalog n [C] *AmE* a box of cards that contain information about something and are arranged in order, especially the cards with book information on them in a library; ▣ **card index** *BrE*

card·hold·er /ˈkɑːdˌhəʊldə $ ˈkɑːrdˌhoʊldər/ n [C] someone who has a CREDIT CARD

car·di·ac /ˈkɑːdi-æk $ ˈkɑːr-/ adj [only before noun] *medical* relating to the heart: *cardiac surgery* | **cardiac arrest/failure** (=when the heart stops working)

car·die /ˈkɑːdi $ ˈkɑːr-/ n [C] *BrE informal* a cardigan

car·di·gan /ˈkɑːdɪgən $ ˈkɑːr-/ also **,cardigan ,sweater** *AmE* n [C] a SWEATER similar to a short coat, fastened at the front with buttons or a zip

car·di·nal[1] /ˈkɑːdənəl $ ˈkɑːr-/ n [C] **1** a priest of high rank in the Roman Catholic Church **2** a North American bird. The male is a bright red colour **3** a CARDINAL NUMBER

cardinal[2] adj [only before noun] very important or basic: *Having clean hands is one of the cardinal rules when preparing food.* | *an issue of cardinal importance*

,cardinal 'number also **cardinal** n [C] a number such as 1, 2, or 3, that shows how many of something there are, but not what order they are in → ORDINAL NUMBER

,cardinal 'point n [C] *BrE technical* one of the four main points (north, south, east, or west) on a COMPASS

,cardinal 'sin n [C] **1** *informal* something bad or stupid that you must avoid doing: *politicians who commit the cardinal sin of ignoring public opinion* **2** a serious SIN in the Christian religion

'card ,index n [C] *BrE* a box of cards that contain information about something and are arranged in order, especially the cards with book information on them in a library; ▣ **card catalog** *AmE*

car·di·o /ˈkɑːdiəʊ $ ˈkɑːrdioʊ/ n [U] *informal* any type of exercise that makes the heart stronger and healthier, for example running: *a combination of cardio, weight training, and kung fu*

cardio- /ˈkɑːdiəʊ, -diə $ ˈkɑːrdioʊ, -diə/ prefix *medical* relating to the heart: *a cardiograph* (=machine that measures movements of the heart) | *cardiovascular* (=the heart and the tubes through which blood flows in your body)

car·di·ol·o·gist /ˌkɑːdiˈɒlədʒɪst $ ˌkɑːrdiˈɑː-/ n [C] *medical* a doctor who studies or treats heart diseases

car·di·ol·o·gy /ˌkɑːdiˈɒlədʒi $ ˌkɑːrdiˈɑː-/ n [U] the medical study of the heart

card·shark /ˈkɑːdʃɑːk $ ˈkɑːrdʃɑːrk/ **card·sharp** /-ʃɑːp $ -ʃɑːrp/ *BrE* n [C] someone who cheats when playing cards in order to make money

'card ,table n [C] a small light table, usually with folding legs, used for playing card games on

'card vote n [C] *BrE* a way of voting at a TRADE UNION meeting in which your vote represents the votes of all the members of your organization

care[1] |S2| |W2| /keə $ ker/ n
1 LOOKING AFTER SB [U] the process of looking after someone, especially because they are ill, old, or very young: *high standards of medical care* | *They shared the care of the children.* | *Care facilities for the elderly are inadequate.* | **in sb's care** (=being looked after by someone) *The children had been left in the care of a babysitter.* | **be under sb's care** (=be officially looked after or treated by someone) *Mentally ill patients will be under the care of a psychiatrist.* → DAY CARE, HEALTH CARE, INTENSIVE CARE; → **tender loving care** at TENDER[1] (5)
2 take care of sb/sth **a)** to look after someone or something: *Who's taking care of the dog while you're away?* | **take care of yourself** *The children are old enough to take care of themselves.* **b)** to deal with all the necessary work, arrangements etc: *Her secretary always took care of the details.* | *Don't worry about your*

accommodation – it's all taken care of. **c)** to pay for something – used when you want to avoid saying this directly: *We'll take care of the fees.*
3 take care **a)** *spoken* used when saying goodbye to family and friends: *Take care! See you next week!* **b)** to be careful: *Take care when driving in icy conditions.* | **take care to do sth** *Take care to ensure that the ladder is steady before you climb it.* | **take care (that)** *Take care that the meat is cooked properly.*
4 KEEPING STH IN GOOD CONDITION [U] the process of doing things to keep something in good condition and working correctly: *With proper care, the washing machine should last for years.* | *advice on skin care*
5 CAREFULNESS [U] when you are careful to avoid damage, mistakes etc: *The note on the box said 'Fragile – handle with care'.* | *The picture had been drawn with great care.*
6 take care over/with sth to spend a lot of time and effort making sure that something is perfect: *Paul always takes great care over his appearance.*
7 in care *BrE* a child who is in care is being looked after by the government, not by their parents: *When he was sent to prison, the children were taken into care.*
8 PROBLEM/WORRY [C,U] *literary* something that causes problems and makes you anxious or sad: *At last I felt free from my cares.* | *Alex looked as though he didn't have a care in the world* (=had no problems or worries). | *a man with the cares of the world on his shoulders* (=with a lot of problems or worries)
9 care of sb *BrE*; **in care of sb** *AmE* used when sending letters to someone at someone else's address; ◨ **c/o**: *Send me the letter care of my uncle.*
10 have a care! *BrE spoken old-fashioned* used to tell someone to be more careful

care² S1 W3 v [I,T]
1 to think that something is important, so that you are interested in it, worried about it etc: [+**about**] *The only thing he seems to care about is money.* | **care what/how/whether etc** *She didn't care what her father thought.* | *'He looked angry.' 'I don't care!'*
2 to be concerned about what happens to someone, because you like or love them; → **caring**: [+**about**] *I care about him and hate to see him hurt like this.* | *She felt that nobody cared.*
3 who cares? *spoken* used to say that something does not worry or upset you because it is not important: *It's rather old and scruffy, but who cares?*
4 see if I care! *spoken* used when you are angry or upset, to say that you do not care about what someone will do: *Go with William, then – see if I care!*
5 sb couldn't care less *spoken* used to say that someone does not care at all about something: *I really couldn't care less what you think!*
6 what does sb care? *spoken* used to say that someone does not care at all about something: *What do I care? It's your responsibility now!*
7 as if I cared! *spoken* used to say that something is not important to you at all: *As if I cared whether he comes with us or not!*
8 for all sb cares *spoken* used when you are angry that someone does not seem concerned about someone or something: *We could be starving for all they care!*
9 not care to do sth *old-fashioned* to not like doing something: *She doesn't care to spend much time with her relatives.* | *I wouldn't care to meet him in a dark alley!* | *I've experienced* **more** *reorganizations* **than I care to remember** (=a lot of them).
10 any ... you care to name/mention any thing of a particular kind: *Virtually any piece of equipment you care to name can be hired these days.*
11 would you care to do sth? *spoken formal* used to ask someone politely whether they want to do something: *Would you care to join us for dinner?*

　care for sb/sth *phr v*
1 to look after someone who is not able to look after themselves; ◨ **take care of**: *He thanked the nurses who*

had cared for him while he was sick. | *The children are being well cared for.*
2 to do things that keep something in good condition: *Instructions on caring for your new sofa are included.*
3 would you care for sth? *spoken formal* used to ask someone politely if they would like something: *Would you care for another drink?*
4 not care for sb/sth *formal* to not like someone or something: *I don't much care for his parents.*

ca·reen /kəˈriːn/ v [I always + adv/prep] *AmE* to move forwards quickly without control, making sudden sideways movements; ◨ **career** *BrE*: [+**down/over/along** etc] *The car careened around the corner.*

ca·reer¹ S2 W2 /kəˈrɪə $ -ˈrɪr/ n [C]
1 a job or profession that you have been trained for, and which you do for a long period of your life: [+**in**] *a career in journalism* | *a teaching career* | *He realized that his acting career was over.* | **career development/ advancement/progression etc** *Career prospects within the company are excellent.* | *a physiotherapist who wanted to make a dramatic* **career change** *by becoming an author* | *Nurses want an improved* **career structure** (=better opportunities to move upwards in their jobs).
2 career soldier/teacher etc someone who intends to be a soldier, teacher etc for most of their life, not just for a particular period of time: *a career diplomat*
3 the period of time in your life that you spend doing a particular activity: *She had not had a very impressive school career up till then.* | *My career as an English teacher didn't last long.* | *Beating the defending champion has to be the highlight of my career.*

career² v [I always + adv/prep] *BrE* to move forwards quickly without control, making sudden sideways movements; ◨ **careen** *AmE*: [+**down/along/towards** etc] *The truck careered down the hill and into a tree.*

ca·reer ˌbreak n [C] a short period of time when you do not work in your usual job or profession, for example because you want to look after your children

ca·reer ˌcounselor n [C] *AmE* a CAREERS OFFICER

ca·reer·ist /kəˈrɪərɪst $ -ˈrɪr-/ adj someone who is careerist considers their career to be more important to them than anything else – often used to show disapproval —**careerism** n [U] —**careerist** n [C]

ca·reers ˌofficer also **ca·reers adˌviser** n [C] *BrE* someone whose job is to give people advice about what jobs and professional training might be suitable for them; ◨ **career counselor** *AmE*

ca·reer ˌwoman n [C] a woman whose career is very important to her, so that she may not want to get married or have children: *a fiercely independent career woman*

care·free /ˈkeəfriː $ ˈker-/ adj having no worries or problems: *He thought back to the carefree days of his childhood.* | *a carefree attitude*

care·ful S1 W2 /ˈkeəfəl $ ˈker-/ adj
1 (be) careful! *spoken* used to tell someone to think about what they are doing so that something bad does not happen: *Be careful – there's broken glass on the floor!*
2 trying very hard to avoid doing anything wrong or to avoid damaging or losing something; ◨ **careless**: *a careful driver* | **careful to do sth** *Be careful to dispose of your litter properly.* | [+**with**] *He was being very careful with the coffee so as not to spill it.* | **careful who/what/ how etc** *I'll be more careful what I say in the future.* | [+**about**] *Mara was careful about what she ate.* | **careful (that)** *We were very careful that he didn't find out.*
3 paying a lot of attention to details, so that something is done correctly and thoroughly: *Any school trip requires careful planning.* | **careful consideration/at-tention/thought** *Careful consideration has been given to all applications.* | **careful analysis/examination/study etc** *careful analysis of the data*
4 careful with money not spending more money than you need to
5 you can't be too careful *spoken* used to say that you

should do everything you can to avoid problems or danger —**carefulness** n [U]

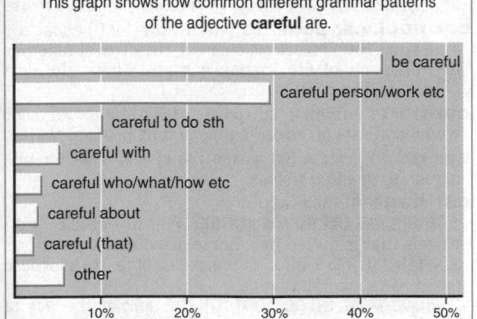

This graph shows how common different grammar patterns of the adjective **careful** are.

- be careful
- careful person/work etc
- careful to do sth
- careful with
- careful who/what/how etc
- careful about
- careful (that)
- other

10%   20%   30%   40%   50%

care·ful·ly [S2] [W2] /'keəfəli $ 'keərfəli/ adv in a careful way; **∎** **carelessly**: *He folded the sheets up carefully.* | **look/listen/think etc carefully** *You need to think very carefully about which course you want to do.* | **carefully planned/chosen/controlled etc** *carefully chosen words*

care·giv·er /'keə,ɡɪvə $ 'ker,ɡɪvər/ n [C] AmE someone who takes care of a child or sick person

'care ,home n [C] BrE a building where people who are old or ill live and are looked after

'care ,label n [C] a small piece of cloth in a piece of clothing that tells you how to wash it

care·less /'keələs $ 'ker-/ adj **1** not paying enough attention to what you are doing, so that you make mistakes, damage things etc; **∎** **careful**: *It was careless of him to leave the door unlocked.* | *a careless mistake* | *careless driving* | [+with] *He's careless with his glasses and has lost three pairs.* | **Careless talk** *can be disastrous for a business.* **2** [usually before noun] natural and not done with any deliberate effort or attention: *He ran a hand through his hair with a careless gesture.* **3** not concerned about something: [+of] *a man careless of his own safety* | *She gave a careless shrug.* ⚠ Do not use **careless** to mean that someone has no worries. Use **carefree**: *They all felt happy and carefree.* —**carelessly** adv —**carelessness** n [U]

'care ,package n [C] AmE a package of food, sweets etc that is sent to someone living away from home, especially a student at college

car·er /'keərə $ 'kerər/ n [C] BrE someone who looks after an old or ill person at home

ca·ress¹ /kə'res/ v [T] **1** especially literary to touch someone gently in a way that shows you love them; **∎** **stroke**: *His hands gently caressed her body.* **2** literary to touch something gently, in a way that seems pleasant or romantic: *Waves caressed the shore.*

caress² n [C] especially literary a gentle touch or kiss that shows you love someone

care·tak·er /'keə,teɪkə $ 'ker,teɪkər/ n [C] **1** BrE someone whose job is to look after a building, especially a school; **∎** **janitor** AmE **2** someone who looks after a house or land while the person who owns it is not there **3 caretaker manager/government/boss etc** a manager, government etc that is in charge for a short period of time until another manager or government is chosen **4** AmE someone who looks after other people, especially a teacher, parent, nurse etc

'care ,worker n [C] BrE someone whose job is to look after people who need care

care·worn /'keəwɔːn $ 'kerwɔːrn/ adj looking sad, worried, and tired: *a careworn expression*

car·go /'kɑːɡəʊ $ 'kɑːrɡoʊ/ n plural **cargos** or **cargoes** [C,U] the goods that are being carried in a ship or plane; **∎** **freight**: [+of] *A ship carrying a cargo of oil has run aground.* | *a cargo plane*

Car·ib·be·an /ˌkærɪ'biːən◂/ adj from or relating to the islands in the Caribbean sea —**Caribbean** n [C]

car·i·bou /'kærɪbuː/ n plural **caribou** [C] a North American REINDEER

car·i·ca·ture¹ /'kærɪkətʃʊə $ -tʃʊr/ n **1** [C] a funny drawing of someone that makes them look silly: [+of] *caricatures of politicians.* **2** [C] a description of someone or something that is only partly true and makes them seem silly: [+of] *The report presents a caricature of the true situation.* **3** [U] the activity of drawing or writing caricatures

caricature² v [T] to draw or describe someone or something in a way that makes them seem silly: **caricature sb/sth as sth** *Scientists are often caricatured as absent-minded professors.*

car·i·ca·tur·ist /'kærɪkətʃʊərɪst $ -tʃʊr-/ n [C] someone who draws or writes caricatures

car·ies /'keəriz $ 'ker-/ n [U] technical decay in someone's teeth; **∎** **cavity**

car·il·lon /kə'rɪljən, 'kærɪljən, $ 'kærəlɑːn, -lən/ n [C] a set of bells in a tower that are controlled from a piano KEYBOARD, or a tune played on these bells

car·ing /'keərɪŋ $ 'ker-/ adj **1** thinking about what other people need or want and trying to help them; → **care**: *a warm and caring man* | *a caring attitude* | *The school aims to educate children in a caring environment.* **2** [only before noun] involving the job of looking after other people: *Like many of **the caring professions**, nursing is very badly paid.* | *More men are taking on a **caring role**.*

car·jack·ing /'kɑː,dʒækɪŋ $ 'kɑːr-/ n [C,U] the crime of using a weapon to force the driver of a car to drive you somewhere or give you their car; → **hijacking** —**carjacker** n [C] —**carjack** v [T]

car·load /'kɑːləʊd $ 'kɑːrloʊd/ n [C] the amount of people or things a car can hold: [+of] *A carload of tourists pulled up and asked for directions.*

car·mine /'kɑːmɪn, -maɪn $ 'kɑːr-/ n [U] literary a dark red colour —**carmine** adj

car·nage /'kɑːnɪdʒ $ 'kɑːr-/ n [U] when a lot of people are killed and injured, especially in a war: *a scene of terrible carnage*

car·nal /'kɑːnl $ 'kɑːrnl/ adj formal **1** relating to sex or someone's body: *carnal desires* **2 carnal knowledge/relations** sexual activity —**carnally** adv

car·na·tion /kɑː'neɪʃən $ kɑːr-/ n [C] a flower that smells sweet. Men often wear a carnation on their jacket on formal occasions → see picture at FLOWER

car·net /'kɑːneɪ $ 'kɑːr-/ n [C] **1** BrE a small book of tickets that you can use on trains, buses etc **2** an official document that allows you to go somewhere, especially to drive across the border into another country for a limited period; → **pass**

car·ni·val /'kɑːnɪvəl $ 'kɑːr-/ n **1** [C,U] a public event at which people play music, wear special clothes, and dance in the streets: *preparations for this year's carnival* | *when it's Carnival in Rio* | *a carnival atmosphere throughout the town* **2** [C] AmE a noisy outdoor event at which you can ride on special machines and play games for prizes; **∎** **funfair** BrE **3** [C] AmE an event at a school, in which students play games for prizes **4 carnival of sth** literary an exciting mixture of things: *Shakespeare's carnival of images*

car·ni·vore /'kɑːnɪvɔː $ 'kɑːrnɪvɔːr/ n [C] **1** an animal that eats flesh; → **herbivore, omnivore** **2** humorous someone who eats meat; → **vegetarian** —**carnivorous** /kɑː'nɪvərəs $ kɑːr-/ adj

car·ob /'kærəb/ n [U] the fruit of a Mediterranean tree, which tastes similar to chocolate

car·ol¹ /'kærəl/ also **Christmas carol** n [C] a traditional Christmas song

carol² v **carolled, carolling** BrE, **caroled, caroling** AmE [I,T] literary to sing or say something in a happy way: *'Goodbye,' carolled Boris happily.*

ca·rot·id ar·te·ry /kəˈrɒtɪd ˌɑːtəri $ -ˈrɑːtɪd ˌɑːr-/ n [C] *medical* one of the two ARTERIES in your neck that supply blood to your head

ca·rouse /kəˈraʊz/ v [I] *literary* to drink a lot, be noisy, and have fun —**carousal** n [C,U]

car·ou·sel also **carrousel** *AmE* /ˌkærəˈsel/ n [C] **1** *especially AmE* a machine with wooden horses on it that turns around and around, which people can ride on for fun **2** the moving belt that you collect your bags from at an airport

carp[1] /kɑːp $ kɑːrp/ v [I] to keep complaining about something in a way that is annoying: [+about] *He always finds something to carp about.*

carp[2] n plural **carp** [C] a large fish that lives in lakes and rivers and can be eaten

car·pal tun·nel syn·drome /ˌkɑːpəl ˈtʌnl ˌsɪndrəʊm $ ˌkɑːr-, -droʊm/ n [U] a medical condition in which you have a lot of pain and weakness in your wrist

car park n [C] *BrE* **1** an area where people can park their cars; ▪ **parking lot** *AmE* **2** an enclosed building in a public place where people can park their cars; ▪ **parking garage** *AmE*

car·pen·ter /ˈkɑːpɪntə $ ˈkɑːrpɪntər/ n [C] someone whose job is making and repairing wooden objects

car·pen·try /ˈkɑːpɪntri $ ˈkɑːr-/ n [U] the skill or work of a carpenter

car·pet[1] S3 W3 /ˈkɑːpɪt $ ˈkɑːr-/ n
1 [C,U] heavy woven material for covering floors or stairs, or a piece of this material; → **carpeting**, **rug**: *My bedroom carpet is green.* | *All the rooms had **fitted** carpets* (=carpets cut to fit the shape of the rooms).
2 a carpet of sth *literary* a thick layer of something on the ground: *a carpet of flowers*
3 be/get called on the carpet *AmE informal* to be criticized by someone in authority because you have done something wrong: *He was called on the carpet by his supervisors to explain his excessive spending.* → MAGIC CARPET; → sweep/brush sth under the carpet at SWEEP[1] (15)

carpet[2] v [T] **1** [usually passive] to cover a floor with carpet: *The building has been carpeted throughout.* **2** [usually passive] *especially BrE informal* to talk in an angry way to someone because they have done something wrong: **carpet sb for sth** *Top officers were carpeted for bullying younger officers.* **3** *literary* if leaves, flowers etc carpet the ground, they cover it in a thick layer: **be carpeted with sth** *The whole garden was carpeted with daffodils.*

car·pet·bag·ger /ˈkɑːpɪtˌbægə $ ˈkɑːrpɪtˌbægər/ n [C] **1** someone from the northern US who went to the southern US after the Civil War in order to make money, especially in a dishonest way **2** someone who moves to a different place to try to be politically successful – used in order to show disapproval **3** *BrE* someone who opens an account at a BUILDING SOCIETY because they think that the building society will soon become a bank, and then they will receive money or SHARES in the bank

carpet-bomb v [T] to drop a lot of bombs over a small area to destroy everything in it —**carpet bombing** n [U]

car·pet·ing /ˈkɑːpɪtɪŋ $ ˈkɑːr-/ n **1** [U] carpets in general, or the material used for making them: *a spacious room with **wall-to-wall carpeting*** (=covering the whole floor) **2** [C] *BrE informal* an occasion when you talk to someone in an angry way because they have done something wrong: *He was called to the manager's office for a carpeting.*

carpet ˌslipper n [C] *BrE old-fashioned* a type of soft shoe that you wear in your house; ▪ **slipper**

carpet ˌsweeper n [C] a simple machine for sweeping carpets, which does not use electricity

car pool, carpool n [C] **1** a group of people who agree to travel together to work, school etc in one car and share the cost **2** a group of cars that a company or organization owns for its workers or members to use

car·pool, car-pool /ˈkɑːpuːl $ ˈkɑːr-/ v [I] *especially AmE* if a group of people carpool, they travel together to work, school etc in one car and share the cost —**carpooling** n [U]

car·port /ˈkɑːpɔːt $ ˈkɑːrpɔːrt/ n [C] a shelter for a car which consists of a roof supported by posts or walls

car·rel /ˈkærəl/ n [C] a small enclosed desk for one person to use in a library

car·riage S3 /ˈkærɪdʒ/ n
1 VEHICLE PULLED BY HORSE [C] a vehicle with wheels that is pulled by a horse, used in the past
2 TRAIN [C] *BrE* one of the parts of a train where passengers sit; ▪ **car** *AmE*
3 MOVEMENT OF GOODS [U] *BrE formal* the act of moving goods from one place to another or the cost of moving them: *Canals in the area were originally built for the carriage of coal.* | *It costs £45.50 including carriage.*
4 MACHINE PART [C] a moving part of a machine that supports or moves another part: *the carriage of a typewriter*
5 POSITION OF BODY [U] *formal* used when describing the position of someone's body as they walk, stand, or sit: *her graceful carriage*
6 FOR MOVING HEAVY OBJECTS [C] something with wheels that is used to move a heavy object, especially a gun → BABY CARRIAGE

carriage clock n [C] a clock inside a glass case with a handle on top

car·riage·way /ˈkærɪdʒweɪ/ n [C] *BrE* one of the two sides of a MOTORWAY or main road, for vehicles travelling in the same direction: *the northbound carriageway of the M1* → DUAL CARRIAGEWAY

car·ri·er /ˈkæriə $ -ər/ n [C] **1** a company that moves goods or passengers from one place to another; → **carry**: *an international carrier* **2** a military vehicle or ship used to move soldiers, weapons etc → AIRCRAFT CARRIER, PEOPLE CARRIER **3** *medical* someone who passes a disease or GENE to other people, especially without being affected by it themselves; → **carry**: *carriers of the lung disease, TB* **4** something used for carrying something; → **carry**: *a baby carrier* **5** *BrE* a carrier bag **6** *AmE* a company that provides a service such as insurance or telephones

carrier ˌbag n [C] *BrE* a bag that you are given in a shop, to carry the things you have bought

carrier ˌpigeon n [C] a PIGEON (=type of bird) that has been trained to carry messages

car·ri·on /ˈkæriən/ n [U] the decaying flesh of dead animals, which is eaten by some animals and birds

car·rot /ˈkærət/ n **1** [C,U] a long pointed orange vegetable that grows under the ground: *grated carrots* | *carrot juice* → see picture at VEGETABLE **2** [C] *informal* something that is offered to someone in order to try and persuade them to do something: *They have refused to sign the agreement despite a carrot of £140 million.* **3** carrot and stick *informal* a way of trying to persuade someone to do something by offering them something good if they do it, and a punishment if they do not: *the government's **carrot and stick approach** in getting young people to find jobs*

car·rot·y /ˈkærəti/ adj *BrE* carroty hair is orange

car·rou·sel /ˌkærəˈsel/ n an American spelling of CAROUSEL

car·ry[1] S1 W1 /ˈkæri/ v carried, carrying, carries
1 LIFT AND TAKE [T] to hold something in your hand or arms, or support it as you take it somewhere: *Gina was carrying a small bunch of flowers.* | *Angela carried the child in her arms.* | *Let me carry that for you.* | *Jack carried his grandson up the stairs.* | **carry sth to sth/sb** *The waiter carried our drinks to the table.*
2 VEHICLE/SHIP/PLANE [T] to take people or things

from one place to another in a vehicle, ship, or plane: *The ship was carrying supplies from the UN World Food Programme.* | *There are more airplanes carrying more people than ever before in the skies.*

3 PIPE/WIRE ETC [T] if a pipe, wire etc carries something such as liquid or electricity, the liquid, electricity etc flows or travels along it: *A drain carries surplus water to the river.* | *The aim is for one wire to carry both television and telephone calls.*

4 MOVE STH [T] to cause something to move along or support something as it moves along: *This stretch of water carries a lot of shipping.* | *The bridge carries the main road over the railway.* | *Pollution was carried inland by the wind.*

5 HAVE WITH YOU [T] to have something with you in your pocket, on your belt, in your bag etc everywhere you go: *I don't carry a handbag. I just carry money in my pocket.* | *All the soldiers carried rifles.* | *He says he's got to carry a knife to protect himself.*

6 HAVE A QUALITY [T] to have something as a particular quality: *Degree qualifications carry international recognition.* | *Few medical procedures carry no risk of any kind.* | *Older managers carry more authority in a crisis.* | *The plan is not likely to carry much weight with* (=have much influence over) *the authorities.* | *If the child believes in what she is saying, she will carry conviction* (=make others believe what she says is true).

7 NEWS/PROGRAMMES [T] if a newspaper, a television or radio broadcast, or a website carries a piece of news, an advertisement etc, it prints it or broadcasts it: *The morning paper carried a story about demonstrations in New York and Washington D.C.* | *The national TV network carries religious programmes.*

8 INFORMATION [T] if something carries information, the information is written on it: *All tobacco products must carry a health warning.* | *goods carrying the label 'Made in the USA'*

9 BE RESPONSIBLE [T] to be responsible for doing something: *Each team member is expected to carry a fair share of the workload.* | *Which minister carries responsibility for the police?* | *Parents carry the burden of ensuring that children go to school.*

10 SHOP [T] if a shop carries goods, it has a supply of them for sale: *The sports shop carries a full range of equipment.*

11 BUILDING [T] if a wall etc carries something, it supports the weight of that thing: *These two columns carry the whole roof.*

12 TAKE SB/STH [T] to take something or someone to a new place, point, or position: **carry sb/sth to sth** *The president wanted to carry the war to the northern states.* | *Blair carried his party to victory in 1997.* | **carry sb/sth into sth** *Clinton carried his campaign into Republican areas.*

13 DISEASE [T] if a person, animal, or insect carries a disease, they can pass it to other people or animals even if they are not ill themselves; → **carrier**: *The disease is carried by a black fly which lives in the rivers.* | *Birds and monkeys can carry disease.*

14 carry insurance/a guarantee etc to have insurance etc: *All our products carry a 12-month guarantee.*

15 be/get carried away to be so excited, angry, interested etc that you are no longer really in control of what you do or say, or you forget everything else: *It's easy to get carried away when you can do so much with the graphics software.* | *I just got carried away because it was such fun.*

16 be carried along (by sth) to become excited about something or determined to do something: *The crowd were carried along on a tide of enthusiasm.* | *You can be carried along by the atmosphere of an auction and spend more than you planned.*

17 CRIME [T] if a crime carries a particular punishment, that is the usual punishment for the crime: *Drink-driving should carry an automatic prison sentence.* | *Murder still carries the death penalty.*

18 SOUND [I] if a sound carries, it goes a long way: *In the winter air, sounds carry clearly.* | *The songs of the*

whales carry through the water over long distances.

19 BALL [I] if a ball carries a particular distance when it is thrown, hit, or kicked, it travels that distance

20 carry sth in your head/mind to remember information that you need, without writing it down: *Alice carried a map of the London Underground in her head.*

21 TUNE [T] to sing a tune using the correct notes: *I sang solos when I was six because I could carry a tune.* | *The highest voice carries the melody.*

22 PERSUADE [T] to persuade a group of people to support you: *He had to carry a large majority of his colleagues to get the leadership.* | *Her appeal to common sense was what finally carried the day* (=persuaded people to support her).

23 VOTE be carried if a suggestion, proposal etc is carried, most of the people at an official meeting vote for it and it is accepted: *The amendment was carried by 292 votes to 246.* | *The resolution was carried unanimously* (=everyone agreed). | *Those in favour of the motion raise your arm. Those against? The motion is carried* (=proposal is accepted).

24 ELECTION [T] *AmE* if someone carries a state or local area in a US election, they win in that state or area: *Cuban Americans play an important role in whether he carries Florida in the fall campaign.*

25 YOUR BODY [T always + adv/prep] to stand and move in a particular way, or to hold part of your body in a particular way: *He had a way of carrying his head on one side.* | **carry yourself** *She carried herself straight and with confidence.*

26 carry the can (for sb/sth) *BrE informal* to be the person who has to take the blame for something even if it was not their fault, or not their fault alone: *He has been left to carry the can for a decision he didn't make.*

27 NOT ENOUGH EFFORT [T] if a group carries someone who is not doing enough work, they have to manage without the work that person should be doing: *We can't afford to carry anyone. Every game is going to be difficult now.*

28 CHILD [I,T] *old-fashioned* if a woman is carrying a child, she is PREGNANT (=has a baby developing inside her)

29 carry all/everything before you *literary* to be completely successful in a struggle against other people

30 carry sth too far/to extremes/to excess to do or say too much about something: *I don't mind a joke, but this is carrying it too far.*

31 WEIGHT [T] to weigh a particular amount more than you should or than you did: *Joe carries only nine pounds more than when he was twenty.*

32 carry a torch for sb to love someone romantically who does not love you: *He's been carrying a torch for your sister for years.*

33 carry the torch of sth to support an important belief or tradition when other people do not: *Leaders in the mountains carried the torch of Greek independence.*

34 as fast as his/her legs could carry him/her as fast as possible: *She ran as fast as her legs could carry her.*

35 ADDING NUMBERS [T] to put a number into the next row to the left when you are adding numbers together → **CARD-CARRYING, CARRIER, CASH AND CARRY;** → **fetch and carry** at FETCH[1] (3)

carry sth ⇔ **forward** *phr v*

1 to succeed in making progress with something: *It will be up to the new team now to carry the work forward.*

2 to include an amount of money in a later set of figures or calculations

carry sth ⇔ **off** *phr v*

1 to do something difficult successfully: *I was flattered to be offered the job but wasn't sure if I could carry it off.*

2 to win a prize: *a film that carried off three Oscars*

carry on *phr v*

1 *especially BrE* to continue doing something: *Sorry, I*

interrupted you. Please carry on. | **carry on doing sth** *You'll have an accident if you carry on driving like that.* | [+**with**] *I want to carry on with my course.* | **carry on as usual/as you are/regardless etc** *For the time being, you're to carry on as normal.*
2 to continue moving: *He stopped and looked back, then carried on down the stairs.* | *Carry straight on until you get to the traffic lights.*
3 carry on sth if you carry on a particular kind of work or activity, you do it or take part in it: *Mr Dean carried on his baking business until he retired.* | *It was so noisy it was hard to* **carry on a conversation.**
4 *spoken* to talk in an annoying way: [+**about**] *I wish everyone would stop carrying on about it.*
5 *old-fashioned* to have a sexual relationship with someone, when you should not: *Lucy confessed to carrying on behind her husband's back.* | [+**with**] *She was carrying on with a neighbour.*
   carry sth ⇔ **out** *phr v*
1 to do something that needs to be organized and planned: *There is a shortage of people to carry out research.* | *A survey is now being carried out nationwide.* | *Turn off the water supply before carrying out repairs.*
2 to do something that you have said you will do or that someone has asked you to do: *Nicholson didn't* **carry out** *his* **threat** *to take legal action.* | *We* **carried out** *her* **instructions** *precisely.* | *Will the government* **carry out** *its* **promise** *to reform the law?*
   carry sth ⇔ **over** *phr v*
1 if something is carried over into a new situation, it continues to exist in the new situation: *The pain and violence of his childhood were carried over into his marriage.*
2 to make an official arrangement to do something or use something at a later time: *Up to five days' holiday can be carried over from one year to the next.*
   carry sb/sth **through** *phr v*
1 to complete or finish something successfully, in spite of difficulties: *I'm determined to carry this through.*
2 carry sb through (sth) to help someone to manage during an illness or a difficult period: *Her confidence carried her through.*

carry² *n* [U] *technical* the distance a ball or bullet travels after it has been thrown, hit, or fired

car·ry·all /ˈkæri-ɔːl $ -ɒːl/ *n* [C] *AmE* a large soft bag; ▣ **holdall** *BrE*; → see picture at BAG

car·ry·cot /ˈkærikɒt $ -kɑːt/ *n* [C] *BrE* a small bed used for carrying a baby

ˈ**carry-on¹** *n* [C]   **1** [usually singular] *BrE spoken* a situation in which someone behaves in a silly or annoying way: *What a carry-on!*   **2** *AmE* a bag that you are allowed to take onto a plane with you → **carry on** at CARRY¹

carry-on² *adj* [only before noun] carry-on bags are ones that you are allowed to take onto a plane with you

ˈ**carry-out** *n* [C] *especially AmE* food that you can take away from a restaurant to eat somewhere else, or a restaurant that sells food like this; ▣ **takeaway** *BrE*

ˈ**carry-,over** *n* [singular]   **1** something you do, or something that happens now, that is the result of a situation that existed in the past: [+**from**] *Some of the problems schools are facing are a carry-over from the previous government's policies.*   **2** an amount of money that has not been used and is available to use later: [+**from**] | *The budget includes a £7 million carry-over from last year.* → **carry over** at CARRY¹

ˈ**car seat** *n* [C]   **1** a special seat for a baby or young child that can be used in a car   **2** a seat in a car: *leather car seats*

car·sick /ˈkɑː,sɪk $ ˈkɑːr-/ *adj* feeling sick because you are travelling in a car —**carsickness** *n* [U]

cart¹ /kɑːt $ kɑːrt/ *n* [C]   **1** a vehicle with no roof that is pulled by a horse and used for carrying heavy things → HANDCART   **2** *AmE* a large wire basket on wheels that

you use in a SUPERMARKET; ▣ **trolley** *BrE*; → see picture at TROLLEY   **3** *AmE* a small table with wheels, used for moving and serving food and drinks; ▣ **trolley** *BrE*   **4** **put the cart before the horse** to do two things in the wrong order → **upset the apple cart** at UPSET² (5)

cart² *v* [T always + adv/prep]   **1** to take something somewhere in a cart, truck etc: **cart sth away** *Household waste is carted away by the city's Sanitation Department.*   **2** *informal* to carry something somewhere, especially that is heavy or difficult to carry: *We carted all the furniture upstairs.*
   cart sb **off/away** *phr v informal* to take someone somewhere, especially to prison or hospital: *He collapsed and had to be carted off to hospital.*

ˈ**car tax** *n* [U] money that people in Britain must pay if they want to drive a car on the roads; ▣ **road tax**

carte blanche /,kɑːt ˈblɑːnʃ $,kɑːrt-/ *n* [U] permission or freedom to do whatever you want: *The new manager will be given carte blanche as long as she can increase the company's profits.* | *She* **had carte blanche** *to produce a film suitable for children.*

car·tel /kɑːˈtel $ kɑːr-/ *n* [C] a group of people or companies who agree to sell something at a particular price in order to prevent competition and increase profits; → **monopoly**: *an illegal drug cartel*

cart·er /ˈkɑːtə $ ˈkɑːrtər/ *n* [C] someone whose job was to drive a CART in the past

cart·horse /ˈkɑːthɔːs $ ˈkɑːrthɔːrs/ *n* [C] a large strong horse, often used for pulling heavy loads

car·ti·lage /ˈkɑːtɫɪdʒ $ ˈkɑːrtɫɪdʒ/ *n* [C,U] a strong substance that can bend, which is around the joints in your body and in your outer ear

cart·load /ˈkɑːtləʊd $ ˈkɑːrtloʊd/ *n* [C] the amount that a CART can hold: [+**of**] *cartloads of hay*

car·tog·ra·phy /kɑːˈtɒɡrəfi $ kɑːrˈtɑː-/ *n* [U] the activity of making maps —**cartographer** *n* [C]

car·ton /ˈkɑːtn $ ˈkɑːrtn/ *n* [C]   **1** a small box made of CARDBOARD or plastic that contains food or a drink: [+**of**] *a carton of fruit juice* | *a milk carton* → see picture at CONTAINER   **2** *especially AmE* a large container with smaller containers of goods inside it: [+**of**] *a carton of cigarettes*

car·toon ⟨S3⟩ /kɑːˈtuːn $ kɑːr-/ *n* [C]
1 a short film that is made by photographing a series of drawings: *cartoon characters such as Donald Duck*
2 a funny drawing in a newspaper or magazine, especially about politicians or events in the news
3 also **cartoon strip** a set of drawings that tell a funny story, especially in a newspaper or magazine; ▣ **comic strip**
4 *technical* a drawing that an artist does before starting to do a painting

car·toon·ist /kɑːˈtuːnɪ̯st $ kɑːr-/ *n* [C] someone who draws cartoons

car'toon ,strip *n* [C] a CARTOON

car·tridge /ˈkɑːtrɪdʒ $ ˈkɑːr-/ *n* [C]   **1** a small container or piece of equipment that you put inside something to make it work: *computer game cartridges* | *an ink cartridge for a printer*   **2** a tube containing explosive powder and a bullet that you put in a gun; ▣ **shell**

ˈ**cartridge ,paper** *n* [U] *BrE* thick strong paper used for drawing on

ˈ**cart track** *n* [C] a narrow road with a rough surface, usually on a farm

cart·wheel /ˈkɑːt-wiːl $ ˈkɑːrt-/ *n* [C]   **1** a movement in which you turn completely over by throwing your body sideways onto your hands while bringing your legs over your head: **do/turn cartwheels** *The children were doing cartwheels in the park.*   **2** the wheel of a CART —**cartwheel** *v* [I]

carve /kɑːv $ kɑːrv/ *v*
1 **MAKE OBJECT OR PATTERN** [T] to make an object or pattern by cutting a piece of wood or stone; → **carving**: **carve sth out of/from sth** *a statue carved from a single block of marble* | *carved wooden chairs*

2 CUT STH INTO A SURFACE [T] to cut a pattern or letter on the surface of something: **carve sth on/in/into sth** *Someone had carved their initials on the tree.*

3 CUT MEAT [I,T] to cut a large piece of cooked meat into smaller pieces using a knife: *Carve the meat into slices.* | *Who's going to carve?*

4 JOB/POSITION/LIFE [T] also **carve out** to succeed in getting the job, position, life etc that you want: *He had carved a niche for himself as a photographer.* | *She carved out a very successful career in the film industry.* | *He moved to San Francisco to carve out a new life for himself.*

5 WATER/WIND [T] if a river, the wind etc carves land or rock, it removes some of it: *The river had carved channels in the limestone rock.* → **not be carved in stone** at STONE[1] (9)

6 REDUCE STH [T always + adv/prep] to reduce the size of something by removing some of it: **carve sth from sth** *The company carved $1 million from its budget.*

carve sb/sth ⇔ **up** *phr v*
1 to divide land, a company etc into smaller parts and share it between people – used especially to show disapproval: *The Ottoman Empire was carved up by Britain and France after World War I.* | *The two companies are attempting to carve up a large slice of America's publishing industry between them.*
2 *BrE informal* to drive past someone in a car and then suddenly move in front of them so that you are too close

carv·er /'kɑːvə $ 'kɑːrvər/ *n* [C] someone who carves wood or stone

car·ver·y /'kɑːvəri $ 'kɑːr- / *n plural* **carveries** [C] *BrE* a restaurant that serves ROAST meat

carve-up *n* [singular] *informal* an arrangement between two or more people, governments etc by which they divide something among themselves even though this is wrong

carv·ing /'kɑːvɪŋ $ 'kɑːr-/ *n* **1** [C] an object or pattern made by cutting a shape in wood or stone for decoration; → **carve 2** [U] the activity or skill of carving something

carving fork *n* [C] a large fork used to hold cooked meat firmly while you are cutting it

carving knife *n* [C] a large knife used for cutting large pieces of meat

car wash *n* [C] a place where there is special equipment for washing cars

car·y·at·id /ˌkæri'ætˌɪd/ *n* [C] *technical* a PILLAR in the shape of a female figure

Cas·a·no·va /ˌkæsə'nəʊvə $ -'noʊ-/ *n* [C] a man who has had sexual relationships with many women

cas·bah /'kæzbɑː/ *n* [C] an ancient Arab city or the market in it

cas·cade¹ /kæ'skeɪd/ *n* [C] **1** a small steep WATERFALL that is one of several together **2** something that hangs down in large quantities: [+of] *Her hair fell over her shoulders in a cascade of curls.*

cascade² *v* [I always + adv/prep] to flow, fall, or hang down in large quantities: *Her thick black hair cascaded down below her waist.* | *Gallons of water cascaded over the side of the bath.*

case¹ [S1] [W1] /keɪs/ *n*
1 EXAMPLE [C] an example of a particular situation or of something happening: [+of] *There were 16 cases of damage to vehicles in the area.* | **in the case of sth** *The amount of fruit in fruit juices must be 6% in the case of berries and 10% in the case of other fruits.* | **in some/many/most etc cases** *In many cases standards have greatly improved.* | *Williams' career is a case in point* (=a clear example of something that you are discussing or explaining). | *This is a classic case* (=typical example) *of poor design.*
2 SITUATION [C usually singular] a situation that exists, especially as it affects a particular person or group: **in sb's case** *Like the others, he produced a written explanation, but in Scott's case this was a 30-page printed booklet.* | *Changing men's and women's traditional*

cases

suitcase

pencil case

violin case

briefcase

C

roles is not easy, but in our case it has been helpful. | **it is the case (that)** *It may be the case that the scheme will need more money.* | *We tend to think of these people as untrustworthy, but that is not the case.* | **in this case** *In this case, several solutions could be tried.* | **in which case** *He won't want to eat it unless he's really hungry, in which case he'll eat almost anything.*
3 (just) in case a) as a way of being safe from something that might happen or might be true: *Take an umbrella, in case it rains.* | *He had his camera ready, just in case he saw something that would make a good picture.* **b)** *AmE* if: *In case I'm late, start without me.*
4 in any case whatever happens or happened: *I don't see why I couldn't do it. In any case, I'm going to try.* | *He's too young to come and in any case I want him to spend the time with Mom.*
5 in that case if that is the situation: *'He didn't want to talk to Sally.' 'In that case why did he agree to meet her?'*
6 REASON/ARGUMENT [C usually singular] a set of reasons why something should happen or be done: *Let me research the facts before I put forward a case.* | [+for] *A group of us met to make our case for more women in the cabinet.* | *There is a strong case* (=very good set of reasons) *for getting parents more involved in the school's activities.*
7 LAW/CRIME [C] **a)** a question or problem that will be dealt with by a law court: *The case will be heard in the High Court.* | *She is keen at all costs to avoid a court case.* | *The lawyers will only be paid if they win the case.* | *He was bound to lose the case.* | [+against] *Marshall has dropped the case against us.* **b)** all the reasons that one side in a legal argument can give against the other side: *The evidence does not support the prosecution's case.* | *The court ruled that we had a case* (=had enough good arguments to go to a law court). **c)** an event or set of events that need to be dealt with by the police in order to find out if a crime has been committed and who committed it: [+of] *Police are investigating a case of armed robbery.* | **on the case** *Around 50 police officers are on the case.*
8 BOX/CONTAINER [C] **a)** a large box or container in which things can be stored or moved: *a packing case* | *a case of wine* **b)** a special box used as a container for holding or protecting something: *a jewellery case* | *Jim put his violin back in its case.* **c)** *BrE* a SUITCASE: *Polly carried her cases upstairs to the bedroom.* → BOOKCASE, BRIEFCASE, PILLOWCASE
9 it's a case of sth *spoken* used before describing a situation: *Everyone can learn, it's just a case of practising.* | *It's a case of too many people and not enough jobs.*
10 DISEASE [C] an example of a disease or a person who has a disease: [+of] *There are thousands of new cases of AIDS in Africa every year.*
11 in case of sth used to describe what you should do in a particular situation, especially on official notices: *In case of fire, break the glass.*
12 GRAMMAR [C] *technical* the way in which the form of a word changes, showing its relationship to other words in a sentence: *case endings*
13 be on sb's case *informal* to be criticizing someone

continuously: *Dad's always on my case about something or other.*
14 be on the case *spoken* if someone says they are on the case, they know about a problem and are going to try to solve it
15 get off my case *spoken* used to tell someone to stop criticizing you or complaining about you: *OK, OK, just get off my case!*
16 PERSON [C] someone who is being dealt with by a doctor, a SOCIAL WORKER, the police etc → BASKET-CASE, NUTCASE → LOWER CASE; → **I rest my case** at REST² (9); → UPPER CASE

> **GRAMMAR (just) in case**
> **in case** is followed by the simple present, the simple past, or 'should': *Write it down in case you forget (NOT in case you will forget).* | *I had a snack, just in case there was no time (NOT in case there would be no time) to eat later.* | *Here's a contact number, in case there should (NOT will/would) be a problem.*
> WORD CHOICE: **in this case, in this respect**
> Do not use **in this/that case** to refer to a particular aspect of something. Use **in this/that respect**: *He supports the death penalty, and in that respect (NOT in that case) I think he is wrong.* | *Computers can search for information much more quickly than humans, and in this respect (NOT in this case) they are more efficient.*

case² *v* [T] **1 be cased in sth** to be completely surrounded by a material or substance: *The reactor will be cased in metal.* → CASING **2 case the joint** *informal* to look around a place that you intend to steal from in order to find out information
case·book /'keɪsbʊk/ *n* [C] a detailed written record kept by a doctor, SOCIAL WORKER, or police officer of the cases they have dealt with
case ,history *n* [C] a detailed record of someone's past illnesses, problems etc that a doctor or SOCIAL WORKER studies
case law *n* [U] *law* a type of law that is based on decisions judges have made in the past
case·load /'keɪsləʊd $ -loʊd/ *n* [C] the number of people a doctor, SOCIAL WORKER etc has to deal with
case·ment /'keɪsmənt/ also **'casement ,window** *n* [C] a window that opens like a door with HINGES at one side
case ,study *n* [C] a detailed account of the development of a particular person, group, or situation that has been studied over a period of time
case work *n* [U] work that a SOCIAL WORKER does which is concerned with the problems of a particular person or family that needs help —**caseworker** *n* [C]
cash¹ S2 W2 /kæʃ/ *n* [U]
1 money in the form of coins or notes rather than cheques, CREDIT CARDS etc: *Cash was taken during a burglary of the apartment.* | **in cash** *The traffic police will accept fines in cash immediately.* | *The shop charges less if the customer **pays in cash**.* → HARD CASH, PETTY CASH
2 money: *Health and education need cash from the government.* | *A phone line to help children in trouble has been closed due to lack of cash.* | *Charity workers must constantly **raise** more **cash** (=collect more money) for the needy.* | *Corporate owners often find themselves **strapped for cash** (=without enough money) to pay taxes.*
3 cash down *BrE*; **cash up front** *AmE* if you pay for something cash down, you pay before you receive it
4 cash on delivery *COD* a payment system in which the customer pays the person who delivers the goods to them
cash² S3 *v* [T]
cash a cheque/postal order/draft etc to exchange a cheque etc for the amount of money it is worth: *Traveller's cheques can be cashed at most hotels for a small charge.* | *Where can I get this cashed?* —**cashable** *adj*

cash in *phr v*
1 to make a profit from a situation in a way that other people think is wrong or unfair: [+on] *The record company was trying to cash in on her fame by releasing early teenage recordings.*
2 cash sth ⇔ in to exchange something such as an insurance POLICY for its value in money
3 cash in your chips to die – used humorously
cash up *BrE*; **cash out** *AmE phr v*
to add up the amount of money received in a shop in a day so that it can be checked

cash ad,vance *n* [C] money that you get from a bank, using a CREDIT CARD: *It seems so easy to get a $100 cash advance every few days at a local ATM machine.*

,cash and 'carry *n* [C] *BrE* a shop where customers representing a business or organization can buy large amounts of goods at cheap prices

cash·back /'kæʃbæk/ *n* [U] **1** a way of getting money at a shop when you use a DEBIT CARD to pay for the things you are buying, in which the shop gives you money which it takes from your bank account: *I got £40 cashback.* **2** a way of reducing the price of a car, piece of furniture etc where the seller says what the price is and offers to give a certain amount of money back to the person who buys it: *Price on the road – £8750. But on top of that, we'll give you £500 cashback.*

cash bar *n* [C] a place at a big party, wedding etc where guests have to pay for their own drinks

cash box *n* [C] a small metal box with a lock that you keep money in

cash card *n* [C] a special plastic card used for getting money from a machine outside a bank

cash cow *n* [C] something that a company sells very successfully and that brings in a lot of money

cash crop *n* [C] a crop grown in order to be sold rather than to be used by the people growing it → **subsistence crop** at SUBSISTENCE (2)

cash desk *n* [C] *BrE* the desk in a shop where you pay

cash 'discount *n* [C] an amount by which a seller reduces a price if the buyer pays immediately or before a particular date

cash dis,penser *n* [C] *BrE* a CASH MACHINE

ca·shew /'kæʃuː, kə'ʃuː/ *n* [C] **1** a small curved nut **2** the tropical American tree that produces the cashew nut

cash flow *n* [singular, U] the movement of money coming into a business as income and going out as wages, materials etc: *We expect a rise in both our production and our cash flow.* | *The builder is unable to pay due to **cash flow problems**.*

cash·ier¹ /kæ'ʃɪə $ -'ʃɪr/ *n* [C] someone whose job is to receive or pay out money in a shop

cashier² *v* [T] to force an officer to leave the army, navy etc because they have done something wrong

,cash-in-'hand *adj* a cash-in-hand payment is made in the form of notes and coins so that there is no record of the payment

cash·less /'kæʃləs/ *adj* done or working without using money in the form of coins and notes: *a cashless pay system* | *the cashless society*

cash ma,chine *n* [C] a machine in or outside a bank, SUPERMARKET, or other public building, from which you can obtain money with a special plastic card

cash·mere /'kæʃmɪə $ 'kæʒmɪr, 'kæʃ-/ *n* [U] a type of fine soft wool: *I wish I could afford a cashmere sweater.*

C

Cash·point /'kæʃpɔɪnt/ *n* [C] *BrE trademark* a CASH MACHINE

'cash ˌregister *n* [C] a machine used in shops to keep the money in and record the amount of money received from each sale; ⊟ **till** *BrE*

'cash-starved *adj* not having as much money as is needed: *cash-starved public services*

'cash-strapped *adj* not having enough money: *cash-strapped governments* | *cash-strapped shoppers*

cas·ing /'keɪsɪŋ/ *n* [C] an outer layer of metal, rubber etc that covers and protects something such as a wire or tyre

ca·si·no /kə'siːnəʊ $ -noʊ/ *n plural* **casinos** [C] a place where people try to win money by playing card games or ROULETTE: *Doesn't that club have a casino upstairs?*

cask /kɑːsk $ kæsk/ *n* [C] a round wooden container used for storing wine or other liquids, or the amount of liquid that it contains: *a cask of rum*

cas·ket /'kɑːskɪt $ 'kæs-/ *n* [C] **1** a small decorated box in which you keep jewellery and other valuable objects **2** *AmE* a COFFIN

cas·sa·va /kə'sɑːvə/ *n* [C,U] a tropical plant with thick roots that you can eat, or the flour made from these roots

cas·se·role¹ /'kæsərəʊl $ -roʊl/ *n* [C] **1** food that is cooked slowly in liquid in a covered dish in the OVEN: *chicken casserole* **2** a deep covered dish used for cooking food in an oven

casserole² *v* [T] to cook food in a casserole

cas·sette /kə'set/ *n* [C] **1** a small flat plastic case containing MAGNETIC TAPE, that can be used for playing or recording sound: *Now available on cassette or CD!* **2** a closed container with photographic film in it, that can be fitted into a camera

cas'sette ˌplayer *n* [C] a piece of electrical equipment used for playing cassettes

cas'sette reˌcorder *n* [C] a piece of electrical equipment used for recording sound or for playing cassettes on; ⊟ **tape recorder**

cas·sock /'kæsək/ *n* [C] a long, usually black, piece of clothing worn by priests

cast¹ W3 /kɑːst $ kæst/ *v past tense and past participle* **cast**

1 cast light on/onto sth to provide new information about something, making it easier to understand: *research findings that cast new light on the origin of our universe* | *The numerous biographies of Baldwin cast little light on the subject.*

2 cast doubt(s) on sth to make people feel less certain about something: *Her documentary casts serious doubt on Gilligan's conviction.*

3 LIGHT AND SHADE [T] *literary* to make light or a shadow appear somewhere: **cast sth over/on/across sth** *The flames cast dancing shadows on the walls.* | *the shade cast by low-hanging branches*

4 cast a shadow/cloud over sth *literary* to make people feel less happy or hopeful about something: *The allegations cast a cloud over the Mayor's visit.* | *Her father's illness cast a shadow over the wedding celebrations.*

5 LOOK [T] *literary* to look quickly in a particular direction: **cast a look/glance at sb/sth** *She cast an anguished look at Guy.* | **cast sb a glance/look** *The young tramp cast him a wary glance.* | *She blushed, casting her eyes down.*

6 cast an eye on/over sth to examine or read something quickly in order to judge whether it is correct, good etc: *Mellor cast an eye over the draft for inaccuracies.* | **cast a critical/expert etc eye** *Tonight, Tim Goodman casts a cynical eye on TV ads.*

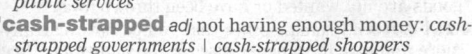

cash machine *BrE/* **ATM** *AmE*

7 cast a vote/ballot to vote in an election: *Barely one in three will bother to cast a ballot on February 26th.* | *To qualify, candidates must get at least 10% of the votes cast.* → CASTING VOTE

8 cast a spell on/over sb a) to attract someone very strongly and to keep their attention completely: *Hong Kong casts a spell over the visitor almost as soon as the aircraft touches down.* **b)** to use magic words or acts to change someone or something: *She's a witch, and she'll cast a spell on you if she catches you.*

9 cast your mind back *literary* to try to remember something that happened in the past: [+to] *Cast your mind back to your first day at school.* | [+over] *He frowned, casting his mind back over the conversation.*

10 cast aspersions on sth/sb *formal* to suggest that someone is not as truthful, honest etc as they seem: *remarks that cast aspersions on the integrity of the jury*

11 METAL [T] to make an object by pouring liquid metal, plastic etc into a MOULD (=hollow container): **cast sth in/from sth** *a statue of a horse cast in bronze*

12 ACTING [T] to choose which people will act particular parts in a play, film etc: **cast sb alongside/opposite sb** (=choose people for the two main roles) *Pfeiffer was expected to be cast alongside Douglas in Basic Instinct.* | **cast sb as sth** *Coppola cast him as Sodapop in The Outsiders.* | **cast sb in a role/a part/the lead** *The producer finally cast Finsh in the male lead.*

13 DESCRIBE [T] to regard or describe someone as a particular type of person: **cast sb as sth** *Clinton had cast himself as the candidate of new economic opportunity.* | *Clarke's trying to cast me in the role of villain here.*

14 THROW [T always + adv/prep] *literary* to throw something somewhere; ⊟ **toss**: *Sparks leapt as he cast more wood on the fire.*

15 FISHING [I,T] to throw a fishing line or net into the water: *There's a trick to casting properly.*

16 SEND AWAY [T always + adv/prep] *literary* to force someone to go somewhere unpleasant: **cast sb into prison/Hell etc** *Memet should, in her opinion, be cast into prison.*

17 cast your net (far and) wide to consider or try as many things as possible in order to find what you want: *We cast our net wide to get the right person for the job.*

18 SKIN when a snake casts its skin, the top layer of skin falls off slowly; ⊟ **shed**

19 cast a shoe if a horse casts a shoe, the shoe falls off by accident

20 cast a horoscope to prepare and write a HOROSCOPE for someone → **the die is cast** at DIE² (3); → **throw in/cast your lot with sb/sth** at LOT² (8); → **cast pearls before swine** at PEARL (4)

cast about/around for sth *phr v*
to try hard to think of the right thing to do or say: *She cast about frantically for an excuse.* | *Telecoms companies are casting around for ways of recouping huge losses.*

cast sb/sth ⇔ **aside** *phr v literary*
to remove or get rid of someone or something because you no longer want or need them: *When Henry became King, he cast aside all his former friends.* | **cast aside inhibitions/doubts etc** *Cast aside your fears!*

cast away *phr v* [usually passive]
to be left alone on a lonely shore or island because your ship has sunk: *If you were cast away on a desert island, what would you miss most?*

cast off *phr v*
1 to untie the rope that fastens your boat to the shore so that you can sail away
2 **cast** sth/sb ⇔ **off** *literary* to remove or get rid of something or someone that you no longer want or need: *His family had cast him off without a penny.*
3 to finish a piece of KNITTING by removing the stitches from the needle to make an edge that will not come undone: **cast sth ⇔ off** *Cast off four stitches.*

C

1 000, 2 000, 3 000, most frequent words in S poken and W ritten English

cast on *phr v*
to start a piece of KNITTING by making the first stitches on the needle: **cast sth ⇔ on** *Cast on 132 stitches.*

cast sb/sth ⇔ out *phr v*
literary to force someone or something to leave a place: *God has cast out the demons from your soul.*

cast sth ⇔ up *phr v literary*
if the sea casts something up, it carries it onto the shore: *A body had been cast up on the rocks.*

cast² *n* [C]
1 ACTORS all the people who perform in a play, film etc: [+of] *Films like 'Ben Hur' have a cast of thousands.* | *the entire cast of 'Les Miserables'* | *an all-star cast* | *a strong supporting cast* (=everyone except the main actors) | *a member of the cast*
2 ON ARM/LEG also **plaster cast** a hard protective case that is put over your arm, leg etc because the bone is broken: *Murray has his leg in a cast.*
3 FOR MAKING A SHAPE a MOULD (=hollow container) into which you pour liquid metal, plastic etc in order to make an object of a particular shape, or the object made in this way: [+of] *Make a cast of the statue.*
4 sb's cast of mind *formal* the way that a person thinks and the type of opinions or mental abilities they have: *Mary was of a far less intellectual cast of mind.*
5 FISHING the act of throwing a fishing line into the water
6 COLOUR *literary* a small amount of a particular colour: *Sage leaves have a silvery cast.*
7 EYE *old-fashioned* a problem with your eye which causes it to look sideways
8 EARTH a small pile of earth that a WORM produces on the surface of the ground

cas·ta·nets /ˌkæstəˈnets/ *n* [plural] a musical instrument made of two small round pieces of wood or plastic that you hold in one hand and knock together, used especially by Spanish dancers

cast·a·way /ˈkɑːstəweɪ $ ˈkæst-/ *n* [C] someone who is left on a lonely shore or island after their ship has sunk

cast 'down *adj* [not before noun] *literary* sad and disappointed: *She could not bear to see him so miserable and cast down.*

caste /kɑːst $ kæst/ *n* [C,U] **1** one of the fixed social classes, which cannot be changed, into which people are born in India: *the caste system* **2** a group of people who have the same position in society

cas·tel·lat·ed /ˈkæstɪleɪtɪd/ *adj technical* built to look like a castle

cast·er, **castor** /ˈkɑːstə $ ˈkæstər/ *n* [C] **1** a small wheel fixed to the bottom of a piece of furniture so that it can move in any direction **2** *BrE* a small container with holes in the top, used to spread sugar, salt etc on food; ▪ **shaker** *AmE*

'caster ˌsugar, **castor sugar** *n* [U] *BrE* sugar with very small grains used for cooking

cast·i·gate /ˈkæstɪgeɪt/ *v* [T] *formal* to criticize or punish someone severely —**castigation** /ˌkæstɪˈgeɪʃən/ *n* [U]

cast·ing /ˈkɑːstɪŋ $ ˈkæstɪŋ/ *n* **1** [U] the process of choosing the actors for a film or play; → **cast**: *a casting director* **2** [C] an object made by pouring liquid metal, plastic etc into a MOULD (=specially shaped container) **3 the casting couch** a situation in which an actress is persuaded to have sex in return for a part in a film, play etc – used humorously

'casting ˌvote *n* [C usually singular] *BrE* the vote of the person in charge of a meeting, which can be used to make a decision when there is an equal number of votes supporting and opposing a proposal

ˌcast 'iron *n* [U] a type of iron that is hard, breaks easily, and is shaped in a MOULD

ˌcast-'iron *adj* **1** a cast-iron excuse/alibi/guarantee etc an excuse etc that is very certain and cannot fail **2** made of cast iron: *a cast-iron frying pan*

cas·tle W3 /ˈkɑːsəl $ ˈkæ-/ *n* [C]
1 also **Castle** a very large strong building, built in the past as a safe place that could be easily defended against attack: *Edinburgh Castle* | *a ruined castle* → see picture at HOUSE
2 one of the pieces used in a game of CHESS. Each player has two castles, which start the game in the corner squares, and can move only forwards or sideways; ▪ **rook**
3 castles in the air plans or hopes that you have that are unlikely ever to come real

'cast-off *adj* [only before noun] cast-off clothes or other goods are not wanted or have been thrown away

'cast-offs *n* [plural] clothes that you do not wear any more and give to someone else: *As the youngest of five kids I was always dressed in other people's cast-offs.*

cast·or /ˈkɑːstə $ ˈkæstər/ *n* another spelling of CASTER

ˌcastor 'oil *n* [U] a thick oil made from the seeds of a plant and used in the past as a medicine to make the BOWELS empty

'castor ˌsugar *n* [U] another spelling of CASTER SUGAR

cas·trate /kæˈstreɪt $ ˈkæstreɪt/ *v* [T] to remove the TESTICLES of a male animal or a man —**castration** /kæˈstreɪʃən/ *n* [U]

cas·u·al /ˈkæʒuəl/ *adj*
1 RELAXED relaxed and not worried, or seeming not to care about something: *a casual manner* | *His eyes were angry, though he sounded casual.* | *Marsha was quite casual about appearing on TV.* | *She had a casual attitude to life.*
2 NOT FORMAL not formal or not for a formal situation; ▪ **formal**: *Jean felt more comfortable in casual clothes.* | *a casual jacket*
3 WORK employed as a temporary worker or working for only a short period of time: *casual labour* | *staff employed on a casual basis* | *Chris has occasional casual work but mostly he is unemployed.*
4 RELATIONSHIP knowing someone or having sex with someone without wanting a close relationship with them; ▪ **serious**: *She will never be more than a casual acquaintance.* | *They had been conducting a casual affair for years.* | *John just wanted casual sex.*
5 WITHOUT ATTENTION without any serious interest or attention: *He gave us a casual glance as he walked by, but didn't stop.* | **To the casual observer** (=to someone who is not looking carefully) *Mary seemed quite calm.*
6 NOT PLANNED [only before noun] happening by chance without being planned: *a casual conversation* | *He made some casual remark* (=one without thinking much about it) *about her holiday.*
7 NOT REGULAR [only before noun] doing something or using something sometimes but not regularly or often; ▪ **occasional**: *a casual drug user* | *The museum is of great interest, both to experts and to casual visitors.*
—**casually** *adv*: *a casually dressed young man* | *'Where do you work?' she asked casually.* | *He walked down the road, casually swinging his bag.* —**casualness** *n* [U]

cas·u·al·ty /ˈkæʒuəlti/ *n plural* **casualties 1** [C] someone who is hurt or killed in an accident or war: *Our aim is to reduce road casualties.* | *thousands of civilian casualties* (=people who are not soldiers who are injured or killed) | *cause/inflict casualties The rebels claim to have inflicted heavy casualties.* **2** [singular] someone or something that suffers as a result of a particular event or situation: [+of] *The Safer City Project is the latest casualty of financial cutbacks.* **3** [U] also **Casualty** *BrE* the part of a hospital that people are taken to when they are hurt in an accident or suddenly become ill; ▪ **Emergency Room** *AmE*: **in casualty** *Rosemary ended up in casualty last night.*

cas·u·is·try /ˈkæʒuɪstri/ *n* [U] *formal* the use of clever but often false arguments to answer moral or legal questions

cat S1 W3 /kæt/ *n* [C]
1 a) a small animal with four legs that people often

keep as a pet. Cats sometimes kill small animals and birds; → **feline**: tabby/ginger/tortoiseshell etc cat (=colours of cats) | *a tom cat* (=a male cat) **b)** also **big cat** a large animal such as a lion or TIGER
2 let the cat out of the bag to tell someone a secret, especially without intending to
3 put/set the cat among the pigeons to do or say something that causes arguments, trouble etc
4 play (a game of) cat and mouse (with sb) to pretend to allow someone to do or have what they want, and then to stop them from doing or having it: *The police played an elaborate game of cat and mouse to trap him.*
5 the cat's whiskers/pyjamas *informal* something or someone that is better than everything else: *I really thought I looked the cat's whiskers in that dress.*
6 like a cat on hot bricks *BrE*, **like a cat on a hot tin roof** *AmE* so nervous or anxious that you cannot keep still or keep your attention on one thing
7 not stand/have a cat in hell's chance (of doing sth) *informal* to not have any chance of succeeding: *His party does not have a cat in hell's chance of ever being returned to government.*
8 when the cat's away (the mice will play) used to say that people will not behave well when the person who has authority over them is not there
9 like the cat that got the cream *BrE*, **like the cat that ate the canary** *AmE informal* very proud or pleased because of something you have achieved or got
10 look like sth the cat dragged/brought in *BrE informal* to look very dirty or untidy → **raining cats and dogs** at RAIN² (1); → **there's not enough room to swing a cat** at ROOM¹ (5)

cat·a·clys·m /'kætəklɪzəm/ *n* [C] *literary* a violent or sudden event or change, such as a serious flood or EARTHQUAKE —**cataclysmic** /ˌkætə'klɪzmɪk‹ / *adj* [usually before noun]

cat·a·comb /'kætəkuːm $ -koʊm/ *n* [C usually plural] an area underground where dead people are buried; ▣ **tomb**

cat·a·falque /'kætəfælk/ *n* [C] *formal* a decorated raised structure on which the dead body of an important person is placed before their funeral

Cat·a·lan /'kætəlæn $ -tl-ən/ *n* [U] a language spoken in part of Spain around Barcelona

cat·a·logue¹ W3 also **catalog** *AmE* /'kætəlɒg $ -lɔːg, -lɑːg/ *n* [C]
1 a complete list of things that you can look at, buy, or use, for example in a library or at an art show: *a mail order catalog* | *an online catalogue*
2 catalogue of mistakes/crimes/cruelty etc a series of mistakes, crimes etc that happen one after the other and never seem to stop: *a catalogue of terrorist crimes* | *an appalling catalogue of errors*

catalogue² also **catalog** *AmE v* [T] **1** to make a complete list of all the things in a group: *The manuscripts have never been systematically catalogued.* **2** to list all the things that are connected with a particular person, event, plan etc: *The report catalogued numerous dangerous work practices.*

ca·tal·y·sis /kə'tælᵻsᵻs/ *n* [U] *technical* the process of making a chemical reaction quicker by adding a catalyst

cat·a·lyst /'kætl-ᵻst/ *n* [C] **1** *technical* a substance that makes a chemical reaction happen more quickly without being changed itself **2** something or someone that causes an important change or event to happen: [+for] *They hope his election will act as a catalyst for reform.* —**catalytic** /ˌkætl'ɪtɪk‹ / *adj*

catalytic con·verter *n* [C] a piece of equipment fitted to a car's EXHAUST system that reduces the amount of poisonous gases the engine sends out

cat·a·ma·ran /ˌkætəmə'ræn/ *n* [C] a sailing boat with two separate HULLS (=the part that goes in the water)

cat·a·pult¹ /'kætəpʌlt/ *n* [C] **1** a large weapon used in former times to throw heavy stones, iron balls etc **2** *BrE* a small stick in the shape of a Y with a thin rubber band fastened over the two ends, used by chil-

dren to throw stones; ▣ **slingshot** *AmE* **3** a piece of equipment used to send an aircraft into the air from a ship

catapult² *v* **1** [T always + adv/prep] to push or throw something very hard so that it moves through the air very quickly: *Sam was catapulted into the air by the force of the blast.* **2 catapult sb to fame/stardom etc** to suddenly make someone very famous: *A remarkable series of events catapulted her into the limelight.*

cat·a·ract /'kætərækt/ *n* [C] **1** a medical condition that causes the LENS of your eye to become white, so that you slowly lose your sight **2** *literary* a large WATERFALL

ca·tarrh /kə'tɑː $ -'tɑːr/ *n* [U] *BrE* an uncomfortable condition in which your body produces a thick liquid that blocks your nose and throat: *After a cold, many patients complain of persistent catarrh.*

ca·tas·tro·phe /kə'tæstrəfi/ *n* **1** [C,U] a terrible event in which there is a lot of destruction, suffering, or death; ▣ **disaster**: environmental/nuclear/economic etc catastrophe *The Black Sea is facing ecological catastrophe as a result of pollution.* | **prevent/avert a catastrophe** *Sudan requires food immediately to avert a humanitarian catastrophe.* **2** [C] an event which is very bad for the people involved; ▣ **disaster**: [+for] *If the contract is cancelled, it'll be a catastrophe for everyone concerned.* —**catastrophic** /ˌkætə'strɒfɪk‹ $ -'strɑː-/ *adj*: *a catastrophic fall in the price of rice* | *The failure of the talks could have catastrophic consequences.* —**catastrophically** /-kli/ *adv*

cat·a·ton·ic /ˌkætə'tɒnɪk‹ $ -'tɑː-/ *adj* not able to move or talk because of an illness, shock etc: catatonic stupor/trance

cat·bird seat /'kætbɜːd ˌsiːt $ -bɜːrd-/ *n* **be (sitting) in the catbird seat** *AmE informal* to be in a position where you have an advantage

'cat ˌburglar *n* [C] a thief who enters a building by climbing up walls, pipes etc

cat·call /'kætkɔːl $ -kɒːl/ *n* [C] a loud whistle or shout expressing disapproval of a speech or performance: *jeers and catcalls from the audience* —**catcall** *v* [I]

catch¹ S1 W1 /kætʃ/ *v past tense and past participle* **caught** /kɔːt $ kɒːt/
1 TAKE AND HOLD a) [I,T] to get hold of and stop an object such as a ball that is moving through the air; → **throw**: *Stephen leapt up and caught the ball in one hand.* | *'Pass me that pen, would you?' 'Here you are. Catch!'* | *The kids were throwing and catching a frisbee down on the beach.* **b)** [T] to suddenly take hold of someone or something with your hand: *He caught her elbow to steady her.* | *Miss Perry caught hold of my sleeve and pulled me back.*
2 FIND/STOP SB [T] **a)** to stop someone after you have been chasing them and not let them get away: *'You can't catch me!' she yelled, running away.* **b)** to find a criminal or enemy and stop them from escaping; ▣ **capture**: *State police have launched a massive operation to catch the murderer.* | *If you go back to the city you're bound to get caught.*
3 SEE SB DOING STH [T] to see someone doing something that they did not want you to know they were doing: **catch sb doing sth** *I caught him reading my private letters.* | *Gemma turned around and caught the stranger looking at her intently.* | **catch sb in the act (of doing sth)** (=catch someone while they are doing something illegal) *The gang was caught in the act of unloading the cigarettes.* | *He was* **caught red-handed** (=as he was doing something wrong) *taking money from the cash register.* | **catch sb at it** *We knew he'd been cheating, but we'd never caught him at it before.*
4 ILLNESS [T] to get an infectious disease: *Anton caught malaria while he was in Mali, and nearly died.* | *Many young people are still ignorant about how HIV is caught.* | **catch sth from/off sb/sth** *In these areas, typhoid and cholera are often caught from contaminated water supplies.* | *I caught chicken pox off my friend at*

school and had to stay home for two weeks. | **catch your death (of cold)** *BrE spoken* (=get a very bad cold) *Don't stand out there in the rain. You'll catch your death.*

5 catch sb by surprise/catch sb off guard also **catch sb napping/unawares, catch sb on the hop** *BrE* to do something or to happen when someone is not expecting it or prepared for it: *Her question caught him off guard.*

6 catch sb with their pants/trousers down to discover that someone is doing something that they should not be doing or has not done something that they should have done: *He's not the first politician to be caught with his pants down, and he won't be the last.*

7 ANIMAL/FISH [T] to trap an animal or fish by using a trap, net, or hook, or by hunting it: *Did you catch any fish?* | *Early settlers caught rabbits and squirrels and even rats in order to survive.*

8 catch a train/plane/bus to get on a train, plane etc in order to travel on it, or to be in time to get on a train, plane etc before it leaves: *I caught the 7.15 train to London.* | *There's a train in now. If you run, you'll just catch it.* | *I have to hurry – I have a bus to catch.*

9 NOT MISS SB/STH [T] to not be too late to do something, see something, talk to someone etc; ➡ miss: *I managed to catch her just as she was leaving.* | *I just caught the last few minutes of the documentary.* | *Tumours like these can be treated quite easily if they're caught early enough.* | catch the post *BrE* (=post letters in time for them to be collected that day)

10 GET STUCK [I,T] if your hand, finger, clothing etc catches or is caught in something, it gets stuck in it accidentally: *His overalls caught in the engine.* | *Her microphone was forever getting caught on her clothes.*

11 catch sb's attention/interest/imagination etc to make you notice something and feel interested in it: *Lucie whistled sharply to catch the other girl's attention.* | *This is a story that will catch the imagination of every child.*

12 not catch sth *spoken* to not hear or understand what someone says: *I'm afraid I didn't catch your name.*

13 HEAR [T] to manage to hear a sound: *I caught the muffled thud of a car door slamming in the street.*

14 catch you later *spoken* used to say goodbye: *'I'll give you a call in a couple days.' 'Okay. Catch you later.'*

15 DO/SEE STH [T] *spoken especially AmE* to go somewhere in order to do or see something: *We could catch a movie* (=go to a movie). | *M Records caught his act and signed him immediately.*

16 catch a ride *AmE spoken* to go somewhere in someone else's car: *I caught a ride as far as Columbus.*

17 you won't catch me doing sth also **you won't catch me somewhere** *spoken* used to say that you would never do something: *I love dancing but you won't catch me being the first on the dance floor!*

18 catch it *informal* to be punished by someone such as a parent or teacher because you have done something wrong: *You'll catch it if Dad finds out where you've been.*

19 catch a glimpse of sb/sth to see someone or something for a very short time: *Fans waited for hours at the airport to catch a glimpse of their idol.*

20 catch sight of sb/sth to suddenly see someone or something that you have been looking for or have been hoping to see: *I caught sight of her in the crowd.*

21 DESCRIBE WELL [T] to show or describe the character or quality of something well in a picture, piece of writing etc; ▣ **capture**: *a novel that catches the mood of post-war Britain*

22 BURN **a)** catch fire if something catches fire, it starts to burn accidentally: *Two farm workers died when a barn caught fire.* **b)** [I] if a fire catches, it starts to burn: *For some reason the charcoal wasn't catching.*

23 catch sb's eye **a)** to attract someone's attention and make them look at something: *Out on the freeway, a billboard caught his eye.* **b)** to look at someone at the same moment that they are looking at you: *Every time she caught his eye, she would glance away embarrassed.*

24 catch yourself doing sth to suddenly realize you are doing something: *Standing there listening to the song, he caught himself smiling from ear to ear.*

25 HIT [T] to hit someone in or on a particular part of their body: *The punch caught him right in the face.*

26 be caught in/without etc sth to be in a situation that you cannot easily get out of or in which you do not have something you need: *We got caught in a rainstorm on the way here.* | *Here's a useful tip if you're caught without a mirror.*

27 catch your breath **a)** to pause for a moment after a lot of physical effort in order to breathe normally again: *Hang on a minute – let me catch my breath!* **b)** to stop breathing for a moment because something has surprised, frightened, or shocked you **c)** to take some time to stop and think about what you will do next after having been very busy or active: *It was an enforced absence from work, but at least it gave me a little time to catch my breath before the final push.*

28 CONTAINER [T] if a container catches liquid, it is in a position where the liquid falls into it: *Place the baking sheet under the muffin pan to catch the drips.*

29 SHINE [T] if the light catches something or if something catches the light, the light shines on it: *The sunlight caught her hair and turned it to gold.*

30 catch the sun *informal* if you catch the sun, your skin becomes red and sometimes sore because of the effects of sunlight: *You've caught the sun on the back of your neck.*

31 WIND [T] if something catches the wind or the wind catches something, it blows on it: *Gary swung the sail round to catch the light wind.*

32 SPORT **a)** [T] to end a player's INNINGS in CRICKET by catching the ball that is hit off their BAT before it touches the ground **b)** [I] to be the CATCHER in a game of baseball

catch at sth *phr v*
to try to take hold of something: *She caught at his arm, 'Hang on. I'm coming with you.'*

catch on *phr v*
1 to become popular and fashionable: *The idea of glasses being a fashion item has been slow to catch on.*
2 to begin to understand or realize something: [+to] *It was a long time before the police caught on to what he was really doing.*

catch sb **out** *phr v*
1 to make someone make a mistake, especially deliberately and in order to prove that they are lying: *The interviewer may try to catch you out.*
2 if something unexpected catches you out, it puts you in a difficult situation because you were not expecting it or not fully prepared for it: *Even the best whitewater rafters get caught out by the fierce rapids here.*

catch up *phr v*
1 to improve and reach the same standard as other people in your class, group etc: *If you miss a lot of classes, it's very difficult to catch up.* | [+with] *At the moment our technology is more advanced, but other countries are catching up with us.*
2 to come from behind and reach someone in front of you by going faster: [+with] *Drive faster – they're catching up with us.* | catch sb up *BrE*: *You go on ahead. I'll catch you up in a minute.*
3 to do what needs to be done because you have not been able to do it until now: [+on] *I have some work to catch up on.* | *I need to catch up on some sleep* (=after a period without enough sleep).
4 to spend time finding out what has been happening while you have been away or during the time you have not seen someone: [+on] *The first thing I did when I got home was to phone up Jo and catch up on all the gossip.* | *I'll leave you two alone – I'm sure you've got a lot of catching up to do.*
5 be/get caught up in sth to be or get involved in something, especially something bad: *I didn't want to get caught up in endless petty arguments.*

catch up with sb *phr v*
1 to finally find someone who has been doing some-

thing illegal and punish them: *It took six years for the law to catch up with them.*
2 if something bad from the past catches up with you, you cannot avoid dealing with it any longer: *At the end of the movie his murky past catches up with him.*

catch² n **1** [C] an act of catching a ball that has been thrown or hit: *Hey! Nice catch!* **2** [C usually singular] *informal* a hidden problem or difficulty: *This deal looks too good to be true – there must be a catch somewhere.* | **the catch is (that)** *The catch is that you can't enter the competition unless you've spent $100 in the store.* **3** [C] a hook or something similar for fastening a door or lid and keeping it shut **4** [C] a quantity of fish that has been caught at one time **5** [U] a simple game in which two or more people throw a ball to each other: *Let's go outside and play catch.* **6 a catch in your voice/throat** a short pause that you make when you are speaking because, you feel upset or are beginning to cry: *There was a catch in Anne's voice and she seemed close to tears.* **7 a (good) catch** someone who is a good person to have a relationship with or to marry because they are rich, attractive etc – often used humorously

catch-all¹ *adj* intended to include all possibilities: *a vague catch-all clause in the contract* | *a catch-all term*

catch·all² /'kætʃɔːl $ -ɒːl/ *n* [C] *AmE* a drawer, cupboard etc where you put any small objects

catch·er /'kætʃə $ -ər/ *n* [C] in baseball, the player behind the BATTER, who catches missed balls; → **pitcher**

catch·ing /'kætʃɪŋ/ *adj* [not before noun] **1** an illness that is catching is easily passed to other people; ⊟ **infectious 2** an emotion or feeling that is catching spreads quickly among people: *Julia's enthusiasm was catching.*

catch·ment ar·e·a /'kætʃmənt ˌeəriə $ -ˌeriə/ *n* [C] **1** *BrE* the catchment area of a school, hospital etc is the area that its students, patients etc come from **2** *technical* the area that a river or lake gets water from

catch·phrase /'kætʃfreɪz/ *n* [C] a short well-known phrase made popular by an entertainer or politician, so that people think of that person when they hear it

Catch-22 /ˌkætʃ twenti'tuː/ *n* [U] an impossible situation that you cannot solve because you need to do one thing in order to do a second thing, but you cannot do the second thing until you have done the first: *It's a Catch-22 situation - without experience you can't get a job and without a job you can't get experience.*

catch·word /'kætʃwɜːd $ -wɜːrd/ *n* [C] a word or phrase that refers to a feature of a situation, product etc that is considered important: *Variety is the catch-word at our latest venue, the Beehive Club.*

catch·y /'kætʃi/ *adj* a catchy tune or phrase is easy to remember: *a catchy song* | *catchy advertising slogans*

cat·e·chis·m /'kætəˌkɪzəm/ *n* [singular] a set of questions and answers about the Christian religion that people learn in order to become full members of a church: *We were taught to recite the catechism.*

cat·e·gor·i·cal /ˌkætəˈɡɒrɪkəl◂ $ -ˈɡɔː-, -ˈɡɑː-/ *adj* [usually before noun] a categorical statement is a clear statement that something is definitely true or false: **categorical denial/assurance etc** *Can you give us a categorical assurance that no jobs will be lost?*

cat·e·gor·i·cal·ly /ˌkætəˈɡɒrɪkli $ -ˈɡɔː-, -ˈɡɑː-/ *adv* in such a sure and certain way that there is no doubt: **categorically deny/refuse etc sth** *He has categorically denied his guilt all along.* | *Are you prepared to* **state categorically** *that her death was caused by lack of food?*

cat·e·go·rize also **-ise** *BrE* /'kætəɡəraɪz/ *v* [T] to put people or things into groups according to the type of person or thing they are; ⊟ **classify:** *The population is categorized according to age, sex, and social group.* | **categorize sth/sb as sth** *Keene doesn't like to be categorized as a socialist.* —**categorization** /ˌkætəɡəraɪˈzeɪʃən $ -rə-/ *n* [C,U]

cat·e·go·ry [S2] [W2] /'kætəɡəri $ -ɡɔːri/ *n plural* **categories** [C] a group of people or things that are all of the same type: **[+of]** *There are five categories of workers.* | *people in the over-45* **age category** | *Seats are available in eight of the 10* **price categories.** | **fall into/belong in/fit into a category** *Voters fall into three* **main categories.** | *Williams' style does not fit easily into the category of jazz.*

ca·ter /'keɪtə $ -ər/ *v* [I,T] to provide and serve food and drinks at a party, meeting etc, usually as a business: **[+for]** *This is the biggest event we've ever catered for.* | *Joan has catered functions for up to 200 people.*

cater for sb/sth also **cater to** sb/sth *phr v* to provide a particular group of people with the things they need or want: *an LA bank catering to Asian businesses* | *Vegetarians are well catered for.* | *Most perfume ads cater to male fantasies.*

ca·ter·er /'keɪtərə $ -ər/ *n* [C] a person or company that provides and serves food and drinks at a party, meeting etc

ca·ter·ing /'keɪtərɪŋ/ *n* [U] the activity of providing and serving food and drinks at parties, meetings etc for money; → **self-catering:** *Who did the catering?* | **catering business/service etc**

cat·er·pil·lar /'kætəˌpɪlə $ -tərˌpɪlər/ *n* [C] a small creature like a WORM with many legs that eats leaves and that develops into a BUTTERFLY or other flying insect

Caterpillar *n* [C] *trademark* also **Caterpillar track** a metal belt made of short connected pieces that is fastened over the wheels of a heavy vehicle to help it to move over soft ground: *a Caterpillar tractor* (=a vehicle fitted with this belt)

cat·er·waul /'kætəwɔːl $ -tərwɒːl/ *v* [I] to make a loud high unpleasant noise like the sound a cat makes —**caterwauling** *n* [U]: *the sound of drunken caterwauling coming from next door*

cat·fight /'kætfaɪt/ *n* [C] *informal* a word for a fight between women, that some people consider offensive

cat·fish /'kætˌfɪʃ/ *n plural* **catfish** [C,U] a type of fish that has WHISKERS (=strong hairs) around its mouth and lives in rivers or lakes

cat flap *BrE*; **pet door** *AmE n* [C] a small hole cut into a door and covered with wood or plastic that moves to allow a pet cat to enter or leave a house

cat·gut /'kætɡʌt/ *n* [U] strong thread made from the INTESTINES of animals and used for the strings of musical instruments

ca·thar·sis /kəˈθɑːsɪs $ -ɑːr-/ *n* [U] *formal* the act or process of removing strong or violent emotions by expressing them through writing, talking, acting etc: *Music is a means of catharsis for me.*

ca·thar·tic /kəˈθɑːtɪk $ -ɑːr-/ *adj formal* helping you to remove strong or violent emotions: *a cathartic experience*

ca·the·dral /kəˈθiːdrəl/ *n* [C] the main church of a particular area under the control of a BISHOP: *St Paul's Cathedral* | **cathedral city** *BrE* (=one with a cathedral)

cath·er·ine wheel /'kæθərɪn wiːl/ *BrE*; **pinwheel** *AmE n* [C] a round flat FIREWORK that spins around as it burns

cath·e·ter /'kæθɪtə $ -ər/ *n* [C] *medical* a thin tube that is put into your body to remove liquids —**catheterize** also **-ise** *v* [T]

cath·ode /'kæθəʊd $ -θoʊd/ *n* [C] *technical* the negative ELECTRODE, marked (-), from which an electric current leaves a piece of equipment such as a BATTERY; ⊟ **anode**

cathode 'ray tube *n* [C] a piece of equipment used in televisions and computers, in which ELECTRONS from the cathode produce an image on a screen

cath·o·lic /'kæθəlɪk/ adj including a very wide variety of things: Whoever lived here before us had **catholic tastes** (=liked a lot of different things). I a catholic collection of records

Catho·lic adj connected with the Roman Catholic Church —**Catholic** n [C] —**Catholicism** /kə'θɒlɪsɪzəm $ kə'θɑː-/ n [U]

cat·house /'kæthaʊs/ n [C] AmE informal a place where men can pay women to have sex with them; ⊟ brothel

cat·kin /'kætkɪn/ n [C] BrE a long soft flower that hangs in groups from the branches of trees such as the WILLOW

'**cat ,litter** also **kitty litter** AmE n [U] a substance like small grey stones that people put in boxes for cats that live indoors, and which the cats use as a toilet

cat·nap /'kætnæp/ n [C] informal a very short sleep: **have/take a catnap** Nomes slept badly, and had to take catnaps during the day. —**catnap** v [I]

cat-o'-nine-tails /ˌkæt ə 'naɪn teɪlz/ n [singular] a whip made of nine knotted strings, used in the past for punishing people

CAT scan·ner /'kæt ˌskænə $ -ər/ n [C] an electronic machine used in a hospital to get an image of the inside of someone's body —**CAT scan** n [C]: Her X-rays and CAT scans were normal.

,**cat's 'cradle** n 1 [U] a game you play by winding string around your fingers to make different patterns 2 [singular] a set of lines, threads etc that form a complicated pattern: The searchlights wove a cat's cradle of light.

Cats eye /'kætsaɪ/ n [C] BrE trademark one of a line of small flat objects fixed in the middle of the road that shine when lit by car lights and guide traffic in the dark

'**cat's paw**, **cats·paw** /'kætspɔː $ -pɒː/ n [C] old-fashioned someone who is used by someone else to achieve something bad

'**cat suit** n [C] a tight piece of women's clothing that covers the body and legs in one piece

cat·sup /'kætsəp/ n an American spelling of KETCHUP

cat·te·ry /'kætəri/ n plural catteries [C] BrE a place where people can pay to leave their pet cats to be cared for while they are away from home

cat·tle /'kætl/ n [plural] cows and BULLS kept on a farm for their meat or milk: herds of cattle I **dairy/beef cattle** I **20/100 etc head of cattle** (=20, 100 etc cattle) I a cattle rancher

'**cattle grid** BrE; '**cattle guard** AmE n [C] a set of bars placed over a hole in the road, so that animals cannot go across but cars can

cat·tle·man /'kætlmən/ n plural cattlemen /-mən/ [C] someone who looks after or owns cattle

'**cattle ,market** also '**cattle ,auction** AmE n [C] 1 a place where cattle are bought and sold 2 informal a beauty competition or a social event where women are judged only by their appearance – used to show disapproval

'**cattle prod** n [C] a type of stick that gives cattle an electric shock when it touches them, used to make them move

'**cattle truck** n [C] a vehicle or part of a train that is used for carrying cattle

cat·ty /'kæti/ adj someone who is catty says unkind things about people —**cattily** adv —**cattiness** n [U]

'**catty-ˌcorner** adv KITTY-CORNER

cat·walk /'kætwɔːk $ -wɒːk/ n [C] 1 a long raised structure that MODELS walk along in a fashion show; ⊟ runway AmE 2 **the catwalk** the business of designing clothes for fashion shows 3 a narrow structure for people to walk on that is high up inside or outside a building

Cau·ca·sian /kɔː'keɪziən $ kɒː'keɪʒən/ n [C] a member of the race of people with white or pale skin —**Caucasian** adj

cau·cus /'kɔːkəs $ 'kɒː-/ n [C] 1 a meeting of the members of a political party to choose people to represent them in a larger meeting, election etc 2 AmE an organized group of people who have similar aims or interests, especially political ones: the chairman of the Congressional Black Caucus

cau·dal /'kɔːdl $ 'kɒːdl/ adj [only before noun] technical relating to an animal's tail

caught /kɔːt $ kɒːt/ the past tense and past participle of CATCH

caul·dron, **caldron** /'kɔːldrən $ 'kɒːl-/ n [C] a large round metal pot for boiling liquids over a fire: a witch's cauldron

cau·li·flow·er /'kɒliˌflaʊə $ 'kɒːliˌflaʊər, 'kɑː-/ n [C,U] a vegetable with green leaves around a firm white centre → see picture at VEGETABLE

,**cauliflower 'ear** n [C] an ear permanently swollen into a strange shape, as a result of an injury

caulk also **calk** AmE /kɔːk $ kɒːk/ v [T] to fill the holes or cracks in a ship with an oily or sticky substance in order to keep water out

caus·al /'kɔːzəl $ 'kɒː-/ adj 1 relating to the connection between two things, where one causes the other to happen or exist; → **cause**: causal relationship/link/factor etc a causal relationship between unemployment and crime 2 technical a causal CONJUNCTION, such as 'because', introduces a statement about the cause of something —**causally** adv

cau·sal·i·ty /kɔː'zælɪti $ kɒː-/ n [U] formal the relationship between a cause and the effect that it has

cau·sa·tion /kɔː'zeɪʃən $ kɒː-/ n [U] formal 1 the action of causing something to happen or exist 2 causality

caus·a·tive /'kɔːzətɪv $ 'kɒː-/ adj formal acting as the cause of something: Smoking is a causative factor in several major diseases.

cause¹ S2 W1 /kɔːz $ kɒːz/ n

1 [C] a person, event, or thing that makes something happen; → **effect**: [+of] Breast cancer is the leading **cause of death** for American women in their forties. I **establish/investigate/discover etc the cause** It's our job to establish the cause of the fire. I **root/underlying etc cause** The cost of the project was enormous, but it was not the fundamental cause of its failure. I **cause and effect** (=the idea that one thing directly causes another) I **die of/from natural causes** (=because of old age or an illness, not an accident, murder etc)
2 [U] a fact that makes it right or reasonable for you to feel or behave in a particular way; ⊟ **reason**: [+for] There is **no cause for alarm**. I The patient's condition is **giving cause for concern**. I The present political climate **gives little cause for optimism**. I **have (good) cause to do sth** His father has good cause to be proud of him. I **with/without good cause** Many people are worried about the economy, and with good cause.
3 [C] an organization, belief, or aim that a group of people support or fight for: [+of] her lifelong devotion to the cause of women's rights I **Nationalist/Republican etc cause** I **champion/further a cause** Since founding Island Records, Blackwell has championed the cause of Jamaican music. I **worthy/good cause** (=an organization that helps people who are ill, old etc, especially a CHARITY) You can get fit, and at the same time raise money for a worthy cause. I Please give generously, it's all in a good cause (=done in order to help people).
4 **have/make common cause (with/against sb)** formal to join with other people or groups in order to oppose an enemy: U.S. officials expect other Western governments to make common cause with them over the arrests.
5 [C] law a case that is brought to a court of law → **lost cause** at LOST² (12)

WORD CHOICE: cause, reason
A **cause** is something such as an action, event, or situation that makes something happen: *The cause of the accident is not known.* | *a determination to tackle the causes of crime*
A **reason** is an explanation for something: *Can you think of any reason why he would behave in this way?* | *There is a good reason (NOT a good cause) for my decision.*
Use **the cause of**, not 'cause for' or 'cause why': *What is the cause of all this unrest?*
⚠ **cause for** is used in some expressions such as **cause for alarm/concern/complaint/optimism/satisfaction**: *There is no cause for concern.* | *His remarks give some cause for hope.*
Use **cause sb to do sth**, not 'cause that sb does sth': *A cat ran into the road, causing her to brake suddenly (NOT causing that she braked suddenly).*

cause² [S1] [W1] v [T] to make something happen, especially something bad: *Heavy traffic is causing delays on the freeway.* | *The fire caused £15,000 worth of damage.* | **cause sth for sb** *The oil spill is causing problems for coastal fisheries.* | **cause concern/uncertainty/embarrassment etc** *The policy changes have caused great uncertainty for the workforce.* | *I'm sorry if I caused any confusion.* | **cause sb trouble/problems etc** *You've caused us all a lot of unnecessary worry.* | *Sorry, I didn't mean to cause offence* (=offend you). | **cause sb/sth to do sth** *What caused you to change your mind?*

cause cé·lè·bre /ˌkəʊz seˈlebrə, ˌkɔːz- $ ˌkɔːz-, ˌkoʊz-/ n plural **causes célèbres** (*same pronunciation*) [C] an event or legal case that a lot of people become interested in, because it is an exciting subject to discuss or argue about: *The case became a cause célèbre among feminists.*

cause·way /ˈkɔːzweɪ $ ˈkɒz-/ n [C] a raised road or path across wet ground or through water

caus·tic /ˈkɔːstɪk $ ˈkɒːs-/ adj **1** a caustic substance can burn through things by chemical action: *caustic soda* (a chemical used for cleaning things) **2** a caustic remark criticizes someone in a way that is unkind but often cleverly humorous: **caustic wit/comments/remark etc** *Eliot appreciated Pound's caustic wit.* —**caustically** /-kli/ adv: *'I can hardly wait,' Sir Trevor replied caustically.*

cau·ter·ize also **-ise** BrE /ˈkɔːtəraɪz $ ˈkɒː-/ v [T] medical to treat a wound or a growth on your body by burning it with hot metal, a LASER, or a chemical

cau·tion¹ /ˈkɔːʃən $ ˈkɒː-/ n **1** [U] the quality of being very careful to avoid danger or risks; → **cautious**: **with caution** *We must proceed with extreme caution.* | *The physician must exercise caution when prescribing anti-depressants.* | **counsel/urge caution** *Many parents are tempted to intervene, but most experts counsel caution.* | **treat/view sth with caution** (=think carefully about something because it might not be true) *Evidence given by convicted criminals should always be treated with the utmost caution.*; → **err on the side of caution** at ERR (1) **2** [C] a warning or piece of advice telling you to be careful: *Although pleased, Henson added a caution that the team still has a long way to go.* | **word/note of caution** *A final word of caution – never try any of this without backing up your system.* **3 throw/cast caution to the winds** literary to stop worrying about danger and to take a big risk: *Throwing caution to the winds, she swung around to face him.* **4** [C,U] BrE a spoken official warning given to someone who has been ARRESTED or who has done something wrong that is not a serious crime: *He was let off with a caution.* | **under caution** *The defendant may make a statement under caution.*

caution² v **1** [I,T] to warn someone that something might be dangerous, difficult etc: **caution (sb) against sth** *Business leaders are cautioning against hasty action that would hamper flexibility.* | **caution (sb) that** *Officials were quick to caution that these remarks did not mean an end to the peace process.* | **caution sb to do sth** *He cautioned them to avoid the forest at night.* **2** [T]

BrE **a)** to warn someone officially that the next time they do something illegal they will be punished: **caution sb for (doing) sth** *She was cautioned for speeding.* **b)** to warn someone officially that what they say to a police officer may be used as EVIDENCE in a court of law

cau·tion·ar·y /ˈkɔːʃənəri $ ˈkɒʃəneri/ adj [usually before noun] giving a warning about what not to do: **cautionary note/comment/words etc** *Most observers were optimistic, yet some sounded a cautionary note.* | **cautionary tale** (=the story of an event that is used to warn people) *a cautionary tale about how not to buy a computer*

cau·tious /ˈkɔːʃəs $ ˈkɒː-/ adj careful to avoid danger or risks; → **caution**: *a cautious driver* | *a cautious approach to the crisis* | *The air-pollution board has reacted with cautious optimism to the announcement.* | **cautious about (doing) sth** *Keller is cautious about making predictions for the success of the program.* —**cautiously** adv: *The government responded cautiously to the move.* —**cautiousness** n [U]

cav·al·cade /ˌkævəlˈkeɪd, ˈkævəlkeɪd/ n [C] a line of people on horses or in cars or carriages moving along as part of a ceremony

cav·a·lier /ˌkævəˈlɪə◂ $ -ˈlɪr◂/ adj [usually before noun] not caring enough about rules, principles, or people's feelings: *The club's owner showed a cavalier attitude to the licensing laws.*

cav·al·ry /ˈkævəlri/ n [plural,U] **1** the part of an army that fights on horses, especially in the past: *The Black Prince led a cavalry charge against them.* **2** the part of a modern army that uses TANKS

cav·al·ry·man /ˈkævəlrimən/ n plural **cavalrymen** /-mən/ [C] a soldier who fights on a horse

cave¹ /keɪv/ n [C] a large natural hole in the side of a cliff or hill, or under the ground: *the entrance to a cave*

cave² v
cave in phr v **1** if the top or sides of something cave in, they fall down or inwards: [+on] *The roof of the tunnel caved in on them.* **2** to finally stop opposing something, especially because someone has persuaded or threatened you: [+to] *The chairman is expected to cave in to pressure from shareholders.*

ca·ve·at /ˈkæviæt, ˈkeɪv-/ n [C] formal a warning that something may not be completely true, effective etc: **caveat that** *She will be offered treatment, with the caveat that it may not work.*

caveat emp·tor /ˌkæviæt ˈemptɔː, ˌkeɪv- $ -tɔːr/ n [U] law the principle that the person who buys something is responsible for checking that it is not broken, damaged etc

cave-in n [C] **1** when the roof of something such as a mine falls in **2** when someone stops opposing something

cave·man /ˈkeɪvmæn/ n plural **cavemen** /-men/ [C] **1** someone who lived in a CAVE many thousands of years ago **2** informal an insulting word for a man who you think is rude, violent etc: *Are you going to give me the macho caveman act?*

cav·er /ˈkeɪvə $ -ər/ n [C] BrE someone who goes into CAVES deep under the ground as a sport; ▤ **spelunker** AmE

cav·ern /ˈkævən $ -ərn/ n [C] a large CAVE

cav·ern·ous /ˈkævənəs $ -ərnəs/ adj literary a cavernous room, space, or hole is very large and deep: *a cavernous dining hall*

cav·i·ar, caviare /ˈkæviɑː $ -ɑːr/ n [U] the preserved eggs of various large fish, eaten as a special very expensive food: *caviare and champagne*

cav·il /ˈkævəl/ v **cavilled, cavilling** BrE, **caviled, caviling** AmE [I] formal to make unnecessary complaints about someone or something: [+at] *They cavilled at our calculations.* —**cavil** n [C,U]

C

cav·ing /ˈkeɪvɪŋ/ n [U] BrE the sport of going into CAVES deep under the ground; ☐ **spelunking** AmE; → see picture at OUTDOOR

cav·i·ty /ˈkævəti/ n plural **cavities** [C] formal a hole or space inside something: Put herbs inside the body cavity of the fish. | I have no cavities (=no holes in my teeth).

'cavity ˌwall n [C] a wall consisting of two walls with a space between them to keep out cold and noise: cavity wall insulation

ca·vort /kəˈvɔːt $ -ɔːrt/ v [I] to jump or dance around in a playful or sexual way: [+about/around] She cavorted about in the shallow water. | [+with] The photograph shows him cavorting with two young women.

caw /kɔː $ kɒ/ n [C] the loud sound made by some types of bird, especially CROWS —**caw** v [I]

cay /kiː, keɪ/ n [C] AmE a very small low island formed of CORAL or sand

cay·enne pep·per /ˌkeɪen ˈpepə $ -ər/ n [U] the red powder made from a PEPPER that has a very hot taste

cay·man /ˈkeɪmən/ n plural **caymans** [C] a South American animal like an ALLIGATOR

CB /ˌsiː ˈbiːˌ/ n [U] Citizens' Band a type of radio communication which people can use to speak to each other over short distances, especially when they are driving

CBE /ˌsiː biː ˈiːˌ/ n [C] Commander of the British Empire an honour given to some British people for things they have done for their country

CBT /ˌsiː biː ˈtiːˌ/ n [U] **1** computer-based testing a way of taking standard tests such as the GRE on a computer **2** computer-based training the use of computers to teach people to do something: CBT software

cc /ˌsiː ˈsiː/ **1** carbon copy to used in a business letter or email to show that you are sending a copy to someone else: To Neil Fry, cc: Anthea Baker, Matt Fox **2** the abbreviation of cubic centimetre or cubic centimetres: a 200cc engine

CCTV /ˌsiː siː tiː ˈviːˌ/ n [U] BrE the written abbreviation of closed circuit television

CD /ˌsiː ˈdiːˌ/ n [C] compact disc a small circular piece of hard plastic on which high quality recorded sound or large quantities of information can be stored

C'D ˌplayer n [C] a piece of equipment used to play COMPACT DISCS → see cture at CAR

CD-R /ˌsiː diː ˈɑː $ -ˈɑːr/ n [C,U] compact disc – recordable a type of CD that you can record music, images, or other information onto, using special equipment on your computer, and that can be recorded onto only once

CD-ROM /ˌsiː diː ˈrɒm $ -ˈrɑːm/ n [C,U] compact disc read-only memory a CD on which large quantities of information can be stored to be used by a computer

CD-RW /ˌsiː diː ɑː ˈdʌbəlju $ -ɑːr-/ n [C,U] compact disc – rewritable a type of CD that you can record music, images, or other information onto, using special equipment on your computer, and that can be recorded onto several times

CDT /ˌsiː diː ˈtiːˌ/ n [U] Craft, Design, and Technology a practical subject studied in British schools

CE BrE; **C.E.** AmE /ˌsiː ˈiːˌ/ Common Era used after a date to show it was after the birth of Christ; ☐ **AD**; → BC

cease¹ W3 /siːs/ v [I,T]
1 formal to stop doing something or stop happening: **cease to do sth** He ceased to be a member of the association. | The things people will do for charity **never cease to amaze me** (=I am always surprised by them). | **cease doing sth** the decision to cease using CFCs in packaging | The rain ceased and the sky cleared. | **cease trading/production/operations etc** (=stop operating a business) The company ceased production at their

Norwich plant last year. | **cease fire!** (=used to order soldiers to stop shooting)
2 cease and desist law to stop doing something → CEASEFIRE; → **wonders will never cease** at WONDER² (5)

cease² n **without cease** formal without stopping

cease·fire /ˈsiːsfaɪə $ -faɪr/ n [C] an agreement to stop fighting for a period of time, especially so that a more permanent agreement can be made: a ceasefire agreement | They have **called** a temporary ceasefire in the region. → ARMISTICE, TRUCE

cease·less /ˈsiːsləs/ adj happening for a long time without stopping: the ceaseless fight against crime —**ceaselessly** adv: The men worked ceaselessly through the night.

ce·dar /ˈsiːdə $ -ər/ n **1** [C] a large EVERGREEN tree with leaves shaped like needles **2** also **cedarwood** [U] the hard red wood of the cedar tree, which smells pleasant

cede /siːd/ v [T] formal to give something such as an area of land or a right to a country or person, especially when you are forced to: **cede sth to sb** Hong Kong was ceded to Britain in 1842. → CESSION

ce·dil·la /sɪˈdɪlə/ n [C] a mark put under the letter 'c' in French and some other languages, to show that it is an 's' sound instead of a 'k' sound. The letter is written 'ç'.

Cee·fax /ˈsiːfæks/ n [U] trademark a service in which the BBC broadcasts written information on television in Britain

cei·lidh /ˈkeɪli/ n [C] an evening entertainment with Scottish or Irish singing and dancing

cei·ling S3 W3 /ˈsiːlɪŋ/ n [C]
1 the inner surface of the top part of a room; → **roof**: rooms with high ceilings | a light hanging from the ceiling
2 the largest number or amount of something that is officially allowed: [+of] a public spending ceiling of £240 bn | **impose/set/put a ceiling (on sth)** The government imposed a ceiling on imports of foreign cars. | **raise/lower the ceiling (on sth)**
3 technical the greatest height an aircraft can fly at or the level of the clouds → GLASS CEILING

ce·leb /səˈleb/ n [C] informal a CELEBRITY: TV celebs

cel·e·brant /ˈseləbrənt/ n [C] formal someone who performs or takes part in a religious ceremony

cel·e·brate W3 /ˈseləbreɪt/ v
1 [I,T] to show that an event or occasion is important by doing something special or enjoyable; → **celebration**: It's Dad's birthday and we're going out for a meal to celebrate. | My folks are celebrating their 50th anniversary. | We hope to give fans something to celebrate this season. | **celebrate Christmas/Thanksgiving etc** How do you usually celebrate New Year?
2 [T] formal to praise someone or something: poems that celebrate the joys of love
3 [T] to perform a religious ceremony, especially the Christian Mass

cel·e·brat·ed /ˈseləbreɪtəd/ adj famous: a celebrated actress | a celebrated legal case

cel·e·bra·tion S3 /ˌseləˈbreɪʃən/ n
1 [C] an occasion or party when you celebrate something: **anniversary/birthday etc celebrations** the lively New Year celebrations in the city centre
2 [singular, U] the act of celebrating: **in celebration of sth** a reception in celebration of the Fund's 70th Anniversary | The show is a celebration of new young talent. | I think this is a **cause for celebration** (=reason to celebrate).

cel·e·bra·to·ry /ˌseləˈbreɪtəri $ ˈseləbrətɔːri/ adj [only before noun] done in order to celebrate a particular event or occasion: Join us for a celebratory drink in the bar.

ce·leb·ri·ty /sɪˈlebrəti/ n plural **celebrities** **1** [C] a famous living person; ☐ **star**: a sporting celebrity | He became a national celebrity. | They had invited a number of *minor celebrities* (=people who are not very famous). **2** [U] *formal* the state of being famous; ⊟ **fame**

ce·ler·i·ac /sə'leriæk/ *n* [U] a large white root vegetable which is a type of CELERY

cel·e·ry /'seləri/ *n* [U] a vegetable with long pale green stems that you can eat cooked or uncooked: *a stick of celery*

ce·les·ti·al /sɪ'lestiəl $ -tʃəl/ *adj* [usually before noun] **1** relating to the sky or heaven: **celestial bodies** (=the sun, moon, stars etc) **2** *literary* very beautiful

cel·i·bate /'selɪbət/ *adj* not married and not having sex, especially because of your religious beliefs; → **virgin**: *Catholic priests are required to be celibate.* —**celibate** *n* [C] —**celibacy** /-bəsi/ *n* [U]: *a vow of celibacy*

cell W1 /sel/ *n* [C]
1 BODY the smallest part of a living thing that can exist independently: **blood/brain/nerve cell** *red blood cells* | *cancer cells* | *Embryos grow by cell division* (=the splitting of cells).
2 PRISON a small room in a prison or police station where prisoners are kept: *He spent a night in the cells at the local police station.* | *the walls of his prison cell*
3 PHONE *AmE* a CELLULAR PHONE; a telephone that you can carry around with you, that works by using a network of radio stations to pass on signals; ⊟ **mobile** *BrE: Call me on my cell if you're running late.*
4 ELECTRIC a piece of equipment for producing electricity from chemicals, heat, or light: *a car powered by electric fuel cells*
5 SECRET GROUP a small group of people who are working secretly as part of a larger political organization: *a terrorist cell*
6 RELIGIOUS a small room in a MONASTERY or CONVENT where someone sleeps
7 INSECT/SMALL ANIMAL a small space that an insect or other small creature has made to live in or use: *the cells of a honeycomb*

cel·lar /'selə $ -ər/ *n* [C] **1** a room under a house or other building, often used for storing things; ⊟ **basement**: *a coal cellar* **2** a store of wine belonging to a person, restaurant etc → SALT CELLAR

cel·list /'tʃelɪst/ *n* [C] someone who plays the cello

cell·mate /'selmeɪt/ *n* [C] someone who shares a prison cell with someone else

cel·lo /'tʃeləʊ $ -loʊ/ *n plural* **cellos** [C] a musical instrument like a large VIOLIN that you hold between your knees and play by pulling a BOW (=special stick) across the strings → see picture at STRINGED INSTRUMENT

Cel·lo·phane /'seləfeɪn/ *n* [U] *trademark* a thin transparent material used for wrapping things

cell·phone, **'cell phone** /'selfəʊn $ -foʊn/ *n* [C] *especially AmE* a cellular telephone; ⊟ **mobile phone** *BrE*

cel·lu·lar /'seljʊlə $ -ər/ *adj* **1** consisting of or relating to the cells of plants or animals **2** a cellular telephone system works by using a network of radio stations to pass on signals: *a cellular network*

cellular 'phone *n* [C] *especially AmE* a telephone that you can carry with you and use in any place; ⊟ **mobile phone** *BrE*; → see picture at MOBILE PHONE

cel·lu·lite /'seljʊlaɪt/ *n* [U] fat that is just below someone's skin and makes it look uneven and unattractive

cel·lu·loid /'seljʊlɔɪd/ *n* [U] **1 on celluloid** on cinema film: *Chaplin's comic genius is preserved on celluloid.* **2** a plastic substance made mainly from CELLULOSE that was used in the past to make photographic film and other objects

cel·lu·lose /'seljʊləʊs $ -loʊs/ *n* [U] **1** the material that the cell walls of plants are made of and that is used to make plastics, paper etc **2** also **cellulose acetate** *technical* a plastic that is used for many industrial purposes, especially making photographic film and explosives

Cel·si·us /'selsiəs/ *n* [U] written abbreviation *C* a scale of temperature in which water freezes at 0° and boils at 100°; ⊟ **Centigrade**: *12° Celsius* (=12 degrees on the Celsius scale) —**Celsius** *adj*

Celt /kelt, selt/ *n* [C] a member of a race of people who lived in ancient Britain and Western Europe before the Romans came, or a person living now whose ANCESTORS were members of this race

Cel·tic /'keltɪk, 'seltɪk/ *adj* relating to the Celts or their languages

ce·ment[1] /sɪ'ment/ *n* [U] **1** a grey powder made from LIME and clay that becomes hard when it is mixed with water and allowed to dry, and that is used in building; → **concrete**: *a bag of cement* **2** a thick sticky substance that becomes very hard when it dries and is used for filling holes or sticking things together

cement[2] *v* [T] **1** also **cement over** to cover something with cement **2** to make a relationship between people, countries, or organizations firm and strong: **cement a relationship/alliance** *They want to cement a good working relationship between the government and trade unions.*

ce'ment ,mixer *n* [C] a machine with a round drum that turns around, into which you put cement, sand, and water to make CONCRETE

cem·e·tery /'semɪtri $ -teri/ *n plural* **cemeteries** [C] a piece of land, usually not belonging to a church, in which dead people are buried; → **graveyard**

cen·o·taph /'senətɑːf $ -tæf/ *n* [C] a MONUMENT built to remind people of soldiers, sailors etc who were killed in a war and are buried somewhere else

cen·sor[1] /'sensə $ -ər/ *n* [C] someone whose job is to examine books, films, letters etc and remove anything considered to be offensive, morally harmful, or politically dangerous; → **censorship**

censor[2] *v* [T] to examine books, films, letters etc to remove anything that is considered offensive, morally harmful, or politically dangerous etc; → **censorship**, **ban**: *The information given to the press was carefully censored by the Ministry of Defence.*

cen·so·ri·ous /sen'sɔːriəs/ *adj formal* criticizing and expressing disapproval: *His tone was censorious.* —**censoriously** *adv* —**censoriousness** *n* [U]

cen·sor·ship /'sensəʃɪp $ -ər-/ *n* [U] the practice or system of censoring something: *the censorship of television programmes*

cen·sure[1] /'senʃə $ -ər/ *n* [U] *formal* the act of expressing strong disapproval and criticism: *a vote of censure*

censure[2] *v* [T] *formal* to officially criticize someone for something they have done wrong: *He was officially censured for his handling of the situation.*

cen·sus /'sensəs/ *n plural* **censuses** [C] **1** an official process of counting a country's population and finding out about the people **2** an official process of counting something for government planning: *a traffic census*

cent S1 W1 /sent/ *n* [C]
1 1/100th of the standard unit of money in some countries. For example, there are 100 cents in one dollar or in one EURO: symbol ¢
2 put in your two cents' worth *AmE* to give your opinion about something, when other people do not want to hear it → **not one red cent** at RED[1] (7)

cen·taur /'sentɔː $ -tɔːr/ *n* [C] a creature in ancient Greek stories with the head, chest, and arms of a man and the body and legs of a horse

cen·te·nar·i·an /,sentɪ'neəriən $ -'ner-/ *n* [C] someone who is 100 years old or older

cen·te·na·ry /sen'tiːnəri $ -'te-, 'sentənəri/ *plural* **centenaries** *especially BrE* also **cen·ten·ni·al** /sen'teniəl/ *especially AmE n* [C] the day or year exactly

C

100 years after a particular event: [+of] *a concert to mark the centenary of the composer's birth*

cen·ter /'sentə $ -ər/ *n, v* the American spelling of CENTRE

centi- /sentɪ/ also **cent-** /sent/ *prefix* [in nouns] **1** a hundred: *a centipede* (=creature with 100 legs) **2** a 100th part of a unit: *a centimetre* (=0.01 metres)

Cen·ti·grade /'sentɪɡreɪd/ *n* [U] written abbreviation *C* CELSIUS —**Centigrade** *adj*

centilitre *BrE*; **centiliter** *AmE* /'sentɪliːtə $ -ər/ *n* [C] written abbreviation *cl* a unit for measuring an amount of liquid. There are 100 centilitres in one litre.

cen·time /'sɒntiːm $ 'sɑːn-/ *n* [C] 1/100th of a FRANC or some other units of money

cen·ti·me·tre S3 *BrE*; **centimeter** *AmE* /'sentɪˌmiːtə $ -ər/ *n* [C] written abbreviation *cm* a unit for measuring length. There are 100 centimetres in one metre

cen·ti·pede /'sentɪpiːd/ *n* [C] a small creature like a WORM with a lot of very small legs

cen·tral S1 W1 /'sentrəl/ *adj*
1 MIDDLE [only before noun, no comparative] in the middle of an area or an object: *He lives in central London.* | *The roof is supported by a central column.* | *Central America/Asia/Europe etc*
2 FROM ONE PLACE [only before noun, no comparative] used about the part of an organization, system etc which controls the rest of it, or its work: *the party's central office* | *the system's central control unit* | *central planning*
3 IMPORTANT more important and having more influence than anything else: [+to] *values which are central to our society* | *Owen played a central role in the negotiations.* | *His ideas were of central importance in the development of the theory.* | *central idea/theme/concern etc Education has become a central issue in public debate.*
4 EASY ACCESS a place that is central is easy to reach because it is near the middle of a town or area: *It's very central, just five minutes walk from the main square.*
5 party/comedy etc central *informal* a place where something is happening a lot: *Tim's house became party central for the band and their friends.*
—**centrally** *adv*: *Our office is centrally situated.* | *All data is held centrally.* —**centrality** /sen'trælɪti/ *n* [U]

central 'bank *n* [C] a national bank that does business with the government, and controls the amount of money available and the general system of banks

central 'government *n* [C,U] *especially BrE* the level of government which deals with national rather than local things; → local government

central 'heating *n* [U] a system of heating buildings in which water or air is heated in one place and then sent around the rest of the building through pipes etc: *the central heating boiler* —**centrally heated** *adj*

cen·tral·is·m /'sentrəlɪzəm/ *n* [U] a way of governing a country or controlling an organization in which one group has power and tells people in other places what to do

cen·tral·ize also **-ise** *BrE* /'sentrəlaɪz/ *v* [T] to organize the control of a country, organization, or system so that everything is done or decided in one place; **≠** decentralize: *plans to centralize the company's European activities* —**centralized** *adj*: *a centralized database* —**centralization** /ˌsentrəlaɪˈzeɪʃən $ -lə-/ *n* [U]

central 'locking *n* [U] *BrE* a system for locking the doors of a car in which all the locks are operated when you turn the key in one lock or use a REMOTE CONTROLLED key

central 'nervous ˌsystem *n* [C] the main part of your NERVOUS SYSTEM, consisting of your brain and your SPINAL CORD

central 'processing ˌunit *n* [C] a CPU

central reser'vation *n* [C] *BrE* a narrow piece of ground that divides the two parts of a MOTORWAY or other main road

cen·tre¹ S1 W1 *BrE*; **center** *AmE* /'sentə $ -ər/ *n*
1 MIDDLE [C usually singular] the middle of a space, area, or object, especially the exact middle: *in the centre (of sth) There was an enormous oak table in the center of the room.* | *The hotel is right in the centre of the village.* | [+of] *Draw a line through the centre of the circle.* | *lines radiating out from the centre* | *chocolates with soft centres*
2 BUILDING [C] a building which is used for a particular purpose or activity: [+for] *the European Centre for Nuclear Research* | *an exhibition at the Community Arts Centre* | *a conference centre*
3 PLACE OF ACTIVITY [C] a place where there is a lot of a particular type of business, activity etc: *business/commercial/financial etc centre a major banking centre* | *It's not exactly a cultural center like Paris.* | [+of/for] *The city became a centre for the paper industry.* | *a center of academic excellence* (=a very good place for education)
4 OF A TOWN [C] *BrE* the part of a town or city where most of the shops, restaurants, cinemas, theatres etc are; **≡** downtown *AmE*: **town/city centre** *shops in the town centre* | *the main route into Leeds city centre*
5 INVOLVEMENT **be at the centre of sth** if a person or thing is at the centre of something that is happening, they are involved in it more than other people or things: *He always seems to be at the centre of things.* | **be at the centre of a row/dispute/controversy etc** *the businessman at the centre of the row over political donations*
6 **be the centre of attention** to be the person that everyone is giving attention to: *Betty just loves being the centre of attention.*
7 **be/take centre stage** if something or someone is centre stage, they have an important position and get a lot of attention: *After his father's death, he was able to rise to power and take centre stage.*
8 POLITICS **the centre** a MODERATE (=middle) position in politics in which you do not support extreme ideas: *The party's new policies show a swing towards the centre.* | **left/right of centre** *Her political views are slightly left of centre.* | **centre-right/centre-left** *a centre-left government*
9 SPORT [C] a player in sports such as football and BASKETBALL who plays in or near the middle of the field or playing area: *the Sonics' six-foot-four-inch center* | **centre forward/half/back etc** (=players in different parts of the middle section of the playing area)
10 **centre of population/urban centre** an area where a large number of people live: *Nuclear installations are built well away from the main centres of population.*

centre² *BrE*; **center** *AmE v* [T] to move something to a position at the centre of something else: *The title isn't quite centred on the page, is it?*

centre around/round sth also **be centred around/round sth** *BrE phr v* if your thoughts, activities etc centre around something or are centred around it, it is the main thing that you are concerned with or interested in: *In the 16th century, village life centred around religion.*

centre on/upon sth also **be centred on/upon sth** *phr v* if your attention centres on something or someone, or is centred on them, you pay more attention to them than anything else: *The debate centred on funding for health services.* | *Much of their work is centred on local development projects.*

cen·tred *BrE*; **centered** *AmE* /'sentəd $ -ərd/ *adj* **1** also **-centred** [only after noun] having a particular person or group as the most important part or FOCUS of something: *a student-centred approach* | *family centered care* **2** feeling calm and in control of your life and feelings: *Julia seems very centred nowadays.*

cen·tre·fold *BrE*; **centerfold** *AmE* /'sentəfəʊld $ -tərfoʊld/ *n* [C] **1** the two pages that face each other in the middle of a magazine or newspaper **2** a picture of a woman with no clothes on that covers the two pages in the middle of a magazine

ˌcentre ˈforward *BrE*; **center forward** *AmE n* [C] an attacking player who plays in the centre of the field in British football

ˌcentre of ˈgravity *n* [singular] the point in any object on which it can balance

cen·tre·piece *BrE*; **centerpiece** *AmE* /ˈsentəpiːs $ -ər-/ *n* **1** [singular] the most important, noticeable, or attractive part of something: [+of] *The centrepiece of Bevan's policy was the National Health Service.* **2** [C] a decoration, especially an arrangement of flowers, in the middle of a table

cen·tri·fu·gal force /ˌsentrɪfjuːgəl ˈfɔːs sen,trɪfˈjuːgəl- $ sen,trɪfˈjuːgəl ˈfɔːrs/ *n* [U] a force which makes things move away from the centre of something when they are moving around it

cen·tri·fuge /ˈsentrɪfjuːdʒ/ *n* [C] a machine that spins a container around very quickly so that the heavier liquids and any solids are forced to the outer edge or bottom

cen·trip·e·tal force /sen,trɪpətl ˈfɔːs $ -ˈfɔːrs/ *n* [U] *technical* a force which makes things move towards the centre of something when they are moving around it

cen·trist /ˈsentrəst/ *adj* having political beliefs that are not extreme; ◨ **moderate** —**centrist** *n* [C]

cen·tu·ri·on /senˈtjʊəriən $ -ˈtʊr-/ *n* [C] an army officer of ancient Rome, who was in charge of about 100 soldiers

cen·tu·ry S1 W1 /ˈsentʃəri/ *n plural* **centuries** [C] **1** one of the 100-year periods measured from before or after the year of Christ's birth: **the 11th/18th/21st etc century** *The church was built in the 13th century.* | **the next/last century** *by the beginning of the next century* | *twentieth-century art forms such as Cubism* | *the story of life on a small farm at* **the turn of the century** (=the beginning of the century) **2** a period of 100 years: *many centuries ago* **3** 100 RUNS scored by one CRICKET player in an INNINGS

CEO /ˌsiː iː ˈəʊ $ -ˈoʊ/ *n* [C] *Chief Executive Officer* the person with the most authority in a large company

ce·ram·ics /sɪˈræmɪks/ *n* **1** [U] the art of making pots, bowls, TILES etc, by shaping pieces of clay and baking them until they are hard → see picture at HANDICRAFT **2** [plural] things that are made this way: *an exhibition of ceramics* —**ceramic** *adj*: *ceramic tiles*

ce·re·al S3 /ˈsɪəriəl $ ˈsɪr-/ *n* **1** [C,U] a breakfast food made from grain and usually eaten with milk: *a bowl of* **breakfast cereal** **2** [C] a plant grown to produce grain, for example wheat, rice etc: *cereal crops* ⚠ Do not confuse with **serial** (=a story broadcast or written in several parts).

cer·e·bel·lum /ˌserəˈbeləm/ *n plural* **cerebellums** *or* **cerebella** /-lə/ [C] *technical* the bottom part of your brain that controls your muscles

cer·e·bral /ˈserəbrəl $ səˈriː-, ˈserə-/ *adj* **1** [only before noun] *medical* relating to or affecting your brain: *a* **cerebral haemorrhage** (=bleeding in the brain) **2** having or involving complicated ideas rather than strong emotions: *a cerebral film*

ˌcerebral ˈpalsy /$ ˌ.. ˈ../ *n* [U] a disease caused by damage to the brain before or during birth which results in difficulties of movement and speech

cer·e·mo·ni·al[1] /ˌserəˈməʊniəl $ -ˈmoʊ-/ *adj* **1** [usually before noun] used in a ceremony or done as part of a ceremony: *the Mayor's ceremonial duties* | *Native American ceremonial robes* **2** if a ceremony in a country or organization is ceremonial, it gives no real power: *the largely ceremonial post of President*

ceremonial[2] *n* [C,U] a special ceremony, or special formal actions: *an occasion for public ceremonial*

cer·e·mo·ni·ous /ˌserəˈməʊniəs $ -ˈmoʊ-/ *adj* done in a formal serious way, as if you were in a ceremony —**ceremoniously** *adv*: *He ceremoniously burnt the offending documents.*

cer·e·mo·ny /ˈserəməni $ -moʊni/ *n plural* **ceremonies** **1** [C] an important social or religious event, when a traditional set of actions is performed in a formal way; → **ceremonial**: *the wedding ceremony* | *a graduation ceremony* | *the opening ceremony of the Olympic Games* **2** [U] the special actions and formal words traditionally used on particular occasions: *The queen was crowned with due ceremony.* **3 without ceremony** in a very informal way, without politeness: *He wished me good luck in the future and left without further ceremony.* → **not stand on ceremony** at STAND¹ (42)

ce·rise /səˈriːs, -ˈriːz/ *n* [U] a bright pinkish-red colour —**cerise** *adj*

cert /sɜːt $ sɜːrt/ *n* **be a (dead) cert** *BrE informal* to be certain to happen or to succeed: *Put your money on Thorpe to win, he's a dead cert.*

cert. **1** the written abbreviation of *certificate* **2** the written abbreviation of *certified*

cer·tain¹ S1 W1 /ˈsɜːtn $ ˈsɜːr-/ *adj* **1** [not before noun] confident and sure, without any doubts; ◨ **sure**: **certain (that)** *I'm absolutely certain that I left the keys in the kitchen.* | *I felt certain that I'd passed the test.* | **certain who/what/how etc** *I'm not certain when it will be ready.* | [+about/of] *Now, are you certain about that?* | *They were watching him. He was certain of it.* **2** if something is certain, it will definitely happen or is definitely true

it is/seems certain (that)
be/appear/look/seem certain to do sth
be certain of (doing) sth
it is not certain whether/how etc
almost/virtually/practically certain
fairly certain
by no means certain/far from certain (=not definite)
certain death

It now **seems certain that** *there will be an election in May.* | *Many people* **look certain to** *lose their jobs.* | *It is wise to apply early to* **be certain of** *obtaining a place.* | *It's not certain where he lived.* | *His re-election was considered* **virtually certain**. | *It is* **by no means certain** *that the deal will be accepted.* | *If they stayed in the war zone they would face* **certain death**.

3 make certain a) to check that something is correct or true; ◨ **make sure**: **make certain (that)** *We need to make certain that it's going to fit first.* **b)** to do something in order to be sure that something will happen; ◨ **make sure**: **make certain (that)** *Secure the edges firmly to make certain that no moisture can get in.* **4 for certain** without doubt; ◨ **for sure**: **know/say (sth) for certain** *I know for certain it's in here somewhere.* | **that's/one thing's for certain** *One thing's for certain, he won't be back.* **5** [only before noun] used to talk about a particular person, thing, group of things etc without naming them or describing them exactly: *The library's only open at certain times of day.* | *I promised to be in a certain place by lunchtime.* | *There are certain things I just can't discuss with my mother.* | **certain kind/type/sort** *the expectation of a certain kind of behaviour* | **in certain circumstances/cases etc** *Extra funding may be available in certain circumstances.* **6 a certain a)** used to say that an amount is not great: *You may need to do* **a certain amount of** *work in the evenings.* | **to a certain extent/degree** (=partly, but not completely) *I do agree with his ideas to a certain extent.* **b)** enough of a particular quality to be noticed: *There's a certain prestige about going to a private school.* **c)** *formal* used to talk about someone you do not know but whose name you've been told: *a certain Mr Franks*

certain² *pron* **certain of sb/sth** *formal* particular people or things in a group: *Certain of the payments were made on Mr Maxwell's authority.*

cer·tain·ly S1 W1 /'sɜːtnli $ 'sɜːr-/ *adv* [sentence adverb]
1 without any doubt; ▤ **definitely**: *I certainly never expected to become a writer.* | *They're certainly not mine.* | **it is certainly true/possible etc** *It is certainly true that there are more courses on offer.* | *The girl was* **almost certainly** *murdered.* | *'Not smoking has made a real difference.' 'It* **most certainly** *has.'*
2 *spoken* used to agree or give your permission: *'I'd like a beer, please' 'Certainly, sir.'* | *'Can I come along?' 'Certainly.'*
3 certainly not *spoken* used to disagree completely or to refuse to give permission: *'May I go?' 'Certainly not!'*

Frequencies of the adverb **certainly** in spoken and written English.

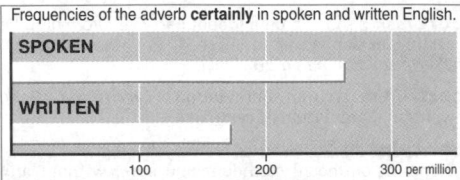

	100	200	300 per million

This graph shows that the adverb **certainly** is more common in spoken English than in written English. This is because it has some special uses in spoken English.

cer·tain·ty /'sɜːtnti $ 'sɜːr-/ *n plural* **certainties 1** [U] the state of being completely certain: **with certainty** *She knew with absolute certainty that he'd say no.* | *The result is impossible to predict with any* **degree of certainty.** **2** [U] the fact that something is certain to happen: **certainty of (doing) sth** *the certainty of being caught* | **certainty that** *There's no certainty that he'll remember.* **3** [C] something that is definitely true or that will definitely happen: *He usually does quite well, but it's not a certainty.* | *The only certainty is that there will need to be major changes.*

cer·ti·fi·a·ble /'sɜːtⅠfaⅠəbəl $ ˌsɜːrtⅠ'faⅠ-/ *adj* **1** *informal* crazy, especially in a way that is dangerous: *If you ask me, that man is certifiable.* **2** *especially AmE* definitely a particular thing: *The guy's a certifiable megastar.* **3** *especially AmE* good enough to be officially approved: *grade A certifiable beef*

cer·tif·i·cate S3 W3 /sə'tⅠfⅠkət $ sər-/ *n* [C]
1 an official document that states that a fact or facts are true: **birth/death/marriage certificate** (=giving details of someone's birth, death, or marriage)
2 an official paper stating that you have completed a course of study or passed an examination: *a degree certificate*

cer·tif·i·cat·ed /sə'tⅠfⅠkeⅠtⅠd $ sər-/ *adj BrE* having successfully completed a training for a profession: *a certificated nurse*

cer·tif·i·ca·tion /sə,tⅠfⅠ'keⅠʃən $ sər-/ *n* **1** [C,U] an official document that says that someone is allowed to do a certain job, that something is of good quality etc: *We successfully completed the certification for open water diving.* **2** [U] the process of giving someone or something an official document that says they are allowed to do a certain job, that something is of good quality etc: [+of] *certification of competence*

certified 'mail *n* [U] *AmE* a way of sending post in which someone records that you have sent it, and the person it is sent to must sign their name to prove they have received it; ▤ **recorded delivery** *BrE*

certified public ac'countant *n* [C] a CPA

cer·ti·fy /'sɜːtⅠfaⅠ $ 'sɜːr-/ *v* **certified, certifying, certifies** [T] **1** to state that something is correct or true, especially after some kind of test: *The accounts were certified by an auditor.* | **certify (that)** *We need to certify that the repairs have been satisfactorily carried out.* | **certify sb dead** (=when a doctor says officially that a person is dead) *BrE: The driver was certified dead at the scene.* **2** to give an official paper to someone which states that they have completed a course of training for a profession; → **certificate: certify sb as**

sth *She was certified as a teacher in 1990.* **3** to officially state that someone is mentally ill

cer·ti·tude /'sɜːtⅠtjuːd $ 'sɜːrtⅠtuːd/ *n* [U] *formal* the state of being or feeling certain about something

ce·ru·le·an /sⅠ'ruːliən/ also **ce,rulean 'blue** *n* [U] *literary* a deep blue colour like a clear sky —**cerulean** *adj*

cer·vi·cal /'sɜːvⅠkəl, sə'vaⅠkəl $ 'sɜːrvⅠkəl/ *adj* **1** related to the neck: *cervical vertebrae* (=the bones in the back of your neck) **2** related to the cervix: *cervical cancer*

cervical 'smear *n* [C] *BrE technical* a test for CANCER of a woman's CERVIX; ▤ **pap smear** *AmE*

cer·vix /'sɜːvⅠks $ 'sɜːr-/ *n* [C] the narrow passage into a woman's UTERUS

ce·sar·e·an /sⅠ'zeəriən $ -'zer-/ *n* another spelling of CAESAREAN

ce·si·um /'siːziəm/ *n* the American spelling of CAESIUM

ces·sa·tion /se'seⅠʃən/ *n* [C,U] *formal* a pause or stop; → **cease**: [+of] *a cessation of hostilities* (=when the fighting stops in a war)

ces·sion /'seʃən/ *n* [C,U] the act of giving up land, property, or rights, especially to another country after a war, or something that is given up in this way; → **cede**: *Spanish cession of the territory in 1818*

cess·pit /'ses,pⅠt/ *n* [C] **1** also **cess·pool** /'sespuːl/ a large hole or container under the ground in which waste from a building, especially from the toilets, is collected **2** a place or situation in which people behave in a bad or immoral way: *For weeks the affair threatened to be a cesspit of scandal.*

ce·ta·cean /sⅠ'teⅠʃən/ *n* [C] *technical* a MAMMAL that lives in the sea, such as a WHALE —**cetacean** *adj*

cf used in writing to introduce something else that should be compared or considered

CFC /ˌsiː ef 'siː/ *n* [C] *chlorofluorocarbon* a gas used in FRIDGES and AEROSOL cans, believed to be responsible for damaging the OZONE LAYER

cha-cha /'tʃɑː ʃɑː/ also **cha-cha-'cha** *n* [C] a dance from South America with small, fast steps

cha·dor /'tʃɑːdɔː, -də $ -dɔːr, -dər/ *n* [C] a long, usually black piece of clothing worn by Muslim women in some countries, which covers the head and body; → **abaya, burqa**

chafe /tʃeⅠf/ *v* **1** [I,T] if a part of your body chafes or if something chafes it, it becomes sore because of something rubbing against it: *Wear a T-shirt under your wetsuit to stop it chafing.* **2** [I] to feel impatient or annoyed: [+at/against/under] *Some hunters are chafing under the new restrictions.* **3** [T] *BrE* to rub part of your body to make it warm

chaff /tʃɑːf $ tʃæf/ *n* [U] **1** the outer seed covers that are separated from grain before it is used as food **2** dried grasses and plant stems that are used for food for farm animals → **separate the wheat from the chaff** at WHEAT (2)

chaf·finch /'tʃæfⅠntʃ/ *n* [C] a common small European bird

cha·grin[1] /'ʃægrⅠn $ ʃə'grⅠn/ *n* [U] annoyance and disappointment because something has not happened the way you hoped: **to sb's chagrin** *The area was declared a wildlife reserve, much to the chagrin of developers.*

chagrin[2] *v* **be chagrined** *formal* to feel annoyed and disappointed: *Dale was chagrined that she wasn't impressed.*

chain[1] S3 W2 /tʃeⅠn/ *n*
1 JOINED RINGS [C,U] a series of metal rings which are joined together in a line and used for fastening things, supporting weights, decoration etc; → **link**: *She had a gold chain around her neck.* | *a length of heavy chain* | *the Mayor's* **chain of office** (=a decoration worn by some British officials at ceremonies) | **pull the chain** (=flush the toilet) *BrE* | *a bicycle chain* (=that

makes the wheels turn); → see picture at BICYCLE

2 CONNECTED EVENTS [C] a connected series of events or actions, especially which lead to a final result: *the* ***chain of events*** *that led to World War I* | *The salesmen are just one* ***link in the chain*** (=part of a process) *of distribution.* | *a rather complicated chain of reasoning* → CHAIN OF COMMAND, FOOD CHAIN

3 SHOPS/HOTELS [C] a number of shops, hotels, cinemas etc owned or managed by the same company or person: [+of] *a chain of restaurants* | **hotel/restaurant/ retail etc chain** *several major UK supermarket chains* → CHAIN STORE

4 CONNECTED LINE [C] people or things which are connected or next to each other forming a line: **mountain/island chain** *the Andean mountain chain* | **chain of atoms/molecules etc** *technical: a chain of amino acids* | *They quickly formed a* ***human chain*** (=a line of people who pass things from one person to the next) *to move the equipment.* | *They sat on the grass making daisy chains* (=flowers tied together).

5 PRISONERS [C usually plural] metal chains fastened to the legs and arms of a prisoner, to prevent them from escaping: **in chains** *He was led away in chains.* | **ball and chain** (=a chain attached to someone's ankle at one end with a heavy metal ball at the other)

6 BUYING A HOUSE [C usually singular] *BrE* a number of people buying houses, where each person must complete the sale of their own house before they can buy the next person's house

chain² *v* **1** [T] to fasten someone or something to something else using a chain, especially in order to prevent them from escaping or being stolen: **chain sb/sth to sth** *a bicycle chained to the fence* | *Four activists chained themselves to the gates.* | **chain sb/sth up** *The elephants were chained up by their legs.* | **chain sb/sth together** *Their hands and feet were chained together.* **2 be chained to sth** to have your freedom restricted because of something you must do: *She felt chained to the kitchen sink.* | *I don't want a job where I'm chained to a desk all day.*

chain gang *n* [C] a group of prisoners chained together to work outside their prison

chain letter *n* [C] a letter sent to several people asking them to send a copy of the letter to several more people

chain-link 'fence *n* [C] a type of fence made of wire twisted together into a diamond pattern

chain mail *n* [U] protective clothing made by joining many small metal rings together, worn by soldiers in the past

chain of com'mand *n* [C] a system in an organization by which decisions are made and passed from people at the top of the organization to people lower down: *Symonds is third in the chain of command.*

chain re'action *n* [C] **1** *technical* a chemical or NUCLEAR reaction which produces energy and causes more reactions of the same kind **2** a series of related events, each of which causes the next: *A sudden drop on Wall Street can set off a chain reaction in other financial markets.*

chain·saw /'tʃeɪnsɔː $ -sɒː/ *n* [C] a tool used for cutting wood, consisting of a circular chain with teeth which is driven by a motor → CIRCULAR SAW; → see picture at SAW

chainsaw

chain-smoke *v* [I,T] to smoke cigarettes one immediately after another —**chain-smoker** *n* [C]

chain stitch *n* [C,U] a way of sewing in which each new stitch is pulled through the last one

chain store also **chain·store** /'tʃeɪnstɔː $ -stɔːr/ *n* [C] one of a group of shops, all of which are owned by one organization; ☐ chain

chairs

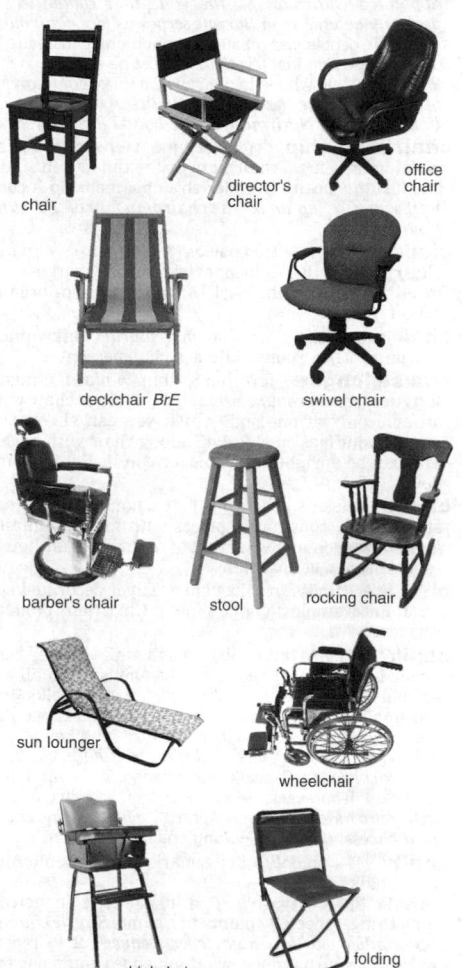

chair

director's chair

office chair

deckchair *BrE*

swivel chair

barber's chair

stool

rocking chair

sun lounger

wheelchair

highchair

folding chair

chair¹ [S1] [W2] /tʃeə $ tʃer/ *n*

1 [C] a piece of furniture for one person to sit on, which has a back, a seat, and four legs: *a table and chairs* | **in/on a chair** *He was sitting in a chair.* | *He sank back into his chair.* | **kitchen chair/garden chair etc**

2 [singular] the position of being in charge of a meeting or committee, or the person who is in charge of it: *Address your questions to the chair, please.* | **be in the chair** *Who will be in the chair at tomorrow's meeting?* | [+of] *He was nominated as chair of the board of governors.*

3 [C] the position of being a university PROFESSOR: [+of] *a new Chair of Medicine*

4 the chair *AmE informal* the ELECTRIC CHAIR

chair² *v* [T] to be the CHAIRPERSON of a meeting or committee: *The commission of inquiry was chaired by a well-known judge.*

chair·lift also **'chair lift** /'tʃeəlɪft $ 'tʃer-/ *n* [C] a line of chairs hanging from a moving wire, used for carrying people up and down mountains, especially to SKI

chair·man [S3] [W1] /'tʃeəmən $ 'tʃer-/ *n plural* **chairmen** /-mən/ [C]

1 someone, especially a man, who is in charge of a meeting or directs the work of a committee or an

organization; → **chairwoman**: [+of] *Potts was appointed chairman of the education committee.* | **deputy/vice chairman** *Barrett serves as vice chairman.* ⚠ Many people use **chairperson** or **chair** instead, to avoid suggesting that this person must be a man.
2 *BrE* someone who is in charge of a large company or organization: *the chairman of British Aerospace* | *Williams has been **chairman of the board** for five years.*

chair·man·ship /ˈtʃeəmənʃɪp $ ˈtʃer-/ *n* [C,U] the position of being a chairman, or the time when someone has this position: **under sb's chairmanship** *A committee was set up under the chairmanship of Edmund Compton.*

chair·per·son /ˈtʃeə,pɜːsən $ ˈtʃer,pɜːr-/ *n plural* **chairpersons** [C] someone who is in charge of a meeting or directs the work of a committee or organization

chair·wom·an /ˈtʃeə,wʊmən/ *n plural* **chairwomen** /-,wɪmɪn/ [C] a woman who is a chairperson

chaise longue /,ʃeɪz ˈlɒŋ $ -ˈlɔːŋ/ *n plural* **chaises longues** *(same pronunciation)* [C] **1** a long chair with an arm only at one end, which you can sit on and stretch your legs out **2** *AmE* a long chair with a back that can be upright for sitting, or can lie flat for lying down

chal·et /ˈʃæleɪ $ ʃæˈleɪ/ *n* [C] **1** a house with a steep sloping roof, common in places with high mountains and snow such as Switzerland **2** *BrE* a small house, especially in a HOLIDAY CAMP

chal·ice /ˈtʃælɪs/ *n* [C] a gold or silver decorated cup used, for example, to hold wine in Christian religious services

chalk¹ /tʃɔːk $ tʃɒːk/ *n* [U] **1** soft white or grey rock formed a long time ago from the shells of small sea animals; ☰ **limestone**: *chalk cliffs* **2** also **chalks** [plural] small sticks of a white or coloured substance like soft rock, used for writing or drawing: *a box of coloured chalks* | *a piece of chalk* | *writing in chalk on the blackboard* **3 chalk and cheese** *BrE* completely different from each other: *The two brothers are **as different as chalk and cheese**.* | *They're **like chalk and cheese**, those two.* → **long chalk** at LONG¹ (21)

chalk² *v* [T + up/on] to write, mark, or draw something with chalk
 chalk sth ⇔ **up** *phr v* **1** to succeed in getting something, especially points in a game: *Seattle chalked up another win last night over Denver.* **2** to record what someone has done, what someone should pay etc: [+to] *You can chalk the drinks up to my account.* **3 chalk it up to experience** *informal* to accept a failure or disappointment calmly and regard it as an experience that you can learn something from

chalk·board /ˈtʃɔːkbɔːd $ ˈtʃɔːkbɔːrd/ *n* [C] *AmE* a BLACKBOARD: *She wrote the day's menu up on a chalkboard.*

chalk·y /ˈtʃɔːki $ ˈtʃɒː-/ *adj* similar to chalk or containing chalk: *white chalky soil* | *There were some chalky bits in the bottom of the drink.* —**chalkiness** *n* [U]

chal·lenge¹ S2 W2 /ˈtʃælɪndʒ/ *n*
1 STH DIFFICULT [C,U] something that tests strength, skill, or ability, especially in a way that is interesting: [+of] *The company is ready to meet the challenges of the next few years.* | **the challenge of doing sth** *I relish the challenge of rebuilding the club.* | **face/take on/accept etc a challenge** (=be ready to deal with one) *Martins now faces the biggest challenge of his career.* | **meet a challenge/rise to a challenge** (=successfully deal with one) *a new and vibrant initiative to meet the challenge of the 21st century* | **intellectual/physical challenge** *the intellectual challenge of postgraduate research*
2 QUESTION STH [C] when someone refuses to accept that someone or something is right and legal: [+to] *a direct challenge to the Governor's authority* | [+from] *The president faces a strong challenge from*

nationalists. | **pose/represent/present a challenge (to sb)** *The strike represented a serious challenge to the government.* | **mount/launch a challenge** *They decided to mount a **legal challenge** to the decision.*
3 COMPETITION [C] when someone tries to win something or invites someone to try to beat them in a fight, competition etc: [+for] *They are ready to mount a challenge for the championship.* | *They **threw down** the **challenge** that he couldn't wash 40 cars in one hour* (=invited him to try to do it). | *The Prime Minister narrowly avoided a **leadership challenge** last year.*
4 STOP [C] a demand from someone such as a guard to stop and give proof of who you are, and an explanation of what you are doing
5 IN LAW [C] *law* a statement made before the start of a court case that a JUROR is not acceptable

challenge² S3 W3 *v* [T]
1 QUESTION STH to refuse to accept that something is right, fair, or legal: *a boy with a reputation for **challenging the authority** of his teachers* | **challenge a view/an idea/an assumption etc** *Viewpoints such as these are strongly challenged by environmentalists.* | *They went to the High Court to **challenge the decision**.* | **challenge sb to do sth** *I challenge Dr. Carver to deny his involvement!*
2 COMPETITION to invite someone to compete or fight against you, or to try to win something; → **challenger**, **dare**: **challenge sb to sth** *After lunch Carey challenged me to a game of tennis.* | [+for] *Liverpool are challenging for the title* (=in a position where they could win).
3 STH DIFFICULT to test the skills or abilities of someone or something; ☰ **stimulate**: *I'm really at my best when I'm challenged.* | **challenge sb to do sth** *Every teacher ought to be challenging kids to think about current issues.*
4 STOP SB to stop someone and demand proof of who they are, and an explanation of what they are doing: *We were challenged by the security guard at the gate.*
5 IN LAW *law* to state before the start of a court case that a JUROR is not acceptable —**challenger** *n* [C]: *Lewis is his main challenger for the world title.*

chal·lenged /ˈtʃælɪndʒd/ *adj* **visually/physically/mentally etc challenged** *AmE* used as a polite expression for describing someone who has difficulty doing things because they are blind etc

chal·leng·ing /ˈtʃælɪndʒɪŋ/ *adj* difficult in an interesting or enjoyable way: *Teaching young children is a challenging and rewarding job.* | *a challenging problem* —**challengingly** *adv*

cham·ber W3 /ˈtʃeɪmbə $ -ər/ *n*
1 ENCLOSED SPACE [C] an enclosed space, especially in your body or inside a machine: *a combustion chamber* | *The heart has four chambers.*
2 ROOM [C] a room used for a special purpose, especially an unpleasant one: **gas/torture chamber** (=used for killing people by gas or for hurting them)
3 MEETING ROOM [C] a large room in a public building used for important meetings: *the council chamber*
4 PARLIAMENT [C] one of the two parts of a parliament or of the US Congress. For example, in Britain the upper chamber is the House of Lords and the lower chamber is the House of Commons
5 PRIVATE ROOM [C] a word used in the past to mean a bedroom or private room: *the Queen's private chambers*
6 chambers [plural] *especially BrE* an office or offices used by BARRISTERS or judges
7 GUN [C] the place inside a gun where you put the bullet

cham·ber·lain /ˈtʃeɪmbəlɪn $ -bər-/ *n* [C] an important official who managed the house of a king or queen in the past

cham·ber·maid /ˈtʃeɪmbəmeɪd $ -ər-/ *n* [C] a female worker whose job is to clean and tidy bedrooms, especially in a hotel

ˈchamber ˌmusic *n* [U] CLASSICAL music written for a small group of instruments

chamber of 'commerce *n plural* **chambers of commerce** [C] a group of business people in a particular town or area, working together to improve trade

chamber ,orchestra *n* [C] a small group of musicians who play CLASSICAL music together

'chamber pot *n* [C] a round container for URINE, used in a bedroom and kept under the bed in the past

cha·me·le·on /kəˈmiːliən/ *n* [C] **1** a LIZARD that can change its colour to match the colours around it **2** someone who changes their ideas, behaviour etc to fit different situations

cham·ois /ˈʃæmwɑː $ ˈʃæmi/ *plural* **chamois** *n* **1** [C] a wild animal like a small goat that lives in the mountains of Europe and southwest Asia **2** also **'chamois ,leather** /ˈʃæmwi leðə $ -ər/ [C,U] soft leather prepared from the skin of chamois, sheep, or goats and used for cleaning or polishing, or a piece of this leather; → **shammy**

cham·o·mile /ˈkæməmaɪl/ *n* another spelling of CAMO-MILE

champ[1] /tʃæmp/ *v* [I,T] *BrE* **1** to bite food in a noisy way; ⬛ **chomp 2 be champing at the bit** to be unable to wait for something patiently

champ[2] *n* [C] *informal* a CHAMPION: *the world champ*

cham·pagne /ʃæmˈpeɪn/ *n* [U] a French white wine with a lot of BUBBLES, drunk on special occasions

cham·pers /ˈʃæmpəz $ -pərz/ *n* [U] *BrE informal* champagne

cham·pi·on[1] [W2] /ˈtʃæmpiən/ *n* [C]
1 someone or something that has won a competition, especially in sport: *the **world** heavyweight boxing champion* | *the Olympic champion* | **reigning/defending champion** (=the champion at the present time)
2 champion of sth/sb someone who publicly fights for and defends an aim or principle, such as the rights of a group of people: *a champion of women's rights*

champion[2] *v* [T] *written* to publicly fight for and defend an aim or principle, such as the rights of a group of people: *She championed the cause of religious freedom.*

cham·pi·on·ship [W2] /ˈtʃæmpiənʃɪp/ *n*
1 [C] also **championships** [plural] a competition to find which player, team etc is the best in a particular sport: *the women's figure skating championships* | *Holland won the European Championship.*
2 [C] the position or period of being a champion; ⬛ **title**: *Warwickshire are the current holders of the cricket championship.*
3 [U + of] *written* the act of championing something or someone

chance[1] [S1] [W1] /tʃɑːns $ tʃæns/ *n*
1 POSSIBILITY [C,U] how possible or likely it is that something will happen, especially something that you want

there's a chance (that) (=it is possible that)
there's every chance (that) (=it is very likely)
some chance
little chance
no chance
a good/fair chance (=something is likely)
a slight/slim/outside chance (=something is unlikely)
a fifty-fifty chance (=the possibility of something happening or not happening is equal)
a million to one chance/a one in a million chance (=something is extremely unlikely to happen)
lessen/minimize/reduce the chance(s) of sth (=make it less likely)
increase/improve the chance(s) of sth (=make it more likely)
chances are (=it is likely)

*There's always **the chance that** something will go wrong.* | [+of] *what are the team's chances of success?* | *She **has a good chance** of a successful recovery.* | *There is **little chance** of her being found alive.* | *The day will be cloudy with **a slight chance** of rain later tonight.* | *He gave the show **a fifty-fifty chance** of survival.* | *It*

was **a million to one chance**, *but it had happened.* | *The operation is performed under local anaesthetic, which **lessens the chances of** infection.* | *How can we **improve** our **chances of** career development?* | ***Chances are** they'll be out when we call.*

2 OPPORTUNITY [C] a time or situation which you can use to do something that you want to do; ⬛ **opportunity**: **chance to do sth** *Ralph was waiting for a chance to introduce himself.* | [+of] *our only chance of escape* | **have/get a chance (to do sth)** *I never get a chance to relax these days.* | *I'm sorry, I haven't had a chance to look at it yet.* | *I can explain everything if you'll just **give me a chance**.* | *You should **take the chance** (=use the opportunity) to travel while you're still young.* | **grab the chance/jump at the chance** (=eagerly and quickly use an opportunity) *If someone invited me over to Florida, I'd jump at the chance.* | *Denise never **misses the chance** of a free meal.* | **a second chance/another chance** *He was given a second chance to prove his abilities.* | *Friday is your **last chance** to see the show before it closes.* | *I'll give you **one last chance** and if you don't bring it on Monday, you'll be in trouble.* | **a chance of a lifetime/a chance in a million** (=a chance that you are very unlikely to have again) *I couldn't pass up going to Japan; it was a chance in a million.* | *Quick! **Now's** your **chance** to ask her, before she leaves.* | *Rick could do really well, **given half a chance** (=if he were given even a small opportunity).*

3 RISK **take a chance** to do something that involves risks: *The rope might break, but that's a chance we'll have to take.* | *After losing $20,000 on my last business venture, I'm **not taking any chances** this time.* | [+on] *He was taking a chance on a relatively new young actor.* | *He decided to take his chances in the boat.*

4 LIKELY TO SUCCEED **sb's chances** how likely it is that someone will succeed: *Ryan will be a candidate in next month's elections, but his chances are not good.* | **sb's chances of doing sth** *England's chances of winning the series have all but disappeared.* | **not fancy/not rate sb's chances** *BrE* (=think someone is unlikely to succeed) *I don't really fancy their chances against such tough opposition.*

5 LUCK [U] the way some things happen without being planned or caused by people; → **fate**: **by chance** *I bumped into her quite by chance in Oxford Street.* | **leave sth to chance** (=to not plan something but just hope that everything will happen as intended) *Dave had thought of every possibility, he was leaving nothing to chance.* | **pure/sheer/blind chance** (=not at all planned) *It was pure chance that they ended up working in the same office in the same town.* | **As chance would have it**, *the one time I wanted to see her, she wasn't in.*

6 stand/have a chance (of sth/of doing sth) if someone or something stands a chance of doing something, it is possible that they will succeed: *If we did move to London, I'd **stand a** much **better chance** of getting a job.* | *Ireland have **an outside chance** (=slight chance) of qualifying for the World Cup.* | *He has **a sporting chance** of promotion* (=a fairly good chance). | *I've given myself **a fighting chance** of getting to the finals* (=a small but real chance if a great effort can be made).

7 by any chance *spoken* used to ask politely whether something is true: *Are you Mrs Grant, by any chance?*

8 any chance of ...? *spoken* used to ask whether you can have something or whether something is possible: *Any chance of a cup of coffee?* | *Any chance of you coming to the party on Saturday?*

9 be in with a chance if a competitor is in with a chance, it is possible that they will win: *I think we're in with a good chance of beating them.*

10 no chance!/fat chance! *spoken* used to emphasize that you are sure something could never happen: *'Maybe your brother would lend you the money?' 'Huh, fat chance!'*

11 on the off chance if you do something on the off chance, you do it hoping for a particular result, although you know it is not likely: *I didn't really expect her to be at home. I just called on the off chance.* → OFF-CHANCE

12 chance would be a fine thing! *BrE spoken* used to mean that the thing you want to happen is very unlikely: *'Do you think you'll get married?' 'Chance would be a fine thing!'* → **game of chance** at GAME¹ (15)

WORD CHOICE: chance, chances, luck

chance means possibility: *There is a small chance he is still alive.* | *You've got a good chance of passing.*

chance also means opportunity: *You will have the chance to meet the star of the show.*

chance also means that something happened by coincidence or was not planned: *It was pure chance that we bought the same shoes.*

Someone's **chances** are the probability that they will do something: *Her chances of finding him after all these years are slim.* | *He aims to win today – what are his chances?*

⚠ Use **chances of doing** sth, not 'chances to do sth': *Your chances of getting (NOT chances to get) a job are as good as anyone's.*

luck is when something good happens without being planned: *He won more through luck than skill.* | *It was such luck that you were there to help me!*

---

chance² *v* **1** [T] to do something that you know involves a risk: *I wasn't sure if I'd got quite enough petrol to get me home, but I decided to chance it.* | *We decided not to chance our luck in the storm.* | *She'd never played before, but she was ready to chance her arm* (=take a risk by doing something which may fail). | **chance doing sth** *I decided to stay where I was. I couldn't chance being seen.* **2** [I] *literary* to happen in a way which is not expected and not planned: **chance to do sth** *She chanced to be passing when I came out of the house.* | *It chanced that we both went to Paris that year.*

chance on/upon/across sb/sth *phr v formal* to find something or meet someone when you are not expecting to: *Henry chanced upon some valuable coins in the attic.*

chance³ *adj* [only before noun] not planned or expected; ☐ **accidental**: **chance meeting/encounter/event etc** *A chance meeting with a journalist changed everything.* | *A chance remark by one of his colleagues got him thinking.*

chan·cel /'tʃɑːnsəl $ 'tʃæn-/ *n* [C] the part of a church where the priests and the CHOIR (=singers) sit

chan·cel·ler·y /'tʃɑːnsələri $ 'tʃæn-/ *n plural* **chancelleries** [C] **1** the building in which a chancellor has his or her office **2** the officials who work in a chancellor's office **3** the offices of an official representative of a foreign country; ☐ **chancery**

chan·cel·lor W3 /'tʃɑːnsələ $ 'tʃænsələr/ *n* [C] **1** the Chancellor of the Exchequer **2 a)** the person who officially represents a British university on special occasions **b)** the person in charge of some American universities **3** the leader of the government or the main government minister of some countries: *Helmut Kohl, the former German Chancellor*

Chancellor of the Ex'chequer *n plural* **Chancellors of the Exchequer** [C] the British government minister in charge of taxes and government spending

chan·ce·ry /'tʃɑːnsəri $ 'tʃæn-/ *n* [singular] **1** especially *BrE* a government office that collects and stores official papers **2** the part of the British system of law courts which deals with EQUITY **3** the offices of an official representative of a foreign country; ☐ **chancellery**

chanc·y /'tʃɑːnsi $ 'tʃænsi/ *adj* not certain, or involving a lot of risk; ☐ **risky**: *Acting professionally is a chancy business.* —**chanciness** *n* [U]

chan·de·lier /ˌʃændə'lɪə $ -'lɪr/ *n* [C] a large round frame for holding CANDLES or lights that hangs from the ceiling and is decorated with small pieces of glass

---

chand·ler /'tʃɑːndlə $ 'tʃændlər/ *n* [C] someone who made or sold CANDLES in the past → SHIP'S CHANDLER

change¹ S1 W1 /tʃeɪndʒ/ *v*

1 BECOME DIFFERENT/MAKE STH DIFFERENT [I,T] to become different, or to make something become different: *Susan has changed a lot since I last saw her.* | *Changing your eating habits is the best way to lose weight.* | *The rules are not going to change overnight* (=change quickly). | *Why do the leaves on trees change colour in the autumn?* | **change (from sth) to sth** *He changed from being a nice lad to being rude and unhelpful.* | [+into] *The hissing sound gradually changed into a low hum.* | **change sb/sth into sth** *A witch had changed him into a mouse.* | **change sth to sth** *Mueller changed his name to Miller when he became a U.S. citizen.* | **changing circumstances/attitudes/conditions etc** *the changing circumstances of the family* | **change drastically/radically/profoundly etc** *Attitudes towards sexuality have radically changed.*

2 START DOING/USING STH DIFFERENT [I,T] to stop doing or using one thing, and start doing or using something else instead; ☐ **switch**: *She changed jobs in May.* | **change (from sth) to sth** *The company has recently changed to a more powerful computer system.* | *The ship changed course and headed south.* | *The company has had to change direction because of developments in technology.* | *Piper awkwardly tried to change the subject* (=talk about something else).

3 REPLACE STH [T] to put or use something new or different in place of something else, especially because it is old, damaged, or broken: *Three boys were changing a tyre by the side of the road.* | *When I lost my keys, I had to change all the locks.* | **change sth (from sth) to sth** *The time of the meeting has been changed from 11 a.m. to 10:30.* | *How often do you change cars* (=buy a new car and sell the old one)?

4 **change your mind** to change your decision, plan, or opinion about something: *Her father tried to get her to change her mind.* | [+about] *If you change your mind about the job, just give me a call.*

5 **change sides** to leave one party, group etc and join an opposing party, group etc: *It's quite rare for politicians to change sides.*

6 CLOTHES **a)** [I,T] to take off your clothes and put on different ones: *Francis came in while Jay was changing.* | *Change your dress – that one looks dirty.* | [+into/out of] *Sara changed into her swimsuit and ran out for a quick swim.* | *You'd better go and get changed.* **b)** [T] to put a clean NAPPY on a baby, or to put clean clothes on a baby or small child: *I bathed him and changed his diaper.* | *Can you change the baby for me while I finish chopping the carrots?*

7 BED [T] to take the dirty SHEETS off a bed and put on clean ones

8 EXCHANGE GOODS [T] *BrE* **a)** to take back to a shop something that you have bought and get something different instead, especially because there is something wrong with it; ☐ **exchange** *AmE*: **change sth for sth** *I bought these gloves for my daughter, but they're too large. Can I change them for a smaller size?* **b)** to give a customer something different instead of what they have bought, especially because there is something wrong with it; ☐ **exchange** *AmE*: *I'm sure the shop will change them for you.*

9 EXCHANGE MONEY [T] **a)** to get smaller units of money that add up to the same value as a larger unit: *Can you change a £20 note?* **b)** to get money from one country for the same value of money from another country: **change sth into/for sth** *I want to change my dollars into pesos, please.*

10 TRAINS/BUSES/AIRCRAFT [I,T] to get off one train, bus, or aircraft and into another in order to continue your journey: [+at] *Passengers for Liverpool should change at Crewe.* | **change trains/buses/planes etc** *I had to change planes in Denver.* | **all change!** (=used to tell passengers to get off a train because it does not go any further)

11 **change hands** if property changes hands, it starts

to belong to someone else: *The house has changed hands three times in the last two years.*
12 change places (with sb) a) to give someone your place and take their place: *Would you mind changing places with me so I can sit next to my friend?* **b)** to take someone else's social position or situation in life instead of yours: *She may be rich, but I wouldn't want to change places with her.*
13 GEAR [I,T] to put the engine of a vehicle into a higher or lower GEAR in order to go faster or slower: **change (into/out of) gear** *Change into second gear as you approach the corner.* | **[+up/down]** *BrE:* *Change down before you get to the hill.*
14 change your tune *informal* to start expressing a different attitude and reacting in a different way, after something has happened: *The question is, will the president change his tune on taxes?*
15 WIND [I] if the wind changes, it starts to blow in a different direction
16 change your spots to change your character completely: *US business has changed its spots in recent years.* → **chop and change** at CHOP¹ (3)

WORD FOCUS: CHANGE
to change something: **alter, adapt, adjust, amend, modify, revise, vary**
to change a system or organization: **restructure, reorganize, reform**
to change something completely: **transform, revolutionize**
to change facts or information, or change what someone has said: **twist, distort, misrepresent**
easily changed: **flexible, adaptable**
impossible to change: **fixed, final, irrevocable**

change sth ⇔ **around** *phr v*
to move things into different positions: *When we'd changed the furniture around, the room looked quite different.*
change over *phr v*
to stop doing or using one thing and start doing or using another: *Complete all the exercises on one leg, then change over.* | **[+to]** *We hope to change over to the new software by next month.*

change² S1 W1 *n*
1 THINGS BECOMING DIFFERENT [C,U] the process or result of something or someone becoming different: *Many people find it hard to cope with change.* | *scientists worried about climatic change* | **[+in]** *changes in the immigration laws* | *A change in personality may mean your teenager has a drug problem.* | **[+of]** *a change of temperature* | *No **major changes** were made to the book.* | **change for the better/worse** (=a change that makes a situation better or worse) *There was a change for the better in the patient's condition.* | **social/political/economic etc change** *the sweeping political changes after the fall of communism* | *She had a **change of heart** (=change in attitude) and decided to stay.* | *Family life has **undergone** dramatic **change** in recent years.*
2 FROM ONE THING TO ANOTHER [C] the fact of one thing or person being replaced by another: *The car needs an oil change.* | **[+of]** *a change of government* | *a change of address* | **change from sth to sth** *the gradual change from grasslands to true desert* | *The government has **made** some major policy **changes**.*
3 PLEASANT NEW SITUATION [singular] a situation or experience that is different from what happened before, and is usually interesting or enjoyable: **[+from]** *The morning was cool; a **welcome change** from the heat of the day before.* | **for a change** *How about dinner out for a change?* | **it/that makes a change** (=used to say that something is better than and different from usual) *'Ron's buying the drinks.' 'That makes a change.'* | **change of scene/air/pace etc** (=when you go to a different place or do something different) *The patients benefit greatly from a change of scenery.*
4 MONEY [U] **a)** the money that you get back when you have paid for something with more money than it costs: *Here's your change, sir.* | **make change** *AmE*

(=give someone change) *Andy was making change for a customer.* **b)** money in the form of coins, not paper money: **in change** *I have about a dollar in change.* | *Matt emptied the **loose change** from his pockets.* | *A beggar asked for some **spare change** (=coins that you do not need).* **c)** coins or paper money that you give in exchange for the same amount of money in a larger unit: **change for £1/$10** *Excuse me, have you got change for a pound?* | **make change** *AmE* (=give someone change) *Can you make change for $20?*
5 small change a) coins you have that do not have a high value: *I only had about a pound in small change.* **b)** used to emphasize that something is a small amount of money when it is compared to a larger amount: *The program costs $20 million a year, small change by Washington standards.*
6 change of clothes/underwear etc an additional set of clothes that you have with you, for example when you are travelling
7 TRAIN/BUS/AIRCRAFT [C] a situation in which you get off one train, bus, or aircraft and get on another in order to continue your journey: *Even with a change of trains, the subway is quicker than a cab at rush hour.*
8 get no change out of sb *BrE spoken* to get no useful information or help from someone: *I wouldn't bother asking Richard – you'll get no change out of him.* → **ring the changes** at RING² (6)

change·a·ble /ˈtʃeɪndʒəbəl/ *adj* likely to change, or changing often: *changeable weather*
changed /tʃeɪndʒd/ *adj* **1 a changed man/woman** someone who has become very different from what they were before, as a result of a very important experience: *Since she stopped drinking, she's a changed woman.* **2** relating to a change in someone's situation: *All organisations need to adapt to changed circumstances.*
change·less /ˈtʃeɪndʒləs/ *adj* never seeming to change: *a changeless desert landscape*
change·ling /ˈtʃeɪndʒlɪŋ/ *n* [C] *literary* a baby that is believed to have been secretly exchanged for another baby by FAIRIES
change of life *n* [singular] the MENOPAUSE
change·o·ver /ˈtʃeɪndʒ₁əʊvə $ -₁oʊvər/ *n* [C] a change from one activity, system, or way of working to another: **changeover (from sth) to sth** *a changeover from military to civilian government*
change purse *n* [C] *AmE* a small bag in which coins are kept; ▪ **purse** *BrE*
changing room *n* [C] *BrE* a room where people change their clothes when they play sports, go swimming etc; ▪ **locker room** *AmE*; → see picture at SPORTS CENTRE
changing table *n* [C] a special piece of furniture that you put a baby on when you change its NAPPY
chan·nel¹ S3 W2 /ˈtʃænl/ *n* [C]
1 TELEVISION a television station and all the programmes that it broadcasts: *the news on Channel 4* | *The kids are watching cartoons on the Disney Channel.* | *What channel is ER on?* | *He **changed channels** to watch the basketball game.*
2 FOR GETTING INFORMATION/GOODS ETC a system or method that you use to send or obtain information, goods, permission etc: *The United States and other countries are working through **diplomatic channels** to find a solution.* | *The new software will be sold through existing **distribution channels.*** | **[+of]** *It is important that we open **channels of communication** with the police.*
3 SEA/RIVER a) an area of water that connects two larger areas of water: *St George's Channel* **b)** the Channel *BrE* the area of water between France and England; ▪ **the English Channel c)** the deepest part of a river, HARBOUR, or sea, especially where it is deep enough to allow ships to sail in

C

4 WATER a passage that water or other liquids flow along: *an irrigation channel*
5 RADIO a particular range of SOUND WAVES which can be used to send and receive radio messages
6 IN A SURFACE a long deep line cut into a surface or a long deep space between two edges; ▤ **groove**: *The sliding doors fit into these plastic channels.*
7 WAY TO EXPRESS YOURSELF a way of expressing your thoughts, feelings, or physical energy: [+for] *Art provides a channel for the children's creativity.*

channel² *v* **channelled, channelling** *BrE*, **channeled, channeling** *AmE* [T] **1** to control and direct something such as money or energy towards a particular purpose; ▤ **direct**: **channel sth into sth** *Most of his energy was channeled into writing and lecturing.* | **channel sth to sb** *Profits are channelled to conservation groups.* | **channel sth through sth** *The famine relief money was channelled through the UN.* **2** to control or direct people or things to a particular place, work, situation etc: **channel sb/sth into sth** *Women were likely to be channeled into jobs as teachers or nurses.* | *Drugs from government pharmacies were being channeled into illegal drug markets.* **3** to cut a long deep line in something: *Water had channelled grooves in the rock.* **4** to send water through a passage: *An efficient irrigation system channels water to the crops.* **5** to allow a spirit to come into your body and speak through you, to tell people a message that you have received in this way: *She claims to channel the spirit of a 2,000-year-old hunter.*

chan·nel·ling *BrE*; **channeling** *AmE* /ˈtʃænl-ɪŋ/ *n* [U] a practice based on the belief that dead people can communicate with living people by making their spirit enter a living person's body and speaking through them —**channeller** *n* [C]

ˈ**channel ˌsurfing**, ˈ**channel ˌhopping** *n* [U] when you change from one television channel to another, only watching a few minutes of any programme

chant¹ /tʃɑːnt $ tʃænt/ *v* [I,T] **1** to repeat a word or phrase again and again: *protestors chanting anti-government slogans* **2** to sing or say a religious song or prayer in a way that involves using only one note or TONE: *a priest chanting the liturgy*

chant² *n* [C] **1** words or phrases that are repeated again and again by a group of people: *Others in the crowd took up the chant* (=began chanting). | [+of] *chants of 'oh no, we won't go'* **2** a regularly repeated tune, often with many words sung on one note, especially used for religious prayers —**chanter** *n* [C]

chan·try /ˈtʃɑːntri $ ˈtʃæn-/ also ˈ**chantry ˌchapel** *n plural* **chantries** [C] a small church or part of a church paid for by someone so that priests can pray for them there after they die

Cha·nu·kah /ˈhɑːnᵿkə $ ˈkɑːnəkə, ˈhɑː-/ *n* HANUKKAH

cha·os /ˈkeɪ-ɒs $ -ɑːs/ *n* [U] **1** a situation in which everything is happening in a confused way and nothing is organized or arranged in order: *The country was plunged into economic chaos.* | **complete/utter/absolute etc chaos** *There was total chaos on the roads.* | **in chaos** *The kitchen was in chaos.* **2** the state of the universe before there was any order

cha·ot·ic /keɪˈɒtɪk $ -ˈɑːtɪk/ *adj* a chaotic situation is one in which everything is happening in a confused way: *a chaotic mixture of images*

chap S3 /tʃæp/ *n*
1 [C] *especially BrE* a man, especially a man you know and like: *a decent sort of chap*
2 **chaps** [plural] protective leather covers worn over your trousers when riding a horse → CHAPPED

chap·ar·ral /ˌʃæpəˈræl/ *n* [U] *AmE* land on which small OAK trees grow close together

chap·book /ˈtʃæpbʊk/ *n* [C] *AmE* a small printed book, usually consisting of writings about literature, poetry, or religion

chap·el /ˈtʃæpəl/ *n* **1** [C] a small church, or a room in a hospital, prison, big church etc in which Christians pray and have religious services **2** [C] a building where Christians who are Nonconformists have religious services **3** [U] *BrE* the religious services held in a chapel: *Bethan goes to chapel every Sunday.* **4** [C] *BrE* the members of a UNION in the newspaper or printing industry

chap·e·rone¹, **chaperon** /ˈʃæpərəʊn $ -roʊn/ *n* [C] **1** an older woman in the past who went out with a young unmarried woman on social occasions and was responsible for her behaviour **2** *AmE* someone, usually a parent or teacher, who is responsible for young people on social occasions: *Three parents went on the school ski trip as chaperones.*

chaperone², **chaperon** *v* [T] to go somewhere with someone as a chaperone

chap·lain /ˈtʃæplᵻn/ *n* [C] a priest or other religious minister responsible for the religious needs of a club, the army, a hospital etc: *the prison chaplain*

chap·lain·cy /ˈtʃæplᵻnsi/ *n plural* **chaplaincies** [C] the job of being a chaplain, or the place where a chaplain works

chapped /tʃæpt/ *adj* chapped lips or hands are sore, dry, and cracked, especially as a result of cold weather or wind —**chap** *v* [T]

chap·py /ˈtʃæpi/ *n plural* **chappies** [C] *BrE* a CHAP

chap·ter S3 W1 /ˈtʃæptə $ -ər/ *n* [C]
1 one of the parts into which a book is divided: *Read Chapter 11 as your homework.* | *This chapter discusses power, and how people use it.*
2 a particular period or event in someone's life or in history: [+of] *We hope that they will join us in opening a new chapter of peace and cooperation.* | [+in] *the noblest chapter in our history*
3 all the priests belonging to a CATHEDRAL, or a meeting of these priests
4 the local members of a large organization such as a club: *the local chapter of the American Legion*
5 **give/quote sb chapter and verse** to give someone exact details about where to find some information
6 a chapter of accidents *BrE* a series of unlucky events coming one after another

chap·ter·house /ˈtʃæptəhaʊs $ -ər-/ *n* [C] a building where the priests belonging to a CATHEDRAL meet

char¹ /tʃɑː $ tʃɑːr/ *v* **charred, charring 1** [I,T] to burn something so that its outside becomes black: *Roast the peppers until the skin begins to char and blister.* → CHARRED **2** [I] *BrE old-fashioned* to work as a cleaner in a house, office, public building etc

char² *n* **1** [C] *BrE old-fashioned* a CHARWOMAN **2** [U] *BrE old-fashioned* tea: *a cup of char*

char·a·banc /ˈʃærəbæŋ/ *n* [C] *BrE old-fashioned* a large comfortable bus used for pleasure trips

char·ac·ter S1 W1 /ˈkærᵻktə $ -ər/ *n*
1 ALL SB'S QUALITIES [C usually singular] the particular combination of qualities that makes someone a particular type of person; → **characteristic**: *He has a cheerful but quiet character.* | *Children grow up with a mixture of character traits* (=character qualities) *from both sides of their family.* | *his temper and other character flaws* (=bad qualities) | **in character/out of character** (=typical or untypical of someone's character) *He swore, which was out of character for him.* | **the English/French etc character** *Openness is at the heart of the American character.* | **character sketch** (=a description of someone's character)
2 PERSON [C] **a)** a person in a book, play, film etc: *Candida is the most interesting character in the play.* | **main/central character** *In the story, the main character has left his girlfriend and baby.* | *Everyone recognizes Disney's cartoon characters.* **b)** a person of a particular type, especially a strange or dishonest one: *a couple of shady characters standing on the corner* | *I'm considered a reformed character these days* (=someone who has stopped doing bad things). **c)** an interesting and unusual person: *Linda was something of a character.*

3 QUALITIES OF STH [singular,U] the particular combination of features and qualities that makes a thing or place different from all others; **◨ nature**: [+of] *The whole character of the school has changed.* | *the unspoilt character of the coast* | **in character** *The southern state became more nationalist in character.*

4 MORAL STRENGTH [U] a combination of qualities such as courage, loyalty, and honesty that are admired and regarded as valuable: *a woman of great character* | *Schools were created to teach reading and mathematics, not moral character.* | *It takes **strength of character** to admit you are wrong.* | *outdoor programs that are meant to be **character building** (=develop good moral qualities)*

5 INTERESTING QUALITY [U] a quality that makes someone or something special and interesting: *a red wine with a meaty character* | *suburban houses that lack character*

6 REPUTATION [U] *formal* the opinion that people have about whether you are a good person and can be trusted: *a man **of** previous **good character*** | *The campaign was accused of **character assassination** (=an unfair attack on someone's character) because of its negative side.* | *His defence called several people as **character witnesses** (=people who think that someone has a good character).* | *Mr Wetherby wrote him a **character reference** (=a statement about his good qualities).*

7 LETTER/SIGN [C] a letter, mark, or sign used in writing, printing, or on a computer: *the Chinese character for horse*

'character ,actor *n* [C] an actor who typically plays unusual characters, rather than the most important characters

char·ac·ter·ise /'kær⦆ktəraɪz/ *v* a British spelling of CHARACTERIZE

char·ac·ter·is·tic¹ [S3] [W2] /ˌkær⦆ktə'rɪstɪk◂/ *n* [C usually plural] a quality or feature of something or someone that is typical of them and easy to recognize: [+of] *a baby discovering the physical characteristics of objects* | **defining/distinguishing characteristic** (=one that separates someone or something from others of the same type) *Violent images are a defining characteristic of his work.*

characteristic² *adj* very typical of a particular thing or of someone's character: *the **highly characteristic** (=very typical) flint walls of the local houses* | [+of] *the qualities that were characteristic of the Nixon administration* —**characteristically** /-kli/ *adv*

char·ac·ter·i·za·tion /ˌkær⦆ktəraɪ'zeɪʃən $ -tərə-/ *n* [C,U] **1** the way in which a writer makes a person in a book, film, or play seem like a real person: *Pilcher's books are full of humour, good characterization, and lively dialogue.* **2** the way in which the character of a real person or thing is described: **characterization of sb/sth as sth** *the characterization of the enemy as 'cruel fanatics'*

char·ac·ter·ize [W3] also **-ise** *BrE* /'kær⦆ktəraɪz/ *v* [T] **1** to describe the qualities of someone or something in a particular way; **◨ portray**: **characterize sb as (being) sth** *The group was characterized as being well-educated and liberal.* **2** to be typical of a person, place, or thing: *Bright colours characterize his paintings.*

char·ac·ter·less /'kær⦆ktələs $ -tər-/ *adj* not having any special or interesting qualities: *a characterless modern building*

cha·rade /ʃə'rɑːd $ ʃə'reɪd/ *n* **1 charades** [U] a game in which one person uses actions and no words to show the meaning of a word or phrase, and other people have to guess what it is **2** [C] a situation in which people behave as though something is true or serious, when it is not really true: *Unless more money is given to schools, all this talk of improving education is just a charade.*

char·broil /'tʃɑːbrɔɪl $ 'tʃɑːr-/ *v* [T] *AmE* to cook food over a very hot charcoal fire —**charbroiled** *adj*

char·coal /'tʃɑːkəʊl $ 'tʃɑːrkoʊl/ *n* **1** [U] a black substance made of burned wood that can be used as FUEL: *cooking over a charcoal fire* **2** [C,U] a stick of this substance used for drawing: *a sketch drawn in charcoal* **3** also **charcoal grey** [U] a dark grey colour —,**charcoal** *adj*

chard /tʃɑːd $ tʃɑːrd/ *n* [U] a vegetable with large leaves

charge¹ [S1] [W1] /tʃɑːdʒ $ tʃɑːrdʒ/ *n*

1 PRICE [C,U] the amount of money you have to pay for goods or services: *Gas charges will rise in July.* | [+of] *an admission charge of $5* | [+for] *There's a 50 pence booking charge for each ticket.* | *Guided tours are provided **at no charge**.* | *Your order will be sent **free of charge** (=at no cost).* | *The shop will fit them for a small **extra charge**.*

2 CONTROL [U] the position of having control or responsibility for a group of people or an activity: **in charge (of sth)** *He asked to speak to the person in charge.* | *the officer in charge of the investigation* | *Stern **put** Travis **in charge of** (=gave him control of) the research team.* | *Owens came in and **took charge of** (=took control of) the situation.* | *A commander in each county was to **have charge of** the local militia.*

3 SB/STH YOU LOOK AFTER a) be in/under sb's charge if someone or something is in your charge, you are responsible for looking after them: *teachers that do their best for the children in their charge* | *The files were left in your charge.* **b)** [C] *formal* someone that you are responsible for looking after: *Sarah bought some chocolate for her three young charges.*

4 CRIME [C] an official statement made by the police saying that they believe someone may be guilty of a crime

on a charge (of sth)
bring/press charges (=state officially that someone is guilty of a crime)
face charges (=be accused of a crime)
drop the charges (=decide to stop making charges)
deny a charge
admit a charge
plead guilty to a charge
be released without charge
be cleared/acquitted of a charge (=when someone is officially not guilty at the end of a trial)
be convicted of a charge (=when someone is found guilty at the end of a trial)

[+against] *He was found guilty of all six charges against him.* | *Phillips was arrested on drug charges.* | *The following morning, he was arrested **on a charge of** burglary.* | *Young appeared in court **on a murder charge**.* | [+of] *Higgins is **facing a charge of** armed robbery.* | *As it was his first offence, the store agreed not to **press charges**.* | *Police **dropped the charges** against him because of insufficient evidence.* | *Nine people have **pleaded guilty to** various **charges**.* | *Green was **cleared of** all **charges** against him.*

5 BLAME [C] a written or spoken statement blaming someone for doing something bad or illegal; **◨ allegation**: **charge that** *the charge that tobacco companies target young people with their ads* | [+of] *a charge of racial discrimination against the company* | **deny/counter a charge** (=say that a charge is untrue) *Wallace denied charges that he had lied to investigators.* | **lay/leave yourself open to a charge of sth** (=be likely to be blamed for something) *The speech laid him open to charges of political bias.*

6 ATTACK [C] an attack in which soldiers or animals move towards someone or something very quickly

7 EFFORT lead the charge to make a strong effort to do something: *It was small businesses that led the charge against health care changes.*

8 ELECTRICITY [U] electricity that is put into a piece of electrical equipment such as a BATTERY: **on charge** (=taking in a charge of electricity) *Leave the battery on charge all night.*

C

9 EXPLOSIVE [C] an explosive put into something such as a bomb or gun

10 STRENGTH OF FEELINGS [singular] the power of strong feelings: *Cases of child abuse have a strong emotional charge.*

11 get a charge out of sth *AmE spoken* to be excited by something and enjoy it very much: *I got a real charge out of seeing my niece take her first steps.*

12 AN ORDER TO DO STH [C] *formal* an order to do something: **charge to do sth** *The old servant fulfilled his master's charge to care for the children.* → **reverse the charges** at REVERSE¹ (6)

charge² S1 W2 *v*

1 MONEY **a)** [I,T] to ask someone for a particular amount of money for something you are selling: *The hotel charges $125 a night.* | **charge sb £10/$50 etc (for sth)** *The restaurant charged us £40 for the wine.* | **charge sth at sth** *Calls will be charged at 44p per minute.* | [+for] *We won't charge for delivery if you pay now.* | **charge rent/a fee/interest etc** *The gallery charges an entrance fee.* **b) charge sth to sb's account/room etc** to record the cost of something on someone's account, so that they can pay for it later: *Wilson charged the drinks to his room.* | *Use a courier and charge it to the department.* **c)** [T] *AmE* to pay for something with a CREDIT CARD: **charge sth on sth** *I charged the shoes on Visa.* | *'How would you like to pay?' 'I'll charge it.'*

2 CRIME [T] to state officially that someone may be guilty of a crime: **charge sb with sth** *Gibbons has been charged with murder.*

3 BLAME SB [T] *formal* to say publicly that you think someone has done something wrong: **charge that** *Demonstrators have charged that the police used excessive force against them.*

4 RUN [I always + adv/prep] to deliberately run or walk somewhere quickly: [+around/through/out etc] *The boys charged noisily into the water.*

5 ATTACK [I,T] to deliberately rush quickly towards someone or something in order to attack them: *Then, with a final effort, our men charged the enemy for the last time.* | [+at/towards/into] *The bear charged towards her at full speed.*

6 ELECTRICITY [I,T] also **charge up** if a BATTERY charges, or if you charge it, it takes in and stores electricity: *The shaver can be charged up and used while travelling.*

7 ORDER SB [T] *formal* to order someone to do something or make them responsible for it: **charge sb with doing sth** *The commission is charged with investigating war crimes.*

8 GUN [T] *old use* to load a gun

9 GLASS [T] *BrE formal* to fill a glass → CHARGED

charge·a·ble /ˈtʃɑːdʒəbəl $ ˈtʃɑːr-/ *adj BrE* **1** needing to be paid for: *Advice will be given as a chargeable service.* **2** something that is chargeable must have tax paid on it: *chargeable assets*

'charge ac·count *n* [C] *AmE* an account you have at a shop that allows you to take goods away with you now and pay later

'charge card *n* [C] a plastic card from a particular shop that you can use to buy goods there and pay for them later; → **credit card**

charged /tʃɑːdʒd $ tʃɑːrdʒd/ *adj* a charged situation or subject makes people feel very angry, anxious, or excited, and is likely to cause arguments or violence: *the charged atmosphere in the room* | *a highly charged debate*

char·gé d'af·faires /ˌʃɑːʒeɪ dæˈfeə $ ˌʃɑːrʒeɪ dæˈfer/ *n plural* **chargés d'affaires** *(same pronunciation)* [C] an official who represents a particular government during the absence of an AMBASSADOR or in a country where there is no ambassador

'charge hand *n* [C] *BrE* a worker in charge of other workers, whose position is below that of a FOREMAN

'charge nurse *n* [C] a nurse who is responsible for the work done in one part of a hospital

charg·er /ˈtʃɑːdʒə $ ˈtʃɑːrdʒər/ *n* [C] **1** a piece of equipment used to put electricity into a BATTERY **2** *literary* a horse that a soldier or KNIGHT rides in battle

'charge sheet *n* [C] a record kept in a police station of the names of people the police have stated may be guilty of a particular crime

char·i·ot /ˈtʃæriət/ *n* [C] a vehicle with two wheels pulled by a horse, used in ancient times in battles and races

char·i·o·teer /ˌtʃæriəˈtɪə $ -ˈtɪr/ *n* [C] the driver of a chariot

cha·ris·ma /kəˈrɪzmə/ *n* [U] a natural ability to attract and interest other people and make them admire you: *He lacks charisma.*

char·is·mat·ic /ˌkærɪzˈmætɪk◂/ *adj* **1** having charisma: *Martin Luther King was a very charismatic speaker.* **2 charismatic church/movement** groups of Christians who believe that God can give them special abilities, for example the ability to cure illness

char·it·a·ble /ˈtʃærɪtəbəl/ *adj* **1** relating to giving help to the poor; ⊠ **uncharitable**; → **charity**: *charitable groups* | *a charitable donation* **2** kind and sympathetic in the way you judge people: *a charitable view of his actions* —**charitably** *adv*

char·i·ty S2 W3 /ˈtʃærɪti/ *n plural* **charities**

1 [C] an organization that gives money, goods, or help to people who are poor, sick etc; → **charitable**: *Several charities sent aid to the flood victims.* | **charity event/walk/concert etc** (=an event organized to collect money for a charity)

2 [U] charity organizations in general: *All the money raised by the concert will go to charity.* | **for charity** *The children raised over £200 for charity.*

3 [U] money or gifts given to help people who are poor, sick etc: *refugees living on charity* | *Her pride wouldn't allow her to accept charity.*

4 [U] *formal* kindness or sympathy that you show towards other people: *Mother Teresa's works of charity* | *Newspaper reports showed him little charity.*

5 charity begins at home a phrase meaning that you should take care of your own family, country etc before you help other people

'charity shop *n* [C] *BrE* a shop that sells used goods that are given to it, in order to collect money for a charity

char·la·dy /ˈtʃɑːˌleɪdi $ ˈtʃɑːr-/ *n plural* **charladies** [C] *BrE old-fashioned* a CHARWOMAN

char·la·tan /ˈʃɑːlətən $ ˈʃɑːr-/ *n* [C] *literary* someone who pretends to have special skills or knowledge – used to show disapproval

Charles·ton /ˈtʃɑːlstən $ ˈtʃɑːrl-/ *n* **the Charleston** a quick dance popular in the 1920s

char·ley horse /ˌtʃɑːli ˈhɔːs $ ˌtʃɑːrli ˈhɔːrs/ *n* [C, singular] *AmE informal* a pain in a large muscle, for example in your leg, caused by the muscle becoming tight; ⊟ **cramp**

char·lie /ˈtʃɑːli $ ˈtʃɑːr-/ *n* [C] *BrE spoken* a stupid person: **feel a right/proper charlie** (=feel very stupid)

charm¹ /tʃɑːm $ tʃɑːrm/ *n* **1** [C,U] a special quality someone or something has that makes people like them, feel attracted to them, or be easily influenced by them – used to show approval; → **charming**: *Robert's boyish charm* | [+of] *the charm of this small Southern city* | *She turned on the charm* (=used her charm) *to everyone she met.* | *The room had no windows and all the charm of a prison cell* (=used to say that something has no charm). **2** [C] a very small object worn on a chain or BRACELET: *a charm bracelet* | *a small gold horseshoe worn as a lucky charm* **3** [C] a phrase or action believed to have special magic powers; ⊟ **spell** **4 work like a charm** to work exactly as you had hoped: *The new sales program has worked like a charm.*

charm² *v* [T]   **1** to attract someone and make them like you, sometimes in order to make them do something for you; → **charming**: *We were charmed by the friendliness of the local people.*   **2** to please and interest someone: *a story that has charmed generations of children*   **3** to gain power over someone or something by using magic

charmed /tʃɑːmd $ tʃɑːrmd/ *adj* **have/lead a charmed life** to be lucky all the time, so that although you are often in dangerous situations nothing ever harms you

,**charmed** '**circle** *n* [singular] *written* a group of people who have special power or influence: *politicians outside the charmed circle*

charm·er /'tʃɑːmə $ 'tʃɑːrmər/ *n* [C] someone who uses their charm to please or influence people: *Even at ten years old, he was a real charmer.* → SNAKE CHARMER

charm·ing /'tʃɑːmɪŋ $ 'tʃɑːr-/ *adj* very pleasing or attractive: *a charming little Italian restaurant* | *Harry can be very charming.* —**charmingly** *adv*

'**charm school** *n* [C] *especially AmE* a school where young women were sometimes sent in the past to learn how to behave politely and gracefully

char·nel house /'tʃɑːnl haʊs $ 'tʃɑːr-/ *n* [C] *literary* a place where the bodies and bones of dead people are stored

charred /tʃɑːd $ tʃɑːrd/ *adj* something that is charred has been burned until it is black: *the charred remains of a body*

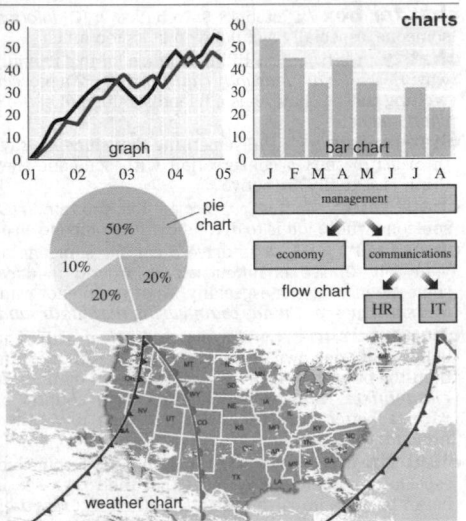

charts

graph

bar chart

pie chart
50%
10%
20%
20%

flow chart
management
economy | communications
HR | IT

weather chart

chart¹ S3 W3 /tʃɑːt $ tʃɑːrt/ *n* [C]
1 information that is clearly arranged in the form of a simple picture, set of figures, GRAPH etc, or a piece of paper with this information on it; ◨ **diagram**: *a chart showing last year's sales* | *a weather chart* | *the theatre's seating chart*
2 the charts the lists, which come out weekly, of the most popular records: *Her new single went straight to number one in the **pop charts**.* | *Brooks again **topped the charts** (=was the most popular).* | **chart hit/success/star etc** *the Beatles' first chart hit*
3 a detailed map, especially of an area of the sea or the stars → BAR CHART, FLOW CHART, PIE CHART

chart² *v* [T]   **1** to record information about a situation or set of events over a period of time, in order to see how it changes or develops: *Scientists have been charting temperature changes in the oceans.*   **2** to make a plan of what should be done to achieve a particular result: *Each team was responsible for making its own decisions and charting its own course.*   **3** to make a map of an area of land, sea, or stars, or to draw lines on a map to show where you have travelled; → **uncharted**

char·ter¹ W3 /'tʃɑːtə $ 'tʃɑːrtər/ *n*
1 [C] a statement of the principles, duties, and purposes of an organization: *the freedoms embodied in the UN charter*
2 [U] the practice of paying money to a company to use their boats, aircraft, etc, or the boat, aircraft etc used in this way: *boats available for charter* | *a charter service*
3 [C] a signed statement from a government or ruler which allows a town, organization, or university to officially exist and have special rights: *The town's charter was granted in 1838.*
4 [singular] *BrE informal* a law or official decision that seems to give someone the right to do something most people consider morally wrong: *Reducing the number of police is just a thieves' charter.*

charter² *v* [T]   **1** to pay a company for the use of their aircraft, boat etc: *We chartered a boat to take us to some of the smaller islands.*   **2** to say officially that a town, organization, or university officially exists and has special rights

char·tered /'tʃɑːtəd $ 'tʃɑːrtərd/ *adj* [only before noun] *BrE* **chartered accountant/surveyor/engineer etc** an ACCOUNTANT, SURVEYOR etc who has successfully completed special examinations

'**charter flight** *n* [C] an aircraft journey that is arranged for a particular group or for a particular purpose, and that usually costs less than an ordinary aircraft journey; → **scheduled flight**

,**charter 'member** *n* [C] *AmE* an original member of a club or organization; ◨ **founder member** *BrE*

'**charter ,school** *n* [C] a school in the US that is run by parents, companies etc rather than by the public school system, but which the state government supports

char·treuse /ʃɑː'trɜːz $ ʃɑːr'truːz/ *n* [U]   **1** a green or yellow alcoholic drink   **2** a bright yellow-green colour

'**chart-,topping** *adj* **chart-topping record/group/hit etc** a record, group etc that has sold the most records in a particular week

char·wom·an /'tʃɑː,wʊmən $ 'tʃɑːr-/ *n plural* **charwomen** /-,wɪmɪn/ [C] *BrE old-fashioned* a woman who works as a cleaner, especially in someone's house

char·y /'tʃeəri $ 'tʃeri/ *adj especially BrE* unwilling to risk doing something: **chary about/of doing sth** *Banks were chary of lending the company more money.*

chase¹ S3 /tʃeɪs/ *v*
1 FOLLOW [I,T] to quickly follow someone or something in order to catch them: *The dogs saw him running and chased him.* | *kids chasing around the house* | **chase sb along/down/up sth etc** *The police chased the suspect along Severn Avenue.* | [+**after**] *A gang of boys chased after her, calling her names.*
2 MAKE SB/STH LEAVE [T always + adv/prep] to make someone or something leave, especially by following them for a short distance and threatening them: **chase sb away/off** *The men were chased off by troops, who fired warning shots.* | **chase sb out of sth** *Anne went to chase the dog out of the garden.*
3 TRY TO GET STH [I,T] to use a lot of time and effort trying to get something such as work or money: *Top graduates from the university are chased by major companies.* | [+**after**] *reporters chasing after a story*
4 HURRY [I always + adv/prep] *BrE* to rush or hurry somewhere: [+**around/up/down etc**] *I was chasing around getting everything organized.*
5 ROMANCE [T] to try hard to make someone notice you and pay attention to you, because you want to have a romantic relationship with them: *'Sometimes a girl wants to be chased,' Amelia said.*
6 METAL [T] *technical* to decorate metal with a special tool: *chased silver*
7 chase the dragon *informal* to smoke the drug HEROIN
chase sb/sth ⇔ down *phr v*

C

to find something or someone that you have been looking for: *We had to chase down everyone we'd sold a bike to.*

chase sb/sth ⇔ **up** *phr v BrE*
1 to remind someone to do something they promised to do for you: *David hasn't paid yet – you'd better chase him up.*
2 to try to make something happen or arrive more quickly, because it has been taking too long: *Can you chase up those photos for me tomorrow?*

chase² *n* **1** [C] the act of following someone or something quickly in order to catch them: *a high-speed car chase* | *Police spotted the car and gave chase* (=chased it). **2** [singular] when you use a lot of time and effort trying to get something: [+after] *the chase after higher-paying jobs* → PAPER CHASE, WILD GOOSE CHASE

chas·er /'tʃeɪsə $ -ər/ *n* [C] a weaker alcoholic drink which is drunk after a strong one, or a stronger alcoholic drink which is drunk after a weak one: *a pint of bitter and a whisky chaser*

chas·m /'kæzəm/ *n* **1** [C] a very deep space between two areas of rock or ice, especially one that is dangerous: *a rope bridge across the chasm* **2** [singular] a big difference between two people, groups, or things: [+between] *the chasm between rich and poor*

chas·sis /'ʃæsi/ *n plural* **chassis** /-siːz/ [C] **1** the frame on which the body, engine, wheels etc of a vehicle are built **2** the landing equipment of a plane

chaste /tʃeɪst/ *adj* **1** *old-fashioned* not having sex with anyone, or not with anyone except your husband or wife; → **celibate, chastity:** *She led a chaste, decent life.* **2** not showing sexual feelings: *a chaste kiss on the cheek* **3** simple and plain in style: *a chaste nightgown* —**chastely** *adv*

chas·ten /'tʃeɪsən/ *v* [T usually passive] *formal* to make someone realize that their behaviour was wrong or mistaken: *Party workers have returned to their home towns, chastened by their overwhelming defeat.* —**chastening** *adj: a chastening experience*

chas·tise /tʃæ'staɪz/ *v* [T] **1** *formal* to criticize someone severely: *'You're a fool,' she chastised herself.* **2** *old-fashioned* to physically punish someone —**chastisement** *n* [C,U]

chas·ti·ty /'tʃæstỊti/ *n* [U] the principle or state of not having sex with anyone, or not with anyone except your husband or wife

chat¹ [S2] /tʃæt/ *n* [C,U] *especially BrE* an informal friendly conversation: [+with] *I've had a long chat with Vinnie.* | [+about] *a chat about the weather* | *She was enjoying their friendly little chat.* | *She used to drop in for a chat quite often.* → BACKCHAT

chat² **chatted, chatting** *v* [I] **1** also **chat away** *especially BrE* to talk in a friendly informal way, especially about things that are not important: *John and I sat up until the early hours chatting.* | [+with/to] *Mary was there, chatting to her mother.* | [+about] *Susie chatted away about her social life.* **2** to communicate with several people in a chat room on the Internet
chat sb ⇔ **up** *phr v BrE informal* to talk to someone in a way that shows you are sexually attracted to them: *I spent the evening chatting up Liz.*

chat·eau /'ʃætəʊ $ ʃæ'toʊ/ *n plural* **chateaux** /-təʊz $ -'toʊz/ [C] a castle or large country house in France → see picture at HOUSE¹

chat·e·laine /'ʃætl-eɪn/ *n* [C] *formal* the female owner, or wife of the owner, of a castle or large country house in France

chat line *n* [C] a telephone service that people call to talk to other people who have called the same service

chat room *n* [C] a place on the Internet where you can write messages to other people and receive messages back from them immediately, so that you can have a conversation while you are ONLINE

chat show *n* [C] *BrE* a television or radio show on which people talk about themselves in reply to questions; ◨ **talk show** *AmE: a TV chat show host* (=person who asks the questions on the show)

chat·tel /'tʃætl/ *n* [C] *law old-fashioned* a piece of personal property that you can move from one place to another: *a society in which women are considered to be chattels* → GOODS AND CHATTELS

chat·ter¹ /'tʃætə $ -ər/ *v* [I] **1** also **chatter away/on** to talk quickly in a friendly way without stopping, especially about things that are not serious or important: *She chattered away happily until she noticed I wasn't listening.* | *She chattered excitedly like a child.* | [+about] *We were chattering about the events of last night.* **2** if birds or monkeys chatter, they make short high sounds **3** if your teeth are chattering, you are so cold or frightened that your teeth are knocking together **4** **the chattering classes** *BrE* educated MIDDLE-CLASS people who like to discuss and have opinions about recent events and situations in society —**chatterer** *n* [C]

chatter² *n* [U] **1** informal talk, especially about things that are not serious or important: [+of] *the excited chatter of the audience* | *Jane's constant chatter was annoying him.* | *gossip and idle chatter* | *She was full of chatter about her new friends.* **2** a series of short high sounds made by some birds or monkeys: [+of] *the chatter of birds* **3** a hard quick repeated sound made by your teeth knocking together or by machines: [+of] *the chatter of the printer*

chat·ter·box /'tʃætəbɒks $ -tərbɑːks/ *n* [C] *informal* someone, especially a child, who talks too much

chat·ty /'tʃæti/ *adj* **1** liking to talk a lot in a friendly way: *He was in an unusually chatty mood.* **2** a piece of writing that is chatty has a friendly informal style: *a chatty letter*

chat-up line *n* [C] *BrE* something that someone says in order to start a conversation with someone they think is sexually attractive

chauf·feur¹ /'ʃəʊfə, ʃəʊ'fɜː $ 'ʃoʊfər, ʃoʊ'fɜːr/ *n* [C] someone whose job is to drive a car for someone else

chauffeur² *v* [T] **1** to drive a car for someone as your job **2** also **chauffeur** sb ⇔ **around** to drive someone in your car, especially when you do not want to: *I spent most of the day chauffeuring the kids around.*

chau·vin·is·m /'ʃəʊvịnɪzəm $ 'ʃoʊ-/ *n* [U] **1** a belief that your own sex is better or more important than the other sex, especially if you are a man: *male chauvinism* **2** a strong belief that your country or race is better or more important than any other: *national chauvinism*

chau·vin·ist /'ʃəʊvịnịst $ 'ʃoʊ-/ *n* [C] **1** someone, especially a man, who believes that their own sex is better or more important than the other sex: *He's a bit of a male chauvinist.* | *a male chauvinist pig* (=an insulting name for a male chauvinist) **2** someone who believes that their own country or race is better or more important than any other —**chauvinist** *adj*

chau·vi·nis·tic /,ʃəʊvị'nɪstɪk◂ $,ʃoʊ-/ *adj* **1** having the belief that your own country or race is better or more important than any other: *a chauvinistic dislike of all things foreign* **2** having the belief that your own sex is better, or more important than the other sex, especially if you are a man —**chauvinistically** /-kli/ *adv*

cheap¹ [S1] [W2] /tʃiːp/ *adj comparative* **cheaper**, *superlative* **cheapest**
1 LOW PRICE not at all expensive, or lower in price than you expected; ◨ **expensive:** *cheap rail fares* | *the cheapest TV on the market* | *Property is cheaper in Spain than here.* | *a cheap shop* (=one that sells goods cheaply) | *The equipment is relatively cheap and simple to use.* | *This coat was dirt cheap informal* (=very cheap). | **cheap and cheerful** *BrE* (=simple and not expensive, but of reasonable quality) *a cheap and cheerful Italian restaurant*
2 BAD QUALITY low in price and quality: *Cheap wine*

gives me a headache. | cheap jewellery | The furniture looked **cheap and nasty**. | a **cheap imitation** of the real thing

3 NOT EXPENSIVE TO USE not costing much to use or to employ; ▣ **inexpensive: cheap to run/use/maintain etc** | Gas appliances are usually cheaper to run than electric ones. | For the employer, a part-time workforce means a **cheap labour** supply.

4 NOT DESERVING RESPECT showing a lack of honesty, moral principles, or sincere feelings, so that you do not deserve respect: She felt cheap and stupid, like a naughty child caught stealing. | You're lying, aren't you? You're so cheap. | His remark was a **cheap shot** at short people. | another **cheap** political **stunt** | It was nothing but a **cheap trick** (=unkind trick).

5 NOT GENEROUS AmE not liking to spend money; ▣ **mean** BrE: She's too cheap to take a cab.

6 cheap thrill excitement that does not take much effort to get: Bella will sleep with anyone for a cheap thrill.

7 life is cheap used to say that it is not important if people die

8 cheap at the price/at any price BrE, **cheap at twice the price** so good, useful, or desirable that the cost is not important —**cheaply** adv: a cheaply furnished room | They lived as cheaply as possible. —**cheapness** n [U]: the relative cheapness of housing

> **WORD FOCUS: words meaning CHEAP**
> **reasonable** not too expensive | **economical** used about cars, systems, or methods that do not cost a lot of money to use | **be good value** to be well worth the price you pay | **be a bargain** to be very cheap

cheap² adv at a low price: Air fares to Africa **don't come cheap** (=are expensive). | I bought this house because it was **going cheap** (=selling for a lower price than usual). | She used to **get** meat **cheap** at the butcher's. | They're selling linen off cheap in Lewis's.

cheap³ n **on the cheap** spending less money than is needed to do something properly: A clean environment cannot be had on the cheap. | holidaying on the cheap

cheap·en /ˈtʃiːpən/ v **1** [I,T] to become or make something become lower in price or value: The good harvest that year cheapened the costs of some raw materials. **2** [T] to make something or someone seem less deserving of respect: She never compromised or cheapened herself.

cheap·o /ˈtʃiːpəʊ $ -oʊ/ adj [only before noun] informal not of good quality and not costing very much: a cheapo camera

cheap·skate /ˈtʃiːpskeɪt/ n [C] informal someone who spends as little money as possible – used to show disapproval: The cheapskate didn't even pay for the cab.

cheat¹ /tʃiːt/ v **1** [I,T] to behave in a dishonest way in order to win or to get an advantage, especially in a competition, game, or examination: He had cheated in the test by using a calculator. | Don't look at my cards – **that's cheating**. | [+at] She always claimed that I cheated at chess.; → see picture at TRICK **2** [T] to trick or deceive someone so that they do not get or keep something they have a right to have: Illegal workers are often cheated by employers. | **cheat sb (out) of sth** a woman who cheated her aged aunt out of her fortune **3 feel cheated** to feel that you have been treated wrongly or unfairly and have not got what you deserve: Young people often feel cheated by their parents without knowing why. **4 cheat death/fate etc** to manage to avoid death or a very bad situation even though it seemed that you would not be able to: The Italian ace cheated death in a spectacular 100 mph crash. **5 be cheated of victory/success etc** if you are cheated of victory, success etc, you do not achieve it because of something unfortunate that happens

cheat on sb phr v to be unfaithful to your husband, wife, or sexual partner by secretly having sex with someone else: The magazine claims that almost half of Britain's women cheat on their partners.

cheat² n [C] **1** someone who is dishonest and cheats: His addiction has turned him into a cheat and a

liar. **2 a cheat** something that is dishonest or unfair **3** a set of instructions given to a computer that make it easier for someone who is playing a computer game to win

check¹ S1 W2 /tʃek/ v

1 FIND OUT [I,T] to do something in order to find out whether something really is correct, true, or in good condition: Check the tiles carefully before you buy them. | A first rule in solving any mystery is to check the facts. | Fill in the cash book carefully and always check your calculations. | **check (that)** Check that all the doors are locked securely. | **check whether/how/who etc** Let me just check whether the potatoes are cooked. | They paused to check how the other climbers were getting on. | **check (sth) for sth** I checked the typing for errors. | Turn the tap on and check for leaks. | **check sth against/with sth** (=compare something with something else to see whether they are the same) You must check the evidence against other sources and decide if it is reliable. | Positive test results are **double checked** (=looked at twice) to make absolutely sure.

2 ASK SB [I,T] to ask someone whether something is correct, true, or allowed: I'm not authorized to give you a refund – I'll have to check first. | **check (that)** Make a phone call to check that you are writing to the right person. | **check whether/how/who etc** I'll call the factory to check whether the beds can be delivered today. | [+with] It's wise to check with your doctor before going on a diet.

3 NOT DO STH [T] to suddenly stop yourself from saying or doing something because you realize it would be better not to: I had to check the urge to laugh out loud. | **check yourself** He grinned, and then checked himself, not wanting to upset Jack.

4 STOP STH [T] to stop something bad from getting worse or continuing to happen: The police are failing to take adequate measures to check the growth in crime.

5 BAGS/CASES ETC [T] AmE, **check in** BrE to leave your bags at an official place so they can be put on a plane or a train, or to take someone's bags in order to do this: Any luggage over five kilos must be checked.

6 MAKE A MARK [T] AmE to make a mark (✓) next to an answer, something on a list etc to show you have chosen it, that it is correct, or that you have dealt with it; ▣ **tick** BrE

7 Check spoken especially AmE say this when someone mentions each thing on a list, to tell them that you have it or have done it: 'Passport?' 'Check.' 'Ticket?' ' Check'.

check in phr v

1 if you check in or are checked in at a hotel or airport, you go to the desk and report that you have arrived: You need to check in two hours before the flight. | [+at] He checked in at the Europa Hotel. | **check sb ⇔ in** Airline employees were checking in passengers. → CHECK-IN

2 check sth ⇔ in to leave your bags at an official place so they can be put on a plane or a train, or to take someone's bags in order to do this: I said goodbye and went to check in my suitcases.

3 AmE to call someone to tell them that you are safe or where you are: He just called to check in and tell them how he was doing.

check sth ⇔ **off** phr v
to write a mark next to something on a list to show that you have chosen it, dealt with it, or made sure that it is correct: One by one he checked them off on his register.

check on sb/sth phr v

1 to make sure that someone or something is safe, is in a satisfactory state, or is doing what they should be doing: Honey, can you go upstairs and check on the kids? | My neighbour comes in once a week to check on things and feed the fish.

2 to try to find out if something is true or correct: He wanted to check on the girl's story.

check out phr v

1 MAKE SURE a) check sth ⇔ out to make sure that

something is actually true, correct, or acceptable; ◧ **investigate**: *I made a phone call to check out his address.* | [+**with**] *Check it out with your boss before you do anything.* **b)** if information checks out, it is proved to be true, correct, or acceptable: *His credit record checks out.*

2 LOOK AT SB/STH check sb/sth ⇔ out to look at someone or something because they are interesting or attractive: *If I hear about a website that sounds interesting, I check it out.* | *Hey, check out that car!*

3 GET INFORMATION check sb ⇔ out *informal* to get information about someone, especially to find out if they are suitable for something: *I'll check them out as potential employers.*

4 HOTEL to leave a hotel after paying the bill: *We checked out at noon.* → CHECKOUT

5 BOOKS check sth ⇔ out *AmE* to borrow a book from a library: *The library allows you to check out six books at a time.*

check sth/sb ⇔ **over** *phr v*
1 to look closely at something to make sure it is correct or acceptable: *They spent the rest of the morning checking over their equipment.*
2 to examine someone to make sure they are healthy: *I'd like the doctor to check you over and do a few tests.*

check up on sb/sth *phr v*
1 to try to find out if someone is doing what they said they would do or what you want them to do: *Don't worry; no-one is going to check up on you.*
2 to make sure that something is true or correct: *Dustin called me to check up on some facts.*

check² S1 W3 *n*
1 FINDING OUT [C] the process of finding out if something is safe, correct, true, or in the condition it should be: [+**on**] *the need for tighter checks on arms sales* | *Conduct regular checks on your water quality.* | **run/carry out/make a check** *I decided to run a check on all personnel.* | *I keep a careful check on my blood pressure.* | **have a check** *BrE*: *Have a check in your bag first and see if it's there.* | *the airport's routine security checks* | *random drug checks* | **health/medical/dental etc check** (=a test done to make sure you are healthy) | **spot check** (=a quick check of one thing among a group of things, that you do without warning) *a spot check on the accounts*
2 keep/hold sb/sth in check keep someone or something under control: *You must learn to keep your emotions in check.* | *attempts to keep global warming in check* | *He made an effort to hold himself in check.*
3 A CONTROL ON STH [C usually singular] something that controls something else and stops it from getting worse, continuing to happen etc: [+**on**] *Higher interest rates will act as a check on public spending.*
4 checks and balances a system that makes it possible for some people or parts of an organization to control the others, so that no particular person or part has too much power or influence
5 PATTERN [C,U] a pattern of squares, especially on cloth: *a shirt with brown and black checks* | **check suit/jacket etc** (=made with cloth patterned with checks) *a blue cotton check dress* → CHECKED
6 FROM YOUR BANK [C] the American spelling of CHEQUE: [+**for**] *a check for $30* | **by check** *Can I pay by check?*
7 IN A RESTAURANT [C] *AmE* a list that you are given in a restaurant showing what you have eaten and how much you must pay; ◧ **bill** *BrE*
8 coat check/hat check *AmE* [C] **a)** a place in a restaurant, theatre etc where you can leave your coat, bag etc to be guarded until you go home **b)** a ticket that you are given so you can claim your things from this place
9 MARK [C] *AmE* a mark (✓) that you put next to an answer to show that it is correct or next to something on a list to show that you have dealt with it; ◧ **tick** *BrE*

10 CHESS [U] the position of the KING (=most important piece) in CHESS where it can be directly attacked by the opponent's pieces

check·book /'tʃekbʊk/ *n* the American spelling of CHEQUEBOOK

'**check card** *n* [C] *AmE* a special plastic card, similar to a CREDIT CARD, that you can use to pay for things directly from your CHECKING ACCOUNT; ◧ **debit card**

checked /tʃekt/ *adj* checked cloth has a regular pattern of differently coloured squares: *a checked blouse*

check·er /'tʃekə $ -ər/ *n* [C] **1** *AmE* someone who works at the CHECKOUT in a SUPERMARKET **2 spell/grammar checker** a computer program that checks whether the spelling of words or the grammar of a sentence is correct **3** someone who makes sure that something is written or done correctly **4 checkers** [U] a game for two players using 12 flat round pieces each and a board with 64 squares, in which the purpose is to take the other player's pieces by jumping over them with your pieces; ◧ **draughts** *BrE* → CHINESE CHEQUERS

check·er·board /'tʃekəbɔːd $ -kərbɔːrd/ *n* [C] *AmE* a board that you play checkers on, with 32 white squares and 32 black squares; ◧ **draughtboard** *BrE*

check·ered also **chequered** *BrE* /'tʃekəd $ -ərd/ *adj* **1** having a pattern made up of squares of two different colours: *a red and white checkered tablecloth* | *a checkered marble floor* **2 have a checkered history/career/past etc** to have had periods of failure as well as successful times in your past: *This is an unusual building with a checkered history.*

'**checkered 'flag** also **chequered flag** *BrE n* [C] a flag covered with black and white squares that is waved at the beginning and end of a motor race

'**check-in** *n* **1** [singular] a place where you report your arrival at an airport, hotel, hospital etc: *the check-in desk* | *Make sure you're at the check-in by 5.30.* **2** [U] the process of reporting your arrival at an airport, hotel, hospital etc: *Ask your travel agent about check-in times.* → **check in** at CHECK¹

'**checking ac·count** *n* [C] *AmE* a bank account that you can take money out of at any time, and for which you are given checks to use to pay for things; ◧ **current account** *BrE* → DEPOSIT ACCOUNT

check·list /'tʃek,lɪst/ *n* [C] a list that helps you by reminding you of the things you need to do or get for a particular job or activity: *The guide contains a useful checklist of points to look for when buying a car.*

check·mate /'tʃekmeɪt/ *n* [C,U] **1** the position of the KING (=most important piece) in CHESS at the end of the game, when it is being directly attacked and cannot escape **2** a situation in which someone has been completely defeated —**checkmate** *v* [T]: *The king is checkmated and the game is over.*

check·out /'tʃek-aʊt/ *n* **1** [C] the place in a SUPERMARKET where you pay for the goods you have collected: *Why can't they have more checkouts open?* | *the checkout assistant* **2** [C,U] the time by which you must leave a hotel room: *Checkout is at noon.* → **check out** at CHECK¹

check·point /'tʃekpɔɪnt/ *n* [C] a place, especially on a border, where an official person examines vehicles or people: *They had to cross five military checkpoints.*

check·room /'tʃek-rʊm, -ruːm/ *n* [C] *AmE* a place in a restaurant, theatre etc where you can leave your coat, bags etc to be guarded; ◧ **cloakroom** *BrE*

check·up, check-up /'tʃek-ʌp/ *n* [C] a general medical examination that a doctor or DENTIST gives you to make sure you are healthy: *It's important to have regular checkups.*

ched·dar /'tʃedə $ -ər/ *n* [U] a firm smooth yellow cheese

cheek¹ W3 /tʃiːk/ *n*
1 [C] the soft round part of your face below each of your eyes: *Lucy stretched up to kiss his cheek.* | *Billy had rosy cheeks and blue eyes.* | *her tear-stained cheeks* | *Julie's cheeks flushed with pleasure at the compliment.* |

red-cheeked/hollow-cheeked/rosy-cheeked etc *a red-cheeked, plump old fellow*
2 [singular,U] *BrE* disrespectful or rude behaviour, especially towards someone in a position of authority: *I've had enough of that boy's cheek.* | **have the cheek to do sth** *He had the cheek to make personal remarks and expect no reaction.* | *She's got a cheek; she just goes on till she gets what she wants.* | *It's a bit of a cheek, asking me to do it for you.* | *What a cheek! Of course I read the instructions!*
3 cheek by jowl (with sb/sth) very close to someone or something else: *an expensive French restaurant cheek by jowl with a cheap clothes shop*
4 turn the other cheek to deliberately avoid reacting in an angry or violent way when someone has hurt or upset you
5 cheek to cheek if two people dance cheek to cheek, they dance very close to each other in a romantic way
6 [C] *informal* one of the two soft fleshy parts of your bottom; ▤ **buttock** → **tongue in cheek** at TONGUE¹ (6) → TONGUE-IN-CHEEK

cheek² v [T] *BrE* to speak rudely or with disrespect to someone, especially to someone older such as your teacher or parents; ▤ **sass** *AmE*: *You can cheek some teachers and they just don't do anything.*

cheek·bone /ˈtʃiːkbəʊn $ -boʊn/ n [C usually plural] one of the two bones above your cheeks, just below your eyes: *She had high cheekbones and green eyes.*

cheek·y /ˈtʃiːki/ adj *BrE* rude or disrespectful, sometimes in a way that is amusing: **cheeky devil/monkey etc** *You did that on purpose, you cheeky little devil!* | *Now don't be cheeky to your elders, young woman.* | *a chubby five-year old with a cheeky grin* —**cheekily** adv: *He grinned cheekily.* —**cheekiness** n [U]

cheep /tʃiːp/ v [I] if a young bird cheeps, it makes a weak, high noise: *baby birds cheeping for food* —**cheep** n [C]

cheer¹ /tʃɪə $ tʃɪr/ n **1** [C] a shout of happiness, praise, approval, or encouragement; ▤ **boo**: *A great cheer went up from the crowd.* | *So let's give a cheer to the kids who passed their exams.* | *The final whistle was greeted with triumphant cheers from players and spectators.* **2 three cheers for sb!** *spoken* used to tell a group of people to shout three times as a way of showing support, happiness, thanks etc: *Three cheers for the birthday girl!* **3** [U] *formal* a feeling of happiness and confidence: *'Hello,' said Auguste cheerily. His good cheer was not returned.* **4** [C] a special CHANT (=phrase that is repeated) that the crowds at a US sports game shout in order to encourage their team to win → CHEERS

cheer² v **1** [I,T] to shout as a way of showing happiness, praise, approval, or support of someone or something: *Everybody cheered when the firemen arrived.* | *The audience was shouting and cheering.* | *The spectators cheered him wildly.* **2** to make someone feel more hopeful when they are worried: *By late afternoon there came news that cheered them all.* | *Government policy towards higher education contains little to cheer university students.* —**cheering** adj: *cheering news*
   cheer sb ⇔ **on** *phr v* to shout encouragement at a person or team to help them do well in a race or competition: *They gathered round the swimming pool and cheered her on.*
   cheer up *phr v* **1** to become less sad, or to make someone feel less sad: *Cheer up! The worst is over.* | *They cheered up when they saw us coming along.* | **cheer** sb ⇔ **up** *Here's a bit of news that will cheer you up.* | *You both need cheering up, I think.* **2 cheer sth** ⇔ **up** to make a place look more attractive: *I bought some posters to cheer the place up a bit.*

cheer·ful /ˈtʃɪəfəl $ ˈtʃɪr-/ adj **1** happy, or behaving in a way that shows you are happy: *She was feeling more cheerful than before.* | *I'm making a real effort to be cheerful despite everything.* | **cheerful voice/smile/manner etc** *'I'm Robyn,' she said with a cheerful smile.* | *It does me good to see a cheerful young face.* **2** something that is cheerful makes you feel happy because it is so bright or pleasant: *a bright, cheerful Italian restaurant* | *There was a cheerful, colourful picture on the wall.* | *The house has a cheerful atmosphere.* **3** tending to be happy most of the time: *She was a cheerful and agreeable companion.* | *Before the accident he had been cheerful and confident.* **4** [only before noun] a cheerful attitude shows that you are willing to do whatever is necessary in a happy way: *a cheerful approach to the job* —**cheerfully** adv: *He smiled cheerfully.* | *'Morning!' she called cheerfully.* —**cheerfulness** n [U] → cheap and cheerful at CHEAP¹ (1)

cheer·i·o S3 /ˌtʃɪəriˈəʊ $ ˌtʃɪriˈoʊ/ *BrE informal* goodbye

cheer·lead·er /ˈtʃɪəˌliːdə $ ˈtʃɪrˌliːdər/ n [C] **1** a member of a team of young women who encourage a crowd to cheer at a US sports game by shouting special words and dancing: *She was a popular cheerleader at the University of Texas.* **2** someone who encourages other people to do something: *She was our cheerleader, teacher, and friend.*

cheerleader

cheer·lead·ing /ˈtʃɪəˌliːdɪŋ $ ˈtʃɪr-/ n [U] **1** the activity of being a cheerleader: *a cheerleading camp for girls* **2** *AmE* the act of loudly supporting an organization, idea etc and not being willing to listen to criticism of it: *The conventions have become nothing but cheerleading rallies for the presidential campaign.*

cheer·less /ˈtʃɪələs $ ˈtʃɪr-/ adj cheerless weather, places, or times make you feel sad, bored, or uncomfortable; ▤ **gloomy**: *This is a cold, cheerless place.* | *The day was grey and cheerless.* —**cheerlessness** n [U]

cheers /tʃɪəz $ tʃɪrz/ interjection **1** used when you lift a glass of alcohol before you drink it, in order to say that you hope the people you are drinking with will be happy and have good health **2** *BrE informal* thank you **3** *BrE informal* goodbye

cheer·y /ˈtʃɪəri $ ˈtʃɪri/ adj happy or making you feel happy: *She gave me a cheery smile.* | *He left them with a cheery wave.* —**cheerily** adv

cheese S2 W3 /tʃiːz/ n [C,U] **1** a solid food made from milk, which is usually yellow or white in colour, and can be soft or hard: *half a kilo of cheese* | *a cheese sandwich* | *Sprinkle with the grated cheese.* | *a selection of English cheeses* | **piece/bit/slice/lump etc of cheese** | **cow's/goat's/sheep's cheese** (=from the milk of a cow etc)
2 (say) cheese! *spoken* used to tell people to smile when you are going to take their photograph → BIG CHEESE; → chalk and cheese at CHALK¹ (3)

cheese·board /ˈtʃiːzbɔːd $ -bɔːrd/ n [C] **1** a board used to cut cheese on **2** a variety of cheeses that are served at the end of a meal: *The meal was finished with the cheeseboard and a dish of fruit.*

cheese·bur·ger /ˈtʃiːzbɜːgə $ -bɜːrgər/ n [C] a HAMBURGER cooked with a piece of cheese on top of the meat

cheese·cake /ˈtʃiːzkeɪk/ n **1** [C,U] a cake made from a mixture containing soft cheese: *a slice of cheesecake* **2** [U] *old-fashioned* photographs of pretty women with few clothes on; → beefcake

cheese·cloth /ˈtʃiːzklɒθ $ -klɒːθ/ n [U] thin cotton cloth used for putting around some kinds of cheeses, and sometimes for making clothes

1 000, 2 000, 3 000, most frequent words in S poken and W ritten English

C

cheesed off /ˌtʃiːzd ˈɒf $ -ˈɒːf/ adj BrE bored and annoyed with something: *You sound really cheesed off.*

cheese-paring n [U] BrE behaviour that shows you are unwilling to give or spend money —**cheese-paring** adj

chees·y /ˈtʃiːzi/ adj **1** tasting like cheese or containing cheese: *cheesy sauces* **2** informal cheap and not of good quality: *a cheesy soap opera* **3** informal not sincere: *a cheesy grin*

chee·tah /ˈtʃiːtə/ n [C] a member of the cat family that has long legs and black spots on its fur, and can run extremely fast → see picture at BIG CAT

chef /ʃef/ n [C] a skilled cook, especially the main cook in a hotel or restaurant: *a master chef* | *a pastry chef* → see picture at OCCUPATION

Chel·sea bun /ˌtʃelsi ˈbʌn/ n [C] BrE a small round sweet cake with dried fruit in it

chem·i·cal¹ S3 W3 /ˈkemɪkəl/ n [C] a substance used in chemistry or produced by a chemical process: **toxic/ hazardous/dangerous chemicals** | *the organic chemicals industry* | *synthetic chemicals*

chemical² W3 adj [only before noun] relating to substances, the study of substances, or processes involving changes in substances: *the chemical composition of bleach* | *a chemical analysis of the soil* —**chemically** /-kli/ adv: *Chemically, the substances are similar.*

chemical engi'neering n [U] the study of machines used in industrial chemical processes —**chemical engineer** n [C]

chemical re'action n [C,U] a natural process in which the atoms of chemicals mix and arrange themselves differently to form new substances: *the chemical reaction between ozone and chlorine*

chemical 'warfare n [U] methods of fighting a war using chemical weapons

chemical 'weapon n [C] a poisonous substance, especially a gas, used as a weapon in war

che·mise /ʃəˈmiːz/ n [C] **1** a piece of women's underwear for the top half of the body **2** a simple dress that hangs straight from a woman's shoulders

chem·ist S3 /ˈkemɪst/ n [C]
1 a scientist who has special knowledge and training in chemistry
2 BrE someone trained to prepare drugs and medicines, who works in a shop; ◰ **pharmacist** AmE
3 BrE a shop where you can buy medicines, beauty products etc; ◰ **pharmacy**; ◰ **drugstore** AmE

chem·is·try S2 /ˈkemɪstri/ n [U]
1 the science that is concerned with studying the structure of substances and the way that they change or combine with each other; → **biochemistry**, **biology**, **physics**
2 if there is chemistry between two people, they like each other and find each other attractive: [+**between**] *It was obvious that there was a very real chemistry between them.*
3 the way substances combine in a particular process, thing, person etc: *a person's body chemistry*

chemistry set n [C] a box containing equipment for children to do simple chemistry at home

chem·ist's /ˈkemɪsts/ n [C] BrE a shop where medicines and TOILETRIES are sold; → **pharmacy**; ◰ **drugstore** AmE

chem·o·ther·a·py /ˌkiːməʊˈθerəpi, ˌke- $ -moʊ-/ n [U] the use of drugs to control and try to cure CANCER

che·nille /ʃəˈniːl/ n [U] twisted thread with a surface like a soft brush, or cloth made from this and used for decorations, curtains etc

cheque S2 BrE; **check** AmE /tʃek/ n [C] a printed piece of paper that you write an amount of money on, sign, and use instead of money to pay for things: [+**for**] *They sent me a cheque for £100.* | **by cheque** *Can I pay by*

cheque? | *You could write her a cheque.* | **cash a cheque** (=get cash in exchange for a cheque) → BLANK CHEQUE, TRAVELLER'S CHEQUE

cheque·book BrE; **checkbook** AmE /ˈtʃekbʊk/ n [C] a small book of cheques that your bank gives you

chequebook 'journalism n [U] BrE when newspapers get material for articles by paying people a lot of money for information about crimes or the private lives of famous people – used to show disapproval

cheque card also **cheque guaran'tee card** n [C] BrE a card given to you by your bank that you must show when you write a cheque, which promises that the bank will pay out the amount written on the cheque; → **cash card**, **check card**

chequ·ered /ˈtʃekəd $ -ərd/ adj a British spelling of CHECKERED

chequered 'flag n a British spelling of CHECKERED FLAG

cheq·uers /ˈtʃekəz $ -ərz/ n → CHINESE CHEQUERS

cher·ish /ˈtʃerɪʃ/ v [T] **1** if you cherish something, it is very important to you: *He was a man who cherished his privacy.* | *I still cherish the memory of that day.* | **cherish a hope/an idea/a dream etc** *a willingness to re-examine cherished beliefs* **2** to love someone or something very much and take care of them well: *In marriage, a man promises to cherish his wife.* | *his most cherished possession*

che·root /ʃəˈruːt/ n [C] a small CIGAR with both ends cut straight

cher·ry S3 /ˈtʃeri/ n plural **cherries**
1 [C] a small round red or black fruit with a long thin stem and a stone in the middle: *a bunch of cherries* | *cherry pie* → see picture at FRUIT
2 a) [C] also **'cherry tree** the tree on which this fruit grows **b)** [U] also **cherrywood** the wood of this tree, used for making furniture
3 [U] also **cherry 'red** a bright red colour —**cherry** adj → **another bite/a second bite at the cherry** at BITE² (8)

cherry bomb n [C] AmE a large round red FIRECRACKER (=small loud explosive)

cher·ry·pick /ˈtʃeripɪk/ v [I,T] to choose the best things or people you want from a group before anyone else has the chance to take them

cherry to'mato n [C] a type of very small TOMATO

cher·ub /ˈtʃerəb/ n [C] **1** an ANGEL shown in works of art as a fat pretty child with small wings **2** informal a young pretty child who behaves very well **3** plural **cherubim** /ˈtʃerəbɪm/ one of the ANGELS who guard the seat where God sits —**cherubic** /tʃəˈruːbɪk/ adj: *a smile of cherubic innocence*

cher·vil /ˈtʃɜːvɪl $ ˈtʃɜːr-/ n [U] a strong-smelling garden plant used as a herb

chess

chess set

chessboard

pawn   knight   bishop   rook/castle   queen   king

chess /tʃes/ n [U] a game for two players, who move their playing pieces according to particular rules across a special board to try to trap their opponent's KING (=most important piece): *They meet fairly often to **play chess**.*

chess·board /ˈtʃesbɔːd $ -bɔːrd/ n [C] a square board with 64 black and white squares, on which you play chess → see picture at CHESS

chess·man /'tʃesmæn/ also **chess·piece** /'tʃes-piːs/ n plural **chessmen** /-men/ [C] any of the 16 black or 16 white playing pieces used in the game of chess

chest S2 W3 /tʃest/ n [C]
1 the front part of your body between your neck and your stomach; → **breast**: Her heart was pounding in her chest. | a hairy chest | **chest pain/infection/injury** He collapsed with severe chest pains. → FLAT-CHESTED
2 a large strong box that you use to store things in or to move your personal possessions from one place to another: a large wooden chest → CHEST OF DRAWERS, TEA CHEST, WAR CHEST; → see picture at BOX
3 get something off your chest to tell someone about something that has been worrying or annoying you for a long time, so that you feel better afterwards

ches·ter·field /'tʃestəfiːld $ -ər-/ n [C] BrE a soft comfortable SOFA, usually covered with leather

chest·nut¹ /'tʃesnʌt/ n **1** [C] a smooth red-brown nut that you can eat: roast chestnuts **2** also **chestnut tree** [C] the tree on which this nut grows **3** [U] a red-brown colour **4** [C] a horse that is red-brown in colour **5 an old chestnut** a joke or story that has been repeated many times **6** [C] a HORSE CHESTNUT → WATER CHESTNUT

chestnut² adj red-brown in colour: her chestnut hair

chest of 'drawers n plural **chests of drawers** [C] especially BrE a piece of furniture with drawers, used for storing clothes; ◨ **dresser** AmE; → see picture at BEDROOM

chest·y /'tʃesti/ adj **1** BrE if you have a chesty cough, or if you are a bit chesty, you have a lot of MUCUS (=thick liquid) in your lungs **2** informal used to describe a woman with large breasts, when you want to avoid saying this directly

chev·ron /'ʃevrən/ n [C] **1** a pattern in a V shape **2** a piece of cloth in the shape of a V which soldiers have on their sleeve to show their rank

chew¹ /tʃuː/ v **1** [I,T] to bite food several times before swallowing it: This meat's so tough I can hardly chew it! | [+at/on] a dog chewing on a bone; → see picture at BITE **2** [I,T] to bite something continuously in order to taste it or because you are nervous: [+on] We gave the dog an old shoe to chew on. | **chew your lip/nails** She chewed her lip and said nothing. | **chew gum/tobacco 3 chew the cud** if a cow or sheep chews the cud, it keeps biting on food it has brought up from its stomach **4 chew the fat** informal to have a long friendly conversation → **bite off more than you can chew** at BITE¹ (10)
chew on sth phr v informal to think carefully about something for a period of time
chew sb ⇔ **out** phr v AmE informal to talk angrily to someone in order to show them that you disapprove of what they have done: John couldn't get the guy to cooperate and so I had to call and chew him out.
chew sth ⇔ **over** phr v to think carefully about something for a period of time: Let me chew it over for a few days.
chew sth ⇔ **up** phr v **1** to damage or destroy something by tearing it into small pieces: Be careful if you use that video recorder. It tends to chew tapes up. **2** to bite something many times with your teeth so that you can make it smaller or softer and swallow it: The dog's chewed up my slippers again.

chew² n [C] **1** the act of biting something many times with your teeth **2** a sweet that you chew **3** a piece of tobacco that you chew but do not swallow

chewing gum n [U] a type of sweet that you chew for a long time but do not swallow

chew·y /'tʃuːi/ adj food that is chewy has to be chewed a lot before it is soft enough to swallow: chewy toffees

chic /ʃiːk/ adj very fashionable and expensive, and showing good judgement of what is attractive and good style: Margaret was looking very chic in blue. | a chic restaurant —**chic** n [U]: the art of comfortable chic

chi·cane /ʃɪ'keɪn/ n [C] BrE an S-shaped bend in a straight road, especially on a track for racing cars

chi·ca·ne·ry /ʃɪ'keɪnəri/ n [U] formal the use of clever plans or actions to deceive people: Clearly there is some chicanery going on.

Chi·ca·no /tʃɪ'kɑːnəʊ $ -noʊ/ n plural **Chicanos** [C] a US citizen who was born in Mexico or whose family came from Mexico; → **Hispanic** —**Chicano** adj

chick /tʃɪk/ n [C] **1** a baby bird: a mother hen with her chicks **2** informal a word meaning a young woman, that some people think is offensive

chick·a·dee /'tʃɪkədi/ n [C] a North American bird with a black head

chick·en¹ S2 /'tʃɪkᵻn/ n
1 [C] a common farm bird that is kept for its meat and eggs; → **hen**, **cock**, **rooster**, **chick**
2 [U] the meat from this bird eaten as food: roast chicken | fried chicken | chicken soup
3 [C] informal someone who is not at all brave; ◨ **coward**: Don't be such a chicken!
4 [U] a game in which children do something dangerous, for example stand on a railway line when a train is coming, and try to be the one who continues doing it for the longest time
5 which came first, the chicken or the egg? used to say that it is difficult or impossible to decide which of two things happened first, or which action is the cause and which is the effect
6 a chicken and egg situation/problem etc a situation in which it is impossible to decide which of two things happened first, or which action is the cause and which is the effect
7 sb's chickens have come home to roost used to say that someone's bad or dishonest actions in the past have caused the problems that they have now → **don't count your chickens before they've hatched** at COUNT¹ (8); → SPRING CHICKEN

chicken² v
chicken out phr v informal to decide at the last moment not to do something you said you would do, because you are afraid: You're not chickening out, are you?

chicken³ adj [not before noun] informal not brave enough to do something; ◨ **cowardly**: Dave's too chicken to ask her out.

'chicken ,feed n [U] an amount of money that is so small that it is almost not worth having: The bank offered to lend us £1,000 but that's chicken feed compared to what we need.

,chicken-fried 'steak n [C,U] AmE a thin piece of BEEF covered in BREADCRUMBS and cooked in hot fat

'chicken ,pox also **chick·en·pox** /'tʃɪkᵻnpɒks $ -pɑːks/ n [U] an infectious illness which causes a slight fever and spots on your skin

'chicken run n [C] an area surrounded by a fence where chickens are kept

chick·en·shit /'tʃɪkᵻnʃɪt/ n [C] AmE informal not polite an offensive word for someone who is not at all brave; ◨ **coward** —**chickenshit** adj

'chicken wire n [U] a type of thin wire net used to make fences for chickens

'chick lit n [U] informal books about young women and the typical problems they have with men, sex, losing weight etc, especially books written by women for women to read – used humorously

chick·pea /'tʃɪkpiː/ n [C] a large brown PEA which is cooked and eaten; ◨ **garbanzo** AmE

chick·weed /'tʃɪkwiːd/ n [U] a garden WEED with small white flowers

chic·o·ry /'tʃɪkəri/ n [U] **1** a European plant whose bitter leaves are eaten in SALADS **2** the roots of this plant, used in coffee or instead of coffee

chide /tʃaɪd/ v [I,T] written to tell someone that you do not approve of something that they have done or said; ◨ **scold**: 'Edward, you are naughty,' Dorothy chided. |

C

chide sb for (doing) sth *She chided him for not responding to her Christmas cards.* | *He swiftly chided himself for such thoughts.*

chief¹ S2 W2 /tʃiːf/ *adj*
1 [only before noun] highest in rank: *He was recently appointed chief economist at the Bank of Scotland.* | *the government's chief medical officer*
2 most important; ▤ main; → chiefly: *One of the chief causes of crime today is drugs.* | *Safety has been, and always will be, our chief concern.* | *The chief reason for this was that people were living longer.* | *his chief rival for the job* | *the prosecution's chief witness* | *She had many reasons for taking the money, but chief among them was revenge.*
3 chief cook and bottle washer someone who does a lot of small jobs to make sure that an event is successful – used humorously

chief² W3 *n* [C]
1 SB IN CHARGE OF AN ORGANIZATION the most important person, or one of the most important people, in a company or organization – used especially in job titles and in news reports: **police/army/fire etc chief** *Los Angeles Police Chief Willie L. Williams* | [+of] *the British Chief of Defence Staff* | *Most health chiefs believe the reforms have gone too far.* | *industry chiefs* | **commander-in-chief/editor-in-chief etc** (=used in job titles for people with the highest rank) *They offered him the position of editor-in-chief.*
2 RULER OF TRIBE the ruler of a tribe: *the Zulu leader, Chief Mangosuthu Buthelezi* | *Native American tribal chiefs*
3 too many chiefs and not enough Indians *BrE* used to say there are too many people saying how something should be done and not enough people doing it
4 great white chief *BrE old-fashioned* the person in charge of a group of people, company, organization etc – used humorously

,chief 'constable *n* [C] a police officer in charge of the police in a large area of Britain

,Chief Ex'ecutive *n* the Chief Executive the President of the US

,chief ex'ecutive ,officer *n* [C] *CEO* the person with the most authority in a large company

,chief in'spector *n* [C] a British police officer of middle rank

,chief 'justice *n* [C] the most important judge in a court of law, especially the US Supreme Court

chief·ly /'tʃiːfli/ *adv* mostly but not completely; ▤ mainly: *The work consists chiefly of interviewing the public.* | *I lived abroad for years, chiefly in Italy.*

,chief of 'staff *n plural* chiefs of staff [C] **1** an officer of high rank in the army, navy etc who advises the officer in charge of a particular military group or operation **2** an official of high rank who advises the person in charge of an organization or government: *the White House chief of staff*

,Chief 'Rabbi *n* the Chief Rabbi the main leader of the JEWISH religion in a country

,chief superin'tendent *n* [C] a British police officer of high rank

chief·tain /'tʃiːftən/ *n* [C] the leader of a tribe or a Scottish CLAN

chif·fon /'ʃifɒn $ ʃɪ'fɑːn/ *n* [U] a soft thin silk or NYLON material that you can see through: *a pink chiffon ballgown*

chi·gnon /'ʃiːnjɒn $ -jɑːn/ *n* [C] hair that is tied in a smooth knot at the back of a woman's head; ▤ bun

chi·hua·hua /tʃɪ'wɑːwə/ *n* [C] a very small dog with smooth hair, originally from Mexico

chil·blains /'tʃɪlbleɪnz/ *n* [plural] painful red areas on your fingers or toes that are caused by cold weather

child S1 W1 /tʃaɪld/ *n plural* children /'tʃɪldrən/ [C]
1 YOUNG PERSON someone who is not yet an adult; ▤ kid: *The hotel is ideal for families with young*

children. | *Your interest and support are important to your child.* | *The film is not suitable for children under 12.* | *I was very happy as a child* (=when I was a child). | **three-year-old child/child of eight etc** *For a child of five this was a terrifying experience.* | *parents with preschool children* (=children who are too young to go to school) | *an agreement to regulate child labour* (=the use of children in industry) | **child killer/victim/prostitute etc** (=a child who is a killer etc) | *the rights of the unborn child* (=a baby that is still inside its mother)
2 SON/DAUGHTER a son or daughter of any age: *I have five children, all happily married.* | *She lives with her husband, Paul, and three grown-up children.* | *Annie had always wanted to get married and have children.* | *Alex is an only child* (=he has no brothers or sisters). | **youngest/eldest child** *especially BrE: Our youngest child, Sam, has just started university.* | **youngest/middle/oldest child** *especially AmE*
3 SB INFLUENCED BY AN IDEA someone who is very strongly influenced by the ideas and attitudes of a particular period of history: [+of] *a real child of the Sixties*
4 SB WHO IS LIKE A CHILD someone who behaves like a child and is not sensible or responsible – used to show disapproval: *She's such a child!*
5 sth is child's play used to say that something is very easy to do: *I've cooked for 200 people before now. So, tonight is child's play by comparison.*
6 children should be seen and not heard an expression meaning that children should be quiet and not talk – used when you disapprove of the way a child is behaving
7 be with child *old use* to be PREGNANT
8 be heavy/great with child *old use* to be nearly ready to give birth

'child a,buse *n* [U] the crime of harming a child physically, sexually, or emotionally

child·bear·ing /'tʃaɪld,beərɪŋ $ -,ber-/ *n* [U] **1** the process of being PREGNANT and giving birth to children: *the trend towards later marriage and childbearing* **2 childbearing age/years** if a woman is of childbearing age or in her childbearing years, she is of an age when it is physically possible for her to have babies

,child 'benefit *n* [U] an amount of money that the British government gives to families with children

child·birth /'tʃaɪldbɜːθ $ -bɜːrθ/ *n* [U] the act of having a baby: **in/during/after childbirth** *His wife died in childbirth.*

child·care /'tʃaɪldkeə $ -ker/ *n* [U] an arrangement in which someone who is trained to look after children cares for them while the parents are at work: *People earning low wages will find it difficult to pay for childcare.* | *I think more women would work if there were better childcare facilities.*

child·hood W3 /'tʃaɪldhʊd/ *n* [C,U] the period of time when you are a child: *I had a very happy childhood.* | **in/during/since (sb's) childhood** *Most infections occur in childhood.* | *She had been writing poems since her childhood.* | **childhood home/friend/experience etc** (=a home etc that you had when you were a child) *Last summer, Jill took me to see her childhood home.* | **childhood memories** (=the memories you have of your childhood) → SECOND CHILDHOOD

child·ish /'tʃaɪldɪʃ/ *adj* **1** [usually before noun] relating to or typical of a child; ▤ adult: *a high childish laugh* | *her childish excitement* **2** behaving in a silly way that makes you seem much younger than you really are – used to show disapproval; ▤ immature; ▤ mature: *Don't be so childish!* | *I wish politicians would stop this childish name-calling.* ⚠ This word is generally used to suggest someone's behaviour is silly or immature. To talk about positive qualities connected with children, use **childlike**. —**childishly** *adv* —**childishness** *n* [U]

child·less /'tʃaɪldləs/ *adj* having no children: **childless couple/woman/marriage** *It was a happy but child-*

less marriage. | *couples who deliberately remain childless* —**childlessness** *n* [U]

child·like /'tʃaɪldlaɪk/ *adj* having qualities that are typical of a child, especially positive qualities such as INNOCENCE and eagerness: *childlike innocence/simplicity/directness* '*You know I love you,' she said with childlike simplicity.* | **childlike delight/wonder/excitement** *The sight filled her with childlike excitement.* | *Standing, she looked less childlike.*

child·min·der /'tʃaɪld,maɪndə $ -ər/ *n* [C] *BrE* someone who is paid to look after young children while their parents are at work —**childminding** *n* [U]

child mo,lester *n* [C] someone who harms children by touching them in a sexual way, or trying to have sex with them —**child molesting** *n* [U]

child 'prodigy *n* [C] a child who is unusually skilful at doing something such as playing a musical instrument

child·proof /'tʃaɪldpruːf/ *adj* something that is childproof is designed to prevent a child from opening, damaging, or breaking it: *a childproof lock*

chil·dren /'tʃɪldrən/ the plural of CHILD

children's home *n* [C] *BrE* a place where children live if their own parents have died or cannot look after them

child sup,port also **maintenance** *BrE n* [U] money that someone pays regularly to their former wife or husband in order to support their children

chil·i /'tʃɪli/ *n* the American spelling of CHILLI

chill¹ /tʃɪl/ *n*   **1** [singular] a feeling of coldness: *There was a slight chill in the air.* | **morning/autumnal/January etc chill** *Suddenly aware of the morning chill, she closed the window.* | [+of] *He sat in the chill of the evening, staring out over the city below.* | *I turned on the heater in the hall* **to take the chill off** *the house* (=to heat it slightly).   **2** [C] a sudden feeling of fear or worry, especially because of something cruel or violent: *The sound of his dark laugh* **sent a chill through** *her.* | **chill of fear/apprehension/disquiet etc** *Fay felt a chill of fear as she watched Max go off with her daughter.* | *There was something in his tone that* **sent a chill down** *Melissa's* **spine** (=made her very frightened).   **3 a)** [C] an illness which causes a slight fever, headache, and SHIVERING (=slight shaking of the body): *Let's get these wet clothes off you before you* **catch a chill.**   **b)** [C usually plural] a feeling of being cold, caused by being ill

chill² *v*   **1** [I,T] if you chill something such as food or drink, or if it chills, it becomes very cold but does not freeze: *a glass of chilled white wine* | *Spoon the mixture into a pudding basin and chill for at least two hours.* | *The longer this salad chills, the better the flavour.*   **2** also **chill out** [I] *informal* to relax completely instead of feeling angry, tired, or nervous: *'Hold it! Just chill for a second, won't you!'* | *I spent the afternoon chilling out in front of the TV.*   **3** [T] to make someone very cold: *The wind blew across her body, chilling her wet skin.* | **chilled to the bone/marrow** (=extremely cold) *Come and sit by the fire – you look chilled to the bone.*   **4** [T] *literary* to suddenly frighten someone, especially by seeming very cruel or violent: *The anger in his face chilled her.* | **chill sb to the bone/chill sb to the marrow/chill sb's blood** (=frighten sb a lot) *He jerked his head round and saw something that chilled his blood.*

chill³ *adj* [usually before noun] unpleasantly cold: *the chill night air* | *a chill wind*

chil·ler /'tʃɪlə $ -ər/ *n* [C] *informal* a film or book that is intended to frighten you

chil·li *BrE*; **chili** *AmE* /'tʃɪli/ *n plural* **chillies** *BrE*; **chilies** *AmE*   **1** [C] also '**chilli pepper** *BrE*; **chili pepper** *AmE* a small thin red or green PEPPER with a very strong hot taste   **2** [U] also **chilli con carne** *BrE*; **chili con carne** *AmE* /-kɒn -kɑːni $ -kɑːn 'kɑːrni/ a spicy dish made with beans, meat, and chillies

chil·ling /'tʃɪlɪŋ/ *adj* something that is chilling makes you feel frightened, especially because it is cruel,

violent, or dangerous: *the chilling sound of wolves howling* —**chillingly** *adv*: *It was chillingly clear that he wanted revenge.*

'**chilli ,powder** *BrE*; **chili powder** *AmE n* [U] a hot-tasting red powder made from dried chillies

'**chill room** *n* [C]   **1** a room in a bar, office etc where people go to play games, listen to music, watch television etc so that they can relax   **2** a website that contains games, pictures, music etc and is designed for people who want to relax or have fun

chill·y /'tʃɪli/ *adj*   **1** chilly weather or places are cold enough to make you feel uncomfortable: **chilly day/night/evening etc** *a chilly November morning* | **chilly wind/breeze/air etc** | *Getting chilly, isn't it?* | *The bathroom's a bit chilly.*   **2** if you feel chilly, you feel uncomfortably cold   **3** unfriendly: *The speech met with a chilly reception.* —**chilliness** *n* [singular, U]

chi·mae·ra /kaɪ'mɪərə, kə- $ -'mɪrə/ *n* another spelling of CHIMERA

chime¹ /tʃaɪm/ *v*   **1** [I,T] if a bell or clock chimes, it makes a ringing sound, especially to tell you what time it is: *The clock in the hall chimed six.*   **2** [I] to be the same as something else or to have the same effect: [+with] *Her views on life didn't quite chime with mine.*

  chime in *phr v* to say something in a conversation, especially to agree with what someone has just said: '*We'll miss you too,' the children chimed in.*

chime² *n*   **1** [C] a ringing sound made by a bell or clock   **2 chimes** [plural] a set of bells or other objects that produce musical sounds, used as a musical instrument or, for example, as a type of doorbell → **WIND CHIMES**

chi·me·ra, chimaera /kaɪ'mɪərə, kə- $ -'mɪrə/ *n* [C]   **1** *formal* something, especially an idea or hope, that is not really possible and can never exist: *trying to present that chimera, 'a balanced view'*   **2** an imaginary creature that breathes fire and has a lion's head, a goat's body, and a snake's tail

chi·me·ri·cal /kaɪ'merɪkəl, kə-/ *adj formal* imaginary or not really possible

chimney

chimney

chim·ney /'tʃɪmni/ *n* [C]   **1** a vertical pipe that allows smoke from a fire to pass out of a building up into the air, or the part of this pipe that is above the roof: *We can't light a fire because the chimney hasn't been swept.* → see picture at ROOF   **2** a tall vertical structure containing a chimney; → **smokestack**: *a factory chimney*   **3** *technical* a narrow opening in tall rocks or cliffs that you can climb up   **4 smoke like a chimney** if someone smokes like a chimney, they smoke a lot of cigarettes or tobacco – used humorously

'**chimney breast** *n* [C] *BrE* the part of a wall in a room that encloses a chimney

'**chimney-piece** *n* [C] *BrE* a decoration, usually made of brick or stone, built above a FIREPLACE

'**chimney pot** *n* [C] *BrE* a short wide pipe made of baked clay or metal, that is attached to the top of a chimney

'**chimney stack** *n* [C] *BrE*   **1** the tall chimney of a building such as a factory; ▪ **smokestack** *AmE*   **2** a group of small chimneys on a roof

'**chimney sweep** *n* [C] someone whose job is to clean chimneys using special long brushes

chim·pan·zee /ˌtʃɪmpænˈziː, -pən-/ also **chimp** /tʃɪmp/ n [C] an intelligent African animal that is like a large monkey without a tail

chin S3 /tʃɪn/ n [C]
1 the front part of your face below your mouth: *He rubbed his chin thoughtfully.*
2 (keep your) chin up! *spoken* used to tell someone to make an effort to stay brave and confident when they are in a difficult situation: *Chin up! It'll be over soon.*
3 take sth on the chin to accept a difficult or unpleasant situation without complaining – used to show approval: *One of our great strengths is our ability to take it on the chin and come out fighting.*

chi·na /ˈtʃaɪnə/ n [U] **1** a hard white substance produced by baking a type of clay at a high temperature: *china teacups* **2** also **chinaware** plates, cups etc made of china: *I'll get my best china out.*

Chi·na·town /ˈtʃaɪnətaʊn/ n [singular,U] an area in a city where there are Chinese restaurants and shops, and where a lot of Chinese people live

chin·chil·la /tʃɪnˈtʃɪlə/ n **1** [C] a small South American animal bred for its fur **2** [U] the pale grey fur of the chinchilla

Chi·nese¹ /ˌtʃaɪˈniːz◂/ n **1** [U] the language used in China **2 the Chinese** [plural] people from China **3** [singular] *BrE informal* a meal of Chinese food, or a restaurant that sells Chinese food: *Do you fancy going out for a Chinese?*

Chinese² *adj* relating to China, its people, or its language

Chinese 'chequers *BrE*; **Chinese checkers** *AmE* n [U] a game in which you move small balls from hole to hole on a board in the shape of a star → see picture at BOARD GAME

Chinese 'lantern n [C] a small box made of thin paper that you put a light inside as a decoration

Chinese 'leaves n [plural] *BrE* a type of CABBAGE eaten especially in East Asia

Chinese 'medicine n [U] a kind of medicine that uses herbs and ACUPUNCTURE

Chinese 'whispers n [U] *BrE* the passing of information from one person to another, and then to others, when the information gets slightly changed each time

chink¹ /tʃɪŋk/ n **1** [C] a small hole in a wall, or between two things that join together, that lets light or air through; ◨ **crack**: [+in] *The sun came through a chink in the curtains.* **2** [C] *BrE* a high ringing sound made by metal or glass objects hitting each other; ◨ **clink**: *the chink of coins* **3 a chink in sb's armour** a weakness in someone's character or in something they have said, that you can use to attack them

chink² v [I,T] *BrE* if glass or metal objects chink, or if you chink them, they make a high ringing sound when they knock together; ◨ **clink**: *They chinked their glasses and drank a toast to the couple.*

Chink n [C] *taboo* a very offensive word for someone from China. Do not use this word.

chin·less /ˈtʃɪnləs/ adj *BrE* lacking courage or determination

chi·nos /ˈtʃiːnəʊz $ -noʊz/ n [plural] loose trousers made from strong woven cotton

chin·strap /ˈtʃɪnstræp/ n [C] a band of cloth under your chin to keep a hat or HELMET in place

chintz /tʃɪnts/ n [U] smooth cotton cloth that is printed with a flowery pattern and used for making curtains, furniture covers etc: *pink chintz curtains*

chintz·y /ˈtʃɪntsi/ adj **1** *BrE* covered with chintz: *a chintzy sofa* **2** *AmE informal* cheap and badly made; ◨ **cheap**: *a chintzy chest of drawers* **3** *AmE informal* unwilling to give people things or spend money; ◨ **stingy**

'chin-up also **chin·up** /ˈtʃɪnʌp/ n [C] *AmE* an exercise in which you hang on a bar and pull yourself up until your chin is above the bar; ◨ **pull-up** *BrE*

chin·wag /ˈtʃɪnwæg/ n [singular] *BrE informal* an informal conversation; ◨ **chat** —**chinwag** v [I]

chip¹ S2 W3 /tʃɪp/ n [C]
1 FOOD **a)** *BrE* [usually plural] a long thin piece of potato cooked in oil; ◨ **French fry** *AmE*: *fish and chips* **b)** *AmE* [usually plural] a thin flat round piece of food such as potato cooked in very hot oil and eaten cold; ◨ **crisp** *BrE*: *They gave us a bag of potato chips.*
2 COMPUTER a small piece of SILICON that has a set of complicated electrical connections on it and is used to store and PROCESS information in computers: *the age of the silicon chip* | *chip technology*
3 PIECE a small piece of wood, stone, metal etc that has been broken off something: *Wood chips covered the floor of the workshop.* | *a chocolate chip cookie* (=one that contains small pieces of chocolate)
4 MARK a small hole or mark on a plate, cup etc where a piece has broken off: [+in] *There's a chip in this bowl.*
5 have a chip on your shoulder to easily become offended or angry because you think you have been treated unfairly in the past
6 when the chips are down *spoken* in a serious or difficult situation, especially one in which you realize what is really true or important: *When the chips are down, you've only got yourself to depend on.*
7 be a chip off the old block *informal* to be very similar to your mother or father in appearance or character
8 GAME [usually plural] a small flat coloured piece of plastic used in games such as POKER or BLACKJACK to represent a particular amount of money
9 SPORT also **chip shot**, **chip kick** a hit in golf, or a kick in football or RUGBY, that makes the ball go high into the air for a short distance
10 have had your chips *BrE informal* to be in a situation in which you no longer have any hope of improvement
11 let the chips fall (where they may) *AmE* to not worry about what the results of a particular action will be: *I decided to tell her my opinion and let the chips fall where they may.* → BLUE CHIP; → **cash in your chips** at CASH IN (3)

chip² v **chipped**, **chipping**
1 ACCIDENTALLY BREAK (STH) [I,T] if you chip something, or if it chips, a small piece of it breaks off accidentally: *Gary fell and chipped one of his front teeth.* | *He chipped a bone in his knee and was carried off the pitch.* | *These plates chip really easily.* | [+off] *The paint had chipped off the gate.*
2 REMOVE STH [I,T always + adv/prep] to remove something, especially something hard that is covering a surface, by hitting it with a tool so that small pieces break off: *Archaeologists were carefully chipping away at the rock.* | *You have to chip the rust off before you start painting.* | *Chip out the plaster with a steel chisel.*
3 SPORT [T] to hit a golf ball or kick a football or a RUGBY ball so that it goes high into the air for a short distance: *United scored just before half-time when Adcock cleverly chipped the ball over the keeper.*
4 POTATOES [T] *BrE* to cut potatoes into thin pieces ready to be cooked in hot oil
chip away at sth *phr v*
to gradually make something less effective or destroy it: *Writers such as Voltaire and Diderot were chipping away at the foundations of society.* | *Fears about the future chipped away at her sense of well-being.*
chip in *phr v*
1 to interrupt a conversation by saying something that adds more detail: [+with] *Other committee members chipped in with suggestions.* | *'It won't be easy,' Jeff chipped in.* | *I'd just like to chip in, Bill, if I might.*
2 if each person in a group chips in, they each give a small amount of money so that they can buy something together: *We all chipped in to buy Amy a graduation present.* | **chip in (with) sth** *52 people in the music industry each chipped in $250 apiece.*

chip·board /ˈtʃɪpbɔːd $ -bɔːrd/ n [U] a type of board made from small pieces of wood pressed together with glue

chip·munk /'tʃɪpmʌŋk/ n [C] a small American animal similar to a SQUIRREL with black lines on its fur

chip·o·la·ta /ˌtʃɪpə'lɑːtə◂/ n [C] BrE a small thin SAUSAGE

chip pan n [C] BrE a deep pan with a wire basket inside used for cooking food in hot oil, especially CHIPS

chipped /tʃɪpt/ adj something that is chipped has a small piece broken off the edge of it: *The nail varnish on her toes was chipped.* | *a chipped saucer* | *a chipped tooth*

chip·per /'tʃɪpə $ -ər/ adj old-fashioned informal happy and active: *You're looking very chipper this morning.*

chip·pings /'tʃɪpɪŋz/ n [plural] BrE small pieces of stone used when putting new surfaces on roads or railway tracks

chip shop also **chippie, chip·py** informal /'tʃɪpi/ n [C] BrE a shop that cooks and sells FISH AND CHIPS and other FRIED food

chi·rop·o·dist /kɪ'rɒpədɪst, ʃɪ- $ -'rɑː-/ n [C] BrE someone who is trained to examine and treat foot injuries and diseases; ▯ **podiatrist** —**chiropody** n [U]

chi·ro·prac·tic /'kaɪrəʊpræktɪk $ -rə-/ n [U] the treatment of physical problems by pressing on and moving the bones in someone's back and joints

chi·ro·prac·tor /'kaɪrəʊˌpræktər $ -rəˌpræktər/ n [C] someone who treats physical problems using chiropractic

chirp /tʃɜːp $ tʃɜːrp/ also **chirrup** BrE v **1** [I,T] if a bird or insect chirps, it makes short high sounds **2** to speak in a happy high voice: *'Yes, all finished,' he chirped.* —**chirp** n [C]

chirp·y /'tʃɜːpi $ 'tʃɜːrpi/ adj happy and active: *You're very chirpy this morning – have you had some good news?* —**chirpily** adv —**chirpiness** n [U]

chir·rup /'tʃɪrəp $ 'tʃɪ-, 'tʃɜː-/ v [I] CHIRP

chis·el¹ /'tʃɪzəl/ n [C] a metal tool with a sharp edge, used to cut wood or stone

chisel² v **chiselled, chiselling** BrE, **chiseled, chiseling** AmE [T] to use a chisel to cut wood or stone into a particular shape: **chisel sth into/from/in etc sth** *Martin chiselled a hole in the door for the new lock.*

chis·elled BrE; **chiseled** AmE /'tʃɪzəld/ adj [usually before noun] if a man has chiselled features, his chin, mouth, nose etc have a strong clear shape: **chiselled features/chin/mouth/nose etc** | *his chiselled good looks*

chit /tʃɪt/ n [C] BrE **1** an official note that shows that you are allowed to have something: *Take the chit to the counter and collect your books.* **2** old-fashioned a young woman who behaves badly and does not respect older people

chit-chat n [U] informal conversation about things that are not very important: *boring social chit-chat*

chit·ter·lings /'tʃɪtəlɪŋz $ -ər-/ also **chit·lings** /'tʃɪtlɪŋz/, **chit·lins** /-lɪnz/ n [plural] the INTESTINE of a pig eaten as food, especially in the southern US

chiv·al·rous /'ʃɪvəlrəs/ adj a man who is chivalrous behaves in a polite, kind, generous, and honourable way, especially towards women —**chivalrously** adv

chiv·al·ry /'ʃɪvəlri/ n [U] **1** behaviour that is honourable, kind, generous, and brave, especially men's behaviour towards women **2** a system of religious beliefs and honourable behaviour that KNIGHTS in the Middle Ages were expected to follow

chives /tʃaɪvz/ n [plural] the long thin green leaves of a plant with purple flowers. Chives taste like onion and are used in cooking

chiv·vy, chivy /'tʃɪvi/ v **chivvied, chivvying, chivvies** [T] BrE informal to try to make someone do something more quickly, especially in an annoying way: **chivvy sb along/up** *Go and see if you can chivvy the kids up a bit.*

chlo·ride /'klɔːraɪd/ n [C,U] a chemical COMPOUND that is a mixture of CHLORINE and another substance: *sodium chloride*

chlo·ri·nate /'klɔːrɪˌneɪt/ v [T] to add chlorine to water to kill BACTERIA

chlo·rine /'klɔːriːn/ n [U] a greenish-yellow gas with a strong smell that is used to keep the water in swimming pools clean. It is a chemical ELEMENT: symbol Cl

chlo·ro·fluo·ro·car·bon /ˌklɔːrəʊfluərəʊ'kɑːbən $ -rəʊfluroʊ'kɑːr-/ n [C] a CFC

chlor·o·form /'klɔːrəfɔːm, 'klɔː- $ 'klɔːrəfɔːrm/ n [U] a liquid that makes you become unconscious if you breathe it —**chloroform** v [T]

chlo·ro·phyll /'klɒrəfɪl, 'klɔː- $ 'klɔː-/ n [U] the green-coloured substance in plants

choc /tʃɒk $ tʃɑːk, tʃɔːk/ n [C,U] BrE informal CHOCOLATE

choc·a·hol·ic /ˌtʃɒkə'hɒlɪk $ ˌtʃɑːkə'hɒ:-, ˌtʃɔːk-/ n [C] another spelling of CHOCOHOLIC

choc·cy /'tʃɒki $ 'tʃɑːki, 'tʃɔːki/ n plural **choccies** [C] BrE spoken a CHOCOLATE (2)

choc-ice n [C] BrE a small block of ICE CREAM covered with chocolate

chock /tʃɒk $ tʃɑːk/ n [C] a block of wood or metal that you put in front of the wheel of a vehicle to prevent it from moving

chock-a-block /ˌtʃɒk ə 'blɒk◂ $ 'tʃɑːk ə ˌblɑːk/ adj [not before noun] BrE completely full of people or things: [+with] *Paris was chock-a-block with tourists.*

chock-'full adj [not before noun] informal completely full of people or things: [+of] *The pond was chock-full of weeds.*

choc·o·hol·ic, chocaholic /ˌtʃɒkə'hɒlɪk $ ˌtʃɑːkə'hɒ:-, ˌtʃɔːk-/ n [C] informal someone who likes chocolate very much and eats a lot of it

choco·late [S2] /'tʃɒklɪt $ 'tʃɑːkələt, 'tʃɔːk-/ n
1 [U] a sweet brown food that you can eat as a sweet or use in cooking to give foods such as cakes a special sweet taste: *a chocolate bar* | *a chocolate cake* | *a packet of chocolate biscuits* | *I prefer milk chocolate to dark chocolate.* → see picture at DESSERT
2 [C] a small sweet that is covered with chocolate: *Would you like a chocolate?* | *a box of chocolates*
3 [C,U] a hot sweet drink made with milk and chocolate, or a cup of this drink: *a mug of hot chocolate* | *Two coffees and one chocolate, please.*
4 [U] a dark brown colour; → see picture at DESSERT

chocolate box adj [only before noun] BrE informal a chocolate box place looks pretty, but in a way that is false because it seems too perfect: *He had grown tired of the chocolate box views.*

chocolate chip 'cookie n [C] a kind of small BISCUIT with small pieces of chocolate in it

choco·lat·ey /'tʃɒklɪti $ 'tʃɑːkələti, 'tʃɔːk-/ adj tasting or smelling of chocolate: *a chocolatey taste*

choice¹ [S1] [W1] /tʃɔɪs/ n
1 [C,U] if you have a choice, you can choose between several things; → **choose**: [+between] *Voters have a choice between three main political parties.* | [+of] *You have a choice of hotel or self-catering accommodation.* | *You have a choice - you can stay here on your own or you can come with us.* | *She was faced with an agonizing choice.* | *We must encourage children to exercise choice and make their own decisions.* | *He has to make some important choices.* | *The booklet is supposed to help parents make informed choices* (=good choices because they have the right information) *for their children.* | *They gave us no choice in the matter.* | *We had no choice but to destroy the animal.* | *You have left me with no choice.*
2 [singular] the range of people or things that you can choose from: *It was a small shop and there wasn't much choice.* | [+of] *There is a choice of four different colours.* | *We offer a wide choice of wines and beers.* | *Consumers these days are spoilt for choice* (=have a lot of things to choose from). BrE
3 [C] the person or thing that someone chooses: [+of]

C

I don't really like her choice of jewellery. | *I think London was a good choice as a venue.*
4 by choice if you do something by choice, you do it because you want to do it and not because you are forced to do it: *She lives alone by choice.*
5 the sth of your choice the person or thing of your choice is the one that you would most like to choose: *Many children are not able to go to the school of their choice.*
6 the sth of choice the thing of choice is the one that people prefer to use: *It is the drug of choice for this type of illness.* → HOBSON'S CHOICE

choice² *adj* **1** [only before noun] *formal* choice food is of very good quality: *choice steak* | *We select only the choicest apples for our pies.* **2 a few choice words/phrases** if you use a few choice words, you say exactly what you mean in an angry way: *He told us what he thought of the idea in a few choice words.*

choir /kwaɪə $ kwaɪr/ *n* [C] **1** a group of people who sing together for other people to listen to; → **choral**: *He joined a church choir at the age of eight.* **2** [usually singular] the part of a church in which a choir sits during religious ceremonies

choir·boy /ˈkwaɪəbɔɪ $ ˈkwaɪr-/ *n* [C] a young boy who sings in a church choir

choir·mas·ter /ˈkwaɪə,mɑːstə $ ˈkwaɪr,mæstər/ *n* [C] someone who teaches a choir to sing together

choke¹ /tʃəʊk $ tʃoʊk/ *v* **1** [I] to be unable to breathe properly because something is in your throat or there is not enough air: [+on] *He choked on a piece of bread.* | *Six people choked to death on the fumes.* **2** [T] if something chokes you, it makes you unable to breathe properly: *I felt as if there was a weight on my chest, choking me.* | *The smoke was choking me.* **3** [T] to prevent someone from breathing by putting your hands around their throat and pressing on it: *His hands were round her throat, choking her.* **4** [I,T] to be unable to talk clearly because you are feeling a strong emotion: [+with] *He was choking with rage.* | *I was too choked with emotion to speak.* | *Her voice was choked with rage.* **5** [T] also **choke sth ⇔ out** to say something with difficulty because you are very upset or angry: *'Get out,' she choked.* **6** [T] also **choke sth ⇔ up** to fill a place so that things cannot move through it: *Weeds were choking the stream.* | **be choked (up) with sth** *The gutters were choked up with leaves.* **7** [I] *informal* to fail at doing something, especially a sport, because there is a lot of pressure on you: *People said I choked, but I just had a bad day on the golf course.* **8** [T] if one plant chokes another, it kills it by growing all around it and taking away its light and room to grow: *Weeds can quickly choke delicate garden plants.* **9 choke a horse** *AmE spoken* if you say that something is big enough to choke a horse, you are emphasizing that it is very big: *a wad of bills big enough to choke a horse*

choke sth ⇔ **back** *phr v* to control your anger, sadness etc so that you do not show it: *He choked back tears as he described what had happened.* | *She choked back a sob.* | *I choked back my anger.*

choke off sth *phr v* to prevent something from happening: *It is feared that higher interest rates might choke off economic recovery.*

choke sth ⇔ **out** *phr v* to say something with difficulty because you are very upset or angry: *His heart hammered as he choked out the words.* | *'No!' she choked out.*

choke up *phr v* **1 choke sth ⇔ up** to fill a place so that things cannot move through it: **be choked up with sth** *The stream was choked up with weeds.* **2 choke sb up** to make someone feel very upset and unable to talk: *This song really chokes me up.* | *I was really choked up when I saw her again.*

choke² *n* [C] **1** a piece of equipment in a vehicle that controls the amount of air going into the engine, and that is used to help the engine start **2** the sound that

someone makes when they cannot breathe properly because something is in their throat or there is not enough air: *She gave a little choke of laughter.*

'choke chain *BrE*; **'choke collar** *AmE n* [C] a chain that is fastened around the neck of a dog to control it

choke·cher·ry /ˈtʃəʊktʃeri $ ˈtʃoʊk-/ *n plural* **chokecherries** [C] a North American tree that produces small sour fruit

choked /tʃəʊkt $ tʃoʊkt/ *adj* [not before noun] *BrE* very upset: *I was really choked when I heard he'd died.*

chok·er /ˈtʃəʊkə $ ˈtʃoʊkər/ *n* [C] a piece of jewellery that fits very tightly around a woman's neck: *a diamond choker*

chol·er /ˈkɒlə $ ˈkɑːlər/ *n* [U] *literary* great anger: *What had brought on this fit of choler?*

chol·e·ra /ˈkɒlərə $ ˈkɑː-/ *n* [U] a serious disease that causes sickness and sometimes death. It is caused by eating infected food or drinking infected water

chol·er·ic /ˈkɒlərɪk $ ˈkɑː-/ *adj literary* bad-tempered or angry: *He was a choleric, ill-tempered man.*

cho·les·te·rol /kəˈlestərɒl $ -roʊl/ *n* [U] a chemical substance found in your blood. Too much cholesterol in your body may cause heart disease.

chomp /tʃɒmp $ tʃɑːmp, tʃɒːmp/ *v* [I] *informal* to eat something: [+on] *She was chomping on a bread roll.* | [+away] *a boy chomping away on a banana* | *British people chomp their way through more than a billion bars of chocolate every year.*

choo-choo /ˈtʃuː tʃuː/ *n* [C] *spoken* a train – used by children or when speaking to children

choose S1 W1 /tʃuːz/ *v past tense* **chose** /tʃəʊz $ tʃoʊz/ *past participle* **chosen** /ˈtʃəʊzən $ ˈtʃoʊ-/ [I,T] **1** to decide which one of a number of things or people you want; → **choice**: *It took us ages to choose a new carpet.* | *A panel of six judges will choose the winner.* | *He chose his words carefully as he spoke.* | *I don't mind which one we have – you choose.* | [+between] *For pudding we could choose between strawberry ice cream and apple tart.* | **choose whether/which/when etc.** *You can choose which method to adopt.* | [+from] *You can choose from a wide range of vehicles.* | **choose to do sth** *I chose to learn German rather than French.* | **choose sb/sth to do sth** *They chose Donald to be their leader.* | **choose sb/sth as sth** *The company has chosen London as its base.* | **choose sb/sth for sth** *Why did you choose me for the job?*
2 to decide to do something because that is what you prefer to do: **choose to do sth** *I chose to ignore his advice.* | *You can, if you choose, invest your money in the stock market.*
3 there is little/nothing to choose between sth used when you think that two or more things are equally good and you cannot decide which is better: *There was little to choose between the two candidates.*

WORD FOCUS: CHOOSE
similar words: **select, pick, appoint, nominate, go for, plump for, opt for**
→ see also **choice¹**, **selection, preference**

This graph shows how common different grammar patterns of the verb **choose** are.

choose sth	
choose to do sth	
choose	
choose between sth	
choose whether/which/when etc	
choose from sth	
other	

10% 20% 30% 40% 50% 60%

choos·y, choosey /ˈtʃuːzi/ *adj informal* someone who is choosy will only accept things that they like a lot or they consider to be very good: [+about] *She's very choosy about clothes.*

chop[1] /tʃɒp $ tʃɑːp/ v **chopped, chopping** [T]   **1** also **chop up** to cut something into smaller pieces: *He went outside to chop some more wood for the fire.* | *Can you chop up some carrots for me?* | *Add two finely chopped onions and a clove of garlic.* | **chop sth into pieces/ chunks etc** *Chop the meat into small cubes.*; → see picture at BREAK   **2** *informal* to reduce an amount of money by a large amount: *He suddenly found that his income had been chopped in half.*   **3 chop and change** *BrE informal* to keep changing your mind: *You can't keep chopping and changing like this!*

chop at sth *phr v* to hit something with a sharp tool in order to cut it: *They chopped at the bushes with their knives.*

chop sth ⇔ **down** *phr v* to make a tree fall down by cutting it with a sharp tool: *A couple of the older trees will have to be chopped down.* | *Large areas of rain-forest are being chopped down every day.*

chop sth ⇔ **off** *phr v* to remove something by cutting it with a sharp tool: *The branch had been chopped off.*

chop[2] n [C]   **1** a small piece of meat on a bone, usually cut from a sheep or pig; → **steak**: *a grilled pork chop* | *a lamb chop*   **2 the chop** *BrE* **a)** if you get or are given the chop, you lose your job: *Six more staff got the chop last week.* | *He was worried that he might be for the chop* (=lose his job).   **b)** if something gets or is given the chop, it is closed or stopped because people do not want to pay for it any more: *We were worried the project might get the chop.* | *Several other factories might now be for the chop* (=likely to be closed or stopped).   **3** a hard downward movement that you make with your hand: *a karate chop*   **4** the act of hitting something with a sharp tool in order to cut it: *With one last chop he split the log in two.*   **5 chops** [plural] *informal* the lower part of the face of a person or animal – used humorously: *Jack was grinning all over his chops.*

chop-'chop *interjection* an expression used when you want someone to hurry: *Come on! Chop-chop!*

chop·per /'tʃɒpə $ 'tʃɑːpər/ n [C]   **1** *BrE* a large knife that you use for cutting large pieces of meat   **2** *informal* a HELICOPTER: *There was a police chopper waiting for us.*   **3** a type of MOTORCYCLE on which the front wheel is further forward than the place where your hands rest   **4 choppers** [plural] *informal* teeth: *a row of huge white choppers*

chopping board n [C] *BrE*; **'chopping block** *AmE* a large piece of wood or plastic that you cut meat or vegetables on when you are cooking → see picture at EAT

chop·py /'tʃɒpi $ 'tʃɑːpi/ adj choppy water has a lot of waves and is not smooth to sail on: *The small boat bobbed about on the choppy water.*

chop·stick /'tʃɒp-stɪk $ 'tʃɑːp-/ n [C usually plural] one of the two thin sticks that you use to eat food in many countries in Asia

chop su·ey /ˌtʃɒp 'suːi $ ˌtʃɑːp-/ n [U] a Chinese dish of meat and vegetables, served with rice

cho·ral /'kɔːrəl/ adj [only before noun] related to music that is sung by a large group of people together; → **choir**: *an evening of choral music*

cho·rale /kɒ'rɑːl $ kə'ræl, -'rɑːl/ n [C] a piece of music praising God, usually sung in a church by a large group of people

chord /kɔːd $ kɔːrd/ n [C]   **1** a combination of several musical notes that are played at the same time and sound pleasant together   **2 strike/touch a chord (with sb)** to do or say something that people feel is familiar or true: *Many of the things she says will strike a chord with other young women.* | *I knew that what he was saying had touched a chord.*   **3** *technical* a straight line join-ing two points on a curve △ Do not confuse with **cord** (=thick string), which has the same pronunciation.

chore /tʃɔː $ tʃɔːr/ n [C]   **1** a small job that you have to do regularly, especially work that you do to keep a house clean: *everyday chores like shopping and housework* | *We share the domestic chores.*   **2** something you have to do that is very boring and unpleas-ant: *I find driving a real chore.*

chor·e·og·raph /'kɒriəgrɑːf, 'kɔː- $ 'kɔːriəgræf/ v [T] to arrange how dancers should move during a performance: *The show is very cleverly choreographed.*

chor·e·og·ra·phy /ˌkɒri'ɒgrəfi, ˌkɔː- $ ˌkɔːri'ɑːg-/ n [U] the art of arranging how dancers should move during a performance —**choreographer** n [C]

chor·is·ter /'kɒrɪstə $ 'kɔːrɪstər, 'kɑː-/ n [C] a singer in a church CHOIR

cho·ri·zo /tʃə'riːzəʊ $ -zoʊ/ n [U] a spicy SAUSAGE made in Spain

chor·tle /'tʃɔːtl $ 'tʃɔːrtl/ v [I] *formal* to laugh because you are amused or pleased about something: *Harry chortled with delight.* —**chortle** n [C]

cho·rus[1] /'kɔːrəs/ n [C]   **1** the part of a song that is repeated after each VERSE: *Everyone joined in the cho-rus.*   **2** a large group of people who sing together; ▣ **choir**: *I sing with the university chorus.*   **3** a piece of music written to be sung by a large group of people: *a recording of the Hallelujah Chorus*   **4** a group of sing-ers, dancers, or actors who act together in a show but do not have the main parts: *New voices are needed to join the chorus for the annual festival in October.*   **5 a chorus of thanks/disapproval/protest etc** something that a lot of people all say at the same time: *The minister was greeted with a chorus of boos.* | *There was a chorus of agreement from the committee.* | *More politicians have now joined in the chorus of com-plaints.*   **6 in chorus** if people say something in cho-rus, they say the same thing at the same time: *'Thank you,' they said in chorus.*

chorus[2] v [T] if people chorus something, they say it at the same time: *'Hurry up!' chorused the girls.*

'chorus girl n [C] a woman who sings and dances with a large group of other women and men in a show or film

'chorus line n [C] a group of people who stand in a straight line and sing and dance together in a show or film

chose /tʃəʊz $ tʃoʊz/ the past tense of CHOOSE

cho·sen /'tʃəʊzən $ 'tʃoʊ-/   **1** the past participle of CHOOSE   **2 the chosen few** a small number of people who are treated as special and better than other people: *information made available only to the chosen few*

chow[1] /tʃaʊ/ n   **1** [U] *old-fashioned informal* food: *I ordered some chow and sat down.*   **2** also **'chow chow** [C] a type of dog with long thick fur that first came from China

chow[2] v

chow down *phr v AmE informal* to eat: *She had to chow down with the others in the cafeteria.*

chow·der /'tʃaʊdə $ -ər/ n [U] a thick soup usually made with fish, vegetables, and milk

chow·der·head /'tʃaʊdəhed $ -ər-/ n [singular] *AmE informal* a stupid person

chow mein /ˌtʃaʊ 'meɪn/ n [U] a Chinese dish made with meat, vegetables, and NOODLES

Christ[1] /kraɪst/ n also **Jesus Christ** the man who is worshipped by Christians as the son of God; → **Chris-tian**: *a follower of Christ*

Christ[2] *interjection* used to express annoyance or sur-prise. Some people think this use is offensive: *Christ! That's hot!*

chris·ten /'krɪsən/ v [T]   **1** to officially give a child its name at a Christian religious ceremony; → **baptize**: *She was christened Sarah.*   **2** to give something or someone a name: *His fans christened him the king of rock.* | *The new plane has been christened the Hawk.*   **3** *informal* to use something for the first time: *We haven't christened the new garden chairs yet.*

Chris·ten·dom /'krɪsəndəm/ n [U] *formal* all the Christian people or countries in the world

C

1 000, 2 000, 3 000, most frequent words in S poken and W ritten English

chris·ten·ing /ˈkrɪsənɪŋ/ n [C] a Christian religious ceremony at which a child is officially given a name and becomes a member of a Christian church; → **baptism**

Chris·tian[1] /ˈkrɪstʃən, -tiən/ n [C] a person who believes in the ideas taught by Jesus Christ

Christian[2] adj **1** related to Christianity: *the Christian religion | the Christian church | a Christian minister* **2** also **christian** behaving in a good, kind way: *That wasn't a very christian thing to do!*

Christian 'era n **the Christian era** the period from the birth of Christ to the present time

Chris·ti·an·i·ty /ˌkrɪstiˈænᵻti/ n [U] the religion based on the life and beliefs of Jesus Christ

Christian name n [C] a person's first name, especially when they are given this name in a Christian religious ceremony: *She didn't like children to call her by her Christian name.*

Christian 'Science n [U] a religion started in America in 1866, which includes the belief that illnesses can be cured by faith —**Christian Scientist** n [C]

Christ·mas /ˈkrɪsməs/ n [C,U] the period of time around 25 December, the day when Christians celebrate the birth of Christ: **at Christmas** *We'll see you at Christmas.* | **over Christmas** *I'll be in Scotland over Christmas.* | *Are you going home for Christmas?* | *a Christmas present | the Christmas holidays | Merry Christmas and a happy New Year everyone!*

Christmas cake n [C,U] a special cake that people eat in Britain at Christmas

Christmas card n [C] a special card that people send to friends and relatives at Christmas

Christmas 'carol n [C] a Christian song that people sing at Christmas

Christmas 'cookie n [C] a special COOKIE that people eat in the US at Christmas

Christmas 'cracker n [C] a tube of coloured paper that two people pull apart at Christmas in Britain for fun. It makes a loud sound as it is pulled apart, and usually contains a small toy

Christmas 'Day n [U] December 25th, the day when most Christians celebrate the birth of Christ: *I always spend Christmas Day with my family.* | *We'll be at home on Christmas Day.*

Christmas 'dinner n [C] a special meal that people eat on Christmas Day

Christmas 'Eve n [U] December 24th, the day before Christmas Day: *We spent Christmas Eve cooking and getting ready for Christmas Day.* | *Unfortunately, I've got to work on Christmas Eve.*

Christmas 'pudding n [C] a special sweet food that contains a lot of dried fruit and is eaten in Britain at the end of the main meal on Christmas Day

Christmas 'stocking n [C] a long sock which children leave in their house on Christmas Eve to be filled with presents

Christ·mas·sy /ˈkrɪsməsi/ adj typical of Christmas: *It looked very Christmassy with lights on the trees.*

Christ·mas·time /ˈkrɪsməstaɪm/ n [U] the period around Christmas

Christmas tree n [C] a FIR tree that people put in their houses and decorate for Christmas

chro·mat·ic /krəʊˈmætɪk, krə- $ kroʊ-, krə-/ adj **1** technical related to a musical scale which consists of SEMITONES: *a chromatic scale | chromatic harmonies* **2** formal related to bright colours

chrome /krəʊm $ kroʊm/ n [U] a type of hard shiny metal: *a chrome candleholder* → see picture at MATERIAL

chrome 'yellow n [U] a very bright yellow colour —**chrome yellow** adj

chro·mi·um /ˈkrəʊmiəm $ ˈkroʊ-/ n [U] a hard blue-white metal that is used to cover metal objects with a shiny silver protective surface. It is a chemical ELEMENT: symbol Cr: *a chromium-plated handrail*

chro·mo·some /ˈkrəʊməsəʊm $ ˈkroʊməsoʊm/ n [C] a part of every living cell that is shaped like a thread and contains the GENES that control the size, shape etc that a plant or animal has

chron·ic /ˈkrɒnɪk $ ˈkrɑː-/ adj **1** a chronic disease or illness is one that continues for a long time and cannot be cured; → **acute**: *chronic arthritis | chronic asthma | chronic heart disease* **2** a chronic problem is one that continues for a long time and cannot easily be solved: *a period of recession and chronic unemployment | There is now a chronic shortage of teachers.* **3** chronic alcoholic/gambler etc someone who has behaved in a particular way for a long time and cannot stop: *He was a chronic alcoholic and unable to hold down a job.* | *a chronic smoker* **4** BrE informal extremely bad: *The food was absolutely chronic.* —**chronically** /-kli/ adv: *patients who are chronically ill | The service has been chronically underfunded for years.*

chronic fa'tigue ˌsyndrome n [U] an illness that makes you feel very tired and weak and can last for a long time

chron·i·cle[1] /ˈkrɒnɪkəl $ ˈkrɑː-/ n [C] a written record of a series of events, especially historical events, written in the order in which they happened: [+of] *He has produced a chronicle of his life during the war years.*

chronicle[2] v [T] to describe events in the order in which they happened: *His life is chronicled in a new biography published last week.* | *The book chronicles the events leading up to the war.*

chron·o·graph /ˈkrɒnəgrɑː $ ˈkrɑːnəgræf/ n [C] a scientific instrument for measuring periods of time

chron·o·log·i·cal /ˌkrɒnəˈlɒdʒɪkəl $ ˌkrɑːnəˈlɑː-/ adj **1** arranged according to when things happened or were made: *We arranged the documents in chronological order.* **2** chronological age a person's chronological age is how old they actually are, rather than how old their mind or body seems —**chronologically** /-kli/ adv: *The paintings are displayed chronologically.*

chro·nol·o·gy /krəˈnɒlədʒi $ -ˈnɑː-/ n plural **chronologies** **1** [U] the order in which events happened in the past: [+of] *It is important to establish the chronology of the events.* **2** [C] an account of events in the order in which they happened: *The book includes a chronology of his life and works.*

chro·nom·e·ter /krəˈnɒmᵻtə $ -ˈnɑːmᵻtər/ n [C] a very exact clock, used for scientific purposes

chrys·a·lis /ˈkrɪsəlᵻs/ n [C] a MOTH or BUTTERFLY at the stage of development when it has a hard outer shell and is changing into its adult form

chry·san·the·mum /krɪˈsænθᵻməm/ n [C] a garden plant with large brightly coloured flowers → see picture at FLOWER

chub /tʃʌb/ n [C] a fish that lives in lakes and rivers

chub·by /ˈtʃʌbi/ adj slightly fat in a way that looks healthy and attractive: *a chubby six-year-old | a baby with round chubby cheeks* —**chubbiness** n [U]

chuck[1] S2 /tʃʌk/ v [T] informal especially BrE **1** to throw something in a careless or relaxed way: **chuck sth on/out of/into etc sth** *Tania chucked her bag down on the sofa.* | *I chucked a few things into a suitcase and left.* | **chuck sb sth** *Chuck me that pen, would you?* **2** to throw something away because you do not want it any more: *I think I might have chucked it by mistake.* **3** also **chuck sth ⇔ in** to leave your job: *You haven't chucked your job, have you?* **4** BrE to end a romantic relationship with someone: *Why did Judy chuck him?* **5** chuck it down to rain very heavily: *It chucked it down all afternoon.* **6** chuck sb under the chin to gently touch someone under their chin in a friendly way

chuck sth ⇔ **away** phr v informal to throw something away because you do not want it any more: *I chucked all my old clothes away when we moved house.*

chuck sb **off** sth *phr v informal*
1 to make someone leave a place or stop using something: *He'll chuck you off his land if he finds you.*
2 chuck yourself off sth to jump from somewhere that is very high: *She tried to chuck herself off the bridge twice last week.*

chuck sb/sth ⟺ **out** *phr v informal*
1 to throw something away because you do not want it any more: *It was broken so I chucked it out.*
2 to make someone leave a place or a job: *Their landlord chucked them out when they couldn't pay the rent.* | [+of] *They got chucked out of the pub for fighting.*

chuck sth ⟺ **in** *phr v*
to leave your job: *He had a job as a driver but he chucked it in.* | *I decided to chuck it all in and go to Australia.*

chuck² *n* **1** [C] part of a machine that holds something firmly so that it does not move **2** [singular] *spoken* a friendly word used to address someone in some parts of Northern England

chuck·le /ˈtʃʌkəl/ *v* [I] to laugh quietly: *What are you chuckling about?* —**chuckle** *n* [C]: *Rosie gave a little chuckle.*

chuck ˈsteak *n* [U] meat that comes from just above the shoulder of a cow

chuck ˌwagon *n* [C] *AmE old-fashioned* a vehicle that carries food for a group of people

chuffed /tʃʌft/ *adj* [not before noun] *BrE informal* very pleased or happy: *He's really chuffed about passing the exam.*

chug /tʃʌɡ/ *v* **chugged, chugging 1** [I always + adv/prep] if a car, train etc chugs somewhere, it moves there slowly, with the engine making a repeated low sound: [+along/up/around etc] *The boat chugged out of the harbour.* **2** [T] also **chug-a-lug** *AmE informal* to drink all of something in a glass or bottle without stopping **3** [I always + adv/prep] to make slow but steady progress: *The economy just keeps chugging along.* —**chug** *n* [C usually singular]

chum /tʃʌm/ *n* **1** [C] *informal old-fashioned* a good friend: *Freddie's an old school chum of mine.* **2** [U] small pieces of oily fish, used to catch other fish

chum·my /ˈtʃʌmi/ *adj informal* friendly: *You and Eric have become quite chummy, haven't you?*

chump /tʃʌmp/ *n* [C] **1** *informal* someone who is silly or stupid, and who is easily deceived **2 chump chop/steak** *BrE* a thick piece of meat with a bone in it

chun·der /ˈtʃʌndə $ -ər/ *v* [I] *informal* to VOMIT

chunk /tʃʌŋk/ *n* [C] **1** a large thick piece of something that does not have an even shape: *ice chunks* | [+of] *a chunk of bread* **2** a large part or amount of something: *The rent takes a large chunk out of my monthly salary.* | [+of] *A huge chunk of the audience got up and left before the end of the show.* **3 a chunk of change** *AmE informal* a large amount of money: *Lurie risked a pretty big chunk of change on the race.*

chunk·y /ˈtʃʌŋki/ *adj* **1** thick, solid, and heavy: *chunky jewellery* → see picture at THICK **2** chunky food has large pieces in it: *chunky peanut butter* **3** someone who is chunky has a broad, heavy body

church [S1] [W1] /tʃɜːtʃ $ tʃɜːrtʃ/ *n*
1 [C] a building where Christians go to worship; → **cathedral**: *a short church service* | *church bells* → see picture at TOWN
2 [U] the religious ceremonies in a church: *Mrs Dobson invited us to dinner after church.* | *My parents go to church every Sunday.* | *at church We didn't see you at church this morning.*
3 [C] also **Church** one of the separate groups within the Christian religion: *the Catholic Church*
4 [singular, U] the institution of the Christian religion, and all the priests and other ministers who are part of it: *the church's attitude towards marriage* | *separation of church and state*

church·go·er /ˈtʃɜːtʃˌɡəʊə $ ˈtʃɜːrtʃˌɡoʊər/ *n* [C] someone who goes to church regularly

church·man /ˈtʃɜːtʃmən $ ˈtʃɜːrtʃ-/ *n plural* **churchmen** /-mən/ [C] a priest; ⊟ **clergyman**

ˌChurch of ˈEngland *n* **the Church of England** also **C of E** the state church in England, the official leader of which is the Queen or King

ˌChurch of ˈScotland *n* **the Church of Scotland** the state church in Scotland

ˈchurch ˌschool *n* [C] a school in Britain that is partly controlled by a church

church·war·den /ˌtʃɜːtʃˈwɔːdn $ ˈtʃɜːrtʃˌwɔːrdn/ *n* [C] someone who looks after church property and money

church·wom·an /ˈtʃɜːtʃˌwʊmən $ ˈtʃɜːrtʃ-/ *n plural* **churchwomen** /-ˌwɪmɪn/ [C] a female priest; ⊟ **clergywoman**

church·yard /ˈtʃɜːtʃjɑːd $ ˈtʃɜːrtʃjɑːrd/ *n* [C] a piece of land around a church where people are buried

churl·ish /ˈtʃɜːlɪʃ $ ˈtʃɜːr-/ *adj formal* not polite or friendly: *It seemed churlish to refuse his invitation.*

churn¹ /tʃɜːn $ tʃɜːrn/ *v* **1** [I] if your stomach churns, you feel sick because you are nervous or frightened: *My stomach was churning on the day of the exam.* **2** [I,T] also **churn up** if water, mud etc churns, or if something churns it, it moves about violently: *We stood on the dock and watched the ocean churn.* **3** [I] if a machine, engine, wheel etc churns, it or its parts begin to move: *I pressed the gas pedal, and slowly the wheels began to churn.* **4** [T] to make milk by using a churn

churn sth ⟺ **out** *phr v* to produce large quantities of something, especially without caring about quality: *She's been churning out novels for twenty years.*

churn sb/sth **up** *phr v* **1 churn** sth ⟺ **up** to damage the surface of the ground, especially by walking on it or driving a vehicle over it: *The lawn had been churned up by the tractor.* **2** to move water, mud etc around violently: **churn** sth ⟺ **up** *The oars had churned up the mud, clouding the water.* **3** *BrE* to make someone upset or angry: *Though she looked calm, in reality she was churned up inside.*

churn² *n* [C] **1** a container used for shaking milk in order to make it into butter **2** also **milk churn** *BrE* a large metal container used to carry milk in

chute

a building chute   a water chute/flume

chute /ʃuːt/ *n* [C] **1** a long narrow structure that slopes down, so that things or people can slide down it from one place to another: *a rubbish chute* | *a laundry chute* | *The pool had several water chutes.* **2** *informal* a PARACHUTE

chut·ney /ˈtʃʌtni/ *n* [U] a mixture of fruits, hot-tasting SPICES, and sugar, that is eaten especially with meat or cheese: *mango chutney*

chutz·pah /ˈhʊtspə/ *n* [U] *informal* a lot of confidence and courage to do something, especially something that might involve being impolite to someone in authority – used to show approval; ⊟ **nerve**: *It took a lot of chutzpah to talk to your boss like that.*

CIA /ˌsiː aɪ ˈeɪ/ *n* **the CIA** *the Central Intelligence Agency* the department of the US government that collects information about other countries, especially secretly

ciao /tʃaʊ/ *interjection informal* used to say goodbye

ci·ca·da /sɪ¹kɑːdə $ sɪ¹keɪdə, -¹kɑː-/ *n* [C] an insect that lives in hot countries, has large transparent wings, and makes a high singing noise

CID /ˌsiː aɪ ¹diː/ *n* **Criminal Investigation Department** the department of the British police that deals with very serious crimes

-cide /saɪd/ *suffix* [in nouns] another form of the suffix -ICIDE: *genocide* (=killing a whole race of people) **—-cidal** [in adjectives] **—-cidally** [in adverbs]

ci·der /¹saɪdə $ -ər/ *n* **1** [C,U] *BrE* an alcoholic drink made from apples, or a glass of this drink; **☐ hard cider** *AmE* **2** [U] *AmE* also **apple cider** a non-alcoholic drink made from apples

ci·gar /sɪ¹gɑː $ -¹gɑːr/ *n* [C] a thick tube-shaped thing that people smoke, and which is made from tobacco leaves that have been rolled up; → **cigarette**

cig·a·rette S2 W3 /ˌsɪgə¹ret $ ¹sɪgəˌret, ˌsɪgə¹ret/ *n* [C] a thin tube of paper filled with finely cut tobacco that people smoke; → **cigar**: *a packet of cigarettes*

ciga¹rette ˌbutt / $ ¹... ˌ.../ also **ciga¹rette end** *BrE n* [C] the part of a cigarette that remains when someone has finished smoking it

ciga¹rette ˌholder / $ ¹... ˌ.../ *n* [C] a narrow tube for holding a cigarette

ciga¹rette ˌlighter / $ ¹... ˌ.../ *n* [C] a small object that produces a flame for lighting cigarettes, CIGARS etc; **☐ lighter**

ciga¹rette ˌpaper / $ ¹... ˌ.../ *n* [C,U] thin paper that people put tobacco in to make their own cigarettes

cig·gy /¹sɪgi/ *n plural* **ciggies** [C] *BrE spoken informal* a cigarette

ci·lan·tro /sɪ¹læntrəʊ $ sɪ¹lɑːntroʊ, -¹læn-/ *n* [U] *AmE* the strong-tasting leaves of a small plant, used especially in Asian and Mexican cooking; **☐ coriander** *BrE*

C in C /ˌsiː ɪn ¹siː/ *n* [C] a COMMANDER IN CHIEF

cinch¹ /sɪntʃ/ *n* [singular] *informal* **1** something that is very easy: *'How was the exam?' 'Oh, it was a cinch!'* | **be a cinch to do sth** *The program is a cinch to install.* **2** *AmE* something that will definitely happen, or someone who will definitely do something: **be a cinch to do sth** *Most observers say the President is a cinch to win re-election.*

cinch² *v* [T] **1** to pull a belt, STRAP etc tightly around something: *a blue dress cinched at the waist by a wide belt* **2** *AmE* to make something certain to happen: *They cinched a place in the play-off.*

cin·der /¹sɪndə $ -ər/ *n* [C usually plural] a very small piece of burnt wood, coal etc: *a cold hearth full of cinders* | *The cake was **burnt to a cinder*** (=completely burnt).

¹cinder block *n* [C] *AmE* a large grey brick used to build houses and other buildings, made from CEMENT and cinders; **☐ breeze-block** *BrE* → see picture at **BLOCK¹**

Cin·der·el·la /ˌsɪndə¹relə/ *n* [C] a person or thing that has been ignored or treated as less important than other people or things: [+of] *Their economy was the Cinderella of the industrialized world.* **—Cinderella** *adj* [only before noun]: *Mental health care has been the Cinderella service for too long.*

cine- /sɪni/ *adj BrE* relating to films or to the film industry: *a cine-projector*

cine cam·e·ra /¹sɪni ˌkæmərə/ *n* [C] *BrE* a camera for making moving films, rather than photographs

cine film /¹sɪni ˌfɪlm/ *n* [U] *BrE* film used in a cine camera

cin·e·ma S3 /¹sɪnɪmə/ *n*
1 [C] *especially BrE* a building in which films are shown; **☐ movie theater** *AmE*: *It's on at the local cinema.* → see picture at **TOWN**
2 the cinema *BrE* if you go to the cinema, you go to a cinema to see a film: *We decided to go to the cinema.*

3 [singular,U] the skill or industry of making films: *a leading figure in Italian cinema*

cin·e·ma·go·er /¹sɪnɪməˌgəʊə $ -ˌgoʊər/ *n* [C usually plural] someone who goes to the cinema to see a film; **☐ moviegoer** *AmE*

cin·e·mat·ic /ˌsɪnɪ¹mætɪk◄ / *adj* relating to films: *a cinematic masterpiece*

cin·e·ma·tog·ra·phy /ˌsɪnɪmə¹tɒgrəfi $ -¹tɑː-/ *n* [U] the skill or study of making films: *with impressive cinematography by Robert Surtees* **—cinematographer** *n* [C]

cin·e·phile /¹sɪnɪfaɪl/ *n* [C] someone who likes films very much and considers them to be a form of art, not just entertainment: *He is a complete cinephile.*

cin·na·mon /¹sɪnəmən/ *n* [U] a sweet-smelling brown substance used for giving a special taste to cakes and other sweet foods: *a cinnamon roll*

ci·pher, cypher /¹saɪfə $ -ər/ *n* **1** [C,U] *formal* a system of secret writing; **☐ code**: *an expert in ciphers* | *messages written in cipher* **2** [C] someone who is not important and has no power or influence: *At work, she was a cipher, a functionary, nothing more.* **3** *literary* [C] the number 0; **☐ zero**

cir·ca /¹sɜːkə $ ¹sɜːr-/ *prep formal* used before a date to show that something happened close to but not exactly on that date: *manuscripts dating from circa 1100*

cir·ca·di·an /sɜː¹keɪdiən $ sɜːr-/ *adj* [only before noun] *technical* relating to a period of 24 hours, used especially when talking about changes in people's bodies: *the body's circadian rhythm*

cir·cle¹ S2 W2 /¹sɜːkəl $ ¹sɜːr-/ *n* [C]
1 SHAPE a completely round shape, like the letter O: *Draw a circle 10cm in diameter.* | *Cut the pastry into circles.*
2 ARRANGED IN CIRCLE a group of people or things arranged in the shape of a circle: *The children stood round in a circle.* | [+of] *a circle of chairs*
3 GROUP OF PEOPLE a group of people who know each other and meet regularly, or who have similar interests or jobs: [+of] *a circle of friends* | **political/legal/literary etc circles** *He's well-known in fashionable circles.* | *Johnson was part of the president's **inner circle*** (=the people who have the most influence).
4 THEATRE *BrE* the upper floor of a theatre, that has seats arranged in curved rows; **☐ balcony** *AmE*
5 go/run around in circles to think or argue about something without deciding anything or making progress
6 come/go full circle also **turn full circle** *BrE* to end in the same situation in which you began, even though there have been changes in the time in between: *Sooner or later, fashion comes full circle.* → **square the circle** at SQUARE³ (5) → VICIOUS CIRCLE

circle² *v* **1** [T] to draw a circle around something: *Circle the correct answer.* **2** [I,T] to move in the shape of a circle around something, especially in the air: *The plane circled the airport before landing.* | [+round/above/over etc] *The pigeons circled above the terrace.*

cir·clet /¹sɜːklɪt $ ¹sɜːr-/ *n* [C] a narrow band of gold, silver, or jewels worn around someone's head or arms

cir·cuit W3 /¹sɜːkɪt $ ¹sɜːr-/ *n* [C]
1 a path that forms a circle around an area, or a journey along this path: *We did a circuit of the old city.*
2 *BrE* a track that cars, MOTORBIKES etc race around
3 the tennis/lecture/cabaret etc circuit all the places that are usually visited by someone who plays tennis etc: *a well-known entertainer on the club circuit*
4 the complete circle that an electric current travels: *an electrical circuit*
5 a regular trip around an area made by a judge or a religious leader, so that a court of law or church can meet in several different places: *a circuit judge* | *a circuit preacher*
6 do circuits *BrE informal* to do CIRCUIT TRAINING → CLOSED CIRCUIT TELEVISION, PRINTED CIRCUIT, SHORT CIRCUIT

circuit board n [C] a board in a piece of electrical equipment that uses thin lines of metal to CONDUCT (=carry) electricity between different points

circuit ,breaker n [C] a piece of equipment that stops an electric current reaching a machine if the machine becomes dangerous

circuit ,court n [C] a court of law that meets in small towns within a particular area whenever a judge visits from a larger town

cir·cu·i·tous /sɜːˈkjuːɪtəs $ sɜːr-/ adj going from one place to another in a way that is longer than the most direct way: a hard, circuitous hike —**circuitously** adv

cir·cuit·ry /ˈsɜːkɪtri $ ˈsɜːr-/ n [U] a system of electric circuits

circuit ,training n [U] BrE a series of many different exercises done quickly after each other, in order to increase your fitness

cir·cu·lar[1] /ˈsɜːkjələ $ ˈsɜːrkjələr/ adj **1** shaped like a circle: a circular table **2** moving around in a circle: a circular bus route **3 circular argument/logic/reasoning** an argument or way of thinking that is not right because the statement it uses to prove that its argument is true can only be true if the original argument is already true —**circularity** /ˌsɜːkjəˈlærəti $ ˌsɜːr-/ n [U]

circular[2] n [C] a printed advertisement, notice etc that is sent to lots of people at the same time

circular 'file n [C] a WASTEPAPER BASKET - used humorously

circular 'saw n [C] an electric tool with a round metal blade that has small sharp parts around the edge, used for cutting wood → see picture at SAW

cir·cu·late /ˈsɜːkjəleɪt $ ˈsɜːr-/ v **1** [I,T] to move around within a system, or to make something do this: Swimming helps to get the blood circulating through the muscles. | Ceiling fans circulated warm air around the room. **2** [I] if information, facts, ideas etc circulate, they become known by many people: Rumours began circulating that the Prime Minister was seriously ill. **3** [T] to send goods, information etc to people: The group circulated petitions calling for a federal law to ban handguns. **4** [I] to talk to a lot of different people in a group, especially at a party

cir·cu·la·tion /ˌsɜːkjəˈleɪʃən $ ˌsɜːr-/ n **1** [singular, U] the movement of blood around your body: Exercise improves the circulation. | good/bad circulation Doctors had to remove her leg because of bad circulation. **2** [U] the exchange of information, money etc from one person to another in a group or society: in/out of circulation Police believe there are thousands of illegal guns in circulation. | The book was taken out of circulation. | remove/withdraw sth from circulation The Treasury Department plans to remove older coins from circulation and replace them with new ones. **3** [C, usually singular] the average number of copies of a newspaper or magazine that are usually sold each day, week, month etc: [+of] The newspaper has a daily circulation of 55,000. **4** [C,U] the movement of liquid, air etc in a system: Let's open the windows and get some circulation in here. **5** in circulation/out of circulation informal when someone takes part or does not take part in social activities at a particular time: Sandy's out of circulation until after her exams.

cir·cu·la·to·ry /ˌsɜːkjəˈleɪtəri, ˈsɜːkjələtəri $ ˈsɜːrkjələtɔːri/ adj [only before noun] relating to the movement of blood around your body: the heart and circulatory system

cir·cum·cise /ˈsɜːkəmsaɪz $ ˈsɜːr-/ v [T] **1** to cut off the skin at the end of the PENIS (=male sex organ) **2** to cut off a woman's CLITORIS (=part of her sex organs)

cir·cum·ci·sion /ˌsɜːkəmˈsɪʒən $ ˌsɜːr-/ n [C,U] the act of circumcising someone, or an occasion when a baby is circumcised as part of a religious ceremony

cir·cum·fer·ence /səˈkʌmfərəns $ sər-/ n [C usually singular, U] the distance or measurement around the outside of a circle or any round shape; → **diameter**,

perimeter, radius: [+of] the circumference of the Earth | in circumference The island is only nine miles in circumference.

cir·cum·flex /ˈsɜːkəmfleks $ ˈsɜːr-/ n [C] a mark placed above a letter in a French word to show its pronunciation, for example, ô

cir·cum·lo·cu·tion /ˌsɜːkəmləˈkjuːʃən $ ˌsɜːr-/ n [C,U] formal the practice of using too many words to express an idea, instead of saying it directly

cir·cum·nav·i·gate /ˌsɜːkəmˈnævɪgeɪt $ ˌsɜːr-/ v [T] to sail, fly, or travel completely around the Earth, an island etc —**circumnavigation** /ˌsɜːkəmnævɪˈgeɪʃən $ ˌsɜːr-/ n [C,U]: circumnavigation of the world

cir·cum·scribe /ˈsɜːkəmskraɪb $ ˈsɜːr-/ v [T] **1** [often passive] formal to limit power, rights, or abilities; ☐ **restrict**: The President's power is circumscribed by Congress and the Supreme Court. **2** technical to draw a line around something: a circle circumscribed by a square

cir·cum·spect /ˈsɜːkəmspekt $ ˈsɜːr-/ adj formal thinking carefully about something before doing it, in order to avoid risk; ☐ **cautious**: The governor was usually circumspect when dealing with the media. —**circumspectly** adv —**circumspection** /ˌsɜːkəmˈspekʃən $ ˌsɜːr-/ n [U]

cir·cum·stance S1 W1 /ˈsɜːkəmstæns, -stəns $ ˈsɜːr-/ n
1 [C usually plural] the conditions that affect a situation, action, event etc: The Soviet Union had been forced by circumstances to sign a pact with Nazi Germany. | I can't imagine a circumstance in which I would be willing to steal. | in ... circumstances The rules can only be waived in exceptional circumstances. | under ... circumstances Prisoners can only leave their cells under certain circumstances (=if particular conditions exist). | He was found dead in suspicious circumstances (=in a way that makes you think something illegal or dishonest has happened). | Unless there are extenuating circumstances, all students must be present on the day of the exam (=reasons which make you feel that it was reasonable for someone to break the usual rules).
2 under no circumstances also **in no circumstances** BrE used to emphasize that something must definitely not happen: Under no circumstances are you to leave the house.
3 under/given the circumstances also **in the circumstances** BrE used to say that a particular situation makes an action, decision etc necessary, acceptable, or true when it would not normally be: It's the best result that could be expected under the circumstances.
4 [U] formal the combination of facts, events etc that influence your life, and that you cannot control: He was a victim of circumstance.
5 circumstances [plural] formal the conditions in which you live, especially how much money you have: economic/financial/personal etc circumstances Whether or not you qualify for a loan will depend on your financial circumstances. | people living in difficult social circumstances | in reduced circumstances old-fashioned (=with much less money than you used to have) → **pomp and circumstance** at POMP

cir·cum·stan·tial /ˌsɜːkəmˈstænʃəl◂ $ ˌsɜːr-/ adj **1** law based on something that appears to be true but is not proven: circumstantial evidence/case The case against McCarthy is based largely on circumstantial evidence. **2** formal including all the details: The book includes a long and circumstantial account of Empson's conversation with the Queen. —**circumstantially** adv

cir·cum·vent /ˌsɜːkəmˈvent $ ˌsɜːr-/ v [T] formal **1** to avoid a problem or rule that restricts you, especially in a clever or dishonest way - used to show disapproval: The company opened an account abroad, in

C

1 000, 2 000, 3 000, most frequent words in S poken and W ritten English

order to circumvent the tax laws. **2** to avoid something by changing the direction in which you are travelling: *We went north in order to circumvent the mountains.* —**circumvention** /-'venʃən/ n [U]

cir·cus /'sɜːkəs $ 'sɜːr-/ n **1** [C] a group of people and animals who travel to different places performing skilful tricks as entertainment: **circus act** (=a trick performed in a circus) | **circus ring** (=a large circular area where tricks are performed) **2** [singular] *informal* a situation in which there is too much excitement or noise: *The first day of school is always such a circus.* | *The trial has turned into a **media circus**.* **3** [C usually singular] *BrE* a round open area where several streets join together, often used in place names: *Piccadilly Circus* **4** [C] a place in ancient Rome where fights, races etc took place, with seats built in a circle

cir·rho·sis /sɪ'rəʊsɪs $ -'roʊ-/ n [U] a serious disease of the LIVER, often caused by drinking too much alcohol

cir·rus /'sɪrəs/ n [U] a form of cloud that is light and shaped like feathers, high in the sky

CIS /ˌsiː aɪ 'es/ n *Commonwealth of Independent States* an association formed by countries that were formerly part of the Soviet Union

cis·sy /'sɪsi/ n plural **cissies** [C] *BrE informal* SISSY

cis·tern /'sɪstən $ -ərn/ n [C] a container in which the supply of water for a building is stored inside the building; ☐ **tank**

cit·a·del /'sɪtədəl, -del/ n [C] **1** a strong FORT (=small castle) built in the past as a place where people could go for safety if their city was attacked; ☐ **fortress** **2** the **citadel of sth** *literary* a place or situation in which an idea, principle, system etc that you think is important is kept safe; ☐ **stronghold**: *the last citadel of freedom*

ci·ta·tion /saɪ'teɪʃən/ n [C] **1** *AmE* a formal statement or piece of writing publicly praising someone's actions or achievements: [+**for**] *a citation for bravery* **2** an official order for someone to appear in court or pay a FINE for doing something illegal: [+**for**] *Turner was issued a traffic citation for reckless driving.* **3** a line taken from a book, speech etc; ☐ **quotation**: *The essay begins with a citation from 'Hamlet'.*

cite /saɪt/ v [T] *formal* **1** to mention something as an example, especially one that supports, proves, or explains an idea or situation: *The judge cited a 1956 Supreme Court ruling in her decision.* | **cite sth as sth** *Several factors have been cited as the cause of the unrest.* **2** to give the exact words of something that has been written, especially in order to support an opinion or prove an idea; ☐ **quote**: *The passage cited above is from a Robert Frost poem.* **3** to order someone to appear before a court of law: **cite sb for sth** *Two managers had been cited for similar infractions.* **4** *BrE* to mention someone by name in a court case: *Sue was cited in the divorce proceedings.* **5** to mention someone because they deserve praise: **cite sb (for sth)** *Garcia was cited for her work with disabled children.*

cit·i·zen S2 W2 /'sɪtɨzən/ n [C]
1 someone who lives in a particular town, country, or state: *We need our schools to teach students to be good citizens.* | *The mayor urged citizens to begin preparing for a major storm.* → SENIOR CITIZEN
2 someone who legally belongs to a particular country and has rights and responsibilities there, whether they are living there or not; → **national**: *At the time, there were over 2000 British citizens living in Iraq.*
3 **second-class citizen** someone who is made to feel unimportant because of the way people treat them

cit·i·zen·ry /'sɪtɨzənri/ n [U] *formal* all the citizens in a particular town, country, or state

citizen's ar'rest n [C] when a person who is not a police officer catches someone and presents them to the police because they have done something illegal: *Brown made a citizen's arrest when a youth attempted to rob an elderly woman.*

Citizens' Band n [U] CB

cit·i·zen·ship /'sɪtɨzənʃɪp/ n [U] **1** the legal right of belonging to a particular country; → **nationality**: **French/US/Brazilian etc citizenship** *I have applied for French citizenship.* | *McGuirk holds dual citizenship* (=the legal right of being a citizen in two countries) *in Ireland and the US.* **2** the ways in which a good citizen behaves, for example being responsible and helping their COMMUNITY: *The schools should be responsible for teaching our children good citizenship.*

cit·ric ac·id /ˌsɪtrɪk 'æsɨd/ n [U] a weak acid found in some fruits such as LEMONS

cit·ron /'sɪtrən/ n [C] a fruit like a LEMON but bigger

cit·ron·el·la /ˌsɪtrə'nelə/ n [U] an oil used for keeping insects away

cit·rus /'sɪtrəs/ n [C] **1** also **'citrus tree** a type of tree that produces citrus fruits **2** also **'citrus fruit** a fruit with thick skin, such as an orange or LEMON —**citrus** adj

cit·y S1 W1 /'sɪti/ n plural **cities** [C]
1 a large important town: *New York City* | *a capital city* | *The nearest big city was St. Louis.* | **city dweller** (=someone who lives in a city) → INNER CITY
2 a) *BrE* a large town, that has been given an official title by a king or queen: *the city of Oxford* **b)** *AmE* a town of any size that has definite borders and powers that were officially given by the state government: *The city of Cleveland celebrated its 200th birthday with fireworks and an outdoor concert.*
3 [usually singular] the people who live in a city: *The city has been living in fear since last week's earthquake.*
4 the City *BrE* the area of London which is Britain's financial centre, and the important institutions there: **City banker/stockbroker etc** (=a banker etc who works in the city)
5 the city *AmE* the government of a city: *The city is working to improve public transportation.*

city 'centre n [C] *BrE* the main shopping or business area in a city; → **downtown** *AmE*

city 'council n [C] the group of elected officials who are responsible for governing a city

'city desk n [C] **1** *BrE* a department of a newspaper that deals with financial news **2** *AmE* a department of a newspaper that deals with local news

'city ˌeditor n [C] **1** also **financial editor** *BrE* a JOURNALIST responsible for the financial news in a newspaper **2** *AmE* a newspaper EDITOR who is responsible for local news

city 'fathers n [plural] the group of people who govern a city

city 'hall n **1** [U] *AmE* the government of a city: *The recycling program simply hasn't been a high priority at City Hall.* **2** [C usually singular] the building a city government uses as its offices

city 'planning n [U] *AmE* the study of the way cities work, so that roads, houses, services etc can be provided effectively; ☐ **town planning** *BrE*

cit·y·scape /'sɪtiskeɪp/ n [C,U] the way a city looks, or the way it looks from a particular place: *the gray New York cityscape*

city 'slicker n [C] someone who lives and works in a city and has no experience of anything outside it – often used to show disapproval

city-'state / $ '.. ,., ,.. './ n [C] an independent state that consists of a city and the surrounding country area, especially in the past: *the city-state of Athens*

cit·y·wide /'sɪtiwaɪd/ adj involving all the areas of a city: *a citywide campaign to fight racism*

civ·ic /'sɪvɪk/ adj [only before noun] **1** relating to a town or city: *Jackson spent the day meeting with local religious and civic leaders.* **2** relating to the people who live in a town or city: *It is your civic duty to vote in the local elections.* | *The local art museum is a source of civic pride* (=people's pride in their own city).

civic 'centre *BrE*; **civic center** *AmE* n [C] **1** *BrE* an area in a city where all the public buildings are **2** *AmE* a large public building where events such as sports games and concerts are held

civ·ics /'sɪvɪks/ n [U] *especially AmE* a school subject dealing with the rights and duties of citizens and the way government works

civ·il S2 W2 /'sɪvəl/ adj
1 [only before noun] relating to the people who live in a country: **civil war/disturbance/unrest etc** (=fighting etc between different groups of people living in the same country) → CIVIL LIBERTY, CIVIL RIGHTS
2 [only before noun] relating to the ordinary people or things in a country that are not part of military, government, or religious organizations: *They were married in a civil ceremony in May.*
3 [only before noun] relating to the laws about the private affairs of citizens, such as laws about business or property, rather than laws about crime; → **civil law**, **criminal**: *Many civil cases can be settled out of court.*
4 polite in a formal but not very friendly way; → **civility**: *Try at least to be civil.*

civil de'fence *BrE*; **civil defense** *AmE* n [U] the organization of ordinary rather than military people to help defend their country from military attack

civil diso'bedience n [U] when people, especially a large group of people, refuse to obey a law in order to protest in a peaceful way against the government

civil engi'neering n [U] the planning, building, and repair of roads, bridges, large buildings etc —**civil engineer** n [C]

ci·vil·ian /sə'vɪljən/ n [C] anyone who is not a member of the military forces or the police: *Many innocent civilians were killed during the war.* —**civilian** adj [only before noun]: *It was difficult to return to civilian life after ten years in the military.*

ci·vil·i·ty /sə'vɪləti/ n *formal* **1** [U] polite behaviour which most people consider normal; → **civil**: *Please have the civility to knock before you enter next time.* **2** civilities [plural] something that you say or do in order to be polite: *We exchanged civilities when we were neighbours, but nothing more.*

civ·i·li·za·tion also **-isation** *BrE* /ˌsɪvəl-aɪ'zeɪʃən $ -vələ-/ n **1** [C,U] a society that is well organized and developed, used especially about a particular society in a particular place or at a particular time; → **civilized**: *modern American civilization* | [+of] *the ancient civilizations of Greece and Rome* **2** [U] all the societies in the world considered as a whole: *The book explores the relationship between religion and civilization.* | *the dawn of civilization* (=the beginning of civilization) **3** [U] a place such as a city where you feel comfortable, especially because it is modern; → **civilized**: *After a week in the mountains all I wanted to do was get back to civilization.*

civ·i·lize also **-ise** *BrE* /'sɪvəl-aɪz/ v [T] **1** to influence someone's behaviour, making or teaching them to act in a more sensible or gentle way: *Andrea was a great civilizing influence on her husband.* **2** to improve a society so that it is more organized and developed, and often more fair or comfortable: *Ellis was credited with civilizing the Texas prison system.*

civ·i·lized also **-ised** *BrE* /'sɪvəl-aɪzd/ adj **1** a civilized society is well organized and developed, and has fair laws and customs; → **civilization**: *Such things should not be allowed to happen in a civilized society.* **2** pleasant and comfortable; → **civilized**: *'This is very civilized,' she said, lying back in the sun with a gin and tonic.* **3** behaving in a polite sensible way instead of getting angry: *Let's try and be civilized about this, shall we?* **4** a civilized hour a time that is not too early in the morning: *Can't we have the meeting at a more civilized hour?*

civil law n [U] the area of law relating to the affairs of private citizens rather than crime; → **criminal law**

civil liberty n [U] also **civil liberties** the right of all citizens to be free to do whatever they want while respecting the rights of other people

civil list n the civil list the sum of money given each year by Parliament to the King or Queen of Britain and members of their family

civil 'rights n [plural] the rights that every person should have, such as the right to vote or to be treated fairly by the law, whatever their sex, race, or religion: **civil rights demonstration/movement etc** *a civil rights leader* → BILL OF RIGHTS

civil 'servant n [C] someone employed in the civil service

civil 'service n the civil service the government departments that manage the affairs of the country

civil 'war n [C,U] a war in which opposing groups of people from the same country fight each other in order to gain political control: *the Spanish civil war*

civ·vies, **civies** /'sɪvɪz/ n [plural] *informal* ordinary clothes, rather than military uniform: *Sam! I didn't recognise you in civvies.*

civ·vy street /'sɪvi striːt/ n [U] *BrE old-fashioned informal* ordinary life as it is lived outside the army, navy, or air force: *I bet your family will be glad to see you when you get back to civvy street.*

CJD /ˌsiː dʒeɪ 'diː/ n [U] the abbreviation of *Creutzfeldt-Jakob disease*

cl *plural* **cl** or **cls** the written abbreviation of *centilitre* or *centilitres*

clack /klæk/ v [I] to make a continuous short hard sound: *the sound of high heels clacking across the courtyard* —**clack** n [singular]: *the clack of typewriters*

clad /klæd/ adj *literary* **1** wearing a particular kind of clothing: [+in] *She felt hot, despite being clad only in a thin cotton dress.* | **warmly/suitably/scantily clad** (=dressed warmly etc) **2 snow-clad/ivy-clad etc** covered in a particular thing: *an armour-clad ship*

clad·ding /'klædɪŋ/ n [U] *especially BrE* a cover of hard material that protects the outside of a building, piece of equipment etc: *decorative timber cladding*

claim¹ S1 W1 /kleɪm/ v
1 TRUTH [T] to state that something is true, even though it has not been proved: **claim (that)** *The company claims that their product 'makes you thin without dieting'.* | **claim to do/be sth** *No responsible therapist will claim to cure your insomnia.* | *I don't claim to be a feminist, but I'd like to see more women in managerial posts.* | **claim to have done sth** *Two young girls claim to have seen the fairies.* | **claim responsibility/credit (for sth)** (=say officially that you are responsible for something that has happened) *The group claimed responsibility for a series of bombings.* | *Opposition leaders will claim victory if the turnout is lower than 50%.* | **claim sb/sth as sth** *A letter appeared in The Times claiming Fleming as the discoverer of penicillin.*
2 MONEY [I,T] to officially demand or receive money from an organization because you have a right to it: **claim sth back** *He should be able to claim the price of the ticket back.* | [+on] *BrE: You can claim on the insurance if you have an accident while on holiday.* | **claim benefit/an allowance/damages etc** *If you're still not satisfied, you may be able to claim compensation.*
3 LEGAL RIGHT [T] to state that you have a right to take or have something that is legally yours: *The majority of those who claim asylum are genuine refugees.* | *Lost property can be claimed between 10 a.m. and 4 p.m.*
4 DEATH [T] if a war, accident etc claims lives, people die because of it – used especially in news reports: *The earthquake has so far claimed over 3000 lives.*
5 ATTENTION [T] if something claims your attention, you notice and consider it carefully: *The military conflict continues to claim our undivided attention.*

claim² S2 W1 n [C]
1 TRUTH a statement that something is true, even though it has not been proved: **claim that** *Gould rejected claims that he had acted irresponsibly.* | **false/extravagant/dubious etc claims** *firms that make false claims about their products* | *They made claims they couldn't live up to.* | *the competing claims of scientists* | **dispute/deny/reject a claim** *The foreign affairs depart-*

ment has denied claims that the men were tortured. | *Evidence to* **support** *these* **claims** *is still lacking.* | **claim to do/be sth** *his claim to be the rightful owner of the painting* | I **make no claim** *to understand the complexities of the situation.*

2 MONEY **a)** an official request for money that you think you have a right to: [+**for**] *claims for compensation* | **reject/uphold/lose etc a claim** *A disabled man has lost his claim for unfair dismissal.* | **make/put in/file a claim** *All claims should be made in writing.* | **pay/wage claim** (=a request from workers for more money) | *Fill in and return the* **claim form** *as soon as it arrives.* **b)** the sum of money you request when you make a claim: *The insurance company cannot* **meet** (=pay) *such enormous* **claims**.

3 RIGHTS a right to do something or to have something, especially because it belongs to you or because you deserve it: [+**to/on**] *Surely they* **have a rightful claim** *on their father's land?* | *The Maldives* **pressed** *its* **claim** *to hold next year's summit.* | *Philip feared Edward would* **lay claim to** *the Scottish crown.* | *the* **competing claims** *of parents and teachers* | **have a claim on sb's time/attention etc** *A woman who has given a man children will always have some claim on his love.*

4 **stake your claim (for sth)** to say that you have a right to own or do something, especially when other people also say they have a right to it: *Tickets are on a 'first come, first served' basis, so stake your claim now.*

5 **sb's/sth's claim to fame** a place or person's claim to fame is the reason why they are famous – often used humorously to mention something that is not very important: *My main claim to fame is that I once shook Elvis's hand.*

6 LAND something such as a piece of land that contains valuable minerals

clai·mant /'kleɪmənt/ *n* [C] someone who claims something, especially money, from the government, a court etc because they think they have a right to it: *benefit claimants*

clair·voy·ant /kleə'vɔɪənt $ kler-/ *n* [C] someone who says they can see what will happen in the future —**clairvoyance** *n* [U]: *the gifts of telepathy and clairvoyance* —**clairvoyant** *adj*

clam¹ /klæm/ *n* [C] **1** a SHELLFISH you can eat that has a shell in two parts that open up: *clam chowder* (=a type of soup) → see picture at SEA FOOD **2** **as happy as a clam** *AmE informal* very happy **3** *AmE informal* someone who does not say what they are thinking or feeling

clam² *v* **clammed, clamming**
clam up *phr v informal* to suddenly stop talking, especially when you are nervous or shy: *A sensitive child is likely just to clam up.*

clam·bake /'klæmbeɪk/ *n* [C] *AmE* an informal outdoor party near the sea, where clams are cooked and eaten

clam·ber /'klæmbə $ -ər/ *v* [I always + adv/prep] to climb or move slowly somewhere, using your hands and feet because it is difficult or steep: [+**over/across** etc] *They clambered over the slippery rocks.* | *We all clambered aboard and the boat pulled out.*

clam·my /'klæmi/ *adj* feeling unpleasantly wet, cold, and sticky: *Get your clammy hands off me!* —**clammily** *adv* —**clamminess** *n* [U]

clam·our¹ *BrE*; **clamor** *AmE* /'klæmə $ -ər/ *n* (singular, U] **1** a very loud noise made by a large group of people or animals: *He shouted over the rising clamour of voices.* **2** the expression of feelings of anger and shock by a large number of people – used especially in news reports: [+**for**] *Trouillot disregarded the growing* **public clamour** *for her resignation.* —**clamorous** *adj*

clamour² *BrE*; **clamor** *AmE v* [I] **1** [always + adv/ prep] to demand something loudly: [+**for**] *The audience cheered, clamoring for more.* | **clamour to do sth** *All his*

friends were clamouring to know where he'd been. **2** to talk or shout loudly: *Children clamored excitedly.*

clamp¹ /klæmp/ *v* [T] **1** [always + adv/prep] to put or hold something in a position so that it cannot move: *She clamped her hands over her ears.* | *Creed opened his mouth to speak, then* **clamped** *it* **shut**. **2** **clamp sanctions/restrictions etc on sb** to put limits on what someone is allowed to do: *The President clamped sanctions on the island after the bomb attack.* **3** [always + adv/prep] to hold two things together, using a clamp: *Clamp the two parts together until the glue dries.* **4** also **wheel-clamp** [usually passive] *BrE* to put a clamp on the wheel of a car so that the car cannot be driven away. This is usually done because the car is illegally parked; ▣ **boot** *AmE*: *He returned, only to discover his car had been clamped.*
clamp down *phr v* to take firm action to stop a particular type of crime: [+**on**] *The police are clamping down on drink-driving offenders.*

clamp² *n* [C] **1** a piece of equipment for holding things together **2** also **wheel clamp** *BrE* a metal object that is fastened to the wheel of a car so that the car cannot be driven away. This is usually done because the car is illegally parked; ▣ **boot** *AmE*

clamp·down /'klæmpdaʊn/ *n* [C usually singular] sudden firm action that is taken to reduce crime: [+**on**] *a clampdown on drug dealers*

clan /klæn/ *n* [C] **1** a large group of families that often share the same name: *the Campbell clan* | *warring clans* **2** *informal* a very large family: *The whole clan will be here over Christmas.*

clan·des·tine /klæn'destɨn/ *adj* done or kept secret: *a clandestine affair* | *clandestine meetings*

clang /klæŋ/ *v* [I,T] if a metal object clangs, or if you clang it, it makes a loud ringing sound: *The gates clanged shut behind her.* —**clang** *n* [singular]

clang·er /'klæŋə $ -ər/ *n* [C usually singular] *BrE informal* a silly or embarrassing mistake: *I can't help noticing the occasional clanger in war films.* | *He's being blamed for* **dropping a** *massive political* **clanger** (=making a silly or embarrassing remark).

clang·our, clangor /'klæŋə $ -ər/ *n* [U] *literary* a loud sound that continues for a long time

clank /klæŋk/ *v* [I] if a metal object clanks, it makes a loud heavy sound: *A tram clanked past.* —**clank** also **clanking** *n* [C]: *the clanking of machinery*

clan·nish /'klænɪʃ/ *adj written* a group of people who are clannish are very close to each other, and seem unfriendly towards strangers: *a small clannish community*

clans·man /'klænzmən/ *n plural* **clansmen** /-mən/ [C] a male member of a CLAN

clans·wom·an /'klænz,wʊmən/ *n plural* **clanswomen** /-,wɪmɪn/ [C] a female member of a CLAN

clap¹ /klæp/ *v* **clapped, clapping** **1** [I,T] to hit your hands against each other many times to make a sound that shows your approval, agreement, or enjoyment; → **applause**: *One man began to clap, and others joined in.* | *The couple were cheered and clapped on their arrival.* | *The audience clapped politely but without much enthusiasm.* **2** [T] if you clap your hands, you hit your hands together a few times to attract someone's attention or to show that you are pleased: *Narouz clapped his hands and a servant entered.* | *Mandy laughed and clapped her hands in delight.* **3** [T] to put your hand on something quickly and firmly: *'Mick!' She clapped her hand over her mouth. 'I'd forgotten!'* | *Ben grinned and clapped me amiably on the shoulder.* **4** **clap eyes on sb/sth** *BrE informal* to see someone or something, especially when you did not expect to: *Mark had loved the house from the moment he clapped eyes on it.* **5** **clap sb in prison/jail/irons** *literary* to suddenly put someone in prison or chains —**clapping** *n* [U]: *Each song was greeted with enthusiastic clapping.*

clap² *n* **1** [singular] the loud sound that you make when you hit your hands together many times to show that you enjoyed something: **give sb a clap** *BrE: Come on everyone, let's give Tommy a clap.* **2** [singular] a sudden loud noise: *an ear-splitting clap of thunder* **3 the clap** *informal* GONORRHEA

clap·board /ˈklæpbɔːd $ ˈklæbərd, ˈklæpbɔːrd/ *n* [C,U] *especially BrE* a set of boards used to cover the outside of a building, or one of these boards: *clapboard houses*

clapped-ˈout *adj BrE* a clapped-out car, machine etc is old and in very bad condition

clap·per /ˈklæpə $ -ər/ *n* [C] **1** the metal part inside a bell that hits it to make it ring **2 run/go/drive etc like the clappers** *BrE informal* to run, drive etc very fast

clap·trap /ˈklæptræp/ *n* [U] *informal* talk that is stupid or shows a lack of knowledge: *romantic claptrap*

clar·et /ˈklærət/ *n* **1** [C,U] red wine from the Bordeaux area of France: *a bottle of claret* **2** [U] a dark red colour —**claret** *adj*

clar·i·fi·ca·tion /ˌklærɪfɪˈkeɪʃən/ *n* [C,U] *formal* the act of making something clearer or easier to understand, or an explanation that makes something clearer: *There have been a number of official changes and clarifications.* | [+on/of] *Email us if you require further clarification on how to order.* | **seek/ask for clarification** *I asked for clarification on the legal position.*

clar·i·fy /ˈklærɪfaɪ/ *v* **clarified, clarifying, clarifies** [T] **1** *formal* to make something clearer or easier to understand; → **clarification**: *clarify issues/a statement/matters etc Could you clarify one or two points for me?* | *Reporters asked him to clarify his position* (=say exactly what his beliefs are) *on welfare reform.* | **clarify how/what etc** *The report aims to clarify how these conclusions were reached.* **2** to make something cleaner or purer by heating it: *clarified butter*

clar·i·net /ˌklærɪˈnet/ *n* [C] a musical instrument like a long black tube, that you play by blowing into it and pressing KEYs to change the notes —**clarinettist** *n* [C]

clar·i·on call /ˈklærɪən ˌkɔːl $ -ˌkɒːl/ *n* [C] *formal* a strong and direct request for people to do something: *This election is a clarion call for our country to face the challenges ahead.*

clar·i·ty /ˈklærəti/ *n* [U] **1** the clarity of a piece of writing, law, argument etc is its quality of being expressed clearly; → **clear**: *Letters may be edited for length and clarity.* | *a lack of clarity in the law on property rights* **2** the ability to think, understand, or remember something clearly; → **clear**: *He had only visited the village once, but remembered it with surprising clarity.* | **clarity of vision/purpose/thought etc** *Churchill's clarity of vision impressed all who knew him.* **3** the quality of being clear and easy to see or hear; → **clear**: *The picture was of such clarity that it could have been a photograph.*

clash¹ /klæʃ/ *v* **1** [I] if two armies, groups etc clash, they start fighting – used in news reports: *Troops clashed near the border.* | [+with] *Police have clashed with demonstrators again today.* **2** [I] if two people or groups clash, they argue because they have very different beliefs and opinions – used in news reports: [+with] *Democrats clashed with Republicans in a heated debate.* | [+over/on] *The two men have clashed over the report's conclusions.* **3** [I] if two colours or designs clash, they look very bad together: [+with] *I can't wear red – it clashes with my hair.* **4** [I] *especially BrE* if two events clash, they happen at the same time in a way that is inconvenient; **conflict** *AmE:* [+with] *The announcement has been delayed to avoid clashing with the Prime Minister's speech.* **5** [I,T] if two pieces of metal clash, or if you clash them, they make a loud ringing sound: *The cymbals clashed.*

clash² *n* [C] **1** a short fight between two armies or groups – used in news reports: *an escalation* (=increase) *of armed clashes along the border* | [+between/with] *violent clashes between police and demonstrators* **2** an argument between two people or groups because they have very different beliefs or opinions – used in news reports: [+between/with] *The*

company's expansion plans could put it in a **head-on clash** with environmentalists. | **personality/culture clash** (=a situation in which two people or groups do not like each other) **3** a sports match between two teams, players etc that is expected to be very exciting – used in sports reports: *The heavyweight clash goes ahead in Las Vegas on 8 May.* **4** a situation in which two events happen at the same time in a way that is inconvenient: *a scheduling clash on TV* **5** a loud sound made by two metal objects hitting each other: *the clash of swords* **6** a combination of two colours, designs etc that look bad together: *a colour clash*

clasp¹ /klɑːsp $ klæsp/ *n* **1** [C] a small metal object for fastening a bag, belt, piece of jewellery etc **2** [singular] a tight hold; **grip**: *the firm clasp of her hand*

clasp² *v* [T] *written* **1** to hold someone or something tightly, closing your fingers or arms around them; **grip**: *A baby monkey clasps its mother's fur tightly.* | **clasp your hands/arms around/behind sth** *Fenella leaned forward, clasping her hands around her knees.* | *She stood with her hands clasped tightly together.* | **clasp sb/sth in your hands/arms** *She clasped the photograph in her hands.* | **clasp sb to your chest/bosom** (=hold someone tightly with your arms) **2** to fasten something with a clasp

class¹ S1 W1 /klɑːs $ klæs/ *n*

1 SOCIAL GROUP a) [C] one of the groups in a society that different types of people are divided into according to their jobs, income, education etc: **professional/landowning/working etc class** *a Marxist view of the ruling classes* | *a member of the landed class* (=people who own land) | **class divisions/differences etc** | *social class inequalities* → LOWER CLASS, MIDDLE CLASS, UPPER CLASS, WORKING CLASS; → **the chattering classes** at CHATTER¹ (4) **b)** [U] the system in which people are divided into these groups: *Defining the concept of class is not an easy task.* | **class system/structure** *The old class system is slowly disappearing.*

2 STUDENTS [C, also + plural verb *BrE*] **a)** a group of students who are taught together; → **classmate**: **in a class** *We're in the same class for math.* | *Gary came top of the class in English.* | *My class are going to the Lake District.* **b)** *AmE* a group of students who finished studying together in the same year; → **classmate**: *a class reunion* | **the class of 1965/2001 etc** (=the group of students who finished in 1965 etc) *The class of '69 spent almost as much time protesting as learning.*

3 TEACHING PERIOD [C,U] a period of time during which someone teaches a group of people, especially in a school; **lesson** *BrE:* **geography/French/cooking etc class** *I missed Bible class last week.* | **in class** (=during the class) *No talking in class!* | *Were you late for class this morning?* | **have a class** *AmE: I have physics class at 9:30 on Tuesdays.*

4 STUDYING [C] a series of classes in a particular subject; **course** *BrE:* [+in] *a class in photography at night school* | **dance/aerobics/Greek etc class** *Dance classes start at 5:15.* | **take/attend/do a class** (=go to a series of classes) *Cindy's taking a class on dealing with stress.* | *He attended evening classes at the local college.*

5 SAME TYPE OF STH [C] a group of people, animals, or things that are considered together because they are similar in some way: [+of] *Have you passed a test for this class of vehicle?*

6 TRAIN/AIRCRAFT ETC [C usually singular] one of the different standards of seats, food etc available on a train, aircraft etc: **first/business/tourist etc class** *We always travel first class.*

7 QUALITY [C] a group into which people or things are divided according to their quality or abilities: **nicer/better etc class of sth** *The port now attracts a wealthier class of visitor.* | **in a class of its own/in a different class** (=better than everything else) *Its sheer versatility puts this computer in a different class.* | *He's not in the same class* (=not as good) *as her at tennis.*

C

8 STYLE/SKILL [U] *informal* a high level of style or skill in something; → **classy: have/show class** *The team showed real class in this afternoon's match.* | *A fountain will give your garden a touch of class.* | **class player/actress etc** | **a class act** *informal* (=someone who is skilful, attractive etc) *Laughton is a class act who's proved his worth in the game.* → HIGH-CLASS, LOW-CLASS
9 UNIVERSITY DEGREE [C] *BrE* one of the three levels of a university degree: *a second class degree*

class² *v* [T often passive] to consider people, things etc as belonging to a particular group, using an official system; ⊟ **classify: class sb/sth as sth** *Heroin and cocaine are classed as hard drugs.*

‚class 'action *n* [C] *AmE* a LAWSUIT arranged by a group of people for themselves and other people with the same problem —**class-action** *adj* [only before noun]: *class-action lawsuits*

‚class 'consciousness *n* [U] *technical* knowledge and understanding of the class system, and of your own and other people's social class

clas·sic¹ W3 /'klæsɪk/ *adj* [usually before noun]
1 TYPICAL having all the features that are typical or expected of a particular thing or situation: **classic example/mistake/case etc** *Too many job hunters make the classic mistake of thinking only about what's in it for them.*
2 ADMIRED admired by many people, and having a value that has continued for a long time: *The Coca-Cola bottle is one of the classic designs of the last century.* | *a collection of classic cars*
3 VERY GOOD of excellent quality: *Roy scored a classic goal in the 90th minute.*
4 TRADITIONAL a classic style of art or clothing is attractive in a simple traditional way; → **classical**: *She chose a classic navy suit for the ceremony.*

classic² *n* [C] **1** a book, play, or film that is important and has been admired for a long time: *'La Grande Illusion' is one of the classics of French cinema.* | **all-time/modern/design etc classic** *The play has become an American classic.* **2** something that is very good and one of the best examples of its kind: *What makes a car a classic?* **3 classics** [plural] the language, literature, and history of Ancient Rome and Greece; → **classicist**: *Judith studied classics at Oxford.*

clas·si·cal W3 /'klæsɪkəl/ *adj*
1 belonging to a traditional style or set of ideas: **classical ballet/dance etc** | *the classical theory of relativity*
2 relating to music that is considered to be important and serious and that has a value that continues for a long time: **classical music/musician/composer etc** *a leading classical violinist* | *a classical repertoire*
3 relating to the language, literature etc of Ancient Greece and Rome: *classical literature* | *a classical scholar* | *classical mythology*
4 also **classic** typical of a particular thing or situation: *the classical argument against democracy* —**classically** /-kli/ *adv*: *a classically trained singer* | *Classically, infection appears in the lower jaw.*

clas·si·cis·m /'klæs‚sɪzəm/ *n* [U] a style of art, literature etc that is simple, regular, and does not show strong emotions; → **realism, romanticism**

clas·si·cist /'klæs‚sɪst/ *n* [C] someone who studies CLASSICS

clas·si·fi·ca·tion /‚klæs‚f‚'keɪʃən/ *n* [C,U] a process in which you put something into the group or class it belongs to, or the group that it belongs to; → **classify**: *the classification of wines according to quality* | *There are five job classifications.*

clas·si·fied /'klæs‚faɪd/ *adj* classified information, documents etc are ones which the government has ordered to be kept secret

‚classified 'ad *n* [C] a small advertisement you put in a newspaper to buy or sell something; ⊟ **small ad** *BrE*; ⊟ **want ad** *AmE*

clas·si·fy /'klæs‚faɪ/ *v* classified, classifying, classifies [T] **1** to decide what group something belongs to; → **classification: classify sth as/under sth** *In law, beer is classified as a food product.* | *We'd classify Drabble's novels under 'Romance'.* | *Families are classified according to the father's occupation.* **2** to regard people or things as belonging to a particular group because they have similar qualities; → **classification**: *As a musician, Cage is hard to classify.* —**classifiable** *adj*

class·less /'klɑːsləs $ 'klæs-/ *adj* [usually before noun] a classless society is one in which people are not divided into different social classes: *Australia is the closest we have to a classless society.* —**classlessness** *n* [U]

class·mate /'klɑːsmeɪt $ 'klæs-/ *n* [C] a member of the same class in a school, college or, in the US, a university

class·room S3 W3 /'klɑːs-rʊm, -ruːm $ 'klæs-/ *n* [C] a room that you have lessons in at a school or college

‚class 'struggle also ‚class 'war *n* [singular, U] in MARXIST THEORY, political opposition and the fight for economic power between CAPITALISTS (=the owners of property, factories etc) and the PROLETARIAT (=the workers)

class·work /'klɑːswɜːk $ 'klæswɜːrk/ *n* [U] school work done by students while they are in a class rather than at home; ◳ **homework**

class·y /'klɑːsi $ 'klæsi/ *adj informal* fashionable and expensive: *classy restaurants*

clat·ter /'klætə $ -ər/ *v* **1** [I] if heavy hard objects clatter, or if you clatter them, they make a loud unpleasant noise: *The tray slipped and clattered to the floor.* **2** [I always + adv/prep] to move quickly and noisily: *children clattering up and down the stairs* —**clatter** *n* [singular, U]: *the clatter of dishes*

clause S3 W2 /klɔːz $ klɒːz/ *n* [C]
1 a part of a written law or legal document covering a particular subject of the whole law or document: *A confidentiality clause was added to the contract.*
2 *technical* a group of words that contains a subject and a verb, but which is usually only part of a sentence

claus·tro·pho·bi·a /‚klɔːstrə'fəʊbiə $ ‚klɒːstrə'foʊ-/ *n* [U] a strong fear of being in a small enclosed space or in a situation that limits what you can do; → **agoraphobia** —**claustrophobic** *adj*: *I get claustrophobic in elevators.* | *a claustrophobic atmosphere*

clav·i·chord /'klævɪkɔːd $ -kɔːrd/ *n* [C] a musical instrument like a piano, that was played especially in the past

clav·i·cle /'klævɪkəl/ *n* [C] *medical* a COLLARBONE

claw¹ /klɔː $ klɒː/ *n* [C] **1** a sharp curved nail on an animal, bird, or some insects: *The cat dug his claws into my leg.* | *lobster claws* → see picture at BIG CAT **2 get your claws into sb a)** if someone gets their claws into another person, they influence them in a harmful way: *The thought of Eloise getting her claws into the child made his blood run cold.* **b)** to say unpleasant things about someone in order to upset them: *Wait till the papers get their claws into him.* **3** the curved end of a tool or machine, used for lifting things: *a claw hammer*

claw² *v* [I,T] **1** to tear or pull at something, using claws or your fingers: [+at] *The cat keeps clawing at the rug.* | *Mary clawed at her husband's sleeve, trying to stop him.* **2 claw your way** to try very hard to reach a place or position, using a lot of effort and determination: **claw your way up/along/back etc** *He clawed his way forward inch by inch.* | *Benson clawed his way back into the lead.*
claw sth ⇔ back *phr v* **1** to get back something that you had lost, by trying very hard: *The company has managed to claw back its share of the market.* **2** *BrE* if a government or organization claws back money it has given to people, it takes it back

clay /kleɪ/ *n* [U] a type of heavy sticky earth that can be used for making pots, bricks etc → **feet of clay** at FOOT[1] (27)

clay 'pigeon ,shooting *n* [U] *BrE* a sport in which you shoot at circles of hard clay that are thrown up into the air; ▪ **skeet shooting** *AmE*

clean[1] W2 /kliːn/ *adj comparative* **cleaner,** *superlative* **cleanest**

1 NOT DIRTY without any dirt, marks etc; ▪ **dirty**

> **keep sth clean**
> **wipe sth clean** (=wipe a cloth over something so it is clean)
> **sweep/scrub etc sth clean** (=rub something hard with a cloth or brush so it is clean)
> **clean and tidy** *especially BrE*
> **neat and clean** *especially AmE*
> **nice and clean**
> **spotlessly/scrupulously clean** (=very clean)
> **as clean as a whistle** (=very clean)

> *Are your hands clean?* | *clean towels* | *Make sure you* **keep** *the wound* **clean.** | *Wipe that sink* **clean** *when you're done.* | *As usual, she left her room* **clean and tidy** *before going to school.* | *a* **spotlessly clean** *kitchen* | *I want you to get those plates* **as clean as a whistle.**

2 PEOPLE/ANIMALS having a clean appearance and habits: *Cats are naturally clean.*

3 ENVIRONMENT containing or producing nothing that is harmful; → **cleanly:** **clean air/water/ energy etc** *the Clean Air Act* | *cleaner fuels*

4 FAIR OR LEGAL a) done in a fair or legal way; ▪ **dirty:** *a clean fight* **b)** showing that you have followed the rules: *a clean driving licence* | *For the last three years, he's had a* **clean record. c)** [not before noun] *informal* not hiding any weapons or illegal drugs: *They searched him at the airport, but he was clean.* **d)** [not before noun] no longer taking illegal drugs: *Dave's been clean for two years now.*

5 NOT OFFENSIVE talk, jokes, behaviour etc that are clean are not offensive or about sex; ▪ **dirty:** *Oh, don't get mad – it's just* **good clean fun!** | **Keep it clean** (=do not offend people with what you say). | **clean living** (=a way of life which is healthy and moral)

6 come clean *informal* to finally tell the truth about something you have been hiding: [+about] *The government should come clean about its plans.*

7 make a clean breast of it to admit that you have done something wrong so that you no longer feel guilty

8 a clean break a complete and sudden separation from a person, organization, or situation: *Den left the next day, needing to* **make a clean break.**

9 clean sheet/slate a record of someone's work, behaviour, performance etc that shows they have not done anything wrong or made any mistakes: *Jed looked forward to starting life again with a clean slate.* | *Lewis has* **kept a clean sheet** *in every game* (=not let the other team score).

10 clean hands if a person, government, organization etc has clean hands, they have done something in a fair or legal way: *Neither side is coming to the negotiating table with completely clean hands.*

11 PAPER a piece of paper that is clean has not yet been used; ▪ **fresh**

12 SMOOTH having a smooth or regular edge or surface; → **cleanly:** *a clean cut* | *Use a clean, simple typeface for signs.*

13 a clean bill of health a report that says you are healthy or that a machine or building is safe: *Inspectors gave the factory a* **clean bill of health.**

14 a clean sweep a) a very impressive victory in a competition, election etc: [+for] *All the polls had pointed to a clean sweep for the Democrats.* | *Hopes that the French would* **make a clean sweep** *at the Games were dashed.* **b)** a complete change in a company or organization, often by removing people

15 TASTE having a fresh pleasant taste: *Add a little lemon juice to give the pasta a cool, clean taste.*

16 clean copy a piece of writing without mistakes or other marks written on it

17 MOVEMENT a clean movement in sport is skilful and exact: *He steadied his arm, hoping for a clean shot.*
—**cleanness** *n* [U] → CLEAN-CUT; → **keep your nose clean** at NOSE[1] (9)

> **WORD FOCUS: CLEAN**
> *very clean:* **spotless, pristine, immaculate, spick and span**

clean[2] S1 W3 *v* → SEE PICTURE ON NEXT PAGE

1 [I,T] to remove dirt from something by rubbing or washing; → **cleanse:** *Your shoes* **need cleaning.** | *Is it* **easy to clean?** | **clean sth down/off** *We clean the machines down at the end of each day.* | **clean sth off/from sth** *He used a tissue to clean his fingerprints off the gun.* → DRY-CLEAN; → **spring-clean** at SPRING-CLEANING

2 [I,T] to clean a building or other people's houses as your job: *Anne comes in to clean twice a week.*

3 clean your teeth *BrE* to make your teeth clean using a TOOTHBRUSH and TOOTHPASTE; ▪ **brush your teeth** *AmE*

4 [T] to remove the inside parts of an animal or bird before cooking it: *Harry caught the fish and cleaned them himself.*

5 clean your plate to eat all your food

> **WORD FOCUS: words meaning CLEAN**
> **wash** with soap and water | **wipe** with a damp cloth | **brush** with a brush to remove the dirt | **polish** by rubbing with a cloth | **scrub** by rubbing hard | **sweep** with a broom | **mop** with water and a mop (a tool with a long handle) | **vacuum** *also* **hoover** *BrE* with a machine that sucks up dust | **disinfect** using chemicals to kill germs | **cleanse** to clean your skin using a special cream | **rinse** to put water on to remove dirt or soap | **dust** to remove dust, for example with a cloth

clean sb/sth **out** *phr v*

1 clean sth ⇔ **out** to make the inside of a room, house etc clean or tidy: *We'd better clean out the attic this week.*

2 clean sb out *informal* if something expensive cleans you out, you spend so much money on it that you now have very little left: *Quite frankly, that trip to Paris cleaned me out.*

3 clean sb/sth out *informal* to steal everything from a place, or all of someone's possessions

clean up *phr v*

1 to make a place completely clean and tidy: *We spent all Saturday morning cleaning up.* | **clean sth** ⇔ **up** *plans to clean up the beaches* | [+after] *John always expects other people to clean up after him* (=to make a place clean after he has used it).

2 to wash yourself after you have got very dirty: **clean yourself up** *Let me just go clean myself up.* | *Dad's upstairs* **getting cleaned up.**

3 clean up your act *informal* to start behaving sensibly and responsibly: *Some companies could face heavy fines if they fail to clean up their act.*

4 *informal* to win a lot of money or make a lot of money in a business deal: *He cleaned up at the races yesterday.*

5 clean sth ⇔ **up** to improve moral standards in a place or organization: *It's high time British soccer* **cleaned up** *its* **image.** → CLEAN-UP

clean[3] *adv* used to emphasize the fact that an action or movement is complete and thorough: **clean away/ through/out** *The thieves got clean away with $300,000 worth of equipment.* | *The car hit her with such force that she was lifted clean off the ground.* | *Sorry, I clean* **forgot** (=completely forgot) *your birthday.*

clean[4] *n* [singular] *BrE* a process in which you clean something: *The car needs a good clean.*

,clean-'cut *adj* someone who is clean-cut looks neat and clean, and appears to have a good moral character: *clean-cut college boys*

clean·er S3 /'kliːnə $ -ər/ *n*

1 [C] *especially BrE* someone whose job is to clean other people's houses, offices etc

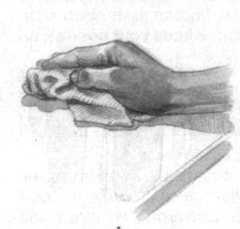

wipe

wipe up

dust

polish

mop

sweep

vacuum

wash up *BrE*/
wash dishes *AmE*

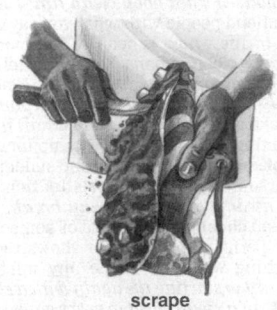

scrape

scrub

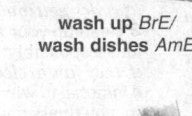

scour

wring

2 [C,U] a machine or substance used for cleaning: *a vacuum cleaner* | *toilet bowl cleaner*
3 the cleaner's a DRY CLEANER'S
4 take sb to the cleaner's *informal* **a)** to cheat someone and to take all their money or possessions **b)** to defeat someone completely: *The Lakers took the Bulls to the cleaner's, winning 96–72.*

clean·ing /'kli:nɪŋ/ *n* [U] the process of job of making a house, office etc clean: *Liz comes on Thursday to **do the cleaning**.* | **cleaning lady/woman** (=a woman who cleans houses, offices etc as her job)

clean·li·ness /'klenlin⅓s/ *n* [U] the practice of keeping yourself or the things around you clean: *a high standard of cleanliness*

clean·ly /'kli:nli/ *adv* **1** quickly and smoothly with a single movement: *The branch snapped cleanly in two.* **2** without producing dirt, pollution etc: *a fuel that burns cleanly without loss of power*

cleanse /klenz/ *v* [T] **1** to make something completely clean: *Use a piece of gauze to cleanse the cut.* | *The water is cleansed and reused.* **2** to remove everything that is bad or immoral from a person's character, an organization, or a place – used especially in news reports: **cleanse sb/sth of sth** *The mayor was elected on a promise to cleanse the city government of corruption.*
→ ETHNIC CLEANSING

cleans·er /'klenzə $ -ər/ *n* [C,U] **1** a substance used for removing dirt or MAKE-UP from your face **2** a substance containing chemicals that is used for cleaning surfaces inside a house, office etc: *cream cleanser for the bathroom*

clean-'shaven *adj* a man who is clean-shaven does not have a BEARD or MOUSTACHE

clean-up also **clean·up** /'kli:nʌp/ *n* [C usually singular] a process by which you get rid of dirt or waste from a place: *The cleanup of the oil spill took months.* | *millions of dollars in clean-up costs*

clear¹ S1 W1 /klɪə $ klɪr/ *adj comparative* **clearer**, *superlative* **clearest**
1 EASY TO UNDERSTAND expressed in a simple and direct way so that people understand; → **clarity**, **clearly:** *clear instructions* | *The question wasn't very clear.* | *It's the clearest guide I've used.* | [+**about**] *The school is clear about its policy on bullying.* | **clear about what/when/how etc** *Be very clear about what jobs should be completed, and by when.* | [+**on**] *The rules are quite clear on the point.* | [+**to**] *It was clear to him that Tolkien was a literary genius.* | **make sth clear** *The bishop made his views clear in a letter to the publisher.* | *How can you make the meaning clearer?* | **make it clear that** *Make it clear that you will not take sides.* | **absolutely/abundantly clear** *Can I make it absolutely clear that we did not intend this to happen?* | *Perhaps I tried to cover too much and didn't **make myself clear*** (=express myself well). | *If you don't understand, it's best to say so and **get things clear**.* | *I catch you smoking again, you're grounded. **Do I make myself clear** (=used when you are angry)?* | **clear picture/idea** (=a good understanding) *The report gave a clear picture of the property's condition.* | *He writes **crystal clear** (=very easy to understand) prose.*
2 IMPOSSIBLE TO DOUBT impossible to doubt, question, or make a mistake about; → **clearly:** *clear evidence of guilt* | *They won by a clear majority.* | **it is clear whether/why/how etc** *It is not yet clear whether he shares these views.* | **it is clear (that)** *It is clear that the drug does benefit some patients.* | *When it became clear that I was going to have a baby, he left me.* | **clear case/example of sth** *a clear case of sexual discrimination*
3 SURE ABOUT STH feeling certain that you know or understand something; → **clearly:** [+**about/on**] *Are you all clear now about what you have to do?* | **clear whether/what/how etc** *I'm still not really clear how this machine works.* | *Let me **get this clear** - you hadn't seen her in three days?* | *a clearer understanding of the issues*
4 THINKING able to think sensibly and quickly; →

clarity, **clearly:** *She felt that her thinking was clearer now.* | *In the morning, with a **clear head**, she'd tackle the problem.*
5 SUBSTANCE/LIQUID easy to see through, rather than coloured or dirty; ▪ **transparent**; ▫ **cloudy**, **opaque:** *clear glass bottles* | *a **crystal clear** mountain lake*
6 WEATHER clean and fresh, without clouds or mist: *a clear June morning* | *The skies were clear and blue.*
7 EYES healthy, very pure in colour, and without any redness: *clear blue eyes*
8 SKIN smooth and without any red spots: *a clear complexion*
9 EASY TO SEE having details, edges, lines etc that are easy to see, or shapes that are easy to recognize; → **clarity:** *a TV with a clear picture and high-quality sound*
10 EASY TO HEAR easy to hear, and therefore easy to understand; → **clarity, clearly:** *a clear speaking voice* | *The radio reception isn't very clear.* | *It's a good recording; the sound is **as clear as a bell*** (=very clear).
11 AFTER TAX a clear amount of profit, wages etc is what is left after taxes have been paid on it; ▪ **net:** *I get £200 a week clear.* | *Sam makes a clear $90,000 per year.*
12 a clear conscience the knowledge that you have done the right thing and should not feel guilty: *I don't think I could vote for him with a clear conscience.* | *She had done what she could and her conscience was clear.*
13 PERIOD OF TIME without any planned activities or events: *Next Monday is clear; how about 10 o'clock?* | *Leave at least one clear day between the flight and any business meetings.*
14 NOT BUSY complete or whole: *Allow three clear days for delivery.*
15 NOT BLOCKED/COVERED not covered or blocked by anything that stops you from doing or seeing what you want: *The roads were fairly clear this morning.* | **clear view/look** *From the top floor you get a clear view of the bay.* | [+**of**] *To prevent fires, the sides of the roads are kept clear of underbrush.*
16 see your way clear (to doing sth) *informal* to have the necessary time or willingness to be able to do something: *We expect good results soon, if the board can see its way clear to continuing funding the project.*
17 be clear of sth to not be touching something, or to be past someone or something: *Wait to cross until the street is clear of cars.* | *The curtains should be a couple of inches clear of the floor.*
18 as clear as mud *spoken* used humorously to say that something is very difficult to understand → ALL CLEAR; → **the coast is clear** at COAST¹ (2) —**clearness** *n* [U]

clear² S1 W2 *v*
1 SURFACE/PLACE [T] to make somewhere emptier or tidier by removing things from it: *Snowplows have been out clearing the roads.* | **clear sth of sth** *Large area of land had been cleared of forest.* | **clear sth from sth** *Workers have been clearing the wreckage from the tracks.* | *Dad **cleared a space*** (=moved things so that there was room) *in the garage for Jim's tools.* | *It's Kelly's turn to **clear the table*** (=remove the dirty plates, forks etc).
2 REMOVE PEOPLE [T] to make people, cars etc leave a place: *Within minutes, police had cleared the area.* | **clear sb/sth from sth** *Crowds of demonstrators were cleared from the streets.*
3 CRIME/BLAME ETC [T usually passive] to prove that someone is not guilty of something: *Rawlings was cleared after new evidence was produced.* | **clear sb of (doing) sth** *Maya was cleared of manslaughter.* | *a long-running legal battle to **clear his name***
4 PERMISSION [T] **a)** to give or get official permission for something to be done: *He was cleared by doctors to resume skating in August.* | **clear sth with sb** *Defence policies must often be cleared with NATO allies first.* **b)** to give official permission for a person, ship, or air-

C

craft to enter or leave a country: *The plane took off as soon as it was cleared.*

5 clear your throat to cough in order to be able to speak with a clear voice

6 WEATHER also **clear up** [I] if the weather, sky, mist etc clears, it becomes better and there is more sun: *The haze usually clears by lunchtime.*

7 LIQUID [I] if a liquid clears, it becomes more transparent and you can see through it: *Wait for the water to clear before adding any fish.*

8 CHEQUE [I,T] if a cheque clears, or if a bank clears it, the bank allows the money to be paid into the account of the person whose name is on the cheque

9 GO OVER/PAST [T] to go over a fence, wall etc without touching it, or to go past or through something and no longer be in it: *The plane barely cleared the fence at the end of the runway.* | *Edwards cleared 18 feet in the pole vault.* | *The plane cleared Chinese airspace.*

10 clear a debt/loan to get rid of a debt by paying what you owe

11 clear your head/mind to stop worrying or thinking about something, or get rid of the effects of drinking too much alcohol: *A good walk might clear my head.*

12 FACE/EXPRESSION [I] *literary* if your face or expression clears, you stop looking worried or angry: *She looked embarrassed, but then her face cleared.*

13 clear the way for sth *written* to make it possible for a process to happen: *This agreement will clear the way for further talks.*

14 SKIN also **clear up** [I] if your skin clears, red marks on it disappear: *The rash has finally cleared.*

15 clear the air to do something to end an argument or bad situation, for example discuss a problem calmly

16 clear (sth through) customs to be allowed to take things through CUSTOMS

17 clear the decks to do all the work that needs to be done before you can do other things: *I'm trying to clear the decks before Christmas.*

18 EARN [T] *informal* to earn a particular amount of money after taxes have been paid on it: *Diane clears £20,000 a year.*

clear sth ⇔ **away** *phr v*
to make a place look tidier by removing things or putting things back where they belong: *When dinner was done and cleared away, Auntie Lou made some tea.* | *Homeowners are clearing away brush near their houses to prevent fires.*

clear off *phr v BrE informal*
to leave a place quickly: *They cleared off when they saw the police coming.* | **clear off!** (=used to tell someone angrily to go away)

clear out *phr v*
1 clear sth ⇔ **out** to make a place tidy by removing things from it and getting rid of them: *I need to clear out my closet.*
2 to leave a place or building quickly: *Wait to get on the train until the people getting off have cleared out.* | **clear out!** *BrE* (=used to tell someone angrily to go away) → **CLEAR-OUT**

clear up *phr v*
1 to make a place look tidier by putting things back where they belong: *I don't mind you using the kitchen as long as you clear up afterwards.* | **clear** sth ⇔ **up** *Adam, clear up this mess before your father sees it.* | [+after] *I get really tired of clearing up after you* (=tidying places that you have made untidy)
2 clear sth ⇔ **up** to explain or solve something, or make it easier to understand: *The White House hopes these problems can be cleared up soon.* | *There are a couple of points we need to clear up before the meeting begins.*
3 if the weather clears up, it gets better
4 if an illness or infection clears up, it disappears

clear³ *adv* **1** away from something, or out of the way: *Firefighters pulled her clear of the wreckage.* | *Please stand clear of the doors.* **2 keep/stay/steer clear (of sb/sth)** to avoid someone or something because of

possible danger or trouble: *If you're a beginner, steer clear of resorts with reputations for difficult skiing.* **3** *informal especially AmE* used to emphasize a long distance: *You can see clear to the hills.* → **loud and clear** at **LOUD²** (2)

clear⁴ *n* **in the clear** not guilty of something: *If Middlemass had spoken to Potter at 8:45, Potter was in the clear.*

clear·ance /ˈklɪərəns $ ˈklɪr-/ *n* **1** [C,U] the process of getting official permission or approval for something: *She'll race if she gets medical **clearance** from her doctor.* | *Morris did not have a **security clearance**.* **2** [C,U] official permission for a plane to take off or land: [+for] *The pilot requested clearance for an emergency landing.* **3** [C,U] the removal of unwanted things from a place: *the clearance of minefields* | **snow/land/slum etc clearance** *flooding caused by forest clearance* **4** [C,U] the amount of space around one object that is needed for it to avoid touching another object: *There was less than a foot's clearance between the ship's sides and the wharf.* **5** [C,U] a process by which a cheque goes from one bank to another **6** [C] an occasion when a player in a game such as football kicks the ball away from his or her GOAL

clearance sale *n* [C] an occasion when goods in a shop are sold cheaply in order to get rid of them

clear-cut¹ *adj* easy to understand or be certain about; ◨ **definite**: *There is not always a clear-cut distinction between right and wrong.*

clear-cut² *n* [C] *AmE* an area of forest that has been completely cut down —**clear-cut** *v* [T]

clear-headed *adj* able to think in a clear and sensible way

clear·ing /ˈklɪərɪŋ $ ˈklɪr-/ *n* [C] a small area in a forest where there are no trees

clearing bank *n* [C] one of the banks in Britain that uses a clearing house when dealing with other banks

clearing house *n* [C] **1** a central office where banks exchange cheques and other financial documents **2** an office that receives and gives out or sells information or goods for several other organizations: *a clearing house for data on comets and asteroids*

clear·ly S1 W1 /ˈklɪəli $ ˈklɪrli/ *adv*
1 [sentence adverb] without any doubt; ◨ **obviously**: *Clearly, ignoring him had been a mistake.*
2 in a way that is easy to see, hear, or understand: *Please speak clearly.* | *The economy was clearly failing.*
3 in a way that is sensible: *I wasn't thinking clearly.*

clear-out *n* [C usually singular] *BrE* a process in which you get rid of unwanted objects or possessions: *I had a clear-out and got rid of a lot of old toys.*

clear-sighted *adj* able to understand a problem or situation well: *a clear-sighted analysis* —**clear-sightedness** *n* [U]

clear·way /ˈklɪəweɪ $ ˈklɪr-/ *n* [C] a road in Britain on which vehicles must not stop

cleat /kliːt/ *n* [C] **1** a small bar with two short arms around which ropes can be tied, especially on a ship **2** [usually plural] a short piece of rubber, metal etc attached to the bottom of a sports shoe; ◨ **stud 3 cleats** [plural] *AmE* a pair of sports shoes with these pieces attached to them, in order to prevent someone from slipping; → **spikes**; → see picture at **FOOTWEAR**

cleav·age /ˈkliːvɪdʒ/ *n* [C,U] **1** the space between a woman's breasts **2** *formal* a difference between two people or things that often causes problems or arguments

cleave /kliːv/ *v past tense* **cleaved**, **clove** /kləʊv $ kloʊv/, *or* **cleft** /kleft/, *past participle* **cleaved**, **cloven** /ˈkləʊvən $ ˈkloʊ-/ *or* **cleft 1** [I,T always + adv/prep] *literary* to cut something into separate parts using a heavy tool, or to be able to be cut in this way: *The wooden door had been cleft in two.* **2** [T] *formal* to divide something into two completely separate parts: *the racial problems that still cleave American society*

3 cleave the air/darkness etc *literary* to move quickly through the air etc: *His fist cleft the air.*

cleave to sb/sth *phr v* **1** *formal* to continue to think that a method, belief, person etc is true or valuable, even when this seems unlikely: *John still cleaves to his romantic ideals.* **2** *literary* to stick to someone or something, or seem to surround them

cleav·er /ˈkliːvə $ -ər/ *n* [C] a heavy knife for cutting up large pieces of meat

clef /klef/ *n* [C] a sign at the beginning of a line of written music to show the PITCH of the notes: **treble/bass clef**

cleft¹ /kleft/ *n* [C] **1** a natural crack in something, especially the surface of rocks or the Earth etc **2** an area on the chin or lip that goes slightly inwards

cleft² *adj* **be (caught) in a cleft stick** *BrE* to be in a very difficult situation in which any action or decision you make will cause problems

cleft³ a past tense and past participle of CLEAVE

cleft 'lip *n* [C] a split in someone's upper lip, that they are born with

cleft 'palate *n* [C] a split in the top of the inside of someone's mouth, that they are born with and that makes it difficult for them to speak clearly

clem·a·tis /ˈklemətɪs, klɪˈmeɪtɪs/ *n* [C,U] a plant that attaches itself to trees, buildings, fences etc as it grows, and that has white or coloured flowers

clem·en·cy /ˈklemənsi/ *n* [U] *formal* forgiveness and less severe punishment for a crime: **grant/give** sb **clemency** *She was granted clemency after killing her violent husband.*

clem·ent /ˈklemənt/ *adj formal* clement weather is neither too hot nor too cold; **▣ mild; ▣ inclement**

clem·en·tine /ˈklemənтiːn, -taɪn/ *n* [C] *BrE* a kind of small, sweet orange

clench /klentʃ/ *v* [T] **1 clench your fists/teeth/jaw etc** to hold your hands, teeth etc together tightly, usually because you feel angry or determined: *Jody was pacing the sidelines, her fists clenched.* **2** to hold something tightly in your hand or between your teeth: *a cigar clenched between his teeth*

cler·gy /ˈklɜːdʒi $ ˈklɜːr-/ *n* **the clergy** [plural] the official leaders of religious activities in organized religions, such as priests, RABBIS, and MULLAHS; → **clerical**: *the power of the clergy in the Middle Ages*

cler·gy·man /ˈklɜːdʒimən $ ˈklɜːr-/ *n plural* **clergymen** /-mən/ [C] a male member of the clergy

cler·gy·wom·an /ˈklɜːdʒi,wʊmən $ ˈklɜːr-/ *n plural* **clergywomen** /-,wɪmɪn/ [C] a female member of the clergy

cler·ic /ˈklerɪk/ *n* [C] a member of the clergy

cler·i·cal /ˈklerɪkəl/ *adj* **1** relating to office work, especially work such as keeping records or accounts: *a clerical error* | *clerical workers* **2** relating to the clergy: *a clerical collar*

clerk¹ /klɑːk $ klɜːrk/ *n* [C] **1** someone who keeps records or accounts in an office: *a clerk in a commercial firm* **2** *AmE* someone whose job is to help people in a shop: *the clerk in the shoe store* **3** *AmE* someone whose job is to help people when they arrive at and leave a hotel: *Leave the keys with the desk clerk.* **4** an official in charge of the records of a court, town council etc **5** *old use* a priest in the Church of England

clerk² *v* [I] *informal especially AmE* to work as a clerk

clerk of 'works *n plural* **clerks of works** [C] *BrE* someone who is in charge of repairs to the buildings in a particular place

clev·er S2 /ˈklevə $ -ər/ *adj* **1** *especially BrE* able to learn and understand things quickly; **▣ intelligent; ▣ smart** *AmE*: *a clever man* | **very/extremely/quite/pretty etc clever** *Lucy is quite clever and does well at school.* **2** able to use your intelligence to get what you want, especially in a slightly dishonest way: *a clever lawyer's tricks*

3 [not before noun] *especially BrE* skilful at doing a particular thing: *Bill's very clever with his hands.* | *his clever ball control* | **clever at doing** sth *He was clever at finding bargains.* **4** done or made in an unusual or interesting way that is very effective: *What a clever little gadget!* | *a clever marketing strategy* **5** *BrE spoken* used jokingly when someone has done something silly or stupid: *'When I got to the library I found I'd left the books at home.' 'That was clever!'* **6 clever clogs/dick** *BrE spoken* used to describe someone who is annoying because they are always right or always think they are right **7 be too clever by half** *BrE spoken* to be clever, and to show that you are clever in a way that annoys other people —**cleverly** *adv* —**cleverness** *n* [U]

cli·ché /ˈkliːʃeɪ $ kliːˈʃeɪ/ *n* [C] an idea or phrase that has been used so much that it is not effective or does not have any meaning any longer: *There is plenty of truth in the cliché that a trouble shared is a trouble halved.* —**clichéd** *adj*

click¹ S3 /klɪk/ *v*
1 [I,T] to make a short hard sound, or make something produce this sound: *The door clicked shut behind me.* | *Mother clicked her tongue* (=made a short sound to show disapproval) *and sighed.* | *Edmund clicked his fingers* (=made a short sound to get someone's attention) *for John to follow him.* | *Sergeant Vogel clicked his heels* (=hit the heels of his shoes together) *and bowed.* | *Twist the lever and the gears click into place.* **2** [I,T] to press a button on a computer MOUSE to choose something from the screen that you want the computer to do, or to press a button on a REMOTE CONTROL: *Choose the image you want by clicking twice.* | *Programs must grab a viewer's attention in the time it takes to click a TV remote.* | [+on] *Children can click on a sentence to hear it read aloud.* **3** [I] *informal* to suddenly understand or realize something: *It's hard work, but one day it will just click.* | *I thought, 'What is he doing?' and then suddenly it all clicked into place* (=I understood how all the events related to each other). **4** [I] *informal* if two people click, they like, understand, and agree with each other: *Petra and I clicked straight away.* **5** [I] *informal* to happen in a good or successful way, especially because people are working together well: *If everything clicks, we should have a good season.*

click² *n* [C] **1** a short hard sound: *The door closed with a click.* **2 the click of a mouse** used to show how quickly something can be done on a computer: *Your photos can be viewed with the click of a mouse.*

click·a·ble /ˈklɪkəbəl/ *adj* if a word or picture that you can see on a computer screen is clickable, it will connect you to more information when you click on it by pressing a button on the computer MOUSE

'click-through *n* [C] an advertisement on the Internet that you can click on for more information, and which allows the advertiser to know how many people are interested enough in their advertisement to do this: *Click-throughs are one of the standard ways to measure the effectiveness of online ads.* | *click-through rates*

cli·ent S3 W1 /ˈklaɪənt/ *n* [C]
1 someone who gets services or advice from a professional person, company, or organization; **▣ customer**: *a meeting with an important client* **2** *technical* a computer on a NETWORK that receives information from a SERVER (=large powerful computer)

cli·en·tele /ˌkliːənˈtel $ ˌklaɪən'tel, ˌkliː-/ *n* [singular] all the people who regularly use a shop, restaurant etc: *The restaurant attracts a young clientele.*

client 'state *n* [C] a country that is dependent on the support and protection of a more powerful country – used in news reports

cliff /klɪf/ n [C] a large area of rock or a mountain with a very steep side, often at the edge of the sea or a river → see picture at COUNTRY

cliff·hang·er /'klɪf,hæŋə $ -ər/ n [C] a situation in a story, film, or a competition that makes you feel very excited or nervous because you do not know what will happen or have to wait a long time to see how it will end: *Tonight's vote may be a cliffhanger.* | *the episode's cliffhanger ending* —**cliffhanging** adj

cli·mac·tic /klaɪ'mæktɪk/ adj forming a very exciting or important part of an event or story, especially near the end of it; → **climax**: *a climatic moment*

cli·mate W3 /'klaɪmɪt/ n
1 [C,U] the typical weather conditions in a particular area: *Los Angeles' warm, dry climate* | **climate change** (=a permanent change in weather conditions)
2 [C] an area with particular weather conditions: *These flowers will not grow in cold climates.*
3 [C usually singular] the general feeling or situation in a place at a particular time: **political/economic/social etc climate** *Small businesses are finding it hard to survive in the present economic climate.* | [+of] *a climate of growing racial intolerance in large cities*

cli·mat·ic /klaɪ'mætɪk/ adj [only before noun] relating to the weather in a particular area: *climatic conditions*

cli·ma·tol·o·gy /,klaɪmə'tɒlədʒi $ -'tɑː-/ n [U] the scientific study of climate —**climatologist** n [C]

cli·max[1] /'klaɪmæks/ n [C usually singular] **1** the most exciting or important part of a story or experience, which usually comes near the end; → **climactic**: [+of] *the climax of his naval career* | [+to] *a thrilling climax to the game* | *The festival reaches its climax with the traditional boat-burning ceremony.* **2** an ORGASM

climax[2] v **1** [I,T] if a situation, process, or story climaxes, it reaches its most important or exciting part: [+in/with] *a series of special events climaxing with a spectacular fireworks show* **2** [I] to have an ORGASM

climb[1] W2 /klaɪm/ v
1 MOVE UP/DOWN [I always + adv/prep, T] to move up, down, or across something using your feet and hands, especially when this is difficult to do: *Harry climbed the stairs.* | *Boys were climbing trees along the river bank.* | [+up/down/along etc] *The wall is too high to climb over.* | *They climbed up into the loft of the old barn.*
2 TEMPERATURE/PRICES ETC [I] to increase in number, amount, or level: *The temperature has climbed steadily since this morning.* | *Inflation climbed 2% last month.* | [+to] *The divorce rate had climbed to almost 30% of all marriages.*
3 WITH DIFFICULTY [I always + adv/prep] to move into, out of, or through something slowly and awkwardly: *The bus pulled in, and we climbed aboard.* | [+through/over/into etc] *John climbed through the window into the kitchen.* | *I turned the TV on and climbed into bed.*
4 PATH/SUN/PLANE [I] to move gradually to a higher position: *The roller coaster climbs 91 feet and reaches speeds of 45 miles an hour.* | [+into/up etc] *The path climbs high into the hills.* | *The plane climbed to 11,600 feet to try to get above the clouds.*
5 SPORT [I,T] to climb mountains or rocks as a sport: *Sir Edmund Hillary was the first man to climb Mount Everest.* | *She loves to hike and climb.* → CLIMBING
6 PLANT [I] to grow up a wall or other structure: **climbing rose/plant**
7 IN A LIST [I,T] to move higher in a list of teams, records etc as you become more popular or successful: [+to] *Their new album has climbed to number 2 in the US charts.*
8 IN YOUR LIFE/JOB [I,T] to move to a better position in your social or professional life: *Steve climbed rapidly in the sales division.* | *men who climbed the career ladder in the 1980s*
9 be climbing the walls spoken to become extremely anxious, annoyed, or impatient: *If I don't get a drink soon, I'll be climbing the walls.*

climb down phr v BrE to admit that you were wrong, especially after being certain that you were right

climb[2] n
1 MOVEMENT UPWARDS [C usually singular] a process in which you move up towards a place, especially while using a lot of effort: *a long, steady climb to the top*
2 INCREASE [C usually singular] an increase in value or amount: *The dollar continued its climb against the yen.* | [+in] *a steady climb in house prices*
3 IMPROVEMENT [C usually singular] the process of improving something, especially your professional or social position: *a slow climb out of the recession* | [+to] *the Labour Party's climb to power*
4 LIST/COMPETITION [singular] a process in which someone or something gets a higher position in a list or in a competition because of being popular or successful: *the Giants' climb from twelfth to fifth in the league* | *the song's steady climb up the charts*
5 ROCK/MOUNTAIN [C] a steep rock, cliff, or mountain you climb up: *one of the hardest rock climbs in the world*

climb-down n [C usually singular] BrE an occasion when you admit that you were wrong: *a humiliating climb-down by the government*

climb·er /'klaɪmə $ -ər/ n [C] **1** someone who climbs as a sport: *a mountain climber* **2** a person or animal that can climb easily: *Monkeys are good climbers.* **3** a plant that grows up a wall or other structure → SOCIAL CLIMBER

climb·ing /'klaɪmɪŋ/ n [U] the sport of climbing mountains or rocks: *a climbing rope* | **rock/mountain climbing** | *He goes climbing nearly every weekend.*

climbing frame n [C] BrE a structure for children to climb on, made from metal bars, wood, or rope; ▣ **jungle gym** AmE

clime /klaɪm/ n [C usually plural] literary a place that has a particular type of CLIMATE: *sunnier climes*

clinch[1] /klɪntʃ/ v **1** [T] to finally agree on something or get something after trying very hard: *a young salesman eager to clinch the deal* | **clinch a match/championship/victory etc** *A last-minute touchdown clinched the game for the Saints.* **2 clinch it** informal if an event, situation, process etc clinches it, it makes someone finally decide to do something that they were already thinking of doing: *We'd talked about moving, and the burglary clinched it for us.* **3** [I] if two people clinch, they hold each other's arms tightly, especially when they are fighting

clinch[2] n [C] **1** a situation in which two people hold each other's arms tightly, especially when they are fighting **2** a situation in which two people who love each other hold each other tightly; ▣ **embrace**

clinch·er /'klɪntʃə $ -ər/ n [C] informal a fact, action, or remark that finally persuades someone to do something, or that ends an argument, discussion, or competition: *Sixsmith scored the clincher after 81 minutes.*

cline /klaɪn/ n [C] technical a series of very small differences in a group of things of the same kind; ▣ **continuum**

cling /klɪŋ/ v past tense and past participle **clung** /klʌŋ/ [I] **1** [always + adv/prep] to hold someone or something tightly, especially because you do not feel safe: [+to/on/at etc] *He wailed and clung to his mother.* | *Passengers clung desperately onto the lifeboats.* **2** [always + adv/prep] to stick to someone or something, or seem to surround them: [+to/around etc] *His wet shirt clung to his body.* | *The smell of cigarette smoke clung to her clothes.* **3** to stay close to someone all the time because you are too dependent on them or do not feel safe – used to show disapproval: *Some children tend to cling on their first day at school.* | *a less clinging wife*

cling on phr v to continue trying to stay in power, in business etc: *Other businesses cling on and hope.*

cling to sth also **cling on to** sth phr v **1** to continue to believe or do something, even though it may not be true or useful any longer: **cling to the hope/belief/idea etc (that)** *He clung to the hope that she would be cured.* **2** to stay in a position of power or stay ahead, when this is difficult, or to try to do this: *an attempt to cling to power*

cling·film /'klɪŋfɪlm/ *n* [U] *BrE trademark* very thin transparent plastic, used to cover food and keep it fresh; **⊟ plastic wrap** *AmE*

cling·y /'klɪŋi/ also **cling·ing** /'klɪŋɪŋ/ *adj* **1** someone who is clingy is too dependent on another person, and will often hold onto them – used to show disapproval: *a shy, clingy child* **2** clingy clothing or material sticks tightly to your body and shows its shape – use this to show approval: *She wore a clingy red dress.*

clin·ic /'klɪnɪk/ *n* [C] **1** a place, often in a hospital, where medical treatment is given to people who do not need to stay in the hospital: **dental/family planning/ antenatal etc clinic** *women attending an antenatal clinic* | *an appointment at an* **outpatient clinic** (=clinic for someone who does not need to stay in a hospital) **2** *especially BrE* a period of time during which doctors give treatment or advice to people with particular health problems: *The baby clinic is held on Monday afternoons.* **3** a meeting during which a professional person gives advice or help to people: *an MP's clinic* | *a free clinic on caring for roses* **4** *AmE* a place where medical treatment is given at a low cost: *the doctors who volunteer at the inner-city clinic* **5** *AmE* a group of doctors who work together and share the same offices; **⊟ practice** **6** an occasion when medical students are taught how to decide what illness a patient has and how to treat it

clin·i·cal W3 /'klɪnɪkəl/ *adj* **1** [only before noun] relating to treating or testing people who are sick: *The drug has undergone extensive* **clinical trials** (=tests to see if it is effective in treating people). | **clinical medicine/experience/training etc** (=medicine etc that deals directly with people, rather than with research or ideas) | *The therapy has helped people with* **clinical depression** (=a strong feeling of sadness, for which you need medical help). **2** relating to a hospital or clinic: *The program gives the students experience in a clinical setting.* **3** considering only the facts and not influenced by personal feelings: *A formal marriage agreement sounds clinical, but it can be a good idea.* **4** a clinical building or room is very plain and clean, but not attractive or comfortable: *The walls were painted a clinical white.* —**clinically** /-kli/ *adv*: *clinically tested drugs*

clinical ther'mometer *n* [C] a THERMOMETER for measuring the temperature of your body

cli·ni·cian /klɪ'nɪʃən/ *n* [C] a doctor who treats and examines people, rather than one who does RESEARCH

clink[1] /klɪŋk/ *v* [I,T] if two glass or metal objects clink, or if you clink them, they make a short ringing sound when they are hit together: *Spoons clinked against the crockery.*

clink[2] *n* [singular] **1** the short ringing sound made by metal or glass objects hitting each other: *the clink of glasses* **2** old-fashioned informal prison

clink·er /'klɪŋkə $ -ər/ *n* **1** [C,U] the hard material like rocks, which is left after coal has been burnt **2** [C] *AmE* a bad note in a musical performance: *The singer hit a real clinker.* **3** [C] *AmE informal* something or someone that is a total failure: *Most of the songs are good, but there are a few clinkers.*

clip[1] /klɪp/ *n*
1 FOR FASTENING [C] a small metal or plastic object that holds or fastens things together: *The wire is held on with a metal clip.* | *a wad of money in a gold clip* → BULLDOG CLIP, PAPERCLIP
2 FILM [C] a short part of a film or television programme that is shown by itself, especially as an advertisement: *clips from the new James Bond film*
3 GUN [C] a container for bullets which passes them quickly into the gun so that they can be fired

4 at a good/rapid/fast etc clip quickly: *Traffic was moving at a good clip.*
5 CUT [singular] *BrE* the act of cutting something to make it shorter or tidier: *I gave the hedge a clip.*
6 a clip round the ear/earhole *BrE informal* a short hit on the side of someone's head
7 NEWSPAPER [C] an article that is cut from a newspaper or magazine for a particular reason
8 $100/50 cents etc a clip *AmE informal* if things cost $100, 50 cents etc a clip, they cost that amount of money each

clip[2] *v* **clipped, clipping**
1 FASTEN [I always + adv/prep, T] to fasten something together or to be fastened together using a clip: **clip sth into/onto etc sth** *A microphone was clipped to his tie.* | *a stack of bills* **clipped together**
2 CUT [T] to cut small amounts of something in order to make it tidier: *The hedges had just been clipped.*
3 CUT FROM NEWSPAPER [T always + adv/prep] to cut an article or picture from a newspaper, magazine etc: **clip sth out of/from sth** *a cartoon clipped from a Minneapolis newspaper*
4 HIT [T] to hit something quickly at an angle, often by accident: *A truck swerved and clipped a parked car.*
5 REDUCE [T] to slightly reduce an amount, quantity etc – used in news reports: **clip sth off/from sth** *Gunnell clipped a second off the world record.*
6 clip sb's wings to restrict someone's freedom, activities, or power
7 clip sb round the ear/earhole *BrE informal* to hit someone quickly on the side of the head
8 TICKET [T] *BrE* to make a hole in a bus or train ticket to show that it has been used; **⊟ punch** *AmE*
9 clip your words to say words in a quick, short, and not very friendly way

'clip art *n* [U] images, photographs, or pictures that are on particular websites, CD-ROMS, and FLOPPY DISKS, and that you can copy and use in your own computer documents

clip·board /'klɪpbɔːd $ -bɔːrd/ *n* [C] **1** a small flat board with a CLIP on top that holds paper so that you can write on it → see picture at OFFICE **2** a part of a computer's MEMORY that stores information when you are moving it from one document to another

clip-'clop *n* [singular] the sound made by a horse as it walks on a hard surface —**clip-clop** *v* [I]

'clip joint *n* [C] *informal* a NIGHTCLUB that charges an unfairly high price for drinks

'clip-on *adj* [only before noun] attached to something with a CLIP: *clip-on earrings* —**clip-on** *n* [C]

clipped /klɪpt/ *adj* **1** cut so that it is short and neat: *a neatly clipped hedge* **2** a clipped voice is quick and clear but not very friendly

clip·per /'klɪpə $ -ər/ *n* **1** clippers [plural] a special tool with two blades, used for cutting small pieces from something: *nail clippers* **2** [C] a fast sailing ship used in the past

clip·ping /'klɪpɪŋ/ *n* [C] **1** an article or picture that has been cut out of a newspaper or magazine; **⊟ cutting: newspaper/press clippings** *old press clippings about movie stars* **2** [usually plural] a small piece cut from something bigger: *hedge clippings*

clique /kliːk/ *n* [C] a small group of people who think they are special and do not want other people to join them – used to show disapproval: [+of] *a ruling clique of officials* | *the cliques formed by high school students*

cliqu·ey /'kliːki/ also **cliqu·ish** /'kliːkɪʃ/ *adj* a cliquey organization, club etc has a lot of cliques or is controlled by them – used to show disapproval

clit·o·ris /'klɪtərɪs/ *n* [C] a small part of a woman's outer sexual organs, where she can feel sexual pleasure

Cllr *BrE* the written abbreviation of *councillor*

cloak[1] /kləʊk $ kloʊk/ *n* **1** [C] a warm piece of clothing like a coat without sleeves that hangs loosely from your shoulders **2** [singular] an organization, activity, or way of behaving that deliberately protects someone or keeps something secret: [+of] *the cloak of secrecy around the country's rulers* | [+for] *The political party is used as a cloak for terrorist activities.* | **under the cloak of sth** *prejudice hiding under the cloak of religion*

cloak² v [T usually passive] **1** to deliberately hide facts, feelings etc so that people do not see or understand them – used especially in news reports: **cloaked in secrecy/mystery** *The talks have been cloaked in secrecy.* **2** *literary* to cover something, for example with darkness or snow: [+in] *hills cloaked in mist* —**cloaked** adj: *The riders were cloaked* (=they wore cloaks).

cloak-and-'dagger adj [usually before noun] very secret and mysterious, and usually involving the work of SPIES: *a cloak-and-dagger operation*

cloak·room /'kləʊkrʊm, -ruːm $ 'kloʊk-/ n [C] **1** a small room where you can leave your coat; ⊟ **coatroom** AmE **2** BrE a room in a public building where there are toilets – used when you want to be polite; ⊟ **rest room** AmE: *Excuse me, where's the ladies' cloakroom?*

clob·ber¹ /'klɒbə $ 'klɑːbər/ v [T] *informal* **1** to hit someone very hard **2** to affect or punish someone or something badly, especially by making them lose money: *The paper got clobbered for libel.* | *The company has been clobbered by falling property prices.* **3** to defeat someone very easily in a way that is embarrassing for the team that loses: *The Dallas Cowboys clobbered the Buffalo Bills last night.*

clobber² n [U] BrE informal someone's possessions, especially their clothes: *Liam's football clobber*

cloche /klɒʃ $ kloʊʃ/ n [C] **1** a hat shaped like a bell, worn by women in the 1920s **2** BrE a glass or transparent plastic cover put over young plants to protect them during cold weather

clocks

stopwatch

grandfather clock

alarm clock

sundial

clock¹ [S2] [W3] /klɒk $ klɑːk/ n [C]
1 an instrument that shows what time it is, in a room or outside on a building: *The clock on the church tower said nine o'clock.* | *I lay there listening to the clock ticking.* | *Mary set her alarm clock for 6:30 am* (=made sure it would ring at 6:30). | *My clock stopped and I didn't wake up in time.* | *I heard the clock strike six.* | **by the hall/kitchen/church etc clock** (=according to a particular clock) *What time is it by the kitchen clock?* | **the clock is slow/fast** (=the clock is showing an earlier or later time than the real time) *The station clock was ten minutes slow.* | **wind (up) a clock** (=turn a key in a clock so that it keeps working) | **set a clock by sth** (=change the time on a clock according to the time on the television, radio etc) *I set my clock by the 6 o'clock news.* | **clock face** (=the front part of a clock) → ALARM

CLOCK, CARRIAGE CLOCK, CUCKOO CLOCK, GRANDFATHER CLOCK; → **watch the clock** at WATCH¹ (8)
2 around the clock also **round the clock** BrE all day and all night without stopping: *Kim has been working round the clock to finish it in time.*
3 put/turn the clock back a) also **set the clock back** AmE to go back to the way things were done in the past instead of doing things in a modern way – used in order to show disapproval: *The new employment bill will put the clock back fifty years.* **b)** to return to a good situation that you experienced in the past or to make someone remember such a situation: *The kids are all grown up now and you can't put the clocks back.*
4 put the clock(s) back/forward BrE to change the time shown on the clock to one hour earlier or later, when the time officially changes
5 the clocks go back/forward BrE the time changes officially to one hour earlier or later: *The clocks go back in October.*
6 against the clock a) if you work against the clock, you work as quickly as you can because you do not have much time: *Everyone is racing against the clock to get things ready in time.* **b)** if you run, swim etc against the clock, you run or swim a particular distance while your speed is measured
7 twenty-four hour clock a system for measuring time in which the hours of the day and night have numbers from 0 to 23
8 start/stop the clock to start or stop measuring how much time is left in a game or sport that has a time limit
9 the clock a) an instrument in a vehicle that measures how far it has travelled: **on the clock** *a car with 43,000 miles on the clock* **b)** an instrument in a vehicle that measures the speed at which it is travelling
10 run out the clock/kill the clock AmE if a team runs out the clock at the end of a game, it tries to keep the ball for the rest of the game so that its opponents cannot get any points → BIOLOGICAL CLOCK, BODY CLOCK, DANDELION CLOCK, TIME CLOCK

clock² v [T] **1** to cover a distance in a particular time, or to reach a particular speed in a race: *Karen won in the 300 metres, clocking 42.9 seconds.* | *the first steam engine to clock 100 miles an hour* **2** to measure or record the time or speed that someone or something is travelling at: **clock sb at/doing sth** *The police clocked him doing between 100 and 110 miles per hour.* **3** BrE informal to notice someone or something, or to look at them carefully: *Did you clock the bloke by the door?* **4** BrE to reduce the number of miles or kilometres shown on the instrument in a car that says how far it has gone, in order to sell the car for more money: *He knew the car had been clocked, but he couldn't prove it.*

clock in/on phr v especially BrE to record on a special card the time you arrive at or begin work; ⊟ **punch** in AmE: *I clock on at 8:30.*
clock off phr v BrE **1** informal to leave work at the end of the day: *What time do you clock off?* **2** to record on a special card the time you stop or leave work: *At this time a lot of service workers would be clocking off.*
clock out phr v especially BrE to record on a special card the time you stop or leave work; ⊟ **punch out** AmE
clock up sth phr v to reach or achieve a particular number or amount: *The Dodgers have clocked up six wins in a row.* | *I clocked up 90,000 miles in my Ford.* | *Councillor Scott has clocked up more than 25 years on the borough council.*

clock-'radio n [C] a machine that is a clock and a radio. You can set the clock to turn the radio on and wake you up.

'clock speed n [C, usually singular] *technical* a measurement of how quickly a computer's CPU (=main controlling part) can deal with instructions: *a clock speed of 1 gigahertz*

clock·watch·ing /'klɒk,wɒtʃɪŋ $ 'klɑːk,wɑːtʃɪŋ-, -,wɒːtʃ-/ n [U] BrE when you often look at a clock to see what time it is because you are bored or want to stop working —**clockwatcher** *n* [C]

clock·wise /ˈklɒk-waɪz $ ˈklɑːk-/ *adv* in the same direction in which the HANDS of a clock move; 🔄 **anticlockwise, counterclockwise**: *Screw the lid on clockwise.* —**clockwise** *adj* → ANTICLOCKWISE, COUNTERCLOCKWISE

clock·work /ˈklɒk-wɜːk $ ˈklɑːk-wɜːrk/ *n* [U] **1** *BrE* clockwork toys, trains, soldiers etc have machinery inside them that makes them move when you turn a key: *mechanical toys powered by clockwork* | *The tape was driven by a clockwork motor.* **2 go/run like clockwork** to happen in exactly the way you had planned: *The concert went like clockwork.* **3 like clockwork** also **(as) regular as clockwork** happening at the same time and in the same way every time: *Matt came round each Friday, regular as clockwork.* **4 with clockwork precision/accuracy** in an extremely exact way

clod /klɒd $ klɑːd/ *n* [C] **1** a lump of mud or earth **2** *informal* a stupid person

clod·hop·per /ˈklɒdˌhɒpə $ ˈklɑːdˌhɑːpər/ *n* [C] **1 clodhoppers** [plural] a pair of heavy strong shoes – used humorously **2** *BrE informal* someone who is awkward and rough

clog¹ /klɒg $ klɑːg/ also **clog up** *v* **clogged, clogging** [I,T] to block something or become blocked: *tourists whose cars clog the roads each summer* | [+**with**] *Over many years, the pipes had got clogged up with grease.* —**clogged** *adj*: *clogged highways*

clog² *n* [C usually plural] a shoe made of wood with a leather top that covers the front of your foot but not your heel → **clever clogs** at CLEVER (6); → **pop your clogs** at POP¹ (12); → see picture at FOOTWEAR

clois·ter /ˈklɔɪstə $ -ər/ *n* [C] **1** [usually plural] a covered passage that surrounds one side of a square garden in a church, MONASTERY etc **2** a building where MONKS or NUNS live

clois·tered /ˈklɔɪstəd $ -ərd/ *adj* **1** protected from the difficulties and demands of ordinary life: *Academics lead a cloistered life.* **2** a cloistered building contains cloisters

clone¹ /kləʊn $ kloʊn/ *n* [C] **1** *technical* an animal or plant produced by scientists from one cell of another animal or plant, so that they are exactly the same **2** *technical* a computer that is built as an exact copy of a more famous computer: *an IBM clone* **3** *informal* someone or something that looks and behaves exactly the same as someone or something else: [+**of**] *She's an exact clone of her sister!*

clone² *v* [T] **1** to make an exact copy of a plant or animal by taking a cell from it and developing it artificially **2** to copy the number of someone else's MOBILE PHONE onto a new CHIP and then use that number on a different telephone, so that the mobile phone's owner receives the telephone bill

clonk /klɒŋk $ klɑːŋk/ *n* [singular] the sound made when a heavy object falls to the ground or hits another heavy object —**clonk** *v* [I,T]

clop /klɒp $ klɑːp/ *v* **clopped, clopping** *v* [I] if a horse clops, its HOOVES make a loud sound as they touch the ground —**clop** *n* [singular]

close¹ S1 W1 /kləʊz $ kloʊz/ *v*

1 SHUT [I,T] to shut something in order to cover an opening, or to become shut in this way; 🔄 **shut**; 🔄 **open**; → **closed**: *Would you mind if I closed the window?* | *She closed the curtains.* | *Let me do the car door – it won't close properly.* | *Beth closed her eyes and tried to sleep.* | *She heard the door close behind her.*

2 MOVE PARTS TOGETHER [I,T] to move the parts of something together so that there is no longer a space between them: *Anne closed her book and stood up.*

3 SHUT FOR PERIOD OF TIME [I,T] also **close up** if a shop or building closes, or you close it, it stops being open to the public for a period of time; 🔄 **open**; 🔄 **shut** *BrE*; → **closed**: *The shops close at six.* | *Harry usually closes the store completely when he goes on vacation.*

4 STOP OPERATING [I,T] also **close down** if a company, shop etc closes, or you close it, it stops operating

permanently; 🔄 **shut down**; → **closed**: *We have reluctantly decided to close the factory.* | *The shop closed down some time last year.*

5 END [I,T] to end or to make something end, especially in a particular way: **close sth with/by etc** *I will now close the meeting by asking you to join me in a final toast.* | [+**with**] *The movie closes with an emotional reunion in Prague.* | **closing remarks** (=something you say at the end of a speech) *In her closing remarks, the judge urged the jury to consider the facts only.*

6 close an account to stop having and using a bank account or other financial account: *My husband closed all my credit card accounts without even asking me.*

7 IN MONEY MARKETS [I always + adv/prep] to be worth a particular amount of money at the end of a day's TRADING (=the buying and selling of shares) on the STOCK EXCHANGE: [+**at**] *The dollar closed at 64p against the pound.* [+**up/down**] *Their shares closed 27p up* (=worth 27p more).

8 close a deal/sale/contract etc to successfully agree a business deal, sale etc

9 OFFER FINISHES [I] to finish on a particular date; 🔄 **end**: *Our special offer closes on June 3.*

10 MAKE DISTANCE/DIFFERENCE SMALLER [I,T] to make the distance or difference between two things smaller: *an attempt to **close the gap** between the rich and poor* | [+**on**] *The other car was closing on us fast.*

11 MAKE STH UNAVAILABLE [T] to make taking part in an activity or using an opportunity no longer possible; → **closed**: *Bidding for the painting will close on Friday.* | *The country has now **closed its borders** to all foreign nationals* (=will not let foreigners in). | *The legislation aims to close a lot of legal loopholes.*

12 be closed if a subject is closed, you are no longer willing to discuss it: *It was a regrettable incident but I now consider the matter closed.*

13 close your doors (to sb) to stop operating permanently: *In 1977 the Skyfame Aircraft Museum closed its doors to the public for the last time.*

14 close your mind to/against sth to refuse to think about something: *She wanted to close her mind to the outside world.*

15 HOLD STH [I always + adv/prep, T] if someone's hands, arms etc close around something, or are closed around something, they hold it firmly: **close (sth) around/round/over etc sth** *Her left hand closed over his arm.* | *She reached for the keys and closed her hand tightly around them.*

16 WOUND also **close up** [I,T] if a wound closes, or if someone closes it, the edges grow together again or are sewn together: *The surgeon closed the incision neatly.*

17 close ranks a) if people close ranks, they join together to protect each other, especially because their group, organization etc is being criticized **b)** if soldiers close ranks, they stand closer together

18 close the book on sth to stop working on something, especially a police operation, because it is not making any progress: *Detectives had closed the book on the Hornsey Murders case three years previously.* → CLOSING DATE, CLOSING TIME; → **close/shut the door on sth** at DOOR (9); → **close your eyes to sth** at EYE¹ (16)

close down *phr v*

1 close sth ⇔ down if a company, shop etc closes down or is closed down, it stops operating permanently: *Paramount closed down its London office in 1968.*

2 *BrE* to stop broadcasting radio or television programmes at the end of the day: *BBC 2 closes down at 12:45 tonight.*

close in *phr v*

1 to move closer to someone or something, especially in order to attack them: *The snake closed in for the kill.* | [+**on/around/upon etc**] *enemy soldiers closing in on them from all sides*

2 if the night, bad weather etc closes in, it becomes darker or gets worse: *The sun had set and dusk was closing in.*

3 if the days close in, they become shorter because it is autumn

close sth ⇔ **off** *phr v*
to separate a road, room etc from the area around it so that people cannot go there or use it: *The roads into the docks were closed off by iron gates.*

close on sb/sth *phr v*
1 to get nearer to someone or something that is moving in front or ahead of you: *The patrol car was rapidly closing on us.*
2 *AmE* to successfully arrange a LOAN, especially in order to buy a house

close sth ⇔ **out** *phr v AmE*
1 to finish in a particular way: *The bond market closed out the week on a strong note.*
2 if a store closes out a type of goods, they sell all of them cheaply: *We're closing out this line of swimwear.*

close up *phr v*
1 close sth ⇔ **up** if a shop or building closes up or is closed up, it stops being open to the public for a period of time: *The resorts are all closed up for the season.*
2 close up shop to stop doing something for a period of time or permanently: *When it rains, there is no alternative but to close up shop.*
3 if a group of people close up, they move closer together
4 close sth ⇔ **up** if a wound closes up or if someone closes it up, the edges grow together again or are sewn together: *The scar is closing up nicely – it'll soon be time to take the stitches out.*
5 to become narrower or to shut: *The flowers close up at night.* | *Occasionally the channel widened then closed up tight again.*
6 to refuse to talk to someone about something: *The moment I said I was a police officer, everyone would close up like a clam.*

close with sb/sth *phr v*
1 to agree a business deal with someone: *It was such a good offer that I closed with him on the spot.*
2 *literary* to move towards someone in order to fight with them

---

WORD CHOICE: close, shut, lock, turn/switch off
In many contexts, the verbs **close** and **shut** can be used in exactly the same way: *Please close OR shut the gate.* | *The windows were all closed OR shut.* | *She closed OR shut her eyes.* | *The store closes OR shuts at 7.*
⚠ Use **close** for a road, border, or airport: *All the crossing points on the border have been closed (NOT shut).*
⚠ Before a noun, use **closed**: *a closed door (NOT shut door)*
⚠ You cannot say 'close someone somewhere'. Use **shut** or **lock** to say that someone is put in a room or building and cannot get out: *They shut her (NOT closed her) in her bedroom.* | *He was locked (NOT closed) in a cell.*
Use **switch off** or **turn off** with electrical things: *Will you turn off (NOT close) the TV?* | *I switched off (NOT closed) all the lights.*

---

close² S1 W1 /kləʊs $ kloʊs/ *adj comparative* **closer**, *superlative* **closest**
1 NEAR not far from someone or something; ⊟ **near**: *If you need to buy bread or milk, the closest shop is about a mile away.* | [+to] *Susan sat on a chair close to the window.* | *I don't mind where we go on vacation as long as it's close to a beach.* | *His eyes were small and close together.* | *There are several accounts of dolphins living in close proximity to humans* (=close to humans). | *The victim had been shot at close range* (=from very close).
2 NEAR IN TIME near to something in time: [+to] *It was close to one-fifteen a.m.* | [+together] *Our birthdays are quite close together.*
3 LIKELY TO HAPPEN seeming very likely to happen

or very likely to do something soon: **close to doing sth** *The two countries are close to signing a peace agreement.* | *We're close to clinching the deal.* | **close to death/tears/despair etc** *The old dog could barely whimper and seemed close to death.* | *The prosecution's main witness was close to tears as she described the events of that night.*
4 LIKE/LOVE if two people are close, they like or love each other very much: *My brother and I are very close.* | [+to] *I felt closer to Rob that evening than ever before.* | *Fiona and I have always been close friends.*
5 SIMILAR very similar to each other: [+to] *When I saw Henry with another woman I felt something close to jealousy.* | *Fitt was the closest thing to a socialist in the party.* | *Their newest model bears a close resemblance to* (=is very similar to) *that of their rival competitor.*
6 CAREFUL [usually before noun] looking at, thinking about, or watching something very carefully; → **closely**: **take/have/get a close look (at sth)** | *She lifted up Jenny's silver medallion to take a closer look.* | **keep a close watch/eye on** (=watch someone or something very carefully) *Don't worry, I'll keep a close eye on the kids.* | *You could have improved your answers by closer attention to detail.*
7 NUMBER/AMOUNT if a number or amount is close to another number or amount, it is not much higher or lower than it: *We don't know the exact figures, but about 10,000 might be a close approximation* (=close to the actual figure). | [+to] *Inflation is close to 7 percent.*
8 COMPETITION/ELECTION ETC finishing or being played, fought etc with both sides almost equal: *It was a close game that could have gone either way.* | **a close second/third etc** (=a finishing position in a competition that is very nearly second, third etc) | *The result is too close to call* (=so close that it is impossible to know who will win).
9 close relation/relative a member of your family such as your brother, sister, parent etc; ⊟ **distant**: *The wedding was attended by close family only.*
10 VERY NEARLY BAD used when you have only just managed to avoid something bad, dangerous, or embarrassing happening: *'Phew, that was close,' Frank said as he swerved to avoid the cyclist.* | **a close call/thing/shave** (=a situation in which something dangerous, embarrassing etc almost happens) *United had a close shave when Liverpool almost scored.*
11 ALMOST very nearly getting, finding, or achieving something: [+to] *At this point, the investigators were closer to the truth than they realized.*
12 keep in close contact/touch if two people keep in close contact, they see, talk to, or write to each other often: *Text messaging enables people to keep in close contact at all times.*
13 WORK/TALK TOGETHER relating to a situation in which people work well with each other or talk to each other often: *He retained very close links with France throughout his life.* | *What we need now is closer cooperation between the club and supporters.*
14 WITH LITTLE SPACE with little or no space around something or between things: *The horses are always eager for exercise after the close confinement of the stables.* | *The shoe is a close fit* (=there is no space around the foot). | *I find it difficult to read such close print* (=with letters printed so close together).
15 close/you're close/that's close *spoken* used to tell someone that they have almost guessed or answered something correctly: *'I reckon he must be about thirty-eight.' 'Close – he was forty last week.'*
16 close to the bone if something someone says is close to the bone, it makes you feel uncomfortable or offends you, especially because it is about something you do not want to admit is true
17 close, but no cigar *spoken* used when something someone does or says is almost correct or successful: *It was close, but no cigar for the Dodgers as they lost to the Reds 4–3.*
18 too close for comfort if something that happens is too close for comfort, it is near enough to make you feel nervous or afraid: *From somewhere too close for comfort*

19 close to home a) if a remark or criticism is close to home, it makes you feel uncomfortable because it is likely to be true: *His comments struck unpleasantly close to home.* **b)** if something unpleasant happens close to home, you are directly affected by it: *It's one thing seeing riots on TV, but when they happen so close to home it's a different matter.*

20 at close quarters if something happens or is done at close quarters, it happens inside a small space or is done from a short distance away: *The troops had been fighting at close quarters.*

21 WEATHER *BrE* uncomfortably warm because there seems to be no air: *The weather that night was hot and close, with a hint of thunder in the distance.*

22 UNWILLING TO TALK ABOUT STH [not before noun] unwilling to tell people about something; **≡ secretive:** [+about] *You're very close about your work, aren't you?*

23 UNWILLING TO SPEND MONEY [not before noun] not generous: [+with] *You won't get a penny out of Jack – he's very close with his money.*

24 a close shave when the hair on someone's face is cut very close to the skin

25 close work work that involves looking at or handling things in a very skilful, detailed, and careful way: *After years of close work, she could hardly see a thing if it was over a yard away.*

26 close vowel *technical* a close vowel is pronounced with only a small space between the tongue and the top of the mouth —**closeness** *n* [U]: *She had never had the physical or emotional closeness that she needed.* → **play your cards close to your chest** at CARD¹ (14)

close³ S3 W2 /kləʊs $ kloʊs/ *adv*

1 not far away; ≡ near: *Come a little closer, so you can see better.* | *Her father lives quite **close by**.* | *They were sitting **close together** on the couch.* | *A variety of good restaurants and cafés are **close at hand** (=very near).* | *James heard footsteps **close behind** him.* | *Ronnie sped off into the distance, with his brother's car following **close behind**.* | **stay/keep close** *We must all stay close.* | **hold/draw sb close** (=hold someone against your body) *He drew her close to him.*

2 close up/up close/close to from only a short distance away: *Now that I could see him close up, I saw that he was very attractive.*

3 close on sth/close to sth *spoken* used to talk about a number, amount etc that is almost exact, but not completely: *a voyage of close on 2000 miles*

4 come close (to doing sth) a) to almost do something: *I tell you, I was so mad I came close to hitting her.* | *She came so close to the finals she must have been bitterly disappointed to go out now.* **b)** to be almost as good as someone or something else: *It's not as good as his last movie, but it comes pretty close.*

5 a close run thing *BrE* a situation in which the people competing with each other are almost equal, so neither of them is more likely to win than the other: *The upcoming election looks likely to be a close run thing.*

6 close on the heels of sth very soon after something else: **come/follow close on the heels of sth** *Yet another scandal followed close on the heels of the senator's resignation.*

7 near to the surface of something: *An electric razor doesn't really shave as close as a blade.*

8 run sb close *BrE* to be almost as successful, skilful etc as someone else: *Last season United ran them close both at home and away.* → **sail close to the wind** at SAIL¹ (6)

close⁴ /kləʊz $ kloʊz/ *n* **1** [singular] *formal* the end of an activity or of a period of time: *At the close of trade, the Dow Jones index was 1.92 points down.* | *The monsoon season was **drawing to a close** (=ending).* | *The event **came to a close** (=finished) with a disco.* | *Finally the meeting was **brought to a close** (=he ended the meeting).* **2** [C usually singular] *BrE* the area and buildings surrounding a CATHE-DRAL

close⁵ /kləʊs $ kloʊs/ *n* [singular] *BrE* used in street names for a road that has only one way in or out: *Take a left turn into Brown's Close.*

close-cropped /ˌkləʊs ˈkrɒpt◂ $ ˌkloʊs ˈkrɑːpt◂/ *adj* close-cropped grass or hair is cut very short

closed S3 /kləʊzd $ kloʊzd/ *adj*

1 not open; **≡ shut; ⇄ open:** *Make sure all the windows are closed.* | *She kept her eyes **tightly closed** .*

2 [not before noun] if a shop, public building etc is closed, it is not open and people cannot enter or use it; **≡ shut; ⇄ open:** *The shops here are closed on Sundays.* | **closed to the public/visitors etc** *The castle is closed to visitors in winter.*

3 restricted to a particular group of people; **⇄ open:** *The golf club has **closed membership**.* | *a **closed meeting*** | *The police have a **closed circle** of suspects.*

4 not willing to accept new ideas or influences; **⇄ open:** *You're facing this situation with a **closed mind**.* | **closed society/world/way of life** *Venetian art in this period was a closed world.*

5 behind closed doors if something happens behind closed doors, it happens in private and the public are not allowed in: *It seems that the deal was made behind closed doors.* | *Football authorities ordered the club to play its next two games behind closed doors after the riots in February.*

6 a closed book (to sb) a subject or problem that someone does not know about or understand: *Mathematics has always been a closed book to me.*

7 a closed set (of sth) a restricted group, or a group that cannot change or grow: *The law is not a closed set of rules and principles.* → **in closed session** at SESSION (2)

closed 'captioned *adj AmE* if a television programme is closed captioned, you are able to read the words that are said at the bottom of your screen, if you have a special piece of equipment attached to your television

closed circuit 'television *n* [U] *CCTV* a system of cameras and television that is used in many public buildings and shopping centres to protect them from crime

closed-'door *adj* [only before noun] closed-door meetings or talks take place secretly

closed e'conomy *n* [C, usually singular] a country that does not trade with any other countries

close·down /'kləʊzdaʊn $ 'kloʊz-/ *n* **1** [C] a situation in which work in a company, factory etc stops, especially permanently; **≡ shutdown 2** [C,U] *BrE* the end of radio or television broadcasts each day

closed 'season *n* [C] *especially AmE* another form of CLOSE SEASON (1)

closed 'shop *n* [C] a company, factory etc where all the workers must belong to a particular TRADE UNION

close-fit·ting /ˌkləʊs ˈfɪtɪŋ◂ $ ˌkloʊs-/ *adj* close-fitting clothes are tight and show the shape of your body

close-knit /ˌkləʊs ˈnɪt◂ $ ˌkloʊs-/ also **closely-'knit** *adj* a close-knit group of people is one in which everyone knows each other well and gives each other support when they need it: *a close-knit community*

close·ly S2 W2 /'kləʊsli/ *adv*

1 very carefully: *The detective **watched** him **closely**, waiting for a reply.* | **closely controlled/guarded/monitored etc** *Political activity is closely controlled.* | *Details of the program are **a closely-guarded secret**.*

2 to a very great degree: *I have been **closely involved** in the work of both committees.* | *The successful applicant will be **working closely** with our international staff.* | *a creature that **closely resembles** a red monkey*

3 closely related/connected/associated etc if two or more things are closely related etc, there is a strong connection between them: *closely related subjects such as physics, chemistry, and maths* | *Her development as a*

C

writer is closely connected with her religion.
4 in a way that is close to other things in time or space: *a flash of lightning, followed closely by thunder* | *We were so closely packed in the elevator I could hardly move.*

close-mouthed /ˌkləʊs ˈmaʊðd◂ ˌ-ˈmaʊθ◂ $ ˌkloʊs-/ also **closed mouthed** /ˌkləʊzd- $ ˌkloʊzd-/ *AmE adj* not willing to say much because you are trying to keep a secret

close-out /ˈkləʊz aʊt $ ˈkloʊz-/ *adj AmE* **closeout sale/price** a sale or price that is intended to get rid of goods cheaply —**closeout** *n* [C]

close-run /ˌkləʊs ˈrʌn◂ $ ˌkloʊs- / *adj* [only before noun] *BrE* in a close-run competition, the winner succeeds by a very small distance or number of points, votes etc: *The Labour Party won the seat, but it was a close-run thing* (=they nearly failed).

close sea·son /ˈkləʊs ˌsiːzən $ ˈkloʊs-/ *n* [C] *BrE* **1** the period each year when particular animals, birds, or fish cannot legally be killed for sport; ➡ **open season**; ⊟ **closed season** *AmE* **2** the period of a year when particular sports are not normally played

close-set /ˌkləʊs ˈset◂ $ ˌkloʊs-/ *adj* close-set eyes are near to each other

clos·et¹ S3 /ˈklɒzɪ̇t $ ˈklɑː-, ˈklɒ:-/ *n* [C]
1 *especially AmE* a cupboard built into the wall of a room from the floor to the ceiling; ➡ **wardrobe**: *a closet full of beautiful clothes*
2 come out of the closet a) to tell people that you are HOMOSEXUAL after hiding the fact; ⊟ **come out b)** to admit something or to start to discuss something that was kept secret before
3 be in the closet *AmE informal* to not tell people that you are HOMOSEXUAL ➔ **WATER CLOSET**; ➔ **a skeleton in the closet** at SKELETON (5)

closet² *adj* **closet homosexual/alcoholic etc** someone who is a HOMOSEXUAL etc but who does not want to admit it: *a closet communist*

closet³ *v* [T usually passive] to shut someone in a room away from other people in order to discuss something private, to be alone etc: **be closeted with sb** | *All morning he'd been closeted with various officials.* | *Don't let her closet herself away in her room.*

close-up /ˈkləʊs ʌp $ ˈkloʊs-/ *n* [C,U] a photograph or part of a film in which the camera seems to have been very close to the picture it took: [+of] *a close-up of her face* | **in close-up** *Much of the movie is shot in close up.*

clos·ing¹ /ˈkləʊzɪŋ $ ˈkloʊ-/ *adj* [only before noun] happening or done at the end of an event or a period of time: **closing remarks/words/ceremony etc** *The judge gave his closing speech to the jury.* | **closing stages/seconds/minutes etc** *in the closing years of his life*

closing² *n* [U] the shutting of a factory, school, hospital etc permanently: [+of] *the closing of an old railway station*

closing date *n* [C] the last date on which it is possible to do something: [+for] *The closing date for applications is 6 August.*

closing time *n* [C,U] the time when a PUB in Britain must stop serving drinks and close

clo·sure /ˈkləʊʒə $ ˈkloʊʒər/ *n* **1** [C,U] when a factory, school, hospital etc has to close permanently: *Several military bases are threatened with closure.* | **factory/hospital/school etc closure** *the problem of school closures* | [+of] *the closure of St Bartholomew's Hospital* **2** [C,U] when a road, bridge etc is closed for a short time so that people cannot use it: *On the M40, there are lane closures near Oxford.* **3** [U] when an event or a period of time is brought to an end, or the feeling that something has been completely dealt with: *Funerals help give people a sense of closure.*

clot¹ /klɒt $ klɑːt/ *v* **clotted, clotting** [I,T] if a liquid such as blood or milk clots, or if something clots it, it becomes thicker and more solid ➔ CLOTTED CREAM

clot² *n* [C] **1** a thick almost solid mass formed when blood or milk dries: *He developed a blood clot on his brain and died.* **2** *BrE informal* a stupid person

cloth /klɒθ $ klɒːθ/ *n* **1** [U] material used for making things such as clothes: **cotton/woollen/silk etc cloth** *a dress of the finest silk cloth* **2** [C] a piece of cloth used for a particular purpose: *She mopped her face with a wet cloth.* | *Is there a clean cloth for the table?* ➔ DISHCLOTH, FACECLOTH, TABLECLOTH **3 man of the cloth** *formal* a Christian priest

cloth cap *n* [C] *BrE* a soft flat cap with a stiff pointed piece at the front

clothe /kləʊð $ kloʊð/ *v* [T usually passive] **1** *formal* to put clothes on your body; ⊟ **dress**: **be clothed in sth** *The King was clothed in a purple gown.* | **fully/partially/scantily etc clothed** *The children lay on the bed, fully clothed and fast asleep.* **2** to provide clothes for yourself or other people: *They could barely keep the family fed and clothed.*

clothes S2 W2 /kləʊðz, kləʊz $ kloʊðz, kloʊz/ *n* [plural] the things that people wear to cover their body or keep warm: *I enjoy shopping for clothes and shoes.* | *What sort of clothes was he wearing?* | **casual clothes** | **put on/take off clothes** *She had a shower and put on clean clothes.* | **change your clothes/change into clean/dry etc clothes** *The kids ran upstairs to change into dry clothes.* | **work/school etc clothes** *men dressed in ordinary street clothes* | *a clothes shop* ➔ **a change of clothes** at CHANGE² (6); ➔ **designer clothes** at DESIGNER²; ➔ PLAIN-CLOTHES

WORD CHOICE: clothes, clothing, garment, cloth
clothes are things that you wear, for example shirts and dresses: *I need some new clothes.* | *Do you ever wear your sister's clothes?*
⚠ **clothes** is always plural and has no singular form: *He was wearing nice clothes* (NOT *a nice clothe/clothes*).
Use **clothing** to talk about a particular type of clothes or when talking about making or selling clothes: *Special protective clothing is worn.* | *a clothing manufacturer*
⚠ This word is not used much in ordinary spoken language: *I went shopping for summer clothes* (NOT *clothing*).
In formal English, you can use **garment** or **piece/item/article of clothing** to refer to one thing you wear: *a long velvet garment* | *a discarded article of clothing*
But it is more usual to name the particular thing you mean: *He was wearing a long coat* (NOT *long garment*).
Cloth is the material that clothes are made from: *a suit made from fine woollen cloth*

clothes basket *n* [C] a large basket for clothes that need to be washed, dried, or IRONED

clothes brush *n* [C] *BrE* a brush used to remove dirt, dust etc from clothes

clothes hanger *n* [C] *BrE* a curved piece of metal, plastic, or wood with a hook on it that you use for hanging clothes; ⊟ **hanger** *AmE*

clothes horse *n* [C] **1** *BrE* a frame that you hang clothes on to dry indoors **2** *AmE informal* a woman who is very interested in clothes and who likes to have many different clothes – used to show disapproval

clothes·line /ˈkləʊðzlaɪn, ˈkləʊz- $ ˈkloʊðz-, ˈkloʊz-/ *n* [C] a long thin rope on which you hang clothes to dry outdoors; ⊟ **washing line** *BrE*

clothes peg *n* [C] *BrE* a wooden or plastic object that you use to fasten wet clothes to a clothesline; ⊟ **clothespin** *AmE*

cloth·i·er /ˈkləʊðiə $ ˈkloʊðiər/ *n* [C] *old-fashioned* someone who makes or sells men's clothes or material for clothes

cloth·ing /ˈkləʊðɪŋ $ ˈkloʊ-/ *n* [U] the clothes that people wear: *the basic necessities such as food and clothing* | **warm/outdoor/waterproof etc clothing** *Lab workers must wear protective clothing.* | **item/article/piece of clothing** *She took only a few items of clothing.* | *Remember to bring a change of clothing.* | **clothing manufacturer/industry/trade etc** *a clothing store*

clotted 'cream n [U] *BrE* very thick cream made by slowly heating milk and taking the cream from the top

clo·ture /ˈkləʊtʃə $ ˈkloʊtʃər/ n [C] *AmE technical* a way of ending an argument over a BILL in the US government and forcing a vote on it

cloud¹ S3 W3 /klaʊd/ n

1 IN THE SKY [C,U] a white or grey mass in the sky that forms from very small drops of water: **heavy/thick/dense etc clouds** *Dark clouds floated across the moon.* | *Heavy clouds had gathered over the summit of Mont Blanc.* | **low/high cloud** *Visibility was bad due to low cloud.* → STORM CLOUD, THUNDERCLOUD

2 IN THE AIR [C] a mass of dust, smoke etc in the air, or a large number of insects flying together: **cloud of dust/smoke/gas etc** *A cloud of steam rose into the air* | *clouds of mosquitoes buzzing around us*

3 PROBLEM [C] something that makes you feel afraid, worried. unhappy etc: **[+of]** *the cloud of economic recession* | **cloud on the horizon** (=something that might spoil a happy situation) *The only cloud on the horizon was her mother's illness.* | *Fears of renewed terrorist attacks* **cast a cloud** *over the event* (=spoilt the happy situation). | *He returned to New York* **under a cloud of** *gloom and despair.*

4 under a cloud (of suspicion) *informal* if someone is under a cloud, people have a bad opinion of them because they think they have done something wrong: *He left the company under a cloud of suspicion.*

5 be on cloud nine *informal* to be very happy about something

6 every cloud has a silver lining used to say that there is something good even in a situation that seems very sad or difficult

7 be/live in cloud-cuckoo-land *BrE* to think that a situation is much better than it really is, in a way that is slightly stupid → **have your head in the clouds** at HEAD¹ (24)

cloud² v **1** [T] to make someone less able to think clearly or make sensible decisions: **cloud sb's judgement/mind/vision etc** *Don't let your personal feelings cloud your judgement.* | *Fear had clouded his vision.* **2** also **cloud over** [I,T] if someone's face or eyes cloud, or if something clouds them, they start to look angry, sad, or worried: *Ann's eyes clouded with the pain.* | *Then suspicion clouded his face.* **3** [T usually passive] to make something less pleasant or more difficult than it should have been: *Her happiness was clouded by having to leave her son behind.* **4 cloud the issue/picture etc** to make a subject or problem more difficult to understand or deal with, especially by introducing unnecessary ideas: *Totally uninformed judgements only cloud the issue.* **5** also **cloud up** [I,T] if glass or a liquid clouds, or if something clouds it, it becomes less clear and more difficult to see through: *Our windows were clouded up with steam.* | *The water clouded and I could no longer see the river bed.* **6** [T] to cover something with clouds: *Thick mist clouded the mountaintops.*

cloud over phr v **1** also **cloud up** *AmE* if the sky clouds over, it becomes dark and full of black clouds **2** if someone's face or eyes cloud over, they start to look angry or sad: *His face clouded over in disappointment.*

cloud·bank /ˈklaʊdbæŋk/ n [C] *BrE* a thick mass of low cloud

cloud·burst /ˈklaʊdbɜːst $ -bɜːrst/ n [C] a sudden short rain storm

cloud·less /ˈklaʊdləs/ adj a cloudless sky is clear and has no clouds in it

cloud·y /ˈklaʊdi/ adj **1** a cloudy sky, day etc is dark because there are a lot of clouds; ◤ clear: *a cloudy night with some light rain* | *Tomorrow, it will be cloudy and cool.* **2** cloudy liquids are not clear: *a rather cloudy wine* **3** cloudy thoughts, memories etc are not very clear or exact

clout¹ /klaʊt/ n **1** [U] *informal* power or the authority to influence other people's decisions: **political/eco-**

283 | **club**

nomic etc clout *people with financial clout* | **the clout to do sth** *Few companies* **have the clout** *to handle such large deals.* | *An official protest could* **carry** *considerable clout.* **2** [C] *BrE informal* a hard blow given with the hand: *He* **gave** *him a* **clout** *round the ear.*

clout² v [T] *informal* to hit someone or something hard: *She clouted the boy across the face.*

clove¹ /kləʊv $ kloʊv/ n [C] **1** one of the separate parts that form a GARLIC plant: **a clove of garlic 2** a black SPICE (=something used to give a special taste to food) with a strong sweet smell

clove² a past tense of CLEAVE

clo·ven /ˈkləʊvən $ ˈkloʊ-/ a past participle of CLEAVE

cloven 'hoof n [C] the type of foot that sheep, cows, and goats have, that is divided into two parts

clo·ver /ˈkləʊvə $ ˈkloʊvər/ n [U] **1** a small plant, usually with three leaves on each stem. If you find one with four leaves, it is thought to bring you luck: *a four-leaf clover* → see picture at FLOWER **2 in clover** *informal* living comfortably because you have plenty of money: *The money* **kept** *him* **in clover** *for years.*

clover·leaf /ˈkləʊvəliːf $ ˈkloʊvər-/ n [C] **1** the leaf of a clover plant **2** a network of curved roads which connect two main roads where they cross

clown¹ /klaʊn/ n [C] **1** someone who wears funny clothes, a red nose, bright MAKE-UP on their face etc, and does silly things to make people laugh, especially at a CIRCUS **2** someone who often makes jokes or behaves in a funny way: *Frankie's a bit of a clown.* | **class clown** (=someone in a school class who behaves in a funny or silly way) **3** a stupid or annoying person: *I can't understand what she sees in that clown.*

clown² v also **clown around/about** [I] to behave in a silly or funny way: *Stop clowning around!*

clown·ish /ˈklaʊnɪʃ/ adj silly or stupid

cloy /klɔɪ/ v [I] if something sweet or pleasant cloys, it begins to annoy you because there is too much of it: *Her sweet submissive smile began to cloy after a while.*

cloy·ing /ˈklɔɪ-ɪŋ/ adj **1** a cloying attitude or quality annoys you because it is too sweet or nice: *cloying sentimentality* **2** cloying food or smells are sweet and make you feel sick: *the thick cloying smell of cheap perfume* —**cloyingly** adv

cloze test /ˈkləʊz test $ ˈkloʊz-/ n [C] a test in which words have been removed from a short piece of writing, and students have to write what they think are the correct words in the empty spaces

club¹ S1 W1 /klʌb/ n [C]

1 FOR AN ACTIVITY OR SPORT **a)** [also + plural verb *BrE*] an organization for people who share a particular interest or enjoy similar activities, or a group of people who meet together to do something they are interested in: **rugby/golf/squash etc club** *Our chess club really needs new members.* | **[+for]** *a club for unemployed young people* | *It costs £15 to* **join the club**. | *She* **belongs to** *a local health* **club**. **b)** the building or place where the members of a particular club meet or play sport: *We could have dinner at the golf club.* → COUNTRY CLUB, FAN CLUB, YOUTH CLUB

2 PROFESSIONAL SPORT [also + plural verb *BrE*] especially *BrE* a professional organization including the players, managers, and owners of a sports team: *Manchester United Football Club*

3 FOR DANCING/MUSIC a place where people go to dance, listen to music, and meet socially: *a jazz club* | *Shall we go to a club?* | *I'm not into the* **club scene** *at all.*

4 TRADITIONAL MEN'S CLUB especially *BrE* **a)** an organization, traditionally for men only, which provides a comfortable place to relax, eat, meet other members, or stay the night: *He always stays at his London club.* **b)** the building where this organization is based

5 book/record/wine etc club an organization which people join in order to buy books, records, wine etc cheaply

6 GOLF also **golf club** a long thin metal stick used in golf to hit the ball → see picture at BAT
7 WEAPON a thick heavy stick used to hit people or things
8 IN CARD GAMES a) **clubs** one of the four SUITS (=types of cards) in a set of playing cards, which has the design of three round black leaves in a group together: **ten/king etc of clubs** *the ace of clubs* b) a card from this suit: *You have to play a club.*
9 in the club BrE old-fashioned if a woman is in the club, she is going to have a baby – used humorously; ▣ **pregnant**
10 join the club also **welcome to the club** AmE spoken used after someone has described a bad situation that they are in, to tell them that you are in the same situation: *'He never listens to me.' 'Join the club.'*

club² *v* **clubbed, clubbing** [T] to hit someone hard with a heavy object: *baby seals being clubbed to death*
   club together *phr v* if people club together, they share the cost of something: *We clubbed together to buy her a present.*

club·ba·ble /ˈklʌbəbəl/ *adj* BrE interesting and good at talking in a friendly and relaxed way with other people

club·bing /ˈklʌbɪŋ/ *n* [U] *informal* the activity of going to NIGHTCLUBS: *She always goes clubbing when she's in New York.* —**clubber** *n* [C]

club·by /ˈklʌbi/ *adj informal* a clubby place is where everyone is very friendly to each other, but people who are outside their group are not very welcome: *the clubby atmosphere of the media*

club class *n* [U] a part of some planes where each seat has more space and more comfort than the usual seat, but is more expensive; ▣ **business class**

club 'foot *n* [C,U] a foot that has been badly twisted since birth and that prevents someone from walking properly —**club-footed** *adj*

club·house /ˈklʌbhaʊs/ *n* [C] a building used by a club, especially a sports club

club·land /ˈklʌb.lænd/ *n* [U] **1** the part of a town which contains a lot of NIGHTCLUBS: *New York's clubland* **2** the most popular NIGHTCLUBS and the people who go to them: *She's rapidly becoming a clubland favourite.*

club 'sandwich *n* [C] a large sandwich consisting of three pieces of bread with two different kinds of cold food between them

club 'soda *n* [C,U] water filled with BUBBLES that is often mixed with other drinks; ▣ **soda water**

cluck¹ /klʌk/ *v* **1** [I] if a chicken clucks, it makes a short low sound **2** [I,T] to express sympathy or disapproval by saying something, or by making a short low noise with your tongue: *Edith clucked her tongue impatiently.* | [+over/around etc] *She stood clucking over the baby.* —**clucking** *adj*: *clucking noises*

cluck² *n* [C usually singular] **1** a low short noise made by chickens **2** a sound made with your tongue, used to show disapproval or sympathy: *a disapproving cluck* **3 dumb/stupid cluck** AmE a stupid person: *You dumb cluck, why'd you tell him?*

clue¹ [S2] /kluː/ *n* [C]
1 an object or piece of information that helps someone solve a crime or mystery: *Police have found a vital clue* (=a very important clue). | [+to/about/as to] *We now have an important clue as to the time of the murder.* | *Archaeological evidence will provide clues about what the building was used for.* | [+in] *This information is a valuable clue in our hunt for the bombers.* | *a desperate search for clues*
2 information that helps you understand the reasons why something happens: [+to/about/as to] *Childhood experiences may provide a clue as to why some adults develop eating disorders.*
3 a piece of information that helps you solve a CROSSWORD

PUZZLE, answer a question etc: *I'll give you a clue, Kevin, it's a kind of bird.*
4 not have a clue (where/why/how etc) *informal* a) to not have any idea about the answer to a question, how to do something, what a situation is etc: *'Do you know how to switch this thing off?' 'I haven't a clue.'* | *Until I arrived here, I hadn't got a clue what I was going to say to her.* b) to be very stupid, or very bad at a particular activity: *Don't let Mike cook you dinner; he hasn't got a clue.* | *I haven't a clue how to talk to girls.* | [+about] *No point asking Jill – she hasn't got a clue about maths.*

clue² *v*
   clue sb ⇔ **in** *phr v informal* to give someone information about something: [+on/about] *Somebody must have clued him in on our sales strategy.*

clued-'up BrE, **clued-'in** AmE *adj informal* knowing a lot about something: [+on/about] *Ask Margaret. She's pretty clued-up about that sort of thing.*

clue·less /ˈkluːləs/ *adj informal* having no understanding or knowledge of something – used to show disapproval: [+about] *Many teachers are clueless about the needs of immigrant students.*

clump¹ /klʌmp/ *n* **1** [C] a group of trees, bushes, or other plants growing very close together: [+of] *a thick clump of grass* | **in a clump** *The roses were planted in clumps across the park.* **2** [C + of] a small mass of something such as earth or mud **3** [U] the sound of someone walking with heavy steps: *I heard the clump of Ralph's boots going up the stairs.*

clump² *v* **1** [I always + adv/prep] to walk with slow noisy steps: [+up/down/along etc] *The kids clumped up the stairs in their boots.* **2** also **clump together** [I,T] if separate objects clump together, or are clumped together, they form a group or solid mass: *This product will cause bacteria and loose dirt to clump together in the water tank.*

clum·sy /ˈklʌmzi/ *comparative* **clumsier,** *superlative* **clumsiest** *adj* **1** moving in an awkward way and tending to make things fall over: *I felt clumsy, shy and awkward at the party.* | *a clumsy attempt to catch the ball* **2** a clumsy object is not easy to use and is often large and heavy **3** a clumsy action or statement is said or done carelessly or badly, and likely to upset someone: *David made a clumsy attempt to comfort us.* | *a clumsy piece of diplomacy* —**clumsily** *adv* —**clumsiness** *n* [U]

clung /klʌŋ/ the past tense and past participle of CLING

clunk /klʌŋk/ *n* [C] a loud sound made when two solid objects hit each other: *the clunk of the car door being shut* —**clunk** *v* [I,T]

clunk·er /ˈklʌŋkə $ -ər/ *n* [C] AmE informal **1** an old car or other machine that does not work well **2** something that is completely unsuccessful because people think it is stupid or wrong

clunk·y /ˈklʌŋki/ *adj* heavy and awkward to wear or use: *clunky old shoes*

clus·ter¹ /ˈklʌstə $ -ər/ *n* [C] **1** a group of things of the same kind that are very close together: [+of] *a cluster of low farm buildings* | *a cluster of red berries* | *a diamond cluster ring* **2** a group of people all in the same place: [+of] *A cluster of children stood around the ice cream van.*

clus·ter² *v* [I,T always + adv/prep] if a group of people or things cluster somewhere, or are clustered somewhere, they form a small group in that place: [+around/together etc] *Reporters clustered around the palace gates for news.* | *Industries in Britain tend to be clustered together.*

cluster ,bomb *n* [C] a bomb that sends out smaller bombs when it explodes —**cluster-bomb** *v* [T]

clutch¹ /klʌtʃ/ *v* **1** [T] to hold something tightly because you do not want to lose it; ▣ **grip, grasp**: *She was clutching a bottle of champagne.* → see picture at HOLD **2** [I,T] also **clutch at sb/sth a)** to suddenly take hold of someone or something because you are frightened, in pain or in danger; ▣ **grab**: *He clutched at a* *pillar for support.* | *Tom fell to the ground clutching his stomach.* **b) clutch at sb's heart** if something clutches at your heart, you suddenly feel fear or nervousness **3 be clutching at straws** *especially BrE* to be trying everything possible to find a solution or hope in a difficult situation, even though it will probably be unsuccessful: *I knew that trying the alternative medicine was just clutching at straws.*

clutch² *n* **1** [C] the PEDAL that you press with your foot when driving a vehicle in order to change GEAR,or the part of the vehicle that this controls → see picture at CAR **2 sb's clutches** [plural] the power, influence, or control that someone has: *a small boy trying to escape from his mother's clutches* | **in sb's clutches** *She'll have him in her clutches soon enough.* **3 clutch of sth** a small group of similar things: *a clutch of eggs* (=the number of eggs laid by a bird at one time) | *a clutch of young mothers* **4** [singular] a tight hold that someone has on something; ⊟ **grip, grasp:** *I shook myself free of her clutch.*

'clutch bag *n* [C] a small bag that women carry in their hand, used especially on formal social occasions

clut·ter¹ /'klʌtə $ -ər/ also **clutter up** *v* [T] **1** to cover or fill a space or room with too many things, so that it looks very untidy: *Piles of books and papers cluttered his desk.* | **be cluttered (up) with sth** *The walls were cluttered with paintings and prints.* **2** to fill your mind with a lot of different things: *the everyday tasks that clutter our lives* —**cluttered** *adj*

clutter² *n* [singular, U] a large number of things that are scattered somewhere in an untidy way; ⊟ **junk:** [+of] *the clutter of soaps, shampoos and towels in the bathroom* | *Could you get rid of some of that clutter in your bedroom?*

cm *plural* **cm** or **cms** the written abbreviation of *centimetre* or *centimetres*

C-note /'si: nəʊt $ -noʊt/ *n* [C] *AmE informal* a 100 dollar note

co- /kəʊ $ koʊ/ *prefix* **1** together with: *to coexist* (=exist together or at the same time) | *coeducation* (=with boys and girls together) **2** doing something with someone else as an equal or with less responsibility: *my co-author* (=someone who wrote the book with me) | *the co-pilot* (=someone who helps a pilot)

c/o the written abbreviation of *care of*, used especially in addresses when you are sending a letter or package to someone who is living in someone else's house: *John Hammond, c/o Mrs Pearce, The Old Rectory, Reepham*

Co. /kəʊ $ koʊ/ **1** the abbreviation of *company*: *James Smith & Co.* **2 and co** *BrE spoken* the other members of a particular group of people: *I can't say I'm looking forward to seeing Angela and co again.* **3** the written abbreviation of *county*: *Co. Durham*

C.O. /ˌsi: 'əʊ◂ $ -'oʊ◂/ *n* [C] *Commanding Officer* an officer who is in charge of a military unit

coach¹ S3 W3 /kəʊtʃ $ koʊtʃ/ *n*
1 **SPORT** [C] someone who trains a person or team in a sport: *a tennis coach* | *the Norwegian national coach* **2** **HELP FOR EXAM** [C] *especially BrE* someone who gives private lessons to someone in a particular subject, especially so that they can pass an examination **3** **BUS** [C] *BrE* a bus with comfortable seats used for long journeys; ⊟ **bus** *AmE*: **by coach** *We went to Paris by coach.* | **on a coach** *She's going to Grimsby on a coach.* | *a coach trip to Scotland* | *The restaurant was full of coach parties* (=groups of people travelling together on a coach). **4** **TRAIN** [C] *BrE* one of the parts of the train in which the passengers sit; ⊟ **car** *AmE* **5** **HORSES** [C] a large carriage pulled by horses and used in the past for carrying passengers **6** **IN PLANE/TRAIN** [U] *AmE* the cheapest type of seats on a plane or train: *We flew coach out to Atlanta.*

coach² *v* [T] **1** to teach a person or team the skills they need for a sport; ⊟ **train;** → **coaching:** *Nigel coaches a cricket team in his spare time.* **2** *especially*

BrE to give someone private lessons in a particular subject, especially so that they can pass an important test; → **coaching: coach sb in/for sth** *The child was coached for stardom by her mother.* **3** to help someone prepare what they should say or do in a particular situation – used to show disapproval; → **coaching: coach sb in/on sth** *The girl must have been carefully coached in what to say in court.*

coach·build·er /'kəʊtʃˌbɪldə $ 'koʊtʃˌbɪldər/ *n* [C] *BrE* someone who builds the main outer structure of a car

'coach house *n* [C] *BrE* a building, similar to a GARAGE, used in the past in Britain for storing a carriage which was pulled by horses

coach·ing /'kəʊtʃɪŋ $ 'koʊ-/ *n* [U] **1** a process in which you teach a person or team the skills they need for a sport; → **coach: tennis/football/rugby etc coaching** | *a coaching session with one of England's leading boxers* **2** the process of helping someone prepare for an important test or prepare what they should say or do in a particular situation; → **coach**

'coaching ˌinn *n* [C] *BrE* a small hotel in Britain used in the past by people travelling in carriages pulled by horses

coach·load /'kəʊtʃləʊd $ 'koʊtʃloʊd/ *n* [C] *BrE* a group of people travelling in a COACH, especially when it is full: [+of] *coachloads of Japanese tourists*

coach·man /'kəʊtʃmən $ 'koʊtʃ-/ *n* [C] *plural* **coachmen** /-mən/ someone who drove a COACH pulled by horses in the past

'coach ˌstation *n* [C] *BrE* the place where people begin or end their journeys on buses that travel a long distance; ⊟ **bus station** *AmE*

coach·work /'kəʊtʃwɜːk $ 'koʊtʃwɜːrk/ *n* [U] *BrE* the main outer structure of a car

co·ag·u·late /kəʊˈægjੁleɪt $ koʊ-/ *v* [I,T] if a liquid coagulates, or something coagulates, it becomes thick and almost solid: *Blood had coagulated around the wound.* —**coagulation** /kəʊˌægjੁˈleɪʃən $ koʊ-/ *n* [U]

coal S3 W2 /kəʊl $ koʊl/ *n*
1 [U] a hard black mineral which is dug out of the ground and burnt to produce heat: *Put some coal on the fire.* | *the coal mining industry* | *a lump of coal*
2 [C usually plural] a piece of coal, especially one that is burning: *Red hot coals glowed in the grate.*
3 [C usually plural] *AmE* a piece of wood or coal that is burning; → **charcoal:** *Grill over hot coals for four to five minutes.*
4 carry/take coals to Newcastle *BrE* to take something to a place where there is already plenty of it available
5 haul/rake/drag sb over the coals to speak angrily to someone because they have done something wrong

coal-'black *adj* very dark black: *coal-black eyes*

'coal ˌbunker *n* [C] *BrE* a small building or large container where coal is stored

'coal ˌcellar *n* [C] a small underground room where coal is stored

co·a·lesce /ˌkəʊəˈles $ ˌkoʊ-/ *v* [I] *formal* if objects or ideas coalesce, they combine to form one single group: [+into/with] *Gradually the different groups of people coalesced into one dominant racial group.* —**coalescence** *n* [U]

coal·face /'kəʊlfeɪs $ 'koʊl-/ *n* *BrE* **1** [C] the part of a coal mine where the coal is cut from the ground **2 at the coalface** where the real work is done, not just talked about: *Academics will be working at the coalface alongside the doctors.*

coal·field /'kəʊlfiːld $ 'koʊl-/ *n* [C] an area where there is coal under the ground

coal-'fired *adj* *BrE* using coal to make something work: *a coal-fired electricity generating station*

---

1 000, 2 000, 3 000, most frequent words in S poken and W ritten English

coal gas n [U] gas produced by burning coal, used especially for electricity and heating → NATURAL GAS

coal hole n [C] BrE a COAL CELLAR

coal·house /'kəʊlhaʊs $ 'koʊl-/ n [C] BrE a small building where coal is stored

co·a·li·tion W3 /,kəʊə'lɪʃən $,koʊə-/ n
1 [C] a union of two or more political parties that allows them to form a government or fight an election together: [+of] *a coalition of democratic forces* | *the centre-right coalition government* | *an emergency meeting of the three coalition parties*
2 [C] a group of people who join together to achieve a particular purpose, usually a political one: [+of] *a coalition of environmental groups*
3 [U] a process in which two or more political parties or groups join together: *He hoped to convert his party members to a belief in coalition.* | **in coalition with sb** *He was working in coalition with other Unionist leaders.*

coal·man /'kəʊlmən $ 'koʊl-/ n plural **coalmen** /-mən/ [C] a man who delivers coal to people's houses

coal mine also **coal pit** BrE n [C] a place from which coal is dug out of the ground —**coal miner** n [C]; → see picture at ENERGY

coal ˌscuttle n [C] BrE a specially shaped container with a handle for carrying coal

coal tar n [U] a thick black sticky liquid made by heating coal without air, from which many drugs and chemical products are made: *coal tar soap*

coarse /kɔːs $ kɔːrs/ adj **1** having a rough surface that feels slightly hard; **☐ rough**; **☐ smooth**: *a jacket of coarse wool* **2** consisting of threads or parts that are thick or large; **☐ fine**: *The coarse sand was hot and rough under her feet.* | *tufts of coarse grass* **3** talking in a rude and offensive way, especially about sex; **☐ crude**: *coarse jokes* —**coarsely** adv: *coarsely ground black pepper* —**coarseness** n [U]

ˌcoarse ˈfishing n [U] BrE the sport of catching fish, except for TROUT or SALMON, in rivers and lakes

coars·en /'kɔːsən $ 'kɔːr-/ v [I,T] **1** to become thicker or rougher, or to make something thicker or rougher: *Hard work had coarsened his hands.* **2** to become or to make someone become less polite in the way they talk or behave: *He's been coarsened by his experience of war.*

coast¹ S3 W3 /kəʊst $ koʊst/ n
1 [C] the area where the land meets the sea; → **coastal**: [+of] *the west coast of Africa* | *We drove along the Pacific coast to Seattle.* | **on the coast** *I used to live in a small village on the coast* (=on the land near the sea). | **off the coast** *a small island off the coast* (=in the sea near the land) *of Scotland* | *the first European to cross Africa coast to coast* | *a deserted stretch of coast*
2 the coast is clear informal if the coast is clear, it is safe for you to do something without being seen or caught

coast² v [I] **1** [usually + adv/prep] if a car or bicycle coasts, it moves without any effort from you or any power from the engine: [+**down/around/along etc**] *Bev coasted downhill on her bicycle.* **2** to not try very hard to do something well – used to show disapproval: *Janey's teacher says she's just coasting at school.* **3** to be successful at something without much effort: *They scored three goals in the first half and from then on United were coasting.* | [+**to/through**] *The Ugandan relay team are coasting to victory.* **4** to sail along the coast while staying close to land

coast·al /'kəʊstl $ 'koʊstl/ adj [only before noun] in the sea or on the land near the coast: *the coastal waters of Britain* | *the coastal path*

coast·er /'kəʊstə $ 'koʊstər/ n [C] **1** a small thin object on which you put a glass, or cup, to protect a table from heat or liquids **2** a ship that sails from port to port along a coast, but does not go further out to sea → ROLLER COASTER

coaster brake n [C] a BRAKE on some types of bicycle that works by moving the PEDALS backwards

coast·guard /'kəʊstɡɑːd $ 'koʊstɡɑːrd/ n **1 the Coastguard** [also + plural verb BrE] the organization that helps swimmers and ships that are in danger around the coast and helps to prevent illegal activities around the coast: *the Coastguard station at Stornoway* | *Contact the Coastguard immediately if you see a boat in trouble.* **2** [C] BrE a member of this organization

Coast Guard n **the Coast Guard** a military organization in the US that is in charge of watching for ships in danger and preventing illegal activities in the ocean

coast·line /'kəʊstlaɪn $ 'koʊst-/ n [C] the land on the edge of the coast, especially the shape of this land as seen from the air: *California's rugged coastline* | *a beautiful stretch of coastline* | **along/around the coastline** *the sandy hills along the coastline of New England*

coat¹ S2 W3 /kəʊt $ koʊt/ n [C]
1 a piece of clothing with long sleeves that is worn over your clothes to protect them or to keep you warm: *Billy! Put your coat on, it's cold outside!* | *The kids took off their coats and threw them on the floor.* | *I need a new winter coat.* | *The lab assistants wear long white coats.* → MORNING COAT
2 AmE a jacket that you wear as part of a suit; **☐ jacket**
3 the fur, wool, or hair that covers an animal's body: *a dog with a glossy coat*
4 a thin layer of a paint or other substance that you spread thinly over the surface of something: [+of] *He applied a light coat of varnish.* → **cut your coat according to your cloth** at CUT¹ (43)

coat² v [T] to cover something with a thin layer of something else: *A layer of snow coated the trees.* | **coat sth with/in sth** *Next, coat the fish with breadcrumbs.*

coat check n [C] AmE a place in a public building where you can leave your coat while you are in the building; **☐ cloakroom** BrE

-coated /kəʊtɪd $ koʊ-/ suffix **1** metal-coated/plastic-coated etc covered with a thin layer of metal, plastic etc → SUGAR-COATED **2** white-coated/fur-coated etc wearing a white coat, fur coat etc

coat ˌhanger n [C] an object that you use to hang up clothes on; **☐ hanger**

coat·ing /'kəʊtɪŋ $ 'koʊ-/ n [C] a thin layer of something that covers a surface: [+of] *a fine coating of dust* | *The tent has a waterproof coating on both sides.*

ˌcoat of ˈarms n plural **coats of arms** [C] a set of pictures or patterns painted on a SHIELD and used as the special sign of a family, town, university etc

coat rack n [C] a board or pole with hooks on it that you hang coats on

coat·room /'kəʊtrʊm, -ruːm $ 'koʊt-/ n [C] AmE COAT CHECK

coat·stand /'kəʊtstænd $ 'koʊt-/ n [C] a tall pole with hooks at the top that you hang coats on

coat·tails /'kəʊt-teɪlz $ 'koʊt-/ n [plural] **1** if you achieve something on someone's coattails, you achieve it because of the other person's power or success: **on sb's coattails** *A number of Republican congressmen were elected on Bush's coattails.* **2** the cloth at the back of a TAILCOAT that is divided into two pieces

coax /kəʊks $ koʊks/ v [T] **1** to persuade someone to do something that they do not want to do by talking to them in a kind, gentle, and patient way: *'Please, Vic, come with us,' Nancy coaxed.* | **coax sb into/out of (doing) sth** *We had to coax Alan into going to school.* | **coax sb to do sth** *We watched the bear coax its cubs to enter the water.* | **coax sb down/out/back etc** *Firefighters managed to coax the man down from the roof.* **2** to make something such as a machine do something by dealing with it in a slow, patient, and careful way: **coax sth out of/from/into etc sth** *He coaxed a fire out of some dry grass and twigs.* | *The driver coaxed his bus through the snow.* —**coaxing** n [U]: *She needs a bit of gentle coaxing.* —**coaxingly** adv

coax sth **out of/from** sb *phr v* to persuade someone to tell you something or give you something: *I managed to coax some money out of Dad.*

cob /kɒb $ kɑːb/ *n* [C] **1** a CORNCOB → **CORN ON THE COB** **2** *BrE* a round LOAF of bread **3** a type of horse that is strong and has short legs **4** a male SWAN

co·balt /ˈkəʊbɔːlt $ ˈkoʊbɒːlt/ *n* [U] **1** a shiny silver-white metal that is often combined with other metals or used to give a blue colour to substances such as glass. It is a chemical ELEMENT: symbol Co **2** also **cobalt blue** a bright blue-green colour —**cobalt** *adj*

cob·ble[1] /ˈkɒbəl $ ˈkɑː-/ *v* [T] *old-fashioned* **1** to repair or make shoes **2** to put COBBLESTONES on a street
cobble sth ⇔ **together** *phr v* to quickly produce or make something that is useful but not perfect: *The diplomats cobbled an agreement together.* | *She cobbled together a tent from a few pieces of string and a sheet.*

cob·ble[2] *n* [C] a cobble-stone

cobble

cob·bled /ˈkɒbəld $ ˈkɑː-/ *adj* a cobbled street is covered with cobblestones

cob·bler /ˈkɒblə $ ˈkɑːblər/ *n* **1** [C,U] cooked fruit covered with a sweet bread-like mixture: *peach cobbler* **2** [C] *old-fashioned* someone who makes and repairs shoes **3 cobblers** [plural] *BrE spoken informal* nonsense: *I've never heard such a load of old cobblers in my life!*

a cobbled street

cob·ble·stone /ˈkɒbəlstəʊn $ ˈkɑːbəlstoʊn/ *n* [C] a small round stone set in the ground, especially in the past, to make a hard surface for a road

co·bra /ˈkəʊbrə $ ˈkoʊ-/ *n* [C] a poisonous African or Asian snake that can spread the skin of its neck to make itself look bigger

cob·web /ˈkɒbweb $ ˈkɑːb-/ *n* [C] **1** a net of sticky threads made by a SPIDER to catch insects, that is inside a building and has not been removed **2 blow/clear the cobwebs away** to do something, especially go outside, in order to help yourself to think more clearly and feel better: *A brisk walk will soon blow the cobwebs away.* —**cobwebbed** *adj*

co·ca /ˈkəʊkə $ ˈkoʊ-/ *n* [U] a South American bush whose leaves are used to make the drug COCAINE

co·caine /kəʊˈkeɪn, kə- $ koʊ-/ *n* [U] a drug, usually in the form of a white powder, that is taken illegally for pleasure or used in some medical situations to prevent pain → CRACK[2] (7)

coc·cyx /ˈkɒksɪks $ ˈkɑːk-/ *n plural* **coccyxes** *or* **coccyges** /kɒkˈsaɪdʒiːz $ ˈkɑːksɪ-/ *technical* the small bone at the bottom of your SPINE; 🮱 **tailbone**

coch·i·neal /ˌkɒtʃʃˈniːl $ ˌkɑː-/ *n* [U] a substance used to give food a red colour

coch·le·a /ˈkɒkliə $ ˈkɑː-/ *n plural* **cochleas** *or* **cochleae** /-li-aɪ/ [C] *technical* a part of the inner ear

cock[1] /kɒk $ kɑːk/ *n* [C]
1 CHICKEN an adult male chicken; 🮱 **rooster** *BrE*; → **hen**: *A cock crowed in the distance.*
2 MALE BIRD *especially BrE* an adult male bird of any kind: *A cock pheasant rose from the hill in front of me.*
3 SEX ORGAN *informal not polite* a PENIS
4 cock and bull story *BrE* a story or excuse that is silly and unlikely but is told as if it were true: *a cock and bull story about the dog eating her homework*
5 OBJECT THAT CONTROLS FLOW something that controls the flow of liquid or gas out of a pipe or container; 🮱 **tap** → BALLCOCK, STOPCOCK
6 MAN *BrE old-fashioned* used by some people when talking to a man they know well → HALF COCKED

cock[2] *v* [T] **1** to lift a part of your body, or hold a part of your body at an angle: *She cocked her head and considered the offer.* | *He cocked a quizzical eyebrow at her.* **2** to pull back the HAMMER of a gun so that it is

ready to be fired **3** to move your hat so that it is at an angle **4 cock an ear/eye** to listen or look very carefully: *The little dog looked up and cocked its ears.* **5 cock a snook at sb/sth** *BrE informal* to show clearly that you do not respect someone or something: *He has always tried to cock a snook at authority.*
cock sth ⇔ **up** *phr v BrE informal not polite* to spoil something by making a stupid mistake or doing it badly: *His secretary cocked up his travelling schedule and he's furious about it.* → COCK-UP

cock·ade /kɒˈkeɪd $ kɑː-/ *n* [C] a small piece of cloth used as a decoration on a hat to show rank, membership of a club etc

cock-a-doo·dle-doo /ˌkɒk ə ˌduːdl ˈduː $ ˌkɑːk-/ *n* [C] the loud sound made by an adult male chicken

cock-a-hoop /ˌkɒk ə ˈhuːp $ ˌkɑːk-/ *adj* [not before noun] *BrE* pleased and excited about something, especially something that you have done: [+at/about/over] *Robert's cock-a-hoop about his new job.*

cock-a-leek·ie /ˌkɒk ə ˈliːki $ ˌkɑːk-/ *n* [U] a type of Scottish soup made with chicken, vegetables, and LEEKS

cock·a·ma·mie /ˌkɒkəˈmeɪmi $ ˌkɑːk-/ *adj AmE informal* a cockamamie story or excuse is not believable or does not make sense: *What cockamamie idea will he think up next?*

cock·a·too /ˌkɒkəˈtuː $ ˈkɑːkətuː/ *n* [C] an Australian PARROT with a lot of feathers on the top of its head

cock·chaf·er /ˈkɒkˌtʃeɪfə $ ˈkɑːkˌtʃeɪfər/ *n* [C] a European BEETLE (=a kind of insect) that damages trees and plants

cock·crow /ˈkɒk-krəʊ $ ˈkɑːk-kroʊ/ *n* [U] *literary* the time in the early morning when the sun rises; 🮱 **dawn**

cocked 'hat *n* [C] *BrE* **1 knock/beat sb/sth into a cocked hat** to be a lot better than someone or something else: *My mother is such a good cook she knocks everybody else into a cocked hat.* **2** a hat with the edges turned up on three sides, worn in the past

cock·e·rel /ˈkɒkərəl $ ˈkɑː-/ *n* [C] a young male chicken

cock·er span·iel /ˌkɒkə ˈspænjəl $ ˌkɑːkər-/ *n* [C] a dog with long ears and long silky fur

cock-'eyed *adj* **1** unlikely to succeed: *The whole idea is completely cock-eyed.* **2** not straight but set at an angle: *I think you put that shelf up cock-eyed.*

cock fight *n* [C] an occasion when two male chickens are made to fight as a sport —**cockfighting** *n* [U]

cock·le /ˈkɒkəl $ ˈkɑː-/ *n* [C] **1** a common European SHELLFISH that is used for food **2 warm the cockles of sb's heart** *especially BrE* to make someone feel happy and full of good feelings towards other people: *Seeing her new baby just warms the cockles of your heart.*

cock·ney, Cockney /ˈkɒkni $ ˈkɑːk-/ *n* **1** [C] someone who comes from the east part of London, and who has a particular way of speaking which is typical of working class people who live there **2** [U] a way of speaking English that is typical of working class people in the east part of London —**cockney** *adj*: *She has a broad cockney accent.*

cock·pit /ˈkɒk.pɪt $ ˈkɑːk-/ *n* [C] **1** the area in a plane, small boat, or racing car where the pilot or driver sits → AIRCRAFT, YACHT **2** a small enclosed area where COCK FIGHTS took place in the past

cock·roach /ˈkɒk-rəʊtʃ $ ˈkɑːk-roʊtʃ/ also **roach** *AmE n* [C] a large black or brown insect that lives in dirty houses, especially if they are warm and there is food to eat

cocks·comb /ˈkɒks-kəʊm $ ˈkɑːks-koʊm/ *n* [C] the red flesh that grows from the top of a male chicken's head

cock·suck·er /ˈkɒkˌsʌkə $ ˈkɑːkˌsʌkər/ *n* [C] *taboo informal* a very insulting word for a man. Do not use this word.

C

cock·sure /ˌkɒkˈʃʊə $ ˌkɑːkˈʃʊr/ adj old-fashioned too confident of your abilities or knowledge, in a way that is annoying to other people: *He seemed rather too cocksure for my liking.*

cock·tail /ˈkɒkteɪl $ ˈkɑːk-/ n [C] **1** an alcoholic drink made from a mixture of different drinks **2 seafood/prawn/lobster cocktail** small pieces of fish, PRAWNS, or LOBSTER served cold with a sauce and eaten as the first part of a meal **3 fruit cocktail** a mixture of small pieces of fruit **4** a mixture of several things which is dangerous, unpleasant, confusing, or exciting: [+of] *a lethal cocktail of painkillers and whisky* | *The book contains a powerful cocktail of romance, family crises and big business.* → MOLOTOV COCKTAIL

cocktail ,bar n [C] an area in a hotel or other place where you can buy cocktails as well as beer and wine

cocktail ,dress n [C] a formal dress for wearing to parties or other evening social events

cocktail ,lounge n [C] a public room in a hotel, restaurant etc, where you can buy alcoholic drinks

cocktail ,party n [C] a party, usually in the early evening, at which alcoholic drinks are served and for which people usually dress formally

cocktail ,shaker n [C] a container in which cocktails are mixed

cocktail stick n [C] a short pointed piece of wood on which small pieces of food are served

cocktail ,waitress n [C] AmE a woman who serves drinks to people sitting at tables in a bar

cock-up n [C] BrE spoken informal something that has been spoiled by someone's stupid mistake or by being done badly: *He's made a monumental cock-up of his first assignment.* | [+over] *There's been a cock-up over the tickets for the football on Saturday.*

cock·y /ˈkɒki $ ˈkɑːki/ adj informal too confident about yourself and your abilities, especially in a way that annoys other people: *He's a cocky little man and I don't like him.* —**cockily** adv —**cockiness** n [U]

co·coa /ˈkəʊkəʊ $ ˈkoʊkoʊ/ n [U] **1** also **cocoa powder** a brown powder made from cocoa beans, used to make chocolate and to give a chocolate taste to foods **2** a sweet hot drink made with cocoa powder, sugar, and milk or water *a cup of cocoa*

cocoa bean n [C] the small seed of a tropical tree which is used to make cocoa

cocoa ,butter n [U] a fat obtained from the seeds of a tropical tree, used in making some COSMETICS

co·co·nut /ˈkəʊkənʌt $ ˈkoʊ-/ n **1** [C] the large brown seed of a tropical tree, which has a hard shell containing white flesh that you can eat and a milky liquid that you can drink: *large tropical gardens of coconut palms* → see picture at FRUIT **2** [U] the white flesh of a coconut, often used in cooking: *desiccated coconut* (=dried coconut)

,coconut 'matting n [U] BrE a rough material used to cover floors that is made from the FIBRES covering a coconut shell

coconut ,milk n [U] the liquid inside a coconut

coconut ,shy n plural **coconut shies** [C] BrE an outdoor game in which you try to knock coconuts off posts by throwing balls at them

co·coon¹ /kəˈkuːn/ n [C] **1** a silk cover that young MOTHS and other insects make to protect themselves while they are growing **2** something that wraps around you completely, especially to protect you: [+of] *The baby peered out of its cocoon of blankets.* **3** a place or situation in which you feel comfortable and safe, and are protected from anything unpleasant: [+of] *She was surrounded by the cocoon of a loving family.*

cocoon² v [T usually passive] to protect or surround someone or something completely, especially so that they feel safe: **be cocooned in sth** *She was cocooned in a reassuring network of friends and relatives.* | Usually *she lay for ages cocooned in her warm bed.* —**cocooned** adj: *a rich, cocooned existence*

cod¹ /kɒd $ kɑːd/ n plural **cod** **1** [C] a large sea fish that lives in the North Atlantic **2** [U] the white flesh of a cod, eaten as food: *Two cod fillets, please.*

cod² adj [only before noun] BrE not real, but intended to look or sound real – often used humorously: *a cod English accent*

COD BrE; **C.O.D.** AmE /ˌsiː əʊ ˈdiː $ -oʊ-/ n [U] **cash on delivery** a payment system in which the customer pays the person who delivers the goods to them

co·da /ˈkəʊdə $ ˈkoʊ-/ n [C] **1** an additional separate part at the end of a piece of music **2** a separate piece of writing at the end of a work of literature or a speech

cod·dle /ˈkɒdl $ ˈkɑːdl/ v [T] to treat someone in a way that is too kind and gentle and that protects them from pain or difficulty: *Don't coddle the child – he's fine!*

code¹ S2 W2 /kəʊd $ koʊd/ n

1 LAWS/BEHAVIOUR [C] a set of rules, laws, or principles that tell people how to behave: *The Torah is the basis for all the Jewish laws and their moral code.* | *Each state in the US has a different criminal and civil code.* | *The judge ruled that there had been no breach of the code.* | *There were plans to introduce a dress code* (=rules about what to wear) *for civil servants.* | **code of conduct/behaviour/ethics** *the strict code of conduct that is so much a part of karate* | **code of practice** (=a set of rules that people in a particular business or profession agree to obey) *The Textile Services Association has drawn up a code of practice endorsed by the Office of Fair Trading.* → HIGHWAY CODE, PENAL CODE

2 SECRET MESSAGE [C,U] a system of words, letters, or symbols that you use instead of ordinary writing, so that the information can only be understood by someone else who knows the system: **in code** *All reports must be sent in code.* | **break/crack a code** (=manage to understand a code) *They didn't realise that we'd broken their secret code.*

3 SYMBOLS GIVING INFORMATION [C] a set of numbers, letters, or symbols that shows what something is or gives information about it: *Goods that you order must have a product code.* | *Every item found on the archaeological dig is given a code number.* → BAR CODE, GENETIC CODE, POSTCODE, ZIP CODE

4 TELEPHONES also **dialling code, STD code** BrE the group of numbers that comes before a telephone number when you are calling from a different area; ▪ **area code** AmE: *What's the code for Aberdeen?*

5 COMPUTERS [C,U] a set of instructions that tell a computer what to do → MACHINE CODE, SOURCE CODE

6 SOUNDS/SIGNALS [C] a system of sounds or signals that represent words or letters when they are sent by machine → MORSE CODE

code² v [T usually passive] **1** to put a set of numbers, letters, or symbols on something to show what it is or give information about it: *Each path is coded to show the level of difficulty.* **2** to put a message into code so that it is secret

cod·ed /ˈkəʊdɪd $ ˈkoʊ-/ adj **1** coded information uses a system of words, letters or symbols instead of ordinary writing so that it can only be understood by someone else who knows the system: *He sent a coded message to CIA headquarters.* **2** having a set of numbers, letters, or symbols to show what something is or give information about it: *The wires are colour coded for easy identification.* **3** coded language expresses your opinion in an indirect way because it will probably offend someone: *They voiced their criticism in coded statements.* **4** technical coded sounds or signals can only be understood by special machines: *coded signals broadcast by the BBC radio transmitters*

co·deine /ˈkəʊdiːn $ ˈkoʊ-/ n [U] a drug used to stop pain

code name n [C] a name that is used to keep someone's or something's real name a secret —**code-name** v [T]: *a crime busting operation code-named Jeeves*

cod·er /ˈkəʊdə $ ˈkoʊdər/ *n* [C] *informal* a computer PROGRAMMER: *a coders' convention*

ˈcode-ˌsharing *n* [U] when two AIRLINE companies sell tickets together and use the same numbers for their flights

ˈcode word *n* [C] **1** a word or phrase that is given a different meaning to its usual meaning, so that it can be used to communicate something secretly **2** a word or expression that you use instead of a more direct one when you want to avoid shocking someone: [+**for**] *'Lively discussion' is a code word for 'arguing'.*

co·dex /ˈkəʊdeks $ ˈkoʊ-/ *n plural* **codices** /-dəsiːz/ [C] *technical* an ancient book written by hand: *a sixth-century codex*

cod·ger /ˈkɒdʒə $ ˈkɑːdʒər/ *n* **old codger** *informal not polite* an offensive word for an old man

co·di·cil /ˈkəʊdəsɪl $ ˈkɑː-/ *n* [C] *law* a document making a change or addition to a WILL (=a legal document saying who you want your money and property to go to when you die)

co·di·fy /ˈkəʊdəfaɪ $ ˈkɑː-/ *v* **codified, codifying, codifies** [T] to arrange laws, principles, facts etc in a system —**codification** /ˌkəʊdəfəˈkeɪʃən $ ˌkɑː-/ *n* [C,U]

cod·ing /ˈkəʊdɪŋ $ ˈkoʊ-/ *n* [U] a system of marking something with letters, symbols etc so that facts about it can be understood by someone who knows the system: *Most petrol stations use* ***colour coding*** *for different types of petrol.* | *A* ***coding system*** *is used to record what is found and when.*

ˌcod-liver ˈoil *n* [U] a yellow oil from a fish that contains a lot of substances that are important for good health

cod·piece /ˈkɒdpiːs $ ˈkɑːd-/ *n* [C] a piece of coloured cloth worn by men in the 15th and 16th centuries to cover the opening in the front of their trousers

cods·wal·lop /ˈkɒdzˌwɒləp $ ˈkɑːdzˌwɑː-/ *n* [U] *BrE informal* nonsense: *What* ***a load of codswallop!***

co·ed¹ /ˌkəʊˈed◂ $ ˈkoʊed/ *adj* **1** using a system in which students of both sexes are educated together: *The university became coed in 1967.* **2** *AmE* a coed place, team etc is used by or includes people of both sexes; ⊟ **mixed** *BrE*

coed² *n* [C] *AmE old fashioned* a woman student at a university

co·ed·u·ca·tion /ˌkəʊedjʊˈkeɪʃən $ ˌkoʊedʒə-/ *n* [U] a system in which students of both sexes are educated together —**coeducational** *adj*

co·ef·fi·cient /ˌkəʊəˈfɪʃənt $ ˌkoʊ-/ *n* [C] *technical* the number by which an unknown quantity is multiplied: *In 8pq, the coefficient of pq is 8.*

co·e·qual /ˌkəʊˈiːkwəl◂ $ ˌkoʊ-/ *adj formal* if people are coequal, they have the same rank, ability, importance etc

co·erce /kəʊˈɜːs $ koʊˈɜːrs/ *v* [T] to force someone to do something they do not want to do by threatening them: **coerce sb into (doing) sth** *The rebels coerced the villagers into hiding them from the army.*

co·er·cion /kəʊˈɜːʃən $ koʊˈɜːrʒən/ *n* [U] the use of threats or orders to make someone do something they do not want to do: *The defendant explained that he had been acting under coercion.*

co·er·cive /kəʊˈɜːsɪv $ koʊˈɜːr-/ *adj formal* using threats or orders to make someone do something they do not want to do: *coercive measures to reduce absenteeism* —**coercively** *adv*

co·ex·ist /ˌkəʊɪgˈzɪst $ ˌkoʊ-/ *v* [I] if two different things coexist, they exist at the same time or in the same place: [+**with**] *great wealth coexisting with extreme poverty*

co·ex·ist·ence /ˌkəʊɪgˈzɪstəns $ ˌkoʊ-/ *n* [U] when two different things or groups of people exist together at the same time or in the same place: [+**of**] *the coexistence of two systems of measurement* | *over fifty years of peaceful coexistence*

C of E /ˌsiː əv ˈiː/ *n BrE* **the C of E** ***the Church of England*** the official church in England, which has the queen or the king as its leader —**C of E** *adj*

cof·fee S1 W2 /ˈkɒfi $ ˈkɒːfi, ˈkɑːfi/ *n*
1 [U] a hot dark brown drink that has a slightly bitter taste: *Do you want a cup of coffee?* | *Do you like your* ***coffee white*** (=with milk) *or* ***black*** (=without milk)*?*
2 [C,U] a cup of coffee: *Who wants a coffee?* | **over coffee** *dinner guests chatting over coffee* (=while drinking coffee) → DECAFFEINATED
3 [U] whole coffee beans, crushed coffee beans, or a powder to which you add water to make coffee: *a jar of coffee* | ***instant coffee*** (=powdered coffee) | *I haven't got any* ***real coffee*** (=coffee beans) *at the moment.*
4 [U] a light brown colour → **wake up and smell the coffee** at WAKE UP (3)

ˈcoffee bar *n* [C] a small restaurant that serves coffee and other non-alcoholic drinks, sandwiches, cakes etc → COFFEE SHOP

ˈcoffee bean *n* [C] the seed of a tropical bush that is used to make coffee

ˈcoffee break *n* [C] a short time when you stop working to have a cup of coffee; ⊟ **tea break** *BrE*

ˈcoffee ˌgrinder *n* [C] a small machine that crushes coffee beans

ˈcoffee house *n* [C] a restaurant that serves coffee, cakes etc

ˈcoffee maˌchine *n* [C] a machine that gives you a cup of coffee, tea etc when you put money in it

cof·fee·mak·er /ˈkɒfiˌmeɪkə $ ˈkɒːfiˌmeɪkər, ˈkɑː-/ *n* [C] an electric machine that makes coffee

ˈcoffee mill *n* [C] a COFFEE GRINDER

ˈcoffee ˌmorning *n* [C] *BrE* a social occasion when a group of people meet in the morning to talk and drink coffee, and usually give money to help a church or another organization

ˈcoffee pot *n* [C] a container from which coffee is served → see picture at POT

ˈcoffee shop *n* [C] **1** *AmE* a restaurant that serves cheap meals **2** *BrE* a place in a large shop or a hotel that serves meals and non-alcoholic drinks

ˈcoffee ˌtable *n* [C] a low table on which you put cups, newspapers etc

ˈcoffee table ˌbook *n* [C] a large expensive book that has a lot of pictures in it and is meant to be looked at rather than read

cof·fer /ˈkɒfə $ ˈkɒːfər, ˈkɑː-/ *n* [C] **1 sb's coffers** the money that an organization, government etc has available to spend: *The money from the exhibition should* ***swell*** *the hospital's* ***coffers*** *a little.* **2** a large strong box used to hold valuable or religious objects

cof·fin /ˈkɒfən $ ˈkɒː-, ˈkɑː-/ *n* [C] a long box in which a dead person is buried or burnt; ⊟ **casket** *AmE* → **a nail in sb's/sth's coffin** at NAIL¹ (3)

cog /kɒg $ kɑːg/ *n* [C] **1** a wheel with small bits sticking out around the edge that fit together with the bits of another wheel as they turn around in a machine **2** one of the small bits that stick out on a cog **3 a cog in the machine/wheel** someone who only has a small unimportant job in a large business or organization

co·gent /ˈkəʊdʒənt $ ˈkoʊ-/ *adj formal* if a statement is cogent, it seems reasonable and correct: **cogent argument/reason/case etc** *a cogent argument for banning the drug* —**cogently** *adv* —**cogency** *n* [U]

cog·i·tate /ˈkɒdʒəteɪt $ ˈkɑː-/ *v* [I + about/on] *formal* to think carefully and seriously about something —**cogitation** /ˌkɒdʒəˈteɪʃən $ ˌkɑː-/ *n* [U]

co·gnac /ˈkɒnjæk $ ˈkoʊ-, ˈkɑː-/ *n* [C,U] a kind of BRANDY (=strong alcoholic drink) made in France, or a glass of this drink

C

cog·nate[1] /'kɒgneɪt $ 'kɑːg-/ adj technical cognate words or languages have the same origin

cognate[2] n [C] technical a word in one language that has the same origin as a word in another language: The German 'Hund' is a cognate of the English 'hound'.

cog·ni·tion /kɒg'nɪʃən $ kɑːg-/ n [U] formal the process of knowing, understanding, and learning something: the regions of the brain that are responsible for memory and cognition

cog·ni·tive /'kɒgnɪtɪv $ 'kɑːg-/ adj formal related to the process of knowing, understanding, and learning something: cognitive psychology —**cognitively** adv

cog·ni·zance, cognisance /'kɒgnɪzəns $ 'kɑːg-/ n [U] formal 1 knowledge or understanding of something 2 **take cognizance of sth** to understand something and consider it when you take action or make a decision

cog·ni·zant, cognisant /'kɒgnɪzənt $ 'kɑːg-/ adj [not before noun] formal if someone is cognizant of something, they know about it and understand it: [+of] He was cognizant of the peculiarities of the case.

co·gno·scen·ti /ˌkɒnjəʊ'ʃenti $ ˌkɑːnjə-/ the cognoscenti formal people who have special knowledge about a particular subject, especially art, literature, or food

cog·wheel /'kɒg-wiːl $ 'kɑːg-/ n [C] a COG

co·hab·it /kəʊ'hæbɪt $ koʊ-/ v [I] to live with another person and have a sexual relationship with them without being married —**cohabitation** /kəʊˌhæbɪ'teɪʃən $ koʊ-/ n [U]

co·here /kəʊ'hɪə $ koʊ'hɪr/ v [I] 1 if ideas, arguments, beliefs, statements etc cohere, they are connected in a clear and reasonable way; → **coherent**: All the details are there and are correct but they don't cohere. 2 if two objects cohere, they stick together

co·her·ence /kəʊ'hɪərəns $ koʊ'hɪr-/ also **co·her·en·cy** /-rənsi/ n [U] 1 when something such as a piece of writing is easy to understand because its parts are connected in a clear and reasonable way: An overall theme will help to give your essay coherence. I He had a coherence of outlook and thought. 2 if a group has coherence, its members are connected or united because they share common aims, qualities, or beliefs: A common religion ensures the coherence of the tribe.

co·her·ent /kəʊ'hɪərənt $ koʊ'hɪr-/ adj 1 if a piece of writing, set of ideas etc is coherent, it is easy to understand because it is clear and reasonable: The three years of the course are planned as a coherent whole. I a coherent account of the incident 2 if someone is coherent, they are talking in a way that is clear and easy to understand: He sounded coherent, but he was too ill to have any idea what he was saying. 3 if a group is coherent, its members are connected or united because they share common aims, qualities, or beliefs: They were never a coherent group. —**coherently** adv: She could not think coherently.

co·he·sion /kəʊ'hiːʒən $ koʊ-/ n [U] 1 if there is cohesion among a group of people, a set of ideas etc, all the parts or members of it are connected or related in a reasonable way to form a whole: a sense of community and social cohesion 2 technical a close relationship, based on grammar or meaning, between two parts of a sentence or a larger piece of writing

co·he·sive /kəʊ'hiːsɪv $ koʊ-/ adj 1 connected or related in a reasonable way to form a whole: a cohesive community 2 uniting people or things: Historically, sport has been a cohesive force in international relations. —**cohesively** adv —**cohesiveness** n [U]

co·hort /'kəʊhɔːt $ 'koʊhɔːrt/ n [C] 1 someone's cohorts are their friends who support them and stay loyal to them – used in order to show disapproval: Mark and his cohorts eventually emerged from the studio. 2 technical a group of people of the same age, social class etc, especially when they are being studied: a cohort of 386 patients aged 65 plus

coif·fure /kwɑː'fjʊə $ -'fjʊr/ n [C] formal the way someone's hair is arranged; ◨ **hairstyle** —**coiffured** or **coiffed** /kwɑːft/ adj

coil[1] /kɔɪl/ also **coil up** v [I,T] to wind or twist into a series of rings, or to make something do this: The snake coiled around the branches of the tree. I Her long hair was coiled up in a plait at the top of her head. I He coiled the rope. —**coiled** adj [only before noun]

coil[2] n [C] 1 a continuous series of circular rings into which something such as wire or rope has been wound or twisted: [+of] a coil of rope 2 one ring of wire, rope etc in a continuous series 3 a wire or a metal tube in a continuous circular shape that produces light or heat when electricity is passed through it: the coil in a light bulb 4 the part of a car engine that sends electricity to the SPARK PLUGS 5 a CONTRACEPTIVE that is a flat curved piece of metal or plastic that is fitted inside a woman's UTERUS; ◨ **IUD**

coin[1] [S3] [W3] /kɔɪn/ n
1 [C] a piece of metal, usually flat and round, that is used as money; → **bill, note**
2 **toss/flip a coin** to choose or decide something by throwing a coin into the air and guessing which side of it will show when it falls: Let's toss a coin to see who goes first.
3 **the other/opposite side of the coin** a different or opposite way of thinking about something: Making the rules is only part of it. How the rules are carried out is the other side of the coin.
4 **two sides of the same coin** two problems or situations that are so closely connected that they are really just two parts of the same thing: Great opportunity and great danger are two sides of the same coin.
5 [U] money in the form of metal coins

coin[2] v [T] 1 to invent a new word or expression, especially one that many people start to use: The word 'aromatherapy' was coined in the 1920s. 2 **to coin a phrase** spoken said in a joking way when you use a very common expression, to show that you know it is used a lot: He'd thought the flight would never — to coin a phrase — get off the ground. 3 **coin money/coin it (in)** BrE informal to earn a lot of money very quickly: BT at its profitable peak was coining it at the rate of £90 a second. 4 to make pieces of money from metal

coin·age /'kɔɪnɪdʒ/ n 1 [U] the system or type of money used in a country: the gold coinage of the Roman empire 2 [C] a word or phrase that has been recently invented: The phrase 'glass ceiling' is a fairly recent coinage. 3 [U] the invention of new words or phrases 4 [U] the making of coins

co·in·cide /ˌkəʊɪn'saɪd $ ˌkoʊ-/ v [I] 1 to happen at the same time as something else, especially by chance; → **coincidence**: [+with] His entry to the party coincided with his marriage. I When our vacations coincided, we often holidayed together. I **planned/timed/arranged to coincide** The show is timed to coincide with the launch of a new book. 2 [not in progressive] if two people's ideas, opinions etc coincide, they are the same; → **coincidence**: The interests of the US and those of the islanders may not coincide. I [+with] The cloth had a natural look which coincided perfectly with the image Laura sought. 3 to meet or be in the same place: The journey coincides in part with the Pennine Way.

co·in·ci·dence /kəʊ'ɪnsɪdəns $ koʊ-/ n 1 [C,U] when two things happen at the same time, in the same place, or to the same people in a way that seems surprising or unusual; → **coincide, coincidental**: 'I'm going to Appleby tomorrow.' 'What a coincidence! I'm going up there too.' I **by coincidence** By coincidence, John and I both ended up at Yale. I **sheer/pure coincidence** (=completely by chance) I didn't set out to find you – it's sheer coincidence that I should walk along the same street. I **not a coincidence/more than coincidence** After the fourth attack on her car she was convinced that the vandalism was more than just coincidence. I seemed to her a **happy coincidence** that Robert should invite her for the weekend.   **2** [singular] formal when two ideas, opinions etc are the same: [+of] a coincidence of interest between the mining companies and certain politicians

co·in·ci·dent /kəʊˈɪnsɪ̩dənt $ koʊ-/ adj formal existing or happening at the same place or time: [+with] The rise of the novel was coincident with the decline of storytelling.

co·in·ci·den·tal /kəʊˌɪnsɪ̩ˈdentl $ koʊ-/ adj happening completely by chance without being planned; → **coincidence: purely/completely/entirely coincidental** Any similarity between this film and real events is purely coincidental. —**coincidentally** adv [sentence adverb]: We have become very profitable. Not coincidentally, we have only half as many employees as we did in 1988.

co·in·sur·ance /ˌkəʊɪnˈʃʊərəns $ ˌkoʊɪnˈʃʊr-/ n [U] AmE **1** a type of insurance in which the payment is split between two people, especially between an employer and a worker: health coinsurance **2** insurance that will only pay for part of the value or cost of something

co·in·sure /ˌkəʊɪnˈʃʊə $ ˌkoʊɪnˈʃʊr-/ v [T] AmE to buy or provide insurance in which the payment is split between two people, or insurance that will only pay for part of the value or cost of something

coir /ˈkɔɪə $ kɔɪr/ n [U] the rough material that covers the shell of a coconut, used for making mats, ropes etc

co·i·tus /ˈkəʊɪ̩təs, ˈkɔɪtəs $ ˈkoʊ-, ˈkɔɪ-/ n [U] technical the act of having sex; ☰ **sexual intercourse** —**coital** adj

coke /kəʊk $ koʊk/ n **1 Coke** [C,U] trademark the drink Coca-Cola, or a bottle, can, or glass of this drink **2** [U] informal cocaine **3** [U] a solid black substance produced from coal and burned to provide heat

col¹ /kɒl $ kɑːl/ n [C] technical a low point between two high places in a mountain range

col² the written abbreviation of **column**

Col. the written abbreviation of **colonel**

co·la /ˈkəʊlə $ ˈkoʊ-/ n [C,U] a brown sweet soft drink or a bottle, can, or glass of this drink: a can of cola → see picture at fast food

col·an·der /ˈkʌləndə, ˈkɒ- $ ˈkʌləndər, ˈkɑː-/ n [C] a metal or plastic bowl with a lot of small holes in the bottom and sides, used to separate liquid from food → see picture at eat

cold¹ [S1] [W1] /kəʊld $ koʊld/ adj comparative **colder**, superlative **coldest**
1 OBJECTS/SURFACES/LIQUIDS/ROOMS something that is cold has a low temperature; ☒ **hot**; → **coldness**: She splashed her face with cold water. | a blast of cold air | We slept on the cold ground. | The house felt cold and empty. | **ice/stone/freezing cold** (=very cold) The radiator is stone cold; isn't the heating working? | **go/get cold** (=become cold) My tea's gone cold. | Come and eat or your dinner will get cold!
2 WEATHER when there is cold weather, the temperature of the air is very low; ☒ **hot**; → **coldness**: It was so cold this morning I had to scrape the ice off my windshield. | The day was bitterly cold. | The hut sheltered her from the cold wind. | **cold winter/evening/January etc** the coldest winter on record | **cold out/outside** It was raining and freezing cold outside. | The weather **gets colder** around the middle of October. | **turn/grow cold** (=become cold or colder, especially suddenly) The nights grew colder.
3 be/feel/look/get cold if you are cold, your body is at a low temperature: Could you turn up the heater, I'm cold. | I feel so cold! | My feet are **as cold as ice** (=very cold).
4 FOOD cold food is cooked but not eaten hot: a plate of cold meats | a cold buffet | Serve the potatoes cold.
5 LACKING FEELING unfriendly or lacking normal human feelings such as sympathy, pity, humour etc; ☒ **warm**; → **coldly, coldness**: Martin was really cold towards me at the party. | His voice was sharp and cold

as ice. | She gave him a cold stare. | a cold, calculated murder
6 get/have cold feet informal to suddenly feel that you are not brave enough to do something you planned to do: The plan failed after sponsors got cold feet.
7 give sb the cold shoulder informal to deliberately ignore someone or be unfriendly to them, especially because they have upset or offended you
8 LIGHT/COLOUR a cold colour or light reminds you of things that are cold; ☒ **warm**; → **coldness**: the cold light of a fluorescent tube
9 in the cold light of day in the morning, when you can think clearly or see something clearly: The house seemed less threatening in the cold light of day.
10 cold (hard) cash AmE money in the form of paper money and coins rather than cheques or credit cards
11 leave sb cold to not feel interested in or affected by something in any way: Opera left him cold.
12 take/need a cold shower used humorously to say that someone is sexually excited and the cold water will stop them feeling that way
13 sb's trail/scent is cold used to say that you cannot find someone because it has been too long since they passed or lived in a particular place: The trail's gone cold. I tracked the boy as far as the factory, but there it ended.
14 IN GAMES [not before noun] used in children's games, to say that someone is far away from the hidden object or answer they are trying to find: You're getting colder!
15 cold facts facts without anything added to make them more pleasant or interesting: Statistics can be merely cold facts.
16 cold steel literary a weapon such as a knife or sword → **in cold blood** at blood¹ (3); → **cold fish** at fish¹ (8); → **blow hot and cold** at blow¹ (21); → **cold comfort** at comfort¹ (7); → **pour cold water over/on** at pour (6); → **a cold sweat** at sweat² (4)

cold² n **1** [C] a common illness that makes it difficult to breathe through your nose and often makes your throat hurt: I've got a bad cold. | Keep your feet dry so you don't **catch a cold** (=become ill). → common cold **2** [U] also **the cold** a low temperature or cold weather: I was shivering with cold. | Don't go out in the cold without your coat! | **you'll catch your death of cold** (=used to warn someone that they may become very ill if they do not keep themselves warm in cold weather) BrE **3 come in from the cold** to become accepted or recognized, especially by a powerful group of people **4 leave sb out in the cold** informal to not include someone in an activity: He chose to favour us one at a time and the others were left out in the cold.

cold³ adv **1** AmE suddenly and completely: Paul stopped cold. 'What was that noise?' **2 out cold** informal unconscious: He drank until he was out cold. | You were **knocked out cold** (=hit on the head so that you became unconscious). **3** without preparation: I can't just get up there and make a speech cold!

cold-ˈblooded adj **1** not showing or involving any emotions or pity for other people's suffering: a cold-blooded killer | cold-blooded murder **2** a cold-blooded animal, such as a snake, has a body temperature that changes with the temperature of the air or ground around it; → **warm-blooded** —**cold-bloodedly** adv —**cold-bloodedness** n [U]

ˌcold ˈcall v [T] to telephone or visit someone you have never met before and try to sell them something —**cold call** n [C] —**cold-calling** n [U]

ˌcold ˈcomfort n [U] if something that is slightly positive is cold comfort to someone who is feeling very bad about a situation, it does not make them feel any better: The drop in the unemployment figures is cold comfort to those still looking for work.

ˈcold cream n [U] a thick white oily cream used for cleaning your face and making it softer

'cold cuts n [plural] thinly cut pieces of cooked meat eaten cold

'cold frame n [C] BrE a box-like structure with sides and a top made of glass or clear plastic, used for keeping young plants warm as they start to grow

'cold front n [C] the front edge of a mass of cold air heading towards a place → WARM FRONT

,cold 'fusion n [U] a type of NUCLEAR FUSION (=the joining together of the centre of two atoms, which releases energy) which some scientists believe can happen at extremely low temperatures, but which other scientists believe is impossible

cold-heart·ed /ˌkəʊld 'hɑːtᵻd◂ $ ˌkoʊld 'hɑːr-/ adj behaving in a way that shows no pity or sympathy: I had no idea you could be so cold-hearted. —**cold-heartedly** adv —**cold-heartedness** n [U]

cold·ly /'kəʊldli $ 'koʊld-/ adv if you do something coldly, you do it without any emotion or warm feeling, making you seem unfriendly; → **cold, coldness: say/speak/reply etc coldly** 'Well, what can I do for you?' he asked coldly. | Janine looked at her coldly.

cold·ness /'kəʊldnᵻs $ 'koʊld-/ n [U] **1** when someone is unfriendly and does not show any warm feelings: There was a certain coldness about him. **2** the state of being cold: [+of] the icy coldness of the water

,cold 'shoulder n **(give sb/get) the cold shoulder** to behave in an unfriendly way towards someone that you know —**cold shoulder** v [T]

'cold snap n [C] a sudden short period of very cold weather

'cold sore n [C] a painful spot on your lip or inside your mouth that is caused by a VIRUS

'cold spell n [C] a period of several days or weeks when the weather is much colder than usual

,cold 'storage n [U] **1** if you keep something such as food in cold storage, you keep it in a cold place so that it will stay fresh and in good condition **2 put sth in cold storage** to not do or use something such as a plan or idea until later in the future: He aims to please even if it means putting his principles in cold storage.

'cold store n [C] BrE a room that is kept very cold and used to store food, especially to keep it fresh

,cold 'turkey n [U] an unpleasant physical condition suffered by people who stop taking a drug that they are ADDICTED to: addicts who are made to go cold turkey

,cold 'war n [singular,U] **1** an unfriendly political relationship between two countries who do not actually fight each other **2 the Cold War** this unfriendly relationship between the US and the Soviet Union after the Second World War

cole·slaw also **cole slaw** AmE /'kəʊlslɔː $ 'koʊlslɔː/ n [U] a SALAD made with thinly cut raw CABBAGE

col·ic /'kɒlɪk $ 'kɑː-/ n [U] if a baby has colic, it has severe pain in its stomach and BOWELS —**colicky** adj

co·li·tis /kəˈlaɪtᵻs/ n [U] an illness in which part of your COLON swells, causing pain

col·lab·o·rate /kəˈlæbəreɪt/ v [I] **1** to work together with a person or group in order to achieve something, especially in science or art; → **collaborator: [+on]** The two nations are collaborating on several satellite projects. | **[+with]** During the late seventies, he collaborated with the legendary Muddy Waters. | **collaborate to do sth** Researchers are collaborating to develop the vaccine. | **collaborate in (doing) sth** Elephants collaborate in looking after their young. **2** to help a country that your country is fighting a war with, especially one that has taken control of your country; → **collaborator: [+with]** Vigilantes began combing the city for anyone known to have collaborated with the enemy.

col·lab·o·ra·tion /kəˌlæbəˈreɪʃən/ n **1** [C,U] when you work together with another person or group to achieve something, especially in science or art: The company is building the centre in collaboration with the

Institute of Offshore Engineering. | **[+between]** a collaboration between the two theatres | **[+with]** The project has involved collaboration with the geography department. **2** [U] when someone gives help to a country that their country is fighting a war with, especially one that has taken control of their country

col·lab·o·ra·tive /kəˈlæbərətɪv $ -reɪ-/ adj **collaborative effort/work/project etc** a job or piece of work that involves two or more people working together to achieve something

col·lab·o·ra·tor /kəˈlæbəreɪtə $ -ər/ n [C] **1** someone who helps their country's enemies, for example by giving them information, when the enemy has taken control of their country; → **collaborate, collaboration:** Their job was to identify enemy collaborators. **2** someone who works with other people or groups in order to achieve something, especially in science or art; → **collaborate, collaboration:** collaborators on a biography of Dickens

col·lage /'kɒlɑːʒ $ kəˈlɑːʒ/ n **1** [C] a picture made by sticking other pictures, photographs, cloth etc onto a surface **2** [U] the art of making pictures in this way

col·la·gen /'kɒlədʒən $ 'kɑː-/ n [U] a PROTEIN found in people and animals. It is often used in beauty products and treatments to make people look younger and more attractive

col·lapse¹ [S3] /kəˈlæps/ v
1 STRUCTURE [I] if a building, wall etc collapses, it falls down suddenly, usually because it is weak or damaged: Uncle Ted's chair collapsed under his weight. | The roof had collapsed long ago.
2 ILLNESS/INJURY [I] to suddenly fall down or become unconscious because you are ill or weak: He collapsed with a heart attack while he was dancing. | Marion's legs collapsed under her.
3 FAIL [I] if a system, idea, or organization collapses, it suddenly fails or becomes too weak to continue: The luxury car market has collapsed. | I thought that without me the whole project would collapse.
4 PRICES [I] if prices, levels, etc collapse, they suddenly become much lower: There were fears that property prices would collapse.
5 SIT/LIE [I] to suddenly sit down, especially because you are very tired or want to relax: I was so exhausted when I got home, I just collapsed on the sofa.
6 FOLD STH SMALLER [I,T] if a piece of furniture or equipment collapses, or if you collapse it, you can fold it so that it becomes smaller: The legs on our card table collapse so we can store it in the closet.
7 MEDICAL [I] if a lung or a BLOOD VESSEL collapses, it suddenly becomes flat, so that it no longer has any air or blood in it

collapse² n
1 BUSINESS/SYSTEM/IDEA ETC [singular, U] a sudden failure in the way something works, so that it cannot continue: **[+of]** the collapse of the Soviet Union | the threat of economic collapse | His business was in danger of collapse.
2 BUILDING/STRUCTURE/FURNITURE ETC [U] when something suddenly falls down: the collapse of an apartment building during the earthquake | The ancient abbey was in imminent danger of collapse.
3 ILLNESS/INJURY [singular, U] when someone suddenly falls down or becomes unconscious because of an illness or injury: The president said he was fine after his collapse yesterday. | She suffered a collapse under anaesthetic.
4 MONEY/PRICES ETC [singular] a sudden decrease in the value of something: the collapse of the stock market | **[+in]** a collapse in the value of pensions

col·lap·si·ble /kəˈlæpsᵻbəl/ adj something collapsible can be folded so that it uses less space: a collapsible chair

col·lar¹ /'kɒlə $ 'kɑːlər/ n [C]
1 CLOTHING the part of a shirt, coat etc that fits around your neck, and is usually folded over: H

2 **CAT/DOG** a narrow band of leather or plastic that is fastened around an animal's neck
3 **INJURED NECK** an object that someone wears around their neck to support it when it has been injured
4 **BUSINESS** a way of making sure that the STOCKS you own do not lose money, even if their price becomes lower
5 **MACHINE** a circular ring that goes round a pipe to make it stronger, especially where two pipes join together
6 **COLOURED FUR/FEATHERS** a band of fur, feathers, or skin around an animal's neck that is a different colour from the rest of the animal → BLUE-COLLAR, DOG COLLAR, WHITE-COLLAR

col·lar[2] *v* [T] **1** to catch someone and hold them so that they cannot escape: *The police collared him less than twenty minutes after the robbery.* **2** to find someone so that you can talk to them, especially when they would prefer to avoid you: *He collared her in the staff room at lunchtime and started telling her about his holiday plans.* **3** **high-collared/open-collared/fur-collared etc** used about clothes that have a particular type of collar: *a high-collared blouse*

col·lar·bone /'kɒləbəʊn $ 'kɑːlərboʊn/ *n* [C] one of the pair of bones that go from the bottom part of your neck to your shoulders → see picture at SKELETON

col·lard greens /ˌkɒləd 'griːnz $ 'kɑːlərd ˌgriːnz/ *n* [plural] *AmE* a vegetable with large green leaves, eaten cooked

col·lar·less /'kɒlələs $ 'kɑːlər-/ *adj* a collarless jacket, shirt etc is one that does not have a collar

'collar stud *n* [C] an object like a button, used to fasten old-fashioned collars to shirts

col·late /kə'leɪt/ *v* [T] **1** *formal* to gather information together, examine it carefully, and compare it with other information to find any differences: *collate information/results/data/figures A computer system is used to collate information from across Britain.* **2** to arrange sheets of paper in the correct order; ▣ **sort** —**collation** /kə'leɪʃən/ *n* [U]

col·lat·e·ral[1] /kə'lætərəl/ *n* [U] property or other goods that you promise to give someone if you cannot pay back the money they lend you; ▣ **security**: *People put up their homes as collateral in order to raise the money to invest in the scheme.* —**collateralize** *AmE v* [T]

collateral[2] *adj* [only before noun] **1** **collateral damage** people who are hurt or killed, or property that is damaged accidentally in a war – used especially by the army, navy etc: *Hitting any non-military targets would risk 'collateral damage'.* **2** relating to something or happening as a result of it, but not as important: *There may be collateral benefits to the scheme.* **3** collateral relatives are members of your family who are not closely related to you

col·league [S3] [W2] /'kɒliːg $ 'kɑː-/ *n* [C] someone you work with, used especially by professional people: *a colleague of mine from the bank* | *She discussed the idea with some of her colleagues.*

col·lect[1] [S1] [W2] /kə'lekt/ *v*
1 **BRING TOGETHER** [T] to get things of the same type from different places and bring them together; → **collection, collector**: *After 25 years of collecting recipes, she has compiled them into a cookbook.* | *The company collects information about consumer trends.* | *We've been out collecting signatures for our petition.*
2 **KEEP OBJECTS** [T] to get and keep objects of the same type, because you think they are attractive or interesting; → **collection, collector**: *Arlene collects teddy bears.*
3 **RENT/DEBTS/TAXES** [T] to get money that you are owed; → **collector**: **collect tax/rent/a debt** *The landlady came around once a month to collect the rent.*
4 **MONEY TO HELP PEOPLE** [I,T] to ask people to give

you money or goods for an organization that helps people: [+**for**] *I'm collecting for Children in Need.*
5 **INCREASE IN AMOUNT** [I,T] if something collects in a place, or you collect it there, it gradually increases in amount: *Rain collected in pools on the road.* | *solar panels for collecting energy from the sun* | *I didn't know what to do with it, so it just sat there collecting dust.*
6 **WIN STH** [T] to receive something because you have won a race, game etc: *Redgrave collected his fifth Olympic gold medal in Sydney.*
7 **collect yourself/collect your thoughts** to make an effort to remain calm and think clearly and carefully about something: *I got there early so I had a few minutes to collect my thoughts before the meeting began.*
8 **TAKE SB/STH FROM A PLACE** [T] especially *BrE* to come to a particular place in order to take someone or something away; ▣ **pick up** *AmE*: *Martin's gone to collect the children from school.* | *I've got to go and collect the book I ordered from the library.*
9 **CROWD** [I] *formal* to come together gradually to form a group of people: *A crowd was beginning to collect around the scene of the accident.*
  collect sth ⇔ **up** *phr v BrE*
  to pick up several things, and put them together: *Can you collect up all the dirty plates and cups?*

collect[2] *adv AmE* **call/phone sb collect** when you telephone someone collect, the person who receives the call pays for it; → **collect call**; ▣ **reverse the charges** *BrE*

col·lect[3] /'kɒlɪkt, -lekt $ 'kɑː-/ *n* [C] a short prayer in some Christian services

col·lect·a·ble /kə'lektəbəl/ also **col·lect·i·ble** /-ʒbəl/ *adj* something that is collectable is likely to be bought and kept as part of a group of similar things, especially because it might increase in value —**collectable** also **collectible** *n* [C]: *shops selling antiques and collectables*

col·lect call *n* [C] *AmE* a telephone call paid for by the person who receives it

col·lect·ed /kə'lektɪd/ *adj* **1** in control of yourself and your thoughts, feelings etc: *She wanted to arrive feeling* **cool, calm, and collected.** **2 collected works/poems/essays/edition** all of someone's books, poems etc printed in one book or set of books: *the Collected Works of Shakespeare*

col·lec·tion [S2] [W1] /kə'lekʃən/ *n*
1 **SET/GROUP** [C] **a)** a set of similar things that are kept or brought together because they are attractive or interesting; → **collect, collector**: *a stamp collection* | *my record collection* | [+**of**] *a collection of Japanese vases* **b)** a group of objects together in the same place: *a collection of empty wine bottles on the back porch*
2 **MONEY** [C] the act of asking people to give you money for an organization that helps people, or during a church service, or the money collected in this way; → **collect**: [+**for**] *Every Christmas we* **have a collection** *for a local charity.* | *We'll be* **taking up a collection** *at the end of tonight's service.*
3 **RENT/DEBTS/TAXES** [U] the act of obtaining money that is owed to you; → **collect, collector**: *a debt collection agency*
4 **BRINGING TOGETHER** [U] the act of bringing together things of the same type from different places to form a group; → **collect**: *a computerized* **data collection** *system*
5 **TAKING STH AWAY** [C,U] the act of taking something from a place; → **collect**: *Garbage collections are made every Tuesday morning.* | *Please collect your purchases from the customer* **collection point.**
6 **FASHION** [C] the clothes designed by a fashion company for a particular season: *Donna Karen's new spring collection*
7 **BOOKS/MUSIC** [C] several stories, poems, pieces of

C

music etc that are in one book or on one record: [+of] *a new collection of Frost's poetry*

8 PEOPLE [C usually singular] a group of people, especially people you think are strange or unusual in some way: [+of] *There was an interesting collection of people at the wedding.*

col'lection ,box *n* [C] a container with a small hole in the top, that people put money for CHARITY into

col'lection ,plate *n* [C] a large, almost flat dish that you put money into during some religious services

col·lec·tive¹ W3 /kə'lektɪv/ *adj* [only before noun] shared or made by every member of a group or society: *a collective decision made by all board members* | *our collective responsibility for the environment*

collective² *n* [C] **1** a group of people who work together to run something such as a business or farm, and who share the profits equally **2** the business or farm that is run by this type of group

col,lective 'bargaining *n* [U] the discussions held between employers and a union in order to reach agreement on wages, working conditions etc

col,lective 'farm *n* [C] a large farm that is owned by the government and controlled by the farm workers

col·lec·tive·ly /kə'lektɪvli/ *adv* as a group: *All members of the cabinet are collectively responsible for decisions taken.* | *Rain, snow and hail are collectively known as precipitation.*

col,lective 'noun *n* [C] technical a noun, such as 'family' or 'flock', that is the name of people or things considered as a unit

col·lec·tiv·is·m /kə'lektɪvɪzəm/ *n* [U] a political system in which all businesses, farms etc are owned by the government —**collectivist** *adj*

col·lec·tiv·ize also **-ise** *BrE* /kə'lektɪvaɪz/ *v* [T] to join privately owned farms or businesses together, so that they can be owned by the government in a Communist political system —**collectivization** /kə,lektɪvaɪ'zeɪʃən $ -və-/ *n* [U]

col·lec·tor /kə'lektə $ -ər/ *n* [C] **1** someone who collects things that are interesting or attractive; → **collect, collection**: *a stamp collector* | *The painting was bought by a private collector.* **2** someone whose job is to collect taxes, tickets, debts etc; → **collect, collection**: *tax/ticket/debt/refuse collector*

col'lector's ,item *n* [C] an object that people want to have because it is interesting or rare, and might become valuable: *Original teddy bears have become real collectors' items.*

col·leen /kɒ'liːn $ kɑː-/ *n* [C] old-fashioned a girl or young woman – used in Ireland

col·lege S1 W2 /'kɒlɪdʒ $ 'kɑː-/ *n*

1 SPECIALIZED EDUCATION [C,U] a school for advanced education, especially in a particular profession or skill: *a teacher training college* | *the London College of Fashion* | *Donna left school and went to art college.* | *at college We were great friends when we were at college.* → SIXTH FORM COLLEGE

2 US UNIVERSITY [C,U] *AmE* a large school where you can study after HIGH SCHOOL and get a degree; ⊟ **university** *BrE*: *Some people who want to go to college still can't get there.* | *in college Fran just finished her freshman year in college.* | *a decline in the number of college students studying history* | *college graduates* | *a college education* | *college campuses* → COMMUNITY COLLEGE, JUNIOR COLLEGE

3 PART OF A UNIVERSITY [C] one of the groups of teachers and students that form a separate part of some universities, especially in Britain: *Trinity College, Cambridge*

4 STUDENTS AND TEACHERS [C also + plural verb *BrE*] the students and teachers of one of these organizations

5 PROFESSIONAL ORGANIZATION [C] a group of people who have special rights, duties, or powers

within a profession or organization: *the American College of Surgeons*

6 NAME OF A SCHOOL [C] *BrE* a word used in the name of some large schools, especially PUBLIC SCHOOLS → ELECTORAL COLLEGE

College 'Boards *n* [plural] *trademark* tests taken by students in order to attend some US universities

col·le·gi·an /kə'liːdʒiən/ *n* [C] a member of a college —**collegian** *adj*

col·le·gi·ate /kə'liːdʒiət/ *adj* **1** relating to college or a college: *collegiate sports* **2** a collegiate university is one that is organized into separate colleges

col·lide /kə'laɪd/ *v* [I] **1** to hit something or someone that is moving in a different direction from you; → **collision**: *A car and a van collided on the motorway.* | [+with] *I ran around the corner, and almost collided with Mrs Laurence.* | *Two trains collided head-on* (=when they were moving directly towards each other). **2** to disagree strongly with a person or group, especially on a particular subject: [+with] *The President has again collided with Congress over his budget plans.* **3** if two very different ideas, ways of thinking etc collide, they come together and produce an interesting result: *Istanbul, where east and west collide*

col·lie /'kɒli $ 'kɑːli/ *n* [C] a middle-sized dog with long hair, kept as a pet or trained to control sheep

col·li·er /'kɒliə $ 'kɑːliər/ *n* [C] *BrE* old-fashioned someone who works in a coal mine

col·lie·ry /'kɒljəri $ 'kɑːl-/ *n* [C] plural **collieries** *BrE* a COAL MINE and the buildings and machinery connected with it

col·li·sion /kə'lɪʒən/ *n* [C,U] **1** an accident in which two or more people or vehicles hit each other while moving in different directions; → **collide**: [+with] *The school bus was involved in a collision with a truck.* | *Two people were killed in a head-on collision* (=between two vehicles that are moving directly towards each other) *on highway 218.* **2** a strong disagreement between two people or groups: [+between] *a collision between the two countries over fishing rights* **3 be on a collision course a)** to be likely to have serious trouble because your aims are very different from someone else's: *The two nations are on a collision course that could lead to war.* **b)** to be moving in a direction in which you will hit something: *an asteroid on a collision course with Earth*

col·lo·cate /'kɒləkeɪt $ 'kɑː-/ *v* [I] technical when words collocate, they are often used together and sound natural together: [+with] *'Enigmatic' collocates with 'smile'.* —**collocate** /-kət/ *n* [C]

col·lo·ca·tion /,kɒlə'keɪʃən $,kɑː-/ *n* [C,U] technical the way in which some words are often used together, or a particular combination of words used in this way: *'Commit a crime' is a typical collocation in English.*

col·lo·qui·al /kə'ləukwiəl $ -'lou-/ *adj* language or words that are colloquial are used mainly in informal conversations rather than in writing or formal speech —**colloquially** *adv*

col·lo·qui·al·is·m /kə'ləukwiəlɪzəm $ -'lou-/ *n* [C] an expression or word used in informal conversation

col·lo·qui·um /kə'ləukwiəm $ -'lou-/ *n* [C] formal a CONFERENCE

col·lo·quy /'kɒləkwi $ 'kɑː-/ *n* [C] formal a conversation → SOLILOQUY

col·lude /kə'luːd/ *v* [I] to work with someone secretly, especially in order to do something dishonest or illegal: [+with] *Several customs officials have been accused of colluding with drug traffickers.* | [+in] *She knew about the plan, and colluded in it.*

col·lu·sion /kə'luːʒən/ *n* [U] a secret agreement that two or more people make in order to do something dishonest

col·ly·wob·bles /'kɒli,wɒbəlz $ 'kɑːli,wɑː-/ *n* **the collywobbles** *BrE* informal an uncomfortable feeling that you get when you are very nervous

co·logne /kə'ləʊn $ -'loʊn/ also **eau de cologne** n [U] a liquid that smells slightly of flowers or plants, that you put on your neck or wrists; → **perfume**

co·lon /'kəʊlən $ 'koʊ-/ n [C] **1** technical the lower part of the BOWELS, in which food is changed into waste matter **2** the sign (:) that is used in writing and printing to introduce an explanation, example, QUOTATION (1) etc; → **semicolon**

colo·nel /'kɜːnl $ 'kɜːr-/ n [C] a high rank in the army, Marines, or the US air force, or someone who has this rank

co·lo·ni·al¹ /kə'ləʊniəl $ -'loʊ-/ adj **1** relating to a country that controls and rules other countries, usually ones that are far away; → **colony**: the struggle against **colonial** rule | Britain was the largest **colonial power**. **2** made in a style that was common in the US in the 18th century: a large colonial house **3** relating to the US when it was under British rule: The town was first established in colonial times.

colonial² n [C] someone who lives in a COLONY but who is a citizen of the country that rules the colony

co·lo·ni·al·is·m /kə'ləʊniəlizəm $ -'loʊ-/ n [U] when a powerful country rules a weaker one, and establishes its own trade and society there; → **colony**, **imperialism**: a legacy of European colonialism

co·lo·ni·al·ist /kə'ləʊniəlɪst $ -'loʊ-/ n [C] a supporter of colonialism —**colonialist** adj: colonialist attitudes

co·lon·ic /kə'lɒnɪk $ -'lɑː-/ adj **1** relating to the COLON **2** **colonic irrigation** the practice of washing someone's COLON with water, which is believed to make them more healthy

col·o·nist /'kɒlənɪst $ 'kɑː-/ n [C] someone who settles in a new colony

col·o·nize also **-ise** BrE /'kɒlənaɪz $ 'kɑː-/ v [T] **1** to establish political control over an area or over another country, and send your citizens there to settle; → **colony 2** if animals or plants colonize an area, large numbers of them start to live there: a dead tree that has been colonized by ants —**colonizer** n [C] —**colonization** /,kɒlənaɪ'zeɪʃən $,kɑːlənə-/ n [U]

col·on·nade /,kɒlə'neɪd $,kɑː-/ n [C] a row of upright stone posts that usually support a roof or row of ARCHES —**colonnaded** adj

col·o·ny /'kɒləni $ 'kɑː-/ n plural **colonies** [C] **1** a country or area that is under the political control of a more powerful country, usually one that is far away; → **colonial**, **colonize**: Algeria was formerly a French colony. → **CROWN COLONY 2** one of the 13 areas of land on the east coast of North America that later became the United States: Connecticut was one of the original colonies. **3** a group of people who are similar in some way and who live together, or the place where they live: an artists' colony | a leper colony **4** a group of animals or plants of the same type that are living or growing together: a seal colony | breeding colonies of rare birds

col·or¹ /'kʌlə $ -ər/ n,v the American spelling of COLOUR

color² v **color me surprised/confused/embarrassed etc** AmE spoken informal used to say that you are very surprised, confused etc by something: 'Color me amazed!' says prize-winner Angela Harris.

col·o·ra·tion /,kʌlə'reɪʃən/ n [U] the colours or pattern of colours on a plant or animal

col·o·ra·tu·ra /,kɒlərə'tʊərə, -'tjʊə- $,kʌlərə'tʊrə/ n **1** [U] a difficult piece of music that is meant to be sung fast **2** [C] a woman, especially a SOPRANO, who sings this type of music

'color ,guard n [C] AmE a group of people who carry flags in an official ceremony

col·or·ize also **colourize** BrE /'kʌləraɪz/ v [T] to add colour to a film that was first made in black and white —**colorization** /,kʌlərɪ'zeɪʃən $ -rə-/ n [U]

'color line n [singular] AmE the set of laws or social customs in some places that prevents people of differ-

ent races from going to the same places or taking part in the same activities; ◨ **colour bar** BrE

co·los·sal /kə'lɒsəl $ kə'lɑː-/ adj used to emphasize that something is extremely large: a colossal statue of the King | a colossal waste of money —**colossally** adv

co·los·sus /kə'lɒsəs $ kə'lɑː-/ n [C] someone or something that is extremely big or extremely important: an intellectual colossus like Leonardo

colour¹ S1 W1 BrE; **color** AmE /'kʌlə $ -ər/ n

1 RED/BLUE/GREEN ETC [C] red, blue, yellow, green, brown, purple etc: What colour dress did you buy? | What colour are his eyes? | The pens come in a wide range of colours. | **light/bright/pastel etc colour** I love wearing bright colours. | **reddish-brown/yellowy-green/deep blue etc colour** The walls were a lovely reddish-brown color.

2 COLOUR IN GENERAL [U] also **colours** the appearance of something as a result of the way it REFLECTS (=throws back) light, especially when its appearance is very bright or is made up of a lot of different colours: Bright bold accessories are the quickest way to **add colour** to a room. | **in colour** The wine was almost pink in colour (=was almost pink). | **blaze/riot/mass of colour** (=lots of different bright colours) In summer the gardens are a blaze of colour. | **a splash of colour** (=a small area of a bright colour) The sky began to slowly **change colour**. | the fall colors (=the colours of the trees in autumn)

3 SB'S RACE [C,U] how dark or light someone's skin is, which shows which race they belong to: Everyone has a right to a job, regardless of their race, sex, or colour. | people of all colors | the continuing battle against **colour prejudice** → COLOURED²

4 **people/women/students etc of color** especially AmE people, women etc who are not white: I'm the only person of color in my class.

5 SUBSTANCE [C,U] a substance such as paint or DYE that makes something red, blue, yellow etc: Wash the garment separately, as the **colour may run** (=come out when washed). | jams that contain no **artificial colours** or preservatives | **lip/nail/eye colour** our new range of eyeshadows and lip colours

6 **in (full) colour** a television programme, film, or photograph that is in colour contains colours such as red, green, and blue rather than just black and white: ◧ **in black and white**: All the recipes in the book are illustrated in full colour.

7 SB'S FACE [U] if you have some colour in your face, your face is pink or red, usually because you are healthy or embarrassed: You look a lot better today. At least you've **got a bit of colour** now. | One of the girls giggled nervously as **colour flooded** her cheeks (=her cheeks suddenly went very pink or red). | He stared at her, the **colour draining** from his face.

8 STH INTERESTING [U] interesting and exciting details or qualities that someone or something has: The old market is lively, **full of colour** and activity. | a travel writer in search of **local colour** | **add/give colour to sth** (=make something more interesting) Intelligent use of metaphors can add colour and style to your writing.

9 **lend/give colour to sth** to make something, especially something unusual, appear likely or true: We now have independent evidence that lends colour to the accusation of fraud.

10 **off colour a)** [not before noun] BrE someone who is off colour is feeling slightly ill **b)** [usually before noun] especially AmE off-colour jokes, stories etc are rude and often about sex

11 **colours** [plural] **a)** the colours that are used to represent a team, school, club, country etc: **club/team/school colours** a peaked cap in the team colours | Australia's **national colours** are gold and green. **b)** BrE a flag, shirt etc that shows that someone or something belongs to or supports a particular team, school, club, or country

C

12 see the colour of sb's money *spoken* to have definite proof that someone has enough money to pay for something: *'A whiskey, please.' 'Let's see the color of your money first.'* → **with flying colours** at FLYING[1] (2); → **nail your colours to the mast** at NAIL[2] (5); → **your true colours** at TRUE[1] (13)

WORD FOCUS: COLOUR

a particular kind of colour: **shade, hint, hue**
words for describing dark colours: **dark, deep, rich**
words for describing light colours: **light, pale, soft, pastel**
words for describing bright colours: **bright, brilliant, vivid, garish** *disapproving,* **gaudy** *disapproving*
having a lot of colours: **colourful, multicoloured** *BrE/* **multicolored** *AmE*

---

colour[2] *BrE;* **color** *AmE v* **1** [T] to change the colour of something, especially by using DYE: *If I didn't colour my hair I'd be totally grey.* | *Colour the icing with a little green food colouring.* | **colour sth red/blue etc** *Sunset came and coloured the sky a brilliant red.* **2** [I,T] also **colour in** to use coloured pencils to put colours inside the lines of a picture: *On the back page is a picture for your child to colour in.* | *She has no idea how to colour a picture – she just scribbles all over it.* **3** [I] *literary* when someone colours, their face becomes redder because they are embarrassed; ◨ **blush:** *Her eyes suddenly met his and she coloured slightly.* **4 colour sb's judgement/opinions/attitudes etc** to influence the way someone thinks about something, especially so that they become less fair or reasonable: *In my position, I can't afford to let my judgement be coloured by personal feelings.*

colour[3] *BrE;* **color** *AmE adj* **colour television/photograph/printer etc** a colour television, photograph etc that produces or shows pictures in colour rather than in black, white, and grey; → **black and white:** *a large color TV* | *Please ask for our free colour brochure.*

col·our·ant *BrE;* **colorant** *AmE* /'kʌlərənt/ *n* [C] a substance used to change the colour of something, especially someone's hair

colour bar *n* [C usually singular] *BrE* a set of laws or social customs that prevents black people from going to the same places or taking part in the same activities as white people; ◨ **color line** *AmE*

colour-blind *BrE;* **color-blind** *AmE adj* **1** unable to see the difference between all or some colours **2** treating people from different races equally and fairly: *The law should be colour-blind.* —**colour-blindness** *n* [U]

colour coded *BrE;* **color coded** *AmE adj* things that are colour coded are marked with different colours so that it is easy to see what they are to be used for

colour-co·ordinated *BrE;* **color-coordinated** *AmE adj* clothes, decorations etc that are colour-coordinated have colours which look good together —**colour-coordi·nation** *n* [U]

col·oured[1] *BrE;* **colored** *AmE* /'kʌləd $ -ərd/ *adj* **1** brightly/highly/richly etc coloured having a bright colour such as red, blue, or yellow etc, or a deep shade of a particular colour, but not black, white, or plain **2** having a colour other than black or white: *coloured glass* | *a cream-coloured sweater* **3** *taboo old-fashioned* a very offensive word used to describe someone who is a member of a race of people with dark or black skin. Do not use this word. **4** used in South Africa to describe someone whose parents or grandparents were not of the same race as each other

coloured[2] *BrE;* **colored** *AmE n* [C] **1** *taboo old-fashioned* a very offensive word for someone who is a member of a race of people with dark or black skin. Do not use this word. **2** a person whose parents or grandparents were not of the same race as each other – used in South Africa

col·our·fast *BrE;* **colorfast** *AmE* /'kʌləfɑːst $ 'kʌlərfæst/ *adj* cloth that is colourfast will not lose its colour when it is washed

col·our·ful *BrE;* **colorful** *AmE* /'kʌləfəl $ -lər-/ *adj* **1** having bright colours or a lot of different colours: *a colourful display of flowers* | *colourful costumes* **2** interesting, exciting, and full of variety: **colourful history/past/career/life** *Charlie Chaplin had a long and colorful career.* | **colourful character/figure** (=someone who is interesting and unusual) **3** colourful language, speech etc uses a lot of swearing —**colourfully** *adv*

col·our·ing *BrE;* **coloring** *AmE* /'kʌlərɪŋ/ *n* **1** [C,U] a substance used to give a particular colour to food: *green food colouring* **2** [U] the activity of putting colours into drawings, or of drawing using CRAYONS, coloured pencils etc: *a children's colouring competition* **3** [U] the colour of someone's skin, hair, and eyes: *Mandy has her mother's fair coloring.* **4** [U] the colours of an animal, bird, or plant

colouring book *BrE;* **coloring book** *AmE n* [C] a book full of pictures that are drawn without colour so that a child can colour them in

col·our·ist *BrE;* **colorist** *AmE* /'kʌlərɪst/ *n* [C] **1** *technical* a painter who uses colour itself as a subject of a painting **2** someone whose job is to DYE people's hair (=change the colour)

col·our·less *BrE;* **colorless** *AmE* /'kʌlələs $ 'kʌlər-/ *adj* **1** having no colour: *a colourless, odourless gas* **2** if your face, hair, eyes, skin, or lips are colourless, they are very pale, usually because you are ill or frightened **3** not interesting or exciting; ◨ **dull:** *his colourless personality* —**colourlessly** *adv*

colour scheme *BrE;* **color scheme** *AmE n* [C] the combination of colours that someone chooses for a room, painting etc

colour supplement *n* [C] *BrE* a magazine printed in colour and given free with a newspaper, especially on Saturdays or Sundays

colt /kəʊlt $ koʊlt/ *n* [C] **1** a young male horse; → **filly** **2** [usually plural] *BrE* a member of a sports team for young people: *our colts team*

col·umn [S2] [W2] /'kɒləm $ 'kɑː-/ *n* [C]
1 a tall solid upright stone post used to support a building or as a decoration
2 a line of numbers or words written under each other that goes down a page; → **row: in a column** *Add up the numbers in each column.* | **[+of]** *a column of figures*
3 an article on a particular subject or by a particular writer that appears regularly in a newspaper or magazine: *He writes a weekly column for 'The Times'.* | **music/science/gardening etc column**
4 one of two or more areas of print that go down the page of a newspaper or book and that are separated from each other by a narrow space: *Turn to Page 5, column 2.* | *'The Sun' devoted 10 column inches to the event* (=their article filled a column ten inches long).
5 something that has a tall thin shape: **[+of]** *a column of smoke*
6 a long moving line of people or things: **[+of]** *a column of marching men* → FIFTH COLUMN, GOSSIP COLUMN, PERSONAL COLUMN, SPINAL COLUMN

col·umn·ist /'kɒləmɪst, -ləmnɪst $ 'kɑː-/ *n* [C] someone who writes articles, especially about a particular subject, that appear regularly in a newspaper or magazine

com /kɒm $ kɑːm/ the abbreviation of **commercial organization**, used in Internet addresses

co·ma /'kəʊmə $ 'koʊ-/ *n* [C,U] someone who is in a coma has been unconscious for a long time, usually because of a serious illness or injury: **be in/go into/come out of a coma** *He went into a coma and died soon afterwards.*

co·ma·tose /'kəʊmətəʊs $ 'koʊmətoʊs/ *adj technical* in a coma

comb[1] /kəʊm $ koʊm/ *n* **1** [C] a flat piece of plastic, metal etc with a row of thin teeth on one side, used for making your hair look tidy; → **brush** **2** [C] a small flat piece of plastic, metal etc with a row of thin teeth on one side, used for keeping your hair back or for decoration   **3** [singular] if you give your hair a comb, you make it tidy using a comb: *Your hair needs a good comb.*   **4** [C] the red piece of flesh that grows on top of a male chicken's head   **5** [C] a HONEYCOMB → FINE-TOOTH COMB

comb² *v* [T]   **1** to make hair look tidy using a comb: *Melanie ran upstairs to* **comb** *her* **hair**.   **2** to search a place thoroughly: **comb sth for sb/sth** *Police are still combing the woods for the missing boy.*

    comb sth ⇔ **out** *phr v* to use a comb to make untidy hair look smooth and tidy: *She sat combing out her hair in front of the kitchen mirror.*

    comb through sth *phr v* to search through a lot of objects or information in order to find a specific thing or piece of information: *We spent weeks combing through huge piles of old documents.*

com·bat¹ /'kɒmbæt $ 'kɑːm-/ *n*   **1** [U] fighting, especially during a war: *Corporal Gierson was killed in combat.* | *We flew over 200* **combat missions**. | *training in* **unarmed combat** (=fighting without weapons) | **mortal combat** (=fighting until one person kills another) | **hand-to-hand combat** (=fighting in which you are close enough to touch your opponent) | **combat aircraft/jacket/boots etc**   **2** [C] a fight or battle

com·bat² /'kɒmbæt, kəm'bæt $ kəm'bæt, 'kɑːmbæt/ *v* **combated, combating** [T] to try to stop something bad from happening or getting worse – used especially in news reports: **combat inflation/crime/racism etc** *In order to combat inflation, the government imposed strict controls on foreign currency.* | *new strategies for combatting terrorism*

'combat fatigue *n* [U] a type of mental illness caused by the terrible experiences of fighting in a war or battle; → **post-traumatic stress disorder**: *These treatment methods enabled 80 percent of combat-fatigue-affected troops to return to duty.*

com·ba·tant /'kɒmbətənt $ kəm'bætnt/ *n* [C] someone who fights in a war

com·ba·tive /'kɒmbətɪv $ kəm'bætɪv/ *adj* ready and willing to fight or argue: *Congress is in a combative mood.* —**combativeness** *n* [U]

com·bats /'kɒmbæts $ 'kɑːm-/ *n* [plural] loose trousers, often with many pockets: *She always wore combats, which were more fashionable than jeans.*

com·bi·na·tion S3 W2 /ˌkɒmbɪ'neɪʃən $ ˌkɑːm-/ *n*   **1** [C,U] two or more different things that exist together or are used or put together; → **combine**: [+of] *A* **combination of factors** *may be responsible for the increase in cancer.* | *A combination of tact and authority was needed to deal with the situation.* | *Certain combinations of sounds are not possible in English.* | **in combination (with sth)** *Some drugs which are safe when taken separately are lethal in combination.*   **2** [C] the series of numbers or letters you need to open a combination lock   **3 winning combination** a mixture of different people or things that work successfully together   **4** [U] *especially AmE* used before a noun to mean that something has more than one purpose or uses more than one method: *a combination nightclub and café* | *new* **combination drug therapies**

ˌcombi'nation ˌlock *n* [C] a lock which can only be opened by using a series of numbers or letters in a particular order → see picture at LOCK²

com·bine¹ S3 W2 /kəm'baɪn/ *v*   **1** [I,T] if you combine two or more different things, or if they combine, they begin to exist or work together; → **combination**: **combine sth with sth** *Augustine was later to combine elements of this philosophy with the teachings of Christianity.* | *Diets are most effective when combined with exercise.* | **combine to do sth** *A number of factors have* **combined** *to create this difficult situation.* | *Ruth hesitated, uncertain of how to combine honesty and diplomacy in her answer.* | **combined**

effect/effects (=the result of two or more different things used or mixed together) *The combined effects of the war and the drought resulted in famine.*   **2** [T] to have two or more different features or qualities at the same time; → **combination**: **combine sth with/and sth** *Good carpet wool needs to combine softness with strength.*   **3** [I,T] if two or more different substances combine, or if you combine them, they mix or join together to produce a new single substance; → **combination**: **combine to do sth** *Different amino acids combine to form proteins.* | *Combine all the ingredients in a large bowl.* | **combine sth with sth** *Steel is produced by combining iron with carbon.*   **4** [T] to do two different activities at the same time: **combine sth with sth** *Many people enjoy combining a holiday with learning a new skill.* | **combine sth and sth** *the problems facing women who wish to combine a career and family* | **combine business with pleasure** (=work and enjoy yourself at the same time)   **5** [I,T] if two or more groups, organizations etc combine, or if you combine them, they join or work together in order to do something: **combine to do sth** *Ten British and French companies combined to form the Channel Tunnel Group.* | *University zoologists and government vets are* **combining forces** (=working together) *to investigate the disease.*

com·bine² /'kɒmbaɪn $ 'kɑːm-/ *n* [C]   **1** also **combine harvester** a machine used by farmers to cut grain, separate the seeds from it, and clean it   **2** a group of people, businesses etc who work together: *The factory was sold to a British combine after the war.*

com·bined /kəm'baɪnd/ *adj* [only before noun]   **1** done, made, or achieved by several people or groups working together; ▤ **joint**: **combined effort/action/operation** *Dinner was a combined effort.*   **2** a combined total is the sum of two or more quantities or figures added together: *Her records have sold a* **combined total** *of 14 million copies.* | *We could only afford a small flat, even on our combined salaries.*

com'bining ˌform *n* [C] *technical* a word that is combined with another word or another combining form to make a new word, for example 'Anglo', meaning 'English', in the word 'Anglo-American'

com·bo /'kɒmbəʊ $ 'kɑːmboʊ/ *n plural* **combos** [C]   **1** a small band that plays JAZZ or dance music: *He played trumpet professionally in a jazz combo.*   **2** a COMBINATION of different things, especially of different types of foods – used especially in product names: *I chose the vegetarian combo.*

com·bus·ti·ble /kəm'bʌstɪbəl/ *adj* able to burn easily: **combustible material/gas etc**

com·bus·tion /kəm'bʌstʃən/ *n* [U]   **1** the process of burning   **2** *technical* chemical activity which uses oxygen to produce light and heat → INTERNAL COMBUSTION ENGINE

com'bustion ˌchamber *n* [C] the enclosed space, for example in an engine, in which combustion happens

come¹ S1 W1 /kʌm/ *v past tense* **came** /keɪm/ *past participle* **come** [I]

    1 MOVE TOWARDS SB/STH to move towards you or arrive at the place where you are; ▤ **go**: *Let me know when they come.* | *Can you* **come here** *for a minute?* | *Come a bit* **closer** *and you'll be able to see better.* | *What time will you be* **coming home**? | [+in/into/out of etc] *There was a knock on the door and a young woman came into the room.* | [+to/towards] *I could see a figure coming towards me.* | [+across/down/up etc] *As they came down the track, the car skidded.* | **come to do sth** *I've come to see Philip.* | **come and do sth** *I'll come and help you move the rest of the boxes.* | *Come and look at this!* | **come running/flying/speeding etc** *Jess came flying round the corner and banged straight into me.* |

come to dinner/lunch *What day are your folks coming to dinner?* | **here comes sb/sth** *spoken* (=used to say that someone or something is coming towards you) *Ah, here comes the bus at last!*

2 GO WITH SB if someone comes with you, they go to a place with you: *We're going for a drink this evening. Would you like to come?* | [+with] *I asked Rosie if she'd like to come with us.* | [+along] *It should be good fun. Why don't you come along?*

3 TRAVEL TO A PLACE to travel to or reach a place: *Which way did you come?* | [+through/across/by way of etc] *They came over the mountains in the north.* | [+from] *Legend has it that the tribe came from across the Pacific Ocean.* | **come by car/train/bus etc** *Will you be coming by train?* | *Have you come far* (=travelled a long way) *today?* | *I've come a long way to see you.* | **come 50/100 etc miles/kilometres** *Some of the birds have come thousands of miles to winter here.*

4 POST if a letter etc comes, it is delivered to you by post; ▤ **arrive**: *A letter came for you this morning.* | *The phone bill hasn't come yet.*

5 HAPPEN if a time or an event comes, it arrives or happens: *At last the day came for us to set off.* | *The moment had come for me to break the news to her.* | *The time will come when you'll thank me for this.* | *Christmas seems to come earlier every year.* | **be/have yet to come** (=used when something has not happened yet but will happen) *The most exciting part is yet to come.* | *I knew he'd be able to take care of himself,* **come what may** (=whatever happens).

6 REACH A LEVEL/PLACE [always + adv/prep] to reach a particular level or place: [+up/down] *She had blonde hair which came down to her waist.* | *The water came up as far as my chest.*

7 BE PRODUCED/SOLD [always + adv/prep] to be produced or sold with particular features: [+in] *This particular sofa comes in four different colours.* | *Cats come in many shapes and sizes.* | [+with] *The computer* **comes complete with** *software and games.*

8 ORDER [always + adv/prep] to be in a particular position in an order, a series, or a list: [+before/after] *P comes before Q in the alphabet.* | **come first/second etc** *She came first in the 200 metres.*

9 come open/undone/loose etc to become open etc: *His shoelace had come undone.* | *The rope came loose.*

10 come to do sth a) to begin to have a feeling or opinion: *He came to think of Italy as his home.* | *I came to believe that he was innocent after all.* **b)** to do something by chance, without planning or intending to do it: *Can you tell me how the body came to be discovered?* | **come to be doing sth** *I often wondered how I came to be living in such a place.*

11 come and go a) to be allowed to go into and leave a place whenever you want: *The students can come and go as they please.* **b)** to keep starting and stopping: *The pain comes and goes.*

12 take sth as it comes to accept something as it happens, without trying to plan for it or change it: *We just take each year as it comes.* | *He takes life as it comes.*

13 have sth coming (to you) *informal* to deserve to be punished or to have something bad happen to you: *I do feel sorry for him, but I'm afraid he had it coming.*

14 as nice/as stupid etc as they come *informal* extremely nice, stupid etc: *My uncle Walter is as obstinate as they come.*

15 for years/weeks/days etc to come used to emphasize that something will continue for a long time into the future: *This is a moment that will be remembered and celebrated for years to come.*

16 in years/days to come in the future: *In years to come, some of the practices we take for granted now will seem quite barbaric.*

17 have come a long way to have made a lot of progress: *Computer technology has come a long way since the 1970s.*

18 come as a surprise/relief/blow etc (to sb) to make someone feel surprised, pleased, disappointed etc: *The decision came as a great relief to us all.* | *The news will* **come as no surprise** *to his colleagues.*

19 come easily/naturally (to sb) to be easy for someone to do: *Public speaking does not come easily to most people.* | *Writing came naturally to her, even as a child.*

20 come of age a) to reach the age when you are legally considered to be an adult: *He'll inherit the money when he comes of age.* **b)** to develop into an advanced or successful form: *Space technology didn't really come of age until the 1950s.*

21 come right out with sth/come right out and say sth *informal* to say something in a very direct way, often when other people think this is surprising: *You came right out and told him? I don't know how you dared!*

22 come clean *informal* to tell the truth about something you have done: [+about] *I think you should come clean about where you were last night.*

23 not know whether you are coming or going *informal* to feel very confused because a lot of different things are happening: *I don't know whether I'm coming or going this week.*

24 come good/right *BrE informal* to end well, after there have been a lot of problems: *Don't worry, it'll all come right in the end.*

25 come to pass *literary* to happen after a period of time: *It came to pass that they had a son.*

26 SEX *informal* to have an ORGASM

SPOKEN PHRASES

27 come in! used to tell someone who has knocked on your door to enter your room, house etc: *She tapped timidly on the door. 'Come in!' boomed a deep voice from inside.*

28 how come? used to ask someone why or how something happened: *How come you've ended up here?* | *'Last I heard, she was teaching in Mexico.' 'How come?'*

29 come to think of it/come to that used to add something that you have just realized or remembered: *Come to think of it, George did seem a bit depressed yesterday.* | *He had never expected to have a wife, or even a girlfriend come to that.*

30 come July/next year/the next day etc used to talk about at a particular time in the future: *Come spring, you'll have plenty of colour in the garden.*

31 come again? used to ask someone to repeat what they have just said

32 don't come the innocent/victim/helpless male etc with me *BrE* used to tell someone not to pretend that they are something they are not in order to get sympathy or help from you: *Don't come the poor struggling artist with me. You're just lazy!*

33 come (now) *old-fashioned* used to comfort or gently encourage someone

34 come, come!/come now *old-fashioned* used to tell someone that you do not accept what they are saying or doing

---

come about *phr v*

1 to happen, especially in a way that is not planned: *The opportunity to get into computing came about quite by accident.* | *I don't know how this confusion has come about.*

2 if a ship comes about, it changes direction

come across *phr v*

1 **come across sb/sth** to meet, find, or discover someone or something by chance: *I came across an old diary in her desk.* | *I've never come across anyone quite like her before.*

2 if an idea comes across well, it is easy for people to understand: *Your point really came across at the meeting.*

3 if someone comes across in a particular way, they seem to have particular qualities; ▤ **come over**: [+as] *He comes across as a very intelligent, sensitive man.* | *She sometimes comes across as being rather arrogant.* | *I don't think I came across very well* (=seemed to have good qualities) *in the interview.*

come across with sth *phr v*

to provide money or information when it is needed:

hoped he might come across with a few facts.

come after sb *phr v*
to look for someone in order to hurt them, punish them, or get something from them: *She was terrified that Trevor would come after her.*

come along *phr v*
1 be coming along *informal* to be developing or making progress; ☰ **progress**: *He opened the oven door to see how the food was coming along.* | *Your English is coming along really well.*
2 to appear or arrive: *A bus should come along any minute now.* | *Take any job opportunity that comes along.*
3 a) to go to a place with someone: *We're going into town – do you want to come along?* **b)** to go somewhere after someone: *You go on ahead – I'll come along later.*
4 come along! a) used to tell someone to hurry up; ☰ **come on**: *Come along! We're all waiting for you!* **b)** used to encourage someone to try harder; ☰ **come on**: *Come along! Don't give up yet!*

come apart *phr v*
1 to split or fall into pieces: *I picked the magazine up and it came apart in my hands.*
2 to begin to fail: *The whole basis of the agreement was coming apart.* | *She felt as if her life was coming apart at the seams* (=failing completely).

come around *phr v*
1 also **come round** *BrE* to come to someone's home or the place where they work in order to visit them; ☰ **come over**: *I'll come around later and see how you are.* | *Why don't you come round for lunch?*
2 also **come round** *BrE* to change your opinion so that you now agree with someone or are no longer angry with them: [+to] *It took him a while to come around to the idea.* | *Don't worry – she'll come round eventually.*
3 also **come round** *BrE* if a regular event comes around, it happens as usual: *By the time the summer came around, Kelly was feeling much better.*
4 *AmE* to become conscious again after you have been unconscious; ☰ **come round** *BrE*: *When she came around her mother was sitting by her bed.* | [+from] *You might feel a little sick when you come around from the anesthetic.*

come at sb/sth *phr v*
1 to move towards someone in a threatening way: *Suddenly, he came at me with a knife.*
2 if images, questions, facts etc come at you, you feel confused because there are too many of them at the same time: *Questions were coming at me from all directions.*
3 *informal* to consider or deal with a problem in a particular way; ☰ **approach**: *We need to come at the problem from a different angle.*

come away *phr v*
1 to become separated from the main part of something; ☰ **come off**: *One of the wires in the plug had come away.* | *I turned some of the pages and they came away in my hand.*
2 to leave a place with a particular feeling or idea: *We came away thinking that we had done quite well.* | [+with] *I came away with the impression that the school was very well run.*

come back *phr v*
1 to return to a particular place or person; ☰ **return**: *My mother was scared that if I left home I'd never come back.* | *Ginny's left me, and there's nothing I can do to persuade her to come back.*
2 to become fashionable or popular again; → **comeback**: *Who'd have thought hippy gear would ever come back!* | *High heels are coming back into fashion.*
3 to appear or start to affect someone or something again; ☰ **return**: *The pain in her shoulder was coming back again.* | *It took a while for my confidence to come back.*
4 if something comes back to you, you remember it or remember how to do it: *As I walked the city streets that evening, the memories came flooding back.* | [+to] *I can't think of her name at the moment, but it'll come back to me.*

5 to reply to someone quickly, often in an angry or unkind way; → **comeback**: [+at] *He came back at me immediately, accusing me of being a liar.*

come before sb/sth *phr v formal*
to be brought to someone in authority, especially a judge in a law court, to be judged or discussed by them: *When you come before the judge, it's best to tell the whole truth.* | *The case is due to come before the courts next month.*

come between sb *phr v*
1 to make people argue and feel angry with each other, when they had been friends before: *Nothing will ever come between us now.* | *I didn't want to come between a husband and wife.*
2 to prevent someone from giving enough attention to something: *She never let anything come between her and her work.*

come by *phr v*
1 to manage to get something that is rare or difficult to get: *How did you come by these pictures?* | *Jobs were hard to come by.*
2 come by (sth) to make a short visit to a place on your way to somewhere else: *He said he'd come by later.* | *I'll come by the house and get my stuff later, OK?*

come down *phr v*
1 a) if a price, level etc comes down, it gets lower: *It looks as if interest rates will come down again this month.* **b)** to accept a lower price: [+to] *He's asking £5000, but he may be willing to come down to £4800.*
2 if someone comes down to a place, they travel south to the place where you are: *Why don't you come down for the weekend sometime?* | [+to] *Are you coming down to Knoxville for Christmas?*
3 to fall to the ground: *A lot of trees came down in the storm.* | *We were still out in the fields when the rain started coming down.*
4 come down on the side of sb/sth also **come down in favour of sb/sth** to decide to support someone or something: *The committee came down in favour of making the information public.*
5 *informal* to start to feel normal again after you have been feeling very happy and excited: *He was on a real high all last week and he's only just come down.*
6 *informal* to stop feeling the effects of a strong drug: *When I came down, I remembered with horror some of the things I'd said.*
7 *BrE old-fashioned* to leave a university after completing a period of study

come down on sb *phr v*
to punish someone or criticize them severely: *We need to come down hard on young offenders.* | *I made the mistake of answering back, and she came down on me like a ton of bricks* (=very severely).

come down to sb/sth *phr v*
1 if a complicated situation or problem comes down to something, that is the single most important thing: *It all comes down to money in the end.*
2 if something old has come down to you, it has been passed between people over a long period of time until you have it: *The text which has come down to us is only a fragment of the original.*

come down with sth *phr v*
to get an illness: *I think I'm coming down with a cold.*

come for sb/sth *phr v*
1 to arrive to collect someone or something: *I'll come for you at about eight o'clock.*
2 to arrive at a place in order to take someone away by force: *Members of the secret police came for him in the middle of the night.*

come forward *phr v*
to offer help to someone, or offer to do something: *So far, only one candidate has come forward.* | *The police are appealing for more witnesses to come forward with information.*

come from sb/sth *phr v*
1 if you come from a place, you were born there or lived there when you were young: *I come from London originally.*

C

2 to be obtained from a place, thing, or person, or to start or be made somewhere: *A lot of drugs come from quite common plants.* | *My information comes from a very reputable source.* | *The idea came from America.*

3 to happen as the result of doing something: **come from doing sth** *Most of her problems come from expecting too much of people.*

4 coming from him/her/you etc *spoken* used to say that someone should not criticize another person for doing something, because they have done the same thing themselves: *You think I'm too selfish? That's rich coming from you!*

5 where sb is coming from *informal* the basic attitude or opinion someone has, which influences what they think, say, or do: *I can see where you're coming from now.*

come in *phr v*
1 if a train, bus, plane, or ship comes in, it arrives at a place: *What time does your train come in?* | [+to] *We come in to Heathrow at nine in the morning.*

2 if money or information comes in, you receive it: *Reports are coming in of a massive earthquake in Mexico.* | *We haven't got enough money coming in.*

3 to be involved in a plan, deal etc: *We need some financial advice – that's where Kate comes in.* | [+on] *You had the chance to come in on the deal.*

4 to join in a conversation or discussion: *Can I come in here and add something to what you're saying?*

5 to become fashionable or popular; ⏣ **go out**: *Trainers really became popular in the 1980s, when casual sportswear came in.*

6 to finish a race: **come in first/second etc** *His horse came in second to last.*

7 if the TIDE comes in, the sea moves towards the land and covers the edge of it; ⏣ **go out**

come in for sth *phr v*
come in for criticism/blame/scrutiny to be criticized, blamed etc for something: *The government has come in for fierce criticism over its handling of this affair.*

come into sth *phr v*
1 to receive money, land, or property from someone after they have died: *She'll come into quite a lot of money when her father dies.*

2 to be involved in something: *Josie doesn't come into the movie until quite near the end.* | *Where do I come into all this?*

3 come into view/sight if something comes into view, you begin to see it: *The mountains were just coming into view.*

4 come into leaf/flower/blossom to start to produce leaves or flowers: *The early roses were just coming into flower.*

5 not come into it *spoken* used to say that something is not important: *Money doesn't really come into it.*

6 come into your own to become very good, useful, or important in a particular situation: *On icy roads, a four-wheel drive vehicle really comes into its own.*

come of sth *phr v*
to happen as a result of something: *I did ask a few questions, but nothing came of it.* | *That's what comes of not practising – you've forgotten everything!*

come off *phr v*
1 come off (sth) to become removed from something: *The label had come off, so there was no way of knowing what was on the disk.*

2 come off (sth) *BrE* to fall off something: *Dyson came off his bike as he rounded the last corner, but wasn't badly hurt.*

3 *informal* if something that has been planned comes off, it happens: *In the end the trip never came off.*

4 *informal* to be successful: *It was a good idea, but it didn't quite come off.* | *The performance on the first night came off pretty well.*

5 come off sth to stop taking a drug that you have been taking regularly: *It wasn't until I tried to come off the pills that I realized I was addicted.*

6 come off best/better/worst etc *BrE* to gain or lose the most, more, the least etc from a situation: *As far as pensions go, it's still women who come off worst.*

7 come off it! *BrE spoken* used to tell someone that you do not believe what they are saying: *Oh come off it! You can't seriously be saying you knew nothing about any of this.*

come on *phr v*
1 come on! *spoken* **a)** used to tell someone to hurry: *Come on, we'll be late!* **b)** used to encourage someone to do something: *Come on, you can do it!* | *Come on, cheer up!* **c)** used to tell someone that you know that what they have just said was not true or right: *Oh come on, don't lie!* **d)** used to make someone angry enough to want to fight you: *Come on, then, hit me!*

2 come on in/over/up etc *spoken* used to tell someone to come in, over, up etc, usually in a friendly way: *Come on in – I've made some coffee.*

3 if a light or machine comes on, it starts working: *A dog started barking and lights came on in the house.*

4 if an illness comes on, you start to be ill with it: *I can feel a headache coming on.*

5 if a television or radio programme comes on, it starts: *Just at that moment, the news came on.*

6 if rain or snow comes on, it starts: *The rain came on just before lunchtime.*

7 to come onto a stage or sports field: *He scored only two minutes after he'd come on.*

8 to improve or make progress: *The children are really coming on now.* | *Your English is coming on really well.*

9 come on sb/sth to find or discover someone or something by chance: *We came on a group of students having a picnic.*

10 come on strong *informal* to make it very clear to someone that you think they are sexually attractive

come on to sb/sth *phr v*
1 to start talking about a new subject: *I'll come on to this question in a few moments.*

2 *informal* if someone comes on to another person, they make it very clear that they are sexually interested in them; → **come-on**: *The way she was coming on to Jack, I'm amazed he managed to get out alive!*

come out *phr v*
1 if something comes out, it is removed from a place: *These stains will never come out!*

2 if information comes out, people learn about it, especially after it has been kept secret: *No doubt the truth will come out one day.* | *It's come out that several ministers received payments from the company.*

3 if a photograph comes out, it shows a clear picture: *I took loads of photographs, but most of them didn't come out.* | *Some of the wedding photos have come out really well.*

4 if a book, record etc comes out, it becomes publicly available: *When is the new edition coming out?*

5 if something comes out in a particular way, that is what it is like after it has been made or produced: *I made a cake, but it hasn't come out very well.* | *The cover has come out a bit too big.*

6 if something you say comes out in a particular way, that is how it sounds or how it is understood: *His words came out as little more than a whisper.* | *That didn't come out the way I meant it to.* | *I tried to explain everything to her, but it came out all wrong* (=not in the way I intended).

7 if someone comes out in a particular way, that is the situation they are in at the end of an event or series of events: *The more experienced team came out on top.* | [+of] *She came out of the divorce quite well.*

8 to be easy to notice: *His right-wing opinions come out quite strongly in his later writings.*

9 to say publicly that you strongly support or oppose a plan, belief etc: [+in favour of] *The board of directors has come out strongly in favour of a merger.* | [+against] *Teachers have come out against the proposed changes.* | *At least he's got the courage to come out and say what he thinks.*

10 if the sun, moon, or stars come out, they appear in the sky: *The sky cleared and the sun came out.*

11 if a flower comes out, it opens: *The snowdrops were just starting to come out.*

12 if someone comes out, they say that they are GAY when this was a secret before: [+to] *That summer, I decided to come out to my parents.*

13 *BrE informal* to refuse to work, as a protest: *Nurses have threatened to come out in support of their pay claim.* | *We decided to come out on strike.*

14 if a young woman came out in the past, she was formally introduced into upper class society at a large formal dance

come out at sth *phr v*
if something comes out at a particular amount, that is the amount it adds up to: *The whole trip, including fares, comes out at $900.*

come out in sth *phr v*
come out in spots/a rash etc if you come out in spots etc, spots appear on your body: *If I eat eggs, I come out in a rash.*

come out of sth *phr v*
1 to no longer be in a bad situation: *There are signs that the country is coming out of recession.*

2 to happen as a result of something: *One or two excellent ideas came out of the meeting.*

3 come out of yourself *informal* to start to behave in a more confident way: *Penny's really come out of herself since she started that course.*

come out with sth *phr v*
to say something, especially something unusual or unexpected: *Some of the things he comes out with are so funny!*

come over *phr v*
1 a) if someone comes over, they visit you at your house: *Do you want to come over on Friday evening?* **b)** if someone comes over, they come to the country where you are: [+to/from] *When did your family first come over to America?*

2 come over sb if a strong feeling comes over you, you suddenly experience it: *A wave of sleepiness came over me.* | *I'm sorry about that – I don't know what came over me* (=I do not know why I behaved in that way).

3 if an idea comes over well, people can understand it easily: *I thought that the points he was making came over quite clearly.*

4 if someone comes over in a particular way, they seem to have particular qualities; ◨ **come across**: *He didn't come over very well* (=seem to have good qualities) *in the interview.* | [+as] *She comes over as a very efficient businesswoman.*

5 come over (all) shy/nervous etc *informal* to suddenly become very shy, nervous etc

come round *phr v BrE*
to COME AROUND

come through *phr v*
1 if a piece of information, news etc comes through, it arrives somewhere: *We're still waiting for our exam results to come through.* | *There is news just coming through of an explosion in a chemical factory.*

2 to be made official, especially by having the correct documents officially approved: *I'm still waiting for my divorce to come through.*

3 come through (sth) to continue to live, be strong, or succeed after a difficult or dangerous time; ◨ **survive**: *If he comes through the operation OK he should be back to normal within a few weeks.* | *It's been a tough time, but I'm sure you'll come through and be all the wiser for it.*

come through with sth *phr v*
to give someone something they need, especially when they have been worried that you would not produce it in time: *Our representative in Hong Kong finally came through with the figures.*

come to *phr v*
1 come to a decision/conclusion/agreement etc to decide something, agree on something etc after considering or discussing a situation; ◨ **reach**: *We came to the conclusion that there was no other way back to the camp.* | *If they don't come to a decision by midnight, the talks will be abandoned.*

2 come to a halt/stop **a)** to slow down and stop; ◨ **stop**: *The train came to a stop just yards from the barrier.* **b)** to stop operating or continuing: *After the election our funding came to an abrupt halt.*

3 come to sth to develop so that a particular situation exists, usually a bad one: *I never thought it would come to this.* | *We need to be prepared to fight, but hopefully it won't come to that* (=that won't be necessary). | *All those years of studying, and in the end it all came to nothing.* | *It's come to something when I'm not allowed to express an opinion in my own house!* | **what is the world/the country etc coming to?** (=used to say that the world etc is in a bad situation)

4 come to sth to add up to a total amount: *That comes to £23.50.* | *The bill came to £48.50.*

5 come to sb if a thought or idea comes to you, you realize or remember something: *The answer came to me in a flash.* | *I've forgotten her name, but maybe it'll come to me later.*

6 to become conscious again after you have been unconscious: *When he came to, he was lying on the floor with his hands tied behind his back.*

7 when it comes to sth *informal* when you are dealing with something or talking about something: *He's a bit of an expert when it comes to computers.*

come under sth *phr v*
1 come under attack/fire/scrutiny etc to be attacked, shot at etc: *The government has come under attack from opposition leaders over proposals to cut health spending.*

2 to be governed or controlled by a particular organization or person: *The organization comes under the authority of the EU.*

3 if a piece of information comes under a particular title, you can find it under that title: *The proposals come under three main headings.*

come up *phr v*
1 if someone comes up to you, they come close to you, especially in order to speak to you: *One of the teachers came up and started talking to me.* | [+to] *A man came up to him and asked for a light.*

2 if someone comes up to a place, they travel north to the place where you are: [+to] *Why don't you come up to New York for the weekend?*

3 if a subject comes up, people mention it and discuss it; ◨ **arise**: *His name came up in the conversation.* | *The subject of salaries didn't come up.*

4 if a problem or difficulty comes up, it appears or starts to affect you; ◨ **arise**: *I'm afraid I'll have to cancel our date – something's come up.* | *The same problems come up every time.*

5 if a job or an opportunity comes up, it becomes available: *A vacancy has come up in the accounts department.*

6 to be dealt with in a law court: *Your case comes up next week.*

7 be coming up to be going to happen soon: *With Christmas coming up, few people have much money to spare.*

8 if the sun or moon comes up, it moves up into the sky where you can see it; ◨ **rise**: *It was six o'clock, and the sun was just coming up.*

9 if a plant comes up, it begins to appear above the ground: *The first spring bulbs are just coming up.*

10 if food comes up, it goes back through your mouth from your stomach after being swallowed; → **vomit**

11 coming (right) up! *spoken* used to say that food or drink will be ready very soon: *'Two martinis, please.' 'Coming up!'*

come up against sth/sb *phr v*
to have to deal with problems or difficulties: *We may find we come up against quite a lot of opposition from local people.* | *You've got no idea of what you're going to come up against.*

come up for sth *phr v*
1 come up for discussion/examination/review etc to be discussed, examined etc: *This matter will come up for discussion at next month's meeting.* | *The regulations come up for review in April.*
2 come up for election/re-election/selection etc to reach the time when people have to vote about whether you should continue in a political position: *The governors come up for re-election next year.*

come upon sb/sth *phr v*
1 to find or discover something or someone by chance: *We came upon a little cottage just on the edge of the wood.*
2 *literary* if a feeling comes upon you, you suddenly feel it: *A wave of tiredness came upon her.*

C

come up to sth/sb *phr v*
1 to reach a particular standard or to be as good as you expected: *This doesn't come up to the standard of your usual work.* | *The resort certainly failed to **come up to expectations**.*
2 be (just) coming up to sth to be nearly a particular time: *It's just coming up to 11 o'clock.*

come up with sth *phr v*
1 to think of an idea, answer etc: *Is that the best excuse you can come up with?* | *We've been asked to come up with some new ideas.*
2 *informal* to produce an amount of money: *We wanted to buy the house but we couldn't come up with the cash.* | *How am I supposed to come up with $10,000?*

> **WORD CHOICE come, go**
> Use **come** for movement towards the place where the speaker is or will be: *Come and see me at my office.* | *I could see them coming down the hill* (getting nearer to me): *When are you coming home* (=to our home) ?
> Use **go** for movement in other directions: *Are you going to Sally's tonight?* | *I wish he would go home* (=to his home, away from me).

come² *n* [U] *informal* a man's SEMEN (=the liquid he produces during sex)

come·back /ˈkʌmbæk/ *n* [C usually singular] **1 make/stage a comeback** if a person, activity, style etc makes a comeback, they become popular again after being unpopular for a long time: *The miniskirt made a comeback in the late 1980s.* **2** a quick reply that is often clever, funny, and insulting; ⊟ **retort**: *I couldn't think of a good comeback.* **3** a way of getting payment or a reward for something wrong or unfair that has been done to you: *Check your contract carefully, or you may have no comeback if something goes wrong.* → **come back** at COME¹

co·me·di·an /kəˈmiːdiən/ *n* [C] **1** someone whose job is to tell jokes and make people laugh: *He started as a **stand-up comedian*** (=someone who tells jokes to an audience). **2** someone who is amusing: *You'll like Matt. He's a real comedian.*

co·me·di·enne /kəˌmiːdiˈen/ *n* [C] a female comedian

come·down /ˈkʌmdaʊn/ *n* [singular] a situation that is not as good, important, interesting etc as the situation you had previously: *The film marks a real comedown for the director.* → **come down** at COME¹

com·e·dy /ˈkɒmədi $ ˈkɑː-/ *n plural* **comedies 1** [U] entertainment that is intended to make people laugh: **comedy writer/series/show/actor etc** | *a career in **stand-up comedy*** (=telling jokes in front of people as a job) **2** [C] a play, film, or television programme that is intended to make people laugh: *a highly successful TV comedy* **3** [U] the quality in something such as a book or play that makes people laugh; ⊟ **humour**; → **tragedy**: *Can't you see the comedy of the situation?* → BLACK COMEDY, SITUATION COMEDY

ˌcomedy of ˈmanners *n plural* **comedies of manners** [C] a play, film, or television programme that shows how silly people's behaviour is or can be

come·ly /ˈkʌmli/ *adj literary old-fashioned* a comely woman is attractive —**comeliness** *n* [U]

ˈcome-on *n* [C usually singular] *informal* something that someone does deliberately to make someone else sexually interested in them: *Rick's the kind of guy who thinks every smile is a come-on.* | **give sb the come-on** (=do something to show you are sexually interested in someone); → **come on to sb/sth** at COME ON (2)

com·er /ˈkʌmə $ -ər/ *n* **all comers** *informal* anyone who wants to take part in an activity, especially a sporting competition: *The contest is open to all comers.* → LATECOMER, NEWCOMER

com·et /ˈkɒmət $ ˈkɑː-/ *n* [C] an object in space like a bright ball with a long tail, that moves around the sun: *Halley's comet*

come·up·pance /kʌmˈʌpəns/ *n* [singular] a punishment or something bad which happens to you that you really deserve: *You'll **get** your **comeuppance** one day!*

com·fort¹ W3 /ˈkʌmfət $ -ərt/ *n*
1 PHYSICAL [U] a feeling of being physically relaxed and satisfied, so that nothing is hurting you, making you feel too hot or cold etc; → **comfortable**, **discomfort**: **built/made/designed for comfort** *All our sports shoes are designed for comfort and performance.* | **too hot/high/tight etc for comfort** (=physically unpleasant for a particular reason) *The temperature was too low for comfort.* | *I dress for comfort, not fashion.* | *Alan was very reluctant to leave the warmth and comfort of the fire.* | **in comfort** *Upstairs is a more intimate bar where guests can relax in comfort.* | *Now you can watch your favorite movies **in the comfort of** your own home.*
2 EMOTIONAL [U] if someone or something gives you comfort, they make you feel calmer, happier, or more hopeful after you have been worried or unhappy; → **comforting**: *Whenever he was upset, he would turn to her for comfort and advice.* | **give/bring/provide/offer comfort** *a book which offers comfort and help to the parents of children with cancer* | *The knowledge that Cara was safe gave him some comfort.* | **great/much/little comfort** *My faith has been a **source of** great **comfort** over the years.* | **take/draw/derive comfort from (doing) sth** *He drew comfort from her warm support.* | **find/take comfort in (doing) sth** *You can take some comfort in the fact that you did your best.* | **it's no/some comfort** *It was no comfort to think he might be as frightened as she was.* | **if it's any comfort** (=used to introduce a statement that you think may make someone feel slightly less worried or unhappy) *Well, if it's any comfort, I don't think he'll try again.*
3 SB/STH THAT HELPS [C] someone or something that helps you feel calmer, happier, or more hopeful after you have been worried or unhappy; → **comforting**: **be a comfort (to sb)** *Louisa's been a **great comfort** to me since Mary died.* | ***It's a comfort** to know there's someone to keep an eye on the kids.*
4 MONEY/POSSESSIONS [U] a way of living in which you have all the money and possessions that you need or want; → **comfortable**: **in comfort** *When Dad died, he left us both enough to **live in comfort** for the rest of our lives.* | *He was used to a life of comfort.*
5 comforts [plural] the things that make your life nicer and more comfortable, especially things that are not necessary: *Modern caravans really do offer **all the comforts of** home.* | *hotels with all the **modern comforts*** (=things such as a television, telephone etc) | **material comforts** (=money and possessions) → CREATURE COMFORTS
6 too close/near for comfort something that is too close for comfort makes you feel worried, unhappy, or uncomfortable, because it is dangerous in some way: *The cars were whizzing past us much too close for comfort.*
7 cold/small comfort a small piece of good news that does not make you feel better about a bad situation: [+**for/to**] *Another drop in the inflation rate was cold comfort yesterday for the 2.74 million jobless.* → COMFORT FOOD, COMFORT ZONE

comfort² *v* [T] to make someone feel less worried, unhappy, or upset, for example by saying kind things to them or touching them; → **comforting:** *Within hours of the news, Helen was on the telephone trying to comfort her heartbroken friend.* | *He longed to take her in his arms and comfort her.* | *Mr Aston's father was last night being comforted by relatives.* | **comfort yourself** *She comforted herself with the thought that it would soon be spring.*

com·fort·a·ble [S2] [W3] /'kʌmftəbəl, 'kʌmfət-$ 'kʌmfərt-, 'kʌmft-/ *adj*
1 FURNITURE/PLACES/CLOTHES ETC making you feel physically relaxed, without any pain or without being too hot, cold etc; → **comfort: comfortable chair/bed/sofa etc** *The bed wasn't particularly comfortable.* | **comfortable room/lounge/hotel etc** *Joyce has a comfortable apartment in Portland.* | **comfortable clothes/shoes/boots etc** *Wear loose, comfortable clothing.* | **comfortable to wear/use/sit on etc** *Linen is very comfortable to wear.*
2 PHYSICALLY RELAXED feeling physically relaxed, without any pain or without being too hot, cold etc; → **comfort:** *I was so comfortable and warm in bed I didn't want to get up.* | *Sit down and **make yourself comfortable**.* | *With difficulty, she rolled her body into a more **comfortable position**.*
3 CONFIDENT [not before noun] confident, relaxed, and not worried: [+with] *She's never felt very **comfortable** with men.* | *In our business, we need people who are comfortable in an unstructured environment.*
4 MONEY having enough money to buy all the things you need or want, without having to worry about how much they cost: **comfortable life/retirement/existence etc** *Jean had been looking forward to a comfortable retirement.*
5 COMPETITION/VOTE [usually before noun] if you have a comfortable win or lead, you win or are leading by a large amount: **comfortable win/victory** *The pair had a comfortable win, beating the German team by nearly three seconds.* | *The bill should pass in the House by a **comfortable margin**.* | *Another penalty from Roberts gave the home team a **comfortable** half-time lead.*
6 ILL/INJURED [not before noun] if someone who is ill or injured is comfortable, they are not in too much pain

com·fort·a·bly /'kʌmftəbli, 'kʌmfət- $ 'kʌmfərt-, 'kʌmft-/ *adv*
1 FURNITURE/PLACES/CLOTHES in a way that makes you feel physically relaxed, without any pain, or without being too hot, cold etc: *The hotel is modern and **comfortably furnished**.* | *his comfortably baggy jeans*
2 PHYSICALLY RELAXED in a way that feels physically relaxed, without any pain, or without being too hot, cold etc: *I was **sitting comfortably** in the lounge, reading a newspaper.*
3 MONEY with enough money to live on without having to worry about paying for things: *She earns enough money to **live comfortably**.* | *His family were **comfortably off** (=fairly rich).*
4 WIN/ACHIEVEMENT easily and without problems: *Davis **won comfortably**, 9–1, 9–3, 9–2.* | *the amount of work you can comfortably deal with*
5 CONFIDENT in a confident and relaxed way: *They were soon chatting comfortably with each other.*

com·fort·er /'kʌmfətə $ -fərtər/ *n* [C] **1** *AmE* a cover for a bed that is filled with a soft warm material such as feathers; ⊟ **duvet** *BrE* **2** someone or something that comforts you

comfort ˌfood *n* [C,U] simple food that makes you feel relaxed and happy

com·fort·ing /'kʌmfətɪŋ $ -fər-/ *adj* making you feel less worried, unhappy, or upset: **it is comforting to think/have/know etc** *It's comforting to know I can call my parents any time.* | *With this **comforting thought**, Harry fell asleep.* | *His voice was strangely comforting.*
—**comfortingly** *adv*

ˈcomfort ˌzone *n* [C usually singular] your comfort zone is the range of activities or situations that you feel happy and confident in

com·fy /'kʌmfi/ *adj informal* comfortable: *a comfy chair*

com·ic¹ /'kɒmɪk $ 'kɑː-/ *adj* amusing you and making you want to laugh; ⊟ **tragic:** *a comic novel* | **comic writer/actress/performer etc** (=someone who writes or performs things that make you laugh) | **comic relief** (=a situation in a serious story that makes you relax a little because it is funny) *The song provides some **comic relief** from the intensity of the scene.*

comic² *n* [C] **1** also **comic book** a magazine for children that tells a story using comic strips **2** someone whose job is to tell jokes and make people laugh; ⊟ **comedian:** *a **stand-up comic***

com·i·cal /'kɒmɪkəl $ 'kɑː-/ *adj* behaviour or situations that are comical are funny in a strange or unexpected way: *The note of pure panic in his voice was almost comical.* —**comically** /-kli/ *adv*

ˈcomic strip *n* [C] a series of pictures drawn inside boxes that tell a story; → **cartoon**

com·ing¹ /'kʌmɪŋ/ *n* **1 the coming of sth/sb** the time when something new begins, especially something that will cause a lot of changes: *With the coming of railways, new markets opened up.* **2 comings and goings** *informal* the movements of people as they arrive and leave places: [+of] *Beds are arranged so that patients can watch the comings and goings of visitors and staff.*

coming² *adj* [only before noun] *formal* happening soon: *the coming winter* → UP-AND-COMING

ˌcoming of ˈage *n* [singular] the point in a young person's life, usually the age of 18 or 21, at which their society considers them to be an adult

com·ma /'kɒmə $ 'kɑːmə/ *n* [C] the mark (,) used in writing and printing to show a short pause or to separate things in a list → INVERTED COMMA → PUNCTUATION MARK

com·mand¹ [W2] /kə'mɑːnd $ kə'mænd/ *n*
1 CONTROL [U] the control of a group of people or a situation: **under sb's command** *troops under the command of General Roberts* | **in command (of sth)** *Lieutenant Peters was now in command.* | *He felt fully in **command of the situation.*** | **take command (of sth)** (=begin controlling a group or situation and making decisions) *The fire officer took command, ordering everyone to leave the building.* | **at sb's command** *Each congressman has a large staff at his command* (=available to be used). | *By 1944, Fletcher **had command of** a B-17 bomber and a 10 man crew.*
2 ORDER [C] an order that should be obeyed: *Shoot when I give the **command**.*
3 COMPUTER [C] an instruction to a computer to do something
4 command of sth knowledge of something, especially a language, or ability to use something: **(have a) good/excellent/poor etc command of sth** *He's studied in the US and has a good command of English.*
5 MILITARY [C also + plural verb *BrE*] **a)** a part of an army, navy etc that is controlled separately and has a particular job: *pilots of the Southern Air Command* **b)** a group of officers or officials who give orders: *the Army High Command* **c)** the group of soldiers that an officer is in control of
6 at your command if you have a particular skill at your command, you are able to use that skill well and easily: *a pianist with the keys at his command*
7 be in command of yourself to be able to control your emotions and thoughts: *Kathleen walked in, tall, slim, confident and in total command of herself.*

command² *v*
1 ORDER [I,T] to tell someone officially to do something, especially if you are a military leader, a king etc: **command sb to do sth** *Captain Picard commanded the*

crew to report to the main deck. | **command that** *The General commanded that the regiment attack at once.*
2 LEAD THE MILITARY [I,T] to be responsible for giving orders to a group of people in the army, navy etc; → **commander**: *He commands the 4th Battalion.*
3 DESERVE AND GET [T] to get something such as respect or attention because you do something well or are important or popular: **command respect/attention/ support etc** *Philip was a remarkable teacher, able to command instant respect.* | **command a high fee/wage/ price etc** *Which graduates command the highest salaries?*
4 CONTROL [T] to control something: *The party that commands a majority of seats in Parliament forms the government.*
5 VIEW [T] if a place commands a view, you can see something clearly from it: *The Ramses Hilton commands a magnificent view of Cairo.*

com·man·dant /ˌkɒmən'dænt $ 'kɑːməndænt/ *n* [C] the army officer in charge of a place or group of people

com·man·deer /ˌkɒmən'dɪə $ ˌkɑːmən'dɪr/ *v* [T] to take someone else's property for your own use, especially during a war: *The local hotel was commandeered for the wounded.*

com·mand·er /kə'mɑːndə $ kə'mændər/ *n* [C] **1** an officer of any rank who is in charge of a group of soldiers or a particular military activity: *the American Commander, General Otis* | *our platoon commander* **2** a high rank in the navy, or someone who holds this rank **3** a British police officer of high rank → **WING COMMANDER**

com·mander in 'chief *n plural* **commanders in chief** [C usually singular] someone of high rank who is in control of all the military organizations in a country or of a specific military activity: *The Queen is Commander in Chief of the British armed forces.*

com·mand·ing /kə'mɑːndɪŋ $ kə'mæn-/ *adj* **1** [only before noun] having the authority or position that allows you to give orders: *a commanding officer* **2** having the confidence to make people respect and obey you – used to show approval: *Papa's commanding presence* **3** a commanding view or position is one from which you can clearly see a long way **4** being in a position from which you are likely to win a race or competition easily: *a commanding lead*

com·mand·ment /kə'mɑːndmənt $ kə'mænd-/ *n* [C] one of the ten rules given by God in the Bible that tell people how they must behave

com'mand ,module *n* [C] the part of a space vehicle from which its activities are controlled

com·man·do /kə'mɑːndəʊ $ kə'mændəʊ/ *n plural* **commandos** *or* **commandoes** **1** [C] a soldier who is specially trained to make quick attacks into enemy areas: *a commando raid* **2 go commando** *AmE spoken* to not wear any underwear – used humorously

com,mand per'formance *n* [C usually singular] a special performance at a theatre that is given for a king, president etc

com'mand post *n* [C] the place from which military leaders and their officers control activities

com·mem·o·rate /kə'meməreɪt/ *v* [T] to do something to show that you remember and respect someone important or an important event in the past: *a parade to commemorate the town's bicentenary* —**commemorative** /kə'memərətɪv/ *adj*: *a commemorative plaque*

com·mem·o·ra·tion /kəˌmemə'reɪʃən/ *n* [U] something that makes you remember and respect someone important or an important event in the past: **in commemoration of sb/sth** *The Prime Minister later attended a service in commemoration of those who died in the war.*

com·mence /kə'mens/ *v* [I,T] *formal* to begin or to start something: *Work will commence on the new build-*

ing immediately. | *Your first evaluation will be six months after you commence employment.* | **[+with]** *The course commences with a one week introduction to Art Theory.* | **commence doing sth** *The planes commenced bombing at midnight.*

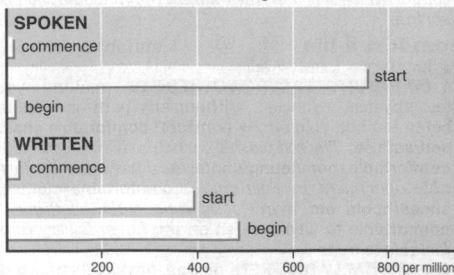

Frequencies of **commence**, **start**, and **begin** in spoken and written English.

This graph shows that in spoken English **start** is the most common of the three verbs. In written English **begin** is the most common. **Commence** is much more formal than **start** and **begin**.

com·mence·ment /kə'mensmənt/ *n formal* **1** [U] the beginning of something: **[+of]** *the commencement of building work* **2** [C,U] *AmE* a ceremony at which university, college, or high school students receive their DIPLOMAS; **⧉ graduation**

com·mend /kə'mend/ *v* [T] *formal* **1** to praise or approve of someone or something publicly: **commend sb for sth** *Inspector Marshall was commended for his professional and caring attitude.* | *The paper was highly commended in the UK Press Awards.* **2** to tell someone that something is good or deserves attention; **⧉ recommend**: *Colleagues, I commend this report to you.* | *Ian McKellen's performance had much to commend it* (=was very good). **3 commend itself (to sb)** *formal* if something commends itself to you, you approve of it: *The plan did not commend itself to the Allies.*

com·mend·a·ble /kə'mendəbəl/ *adj formal* deserving praise: *Your enthusiasm is highly commendable.* | *Baldwin answered with commendable honesty.* —**commendably** *adv*

com·men·da·tion /ˌkɒmən'deɪʃən $ ˌkɑː-/ *n* [C,U] *formal* an official statement praising someone, especially someone who has been brave or very successful

com·men·su·rate /kə'menʃərət/ *adj* matching something in size, quality, or length of time: **[+with]** *Salary will be commensurate with age and experience.*

com·ment¹ [S1] [W2] /'kɒment $ 'kɑː-/ *n*
1 [C,U] an opinion that you express about someone or something; **⧉ remark**: *Does anyone have any questions or comments?* | **[+on/about]** *his comments about asylum seekers* | *He was fined for making abusive comments to the referee.* | **fair comment** (=criticism that is reasonable or deserved)
2 [U] criticism or discussion of something someone has said or done: *The speech received much comment in the press.* | **no comment** (=used by people in public life when they do not want to answer questions)
3 be a comment on sth to be a sign of the bad quality of something: *The number of adults who cannot read is a sad comment on the quality of our schools.*

comment² [S2] [W3] *v* [I,T] to express an opinion about someone or something; **⧉ remark**: **[+on]** *People were always commenting on my sister's looks.* | **comment that** *Morrison's lawyer commented that the decision was 'outrageous'.*

com·men·ta·ry /'kɒməntəri $ 'kɑːmənteri/ *n plural* **commentaries** [C,U] **1** a spoken description of an event, given while the event is happening, especially on the television or radio: *Commentary is by Tom Ferris.* | **[+on]** *We'll be bringing you full commentary on the game between Notts and Brescia.* | **running commentary** (=a continuous description of something) **2** some thing such as a book or article that explains or discusses a book, poem, idea etc: *political commentary* **3** be a sad/tragic/devastating etc **commentary on sth** to be a sign of how bad a particular situation is: *The incident was a sad commentary on British football.*

com·men·tate /'kɒmənteɪt $ 'kɑː-/ v [I + on] to describe an event such as a sports game on television or radio

com·men·ta·tor /'kɒmənteɪtə $ 'kɑːmənteɪtər/ n [C] **1** someone who knows a lot about a particular subject, and who writes about it or discusses it on the television or radio: *political commentators* **2** someone on television or radio who describes an event as it is happening: *a sports commentator*

com·merce /'kɒmɜːs $ 'kɑːmɜːrs/ n [U] the buying and selling of goods and services; ▣ **trade**: *measures promoting local commerce and industry* → CHAMBER OF COMMERCE, E-COMMERCE

com·mer·cial¹ [S2] [W2] /kə'mɜːʃəl $ -ɜːr-/ adj
1 related to business and the buying and selling of goods and services: *Our top priorities must be profit and commercial growth.*
2 related to the ability of a product or business to make a profit: *Gibbons failed to see the commercial value of his discovery.* | **commercial success/failure** *The film was a huge commercial success.*
3 [only before noun] a commercial product is one that is produced and sold in large quantities
4 more concerned with money than with quality: *I used to like their music but they've become very commercial.*
5 commercial radio/TV/channel etc radio or television broadcasts that are produced by companies that earn money through advertising

commercial² [S3] n
1 [C] an advertisement on television or radio: *a soap powder commercial*
2 commercial break the time when advertisements are broadcast during a television or radio programme

com·mer·cial·is·m /kə'mɜːʃəlɪzəm $ -ɜːr-/ n [U] the principle or practice of being more concerned with making money from buying and selling goods than you are about their quality – used to show disapproval: *the commercialism of modern culture*

com·mer·cial·ize also **-ise** BrE /kə'mɜːʃəlaɪz $ -ɜːr-/ v [T] **1** [usually passive] to be more concerned with making money from something than about its quality – used to show disapproval: *Christmas has become so commercialized.* **2** to sell something completely new to the public for the first time: *Some space launches will be commercialized to help pay for more space research.* —**commercialization** /kə,mɜːʃəlaɪ'zeɪʃən $ -,mɜːrʃələ-/ n [U]

com·mer·cial·ly /kə'mɜːʃəli $ -ɜːr-/ adv **1** considering whether a business or product is making a profit: *The project is no longer commercially viable* (=certain to make money). | [sentence adverb] *Commercially, the movie was a flop.* **2** produced or used in large quantities as a business: *commercially farmed land* **3** if a new product is commercially available, you can buy it in shops: *the world's first commercially available 3-D computer screen*

com,mercial 'traveller n [C] BrE old-fashioned someone who travels from place to place selling goods for a company; ▣ **sales representative**

com·mie /'kɒmi $ 'kɑː-/ n [C] informal an insulting word for a COMMUNIST

com·min·gle /kə'mɪŋɡəl/ v **1** [I,T] formal to mix together, or to make different things do this: *Many towns allow recyclable items to be commingled for collection in a single container.* **2** [T] AmE technical if a financial organization commingles money, it mixes its own money with money that belongs to its customers or to another part of the business, usually in an illegal

way: **commingle sth with sth** *The company faces charges that it commingled its own funds with customer funds.* —**commingling** n [U]

com·mis·e·rate /kə'mɪzəreɪt/ v [I + with] formal to express your sympathy for someone who is unhappy about something

com·mis·e·ra·tion /kə,mɪzə'reɪʃən/ n [plural, U] formal a feeling of sympathy for someone when something unpleasant has happened to them: *Congratulations to the winners, commiserations to the losers.* → CONDOLENCE

com·mis·sar·i·at /,kɒmɪ'seəriət $,kɑːmɪ'ser-/ n [C] a military department that is responsible for supplying food

com·mis·sa·ry /'kɒmɪsəri $ 'kɑːmɪseri/ n plural **commissaries** [C] **1** BrE an officer in the army who is in charge of food supplies **2** AmE a shop that supplies food and other goods in a military camp **3** AmE a place where you can eat in a large organization such as a film STUDIO, factory etc

com·mis·sion¹ [S1] [W1] /kə'mɪʃən/ n
1 [C] a group of people who have been given the official job of finding out about something or controlling something: *The Government set up a commission to investigate allegations of police violence.* | [+on] *the Royal Commission on Environmental Pollution*
2 [C,U] an extra amount of money that is paid to a person or organization according to the value of the goods they have sold or the services they have provided: *The dealer takes a 20% commission on the sales he makes.* | **on commission** *He sold cosmetics on commission.*
3 [C] a request for an artist, designer, or musician to make a piece of art or music, for which they are paid: *a commission from the Academy for a new sculpture*
4 [C] the position of an officer in the army, navy etc
5 [U] formal the commission of a crime is the act of doing it
6 out of commission a) not working or not available for use: *One of the ship's anchors was out of commission.* **b)** informal ill or injured, and unable to work
7 in commission available to be used: *The operating theatres will be back in commission next week.*

commission² v **1** [T] to formally ask someone to write an official report, produce a work of art for you etc: *The report was commissioned by the Welsh Office.* | **commission sb to do sth** *Macmillan commissioned her to illustrate a book by Spike Milligan.* **2 be commissioned (into sth)** to be given an officer's rank in the army, navy etc: *He was commissioned into the Royal Engineers.*

com·mis·sion·aire /kə,mɪʃə'neə $ -'ner/ n [C] BrE someone whose job is to stand at the entrance to a hotel or theatre wearing a uniform and help people; ▣ **doorman**

com,missioned 'officer n [C] a military officer who has a commission

com·mis·sion·er /kə'mɪʃənə $ -ər/ n [C] **1** someone who is officially in charge of a government department in some countries **2** the head of the police department in some parts of the US **3** a member of a commission

com,missioner for 'oaths n [C] BrE a lawyer who may legally be a WITNESS to particular legal documents

com·mit [S2] [W2] /kə'mɪt/ v committed, committing
1 CRIME [T] to do something wrong or illegal: *Women commit fewer crimes than men.* | **commit murder/rape/arson etc** *Brady committed a series of brutal murders.*
2 commit suicide to kill yourself deliberately
3 commit adultery if a married person commits adultery, they have sex with someone who is not their husband or wife
4 SAY YOU WILL DO STH [I,T] to say that someone will

C

definitely do something or must do something: **commit sb to doing sth** *He has clearly committed his government to continuing down the path of economic reform.* | **commit sb to sth** *Meeting them doesn't commit us to anything.* | **commit yourself** *I'd committed myself and there was no turning back.* | **commit yourself to (doing) sth** *The banks have committed themselves to boosting profits by slashing costs.*

5 RELATIONSHIP [I,T] to give someone your love or support in a serious and permanent way: *Anna wants to get married, but Bob's not sure he wants to commit.* | [+to] *He has not yet committed to any of the candidates.*

6 MONEY/TIME [T] to decide to use money, time, people etc for a particular purpose: **commit sth to sth** *A lot of money has been committed to this project.*

7 FOR TRIAL [T] *BrE* to send someone to be tried in a court of law: *The two men* **were committed for trial** *at Bristol Crown Court.*

8 PRISON/HOSPITAL [T] to order someone to be put in a hospital or prison: **commit sb to sth** *The judge committed him to prison for six months.*

9 commit sth to memory *formal* to learn something so that you remember it; ▣ **memorize**

10 commit sth to paper *formal* to write something down → COMMITTED

com·mit·ment S2 W2 /kəˈmɪtmənt/ *n*
1 [C] a promise to do something or to behave in a particular way: *Are you ready to* **make** *a long-term* **commitment**? | [+to] *Our company has a commitment to quality and customer service.*
2 [U] the hard work and loyalty that someone gives to an organization, activity etc: *I was impressed by the energy and commitment shown by the players.* | [+to] *Her commitment to work is beyond question.*
3 [C] something that you have promised you will do or that you have to do: *Will the job fit in with your* **family commitments**?
4 [C] an amount of money that you have to pay regularly: *I had a lot of financial commitments.*
5 [C,U] the use of money, time, people etc for a particular purpose: *commitments of food and medical aid of over $4 billion*

com·mit·tal /kəˈmɪtl/ *n* [C,U] **1** the process in which a court sends someone to a mental hospital or prison **2** *formal* the burying or CREMATING of a dead person

com·mit·ted /kəˈmɪtɪd/ *adj* willing to work very hard at something: *The party has a core of committed supporters.* | [+to] *We are fully committed to Equal Opportunity policies.*

com·mit·tee S3 W1 /kəˈmɪti/ *n* [C also + plural verb *BrE*] a group of people chosen to do a particular job, make decisions etc: [+of] *the International Committee of the Red Cross* | [+on] *a Ministerial committee on security affairs* | **on a committee** *He's on the finance committee.* | *a committee meeting* | *committee members* → SELECT COMMITTEE; → standing committee at STANDING¹ (1)

com·mode /kəˈməʊd $ -ˈmoʊd/ *n* [C] **1** a piece of furniture shaped like a chair that can be used as a toilet **2** an old-fashioned piece of furniture with drawers or shelves **3** *AmE* a word meaning 'toilet' used by people who do not like saying 'toilet'

com·mo·di·ous /kəˈməʊdiəs $ -ˈmoʊ-/ *adj formal* a house or room that is commodious is very big

com·mod·i·ty /kəˈmɒdɪti $ kəˈmɑː-/ *n plural* **commodities** [C] **1** a product that is bought and sold: *agricultural commodities* | *Commodity prices fell sharply.* **2** *formal* a useful quality or thing: *Time is a precious commodity.*

com·mo·dore /ˈkɒmədɔː $ ˈkɑːmədɔːr/ *n* [C] **1** a high rank in the navy, or someone who has this rank **2** the CAPTAIN in charge of a group of ships that are carrying goods

com·mon¹ S1 W1 /ˈkɒmən $ ˈkɑː-/ *adj*
1 HAPPENING OFTEN happening often and to many people or in many places; ▣ **rare**: *Heart disease is one of the commonest causes of death.* | [+among] *Bad dreams are fairly common among children.* | **it's common for sb to do sth** *It's common for new fathers to feel jealous of the baby.* ⚠ Do not say 'It is common that...': *It is common for children to be afraid (NOT It is common that children are afraid) of the dark.*
2 A LOT existing in large numbers; ▣ **rare**: *Daisies are very common flowers.*
3 SAME/SIMILAR [usually before noun, no comparative] common aims, beliefs, ideas etc are shared by several people or groups: *people working towards a common goal* | *countries that share a common language* | [+to] *a theme that is common to all her novels*
4 common ground facts, features, or beliefs that are shared by people or things that are very different: [+between] *There is a great deal of common ground between management and trade unions on this issue.*
5 SHARED BY EVERYONE [no comparative] belonging to or shared by everyone in a society: [+to] *These problems are common to all societies.* | *Joe was chosen as captain* **by common consent** (=with everyone's agreement).
6 common knowledge something everyone knows: *It* **is common knowledge that** *travel broadens the mind.*
7 the common good the advantage of everyone: *They work together for the common good.*
8 common practice a usual or accepted way of doing things: *It was common practice for families to attend church together.*
9 ORDINARY [only before noun, no comparative] ordinary and not special in any way: *common salt* | *The twentieth century was called the century of* **the common man** (=ordinary people). | *He insists that he is a revolutionary not a common criminal.*
10 common courtesy/decency/politeness a polite way of behaving that you expect from people: *It would be common courtesy to return their hospitality.*
11 common or garden *BrE* ordinary; ▣ **garden-variety** *AmE*: *a common or garden dispute*
12 make/find common cause (with/against sb) *formal* to join with other people or groups in order to achieve something: *France and Russia made common cause against Britain.*
13 common touch the ability of someone in a position of power or authority to talk to and understand ordinary people – used to show approval: *He's made it to the top without losing the common touch.*
14 SOCIAL CLASS *BrE old-fashioned* an offensive word used for describing someone from a low social class

common² *n* **1** have sth in common (with sb) to have the same interests, attitudes etc as someone else: *I found I* **had a lot in common with** *these people.* | *four women with almost* **nothing in common** **2** have sth in common (with sth) if objects or ideas have something in common, they share the same features: *The two games* **have much in common.** **3** in common with sb/sth in the same way as someone or something else: *In common with a lot of other countries, we're in an economic recession.* **4** [C] a large area of open land in a town or village that people walk or play sport on: *Boston Common*

com·mo·nal·i·ty /ˌkɒməˈnælɪti $ ˌkɑː-/ *n* [U] *formal* the fact of having things in common

common 'cold *n* [C] a slight illness in which your throat hurts and it is difficult to breathe normally; ▣ **cold**

common 'currency *n* [U] used to say that something is used by a lot of people or accepted by everyone: *Words like 'spliff' and 'blunt' have become common currency.*

common de'nominator *n* [C] **1** an attitude or quality that all the different members of a group have: *The common denominator of both types of novel is the vulnerable, threatened heroine.* **2** the lowest common

denominator the least attractive, least intelligent people or features in a situation: *trashy TV programs that appeal to the lowest common denominator* **3** technical a number that can be divided exactly by all the DENOMINATORS (=bottom number) in a set of FRACTIONS

com·mon·er /'kɒmənə $ 'kɑːmənər/ *n* [C] someone who is not a member of the NOBILITY

common ,land *n* [U] *BrE* lands that belongs to or can be used by everyone living in an area

common 'law *n* [U] the system of laws that has developed from customs and the decisions of judges rather than from laws made by Parliament; → **statute law**

common-law *adj* [only before noun] **1 common-law marriage/husband/wife** a relationship that is considered to be a marriage because the man and woman have lived together for a long time **2** according to or related to common law: **common law rules/courts/rights etc**

com·mon·ly W3 /'kɒmənli $ 'kɑː-/ *adv* **1** usually or by most people; ▣ **widely**: *Sodium chloride is more commonly known as salt.* | *a commonly used industrial chemical* **2** often, in many places, or in large numbers; ▣ **widely**: *Lung cancer is the most commonly found cancer in men.* | *commonly available software packages*

common 'noun *n* [C] in grammar, a common noun is any noun that is not the name of a particular person, place, or thing. For example, 'book, 'sugar', and 'stuff' are common nouns; → **proper noun, noun**

com·mon·place[1] /'kɒmənpleɪs $ 'kɑː-/ *adj* happening or existing in many places, and therefore not special or unusual: *Car thefts are commonplace in this part of town.*

commonplace[2] *n* [C usually singular] **1** something that happens or exists in many places, so that it is not unusual: *Women's groups have become a commonplace.* **2** something that has been said so often that it is no longer interesting or original **3 the commonplace** something that is ordinary or boring; ▣ **the everyday**: *Moore took as his main theme the mystery of the commonplace.*

common room *n* [C] *BrE* a room in a school or college that a group of teachers or students use when they are not teaching or studying

Com·mons /'kɒmənz $ 'kɑː-/ *n* **the Commons** the larger and more powerful of the two parts of the British parliament, whose members are elected by citizens; → **the Lords**: *The Government has a huge majority in the Commons.*

common 'sense *n* [U] the ability to behave in a sensible way and make practical decisions: *Use your common sense for once!* | *a common-sense approach to education*

com·mon·wealth /'kɒmənwelθ $ 'kɑː-/ *n* **1 the Commonwealth** an organization of about 50 countries that were once part of the British EMPIRE: *the Commonwealth Games* **2** [C] an association of countries with political or economic connections: [+of] *a commonwealth of nations* **3** [C] *AmE* the official legal title of some US states

com·mo·tion /kə'məʊʃən $ -'moʊ-/ *n* [singular, U] sudden noisy activity: *They heard a commotion downstairs.* | *Everyone looked to see what was causing the commotion.*

comms /kɒmz $ kɑːmz/ *n* [plural] *BrE technical* **communications** used when talking about computer programs that allow communication between different computers; ▣ **communications software** *AmE*

com·mu·nal /'kɒmjʊnəl, kə'mjuːnl $ 'kɑː-/ *adj* **1** shared by a group of people or animals, especially a group who live together: *a communal bathroom* **2** involving people from many different races, religions, or language groups: *the worst communal* violence in two years **3** relating or belonging to all the people living in a particular COMMUNITY: *crops grown on communal land*

com·mune[1] /'kɒmjuːn $ 'kɑː-, kə'mjuːn/ *n* [C] **1** a group of people who live together and who share the work and their possessions: *a hippie commune* **2** the smallest unit of local government in countries such as France and Belgium **3** a group of people in a Communist country who work as a team on a farm, and give what they produce to the state

com·mune[2] /kə'mjuːn/ *v*
  commune with sb/sth *phr v formal* **1** to communicate with a person, god, or animal, especially in a mysterious, SPIRITUAL way **2 commune with nature** to spend time outside in a natural place, enjoying it in a quiet peaceful way: *Take time to relax and commune with nature.*

com·mu·ni·ca·ble /kə'mjuːnɪkəbəl/ *adj formal* **1** a communicable disease can be passed on to other people; ▣ **infectious** **2** able to be communicated: *Some experiences are communicable only through symbols.*

com·mu·ni·cant /kə'mjuːnɪkənt/ *n* [C] someone who receives COMMUNION regularly in the Christian church

com·mu·ni·cate S3 W3 /kə'mjuːnɪkeɪt/ *v*
1 EXCHANGE INFORMATION [I,T] to exchange information or conversation with other people, using words, signs, writing etc: *We communicated mostly by e-mail.* | [+with] *People use more than words when they communicate with each other.* | **communicate sth to sb** *The decision was communicated to our staff late in 1998.*
2 TELL PEOPLE STH [I,T] to express your thoughts and feelings clearly, so that other people understand them: *A baby communicates its needs by crying.* | **communicate sth to sb** *Without meaning to, she communicated her anxiety to her child.* | *His enthusiasm communicated itself to the voters.* | *A teacher must be able to* **communicate effectively** *to students.*
3 UNDERSTAND [I] if two people communicate, they are able to talk about and understand each other's feelings or desires: *Many couples make themselves miserable by not communicating.* | [+with] *Parents sometimes find it difficult to communicate with their teenage children.*
4 DISEASE [T usually passive] to pass a disease from one person or animal to another; → **communicable**
5 ROOMS [I] if rooms or parts of a building communicate, you can get directly to one from the other: *communicating doors*

com·mu·ni·ca·tion S2 W1 /kə,mjuːnɪ'keɪʃən/ *n*
1 [U] the process by which people exchange information or express their thoughts and feelings: *Good communication is vital in a large organization.* | *Radio was the pilot's only means of communication.*
2 communications a) [plural] ways of sending information, especially using radio, telephone, or computers: *Modern communications are enabling more people to work from home.* **b)** [plural] roads, railways etc that are used for travelling and sending goods: [+with] *Paris has good communications with many European cities.* **c)** [U] the study of using radio, television, cinema etc to communicate: *a diploma in communications*
3 [U] the way people express themselves so that other people will understand: *a week's course in improving* **communication skills** | *There has been a* **breakdown in communication** (=failure).
4 be in communication with sb *formal* to talk or write to someone regularly
5 [C] *formal* a letter, message, or telephone call: *a communication from the Ministry of Defence*

com,muni'cation ,cord *n* [C] *BrE* a chain that a passenger can pull to stop a train in an EMERGENCY (=a sudden dangerous situation)

C

com·mu·ni·ca·tions ,satellite n [C] a SATELLITE that is used to send radio, television, and telephone signals around the world

com·mu·ni·ca·tive /kə'mjuːnɪkətɪv $ -keɪtɪv/ adj **1** able to talk easily to other people: *Tom wasn't very communicative – he kept himself to himself.* **2** relating to the ability to communicate, especially in a foreign language: *students' communicative skills*

com·mu·ni·ca·tor /kə'mjuːnɪkeɪtə $ -ər/ n [C] someone who is able to express ideas or their feelings clearly to other people: *She's a skilled communicator.*

com·mu·nion /kə'mjuːnjən/ n **1 Communion** [U] also **Holy Communion** the Christian ceremony in which people eat bread and drink wine as signs of Christ's body and blood **2** [U] formal a special relationship with someone or something which makes you feel that you understand them very well: [+with] *Prayer is a form of communion with God.* **3** [C] formal a group of people or organizations that share the same religious beliefs; ◘ **denomination**: *He belongs to the Anglican communion.*

com·mu·ni·qué /kə'mjuːnɪkeɪ $ kə,mjuːnɪ'keɪ/ n [C] an official report or announcement: *A communiqué was issued by NATO Defence Ministers.*

com·mu·nis·m, Communism /'kɒmjənɪzəm $ 'kɑː-/ n [U] **1** a political system in which the government controls the production of all food and goods, and there is no privately owned property; → **capitalism, socialism 2** the belief in this political system

com·mu·nist¹, Communist /'kɒmjənɪst $ 'kɑː-/ n [C] someone who is a member of a political party that supports communism, or who believes in communism; → **capitalist, socialist**

communist², Communist adj relating to communism; → **capitalist, socialist**: *a communist country | a communist regime*

'Communist ,bloc n **the Communist bloc** the group of countries in Eastern Europe that had Communist governments and were controlled by the former Soviet Union

com·mu·ni·ty [S1] [W1] /kə'mjuːnɪti/ n plural **communities**
1 [C, also + plural verb BrE] the people who live in the same area, town etc: *The new arts centre will serve the whole community.* | *community education programmes* | **community relations/affairs/needs etc** *We meet once a month to discuss community problems.* | **community groups/leaders etc** *Community leaders met to discuss the proposed golf course.* | **community spirit** (=the desire to be friendly with and help other people who live in the same community)
2 [C] a group of people who have the same interests, religion, race etc: *different ethnic communities* | **the gay/black/Asian etc community** *the gay community in San Francisco* | **the business/academic/scientific etc community**
3 the community society and the people in it: *The trend is towards reintegrating mentally ill people into the community.* | **the international community** (=all the countries of the world) *The President appealed to the international community for aid for the flood victims.*
4 sense of community the feeling that you belong to a community
5 [C] a group of plants or animals that live in the same environment: *Communities of otters are slowly returning to British rivers.*

com'munity ,centre BrE; **community center** AmE n [C] a place where people from the same area can go for social events, classes etc

com'munity ,chest n [C] AmE old use money that is collected by the people and businesses in an area to help poor people

com'munity ,college n [C] **1** a SECONDARY SCHOOL in the UK that students from the local area can go to, and which also has classes for adults **2** a college in the US

that students can go to for two years in order to learn a skill or prepare for university; ◘ **junior college**

com'munity ,property n [U] law property that is considered to be owned equally by both a husband and wife in US law

com,munity 'service n [U] work that is not paid that someone does to help other people, sometimes as punishment for a crime

com·mu·ta·tion /,kɒmjʊ'teɪʃən $,kɑː-/ n [C,U] law a reduction in how severe a punishment is: *Activists are campaigning for a commutation of Pollard's sentence.*

com·mute¹ /kə'mjuːt/ v **1** [I] to regularly travel a long distance to get to work: [+to/from/between] *Jim commutes to Manhattan every day.* **2 commute a sentence (to sth)** technical to change the punishment given to a criminal to one that is less severe: *Baldry's 20-year prison sentence was commuted to three years.* **3 commute sth for/into sth** technical to exchange one thing, especially one kind of payment, for another: *He commuted his pension for a lump sum.*

commute² n [C usually singular] the journey to work every day: *My morning commute takes 45 minutes.*

com·mut·er /kə'mjuːtə $ -ər/ n [C] someone who travels a long distance to work every day

com'muter ,belt n [C] BrE an area around a large city, from which many people travel to work every day

comp¹ /kɒmp $ kɑːmp/ n [C] informal **1** AmE a ticket for a play, sports game etc that is given away free **2** BrE a COMPREHENSIVE SCHOOL

comp² v [T] AmE spoken to give something such as a ticket away free

com·pact¹ /kəm'pækt, 'kɒmpækt $ kəm'pækt/ adj **1** small, but arranged so that everything fits neatly into the space available – used to show approval: *The compact design of the machine allows it to be stored easily.* | *The students' rooms were compact, with a desk, bed, and closet built in.* **2** packed or put together firmly and closely: *The bushes grew in a compact mass.* **3** small, but solid and strong: *a short compact-looking man* —**compactly** adv —**compactness** n [U]

com·pact² /'kɒmpækt $ 'kɑːm-/ n [C] **1** a small flat container with a mirror, containing powder for a woman's face **2** a COMPACT CAMERA **3** AmE a small car **4** formal an agreement between countries or people: *A compact was negotiated between the company and the union.*

com·pact³ /kəm'pækt/ v [T] to press something together so that it becomes smaller or more solid: *compacted earth*

,compact 'camera n [C] a small camera with a LENS that cannot be removed

,compact 'disc n [C,U] **CD** a small circular piece of hard plastic on which high-quality recorded sound or large quantities of information can be stored: *The new album is available on vinyl, cassette, or compact disc.*

,compact 'disc ,player n [C] a CD PLAYER

com·pan·ion [W3] /kəm'pænjən/ n [C]
1 someone you spend a lot of time with, especially a friend: *For ten years he had been her constant companion.* | *His dog became his closest companion.* | *a travelling companion* | **dinner/drinking companion**
2 one of a pair of things that go together or can be used together: [+to] *This book is a companion to Professor Farrer's first work.* | **companion volume/piece etc** *The Encyclopedia of Gardening is a companion volume to the Encyclopedia of Plants and Flowers.*
3 used in the titles of books about a particular subject: *A Companion to Japanese Literature*
4 someone, especially a woman, who is paid to live or travel with an older person

com·pan·ion·a·ble /kəm'pænjənəbəl/ adj literary friendly and pleasant to be with: *They sat together in companionable silence.* —**companionably** adv

com·pan·ion·ship /kəm'pænjənʃɪp/ n [U] when you are with someone you enjoy being with, and are not alone: *When Stan died, I missed his companionship.*

com·pan·ion·way /kəmˈpænjənweɪ/ n [C] technical the steps going from one DECK (=level) of a ship to another deck

com·pa·ny S1 W1 /ˈkʌmpəni/ n plural **companies**
1 BUSINESS [C also + plural verb BrE] a business organization that makes or sells goods or services; ⊟ **business, firm**

run a company
set up/start a company
join a company (=become an employee)
a company goes bust/bankrupt (=stops doing business because it has lost too much money)
record/oil/insurance/phone etc company
multinational company (=one that has offices in different countries)
company policy
company director/executive

Which company do you work for? | *The company are hoping to expand their operations abroad.* | *In ten years, Jeff went from working in the mailroom to **running** the company.* | *The company was **set up** just after the war.* | ***Insurance companies** say they investigated 43,000 cases of fraud last year.* | *I called the **phone company** about the bill.* | *an independent **record company*** | *a **multinational company** specializing in sports equipment* | *a final draft of the **company policy** on the use of email for private purposes* | *Once again, **company directors** have awarded themselves a massive pay increase.* → LIMITED COMPANY, PARENT COMPANY, PUBLIC COMPANY

2 OTHER PEOPLE [U] when you are with other people and not alone: *The two men **enjoy each other's company**.* | *Rita's husband is away for the week, so I thought I'd go over and **keep her company** (=be with her so that she doesn't feel lonely).* | *Come over for dinner – I **could use the company** (=would like to be with people).* | *James is **good company** (=a cheerful person who is enjoyable to be with).* | **as company** *Bessie was glad to have the dog **as company**.* | **in sb's company** (=with someone) *I felt nervous in the company of such an important man.* | **in company with sb** (=together with another person or group) *He's performing in company with saxophonist Ernie Watts.*
3 GUESTS [U] people who are visiting you in your home: *It looks like the Hammills **have company**.* | *We're **expecting company** this evening.*
4 FRIENDS [U] your friends or the group of people you spend time with: *People judge you by **the company** you **keep** (=the people you spend time with).* | *Things began to go wrong when he got into **bad company**.*
5 PERFORMERS [C] a group of actors, dancers, or singers who work together: *a **theatre company*** | *a **touring company*** | *the Kirov Ballet Company*
6 be in good company used to tell someone who has made a mistake that they should not be embarrassed because some important or respected people have made the same mistake: *If you can't program the video recorder, you're in good company.*
7 GROUP [U] formal a group of people who are together in the same place, often for a particular purpose or for social reasons: *He glanced around at the **assembled company**.* | *Some jokes are just not appropriate to tell **in mixed company** (=in a group of both men and women).* | **in company** (=when surrounded by other people, especially at a social occasion) *Parents should teach their children how to behave in company.*
8 sb and company informal used after a person's name to mean that person and their friends: *This has not stopped Senator Biden and company from trying to make it an issue in the election.*
9 ARMY [C] a group of about 120 soldiers who are usually part of a larger group
10 two's company, three's a crowd used to suggest that two people would rather be alone together than have other people with them → **part company** at PART² (4); → **present company excepted** at PRESENT¹ (7)

WORD FOCUS: COMPANY
similar words: **firm, business**
a big company: **corporation, multinational, conglomerate**
an Internet company: **dot-com**
a company that is owned by a larger company: **subsidiary, affiliate**
abbreviations used in company names: **Ltd** (Limited) | **Co.** (Company) | **Corp.** (Corporation) | **PLC** (Public Limited Company) BrE, **Pty.** (Proprietary) used in Australia and South Africa
→ see also start-up³

company 'car n [C] a car that your employer gives you while you work for them
company 'law n [U] law the laws relating to the way in which companies operate
company 'secretary n plural **company secretaries** [C] someone with a high position in a company who deals with ADMINISTRATIVE and legal matters
com·pa·ra·ble /ˈkɒmpərəbəl $ ˈkɑːm-/ adj **1** similar to something else in size, number, quality etc, so that you can make a comparison; → **compare, comparison**: *A car of **comparable size** would cost far more abroad.* | **comparable figures/data/results** *comparable figures for the same period of time last year* | **[+with/to]** *The planet Pluto is **comparable in size** to the moon.* **2** being equally important, good, bad etc: *These two artists just aren't comparable.* | **[+with/to]** *His poetry is hardly comparable with Shakespeare's.* —**comparability** /ˌkɒmpərəˈbɪlɪti $ ˌkɑːm-/ n [U]
com·pa·ra·bly /ˈkɒmpərəbli $ ˈkɑːm-/ adv in a similar way or to a similar degree: *comparably priced products*
com·par·a·tive¹ /kəmˈpærətɪv/ adj **1 comparative comfort/freedom/wealth etc** comfort etc that is quite good when compared to how comfortable, free, or rich etc something or someone else is; ⊟ **relative**: *After a lifetime of poverty, his last few years were spent in **comparable comfort**.* | *She didn't want to leave the **comparative safety** of the shelter.* **2 comparative study/analysis etc** a study etc that involves comparing something to something else: *a comparative study of the US and British steel industries* **3 comparative beginner/newcomer etc** someone who is not really a beginner etc, but who seems to be one when compared to other people who have lived or worked somewhere for a long time: *After living here five years, we're still considered comparative newcomers.* **4 comparative figures/data** comparative figures etc are similar to other figures, so that you can make a comparison: *Comparative figures for last year clearly show how sales have declined.* **5** technical the comparative form of an adjective or adverb shows an increase in size, quality, degree etc when it is considered in relation to something else. For example, 'bigger' is the comparative form of 'big', and 'more slowly' is the comparative form of 'slowly'; → superlative
comparative² n **the comparative** technical the form of an adjective or adverb that shows an increase in size, degree etc when something is considered in relation to something else. For example, 'bigger' is the comparative of 'big', and 'more slowly' is the comparative of 'slowly'; → **the superlative**
com·par·a·tive·ly /kəmˈpærətɪvli/ adv as compared to something else or to a previous state; ⊟ **relatively**: *a **comparatively small** number of people* | *Comparatively few books have been written on the subject.* | *Crime on the island is **comparatively rare**.* | *Comparatively speaking, this part of the coast is still unspoiled.*
com·pare¹ S1 W1 /kəmˈpeə $ -ˈper/ v
1 [T] to examine or judge two or more things in order to show how they are similar to or different from each other; → **comparison, comparative**: *The report compares the different types of home computer available.* |

compare sth/sb with sth/sb *The police compared the suspect's fingerprints with those found at the crime scene.* | **compare sth/sb to sth/sb** *Davies' style of writing has been compared to Dickens'.* | **compare and contrast** (=an expression used when telling students to write about the things that are similar or different in works of literature or art) *Compare and contrast the main characters of these two novels.*
2 compared to/with sth used when considering the size, quality, or amount of something in relation to something similar: *a 20% reduction in burglary compared with last year* | *Compared to our small flat, Bill's house seemed like a palace.*
3 [I] to be better or worse than something else: **compare (favourably/unfavourably) with sth** *The quality of English wines can now compare with wines from Germany.* | *How does life in Britain compare with life in the States?* | *The imported fabric is 30% cheaper and compares favourably* (=is as good) *in quality.*
4 sth doesn't/can't compare (with sth) if something does not compare with something else, it is not as good, large etc: *The rides at the fair just can't compare with the rides at Disneyland.*
5 compare notes (with sb) *informal* to talk to someone in order to find out if their experience of something is the same as yours: *Leading scientists got together in Paris to compare notes on current research.*

compare² *n* **beyond/without compare** *literary* a quality that is beyond compare is the best of its kind: *a beauty and an elegance beyond compare*

com·pa·ri·son S3 W2 /kəm'pærɪsən/ *n*
1 COMPARING [U] the process of comparing two or more people or things; → **compare**, **comparative**: [+with] *Comparison with his previous movies shows how Lee has developed as a director.* | **in comparison (with/to sth)** *In comparison to other recent video games, this one isn't very exciting.* | *He was a loud friendly man. In comparison, his brother was rather shy.* | **by comparison (with sth)** *By comparison with other European countries, car prices in the UK are very high.* | *After months of living in a tropical climate, Spain seemed cool by comparison.* | **for comparison (with sth)** *These figures are provided for comparison with the results of previous studies.* | *He showed us the original text for comparison.* | *Her paintings* **invite comparison** *with those of the early Impressionists* (=they remind you of them). | **stand/bear comparison** (=is as good as someone or something else) *Irving's work bears comparison with the best of the modern novelists.* | **on comparison** *BrE* (=after you have compared two things to see if they are similar or different) *On comparison, the Renault was the more reliable of the two cars.*
2 JUDGMENT [C] a statement or examination of how similar or different two people or things are: [+of] *a comparison of pollution levels in Chicago and Detroit* | [+between] *The article* **makes** *a* **comparison** *between the two poems.*
3 BE LIKE STH [C] a statement that someone or something is like someone or something else: **(make/draw) a comparison between sb/sth** (=show the similarities between two people or things) *The writer draws comparisons between the two presidents.* | *You can't make a comparison between American and Japanese schools – they're too different.*
4 there's **no comparison** *spoken* used when you think that someone or something is much better than someone or something else: [+between] *There's just no comparison between canned vegetables and fresh ones.*
5 GRAMMAR [U] a word used in grammar meaning the way an adverb or adjective changes its form to show whether it is COMPARATIVE or SUPERLATIVE

com'parison-ˌshop *v* [I] to go to different shops in order to compare the prices of things, so that you can buy things for the cheapest possible price
—**comparison shopping** *n* [U]

com·part·ment /kəm'pɑːtmənt $ -ɑːr-/ *n* [C] **1** a smaller enclosed space inside something larger: *The bag is divided into* **separate compartments.** | *The* **engine compartment** *is soundproofed.* | *She kept the money hidden in a secret compartment in her briefcase.* → GLOVE COMPARTMENT **2** one of the separate areas into which a plane, ship, or train is divided: *a* **first-class compartment**

com·part·men·tal·ize also **-ise** *BrE* /ˌkɒmpɑːt'mentl-aɪz $ kəm,pɑːrt-/ *v* [T] to divide something into separate areas or groups: *Women are better than men at compartmentalizing their lives.* —**compartmentalized** *adj* —**compartmentalization** /ˌkɒmpɑːt,mentl-aɪ'zeɪʃən $ kəm,pɑːrtmentl-ə-/ *n* [U]

com·pass /'kʌmpəs/ *n* **1** [C] an instrument that shows directions and has a needle that always points north: *a map and compass* | **compass points/points of the compass** (=the marks on a compass that show you north, south, east, west etc); → see picture at MEASUREMENT **2** [C] also **compasses** a V-shaped instrument with one sharp point and a pen or pencil at the other end, used for drawing circles or measuring distances on maps → see picture at MATHEMATICS **3** [U] *formal* the area or range of subjects that someone is responsible for or that is discussed in a book: [+of] *Within the brief compass of a single page, the author covers most of the major points.*

'compass rose *n* [singular] *technical* a symbol that consists of a circle with a pointed star in it, which is printed on maps and shows which direction is north, south, east, west etc

com·pas·sion /kəm'pæʃən/ *n* [U] a strong feeling of sympathy for someone who is suffering, and a desire to help them: [+for] *compassion for the sick* | **feel/show/have compassion** *Did he feel any compassion for the victim of his crime?* | **with compassion** *Lieberman explores this sensitive topic with compassion.* | *I was shocked by the doctor's* **lack of compassion.**

com·pas·sion·ate /kəm'pæʃənət/ *adj* feeling sympathy for people who are suffering: *a caring, compassionate man* | *I allowed him to go home* **on compassionate grounds.** | *One measure of a civilized and compassionate society is how well it treats its prison population.* —**compassionately** *adv*

com,passionate 'leave *n* [U] special permission to have time away from work because one of your relatives has died or is very ill

com'passion fatˌigue *n* [U] if you are suffering from compassion fatigue, you have stopped feeling sympathy for people and do not want to give any more money to help them, because you have seen so many reports on television, in newspapers etc about other groups of people who are in trouble: *Some donors, battered by so many appeals for help, may find themselves battling compassion fatigue.*

com·pat·i·bil·ity /kəm,pætɪ'bɪləti/ *n* [U] **1** *technical* the ability of one piece of computer equipment to be used with another one, especially when they are made by different companies: [+with] *the system's compatibility with Windows software* **2** the ability to exist or be used together without causing problems: *compatibility of flavours* **3** the ability to have a good relationship with someone because you have similar interests, ideas etc: *sexual compatibility*

com·pat·i·ble¹ /kəm'pætɪbəl/ *adj* **1** if two pieces of computer equipment are compatible, they can be used together, especially when they are made by different companies; → **compatibility**: *The new software is* **IBM compatible** (=can be used with IBM computers). **2** able to exist or be used together without causing problems; → **compatibility**: [+with] *Stephen's political views often weren't compatible with her own.* **3** two people that are compatible are able to have a good relationship because they have similar opinions or interests; → **compatibility**

compatible² n [C] technical a piece of computer equipment that can be used in or with another piece of equipment, especially one made by a different company: *Most programs work with IBM compatibles.*

com·pat·ri·ot /kəm'pætriət $ -'peɪt-/ n [C] someone who was born in or is a citizen of the same country as someone else: **sb's compatriot** *Schmidt defeated his compatriot Hausmann in the quarter final.*

com·pel /kəm'pel/ v **compelled**, **compelling** [T] **1** to force someone to do something; → **compulsion**: **compel sb to do sth** *The law will compel employers to provide health insurance.* | *She felt compelled to resign because of the scandal.* **2** formal to make people have a particular feeling or attitude; → **compulsion**: *His performance compelled the audience's attention.*

com·pel·ling /kəm'pelɪŋ/ adj **1 compelling reason/ argument/case etc** an argument etc that makes you feel certain that something is true or that you must do something about it: *Lucy had no compelling reason to go into town.* | *The court was presented with compelling evidence that she'd murdered her husband.* **2** very interesting or exciting, so that you have to pay attention: *His life makes a compelling story.* **3 compelling need/desire/urge (to do sth)** a strong need, desire etc to do something, making you feel that you must do it: *He felt a compelling need to tell someone about his idea.* —**compellingly** adv

com·pen·di·um /kəm'pendiəm/ n plural **compendiums** or **compendia** /-diə/ [C] **1** formal a book that contains a complete collection of facts, drawings etc on a particular subject: *a cricketing compendium* **2** BrE a set of different BOARD GAMES in a box

com·pen·sate /'kɒmpənseɪt $ 'kɑːm-/ v **1** [I] to replace or balance the effect of something bad: *Because my left eye is so weak, my right eye has to work harder to compensate.* | [+for] *Her intelligence more than compensates for her lack of experience.* **2** [T] to pay someone money because they have suffered injury, loss, or damage: *the government's promise to compensate victims of the flood* | **compensate sb for sth** *The firm will compensate workers for their loss of earnings.*

com·pen·sa·tion W3 /ˌkɒmpən'seɪʃən $ ˌkɑːm-/ n **1** [U] money paid to someone because they have suffered injury or loss, or because something they own has been damaged: [+for] *compensation for injuries at work* | [+from] *She received compensation from the government for the damage caused to her property.* | **in compensation** *The jury awarded Tyler $1.7 million in compensation.* | **as compensation** *The workers were given 30 days' pay as compensation.* | *People who are wrongly arrested may be* **paid compensation**. | **demand/seek/claim compensation** *The parents are seeking compensation for birth defects caused by the drug.* | **award/grant compensation** *The court awarded Jamieson £30,000 compensation.* **2** [C,U] something that makes a bad situation better: *One of the few compensations of losing my job was seeing more of my family.* | **by way of compensation** (=in order to make a situation better) *By way of compensation he offered to take her out for a meal.* **3** [C,U] when someone behaves in a particular way in order to replace something that is missing or to balance the bad effects of something: [+for] *Linda's aggressiveness is just a compensation for her feelings of insecurity.* | **as compensation (for sth)** *Lip-reading can act as compensation for loss of hearing.* **4** [U] AmE the money someone is paid for doing their job

com·pen·sa·to·ry /ˌkɒmpən'seɪtəri◂ $ kəm'pensəˌtɔːri/ adj [usually before noun] formal **1** compensatory payments are paid to someone who has been harmed or hurt in some way: *She was awarded a large sum in* **compensatory damages**. **2** intended to reduce the bad effects of something: *Workers are given a compensatory day off when a national holiday falls on a weekend.*

com·pere /'kɒmpeə $ 'kɑːmper/ n [C] BrE someone who introduces the people who are performing in a television programme, theatre show etc; ☐ **host** AmE —**compere** v [I,T]: *Ballentine will compere the show.*

com·pete S3 W3 /kəm'piːt/ v [I]
1 BUSINESS if one company or country competes with another, it tries to get people to buy its goods or services rather than those available from another company or country; → **competition, competitor, competitive**: [+with/against] *They found themselves competing with foreign companies for a share of the market.* | *The Renault Clio competes against such cars as the Peugeot 206.* | [+for] *The stores have to compete for customers in the Christmas season.* | [+in] *The company must be able to compete in the international marketplace.* | **compete to do sth** *Several advertising agencies are competing to get the contract.* | **can't compete (with sth)** (=be unable to be more successful) *Small, independent bookstores simply can't compete with the big national chains.*
2 PERSON to try to gain something and stop someone else from having it or having as much of it; → **competition, competitive**: [+for] *She and her sister are always competing for attention.* | [+against] *I had to compete against 19 other people for the job.* | [+with] *As a stepmother, don't even try to compete with the children's mother for their love.*
3 IN A COMPETITION to take part in a competition or sports event; → **competitor**: [+in/at] *How many runners will be competing in the marathon?* | *Professional athletes may now compete at the Olympics.* | [+against] *Edwards will be competing against his closest rival Olsson in the triple jump.*
4 sb/sth can't compete with sb/sth to not be as interesting, attractive etc as someone or something else: *Melinda was plain and knew she couldn't compete with her sister where boys were concerned.*

com·pe·tence /'kɒmpɪtəns $ 'kɑːm-/ n **1** [U] also **competency** the ability to do something well; ☐ **incompetence**: [+in] *Students will gain competence in a wide range of skills.* | [+of] *He questioned the competence of the government.* | **professional/linguistic/ technical etc competence** *Doctors have to constantly update their knowledge in order to maintain their professional competence.* **2** [U] law the legal power of a court of law to hear and judge something in court, or of a government to do something: **be within the competence of sth** *Many legal issues are within the competence of individual states rather than the federal government.* **3** [C] also **competency** formal a skill needed to do a particular job: *Typing is considered by most employers to be a basic competence.*

com·pe·tent /'kɒmpɪtənt $ 'kɑːm-/ adj **1** having enough skill or knowledge to do something to a satisfactory standard; ☐ **incompetent**: *A competent mechanic should be able to fix the problem.* | **very/ highly/extremely competent** *She's a highly competent linguist.* | **competent to do sth** *I don't feel competent to give an opinion at the moment.* | *He is the only party leader competent enough to govern this country.* **2** satisfactory but not especially good: *The workmen did a competent job.* **3** technical having normal mental abilities: *We believe the patient was not* **mentally competent**. | *A psychiatrist said McKibben was* **competent to stand trial**. **4** [not before noun] law having the legal power to deal with something in a court of law: **competent to do sth** *This court is not competent to hear your case.* —**competently** adv

com·pet·ing /kəm'piːtɪŋ/ adj [only before noun] **1** competing stories, ideas etc cannot all be right or accepted: *Several people gave* **competing accounts** *of the accident.* | *a compromise between competing interests within the organization* | *competing claims* **2 competing products/brands/companies etc** products etc that are trying to be more successful than each other

com·pe·ti·tion S1 W1 /ˌkɒmpəˈtɪʃən $ ˌkaːm-/ n
1 [U] a situation in which people or organizations try to be more successful than other people or organizations; → **compete, competitor**: [+for] *Competition for the job was intense.* | [+between/among] *Sometimes there's a lot of competition between children for their mother's attention.* | *This price reduction is due to competition among suppliers.* | [+in] *competition in the automobile industry* | **fierce/stiff/intense etc competition** *There is fierce competition between the three leading soap manufacturers.* | **be in competition with sb/sth** *Government departments are in direct competition with each other for limited resources.* | **in the face of competition (from sb/sth)** (=in a situation where you are competing with someone or something) *Small grocery stores are going out of business in the face of stiff competition from the large supermarket chains.*
2 [singular, U] the people or groups that are competing against you, especially in business or in a sport; → **compete, competitor**: *Going to trade fairs is an ideal opportunity to size up* **the competition.** | **no/not much/ little etc competition** (=no one who is likely to be better than you) *Jones is certain to win the race; there's just no competition.* | **a lot of/considerable/fierce etc competition** *The team overcame fierce competition for their place in the finals.* | **foreign/international competition** (=companies from other countries that you are competing with) *Japanese PC makers now face foreign competition in their home market.*
3 [C] an organized event in which people or teams compete against each other; → **competitor**

> **enter a competition** (=take part in a competition)
> **hold/run/launch a competition** (=organize a competition)
> **win/lose a competition**
> **be out of a competition** (=no longer be in a competition)
> **knock sb out of a competition** (=defeat someone so that they can no longer take part in the competition)
> **a knockout competition** *BrE* (=one in which if you lose a game, you are no longer in the competition)
> **the winner of a competition**

a photography competition | **competition to do sth** *a competition to find a designer for the new airport building* | *Teams from high schools all over the state have* **entered** *the* **competition.** | *The* **competition** *will be* **held** *in Copenhagen next year.* | *Who* **won** *the* **competition?** | *With France and Germany* **out of the competition,** *England have a great chance to win.* | *Liverpool were* **knocked out of the competition** *in the third round.*

com·pet·i·tive S2 W3 /kəmˈpetətɪv/ adj
1 determined or trying very hard to be more successful than other people or businesses; → **compete, competitor**: *Some US industries are not as competitive as they have been in the past.* | *The team seems to have lost its* **competitive edge** *recently* (=its ability to compete well).
2 relating to competition; → **compete, competitor**: *Competitive sports encourage children to work together as a team.* | **highly/fiercely/intensely etc competitive** *Advertising is an intensely competitive business.*
3 products or prices that are competitive are cheaper than others but still of good quality: *The hotel offers a high standard of service at competitive rates.* —**competitively** adv

com·pet·i·tive·ness /kəmˈpetətɪvnəs/ n [U] **1** the ability of a company, country, or a product to compete with others: *New machinery has enhanced the company's productivity and competitiveness.* | *Europe's competitiveness in international markets* **2** the desire to be more successful than other people: *Her enthusiasm and competitiveness rubbed off on everyone.*

com·pet·i·tor /kəmˈpetətə $ -ər/ n [C] **1** a person, team, company etc that is competing with another:

Last year they sold twice as many computers as their competitors. | **major/main competitors** *The company's four major competitors have nothing to rival the new product.* **2** someone who takes part in a competition: *Two of the competitors failed to turn up for the race.*

com·pi·la·tion /ˌkɒmpəˈleɪʃən $ ˌkaːm-/ n **1** [C] a book, list, record etc which consists of different pieces of information, songs etc: [+of] *a compilation of love songs* | **compilation CD/album/tape** **2** [U] the process of making a book, list, record etc from different pieces of information, songs etc: *dictionary compilation*

com·pile /kəmˈpaɪl/ v [T] **1** to make a book, list, record etc, using different pieces of information, music etc; → **compilation**: *The document was compiled by the Department of Health* | **compile sth from/for sth** *The report was compiled from a survey of 5000 households.* **2** technical to put a set of instructions into a computer in a form that it can understand and use

com·pil·er /kəmˈpaɪlə $ -ər/ n [C] **1** someone who collects different pieces of information to be used in a book, report, or list **2** technical a set of instructions in a computer that changes a computer language known to the computer user into the form needed by the computer

com·pla·cen·cy /kəmˈpleɪsənsi/ n [U] a feeling of satisfaction with a situation or with what you have achieved, so that you stop trying to improve or change things – used to show disapproval: *Doctors have warned against complacency in fighting common diseases.* | *Despite yesterday's win, there is clearly no room for complacency if the team want to stay top of the league.*

com·pla·cent /kəmˈpleɪsənt/ adj pleased with a situation, especially something you have achieved, so that you stop trying to improve or change things – used to show disapproval: *There's a danger of becoming complacent if you win a few games.* | *a* **complacent attitude** *towards the problem* | [+about] *We simply cannot afford to be complacent about the future of our car industry.* —**complacently** adv

com·plain S2 W3 /kəmˈpleɪn/ v
1 [I,T not in passive] to say that you are annoyed, not satisfied, or unhappy about something or someone; → **complaint**: *Residents are complaining because traffic in the area has increased.* | *'You never ask my opinion about anything,' Rod complained.* | **complain (that)** *She complained that no one had been at the airport to meet her.* | [+about] *She often complains about not feeling appreciated at work.* | [+of] *Several women have complained of sexual harassment.* | [+to] *Neighbours complained to the police about the dogs barking.* | *Employees* **complained bitterly** *about working conditions.*
2 (I/you/he etc) **can't complain** spoken used to say that a situation is satisfactory, even though there may be a few problems: *I make a good living. I can't complain.*
complain of sth phr v formal
to say that you feel ill or have a pain in a part of your body: *Dan's been complaining of severe headaches.*

com·plain·ant /kəmˈpleɪnənt/ n [C] law someone who makes a formal complaint in a court of law; ☐ **plaintiff**

com·plaint S2 W3 /kəmˈpleɪnt/ n
1 [C,U] a statement in which someone complains about something: *The sales assistants are trained to deal with* **customer complaints** *in a friendly manner.* | *A* **common complaint** *among air passengers is that not enough leg room is provided.* | **formal/official complaint** | [+about] *Keating was dismissed after complaints about the quality of his work.* | [+of] *complaints of police brutality* | [+from/to] *complaints from local residents* | *a complaint to the Advertising Standards Authority* | [+against] *All complaints against police officers are carefully investigated.* | **complaint that** *We are concerned by complaints that children are being bullied.* | *If you wish to* **make a complaint,** *you should see the manager* (=complain formally to someone). | **have/receive a complaint** *The BBC received a stream of*

complaints about the programme. | **Complaints are dealt with** by the customer services department. | The Council received over 10,000 **letters of complaint**. | **file/lodge/submit a complaint** (=complain officially to someone) She went to the city council and lodged a complaint. | **reason/cause/grounds for complaint** Anyone dismissed because of their race has legitimate grounds for complaint. | a **complaints procedure** (=a system for dealing with complaints)
2 [C] something that you complain about: Our main complaint was the poor standard of service. | My only complaint is that the price is rather high.
3 [C] formal an illness that affects a particular part of your body: He is having treatment for a **chest complaint**.

com·plai·sance /kəm'pleɪzəns/ n [U] formal willingness to do what pleases other people —**complaisant** adj —**complaisantly** adv

com·plect·ed /kəm'plektᵻd/ adj AmE **light/fair/dark complected** having light or dark skin

com·ple·ment¹ /'kɒmpləmənt $ 'kɑːm-/ n [C]
1 someone or something that emphasizes the good qualities of another person or thing: [+to] This wine would be a nice complement to grilled dishes. **2** the number or quantity needed to make a group complete: [+of] Each new cell will carry its **full complement** of chromosomes. **3** technical a word or phrase that follows a verb and describes the subject of the verb. In 'John is cold' and 'John became chairman', 'cold' and 'chairman' are complements.

com·ple·ment² /'kɒmpləment $ 'kɑːm-/ v [T] to make a good combination with someone or something else: John and Bob complemented each other extremely well. | The dark red walls complement the red leather chairs.

com·ple·men·ta·ry /ˌkɒmplə'mentᵊri◂ $ ˌkɑːm-/ adj **1** complementary things go well together, although they are usually different: The computer and the human mind have different but complementary abilities. **2** technical complementary colours of light are very different and combine to make white **3** technical two angles that are complementary add up to 90 degrees —**complementarity** /ˌkɒmpləmen'tærᵊti $ ˌkɑːm-/ n [U]

complementary 'medicine n [U] especially BrE complementary medicine uses treatments that are not part of traditional Western medicine: acupuncture and other complementary therapies

com·plete¹ S2 W1 /kəm'pliːt/ adj
1 [usually before noun] used to emphasize that a quality or situation is as great as it could possibly be; **= total**: The police were in **complete control** of the situation. | Their engagement came as a **complete surprise** to me. | This is a **complete waste of time**. | a **complete fool/idiot etc** Meg realized she'd been a complete fool. | a **complete stranger** | The darkness was almost complete.
2 including all parts, details, facts etc and with nothing missing; **= whole**; ≠ **incomplete**: a complete set of china | The list below is not complete. | **the complete works of** Shakespeare (=a book, CD etc containing everything Shakespeare wrote)
3 [not before noun] finished; ≠ **incomplete**: Work on the new building is nearly complete.
4 complete with sth having particular equipment or features: The house **comes complete with** swimming pool and sauna. —**completeness** n [U]: For the sake of completeness I should mention one further argument.

complete² S2 W1 v [T]
1 to finish doing or making something, especially when it has taken a long time: The students have just completed their course. | The building took two years to complete.
2 to make something whole or perfect by adding what is missing: The child's task was to complete the sentences. | I need one more stamp to complete the set.
3 to write the information that is needed on a form;

☰ fill out: In all, more than 650 people completed the questionnaire. | Send your completed form to the following address.

com·plete·ly S1 W2 /kəm'pliːtli/ adv to the greatest degree possible; **= totally**: I completely forgot that it was his birthday yesterday. | He had never completely recovered from his illness. | a completely new range of low-cost computers | I'm not completely sure. | Portuguese is pronounced completely differently from Spanish.

com·ple·tion /kəm'pliːʃən/ n [U] **1** the state of being finished: The new houses are **nearing completion** (=almost finished). | The project has a **completion date** of December 22nd. **2** the act of finishing something: [+of] The job is subject to your satisfactory completion of the training course. | **on completion (of sth)** On completion of the building, they make a final inspection. **3** law the final point in the sale of a house, when all the documents have been signed and all the money paid

com·plex¹ S3 W2 /'kɒmpleks $ ˌkɑːm'pleks◂/ adj
1 consisting of many different parts and often difficult to understand; **= complicated**; ≠ **simple**: a **complex system** of highways | Photosynthesis is a **highly complex** process. | Peter seemed to have an instant understanding of the most complex issues. | It was a very complex relationship between two complex people.
2 technical a complex word or sentence contains a main part and one or more other parts; → **compound**

com·plex² /'kɒmpleks $ 'kɑːm-/ n [C] **1** a group of buildings, or a large building with many parts, used for a particular purpose: The town has one of the best **leisure complexes** in the country. | a three-story apartment complex **2** a complex of sth formal a large number of things which are closely related: China was a complex of different societies. **3** an emotional problem in which someone is unnecessarily anxious about something or thinks too much about something: I used to **have a complex about** my looks. → INFERIORITY COMPLEX, OEDIPUS COMPLEX, PERSECUTION COMPLEX

com·plex·ion /kəm'plekʃən/ n **1** [C] the natural colour or appearance of the skin on your face: Drinking lots of water is good for the complexion. | **pale/fair/ruddy etc complexion** (=a pale, fair, red etc face) | **fair-complexioned/smooth-complexioned etc** She was fair-complexioned with pale blonde hair. **2** [singular] the general character or nature of something: Crime has risen everywhere, under governments of every political complexion. **3 put a different/new/fresh complexion on sth** to make a situation or event seem different: This document puts a different complexion on the matter.

com·plex·i·ty /kəm'pleksᵻti/ n plural **complexities 1** [U] the state of being complicated: [+of] There is increasing recognition of the complexity of the causes of poverty. | a design of great complexity **2** [C usually plural] one of the many details or features of something that make it hard to understand or deal with: [+of] The complexities of economics are clearly and entertainingly explained.

com·pli·ance /kəm'plaɪəns/ n [U] formal when someone obeys a rule, agreement, or demand; → **comply**: **in compliance with sth** He changed his name to Lee in 1815 in compliance with his uncle's will. | [+with] Patients should have a history of good compliance with treatment. | **ensure/secure/enforce compliance** The staff involved should be monitored to ensure compliance with the policy.

com·pli·ant /kəm'plaɪənt/ adj **1** willing to obey or to agree to other people's wishes and demands; → **comply**: For years I had tried to be a compliant and dutiful wife. **2** made or done according to particular rules or standards; → **comply**: [+with] Future versions will be fully compliant with the industry standard.

drive through hard rock. **2** [I,T] to make a computer FILE smaller by using a special computer PROGRAM, which makes the file easier to store or send, or to become smaller in this way: *The program compresses any data saved to the disk.* **3** [T] to write or express something using fewer words; ▤ **condense: compress sth into sth** *In this chapter we compress into summary form the main issues discussed so far.* **4** [T] to reduce the amount of time that it takes for something to happen or be done: **compress sth into sth** *Many couples want to compress their childbearing into a short space of time in their natural life.* —**compressible** *adj* —**compression** /-'preʃən/ *n* [U]: *data compression*

com·press² /'kɒmpres $ 'kɑːm-/ *n* [C] a small thick piece of material that you put on part of someone's body to stop blood flowing out or to make it less painful: **cold/hot compress** *Apply a cold compress to the injury.*

com·pres·sor /kəm'presə $ -ər/ *n* [C] a machine or part of a machine that compresses air or gas

com·prise [W3] /kəm'praɪz/ *v* [not in progressive] *formal* **1** [linking verb] to consist of particular parts, groups etc: *The house comprises two bedrooms, a kitchen, and a living room.* | **be comprised of sb/sth** *The committee is comprised of well-known mountaineers.* **2** [T] to form part of a larger group of people or things; ▤ **constitute, make up:** *Women comprise a high proportion of part-time workers.*

com·pro·mise¹ /'kɒmprəmaɪz $ 'kɑːm-/ *n* **1** [C,U] an agreement that is achieved after everyone involved accepts less than what they wanted at first, or the act of making this agreement: *Compromise is an inevitable part of marriage.* | *To stop the argument they decided on a compromise.* | [+**with**] *Fresh attempts at compromise with the legislature were also on the agenda.* | [+**between**] *a compromise between government and opposition* | *If moderates fail to* **reach a compromise**, *the extremists will dominate the agenda.* | *Everyone has to be prepared to* **make compromises.** **2** [C] a solution to a problem in which two things or situations are changed slightly so that they can exist together: [+**between**] *a happy compromise between the needs of family and work*

compromise² *v* **1** [I] to reach an agreement in which everyone involved accepts less that what they wanted at first: *She admitted that she was unable to compromise.* | [+**with**] *His work-mates demanded that he never compromise with the bosses.* | [+**on**] *The new regime was prepared to compromise on the oil dispute.* **2** [T] to do something which is against your principles and which therefore seems dishonest or shameful: **compromise your principles/standards/integrity etc** *As soon as you compromise your principles you are lost.* | **compromise yourself** *She had already compromised herself by accepting his invitation.*

com·pro·mis·ing /'kɒmprəmaɪzɪŋ $ 'kɑːm-/ *adj* proving that you have done something morally wrong or embarrassing, or making it seem as if you have done so: **compromising position/situation** *The doctor was found in a compromising position with a nurse* (=having sex with her). | **compromising letter/photograph/ picture etc** *A large number of compromising letters fell into the hands of investigators.*

comp·trol·ler /kən'trəʊlə, kəmp- $ -'troʊlər/ *n* [C] *formal* an official title for a CONTROLLER

com·pul·sion /kəm'pʌlʃən/ *n* **1** [C] a strong and unreasonable desire to do something; → **compel:** *The desire to laugh became a compulsion.* | **compulsion to do sth** *Leith felt an overwhelming compulsion to tell him the truth.* | *the compulsion to smoke or eat too much* **2** [singular, U] the act of forcing or influencing someone to do something they do not want to do; → **compel: under (no) compulsion to do sth** *Owners are under no compulsion to sell their land.* | *The use of compulsion in psychiatric care cannot be justified.*

com·pul·sive /kəm'pʌlsɪv/ *adj* **1** compulsive behaviour is very difficult to stop or control, and is often a result of or a sign of a mental problem; → **obsessive: compulsive gambling/overeating/spending etc** *Compulsive overspending in these days of credit cards has become more common.* **2 compulsive overeater/gambler/spender/liar etc** someone who has such a strong desire to eat too much etc that they are unable to control it: *a help group for compulsive overeaters* **3** a book, programme etc that is compulsive is so interesting that you cannot stop reading or watching it: **compulsive reading/viewing** *'Gardening World' is compulsive viewing for gardeners.* —**compulsively** *adv* —**compulsiveness** *n* [U]

com·pul·so·ry /kəm'pʌlsəri/ *adj* something that is compulsory must be done because it is the law or because someone in authority orders you to; ▤ **mandatory;** → **voluntary:** *the threat of compulsory redundancies* | *compulsory schooling/education 11 years of compulsory education* | *Car insurance is compulsory.* —**compulsorily** *adv*

com·punc·tion /kəm'pʌŋkʃən/ *n* [U usually in negatives] *formal* a feeling that you should not do something because it is bad or wrong: **have/feel no compunction about (doing) sth** *He had no compunction about interfering in her private affairs.* | *They used their tanks against the leftists* **without compunction.**

com·pu·ta·tion /ˌkɒmpjʊˈteɪʃən $ ˌkɑːm-/ *n* [C,U] *formal* the process of calculating or the result of calculating: *the computation of the monthly statistics* —**computational** *adj: computational linguistics*

com·pute /kəm'pjuːt/ *v* [I,T] *formal* to calculate a result, answer, sum etc: *Final results had not yet been computed.*

com·put·er [S1] [W1] /kəm'pjuːtə $ -ər/ *n* [C] an electronic machine that stores information and uses programs to help you find, organize, or change the information: *A message flashed up on my* **computer screen.** | *recent problems with hospital* **computer systems** | **on computer** *The information is stored on computer.* | **by computer** *Shoppers can send in their orders by computer and pick up their goods later.* | **computer software/program/application** *the latest computer software* | **computer games** (=games that you play on a computer) *for children* | *the use of* **computer graphics** (=pictures and images created by computers) *in film* | *the development of* **computer technology** | *the* **computer industry** | *a huge global* **computer network** → see picture at OFFICE

WORD FOCUS: COMPUTER
people who work with computers: **user, programmer, web designer, IT person, software engineer, (systems) analyst, administrator, webmaster, helpdesk, techie** *informal,* **geek** *disapproving informal*
someone who tries to break into a computer system: **hacker, cracker**
things you do with your computer: **start up/power up** your computer | **open** a file or document | **enter** information | **click on** an icon | **cut and paste** pieces of text | **copy** files or programs | **scroll up and down** the page | **delete** things you do not want | **download** files or pictures from the Internet | **burn** CDs or DVDs | **close** a file or document | **save** your work | **shut down** your computer
computer problems: **bug, virus, error, corrupted file/ data, crash, worm**
→ Internet, email, personal computer, laptop, palmtop, pda

com,puter-aided de'sign *n* [U] CAD
com,puter-aided manu'facturing *n* [U] CAM
com·put·er·ate /kəm'pjuːtərət/ *adj* able to use a computer well: *Students need to be computerate as well as literate.*

com·put·er·ize also **-ise** *BrE* /kəm'pjuːtəraɪz/ *v* [T] to use a computer to control the way something is done, to store information etc: *a scheme to computerize the library service* | *a* **computerized system** *for compiling* the weekly charts of record sales | *computerized information* | *a computerized database* —**computerization** /kəm‚pjuːtəraɪˈzeɪʃən $ -rə-/ n [U]: *the computerization of the printing industry*

com‚puter-'literate adj able to use a computer: *Nowadays, all graduates are computer-literate.* —**computer literacy** n [U]

com‚puter 'modelling n [U] the use of computer images that are models of real things, used to help improve the way that something is designed or to solve a problem: *computer modelling of the city's traffic flow*

com‚puter 'science n [U] the study of computers and what they can do: *a BSc in Computer Science*

com‚puter 'virus n [C] a set of instructions secretly put into a computer, usually spread through emails, which can destroy information stored on the computer

com·put·ing /kəmˈpjuːtɪŋ/ n [U] the use of computers as a job, in a business etc: *Have you ever done any computing?* | *computing facilities for language research*

com·rade /ˈkɒmrɪ̱d, -reɪd $ ˈkɑːmræd/ n [C] **1** formal a friend, especially someone who shares difficult work or danger: *He misses his comrades from his days in the Army.* **2** SOCIALISTS or COMMUNISTS often call each other 'comrade', especially in meetings: *Comrades, please support this motion.* —**comradely** adj

‚**comrade in 'arms** n plural **comrades in arms** [C] someone who has fought with you or worked with you to achieve particular aims

com·rade·ship /ˈkɒmrɪ̱dʃɪp, -reɪd- $ ˈkɑːmræd-/ n [U] formal friendship and loyalty among people who work together, fight together etc: *It was the spirit of comradeship that made victory possible.*

con¹ /kɒn $ kɑːn/ v **conned, conning** [T] informal **1** to get money from someone by deceiving them: **con sb out of sth** *He conned me out of £300.* **2** to persuade someone to do something by deceiving them: **con sb into doing sth** *You had no right to con me into thinking I could trust you.*

con² n [C] informal **1** a trick to get someone's money or make them do something: *a con to make people pay for goods they hadn't actually received* **2** a prisoner → MOD CONS; → **the pros and cons** at PRO¹ (3)

con- /kən, kɒn $ kən, kɑːn/ prefix together; ▣ with: *a confederation* | *to conspire* (=plan together)

Con BrE the written abbreviation of **Conservative**, in British politics: *Sir Teddy Taylor (Con)*

'**con ‚artist** n [C] informal someone who tricks or deceives people in order to get money from them

con·cat·e·na·tion /kɒn‚kætɪ̱ˈneɪʃən $ kɑːn-/ n [C,U] formal a series of events or things joined together one after another: [+of] *a strange concatenation of events*

con·cave /ˌkɒnˈkeɪv◂, kən- $ ‚kɑːnˈkeɪv◂, kən-/ adj a concave surface is curved inwards in the middle; ▣ **convex**: *a concave lens*

con·cav·i·ty /kənˈkævɪ̱ti/ n plural **concavities** formal **1** [U] the state of being concave **2** [C] a place or shape that is curved inwards

con·ceal /kənˈsiːl/ v [T] formal **1** to hide something carefully: *The shadows concealed her as she crept up to the house.* | *The path was concealed by long grass.* | *a concealed weapon* **2** to hide your real feelings or the truth: *She tried to conceal the fact that she was pregnant.* | **conceal sth from sb** *She was taking drugs and trying to conceal it from me.* —**concealment** n [U]: *deliberate concealment of his activities*

con·cede /kənˈsiːd/ v **1** ADMIT STH IS TRUE [I,T] to admit that something is true or correct, although you wish it were not true; → **concession**: *'That's the only possible solution.' 'Yes, I suppose so,' Charles conceded.* | **concede (that)** *I conceded that I had made a number of errors.* **2** ADMIT DEFEAT [I,T] to admit that you are not going to win a game, argument, battle etc; → **concession**: *The Georgian forces defended the capital but were finally obliged to concede.* | *In May 1949, Stalin conceded*

defeat and reopened land access to Berlin. **3** concede a goal/point/penalty to not be able to stop your opponent from getting a GOAL during a game: *The team has conceded only 19 goals in 28 games.* **4** GIVE STH AS A RIGHT [T] to give something to someone as a right or PRIVILEGE, often unwillingly; → **concession**: **concede sth to sb** *The king finally agreed to concede further powers to Parliament.* | *Finally the company conceded wage increases to their workers.*

con·ceit /kənˈsiːt/ n **1** [U] an attitude that shows you have too high an opinion of your own abilities or importance; ▣ **conceitedness**: *The conceit of the woman!* **2** [C] technical an unusual way of showing or describing something in a play, film, work of art etc: *His sermons were full of puns and conceits.*

con·ceit·ed /kənˈsiːtɪ̱d/ adj someone who is conceited thinks they are very clever, skilful, beautiful etc – used to show disapproval: *You're the most conceited, selfish person I've ever known.* —**conceitedly** adv —**conceitedness** n [U]

con·ceiv·a·ble /kənˈsiːvəbəl/ adj able to be believed or imagined; ▣ **inconceivable**: *It is conceivable that you may get full compensation, but it's not likely.* | *We were discussing the problems from every conceivable angle.* —**conceivably** adv: *Conceivably, interest rates could rise very high indeed.*

con·ceive /kənˈsiːv/ v **1** [I,T] formal to imagine a particular situation or to think about something in a particular way. **(cannot) conceive of (doing) sth** *Many people can't conceive of a dinner without meat or fish.* | **conceive that** *He could not conceive that anything really serious could be worrying his friend.* | **conceive what/why/how etc** *I can hardly conceive what it must be like here in winter.* | **conceive of sth/sb as sth** *Language may be conceived of as a process which arises from social interaction.* **2** [T] to think of a new idea, plan etc and develop it in your mind: *Scientists first conceived the idea of the atomic bomb in the 1930's.* **3** [I,T] to become PREGNANT: *fertility treatment for women who have difficulty conceiving*

con·cen·trate¹ S2 W2 /ˈkɒnsəntreɪt $ ˈkɑːn-/ v **1** [I] to think very carefully about something that you are doing; → **concentration**: *Now please concentrate.* | *Adrian was finding it difficult to concentrate.* | [+on] *I quiet – let me concentrate on my homework.* **2** [I,T] to be present in large numbers or amounts somewhere, or to cause people or things to be present in large numbers or amounts somewhere; → **concentration**: **concentrate sth in/at sth** *Italian industry is concentrated mainly in the north.* | *Construction of the aircraft is being concentrated at Prestwick.* | [+in/at] *Women concentrate in a small number of occupations.* **3** sth concentrates the mind if something concentrates the mind, it makes you think very clearly: *Relaxing in a Jacuzzi concentrates the mind wonderfully.* **4** [T] to make a substance or liquid stronger by removing some of the water from it; → **concentrated** **concentrate (sth) on** sth phr v to give most of your attention or effort to one thing: *Doctors are aiming to concentrate more on prevention than cure.* | **concentrate your efforts/attention/energy/ mind etc on sth** *I'm concentrating my efforts on writing my autobiography.*

concentrate² n [C,U] a substance or liquid which has been made stronger by removing most of the water from it: *orange juice concentrate*

con·cen·trat·ed /ˈkɒnsəntreɪtɪ̱d $ ˈkɑːn-/ adj **1** a concentrated liquid or substance has been made stronger by removing water from it: *concentrated orange juice* | *a concentrated cream detergent* **2** [only before noun] showing a lot of effort or determination: *He made a concentrated effort to improve his work.*

con·cen·tra·tion S3 W2 /ˌkɒnsənˈtreɪʃən $ ‚kɑːn-/ n **1** [U] the ability to think about something carefully or

for a long time; → **concentrate**: *She needed all her* **powers of concentration** *to stop herself from slipping on the icy road.* | *Lack of concentration was a real problem.* | *I* **lost** *my* **concentration** *and fell asleep.*
2 [U] a process in which you put a lot of attention, energy etc into a particular activity; → **concentrate**: **concentration on (doing) sth** *concentration on your health* | *concentration on providing quality value and service*
3 [C,U] a large amount of something in a particular place or among particular people; → **concentrate**: [+of] *the concentration of greenhouse gases in the atmosphere* | *the concentration of power in the hands of a few* | *the effect on trees of* **high concentrations** *of sulphur dioxide around industrial areas* | *people with blood alcohol concentrations above the limit*
4 [C] *technical* the amount of a substance contained in a liquid; → **concentrate**: **high/low concentrations** *Additives are expensive but are used in very low concentrations.* | [+of] *allowable concentrations of pesticides in drinking water*

,**concen'tration** ,**camp** *n* [C] a prison where political prisoners and other people who are not soldiers are kept and treated cruelly, especially during a war

con·cen·tric /kən'sentrɪk/ *adj* having the same centre; → **eccentric**: *concentric circles*

con·cept S3 W2 /'kɒnsept $ 'kɑːn-/ *n* [C] an idea of how something is, or how something should be done: [+of] *the concept of total patient care* | *the concept of infinite space* | **concept that** *the concept that we are citizens of one world* | *a* **new concept** *in business travel* | *our* **basic concepts** *of decent human behaviour* | *It's very simple, once you* **grasp** *the* **concept**.

con·cep·tion /kən'sepʃən/ *n* **1** [C,U] an idea about what something is like, or a general understanding of something; → **concept**: [+of] *the conception of parliamentary democracy* | *changing conceptions of the world* | **have (no) conception of sth** *They have no conception of what women really feel and want.* **2** [U] a process in which someone forms a plan or idea; → **conceive**: *the original conception of the book* **3** [C,U] the process by which a woman or female animal becomes PREGNANT, or the time when this happens; → **conceive**: *the moment of conception*

con·cep·tu·al /kən'septʃuəl/ *adj formal* dealing with ideas, or based on them: *the conceptual framework of the play* —**conceptually** *adv*

con,ceptual 'art *n* [U] *technical* art in which the main aim of the artist is to show an idea, rather than to represent actual things or people

con·cep·tu·al·ize also **-ise** *BrE* /kən'septʃuəlaɪz/ *v* [I,T] to form an idea: *How do older people conceptualize their health?* —**conceptualization** /kən,septʃuəlaɪ'zeɪʃən $ -lə-/ *n* [C,U]

con·cern¹ S1 W1 /kən'sɜːn $ -ɜːrn/ *n*
1 WORRY a) [U] a feeling of worry about something important: *The recent rise in crime is a matter of considerable public concern.* | [+for] *our concern for human rights* | [+about/over/with] *the rise of concern about the environment* | *the growing concern over inflation* | *concern with worsening law and order* | **concern that** *increased concern that the war could continue for a long time* | **be a cause for concern/cause concern** *The activities of the far right have been a cause for concern for a while now.* | *In her last days the poet* **expressed concern** *for her father.* **b)** [C] something that worries you: *One of the concerns that people have is the side effects of treatment.* | *Education remains the electorate's main concern.* | *the* **concerns expressed** *by parents*
2 STH IMPORTANT [C,U] something that is important to you or that involves you: *His main concern is to be able to provide for his family.* | [+for] *The consumer has become a major concern for this government.* | **of concern to sb** *topics of concern to television viewers*

3 FEELING FOR SB [singular, U] a feeling of wanting someone to be happy and healthy: *He was moved by her obvious concern.* | [+for] *parents' loving concern for their children*
4 sb's concern if something is your concern, you are responsible for it: *The money side of the business is your concern.*
5 not sb's concern/none of sb's concern if something is not your concern, you are not interested in it and you do not need to worry about it or become involved in it: *His affairs were none of her concern.*
6 BUSINESS [C] a business or company: *The restaurant is a family concern.* | *We will continue to run the company as* **a going concern** (=a business that is financially successful).

con·cern² W3 *v* [T]
1 [not in passive] if a story, book, report etc concerns someone or something, it is about them: *This study concerns couples' expectations of marriage.* | *The report concerns the drug traffic on the Mexican-US border.*
2 to make someone feel worried or upset: *Issues like food additives do concern me.*
3 [not in passive] if an activity, situation, rule etc concerns you, it affects you or involves you: *The tax changes will concern large corporations rather than small businesses.*
4 concern yourself with/about sth *formal* to become involved in something because you are interested in it or because it worries you: *He told them not to concern themselves about him.* | *He loved his wife, and concerned himself with her needs and desires.*
5 to whom it may concern an expression written at the beginning of a formal letter when you do not know the name of the person you want to communicate with

con·cerned S1 W1 /kən'sɜːnd $ -ɜːrnd/ *adj*
1 INVOLVED [not before noun] involved in something or affected by it: *Divorce is very painful, especially when children are concerned.* | *Some of the farmers concerned suffer particularly from the low prices.* | *We are trying to reach an agreement with* **all concerned** (=everyone who is involved or affected). | [+with] *all the people concerned with children's education* | [+in] *There was no evidence that he was concerned in any criminal activity.*
2 WORRIED worried about something: [+about] *She is concerned about how little food I eat.* | [+for] *He called the police because he was concerned for Gemma's safety.* | **concerned (that)** *Pamela was concerned that her schoolwork had deteriorated despite her hard work.* | *The drug came under strong attack from concerned professional observers.*
3 as far as sb is concerned *spoken* used to show what someone's opinion on a subject is or how it affects them: *As far as Americans are concerned, a lot of our hotels are below average.* | *As far as I'm concerned, you can forget about it.*
4 as far as sth is concerned also **where sth is concerned** *spoken* used to show which subject or thing you are talking about: *As far as traffic is concerned there are no delays at the moment.*
5 THINK STH IS IMPORTANT [not before noun] believing that something is important: [+with] *Many politicians are more concerned with power and control than with the good of the people.* | **concerned to do sth** *Mr Quinn is simply concerned to hold on to his job.*
6 LOVE/CARE caring about someone and whether they are happy and healthy: [+for/about] *He was genuinely concerned for the children.*
7 concerned with sb/sth if a book, story etc is concerned with a person, subject etc, it is about that subject: *This chapter is concerned with the mental health of older people.*

con·cern·ing W3 /kən'sɜːnɪŋ $ -ɜːr-/ *prep* about or relating to: *calls from young children concerning lost pets* | *the facts concerning Marr's car crash*

con·cert S3 W3 /'kɒnsət $ 'kɑːnsərt/ *n* [C]
1 a performance given by musicians or singers: *a rock concert* | *live concert performances* | *a concert of French choral music* | *We were* **going to** *a* **concert** *in Bath*

Abbey. | *He gave a concert at the opera house.*
2 in concert (with sb) a) *formal* people who do something in concert do it together after having agreed on it: *Britain has to pursue policies in concert with other EU members.* | *It appeared that both the accused were* ***acting in concert*** *in the attack upon the deceased.* **b)** playing or singing at a concert: *They're appearing in concert tonight at the Royal Concert Hall.*

con·cert·ed /kən'sɜːtɪd $ -ɜːr-/ *adj* **concerted effort/action/attack etc** a concerted effort etc is done by people working together in a carefully planned and very determined way: *Libraries have* ***made*** *a* ***concerted effort*** *to attract young people.* —**concertedly** *adv*

con·cert·go·er /'kɒnsət,ɡəʊə $ 'kɑːnsərt,ɡoʊər/ *n* [C] someone who often goes to concerts, or someone who is at a particular concert

'**concert hall** *n* [C] a large public building where concerts are performed

con·cer·ti·na¹ /,kɒnsə'tiːnə $,kɑːnsər-/ *n* [C] a musical instrument like a small ACCORDION, that you hold in both hands and play by pressing in from each side

concertina² *v* [I] *BrE* if something concertinas, it folds together on itself: *His too-long trousers concertinaed around his feet.*

con·cert·mas·ter /'kɒnsət,mɑːstə $ 'kɑːnsərt-,mæstər/ *n* [C] the most important VIOLIN player in an ORCHESTRA

con·cer·to /kən'tʃɜːtəʊ $ -'tʃertoʊ/ *n plural* **concertos** [C] a piece of CLASSICAL music, usually for one instrument and an ORCHESTRA

con·ces·sion /kən'seʃən/ *n*
1 STH YOU ALLOW SB [C] something that you allow someone to have in order to end an argument or a disagreement; → **concede**: [+to] *a policy of no concessions to terrorists* | *The British were not prepared to* ***make*** *any* ***concessions.*** | [+on] *his readiness to make concessions on many of the issues raised* | [+from] *We will try to force further concessions from the government.* | **major/important/substantial concession** *The committee has* ***won*** *a number of major* ***concessions*** *from the prison authorities.*
2 A RIGHT [C,U] a special right that a particular person or group of people is allowed to have, for example by the government or an employer, or the act of giving or allowing something as a right: *the ending of* ***tax concessions*** *for home owners* | *the import/export* ***concessions*** *that had been* ***granted*** *to the island* | [+of] *the concession of autonomy to the universities*
3 PRICE REDUCTION [C] *BrE* a reduction in the price of tickets, FEES etc for certain groups of people, for example old people or children; ▣ **reduction**: *To qualify for travel concessions you have to be 60.* | *Open daily, adults £4, concessions £2* (=people who have the right to a concession pay £2).
4 CHANGE OF BEHAVIOUR [C] a change in your behaviour that you make because of a particular situation or idea: *He took off his jacket* ***as a concession*** *to the heat.* | *He* ***made*** *no* ***concessions*** *to fashion.*
5 BUSINESS [C] *AmE* **a)** the right to have a business in a particular place, especially in a place owned by someone else: *The company owns valuable logging and mining concessions.* **b)** a small business that sells things in a place owned by someone else: *Joe runs a hamburger concession in the mall.*
6 THINGS SOLD concessions [plural] *AmE* the things sold at a concession stand

con·ces·sion·aire /kən,seʃə'neə $ -'ner/ *n* [C] someone who has been given the right to have a business in a particular place, especially in a place owned by someone else

con·ces·sion·ar·y /kən'seʃənəri $ -neri/ *adj*
1 given as a concession **2** *BrE* specially reduced in price, for example for old people or children: *a concessionary fares scheme for pensioners*

con'cession ,stand *n* [C] *AmE* a small business that sells food, drinks, or other things at sports events, theatres etc

conch /kɒntʃ, kɒŋk $ kɑːntʃ, kɑːŋk/ *n* [C] the large twisted shell of a tropical sea animal that looks like a SNAIL

con·ci·erge /'kɒnsieəʒ $,kɑːnsi'erʒ/ *n* [C] **1** someone in a hotel whose job is to help guests by telling them about places to visit, restaurants to eat in etc **2** someone who looks after a block of apartments and who checks who is going in and coming out, especially in France

con·cil·i·ate /kən'sɪlieɪt/ *v* [I,T] *formal* to do something to make people more likely to stop arguing, especially by giving them something they want: *proposals designed to conciliate the unions* —**conciliator** *n* [C]

con·cil·i·a·tion /kən,sɪli'eɪʃən/ *n* [U] *formal* the process of trying to get people to stop arguing and agree; → **reconciliation**: *conciliation talks between the two sides*

con·cil·i·a·tory /kən'sɪliətəri $ -tɔːri/ *adj* doing something that is intended to make someone stop arguing with you: **conciliatory approach/tone/gesture etc** *Perhaps you should adopt a more conciliatory approach.* | *Brooks felt in no mood to be conciliatory.*

con·cise /kən'saɪs/ *adj* **1** short, with no unnecessary words; ▣ **brief**: *Your summary should be as* ***clear and concise*** *as possible.* **2** [only before noun] shorter than the original book on which something is based: *the Concise Dictionary of Spoken Chinese* —**concisely** *adv* —**conciseness** *n* [U]

con·clave /'kɒŋkleɪv $ 'kɑːŋ-/ *n* [C] *formal* a private and secret meeting

con·clude S3 W2 /kən'kluːd/ *v*
1 [T] to decide that something is true after considering all the information you have; → **conclusion**: **conclude that** *The report concluded that the school should be closed immediately.* | **conclude from sth that** *Richardson concluded from his studies that equality between the sexes is still a long way off.*
2 [T] *formal* to complete something you have been doing, especially for a long time: *When the investigation is concluded, the results will be sent to the US Attorney's office.* | *Francis, having concluded his business with James, left for Miami.*
3 [I,T] to end something such as a meeting, book, event, or speech by doing or saying one final thing: [+with] *Each chapter concludes with a short summary.* | **conclude by doing sth** *She concluded by saying she was proud to be from Salford.* | **To conclude**, *I'd like to express my thanks to my family.* | *'So now', she concluded, 'I'm trying to bring some order to the garden.'*
4 conclude an agreement/treaty/contract etc to finish arranging an agreement etc successfully: *That same year, France concluded a trading agreement with Spain.*

con·clu·ding /kən'kluːdɪŋ/ *adj* **concluding remark/section/stage etc** the last remark etc in an event or piece of writing: *the concluding section of Chapter 6*

con·clu·sion S2 W2 /kən'kluːʒən/ *n*
1 [C] something you decide after considering all the information you have; → **conclude**

> **come to a conclusion/reach a conclusion** (=decide something)
> **draw a conclusion (from sth)** (=decide something because of information you have)
> **lead to/point to/support the conclusion that** (=make you decide that)
> **jump to conclusions** (=decide something too quickly, without knowing all the facts)
> **logical conclusion**
> **firm conclusion**
> **inescapable conclusion** (=the conclusion that you must come to)

These are the report's main conclusions. | **conclusion (that)** *I soon* ***came to the conclusion that*** *she was lying.* | *It is still too early to* ***reach a conclusion*** *on this point.* | *There are perhaps two main* ***conclusions*** *to be* ***drawn*** *from the above discussion.* | *All the evidence*

pointed to the conclusion that he was guilty. | *It's important not to jump to conclusions.* | *The police came to the inescapable conclusion that the children had been murdered.*
2 [C] *formal* the end or final part of something; ◧ **end**: [+of] *At the conclusion of the meeting, little progress had been made.*
3 in conclusion used in a piece of writing or a speech to show that you are about to finish what you are saying; ◧ **finally**: *In conclusion, I would like to say how much I have enjoyed myself today.*
4 [U] the final arrangement of an agreement, a business deal etc: [+of] *celebrating the conclusion of a peace treaty*
5 be a foregone conclusion to be certain to happen, even though it has not yet officially happened: *The outcome of the battle was a foregone conclusion.*

con·clu·sive /kənˈkluːsɪv/ *adj* showing that something is definitely true; ◪ **inconclusive**: **conclusive proof/evidence/findings etc** *The investigation failed to provide any conclusive evidence.* —**conclusively** *adv*

con·coct /kənˈkɒkt $ -ˈkɑːkt/ *v* [T]   **1** to invent a clever story, excuse, or plan, especially in order to deceive someone: *John concocted an elaborate excuse for being late.*   **2** to make something, especially food or drink, by mixing different things, especially things that are not usually combined: *Jean concocted a great meal from the leftovers.*

con·coc·tion /kənˈkɒkʃən $ -ˈkɑːk-/ *n* [C] something, especially a drink or food, made by mixing different things, especially things that are not usually combined: *He sipped the concoction cautiously.*

con·com·i·tant¹ /kənˈkɒmɪtənt $ -ˈkɑː-/ *adj formal* existing or happening together, especially as a result of something: *war with all its concomitant sufferings* —**concomitantly** *adv*

concomitant² *n* [C] *formal* something that often or naturally happens with something else: [+of] *Deafness is a frequent concomitant of old age.*

con·cord /ˈkɒŋkɔːd $ ˈkɑːŋkɔːrd/ *n* [U]   **1** *formal* the state of having a friendly relationship, so that you agree on things and live in peace; ◪ **discord**   **2** *technical* in grammar, concord between words happens when they match correctly, for example when a plural noun has a plural verb following it

con·cor·dance /kənˈkɔːdəns $ -ɔːr-/ *n*   **1** [C] an alphabetical list of all the words used in a book or set of books, with information about where they can be found and usually about how they are used: *a Shakespeare concordance* | [+to] *a concordance to the Bible*   **2** [C] a list of all the words in a book, magazine etc, held on a computer DATABASE, showing every example of a particular word in the book etc: *concordance lines*   **3** [U] *formal* the state of being similar to something else or in agreement with it: *the concordance between the proposals*

con·cor·dant /kənˈkɔːdənt $ -ɔːr-/ *adj formal* being in agreement or having the same regular pattern

con·course /ˈkɒŋkɔːs $ ˈkɑːŋkɔːrs/ *n* [C]   **1** a large hall or open place in a building such as an airport or train station   **2** *formal* a large crowd that has gathered together: [+of] *an immense concourse of spectators*

con·crete¹ 🔊 /ˈkɒŋkriːt $ kɑːnˈkriːt/ *adj*
1 made of concrete: *a concrete floor*
2 definite and specific; → **abstract**: *What does that mean in concrete terms?* | *the lack of any concrete evidence* | *a dialogue about concrete issues and problems* —**concretely** *adv*

con·crete² /ˈkɒŋkriːt $ ˈkɑːŋ-/ *n* [U] a substance used for building that is made by mixing sand, very small stones, CEMENT, and water → see picture at MATERIAL

con·crete³ /ˈkɒŋkriːt $ ˈkɑːŋ-/ *v* [T] to cover something such as a path, wall etc with concrete

concrete ˈjungle *n* [C usually singular] an unpleasant area in a city that is full of big ugly buildings and has no open spaces

ˈconcrete ˌmixer *n* [C] a CEMENT MIXER

con·cu·bine /ˈkɒŋkjʊbaɪn $ ˈkɑːŋ-/ *n* [C] a woman in the past who lived with and had sex with a man who already had a wife or wives, but who was socially less important than the wives

con·cur /kənˈkɜː $ -ˈkɜːr/ *v* **concurred, concurring** [I] *formal*   **1** to agree with someone or have the same opinion as them: [+with] *The committee largely concurred with these views.*   **2** to happen at the same time; ◧ **coincide**: **concur to do sth** *Everything concurred to produce the desired effect.*

con·cur·rence /kənˈkʌrəns $ -ˈkɜːr-/ *n formal*   **1** [C] an example of events, actions etc happening at the same time: [+of] *a strange concurrence of events*   **2** [U] agreement: [+with] *Jules expressed his concurrence with the suggestion.*

con·cur·rent /kənˈkʌrənt $ -ˈkɜːr-/ *adj*   **1** existing or happening at the same time: *The exhibition reflected concurrent developments abroad.*   **2** *formal* in agreement: [+with] *My opinions are concurrent with yours.* —**concurrently** *adv*: *Because his prison sentences run concurrently, he could be free in two years.*

con·cuss /kənˈkʌs/ *v* [T usually passive] if you are concussed, something hits you on the head, making you lose consciousness or feel sick for a short time: *He was concussed by the blast.*

con·cus·sion /kənˈkʌʃən/ *n*   **1** [U] *BrE*, [C] *AmE* a small amount of damage to the brain that makes you lose consciousness or feel sick for a short time, usually caused by something hitting your head: **with (a) concussion** *He was rushed into hospital with concussion.* | *I had a concussion and a lot of scrapes and bruises.*   **2** [C usually singular] a violent shaking movement, caused by the very loud sound of something such as an explosion: *The ground shuddered and heaved with the concussion of the blast.*

con·demn /kənˈdem/ *v* [T]
1 DISAPPROVE to say very strongly that you do not approve of something or someone, especially because you think it is morally wrong: *Politicians were quick to condemn the bombing.* | **condemn sth/sb as sth** *The law has been condemned as an attack on personal liberty.* | **condemn sb/sth for (doing) sth** *She knew that society would condemn her for leaving her children.*
2 PUNISH to give someone a severe punishment after deciding they are guilty of a crime: **condemn sb to sth** *He was found guilty and condemned to death.*
3 FORCE TO DO STH if a particular situation condemns someone to something, it forces them to live in an unpleasant way or to do something unpleasant: **condemn sb to (do) sth** *people condemned to a life of poverty* | *His occupation condemned him to spend long periods of time away from his family.*
4 NOT SAFE to state officially that something is not safe enough to be used: *an old house that had been condemned* | **condemn sth as sth** *The pool was closed after being condemned as a health hazard.*

con·dem·na·tion /ˌkɒndəmˈneɪʃən, -dem- $ ˌkɑːn-/ *n* [C,U] an expression of very strong disapproval of someone or something, especially something you think is morally wrong: [+of] *There was widespread international condemnation of the bombing.*

con·dem·na·to·ry /kənˈdemnətəri, ˌkɒndemˈneɪtəri $ kənˈdemnətɔːri/ *adj* expressing strong disapproval: *my father's condemnatory attitude*

con·demned /kənˈdemd/ *adj* [only before noun]   **1** a condemned person is going to be punished by being killed   **2** a condemned building is officially not safe to live in or use

conˈdemned ˌcell *n* [C] *BrE* a room for a prisoner who was going to be punished by death; → **death row**

con·den·sa·tion /ˌkɒndenˈseɪʃən, -dən- $ ˌkɑːn-/ *n*   **1** [U] small drops of water that are formed when steam or warm air touches a cold surface: *There was a* *lot of condensation on the windows.* **2** [U] *technical* when a gas becomes a liquid **3** [C,U] *formal* the act of making something shorter

con·dense /kən'dens/ *v* **1** [I,T] if a gas condenses, or is condensed, it becomes a liquid: *the mist which condensed on every cold surface* | [**+into**] *The gaseous metal is cooled and condenses into liquid zinc.* **2** [T] to make something that is spoken or written shorter, by not giving as much detail or using fewer words to give the same information: **condense sth into sth** *This whole chapter could be condensed into a few paragraphs.* **3** [T] to make a liquid thicker by removing some of the water: ***condensed soup***

con,densed 'milk *n* [U] a type of thick sweet milk sold in cans

con·dens·er /kən'densə $ -ər/ *n* [C] **1** a piece of equipment that makes a gas change into a liquid **2** a machine for storing electricity, especially in a car engine

con·de·scend /ˌkɒndɪ'send $ ˌkɑːn-/ *v* [I] **1** to behave as if you think you are better, more intelligent, or more important than other people – used to show disapproval: [**+to**] *Take care not to condescend to your readers.* **2** to do something in a way that shows you think it is below your social or professional position – used to show disapproval: **condescend to do sth** *'Yes. I know,' Clara said, condescending to look at Rose for the first time.* —**condescension** /-'senʃən/ *n* [U]

con·de·scend·ing /ˌkɒndɪ'sendɪŋ◂ $ ˌkɑːn-/ *adj* behaving as though you think you are better, more intelligent, or more important than other people – used to show disapproval: *Professor Hutter's manner is extremely condescending.* —**condescendingly** *adv*

con·di·ment /'kɒndəmənt $ 'kɑːn-/ *n* [C] *formal* a powder or liquid, such as salt or KETCHUP, that you use to give a special taste to food

con·di·tion¹ S1 W1 /kən'dɪʃən/ *n*

1 SITUATION conditions [plural] the situation in which people live or work, especially the physical things that affect the quality of their lives: *Conditions in the prison were atrocious.* | **living/working conditions** *an attempt to improve living conditions for the working classes* | ***Poor working conditions** lead to demoralized and unproductive employees.* | **in appalling/overcrowded/dreadful etc conditions** *These children work 70 metres below ground in appalling conditions.* | *In May, staff went on strike, demanding better **pay and conditions**.*

2 WEATHER conditions [plural] the weather at a particular time, especially when you are considering how this affects people: *The conditions during the first half of the match were appalling.* | **cold/windy/icy etc conditions** *In cold conditions you'll need a sleeping bag with a hood.* | *the worsening weather conditions*

3 THINGS AFFECTING SITUATION conditions [plural] all the things that affect the way something happens: **under ... conditions** *Under normal conditions, people will usually do what requires least effort.* | *Under these conditions, the fire can be rapidly controlled.* | *Profits increased by £1.5m, despite the difficult economic conditions.* | *The combination of rain and greasy surfaces made driving conditions treacherous.*

4 STATE [singular, U] the state that something is in, especially how good or bad its physical state is: **in (a) good/poor/excellent/terrible etc condition** *The car has been well maintained and is in excellent condition.* | *The house was in a terrible condition.* | [**+of**] *The condition of nuclear plants is a matter of great concern.*

5 HEALTH/FITNESS [singular, U] how healthy or fit you are: *She is being treated at Walton Hospital, where her condition is described as 'satisfactory'.* | **in (a) critical/stable/satisfactory condition** *One of the victims was in a critical condition after suffering severe burns.* | **physical/mental condition** *If you are uncertain about your physical condition, check with your doctor before trying these exercises.* | *'I'm so **out of condition** (=unfit),' she panted.* | *an athlete **in peak condition*** | **in no condition to do sth** (=too drunk, ill, or upset to be able to do something) *I was in no condition to cope with a train journey.* | *Mark can't possibly drive home **in that condition*** (=when he is so drunk, ill, or upset).

6 AGREEMENT/CONTRACT [C] something that you must agree to in order for something to happen, especially when this is included in a contract

lay down/impose/set conditions (=say what must be done)
strict condition
meet/satisfy/fulfil a condition (=do what has been agreed)
terms and conditions (=what a contract says must be done)
on condition that/on one condition (=only if a particular thing is agreed to)
subject to conditions (=if particular things are agreed to)

*She **laid down** only one **condition**: that her name not be revealed.* | [**+for**] *There were **strict conditions** for letting us use their information.* | *The bank agreed to extend the loan if **certain conditions** were **met**.* | *A statement of your **terms and conditions** of employment can be found in the Personnel Handbook.* | *He was released on bail **on condition that** he did not go within half a mile of his mother's address.* | *The application was approved, **subject to** certain **conditions**.*

7 FOR STH TO HAPPEN [C] something that must exist or happen first, before something else can happen: [**+for/of**] *Our goal is to create the conditions for a lasting peace.* | *Investment is a **necessary condition** of economic growth.*

8 ILLNESS [C] an illness or health problem that affects you permanently or for a very long time: *People **suffering from this condition** should not smoke.* | **heart/lung etc condition** *She has a serious heart condition.* | *Was he being treated for any **medical condition**?*

9 SITUATION OF GROUP [singular] *formal* the situation or state of a particular group of people, especially when they have problems and difficulties: *Few people can really appreciate the condition of the poor in our cities.* | *All my paintings are ultimately about the **human condition**.*

10 NEVER on no condition never: *On no condition should untrained personnel use the equipment.*

condition² *v* **1** [T] to make a person or an animal think or behave in a certain way by influencing or training them over a period of time; → **conditioning**: *People are conditioned by the society in which they live.* | **condition sb to do sth** *Many women are conditioned from birth to be accepting rather than questioning.* **2** [T] *formal* to control or decide the way in which something can happen or exist; **=** **determine**: *What I buy is conditioned by the amount I earn.* **3** [I,T] to keep hair or skin healthy by putting a special liquid on it; → **conditioner**: *a shampoo that washes and conditions all in one*

con·di·tion·al¹ /kən'dɪʃənəl/ *adj* **1** if an offer, agreement etc is conditional, it will only be done if something else happens first; **≠** **unconditional**: *a conditional acceptance* | [**+on/upon**] *His agreement to buy our house was conditional on our leaving all the furniture in it.* **2** in grammar, a conditional sentence is one that begins with 'if' or 'unless' and expresses something that must be true or happen before something else can be true or happen —**conditionally** *adv*

conditional² *n* [C] a sentence or CLAUSE that is expressed in a conditional form

con,ditional 'discharge *n* [C usually singular] a judgment made by a court that allows someone who has done something illegal not to be punished if they obey rules set by the court

con·di·tion·er /kən'dɪʃənə $ -ər/ *n* [C,U] **1** a liquid that you put onto your hair after washing it to make it

C

softer **2** BrE a liquid that you wash clothes in to make them softer; ⬛ **softener** AmE

con·di·tion·ing /kənˈdɪʃənɪŋ/ n [U] the process by which people or animals are trained to behave in a particular way when particular things happen: *Social conditioning makes crying more difficult for men.* → AIR CONDITIONING

con·do /ˈkɒndəʊ $ ˈkɑːndoʊ/ n plural **condos** [C] AmE informal a CONDOMINIUM

con·do·lence /kənˈdəʊləns $ -ˈdoʊ-/ n [C usually plural, U] sympathy for someone who has had something bad happen to them, especially when someone has died: *a letter of condolence* | **send/offer your condolences** (=formally express your sympathy when someone has died)

con·dom /ˈkɒndəm $ ˈkɑːn-, ˈkʌn-/ n [C] a thin rubber bag that a man wears over his PENIS (=sex organ) during sex, to prevent a woman having a baby or to protect against disease

con·do·min·i·um /ˌkɒndəˈmɪniəm $ ˌkɑːn-/ n [C] especially AmE **1** one apartment in a building with several apartments, each of which is owned by the people living in it **2** a building containing several of these apartments

con·done /kənˈdəʊn $ -ˈdoʊn/ v [T] to accept or forgive behaviour that most people think is morally wrong: *I cannot condone the use of violence under any circumstances.*

con·dor /ˈkɒndɔː $ ˈkɑːndər, -dɔːr/ n [C] a very large South American VULTURE (=a bird that eats dead animals)

con·du·cive /kənˈdjuːsɪv $ -ˈduː-/ adj **be conducive to sth** formal if a situation is conducive to something such as work, rest etc, it provides conditions that make it easy for you to work etc: *an environment conducive to learning*

con·duct¹ S3 W2 /kənˈdʌkt/ v
1 CARRY OUT [T] to carry out a particular activity or process, especially in order to get information or prove facts: **conduct a survey/investigation/review etc** *We are conducting a survey of consumer attitudes towards organic food.* | **conduct an experiment/a test** *Is it really necessary to conduct experiments on animals?* | **conduct a campaign** *They conducted a campaign of bombings and assassinations.* | **conduct an interview** *The interview was conducted in English.* | *The memorial service was conducted by the Rev. David Prior.* | *It was the first time that I had conducted business in Brazil.*
2 MUSIC [I,T] to stand in front of a group of musicians or singers and direct their playing or singing; → **conductor**: **conduct an orchestra/choir** *The orchestra is conducted by John Williams.* | *Who will be conducting?*
3 BEHAVE **conduct yourself** formal to behave in a particular way, especially in a situation where people judge you by the way you behave: *He was a player who always conducted himself impeccably, both on and off the field.*
4 ELECTRICITY/HEAT [T] if something conducts electricity or heat, it allows electricity or heat to travel along or through it; → **conductor**: *Aluminium, being a metal, readily conducts heat.*
5 SHOW SB STH [T always + adv/prep] formal to take or lead someone somewhere: **conduct sb to sth** *On arrival, I was conducted to the commandant's office.* | **conducted tour (of sth)** (=a tour of a building, city, or area with someone who tells you about that place) *a conducted tour of Berlin*

con·duct² W3 /ˈkɒndʌkt $ ˈkɑːn-/ n [U] formal
1 the way someone behaves, especially in public, in their job etc; ⬛ **behaviour**: *The Senator's conduct is being investigated by the Ethics Committee.* | *an inquiry into the conduct of the police* | **ethical/professional etc conduct** *the Law Society's Code of Professional Conduct* | **improper/violent/offensive etc conduct** | *He*

was arrested for **disorderly conduct** (=noisy violent behaviour).
2 conduct of sth the way in which an activity is organized and carried out: *complaints about the conduct of the elections* | *Disclosure of information would compromise the proper conduct of the investigation.*

con·duc·tion /kənˈdʌkʃən/ n [U] the passage of electricity through wires, heat through metal, water through pipes etc

con·duc·tive /kənˈdʌktɪv/ adj able to conduct electricity, heat etc: *Copper is a very conductive metal.* —**conductivity** /ˌkɒndʌkˈtɪvˌti $ ˌkɑːn-/ n [U]

con·duc·tor /kənˈdʌktə $ -ər/ n [C] **1** someone who stands in front of a group of musicians or singers and directs their playing or singing **2** BrE someone whose job is to collect payments from passengers on a bus **3** AmE someone who is in charge of a train and collects payments from passengers or checks their tickets; ⬛ **guard** BrE **4** something that allows electricity or heat to travel along it or through it: *Wood is a poor conductor of heat.* → LIGHTNING CONDUCTOR

con·duit /ˈkɒndjuːɪt, -dɪt $ ˈkɑːnduːɪt/ n [C] **1** technical a pipe or passage through which water, gas, a set of electric wires etc passes **2** formal a connection between two things that allows people to pass ideas, news, money, weapons, drugs etc from one place to another: [+for] *Drug traffickers have used the country as a conduit for shipments to the U.S.*

cone¹ /kəʊn $ koʊn/ n [C] **1** a solid or hollow shape that is round at one end, has sloping sides, and has a point at the other end, or something with this shape **2** an object shaped like a large cone that is put on a road to prevent cars from going somewhere or to warn drivers about something **3** the fruit of a PINE or FIR tree; → **conifer 4** a piece of thin cooked cake, shaped like a cone, that you put ICE CREAM in, or a cone like this with ice cream in it **5** technical a CELL in your eye that is shaped like a cone, that helps you see light and colour; → **rod**

cone² v
cone sth ⇔ **off** phr v BrE to put a row of orange CONES around an area to prevent people or cars from going there, for example during building work

con·fec·tion /kənˈfekʃən/ n [C] formal **1** a beautifully prepared sweet food **2** something, especially a piece of clothing or a building, that is very delicate and complicated, or has a lot of decoration: [+of] *a dreamy confection of pink beads and satin* **3** something such as a film or song that is not serious or important

con·fec·tion·er /kənˈfekʃənə $ -ər/ n [C] someone who makes or sells sweets, cakes etc

con'fectioner's ˌsugar n [U] AmE a kind of sugar that is very powdery; ⬛ **icing sugar** BrE

con·fec·tion·e·ry /kənˈfekʃənəri $ -neri/ n [U] sweets, chocolates etc

con·fed·e·ra·cy /kənˈfedərəsi/ n plural **confederacies** [C] a confederation

con·fed·e·rate /kənˈfedərˌt/ n [C] **1** formal someone who helps someone else do something, especially something secret or illegal; ⬛ **accomplice**: *The young woman was his confederate, of course.* **2** a member of a confederacy —**confederate** adj

con·fed·e·ra·tion /kənˌfedəˈreɪʃən/ n [C] a group of people, political parties, or organizations that have united for political purposes or trade

con·fer /kənˈfɜː $ -ˈfɜːr/ v conferred, conferring formal **1** [I] to discuss something with other people, so that everyone can express their opinions and decide on something: [+with] *Franklin leant over and conferred with his attorneys.* **2** confer a title/degree/honour etc to officially give someone a title etc, especially as a reward for something they have achieved: [+on/upon] *An honorary degree was conferred on him by the University.* —**conferment** n [C,U]

con·fe·rence S3 W1 /ˈkɒnfərəns $ ˈkɑːn-/ n [C]
1 a large formal meeting where a lot of people discuss

important matters such as business, politics, or science, especially for several days: *Representatives from over 100 countries **attended** the International Peace Conference in Geneva.* | [+on] *a UN conference on the environment* | **hold a conference** (=have a conference) | **conference centre/facilities/hall etc** → PRESS CONFERENCE
2 a private meeting for a few people to have formal discussions: [+with] *After a brief conference with his aides, he left for the airport.* | **conference room/table etc** *The meeting will be held in the conference room at 10 am.* | **in conference** *Mr Dickson is in conference.*
3 *AmE* a group of teams that play against each other to see who is the best: *the Western Conference finals*

conference ˌcall *n* [C] a telephone call in which several people in different places can all talk to each other

con·fess /kənˈfes/ *v* [I,T] **1** to admit, especially to the police, that you have done something wrong or illegal; → **confession**: **confess to (doing) sth** *Edwards confessed to being a spy for the KGB.* | *Occasionally people confess to crimes they haven't committed just to get attention.* | **confess (that)** *My husband confessed he'd been having an affair with a woman in his office.* | *Torture was used and Fian confessed.* **2** to admit something that you feel embarrassed about; → **confession**: **confess (that)** *Marsha confessed that she didn't really know how to work the computer.* | **confess to (doing) sth** *He confessed to having a secret admiration for his opponent.* | **I (have to/must) confess** (=used when admitting something you feel slightly embarrassed about) *I must confess I don't visit my parents as often as I should.* **3** to tell a priest or God about the wrong things you have done so that you can be forgiven; → **confession**: *He knelt and **confessed** his **sin**.*

con·fessed /kənˈfest/ *adj* [only before noun] having admitted publicly that you have done something: *a confessed criminal* → SELF-CONFESSED

con·fes·sion /kənˈfeʃən/ *n* **1** [C] a statement that you have done something wrong, illegal, or embarrassing, especially a formal statement: *Sanchez's confession was read out to the court.* | [+of] *a confession of adultery* | *At 3 a.m. Higgins broke down and **made** a full confession.* | *I **have a confession** - I like Britney Spears' music.* **2** [C,U] when you tell a priest or God about the bad things that you have done: *You must **go to** confession.* | *a priest who **hears** confession* **3** [C] *formal* a statement of what your religious beliefs are: [+of] *a confession of faith*

con·fes·sion·al[1] /kənˈfeʃənəl/ *n* [C] a place in a church, usually an enclosed room, where a priest hears people make their confessions

confessional[2] *adj* confessional speech or writing contains private thoughts or feelings that you would normally keep secret

con·fes·sor /kənˈfesə $ -ər/ *n* [C] *formal* the priest who someone regularly makes their confession to

con·fet·ti /kənˈfeti/ *n* [U] small pieces of coloured paper that you throw into the air over people who have just got married or at events such as parties, PARADES etc

con·fi·dant /ˈkɒnfɪdænt, ˌkɒnfɪˈdænt, -ˈdɑːnt $ ˈkɑːnfɪdænt/ *n* [C] someone you tell your secrets to or who you talk to about personal things

con·fi·dante /ˈkɒnfɪdænt, ˌkɒnfɪˈdænt, -ˈdɑːnt $ ˈkɑːnfɪdænt/ *n* [C] a female confidant

con·fide /kənˈfaɪd/ *v* [T] **1** to tell someone you trust about personal things that you do not want other people to know: **confide to sb that** *He confided to his friends that he didn't have much hope for his marriage.* **2** *formal* to give something you value to someone you trust so they look after it for you: **confide sth to sb** *He confided his money to his brother's safekeeping.*
  confide in sb *phr v* to tell someone about something very private or secret, especially a personal problem, because you feel you can trust them: *I've never felt able to confide in my sister.*

con·fi·dence S2 W2 /ˈkɒnfɪdəns $ ˈkɑːn-/ *n*
1 FEELING SB/STH IS GOOD [U] the feeling that you can trust someone or something to be good, work well, or produce good results

> **lack of confidence**
> **have confidence in sb/sth**
> **have every/complete/absolute confidence in sb/sth**
> **lose (your) confidence in sb/sth**
> **gain/win sb's confidence**
> **increase confidence (in sb/sth)**
> **inspire confidence (in sb/sth)** (=make people have confidence)
> **restore confidence (in sb/sth)** (=bring back people's confidence)
> **destroy/shatter (sb's) confidence (in sb/sth)**
> **undermine (sb's) confidence (in sb/sth)** (=make someone have less confidence)
> **public confidence**
> **business confidence** (=when businesses think the economic situation is good)
> **consumer confidence** (=when ordinary people think the economic situation is good)

[+in] *Our first priority is to maintain the customer's confidence in our product.* | *The survey reveals a general **lack of confidence** in the police.* | *She **had complete confidence** in the young nurse.* | *Opinion polls show that voters have **lost confidence** in the administration.* | *the school's campaign to **win back the confidence** of local parents* | *The Bank immediately took action to **restore confidence**.* | *These miscarriages of justice have **undermined confidence** in our legal system.* | ***Public confidence** in the government is at an all-time low.* | *Surveys indicate an improvement in **business confidence**.*

2 BELIEF IN YOURSELF [U] the belief that you have the ability to do things well or deal with situations successfully: [+in] *Minton is an outstanding boxer, with tremendous confidence in his own ability.* | *I didn't **have** any **confidence** in myself.* | **lack confidence/be lacking in confidence** *She's a good student, but she lacks confidence.* | *Living on her own in a foreign country for a year **gave** her a lot of **confidence**.* | **confidence to do sth** *Good training will give a beginner the confidence to enjoy skiing.* | **gain (in)/lose confidence** *You do lose confidence when you spend years and years at home with children.* | **sb's confidence is growing/sb is growing in confidence** *I felt I was doing well and my confidence began to grow.* | **boost/increase etc sb's confidence** (=make someone feel more confident) | **shake/damage etc sb's confidence** (=make someone feel less confident) *Julie's confidence was badly shaken by her car accident.* | **with confidence** *Our goal is to prepare students to go into the business world with confidence.*
3 FEELING STH IS TRUE [U] the feeling that something is definite or true: **say/speak/predict etc with confidence** *How can anyone say with confidence that the recession is over?* | [+in] *I have complete confidence in Mr Wright's analysis of the situation.* | **have confidence (that)** *I have every confidence that the job will be completed satisfactorily on time.*
4 gain/win/earn sb's confidence if you gain someone's confidence, they begin to trust you: *After a discouraging start, the young priest had begun to win the confidence of the villagers.*
5 KEEP INFORMATION SECRET [U] if you tell someone something in confidence, you tell them something on the understanding that they will not tell anyone else; → **confide**: **in confidence** *I'll tell you about Moira – in confidence, of course.* | **in strict/the strictest confidence** *Any information given during the interview will be treated in the strictest confidence.* | **breach of confidence** (=when someone tells someone something that they were told in confidence) *Lawyers are satisfied that no breach of confidence took place.*
6 take sb into your confidence to tell someone your secrets or private or personal details about your life:

C

Elsa took me into her confidence and told me about some of the problems she was facing.
7 **A SECRET** [C] a secret or a piece of information that is private or personal: **share/exchange confidences** *They spent their evenings drinking wine and sharing confidences.* | *I have never **betrayed** a **confidence**.* → VOTE OF CONFIDENCE, VOTE OF NO CONFIDENCE

'confidence-,building *adj* a confidence-building event, activity etc increases your confidence: *the use of **confidence-building exercises** to assist adults to return to the labour market*

'confidence ,trick *n* [C] a dishonest trick played on someone in order to get their money; ◨ **con** —**confidence trickster** *n* [C]

con·fi·dent S2 W3 /'kɒnfɪdənt $ 'kɑːn-/ *adj*
1 [not before noun] sure that something will happen in the way that you want or expect: **confident (that)** *We are confident next year's profits will be higher.* | *He is quietly confident that there will be no problems this time.* | [+of] *The Prime Minister appeared relaxed and confident of winning an overall majority.* | *The company is confident of success.* | [+about] *I feel quite confident about the future.*
2 sure that you have the ability to do things well or deal with situations successfully: *Despite her disability, Philippa is very confident.* | [+about] *I feel much more confident about myself and my abilities these days.* | **confident smile/voice/manner** etc *He began to read in a calm, confident voice.*
3 sure that something is true: **confident (that)** *We are confident we have done nothing wrong.* | *He began to feel confident that Zaborski was only guessing.* | *It is not possible to give a confident answer to the question whether the delay was unreasonable.* ⚠ Do not confuse with the noun **confidant** (=someone you tell secrets or personal things to). —**confidently** *adv* → SELF-CONFIDENT

WORD FOCUS: CONFIDENT
confident about your abilities: **confident, self-confident, sure of yourself, assured, poised**
too confident: **overconfident, cocky, brash**
not confident: **lack confidence, be insecure, be unsure of yourself**

con·fi·den·tial /,kɒnfɪ'denʃəl◂ $,kɑːn-/ *adj* **1** spoken or written in secret and intended to be kept secret: *a confidential government report* | *Doctors are required to **keep** patients' records completely **confidential**.* | *The information will be regarded as **strictly confidential** (=completely confidential).* **2** a confidential way of speaking or behaving shows that you do not want other people to know what you are saying: *His voice sank into a confidential whisper.* —**confidentially** *adv*

con·fi·den·ti·al·i·ty /,kɒnfɪ,denʃi'æləti $,kɑːn-/ *n* [U] a situation in which you trust someone not to tell secret or private information to anyone else: *The relationship between attorneys and their clients is based on confidentiality.* | **breach of confidentiality** (=when someone gives away information they have promised to keep secret) *It is a breach of confidentiality for a priest to reveal what someone has said in the confessional.*

con·fid·ing /kən'faɪdɪŋ/ *adj* behaving in a way that shows you want to tell someone about something that is private or secret: *Her tone was suddenly confiding.* —**confidingly** *adv*: *He leant forward confidingly.*

con·fig·u·ra·tion /kən,fɪgə'reɪʃən, -gjʊ- $ -gjʊ-/ *n* [C,U] **1** *formal* or *technical* the shape or arrangement of the parts of something; ◨ **layout**: [+of] *the configuration of pistons in an engine* **2** *technical* the combination of equipment needed to run a computer system

con·fig·ure /kən'fɪgə $ -gjər/ *v* [T] *technical* to arrange something, especially computer equipment, so that it works with other equipment

con·fine W3 /kən'faɪn/ *v* [T]
1 **LIMIT** to keep someone or something within the limits of a particular activity or subject; ◨ **restrict**:

confine sth to sth *The police cadet's duties were confined to taking statements from the crowd.* | *We confined our study to 10 cases.* | **confine yourself to (doing) sth** *Owen did not confine himself to writing only one type of poem.*
2 **KEEP SB IN A PLACE** to keep someone in a place that they cannot leave, such as a prison: **confine sb to sth** *Any soldier who leaves his post will be confined to barracks* (=made to stay in the barracks). | **be confined in sth** *He was allegedly confined in a narrow, dark room for two months.*
3 **STOP STH SPREADING** to stop something bad from spreading to another place: **confine sth to sth** *Firefighters managed to confine the fire to the living room.*
4 **STAY IN ONE PLACE** [usually passive] if you are confined to a place, you have to stay in that place, especially because you are ill: *Vaughan is **confined to** a **wheelchair**.* | *She's **confined to bed** with flu.*

con·fined /kən'faɪnd/ *adj* **1** **be confined to sb/sth** to exist in or affect only a particular place or group: *The risk of infection is confined to groups such as medical personnel.* **2** a confined space or area is one that is very small: *It wasn't easy to sleep in such a confined space.*

con·fine·ment /kən'faɪnmənt/ *n* **1** [U] *formal* the act of putting someone in a room, prison etc that they are not allowed to leave, or the state of being there: *They were held in confinement for three weeks.* | *He visited prisoners at their place of confinement.* → SOLITARY CONFINEMENT **2** [C,U] *old-fashioned* or *formal* the time when a woman gives birth to a baby: *the pros and cons of home versus hospital confinement*

con·fines /'kɒnfaɪnz $ 'kɑːn-/ *n* [plural] limits or borders: **within/beyond the confines of sth** *within the confines of the prison*

con·firm S2 W2 /kən'fɜːm $ -ɜːrm/ *v* [T]
1 to show that something is definitely true, especially by providing more proof: *New evidence has confirmed the first witness's story.* | *To confirm my diagnosis I need to do some tests.* | **confirm that** *Research has confirmed that the risk is higher for women.* | **confirm what** *The new results confirm what most of us knew already.*
2 to say that something is definitely true: *The President refused to confirm the rumor.* | *Managers have so far refused to **confirm or deny** reports that up to 200 jobs are to go.* | **confirm that** *Walsh confirmed that the money had been paid.* | **confirm what** *My brother will confirm what I have told you.*
3 to tell someone that a possible arrangement, date, or situation is now definite or official: *Could you confirm the dates we discussed?* | *Smith was confirmed as the club's new manager yesterday.* | **confirm a booking/reservation/appointment** *I am writing to confirm a booking for a single room for the night of 6 June.*
4 to make you believe that your idea or feeling is right: **confirm your fears/doubts/suspicions** etc *This just confirms my worst fears.* | **confirm you in your belief/opinion/view** etc **(that)** (=make you believe something more strongly) *The expression on his face confirmed me in my suspicions.*
5 **be confirmed** to be made a full member of the Christian church in a special ceremony

con·fir·ma·tion /,kɒnfə'meɪʃən $,kɑːnfər-/ *n* [C,U] **1** a statement, document etc that says that something is definitely true: [+of] *There has still been no **official confirmation** of the report.* | **confirmation that** *verbal confirmation that payment has been made* **2** a letter etc that tells you that an arrangement, date, time etc is now definite: *Most hotels require confirmation from a prospective guest in writing.* **3** a religious ceremony in which someone is made a full member of the Christian church

con·firmed /kən'fɜːmd $ -ɜːr-/ *adj* **a confirmed bachelor/atheist/vegetarian** etc someone who seems completely happy with the way of life they have chosen

con·fis·cate /'kɒnfɪskeɪt $ 'kɑːn-/ *v* [T] to officially take private property away from someone, usually as a punishment: *Miss Williams confiscated all our sweets.* | *Many opposition supporters had their goods confis-*

cated. —**confiscation** /ˌkɒnfɪ̈'skeɪʃən $ ˌkɑːn-/ *n* [C,U]: *the confiscation of pornographic material*

con·fla·gra·tion /ˌkɒnflə'greɪʃən $ ˌkɑːn-/ *n* [C] *formal* **1** a very large fire that destroys a lot of buildings, forests etc **2** a violent situation or war

con·flate /kən'fleɪt/ *v* [T] *formal* to combine two or more things to form a single new thing: *He conflates two images from Kipling's short stories in the film.* —**conflation** /-'fleɪʃən/ *n* [C,U]

con·flict¹ S2 W2 /'kɒnflɪkt $ 'kɑːn-/ *n*
1 [C,U] a state of disagreement or argument between people, groups, countries etc: [+**over**] *conflicts over wage settlements* | [+**between**] *the conflict between tradition and innovation* | **in conflict (with sb)** *normal kids who are in conflict with their parents* | **political/social/industrial conflict** *social and political conflict in the 1930s* | *the threat of industrial conflict in the coalfields* | *Marx points out the potential conflicts below the surface of society.* | *His views on the literal truth of the Bible brought him into conflict with other Christian leaders.* | *Doctors exercise considerable power and often come into conflict with politicians.* | *a lawyer specializing in conflict resolution*
2 [C,U] fighting or a war: **armed/military/violent conflict** *For years the region has been torn apart by armed conflicts.* | *UN troops intervened to avert a threat of violent conflict.* | *efforts to resolve the conflict*
3 [C,U] a situation in which you have to choose between two or more opposite needs, influences etc: *As women increasingly went out to work, the possibility of a conflict of loyalties became stronger.* | [+**between**] *a conflict between the demands of one's work and one's family* | **in conflict (with sth)** *The principles of democracy are sometimes in conflict with political reality.*
4 [C,U] a situation in which you have two opposite feelings about something: *a state of inner conflict*
5 [C] *AmE* something that you have to do at the same time that someone wants you to do something else: *Sorry, I have a conflict on Friday. Can we make it Monday?*
6 conflict of interest/interests a) a situation in which you cannot do your job fairly because you will be affected by the decision you make: *There is a growing conflict of interest between her position as a politician and her business activities.* **b)** a situation in which different people want different things

con·flict² /kən'flɪkt/ *v* [I] if two ideas, beliefs, opinions etc conflict, they cannot exist together or both be true: [+**with**] *new evidence which conflicts with previous findings* | **conflicting opinions/demands/interests etc** *I had been given a great deal of conflicting advice.* | *There are conflicting views about what caused the accident.*

con·flict·ed /kən'flɪktɪ̈d/ *adj AmE* **be/feel conflicted (about sth)** to be confused about what choice to make, especially when the decision involves strong beliefs or opinions: *Many mothers today feel conflicted about working outside the home.*

con·flu·ence /'kɒnfluəns $ 'kɑːn-/ *n* [singular] **1** *technical* the place where two or more rivers flow together **2** *formal* a situation in which two or more things combine or happen at the same time: [+**of**] *a confluence of unhappy events*

con·form /kən'fɔːm $ -ɔːrm/ *v* [I] **1** to behave in the way that most other people in your group or society behave; → **conformist**: *the pressure on schoolchildren to conform* | [+**to/with**] *people who do not conform to traditional standards of behaviour* **2** to obey a law, rule etc: [+**to/with**] *Students can be expelled for refusing to conform to school rules.* | *All new buildings must conform with the regional development plan.* | *products which conform to international safety standards* **3 conform to a pattern/model/ideal etc** to be similar to what people expect or think is usual: *Joseph does not conform to the stereotype of a policeman.*

con·for·ma·tion /ˌkɒnfɔː'meɪʃən $ ˌkɑːnfɔːr-/ *n* [C,U] *technical* the shape of something or the way in which it is formed: *the conformation of the earth*

con·form·ist /kən'fɔːmɪ̈st $ -ɔːr-/ *adj* thinking and behaving like everyone else, because you do not want to be different, or forcing people to do this – often used to show disapproval; → **nonconformist**: *a country with a conformist education system* —**conformist** *n* [C]

con·for·mi·ty /kən'fɔːmɪ̈ti $ -ɔːr-/ *n* [U] **1** behaviour that obeys the accepted rules of society or a group, and is the same as that of most other people: *an emphasis on conformity and control* | [+**to**] *conformity to social expectations* **2 in conformity with sth** *formal* in a way that obeys rules, customs etc: *We must act in conformity with local regulations.*

con·found /kən'faʊnd/ *v* [T] **1** to confuse and surprise people by being unexpected: *His amazing recovery confounded the medical specialists.* **2** to prove someone or something wrong: **confound the critics/pundits/experts etc** *United's new striker confounded the critics with his third goal in as many games.* **3** *formal* to defeat an enemy, plan etc **4** *formal* if a problem etc confounds you, you cannot understand it or solve it: *Her question completely confounded me.* **5 confound it/him/them etc** *old-fashioned* used to show that you are annoyed with someone or something

con·found·ed /kən'faʊndɪ̈d/ *adj* [only before noun] *old-fashioned* used to show that you are annoyed: *That confounded dog has run away again!*

con·front /kən'frʌnt/ *v* [T] **1** if a problem, difficulty etc confronts you, it appears and needs to be dealt with: *The problems confronting the new government were enormous.* | **be confronted with sth** *Customers are confronted with a bewildering amount of choice.* **2** to deal with something very difficult or unpleasant in a brave and determined way: *We try to help people confront their problems.* **3** to face someone in a threatening way, as though you are going to attack them: *Troops were confronted by an angry mob.* **4** to ACCUSE someone of doing something, especially by showing them the proof: **confront sb with/about sth** *I confronted him with my suspicions, and he admitted everything.* | *I haven't confronted her about it yet.*

con·fron·ta·tion /ˌkɒnfrən'teɪʃən $ ˌkɑːn-/ *n* [C,U] **1** a situation in which there is a lot of angry disagreement between two people or groups: *She had stayed in her room to avoid another confrontation.* | [+**with/between**] *an ideological confrontation between conservatives and liberals* **2** a fight or battle: **military/violent/armed confrontation** *Japan seemed unlikely to risk military confrontation with Russia.*

con·fron·ta·tion·al /ˌkɒnfrən'teɪʃənəl◂ $ ˌkɑːn-/ *adj* likely to cause arguments or make people angry: *a confrontational style of management*

con·fuse /kən'fjuːz/ *v* [T] **1** to make someone feel that they cannot think clearly or do not understand: *I understand the text but the diagrams are confusing me.* **2** to think wrongly that a person or thing is someone or something else: *People might well confuse the two products.* | **confuse sb/sth with sb/sth** *I always confuse you with your sister – you look so alike.* | *Donald Regan, not to be confused with former President Ronald Reagan* **3 confuse the issue/matter/argument etc** to make it even more difficult to think clearly about a situation or problem or to deal with it: *He kept asking unnecessary questions which only confused the issue.*

con·fused S3 /kən'fjuːzd/ *adj*
1 unable to understand or think clearly what someone is saying or what is happening: *I'm totally confused. Could you explain that again?* | [+**about**] *If you're confused about anything, phone my office.* | *All the corridors looked the same and he felt thoroughly confused.*
2 not clear or not easy to understand: *Witness statements presented a confused picture of the incident.* | *a lot of confused ideas* —**confusedly** /-'fjuːzɪ̈dli/ *adv*

C

con·fus·ing S3 /kənˈfjuːzɪŋ/ adj unclear and difficult to understand: *The instructions were really confusing.* | *It was a very confusing situation.* —**confusingly** adv

con·fu·sion S3 W3 /kənˈfjuːʒən/ n
1 [C,U] when you do not understand what is happening or what something means because it is not clear: [+**about/over/as to**] *There was some confusion as to whether we had won or lost.* | **create/lead to confusion** *This complicated situation has led to* **considerable confusion.**
2 [C,U] a situation in which someone wrongly thinks that a person or thing is someone or something else: *To avoid confusion, the teams wore different colours.* | [+**between**] *There is a confusion in the public mind between psychology and psychiatry.*
3 [U] a feeling of not being able to think clearly what you should say or do, especially in an embarrassing situation: *His confusion at meeting her there was quite apparent.* | **in confusion** *Matt stared at her in confusion.*
4 [C,U] a very confusing situation, that usually has a lot of noise and action, so that it is difficult for someone to understand it or control it: *a scene of indescribable confusion* | [+**of**]: *There was a confusion of shouts and orders as the ship prepared to depart.*

con·fute /kənˈfjuːt/ v [T] *formal* to prove that a person or an argument is completely wrong

con·ga /ˈkɒŋgə $ ˈkaːŋgə/ n [C] a dance in which people dance in a line, holding on to the person in front of them → see picture at DRUM

con·geal /kənˈdʒiːl/ v [I] if a liquid such as blood congeals, it becomes thick or solid: *a pan full of congealed fat*

con·ge·ni·al /kənˈdʒiːniəl/ adj **1** pleasant in a way that makes you feel comfortable and relaxed: **congenial atmosphere/surroundings/environment** *The department provides a congenial atmosphere for research.* | *Frank was a very congenial colleague.* | [+**to**] *The summers out here are not congenial to the average North European.* **2** suitable for something: *Compost provides congenial conditions for roots to develop.* —**congeniality** /kənˌdʒiːniˈælɪti/ n [U]

con·gen·i·tal /kənˈdʒenɪtl/ adj [usually before noun] **1** a congenital medical condition or disease has affected someone since they were born: *congenital abnormalities* | *a congenital defect* **2** a congenital quality is one that has always been part of your character and is unlikely to change: *He's a* **congenital liar.** | *her congenital inability to make decisions* —**congenitally** adv

con·ger eel /ˌkɒŋgər ˈiːl $ ˈkaːŋgər iːl/ n [C] a large fish that looks like a snake

con·ges·ted /kənˈdʒestɪd/ adj **1** full of traffic: *congested airspace* | *The roads out of Cornwall were* **heavily congested** (=very congested). **2** a part of your body that is congested is very full of liquid, usually blood or MUCUS —**congestion** /-ˈdʒestʃən/ n [U]: *traffic congestion*

con'gestion ˌcharging n [U] *BrE* a way of reducing traffic in city centres by charging drivers money to enter; ◼ **road pricing:** *Plans to introduce congestion charging were dropped until after the election.*

con·glom·e·rate /kənˈglɒmərɪt $ -ˈglɑː-/ n **1** [C] a large business organization consisting of several different companies that have joined together: *an international conglomerate* | **industrial/financial/media etc conglomerate** **2** [C,U] *technical* a rock consisting of different sizes of stones held together by clay **3** [C] *formal* a group of things gathered together

con·glom·e·ra·tion /kənˌglɒməˈreɪʃən $ -ˌglɑː-/ n [C] *formal* a group of different things gathered together: [+**of**] *the loose conglomeration of artists known as L'École de Paris*

con·grats /kənˈgræts/ n [plural] *informal* CONGRATULATIONS

con·grat·u·late /kənˈgrætʃʊleɪt/ v [T] **1** to tell someone that you are happy because they have achieved something or because something nice has happened to them: *He never even stopped to congratulate me.* | **congratulate sb on sth** *She congratulated me warmly on my exam results.* | **congratulate sb for (doing) sth** *All three are to be congratulated for doing so well.* **2** **congratulate yourself (on sth)** to feel pleased and proud of yourself because you have achieved something or something good has happened to you: *I congratulated myself on my good fortune.* —**congratulatory** /kənˌgrætʃʊˈleɪtəri $ -ˈgrætʃʊlətɔːri/ adj: *congratulatory messages*

con·grat·u·la·tion S3 /kənˌgrætʃʊˈleɪʃən/ n [U]
1 **congratulations a)** used when you want to congratulate someone: *'I've just passed my driving test!' 'Congratulations!'* | [+**on**] *Congratulations on a superb performance!* **b)** words saying you are happy that someone has achieved something: *Give Oscar my congratulations.*
2 when you tell someone that you are happy because they have achieved something or because something nice has happened to them: *letters of congratulation*

con·gre·gate /ˈkɒŋgrɪgeɪt $ ˈkaːŋ-/ v [I] to come together in a group: *Crowds began to congregate to hear the President's speech.*

con·gre·ga·tion /ˌkɒŋgrɪˈgeɪʃən $ ˌkaːŋ-/ n [C also + plural verb] *BrE* **1** a group of people gathered together in a church: *The congregation knelt to pray.* **2** the people who usually go to a particular church: *Several members of the congregation are away.*

Con·gre·ga·tion·al·is·m /ˌkɒŋgrɪˈgeɪʃənəlɪzəm $ ˌkaːŋ-/ n [U] a type of Christianity in which each congregation is responsible for making its own decisions —**Congregational** adj —**Congregationalist** n [C]

con·gress /ˈkɒŋgres $ ˈkaːŋgrɪs/ n **1** [C,U] a formal meeting of representatives of different groups, countries etc, to discuss ideas, make decisions etc: *a congress of the ruling Labor Party* **2** [C] the group of people chosen or elected to make the laws in some countries **3** **Congress** the group of people elected to make laws in the US, consisting of the Senate and the House of Representatives: *The President has lost the support of Congress.* **4** [singular] used in the names of political parties: *Gandhi's Congress Party* —**congressional** /kənˈgreʃənəl/ adj [only before noun]: *a congressional committee*

con·gress·man /ˈkɒŋgrɪsmən $ ˈkaːŋ-/ n *plural* **congressmen** /-mən/ [C] a man who is a member of a congress, especially the US House of Representatives

con·gress·wom·an /ˈkɒŋgrɪs,wʊmən $ ˈkaːŋ-/ n *plural* **congresswomen** /-,wɪmɪn/ [C] a woman who is a member of a congress, especially the US House of Representatives

con·gru·ent /ˈkɒŋgruənt $ ˈkaːŋ-/ adj **1** *formal* fitting together well **2** *technical* congruent TRIANGLES are the same size and shape —**congruence** n [U]

con·i·cal /ˈkɒnɪkəl $ ˈkaː-/ adj shaped like a CONE: *huts with conical roofs*

co·ni·fer /ˈkəʊnɪfə, ˈkɒ- $ ˈkaːnəfər, ˈkoʊ-/ n [C] a tree such as a PINE or FIR that has leaves like needles and produces brown CONES that contain seeds. Most types of conifer keep their leaves in winter —**coniferous** /kəˈnɪfərəs $ koʊ-, kə-/ adj: *coniferous forests*

conj. also **conj** *BrE* the written abbreviation of *conjunction*

con·jec·ture¹ /kənˈdʒektʃə $ -ər/ n *formal* **1** [U] when you form ideas or opinions without having very much information to base them on: *What she said was* **pure conjecture.** | *There has been some conjecture about a possible merger.* **2** [C] an idea or opinion formed by guessing; ◼ **guess, hypothesis:** *My results show that this conjecture was, in fact, correct.* —**conjectural** adj

conjecture² v [I,T] *formal* to form an idea or opinion without having much information to base it on:

◨ **guess: conjecture that** *It seems reasonable to conjecture that these conditions breed violence.*

con·join /kənˈdʒɔɪn/ *v* [I,T] *formal* to join together, or to make things or people do this

con·joined ˈtwins *n* [plural] two people who are born with their bodies joined to each other

con·ju·gal /ˈkɒndʒʊ̩gəl $ ˈkɑːn-/ *adj* [only before noun] *formal* **1** relating to marriage: *conjugal love* **2 conjugal visit** a private meeting between a prisoner and his or her wife or husband, during which they are allowed to have sex

con·ju·gate /ˈkɒndʒʊ̩geɪt $ ˈkɑːn-/ *v* **1** [I] if a verb conjugates, it has different forms to show different tenses etc: *The verb 'to go' conjugates irregularly.* **2** [T] if you conjugate a verb, you state the different forms that it can have

con·ju·ga·tion /ˌkɒndʒʊ̩ˈgeɪʃən $ ˌkɑːn-/ *n* [C] **1** the way that a particular verb conjugates **2** a set of verbs in languages such as Latin that conjugate in the same way

con·junc·tion /kənˈdʒʌŋkʃən/ *n* **1 in conjunction with sb/sth** working, happening, or being used with someone or something else: *The worksheets are designed to be used in conjunction with the new course books.* **2** [C] a combination of different things that have come together by chance: [+of] *a happy conjunction of events* **3** [C] *technical* a word such as 'and', 'but', or 'because' which joins parts of a sentence

con·junc·ti·vi·tis /kənˌdʒʌŋktɪˈvaɪt̩s/ *n* [U] a painful and infectious disease of the eye that makes it red

con·junc·ture /kənˈdʒʌŋktʃə $ -ər/ *n* [C] *formal* a combination of events or situations, especially one that causes problems: *the historic conjuncture from which Marxism arose*

con·jure /ˈkʌndʒə $ ˈkɑːndʒər, ˈkʌn-/ *v* **1** [I,T] to perform clever tricks in which you seem to make things appear, disappear, or change by magic: *The magician conjured a rabbit out of his hat.* **2** [T] to make something appear or happen in a way which is not expected: *He has conjured victories from worse situations than this.* **3 a name to conjure with** the name of a very important person

conjure sth ⇔ **up** *phr v* **1** to bring a thought, picture, idea, or memory to someone's mind: **conjure up images/pictures/thoughts etc (of sth)** *Dieting always seems to conjure up images of endless salads.* **2** to make something appear when it is not expected, as if by magic: *Somehow we have to conjure up another $10,000.* **3** to make the soul of a dead person appear by saying special magic words

con·jur·er, **conjuror** /ˈkʌndʒərə $ ˈkɑːndʒərər, ˈkʌn-/ *n* [C] someone who entertains people by performing clever tricks in which things seem to appear, disappear, or change by magic; ◨ **magician**

con·jur·ing /ˈkʌndʒərɪŋ $ ˈkɑːn-, ˈkʌn-/ *n* [U] the skill of performing clever tricks in which you seem to make things appear, disappear, or change by magic; ◨ **magic**: *He did conjuring tricks for the children.*

conk¹ /kɒŋk $ kɑːŋk, kɔːŋk/ *n* [C] *BrE informal* a nose

conk² *v* [T] *informal* to hit someone hard, especially on the head

conk out *phr v informal* **1** if a machine or car conks out, it suddenly stops working: *Our car conked out on the way home.* **2** if someone conks out, they fall asleep because they are very tired: *I got home from work and I just conked out on the sofa.*

con·ker /ˈkɒŋkə $ ˈkɑːŋkər/ *n* **1** [C] the large brown shiny seed of the HORSE CHESTNUT tree **2 conkers** [U] *BrE* a children's game in which conkers are hung from pieces of string and you try to break the other person's conker by hitting it with your own

con·man /ˈkɒnmæn $ ˈkɑːn-/ *n plural* **conmen** /-men/ [C] *informal* someone who tries to get money from people by tricking them; → **con**

con·nect S2 W2 /kəˈnekt/ *v*

1 JOIN THINGS [T] to join two or more things together:

---

connect sth to/with sth *The railway link would connect Felixstowe with Fishguard.* | *Connect the speakers to the CD player.* | *We'd like two rooms with connecting doors* (=doors that join the rooms).

2 RELATIONSHIP [T] to realize or show that a fact, event, or person is related to something: *She did not connect the two events in her mind.* | **connect sb/sth with sth** *There is little evidence to connect them with the attack.*

3 ELECTRICITY/TELEPHONE ETC [I,T] to join something to the main supply of electricity, gas, or water, or to a telephone or computer network; ◨ **disconnect**: [+to] *Click here to connect to the Internet.* | *Has the phone been connected yet?* | *The power supply should be connected by a qualified electrician.*

4 TRANSPORT [I] if one train, flight etc connects with another, it arrives just before the other one leaves so that you can continue your journey: *I missed the connecting flight.* | [+with/to] *This train connects with the one to Glasgow.* | *From Toronto you can connect to all other Air Canada destinations.*

5 TELEPHONES [T] to join two telephone lines so that two people can speak: *Please hold the line. I'm trying to connect you.*

6 HIT STH [I] to succeed in hitting someone or something: *He swung at the ball, but didn't connect.*

7 UNDERSTAND PEOPLE [I] *especially AmE* if people connect, they feel that they like each other and understand each other: [+with] *They valued her ability to empathize and connect with others.*

connect sth ⇔ **up** *phr v* to join something to the main supply of electricity, gas, or water, to the telephone network, or to another piece of equipment: *Is the washing machine connected up yet?* | [+with] *The autopilot can be connected up with the flight recorder.*

con·nect·ed /kəˈnekt̩d/ *adj* **1 JOINED** to be joined to something else or joined to a large system or network: [+to] *The light is connected to a timer.* | *a computer connected to the Internet* | [+by] *a series of artificial lakes connected by waterfalls* **2 RELATIONSHIP** if two facts, events, people etc are connected, there is some kind of relationship between them: [+with] *problems connected with drug abuse* | *everyone connected with the film industry* | *Mr Edelson was closely connected with Trinity College.* **3 well connected** having important or powerful friends or relatives

con·nect·ed·ness /kəˈnekt̩dn̩s/ *n* [U] **1** the feeling people have that they are members of a group in society and that they share particular qualities with other members of that group: *Human beings have a need for both independence and connectedness.* **2** the degree to which people are connected by electronic technology such as the Internet and e-mail: [+between/with] *Communication technology has increased the connectedness between physicians and patients.*

con·nec·tion S3 W2 /kəˈnekʃən/ *n*

1 RELATIONSHIP [C] the way in which two facts, ideas, events etc are related to each other, and one is affected or caused by the other; ◨ **link**

have a connection (with/to sth)
establish a connection (between two things) (=prove or discover a link)
make a connection (between two things) (=realize there is a link)
there is a connection (between two things)
see a connection (=realize there is a connection)
close/direct connection
causal connection (=when one thing causes the other)
tenuous/loose connection (=one that is not at all close)

[+between] *the causal connection between smoking and cancer* | *There is a connection between pollution and the death of trees.* | [+with] *Mr O'Hara had no known connection with terrorist activity.* | [+to] *Will-*

C

*iams apparently **has** no **connection** to the case.* | *Police have so far failed to **establish a connection** between the two murders.* | *The evidence was there in the file but no one **made the connection**.* | *Students often **see** little **connection** between school and the rest of their lives.* | *He demonstrated the **close connection** between social conditions and health.*
2 JOINING [C,U] when two or more things are joined together or when something is joined to a larger system or network: *a digital telephone connection via satellite* | *They're offering free Internet connection.* | [+to] *The socket allows connection to a PC.* | *There's a £25 connection charge* (=money you pay to be connected to a service such as telephones, electricity etc).
3 in connection with sth concerning or involving something: arrest/charge/question etc sb in connection with a crime *Two men have been arrested in connection with the attack.* | *visits made to Spain in connection with her business* | *his work in connection with refugees*
4 ELECTRICAL WIRE [C] a wire or piece of metal joining two parts of a machine or electrical system: *an electrical connection* | *My radio isn't working properly – I think it's got a **loose connection*** (=wires which are not joined correctly).
5 TRAIN/FLIGHT ETC [C] a train, bus, or plane which is arranged to leave at a time which allows passengers from an earlier train, bus, or plane to use it to continue their journey: [+to] *If this train gets delayed we'll miss our connection to Paris.*
6 ROAD/RAILWAY ETC [C] a road, railway etc that joins two places and allows people to travel between them: *Cheshunt has good rail connections to London.*
7 PEOPLE connections [plural] **a)** people who you know who can help you, especially because they are in positions of power: *connections in high places* | *We have good connections in the advertising industry.* **b)** people who are related to you, but not very closely: *He is English, but has Irish connections.* | *the network of family connections in Italy*

con·nect·ive /kə'nektɪv/ n [C] a word that joins parts of a sentence

con'nective ,tissue n [U] parts of the body such as muscle or fat that exist between or join organs and other body parts

con·nec·tiv·i·ty /ˌkɒnek'tɪv1ti $ ˌkɑː-/ n [U] technical the ability of computers and other electronic equipment to connect with other computers or programs: *a growing demand for high-speed connectivity* | *Internet connectivity software*

con·nec·tor /kə'nektə $ -ər/ n [C] an object which is used to join two pieces of equipment together

con·ne·xion /kə'nekʃən/ n a British spelling of CON-NECTION

'conning ,tower n [C] technical the structure on top of a SUBMARINE (=underwater ship)

con·nip·tion /kə'nɪpʃən/ also **con'niption ,fit** n [C] AmE old-fashioned a way of behaving which shows that you are very angry: *My mother **threw a conniption fit** when I didn't come home till two in the morning.*

con·nive /kə'naɪv/ v [I] **1** to not try to stop something wrong from happening: [+at] *He would not be the first politician to connive at a shady business deal.* **2 connive (with sb) to do sth** to work secretly with someone to achieve something, especially something wrong; ☰ **conspire**: *They connived with their mother to deceive me.* —**connivance** n [U]: *We could not have escaped without the connivance of the guards.*

con·niv·ing /kə'naɪvɪŋ/ adj a conniving person secretly tries to gain something or harm someone – used to show disapproval

con·nois·seur /ˌkɒnə'sɜː $ ˌkɑːnə'sɜːr/ n [C] someone who knows a lot about something such as art, food, or music: *a wine connoisseur* | [+of] *Fry was a connoisseur of Renaissance art.*

con·no·ta·tion /ˌkɒnə'teɪʃən $ ˌkɑː-/ n [C] a quality or an idea that a word makes you think of that is more than its basic meaning; → **denotation**: [+of] *The word 'professional' has connotations of skill and excellence.* | *a negative connotation* —**connotative** /'kɒnəteɪtɪv $ 'kɑːn-, kə'noʊtətɪv/ adj

con·note /kə'nəʊt $ -'noʊt/ v [T] formal if a word connotes something, it makes you think of qualities and ideas that are more than its basic meaning; → **denote**: *The word 'plump' connotes cheerfulness.*

con·nu·bi·al /kə'njuːbiəl $ -'nuː-/ adj connubial bliss formal the state of being happily married: *living in connubial bliss*

con·quer /'kɒŋkə $ 'kɑːŋkər/ v **1** [I,T] to get control of a country by fighting: *The Normans conquered England in 1066.* | *Egypt was conquered by the Persian king Kambyses.* **2** [I,T] to defeat an enemy: *The Zulus conquered all the neighbouring tribes.* **3** [T] to gain control over something that is difficult, using a lot of effort: conquer your nerves/fear *She was determined to conquer her fear of flying.* | *efforts to conquer inflation* | *drugs to conquer the disease* **4** [T] to succeed in climbing to the top of a mountain when no one has ever climbed it before: *an attempt to conquer the peaks of Everest* **5** [T] to become very successful in a place: *In the last few years, the company has succeeded in conquering the European market.* —**conqueror** n [C] —**conquering** adj: *conquering heroes*

con·quest /'kɒŋkwest $ 'kɑːŋ-/ n **1** [singular, U] the act of getting control of a country by fighting: *the Norman Conquest* (=the conquest of England by the Normans) | [+of] *the Spanish conquest of the Inca Empire* **2** [C] land that is won in a war: *French conquests in Asia* **3** [C] someone that you have persuaded to love you or to have sex with you – often used humorously: *He boasts about his many conquests.* **4** when you gain control of or deal successfully with something that is difficult or dangerous: [+of] *the conquest of space*

con·quis·ta·dor /kɒn'kwɪstədɔː $ kɑːn'kiːstədɔːr/ n [C] one of the Spanish conquerors of Mexico and Peru in the 18th century

con·san·guin·i·ty /ˌkɒnsæŋ'gwɪn₃ti $ ˌkɑːn-/ n [U] formal when people are members of the same family

con·science /'kɒnʃəns $ 'kɑːn-/ n [C,U] **1** the part of your mind that tells you whether what you are doing is morally right or wrong: guilty/troubled conscience (=a guilty feeling, because you have done something wrong) *It was his guilty conscience that made him offer to help.* | *Well, at least I can face them all with a **clear conscience*** (=when you know that you have done nothing wrong). | *a film with a **social conscience*** (=a moral sense of how society should be) | **prisoner of conscience** (=someone who is in prison because of their political or religious beliefs) | *I can't tell you what to do – it's a **matter of conscience*** (=something that you must make a moral judgment about). | *a **crisis of conscience** among medical staff* (=a situation in which it is very difficult to decide what is the right thing to do) | *The dog's sad look **pricked** her **conscience*** (=made her feel guilty) *and she took him home.* ⚠ Do not confuse with **consciousness** (=the condition of being awake and aware of thoughts and feelings). **2** a guilty feeling that you have about something bad you have done: twinge/pang of conscience *Ian felt a pang of conscience at having misjudged her.* | **have no conscience (about sth)** (=not feel guilty about something) *They've no conscience at all about cheating.* **3 on your conscience** if you have something on your conscience, it makes you feel guilty: *He didn't want somebody's death on his conscience.* | *Could you live with that on your conscience?* **4 not in (all/good) conscience** formal if you cannot in all conscience do something, you cannot do it because you think it is wrong: *I couldn't in all conscience tell him that his job was safe.*

'conscience-,stricken *adj* feeling very guilty about something that you have done wrong: *Kate hurried home, conscience-stricken at leaving her mother alone.*

con·sci·en·tious /ˌkɒnʃiˈenʃəs◂ $ ˌkɑːn-/ *adj* careful to do everything that it is your job or duty to do: *A conscientious teacher may feel inclined to take work home.* | *a conscientious and hard-working student* —**conscientiously** *adv* —**conscientiousness** *n* [U]: *his conscientiousness and loyalty to the company*

conscientious ob'jector *n* [C] someone who refuses to become a soldier because of their moral or religious beliefs → DRAFT DODGER

con·scious S2 W3 /ˈkɒnʃəs $ ˈkɑːn-/ *adj*
1 AWARE [not before noun] noticing or realizing something; ⬛ **aware: conscious of (doing) sth** *I became conscious of someone watching me.* | *I was very conscious of the fact that I had to make a good impression.* | **conscious that** *She was conscious that Marie was listening to every word.*
2 AWAKE awake and able to understand what is happening around you; ⬛ **unconscious:** *The driver was still conscious when the ambulance arrived.*
3 conscious effort/decision/attempt etc an effort etc that is deliberate and intended: *Vivien had made a conscious effort to be friendly.*
4 CONCERNED thinking a lot about or concerned about something: **politically/environmentally/socially etc conscious** *environmentally conscious consumers* | **health-conscious/fashion-conscious etc** *Many employers are becoming more safety-conscious.* | [+of] *She was very conscious of security.* → SELF-CONSCIOUS
5 THOUGHTS conscious thoughts, memories etc are ones which you know about; → **subconscious:** *the conscious mind* | *Without conscious thought, she instinctively placed a hand on his arm.* | *It affects the audience at a deeper, less conscious level.* —**consciously** *adv: She was probably not consciously aware of the true nature of her feelings.*

con·scious·ness W3 /ˈkɒnʃəsnᵻs $ ˈkɑːn-/ *n*
1 [U] the condition of being awake and able to understand what is happening around you: *David* **lost consciousness** (=went into a deep sleep) *at eight o'clock and died a few hours later.* | *She could faintly hear voices as she began to* **regain consciousness** (=wake up).
2 [C,U] your mind and your thoughts: *The painful memories eventually faded from her consciousness.* | *Hypnosis is an altered* **state of consciousness.** | *research into* **human consciousness**
3 [C] someone's ideas, feelings, or opinions about politics, life etc: *The experience helped to change her political consciousness.*
4 [U] when you know that something exists or is true; ⬛ **awareness:** *This will increase* **public consciousness** *of the pollution issue.* → STREAM OF CONSCIOUSNESS

'consciousness ,raising *n* [U] the process of making people understand and care more about a moral, social, or political problem, especially by giving them information

cons·cript¹ /kənˈskrɪpt/ *v* [T] **1** to make someone join the army, navy etc; ⬛ **draft** *AmE:* **conscript sb into sth** *Young Frenchmen were conscripted into the army and forced to fight in Algeria.* **2** to make someone become a member of a group or take part in a particular activity; ⬛ **recruit**

con·script² /ˈkɒnskrɪpt $ ˈkɑːn-/ *n* [C] someone who has been made to join the army, navy etc; ⬛ **draftee** *AmE: a young army conscript*

con·scrip·tion /kənˈskrɪpʃən/ *n* [U] when people are made to join the army, navy etc; ⬛ **draft**

con·se·crate /ˈkɒnsᵻkreɪt $ ˈkɑːn-/ *v* [T] **1** to officially state in a special religious ceremony that a place or building is holy and can be used for religious purposes: *The bones will be reburied in* **consecrated ground.** **2** to officially state in a special religious ceremony that someone is now a priest, BISHOP etc —**consecration** /ˌkɒnsᵻˈkreɪʃən $ ˌkɑːn-/ *n* [U]

con·sec·u·tive /kənˈsekjᵿtɪv/ *adj* consecutive numbers or periods of time follow one after the other without any interruptions: *It had rained for four consecutive days.* | *Can they win the title for the third consecutive season?* —**consecutively** *adv: Number the pages consecutively.*

con·sen·su·al /kənˈsenʃuəl/ *adj formal* **1** involving the agreement of all or most people in a group: *a consensual style of management* **2** consensual sexual activity is wanted and agreed to by the people involved

con·sen·sus /kənˈsensəs/ *n* [singular, U] an opinion that everyone in a group agrees with or accepts: [+on/about] *a lack of consensus about the aims of the project* | **consensus that** *There is a consensus among teachers that children should have a broad understanding of the world.* | *The EU Council of Finance Ministers failed to* **reach a consensus** *on the pace of integration.* | *the current* **consensus of opinion** | *The* **general consensus** *was that technology was a good thing.* | *the* **consensus politics** *of the fifties*

con·sent¹ W3 /kənˈsent/ *n* [U]
1 permission to do something

> with/without sb's consent
> give/grant (your) consent
> refuse/withhold (your) consent
> obtain (sb's) consent
> **prior consent** (=consent before something can happen)
> written consent
> **verbal consent** (=spoken consent)
> **parental consent** (=consent from someone's parents)
> **informed consent** (=consent based on full information about what will happen)
> **tacit consent** (=consent given without being actually spoken)

> *He took the car* **without** *the owner's* **consent.** | *Her parents* **gave** *their* **consent** *to the marriage.* | *A patient can* **refuse consent** *for a particular treatment at any time.* | *Most owners are happy to have their names used for publicity if this is done with their* **prior consent.** | **Informed consent** *was obtained from all participants before the study began.* → AGE OF CONSENT

2 agreement about something; → **dissent:** *The chairman was elected* **by common consent** (=with most people agreeing). | *divorce* **by mutual consent** (=by agreement between both the people involved)

consent² *v* [I] to give your permission for something or agree to do something: [+to] *Her father reluctantly consented to the marriage.* | **consent to do sth** *He rarely consents to do interviews.*

con,senting 'adult *n* [C] *law* someone who is considered to be old enough to decide whether they want to have sex → AGE OF CONSENT

con·se·quence S3 W2 /ˈkɒnsᵻkwəns $ ˈkɑːnsᵻkwens/ *n*
1 [C] something that happens as a result of a particular action or set of conditions: [+of] *Many believe that poverty is a direct consequence of overpopulation.* | [+for] *Our findings have far-reaching consequences for researchers.* | **dire/disastrous/serious etc consequences** *Errors in forecasting can have dire consequences.* | **with ... consequences** *He ate some poisonous mushrooms, with fatal consequences.* | **take/suffer/face the consequences (of sth)** (=accept the bad results of something you have done) *He broke the law, and now he must face the consequences of his actions.*
2 as a consequence (of sth)/in consequence (of sth) *formal* as a result of something: *Animals have died as a consequence of coming into contact with this chemical.* | *She was over the age limit and, in consequence, her application was rejected.*
3 of little/no/any etc consequence *formal* not very

important or valuable: [+**to**] *Your opinion is of little consequence to me.* | *I don't suppose it is of any consequence now.*

con·se·quent /ˈkɒnsɪ̈kwənt $ ˈkɑːn-/ *adj* [usually before noun] *formal* happening as a result of a particular event or situation: *the rise in inflation and consequent fall in demand* → SUBSEQUENT

con·se·quen·tial /ˌkɒnsɪ̈ˈkwenʃəl $ ˌkɑːn-/ *adj* [usually before noun] *formal* **1** happening as a direct result of a particular event or situation: *redundancy and the consequential loss of earnings* **2** important; ▣ **significant**; ◪ **inconsequential**: *a consequential decision* —**consequentially** *adv*

con·se·quent·ly W3 /ˈkɒnsɪ̈kwəntli $ ˈkɑːnsɪ̈-kwentli/ *adv* [sentence adverb] as a result: *Most computer users have never received any formal keyboard training. Consequently, their keyboard skills are inefficient.* | *The molecules are absorbed into the bloodstream and consequently affect the organs.*

con·ser·van·cy /kənˈsɜːvənsi $ -ɜːr-/ *n formal* **1** [singular] a group of officials who control and protect an area of land, a river etc: *the Thames Conservancy* **2** [U] the protection of natural things such as animals, plants, forests etc; ▣ **conservation**

con·ser·va·tion S3 W3 /ˌkɒnsəˈveɪʃən $ ˌkɑːnsər-/ *n* [U]
1 the protection of natural things such as animals, plants, forests etc, to prevent them being spoiled or destroyed; ▣ **preservation**; → **conserve**: *wildlife conservation* | *a local conservation group* | [+**of**] *conservation of the countryside*
2 when you prevent something from being lost or wasted; → **conserve**: *energy conservation* | [+**of**] *Recycling is an important part of the conservation of resources.*

conser'vation area *n* [C] **1** an area where animals and plants are protected **2** *BrE* an area where interesting old buildings are protected and new buildings are carefully controlled

con·ser·va·tion·ist /ˌkɒnsəˈveɪʃənɪ̈st $ ˌkɑːnsər-/ *n* [C] someone who works to protect animals, plants etc or to protect old buildings —**conservationism** *n* [U]

con·ser·va·tis·m /kənˈsɜːvətɪzəm $ -ɜːr-/ *n* [U] **1** dislike of change and new ideas: *people's innate conservatism in matters of language* **2** also **Conservatism** the political belief that society should change as little as possible **3** **Conservatism** the political beliefs of the British Conservative Party

con·ser·va·tive¹ /kənˈsɜːvətɪv $ -ɜːr-/ *adj* **1** not liking changes or new ideas: *a very conservative attitude to education* | *conservative views* **2** **Conservative** belonging to or concerned with the Conservative Party in Britain: *Conservative policies* | *a Conservative MP* **3** not very modern in style, taste etc; ▣ **traditional**: *a dark conservative suit* **4** a **conservative estimate/guess** a guess which is deliberately lower than what the real amount probably is: *At a conservative estimate, the holiday will cost about £1500.*
—**conservatively** *adv*: *a fortune conservatively estimated at 2 million dollars* | *He was conservatively dressed in a dark business suit.*

conservative² *n* [C] **1** **Conservative** someone who supports or is a member of the Conservative Party in Britain **2** someone who does not like changes in politics, ideas, or fashion: *an argument between reformers and conservatives in the organization*

Con'servative Party *n* the **Conservative Party** a British political party on the RIGHT

con·ser·va·toire /kənˈsɜːvətwɑː $ -ˈsɜːrvətwɑːr/ *n* [C] *BrE* a school where people are trained in music or acting; ▣ **conservatory** *AmE*

con·ser·va·to·ry /kənˈsɜːvətəri $ -ˈsɜːrvətɔːri/ *n* plural **conservatories** [C] **1** *BrE* a room with glass walls and a glass roof, where plants are grown, that is

usually added on to a house **2** *AmE* a school where people are trained in music or acting; ▣ **conservatoire** *BrE*

con·serve¹ /kənˈsɜːv $ -ɜːrv/ *v* [T] **1** to protect something and prevent it from changing or being damaged; ▣ **preserve**: *We must conserve our woodlands for future generations.* | *efforts to conserve fish stocks* **2** to use as little water, energy etc as possible so that it is not wasted: *systems designed to conserve energy*

con·serve² /ˈkɒnsɜːv $ ˈkɑːnsɜːrv/ *n* [C,U] *formal* fruit that is preserved by being cooked with sugar; ▣ **jam**: *strawberry conserve*

con·sid·er S1 W1 /kənˈsɪdə $ -ər/ *v*
1 THINK ABOUT [I,T] to think about something carefully, especially before making a choice or decision: **consider doing sth** *I seriously considered resigning* (=almost actually resigned). | **consider the possibility of (doing) sth** *Have you considered the possibility of retraining?* | **consider whether (to do sth)** *We are considering whether to change our advice to tourists.* | **consider where/how/why etc** *We're still considering where to move to.* | *We will have to **consider** your offer carefully.* | **be considering your position** *formal* (=deciding whether or not to leave your job)
2 OPINION [T] to think of someone or something in a particular way or to have a particular opinion: **consider (that)** *The local authority considered that the school did not meet requirements.* | **consider sb/sth (to be) sth** *A further increase in interest rates is now considered unlikely.* | *Liz Quinn was considered an excellent teacher.* | *They consider themselves to be Europeans.* | *I consider it a great honour to be invited.* | **consider it necessary/important etc to do sth** *I did not consider it necessary to report the incident.* | **consider sb/sth to do sth** *The campaign was considered to have failed.* | **consider yourself lucky/fortunate** (=believe you are lucky etc) *Consider yourself lucky you weren't in the car at the time.* | **consider yourself (to be) sth** (=think of yourself as a particular type of person) *They consider themselves to be middle class.*
3 PEOPLE'S FEELINGS [T] to think about someone or their feelings, and try to avoid upsetting them; → **considerate**: *You've got to learn to consider other people!* | *You never once considered my feelings in all this, did you?*
4 IMPORTANT FACT [I,T] to think about an important fact relating to something when making a judgment; → **considering**: *It's not surprising **when you consider that** he only arrived 6 months ago.* | *All things considered, I'm sure we made the right decision.*
5 DISCUSS [T] to discuss something such as a report or problem, so that you can make a decision about it: *The committee has been considering the report.*
6 LOOK AT [T] *formal* to look at someone or something carefully: *Henry considered the sculpture with an expert eye.*
7 **Consider it done** *spoken* used to say yes very willingly when someone asks you to do something for them: *'Could you drive me to the airport tomorrow?' 'Consider it done.'* → **all things considered** at THING (22)

con·sid·er·a·ble S2 W1 /kənˈsɪdərəbəl/ *adj* fairly large, especially large enough to have an effect or be important; → **inconsiderable**: **considerable amount/number etc of sth** *We've saved a considerable amount of money.* | *Michael has already spent considerable time in Barcelona.* | *issues of considerable importance* | *The series has aroused considerable interest.*

con·sid·er·a·bly S3 W3 /kənˈsɪdərəbli/ *adv* much or a lot: *It's considerably colder today.* | *Conditions have improved considerably over the past few years.*

con·sid·er·ate /kənˈsɪdərɪ̈t/ *adj* always thinking of what other people need or want and being careful not to upset them; ◪ **inconsiderate**: *He was always kind and considerate.* | **it is considerate of sb (to do sth)** *It was very considerate of you to let us know you were going to be late.* | [+**towards**] *As a motorist, I try to be considerate towards cyclists.* —**considerately** *adv*

con·sid·e·ra·tion ⬚S1 ⬚W2 /kən,sɪdə'reɪʃən/ *n*
1 [U] *formal* careful thought and attention, especially before making an official or important decision: *proposals put forward for consideration* | **under consideration** *There are several amendments under consideration.* | **due/serious/proper etc consideration** *After due consideration, I have decided to tender my resignation.* | **give sth careful/full etc consideration** *We would have to give serious consideration to banning it altogether.* | **deserve/merit consideration** *These plans definitely merit further consideration.*
2 take sth into consideration to remember to think about something important when you are making a decision or judgement: *We will take your recent illness into consideration when marking your exams.*
3 [C] a fact that you think about when you are making a decision: *Political rather than economic considerations influenced the location of the new factory.*
4 [U] the quality of thinking about other people's feelings and being careful not to upset them: [+for] *The murdered woman's name has not been released, out of consideration for her parents.* | *They've got no **consideration for others**.* | *Show* some *consideration!*
5 [singular, U] *formal* a payment for something, especially a service: *I might be able to help you, for a small consideration.* | *a payment* **in consideration of** (=as payment for) *their services*

con·sid·ered /kən'sɪdəd $ -ərd/ *adj* [only before noun] a considered opinion, reply, judgment etc is one that you have thought about carefully: *He hadn't had time to form a **considered opinion**.* | *The committee is meeting to prepare a **considered response** to the problem.* → ILL-CONSIDERED

con·sid·er·ing[1] /kən'sɪdərɪŋ/ *prep, conjunction* used to say that you are thinking about a particular fact when you are giving your opinion: *Considering the strength of the opposition, we did very well to score two goals.* | **considering (that)** *I think we paid too much for the house, considering that we needed to get the roof repaired.* | **considering who/how etc** *John did quite well in his exams, considering how little he studied.*

considering[2] *adv spoken* used after you have given an opinion, to say that something is true in spite of a situation that makes it seem surprising: *He didn't look too tired, considering.*

con·sign /kən'saɪn/ *v* [T] *formal* to send something somewhere, especially in order to sell it
    consign sb/sth to sth *phr v formal* **1** to make someone or something be in a particular situation, especially a bad one: *It was a decision which consigned him to political obscurity.* | **consign sb/sth to the dustbin/scrapheap/rubbish heap etc** *BrE: Many older people feel they have been consigned to the medical scrapheap.* **2** to put something somewhere, especially in order to get rid of it: *The shoes looked so tatty that I consigned them to the back of the cupboard.*

con·sign·ee /,kɒnsaɪ'niː, -sᵻ- $,kɑːn-/ *n* [C] *technical* the person that something is delivered to

con·sign·ment /kən'saɪnmənt/ *n* **1** [C] a quantity of goods that are sent somewhere, especially in order to be sold: [+of] *a large consignment of clothes* **2 on consignment** goods that are on consignment are being sold for someone else for a share of the profit **3** [U] when someone sends or delivers something

con'signment ,shop *n* [C] *AmE* a shop where you take things you do not want, so the shop can sell them and give you a share of the profit

con·sign·or /kən'saɪnə $ -ər/ *n* [C] *technical* the person who sends goods to someone else

con·sist ⬚W3 /kən'sɪst/ *v*
    consist in sth *phr v* [not in progressive] *formal* to be based on or depend on something: *Happiness does not consist in how many possessions you own.*
    consist of sth *phr v* [not in progressive] to be formed from two or more things or people: *The buffet consisted of several different Indian dishes.* | **consist mainly/largely/primarily of sb/sth** *The audience*

consisted mainly of teenagers. | **consist entirely/solely of sb/sth** *The area does not consist entirely of rich people, despite popular belief.*

con·sis·ten·cy /kən'sɪstənsi/ *n plural* **consistencies** [C,U] **1** the quality of always being the same, doing things in the same way, having the same standards etc – used to show approval; 🔁 **inconsistency**: [+in] *Consumer groups are demanding greater consistency in the labelling of food products.* | [+of] *Consistency of performance depends on several factors.* | [+between/among] *There are checks to ensure consistency between interviewers.* **2** how thick, smooth etc a substance is: [+of] *Beat the mixture until it has the consistency of thick cream.*

con·sis·tent ⬚S3 ⬚W3 /kən'sɪstənt/ *adj*
1 always behaving in the same way or having the same attitudes, standards etc – usually used to show approval; 🔁 **inconsistent**: *She's one of the team's most consistent players.* | [+in] *We need to be consistent in our approach.*
2 continuing to happen or develop in the same way: *a consistent improvement in the country's economy*
3 a consistent argument or idea does not have any parts that do not match other parts; 🔁 **inconsistent**: *The evidence is not consistent.*
4 be consistent with sth if a fact, idea etc is consistent with another one, it seems to match it: *Her injuries are consistent with having fallen from the building.* | *The results are consistent with earlier research.* —**consistently** *adv: consistently high performance*

con·so·la·tion /,kɒnsə'leɪʃən $,kɑːn-/ *n* [C,U] something that makes you feel better when you are sad or disappointed: [+for/to] *The only consolation for the team is that they get a chance to play the game again.* | *If it's any consolation, things do get easier as the child gets older.* | *He **had the consolation of** knowing that he couldn't have done any better.* | **be little/no consolation** *The fact that there has been a reduction in crime is little consolation to victims of crime.*

conso'lation prize *n* [C] a prize that is given to someone who has not won a competition: *Ten runners-up received a T-shirt as a consolation prize.*

con·sol·a·to·ry /kən'sɒlətəri, -'səʊlə- $ -'soʊlətɔːri, -'sɑː-/ *adj formal* intended to make someone feel better

con·sole[1] /kən'səʊl $ -'soʊl/ *v* [T] to make someone feel better when they are feeling sad or disappointed; → **consolation**: *No one could console her when Peter died.* | **console yourself with sth** *She consoled herself with the fact that no one else had done well in the exam either.* | **console yourself that** *He consoled himself that he would see Kate again soon.*

con·sole[2] /'kɒnsəʊl $ 'kɑːnsoʊl/ *n* [C] **1** a flat board that contains the controls for a machine, piece of electrical equipment, computer etc → see picture at BEDROOM **2** a special cupboard for a television, computer etc

con·sol·i·date /kən'sɒlᵻdeɪt $ -'sɑː-/ *v* [I,T] **1** to strengthen the position of power or success that you have, so that it becomes more effective or continues for longer: *The company has **consolidated** its **position** as the country's leading gas supplier.* | *The team consolidated their lead with a third goal.* **2** to combine things in order to make them more effective or easier to deal with: *We consolidate information from a wide range of sources.* | *They took out a loan to consolidate their debts.* | *The company is planning to consolidate its business activities at a new site in Arizona.* —**consolidation** /kən,sɒlᵻ'deɪʃən $ -,sɑː-/ *n* [C,U]: *the consolidation of political power*

con·som·mé /kən'sɒmeɪ, 'kɒnsəmeɪ $,kɑːnsə'meɪ/ *n* [U] clear soup made from meat or vegetables

con·so·nant[1] /'kɒnsənənt $ 'kɑːn-/ *n* [C] **1** a speech sound made by partly or completely stopping the flow of air through your mouth; → **vowel 2** a letter that represents a consonant sound. The letters 'a', 'e', 'i', 'o', 'u', and sometimes 'y' represent vowels, and all the other letters are consonants

consonant² *adj* **1** be consonant with sth *formal* to match or exist well with something else: *This policy is scarcely consonant with the government's declared aims.* **2** *technical* relating to a combination of musical notes that sounds pleasant; **□ dissonant** —**consonance** *n* [U]: *a religion in consonance with Christianity*

con·sort¹ /ˈkɒnsɔːt $ ˈkɑːnsɔːrt/ *n* [C] **1** the wife or husband of a ruler → **PRINCE CONSORT** **2** a group of people who play very old music, or the group of old-fashioned instruments they use **3 in consort (with sb)** *formal* doing something together with someone

con·sort² /kənˈsɔːt $ -ɔːrt/ *v*
consort with sb *phr v formal* to spend time with someone that other people do not approve of: *a man who regularly consorted with prostitutes*

con·sor·ti·um /kənˈsɔːtiəm $ -ɔːr-/ *n plural* **consortia** /-tiə/ or **consortiums** [C] a group of companies or organizations who are working together to do something: *a consortium of oil companies* | *The aircraft will be built by a European consortium.*

con·spic·u·ous /kənˈspɪkjuəs/ *adj* **1** very easy to notice; **□ inconspicuous**: *The notice must be displayed in a conspicuous place.* | *a bird with conspicuous white markings* | *I felt very conspicuous in my red coat.* **2** conspicuous success, courage etc is very great and impressive: *He had represented Italy with conspicuous success.* | *The award is given for notable or conspicuous achievement in science.* **3 be conspicuous by your/its absence** used to say that someone or something is not somewhere where they were expected to be: *a group that were conspicuous by their absence from the awards ceremony*

con,spicuous con'sumption *n* [U] the act of buying a lot of things, especially expensive things that are not necessary, in order to IMPRESS other people and show them how rich you are

con·spi·ra·cy /kənˈspɪrəsi/ *n plural* **conspiracies** [C,U] **1** a secret plan made by two or more people to do something that is harmful or illegal; → **conspire**: **conspiracy to do sth** *He was charged with conspiracy to commit criminal damage.* | [+against] *a conspiracy against the government* | *There were many **conspiracy theories** (=beliefs that something is the result of a conspiracy) surrounding Princess Diana's death.* **2 conspiracy of silence** an agreement not to talk about something, even though it should not be a secret: *There's often a conspiracy of silence surrounding bullying in schools.*

con·spi·ra·tor /kənˈspɪrətə $ -ər/ *n* [C] someone who is involved in a secret plan to do something illegal

con·spi·ra·to·ri·al /kənˌspɪrəˈtɔːriəl/ *adj* **1** a conspiratorial expression, voice, or manner suggests you are sharing a secret with someone: *His voice became low and conspiratorial.* | *Natasha whispered to Maggie in a conspiratorial tone.* | **conspiratorial whisper/smile/wink etc** *Britta gave him a conspiratorial smile.* **2** relating to a conspiracy —**conspiratorially** *adv*

con·spire /kənˈspaɪə $ -ˈspaɪr/ *v* [I] **1** to secretly plan with someone else to do something illegal; → **conspiracy**: **conspire (with sb) to do sth** *All six men admitted conspiring to steal cars.* | [+against] *There was some evidence that he had been conspiring against the government.* **2** if events conspire to do something, they happen at the same time and make something bad happen: **conspire to do sth** *Pollution and neglect have conspired to ruin the city.* | [+against] *Emily felt that everything was conspiring against her.*

con·sta·ble /ˈkʌnstəbəl $ ˈkɑːn-/ *n* [C] **1** a British police officer of the lowest rank **2** in the US, someone

who has some of the powers of a police officer and can send legal documents that order someone to do something

con·stab·u·la·ry /kənˈstæbjʊ̈ləri $ -leri/ *n plural* **constabularies** [C] the police force of a particular area or country

con·stan·cy /ˈkɒnstənsi $ ˈkɑːn-/ *n* [U] *formal* **1** the quality of staying the same even though other things change: [+of] *constancy of temperature* **2** loyalty and faithfulness to a particular person

con·stant¹ S2 W2 /ˈkɒnstənt $ ˈkɑːn-/ *adj*
1 happening regularly or all the time: *There was a **constant stream of** visitors to the house.* | *Amy lived in constant fear of being attacked.* | *He kept in constant contact with his family while he was in Australia.*
2 staying the same: *The truck was travelling at a fairly constant speed.*
3 *literary* loyal and faithful: *a constant friend*

constant² *n* [C] **1** *technical* a number or quantity that never changes **2** *formal* something that stays the same even though other things change → **VARIABLE²**

con·stant·ly S3 W3 /ˈkɒnstəntli $ ˈkɑːn-/ *adv* all the time, or very often: *He talked constantly about his work.* | *The English language is **constantly changing**.*

con·stel·la·tion /ˌkɒnstəˈleɪʃən $ ˌkɑːn-/ *n* [C] **1** a group of stars that forms a particular pattern and has a name: *a star in the constellation of Orion* **2 a constellation of sth** *literary* a group of people or things that are similar: *a constellation of ideas*

con·ster·na·tion /ˌkɒnstəˈneɪʃən $ ˌkɑːnstər-/ *n* [U] a feeling of worry, shock, or fear: *The government's plans have **caused** considerable **consternation** among many Americans.* | *A new power station is being built **much to the consternation of** environmental groups* (=they are very worried about it). | **in consternation** *He looked at her in consternation.*

con·sti·pa·tion /ˌkɒnstɪ̈ˈpeɪʃən $ ˌkɑːn-/ *n* [U] the condition of having difficulty in getting rid of solid waste from your body; → **diarrhoea** —**constipated** /ˈkɒnstɪ̈peɪtɪ̈d $ ˈkɑːn-/ *adj*

con·sti·tu·en·cy W3 /kənˈstɪtʃuənsi/ *n plural* **constituencies** [C]
1 *BrE* an area of a country that elects a representative to a parliament: *a rural constituency* | *constituency boundaries* | *He represents the Essex constituency of Epping Forest.*
2 [also + plural verb *BrE*] the people who live and vote in a particular area
3 any group that supports or is likely to support a politician or a political party: *The trade unions were no longer the constituency of the Labour Party alone.*

con·sti·tu·ent¹ /kənˈstɪtʃuənt/ *n* [C] **1** someone who votes in a particular area **2** one of the substances or things that combine to form something: [+of] *Sodium is one of the constituents of salt.*

constituent² *adj* [only before noun] *formal* being one of the parts of something: *the EU and its constituent members*

con,stituent as'sembly *n* [C] a group of elected representatives that have the power to write or change their country's constitution

con·sti·tute W3 /ˈkɒnstɪ̈tjuːt $ ˈkɑːnstɪ̈tuːt/ *v*
1 [linking verb, not in progressive] to be considered to be something: *Failing to complete the work constitutes a breach of the employment contract.* | *The rise in crime constitutes a threat to society.*
2 [linking verb, not in progressive] if several people or things constitute something, they are the parts that form it: *We must redefine what constitutes a family.*
3 [T usually in passive] *formal* to officially form a group or organization: *The Federation was constituted in 1949.*

con·sti·tu·tion W2 /ˌkɒnstɪ̈ˈtjuːʃən $ ˌkɑːnstɪ̈ˈtuː-/ *n* [C]
1 also **Constitution** a set of basic laws and principles that a country or organization is governed by: *The*

2 your health and your body's ability to fight illness: **(have) a strong/good/weak etc constitution** *She's got a strong constitution – she'll recover in no time.*
3 *formal* the parts or structure of something: [+of] *What's the chemical constitution of the dye?*

con·sti·tu·tion·al¹ W3 /ˌkɒnstɪˈtjuːʃənəl◂ $ ˌkɑːnstəˈtuː-/ *adj*
1 officially allowed or limited by the system of rules of a country or organization: *a constitutional right to privacy* | *a constitutional monarchy* (=a country ruled by a king or queen whose power is limited by a constitution)
2 connected with the constitution of a country or organization: *a constitutional crisis* | **constitutional reform/change/amendment** *a proposal for constitutional reform*
3 relating to someone's health, physical ability, or character —**constitutionally** *adv*: *a constitutionally guaranteed right* | *He was constitutionally incapable of dealing with conflict.*

constitutional² *n* [C] *old-fashioned* a walk you take because it is good for your health

con·sti·tu·tion·al·is·m /ˌkɒnstɪˈtjuːʃənəlɪzəm $ ˌkɑːnstəˈtuː-/ *n* [U] the belief that a government should be based on a constitution —**constitutionalist** *n* [C]

con·sti·tu·tion·al·i·ty /ˌkɒnstɪˌtjuːʃəˈnæləti $ ˌkɑːnstəˌtuː-/ *n* [U] the quality of being acceptable according to a constitution: *A decision on the proposal's constitutionality still has to be made.*

con·strain /kənˈstreɪn/ *v* [T] **1** to stop someone from doing what they want to do: **constrain sb from doing sth** *Financial factors should not constrain doctors from prescribing the best treatment for patients.* **2** to limit something: *Poor soil has constrained the level of crop production.* | *Women's employment opportunities are often severely constrained by family commitments.*

con·strained /kənˈstreɪnd/ *adj* **be/feel constrained to do sth** to feel that you must do something: *He felt constrained to accept the invitation.*

con·straint W3 /kənˈstreɪnt/ *n*
1 [C] something that limits your freedom to do what you want; ◨ **restriction**: [+on] *Constraints on spending have forced the company to rethink its plans.* | *the constraints of family life* | **financial/environmental/political etc constraints** *There have been financial and political constraints on development.* | **impose/place constraints on sb/sth** *constraints imposed on teachers by large class sizes*
2 [U] control over the way people are allowed to behave, so that they cannot do what they want: *freedom from constraint*

con·strict /kənˈstrɪkt/ *v* **1** [I,T] to make something narrower or tighter, or to become narrower or tighter: *Caffeine constricts the blood vessels in your body.* | *Linda's throat constricted and she started to cry.* **2** [T] to limit someone's freedom to do what they want: *Fear of crime constricts many people's lives.* —**constricted** *adj* —**constriction** /-ˈstrɪkʃən/ *n* [C,U]

con·struct¹ W3 /kənˈstrʌkt/ *v* [T]
1 to build something such as a house, bridge, road etc: *There are plans to construct a new road bridge across the river.* | **construct sth from/of/in sth** *skyscrapers constructed entirely of concrete and glass*; → see picture at ASSEMBLE
2 to form something such as a sentence, argument, or system by joining words, ideas etc together: *Boyce has constructed a new theory of management.*
3 *technical* to draw a mathematical shape: *Construct a square with sides of 5cm.*

con·struct² /ˈkɒnstrʌkt $ ˈkɑːn-/ *n* [C] *formal* **1** an idea formed by combining several pieces of information or knowledge **2** something that is built or made

con·struc·tion S3 W2 /kənˈstrʌkʃən/ *n*
1 **BUILDING STH** [U] the process of building things

such as houses, bridges, roads etc: [+of] *the construction of a new airport* | **under construction** (=being built) *The hotel is currently under construction.* | *a road construction project* | *construction workers*
2 **MAKING STH FROM MANY PARTS** [U] the process of making something using many parts: *Work out the exact design before you start construction.*
3 **WAY STH IS MADE** [U] the materials used to build or make something, or its design and structure: *The houses were partly timber in construction.* | *External doors should be of robust construction.*
4 **A BUILDING/STRUCTURE** [C] *formal* something that has been built: *a strange construction made of wood and glass*
5 **GRAMMAR** [C] the way in which words are put together in a sentence, phrase etc: *difficult grammatical constructions*
6 **IDEAS/KNOWLEDGE** [U] the process of forming something from knowledge or ideas: *the construction of sociological theory*
7 **put a construction on sth** *formal* to think that a statement has a particular meaning or that something was done for a particular reason: *The judge put an entirely different construction on his remarks.*
—**constructional** *adj*

con·struc·tive /kənˈstrʌktɪv/ *adj* useful and helpful, or likely to produce good results: *The meeting was very constructive.* | *We welcome any constructive criticism.*
—**constructively** *adv*

con·structive dis·mis·sal *n* [C,U] *BrE* when your employer changes your job or working conditions so you feel forced to leave your job

con·struc·tor /kənˈstrʌktə $ -ər/ *n* [C] a company or person that builds things

con·strue /kənˈstruː/ *v* [T usually in passive] to understand a remark or action in a particular way; → **misconstrue**: **construe sth as sth** *comments that could be construed as sexist* | *The term can be construed in two different ways.*

con·sul /ˈkɒnsəl $ ˈkɑːn-/ *n* [C] a government official who is sent to live in a foreign city in order to help people from his or her own country who are living or staying there; → **ambassador**: *the British Consul in Geneva* —**consular** /ˈkɒnsjʊlə $ ˈkɑːnsələr/ *adj*: *a consular official*

con·su·late /ˈkɒnsjʊlət $ ˈkɑːnsələt/ *n* [C] the building in which a consul lives and works; → **embassy**

con·sult S3 W3 /kənˈsʌlt/ *v*
1 [I,T] to ask for information or advice from someone because it is their job to know something: *If symptoms persist, consult a doctor without delay.* | **consult sb about sth** *An increasing number of people are consulting their accountants about the tax laws.* | [+with] *I need to consult with my lawyer.*
2 [I,T] to discuss something with someone so that you can make a decision together: *I can't believe you sold the car without consulting me!* | [+with] *The President consulted with European leaders before taking action.*
3 [T] to look for information in a book, map, list etc: *Have you consulted a dictionary?*

con·sul·tan·cy /kənˈsʌltənsi/ *n* plural **consultancies** **1** [C] a company that gives advice on a particular subject: *a management consultancy* | *a consultancy firm* **2** [U] advice that a company is paid to provide: *consultancy fees*

con·sul·tant S3 W3 /kənˈsʌltənt/ *n* [C]
1 someone whose job is to give advice on a particular subject: *a management consultant*
2 *BrE* a hospital doctor of a very high rank who has a lot of knowledge about a particular area of medicine

con·sul·ta·tion S3 W3 /ˌkɒnsəlˈteɪʃən $ ˌkɑːn-/ *n*
1 [C,U] a discussion in which people who are affected by or involved in something can give their opinions: [+with] *The decision was reached after consultation*

C

1 000, 2 000, 3 000, most frequent words in S poken and W ritten English

with parents and teachers. | [+**between**] *He's calling for urgent consultations between the government and the oil industry to resolve the problem.* | **in consultation with sb** *The plans were drawn up in consultation with engineers.* | **consultation process/exercise/period** *There will be a public consultation exercise to ask for people's views.* | **consultation paper/document**
2 [C] a meeting with a professional person, especially a doctor, for advice or treatment: *A follow-up consultation was arranged for two weeks' time.*
3 [U] the process of getting advice from a professional person: *Trained parenting experts are available for consultation by telephone.*
4 [U] the process of looking for information or help in a book: *Leaflets were regularly displayed for consultation by students.*

con·sul·ta·tive /kən'sʌltətɪv/ *adj* [usually before noun] providing advice and suggesting solutions to problems: *a consultative document*

con·sult·ing[1] /kən'sʌltɪŋ/ *n* [U] the service of providing advice to companies

consulting[2] *adj* [only before noun] providing advice to companies: *a major international consulting firm*

con'sulting ,room *n* [C] a room where a doctor sees patients

con·sum·a·ble /kən'sjuːməbəl $ -'suːm-/ *adj* consumable goods are intended to be used and then replaced

con·sum·a·bles /kən'sjuːməbəlz $ -'suːm-/ *n* [plural] goods that are intended to be used and then replaced: *consumables such as printer ribbons and disks*

con·sume /kən'sjuːm $ -'suːm/ *v* [T]　**1** to use time, energy, goods etc; → **consumption**: *Only 27% of the paper we consume is recycled.* | *A smaller vehicle will consume less fuel.*　**2** *formal* to eat or drink something; → **consumer, consumption**: *Alcohol may not be consumed on the premises.*　**3** *literary* if a feeling or idea consumes you, it affects you very strongly, so that you cannot think about anything else: *She was scared by the depression which threatened to consume her.* | **be consumed with sth** *He was consumed with guilt after the accident.*　**4** *formal* if fire consumes something, it destroys it completely → **TIME-CONSUMING**

con·sum·er [S2] [W2] /kən'sjuːmə $ -'suːmər/ *n* [C] someone who buys and uses products and services; → **consumption, producer**: *Consumers will soon be paying higher airfares.* | *It will offer a wider choice of goods for the consumer* (=consumers in general). | **Consumer demand** *led to higher imports of manufactured goods.* | **Consumer spending** *was down by 0.1% last month.* | *sources of consumer advice* (=advice for consumers)

con,sumer 'confidence *n* [U] the level of people's satisfaction with the economic situation, which is shown by how much money they spend: *Consumer confidence reached an all-time low in September.*

con,sumer 'durables *n* [plural] *BrE* large things such as cars, televisions, or furniture that you do not buy often

con'sumer ,goods *n* [plural] goods that people buy for their own use, rather than goods bought by businesses and organizations; → **capital goods**

con'sumer ,group *n* [C] an organization that makes sure that CONSUMERS are treated fairly and that products are safe

con·sum·er·ism /kən'sjuːmərɪzəm $ -'suː-/ *n* [U]　**1** the belief that it is good to buy and use a lot of goods and services – often used to show disapproval: *the growth of consumerism*　**2** actions to protect people from unfair prices, advertising that is not true etc —**consumerist** *adj*

con,sumer 'price ,index *n* [C] a list of the prices of products that shows how much prices have increased during a particular period of time

con'sumer so,ciety *n* [C] a society in which buying goods and services is considered to be very important

con·sum·ing /kən'sjuːmɪŋ $ -'suː-/ *adj* [only before noun] a consuming feeling is so strong that you think of little else: *a consuming hatred* | **consuming interest/ passion** (=a strong feeling of interest, or something you are extremely interested in) *During this period, politics became his consuming interest.*

-consuming /kənsjuːmɪŋ $ -suː-/ *suffix* using a lot of something such as time, energy, or space: *a time-consuming job* | *energy-consuming labour*

con·sum·mate[1] /kən'sʌmɪt, 'kɒnsəmɪt/ *adj* [only before noun] *formal*　**1** showing a lot of skill: *a great performance from a consummate actor* | *He won the race* **with consummate ease** (=very easily). | *De Gaulle conducted his strategy* **with consummate skill.**　**2** used to emphasize how bad someone or something is: *his consummate lack of tact* | *The man's a consummate liar.* —**consummately** *adv*

con·sum·mate[2] /'kɒnsəmeɪt $ 'kɑːn-/ *v* [T] *formal*　**1** to make a marriage or relationship complete by having sex　**2** to make something complete, especially an agreement

con·sum·ma·tion /ˌkɒnsə'meɪʃən $ ˌkɑːn-/ *n* [singular, U] *formal*　**1** when people make a marriage or relationship complete by having sex　**2** the point at which something is complete or perfect: *the consummation of his ambitions*

con·sump·tion [W3] /kən'sʌmpʃən/ *n* [U]
1 **AMOUNT USED** the amount of energy, oil, electricity etc that is used; → **consume**: *energy/fuel etc* **consumption** *dramatic rises in fuel consumption* | *Vigorous exercise increases oxygen consumption.*
2 **FOOD/DRINK a)** *formal* the act of eating or drinking; → **consume**: [+**of**] *The consumption of alcohol on the premises is forbidden.* | **fit/unfit for human consumption** (=safe or not safe to eat) *The meat was declared unfit for human consumption.* **b)** the amount of a substance that people eat, drink, smoke etc: *alcohol/tobacco/caffeine etc* **consumption** *The Government wants to reduce tobacco consumption by 40%.*
3 **BUYING** the act of buying and using products; → **consume, consumer**: *art intended for* **mass consumption** (=to be bought, seen etc by lots of people) | *China's austerity program has cut* **domestic consumption** (=when products are bought in the country where they were produced). | **conspicuous consumption** (=when people buy expensive products to prove they are rich)
4 **for general/public/private etc consumption** intended to be heard or read only by a particular group of people: *secret policy documents that are not for public consumption*
5 *old-fashioned* TUBERCULOSIS

con·sump·tive /kən'sʌmptɪv/ *n* [C] *old-fashioned* someone with TUBERCULOSIS —**consumptive** *adj*

cont. a written abbreviation of *continued*

con·tact[1] [S3] [W2] /'kɒntækt $ 'kɑːn-/ *n*
1 **COMMUNICATION** [U] communication with a person, organization, country etc: [+**with/between**] *There is very little contact between the two tribes.* | *Few people* **have** *daily* **contact with** *mentally disabled people.* | **be/get/stay/keep in contact (with sb)** *We stay in contact by email.* | *We'd like to* **make contact with** *other schools in the area.* | *The children* **lost contact** *with their families* (=they no longer see them because they do not know where to find them). | *the ship's failure to make* **radio contact** | *She* **put** *me* **in contact with** *an expert in the field* (=she gave me their name, telephone number etc). | **face-to-face/social/personal contact** (=talking to someone who is with you) *There is little* **personal contact** *with customers.* | *staff who have* **direct contact** *with the patient* | *The town is cut off from contact with the outside world.*
2 **TOUCH** [U] when two people or things touch each

other: [+with/between] *Children need physical contact with a caring adult.* | *The disease spreads by sexual contact between infected animals.* | **in contact with sth** *For a second, his hand was in contact with mine.* | *When water comes into contact with air, carbon dioxide is released.* | **on contact (with sth)** *The bomb exploded on contact* (=at the moment it touched something).
3 EXPERIENCE [U] when you meet someone or experience a particular kind of thing: *Everyone who came into contact with Di felt better for knowing her.* | *Pat's job brings her into contact with the problems people face when they retire.*
4 PERSON [C usually plural] a person you know who may be able to help or advise you: *He has a lot of contacts in the media.* | *a worldwide network of contacts* | **business/personal contacts**
5 contacts [plural] a situation in which you can communicate easily with a group, country etc: [+with/between] *We have good contacts with the local community.* | *He goes to great lengths to maintain these contacts.* | *the establishment of diplomatic contacts*
6 point of contact a) a place you go to or a person you meet when you ask an organization for help: **first/initial point of contact** *Primary health care teams are the first point of contact for users of the service.* **b)** a way in which two different things are related: *finding a point of contact between theory and practice* **c)** the part of something where another thing touches it: *The sting causes swelling at the point of contact.*
7 ELECTRICAL [C] an electrical part that completes a CIRCUIT when it touches another part
8 EYES [C] *informal* a contact lens → **eye contact** at EYE¹ (5)

contact² S3 W2 *v* [T] to write to or telephone someone: *Give the names of two people who can be contacted in an emergency.* | *Please do not hesitate to contact me if you have any queries.* —**contactable** *adj* [not before noun]: *A mobile phone makes you contactable wherever you are.*

contact³ *adj* [only before noun] **1 contact number/ address/details** a telephone number or address where someone can be found if necessary: *If you are baby-sitting, make sure you have a contact number for the parents.* **2 contact explosives** or chemicals become active when they touch something: *contact poisons*

contact ,lens *n* [C] a small round piece of plastic that you put on your eye to help you see clearly

contact ,sport *n* [C] a sport such as AMERICAN FOOTBALL, RUGBY etc in which players have physical contact with each other

con·ta·gion /kən'teɪdʒən/ *n* **1** [U] *technical* a situation in which a disease is spread by people touching each other: *The danger of contagion is very small.* **2** [C] *technical* a disease that can be passed from person to person by touch **3** [singular] *formal* a feeling or attitude that spreads quickly between people or places: *a contagion of fear that spread from city to city*

con·ta·gious /kən'teɪdʒəs/ *adj* **1** a disease that is contagious can be passed from person to person by touch **2** a person who is contagious has a disease that can be passed to another person by touch: *The patient is still highly contagious.* **3** if a feeling, attitude, or action is contagious, other people are quickly affected by it and begin to have it or do it: *her contagious enthusiasm* —**contagiousness** *n* [U]

con·tain S2 W1 /kən'teɪn/ *v* [T]
1 CONTAINER/PLACE if something such as a bag, box, or place contains something, that thing is inside it: *The thieves stole a purse containing banknotes.* | *The museum contains a number of original artworks.*
2 WRITING/SPEECH if a document, book, speech etc contains something, that thing is included in it: *The letter contained information about Boulestin's legal affairs.* | **be contained in/within sth** *The proposed changes are contained in a policy statement.*
3 SUBSTANCE if a substance contains something, that thing is part of it: *This product may contain nuts.*

4 CONTROL FEELINGS to control strong feelings of anger, excitement etc: *Jane couldn't contain her amusement any longer.* | **contain yourself** *He was so excited he could hardly contain himself.*
5 STOP STH to stop something from spreading or escaping: *Doctors are struggling to contain the epidemic.* | *measures aimed at containing political opposition* → SELF-CONTAINED
6 MATHS *technical* to surround an area or an angle: *How big is the angle contained by these two sides?*

con·tain·er /kən'teɪnə $ -ər/ *n* [C] **1** something such as a box or bowl that you use to keep things in: *ice cream in plastic containers* **2** a very large metal box in which goods are packed to make it easy to lift or move them onto a ship or vehicle: *a container ship*

con·tain·ment /kən'teɪnmənt/ *n* [U] *formal* the act of keeping something under control, stopping it becoming more powerful etc: *containment of public expenditure* | *political containment of member states*

con·tam·i·nant /kən'tæmɪnənt/ *n* [C] *formal* a substance that makes something dirty: *environmental contaminants*

con·tam·i·nate /kən'tæmɪneɪt/ *v* [T] **1** to make a place or substance dirty or harmful by putting something such as chemicals or poison in it: *Drinking water supplies are believed to have been contaminated.* **2** to influence something in a way that has a bad effect: *He claims the poster ads have 'contaminated Berlin's streets'.* —**contamination** /kən,tæmɪ'neɪʃən/ *n* [U]: *radioactive contamination*

con·tam·i·nat·ed /kən'tæmɪneɪtɪd/ *adj* water, food etc that is contaminated has had a harmful substance added to it: **contaminated food/blood/water supplies** etc *Several outbreaks of infection have been traced to contaminated food.*

contd. a written abbreviation of **continued**

con·tem·plate /'kɒntəmpleɪt $ 'kɑːn-/ *v* **1** [T] to think about something that you might do in the future; ◨ **consider**: *He had even contemplated suicide.* | **contemplate doing sth** *Did you ever contemplate resigning?* **2** [I] to accept the possibility that something is true: **too dreadful/horrifying etc to contemplate** *The thought that she might be dead was too terrible to contemplate.* **3** [I,T] to think about something seriously for a period of time; ◨ **consider**: *Jack went on vacation to contemplate his future.* | **contemplate what/whether/how etc** *She sat down and contemplated what she had done.* | **contemplate your navel** (=think so much about your own life that you do not notice other important things – used humorously) **4** [T] to look at someone or something for a period of time in a way that shows you are thinking: *He contemplated her with a faint smile.*

con·tem·pla·tion /,kɒntəm'pleɪʃən $,kɑːn-/ *n* [U] quiet, serious thinking about something: *The monks spend an hour in contemplation each morning.*

con·tem·pla·tive¹ /kən'templətɪv, 'kɒntəmpleɪtɪv $ kən-, 'kɑːntem-/ *adj* spending a lot of time thinking seriously and quietly: *a contemplative mood* —**contemplatively** *adv*

contemplative² *n* [C] *formal* someone who spends their life thinking deeply about religious matters

con·tem·po·ra·ne·ous /kən,tempə'reɪniəs/ *adj* *formal* happening or done in the same period of time; ◨ **contemporary**: [+with] *Built in the 13th century, the chapels are contemporaneous with many of the great Gothic cathedrals.* —**contemporaneously** *adv* —**contemporaneity** /kən,tempərə'niːɪti/ *n* [U]

con·tem·po·ra·ry¹ W2 /kən'tempərəri, -pəri $ -pəreri/ *adj*
1 belonging to the present time; ◨ **modern**: **contemporary music/art/dance etc** *an exhibition of contemporary Japanese prints* | *life in contemporary Britain*
2 happening or done in the same period of time:

[+**with**] *The wall hangings are thought to be roughly contemporary with the tiled floors.*

contemporary² *n plural* **contemporaries** [C] someone who lived or was in a particular place at the same time as someone else: **sb's contemporaries** *Oswald was much admired by his contemporaries at the Academy.*

con·tempt /kən'tempt/ *n* [U] **1** a feeling that someone or something is not important and deserves no respect: [+**for**] *The* **contempt** *he felt for his fellow students was obvious.* | **utter/deep contempt** *The report shows* **utter contempt** *for women's judgement.* | **open/ undisguised contempt** *She looked at him with undisguised contempt.* | *The public is* **treated with contempt** *by broadcasters.* | *How could she have loved a man who so clearly* **held** *her* **in contempt?** | **beneath contempt** *That sort of behaviour is simply beneath contempt* (=does not deserve respect or attention). **2** *law* disobedience or disrespect towards a court of law: *He was jailed for 7 days for* **contempt of court.** | **in contempt of sth** *He was found in contempt of the order.* **3** complete lack of fear about something: [+**for**] *his contempt for danger*

con·temp·ti·ble /kən'temptⱼbəl/ *adj literary* not deserving any respect at all; ▤ **despicable**: *They were portrayed as contemptible cowards.*

con·temp·tu·ous /kən'temptʃuəs/ *adj* showing that you think someone or something deserves no respect: *Benedict threw her a contemptuous glance.* | [+**of**] *He was* **openly contemptuous** *of his elder brother.* —**contemptuously** *adv*

con·tend /kən'tend/ *v* **1** [I] to compete against someone in order to gain something: [+**for**] *Three armed groups are contending for power.* | *Inevitably, fights break out between the members of contending groups.* **2** [T] to argue or state that something is true:

contend (that) *Some astronomers contend that the universe may be younger than previously thought.*

contend with sth *phr v* to have to deal with something difficult or unpleasant: *The rescue team also had bad weather conditions* **to contend with**.

con·tend·er /kən'tendə $ -ər/ *n* [C] someone or something that is in competition with other people or things: [+**for**] *a contender for the Democratic nomination* | **serious/strong/leading etc contender** *Her new album has to be a strong contender for the Album of the Year award.*

con·tent¹ [S2] [W2] /'kɒntent $ 'kɑːn-/ *n*
1 contents [plural] **a)** the things that are inside a box, bag, room etc: [+**of**] *The customs official rummaged through the contents of his briefcase.* | *Most of the gallery's contents were damaged in the fire.* | **contents insurance** (=insurance for things such as furniture that you have in your house) **b)** the things that are written in a letter, book etc: [+**of**] *She kept the contents of the letter a secret.* | *The program automatically creates a* **table of contents** (=a list at the beginning of a document that shows the different parts into which it is divided). | *He cast his eye down the* **contents page**.
2 [singular] the amount of a substance that is contained in something, especially food or drink: **fat/protein/ alcohol etc content** *the fat content of cheese* | *water with a low salt content*
3 [singular, U] the ideas, facts, or opinions that are contained in a speech, piece of writing, film, programme etc: *The content of the media course includes scripting, editing and camera work.*
4 [singular, U] the information contained in a website considered separately from the software that makes the website work: *The graphics are brilliant. It's just a shame the content is so poor.*

con·tent² [W3] /kən'tent/ *adj* [not before noun]
1 happy and satisfied: *Andy was a good husband, and Nicky was clearly very content.* | [+**with**] *We'll be content*

container

a packet of cheese

a tube of toothpaste

a bag of crisps

a box of matches

a sachet of tomato sauce

a tub of margarine

a carton of milk

a jar of pickles

an oil drum

a tin of beans

a can of cola

a beer barrel

a pot of honey

a tin of tuna

with a respectable result in tomorrow's match.

2 content (for sb) to do sth willing to do or accept something, rather than doing more: *She sat quietly, content to watch him working.* | *He seemed **quite content** to let Steve do the talking.* | *Dr Belson had been **more than content** for them to deal with any difficulties.*

3 not content with sth used to emphasize that someone wants or does more than something: *Not content with her new car, Selina now wants a bike for trips into the city centre.*

content³ *n* [U] **1** *literary* a feeling of quiet happiness and satisfaction **2 do sth to your heart's content** to do something as much as you want: *She took refuge in the library, where she could read to her heart's content.*

content⁴ *v* [T] **1 content yourself with (doing) sth** to do or have something that is not what you really wanted, but is still satisfactory: *Mr Lal has been asking for more responsibility, but has **had to content** himself **with** a minor managerial post.* **2** *formal* to make someone feel happy and satisfied: *I was no longer satisfied with the life that had hitherto contented me.*

con·tent·ed /kənˈtentɪd/ *adj* happy and satisfied because your life is good; ⊟ **discontented**: *I felt warm, cosy and contented.* | *They lapsed into a contented silence* —**contentedly** *adv*: *He smiled contentedly.*

con·ten·tion /kənˈtenʃən/ *n* **1** [C] *formal* a strong opinion that someone expresses: **sb's contention that** *Her main contention is that doctors should do more to encourage healthy eating.* **2** [U] *formal* argument and disagreement between people: **source/area/point of contention** *The issue of subsidies is a source of contention in Europe.*; → **bone of contention** at BONE¹ (5) **3 in contention** having a chance of winning something: *A goal from Hodge **kept** England **in contention**.* **4 out of contention** no longer having a chance of winning something: *Injury has **put** him **out of contention** for the title.*

con·ten·tious /kənˈtenʃəs/ *adj* **1** causing a lot of argument and disagreement between people: **contentious issue/area/subject etc** *Animal welfare did not become a contentious issue until the late 1970s.* **2** someone who is contentious often argues with people —**contentiously** *adv*

con·tent·ment /kənˈtentmənt/ *n* [U] the state of being happy and satisfied; ⊟ **discontent**: *He gave a **sigh of contentment**, and fell asleep.* | *a feeling of **deep contentment***

con·test¹ /ˈkɒntest $ ˈkɑːn-/ *n* [C]
1 a competition or a situation in which two or more people or groups are competing with each other

hold a contest
enter a contest (=start taking part in one)
win/lose a contest
beauty contest (=a competition to find the most beautiful person)
talent contest (=a competition to find the best performer)
popularity contest (=a situation in which people decide which person they like the most)
unequal contest *BrE* (=when one person has a much greater chance of winning)
fair contest (=when everyone has the same chance of winning)
close contest (=when someone wins by only a very small amount)
leadership contest (=when two politicians compete to become the leader of their party)

[**+for**] *the bitter contest for the Republican presidential nomination* | *Stone decided to **hold a contest** to see who could write the best song.* | *I only **entered** the **contest** for fun.* | *It is clear that the election will be a **close contest**.* | [**+between/against**] *the 1960 contest between Kennedy and Nixon* | *the 1975 Liberal **leadership contest***

2 no contest *informal* **a)** *spoken* used to say that someone or something is the best of its kind: *I think*

---

you're the best rider here, no contest. **b)** if a victory is no contest, it is very easy to achieve
3 plead no contest *law* to state that you will not offer a defence in a court of law for something wrong you have done

con·test² /kənˈtest/ *v* [T] *formal* **1** to say formally that you do not accept something or do not agree with it: *His brothers are contesting the will.* **2** to compete for something or to try to win it: *His wife is contesting a seat on the council.*

con·tes·tant /kənˈtestənt/ *n* [C] someone who competes in a contest

con·text [S3] [W1] /ˈkɒntekst $ ˈkɑːn-/ *n* [C,U]
1 the situation, events, or information that are related to something and that help you to understand it: **political/social/historical etc context** *the political context of the election* | **place/put/see etc sth in context** *To appreciate what these changes will mean, it is necessary to **look at** them **in context**.* | **in the context of sth** *These incidents are best understood in the **broader context** of developments in rural society.*
2 the words that come just before and after a word or sentence and that help you understand its meaning: *The meaning of 'mad' depends on its context.*
3 take/quote sth out of context to repeat part of what someone has said or written without describing the situation in which it was said, so that it means something quite different: *His comments, taken out of context, seem harsh.*

con·tex·tu·al /kənˈtekstʃuəl/ *adj* [usually before noun] relating to a particular context: **contextual information/factors etc** —**contextually** *adv*

con·tex·tu·al·ize also **-ise** *BrE* /kənˈtekstʃuəlaɪz/ *v* [T] *formal* to consider something together with the situation, events, or information related to it, rather than alone: *The essays seek to contextualise Kristeva's writings.*

con·tig·u·ous /kənˈtɪɡjuəs/ *adj formal* next to something, or next to each other: *America's 48 contiguous states* —**contiguously** *adv* —**contiguity** /ˌkɒntɪˈɡjuːɪti $ ˌkɑːn-/ *n* [U]

con·ti·nence /ˈkɒntɪnəns $ ˈkɑːn-/ *n* [U] **1** *medical* the ability to control your BOWELS and BLADDER; ⊟ **incontinence 2** *old-fashioned* the ability to control your sexual desires

con·ti·nent¹ /ˈkɒntɪnənt $ ˈkɑːn-/ *n* [C] **1** a large mass of land surrounded by sea: *the continents of Asia and Africa* **2 the Continent** *BrE old-fashioned* Western Europe, not including Britain

continent² *adj* **1** *medical* able to control your BOWELS and BLADDER; ⊟ **incontinent 2** *old-fashioned* able to control your sexual desires

con·ti·nen·tal /ˌkɒntɪˈnentl◂ $ ˌkɑːn-/ *adj* **1 a) the continental United States** all the states of the US except Alaska and Hawaii **b) continental Europe/Asia etc** all the countries of Europe, Asia etc that are not on islands **2** relating to a large mass of land: *the warming-up of continental interiors* **3** typical of the warmer countries in Western Europe: *a continental-style café* **4** *BrE old-fashioned* belonging to or in the European continent, not including Britain: *continental holidays*

continental 'breakfast *n* [C] a breakfast consisting of coffee and bread with butter and JAM; → **English breakfast**

continental 'drift *n* [U] the very slow movement of the CONTINENTS across the Earth's surface

continental 'quilt *n* [C] *BrE* a DUVET

continental 'shelf *n plural* **continental shelves** [C] *technical* the edge of a CONTINENT where it slopes down steeply to the bottom of the ocean

con·tin·gen·cy /kənˈtɪndʒənsi/ *n plural* **contingencies** [C] **1** an event or situation that might happen in the future, especially one that could cause problems: *a contingency plan* | *Add up your outgoings, putting on a bit more for contingencies.* **2 contingency fee** an amount of money that a lawyer in the US will be paid only if the person they are advising wins in court

con·tin·gent[1] /kənˈtɪndʒənt/ *adj formal* depending on something that may happen in the future: [+on/upon] *Further investment is contingent upon the company's profit performance.*

contingent[2] *n* [C also + plural verb *BrE*] **1** a group of people who all have something in common, such as their nationality, beliefs etc, and who are part of a larger group: *Has the Scottish contingent arrived yet?* **2** a group of soldiers sent to help a larger group: [+of] *A large contingent of troops was dispatched.*

con·tin·u·al /kənˈtɪnjuəl/ *adj* [only before noun] **1** continuing for a long time without stopping: *five weeks of continual rain* | *the Japanese business philosophy of continual improvement* **2** repeated many times, often in a way that is harmful or annoying: *She has endured house arrest and continual harassment by the police.* —**continually** *adv*: *We are continually reassessing the situation.*

> **WORD CHOICE: continual, continuous**
> **continual** and **continuous** are both used to describe things that continue without stopping: *continual rain* | *a continuous fall in unemployment since 1998*
> Use **continuous** to describe things that go on without a break: *I had six continuous hours of meetings.* | *a continuous line of trees*
> Use **continual** to describe things which happen repeatedly: *his continual attempts to intervene*
> Use **continual** when the thing that is happening is annoying or bad: *She was fed up with the continual arguments.*

con·tin·u·ance /kənˈtɪnjuəns/ *n* [singular, U] *formal* the state of continuing for a long period of time: *the continuance in power of the Nationalist party*

con·tin·u·a·tion /kənˌtɪnjuˈeɪʃən/ *n* **1** [C] something that continues or follows something else that has happened before, without a stop or change: [+of] *The present economic policy is a continuation of the earlier one.* **2** [U] the continuation of something is the fact that it continues to exist or happen: [+of] *measures to ensure the continuation of food supplies* **3** [C] something that joins something else as if it were part of it: [+of] *The Baltic Sea is a continuation of the North Sea.*

continu·ation ˌschool *n* [C] *AmE* a school for children who cannot study at high school because they have social problems

con·tin·ue [S1] [W1] /kənˈtɪnjuː/ *v*
1 [I,T] to not stop happening, existing, or doing something; → **continuous, continual, discontinue**: *continue to do sth Sheila continued to work after she had her baby.* | *He will be continuing his education in the US.* | *I felt too sick to continue.* | **continue unabated/apace/unchecked** (=continue at the same high speed or level) *The flood of refugees continued unabated.* | [+with] *He was permitted to continue with his work while in prison.* | [+for] *The strike continued for another four weeks.* | **continue doing sth** *Most elderly people want to continue living at home for as long as they can.*
2 [I,T] to start again, or start doing something again, after an interruption; ◨ **resume**: *After a brief ceasefire, fighting continued.* | *Rescue teams will continue the search tomorrow.* | **continue doing sth** *He picked up his book and continued reading.*
3 [I] to go further in the same direction: [+down/along/into etc] *We continued along the road for some time.* | *The road continues northwards to the border.*
4 [I] to stay in the same job, situation etc: [+as] *Miss Silva will continue as publishing director.*
5 [I,T] to say more after an interruption: *'And so', he continued, 'we will try harder next time.'*

6 to be continued used at the end of part of a story, a television show etc to tell people that the story has not finished yet

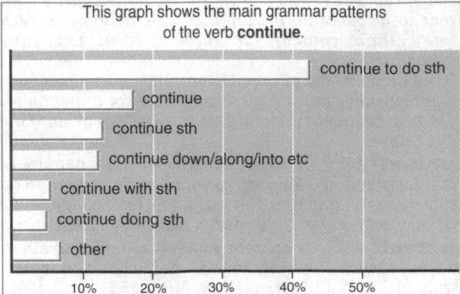

This graph shows the main grammar patterns of the verb **continue**.

con·tin·ued /kənˈtɪnjuːd/ *adj* [only before noun] continuing to happen or exist for a long time, or happening many times: *threats to the continued existence of the species* | *continued press speculation*

con·tinuing eduˈcation *n* [U] training and education for adults that takes place outside the formal education system, usually in classes in the evenings

con·ti·nu·i·ty /ˌkɒntɪˈnjuːɪti $ ˌkɑːntɪˈnuː-/ *n* [U] **1** the state of continuing for a period of time without problems, interruptions, or changes: *We should ensure continuity of care between hospital and home.* **2** *technical* the organization of a film or television programme to make it seem that the action happens without pauses or interruptions

conti·ˈnuity anˌnouncer *n* [C] someone on the radio or television who says what programme is being broadcast next, or gives information about future programmes

con·tin·u·o /kənˈtɪnjuːəʊ $ -oʊ/ *n plural* **continuos** [C] *technical* a musical part consisting of a line of low notes with figures showing the higher notes that are played with them

con·tin·u·ous [S2] [W3] /kənˈtɪnjuəs/ *adj*
1 continuing to happen or exist without stopping; → **continue**: *continuous economic growth* | *a continuous flow of information*
2 something such as a line that is continuous does not have any spaces or holes in it
3 continuous assessment *BrE* a way of judging a student's work by looking at what they have achieved during the year rather than testing them in an examination
4 *technical* the continuous form of a verb shows that an action is continuing. In English, this is formed by the verb 'be', followed by a PRESENT PARTICIPLE, as in 'I was waiting for the bus.' —**continuously** *adv*: *UMNO had ruled Malaysia continuously since independence.*

con·tin·u·um /kənˈtɪnjuəm/ *n plural* **continuums** *or* **continua** /-njuə/ [C] *formal* a scale of related things on which each one is only slightly different from the one before: *The Creole language is really various dialects arranged on a continuum.* | *All the organisms in an ecosystem are part of an evolutionary continuum.*

con·tort /kənˈtɔːt $ -ɔːrt/ *v* [I,T] if you contort something, or if it contorts, it twists out of its normal shape and looks strange or unattractive: [+with/in] *His face was contorted with rage.* | *His body contorted in agony*

con·tor·tion /kənˈtɔːʃən $ -ɔːr-/ *n* **1** [C] a twisted position or movement that looks surprising or strange *I could not force my body into the contortions required by classical ballet.* | *facial contortions* **2** [U] when something is twisted so that it does not have its normal shape: *involuntary muscle contortion* **3** [C] something difficult you have to do in order to achieve something *He went through a series of amazing contortions to get Karen a work permit.*

con·tor·tion·ist /kənˈtɔːʃənˌɪst $ -ɔːr-/ *n* [C] someone who twists their body into strange positions in order to entertain people

con·tour /'kɒntʊə $ 'kɑːntʊr/ n [C] **1** the shape of the outer edges of something such as an area of land or someone's body: *the contours of the hills | the contours of her face* **2** also **contour line** a line on a map that shows points that are of equal heights above sea level

con·toured /'kɒntʊəd $ 'kɑːntʊrd/ adj **1** a contoured surface or object has been made with curves in it: *contoured seats* **2** contoured land has some parts higher than others

contra- /kɒntrə $ kɑːn-/ prefix acting against something, or opposite to something: *contraceptive devices* (=against conception)

con·tra·band /'kɒntrəbænd $ 'kɑːn-/ n [U] goods that are brought into a country illegally, especially to avoid tax: *a cargo of contraband* —**contraband** adj: *contraband cigarettes*

con·tra·bass /ˌkɒntrə'beɪs $ ˌkɑːn-/ n [C] a DOUBLE BASS

con·tra·cep·tion /ˌkɒntrə'sepʃən $ ˌkɑːn-/ n [U] the practice of preventing a woman from becoming PREGNANT when she has sex, or the methods for doing this; ▣ **birth control**: *The pill is a popular method of contraception.*

con·tra·cep·tive /ˌkɒntrə'septɪv‹ $ ˌkɑːn-/ n [C] a drug, object, or method used to prevent a woman from becoming PREGNANT when she has sex: *free contraceptives* —**contraceptive** adj [only before noun]: *a contraceptive device*

con·tract¹ [S2] [W1] /'kɒntrækt $ 'kɑːn-/ n [C]
1 an official agreement between two or more people, stating what each will do

> enter into/make a contract (with sb)
> sign a contract (with sb)
> agree a contract
> a contract to do sth
> end/terminate a contract (with sb)
> break a contract (with sb) (=do something that is not allowed by your contract)
> win/be awarded a contract (=gain a contract to do work for someone)
> renew sb's contract (=make a new contract with someone)
> fulfil BrE /fulfill AmE a contract (=do what you have agreed to do)
> on a contract/under contract (=working for someone with whom you have a contract)
> the terms of a contract
> one-/two-/ten- etc year contract
> be in breach of a contract (=having done something not allowed by your contract)
>
> *Read the contract carefully before you sign it. | [+with/between] Tyler has agreed a seven-year contract with a Hollywood studio. | a three-year contract to provide pay telephones at local restaurants | His contract is to be terminated by mutual consent. | What are the legal consequences of breaking a contract? | The contract was awarded to builders John Worman Ltd. | Mr Venables informed me the club would not be renewing my contract. | The firm operates schools under contract to state education authorities. | Employees who refuse to relocate are in breach of contract.*

2 subject to contract if an agreement is subject to contract, it has not yet been agreed formally by a contract
3 *informal* an agreement to kill a person for money: *They put a contract out on him and he's in hiding.*

con·tract² /kən'trækt/ v **1** [I] to become smaller or narrower; ▣ **expand**: *Metal contracts as it cools. | The economy has contracted by 2.5%.* **2** [T] *formal* to get an illness: *Two-thirds of the adult population there has contracted AIDS.* **3** [I,T] to sign a contract in which you agree formally that you will do something or someone will do something for you: *contract (sb) to do sth They are contracted to work 35 hours a week. | the company that had been contracted to build the models | contract (with) sb for sth Doctors control their budgets and contract with hospitals for services. | contract a*

marriage/alliance etc (=agree to marry someone, form a relationship with them etc) *Most of the marriages were contracted when the brides were very young.*

contract³ /'kɒntrækt $ 'kɑːn-/
contract in phr v BrE **1 contract sb/sth ⇔ in** to arrange for a person or company outside your own organization to come in and do a particular job: *We contract in cleaning services.* **2** *formal* to agree officially to take part in something: *The rules require all members to contract in.*
contract out phr v **1 contract sth ⇔ out** to arrange to have a job done by a person or company outside your own organization: [+to] *The company has contracted the catering out to an outside firm.* **2** BrE to agree officially not to take part in something such as a PENSION PLAN

contract 'bridge n [U] a form of the card game BRIDGE, in which one of the two pairs says how many TRICKS they will try to win

con·trac·tion /kən'trækʃən/ n **1** [C] *medical* a very strong and painful movement of a muscle, especially the muscles around the WOMB during birth **2** [U] the process of becoming smaller or narrower: *the contraction of metal as it cools* **3** [C] a shorter form of a word or words: *'Haven't' is a contraction of 'have not'.*

con·trac·tor /kən'træktə $ 'kɑːntræktər/ n [C] a person or company that agrees to do work or provide goods for another company: *a roofing contractor*

con·trac·tu·al /kən'træktʃuəl/ adj [only before noun] agreed in a contract: *Tutors have a contractual obligation to research and publish.* —**contractually** adv

con·tra·dict /ˌkɒntrə'dɪkt $ ˌkɑːn-/ v **1** [I,T] to disagree with something, especially by saying that the opposite is true: *Deborah opened her mouth to contradict, but closed it again. | Dad just can't bear to be contradicted. | The article flatly contradicts their claims.* **2** [T] if one statement, story etc contradicts another, the facts in it are different so that both statements cannot be true: *The witness statements contradict each other and the facts remain unclear.* **3 contradict yourself** to say something that is the opposite of what you said before: *Within five minutes he had contradicted himself twice.*

con·tra·dic·tion /ˌkɒntrə'dɪkʃən $ ˌkɑːn-/ n **1** [C] a difference between two statements, beliefs, or ideas about something that means they cannot both be true: *apparent contradictions in the defendant's testimony |* [+between] *a contradiction between the government's ideas and its actual policy* **2** [U] the act of saying that someone else's opinion, statement etc is wrong or not true: *You can say what you like without fear of contradiction.* **3 a contradiction in terms** a combination of words that seem to be the opposite of each other, with the result that the phrase has no clear meaning: *'Permanent revolution' is a contradiction in terms.* **4** in **(direct) contradiction to sth** in a way that is opposite to a belief or statement: *Your behaviour is in direct contradiction to the principles you claim to have.*

con·tra·dic·to·ry /ˌkɒntrə'dɪktəri‹ $ ˌkɑːn-/ adj two statements, beliefs etc that are contradictory are different and therefore cannot both be true or correct: **contradictory messages/statements/demands etc** *The public is being fed contradictory messages about the economy.*

con·tra·dis·tinc·tion /ˌkɒntrədɪ'stɪŋkʃən $ ˌkɑːn-/ n [C] **in contradistinction to sth** *formal* in contrast to or compared to something: *plants in contradistinction to animals*

con·tra·flow /'kɒntrəfləʊ $ 'kɑːntrəfloʊ/ n [C,U] BrE a temporary arrangement on a road that is being repaired, that makes traffic travelling in both directions use only one side of the road: *A contraflow is in operation between Junctions 6 and 12.*

con·trail /'kɒntreɪl $ 'kɑːn-/ n [C] a line of white steam made in the sky by a plane

con·tra·in·di·ca·tion /ˌkɒntrəˌɪndɪˈkeɪʃən $ ˌkɑːn-/ n [C] *medical* a medical reason for not giving someone a particular medicine or drug —**contraindicate** /ˌkɒntrəˈɪndɪkeɪt $ ˌkɑːn-/ v [T usually passive]: *In this situation, steroids are contraindicated.*

con·tral·to /kənˈtræltəʊ $ -toʊ/ n plural **contraltos** **1** [C] the lowest female singing voice, or a woman with a voice like this **2** [singular] the part of a musical work that is written for a contralto voice

con·trap·tion /kənˈtræpʃən/ n [C] a piece of equipment or machinery that looks funny, strange, and unlikely to work well: *a bizarre contraption*

con·tra·ri·wise /kənˈtreəriwaɪz, ˈkɒntrəriwaɪz $ ˈkɑːntreri-/ adv *BrE* in the opposite way or direction; ▣ **conversely**

con·tra·ry¹ /ˈkɒntrəri $ ˈkɑːntreri/ n **1 on the contrary/quite the contrary** used to add to a negative statement, to disagree with a negative statement by someone else, or to answer no to a question: *It wasn't a good thing; on the contrary it was a huge mistake.* | *'I suppose your wife doesn't understand you.' 'On the contrary, she understands me very well.'* | *'Are they happy?' 'No, no, quite the contrary.'* **2 evidence/statements etc to the contrary** something showing or saying the opposite: *Unless there is evidence to the contrary, we ought to believe them.* | *He continued to drink despite advice to the contrary.* **3 the contrary** *formal* the opposite of what has been said or suggested

contrary² adj **1** contrary ideas, opinions, or actions are completely different and opposed to each other: *Two contrary views emerged.* | *The men shouted contrary orders.* | [+to] *The government's actions are contrary to the public interest.* **2 contrary to popular belief/opinion** used to say that something is true even though people believe the opposite: *Contrary to popular belief, a desert can be very cold.* **3** *formal* a contrary wind is not blowing in the direction you want to sail

con·tra·ry³ /kənˈtreəri $ ˈkɑːntreri, kənˈtreri/ adj someone who is contrary deliberately does different things from other people: *Evans was his usual contrary self.* —**contrariness** n [U]

con·trast¹ W2 /ˈkɒntraːst $ ˈkɑːntræst/ n **1** [C,U] a difference between people, ideas, situations, things etc that are being compared: *While there are similarities in the two cultures, there are also great contrasts.* | [+between] *the economic and social contrasts between the poor and the rich* | [+with] *The marble is smooth and polished, making a strong contrast with the worn stonework around it.* | **by contrast (to/with)** *The birth rate for older women has declined, but, by contrast, births to teenage mothers have increased.* | **in contrast (to/with)** *The stock lost 60 cents a share, in contrast to last year, when it gained 21 cents.* | **(in) stark/marked/sharp etc contrast to sth** *The winter heatwave in California is a stark contrast to the below-freezing temperatures on the East Coast.* | *The spirited mood on Friday was in sharp contrast to the tense atmosphere last week.* | *The approach to learning at this school stands in marked contrast to the traditional methods used at other schools nearby.* **2** [C] something that is very different from something else: *The wine used in the sauce is quite sweet, so add dried thyme as a contrast.* | [+to] *The red stems of this bush provide a contrast to the drab brown of the rest of the winter garden.* **3** [U] the degree of difference between the light and dark parts of a television picture, X-RAY, PHOTOCOPY etc: *This button adjusts the contrast.* | *The chemical heightens contrast between different kinds of tissue in the breast.* **4** [U] the differences in colour, or between light and dark, that an artist uses in paintings or photographs to make a particular effect: *The artist has used contrast marvelously in his paintings.*

con·trast² /kənˈtraːst $ -ˈtræst/ v **1** [I] if two things contrast, the difference between them is very easy to see and is sometimes surprising: [+with] *The snow was icy and white, contrasting with the brilliant blue sky.* | **contrast sharply/strikingly with sth** (=be extremely different from something) *These results contrast sharply with other medical tests carried out in Australia.* **2** [T] to compare two things, ideas, people etc to show how different they are from each other: **contrast sth with sth** *In another passage, Melville again contrasts the land with the sea.* | *an essay* **comparing and contrasting** (=showing how two things are similar and different) *Verdi and Wagner and their operas*

con·tras·ting /kənˈtraːstɪŋ $ -ˈtræs-/ adj two or more things that are contrasting are different from each other, especially in a way that is interesting or attractive: *a blue shirt with a contrasting collar*

con·tra·vene /ˌkɒntrəˈviːn $ ˌkɑːn-/ v [T] *formal* to do something that is not allowed according to a law or rule; ▣ **violate**: *Some portions of the bill may contravene state law.*

con·tra·ven·tion /ˌkɒntrəˈvenʃən $ ˌkɑːn-/ n [C,U] when someone does something that is not allowed by a law or rule; ▣ **violation**: [+of] *Sending the troops was a contravention of the treaty.* | **in contravention of sth** (=in a way not allowed by a rule or law) *Several of the girls were wearing trousers, in contravention of the school rules on dress.*

con·tre·temps /ˈkɒntrətɒŋ $ ˈkɑːntrətaːn/ n plural **contretemps** [C] an argument or disagreement – often used humorously

con·trib·ute S2 W2 /kənˈtrɪbjuːt/ v **1** [I,T] to give money, help, ideas etc to something that a lot of other people are also involved in: [+to/towards] *City employees cannot contribute to political campaigns.* | **contribute sth to/towards sth** *The volunteers contribute their own time to the project.* **2** [I] to help to make something happen: *Stress is a* **contributing factor** *in many illnesses.* | [+to] *Alcohol contributes to 100,000 deaths a year in the US.* | **contribute substantially/significantly/greatly etc to sth** *Enya's success has contributed substantially to the current interest in Celtic music.* **3** [I,T] to write articles, stories, poems etc for a newspaper or magazine; → **contributor**: [+to] *one of several authors contributing to the book*

con·tri·bu·tion S2 W2 /ˌkɒntrɪˈbjuːʃən $ ˌkɑːn-/ n **1** [C] something that you give or do in order to help something be successful: [+to/towards] *Einstein was awarded the Nobel Prize for his contribution to Quantum Theory.* | *The school sees its job as preparing students to* **make a contribution** *to society.* | **significant/substantial/valuable etc contribution** *Wolko made outstanding contributions to children's medicine.* **2** [C] an amount of money that you give in order to help pay for something: *a campaign contribution* | [+of] *A contribution of £25 will buy 15 books.* | [+to/towards] *Contributions to charities are tax deductible.* | *You can* **make** *annual* **contributions** *of up to $1000 in education savings accounts.* **3** [C] a regular payment that you make to your employer or to the government to pay for things that you will receive when you are no longer working, for example health care, a PENSION etc: *income tax and national insurance contributions* | [+to] *Have you been* **making** *regular* **contributions** *to a pension plan?* **4** [C] a piece of writing, a song, a speech etc that forms part of a larger work such as a newspaper, book, broadcast, recording etc: [+from] *a magazine with contributions from well-known travel writers* | *a Christmas album featuring contributions from Carly Simon, Amy Grant, and others* **5** [U] when you give money, time, help etc: *All the money has been raised by voluntary contribution.*

con·trib·u·tor /kənˈtrɪbjᵿtə $ -ər/ n [C] **1** someone who gives money, help, ideas etc to something that a lot of other people are also involved in: *campaign contributors* | [+to] *Dr Win was a major contributor to the research.* **2** someone who writes a story, song, speech etc that forms part of a larger work such as a newspaper, book, broadcast, recording etc: [+**to**] *a regular contributor to Time magazine* **3** *formal* someone or something that helps to cause something to happen: [+**to**] *Cars are still one of the principal contributors to air pollution.*

con·trib·u·to·ry /kənˈtrɪbjᵘtəri $ -tɔːri/ *adj* **1** [only before noun] being one of the causes of a particular result: *Smoking is a* **contributory factor** *in lung cancer.* **2** a contributory PENSION or insurance plan is one that is paid for by the workers as well as by the company they work for; ◱ **noncontributory**

con·tributory 'negligence *n* [U] *law* failure to take enough care to avoid or prevent an accident, so that you are partly responsible for any loss or damage caused

con trick *n* [C] a CONFIDENCE TRICK

con·trite /ˈkɒntraɪt $ ˈkɑːn-/ *adj formal* feeling guilty and sorry for something bad that you have done: *a contrite apology* —**contritely** *adv* —**contrition** /kənˈtrɪʃən/ *n* [U]

con·triv·ance /kənˈtraɪvəns/ *n formal* **1** [C] something that is artificial or does not seem natural, but that helps something else to happen – usually used to show disapproval: *A ridiculous series of plot contrivances moves the film along.* **2** [C,U] a plan or trick to make something happen or get something for yourself, or the practice of doing this: *Harriet's matchmaking contrivances* **3** [C] a machine or piece of equipment that has been made for a special purpose: *a steam-driven contrivance used in 19th century clothing factories*

con·trive /kənˈtraɪv/ *v* [T] **1** *formal* to succeed in doing something in spite of difficulties: **contrive to do sth** *Schindler contrived to save more than 1,000 Polish Jews from the Nazis.* **2** to arrange an event or situation in a clever way, especially secretly or by deceiving people: *The lawsuit says oil companies contrived the oil shortage in the 1970s.* **3** to make or invent something in a skilful way, especially because you need it suddenly: *In 1862, a technique was contrived to take a series of photographs showing stages of movement.*

con·trived /kənˈtraɪvd/ *adj* seeming false and not natural: *The characters are as contrived as the plot.*

con·trol¹ |S1| |W1| /kənˈtrəʊl $ -ˈtroʊl/ *n*
1 MAKE SB/STH DO WHAT YOU WANT [U] the ability or power to make someone or something do what you want or make something happen in the way you want

> **have control (over/of sth)**
> **take/gain control (of/over sth)**
> **fight/struggle for control (of/over sth)**
> **lose control (of/over sth)**
> **be under control**
> **keep sth under control** (=keep something happening in the way you want)
> **get/go out of control** (=stop happening in the way you want)
> **beyond/outside sb's control** (=impossible for someone to control)
> **full/total control**

The disease robs you of muscle control. | [+**of/over**] *Babies are born with very little control over their movements.* | *Artists like to* **have** *some* **control over** *where their works are hung in a gallery.* | *She's a good teacher who* **has control of** *her class.* | *Students are encouraged to* **take control of** *their own learning, rather than just depending on the teacher.* | *Excessive drinking can make you* **lose control of** *your own life.* | *'Do you need any help?' 'No. It's* **under control,** *thanks.'* | *Dogs are allowed on the trails if they are* **kept under control.** | *The car* **spun out of control** *and hit a tree.* | *Flight delays do occur, for reasons that are* **outside our control.**

2 POWER [U] the power to make the decisions about how a country, place, company etc is organized or what it does: *The press was freed from political control.* | [+**of**] *Jordan asked for editorial control of the project.* | **in control (of sth)** *Anti-government forces are still in control of the area.* | *By the end of the year, the rebels* **had**

control over *the northern territories.* | *The Johnson family* **has** *effective* **control of** *the company, owning almost 60% of the shares.* | *China* **gained control of** *the island in 1683.* | *His son is being trained to* **take control** *of the family business.* | *The Democrats* **lost control of** *Congress in the last election.* | **under the control of sb** *The college was under the control of a group of trustees.* | *The whole of this area* **came under** *Soviet control after World War II.* | *The Conservatives are hoping to* **regain control of** *the city council.*

3 WAY OF LIMITING STH [C,U] an action, method, or law that limits the amount or growth of something, especially something that is dangerous: *pest control* | [+**of**] *the control of inflation* | [+**on**] *The authorities imposed strict controls on the movement of cattle.* | *an agreement on* **arms control** (=control of the amount of weapons a country has) | **under control** *Firefighters* **had** *the blaze* **under control** *by 9:44 p.m.* | *Shea used diet and exercise to* **bring** *her weight* **under control.** | *The Federal Reserve Bank raised interest rates to* **keep** *inflation* **under control.** | **rent/price/wage etc controls** *Rent controls ensured that no one paid too much for housing.* | **tight/rigid controls** (=strict controls) *The government favours the introduction of tighter controls on immigration.* | *Police used fire hoses and dogs for* **crowd control.**

4 ABILITY TO STAY CALM [U] the ability to remain calm even when you feel very angry, upset, or excited: *There were sudden tears in his eyes and he paused, fighting for control.* | *Davidson* **lost control of himself** *and started yelling.* | *Small children can't be expected to have the same* **self-control** (=ability to control their emotions and behaviour) *as an adult.* | **under control** *Her voice is under control, but she is almost shaking with anger.* | **in control** *I felt calm and in control.*

5 MACHINE/VEHICLE [C] the thing that you press or turn to make a machine, vehicle, television etc work: *the TV remote control* | *the volume control on the radio* | *a car with manual controls* | **at the controls** (=controlling a vehicle or aircraft) *Belton, at the controls, made a perfect landing.*

6 PEOPLE WHO ORGANIZE ACTIVITY [singular, U] the people who direct an activity or who check that something is done correctly, the place where this is done, or the process of doing it: *air-traffic control* | *Please stop at passport control.* | *computers used for stock control*

7 SCIENTIFIC TEST [C] **a)** a person, group etc against which you compare another person or group that is very similar, in order to see if a particular quality is caused by something or happens by chance: **control group/population/sample etc** *A control group of non-smoking women were compared to four groups of women smokers.* **b)** a thing that you already know the result for that is used in a scientific test, in order to show that your method is working correctly → CON-TROLLED EXPERIMENT

8 COMPUTER also **control key** [singular] a particular button on a computer that allows you to do certain operations: *Press control and F2 to exit.* → BIRTH CONTROL, QUALITY CONTROL, REMOTE CONTROL

control² |S2| |W1| *v* **controlled, controlling** [T]
1 POWER to have the power to make the decisions about how a country, place, company etc is organized or what it does: *The Democrats continued to control the Senate until last year.* | *a huge company controlling half the world's coffee trade* | **Labour-/Republican-/Democrat- etc controlled** *a Conservative-controlled council*

2 LIMIT to limit the amount or growth of something, especially something that is dangerous: *a chemical used to control weeds* | *an economic plan to control inflation* | *Development in areas of outstanding natural beauty is strictly controlled.* | *Strict measures were*

C

taken to control the spread of foot and mouth disease.
3 MAKE SB/STH DO WHAT YOU WANT to make someone or something do what you want, or make something happen in the way that you want: *Police had to be called in to control the crowds.* | *a skilled rider controlling a spirited horse* | *a controlling parent*
4 EMOTION if you control your emotions, your voice, your expression etc, you succeed in behaving calmly and sensibly, even though you feel angry, upset, or excited: *Sarah took a deep breath, trying to control her anger.* | *He controlled the urge to laugh.* | **control yourself** *Newman controlled himself with an effort.*
5 MACHINE/PROCESS/SYSTEM to make a machine, process, or system work in a particular way: *a radio-controlled toy car* | *A thermostat controls the temperature in the building.* | **control how/what/which etc** *The valves in the heart control how quickly the blood is pumped around the body.*
6 CHECK STH to make sure that something is done correctly; ▤ **check**, **monitor**: *The company strictly controls the quality of its products.*

> **WORD CHOICE: control, manage, run, be in charge**
> To **control** something means to have the power to make it work in the way that you want, usually without anyone else being able to stop you: *The army controls the north of the country.* | *With 75% of the shares, he effectively controls the company.*
> To **manage** something means to organize the way that it works, often with responsibility for other people's work: *She manages a team of software developers.* | *David managed a small bookstore.*
> To **run** something such as a business means to organize it and take the important decisions about how it works, perhaps as the owner of the business: *I run my own cleaning business.* | *Louise will be running the project.*
> To **be in charge** means to have responsibility for a situation or activity and decide what happens in it: *When the Director is away, her deputy is in charge.* | *He's in charge of marketing.*
> WORD CHOICE: **control, check, inspect, examine, test, monitor**
> ⚠ Do not use **control** to mean 'check' or 'test'. Use one of the following verbs:
> **check** or **inspect** means to look at something carefully to see if it is correct, safe, or legal: *Your passports will be checked on arrival.* | *Safety officers inspected the building.*
> **examine** means to look at something very carefully in order to find out more about it: *Experts who examined the letter declared it a fake.*
> **test** means to carry out an experiment or process in order to find out what qualities something has: *They test blood samples for drugs.* | *Every car is tested to ensure that it meets high safety standards.*
> **monitor** means to keep checking or testing something over a period of time to see if it changes: *Her heart rate is being monitored.* | *This device monitors room temperature and humidity.*

con·trol ,freak *n* [C] *informal* someone who is too concerned about controlling all the details in every situation they are involved in

con'trol ,key *n* [C] a particular button on a computer that allows you to do certain operations

con·trol·la·ble /kən'trəʊləbəl $ -'troʊl-/ *adj* able to be controlled: *Diabetes is a serious but controllable disease.*

con·trolled /kən'trəʊld $ -'troʊld/ *adj* **1** deliberately done in a particular way, or made to have particular qualities: *a test held under controlled conditions* | *a controlled explosion* **2** limited by a law or rule: *Access to the site is closely controlled.* | *a police search for* **controlled drugs** (=a drug that is illegal to have without permission from a doctor) **3** calm and not showing emotion, even if you feel angry, afraid etc: *a controlled, authoritative voice*

con,trolled ex'periment *n* [C] a scientific test done in a place where you can control all the things that might affect the test: *a controlled experiment to determine the effects of light on plant growth*

con,trolled 'substance *n* [C] *law* a drug that is illegal to possess or use without permission from a doctor: *an arrest for the possession and sale of controlled substances*

con·trol·ler /kən'trəʊlə $ -'troʊlər/ *n* [C] **1** someone who is in charge of a particular system, organization, or part of an organization: *air-traffic controllers* **2** also **comptroller** *formal* someone who is in charge of the money received or paid out by a company or government department

con,trolling 'interest *n* [C usually singular] if you have a controlling interest in a company, you own enough SHARES to be able to make decisions about what happens to the company: **[+in]** *The firm paid over $10 million for a controlling interest in five hotels.*

con'trol room *n* [C] the room that a process, service, large machine, factory etc is controlled from: *the submarine's control room*

con'trol ,tower *n* [C] a tall building at an airport from which people direct the movement of aircraft on the ground and in the air

con·tro·ver·sial /ˌkɒntrə'vɜːʃəl◂ $ ˌkɑːntrə'vɜːr-/ *adj* causing a lot of disagreement, because many people have strong opinions about the subject being discussed: *the controversial issue of welfare reform* | *a* **highly controversial** (=very controversial) *plan to flood the valley in order to build a dam* | *He is a* **controversial figure** (=person who does controversial things) *in the art world.* —**controversially** *adv*

con·tro·ver·sy /ˈkɒntrəvɜːsi, kən'trɒvəsi $ ˈkɑːntrəvɜːrsi/ *n plural* **controversies** [C,U] a serious argument about something that involves many people and continues for a long time: *a political controversy* | *the* **controversy surrounding** *Skinner's theories* | **cause/provoke/arouse controversy** *The judges' decision provoked controversy.* | **[+over/about]** *the controversy over campaign-finance issues* | **Controversy arose** (=began) *over the use of the chemicals on fruit and vegetables.*

con·tu·sion /kən'tjuːʒən $ -'tuː-/ *n* [C,U] *medical* a BRUISE or BRUISING —**contused** *adj*

co·nun·drum /kə'nʌndrəm/ *n* [C] **1** a confusing and difficult problem: *the conundrum of our purpose on earth* **2** a trick question asked for fun; ▤ **riddle**

con·ur·ba·tion /ˌkɒnɜː'beɪʃən $ ˌkɑːnɜːr-/ *n* [C] *formal* a group of towns that have spread and joined together to form an area with a high population, often with a large city as its centre

con·va·lesce /ˌkɒnvə'les $,kɑːn-/ *v* [I] to spend time getting well after an illness; ▤ **recover**: *the time needed to convalesce after an operation*

con·va·les·cence /ˌkɒnvə'lesəns $,kɑːn-/ *n* [singular] the length of time a person spends getting well after an illness: *a long and painful convalescence*

con·va·les·cent /ˌkɒnvə'lesənt◂ $,kɑːn-/ *n* [C] someone who is spending time getting well after an illness —**convalescent** *adj*

,conva'lescent ,home also **,conva'lescent ,hospital** *n* [C] a place where people stay when they need care from doctors and nurses, but are not sick enough to be in a hospital; → **nursing home**

con·vect /kən'vekt/ *v* [I] *technical* to move heat by convection

con·vec·tion /kən'vekʃən/ *n* [U] *technical* the movement in a gas or liquid caused by warm gas or liquid rising, and cold gas or liquid sinking

con'vection ,oven *n* [C] a special OVEN that makes hot air move around inside it so that all the parts of the food get the same amount of heat

con·vec·tor /kən'vektə $ -ər/ also **con'vector ,heater** *n* [C] *BrE* an electrical heater that uses hot air

con·vene /kən'viːn/ *v* [I,T] if a group of people convene, or someone convenes them, they come together, especially for a formal meeting: *a report by experts convened by the National Institutes of Health*

con·ven·er, **convenor** /kən'viːnə $ -ər/ *n* [C] **1** someone who arranges for people to meet at a formal meeting **2** *BrE* an important official for a TRADE UNION at a factory or office

con·ve·ni·ence /kən'viːniəns/ *n* **1** [U] the quality of being suitable or useful for a particular purpose, especially by making something easier or saving you time: *Ready meals sell well because of their convenience.* | **the convenience of doing sth** *Most of us like the convenience of using credit cards to buy things.* | **for convenience** *For convenience, the German translation is printed below.* **2** [U] what is easiest and best for a particular person: **at sb's convenience** (=at a time that is best and easiest for someone) *These meals can be prepared in advance, and served at your convenience.* | **for sb's convenience** *For your convenience, the bank is open until 7 p.m.* | *Services should be run to suit the convenience of the customer, not the staff.* **3** [C] something that is useful because it saves you time or means that you have less work to do: *The supermarket offers a bag-packing service, as a convenience to customers.* | *a hotel with all the modern conveniences, including Internet access* **4** **at your earliest convenience** *formal* as soon as possible – used in letters: *We should be grateful if you would reply at your earliest convenience.* **5** [C usually plural] also **public convenience** *formal* a public toilet **6 a marriage of convenience** a marriage that has been agreed for a particular purpose, not because the two people love each other: *In the past most royal marriages were marriages of convenience, arranged for political reasons.*

con'venience ,food *n* [C,U] food that is partly or completely prepared already and that is sold frozen or in cans, packages etc, so that it can be prepared quickly and easily: *We eat too little fresh food, relying instead on convenience foods.*

con'venience ,store *n* [C] a shop where you can buy food, alcohol, magazines etc, that is often open 24 hours each day

con·ve·ni·ent S3 /kən'viːniənt/ *adj* **1** useful to you because it saves you time, or does not spoil your plans or cause you problems: *Mail-order catalogs are a convenient way to shop.* | *My secretary will call you to arrange a convenient time to meet.* | [+for] *Is three o'clock convenient for you?* | **convenient to do sth** *It is simple and convenient to use.* **2** close and easy to reach: *The bus stop around the corner is probably the most convenient.* | [+for] *BrE*[+to] *AmE*: *restaurants convenient for shops and theatres* → INCONVENIENT

con·ve·ni·ent·ly /kən'viːniəntli/ *adv* **1** in a way that is useful to you because it saves you time or does not spoil your plans or cause you problems: *Conveniently, her parents are often willing to babysit.* | *At that time, ice cream couldn't be conveniently bought in a store.* **2** in a place that is close or easily reached: *The hotel is conveniently located near the airport.* **3** if someone has conveniently forgotten, ignored, lost etc something, they deliberately do this because this helps them to avoid a problem or to get what they want: *You conveniently forgot to tell me she was Nick's sister.*

con·ve·nor /kən'viːnə $ -ər/ *n* [C] another spelling of CONVENER

con·vent /'kɒnvənt $ 'kɑːnvent/ *n* [C] a building or set of buildings where NUNS live → CONVENT SCHOOL

con·ven·tion W2 /kən'venʃən/ *n*
1 [C] a large formal meeting for people who belong to the same profession or organization or who have the same interests: *a teachers' convention* | *the city's new convention center* | *a convention for science fiction fans* **2** [C] a formal agreement, especially between countries, about particular rules or behaviour; ◘ **pact**, **treaty**: [+on] *the European convention on human rights*

3 [C,U] behaviour and attitudes that most people in a society consider to be normal and right; ◘ **custom**: *Playing together teaches children social conventions such as sharing.* | *They defied the conventions of the time by living together without being married.* | **by convention** *By convention, the bride's father gives her away at her wedding.* **4** [C] a method or style often used in literature, art, the theatre etc to achieve a particular effect: *the conventions of the nineteenth century novel*

con·ven·tion·al W3 /kən'venʃənəl/ *adj*
1 [only before noun] a conventional method, product, practice etc has been used for a long time and is considered the usual type: *Internet connections through conventional phone lines are fairly slow.* | *Bake for 20 minutes in a conventional oven; 8 in a microwave.* **2** always following the behaviour and attitudes that most people in a society consider to be normal, right, and socially acceptable, so that you seem slightly boring: *a strong believer in conventional morals* | [+in] *He is conventional in his approach to life.* **3 (the) conventional wisdom** the opinion that most people consider to be normal and right, but that is sometimes shown to be wrong: *As traffic grew, the conventional wisdom was that roads should be widened to make room.* **4** [only before noun] conventional weapons and wars do not use NUCLEAR explosives or weapons: *conventional forces* **5 conventional medicine** the usual form of medicine practised in most European and North American countries; ◘ **western medicine**—**conventionally** *adv* —**conventionality** /kən,venʃə'næl̩ti/ *n* [U]

con·ven·tion·eer /kən,venʃə'nɪə $ -'nɪr/ *n* [C] *especially AmE written* someone who attends a convention

'convent ,school *n* [C] a school for girls that is run by Roman Catholic NUNS

con·verge /kən'vɜːdʒ $ -'vɜːrdʒ/ *v* [I] **1** to come from different directions and meet at the same point to become one thing; ◘ **diverge**: *The two rivers converge into one near Pittsburgh.* **2** if groups of people converge in a particular place, they come there from many different places and meet together to form a large crowd: [+on] *Reporters converged on the scene.* **3** if different ideas or aims converge, they become the same; ◘ **diverge**: *Cultural beliefs about the role of women converge with government policies.* —**convergent** *adj*: *The member states should start to have more convergent policies.*

con·ver·sant /kən'vɜːsənt $ -ɜːr-/ *adj* [not before noun] **1** *formal* having knowledge or experience of something: [+with] *Staff members are conversant with the issues.* **2** *AmE* able to hold a conversation in a foreign language, but not able to speak it perfectly: [+in] *Kim was conversant in Russian.*

con·ver·sa·tion S1 W2 /,kɒnvə'seɪʃən $,kɑːnvər-/ *n* [C,U] an informal talk in which people exchange news, feelings, and thoughts

have/hold a conversation (with sb)
carry on a conversation (with sb) (=have a conversation)
get into (a) conversation (with sb) (=start having a conversation)
make (polite) conversation (with sb) (=talk to someone in order to be polite)
engage sb in conversation
(a) conversation turns to sth (=people start talking about something)
deep in conversation (=very involved in conversation)
snatches of conversation (=small parts of a conversation)
topic of conversation
a private conversation

a telephone conversation | *Children quickly get bored by adult conversation.* | [+with] *a short conversation with the teacher* | [+**about**] *a conversation about family and friends* | *They* **had** *a short* **conversation** *in German and seemed to be disagreeing about something.* | *It's impossible to* **carry on a conversation** *with all this noise in the background.* | *'Did you have a good journey?' he said, trying to* **make conversation.** | *He was silent, no matter how hard Sofia tried to* **engage** *him* **in conversation.** | *After a while, the* **conversation turned to** *a friend's coming wedding.* | *They were* **deep in conversation,** *relaxed and smiling.* | *He could hear* **snatches of conversation** *from across the room.*

con·ver·sa·tion·al /ˌkɒnvəˈseɪʃənəl◂ $ ˌkɑːnvər-/ *adj* **1** a conversational style, phrase etc is informal and commonly used in conversation: *The article was written in straightforward, almost conversational language.* **2** relating to conversation: *lessons in conversational German* —**conversationally** *adv*

con·ver·sa·tion·al·ist /ˌkɒnvəˈseɪʃənəlᵻst $ ˌkɑːnvər-/ *n* [C] someone who talks about intelligent, amusing, and interesting things

conver'sation ,piece *n* [C] something that provides a subject for conversation – often used humorously about objects that seem very strange or ugly

con·verse¹ /kənˈvɜːs $ -ˈvɜːrs/ *v* [I] *formal* to have a conversation with someone: [+**with**] *She enjoyed the chance to converse with someone who spoke her language.*

con·verse² /ˈkɒnvɜːs $ ˈkɑːnvɜːrs/ *n formal* **the converse** the converse of a fact, word, statement etc is the opposite of it: *Some teachers welcomed the change; but for the majority of teachers,* **the converse was true.**

con·verse³ /ˈkɒnvɜːs $ kənˈvɜːrs/ *adj formal* opposite: *a converse example*

con·verse·ly /ˈkɒnvɜːsli, ˈkɒnvɜːsli $ kənˈvɜːrsli, ˈkɑːnvɜːrsli/ *adv* used when one situation is the opposite of another: *American consumers prefer white eggs;* **conversely,** *British buyers like brown eggs.*

con·ver·sion /kənˈvɜːʃən $ -ˈvɜːrʒən/ *n* [C,U] **1** when you change something from one form, purpose, or system to a different one: [+**into**] *The warehouse was undergoing conversion into apartments.* | [+**of**] *the conversion of waste into usable products* | [+**to**] *The British conversion to the metric system took place in the 1970s.* | **house/barn/loft etc conversion** *BrE* (=when you change the use of a house, barn etc, so that it becomes apartments, a house, a room etc) **2** when someone changes from one religion or belief to a different one: [+**to**] *a conversion to vegetarianism* | [+**from**] *Newman's conversion from Anglicanism to Catholicism* **3** a way of scoring extra points in RUGBY or AMERICAN FOOTBALL

con'version ,course *n* [C] *BrE* a course for students who have some knowledge of a subject, but who need slightly different or more knowledge in order to do something: *A qualified pilot would still need a conversion course to fly microlight aircraft.*

con·vert¹ W3 /kənˈvɜːt $ -ˈvɜːrt/ *v* **1 a)** [T] to change something into a different form of thing, or to change something so that it can be used for a different purpose or in a different way: **convert sth to/into sth** *They converted the spare bedroom into an office.* | *The stocks can be easily converted to cash.* | *a 19th century* **converted barn** (=barn changed into a house) **b)** [I] to change into a different form of thing, or change into something that can be used for a different purpose or in a different way: [+**to/into**] *a sofa that converts into a bed* | *In the process, the light energy converts to heat energy.*
2 a) [T] to persuade someone to change to a different religion: **convert sb to sth** *European missionaries converted thousands to Christianity.* **b)** [I] to change to a different religion: [+**to**] *She converted to Catholicism.*
3 a) [I] to change to a different set of ideas, principles, or ways of doing something: [+**to**] *people who have recently converted to vegetarianism* **b)** [T] to persuade

someone to change to a different set of ideas, principles, or ways of doing something: **convert sb to sth** *She succeeded in converting me to her point of view.* | **newly/freshly converted** *newly converted feminists*
4 [I,T] to make a conversion in RUGBY or AMERICAN FOOTBALL → **preach to the converted** at PREACH (4)

con·vert² /ˈkɒnvɜːt $ ˈkɑːnvɜːrt/ *n* [C] someone who has been persuaded to change their beliefs and accept a particular religion or opinion: [+**to**] *a convert to Christianity* | *recent converts to the cause*

con·vert·er, convertor /kənˈvɜːtə $ -ˈvɜːrtər/ *n* [C] a piece of equipment that changes the form of something, especially so that it can be more easily used: *a converter that allows you to view digital television on your old TV* → CATALYTIC CONVERTER

con·ver·ti·ble¹ /kənˈvɜːtᵻbəl $ -ˈvɜːr-/ *adj* **1** an object that is convertible can be folded or arranged in a different way so that it can be used as something else: *a convertible sofa* **2** *technical* able to be exchanged for the money of another country: *a convertible currency* **3** *technical* a financial document such as an insurance arrangement or a BOND that is convertible can be exchanged for money, STOCKS etc —**convertibility** /kənˌvɜːtᵻˈbɪlᵻti $ -ˈvɜːr-/ *n* [U]

convertible² *n* [C] a car with a soft roof that you can fold back or remove; → **hardtop, cabriolet**

con·vex /ˌkɒnˈveks◂, kən-, ˈkɒnveks $ ˌkɑːnˈveks◂, kən-,ˈkɑːnveks/ *adj* curved outwards, like the surface of the eye; ⊞ **concave:** *a convex lens* | *a convex mirror* —**convexly** *adv* —**convexity** /kənˈveksᵻti/ *n* [C,U]

con·vey /kənˈveɪ/ *v* [T] **1** to communicate or express something, with or without using words: *All this information can be conveyed in a simple diagram.* | *Ads* **convey the message** *that thin is beautiful.* | *He was sent to* **convey a message** *to the U.N. Secretary General.* | **convey sth to sb** *I want to convey to children that reading is one of life's greatest treats.* | **convey a sense/an impression/an idea etc** *You don't want to convey the impression that there's anything illegal going on.* **2** *formal* to take or carry something from one place to another: *Your luggage will be conveyed to the hotel by taxi.* **3** *law* to legally change the possession of property from one person to another

con·vey·ance /kənˈveɪəns/ *n* **1** [C] *formal* a vehicle: *Wheeled conveyances of any kind are not allowed in the park.* **2** [U] *formal* when you take something from one place to another: *the conveyance of goods* **3** [U] when you communicate or express something, with or without using words: *Facial expressions are part of the conveyance of meaning.* **4** [C] *law* a legal document that gives land, property etc to one person from another

con·vey·anc·ing /kənˈveɪənsɪŋ/ *n* [U] *BrE* the work done, usually by a lawyer, to change the possession of property, especially a house, from one person to another —**conveyancer** *n* [C]

con·vey·or, conveyer /kənˈveɪə $ -ər/ *n* [C] **1** a person or thing that carries or communicates something: *the conveyer of good news* **2** a conveyor belt

con'veyor belt *n* [C] a long continuous moving band of rubber, cloth, or metal, used in a place such as a factory or airport to move things from one place to another: *We lifted our baggage from the conveyor belt.*

con·vict¹ /kənˈvɪkt/ *v* [T] to prove or officially announce that someone is guilty of a crime after a TRIAL in a law court; ⊞ **acquit: convict sb of sth** *She was convicted of shoplifting.* | **convict sb on sth** *He was* **convicted on** *fraud* **charges.** | *a convicted murderer*

con·vict² /ˈkɒnvɪkt $ ˈkɑːn-/ *n* [C] someone who has been proved to be guilty of a crime and sent to prison: *an escaped convict*

con·vic·tion W3 /kənˈvɪkʃən/ *n*
1 [C] a very strong belief or opinion: **religious/political etc convictions** *a woman of strong political convictions* | **deep/strong conviction** *The Dotens have a deep conviction that marriage is for life.* | **conviction that** *The students possess the conviction that they can

2 [U] the feeling of being sure about something and having no doubts: **with/without conviction** *He was able to say with conviction that he had changed.* | *'No,' she said, without conviction.* | *It was a reasonable explanation, but his voice* **lacked** *conviction.* | *It took her so much effort to speak that what she said* **carried** *great conviction* (=showed she felt sure of what she said).
3 [C,U] a decision in a court of law that someone is guilty of a crime, or the process of proving that someone is guilty: **acquittal:** *They had no previous convictions.* | *Applicants are checked for criminal convictions.* | [+**for**] *This was her third conviction for theft.* | *the trial and conviction of Jimmy Malone* → **have the courage of your convictions** at COURAGE (2)

con·vince [S3] [W3] /kən'vɪns/ v [T]
1 to make someone feel certain that something is true: *Her arguments didn't convince everyone, but changes were made.* | **convince sb (that)** *Baker had to convince jurors that his client had been nowhere near the scene of the murder.* | **convince sb of sth** *The officials were eager to convince us of the safety of the nuclear reactors.*
2 to persuade someone to do something; **persuade:** **convince sb to do sth** *I've been trying to convince Jean to come with me.*

con·vinced /kən'vɪnst/ adj **1** [not before noun] feeling certain that something is true: *Molly agreed, but she did not sound very convinced.* | **be convinced (that)** *I was convinced that we were doing the right thing.* | [+**of**] *Researchers are convinced of a genetic cause for the disease.* | **firmly/totally/fully etc convinced** *Herschel was firmly convinced of the possibility of life on other planets.* **2 convinced Muslim/Christian etc** someone who believes very strongly in a particular religion

con·vinc·ing /kən'vɪnsɪŋ/ adj **1** making you believe that something is true or right: *convincing evidence of his guilt* | **wholly/utterly/totally etc convincing** *Courtenay played the role in an utterly convincing way.* **2 convincing victory/win** an occasion when a person or team wins a game by a lot of points —**convincingly** adv

con·viv·i·al /kən'vɪviəl/ adj formal friendly and pleasantly cheerful: *a convivial atmosphere* —**convivially** adv —**conviviality** /kən,vɪvi'æləti/ n [U]

con·vo·ca·tion /,kɒnvə'keɪʃən $,kɑːn-/ n **1** [C usually singular] formal a large formal meeting of a group of people, especially church officials **2** [U] formal the process of arranging for a large meeting to be held **3** [C usually singular] AmE the ceremony held when students have finished their studies and are leaving a college or university

con·voke /kən'vəʊk $ -'voʊk/ v [T] formal to tell people that they must come together for a formal meeting: *Separate meetings had been convoked by the two opposing factions.*

con·vo·lut·ed /'kɒnvəluːtɪd $ 'kɑːn-/ adj **1** complicated and difficult to understand: *long paragraphs and convoluted sentences* | *The argument is rather convoluted.* **2** formal having many twists and bends: *a tightly-coiled convoluted tube*

con·vo·lu·tion /,kɒnvə'luːʃən $,kɑːn-/ n [C usually plural] **1** the complicated details of a story, explanation etc, which make it difficult to understand: [+**of**] *the endless convolutions of the plot* **2** a fold or twist in something which has many of them: [+**of**] *the many convolutions of the small intestine*

con·voy¹ /'kɒnvɔɪ $ 'kɑːn-/ n [C] a group of vehicles or ships travelling together, sometimes in order to protect one another: [+**of**] *The British left in a convoy of 20 cars.* | **in convoy** *We drove in convoy in case their car broke down again.* | *a military convoy* | **aid/relief/food etc convoy**

convoy² v [T] to travel with something in order to protect it: *American destroyers helped to convoy much-needed supplies to Britain in 1917.*

con·vulse /kən'vʌls/ v **1** [I] if your body or a part of it convulses, it moves violently and you are not able to

control it: *He sat down, his shoulders convulsing with sobs.* **2 be convulsed with laughter/anger etc** to be laughing so much or feel so angry that you shake and are not able to stop yourself **3** [T] if something such as a war convulses a country, it causes a lot of problems or confusion: *A wave of nationalist demonstrations convulsed the country in 1919.*

con·vul·sion /kən'vʌlʃən/ n [C] **1** a shaking movement of your body that you cannot control, which happens because you are ill; **seizure:** *His temperature was very high and he* **went into convulsions**. **2** [usually plural] a great change that affects a country: *the 19th-century political convulsions in France* **3 be in convulsions** to be laughing a lot

con·vul·sive /kən'vʌlsɪv/ adj [usually before noun] a convulsive movement or action is sudden, violent, and impossible to control: *a convulsive sob* —**convulsively** adv: *Con's body jerked convulsively.*

co·ny, coney /'kəʊni $ 'koʊni/ n plural **conies** or **coneys 1** [C] old use a rabbit **2** [U] rabbit fur used for making coats

coo¹ /kuː/ v **1** [I] when DOVES or PIGEONS coo, they make a low soft cry **2** [I,T] to make soft quiet sounds, or to speak in a soft quiet way: *'Darling,' she cooed.* | *a cooing voice* —**coo** n [C] → **bill and coo** at BILL² (3)

coo² interjection BrE used to express surprise: *Coo! That must have cost a lot!*

cook¹ [S2] /kʊk/ v
1 [I,T] to prepare food for eating by using heat: *Where did you learn to cook?* | *Cook the sauce over a low heat for 10 minutes.* | **cook a meal/dinner/breakfast etc** *I'm usually too tired to cook an evening meal.* | **cook sth for supper/lunch/dinner etc** *He was cooking rice for supper.* | **cook sb sth** *She cooked them all a good dinner every night.* | **cook (sth) for sb** *I promised I'd cook for them.* | *slices of cooked ham* | *a cooked breakfast*
2 [I] to be prepared for eating by using heat: *He could smell something delicious cooking.* | *Hamburgers were cooking in the kitchen.*
3 cook the books to dishonestly change official records and figures in order to steal money or give people false information: *The Government was cooking the books and misleading the public over unemployment.*
4 be cooking informal to be being planned in a secret way: *They've got something cooking, and I don't think I like it.*
5 be cooking (with gas) spoken used to say that someone is doing something very well: *The band's really cooking tonight.*

WORD FOCUS: words meaning COOK
fry (in oil) | **boil** (in hot water) | **bake** (bread and cakes in an oven) | **roast** (meat or vegetables in an oven) | **microwave** (using a microwave oven) | **grill/broil** AmE (using a grill) | **steam, toast, simmer, poach, barbecue, stir-fry, saute, chargrill**
raw (not cooked) | **rare** (used about meat that has been cooked for a short time) | **well-done** (used about meat that has been cooked for a long time)
→ see also cookbook, recipe, culinary

---

cook sth ⇔ **up** phr v
1 to prepare food, especially quickly: *Every night he cooked up a big casserole.*
2 informal to invent an excuse, reason, plan etc, especially one that is slightly dishonest or unlikely to work: *the plan that Graham and Dempster had cooked up*

cook² n [C] **1** someone who prepares and cooks food as their job; **chef:** *He works as a cook in a local restaurant.* **2 be a good/wonderful/terrible etc cook** to be good or bad at preparing and cooking food **3 too many cooks (spoil the broth)** used when you think there are too many people trying to do the same job at the same time, so that the job is not done well → **chief cook and bottle-washer** at CHIEF¹ (3)

cook·book /'kʊkbʊk/ n [C] AmE a book that tells you how to prepare and cook food; ▣ **cookery book** BrE

cook-'chill adj [only before noun] BrE cook-chill foods have already been cooked when you buy them, and are stored at a low temperature, but not frozen

cook·er /'kʊkə $ -ər/ n [C] BrE **1** a large piece of equipment for cooking food on or in; ▣ **stove** AmE: a gas cooker **2** a fruit, especially an apple, that is suitable for cooking but not for eating raw

cook·e·ry /'kʊkəri/ n [U] BrE the art or skill of cooking: a one-year cookery course | French cookery

cookery book n [C] BrE a book that tells you how to prepare and cook food; ▣ **cookbook** AmE: a recipe from a cookery book

cook·house /'kʊkhaʊs/ n [C] old-fashioned an outdoor kitchen where you cook food, especially in a military camp

cook·ie /'kʊki/ n [C] **1** especially AmE a small flat sweet cake; ▣ **biscuit** BrE: a glass of milk and a cookie | a chocolate chip cookie **2 tough/smart cookie** informal someone who is clever and successful, and knows how to get what they want **3 that's the way the cookie crumbles** informal said when something bad has happened and you must accept things the way they are, even though you do not want to **4** technical information that a website leaves in your computer so that the website will recognize you when you use it again **5** AmE old-fashioned an attractive young woman

cookie cutter¹ n [C] AmE an instrument that cuts cookies into special shapes before you bake them

cookie cutter² adj [only before noun] AmE almost exactly the same as other things of the same type, and not very interesting: the cookie cutter approach of the urban renewal programme

cookie sheet n [C] AmE a flat piece of metal that you bake food on; ▣ **baking tray** BrE

cook·ing¹ [S3] /'kʊkɪŋ/ n [U]
1 the act of making food and cooking it: My mother does all the cooking. | I love cooking.
2 food made in a particular way or by a particular person: My compliments on your cooking. | Indian cooking | simple, basic **home cooking** (=good food like the food you get in your own home)

cooking² adj [only before noun] suitable for or used in cooking: The rooms all have **cooking facilities** (=there is cooking equipment in the rooms). | **cooking pot/utensils/equipment etc** | cooking apples

cooking apple n [C] an apple that is usually cooked, rather than eaten raw; → **eating apple**

cooking oil n [U] oil from plants, such as SUNFLOWERS or OLIVES, used in cooking

cook·out /'kʊk-aʊt/ n [C] AmE informal a party or occasion when a meal is cooked and eaten outdoors: a cookout on the beach

cook·ware /'kʊkweə $ -wer/ n [U] containers and equipment used for cooking

cool¹ [W3] /kuːl/ adj comparative **cooler**, superlative **coolest**
1 TEMPERATURE low in temperature, but not cold, often in a way that feels pleasant: She swam out into the cool water. | The evening air was cool. | Relax in the sun with a cool drink. | the cooler weather of September
2 CLOTHING clothing that is cool is made of thin material so that you do not become too hot: a cool cotton dress
3 CALM calm and not nervous, upset, or excited: **keep/stay cool** his ability to keep cool in a crisis | She looks efficient and **as cool as a cucumber**. | Outwardly she is **cool, calm and collected**. | a **cool customer** (=someone who always behaves calmly) | Keep a **cool head** (=stay calm).
4 APPROVAL informal very attractive, fashionable, interesting etc in a way that people admire – used in

order to show approval: She's pretty cool. | You look cool in denim. | Cool bike! | 'I'm thinking of studying abroad.' 'Really? Cool.'
5 AGREEMENT spoken used to say that you agree with something, that you understand it, or that it does not annoy you: OK, Ryan, **that's cool**, I can handle that. | 'I just have to go, you know.' 'It's all right, **it's cool**.' | 'I'm finished.' 'Cool.' | [+about] My mum was cool about whatever I wore. | **sth is cool with sb** Would Friday be cool with you guys? | **sb is cool with sth** 'Do you want to come over to my house and watch a video tonight?' 'I'm cool with that.'
6 NOT FRIENDLY behaving in a way that is not as friendly as you expect: My proposal met with a **cool response**. | Luke gave her a **cool look**.
7 COLOUR a cool colour is one, such as blue or green, that makes you think of cool things
8 a cool million/hundred thousand etc informal a surprisingly large amount of money: He earns a cool half million every year. —**coolness** n [U]: the coolness of the nights —**coolly** adv: She nodded coolly and walked out.

cool² [S3] v
1 [I,T] also **cool down** to make something slightly colder, or to become slightly colder: The air conditioning doesn't seem to be cooling the room much. | Allow the biscuits to cool for five minutes. | a cooling breeze
2 [I] if a feeling, emotion, or relationship cools, it becomes less strong: The affair had cooled, on her side at least. | When tempers had cooled, he apologized.
3 cool it spoken **a)** used to tell someone to stop being angry, violent etc: Come on now – calm down, cool it. **b)** to stop putting as much effort into something, or pressure on someone, as you have been: He was getting more serious about her. It was time to cool it.
4 cool your heels to be forced to wait: I'll put him in a cell to cool his heels for a bit.

cool down phr v
1 to make something slightly colder, or to become slightly colder: The air has cooled down a little now. | **cool sb/sth ⇔ down** A glass of lemonade will cool you down.
2 to become calm after being angry: After I cooled down I realized I had been wrong.

cool off phr v
1 to return to a normal temperature after being hot: Cool off with an iced drink. | By late autumn Mediterranean islands have cooled off, and can have rainy days.
2 to become calm after being angry: He slammed the door and went for a walk to cool off.

cool³ n **1 the cool** a temperature that is pleasantly cold: [+of] They went for a stroll **in the cool of the evening**. **2 keep your cool** to remain calm in a frightening or difficult situation: I must keep my cool, she thought; losing my temper isn't going to help. **3 lose your cool** to stop being calm in an annoying or frightening situation: Kenneth finally lost his cool with a photographer, and threatened to hit him.

cool⁴ adv **play it cool** to behave in a calm way because you do not want someone to know that you are really nervous, angry etc: She would not show him how upset she was. It was always smarter to play it cool.

coo·lant /'kuːlənt/ n [C,U] technical a liquid or gas used to cool something, especially an engine

cool·box /'kuːlbɒks $ -bɑːks/ also **cool·bag** /'kuːlbæg/ n [C] BrE a container that keeps food and drink cool and fresh, used on a PICNIC; ▣ **cooler** AmE

cool·er /'kuːlə $ -ər/ n [C] **1** a container in which something, especially drinks, is cooled or kept cold: Mike went to fetch a bottle of wine from the cooler. **2** AmE a coolbox **3** AmE a machine that provides AIR CONDITIONING **4 the cooler** informal prison

cool-'headed adj not easily excited or upset: We need a quick-thinking, cool-headed person for the job.

coo·lie /'kuːli/ n [C] taboo old-fashioned a very offensive word for an unskilled worker who is paid very low wages, especially in parts of Asia. Do not use this word.

cooling-'off ,period n [C] **1** BrE a period of time after you have signed some types of sales agreement, when you can change your mind about buying something: *Customers signing new life policies will have a cooling-off period of 14 days in which to cancel.* **2** a period of time when two people or groups who are arguing about something can go away and think about how to improve the situation

cooling ,system n [C] a system for keeping the temperature in a machine, engine etc low: *a fault in the power station's cooling system*

cooling ,tower n [C] a large round tall building, used in industry for making water cool

coon /ku:n/ n [C] informal **1** AmE a RACCOON **2** taboo a very offensive word for a black person. Do not use this word.

coon·skin /'ku:nskɪn/ adj made from the skin of a RACCOON: *pictures of traders in coonskin caps*

co-op S3 /'kəʊɒp $ 'koʊɑːp/ n [C] a COOPERATIVE

coop /ku:p/ n [C] a building for small animals, especially chickens

,cooped 'up adj [not before noun] having to stay for a period of time in a place that is too small: *It isn't good for you to be cooped up in the house all day.*

coo·per /'ku:pə $ -ər/ n [C] someone who makes BARRELS

co·op·e·rate also **co-operate** BrE /kəʊ'ɒpəreɪt $ koʊ'ɑːp-/ v [I] **1** to work with someone else to achieve something that you both want: [+in/on] *The two universities are to cooperate in the development of a new industrial process.* | *They **agreed to co-operate** with Brazil on a programme to protect the rain-forests.* | [+with] *Leopards cooperate with each other when hunting game.* | *As chairman I was anxious to co-operate with Mr Baker as far as possible.* | *The church seeks to **cooperate closely** with local schools.* | **cooperate to do sth** *Both sides agreed to co-operate to prevent illegal fishing in the area.* **2** to do what someone wants you to do: [+with] *I will advise my client to **cooperate fully** with the police.* | *If you **refuse to co-operate**, I shall kill you.*

co·op·e·ra·tion S3 W2 also **co-operation** BrE /kəʊ,ɒpə'reɪʃən $ koʊ,ɑːp-/ n [U] **1** when you work with someone to achieve something that you both want: [+with] *political co-operation with Britain* | **in cooperation with sb** *A study was undertaken in co-operation with oil companies.* | *Burglar alarm companies claim they work in **close co-operation** with the police.* | [+between] *the lack of effective co-operation between industry and higher education* | *the need to strengthen **international co-operation*** **2** willingness to do what someone asks you to do: *Have your passports ready, and thank you for your cooperation.* | *Your **full cooperation** is requested.*

co·op·e·ra·tive¹ also **co-operative** BrE /kəʊ'ɒpərətɪv $ koʊ'ɑːp-/ adj **1** willing to cooperate; ☐ **helpful**; ☐ **uncooperative**: *He was doing his best to be cooperative.* | *a cooperative witness* **2** made, done, or operated by people working together: *a co-operative venture between the City Council and the police* **3** a cooperative store, bank etc is operated by people working together as a cooperative: *a co-operative store in a provincial town* —**cooperatively** adv

cooperative² also **co-operative** BrE n [C] a business or organization owned equally by all the people working there; ☐ **co-op**: *a women-only housing co-operative* | *a workers' co-operative*

co·opt also **co-opt** BrE /kəʊ'ɒpt $ koʊ'ɑːpt/ v [T] formal **1** BrE to make someone a member of a group, committee etc, by the agreement of all the members: *The committee may co-opt additional members for special purposes.* | **coopt sb onto/into/to sth** *She was coopted onto the county education committee.* **2** to persuade someone to help or support you: **coopt sb to do sth** *Social scientists were co-opted to work with the development agencies.* | *Nan was coopted into the kitchen to make pastry.*

co·or·di·nate¹ also **co-ordinate** BrE /kəʊ'ɔ:dɪneɪt $ koʊ'ɔ:r-/ v **1** [T] to organize an activity so that the people involved in it work well together and achieve a good result: *The agencies are working together to co-ordinate policy on food safety.* | *a co-ordinated approach to economic and social questions* **2** [T] to make the parts of your body move and work together well: *Her movements were beautifully co-ordinated.* | *I couldn't get my brain to function or coordinate my muscles.* **3** [I,T] if clothes, decorations etc coordinate, or if you coordinate them, they look good together because they have similar colours and styles: *Don't be afraid to mix colours, as long as they co-ordinate.* | *You might coordinate your curtains and cushions.* | [+with] *The cooker is green, to co-ordinate with the kitchen.*

co·or·din·ate² also **co-ordinate** BrE /kəʊ'ɔ:dɪnət $ koʊ'ɔ:r-/ n [C] **1** technical one of a set of numbers which give the exact position of a point on a map, computer screen etc **2** coordinates [plural] things such as clothes that can be worn or used together because their colours match or their styles are similar: *Matching bag and accessories provide a complete ensemble of colour coordinates.*

coordinate³ also **co-ordinate** BrE adj technical **1** equal in importance or rank in a sentence; → **subordinate**: *coordinate clauses joined by 'and'* **2** involving the use of coordinates

co,ordinating con'junction n [C] a word such as 'and' or 'but' which joins two words, groups, or CLAUSES which are equal in importance or rank; → **subordinating conjunction**

co·or·di·na·tion also **co-ordination** BrE /kəʊ,ɔ:dɪ'neɪʃən $ koʊ,ɔ:r-/ n [U] **1** the way in which your muscles move together when you perform a movement: *Too much alcohol affects your coordination.* **2** the organization of people or things so that they work together well: [+of] *the coordination of our economic policies* | [+between] *co-ordination between central and local government*

co·or·di·na·tor /kəʊ'ɔ:dɪneɪtə $ koʊ'ɔ:rdɪneɪtər/ n [C] someone who organizes the way people work together in a particular activity

coot /ku:t/ n [C] **1** a small black and white water bird with a short beak **2** old coot AmE informal an old man who you think is strange or unpleasant: *a miserable, mean old coot*

cop¹ S3 /kɒp $ kɑ:p/ n [C]
1 informal a police officer: *the local cop* | *a narcotics cop* | *He pulled out his badge and said he was a cop.*
2 not be much cop BrE informal to not be very good: *They say he's not much cop as a coach.*
3 it's a fair cop BrE spoken used humorously when someone has discovered that you have done something wrong and you want to admit it

cop² v copped, copping [T] spoken informal **1** cop it BrE a) to be punished or spoken to angrily because you have done something wrong: *You'll cop it when Mum finds out!* b) to be killed **2** BrE to receive something, especially something that you do not want: *I copped all the blame for what happened.* **3** cop hold of sth BrE used to tell someone to hold something: *Cop hold of the other end, will you?* **4** cop an attitude AmE to behave in a way that is not nice, especially by showing that you think you are better or more intelligent than other people **5** cop a feel AmE to touch someone in a sexual way when they do not want you to **6** cop a plea AmE to agree to say you are guilty of a crime in order to receive a less severe punishment: *Dunn copped a plea to avoid going to jail.* **7** cop a buzz AmE to feel the effects of taking illegal drugs or drinking alcohol

cop off phr v BrE informal to meet someone and start a sexual relationship with them: [+with] *The hero falls in love with Dee but eventually cops off with the more desirable Clare.*

cop out phr v informal to not do something that

someone thinks you should do: *As far as I'm concerned, she's copped out and joined the rat race.* → COP-OUT

cope¹ S2 W2 /kəʊp $ koʊp/ *v* [I]
1 to succeed in dealing with a difficult problem or situation: *Sometimes I find it hard to cope.* | *He coped quite well as manager while still captaining the team.* | [+**with**] *She feared she wouldn't be able to cope with two new babies.* | *Local authorities have to cope with the problems of homelessness.*
2 if a system or machine copes with a particular type or amount of work, it does it: [+**with**] *No system is designed to cope with the floods we have had this year.* | *My computer can cope with huge amounts of data.*

cope² *n* [C] a long loose piece of clothing worn by priests on special occasions

cop·i·er /'kɒpiə $ 'kɑːpiər/ *n* [C] a machine that makes exact copies of writing or pictures on paper by photographing them; ▪ **photocopier**

co-,pi·lot *n* [C] a pilot who shares the control of an aircraft with the main pilot

cop·ing /'kəʊpɪŋ $ 'koʊ-/ *n* [C,U] a layer of rounded stones or bricks at the top of a wall or roof

co·pi·ous /'kəʊpiəs $ 'koʊ-/ *adj* [usually before noun] existing or being produced in large quantities: *He could drink copious amounts of beer without ill effect.* | *She listened to me and took copious notes.* —**copiously** *adv*: *Then she wept copiously.*

cop-out *n* [C] *informal* something you do or say in order to avoid doing or accepting something: *There is plenty to do on your own doorstep; to look further is a cop-out.*

cop·per /'kɒpə $ 'kɑːpər/ *n* **1** [U] a soft reddish-brown metal that allows electricity and heat to pass through it easily, and is used to make electrical wires, water pipes etc. It is a chemical ELEMENT: symbol Cu **2 coppers** [plural] *BrE* money of low value made of copper or BRONZE: *He offered to do the job for a few coppers.* **3** [C] a reddish-brown colour: *her copper hair* **4** [C] *BrE informal* a police officer —**coppery** *adj*: *coppery skin*

copper 'beech *n* [C] a large European tree with purple-brown leaves

copper-'bottomed *adj* able to be depended on: *a copper-bottomed guarantee*

cop·per·head /'kɒpəhed $ 'kɑːpər-/ *n* [C] a poisonous yellow and brown North American snake

cop·per·plate /'kɒpəpleɪt $ 'kɑːpər-/ *n* [U] neat regular curving handwriting with the letters all joined together in a very specific style, used especially in the past

cop·pice¹ /'kɒpɪs $ 'kɑː-/ *n* [C] a copse

coppice² *v* [T] to cut a tree down so that useful new wood will grow from the bottom

copse /kɒps $ kɑːps/ also **coppice** *n* [C] a group of trees or bushes growing close together

cop shop *n* [C] *BrE informal* a POLICE STATION

cop·ter /'kɒptə $ 'kɑːptər/ *n* [C] *AmE* a HELICOPTER

cop·u·la /'kɒpjʊlə $ 'kɑːp-/ *n* [C] *technical* a type of verb that connects the subject of a sentence to its COMPLEMENT, for example 'seem' in the sentence 'The house seems big'; ▪ **linking verb**

cop·u·late /'kɒpjʊleɪt $ 'kɑːp-/ *v* [I + with] *technical* to have sex —**copulation** /,kɒpjʊ'leɪʃən $,kɑːp-/ *n* [U]

cop·y¹ S1 W2 /'kɒpi $ 'kɑːpi/ *n plural* **copies**
1 [C] something that is made to be exactly like another thing: [+**of**] *She forwarded them a copy of her British passport.* | *This chair is a copy of an original design.* | *Be sure to make copies of all the documents.* | *back-up copies of your files*
2 [C] one of many books, magazines, records etc that are all exactly the same: [+**of**] *We have six copies of the movie to give away.* | *a copy of the local newspaper* | *The hardback costs £16.99 a copy.* | *The record sold a million copies.* | *Free copies are available on request.*

3 [U] *technical* something written in order to be printed in a newspaper, magazine, advertisement etc: *Now that I've seen the finished copy, I'm delighted.*
4 good copy *informal* interesting news: *The interviews made good copy and helped with the film's publicity.* → FAIR COPY, HARD COPY, SOFT COPY

copy² S2 *v* **copied, copying, copies**
1 [I,T] to deliberately make or produce something that is exactly like another thing: *Could you copy this letter and send it out, please?* | *To copy a file, press F3.* | **copy (sth) from sth** *a design copied from an 18th century wallpaper* | *The pupils just copy from textbooks and learn facts.* | **copy sth into sth** *He copied the number into his notebook* (=wrote the same number there).
2 [T] to deliberately do something that someone else has done or behave like someone else: *Children often copy what they see on television.* | *I found myself copying him and his mannerisms.*
3 [I,T] to cheat in an examination, schoolwork etc by looking at someone else's work and writing the same thing as they have: [+**from**] *Jeremy had copied from the girl next to him.*

copy sth ⇔ down *phr v*
to write something down exactly as it was said or written: *I think I must have copied your number down wrong.*

copy sb in *phr v*
to send someone a copy of an e-mail message you are sending to someone else: [+**on**] *Can you copy me in on the memo you're sending to Chris?*

copy sth ⇔ out *phr v*
to write something again exactly as it is written in the document that you are looking at: *The monks copied their manuscripts out by hand.*

copy sth ⇔ up *phr v BrE*
to write something again in a better or neater form: *It is important to copy up your notes soon after the lecture.*

cop·y·book /'kɒpibʊk $ 'kɑː-/ *adj* [only before noun] completely suitable or correct: *a copybook answer*

cop·y·cat¹ /'kɒpikæt $ 'kɑː-/ *n* [C] *informal* someone who copies other people's clothes, behaviour, work etc – used by children to show disapproval

copycat² *adj* **copycat crime/attack etc** a crime, attack etc which is similar to a famous crime that another person has committed: *Crime reports in newspapers often encourage copycat crimes.*

copy ,editor *n* [C] someone whose job is to make sure that the words in a book, newspaper etc are correct and ready to be printed —**copy-edit** *v* [I,T]

cop·y·ist /'kɒpi-ɪst $ 'kɑː-/ *n* [C] someone who made written copies of documents, books etc in the past

cop·y·right /'kɒpiraɪt $ 'kɑː-/ *n* [C,U] the legal right to be the only producer or seller of a book, play, film, or record for a specific length of time: *Who owns the copyright of this book?* | *The database will be protected by copyright.* | **infringement/breach of copyright** (=when you break the copyright laws) —**copyright** *adj*: *copyright material* —**copyright** *v* [T]

cop·y·writ·er /'kɒpi,raɪtə $ 'kɑːpi,raɪtər/ *n* [C] someone who writes the words for advertisements

coq au vin /,kɒk əʊ 'væn $,koʊk oʊ-/ *n* [U] chicken cooked in red wine

coq·ue·try /'kɒkɪtri $ 'koʊ-/ *n plural* **coquetries** [C,U] *literary* behaviour that is typical of a coquette

co·quette /kəʊ'ket, kɒ- $ koʊ-/ *n* [C] *literary* a woman who frequently tries to attract the attention of men without having sincere feelings for them; ▪ **flirt** —**coquettish** *adj* —**coquettishly** *adv*

cor /kɔː $ kɔːr/ *interjection BrE spoken* used when you are very surprised or impressed by something

cor- /kə, kɒ $ kə, kɔːr, kɑːr/ *prefix* the form used for CON-before r: *to correlate* (=connect together)

cor·a·cle /'kɒrəkəl $ 'kɔː-, 'kɑː-/ *n* [C] a small round boat that you move with a PADDLE

cor·al[1] /ˈkɒrəl $ ˈkɔː-, ˈkɑː-/ n [U] a hard red, white, or pink substance formed from the bones of very small sea creatures, which is often used to make jewellery

coral[2] adj pink or reddish-orange in colour

coral 'reef n [C] a line of hard rocks formed by coral, found in warm sea water that is not very deep

cor an·glais /ˌkɔːr ˈɒŋgleɪ $ -ɒːŋˈgleɪ/ n plural **cors anglais** (same pronunciation) [C] BrE a long wooden musical instrument which is like an OBOE but with a lower sound; ▣ **English horn** AmE

cor bli·mey /ˌkɔː ˈblaɪmi $ ˌkɔːr-/ also **blimey** interjection BrE old-fashioned used to express surprise

cord[1] /kɔːd $ kɔːrd/ n **1** [C,U] a piece of thick string or thin rope: The robe was held at the waist by a cord. | He pulled explosives and some tangled cord from his bag. **2 cords** [plural] trousers made from a thick strong cotton cloth with thin raised lines on it **3** [C,U] an electrical wire or wires with a protective covering, usually for connecting electrical equipment to the supply of electricity: the phone cord | an extension cord **4** [C] AmE a specific quantity of wood cut for burning in a fire: We use three cords of wood in a winter. → **cut the cord** at CUT[1] (40); → COMMUNICATION CORD, SPINAL CORD, UMBILICAL CORD, VOCAL CORDS

cord[2] adj cord clothes are made from CORDUROY: green cord trousers

cord·age /ˈkɔːdɪdʒ $ ˈkɔːr-/ n [U] rope or cord in general, especially on a ship

cor·di·al[1] /ˈkɔːdiəl $ ˈkɔːrdʒəl/ n [C,U] **1** BrE sweet fruit juice that you add water to before you drink it: lime cordial **2** AmE old-fashioned a strong sweet alcoholic drink; ▣ **liqueur**: an after-dinner cordial

cordial[2] adj friendly but quite polite and formal: The talks were conducted in a cordial atmosphere. —**cordiality** /ˌkɔːdiˈæləti $ ˌkɔːrdʒiˈæ-, ˌkɔːrˈdʒæ-/ n [U]

cor·di·al·ly /ˈkɔːdiəli $ ˈkɔːrdʒəli/ adv **1** in a friendly but polite and formal way: You are cordially invited to our wedding on May 9. **2 cordially dislike/ loathe etc** to dislike someone or something very strongly

cor·dite /ˈkɔːdaɪt $ ˈkɔːr-/ n [U] an explosive used in bullets and bombs

cord·less /ˈkɔːdləs $ ˈkɔːrd-/ adj a piece of equipment that is cordless is not connected to its power supply by wires: a cordless phone | a cordless drill

cor·don[1] /ˈkɔːdn $ ˈkɔːrdn/ n [C] a line of police officers, soldiers, or vehicles that is put around an area to stop people going there: [+of] A cordon of police surrounded the building. | [+around] the security cordon around the capital

cordon[2] v

cordon sth ⇔ **off** phr v to surround and protect an area with police officers, soldiers, or vehicles: Police cordoned off the street where the murder took place.

cor·don bleu /ˌkɔːdɒn ˈblɜː $ ˌkɔːrdɔːn ˈbluː/ adj [only before noun] relating to cooking of very high quality: a cordon bleu chef

cor·du·roy /ˈkɔːdʒ⅃rɔɪ, -djⅣ- $ ˈkɔːrdə-/ n [U] a thick strong cotton cloth with thin raised lines on it, used for making clothes: a corduroy jacket

core[1] [W3] /kɔː $ kɔːr/ n [C]
1 FRUIT the hard central part of a fruit such as an apple: Remove the cores, and bake the apples for 40 minutes. → see picture at FRUIT
2 MOST IMPORTANT PART the most important or central part of something: [+of] The core of the book focuses on the period between 1660 and 1857. | Debt is **at the core of** the problem.
3 PEOPLE a number of people who form a group which is very important to an organization: The business needs a new core of trained administrators. | a core group of clients → HARD CORE
4 to the core extremely or completely: **shaken/ shocked/thrilled to the core** When I heard the news, I was shaken to the core. | That woman is **rotten to the core**! | He was a bureaucrat to the core.
5 PLANET the central part of the Earth or any other PLANET → see picture at GLOBE
6 NUCLEAR REACTOR the central part of a NUCLEAR REACTOR

core[2] adj **1 core curriculum/subjects/skills etc** subjects that have to be studied at a school or college: the national core curriculum | the core subjects of English, maths, and science | Schools have to deliver the core skills. **2 core business/activities/operations etc** the main business or activities of a company or organization: The core business of airlines is flying people and cargo from place to place. | the company's core product **3 core values/beliefs** the values or beliefs that are most important to someone: the core values of American liberalism, such as taxing the rich to help the poor

core[3] v [T] to remove the centre from a fruit

co·re·li·gion·ist /ˌkəʊrⅢˈlɪdʒənⅢst $ ˌkoʊ-/ n [C] formal someone who is a member of the same religion as you

cor·er /ˈkɔːrə $ -ər/ n [C] a specially shaped knife for taking the hard centres out of fruit

co·res·pon·dent /ˌkəʊrⅢˈspɒndənt $ ˌkoʊrⅢˈspɑːn-/ n [C] someone whose name is given in a DIVORCE because they have had sex with the wife or husband of the person who wants the divorce; → **respondent**

cor·gi /ˈkɔːgi $ ˈkɔːrgi/ n [C] a small dog with short legs and a pointed nose

co·ri·an·der /ˌkɒriˈændə $ ˌkɔːriˈændər/ n [U] BrE a herb, used especially in Asian cooking; ▣ **cilantro** AmE

cork[1] /kɔːk $ kɔːrk/ n **1** [U] the BARK (=outer part) of a tree from southern Europe and North Africa, used to make things: a cork bulletin board **2** [C] a long round piece of cork which is put into the top of a bottle, especially a wine bottle, to keep liquid inside

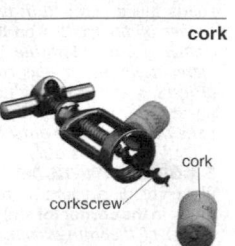
cork

cork

corkscrew

cork[2] v [T] to close a bottle by blocking the hole at the top tightly with a long round piece of cork; ▣ **uncork**

cork·age /ˈkɔːkɪdʒ $ ˈkɔːr-/ n [U] BrE the charge made by a hotel or restaurant for allowing people to bring in their own alcoholic drinks

corked /kɔːkt $ kɔːrkt/ adj corked wine tastes bad because a fault in the cork has allowed air into the bottle

cork·er /ˈkɔːkə $ ˈkɔːrkər/ n [C] BrE old-fashioned someone or something you think is very good —**corking** adj

cork·screw[1] /ˈkɔːkskruː $ ˈkɔːrk-/ n [C] a tool made of twisted metal that you use to pull a CORK out of a bottle → see picture at CORK

corkscrew[2] adj [only before noun] twisted or curly; ▣ **spiral**: corkscrew curls

cor·mo·rant /ˈkɔːmərənt $ ˈkɔːr-/ n [C] a large black sea bird which has a long neck and eats fish

corn [S3] /kɔːn $ kɔːrn/ n
1 [U] BrE plants such as wheat, BARLEY, and OATS or their seeds: fields of corn | an **ear of corn** (=the top part of this plant where the seeds grow)
2 [U] **a)** AmE a tall plant with large yellow seeds that grow together on a COB (=long hard part), which is cooked and eaten as a vegetable or fed to animals; ▣ **maize** BrE: All our chickens are fed on corn. → CORN ON THE COB **b)** the seeds of this plant → SWEETCORN
3 [C] a painful area of thick hard skin on your foot

[1] 000, [2] 000, [3] 000, most frequent words in [S] poken and [W] ritten English

C

corn·ball /'kɔːnbɔːl $ 'kɔːrnbɒːl/ adj [only before noun]
AmE informal cornball humour is extremely simple,
old-fashioned, and silly: Country and Western songs
always have such cornball titles.

corn bread n [U] bread made from CORNMEAL

corn chip n [C] crushed MAIZE formed into a small flat
piece, cooked in oil, and eaten cold, especially in the US

corn·cob /'kɔːnkɒb $ 'kɔːrnkɑːb/ also **cob** n [C] the
hard part of a corn plant that the yellow seeds grow on

corn·crake /'kɔːnkreɪk $ 'kɔːrn-/ n [C] a European
bird with a loud sharp cry

corn dolly n [C] BrE a figure made in the past from
wheat plants to celebrate the HARVEST

cor·ne·a /'kɔːniə $ 'kɔːr-/ n [C] the transparent pro-
tective covering on the outer surface of your eye
—**corneal** adj

corned beef /ˌkɔːnd 'biːf◂ $ ˌkɔːrnd-/ n [U] **1** BrE
BEEF that has been cooked and preserved in a
can **2** AmE BEEF that has been covered in salt water
and spices to preserve it

cor·ner[1] S1 W2 /'kɔːnə $ 'kɔːrnər/ n
1 WHERE TWO LINES/EDGES MEET [C] the point at
which two lines or edges meet: He pulled a dirty
handkerchief out by its corner and waved it at me. |
[+of] Their initials were sewn on the corner of every
pillow. | **in the corner (of sth)** The TV station's name
appears in the corner of the screen. | **on the corner (of
sth)** Jessie sat on the corner of her bed. | **three-
cornered/four-cornered etc** a three-cornered hat
2 ROAD [C usually singular] **a)** the point where two
roads meet: [+of] Ruth walked with her as far as the
corner of the road. | **on the corner** The hotel is on the
corner of 5th and Maine. | **at the corner** Several women
were standing at the corner, talking to two police
officers. | kids hanging around on **street corners b)** a
point in a road where it turns sharply: He had tried to
take the corner too quickly, and had lost control of the
car. | The petrol station is **around the corner**.
3 CORNER OF A ROOM/BOX [C usually singular] the
place inside a room or box where two walls or sides
meet: **in the corner (of sth)** There was an old piano in the
corner of the living room. | **corner table/seat** I reserved
a corner table in my favourite restaurant.
4 MOUTH/EYE [C] the sides of your mouth or eyes: A
tear appeared in the corner of his eye.
5 DIFFICULT SITUATION [singular] a difficult situation
that you cannot easily escape from: **back/box/force/
push sb into a corner** (=put someone into a situation
where they do not have any choices about what to do)
Don't let your enemies back you into a corner. | The
writers have **painted themselves into a corner** by
killing off all the most popular characters in the first
series. | He found himself in a **tight corner** (=a very
difficult situation) looking for a way to get out.
6 SPORTS [C] **a)** a kick that one team is allowed to
take from one of the corners of their opponent's end of
the field **b)** any of the four corners of the area in which
the competitors fight in BOXING or WRESTLING, especially
one of the two corners where the competitors go in
between ROUNDS
7 DISTANT PLACE [C] a distant place in another part
of the world: [+of] She's gone off to work in some remote
corner of the world. | People came from **the four corners
of the world** (=from lots of different places) to make
America their new home.
8 see sth out of the corner of your eye to notice
something accidentally, without turning your head
towards it or looking for it: Out of the corner of her eye
she saw the dog running towards her.
9 (just) around/round the corner **a)** near: There's a bus
stop just around the corner. **b)** likely to happen soon:
Economic recovery is just around the corner.
10 turn the corner to start to become successful or to
feel better or happier, after a time when you have been
unsuccessful, ill, or unhappy: We knew Dad had turned

the corner when he started complaining about the hospital food.
11 fight your corner/fight sb's corner BrE to try very
hard to defend yourself in a discussion or argument,
or to do this for someone else: My line manager supports me, and says she's willing to fight my corner.
12 cut corners to save time, money, or energy by doing
things quickly and not as carefully as you should:
Don't try to cut corners when you're decorating.
13 cut a corner to go across the corner of something,
especially a road, instead of staying next to the edges
14 have/get a corner on sth to be the only company,
organization etc that has a particular product, ability,
advantage etc: London does not have a corner on film
festivals. | The company admitted reducing prices to **get
a corner on the market**. → KITTY-CORNER

corner[2] v **1** [T] to force a person or animal into a
position from which they cannot easily escape: Once
the dog was cornered, he began to growl. **2** [T] to go to
someone who is trying to avoid you, and make them
listen to you: Later, he cornered Jenny on the stairs and
asked her what was wrong. **3** **corner the market** to
gain control of the whole supply of a particular kind of
goods: They've been trying to corner the market by
buying up all the wheat in sight. **4** [I] if a car corners,
it goes around a corner or bend in the road

corner shop n [C] BrE a small shop near houses, that
sells food, cigarettes, and other things needed every
day; → **convenience store**

cor·ner·stone /'kɔːnəstəʊn $ 'kɔːrnərstoʊn/ n
[C] **1** something that is extremely important because
everything else depends on it: [+of] The magazine
became the cornerstone of McFadden's publishing
empire. **2** a stone at one of the bottom corners of a
building, often put in place at a special ceremony;
☐ foundation stone

cor·net /'kɔːnɪt $ kɔːr'net/ n [C] **1** a musical instru-
ment like a small TRUMPET **2** BrE a container made of
very thin cake, that you hold in your hand and eat ICE
CREAM from; **☐ cone**

corn ex·change n [C] BrE a place where corn used to
be bought and sold

corn·flakes /'kɔːnfleɪks $ 'kɔːrn-/ n [plural] small flat
pieces of crushed corn, usually eaten at breakfast with
milk

corn·flour /'kɔːnflaʊə $ 'kɔːrnflaʊr/ n [U] BrE fine
white flour made from CORN (2), used in cooking to make
soups and sauces thicker; **☐ cornstarch** AmE

corn·flow·er /'kɔːnflaʊə $ 'kɔːrnflaʊər/ n [C] a wild
plant with blue flowers

cor·nice /'kɔːnɪs $ 'kɔːr-/ n [C] wood or PLASTER that
runs along the top edge of a wall, used for decoration:
A carved cornice runs around the high-ceilinged room.

cor·niche /kɔː'niːʃ $ kɔːr-/ n [C] a road built along a
coast

Cor·nish pas·ty /ˌkɔːnɪʃ 'pæsti $ ˌkɔːr-/ n [C] a
folded piece of PASTRY, baked with meat and potatoes in
it, for one person to eat

corn liquor n [U] AmE CORN WHISKEY

corn·meal /'kɔːnmiːl $ 'kɔːrn-/ n [U] a rough type of
flour made from dried crushed CORN (2)

corn on the cob n [U] the top part of a CORN (2) plant
on which yellow seeds grow, cooked and eaten as a
vegetable → see picture at VEGETABLE

corn pone /'kɔːn pəʊn $ 'kɔːrn poʊn/ n [U] a kind of
American bread made from cornmeal

corn·rows /'kɔːnrəʊz $ 'kɔːrnroʊz/ n [plural] a way of
having your hair in small tight PLAITS in lines along your
head

corn·starch /'kɔːnstɑːtʃ $ 'kɔːrnstɑːrtʃ/ n [U] AmE
CORNFLOUR

corn syrup n [U] a very sweet thick liquid made from
CORN (2), used in cooking

cor·nu·co·pi·a /ˌkɔːnjʊˈkəʊpiə $ ˌkɔːrnəˈkoʊ-/ n [sin-
gular] **1** a container in the shape of an animal's horn,
full of fruit and flowers, used to represent a time when

there are large supplies of food　**2** *literary* a lot of good things: [+of] *a cornucopia of delights*

'corn ˌwhiskey also **corn liquor** *n* [U] a strong alcoholic drink made from CORN (2)

corn·y /'kɔːni $ 'kɔːrni/ *adj* too silly and repeated too often to be funny or interesting: *corny jokes* | *I know it sounds corny, but I dream about her every night.*

co·rol·la·ry /kə'rɒləri $ 'kɔːrəleri, 'kɑː-/ *n plural* **corollaries** [C] *formal* something that is the direct result of something else: [+of/to] *Is social inequality the inevitable corollary of economic freedom?*

co·ro·na /kə'rəʊnə $ -'roʊ-/ *n* [C] the shining circle of light seen around the sun when the moon passes in front of it in an ECLIPSE

cor·o·na·ry¹ /'kɒrənəri $ 'kɔːrəneri, 'kɑː-/ *adj* relating to the heart; 🔲 **cardiac**: *coronary disease*

coronary² *n plural* **coronaries** [C] *informal* if someone has a coronary, their heart suddenly stops working because the flow of blood to it has been blocked by a small piece of solid blood; 🔲 **heart attack**

ˌcoronary 'artery *n* [C] one of the two ARTERIES that supply blood to the heart

ˌcoronary throm'bosis *n* [C,U] a disease which causes someone's heart to suddenly stop working, because the flow of blood to it has been blocked by a small piece of solid blood; 🔲 **coronary**

cor·o·na·tion /ˌkɒrə'neɪʃən◂ $ ˌkɔː-, ˌkɑː-/ *n* [C] the ceremony at which someone is officially made king or queen

cor·o·ner /'kɒrənə $ 'kɔːrənər, 'kɑː-/ *n* [C] an official whose job is to discover the cause of someone's death, especially if they died in a sudden or unusual way: *The coroner recorded a verdict of death by natural causes.* | *The coroner's court heard how Mr Banner had been shot twice in the head.*

cor·o·net /'kɒrənˌt $ ˌkɒrə'net, ˌkɑː-/ *n* [C] a small CROWN worn by princes or other members of a royal family, especially on formal occasions

Corp. /kɔːp $ kɔːrp/　**1** the abbreviation of *corporation*: *Microsoft Corp.*　**2** the abbreviation of *corporal*

cor·po·ra /'kɔːpərə $ 'kɔːr-/ *a plural of* CORPUS

cor·po·ral /'kɔːpərəl $ 'kɔːr-/ *n* [C] a low rank in the army, air force etc

ˌcorporal 'punishment *n* [U] punishment that involves hitting someone, especially in schools and prisons; → **capital punishment**: *Corporal punishment was abolished in Britain in 1986.*

cor·po·rate W2 /'kɔːpərˌt $ 'kɔːr-/ *adj* [only before noun]
1 belonging to or relating to a corporation: *The company is moving its corporate headquarters* (=main offices) *from New York to Houston.* | *Vince is vice-president of corporate communications.* | *Corporate America is not about to be converted to the environmentalist cause.* | *changing the corporate culture* (=the way that people in a corporation think and behave) *to accept family-friendly policies* | *an advertising campaign intended to reinforce our corporate identity* (=the way a company presents itself to the public) | *the yacht can be hired for corporate hospitality* (=entertainment provided by companies for their customers)
2 shared by or involving all the members of a group: *corporate responsibility*
3 used to describe a group of organizations that form a single group: *The university is a corporate body made up of several different colleges.* —**corporately** *adv*

cor·po·ra·tion S3 W2 /ˌkɔːpə'reɪʃ ən $ ˌkɔːr-/ *n* [C]
1 a big company, or a group of companies acting together as a single organization: *He works for a large American corporation.* | *multinational corporations* | *the Siemens Corporation* | **corporation tax** (=tax that companies have to pay on their profits)
2 an organization or group of organizations that work together for a particular purpose and are officially recognized as one: *the New Orleans Citywide Develop-*

ment Corporation | *a housing corporation*
3 *BrE old use* a group of people elected to govern a town or city; 🔲 **council**

cor·po·ra·tis·m /'kɔːpərətɪzəm $ 'kɔːr-/ *n* [U] the power and influence that large corporations have

cor·po·re·al /kɔː'pɔːriəl $ kɔːr-/ *adj formal*　**1** relating to the body, rather than to the mind, feelings, or spirit; 🔲 **physical**: *corporeal desires*　**2** existing in a physical form and able to be touched

corps /kɔː $ kɔːr/ *n plural* **corps** /kɔːz $ kɔːrz/ [C]　**1** a group in an army with special duties and responsibilities: *the medical corps* | *the U.S. Army Corps of Engineers*　**2** a group of people who work together to do a particular job: *the president's press corps* | *the diplomatic corps*　**3** *technical* a trained army unit made of two or more DIVISIONS (=groups of soldiers) ⚠ Do not confuse with **corpse** (=dead body) which has a different pronunciation /kɔːps $ kɔːrps/.

corpse /kɔːps $ kɔːrps/ *n* [C] the dead body of a person; 🔲 **body**: *The corpse was found by children playing in the woods.*

cor·pu·lent /'kɔːpjʊlənt $ 'kɔːr-/ *adj formal* fat —**corpulence** *n* [U]

cor·pus /'kɔːpəs $ 'kɔːr-/ *n plural* **corpuses** *or* **corpora** /-pərə/ [C]　**1** *formal* a collection of all the writing of a particular kind or by a particular person: *the entire corpus of Shakespeare's works*　**2** *technical* a large collection of written or spoken language, that is used for studying the language: *a corpus of spoken English* → HABEAS CORPUS

cor·pus·cle /'kɔːpəsəl, kɔː'pʌ- $ 'kɔːrpə-/ *n* [C] one of the red or white cells in the blood

cor·ral¹ /kə'rɑːl $ kə'ræl/ *n* [C] a fairly small enclosed area where cattle, horses etc can be kept temporarily, especially in North America

corral² *v* **corralled, corralling** *BrE*, **corraled, corraling** *AmE* [T]　**1** to make animals move into a corral: *They corralled the cattle before loading them onto the truck.*　**2** to keep people in a particular area, especially in order to control them: *Once at the airport, we were herded to the gate and corralled into a small room.*

cor·rect¹ S1 W2 /kə'rekt/ *adj*
1 having no mistakes; 🔲 **right**; 🔲 **incorrect**: *If my calculations are correct, we're about 10 miles from Exeter.* | *Score one point for each correct answer.* | *You are absolutely correct, the Missouri is the longest river in the US.* | **factually/grammatically/anatomically etc correct** *The sentence is grammatically correct, but doesn't sound natural.*
2 suitable and right for a particular situation: *What's the correct procedure in cases like this?* | *When lifting heavy weights, it is very important that your back is in the correct position.*
3 correct behaviour is formal and polite: *It was not considered correct for young ladies to go out on their own.* —**correctly** *adv*: *If I remember correctly, he's Spanish.* | *We must make sure that things are done correctly.* —**correctness** *n* [U]

correct² S3 *v* [T]
1 to make something right or to make it work the way it should: *Some eyesight problems are relatively easy to correct.* | *You have the right to see a copy of your file, and to correct any mistakes you may find.*
2 to show someone that something is wrong, and make it right: *Correct my pronunciation if it's wrong.* | *'She's in Ireland now.' 'She was,' Farrell corrected him.* | **correct yourself** *'I,' Lady Deverill corrected herself, 'we are very happy here.'*
3 if a teacher corrects a student's written work, he or she writes marks on it to show the mistakes in it
4 correct me if I'm wrong *spoken* used when you are not sure that what you are going to say is true or not: *Correct me if I'm wrong, but didn't you say you'd never met him before?*

5 I stand corrected *formal spoken* used to admit that something you have said is wrong after someone has told you it is wrong

cor·rec·tion /kəˈrekʃən/ n **1** [C] a change made in something in order to make it right or better: *I just need to make a few corrections, and then we can send it to the printer.* **2** [U] *spoken* used to say that what you have just said is wrong and you want to change it: *That will basically cover fifty...correction sixty percent of all charges.* **3** [U] the act of changing something in order to make it right or better: *Please hand in your papers for correction.* **4** [U] *old-fashioned* punishment for people who have done something wrong or illegal

cor·rec·tion·al /kəˈrekʃənəl/ adj [only before noun] *technical* relating to the punishment of criminals: **correctional facility/institution/centre** (=a prison)

corˈrection ˌfluid n [U] a special white liquid used for covering mistakes made when writing something

cor·rec·ti·tude /kəˈrektɪtjuːd $ -tuːd/ n [U] *formal* correctness of behaviour

cor·rec·tive¹ /kəˈrektɪv/ adj [usually before noun] intended to make something right or better again: *corrective surgery* | **corrective action/measures** *corrective measures to deal with the country's serious economic decline*

corrective² n [C usually singular] *formal* something that is intended to correct a fault or mistake: [+to] *The biography is a useful corrective to the myths that have grown up around this man.*

cor·rel·ate¹ /ˈkɒrəleɪt $ ˈkɔː-, ˈkɑː-/ v [I,T] if two or more facts, ideas etc correlate or if you correlate them, they are closely connected to each other or one causes the other: [+with] *Poverty and poor housing correlate with a shorter life expectancy.* | **correlate strongly/significantly/closely** *Lack of prenatal care correlates strongly with premature birth.*

cor·re·late² /ˈkɒrələt $ ˈkɔː-, ˈkɑː-/ n [C] either of two things that correlate with each other

cor·re·la·tion /ˌkɒrəˈleɪʃən $ ˌkɔː-, ˌkɑː-/ n [C,U] a connection between two ideas, facts etc, especially when one may be the cause of the other: [+between] *Researchers found a strong correlation between urban deprivation and poor health.* | **strong/high/close/significant etc correlation** *There is a direct correlation between the best-known brands and the best-selling brands.* | [+with] *There was also some correlation with social class.*

cor·rel·a·tive /kəˈrelətɪv/ adj *formal* two or more facts, ideas etc that are correlative are closely related or dependent on each other: *rights and their correlative responsibilities* —**correlative** n [C]

cor·re·spond /ˌkɒrəˈspɒnd $ ˌkɔːrəˈspɑːnd, ˌkɑː-/ v [I] **1** if two things or ideas correspond, the parts or information in one relate to the parts or information in the other: *The two halves of the document did not correspond.* | [+with/to] *The numbers correspond to points on the map.* **2** to be very similar to or the same as something else: [+to] *The French 'baccalauréat' exam roughly corresponds to British A levels.* | **correspond closely/exactly/precisely to sth** *The description of these events corresponds closely to other accounts written at the time.* **3** to write letters to someone and receive letters from them: *For the next three years they corresponded regularly.* | [+with] *She stopped corresponding with him after the death of her mother.*

cor·re·spon·dence /ˌkɒrəˈspɒndəns $ ˌkɔːrəˈspɑːn-, ˌkɑː-/ n [U] **1** the letters that someone sends and receives, especially official or business letters: *A secretary came in twice a week to deal with his correspondence.* **2** the process of sending and receiving letters: *The magazine is unable to enter into any correspondence on medical matters.* | **(be in) correspondence with sb** *He had been in correspondence with her for several years before they finally met.* | *All correspondence between us must cease.* **3** a relation-

ship or connection between two or more ideas or facts: [+between] *There was no correspondence between the historical facts and Johnson's account of them.*

correˈspondence ˌcourse n [C] a course of lessons in which the student works at home and sends completed work to their teacher by post: *I'm taking a correspondence course in business studies.*

cor·re·spon·dent /ˌkɒrəˈspɒndənt $ ˌkɔːrəˈspɑːn-, ˌkɑː-/ n [C] **1** someone who is employed by a newspaper or a television station etc to report news from a particular area or on a particular subject; → **reporter**: **political/foreign/legal etc correspondent** *the political correspondent for The Times* | *Our correspondent in South Africa sent this report.* **2** someone who writes letters: *I'm not a very good correspondent, I'm afraid.*

cor·re·spon·ding /ˌkɒrəˈspɒndɪŋ◂ $ ˌkɔːrəˈspɑːn-, ˌkɑː-/ adj [only before noun] **1** caused by or connected with something you have already mentioned: *The war, and the corresponding fall in trade, have had a devastating effect on the country.* **2** having similar qualities or a similar size, position etc to something else; ■ **equivalent**: *Sales are up 10% on the corresponding period last year.* —**correspondingly** adv: *As his political power has shrunk, he has grown correspondingly more dependent on the army.*

cor·ri·dor S2 W3 /ˈkɒrɪdɔː $ ˈkɔːrɪdər, ˈkɑː-/ n [C] **1** a long narrow passage on a train or between rooms in a building, with doors leading off it: **in the corridor** *We had to wait outside in the corridor until our names were called.* | **down/along the corridor** *She hurried down the corridor.* | *Go down here and the bathroom's at the end of the corridor.* **2** a narrow area of land between cities or countries that has different qualities or features from the land around it: *the industrial corridor that connects Queretaro with Mexico City* **3 corridors of power** the places where important government decisions are made

cor·rie /ˈkɒri $ ˈkɔː- ˈkɑː-/ n [C] *BrE technical* a deep bowl-shaped area on a mountain

cor·rob·o·rate /kəˈrɒbəreɪt $ kəˈrɑː-/ v [T] *formal* to provide information that supports or helps to prove someone else's statement, idea etc: *We now have new evidence to corroborate the defendant's story.* | *Experiments elsewhere corroborate these results.* —**corroboration** /kəˌrɒbəˈreɪʃən $ -ˌrɑː-/ n [U] —**corroborative** /kəˈrɒbərətɪv $ -ˈrɑːbəreɪ-/ adj: *corroborative evidence*

cor·rode /kəˈrəʊd $ -ˈroʊd/ v [I,T] **1** if metal corrodes, or if something corrodes it, it is slowly destroyed by the effect of water, chemicals etc: *Higher levels of pollution have started to corrode pipes.* **2** *written* to gradually make something weaker or destroy it completely: *Corruption has corroded our confidence in the police force.*

cor·ro·sion /kəˈrəʊʒən $ -ˈroʊ-/ n [U] the gradual destruction of metal by the effect of water, chemicals etc or a substance such as RUST produced by this process: *They are sprayed with oil to prevent corrosion.* | *Check for signs of corrosion.*

cor·ro·sive /kəˈrəʊsɪv $ -ˈroʊ-/ adj **1** a corrosive liquid such as an acid can destroy metal, plastic etc: *a highly corrosive substance* **2** *written* gradually making something weaker, and possibly destroying it; ■ **damaging**: *the corrosive effect of money in modern politics*

cor·ru·gated /ˈkɒrəɡeɪtɪd $ ˈkɔː-, ˈkɑː-/ adj in the shape of waves or folds, or made like this in order to give something strength: *corrugated cardboard*

cor·rupt¹ /kəˈrʌpt/ adj **1** using your power in a dishonest or illegal way in order to get an advantage for yourself; ⊠ **incorruptible**: *Corrupt judges have taken millions of dollars in bribes.* **2** immoral or dishonest: *a corrupt society* | *officials engaged in corrupt practices* **3** something that is corrupt is not pure or has been damaged or partly ruined: *corrupt data* —**corruptly** adv —**corruptness** n [U]

corrupt² *v* [T] **1** to encourage someone to start behaving in an immoral or dishonest way: *Young prisoners are being corrupted by the older, long-term offenders.* | *They say power corrupts.* **2** to change the traditional form of something, such as a language, so that it becomes worse than it was: *The culture has been corrupted by Western influences.* **3** to change the information in a computer, so that the computer does not work properly any more: *a virus which corrupts the data on your hard drive* —**corruptible** *adj* —**corruptibility** /kə,rʌptɨ'bɪlɨti/ *n* [U]

cor·rup·tion /kə'rʌpʃən/ *n* **1** [U] dishonest, illegal, or immoral behaviour, especially from someone with power: *officials charged with bribery and corruption* | *The investigation uncovered **widespread corruption** within the police force.* | **political/official corruption** **2** [C usually singular] *technical* a changed form of something, for example a word: *The word 'Thursday' is a corruption of 'Thor's Day'.*

cor·sage /kɔː'sɑːʒ $ kɔːr-/ *n* [C] a group of small flowers that a woman fastens to her clothes on a special occasion such as a wedding

cor·set /'kɔːsɨt $ 'kɔːr-/ *n* [C] a piece of tight-fitting underwear that women wore especially in the past to make them look thinner

cor·tege /kɔː'teɪʒ $ kɔːr'teʒ/ *n* [C] a line of people or cars that move along slowly in a funeral

cor·tex /'kɔːteks $ 'kɔːr-/ *n plural* **cortices** /-tɨsiːz/ [C] the outer layer of an organ in your body, especially your brain —**cortical** /'kɔːtɪkəl $ 'kɔːr-/ *adj*

cor·ti·sone /'kɔːtɨzəʊn $ 'kɔːrtɨsoʊn/ *n* [U] a HORMONE that is used especially in the treatment of injuries and diseases such as ARTHRITIS: *a cortisone injection*

cor·us·ca·ting /'kɒrəskeɪtɪŋ $ 'kɔː-, 'kɑː-/ *adj literary* attractive and having a lot of energy, or shining brightly: *a play with scenes of coruscating brilliance*

cos¹ [S1] **'cos** /kəz/ *conjunction BrE spoken informal* because: *I don't get out much now cos of the children.*

cos² /kɒz $ kɑːz/ *technical* the written abbreviation of *cosine*

cosh¹ /kɒʃ $ kɑːʃ/ *n* [C] a heavy weapon in the shape of a short thick pipe

cosh² *v* [T] to hit someone with a cosh

co·sig·na·to·ry /,kəʊ'sɪgnətəri $,koʊ'sɪgnətɔːri/ *n plural* **cosignatories** [C] one of a group of people who sign a legal document for their department, organization, country etc: *Both cosignatories must sign the cheque.*

co·sine /'kəʊsaɪn $ 'koʊ-/ *n* [C] *technical* the measurement of an ACUTE angle in a TRIANGLE with a RIGHT ANGLE, that is calculated by dividing the length of the side next to it by the length of the HYPOTENUSE; → **sine**

cos·met·ic /kɒz'metɪk $ kɑːz-/ *adj* **1** dealing with the outside appearance rather than the important part of something; **⊟** **superficial**: *We're making a few cosmetic changes to the house before we sell it.* | *Many MPs denounced the resolution as a **cosmetic exercise** (=something which will look good, but have no real effect).* **2** intended to make your hair, skin, body etc look more attractive: *the cosmetic industry* | *cosmetic products* | *Are you on the diet for health or cosmetic reasons?*

cos·met·ics /kɒz'metɪks $ kɑːz-/ *n* [plural] creams, powders etc that you use on your face and body in order to look more attractive; → **make-up**: *a range of cosmetics and toiletries*

cos,metic 'surgery *n* [U] medical operations that improve your appearance after you have been injured, or because you want to look more attractive

cos·mic /'kɒzmɪk $ 'kɑːz-/ *adj* **1** relating to space or the universe **2** extremely large: *a scandal of cosmic proportions* —**cosmically** /-kli/ *adv*

,cosmic 'ray *n* [C usually plural] a stream of RADIATION reaching the Earth from space

cos·mog·o·ny /kɒz'mɒgəni $ kɑːz'mɑː-/ *n plural* **cosmogonies** [C,U] the origin of the universe, or a set of ideas about this

cos·mol·o·gy /kɒz'mɒlədʒi $ kɑːz'mɑː-/ *n* [U] the science of the origin and structure of the universe, especially as studied in ASTRONOMY

cos·mo·naut /'kɒzmənɔːt $ 'kɑːzmənɔːt/ *n* [C] an ASTRONAUT from the former Soviet Union

cos·mo·pol·i·tan¹ /,kɒzmə'pɒlɨtən $,kɑːzmə-'pɑː-/ *adj* **1** a cosmopolitan place has people from many different parts of the world – use this to show approval: *a vibrant, cosmopolitan city* | *a lively hotel with a cosmopolitan atmosphere* **2** a cosmopolitan person, belief, opinion etc shows a wide experience of different people and places: *Brigitta has such a cosmopolitan outlook on life.*

cosmopolitan² *n* [C] someone who has travelled a lot and feels at home in any part of the world

cos·mos /'kɒzmɒs $ 'kɑːzməs/ *n* **the cosmos** the whole universe, especially when you think of it as a system

cos·set /'kɒsɨt $ 'kɑː-/ *v* [T] to give someone as much care and attention as you can, especially too much: *He cosseted her with flowers and champagne.*

cost¹ [S1] [W1] /kɒst $ kɒːst/ *n*
1 [C] the amount of money that you have to pay in order to buy, do, or produce something

pay the cost of sth
meet/bear the cost (of sth) (=pay for something)
cover the cost (of sth) (=pay for all of something)
the cost of doing sth
at a cost of $10/$100 etc
high/low cost
full/total cost
extra/additional cost
rising/escalating cost
at no extra cost (to sb)
labour/transport/legal etc costs
running/operating costs (=what it costs to organize an event or run a business)

[+of] *the cost of accommodation* | *I offered to **pay the cost of** the taxi.* | *Insurance to **cover the cost of** a funeral is possible.* | *This doesn't include **the cost of** repairing the damage.* | *The new building's going up **at a cost of** $82 million.* | *low cost housing* | *the **high cost** of production* | *A cassette/radio is included **at no extra cost**.* | *The funds will just cover the museum's **running costs**.* → COST OF LIVING

2 costs [plural] **a)** the money that you must regularly spend in order to run a business, a home, a car etc: **reduce/cut costs** *We have to cut costs in order to remain competitive.* | *At this rate we'll barely **cover** our **costs** (=make enough money to pay for the things we have bought).* | *the travel **costs incurred** in attending the meeting (=money you have to spend)* | *Because of the engine's efficiency the car has very low **running costs** (=the cost of owning and using a car or machine).* **b)** also **court costs** the money that you must pay to lawyers etc if you are involved in a legal case in court, especially if you are found guilty: *Bellisario won the case and was awarded costs.* | *He was fined £1000 and ordered to pay costs of £2200.*

3 [C,U] something that you lose, give away, damage etc in order to achieve something: **at (a) cost to sb** *She had kept her promise to Christine, but at what cost to herself?* | **social/environmental etc cost** *the environmental cost of such mining projects* | *They need to weigh up the **costs and benefits** (=disadvantages and advantages) of regulation.* | *He's determined to win, **whatever the cost** (=no matter how much work, money, risk etc is* needed). | *We must avoid a scandal at all costs* (=whatever happens).

4 [singular] *especially AmE* the price that someone pays for something that they are going to sell; ☐ **cost price**: **at cost** *His uncle's a car dealer and let him buy the car at cost* (=without making a profit).

5 know/find out/learn etc sth to your cost to realize something is true because you have had a very unpleasant experience: *Driving fast in wet conditions is dangerous, as my brother discovered to his cost!* → **count the cost** at COUNT[1] (10)

WORD CHOICE: cost, costs, price, charge, fee, fare
Use **cost** to talk about paying for services and activities, rather than objects: *The total cost of the trip was under $500.* | *I worked out the cost of the repairs.*
Your **costs** are the amount of money you have to spend in order to run a business or to do a particular activity: *The shop was not making enough money to cover its costs.*
Use **price** to mean the amount of money that you must pay for something in a place such as a shop or restaurant: *We are cutting all our prices (NOT costs) by 50% for one day only!* | *We were shocked by the price of a cup of coffee in London.*
A **charge** is the amount you have to pay to have a particular service or use something: *For a small charge we will also make your hotel reservations.*
A **fee** is the amount you have to pay to enter or join something: *The gallery charges no entrance fee.* | *The fee for membership is £25 per year.* It is also the amount you have to pay for a professional service: *The lawyer explained her fees.*
A **fare** is the amount you have to pay to travel somewhere by bus, train, plane etc: *I need some money for my bus fare.* | *His parents paid his fare to Sydney.*

---

cost² [S1] [W2] *v*
1 *past tense and past participle* **cost** [linking verb] to have a particular price: *A full day's activities will cost you £45.* | *His proposals could cost the taxpayer around £8 billion a year.* | *How much would it cost us to replace?* | **not cost sb a penny** (=cost nothing) *It won't cost you a penny for the first six months.* | **cost a (small) fortune/a pretty penny** (=have a very high price) *It's costing us a fortune in phone bills.* | **cost a bomb/a packet** *BrE* (=have a very high price) *What a fantastic dress. It must have cost a bomb!* | *Lighting can change the look of a room and needn't* **cost the earth** (=have a price which is too high). | *Getting that insured is going to* **cost you an arm and a leg** (=have a very high price).
2 cost sb their job/life/marriage etc when something makes you lose your job etc: *Joe's brave action cost him his life.* | *His strong stand on the issue could have cost him his job.* | *Bad management could be costing this club a chance at the title.*
3 cost sb dear/dearly to make someone suffer a lot or to lose something important: *A couple of missed chances in the first half cost them dear.* | *The scandal has cost Nicholson dearly.*
4 *past tense and past participle* **costed** [T usually passive] to calculate the total price of something or decide how much the price of something should be: *We'll get the plan costed before presenting it to the board.*
5 it will cost you *spoken* used to say that something will be expensive: *Tickets are available, but they'll cost you!*

co-star¹ /'kəʊ stɑː $ 'koʊ stɑːr/ *n* [C] one of two or more famous actors who appear together in a film or play

co-star² *v* **co-starred, co-starring** [I] to be working in a film or play with other famous actors: [+with/in] *She's co-starring in a TV version of the 1960s thriller.* | *He co-starred with Bruce Willis in the movie Die Hard.*

cost-benefit *n* **cost-benefit analysis/study/approach** *technical* a way of calculating the methods or plans that will bring you the most BENEFITS (=advantages or help) for the smallest cost, especially in business

cost-ef,fective, cost effective *adj* bringing the best possible profits or advantages for the lowest possible costs: **cost effective way of doing sth** *the most cost-effective way of reducing carbon dioxide emissions* | *The procedure is quick, easy to use and cost effective.* —**cost-effectively** *adv* —**cost-effectiveness** *n* [U]

cos-ter-mon-ger /'kɒstə,mʌŋgə $ 'kɑːstər ,mɑːŋgər, -,mʌŋ-/ *BrE old-fashioned n* [C] someone who sells fruit and vegetables in the street

cost-ing /'kɒstɪŋ $ 'kɔːst-/ *n* [C,U] the process of calculating the cost of a future business activity, product etc, or the calculation itself: *the planning and costing of staffing levels* | *We were asked to prepare detailed costings for the scheme.*

cost-ly /'kɒstli $ 'kɔːstli/ *adj* **1** very expensive, especially wasting a lot of money: *a complex and costly procedure* | *Such a database would be extremely costly to set up.* **2** something that is costly causes a lot of problems or trouble: *His delay in making a decision could* **prove costly** *in the long run.* —**costliness** *n* [U]

cost of 'living *n* **the cost of living** the amount of money you need to pay for the food, clothes etc you need to live: *Average wages have increased in line with the cost of living.*

cost 'price *n* [U] the price that someone pays for something that they are going to sell

cos-tume /'kɒstjʊm $ 'kɑːstuːm/ *n* **1** [C] a set of clothes worn by an actor or by someone to make them look like something such as an animal, famous person etc; → **outfit**: *The film featured lavish costumes and spectacular sets.* | *Hallowe'en costumes* **2** [C,U] clothes that are typical of a particular place or period of time in the past: *The dancers were all in* **national costume**. | *performers dressed in* **period costume** (=the clothes of a period of history) **3** [C] *BrE* a SWIMMING COSTUME

costume ,drama *n* [C] a play that is about a particular time in history, in which people wear costumes from that time

costume ,jewellery *n* [U] cheap jewellery that is often designed to look expensive

co-sy¹ *BrE*; **cozy** *AmE* /'kəʊzi $ 'koʊzi/ *adj* **1** a place that is cosy is small, comfortable, and warm: *The living room was* **warm and cosy**. **2** a situation that is cosy is comfortable and friendly: *a cosy chat* **3** having a close connection or relationship, especially one you do not approve of: *He was accused of being too cosy with some clients.* —**cosily** *adv* —**cosiness** *n* [U]

cosy² *n plural* **cosies** [C] *BrE* a covering for a TEAPOT that keeps the tea inside from getting cold too quickly: *a tea cosy*

cot /kɒt $ kɑːt/ *n* [C] **1** *BrE* a small bed with high sides for a baby or young child; ☐ **crib** *AmE*; → see picture at BED **2** *AmE* a CAMP BED

cot ,death *n* [C] *BrE* the sudden and unexpected death of a baby while it is sleeping; ☐ **crib death** *AmE*

co-te-rie /'kəʊtəri $ 'koʊ-/ *n* [C] *formal* a small group of people who enjoy doing the same things together, and do not like including others; → **clique**

co-ter-mi-nous /kəʊ'tɜːmɪnəs $ koʊ'tɜːr-/ *adj technical* **1** *formal* having the same pattern or features **2** coterminous countries share the same border

cot-tage [S2] [W3] /'kɒtɪdʒ $ 'kɑː-/ *n* [C] a small house in the country: *a country cottage* | *We're staying in a holiday cottage in Dorset.*

cottage 'cheese / $ '.. ./ *n* [U] soft white cheese made from sour milk

cottage 'hospital *n* [C] a small hospital, usually in a country area

cottage 'industry *n* [C] an industry that consists of people working at home: *Hand weaving is a flourishing cottage industry in the region.*

cot-tag-er /'kɒtɪdʒə $ 'kɑːtɪdʒər/ *n* [C] a person in the past who lived in a cottage

cot·tag·ing /'kɒtɪdʒɪŋ $ 'kɑː-/ *n* [U] *BrE informal* when a HOMOSEXUAL man goes to a public toilet with the intention of meeting other men for sex

cot·ton¹ /'kɒtn $ 'kɑːtn/ *n* [U] *BrE* **1** cloth or thread made from the white hair of the cotton plant: *a white cotton shirt* | *Made from 100% cotton.* → see picture at MATERIAL **2** a plant with white hairs on its seeds that are used for making cotton cloth and thread **3** *BrE* thread used for sewing: *a needle and cotton* | *a cotton reel* (=small round tube which cotton thread is wound around) **4** *AmE* COTTON WOOL

cotton² *v*

cotton on *phr v informal* to begin to understand something; → **realize**: *It took me a while to cotton on.* | [+to] *Sarah soon cottoned on to what he was trying to do.*

cotton to sb/sth *phr v AmE informal* to begin to like a person, idea etc: *I didn't cotton to her at first, but she's really nice.*

'cotton bud *n* [C] *BrE* a small thin stick with COTTON WOOL at each end, used for cleaning places that are hard to reach, such as inside your ears; ⊟ **Q-tip** *AmE*

'cotton ,candy *n* [U] *AmE* CANDYFLOSS

'cotton gin *n* [C] a machine that separates the seeds of a cotton plant from the cotton

'cotton-,picking *adj* [only before noun] *especially AmE old-fashioned* used to emphasize that you are annoyed or surprised: *Mind your own cotton-picking business!*

cot·ton·wood /'kɒtnwʊd $ 'kɑː-/ *n* [C,U] a North American tree with seeds that look like white cotton

,cotton 'wool *n* [U] *BrE* **1** a soft mass of cotton that you use especially for cleaning and protecting wounds: *She put some disinfectant on a piece of cotton wool and dabbed it on her cheek.* **2 wrap sb (up) in cotton wool** to protect someone completely from the dangers, difficulties etc of life: *You can't wrap those kids in cotton wool all their lives.*

couch¹ /kaʊtʃ/ *n plural* **couches** [C] **1** a comfortable piece of furniture big enough for two or three people to sit on; ⊟ **sofa**, **settee**: *Tom offered to sleep on the couch.* → see picture at SOFA **2** a long narrow bed for a doctor's or PSYCHIATRIST's patients to lie on

couch² *v* **be couched in sth** *formal* to be expressed in a particular way: *The offer was couched in legal jargon.*

cou·chette /kuːˈʃet/ *n* [C] *BrE* a narrow bed that folds down from the wall in a train, or a comfortable seat on a night train or boat; → **sleeping car**

'couch po,tato *n* [C] someone who spends a lot of time sitting and watching television

cou·gar /'kuːgə, -gɑː $ -gər, -gɑːr/ *n* [C] a large brown wild cat from the mountains of Western North America and South America; ⊟ **mountain lion**

cough¹ /kɒf $ kɒːf/ *v* [I] **1** to suddenly push air out of your throat with a short sound, often repeatedly: *Matthew coughed and cleared his throat.* | *I think I'm getting a cold or flu – I've been coughing and sneezing all day.* **2** to make a sudden sound like someone coughing: *The engine coughed and spluttered, then stopped altogether.*

cough up *phr v* **1** *informal* to give someone money, information etc when you do not really want to: *Come on, cough up.* | **cough sth** ⇔ **up** *Insurance companies had to cough up £10 million in storm damage claims.* **2 cough sth** ⇔ **up** to push something out of your throat or lungs into your mouth: *You must go to the doctor if you're coughing up blood.*

cough² *n* **1** [C] the action or sound made when you cough: *Stuart gave an embarrassed cough.* **2** [U] a medical condition that makes you cough a lot: *She's got a terrible smoker's cough.* | **dry/persistent/ticklish etc cough** *Symptoms include a sore throat and dry, persistent cough.*

'cough ,mixture also **'cough ,syrup** or **'cough ,medicine** *n* [U] a thick, usually sweet, liquid containing medicine that helps you to stop coughing

could S1 W1 /kəd; *strong* kʊd/ *modal verb negative short form* **couldn't**

1 PAST ABILITY used as the past tense of 'can' to say what someone was able to do or was allowed to do in the past: *By the time she was eight, she could read Greek and Latin.* | *In those days you could buy a box of cigars for a dollar.* | *Could you hear what I was saying?* | *I couldn't get tickets after all, they were sold out.* | *I knew I couldn't afford the rent.* | *The teacher said we could all go home.*
2 POSSIBILITY **a)** used to say that something is possible or might happen: *Most accidents in the home could be prevented.* | *It could be weeks before we get a reply.* | *If you're not careful, you could get into even worse trouble.* | *A faulty connection could easily* (=would be likely to) *cause a fire.* **b)** used to say that something was a possibility in the past, but did not actually happen: *Somebody could have been killed.* | *I could have warned you if I had known where you were.* | *He could have escaped, but he chose to stand and fight.*
3 EMPHASIZING YOUR FEELINGS *spoken* used to emphasize how happy, angry etc you are by saying how you want to express your feelings: *Sometimes he irritates me so much I could scream.* | *I was so angry I could have killed her.* | *I was so relieved I could have kissed them all.*
4 REQUESTING *spoken* used to make a polite request: *Could you help me with these boxes?* | *Could I have a drink of water, please?* | *How about Sam? Could he come along too?* | *I wonder if I could just ask you to sign this.*
5 SUGGESTING *spoken* used to suggest doing something: *You could ask your doctor for a check-up.* | *You could always try phoning her at the office.* | *Maybe we could get together sometime next week?* | *Couldn't you get one of your friends to help you?*
6 ANNOYANCE *spoken* used to show that you are annoyed about someone's behaviour: *You could have told me you were going to be late* (=you should have told me but you did not)! | *You could at least say that you're sorry.* | *How could you be so stupid!*
7 couldn't be better/worse/more pleased etc used to emphasize how good, bad etc something is: *Their lifestyles couldn't be more different.* | *'How are things?' 'Fine! Couldn't be better.'* | *Ordering on-line couldn't be simpler.*
8 I couldn't *BrE spoken* used to politely say that you do not want any more food or drink: *'Would you like another piece of pie?' 'Oh, no thanks, I couldn't.'*
9 could do with sth *spoken* to need or want something: *I could do with a hot drink.* → **could do worse (than)** at WORSE¹ (5); → **couldn't care less** at CARE² (5); → **couldn't agree more** at AGREE (1)

couldst /kʊdst/ *v old use* **thou couldst** words meaning 'you could'

cou·lis /'kuːli/ *n plural* **coulis** /'kuːliz/ [C] a thin fruit sauce

coun·cil S2 W1 /'kaʊnsəl/ *n* [C]
1 a group of people that are chosen to make rules, laws, or decisions, or to give advice: *the council for civil liberties* | *the UN Security Council*
2 the organization that is responsible for local government in a particular area in Britain: **local council** *elections* | *He sent a letter to the council to complain about the noise.* | **County/District/City etc Council** *Northampton Borough Council* | **council leader/officer/worker etc** | **council chamber/offices**
3 a group of people elected to the government of a city in the US: *the Los Angeles city council*

'council es,tate *n* [C] *BrE* an area in a town or city with streets of council houses

'council house also **'council flat** *n* [C] *BrE* a house or FLAT in Britain that is provided by the local council for a very low rent

coun·cil·lor S3 W3 *BrE*, **councilor** *AmE* /'kaʊnsələ $ -ər/ *n* [C] a member of a council: *Write to your local councillor to complain.* ⚠ Do not confuse with **counsellor** (=person whose job is to help you talk about and deal with your problems).

C

coun·cil·man /ˈkaʊnsəlmən/ *n plural* **councilmen** /-mən/ [C] *AmE* a man who is a member of the government of a city in the US

,**council of 'war** *n plural* **councils of war** [C] a meeting to decide how to deal with a particular problem – used humorously

'**council ,tax** *n* [singular, U] *BrE* a tax which every home in Britain has to pay to local government, based on the area and the value of the house, FLAT etc

coun·cil·wom·an /ˈkaʊnsəl,wʊmən/ *n plural* **councilwomen** /-,wɪmɪn/ [C] *AmE* a woman who is a member of the government of a city in the US

coun·sel¹ /ˈkaʊnsəl/ *n* [U] **1** a type of lawyer who represents you in court: [+**for**] *The judge asked counsel for the defence to explain.* **2 keep your own counsel** written to keep your plans, opinions etc secret **3** *literary* advice

counsel² *v* **counselled, counselling** *BrE*, **counseled, counseling** *AmE* [T] **1** *formal* to advise someone: **counsel sb to do sth** *She counselled them not to accept this settlement.* **2** to listen and give support to someone with problems: *a new unit to counsel alcoholics*

coun·sel·ling *BrE*, **counseling** *AmE* /ˈkaʊnsəlɪŋ/ *n* [U] advice and support given by a counsellor to someone with problems, usually after talking to them: *advice and counselling for people with disabilities* | **group/bereavement/debt etc counselling** *a debt counselling service* | [+**for**] *She's been undergoing counseling for depression.*

coun·sel·lor *BrE*, **counselor** *AmE* /ˈkaʊnsələ $ -ər/ *n* [C] someone whose job is to help and support people with problems: *Have you thought of seeing a counsellor?* | **student/marriage guidance/stress etc counsellor**

count¹ S1 W3 /kaʊnt/ *v*
1 FIND THE TOTAL also **count up** [T] to calculate the total number of things or people in a group: *I was amazed at the number of plants – I counted 147.* | **count (up) how many** *Count up how many ticks are in each box.*
2 SAY NUMBERS also **count up** [I] to say numbers in order, one by one or in groups: [+**to**] *Sarah can count up to five now.* | **count by twos/fives etc** *It's quicker to count by tens* (=saying 10, 20, 30 ...).
3 BE ALLOWED [I,T] to be allowed or accepted, or to allow or accept something, according to a standard, set of ideas, or set of rules: *A linesman had his flag up so the kick did not count.* | [+**as**] *Locally produced sales by American firms in Japan do not count as exports.* | *Today's session is counted as training, so you will get paid.* | [+**towards**] *Results from the two rounds count towards championship points.*
4 INCLUDE [T] to include someone or something in a total: *There are more than two thousand of us, **not counting** the crew.* | **count sb/sth among sth** *I count Jules and Ady among my closest friends.*
5 CONSIDER STH [T] to consider someone or something in a particular way: **count sb/sth as sth** *I don't count him as a friend anymore.* | *You should count yourself **lucky** that you weren't hurt.*
6 IMPORTANT [I not in progressive] to be important or valuable: *First impressions really do count.* | [+**for**] *His promises don't count for much.* | *His overseas results count for nothing.*
7 I/you can count sb/sth on (the fingers of) one hand *spoken* used to emphasize how small the number of something is: *The number of cougar attacks on humans can be counted on the fingers of one hand.*
8 don't count your chickens (before they're hatched) *spoken* used to say that you should not make plans that depend on something good happening, because it might not: *I wouldn't count your chickens, Mr Vass. I've agreed to sign the contract, but that's all.*
9 count your blessings *spoken* used to tell someone to be grateful for the good things in their life
10 count the cost to start having problems as a result

of your earlier decisions or mistakes: *We're now counting the cost of not taking out medical insurance.*
11 who's counting? used to say that you are not worried about the number of times something happens – often used humorously: *Apparently the next Star Trek film (number six, but who's counting?) will definitely be the last.*
12 count sheep to imagine a line of sheep jumping over a fence, one at a time, and count them as a way of getting to sleep → **stand up and be counted** at STAND¹ (5); → **it's the thought that counts** at THOUGHT² (12)
  count down *phr v*
to count the number of days, minutes etc until a particular moment or event: **count sth ⇔ down** *We are counting down the days to the end of this tour.*
  count sb in *phr v*
to include someone in an activity: *When the game gets started, you can count me in.*
  count on/upon sb/sth *phr v*
1 to depend on someone or something, especially in a difficult situation: *You can count on me.* | *With luck, you might cover your costs, but don't count on it.* | **count on (sb/sth) doing sth** *We're all counting on winning this contract.* | *They were counting on him not coming out of hospital.* | **count on sb/sth to do sth** *You can count on Dean to ruin any party.*
2 to expect something: *The presence of Paula was one thing he hadn't counted on.* | **count on (sb/sth) doing sth** *We didn't count on so many people being on vacation.*
  count sb/sth out *phr v*
1 to not include someone or something in an activity: *I'm sorry, you'll have to count me out tonight.*
2 to decide that someone or something is not important or worth considering: *I wouldn't count him out. If anybody can make a comeback, he can.*
3 **count sth ⇔ out** to put things down one by one as you count them: *The teller counted out ten $50 bills.*

count² S2 W3 *n* [C]
1 TOTAL the process of counting, or the total that you get when you count things: *Hold your breath for a count of 10.*
2 MEASUREMENT a measurement that shows how much of a substance is present in a place, area etc that is being examined: *The **pollen count** is high today.*
3 lose count to forget a number you were calculating or a total you were trying to count: [+**of**] *There have been so many accidents here, the police have lost count.*
4 keep count to keep a record of the changing total of something over a period of time: [+**of**] *I never manage to keep count of what I spend on my credit card.*
5 on all/several/both etc counts in every way, in several ways etc: *It was important that they secure a large and widespread audience. They failed on both counts.*
6 at the last count according to the latest information about a particular situation: *At the last count, I had 15 responses to my letter.*
7 be out for the count a) to be in a deep sleep **b)** if a BOXER is out for the count, he has been knocked down for ten seconds or more
8 LAW *technical* one of the crimes that someone is charged with: *Davis was found not guilty on **all counts.*** | **count of theft/burglary/murder etc** *He was charged with two counts of theft.*
9 RANK/TITLE a European NOBLEMAN with a high rank

count·a·ble /ˈkaʊntəbəl/ *adj* a countable noun has both a singular and a plural form; → **count noun**; 🔁 **uncountable**

count·down /ˈkaʊntdaʊn/ *n* [C usually singular] **1** the period of time before something happens, such as a spacecraft being LAUNCHED, when someone counts backwards until the event happens **2** the period of time before an important event, when people become more and more excited about it: [+**to**] *the countdown to the World Cup*

coun·te·nance¹ /ˈkaʊntˈnəns/ *n* [C] *literary* your face or your expression: *All colour drained from her countenance.*

countenance² v [T] *formal* to accept, support, or approve of something: **countenance {sb} doing sth** *I will not countenance you being rude to Dr Baxter.*

coun·ter¹ [S3] /'kaʊntə $ -ər/ n [C]
1 the place where you pay or are served in a shop, bank, restaurant etc: *He wondered if the girl behind the counter recognised him.*
2 *AmE* a long flat surface on top of a piece of furniture, especially in a kitchen; ☐ **worktop** *BrE*
3 **over the counter** drugs, medicines etc that are bought over the counter are ones that you can buy in a shop without a PRESCRIPTION from a doctor
4 **under the counter** if you buy something under the counter, you buy it secretly and usually illegally: *It's risky, but you can get alcohol under the counter.*
5 a small object that you use in some games that are played on a board
6 a piece of electrical equipment that counts something: *Set the video counter to zero before you press play.*
→ GEIGER COUNTER
7 a computer program that counts the number of people that have visited a website
8 an action that tries to prevent something bad from happening, or an argument that is used to prove that something is wrong: [+to] *The road blocks were a counter to terrorist attacks in that area.*

counter² v **1** [I,T] to say something in order to try to prove that what someone said was not true or as a reply to something: *'I could ask the same thing of you,' she countered.* | **counter an argument/an allegation/a criticism etc** *He was determined to counter the bribery allegations.* **2** [T] to do something in order to prevent something bad from happening or to reduce its bad effects: *There are steps you can take to counter the effects of stress.*

counter³ adj, adv **be/run/go counter to sth** to be the opposite of something: *Some actions by the authorities ran counter to the president's call for leniency.*

counter- /'kaʊntə $ -tər/ prefix **1** the opposite of something; *a counterproductive thing to do* (=producing results opposite to what you wanted) **2** done or given as a reaction to something, especially to oppose it: *claims and counterclaims* **3** matching something: *my counterpart in the American system* (=someone who has the same job that I have)

coun·ter·act /,kaʊntər'ækt/ v [T] to reduce or prevent the bad effect of something, by doing something that has the opposite effect: *They gave him drugs to counteract his withdrawal symptoms.* —**counteraction** /-'ækʃən/ n [C,U]

coun·ter·at·tack /'kaʊntərə,tæk/ n [C] an attack you make against someone who has attacked you, in a war, sport, or argument —**counterattack** v [I,T]

coun·ter·bal·ance /,kaʊntə'bæləns $ -tər-/ v [T] to have an equal and opposite effect to something such as a change, feeling etc: *Riskier investments tend to be counterbalanced by high rewards.* —**counterbalance** /'kaʊntə,bæləns $ -tər-/ n [C]

coun·ter·charge /'kaʊntə,tʃɑːdʒ $ -tər,tʃɑːrdʒ/ n [C] a statement that says someone has done something wrong, made after they have said that you have done something wrong

coun·ter·clock·wise /,kaʊntə'klɒkwaɪz $ -tər'klɑːk-/ adv *AmE* ANTICLOCKWISE → CLOCKWISE

coun·ter·cul·ture /'kaʊntə,kʌltʃə $ -tər,kʌltʃər/ n [U] the art, beliefs, behaviour etc of people who are against the usual or accepted behaviour, art etc of society: *the counterculture revolution of the late 1960s*

counter-'espionage n [U] the process of trying to stop someone SPYING on your country

coun·ter·feit¹ /'kaʊntəfɪt $ -tər-/ adj made to look exactly like something else, in order to deceive people; ☐ **fake**: **counterfeit currency/money etc** *counterfeit £10 notes* | **counterfeit goods/software etc**

counterfeit² v [T] to copy something exactly in order to deceive people; ☐ **fake**: *They admitted counterfeiting documents.*

coun·ter·foil /'kaʊntəfɔɪl $ -tər-/ n [C] the part of something such as a cheque or ticket that you keep as a record

coun·ter·in·sur·gen·cy /,kaʊntərɪn'sɜːdʒənsi $ -ɜːr-/ n [U] military action against people who are fighting against their own country's government

coun·ter·in·tel·li·gence /,kaʊntərɪn'telɪdʒəns/ n [U] action that a country takes in order to stop other countries discovering its secrets

coun·ter·mand /,kaʊntə'mɑːnd, 'kaʊntəmɑːnd $,kaʊntər'mænd/ v [T] *formal* to officially tell people to ignore an order, especially by giving them a different one: *Terrorists tried to force him to countermand the order to attack.*

coun·ter·mea·sure /'kaʊntəmeʒə $ -tərmeʒər/ n [C usually plural] an action taken to prevent another action from having a harmful effect: *new countermeasures against terrorism*

coun·ter·pane /'kaʊntəpeɪn $ -ər-/ n [C] *old-fashioned* a BEDSPREAD

coun·ter·part /'kaʊntəpɑːt $ -tərpɑːrt/ n [C] someone or something that has the same job or purpose as someone or something else in a different place: **sb's counterpart** *Belgian officials are discussing this with their French counterparts.*

coun·ter·point /'kaʊntəpɔɪnt $ -ər-/ n **1** [U] the combination of two or more tunes played together so that they sound like one tune: **in counterpoint to sth** *The viola is exactly in counterpoint to the first violin.* **2** [C] a tune that is one part of counterpoint **3** [C,U] when two things that are different are compared in an interesting or pleasant way: [+to] *I have used my interviews with parents as a counterpoint to a professional judgement.*

coun·ter·pro·duc·tive /,kaʊntəprə'dʌktɪv $ -tər-/ adj achieving the opposite result to the one that you want: *Sending young offenders to prison can be counterproductive.*

counter-revo'lution n [C,U] political or military actions taken to get rid of a government that is in power because of a previous REVOLUTION —**counter-revolutionary** n [C] —**counter-revolutionary** adj

coun·ter·sign /'kaʊntəsaɪn $ -ər-/ v [T] to sign a paper that has already been signed by someone else: *The note must be countersigned by a doctor.*

coun·ter·ten·or /,kaʊntə'tenə $ 'kaʊntər,tenər/ n [C] a man who is trained to sing with a very high voice

counter-'terrorist adj **counter-terrorist operation/team/unit etc** a plan or group that tries to prevent the activities of violent political groups —**counter-terrorism** n [U] —**counter-terrorist** n [C]

coun·ter·vail·ing /,kaʊntə'veɪlɪŋ $ -ər-/ adj *formal* with an equally strong but opposite effect

coun·tess /'kaʊntɪs/ n [C] a woman with the same rank as an EARL or a COUNT² (9)

'counting house n [C] an office where accounts and money were kept in the past

count·less /'kaʊntləs/ adj [usually before noun] too many to be counted: *a famous film clip which has been shown countless times*

'count noun n [C] a noun that has both a singular and plural form and can be used with 'a' or 'an' → NOUN

coun·tri·fied /'kʌntrɪfaɪd/ adj typical of the countryside, or made to seem typical of the countryside: *the countrified existence of the newly rich*

coun·try¹ [S1] [W1] /'kʌntri/ n plural **countries**
1 [C] an area of land that is controlled by its own government, president, king etc; → **nation**: *the Scandinavian countries* | *developing countries* | *Finding a doctor can be difficult in a foreign country.* → MOTHER COUNTRY
2 the country a) land that is outside towns and cities,

C

including land used for farming; ◘ **the countryside**: **in the country** *I've always wanted to live in the country.* **b)** all the people who live in a particular country: *The President has the support of the country.*
3 [U] an area of land that is suitable for a particular activity, has particular features or that is connected with a particular person or people: *The Peak District is good walking country.* | *mountainous country* | *the rugged moors of Brontë country*
4 [U] country and western music: *I'm a big fan of country.*
5 go to the country BrE if a Prime Minister goes to the country, they ask for a GENERAL ELECTION to be held

country² *adj* [only before noun] **1** belonging to or connected with the countryside; ◘ **rural**; ◙ **urban**: *They much preferred country life to life in the city.* **2** relating to country and western music: *a country singer*

,**country and** '**western** *n* [U] *formal* popular music in the style of music from the southern and western US

,**country 'bumpkin** *n* [C] someone who is considered to be stupid because they are from an area outside towns and cities; ◘ **yokel**

'**country ,club** *n* [C] a sports and social club, especially one for rich people

,**country 'cousin** *n* [C] someone who does not have a lot of experience and is confused by busy city life

,**country 'dancing** *n* [U] a traditional form of dance in which pairs of dancers move in rows and circles

,**country 'house** *n* [C] BrE a large house in the countryside, especially one that is of historical interest; → **stately home**

coun·try·man /'kʌntrimən/ *n* [C] *plural* **countrymen** /-mən/ **1** sb's **countryman** someone from your own country; ◘ **compatriot**: *It was two years since I'd seen any fellow countrymen.* **2** BrE a man who lives in the country rather than in a town or city

'**country ,music** *n* [U] COUNTRY AND WESTERN

,**country 'seat** *n* [C] BrE the countryside house of someone who is rich and owns land

coun·try·side S2 W3 /'kʌntrisaɪd/ *n* [U] land that is outside cities and towns; ◘ **the country**: *The house had lovely views over open countryside.* | **in the countryside** *people who live in the countryside*

coun·try·wide /'kʌntriwaɪd/ *adj* happening or existing in all parts of a country; ◘ **nationwide** —**countrywide** *adv*

coun·try·wom·an /'kʌntri,wumən/ *n plural* **countrywomen** /-,wɪmɪn/ [C] BrE a woman who lives in the country rather than in a town or city

coun·ty S1 W2 /'kaʊnti/ *n plural* **counties** [C] an area of a state or country that has its own government to deal with local matters: *Fairfax County, Virginia*

,**county 'council** *n* [C] a group of people who are elected to the local government of a county, especially in Britain: *Kent County Council*

,**county 'court** *n* [C] a local court of law. In Britain county courts deal with private quarrels between people rather than with serious crimes. In the US they also deal with less important criminal cases

,**county 'fair** *n* [C] AmE an event that happens each year in a particular county, with games and competitions for the best farm animals, cooking etc

,**county 'town** BrE; ,**county 'seat** AmE *n* [C] the town in a county where its government is

coup /kuː/ *n* [C] **1** a sudden and sometimes violent attempt by citizens or the army to take control of the government; ◘ **coup d' état**: *Haiti's first elected president was deposed in a violent military coup.* | *a coup attempt by junior officers* | *He evaded capture after the failed coup.* **2** an achievement that is extremely impressive because it was very difficult: *Getting a former professional player as coach was a major coup for the club.*

coup de grâce /,kuː də 'grɑːs/ *n* [singular] **1** an action or event that ends or destroys something that has gradually been getting weaker **2** a hit or shot that kills someone or something

coup d'état /,kuː deɪ'tɑː $ -de'tɑː/ *n plural* **coups d'état** *(same pronunciation)* [C] a COUP

cou·pé /'kuːpeɪ $ kuː'peɪ/ *n* [C] a car with two doors and a sloping back; → **sports car**

cou·ple¹ S1 W1 /'kʌpəl/ *n*
1 a couple a) two things or people of the same kind: [+of] *There are a couple of girls waiting for you.* **b)** a small number of things: *I just need to make a couple more calls.* | [+of] *You'll be all right in a couple of days.*
2 [C] two people who are married or are having a sexual or romantic relationship: *a newly married couple* | *the couple next door*

couple² *v* **1** [T] to join or fasten two things together: **couple sth to sth** *Each element is mathematically coupled to its neighbours.* **2** [I] *formal* to have sex
couple sth with sth *phr v* [usually passive] if one thing is coupled with another, the two things happen or exist together and produce a particular result; ◘ **combine**: *Lack of rain coupled with high temperatures caused the crops to fail.*

coup·let /'kʌplət/ *n* [C] two lines of poetry, one following the other, that are the same length: *rhyming couplets*

coup·ling /'kʌplɪŋ/ *n* [C] **1** something that connects two things together, especially two vehicles **2** when two things are joined or connected; ◘ **combination**: *an attractive coupling of two Slavonic Dances* **3** *formal* an act of having sex

cou·pon /'kuːpɒn $ -pɑːn/ *n* [C] **1** a small piece of printed paper that gives you the right to pay less for something or get something free: *The coupon entitles you to 10 cents off your next purchase.* **2** a printed form, used when you order something, enter a competition etc: *To order, fill in the coupon on page 154.*

cour·age S3 /'kʌrɪdʒ $ 'kɜːr-/ *n* [U]
1 the quality of being brave when you are in danger, in pain, in a difficult situation etc; → **bravery**; ◙ **cowardice**: *Sue showed great courage throughout her illness.* | **courage to do sth** *Gradually I lost the courage to speak out about anything.* | *He did not have the courage to tell Nicola that he was ending their affair.* | **summon/pluck up the courage (to do sth)** (=try to make yourself be brave enough to do something) *I plucked up the courage to go out by myself.* | *Driving again after his accident must have taken a lot of courage* (=needed courage).
2 have the courage of your (own) convictions to be brave enough to say or do what you think is right even though other people may not agree or approve → DUTCH COURAGE

cou·ra·geous /kə'reɪdʒəs/ *adj* brave: *He was wrong, and courageous enough to admit it.* | *a courageous decision* —**courageously** *adv*

cour·gette /kʊə'ʒet $ kʊr-/ *n* [C] a long vegetable with dark green skin; ◘ **zucchini** AmE

cou·ri·er¹ /'kʊriə $ -ər/ *n* [C] **1** a person or company that is paid to take packages somewhere → see picture at OCCUPATION **2** BrE *old-fashioned* a REP

courier² *v* [T] to send something somewhere using a courier

course¹ S1 W1 /kɔːs $ kɔːrs/ *n*
1 of course a) used to show that what you are saying is expected or already known and so not surprising: *You can pay by cheque, assuming of course you have a valid cheque card.* | *Of course there are exceptions to every rule.* **b)** also **course** *informal spoken* used to say yes or to give permission politely: *'Can I have a word with you?' 'Of course.'* | *'Can you give me a lift?' 'Course, no problem.'* **c)** also **course** *spoken* used to emphasize that what you are saying is true or correct: *Of course he'll come!* | **well/but of course** *Well of course I love you.*
2 of course not also **course not** *spoken informal* used to say very strongly that something is not true or correct:

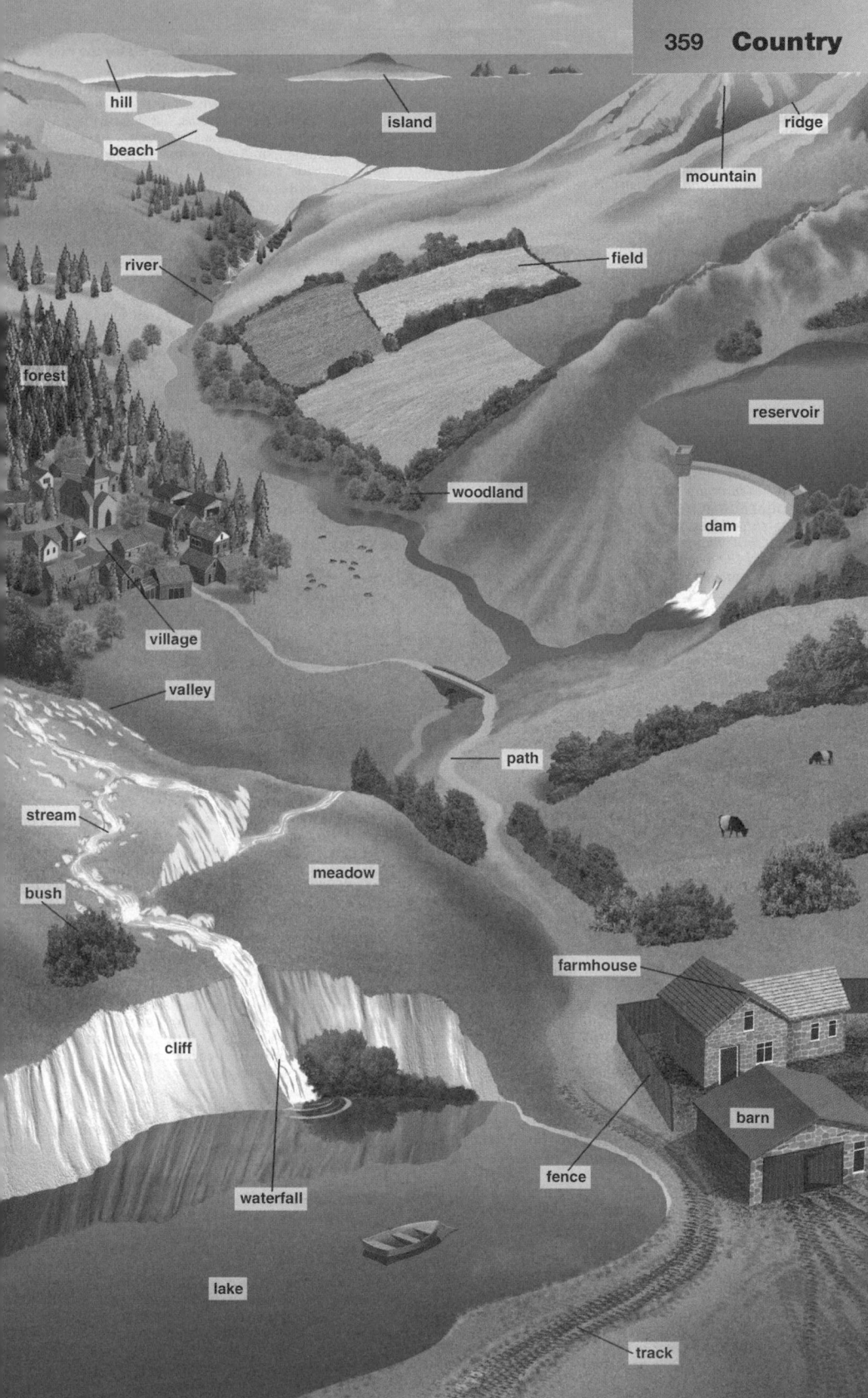

hill

island

ridge

beach

mountain

river

field

forest

reservoir

woodland

dam

village

valley

path

stream

meadow

bush

farmhouse

cliff

barn

waterfall

fence

lake

track

He asked his father if it was true. ' Of course not,' Jack said. | 'You don't mind if I call her?' 'No, course not.'
3 EDUCATION [C] **a)** a series of lessons in a particular subject; ⊟ **class** *AmE*: **do a course** *BrE* **take a course** *Andy's doing a one-year journalism course.* | [+**on/in**] *a course on architecture* | *I'm taking a course in graphic design.* | *73 candidates* **enrolled on the course.** | *For details, contact your* **course tutor. b)** *BrE* a period of study in a particular subject, especially at university; ⊟ **program** *AmE*: **take/follow a course** *Students following the Honours course are expected to study Islamic History.* | **degree/postgraduate etc course** *entry qualifications for degree-level courses* | **taught course** (=one which has formal lectures, rather than one in which a student studies alone) ⚠ **course** is never followed by 'of': *a course in English (NOT of English)* → CORRESPONDENCE COURSE, CRASH COURSE, REFRESHER COURSE, SANDWICH COURSE
4 TIME [singular] a period of time or process during which something happens: **during/in/throughout/over the course of sth** *During the course of our conversation, it emerged that Bob had been in prison.* | *Over the course of the next few years, the steel industry was reorganized.* | **in the course of doing sth** *In the course of researching customer needs, we discovered how few families have adequate life insurance.*
5 DEVELOPMENT [singular] the usual or natural way that something changes, develops, or is done: [+**of**] *forces that shape the course of evolution* | *Meeting Sally changed the whole* **course of his life.** | **in the normal/ natural/ordinary course of events** *In the normal course of events, a son would inherit from his father.* | **take/run its course** (=develop in the usual way and reach a natural end) *Relax and let nature* **take its course.** | *It seems the boom in World Music has run its course.* | *Gorbachev* **changed the course of** *Soviet history.*
6 PLANS [singular, U] the general plans someone has to achieve something or the general way something is happening: *They will go to any lengths to get the White House to* **change course.** | *He will* **steer a middle course** *between pacifism and revolution.* | *As long as the economy* **stays on course,** *the future looks rosy.*
7 ACTIONS [C usually singular] an action or series of actions that you could take in order to deal with a particular situation: *I agreed that this was the only sensible* **course of action.** | **take/decide on a course** *The judge took the only course of action open to him.*
8 DIRECTION [C usually singular, U] the planned direction taken by a boat or plane to reach a place: *The plane* **changed course** *to avoid the storm.* | **on/off course** (=going in the right or wrong direction) *The ship was* **blown off course.** | *The aircraft was almost 10 miles off course.* | *She tightened the mainsail while* **holding the course** (=travelling in the same direction as planned).
9 **on course** likely to achieve something because you have already had some success: [+**for**] *If he wins today, he's on course for the Grand Slam.* | **on course to do sth** *We're* **back on course** *to qualify for the championship.*
10 MEAL [C] one of the separate parts of a meal: **three-course/five-course etc meal** *The ticket includes entry and a four-course meal.* | **first/second/main etc course** *We had fish for the main course.*
11 SPORT [C] an area of land or water where races are held, or an area of land designed for playing golf: *a particularly difficult course* | *an 18-hole course* → ASSAULT COURSE, OBSTACLE COURSE (1)
12 MEDICAL TREATMENT [C] *especially BrE* an amount of medicine or medical treatment that you have regularly for a specific period of time: **course of injections/drugs/treatment etc** *a course of antibiotics*
13 **in (the) course of time** after some or enough time has passed; ⊟ **eventually**: *She'll get used to school in the course of time.*
14 RIVER [C] the direction a river moves in: *The course of the water was shown by a line of trees.*
15 WALL [C] a layer of bricks, stone etc in a wall: *a damp-proof course* → **as a matter of course** at MATTER¹

(20); → **par for the course** at PAR (3); → **stay the course** at STAY¹ (7); → **in due course** at DUE¹ (4)

course² *v* **1** [I always + adv/prep] *literary* if a liquid or electricity courses somewhere, it flows there quickly: *Tears coursed down his cheeks.* **2** [I always + adv/prep] *literary* if a feeling courses through you, you feel it suddenly and strongly: *His smile sent waves of excitement coursing through her.* **3** [I,T] to chase rabbits with dogs as a sport

course·book /'kɔːsbʊk $ 'kɔːrs-/ *n* [C] *BrE* a book that students use regularly during a set of lessons on a particular subject; ⊟ **textbook**

course·ware /'kɔːsweə $ 'kɔːrswer/ *n* [U] computer software that is designed to teach people a particular subject

course·work /'kɔːswɜːk $ 'kɔːrswɜːrk/ *n* [U] work that students do during a course of study, rather than in examinations, and that forms part of their final mark

court¹ S1 W1 /kɔːt $ kɔːrt/ *n*
1 FOR DECIDING ABOUT A LEGAL CASE [C,U] the place where a trial is held, or the people there, especially the judge and the JURY who examine the evidence and decide whether someone is guilty or not guilty

> court of law
> court case
> appear in court
> go to court
> take sb to court (=bring a legal case against someone)
> bring a case to court
> a case comes to court
> settle sth out of court (=reach an agreement about a dispute without using the court)
> be thrown out of court (=a judge refuses to consider a case)
> a case is heard in court (=a case is dealt with by a court)
> the court (=the judge, the jury, and the other people in a court)
> criminal court (=a court where cases about crimes are heard)
> civil court (=a court where cases about civil disagreements are heard)

A crowd of reporters had gathered outside the court. | *It could not be proved in a* **court of law.** | *The* **court case** *lasted six weeks.* | *Four people will* **appear in court** *today, charged with possessing explosives.* | *I'd rather resolve our differences without* **going to court.** | *She threatened to* **take the magazine to court** *if they didn't publish an immediate apology.* | *We hadn't enough evidence to* **bring the case to court.** | *Victims are often not told when a case* **comes to court.** | *In the end the matter was* **settled out of court.** | *The case was* **thrown out of court.** | *The* **court** *ruled that no compensation was due.* | *The* **court** *upheld the earlier decision* (=decided that the earlier decision was correct). | *Dr Porter told* **the court** *that the postmortem revealed signs of strangulation.* → COUNTY COURT, CROWN COURT, HIGH COURT, KANGAROO COURT, MAGISTRATES' COURT, SMALL CLAIMS COURT, STATE COURT, SUPREME COURT, TRIBUNAL

2 FOR PLAYING A SPORT [C] an area made for playing games such as tennis; → **field, pitch: squash/ tennis/basketball etc court** *Can you book a squash court for tomorrow?* | **on court** *The players are due on court in an hour.;* → see picture at SPORTS CENTRE
3 KING/QUEEN **a)** [C] the place where a king or queen lives and works: *the* **royal courts** *of Europe* **b) the court** the king, queen, their family, and their friends, advisers etc: *Several members of the court were under suspicion.* | *There was a taste in* **court circles** *for romantic verse.* | **Court officials** *denied the rumours.*
4 **hold court** *formal* to speak in an interesting, amusing, or forceful way so that people gather to listen: [+**to**] *Dylan was holding court upstairs to a group of fans.*
5 **pay court to sb** *old-fashioned* to give someone a lot of attention to try and make them like you

6 AREA NEXT TO A BUILDING [C] a COURTYARD → **the ball is in sb's court** at BALL[1] (7); → **be laughed out of court** at LAUGH[1] (6); → FOOD COURT

WORD FOCUS: COURT
people in a court of law: **judge, magistrate, jury, defence** *BrE*/**defense** *AmE*, **prosecution, defendant, witness, attorney, lawyer, barrister** *BrE*, **solicitor** *BrE*, **district attorney** *AmE*
what happens in a court case: At the beginning of the trial, the person who is accused **pleads guilty** or **not guilty** to the **charges** against them. The lawyers for the prosecution try to **prove** that the defendant is guilty, and the lawyers for the defence try to prove that their client is innocent. The judge and the jury **examine the evidence** and listen to the **testimony** of the witnesses. At the end of the trial, the judge then **sums up** the case, and the jury then **gives their verdict**. If the person is **found guilty**, the judge **sentences** them to a period of time in prison, or orders them to pay a **fine**. If the person is **found not guilty**, they are **released**.
→ see also crime, criminal

court² *v* [T] **1** to try hard to please someone, especially because you want something from them: *His campaign team have assiduously courted the media.* **2 court danger/death etc** *formal* to behave in a way that makes danger etc more likely: *To have admitted this would have courted political disaster.* **3 be courting** *old-fashioned* if a man and a woman are courting, they are having a romantic relationship and may get married: *That was back in the 1960s when we were courting.* **4** *old-fashioned* if a man courts a woman, he spends time being nice to her because he hopes to marry her

court card *n* [C] *BrE* the king, queen, or JACK in a set of playing cards; ▣ **face card** *AmE*

court corre·spondent *n* [C] *BrE* someone who reports the news relating to a royal family for a newspaper or television company

court costs *n* [plural] the costs of taking a case to court: *You could be ordered to pay court costs.*

cour·te·ous /'kɜːtiəs $ 'kɜːr-/ *adj* polite and showing respect for other people; ▣ **discourteous**: *The staff are always courteous and helpful.* | *a courteous reply*

cour·te·san /ˌkɔːtɪˈzæn $ 'kɔːrtəzən/ *n* [C] a woman who had sex with rich or important men for money in the past; → **prostitute**

cour·te·sy¹ /'kɜːtɪsi $ 'kɜːr-/ *n plural* **courtesies** **1** [U] polite behaviour and respect for other people; ▣ **politeness**; ▣ **discourtesy**: *It's a matter of common courtesy to acknowledge letters.* | **have the courtesy to do sth** *He didn't even have the courtesy to call and say he couldn't come.* **2** [C] something you do or say to be polite: *The two men exchanged courtesies before getting down to business.* **3 (by) courtesy of sb** by someone's permission or kindness, rather than by paying them: *photographs supplied courtesy of Blenheim Palace* **4 (by) courtesy of sth** if one thing happens courtesy of another, the second thing caused the first: *Healy received a deep cut on his left hand, courtesy of Nicol's ice skate.* **5 do sb the courtesy of doing sth** to be polite enough to do something for someone: *At least do me the courtesy of telling the truth.*

courtesy² *adj* [only before noun] **1** provided free to a customer by a company: **courtesy bus/taxi/car/phone etc** *The hotel runs a courtesy bus from the airport.* | *Most reviewers receive a courtesy copy of the book.* **2 courtesy visit/call** a visit etc done to be polite or show respect: *Our captain put in a courtesy visit during dinner.*

court·house /'kɔːthaʊs $ 'kɔːrt-/ *n* [C] *AmE* a building containing law courts and government offices

court·ier /'kɔːtiə $ 'kɔːrtɪr/ *n* [C] someone in the past with an important position at a royal court

court·ly /'kɔːtli $ 'kɔːrtli/ *adj* graceful and polite: *a tall man with courtly manners* —**courtliness** *n* [U]

court-'martial¹ / $ '. ˌ../ *n* [C,U] a court that judges soldiers etc who may have broken military law, or an occasion when this judgment is made: *Navy commanders recommended that he be tried by court-martial.*

court-martial² *v* **court-martialled, court-martialling** *BrE*, **court-martialed, court-martialing** *AmE* [T] to hear and judge someone's case in a military court: *The drill instructor was court-martialed for having sex with a trainee.*

Court of Ap'peal *n* [singular] the highest law court in Britain apart from the HOUSE OF LORDS

Court of Ap'peals *n* [singular] one of 12 law courts in the US that deals with cases when people are not satisfied with the judgment given by a lower court; → **appellate court**

court of in'quiry *n plural* **courts of inquiry** [C] *BrE* a group of people chosen to discover the facts about something such as a serious accident; → **grand jury**

court of 'law also **law court** *n plural* **courts of law** [C] a place where law cases are judged; ▣ **court**

court 'order *n* [C] an order or decision made by a law court: *His computer was seized under a court order.*

court re'porter *n* [C] someone whose job is to record everything that is said during a court case

court·room /'kɔːtruːm, -rʊm $ 'kɔːrt-/ *n* [C] a room in a law court where cases are judged

court·ship /'kɔːt-ʃɪp $ 'kɔːrt-/ *n* **1** [C,U] the period of time during which a man and woman have a romantic relationship before marrying **2** [U] special behaviour used by animals to attract each other for sex: *courtship rituals*

court shoe *n* [C] *BrE* a type of plain formal shoe worn by women; ▣ **pump** *AmE*

court·yard /'kɔːtjɑːd $ 'kɔːrtjɑːrd/ *n* [C] an open space that is completely or partly surrounded by buildings: *the castle courtyard*

cous·cous /'kʊskəs/ *n* [U] a type of North African food made of crushed wheat

cous·in S3 /'kʌzən/ *n* [C]
1 the child of your UNCLE or AUNT → FIRST COUSIN, KISSING COUSIN, SECOND COUSIN
2 something that has the same origins as something else: [+of/to] *a drug that is a chemical cousin to amphetamines* | **close/distant cousin** *The Alaskan brown bear is a close cousin of the grizzly bear.*
3 someone or something that is similar to someone or something else: *His avant-garde music, sometime cousin to jazz, had limited appeal.*

cou·ture /kuːˈtjʊə $ -'tʊr/ also **haute-couture** *n* [U] the design and production of expensive and fashionable clothes, or the clothes themselves: *a couture collection*

cove /kəʊv $ koʊv/ *n* [C] **1** part of the coast where the land curves round so that the sea is partly surrounded by land; → **bay**: *The last fishing boats left the cove.* **2** *BrE old-fashioned* a man

cov·en /'kʌvən/ *n* [C] a group or meeting of WITCHES

cov·e·nant /'kʌvənənt/ *n* [C] a legal agreement in which someone promises to pay a person or organization an amount of money regularly; → **endowment** —**covenant** *v* [I,T]: *He covenanted to pay £30 a month into the fund.*

Cov·en·try /'kɒvəntri, 'kʌv- $ 'kʌv-, 'kɑːv-/ *n* **send sb to Coventry** *BrE* to refuse to speak to someone in order to punish them, show disapproval etc

cov·er¹ S1 W1 /'kʌvə $ -ər/ *v* [T]
1 HIDE/PROTECT also **cover up** to put something over or be over something in order to hide, close, or protect it: *Cover the pot and bake for an hour.* | *She wore a low-cut dress, partly covered by a thin shawl.* | **cover sth with sth** *Dan covered his face with his hands.*
2 LAYER if something covers a surface, it forms a

layer over it: *Grey mould covered the walls.* | *Much of the country is covered by snow.* | **cover sth with/in sth** *The bulletin board was covered with messages.* | *The eruption of the volcano covered states as far away as Montana in a fine layer of ash.*

3 INCLUDE to include or deal with a particular subject or group of things: *The course covers all aspects of business and law.* | *Are there any areas you feel are not covered adequately in the book?* | *'Exercise' is a word which covers a vast range of activities.* | *We need more time to cover so much* **ground** (=include so many things). | *pollutants that are not covered by the Kyoto agreement*

4 DISTANCE to travel a particular distance: *They were hoping to cover 40 miles yesterday.* | *A leopard can cover a lot of* **ground** *very quickly.*

5 AREA to spread over an area: *The city covers 25 square miles.*

6 NEWS to report the details of an event for a newspaper or a television or radio programme: *I'd just returned from covering the Cambodian war.*

7 MONEY if a sum of money covers the cost of something, it is enough to pay for it: *The award should be enough to cover her tuition fees.* | *Airlines are raising fares to cover the rising costs of fuel.*

8 INSURANCE if your insurance covers you or your possessions, it promises to pay you money if you have an accident, something is stolen etc: *Most policies cover accidental damage to pipes.* | *The treatment wasn't covered by her healthcare insurance.* | **cover sb against/for sth** *Are we covered for theft?* | **cover sb to do sth** *He thought he was covered to drive the vehicle.*

9 GUNS a) to protect someone by being ready to shoot anyone who attacks them: *I'll make for the door – cover me, will you?* **b)** to aim a gun at a person or a place where people might be, in order to prevent them from moving or escaping: *He stepped into the doorway and swung the gun up to cover the corridor.*

10 SPORT to stay close to a member of the opposing team or a part of the field in order to prevent your opponents from gaining points

11 MUSIC to perform or record a song that was originally recorded by another artist: *They've covered several hits from the 1980s.*

12 cover (all) the bases to make sure you can deal with any situation or problem so that nothing bad happens: *Parents are already stressed trying to cover the bases at home and at work.*

13 cover yourself (against sth) also **cover your back**; **cover your butt/ass** *AmE* to do things in a way that will prevent people from blaming or criticizing you: *Doctors are concerned to cover themselves against charges of negligence.* | *He copied Stella in on the email just to cover his back.*

14 cover your tracks to try to hide something you have done so that other people do not find out: *He started to destroy documents to cover his tracks.*

cover for sb *phr v*
1 to do the work that someone else usually does, because they are not there: *Who's covering for you while you're away?*
2 to prevent someone from getting into trouble by lying for them, especially about where they are or what they are doing

cover sth ⇔ **over** *phr v*
to put something on top of something else so that it is completely hidden: *The female lays a single egg and covers it over.*

cover up *phr v*
1 **cover** sth ⇔ **up** to put something over something else so that it cannot be seen: *Her legs were so swollen she had to cover them up.*
2 **cover** sth ⇔ **up** to prevent people from discovering mistakes or unpleasant facts; → **whitewash**: *The whole thing was covered up and never reached the papers.* | *Mum is worried, but she covers it up by joking.* →
COVER-UP

3 cover up for sb to protect someone by hiding unpleasant facts about them: *They covered up for Kirk by refusing to answer any questions.*
4 to put clothes, BLANKETS etc over yourself in order to hide or protect your body, or to keep yourself warm: *Cover up, or stay out of the sun.* | **cover yourself up** *Hastily, she covered herself up with the towel.*

cover² S1 W2 *n*
1 PROTECTION [C] something that is put on top of something else to protect it; → **lid**: *a blue duvet cover* | *a plastic cover* | *A* **dust cover** (=to keep dirt etc off) *hung over the painting.* → see picture at LID

2 BOOKS [C] the outer front or back part of a magazine, book etc: *His photo's on the cover of Newsweek again.* | **front/back cover** *an advertisement on the back cover* | *I read the magazine from cover to cover* (=all of it). | **cover photo/shot/picture** (=picture on the front cover) *The cover shot was of three guys in army kit.*

3 BED the **covers** [plural] the sheets etc that you put over yourself when you are in bed: *The covers had slipped off in the night.*

4 SHELTER [U] shelter or protection from bad weather or attack: **run/dive for cover** *He was shot in the head as he ran for cover.* | *We were forced to* **take cover** *in a barn.* | *Three soldiers* **broke cover** (=left the place where they were hiding).

5 INSURANCE [U] *BrE* the protection an insurance gives you, so that it pays you money if you are injured, something is stolen etc; ▤ **coverage** *AmE*: *temporary medical cover* | [+**against/for**] *cover against fire and theft*

6 WAR [U] military protection and support given to aircraft, ships etc that are likely to be attacked: *fighters used as cover for ground troops*

7 PLANTS [U] trees and plants that grow in large numbers on a piece of land: *Once the forest cover is felled, rains wash away the soil.* | *With its spreading stems, ivy makes good* **ground cover**.

8 WEATHER [U] clouds, snow etc that partly hide the sky or the ground: **cloud/snow/fog etc cover** *Cloud cover in the morning should clear later.*

9 WORK [U] an arrangement in which people do a job or provide a service, especially because the people who normally do it are not there; → **backup**: *It's your responsibility to arrange adequate cover for holiday periods.* | *night-time ambulance cover*

10 MUSIC also **cover version** [C] a new recording of a song, piece of music etc that was originally recorded by a different artist: *She's opted to* **do** *a* **cover version** *for her first single.*

11 SECRET [C usually singular] behaviour or activities that seem normal or honest but are being used to hide something bad or illegal: [+**for**] *The gang used the shop as a cover for drug deals.* | *All that toughness is just a cover for his inability to show affection.*

12 under cover a) pretending to be someone else in order to do something secretly: *She was* **working under cover** *to get information on drug gangs.* **b)** under a roof or other structure: *The aircraft is displayed under cover in the USAF Gallery.*

13 under (the) cover of darkness/night *literary* hidden by the darkness of night: *They escaped under cover of darkness.*

14 under plain cover/under separate cover if a letter etc is sent under plain cover or under separate cover, it is sent in a plain envelope or a separate envelope: *The bill will be sent to you later under separate cover.*

cov·er·age /ˈkʌvərɪdʒ/ *n* [U] **1** when a subject or event is reported on television or radio, or in newspapers: **media/press etc coverage** *The allegations received widespread media coverage.* | **live coverage** *of the match* (=the match is broadcast at the same time that it is happening) **2** *AmE* the protection an insurance company gives you, so that it pays you money if you are injured, something is stolen etc; ▤ **cover** *BrE*: *health care coverage* **3** the range of subjects and facts included in a book, programme, class etc: [+**of**] *Prestel's website provides good coverage of the subject.*

4 when something affects or covers a particular area or group of things: *More satellites are needed to provide telephone coverage in remote areas.*

cov·er·alls /'kʌvərɔːlz $ -ɒːlz/ *n* [plural] *AmE* a piece of clothing that you wear over all your clothes to protect them; ⊟ **overalls** *BrE*

'**cover charge** *n* [C] money that you have to pay in a restaurant in addition to the cost of the food and drinks, especially when there is a band or dancing

cov·ered /'kʌvəd $ -ərd/ *adj* **1** having a roof: *a covered arena* **2** having a layer of something on top: *snow-covered hills*

'**cover girl** *n* [C] an attractive young woman whose photograph is on the front cover of a magazine

cov·er·ing /'kʌvərɪŋ/ *n* **1** [singular] something that covers or hides something: *a light covering of snow* **2 coverings** [plural] a layer of something such as paper, wood, or cloth used to cover walls, floors etc: *colourful wall coverings*

,**covering** '**letter** *n* [C] *BrE* a letter that you send with documents or a package that gives information about its contents; ⊟ **cover letter** *AmE*: *Send your CV and a covering letter to the address below.*

cov·er·let /'kʌvəlꜞt $ -vər-/ *n* [C] *old-fashioned* a cloth cover for a bed; ⊟ **bedspread**

'**cover ,letter** *n* [C] *AmE* a covering letter

'**cover note** *n* [C] *BrE* a document that proves you have car insurance

'**cover ,price** *n* [C, usually singular] the price printed on the front of a book, magazine etc: *10p of the cover price goes directly to charity.*

'**cover ,story** *n* [C] the main story that appears with a picture on the front cover of a newspaper or magazine

cov·ert¹ /'kʌvət, 'kəʊvɜːt $ 'koʊvərt/ *adj* secret or hidden; ⊡ **overt**: *covert operations against the government*

covert² *n* [C] a group of thick bushes where animals can hide

'**cover-up** *n* [C] an attempt to prevent the public from discovering the truth about something; → **whitewash**: *He accused the government of a cover-up.* → **COVER UP** (2)

cov·et /'kʌvꜞt/ *v* [T] *formal* to have a very strong desire to have something that someone else has: *The Michelin Awards are coveted by restaurants all over the world.*

cov·et·ous /'kʌvꜞtəs/ *adj formal* having a very strong desire to have something that someone else has: *They began to cast covetous eyes on their neighbours' fields.* —**covetously** *adv* —**covetousness** *n* [U]

cow¹ [S2] /kaʊ/ *n* [C]
1 a large female animal that is kept on farms and used to produce milk or meat; → **bull**
2 a male or female animal of this type; → **bull**: *a herd of cows*
3 the female of some large animals, such as the ELEPHANT or the WHALE; → **bull**
4 *BrE spoken not polite* an offensive word for a woman who you think is stupid or unpleasant
5 have a cow *informal* to be very angry or surprised about something
6 till the cows come home *informal* for a very long time, or for ever → **CASH COW, MAD COW DISEASE, SACRED COW**

cow² *v* [T usually passive] to frighten someone in order to make them do something: **cow sb into sth** *The protesters had been cowed into submission by the police.*

cow·ard /'kaʊəd $ -ərd/ *n* [C] someone who is not at all brave: *Try it. Don't be such a coward.* —**cowardly** *adj*: *a cowardly attack on a defenceless man*

cow·ard·ice /'kaʊədꜞs $ -ər-/ also **cow·ard·li·ness** /'kaʊədlinꜞs $ -ərd-/ *n* [U] lack of courage; ⊡ **bravery**: *cowardice in the face of danger*

cow·bell /'kaʊbel/ *n* [C] a small bell → see picture at BELL

cow·boy /'kaʊbɔɪ/ *n* [C] **1** in the US, a man who rides a horse and whose job is to care for cattle **2** *BrE*

someone who is dishonest in business, or who produces very bad quality work: *a firm of cowboy builders* **3 cowboys and Indians** a game played by children who fight while pretending to be cowboys and Native Americans

'**cowboy ,hat** *n* [C] a hat with a wide circular edge and a soft round top; → **Stetson**

cow·catch·er /'kaʊ,kætʃə $ -ər/ *n* [C] a piece of metal on the front of a train that pushes things off the track

'**cow chip** *n* [C] *AmE* a round flat mass of dry solid waste from a cow; ⊟ **cow pat**

cow·er /'kaʊə $ -ər/ *v* [I] to bend low and move back because you are frightened: [+**back/against/under etc**] *He cowered against the wall.*

cow·girl /'kaʊgɜːl $ -gɜːrl/ *n* [C] in the US, a woman who rides a horse and whose job is to care for cattle

cow·hand /'kaʊhænd/ *n* [C] someone whose job is to care for cattle; → **rancher**

cow·hide /'kaʊhaɪd/ *n* [C,U] the skin of a cow or the leather made from it

cowl /kaʊl/ *n* [C] **1** a large HOOD that covers your head and shoulders: *a monk in a dark habit and cowl* **2** a cover for a CHIMNEY

cow·lick /'kaʊ,lɪk/ *n* [C] hair that sticks up on your head

cow·ling /'kaʊlɪŋ/ *n* [C] a metal cover for an aircraft engine

,**cowl 'neck** *n* [C] the neck on a piece of clothing that falls in folds at the front

co-work·er /,kəʊ 'wɜːkə $ 'koʊ ,wɜːrkər/ *n* [C] someone who works with you and has a similar position; ⊟ **colleague**

cow·pat /'kaʊpæt/ *n* [C] a round flat mass of solid waste from a cow; ⊟ **cow chip** *AmE*

,**cow 'pie** *n* [C] *AmE informal* a COW CHIP

cow·poke /'kaʊpəʊk $ -poʊk/ *n* [C] *AmE old-fashioned* a COWBOY

cow·rie /'kaʊri/ *n* [C] a small shiny shell that was used in the past as money in parts of Africa and Asia

cow·shed /'kaʊʃed/ *n* [C] a building where cows are kept

cow·slip /'kaʊ,slɪp/ *n* [C] a small European wild plant with sweet smelling yellow flowers

cox /kɒks $ kɑːks/ *n* [C] someone who controls the direction of a rowing boat, especially in races —**cox** *v* [T]

cox·comb /'kɒkskəʊm $ 'kɑːkskoʊm/ *n* [C] *old-fashioned* a stupid man who is too proud of his clothes and appearance

cox·swain /'kɒksən, -sweɪn $ 'kɑːk-/ *n* [C] a cox

coy /kɔɪ/ *adj* **1** shy or pretending to be shy in order to attract people's interest: *She gave him a coy smile.* **2** unwilling to give information about something; ⊡ **open**: [+**about**] *Tania was always coy about her age.* —**coyly** *adv* —**coyness** *n* [U]

coy·ote /'kɔɪ-əʊt, kɔɪ'əʊti $ 'kaɪ-oʊt, kaɪ'oʊti/ *n* [C] a small wild dog that lives in North West America and Mexico

coy·pu /'kɔɪpuː/ *n* [C] an animal like a BEAVER, kept on farms for its fur

coz /kʌz, kəz $ kɒːz, kəz / *conjunction BrE informal* because

coz·en /'kʌzən/ *v* [T] *old-fashioned* to trick or deceive someone

co·zy /'kəʊzi $ 'koʊ-/ *adj* the usual American spelling of COSY

coz·zie /'kɒzi $ 'kɑː-/ *n* [C] *BrE informal* a SWIMMING COSTUME

CPA /,siː piː 'eɪ/ *n* [C] *AmE* **Certified Public Accountant** an ACCOUNTANT who has passed all his or her examinations

CPR /ˌsiː piː ˈɑː $ -ˈɑːr/ n [U] *cardiopulmonary resuscitation* when you breathe into someone's mouth and press repeatedly on their chest in order to make them breathe again and make their heart start beating again after it has stopped

CPU /ˌsiː piː ˈjuː/ n [C] *technical* **central processing unit** the part of a computer that controls what it does

crab /kræb/ n **1** [C] a sea animal with a hard shell, five legs on each side, and two large CLAWS; → **crustacean 2** [U] the flesh of this animal that you can cook and eat: *crab meat* | *dressed crab* (=prepared for eating) **3 crabs** [plural] *informal* a medical condition in which a type of LOUSE (=insect) is in the hair around sexual organs **4** [singular] *AmE informal* someone who becomes annoyed easily about unimportant things

ˈcrab ˌapple n [C] a small sour apple, or the tree it grows on

crab·bed /ˈkræbɪd/ adj *literary* writing which is crabbed is small, untidy, and difficult to read

crab·by /ˈkræbi/ adj easily annoyed by unimportant things; **☒ bad-tempered**: *a crabby old man* | *You're a bit crabby this morning.*

crab·grass /ˈkræbɡrɑːs $ -ɡræs/ n [U] *AmE* a kind of rough grass

crab·wise /ˈkræbwaɪz/ also **crab·ways** /-weɪz/ adv sideways: *I moved crabwise along the edge of the cliff.*

crack¹ [S3] /kræk/ v
1 BREAK [I,T] to break or to make something break, either so that it gets lines on its surface, or so that it breaks into pieces: *Don't put boiling water in the glass or it will crack.* | *Concrete is liable to crack in very cold weather.* | *He picked up a piece of rock and cracked it in half.* | *She fell and cracked a bone in her leg.* | *He cracked a couple of eggs into a pan.*
2 SOUND [I,T] to make a quick loud sound like the sound of something breaking, or to make something do this: *Thunder cracked overhead.* | *He cracked his whip and galloped off.* | *Dennis rubbed his hands together and* **cracked his knuckles**.
3 HIT [T] to hit someone or something hard: **crack sth on sth** *I slipped and cracked my head on the door.* | *She cracked him* **over the head** *with a hammer.*
4 NOT BE ABLE TO CONTINUE [I] to be unable to continue doing something because there is too much pressure and you do not have the mental strength to continue: [+under] *Some young executives crack under the pressure of having to meet tough sales targets every month.* | *He cracked under interrogation and confessed.*
5 VOICE [I] if your voice cracks, it starts to sound different because you are feeling strong emotions: *His voice cracked slightly as he tried to explain.*
6 SOLVE/UNDERSTAND [T] to find the answer to a problem or manage to understand something that is difficult to understand; **☒ solve**: *I think we've* **cracked the problem** *of the computer crashing all the time.* | *It took them nearly two months to* **crack the code**. | *This new evidence could help detectives to* **crack the case**.
7 STOP SB [T] *informal* to stop a person from being successful: *His political enemies have never managed to crack him.*
8 OPEN A SAFE [T] to open a SAFE illegally in order to steal the things inside it
9 COMPUTER [T] to illegally copy computer software or change free software which may lack certain features of the full VERSION, so that the free software works in the same way as the full version: *You can find out how to crack any kind of software on the web.*
10 crack it *BrE informal* to manage to do something successfully: *I think we've cracked it!* | *He seems to have got it cracked.*
11 crack a joke *informal* to tell a joke: *He kept cracking jokes about my appearance.*
12 crack open a bottle *BrE informal* to open a bottle of alcohol for drinking: *We cracked open a few bottles.*
13 get cracking *informal* to start doing something or

going somewhere quickly: *I think we need to get cracking if we're going to catch this train.*
14 crack the whip *informal* to make people work very hard
15 sth is not all/everything it's cracked up to be *informal* used to say that something is not as good as people say it is: *I thought the film was OK, but it's not all it's cracked up to be.*

crack down *phr v*
to become more strict in dealing with a problem and punishing the people involved: [+on] *The government is determined to crack down on terrorism.* | *The police are* **cracking down hard** *on violent crime.* → CRACKDOWN

crack into sth *phr v*
to secretly enter someone else's computer system, especially in order to damage the system or steal the information stored on it; → **hack**: *A teenager was accused of cracking into the company's network.*

crack on *phr v BrE informal*
to continue working hard at something in order to finish it: [+with] *I need to crack on with my project work this weekend.*

crack up *phr v informal*
1 crack (sb) up to laugh a lot at something, or to make someone laugh a lot: *Everyone in the class just cracked up.* | *She's so funny. She cracks me up.*
2 to become unable to think or behave sensibly because you have too many problems or too much work: *I was beginning to think I was cracking up!*

crack² n
1 GAP [C] a very narrow space between two things or two parts of something: [+between] *He squeezed into a crack between two rocks.* | [+in] *He could see them through a crack in the door.* | *She opened the door* **a crack** *and peeped into the room.*
2 BREAK [C] a thin line on the surface of something when it is broken but has not actually come apart: [+in] *There were several small cracks in the glass.*; → see picture at HOLE
3 WEAKNESS [C] a weakness or fault in an idea, system, or organization: [+in] *The cracks in their relationship were starting to show.* | *The first* **cracks** *are beginning to* **appear** *in the economic policy.*
4 SOUND [C] a sudden loud sound like the sound of a stick being broken: **loud/sharp crack** *There was a sharp crack as the branch broke off.* | [+of] *We could hear the crack of gunfire in the distance.* | *a crack of thunder*
5 JOKE [C] *informal* a clever joke or rude remark: [+about] *I didn't like his crack about her being overweight.* | *He's always* **making cracks** *about how stupid I am.*
6 ATTEMPT [C] *informal* an attempt to do something; **☒ shot**: [+at] *I'd like a* **crack at** *climbing that mountain.* | *The competition's open to anyone – why don't you* **have a crack**?
7 DRUG [U] an illegal drug that some people take for pleasure: *crack addicts*
8 BODY [C] *informal* the space between someone's BUTTOCKS
9 a crack on the head a hard hit on the head: *You've had a nasty crack on the head and you need to rest.*
10 a crack in sb's voice a change in someone's voice because they are feeling very upset: *He noticed the crack in her voice as she tried to continue.*
11 the crack of dawn very early in the morning: **at the crack of dawn** *We were up at the crack of dawn.*
12 COMPUTER [C] a piece of information or computer CODE that lets you illegally change free software which may lack certain features of the full VERSION, so that the free software works in the same way as the full version
13 a fair crack of the whip *BrE informal* the same chance as other people to do something: *They feel they haven't been* **given a fair crack of the whip**.

crack³ adj [only before noun] **1** with a lot of experience and skill: *crack troops* | *a crack regiment* | *a crack sportsman* **2 crack shot** someone who is able to shoot a weapon very well and hit the thing they are aiming at

'crack ,baby n [C] plural **crack babies** a baby that is born with medical and mental problems because its mother regularly smoked the illegal drug CRACK before the baby was born

crack·down /'krækdaʊn/ n [C usually singular] action that is taken to deal more strictly with crime, a problem, protests etc: [+on/against] *a military crackdown on pro-democracy demonstrations | the government's crackdown against drugs* → **crack down** at CRACK¹

cracked /krækt/ adj **1** something that is cracked has one or more lines on the surface because it is damaged but not completely broken: *The mirror was cracked and dirty. | dry, cracked lips | He escaped with a cracked rib and bruising.* **2** someone's voice that is cracked sounds rough and uncontrolled **3** [not before noun] informal slightly crazy

crack·er /'krækə $ -ər/ n [C] **1** a hard dry type of bread in small flat shapes, that is often eaten with cheese **2** also **Christmas cracker** a decorated paper tube that makes a small exploding sound when you pull it apart. Crackers contain a small gift, a paper hat, and a joke, and are used at Christmas in Britain. **3** a FIRECRACKER **4** BrE spoken something that is very good or funny: *That was a cracker of a goal.* **5** someone who illegally breaks into a computer system in order to steal information or stop the system from working properly; ⊟ **hacker**: *computer crackers* **6** BrE old-fashioned informal a very attractive woman

crack·ers /'krækəz $ -ərz/ adj [not before noun] crazy: *You lent him all that money? You must be crackers!*

crack·head /'krækhed/ n [C] informal someone who uses the illegal drug CRACK

'crack house n [C] a place where the illegal drug CRACK is sold, bought, and smoked

crack·ing /'krækɪŋ/ adj [only before noun] BrE informal very good, exciting etc; ⊟ **great**: *We've got two cracking games to look forward to.*

crack·le /'krækəl/ v [I] to make repeated short sounds like something burning in a fire: *logs crackling on the fire | An announcement crackled over the tannoy.* —**crackle** n [C] —**crackly** adj

crack·ling /'kræklɪŋ/ n **1** [singular, U] the sound made by something when it crackles: *There was silence except for the crackling of the fire.* **2** [U] BrE the hard skin on a piece of pig meat when it has been cooked for a long time **3** **cracklings** [plural] AmE pieces of skin, usually from a pig or chicken, that have been cooked in hot oil and are eaten cold

crack·pot /'krækpɒt $ -pɑːt/ n [C] someone who is slightly crazy —**crackpot** adj: *crackpot schemes*

'crack-up n [C] **1** a NERVOUS BREAKDOWN **2** AmE an accident involving one or more vehicles → **crack up** at CRACK¹

cra·dle¹ /'kreɪdl/ n **1** [C] a small bed for a baby, especially one that moves gently from side to side; → **cot**: *She rocked the cradle to quieten the child.* **2** **the cradle of sth** formal the place where something important began: *Athens is often regarded as the cradle of democracy.* **3** **from (the) cradle to (the) grave** all through your life: *From cradle to grave, the car marks every rite of American passage.* **4** [singular] the beginning of something: *Like most Catholic children, he had heard stories of Ireland from the cradle.* **5** [C] a structure that is used to lift something heavy up or down: *a window-cleaner's cradle* **6** [C] the part of a telephone where you put the RECEIVER when you are not using it: *She replaced the receiver on the cradle.* → CAT'S CRADLE; → **rob the cradle** at ROB (5)

cradle² v [T] **1** to hold something gently, as if to protect it: *John cradled the baby in his arms.* **2** to hold a telephone RECEIVER by putting it between your ear and your shoulder: *She hunched over the desk, telephone cradled at her neck.*

'cradle-,robber also **'cradle-,snatcher** BrE n [C] someone who has a romantic relationship with some-

one who is much younger – used to show disapproval; → **sugar daddy, toy boy** —**cradle-rob**; **cradle-snatch** BrE v [I]

craft¹ S3 /krɑːft $ kræft/ n **1** plural **crafts** [C] a job or activity in which you make things with your hands, and that you usually need skill to do; → **handicraft**: *traditional rural crafts | arts and crafts* **2** plural **craft** [C] **a)** a small boat **b)** an aircraft or spacecraft **3** [C] formal a profession, especially one needing a special skill: *The musician spends years perfecting his craft.* **4** [U] skill in deceiving people: *Craft and cunning were necessary for the scheme to work.* → LANDING CRAFT

craft² v [T usually passive] to make something using a special skill, especially with your hands: *Each doll is crafted individually by specialists. | a **hand-crafted** silver cigar case*

-craft /krɑːft $ kræft/ suffix [in nouns] **1** a vehicle of a particular type: *a spacecraft | a hovercraft | several aircraft* **2** skill of a particular kind: *statecraft* (=skill in government) | *stagecraft* (=skill in acting, directing etc in plays)

'craft knife n plural **craft knives** [C] BrE a very sharp knife used for cutting paper, thin wood etc

crafts·man /'krɑːftsmən $ 'kræfts-/ n plural **craftsmen** /-mən/ [C] someone who is very skilled at a particular CRAFT

crafts·man·ship /'krɑːftsmənʃɪp $ 'kræfts-/ n [U] **1** very detailed work that has been done using a lot of skill, so that the result is beautiful: *The carving is a superb piece of craftsmanship.* **2** the special skill that someone uses to make something beautiful with their hands: *Salisbury Cathedral is remarkable for its high standard of craftsmanship.*

crafts·wom·an /'krɑːfts,wʊmən $ 'kræfts-/ n plural **craftswomen** /-,wɪmɪn/ [C] a woman who is very skilled at a particular CRAFT

craft·y S2 /'krɑːfti $ 'kræf-/ adj comparative **craftier**, superlative **craftiest** good at getting what you want by clever planning and by secretly deceiving people; ⊟ **cunning, sly**: *He's a crafty old devil.* —**craftily** adv —**craftiness** n [U]

crag /kræg/ n [C] a high and very steep rough rock or mass of rocks

crag·gy /'krægi/ adj **1** a mountain that is craggy is very steep and covered in rough rocks: *the craggy peaks of the Sierra Madre* **2** having a face with many deep lines on it: *his thin craggy face*

cram /kræm/ v **crammed, cramming** **1** [T always + adv/prep] to force something into a small space: *cram sth into/onto etc sth Jill crammed her clothes into the bag. | A lot of information has been crammed into this book.* **2** [I always + adv/prep] if a lot of people cram into a place or vehicle, they go into it so it is then full: [+in/into] *We all crammed in and Pete started the car. | 36,000 spectators crammed into the stadium to see the game.* **3** [T] especially AmE if a lot of people cram a place, they fill it: *Thousands of people crammed the mall Sunday.* **4** [I] to prepare yourself for an examination by learning a lot of information quickly; ⊟ **swot** BrE: *She's been cramming hard all week. |* [+for] *I have to cram for my chemistry test tomorrow.*

cram sth ⇔ **in** also **cram sth into sth** phr v to do a lot of activities in a short period of time; ⊟ **pack in**: *We crammed in as much sightseeing as possible during our stay in New York.*

crammed /kræmd/ adj **crammed with/crammed full of sth** completely full of things or people; ⊟ **packed**: *The guide is crammed full of useful information. | The streets were crammed with people.*

cram·mer /ˈkræmə $ -ər/ n [C] BrE a special school that prepares people quickly for examinations

cramp[1] /kræmp/ n **1** [C,U] a severe pain that you get in part of your body when a muscle becomes too tight, making it difficult for you to move that part of your body: *Several players were suffering from cramp.* | *muscle cramps* | **have/get (a) cramp** *One of the swimmers got cramp and had to drop out of the race.* → WRITER'S CRAMP **2 (stomach) cramps** [plural] severe pains in the stomach, especially the ones that women get when they MENSTRUATE

cramp[2] v **1** [T] to prevent the development of someone or something; ■ **hinder, restrict**: *Stricter anti-pollution laws may cramp economic growth.* **2 cramp sb's style** informal to prevent someone from behaving in the way they want to: *Paul said he didn't want Sarah to come along because she cramps his style.* **3** [I,T] also **cramp up** to get or cause cramp in a muscle: *He cramped in the last 200 metres of the race.* | *Sitting still for so long had cramped her muscles.*

cramped /kræmpt/ adj **1** a cramped room, building etc does not have enough space for the people in it; → **crowded**: *The kitchen was small and cramped.* | *a cramped apartment* | *The troops slept in* **cramped conditions** *with up to 20 in a single room.* → see picture at SPACIOUS **2** also **cramped up** unable to move properly and feeling uncomfortable because there is not enough space: *cramped muscles* **3** writing that is cramped is very small and difficult to read

cram·pon /ˈkræmpɒn $ -pɑːn/ n [C usually plural] a piece of metal with sharp points that mountain climbers fasten under their boots to stop them slipping on ice or snow

cran·ber·ry /ˈkrænbəri $ -beri/ n plural **cranberries** [C] a small red sour fruit: *cranberry sauce*

crane[1] /kreɪn/ n [C] **1** a large tall machine used by builders for lifting heavy things; → **hoist 2** a tall water bird with very long legs

crane[2] v [I,T always + adv/prep] to look around or over something by stretching or leaning: **crane forward/over** etc *The children craned forward to see what was happening.* | *He* **craned his neck** *above the crowd to get a better view.*

crane fly n plural **crane flies** [C] BrE a flying insect with long legs; ■ **daddy longlegs**

cra·ni·um /ˈkreɪniəm/ n plural **craniums** or **crania** /-niə/ [C] technical the part of your head that is made of bone and covers your brain —**cranial** adj

crank[1] /kræŋk/ n [C] **1** a handle on a piece of equipment, that you can turn in order to move something **2** informal someone who has unusual ideas and behaves strangely: *Zoff was originally dismissed as a crank, but his theories later became very influential.* **3 crank call/letter** a telephone call or letter in which someone says annoying things **4** AmE informal someone who easily gets angry or annoyed with people

crank[2] v also **crank up** [T] to make something move by turning a crank: *Try* **cranking the engine**.
  crank sth ⇔ **up** phr v informal to make the sound of something, especially music, louder: *We* **cranked up** *the volume.*
  crank sth ⇔ **out** phr v to produce a lot of something very quickly: *He cranked out three novels last year.*

crank·shaft /ˈkræŋkʃɑːft $ -ʃæft/ n [C] a long piece of metal in a vehicle that is connected to the engine and helps to turn the wheels

crank·y /ˈkræŋki/ adj **1** BrE informal strange; → **eccentric, weird**: *Organic farming is no longer thought of as cranky.* **2** informal bad-tempered: *I was feeling tired and cranky.* —**crankiness** n [U]

cran·ny /ˈkræni/ n plural **crannies** [C] a small narrow hole in a wall or rock: *The toad hid itself in a cranny in the wall.* → **nook and cranny** at NOOK (3)

crap[1] /kræp/ n spoken not polite **1** [U] something someone says that you think is completely wrong or untrue; ■ **rubbish**: *You don't believe all that crap, do you?* | **load/pile of crap** also **bunch of crap** AmE: *That's a bunch of crap! I never said that.* | *He came out with a load of crap about how he'd tried to call me yesterday.* | *Greg's* **full of crap** (=often says things that are completely wrong). | **cut the crap** (=used to tell someone to stop saying things that are completely wrong) *Just cut the crap and tell me what really happened.* **2** [U] something that is very bad or is of bad quality; ■ **rubbish**: *They sell a lot of stuff cheap, but most of it is crap.* | **load/pile of crap** also **bunch of crap** AmE: *The game was a load of crap.* **3** [U] things that are useless or unimportant: *What is all this crap doing on my desk?* **4** [U] bad or unfair treatment: **take/stand for/put up with crap** (=to allow someone to treat you badly) *I'm not going to take any more of this crap!* | *I* **don't need this** kind of **crap** (=used when you are angry about the way someone is behaving towards you). | *I'm tired of you* **giving me crap** (=saying bad things) about my long hair. **5** [U] solid waste that is passed from your BOWELS **6** [singular] the act of passing solid waste from your BOWELS: **take a crap** also **have a crap** BrE **7 craps** [plural] AmE a game played for money in the US, using two DICE: **shoot craps** (=to play this game)

crap[2] adj BrE spoken not polite very bad: *a crap film* | *I've had such a crap day.* | [+at] *I'm really crap at tennis.*

crap[3] v **crapped, crapping** [I] informal not polite to pass waste matter from your BOWELS

crap·per /ˈkræpə $ -ər/ n informal not polite **the crapper** a toilet

crap·py /ˈkræpi/ adj informal not polite very bad: *a crappy hotel*

crash[1] /kræʃ/ v
1 CAR/PLANE ETC [I,T] to have an accident in a car, plane etc by violently hitting something else; → **collide**: *The jet crashed after take-off.* | *The plane crashed into a mountain.* | **crash a car/bus/plane** etc *He was drunk when he crashed the car.*
2 HIT SB/STH HARD [I,T always + adv/prep] to hit something or someone extremely hard while moving, in a way that causes a lot of damage or makes a lot of noise: [+into/through etc] *A brick crashed through the window.* | *We watched the waves crashing against the rocks.* | *The plates* **went crashing** *to the ground.* | *A large branch* **came crashing down**.
3 LOUD NOISE [I] to make a sudden loud noise: *Thunder crashed and boomed outside.*
4 COMPUTER [I,T] if a computer crashes, or if you crash the computer, it suddenly stops working: *The system crashed and I lost three hours' worth of work.*
5 FINANCIAL [I] if a STOCK MARKET or SHARES crash, they suddenly lose a lot of value
6 SPORT [I] BrE to lose very badly in a sports event: *Liverpool* **crashed** *to their worst defeat of the season.*
7 SLEEP [I] spoken **a)** to stay at someone's house for the night: *Can I crash at your place on Saturday night?* **b)** also **crash out** to go to bed, or go to sleep very quickly, because you are very tired: *I crashed out on the sofa this afternoon.*
8 PARTY [T] informal to go to a party that you have not been invited to: *We crashed Joe's party yesterday.*
9 crashing bore BrE old-fashioned someone who is very boring

crash[2] S3 n [C]
1 an accident in which a vehicle violently hits something else; → **collision**: **plane/car etc crash** *41 people were killed in the plane crash.* | *the Clapham rail crash* | *a* **fatal crash** | *a* **head-on crash** *between two trains* | *a* **crash victim**
2 a sudden loud noise made by something fall-

crash
dent
a crashed car

ing, breaking etc: *I heard a loud crash.* | **with a crash** *The branch came down with a crash.* | [+of] *a crash of thunder*

3 an occasion when a computer or computer system suddenly stops working

4 an occasion on which the STOCKS and SHARES in a STOCK MARKET suddenly lose a lot of value: *the stock market crash of October 1987*

crash ,barrier *n* [C] *BrE* a strong fence or wall built to keep cars apart or to keep them away from people, in order to prevent an accident

crash course *n* [C] a course in which you learn a lot about a particular subject in a very short period of time: [+in] *a crash course in Spanish*

crash ,diet *n* [C] an attempt to lose a lot of weight quickly by strictly limiting how much you eat

crash ,helmet *n* [C] a very strong hard hat that protects your head, and is worn by racing car drivers, people riding MOTORCYCLES etc

crash 'landing, crash-landing *n* [C] an occasion when a pilot has to bring a plane down to the ground in a rougher and more dangerous way than usual because the plane has a problem: *He was forced to make a crash-landing in the middle of the desert.* —**crash-land** *v* [I,T]

crass /kræs/ *adj* behaving in a stupid and offensive way which shows that you do not understand or care about other people's feelings; → **insensitive**: *a crass remark* | *an act of cross stupidity* —**crassly** *adv*

-crat /kræt/ *suffix* [in nouns] another form of the suffix -OCRAT

crate¹ /kreɪt/ *n* [C] **1** a large box made of wood or plastic that is used for carrying fruit, bottles etc: [+of] *a crate of beer;* → see picture at BOX **2** *old-fashioned* a very old car or plane that does not work very well

crate² also **crate up** *v* [T] to pack things into a crate

cra·ter /'kreɪtə $ -ər/ *n* [C] **1** a round hole in the ground made by something that has fallen on it or by an explosion: *craters on the moon's surface* → see picture at HOLE **2** the round open top of a VOLCANO → see picture at VOLCANO

cra·vat /krə'væt/ *n* [C] a wide piece of loosely folded material that men wear around their necks; → **tie**

crave /kreɪv/ *v* [T] to have an extremely strong desire for something: *She's an insecure child who craves attention.*

cra·ven /'kreɪvən/ *adj formal* completely lacking courage; → **cowardly**: *He had a craven fear of flying.* —**cravenly** *adv*

crav·ing /'kreɪvɪŋ/ *n* [C] an extremely strong desire for something; → **longing**: [+for] *She had a craving for some chocolate.*

craw /krɔː $ krɒ/ *n* [C] → **stick in your craw** at STICK¹ (11)

craw·fish /'krɔːˌfɪʃ $ 'krɒː-/ *n plural* **crawfish** [C] a CRAYFISH

crawl¹ /krɔːl $ krɒːl/ *v* [I] **1** to move along on your hands and knees with your body close to the ground: [+along/across etc] *The baby crawled across the floor.* **2** if an insect crawls, it moves using its legs: [+over/up etc] *There's a bug crawling up your leg.* **3** crawl into/out of bed to get into or out of bed slowly because you are very tired: *We crawled into bed at 2 am.* **4** if a vehicle crawls, it moves forward very slowly: [+along etc] *The traffic was crawling along.* **5** *BrE informal* to be too pleasant or helpful to someone in authority, especially because you want them to help you – used in order to show disapproval: [+to] *She's always crawling to the boss.* **6** be crawling with sth to be completely covered with insects, people etc: *The floor was crawling with ants.* | *The whole place was crawling with cops.* **7** crawl the Net/web if a computer program crawls the Net, it quickly searches the Internet to find the particular information you need; → **spider**: *robots that crawl the net searching out e-mail addresses for junk mailing*

crawl² *n* [singular] **1** a very slow speed: *The traffic had slowed to a crawl.* **2 the crawl** a way of swimming in which you lie on your stomach and move one arm, and then the other, over your head; → **backstroke, breaststroke, butterfly;** → see picture at SWIMMING

'crawler ,lane *n* [C] *BrE* a special part of a road that can be used by slow vehicles so that other vehicles can go past; → **fast lane**

cray·fish /'kreɪˌfɪʃ/ *n plural* **crayfish** [C,U] a small animal like a LOBSTER that lives in rivers and streams, or the meat from this animal

cray·on¹ /'kreɪən, -ɒn $ -ɑːn, -ən/ *n* [C] a stick of coloured WAX or CHALK that children use to draw pictures

crayon² *v* [I,T] to draw something with a crayon

craze /kreɪz/ *n* [C] a fashion, game, type of music etc that becomes very popular for a short time; ◻ **fad**: [+for] *She started a craze for this type of jewellery.* | *At that time, scooters were the latest craze.* | **fitness/dance/fashion etc craze** *The jogging craze began in the 1970s.*

crazed /kreɪzd/ *adj* behaving in a wild and uncontrolled way like someone who is mentally ill: **crazed with grief/pain/fear etc** *He was crazed with grief after the death of his mother.* | *The old woman had a crazed expression on her face.* | *a crazed killer*

cra·zy¹ [S3] [W3] /'kreɪzi/ *adj comparative* **crazier**, *superlative* **craziest**

1 STRANGE very strange or not sensible; ◻ **mad**: *The neighbours must think we're crazy.* | *It's an absolutely crazy idea.* | *I know this idea sounds crazy, but it may be worth a try.* | **crazy to do sth** *It'd be crazy to go out in this rain.* | *I must have been crazy to agree to this.* | *He often works 12 hours a day – it's crazy.*

2 crazy about sb/sth liking someone very much, or very interested in something: *He's crazy about her.* | *Dan's crazy about football.*

3 ANGRY angry or annoyed: *Turn that music down. It's driving me crazy* (=really annoying me)! | *Dad will go crazy when he hears about this.*

4 like crazy very much or very quickly: *We're going to have to work like crazy to get this finished on time.*

5 go crazy to do something too much, in a way that is not usual or sensible, especially because you are excited: *Don't go crazy and spend it all at once.*

6 MENTALLY ILL mentally ill; ◻ **mad**: *I feel so alone, sometimes I wonder if I'm going crazy.* —**crazily** *adv* —**craziness** *n* [U]

crazy² *n plural* **crazies** [C] *informal especially AmE* someone who is crazy

crazy 'golf *n* [U] *BrE* a golf game, played for fun outdoors, in which you hit a small ball through passages, over bridges and small hills etc; ◻ **miniature golf**

crazy 'paving *n* [U] *BrE* pieces of stone of different shapes fitted together to make a path or flat area

crazy 'quilt *n* [C] a cover for a bed, made from small pieces of cloth of different shapes and colours that have been sewn together

creak /kriːk/ *v* [I] if something such as a door, wooden floor, old bed, or stair creaks, it makes a long high noise when someone opens it, walks on it, sits on it etc: *The floorboards creaked as she walked across the room.* | *The door creaked open.* —**creak** *n* [C]

creak·y /'kriːki/ *adj* **1** something such as a door, floor, or bed that is creaky creaks when you open it, walk on it, sit on it etc, especially because it is old and not in good condition: *creaky stairs* **2** an organization, company etc that is creaky uses old-fashioned methods and does not work very well: *creaky state-owned factories* —**creakily** *adv* —**creakiness** *n* [U]

cream¹ /kriːm/ *n* **1** [U] a thick yellow-white liquid that rises to the top of milk: *fresh cream* | *strawberries and cream* **2** [U] a pale yellow-white colour **3** [C,U] used in the names of foods containing cream or something similar to it: *cream of chicken soup* **4** [C,U] a thick smooth substance that you put on your skin to make it feel soft, treat a medical condition etc; → **lotion**: *sun cream* | *face cream* **5 the cream of sth** the best people or things from a group: *the cream of Europe's athletes* | *The students at this college are the **cream of the crop** (=the best of all).*

cream² *adj* pale yellow-white in colour: *a cream-coloured carpet*

cream³ *v* [T] **1** to mix foods together until they become a thick soft mixture: *Cream the butter and sugar together.* | *creamed potatoes* **2** *AmE informal* to hit someone very hard or easily defeat someone in a game, competition etc: *We got creamed 45–6.*

cream sb/sth ⇔ off *phr v especially BrE* to choose the best people or things from a group, especially so that you can use them for your own advantage: *The best students are creamed off by the large companies.*

cream 'cheese / $ '. ./ *n* [U] a type of soft white smooth cheese

cream 'cracker *n* [C] *BrE* a light BISCUIT often eaten with cheese

cream·er /'kri:mə $ -ər/ *n* **1** [U] a white liquid or powder that you can use instead of milk or cream in coffee or tea **2** [C] a small container for holding cream

cream·e·ry /'kri:məri/ *n plural* **creameries** [C] *old-fashioned* a place where milk, butter, cream, and cheese are produced or sold; → **dairy**

cream 'tea *n* [C,U] *BrE* a small meal eaten in Britain, with small cakes and tea

cream·y /'kri:mi/ *adj comparative* **creamier**, *superlative* **creamiest 1** thick and smooth like cream: *Beat the mixture until smooth and creamy.* | *a soft cheese with a creamy texture* **2** containing cream: *creamy milk* **3** pale yellow-white in colour

crease¹ /kri:s/ *n* **1** [C] a line on a piece of cloth, paper etc where it has been folded, crushed, or pressed: *She **smoothed** the creases from her skirt.* | *I'll have to iron out the creases.* **2** [C] a fold in someone's skin: *the creases on his forehead* **3** [singular] the line where the player has to stand to hit the ball in CRICKET

crease² *v* [I,T] to become marked with a line or lines, or to make a line appear on cloth, paper etc by folding or crushing it; → **crumple**: *Don't sit on my newspaper. You'll crease it!* | *These trousers crease really easily.* | *A worried frown creased her forehead.* —**creased** *adj*: *This shirt is too creased to wear.*

crease (sb) up *phr v BrE spoken* to laugh a lot, or to make someone laugh a lot: *She really creases me up!*

cre·ate [S1] [W1] /kri'eɪt/ *v* [T] **1** to make something exist that did not exist before: *Some people believe the universe was created by a big explosion.* | *Her behaviour is creating a lot of problems.* | *The new factory is expected to create more than 400 new jobs.* **2** to invent or design something: *This dish was created by our chef Jean Richard.* | *Philip Glass created a new kind of music.* | *The software makes it easy to create colourful graphs.* **3 create sb sth** *BrE* to officially give someone a special rank or title: *James I created him Duke of Buckingham.*

cre·a·tion [S3] [W2] /kri'eɪʃən/ *n* **1** [U] the act of creating something: [+of] *The plan should result in the creation of 2000 new jobs.* | *the creation of a single European currency* | *a **job creation** scheme* **2** [C] something that has been created: *The dress is a stunning creation in green, gold, and white.* | *Most countries have systems of government that are relatively modern creations.* **3 the Creation** the act by God, according to the Bible, of making the universe, including the world and everything in it **4** [U] *literary* the whole universe and all living things

cre·a·tion·ist /kri'eɪʃənɪ̯st/ *n* [C] someone who believes that God created the universe in the way described in the Bible —**creationism** *n* [U] —**creationist** *adj*

cre·a·tive¹ [S3] [W3] /kri'eɪtɪv/ *adj* **1** involving the use of imagination to produce new ideas or things: *This job is so boring. I wish I could do something more creative.* | *I teach **creative writing** at Trinity College.* | *the **creative process** of writing a poem* | *Diaghilev did his great **creative work** in France.* | *a **creative solution** to the problem* **2** someone who is creative is very good at using their imagination to make things; → **inventive**: *You're so creative! I could never make my own clothes.* —**creatively** *adv* —**creativeness** *n* [U]

creative² *n* [C] *informal* someone such as a writer or artist who uses their imagination or skills to make things

cre,ative ac'counting *n* [U] the process of using unusual but not illegal ways to change business accounts to make them look better than they really are

cre·a·tiv·i·ty /ˌkri:eɪˈtɪvɪ̯ti/ *n* [U] the ability to use your imagination to produce new ideas, make things etc: *artistic creativity* | *Teachers have been attacked for stifling creativity in their pupils.* | *Editors complain about the lack of creativity in the ideas put to them.*

cre·a·tor /kri'eɪtə $ -ər/ *n* **1** [C] someone who made or invented a particular thing; → **inventor**: [+of] *Walt Disney, the creator of Mickey Mouse* **2 the Creator** God

crea·ture [W3] /'kri:tʃə $ -ər/ *n* [C]
1 LIVING THING anything that is living, such as an animal, fish, or insect, but not a plant: *The first **living creature** sent into space was a dog named Laika.* | **creatures of the deep** (=animals and fish that live in the ocean)
2 IMAGINARY OR STRANGE an imaginary animal or person, or one that is very strange and frightening: *creatures from outer space*
3 a creature of habit someone who always does things in the same way or at the same time
4 STH MADE OR INVENTED *formal* something, especially something bad, that was made or invented by a particular person or organization: [+of] *The poll tax was a creature of the Government.*
5 SB CONTROLLED BY STH someone who is controlled or influenced a lot by something: [+of] *He was a creature of the military government.*
6 beautiful/stupid/adorable etc creature *literary* someone who has a particular character or quality: *He was the most beautiful creature Dot had ever seen.*

creature 'comforts *n* [plural] all the things that make life more comfortable and enjoyable, such as good food, a warm house, and comfortable furniture; → **mod cons**

cre·che, **crèche** /kreʃ $ kreʃ, kreɪʃ/ *n* [C] **1** *BrE* a place where babies are looked after while their parents are at work; ▤ **day care center** *AmE* **2** *AmE* a model of the scene of Jesus Christ's birth, placed in churches and homes at Christmas; ▤ **crib** *BrE*

cre·dence /'kri:dəns/ *n* [U] *formal* the acceptance of something as true: **give credence to sth** (=to believe or accept something as true) *I don't give any credence to these rumors.* | **gain credence** (=to become more widely accepted or believed) *His ideas quickly gained credence among economists.* | **lend credence to sth** (=to make something more believable) *The DNA results lend credence to Hausmann's claims of innocence.*

cre·den·tialed /krɪ'denʃəld/ *adj* someone who is credentialed is legally allowed to do a particular job, because they have done the right type of training: *a newly credentialed teacher*

cre·den·tials /krɪ'denʃəlz/ *n* [plural] **1** someone's education, achievements, experience etc that prove they have the ability to do something: [+for/as] *She had excellent credentials for the job.* | *There are doubts over his credentials as a future Prime Minister.* | *He spent the first part of the interview trying to **establish** his creden-*

tials *as a financial expert.* | *Her* **academic credentials** *include an MA and a PhD.* **2** a letter or other document which proves your good character or your right to have a particular position: *The commissioner presented his credentials to the State Department.*

cred·i·bil·i·ty /ˌkredɪ̬ˈbɪlɪ̬ti/ *n* [U] **1** the quality of deserving to be believed and trusted: **damage/undermine sb's credibility (as sth)** *The scandal has damaged his credibility as a leader.* | **[+of]** *There are serious questions about the credibility of these reports.* | **gain/lose credibility** *Predictions of economic recovery have now lost all credibility.* **2 credibility gap** the difference between what someone says and what they do: *a credibility gap between the Government's promises and their achievements*

cred·i·ble /ˈkredɪ̬bəl/ *adj* deserving or able to be believed or trusted: **credible explanation/story/account** etc *He was unable to give a credible explanation for his behaviour.* | *Her excuse was barely credible.* | **credible threat/challenge/force etc** *Can Thompson make a credible challenge for the party leadership?* | *a* **credible alternative** *to nuclear power* —**credibly** *adv*

cred·it¹ [S2] [W2] /ˈkredɪ̬t/ *n*
1 **DELAYED PAYMENT** [U] an arrangement with a shop, bank etc that allows you to buy something and pay for it later: **on credit** *56 per cent of new cars were bought on credit.* | *Several stores are offering* **interest-free credit** (=credit with no INTEREST charges). | *a* **credit agreement** | *What's the* **credit limit** *on your Visa card?* | **credit facilities** (=the opportunity to buy something on credit)
2 **PRAISE** [U] approval or praise that you give to someone for something they have done: **[+for]** *Credit for this win goes to everybody in the team.* | *They never* **give** *Gene any* **credit** *for all the extra work he does.* | **take/claim/deserve etc (the) credit** *She deserves credit for trying her best.* | **to sb's credit** (=used to say that someone has done something good) *To Jamie's credit, he remained calm.* | *Credit must go to Fiona for making sure everything ran smoothly.*
3 **be a credit to sb/sth** also **do sb/sth credit** to behave so well or be so successful that your family, team etc are proud of you: *She's a credit to her profession.* | *Your children really do you credit.*
4 **have sth to your credit** to have achieved something: *She already has two successful novels to her credit.*
5 **in credit** if you are in credit, you have money in your bank account: *There are no bank charges if you stay in credit.*
6 **the credits** [plural] a list of all the people involved in making a film or television programme, which is shown at the beginning or end of it
7 **on the credit side** used to talk about the good things about someone or something: *On the credit side, the book is extremely well-researched.*
8 **UNIVERSITY** [C] a successfully completed part of a course at a university or college: *I don't have enough credits to graduate.*
9 **AMOUNT OF MONEY** [C] an amount of money that is put into someone's bank account or added to another amount; [F] **debit:** *The company promised to provide credits to customers who had been charged too much.*
10 **TRUE/CORRECT** [U] the belief that something is true or correct: *The witness's story* **gained credit** *with the jury.*

credit² *v* [T not in progressive] **1** to add money to a bank account; [F] **debit: [+to]** *The cheque has been credited to your account.* | **[+with]** *For some reason my account's been credited with an extra $76.* **2 credit sb with (doing) sth** to believe or admit that someone has a quality, or has done something good: *Do credit me with a little intelligence!* | *Evans is credited with inventing the system.* **3 be credited to sb/sth** if something is credited to someone or something, they have achieved it or are the reason for it: *Much of Manchester United's success can be credited to their manager.* **4** *formal* to believe that something is true: **difficult/hard/impossible etc to credit** *We found his statement hard to credit.*

cred·it·a·ble /ˈkredɪ̬təbəl/ *adj* [usually before noun] deserving praise or approval: *The team produced a* **creditable performance.** | *She did a* **creditable job** *of impersonating the singer Mariah Carey.* —**creditably** *adv*

'credit ac,count *n* [C] *BrE* an account with a shop which allows you to take goods and pay for them later; [F] **charge account** *AmE*

'credit card *n* [C] a small plastic card that you use to buy goods or services and pay for them later: *We accept all major credit cards.*

'credit note *n* [C] *BrE* a document given to a customer who is owed money, for example because they have returned goods

cred·i·tor /ˈkredɪ̬tə $ -ər/ *n* [C] a person, bank, or company that you owe money to; [F] **debtor**

'credit ,rating *n* [C] a judgment made by a bank or other company about how likely a person or business is to pay their debts

'credit ,voucher *n* [C] a credit note

cred·it·wor·thy /ˈkredɪ̬t₁wɜːði $ -ˌwɜːr-/ *adj formal* considered to be safe to lend money to: *creditworthy borrowers* —**creditworthiness** *n* [U]

cre·do /ˈkriːdəʊ, ˈkreɪ- $ -doʊ/ *n plural* **credos** [C] a formal statement of the beliefs of a particular person, group, religion etc: *American Express is emphasizing its 'the customer is first' credo.*

cre·du·li·ty /krɪˈdjuːlɪ̬ti $ -ˈduː-/ *n* [U] *formal* willingness or ability to believe that something is true: *Advertisers were accused of exploiting consumers' credulity.* | **strain/stretch credulity** (=seem very difficult to believe) *It strained credulity to believe that a nuclear war would not lead to the destruction of the planet.*

cred·u·lous /ˈkredjɵləs $ -dʒə-/ *adj formal* always believing what you are told, and therefore easily deceived; [F] **gullible:** *Quinn charmed credulous investors out of millions of dollars.*

creed /kriːd/ *n* [C] **1** a set of beliefs or principles: *Marxism has never been weaker as a* **political creed.** | *a* **religious creed** | *people of all colours and creeds* **2 the Creed** a formal statement of belief spoken in certain Christian churches

creek /kriːk/ *n* [C] **1** *AmE, AusE* a small narrow stream or river **2** *BrE* a long narrow area of water that flows from the sea into the land **3 be up the creek (without a paddle)** *spoken* also **be up shit creek (without a paddle)** *not polite* to be in a very difficult situation: *If I don't get my passport by Friday, I'll be up the creek.*

creel /kriːl/ *n* [C] a FISHERMAN'S basket for carrying fish

creep¹ /kriːp/ *v past tense and past participle* **crept** /krept/ [I always + adv/prep] **1** to move in a quiet, careful way, especially to avoid attracting attention: **[+into/over/around etc]** *Johann would creep into the gallery to listen to the singers.* | *He crept back up the stairs, trying to avoid the ones that creaked.* **2** if something such as an insect, small animal, or car creeps, it moves slowly and quietly; → **crawl: [+down/along/away etc]** *a caterpillar creeping down my arm* **3** to gradually enter something and change it: **[+in/into/over etc]** *Funny how religion is creeping into the environmental debate.* **4** if a plant creeps, it grows or climbs up or along a particular place: **[+up/over/around etc]** *ivy creeping up the walls of the building* **5** if mist, clouds etc creep, they gradually fill or cover a place: **[+into/over etc]** *Fog was creeping into the valley.* **6** *BrE informal* to be insincerely nice to someone, especially someone in authority, in order to gain an advantage for yourself: **creep (up) to sb** *I'm not the kind of person to creep to anybody.* **7 sb/sth makes my flesh creep** used to say that someone or something makes you feel strong dislike or fear: *His glassy stare made my flesh creep.*

---

[1] 000, [2] 000, [3] 000, most frequent words in [S]poken and [W]ritten English

creep up on sb/sth *phr v* **1** to surprise someone by walking up behind them silently: *Don't yell – let's creep up on them and scare them.* **2** if a feeling or idea creeps up on you, it gradually increases: *The feeling she had for Malcolm had crept up on her and taken her by surprise.* **3** to seem to come sooner than you expect: *Somehow, the end of term had crept up on us.*

creep² *n* [C] **1** *informal especially AmE* someone who you dislike extremely: *Get lost, you little creep!* **2** *BrE informal* someone who tries to make you like them or do things for them by being insincerely nice to you: *Don't try and flatter her – she doesn't approve of creeps.* **3 give sb the creeps** if a person or place gives you the creeps, they make you feel nervous and a little frightened, especially because they are strange: *That house gives me the creeps.* **4 mission/cost/grade etc creep** when something gradually starts to go beyond what it was intended to deal with or include: *He denied that giving civilian tasks to the NATO forces was a case of mission creep.*

creep·er /ˈkriːpə $ -ər/ *n* [C] a plant that grows up trees or walls, or along the ground → VIRGINIA CREEPER

creep·y /ˈkriːpi/ *adj informal* making you feel nervous and slightly frightened: *There's something creepy about the way he looks at me.* | *The whole place feels creepy.*

creepy-ˈcrawly *n plural* **creepy-crawlies** [C] *informal* an insect, especially one that you are frightened of

cre·mate /krɪˈmeɪt $ ˈkriːmeɪt/ *v* [T] to burn the body of a dead person at a funeral ceremony —**cremation** /krɪˈmeɪʃən/ *n* [C,U]

crem·a·to·ri·um /ˌkreməˈtɔːriəm $ ˌkriː-/ also **crem·a·to·ry** /ˈkremətəri $ ˈkriːmətɔːri/ *n plural* **crematoriums, crematoria** /-riə/ [C] a building in which the bodies of dead people are burned at a funeral ceremony

crème car·a·mel /ˌkrem ˈkærəməl, -mel/ *n plural* **crèmes caramels** [C,U] *BrE* a sweet food made from milk, eggs, and sugar

crème de la crème, creme de la creme /ˌkrem də laː ˈkrem/ *n* [singular] the very best of a kind of thing or group of people: *Oxford and Cambridge are often seen as the crème de la crème of British universities.*

crème de menthe /ˌkrem də ˈmɒnθ $ -ˈmɑːnt/ *n* [U] a strong sweet green alcoholic drink

cre·ole /ˈkriːəʊl $ -oʊl/ *n* **1** [C,U] a language that is a combination of a European language with one or more other languages; → **pidgin** **2 Creole** [C] **a)** someone whose family was originally from both Europe and Africa **b)** someone whose family were originally French SETTLERS in the southern US **3** [U] food prepared in the spicy strong-tasting style of the southern US: *shrimp creole* —**creole** *adj*

cre·o·sote /ˈkriːəsəʊt $ -soʊt/ *n* [U] a thick brown oily liquid used for preserving wood —**creosote** *v* [T]

crepe, crêpe /kreɪp/ *n* **1** [U] a type of light soft thin cloth, with very small folded lines on its surface, made from cotton, silk, wool etc **2** a very thin PANCAKE **3** [U] tightly pressed rubber used especially for making the bottoms of shoes: *crepe-soled shoes*

crepe ˈpaper /ˈ. ˌ.../ *n* [U] a type of thin brightly coloured paper that stretches slightly and is used for making decorations

crept /krept/ the past tense and past participle of CREEP

cre·scen·do /krɪˈʃendəʊ $ -doʊ/ *n plural* **crescendos** [C] **1** if a sound or a piece of music rises to a crescendo, it gradually becomes louder until it is very loud; ☒ **diminuendo**: *The shouting rose to a deafening crescendo.* | *The curtains opened as the music reached a crescendo.* **2** if an activity or feeling reaches a crescendo, it gradually becomes stronger until it is very strong: *The campaign reached its crescendo in the week of the election.*

cres·cent /ˈkresənt, ˈkrez-/ *n* [C] **1** a curved shape that is wider in the middle and pointed at the ends: *a*

small crescent of pastry topped with cheese | *a* **crescent moon** **2** the curved shape that is used as a sign of the Muslim religion **3** a street with a curved shape – often used in the names of streets

cress /kres/ *n* [U] a small plant with round green leaves that are eaten raw; → **mustard**: *Sprinkle some finely chopped cress over the top.*

crest¹ /krest/ *n* [C] **1** the top or highest point of something such as a hill or a wave: [+of] *It took us over an hour to reach the crest of the hill.* **2** a special picture that is used as a sign of a family, town, school, or organization; → **coat of arms: school/family crest** **3** a group of feathers that stick up on the top of a bird's head: *exotic birds with colourful crests* **4** a decoration of long bright feathers that soldiers wore in the past on top of their hats **5 be on/riding the crest of a wave** to be very successful: *a young film director who is on the crest of a wave at the moment*

crest² *v* [T] *formal* to reach the top of a hill or mountain: *They crested a wooded hill shortly before sunset.*

crest·ed /ˈkrestɪd/ *adj* **1** a crested bird has a crest on its head **2** marked with the crest of a family, town, school, or organization: *crested notepaper*

crest·fal·len /ˈkrest,fɔːlən $ -,fɒːl-/ *adj* looking disappointed and upset: *He came back looking crestfallen.*

Cre·ta·ceous /krɪˈteɪʃəs/ *adj* the Cretaceous period was the time long ago when rocks containing CHALK were formed

cret·in /ˈkretɪn $ ˈkriːtn/ *n* [C] *informal* an offensive word for someone who is extremely stupid

Creutz·feldt-Jak·ob dis·ease /ˌkrɔɪtsfelt ˈjækɒb dɪˌziːz $ -ˈjɑːkoʊb-/ *n* [U] *CJD* a very serious disease that kills people and that may be caused by eating BEEF that is infected with BSE

cre·vasse /krɪˈvæs/ *n* [C] a deep open crack in the thick ice on a mountain

crev·ice /ˈkrevɪs/ *n* [C] a narrow crack in the surface of something, especially in rock: *small creatures that hide in crevices in the rock*

crew¹ ⒮ ⒲ /kruː/ *n* **1** [C] all the people who work on a ship or plane: *The plane crashed, killing two of the crew and four passengers.* | [+of] *He joined the crew of a large fishing boat.* | *a crew member* **2** [C] a group of people working together with special skills: *a TV camera crew* → GROUND CREW **3** [singular] a group of people or friends – often used to show disapproval: *a motley crew of students* | *Do you still hang out with the same crew?* **4** [C] a team of people who compete in ROWING races: *Who will be on the college crew?* **5** [C] *informal* a group of musicians, especially in GARAGE music

crew² *v* [I,T] to be part of the crew on a boat: *The boat is crewed by ten men.*

crew cut *n* [C] a very short hair style for men → see picture at HAIRSTYLE

crew·man /ˈkruːmən/ *n plural* **crewmen** /-mən/ [C] a member of the crew on a boat or ship

crew neck *n* [C] a plain round neck on a SWEATER or shirt, or a sweater or shirt with this type of neck

crib¹ /krɪb/ *n* **1** [C] *AmE* a bed for a baby or young child, with bars on the side to stop the baby from falling out; ▣ **cot** *BrE* **2** [C] *BrE* a bed with high sides for a very young baby, which you can move gently from side to side; ▣ **cradle** **3** [C] a wooden frame in which you put food for animals such as cows and horses **4** [C] *BrE* a model of the scene of Jesus' birth, often placed in churches and homes at Christmas; → **Nativity** **5** [C] *BrE informal* a book or piece of paper with information or answers to questions, which students sometimes use dishonestly in examinations **6** [C] *AmE spoken* the place where someone lives: *sb's crib I'm not at my crib, I'm at Jed's house.* **7** [U] the card game of cribbage

crib² v **cribbed**, **cribbing** [I,T] *especially BrE* to copy school or college work dishonestly from someone else: **crib sth off/from sb** *He didn't want anyone to crib the answers from him.*

crib·bage /'krɪbɪdʒ/ also **crib** n [U] a card game in which players show how many points they have by putting small pieces of wood in holes in a small board

crib death n [C] *AmE* the sudden and unexpected death of a baby while it is asleep; ▤ **cot death** *BrE*

crick¹ /krɪk/ n [C] a pain in the muscles in your neck or back that is caused by the muscles becoming stiff: **a crick in your back/neck** *He was getting a crick in his neck from leaning out of the window for so long.*

crick² v [T] to hurt your back or neck by bending or moving in a way that makes the muscles become stiff: *I cricked my back bending to pick up the suitcase.*

crick·et S3 W3 /'krɪkɪt/ n
1 [U] a game between two teams of 11 players in which players try to get points by hitting a ball and running between two sets of three sticks
2 [C] a small brown insect that can jump, and that makes a rough sound by rubbing its wings together

crick·et·er /'krɪkɪtə $ -ər/ n [C] *BrE* someone who plays cricket; → **batsman**, **bowler**, **fielder**: *Her father was a very good cricketer.*

cri·er /'kraɪə $ -ər/ n [C] a TOWN CRIER

cri·key /'kraɪki/ interjection *BrE spoken* used to show that you are surprised or annoyed: *Crikey, I'm late!*

crime S2 W2 /kraɪm/ n
1 [U] illegal activities in general

commit crime
combat/fight crime
turn to crime (=start committing crimes)
crime rate (=the amount of crime that happens somewhere)
crime figures/statistics
crime prevention
violent crime
serious crime
petty crime (=crime that is not very serious)
car crime *BrE*
street crime
victim of crime
juvenile/youth crime (=by children and teenagers)
tough on crime (=always punishing crime severely)

We moved here ten years ago because there was very little crime. | *Women* **commit** *far less* **crime** *than men.* | *Police officers are being given new powers to help* **combat crime**. | *the reasons why people* **turn to crime** | *The town has a relatively low* **crime rate**. | *The latest* **crime figures** *show a drop in the number of robberies.* | *We need to focus more on* **crime prevention**. | **Violent crime** *is on the increase in the city.* | *There has been a rise in* **serious crime** *in the area.* | *He became involved in* **petty crime** *as a teenager.* | *a police crackdown on* **car crime** | **Street crime** *was rising rapidly in the Russian capital.* | *a new support group for* **victims of crime** | *Politicians are trying to appear* **tough on crime**. | *the latest novel by crime writer Ed McBain*

⚠ Do not say 'make/do (a) crime'. Use **commit**: *Young men are more likely to commit crime. She has committed a terrible crime.*

2 [C] an illegal action, which can be punished by law: *He insisted that he had not* **committed** *any* **crime**. | *Rape is a very* **serious crime**. | *men who have been found guilty of* **violent crimes** | [+against] *Crimes against the elderly are becoming more common.* | *The City Council* **made it a crime** *to drink alcohol in the street.* | *Police are still busy hunting for clues at* **the scene of the crime** (=where the crime happened).
3 a life of crime when someone spends their life stealing and committing other crimes, in order to get money to live
4 the perfect crime a crime that no one knows has been committed, so no one can be punished for it

5 crime of passion a crime, especially murder, caused by sexual jealousy
6 crime against humanity a crime of cruelty against large numbers of people, especially in a war
7 crime doesn't pay used to say that crime does not give you any advantage, because you will be caught and punished – used when warning people not to get involved in crime
8 [singular] something that someone is blamed or criticized for doing – use this when you think someone is treated very unfairly; → **sin**: *My only crime is that I fell in love with another girl.* | *Johnson's* **biggest crime** *was that he told the truth.*
9 it's a crime *spoken* said when you think something is very wrong, and someone should not do it: *It would be a crime to waste all that good food.* → **partners in crime** at PARTNER¹ (5); → WHITE-COLLAR (2)

WORD FOCUS: **CRIME**
crimes that involve stealing things: **robbery, burglary, theft, shoplifting, fraud, carjacking**
crimes that involve attacking people: **assault, mugging, murder, rape**
someone who commits crimes: **criminal, thief, crook, burglar, mugger, robber, pickpocket, rapist, offender, lawbreaker**
→ see also criminal, offence, felony, misdemeanour, organized crime, war crime

crime wave n [singular] a sudden large increase in the amount of crime in an area: *More police officers are being brought in to help tackle the current crime wave.*

crim·i·nal¹ S3 W2 /'krɪmɪnəl/ adj
1 relating to crime: *Experts cannot agree on the causes of* **criminal behaviour**. | *I was sure he was involved in some kind of* **criminal activity**. | *She has not committed a* **criminal offence** (=a crime). | *He was arrested and charged with* **criminal damage** (=damaging someone's property illegally). | *The doctor was found guilty of* **criminal negligence** (=not taking enough care to protect people in your work).
2 relating to the part of the legal system that is concerned with crime; → **civil**: *The case will be tried in a* **criminal court**. | *We no longer have any faith in the* **criminal justice system**. | *The police are investigating the matter, and he may face* **criminal charges** (=he may be officially accused of a crime). | *She usually deals with serious* **criminal cases**. | *a* **criminal lawyer**
3 wrong, dishonest, and unacceptable: *It seems criminal that teachers are paid so little money.* —**criminally** *adv*: *a hospital for the criminally insane* —**criminality** /ˌkrɪmɪ'næləti/ n [U]

criminal² n [C] someone who is involved in illegal activities or has been proved guilty of a crime: *Police have described the man as a violent and dangerous criminal.* | *a* **convicted criminal** (=someone who has been found guilty of a crime) | *The new law will ensure that* **habitual criminals** (=criminals who commit crimes repeatedly) *receive tougher punishments than first-time offenders.* | *Teenagers should not be sent to prison to mix with* **hardened criminals** (=criminals who have committed a lot of crimes and will never stop committing crimes).

crim·i·nal·ize also **-ise** *BrE* /'krɪmɪnəl-aɪz/ v [T] to make something illegal, or to say that someone is a criminal because of something they have done; ▤ **decriminalize**: *The government has introduced new legislation to criminalize computer hacking.*

criminal law n [U] laws concerning crimes and their punishments; → **civil law**, **common law**: *There was not enough evidence to bring a prosecution under the criminal law.*

criminal record n [C] an official record kept by the police of any crimes a person has committed: *He already* **had a criminal record**.

crim·i·nol·o·gy /ˌkrɪmɪˈnɒlədʒi $ -ˈnɑː-/ *n* [U] the scientific study of crime and criminals —**criminologist** *n* [C]

crimp /krɪmp/ *v* [T] **1** to press cloth, paper etc into small regular folds: *Use a hot iron to crimp the edges.* **2** to make your hair slightly curly by using a special heated tool: *a young woman with crimped blonde hair*

crim·son¹ /ˈkrɪmzən/ *adj* **1** deep red in colour: *The leaves turn crimson in autumn.* | *a crimson dress* **2** if you go crimson, your face becomes red because you are very angry or embarrassed: **go/turn/flush/blush crimson** *The boy blushed crimson.* | [+with] *Her face was crimson with embarrassment.* —**crimson** *n* [U]

crimson² *v* [I] *literary* if your face crimsons, it becomes red because you are embarrassed; ◘ **blush**: *Rachel crimsoned and sat down.*

cringe /krɪndʒ/ *v* [I] **1** to move away from someone or something because you are afraid: *A stray dog was cringing by the door.* | *She cringed away from him.* **2** to feel embarrassed by something that you have said or done because you think it makes you seem silly; → **wince**: [+at] *She cringed at the sound of her own voice.* | *It makes me cringe when I think how stupid I was.*

crin·kle¹ /ˈkrɪŋkəl/ also **crinkle up** *v* [I,T] **1** if you crinkle part of your face, or if it crinkles, you move it so that small lines appear on it: *His mouth crinkled into a smile.* | *He smiled boyishly, crinkling his eyes.* | *Her face crinkled up in disgust.* **2** to become covered with small folds, or make something do this: *The heat was beginning to make the cellophane crinkle.* —**crinkled** *adj*: *The pages were brown and crinkled.*

crinkle² *n* [C] a thin fold, especially in your skin or on cloth, paper etc: *The first crinkles of age were beginning to appear round her eyes.*

crinkle-cut *adj* crinkle-cut vegetables have been cut into long pieces with gentle curves along the edges: *a bag of frozen crinkle-cut chips*

crin·kly /ˈkrɪŋkli/ *adj* **1** having a lot of small lines or folds: *She looked fondly at his crinkly face.* | *He smiled his nice, crinkly smile.* | *The paper was brown and crinkly at the edges.* **2** hair that is crinkly is stiff and curly: *He had blue eyes and crinkly fair hair.*

crin·o·line /ˈkrɪnəlɪn/ *n* [C] a round frame that was worn in the past under a woman's skirt to support it and hold it away from her body

cripes /kraɪps/ *interjection old-fashioned* used to express surprise or anger

crip·ple¹ /ˈkrɪpəl/ *n* [C] **1** *old-fashioned* someone who is unable to walk properly because their legs are damaged or injured – now considered offensive; → **disabled 2 emotional cripple** *informal* someone who cannot express their feelings to other people – used to show disapproval

cripple² *v* [T] **1** *old-fashioned* to hurt someone badly so that they cannot walk properly; ◘ **disable**: *She was crippled in a car accident.* **2** to damage something badly so that it no longer works or is no longer effective: *The industry is being crippled by high interest rates.* —**crippled** *adj*: *The pilot guided the crippled helicopter to the ground.*

crip·pling /ˈkrɪplɪŋ/ *adj* **1** causing so much damage or harm that something no longer works or is no longer effective: *the crippling effects of war on the economy* **2** a crippling disease or condition causes severe pain and makes it difficult or impossible for someone to walk

cri·sis S2 W2 /ˈkraɪsɪs/ *n plural* **crises** /-siːz/ [C,U] **1** a situation in which there are a lot of problems that must be dealt with quickly so that the situation does not get worse or more dangerous; → **emergency**

economic/financial/political crisis
deal with/handle a crisis
energy/oil/housing crisis
debt/budget crisis
a crisis erupts/arises
a major/severe crisis
resolve/solve/defuse a crisis
avert a crisis
in/during a crisis
be in crisis
crisis management (=dealing with a crisis)

The country now faces an **economic crisis**. | *The Prime Minister was criticized for the way in which he* **handled the crisis**. | *the current* **debt crisis** | *a* **major political crisis** | *I was relieved that we had* **averted** *yet another financial crisis.* | *Oil companies were heavily criticized when they made large profits* **during** *the oil* **crisis** *of the 1970s.* | *The car industry is now* **in crisis**. | *He doesn't seem to be very good at* **crisis management**.

2 a time when a personal emotional problem or situation has reached its worst point: *an emotional crisis* | *In times of crisis, you find out who your real friends are.* | *He seems to be* **going through** *a crisis.* | *She has reached a* **crisis point** *in her career.* | *Both parties experienced an* **identity crisis** (=feeling of uncertainty about their purpose) *at the end of the '90s.*
3 crisis of confidence a situation in which people no longer believe that a government or an economic system is working properly, and will no longer support it or work with it: *There seems to be a crisis of confidence in the economy.*
4 crisis of conscience a situation in which someone feels worried or uncomfortable because they have done something which they think is wrong or immoral → MIDLIFE CRISIS

crisp¹ /krɪsp/ *n* [C] *BrE* a very thin flat round piece of potato that is cooked in oil and eaten cold; → **chip**; ◘ **potato chip** *AmE*: *a packet of crisps*

crisp² *adj*
1 HARD something that is crisp is hard, and makes a pleasant sound when you break it or crush it: *She kicked at the crisp leaves at her feet.* | *He stepped carefully through the crisp, deep snow.*
2 FOOD food that is crisp is pleasantly hard or firm when you bite it; ◘ **crispy**; ◙ **soggy**: *a crisp green salad* | *a crisp, juicy apple* | *Cook the pastry until it is crisp and golden.* | *The meat should be nice and crisp on the outside.*
3 PAPER/CLOTH paper or cloth that is crisp is fresh, clean, and new; ◘ **fresh**: *a crisp, new five dollar bill* | *crisp cotton sheets.*
4 WEATHER weather that is crisp is cold and dry; ◙ **humid**: *The air was fresh and crisp.* | *a crisp, clear autumn day* | *The weather remained crisp and dry.*
5 PEOPLE if someone behaves or speaks in a crisp way, they are confident, polite, and firm, but not very friendly: *Her tone was crisp and businesslike.*
6 PICTURE/SOUND a picture or sound that is crisp is clear; ◙ **sharp**: *an old recording that still sounds remarkably crisp* —**crisply** *adv*: *'Take a seat,' she said crisply.* —**crispness** *n* [U]

crisp³ *v* [I,T] to become crisp or make something become crisp by cooking or heating it: *Cook the chicken until the skin is nicely crisped.*

crisp·bread /ˈkrɪspbred/ *n* [C,U] a thin dry BISCUIT with a salty taste

crisp·y /ˈkrɪspi/ *adj* food that is crispy is pleasantly hard on the outside: *a piece of crispy fried bread*

criss·cross¹, **criss-cross** $ -krɒːs/ *v* **1** [I,T] to make a pattern of straight lines that cross each other: *Railway lines crisscross the countryside.* **2** [T] to travel many times from one side of an area to another: *They spent the next two years crisscrossing the country by bus.*

crisscross², **criss-cross** *n* [C] a pattern made up of a lot of straight lines that cross each other; → **zigzag**

Inside the box was a crisscross of wires. —**crisscross**
adj: a crisscross pattern of streets

cri·te·ri·on W2 /kraɪ'tɪəriən $ -'tɪr-/ *n plural* **criteria**
/-riə/ [C usually plural] a standard that you use to judge
something or make a decision about something: *the
criteria we use to select candidates* | [+**for**] *the criteria
for measuring how good schools are* | *Academic ability is
not the sole problem for admission to the college.* | *a set
of criteria for identifying people who are genuinely ill
and unable to work* | **meet/satisfy/fulfil criteria** *To
qualify for a grant, students must satisfy certain criteria.*

crit·ic W3 /'krɪtɪk/ *n* [C]
1 someone whose job is to make judgments about the
good and bad qualities of art, music, films etc;
◼ **reviewer**: **music/art/film/theatre/literary critic** *a
review by the theatre critic of the Sunday Times*
2 someone who criticizes a person, organization, or
idea: [+**of**] *Critics of the scheme have said that it will not
solve the problem of teenage crime.* | **fierce/outspoken
critic** *He has always been an outspoken critic of the
government.*
3 armchair critic someone who criticizes other people
but who does not have any proper experience of the
activity the other people are doing

WORD CHOICE critic, review, criticism, critique
⚠ Do not use **critic** to refer to something that a critic
says or writes.
A **review** is the usual word for a short article that a critic
writes in a newspaper or magazine: *His first novel got
wonderful reviews.* | *Have you read the reviews of her
play?*
criticism is the activity of publishing opinions about
things such as books and films, or a group of essays,
lectures etc on this subject: *a collection of literary
criticism*
A **critique** is a detailed explanation of the problems of
something such as a set of political ideas, in the form of
a speech, book, article etc: *He wrote a critique of
capitalism.*

---

crit·i·cal S2 W2 /'krɪtɪkəl/ *adj*
1 CRITICIZING if you are critical, you criticize someone or something: [+**of**] *Many economists are critical of
the government's economic policies.* | *Many parents are
strongly critical of the school.* | *He made some highly
critical remarks.*
2 IMPORTANT something that is critical is very
important because what happens in the future depends
on it; ◼ **crucial**: [+**to**] *These talks are critical to the
future of the peace process.* | *It is absolutely critical for
us to know the truth.* | *Foreign trade is of critical
importance to the economy.*
3 SERIOUS/WORRYING a critical time or situation is
serious and worrying because things might suddenly
become much worse: *The fighting has stopped, but the
situation is still critical.* | *changes that took place
during the critical period at the end of the war*
4 ILL so ill that you might die: *He is still in a critical
condition in hospital.* | *She is in intensive care, where
she remains critical but stable.*
5 the critical list a) the list of patients in a hospital who
are so ill that they might die: **on the critical list** *Two of
the victims were still on the critical list Sunday night.* |
take sb off the critical list *He was taken off the critical
list and is now in a stable condition.* **b)** if a system, plan,
company etc is on the critical list, it is having severe
problems and might fail soon
6 MAKING JUDGMENTS making careful judgments
about how good or bad something is: *His book provides
a critical analysis of the television industry in Britain.* |
She looked round the room with a critical eye.
7 ART/LITERATURE according to critics who give
judgments about art, films, theatre, and books: *The
book came out last year to great critical acclaim*
(=critics said it was very good). | *Her first play was a
critical success* (=critics said it was good).

crit·i·cally /'krɪtɪkli/ *adv*
1 critically ill/injured so ill or so badly injured that you
might die; → **fatally**: *10 people died and 30 were criti-
cally injured in a rail crash yesterday.* | *She is still
critically ill in hospital.*
2 IMPORTANT in a way that is very important; ◼ **cru-
cially**: *The success of the project depends critically on
the continuation of this funding.* | *This is a critically
important meeting.*
3 SERIOUS/WORRYING in a way that is very serious
and worrying; ◼ **dangerously**: *Food supplies are at a
critically low level.*
4 CRITICIZING in a way that shows you are criticizing
someone or something: *Mike looked at her critically.* |
*He has spoken critically of the government's refusal to
support the industry.*
5 MAKING JUDGMENTS thinking about something
and giving a careful judgment about how good or bad it
is: *We teach students to think critically about the texts
they are reading.*
6 ART/LITERATURE according to critics who give
judgments about art, films, theatre, and books: *The
play was critically acclaimed* (=praised by critics)
when it opened in London last month.

critical 'mass *n* [C,U] **1** the amount of a substance
that is necessary for a NUCLEAR CHAIN REACTION to
start **2** the smallest number of people or things that
are needed in order for something to happen or be
possible: *How can we get a critical mass of people
involved to keep the club running?*

critical 'path *n* [C] a way of planning and organizing
a large piece of work so that there will be few delays
and the cost will be as low as possible: *Costs can be
calculated once the critical path has been established.*

crit·i·cis·m S2 W2 /'krɪtᵻsɪzəm/ *n* [C,U]
1 remarks that say what you think is bad about someone or something; ◼ **praise**

---

strong/severe/harsh criticism
widespread criticism (=when a lot of people criticize
something)
public criticism
constructive criticism (=criticism aimed at helping
someone improve)
direct/level criticism at sb (=criticize someone)
come in for/attract/draw criticism (=be criticized)
face criticism
accept/take criticism (=accept criticism and learn
from it)
provoke criticism (=make people criticize something)
a storm/barrage of criticism (=a lot of criticism)

[+**of**] *My main criticism of the scheme is that it does
nothing to help families on low incomes.* | *Despite
strong criticism, the new system is still in place.* |
There has been widespread criticism of the decision. |
We try to give students constructive criticism. |
*Another criticism levelled at him was that his teach-
ing methods were old-fashioned.* | *The government's
economic strategy has attracted a lot of criticism.* |
You must learn to accept criticism. | *Many employees
find it hard to take even mild criticism.* | *His actions
provoked severe criticism from civil rights groups.* |
the storm of criticism that followed his announcement

2 writing which expresses judgments about the good
or bad qualities of books, films, music etc: *literary
criticism*

crit·i·cize S3 W3 also **-ise** *BrE* /'krɪtᵻsaɪz/ *v*
1 [I,T] to express your disapproval of someone or
something, or to talk about their faults; ◼ **praise**: *Ron
does nothing but criticize and complain all the time.* | **be
strongly/sharply/heavily criticized** *The decision has
been strongly criticized by teachers.* | *The new law has
been widely criticized.* | **criticize sb/sth for (doing) sth**
He has been criticized for incompetence. | *Doctors have
criticized the government for failing to invest enough in*

---

1 000, 2 000, 3 000, most frequent words in S poken and W ritten English

the health service. | **criticize sb/sth as sth** *The report has been criticized as inaccurate and incomplete.*
2 [T] *formal* to express judgments about the good and bad qualities of something: *We look at each other's work and criticize it.*

WORD FOCUS: CRITICIZE

to criticize someone or something very strongly: **attack, lay into, tear sb/sth to shreds, pillory, pan**
to criticize someone unfairly: **put sb down, slag sb off** *BrE informal,* **talk about sb behind their back, bitch about** *informal*
to criticize small details: **pick holes**

---

cri·tique¹ /krɪˈtiːk/ *n* [C,U] a detailed explanation of the problems of something such as a set of political ideas; → **evaluation**: [+of] *a major new critique of his work* | *a critique of modern economic theory*

critique² *v* [T] *formal* to say how good or bad a book, play, painting, or set of ideas is; → **evaluate**: *He offered to critique our plans.*

crit·ter /ˈkrɪtə $ -ər/ *n* [C] *AmE spoken* a creature, especially an animal

croak¹ /krəʊk $ kroʊk/ *v* **1** [I] to make a deep low sound like the sound a FROG makes **2** [I,T] to speak in a low rough voice, as if you have a sore throat: *'Help!' she croaked, her throat dry with fear.* **3** [I] *informal* to die

croak² *n* [C] **1** the sound that a FROG makes **2** a low rough sound made in a person's or animal's throat: *The words came out as a dry croak.* —**croaky** *adj*

cro·chet /ˈkrəʊʃeɪ $ kroʊˈʃeɪ/ *v* [I,T] to make clothes etc from wool or cotton, using a special needle with a hook at one end; → **knit** —**crochet** *n* [U] —**crocheting** *n* [U]

crock /krɒk $ krɑːk/ *n* [C] **1** *old use* a clay pot **2 crocks** *BrE informal* old-fashioned cups, dishes, plates etc **3 a crock (of shit)** *AmE spoken* something that is unbelievable, unfair, untrue etc

crocked /krɒkt $ krɑːkt/ *adj* [not before noun] **1** *BrE* old-fashioned injured or broken **2** *AmE spoken* drunk: *Kitty got totally crocked last night.*

crock·e·ry /ˈkrɒkəri $ ˈkrɑː-/ *n* [U] *BrE* cups, dishes, plates etc; → **cutlery**: *a stack of dirty crockery*

croc·o·dile /ˈkrɒkədaɪl $ ˈkrɑː-/ *n* **1** [C] a large REPTILE with a long mouth and many sharp teeth that lives in lakes and rivers in hot wet parts of the world; → **alligator**; → see picture at REPTILE **2** [U] the skin of this animal, used for making things such as shoes: *a crocodile briefcase* **3** [C] *BrE* a long line of people, especially school children, walking in pairs **4 crocodile tears** if someone sheds crocodile tears, they seem sad, sorry, or upset, but they do not really feel this way: *They weep crocodile tears for the poor, but are basically happy with things as they are.*

cro·cus /ˈkrəʊkəs $ ˈkroʊ-/ *n* [C] a small purple, yellow, or white flower that appears in early spring

croft /krɒft $ krɒːft/ *n* [C] *BrE* a very small farm in Scotland

croft·er /ˈkrɒftə $ ˈkrɒːftər/ *n* [C] *BrE* someone who lives and works on a croft in Scotland

croft·ing /ˈkrɒftɪŋ $ ˈkrɒːf-/ *n* [U] the system of farming on crofts in Scotland

crois·sant /ˈkwɑːsɒŋ $ krɒːˈsɑːnt/ *n* [C] a piece of bread, shaped in a curve and usually eaten for breakfast → see picture at BREAD

crone /krəʊn $ kroʊn/ *n* [C] *not polite* an ugly or unpleasant old woman

cro·ny /ˈkrəʊni $ ˈkroʊni/ *n plural* **cronies** [C usually plural] one of a group of people who spend a lot of time with each other – used to show disapproval: **sb's cronies** *the senator's political cronies.*

cro·ny·i·sm /ˈkrəʊni-ɪzəm $ ˈkroʊ-/ *n* [U] the practice of unfairly giving the best jobs to your friends when you are in a position of power – used to show disapproval

crook¹ /krʊk/ *n* [C] **1** *informal* a dishonest person or a criminal: *The crooks got away across the park.* **2** a long stick with a curved end, used by people who look after sheep **3 the crook of your arm** the part of your arm where it bends

crook² *v* [T] if you crook your finger or your arm, you bend it

crook·ed /ˈkrʊkɪd/ *adj* **1** bent, twisted, or not in a straight line; **≠** **straight**: **crooked smile/grin** *His lips curled into a crooked smile.* | *Your tie's crooked.* | *narrow crooked streets* **2** dishonest: *a crooked cop* —**crookedly** *adv* —**crookedness** *n* [U]

croon /kruːn/ *v* [I,T] to sing or speak in a soft gentle voice, especially about love: *Sinatra crooning mellow tunes* | *'My child,' Sarah crooned.* —**crooner** *n* [C]

crop¹ W3 /krɒp $ krɑːp/ *n* [C]
1 a plant such as wheat, rice, or fruit that is grown by farmers and used as food; → GM: *The main crops were oats and barley.* | **crop production** | *crops grown for market* → CASH CROP
2 the amount of wheat, fruit, rice etc that is produced in a season; **≡** **harvest**: [+of] *this season's crop of quality pears* | *Fruit growers are gathering in a* **bumper crop** (=a very large amount of something produced in a season). | *increased* **crop yields**
3 crop of sb/sth a group of people that arrive or things that happen at the same time: [+of] *South Korea's present crop of elected politicians*
4 a short whip used in horse riding
5 the part under a bird's throat where food is stored
6 a very short HAIRSTYLE
7 crop of dark hair/blonde curls etc hair that is short, thick, and attractive: *his reddish crop of shining hair*

crop² *v* **cropped, cropping** **1** [T] to cut someone's hair short: *Stella had had her hair* **closely cropped.** **2** [T] to cut a part off a photograph or picture so that it is a particular size or shape **3** [T] if an animal crops grass or other plants, it makes them short by eating them **4** [I] *BrE* if a plant crops, it produces fruit, grain etc: *My strawberries crop in June or July.*

crop up *phr v* **1** if a problem crops up, it happens or appears suddenly and in an unexpected way; **≡** **arise** **2** if something such as a name or a subject crops up, it appears in something you read or hear; **≡** **come up**: *Your name kept cropping up in conversation.*

'crop ˌcircle *n* [C] a pattern that appeared in British farm fields, which some people believe were made by creatures from another world

'crop-ˌdusting *n* [U] *AmE* CROP-SPRAYING

crop·per /ˈkrɒpə $ ˈkrɑːpər/ **come a cropper** *BrE informal* **a)** to fail in something, especially unexpectedly: *Swedish investors have come a cropper in London.* **b)** to accidentally fall from a horse, bicycle etc: *She came a cropper on the ski slopes.*

'crop roˌtation *n* [U] the practice of changing the crops that you grow in a field each year to preserve the good qualities in the soil

'crop-ˌspraying *n* [U] *BrE* the practice of dropping chemicals from a plane onto crops in order to kill insects; **≡** **crop-dusting** *AmE*

'crop top *n* [C] a type of women's shirt that does not cover the stomach

cro·quet /ˈkrəʊkeɪ, -ki $ kroʊˈkeɪ/ *n* [U] a game played on grass in which players hit balls with wooden MALLETS (=long-handled hammers) so that they roll under curved wires

cro·quette /krəʊˈket $ kroʊ-/ *n* [C] a piece of crushed meat, fish, potato etc that is made into a small round piece, covered in BREADCRUMBS, and cooked in oil

cro·sier /ˈkrəʊʒə, -ʒə $ -ʒər/ *n* [C] a CROZIER

cross¹ S2 W2 /krɒs $ krɒːs/ *v*
1 GO FROM ONE SIDE TO ANOTHER [I,T] to go or stretch from one side of something such as a road, river, room etc to the other: [+to] *He crossed to the*

window. | **cross (over) the road/street/river etc** *It's easy to have an accident just crossing the road.* | *He was hit by a car when he tried to cross over the road near Euston station.* | **cross the Atlantic/the Channel etc** *the first steamship to cross the Atlantic* | *An old bridge crosses the river.* | [+**over**] *She crossed over to sit beside Dot.*

2 CROSS A LINE ETC [T] if you cross a line, track etc you go over and beyond it: *He raised his arms in triumph as he crossed the line for his 100-metres win.*

3 TWO ROADS/LINES ETC [I,T] if two or more roads, lines, etc cross, or if one crosses another, they go across each other: *The by-pass crosses Wilton Lane shortly after a roundabout.*

4 LEGS/ARMS/ANKLES [T] if you cross your legs, arms, or ANKLES, you put one on top of the other: *She was sitting on the floor with her legs crossed.*

5 cross sb's mind [usually in negatives] if you say that an idea, thought etc never crossed your mind, you mean that you did not think of it; ☰ **occur to sb**: *It didn't cross her mind that she might be doing something illegal.* | **the thought has (never) crossed my mind** (=used to tell someone you have thought of the thing they are suggesting, or have never thought of it)

6 cross sb's face *written* if an expression crosses someone's face, it appears on their face: *A look of surprise crossed her face.*

7 cross your fingers used to say that you hope something will happen in the way you want: *She hung the washing out, then crossed her fingers for a dry day.* | *The exam's at two. Will you keep your fingers crossed for me?*

8 BREED OF PLANT/ANIMAL [T] to mix two or more different breeds of animal or plant to form a new breed; → **crossbreed**: *a flower produced by crossing several different varieties* | **cross sth with sth** *These cattle were crossed with horned animals from the highlands.*

9 sb's paths cross also **cross paths** if two people's paths cross, or if they cross paths, they meet, usually without expecting it: *If our paths crossed I usually ignored her.* | *We didn't cross paths again until 2001.*

10 cross that bridge when you come to it used to say that you will not think or worry about something until it actually happens

11 cross my heart (and hope to die) *spoken informal* used to say that you promise that you will do something, or that what you are saying is true

12 MAKE SB ANGRY [T] to make someone angry by opposing their plans or orders: *He hated anyone who crossed him.*

13 SPORT [I,T] to kick, throw, or hit the ball across the playing area in a sport such as football, HOCKEY etc

14 CHEQUE [T] *BrE* to draw two lines across a cheque to show that it must be paid into the bank account of the person whose name is on it

15 LETTERS [I] if two letters about the same subject cross in the post, each was sent before the other was received

16 cross swords (with sb) to argue with someone: *I've crossed swords with him on a number of issues.*

17 cross yourself to move your hand across your upper body in the shape of a cross as a sign of the Christian faith

18 cross sb's palm with silver *especially BrE* to give money to someone when you want them to tell your FORTUNE → **dot the i's and cross the t's** at DOT² (4); → **cross the Rubicon** at RUBICON

cross sth ⇔ **off** also **cross sth off sth** *phr v* to draw a line through one or more things on a list because you have dealt with them or they are not needed any more: *Whenever I buy something, I cross it off the list.*

cross sth ⇔ **out** *phr v* to draw a line or lines through something you have written or drawn, usually because it is wrong: *I crossed out 'Miss' and wrote 'Ms'.*

cross over *phr v*
1 if an entertainer crosses over from one area of

entertainment to another, they become successful in the second one as well as the first → CROSSOVER (2)
2 *BrE old use* to die

cross² S3 W3 *n* [C]
1 MIXTURE OF THINGS a mixture of two things, breeds, or qualities: [+**between**] *The tour manager's role is a cross between hostess and courier.* | *Their dog is a cross between two well-known breeds.*
2 MARK ON PAPER *especially BrE* **a)** a mark (x or +) used on paper, to represent where something is, or where something should be: *I've put a cross on the map to mark where our street is.* | *Please sign your name by the cross.* **b)** a mark (x) on paper to show that something that has been written or printed is not correct: *My homework got a lot more ticks than crosses.* **c)** a mark (x or +) used by someone who cannot write, in order to sign their name
3 CHRISTIAN SIGN a) **the cross** the cross that Jesus Christ died on: *Christians believe that Jesus died on the cross for our sins.* **b)** an object, picture, or mark in the shape of a cross, used as a sign of the Christian faith or for decoration: *Pauline wore a tiny gold cross.*
4 PUNISHMENT an upright post of wood with another crossing it near the top, that people in the past were fastened to with nails and left to die on as a punishment
5 MILITARY AWARD a decoration in the shape of a cross that is given to someone as an honour, especially for military courage: *He was awarded the George Cross.*
6 SPORT a) a kick or hit of the ball in a sport such as football, HOCKEY etc, that goes across the field **b)** a way of hitting someone in the sport of BOXING, in which your arm goes over theirs as they try to hit you: *He caught his opponent with a right cross to the chin.*
7 PROBLEM if you describe something as the cross that someone has to bear, you mean it is a problem that makes them very unhappy or worried, and that continues for a long time: *I feel sorry for you, but we all have our crosses to bear.* → **the sign of the Cross** at SIGN¹ (10)

cross³ S2 *adj* [usually before noun] *especially BrE* angry or annoyed: **get/be cross (with sb)** *She gets cross when he goes out drinking.* | *Sometimes I get very cross with the children.* | [+**at/about**] *She was cross at being interrupted.* —**crossly** *adv*

cross- /krɒs $ krɒːs/ *prefix* **1** going from one side to the other: *a cross-Channel ferry* (=sailing from Britain to France) **2** going between two things and joining them: *cross-cultural influences*

cross·bar /ˈkrɒsbɑː $ ˈkrɒːsbɑːr/ *n* [C] **1** a bar that joins two upright posts, especially two GOALPOSTS **2** the metal bar between the seat and the HANDLEBARS on a man's bicycle → see picture at BICYCLE

cross·bones /ˈkrɒsbəʊnz $ ˈkrɒːsbəʊnz/ *n* [plural] → SKULL AND CROSSBONES

ˈcross-ˌborder *adj* [only before noun] relating to activity across a border between two countries: **cross-border trade/business etc** | **cross-border attack/raid**

cross·bow /ˈkrɒsbəʊ $ ˈkrɒːsbəʊ/ *n* [C] a weapon like a small BOW attached to a longer piece of wood, used for shooting ARROWS with a lot of force

cross·breed¹ /ˈkrɒsbriːd $ ˈkrɒːs-/ *v past tense and past participle* **crossbred** /-bred/ [I,T] if one breed of plant or animal crossbreeds with another, or if you crossbreed them, they breed, producing a new type of plant or animal —**crossbred** /-bred/ *adj*

crossbreed² *n* [C] an animal or plant that is a mixture of breeds; → **hybrid**

ˌcross-ˈcheck *v* [I,T] to make certain that something is correct by using a different method to check it again —**ˈcross-check** *n* [C]

ˌcross-ˈcountry¹ *adj* [only before noun] **1** across fields or not along main roads: *cross-country running* | *We took a cross-country route instead of the motor-*

way. **2** from one part of the country to the other: *cross-country flights* —**cross-country** *adv*: *We rode cross-country to the village.*

cross-country[2] *n plural* **cross-countries** [C,U] a race that involves running or SKIING across countryside and fields, not on a track, or the sport of doing this → see picture at OUTDOOR

,**cross-'cultural** *adj* [only before noun] belonging to or involving two or more different societies, countries, or CULTURES; → **multicultural**: *cross-cultural communication*

'**cross-,current** *n* [C] a current in the sea, a river etc that moves across the general direction of the main current

,**cross-'dressing** *n* [U] *BrE* the practice of wearing the clothes of the opposite sex, especially for sexual pleasure; → **transvestite** —**cross-dresser** *n* [C]

crossed /krɒst $ krɔːst/ *adj* if a telephone line is crossed, it is connected by mistake to two or more telephones, so that you can hear other people's conversations: *I phoned him up and got a crossed line.*

,**crossed 'cheque** *n* [C] a cheque in Britain that has two lines across it showing that it must be paid into a bank account

,**cross-ex'amine** *v* [T] to ask someone questions about something that they have just said, to see if they are telling the truth, especially in a court of law —,**cross-exami'nation** *n* [C,U]: *He broke down under cross-examination.*

,**cross-'eyed** / $ '. ./ *adj* having eyes that both look in towards the nose

,**cross-'fertilize** also **-ise** *BrE* *v* [T] **1** to combine the male sex cells from one type of plant with female sex cells from another **2** to influence someone or something with ideas from other areas: *In a university students live together, encourage, support and cross-fertilise each other.* —,**cross-fertili'zation** *n* [U]

cross·fire /'krɒsfaɪə $ 'krɔːsfaɪr/ *n* [U] **1** bullets from two or more opposite directions that pass through the same area: *Doctors who tried to help the wounded were caught in the crossfire.* | **in crossfire** *Many civilians were killed in crossfire.* **2** situation in which people are arguing, and the results of this affect other people who are not directly involved: *During a divorce, kids often get caught in the crossfire.*

,**cross-'grained** *adj* wood that is cross-grained has lines that go across it instead of along it

'**cross-,hatching** *n* [U] lines drawn across part of a picture, DIAGRAM etc to show that something is made of different material, or to produce the effect of shade

cross·ing /'krɒsɪŋ $ 'krɔː-/ *n* [C] **1** a place where you can safely cross a road, railway, river etc: *You must give way to any pedestrians on the crossing.* → LEVEL CROSSING, PEDESTRIAN CROSSING, PELICAN CROSSING, ZEBRA CROSSING **2** a place where two lines, roads, tracks etc cross: *Turn left at the first crossing.* **3** a journey across the sea, a lake, or a river: *The crossing was rough.*

cross-legged /,krɒs 'legd◄, -'legd◄ $ 'krɔːs ,legd, -,legd/ *adv* in a sitting position with your knees wide apart and one foot on top of the other: *We sat cross-legged on the floor.* —**cross-legged** *adj*

cross·o·ver /'krɒsəʊvə $ 'krɔːsoʊvər/ *n* **1** [C] the change a popular performer makes from working in one area of entertainment to another: *Madonna has made a crossover from rock music to the movies.* **2** [C,U] the fact of liking, using, or supporting different types of things or groups: *There is not much crossover between readers of modern and historical romances.* → CROSS OVER (1)

cross·piece /'krɒspiːs $ 'krɔːs-/ *n* [C] something that lies across another thing, especially in a building, on a railway track etc

,**cross-'purposes** *n* **at cross-purposes** if two people are at cross-purposes, they do not understand each other because they are talking about different things but fail to realize this: *I think we're talking at cross-purposes.*

,**cross-re'fer** *v* **cross-referred, cross-referring** [I,T] to tell a reader to look in another place in the book they are reading, so that they can get further information [+to/from] *The author cross-refers to his other books.*

,**cross-'reference** / $ '. ,.../ *n* [C,U] a note that tells the reader of a book to go to another place in the book to get further information: *The book has clear cross references and a good index.* —**cross-reference** *v* [T]

cross·roads /'krɒsrəʊdz $ 'krɔːsroʊdz/ *n plural* **crossroads** [C] **1** a place where two roads meet and cross each other; → **junction, T-junction**: **at the crossroads** *Turn left at the next crossroads.* | *The car was approaching the crossroads.* **2** a time when someone has to make very important decisions which will affect their future: **at a crossroads** *Now farming is at a crossroads in the European Community.* | *a career crossroads* **3** an important or central place: **at the crossroads** *The city was ideally situated at the crossroads to the great trade centres of Europe.*

'**cross-,section** *n* [C] **1** something that has been cut in half so that you can look at the inside, or a drawing of this: [+of] *a cross-section of a plant stem* | **in cross-section** *The roof beams were 50 centimetres square in cross-section.* **2** a group of people or things that is typical of a much larger group; → **sample**: [+of] *a wide cross-section of the taxpaying population*

,**cross-'selling** *n* [U] when one company helps to sell another company's products by, for example, advertising the second company's products at the same time as its own

'**cross-stitch** *n* [C,U] a stitch in a cross shape used in decorative sewing

'**cross street** *n* [C] a smaller street that crosses another street

cross·town also **cross-town** /'krɒstaʊn $ 'krɔːs-/ *adj* [only before noun] moving in a direction across a town or city: *a crosstown bus*

,**cross-'trainer** *n* [C usually plural] a type of shoe that can be worn for playing different types of sports

,**cross-'training** *n* [U] **1** an exercise programme that includes many different kinds of exercise, so that all of your muscles are used: *Cross-training helps you add variety to your workouts.* **2** when people in a company learn about each other's jobs, so that they understand each other better and work together better as a team: *Cross-training is a vital part of job rotation.* —**cross-train** *v* [I]

cross·walk /'krɒswɔːk $ 'krɔːswɒːk/ *n* [C] *AmE* a specially marked place for people to walk across a street; ▤ **pedestrian crossing** *BrE*

cross·wind /'krɒs,wɪnd $ 'krɔːs-/ *n* [C] a wind that blows across the direction that you are moving in

cross·wise /'krɒs,waɪz $ 'krɔːs-/ *adv* **1** from one corner of something to the opposite corner: *Halve the potatoes crosswise.* **2** two things that are placed crosswise are arranged to form the shape of an 'x'

cross·word /'krɒswɜːd $ 'krɔːswɜːrd/ also '**crossword ,puzzle** *n* [C] a word game in which you write the answers to questions in a pattern of numbered boxes: *I like to sit down and do the crossword.*

crotch /krɒtʃ $ krɑːtʃ/ also **crutch** *BrE* *n* [C] the part of your body between the tops of your legs, or the part of a piece of clothing that covers this; → **groin**

crotch·et /'krɒtʃɪt $ 'krɑː-/ *n* [C] *BrE* a musical note which continues for a quarter of the length of a SEMI-BREVE; ▤ **quarter note** *AmE*; → **minim, quaver**

crotch·et·y /'krɒtʃɪti $ 'krɑː-/ *adj* easily annoyed or made slightly angry; ▤ **grumpy**: *a crotchety old man*

crouch /kraʊtʃ/ *v* [I] **1** also **crouch down** to lower your body close to the ground by bending your knees completely; → **squat**: *He crouched in the shadows near the doorway.* | *Paula crouched down and held her hands out to the fire.* **2** to bend over something so that you are very near to it; → **lean**: [+**over**] *a young girl crouched over a book* —**crouch** *n* [C]: *She dropped to the ground in a crouch.*

croup /kruːp/ *n* [U] an illness in children which makes them cough and have difficulty breathing

crou·pi·er /ˈkruːpiə $ -ər/ *n* [C] someone whose job is to collect and pay out money where people play cards, ROULETTE etc for money at a CASINO

crou·ton /ˈkruːtɒn $ -taːn/ *n* [C usually plural] a small square piece of CRISP bread that is served with soup or on SALAD

crow¹ /krəʊ $ krəʊ/ *n*   **1** [C] a large shiny black bird with a loud cry   **2** [singular] the loud sound a COCK makes   **3 as the crow flies** in a straight line: *ten miles from here as the crow flies* → **eat crow** at EAT (7)

crow² *v* [I]   **1** if a COCK crows, it makes a loud high sound   **2** to talk about what you have done in a very proud way – used to show disapproval: [+**over/about**] *He was crowing over winning the bet.*   **3** *written* if someone, especially a baby, crows, they make a noise that shows they are happy: *Ben rushed to his father, crowing with pleasure.*

crow·bar /ˈkrəʊbɑː $ ˈkrəʊbɑːr/ *n* [C] a heavy iron bar used to lift something or force it open

crowd¹ [S2] [W2] /kraʊd/ *n*
1 [C] a large group of people who have gathered together to do something, for example to watch something or protest about something: [+**of**] *a crowd of angry protesters* | *a crowd of 30,000 spectators* | *There were crowds of shoppers in the street.* | *A vast **crowd gathered** in the main square.* | *She **mingled with the crowd** of guests, exchanging greetings.* | *Saturday's game was watched by a **capacity crowd** (=the maximum number of people that a sports ground etc can hold).* | *Troops fired tear gas and shots to **disperse a crowd** of 15,000 demonstrators.* → see picture at AUDIENCE
2 [singular] *informal* a group of people who know each other, work together etc: *I didn't know him; he wasn't one of the usual crowd.*
3 the crowd ordinary people, not unusual in any way: *You have to do things exceptionally well to **stand out from the crowd** (=be different from ordinary people).* | *He wanted to go unnoticed, to be **one of the crowd**.*

crowd² *v*   **1** [I always + adv/prep] if people crowd somewhere, they gather together in large numbers, filling a particular place: [+**into**] *Hundreds of people crowded into the church for the funeral.* | [+**round/ around**] *We all crowded round the table.* | **be crowded together** *the rapid spread of infection in areas where people are crowded together*   **2** [T] if people or things crowd a place, there are a lot of them there: *Holidaymakers crowded the beaches.* | *Range after range of mountains crowd the horizon.*   **3** [T] if thoughts or ideas crowd your mind or memory, they fill it, not allowing you to think of anything else: *Strange thoughts and worries were crowding his mind.*   **4** [T] **a)** to make someone angry by moving too close to them: *Stop crowding me – there's plenty of room.* **b)** *especially AmE* to make someone angry or upset by making too many unfair demands on them

crowd in *phr v* if problems or thoughts crowd in on you, you cannot stop thinking about them: [+**on**] *She shut her mind against the fears that were crowding in on her.*

crowd sb/sth ⇔ **out** *phr v* to force someone or something out of a place or situation: *Supermarket chains have crowded out the smaller shops.*

crowd·ed /ˈkraʊdɨd/ *adj* too full of people or things: *a crowded room* | *a crowded street* | *The train was very crowded, and we had to stand.* | [+**with**] *The narrow roads were crowded with holiday traffic.*

crowd ˌpleaser also **crowd-pleaser** *n* [C] an actor, politician, or sportswoman etc who always pleases an AUDIENCE (=people watching a performance)

crown¹ [S3] [W3] /kraʊn/ *n*
1 HAT FOR KING/QUEEN [C] **a)** a circle made of gold and decorated with jewels, worn by kings and queens

on their heads **b)** a circle, sometimes made of things such as leaves or flowers, worn by someone who has won a special honour
2 COUNTRY'S RULER the crown **a)** the position of being king or queen: *The treaty of Troyes made Henry V heir to the crown of France.* **b)** the government of a country such as Britain that is officially led by a king or queen: *He has retired from the service of the Crown.*
3 TOOTH [C] an artificial top for a damaged tooth
4 HEAD [usually singular] the top part of a hat or someone's head: [+**of**] *auburn hair piled high on the crown of her head* | *a hat with a high crown*
5 HILL [usually singular] the top of a hill or something shaped like a hill: [+**of**] *They drove to the crown of Zion hill and on into town.* | *The masonry at the crown of the arch is paler than on either curve.*
6 SPORTS [usually singular] the position you have if you have won an important sports competition: *Can she retain her Wimbledon crown?* | *He went on to win the world crown in 2001.*
7 MONEY [C] **a)** the standard unit of money in some European countries: *Swedish crowns* **b)** an old British coin. *Four crowns made a pound.*
8 PICTURE [C] a mark, sign, BADGE etc in the shape of a crown, used especially to show rank or quality

crown² *v* [T]   **1** to place a crown on the head of a new king or queen as part of an official ceremony in which they become king or queen; → **coronation**: *Louis was crowned at Reims in 814.* | **crown sb (as) king/queen etc** *In 1896 Nicholas was crowned as tsar.*   **2** to make something perfect or complete, by adding an achievement etc: **crown sb with sth** *a long career crowned with a peaceful retirement*   **3 be crowned with sth** *literary* having something on top: *Almost every hill is crowned with a little walled village.*   **4** to put a protective top on a damaged tooth   **5** *informal* to hit someone on the head

crown ˈcolony *n* [C] a COLONY controlled by the British government

Crown Court *n* [C,U] a court of law in Britain that deals with serious criminal cases and is higher than a Magistrates' Court

crowned ˈhead *n* [C usually plural] a king or queen: *All the crowned heads of Europe were present.*

crown·ing /ˈkraʊnɪŋ/ *adj* [always before noun] used to describe something that makes something complete or perfect, or is the best feature of something: *The hotel's crowning glory was a stunning roof garden.* | *his crowning achievement*

crown ˈjewel *n* [C]   **1 the crown jewels** the crown, sword, jewels etc worn by a king or queen for official ceremonies   **2** the best or most valuable thing that a person or place has: *Innsbruck's crown jewel is the old town centre.*

crown ˈprince *n* [C] the son of a king or queen, who is expected to become the next king

crown ˈprincess / $ ˌ. ˈ../ *n* [C] the daughter of a king or queen, who is expected to become the next queen

crow's feet *n* [plural] the very small lines that form in the skin near the eyes of older people

crow's nest *n* [C] a small box at the top of a ship's MAST from which someone can watch for danger, land etc

cro·zier, crosier /ˈkrəʊziə, -ʒə $ -ʒər/ *n* [C] a long stick with a decorative curved end, carried by a BISHOP

CRT /ˌsiː ɑː ˈtiː $ -ɑːr-/ *n* [C] the abbreviation of **cathode ray tube**

cru·cial [S3] [W2] /ˈkruːʃəl/ *adj* something that is crucial is extremely important, because everything else depends on it: [+**to**] *This aid money is crucial to the government's economic policies.* | **crucial in/to doing sth** *The work of monks was crucial in spreading*

Christianity. | **play a crucial role/part in sth** *The city of Mycenae played a crucial role in the history of Greece.* | *The conservation of tropical forests is of crucial importance.* —**crucially** adv

cru·ci·ble /'kru:sɪbəl/ n [C] a container in which substances are heated to very high temperatures

cru·ci·fix /'kru:sɪfɪks/ n [C] a cross with a figure of Christ on it

cru·ci·fix·ion /ˌkru:sɪ'fɪkʃən/ n **1** [C,U] in past times, the act of killing someone by fastening them to a cross and leaving them to die **2 the Crucifixion** the death of Christ on the cross **3** [C] also **Crucifixion** a picture or other object representing Christ on the cross

cru·ci·form /'kru:sɪfɔ:m $ -fɔ:rm/ adj formal shaped like a cross

cru·ci·fy /'kru:sɪfaɪ/ v **crucified, crucifying, crucifies** [T] **1** to kill someone by fastening them to a cross **2** to criticize someone severely and cruelly for something they have done, especially in public

crud /krʌd/ n [U] informal something unpleasant to look at, smell, taste etc: *I can't eat this crud!* —**cruddy** adj

crude[1] /kru:d/ adj **1** not exact or without any detail, but generally correct and useful; → **approximate**: *a crude estimate of the population available for work* **2** not developed to a high standard, or made with little skill: *a crude wooden bridge* | *crude workmanship* **3** offensive or rude, especially in a sexual way; ☐ **vulgar**: *crude pictures* | *His language was often crude.* **4** [only before noun] crude oil, rubber etc is in its natural or raw condition before it is treated with chemicals **5 in crude terms** expressed in a simple way: *Private morality, in crude terms, is not the law's business.* —**crudely** adv: *crudely built shacks* —**crudeness** n [U] —**crudity** n [C,U]

crude[2] also **crude 'oil** n [U] oil that is in its natural condition, as it comes out of an OIL WELL, before it is made more pure or separated into different products: *1000 barrels of crude*

cru·el S3 /'kru:əl/ adj
1 making someone suffer or feel unhappy: *His death was a cruel blow.* | *Sometimes life seems unbearably cruel.*
2 deliberately hurting people or animals; ☐ **kind**: *The prisoner was a hard, cruel man.* | *cruel jokes about mothers-in-law* | *It was a cruel, tactless thing to say.* | [+to] *She was often cruel to her sister.*
3 be cruel to be kind to do something to someone that will make them upset or unhappy in order to help them in another way —**cruelly** adv: *He was cruelly neglected by his parents.*

cru·el·ty /'kru:əlti/ n plural **cruelties 1** [C,U] behaviour or actions that deliberately cause pain to people or animals; ☐ **kindness**: *The children had suffered cruelty and neglect.* | *There was a hint of cruelty in Brian's smile.* | [+to] *cruelty to animals* | [+of] *the cruelty of the slave trade* | *The deliberate cruelty of his words cut her like a knife.* | *the cruelties of war* **2** [U] the unfairness of something that happens: *the cruelty of life*

cru·et /'kru:ɪt/ n [C] a thing that holds the containers for salt, pepper, oil, or VINEGAR on a table

cruise[1] /kru:z/ v **1** [I,T] to sail along slowly, especially for pleasure: *We were cruising in the Caribbean all winter.* | *an evening spent cruising the River Seine* **2** [I usually + adv/prep] to move at a steady speed in a car, aircraft etc: *We were cruising along at 50 miles per hour.* | *We fly at a cruising speed of 500 mph.* **3** [I,T] to drive a car slowly through a place with no particular purpose: *They cruised up and down the coast road.* **4** [I] informal to do something well or successfully, without too much effort: [+to] *The horse cruised to a three-length win.* **5** [I,T] informal to go to a bar or other public place, looking for a sexual partner: *We went cruising the singles bars.*

cruise[2] n [C] **1** a holiday on a large ship: *a Mediterranean cruise* | [+around] *a cruise around the world*; → see picture at TRIP **2** a journey by boat for pleasure

'cruise con·trol n [C] a piece of equipment in a car that makes it go at a steady speed

'cruise ,liner n [C] a large ship for cruising

,cruise 'missile n [C] a large explosive weapon that flies close to the ground and can be aimed at something hundreds of kilometres away

cruis·er /'kru:zə $ -ər/ n [C] **1** a large fast ship used by the navy: *a battle cruiser* **2** a boat used for pleasure **3** AmE a police car

cruis·er·weight /'kru:zəweɪt $ -zər-/ n [C] a BOXER who weighs less than 86.18 kilograms, and who is heavier than a LIGHT HEAVYWEIGHT but lighter than a HEAVYWEIGHT

'cruise ship n [C] a large ship with restaurants, bars etc that people have holidays on

cruis·ing /'kru:zɪŋ/ n [U] AmE **1** the activity of taking a holiday on a cruise ship **2** when young people drive cars slowly down a particular street as a way of being with their friends: *a sign saying 'No cruising'* **3** when someone looks for sexual partners in bars, restaurants, on the street etc

crumb /krʌm/ n [C] **1** a very small piece of dry food, especially bread or cake: *She stood up to brush the crumbs off her uniform.* | *Coat with bread crumbs and bake.* **2** a very small amount of something: **crumb of comfort/hope/affection etc** *There was only one crumb of comfort – Alex hadn't said anything to Jeff.*

crum·ble[1] /'krʌmbəl/ v **1** [I] also **crumble away** if something, especially something made of stone or rock, is crumbling, small pieces are breaking off it: *The old stonework was crumbling away.* | *crumbling colonial buildings* **2** [I,T] to break apart into lots of little pieces, or make something do this: *The fall leaves crumbled in my fingers.* | *¼ cup crumbled goat's cheese* **3** [I] also **crumble away** to lose power, become weak, or fail: *The Empire began to crumble during the 13th century.* | *our crumbling economy* → **that's the way the cookie crumbles** at COOKIE (3)

crumble[2] n [U] BrE a sweet dish of fruit covered with a dry mixture of flour, butter, and sugar and baked: *apple crumble*

crum·bly /'krʌmbli/ adj something that is crumbly breaks easily into small pieces: *a nice, crumbly cheese* | *the garden's crumbly black soil*

crumbs /krʌmz/ interjection BrE old-fashioned used to express surprise

crum·my /'krʌmi/ adj informal of bad quality or unpleasant: *We were staying in this really crummy hotel.* | *a crummy job*

crum·pet /'krʌmpɪt/ n BrE **1** [C] a small round bread with holes in one side, eaten hot with butter **2** [U] informal not polite an offensive word for someone who is sexually attractive

crum·ple /'krʌmpəl/ v **1** [I,T] also **crumple up** to crush something so that it becomes smaller and bent, or to be crushed in this way: *Dan tore the page out, crumpled it, and threw it in the wastepaper basket.* → see picture at FOLD **2** [I] if your face crumples, you suddenly look sad or disappointed, as if you might cry **3** [I] if your body crumples, you fall down in an uncontrolled way: [+to] *The blow hit him in the head and he crumpled to the ground.*

crum·pled /'krʌmpəld/ adj **1** also **crumpled up** crushed into a smaller bent shape: *Tom flattened the crumpled paper against his knee.* **2** cloth or clothing that is crumpled has a lot of lines or folds in it: *an old man with untidy hair and a crumpled suit* **3** someone who is crumpled somewhere is lying still in a strange position after they have fallen

crunch[1] /krʌntʃ/ n **1** [singular] a noise like the sound of something being crushed: *The only sound was the crunch of tyres on gravel.* **2** [C, singular] AmE a difficult situation caused by a lack of something, especially money or time: *Three new teachers were hired to help ease the crunch.* | **cash/budget/financial etc crunch** *Cost cutting had enabled the organization to survive a previous cash crunch.* **3 the crunch** also **crunch time** *AmE* an important time, especially one when a difficult decision has to be made: *The crunch came when my bank asked for my credit card back.* | *When it came to the crunch, she couldn't agree to marry him.* **4** [C] an exercise in which you lie on your back and lift your head and shoulders off the ground to make your stomach muscles strong; ▤ **sit-up**

crunch² *v* **1** [I] to make a sound like something being crushed: *Their boots crunched loudly on the frozen snow.* **2** [I always + adv/prep, T] to eat hard food in a way that makes a noise: [+**on**] *The dog was crunching on a bone.* **3 crunch (the) numbers** to do a lot of calculations in order to reach an answer: *The computer will crunch all the numbers to determine the final score.*

crunch·y /ˈkrʌntʃi/ *adj* food that is crunchy is firm and makes a noise when you bite it – usually used to show approval: *a delicious crunchy salad* —**crunchiness** *n* [U]

cru·sade¹ /kruːˈseɪd/ *n* [C] **1** a determined attempt to change something because you think you are morally right; → **campaign**: [+**against/for**] *He seems to be running a one-man crusade against cigarette smoking.* **2** also **Crusade** one of a series of wars fought in the 11th, 12th, and 13th centuries by Christian armies trying to take Palestine from the Muslims

crusade² *v* [I] to take part in a crusade: [+**against/for**] *He continued to crusade for free education for all.* —**crusader** *n* [C]

crush¹ /krʌʃ/ *v* [T] **1** to press something so hard that it breaks or is damaged: *His leg was crushed in the accident.* | *Two people were crushed to death in the rush to escape.* → see picture at SQUEEZE **2** to press something in order to break it into very small pieces or into a powder: *Crush two cloves of garlic.* **3 crush a rebellion/uprising/revolt etc** to use severe methods to stop people from fighting you or opposing you; ▤ **put down**: *The revolution was crushed within days.* **4 crush sb's hopes/enthusiasm/confidence etc** to make someone lose all hope, confidence etc **5** to make someone feel extremely upset or shocked: *Sara was crushed by their insults.*

crush on sb *phr v AmE informal* to have a feeling of romantic love for someone, especially someone you do not know well: *a guy in my class that I'm crushing on*

crush² *n* **1** [singular] a crowd of people pressed so close together that it is difficult for them to move: *There's always such a crush on the train in the mornings.* **2** [C] a strong feeling of romantic love for someone, especially one that a young person has for someone older who they do not know well; → **infatuation**: *She had a huge crush on her geography teacher.* | *It's just a schoolgirl crush.* **3** [C] *AmE informal* someone who you have a feeling of romantic love for, but who you do not know well: *a first date with your crush*

crush·ing /ˈkrʌʃɪŋ/ *adj* [usually before noun] **1** very hard to deal with, and making you lose hope and confidence: *The Eighth Army had suffered a crushing defeat.* | *Failing his final exams was a crushing blow* (=made him lose hope and confidence). | *the crushing burden of debt* **2** a crushing remark, reply etc contains a very strong criticism —**crushingly** *adv*: '*That's fairly obvious,*' *she replied crushingly.*

crust /krʌst/ *n* [C,U] **1** the hard brown outer surface of bread: *sandwiches with the crusts cut off* **2** the baked outer part of foods such as PIES or PIZZAS: *a thin crust pizza* **3** a thin hard dry layer on the surface of something: *A hard gray crust had formed on the bottom of the tea kettle.* **4** the hard outer layer of the Earth: *deep within the Earth's crust* → see picture at GLOBE → **earn a crust** at EARN (1); → UPPER CRUST

crus·ta·cean /krʌˈsteɪʃən/ *n* [C] *technical* an animal such as a LOBSTER or a CRAB that has a hard outer shell and several pairs of legs, and usually lives in water —**crustacean** *adj*

crust·ed /ˈkrʌstᵻd/ *adj* having a thin hard dry layer on the surface: [+**with**] *old boots crusted with mud*

crust·y /ˈkrʌsti/ *adj* **1** bread that is crusty is pleasant to eat because it has a hard CRUST: *a crusty baguette* **2** *informal* someone who is crusty is bad-tempered; ▤ **grumpy**: *a crusty old man* **3** having a thin dry hard layer of something on the surface: *The lake was ringed by crusty salt deposits.*

crutch /krʌtʃ/ *n* [C] **1** [usually plural] one of a pair of long sticks that you put under your arms to help you walk when you have hurt your leg: (=use crutches) *I was on crutches for three months after the operation.* **2** something that gives someone support or help, especially something that is not really good for them: *As things got worse at work, he began to use alcohol as a crutch.* **3** *BrE* the part of your body between the tops of your legs; ▤ **crotch**

crux /krʌks/ *n* **the crux** the most important part of a problem, question, argument etc: [+**of**] *The crux of the matter is how do we prevent a flood occurring again?* | *The crux of the problem lay in the lack of equipment.*

cry¹ [S2] [W2] /kraɪ/ *v past tense and past participle* **cried**, *present participle* **crying**, *third person singular* **cries**
1 PRODUCE TEARS [I] to produce tears from your eyes, usually because you are unhappy or hurt: *Don't cry, Laura. It'll be OK.* | *Upstairs, a baby began to cry.* | *Jamie looked like he'd been crying.* | *I just couldn't stop crying.* | *That film always makes me cry.* | [+**over/about**] *I am too old to be crying over some young guy.* | [+**with/in**] *She felt like crying with frustration.* | [+**for**] *She could hear him crying for his mother.* | **cry your eyes/heart out** (=be extremely sad and cry a lot) | *Oliver, alone, began to cry bitterly* (=cry a lot). | **cry yourself to sleep** (=cry until you fall asleep)
2 SAY LOUDLY [T] *written* to shout or say something loudly; ▤ **cry out**: '*Stop!*' *she cried.* | *It was painful, and made me cry aloud.* | [+**to**] '*Goodbye then!*' *he cried to her.* | [+**for**] *I could hear voices crying for help.*
3 cry over spilt milk to waste time feeling sorry about an earlier mistake or problem that cannot be changed: *It's no use crying over spilt milk.*
4 for crying out loud *spoken* used when you feel annoyed or impatient with someone: *For crying out loud, stop nagging!*
5 cry foul to protest because you think something is wrong or not fair: *When the ads appeared, it was the Democrats' turn to cry foul.*
6 ANIMALS/BIRDS [I] if animals or birds cry, they make a loud sound: *I could hear gulls crying and the soft whisper of the sea.*
7 cry wolf to ask for help when you do not need it, so that people do not believe you when you really need help
8 cry into your beer *informal* to feel too much pity for yourself, especially because you think you have been treated unfairly → **not know whether to laugh or cry** at LAUGH¹ (3); → **cry for the moon** at MOON¹ (4); → **a shoulder to cry on** at SHOULDER¹ (5)

be in tears to be crying | **burst into tears** to suddenly start crying | **break down (in tears)** to suddenly cry a lot, after trying not to cry | **sob** to cry noisily, with sudden noisy breaths | **weep** *especially written* to cry a lot for a long time | **bawl** if a baby bawls, it cries very loudly | **have tears in your eyes** to be about to cry | **your eyes water** you start to cry, especially because you have been cutting up onions or there is a lot of smoke

cry off *phr v BrE*
to say that you cannot do something that you have already promised to do; → **cancel**: *Leah and I were*

C

going to go to Morocco together, but at the last moment she cried off.

cry out *phr v*

1 to make a loud sound of fear, shock, pain etc: [+in/with] *Even the smallest movement made him cry out in pain.* | *John tightened his grip until she cried out.*

2 to shout or say something loudly: *'Why are you doing this?' she cried out suddenly.* | [+for] *I felt too terrified to even cry out for help.*

3 be crying out for sth *informal* to need something urgently: *The kitchen is crying out for a coat of paint.* | *My parents had divorced and I was crying out for love.*

cry² W3 *n plural* **cries**

1 SOUND EXPRESSING EMOTION [C] a loud sound expressing a strong emotion such as pain, fear, or pleasure: *a baby's cry* | **cry of pain/alarm/delight etc** *Alice leapt to one side with a cry of alarm.* | **let out/give a cry** *The stone hit him on the forehead and he gave a sharp cry.*

2 SHOUT [C] a shouted word or phrase: [+of] *At last, there was a cry of 'Silence!', and everyone looked towards the door.* | [+for] *Fortunately, a passerby heard his cries for help.*

3 TEARS [singular] *especially BrE* a period of time during which tears come out of your eyes, usually because you are unhappy: *It's good to **have a cry** sometimes.* | *I felt much better after I'd had **a good cry*** (=cried for a long time).

4 cry for help something someone says or does that shows that they are very unhappy and need help: *I think taking the pills was a cry for help.*

5 PHRASE [C] a phrase that is used to unite people in support of a particular action or idea; ▪ **slogan**: *'Land and Liberty' was the **rallying cry** of revolutionary Mexico.* → BATTLE CRY (1), WAR CRY

6 ANIMAL/BIRD [C] a sound made by a particular animal: *the cries of seagulls overhead* → **be a far cry from sth** at FAR² (5); → **in full cry** at FULL¹ (22); → HUE AND CRY

cry·ba·by /ˈkraɪˌbeɪbi/ *n plural* **crybabies** [C] someone, especially a child, who cries too often without good reason – used to show disapproval: *Don't be such a crybaby!*

cry·ing¹ /ˈkraɪ-ɪŋ/ *adj* **1** it's a crying shame *spoken* used to say that something is very sad or upsetting: *It would be a crying shame if the village shop closed down.* **2** crying need for sth a serious need for something: *There is a crying need for a place where our young people can meet.*

crying² *n* [U] when someone produces tears from their eyes, usually because they are unhappy or hurt: *As he neared her tent he heard the sound of crying.*

cry·o·gen·ics /ˌkraɪəˈdʒenɪks/ *n* [U] the scientific study of very low temperatures —**cryogenic** *adj*

crypt /krɪpt/ *n* [C] a room under a church, used in the past for burying people; → **vault**

cryp·tic /ˈkrɪptɪk/ *adj* having a meaning that is mysterious or not easily understood: **cryptic remark/comment/statement etc** *a cryptic note at the end of the letter* —**cryptically** /-kli/ *adv*

crypto- /krɪptəʊ, -tə $ -toʊ, -tə/ *prefix formal* secret or hidden: *a crypto-Communist*

cryp·tog·ra·phy /krɪpˈtɒɡrəfi $ -ˈtɑː-/ *n* [U] the study of secret writing and CODES —**cryptographer** *n* [C]

crys·tal /ˈkrɪstl/ *n* **1** [U] very high quality clear glass: *a set of six crystal glasses* **2** [C] a small regular-shaped piece of a substance, formed naturally when this substance becomes solid: *ice crystals* | *copper sulphate crystals* **3** [C,U] rock that is clear, or a piece of this **4** [C] *AmE* the clear cover on a clock or watch

crystal 'ball *n* [C] a glass ball that you can look into, which some people believe can show what is going to happen in the future

crystal 'clear *adj* **1** very clearly stated and easy to understand: *I want to make one thing crystal clear – I do*

not agree with these proposals. **2** completely clean and clear: *the crystal clear water of the lake*

crys·tal·line /ˈkrɪstəlaɪn, -liːn $ -lən/ *adj* **1** made of crystals **2** very clear or transparent, like crystal

crys·tal·lize also **-ise** *BrE* /ˈkrɪstəlaɪz/ *v* **1** [I,T] if a liquid crystallizes, it forms CRYSTALS: *The liquid will crystallize at 50 degrees centigrade.* **2** [I,T] if an idea, plan etc crystallizes or is crystallized, it becomes very clear in your mind: *Inside her a thought was crystallizing.* —**crystallization** /ˌkrɪstəlaɪˈzeɪʃən $ -lə-/ *n* [U]

crys·tal·lized also **crystallised** *BrE* /ˈkrɪstəlaɪzd/ *adj* crystallized fruit, GINGER, or flowers are made by a special process which covers them with sugar

CSE /ˌsiː es ˈiː/ *n* [C,U] **Certificate of Secondary Education** an examination in a range of subjects that was done by students in schools in England and Wales before 1988, usually at the age of 15 or 16; → GCSE

C-section /ˈsiː ˌsekʃən/ *n* [C] *AmE informal* a CAESAREAN

CS gas /ˌsiː es ˈɡæs/ *n* [U] *BrE* TEAR GAS

ct *BrE*, **ct.** *AmE* the written abbreviation of **carat**: *a 24ct gold necklace*

CT scan /ˌsiː ˈtiː skæn, ˈkæt skæn/ *n* [C] another name for a CAT SCAN

cu *BrE*, **cu.** *AmE* the written abbreviation of **cubic**: *40 cu feet*

cub /kʌb/ *n* [C] **1** the baby of a wild animal such as a lion or a bear: *a five-month old lion cub* | *a tiger and her cubs* **2** the Cubs the CUB SCOUT organization **3** a member of the CUB SCOUTS organization → CUB REPORTER

cub·by·hole /ˈkʌbihəʊl $ -hoʊl/ *n* [C] a very small space or room, used especially for storing things

cube¹ /kjuːb/ *n* [C] **1** a solid object with six equal square sides: *a sugar cube* | *an ice cube* | *Cut the meat into small cubes.* **2** the cube of sth the number you get when you multiply a number by itself twice, for example 4 x 4 x 4 = 64, so the cube of 4 is 64 **3** *AmE spoken* a CUBICLE

cube² *v* [T] **1** to multiply a number by itself twice: *4 cubed is 64* **2** to cut food into cubes

cube 'root /ˈ $ ˈ . ./ *n* [C] the cube root of a particular number is the number that, when multiplied by itself twice will give that number: *4 is the cube root of 64*

cu·bic /ˈkjuːbɪk/ *adj* relating to a measurement of space which is calculated by multiplying the length of something by its width and height; → **square**: **cubic centimetre/metre/inch etc** *75,000 million cubic metres of gas* | *the cubic capacity of an engine*

cu·bi·cle /ˈkjuːbɪkəl/ *n* [C] a small part of a room that is separated from the rest of the room: *a shower cubicle* | *office workers in their cubicles* → see picture at SPORTS CENTRE

cub·is·m /ˈkjuːbɪzəm/ *n* [U] a 20th century style of art, in which objects and people are represented by GEOMETRIC shapes —**cubist** *adj*: *cubist paintings* —**cubist** *n* [C]

cu·bit /ˈkjuːbɪt/ *n* [C] an ancient unit for measuring length, equal to the length of your arm between your wrist and your elbow

cub re'porter *n* [C] a young newspaper or television REPORTER without much experience

'Cub ˌScout *n* [C] **1** the Cub Scouts the part of the SCOUT organization for younger children **2** a young child who is a member of this organization; → Girl Scout, boy scout

cuck·old¹ /ˈkʌkəld, ˈkʌkəʊld $ -kəld/ *n* [C] *old use* an insulting word for a man whose wife has been having sex with another man

cuckold² *v* [T] *old use* if a wife or her LOVER cuckold her husband, they have sex with each other

cuck·oo¹ /ˈkʊkuː $ ˈkuːkuː, ˈkʊ-/ *n* [C] a grey European bird that puts its eggs in other birds' NESTS and that makes a sound that sounds like its name

cuckoo² *adj* [not before noun] *informal* crazy or silly: *You're completely cuckoo!*

cuckoo clock *n* [C] a clock with a wooden bird inside that comes out every hour and makes a sound

cu·cum·ber /ˈkjuːkʌmbə $ -ər/ *n* [C,U] a long thin round vegetable with a dark green skin and a light green inside, usually eaten raw → **cool as a cucumber** at COOL¹ (3); → see picture at VEGETABLE

cud /kʌd/ *n* [U] food that a cow or similar animal has chewed, swallowed, and brought back into its mouth to chew a second time: *a cow chewing its cud*

cud·dle¹ /ˈkʌdl/ *v* [I,T] to hold someone or something very close to you with your arms around them, especially to show that you love them; → **hug**: *Dawn and her boyfriend were cuddling on the sofa.*
   cuddle up *phr v* to lie or sit very close to someone or something: [+to/together] *The children cuddled up to each other for warmth.*

cuddle² *n* [singular] an act of cuddling someone; → **hug**: *Come over here and let me give you a cuddle.*

cud·dly /ˈkʌdli/ *adj* **1** a person or animal that is cuddly makes you want to cuddle them: *He is the most affectionate and cuddly dog I have ever known.* **2** [only before noun] cuddly toys are soft toys designed for children to cuddle

cud·gel /ˈkʌdʒəl/ *n* **1** [C] a short thick stick used as a weapon **2 take up the cudgels (on behalf of sb/sth)** *formal* to start to fight for an idea that you believe in

cue¹ /kjuː/ *n* [C] **1** an action or event that is a signal for something else to happen: [+for] *Our success was the cue for other companies to press ahead with new investment.* | *sb's cue to do sth I think that's my cue to explain why I'm here.* **2** a word, phrase, or action in a play that is a signal for the next person to speak or act: *She stood nervously in the wings waiting for her cue.* | **miss your cue** (=not speak or act when you are supposed to) **3 (right/as if) on cue** happening or done at exactly the right moment: *And then, on cue, the weather changed.* | *As if on cue, Sam arrived.* **4 take your cue from sb** to use someone else's actions or behaviour to show you what you should do or how you should behave: *With interest rates, the smaller banks will take their cue from the Federal Bank.* **5** a long straight wooden stick used for hitting the ball in games such as BILLIARDS and POOL → see picture at POOL

cue² *v* [T] to give someone a sign that it is the right moment for them to speak or do something, especially during a performance: *The studio manager will cue you when it's your turn to come on.*
   cue sth ⇔ **up** *phr v* to make a CASSETTE, VIDEO, or CD be exactly in the position you want it to be in, so that you can play something immediately when you are ready: *The videotape's cued up and ready to go!*

cue ball *n* [C] the ball which a player hits with the cue in a game such as BILLIARDS → see picture at POOL

cuff¹ /kʌf/ *n* [C] **1** the end of a sleeve **2** *AmE* a narrow piece of cloth turned upwards at the bottom of a trouser leg; ◨ **turn-up** *BrE* **3** an action in which you hit someone lightly on the head with your hand open **4 cuffs** [plural] HANDCUFFS → OFF-THE-CUFF

cuff² *v* [T] **1** to hit someone lightly, especially in a friendly way: *She cuffed him playfully on the side of the head.* **2** to put HANDCUFFS on someone

cuff link *n* [C] a small piece of jewellery that a man can use to fasten his shirt cuffs

cui·sine /kwɪˈziːn/ *n* [U] **1** a particular style of cooking: *French cuisine | vegetarian cuisine* | [+of] *the traditional cuisine of the Southwest* **2** the food cooked in a particular restaurant or hotel, especially when it is very good: *Enjoy the delicious cuisine created by our award-winning chef.* → HAUTE CUISINE

cul-de-sac /ˈkʌl də ˌsæk, ˈkʊl- $ ˌkʌl də ˈsæk, ˌkʊl-/ *n* [C] **1** a road which is closed at one end, so that there is only one way in and out **2** an unhelpful situation in which you cannot make any more progress: *These ideas lead us into a philosophical cul-de-sac.*

cu·li·na·ry /ˈkʌlɪnəri $ ˈkʌlɪneri, ˈkjuːl-/ *adj* [only before noun] *formal* relating to cooking: *culinary skills |*

mushrooms dried for culinary use | *the region's **culinary delights** (=food that tastes very good)*

cull¹ /kʌl/ *v* **1** [I,T] to kill some animals of a group, usually the weakest ones, especially so that the size of the group does not increase too much **2** [T] *formal* to find or choose information from many different places: **cull sth from sth** *The data had been culled from a variety of sources.*

cull² *n* [C] the act of killing the weakest animals in a group, especially so that the size of the group does not increase too much

cul·len·der /ˈkʌləndə $ -ər/ another spelling of COLANDER

cul·mi·nate /ˈkʌlmɪneɪt/
   culminate in/with sth *phr v* if a process culminates in or with a particular event, it ends with that event: *A series of events for teachers and students will culminate in a Shakespeare festival next year.*

cul·mi·na·tion /ˌkʌlmɪˈneɪʃən/ *n* [U] **the culmination of sth** something, especially something important, that happens at the end of a long period of effort or development: *This little book represented the culmination of 15 years' work.*

cu·lottes /kjuːˈlɒts $ kjʊˈlɑːts/ *n* [plural] women's trousers which stop at the knee and are shaped to look like a skirt

cul·pa·ble /ˈkʌlpəbəl/ *adj* **1** *formal* deserving blame: *Both parties were held to be to some extent culpable.* **2** *law* a culpable action is one that is considered criminal: **culpable homicide/negligence etc** *He pleaded guilty to culpable homicide.* —**culpably** *adv* —**culpability** /ˌkʌlpəˈbɪləti/ *n* [U]

cul·prit /ˈkʌlprət/ *n* [C] **1** the person who is guilty of a crime or doing something wrong; → **victim**: *Police finally managed to catch the culprit.* **2** *informal* the reason for a particular problem or difficulty: *High production costs are **the main culprit**.*

cult¹ /kʌlt/ *n* **1** [C] an extreme religious group that is not part of an established religion: *Anyone who betrayed the cult could be punished by death.* **2** [C] a fashionable belief, idea, or attitude that influences people's lives: [+of] *Diet, exercise ... It's all part of this cult of self-improvement.* **3** [singular] a group of people who are very interested in a particular thing: *O'Brien has a cult of devoted readers.* **4** [C,U] *formal* a system of religious beliefs and practices → PERSONALITY CULT

cult² *adj* [only before noun] **cult film/band/figure etc** a film, music group etc that has become very popular but only among a particular group of people: *the 1980s cult movie 'The Gods Must Be Crazy'* | *The actor James Dean acquired the status of a cult hero.*

cul·ti·va·ble /ˈkʌltɪvəbəl/ *adj* land which is cultivable can be used to grow crops

cul·ti·vate /ˈkʌltɪveɪt/ *v* [T] **1** to prepare and use land for growing crops and plants: *The land was too rocky to cultivate.* **2** *formal* to plant and take care of a particular crop; ◨ **grow**: *We cultivated maize and watermelons.* **3** to work hard to develop a particular skill, attitude, or quality: *Try to cultivate a more relaxed and positive approach to life.* | *The company has been successful in cultivating a very professional image.* **4** to make an effort to develop a friendly relationship with someone, especially someone who can help you: *Professor Gladwyn would be an acquaintance worth cultivating.*

cul·ti·vat·ed /ˈkʌltɪveɪtɪd/ *adj* **1** someone who is cultivated is intelligent and knows a lot about music, art, literature etc: *a **highly cultivated** man* **2** cultivated land is land that is used for growing crops or plants: *cultivated fields* **3** [only before noun] cultivated crops or plants are ones grown by people; ◨ **wild**: *cultivated mushrooms*

cul·ti·va·tion /ˌkʌltɪ̥'veɪʃən/ *n* [U] **1** the preparation and use of land for growing crops: *different methods of soil cultivation* | **under cultivation** *These fields have been under cultivation* (=used for growing crops) *for years.* **2** the planting and growing of plants and crops: *Terraces for rice cultivation covered the hillsides.* | **[+of]** *the successful cultivation of tobacco* **3** the deliberate development of a particular quality or skill

cul·ti·va·tor /'kʌltɪ̥veɪtə $ -ər/ *n* [C] **1** *formal* someone who grows crops or plants, especially a farmer **2** a tool or machine that is used to prepare land for growing crops

cul·tu·ral W2 /'kʌltʃərəl/ *adj* [usually before noun] **1** belonging or relating to a particular society and its way of life: *the very real historical and **cultural differences** between our two societies* | *the desire to maintain a distinct **cultural identity*** | *It is important to look at the political and **cultural context** in which the novel was written.* | *people who share the same **cultural background*** | **cultural heritage/traditions etc** (=ideas, customs etc that have existed in a particular society for a long time) *Japan's unique cultural heritage* → MULTICULTURAL
 2 relating to art, literature, music etc: *the city's rich and varied **cultural life*** | *Students need to have time for relaxation and **cultural activities**, as well as for academic work.* | *In the later Middle Ages, Prague was an important **cultural centre** (=a place, usually a big city, where a lot of artistic and musical events happen).*

cul·tu·ral·ly /'kʌltʃərəli/ *adv* **1** in a way that is related to the ideas, beliefs, or customs of a society: *Teaching materials need to be culturally appropriate.* | [sentence adverb]: *Historically and culturally, Britain has always been linked to the continent.* **2** in a way that is related to art, music, literature etc: *The French are a culturally sophisticated people.* | [sentence adverb]: *Culturally, the city has a lot to offer.*

cul·ture¹ S2 W1 /'kʌltʃə $ -ər/ *n*
 1 IN A SOCIETY [C,U] the beliefs, way of life, art, and customs that are shared and accepted by people in a particular society: *We speak Danish at home so that the boys don't lose touch with their language and culture.* | *In our culture, it is rude to ask someone how much they earn.* | *I love working abroad and meeting people from different cultures.* | **Western/American/Japanese etc culture** *A brief history of Western culture.* | **modern/contemporary culture** *Business is one of the major forces in modern culture.*
 2 IN A GROUP [C,U] the attitudes and beliefs about something that are shared by a particular group of people or in a particular organization: *Every government department has its own particular culture.* | **corporate/business/company culture** *Changing the corporate culture is a long and difficult process.* | **[+of]** *In the field of drug development, the culture of secrecy is deep and strong.* | *modern American **youth culture*** | *the **drug culture** that is destroying so many young lives today* | *the German political culture* → SUBCULTURE
 3 ART/MUSIC/LITERATURE [U] activities that are related to art, music, literature etc: *If it's culture you're looking for, the city has plenty of museums and art galleries.* | *the Italian Ministry of Culture* | **popular culture** (=the music, books, films etc that are liked by a lot of people)
 4 SOCIETY [C] a society that existed at a particular time in history: *This technique was then adapted and refined by the more sophisticated cultures of the ancient world.* | *primitive cultures*
 5 MEDICINE/SCIENCE [C,U] *technical* BACTERIA or cells grown for medical or scientific use, or the process of growing them: *It takes two to three weeks to grow the culture from which the presence of handicap can be detected.* | *The laboratories have extensive **tissue culture** facilities.*

6 CROPS [U] *technical* the practice of growing crops: *clearing forest for rice culture*

culture² *v* [T] *technical* to grow BACTERIA or cells for medical or scientific use

cul·tured /'kʌltʃəd $ -ərd/ *adj* intelligent, polite, and interested in art, literature, music etc: *a well-read and cultured woman* | *His voice was cultured and unmistakably English.*

ˌcultured 'pearl *n* [C] a PEARL that has been grown artificially

'culture ˌshock *n* [singular, U] the feeling of being confused or anxious that you get when you visit a foreign country or a place that is very different from the one you are used to: *India is where I first experienced real culture shock.* | *Moving to London was a bit of a culture shock after ten years of living in the country.*

cul·vert /'kʌlvət $ -ərt/ *n* [C] a pipe that takes a stream under a road, railway line etc

cum /kʊm, kʌm/ *prep* used between two nouns to show that something has two purposes: *a kitchen-cum-dining room* | *a lunch-cum-business meeting*

cum·ber·some /'kʌmbəsəm $ -bər-/ *adj* **1** a process or system that is cumbersome is slow and difficult: *Doctors are complaining that the system is cumbersome and bureaucratic.* | *cumbersome procedures* **2** heavy and difficult to move: *a large cumbersome machine* **3** words or phrases that are cumbersome are long or complicated

cum·in /'kʌmɪ̥n, 'kjuː- $ 'kʌmɪ̥n, 'kuː-, 'kjuː-/ *n* [U] the seeds of a plant that have a sweet smell and are used especially in Mexican and Indian cooking, or the plant that they grow on

cum lau·de /kʊm 'laʊdeɪ, kʌm 'lɔːdi $ kʊm 'laʊdi/ *adv AmE* **with honours** if you GRADUATE cum laude, you finish a university degree and are given official praise for special achievement → MAGNA CUM LAUDE, SUMMA CUM LAUDE

cum·mer·bund /'kʌməbʌnd $ -ər-/ *n* [C] a wide piece of cloth that a man wears around his waist as part of a special suit worn on very formal occasions

cu·mu·la·tive /'kjuːmjᵿlətɪv $ -leɪtɪv/ *adj* increasing gradually as more of something is added or happens: *Learning is a cumulative process.* | **cumulative effect (of sth)** *Depression is often caused by the cumulative effects of stress and overwork.*

cu·mu·lus /'kjuːmjᵿləs/ *n* [C,U] a thick white cloud with a flat bottom edge

cu·nei·form /'kjuːnɪfɔːm, 'kjuːnɪ-ᵿfɔːm $ kjuː'niːəfɔːrm/ *adj* relating to the writing used by the people of ancient Mesopotamia —**cuneiform** *n* [U]

cun·ni·lin·gus /ˌkʌnɪ'lɪŋɡəs/ *n* [U] *technical* the act of touching the female sex organs with the lips and tongue in order to give sexual pleasure; → fellatio

cun·ning¹ /'kʌnɪŋ/ *adj* **1** someone who is cunning is clever and good at deceiving people in order to get what they want; ▪ **crafty**: *a cunning opponent* **2** behaviour or actions that are cunning are clever but dishonest and unfair, and are used to get what you want: *a cunning plan* **3** a cunning object or piece of equipment is clever and unusual: *a cunning little device for keeping out draughts* **4** *AmE old-fashioned* attractive: *a cunning little dress* —**cunningly** *adv*

cunning² *n* [U] the ability to achieve what you want by deceiving people in a clever way: *the tiger's ferocity and cunning* | *She would use **low cunning** (=unpleasant dishonest methods) to win people's sympathy.*

cunt /kʌnt/ *n* [C] *taboo informal* **1** a stupid or unpleasant person **2** a woman's VAGINA (=sex organ)

eggcup

coffee cup

cup and saucer

mug

C

cup¹ S1 W1 /kʌp/ n

1 FOR DRINKING [C] a small round container, usually with a handle, that you use to drink tea, coffee etc ; → **saucer**: *Mathew picked up the cup and sipped his coffee.* | *She put her cup and saucer down on the table.* | **tea/coffee cup** *Helen took the coffee cups into the kitchen.* | **paper/plastic/china etc cup** *They drank cheap wine from plastic cups.*

2 DRINK [C] the liquid contained inside a cup: [+of] *Let's go and have a cup of coffee.* | *Will you stay for a cup of tea?* | *Would you like another cup?*

3 AMOUNT OF LIQUID/FOOD [C] **a)** a unit used in the US for measuring food or liquid in cooking, equal to eight FLUID OUNCES or 237 MILLILITRES: *Mix the butter with 1 cup of powdered sugar until light and fluffy.* **b)** **cupful** /'kʌpful/ the amount of liquid or food that a cup can hold: *Breakfast consisted of half a cup of milk and a dry biscuit.*

4 SPORT COMPETITION a) [C] a specially shaped silver container, often with two handles, that is given as a prize in a competition, especially a sports competition: *The president of the club came to present the cup to the winners.* **b)** [singular] a sports competition in which a cup is given as a prize: *They've won the European Cup twice.* | *Germany's World Cup team*

5 ROUND THING [C] something round and hollow that is shaped like a cup: *The flowers' white petals contrast handsomely with their lemon-yellow cups.* | *acorn cups* | [+of] *She held it in the cup of her hand.*

6 GOLF [C] AmE a hole in the ground that you have to try to hit the ball into in the game of golf

7 CLOTHING [C] **a)** the part of a BRA that covers a woman's breast **b)** AmE a JOCKSTRAP

8 ALCOHOL [C,U] BrE a mixed alcoholic drink: *He's gone to get me some fruit cup.* | *a glass of champagne cup*

9 not be your cup of tea *spoken* to not be the type of thing that you like: *Jazz just isn't my cup of tea – I prefer classical music.*

10 in your cups BrE old-fashioned drunk, or when drunk: *By the time Anthony arrived, Richard was already deep in his cups.* → EGGCUP

cup² v **cupped, cupping** [T] **1** to hold something in your hands, so that your hands form part of a circle around it: *He cupped her face in his hands and kissed her.* | *Luke was sitting at his desk, one hand cupping his chin.* **2 cup your hand(s)** to make a shape like a cup with your hand or hands: *He struck a match and cupped his hand around the flame.*

cup·board S2 /'kʌbəd $ -ərd/ n [C] a piece of furniture with doors, and sometimes shelves, used for storing clothes, plates, food etc; → **closet, wardrobe:** *It's in the kitchen cupboard.* | *The cupboard doors were open.* → AIRING CUPBOARD; → **skeleton in the cupboard** at SKELETON (5); → see picture at EAT

cup·cake /'kʌpkeɪk/ n [C] a small round cake

'cup ,final n [C] the last and most important game in a competition, especially a football competition

cup·ful /'kʌpful/ n [C] the amount that a cup can hold

cu·pid /'kju:pɪd/ n **1** [singular] the Roman god of sexual love, represented as a beautiful boy with wings who is carrying a BOW and ARROW **2** [C] an image of this god, used to represent love **3 play cupid** to try to arrange for two people to fall in love with each other: *She vowed never to play cupid again.*

cu·pid·i·ty /kju'pɪdɪti/ n [U] formal very strong desire for something, especially money or property; ▤ **greed:** *the cupidity of some businessmen*

cu·po·la /'kju:pələ/ n [C] a round structure on the top of a building, that is shaped like an upside down bowl: *a golden edifice with an onion-shaped cupola*

cup·pa /'kʌpə/ n [C] BrE spoken a cup of tea: *I'm dying for a cuppa!*

'cup tie n [C] a game between two teams in a competition in which only the winning team will play any more games: *Saturday's FA Cup tie against Spurs*

cur /kɜ: $ kɜ:r/ n [C] old-fashioned an unfriendly dog, especially one that is a mix of several breeds

cur·a·ble /'kjʊərəbəl $ 'kjʊr-/ adj an illness that is curable can be cured; ▤ **incurable**

cu·ra·çao /ˌkjʊərəsəʊ $ 'kjʊrəsoʊ/ n [U] a strong thick alcoholic drink that tastes of oranges

cu·ra·cy /'kjʊərəsi $ 'kjʊr-/ n plural **curacies** [C] the job or position of a curate, or the period of time that someone has this position

cu·rate /'kjʊərɪt $ 'kjʊr-/ n [C] **1** a priest of the lowest rank, whose job is to help the priest who is in charge of an area **2 curate's egg** BrE something that has good and bad parts: *The book is something of a curate's egg.*

cu·ra·tive /'kjʊərətɪv $ 'kjʊr-/ adj able to, or intended to cure illness; → **heal:** *the spring's alleged curative properties* —**curative** n [C]: *This herb was once thought to be a curative.*

cu·ra·tor /kjʊ'reɪtə $ -ər/ n [C] someone who is in charge of a MUSEUM or ZOO: *He's Curator of Prints at the Metropolitan.*

curb¹ /kɜ:b $ kɜ:rb/ v [T] to control or limit something in order to prevent it from having a harmful effect: *measures to curb the spread of the virus*

curb² n [C] **1** an influence which helps to control or limit something: [+on] *We are trying to keep a curb on their activities.* **2** AmE the raised edge of a road, between where people can walk and cars can drive; ▤ **kerb** BrE; → **pavement, sidewalk**

curd /kɜ:d $ kɜ:rd/ n [U] also **curds** [plural] the thick substance that forms in milk when it becomes sour; → **whey** → BEAN CURD

cur·dle /'kɜ:dl $ 'kɜ:rdl/ v [I,T] **1** to become thicker or form curd, or to make a liquid do this: *Milk may curdle in warm weather.* **2 make your blood curdle** to make you very frightened → BLOODCURDLING

cure¹ /kjʊə $ kjʊr/ n [C] **1** a medicine or medical treatment that makes an illness go away: [+for] *There is still no cure for AIDS.* **2** something that solves a problem, or improves a bad situation; → **solution:** [+for] *There is no easy cure for loneliness.* **3** the act of making someone well again after an illness: *The new treatment effected a miraculous cure.*

cure² v [T] **1** to make an illness or medical condition go away: *Many types of cancer can now be cured.* | *an operation that can cure short-sightedness in 15 minutes* **2** to make someone well again after they have been ill; → **heal:** *She had some acupuncture treatment which seems to have cured her.* | **cure sb of sth** *90% of patients can be cured of the disease.* **3** to solve a problem, or improve a bad situation: *Attempts to cure unemployment have so far failed.* **4 cure sb of sth** to make someone stop behaving in a particular way or stop them having a particular feeling or attitude:

Nothing could cure her of her impatience with Anna. **5** to preserve food, tobacco etc by drying it, hanging it in smoke, or covering it with salt: *cured ham*

'cure-all *n* [C] something that people think will cure any problem or illness: [+for] *Investment is not a cure-all for every economic problem.*

cur·few /'kɜːfjuː $ 'kɜːr-/ *n* [C,U] **1** a law that forces people to stay indoors after a particular time at night, or the time people must be indoors: *The government **imposed** a night-time **curfew** throughout the country.* | *The **curfew was lifted** (=ended) on May 6th.* | *The whole town was **placed under curfew.*** | *Anyone found in the streets after curfew was shot.* **2** *AmE* the time, decided by a parent, by which a child must be home or asleep in the evening

cu·ri·o /'kjʊəriəʊ $ 'kjʊrioʊ/ *n plural* **curios** [C] a small object that is interesting because it is beautiful or rare

cu·ri·os·i·ty /ˌkjʊəri'ɒsɪti $ ˌkjʊri'ɑːs-/ *n plural* **curiosities**
1 [singular, U] the desire to know about something

satisfy sb's curiosity
arouse sb's curiosity (=make people want to know about something)
out of curiosity (=because of curiosity)
with curiosity
natural curiosity
intellectual/scientific curiosity
idle curiosity (=wanting to know about something for no particular reason)
be burning with curiosity (=want to know about something very much)

*I opened the packet just to **satisfy my curiosity.*** | *The news **aroused** a lot of **curiosity** among local people.* | *She decided to follow him **out of curiosity.*** | *Margaret looked at him **with curiosity.*** | [+about] *Children have a **natural curiosity** about the world around them.* | *a man of immense **intellectual curiosity*** | *It was **idle curiosity** that made me ask.*

2 [C] someone or something that is interesting because they are unusual or strange: *a house full of old maps and other curiosities* | *In the past, men who wanted to work with children were regarded as something of a curiosity.* | *It's not worth much, but I kept it for its curiosity value.*
3 curiosity killed the cat used to tell someone not to ask too many questions about something

cu·ri·ous S3 /'kjʊəriəs $ 'kjʊr-/ *adj*
1 wanting to know about something; → **inquisitive**: *Puppies are naturally curious.* | [+about] *He was curious about how she would react.* | **curious to know/see/hear etc** *Mandy was curious to know what happened.* | **curious look/glance** *Her shouting attracted some curious glances from other people in the restaurant.*
2 strange or unusual: *He felt a curious mixture of excitement and panic.* | *a curious coincidence* | *It's curious that she left without saying goodbye.* —**curiously** *adv*: *'What have you got in there?' Felix asked curiously.* | *She felt curiously calm.*

curl¹ /kɜːl $ kɜːrl/ *v* [I,T] **1** to form a twisted or curved shape, or to make something do this: *Mary was busy curling her hair.* | [+around/round] *Ivy curled round the tree.* **2** [always + adv/prep] to move, forming a twisted or curved shape, or to make something do this: [+across/along etc] *Morning mists curled across the river.* | **curl sth around/round/over etc sth** *He curled his arm around Claudia's waist.* **3** if you curl your lip, or if your lip curls, you move it upwards and sideways, to show that you disapprove of someone or something: *Her lip curled in contempt.* → **make sb's toes curl** at **TOE¹** (5); → **make your hair curl** at **HAIR** (9)
curl up *phr v* **1** to move so that you are lying or sitting with your arms and legs bent close to your body: *I just wanted to curl up and go to sleep.* | *Sarah was curled up on the sofa.* **2** if something flat curls up,

its edges start to become curved and point upwards: *The letter was now yellow and beginning to curl up.*

curl² *n* **1** [C] a piece of hair that hangs in a curved shape: *a little boy with beautiful blonde curls* **2** [singular, U] the ability of your hair to form curls: *Use a diffuser to maximise the volume and curl of your hair.* | *hair that has a natural curl* **3** [C] something in the shape of a curve: *Decorate the cake with chocolate curls.* | [+of] *A curl of smoke rose from her cigarette.* **4** [C] an exercise in which you repeatedly bend your arms, legs, or stomach in order to make your muscles strong **5 curl of sb's lip/mouth** a sideways and upwards movement of your lip or mouth, showing that you disapprove of someone or something

curl·er /'kɜːlə $ 'kɜːrlər/ *n* [C] a small plastic or metal tube used for making hair curl; ⊟ **roller**: *Her hair was in curlers.*

cur·lew /'kɜːljuː $ 'kɜːrluː/ *n* [C] a bird with long legs and a long beak that lives near water

curl·ing /'kɜːlɪŋ $ 'kɜːr-/ *n* [U] a sport played on ice, in which players slide flat heavy stones towards a marked place

'curling ˌtongs *BrE n* [plural] **'curling ˌiron** *AmE n* a piece of electrical equipment that you heat and use to put curls in your hair

curl·y S3 /'kɜːli $ 'kɜːrli/ *adj*
1 having a lot of curls; ⊟ **straight**: *long dark curly hair* **2** *BrE* curved in shape: *cows with curly horns* —**curliness** *n* [U]

cur·mud·geon /kɜː'mʌdʒən $ kɜːr-/ *n* [C] *old-fashioned* someone who is often annoyed or angry, especially an old person

cur·rant /'kʌrənt $ 'kɜːr-/ *n* [C] **1** a small dried GRAPE used especially in baking cakes; → **raisin, sultana** **2** a small round red or black BERRY → **BLACKCURRANT, REDCURRANT**

cur·ren·cy W2 /'kʌrənsi $ 'kɜːr-/ *n plural* **currencies**
1 [C,U] the system or type of money that a country uses: *The bank can supply you with **foreign currency.*** | *There are moves towards a **single currency** in Europe.* | *The **local currency** is the Swiss franc.* → **HARD CURRENCY**
2 [U] the state of being accepted or used by a lot of people: *The argument has received **wide currency.*** | *Marxism began to **gain currency.*** | *The idea was **common currency** in European political life.*

cur·rent¹ S1 W1 /'kʌrənt $ 'kɜːr-/ *adj* [only before noun] happening or existing now: *the current President* | *In its current state, the house would be worth £200,000.*

current² *n* [C] **1** a continuous movement of water in a river, lake, or sea; → **tide**: **ocean/sea/tidal etc current** | *Strong currents can be very dangerous for swimmers.* **2** a continuous movement of air: *Some birds use warm **air currents** to help them fly.* | [+of] *currents of warm air rising from the plain* **3** a flow of electricity through a wire: *an electrical current* → **ALTERNATING CURRENT, DIRECT CURRENT** **4** an idea, feeling, or opinion that a particular group of people has: *The committee reflects the different political currents within the organization.* | [+of] *There was an underlying current of discontent among teachers.* ⚠ Do not confuse with **currant** (=small dried fruit).

'current acˌcount *n* [C] *BrE* a bank account that you can take money out of at any time; ⊟ **checking account** *AmE*

ˌcurrent afˈfairs *n* [U] important political events or other events in society that are happening now

cur·rent·ly S2 W2 /'kʌrəntli $ 'kɜːr-/ *adv* at the present time: *The brochure shows the products that are currently available.* | *He is currently working on his first novel.*

cur·ric·u·lar /kə'rɪkjʊlə $ -ər/ *adj* [only before noun] relating to the curriculum of a school: *curricular changes*

cur·ric·u·lum W2 /kə'rɪkjʊləm/ *n plural* **curricula** /-lə/, *or* **curriculums** [C] the subjects that are taught by a school, college etc, or the things that are studied in a particular subject: *Languages are an essential part of the school curriculum.* | *curriculum planning* | **on the curriculum** *BrE: IT is now on the curriculum in most schools.* | **in the curriculum** *AmE: Students are exempt from some classes in the curriculum for religious reasons.*; → **syllabus**

curriculum vi·tae /kəˌrɪkjᵿləm ˈviːtaɪ/ *n* [C] **1** a formal British expression for **CV**; ☐ **resume** *AmE* **2** *AmE* a short written description of a university teacher's previous jobs and work, that they send when looking for a new teaching job

cur·ried /ˈkʌrid $ ˈkɜːr-/ *adj* [only before noun] cooked with hot spices: *curried lamb*

cur·ry¹ /ˈkʌri $ ˈkɜːri/ *n plural* **curries** [C,U] a type of food from India, consisting of meat or vegetables in a spicy sauce: *chicken curry*

curry² *v past tense and past participle* **curried**, *present participle* **currying**, *third person singular* **curries** **curry favour (with sb)** to try to make someone like you or notice you in order to get something that you want – used to show disapproval: *a businessman who made several attempts to curry favour with politicians*

curry ˌpowder *n* [U] a mixture of spices, used in cooking to give food a spicy taste

curse¹ /kɜːs $ kɜːrs/ *v* **1** [I] to swear: *Gilbert was cursing under his breath.* **2** [T] to say or think bad things about someone or something because they have made you angry: *He cursed his bad luck in arriving just after she'd left.* | **curse sb/sth for (doing) sth** *Elsa cursed herself for believing his lies.* **3** [T] to ask God or a magical power to harm someone

curse sb ⇔ out *phr v AmE informal* to swear at someone who has made you angry

curse² *n* [C] **1** a swear word or words that you say because you are very angry: *He muttered a curse under his breath.* **2** a word or sentence used to ask God or a magical power to do something bad to someone or something: *He believed that someone had* **put a curse on** *the house.* **3** something that causes trouble, harm etc: [+of] *Noise is one of the curses of modern-day life.* **4 the curse** *old-fashioned a* MENSTRUAL PERIOD

curs·ed /ˈkɜːsᵻd $ ˈkɜːr-/ *adj* **1 be cursed with/by sth** to be affected by something bad: *The museum has been cursed by financial problems since it opened.* **2** *literary* suffering as a result of a punishment by God or a god

cur·sive /ˈkɜːsɪv $ ˈkɜːr-/ *adj* written in a style of writing with the letters joined together: *cursive script* —**cursively** *adv*

cur·sor /ˈkɜːsə $ ˈkɜːrsər/ *n* [C] a mark that can be moved around a computer screen to show where you are working

cur·so·ry /ˈkɜːsəri $ ˈkɜːr-/ *adj* done very quickly without much attention to details: **cursory glance/look** *Even a cursory glance at the figures will tell you that sales are down this year.* | **cursory examination/inspection** *a cursory examination of the evidence* —**cursorily** *adv*

curt /kɜːt $ kɜːrt/ *adj* using very few words in a way that seems rude: *With a curt nod, he turned away and sat down.* | *a curt note* —**curtly** *adv* —**curtness** *n* [U]

cur·tail /kɜːˈteɪl $ kɜːr-/ *v* [T] *formal* to reduce or limit something: *The new law will curtail police powers.* | **severely/drastically curtail** *Budget cuts have drastically curtailed training programs.* —**curtailment** *n* [C,U]

cur·tain¹ S2 W3 /ˈkɜːtn $ ˈkɜːrtn/ *n* [C] **1** a piece of hanging cloth that can be pulled across to cover a window, divide a room etc: *red velvet curtains* | **draw/close/pull the curtains** *Ella drew the curtains and switched the light on.* | **draw back/open the curtains** *Shall I open the curtains?* **2** a sheet of heavy material that comes down at the front of the stage in a theatre: **the curtain goes up/rises** *Before the curtain went up, the dancers took their places on stage.* | **the curtain comes down/falls** **3** *written* a thick layer of something that stops anything

behind it from being seen: [+of] *a curtain of smoke* **4 bring down the curtain on sth** *informal* to cause or mark the end of a situation or period of time: *The decision brought down the curtain on a 30-year career.* **5 (it'll) be curtains for sb/sth** *informal* used to say that someone will die or that something will end

curtain² *v*

curtain sth ⇔ off *phr v* to separate one area, room etc from another by hanging a curtain between them: *The room was curtained off by red drapes.*

ˈcurtain call *n* [C] the time at the end of a performance when the actors come to the front of the stage to receive APPLAUSE

cur·tained /ˈkɜːtnd $ ˈkɜːr-/ *adj* [only before noun] a curtained window or door has a curtain hanging across it

ˈcurtain hook *n* [C] a small hook that is joined to the top of a curtain so that you can hang it up

ˈcurtain rail *n* [C] a long piece of plastic or metal that you hang a curtain on

ˈcurtain ˌraiser *n* [C] an event such as a performance or sports event that happens before a more important one: *A local team are playing as a curtain raiser to the game between England and Italy.*

curt·sy, curtsey /ˈkɜːtsi $ ˈkɜːr-/ *v past tense and past participle* **curtsied**, *present participle* **curtsying**, *third person singular* **curtsies** [I] if a woman curtsies, she bends her knees with one foot in front of the other as a sign of respect for an important person; → **bow** —**curtsy** *n* [C]

cur·va·ceous /kɜːˈveɪʃəs $ kɜːr-/ *adj* having an attractively curved body shape – used about women: *a tall, curvaceous young woman*

cur·va·ture /ˈkɜːvətʃə $ ˈkɜːrvətʃər/ *n* [C,U] *technical* the state of being curved, or the degree to which something is curved: [+of] *the curvature of the Earth's surface* | *He suffered from curvature of the spine.*

curve¹ S3 W3 /kɜːv $ kɜːrv/ *n* [C]
1 a line that gradually bends like part of a circle: [+of] *the curve of her hips* | *a sweeping curve of railroad track*
2 a line on a GRAPH that gradually bends and represents a change in the amount or level of something: *The curve illustrates costs per capita.* | **demand/supply curve** *The market demand curve has increased.*
3 a bend in a road, river etc: *The car took the curve much too quickly.*
4 also **curve ball** in baseball, a ball that spins and moves in a curve when it is thrown, so that it is difficult to hit
5 throw sb a curve *AmE* to surprise someone with a question or problem that is difficult to deal with → LEARNING CURVE

curve² *v* [I,T] to bend or move in the shape of a curve, or to make something do this: *The track curved round the side of the hill.* | *A smile curved her lips.*

curved /kɜːvd $ kɜːrvd/ *adj* having a shape that is like a curve and not straight: *a curved wall*

curv·y /ˈkɜːvi $ ˈkɜːrvi/ *adj* **1** having a shape with several curves: *a curvy line* **2** a woman who is curvy is attractive because her body has a lot of curves

cush·ion S3 /ˈkʊʃən/ *n* [C]
1 a cloth bag filled with soft material that you put on a chair or the floor to make it more comfortable; → **pillow**: *a velvet cushion* | *a cushion cover*
2 something that stops one thing from hitting another thing: *Good sports shoes should provide a cushion when running.*
3 [usually singular] something, especially money, that prevents you from being immediately affected by a bad situation: [+against] *Savings can act as a cushion against unemployment.*

C

4 the soft rubber edge of the table used for playing BILLIARDS or SNOOKER → see picture at POOL

cushion² v [T] **1** to make the effect of a fall or hit less painful, for example by having something soft in the way: *His landing was cushioned by the fresh snow that had fallen.* **2** to protect someone from an unpleasant situation or the unpleasant effects of something: **cushion the blow/impact (of sth)** *generous leaving allowances to help cushion the blow of redundancy* | **cushion sb from/against sth** *Parents today often feel their children should be cushioned from the outside world.*

cush·ion·ing /ˈkʊʃənɪŋ/ n [U] something soft that protects someone or something when they hit a surface: *A special pad in the heel offers good cushioning as you walk.*

cush·y /ˈkʊʃi/ adj a cushy job or life is very easy and does not need much effort: *I wish I had a nice cushy job like her.* | *a very cushy number* (=an easy job or life)

cusp /kʌsp/ n **1** [C] technical the point formed where two curves join **2 be on the cusp of sth** [singular] to be at the time when a situation or state is going to change: *The country was on the cusp of economic expansion.* **3 on the cusp** someone who was born on the cusp was born near the time when one STAR SIGN ends and another begins

cuss /kʌs/ v [I,T] BrE old-fashioned, AmE spoken to swear because you are annoyed by something
cuss sb ⇔ **out** phr v AmE spoken to swear and shout at someone because you are angry: *She got mad and started cussing him out.*

'cuss word n [C] old-fashioned a rude word that you use because you are angry

cus·tard /ˈkʌstəd $ -ərd/ n **1** [U] a sweet yellow sauce that is made with milk, sugar, eggs, and flour **2** [C,U] a soft baked mixture with milk, sugar, and eggs

,custard 'pie n [C] a PIE filled with a substance that looks like custard, which people throw at each other as a joke in films, on television etc

cus·to·di·al /kʌˈstəʊdiəl $ -ˈstoʊ-/ adj relating to the custody of someone, especially a child: *custodial care*

cus,todial 'sentence n [C] BrE a period of time that someone has to spend in prison as a punishment

cus·to·di·an /kʌˈstəʊdiən $ -ˈstoʊ-/ n [C] **1** someone who is responsible for looking after something important or valuable: [+of] *Farmers are custodians of the land for the next generation.* **2** especially AmE someone who looks after a public building: *a custodian at the stadium* **3 custodian of tradition/moral values etc** someone who tries to protect a traditional set of beliefs, attitudes etc

cus·to·dy /ˈkʌstədi/ n [U] **1** the right to take care of a child, given to one of their parents when they have DIVORCED: [+of] *He got custody of his son after the divorce.* | *It is usually the mother who is **awarded custody** (=legally allowed to have custody).* | *a dispute over who should **have custody of** the children* | *The couple will retain **joint custody** (=they will both have custody) of their daughters.* | *Allen is fighting a bitter **custody battle** over his three children.* **2** when someone is kept in prison until they go to court, because the police think they have committed a crime: *The committee is looking at alternatives to custody.* | **in custody** *Police are investigating the death of a man in custody.* | **hold/keep sb in custody** *A man is being held in police custody in connection with the murder.* | **remand sb in custody** BrE (=send someone to prison to wait until they go to court) *A man has been remanded in custody charged with the murder of a schoolgirl.* | *She was **taken into custody** as a suspect.* **3** formal when someone is responsible for keeping and looking after something: *Managers are responsible for the safe custody and retention of records.* | *The collection of art books is now **in the custody of** the university.*

cus·tom¹ W3 /ˈkʌstəm/ n

1 [C,U] something that is done by people in a particular society because it is traditional : **local/ancient/French etc custom** *The guide offers information on local customs.* | **it is the custom (for sb) to do sth** *It's the custom for the bride's father to pay for the wedding.* | **the custom of doing sth** *The custom of naming women after flowers is becoming less common.*

2 [singular] formal something that you usually do every day, or in a particular situation: *He awoke early, as was his custom.*

3 customs [plural] **a)** the place where your bags are checked for illegal goods when you go into a country; → immigration: *She was stopped at customs and questioned.* | *It took ages to **clear customs** (=be allowed through customs) but then we were out of the airport quite quickly.* | *You won't be able to take that **through customs.*** **b)** the government department that checks goods coming into a country and collects any taxes on them: *customs officers* | *the US customs service*

4 [U] formal the practice of regularly using a particular shop or business: *an advertisement to attract more custom* | *Smaller shops lose a lot of custom when supermarkets open nearby.*

custom² adj [only before noun] especially AmE custom products or services are specially designed and made for a particular person: *His son operates a custom furniture business.*

custom- /ˈkʌstəm/ prefix **custom-made/custom-built/custom-designed etc** made, built etc for a particular person: *He always wore custom-made suits.* | *custom-ordered vehicles*

cus·tom·a·ry /ˈkʌstəməri $ -meri/ adj **1** something that is customary is normal because it is the way something is usually done; ▣ usual: **it is customary (for sb) to do sth** *In some cultures it is customary for the bride to wear white.* **2** [only before noun] someone's customary behaviour is the way they usually do things; ▣ usual: *Barbara answered with her customary enthusiasm.* —**customarily** /ˈkʌstəmər.li $ ˌkʌstəˈmer.li/ adv

cus·tom·er S1 W1 /ˈkʌstəmə $ -ər/ n [C]

1 someone who buys goods or services from a shop, company etc: *We aim to offer good value and service to all our customers.* | *We've had several letters from satisfied customers.* | **customer service/care** *Many of the banks offer a poor level of customer service.* | *He's one of our **regular customers**.* | **best/biggest/largest customer** (=the person or company who uses a shop or company the most)

2 awkward/tricky/tough etc customer someone who is difficult to deal with because they behave in a deliberately unhelpful way → **cool customer** at COOL¹ (3)

> **WORD CHOICE: customer, client, patron, shopper, consumer**
>
> **Customer** is the most general word. A **customer** is someone who buys something from a particular shop. People who pay to use something such as a transport service can also be called **customers**: *A customer came in and bought several jackets.* | *Customers are advised that the next train is delayed.*
> A **client** is someone who pays for a service: *a hairdresser and her clients*
> A **patron** of a particular restaurant, bar etc is someone who eats or drinks there. This is a fairly formal word and it is more usual to use **customer**: *Patrons are asked to refrain from smoking.*
> A **shopper** is someone who is involved in the activity of buying things from shops: *The street was crowded with shoppers.*
> A **consumer** is anyone who pays for goods and services. This word is used especially when you are talking about people's rights: *Consumers have a right to know what they are buying.*

,customer 'services n [U] the part of a company or business that deals with questions, problems etc that customers have: *You should call customer services and complain.* | *He's customer services manager at the store.*

cus·tom·iz·a·ble /ˈkʌstəmaɪzəbəl $ ˌkʌstəˈmaɪz-/ *adj* able to be changed in order to be suitable for a particular object or situation: *Download free, customizable business forms from Entrepreneur.com.*

cus·tom·ize also **-ise** *BrE* /ˈkʌstəmaɪz/ *v* [T] to change something to make it more suitable for you, or to make it look special or different from things of a similar type: *a customized car*

Customs and Excise *n* the department of the British government that is responsible for collecting tax on goods that are being bought or sold, or goods that have been brought into the country

cut¹ S1 W1 /kʌt/ *v past tense and past participle* **cut**, *present participle* **cutting**

1 REDUCE [T] to reduce the amount of something: *They're introducing CCTV cameras in an attempt to cut street crime in the area.* | *You need to cut the amount of fat and sugar in your diet.* | *Scientists are warning that unless carbon emissions are cut, we could be heading for an environmental catastrophe.* | *700 jobs will be lost in order to* **cut costs** *and boost profits.* | *The major aviation companies need to* **cut prices** *if they are to compete with budget airlines.* | **cut sth by £1 million/$5 billion/half etc** *The welfare budget has been cut by $56 billion.* | **cut sth off sth** *A new direct service will cut two hours off the flying time between London and Seoul.* | *Staffing levels had already been* **cut to the bone** (=reduced to the lowest level possible).

2 DIVIDE STH WITH A KNIFE, SCISSORS ETC [I,T] to divide something or separate something from its main part, using scissors, a knife etc: *Do you want me to cut the cake?* | *The telephone wires had been cut minutes before the assault.* | **cut sth with sth** *Jane cut the cord with a knife.* | **cut sb sth** *Can you cut me a piece of bread, please?* | [+along/across/round etc] *Using a pair of scissors, cut carefully along the dotted lines.* | [+through] *We'll need a saw that will cut through metal.* | **cut sth in half/in two** *Cut the orange in half.* | **cut sth into slices/chunks/pieces etc** (=make something into a particular shape by cutting) *Cut the carrots into thin strips.* | **cut sth to size/length** (=cut something so that it is the size you need) *The curtain pole can be cut to length.* → CUT AWAY, CUT OFF, CUT OUT, CUT UP

3 MAKE STH SHORTER WITH A KNIFE ETC [T] to make something shorter with a knife, scissors etc, especially in order to make it neater: *For reasons of hygiene, we had to cut our fingernails really short.* | **cut the lawn/grass/hedge etc** *From outside the open window came the sound of someone cutting the hedge.* | **have/get your hair cut** *Isn't it about time you got your hair cut?*

4 REMOVE PARTS FROM FILM ETC [T] to remove parts from a film, book, speech etc, for example because it is too long or might offend people: *The original version was cut by more than 30 minutes.*

5 MAKE A HOLE/MARK [I,T] to make a hole or mark in the surface of something, or to open it using a sharp tool: [+into] *The blade cut deep into the wood.* | **cut sth into sth** *Strange letters had been cut into the stone.* | *Cut a hole in the middle of the paper.* | *Cut open the chillies and remove the seeds.*

6 INJURE [T] to injure yourself on something sharp that breaks the skin and makes you bleed: **cut your finger/knee/hand etc** *I noticed he'd cut his finger quite badly.* | **cut yourself (on sth)** *Marcie said she'd cut herself on a broken glass.* | *That knife's extremely sharp! Mind you don't cut yourself.* | *On Eric's chin was a scrap of cotton wool where he'd* **cut** *himself* **shaving.** | *She fell and* **cut** *her head* **open.**

7 MAKE/FORM STH BY CUTTING [T] to make or form something from a solid piece of wood, metal etc using a sharp tool: *I'll get a spare key cut for you.* | **cut sth from sth** *The chair had been cut from the trunk of a tree.*

8 LET SB GET FREE [T] to cut something such as metal or rope in order to let someone escape from where they are trapped: **cut sb from sth** *She had to be*

cut from the wreckage of her car. | *He was in the vehicle for an hour before he was* **cut free.**

9 TOOL/MATERIAL [I] if a tool cuts well, badly etc, it cuts things well or badly etc: *professional quality tools that cut efficiently and smoothly*

10 CLOTHES [T usually passive] if a piece of clothing is cut in a particular way, that is the way it is designed and made: *The T-shirt is cut fairly low at the neck.*

11 ON COMPUTER [I,T] to remove something from a document or FILE on a computer: *To cut text, press Control + C.* | *Cut and paste* *the picture into a new file* (=remove it and then make it appear in a new file).

12 GO A QUICK WAY [I always + adv/prep] to get to somewhere by a quicker and more direct way than the usual way; → **shortcut**: [+through/down/across etc] *I usually cut through the car park to get to work.* | *Let's cut across the field.*

13 DIVIDE AN AREA [I,T] to divide an area into two or more parts: **cut sth in/into sth** *The river cuts the whole region in two.* | [+through] *The new road will cut through a conservation area.*

14 PLAYING CARDS [I,T] to divide a pack of cards into two: *First cut the pack, and then deal the cards*

15 MUSIC [T] to produce a CD, song etc for people to buy: *The band cut their first single in 2001.*

16 CROPS [T] to take the top part off crops such as wheat before gathering them

17 cut a deal to make a business deal: *A French company has reportedly cut a deal to produce software for government agencies.*

18 cut (sb) a check *AmE informal* to write a CHECK for a particular amount of money and give it to someone: *When the damage assessor called, he cut a check for $139.*

19 Cut! *spoken* said by the DIRECTOR of a film to tell people to stop acting, filming etc

20 PUT A FILM TOGETHER [T] to put the parts of a film together so that they make a continuous story, and get rid of the parts you do not want

21 cut in line *AmE* to unfairly go in front of other people who are waiting to do something

22 cut class/school *AmE informal* to deliberately not go to a class that you should go to: *She started cutting classes.*

23 cut your teeth (on sth) to get your first experience of doing something and learn the basic skills: *Both reporters cut their journalistic teeth on the same provincial newspaper.*

24 cut corners to do something in a way that saves time, effort, or money, but that also results in it not being done properly: *There's always a temptation to cut corners when you're pushed for time, but it's not usually worth it.*

25 cut sth short to stop doing something earlier than you planned: *The band has cut short its US concert tour.* | *Her athletic career was cut short by a leg injury.*

26 cut sb short to stop someone from finishing what they wanted to say: *I tried to explain, but he cut me short.*

27 cut the ... *spoken* an impolite way of telling someone to stop doing something because it is annoying you: *Cut the sarcasm, Jane, and tell me what really happened!* | *Cut the crap* (=stop saying something that is not true)! *I saw his car outside your house.*

28 cut sb dead to deliberately ignore someone when you meet them: *I saw Ian in town but he cut me dead.*

29 cut your losses to stop doing something that is failing, so that you do not waste any more money, time, or effort: *He decided to cut his losses and sell the business.*

30 LINE [T] if a line cuts another line, they cross each other at a particular point

31 TOOTH [T] if a baby cuts a tooth, the tooth starts to grow

32 cut sb to the quick/bone *literary* to upset someone very much by saying something cruel: *His mockery frightened her and cut her to the bone.*

33 cut to the chase *informal* to immediately start

dealing with the most important part of something

34 cut a fine/strange etc figure *literary* to have an impressive, strange etc appearance: *Mason cuts a battered but defiant figure.*

35 cut your own throat to behave in a way that will cause harm to yourself, especially because you are very offended or angry about something: *He'd just be cutting his own throat if he left now.*

36 (it) cuts both ways *spoken* used to say that something has two effects, especially a good effect and a bad one: *The higher the interest rate, the greater the financial risk – which, of course, cuts both ways.*

37 cut the ground from under sb's feet to make someone or their ideas seem less impressive by having better ideas yourself or doing something before they do

38 cut and run *informal* to avoid a difficult situation by leaving suddenly: *Although the company has faced financial difficulties, they do not intend to cut and run.*

39 cut no ice/not cut much ice if something cuts no ice with someone, it will not persuade them to change their opinion or decision: *It's unlikely that these arguments will cut much ice with Democrats.*

40 cut the (umbilical) cord to stop being too dependent on someone, especially your parents

41 not cut the mustard *informal* to not be good enough: *Other magazines have tried to copy the formula but have never quite cut the mustard.*

42 DRUGS [T usually passive] to mix an illegal drug such as HEROIN with another substance

43 cut your coat according to your cloth to spend only as much money as you can afford

44 to cut a long story short *spoken* used to say that you are only going to mention the main facts of something: *To cut a long story short, he threw them out of the house.*

45 cut it/things fine; cut it close *AmE* to leave yourself just enough time to do something: *Even in normal traffic, 20 minutes to get to the airport is cutting it fine.*

46 not cut it *informal* to not be good enough to do something: *Players who can't cut it soon quit the team.*

47 cut a swathe through sth *literary* to cause a lot of damage in a place or among a group of people: *A series of bribery scandals has cut a swathe through the government.*

48 you could cut the atmosphere with a knife *informal* used to say that everyone in a place is very annoyed or angry with each other and this is very easy to notice

---

WORD FOCUS: words meaning CUT

chop to cut vegetables, meat, or wood into pieces | **slice** to cut bread, vegetables, or meat into thin pieces | **dice** to cut vegetables into small pieces | **peel** to cut the outside part off an onion, apple etc | **grate** to cut cheese or vegetables into small pieces by rubbing them against a special tool | **carve** to cut pieces from a large piece of meat | **saw** to cut wood using a special tool called a saw | **chop down** to cut down a tree, using an axe | **snip** to cut something quickly using scissors | **shave** to remove hair from your face or body | **trim** to remove small parts of something to make it look neat | **mow** to cut grass | **prune** to cut off the top part of plants, in order to make them grow better
→ see also slit, slash, graze, gash, amputate

---

cut across sth *phr v*
if a problem or feeling cuts across different groups of people, they are all affected by it: *Domestic violence seems to cut across most social divisions.*

cut sth ⇔ **away** *phr v*
to remove unwanted or unnecessary parts from something by cutting it: *Cut away all the dead wood.*

cut back *phr v*
1 to reduce the amount, size, cost etc of something: [+**on**] *Several major hospitals are cutting back on staff at the moment.* | **cut sth** ⇔ **back** *Education spending cannot be cut back any further.* | *Richer countries must do more to cut back carbon emissions.* → CUTBACK
2 cut sth ⇔ **back** to remove the top part of a plant in

order to help it to grow: *Cut back the shoots in spring to encourage bushier growth.*
3 to eat, drink, or use less of something, especially in order to improve your health: [+**on**] *Try to cut back on foods containing wheat and dairy products .*

cut down *phr v*
1 REDUCE to reduce the amount of something: **cut sth** ⇔ **down** *Installing double-glazing will cut down the noise from traffic.* | [+**on**] *By getting the design right, you can cut down on accidents.*
2 EAT/USE LESS to eat, drink, or use less of something, especially in order to improve your health: *I've always smoked, but I'm trying to cut down.* | [+**on**] *Cut down on fatty foods and alcohol if you want to lose weight.*
3 TREE **cut sth** ⇔ **down** to cut through the main part of a tree so that it falls on the ground
4 KILL **cut sb** ⇔ **down** *literary* to kill or injure someone, especially in a battle: *Hundreds of men were cut down by crossbow fire.*
5 REDUCE LENGTH **cut sth** ⇔ **down** to reduce the length of something such as a piece of writing: *Your essay's too long – it needs cutting down a little.*
6 cut sb down to size to make someone realize that they are not as important, successful etc as they think they are

cut in *phr v*
1 INTERRUPT to interrupt someone who is speaking by saying something: *'What shall I do?' Patrick cut in again.* | [+**on**] *Sorry to cut in on you, but there are one or two things I don't understand.*
2 DRIVING to suddenly drive in front of a moving car in a dangerous way: [+**on**] *She cut in on a red Ford, forcing the driver to brake heavily.*
3 MACHINE if a part of a machine cuts in, it starts to operate when it is needed: *The safety device cuts in automatically.*
4 INCLUDE SB **cut sb in** *informal* to allow someone to take part in a plan or to make money from it: [+**on**] *Come on, Joey, you said you were going to cut me in on this one!*

cut sb/sth **off** *phr v*
1 SEPARATE **cut sth** ⇔ **off** to separate something by cutting it away from the main part: *One of his fingers was cut off in the accident.* | **cut sth off sth** *Cut the fat off the meat.*
2 STOP SUPPLY **cut sth** ⇔ **off** to stop the supply of something such as electricity, gas, water etc: *The gas had been cut off.* | *The US has threatened to cut off economic and military aid.*
3 get cut off to suddenly not be able to hear someone that you were speaking to on the telephone: *I don't know what happened – we just got cut off.*
4 be cut off a) if a place is cut off, people cannot leave it or reach it: *In winter, the town is often cut off by snow.* **b)** to be a long way from other places and be difficult to get to: *Accessible only by air, the town is cut off from the rest of the country.* **c)** if someone is cut off, they are lonely and not able to meet many other people: *Many older people feel cut off and isolated.*
5 STOP BEING FRIENDLY **cut sb** ⇔ **off** to stop having a friendly relationship with someone: *Julia had been completely cut off by all her family and friends.* | **cut yourself off (from sb)** *After his wife died, he cut himself off completely from the rest of the world.*
6 INTERRUPT to interrupt someone and stop them from finishing what they were saying: *Emma cut him off in mid-sentence.*
7 PREVENT STH **cut sb off from sth** to prevent someone from having something that they need or want: *The project aims to ensure that poorer people are not cut off from the benefits of computer technology.*
8 MONEY/PROPERTY to refuse to let someone receive your money or property, especially when you die: *My parents threatened to **cut me off without a penny** if I married him.*
9 DRIVING **cut sb** ⇔ **off** *AmE* to suddenly drive in front of a moving car in a dangerous way: *A man in a station wagon cut me off on the freeway.*

C

10 cut off your nose to spite your face to do something because you are angry, even though it will harm you

cut out *phr v*

1 REMOVE STH cut sth ⇔ out to remove something by cutting round it: *The cancerous cells had to be cut out.* | [+of] *Billy showed me the article he'd cut out of the magazine*

2 CUT A SHAPE cut sth ⇔ out to cut a shape from a piece of paper, cloth etc: *The children were cutting out squares from the scraps of material.*

3 STOP STH HAPPENING cut sth ⇔ out to stop something from happening or existing: *The idea behind these forms is to cut out fraud.* | *A catalytic converter will cut out 90% of carbon monoxide emissions.*

4 STOP DOING/EATING STH cut sth ⇔ out to stop doing or eating something, especially because it might be bad for your health: *The current advice to pregnant women is to cut out alcohol.*

5 FROM WRITING cut sth ⇔ out to remove something from a piece of writing, especially because it might offend people: *I would cut out that last bit about racial prejudice.*

6 cut it/that out *spoken* used to tell someone to stop doing something because it is annoying you: *Hey, you guys, cut it out – Mom's trying to get some sleep.*

7 NOT INVOLVE SB cut sb ⇔ out to stop someone from doing something or being involved in something: *The new rules will cut out 25% of people who were previously eligible to vote.*

8 be cut out for sth also **be cut out to be sth** [usually in questions and negatives] to have the qualities that you need for a particular job or activity: *In the end, I decided I wasn't cut out for the army.* | *Are you sure you're really cut out to be a teacher?*

9 ENGINE if an engine or machine cuts out, it suddenly stops working: *The engine cut out halfway across the lake.*

10 LIGHT/VIEW cut sth ⇔ out to prevent light, sound etc from reaching somewhere: *You'll need sunglasses that will cut out harmful UV rays from the sun.*

11 cut sb out to prevent someone from getting something, especially your money after your death: *Em's father decided to cut her out of his will.* → **have your work cut out** at WORK² (15); → **cut out the middleman** at MIDDLEMAN

cut through sth *phr v*

1 *written* to move or pass easily through water or air: *The boat cut effortlessly through the water.*

2 to quickly and easily deal with something that is confusing or difficult: *You need someone to help you cut through all the irritating legal jargon.*

3 *literary* if a sound cuts through silence or noise, it is heard because it is loud: *A piercing shriek cut through the silence.*

cut up *phr v*

1 CUT INTO PIECES cut sth ⇔ up to cut something into small pieces: *Could you cut the pizza up, please?* | [+into] *He cut the paper up into little pieces.*

2 DRIVING cut sb/sth ⇔ up *BrE* to suddenly drive in front of a moving vehicle in a dangerous way: *Some idiot cut me up on the motorway.*

3 BEHAVE BADLY *AmE informal* to behave in a noisy or rude way

4 cut up rough *BrE informal* to react in an angry or violent way: *Careful how you approach him – he can cut up a bit rough if he's got a mind to.*

5 CRITICIZE cut sb ⇔ up *informal* to criticize someone in an unpleasant way → CUT UP

cut² S2 W2 *n* [C]

1 REDUCTION [usually plural] a reduction in the size or amount of something, especially the amount of money that is spent by a government or company: *There will be cuts across all levels of the company.* | [+in] *Cuts in public spending mean that fewer people can go on to higher education.* | *The decision to **make cuts** in health care provision has been widely criticized.* | **tax/pay/job etc cuts** *A shorter working week will mean pay cuts for millions of workers.* | *The building plans could be hit by*

*possible **spending cuts**.* | [+of] *A cut of 1% in interest rates was announced yesterday.*

2 SKIN WOUND a wound that is caused when something sharp cuts your skin: *That's quite a nasty cut – you ought to get it seen to by a doctor.* | *The driver escaped with minor **cuts and bruises**.*

3 HOLE/MARK a narrow hole in or mark in the surface of something, made by a sharp tool or object: *Make a small cut in the paper.*

4 HAIR [usually singular] **a)** an act of cutting someone's hair; ⊟ **haircut**: *How much do they charge for a cut and blow-dry?* **b)** the style in which your hair is cut; ⊟ **haircut**: *a short stylish cut*

5 CLOTHES [usually singular] the style in which clothes have been made: *I could tell by the cut of his suit that he wasn't a poor man.*

6 SHARE OF STH [usually singular] someone's share of something, especially money: [+of] *She was determined to claim her cut of the winnings.*

7 REMOVAL FROM FILM an act of removing a part from a film, play, piece of writing etc, or a part that has been removed

8 FILM [usually singular] the process of putting together the different parts of a film and removing the parts that will not be shown: *Spielberg himself oversaw the final cut.*

9 the cut and thrust of sth the exciting but sometimes difficult or unpleasant way that something is done: *the cut and thrust of political debate*

10 be a cut above sth to be much better than someone else or something else: *The movie is a cut above recent thrillers.* | *He proved himself to be **a cut above the rest** in last week's competition.*

11 MEAT a piece of meat that has been cut to a size suitable for cooking or eating: *Long slow cooking is more suitable for cheaper cuts of meat.*

12 ROAD *AmE* a road that has been made through a hill → COLD CUTS, POWER CUT, SHORT CUT

cut and 'dried *adj* a situation, decision, result etc that is cut and dried cannot now be changed: *I don't think the plan is as cut and dried as people think.*

cut·a·way /ˈkʌtəwei/ *adj* a cutaway model, drawing etc is open on one side so that you can see the details inside it —**cutaway** *n* [C]

cut·back /ˈkʌtbæk/ *n* [C usually plural] a reduction in something, such as the number of workers in a company or the amount of money a government or company spends: *The shortage of teachers was blamed on government cutbacks.* | [+in] *cutbacks in funding for libraries* | *A fall in donations has forced the charity to **make cutbacks.*** | **sharp/drastic/severe cutback** *sharp cutbacks in the military budget* → CUT BACK (1)

cute S3 /kjuːt/ *adj*

1 very pretty or attractive: *a cute little puppy* | *The baby's so cute.* | *That's a really cute outfit.*

2 *especially AmE* sexually attractive: *Tell us about this cute guy you met!*

3 *especially AmE* clever in a way that can seem rude: *Their lawyer tried a cute trick.* —**cutely** *adv* —**cuteness** *n* [U]

cute·sy /ˈkjuːtsi/ *adj* too pretty or clever in a way you think is annoying: *She spoke in a tiny cutesy voice.*

cute·y /ˈkjuːti/ *n* another spelling of CUTIE

cut 'glass *n* [U] glass that has patterns cut into its surface: *a cut glass decanter*

cu·ti·cle /ˈkjuːtɪkəl/ *n* [C] the area of hard skin around the base of your nails

cut·ie, cutey /ˈkjuːti/ *n* [C] *spoken* someone who is attractive and nice: *Mark is such a cutie!*

cut·lass /ˈkʌtləs/ *n* [C] a short sword with a curved blade, used by SAILORS or PIRATES in the past

cut·ler /ˈkʌtlə $ -ər/ *n* [C] *old-fashioned* someone who makes or sells cutlery

C

cut·le·ry /ˈkʌtləri/ n [U] *especially BrE* knives, forks, and spoons that you use for eating and serving food; → crockery; ◻ **silverware** *AmE*

cut·let /ˈkʌtl̩t/ n [C] **1** a small flat piece of meat on a bone: *a lamb cutlet* **2 vegetable/nut etc cutlet** *BrE* small pieces of vegetables, nuts etc that are pressed together into a flat piece and cooked

ˈ**cut-off, cut·off** /ˈkʌtɒf $ -ɔːf/ n **1** [C usually singular] a limit or level at which you stop doing something; → **deadline: cut-off date/point/score etc** (=the date etc when you stop doing something) *The cut-off date for registration is July 2.* **2** [C usually singular] when you completely stop doing something or supplying something: [+of] *A full-scale cut-off of US aid would be a disaster.* **3 cutoffs** or **cut-off jeans/trousers etc** [plural] short trousers that you make by cutting off the bottom part of a pair of trousers

cut·out /ˈkʌtaʊt/ n [C] **1** the shape of a person, object etc that has been cut out of wood or paper; → **silhouette 2** a piece of equipment that stops a machine that is not working properly

ˌ**cut-ˈprice** also ˌ**cut-ˈrate** *especially AmE adj* **1** cut-price goods or services are cheaper than usual: *cut-price toys | a travel operator offering cut-price deals* **2** a cut-price shop sells goods at reduced prices: *cut-price supermarkets*

cut·ter /ˈkʌtə $ -ər/ n [C] **1** [often plural] a tool that is used for cutting something: *wire cutters | a pastry cutter* **2** someone whose job is to cut something: *a diamond cutter* **3** a small ship

ˈ**cut-throat, cut·throat** /ˈkʌtθrəʊt $ -θroʊt/ adj [usually before noun] a cut-throat activity or business involves people competing with each other in an unpleasant way: *Cut-throat competition is keeping prices low. | the cut-throat world of advertising*

ˌ**cut-throat ˈrazor** n [C] *BrE* a RAZOR with a very long sharp blade, used especially in the past

cut·ting[1] /ˈkʌtɪŋ/ n [C] **1** a stem or leaf that is cut from a plant and put in soil or water to grow into a new plant **2** *BrE* an article that has been cut from a newspaper or magazine; ◻ **clipping: press/newspaper cuttings** *Margot sent him some press cuttings about the wedding.* **3** *BrE* a passage that has been dug through high ground for a railway, road etc; ◻ **cut** *AmE*

cutting[2] *adj* unkind and intended to upset someone: *a cutting remark*

ˈ**cutting board** n [C] *BrE* a piece of wood or plastic that you cut meat or vegetables on; ◻ **chopping board**

ˌ**cutting ˈedge** n **1 the cutting edge (of sth)** the newest and most exciting stage in the development of something: **at the cutting edge (of sth)** *research that's at the cutting edge of genetic science | The deck represents the cutting edge in CD reproduction.* **2** [singular] an advantage over other people or things: *The team are relying on Gregg to give them a cutting edge.* —ˈ**cutting-edge** adj: *cutting-edge scientific discoveries*

ˈ**cutting room** n [C] a room where the different parts of a film are cut apart and put into the correct order, to make the final form of the film

cut·tle·fish /ˈkʌtl̩ˌfɪʃ/ n plural **cuttlefish** [C] a sea creature with ten soft arms

ˌ**cut ˈup** also **cut-up** adj [not before noun] **1** *informal* very upset about something that has happened: [+about] *He was very cut up about Stephen dying.* **2 be badly cut up** to have a lot of injuries because you have been in an accident or fight

ˈ**cut-up** n [C] *AmE informal* someone who makes other people laugh by doing amusing things, especially in a situation when they should not do this

cuz /kəz, kʌz/ conjunction *AmE spoken* a short form of 'because'; ◻ **cos** *BrE*: *'Why?' 'Cuz I said so!'*

CV /ˌsiː ˈviː/ n [C] *curriculum vitae* a short written document that lists your education and previous jobs, which you send to employers when you are looking for a job; ◻ **resume** *AmE*

cwt *BrE*; **cwt.** *AmE* the written abbreviation of *hundredweight*

-cy /si/ suffix [in nouns] **1** the state or quality of being something: *accuracy | bankruptcy* **2** a particular rank or position: *a baronetcy*

cy·an /ˈsaɪən $ ˈsaɪˌæn, -ən/ adj *technical* having a dark greenish-blue colour —**cyan** n [U]

cy·a·nide /ˈsaɪənaɪd/ n [U] a very strong poison

cyber- /saɪbə $ -ər/ prefix relating to computers, especially to messages and information on the Internet: *cyber-shoppers*

cy·ber·crime, cyber crime /ˈsaɪbəkraɪm $ -bər-/ n [C,U] criminal activity that involves the use of computers or the Internet

cy·ber·fraud /ˈsaɪbəfrɔːd $ -bərfrɒːd/ n [U] the illegal act of deceiving people on the Internet in order to gain money, power etc

cy·be·ri·a /saɪˈbɪəriə $ -ˈbɪr-/ n [U] CYBERSPACE

cy·ber·land /ˈsaɪbəlænd $ -bər-/ n [U] activity that involves the Internet and the people who use it

cy·ber·net·ics /ˌsaɪbəˈnetɪks $ -bər-/ n [U] the scientific study of the way in which information is moved and controlled in machines, the brain, and the NERVOUS SYSTEM —**cybernetic** adj

cy·ber·punk /ˈsaɪbəpʌŋk $ -bər-/ n [U] stories about imaginary events relating to computer science, usually set in the future —**cyberpunk** adj [only before noun]

cy·ber·sick·ness /ˈsaɪbəˌsɪknəs $ -bər-/ n [U] a feeling of illness caused by using a computer for long periods of time or being in a room with a lot of computers – used humorously

cy·ber·space /ˈsaɪbəspeɪs $ -bər-/ n [U] all the connections between computers in different places, considered as a real place where information, messages, pictures etc exist: *Students are discovering the endless amount of information in cyberspace.*

cy·ber·squat·ter /ˈsaɪbəˌskwɒtə $ -bərˌskwɑːtər/ n [C] someone who officially records the names of companies that they do not own or work for as DOMAIN NAMES on the Internet in order to sell these names to companies for profit —**cybersquatting** n [U]

cy·ber·stalk·ing /ˈsaɪbəˌstɔːkɪŋ $ -bərˌstɒːk-/ n [U] the illegal use of the Internet, email, or other electronic communication systems to follow someone or threaten them: *The state's first cyberstalking laws went into effect a little over a year ago.* —**cyberstalker** n [C]

cy·ber·ter·ror·ist /ˈsaɪbəˌterərɪ̩st $ -bər-/ n [C] someone who uses the Internet to damage computer systems, especially for political purposes: *Such a strategic attack, mounted by cyberterrorists, would shut down everything from power stations to air traffic control centres.* —**cyberterrorism** n [U]

cy·ber·wid·ow /ˈsaɪbəˌwɪdəʊ $ -bərˌwɪdoʊ/ n [C] *informal* the wife of a man who spends a lot of time working or playing on his computer – used humorously

cy·borg /ˈsaɪbɔːg $ -bɔːrg/ n [C] a creature that is partly human and partly machine

cyc·la·men /ˈsɪkləmən/ n plural **cyclamen** [C] a plant with pink, red, or white flowers

cy·cle[1] S3 W3 /ˈsaɪkəl/ n [C]
1 a number of related events that happen again and again in the same order: *a woman's menstrual cycle |* [+of] *the cycle of the seasons | Sometimes the only way to break the cycle of violence in the home is for the wife to leave.* → LIFE CYCLE; → **vicious cycle** at VICIOUS CIRCLE
2 *especially BrE* a bicycle or MOTORCYCLE: *a map showing cycle routes*
3 the period of time needed for a machine to finish a process: *This washing machine has a 50-minute cycle.*
4 a group of songs, poems etc that are all about a particular important event

cycle² v **1** [I] especially BrE to travel by bicycle; ⊟ **bike** AmE: [+**to/down/home etc**] Do you cycle to work? **2** [I,T] AmE to go through a series of related events again and again, or to make something do this: The water is cycled through the machine and reused.

'**cycle lane** n [C] BrE a part of a wide road that only bicycles are allowed to use

'**cycle path** n [C] BrE a path for bicycles, for example beside a road or in a park

cy·cle·way /'saɪkəlweɪ/ n [C] BrE a road or path, sometimes a long one, for bicycles

cy·clic /'saɪklɪk/ also **cyc·li·cal** /'sɪklɪkəl, 'saɪ-/ adj happening in cycles: cyclical changes in the economy —**cyclically** /-kli/ adv

cy·cling /'saɪklɪŋ/ n [U] especially BrE the activity of riding a bicycle

'**cycling shorts** n [plural] especially BrE a pair of short trousers made out of cloth that stretches

cy·clist /'saɪklɪ̣st/ n [C] someone who rides a bicycle

cy·clone /'saɪkləʊn $ -kloʊn/ n [C] a very strong wind that moves very fast in a circle; → **hurricane, typhoon**

Cy·clops /'saɪklɒps $ -klɑːps/ n [singular] a very big man in ancient Greek stories who only had one eye in the middle of his forehead

cyg·net /'sɪgnɪ̣t/ n [C] a young SWAN

cyl·in·der /'sɪlɪ̣ndə $ -ər/ n [C] **1** a shape, object, or container with circular ends and long straight sides; → **tube**: The gases are stored in cylinders. **2** the tube within which a PISTON moves forwards and backwards in an engine: a four-cylinder engine **3 be firing/running on all cylinders** informal to be operating or performing very well: In this book, the author is firing on all cylinders.

cy·lin·dri·cal /sɪ̣'lɪndrɪkəl/ adj in the shape of a cylinder: a cylindrical oil tank

cym·bal /'sɪmbəl/ n [C] a musical instrument in the form of a thin round metal plate, which you play by hitting it with a stick or by hitting two of them together: the clash of cymbals → see picture at DRUM

cyn·ic /'sɪnɪk/ n [C] someone who is not willing to believe that people have good, honest, or sincere reasons for doing something: Even **hardened cynics** believe the meeting is a step towards peace. —**cynicism** /-sɪzəm/ n [U]

cyn·i·cal /'sɪnɪkəl/ adj **1** unwilling to believe that people have good, honest, or sincere reasons for doing something: a cynical view of human nature | [+**about**] The public is cynical about election promises. **2** not caring that something might not be morally right, might hurt someone etc, when you are trying to get something for yourself: a cynical disregard for international agreements —**cynically** /-kli/ adv

cy·pher /'saɪfə $ -ər/ n another spelling of CIPHER

cy·press /'saɪprɪ̣s/ n [C] a tree with dark green leaves and hard wood, which does not lose its leaves in winter

Cy·ril·lic /sɪ̣'rɪlɪk/ adj the Cyrillic alphabet is the one used for Russian, Bulgarian, and some other Slavonic languages

cyst /sɪst/ n [C] a lump containing liquid that grows in your body or under your skin, and that sometimes needs to be removed; → **boil**

cystic fi·bro·sis /ˌsɪstɪk faɪ'brəʊsɪ̣s $ -'broʊ-/ n [U] a serious medical condition, especially in children, in which breathing and DIGESTING food is very difficult

cyst·i·tis /sɪ'staɪtɪ̣s/ n [U] an infection of the BLADDER that especially affects women

cy·tol·o·gy /saɪ'tɒlədʒi $ -'tɑː-/ n [U] the scientific study of cells from living things —**cytologist** n [C]

czar /zɑː $ zɑːr/ n [C] **1** another spelling of TSAR **2 banking/drug/health etc czar** AmE someone who is very powerful in a particular job or activity

cza·ri·na /zɑː'riːnə/ n another spelling of TSARINA

C

D, d

D, **d** /diː/ *plural* **D's, d's** *n* **1** [C,U] the fourth letter of the English alphabet **2** [C,U] the second note in the musical SCALE of C MAJOR or the musical KEY based on this note **3** [C] a mark given to a student's work to show that it is not very good: *I got a D in history last semester.* **4** the number 500 in the system of ROMAN NUMERALS → **D AND C**

d. also **d** *BrE* **1** the written abbreviation of *died*: *John Keats d. 1821* **2** the written abbreviation of *penny* or *pence* in the system of money used in Britain before 1971

d' /d/ the short form of 'do': *D'you know how many people are going to be there?*

-d /d, t/ *suffix* the form used for -ED after 'e': *baked*

-'d /d/ **1** the short form of 'would': *I asked if she'd be willing to help.* **2** the short form of 'had': *Nobody knew where he'd gone.* **3** the short form of 'did': *Where'd you get that?*

D.A. /ˌdiː ˈeɪ/ *n* [C] the abbreviation of *district attorney*

dab¹ /dæb/ *n* [C] **1** a small amount of something that you put onto a surface: [+of] *a dab of butter* **2** a light touch with your hand, a cloth etc: *She wiped her tears away with a dab of her handkerchief.* **3** be a dab hand at/with sth *BrE informal* to be very good at a particular activity **4** a small flat fish **5** dabs [plural] *BrE old-fashioned* your FINGERPRINTS

dab² *v* **dabbed, dabbing** **1** [I,T] to touch something lightly several times, usually with something such as a cloth: *She dabbed her eyes with a handkerchief.* | [+at] *He dabbed at his bleeding lip.* **2** [T] to put a substance onto something with quick light movements of your hand: **dab sth on/onto etc sth** *She hastily dabbed some cream on her face.*

dab·ble /ˈdæbəl/ *v* **1** [I] to do something or be involved in something in a way that is not very serious: [+in/at/with] *people who dabble in painting as a way of relaxing* **2** [T] *BrE* to move your hands, feet etc about in water: **dabble sth in sth** *children dabbling their feet in the sea*

dach·a /ˈdætʃə $ ˈdɑː-/ *n* [C] a large country house in Russia

dachs·hund /ˈdæksənd, -sʊnd/ *n* [C] a type of small dog with short legs and a long body

Dac·ron /ˈdækrɒn $ ˈdeɪkrɑːn/ *n* [U] a type of cloth that is not made from natural materials

dac·tyl /ˈdæktɪl $ -tl/ *n* [C] a repeated sound pattern in poetry, consisting of one long sound followed by two short sounds, as in the word 'carefully' —**dactylic** /dækˈtɪlɪk/ *adj*

dad [S1] [W2] /dæd/ *n* [C] father: *She lives with her mom and dad.* | *Dad, will you help me?*

dad·dy [S1] /ˈdædi/ *n plural* **daddies** [C] father – used especially by children or when speaking to children: *Daddy's home!* → **SUGAR DADDY**

daddy long·legs /ˌdædi ˈlɒŋlegz $ -ˈlɔːŋ-/ *n* [C] a flying insect with six long legs

da·do /ˈdeɪdəʊ $ -doʊ/ *n plural* **dadoes** [C] the lower part of a wall in a room, especially when it is decorated differently from the upper part of the wall

dae·mon /ˈdiːmən/ *n* [C] a creature in ancient Greek stories that is half a god and half a man; → **demon**

daf·fo·dil /ˈdæfədɪl/ *n* [C] a tall yellow spring flower with a tube-shaped part in the middle

daf·fy /ˈdæfi/ *adj informal* silly or crazy in an amusing way

daft /dɑːft $ dæft/ *adj especially BrE* **1** silly: *a daft idea* | *Me, jealous? Don't be daft* (=that is a silly idea). | *She's as daft as a brush* (=extremely silly). **2** be daft about sth to be extremely interested in something: *Tony's still daft about cars!* —**daftness** *n* [U]

dag·ger /ˈdægə $ -ər/ *n* [C] **1** a short pointed knife used as a weapon **2** look daggers at sb *informal* to look at someone angrily **3** be at daggers drawn if two people are at daggers drawn, they are extremely angry with each other → **CLOAK-AND-DAGGER**

da·go /ˈdeɪgəʊ $ -goʊ/ *n plural* **dagos** [C] *taboo* a very offensive word for someone from Spain, Italy, or Portugal. Do not use this word.

da·guer·ro·type /dəˈgerəʊtaɪp $ -rə-/ *n* [C,U] an old type of photograph, or the process used to make it

dahl /dɑːl/ *n* [C,U] an Indian dish made with beans, PEAS, or LENTILS

dah·li·a /ˈdeɪliə $ ˈdæliə/ *n* [C] a large garden flower with a bright colour

dai·ly¹ [S3] [W2] /ˈdeɪli/ *adj* [only before noun] **1** happening or done every day: *daily flights to Miami* **2** daily life the ordinary things that you usually do or experience **3** relating to a single day: *the daily rate of pay*

daily² *adv* happening or done every day: *The zoo is open daily.*

daily³ *n plural* **dailies** [C] **1** also **daily paper** a newspaper that is printed and sold every day, or every day except Sunday **2** *BrE old-fashioned* also **daily help** someone, especially a woman, who is employed to clean someone's house **3** dailies [plural] *AmE* the prints of a film as it is being made, which are looked at every day after filming ends; ◻ **rushes** *BrE*

dain·ty¹ /ˈdeɪnti/ *adj comparative* **daintier**, *superlative* **daintiest** **1** small, pretty, and delicate: *a dainty gold chain* | *a child with dainty features* **2** moving or done in a careful way, using small movements: *a dainty walk* —**daintily** *adv* —**daintiness** *n* [U]

dainty² *n plural* **dainties** [C] *old-fashioned* something small that is good to eat, especially something sweet such as a cake

dai·qui·ri /ˈdaɪkɪri, ˈdæk-/ *n* [C] a sweet alcoholic drink made with RUM and fruit juice

dai·ry /ˈdeəri $ ˈderi/ *n plural* **dairies** [C] **1** a place on a farm where milk is kept and butter and cheese are made **2** a company which sells milk and sometimes makes other things from milk, such as cheese **3** dairy products/produce milk, butter, cheese etc

'dairy ˌcattle *n* [plural] cattle that are kept to produce milk rather than for their meat

'dairy ˌfarm *n* [C] a farm that has cows and produces and sells milk

dai·ry·maid /ˈdeərimeɪd $ ˈder-/ *n* [C] a woman who worked in a dairy in the past

dai·ry·man /ˈdeərimən $ ˈderimən, -mæn/ *n plural* **dairymen** /-mən $ -mən, -men/ [C] a man who works in a dairy

da·is /ˈdeɪs, deɪs/ *n* [singular] a low stage in a room that you stand on when you are making a speech or performing, so that people can see and hear you

dai·sy /ˈdeɪzi/ *n plural* **daisies** [C] **1** a white flower with a yellow centre → see picture at FLOWER **2** be pushing up (the) daisies to be dead – used humorously → **fresh as a daisy** at FRESH (11)

'daisy ˌchain *n* [C] daisies attached together into a string that you can wear around your neck or wrist

Dal·ai La·ma /ˌdælaɪ ˈlɑːmə $ ˌdɑː-/ *n* [C] the leader of the Tibetan Buddhist religion

dale /deɪl/ *n* [C] a valley – used in the past or in the names of places, especially in the North of England

dal·li·ance /ˈdæliəns/ *n* [C,U] *literary* a romantic or sexual relationship between two people that is not considered serious

dal·ly /ˈdæli/ *v* **dallied, dallying, dallies** [I] to waste time, or do something very slowly: *Don't dally along the* *way! We haven't got much time.*

dally with sb/sth *phr v* **1** to do something or think about something, but not in a very serious way: *They've dallied with the idea of touring round the world.* **2** *old-fashioned* to have a romantic relationship with someone, but not in a serious way

Dal·ma·tian, dalmatian /dæl'meɪʃən/ *n* [C] a large dog with short white hair and black or brown spots

dam¹ /dæm/ *n* [C] **1** a special wall built across a river or stream to stop the water from flowing, especially in order to make a lake or produce electricity → see picture at ENERGY; → see picture at COUNTRY **2** *technical* the mother of a four-legged animal, especially a horse; → **sire**

dam² *v* dammed, damming [T] also **dam up 1** to stop the water in a river or stream from flowing by building a special wall across it **2** to stop something from being expressed or continuing: *Once she allowed her anger to show, it could not be dammed up again.*

dam·age¹ S2 W2 /'dæmɪdʒ/ *n*

1 PHYSICAL HARM [U] physical harm that is done to something or to a part of someone's body, so that it is broken or injured

do/cause damage
serious/severe/extensive damage
irreparable/irreversible/permanent damage (=damage
  that cannot be repaired)
minor damage
accidental damage
brain/liver/lung etc damage
flood/storm/fire etc damage (=damage caused by a
  flood, storm, fire etc)

[+to] *damage to property* | *These chemicals have been found to **cause** serious environmental **damage**.* | *The earthquake caused **extensive** structural **damage**.* | *His eyesight may have suffered **irreparable damage**.* | *The other ship sustained only **minor damage**.* | *The insurance covers **accidental damage** to the vehicle.* | *There may be permanent **brain damage**.* | *the need to reduce **flood damage***

2 EMOTIONAL HARM [U] harm caused to someone's emotions or mind: *The death of a parent can cause long-lasting **psychological damage**.*

3 BAD EFFECT [U] a bad effect on something: [+to] *The damage to his reputation was considerable.* | *The closure of the factory will cause severe damage to the local economy.* | **damage limitation/control** *the attempts at political damage control during the scandal*

4 damages [plural] *law* money that a court orders someone to pay to someone else as a punishment for harming them or their property; → **compensation**: *The court awarded him £15,000 in damages.*

5 the damage is done used to say that something bad has happened which makes it impossible to go back to the way things were before it happened: *She immediately apologized, but the damage was done.*

6 what's the damage? *spoken* used humorously to ask how much you have to pay for something

damage² S3 W3 *v* [T]

1 to cause physical harm to something or to part of someone's body: *insects that damage crops* | **badly/severely/seriously damage** *Smoking can severely damage your health.* | *a shampoo for dry or damaged hair*

2 to have a bad effect on something or someone in a way that makes them weaker or less successful: *The changes in share values have damaged investor confidence.* | *emotionally damaged children*

WORD CHOICE: damage, hurt, injure, wound
Damage means to cause physical harm to a thing or to a part of your body: *Fires can damage crops and animals.* | *He damaged a knee ligament playing rugby.* You do not usually talk about damaging a person. Use **hurt**, **injure**, or **wound** instead: *He was hurt in a climbing accident (NOT He was damaged in a climbing accident).* However, you can talk about damaging an unborn child: *German measles in pregnancy can damage your baby.* Use **hurt** or **injure** to talk about people suffering physical

harm as a result of an accident, earthquake, hurricane etc: *No one was hurt in the car crash.* | *We hoped he wasn't seriously injured.*
⚠ Do not say 'injure someone's health'. Say '**damage someone's health**'.
Use **wound** to talk about someone being hurt by a weapon such as a gun or a knife: *He shot dead three people and wounded several others.* | *a wounded soldier*

---

dam·ag·ing /'dæmɪdʒɪŋ/ *adj* **1** causing physical harm to someone or something: *the damaging effects of sunlight* **2** affecting someone or something in a bad way: *damaging criticism of his policies* | [+to] *The loss of jobs was damaging to morale.*

dam·ask /'dæməsk/ *n* [U] a type of cloth with a pattern woven into it, often used to cover furniture: *a damask tablecloth*

dame /deɪm/ *n* [C] **1** *AmE old-fashioned informal* a woman **2** *BrE* a humorous female character in a PANTOMIME (=a special play at Christmas) who is played by a man

Dame *n* a British title given to a woman as an honour for achievement or for doing good things: *Dame Judi Dench*

dam·mit /'dæmɪt/ *interjection not polite* a way of spelling 'damn it'

damn¹ /dæm/ *interjection not polite* **1** used when you are very annoyed or disappointed: *Damn! I've locked my keys in the car.* **2** used when something is impressive or surprising: *Damn, she's old.*

damn² *adv* [+ adj/adv] *informal not polite* **1** used to emphasize a statement: *Everything was so damn expensive.* | *The band sounded pretty damn good.* | *I'll damn well do as I please.* | *You know damn well what I'm talking about.* | *He damn near (=almost) drowned.* | 'It isn't easy.' '**Damn right**, it's not.' **2 damn all** *especially BrE* nothing at all: *He knows damn all about cars.*

damn³ S2 *adj* [only before noun] *spoken not polite*
1 used when you are angry or annoyed with someone or something: *Turn off the damn TV!*
2 used to emphasize something negative: *It's a damn shame he left her.*
3 not a damn thing nothing at all: *There's not a damn thing you can do about it.*
4 a damn sight more/better etc a lot more, a lot better etc: *He's as smart as you or me and a damn sight tougher.*

damn⁴ *v* [T] **1 damn it/you etc!** *spoken not polite* used when you are extremely angry or annoyed with someone or something: *Damn it, be careful with that!* | *Stop, damn you!* | *Damn that telephone!* **2 (I'll be/I'm) damned if ...** *spoken not polite* used to make a negative statement in a strong way: 'Where's Wally?' 'Damned if I know.' (=I don't know) | *I'll be damned if I can find my keys (=I can't find them).* | *I'll be damned if I let him in the house (=I won't let him in).* **3 I'll be damned** *spoken not polite* used when you are surprised: *I'll be damned! I haven't seen him for years!* **4 damn the consequences/expense/calories etc** *spoken* used to say that you are going to do something, even though it might have bad results: *The time has come for me to speak out, and damn the consequences.* **5 be damned** to be given the punishment of going to HELL after you die **6** to state that something is very bad: *The critics damned the play on the first night.* | **damn (sb/sth) with faint praise** (=show that you think someone or something is not good by only praising them a little) **7 damned if you do, damned if you don't** *spoken* used to say that whatever you say or do will be considered wrong → **(as) near as damn it** at NEAR¹ (8)

damn⁵ *n spoken not polite* **1 not give a damn (about sb/sth)** to not care at all about someone or something: *I* *don't give a damn about her.* **2 be not worth a damn** to have no value at all: *Her promise isn't worth a damn.*

dam·na·ble /'dæmnəbəl/ *adj old-fashioned* very bad or annoying: *This damnable heat!* —**damnably** *adv*

dam·na·tion[1] /dæm'neɪʃən/ *n* [U] when someone is punished by being sent to HELL after their death, or the state of being in hell for ever

damnation[2] *interjection old-fashioned* used when you are very angry or annoyed

damned[1] /dæmd/ *adj, adv* another form of 'damn', used especially in writing

damned[2] *n* **the damned** the people who God will send to HELL when they die because they have been so bad

damned·est /'dæmdˌst/ *adj spoken not polite* **1 do/try your damnedest** to try very hard to do something: *I'll do my damnedest to fix it, but I can't promise anything.* **2** [only before noun] used to emphasize that something is unusual, surprising etc: *It was the damnedest thing you ever saw!*

damn-fool *adj* [only before noun] very stupid: *a damn-fool mistake*

damn·ing /'dæmɪŋ/ *adj* proving or showing that someone has done something very bad or wrong: *damning evidence of her treachery* | *a damning report*

Dam·o·cles /'dæməkliːz/ → **sword of Damocles** at SWORD (2)

damp[1] /dæmp/ *adj* **1** slightly wet, often in an unpleasant way: *Wipe the leather with a damp cloth.* | *a cold, damp day* **2 damp squib** *BrE informal* something that is intended to be exciting, effective etc, but which is disappointing —**dampness** *n* [U] —**damply** *adv*

> **WORD CHOICE: damp, moist, humid**
> Use **damp** especially to say that something is slightly wet in an unpleasant way: *The room was cold and damp.*
> Use **moist** to say that something is slightly wet in a pleasant way or in the way it should be: *She took a mouthful of the delicious moist cake.* | *rich, moist soil*
> Use **humid** to talk about the weather or the air when it is slightly wet and makes you feel uncomfortable: *the hot humid atmosphere of a greenhouse*

damp[2] *n* [U] *BrE* water in walls or in the air that causes things to be slightly wet: *Damp had stained the walls.*

damp[3] *v* [T] to dampen something
damp sth ⇔ **down** *phr v* to make a fire burn more slowly, often by covering it with ASH

damp course *n* [C] *BrE* a layer of material which is put into the bottom of a wall to prevent water rising through it

damp·en /'dæmpən/ *v* [T] **1** to make something slightly wet; ▣ **moisten** **2** also **dampen down** *BrE* to make something such as a feeling or activity less strong: *The light rain dampened the crowd's enthusiasm.* | *Raising interest rates might dampen the economy.* **3** to make a sound or movement less loud or strong: *The spring dampens the shock of the impact.*

damp·er /'dæmpə $ -ər/ *n* [C] **1 put a damper on sth** to make something less enjoyable, active, or great than it could have been: *A couple of knee injuries put a damper on his football career.* **2** a type of small metal door that is opened or closed in a STOVE or FURNACE, to control the air reaching the fire so that it burns more or less strongly **3** a piece of equipment that stops a movement from being too strong **4** a piece of equipment that stops a piano string from making a sound

damp-proof ,course *n* [C] *BrE* a DAMP COURSE

dam·sel /'dæmzəl/ *n* [C] *old use* **1** a young woman who is not married **2 damsel in distress** a young woman who needs help or protection – used humorously

dam·son /'dæmzən/ *n* [C] a small bitter purple PLUM

dance[1] S2 W3 /dɑːns $ dæns/ *n*
1 [C] a special set of movements performed to a particular type of music: *The waltz is an easy dance to learn.* | **folk/traditional dance** *the traditional dances and music of Russia*
2 [C] a social event or party where you dance: *Are you going to the dance this weekend?* | *the school dance*
3 [C] an act of dancing: *Claire **did a little dance** of excitement.* | **have a dance** *especially BrE*: *Let's have another dance.*
4 [C] a piece of music which you can dance to: *The band was playing a slow dance.*
5 [U] the activity or art of dancing: *modern dance* | *dance and movement classes* → **song and dance about sth** at SONG (4); → **lead sb a dance** at LEAD[1] (19)

dance[2] S3 *v*
1 [I,T] to move your feet and body in a way that matches the style and speed of music: *Come on, let's dance.* | [+to] *They danced to Ruby Newman's orchestra* (=the orchestra was playing). | [+with] *The bride danced with her father.* | **dance a waltz/rumba/tango etc**
2 [I,T] to dance in performances, especially in BALLET: *danced with the Boston Repertory Ballet.* | *Nakamura dances several solos in this production.*
3 [I] *literary* to move up, down, and around quickly: *Pink and white balloons danced in the wind.*
4 dance to sb's tune to do what someone wants you to do – used to show disapproval: *At that time, Eastern bloc countries danced to the Soviet tune.*
5 dance attendance on sb to do everything possible in order to please someone: *a movie star with several young men dancing attendance on her* —**dancing** *n* [U]: *the beauty of her dancing*

dance band *n* [C] a group of musicians who play music that you dance to

dance floor *n* [C] a special floor in a restaurant, hotel etc for people to dance on

dance hall *n* [C] a large public room where people paid to go and dance in the past

danc·er /'dɑːnsə $ 'dænsər/ *n* [C] **1** someone who dances as a profession: *The dancer's technique is strong.* | **ballet/ballroom/flamenco etc dancer** *Margot Fonteyn, the famous British ballet dancer* **2** someone who dances: *the dancers on the floor* | **good/bad dancer** *Dave's a good dancer.*

D and C /ˌdiː ən 'siː/ *n* [C] a medical operation to clean out the inside of a woman's UTERUS

dan·de·li·on /'dændɪlaɪən/ *n* [C] a wild plant with a bright yellow flower which later becomes a white ball of seeds that are blown away in the wind

dandelion ,clock *n* [C] *BrE* the soft ball of white seeds that grows on the dandelion plant

dan·der /'dændə $ -ər/ *n* **get sb's dander up** to make someone angry – often used humorously

dan·di·fied /'dændɪfaɪd/ *adj old-fashioned* a man who is dandified wears very fashionable clothes in a way that shows he cares too much about his appearance

dan·dle /'dændl/ *v* [T] *old-fashioned* to play with a baby or small child by moving them up and down in your arms or on your knee

dan·druff /'dændrəf, -drʌf/ *n* [U] small pieces of dead skin from someone's head that can be seen in their hair or on their shoulders

dan·dy[1] /'dændi/ *n plural* **dandies** [C] *old-fashioned* a man who spends a lot of time and money on his clothes and appearance

dandy[2] *adj especially AmE* very good – often used in a slightly humorous way: *We're at our hotel, and everything is **fine and dandy**.*

Dane /deɪn/ *n* [C] someone from Denmark

dang /dæŋ/ *interjection especially AmE* a word meaning DAMN that people use because it is less offensive —**dang** *adj, adv* —**dang** *v* [T]

dan·ger S2 W2 /'deɪndʒə $ -ər/ *n*
1 [U] the possibility that someone or something will be harmed, destroyed, or killed: *Danger! No boats beyond*

this point. | **in danger** *The refugees believe that their lives are in danger.* | *I don't want to* **put** *you* **in danger.** | [+**of**] *The danger of a fire in the home increases during the holidays.* | **be in danger of (doing) sth** *The bridge was in danger of collapsing.* | **grave/great/real/serious etc danger** *The condor was in grave danger of extinction.* | [+**from**] *The public was not aware of the danger from nuclear tests in Nevada.* | **out of danger** *The patient is now out of danger.* | *Pedestrians on this road* **face** *constant* **danger** *from cars.*
2 [C,U] the possibility that something bad will happen: **be in danger of (doing) sth** *The party is in danger of being defeated in the next election.* | **danger that** *There is a danger that museums will attempt to entertain rather than educate.* | **the danger of (doing) sth** *to guard against the danger of becoming isolated*
3 [C] something or someone that may harm or kill you: *the dangers that abound in the region* | [+**of**] *Children need to be educated about the dangers of drug use.* | **be a danger to sb/sth** *The wreck is a danger to other ships.*
4 there's no danger of sth used to say that something will not happen: *There's no danger of Darren ever getting up early.*
5 be on the danger list *BrE* to be so ill that you may die

'danger ,money *BrE*; **'danger ,pay** *AmE n* [U] additional money that you are paid for doing dangerous work

dan·ger·ous [S2] [W2] /ˈdeɪndʒərəs/ *adj*
1 able or likely to harm or kill you; → **harmful**: *laws about dangerous dogs* | *Some of these prisoners are extremely dangerous.* | **It's dangerous** *for a woman to walk alone at night.* | [+**for**] *The crumbling sidewalks are dangerous for old people.* | [+**to**] *The virus is probably not dangerous to humans.* | **highly/very dangerous** *The aircraft caught fire, a highly dangerous situation.* | *The powdered milk was not as good as breast milk, and was* **downright dangerous** (=actually dangerous) *when it was mixed with unclean water.*
2 involving a lot of risk, or likely to cause problems; ▣ **risky**: *The business is in a dangerous financial position.* | *a politically dangerous strategy*
3 dangerous ground/territory a situation or subject that could make someone very angry or upset: *Teachers can be on dangerous ground if they discuss religion.*
—**dangerously** *adv*: *people who drive dangerously*

WORD FOCUS: DANGEROUS
similar words: **hazardous, risky, treacherous, perilous** *literary*

dan·gle /ˈdæŋɡəl/ *v* **1** [I,T] to hang or swing loosely, or to make something do this: [+**from**] *A light bulb dangled from a wire in the ceiling.* | **dangle sth in/over etc sth** *I dangled my feet in the clear blue water.* **2** [T] to offer something good to someone, in order to persuade them to do something: **dangle sth in front of sb/before sb** *A good pay package and a company car were dangled in front of her.*

Da·nish¹ /ˈdeɪnɪʃ/ *n* **1** [U] the language used in Denmark **2** [C] *AmE* a very sweet cake made of light PASTRY; ▣ **Danish pastry**

Danish² *adj* relating to Denmark, its people, or its language

,Danish 'pastry *n* [C] a small fairly flat sweet cake, often with fruit inside

dank /dæŋk/ *adj* unpleasantly wet and cold: *a dank prison cell* —**dankness** *n* [U]

dap·per /ˈdæpə $ -ər/ *adj* a man who is dapper is nicely dressed, has a neat appearance, and is usually small or thin: *a dapper little man in a grey suit*

dap·ple /ˈdæpəl/ *v* [T] *literary* to mark something with spots of colour, light, or shade

dap·pled /ˈdæpəld/ *adj* marked with spots of colour, light, or shade: *the dappled shade of the trees*

,dapple-'grey *BrE*; **dapple-gray** *AmE n* [C] a horse that is grey with spots of darker grey

---

Darby and Joan /ˌdɑːbi ən ˈdʒəʊn $ ˌdɑːrbi ən ˈdʒoʊn/ *n BrE* **like Darby and Joan** used humorously when talking about an old husband and wife who live very happily together

dare¹ [W3] /deə $ der/ *v, modal verb*
1 [I not in progressive] to be brave enough to do something that is risky or that you are afraid to do – used especially in questions or negative sentences: *He wanted to ask her, but he didn't dare.* | *'I'll tell Dad.' 'You wouldn't dare!'* | **dare (to) do sth** *I daren't go home.* | *Only a few journalists dared to cover the story.* | *She hardly dared hope that he was alive.* | *Dare we admit this?*
2 how dare you *spoken* said to show that you are very angry and shocked about what someone has done or said: *How dare you accuse me of lying!*
3 don't you dare! *spoken* said to warn someone not to do something because it makes you angry: *Don't you dare talk to me like that!*
4 [T] to try to persuade someone to do something dangerous or embarrassing as a way of proving that they are brave: **dare sb to do sth** *One night they dared Frank to steal a bottle of his father's whiskey.* | *So jump, then.* **I dare you.**
5 dare I say/suggest *spoken formal* used when saying something that you think people may not accept or believe: *I thought the play was, dare I say it, boring.*
6 I dare say also **I daresay** *spoken especially BrE* used when saying or agreeing that something may be true: *I dare say things will improve.*

dare² *n* [C] something dangerous that you have dared someone to do: **for a dare** *BrE*/**on a dare** *AmE* (=because someone has dared you to) *She ran across a busy road for a dare.*

dare·dev·il /ˈdeədevəl $ ˈder-/ *n* [C] someone who likes doing dangerous things —**daredevil** *adj*

daren't /deənt $ dernt/ *especially BrE* the short form of 'dare not'

dare·say /ˌdeəˈseɪ $ ˈdeɪrseɪ/ → **I daresay** at DARE¹ (6)

dar·ing¹ /ˈdeərɪŋ $ ˈder-/ *adj* **1** involving a lot of risk or danger, or brave enough to do risky things: *a daring rescue attempt* **2** new or unusual in a way that may shock people: *a daring new building* —**daringly** *adv*

daring² *n* [U] courage that makes you willing to take risks: *a plan of great daring*

dark¹ [S2] [W1] /dɑːk $ dɑːrk/ *adj comparative* **darker**, *superlative* **darkest**
1 NO LIGHT if it is dark, there is little or no light; ▣ **light**: *The church was dark and quiet.* | *the dark winter days* | *Suddenly, the room* **went dark** (=became dark). | *It gets dark* (=night begins) *about ten o'clock during the summer.* | *It was still dark* (=was night) *when we boarded the train.* | *It was* **pitch dark** (=completely dark) *in the attic.*
2 COLOUR quite close to black in colour; ▣ **light, pale**: *There were dark clouds in the sky.* | *men in dark suits* | *a slightly darker colour* | **dark blue/green/pink etc** *a dark blue dress*
3 HAIR/EYES/SKIN someone who is dark has hair, eyes, or skin that is brown or black in colour; ▣ **fair**: *a tall, dark man* | *John's dark skin and eyes*
4 MYSTERIOUS mysterious or secret: *a dark secret* | **keep sth dark** *BrE* (=keep something secret) *Apparently, he has a son, but he's kept that very dark.*
5 EVIL evil or threatening: *There was a darker side to his character.* | *a place where so many dark deeds had been committed* | *the dark forces of the universe*
6 UNHAPPY TIME a dark time is unhappy or without hope: *the dark days of the war* | *Even in the darkest moments, I still had you, my love.*
7 FEELINGS/THOUGHTS if you have dark feelings or thoughts, you are very sad or worried: *a dark depression* | *her darkest fears*
8 HUMOUR dark humour deals with things that are

bad or upsetting in a funny way; ▣ **black**: *the dark humor common in difficult situations*
9 darkest Africa/South America etc *old-fashioned* the parts of Africa etc about which we know very little

dark² *n* **1** the dark when there is no light, especially because the sun has gone down: *my childish fear of the dark* | **in the dark** *I turned off the light and lay there in the dark.* | *We stood outside in the **pitch dark*** (=when there is no light at all). **2 after/before/until dark** after, before, or until the sun goes down at night: *I want you home before dark.* **3 in the dark** *informal* knowing nothing about something important, because you have not been told about it: *We're in the dark just as much as you are.* | *College officials were **kept in the dark** about the investigation.* → **a shot in the dark** at SHOT¹ (10)

Dark Ages *n* **1 the Dark Ages** the period in European history from 476 AD to about 1000 AD **2** a time when attitudes, knowledge, technology etc were not as modern or developed as they are now: *Richard is stuck in the Dark Ages when it comes to his attitudes towards women.*

dark·en /'dɑːkən $ 'dɑːr-/ *v* **1** [I,T] to become dark, or to make something dark: *The sky darkened and a few drops of rain fell.* | *a darkened theater* | *The evening shadows darkened the room.* **2** [I,T] to become less hopeful or positive, or to make something like this: *As he got drunker, his mood darkened.* **3** [I] if someone's face darkens, they start to look angry: *The captain's face darkened as he read.* **4 never darken my door again** *old-fashioned* said when you do not want to see someone again – now used humorously

dark glasses *n* [plural] glasses with dark glass in them that you wear to protect your eyes from the sun or to hide your eyes; → **sunglasses**

dark horse *n* [C] **1** someone who is not well known, and who surprises people by winning a competition: *In the 1955 golf championship, dark horse Jack Fleck defeated Ben Hogan.* **2** *BrE* someone who does not tell people much about themselves, but who has surprising qualities or abilities: *She's a dark horse. I didn't know she'd written a novel.*

dark·ie /'dɑːki $ 'dɑːr-/ *n* [C] *taboo old-fashioned* a very offensive word for a black person. Do not use this word.

dark·ly /'dɑːkli $ 'dɑːrk-/ *adv* **1** in a sad, angry, or threatening way: *Fred scowled darkly at her.* **2** having a dark colour: *a darkly handsome young man* **3 darkly funny/humorous/comic** dealing with something that is bad or upsetting in a funny way: *a darkly comic look at illness*

dark·ness W3 /'dɑːknᵻs $ 'dɑːrk-/ *n* [U]
1 when there is no light: *the long hours of darkness during winter* | **in darkness** *The lamp suddenly went out, leaving us in darkness.* | **total/pitch/complete darkness** *The room was in total darkness.* | *We lit our campfire **as darkness fell*** (=it became night). | *He stared out the window at **the gathering darkness*** (=the night slowly coming).
2 evil or the devil: *His smooth manner covered a heart of darkness.* | **the forces/powers of darkness** (=the devil or evil people)
3 the dark quality of a colour: *the darkness of the lenses*

dark·room /'dɑːkruːm, -rʊm $ 'dɑːrk-/ *n* [C] a special room with only red light or no light, where film from a camera is made into photographs

dar·ling¹ S2 /'dɑːlɪŋ $ 'dɑːr-/ *n*
1 *spoken* used when speaking to someone you love: *Look, darling, there's Mary.*
2 [C] someone who is very nice: *You really are a darling, Barney.*
3 the darling of sth the most popular person or thing in a particular group or area of activity: *She's the darling of the fashion world.*

darling² *adj* [only before noun] **1** used of someone you love very much: *my two darling daughters* **2** *spoken* used when you think someone or something is attractive: *What a darling little house!*

darn¹ /dɑːn $ dɑːrn/ also **darn it/him/them etc** *interjection AmE informal* used to show that you are annoyed or disappointed; ▣ **damn**: *Darn! I forgot my keys!* | *Darn it! I'll have to do it all myself!*

darn² also **darned** *adj spoken informal* **1** used to emphasize how bad, stupid, unfair etc someone or something is; ▣ **damn**: *The darn fool got lost on the way.* **2 a darn sight better/harder etc** a lot better, harder etc; ▣ **damn**: *He'd earn a darn sight more money there.* —**darn** also **darned** *adv*: *It was a darned good movie.*

darn³ *v* [T] to repair a hole in a piece of clothing by stitching wool over it: *Her cardigan had been darned at the elbows.*

darn⁴ *n* [C] a place where a hole in a piece of clothing has been repaired neatly with wool

darned /dɑːnd $ dɑːrnd/ *adj spoken informal* **1 I'll be darned!** used when you are surprised about something: *Did they really? I'll be darned!* **2 I'll be darned if ...** used to emphasize that you will not allow something to happen **3 darned if I know** used to emphasize that you do not know something

dart¹ /dɑːt $ dɑːrt/ *v* **1** [I always + adv/prep] to move suddenly and quickly in a particular direction: *Jill darted forward and pulled him away from the fire.* **2** [I,T] *literary* to look at someone or something very quickly: *Tom darted a terrified glance over his shoulder at his pursuers.*

dart² *n* **1** [C] a small pointed object that is thrown or shot as a weapon, or one that is thrown in the game of darts: *a poisoned dart* **2 darts** [U] a game in which darts are thrown at a round board with numbers on it **3** [singular] a sudden quick movement in a particular direction: *The prisoner **made a dart for** the door.* **4 dart of guilt/panic/pain etc** a very sudden, sharp feeling: *It sent a dart of terror through her.* **5** [C] a small fold put into a piece of clothing to make it fit better

dart·board /'dɑːtbɔːd $ 'dɑːrtbɔːrd/ *n* [C] a round board used in the game of darts

dash¹ /dæʃ/ *v* **1** [I always + adv/prep] to go or run somewhere very quickly: *Olive dashed into the room, grabbed her bag, and ran out again.* **2 dash sb's hopes** to disappoint someone by telling them that what they want is not possible: *Hopkins' hopes were dashed when his appeal was denied.* **3 (I) must dash/(I) have to dash** *BrE spoken* used to tell someone that you must leave quickly: *Anyway, I must dash – I said I'd meet Daniel at eight.* **4** [I,T always + adv/prep] *written* to throw or push something violently against something, especially so that it breaks: **dash sth against/on sth** *The ship was dashed against the rocks.* | [+against] *Waves were dashing against the sea wall.* **5 dash it (all)!** *BrE old-fashioned* used to show that you are slightly annoyed or angry about something
dash off *phr v* **1** to leave somewhere very quickly: *Harry dashed off before she had a chance to thank him.* **2 dash sth ⇔ off** to write or draw something very quickly: *She dashed off a quick letter.*

dash² *n*
1 SMALL AMOUNT [singular] **a)** a small amount of a substance that is added to something else: [+of] *Add salt, pepper and a dash of vinegar.* **b)** a small amount of a quality that is added to something else: [+of] *Add a dash of romance to your life with a trip to Paris.*
2 RUN QUICKLY [C usually singular] an occasion when someone runs somewhere very quickly in order to get away from something or someone, or in order to reach them: **make a dash for sth** *He made a dash for the door.* | *The prisoners made a dash for freedom.* | *It's pouring with rain – we'll have to **make a dash for it**.* | *When the alarm went there was a **mad dash** for the exit.*
3 LINE [C] a line [–] used in writing to separate two

closely related parts of a sentence, as for example, in the sentence 'Go home – they're waiting for you.'; → **hyphen**

4 SOUND [C] a long sound or flash of light used for sending messages in MORSE CODE → **dot**

5 CAR [C] AmE a DASHBOARD

6 STYLE [U] old-fashioned style, energy, and courage in someone such as a soldier

7 cut a dash old-fashioned to look very impressive and attractive in particular clothes: With her new image, she'll certainly cut a dash on her holiday cruise.

dash·board /ˈdæʃbɔːd $ -bɔːrd/ n [C] the part in front of the driver in a car that has the controls on it → see picture at **CAR**

dash·ing /ˈdæʃɪŋ/ adj a man who is dashing wears nice clothes and is very attractive and confident: a dashing young doctor —**dashingly** adv

dast·ard·ly /ˈdæstədli $ -ərd-/ adj old-fashioned very cruel or evil: tales of pirates and their dastardly deeds

DAT /dæt/ n [U] digital audio tape a system used to record sound or information in DIGITAL form

da·ta S1 W1 /ˈdeɪtə, ˈdɑːtə/ n [plural,U]
1 information or facts: The research involves collecting data from two random samples. | [+on] data on pesticide use | experimental/historical/statistical etc data detailed research data
2 information in a form that can be stored and used, especially on a computer: It's possible to store a lot more data on a DVD. | data storage/transfer/retrieval

data ,bank n [C] a database

da·ta·base S2 W2 /ˈdeɪtəˌbeɪs/ n [C] a large amount of data stored in a computer system so that you can find and use it easily: customer details held on a database | database system/software/application etc

data ,mining n [U] the process of using a computer to examine large amounts of information about customers, in order to discover things about them that are not easily seen or noticed

data ,processing n [U] the use of computers to store and organize information, especially in business

date¹ S1 W1 /deɪt/ n [C]
1 DAY a particular day of the month or year, especially shown by a number: The date on the letter was 30th August 1962. | What's today's date? | [+of] What's the date of the next meeting? | date of birth/birth date (=the day you were born) Please write your name, address, and date of birth on the form. | date of publication/issue/delivery etc You should apply at least 8 weeks before your date of departure. | set/decide on/fix a date (=choose a particular day for something) Have you set a date for the wedding? | The closing date (=last day you can do something) for applications is 10th Sept.
2 at a later/future date formal at some time in the future; ▣ later: The details will be agreed at a later date.
3 to date up to now: The cost of the work to date has been about £150 million. | Her best performance to date was her third place at the World Junior Championships.
4 ROMANTIC MEETING a) an occasion when you go out with someone that you like in a romantic way: [+with] I've got a date with Andrea tomorrow night. | I felt like a teenager going out on a first date. → BLIND DATE **b)** AmE someone that you have a date with: sb's date Can I bring my date to the party?
5 ARRANGEMENT TO MEET SB a time arranged to meet someone, especially socially: Let's make a date to come over and visit.
6 FRUIT a sweet sticky brown fruit with a long hard seed inside → CLOSING DATE; → expiry date at EXPIRY (2); → OUT-OF-DATE, SELL-BY DATE, UP-TO-DATE

date² S3 W3 v
1 WRITE DATE [T] to write or print the date on something: a newspaper dated November 23, 1963 | Make sure you sign and date it at the bottom.
2 FIND AGE [T] to find out when something old was

made or formed: The rocks are dated by examining the fossils found in the same layer. | radiocarbon dating
3 OLD-FASHIONED [I] if clothing, art etc dates, it begins to look old-fashioned: His designs are so classic, they've hardly dated at all. → DATED
4 RELATIONSHIP [T] AmE to have a romantic relationship with someone; ▣ go out with: Is he still dating Sarah?
5 SHOW SB'S AGE [T] if something that you say, do, or wear dates you, it shows that you are fairly old: Yes, I remember the moon landings – that dates me, doesn't it?

date from sth also **date back to** sth phr v to have existed since a particular time in the past: The church dates from the 13th century.

date·book /ˈdeɪtbʊk/ n [C] AmE a small book in which you write things you must do, addresses, telephone numbers etc; ▣ diary

dat·ed /ˈdeɪtᵻd/ adj old-fashioned: That dress looks a bit dated now. → out-of-date

date·line /ˈdeɪtlaɪn/ n [singular] the INTERNATIONAL DATE LINE

date rape n [C,U] a RAPE that is committed by someone the woman has met in a social situation

date stamp n [C] **a)** an object used for printing the date on documents **b)** the mark that it makes

dating ,agency also **dating ,service** n [C] a business that helps people to meet other people in order to have a romantic relationship

da·tive /ˈdeɪtɪv/ n [C usually singular] a particular form of a noun in some languages such as Latin and German, which shows that the noun is the INDIRECT OBJECT of a verb

daub¹ /dɔːb $ dɒːb/ v [T] to put paint or a soft substance on something without being very careful: soldiers' faces daubed with black mud

daub² n **1** [C] a small amount of a soft or sticky substance: [+of] a daub of paint **2** [U] technical mud or clay used for making walls → wattle and daub at WATTLE (1)

daugh·ter S1 W1 /ˈdɔːtə $ ˈdɒːtər/ n [C] someone's female child: She's got two daughters and one son. | our eldest daughter | [+of] the daughter of Labour MP Tony Benn

daughter-in-law n plural daughters-in-law [C] your son's wife

daugh·ter·ly /ˈdɔːtəli $ ˈdɒːtər-/ adj behaving in a way that a daughter is expected to behave

daunt /dɔːnt $ dɒːnt/ v [T usually passive] **1** to make someone feel afraid or less confident about something: He felt utterly daunted by the prospect of moving to another country. | Don't be daunted by all the technology. **2** nothing daunted old-fashioned used to say that someone continues or starts to do something in spite of difficulties: It was steep but, nothing daunted, he started climbing.

daunt·ing /ˈdɔːntɪŋ $ ˈdɒːn-/ adj frightening in a way that makes you feel less confident: The trip seemed rather daunting for a young girl. | He's got the daunting task of following in Ferguson's footsteps. | the daunting prospect of asking for a loan

daunt·less /ˈdɔːntləs $ ˈdɒːnt-/ adj confident and not easily frightened: dauntless optimism

daw·dle /ˈdɔːdl $ ˈdɒː-/ v [I] to take a long time to do something or walk somewhere: Don't dawdle – we're late already! | [+over] I dawdled over a second cup of coffee. —**dawdler** n [C]

1 000, 2 000, 3 000, most frequent words in S poken and W ritten English

dawn

dawn

dusk

dawn¹ /dɔːn $ dɒːn/ *n* [C,U]   **1** the time at the beginning of the day when light first appears; ▤ **daybreak**; → **dusk**: *at dawn The first boats set off at dawn.* | *When dawn broke* (=the first light of the day appeared), *we were still 50 miles from Calcutta.* | *I was up at the crack of dawn* (=very early in the morning) *to get the plane.* | *We worked from dawn to dusk* (=through the whole day while it is light). | *the cold light of dawn*   **2** the **dawn of civilization/time etc** the time when something began or first appeared: *People have been falling in love since the dawn of time.*   **3** a **false dawn** something that seems positive or hopeful but really is not: *There was talk of share prices recovering, but that was just a false dawn.*

dawn² *v* [I]   **1** if day or morning dawns, it begins: *The morning dawned fresh and clear after the storm.*   **2** literary if a period of time or situation dawns, it begins: *The age of Darwin had dawned.*   **3** formal if a feeling or idea dawns, you have it for the first time: *It began to dawn that something was wrong.*

dawn on sb *phr v* if a fact dawns on you, you realize it for the first time: *Then the ghastly truth dawned on me.* | *It dawned on me that Joanna had been right all along.*

,**dawn 'chorus** *n* the **dawn chorus** the sound of many birds singing at dawn

,**dawn 'raid** *n* [C] an attack or operation by soldiers or police that happens very early in the morning

day S1 W1 /deɪ/ *n*
1 24 HOURS [C] a period of 24 hours: *We spent three days in Paris.* | *'What day is it today?' 'Friday.'* | *He left two days ago.* | *I'll call you in a couple of days.* | *The following day, a letter arrived.* | **on a/the following/that etc day** (=during a particular day) *Over 10,000 soldiers died on that one day in January.* | *What really happened on that day so long ago?* | *I saw Jane the day before yesterday.* | *We're leaving for New York the day after tomorrow.* | *Women generally use up about 2000 calories a day* (=each day). | *I got an email from Jo the other day* (=a few days ago).
2 NOT NIGHT [C,U] the period of time between when it gets light in the morning and when it gets dark; ▤ **night**: *She only leaves her house during the day.* | *It was a cold blustery day.* | *Kept in that dark cell, I could no longer tell whether it was day or night.* | **on a/that/the following etc day** *She first met Steve on a cold but sunny day in March.* | **by day** (=during the day) *Owls usually sleep by day and hunt by night.* | *The day dawned* (=started) *bright and clear.*
3 WHEN YOU ARE AWAKE [C usually singular] the time during the day when you are awake and active: *His day begins at six.* | *Jackie starts the day with a few gentle exercises.* | *Sometimes I feel I just can't face another day.* | *'See you later,' said the girl, 'Have a nice day.'* (=used in a friendly way when you say goodbye to someone) | *It's been a long day* (=used when you have been awake and busy for a long time). | **all day (long)** (=during the whole time you are awake) *I've been studying all day. I'm beat!* ⚠ Do not say **all the day**. Say **all day**.

4 TIME AT WORK [C] the time you spend doing your job during a 24-hour period: *I work a ten-hour day.* | *Rail workers are campaigning for a shorter working day.* | *I've got a day off* (=a day when I do not have to go to work) *tomorrow.*
5 PAST [C] used to talk about a time in the past: *I knew him pretty well from his days as a DJ in the Bounty Club* (=from when he was a DJ). | *I always used to do the cooking in the early days of our marriage.* | *Not much was known about the dangers of smoking in those days* (=then). | *They were very much opposed to the government of the day* (=that existed then). | **One day** (=on a day in the past), *a mysterious stranger called at the house.* | **From day one** (=from the beginning), *I knew I wouldn't get on with him.* | **In my day** (=in the past, when I was young), *kids used to have some respect for their elders.* | **in sb's student/army/childhood etc days** (=in the past when someone was a student etc) *I used to run six miles a day in my army days.* | **those were the days** *spoken* (=used to talk about a time in the past you think was better than now) *We used to stay in bed all morning and party all night. Those were the days!*
6 NOW [C] used to talk about the situation that exists now: *I don't do much exercise these days* (=now). | *It's incredible that such attitudes still exist in this day and age* (=used to express disapproval that something still exists now). | **To this day** (=until and including now), *he denies any involvement in the crime.* | **up to/until/to the present day** (=until and including now) *This tradition has continued right up until the present day.*
7 FUTURE [C] used to talk about a time in the future: **one day/some day** (=some time in the future) *I'd like to go and visit the States one day.* | *Some day we might get him to see sense.* | **One of these days** (=some time soon) *I'm going to walk right out of here and never come back.* | *Kelly's expecting the baby any day now* (=very soon). | **The day will come** (=the time will come) *when he won't be able to care for himself any more.*
8 sb's/sth's **day** a successful period of time in someone's life or in something's existence: *Your grandfather was a famous radio personality in his day* (=at the time he was most successful). | *Don't be too disappointed you didn't win – your day will come* (=you will be successful in the future). | *Game shows like that have had their day* (=were successful in the past, but are not any more).
9 Independence/election/Christmas etc **day** a day on which a particular event or celebration takes place: *Rioting broke out just three days before polling day.*
10 five/three/nine etc **years to the day** exactly five years etc: *It's two years to the day since he died.*
11 sb's **days** someone's life: *She ended her days in poverty.*
12 sb's/sth's **days are numbered** used to say that someone or something will not exist for much longer: *It seems that the hospital's days are numbered.*
13 **day after day** also **day in day out** continuously for a long time in a way that is annoying or boring: *I couldn't stand sitting at a desk day after day.*
14 **from day to day** also **from one day to the next** if a situation changes from day to day or from one day to the next, it changes often: *I never know from day to day what I'm going to be doing.* | *His moods swung wildly from one day to the next.* → **DAY-TO-DAY**; → **live from day to day** at LIVE¹ (5)
15 **day by day** slowly and gradually: *Her health was improving day by day.*
16 **night and day** also **day and night** all the time; ▤ **continuously**: *Being together night and day can put a great pressure on any relationship.*
17 **day out** *especially BrE* a trip you make for pleasure on a particular day: *A visit to the caves makes a fascinating and exciting day out for all the family.*
18 **have an off day** to be less successful or happy than usual, for no particular reason: *Even the greatest athletes have their off days.*
19 **make sb's day** to make someone very happy: *Hearing her voice on the phone really made my day.*
20 soup/dish/fish etc **of the day** a soup, meal etc that a

restaurant serves on a particular day in addition to the meals they always offer

21 be all in a day's work if something difficult, unpleasant, or unusual is all in a day's work for someone, it is a normal part of their job

22 take each day as it comes also **take it one day at a time** to deal with something as it happens and not worry about the future: *Since I had the accident, I've learned to take each day as it comes.*

23 the day of reckoning a time when you have to deal with the unpleasant results of something you did in the past

SPOKEN PHRASES

24 it's (just) one of those days used to say that everything seems to be going wrong on this particular day

25 it's not sb's day used when several unpleasant things have happened to someone in one day: *It really wasn't Chris's day – he overslept and then his car broke down.*

26 make a day of it *BrE* to spend all day doing something for pleasure: *If the weather's nice, we'll make a day of it and take a picnic.*

27 that'll be the day used to say that you think something is very unlikely to happen: *'Bill says he's going to start going to the gym.' 'That'll be the day!'*

28 not have all day used to say that you want someone to do something faster because you do not have enough time to wait for them to finish: *Hurry up! I haven't got all day!*

29 it's not every day (that) used to say that something does not happen often and is therefore very special: *Let's go out and celebrate. After all, it's not every day you get a new job.*

30 be on days to work during the day at a job you sometimes have to do at night: *I'm on days this week.*

31 40/50/60 etc if he's/she's a day used to emphasize that someone is at least as old as you are saying: *She's ninety if she's a day.*

→ **at the end of the day** at END¹ (12); → **call it a day** at CALL¹ (10); → **carry the day** at CARRY¹ (22); → **the early days** at EARLY¹ (1); → **every day (has) its day** at DOG¹ (11); → **the good old days** at OLD (8); → **HALF DAY**; → **have a field day** at FIELD DAY (1); → **it's early days** at EARLY¹ (3); → **it's (a little) late in the day** at LATE¹ (8); → **it's sb's lucky day** at LUCKY (5); → **(live to) see the day** at SEE¹ (23); → **name the day** at NAME² (6); → **OPEN DAY**; → **save the day** at SAVE¹ (12); → SPEECH DAY, SPORTS DAY

'day boy *n* [C] *BrE* a boy DAY PUPIL

day·break /'deɪbreɪk/ *n* [U] the time of day when light first appears: *We arrived in Cairo at daybreak.*

'day camp *n* [C] *AmE* a place where children can go in the day during the school holidays to do sports, art etc

'day care, day·care /'deɪkeə $ -ker/ *n* [U] when babies or young children, or sick or old people are looked after during the day, especially while their family members are at work: **day care centre/services/facilities** *subsidized day care facilities* | [+for] *Local authorities may provide day care for under fives.* | *a day care centre for the elderly*

'day ˌcentre *n* [C] *BrE* a place where sick or old people or people who have a particular problem can go during the day to be looked after, to meet other people, or to get help: [+for] *a local day centre for homeless people*

day·dream¹ /'deɪdriːm/ *v* [I] to think about something pleasant, especially when this makes you forget what you should be doing; → **dream**: [+about] *What are you daydreaming about? There's work to be done.*
—**daydreamer** *n* [C]; → see picture at NIGHTMARE

daydream² *n* [C] pleasant thoughts you have while you are awake that make you forget what you are doing; → **dream**

'day girl *n* [C] *BrE* a girl DAY PUPIL

Day-Glo /'deɪɡləʊ $ -ɡloʊ/ *adj trademark* having a very bright orange, green, yellow, or pink colour: *Day-Glo orange posters*

'day job *n* [C] your normal job which you earn most of your money from doing, especially as opposed to another interest: *I'd love to be a professional writer, but I'm not giving up my day job just yet.*

day·light /'deɪlaɪt/ *n* [U] **1** the light produced by the sun during the day: **in daylight** *They're shy animals and don't often come out in daylight.* | *The park is open to the public during daylight hours.* | *If possible, it's better to work in natural daylight.* → **in broad daylight** at BROAD¹ (7) **2 (put) daylight between yourself and sb** *informal* if you put daylight between yourself and someone else, you make the distance or difference between you larger: *Now the team need to put some daylight between themselves and their rivals for the championship.* **3 scare/frighten the (living) daylights out of sb** *informal* to frighten someone a lot: *It scared the living daylights out of me when the flames shot out.* **4 beat/knock the (living) daylights out of sb** *informal* to hit someone a lot and seriously hurt them **5 daylight robbery** *BrE informal* a situation in which something costs you a lot more than is reasonable: *£2.50 for a cup of coffee? It's daylight robbery!*

daylight 'saving time also **ˌdaylight 'savings** *n* [U] the time during the summer when clocks are one hour ahead of standard time → BRITISH SUMMER TIME

'day ˌnursery *n* [C] a place where small children can be looked after while their parents are at work

'day off *n plural* **days off** [C] a day when you do not go to work, school etc because you have a holiday or because you are sick: *On my days off, you'll usually find me out in the back garden.* | **take/have a day off** *I'm taking a few days off before the wedding.*

ˌday of 'judgement *n* **the day of judgement** JUDGMENT DAY

'day ˌpupil *n* [C] *BrE* a student who goes to a BOARDING SCHOOL but who lives at home

ˌday re'lease *n* [U] *BrE* a system that allows workers to spend one day a week studying a subject at a college

ˌday re'turn *n* [C] *BrE* a train or bus ticket that lets you go somewhere at a cheaper price than usual, if you go there and back on the same day

'day room *n* [C] a room in a hospital where patients can go to read, watch television etc

'day school *n* [C,U] a school where the students go home in the evening rather than one where they live → BOARDING SCHOOL

day·time /'deɪtaɪm/ *n* [U] the time during the day between the time when it gets light and the time when it gets dark: **in/during the daytime** *I can't sleep in the daytime.* | *Can I take your daytime telephone number* (=the number of the telephone you use during the day)? | *daytime television*

day-to-'day *adj* [only before noun] **1 day-to-day work/business/life etc** day-to-day jobs or activities are ones that you do every day as a normal part of your life, your job etc: *The manager is responsible for the day-to-day running of the hotel.* **2** planning for only one day at a time, usually because you are unable to plan for longer: *I see a counsellor and can now handle life on a day-to-day basis.*

'day ˌtrading *n* [U] the activity of using a computer to buy and sell SHARES on the Internet, often buying and selling very quickly to make a profit out of small price changes —**day trader** *n* [C]

'day trip *n* [C] *BrE* a visit to an interesting place where you go there and come back the same day: [+to] *I remember my grandparents taking me on a day trip to Blackpool.* —**day tripper** *n* [C]

daze /deɪz/ *n* **in a daze** feeling confused and not able to think clearly: *She wandered round in a daze, not sure what to do.*

dazed /deɪzd/ *adj* unable to think clearly, es... because of a shock, accident etc: *Dazed surviv...*

D

gered from the wreckage. | **dazed look/expression etc**
Her face was very pale and she wore a dazed expression.

daz·zle /ˈdæzəl/ v [T] **1** if a very bright light dazzles
you, it stops you from seeing properly for a short time:
a deer dazzled by the headlights **2** to make someone
feel strong admiration: *As children, we were dazzled by
my uncle's good looks and charm.* —**dazzle** n [U]

daz·zling /ˈdæzəlɪŋ/ adj **1** a light that is dazzling is
very bright and makes you unable to see properly for a
short time **2** very impressive and attractive: *a dazzling display of football skills*

dB the written abbreviation of *decibel* or *decibels*

DC /ˌdiː ˈsiː/ the abbreviation of *direct current*; → AC

D.C. the abbreviation of *District of Columbia* in the
US

DDT /ˌdiː diː ˈtiː/ n [U] a chemical used to kill insects
that harm crops

de- /diː, dɪ/ prefix **1** shows an opposite: *deindustrial-
ization* (=becoming less industrial) **2** shows that
something is removed: *Debone the fish* (=remove its
bones). | *The king was dethroned* (=removed from
power). **3** shows that something is reduced: *The government have devalued the currency.*

dea·con /ˈdiːkən/ n [C] a religious official, in some
Christian churches, who is just below the rank of a
priest

dea·coness /ˌdiːkəˈnes $ ˈdiːkənəs/ n [C] a female
religious official, in some Christian churches, who is
just below the rank of a priest

de·ac·ti·vate /diːˈæktɪveɪt/ v [T] to switch something, especially a piece of equipment, off or to stop it
from being used any more; ⊟ **activate**: *You need to type
in a code number to deactivate the alarm.*

dead¹ S1 W1 /ded/ adj [no comparative]
1 NOT ALIVE no longer alive

a dead body
be shot dead
be found dead
be feared/presumed dead
drop dead (=die suddenly)
clinically dead (=dead based on medical checks)
dead on arrival (=dead when arriving at a hospital)
pronounce sb dead (=a doctor says that someone is dead after checking their body)
leave sb for dead (=leave someone because you think they are dead)
stone dead/dead as a doornail informal (=dead, with no signs of life)
more dead than alive (=very badly hurt or ill and almost dead)
long dead/dead and gone (=dead for a long time)

Her mother had been dead for ten years. | *Police are
trying to contact the family of the dead man.* | *a pile of
dead leaves* | *the **dead body** of a young soldier* | *Two
men were **shot dead** by terrorists.* | *Magnus was **found
dead** in his car.* | *One man is still missing, presumed
dead.* | *He was out playing golf when he suddenly had
a heart attack and **dropped dead**.* | *She was **pro-
nounced dead on arrival** at the hospital.* | *His fellow
climbers had **left** him **for dead** on the mountain.* | *We
didn't know if she was dead or alive.* | *When they found
him he was **more dead than alive**.* | *Her parents were
long dead.*

⚠ Do not confuse **dead**, which is an adjective, with **died**,
which is the past tense and past participle of the verb **die**:
The man was already dead (NOT *The man was already
died*).

2 NOT WORKING [not before noun] not working
because there is no power: *I picked up the phone but
...covered the line was dead.* | *Suddenly the radio went
...d.* | *I think the batteries are dead.*

3 READY USED already used: *a small pile of dead
...es* | **dead glass/bottle** (=one that someone has
...d drinking from in a bar or restaurant)

4 BORING [not before noun] a place that is dead
boring because there is nothing interesting or excitin...
happening there: *This place is dead after nine o'clock.*

5 NOT ACTIVE/USED not active or being used: *The
luxury car market has been dead in recent months.*

6 ARM/LEG ETC [not before noun] a part of your body
that is dead has no feeling in it, especially because the
blood supply to it has been stopped: *When I got up my
foot had **gone dead** where I'd been sitting on it.*

7 NO EMOTION [not before noun] showing no emotion
or sympathy: *Jennie's eyes were cold and dead.*

8 TIRED [not before noun] spoken very tired: *I can't go
out tonight. I'm absolutely dead!* | *She was **dead on** her
feet and didn't have the energy to argue* (=used when
someone keeps going even though they are very tired).

9 be dead to the world to be very deeply asleep or
unconscious: *Better leave Craig – he's dead to the world.*

10 USED FOR EMPHASIS [only before noun] completely or exactly – used to emphasize what you are
saying: *We all sat waiting in **dead silence*** (=complete
silence). | *The train came to a **dead stop*** (=it stopped
completely). | *The arrow hit the **dead centre** of the
target* (=the exact centre). | *I've given the whole thing up
as a **dead loss*** (=completely useless or a complete
failure). | *John tells me it's a **dead cert**, we can't lose
(=something which will certainly happen, win, suc-
ceed etc).* | *He fell to the floor **in a dead faint*** (=com-
pletely unconscious).

11 over my dead body spoken used to say that you are
determined to not allow something to happen: *You'll
marry him over my dead body!*

12 I wouldn't be seen/caught dead spoken used to say
that you would never wear particular clothes, go to
particular places, or do particular things, because you
would feel embarrassed: [+in/on/with etc] *I wouldn't be
seen dead in a dress like that!*

13 IN SERIOUS TROUBLE spoken in serious trouble:
if ... I'm dead/you're dead etc *If Mum finds out about
this, I'm dead.* | *You're **in dead trouble** now* (=in very
serious trouble)! | *One word of this to Sam and you're
dead meat* (=you are in serious trouble and someone is
very angry with you)!

14 be dead and buried an argument, problem, plan etc
that is dead and buried is not worth considering again:
*The old argument about whether the UK should be a
member of the EU should now be dead and buried .*

15 be dead in the water informal if a plan or idea is dead
in the water, it is unlikely to continue successfully

16 drop dead! spoken used to rudely and angrily tell
someone to go away and leave you alone

17 dead language a dead language, for example Latin
or Ancient Greek, is no longer used by ordinary people
→ **living language** at LIVING¹ (1)

18 the dead hand of sth something which stops or
slows your progress, especially a strong influence: *the
dead hand of local government bureaucracy*

19 PLANET a dead PLANET has no life on it

20 IN SPORT when the ball is dead in some games, it
is no longer on the playing area → **(as) dead as a dodo**
at DODO (3) → DEAD RINGER —**deadness** n [U]

dead² S3 adv informal

1 completely: **dead right/wrong** *'It's a crazy idea.'
'You're dead right!'* | **dead straight/flat** *The road was
dead straight.* | **dead quiet/calm/still** *Everything sud-
denly went dead still.* | **be dead (set) against sth**
(=completely disagree with something) *Her family
were dead against the marriage.* | *He was obviously
dead drunk.* | *When he saw her, he **stopped dead in his
tracks*** (=suddenly stopped moving completely).

2 spoken very: *He was **dead good-looking**.* | *It sounded
dead boring.* | **dead beat/tired** (=very tired)

3 [+ adj/adv] directly or exactly: *I stared **dead ahead** at
the doorway.* | *The bus arrived **dead on time**.*

dead³ n **1 the dead** [plural] people who have died:
Families on both sides buried their dead. | **the dead and
injured/wounded/dying** *Most of the dead and injured
had been passengers on the bus.* **2 the dead of night/
winter** the middle of the night or the middle of the

deal

winter: *creeping around in the dead of night* **3 rise/ come back/return from the dead** to become alive again after dying: *Christ rose from the dead.*

dead·beat /ˈdedbiːt/ *n* [C] **1** someone who is lazy and has no plans in life **2** someone who avoids paying their debts

dead·bolt /ˈdedbəult $ -boult/ *n* [C] a strong lock often used on doors

dead ˈduck *n* a dead duck *informal* a plan, idea etc that is not worth considering because it is very likely to fail: *He admitted that the whole project was a dead duck.*

dead·en /ˈdedn/ *v* [T] to make a feeling or sound less strong: *medicine to deaden the pain*

dead ˈend *n* [C] **1** a street with no way out at one end **2** a situation from which no more progress is possible: **come to/reach a dead end** *The negotiations have reached a dead end.* **3 dead-end job** a job with low wages and no chance of progress

dead·head /ˈdedhed/ *v* [T] to remove the dead or dying flowers from a plant

dead ˈheat *n* [C] a situation during or at the end of a race or competition in which two or more competitors have the same number of points etc, have reached the same level, or have taken the same time to complete a particular distance

dead ˈletter *n* [C] **1** a law, idea etc that still exists but that people no longer obey **2** a letter that cannot be delivered or returned

dead·line /ˈdedlaɪn/ *n* [C] a date or time by which you have to do or complete something: [+for] *The deadline for applications is May 27th.* | [+of] *It has to be in before the deadline of July 1st.* | **meet/miss a deadline** (=have or not have something finished on time) *working under pressure to meet a deadline* | **set/impose a deadline** *They've set a deadline of Nov 5.* | **tight/strict deadline** (=a deadline that is difficult)

dead·lock /ˈdedlɒk $ -lɑːk/ *n* [singular, U] **1** a situation in which a disagreement cannot be settled; ▤ **stalemate**: *The talks have reached a complete deadlock.* | *a last-ditch effort to break the deadlock* | *Negotiations ended in deadlock.* **2** *BrE* a DEADBOLT —**deadlocked** *adj*: *Talks between management and unions remain deadlocked over the issue of possible redundancies.*

dead·ly¹ /ˈdedli/ *adj*
1 VERY DANGEROUS likely to cause death; ▤ **lethal**: *a deadly poison* | *a deadly weapon* | **deadly disease/virus**
2 deadly enemy someone who will always be your enemy and will try to harm you as much as possible: *The two rapidly became deadly enemies.*
3 COMPLETE complete or total: *We sat in deadly silence.* | *He was in deadly earnest* (=completely serious).
4 VERY EFFECTIVE causing harm in a very effective way: *She hit the target with deadly accuracy.*
5 LIKE DEATH [only before noun] like death in appearance: *His face had a deadly paleness.*

deadly² *adv* **deadly serious/dull/boring etc** very serious, dull etc: *I'm deadly serious, this isn't a game!*

deadly ˈnightshade *n* [C,U] a poisonous European plant; ▤ **belladonna**

dead·pan /ˈdedpæn/ *adj* sounding and looking completely serious when you are saying or doing something funny: **deadpan voice/expression etc** *deadpan humour*

dead ˈreckoning *n* [U] calculating the position of a ship or aircraft without using the sun, moon, or stars

dead ˈringer *n* [C] someone who looks exactly like someone else: [+for] *Dave's a dead ringer for Paul McCartney.*

dead·weight, dead weight /ˈdedweɪt/ *n* [singular] **1** something that is very heavy and difficult to carry **2** someone or something that prevents you from making progress or being successful

dead ˈwood, dead·wood /ˈdedwʊd/ *n* [U]
1 people or things within an organization which are no longer useful or needed **2** branches of a tree which are no longer alive

deaf W3 /def/ *adj*
1 physically unable to hear anything or unable to hear well; → **hearing impaired**: *communication between deaf and hearing people* | *I think Mum's going a bit deaf.* | *She's* **deaf and dumb** (=unable to hear or speak) *and communicates using sign language.* | *Tom was born* **profoundly deaf** (=completely deaf). | **stone deaf/deaf as a post** *informal* (=completely deaf) → HARD OF HEARING, TONE-DEAF
2 the deaf [plural] people who are deaf: *a school for the deaf*
3 be deaf to sth *literary* to be unwilling to hear or listen to something: *She was deaf to his pleas.*
4 turn a deaf ear (to sth) to be unwilling to listen to what someone is saying or asking: *The factory owners turned a deaf ear to the demands of the workers.*
5 fall on deaf ears if advice or a warning falls on deaf ears, everyone ignores it —**deafness** *n* [U]

deaf·en /ˈdefən/ *v* [T usually passive] **1** if a noise deafens you, it is so loud that you cannot hear anything else **2** to make someone go deaf

deaf·en·ing /ˈdefənɪŋ/ *adj* **1** very loud: *a deafening roar* **2 deafening silence** a complete silence, when it is uncomfortable or you are expecting someone to say something

deaf ˈmute *n* [C] *old-fashioned, not polite* someone who is unable to hear or speak

deal¹ S1 W1 /diːl/ *n*
1 AGREEMENT [C] an agreement or arrangement, especially in business or politics, that helps both sides involved

make/do a deal
strike/cut a deal (=make a deal)
negotiate a deal
close/clinch a deal (=successfully complete a deal)
get a good deal (on sth) (=buy something at a good price)
business deal
pay deal
sth is a done deal *informal* (=something has been completely and finally agreed)

They **made a deal** *to sell the land to a property developer.* | [+with] *rumors that the company had* **struck a deal** *with Microsoft to market its products* | [+between] *Twelve US soldiers were released after a deal between the army and the guerillas.* | *Cash incentives worth almost £45 million helped to* **clinch the deal**. | *You can get some really* **good deals** *on the internet.* | *She and Branson have been discussing a possible* **business deal** *together.* | *The merger is still far from being* **a done deal**. | *a new band signing a major record deal*

2 a great deal also **a good deal** a large quantity of something; ▤ **a lot**: [+of] *It took a great deal of time and effort.* | *His work has been attracting a great deal of attention.* | **a great deal more/less etc** (=a lot more, less etc) *He knew a good deal more than I did.* | *She's married to a man a good deal older than herself.* ⚠ Only use **a great/good deal of** with uncountable nouns: *a great deal of time/money/work/interest/information*
3 TREATMENT [C usually singular] treatment of a particular type that is given or received: **a better/fairer etc deal** *a better deal for nurses* | *The prime minister promised farmers a* **new deal** (=a new and fairer system). | **a rough/raw deal** (=unfair treatment) *Women tend to get a raw deal from employers.*
4 it's a deal *spoken* used to say that you agree to do something: *OK, it's a deal.*
5 CARDS [singular] when you give out cards to players in a card game; → **dealer**: *It's your deal, Alison.*

▯**1** 000, ▯**2** 000, ▯**3** 000, most frequent words in ▯**S** poken and ▯**W** ritten English

6 WOOD [U] *BrE* FIR or PINE wood used for making things: *a deal table*

7 a deal of sth *old-fashioned* a large amount of something → BIG DEAL

deal² S1 W1 *v past tense and past participle* **dealt** /delt/

1 [I,T] also **deal sth** ⇔ **out** to give playing cards to each of the players in a game: *Whose turn is it to deal?*

2 [I] *informal* to buy and sell illegal drugs: *Many users end up dealing to support their habit.*

3 deal a blow (to sb/sth) to cause harm to someone or something – used in news reports: **deal a heavy/severe/serious etc blow** *The sanctions have dealt a severe blow to the local tourism industry.* | *This will deal a blow to consumer confidence.*

deal in *phr v*
1 deal in sth to buy and sell a particular type of product; → **dealer**: **deal in shares/securities etc** *investors dealing in stocks and shares* | **deal in drugs/stolen goods etc** *He then began dealing in heroin.* | **deal in antiques/second-hand books etc**
2 deal in sth to be interested or involved in something: *As a scientist, I do not deal in speculation.*
3 deal sb in to include someone in a game of cards

deal sth ⇔ **out** *phr v*
1 to give playing cards to each of the players in a game: *I began dealing out the cards.*
2 to decide what kind of punishment someone will get

deal with sb/sth *phr v*
1 to take the necessary action, especially in order to solve a problem; 🔲 **handle**: *an effective strategy for dealing with disruptive pupils* | *Don't worry, I'll deal with this.* | **deal with a problem/issue/matter etc** *The council has failed to deal with the problem of homelessness in the city.* | **deal effectively/adequately etc with sth** *They should deal properly and fairly with any complaint.*
2 if a book, speech etc deals with a particular subject, it is about that subject: *These ideas are dealt with more fully in Chapter Four.*
3 to do business with someone or have a business connection with someone: *Most travel agents do not deal directly with these companies.*
4 to succeed in controlling your feelings about an emotional problem so that it does not affect your life; 🔲 **cope with**: *How's he dealing with the whole thing?*

deal·er W3 /'di:lə $ -ər/ *n* [C]
1 someone who buys and sells a particular product, especially an expensive one: **car/antique/art etc dealer** | [+in] *a dealer in modern art*
2 someone who sells illegal drugs
3 someone who gives out playing cards in a game

deal·er·ship /'di:ləʃɪp $ -ər-/ *n* [C] a business that sells a particular company's product, especially cars

deal·ing /'di:lɪŋ/ *n* **1 dealings** [plural] the business activities or relationships that someone is involved in: *an investigation of his financial dealings* | [+with] *She is ruthless in her dealings with competitors.* | *We've had dealings with him in the past.* **2** [U] the activity of buying, selling, or doing business with people: *penalties for drug dealing* | **plain/honest/fair dealing** (=a particular way of doing business) *a reputation for fair dealing* → **insider dealing** at INSIDER TRADING; → WHEELING AND DEALING

dealt /delt/ the past tense and past participle of DEAL

dean /di:n/ *n* [C] **1** a priest of high rank in the Christian church who is in charge of several priests or churches **2** someone in a university who is responsible for a particular area of work: *the admissions dean* **3** *AmE* someone with a lot of experience of a particular job or subject; 🔲 **doyen** *BrE*: [+of] *Neier is the dean of American human rights activism.*

dean·e·ry /'di:nəri/ *n plural* **deaneries** [C] the area controlled by a dean or the place where a dean lives

'dean's list *n* [C] *AmE* a list of the best students at a university

dear¹ S1 /dɪə $ dɪr/ *interjection* **Oh dear** used to show that you are surprised, upset, or annoyed because something bad has happened: *Oh dear, I've broken the lamp.* | *'I think I'm getting a cold.' 'Oh dear!'*

dear² S2 *n* [C]
1 used when speaking to someone you love: *How did the interview go, dear?*
2 *spoken* used by an older person when speaking in a friendly way to someone who is younger: *Can I help you, dear?* | *Come along, my dear, take a seat.*
3 *BrE spoken* someone who is kind and helpful: *Be a dear and make me a coffee.*
4 old dear *BrE* a fairly rude expression meaning an old woman

dear³ S2 W2 *adj comparative* **dearer**, *superlative* **dearest**
1 Dear used before someone's name or title to begin a letter: *Dear Sir or Madam, ...* | *Dear Mrs. Wilson, ...* | *Dear Meg, ...*
2 *BrE* expensive; 🔲 **cheap**: *Cars are 59% dearer in Britain than in Europe.*
3 *formal* a dear friend or relative is very important to you and you love them a lot: *Mark became a dear friend.* | **be dear to sb** *His sister was very dear to him.*
4 hold sth dear to think that something is very important: *Household economy was something my mother held very dear.*
5 dear old... *BrE spoken* used to describe someone or something in a way that shows your love or liking of them; 🔲 **good old**: *Here we are, back in dear old Manchester!*
6 for dear life *written* if you run, fight, hold on etc for dear life, you do it as fast or as well as you can because you are afraid: *She grasped the side of the boat and hung on for dear life.*
7 the dear departed *BrE literary* a person you love who has died

dear⁴ *adv* **cost sb dear** *written* to cause a lot of trouble and suffering for someone: *Carolyn's marriage to Pete cost her dear.*

dear·est /'dɪərɪ̈st $ 'dɪr-/ *n spoken* used when speaking to someone you love

dear·ie, **deary** /'dɪəri $ 'dɪr-/ *n spoken informal* **1** used when speaking to someone you love **2 dearie me** *old-fashioned* used when you are surprised or sad about something

,dear 'John ,letter *n* [C] *old-fashioned* a letter that a man receives from his wife or girlfriend that tells him she no longer loves him

dear·ly /'dɪəli $ 'dɪrli/ *adv* **1** very much: *James loved her dearly.* | *I would dearly like to know what she said.* **2** in a way that involves a lot of suffering, damage, trouble etc: *The weakness in their defense has already cost them dearly this season.* | *Ordinary people are paying dearly for the mistakes of this administration.* **3 dearly beloved** *spoken* used by a priest or minister at the beginning of a Christian service

dearth /dɜːθ $ dɜːrθ/ *n* [singular] a lack of something: [+of] *a dearth of job opportunities*

dear·y /'dɪəri $ 'dɪri/ *n* another spelling of DEARIE

death S1 W1 /deθ/ *n*
1 a) [U] the end of the life of a person or animal; 🔲 **birth**: [+of] *The death of his mother came as a tremendous shock.* | *Cancer is the leading cause of death in women.* | *How Danielle met her death* (=died) *will probably never be known.* | *His friend was close to death.* | *His family are still mourning John's tragic death.* | *the anniversary of Lenin's death* | **bleed/burn/starve etc to death** *a homeless man who froze to death* | **beat/stab/shoot etc sb to death** *The 76-year-old pensioner was beaten to death.* | **put/sentence/condemn sb to death** (=kill someone or decide they should be killed as an official punishment) *Legend has it that Sarah was put to death for practising witchcraft.* | *Members of the family have received **death threats**.* | *He remained*

*esident until his **untimely death** (=death at a surprisingly young age) in 1917.* | *Two of the passengers managed to **escape death*** (=avoid being killed). **b)** [C] a particular case when someone dies; ⧫ **birth**: *a campaign to reduce the number of traffic deaths* | [+**from**] *deaths from cancer* | *I heard there'd been a **death in the family**.*
2 the death of sth the permanent end of something; ⧫ **birth**: *The latest bombing is the death of all our hopes.* | *These regulations could **spell the death** (=lead to the end) of the American car industry.*
3 to death *informal* **a)** used to emphasize that a feeling or emotion is very strong: **be bored/scared/frightened etc to death** *She was scared to death of what might happen next.* | *I'm absolutely **sick to death of** it* (=very angry, bored, or unhappy about something). | **bore/scare/love etc sb to death** *He drove at a speed which frightened Leonora to death.* | *She used to worry me to death.* **b)** used to say that an action is continued with a lot of effort and for as long as possible: *They just **work you to death** in that place.*
4 do sth to death *informal* to perform or present an idea, joke etc so often that people become tired of it: *Most of his material has been done to death by numerous comedians.*
5 to the death a) until someone is dead: *They will **fight to the death** rather than give an inch of ground.* | *soldiers locked in a bitter struggle to the death* **b)** until you achieve something even if it means that you suffer: *The leadership election has become a fight to the death.*
6 Death a creature that looks like a human SKELETON, used in paintings, stories etc to represent the fact that people die
7 be at death's door to be very ill and likely to die
8 look/feel like death warmed up *BrE*; **look/feel like death warmed over** *AmE informal* to look or feel very ill or tired
9 you'll catch your death (of cold) *spoken old-fashioned* used to warn someone that they are likely to become ill because they are wet or cold
10 sb will be the death of me *spoken old-fashioned* used to say that someone is causing you a lot of worry and problems: *That boy will be the death of me!* ⧫ BLACK DEATH; → **kiss of death** at KISS² (3); → **life and death** at LIFE (10)

death·bed /ˈdeθbed/ *n* [C usually singular] the bed on which someone dies or is dying: **on your deathbed** *On her deathbed, Miriam's mother reveals that she never knew her father.* | **deathbed confession/conversion etc** (=made when you are dying) *The disease allowed no time for a deathbed repentance.*

'death blow *n* [singular] an action or event that makes something fail or end; → **death knell**: *His decision to leave the show has **delivered a death blow** to the series.*

'death camp *n* [C] a place where large numbers of prisoners are killed or die, usually in a war

'death cer,tificate *n* [C] a legal document, signed by a doctor, that states the time and cause of someone's death; → **birth certificate**

'death-de,fying *adj* [only before noun] a death-defying action is very dangerous: *death-defying film stunts*

'death ,duties *n* [plural] *BrE old-fashioned* INHERITANCE TAX

'death knell *n* [singular] a sign that something will soon fail or stop existing; → **death blow**: **(sound/strike/toll) the death knell for/of sth** *The loss of Georgia would sound the death knell of Republican hopes.*

death·less /ˈdeθləs/ *adj* **deathless prose/verse/lines etc** writing that is very bad or boring – used humorously

death·ly /ˈdeθli/ *adj, adv* reminding you of death or of a dead body: **deathly cold/white/pale** *She was deathly pale, and looked as if she might faint.* | **a deathly hush/silence** (=complete silence) *A deathly hush fell over the room.*

'death mask *n* [C] a model of a dead person's face, made by covering their face with a soft substance and letting it become hard

'death ,penalty *n* [singular] the legal punishment of death; → **capital punishment**: *Three Britons are facing the death penalty for spying.*

'death rate *n* [C] **1** the number of deaths for every 100 or every 1000 people in a particular year and in a particular place; → **birth rate 2** the number of deaths each year from a particular disease or in a particular group: *childhood death rates*

'death ,rattle *n* [C] a noise that sometimes comes from the throat or chest of someone who is dying

death row /,deθ ˈrəʊ $ -ˈroʊ/ *n* [U] the part of a prison where prisoners who will be punished by being killed are kept: **on death row** *a murderer on death row*

'death ,sentence *n* [C] **1** the official punishment of death, ordered by a judge: *He received a **death sentence**.* | *Premeditated murder **carries** (=is punished by) the death sentence.* **2** something such as an illness that makes you sure you will die: *Cancer is no longer a death sentence.* **3** an action or decision that is very harmful to someone or something: *In 1987, the government **passed** a **death sentence on** the river by granting permission for the new dam.*

'death's head *n* [C] *literary* a human SKULL, used as a sign of death

'death squad *n* [C] a group of people who have been ordered to kill someone's political opponents

'death throes *n* [plural] **1** the final stages before something fails or ends: *The peace pact seems to be **in its death throes**.* **2** sudden violent movements that people sometimes make when they are dying

'death toll *n* [C usually singular] the total number of people who die in an accident, war etc: *As the unrest continued, the **death toll rose**.* | *The official **death toll stands at** 53.*

'death trap *n* [C] *informal* a vehicle, building, piece of equipment etc that is in very bad condition and might injure or kill someone: *A car with tires in this condition is simply a death trap.*

'death ,warrant *n* [C] **1** an official document stating that someone is to be killed as a punishment **2** something that is likely to cause you very serious trouble, or even your death: *By indulging in casual sex, many teenagers could be **signing** their **own death warrants**.*

'death wish *n* [singular] a desire to die: *Before I did the jump, people would ask if I **had a death wish**.*

deb /deb/ *n* [C] *informal* a DEBUTANTE

de·ba·cle, débâcle /deɪˈbɑːkəl, dɪ-/ *n* [C] an event or situation that is a complete failure: *the debacle of the 1994 elections*

de·bar /dɪˈbɑː $ -ˈbɑːr/ *v* **debarred, debarring** [T usually passive] *formal* to officially prevent someone from doing something; ⧫ **ban**: **debar sb from (doing) sth** *All five men were debarred from entering France for three years.*

de·bark /dɪˈbɑːk $ -ˈbɑːrk/ *v* [I] to DISEMBARK (=get off a ship): [+**from**] *I remember how glad I felt debarking from a ship in Bremerhaven after six days on the ocean.*

de·base /dɪˈbeɪs/ *v* [T] *formal* to make someone or something lose its value or people's respect: *The medical profession has been debased by these revelations.* | **debase yourself** *actors who debased themselves by participating in the show* | **debase a currency/coinage** (=reduce its value) —**debasement** *n* [C,U]: *currency debasement*

de·bat·a·ble /dɪˈbeɪtəbəl/ *adj* things that are deba...able are not certain because people have differ... opinions about them: *a **debatable point** | it is de**... able whether/how etc** It's debatable whether this bo... as good as her last.* | *Whether the object was us... rituals is **highly debatable**.*

de·bate¹ [S1] [W2] /dɪ'beɪt/ n

1 [C,U] discussion of a particular subject that often continues for a long time and in which people express different opinions

heated/fierce/intense debate (=one in which people express strong and very different opinions)
widespread debate
lively debate
public debate
a debate rages (=it happens over a period of time and people have strong feelings about it)
long-running debate
ongoing debate (=continuing debate)
provoke/trigger/spark off a debate (=cause a debate)

the gun-control debate in the US | The new drug has become the subject of **heated debate** within the medical profession. | [+over/about] There has been **widespread public debate** over the introduction of genetically modified food. | There was much **lively debate** about whether women should spend more time in the home. | A fierce **debate raged** over which artist's work should be chosen for the prize. | [+between] the **ongoing debate** between environmentalists and the road-building lobby over the future of our countryside | Nuclear power has always been a topic that has **sparked off** considerable **debate**.

2 [C,U] a formal discussion of a particular problem, subject etc in which people express different opinions, and sometimes vote on them: [+on/over/about] a debate on legalized gambling | a **televised debate** | have/hold/conduct a debate It would have been better to hold the debate during the day. | be under debate What topics are under debate in Congress this week?
3 be open to debate also **be a matter for debate** if an idea is open to debate, no one has proved yet whether it is true or false; ◻ debatable: Whether that would have made any difference is open to debate.
debate² v [I,T] **1** to discuss a subject formally when you are trying to make a decision or find a solution: The issue will be debated on Tuesday. | debate whether/what/how etc Meanwhile, philosophers debate whether it's right to clone an individual. | debate (sth) with sb an invitation to debate with William on the future of democracy | His conclusions are hotly debated (=argued about strongly). **2** to consider something carefully before making a decision: debate with yourself I debated with myself whether I should tell anyone. | debate who/what/how etc I'm still debating what to do. | debate doing sth For a moment Mary debated telling Rick the truth.
de·bat·er /dɪ'beɪtə $ -ər/ n [C] someone who speaks in a formal debate
de·bauched /dɪ'bɔːtʃt $ -'bɒːtʃt, -'bɑːtʃt/ adj formal someone who is debauched behaves in a bad or immoral way, for example by drinking too much alcohol, taking drugs, or having sex with many people
de·bauch·e·ry /dɪ'bɔːtʃəri $ dɪ'bɒː-, dɪ'bɑː-/ n [U] formal immoral behaviour involving drugs, alcohol, sex etc: a life of debauchery
de·ben·ture /dɪ'bentʃə $ -ər/ n [C] technical an official document produced by a company showing how much INTEREST it will pay on a LOAN (=money it has borrowed)
de·bil·i·tate /dɪ'bɪlɪteɪt/ v [T] formal **1** to make someone ill and weak **2** to make an organization or system less effective or powerful: Progress has been debilitated by a refusal to share ideas. —debilitating adj: a debilitating disease
de·bil·i·ty /dɪ'bɪlɪti/ n plural debilities [C,U] formal weakness, especially as the result of illness; → disability: physical and mental debility
deb·it¹ /'debɪt/ n [C] **1** technical a decrease in the amount of money in a bank account, for example because you have taken money out of it; ◻ credit; → direct debit **2** technical a record in financial

accounts that shows money that has been spent or that is owed; ◻ credit **3 on the debit side** used to say that something is a disadvantage in a particular situation, especially after you have described the advantages: Bikes are easy to park, but on the debit side can be dangerous in traffic.
debit² v [T] technical **1** to take money out of a bank account; ◻ credit: debit sth from sth The sum of £25 has been debited from your account. **2** to record in financial accounts the money that has been spent or that is owed: debit sth against/to sth Purchases are debited against the client's account.
'debit card n [C] a plastic card with your signature on that you can use to pay for things. The money is taken directly from your bank account → CASH CARD, CHEQUE CARD, CREDIT CARD
'debit note; **'debit re,ceipt** AmE n [C] a written record showing that a customer owes money to a company
deb·o·nair /,debə'neə◂ $ -'ner/ adj old-fashioned a man who is debonair is fashionable and confident
de·brief /,diː'briːf/ v [T] to ask someone questions about a job they have just done or an experience they have just had, in order to gather information; → brief: The returning bomber crews were debriefed. —debriefing n [U]: a debriefing session
deb·ris /'debriː, 'deɪ- $ də'briː, deɪ-/ n [U] **1** the pieces of something that are left after it has been destroyed in an accident, explosion etc: She was hit by flying debris from the blast. **2** technical pieces of waste material, paper etc: plant/garden/industrial etc debris Clean the ventilation ducts to remove dust and insect debris.
debt [S2] [W2] /det/ n
1 [C] a sum of money that a person or organization owes: [+of] This over-ambitious strategy has saddled them with debts of around $3,000,000. | pay (off)/repay/clear/settle etc a debt He had enough money to pay off his father's outstanding debts. | Romania is paying more and more to Western banks simply to service the debt (=pay it). | run up/amass debts students who run up huge debts
2 [U] when you owe money to someone; ◻ credit: in debt (to sb) Nearly half the students said they were in debt. | The band will be in debt to the record company for years. | £200/$1000 etc in debt A rash business decision left him $600 in debt. | get/run/fall etc into debt The club sank deeper into debt. | be heavily/deeply in debt (=owe a lot of money)
3 [C usually singular] the degree to which you have learned from or been influenced by someone or something else: [+to] Braque acknowledged his debt to Impressionist painting.
4 debt of gratitude/thanks the fact of being grateful to someone who has helped you: I owe a debt of gratitude to my tutors. → BAD DEBT, NATIONAL DEBT
'debt col,lector n [C] someone whose job is to get back the money that people owe
debt·or /'detə $ -ər/ n [C] technical a person, group, or organization that owes money; ◻ creditor
'debt re,lief n [U] an arrangement in which very poor countries do not have to pay back all the money that has been lent to them by richer countries
'debt-,ridden adj [usually before noun] debt-ridden countries or organizations owe so much money they cannot pay the money back
de·bug /,diː'bʌg/ v debugged, debugging [T] **1** to remove the BUGS (=mistakes) from a computer program; → disinfect **2** to remove secret listening equipment from a place —debugging n [U]
de·bunk /,diː'bʌŋk/ v [T] to show that an idea or belief is false: His claims were later debunked by fellow academics. —debunker n [C]
de·but¹ /'deɪbjuː, 'deb- $ deɪ'bjuː, dɪ-/ n [C] the first public appearance of an entertainer, sports player etc or of something new and important: sb's debut He

made his Major League **debut** as shortstop. | **film/ acting/directorial etc debut** His Broadway debut was 'The Scarlet Pimpernel'. | **debut album/CD/single etc** Their debut album was recorded in 1991. | **debut match/ performance etc** He scored in his debut match for the club.

debut² v **1** [I] to appear in public or become available for the first time: The show will debut next Monday at 8.00pm. **2** [T] to introduce a product to the public for the first time; → **release**; ▤ **launch**: Ralph Lauren debuted his autumn collection in Paris last week.

deb·u·tante /'debjʊtɑːnt/ also **deb** informal n [C] a young rich UPPER-CLASS woman who starts going to fashionable events as a way of being introduced to upperclass society

Dec. also **Dec** BrE the written abbreviation of December

deca- /dekə/ prefix [in nouns] ten: a decalitre (=10 litres) | the decathlon (=a sports competition with 10 different events) → DECI-

dec·ade S3 W2 /'dekeɪd, de'keɪd/ n [C] a period of 10 years

dec·a·dence /'dekədəns/ n [U] behaviour that shows that someone has low moral standards and is more concerned with pleasure than serious matters

dec·a·dent /'dekədənt/ adj having low moral standards and being more concerned with pleasure than serious matters: Pop music was condemned as decadent and crude. —**decadently** adv

de·caf, decaff /'diːkæf/ n [U] informal decaffeinated coffee

de·caf·fein·a·ted /diːˈkæfɪneɪtᵻd/ adj coffee or tea that is decaffeinated does not contain CAFFEINE (=the substance that keeps you awake)

de·cal /'diːkæl, 'de- $ diːˈkæl, 'dekəl/ n [C] AmE a piece of paper with a pattern or picture on it that you stick on a surface; ▤ **transfer** BrE

de·camp /dɪˈkæmp/ v [I] formal to leave a place quickly: [+to/from] The wealthier inhabitants decamped to the suburbs.

de·cant /dɪˈkænt/ v [T] to pour liquid, especially wine, from one container into another: **decant sth into sth** Never decant cleaning products into old pop bottles.

de·cant·er /dɪˈkæntə $ -ər/ n [C] a container used for serving alcoholic drinks: a crystal decanter

de·cap·i·tate /dɪˈkæpɪteɪt/ v [T] to cut off someone's head: a decapitated body —**decapitation** /dɪˌkæpɪˈteɪʃən/ n [C,U]

de·cath·lon /dɪˈkæθlɒn, -lən $ -lɑːn, -lən/ n [singular] a sports competition with 10 different events; → **pentathlon, triathlon**

de·cay¹ /dɪˈkeɪ/ v **1** [I,T] to be slowly destroyed by a natural chemical process, or to make something do this; → **rot**: Her body was already starting to decay. | Most archaeological finds are broken, damaged, or decayed. | decaying organic matter **2** [I] if buildings, structures, or areas decay, their condition gradually becomes worse: Hundreds of historic buildings are being allowed to decay. | Britain's decaying inner cities **3** [I] if traditional beliefs, standards etc decay, people do not believe in them or support them any more; ▤ **decline**: In Orthodox Europe, mass religion seems to have decayed less.

decay² n [U] **1** the natural chemical change that causes the slow destruction of something: old cars in various **stages of decay** | tooth decay **2** the gradual destruction of buildings, structures etc because they have not been cared for: poverty and urban decay | **fall into (a state of) decay** During the war, the area fell into decay. **3** the gradual destruction of ideas, beliefs, social or political systems etc: moral and spiritual decay

de·cease /dɪˈsiːs/ n [U] law death: On your decease, the house passes to your wife.

de·ceased /dɪˈsiːst/ n law **the deceased** someone who has died, especially recently: The deceased left a large sum of money to his children.

de·ceit /dɪˈsiːt/ n [C,U] behaviour that is intended to make someone believe something that is not true: an atmosphere of hypocrisy and deceit | **deliberate/calculated/outright deceit**

de·ceit·ful /dɪˈsiːtfəl/ adj someone who is deceitful tells lies in order to get what they want: His manner was sly and deceitful. —**deceitfully** adv: His lawyer argued that his client had not **acted deceitfully**. —**deceitfulness** n [U]

de·ceive /dɪˈsiːv/ v [T] **1** to make someone believe something that is not true; ▤ **trick**; → **deception**: He had been deceived by a young man claiming to be the son of a millionaire. | **deceive sb into doing sth** He tried to deceive the public into thinking the war could still be won. | **deceive sb about sth** I wouldn't deceive you about anything as important as this. **2 deceive yourself** to refuse to believe that something is true because the truth is unpleasant: I thought she loved me, but I was deceiving myself. | **deceive yourself that** He didn't deceive himself that he and Ruth could remain friends. **3** to give someone a wrong belief or opinion about something: Don't be deceived by the new cover – this is a rehash of old hits. —**deceiver** n [C]

de·cel·e·rate /ˌdiːˈseləreɪt/ v [I] formal to go slower, especially in a vehicle; ▤ **slow down**; ◫ **accelerate** —**deceleration** /ˌdiːseləˈreɪʃən/ n [U]: a deceleration in economic growth

De·cem·ber /dɪˈsembə $ -ər/ n [C,U] written abbreviation **Dec.** the 12th month of the year, between November and January: **next/last December** Last December they visited Prague. | **in December** We got married in December. | **on December 6th** Jake's birthday is on December 6th. | **on 6th December** BrE: The event was to take place on 6th December. | **December 6** AmE: Her letter arrived December 6.

de·cen·cy /'diːsənsi/ n **1** [U] polite, honest, and moral behaviour and attitudes that show respect for other people: a judgment reflecting the decency and good sense of the American people | **common/human/public decency** (=standards of behaviour that are expected of everyone) The film was banned on the grounds of public decency. | Is there no **sense of decency** left in this country? | If they're going to charge people a fee, they ought to at least **have the decency to** tell them in advance. **2 decencies** [plural] old-fashioned standards of acceptable behaviour

de·cent S2 /'diːsənt/ adj

1 [usually before noun] of a good enough standard or quality: a decent salary | Don't you have a decent jacket? | a house with a **decent-sized** yard | Their in-flight magazine is actually halfway decent (=quite good).

2 following moral standards that are acceptable to society; → **decency**: **decent citizens/people/folk etc** The majority of residents here are decent citizens. | a decent burial | Paul visited the local bars more frequently than was decent for a senior lecturer. | The chairman **did the decent thing** (=did what people thought he ought to) and resigned.

3 [usually before noun] treating people in a fair and kind way: I decided her father was a decent guy after all. | **It was decent of** you to show up today.

4 wearing enough clothes so that you do not show too much of your body – used humorously: Are you decent? Can I come in? —**decently** adv

de·cen·tral·ize also **-ise** BrE /ˌdiːˈsentrəlaɪz/ v [I,T] to move parts of a government, organization etc from a central place to several different smaller ones; ◫ **centralize**: Many firms are decentralizing their operations. —**decentralized** adj: a decentralized economy —**decentralization** /diːˌsentrəlaɪˈzeɪʃən $ -lə-/ n [U]

de·cep·tion /dɪˈsepʃən/ n [C,U] the act of deliberately making someone believe something that is not true; → **deceive**: *She didn't have the courage to admit to her deception.* | *He was convicted of obtaining money by deception.*

de·cep·tive /dɪˈseptɪv/ adj **1** something that is deceptive seems to be one thing but is in fact very different: *Some snakes move with deceptive speed* (=move faster than you think or expect). | *Gwen's students may look angelic, but appearances can be deceptive.* **2** intended to make someone believe something that is not true: *misleading and deceptive adverts* | *deceptive practices* —**deceptively** adv

deci- /desɪ/ prefix [in nouns] a 10th part of a unit: *a decilitre* (=0.1 litres) → **DECA-**

dec·i·bel /ˈdesɪˌbel,-bəl/ n [C] written abbreviation *dB* a unit for measuring the loudness of sound: *noise levels exceeding 85 decibels*

de·cide ⟨S1⟩ ⟨W1⟩ /dɪˈsaɪd/ v
1 [I,T] to make a choice or judgment about something, especially after considering all the possibilities or arguments; → **decision**: *Has anything been decided yet?* | **decide to do sth** *Tina's decided to go to Prague for her holidays.* | **decide (that)** *It was decided that four hospitals should close.* | **decide who/what/whether etc** *I can't decide whether I like him or not.* | *People have a right to decide how to spend their own money.* | **decide between sth** *A meeting was called to decide between the three candidates.* | **decide for yourself** (=make your own decision) *You must decide for yourself.* | *The trainees decide among themselves what programs to take.* | **decide against/in favour of (doing) sth** *He eventually decided against telling Georgina.* | *After a long discussion, they decided in favour of* (=chose) *the younger applicant.*
2 [T] to influence a situation or event so that a particular result is produced: *It was the penalty kick that decided the match.*
3 [T] to be the reason for someone making a particular choice: *Taxes could be the deciding factor for millions of floating voters.* | **decide sb to do sth** *The look he gave her decided her not to ask.*
4 [I,T] law to make an official or legal judgment: *The Commission will have the power to decide disputes.* | **decide in favour of/against sb** *If the Parole Board decides in his favour, the prisoner will be released.*
  decide on/upon sth phr v
to choose something or someone after thinking carefully: *Have you decided on a date for the wedding?*

de·cid·ed /dɪˈsaɪdɪd/ adj [only before noun] formal definite and easily noticed: *a decided change for the better*

de·cid·ed·ly /dɪˈsaɪdɪdli/ adv **1** [+ adj/adv] definitely or in a way that is easily noticed: *Cole's style is decidedly more formal than the previous manager's.* **2** BrE written in a way that shows that you are very sure about a decision: *'I'm not going to do it,' said Margaret decidedly.*

de·cid·er /dɪˈsaɪdə $ -ər/ n [C usually singular] the last part of a game or competition, which will show who the winner is: *This next round will be the decider.*

de·cid·u·ous /dɪˈsɪdʒuəs/ adj deciduous trees lose their leaves in winter; ☒ **evergreen**

dec·i·mal[1] /ˈdesɪməl/ n [C] a FRACTION (=a number less than 1) that is shown as a FULL STOP followed by the number of TENTHS, HUNDREDTHS etc. The numbers 0.5, 0.175, and 0.661 are decimals

decimal[2] adj a decimal system is based on the number 10: *changing to a decimal system* | *calculations accurate to three decimal places* (=one of the numbers after the full stop in a decimal)

dec·i·mal·iza·tion also **-isation** BrE /ˌdesɪməlaɪˈzeɪʃən $ ˌdesɪmələ-/ n [U] the process of changing to a decimal system of money or measurement —**decimalize** /ˈdesɪməlaɪz $ ˈdesəmə-/ v [I,T]

decimal ˈpoint n [C] the FULL STOP in a decimal, used to separate whole numbers from TENTHS, HUNDREDTHS etc

dec·i·mate /ˈdesɪmeɪt/ v [T] to destroy a large part of something: *The population has been decimated by disease.* —**decimation** /ˌdesɪˈmeɪʃən/ n [U]

de·ci·pher /dɪˈsaɪfə $ -ər/ v [T] **1** to find the meaning of something that is difficult to read or understand; → **indecipherable**: *She studied the envelope, trying to decipher the handwriting.* **2** to change a message written in a CODE into ordinary language so that you can read it; ☒ **decode** —**decipherment** n [U]

de·ci·sion ⟨S1⟩ ⟨W1⟩ /dɪˈsɪʒən/ n
1 [C] a choice or judgment that you make after a period of discussion or thought

> **make a decision**
> **take a decision** (=make an important decision, especially after considering carefully)
> **reach/come to a decision**
> **a big/major decision**
> **a difficult/hard/tough etc decision**
> **decision to do sth**
> **the right/wrong decision**
> **reverse/overturn a decision** (=officially change an earlier decision)
> **sb's decision is final** (=it cannot be changed)
> **a snap decision** (=one made extremely quickly)

> *Do you ever wonder if you **made** the right **decision**?* | *No final **decision** has been **taken**, but it seems likely that the two companies could merge in the near future.* | [+about/on] *We finally **came to a** firm **decision** on the matter.* | *They can help with decisions about where to invest your money.* | *I need to think about it. It's a **big decision**.* | *All managers face **tough decisions** at one time or another.* | *She refused to discuss her **decision to** quit the group.* | [+as to which/whether/who etc] *Viewers make the final decision as to who should be eliminated from the competition.* | *The Supreme Court has **overturned** the lower court's **decision**.* | *The judges' **decision** is **final**.* | *She made a **snap decision**, which was to have fatal consequences.* | *What were the reasons behind your decision?*

2 [U] the quality someone has that makes them able to make choices or judgments quickly and confidently; ☒ **indecision**: *the ability to act with speed and decision* **3** [U] the act of deciding something: *The Court has the ultimate power of decision.*

de·ˈcision-ˌmaker n [C usually plural] a person in a large organization who is responsible for making important decisions: *the corporation's key decision-makers*

de·ˈcision-ˌmaking n [U] the process of making important decisions: *attempts to involve workers in decision-making*

de·ci·sive /dɪˈsaɪsɪv/ adj **1** an action, event etc that is decisive has a big effect on the way that something develops: **decisive factor/effect/influence etc** *Women can **play a decisive role** in the debate over cloning.* | **decisive action/steps** *We will **take decisive steps** towards political union with Europe.* **2** someone who is decisive is good at making decisions quickly and with confidence; ☒ **indecisive**: *a decisive leader* | *a talent for quick **decisive action*** **3** definite and clear in a way that leaves no doubt: **decisive victory/result/defeat etc** | *The answer was a decisive no.* —**decisively** adv: *Yet again, we have failed to act decisively.* —**decisiveness** n [U]: *military decisiveness* | *the speed and decisiveness of his victory*

deck[1] /dek/ n [C]
1 ON A SHIP a) the outside top level of a ship that you can walk on or sit on: *Let's go up on deck.* | **above/below deck** *Peter stayed below deck.* **b)** one of the different levels on a ship: **main/passenger/car etc deck** *a staircase leading to the passenger deck*
2 ON A BUS, PLANE ETC one of the levels on a bus, plane etc: **lower/upper etc deck** *I managed to find a seat on the upper deck.* | *Eddie returned to the flight deck*

(=the part of an aircraft where the pilot sits). → DOUBLE-DECKER (1), SINGLE-DECKER
3 AT THE BACK OF A HOUSE AmE a wooden floor built out from the back of a house, where you can sit and relax outdoors; → **decking**: deck furniture
4 MUSIC a piece of equipment used for playing music tapes, records etc: cassette/tape/record deck
5 CARDS a set of playing cards; ▭ pack BrE: Irene shuffled the deck. | a deck of cards → all hands on deck at HAND¹ (38); → clear the decks at CLEAR² (17); → hit the deck at HIT¹ (17)

deck² v [T] **1** also **deck sth out** [usually passive] to decorate something with flowers, flags etc: deck sth (out) with sth The street was decked with flags for the royal wedding. **2** informal to hit someone so hard that they fall over: Gerry just swung round and decked him.

deck·chair /'dektʃeə $ -tʃer/ n [C] BrE a folding chair with a long seat made of cloth, used especially on the beach → see picture at CHAIR

deck·hand /'dekhænd/ n [C] someone who works on a ship, cleaning and doing small repairs

deck·ing /'dekɪŋ/ n [U] a wooden floor next to a house or in a garden

deck shoe n [C] a flat shoe made of CANVAS (=heavy cloth)

de·claim /dɪ'kleɪm/ v [I,T] written to speak loudly, sometimes with actions, so that people notice you —**declamation** /ˌdeklə'meɪʃən/ n [C,U]

de·clam·a·to·ry /dɪ'klæmətəri $ -tɔːri/ adj declamatory speech or writing expresses feelings and opinions very strongly: a declamatory style

dec·la·ra·tion W3 /ˌdeklə'reɪʃən/ n [C,U]
1 an important official statement about a particular situation or plan, or the act of making this statement: a ceasefire declaration | Under Islamic law it was possible to divorce by simple declaration. | [+of] the declaration of war
2 an official or serious statement of what someone believes: [+of] the United Nations Declaration of Human Rights | declarations of undying love
3 a statement in which you officially give information about yourself: a declaration of taxable earnings

de·clar·a·tive /dɪ'klærətɪv/ adj a declarative sentence has the form of a statement

de·clare W2 /dɪ'kleə $ -'kler/ v
1 STATE OFFICIALLY [T] to state officially and publicly that a particular situation exists or that something is true: A state of emergency has been declared. | declare that The court declared that Brown's case should be reviewed. | declare sth (to be) sth Several countries wanted Antarctica to be declared a 'world park'. | The city was declared to be in a state of siege. | I declare you man and wife. | declare sth illegal/invalid etc The war was declared illegal by the International Court of Justice. | Mr Steel has been **declared bankrupt** (=it has been officially stated that he cannot pay his debts.) | We celebrate September 16, the day when Mexico **declared independence** from Spain (=officially stated that it was no longer ruled by Spain).
2 STATE WHAT YOU THINK [T] to say publicly what you think or feel: 'It's not fair,' Jane declared. | He **declared** his **intention** to stand for president. | declare that Carol held a press conference and declared that she was innocent. | declare yourself (to be) sth Edward declared himself angry and frustrated.
3 declare war (on sb/sth) a) to state officially that you are at war with another country **b)** informal to say that something is wrong and that you will do everything you can to stop it: Angry residents have declared war on the owners of the factory.
4 MONEY/PROPERTY ETC [T] **a)** to state on an official government form how much money you have earned, what property you own etc: All tips are counted as part of your earnings and must be declared. **b)** to tell a CUSTOMS official that you are carrying goods on which you should pay tax when you enter a country
5 declare an interest to tell people that you are con-

nected with something that is being discussed: I should, at this point, declare an interest: I own shares in the company.
6 CRICKET [I] to choose to end your team's turn before all your players have BATTED
declare against sb/sth phr v
to state that you oppose someone or something
declare for sb/sth phr v
to state that you support someone or something

de·clared /dɪ'kleəd $ -'klerd/ adj stated officially and publicly: **declared aim/objective/intention etc** It is their declared intention to increase taxes.

de·clas·si·fied /ˌdiː'klæsˌfaɪd/ adj official information that is declassified was secret but is not secret any more; → classified —**declassify** v [T]

de·clen·sion /dɪ'klenʃən/ n [C] **1** the set of various forms that a noun, PRONOUN, or adjective can have according to whether it is the SUBJECT, OBJECT etc of a sentence in a language such as Latin or German **2** a particular set of nouns etc that all have the same set of forms

de·cline¹ W2 /dɪ'klaɪn/ n [singular, U] a decrease in the quality, quantity, or importance of something: [+in] There has been a decline in the size of families. | [+of] the decline of manufacturing | **rapid/sharp/steep/dramatic** decline a rapid decline in unemployment | **steady/gradual/long-term** decline The island's population initially numbered 180, but there was a gradual decline until only 40 people were left. | the social and **economic decline** faced by many cities | **in decline** There's a widely held belief that educational standards are in decline (=falling). | **fall/go etc into decline** The port fell into decline (=became less important and less busy) in the 1950s.

decline² W3 v
1 DECREASE [I] to decrease in quantity or importance: Spending on information technology has declined. | Car sales have declined by a quarter. | After the war, the city declined in importance.
2 SAY NO [I,T] formal to say no politely when someone invites you somewhere, offers you something, or wants you to do something: Offered the position of chairman, Smith declined, preferring to keep his current job. | Mary declined a hot drink and went to her room. | **decline an offer/invitation etc** Mary declined Jay's invitation to dinner. | **decline to do sth** The court declined to review her case. | The minister **declined to comment** (=refused to speak to people who report the news) about the progress of the peace talks.
3 BECOME WORSE [I] to become gradually worse in quality; ▭ deteriorate: Her health has been declining progressively for several months. | Qualified staff are leaving and standards are declining.
4 sb's declining years formal the last years of someone's life
5 GRAMMAR a) [I] if a noun, PRONOUN, or adjective declines, its form changes according to whether it is the SUBJECT, OBJECT etc of a sentence **b)** [T] if you decline a noun, PRONOUN, or adjective, you show the various forms that it can take —**declining** adj: declining attendance at baseball games

de·code /ˌdiː'kəʊd $ -'koʊd/ v [T] **1** to discover the meaning of a message written in a CODE (=a set of secret signs or letters); ▭ decipher **2** if a computer decodes DATA, it receives it and changes it into a form that can ▮ used by the computer or understood by a pers ▮ **encode**: The software decodes the informc ▮ embedded in the satellite broadcasts. **3** to receive ▮ tronic or DIGITAL signals and change them into a ▮ and sound for a television or radio; ▮ **encode** ▮ ing boxes for your TV set **4** technical to ur ▮ the meaning of a word rather than use ▮ express meaning; ▮ **encode**

de·cod·er /ˌdiː'kəʊdə $ -'koʊdər/ n [C ▮ electronic equipment that receives ▮ changes it for another machine to use ▮ put pictures and sound onto your tele ▮

dé·colle·tage /ˌdeɪkɒl'tɑːʒ $ deɪˌkɑːlə'tɑːʒ/ n [U] the top edge of a woman's dress that is cut very low to show part of her shoulders and breasts —**décolleté** /deɪ'kɒlteɪ $ ˌdeɪkɑːlə'teɪ/ adj

de·col·o·nize also **-ise** BrE /ˌdiː'kɒlənaɪz $ -'kɑː-/ v [T] to make a former COLONY politically independent —**decolonization** /diːˌkɒlənaɪ'zeɪʃən $ -ˌkɑːlənə-/ n [U]

de·com·miss·ion /ˌdiːkə'mɪʃən/ v [T] to stop using a ship, weapon, etc NUCLEAR REACTOR and to take it to pieces

de·com·pose /ˌdiːkəm'pəʊz $ -'poʊz/ v [I,T] **1** to decay or make something decay: a partially decomposed body **2** technical to divide into smaller parts, or to make something do this —**decomposition** /ˌdiːkɒmpə'zɪʃən $ -kɑːm-/ n [U]

de·com·press /ˌdiːkəm'pres/ v [T] **1** to reduce the pressure of air on something **2** technical to change the information in a computer document back into a form that can be easily read or used, when the information was stored on the computer in a special form that used less space on the computer's memory: Most Macintosh computers can decompress files automatically. —**decompression** /-'preʃən/ n [U]

decom'pression ˌchamber n [C] a special room where people go after they have been deep under the sea, so that their bodies can slowly return to normal air pressure

decom'pression ˌsickness n [U] a dangerous medical condition that people get when they come up from deep under the sea too quickly; ◨ **the bends**

de·con·gest·ant /ˌdiːkən'dʒestənt◂/ n [C,U] medicine that you can take if you have a cold, to help you breathe more easily

de·con·struc·tion /ˌdiːkən'strʌkʃən/ n [U] a method used in PHILOSOPHY and the criticism of literature which claims that there is no single explanation of the meaning of a piece of writing —**deconstruct** /-'strʌkt/ v [T]

de·con·tam·i·nate /ˌdiːkən'tæmɪ̩neɪt/ v [T] to remove a dangerous substance from somewhere; → **contamination**: It may cost over $5 million to decontaminate the whole site. —**decontamination** /ˌdiːkəntæmɪ̩'neɪʃən/ n [U]

de·cor /'deɪkɔː $ -kɔːr/ n [C usually singular, U] the way that the inside of a building is decorated: The decor is a mix of antique and modern.

dec·o·rate [S3] /'dekəreɪt/ v
1 [I,T] BrE to paint the inside of a room, put special paper on the walls etc: The bathroom is decorated in green and yellow. | We plan to spend the weekend decorating.
2 [T] to make something look more attractive by putting something pretty on it: Children's pictures decorated the walls of the classroom. | **decorate sth with sth** an old-fashioned dress decorated with ribbons and lace

decorating the home

decorating the Christmas tree

[T] to give someone a MEDAL as an official sign of [hon]our: **decorate sb for sth** soldiers decorated for [braver]y —**decorating** n [U]

[deco]**ra·tion** [S3] /ˌdekə'reɪʃən/ n
[usu]ally plural] something pretty that you put onto [somethin]g else in order to make it more attractive: [...] decorations | cake decorations
[sty]le in which something is decorated: He is [...] Islamic decoration. | for decoration a box [of flo]wers glued to it for decoration
[BrE] you paint or put special paper on the

inside walls, ceiling etc of a house or building
4 [C] something such as a MEDAL that is given to someone as an official sign of honour

dec·o·ra·tive /'dekərətɪv $ 'dekərə-, 'dekəreɪ-/ adj pretty or attractive, but not always necessary or useful: a decorative panel above the door —**decoratively** adv

dec·o·ra·tor /'dekəreɪtə $ -ər/ n [C] especially BrE someone who paints houses and puts paper on the walls as their job; → **interior designer**; → see picture at OCCUPATION

dec·o·rous /'dekərəs/ adj formal having the correct appearance or behaviour for a particular occasion —**decorously** adv: A servant was hovering decorously behind them.

de·co·rum /dɪ'kɔːrəm/ n [U] formal behaviour that shows respect and is correct for a particular situation, especially a formal occasion: He was disciplined for breaching the Senate's rules of decorum.

de·coy /'diːkɔɪ/ n [C] **1** someone or something that is used to trick someone into going somewhere or doing something, so that you can catch them, attack them etc: Officer Langley acted as a decoy to catch the rapist. **2** a model of a bird used to attract wild birds so that you can watch them or shoot them —**decoy** /dɪ'kɔɪ/ v [T]

de·crease¹ /dɪ'kriːs/ v [I,T] to become less or go down to a lower level, or to make something do this; → **reduce**; ◨ **increase**: Average house prices decreased by 13% last year. | [+to] By 1881, the population of Ireland had decreased to 5.2 million. | [+from] The North's share of the world's energy consumption is expected to decrease from 70% to 60%. | [+in] Attacks of asthma decrease in frequency through early adult life. | The government wants to decrease population growth.

de·crease² /'diːkriːs/ n [C,U] the process of becoming less, or the amount by which something becomes less; ◨ **increase**; ◨ **reduction**: [+in] Teachers reported decreases in drug use and verbal abuse of teachers. | [+of] There has been a steady decrease of temperature.

de·cree¹ /dɪ'kriː/ n [C] **1** an official order or decision, especially one made by the ruler of a country: The Emperor **issued** the **decree** repealing martial law. **2** a judgment in a court of law

decree² v [T] to make an official judgment or give an official order: **decree (that)** The King decreed that there should be an end to the fighting.

de·cree ˈabsolute n [singular] BrE an order by a court of law which officially ends a marriage

decree ni·si /dɪˌkriː 'naɪsaɪ/ n [singular] BrE an order by a court of law that a marriage will end at a particular time in the future unless there is a good reason not to end it

de·crep·it /dɪ'krepɪ̩t/ adj old and in bad condition: The buildings were in a decrepit state. —**decrepitude** n [U]

de·crim·in·a·lize also **-ise** BrE /diː'krɪmɪ̩nəlaɪz/ v [T] to state officially that something is not illegal any more: the campaign to decriminalize cannabis —**decriminalization** /diːˌkrɪmɪ̩nəlaɪ'zeɪʃən $ -lə-/ n [U]

de·cry /dɪ'kraɪ/ v decried, decrying, decries [T] formal to state publicly that you do not approve of something; ◨ **condemn**

de·crypt /diː'krɪpt/ v [T] to change a message or information on a computer back into a form that can be read, when someone has sent it to you in a type of computer CODE; → **encrypt**: Only certain employees will be able to decrypt sensitive documents. —**decryption** /diː'krɪpʃən/ n [U]

ded·i·cate /'dedɪ̩keɪt/ v [T] **1** to give all your attention and effort to one particular thing: **dedicate yourself/your life to sth** The actress now dedicates herself to children's charity work. **2** to say at the beginning of a book or film, or before a piece of music, that it has been written, made, or performed for someone that you love or respect: **dedicate sth to sb** The book was dedicated to *her husband.* **3** to state in an official ceremony that a building will be given someone's name in order to show respect for them **4** to use a place, time, money etc only for a particular purpose: **dedicate sth to/for sth** *The company dedicated $50,000 for the study.*

ded·i·cat·ed /'dedₐkeɪtₒd/ *adj* **1** someone who is dedicated works very hard at what they do because they care a lot about it: *a dedicated and thoughtful teacher* | *She is a dedicated socialist.* | [+**to**] *The Woodland Trust is dedicated to preserving our native woodland.* **2** [only before noun] made for or used for only one particular purpose: *a dedicated graphics processor*

ded·i·ca·tion /ˌdedₐkeɪʃən/ *n* **1** [U] hard work or effort that someone puts into a particular activity because they care about it a lot: *To reach a high level of skill requires talent, dedication, and a lot of hard work.* | [+**to**] *I admire his dedication to the job.* **2** [C] an act of dedicating something to someone, or a ceremony where this is done **3** [C] the words used at the beginning of a book, film, or piece of music, thanking someone or saying that book etc has been written to show respect for them

de·duce /dɪ'djuːs $ dɪ'duːs/ *v* [T] *formal* to use the knowledge and information you have in order to understand something or form an opinion about it: **deduce that** *From her son's age, I deduced that her husband must be at least 60.* | [+**from**] *What did Darwin deduce from the presence of these species?* —**deducible** *adj*

de·duct /dɪ'dʌkt/ *v* [T] to take away an amount or part from a total; ▣ **subtract**: **deduct sth from sth** *The payments will be deducted from your salary.* —**deductible** *adj: Interest charges are tax deductible.*

de·duc·tion /dɪ'dʌkʃən/ *n* [C,U] **1** the process of using the knowledge or information you have in order to understand something or form an opinion, or the opinion that you form: *Children will soon make deductions about the meaning of a word.* **2** the process of taking away an amount from a total, or the amount that is taken away: *After deductions for tax etc, your salary is about £700 a month.*

de·duc·tive /dɪ'dʌktɪv/ *adj* using the knowledge and information you have in order to understand or form an opinion about something: *deductive reasoning*

deed /diːd/ *n* [C] **1** *formal* something someone does, especially something that is very good or very bad: *After the morning's good deeds he deserved a rest.* | *She tried to strangle his baby and her lover helped her finish the evil deed.* **2** *law* an official paper that is a record of an agreement, especially an agreement concerning who owns property: *a mortgage deed* **3 in deed** in what you do: *Everyone sins at some time, in thought if not in deed.* **4 your good deed for the day** something kind or helpful that you do – used humorously

'deed poll *n* [C,U] a legal document signed by only one person, for example in order to officially change your name: *Steve changed his name by deed poll to Elvis Presley-Smith.*

dee·jay /'diːdʒeɪ/ *n* [C] *informal* a DISC JOCKEY —**deejay** *v* [I]

deem /diːm/ *v* [T not in progressive] *formal* to think of something in a particular way or as having a particular quality; ▣ **consider**: **deem that** *They deemed that he was no longer capable of managing the business.* | **deem sth necessary/appropriate etc** *They were told to take whatever action they deemed necessary.* | **be deemed to be sth** *They were deemed to be illegal immigrants.* | **be deemed to do sth** *UK plans were deemed to infringe EU law.*

deep¹ ▣ ▣ /diːp/ *adj comparative* **deeper**, *superlative* **deepest**
1 GOING FAR DOWN **a)** going far down from the top or from the surface; ▣ **shallow**: *The castle is on an island surrounded by a deep lake.* | *The swimming pool has a deep end and a shallow end for kids.* | *We'll take the boat out into deep water where we can dive.* | *a deep narrow valley* **b)** you use deep to say what distance something goes down from the top or surface: **2 metres/6 feet etc**

deep *Dig a hole around 12 inches deep.* | **ankle-deep/ waist-deep etc** *In places, the snow was waist-deep* (=deep enough to reach a person's waist). → KNEE-DEEP
2 GOING FAR IN going far in from the outside or from the front edge of something: *a deep wound* | *She was sitting in a deep leather chair.*
3 SERIOUS serious or severe: *Despite the peace process, there are deep divisions in the community.* | *The country is in a deep recession.* | *Evan would be in deep trouble if he was caught.*
4 BREATH a deep breath or SIGH is one in which you breathe a lot of air in or out: *She stopped and took a deep breath.* | *Tom gave a deep sigh of relief.*
5 FEELING/BELIEF a deep feeling, belief etc is very strong and sincere; ▣ **profound**: *May I express my deepest sympathy.* | *The letters show her deep affection for him.* | *He has a deep understanding of the environment.*
6 SOUND a deep sound is very low: *Her laugh was deep and loud.* | *I love that deep bass line.*
7 COLOUR a deep colour is dark and strong; ▣ **light**, **pale**: *She gazed at him with wide deep blue eyes.* | *The berries are a deep red colour.*
8 DIFFICULT TO UNDERSTAND important but complicated or difficult to understand: *These problems are too deep for me.* | *There is a deep issue of principle involved.*
9 SLEEP if someone is in a deep sleep, it is difficult to wake them: *He lay down and fell into a deep sleep.*
10 deep in thought/conversation etc thinking so hard or paying attention to something so much that you do not notice anything else that is happening around you
11 deep in debt owing a lot of money
12 a deep impression a strong effect or influence that remains for a long time: *What he said made a deep impression on me.*
13 PERSON a deep person is serious and intelligent, but is hard to know well: *Henry has always been a deep one. He keeps his views to himself.*
14 be in deep shit *spoken not polite* to be in a bad situation because of something you have done
15 be in deep water to be in trouble or in a difficult or serious situation: *The company is in deep water over their refusal to reduce prices.*
16 BALL GAMES a deep ball is hit, thrown, or kicked to a far part of the sports field
17 jump/be thrown in at the deep end to choose to do or be made to do a very difficult job without having prepared for it: *She decided to jump in at the deep end, buy a farm, and teach herself.*
18 go off at the deep end *informal* to become angry suddenly and violently, usually when there is not a good reason

deep² ▣ *adv*
1 [always + adv/prep] a long way into or below the surface of something: *Some bones were hidden deep beneath the ground.* | *The railway tunnel led deep under the mountains.* | *We were deep in a tropical rainforest* (=far from the edge of the forest). | *Tom stared deep into her eyes.* | *They talked deep into the night* (=very late).
2 deep down a) if you know or feel something deep down, you secretly know or feel it even though you do not admit it: *He knew, deep down, that he would have to apologise.* **b)** if someone is good, evil etc deep down, that is what they are really like even though they usually hide it: *Deep down, she is a very caring person.*
3 two/three etc deep if things or people are two deep, three deep etc, there are two, three etc rows or layers of things or people: *People were standing four deep at the bar.*
4 run/go deep if a feeling such as hatred or anger runs deep in someone, they feel it very strongly, especially because of something that has happened in the past: *The prejudice runs deep and we need to understand the fears behind it.*

▣ 000, ▣ 000, ▣ 000, most frequent words in ▣ poken and ▣ ritten English

D

5 be in (too) deep *informal* to be very involved in a situation, especially so that it causes you problems → **still waters run deep** at STILL² (5)

deep³ *n* **the deep** *literary* the sea

deep·en /ˈdiːpən/ *v*
1 GET WORSE [I] if a serious situation deepens, it gets worse – used especially in news reports: *The recession continues to deepen.* | *a deepening international crisis*
2 BECOME STRONGER [I,T] to become stronger or greater, or to make something stronger or greater: *Jeanne liked Simon as a friend but she did not want the relationship to deepen.* | *The idea only deepened his gloom.* | *The mystery deepened* (=became even more mysterious). | *Students explore new ideas as they deepen their understanding* (=understand more) *of the subject.*
3 EXPRESSION ON SB'S FACE [I] *literary* if someone's smile or FROWN deepens, they smile even more or frown even more: *Her worried frown deepened.*
4 WATER [I,T] if water deepens, or if someone deepens it, it becomes deeper: *The river deepens beyond the town.* | *The harbour has been deepened to take bigger boats.*
5 COLOUR [I] *literary* if light or a colour deepens, it becomes darker: *The twilight deepened.*
6 SOUND [I] if a sound deepens, it becomes lower: *His voice deepened as he relaxed.*
7 BREATH [I] if your breathing deepens, you take more air into your lungs

,deep ˈfreeze / $ ˈ. ./ *n* [C] a large metal box in which food can be stored at very low temperatures for a long time; ▤ **freezer**

ˈdeep fry *v* [T] to cook food under the surface of hot fat or oil

deep·ly W3 /ˈdiːpli/ *adv*
1 used to emphasize that a belief, feeling, opinion etc is very strong, important, or sincere: *Her lies hurt my father deeply.* | *She is deeply upset.* | *He loves her deeply.* | *Teachers are deeply divided on this issue.* | *deeply held religious beliefs*
2 in a serious, careful way: *Most doctors think deeply about what their patients want.*
3 a long way into something: [+into] *John kept sinking more deeply into the mud.*
4 breathe deeply to take a large breath of air into your lungs
5 sleep deeply to be in a deep sleep, from which it is hard to wake up

,deep-ˈrooted also ,deeply ˈrooted *adj* a deep-rooted habit, idea, belief etc is so strong in a person or society that it is very difficult to change or destroy it; → **deep-seated**: *a deep-rooted suspicion of lawyers*

ˈdeep-sea *adj* [only before noun] deep-sea fishing or DIVING is done in the deep part of the sea, far away from land

,deep-ˈseated *adj* a deep-seated attitude, feeling, or idea is strong and is very difficult to change; → **deep-rooted**: *a deep-seated fear of failure*

,deep-ˈset *adj* deep-set eyes seem to be further back into the face than most people's

,deep ˈsix *v* [T] *AmE informal* to decide not to use something such as a plan

,Deep ˈSouth *n* **the Deep South** the most southern states of the US

,deep vein thromˈbosis *n* [U] *medical* DVT a serious illness which happens when a small amount of blood becomes very thick and causes the heart to stop beating properly. This sometimes happens to people who have been on long plane journeys, because they have been sitting still for so long

deer /dɪə $ dɪr/ *n plural* **deer** [C] a large wild animal that can run very fast, eats grass, and has horns

deer·stalk·er /ˈdɪəˌstɔːkə $ ˈdɪrˌstɒːkər/ *n* [C] a type of soft hat with pieces of cloth that cover your ears

de·face /dɪˈfeɪs/ *v* [T] to spoil the surface or appearance of something, especially by writing on it or breaking it: *Most of the monuments had been broken or defaced.* —**defacement** *n* [U]

de fac·to /ˌdeɪ ˈfæktəʊ $ dɪ ˈfæktoʊ, ˌdeɪ-/ *adj formal* really existing although not legally stated to exist; → **de jure**: *a de facto state of war* —**de facto** *adv*

def·a·ma·tion /ˌdefəˈmeɪʃən/ *n* [U] the act of defaming someone: *He sued the newspaper for defamation of character.*

de·fame /dɪˈfeɪm/ *v* [T] to write or say bad or untrue things about someone or something, so that people will have a bad opinion of them —**defamatory** /dɪˈfæmətəri $ -tɔːri/ *adj*

de·fault¹ /dɪˈfɔːlt $ -ˈfɒːlt/ *n* **1 by default a)** if you win a game, competition etc by default, you win it because your opponent did not play or because there were no other competitors **b)** if something happens by default, it happens because you did not do anything to change it **2** [C,U] *formal* failure to pay money that you owe at the right time: **in default** *The company is in default on its loan agreement.* | [+in] *The bank can seize the asset in the event of a default in payment.* | *the risk of default by borrowers* **3** [U] *law* failure to do something that you are supposed to do according to the law or because it is your duty **4** [C usually singular] *technical* the way in which things are arranged on a computer screen unless you decide to change them: *You can change the default settings to suit your needs.* **5 in default of sth** *formal* because of the lack or absence of something

default² *v* [I] **1** to fail to pay money that you owe at the right time: [+on] *He defaulted on his child support payments.* **2** to not do something that you are supposed to do, especially that you are legally supposed to do —**defaulter** *n* [C]

de·feat¹ W3 /dɪˈfiːt/ *n* [C,U]
1 failure to win or succeed

admit/accept/concede defeat
suffer a defeat (=experience a defeat)
a heavy/humiliating/crushing/resounding defeat
a narrow defeat (=by only a small amount)
inflict a defeat on sb

*She was a woman who hated to **admit defeat**.* | *The Democratic Party candidate has already **conceded defeat**.* | [+in] *The socialist party **suffered** a **crushing defeat** in the French elections.* | *The captain offered no excuses for his team's **humiliating defeat**.* | *Italy's **narrow defeat** in their game with Germany* | *They **inflicted** a heavy **defeat on** the Government's plans to tighten asylum controls.*

2 victory over someone or something: [+of] *The defeat of the army was followed by the establishment of constitutional government.*

defeat² *v* [T] **1** to win a victory over someone in a war, competition, game etc; ▤ **beat**: *They hoped to defeat the enemy at sea.* | *defeat sb by sth Newcastle were defeated by 3 goals to 2.* **2** if something defeats you, you cannot understand it and therefore cannot answer or deal with it; ▤ **beat**: *It was the last question on the paper that defeated me.* **3** to make something fail: **defeat the object/purpose (of the exercise)** *Don't let your arms relax as that would defeat the object of the exercise.*

de·feat·ed /dɪˈfiːtɪd/ *adj* sad and unable to deal with problems: *He looked lost and defeated.*

de·feat·ist /dɪˈfiːtɪst/ *n* [C] someone who believes that they will not succeed —**defeatist** *adj*: *a defeatist attitude* —**defeatism** *n* [U]

def·e·cate /ˈdefɪkeɪt/ *v* [I] *formal* to get rid of waste matter from your BOWELS —**defecation** /ˌdefɪˈkeɪʃən/ *n* [U]

de·fect¹ /ˈdiːfekt, dɪˈfekt/ *n* [C] a fault or a lack of something that means that something or someone is not perfect: *All the cars are tested for defects before they leave the factory.* | *a genetic defect*

defect² /dɪˈfekt/ v [I] to leave your own country or group in order to go to or join an opposing one: [+**to/from**] *a Russian actor who defected to the West* —**defector** n [C] —**defection** /dɪˈfekʃən/ n [C,U]

de·fec·tive /dɪˈfektɪv/ adj not made properly, or not working properly; ▤ **faulty**: *The disease is caused by a defective gene.* | *defective products*

de·fence ⸂C2⸃ ⸂W1⸃ *BrE*; **defense** *AmE* /dɪˈfens/ n
1 PROTECTION a) [U] the act of protecting something or someone from attack: [+**of**] *In Britain, the defence of the country has historically been left to the navy.* | *a firm commitment to the defense of human rights* | *The first line of defence is a smoke detector.* **b)** [C] something that can be used to protect something or someone from attack: *The area's flood defences need repair.* | [+**against**] *The immune system is the body's defence against infection.* → SELF-DEFENCE
2 MILITARY a) [U] all the systems, people, materials etc that a country uses to protect itself from attack: *calls for a national debate on defence* | *the Defense Department* **b)** **defences** *BrE*; **defenses** *AmE* [plural] all the armies, weapons, structures etc that are available to defend a place: *The invading army easily overcame the town's defences.*
3 AGAINST CRITICISM [C,U] something that you say or do in order to support someone or something that is being criticized: **in sb's/sth's defence** *Jean wrote a letter to the paper in Angela's defense.* | [+**of**] *a philosophical defence of nationalism* | **come/leap to sb's defence** *Evelyn Waugh came to Wilson's defence and acknowledged the brilliance of the book's themes.*
4 IN A LAW COURT a) [C] the things that are said in a court of law to prove that someone is not guilty of a crime: *Major has a good defence and believes he will win the case.* | *a defence lawyer* **b) the defence** all the lawyers who try to prove in a court of law that someone is not guilty of a crime: *The defense called only one witness.* → PROSECUTION (2)
5 EMOTIONS [C] something you do or a way of behaving that prevents you from seeming weak or being hurt by others: *Liz dropped her defences and began to relax.*
6 SPORT [C] *BrE* the players in a game whose main job is to try to prevent the other team from getting points

de·fence·less *BrE*, **defenseless** *AmE* /dɪˈfensləs/ adj weak and unable to protect yourself from attack or harm: *a defenceless old lady*

de'fence ˌmechanism *BrE*, **defense mechanism** *AmE* n [C] **1** a process in your brain that makes you forget things that are painful for you to think about **2** a reaction in your body that protects you from an illness or danger

de·fend ⸂S3⸃ ⸂W3⸃ /dɪˈfend/ v
1 [I,T] to do something in order to protect someone or something from being attacked: *a struggle to defend our homeland* | **defend sth against/from sth** *the need to defend democracy against fascism* | **defend yourself (against/from sth)** *advice on how women can defend themselves from sex attackers* | [+**against**] *We need to defend against military aggression.*
2 [T] to use arguments to protect something or someone from criticism, or to prove that something is right: *She was always defending her husband in front of their daughter.* | *Students should be ready to explain and defend their views.* | **defend sb against/from sb/sth** *He defended his wife against rumours and allegations.* | **defend yourself (against/from sth)** | *Cooper wrote to the journal immediately, defending himself.*
3 [T] to do something in order to stop something from being taken away or in order to make it possible for something to continue: *the workers' attempts to defend their interests* | *We are defending the right to demonstrate.*
4 [I,T] to protect your own team's end of the field in a game such as football, in order to prevent your opponents from getting points: *Bournemouth defended well throughout the game.*
5 [T] to take part in a competition that you won the last time it was held, and try to win it again: *The world*

heavyweight champion was defending his title. | *the defending champion* | *He is defending a Labour majority of 5,000.*
6 [I,T] to be a lawyer for someone who has been charged with a crime; → **prosecute**: *He had top lawyers to defend him.* | *Howard, defending, said Thompson had been drinking heavily.*

de·fen·dant ⸂W2⸃ /dɪˈfendənt/ n [C] the person in a court of law who has been ACCUSED of doing something illegal; → **plaintiff**; ▤ **prisoner** *AmE*: *We find the defendant not guilty.*

de·fend·er /dɪˈfendə $ -ər/ n [C] **1** one of the players in a game such as football who have to defend their team's GOAL from the opposing team: *It's his fourth season as an Arsenal defender.* **2** someone who defends a particular idea, belief, person etc: *He presented himself as a defender of democracy.*

de·fense¹ /dɪˈfens/ n the American spelling of DEFENCE

de·fense² /dɪˈfens $ ˈdiːfens/ n [C,U] *AmE* the players in a game of football etc whose main job is to try to prevent the other team from getting points

de·fen·si·ble /dɪˈfensɪbəl/ adj **1** a defensible opinion, idea, or action seems reasonable, and you can easily support it; ▤ **indefensible**: *a morally defensible prison system* **2** a defensible building or area is easy to protect against attack —**defensibly** adv

de·fen·sive¹ /dɪˈfensɪv/ adj **1** used or intended to protect someone or something against attack; ▤ **offensive**: *The prince drew up his forces in a strong defensive position.* | *The rockets are a purely defensive measure against nuclear attack.* **2** behaving in a way that shows you think someone is criticizing you even if they are not: *She despised herself for sounding so defensive.* | *a reserved and defensive manner* **3** *AmE* relating to stopping the other team from getting points in a game; ▤ **offensive**: *defensive play* —**defensively** adv —**defensiveness** n [U]

defensive² n **1 on/onto the defensive** behaving in a way that shows that you think that someone is criticizing you even if they are not: *In his presence, she was constantly on the defensive.* **2 put/force sb on the defensive** if you put someone on the defensive in an argument, you attack them so that they are in a weaker position: *an issue that is sure to put the White House on the defensive*

de·fer /dɪˈfɜː $ -ˈfɜːr/ v **deferred, deferring** [T] to delay something until a later date; ▤ **put back**: **defer sth until/to sth** *Further discussion on the proposal will be deferred until April.* | *The committee deferred their decision.* —**deferment** n [C,U] —**deferral** n [C,U]

defer to sb/sth phr v *formal* to agree to accept someone's opinion or decision because you have respect for that person: *I will defer to your wishes.*

def·er·ence /ˈdefərəns/ n [U] *formal* polite behaviour that shows that you respect someone and are therefore willing to accept their opinions or judgment: [+**to**] *Lewis was annoyed that Adam did not show enou[gh] respect and deference to him.* | **out of/in deference to** (=because you respect someone's beliefs, opinio[ns]) *They were married in church out of deference [to] parents' wishes.* —**deferential** /ˌdefəˈrenʃəl[◂] erential treatment* —**deferentially** adv

de·fi·ance /dɪˈfaɪəns/ n [U] behaviour th[at shows you] refuse to do what someone tells you to [do, especially] because you do not respect them; → **def[iant]** *defiance Running away was an act o[f defiance against] his parents.* | **in defiance (of sth)** [...] *drinking in the streets, in flagrant [defiance ...] Her fists clenched in defiance.*

de·fi·ant /dɪˈfaɪənt/ adj cle[arly refusing to do what] someone tells you to do: *Mar[...] in a defiant gesture.* —**def[iantly ...]**

de·fib·ril·la·tor /diːˈfɪbrᵻleɪtə $ -ər/ n [C] a machine that gives the heart an electric shock to make it start beating again after a heart attack

de·fi·cien·cy /dɪˈfɪʃənsi/ n plural **deficiencies** [C,U] formal **1** a lack of something that is necessary; ▤ **shortage**: [+of] a deficiency of safe play areas for children | **iron/vitamin etc deficiency** Some elderly people suffer from iron deficiency in their diet. **2** a weakness or fault in something: [+in] There are deep deficiencies in this law.

de·fi·cient /dɪˈfɪʃənt/ adj formal **1** not containing or having enough of something: Women who are dieting can become iron deficient. | [+in] patients who were deficient in vitamin C **2** not good enough: Our prisons are our most deficient social service.

def·i·cit /ˈdefᵻsᵻt/ n [C] the difference between the amount of something that you have and the higher amount that you need; → **shortfall**: the country's widening **budget deficit** | the US's foreign **trade deficit** | [+of] a deficit of £2.5 million | [+in] Many countries have a big deficit in food supply. | **in deficit** The US balance of payments was in deficit.

de·file¹ /dɪˈfaɪl/ v [T] formal to make something less pure and good, especially by showing no respect: Hallam's tomb had been defiled and looted.

de·file² /dɪˈfaɪl, ˈdiːfaɪl/ n [C] formal a narrow passage, especially through mountains

de·fine S3 W2 /dɪˈfaɪn/ v [T]
1 to describe something correctly and thoroughly, and to say what standards, limits, qualities etc it has that make it different from other things: the ability to define clients' needs | The duties of the post are difficult to define. | **clearly/well defined** The tasks will be clearly defined by the tutor. | **define sth as sth** 70% of the workers can be defined as low-paid.
2 to explain exactly the meaning of a particular word or idea; → **definition**: I'll now try to define the term 'popular culture'. | **define sth as sth** A budget is defined as 'a plan of action expressed in money terms'. | Define precisely what you mean by 'crime'.
3 to show the edge or shape of something clearly; → **definition**: The bird has **sharply defined** black and rust markings. —**definable** adj

def·i·nite S3 /ˈdefᵻnᵻt, ˈdefənᵻt/ adj
1 clearly known, seen, or stated; ▤ **clear**: It's impossible for me to give you a definite answer. | We need to record sufficient data to enable definite conclusions to be reached. | He'd shown definite signs of resigning himself to the situation.
2 a definite arrangement, promise etc will happen in the way that someone has said; → **indefinite**: Fix a definite date for the delivery of your computer.
3 [not before noun] saying something very firmly so that people understand exactly what you mean: [+about] She's not definite about retiring from the game.

definite 'article n [C usually singular] **1** the word 'the' in English → **INDEFINITE ARTICLE 2** a word in another language that is like 'the'

def·i·nite·ly S1 /ˈdefᵻnᵻtli, ˈdefənᵻtli/ adv without ˌny doubt; ▤ **certainly**: 'Do you reckon Margot will be ˌre?' 'Definitely not.' | The hotel fitness centre is ˌitely worth a visit. | I definitely need a holiday.

ˌi·tion S3 W2 /ˌdefᵻˈnɪʃən/ n
ˌphrase or sentence that says exactly what a ˌase, or idea means; → **define**: a dictionary ˌ[+of] There are many definitions of the word ˌ **definition of sth as sth** the definition of

ˌ something has a particular quality by ˌ have that quality because all things ˌit: People say that students are by ˌnd impatient.

ˌhapes, or sound that something ˌs high definition television |

de·fin·i·tive /dɪˈfɪnᵻtɪv/ adj **1** [usually before noun] a definitive book, description etc is considered to be the best and cannot be improved: **definitive study/work/ guide etc** the definitive study of Victorian railway stations **2** a definitive agreement, statement etc is one that will not be changed: a definitive agreement to buy the company —**definitively** adv

de·flate /ˌdiːˈfleɪt, dɪ-/ v **1** [I,T] if a tyre, BALLOON etc deflates, or if you deflate it, it gets smaller because the gas inside it comes out; ▤ **inflate**; → **go down, let down 2** [T] to make someone feel less important or less confident: She was deflated when Fen made no comment on her achievement. **3** [T] to show that a statement, argument etc is wrong: Simkin hoped to find a way to deflate his opponent's argument. **4** [I,T] technical to change economic rules or conditions in a country so that prices fall or stop rising

de·fla·tion /diːˈfleɪʃən/ n [U] technical a reduction in the amount of money in a country's ECONOMY, so that prices fall or stop rising; → **inflation** —**deflationary** adj: the government's deflationary policies

de·flect /dɪˈflekt/ v **1** [I,T] if someone or something deflects something that is moving, or if it deflects, it turns in a different direction: Connor **deflected** the **blow** with his left forearm. **2** [T] to do something to stop people paying attention to you, criticizing you etc: **deflect sth (away) from sth** his attempts to **deflect attention** away from his private life | The committee is seeking to **deflect criticism** by blaming me. **3** [T] to take someone's attention away from something: **deflect sb from (doing) sth** Nothing can deflect me from reaching my goal.

de·flec·tion /dɪˈflekʃən/ n [C,U] **1** the action of making something change its direction: [+of] the deflection of the missile away from its target **2** technical the degree to which the moving part on a measuring instrument moves away from zero

de·flow·er /ˌdiːˈflaʊə, dɪ- $ -ər/ v [T] literary to have sex with a woman who has never had sex before

de·fog /diːˈfɒɡ $ -ˈfɑːɡ, -ˈfɒːɡ/ v **defogged, defogging** [T] AmE to remove mist from the windows inside a car, by using heat; ▤ **demist** BrE

de·fo·li·ant /diːˈfəʊliənt $ -ˈfoʊ-/ n [C,U] formal a chemical substance, used especially in war, that makes all the leaves of plants drop off

de·fo·li·ate /diːˈfəʊlieɪt $ -ˈfoʊ-/ v [T] formal to use defoliant on a plant or tree

de·for·es·ta·tion /diːˌfɒrᵻˈsteɪʃən $ -ˌfɔː-,-,ˌfɑː-/ n [U] the cutting or burning down of all the trees in an area: the deforestation of the tropics —**deforest** /diːˈfɒrᵻst $ -ˈfɔː-, -ˈfɑː-/ v [T usually passive]

de·form /dɪˈfɔːm $ -ɔːrm/ v [I,T] if you deform something, or if it deforms, its usual shape changes so that its usefulness or appearance is spoiled: Wearing badly-fitting shoes can deform your feet.

de·for·ma·tion /ˌdiːfɔːˈmeɪʃən $ -ɔːr-/ n [C,U] technical a change in the usual shape of something, especially one that makes it worse, or the process of changing something's shape

de·formed /dɪˈfɔːmd $ -ɔːrmd/ adj something that is deformed has the wrong shape, especially because it has grown or developed wrongly: the deformed toe on his right foot

de·for·mi·ty /dɪˈfɔːmᵻti $ -ɔːr-/ n plural **deformities** [C,U] a condition in which part of someone's body is not the normal shape: a hip deformity

de·fraud /dɪˈfrɔːd $ -ˈfrɒːd/ v [T] to trick a person or organization in order to get money from them: **defraud sb of sth** She defrauded her employers of thousands of pounds. | He faces charges of theft and **conspiracy to defraud** (=a secret plan to cheat someone, made by two or more people).

de·fray /dɪˈfreɪ/ v **defray costs/expenses** formal to give someone back the money that they have spent on something: The proceeds from the competition help to defray the expenses of the evening.

de·frock /ˌdiːˈfrɒk $ -ˈfrɑːk/ v [T] to officially remove a priest from his or her job because he or she did something wrong —**defrocked** adj

de·frost /ˌdiːˈfrɒst $ -ˈfrɒːst/ v **1** [I,T] if frozen food defrosts, or if you defrost it, it gets warmer until it is not frozen; → **melt, thaw 2** [I,T] if a FREEZER or REFRIGERATOR defrosts, or if you defrost it, it is turned off so that the ice inside it melts **3** [T] AmE to remove ice from inside the windows of a car by using heat or warm air

deft /deft/ adj written **1** a deft movement is skilful, and often quick: He sketched her with quick, deft strokes. | deft footwork **2** skilful at doing something: his deft chairmanship of the company —**deftly** adv —**deftness** n [U]

de·funct /dɪˈfʌŋkt/ adj formal not existing any more, or not useful any more: the now-defunct nuclear reactor

de·fuse /ˌdiːˈfjuːz/ v [T] **1** to improve a difficult or dangerous situation, for example by making people less angry or by dealing with the causes of a problem: **defuse a situation/crisis/row etc** Beth's quiet voice helped to defuse the situation. | **defuse tension/anger** etc The agreement was regarded as a means of defusing ethnic tensions. **2** to remove the FUSE from a bomb in order to prevent it from exploding

de·fy /dɪˈfaɪ/ v **defied, defying, defies** [T] **1** to refuse to obey a law or rule, or refuse to do what someone in authority tells you to do; → **defiance**: people who openly defy the law **2 defy description/analysis/belief etc** to be almost impossible to describe or understand: The beauty of the scene defies description. **3 defy logic/the odds etc** to not happen according to the principles you would expect: a 16-week premature baby who defied the odds and survived **4 I defy sb to do sth** spoken formal used when you ask someone to do something that you think is impossible: I defy anyone to prove otherwise.

deg. also **deg** BrE the written abbreviation of **degree** or **degrees**

de·gen·e·rate[1] /dɪˈdʒenəreɪt/ v [I] to become worse: [+into] The conference degenerated into a complete fiasco. —**degeneration** /dɪˌdʒenəˈreɪʃən/ n [U]

de·gen·e·rate[2] /dɪˈdʒenərɪt/ adj formal morally unacceptable: The painting was condemned as 'degenerate'.

degenerate[3] n [C] someone whose behaviour is considered to be morally unacceptable

de·gen·e·ra·tive /dɪˈdʒenərətɪv/ adj a degenerative illness gradually gets worse and cannot be stopped; → **progressive**

deg·ra·da·tion /ˌdegrəˈdeɪʃən/ n **1** [C,U] an experience or situation that makes you feel ashamed and angry: a life of poverty and degradation **2** [U] the process by which something changes to a worse condition

de·grade /dɪˈɡreɪd/ v **1** [T] to treat someone without respect and make them lose respect for themselves: a movie that degrades women | **degrade yourself (by doing sth)** How can you degrade yourself by writing such trash? **2** [T] to make a situation or the condition of something worse: The dolphin's habitat is being rapidly degraded. **3** [I,T] technical if a substance, chemical etc degrades, or if something degrades it, it changes to a simpler form —**degradable** adj

de·grad·ing /dɪˈɡreɪdɪŋ/ adj a degrading experience, event etc is unpleasant and makes you lose respect for yourself: [+to] Pornography is degrading to women and to the men that look at it. | the **degrading treatment** that the prisoners receive in jail

de·gree S3 W1 /dɪˈɡriː/ n

1 [C] written abbreviation **deg.** a unit for measuring temperature. It can be shown as a symbol after a number. For example, 70° means 70 degrees: Preheat the oven to 425 degrees. | **20 degrees Celsius/70 degrees Fahrenheit/1 degree Centigrade etc** The temperature dropped to five degrees Centigrade.

2 [C] written abbreviation **deg.** a unit for measuring the size of an angle. It can be shown as a symbol after a number. For example, 18° means 18 degrees: Then the cylinder is rotated 180 degrees.

3 [C,U] the level or amount of something: [+of] 1960s Britain was characterised by a greater degree of freedom than before. | Newspapers vary in **the degree to which** they emphasize propaganda rather than information.

4 to a degree also **to some degree/to a certain degree** partly: To a degree, it is possible to educate oneself. | We're all willing to support him to some degree.

5 [C] a course of study at a university or college, or the QUALIFICATION that is given to you when you have successfully completed the course: [+in] a degree in Economics | Applicants must **have a degree** in Engineering. | an Honours degree

6 by degrees very slowly; 🔲 **gradually**: By degrees, Huy forced himself into a sitting position.

de·hu·man·ize also **-ise** BrE /ˌdiːˈhjuːmənaɪz/ v [T] to treat people so badly that they lose their good human qualities: War dehumanizes people. —**dehumanizing** adj —**dehumanization** /diːˌhjuːmənaɪˈzeɪʃən $ -nə-/ n [U]

de·hy·drate /ˌdiːhaɪˈdreɪt $ diːˈhaɪdreɪt/ v **1** [T] to remove the liquid from a substance such as food or a chemical; → **rehydrate, hydrate**: The substance is dehydrated and stored as powder. **2** [I,T] to lose too much water from your body, or to make this happen: Alcohol dehydrates the body. —**dehydrated** adj —**dehydration** /ˌdiːhaɪˈdreɪʃən/ n [U]

de-ice /ˌdiːˈaɪs/ v [T] to remove the ice from something, especially an aircraft

de·i·fy /ˈdiːɪfaɪ, ˈdeɪ-/ v **deified, deifying, deifies** [T] to treat someone or something with extreme respect and admiration —**deification** /ˌdiːɪfɔ̩ˈkeɪʃən, ˌdeɪ-/ n [U]

deign /deɪn/ v **deign to do sth** to do something that you think you are really too important to do – often used humorously: Travis called after her, but she didn't deign to answer.

de·is·m /ˈdeɪ-ɪzəm, ˈdiː-/ n [U] the belief in a God who made the world but has no influence on human lives; → **theism**

de·i·ty /ˈdeɪɪti, ˈdiː-/ n plural **deities** [C] a god or GODDESS: the deities of ancient Greece

dé·jà vu /ˌdeɪʒɑː ˈvjuː $ -ˈvuː/ n [U] the feeling that what is happening now has happened before in exactly the same way: a strange **sense of déjà vu**

de·ject·ed /dɪˈdʒektɪ̩d/ adj unhappy, disappointed, or sad: The unemployed stood at street corners, dejected. —**dejectedly** adv —**dejection** /dɪˈdʒekʃən/ n [U]

de ju·re /ˌdiː ˈdʒʊəri, ˌdeɪ ˈdʒʊəreɪ $ -ˈdʒʊr-/ adj, adv technical true or right because of a law; → **de facto**

de·lay[1] S2 W3 /dɪˈleɪ/ n

1 [C] when someone or something has to wait, or the length of the waiting time: Sorry for the delay, Mr Weaver. | [+in] Why was there a delay in warning the public? | [+of] a delay of about an hour | **long/considerable/slight etc delay** Long delays are expected on the motorways.

2 [U] when something does not happen or start when it should do: **without delay** They must restore normal services without delay. | There can be no excuse for any **further delay**.

delay[2] S3 v

1 [I,T] to wait until a later time to do something: Don't delay – send off for the information now. | He **delayed** his **decision** on whether to call an election. | **delay sth until sth** The opening of this section of the road is delayed until September. | **delay sth for sth** Our meeting was delayed for ten minutes. | **delay doing sth** Big companies often delay paying their bills.

2 [T] to make someone or something late: **seriously/ badly/slightly etc delayed** *The flight was badly delayed because of fog.* —**delayed** *adj*

de·layed-'action *adj* [only before noun] designed to work or start only after a fixed period of time has passed: *a delayed-action bomb*

de'laying ˌtactic *n* [C usually plural] something you do deliberately in order to delay something so that you gain an advantage for yourself

de·lec·ta·ble /dɪˈlektəbəl/ *adj formal* **1** extremely pleasant to taste or smell; **=** **delicious**: *Delectable smells rose from the kitchen.* **2** used, often humorously, to describe a very attractive woman —**delectably** *adv*

de·lec·ta·tion /ˌdiːlekˈteɪʃən/ *n* [U] *formal* if you do something for someone's delectation, you do it to give them enjoyment, pleasure, or amusement

del·e·gate¹ /ˈdelɪɡət/ *n* [C] someone who has been elected or chosen to speak, vote, or take decisions for a group; → **representative**: *Around 350 delegates attended the conference.*

del·e·gate² /ˈdelɪɡeɪt/ *v* **1** [I,T] to give part of your power or work to someone in a lower position than you: *A good manager knows when to delegate.* | *It takes experience to judge correctly how much power should be delegated.* | **delegate sth to sb** *Minor tasks should be delegated to your assistant.* **2** [T] to choose someone to do a particular job, or to be a representative of a group, organization etc: **delegate sb to do sth** *I was delegated to find a suitable conference venue.*

del·e·ga·tion /ˌdelɪˈɡeɪʃən/ *n* **1** [C] a group of people who represent a company, organization etc: [+**to**] *the head of the American delegation to the United Nations* | [+**of**] *a delegation of government officials* | *A trade delegation will visit Kuwait.* **2** [U] the process of giving power or work to someone else so that they are responsible for part of what you normally do: [+**of**] *the delegation of authority*

de·lete /dɪˈliːt/ *v* [T] to remove something that has been written down or stored in a computer: *His name was deleted from the list.* | *I seem to have deleted a file by mistake.*

del·e·ter·i·ous /ˌdelɪˈtɪəriəs◂ $ -ˈtɪr-/ *adj formal* damaging or harmful: *the deleterious effects of smoking*

de·le·tion /dɪˈliːʃən/ *n* **1** [U] when you remove something from a piece of writing or from a computer's memory: [+**of**] *the deletion of unwanted files* **2** [C] a letter or word that has been removed from a piece of writing

del·i /ˈdeli/ *n* [C] a DELICATESSEN

de·lib·e·rate¹ /dɪˈlɪbərət/ *adj* **1** intended or planned; **≠** **unintentional**; **=** **intentional**: *a deliberate attempt to humiliate her* | *The attack on him was quite deliberate.* **2** deliberate speech, thought, or movement is slow and careful: *He approached her with slow, deliberate steps.* —**deliberateness** *n* [U]

de·lib·e·rate² /dɪˈlɪbəreɪt/ *v* [I] to think about something very carefully: *The jury deliberated for four days before acquitting him.* | [+**on/about/over**] *There was silence while she deliberated on his words.*

de·lib·er·ate·ly S3 W3 /dɪˈlɪbərətli/ *adv* **1** done in a way that is intended or planned; **=** **on purpose, intentionally**: *He was deliberately trying to upset her.* **2** done or said in a slow careful way: *He shook his head slowly and deliberately.*

de·lib·e·ra·tion /dɪˌlɪbəˈreɪʃən/ *n* **1** [C,U] careful consideration or discussion of something: *After much deliberation, first prize was awarded to Derek Murray.* | [+**of**] *the deliberations of committee meetings* **2** [U] *formal* if you speak or move with deliberation, you speak or move slowly and carefully

de·lib·e·ra·tive /dɪˈlɪbərətɪv $ -bəreɪtɪv/ *adj formal* existing for the purpose of discussing or planning something

del·i·ca·cy /ˈdelɪkəsi/ *n plural* **delicacies** **1** [C] something good to eat that is expensive or rare: *Snails are considered a delicacy in France.* **2** [U] a careful and sensitive way of speaking or behaving so that you do not upset anyone; **=** **tact**: *He carried out his duties with great delicacy and understanding.* **3** [U] the quality of being easy to harm or damage

del·i·cate /ˈdelɪkət/ *adj* **1** needing to be dealt with carefully or sensitively in order to avoid problems or failure: *There's something I have to speak to you about – it's a delicate matter.* | *delicate negotiations* **2** easily damaged or broken; **=** **fragile**: *delicate hand-cut glass* | *The sun can easily damage a child's delicate skin.* **3** old-fashioned someone who is delicate is hurt easily or easily becomes ill: *a delicate child* **4** a part of the body that is delicate is attractive and graceful: *Her wrists and ankles were slim and delicate.* | *her delicate features* **5** made skilfully and with attention to the smallest details: *a plate with a delicate pattern of leaves* **6** a taste, smell, or colour that is delicate is pleasant and not strong: *The wine has a dry delicate flavour.* | *a delicate pink* —**delicately** *adv* → INDELICATE

del·i·cates /ˈdelɪkəts/ *n* [plural] clothes that are made from material that needs careful treatment

del·i·ca·tes·sen /ˌdelɪkəˈtesən/ *n* [C] a shop that sells high quality cheeses, SALADS, cooked meats etc

de·li·cious /dɪˈlɪʃəs/ *adj* **1** very pleasant to taste or smell: *'The meal was absolutely delicious,' she said politely.* | *the delicious smell of new-mown grass* **2** *literary* extremely pleasant or enjoyable —**deliciously** *adv*: *deliciously spicy meat*

de·light¹ /dɪˈlaɪt/ *n* **1** [U] a feeling of great pleasure and satisfaction: **with/in delight** *The kids were screaming with delight.* | **to sb's delight/to the delight of sb** *To the delight of his proud parents, he has made a full recovery.* | **squeal/gasp/cry etc of delight** *She gave a little gasp of delight.* **2** [C] something that makes you feel very happy or satisfied: **the delights of sth** *a chance to sample the delights of nearby Vienna* | **it is a delight to do sth** *It was a delight to see him so fit and healthy.* **3** **take delight in (doing) sth** to enjoy something very much, especially something you should not do: *Chris takes great delight in teasing his sister.*

delight² *v* [T] to give someone great satisfaction and enjoyment: *Her fabulous recipes will delight anyone who loves chocolate.* | **delight sb with sth** *He is delighting audiences with his wit and humour.*

delight in sth *phr v* [T not in passive] to enjoy something very much, especially something that other people think is not nice: *He delights in complicating everything.* | *She delighted in interesting conversation.*

de·light·ed S2 /dɪˈlaɪtɪd/ *adj* very pleased and happy: **delighted to do sth** *Sandy will be delighted to see you.* | **delighted (that)** *I'm delighted that we have settled the matter.* | [+**with/by/at**] *She was delighted with her new home.* | *I am delighted by the result.* | *Her screams of delighted laughter filled the air.* ⚠ Do not say 'very delighted'. Say **absolutely delighted**. —**delightedly** *adv*

de·light·ful /dɪˈlaɪtfəl/ *adj* very pleasant: *a delightful little girl* | *The whole house is delightful.* —**delightfully** *adv*: *a movie that's full of delightfully comic moments*

de·lim·it /dɪˈlɪmɪt/ *v* [T] *formal* to set or say exactly what the limits of something are —**delimitation** /dɪˌlɪmɪˈteɪʃən/ *n* [C,U]

de·lin·e·ate /dɪˈlɪnieɪt/ *v* [T] *formal* **1** to describe or draw something carefully so that people can understand it: *The document delineates your rights and your obligations.* **2** to make the borders between two areas very clear: *The boundaries of these areas should be clearly delineated.* —**delineation** /dɪˌlɪniˈeɪʃən/ *n* [U]

•lin·quen·cy /dɪˈlɪŋkwənsi/ n plural **delinquen-cies** [C,U] illegal or immoral behaviour or actions, especially by young people: *the ever-rising statistics of delinquency and crime*

de·lin·quent[1] /dɪˈlɪŋkwənt/ adj **1** behaving in a way that is illegal or that society does not approve of; → **criminal**: **delinquent girls/boys/children/teenagers 2** technical a delinquent debt, account etc has not been paid on time: *the recovery of delinquent loans*

delinquent[2] n [C] someone, especially a young person, who breaks the law or behaves in ways their society does not approve of: *Deanes writes and lectures about teenage delinquents.* → JUVENILE DELINQUENT

de·lir·i·ous /dɪˈlɪriəs/ adj **1** talking continuously in an excited or anxious way, especially because you are ill: *He suffered an attack of malaria and was delirious.* **2** extremely excited or happy: [+with] *He was delirious with joy.* —**deliriously** adv

de·lir·i·um /dɪˈlɪriəm/ n **1** [U] a state in which someone is delirious, especially because they are very ill: *Before she died she had fits of delirium.* **2** [singular,U] extreme excitement

delirium trem·ens /dɪˌlɪriəm ˈtremənz $ -ˈtriː-/ n [U] medical the DT's

de·liv·er S2 W2 /dɪˈlɪvə $ -ər/ v
1 TAKE STH SOMEWHERE [I,T] to take goods, letters, packages etc to a particular place or person: *The morning mail has just been delivered.* | *Do you deliver on Saturdays?* | **deliver sth to sb** *They set off to deliver supplies to an isolated village.* | *I'm having some flowers delivered for her birthday.*
2 deliver a speech/lecture/address etc to make a speech etc to a lot of people: *The king delivered a televised speech to the nation on Nov 5.*
3 DO STH YOU SHOULD DO [I,T] to do or provide the things you are expected to, because you are responsible for them or they are part of your job: *the costs of delivering adequate nursing care* | *the failure of some services to **deliver the goods** (=do what they have promised)* | *The company will **deliver on its promises**.*
4 BABY [T] to help a woman give birth to her baby, or to give birth to a baby: *They rushed her to hospital where doctors delivered her baby.*
5 BLOW/SHOCK ETC [T] to give something such as a blow, shock, or warning to someone or something: *He delivered a strong warning about the dangers facing the government.*
6 deliver a judgment/verdict to officially state a formal decision or judgment: *The jury delivered a verdict of unlawful killing.*
7 PERSON [T] formal to put someone into someone else's control: **deliver sb to sb** *Sharett had betrayed him and delivered him to the enemy.*
8 VOTES [T] especially AmE to get the votes or support of a particular group of people in an election: *He cannot deliver the Latino vote.*
9 MAKE SB FREE OF STH [T] literary or biblical to help someone escape from something bad or evil: **deliver sb from sth** *'Deliver us from evil,' she prayed.* —**deliverer** n [C]
deliver sth ⇔ **up** phr v formal
to give something to someone else: *A bankrupt must deliver up all his books, papers and records.*

de·liv·er·a·ble /dɪˈlɪvərəbəl/ n [C usually plural] technical something that a company has promised to have ready for a customer, especially parts of computer systems: *software deliverables*

de·liv·er·ance /dɪˈlɪvərəns/ n [U + from] formal the state of being saved from harm or danger; → **salvation**, rescue

de·liv·er·y S2 W3 /dɪˈlɪvəri/ n plural **deliveries**
1 [C,U] the act of bringing goods, letters etc to a particular person or place, or the things that are brought: *Most Indian restaurants offer free delivery.* | *You can expect delivery in a week to ten days.* | *fresh milk deliveries* | [+of] *deliveries of food and supplies* | **on delivery** (=when something is delivered) *The restau-*

*rant pays **cash on delivery** for fish, which the local fishermen like.*
2 take delivery of sth to officially accept something large that you have bought: *We expect to take delivery of the aircraft sometime in June.*
3 [C] the process of giving birth to a child; → **labour**: *Mrs Howell had an easy delivery.* | *Liz was taken to the **delivery room** (=a room in a hospital for births) immediately.*
4 [U] the way in which someone speaks in public: *You'll have to work on your delivery.*

de·livery ˌman n [C] a man who delivers goods to people

dell /del/ n [C] literary a small valley with grass and trees

de·louse /ˌdiːˈlaʊs/ v [T] to remove lice (LOUSE) or similar animals from someone's hair, clothes etc

del·ta /ˈdeltə/ n [C] **1** the fourth letter of the Greek alphabet **2** an area of low land where a river spreads into many smaller rivers near the sea: *the Nile delta*

de·lude /dɪˈluːd/ v [T] to make someone believe something that is not true; ▤ **deceive**: *I was angry with him for trying to delude me.* | **delude sb/yourself into doing sth** *It is easy to delude yourself into believing you're in love.* | *Don't be deluded into thinking your house is burglarproof.*

del·uge[1] /ˈdeljuːdʒ/ n [C] **1** [usually singular] a large amount of something such as letters or questions that someone gets at the same time; ▤ **flood**: [+of] *Viewers sent a deluge of complaints about the show.* **2** formal a large flood, or period when there is a lot of rain; ▤ **flood**

deluge[2] v [T] **1** [usually passive] to send a very large number of letters, questions etc to someone all at the same time; ▤ **flood**: **be deluged with sth** *He was deluged with phone calls from friends and colleagues, congratulating him.* **2** formal to cover something with a lot of water; ▤ **flood**

de·lu·sion /dɪˈluːʒən/ n **1** [C,U] a false belief about yourself or the situation you are in: **under a delusion (that)** *He is under the delusion that I am going to cheat him.* **2 delusions of grandeur** the belief that you are much more important or powerful than you really are —**delusive** /-sɪv/ adj —**delusional** adj

de·luxe /dɪˈlʌks $ -ˈlʊks/ adj [usually before noun] of better quality and more expensive than other things of the same type; → **luxury**: *a deluxe hotel* | *The deluxe model costs a lot more.*

delve /delv/ v [I] **1** to try to find more information about someone or something: [+into] *research that delves deeply into this issue* **2** [always + adv/prep] to search for something by putting your hand deeply into a bag, container etc: [+into/in] *He delved into his pocket and brought out a notebook.*

Dem. the written abbreviation of **Democrat** or **Democratic**

de·mag·ne·tize also **-ise** BrE /ˌdiːˈmægnətaɪz/ v [T] to take away the MAGNETIC qualities of something; ▤ **magnetize**

dem·a·gogue /ˈdeməgɒg $ -gɑːg/ n [C] a political leader who tries to make people feel strong emotions in order to influence their opinions – used to show disapproval —**demagogy**, **demaguery** n [U] —**demagogic** /ˌdeməˈgɒgɪk $ -ˈgɑː-/ adj

de·mand[1] S1 W1 /dɪˈmɑːnd $ dɪˈmænd/ n
1 [singular, U] the need or desire that people have f particular goods and services: *Food production is s increasing faster than demand.* | [+for] *the deman new housing* | **huge/great/strong etc demand** *The huge demand for new cars.* | *the **growing demc** pasta in the UK* | **in demand** *He was a successful much in demand.* | *We rely on new sources of **meet demand**.* | *strong **consumer demand** →* DEMAND
2 [C] a very firm request for somethir

believe you have the right to get: *demonstrations in support of the nationalists' demands* | [+**for**] *their demand for higher salaries* | **demand that** *demands that he should resign*

3 demands [plural] the difficult, annoying, or tiring things that you need to do, or a skill you need to have: [+**of**] *the demands of modern life* | [+**on**] *The curriculum makes great demands on the teacher.* | *There are heavy demands on people's time these days.* | **place/put demands on/upon sb/sth** *the increased demands placed on police officers*

4 popular demand when a lot of people have asked for something to be done, performed etc: **by/due to popular demand** (=because of popular demand) *The exhibition will run for an extra week, due to popular demand.*

5 on demand *formal* whenever someone asks: *Should you feed your baby on demand, or stick to a timetable?*

demand² W2 v [T]
1 to ask for something very firmly, especially because you think you have a right to do this: *Angry demonstrators demanded the resignation of two senior officials.* | **demand to know/see/have etc sth** *I demand to know what's going on.* | **demand that** *They demanded that the military government free all political prisoners.* | **demand sth of sb** *It seemed that no matter what she did, more was demanded of her.* | *'Where are you going?' she demanded angrily.* ⚠ Do not say 'demand for something'. Say **demand something**: *I demand my money back!* (NOT *I demand for my money back!*)
2 if one thing demands another, it needs that thing in order to happen or be done successfully: *Too many things demanded his attention at the same time.* | *It's a desperate situation demanding a desperate remedy.*

de·mand·ing S3 /dɪˈmɑːndɪŋ $ dɪˈmæn-/ *adj*
1 needing a lot of ability, effort, or skill: *a demanding job* | **physically/emotionally/intellectually etc demanding** *Climbing is physically demanding.*
2 expecting a lot of attention or expecting to have things exactly the way you want them, especially in a way that is not fair: *Her mother could be very demanding at times.*

de·mar·cate /ˈdiːmɑːkeɪt $ dɪˈmɑːr-/ *v* [T] *formal* to decide or mark the limits of an area, system etc

de·mar·ca·tion /ˌdiːmɑːˈkeɪʃən $ -ɑːr-/ *n* [U] *formal* **1** the point at which one area of work, responsibility etc ends and another begins: [+**between**] *traditional lines of demarcation between medicine and surgery* **2** the process of deciding on or marking the border between two areas of land: [+**of**] *the exact demarcation of the north-south boundary*

de·mean /dɪˈmiːn/ *v* [T] to do something that makes people lose respect for someone or something; → **degrade**: *language that demeans women* | **demean yourself (by doing sth)** *I wouldn't demean myself by begging him for a job.*

de·mean·ing /dɪˈmiːnɪŋ/ *adj* showing less respect for someone than they deserve, or making someone feel embarrassed or ashamed; → **degrading**: [+**to**] *policies demeaning to women* | *I refuse to do demeaning work.*

de·mea·nour *BrE*, **demeanor** *AmE* /dɪˈmiːnə $ -ər/ *n* [singular, U] *formal* the way someone behaves, dresses, speaks etc that shows what their character is like: *his quiet, reserved demeanour*

de·men·ted /dɪˈmentɪd/ *adj* **1** crazy or behaving in a very strange way: *She was almost demented with grief.* **2** *old-fashioned* suffering from dementia

de·men·tia /dɪˈmenʃə, -ʃiə $ -tʃə/ *n* [U] an illness that affects the brain and memory, and makes you gradually lose the ability to think and behave normally

dem·e·ra·ra sug·ar /ˌdeməreərə ˈʃʊgə $ -rerə -/ *n* [U] *BrE* a type of rough brown sugar

de·merge /diːˈmɜːdʒ $ -ˈmɜːrdʒ/ *v* [I,T] *technical* to make part of a large company into a separate company: *After the takeover, several subsidiary companies demerged.*

de·mer·it /diːˈmerɪt/ *n* [C] **1** *formal* a bad quality feature of something: [+**of**] *The merits and demerits* (=the good and bad qualities) *of this argument have been explored.* **2** *AmE* a mark showing that a student has behaved badly at school; → **merit**

de·mesne /dɪˈmeɪn/ *n* [C] in the past, a very big house and all the land that belonged to it

demi- /demi/ *prefix* half; → **semi-**: *a demisemiquaver* (=very short musical note)

dem·i·god /ˈdemigɒd $ -gɑːd/ *n* [C] **1** someone who is so important and powerful that they are treated like a god **2** a man in ancient stories, who is half god and half human: *demigods such as Hercules*

dem·i·john /ˈdemidʒɒn $ -dʒɑːn/ *n* [C] *BrE* a large bottle with a short narrow neck, used for making wine

de·mil·i·ta·rize also **-ise** *BrE* /ˌdiːˈmɪlɪtəraɪz/ *v* [usually passive] to remove the weapons, soldiers etc from a country or area so that there can be no fighting there: *the demilitarized zone between the two countries* —**demilitarization** /diːˌmɪlɪtəraɪˈzeɪʃən $ -rə-/ *n* [U]

de·min·ing /diːˈmaɪnɪŋ/ *n* [U] the process of removing LANDMINES from an area of land

de·mise /dɪˈmaɪz/ *n* [U] **1** *formal* the end of something that used to exist: [+**of**] *the imminent demise* (=happening soon) *of the local newspaper* **2** *formal or law* death: *the mystery surrounding Elena's untimely demise* (=when death happens sooner than is normal or expected) —**demise** *v* [I]

de·mist /ˌdiːˈmɪst/ *v* [T] *BrE* to remove mist from a car window, by using heat; ▤ **defog** *AmE* —**demister** *n* [C]

dem·o¹ /ˈdeməʊ $ -moʊ/ *n* plural **demos** [C] **1** a recording containing an example of someone's music that is sent to a record company so that they can decide whether to produce it or not: *a demo tape* **2** *BrE informal* an event at which a large group of people publicly protest about something; ▤ **demonstration** *Police stood by to stop any pro-independence demos.* **3** an explanation of how something works; ▤ **demonstration** **4 a)** *AmE* an example of a product that is used to show what it is like or how it works: *demo homes on the new development* **b)** a computer program that shows what a new piece of software will be able to do when it is ready to be sold: *Click here to download a demo of the new version of our personal finance software.*

demo² *v* [T] *informal* to show or explain how something works or is done, especially new computer equipment: ▤ **demonstrate**: *They're going to demo some of the new software at this year's Mac convention.*

de·mob /diːˈmɒb $ -ˈmɑːb/ *v* **demobbed, demobbing** [T] *BrE* to demobilize soldiers etc

de·mo·bi·lize also **-ise** *BrE* /diːˈməʊbɪlaɪz $ -ˈmoʊ-/ *v* [T usually passive] to send home the members of an army, navy etc, especially at the end of a war: *programmes to help demobilized soldiers fit into civilian life* —**demobilization** /diːˌməʊbɪlaɪˈzeɪʃən $ -ˌmoʊbələ-/ *n* [U]

de·moc·ra·cy W2 /dɪˈmɒkrəsi $ dɪˈmɑː-/ *n* plural **democracies**
1 [U] a system of government in which every citizen in the country can vote to elect its government officials: *a return to democracy after 16 years of military rule*
2 [C] a country that has a government which has been elected by the people of the country: *a parliamentary democracy* | *Western democracies*
3 [U] a situation or system in which everyone is equal and has the right to vote, make decisions etc; → **democratic**: *democracy within the trade unions*

democrat /ˈdeməkræt/ *n* [C] someone who believes in democracy, or works to achieve it

Dem·o·crat *n* [C] a member or supporter of the Democratic Party of the US

dem·o·crat·ic W2 /ˌdeməˈkrætɪk◂/ *adj*
1 controlled by representatives who are elected by the people of a country: *a democratic government* | *the role of the media in the democratic process*

organized according to the principle that everyone ...as a right to be involved in making decisions: *a democratic management style*

3 organized according to the principle that everyone in a society is equally important, no matter how much money they have or what social class they come from: *a democratic society*

4 also **Democratic** belonging to or supporting the Democratic Party of the US: *the Democratic nominee for the presidency* —**democratically** /-kli/ *adv*: *democratically elected councils*

Demo'cratic ˌParty *n* the Democratic Party one of the two main political parties of the US; → **the Republican Party**

de·moc·ra·tize also **-ise** *BrE* /dɪ'mɒkrətaɪz $ dɪ'mɑː-/ *v* [T] to change the way in which a government, company etc is organized, so that it is more democratic: *efforts to democratize school management structures* —**democratization** /dɪˌmɒkrətaɪ'zeɪʃən $ dɪˌmɑːkrətə-/ *n* [U]

dem·o·graph·ic /ˌdemə'græfɪk◂/ *n* **1** demographics [plural] information about a group such as the people who live in a particular area: *the demographics of a newspaper's readership* **2** [C] a part of the population that is considered as a group, especially by advertisers who want to sell things to that group: *the 21–40 demographic* —**demographic** *adj*: *demographic change*

de·mog·ra·phy /dɪ'mɒɡrəfi $ -'mɑː-/ *n* [U] the study of human populations and the ways in which they change, for example the study of how many births, marriages and deaths happen in a particular place at a particular time —**demographer** *n* [C]

de·mol·ish /dɪ'mɒlɪʃ $ dɪ'mɑː-/ *v* [T] **1** to completely destroy a building: *The entire east wing of the building was demolished in the fire.* **2** to prove that an idea or opinion is completely wrong: *He demolished my argument in minutes.* **3** to end or ruin something completely: *These ants can demolish large areas of forest.* **4** to defeat someone very easily: *Miami demolished Texas 46–3.* **5** *especially BrE informal* to eat all of something very quickly: *He demolished a second helping of pie.* —**demolition** /ˌdemə'lɪʃən/ *n* [C,U]

demo'lition ˌjob *n* [C] **1** an act of criticizing someone severely or telling other people things about them which may be unfair or untrue, in order to harm them or to cause people to have a bad opinion of them: *He accused opposition leaders of doing a demolition job on the President.* **2** an event, especially a sports event, in which one person or team defeats the other one very easily: [+against] *Currie led the team with 55 points in the demolition job against Ireland.*

de·mon /'diːmən/ *n* [C] **1** an evil SPIRIT or force: *He was speeding down the motorway as if pursued by a demon.* **2** [usually plural] something that makes you anxious and causes you problems: *She struggled with her husband's demons of addiction and alcoholism.* **3** someone who is very good at something – often used humorously: *a demon cook* **4** the demon drink *BrE* alcoholic drink – often used humorously → DAEMON

de·mo·ni·a·cal /ˌdiːmə'naɪəkəl/ also **de·mo·ni·ac** /dɪ'məʊniæk $ -'moʊ-/ *adj formal* wild, uncontrolled, and evil: *Fear gripped her at the demoniacal glint in his dark eyes.* —**demoniacally** /-kli/ *adv*

de·mon·ic /dɪ'mɒnɪk $ dɪ'mɑː-/ *adj* **1** wild and cruel: *demonic laughter* **2** relating to a demon: *the demonic forces in the universe* —**demonically** /-kli/ *adv*

de·mon·stra·ble /dɪ'mɒnstrəbəl, 'demən- $ dɪ'mɑːn-/ *adj formal* able to be shown or proved: *We must provide demonstrable improvements in health services.* —**demonstrably** *adv*: *These conclusions are demonstrably wrong.*

dem·on·strate [W2] /'demənstreɪt/ *v*

1 [T] to show or prove something clearly: *The study demonstrates the link between poverty and*

malnutrition. | **demonstrate that** *Hitchcock's films demonstrate that a British filmmaker could learn from Hollywood.* | **demonstrate how/what/why etc** *This section will attempt to demonstrate how the Bank of England operates.* | *The government now has an opportunity to* **demonstrate** *its* **commitment** *to reform.*

2 [T] to show or describe how to do something or how something works: **demonstrate how** *They'll be demonstrating how to handle modern, high performance cars.* | *Instructors should demonstrate new movements before letting the class try them.*

3 [I] to protest or support something in public with a lot of other people: *Supporters demonstrated outside the courtroom during the trial.* | [+against] *What are they demonstrating against?*

4 [T] to show that you have a particular ability, quality, or feeling: *He has demonstrated an ability to meet deadlines.*

demonstration D

demonstration

procession

riot

dem·on·stra·tion [S3] [W3] /ˌdemən'streɪʃən/ *n* [C]

1 an event at which a large group of people meet to protest or to support something in public: **peaceful/violent demonstration** *Police opened fire on a peaceful demonstration.* | *The proposals sparked* **mass demonstrations**. | [+against] *a demonstration against the government's educational policies* | **stage/hold a demonstration** *Supporters staged a demonstration outside the US embassy.*

2 an act of explaining and showing how to do something or how something works: [+of] *He gave a practical* **demonstration** *of the boat's military potential.* | *a cookery demonstration*

3 *formal* an action that proves that someone or something has a particular ability, quality, or feeling: [+of] *The high level of calls is a* **clear demonstration of** *the need for this service.* | *a physical demonstration of affection*

de·mon·stra·tive /dɪ'mɒnstrətɪv $ dɪ'mɑːn-/ willing to show that you care about someone: *mother wasn't demonstrative; she never hugged* —**demonstratively** *adv*

de·monstrative 'pronoun *n* [C] one of the words 'this', 'that', 'these', and 'those'

dem·on·stra·tor /'demənstreɪtə $ -ər/ *n* [C] **1** someone who takes part in a demonstration: *anti-war demonstrators* **2** someone who shows people how to do something or how something works

de·mor·al·ize also **-ise** *BrE* /dɪ'mɒrəlaɪz $ dɪ'mɔː-, dɪ'mɑː-/ *v* [T] to reduce or destroy someone's courage or confidence: *The illness demoralized him and recovery took several weeks.* —**demoralized** *adj*: *The refugees were cold, hungry, and demoralized.* —**demoralizing** *adj*: *the demoralizing effects of unemployment* —**demoralization** /dɪ,mɒrəlaɪ'zeɪʃən $ -,mɔːrələ-, -,mɑː-/ *n* [U]

de·mote /dɪ'məʊt $ -'moʊt/ *v* [T usually in passive] to make someone's rank or position lower or less important; **☒ promote**: *The sergeant was demoted to private.* —**demotion** /-'məʊʃən $ -'moʊ-/ *n* [C,U]

de·mot·ic /dɪ'mɒtɪk $ -'mɑː-/ *adj* formal used by or popular with most ordinary people

de·mo·ti·vat·ing /diː'məʊtɪ̈veɪtɪŋ $ -'moʊ-/ *adj* making someone less eager or willing to do their job: *Tasks that do not challenge you can be very demotivating.* —**demotive** *v* [T]

de·mur[1] /dɪ'mɜː $ -'mɜːr/ *v* **demurred, demurring** [I] to express doubt about or opposition to a plan or suggestion: *They demurred politely, but finally agreed to stay.*

demur[2] *n* [U] disagreement or disapproval: **without demur** *I agreed to this without demur.*

de·mure /dɪ'mjʊə $ -'mjʊr/ *adj* **1** quiet, serious, and well-behaved – used especially about women in the past: *Old photos of Maggie show her young and demure.* **2** demure clothes do not show much of a woman's body: *a demure white dress* —**demurely** *adv*

de·mys·ti·fy /ˌdiː'mɪstɪ̈faɪ/ *v* **demystified, demystifying, demystifies** [T] to make a subject that seems difficult or complicated easier to understand, especially by explaining it in simpler language: *This book attempts to demystify the male worlds of plumbing and carpentry.* —**demystification** /diːˌmɪstɪ̈fɪ'keɪʃən/ *n* [U]

den /den/ *n* [C] **1** the home of some animals, for example lions or FOXES **2** a place where secret or illegal activities take place: *corrupt gambling dens* | *a den of thieves* **3** an enclosed and secret place where children play **4** especially *AmE* a room in a house where people relax, watch television etc **5** *BrE* old-fashioned a small room in a house where people can work, read etc without being interrupted: *Father retreated to his den.* **6** **den of iniquity** a place where activities that you think are immoral or evil happen – often used humorously: *Her mother was convinced that London was a den of iniquity.*

de·na·tion·al·ize also **-ise** *BrE* /diː'næʃənəlaɪz/ *v* [T] to sell a business or industry that is owned by the state, so that it is then owned privately; **☒ privatize**; **☒ nationalize** —**denationalization** /diːˌnæʃənəlaɪ'zeɪʃən $ -lə-/ *n* [U]

de·ni·al /dɪ'naɪəl/ *n* **1** [C,U] a statement saying that something is not true; → **deny**: [+of] *The government issued an official denial of the rumour.* | **denial that** *denials that border security had not been strict enough* **2** [U] when someone refuses to allow someone else to have or to do something: [+of] *protests against the denial of human rights* **3** [U] a condition in which you refuse to admit or believe that something bad exists or has happened: **in denial** *His girlfriend is in denial, and refuses to admit that he will soon die.*

·i·er /'deniə $ -ər/ *n* [U] a unit for measuring how ⁓NYLON, silk etc thread is: **10-/15-/20- etc denier** *a ⁓f 15-denier tights*

den·i·grate /'denɪ̈greɪt/ *v* [T] to say things to ma⁓ someone or something seem less important or goo⁓ *people who denigrate their own country* —**denigratio⁓** /ˌdenɪ̈'greɪʃən/ *n* [U]

den·im /'denɪ̈m/ *n* [U] a type of strong cotton clot⁓ used especially to make JEANS

den·i·zen /'denɪ̈zən/ *n* [C + of] literary an animal⁓ plant, or person that lives or is found in a particula⁓ place

de·nom·i·nate /dɪ'nɒmɪ̈neɪt $ dɪ'nɑː-/ *v* [T usuall⁓ passive] *technical* to officially set the value of some⁓ thing according to one system or type of money

de·nom·i·na·tion /dɪˌnɒmɪ̈'neɪʃən $ dɪˌnɑː-/ *n* [C] **1** a religious group that has slightly differen⁓ beliefs from other groups within the same religion⁓ *Christians of all denominations* **2** *technical* the valu⁓ shown on a coin, paper money, or a stamp

de·nom·i·na·tion·al /dɪˌnɒmɪ̈'neɪʃənəl $ dɪˌnɑː-/ *adj* relating or belonging to a particular religiou⁓ denomination

de·nom·i·na·tor /dɪ'nɒmɪ̈neɪtə $ dɪ'nɑːmɪ̈neɪtər/ *n* [C] *technical* the number below the line in a FRACTION; → **numerator** → **lowest common denominator** at COMMO⁓ DENOMINATOR (2)

de·note /dɪ'nəʊt $ -'noʊt/ *v* [T] *formal* **1** to mea⁓ something; → **connote**: *What does the word 'curricu⁓ lum' denote that 'course' does not?* **2** to represent or b⁓ a sign of something; **☒ indicate**: *Crosses on the ma⁓ denote villages.* —**denotative** *adj* —**denotatio⁓** /ˌdiːnəʊ'teɪʃən $ -noʊ-/ *n* [C]

de·noue·ment /deɪ'nuːmɒŋ $ ˌdeɪnuː'mɑːŋ/ *n* [C⁓ *formal* the exciting last part of a story or play: *The plo⁓ takes us to Paris for the denouement of the story.*

de·nounce /dɪ'naʊns/ *v* [T] **1** to express stron⁓ disapproval of someone or something, especially i⁓ public; → **denunciation**: *Amnesty Internationa⁓ denounced the failure by the authorities to take action.* **denounce sb/sth as sth** *He denounced the election as ⁓ farce.* **2** to give information to the police or othe⁓ authority about someone's illegal political activities⁓ **denounce sb to sb** *She denounced him to the secre⁓ police.*

dense /dens/ *adj* **1** made of or containing a lot ⁓ things or people that are very close together; **☒ thick⁓ dense undergrowth/forest/woodland/jungle etc** *A na⁓ row track wound steeply up through dense forest.* | ⁓ *dense rurally-based population* **2** difficult to se⁓ through or breathe in: **dense fog/smoke/cloud** *dens⁓ black smoke* **3** *informal* not able to understand thing⁓ easily; **☒ stupid**: *Am I being dense? I don't quite under⁓ stand.* **4** a dense piece of writing is difficult to under⁓ stand because it contains a lot of information or use⁓ complicated language **5** *technical* a substance that i⁓ dense has a lot of MASS in relation to its size: *Water ⁓ eight hundred times denser than air.* —**densely** *adv*: ⁓ *densely populated area* —**denseness** *n* [U]

den·si·ty /'densɪ̈ti/ *n* [U] **1** the degree to which a⁓ area is filled with people or things: [+of] *the size an⁓ density of settlements* | *areas of high population den⁓ sity* **2** *technical* the relationship between the MASS ⁓ something and its size

dent[1] /dent/ *n* [C] **1** a hollow area in the surface ⁓ something, usually made by something hitting it: [+in⁓ *There was a large dent in the passenger door*; → see⁓ picture at CRASH **2** a reduction in the amount of some⁓ thing: [+in] *The trip made a big dent in our savings.* | *Eight years of effort have hardly put a dent in dru⁓ trafficking.*

dent[2] *v* **1** [I,T] if you dent something, or if it dents⁓ you hit or press it so that its surface is bent inwards: *N⁓ one was injured, but the car was scratched an⁓ dented.* **2** [T] to damage or harm something: *Th⁓ scandal has dented his reputation.*

den·tal /'dentl/ *adj* [only before noun] relating to you⁓ teeth: **dental treatment/care** *Dental care was free in th⁓ 60s.* | **dental disease/problems/decay etc**

dental 'floss *n* [U] thin strong string that you use for cleaning between your teeth

dental 'hygienist *n* [C] someone who works with a dentist and cleans people's teeth, or gives them advice about how to look after their teeth

dental nurse *n* [C] someone whose job is to help a dentist

dental ,surgeon *n* [C] a dentist who can perform operations in the mouth

den·tine /'denti:n/ also **den·tin** /'dentɪn/ *n* [U] the type of bone that your teeth are made of

den·tist /'dentɪst/ *n* [C] someone whose job is to treat people's teeth: **the dentist/the dentist's** (=the place where a dentist works) *I'm going to the dentist this afternoon.* → see picture at OCCUPATION

den·tis·try /'dentɪstri/ *n* [U] the medical study of the mouth and teeth, or the work of a dentist

den·tures /'dentʃəz $ -ərz/ *n* [plural] a set of artificial teeth worn by someone who does not have their own teeth any longer; ⊟ **false teeth**

de·nude /dɪ'nju:d $ dɪ'nu:d/ *v* [T usually passive] *formal* **1** to remove the plants and trees that cover an area of land: *a hillside denuded in a fire* **2** to take something away from someone or something: **denude sb/sth of sth** *The fact that people have left farm work has denuded many villages of their working populations.* —**denudation** /,di:nju:'deɪʃən $ -nu:-/ *n* [U]

de·nun·ci·a·tion /dɪ,nʌnsi'eɪʃən/ *n* [C] a public statement in which you criticize someone or something

de·ny S2 W2 /dɪ'naɪ/ *v* **denied, denying, denies** [T]
1 SAY STH IS NOT TRUE to say that something is not true, or that you do not believe something; → **denial**: **deny (that)** *I've never denied that there is a housing problem.* | *I can't deny her remarks hurt me.* | **deny doing sth** *Two men have denied murdering a woman at a remote picnic spot.* | **strongly/vehemently/strenuously etc deny sth** *Jackson vehemently denied the allegations.* | *The government **denied the existence of** poverty among 16- and 17-year-olds.* | **deny a charge/allegation/claim** *The men have denied charges of theft.*
2 NOT ALLOW to refuse to allow someone to have or do something: *landowners who deny access to the countryside* | **deny sb sth** *She could deny her son nothing.* | **deny sth to sb** *This is the only country in Europe to deny cancer screening to its citizens.*
3 there's no denying (that/sth) *spoken* used to say that it is very clear that something is true: *There's no denying that this is an important event.*
4 FEELINGS to refuse to admit that you are feeling something: *Emotions can become destructive if they are suppressed and denied.*
5 deny yourself (sth) to decide not to have something that you would like, especially for moral or religious reasons: *He denied himself all pleasures and luxuries.*

de·o·do·rant /di:'əʊdərənt $ -'oʊ-/ *n* [C,U] a chemical substance that you put on the skin under your arms to stop you from smelling bad; → **antiperspirant**

de·o·do·rize also **-ise** *BrE* /di:'əʊdəraɪz $ -'oʊ-/ *v* [T] to remove a bad smell or to make it less noticeable

de·part /dɪ'pɑ:t $ -ɑ:rt/ *v* **1** [I,T] to leave, especially when you are starting a journey; → **departure**: [+from] *ocean liners arriving at and departing from the island* | [+for] *Dorothy departed for Germany last week.* | *Flights by Air Europe depart Gatwick on Tuesdays.* **2 depart this life** *formal* to die **3** [I] to start to use new ideas or do something in a different way; → **departure**: [+from] *It's revolutionary music; it departs from the old form and structures.* | *In his speech, the President departed from his text only once.* **4** [I,T] to leave an organization or job; → **departure**: *the company's departing chairman*

de·part·ed /dɪ'pɑ:tɪd $ -ɑ:r-/ *adj* [only before noun] dead – used in order to avoid saying the word 'dead': *his dear departed wife*

419   **depend**

de·part·ment S3 W1 /dɪ'pɑ:tmənt $ -ɑ:r-/ *n* [C]
1 one of the groups of people who work together in a particular part of a large organization such as a hospital, university, company, or government: *the personnel department* | *the English department* | [+of] *the Department of the Environment*
2 an area in a large shop where a particular type of product is sold: *the toy department*
3 be sb's department *spoken* if something is someone's department, they are responsible for it or know a lot about it: *I'll see what I can do, but it's not really my department.*
4 *spoken* a particular part of someone's character, or a particular part of a larger activity or subject: *Dave was a little lacking in the trustworthiness department.*
—**departmental** /,di:pɑ:t'mentl◂ $ -ɑ:r-/ *adj*: *a departmental meeting* → FIRE DEPARTMENT, POLICE DEPARTMENT

de·part·men·ta·lize also **-ise** *BrE* /,di:pɑ:t'mentlaɪz $ -ɑ:r-/ *v* [T] to divide something into different departments

de'partment ,store *n* [C] a large shop that is divided into separate departments, each selling a different type of goods → see picture at TOWN

de·par·ture W3 /dɪ'pɑ:tʃə $ -'pɑ:rtʃər/ *n*
1 [C,U] an act of leaving a place, especially at the start of a journey; ⊟ **arrival**: [+for] *I saw Simon shortly before his departure for Russia.* | [+of] *There was a delay in the departure of our plane.* | [+from] *Mozart's departure from Paris in September 1778*
2 [C,U] an act of leaving an organization or position: [+from] *He refused to discuss his departure from the government.*
3 [C] a flight, train etc that leaves at a particular time: *There are several departures for New York every day.*
4 [C] a way of doing something that is different from the usual, traditional, or expected way: [+from] *Their new designs represent a departure from their usual style.* | **radical/major/significant etc departure** (=a big change) *This would be a radical departure from the subsidy system.*

de'parture ,lounge *n* [C] the place at an airport where people wait until their plane is ready to leave

de'partures ,board *n* [C] a board in an airport or station that shows the times at which planes or trains leave

de·pend S1 W2 /dɪ'pend/ *v*
it/that depends *spoken* used to say that you cannot give a definite answer to something because your answer will be affected by something else: *'How long are you staying?' 'I don't know; it depends.'* | **it depends who/what/how/whether etc** *You may take several months to reach your target weight – it depends how much you want to lose.*

depend on/upon sb/sth *phr v*
1 if something depends on something else, it is directly affected or decided by that thing: *The length of time spent exercising depends on the sport you are training for.* | **depend on how/what/whether etc** *Choosing the right bike depends on what you want to use it for.* | **depending on sth** *The expenses you claim can vary enormously, depending on travel distances involved.*
2 to need the support, help, or existence of someone or something in order to exist, be healthy, be successful etc; ⊟ **rely on**: *The country depends heavily on its tourist trade.* | *We depend entirely on donations from the public.* | **depend on sb/sth for sth** *Many women have to depend on their husbands for their state pension.* | **depend on sb/sth to do sth** *I'm depending on you to tell me everything.* | **depend on sb/sth doing sth** *We're depending on him finishing the job by Friday.*
3 to trust or have confidence in someone or something: *You can depend on Jane – she always keeps her promises.* ⚠ Do not say that one thing 'is depend on' another. Say one thing **is dependent on** another.

2 someone whose job is to help a SHERIFF in the US
3 a member of parliament in some countries, for example France

de·rail /ˌdiːˈreɪl, dɪ-/ v **1** [I,T] if a train derails or something derails it, it goes off the tracks **2** [T] to spoil or interrupt a plan, agreement etc: *a mistake that might derail the negotiations* —**derailment** n [C,U]

de·ranged /dɪˈreɪndʒd/ adj someone who is deranged behaves in a crazy or dangerous way, usually because they are mentally ill: *a deranged gunman* —**derangement** n [C,U]

der·by /ˈdɑːbi $ ˈdɜːrbi/ n plural derbies [C] **1 Derby** used in the names of some well-known horse races: *the Kentucky Derby | the Derby BrE* (=a famous race in England) **2** *BrE* a sports match between two teams from the same area or city **3** *especially AmE* a man's hard round hat that is usually black; ⊟ **bowler** *BrE* **4** a particular type of race or competition: *a donkey derby*

de·reg·u·late /ˌdiːˈreɡjᵿleɪt/ v [T usually passive] to remove government rules and controls from some types of business activity: *industries that have been deregulated* —**deregulation** /ˌdiːˌreɡjᵿˈleɪʃən/ n [U]

der·e·lict¹ /ˈderᵻlɪkt/ adj a derelict building or piece of land is in very bad condition because it has not been used for a long time

derelict² n [C] someone who has no money or home, lives on the streets, and is very dirty – used to show disapproval

der·e·lic·tion /ˌderᵻˈlɪkʃən/ n **1 dereliction of duty** *formal* when someone fails to do what they should do as part of their job **2** [U] the state of being derelict: *areas of industrial dereliction*

de·ride /dɪˈraɪd/ v [T] *formal* to make remarks or jokes that show you think someone or something is silly or useless; ⊟ **mock**: *You shouldn't deride their efforts.* | **deride sb as sth** *The party was derided as totally lacking in ideas.*

de ri·gueur /də riːˈɡɜː $ -ˈɡɜːr/ adj [not before noun] considered to be necessary if you want to be accepted, fashionable etc – used humorously: *the gleaming white teeth that are de rigueur for movie stars*

de·ri·sion /dɪˈrɪʒən/ n [U] when you show that you think someone or something is stupid or silly: *His speech was greeted with derision by opposition leaders.*

de·ri·sive /dɪˈraɪsɪv/ adj showing that you think someone or something is stupid or silly: *derisive laughter* —**derisively** adv

de·ri·so·ry /dɪˈraɪsəri/ adj **1** an amount of money that is derisory is so small that it is not worth considering seriously: *Unions described the pay offer as derisory.* **2** DERISIVE

de·riv·a·ble /dɪˈraɪvəbəl/ adj [+from] something that is derivable can be calculated from something else

der·i·va·tion /ˌderᵻˈveɪʃən/ n [C,U +of] *technical* the origin of something, especially a word

de·riv·a·tive¹ /dɪˈrɪvətɪv/ n [C] **1** something that has developed or been produced from something else: [+of] *Heroin is a derivative of morphine.* **2** a type of financial INVESTMENT: *the derivatives market*

derivative² adj not new or invented, but copied or taken from something else – used to show disapproval: *a derivative text*

de·rive /dɪˈraɪv/ v **1** [T] to get something, especially an advantage or a pleasant feeling, from something: **derive sth from sth** *Medically, we will derive great benefit from this technique.* | **derive pleasure/enjoyment etc** *Many students derived enormous satisfaction from the course.* **2** also **be derived** [I,T] to develop or come from something else: [+from] *This word is derived from Latin.* | *patterns of behaviour that derive from basic beliefs* **3** [T] *technical* to get a chemical substance from another substance: **be derived from sth** *The enzyme is derived from human blood.*

der·ma·ti·tis /ˌdɜːməˈtaɪtᵻs $ ˌdɜːr-/ n [U] a disease of the skin that causes redness, swelling, and pain

der·ma·tol·o·gy /ˌdɜːməˈtɒlədʒi $ ˌdɜːrməˈtɑː-/ n [U] the part of medical science that deals with skin diseases and their treatment —**dermatologist** n [C]

de·rog·ate /ˈderəɡeɪt/ v
derogate from sth phr v *formal* to make something seem less important or less good

de·rog·a·to·ry /dɪˈrɒɡətəri $ dɪˈrɑːɡətɔːri/ adj derogatory remarks, attitudes etc are insulting and disapproving: *Their conversation contained a number of derogatory racial remarks.*

der·rick /ˈderɪk/ n [C] **1** a tall machine used for lifting heavy weights, especially on ships **2** a tall tower built over an oil well, used to raise and lower the DRILL

der·rière /ˈderieə $ ˌderiˈer/ n [C] your BUTTOCKS - used humorously

der·ring-do /ˌderɪŋ ˈduː/ n deeds/acts etc of derring-do very brave actions like the ones that happen in adventure stories – used humorously

der·vish /ˈdɜːvɪʃ $ ˈdɜːr-/ n [C] a member of a Muslim religious group, some of whom dance fast and spin around as part of a religious ceremony

de·sal·i·na·tion /ˌdiːˌsælᵻˈneɪʃən/ n [U] *technical* the process of removing salt from sea water so that people can use it —**desalinate** /diːˈsælᵻneɪt/ v [T]

de·scale /ˌdiːˈskeɪl/ v [T] *BrE* to remove the white substance that forms on the inside of pipes, KETTLES etc

des·cant /ˈdeskænt/ n [C,U] a tune that is played or sung above the main tune in a piece of music

de·scend /dɪˈsend/ v **1** [I,T] *formal* to move from a higher level to a lower one; ⊟ **ascend**: *Our plane started to descend.* | *I heard his footsteps descending the stairs.* | [+to/into etc] *The path continues for some way before descending to Garsdale Head.* ⚠ It is more usual to say **go down** or **come down**. **2** [I] *literary* if darkness, silence, a feeling etc descends, it becomes dark etc or you start to feel something, especially suddenly: [+on/upon/over] *Total silence descended on the room.* | *An air of gloom descended over the party headquarters.* **3 in descending order (of sth)** numbers, choices etc that are in descending order are arranged from the highest or most important to the lowest or least important: *The hotels are listed in descending order of price.*
descend from sb/sth phr v **1 be descended from sb** to be related to a person or group who lived a long time ago: *She claims to be descended from Abraham Lincoln.* | *The people here are descended from the Vikings.* **2** to have developed from something that existed in the past: *ideas that descend from those of ancient philosophers*
descend on/upon sb/sth phr v if a large number of people descend on a person or a place, they come to visit or stay, especially when they are not very welcome: *Millions of tourists descend on the area every year.*
descend to sth phr v to behave or speak in an unpleasant way, which is not the way you usually behave: *Surely he wouldn't descend to such a mean trick?* | **descend to sb's level** (=behave or speak as badly as someone else) *Other people may gossip, but don't descend to their level.*

de·scen·dant /dɪˈsendənt/ n [C] **1** someone who is related to a person who lived a long time ago, or to a family, group of people etc that existed in the past; → **ancestor**: **sb's descendants/the descendants of sb** *The coastal areas were occupied by the descendants of Greek colonists.* | *He was a direct descendant of Napoleon Bonaparte.* **2** something that has developed from something else: [+of] *Quechua is a descendant of the Inca language.*

de·scent /dɪˈsent/ n **1** [C,U] *formal* the process of going down; ⊟ **ascent**: *Passengers must fasten their seat belts prior to descent.* | [+from/to] *The descent to Base Camp took about two days.* **2** [U] your family igins, especially your nationality or relationship to ~~s~~omeone important who lived a long time ago: **of Russian/Italian etc descent** *young men and women of Asian descent* | [+**from**] *The emperor **claimed descent** from David.* | **by descent** *They're Irish by descent.* **3** [C] a path or road that goes down a slope; ⊞ **ascent**: *There is no direct descent from the summit.* **4** [singular] a gradual change towards behaviour or a situation that is very bad: **descent into alcoholism/chaos/madness etc** *the story of his descent into drug abuse* **5** [singular] *BrE* a sudden unwanted visit or attack: *the descent on the town by a motorcycle gang*

de·scribe S1 W1 /dɪˈskraɪb/ v [T]
1 to say what something or someone is like by giving details about them: *The police asked her to describe the two men.* | *An alternative approach to the problem is described in Chapter 3.* | **describe sb/sth as (being/having) sth** *After the operation her condition was described as comfortable.* | *The youth is described as being 18 to 19 years old.* | **describe how/why/what etc** *It's difficult to describe how I feel.* | **describe sth to sb** *So describe this new boyfriend to me!* | **describe doing sth** *He described finding his mother lying on the floor.*
2 describe a circle/an arc etc *formal* to make a movement which forms the shape of a circle etc: *Her hand described a circle in the air.*

de·scrip·tion S2 W2 /dɪˈskrɪpʃən/ n [C,U]
1 a piece of writing or speech that gives details about what someone or something is like: *Berlin sounds fascinating from your description.* | [+**of**] *The writer began with a description of the area.* | *The police have issued a **detailed description** of the missing woman.* | *an **accurate description** of the event* | *I checked my **job description**.* | **give/provide etc a description** *The booklet gives a brief description of each place.* | **brief/short/full/complete description** *Your insurance company will need a full description of the stolen property.* | *The guide gives a **general description** of the island.* | **fit/match/answer a description** (=be like the person or thing described) *He matches the description of the attacker.*
2 be beyond/past description to be too good, bad, big etc to be described easily: *The death and destruction were beyond description.*
3 of every/some/any etc description also **of all descriptions** people or things of every type, some type etc: *People of all descriptions came to see the show.*

de·scrip·tive /dɪˈskrɪptɪv/ adj **1** giving a description of something: *the descriptive passages in the novel* **2** *technical* describing how the words of a language are actually used, rather than saying how they ought to be used; ⊞ **prescriptive** —**descriptively** adv

des·e·crate /ˈdesɪkreɪt/ v [T] to spoil or damage something holy or respected —**desecration** /ˌdesɪˈkreɪʃən/ n [U]

de·seg·re·gate /diːˈsegrɪgeɪt/ v [T] to end a system in which people of different races are kept separate; → **integrate**; ⊞ **segregate** —**desegregation** /ˌdiːsegrɪˈgeɪʃən $ diːˌseg-/ n [U]

de·sel·ect /ˌdiːsəˈlekt/ v [T] **1** to remove something from a list of choices on a computer **2** *BrE* if members of a political party deselect an existing Member of Parliament, they refuse to choose him or her as a CANDIDATE at the next election —**deselection** /-ˈlekʃən/ n [U]

de·sen·si·tize also **-ise** *BrE* /diːˈsensɪtaɪz/ v [T] to make someone react less strongly to something by making them become used to it: **desensitize sb to sth** *Does TV desensitize people to violence?* —**desensitization** /diːˌsensɪtaɪˈzeɪʃən $ -tə-/ n [U]

des·ert¹ /ˈdezət $ -ərt/ n **1** [C,U] a large area of land where it is always very hot and dry, and there is a lot of sand: *the Sahara Desert* | *This area of the country is mostly desert.* | **in the desert** *The plane crash-landed in the desert.* **2** [C] a place where there is no activity or

where nothing interesting happens: *The railroad yard was a desert now.* △ Do not confuse **desert** and **dessert** although they have similar spellings.

de·sert² /dɪˈzɜːt $ -ˈzɜːrt/ v **1** [T] to leave someone or something and no longer help or support them; ⊟ **abandon**: *Helen was deserted by her husband.* | *Many of the party's traditional voters deserted it at the last election.* | *The price rise caused many readers to desert the magazine.* | **desert sb for sb** *He deserted her for another woman.* **2** [T] to leave a place so that it is completely empty; ⊟ **abandon**: *The birds have deserted their nest.* **3** [I] to leave the army, navy etc without permission: *Several hundred soldiers have deserted.* **4** [T] if a feeling, quality, or skill deserts you, you no longer have it, especially at a time when you need it: *Mike's confidence seemed to have deserted him.*

de·sert·ed /dɪˈzɜːtɪd $ -ɜːr-/ adj **1** empty and quiet because no people are there: *The streets were deserted.* | *The old mine now stands completely deserted.* **2 deserted wife/husband/child etc** a wife etc who has been left by her husband etc

de·sert·er /dɪˈzɜːtə $ -ˈzɜːrtər/ n [C] a soldier who leaves the army, navy etc without permission

de·sert·i·fi·ca·tion /dɪˌzɜːtɪfɪˈkeɪʃən $ -ˌzɜːr-/ n [U] *technical* the process by which useful land, especially farm land, changes into desert

de·ser·tion /dɪˈzɜːʃən $ -ɜːr-/ n **1** [C,U] the act of leaving the army, navy etc without permission **2** [U] *law* the act of leaving your wife or husband because you do not want to live with them any longer

‚desert ˈisland n [C] a small tropical island that is far away from other places and has no people living on it

de·serts /dɪˈzɜːts $ -ˈzɜːrts/ n **get/receive your (just) deserts** to be punished in a way that you deserve: *Offenders should receive their just deserts.*

de·serve S2 W3 /dɪˈzɜːv $ -ɜːrv/ v [T]
1 to have earned something by good or bad actions or behaviour: *What have I done to deserve this?* | **deserve to do sth** *We didn't deserve to win.* | **richly/fully/thoroughly etc deserve sth** *the success he so richly deserves* | *I'm sorry for the kids. They **deserve better** (=deserve to be treated in a better way).* | **deserve a rest/break/holiday etc** *I think we deserve a rest after all that hard work.* | *Ledley **deserves** a **place** in the team.* | *Paula deserves a special **mention** for all the help she has given us.* | *I would never hit anyone, even if they deserved it.* | *What has he done to **deserve** this **punishment**?* | **deserve all/everything you get** (=deserve any bad things that happen to you) *He deserves all he gets for being so dishonest.* | *People who are sent to prison for drunk-driving **get what they deserve**.*
2 deserve consideration/attention etc if a suggestion, idea, or plan deserves consideration, attention etc, it is good enough to be considered, paid attention to etc; ⊟ **merit**: *This proposal deserves serious consideration.*
3 sb deserves a medal *spoken* used to say that you admire the way someone dealt with a situation or problem: [+**for**] *You deserve a medal for putting up with Ian's constant demands.*

de·served /dɪˈzɜːvd $ -ˈzɜːrvd/ adj earned because of good or bad behaviour, skill, work etc: *He has a **well-deserved** reputation as a reliable worker.* | *a **deserved** win/victory/success etc Larsson's goal gave Celtic a deserved victory.*

de·serv·ed·ly /dɪˈzɜːvɪdli $ -ɜːr-/ adv **1** in a wa~~y~~ that is right or deserved: **deservedly popular/we~~ll~~-known/famous etc** *Bistro Roti is a deservedly pop~~ular~~ restaurant.* | *Arsenal were **deservedly beaten** 2~~-~~ Leeds.* **2 (and) deservedly so** used to say tha~~t~~ agree that something is right and deserved: ~~H~~ *widely respected in the music world, and deser~~ve~~*

de·serv·ing /dɪˈzɜːvɪŋ $ -ɜːr-/ adj **1** nee~~ding~~ and support, especially financial support: **causes/cases** *The National Lottery pro~~vides~~*

money for deserving causes. **2 be deserving of sth** *formal* to deserve something: *Some criminals are more deserving of their punishment than others.*

des·ic·cat·ed /ˈdesɪkeɪtɪd/ *adj technical* **1** desiccated food has been dried in order to preserve it **2** completely dry: *desiccated soil*

des·ic·ca·tion /ˌdesɪˈkeɪʃən/ *n* [U] *technical* the process of becoming completely dry

de·sid·e·ra·tum /dɪˌzɪdəˈrɑːtəm, -ˈreɪ-, -ˌsɪd- $ dɪˌsɪdəˈreɪtəm, -ˈrɑː-/ *n plural* **desiderata** /-tə/ [C] *formal* something that is wanted or needed

de·sign¹ S3 W1 /dɪˈzaɪn/ *n*
1 PROCESS OF PLANNING [U] the art or process of making a drawing of something to show how you will make it or what it will look like: *The new plane is in its final design stage.* | *the design process* | *the design team* | *a course in* **graphic design** | *computer-aided design*
2 ARRANGEMENT OF PARTS [C,U] the way that something has been planned and made, including its appearance, how it works etc: *The car's design has been greatly improved.* | [+of] *the design of the new building* | *Some changes have been made to the computer's basic design.* | *a* **design fault** | *The electric windows are an important* **design feature** *of this model.*
3 PATTERN [C] a pattern for decorating something: *a floral design* | *Vinyl flooring is available in a wide range of designs.*
4 DRAWING [C] a drawing that shows how something will be made or what it will look like: [+for] *the design for the new sports centre*
5 INTENTION [C,U] a plan that someone has in their mind: **by design** (=intentionally) *We shall never know whether this happened by accident or by design.* | *He has some* **grand designs** *for the company.*
6 have designs on sth to want something for yourself, especially because it will bring you money: *Several developers have designs on the property.*
7 have designs on sb *formal* to want a sexual relationship with someone: *It soon became obvious that he had designs on her.*

design² S3 W1 *v* [T]
1 to make a drawing or plan of something that will be made or built: *The tower was designed by Gilbert Scott.* | **design sth for sth** *She designed a new logo for the company.* | **well/badly etc designed** *a badly designed office* | **specially designed** *software*
2 [usually passive] to plan or develop something for a specific purpose: **design sth to do sth** *These exercises are designed to strengthen muscles.* | **be designed for sb/sth** *The course is designed for beginners.* | **be designed as sth** *The book is designed as a reference manual.*

des·ig·nate¹ /ˈdezɪgneɪt/ *v* [T usually passive] **1** to choose someone or something for a particular job or purpose: **be designated sth** *The lake was recently designated a conservation area.* | **designate sth as/for sth** *Funds were designated for projects in low-income areas.* | **designate sb to do sth** *She has been designated to take over the position of treasurer.* **2** to represent or refer to something using a particular sign, name etc: *Buildings are designated by red squares on the map.*

des·ig·nate² /ˈdezɪgnɪt, -neɪt/ *adj* [only after noun] *formal* used after the name of an official job to show that someone has been chosen for that job but has not yet officially started work: *the director designate*

ᵉsignated ˈdriver *n* [C] someone who agrees not to drink alcohol when a group of friends go out ᵗether to a party, bar etc so that he or she can drive ᵉother safely to and from home

ᵐnated ˈhitter *n* [C] a baseball player who ᵉs the PITCHER when it is the pitcher's turn to hit

ᵃ·tion /ˌdezɪgˈneɪʃən/ *n formal* **1** [U] the ᵒsing someone or something for a particular

purpose, or of giving them a particular descriptiᵒ [+as] *the designation of Stansted as the third Londoᵣ airport* **2** [C] a name or title: *Her official designatioᵣ is Systems Manager.*

de·sign·er¹ W3 /dɪˈzaɪnə $ -ər/ *n* [C] someone whose job is to make plans or patterns for clothes, furniture, equipment etc: *an* **interior designer** | *a* **software designer** | **dress/fashion designer**

designer² *adj* [only before noun] made by a well-known and fashionable designer: **designer clothes/jeans/suits etc** | **designer label** (=an expensive brand from a well-known designer)

ˈdesigner ˌdrug *n* [C] an illegal drug that has an exciting or relaxing effect, and is taken for pleasure

de·sir·a·ble /dɪˈzaɪərəbəl $ -ˈzaɪr-/ *adj* **1** *formal* something that is desirable is worth having or doing: *The ability to speak a foreign language is* **highly desirable.** | *a desirable neighborhood* | **It is desirable that** *you should have some familiarity with computers.* | *It is desirable to keep the cost as low as possible.* **2** *literary* sexually attractive: *a desirable young woman* —**desirably** *adv* —**desirability** /dɪˌzaɪərəˈbɪləti $ -ˌzaɪr-/ *n* [U]

de·sire¹ /dɪˈzaɪə $ -ˈzaɪr/ *n* **1** [C,U] a strong hope or wish: **desire to do sth** *a* **strong desire** *to win* | [+for] *a desire for knowledge* | **desire that** *It was Harold's desire that he should be buried next to his wife.* | **express/show a desire** *She expressed a desire to visit us.* | **have no desire to do sth** (=used to emphasize that you do not want to do something) *I have no desire to cause any trouble.* | **overwhelming/burning desire** (=very strong desire) *Paul had a burning desire to visit India.* **2** [U] *formal* a strong wish to have sex with someone: *female* **sexual desire** | [+for] *He tried to hide his desire for her.* → **your heart's desire** at HEART (23)

desire² *v* [T not in progressive] **1** *formal* to want something very much: *The hotel has* **everything you could** *possibly* **desire.** | **desire to do sth** *He desired to return to Mexico.* | *Add lemon juice* **if desired.** **2** *literary* to want to have sex with someone —**desired** *adj*: *His remarks* **had the desired effect.**

de·sir·ous /dɪˈzaɪərəs $ -ˈzaɪr-/ *adj* [not before noun] *formal* wanting something very much: [+of] *He became restless and desirous of change.*

de·sist /dɪˈzɪst, dɪˈsɪst/ *v* [I] *formal* to stop doing something: *We hope that the military regime will desist from its acts of violence.* → **cease and desist** at CEASE¹ (2)

desk S2 W2 /desk/ *n* [C]
1 a piece of furniture like a table, usually with drawers in it, that you sit at to write and work: *Marie was sitting at her desk.* → see picture at TABLE; → see picture at OFFICE
2 a place where you can get information or a particular service in a hotel, airport etc: *the reception desk* | *the* **check-in desk**
3 an office that deals with a particular subject, especially in newspapers or television: **the news/sports desk**

ˈdesk clerk *n* [C] someone who works at the main desk in a hotel

de·skill /ˌdiːˈskɪl/ *v* [T] to remove or reduce the need for skill in a job, usually by changing to machinery —**deskilling** *n* [U]

ˈdesk job *n* [C] a job that involves working mostly at a desk in an office

ˈdesk ˌtidy *n plural* **desk tidies** [C] *BrE* a container for putting pens, pencils etc in, that you keep on your desk

desk·top /ˈdesktɒp $ -tɑːp/ *n* [C] **1** the main area on a computer where you can find the ICONS that represent programs, and where you can do things to manage the information on the computer **2** the top surface of a desk

ˌdesktop comˈputer *n* [C] a computer that is small enough to be used on a desk → LAPTOP

ˌdesktop ˈpublishing *n* [U] *DTP* the work of arranging the writing and pictures for a magazine, small book etc, using a computer and special software

des·o·late¹ /'desələt/ adj **1** a place that is desolate is empty and looks sad because there are no people there: *a desolate landscape* **2** someone who is desolate feels very sad and lonely —**desolately** adv —**desolation** /ˌdesə'leɪʃən/ n [U]

des·o·late² /'desəleɪt/ v [T usually passive] literary to make someone feel very sad and lonely: *David was desolated by his wife's death.* —**desolated** adj

de·spair¹ /dɪ'speə $ -'sper/ n [U] **1** a feeling that you have no hope at all: **in despair** *She killed herself in despair.* | **the depths of despair** (=very strong feelings of despair) | *The noise from the neighbours used to drive him to despair.* | **to the despair of sb** *To the despair of the workers, the company announced the closure of the factory.* **2** **be the despair of sb** old-fashioned to make someone feel very worried, upset, or unhappy: *She is the despair of her teachers.*

despair² v [I] formal to feel that there is no hope at all: *Despite his illness, Ron never despaired.* | **despair of (doing) sth** *He despaired of ever finding her.* | **despair of sb** *My teachers began to despair of me.*

de·spair·ing /dɪ'speərɪŋ $ -'sper-/ adj showing a feeling that you have no hope at all: **despairing cry/look/ sigh etc** *She gave me a last despairing look.* —**despairingly** adv

de·spatch /dɪ'spætʃ/ another spelling of DISPATCH

des·pe·ra·do /ˌdespə'rɑːdəʊ $ -doʊ/ n plural **desperadoes** or **desperados** [C] old-fashioned a violent criminal who is not afraid of danger

des·per·ate [W3] /'despər‚t/ adj
1 willing to do anything to change a very bad situation, and not caring about danger: *I had no money left and was desperate.* | *Time was running out and we were getting desperate.* | *the missing teenager's desperate parents* | [+with] *She was desperate with fear.*
2 needing or wanting something very much: [+for] *The team is desperate for a win.* | *I was desperate for a cigarette.* | **desperate to do sth** *He was desperate to get a job.*
3 a desperate situation is very bad or serious: *a desperate shortage of doctors* | *We're in desperate need of help.*
4 a desperate action is something that you only do because you are in a very bad situation: **desperate attempt/bid/effort** *She made a desperate attempt to escape.* | *We had to resort to desperate measures.* | **desperate battle/struggle/fight** *a desperate struggle to rescue the men*

des·pe·rate·ly /'despər‚tli/ adv **1** in a desperate way: *The doctors **tried desperately** to save her life.* | *He looked round desperately for someone to help him.* **2** very or very much: **desperately want/need** *The crops desperately need rain.* | **desperately poor/ill/ tired etc** *He was desperately ill with a fever.* | **desperately unhappy/lonely/worried etc**

des·per·a·tion /ˌdespə'reɪʃən/ n [U] the state of being desperate: *a look of desperation* | **in/out of desperation** *She resorted to stealing food out of desperation.* | *In desperation, we had to borrow the money.*

des·pic·a·ble /dɪ'spɪkəbəl, 'despɪ-/ adj extremely bad, immoral, or cruel: *It's despicable the way he treats those kids.* | *a despicable act of terrorism* | *a despicable crime* —**despicably** adv

de·spise /dɪ'spaɪz/ v [T not in progressive] to dislike and have a low opinion of someone or something: *She despised her neighbours.*

de·spite [S2] [W1] /dɪ'spaɪt/ prep
1 used to say that something happens or is true even though something else might have prevented it; **in spite of**: *Despite all our efforts to save the school, the authorities decided to close it.* | **despite the fact (that)** *She went to Spain despite the fact that her doctor had told her to rest.*
2 **despite yourself** if you do something despite yourself, you do it although you did not intend to: *Liz realized that, despite herself, she cared about Edward.*

de·spoil /dɪ'spɔɪl/ v [T] literary **1** to make a place much less attractive by removing or damaging things; → **spoil** **2** to steal from a place or people using force, especially in a war

de·spon·dent /dɪ'spɒndənt $ dɪ'spɑːn-/ adj extremely unhappy and without hope: *Gill had been out of work for a year and was getting very despondent.* | [+about] *He was becoming increasingly despondent about the way things were going.* —**despondency** n [U] —**despondently** adv

des·pot /'despɒt, -ət $ 'despət, -ɑːt/ n [C] someone, especially a ruler, who uses power in a cruel and unfair way; ▯ **tyrant** —**despotic** /de'spɒtɪk $ -'spɑː-/ adj —**despotically** /-kli/ adv

des·pot·is·m /'despətɪzəm/ n [U] rule by a despot

des res /ˌdez 'rez/ n [C] BrE informal a house that a lot of people admire and would like to live in – sometimes used humorously

desserts

chocolate gateau

strawberry tart

apple pie

ice cream

des·sert /dɪ'zɜːt $ -ɜːrt/ n [C,U] sweet food served after the main part of a meal: **for dessert** *What are we having for dessert?*

des·sert·spoon /dɪ'zɜːtspuːn $ -'zɜːrt-/ n [C] BrE **1** a spoon that is larger than a TEASPOON but smaller than a TABLESPOON **2** also **dessertspoonful** /-fʊl/ the amount that a dessertspoon can hold, used as a unit for measuring food or liquid in cooking: [+of] *Add a dessertspoonful of dry mustard.*

des'sert wine n [C,U] a sweet wine served with dessert

de·sta·bil·ize also **-ise** BrE /diː'steɪb‚laɪz/ v [T] to make something such as a government or ECONOMY become less successful or powerful, or less able to control events: *an attempt to destabilize the government* —**destabilization** /diːˌsteɪb‚laɪ'zeɪʃən $ -lə-/ n [U]

des·ti·na·tion /ˌdest‚'neɪʃən/ n [C] the place that someone or something is going to: **sb's destination** *Allow plenty of time to get to your destination.* | **holiday/ tourist destination** *Maui is a popular tourist destination.*

des·tined /'dest‚nd/ adj **1** [not before noun] seeming certain to happen at some time in the future: [+for] *She seemed destined for a successful career.* | **destined to do sth** *We were destined never to meet again.* **2** **destined for sth** to be travelling to a particular place, or intended to go there: *The flight was destined for Cairo.* **3** [only before noun] literary a destined person or thing is one that you will have in the future: *the King's destined bride*

des·ti·ny /'dest‚ni/ n plural **destinies 1** [C usually singular] the things that will happen to someone in the future, especially those that cannot be changed or controlled; ▯ **fate**: **sb's destiny** *Nancy wondered whether it was her destiny to live in England and marry*

Melvyn. **2** [U] the power that some people believe decides what will happen to them in the future: *She always had a strong sense of destiny.*

des·ti·tute /ˈdestɪtjuːt $ -tuːt/ *adj* **1** having no money, no food, no home etc: *The floods left many people destitute.* **2 be destitute of sth** *literary* to be completely without something: *a man who is destitute of compassion* —**destitution** /ˌdestɪˈtjuːʃən $ -ˈtuː-/ *n* [U]

de·stroy [S2] [W2] /dɪˈstrɔɪ/ *v* [T]
1 to damage something so badly that it no longer exists or cannot be used or repaired; → **destruction: completely/totally destroy** *The school was completely destroyed by fire.* | *companies that are polluting and destroying the environment* | **destroy sb's confidence/ hope/faith etc**
2 if something destroys someone, it ruins their life completely: *The scandal destroyed Simmons and ended his political career.*
3 *informal* to defeat an opponent easily: *The Bears destroyed the Detroit Lions 35–3.*
4 to kill an animal, especially because it is ill or dangerous: *One of the bulls had to be destroyed.*

WORD CHOICE: destroy, ruin, spoil
Destroy means to damage something so badly that it no longer exists or people can no longer use it: *The earthquake destroyed even the tallest buildings.* | *The rainforests are being destroyed at a frightening rate.* If you **ruin** or **spoil** something, it still exists, but it has lost all its good qualities or features. **Ruin** is stronger than **spoil**: *The rain ruined my hair.* | *I don't want to spoil your day.*

---

de·stroy·er /dɪˈstrɔɪə $ -ər/ *n* [C] **1** a small fast military ship with guns **2** someone or something that destroys things or people

de·struc·tion [W3] /dɪˈstrʌkʃən/ *n* [U] the act or process of destroying something or of being destroyed; → destroy: [+of] *the destruction of the rainforest* | **weapons of mass destruction** | **the environmental destruction** *caused by the road building programme* | *The floods brought **death and destruction** to the area.*

de·struc·tive /dɪˈstrʌktɪv/ *adj* causing damage to people or things; → **destroy:** *the destructive power of modern weapons* | [+to] *What is good for the individual can be destructive to the family.* —**destructively** *adv* —**destructiveness** *n* [U]

des·ul·to·ry /ˈdesəltəri, ˈdez- $ -tɔːri/ *adj formal* done without any particular plan or purpose: *They talked briefly in a desultory manner.* —**desultorily** /ˈdesəltərɪli, ˈdez- $ -tɔːrɪli/ *adv*

Det. also **Det** *BrE* the written abbreviation of *detective*

de·tach /dɪˈtætʃ/ *v* **1** [I,T] if you detach something, or if it detaches, it becomes separated from the thing it was attached to; ≠ **attach: detach sth from sth** *You can detach the hood from the jacket.* | *Please detach and fill out the application form.* **2 detach yourself from sb/sth** to try to be less involved in or less concerned about a situation: *Doctors have to detach themselves from their feelings.*

de·tach·a·ble /dɪˈtætʃəbəl/ *adj* able to be removed and put back; ≡ **removable:** *The coat has a detachable lining.*

de·tached /dɪˈtætʃt/ *adj* **1** not reacting to or becoming involved in something in an emotional way; ≠ **involved:** *Try to take a more detached view.* | [+from] *He appeared totally detached from the horrific nature of his crimes.* | **detached way/manner** *She described what had happened in a cold and detached manner.* **2** *especially BrE* a detached house or garage is not joined to another building → SEMI-DETACHED, TERRACED HOUSE

de·tach·ment /dɪˈtætʃmənt/ *n* **1** [U] the state of not reacting to or being involved in something in an emotional way; ≠ **involvement:** [+from] *He felt a sense of detachment from what was happening around him.* **2** [C] a group of soldiers who are sent away from a larger group to do a special job **3** [singular, U] *formal* when something becomes separated from something else: [+of] *detachment of the retina*

de·tail¹ [S2] [W1] /ˈdiːteɪl $ dɪˈteɪl/ *n*
1 [C] a single feature, fact, or piece of information about something: [+of] *She told me every detail of her trip.* | **down to the smallest/last detail** (=completely) *Todd had planned the journey down to the smallest detail.*
2 [U] all the separate features and pieces of information about something: **in detail** *He described the process in detail* (=using a lot of details). | *This issue will be discussed in more detail in Chapter 5.* | *McDougal was reluctant to go into detail* (=give a lot of details) *about the new deal.* | *Editing requires great attention to detail.* | *the fine detail of the plan* | **have an eye for detail** (=be skilled at noticing details) | *Photographers need to have an eye for detail.*
3 details [plural] information that helps to complete what you know about something: [+of] *Full details of the incident were recently revealed.* | [+about] *She refused to give any details about what had happened.* | *Details of the course can be found on our website.* | **further/more details** *For further details, contact the personnel department.*
4 [singular, U] *technical* a specific duty in the army, or the person or group with that duty: *the security detail*

detail² *v* [T] **1** to list things or give all the facts or information about something: *The report details the progress we have made over the last year.* **2 detail sb to (do) sth** to officially order someone, especially soldiers, to do a particular job: *Four soldiers were detailed to guard duty.* **3** *AmE* to clean a car very thoroughly, inside and out; ≡ **valet** *BrE*

de·tailed [W2] /ˈdiːteɪld $ dɪˈteɪld/ *adj*
1 containing or including a lot of information or details: **detailed description/account/analysis etc** *a detailed study of crime in Seattle* | *More detailed information is available on request.*
2 having a lot of decorations or small features that are difficult to produce: *a beautifully detailed carving*

de·tail·ing /ˈdiːteɪlɪŋ $ dɪˈteɪlɪŋ/ *n* [U] **1** decorations that are added to something such as a car or piece of clothing **2** *AmE* the process of cleaning a car very thoroughly, inside and out; ≡ **valeting** *BrE*

de·tain /dɪˈteɪn/ *v* [T] **1** to officially prevent someone from leaving a place: *Two suspects have been detained by the police for questioning.* | *She was detained in hospital with a suspected broken leg.* **2** [usually passive] *formal* to stop someone from leaving as soon as they expected; ≡ **delay:** *He was detained in Washington on urgent business.*

de·tain·ee /ˌdiːteɪˈniː/ *n* [C] *formal* someone who is officially kept in a prison, usually because of their political views

de·tect [W3] /dɪˈtekt/ *v* [T] to notice or discover something, especially something that is not easy to see, hear etc: *Many forms of cancer can be cured if detected early.* | **difficult/impossible/easy/possible etc to detect** | **detect a change/difference** *Dan detected a change in her mood.* | **detect a note of sarcasm/irony/ excitement etc** *Do I detect a note of sarcasm in your voice?* —**detectable** *adj*

de·tec·tion /dɪˈtekʃən/ *n* [U] when something is found that is not easy to see, hear etc, or the process of looking for it: [+of] *Early detection of the disease is vital.* | **escape/avoid detection** *By flying low, the plane avoided detection by enemy radar.*

de·tec·tive [W3] /dɪˈtektɪv/ *n* [C]
1 a police officer whose job is to discover information about crimes and catch criminals → STORE DETECTIVE
2 also **private detective** someone who is paid to discover information about someone or something: *She hired a detective to find out if her husband was having an affair.*

detective work efforts to discover information, find out how something works, answer a difficult question etc: *It took a lot of detective work to discover the cause of the problem.*
4 detective story/novel etc a story etc about a crime, often a murder, and a detective who tries to find out who did it

de·tec·tor /dɪˈtektə $ -ər/ n [C] a machine or piece of equipment that finds or measures something: *a smoke detector* | *a metal detector* → LIE DETECTOR

dé·tente, detente /ˈdeɪtɒnt, deɪˈtɑːnt $ deɪˈtɑːnt/ n [U] a time or situation in which two countries that are not friendly towards each other agree to behave in a more friendly way

de·ten·tion /dɪˈtenʃən/ n **1** [U] the state of being kept in prison: *in detention Willis was held in detention for five years.* **2** [C,U] a punishment in which children who have behaved badly are forced to stay at school for a short time after the others have gone home: *in detention She was always getting put in detention.*

de'tention ˌcentre *BrE*; **detention center** *AmE* n [C] a prison, often for a particular type of person

de·ter /dɪˈtɜː $ -ˈtɜːr/ v **deterred, deterring** [T] to stop someone from doing something, by making them realize it will be difficult or have bad results; → **deterrent**: *The company's financial difficulties have deterred potential investors.* | **deter sb from (doing) sth** *The security camera was installed to deter people from stealing.* ⚠ Do not say 'deter someone to do something'. Say **deter someone from doing something.**

de·ter·gent /dɪˈtɜːdʒənt $ -ɜːr-/ n [C,U] a liquid or powder used for washing clothes, dishes etc

de·te·ri·o·rate /dɪˈtɪəriəreɪt $ -ˈtɪr-/ v [I] **1** to become worse: *Ethel's health has deteriorated.* | *America's deteriorating economy* **2 deteriorate into sth** to develop into a bad or worse situation: *The argument deteriorated into a fight.* —**deterioration** /dɪˌtɪəriˈreɪʃən $ -ˌtɪr-/ n [U]

de·ter·mi·nant /dɪˈtɜːmɪnənt $ -ɜːr-/ n [C] *formal* something that strongly influences what you do or how you behave: [+of] *Social class is a major determinant of consumer spending patterns.*

de·ter·mi·nate /dɪˈtɜːmɪnɪt $ -ɜːr-/ adj *formal* definite or with an exact limit; **ⓕ indeterminate**: *a determinate prison sentence of five years*

de·ter·mi·na·tion W3 /dɪˌtɜːmɪˈneɪʃən $ -ɜːr-/ n
1 [U] the quality of trying to do something even when it is difficult: **determination to do sth** *Yuri shows great determination to learn English.* | *his dogged determination* (=very strong determination) *to succeed* **2** [C,U] *formal* the act of deciding something officially: [+of] *the determination of government policy* **3** [C] *formal* the act of finding the exact level, amount, or cause of something: [+of] *accurate determination of the temperature*

de·ter·mine W1 /dɪˈtɜːmɪn $ -ɜːr-/ v [T]
1 to find out the facts about something; **ⓕ establish**: *Investigators are still trying to determine the cause of the fire.* | **determine how/what/who etc** *The aim of the inquiry was to determine what had caused the accident.* | **determine that** *Experts have determined that the signature was forged.*
2 if something determines something else, it directly influences or decides it: *The amount of available water determines the number of houses that can be built.* | *The age of a wine is a determining factor as to how it tastes.* | **determine how/whether/what etc** *How hard the swimmers work now will determine how they perform in the Olympics.*
3 to officially decide something: *The date of the court case has not yet been determined.* | **determine how/ what/who etc** *The tests will help the doctors determine what treatment to use.*
4 determine to do sth *formal* to decide to do something: *We determined to leave at once.*

de·ter·mined W3 /dɪˈtɜːmɪnd $ -ɜːr-/ adj
1 having a strong desire to do something, so that you will not let anyone stop you: *Gwen is a very determined woman.* | **determined to do sth** *She was determined to win.* | **determined (that)** *He was determined that the same mistakes would not be repeated.*
2 showing determination, especially in a difficult situation: **determined attempt/effort** *She was making a determined effort to give up smoking.* | *The library was closed down despite determined opposition.*

de·ter·min·er /dɪˈtɜːmɪnə $ -ˈtɜːrmənər/ n [C] *technical* a word that is used before a noun in order to show which thing you mean. In the phrases 'the car' and 'some cars', 'the' and 'some' are determiners

de·ter·min·is·m /dɪˈtɜːmɪnɪzəm $ -ɜːr-/ n [U] the belief that what you do and what happens to you are caused by things that you cannot control —**deterministic** /dɪˌtɜːmɪˈnɪstɪk $ -ɜːr-/ adj

de·ter·rent /dɪˈterənt $ -ˈtɜːr-/ n [C] **1** something that makes someone less likely to do something, by making them realize it will be difficult or have bad results: *The small fines for this type of crime do not act as much of a deterrent.* | [+to/for/against] *Window locks are an effective deterrent against burglars.* | *the deterrent effect of prison sentences* **2 nuclear deterrent** the NUCLEAR weapons that a country has in order to prevent other countries from attacking it —**deterrence** n [U]

de·test /dɪˈtest/ v [T not in progressive] *formal* to hate something or someone very much: *Liz and Mo detested each other.* —**detestation** /ˌdiːteˈsteɪʃən/ n [U]

de·test·a·ble /dɪˈtestəbəl/ adj *formal* very bad, and deserving to be criticized or hated: *a detestable little man* —**detestably** adv

de·throne /dɪˈθrəʊn $ -ˈθroʊn/ v [T] **1** to remove a king or queen from power **2** to remove someone from a position of authority or importance: *an attempt to dethrone the senator* | *Douglas dethroned Tyson in a fight that shook the boxing world.* —**dethronement** n [U]

det·o·nate /ˈdetəneɪt/ v [I,T] to explode or to make something explode —**detonation** /ˌdetəˈneɪʃən/ n [U]

det·o·na·tor /ˈdetəneɪtə $ -ər/ n [C] a piece of equipment used to make a bomb etc explode

de·tour¹ /ˈdiːtʊə $ -tʊr/ n [C] **1** a way of going from one place to another that is longer than the usual way: **make/take a detour** *We took a detour to avoid the town centre.* **2** *AmE* a different road for traffic when the usual road cannot be used; **ⓕ diversion** *BrE*

detour² v [I,T] *AmE* to make a detour

de·tox¹ /ˈdiːtɒks $ -tɑːks/ n [U] **1** *informal* special treatment to help people stop drinking alcohol or taking drugs; **ⓕ rehab**: *in detox She spent a month in detox.* **2** when you do not eat solid food or only drink special liquids for a period of time, which is thought to remove harmful substances from your body

detox² v [I] *informal* **1** if someone detoxes, they are given special treatment at a hospital to help them stop drinking alcohol or taking drugs **2** to not eat solid food or only drink special liquids for a period of time, which is thought to remove harmful substances from your body

de·tox·i·fi·ca·tion /ˌdiːtɒksɪfɪˈkeɪʃən $ -ˌtɑːk-/ n [U] **1** the process of removing harmful chemicals or poison from something **2** detox —**detoxify** /diːˈtɒksɪfaɪ $ -ˈtɑːk-/ v [T]

de·tract /dɪˈtrækt/ v
detract from sth *phr v* [not in progressive] to make something seem less good: *One mistake is not going to detract from your achievement.*

de·trac·tor /dɪˈtræktə $ -ər/ n [C] someone who says bad things about someone or something, in order to make them seem less good than they really are: *sb's*

detractors *Even the President's detractors admit that the decision was the right one.*

det·ri·ment /'detrₐmənt/ *n* [U] *formal* harm or damage: **to the detriment of sth** (=resulting in harm or damage to something) *He worked very long hours, to the detriment of his marriage.*

det·ri·men·tal /ˌdetrₐ'mentl◂/ *adj formal* causing harm or damage; ▤ **damaging**: [+to] *Smoking is detrimental to your health.* | *the **detrimental effect** of pollution on the environment* —**detrimentally** *adv*

de·tri·tus /dɪ'traɪtəs/ *n* [U] *formal* pieces of waste that remain after something has been broken up or used

deuce /djuːs $ duːs/ *n* **1** [U] the situation in tennis when both players have 40 points, after which one of the players must win two more points to win the game **2** [C] *AmE* a playing card with the number two on it **3 what/how etc the deuce ...?** *old-fashioned spoken* used to add force to a question: *What the deuce is going on?*

D

Deutsch·mark /'dɔɪtʃmɑːk $ -mɑːrk/ also **mark** *n* [C] the standard unit of money used in Germany before the EURO

de·val·ue /diː'væljuː/ *v* **1** [I,T] *technical* to reduce the value of one country's money when it is exchanged for another country's money: *Nigeria has just devalued its currency.* **2** [T] to make someone or something seem less important or valuable: *History has tended to devalue the contributions of women.* —**devaluation** /diːˌvæljuˈeɪʃən/ *n* [C,U]: *the devaluation of the pound*

dev·a·state /'devəsteɪt/ *v* [T] **1** to make someone feel extremely shocked and sad: *Rob was devastated by the news of her death.* **2** to damage something very badly or completely: *The city centre was devastated by the bomb.* —**devastation** /ˌdevə'steɪʃən/ *n* [U]

dev·a·stat·ed /'devəsteɪtₐd/ *adj* feeling extremely shocked and sad: *She was left feeling totally devastated.*

dev·a·stat·ing /'devəsteɪtɪŋ/ *adj* **1** badly damaging or destroying something: **devastating effect/impact** *Acid rain has a devastating effect on the forest.* | **devastating results/consequences** *The oil spill has had devastating consequences for local wildlife.* | *It will be a **devastating blow** for the town if the factory closes.* **2** making someone feel extremely sad or shocked: *He was in Nice when he heard the **devastating** news.* | *Long-term unemployment can be devastating.* **3** very impressive or effective: *In a devastating display of military muscle, soldiers seized the town yesterday.* **4** *literary* extremely attractive: *a devastating smile* —**devastatingly** *adv*: *a devastatingly attractive man*

de·vel·op S3 W1 /dɪ'veləp/ *v*
1 GROW [I,T] to grow or change into something bigger, stronger, or more advanced, or to make someone or something do this; → **advance**: *Knowledge in the field of genetics has been developing very rapidly.* | *Corsica has developed its economy around the tourist industry.* | [+into] *Chicago developed into a big city in the late 1800s.* | [+from] *It's hard to believe that a tree can develop from a small seed.* | *exercises to **develop muscle** strength*
2 NEW IDEA/PRODUCT [T] to design or make a new idea, product, system etc over a period of time: *Scientists are developing new drugs to treat arthritis.* | *She should have developed her own style instead of copying him.* | *Researchers are developing technology for the US military.*
3 FEELING [T] to start to have a feeling or quality that then becomes stronger: *He had developed a certain affection for me.* | **develop a sense/awareness/knowledge of sth** *The children are beginning to develop a sense of responsibility.* | *It was in college that he **developed a taste for** (=started to like) rugby football.*
4 SKILL/ABILITY [I,T] if you develop a skill or ability, or if it develops, it becomes stronger or more advanced: *The course is designed to help students develop their speaking skills.*
5 DISEASE [I,T] if you develop a disease or illness, or it develops, you start to have it: *Some alcoholics develop liver disease.* | *Pneumonia can develop very quickly.*
6 FAULT/PROBLEM [T] to begin to have a physical fault: *The oil tank had developed a small crack.* | *The plane developed engine trouble and was forced to land.*
7 PROBLEM/DIFFICULTY [I] if a problem or difficult situation develops, it begins to happen or exist, or it gets worse: *Trouble is developing in the cities.* | [+into] *Regional clashes could develop into larger quarrels.*
8 IDEA/ARGUMENT [T] to make an argument or idea clearer, by studying it more or by speaking or writing about it in more detail: *We will develop a few of these points in the seminar.*
9 LAND [T] to use land for the things that people need, for example by taking minerals out of it or by building on it: *We would like to see the land developed for low-cost housing.*
10 PHOTOGRAPHY [I,T] to make a photograph out of a photographic film, using chemicals: *Did you ever get the pictures developed?*

de·vel·oped /dɪ'veləpt/ *adj* **1** a developed country is one of the rich countries of the world with many industries, comfortable living for most people, and usually an elected government; → **developing**, **underdeveloped**: *energy consumption in the developed world* | **developed countries/nations** | *The charity works with children in less developed countries.* **2** a developed sense, system etc, is better, larger, or more advanced than others: *Dogs have a **highly developed** sense of smell.* | *plants with **well developed** root systems* | *Labour has a more **fully developed** programme for the unemployed.*

de·vel·op·er /dɪ'veləpə $ -ər/ *n* **1** [C] a person or company that makes money by buying land and then building houses, factories etc on it: *a Florida **property developer*** **2** [C] a person or an organization that works on a new idea, product etc to make it successful: *software developers* **3** [C,U] a chemical substance used for making images appear on film or photographic paper → **late developer** at LATE¹ (7)

de·vel·op·ing /dɪ'veləpɪŋ/ *adj* **1** a developing country is a poor country that is trying to increase its industry and trade and improve life for its people; → **developed**, **underdeveloped**: **developing countries/nations** *aid to developing countries* | *poverty and hunger in the **developing world*** | **developing economies/markets** *the developing economies in Eastern Europe* **2** growing or changing: *the growth of the developing embryo* | *a developing crisis in Washington*

de·vel·op·ment W1 /dɪ'veləpmənt/ *n*
1 GROWTH [U] the process of gradually becoming bigger, better, stronger, or more advanced: *child development* | [+of] *a course on the development of Greek thought* | **professional/personal development** *opportunities for professional development*
2 ECONOMIC ACTIVITY [U] the process of increasing business, trade, and industrial activity: **economic/industrial/business etc development** *economic development in Russia*
3 EVENT [C] a new event or piece of news that changes a situation: *recent political developments in the former Soviet Union* | *We will **keep** you **informed of** developments.*
4 NEW PLAN/PRODUCT [U] the process of working on a new product, plan, idea etc to make it successful: *The funds will be used for marketing and **product development**.* | **under/in development** *Spielberg has several interesting projects under development.*
5 IMPROVEMENT [C] a change that makes a product, plan, idea etc better: *There have been significant computer developments during the last decade.*
6 BUILDING PROCESS [U] the process of planning and building new houses, streets etc on land: **for development** *The land was sold for development.*
7 HOUSES/OFFICES ETC [C] a group of new buildings

that have all been planned and built together on the same piece of land: *a new* **housing development**

de·vel·op·men·tal /dɪˌveləpˈmentl/ *adj* relating to the development of someone or something: *the* **developmental stages** *of childhood* | *Higher education is a continuing* **developmental process**. —**developmentally** *adv*

de·vi·ance /ˈdiːviəns/ also **de·vi·an·cy** /ˈdiːviənsi/ *n* [U] when something is different, especially in a bad way, from what is considered normal: *sexual deviance*

de·vi·ant /ˈdiːviənt/ *adj* different, in a bad way, from what is considered normal: *deviant behaviour* —**deviant** *n* [C]: *a sexual deviant*

de·vi·ate¹ /ˈdiːvieɪt/ *v* [I] to change what you are doing so that you are not following an expected plan, idea, or type of behaviour: [+**from**] *The plane had to deviate from its normal flight path.*

de·vi·ate² /ˈdiːviɪt/ *adj formal* DEVIANT

de·vi·a·tion /ˌdiːviˈeɪʃən/ *n* **1** [C,U] a noticeable difference from what is expected or acceptable: [+**from**] *There must be no deviation from the normal procedure.* **2** [C] *technical* the difference between a number or measurement in a SET and the average of all the numbers or measurements in that set → STANDARD DEVIATION

de·vice W2 /dɪˈvaɪs/ *n* [C]
1 a machine or tool that does a special job; ▪ gadget: *modern labour-saving devices* | **device for doing sth** *a device for separating metal from garbage* | **device to do sth** *The company makes devices to detect carbon monoxide.*
2 a special way of doing something that makes it easier to do: **device for doing sth** *Testing yourself with information on cards is a useful device for studying.* | *a memory device*
3 a plan or trick, especially for a dishonest purpose: **device to do sth** *Their proposal was only a device to confuse the opposition.*
4 a bomb or other explosive weapon: **explosive/ nuclear/incendiary etc device**
5 the special use of words in literature, or of words, lights etc in a play, to achieve an effect: *Metaphor is a common literary device.* → **leave sb to their own devices** at LEAVE¹ (4)

dev·il /ˈdevəl/ *n* **1** the devil also **the Devil** the most powerful evil SPIRIT in some religions, especially in Christianity; ▪ Satan **2** [C] an evil SPIRIT; ▪ demon: *The villagers believed a devil had taken control of his body.* **3** speak of the devil also talk of the devil *BrE spoken* used when someone you have just been talking about walks into the room where you are **4** poor/ lucky/handsome etc devil *spoken* used to talk about someone who you feel sorry for, who is lucky etc: *What on earth is wrong with the poor devil?* **5** little/old devil *spoken* used to talk about a child or an older man who behaves badly, but who you like: *He's a naughty little devil.* | *I really miss the old devil.* **6** be a devil *BrE spoken* used to persuade someone to do something they are not sure they should do: *Go on, be a devil, have another gin and tonic.* **7** what/who/why etc the devil? *old-fashioned spoken* used to show that you are surprised or annoyed: *How the devil should I know what she's thinking?* **8** a devil of a time/job etc *old-fashioned spoken* a difficult or unpleasant time, job etc: *We had a devil of a job trying to get the carpet clean again.* **9** go to the devil! *old-fashioned spoken* used to tell someone rudely to go away or stop annoying you **10** do sth like the devil *old-fashioned spoken* to do something very fast or using a lot of force: *They rang the bell and ran like the devil.* **11** better the devil you know (than the devil you don't) used to say that it is better to deal with someone or something you know, even if you do not like them, than to deal with someone or something new that might be worse **12** between the devil and the deep blue sea in a difficult situation because there are only two choices you can make and both of them are unpleasant **13** ... and the devil take

the hindmost used to say that everyone in a situation only cares about what happens to themselves and does not care about other people → DEVIL'S ADVOCATE

dev·il·ish /ˈdevəlɪʃ/ *adj* **1** *literary* very bad, difficult, or unpleasant: *devilish schemes to cheat people* **2** seeming likely to cause trouble, but in a way that is amusing or attractive: *Dalton looked at her with a devilish grin.*

dev·il·ish·ly /ˈdevəlɪʃli/ *adv* [+ adj/adv] *old-fashioned* very – used to show that you think something is annoying or bad: *a devilishly difficult task*

dev·illed *BrE*; **deviled** *AmE* /ˈdevəld/ *adj* devilled food is cooked with very hot pepper: *deviled eggs*

devil-may-ˈcare *adj* happy and willing to take risks: *a devil-may-care attitude to life*

dev·il·ment /ˈdevəlmənt/ also **dev·il·ry** /ˈdevəlri/ *n* [U] *literary* wild or bad behaviour that causes trouble: *eyes blazing with devilment*

devil's ˈadvocate *n* [C] someone who pretends to disagree with you in order to have a good discussion about something: *He would play devil's advocate with anyone.*

devil's food ˌcake *n* [C,U] *AmE* a type of chocolate cake

de·vi·ous /ˈdiːviəs/ *adj* **1** using dishonest tricks and deceiving people in order to get what you want; → deceitful: *a devious politician* **2** *formal* not going in the most direct way to a place: *a devious route* —**deviously** *adv* —**deviousness** *n* [U]

de·vise /dɪˈvaɪz/ *v* [T] to plan or invent a new way of doing something: *She* **devised a method** *for quicker communications between offices.*

de·void /dɪˈvɔɪd/ *adj formal* **be devoid of sth** to be completely lacking in something: *His face was devoid of any warmth or humour.*

de·vo·lu·tion /ˌdiːvəˈluːʃən/ *n* [U] when a national government gives power to a group or organization at a lower or more local level —**devolutionist** *adj* —**devolutionist** *n* [C]

de·volve /dɪˈvɒlv $ dɪˈvɑːlv/ *v formal* **1** [I,T] if you devolve responsibility, power etc to a person or group at a lower level, or if it devolves on them, it is given to them: **devolve sth to sb/sth** *The federal government has devolved responsibility for welfare to the states.* | [+**on/ upon**] *Half of the cost of the study will devolve upon the firm.* **2** [I,T] if land, money etc devolves to someone, it becomes their property when someone else dies

de·vote /dɪˈvəʊt $ -ˈvoʊt/ *v* [T] **1** to use all or most of your time, effort etc in order to do something or help someone; ▪ dedicate: **devote your time/energy/atten- tion etc to sth** *He wanted to devote his energies to writing films.* | **devote yourself to sth** *She devoted herself full-time to her growing business.* **2** to use a particular area, period of time, or amount of space for a specific purpose: **devote sth to sth** *The meeting will be devoted to health and safety issues.*

de·vot·ed /dɪˈvəʊtɪd $ -ˈvoʊ-/ *adj* **1** giving someone or something a lot of love and attention: *a devoted father* | [+**to**] *Isabella was devoted to her brother.* **2** dealing with, containing, or being used for only one thing; ▪ dedicated: [+**to**] *a museum devoted to photography* **3** strongly supporting someone or something because you admire or enjoy them: *Beckham's devoted fans* | *The journal had a devoted following of around 1000 subscribers.* —**devotedly** *adv*

dev·o·tee /ˌdevəˈtiː/ *n* [C] **1** someone who enjoys or admires someone or something very much: [+**of**] *a devotee of 1930s films* **2** a very religious person: *a Sikh devotee*

de·vo·tion /dɪˈvəʊʃən $ -ˈvoʊ-/ *n* **1** [U] the strong love that you show when you pay a lot of attention to someone or something: [+to] *Alanna has always shown intense devotion to her children.* **2** [U] the loyalty that you show towards a person, job etc, especially by working hard; → **dedication**: [+to] *the soldier's courage and devotion to duty* | *his integrity and devotion to his patients* **3** [U] strong religious feeling **4 devotions** [plural] prayers and other religious acts

de·vo·tion·al /dɪˈvəʊʃənəl $ -ˈvoʊ-/ *adj* relating to or used in religious services: *devotional music*

de·vour /dɪˈvaʊə $ -ˈvaʊr/ *v* [T] **1** to eat something quickly because you are very hungry: *The boys devoured their pancakes.* **2** to read something quickly and eagerly, or watch something with great interest: *He devoured science fiction books as a teenager.* **3 be devoured by sth** to be filled with a strong feeling that seems to control you: *Cindy felt devoured by jealousy.* **4** *literary* to destroy someone or something: *Her body had been almost entirely devoured by the disease.* **5** to use up all of something: *a job that devours all my energy*

de·vout /dɪˈvaʊt/ *adj* **1** someone who is devout has a very strong belief in a religion: *a devout Catholic* **2** *formal* a devout hope or wish is one that you feel very strongly: *It is my devout hope that we can work together in peace.* —**devoutly** *adv*

dew /djuː $ duː/ *n* [U] the small drops of water that form on outdoor surfaces during the night

dew·drop /ˈdjuːdrɒp $ ˈduːdrɑːp/ *n* [C] a single drop of dew: *dewdrops sparkling in the morning sunlight*

dew·fall /ˈdjuːfɔːl $ ˈduːfɒl/ *n* [U] *AmE* the forming of dew or the time when dew begins to appear

dew·y /ˈdjuːi $ ˈduːi/ *adj* wet with drops of DEW: *The dewy woodland was solitary and still.*

,dewy-ˈeyed *adj* having eyes that are slightly wet with tears

dex·ter·i·ty /dekˈsterɪti/ *n* [U] **1** skill and speed in doing something with your hands: *Computer games can improve children's manual dexterity.* **2** skill in using words or your mind: *his charm and verbal dexterity*

dex·ter·ous /ˈdekstərəs/ also **dextrous** *adj* **1** skilful and quick when using your hands: *dextrous use of the needle* **2** skilful in using words or your mind: *his dexterous accounting abilities* —**dexterously** *adv*

dex·trose /ˈdekstrəʊz, -strəʊs $ -stroʊz, -stroʊs/ *n* [U] a type of sugar that is in many sweet fruits

dex·trous /ˈdekstrəs/ *adj* another spelling of DEXTEROUS

di- /daɪ, dɪ/ *prefix* two, twice, or double: *A diphthong is a vowel made up of two sounds.* → SEMI-, BI-, TRI-

di·a·be·tes /ˌdaɪəˈbiːtiːz, -tɪs/ *n* [U] a serious disease in which there is too much sugar in your blood

di·a·bet·ic¹ /ˌdaɪəˈbetɪk◂/ *adj* **1** having diabetes: *Sarah is diabetic.* **2** caused by diabetes: *a diabetic coma* **3** produced for people who have diabetes: *diabetic chocolate*

diabetic² *n* [C] someone who has diabetes

di·a·bol·i·cal /ˌdaɪəˈbɒlɪkəl◂ $ -ˈbɑː-/ *adj* **1** also **di·a·bol·ic** /ˌdaɪəˈbɒ◂lɪk $/ evil or cruel: *diabolical abuse* **2** *BrE informal* extremely unpleasant or bad: *The toilets were in a diabolical state.* —**diabolically** /-kli/ *adv*

di·a·crit·ic /ˌdaɪəˈkrɪtɪk/ *n* [C] *technical* a mark placed over, under, or through a letter in some languages, to show that the letter should be pronounced differently from the same letter without a mark —**diacritical** *adj*: *diacritical marks*

di·a·dem /ˈdaɪədem/ *n* [C] *literary* a circle of jewels that a queen, princess etc wears on her head

di·ag·nose /ˈdaɪəgnəʊz $ -noʊs/ *v* [T] to find out what illness someone has, or what the cause of a fault is, after doing tests, examinations etc: **diagnose sb as (having) sth** *Joe struggled in school before he was diagnosed as dyslexic.* | **diagnose sth as sth** *The illness was*

diagnosed as mumps.* | **diagnose sb with sth** *She wa diagnosed with breast cancer.*

di·ag·no·sis /ˌdaɪəgˈnəʊsɪs $ -ˈnoʊ-/ *n plural* **diag noses** /-siːz/ [C,U] the process of discovering exactl what is wrong with someone or something, by examin ing them closely; → **prognosis**: [+of] *diagnosis of kic ney disease* | *An exact diagnosis can only be made b obtaining a blood sample.*

di·ag·nos·tic /ˌdaɪəgˈnɒstɪk◂ $ -ˈnɑː-/ *adj* relating t or used for discovering what is wrong with someone c something: **diagnostic tests/tools** *Doctors depend o accurate diagnostic tools.*

di·ag·o·nal /daɪˈægənəl/ *adj* **1** a diagonal line i straight and joins two opposite corners of a flat shape usually a square; → **horizontal, vertical 2** followin a sloping angle: *diagonal parking spaces* —**diagonal** [C] —**diagonally** *adv*: *The path goes diagonally acros the field.*

di·a·gram¹ /ˈdaɪəgræm/ *n* [C] a simple drawing c plan that shows exactly where something is, wha something looks like, or how something works: [+of] *diagram of the heating system* —**diagrammati** /ˌdaɪəgrəˈmætɪk◂/ *adj* —**diagrammatically** /-kli/ ac

diagram² *v* **diagrammed, diagramming** [T] to shov or represent something in a diagram

dial¹ /ˈdaɪəl/ *n* [C] **1** the round part of a clock, watcr machine etc that has numbers that show you the tim or a measurement: *The lighted dial of her watch sai 1.20.* | *She looked at the dial to check her speed.* **2** th part of a piece of equipment such as a radio or THERM STAT that you turn around to do something, such as fin a different station or change the temperature: *The dia on the heater was set to 'HOT'.* **3** the wheel on a older telephone with numbered holes for your finger that you move around in order to make a call

dial² *v* **dialled, dialling** *BrE*, **dialed, dialing** *AmE* [I,T to press the buttons or turn the dial on a telephone i order to make a telephone call: *I think I dialed th wrong number.*

di·a·lect /ˈdaɪəlekt/ *n* [C,U] a form of a languag which is spoken only in one area, with words o grammar that are slightly different from other forms c the same language; → **accent: Chinese/Yorkshire/Bel fast etc dialect** *The people up there speak a Tibetar dialect.* | *the local dialect*

di·a·lec·tic /ˌdaɪəˈlektɪk/ also **dialectics** *n* [U] *for mal* a method of examining and discussing ideas ir order to find the truth, in which two opposing ideas ar compared in order to find a solution that includes them both —**dialectical** *adj*

'dialling code *n* [C] *BrE* the numbers at the beginnin of a telephone number that represent a specific area o a city or country; ◨ **area code** *AmE*

'dialling tone *n* [C] *BrE* the sound you hear when you pick up the telephone that lets you know that you ca make a call; ◨ **dial tone** *AmE*

di·a·logue also **dialog** *AmE* /ˈdaɪəlɒg $ -lɒːg, -lɑːg/ ∩ [C,U] **1** a conversation in a book, play, or film: *c boring movie full of bad dialogue* | *Students were asked tc read simple dialogues out loud.* **2** *formal* a discussior between two groups, countries etc: [+between/with *There is a need for constructive dialogue between lead ers.* → MONOLOGUE

'dialogue ˌbox *BrE*; **'dialog box** *AmE n* [C] a box that appears on your computer screen when the program you are using needs to ask you a question before it car continue to do something. You CLICK on one part of the box to give your answer.

'dial tone *n* [C] *AmE* the sound you hear when you pick up the telephone that lets you know that you can make a call; ◨ **dialling tone** *BrE*

'dial-up *adj* [only before noun] relating to a telephone line that is used to send information from one com puter to another: *a dial-up connection* —**dial-up** *n* [C

di·al·y·sis /daɪˈælɪsɪs/ *n* [U] the process of takin harmful substances out of someone's blood using a

di·a·mant·é /ˌdiːə'mɒnteɪ◂ $ ˌdiːəmɑːn'teɪ◂/ adj decorated with artificial DIAMONDS: a diamanté necklace

di·am·e·ter /daɪ'æm₁tə $ -ər/ n [C] a straight line from one side of a circle to the other side, passing through the centre of the circle, or the length of this line: **3 inches/1 metre etc in diameter** Draw a circle six centimetres in diameter. | [+of] The diameter of the Earth is about 13,000 km.

di·a·met·ri·cally /ˌdaɪə'metrɪkli/ adv **diametrically opposed/opposite** completely different and opposite: The two ideas are diametrically opposed.

di·a·mond /'daɪəmənd/ n **1** [C,U] a clear, very hard valuable stone, used in jewellery and in industry: a diamond engagement ring **2** [C] a shape with four straight but sloping sides of equal length, with one point facing directly up and the other directly down: Cut the cookie dough into diamonds. **3 a)** diamonds one of the four SUITS (=types of cards) in a set of playing cards, which has the design of a red diamond shape on it: **two/queen etc of diamonds** the ace of diamonds **b)** [C] a card from this suit: You have to play a diamond. **4** [C] **a)** the area in a baseball field that is within the diamond shape formed by the four BASES **b)** the whole playing field used in baseball

diamond anni'versary n [C] the date that is exactly 60 years after the date when two people were married or after some other important date

diamond in the 'rough n [C] AmE someone who behaves in a slightly rude way, but is really kind and generous; ▤ **rough diamond** BrE

diamond 'jubilee n [C] the date that is exactly 60 years after the date of an important event, especially of someone becoming a king or queen → GOLDEN JUBILEE, SILVER JUBILEE

diamond ˌlane n [C] AmE a special LANE on a road or street that is marked with a diamond shape and can be used only by buses, taxis etc and sometimes private cars with more than one passenger

diamond 'wedding n [C] BrE the date that is exactly 60 years after the date when two people were married

di·a·per S3 /'daɪəpə $ 'daɪpər/ n [C] AmE a piece of soft cloth or soft paper that is put between a baby's legs and fastened around its waist to hold liquid and solid waste; ▤ **nappy** BrE: Wait a minute while I change her diaper.

diaper ˌrash n [U] AmE sore skin between a baby's legs and on its BUTTOCKS, caused by a wet diaper; ▤ **nappy rash** BrE

di·aph·a·nous /daɪ'æfənəs/ adj literary diaphanous cloth is so thin that you can almost see through it

di·a·phragm /'daɪəfræm/ n [C] **1** the muscle that is between your lungs and your stomach, and that you use when you breathe **2** a round rubber object that a woman can put inside her VAGINA to stop her from getting PREGNANT **3** technical a thin round object, especially in a telephone or LOUDSPEAKER, that is moved by sound or that moves when it produces sound **4** technical a round flat part inside a camera that controls the amount of light that enters the camera

di·a·rist /'daɪərɪst $ 'daɪr-/ n [C] someone who writes a diary, especially one that is later sold

di·ar·rhoea BrE, **diarrhea** AmE /ˌdaɪə'rɪə/ n [U] an illness in which waste from the BOWELS is watery and comes out often

di·a·ry /'daɪəri $ 'daɪri/ n plural **diaries** [C] **1** a book in which you write down the things that happen to you each day; ▤ **journal**: Inge kept a diary (=wrote in a diary) during the war years. | **diary entry** (=what you have written for a particular day) **2** especially BrE a book with separate spaces for each day of the year, in which you write down the meetings, events etc that are planned for each day; ▤ **calendar** AmE: Did you put the meeting date **in your diary**?

di·as·po·ra /daɪ'æspərə/ n [C] **1 the Diaspora** the movement of the Jewish people away from ancient Palestine, to settle in other countries **2** the spreading of people from a national group or culture to other areas: the African diaspora

di·a·ton·ic scale /ˌdaɪətɒnɪk 'skeɪl $ -tɑː-/ n **the diatonic scale** a set of eight musical notes that uses a particular pattern of spaces between the notes

di·a·tribe /'daɪətraɪb/ n [C] formal a long speech or piece of writing that criticizes someone or something very severely: [+against] a diatribe against contemporary American civilization

dibs /dɪbz/ n [plural] AmE informal the right to have, use, or do something: Freshmen **have first dibs on** dormitory rooms.

dice¹ /daɪs/ n **1** [plural] singular **die** one or more small blocks of wood, plastic etc that have six sides with a different number of spots on each side, used in games: **throw/roll the dice** It's your turn to roll the dice. ⚠ **Die** is singular and **dice** is plural, but many people use **dice** when they are talking about a single **die**. **2** [U] any game of chance that is played with dice **3 the dice are loaded** the situation is arranged so that a particular person will win or gain an advantage **4 no dice** especially AmE old-fashioned spoken used to refuse to do something or to say that something is not possible: 'Can I borrow some cash?' 'Sorry, no dice.' **5 a throw of the dice** something you do that you hope will have an effect on a situation, but is not certain to do so: a last desperate **throw of the dice** to try and win his wife back

dice² v **1** also **dice sth ⇔ up** [T] to cut food into small square pieces: diced carrots **2 dice with death** to put yourself in a very dangerous situation

dic·ey /'daɪsi/ adj informal slightly dangerous and uncertain: The future looks pretty dicey for small businesses.

di·chot·o·my /daɪ'kɒtəmi $ -'kɑː-/ n plural **dichotomies** [C] formal the difference between two things or ideas that are completely opposite: [+between] a dichotomy between his public and private lives

dick¹ /dɪk/ n [C] **1** informal not polite a PENIS **2** spoken not polite an offensive word for a stupid annoying person, especially a man: He's acting like a complete dick. **3** AmE old-fashioned a PRIVATE DETECTIVE → **clever dick** at CLEVER (6); → SPOTTED DICK

dick² v

dick sb **around** phr v AmE spoken not polite to cause a lot of problems for someone, especially by changing your mind a lot or preventing them from getting what they want: The phone company's been dicking me around for three months.

dick·ens /'dɪkɪnz/ n spoken old-fashioned **1 what/ who/where the dickens ...?** used when asking a question to show that you are very surprised or angry: What the dickens is the matter with her? **2 as pretty/ smart etc as the dickens** AmE very pretty, clever etc: Isn't she as cute as the dickens!

Dic·ken·si·an /dɪ'kenziən/ adj Dickensian buildings, living conditions etc are poor, dirty, and unpleasant: a single mother living in a Dickensian block of flats

dick·er /'dɪkə $ -ər/ v [I] informal especially AmE to argue about or discuss the details of a sale, agreement etc: [+about/over] Politicians in Washington are still dickering over the budget.

dick·ey /'dɪki/ n another spelling of DICKY²

dick·head /'dɪkhed/ n [C] spoken not polite an offensive word for a stupid annoying person, especially a man: Don't be such a dickhead!

dick·y¹ /'dɪki/ adj BrE old-fashioned weak, and likely to break or not work properly: **dicky heart/ticker** (=a heart that is weak and not very healthy)

dicky², **dickey** n [C] a false shirt front or collar worn under a suit or dress

dick·y·bird /'dɪkibɜːd $ -bɜːrd/ n [C] BrE informal **1** a small bird – used by or when speaking to children **2 not hear a dickybird** to not hear any news about someone or something: *'Have you heard from them since they moved?' 'No, not a dickybird.'*

dic·ta /'dɪktə/ a plural of DICTUM

Dic·ta·phone /'dɪktəfəʊn $ -foʊn/ n [C] trademark an office machine on which you can record speech so that someone can listen to it and TYPE it later

dic·tate¹ /dɪk'teɪt $ 'dɪkteɪt/ v **1** [I,T] to say words for someone else to write down: **dictate a letter/memo etc to sb** *She's dictating a letter to her secretary right now.* **2** [I,T] to tell someone exactly what they must do or how they must behave: **[+to]** *The media cannot be allowed to dictate to the government.* | **dictate who/ what/how etc** *Can they dictate how the money will be spent?* | *Federal funds have to be used as dictated by Washington.* | **dictate that** *Islamic custom dictates that women should be fully covered.* | *The US government attempted to dictate the terms of the agreement.* **3** [T] to control or influence something; **⧉ determine: dictate what/how etc** *Funds dictate what we can do.* | **dictate that** *The laws of physics dictate that what goes up must come down.* | *The massive publicity dictated a response from the city government.*

dic·tate² /'dɪkteɪt/ n [C] an order, rule, or principle that you have to obey: **[+of]** *teenagers following the dictates of fashion*

dic·ta·tion /dɪk'teɪʃən/ n **1** [U] when you say words for someone to write down: *There were no secretaries available to take dictation* (=write down what someone is saying). **2** [C] a piece of writing that a teacher reads out to test your ability to hear and write the words correctly: *I hate doing French dictations.*

dic·ta·tor /dɪk'teɪtə $ 'dɪkteɪtər/ n [C] **1** a ruler who has complete power over a country, especially one whose power has been gained by force: *the downfall of the hated dictator* **2** someone who tells other people what they should do, in a way that seems unreasonable: *a real little dictator*

dic·ta·to·ri·al /ˌdɪktə'tɔːriəl◂/ adj **1** a dictatorial government or ruler has complete power over a country: *dictatorial regimes* **2** a dictatorial person tells other people what to do in an unreasonable way: *Professor Clement's dictatorial attitude* **—dictatorially** adv

dic·ta·tor·ship /dɪk'teɪtəʃɪp $ -teɪtər-/ n **1** [C,U] government by a ruler who has complete power **2** [C] a country that is ruled by one person who has complete power

dic·tion /'dɪkʃən/ n [U] **1** the way in which someone pronounces words: **clear/perfect/good etc diction** *She had perfect diction.* **2** the choice and use of words and phrases to express meaning, especially in literature

dic·tion·a·ry /'dɪkʃənəri $ -neri/ n plural **dictionaries** [C] **1** a book that gives a list of words in alphabetical order and explains their meanings in the same language, or another language: *a German – English dictionary* **2** a book that explains the words and phrases used in a particular subject: *a science dictionary*

dic·tum /'dɪktəm/ n plural **dictums** or **dicta** /-tə/ [C] **1** a formal statement of opinion by someone who is respected or has authority **2** a short phrase that expresses a general rule or truth: *Descartes' famous dictum: 'I think; therefore, I am'*

did /dɪd/ the past tense of DO

di·dac·tic /daɪ'dæktɪk, dɪ-/ adj **1** speech or writing that is didactic is intended to teach people a moral lesson: *His novel has a didactic tone.* **2** someone who is didactic is too eager to teach people things or give instructions **—didactically** /-kli/ adv

did·dle /'dɪdl/ v [T] BrE informal to get money from someone by deceiving them: **diddle sb out of sth** *They'll diddle you out of your last penny if you let them.*

did·dly /'dɪdli/ also **did·dly·squat** /ˌdɪdli'skwɒt $ 'dɪdliskwɑːt/ AmE informal n **not know/mean diddly** to know or mean nothing at all: *Brad? He doesn't know diddly about baseball.*

did·ge·ri·doo /ˌdɪdʒəri'duː/ n [C] a long wooden musical instrument, played especially in Australia

did·n't /'dɪdnt/ the short form of 'did not': *You saw him, didn't you?* | *I didn't want to go.*

didst /dɪdst/ thou didst old use you did

die¹ S1 W1 /daɪ/ v died, dying, dies [I]
1 BECOME DEAD to stop living and become dead: *He died in 1985 at the age of 76.* | *Her father died suddenly in an accident when she was only ten.* | **[+of/from]** *The animals died of starvation in the snow.* | *patients who are dying from cancer* | *She died peacefully in her sleep at the age of 98.* | **die for sth** (=be killed while fighting to defend something) *Do you believe in anything enough to die for it?* | **die young/happy/poor** *She died young, at the age of 27.* | *The bullet went straight through his head, and he died instantly.* | **to your dying day/until the day you die** (=until you die) *It must remain a secret until the day I die.* | **sb's dying breath/wish** (=someone's last breath or wish) *It was his dying wish that the house be opened to the public.* | **die a hero/ martyr/rich man etc** *My uncle died a hero.* | **die a natural/violent/agonizing death** *Did she die a natural death* (=did she die naturally, or did someone kill her?)?
2 DISAPPEAR to disappear or stop existing: *Our love will never die.* | *The family name will die with him* (=disappear when he dies). | *He's one of a dying breed* (=a type of person that is no longer common).
3 MACHINES informal to stop working; **⧉ break down:** *The engine spluttered and died.* | **die on sb** (=stop working while they are using it) *The mower just died on me.*
4 be dying for sth/to do sth spoken to want something very much: *I'm dying for a cup of tea.* | *She was dying to ask where he'd got it.* | *I'm dying to see what it is.*
5 be dying of hunger/thirst/boredom spoken to be very hungry, thirsty, bored etc: *Do you fancy a cup of tea? I'm dying of thirst.*
6 I nearly died/I could have died spoken used to say that you felt very surprised or embarrassed: *I nearly died when I saw it was my ex-husband!*
7 die of embarrassment/shame to be very embarrassed or ashamed: *The room was such a mess, I just died of embarrassment.*
8 I'd rather die spoken used to say very strongly that you do not want to do something: *I'd rather die than work for him!*
9 in the dying minutes/seconds/moments (of sth) during the last minutes or seconds before the end of something: *United scored an equaliser in the dying minutes of the game.*
10 old habits/traditions/customs die hard used to say that it takes a long time to change to a new way of doing something
11 never say die spoken used to encourage someone to continue doing something that is difficult
12 die a/the death informal to gradually fail or be forgotten: *The rumour gradually died a death.*
13 die laughing spoken to laugh a lot: *We nearly died laughing when he told us.*
14 to die for informal extremely nice, attractive, or desirable: *She had hair to die for.*

WORD FOCUS: DIE
a ceremony for someone who has died: **funeral** a ceremony at which someone who has died is buried or burned | **burial** when someone's body is put into the ground | **cremation** when someone's body is burned | **hearse** a large car that takes the body to the funeral | **coffin** a box in which someone is buried or carried to the funeral | **grave** the place where someone is buried | **graveyard/cemetery** an area where dead people are

buried | **undertaker** someone who arranges funerals | **the mourners** the people at a funeral
→ see also death, widow, widower, orphan, bereaved, will², obituary

die away *phr v*
if sound, wind, or light dies away, it becomes gradually weaker until you cannot hear, feel, or see it: *Her voice died away as she saw the look on David's face.* | *She waited until the footsteps had died away.*

die back *phr v*
if a plant dies back, it dies above the ground but remains alive at its roots

die down *phr v*
if something dies down, it becomes less strong, active, or violent: *Don't worry, the gossip will soon die down.* | *when the excitement had died down*

die off *phr v*
if a group of people or animals die off, they die one by one until there are no more of them

die out *phr v*
to disappear or stop existing completely: *The wild population of koalas is in danger of dying out.* | *There will be outbreaks of rain, gradually dying out in the afternoon.*

die² *n* [C] **1** a metal block used to press or cut something into a particular shape **2** a DICE **3 the die is cast** used to say that a decision has been taken and cannot now be changed

die ,casting *n* [U] the process of making metal objects by forcing liquid metal into a hollow container with a particular shape, and then allowing it to become hard

die·hard /'daɪhɑːd $ -hɑːrd/ *n* [C] someone who opposes change and refuses to accept new ideas —**diehard** *adj: a few diehard fans* → **old habits die hard** at DIE¹ (9)

die·sel /'diːzəl/ *n* **1** [U] a type of heavy oil used instead of petrol in engines, especially in trucks, buses, and trains: *a 1.9 litre diesel engine* | **diesel car/truck etc 2** [C] *informal* a vehicle that uses diesel

diesel ,fuel also **'diesel oil** *n* [U] DIESEL

di·et¹ S3 W2 /'daɪət/ *n*
1 [C,U] the kind of food that a person or animal eats each day: **balanced/healthy/poor etc diet** *It is important to have a balanced, healthy diet.* | *the effects of poor diet and lack of exercise* | **vegetarian/high-fibre/Western etc diet** | [+of] *They exist on a diet of fish.* | *Bamboo is the panda's* **staple diet** (=main food). | **in sb's diet** *the importance of vitamins and minerals in your diet*
2 [C] a limited range and amount of food that you eat when you want to get thinner: **go/be on a diet** *Lyn always seems to be on a diet.*
3 [C] a limited type of food and drink that someone is allowed because they have a health problem: *a salt-free diet*
4 a diet of sth too much of an activity that you think is boring or has bad effects: *Kids today are raised on a constant diet of pop music and television.*
5 [C] *old-fashioned* an official meeting to discuss political or church matters

diet² *v* [I] to limit the amount and type of food that you eat, in order to become thinner; **slim**

diet³ *adj* [only before noun] diet drinks or foods contain less sugar or fat than ordinary ones: *a diet soda*

di·e·ta·ry /'daɪətəri $ -teri/ *adj* related to the food someone eats; → **nutritional**: *special dietary requirements*

di·et·er /'daɪətə $ -ər/ *n* [C] someone who is trying to become thinner by controlling what they eat

di·e·tet·ics /ˌdaɪə'tetɪks/ *n* [U] the science that is concerned with what people eat and drink and how this affects their health

di·e·ti·cian, dietitian /ˌdaɪə'tɪʃən/ *n* [C] someone who is trained to give people advice about what it is healthy for them to eat and drink

dif·fer W3 /'dɪfə $ -ər/ *v* [I]
1 to be different from something in some way: *The two systems differ in many respects.* | [+**from**] *People differ from one another in their ability to handle stress.* | [+**between**] *The symptoms did not differ between the two groups.* | **differ widely/greatly/significantly etc** *We soon found that prices differed enormously.* | *Experts have* **differing views** *on the subject.*
2 if two people or groups differ about something, they have opposite opinions; **disagree**: [+**about/on/over**] *The two lawyers differed about how to present the case.*
3 agree to differ to stop arguing with someone and accept that you will never agree
4 I beg to differ *spoken formal* used to say that you disagree with someone

dif·fe·rence S1 W1 /'dɪfərəns/ *n*
1 [C,U] a way in which two or more people or things are not like each other; **similarity**

> **big/major/important/significant difference**
> **small/minor difference**
> **subtle difference** (=not obvious)
> **marked difference** (=very noticeable)
> **there's no difference** (=they are the same)
> **there's very little difference** (=they are very similar)
> **there's a world of difference** (=they are very different)
> **know/can tell the difference** (=be able to recognize the difference)
> **spot the difference** (=notice the difference)
>
> [+**between**] *The main difference between the groups was age.* | *There's a* **big difference** *between knowing that something is true, and being able to prove it.* | [+**in**] *Researchers found a number of* **important differences** *in the way boys and girls learn.* | *There was a* **marked difference** *in his behavior toward me.* | *There was certainly* **no difference** *between them in terms of intelligence.* | *There is* **very little difference** *between the parties on green issues.* | *There's a* **world of difference** *between us.* | *Do children* **know the difference** *between right and wrong?* | *See if you can* **spot the difference** *between these two pictures.* | *Class differences still play an important role in society.*

2 [singular, U] the amount by which one thing is greater or smaller than another: **difference in age/size etc** *There's not much difference in price.* | *There's a five-hour* **time difference** *between London and New York.* → **split the difference** at SPLIT¹ (9)
3 make a/the difference to have an important effect or influence on something or someone: *Whatever she did, it made no difference.* | [+**to**] *One more person wouldn't make any difference to the arrangements.* | [+**between**] *It could make the difference between missing your train and getting to work on time.* | *Having a good teacher has* **made all the difference** *for Alex* (=had an important influence).
4 it makes no difference to sb used to say that it does not matter to someone which thing happens, is chosen etc: *Morning or afternoon. It makes no difference to me.*
5 our/your/their differences disagreements: *We've* **had** *our* **differences** *in the past, but we get on OK now.* | **settle/resolve your differences** (=agree not to argue any more)
6 difference of opinion a slight disagreement: *There have been some differences of opinion as to exactly how the money should be spent.*
7 with a difference *informal* used to describe something which is interesting or unusual, especially in a good way: *an adventure holiday with a difference*

dif·fe·rent S1 W1 /'dɪfərənt/ *adj*
1 not like something or someone else, or not like before; **similar**

D

very/quite different
completely/totally/entirely different
radically different (=very different)
significantly/markedly different (=different in a very noticeable way)
slightly different
subtly different (=different in a way that is not easy to notice)
refreshingly different (=different in a good way)
no different (from/to sth)
a different world (=a very different situation or environment)

[+from] *Our sons are **very different** from each other.* | [+to] *Her jacket's different to mine.* | [+than] *AmE: He seemed different than he did in New York.* | *The place looks **completely different** now.* | *They decided to try a **radically different** approach.* | *We found women had **significantly different** political views from men.* | *a **slightly different** way of doing things* | *What actually happened was **subtly different** from the PR people's version.* | *The show is **refreshingly different** from most exhibitions of modern art.* | *The publishing business is **no different** from any other business in this respect.* | *It's **a different world** here in London.*

⚠ In spoken British English, **different from** and **different to** are both common, but teachers prefer **different from**. **Different than** is also used in American English and occasionally in British English. Do not say **different of**.
2 [only before noun] used to talk about two or more separate things of the same basic kind; ◱ **various**: *Different people reacted in **different ways**.* | **different types/kinds etc** *There are many different types of fabric.* | *I looked in lots of different books but couldn't find anything about it.*
3 [only before noun] another: *I think she's moved to a different job now.*
4 *spoken* unusual, often in a way that you do not like: *'What did you think of the film?' 'Well, it was certainly different.'* —**differently** *adv: I didn't expect to be treated any differently from anyone else.* | *Things could have turned out quite differently.*

dif·fe·ren·tial[1] /ˌdɪfəˈrenʃəl◂/ *n* [C] **1** *formal* a difference between things, especially between the wages of people doing different types of jobs in the same industry or profession: **pay/wage/salary differential 2** *technical* a differential gear

differential[2] *adj* based on or depending on a difference: *differential rates of pay* | *differential treatment of part-time and full-time staff*

ˌdifferential ˈcalculus *n* [U] a way of measuring the speed at which an object is moving at a particular moment

ˌdifferential ˈgear *n* [C] *technical* an arrangement of GEARS that allows one back wheel of a car to turn faster than the other when the car goes around a corner

dif·fe·ren·ti·ate /ˌdɪfəˈrenʃieɪt/ *v* **1** [I,T] to recognize or express the difference between things or people; ◱ **distinguish**: [+between] *It's important to differentiate between fact and opinion.* | **differentiate sth from sth** *It's sometimes hard to differentiate one sample from another.* **2** [T] to be the quality, feature etc that makes one thing or person clearly different from another; ◱ **distinguish**: *What differentiates these two periods of history?* | **differentiate sth from sth** *Its unusual nesting habits differentiate this bird from others.* **3** [I] to behave differently towards someone or something, especially in an unfair way; ◱ **discriminate**: [+between] *a policy which differentiates between men and women* —**differentiation** /ˌdɪfərenʃiˈeɪʃən/ *n* [U]: *socio-economic differentiation*

dif·fi·cult[S1][W1] /ˈdɪfɪkəlt/ *adj*
1 hard to do, understand, or deal with; ◲ **easy**: *a difficult question* | *an immensely difficult task* | *Was the exam very difficult?* | *It's difficult to see how more savings can be made.* | **difficult (for sb) to understand/**

find/obtain etc *That's rather difficult for me to explain.* | *He's **finding it difficult** to get a job.*
2 involving a lot of problems and causing a lot of trouble or worry: *a difficult situation* | *Things are a bit difficult at home at the moment.* | *There could be difficult times ahead.* | **make life/things difficult for sb** (=cause problems for someone) *She's doing everything she can to make life difficult for him.*
3 someone who is difficult never seems pleased or satisfied; ◱ **awkward**: *Don't be so difficult!* | *a difficult customer*

WORD FOCUS: DIFFICULT
difficult to do: **hard, tough, challenging, daunting**
difficult and needing a lot of physical effort: **tough, strenuous, back-breaking, gruelling, arduous, punishing**
difficult to deal with or talk about: **tricky, awkward, delicate, sensitive, touchy**
words for describing a difficult person: **awkward, trying**
words for describing difficult conditions: **adverse, hostile**

dif·fi·cul·ty[S1][W1] /ˈdɪfɪkəlti/ *n plural* **difficulties**
1 [U] if you have difficulty doing something, it is difficult for you to do: **have/experience difficulty (in) doing sth** *They had **great difficulty** in finding a replacement.* | **with/without difficulty** *He got to his feet **with difficulty**.* ⚠ Do not say that someone 'has difficulty to do something'. Say that someone **has difficulty doing something** or **has difficulty in doing something**.
2 [C usually plural] a problem or something that causes trouble

have/experience/encounter difficulties
run/get into difficulties (=experience difficulties)
difficulties arise
overcome difficulties
cause difficulties (for sb)
be fraught with/beset by difficulties (=involve a lot of difficulties)
practical difficulties
mechanical/technical difficulties
financial difficulties (=a bad financial situation)
breathing difficulties
behavioural difficulties (=bad behaviour)
marital difficulties (=problems between a husband and wife)

[+with] *There are several difficulties with this theory.* | *If you **have** any **difficulties**, give me a call.* | *The project soon **ran into difficulties**.* | ***Difficulties** can **arise** when there is more than one defendant.* | *We're confident that the legal **difficulties** can be **overcome**.* | *The rearrangement of school classes may **cause** timetabling **difficulties**.* | *Their ten years of marriage have **been fraught with difficulties**.* | *the **practical difficulties** of prosecuting alleged war criminals* | *The broadcast was delayed because of **technical difficulties**.* | *She developed **breathing difficulties** during the night.*
3 [U] if you are in difficulty, you are in a situation in which you have problems: **in difficulty** *The business is in financial difficulty.* | **get/run into difficulty** (=get into a difficult situation) *She soon got into difficulty with debt.*
4 [U] the quality of being difficult to do: **the difficulty of (doing) sth** *the difficulty of solving such problems*
5 [U] how difficult something is: *The tests vary in difficulty.* → LEARNING DIFFICULTIES

dif·fi·dent /ˈdɪfɪdənt/ *adj* shy and not wanting to make people notice you or talk about you: **diffident manner/smile/voice etc** | [+about] *He was diffident about his own success.* —**diffidently** *adv* —**diffidence** *n* [U]

dif·fract /dɪˈfrækt/ *v* [T] *technical* to bend light or sound waves as they pass around something or through a hole; → **refract** —**diffraction** /dɪˈfrækʃən/ *n* [U]

dif·fuse[1] /dɪˈfjuːz/ *v* **1** [I,T] to make heat, light, liquid etc spread through something, or to spread like this: [+through/into/across] *The pollutants diffuse into the soil.* **2** [I,T] to spread ideas or information among a lot of people, or to spread like this: *Their ideas diffused quickly across Europe.* **3** [T] to make a bad feeling or situation less strong or serious: *an attempt to diffuse his anger* —**diffusion** /dɪˈfjuːʒən/ *n* [U]

dif·fuse² /dɪˈfjuːs/ *adj* **1** spread over a large area: *The organization is large and diffuse.* **2** using a lot of words and not explaining things clearly and directly: *His writing is diffuse and difficult to understand.* —**diffuseness** *n* [U]

dig

dig   burrow

dig¹ [S3] /dɪg/ *v past tense and past participle* **dug** /dʌg/ *present participle* **digging**
1 [I,T] to move earth, snow etc, or to make a hole in the ground, using a SPADE or your hands: **dig a hole/trench/grave etc** *They dig a small hole in the sand to bury their eggs.* | [+**down**] *Dig down about 6 inches.* | [+**for**] *birds digging for worms*
2 [T] to remove something, especially vegetables, from the ground using a SPADE: *freshly dug carrots*
3 [I,T always + adv/prep] to put your hand into something, especially in order to search for something: *She dug around in her bag for a pen.* | *He dug his hands deep into his pockets.*
4 dig your heels in to refuse to do something in spite of other people's efforts to persuade you
5 dig deep to use something which you have, especially money or effort, which you would not normally need: *With one man sent off, the team had to dig deep and hang on for a draw.*
6 dig a hole for yourself also **dig yourself into a hole** to get yourself into a difficult situation by doing or saying the wrong thing
7 dig sb out of trouble/a mess/a hole etc to help a person or organization get out of trouble
8 dig your own grave to do something that will cause serious problems for you in the future
9 [T] *old-fashioned* to like something: *I dig that hat!*
dig in *phr v*
1 dig sth ⇔ **in** also **dig sth into sth** to mix something into soil by digging: *Dig some fertiliser into the soil first.*
2 also **dig (sth) into sth** to push a hard or pointed object into something, especially someone's body, or to press into something: *She dug her finger nails into his arm.* | **dig sth** ⇔ **in** *He dug his spurs in and urged his horse on.* | *I could feel one of the hooks digging in.*
3 if a group of people, especially soldiers, dig in, they make a protected place for themselves or prepare for a difficult situation: *The troops dug in along the defensive line.* | *We just have to dig in and hope we can turn things around.*
4 also **dig into sth** *informal* to start eating food that is in front of you: *Go in – dig in!* | *He was already digging into his pie and chips.*
dig into sth *phr v*
1 to start using a supply of something, especially money: *I'm going to have to dig into my savings again.*
2 to try to find out about something unknown or secret: *He had been digging into her past.* → DIG IN

dig sth ⇔ **out** *phr v*
1 to get something out of earth, snow etc using a SPADE or your hands: [+**of**] *We had to dig the car out of a snow drift.*
2 to find something you have not seen for a long time, or that is not easy to find: *I must remember to dig out that book for you.*
dig sth ⇔ **up** *phr v*
1 to remove something from the earth using a SPADE: *I'll dig up that plant and move it.*
2 to remove the surface of an area of ground, road etc, or to make holes in it: *They're digging up the road just outside my flat.*
3 to find hidden or forgotten information by careful searching: *They tried to dig up something from his past to spoil his chances of being elected.*

dig² *n* [C] **1** a joke or remark that you make to annoy or criticize someone: [+**at**] *He couldn't resist a dig at the referee.* | *Here was a chance to **have a dig** at trade unionists.* **2 give sb a dig** to push someone quickly and lightly with your finger or elbow: *Ginnie gave her sister a dig in the ribs.* **3** an organized process of digging in order to find ancient objects for study: *an archaeological dig* **4 digs** [plural] *BrE old-fashioned* a room that you pay rent to live in: **in digs** *He's 42 and still living in digs.*

di·gest¹ /daɪˈdʒest, dɪ-/ *v* [T] **1** to change food that you have just eaten into substances that your body can use: *Most babies can digest a wide range of food easily.* → INGEST **2** to understand new information, especially when there is a lot of it or it is difficult to understand: *I struggled to digest the news.*

di·gest² /ˈdaɪdʒest/ *n* [C] a short piece of writing that gives the most important facts from a book, report etc

di·gest·i·ble /daɪˈdʒestɪbəl, dɪ-/ *adj* food that is digestible can be easily digested; ▣ **indigestible**

di·ges·tion /daɪˈdʒestʃən, dɪ-/ *n* **1** [U] the process of digesting food **2** [C] your ability to digest food easily: *Too much tea is bad for your digestion.*

di·ges·tive /daɪˈdʒestɪv, dɪ-/ *adj* [only before noun] connected with the process of digestion: **digestive system/organs/juices etc**

di,gestive 'biscuit also **digestive** *n* [C] a type of plain slightly sweet BISCUIT that is popular in Britain

dig·ger /ˈdɪgə $ -ər/ *n* [C] a large machine that digs and moves earth → GOLD DIGGER

dig·gings /ˈdɪgɪŋz/ *n* [plural] a place where people are digging holes in the ground

di·gi·cam /ˈdɪdʒɪkæm/ *n* [C] a type of camera that can store pictures in a DIGITAL form which can be put into a computer, rather than on film

di·git /ˈdɪdʒɪt/ *n* [C] **1** one of the written signs that represent the numbers 0 to 9: **three-digit/four-digit etc number** *4305 is a four-digit number.* **2** *technical* a finger or toe

di·gi·tal /ˈdɪdʒɪtl/ *adj* **1** using a system in which information is recorded or sent out electronically in the form of numbers, usually ones and zeros: *digital TV* | *a digital signal* | *a **digital camera*** | *digital recording* | **digital cassette/audiotape etc** *a recording on digital audiotape;* → see picture at BEDROOM **2** giving information in the form of numbers; → **analogue**: *a **digital watch*** **3** *formal* relating to the fingers and toes —**digitally** *adv*

,digital 'signature *n* [C] information on an electronic message that proves who the person sending the message is

,digital 'television *n* **1** also **digital** [U] a system of broadcasting using digital signals; → **analogue**, **cable 2** [C] a television which can receive digital broadcasts

di·gi·tize also **-ise** *BrE* /ˈdɪdʒɪtaɪz/ *v* [T] to put information into a digital form

D

dig·ni·fied /'dɪgnɪfaɪd/ *adj* behaving in a calm and serious way, even in a difficult situation, which makes people respect you: *a dignified old lady* | *She made a dignified departure.*

dig·ni·fy /'dɪgnɪfaɪ/ *v* **dignified, dignifying, dignifies** [T] to make something or someone seem better or more important than they really are, especially by using a particular word to describe them: **dignify sb/sth with sth** *I cannot dignify him with the name 'physician'.*

dig·ni·ta·ry /'dɪgnɪtəri $ -teri/ *n plural* **dignitaries** [C] someone who has an important official position; ≈ VIP: *Flowers were presented to visiting dignitaries.*

dig·ni·ty /'dɪgnɪti/ *n* [U] **1** the ability to behave in a calm controlled way even in a difficult situation: **with dignity** *The family faced their ordeal with dignity and courage.* | *an appearance of quiet dignity* **2** your dignity your sense of your own value or importance: **retain/lose your dignity** *Old people need to retain their dignity and independence.* | *Arguing **was beneath** her dignity* (=was something she thought she was too important to do). **3** the fact of being respected or deserving respect: **with dignity** *Patients should be allowed to die with dignity.* | *Prisoners should be treated with regard for **human dignity.*** **4** a calm and serious quality: [+of] *the dignity of the occasion* **5 stand on your dignity** *formal* to demand to be treated with proper respect

di·gress /daɪ'gres/ *v* [I] to talk or write about something that is not your main subject: *Do you mind if I digress for a moment?* —**digression** /daɪ'greʃən/ *n* [C,U]: *After several long digressions he finally reached the interesting part of the story.*

dike /daɪk/ *n* another spelling of DYKE

dik·tat /dɪk'tæt/ *n* [C,U] an order that is forced on people by a ruler or government: *government by diktat*

di·lap·i·dat·ed /dɪ'læpədeɪtɪd/ *adj* a dilapidated building, vehicle etc is old and in very bad condition; → **derelict** —**dilapidation** /dɪ,læpɪ'deɪʃən/ *n* [U]

di·late /daɪ'leɪt/ *v* [I,T] if a hollow part of your body dilates or if something dilates it, it becomes wider; ◆ **contract**: *dilated pupils* —**dilation** /daɪ'leɪʃən/ *n* [U]

dilate on/upon sth *phr v formal* to speak or write a lot about something: *He dilated upon their heroism.*

dil·a·to·ry /'dɪlətəri $ -tɔːri/ *adj formal* slow in doing something

dil·do /'dɪldəʊ $ -doʊ/ *n plural* **dildos** [C] an object shaped like a male sex organ that a woman can use for sexual pleasure

di·lem·ma /dɪ'lemə, daɪ-/ *n* [C] a situation in which it is very difficult to decide what to do, because all the choices seem equally good or equally bad: *a moral dilemma* | **in a dilemma** *I'm in a dilemma about this job offer.* | *This **placed** Robert Kennedy **in a dilemma.*** | *Many women are **faced with** the dilemma of choosing between work and family commitments.* → **be on the horns of a dilemma** at HORN[1] (6)

dil·et·tan·te /,dɪlɪ'tænti $ -'tɑːnti/ *n* [C] someone who is not serious about what they are doing or does not study a subject thoroughly —**dilettante** *adj* [only before noun]

dil·i·gent /'dɪlɪdʒənt/ *adj* someone who is diligent works hard and is careful and thorough: *a diligent student* —**diligently** *adv*: *They worked diligently all morning.* —**diligence** *n* [U]

dill /dɪl/ *n* [U] a type of herb

dill 'pickle *n* [C] a whole CUCUMBER which has been preserved in VINEGAR

dil·ly-dal·ly /'dɪli ,dæli/ *v* **dilly-dallied, dilly-dallying, dilly-dallies** [I] to waste time, because you cannot decide about something: *Don't dilly-dally, just get on with it!*

di·lute¹ /daɪ'luːt $,dɪ'luːt, daɪ-/ *v* [T] **1** to make a liquid weaker by adding water or another liquid; →

water down: *diluted fruit juice* | **dilute sth with/in sth** *Dilute the paint with a little oil.* **2** to make a quality, belief etc weaker or less effective; → **water down**: *an attempt to dilute the proposals* —**dilution** /daɪ'luːʃən/ *n* [C,U]: *Any dilution of standards must be resisted.*

di·lute² *adj* a dilute liquid has been made weaker by the addition of water or another liquid: *dilute hydrochloric acid*

dim¹ /dɪm/ *adj comparative* **dimmer,** *superlative* **dimmest**
1 DARK fairly dark or not giving much light, so that you cannot see well; ◆ **bright**: *in the dim light of the early dawn* | *a dim glow*
2 SHAPE a dim shape is one which is not easy to see because it is too far away, or there is not enough light: *The dim outline of a building loomed up out of the mist.*
3 take a dim view of sth to disapprove of something: *Miss Watson took a dim view of Paul's behaviour.*
4 dim recollection/awareness etc a memory or understanding of something that is not clear in your mind; ≈ **vague**: *Laura had a dim recollection of someone telling her this before.*
5 EYES *literary* dim eyes are weak and cannot see well: *Isaac was old and his eyes were dim.*
6 FUTURE CHANCES if your chances of success in the future are dim, they are not good: *Prospects for an early settlement of the dispute are dim.*
7 in the dim and distant past a very long time ago – used humorously
8 NOT INTELLIGENT *informal* not intelligent: *You can be really dim sometimes!* —**dimly** *adv*: *a dimly lit room* | *She was only dimly aware of the risk.* —**dimness** *n* [U]

dim² *v* **dimmed, dimming** **1** [I,T] if a light dims, or if you dim it, it becomes less bright: *The lights in the theatre began to dim.* **2** [I,T] if a feeling, quality etc dims or is dimmed, it grows weaker or less: *Even the rain could not dim their enthusiasm.* | *Hopes of a peaceful settlement have dimmed.* **3 dim your headlights/lights** *AmE* to lower the angle of the front lights of your car, especially when someone is driving towards you; ≈ **dip** *BrE*

dime /daɪm/ *n* [C] **1** a coin of the US and Canada, worth one tenth of a dollar **2 a dime a dozen** *AmE informal* very common and not valuable; ≈ **ten a penny** *BrE*: *PhDs are a dime a dozen nowadays.*

'dime ,novel *n* [C] *AmE* a cheap book with a story that contains a lot of exciting events

di·men·sion W3 /daɪ'menʃən, dɪ-/ *n* [C]
1 a part of a situation or a quality involved in it; ≈ **aspect**: [+of] *the moral dimension of world politics* | **add a new/an extra/another etc dimension (to sth)** *His coaching has added another dimension to my game.* | **political/social/economic etc dimension** *It is important to keep in mind the historical dimension to these issues.* | *You can have a **spiritual dimension** to your life without being religious.*
2 [usually plural] the length, height, width, depth, or DIAMETER of something: *a rectangle with the dimensions 5cm x 2cm* | [+of] *We'll need to know the exact dimensions of the room.*
3 a direction in space that is at an angle of 90 degrees to two other directions: *A diagram represents things in only two dimensions.* → **FOURTH DIMENSION, THREE-DIMENSIONAL** (1), **TWO-DIMENSIONAL** (1)
4 dimensions [plural] how great or serious a problem is: *We're heading for a catastrophe of enormous dimensions.*

'dime store *n* [C] *AmE* a shop that sells many different kinds of cheap goods, especially for the house

di·min·ish /dɪ'mɪnɪʃ/ *v* **1** [I,T] to become or make something become smaller or less; ≈ **reduce**: *The party's share of the electorate has diminished steadily.* | *These drugs diminish blood flow to the brain.* **2** [T] to deliberately make someone or something appear less important or valuable than they really are: *Don't let him diminish your achievements.* | *But that's not to* diminish the importance of his discoveries. **3 diminishing returns** when the profits or advantages you are getting from something stop increasing in relation to the effort you are making

di,minished responsi'bility also **di,minished ca'pacity** AmE n [U] law when someone is not considered to be responsible for their actions because they are mentally ill

di·min·u·en·do /dɪ̩mɪnjuˈendəʊ $ -doʊ/ n plural **diminuendos** [C] a part in a piece of music where it becomes gradually quieter; **ⓕ crescendo** —**diminuendo** adj, adv

dim·i·nu·tion /ˌdɪmɪ̩ˈnjuːʃən $ -ˈnuː-/ n [C,U] formal a reduction in the size, number, or amount of something: [+of/in] a diminution in value

di·min·u·tive¹ /dɪ̩ˈmɪnjɪ̩tɪv/ adj small: a shy diminutive man

diminutive² n [C] a word formed by adding a diminutive suffix

di,minutive 'suffix n [C] technical an ending that is added to a word to express smallness, for example 'ling' added to 'duck' to make 'duckling'

dim·mer /ˈdɪmə $ -ər/ also **'dimmer ,switch** n [C] an electric light switch that can change the brightness of the light

dim·ple /ˈdɪmpəl/ n [C] **1** a small hollow place on your skin, especially one on your cheek or chin when you smile **2** a small hollow place in a surface —**dimpled** adj: dimpled cheeks

dim·wit /ˈdɪmwɪt/ n [C] spoken a stupid person —**dim-'witted** adj

din¹ /dɪn/ n [singular] a loud unpleasant noise that continues for a long time: [+of] The din of the engines was deafening. | **above the din** Ged was trying to make himself heard above the din.

din² v **dinned, dinning**
din sth **into** sb phr v to make someone learn and remember something by saying it to them many times: Respect for our elders was dinned into us at school.

di·nar /ˈdiːnɑː $ dɪˈnɑːr, ˈdiːnɑːr/ n [C] the standard unit of money in Yugoslavia and some Middle Eastern countries

dine /daɪn/ v [I] formal to eat dinner: He was dining with friends at the Ritz. → **wine and dine** sb at WINE²
dine on/off sth phr v formal to eat a particular kind of food for dinner, especially expensive food: We dined on lobster and strawberries.
dine out phr v **1** formal to eat dinner in a restaurant or in someone else's house; → **eat out**: They would dine out together once a month. **2 dine out on** sth BrE informal to keep using a story about something that has happened to you, in order to entertain people at meals

din·er /ˈdaɪnə $ -ər/ n [C] **1** someone who is eating in a restaurant **2** especially AmE a small restaurant that serves cheap meals

di·nette /daɪˈnet/ n [C] AmE a small area, usually in or near the kitchen, where people eat meals

ding-a-ling /ˈdɪŋ ə lɪŋ/ also **ding·bat** /ˈdɪŋbæt/ n [C] AmE spoken a stupid person: Some ding-a-ling parked too close to us.

ding-dong /ˈdɪŋ dɒŋ $ -dɔːŋ/ n **1** [U] the noise made by a bell **2** [singular] BrE spoken a noisy argument: They were having a real ding-dong in the kitchen. **3** [C] AmE spoken a stupid person

din·ghy /ˈdɪŋi, ˈdɪŋgi/ n plural **dinghies** [C] a small open boat used for pleasure, or for taking people between a ship and the shore → **RUBBER DINGHY**

din·go /ˈdɪŋgəʊ $ -goʊ/ n plural **dingoes** [C] an Australian wild dog

din·gy /ˈdɪndʒi/ adj comparative **dingier**, superlative **dingiest** dark, dirty, and in bad condition: a dingy room | a dingy side-street —**dinginess** n [U]

'dining car n [C] a carriage on a train where meals are served; **ⓔ restaurant car**

'dining room n [C] a room where you eat meals in a house or hotel

'dining ,table n [C] a table at which you eat meals → **DINNER TABLE**

din·kum /ˈdɪŋkəm/ adj **fair dinkum** spoken informal fair or honest – used in Australian English

din·ky /ˈdɪŋki/ adj informal **1** BrE small and attractive: a dinky little bag **2** AmE too small and often not very nice: It was a really dinky hotel room.

din·ner S1 W2 /ˈdɪnə $ -ər/ n
1 [C,U] the main meal of the day, eaten in the middle of the day or the evening: **to dinner** Perhaps we should **invite** them **to dinner**. | **for dinner** We're having fish for dinner tonight. | What time do you usually **have dinner?** | We **eat dinner** at about seven. | a three course dinner | **school dinners** BrE (=meals provided in the middle of the day at school) | **dinner money** BrE (=money children are given to pay for their meal at school) | **Sunday/Christmas/Thanksgiving dinner** (=special meal eaten on Sunday, at Christmas, at Thanksgiving etc) | dinner guests
2 [C] a formal occasion when an evening meal is eaten, often to celebrate something: The Club's annual dinner will be held in November. → **dog's dinner** at DOG¹ (9); → **more sth than you've had hot dinners** at HOT¹ (30); → TV DINNER

WORD CHOICE: dinner, supper, tea, lunch
In Britain, the main meal of the day is **dinner** and it is usually eaten in the evening. Some people call this meal **supper**, but to others supper is a very small meal that is eaten just before they go to bed. Some people call this main evening meal **tea**, but to others tea is a small meal that is eaten in the afternoon.
Some people use **dinner** to refer to the meal they eat in the middle of the day, but if you want to be clear that you are referring to this meal, use **lunch**.

'dinner ,dance n [C] a social event in the evening, that includes a formal meal and music for dancing

'dinner ,jacket n [C] BrE a black or white jacket worn by men on very formal occasions, usually with a BOW TIE

'dinner ,lady n [C] BrE a woman who serves meals to children at school

'dinner ,party n [C] a social event when people are invited to someone's house for an evening meal

'dinner ,service also **'dinner set** n [C] a complete set of plates, dishes etc, used for serving a meal

'dinner ,table n **the dinner table a)** an occasion when people are eating dinner together: It wasn't a very suitable conversation for the dinner table. **b)** the table at which people eat dinner → **DINING TABLE**

'dinner ,theater n [C,U] AmE a restaurant in which you see a play after your meal, or this type of entertainment

din·ner·time /ˈdɪnətaɪm $ -ər-/ n [U] the time when you usually have dinner, especially in the middle of the day: Do you want to go for a drink at dinnertime?

di·no·saur /ˈdaɪnəsɔː $ -sɔːr/ n [C] **1** one of a group of REPTILES that lived millions of years ago **2** informal someone or something that is old-fashioned and no longer effective or suitable for modern times: lengthy speeches by some of the party's dinosaurs

dint /dɪnt/ n **by dint of (doing)** sth by using a particular method: By dint of hard work and persistence, she had got the job of manager.

di·o·cese /ˈdaɪəsɪs/ n [C] the area under the control of a BISHOP in some Christian churches —**diocesan** /daɪˈɒsɪsən $ -ˈɑː-/ adj

di·ode /ˈdaɪəʊd $ -oʊd/ n [C] technical a piece of electrical equipment that makes an electrical current flow in one direction

1 000, 2 000, 3 000, most frequent words in S poken and W ritten English

di·ox·ide /daɪˈɒksaɪd $ -ˈɑːk-/ n [C,U] a chemical COM-POUND that contains two atoms of oxygen and one atom of another chemical ELEMENT → CARBON DIOXIDE

di·ox·in /daɪˈɒksɪ̰n $ -ˈɑːk-/ n [C,U] a very poisonous chemical used in industry and farming

dip¹ /dɪp/ v dipped, dipping
1 PUT STH IN LIQUID [T] to put something into a liquid and lift it out again: **dip sth in/into sth** He dipped his hand in the water. | Dip the strawberries into melted chocolate.
2 MOVE DOWN [I,T] to move down, or to make something move down, usually for just a short time: We watched the sun **dip** below the horizon. | She **dipped** her head and spoke into the microphone.
3 BECOME LESS [I] if an amount or level dips, it becomes less, usually for just a short time; ◧ fall: Profits dipped slightly last year. | Temperatures dipped to -10°C last night.
4 ROAD/PATH [C] if land or a road or path dips, it slopes down and then goes up again
5 dip your headlights/lights BrE to lower the angle of the front lights of your car when someone is driving towards you
6 ANIMALS [T] to put animals in a chemical that kills insects on their skin → SKINNY-DIPPING
  dip into sth phr v
1 to read short parts of a book, magazine etc, but not the whole thing: It's the kind of book you can dip into now and again.
2 to use some of an amount of money that you have: Medical bills forced her to **dip into** her **savings**. | Parents are being asked to **dip into** their **pockets** for new school books (=use their own money to pay for them).
3 to put your hand into a bag or box in order to take out one of the things inside: On her lap was a bag of candy which she kept dipping into.

dip² n
1 SWIM [C] informal a quick swim: Are you coming in for a dip? | **take/have a dip** Let's take a dip in the lake before lunch.
2 DECREASE [C] a slight decrease in the amount of something: [+in] an unexpected dip in profits
3 FOOD [C,U] a thick mixture that you can dip food into before you eat it: sour cream and onion dip
4 IN A SURFACE [C] a place where the surface of something goes down suddenly, then goes up again: [+in] a dip in the road
5 FOR ANIMALS [C,U] a chemical that kills insects on sheep and other animals: **sheep dip**
6 PERSON [C] AmE spoken a stupid person
7 a dip into sth a quick look at information, a book, magazine etc: People interested in history would enjoy a dip into this book. → LUCKY DIP

Dip BrE the written abbreviation of **diploma**

diph·ther·i·a /dɪfˈθɪəriə, dɪp- $ -ˈθɪr-/ n [U] a serious infectious throat disease that makes breathing difficult

diph·thong /ˈdɪfθɒŋ, ˈdɪp- $ -θɔːŋ/ n [C] technical a vowel sound made by pronouncing two vowels quickly one after the other. For example, the vowel sound in 'main' is a diphthong.

di·plo·ma /dɪˈ̰pləʊmə $ -ˈploʊ-/ n [C] **1** BrE a document showing that someone has successfully completed a course of study or passed an examination: I'm hoping to **get** my teaching **diploma** this year. | [+in] a diploma in catering **2** AmE a document showing that a student has successfully completed their HIGH SCHOOL or university education: **high school/college diploma**

di·plo·ma·cy /dɪˈ̰pləʊməsi $ -ˈploʊ-/ n [U] **1** the job or activity of managing the relationships between countries: international diplomacy **2** skill in dealing with people without upsetting them: The job requires tact and diplomacy. → **gunboat diplomacy** at GUNBOAT (2)

dip·lo·mat /ˈdɪpləmæt/ n [C] **1** someone who officially represents their government in a foreign coun-

try; → **ambassador**: French diplomats **2** someone who is good at dealing with people without upsetting them

dip·lo·mat·ic /ˌdɪpləˈmætɪk◂/ adj **1** relating to or involving the work of diplomats: Diplomatic efforts to end the fighting began on Oct 25. **2** diplomatic relations/ties the arrangement between two countries that each should keep representatives at an EMBASSY in the other's country: **establish/break off diplomatic relations** The two countries established diplomatic relations last year. **3** dealing with people politely and skilfully without upsetting them; ◧ **tactful**: They were always very diplomatic with awkward clients. | a diplomatic answer —**diplomatically** /-kli/ adv: Maria handled the situation very diplomatically.

diplomatic 'bag n [C] a bag or container used for sending official government documents to diplomats working abroad

diplo'matic ,corps n [U] all the diplomats working in a particular country

diplomatic im'munity n [U] a diplomat's special rights in the country where they are working, which protect them from local taxes and PROSECUTION

Diplo'matic ,Service n the Diplomatic Service the British government department that sends people to represent Britain in other countries

di·plo·ma·tist /dɪˈ̰pləʊmətɪ̰st $ -ˈploʊ-/ n [C] old-fashioned a DIPLOMAT

dip·per /ˈdɪpə $ -ər/ n [C] **1** a small bird that finds its food in streams **2** a large spoon with a long handle, used for taking liquid out of a container → BIG DIPPER

dip·py /ˈdɪpi/ adj informal silly or crazy

dip·shit /ˈdɪpʃɪt/ n [C] AmE spoken not polite an offensive word for a stupid person

dip·so·ma·ni·ac /ˌdɪpsəˈmeɪniæk/ n [C] BrE old-fashioned someone who has a very strong desire for alcohol, which they cannot control; ◧ **alcoholic**

dip·stick /ˈdɪpˌstɪk/ n [C] **1** a stick for measuring the amount of liquid in a container, especially the amount of oil in a car's engine **2** spoken a stupid person

dip·tych /ˈdɪptɪk/ n [C] a picture made in two parts which can be closed like a book → TRIPTYCH

dire /daɪə $ daɪr/ adj **1** extremely serious or terrible: warnings of **dire consequences** that often don't come true | The country is **in dire need of** food aid. | The situation looked dire. **2** be in dire straits to be in an extremely difficult or serious situation: Everyone agrees the sport is in dire straits. **3** dire warning/prediction/forecast a warning about something terrible that will happen in the future: Last night there were dire warnings of civil war.

di·rect¹ S2 W1 /dɪˈrekt, daɪˈrekt◂/ adj
1 WITHOUT INVOLVING OTHERS done without any other people, actions, processes etc coming between; ◧ **indirect**: Experienced users have direct access to the main data files. | I'm not in **direct contact** with them. | Few policy-makers have had direct experience of business. | **direct effect/impact/influence etc** Educational level has a sizeable direct effect on income. | **direct link/connection/relationship etc** There is a direct link between poverty and ill-health. | **direct result/consequence** The decision to close the hospital is a direct result of Government health policy.
2 FROM ONE PLACE TO ANOTHER going straight from one place to another without stopping or changing direction; ◧ **indirect**: Which is the most **direct route** to London? | a direct flight to New York
3 EXACT [only before noun] exact or total: Weight increases **in direct proportion to** mass. | For Lawrence, in direct contrast to Adam, everything seemed to come so easily. | a **direct quote** (=exact words) from the book
4 BEHAVIOUR/ATTITUDE saying exactly what you mean in an honest clear way; ◧ **indirect**: Women often feel men are too direct and not sympathetic enough. |

Now, let me ask you a **direct question**, *and I expect a* **direct answer***.*

5 direct descendant someone who is related to someone else through their parents and grandparents, not through their AUNTS, UNCLES etc: [+of] *She claimed to be a direct descendant of Wordsworth.*

6 direct hit an occasion on which something such as a bomb hits a place exactly, causing a lot of damage: *During the war, the cathedral **suffered** many **direct hits***. | *One of the bombers **scored a direct hit**.*

7 direct heat/sunlight strong heat or light that someone or something is not protected from; ⬛ **indirect**: *Never change the film in direct sunlight.* → DIRECTLY, DIRECTNESS

direct² S2 W2 *v*

1 AIM [T always + adv/prep] to aim something in a particular direction or at a particular person, group etc: **direct sth at/towards etc sth** *The machine directs an X-ray beam at the patient's body.* | *The new route directs lorries away from the town centre.* | *I'd like to **direct your attention** to paragraph four.* | *I want to **direct** my **efforts** more towards my own projects.*

2 BE IN CHARGE [T] to be in charge of something or control it: *Mr Turner was directing the investigation from a very early stage.* | *The choir was directed by Sir David Willcocks.*

3 FILM/PLAY [I,T] to give the actors in a play, film, or television programme instructions about what they should do: *The play was directed by Frank Hauser.*

4 WAY/ROUTE [T] *formal* to tell someone how to get to a place: **direct sb to sth** *Could you direct me to Trafalgar Square, please?*

5 TELL SB TO DO STH [T] *formal* to tell someone what they should do; ⬛ **order**: **direct sb to do sth** *The judge directed the jury to find Mr Baggs not guilty.* | **direct that** *He directed that his body should be buried in Upton, Northamptonshire.*

WORD CHOICE: direct, take, guide, lead

If you **direct** someone somewhere, you tell them which way to go to get there, but you do not go with them: *He directed me to a hotel near the airport (NOT He guided me to a hotel near the airport).*

⚠ Do not say that you direct something in a particular direction. Say that you **point** something in a particular direction: *He pointed the gun at the policeman (NOT He directed the gun at the policeman).*

If you **take**, **guide**, or **lead** someone somewhere, you go with them there: *I'll take you to the airport.* Use **guide** especially to talk about helping someone along a difficult route: *They guided me through a maze of one-way streets.* Use **lead** to talk about going in front of someone who is following you: *The waiter led us to a table in the corner.*

---

direct³ *adv* **1** without stopping or changing direction; ⬛ **directly**: *Can we fly direct to Chicago, or do we stop in Salt Lake City first?* **2** without dealing with anyone else first; ⬛ **directly**: *Esther decided to contact the manager direct.* | *It is usually cheaper to buy the goods direct from the wholesaler.*

di,rect 'access *n* [U] *technical* the ability to obtain DATA directly from a computer FILE without starting from the beginning

di,rect 'action *n* [U] an action such as a STRIKE or a protest that is intended to make a government or company change something immediately: *Peaceful direct action by pressure groups has a powerful effect on public opinion.*

di,rect 'current *n* [U] *DC* a flow of electricity that moves in one direction only; → **alternating current**

di,rect 'debit *n* [C,U] *BrE* an instruction you give your bank to pay money directly out of your account regularly to a particular person or organization

di,rect de'posit *n* [U] a method of paying someone's wages directly into their bank account —**direct deposit** *v* [T]

di,rect 'discourse *n* [U] *AmE technical* DIRECT SPEECH

di·rec·tion S1 W1 /dɪˈrekʃən, daɪ-/ *n*

1 TOWARDS [C] the way something or someone moves, faces, or is aimed: *Which **direction** did they go in?* | **in the direction of sth** *The suspects were last seen heading in the direction of Miami.* | **in sb's direction** *Tony glanced in her direction and their eyes met.* | *The girls pointed **in the opposite direction**.* | *On seeing me, Maurice **changed direction** and went along the wharf instead.* | *As shots rang out, the crowd ran screaming **in all directions**.* | **from the direction of sth** *There was a loud scream from the direction of the children's pool.* | **in a southerly/easterly etc direction** *Continue in a southerly direction until you reach the road.*

2 directions [plural] **a)** instructions about how to get from one place to another: *A very helpful woman **gave** me **directions** to the police station.* **b)** instructions about what to do: *Be sure you **read the directions** before using any piece of equipment.*

3 WAY STH DEVELOPS [C] the general way in which someone or something changes or develops: *We are happy with the **direction** the club is **taking**.* | **move/head/go in the right direction** *I believe that things are heading in the right direction in South Africa.* | **new/different/exciting etc direction** *The company is hoping to extend its operations in new directions.*

4 CONTROL [U] control, management, or advice: **under sb's direction** *Under Thompson's direction, the college has developed an international reputation.*

5 WHERE FROM OR WHERE TO [C] where something comes from or where something leads: **in a direction** *The evidence all points in this direction.* | **from a direction** *Help came from a wholly unexpected direction.*

6 PURPOSE [U] a general purpose or aim: *Her mother felt that Rachel's life **lacked direction**.*

7 FILM/PLAY [U] the instructions given to the actors and other people working on a film, play etc ; → **a step in the right direction** at STEP¹ (2)

di·rec·tion·al /dɪˈrekʃənəl, daɪ-/ *adj technical* **1** relating to the direction in which something is pointing or moving **2** a directional piece of equipment receives or gives out radio signals from some directions more strongly than others

di·rec·tion·less /dɪˈrekʃənləs, daɪ-/ *adj* lacking a clear direction or aim: *I felt directionless and lost.*

di·rec·tive¹ /dɪˈrektɪv, daɪ-/ *n* [C] an official order or instruction: [+on] *proposals for **implementing** the EU **directive** on paternity leave*

directive² *adj formal* giving instructions: *The team leader will have a less directive role.*

di·rect·ly¹ S2 W2 /dɪˈrektli, daɪ-/ *adv*

1 with no other person, action, process etc between; ⬛ **indirectly**: *The new property tax law won't **directly** affect us.* | *We hope to bring together the countries **directly involved** in the conflict.* | [+to/from] *Application for admission to this course should be made directly to the University.*

2 exactly in a particular position or direction; ⬛ **right**: **directly in front of/behind/under etc sth** *It was a small house, directly behind the church.* | *The girl was sitting directly opposite him.* | *Have you noticed how he never looks directly at you?*

3 speak/ask/answer etc directly to say exactly what you mean without trying to hide anything: *Jeff has a job in mind, but refuses to say directly what it is.*

4 *BrE old-fashioned* very soon: *He should be here directly, if you don't mind waiting.*

5 *BrE old-fashioned* immediately

directly² *conjunction BrE old-fashioned* as soon as: *I came directly I got your message.*

di,rect 'mail *n* [U] advertisements that are sent by post to many people

di,rect 'marketing *n* [U] the business of selling things directly to people by post or telephone rather than in shops

di,rect 'method *n* [singular, U] a method of teaching a foreign language without using the student's own language

di·rect·ness /dɔ'ˈrektnɪs, daɪ-/ *n* [U] the quality of being clear, plain, or easy to understand: *She has a childlike enthusiasm and directness.* | [+of] *The direct-ness of the question startled me.*

,**direct 'object** *n* [C] *technical* in grammar, the person or thing that is affected by the action of a TRANSITIVE verb, for example 'Mary' in the statement 'I saw Mary' → INDIRECT OBJECT

di·rec·tor W1 /dɔ'ˈrektə, daɪ- $ -ər/ *n* [C]
1 someone who controls or manages a company; → **executive**: [+of] *a former director of Gartmore Pensions Ltd* | *The company is run by a board of directors* (=a group of directors).
2 someone who is in charge of a particular activity or organization: [+of] *the director of education for Norfolk* | **finance/marketing/sales etc director** (=the person in charge of the financial department etc)
3 the person who gives instructions to the actors and other people working on a film or play; → **producer**; → MANAGING DIRECTOR, NON-EXECUTIVE DIRECTOR; → see picture at CHAIR

di·rec·tor·ate /dɔ'ˈrektərət, daɪ-/ *n* [C] **1** the group of directors who run a company; **□ board** **2** a department of a government or large organization in charge of a particular area or activity: *the regional directorate of education*

di,rector-'general *n* [C] *BrE* the person in charge of a large public organization: *the Director-General of Fair Trading*

di·rec·to·ri·al /ˌdaɪrekˈtɔːriəl/ *adj* [only before noun] relating to the work of a film or theatre director: *De Niro's directorial debut, Tales of the Bronx*

Di,rector of 'Studies *n* [C] a teacher in a British university or language school who is in charge of organizing the students' programmes of study

di'rector's ,cut *n* [C] a film containing all the parts that the director wanted to include, that usually appears after the film has been shown in cinemas without those parts

di·rec·tor·ship /dɔ'ˈrektəʃɪp, daɪ- $ -ər-/ *n* [C] the position of being a director of a company or organization: **under the directorship of sb** *The Institute was established in 1960 under the directorship of Professor Leon Radzinowicz.*

di·rec·to·ry /daɪˈrektəri, dɔ-/ *n plural* **directories** [C] **1** a book or list of names, facts etc, usually arranged in alphabetical order: *I couldn't find your number in the telephone directory.* | *a new business directory* **2** a place in a computer where FILES or programs are organized

di,rectory en'quiries *BrE*; **di,rectory as'sistance** *AmE n* [U] a service on the telephone network that you can use to find out someone's telephone number

di,rect 'speech *n* [U] speech reported using the actual words spoken, as in " 'I don't want to go,' said Julie." → INDIRECT SPEECH, REPORTED SPEECH

di,rect 'tax *n* [C,U] a tax, such as income tax, which is collected from the person who pays it, rather than a tax on goods or services; → **indirect tax** —**di,rect tax'ation** *n* [U]

di,rect-to-con'sumer *adj* [only before noun] direct-to-consumer advertising is aimed at the customer who will buy the product rather than the shops where it will be sold

dirge /dɜːdʒ $ dɜːrdʒ/ *n* [C] **1** a slow sad song sung at a funeral **2** a song or piece of music that is too slow and boring

dir·i·gi·ble /'dɪrɪdʒɪbəl, dɔ'ˈrɪ-/ *n* [C] an AIRSHIP

dirk /dɜːk $ dɜːrk/ *n* [C] a heavy pointed knife used as a weapon in Scotland in the past

dirt S3 /dɜːt $ dɜːrt/ *n* [U]
1 any substance that makes things dirty, such as mud or dust: *You should have seen the dirt on that car!* | *His face and hands were black with dirt.* | *a patch of grass, covered in dog dirt* (=waste from a dog's bowels)
2 *especially AmE* earth or soil: *Michael threw his handful of dirt onto the coffin.* | **in (the) dirt** *The children had been sitting in the dirt.*
3 *informal* information about someone's private life or activities which could give people a bad opinion of them if it became known: *The newspapers had been digging up dirt on the President.*
4 talk, writing, a film etc that is considered bad or immoral because it is about sex → **dish the dirt** at DISH²; → **hit/strike paydirt** at PAYDIRT; → **hit the dirt** at HIT¹ (17); → **treat sb like dirt** at TREAT¹ (1)

dirt·bag /'dɜːtbæg $ 'dɜːrt-/ *n* [C] *informal especially AmE* someone who is very unpleasant and immoral

'**dirt bike** *n* [C] a small MOTORCYCLE for young people, usually ridden on rough paths or fields

,**dirt 'cheap** *adj, adv informal* extremely cheap: *Such cheap goods obviously rely on dirt cheap labor.* | *I got these shoes dirt cheap.*

'**dirt-,disher** *n* [C] *AmE informal* a DISHER

'**dirt ,farmer** *n* [C] *AmE* a poor farmer who works to feed himself and his family, without paying anyone else to help

,**dirt 'poor** *adj informal* extremely poor

'**dirt road** *n* [C] a road made of hard earth

'**dirt track** *n* [C] **1** a road or path made of hard earth **2** a track used for MOTORCYCLE races

dirt·y¹ S2 W3 /'dɜːti $ 'dɜːr-/ *adj comparative* **dirtier**, *superlative* **dirtiest**
1 NOT CLEAN covered in or marked by an unwanted substance; **□ clean**: *a stack of dirty dishes in the sink* | *How did you get so dirty?* | **dirty clothes/washing/laundry** *She circled the bedroom, picking up dirty clothes.*
2 SEX relating to sex, in a way that is considered immoral or unpleasant: *kids telling dirty jokes* | *a dirty magazine* | *She looked at me as if I had said a dirty word.* | **have a dirty mind** *BrE* (=think about sex a lot) | **dirty weekend** *BrE* (=a weekend when a man and woman who are not married to each other go away to have sex)
3 BAD/IMMORAL used to emphasize that you think someone or something is bad, dishonest, or immoral: *You're a dirty liar!* | *a dirty fighter* | *you and your dirty little deals* | **do the dirty on sb** *BrE* (=treat someone in a way that is unfair or dishonest) | *What a dirty rotten trick!*
4 sth is a dirty word if something is a dirty word, people believe it is a bad thing even if they do not know or think much about it; **□ swear word**: *'Liberal' has somehow become a dirty word in America.*
5 **give sb a dirty look** to look at someone in a very disapproving way: *Susan gave her brother a dirty look.*
6 **dirty trick** a dishonest or unfair action, especially done by a government, company, or organization: *political dirty tricks*
7 **wash your dirty linen/laundry** also **air your dirty laundry** *AmE* to discuss something embarrassing or bad about yourself where everyone can see, know, or hear: *The divorce has meant airing their dirty laundry in court.*
8 **do sb's dirty work** to do an unpleasant or dishonest action for someone, so that they do not have to do it themselves: *I'm not talking to him; you do your own dirty work!*
9 **it's a dirty job, but someone has to do it** used to say that something is unpleasant to do, but that it is necessary – often used humorously
10 DRUGS *AmE informal* containing or possessing illegal drugs
11 **dirty bomb** a bomb that contains a RADIOACTIVE substance which makes the bomb more dangerous than bombs containing only traditional explosives

12 SPORT a dirty sports event is one in which people competing in the event have illegally used drugs to improve their performance: *Many people think that the race has been a dirty event for years.* —**dirtily** adv

> **WORD FOCUS: DIRTY**
> *similar words:* **filthy, grubby, grimy, mucky** *BrE,* **muddy, greasy, dusty, soiled, contaminated, polluted**

dirty[2] *adv informal* **1 play dirty** to behave in a very unfair and dishonest way, especially in a competition or game: *a team that plays dirty* **2 talk dirty** to talk about sex using offensive words **3 dirty great/dirty big** *BrE spoken* extremely big: *a dirty great snake*

dirty[3] *v* **dirtied, dirtying, dirties** [I,T] **1** to make something dirty **2** to make someone feel or seem bad, dishonest, or immoral: *The army's actions dirtied its reputation.* **3 dirty your hands** to do hard physical work, in which your hands become dirty

dirty old 'man *n* [C] *informal* an older man who is too sexually interested in younger women – used to show disapproval

dis- /dɪs/ *prefix* **1** shows an opposite or negative: *I disapprove* (=do not approve) | *dishonesty* (=lack of honesty) **2** [in verbs] shows the stopping or removing of a condition: *Disconnect the machine.* | *Disinfect the wound.*

dis·a·bil·i·ty /ˌdɪsəˈbɪləti/ *n plural* **disabilities 1** [C] a physical or mental condition that makes it difficult for someone to use a part of their body properly, or to learn normally: **with a disability** *Public places are becoming more accessible to people with disabilities.* | **learning/physical/mental etc disability** *children with* **severe** *learning* **disabilities 2** [U] when you have a physical or mental disability: *learning to cope with disability* **3** [U] *AmE* money that is given by the government to people who have physical disabilities: **on disability** *Evans lives on disability because of an accident that left her paralyzed.*

dis·a·ble /dɪsˈeɪbəl/ *v* [T] **1** [usually passive] to make someone unable to use a part of their body properly: *Carter was permanently disabled in the war.* **2** to deliberately make a machine or piece of equipment impossible to use: *The virus will disable your computer.* —**disablement** *n* [C,U] —**disabling** *adj: a disabling injury*

dis·a·bled W3 /dɪsˈeɪbəld/ *adj* **1** someone who is disabled cannot use a part of their body properly, or cannot learn easily; → **handicapped**: *a support group for parents of disabled children* | *a* **severely** *disabled polio patient* | **physically/mentally disabled** *If you are elderly or physically disabled, massage can be beneficial.* | *teachers who work with* **learning disabled** *children* (=children who have problems learning) | **disabled parking/toilet/access etc** (=for physically disabled people) **2 the disabled** [plural] people who are disabled: *The theatre has good access for the disabled.*

dis·a·buse /ˌdɪsəˈbjuːz/ *v* [T] *formal* to persuade someone that what they believe is not true: **disabuse sb of sth** *I tried to disabuse him of that notion.*

dis·ad·van·tage[1] /ˌdɪsədˈvɑːntɪdʒ $ -ˈvæn-/ *n* [C,U] something that causes problems, or that makes someone or something less likely to be successful or effective; **▪** **advantage**

> **big/major/serious/grave disadvantage**
> **advantages and disadvantages**
> **be at a disadvantage** (=have a disadvantage)
> **put/place sb at a disadvantage**
> **the advantages/benefits outweigh the disadvantages** (=there are more advantages than disadvantages)
> **social/economic/educational disadvantage** (=a situation in which someone has a much lower social, economic, or educational level than other people)

[**+of**] *The main disadvantage of the material is that it fades in strong sunlight.* | [**+to**] *There are some* **big disadvantages** *to marriage – you do lose a lot of your freedom.* | *Both methods have their* **advantages and**

disadvantages. | *Anyone who can't use a computer is* **at a disadvantage** *these days.* | *The new rules may* **put** *European farmers* **at a disadvantage.** | *The* **benefits** *of the system far* **outweigh the disadvantages.** | *Criminal behaviour can be linked to* **economic disadvantage.**

disadvantage[2] *v* [T] to make someone less likely to be successful or to put them in a worse situation than others

dis·ad·van·taged /ˌdɪsədˈvɑːntɪdʒd◂ $ -ˈvæn-/ *adj* **1** having social problems, such as a lack of money or education, which make it difficult for you to succeed: *disadvantaged areas of the city* **2 the disadvantaged** [plural] people who are disadvantaged: *health programs for the disadvantaged*

dis·ad·van·ta·geous /ˌdɪsædvənˈteɪdʒəs, -ˈvæn-/ *adj* [+ to/for] *formal* unfavourable and likely to cause problems for you; **▪** **advantageous** —**disadvantageously** *adv*

dis·af·fec·ted /ˌdɪsəˈfektɪd◂/ *adj formal* not satisfied with your government, leader etc, and therefore no longer loyal to them or no longer believing they can help you: *the disaffected youth from poor neighborhoods* —**disaffection** /-ˈfekʃən/ *n* [U]

dis·af·fil·i·ate /ˌdɪsəˈfɪlieɪt/ *v* [I,T + from] *formal* if an organization disaffiliates from another organization or is disaffiliated from it, it breaks the official connection it has with it; **▪** **affiliate** —**disaffiliation** /ˌdɪsəfɪliˈeɪʃən/ *n* [U]

dis·a·gree S2 /ˌdɪsəˈɡriː/ *v* [I] **1** to have or express a different opinion from someone else; **▪** **agree**: [**+with**] *He is tolerant of those who disagree with him.* | [**+about/on/over**] *Experts disagree on how much the program will cost.* | *Barr* **strongly disagreed** *with Kronfeld's statement.* **2** if statements, numbers, or reports about the same event or situation disagree, they are different from each other; **▪** **agree**: *The statements of several witnesses disagree.*

> **disagree with** sb *phr v*
> if something such as food or weather disagrees with you, it has a bad effect on you or makes you ill: *Seafood always disagrees with me.*

dis·a·gree·a·ble /ˌdɪsəˈɡriːəbəl◂/ *adj formal* **1** not at all enjoyable or pleasant; **▪** **agreeable**: *a disagreeable job* | [**+to**] *The conversation was disagreeable to him.* **2** unfriendly and bad-tempered; **▪** **agreeable**: *a rude, disagreeable woman* —**disagreeably** *adv*

dis·a·gree·ment /ˌdɪsəˈɡriːmənt/ *n* **1** [C,U] a situation in which people express different opinions about something and sometimes argue; **▪** **agreement**: *We've* **had a few disagreements**, *but we're still good friends.* | [**+about/over/as to/on**] *disagreements about who will be allowed to vote* | [**+among/between**] *There were disagreements among doctors about the best way to treat the disease.* | [**+with**] *Connor's disagreements with school administrators* | **sharp/fundamental/profound etc disagreement** (=serious disagreement) | **be in disagreement** (=disagree) *Scientists are in disagreement about the significance of the data.* **2** [U] differences between two statements, reports, numbers etc that ought to be similar; **▪** **agreement**: [**+between**] *There is disagreement between these two estimates.*

dis·al·low /ˌdɪsəˈlaʊ/ *v* [T] to officially refuse to accept something, because a rule has been broken; **▪** **allow**: *Manchester United had a goal disallowed for being offside.*

dis·ap·pear S2 W2 /ˌdɪsəˈpɪə $ -ˈpɪr/ *v* [I] **1** to become impossible to see any longer; **▪** **vanish**; **▪** **appear**: [**+behind/under/into etc**] *The sun had disappeared behind a cloud.* | **disappear from view/sight** *David watched her car until it disappeared from view.* |

D

At this point the path seemed to **disappear altogether** (=disappear completely).
2 to be lost, or to become impossible to find; ▤ **vanish**: *The two girls disappeared while walking home from school.* | *My keys have disappeared again.* | **disappear without trace** *BrE*/**without a trace** *AmE* (=without any way of finding them) *75,000 soldiers simply disappeared without trace.*
3 to stop existing: *The rain forest may disappear forever.*

dis·ap·pear·ance /ˌdɪsəˈpɪərəns $ -ˈpɪr-/ *n* [C,U] **1** when someone or something becomes impossible to see or find: *Police are investigating the woman's disappearance.* **2** when something stops existing; → **extinction**: *the disappearance of ancient forests*

dis·ap·point /ˌdɪsəˈpɔɪnt/ *v* [I,T] **1** to make someone feel unhappy because something they hoped for did not happen or was not as good as they expected: *I hated to disappoint her.* | *Great things were expected of this band, and they didn't disappoint.* **2 disappoint sb's hopes/expectations/plans** to prevent something from happening that someone hoped for or expected: *The Berlin settlement of 1878 disappointed Russian hopes in the Balkans.*

dis·ap·point·ed /ˌdɪsəˈpɔɪntɪd◂/ *adj* unhappy because something you hoped for did not happen, or because someone or something was not as good as you expected: *Dad seemed more disappointed than angry.* | *disappointed customers* | [+at/with/about] *Local residents were disappointed with the decision.* | **disappointed (that)** *I was disappointed that we played so well yet still lost.* | [+in] *I'm very disappointed in you.* | **bitterly/deeply/terribly disappointed** *The girl's parents were bitterly disappointed at the jury's verdict.* | **disappointed to hear/see/find etc** *Visitors were disappointed to find the museum closed.*

dis·ap·point·ing /ˌdɪsəˈpɔɪntɪŋ◂/ *adj* not as good as you hoped or expected: *disappointing profit figures* | *The Lakers' loss in the playoffs was very disappointing.* —**disappointingly** *adv*

dis·ap·point·ment /ˌdɪsəˈpɔɪntmənt/ *n* **1** [U] a feeling of unhappiness because something is not as good as you expected, or has not happened in the way you hoped: *He could see the disappointment in her eyes.* | **to sb's (great) disappointment** *To Edward's disappointment, Gina never turned up at the party.* | [+at/with/over etc] *the managers' disappointment with the results* | *Several people* **expressed disappointment** *at the delay.* | **disappointment that** *her disappointment that she hadn't been picked* | *She was unable to hide her* **bitter disappointment.** **2** [C] someone or something that is not as good as you hoped or expected: *The movie was kind of a disappointment.* | **great/bitter disappointment** *The loss was a bitter disappointment.* | [+to] *She felt she was a disappointment to her family.* | [+for] *The team's performance has been a disappointment for the fans.*

dis·ap·pro·ba·tion /ˌdɪsæprəˈbeɪʃən/ *n* [U] *formal* disapproval of someone or something because you think they are morally wrong; ▤ **approbation**

dis·ap·prov·al /ˌdɪsəˈpruːvəl/ *n* [U] an attitude that shows you think that someone or their behaviour, ideas etc are bad or not suitable; ▤ **approval**: [+of] *strong disapproval of the country's human rights record* | **with/in disapproval** *Baxter eyed our clothes with obvious disapproval.* | *Clarissa shook her head in disapproval.*

dis·ap·prove /ˌdɪsəˈpruːv/ *v* **1** [I] to think that someone or their behaviour, ideas etc are bad or wrong; ▤ **approve**: *I knew my parents would disapprove, but I went anyway.* | [+of] *I disapprove of diets; it's better to eat sensibly.* | *She family* **strongly disapproved** *of her behaviour.* **2** [T] *formal* to not agree to something that has been suggested; ▤ **approve**: *The board of directors disapproved the sale.*

dis·ap·prov·ing /ˌdɪsəˈpruːvɪŋ◂/ *adj* showing that you think someone or something is bad or wrong; ▤ **approving**: *a disapproving frown* —**disapprovingly** *adv*

dis·arm /dɪsˈɑːm $ -ˈɑːrm/ *v* **1** [I] to reduce the size of your army, navy etc, and the number of your weapons; ▤ **arm**: *Getting the rebels to disarm will not be easy.* **2** [T] to take away someone's weapons; ▤ **arm**: *Captured soldiers were disarmed and put into camps.* **3** [T] to make someone feel less angry or disapproving of you, and more friendly; → **disarming**: *His tact and political skills disarmed his critics.* **4** [T] to take the explosives out of a bomb, MISSILE etc

dis·ar·ma·ment /dɪsˈɑːməmənt $ -ˈɑːr-/ *n* [U] when a country reduces the number of weapons it has, or the size of its army, navy etc: *a commitment to worldwide* **nuclear disarmament**

dis·arm·ing /dɪsˈɑːmɪŋ $ -ˈɑːr-/ *adj* making you feel less angry or disapproving towards someone, and more friendly: *a disarming sense of humor* —**disarmingly** *adv*

dis·ar·range /ˌdɪsəˈreɪndʒ/ *v* [T] *formal* to make something untidy

dis·ar·ray /ˌdɪsəˈreɪ/ *n* [U] *formal* the state of being untidy or not organized: **in disarray** *This left the Liberal Party in total disarray.* | **throw sth into disarray/fall into disarray** *The delay threw the entire timetable into disarray.*

dis·as·so·ci·ate /ˌdɪsəˈsəʊʃieɪt, -sieɪt $ -ˈsoʊ-/ *v* [T] another spelling of DISSOCIATE

di·sas·ter ▤S2 ▤W3 /dɪˈzɑːstə $ dɪˈzæstər/ *n* [C,U]
1 a sudden event such as a flood, storm, or accident which causes great damage or suffering; → **catastrophe**

> air disaster
> nuclear disaster
> natural disaster (=caused by nature)
> ecological/environmental disaster (=one that causes great damage to nature)
> end in disaster
> spell disaster (=mean that there will be disaster)
> disaster strikes (=it happens)
> on the brink of disaster
> prevent/avert a disaster
> sth is a disaster waiting to happen

One hundred and twenty people died in China's worst **air disaster**. | *the economic consequences of the Chernobyl* **nuclear disaster** | [+for] *The oil spill was a disaster for Alaskan sea animals.* | *The 1987 hurricane was the worst* **natural disaster** *in England for decades.* | *Their expedition nearly* **ended in disaster**, *when one of the climbers slid off the mountain.* | *The drought could* **spell disaster** *for wildlife.* | **Disaster struck** *when two men were killed during their parachute jumps.* | *The peace process was* **on the brink of disaster.** | *Luckily the pilot saw the other plane just in time, and a* **disaster was narrowly averted.**

2 something that is very bad or a failure, especially when this is very annoying or disappointing: **sth is a complete/total/disaster** *Because of the weather, the parade was a total disaster.* | *The evening was an* **unmitigated disaster** (=a complete failure). | [+for] *The cuts in funding will be a disaster for the schools.* | *Five small boys on skis* **is a recipe for disaster** (=is very likely to end badly).

di'saster ˌarea *n* [C] **1** a place where a flood, storm, fire etc has happened and caused a lot of damage: *The town was* **declared a disaster area** (=officially called a disaster area) *after the floods.* **2** *informal* a place that is very untidy or dirty: *The kitchen is a disaster area.*

di·sas·trous /dɪˈzɑːstrəs $ dɪˈzæ-/ *adj* very bad, or ending in failure: *a disastrous first marriage* | **disastrous effects/consequences/results** *Climate change could have disastrous effects on Earth.* | *The move* **proved disastrous** (=was disastrous) *for the company.* —**disastrously** *adv*

dis·a·vow /ˌdɪsəˈvaʊ/ v [T] *formal* to say that you are not responsible for something, that you do not know about it, or that you are not involved with it —**disavowal** n [C,U]

dis·band /dɪsˈbænd/ v [I,T] to stop existing as an organization, or to make something do this

dis·bar /dɪsˈbɑː $ -ˈbɑːr/ v **disbarred**, **disbarring** [T] to make a lawyer leave the legal profession; → **debar**

dis·be·lief /ˌdɪsbɪˈliːf/ n [U] a feeling that something is not true or does not exist; → **unbelief**, **belief**: *The reaction to the murders was one of shock and disbelief.* | *in/with disbelief Rosie stared in disbelief.*

dis·be·lieve /ˌdɪsbɪˈliːv/ v [I,T] *formal* to not believe something or someone: *I see no reason to disbelieve him.* —**disbelieving** adj

dis·burse /dɪsˈbɜːs $ -ɜːrs/ v [T] *formal* to pay out money, especially from a large sum that is available for a special purpose —**disbursement** n [C,U]

disc S3 also **disk** especially AmE /dɪsk/ n [C]
1 a round flat shape or object: *three keys attached to a metal disc*
2 a COMPACT DISC
3 a record that you play on a RECORD PLAYER
4 BrE a computer DISK: **on disc** *The report form is available on disc from Personnel.*
5 a flat piece of CARTILAGE between the bones of your back: *He retired early because of a slipped disc* (=one that has moved out of its correct place). → DISC BRAKES, DISC JOCKEY, DISK DRIVE, LASER DISK

dis·card¹ /dɪsˈkɑːd $ -ɑːrd/ v **1** [T] to get rid of something; ▣ **throw away**: *Discard any old cleaning materials.* | *discarded paper* **2** [I,T] to put down unwanted cards in a card game

dis·card² /ˈdɪskɑːd $ -ɑːrd/ n [C] an unwanted card that is put down in a card game

'disc brakes n [plural] BRAKES that work by two hard surfaces pressing against a DISC in the centre of a car wheel

di·scern /dɪˈsɜːn $ -ɜːrn/ v [T not in progressive] *formal* **1** to notice or understand something by thinking about it carefully: *discern what/where/why etc Officials were keen to discern how much public support there was.* **2** to be able to see something by looking carefully; ▣ **perceive**: *We could just discern a town in the distance.* —**discernible** adj —**discernibly** adv

di·scern·ing /dɪˈsɜːnɪŋ $ -ɜːr-/ adj showing the ability to make good judgments, especially about art, music, style etc; ▣ **discriminating**: *an ideal tour for the discerning traveller* | **the discerning eye/ear** (=someone who can make good judgments about art or music)

di·scern·ment /dɪˈsɜːnmənt $ -ɜːr-/ n [U] *formal* **1** the ability to make good judgments about people or about art, music, style etc: *the woman's taste and discernment* **2** when you notice or understand something: *the discernment of opportunities*

dis·charge¹ /dɪsˈtʃɑːdʒ $ -ɑːr-/ v
1 SEND SB AWAY [T] to officially allow someone to leave somewhere, especially the hospital or the army, navy etc, or to tell them that they must leave: *Hospitals now tend to discharge patients earlier than in the past.* | *The judge discharged the jury.* | **discharge sb from sth** *Several of the recruits were discharged from the Army due to medical problems.* | **discharge yourself** BrE (=leave hospital before your treatment is complete) | **conditionally discharge sb** BrE (=let someone leave prison if they obey particular rules) *Dunning was conditionally discharged for two years.*
2 GAS/LIQUID/SMOKE ETC [I always + adv/prep, T] to send out gas, liquid, smoke etc, or to allow it to escape: **discharge sth into sth** *Sewage is discharged directly into the sea.* | [+into] *Rainwater collects here and then discharges into the river Kennett.*
3 SHOOT [T] *formal* to fire a gun or shoot an ARROW etc: *A soldier accidentally discharged his weapon.*
4 DUTY/RESPONSIBILITY/DEBT ETC [T] *formal* to do or pay what you have a duty to do or pay: **discharge**

your duties/responsibilities/obligations etc *The trustees failed to discharge their duties properly.*
5 ELECTRICITY [I,T] if a piece of electrical equipment discharges, or if it is discharged, it sends out electricity
6 A WOUND [I,T] if a wound or body part discharges a substance such as PUS (=infected liquid), the substance slowly comes out of it
7 GOODS/PASSENGERS [T] *formal* to take goods or passengers off a ship, plane etc

dis·charge² /ˈdɪstʃɑːdʒ $ -tʃɑːrdʒ/ n *formal* **1** [U] when you officially allow someone to leave somewhere, especially the hospital or their job in the army, navy etc: [+from] *Nurses visit the mother and baby for two weeks after their discharge from the hospital.* → DISHONOURABLE DISCHARGE, HONORABLE DISCHARGE **2** [C,U] when gas, liquid, smoke etc is sent out, or the substance that is sent out: [+of] *the discharge of toxic waste into the sea* **3** [C,U] when a substance slowly comes out of a wound or part of your body, or the substance that comes out **4** [C,U] electricity that is sent out by a piece of equipment, a storm etc **5** [U] when someone performs a duty or pays a debt: [+of] *the discharge of the college's legal responsibilities* **6** [U] when someone shoots a gun

di·sci·ple /dɪˈsaɪpəl/ n [C] **1** someone who believes in the ideas of a great teacher or leader, especially a religious one: [+of] *He was also an avid reader and a disciple of Tolstoy.* **2** one of the first 12 men to follow Christ —**discipleship** n [U]

dis·ci·pli·nar·i·an /ˌdɪsɪpləˈneəriən $ -ˈner-/ n [C] someone who believes people should obey orders and rules, and who makes them do this: *Dad was a strict disciplinarian.*

dis·ci·pli·na·ry /ˈdɪsɪplɪnəri, ˌdɪsɪˈplɪ- $ ˈdɪsɪpləneri/ adj relating to the punishment of someone who has not obeyed rules, or to trying to make people obey rules: *The investigation led to* **disciplinary action** (=things you do to punish someone) *against two officers.* | **disciplinary hearing/committee** (=a meeting or group that decides if someone should be punished)

dis·ci·pline¹ S3 W2 /ˈdɪsɪplɪn/ n
1 [U] a way of training someone so that they learn to control their behaviour and obey rules: *The book gives parents advice on discipline.* | *serious* **discipline problems** *in the police force*
2 [U] the ability to control your own behaviour, so that you do what you are expected to do: *Working from home requires a good deal of discipline.* → SELF-DISCIPLINE
3 [C,U] a way of training your mind or learning to control your behaviour: *Martial arts teach respect, discipline, and cooperation.* | [+for] *Learning poetry is a good discipline for the memory.*
4 [C] an area of knowledge or teaching, especially one such as history, chemistry, mathematics etc that is studied at a university

discipline² v [T] **1** to punish someone in order to keep order and control: *The officers were later disciplined.* **2** to teach someone to obey rules and control their behaviour: *Different cultures have different ways of disciplining their children.* **3** **discipline yourself (to do sth)** to control the way you work, how regularly you do something etc, because you know it is good for you: *Try to discipline yourself to write every day.*

dis·ci·plined /ˈdɪsɪplɪnd/ adj obeying rules and controlling your behaviour: *skilled and disciplined workers*

'disc jockey n [C] *DJ* someone whose job is to play the music on a radio show or in a club where you can dance

dis·claim /dɪsˈkleɪm/ v [T] *formal* to state, especially officially, that you are not responsible for something, that you do not know about it, or that you are not involved with it; ▣ **deny**: **disclaim responsibility/knowledge etc** *Martin disclaimed any responsibility for his son's actions.*

D

dis·claim·er /dɪsˈkleɪmə $ -ər/ n [C] a statement that you are not responsible for or involved with something, or that you do not know about it – used especially in advertising or legal agreements

dis·close /dɪsˈkləʊz $ -ˈkloʊz/ v [T] formal **1** to make something publicly known, especially after it has been kept secret; **≡ reveal**: *Some companies have already voluntarily disclosed similar information.* | *He refused to disclose the identity of the politician.* | **disclose that** *It was disclosed that £3.5 million was needed to modernize the building.* **2** to show something by removing the thing that covers it; **≡ reveal**

dis·clo·sure /dɪsˈkləʊʒə $ -ˈkloʊʒər/ n [C,U] a secret that someone tells people, or the act of telling this secret: *the disclosure of private medical information*

dis·co /ˈdɪskəʊ $ -koʊ/ n plural **discos 1** [C] a place or social event at which people dance to recorded popular music: *the school disco* **2** [U] a type of dance music that was first popular in the 1970s

dis·col·or /dɪsˈkʌlə $ -ər/ v the American spelling of DISCOLOUR

dis·col·o·ra·tion /dɪsˌkʌləˈreɪʃən/ n **1** [U] the process of becoming discoloured **2** [C] a place on the surface of something where it has become discoloured

dis·col·our BrE; **discolor** AmE /dɪsˈkʌlə $ -ər/ v [I,T] to change colour, or to make something change colour, so that it looks unattractive: *Once cut, apples quickly discolour.*

dis·com·bob·u·lat·ed /ˌdɪskəmˈbɒbjᵘleɪtᵻd $ -ˈbɑːb-/ adj completely confused – used humorously

dis·com·fit /dɪsˈkʌmfᵻt/ v [T] formal to make someone feel slightly uncomfortable, annoyed, or embarrassed: *He was discomfited by her silence.* —**discomfiture** n [U]

dis·com·fort /dɪsˈkʌmfət $ -ərt/ n **1** [U] a feeling of slight pain or of being physically uncomfortable: *If the exercise causes discomfort, stop immediately.* **2** [U] a feeling of embarrassment, shame, or worry: *To her discomfort, he laughed.* **3** [C] something that makes you feel uncomfortable or gives you a slight pain: *the discomforts of air travel*

dis·com·pose /ˌdɪskəmˈpəʊz $ -ˈpoʊz/ v [T] formal to make someone feel worried and no longer calm; **≡ disturb** —**discomposure** /-ˈpəʊʒə $ -ˈpoʊʒər/ n [U]

dis·con·cert /ˌdɪskənˈsɜːt $ -ɜːrt/ v [T] to make someone feel slightly confused, embarrassed, or worried —**disconcerted** adj: *a disconcerted look*

dis·con·cert·ing /ˌdɪskənˈsɜːtɪŋ $ -ɜːr-/ adj making you feel slightly confused, embarrassed, or worried: *a disconcerting question* —**disconcertingly** adv

dis·con·nect¹ /ˌdɪskəˈnekt/ v **1** [T] to remove the supply of power, gas, water etc from a machine or piece of equipment; **≡ connect**: **disconnect sth from sth** *Always disconnect the machine from the mains first.* | *The family agreed to disconnect her life support system.* **2** [I,T] to separate something from the thing it is connected to, or to become separated; **≡ connect**: [+from] *Two freight cars disconnected from the train engine.* | **disconnect sth from sth** *Disconnect part A from part D.* **3** [T] to officially stop supplying a service, such as water, telephone, electricity, or gas, to a house or other building; **≡ connect**: *Eleven percent of households were disconnected for non-payment of bills.* **4** [I,T] if you disconnect or become disconnected from your feelings, family, society etc, you no longer feel as though you belong or have a relationship with them: [+from] *Divorced men can too easily become disconnected from their children.* **5** [T] to break the telephone connection between two people; **≡ connect** —**disconnection** /-ˈnekʃən/ n [C,U]

disconnect² n [singular] when two people or groups no longer understand or have a relationship with each other: *the disconnect between the ordinary public and the concerns of politicians*

dis·con·nect·ed /ˌdɪskəˈnektᵻd◂ / adj disconnected thoughts or ideas do not seem to be related to each other; **≡ unrelated**

dis·con·so·late /dɪsˈkɒnsəlᵻt $ -ˈkɑːn-/ adj formal extremely sad and hopeless: *He was disconsolate after his divorce.* —**disconsolately** adv

dis·con·tent /ˌdɪskənˈtent/ also **dis·con·-tent·ment** /-ˈtentmənt/ n [U] a feeling of being unhappy and not satisfied with the situation you are in; **⚹ contentment**: [+with] *Discontent with the current government is strong.* | [+at/over] *There is widespread discontent at the quality of education.* | *Perhaps she sensed my growing discontent.*

dis·con·tent·ed /ˌdɪskənˈtentᵻd◂ / adj unhappy or not satisfied with the situation you are in; **⚹ contented**: [+with] *She became increasingly discontented with her work.* —**discontentedly** adv

dis·con·tin·ue /ˌdɪskənˈtɪnjuː/ v [T] to stop doing, producing, or providing something: *Bus route 51 is being discontinued.* | *a discontinued china pattern* —**discontinuation** /ˌdɪskəntɪnjuˈeɪʃən/ n [U] —**discontinuance** /ˌdɪskənˈtɪnjuəns/ n [U]

dis·con·ti·nu·i·ty /ˌdɪskɒntᵻˈnjuːᵻti $ -kɑːntᵻˈnuː-/ n plural **discontinuities 1** [C] a sudden change or pause in a process: [+between] *the policy discontinuities between the present and previous governments* **2** [U] when a process is not continuous: *discontinuity in economic development*

dis·con·tin·u·ous /ˌdɪskənˈtɪnjuəs◂ / adj formal not continuous

dis·cord /ˈdɪskɔːd $ -ɔːrd/ n **1** [U] formal disagreement or arguing between people: *marital discord* | *discord within NATO* **2** [C,U] an unpleasant sound made by a group of musical notes that do not go together well; **→ harmony**

dis·cord·ant /dɪsˈkɔːdənt $ -ɔːr-/ adj **1** formal a discordant sound is unpleasant because it is made up of musical notes that do not go together well **2** literary strange, wrong, or unsuitable in relation to everything around; **⚹ harmonious**: *The modern decor strikes a discordant note in this 17th century building.* **3** formal not in agreement: *discordant results from the experiment*

dis·co·theque /ˈdɪskətek, ˌdɪskəˈtek/ n [C] especially BrE a DISCO

dis·count¹ [S3] /ˈdɪskaʊnt/ n [C] a reduction in the usual price of something: **10% discount/discount of 25% etc** *Members get a 15% discount.* | **at a discount** *Employees can buy books at a discount.* | [+on] *The Young Persons Railcard gives you a discount on rail travel.* | **offer/give sb a discount** | **discount price/fare** *discount airfares to Europe* | **discount store/shop/warehouse** (=a place where you can buy goods cheaply)

dis·count² /dɪsˈkaʊnt $ ˈdɪskaʊnt/ v [T] **1** to regard something as unlikely to be true or important: *Experts discounted the accuracy of the polls.* | *General Hausken had not discounted the possibility of an aerial attack.* **2** to reduce the price of something: *Games were discounted to as little as $5.*

dis·count·er /ˈdɪskaʊntə $ -ər/ n [C] a shop or person that sells goods cheaply

discount rate n [C usually singular] the interest rate that a country's CENTRAL BANK charges to other banks

dis·cour·age /dɪsˈkʌrɪdʒ $ -ˈkɜːr-/ v [T] **1** to persuade someone not to do something, especially by making it seem difficult or bad; **⚹ encourage**: *attempts to discourage illegal immigration* | **discourage sb from doing sth** *My father is a lawyer, and he discouraged me from entering the field.* △ Do not say 'discourage someone to do something'. Say **discourage someone from doing something**. **2** to make someone less confident or less willing to do something; **≡ demoralize**; **⚹ encourage**: *You should not let one failure discourage you.* **3** to make something less likely to happen; **⚹ encourage**: *Aspirin may discourage tumour growth in some types of cancer.*

dis·cour·aged /dɪsˈkʌrɪdʒd $ -ˈkɜːr-/ adj no longer having the confidence you need to continue doing something; ⊟ **demoralized**: A lot of players get discouraged and quit.

dis·cour·age·ment /dɪsˈkʌrɪdʒmənt $ -ˈkɜːr-/ n **1** [U] when you no longer feel confident or willing to do something: In research, times of discouragement alternate with times of great achievement. **2** [U] when you try to persuade someone not to do something, especially by making it seem difficult or bad: the discouragement of smoking **3** [C] something that discourages you

dis·cour·a·ging /dɪsˈkʌrɪdʒɪŋ $ -ˈkɜːr-/ adj making you lose the confidence or determination you need to continue doing something: The results were discouraging. —**discouragingly** adv

dis·course[1] W3 /ˈdɪskɔːs $ -ɔːrs/ n formal **1** [C] a serious speech or piece of writing on a particular subject: [+on/upon] a discourse on art **2** [U] serious conversation or discussion between people: Candidates should engage in serious political discourse. **3** [U] the language used in particular types of speech or writing: a study of spoken discourse

dis·course[2] /dɪsˈkɔːs $ -ɔːrs/ v **discourse on/upon** sth phr v formal to make a long formal speech about something, or to discuss something seriously

dis·cour·te·ous /dɪsˈkɜːtiəs $ -ɜːr-/ adj formal not polite, and not showing respect for other people; ⊟ **rude**, **impolite**: It would be discourteous to ignore his request. —**discourteously** adv

dis·cour·te·sy /dɪsˈkɜːtəsi $ -ɜːr-/ n plural **discourtesies** [C,U] formal an action or behaviour that is not polite or does not show respect

dis·cov·er S2 W1 /dɪsˈkʌvə $ -ər/ v [T] **1** to find someone or something, either by accident or because you were looking for them: The body was discovered in a field. | Forest Service crews often discover campfires that have not been put out completely. **2** to find out something that you did not know about before: The exercises let students discover math concepts on their own. | **discover (that)** She discovered that she was pregnant. | **discover who/what/how** etc His friends were shocked to discover how ill he was. **3** if someone discovers a new place, fact, substance etc, they are the first person to find it or know that it exists: The Curies are best known for discovering radium. **4** to notice or try something for the first time and start to enjoy it: At fourteen, Louise discovered boys. **5** to notice someone who is very good at something and help them to become successful and well-known: a band that's waiting to be discovered —**discoverer** n [C]

dis·cov·e·ry W3 /dɪsˈkʌvəri/ n plural **discoveries** **1** [C] a fact or thing that someone finds out about, when it was not known about before: recent archaeological discoveries | [+about] The Hubble Telescope has allowed astronomers to **make** significant **discoveries** about our galaxy. | **discovery that** the discovery that bees can communicate with each other **2** [U] when someone discovers something: [+of] the discovery of oil in Alaska

dis·cred·it[1] /dɪsˈkredɪt/ v [T] **1** to make people stop respecting or trusting someone or something: The company's lawyers tried to discredit her testimony. **2** to make people stop believing in a particular idea: Some of Freud's theories have now been discredited.

discredit[2] n [U] the loss of other people's respect or trust: **to sb's discredit** To his discredit, he knew about the problem but said nothing. | **bring discredit on/upon/to sb/sth** The behaviour of fans has brought discredit on English football.

dis·cred·it·a·ble /dɪsˈkredɪtəbəl/ adj formal bad or wrong, and making people lose respect for you or trust in you: discreditable dealings

di·screet /dɪˈskriːt/ adj **1** careful about what you say or do, so that you do not offend, upset, or embarrass people or tell secrets; ⊟ **indiscreet**: He assured her that he would be discreet. | I stood back at a discreet distance. **2** small and showing good taste or judgment – use this to show approval: discreet jewelry —**discreetly** adv

di·screp·an·cy /dɪˈskrepənsi/ n plural **discrepancies** [C,U] a difference between two amounts, details, reports etc that should be the same: [+in] Police found discrepancies in the two men's reports. | [+between] There is a large discrepancy between the ideal image of motherhood and the reality.

di·screte /dɪˈskriːt/ adj clearly separate: The change happens in a series of discrete steps. —**discretely** adv —**discreteness** n [U]

di·scre·tion /dɪˈskreʃən/ n [U] **1** the ability and right to decide exactly what should be done in a particular situation: **at sb's discretion** (=according to someone's decision) The awards are made at the discretion of the committee. | Promotions are **left to the discretion** of the supervisor. | [+over/as to] People want to have more discretion over their working hours. | **use/exercise your discretion** The judge exercised his discretion rightly to admit the evidence. | **discretion to do sth** The committee has the absolute discretion to refuse applications. **2** the ability to deal with situations in a way that does not offend, upset, or embarrass people or tell any of their secrets: British newspapers no longer feel they must treat the royal family with discretion. **3 discretion is the better part of valour** used to say that it is better to be careful than to take unnecessary risks

di·scre·tion·a·ry /dɪˈskreʃənəri $ -neri/ adj not controlled by strict rules, but decided on by someone in a position of authority: the court's **discretionary powers** | **discretionary award/grant/fund** etc

dis·cretionary 'income n [U] the money remaining from your income after your bills have been paid, which can be spent on entertainment, holidays etc

di·scrim·i·nate /dɪˈskrɪmɪneɪt/ v **1** [I] to treat a person or group differently from another in an unfair way: [+against] Under federal law, it is illegal to discriminate against minorities and women. | **discriminate on the grounds/basis of sth** It was found that the company still discriminated on the basis of race in promotions. **2** [I,T] to recognize a difference between things; ⊟ **differentiate**: [+between] Newborn babies can discriminate between a man's and a woman's voice. | **discriminate sth from sth** the process of learning to discriminate fact from opinion

di·scrim·i·nat·ing /dɪˈskrɪmɪneɪtɪŋ/ adj able to judge what is of good quality and what is not; ⊟ **discerning**: a book that will appeal to discriminating readers

di·scrim·i·na·tion /dɪˌskrɪmɪˈneɪʃən/ n [U] **1** the practice of treating one person or group differently from another in an unfair way: laws to prevent discrimination | [+against] widespread discrimination against older people in the job market | [+in favour of] discrimination in favour of university graduates | **racial/sex/religious** etc **discrimination** (=treating someone unfairly because of their race, sex etc) → POSITIVE DISCRIMINATION, REVERSE DISCRIMINATION **2** the ability to recognize the difference between two or more things, especially the difference in their quality: shape discrimination

di·scrim·in·a·to·ry /dɪˈskrɪmɪnətəri $ -tɔːri/ adj treating a person or a group of people differently from other people, in an unfair way: discriminatory hiring practices

⊡ 1 000, 2 000, 3 000, most frequent words in S poken and W ritten English

di·scur·sive /dɪˈskɜːsɪv $ -ɜːr-/ *adj formal* discussing many different ideas, facts etc, without always having a clear purpose: *a long, discursive article* —**discursively** *adv*

dis·cus /ˈdɪskəs/ *n* [C] **1** a heavy flat circular object which is thrown as far as possible as a sport **2 the discus** the sport of throwing this object

di·scuss S3 W1 /dɪˈskʌs/ *v* [T]
1 to talk about something with another person or a group in order to exchange ideas or decide something: *Littman refused to discuss the case publicly.* | *If you would like to discuss the matter further, please call me.* | **discuss sth with sb** *Pupils should be given time to discuss the book with their classmates.* | **discuss what/ who/where etc** *Your accountant will discuss with you how to complete these forms.*
2 to talk or write about something in detail and consider different ideas or opinions about it: *This topic will be discussed in Chapter 4.*

di·scus·sion W1 /dɪˈskʌʃən/ *n* [C,U]
1 when you discuss something: *class discussions* | *the topics suggested for discussion* | [+of] *the discussion of important issues* | [+about] *high-level discussions about trade and commerce* | [+with] *The embassy will continue discussions with the Chinese government.* | *We have had discussions about her legal situation.* | **under discussion** (=being discussed) *The project is under discussion as a possible joint venture between the two space agencies.*
2 a piece of writing about a subject that considers different ideas or opinions about it: [+of] *the report's discussion of the legislation*

di'scussion ,list *n* [C] a place on the Internet where people can write and receive messages in order to share ideas and information about a particular subject: *the Mercedes-Benz discussion list*

dis·dain¹ /dɪsˈdeɪn/ *n* [U] *formal* a complete lack of respect that you show for someone or something because you think they are not important or good enough: **with disdain** *She watched me with disdain.* | *a look of complete disdain* | [+for] *his disdain for capitalism*

disdain² *v formal* **1** [T] to have no respect for someone or something, because you think they are not important or good enough: *Childcare was seen as women's work, and men disdained it.* **2 disdain to do sth** to refuse to do something because you are too proud to do it: *Butler disdained to reply.*

dis·dain·ful /dɪsˈdeɪnfəl/ *adj formal* showing that you do not respect someone or something, because you think that they are not important or good enough: *a disdainful look* | [+of] *university professors who are disdainful of popular entertainment* —**disdainfully** *adv*

dis·ease S3 W1 /dɪˈziːz/ *n*
1 [C,U] an illness which affects a person, animal, or plant

have/suffer from a disease
heart/liver/brain etc disease
a disease of the brain/stomach etc
catch a disease
contract a disease *formal* (=catch a disease)
a disease spreads/the spread of a disease
infectious/contagious disease (=one that spreads quickly from one person to another)
a fatal/deadly disease (=one that causes death)
an incurable disease (=one that cannot be cured)
a degenerative disease (=one that gradually gets worse and worse)
a cure for a disease
the symptoms of a disease (=the things that show that someone has it)

*She **suffers from** a rare **disease** of the brain.* | **Heart disease** *runs in our family.* | *filthy conditions that cause disease* | *She **contracted the disease** while she*

was abroad on holiday. | *The government has taken steps to halt **the spread of the disease**.* | *vaccinations against **infectious diseases** such as measles* | *'Mad cow disease' is a **fatal** degenerative **disease** of the nervous system.* | *The first **symptoms of the disease** are vomiting and a slight fever.*
2 [C] something that is seriously wrong with society or with someone's mind, behaviour etc: *Loneliness is a disease of our urban communities.* —**diseased** *adj: diseased muscles* | *a diseased plant*

dis·em·bark /ˌdɪsɪmˈbɑːk $ -ɑːrk/ *v* **1** [I] to get off a ship or aircraft; ➡ **embark 2** [T] to put people or goods onto the shore from a ship —**disembarkation** /ˌdɪsembɑːˈkeɪʃən $ -bɑːr-/ *n* [U]

dis·em·bod·ied /ˌdɪsɪmˈbɒdid◂ $ -ˈbɑː-/ *adj* **1** existing without a body or separated from a body: *disembodied spirits* **2** a disembodied sound or voice comes from someone who cannot be seen

dis·em·bow·el /ˌdɪsɪmˈbaʊəl/ *v* **disembowelled, disembowelling** [T] to remove someone's BOWELS —**disembowelment** *n* [U]

dis·en·chant·ed /ˌdɪsɪnˈtʃɑːntɪd $ -ˈtʃænt-/ *adj* disappointed with someone or something, and no longer believing that they are good; ➡ **disillusioned**: [+with] *By that time I was becoming disenchanted with the whole idea.* —**disenchantment** *n* [U]: *Voters have expressed growing disenchantment with the government.*

dis·en·fran·chise /ˌdɪsɪnˈfræntʃaɪz/ *v* [T] to take away someone's rights, especially their right to vote —**disenfranchisement** /-tʃɪzmənt $ -tʃaɪz-/ *n* [U]

dis·en·fran·chised /ˌdɪsɪnˈfræntʃaɪzd/ *adj* not having any rights, especially the right to vote, and not feeling part of society

dis·en·gage /ˌdɪsɪnˈɡeɪdʒ/ *v* **1** [T] to move so that you are not touching or holding someone: **disengage yourself** *Sally found it difficult to disengage herself from his embrace.* **2** [I,T] if you disengage something, especially a part of a machine, or if it disengages, you make it move away from another part that it was connected to; ➡ **engage**: *Disengage the gears when you park the car.* | *He tapped in the code and the lock disengaged.* **3** [I] to stop being involved or interested in something: [+from] *Too many young people disengage from learning.* **4** [I,T] if two armies disengage, they stop fighting; ➡ **engage** —**disengagement** *n* [U]

dis·en·gaged /ˌdɪsɪnˈɡeɪdʒd/ *adj* not involved with or interested in something or someone, and feeling separate from them; ➡ **engaged**: *teenagers who are depressed or disengaged from their families*

dis·en·tan·gle /ˌdɪsɪnˈtæŋɡəl/ *v* [T] **1** to separate different ideas or pieces of information that have become confused together: *It's very difficult to disentangle fact from fiction in what she's saying.* **2 disentangle yourself (from sb/sth)** to escape from a difficult situation that you are involved in: *She had just disentangled herself from a long relationship.* **3** to remove knots from ropes, strings etc that have become twisted or tied together **4** to separate something from the things that are twisted around it

dis·e·qui·lib·ri·um /ˌdɪsekwɪˈlɪbriəm, ˌdɪsiː-/ *n* [U] a lack of balance in something

dis·es·tab·lish /ˌdɪsɪˈstæblɪʃ/ *v* [T] *formal* to officially decide that a particular church is no longer the official church of your country

dis·fa·vour *BrE*; **disfavor** *AmE* /dɪsˈfeɪvə $ -ər/ *n* [U] a feeling of dislike and disapproval; ➡ **favour**: **with disfavour** *The job creation program is **looked upon with disfavour** by the local community.* | *Coal **fell into disfavour** because burning it caused pollution.*

dis·fig·ure /dɪsˈfɪɡə $ -ˈfɪɡjər/ *v* [T] to spoil the appearance that something naturally has: *His face had been disfigured in an accident.* —**disfigured** *adj* —**disfigurement** *n* [C,U] —**disfiguring** *adj: a disfiguring disease*

dis·fran·chise /dɪsˈfræntʃaɪz/ v [T] to DISENFRANCHISE someone

dis·gorge /dɪsˈɡɔːdʒ $ -ɔːrdʒ/ v **1** [T] *literary* if a vehicle or building disgorges people, they come out of it in a large group: *Cars drew up to disgorge a wedding party.* **2** [T] if something disgorges what was inside it, it lets it pour out: *Chimneys were disgorging smoke into the air.* **3** [I,T] if a river disgorges, it flows into the sea: *The Mississippi disgorges its waters into the Gulf of Mexico.* **4** [T] *formal* to give back something that you have taken illegally **5** [T] *formal* to bring food back up from your stomach through your mouth

dis·grace¹ /dɪsˈɡreɪs/ n **1** [U] the loss of other people's respect because you have done something they strongly disapprove of: *Smith faced total public disgrace after the incident.* | **in disgrace** *Toranaga sent us away in disgrace.* | *His actions* **brought disgrace on** *the family.* | *There was* **no disgrace** *in finishing fourth.* **2 be a disgrace** used to say that something or someone is so bad or unacceptable that the people involved with them should feel ashamed: *The UK rail system is a national disgrace.* | [+to] *You are a disgrace to the medical profession.* | **absolute/utter disgrace** *It's* **an** *absolute* **disgrace,** *the way he treats his wife.*

disgrace² v [T] to do something so bad that you make other people feel ashamed: *How could you disgrace us all like that?* | **disgrace yourself (by doing sth)** *I'm not the one who disgraced herself at the wedding!* | **be (publicly) disgraced** (=be made to feel ashamed, especially in public)

dis·grace·ful /dɪsˈɡreɪsfəl/ adj bad, embarrassing, or unacceptable: *It's a disgraceful waste of taxpayers' money.* | **absolutely/utterly etc disgraceful** *Their behaviour was absolutely disgraceful.* | **It is disgraceful that** *anyone should have to live in such conditions.* —**disgracefully** adv

dis·grun·tled /dɪsˈɡrʌntld/ adj annoyed or disappointed, especially because things have not happened in the way that you wanted: *a disgruntled client*

dis·guise¹ /dɪsˈɡaɪz/ v [T] **1** to change someone's appearance so that people cannot recognize them: **disguise yourself as sb/sth** *Maybe you could disguise yourself as a waiter and sneak in there.* | *He escaped across the border disguised as a priest.* **2** to change the appearance, sound, taste etc of something so that people do not recognize it: *There's no way you can disguise that southern accent.* | **disguise sth as sth** *a letter bomb disguised as a musical greetings card* **3** to hide a fact or feeling so that people will not notice it: *Try as he might, Dan couldn't disguise his feelings for Katie.* | **disguise the fact (that)** *There's no disguising the fact that business is bad.* | *The speech was seen by many as a* **thinly disguised** *attack on the president.*

disguise² n **1** [C,U] something that you wear to change your appearance and hide who you are, or the act of wearing this: *His disguise didn't fool anyone.* | *She wore dark glasses in an absurd attempt at disguise.* **2 in disguise a)** wearing a disguise: *The woman in the park turned out to be a police officer in disguise.* **b)** made to seem like something else that is better: *'Tax reform' is just a tax increase in disguise.* → **blessing in disguise** at BLESSING (4)

dis·gust¹ /dɪsˈɡʌst, dɪz-/ n [U] **1** a strong feeling of dislike, annoyance, or disapproval: **with disgust** *Joan looked at him with disgust.* | **in disgust** *Sam threw his books down in disgust and stormed out of the room.* | **to sb's disgust** *Much to my disgust, I found that there were no toilets for the disabled.* | [+with] *Nelson's disgust with US politics* | [+at] *The fans didn't hide their disgust at the umpire's decision.* **2** a very strong feeling of dislike that almost makes you sick, caused by something unpleasant: *He reached into the bin with a look of disgust on his face.* | **with disgust** *Edward tasted the thin, sour wines with disgust.*

disgust² v [T] **1** to make someone feel very annoyed or upset about something that is not acceptable: *Many parents claimed to be disgusted by the amount of vio-*

lence in the film.* | **be disgusted to find/hear/see etc** *Dear Sir, I was disgusted to see the picture on page one of Sunday's feature section.* **2** to be so unpleasant that it makes you feel almost sick: *The thought of dissecting a frog disgusts me.*

dis·gust·ed /dɪsˈɡʌstɪd, dɪz-/ adj very annoyed or upset by something that is not acceptable: *Disgusted onlookers claimed the driver was more concerned about his car than about the victim.* | [+at/by/with] *Most locals are disgusted by the anti-foreigner violence.* | **disgusted that** *Animal welfare workers were disgusted that anyone could do this to a puppy.*

dis·gust·ing [S2] /dɪsˈɡʌstɪŋ, dɪz-/ adj **1** extremely unpleasant and making you feel sick; ▤ **revolting**: *Rubbish was piled everywhere – it was disgusting.* | *Smoking is a really disgusting habit.* **2** shocking and unacceptable: *Sixty pounds for a thirty-minute consultation. I think that's disgusting!* | *That's a disgusting thing to say.* —**disgustingly** adv: *They're disgustingly rich.*

dish¹ [S3] /dɪʃ/ n [C] **1** a flat container with low sides, for serving food from or cooking food in; → **bowl**: *a serving dish* | *an oven-proof dish* | [+of] *a large dish of spaghetti* **2 the dishes** all the plates, cups, bowls etc that have been used to eat a meal and need to be washed: **do/wash the dishes** *I'll just do the dishes before we go.* **3** food cooked or prepared in a particular way as a meal: *a wonderful pasta dish* | *The menu includes a wide selection of vegetarian dishes.* | *This soup is substantial enough to serve as a* **main dish** (=the biggest part of a meal). **4** something that is shaped like a dish: *a soap dish* **5** *informal old-fashioned* someone who is sexually attractive → SIDE DISH, SATELLITE DISH

dish² v [I,T] *informal* to give a lot of information about something or someone, especially something that would usually be secret or private: [+on] *She's ready to dish on boys, beauty, and break-ups in her new column.* | **dish the dirt** (=tell people shocking things about someone's private life)

dish sth ⇔ **out** *phr v* **1** to give something to various people in a careless way: *We'll probably dish out some leaflets there too.* | *Paul still tends to dish out unwanted advice.* **2** to serve food to people: *Sam's dishing out sandwiches if you want one.* **3 sb can dish it out but they can't take it** used to say that someone often criticizes other people, but does not like being criticized

dish sth ⇔ **up** *phr v* to put food for a meal into dishes, ready to be eaten: *Could you dish up the vegetables?*

dis·har·mo·ny /dɪsˈhɑːməni $ -ɑːr-/ n [U] disagreement about important things which makes people be unfriendly to each other

dish·cloth /ˈdɪʃklɒθ $ -klɒːθ/ n [C] a cloth used for washing dishes

dis·heart·ened /dɪsˈhɑːtnd $ -ɑːrtnd/ adj *formal* disappointed, so that you lose hope and the determination to continue doing something: *If young children don't see quick results they grow disheartened.* —**dishearten** v [T]

dis·heart·en·ing /dɪsˈhɑːtn-ɪŋ $ -ɑːr-/ adj making you lose hope and determination: **it is disheartening to hear/see etc sth** *It's disheartening to see what little progress has been made.* —**dishearteningly** adv

dish·er /ˈdɪʃə $ -ər/ also **dirt-disher** n [C] AmE *informal* someone who enjoys telling people a lot of information about other people's behaviour and private lives; ▤ **gossip**: *the movie role of the light-hearted Hollywood disher*

di·shev·elled *BrE*; **disheveled** *AmE* /dɪˈʃevəld/ adj if someone's appearance or their clothes, hair etc is dishevelled, they look very untidy: *Pam arrived late, dishevelled and out of breath.*

D

dis·hon·est /dɪsˈɒnⁱst $ -ˈɑː-/ adj not honest, and so deceiving or cheating people; ⊟ **honest**: *dishonest traders* | *People on welfare are wrongly seen as lazy or dishonest.* —**dishonestly** adv: *A person is guilty of theft if he or she dishonestly obtains property.*

dis·hon·est·y /dɪsˈɒnⁱsti $ -ˈɑː-/ n [U] behaviour in which you deceive or cheat people; ⊟ **honesty**

dis·hon·our¹ BrE; **dishonor** AmE /dɪsˈɒnə $ -ˈɑːnər/ n [U] loss of respect from other people, because you have behaved in a morally unacceptable way; ⊟ **honour**: *You've brought enough dishonour on your family already without causing any more trouble.*

dishonour² BrE; **dishonor** AmE v [T] **1** formal to make your family, country, profession etc lose the respect of other people: *He dishonored the uniform and did not deserve to be a marine.* **2** if a bank dishonours a cheque, it refuses to pay out money for it; ⊟ **honour 3** to refuse to keep an agreement or promise; ⊟ **honour**: *Union leaders accused management of dishonouring existing pay agreements.*

dis·hon·our·a·ble BrE; **dishonorable** AmE /dɪsˈɒnərəbəl $ -ˈɑː-/ adj not morally correct or acceptable; ⊟ **honourable**: *Surrender was seen as dishonourable.*

dis,honourable 'discharge BrE; **dishonorable discharge** AmE n [C,U] an order to someone to leave the army, navy etc, because they have behaved in a morally unacceptable way

dish·pan /ˈdɪʃpæn/ n [C] AmE a large bowl in which you wash dishes, plates etc

dish·rag /ˈdɪʃræg/ n [C] AmE a DISHCLOTH

'dish ,towel n [C] AmE a cloth used for drying dishes

dish·wash·er /ˈdɪʃˌwɒʃə $ -ˌwɒːʃər, -ˌwɑː-/ n [C] **1** a machine that washes dishes **2** especially AmE someone whose job is to wash dirty dishes, plates etc, especially in a restaurant

dish·wash·ing liq·uid /ˈdɪʃwɒʃɪŋ ˌlɪkwⁱd $ -wɒː-, -wɑː-/ n [U] AmE liquid soap used to wash dishes; ⊟ **washing-up liquid** BrE

dish·wa·ter /ˈdɪʃˌwɔːtə $ -ˌwɒːtər, -ˌwɑː-/ n [U] **1** dirty water that dishes have been washed in **2** informal if you say that tea or coffee tastes like dishwater, you mean that it tastes unpleasantly weak

dish·y /ˈdɪʃi/ adj old-fashioned informal sexually attractive

dis·il·lu·sion /ˌdɪsⁱˈluːʒən/ v [T] to make someone realize that something which they thought was true or good is not really true or good: *I hate to disillusion you, but I don't think she's coming back.* —**disillusionment** n [U]

dis·il·lu·sioned /ˌdɪsⁱˈluːʒəndꞏ/ adj disappointed because you have lost your belief that someone is good, or that an idea is right; ⊟ **disenchanted**: [+by/with] *As she grew older, Laura became increasingly disillusioned with politics.*

dis·in·cen·tive /ˌdɪsⁱnˈsentɪv/ n [C] something that makes people less willing to do something; ⊟ **incentive**: *disincentive to (doing/do) sth High interest rates can be a disincentive to expanding a business.*

dis·in·cli·na·tion /ˌdɪsɪŋklⁱˈneɪʃən/ n [U] a lack of willingness to do something; ⊟ **inclination**: *the increasing disinclination of farm workers' children to consider a job in farming*

dis·in·clined /ˌdɪsɪnˈklaɪnd/ adj **be/feel disinclined to do sth** formal to be unwilling to do something; ⊟ **reluctant**: *I was disinclined to talk to Stephen about it.*

dis·in·fect /ˌdɪsⁱnˈfekt/ v [T] **1** to clean something with a chemical that destroys BACTERIA: *First use some iodine to disinfect the wound.* | *Disinfect the area thoroughly.* **2** to run a special computer program to get rid of a computer VIRUS

dis·in·fec·tant /ˌdɪsⁱnˈfektənt/ n [C,U] a chemical or a cleaning product that destroys BACTERIA; → **antiseptic**

dis·in·for·ma·tion /ˌdɪsɪnfəˈmeɪʃən $ -fər-/ n [U] false information which is given deliberately in order to hide the truth or confuse people, especially in political situations; → **misinformation**: *government disinformation about the effects of nuclear testing*

dis·in·gen·u·ous /ˌdɪsⁱnˈdʒenjuəsꞏ/ adj formal not sincere and slightly dishonest; ⊟ **ingenuous**: *Keeping the details of the tax changes vague is disingenuous.* —**disingenuously** adv

dis·in·her·it /ˌdɪsⁱnˈherⁱt/ v [T] to take away from someone, especially your son or daughter, their legal right to receive your money or property after your death; → **inherit, will**

dis·in·te·grate /dɪsˈɪntⁱgreɪt/ v **1** [I,T] to break up, or make something break up, into very small pieces: *The whole plane just disintegrated in mid-air.* **2** [I] to become weaker or less united and be gradually destroyed: *a society disintegrating under economic pressures* —**disintegration** /dɪsˌɪntⁱˈgreɪʃən/ n [U]: *the disintegration of the Soviet empire into separate republics*

dis·in·ter /ˌdɪsɪnˈtɜː $ -ˈtɜːr/ v **disinterred, disinterring** [T] formal **1** to dig and remove a dead body from a GRAVE; ⊟ **inter 2** to find or use something that has been lost or not used for a long time: *She disinterred two frozen TV dinners from the freezer.*

dis·in·terest /dɪsˈɪntrⁱst/ n [U] **1** a lack of interest: [+in] *The exception to Balfour's disinterest in social issues was education.* **2** when you are able to judge a situation fairly because you are not involved in it

dis·in·terest·ed /dɪsˈɪntrⁱstⁱd/ adj **1** able to judge a situation fairly because you are not concerned with gaining any personal advantage from it; ⊟ **objective, impartial, unbiased**: *A lawyer should provide disinterested advice.* **2** not interested. Many teachers think that this is not correct English; → **uninterested** —**disinterestedly** adv

dis·in·vest·ment /ˌdɪsⁱnˈvestmənt/ n [C,U] technical the process of taking your money out of a company by selling your SHARES in it; ⊟ **investment**

dis·joint·ed /dɪsˈdʒɔɪntⁱd/ adj **1** something, especially a speech or piece of writing, that is disjointed has parts that do not seem well connected or are not arranged well: *disjointed fragments of information* **2** a disjointed activity or system is one in which the different parts do not work well together: *Burley was critical of his team's disjointed performance.*

dis·junc·tion /dɪsˈdʒʌŋkʃən/ also **dis·junc·ture** /dɪsˈdʒʌŋktʃə $ -ər/ n [C usually singular] formal a difference between two things that you would expect to be in agreement: *a disjunction between the skills taught in schools and the skills demanded by employers*

dis·junc·tive /dɪsˈdʒʌŋktɪv/ adj technical a disjunctive CONJUNCTION expresses a choice or opposition between two ideas. For example, 'or' is a disjunctive conjunction.

disk S2 W3 /dɪsk/ n [C]
1 a small flat piece of plastic or metal which is used for storing computer or electronic information → see picture at BEDROOM
2 the usual American spelling of DISC → COMPACT DISC, FLOPPY DISK, HARD DISK, LASER DISK

'disk drive n [C] a piece of equipment in a computer system that is used to get information from a disk or to store information on it

dis·kette /dɪsˈket $ ˈdɪskET/ n [C] a FLOPPY DISK

dis·like¹ /dɪsˈlaɪk/ v [T not in progressive] to think someone or something is unpleasant and not like them; ⊟ **like**: *Why do you dislike her so much?* | **dislike doing sth** *I dislike being the centre of attention.*

dis·like² /dɪsˈlaɪk, ˈdɪslaɪk/ n **1** [C,U] a feeling of not liking someone or something; ⊟ **liking**: [+of] *She shared her mother's dislike of housework.* | [+for] *Truman had a strong dislike for communism.* | **intense/acute/violent etc dislike** (=very strong dislike) *His colleagues regarded him with intense dislike.* | *When the* two men met, they **took an instant dislike to** each other (=they disliked each other immediately). **2 dislikes** [plural] the things that you do not like: *A good hotel manager should know his regular guests' **likes and dislikes**.*

dis·lo·cate /ˈdɪsləkeɪt $ -loʊ-/ v [T] **1** to move a bone out of its normal position in a joint, usually in an accident: *I dislocated my shoulder playing football.* **2** *formal* to spoil the way in which a plan, system, or service is arranged, so that it cannot work normally; ◨ **disrupt**: *Communications were temporarily dislocated by the bad weather.* —**dislocated** *adj: a dislocated elbow* —**dislocation** /ˌdɪslə'keɪʃən $ -loʊ-/ n [C,U]: *The 1930s was a period of economic dislocation.*

dis·lodge /dɪsˈlɒdʒ $ -ˈlɑːdʒ/ v [T] **1** to force or knock something out of its position: *Ian dislodged a few stones as he climbed up the rock.* **2** to make someone leave a place or lose a position of power: *the revolution that failed to dislodge the British in 1919*

dis·loy·al /dɪsˈlɔɪəl/ adj doing or saying things that do not support your friends, your country, or the group you belong to; ◨ **loyal**: [+to] *He felt he had been disloyal to his friends.* —**disloyalty** n [U]

dis·mal /ˈdɪzməl/ adj **1** if a situation or a place is dismal, it is so bad that it makes you feel very unhappy and hopeless: *The future looks pretty dismal right now.* | *a dismal, grey afternoon* **2** bad and unsuccessful: *The team's record so far is pretty dismal.* | *Her scheme was a dismal failure.* —**dismally** adv

dis·man·tle /dɪsˈmæntl/ v [T] **1** to take a machine or piece of equipment apart so that it is in separate pieces: *Chris dismantled the bike in five minutes.* **2** to gradually get rid of a system or organization: *an election promise to dismantle the existing tax legislation*

dis·may¹ /dɪsˈmeɪ/ n [U] the worry, disappointment, or unhappiness you feel when something unpleasant happens: **with/in dismay** *They stared at each other in dismay.* | **to sb's dismay** *I found to my dismay that I had left my notes behind.* | *The thought of leaving **filled** him **with dismay**.*

dismay² v [T] to make someone feel worried, disappointed, and upset: *The poor election turnout dismayed politicians.*

dis·mayed /dɪsˈmeɪd/ adj worried, disappointed, and upset when something unpleasant happens: **dismayed to see/discover/learn etc** *Ruth was dismayed to see how thin he had grown.* | [+at/by] *They were dismayed at the cost of the repairs.* | **dismayed that** *We are dismayed that the demonstration was allowed to take place.*

dis·mem·ber /dɪsˈmembə $ -ər/ v [T] **1** to cut a body into pieces or tear it apart **2** *formal* to divide a country, area, or organization into smaller parts —**dismemberment** n [U]

dis·miss W3 /dɪsˈmɪs/ v [T] **1** to refuse to consider someone's idea, opinion etc, because you think it is not serious, true, or important: *The government has dismissed criticisms that the country's health policy is a mess.* | **dismiss sth as sth** *He just laughed and dismissed my proposal as unrealistic.* | *It's an idea that shouldn't be **dismissed out of hand** (=dismissed immediately and completely).* **2** to remove someone from their job; ◨ **fire, sack**: **dismiss sb from sth** *Bryant was unfairly dismissed from his post.* | **dismiss sb for sth** *Employees can be dismissed for sending obscene emails.* **3** *formal* to tell someone that they are allowed to go, or are no longer needed: *The class will be dismissed early today.* **4** if a judge dismisses a court case, he or she stops it from continuing: *The case was dismissed owing to lack of evidence.* **5** to end the INNINGS of a player or team in the game of CRICKET

dis·miss·al /dɪsˈmɪsəl/ n **1** [C,U] when someone is removed from their job: *Wilson was claiming compensation for **unfair dismissal**.* | *No dismissals have been announced yet.* **2** [U] when someone decides or says

that something is not important, serious, or true: *Gill's dismissal of the book as '386 pages of rubbish'* **3** [C,U] a decision by a judge to stop a court case

dis·miss·ive /dɪsˈmɪsɪv/ adj refusing to consider someone or something seriously: [+of] *Some historians have been dismissive of this argument.* | **dismissive gesture/wave/shrug etc** *Cath spread both hands in a dismissive gesture.* —**dismissively** adv

dis·mount /dɪsˈmaʊnt/ v *formal* **1** [I + from] to get off a horse, bicycle, or MOTORCYCLE; ◨ **mount** **2** [T] to take something, especially a gun, out of its base or support

dis·o·be·di·ent /ˌdɪsə'biːdiənt◂, ˌdɪsəʊ- $ ˌdɪsə-, ˌdɪsoʊ-/ adj deliberately not doing what you are told to do by your parents, teacher, etc; ◨ **obedient** —**disobedience** n [U] → CIVIL DISOBEDIENCE

dis·o·bey /ˌdɪsə'beɪ, ˌdɪsəʊ- $ ˌdɪsə-, ˌdɪsoʊ-/ v [I,T] to refuse to do what someone with authority tells you to do, or refuse to obey a rule or law; ◨ **obey**: *punishment for disobeying orders*

dis·or·der W3 /dɪsˈɔːdə $ -ˈɔːrdər/ n
1 [C] *medical* a mental or physical illness which prevents part of your body from working properly: **a disorder of the brain/liver/digestive system etc** *He suffers from a rare disorder of the liver.* | **a stomach/lung/heart etc disorder** | **a mental/psychiatric disorder** *people with mental disorders* | **severe eating disorders** *such as bulimia and anorexia*
2 [U] a situation in which a lot of people behave in an uncontrolled, noisy, or violent way in public: **civil/public/crowd disorder** *A number of stadiums were closed because of crowd disorder.*
3 [U] a situation in which things or people are very untidy or disorganized; ◨ **order**: **in/into disorder** *Everything was in disorder, but nothing seemed to be missing.* | *His whole system was **thrown into disorder**.*

dis·or·dered /dɪsˈɔːdəd $ -ˈɔːrdərd/ adj **1** not tidy, planned, or arranged in order: *her grey, disordered hair* **2** if someone is mentally disordered, their mind is not working in a normal and healthy way

dis·or·der·ly /dɪsˈɔːdəli $ -ˈɔːrdər-/ adj *formal* **1** untidy or without any order; ◨ **orderly**: *clothes left in a disorderly heap* **2** behaving in a noisy violent way and causing trouble in a public place: **disorderly conduct/behaviour** *He was arrested for disorderly conduct.* | *Bell denied being **drunk and disorderly**.*

dis·or·gan·ized also **-ised** *BrE* /dɪsˈɔːɡənaɪzd $ -ˈɔːr-/ adj **1** not arranged or planned in a clear order, or lacking any kind of plan or system; ◨ **well-organized**: *The conference was completely disorganized.* **2** someone who is disorganized is very bad at arranging or planning things; ◨ **organized**: *He's an extremely disorganized person.* → UNORGANIZED

dis·or·i·ent·ed /dɪsˈɔːrientᵻd/ also **dis·or·i·en·tat·ed** /dɪsˈɔːrienteɪtᵻd/ *BrE* adj **1** confused and not understanding what is happening around you **2** confused about where you are or which direction you should go: *When he emerged into the street, he was completely disoriented.*

dis·or·i·ent·ing /dɪsˈɔːrientɪŋ/ also **dis·or·i·en·tat·ing** /dɪsˈɔːrienteɪtɪŋ/ *BrE* adj **1** making someone not know where they are or which direction they should go: *a disorientating maze of corridors* **2** confusing you and making you not certain about what is happening around you: *Lack of sleep can be disorienting.* —**disorient** also **disorientate** *BrE* v [T] —**disorientation** /dɪsˌɔːrien'teɪʃən/ n [U]

dis·own /dɪsˈəʊn $ -ˈoʊn/ v [T not in progressive] to say that you no longer want to be connected with someone or something, especially a member of your family or something that you are responsible for: *Frankly, I'm not surprised her family disowned her.* | *Since 1960, Kubrick has virtually disowned the film.*

di·spar·age /dɪˈspærɪdʒ/ v [T] *formal* to criticize someone or something in a way that shows you do not think they are very good or important: *Matcham's theatres were widely disparaged by architects.* —**disparagement** n [C,U]

di·spar·a·ging /dɪˈspærɪdʒɪŋ/ adj criticizing someone or something, and showing that you do not think they are very good or important: **disparaging remarks/comments** *She made some disparaging remarks about the royal family.* —**disparagingly** adv

dis·pa·rate /ˈdɪspərət/ adj *formal* consisting of things or people that are very different and not related to each other: *a meeting covering many disparate subjects* | *the difficulties of dealing with disparate groups of people*

di·spar·i·ty /dɪˈspærəti/ n plural **disparities** [C,U] *formal* a difference between two or more things, especially an unfair one; → **parity**: [+in/between] *We are still seeing a disparity between the rates of pay for men and women.*

dis·pas·sion·ate /dɪsˈpæʃənət/ adj not influenced by personal emotions and therefore able to make fair decisions; ▣ **impartial**: *a dispassionate view of the situation* —**dispassionately** adv

di·spatch¹ , **despatch** /dɪˈspætʃ/ v [T] **1** *formal* to send someone or something somewhere for a particular purpose: **dispatch sb/sth to sb/sth** *A reporter was dispatched to Naples to cover the riot.* | *Goods are normally dispatched within 24 hours.* **2** to deal with someone or to finish a job quickly and effectively: *She dispatched* (=beat) *her opponent 6–2, 6–1.* **3** old-fashioned to deliberately kill a person or animal

dispatch² , **despatch** n **1** [C] a message sent between military or government officials: *a dispatch from headquarters* **2** [C] a report sent to a newspaper from one of its writers who is in another town or country **3** [singular] the act of sending people or things to a particular place: *the dispatch of warships to the region* **4** **with dispatch** *formal* if you do something with dispatch, you do it well and quickly → **mentioned in dispatches** at MENTION¹ (4)

di'spatch box n *BrE* **1** the dispatch box a box on a central table in the British Parliament, which important members of parliament stand next to when they make speeches **2** [C] a box for holding official papers

di·spatch·er /dɪˈspætʃə $ -ər/ n [C] *AmE* someone whose job is to send out vehicles such as taxis or AMBULANCES to places where they are needed

di'spatch ˌrider n [C] *BrE* someone whose job is to take messages or packages by MOTORCYCLE

di·spel /dɪˈspel/ v **dispelled, dispelling** [T] to make something go away, especially a belief, idea, or feeling: *We want to **dispel** the **myth** that you cannot eat well in Britain.* | *Light poured into the hall, dispelling the shadows.*

di·spen·sa·ble /dɪˈspensəbəl/ adj not necessary or important and so easy to get rid of; ▣ **indispensable**: *Part-time workers are considered dispensable.*

di·spen·sa·ry /dɪˈspensəri/ n plural **dispensaries** [C] a place where medicines are prepared and given out, especially in a hospital → PHARMACY

dis·pen·sa·tion /ˌdɪspənˈseɪʃən, -pen-/ n **1** [C,U] special permission from someone in authority, especially a religious leader, to do something that is not usually allowed: *Caroline's marriage was annulled by **special dispensation** from the church.* **2** [U] *formal* the act of providing people with something as part of an official process: [+of] *the dispensation of justice* **3** [C] *formal* a religious or political system that has control over people's lives at a particular time

di·spense /dɪˈspens/ v [T] *formal* **1** to give something to people, especially in fixed amounts; ▣ **give out**: **dispense sth to sb** *Villagers dispensed tea to people involved in the accident.* | *a machine for dispensing cash* **2** to officially provide something for people:

dispense justice (=decide whether or not someone is guilty of a crime and what punishment they should receive) **3** to officially prepare and give medicines to people

dispense with sth *phr v formal* to not use or do something that people usually use or do, because it is not necessary: *Ann suggested that they dispense with speeches altogether at the wedding.* | **dispense with sb's services** (=no longer employ someone) | *Let's **dispense with the formalities** (=speak openly and directly), shall we?*

di·spens·er /dɪˈspensə $ -ər/ n [C] a machine which provides a particular amount of a product or substance when you press a button or put money into it: *a paper towel dispenser* → CASH DISPENSER

di'spensing ˌchemist n [C] *BrE* a CHEMIST or PHARMACIST

di·sper·sal /dɪˈspɜːsəl $ -ɜːr-/ n [C,U] the process of spreading things over a wide area or in different directions: *the role of birds in the dispersal of seeds*

di·sperse /dɪˈspɜːs $ -ɜːrs/ v [I,T] **1** if a group of people disperse or are dispersed, they go away in different directions: *Police used tear gas to disperse the crowd.* **2** if something disperses or is dispersed, it spreads in different directions over a wide area: *The clouds dispersed as quickly as they had gathered.*

di·sper·sion /dɪˈspɜːʃən $ -ˈspɜːrʒən/ n [U] DISPERSAL

di·spir·ited /dɪˈspɪrɪtɪd/ adj someone who is dispirited does not feel as hopeful, eager, or interested in something as they were in the past: *At last, dispirited and weary, they gave up the search.* —**dispiritedly** adv

dis·place /dɪsˈpleɪs/ v [T] **1** to take the place or position of something or someone; ▣ **replace**: *Coal has been displaced by natural gas as a major source of energy.* | *immigrants who displace US workers in the job market* **2** to make a group of people or animals have to leave the place where they normally live: *Fifty thousand people have been displaced by the fighting.* **3** to force something out of its usual place or position: *The water displaced by the landslides created a tidal wave.* —**displaced** adj

dis·placed ˈperson n plural **displaced persons** [C] *technical* someone who has been forced to leave their country because of war or cruel treatment; ▣ **refugee**

dis·place·ment /dɪsˈpleɪsmənt/ n **1** [U] *formal* when a group of people or animals are forced to leave the place where they usually live **2** [singular] *technical* the weight or VOLUME of liquid that something replaces when it floats in that liquid – used especially to describe how heavy something such as a ship is

di·splay¹ W2 /dɪˈspleɪ/ n [C]

1 OBJECTS an arrangement of things for people to look at or buy: [+of] *a superb display of African masks* | *a dazzling display* (=very good display) *of flowers* | *The **window display** caught her eye.* | **display cases** *containing old photographs*

2 ENTERTAINMENT a public performance of something that is intended to entertain people: *a fireworks display* | [+of] *a display of juggling*

3 **on display a)** something that is on display is in a public place where people can look at it; ▣ **on show**: *Mapplethorpe's photographs were first **put on display** in New York.* | **be/go on display** *One of the world's oldest cars has gone on display in Brighton today.* **b)** if a quality, feeling, or skill is on display, it is very clear and easy to notice: *The musical talent on display is extremely impressive.*

4 display of affection/emotion/aggression etc an occasion when someone clearly shows a particular feeling, attitude, or quality: *Unprovoked displays of aggression cannot be tolerated.*

5 ON EQUIPMENT a part of a piece of equipment that shows information, for example a computer screen: *This time the display flashed a red warning signal.*

display² W2 v

1 [T] to show something to people, or put it in a place where people can see it easily: *shop windows displaying*

the latest fashions | *All the exam results will be dis-played on the noticeboard.*
2 [T] to clearly show a feeling, attitude, or quality by what you do or say: *She displayed no emotion on the witness stand.* | *ten piano pieces, each written to display the talents of individual players*
3 [T] if a computer or something similar displays information, it shows it on its screen: *I pressed 'return' and an error message was displayed.*
4 [I] if a male bird or animal displays, it behaves in a particular way as a signal to other birds or animals, especially to attract a female

dis·pleased /dɪsˈpliːzd/ *adj formal* annoyed or not satisfied; ✷ **pleased**: *He looked extremely displeased.* | [+with] *City officials are displeased with the lack of progress.* —**displease** v [T] —**displeasing** *adj*

dis·plea·sure /dɪsˈpleʒə $ -ər/ n [U] *formal* the feeling of being annoyed or not satisfied with someone or something; ✷ **annoyance**: [+at/with] *Their displeasure at being kept waiting was clear.* | **incur sb's displeasure** (=make someone displeased)

dis·port /dɪˈspɔːt $ -ɔːrt/ v [T] **disport yourself** *old-fashioned* to amuse yourself by doing things that are active and enjoyable – used humorously

dis·pos·a·ble /dɪˈspəʊzəbəl $ -ˈspoʊ-/ *adj* **1** intended to be used once or for a short time and then thrown away: *disposable nappies* **2** available to be used: *disposable resources* —**disposable** n [C]

dis,posable 'income n [U] the amount of money you have left to spend after you have paid your taxes, bills etc

dis·pos·al /dɪˈspəʊzəl $ -ˈspoʊ-/ n **1** [U] when you get rid of something: [+of] *the safe disposal of radioactive waste* | **bomb disposal** experts **2** **at sb's disposal** available for someone to use: *Tanner had a lot of cash at his disposal.* | **sb is at your (complete) disposal** (=someone is ready to help you in any way) **3** [C] *AmE* a small machine under the kitchen SINK which breaks vegetable waste into small pieces; ✷ **waste disposal 4** [U] *technical* the sale of something you own such as a house, a business, or land: *The profit or loss on the disposal of an asset must be accounted for.* **5** [U] *formal* the way in which an amount of money is used: *The Commission has complete control over the disposal of the funds.*

dis·pose /dɪˈspəʊz $ -ˈspoʊz/ v [T always + adv/prep] *formal* to arrange things or put them in their places: *Chinese vases are disposed around the gallery.*
dispose of sth *phr v* **1** to get rid of something, especially something that is difficult to get rid of: *an incinerator built to dispose of toxic waste* **2** to sell something, especially part of a business: *I am still not sure how best to dispose of the shares.* **3** *formal* to deal with something such as a problem or question successfully: *Your idea at least disposes of the immediate problem.* **4** to defeat an opponent: *Two goals by Raul disposed of Barcelona.*
dispose sb **to/towards** sth *phr v formal* to make someone more likely to have particular feelings or thoughts: *The body releases a chemical that disposes you towards sleep.*

dis·posed /dɪˈspəʊzd $ -ˈspoʊzd/ *adj formal* **1** **be well/favourably/kindly disposed (to/towards sb/sth)** to like or approve of someone or something: *Management is favourably disposed to the idea of job-sharing.* **2** **be/feel/seem etc disposed to do sth** *formal* to want or be willing to do something: *Jon disagreed, but did not feel disposed to argue.* **3** **be disposed to sth** *formal* to have a tendency towards something: *a man disposed to depression*

dis·po·si·tion /ˌdɪspəˈzɪʃən/ n *formal* **1** [C usually singular] a particular type of character which makes someone likely to behave or react in a certain way; ✷ **temperament**: **of a nervous/sociable/sensitive etc disposition** (=having a nervous etc character) *The film is not suitable for people of a nervous disposition.* | **have a cheerful/sunny etc disposition** (=have a happy char-

acter) **2** [singular] a tendency or willingness to behave in a particular way; ✷ **inclination**: **have/show a disposition to do sth** *Neither side shows the slightest disposition to compromise.* | [+towards] *Most children have a disposition towards obedience.* **3** [C usually singular] the position or arrangement of something in a particular place: [+of] *a map showing the disposition of American forces* **4** [U] *formal* the way in which something is dealt with or used: [+of] *A solicitor advised him as to the disposition of the money.* **5** [C,U] *law* the act of formally giving property to someone: *the disposition of assets on death*

dis·pos·sess /ˌdɪspəˈzes/ v [T usually passive] to take property or land away from someone: **be dispossessed of sth** *Many black South Africans had been dispossessed of their homes.* —**dispossession** /-ˈzeʃən/ n [U]

dis·pos·sessed /ˌdɪspəˈzest◂/ n **the dispossessed** people who have had property or land taken away

dis·pro·por·tion /ˌdɪsprəˈpɔːʃən $ -ɔːr-/ n [C,U] *formal* a situation in which two or more things are not equal in amount, level etc: *a dangerous disproportion between production and consumption*

dis·pro·por·tion·ate /ˌdɪsprəˈpɔːʃənɪt◂ $ -ɔːr-/ *adj* too much or too little in relation to something else: *the disproportionate amount of money being spent on defence* —**disproportionately** *adv*

dis·prove /dɪsˈpruːv/ v [T] to show that something is wrong or not true; ✷ **prove**: *These figures disproved Smith's argument.* —**disproof** /-ˈpruːf/ n [C,U] *formal*

di·sput·a·ble /dɪˈspjuːtəbəl, ˈdɪspjʊ-/ *adj* something that is disputable is not definitely true or right, and therefore is something that you can argue about; ✷ **indisputable**

dis·pu·ta·tion /ˌdɪspjʊˈteɪʃən/ n [C,U] *formal* a discussion about a subject which people cannot agree on

dis·pu·ta·tious /ˌdɪspjʊˈteɪʃəs/ *adj formal* tending to argue; ✷ **argumentative**

dis·pute¹ W2 /dɪˈspjuːt, ˈdɪspjuːt/ n [C,U]
1 a serious argument or disagreement

be involved in a dispute
get into a dispute (=become involved)
settle/resolve a dispute
bitter dispute
long-running dispute (=one that lasts a long time)
political/legal dispute
pay dispute
industrial dispute *BrE* **labor** dispute *AmE* (=between workers and employers)
territorial dispute (=about land)
domestic dispute (=between a couple who live together)
be in dispute with sb (=be involved in a dispute)
a dispute **arises** (=it starts)

[+with] *The firm is involved in a legal dispute with a rival company.* | [+over] *He got into a dispute over a taxi fare.* | *Every effort was made to settle the dispute, but without success.* | [+between] *the bitter border dispute between the countries* | *A long-running pay dispute is disrupting rail services.* | *The coal industry was plagued by industrial disputes.* | *The police don't usually like to intervene in domestic disputes.* | *The miners were in dispute with their employers over pay.* | *A dispute arose over who was to be the next king.*

2 be beyond dispute if something is beyond dispute, everyone agrees that it is true or that it really happened: *It is beyond dispute that advances in medicine have enabled people to live longer.*

3 be open to dispute if something is open to dispute, it is not completely certain and not everyone agrees about it: *His interpretation of the poem is open to dispute.*

4 be in dispute if something is in dispute, people are arguing about it: *The facts of the case are still in dispute.*

dis·pute[2] /dɪˈspjuːt/ v **1** [T] to say that something such as a fact or idea is not correct or true: *The main facts of the book have never been disputed.* | **dispute that** *Few would dispute that travel broadens the mind.* **2** [I,T] *formal* to argue or disagree with someone: **dispute (sth) with sb** *Hazlitt, though much younger, was soon disputing with Wordsworth on equal terms.* | *What happened next is **hotly disputed**.* **3** [T] to try to get control of something or win something: *Soviet forces disputed every inch of ground.*

dis·qual·i·fy /dɪsˈkwɒlɪ̩faɪ $ -ˈkwɑː-/ v **disqualified, disqualifying, disqualifies** [T usually passive] **1** to stop someone from taking part in an activity because they have broken a rule; **ꙍ ban**: **disqualify sb from (doing) sth** *He was **disqualified from driving**.* **2** to unfairly prevent someone from doing a job or taking part in an activity; **ꙍ exclude**: **disqualify sb from (doing) sth** *a system which disqualifies the poor from education* —**disqualification** /dɪs̩kwɒlɪ̩fɪ̩ˈkeɪʃən $ -̩kwɑː-/ n [C,U]: *automatic disqualification*

dis·qui·et /dɪsˈkwaɪət/ n [U] *formal* anxiety or unhappiness about something: [+over/about/at] *public disquiet over deaths in police custody* | [+among] *His appointment **caused disquiet** among members.* | *express/voice your disquiet The union has voiced its disquiet about the way the protest was handled.*

dis·qui·et·ing /dɪsˈkwaɪətɪŋ/ adj *formal* causing anxiety: *He found Jean's manner disquieting.*

dis·qui·si·tion /̩dɪskwɪˈzɪʃən/ n [C] *formal* a long speech or written report

dis·re·gard[1] /̩dɪsrɪˈɡɑːd $ -ɑːrd/ v [T] to ignore something or treat it as unimportant: *He ordered the jury to disregard the witness's last statement.* | *Mark totally disregarded my advice.*

disregard[2] n [singular, U] when someone ignores something that they should not ignore: [+for/of] *his disregard for her feelings* | **total/reckless/complete/ flagrant etc disregard** *Local councillors accused the terrorists of **showing** a complete **disregard** for human life.* | **in disregard of sth** *He said the bombing was in complete disregard of the Geneva Convention.*

dis·re·pair /̩dɪsrɪˈpeə $ -ˈper/ n [U] buildings, roads etc that are in disrepair are in bad condition because they have not been cared for: *buildings allowed to **fall into disrepair*** | *The castle is **in a state of disrepair**.*

dis·rep·u·ta·ble /dɪsˈrepjɵ̩təbəl/ adj considered to be dishonest, bad, illegal etc; **ꙍ reputable**: *disreputable behavior* | *a disreputable neighbourhood*

dis·re·pute /̩dɪsrɪˈpjuːt/ n [U] a situation in which people no longer admire or trust someone or something: *He faces six charges of **bringing** the game **into disrepute**.* | *This theory **fell into disrepute** in the fifties.*

dis·re·spect[1] /̩dɪsrɪˈspekt/ n [singular, U] lack of respect for someone or something; **ꙍ respect**: [+for] *disrespect for the law* | *Damien has always had a **healthy disrespect** (=that you think is good) for media opinion.* | *It was said on the spur of the moment and I **meant no disrespect** to anybody.* | *No disrespect to Phil, but the team has performed better since he left* (=used to show you are not criticizing someone). —**disrespectful** adj —**disrespectfully** adv

disrespect[2] v [T] to say or do things that show a lack of respect for someone: *Hicks accused Williams of disrespecting him at a record company party.*

dis·robe /dɪsˈrəʊb $ -ˈroʊb/ v [I] *formal* to remove your clothes

dis·rupt /dɪsˈrʌpt/ v [T] to prevent something from continuing in its usual way by causing problems: *Traffic was disrupted by a hoax bomb.* | *Climate change could disrupt the agricultural economy.*

dis·rup·tion /dɪsˈrʌpʃən/ n [C,U] a situation in which something is prevented from continuing in its usual way: *The strike **caused widespread disruption**.*

dis·rup·tive /dɪsˈrʌptɪv/ adj causing problems and preventing something from continuing in its usual way: [+to] *Night work can be very disruptive to home life.* | *Mike's parents thought I was **a disruptive influence** (=a person who causes disruption).* | *ways to handle **disruptive pupils*** —**disruptively** adv

diss /dɪs/ v [T] *informal* to say unkind things about someone you know

dis·sat·is·fac·tion /dɪ̩sætɪsˈfækʃən, dɪs̩sæ-/ n [U] a feeling of not being satisfied; **ꙍ satisfaction**: [+with] *30% of customers **expressed dissatisfaction** with the service.*

dis·sat·is·fied /dɪsˈsætɪs̩faɪd, dɪs̩sæ-/ adj not satisfied because something is not as good as you had expected; **ꙍ satisfied**: *dissatisfied clients* | [+with] *If you are dissatisfied with this product, please return it.*

dis·sect /dɪˈsekt, daɪ-/ v [T] **1** to cut up the body of a dead animal or person in order to study it **2** to examine something carefully in order to understand it: *books in which the lives of famous people are dissected* **3** to divide an area of land into several smaller pieces: *fields dissected by small streams* —**dissection** /-ˈsekʃən/ n [C,U]

dis·sem·ble /dɪˈsembəl/ v [I,T] *literary* to hide your true feelings, thoughts etc

dis·sem·i·nate /dɪˈsemɪ̩neɪt/ v [T] *formal* to spread information or ideas to as many people as possible: *Her findings have been **widely disseminated**.* —**dissemination** /dɪ̩semɪˈneɪʃən/ n [U]: *the dissemination of information*

dis·sen·sion /dɪˈsenʃən/ n [C,U] disagreement among a group of people: [+in/within/between/among] *This move **sowed dissension** within the party ranks.* | *The Labour Party was torn by **internal dissensions**.*

dis·sent[1] /dɪˈsent/ n **1** [U] refusal to agree with an official decision or accepted opinion; **ꙍ opposition**; → **consent, assent**: *the ruthless suppression of political dissent* | *These **voices of dissent** grew louder and louder.* **2** [C] *law* a statement by a judge giving their reasons for disagreeing with the other judges in a law case

dissent[2] v [I] **1** to say that you disagree with an official decision or accepted opinion: [+from] *Few historians would dissent from this view.* | *There are some **dissenting voices** (=people who do not agree) among the undergraduates.* **2** *law* if a judge dissents, they say formally that they do not agree with the other judges in a law case

dis·sent·er /dɪˈsentə $ -ər/ n [C] **1** a person or organization that disagrees with an official decision or accepted opinion: *Political dissenters were imprisoned.* **2** also **Dissenter** someone in the past who did not accept the beliefs of the established Protestant church in Western Europe; **ꙍ non-conformist**

dis·ser·ta·tion /̩dɪsəˈteɪʃən $ ̩dɪsər-/ n [C] a long piece of writing on a particular subject, especially one written for a university degree

dis·ser·vice /dɪsˈsɜːvɪ̩s, dɪsˈsɜː- $ -ˈsɜːr-/ n **do sb/sth a disservice** also **do a disservice to sb/sth** to do something that gives other people a bad opinion of someone or something: *The fans have done the game a great disservice.*

dis·si·dent /ˈdɪsɪ̩dənt/ n [C] someone who publicly criticizes the government in a country where this is punished: *a prominent political dissident* —**dissident** adj [only before noun]: *dissident writers* —**dissidence** n [U]

dis·sim·i·lar /dɪˈsɪmɪ̩lə, dɪsˈsɪ- $ -ər/ adj not the same; **ꙍ similar**: [+to] *Madonna's career is **not dissimilar to** (=is quite similar to) Cher's.* —**dissimilarity** /dɪ̩sɪmɪˈlærɪ̩ti, dɪs̩sɪ-/ n [C,U]: *dissimilarities between the US and Britain*

dis·sim·u·late /dɪˈsɪmjɵ̩leɪt/ v [I,T] *formal* to hide your true feelings or intentions, especially by lying

dis·si·pate /ˈdɪsɪ̩peɪt/ v *formal* **1** [I,T] to gradually become less or weaker before disappearing completely, or to make something do this: *As he thought it over, his anger gradually dissipated.* | *Little by little, the smoke was dissipated by the breeze.* **2** [T] to waste something valuable such as time, money, or energy: *His savings were soon dissipated.*

dis·si·pat·ed /ˈdɪsɪpeɪtɪd/ *adj formal* spending too much time enjoying physical pleasures such as drinking alcohol in a way that is harmful

dis·si·pa·tion /ˌdɪsɪˈpeɪʃən/ *n* [U] *formal* **1** the process of making something gradually weaker or less until it disappears: *the dissipation of heat* **2** the enjoyment of physical pleasures in a way that is harmful: *a life of dissipation* **3** the act of wasting money, time, energy etc: *the dissipation of resources*

dis·so·ci·ate /dɪˈsəʊʃieɪt, -sieɪt $ -ˈsoʊ-/ *v* [T] **1** to do or say something to show that you do not agree with the views or actions of someone with whom you had a connection: **dissociate yourself from sth** *I wish to dissociate myself from Mr Irvine's remarks.* **2** *technical* to regard two things or people as separate and not connected to each other; 🔁 **associate** —**dissociation** /dɪˌsəʊʃiˈeɪʃən -siˈeɪ- $ -ˌsoʊ-/ *n* [U]

dis·so·lute /ˈdɪsəluːt/ *adj* having an immoral way of life, for example drinking too much alcohol or having sex with many people

dis·so·lu·tion /ˌdɪsəˈluːʃən/ *n* [U] **1** the act of formally ending a parliament, business, or marriage; → **dissolve**: *The president announced the dissolution of the National Assembly.* **2** the act of breaking up an organization, institution etc so that it no longer exists: *the dissolution of the monasteries* **3** the process by which something gradually becomes weaker and disappears: *the eventual dissolution of class barriers*

dis·solve /dɪˈzɒlv $ dɪˈzɑːlv/ *v*
1 BECOME PART OF LIQUID [I,T] if a solid dissolves, or if you dissolve it, it mixes with a liquid and becomes part of it: *Stir until the sugar dissolves.* | [+in] *Sugar dissolves in water.* | **dissolve sth in sth** *Dissolve the tablet in water.*
2 END [T] to formally end a parliament, business arrangement, marriage etc: *The monarch had the power to dissolve parliament.*
3 EMOTION **dissolve into/in laughter/tears** etc to start laughing or crying: *She dissolved into fits of laughter.*
4 BECOME WEAKER [I,T] to gradually become smaller or weaker before disappearing, or to make something do this: *Her enthusiasm dissolved his shyness.* | *A few clouds formed briefly before dissolving again.*

dis·so·nance /ˈdɪsənəns/ *n* **1** [C,U] *technical* a combination of notes that sound strange because they are not in HARMONY; 🔁 **consonance** **2** [U] *formal* lack of agreement —**dissonant** *adj*

dis·suade /dɪˈsweɪd/ *v* [T] to persuade someone not to do something; 🔁 **persuade**: **dissuade sb from (doing) sth** *a campaign to dissuade young people from smoking* —**dissuasion** /dɪˈsweɪʒən/ *n* [U]

dis·taff /ˈdɪstɑːf $ -stæf/ *n* [C] a stick, used in the past for spinning wool

dis·tance¹ S2 W2 /ˈdɪstəns/ *n*
1 AMOUNT OF SPACE [C,U] the amount of space between two places or things: [+from/between] *the distance from Chicago to Detroit* | *Measure the distance between the two points.* | **short/long/considerable/great distance** | *The cottage is* **some distance** (=quite a long distance) *from the road.* | **at a distance of 2 feet/10 metres** etc *A shark can smell blood at a distance of half a kilometer.* | *Some members* **travelled** *a considerable distance to attend the meeting.* | *She felt she had to* **put some distance between** *herself and the house* (=go quite a long way away from it). | **within walking/striking/commuting** etc **distance (of sth)** *If you are within striking distance of Speyside, visit the lakes.* | **stopping/braking distance** (=the distance you travel in a car after pressing the brakes before the car stops)
2 FAR AWAY [singular] used to talk about a situation when something is far away from you in space or time:

in the distance *Church bells rang in the distance* (=they were far away). | **at/from a distance** *We watched from a* **safe distance** (=we were far away).
3 UNFRIENDLY FEELING [singular] a situation in which two people do not have a close friendly relationship: [+between] *There was still a distance between me and my father.*
4 keep your distance a) to stay far enough away from someone or something to be safe: *A lighthouse on the cliff warns ships to keep their distance.* **b)** also **keep sb at a distance** to avoid becoming too friendly with someone: *The neighbours tend to keep their distance.*
5 go the (full) distance *informal* to finish something you have started: *Do you think Greg will go the distance this time?* → LONG-DISTANCE, MIDDLE DISTANCE

distance² *v* **distance yourself (from sth)** to say that you are not involved with someone or something, especially to avoid being connected with them: *The UNO has firmly distanced itself from the anti-government movement.*

'distance ˌlearning *n* [U] a method of study that involves working at home and sending your work to your teacher

dis·tant W3 /ˈdɪstənt/ *adj*
1 FAR AWAY far away in space or time: *the sound of distant gunfire.* | *Her honeymoon seemed a* **distant memory.** | *That affair was* **in the dim and distant past** (=a long time ago). | *The President hopes to visit Ireland* **in the not too distant future** (=quite soon). | [+from] *stars that are distant from our galaxy*
2 NOT FRIENDLY unfriendly: *After the quarrel Sue remained cold and distant.*
3 NOT CONCENTRATING thinking deeply about something private, rather than about what is happening around you: *Geri had a distant look in her eyes.*
4 RELATIVE [only before noun] not closely related to you; 🔁 **close**: *a distant cousin*
5 distant from sth different from something or not closely connected with it: *The reality of independence was distant from the hopes they had had.* —**distantly** *adv*: *We are distantly related.*

dis·taste /dɪsˈteɪst/ *n* [U] a feeling that something or someone is unpleasant or morally offensive: [+for] *her distaste for any form of compromise*

dis·taste·ful /dɪsˈteɪstfəl/ *adj* unpleasant or morally offensive: *What follows is John's story. Parts of it may seem distasteful, even shocking.*

dis·taste·ful·ly /dɪsˈteɪstfəli/ *adv written* feeling or showing distaste: *She looked distastefully at the overflowing bin.*

dis·tem·per /dɪsˈtempə $ -ər/ *n* [U] **1** a serious infectious disease that affects animals, especially dogs **2** *BrE* a type of paint that you mix with water to paint walls

dis·tend /dɪˈstend/ *v* [I,T] *formal* to swell or make something swell because of pressure from inside —**distended** *adj*: *a distended stomach* —**distension** /-ˈtenʃən/ *n* [U] *technical*

dis·till, distil /dɪˈstɪl/ *v* **distilled, distilling** [T] **1** to make a liquid such as water or alcohol more pure by heating it so that it becomes a gas and then letting it cool. Drinks such as WHISKY are made this way: *distilled water* **2** to remove a chemical substance from a plant, for example by heating or pressing it **3** to get the main ideas or facts from a much larger amount of information: **distill sth into sth** *The notes I had brought back were waiting to be distilled into a book.* —**distillation** /ˌdɪstɪˈleɪʃən/ *n* [C,U]

dis·til·ler /dɪˈstɪlə $ -ər/ *n* [C] a person or company that makes strong alcoholic drinks such as WHISKY

dis·til·le·ry /dɪˈstɪləri/ *n plural* **distilleries** [C] a factory where strong alcoholic drink such as WHISKY is produced

dis·tinct W3 /dɪˈstɪŋkt/ adj
1 clearly different or belonging to a different type: *two entirely distinct languages* | distinct **types/groups/categories etc** *There are four distinct types.* | [+**from**] *The learning needs of the two groups are quite distinct from each other.*
2 as distinct from sth used to make it clear that you are not referring to a particular kind of thing, but to something else: *a movie star, as distinct from an actor*
3 something that is distinct can clearly be seen, heard, smelled etc: *The outline of the ship became more distinct.*
4 [only before noun] a distinct possibility, feeling, quality etc definitely exists and cannot be ignored: *I got the distinct impression he was trying to make me angry.* | *There is a distinct possibility that this will eventually be needed.* | *the distinct lack of enthusiasm from my sister*

dis·tinc·tion S3 W2 /dɪˈstɪŋkʃən/ n
1 DIFFERENCE [C,U] a clear difference or separation between two similar things: [+**between**] *the distinction between formal and informal language* | **clear/sharp distinction** *There is often no clear distinction between an allergy and food intolerance.* | **make/draw a distinction** *The Act makes no distinction between children and adults* (=it treats them as if they were the same).
2 EXCELLENCE [U] the quality of being excellent and important: *No one today doubts Eliot's distinction as a poet.*
3 BEING SPECIAL [singular] the quality of being special in some way: **have/earn/achieve etc the distinction of doing sth** *At that time, it had the distinction of being the largest bridge in the UK.* | *The US enjoys the dubious distinction of being the lawsuit capital of the world.*
4 RESULT [C,U] a special mark given to a student whose work is excellent: **with distinction** *He obtained a law doctorate with distinction.*

dis·tinc·tive /dɪˈstɪŋktɪv/ adj having a special quality, character, or appearance that is different and easy to recognize: *a rock band with a distinctive sound* —**distinctively** adv —**distinctiveness** n [U]

dis·tinct·ly /dɪˈstɪŋktli/ adv **1** clearly: *Speak clearly and distinctly.* | *He distinctly remembered the day his father left.* **2** very: *Paul was left feeling distinctly foolish.* | **distinctly uncomfortable/uneasy/unhappy etc 3** used to say that something has a particular quality or character that is easy to recognize: *dishes with a distinctly Jewish flavor*

dis·tin·guish S3 W3 /dɪˈstɪŋgwɪʃ/ v
1 [I,T] to recognize and understand the difference between two or more things or people; ▤ **differentiate:** [+**between**] *His attorney argued that Cope could not distinguish between right and wrong.* | **distinguish sb/sth from** *a method of distinguishing cancer cells from normal tissue*
2 [T not in progressive] to be the thing that makes someone or something different or special: **distinguish sb/sth from** *The factor that distinguishes this company from the competition is customer service.* | **distinguishing feature/mark/characteristic** *The main distinguishing feature of this species is the leaf shape.*
3 [T not in progressive] *written* to be able to see the shape of something or hear a particular sound: *The light was too dim for me to distinguish anything clearly.*
4 distinguish yourself to do something so well that people notice and remember you: *He distinguished himself on several occasions in the civil war.*

dis·tin·guish·a·ble /dɪˈstɪŋgwɪʃəbəl/ adj easy to recognize as being different from something else: [+**from**] *The fake was barely distinguishable from the original painting.* | **barely/hardly/scarcely distinguishable** | **clearly/easily/readily distinguishable** *The cheese is easily distinguishable by its colour.*

dis·tin·guished /dɪˈstɪŋgwɪʃt/ adj **1** successful, respected, and admired: *a long and distinguished career* **2** dressed in neat and attractive clothes that are worn by adults, not looking like a young person: *a tall distinguished figure in a dark suit*

dis·tort /dɪˈstɔːt $ -ɔːrt/ v **1** [I,T] to change the appearance, sound, or shape of something so that it is strange or unclear: *Tall buildings can distort radio signals.* **2** [T] to report something in a way that is not completely true or correct: *His account was badly distorted by the press.* **3** [T] to change a situation from the way it would naturally be: *an expensive subsidy which distorts the market* —**distorted** adj: *His face was distorted in anger.* —**distortion** /dɪˈstɔːʃən $ -ɔːr-/ n [C,U]: *a gross distortion of the facts*

dis·tract /dɪˈstrækt/ v [T] to take someone's attention away from something by making them look at or listen to something else: *Try not to distract the other students.* | **distract sb/sth from sth** *Coverage of the war was used to distract attention from other matters.* —**distracting** adj

dis·tract·ed /dɪˈstræktɪd/ adj anxious and unable to think clearly —**distractedly** adv

dis·trac·tion /dɪˈstrækʃən/ n **1** [C,U] something that stops you paying attention to what you are doing: *I study in the library as there are too many distractions at home.* | [+**from**] *Demands for equality were seen as a distraction from more serious issues.* **2 drive sb to distraction** to continue annoying or upsetting someone very much: *The baby's constant crying drove me to distraction.* **3** [C] *old-fashioned* a pleasant activity

dis·traught /dɪˈstrɔːt $ -ˈstrɒːt/ adj so upset and worried that you cannot think clearly: *Relatives are tonight comforting the distraught parents.*

dis·tress¹ /dɪˈstres/ n [U] **1** a feeling of extreme unhappiness: *Luke's behaviour caused his parents great distress.* | **in distress** *The girl was crying and clearly in distress.* **2** suffering and problems caused by a lack of money, food etc: *acute financial distress* | **in distress** *charities that aid families in distress* **3** *formal* great physical pain **4** a situation when a ship, aircraft etc is in danger and needs help: *We picked up a distress signal 6 km away.* | **in distress** *The ship is in distress and taking on water.*

distress² v [T] to make someone feel very upset: *The dream had distressed her greatly.*

dis·tressed /dɪˈstrest/ adj **1** very upset: **deeply/visibly distressed** *Hannah was deeply distressed by the news.* | [+**at/by**] *My client is very distressed at the treatment she received from your officers.* | **distressed to find/hear/see/learn etc sth** *She was distressed to see he was crying.* **2** *technical* in a lot of pain: *The animal was clearly distressed.* **3** distressed furniture or clothes have been made to look older than they really are **4** *formal* having very little money: *a family living in distressed circumstances*

dis·tress·ing /dɪˈstresɪŋ/ also **dis·tress·ful** /dɪˈstresfəl/ adj making you feel very upset: *a distressing experience* —**distressingly** adv

dis·trib·ute W3 /dɪˈstrɪbjuːt/ v [T]
1 to share things among a group of people, especially in a planned way; ▤ **give out: distribute sth among/to sb** *Clothes and blankets have been distributed among the refugees.* | *a man distributing leaflets to passers-by*
2 to supply goods to shops and companies so that they can sell them: *Milk is distributed to the local shops by Herald's Dairies.*
3 to spread something over a large area: *Make sure the weight of the load is evenly distributed.*
4 be distributed to exist in different parts of an area or group: **be widely/evenly distributed** *This species of dolphin is widely distributed throughout the world.* | *The population is distributed in a very uneven pattern.*

dis·tri·bu·tion W2 /ˌdɪstrɪˈbjuːʃən/ n
1 [U] the act of sharing things among a large group of people in a planned way: [+**of**] *the distribution of aid supplies*
2 [U] when goods are supplied to shops and companies for them to sell: *a distribution centre*

3 [C,U] the way in which something exists in different amounts in different parts of an area or group: *population distribution* | [+of] *the highly unequal distribution of economic power*

dis·trib·u·tive /dɪ'strɪbjˣtɪv/ *adj* [usually before noun] connected with distribution: *distributive costs*

dis·trib·u·tor /dɪ'strɪbjˣtə $ -ər/ *n* [C] **1** a company or person that supplies shops and companies with goods **2** the part of an engine that sends an electric current to the SPARK PLUGS

dis·trib·u·tor·ship /dɪ'strɪbjˣtəʃɪp $ -ər-/ *n* [C] a company that has an arrangement to sell the products of another company: *the UK distributorship for Sol lighting products*

dis·trict S3 W2 /'dɪstrɪkt/ *n* [C]
1 an area of a town or the countryside, especially one with particular features: **rural/financial/theatre etc district** *a house in a pleasant suburban district*
2 an area of a country, city etc that has official borders: *a postal district*

district at'torney *n* [C] a lawyer in the US who works for the government in a particular area and who is responsible for bringing people who may be criminals to court

district 'council *n* [C] *BrE* a group of people elected to organize local services such as education, health services etc in a particular area

district 'court *n* [C] a US court of law which deals with cases involving national rather than state law

district 'nurse *n* [C] *BrE* a nurse who visits people in their own homes

dis·trust¹ /dɪs'trʌst/ *n* [U] a feeling that you cannot trust someone; → **mistrust**: *Local people regard the police with suspicion and distrust.* | [+of] *Dylan's **deep distrust** of journalists made him difficult to interview.* —**distrustful** *adj*

distrust² *v* [T] to not trust someone or something; ⟺ **trust**: *She had every reason to distrust him.*

dis·turb /dɪ'stɜːb $ -ɜːrb/ *v* [T]
1 INTERRUPT to interrupt someone so that they cannot continue what they are doing: *Sorry to disturb you, but I have an urgent message.* | *The thieves fled when they were disturbed by a neighbour.* | **Do not disturb** (=a sign you put on a door so that people will not interrupt you).
2 WORRY to make someone feel worried or upset: *What disturbs you most about this latest development?*
3 MOVE to move something or change its position: *If you find a bird's nest, never disturb the eggs.* | *I promise not to **disturb anything**.*
4 CHANGE to change a normal situation in a way that causes problems: *My hormone balance is disturbed by my pregnancy.* | *New procedures often disturb the comfortable habits of the workforce.*
5 **disturb the peace** *law* to behave in a noisy and unpleasant way in public

dis·turb·ance /dɪ'stɜːbəns $ -ɜːr-/ *n* **1** [C,U] *formal* a situation in which people behave violently in public: *There were disturbances in the crowd as fans left the stadium.* | **create/cause a disturbance** | *army training on controlling **civil disturbance*** **2** [C,U] something that interrupts what you are doing, or the act of making this happen: *We arrange the work so there's as little disturbance as possible.* | [+to] *When a helicopter lands, it can **cause a disturbance** to local residents.* **3** [U] a medical condition in which someone is mentally ill and does not behave normally: *a history of mental disturbance*

dis·turbed /dɪ'stɜːbd $ -ɜːrbd/ *adj* **1** not behaving normally because of a mental condition: **mentally/emotionally disturbed** *the care of emotionally **disturbed** children* | *while the balance of his mind was disturbed* **2** worried or upset: [+by/about/at] *Police are very disturbed about the latest trend.* | **seriously/deeply/greatly etc disturbed** | **disturbed to find/see/discover/learn etc** *She was disturbed to learn he had bought a motorbike.* | **disturbed that** *I'm disturbed that so many*

of the students appear to be illiterate. **3 disturbed sleep** sleep that is interrupted

dis·turb·ing /dɪ'stɜːbɪŋ $ -ɜːr-/ *adj* worrying or upsetting: *a disturbing increase in the crime rate* —**disturbingly** *adv*

dis·u·nited /ˌdɪsjuː'naɪtˣd/ *adj* people who are disunited are in the same organization, country, or group but cannot agree or work with each other

dis·u·ni·ty /dɪs'juːnˣti/ *n* [U] a situation in which a group of people cannot agree or work with each other: *Disunity destroyed the Republicans at the polls.*

dis·use /dɪs'juːs/ *n* [U] a situation in which something is no longer used: *The building eventually fell into disuse.*

dis·used /ˌdɪs'juːzd◂/ *adj* [usually before noun] a disused building, railway, mine etc is no longer used

ditch¹ /dɪtʃ/ *n* [C] a long narrow hole dug at the side of a field, road etc to hold or remove unwanted water → LAST-DITCH

ditch² *v* **1** [T] *informal* to stop having something because you no longer want it: *The government has ditched plans to privatise the prison.* **2** [T] *informal* to end a romantic relationship with someone: *Meg and Neil were due to marry, but she ditched him.* **3** [T] *AmE spoken informal* to not go to school, a class etc when you should; ⟺ **skip** *BrE*: *Did you ditch class today?* **4** [T] *AmE spoken informal* to leave someone you are with in a place without telling them you are going **5** [I,T] to land an aircraft in a controlled crash into water: *Two balloonists who ditched during the race were rescued by helicopter.*

ditch·wa·ter /'dɪtʃwɔːtə $ -wɒːtər, ˌwɑː-/ *n* **as dull as ditchwater** *BrE* very boring

dith·er /'dɪðə $ -ər/ *v* [I] to keep being unable to make a final decision about something: [+over/about/between] *He accused the government of dithering over the deal.* | **Stop dithering, girl, and get on with it!** —**ditherer** *n* [C]

di·tran·si·tive /ˌdaɪ'trænsˣtɪv, -zˣ-/ *adj* a ditransitive verb has an INDIRECT OBJECT and a DIRECT OBJECT. 'Give' in the sentence 'Give me the book' is ditransitive.; → **intransitive, transitive**

dit·sy /'dɪtsi/ *adj* another spelling of DITZY

dit·to¹ /'dɪtəʊ $ -toʊ/ *adv spoken informal* **1** used to say that you have exactly the same opinion as someone else: *'I hated school.' 'Ditto.'* **2** used to say that what is true of one thing is also true of another: *Where should she go? Mississippi? Too hot. Ditto Alabama.*

ditto² also **'ditto mark** *n plural* **dittoes** [C] *written* a mark (″) that you write immediately under a word in a list to show that the same word is repeated

dit·ty /'dɪti/ *n plural* **ditties** [C] a short simple poem or song – used humorously

dit·zy, ditsy /'dɪtsi/ *adj AmE informal* silly or stupid, and likely to forget things easily —**ditz** *n* [C]

di·u·ret·ic /ˌdaɪjʊ'retɪk◂/ *n* [C] *medical* a substance that increases the flow of URINE —**diuretic** *adj*

di·ur·nal /daɪ'ɜːnəl $ -'ɜːr-/ *adj technical* **1** happening or active in the daytime; ⟺ **nocturnal** **2** happening every day

Div. also **Div** *BrE n* the written abbreviation of *division*

di·va /'diːvə/ *n* [C] a very successful and famous female singer: *opera diva Jessye Norman*

di·van /dɪ'væn $ 'daɪvæn/ *n* [C] **1** a bed with a thick base **2** a long low soft seat without a back or arms

dive¹ /daɪv/ *v past tense* **dived** also **dove** /dəʊv $ doʊv/ *AmE, past participle* **dived** [I]
1 JUMP INTO WATER to jump into deep water with your head and arms going in first: [+into/off etc] *The snaps show the TV presenter as she dives into a pool.* | *Diving off the cliffs is dangerous.*
2 SWIM UNDER WATER to swim under water using special equipment to help you breathe: *The first time*

D

you dive on a coral reef is an experience you will never forget.

3 GO DEEPER/LOWER to travel down through the air or through water to a lower level: *The submarine began to dive.* | *The aircraft appeared to dive vertically towards the crowd.*

4 MOVE QUICKLY [always + adv/prep] to move or jump quickly in a particular direction or into a particular place: *Jackson dived after the ball.* | *We dived into a shop to avoid the rain.* | *The soldiers were diving for cover* (=to protect themselves behind something).

5 dive into your bag/pocket etc to put your hand quickly in your bag, pocket etc in order to get something out: *He dived into his pocket and produced a packet of cigarettes.*

6 NUMBERS if numbers, prices etc dive, they suddenly become much lower than before: *The dollar dived against the yen in Tokyo today.*

dive in *phr v*
to start doing something eagerly: *Harvey dived in with several questions.*

dive² *n* [C]
1 SUDDEN MOVEMENT a sudden movement in a particular direction or into a particular place: *She made a dive for the bathroom.*
2 SUDDEN FALL a sudden fall in the amount, value, or success of something: *The news put shares in a dive.* | *The team's fortunes have taken a dive this year.*
3 MOVEMENT DOWNWARDS when something moves down through the air or water: *Thankfully, the pilot managed to pull out of the dive and regain control.* | **steep/vertical dive**
4 JUMP a jump into deep water with your head and arms going in first
5 SWIM the act of going under water to swim, using special equipment to help you breathe
6 PLACE *informal* a bar, club etc that is cheap and dirty

dive-bomb *v* [I,T] if an aircraft dive-bombs a place, it drops bombs on it —**dive-bomber** *n* [C]

div·er /ˈdaɪvə $ -ər/ *n* [C] **1** someone who swims or works under water using special equipment to help them breathe **2** someone who jumps into water with their head and arms first

di·verge /daɪˈvɜːdʒ, dɪ̯- $ -ɜːrdʒ/ *v* [I] **1** if similar things diverge, they develop in different ways and so are no longer similar: *The two species diverged millions of years ago.* | *Global growth rates are diverging markedly.* **2** if opinions, interests etc diverge, they are different from each other: [+from] *Here Innocent's views diverged from Gregory's.* **3** if two lines or paths diverge, they separate and go in different directions; **↔** converge —**divergence** *n* [C,U]: *divergence between the US and Europe* —**divergent** *adj*: *divergent views*

di·verse /daɪˈvɜːs $ dɪ̯ˈvɜːrs, daɪ-/ *adj* very different from each other: *subjects as diverse as pop music and archaeology* —**diversely** *adv*

di·ver·si·fy /daɪˈvɜːsɪ̯faɪ $ dɪ̯ˈvɜːr-, daɪ-/ *v* diversified, diversifying, diversifies **1** [I,T] if a business, company, country etc diversifies, it increases the range of goods or services it produces: [+(away) from] *farmers forced to diversify away from their core business* | [+into] *The company is planning to diversify into other mining activities.* | *We need to diversify the economy.* **2** [I,T] to change something or to make it change so that there is more variety: *User requirements have diversified over the years.* **3** [I] *technical* to put money into several different types of INVESTMENT instead of only one or two: [+into] *Spread the risk by diversifying into dollar bonds.* —**diversification** /daɪˌvɜːsɪ̯fɪˈkeɪʃən $ dɪ̯ˌvɜːr-, daɪ-/ *n* [U]: *diversification of the rural economy*

di·ver·sion /daɪˈvɜːʃən, dɪ̯- $ -ɜːrʒən/ *n* **1** [C,U] a change in the direction or use of something, or the act of changing it: [+of] *a campaign to halt the diversion of*

the river | *the diversion of funds into the military budget* **2** [C,U] an enjoyable activity that you do to stop yourself from becoming bored **3** [C] something that stops you from paying attention to what you are doing or what is happening: *Two prisoners created a diversion to give the men time to escape.* **4** [C] *BrE* a different way that traffic is sent when the usual roads are closed

di·ver·sion·a·ry /daɪˈvɜːʃənəri, dɪ̯- $ -ˈvɜːrʒəneri/ *adj written* intended to take someone's attention away from something: *Most children are skilled in diversionary tactics.*

di·ver·si·ty /daɪˈvɜːsɪ̯ti, dɪ̯- $ -ɜːr-/ *n* **1** [U] the fact of including many different types of people or things: **cultural/ethnic/linguistic etc diversity** *The curriculum will take account of the ethnic diversity of the population.* **2** [singular] a range of different people, things, or ideas; **▤** variety: [+of] *a diversity of opinions*

di·vert /daɪˈvɜːt, dɪ̯- $ -ɜːrt/ *v* [T] **1** to change the use of something such as time or money: **divert sth into/to/(away) from etc sth** *The company should divert more resources into research.* | *Officials diverted revenue from arms sales to the rebels.* **2** to change the direction in which something travels: **divert a river/footpath/road etc** *Canals divert water from the Truckee River into the lake.* | *The high street is closed and traffic is being diverted.* **3** if you divert your telephone calls, you arrange for them to go directly to another number, for example because you are not able to answer them yourself for some time: *Remember to divert your phone when you are out of the office.* **4** to deliberately take someone's attention from something by making them think about or notice other things: **divert (sb's) attention (away from sb/sth)** *The crime crackdown is an attempt to divert attention from social problems.* | *He'd been trying to divert suspicion away from himself.* **5** *formal* to amuse or entertain someone

di·vert·ing /daɪˈvɜːtɪŋ, dɪ̯- $ -ɜːr-/ *adj formal* entertaining and amusing: *a mildly diverting film*

di·vest /daɪˈvest, dɪ̯-/ *v* [I,T] *technical* if a company divests, it sells some of its ASSETS, INVESTMENTS etc: *pressure on hospitals to divest tobacco-related stocks*

divest sb of sth *phr v formal* **1 divest yourself of sth** to sell or give away something you own: *Dad had long since divested himself of anything valuable.* **2 divest yourself of sth** to remove something you are wearing or carrying: *Pedro divested himself of his overcoat.* **3** to take something away from someone: *The king was divested of all his wealth and power.*

di·vest·ment /daɪˈvestmənt/ *n* [C,U] *technical* another word for DISINVESTMENT

di·vide¹ [S1] [W2] /dɪ̯ˈvaɪd/ *v*
1 [I,T] if something divides, or if you divide it, it separates into two or more parts: **divide sth into sth** *Scientists traditionally divide the oceans into zones.* | *The book is divided into six sections.* | [+into] *Here, the river divides into three channels.*
2 KEEP SEPARATE also **divide off** [T] to keep two areas separate from each other: *The Wall used to divide East and West Berlin.* | **divide sth from sth** *Only a thin curtain divided her cabin from his.*
3 SHARE also **divide up** [T] to separate something into parts and share them between people: **divide sth between/among sb/sth** *The money will be divided equally among the charities.*
4 SPEND TIME/ENERGY [T] if you divide your time, energy etc between different activities or places, you spend part of your time doing each activity or in each place: **divide sth between sth/sb** *She divides her time between New York and Paris.*
5 MATHEMATICS a) [T] to calculate how many times one number contains a smaller number; **→** multiply: **divide sth by sth** *If you divide 21 by 3, you get 7.* | *'What's six divided by three?' 'Two'.* **b)** [I] to be contained exactly in a number one or more times: [+into] *8 divides into 64.*
6 DISAGREE [T] to make people disagree so that they form groups with different opinions: *The issue of*

*cloning has **sharply divided** voters.*
7 divide and rule/conquer to defeat or control people by making them argue with each other instead of opposing you
8 divided loyalties a feeling you have when two people you like have argued and you are not sure which person you should support: *Divorce is an agony of divided loyalties for children.* —**divided** *adj*: *a deeply divided society* | *The committee was divided over the proposal.*

divide² *n* [C usually singular] **1** a strong difference between the beliefs or way of life of groups of people, that may make them hate each other: *The North/South divide is characteristic of Britain.* | **cultural/political/racial etc divide** *people on both sides of the political divide* **2** *AmE* a line of high ground between two river systems; ⊟ **watershed**

di‚vided 'highway *n* [C] *AmE* a main road with two lines of traffic travelling in each direction, separated by a piece of land; ⊟ **dual carriageway** *BrE*

div‧i‧dend [W3] /ˈdɪvɪˌdənd, -dend/ *n* [C]
1 a part of a company's profit that is divided among the people with SHARES in the company
2 *BrE* prize money offered in a national competition called the FOOTBALL POOLS which people can win by correctly guessing the results of football games
3 *technical* a number that is to be divided by another number
4 pay/bring dividends to be very useful and bring a lot of advantages, especially later in the future: *Good eating habits will pay dividends later on in life.*

di‧vid‧er /dɪˈvaɪdə $ -ər/ *n* [C] **1** something that divides something else into parts: *a room divider* | *alphabetical file dividers* **2** *AmE* a piece of land that separates traffic travelling in opposite directions on a main road; ⊟ **reservation** *BrE*: *Police saw his Mercedes speeding along the center divider.* **3 dividers** [plural] an instrument used for measuring or marking lines or angles, consisting of two pointed pieces of metal joined together at the top → see picture at MATHEMATICS

di'viding ‚line *n* [C usually singular] the difference between two similar things: [+**between**] *What's the dividing line between normal drinking and addiction?*

div‧i‧na‧tion /ˌdɪvɪˈneɪʃən/ *n* [U] the ability to say what will happen in the future, or the act of doing this

di‧vine¹ /dɪˈvaɪn/ *adj* **1** coming from or relating to God or a god: **divine intervention/providence/revelation/guidance etc** *faith in divine providence* | *divine power* | *divine love* **2** *old-fashioned* very pleasant or good

divine² *v* **1** [T] *literary* to discover or guess something: **divine that** *Somehow, the children had divined that he was lying.* **2** [I] to search for underground water or minerals using a Y-shaped stick: *a divining rod* (=the stick used for this) —**diviner** *n* [C]

di‚vine 'right *n* [singular] **1** the right given to a king or queen by God to rule a country, that in former times could not be opposed **2** *informal* the right to do what you want without having to ask permission: *Being my wife doesn't **give you the divine right to** read my mail.*

div‧ing /ˈdaɪvɪŋ/ *n* [U] **1** the sport of swimming under water using special equipment to help you breathe: *We **went diving** on the coral reef.* **2** the activity of jumping into water with your head and arms first → SCUBA DIVING

diving bell *n* [C] a metal container that is open at the bottom and filled with air under pressure, in which people can work under water

diving board *n* [C] a board above the edge of a SWIMMING POOL which people DIVE from → see picture at SPORTS CENTRE

di‧vin‧i‧ty /dɪˈvɪnɪti/ *n plural* **divinities 1** [U] *AmE* the study of God and religious beliefs; ⊟ **theology** *BrE*: *a graduate of Harvard divinity school* **2** [U] the quality or state of being a god **3** [C] a god

di‧vis‧i‧ble /dɪˈvɪzɪbəl/ *adj* [not before noun] able to be divided, for example by a number: [+**by**] *6 is divisible by 3.* | [+**into**] *The nervous system is divisible into three parts.*

di‧vi‧sion [S3] [W1] /dɪˈvɪʒən/ *n*
1 SEPARATING [C,U] the act of separating something into two or more different parts, or the way these parts are separated or shared: **division of sth between/among/into sth** *the division of words into syllables* | *the traditional division of labour* (=the way that particular tasks are shared) *between husband and wife*
2 DISAGREEMENT [C,U] disagreement among the members of a group that makes them form smaller opposing groups: **division between/within/among sth** *Can he heal the **deep divisions** among Republican ranks?* | **racial/class/gender etc division** *The old class divisions had begun to break down.* | *The Army was plagued by **internal divisions**.*
3 MATHEMATICS [U] the process of finding out how many times one number is contained in another; → **multiplication, long division**
4 PART OF AN ORGANIZATION [C] a group that does a particular job within a large organization: *the Computer Services Division*
5 MILITARY [C] a large military group: *a tank division*
6 SPORT [C] one of the groups of teams that a sports competition is divided into, often based on the number of games they have won: **the Premier/First/Second/Third/Fourth Division** *a second-division club*
7 IN PARLIAMENT [C] a process in which members of the British parliament vote for something by dividing into groups: *MPs **forced a division** on the bill.* | *Some members supported the opposition in the **division lobbies** (=the rooms where the vote takes place).*

di‧vi‧sion‧al /dɪˈvɪʒənəl/ *adj* [only before noun] relating to one of the parts into which a large organization, group etc is divided: *divisional headquarters*

di‧vi‧sive /dɪˈvaɪsɪv/ *adj* causing a lot of disagreement between people: *The strike was a **divisive issue** in the community.* | **socially/economically/politically etc divisive** *socially divisive policies*

di‧vi‧sor /dɪˈvaɪzə $ -ər/ *n* [C] *technical* the number by which another number is to be divided

di‧vorce¹ [S3] /dɪˈvɔːs $ -ɔːrs/ *n*
1 [C,U] the legal ending of a marriage; → **separation**: *Why doesn't she **get a divorce**? | In Britain, one in three marriages **ends in divorce**.* | **file/sue/petition for divorce** (=start the legal divorce process) *His wife had threatened to **start divorce proceedings**.* | *the rise in the **divorce rate** | She received the house as part of the **divorce settlement** (=the amount of money, property etc each person receives in a divorce case).* | *The Act extended the **grounds** (=legal reasons) **for divorce**.*
2 [C usually singular] *formal* the fact of separating two related things: [+**between**] *the divorce between theory and method*

divorce² *v* **1** [I,T] if someone divorces their husband or wife, or if two people divorce, they legally end their marriage; → **separate**: *David's parents divorced when he was six.* | *My father threatened to divorce her.* **2** [T] *formal* to separate two ideas, subjects etc completely: **divorce sth from sth** *It is difficult to divorce sport from politics.* **3** [T] to stop being involved in an activity, organization, situation etc: **divorce yourself from sth** *Our society has divorced itself from religion.*

di‧vorced /dɪˈvɔːst $ -ɔːrst/ *adj* **1** no longer married to your wife or husband: *Are you married, single, or divorced?* | *a divorced woman* | [+**from**] *Anne is divorced from Simon's father.* | *My parents are **getting divorced**.* **2** separate from and not connected in any way to an idea, subject etc: [+**from**] *His ideas are completely **divorced from reality**.*

D

di·vor·cée /dɪ¹ˌvɔːˈsiː: $ dɪ²ˌvɔːrˈseɪ/ n [C]   **1** *AmE old-fashioned* a woman who is divorced   **2** *BrE* a man or woman who is divorced

div·ot /ˈdɪvət/ n [C] a small piece of earth and grass that you dig out accidentally while playing a sport such as GOLF or POLO

di·vulge /daɪˈvʌldʒ, dɪ¹-/ v [T] *formal* to give someone information that should be secret; ◨ **reveal**: divulge information/secrets/details etc (to sb) *It is not company policy to divulge personal details of employees.* | **divulge that** *Clare divulged that she was recovering from a nervous breakdown.* | **divulge what/where etc** *The Pentagon refused to divulge what type of plane it was.*

div·vy[1] /ˈdɪvi/ n *plural* **divvies** [C] *BrE informal* a stupid person

divvy[2] v **divvied, divvying, divvies**
  divvy sth ⇔ **up** *phr v informal* to share something between several people: *We can divvy up the profits between us.*

Di·wa·li /dɪˈwɑːli/ also **Di·va·li** /-ˈvɑːli/ n [U] a Hindu FESTIVAL that is celebrated in the autumn

Dix·ie /ˈdɪksi/ n *informal* the southern states of the US that fought against the northern states in the Civil War

Dix·ie·land /ˈdɪksilænd/ n [U] a type of traditional JAZZ music

DIY /ˌdiː aɪ ˈwaɪ/ n [U] *BrE* **do-it-yourself** the activity of making or repairing things yourself instead of buying them or paying someone else to do it

diz·zy /ˈdɪzi/ adj   **1** feeling unable to stand steadily, for example because you are looking down from a high place or because you are ill: *The heat and the champagne made him feel dizzy.* | *She started to suffer from dizzy spells* (=a short period when you feel dizzy). | [+with] *Ruth felt dizzy with relief.*   **2 the dizzy heights (of sth)** an important position – used humorously: *Naomi had reached the dizzy heights of manageress.*   **3** *informal* stupid and forgetful: *a dizzy blonde*   **4** very busy and exciting: *Hong Kong buzzes from dawn to dusk at a dizzy pace.* —**dizziness** n [U]: *headaches, dizziness, and vomiting* —**dizzily** adv

diz·zy·ing /ˈdɪzi-ɪŋ/ adj making you feel dizzy: *The riverbank rushed towards her with dizzying speed.*

DJ /ˌdiː ˈdʒeɪ◂/ n [C] **disc jockey** someone who plays records on a radio show or in a club where you can dance

djinn /dʒɪn/ n [C] a magical person in Islamic stories who has special powers; ◨ **genie**

DNA /ˌdiː en ˈeɪ◂/ n [U] **deoxyribonucleic acid** a substance that carries GENETIC information in the cells of the body: **DNA testing/profiling/fingerprinting/evidence etc** (=processes that examine DNA samples to help discover who has committed a crime) *The men will undergo voluntary DNA testing of their saliva.*

DNA 'profiling n [U] the act of examining the DNA found where a crime has happened and the DNA of people who may have committed the crime, in order to find out who is responsible

do[1] S1 W1 /duː/ *auxiliary verb past tense* **did** /dɪd/ *past participle* **done** /dʌn/ *third person singular* **does** /dəz; *strong* dʌz/
  1 a) used with another verb to form questions or negatives: *Do you like bananas?* | *I don't feel like going out tonight.* | *Ian didn't answer.* | *Where do you live?* | *Doesn't Rosie look wonderful!* | *Don't listen to her!* **b)** *spoken* used to form QUESTION TAGS (=short questions that you add to the end of statements): *You know Tony, don't you?* | *She didn't understand, did she?*
  2 used instead of repeating a verb that has already been used: *'Will Kay come?' 'She may do.'* | *So now you know as much as I do.* | *'You forgot all about it.' 'No, I didn't.'* | *'I want to go home.' 'So do I.'* | *I didn't believe the story and neither did he.*
  3 used to emphasize the main verb in a sentence: *Do be careful.* | *You do look nice in that hat.* | *I do think she's behaved badly.* | *'You should have warned me.' 'But I did warn you.'* | *He owns, or did own* (=emphasizing past tense), *a yacht.*
  4 *spoken* used when politely offering someone something: *Do have another sandwich.*

do[2] S1 W1 *v past tense* **did**, *past participle* **done**, *third person singular* **does**
  1 ACTION/ACTIVITY [T] to perform an action or activity: *Have you done your homework yet?* | *You need to do more exercise.* | *It's a pleasure doing business with you.* | *I didn't know what to do.* | *All he does is sit in front of the television all day.* | **do something/nothing/anything etc** *We should do something to help him.* | *It all happened so quickly that I couldn't do anything about it.* | *bored teenagers with nothing to do* | **do the laundry/ironing/dishes etc** *It's your turn to do the dishes.*
  2 SUCCEED [I] used to ask or talk about how successful someone is at something: **do well/badly** *Students are under considerable pressure to do well.* | **how sb/sth is doing (with/in sth)** *You should get promoted after about a year, depending on how you're doing.* | *How's he doing in trying to give up smoking?*
  3 HAVE AN EFFECT [T] to have a particular effect on something or someone: *The scandal will do serious damage to his reputation.* | *This will do nothing for* (=will not improve) *Jamie's confidence.* | *The colour does nothing for her* (=does not improve her appearance). | *Getting the job has done a lot for* (=had a good effect on) *her self-esteem.* | *A week in the countryside will do you good* (=make you feel better). | *Exercise can do wonders for* (=have a very good effect on) *body, mind, and spirit.*
  4 JOB [T] to have a particular job: *What do you want to do after you leave school?* | *What do you do for a living* (=as your job)? | *I don't like her but she's very good at what she does.*
  5 ENOUGH/ACCEPTABLE [I,T not in progressive] used to say that something will be enough or be acceptable: *We don't have a lot of wine for the party, but it should just about do.* | *I can't find my black shoes so these will have to do.* | *A few sandwiches will do me for lunch.* | *It won't do* (=it is not acceptable) *to say that the situation couldn't have been avoided.*
  6 what sb will do for sth used to talk about what arrangements someone has made to get something they need: *What will you do for money if you leave your job?* | *I'm not sure what we'll do for transport yet.*
  7 what is sb/sth doing? *spoken* used to ask why someone or something is in a particular place or doing a particular thing, especially when you are surprised or annoyed by this: *What's my coat doing on the floor?* | *What are you doing walking around at this time of night?* | *What on earth do you think you're doing?*
  8 do your/sb's hair/nails/make-up etc to do something that improves your appearance or someone else's appearance: *It must take her ages to do her make-up in the mornings.* | *Who does your hair?*
  9 SPEND TIME [T] *informal* to spend a period of time doing something: *She did a year backpacking around the world.* | *Oh yes, I certainly did my time in the army* (=spent time in the army).
  10 STUDY [T not in passive] *BrE* to study a particular subject in a school or university: *I did French for five years.*
  11 COOK [T] to cook a particular type of food: *I was thinking of doing a casserole tonight.*
  12 do 10 miles/20 kms etc to achieve a particular distance, speed etc: *We did 300 kilometres on the first day.* | *The car can do 120 mph.*
  13 PROVIDE A SERVICE [T] to provide a particular service or sell a particular product: *They do interior and exterior design.* | *We don't do food after two o'clock.*
  14 PERFORM A PLAY [T] to perform a particular play, show etc: *We did 'Guys and Dolls' last year.*
  15 DECORATE [T] to paint or decorate a room, house etc: *How are you going to do your living room?*
  16 BEHAVE [I] to behave in a particular way: *In the*

evenings students are free to **do as they please** (=do what they want). | *I wish you'd* **do as you're told** (=do what you are told to do)*!*

17 sb doesn't do nice/funny/sensible etc *spoken informal* used humorously to say that someone cannot or does not behave in a particular way: *Sensible? I don't do sensible.*

18 COPY BEHAVIOUR [T] to copy someone's behaviour or the way they talk, especially in order to entertain people: *He does a brilliant George Bush* (=copies him in a very funny way).

19 do lunch/do a movie etc *informal* to have lunch, go to see a film etc with someone: *Let's do lunch next week.*

20 DRUGS [T] *informal* to use an illegal drug: *He says he's never done hard drugs in his life.*

21 VISIT [T] to visit a particular place, especially as a tourist: *Let's do the Eiffel Tower today.*

22 that'll do! *spoken* used to tell a child to stop behaving badly

23 that does it! *spoken* used to say angrily that you will not accept a situation any more: *Right, that does it! I'm not going to listen to any more of this!*

24 that should do it *also* **that ought to do it** *spoken* used to say that you will have finished doing something if you just do one more thing: *I've just got to prepare the dessert and that should do it.*

25 do it *informal* to have sex – used humorously or when you want to avoid saying the word 'sex'

26 sb would do well to do sth used to advise someone that they should do something: *Most people would do well to reduce the amount of salt in their diet.*

27 PUNISH [T] *BrE spoken* to punish or attack someone → be/get done at DONE² (8)

28 DECEIVE [T] *BrE informal* to deceive or trick someone → be done at DONE² (7)

29 what's doing ...? *spoken* used to ask what is happening: *What's doing at your place tonight?*

30 do or die used to say that someone is determined to do something very brave or dangerous even if they die attempting it

31 how (are) you doing? *spoken* used when you meet someone to ask them if they are well, happy etc: *Hi Bob, how you doing?*

32 what can I do you for? *spoken* used humorously to ask someone how you can help them, especially when you are trying to sell them something

33 do well by sb to treat someone well: *His relations always did pretty well by him.* → DOING → DONE²; → do your bit at BIT² (8); → how do you do at HOW (11); → nothing doing at NOTHING¹ (14); → do sb proud at PROUD (5); → do sth to death at DEATH (4); → CAN-DO

do away with sb/sth *phr v*
1 to get rid of something or stop using it: *People thought that the use of robots would do away with boring low-paid factory jobs.*
2 *informal* to kill someone

do sb ⇔ **down** *phr v*
to criticize someone, especially in an unfair way: *I know you don't like him, but there's no need to keep doing him down in front of the boss.*

do for sb/sth *phr v BrE informal*
to kill someone or harm something or someone very badly: *Working 100 hours a week nearly did for me.* → be done for at DONE² (3)

do sb **in** *phr v informal*
1 to kill someone: *He was planning to do himself in.*
2 to make someone feel extremely tired: *That walk really did me in.* → done in at DONE² (4)

do sth ⇔ **out** *phr v BrE*
1 to make a room look nice by decorating it: *The room was beautifully done out in pastel colours.*
2 *informal* to clean a room or cupboard thoroughly

do sb **out of** sth *phr v informal*
to dishonestly stop someone from getting or keeping something, especially something they have a right to have: *Are you trying to do me out of a job?*

do sb/sth **over** *phr v*
1 do sth ⇔ over *especially AmE* to make a place look attractive by decorating it: *The whole apartment had*

been done over in an Art Deco style.
2 *AmE* to do something again, especially because you did it wrong the first time: *If you make too many mistakes, you'll have to do it over.*
3 do sth ⇔ over *BrE spoken informal* to steal things from a building
4 *BrE spoken informal* to attack and injure someone

do up *phr v*
1 to fasten something, or to be fastened in a particular way: **do sth** ⇔ **up** *Do up your coat or you'll get cold.* | *a skirt which does up at the back*
2 do sth ⇔ up to repair an old building or car, or to improve its appearance: *They did up an old cottage in the Scottish Highlands.*
3 do sth ⇔ up to decorate something in a particular way: *The apartment was done up in Viennese style.*
4 do sth ⇔ up to wrap something in paper
5 do yourself up to make yourself look neat and attractive: *Sue spent ages doing herself up.*

do with sth *phr v*
1 could do with sth *spoken* to need or want something: *I could have done with some help this morning.*
2 have/be to do with sb/sth to be about something, be related to something, or be involved with something: *Their conversation had been largely to do with work.* | *I'm sorry about the accident, but it's* **nothing to do with** *me* (=I am not involved in any way). | *This question* **doesn't have anything to do with** *the main topic of the survey.* | *I'm sure her problems* **have something to do with** *what happened when she was a child.*
3 what to do with yourself how to spend your time: *She didn't know what to do with herself after she retired.*
4 what sb should do with sth/what to do with sth etc used to ask or talk about how someone should deal with something: *What shall I do with these papers?* | *I wouldn't know what to do with a newborn baby.*
5 what has sb done with sth? *spoken* used to ask where someone has put something: *What have you done with the remote for the TV?*
6 what is sb doing with sth? used to ask why someone has something: *What are you doing with my diary?*
7 I can't be doing with sth *BrE spoken* used to say that you are annoyed by something and do not want to have to think about it: *I can't be doing with all this right now.*

do without *phr v*
1 do without (sth) to live or do something without a particular thing: *I don't have any sugar so you'll have to do without.* | *You can do without a carpet but you've got to have somewhere to sit.*
2 can do without sth used to say that something is annoying you or causing you problems: *You can do without all that hassle.* | *Those are the type of stupid remarks I can do without.*

do³ *n plural* **dos** *or* **do's** [C] **1** *informal* a party or other social event: *We're having a do to celebrate his 30th birthday.* **2** dos and don'ts *also* **do's and don'ts** things that you should and should not do in a particular situation: *The booklet lists the dos and don'ts of caring for dogs.* **3** *AmE informal* a HAIRDO

do⁴, doh /dəʊ $ doʊ/ *n* [singular, U] the first note in the musical SCALE according to the SOL-FA system

D.O.A. /ˌdiː əʊ 'eɪ $ -oʊ-/ *adj* **dead on arrival** used when someone is said by a doctor to be dead when they are brought to a hospital

do·a·ble /'duːəbəl/ *adj* [not before noun] *spoken informal* able to be done or completed: *We've got to think first whether this plan is doable.*

d.o.b. the written abbreviation of *date of birth*

doc /dɒk $ dɑːk/ *n* [C] *informal* a doctor

do·cent /dəʊ'sent $ doʊ-/ *n* [C] *AmE* someone who guides visitors through a MUSEUM, church etc

do·cile /'dəʊsaɪl $ 'dɑːsəl/ *adj* quiet and easily controlled: *Labradors are gentle, docile dogs.* —**docilely** *adv* —**docility** /dəʊ'sɪləti $ dɑː-/ *n* [U]

dock¹ /dɒk $ dɑːk/ *n* **1** [C] a place in a port where ships are loaded, unloaded, or repaired; → **dry dock:** *A crowd was waiting at the dock to greet them.* | **in dock** *The ship is in dock for repairs.* | **2 the docks** [plural] the area of a port where there are docks: *James arrived at the docks expecting to see a luxury liner.* **3** [C] *AmE* a JETTY **4 the dock** the part of a law court where the person who is charged with a crime stands: **in the dock** *Three defendants stood in the dock.* **5 in the dock** *especially BrE* thought to have done something dishonest, harmful, or wrong: *These chemicals remain in the dock until we have more scientific evidence.* **6** [C,U] a plant with thick green leaves that grows wild in Britain: *a dock leaf*

dock² *v*
1 SHIPS [I,T] if a ship docks, or if the captain docks it, it sails into a dock so that it can unload: [+at/in] *We docked at Rangoon the next morning.*
2 dock sb's **wages/pay/salary** to reduce the amount of money you pay someone as a punishment: *The company has threatened to dock the officers' pay.*
3 COMPUTERS [T] to connect two computers using an electrical wire: **dock sth to/into/with sth** *Users can dock a laptop to their desktop setup.*
4 SPACECRAFT [I + with] if two spacecraft dock, they join together in space
5 ANIMALS [T] to cut an animal's tail short

dock·er /ˈdɒkə $ ˈdɑːkər/ *n* [C] *BrE* someone whose job is loading and unloading ships; ▤ **longshoreman** *AmE*

dock·et /ˈdɒkɪt $ ˈdɑː-/ *n* [C] **1** *technical* a short document giving details of goods that are delivered **2** *AmE law* a list of legal cases that will be heard in a particular court **3** *AmE* a list of things that are to be discussed or done; ▤ **agenda:** *What's on the docket for tomorrow's meeting?*

dock·land /ˈdɒklənd, -lænd $ ˈdɑːk-/ also **docklands** *n* [U] the area of a port where there are docks: *a dockland development*

dock·side /ˈdɒksaɪd $ ˈdɑːk-/ *n* [singular] the edge of the land that is next to the water in a port

dock·work·er /ˈdɒkˌwɜːkə $ ˈdɑːkˌwɜːrkər/ *n* [C] someone whose job is loading and unloading ships

dock·yard /ˈdɒkjɑːd $ ˈdɑːkjɑːrd/ *n* [C] a place where ships are repaired or built

doc·tor¹ S2 W1 /ˈdɒktə $ ˈdɑːktər/ *n* [C]
1 written abbreviation *Dr* someone who is trained to treat people who are ill: *She was treated by her local doctor.* | *You should consult your family doctor for further advice.* | **go to/see/visit a doctor** *I'd like to make an appointment to see Dr Pugh.* | *His doctor prescribed him some antibiotics.* (=ordered drugs for him by writing an official note) | **the doctor's** *informal* (=the place where your doctor works) *'Where's Sandy today?' 'I think she's at the doctor's.'* | *a busy doctor with over 2000 patients on her list* → see picture at OCCUPATION
2 someone who holds the highest level of degree given by a university: *a Doctor of Law*

WORD FOCUS: DOCTOR
similar words: **physician** *especially AmE,* **GP** *BrE,* **consultant, registrar**
a doctor who does operations: **surgeon**
a doctor who treats mental illnesses: **psychiatrist, psychotherapist, shrink** *informal*
a doctor who treats people's teeth: **dentist, orthodontist**
a doctor who treats animals: **vet, veterinarian** *especially AmE*
someone who is training to be a doctor: **medical student, intern** *AmE*
the place where you go to see your doctor: **surgery** *BrE,* **office** *AmE*

doctor² *v* [T] **1** to dishonestly change something in order to gain an advantage: *He had doctored his passport to pass her off as his daughter.* | *There are concerns that some players have been doctoring the ball.* **2** to add something harmful to food or drink: *Paul sus-*

pected that his drink had been doctored. **3** to remove part of the sex organs of an animal to prevent it from having babies; ▤ **neuter:** *You should have your cat doctored.* **4** to give someone medical treatment, especially when you are not a doctor: *Bill doctored the horses with a strong-smelling ointment.*

doc·tor·al /ˈdɒktərəl $ ˈdɑːk-/ *adj* [only before noun] done as part of work for the university degree of doctor: *a doctoral thesis*

doc·tor·ate /ˈdɒktərɪt $ ˈdɑːk-/ *n* [C] a university degree of the highest level: [+in] *She received her doctorate in history in 1998.*

Doctor of Phi'losophy *n* [C] a PHD

doc·tri·naire /ˌdɒktrɪˈneə $ ˌdɑːktrɪˈner/ *adj formal* certain that your beliefs or opinions are correct and unwilling to change them: *The party followed an increasingly doctrinaire course.*

doc·trine /ˈdɒktrɪn $ ˈdɑːk-/ *n* **1** [C,U] a set of beliefs that form an important part of a religion or system of ideas: *traditional doctrines of divine power* | *Marxist doctrine* **2 Doctrine** [C] *AmE* a formal statement by a government about their future plans: *the announcement of the Truman Doctrine* —**doctrinal** /dɒkˈtraɪnl $ ˈdɑːktrɪnl/ *adj*

doc·u·dra·ma /ˈdɒkjʊˌdrɑːmə $ ˈdɑːkjuˌdrɑːmə, -ˌdræmə/ *n* [C] a film on television which shows real events in the form of a story

doc·u·ment¹ W2 /ˈdɒkjəmənt $ ˈdɑːk-/ *n* [C]
1 a piece of paper that has official information on it
2 a piece of written work that is stored on a computer; → **file**

doc·u·ment² /ˈdɒkjəment $ ˈdɑːk-/ *v* [T] **1** to write about something, film it, or take photographs of it, in order to record information about it: **document how/what etc** *His research will document how the debt crisis occurred.* **2** to support an opinion, argument etc with recorded facts: **be well/extensively/poorly etc documented** *It is well documented that men die younger than women.*

doc·u·men·ta·rist /ˌdɒkjʊˈmentərɪst $ ˌdɑːk-/ *n* [C] someone whose job is to make documentaries

doc·u·men·ta·ry¹ /ˌdɒkjʊˈmentəri $ ˌdɑːk-/ *n plural* **documentaries** [C] a film or television or a radio programme that gives detailed information about a particular subject: [+on/about] *A local film crew is making a documentary about volcanoes.*

documentary² *adj* [only before noun] **1** documentary films, programmes, photographs etc give or show information about a particular subject: *documentary films* **2** consisting of or written on documents: **documentary evidence/proof** *One of the most useful sources of documentary evidence is maps.*

doc·u·men·ta·tion /ˌdɒkjəmənˈteɪʃən, -men- $ ˌdɑːk-/ *n* **1** [U] official documents, reports etc that are used to prove that something is true or correct: *Applicants must provide supporting documentation.* **2** [C,U] the act of recording information in writing, on film etc: [+of] *a careful documentation of the costs*

doc·u·soap /ˈdɒkjʊsəʊp $ ˈdɑːkjʊsoʊp/ *n* [C] *BrE* a television programme that shows what happens in the daily lives of real people

dod·der·ing /ˈdɒdərɪŋ $ ˈdɑː-/ *adj* shaking slightly and walking with difficulty because of old age: *a doddering old man* —**dodder** *v* [I]

dod·dery /ˈdɒdəri $ ˈdɑː-/ *adj BrE* weak and not able to do things easily because of old age: *Some of the patients are a bit doddery.*

dod·dle /ˈdɒdl $ ˈdɑːdl/ *n* **be a doddle** *BrE informal* to be very easy: *The exam was a doddle!*

dodge¹ /dɒdʒ $ dɑːdʒ/ *v* **1** [I,T] to move quickly to avoid someone or something: *He ran across the courtyard, dodging a storm of bullets.* | [+between/through/into etc] *Helen clutched Edward's arm as they dodged through the traffic.* **2** [T] to deliberately avoid discussing something or doing something; ▤ **evade:**

dodge an issue/question *Senator O'Brian skillfully dodged the crucial question.* | **draft dodging** (=when someone avoids an order to join the army, navy etc)

dodge² *n* [C] *informal* something dishonest that is done to avoid a rule or law: *Businesses are investing in tree plantations as a **tax dodge** (=a way of avoiding paying tax).

dodg·em car /'dɒdʒəm ˌkɑː $ 'dɑːdʒəm ˌkɑːr/ *n* [C] *BrE* a car used on the dodgems; ▯ **bumper car** *AmE*

dodg·ems /'dɒdʒəmz $ 'dɑː-/ *n BrE* **the dodgems** a ride at a FUNFAIR in which people drive small electric cars in an enclosed area, trying to hit other cars

dodg·er /'dɒdʒə $ 'dɑːdʒər/ *n* [C] **tax/draft dodger** someone who uses dishonest methods to avoid paying taxes or serving in the army, navy etc

dodg·y /'dɒdʒi $ 'dɑː-/ *adj BrE informal* **1** not working properly or not in good condition: *Norton Disk Doctor can perform miracles on a dodgy hard disk.* | *Simon was rushed to hospital after eating what must have been dodgy prawns.* **2** seeming to be false, dishonest, or not to be trusted: *One girl thought the men looked dodgy.* | *dodgy share dealings* **3** involving risk or danger: *There were a few dodgy moments.*

do·do /'dəʊdəʊ $ 'doʊdoʊ/ *n plural* **dodos** [C] **1** a large bird that was unable to fly and no longer exists **2** *AmE informal* a stupid person **3 (as) dead as a dodo** completely dead or inactive, or no longer used

doe /dəʊ $ doʊ/ *n* [C] **1** a female rabbit or DEER; → **buck**, **stag** **2 doe eyes** large attractive eyes: *a pretty girl with big brown doe eyes*

do·er /'duːə $ -ər/ *n* [C] *informal* someone who does things instead of just thinking or talking about them: *Dole is a doer, not a talker.*

does /dəz; *strong* dʌz/ the third person singular of the present tense of DO

does·n't /'dʌzənt/ the short form of 'does not'

doff /dɒf $ dɑːf, dɔːf/ *v* [T] *old-fashioned* to remove the hat you are wearing as a sign of respect

dog¹ S1 W1 /dɒg $ dɒːg/ *n* [C]
1 ANIMAL a common animal with four legs, fur, and a tail. Dogs are kept as pets or trained to guard places, find drugs etc; → **puppy**: *I could hear a dog barking.* | *a pack of **stray dogs*** | *What **breed of dog** is she?*
2 MALE ANIMAL a male dog, FOX, or WOLF; → **bitch**
3 WOMAN *informal not polite* an offensive word meaning an unattractive woman
4 dog eat dog when people compete against each other and will do anything to get what they want: *It's a **dog eat dog world** out there.*
5 be going to the dogs *informal* if a country or organization is going to the dogs, it is getting worse and will be difficult to improve
6 DISHONEST *informal not polite* an offensive word for an unpleasant or dishonest man: *You **dirty dog!***
7 a dog's life *spoken* a life that is difficult and unpleasant, with very little pleasure: *His wife's a nag who **leads him a dog's life** (=makes his life unpleasant).*
8 make a dog's breakfast of sth *BrE informal* to do something very badly: *The orchestra made a complete dog's breakfast of the fourth movement.*
9 a dog's dinner *BrE informal* something that is meant to be impressive or fashionable but that other people think is not: *She was **dressed up like a dog's dinner**.*
10 not have a dog's chance *BrE informal* to have no chance of being successful
11 every dog has its/his day used to say that even the most unimportant person has a time in their life when they are successful and important
12 like a dog with two tails *BrE informal* very pleased and happy because something good has happened
13 FEET **dogs** [plural] *AmE informal* feet: *Boy, my dogs really hurt.*
14 POOR QUALITY *AmE informal* something that is of very poor quality
15 dog and pony show *AmE* an event that has only been organized so that people can admire it and think that it is impressive, not for any real purpose

16 be the dog's bollocks *BrE informal* a very rude expression used to say that something is very good
17 the dogs *BrE informal* a sports event consisting of a series of races for dogs
18 put on the dog *AmE old-fashioned* to pretend to be richer, more clever etc than you really are → **the hair of the dog** at HAIR (13); → SHAGGY DOG STORY; → **as sick as a dog** at SICK¹ (1); → **let sleeping dogs lie** at SLEEP¹ (6); → **the tail wagging the dog** at TAIL¹ (11); → TOP DOG; → **treat someone like a dog** at TREAT¹ (1)

dog² *v* **dogged**, **dogging** [T] **1** if a problem or bad luck dogs you, it causes trouble for a long time: *He has been dogged by injury all season.* **2** to follow close behind someone

dog·cart /'dɒgkɑːt $ 'dɒːgkɑːrt/ *n* [C] **1** a vehicle with two wheels and seats that is pulled by a horse **2** a small vehicle pulled by a dog

dog·catch·er /'dɒgˌkætʃə $ 'dɒːgˌkætʃər/ *n* [C] a DOG WARDEN

'dog ˌcollar *n* [C] **1** a piece of thin leather that you fasten around a dog's neck **2** *informal* a stiff round white collar worn by priests

'dog days *n* [plural] **1** the hottest days of the year **2** a period of time when something is not successful: *Few opera houses survived the dog days of the 1980s.*

dog-eared /'dɒg ɪəd $ 'dɒːg ɪrd/ *adj* dog-eared books or papers have been used so much that the corners are turned over or torn: *a dog-eared novel*

'dog-end *n* [C] *BrE* the small part of a cigarette left after it has been smoked

dog·fight /'dɒgfaɪt $ 'dɒːg-/ *n* [C] **1** an organized fight between dogs **2** a fight between armed aircraft

dog·fish /'dɒgfɪʃ $ 'dɒːg-/ *n plural* **dogfish** or **dogfishes** [C] a type of small SHARK

dog·ged /'dɒgɪd $ 'dɒː-/ *adj* dogged behaviour shows that you are very determined to continue doing something: *a **dogged determination** to succeed* —**doggedly** *adv* —**doggedness** *n* [U]

dog·ge·rel /'dɒgərəl $ 'dɒː-, 'dɑː-/ *n* [U] poetry that is silly or funny and not intended to be serious

dog·gie /'dɒgi $ 'dɒː-/ *n* [C] another spelling of DOGGY

dog·gone /'dɒgɒn $ 'dɒːgɒːn/ *v* **doggone it** *AmE spoken old-fashioned* used when you are slightly annoyed about something —**doggone** *adj, adv*: *What are those doggone kids doing in my yard?*

dog·gy¹, **doggie** /'dɒgi $ 'dɒːgi/ *n plural* **doggies** [C] a dog – used by or to children

doggy² *adj informal* **1** like or relating to dogs: *doggy noises from the shed* **2 doggy style/fashion** a way of having sex in which a man has a position behind his partner

'doggy bag *n* [C] a small bag for taking home the food that is left over from a meal in a restaurant

'doggy ˌpaddle *n* [singular,U] DOG PADDLE

dog·house /'dɒghaʊs $ 'dɒːg-/ *n* **1 be in the doghouse** *informal* to be in a situation in which someone is annoyed with you because of something you have done **2** [C] *AmE* a small house outdoors for a dog to sleep in

dog·leg /'dɒgleg $ 'dɒːg-/ *n* [C] a place where a road, path etc suddenly changes direction

dog·ma /'dɒgmə $ 'dɒːgmə, 'dɑːgmə/ *n* [C,U] a set of firm beliefs held by a group of people who expect other people to accept these beliefs without thinking about them: **religious/political/ideological etc dogma** *the rejection of political dogma*

dog·mat·ic /dɒgˈmætɪk $ dɒːg-, dɑːg-/ *adj* someone who is dogmatic is completely certain of their beliefs and expects other people to accept them without arguing: *Her staff find her bossy and dogmatic.* —**dogmatically** /-kli/ *adv* —**dogmatism**

D

/'dɒgmətɪzəm $ 'dɔːg-, 'dɑːg-/ n [U]: *the narrow dogmatism of the past* —**dogmatist** n [C]

do-good·er /du: 'gʊdə $ -ər/ n [C] someone who helps people who are in bad situations, but who is annoying because their help is not needed – used to show disapproval: *I've got very little time for interfering do-gooders.*

'dog ,paddle also **doggy paddle** n [singular,U] a simple way of swimming by moving your legs and arms up and down

dogs·bod·y /'dɒgz,bɒdi $ 'dɔːgz,bɑːdi/ n plural **dogsbodies** [C] BrE someone who has to do all the small boring jobs that no one else wants to do: *I spent the summer helping out as a general dogsbody on the local paper.*

dog·sled /'dɒgsled $ 'dɔːg-/ n [C] a SLEDGE (=a vehicle that travels over snow) that is pulled by dogs

'dog tag n [C] AmE a small piece of metal that soldiers wear on a chain around their necks with their name, blood type etc written on it

dog-'tired adj informal very tired

'dog ,warden n [C] BrE someone whose job is to collect dogs without owners

doh, do /dəʊ $ doʊ/ n [singular, U] the first or eighth note in the SOL-FA musical SCALE

d'oh /dəʊ, dɜː $ dʌ, doʊ/ interjection spoken used humorously when you have just realized that you have done or said something stupid

DoH /,diː əʊ 'eɪtʃ $ -oʊ-/ n BrE **the DoH** the abbreviation of the *Department of Health*

doi·ly /'dɔɪli/ n plural **doilies** [C] a circle of paper or cloth with a pattern of holes in it that you put under things to protect the surface below, or for decoration

do·ing /'duːɪŋ/ n **1 be sb's (own) doing** if something bad is someone's doing, they did or caused it: *If you fall into this trap, it will be all your own doing.* **2 take some doing** informal to be hard work: *We had to be on the parade ground for 5.30 a.m. and that took some doing.* **3 doings** [plural] events, activities etc that someone is involved in: *Supper is a family get-together, where the doings of the day are talked about.*

,do-it-your'self n [U] DIY

dol·drums /'dɒldrəmz $ 'doʊl-, 'dɑːl-, 'dɔːl-/ n [plural] informal **a)** if an industry, company, activity etc is in the doldrums, it is not doing well or developing: **in the doldrums** *The property market has been in the doldrums for months.* | *Recent economic doldrums have damaged the rural west.* **b)** if you are in the doldrums, you are feeling sad: *Fay is in the doldrums today.*

dole¹ /dəʊl $ doʊl/ n [U] informal **1** BrE money given by the government in Britain to people who are unemployed: **be/go on the dole** (=be unemployed and receiving money from the government) *Too many young people are still on the dole.* | *The number claiming dole went up by 3,500.* **2 the dole queue/dole queues** BrE the number of people who are unemployed and claiming money from the government, or a line of people waiting to claim this money each week: *As two factories closed today, 500 people joined the dole queue.* | *Meanwhile, dole queues lengthened.* **3 the dole** AmE money given by the government in the US to people who need financial help; ▣ **welfare**: **on the dole** *people on the public dole*

dole² v

dole sth ⇔ **out** phr v informal to give something such as money, food, advice etc to more than one person: [+to] *Vera was doling out candy to all the kids.*

dole·ful /'dəʊlfəl $ 'doʊl-/ adj formal very sad: *a doleful song about lost love* —**dolefully** adv

doll¹ [S3] /dɒl $ dɑːl, dɔːl/ n **1** [C] a child's toy that looks like a small person or baby: *a small wooden doll* **2** [C] old-fashioned informal a word meaning an attractive young woman – now usually considered offensive:

Hey, doll, why don't you get me a cup of coffee? **3** [singular] AmE informal a very nice person: *Thanks, you're a doll.*

doll² v informal

doll yourself **up** phr v informal if a woman dolls herself up, she puts on attractive clothes and MAKE-UP, especially before going out to a party, club etc: *Maggie was in her room, dolling herself up.* | **be/get dolled up (for sth)** *The girls were all dolled up for a party.*

dol·lar [S1] [W3] /'dɒlə $ 'dɑːlər/ n [C] **1** the standard unit of money in the US, Canada, Australia, and some other countries, divided into 100 CENTS; symbol $: *It cost three dollars.* | *a ten-dollar bill* **2 the dollar** the value of US money in relation to the money of other countries: *The pound has risen against the dollar* (=increased in value in relation to the dollar). → **you can bet your bottom dollar** at BET¹ (4) → **feel/look like a million dollars** at MILLION (4)

dol·lar·i·za·tion /,dɒləraɪ'zeɪʃən $ -rə-/ n [U] technical a situation in which countries outside the US want to use the dollar rather than their own country's money

,dollars-and-'cents adj [only before noun] AmE financial: *From a dollars-and-cents point of view, this idea just won't work.*

doll·house /'dɒlhaʊs $ 'dɑːl-, 'dɔːl-/ n [C] AmE a DOLL'S HOUSE

dol·lop /'dɒləp $ 'dɑː-/ n [C] informal **1** a small amount of soft food, usually dropped from a spoon [+of] *a dollop of thick cream* **2** an amount of something: [+of] *a big dollop of luck* —**dollop** v [T]

'doll's house n [C] BrE a small toy house with furniture inside; ▣ **dollhouse** AmE

dol·ly /'dɒli $ 'dɑːli, 'dɔːli/ n plural **dollies** [C] **1** a DOLL - used especially by children **2** technical a flat frame on wheels used for moving heavy objects

'dolly bird n [C] BrE old-fashioned informal a pretty young woman, especially one who wears fashionable clothes

dol·men /'dɒlmen, -mən $ 'doʊlmən, 'dɒːl-, 'dɑːl-/ n [C] technical two or more large upright stones supporting a large flat piece of stone, built in ancient times

dol·our BrE; **dolor** AmE /'dɒlə $ 'doʊlər/ n [U] literary great sadness

dol·phin /'dɒlfᵻn $ 'dɑːl-, 'dɔːl-/ n [C] a very intelligent sea animal like a fish with a long grey pointed nose

'dolphin-safe adj dolphin-safe fish is caught in a way that does not harm or kill dolphins: *dolphin-safe tuna*

dolt /dəʊlt $ doʊlt/ n [C] old-fashioned a silly or stupid person —**doltish** adj

-dom /dəm/ suffix **1** [in U nouns] the state of being something: *freedom* | *boredom* **2** [in C nouns] **a)** an area ruled in a particular way: *a kingdom* **b)** a particular rank: *a dukedom* → OFFICIALDOM

do·main /də'meɪn, dəʊ- $ də-, doʊ-/ n [C] formal **1** an area of activity, interest, or knowledge, especially one that a particular person, organization etc deals with: **outside/within the domain of sth/sb** *This problem is outside the domain of medical science.* | *Looking after the house was viewed as a woman's domain.* → PUBLIC DOMAIN **2** an area of land owned and controlled by one person or government, especially in the past: *the extent of the royal domain* **3** technical the set of possible quantities by which something can vary in mathematics **4** a domain name

do'main ,name n [C] the first part of a website's address, which usually begins with 'www.' and ends with '.com', '.org', '.uk', or other letters that show which country the website is from

dome /dəʊm $ doʊm/ n [C] **1** a round roof on a building **2** a shape or building like a ball cut in half

domed /dəʊmd $ doʊmd/ adj covered with a dome or shaped like a dome: *a high domed ceiling*

do·mes·tic¹ [W2] /də'mestɪk/ adj **1** relating to or happening in one particular country

and not involving any other countries: **domestic market/economy/demand** etc *the booming domestic economy* | *US foreign and domestic policy* | *our nation's domestic affairs* | *Domestic flights* (=flights that stay inside a particular country) *go from Terminal 1*.
2 [only before noun] relating to family relationships and life at home: *Unfortunately his domestic life wasn't very happy.* | **domestic tasks/chores/responsibilities** etc *Nowadays there is more sharing of domestic chores.* | *families that can afford domestic help* (=help with cleaning, washing etc) | *an organization that supports women facing domestic violence* (=violence in a family, especially from a husband to his wife)
3 used in people's homes: *a new tax on domestic fuel* | *domestic appliances such as washing machines*
4 someone who is domestic enjoys spending time at home and is good at cooking, cleaning etc: *No, I'm not very domestic.*
5 [only before noun] a domestic animal lives on a farm or in someone's home: *cats, dogs and other domestic pets* —**domestically** /-kli/ *adv*: *domestically produced coal*

domestic² *n* [C] **1** *old-fashioned* a servant who works in a large house **2** *BrE informal* a fight between members of a family in their home: *It sounded like the neighbours were having a bit of a domestic.*

do·mes·ti·cate /dəˈmestɪˌkeɪt/ *v* [T] to make an animal able to work for people or live with them as a pet; → **tame** —**domestication** /dəˌmestɪˈkeɪʃən/ *n* [U]

do·mes·ti·cat·ed /dəˈmestɪˌkeɪtɪd/ *adj* **1** domesticated animals are able to work for people or live with them as pets **2** someone who is domesticated enjoys spending time at home and doing work in the home: *Ray's very domesticated and even likes baking cakes.*

do·mes·tic·i·ty /ˌdəʊmeˈstɪsɪti $ ˌdoʊ-/ *n* [U] life at home with your family: *a scene of happy domesticity*

do,mestic 'partner *n* [C] *AmE* someone who you live with and have a sexual relationship with, but who you are not married to

do,mestic 'science *n* [U] *BrE old-fashioned* the study of cooking, sewing etc, taught as a subject at school; ▣ **home economics**

do,mestic 'service *n* [U] *formal* the work of a servant in a large house

dom·i·cile /ˈdɒmɪˌsaɪl $ ˈdɑː-, ˈdoʊ-/ *n* [C] *formal* the place where someone lives: *Military service entails frequent changes of domicile.*

dom·i·ciled /ˈdɒmɪˌsaɪld $ ˈdɑː-, ˈdoʊ-/ *adj formal* be domiciled in to live in a particular place

dom·i·cil·i·a·ry /ˌdɒmɪˈsɪliəri $ ˌdɑːmɪˈsɪlieri, ˌdoʊ-/ *adj* [only before noun] *formal* **domiciliary services/care/visits** etc services, care etc in someone's home

dom·i·nance /ˈdɒmɪnəns $ ˈdɑː-/ *n* [U] the fact of being more powerful, more important, or more noticeable than other people or things; → **dominate**: [+of] *the continuing dominance of the army in Uganda* | **political/economic/cultural** etc **dominance** *the economic and political dominance of Western countries* | [+over] *television's dominance over other media*

dom·i·nant¹ W3 /ˈdɒmɪnənt $ ˈdɑː-/ *adj*
1 more powerful, important, or noticeable than other people or things; → **dominate**: *The dominant male gorilla is the largest in the group.* | *Japan became dominant in the mass market during the 1980s.* | *its dominant position within the group*
2 controlling or trying to control other people or things – used to show disapproval; ▣ **domineering**: *a dominant personality*
3 *technical* a dominant GENE causes a child to have a particular physical feature or illness, even if it has been passed on from only one parent; → **recessive**: *The disease is under the control of a single dominant gene.*

dominant² *n* [singular] *technical* the fifth note of a musical SCALE of eight notes

dom·i·nate W3 /ˈdɒmɪˌneɪt $ ˈdɑː-/ *v*
1 [I,T] to control someone or something or to have more importance than other people or things: *The industry is dominated by five multinational companies.* | *New Orleans dominated throughout the game.* | *Her loud voice totally dominated the conversation.* | *Education issues dominated the election campaign.*
2 [T] to be larger and more noticeable than anything else in a place: *The cathedral dominates the city.* —**dominating** *adj*: *his dominating characteristic* —**domination** /ˌdɒmɪˈneɪʃən $ ˌdɑː-/ *n* [U]: *the desire for political domination*

dom·i·na·trix /ˌdɒmɪˈneɪtrɪks $ ˌdɑː-/ *n* [C] a woman who is the stronger partner in a SADOMASOCHISTIC sexual relationship

dom·i·neer·ing /ˌdɒmɪˈnɪərɪŋ◂ $ ˌdɑːmɪˈnɪr-/ *adj* someone who is domineering tries to control other people without considering their feelings or ideas – used to show disapproval: *a domineering mother* —**domineer** *v* [I]

Do·min·i·can /dəˈmɪnɪkən/ *n* [C] a member of a Christian religious group who leads a holy life —**Dominican** *adj*

do·min·ion /dəˈmɪnjən/ *n* **1** [U] *literary* the power or right to rule people or control something: **have/hold dominion over sb/sth** *Alexander the Great held dominion over a vast area.* **2** [C] *formal* the land owned or controlled by one person or a government: *the king's dominions* **3** also **Dominion** [C] *old-fashioned* a country belonging to the British EMPIRE or COMMONWEALTH; → **colony, protectorate**: *opinion both at home and in the dominions*

dom·i·no /ˈdɒmɪˌnəʊ $ ˈdɑːmɪˌnoʊ/ *n plural* **dominoes** **1** [C] one of a set of small flat pieces of wood, plastic etc, with different numbers of spots, used for playing a game **2 dominoes** [U] the game played using dominoes **3 domino effect** a situation in which one event or action causes several other things to happen one after the other

don¹ /dɒn $ dɑːn/ *n* [C] **1** *BrE* a university teacher, especially one who teaches at the universities of Oxford or Cambridge **2** *informal* the leader of a Mafia organization

don² *v* **donned, donning** [T] *literary* to put on a hat, coat etc

do·nate /dəʊˈneɪt $ ˈdoʊneɪt/ *v* [I,T] **1** to give something, especially money, to a person or an organization in order to help them: **donate sth to sb/sth** *Last year he donated $1,000 to cancer research.* **2** to allow some blood or a body organ to be removed from your body so that it can be used in a hospital to help someone who is ill or injured: *people who volunteer to donate blood*

do·na·tion /dəʊˈneɪʃən $ doʊ-/ *n* **1** [C] something, especially money, that you give to a person or an organization in order to help them: [+to/from] *Would you like to* **make a donation** (=give money) *to our charity appeal?* | *There have been generous donations from EEC funds.* **2** [U] the act of giving something, especially money, to help a person or an organization: [+of] *the donation of a quarter of a million pounds* | **blood/organ donation**

done¹ /dʌn/ the past participle of DO

done² *adj* [not before noun, no comparative]
1 FINISHED finished or completed; ▣ **finished**: *The job's nearly done.* | **sb is done (with sth)** *someone has finished doing or using something* *As soon as I'm done, I'll give you a call.* | *Are you done with this magazine?* | *I'll be glad when the exams are* **over and done with** (=completely finished).
2 COOKED cooked enough to eat; → **overdone, underdone**: *Is the pasta done yet?*
3 be done for *informal* to be in serious trouble or likely to fail: *If we get caught, we're done for.*
4 done in *informal* extremely tired: *Sit down – you look done in.*

5 be done also be the done thing *BrE* to be socially acceptable: *Showing affection in public just isn't done in Japan.*

6 be done with it; have done with it *BrE* used to tell someone to stop thinking about or trying to decide something because they have already done this enough: *Just buy it and have done with it!*

7 be done *BrE informal* to be deceived or cheated: *If you paid £50, you were done, mate!*

8 be/get done *BrE informal* to be caught by the police for doing something illegal, but usually not too serious: [+for] *I got done for speeding last night.*

9 a done deal *informal* an agreement that has been made and cannot be changed: *The merger is far from a done deal.* → be hard done by at HARD² (6)

done³ *interjection* used to agree to and accept the conditions of a deal: *'I'll give you $90 for it.' 'Done!'*

Don Juan /ˌdɒn ˈhwɑːn, -ˈwɑːn, -ˈdʒuːən $ ˌdɑːn-/ n [C] a man who is good at persuading women to have sex with him

don·key /ˈdɒŋki $ ˈdɑːŋki/ n **1** [C] a grey or brown animal like a horse, but smaller and with long ears **2** donkey's years *BrE spoken* a very long time: **for donkey's years** *I've had this jacket for donkey's years.*

donkey jacket n [C] *BrE* a short thick coat, usually very dark blue, with a piece of leather or plastic across the shoulders

don·key·work /ˈdɒŋkiwɜːk $ ˈdɑːŋkiwɜːrk/ n [U] *BrE* the hard boring work that is part of a job or project: *Why do I always have to do the donkeywork?*

don·nish /ˈdɒnɪʃ $ ˈdɑːnɪʃ/ *adj BrE* clever, serious, and more interested in ideas than real life

do·nor /ˈdəʊnə $ ˈdoʊnər/ n [C] **1** a person, group etc that gives something, especially money, to help an organization or country: *We urgently need more assistance from donor countries* (=countries that give money, food etc to help in poor countries or disaster areas). | *An anonymous donor* (=whose name is unknown) *has given £500 towards the restoration fund.* **2** someone who gives blood or a body organ so that it can be used in the medical treatment of someone else: *Some patients die before a suitable donor is found.* | **blood/organ/kidney etc donor** *the shortage of blood donors*

donor card n [C] a card that you carry to show that when you die a doctor can take parts of your body to use in the medical treatment of someone else

do-nothing *adj* [only before noun] *BrE informal* lazy or unwilling to make any changes, especially in politics: *the do-nothing government of the last few years*

don't /dəʊnt $ doʊnt/ **1** the short form of 'do not': *Don't worry!* | *You know him, don't you?* → dos and don'ts at DO³ (2) **2** *spoken* an incorrect short form of 'does not': *She don't like it.*

do·nut /ˈduːnʌt $ ˈdoʊ-/ n *especially AmE* another spelling of DOUGHNUT

doo·dah /ˈduːdɑː/ *BrE*; **doo·dad** /ˈduːdæd/ *AmE* n [C] *informal* a small object whose name you have forgotten or do not know: *Where's the doodah to turn off the TV?*

doo·dle /ˈduːdl/ v [I] to draw shapes, lines, or patterns without really thinking about what you are doing: *Brad was doodling on a sheet of paper.* —**doodle** n [C]

doo·hick·ey /ˈduːˌhɪki/ n [C] *AmE informal* a small object whose name you have forgotten or do not know, especially a part of a machine

doo·lal·ly /duːˈlæli/ *adj BrE spoken* crazy

doom¹ /duːm/ v [T usually passive] to make someone or something certain to fail, die, be destroyed etc: **be doomed to failure/defeat/extinction etc** *Many species are doomed to extinction.* | *The plan was doomed from the start.* | **be doomed to do sth** *We are all doomed to die in the end.* —**doomed** *adj*: *passengers on the doomed flight*

doom² n [U] something very bad that is going to happen, or the fact that it is going to happen: *A sense of impending doom* (=coming very soon) *gripped her.* | **sense/feeling of doom** | **spell doom for sth** (=mean that something will be unable to continue or survive) *The recession spelled doom for many small businesses.* | *Thousands of soldiers met their doom* (=died) *on this very field.* | **doom and gloom/gloom and doom** (=when there seems to be no hope for the future) *Despite these poor figures, it's not all doom and gloom.*

doom-laden *adj BrE* saying or making you feel that something very bad is going to happen soon: *documentaries full of doom-laden predictions*

doom·say·er /ˈduːmˌseɪə $ -ər/ *especially AmE* also **doomster** *BrE* n [C] someone who says that bad things are going to happen

Dooms·day /ˈduːmzdeɪ/ n [U] **1** till/until Doomsday *informal* for a very long time: *You could wait till Doomsday and he'd never show up.* **2** the last day of the Earth's existence, when everything will be destroyed according to some religions: **doomsday scenario** (=a description of a very bad and hopeless situation)

doom·ster /ˈduːmstə $ -ər/ n [C] *BrE informal* a DOOMSAYER

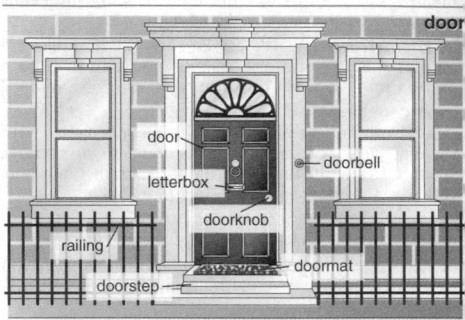

door

door | doorbell | letterbox | doorknob | railing | doormat | doorstep

door S1 W1 /dɔː $ dɔːr/ n [C]

1 the large flat piece of wood, glass etc that you open and close when you go into or out of a building, room, vehicle etc, or when you open a cupboard; → gate **open/close/shut the door** *Could you open the door for me?* | **the door swung/flew/burst etc open** *The door flew open and Ruth stormed in.* | **slam the door** (=shut it loudly, usually because you are angry) | **front/back/side door** (=at the front, back etc of a house) *Is the back door shut?* | **the main door** (=at the front entrance) *of the cathedral* | **kitchen/bathroom/bedroom etc door** *Don't forget to lock the garage door.* | *Can you answer the door* (=open it after someone has knocked or pressed the bell)? | **get the door** *AmE* (=open or close it for someone) *Here, let me get the door for you.* | **knock on/at the door** *Knock on the door and see if they're home.* | **cupboard/fridge etc door** *Mary slid back the closet door.* | **door handle/knob** *brass door handles* → FIRE DOOR, FRENCH DOORS, REVOLVING DOOR (1), SLIDING DOOR, STAGE DOOR, SWING DOOR, TRAPDOOR; → see picture at CAR

2 the space made by an open door; ≡ doorway: **in/out (of)/through the door** *Rick turned and ran out of the door.* | *I glanced through the open door.*

3 at the door if someone is at the door, they are waiting for you to open the door of a building so they can come inside: *There's somebody at the front door.*

4 out of doors outside; ≡ outdoors: *I prefer working out of doors.*

5 show/see sb to the door to take someone to the main way out of a building: *My secretary will show you to the door.*

6 two/three etc doors away/down/up used to say how many houses or buildings there are between your house, office etc and another building: [+from] *Patrick lived two doors away from me.*

7 (from) door to door a) *especially BrE* from one place to another: *How long is the journey, door to door?* **b)** going

to each house in a street or area to sell something, collect money, or ask for votes: *Joe sold vacuum cleaners door to door for years.* → DOOR-TO-DOOR
8 be on the door to work at the entrance to a theatre, club etc, collecting tickets
9 shut/close the door on sth to make something impossible: *The accident shut the door on her ballet career.* → **at death's door** at DEATH (7); → **behind closed doors** at CLOSED (5); → **get in through the back door** at BACK DOOR (2); → **lay sth at sb's door** at LAY² (19); → NEXT DOOR; → **open doors (for sb)** at OPEN² (16); → OPEN-DOOR POLICY; → **open the door to sth** at OPEN² (16); → **show sb the door** at SHOW¹ (20)

door·bell /'dɔːbel $ 'dɔːr-/ n [C] a button outside a house that makes a sound when you push it so that people inside know you are there: *ring the doorbell* (=push the button); → see picture at DOOR

do-or-'die adj [only before noun] very determined: *a do-or-die attitude*

door·jamb /'dɔːdʒæm $ 'dɔːr-/ n [C] especially AmE a DOORPOST

door·keep·er /'dɔːˌkiːpə $ 'dɔːrˌkiːpər/ n [C] someone who guards the main door of a large building and lets people in and out

door·knob /'dɔːnɒb $ 'dɔːrnɑːb/ n [C] a round handle that you turn to open a door → see picture at DOOR

door·knock·er /'dɔːˌnɒkə $ 'dɔːrˌnɑːkər/, also **knocker** n [C] a heavy metal ring or bar on a door that you use to knock with

door·man /'dɔːmæn, -mən $ 'dɔːr-/ n plural **doormen** /-men, mɒn/ [C] a man who usually wears a uniform and works in a hotel, club etc letting people into the building, helping people find taxis etc; → **porter**

door·mat /'dɔːmæt $ 'dɔːr-/ n [C] **1** a piece of material inside or outside a door for you to clean your shoes on → see picture at DOOR **2** informal someone who lets other people treat them badly and never complains: *Don't let him treat you like a doormat.*

door·nail /'dɔːneɪl $ 'dɔːr-/ n **(as) dead as a doornail** informal completely dead

door·post /'dɔːpəʊst $ 'dɔːrpoʊst/ n [C] one of two upright posts on either side of a doorway

door prize n [C] AmE a prize given to someone who has the winning number on their ticket for a show, dance etc

door·step¹ /'dɔːstep $ 'dɔːr-/ n [C] **1** a step just outside a door to a house or building: **on the doorstep** *He stood on the doorstep, straightening his tie.* | *the front doorstep;* → see picture at DOOR **2 on sb's/the doorstep a)** very near someone's home: *Wow! You've got the beach right on your doorstep!* **b)** at someone's home: *I got a bit of a shock when he just turned up on the doorstep.* **3** BrE informal a very thick piece of bread

doorstep² v **doorstepped, doorstepping** [I,T] BrE if politicians or JOURNALISTS doorstep people, they visit people at their homes in order to get votes or information – often used to show disapproval: *Journalists had doorstepped the couple and their neighbours.*

door·stop /'dɔːstɒp $ 'dɔːrstɑːp/ / also **door·stop·per** /-ˌstɒpə $ -ˌstɑːpər/ BrE n [C] **1** something you put under or against a door to keep it open **2** a rubber object fastened to a wall to stop a door hitting it when it opens

door-to-'door adj [only before noun] visiting each house in a street or area, usually to sell something, collect money, or ask for votes: *a door-to-door salesman* → **door to door** at DOOR (7)

door·way /'dɔːweɪ $ 'dɔːr-/ n [C] the space where a door opens into a room or building: **in the doorway** *There was Paolo, standing in the doorway.*

doo·zy /'duːzi/ n plural **doozies** also **doozie** AmE informal something that is extremely good, bad, strange, big etc: *I've heard lies before, but that one was a real doozy!*

dope¹ /dəʊp $ doʊp/ n informal **1** [U] a drug that is not legal, especially MARIJUANA: *Jeff used to smoke dope all the time.* **2** [C] spoken a stupid person; ◫ **idiot**: *What a dope!* **3 dope test** a test given to people or animals taking part in a sport, to see if they have taken or have been given a drug to improve their performance **4 the dope (on sb/sth)** new information about someone or something, especially information that not many people know: *What's the dope on the new guy?*

dope² v [T usually passive] **1** also **dope sb up** to give a person or an animal a drug, often in their food or drink, to make them unconscious: *The girl had been doped and kidnapped.* **2** to give an animal a drug that makes it perform better in a race **3 be doped (up)** BrE to be unable to think or behave normally, because of the effects of drugs or alcohol: [+on] *She was doped up on drink and drugs most of the time.*

dope³ adj AmE informal very good: *Check out our dope new album.*

dope·head /'dəʊphed $ 'doʊp-/ n [C] informal someone who takes a lot of illegal drugs

dop·ey also **dopy** BrE /'dəʊpi $ 'doʊpi/ adj informal **1** thinking or reacting slowly, as if you have taken a drug: *She's still a little dopey from the anaesthetic.* **2** slightly stupid: *a dopey grin*

dop·ing /'dəʊpɪŋ $ 'doʊ-/ n [U] the practice of using drugs to improve performance in a sport: **doping scandal/ban/test** etc **doping offences**

dop·pel·gang·er /'dɒpəlgæŋə, -geŋ- $ 'dɑːpəlgæŋər/ n [C] **1** sb's doppelganger someone who looks exactly like someone else; ◫ **double 2** an imaginary spirit that looks exactly like a living person

do·py /'dəʊpi $ 'doʊpi/ adj a British spelling of DOPEY

Dor·ic /'dɒrɪk $ 'dɔː-, 'dɑː-/ adj in the oldest and simplest of the Greek building styles; → **Ionic**: *a Doric column*

dork /dɔːk $ dɔːrk/ n [C] informal someone who you think is or looks stupid —**dorky** adj

dorm /dɔːm $ dɔːrm/ n [C] informal a DORMITORY

dor·mant /'dɔːmənt $ 'dɔːr-/ adj not active or not growing at the present time but able to be active later; ◪ **active**: **lie/remain dormant** *The seeds remain dormant until the spring.* | *a huge dormant volcano* —**dormancy** n [U]

dor·mer /'dɔːmə $ 'dɔːrmər/, **'dormer ,window** BrE n [C] a window built into a roof, so that it sticks out from the roof → SKYLIGHT

dor·mi·to·ry /'dɔːmɪtəri $ 'dɔːrmɪ̩tɔːri/ n plural **dormitories** [C] **1** especially BrE a large room for several people to sleep in, for example in a BOARDING SCHOOL or HOSTEL **2** AmE a large building at a college or university where students live; ◫ **hall of residence** BrE

'dormitory ,town n [C] BrE a town that is near a city with more work opportunities, so that many people who live there travel to work in the city every day; ◫ **bedroom community/suburb** AmE

dor·mouse /'dɔːmaʊs $ 'dɔːr-/ n plural **dormice** [C] a small European mouse with a long furry tail

dor·sal /'dɔːsəl $ 'dɔːr-/ adj [only before noun] on or relating to the back of an animal or fish: *a shark's dorsal fin*

do·ry /'dɔːri/ n plural **dories 1** [C] a rowing boat that has a flat bottom and is used for fishing **2** [C,U] a flat sea fish that can be eaten, or the flesh of this fish

DOS /dɒs $ dɑːs/ n [U] technical **Disk Operating System** software that is loaded onto a computer system to make all the different parts work together

dos·age /'dəʊsɪdʒ $ 'doʊ-/ n [C usually singular] the amount of a medicine or drug that you should take at one time, especially regularly: **high/low dosage** | [+of] *He was recommended a high dosage of morphine.* | **increase/reduce the dosage** | *The daily dosage is steadily reduced over several weeks.*

dose¹ /dəʊs $ doʊs/ *n* [C] **1** the amount of a medicine or a drug that you should take: [+of] *Never exceed the recommended dose of painkillers.* | **high/low dose** *Start with a low dose and increase it.* **2** an amount of something that you do or experience at one time, especially something unpleasant: **a bad/mild dose of flu** *BrE* (=making you feel very ill or only slightly ill) *Dave had a bad dose of flu.* | **lethal/fatal dose (of sth)** (=an amount that kills) *a lethal dose of radiation* | *I quite like Jamie **in small doses*** (=in limited amounts but not a lot or often). **3 like a dose of salts** *BrE informal* very quickly and easily: *The cleaners **went through** the house **like a dose of salts**.*

dose² *v* [T] also **dose up** to give someone medicine or a drug: **dose sb/yourself with sth** *Sumi dosed herself up with aspirin and went to bed.*

dosh /dɒʃ $ dɑːʃ/ *n* [U] *BrE informal* money

do-si-do /ˌdəʊ si ˈdəʊ $ ˌdoʊ si ˈdoʊ/ *n* [singular] an action in COUNTRY DANCING in which partners move around each other with their backs towards each other —**do-si-do** *v* [I]

doss¹ /dɒs $ dɑːs/ *v* [I] *BrE informal* also **doss down** to sleep somewhere that is not your usual place, or not a real bed: *I dossed down on the couch downstairs.*

doss around/about *phr v* to spend your time in a lazy way, doing very little: *We just dossed around all day Saturday.*

doss² *n BrE informal* **a doss** work that does not need much effort: *This job's a real doss.*

doss·er /ˈdɒsə $ ˈdɑːsər/ *n* [C] *BrE informal* **1** someone who has nowhere to live, and sleeps in the street or in cheap HOSTELS **2** someone who is very lazy

doss house *n* [C] *BrE informal* a place where people who have nowhere to live can stay cheaply; ⊟ **flop-house** *AmE*

dos·si·er /ˈdɒsieɪ $ ˈdɔːsjeɪ, ˈdɑː-/ *n* [C] a set of papers containing detailed, usually secret information about a person or subject; ⊟ **file**: [+on] *A firm of detectives produced a dossier on his activities.*

dot¹ [S2] /dɒt $ dɑːt/ *n* [C]
1 a small round mark or spot: *a pattern of dots on the screen*
2 on the dot *informal* exactly on time or at a particular time: *I'll be there on the dot.* | **at three o'clock/seven thirty etc on the dot** (=at exactly 3:00/7:30 etc) *Mr Green arrived at six **on the dot**.*
3 something that looks like a small spot because it is so far away: *The plane was just **a dot on the horizon**.*
4 a short sound or flash of light used when sending messages in MORSE CODE; → **dash**; → **the year dot** at YEAR (13)

dot² *v* dotted, dotting [T] **1** to mark something by putting a dot on it or above it: *She never dots her i's.* **2** [usually passive] if an area is dotted with things, there are a lot of them there but they are spread far apart: **be dotted with sth** *The lake was dotted with sailboats.* | **be dotted about/around sth** *The company has over 20 stores dotted around the country.* | *Brilliant red poppies dotted the field.* **3** to put a very small amount of something on a surface, especially in several places: **dot sth with sth** *Dot the apples with butter.* **4 dot the i's and cross the t's** *informal* to pay careful attention to all the details when you are finishing something

do·tage /ˈdəʊtɪdʒ $ ˈdoʊ-/ *n* **in your dotage** in your old age

dot-com, dot.com, dot com /ˌdɒt ˈkɒm $ ˌdɑːt ˈkɑːm/ *adj* [only before noun] *informal* relating to a person or company whose business is done using the Internet or involves the Internet: *a dot-com company* | *dot-com millionaires* —**dot-com** *n* [C]: *Several of the leading dot-coms saw their share prices slide yesterday.*

dote /dəʊt $ doʊt/ *v*
dote on/upon sb *phr v* to love someone very much, and show this by your actions: *Everyone doted on Sally,*

the only girl in the family. —**doting** *adj* [only before noun]: *a doting parent* —**dotingly** *adv*

doth /dʌθ/ *old use* a form of 'does'

'dot-matrix ˌprinter *n* [C] a machine connected to a computer that prints letters, numbers etc using many small DOTS

dotted 'line *n* [C] a series of printed or drawn DOTS that form a line → **sign on the dotted line** at SIGN² (4)

dot·ty /ˈdɒti $ ˈdɑːti/ *adj old-fashioned informal* **1** slightly crazy **2 dotty about sb/sth** liking or loving someone or something very much: *Gemma's dotty about horses.*

dou·ble¹ [S1] [W2] /ˈdʌbəl/ *adj* [usually before noun]
1 OF TWO PARTS consisting of two parts that are similar or exactly the same: *a double sink* | *a double wardrobe* | *the great double doors of the cathedral* | *Don't park your car on double yellow lines.*
2 TWO DIFFERENT USES combining or involving two things of the same type: *a double murder case* | *A lot of the jokes were based on **double meaning**.*
3 TWICE AS BIG twice as big, twice as much, or twice as many as usual: *a double whisky* | *The city was enclosed by walls of double thickness.*
4 FOR TWO PEOPLE made for two people or things to use; → **single**: *Do you need a double bed or two singles?* | *a double room* | *a double garage*
5 TWO LETTERS/NUMBERS *BrE spoken* used to say that a particular letter or number is repeated: *My name's Robbins with a double 'b'.* | *The number is 86 double 2* (=86922).
6 FLOWER a double flower has more than the usual number of PETALS → **DOUBLY**

double² *n*
1 TWICE THE SIZE [C,U] something that is twice as big, as much etc as usual or as something else: *Scotch and water, please – make it a double.* | *'They offered me £10,000.' 'I'll give you double.'*
2 ROOM [C] a room for two people in a hotel; → **single**: *A double costs $95 a night.*
3 TENNIS **doubles** [U] a game played between two pairs of players, especially in tennis; → **singles**: *the men's doubles* → **MIXED DOUBLES**
4 BASEBALL [C] a hit in baseball which allows the BATTER to reach second BASE: *Walker led the inning with a double.*
5 SIMILAR PERSON **sb's double** someone who looks very like someone else: *She's her mother's double.*
6 IN FILMS [C] an actor who takes the place of a more famous actor in a film, especially because the acting involves doing something dangerous: *I think they used a double in the shower scene.*
7 at the double *BrE*, **on the double** *AmE informal* very quickly and without any delay: *He was told to get back to Washington on the double.*
8 double or quits *BrE*; **double or nothing** *AmE* a situation in a game when you must do something that could either win you twice as much money or make you lose it all

double³ *v* **1** [I,T] to become twice as big or twice as much, or to make something twice as big or twice as much: **double in size/number/value etc** *Within two years the company had doubled in size.* | *The church has doubled its membership in the last five years.* | **double the size/number/amount etc (of sth)** *A promise was given to double the number of police on duty.* **2** [T] also **double over/up** to fold something in half: *Take a sheet of paper and double it over.* **3** [I] to hit the ball far enough to get to second BASE in a game of baseball

double as sb/sth *phr v* to have a second use, job, or purpose as a particular thing: *The school doubled as a hospital during the war.*

double back *phr v* to turn around and go back the way you have come: *The driver doubled back and headed for Howard Bay.* | **double back on yourself** *We kept getting lost and having to double back on ourselves*

double up *phr v* **1** also **double over** to suddenly bend over at the waist because you are laughing so much or are in pain: *Emilio doubled over, grabbing his* leg. | **be doubled up/over with laughter/pain** etc *Both the girls were doubled up with laughter.* **2** to share something, especially a bedroom: [+**with**] *You'll have to double up with Susie while your aunt is here.*

double⁴ *adv* **be bent double** to be bent over a long way: *The trees were almost bent double in the wind.* → see **double** at SEE¹ (29)

double⁵ *predeterminer* twice as big, twice as much, or twice as many: **double the amount/number/size** etc *We'll need double this amount for eight people.* | *The value of the house is double what it was.*

double act *n* [C] two actors, especially COMEDIANS, who perform together

double 'agent *n* [C] someone who finds out an enemy country's secrets for their own country but who also gives secrets to the enemy; → **spy**

double-'barrelled *BrE*; **double-barreled** *AmE* **1** a double-barrelled gun has two places where the bullets come out **2** *BrE* a double-barrelled family name has two parts **3** *AmE* very strong or using a lot of force: *a double-barreled attack*

double bass /ˌdʌbəl 'beɪs/ also **bass** *n* [C] a very large musical instrument shaped like a VIOLIN that the musician plays standing up

double 'bed *n* [C] a bed made for two people to sleep in → see picture at BED

double 'bill *n* [C] a cinema, theatre, concert etc performance in which you can see two films, plays etc, one after the other

double 'bind *n* [C usually singular] a situation in which any choice you make will have bad results

double-'blind *adj technical* a double-blind scientific test or study compares two groups in which neither the scientists nor the people being studied know which group is being tested and which group is not

double 'bluff *n* [C] an attempt to deceive someone by telling them the truth, hoping that they will think you are lying

double 'boiler *n* [C] a pot for cooking food, consisting of one pan resting on top of another pan with hot water in it

double-'book *v* [I,T] to promise the same seat in a theatre, on a plane etc to more than one person by mistake —**double-booking** *n* [U]

double-'breasted *adj* a double-breasted jacket, coat etc has two sets of buttons; → **single-breasted**

double-'check *v* [I,T] to check something again so that you are completely sure it is correct, safe etc

double 'chin *n* [C] a fold of loose skin under someone's chin that looks like a second chin

double-'click *v* [I,T] to press a button on a computer mouse twice in order to send an instruction to the computer

double 'cream *n* [U] *BrE* very thick cream; → **single cream**

double-'cross *v* [T] to cheat someone, especially after you have agreed to do something dishonest with them —**double cross** *n* [C] —**double-crosser** *n* [C]

double 'date *n* [C] *old-fashioned* an occasion when two COUPLES meet to go to a film, restaurant etc together —**double-date** *v* [I,T]

double 'dealer *n* [C] *BrE informal* someone who deceives other people —**double dealing** *n* [U]

double-deck·er /ˌdʌbəl 'dekə◂ $ -ər◂/ *n* [C] **1** a bus with two levels; → **single-decker 2** a sandwich made with three pieces of bread and two layers of food —**double-decker** *adj* [only before noun]

double-'digit *adj* [only before noun] *especially AmE* relating to the numbers 10 to 99; ◧ **double-figure** *BrE*: *double-digit inflation*

double 'digits *n* [plural] *AmE* the numbers from 10 to 99; ◧ **double figures**: *Sam's team scored in the double digits in nine out of ten games.*

double-'dip *v* [I] *AmE* to get money from two places at once, usually in a way that is not legal or not fair

double-'Dutch *n* [U] **1** *BrE informal* speech or writing that you cannot understand; ◧ **nonsense 2** *AmE* a game in which one child jumps over two long ropes that are being swung around by other children

double 'duty *n* **do double duty** to do more than one job or be useful for more than one thing at the same time: [+**as**] *The sofa does double duty as a guest bed.*

double-'edged *adj* **1 a double-edged sword/ weapon** something that seems to be good, but that can have a bad effect: *Being famous is often a double-edged sword.* **2** having two different parts: *a double-edged attack on global warming* **3** a double-edged remark has two possible meanings, one of which is not very nice: *It sounded like a double-edged comment.* **4** with two cutting edges: *a double-edged knife*

double en·ten·dre /ˌduːblɒn'tɒndrə $ -blɑːn'tɑːn-/ *n* [C] a word or phrase that may be understood in two different ways, one of which is often sexual

double 'fault *n* [C] two mistakes, one after another, when you are SERVING in tennis, which make you lose a point

double 'feature *n* [C] *AmE* **1** a cinema performance in which two films are shown one after the other; ◧ **double bill** *BrE* **2** a video with two films on it

double-'figure *adj* [only before noun] *BrE* relating to the numbers 10 to 99; ◧ **double-digit** *AmE*: *Almost all leading shares had double-figure gains.*

double 'figures *n* [plural] the numbers from 10 to 99; ◧ **double digits** *AmE*: **in double figures** *King's was the only other score in double figures.* | **approach/reach/go into** etc **double figures** *The death toll is thought to have reached double figures.*

double 'first *n* [C usually singular] a British university degree in which a student reaches the highest standard in two subjects

double 'glazing *n* [U] *BrE* glass on a window or door in two separate sheets with a space between them, used to keep noise out and heat in —**double-glaze** *v* [T]

double-'header *n* [C] two baseball games played one after the other

double 'helix *n* [C] *technical* a shape consisting of two parallel SPIRALS that twist around the same centre, found especially in the structure of DNA

double in'demnity *n* [U] *AmE law* a feature of a life insurance POLICY that allows double the value of the contract to be paid in the case of death by accident

double 'jeopardy *n* [U] *law* when someone is taken to court a second time for the same crime, in some unusual situations

double-'jointed *adj* able to move the joints in your fingers, arms etc backwards as well as forwards

double 'life *n* [C] if someone lives a double life, they deceive people by having two separate homes, families, or sets of activities, one of which they keep secret: **lead/live a double life** *Marje had no idea that her husband was leading a double life with another woman.*

double 'negative *n* [C] two negative words used in one sentence when only one is needed in correct English grammar, for example in the sentence 'I don't want nobody to help me!'

double-'park *v* [I,T] to leave a vehicle on a road beside another vehicle that is already parked there

double 'play *n* [C] the action of making two runners in a game of baseball have to leave the field by throwing the ball quickly from one BASE to another before the runners reach either one

double 'quick *adv BrE informal* as quickly as possible: *Call an ambulance double quick!* —**double-quick** *adj* [only before noun]: *Lunch was produced in double-quick time.*

double-'sided *adj* something such as tape or paper that is double-sided has something on both surfaces: *Stick down the edge of the carpet with double-sided sticky tape.*

doub·le·speak /'dʌbəl,spiːk/ n [U] BrE speech that is complicated and can have more than one meaning, sometimes used deliberately to deceive or confuse people; ◨ **double-talk**

double 'standard n [C] a rule, principle etc that is unfair because it treats one group of people more severely than another in the same situation

doub·let /'dʌblət/ n [C] a man's tight jacket, worn in Europe from about 1400 to the middle 1600s

double 'take n [C] **do a double take** to look at someone or something again because you are very surprised by what you saw or heard

'double-talk n [U] speech that is complicated and can have more than one meaning, sometimes used deliberately to deceive or confuse people; ◨ **double-speak** BrE: legal double-talk

doub·le·think /'dʌbəl,θɪŋk/ n [U] BrE a dishonest belief in two opposing ideas at the same time

double 'time n [U] double pay given to someone when they work at a time when people do not normally work

'double-time adj, adv especially AmE very quick or as quickly as possible: Get upstairs and clean your room – double-time!

double 'vision n [U] a medical condition in which you see two objects instead of one all the time, for example after an accident

double 'whammy n [C] two bad things that happen together or one after the other: the double whammy of higher prices and more taxes

dou·bloon /dʌ'bluːn/ n [C] a gold coin used in the past in Spain and Spanish America

doub·ly /'dʌbli/ adv **1** [+ adj] much more than usual: Be doubly careful when driving in fog. **2** in two ways or for two reasons: You are doubly mistaken.

doubt¹ S1 W1 /daʊt/ n

1 [C,U] a feeling of being not sure whether something is true or right

have (your) doubts
have no doubts at all
raise doubts (=make people have doubts)
express/voice doubts (=say that you have doubts)
nagging/lingering doubt (=a doubt that does not go away)
serious/grave doubts
an element of doubt (=a slight doubt)
there is little/some/no doubt (that) (=used to talk about how certain you are about something)
not the slightest doubt (=no doubt at all)
without a shadow of a doubt (=with no doubt at all)
cast/throw doubt on sth (=make someone feel uncertain about something)

Ally was confident that we would be ready on time, but I **had my doubts**. | [+about] Elizabeth **had no doubts at all** about his ability to do the job. | The incident **raises doubts** about the safety of nuclear power. | The meeting will provide people with an opportunity to **voice** any **doubts** they may have about the proposals. | There was still one little **nagging doubt** at the back of his mind. | [+as to whether/what etc] Some government ministers had **serious doubts** as to whether the policy would work. | There is **an element of doubt** as to whether the deaths were accidental. | **There's no doubt** that one day a cure will be found. | **There is little doubt** he was the killer. | She knew, **without a shadow of a doubt**, that this was where she wanted to be. | The prosecution tried to **cast doubt on** her character as a witness.

2 no doubt used when you are saying that you think something is probably true: No doubt you'll have your own ideas. | She was a top student, **no doubt about it** (=it is certainly true).

3 if/when (you're) in doubt used when advising someone what to do if they are uncertain about something:

If in doubt, consult your doctor.
4 be in doubt if something is in doubt, it may not happen, continue, exist, or be true: The future of the peace talks is in doubt.
5 beyond doubt if something is beyond doubt, it is completely certain: The prosecution must prove **beyond reasonable doubt** that the accused is guilty of the crime. | **put the game/result/match beyond doubt** (=do something which makes it certain that a particular player or team will win a match) Ferdinand's second goal put the game beyond doubt.
6 without doubt used to emphasize an opinion: Sally was without doubt one of the finest swimmers in the school.
7 open to doubt something that is open to doubt has not been proved to be definitely true or real: The authenticity of the relics is open to doubt. → SELF-DOUBT; → give sb/sth the benefit of the doubt at BENEFIT¹ (4)

doubt² S2 v [T not in progressive]
1 to think that something may not be true or that it is unlikely: Kim never doubted his story. | **doubt (that)** doubt we'll ever see him again. | **doubt if/whether** You can complain, but I doubt if it'll make any difference. 'Do you think there'll be any tickets left?' ' **I doubt it** (= don't think so).'
2 to not trust or have confidence in someone: I never doubted myself. I always knew I could play tennis at this level. | She loved him, and had never doubted him. | I have no reason to **doubt** his **word** (=think that he is lying). —**doubter** n [C]

doubt·ful /'daʊtfəl/ adj **1** probably not true or not likely to happen: Prospects for a lasting peace remain doubtful. | **it is doubtful if/whether** It was doubtful whether the patient would survive the operation. | **it is doubtful that** It is doubtful that the missing airmen will ever be found. **2** not sure that something is true or right: 'Everything's going to be all right, you'll see. Jenny looked **doubtful**. | [+if/whether] I'm still doubtful whether I should accept this job. | **doubtful about (doing) sth** At first we were doubtful about employing Charlie. **3** unlikely to be successful: Already the whole scheme was looking increasingly doubtful. **4** probably not good; ◨ **dubious**: Here the tap water is of doubtful quality. —**doubtfully** adv

doubt·ing Thom·as /,daʊtɪŋ 'tɒməs $ -'tɑːm-/ n [singular] someone who does not always believe things until they have seen proof of them

doubt·less /'daʊtləs/ adv used when saying that something is almost certain to happen or be true: Doubtless there would be dozens of photographers waiting for her.

douche /duːʃ/ n [C usually singular] a mixture of water and something such as VINEGAR, that a woman puts into her VAGINA to wash it, or the object that she uses to do this —**douche** v [I,T]

dough /dəʊ $ doʊ/ n **1** [singular, U] a mixture of flour and water ready to be baked into bread, PASTRY etc → see picture at BREAD **2** [U] informal money

dough·nut /'dəʊnʌt $ 'doʊ-/ n [C] a small round cake often in the form of a ring → see picture at DESSERT

dough·ty /'daʊti/ adj [only before noun] literary brave and determined

dough·y /'dəʊi $ 'doʊi/ adj **1** looking and feeling like dough **2** doughy skin is pale and soft and looks unhealthy

dour /dʊə, 'daʊə $ daʊr, dʊr/ adj **1** serious, never smiling, and unfriendly **2** a dour place is one that is plain and dull, and where people do not have any fun —**dourly** adv

douse, dowse /daʊs/ v [T] **1** to stop a fire from burning by pouring water on it **2** [+ with/in] to cover something in water or other liquid

dove¹ /dʌv/ n [C] **1** a kind of small white PIGEON (=bird) often used as a sign of peace **2** someone in politics who prefers peace and discussion to war ◨ **hawk**

dove² /dəʊv $ doʊv/ AmE a past tense of DIVE

dove·cot, **dove·cote** /'dʌvkɒt $ -kɑːt/ *n* [C] a small house built for doves to live in

dove·tail¹ /'dʌvteɪl/ *v* **1** [I,T] to fit together perfectly or to make two plans, ideas etc fit together perfectly: [+with] *My vacation plans dovetail nicely with Joyce's.* **2** [T + together] to join two pieces of wood by means of dovetail joints

dovetail² also **,dovetail 'joint** *n* [C] a type of JOINT fastening two pieces of wood together

dov·ish /'dʌvɪʃ/ *adj* preferring peace and discussion to war; → **hawkish**

dow·a·ger /'daʊədʒə $ -ər/ *n* [C] **1** a woman from a high social class who has land or a title from her dead husband: *the dowager Duchess of Devonshire* **2** *informal* a respected and impressive old lady

dow·dy /'daʊdi/ *adj* **1** a dowdy woman is not attractive, because she wears dull and unfashionable clothes **2** dowdy things are dull, unattractive, and unfashionable: *a dowdy dress*

dow·el /'daʊəl/ *n* [C] a wooden pin for holding two pieces of wood, metal, or stone together

dow·el·ling /'daʊəlɪŋ/ *n* [U] wood in the shape of a round rod, cut up to make dowels

Dow Jones In·dex /,daʊ 'dʒəʊnz ,ɪndeks $ -'dʒəʊnz-/ also **,Dow 'Jones ,Average** *n* the Dow Jones Index a daily list of prices of shares on the American Stock Exchange, based on the daily average prices of 30 industrial shares; → **the FTSE Index**

down¹ S1 W1 /daʊn/ *adv, prep, adj*
1 TO A LOWER POSITION to or towards a lower place or position; ⮕ **up**: *David bent down to tie his shoelace.* | *Get down off the table.* | *Tears were streaming down my face.* | *The sun was going down and it would soon be dark.* | *They came running down the stairs.* | *She stood on a balcony looking down into the courtyard.* | *Glancing down the list of runners, I noticed a familiar name.* | *Her flowing black hair came down to her waist.* | *Ken fell asleep face down* (=with his face towards the ground) *on the couch.*
2 IN A LOWER PLACE in a lower place or position; ⮕ **up**: *We heard the sound of laughter down below.* | *The bathroom is down those stairs.* | *Halfway down the page, there was the item I was looking for.*
3 TO LIE/SIT into a sitting or lying position: *Please sit down.* | *I think I'll go and lie down for a while.*
4 ALONG at or to a place that is further along something such as a road or path: *A young man came hurrying down the street.* | *She looked down the road to see if anyone was coming.* | *There is a pleasant little cafe bar a hundred yards down the road.* | *The bus stop is a bit further down on the left-hand side.*
5 SOUTH in or towards the south; ⮕ **up**: *They drove all the way down from Boston to Miami.* | *They sailed down the east coast of Africa.* | *Now he's bought a villa down south.* | *a trip down Mexico way*
6 SOMEWHERE LOCAL at or to a place that is not far away: *She's just gone down to the shops.* | *I saw her down at the station this morning.*
7 RIVER away from the place where a river starts; ⮕ **up**: *Chunks of ice came floating down the river.*
8 FASTENED TO A SURFACE used with verbs that mean 'fasten' to show that something is fastened firmly to the surface or object below it: *The coffin lid had been nailed down.*
9 LESS at or towards a level or amount that is less; ⮕ **up**: *Keep your speed down.* | *House prices have come down in recent months.* | *Turn the radio down.* | [+to] *Sharif cut his report down to only three pages.*
10 LOSING losing to an opponent by a certain number of points: **two goals down/three points down etc** *Swindon were six points down at one stage.*
11 WRITTEN used with verbs that mean 'write' to show that you write something on paper or in a book: *I'll write down the address for you.* | *Start by jotting down a few ideas.* | *Let's put you down as self-employed.*
12 ON A LIST if you are down for something, your name is on a list of people who want to do something or

469   **down-**

are intended to do something: [+for] *Purvis is down for the 200 metre freestyle event.* | *We've already put his name down for nursery school.* | **down to do sth** *I've got you down to do the table decorations.*
13 TO LATER TIMES from an earlier time in history to a later time or to people who are born in later times: *a person whose words and actions have inspired millions of people down the centuries* | *This knowledge was handed down in the family from father to son.* | *The story has been passed down the generations for a thousand years.* | [+to] *traditions that have come down to us from medieval times*
14 PAID IMMEDIATELY paid to someone immediately: *A top quality freezer for only £20 down and £5 a week for a year.*
15 EVERY PART from top to bottom: *I want you to wash my car down.*
16 SWALLOWED in or into your stomach as a result of swallowing: *Meg's been very ill and can't keep her food down.* | *He gulped down the coffee.*
17 SAD unhappy or sad: *Andy's been feeling down lately.*
18 COMPUTER if a computer is down, it is not working; ⮕ **up**
19 be down to sb if an action or decision is down to you, it is your responsibility: *It's down to me to make sure that everyone is happy.* → **be up to sb** at **UP¹** (19b)
20 be down to sb/sth to be the result of one person's actions or one particular thing: *Chris's success is all down to him.*
21 be down to your last pound/dollar/litre etc to be left with only a small amount of something: *We're down to our last five dollars.*
22 down to sth/sb including everything or everyone, even the smallest thing or the least important person: *Everyone uses the cafeteria, from the managing director down to the office boy.* | *The plans were all complete down to the last detail.*
23 be/go down with sth to have a particular illness: *Jane's gone down with flu.*
24 Down with sb/sth *spoken* used to say that you strongly oppose a government, leader etc and want them to lose their power: *Down with the government!*
25 be down on sb/sth *informal* to have a severe attitude towards someone or something, especially when this is unfair: *Why is Mark so down on her at the moment?*
26 LEAVING UNIVERSITY *BrE* used to say that someone leaves or has left a university at the end of a period of study: [+from] *Sarah came down from Oxford in 1966.*
27 COMPLETED already done or completed: *Well, you've passed your second test, so it's two down and four more to go.*
28 down under *informal* in or to Australia or New Zealand
29 Down! *spoken* used to tell a jumping dog to get down
30 be down with sb *spoken informal* to be friends with someone → **be down on your luck** at **LUCK¹** (17)

down² *v* [T] **1** to drink or eat something quickly: *He downed the coffee in one gulp.* **2** to knock or force someone to the ground: *O'Malley downed his opponent in the first round.* **3 down tools** *BrE* to stop working, especially because you are taking part in a STRIKE (=protest about pay or conditions by stopping work)

down³ *n* **1** [U] soft hair like a baby's **2** [U] the soft fine feathers of a bird **3** [C] one of the four chances that an American football team has to move forward when it is their turn to have the ball **4 the downs** low round hills covered with grass, as in the south of England **5 have a down on sb** *BrE informal* to dislike or have a bad opinion of someone: *For some reason, Malcolm had a down on the whole teaching profession.* → **ups and downs** at **UP²** (1)

down- /daʊn/ *prefix* **1** at or towards the bottom or end of something; → **up-**: *downstairs* | *downriver*

1 000, 2 000, 3 000, most frequent words in S spoken and W written English

D

(=nearer to where it goes into the sea) **2** used to show that something is being made smaller or less important; → **up-**: *to downgrade a job* (=make it less important) | *to downsize a company* (=reduce the number of jobs in it) **3** used to show that something is bad or negative; → **up-**: *the downside of a situation* (=the negative part of it) | *down-market products* (=low quality products)

down-and-'out¹ *adj* **1** having no luck or money: *a down-and-out actor* **2** having no home and living on the street

down-and-'out² *n* [C] *BrE* someone who has no home and who lives on the street

down-at-'heel *adj BrE* unattractive and not well cared for, because of a lack of money: *The town today is a shabby, down-at-heel place.*

down·beat¹ /'daʊnbiːt/ *adj* not showing any strong feelings, especially not happy ones; ⊟ **upbeat**: *Al was surprisingly downbeat about the party.*

downbeat² *n* [C] **1** the first note in a BAR of music **2** the movement a CONDUCTOR makes to show when this note is to be played or sung

down·cast /'daʊnkɑːst $ -kæst/ *adj* **1** sad or upset because of something bad that has happened **2** downcast eyes are looking down: *Penelope sat silently, her eyes downcast.*

down·er /'daʊnə $ -ər/ *n informal* **1** [C] a drug that makes you feel very relaxed or sleepy; → **upper** **2** [singular] a person or situation that stops you feeling happy: *The weather was a bit of a downer.* **3 be on a downer** *BrE* to be sad or experiencing a series of sad events: *What's up with Ruth? She's been on a downer all week.*

down·fall /'daʊnfɔːl $ -fɒːl/ *n* [singular] **1** complete loss of your money, moral standards, social position etc, or the sudden failure of an organization: *the scandal that led to the president's downfall* **2** something that causes a complete failure or loss of someone's money, moral standards, social position etc: *be sb's downfall* *an addiction to gambling that proved to be her downfall*

down·grade /'daʊngreɪd/ *v* [T] **1** to make a job less important, or to move someone to a less important job; ⊟ **upgrade** **2** to make something seem less important or valuable than it is: *Police often downgrade the seriousness of violence against women in the home.* **3** to state that something is not as serious as it was: *Hurricane Bob has been downgraded to a tropical storm.*

down·heart·ed /ˌdaʊnˈhɑːtɪ̯d◂ $ -ɑːr-/ *adj* feeling sad and disappointed, especially because you have tried to achieve something but have failed: *When no replies came, I began to feel downhearted.*

down·hill¹ /ˌdaʊnˈhɪl◂/ *adv* **1** towards the bottom of a hill or towards lower land; ⊟ **uphill**: *I was going downhill and my brakes failed.* **2 go downhill** if a situation goes downhill, it gets worse; ⊟ **deteriorate**: *Grandma fell and broke her leg, and she went downhill quite rapidly after that.*

downhill² *adj* **1** on a slope that goes down to a lower point; ⊟ **uphill**: *downhill skiing* | *It's a long walk back, but at least it's all downhill.* **2 be all downhill (from here)/be downhill all the way (from here)** to be easy to do, because you have already done the hard part: *The worst is over – it's all downhill from here.*

down-home *adj* [only before noun] *AmE* typical of the simple values and customs of people who live in the country, especially in the southern US; → **homely**: *down-home family recipes*

Dow·ning Street /'daʊnɪŋ striːt/ *n* the government or Prime Minister of Great Britain: *Downing Street declined to comment on the allegations.*

down·load¹ /ˌdaʊnˈləʊd $ 'daʊnloʊd/ *v* [T] to move information or programs from a computer network to a small computer: *games that can be downloaded free from the Internet*

down·load² /'daʊnləʊd $ -loʊd/ *n* [C] a computer FILE or program that has been downloaded, or the process of downloading it: *We've got reviews and downloads of the latest business software.*

down·load·a·ble /ˌdaʊnˈləʊdəbəl $ 'daʊnloʊd-/ *adj* if a computer program or FILE is downloadable, you are allowed to copy it from a computer network onto your own computer

down·mar·ket¹ /ˌdaʊnˈmɑːkɪ̯t◂ $ -ɑːr-/ *adj BrE* downmarket goods or services are cheap and not of very good quality; ⊟ **downscale** *AmE*; ⊟ **upmarket**: *downmarket tabloid newspapers* | *The company wanted to break away from its traditional, downmarket image.*

downmarket² *adv BrE* **1 go/move downmarket** to start buying or selling cheaper goods or services **2 take sth downmarket** to change a product or service so that it is cheaper and more popular – used to show disapproval: *He was accused of taking the radio station downmarket in order to compete with commercial stations.*

down 'payment *n* [C] a payment you make when you buy something that is only part of the full price, with the rest to be paid later: *We've almost got enough money to make a down payment on a house.*

down·play /ˌdaʊnˈpleɪ $ 'daʊnpleɪ/ *v* [T] to make something seem less important than it really is; ⊟ **play down**: *White House officials attempted to downplay the President's role in the affair.*

down·pour /'daʊnpɔː $ -pɔːr/ *n* [C usually singular] a lot of rain that falls in a short time

down·right /'daʊnraɪt/ *adv* [+ adj/adv] used to emphasize that something is completely bad or untrue: *Jed's just downright lazy.* | *It's downright disgusting.* —**downright** *adj* [only before noun]: *That's a downright lie!*

down·riv·er /daʊnˈrɪvə $ -ər/ *adv* in the direction that the water in a river is flowing; ⊟ **upriver**; → **downstream**: *The bridge was another mile downriver.*

down·scale¹ /'daʊnskeɪl/ *adj AmE* downscale goods or services are cheap and not of very good quality

down·scale² /ˌdaʊnˈskeɪl $ 'daʊnskeɪl/ *v* [I,T] *AmE* to sell or buy cheaper goods of lower quality

down·shift /ˌdaʊnˈʃɪft $ 'daʊnʃɪft/ *v* [I] **1** to put the engine of a vehicle into a lower GEAR in order to go slower **2** if someone downshifts, they choose to do a less important or difficult job, so that they do not have to worry about their work and have more time to enjoy their life

down·side /'daʊnsaɪd/ *n* **the downside** the negative part or disadvantage of something: *Digital cell phones offer more security, but the downside is that they have less power.* | [+of] *The downside of the book is that it is written in a rather boring style.*

down·size /'daʊnsaɪz/ *v* [I,T] if a company or organization downsizes, it reduces the number of people it employs in order to reduce costs: *The airline has downsized its workforce by 30%.* —**downsizing** *n* [U]

down·spout /'daʊnspaʊt/ *n* [C] *BrE* a pipe that carries water away from the roof of a building

'Down's ˌsyndrome *n* [U] a condition that someone is born with, that stops them from developing in a normal way, both mentally and physically

down·stage /ˌdaʊnˈsteɪdʒ◂/ *adv* towards or near the front of the stage in a theatre; ⊟ **upstage** —**downstage** *adj*

down·stairs [S2] /ˌdaʊnˈsteəz $ -ˈsterz/ *adv* **1** towards or on a lower floor of a building, especially a house; ⊟ **upstairs**: *Rosie ran downstairs to answer the door.* | *Charles was downstairs in the kitchen.* **2 the downstairs** the rooms on the ground floor in a house: *We have still got to paint the downstairs.* —**downstairs** *adj*: *a downstairs bathroom*

down·state /'daʊnsteɪt/ adj [only before noun] AmE in or from the southern part of a state; **upstate**: *A downstate judge was called in to hear the case.* —**down·state** /ˌdaʊn'steɪt/ adv

down·stream /ˌdaʊn'striːm/ adv in the direction that the water in a river or stream is flowing; **upstream**; → **downriver**: *a boat drifting downstream*

down·time /'daʊntaɪm/ n [U] **1** the time when a computer is not working **2** also **down time** informal a period of time when you have finished what you were doing, and you can relax or do something that you had not originally planned to do: *Often, during semesters, you have down time when you can do some exercise.* —**downtime** adj: *downtime activities for teachers*

down-to-'earth adj practical and direct in a sensible honest way: *Fran's a very friendly, down-to-earth person.* | *a chef with a very down-to-earth approach to cooking*

down·town S3 W3 /ˌdaʊn'taʊn/ adv to or in the centre or main business area of a town or city; → **uptown**: *I have to go downtown later.* —**downtown** adj [only before noun]: *downtown restaurants* | *She works for a law firm in downtown Miami.*

down·trod·den /'daʊnˌtrɒdn $ -ˌtrɑː-/ adj downtrodden people are treated badly and without respect by people who have power over them

down·turn /'daʊntɜːn $ -tɜːrn/ n [C usually singular] a period or process in which business activity, production etc is reduced and conditions become worse; **upturn**: *America's current economic downturn* | [+in] *a downturn in the auto industry*

down·ward /'daʊnwəd $ -wərd/ adj [only before noun] **1** moving or pointing towards a lower position; **upward**: *a gentle downward slope* **2** moving to a lower level; **upward**: *Share prices continued their downward trend.* | *She was caught in a downward spiral of drink and drugs.* → DOWNWARDS

downwardly com'patible adj computer software that is downwardly compatible can be used on older computers as well as very new ones

downwardly 'mobile adj someone who is downwardly mobile is becoming poorer; **upwardly mobile**

down·wards /'daʊnwədz $ -wərdz/ also **downward** adv **1** towards a lower level or position; **upwards**: *Nina glanced downwards.* | *Hold out your hands with your palms facing downwards.* | *The body was lying face downwards* (=with the front of the body on the floor). **2** used when a number or amount becomes smaller; **upwards**: *The death toll was later revised downwards to 689.* **3 from the chairman/president/top etc downwards** used to mean that people of all levels in an organization, country etc are affected by something: *Everyone from the chairman downwards is taking a pay cut.*

down·wind /ˌdaʊn'wɪnd/ adv in the direction that the wind is moving; **upwind**

down·y /'daʊni/ adj covered in or filled with soft fine hair or feathers: *the baby's downy head*

dow·ry /'daʊəri $ 'daʊri/ n plural **dowries** [C] property and money that a woman gives to her husband when they marry in some societies

dowse¹ /daʊz/ v [I + for] to look for water or minerals under the ground using a special stick that points to where they are

dowse² /daʊs/ v [T] another spelling of DOUSE

dows·er /'daʊzə $ -ər/ n [C] someone who dowses for water or minerals

dowsing rod /'daʊzɪŋ ˌrɒd $ -ˌrɑːd/ n [C] a special stick in the shape of a Y used by a dowser

doy·en /'dɔɪən/ n [C] the oldest, most respected, or most experienced member of a group: [+of] *the doyen of sports commentators*

doy·enne /dɔɪ'en/ n [C] the oldest, most respected, or most experienced woman in a group: [+of] *the doyenne of piano teachers in the city*

doz. also **doz** BrE n the written abbreviation of *dozen*

doze /dəʊz $ doʊz/ v [I] to sleep lightly for a short time: *Grandad was dozing in his chair.* —**doze** n [singular]

doze off phr v to go to sleep, especially when you did not intend to; **drop off**, **nod off**: *I must have dozed off.*

doz·en S2 W3 /'dʌzən/ number plural **dozen** or **dozens** written abbreviation **doz.**
1 twelve: *a dozen eggs* | **two/three/four etc dozen** (=24, 36, 48 etc) *The number of deaths has risen to more than two dozen.* | **dozens of people/companies/cars etc** (=but not hundreds or thousands) *According to a government spokesman, dozens of people were killed.* | *Chris, Helen, and half a dozen others went on holiday together.* | **A dozen or so** (=about 12) *cars were parked near the entrance.*
2 informal a lot of: **a dozen** *I've heard this story a dozen times before.* | **dozens of sth** *She's had dozens of boyfriends.* | *We collected dozens and dozens of shells on the beach.* → BAKER'S DOZEN; → **a dime** (2); → **nineteen to the dozen** at NINETEEN (2); → **six of one and half a dozen of another** at SIX (4)

doz·y /'dəʊzi $ 'doʊ-/ adj **1** not feeling very awake **2** BrE informal slow to understand things; **stupid**: *Those kids are really dozy sometimes!*

DP /ˌdiː 'piː/ n [U] technical the abbreviation of *data processing*

D.Phil. also **DPhil** BrE /ˌdiː 'fɪl/ n [C] *Doctor of Philosophy* a university degree of a very high level, which involves doing advanced RESEARCH; **PhD**

dpi /ˌdiː piː 'aɪ/ *dots per inch* a way of measuring how much ink is put on the page by a PRINTER

DPP /ˌdiː piː 'piː/ n the DPP the abbreviation of *the Director of Public Prosecutions*

Dr BrE; **Dr.** AmE **1** the written abbreviation of *doctor* **2** the written abbreviation of *drive*: *88 Park Dr*

drab /dræb/ adj **1** not bright in colour, especially in a way that stops you from feeling cheerful; **dull**: *The walls were painted a drab green.* **2** boring: *people forced to live grey, drab existences in ugly towns* —**drabness** n [U] → DRIBS AND DRABS

drach·ma /'drækmə/ n plural **drachmas** or **drachmae** /-miː/ [C] the standard unit of money used in Greece before the EURO

dra·co·ni·an /drə'kəʊniən $ -'koʊ-/ adj very strict and cruel: *draconian measures/controls/penalties etc draconian measures to control population growth*

draft¹ S2 W3 /drɑːft $ dræft/ n [C]
1 PIECE OF WRITING a piece of writing or a plan that is not yet in its finished form: *the rough draft of his new novel* | *I read the first draft and thought it was very good.* | *All parties eventually approved the final draft* (=finished form) *of the peace treaty.*
2 MILITARY the draft AmE a) a system in which people are ordered to join the army, navy etc, especially during a war; **conscription** b) the group of people who are ordered to do this
3 MONEY especially BrE a written order for money to be paid by a bank, especially from one bank to another
4 SPORTS AmE a system in which professional teams choose players from colleges to join their teams
5 COLD AIR/BEER the American spelling of DRAUGHT

draft² v [T]
1 PIECE OF WRITING to write a plan, letter, report etc that will need to be changed before it is in its finished form: *Eva's busy drafting her speech for the conference.*
2 MILITARY [usually passive] to order someone to join the army, navy etc, especially during a war; **conscript**: *be drafted into sth My dad was eighteen when he got drafted into the army.*
3 SPORTS AmE to choose a college player to join a

professional team: *Craigwell was drafted by the Chicago Blackhawks.*

draft sb ⇔ **in** also **draft sb into sth** *phr v*
to ask or order someone to work in a place where they do not normally work: *Extra staff were drafted in to deal with the Christmas rush.* | *Hundreds of police have been drafted into the area.*

draft³ *adj* **1** draft proposal/copy/version etc a piece of writing that is not yet in its finished form **2** the American spelling of DRAUGHT

'**draft board** *n* [C] the committee that decides who will be drafted into the army, navy etc

'**draft card** *n* [C] a card sent to someone telling them they have been drafted into the army, navy etc

'**draft ,dodger** *n* [C] someone who illegally avoids joining the army, navy etc, even though they have been ordered to join

draft·ee /drɑːfˈtiː $ dræf-/ *n* [C] someone who has been drafted into the army, navy etc

draft·er /'drɑːftə $ 'dræftər/ *n* [C] a draftsman

drafts·man /'drɑːftsmən $ 'dræfts-/ *n plural* **drafts-men** /-mən/ [C] **1** also **drafter** someone who puts a suggested law or a new law into the correct words **2** the American spelling of DRAUGHTSMAN

draft·y /'drɑːfti $ 'dræfti/ *adj* the American spelling of DRAUGHTY

drag¹ S3 W3 /dræg/ *v* **dragged**, **dragging**
1 PULL STH [T] to pull something along the ground, often because it is too heavy to carry: drag sth **away/along/through** etc *Inge managed to drag the table into the kitchen.*
2 PULL SB [T always + adv/prep] to pull someone somewhere where they do not want to go, in a way that is not gentle: *He grabbed her arm and dragged her into the room.*
3 drag yourself to/into/out of etc sth *informal* to move somewhere with difficulty, especially because you are ill, tired, or unhappy: *I dragged myself out of bed and into the bathroom.* | *Can you drag yourself away from* (=stop watching) *the TV for a minute?*
4 PERSUADE SB TO COME [T always + adv/prep] *informal* if you drag someone somewhere, you persuade or force them to come with you when they do not want to: *Mom dragged us to a classical music concert.*
5 COMPUTER [T] to move words, pictures etc on a computer screen by pulling them along with the MOUSE: *You can **drag and drop** text like this.*
6 BE BORING [I] if time or an event drags, it seems to go very slowly because nothing interesting is happening: *Friday afternoons always drag.*
7 TOUCH THE GROUND [I] if something is dragging along the ground, part of it is touching the ground as you move: [+along/in/on] *Your coat's dragging in the mud.*
8 drag your feet/heels *informal* to take too much time to do something because you do not want to do it: *The authorities are dragging their feet over banning cigarette advertising.*
9 drag a lake/river etc to look for something in a lake, river etc by pulling a heavy net along the bottom: *The police are dragging the lake for the missing girl's body.*
10 drag sb's name through the mud to tell people about the bad things that someone has done, so that they will have a bad opinion of them
11 drag sb through the courts to force someone to go to a court of law, especially in order to make them have a bad experience because you are angry with them
12 drag sb kicking and screaming into sth to force someone to do something that they do not want to – used humorously: *The party will have to be dragged kicking and screaming into the 21st century.*
13 look as if you've been dragged through a hedge backwards to look very untidy – used humorously
14 INJURED LEG/FOOT [T] if you drag your leg, foot etc, you cannot lift it off the ground as you walk

because it is injured: *a bird dragging its broken wing*
drag sb/sth ⇔ **down** *phr v*
1 to make someone feel unhappy and weak: *Joe's been ill for weeks now – it's really dragging him down.*
2 to make the price, level, or quality of something go down: *Declining prices for aluminium have dragged down the company's earnings.*
3 if someone or something bad drags you down, they make you become worse or get into a worse situation: *Don't let them drag you down to their level.*
drag sb/sth **into** sth also **drag sb/sth** ⇔ **in** *phr v*
1 to make someone get involved in an argument, war or other unpleasant situation that they do not want to be involved in: *I'm sorry to drag you into this mess.*
2 to talk about something when you are having a discussion or argument, even though it is not connected with it: *Don't drag my past into this!*
drag on *phr v*
if an event or situation drags on, it continues for too long: [+for] *an expensive court battle that could drag on for years*
drag sth ⇔ **out** *phr v*
to make an event or situation last longer than is necessary: *Neither of them wanted to drag the divorce out longer than they had to.*
drag sth **out of** sb *phr v*
to make someone tell you something when they had not intended to tell you or were not supposed to tell you: *Police finally dragged a confession out of him.*
drag sb/sth ⇔ **up** *phr v*
1 to mention an unpleasant or embarrassing story from the past, even though it upsets someone: *Why do you have to drag that up again?*
2 be dragged up *BrE* if a child is dragged up, their parents do not teach them to behave properly – used humorously: *Those children have been dragged up, not brought up!*

drag² *n* **1** a drag *informal* **a)** something or someone that is boring: *Don't be such a drag! Come to the party.* **b)** something that is annoying and continues for a long time: *It's a **real drag** having to travel so far to work every day.* **2** be a drag on sb/sth to make it hard for someone to make progress towards what they want: *Any slowdown in the economy is going to be a drag on the President's re-election campaign.* **3** [C] the act of breathing in smoke from your cigarette: *Frank **took a drag** on his cigarette.* **4** in drag wearing clothes worn by the opposite sex, especially to entertain people: *The whole performance is done in drag.* **5** [U] the force of air that pushes against an aircraft or a vehicle that is moving forward: *The car's rounded edges reduce drag.* **6** the main drag *AmE informal* the biggest or longest street that goes through a town: *Our hotel is right on the main drag.*

drag·net /'drægnet/ *n* [C] **1** a system in which the police look for criminals, using very thorough methods **2** a net that is pulled along the bottom of a river or lake, to bring up things that may be there

drag·on /'drægən/ *n* [C] **1** a large imaginary animal that has wings and a long tail and can breathe out fire **2** a woman who behaves in an angry, unfriendly way → chase the dragon at CHASE¹ (7)

drag·on·fly /'drægənflaɪ/ *n plural* **dragonflies** [C] a brightly-coloured insect with a long thin body and transparent wings which lives near water → see picture at INSECT

dra·goon¹ /drəˈguːn/ *n* [C] a soldier in past times who rode a horse and carried a gun and sword

dragoon² *v*
dragoon sb **into** sth *phr v* to force someone to do something they do not want to do: dragoon sb into doing sth *Monica was dragooned into being on the committee.*

'**drag queen** *n* [C] *informal* a HOMOSEXUAL man who dresses as a woman, especially to entertain people

'**drag race** *n* [C] a car race over a very short distance
—**drag racing** *n* [U]

drag·ster /'drægstə $ -ər/ *n* [C] a car used in drag races that is long, narrow, and low

drain¹ /dreɪn/ *v*

1 LIQUID a) [T] to make the water or liquid in something flow away: *The swimming pool is drained and cleaned every winter.* | **drain sth from sth** *Brad drained all the oil from the engine.* | *Can you drain the spaghetti, please* (=pour away the water from the pan)*?* **b)** [I always + adv/prep] if liquid drains away, it flows away: [+**away/off/from**] *I watched the bath water drain away.* **c)** [I] if something drains, the liquid that is in it or on it flows away and it becomes dry: *Open ditches drain very efficiently.* | *She washed up and left the dishes to drain.* | **well-drained/poorly-drained** soil (=soil from which water flows away quickly or slowly) *This plant needs rich, well-drained soil.*

2 MAKE SB TIRED [T] to make someone feel very tired and without any energy: *Working with children all day really drains you.*

3 USE TOO MUCH [T] to use too much of something, especially money, so that there is not enough left: *Huge imports were draining the country's currency reserves.*

4 the colour/blood drains from sb's face/cheeks used to say that someone's face becomes very pale, because they are frightened or shocked: *When the verdict was read out, all the colour drained from Zelda's cheeks.*

5 drain a glass/cup etc *written* to drink all the liquid in a glass, cup etc: *Hannah drained her mug in one gulp.*

drain away *phr v*
if something drains away, it is reduced until there is none left: *I watched the light drain away.* | **anger/confidence/tension/hope etc drains away** *Sally felt her anger drain away.*

drain sth ⇔ **off** *phr v*
to make water or a liquid flow off something, leaving it dry: *After cooking the meat, drain off the excess fat.*

drain² *n* [C] **1** especially *BrE* a pipe that carries water or waste liquids away: *The flood was caused by a* **blocked drain.** | *There's a problem with* **the drains.** **2** *BrE* the frame of metal bars over a drain where water etc can flow into it; ▉ **grate** *AmE* **3** *AmE* the hole in the bottom of a bath or SINK that water flows out through; ▉ **plughole** *BrE* **4 a drain on sth** something that continuously uses a lot of time, money etc: *The war was an enormous* **drain on** *the country's resources.* **5 down the drain** *informal* **a)** if time, effort, or money goes down the drain, it is wasted or produces no results: *Well that's it. 18 months' work down the drain.* **b)** if an organization, country etc goes down the drain, it becomes worse or fails: *That's why this country's going down the drain!* → BRAIN DRAIN; → **laugh like a drain** at LAUGH¹ (1)

drain·age /'dreɪnɪdʒ/ *n* [U] the process or system by which water or waste liquid flows away: *A handful of pebbles in the bottom of a flowerpot will help drainage.* | *a plan to improve the town's drainage system*

'drain board *n* an American word for DRAINING BOARD

drained /dreɪnd/ *adj* very tired and without any energy: *Suddenly, she felt totally drained.* | *I felt depressed and completely drained of energy.*

'draining board also **drain board** *AmE n* [C] a slightly sloping area next to a kitchen SINK where you put wet dishes to dry

drain·pipe /'dreɪnpaɪp/ *n* [C] **1** *BrE* a pipe that carries rain water away from the roof of a building **2** *AmE* a pipe that carries waste water away from buildings

,drainpipe 'trousers *n* [plural] tight trousers with narrow legs

drake /dreɪk/ *n* [C] a male duck → DUCKS AND DRAKES

dram /dræm/ *n* [C] a small alcoholic drink, especially WHISKY - used especially in Scotland

dra·ma W3 /'drɑːmə $ 'drɑːmə, 'dræmə/ *n*
1 [C,U] a play for the theatre, television, radio etc, usually a serious one, or plays in general; → **comedy**: *the great traditions of ancient Greek drama* | *a* **TV/television/radio drama** *the award-winning TV drama*

'Prime Suspect' | *a new* **drama series** *for Saturday nights* | *a drama critic* | *a* **courtroom drama** (=one that takes place in a court of law) | *a lavish* **costume drama** (=one about events in a past century) | *He plays a Russian spy in the* **comedy drama** *'Sleepers'.*
2 [U] acting - used when talking about it as a subject to study or teach: *young actors coming out of* **drama school** | *our drama teacher*
3 [C,U] an exciting event or set of events, or the quality of being exciting: *Maggie's life is always full of drama.* | *accidents, burst pipes, and other domestic dramas* | *a night of* **high drama** (=very exciting events) | *the drama of the moment*
4 make a drama out of sth to become upset about a small problem and make it seem worse than it really is: *Brian always makes such a drama out of everything.*
5 drama queen a woman or HOMOSEXUAL man who tends to behave as if situations are worse than they really are - used to show disapproval

dra·mat·ic /drə'mætɪk/ *adj* **1** great and sudden: **dramatic change/shift/improvement** *Computers have brought dramatic changes to the workplace.* | **dramatic increase/rise/fall/drop/reduction etc** *Universities have suffered a dramatic drop in student numbers.* | **dramatic effect/results** *A serious accident can have a dramatic effect on your family's finances.* **2** exciting or impressive: *A superb goal by Owen earned United a dramatic victory yesterday.* | *Some of the most* **dramatic events** *in American history happened here.* | *the* **dramatic scenery** *of the Grand Canyon* **3** connected with acting or plays: *the amateur dramatic society* | *the dramatic arts* **4** intended to be impressive, so that people notice: *She needed a stunning dress to help her make a dramatic entrance.* | *Tristan threw up his hands in a* **dramatic gesture.** —**dramatically** /-kli/ *adv*: *Output has increased dramatically.*

dra,matic 'irony *n* [U] when the people watching a play know something that the characters do not, and can understand the real importance or meaning of what is happening

dra·mat·ics /drə'mætɪks/ *n* [plural] behaviour that shows too much emotion, and is annoying or does not seem sincere: *Rex had no time for her dramatics, and left the room.* → **amateur dramatics** at AMATEUR

dram·a·tis per·so·nae /ˌdræmətɪs pɜː'səʊnaɪ, pə'səʊni: $ -pər'səʊni:/ *n* [plural] *formal* the characters in a play; → **cast**

dram·a·tist /'dræmətɪst/ *n* [C] someone who writes plays, especially serious ones; ▉ **playwright**

dram·a·tize also **-ise** *BrE* /'dræmətaɪz/ *v* [T] **1** to make a book or event into a play or film: *a novel dramatized for television* **2** to make a situation seem more exciting, terrible etc than it really is: *Why do you have to dramatize everything?* **3** to make something more noticeable; ▉ **highlight**: *This incident dramatized the difficulties involved in the project.* —**dramatization** /ˌdræmətaɪ'zeɪʃən $ -tə-/ *n* [C,U]

drank /dræŋk/ the past tense of DRINK

drape /dreɪp/ *v* [T] **1** to put something somewhere so that it hangs or lies loosely: **drape sth over/around/across sth** *He took off his coat and draped it over a chair.* | *Mina lay back, her arms draped lazily over the cushions.* **2** to cover or decorate something with a cloth: **drape sth over/around sth** *Jack emerged with a towel draped around him.* | **drape sth with/in sth** *The soldiers' coffins were draped with American flags.*

drap·er /'dreɪpə $ -ər/ *n* [C] *BrE old-fashioned* someone who sells cloth, curtains etc

drap·er·y /'dreɪpəri/ *n* **1** [U] cloth arranged in folds: *a table covered with drapery* **2 draperies** [plural] *AmE* long heavy curtains **3** [U] *BrE* cloth and other goods sold by a draper: *a drapery business*

drapes /dreɪps/ *n* [plural] *AmE* long heavy curtains

---

dras·tic /'dræstɪk/ *adj* extreme and sudden: **drastic action/measures** *NATO threatened drastic action if its terms were not met.* | **drastic cuts** *in government spending* | **Drastic changes** *are needed if environmental catastrophe is to be avoided.* —**drastically** /-kli/ *adv*: *The size of the army was drastically cut.*

drat /dræt/ *interjection old-fashioned* used to show you are annoyed —**dratted** *adj*

draught¹ /drɑːft $ dræft/ *n* [C] *BrE*
1 AIR cold air that moves through a room and that you can feel; ☐ **draft** *AmE*: *Can you close the window? I'm **in a draught**.*
2 BEER **on draught** beer that is on draught is served from a large container rather than a bottle; ☐ **on draft** *AmE*
3 GAME **a)** **draughts** [U] a game played by two people, each with 12 round pieces, on a board of 64 squares; ☐ **checkers** *AmE* **b)** one of the round pieces used in the game of draughts; ☐ **checker** *AmE*; → see picture at BOARD GAME
4 MEDICINE *old use* a medicine that you drink: *a sleeping draught*
5 SHIP *technical* the depth of water needed by a ship so that it will not touch the bottom of the sea, a river etc; ☐ **draft** *AmE*
6 SWALLOW *written* the act of swallowing liquid, or the amount of liquid swallowed at one time; ☐ **draft** *AmE*: *Mick took a long draught of lager.*

draught² *BrE*; **draft** *AmE adj* [only before noun] **1** draught beer is served from a large container rather than a bottle **2** a draught animal is used for pulling heavy loads

draught·board /'drɑːftbɔːd $ 'dræftbɔːrd/ *n* [C] *BrE* a board with 64 squares on which the game of draughts is played; ☐ **checkerboard** *AmE*

'draught ex,cluder *n* [C,U] *BrE* material that you put around the edge of windows and doors to stop cold air from coming into the house

draughts·man *BrE*; **draftsman** *AmE* /'drɑːftsmən $ 'dræfts-/ *n plural* **draughtsmen** /-mən/ [C] **1** someone whose job is to draw all the parts of a new building or machine that is being planned **2** someone who draws well

draughts·man·ship *BrE*; **draftsmanship** *AmE* /'drɑːftsmənʃɪp $ 'dræfts-/ *n* [U] the skill of drawing or the ability to draw well

draugh·ty *BrE*; **drafty** *AmE* /'drɑːfti $ 'dræfti/ *adj* a draughty room or building has cold air blowing through it: *a draughty old house*

draw¹ S1 W1 /drɔː $ drɒː/ *v past tense* **drew** /druː/ *past participle* **drawn** /drɔːn $ drɒːn/
1 PICTURE [I,T] to produce a picture of something using a pencil, pen etc: *Katie had drawn a cottage with a little stream running next to it.* | *She asked the little girl to **draw a picture** of the man she'd spoken to.* | *Keith was drawing a complicated-looking graph.* | *I've never been able to draw very well.* | **draw sb sth** *Can you draw me a map of how to get there?*
2 **draw (sb's) attention** to make someone notice something: [+to] *I have been asked to draw your attention to the following points.* | *A dark house can **draw attention to the fact that** the house is empty.* | **draw attention to yourself** *He didn't want to draw attention to himself.* | *The case drew international attention.*
3 **draw a conclusion** to decide that a particular fact or principle is true according to the information you have been given: [+from] *It would be unwise to draw firm conclusions from the results of a single survey.*
4 **draw a comparison/parallel/distinction etc** to compare two people or things and show how they are similar or different: [+between] *The author draws a comparison between East and West Germany and the North-South divide in England.* | *The report draws a distinction between various forms of health care.*
5 GET A REACTION [T] to get a particular kind of

reaction from someone: **draw sth from sb** *His remarks drew an angry response from Democrats.* | **draw praise/criticism** *The movie drew praise from critics.*
6 ATTRACT [T] to attract someone or make them want to do something: **draw sb to sth** *What first drew you to teaching?* | *Beth felt strangely drawn to this gentle stranger.* | *The festival is likely to **draw huge crowds.***
7 GET STH YOU NEED [T] to get something that you need or want from someone or something: **draw sth from sth** *I drew a lot of comfort from her kind words.* | *Plants draw nourishment from the soil.*
8 GIVE INFORMATION **be drawn** [usually in negatives] to give information in reply to questions about something: *She refused to be drawn on the subject of her divorce.*
9 MOVE [I always + adv/prep] to move in a particular direction: *She drew away, but he pulled her close again.* | *The boat drew alongside us and a man appeared on the deck.* | *I arrived just as the train was drawing into the station.*
10 **draw near/closer** to become closer in time or space: *Maria grew anxious as the men drew closer.* | *Christmas is drawing near.*
11 **draw level** to move into a position where you are equal to someone else in a race, game, or competition: *Black drew level with the other runners.*
12 PULL SB/STH [T always + adv/prep] to move someone or something in a particular direction by pulling them gently: **draw sb/sth aside/up/across etc** *Bobby drew a chair up to the table.* | *Hussain drew me aside to whisper in my ear.* | **draw the curtains/a blind etc** (=close them by pulling them gently)
13 PULL A VEHICLE [T] if an animal draws a vehicle, it pulls it along: *a carriage drawn by six horses* | *an ox-drawn cart*
14 TAKE STH OUT [T] to take something out of a container, pocket etc: **draw sth out/from sth** *Ali reached into his pocket and drew out a piece of paper.* | **draw a gun/sword/weapon etc** *Maria drew her gun nervously and peered out into the gloom.*
15 **draw a line (between sth)** to think or show that one thing is different from another: *Adolescents often use drugs simply to try to draw a line between their own and their parents' way of life.*
16 **draw the line (at sth)** to allow or accept something up to a particular point, but not beyond it: *I don't mind doing some gardening but I draw the line at digging.*
17 **where do you draw the line?** *spoken* used to say it is impossible to decide at which point an acceptable limit has been reached: *Some say 50 is too old to have a baby, but where do you draw the line?*
18 **draw a line under sth** to say that something is completely finished and you will not think about it again: *I just want to draw a line under the relationship and move on.*
19 **draw sb's eye (to sth)** if something draws your eye, it makes you notice it: *My eye was drawn to a painting on the wall.*
20 FROM A BANK also **draw out** [T] to take money from your bank account; ☐ **withdraw**: *Hughes had drawn $8000 in cash from a bank in Toronto.*
21 RECEIVE MONEY [T] to receive an amount of money regularly from a government or financial institution: *How long have you been drawing unemployment benefit?* | *I'll be **drawing my pension** before he'll ever get around to asking me to marry him!*
22 **draw a cheque (on sth)** *BrE*, **draw a check (on sth)** *AmE* to write a cheque for taking money out of a particular bank account
23 BREATHE [I,T] to take air or smoke into your lungs: *She **drew a deep breath**.* | *Ruth paused to **draw breath**, her voice barely hiding her excitement.* | *He lit his pipe and drew deeply.*
24 **draw breath** to find time to have a rest when you are busy: *I've hardly had a moment to draw breath.*
25 TAKE LIQUID FROM STH [T] **a)** to take a liquid from something such as a BARREL or TAP **b)** to take water from a WELL

26 FIRE [I] if a fire or CHIMNEY draws, it lets the air flow through to make the fire burn well

27 CHOOSE [I,T] to choose by chance a card, ticket etc that will win a prize: *The winning ticket will be drawn at the Christmas Party.*

28 draw lots/straws to decide who will do something by taking pieces of paper out of a container or choosing STRAWS of hidden lengths: *We drew lots to see who would go first.*

29 draw the short straw used to say that someone has been unlucky because they were chosen to do something that no one else wanted to do: *He drew the short straw and had to drive everyone to the party.*

30 GAME [I,T] especially BrE to finish without either side winning in a game such as football; ☐ tie: *They drew 3–3.* | [+with] *Liverpool drew with Juventus.*

31 be drawn against sb BrE to be chosen by chance to play or compete against someone: *England have been drawn against France in next month's game.*

32 draw a blank informal to be unsuccessful in finding information or the answer to a problem: *All his investigations have drawn a blank so far.*

33 draw to a halt/stop if a vehicle draws to a halt or stop, it slows down and stops

34 draw to a close/end to end: *Festival-goers began to drift off as the evening drew to an end.*

35 draw a veil over sth to deliberately keep something unpleasant or embarrassing from being known: *I'd rather draw a veil over what happened last night.*

36 draw blood **a)** to make someone bleed: *The dog bit her so hard that it drew blood.* **b)** to make someone angry or embarrass them in an argument, especially a public one: *Barker sought to draw blood by mentioning his rival's weakness of character.*

37 draw a bow to bend a BOW by pulling back the string in order to shoot an ARROW

38 SHIP [T] technical if a ship draws a particular depth, it needs that depth of water to float in → **be at daggers drawn** at DAGGER (3)

draw back phr v
1 to move backwards, especially because you are frightened or surprised: *Suddenly, she drew back, startled.* | **draw back in horror/shock/fear etc** *She peeped into the box and drew back in horror.*
2 to decide not to do something, especially because you think it would be bad for you; ☐ withdraw: [+from] *In the end the government drew back from their extreme standpoint.*

draw in phr v
1 BrE if the days or nights draw in, it starts to get dark earlier in the evening because winter is coming: *In October the nights start drawing in.*
2 draw sb ⇔ in to get someone involved in something: *We should use the demonstration as an opportunity to draw more supporters in.* | *Despite himself, he found himself being drawn in by the man's warmth and ease.*
3 draw in your horns BrE to spend less money because you have financial problems

draw sb into sth phr v
to make someone become involved in something, especially when they do not want to be involved: *He tried to draw her into conversation.* | *She found herself drawn into a disagreement between two of her neighbours.*

draw sth ⇔ off phr v
to remove some liquid from a larger supply: *The cold water is heated as it is drawn off.*

draw on phr v
1 draw on/upon sth to use information, experience, knowledge etc for a particular purpose: *His work draws heavily on learning theories of the 1980s.* | *She has 20 years' teaching experience to draw on.*
2 draw on sth to use part of a supply of something such as money: *I had to draw on my savings to pay for the repairs.*
3 draw on a cigarette/cigar etc to breathe in smoke from a cigarette etc
4 BrE formal if a period of time or an event draws on, it comes closer to its end: *Winter is drawing on.* | *As the journey drew on, he started to feel tired.*

draw out phr v
1 draw sth ⇔ out to take money from your bank account
2 draw sb ⇔ out to make someone feel less shy and more willing to talk: *She just needed someone to draw her out and take an interest in her.*
3 draw sth ⇔ out formal to mention a particular piece of information and explain it clearly and in detail: *There are two major themes to be drawn out in this discussion.*
4 draw sth ⇔ out to make an event last longer than usual: *The final question drew the meeting out for another hour.* → DRAWN-OUT
5 BrE if the days or nights draw out, it stays light until later in the evening because summer is coming

draw up phr v
1 draw sth ⇔ up to prepare a written document, such as a list or contract: ***Draw up a list** of all the things you want to do.* | **draw up plans/proposals** *He was asked to draw up proposals for reforming the law.* | *The contract was drawn up last year.*
2 if a vehicle draws up, it arrives somewhere and stops: *A taxi drew up at the gate.*
3 draw up a chair to move a chair closer to someone or something
4 draw yourself up (to your full height) to stand up very straight because you are angry or determined about something: *He drew himself up and said, 'This has gone far enough'.*
5 draw your knees up to bring your legs closer to your body: *Ruth sat, knees drawn up under her chin, and waited.*

draw² n [C] **1** the final result of a game or competition in which both teams or players have the same number of points; ☐ tie: *The match **ended in a draw**.* **2** an occasion when someone or something is chosen by chance, especially the winning ticket in a LOTTERY, or the teams who will play against each other in a competition: *England has been selected to play Germany in the draw for the first round of the World Cup.* **3** BrE a competition in which people whose names or tickets are chosen by chance win money or prizes: *Congratulations! You have been entered into our £100,000 **prize draw**!* **4** a performer, place, event etc that a lot of people come to see: *It is hoped that the new art gallery will be a big draw for visitors.* **5** when you breathe in smoke from a cigarette; ☐ drag: *Maltravers took a long draw on his cigarette.* → **the luck of the draw** at LUCK¹ (18); → **quick on the draw** at QUICK¹ (9)

draw·back /'drɔːbæk $ 'drɒ:-/ n [C] a disadvantage of a situation, plan, product etc: *It's a great city – the only drawback is the weather.* | **drawback of/to (doing) sth** *The main drawback to these products is that they tend to be too salty.*

draw·bridge /'drɔːbrɪdʒ $ 'drɒ:-/ n [C] a bridge that can be pulled up to stop people from entering a castle, or to let ships pass → see picture at BRIDGE

drawer S3 /drɔː $ drɒːr/ n [C]
1 part of a piece of furniture, such as a desk, that you pull out and push in and use to keep things in: *She took a file from her **desk drawer**.* | *The scissors are in the **kitchen drawer** (=drawer in a piece of kitchen furniture).* | **top/bottom/right-hand/left-hand drawer** *He opened the top drawer of his desk, and took out a brown envelope.* | **sock/cutlery drawer** (=one for keeping socks, or knives, forks etc in) → BOTTOM DRAWER, CHEST OF DRAWERS, TOP-DRAWER; → see picture at OFFICE
2 drawers [plural] old-fashioned underwear that women and girls wear between their waist and the tops of their legs; ☐ knickers

draw·ing S2 W2 /'drɔːɪŋ $ 'drɒː-/ n
1 [C] a picture that you draw with a pencil, pen etc: [+of] *a drawing of Canterbury Cathedral*
2 [U] the art or skill of making pictures, plans etc with a pen or pencil: *I've never been very good at drawing.*
3 [C] AmE a competition in which people whose names

or tickets are chosen by chance win money or prizes; ◪ **draw** BrE: *The church social will include a buffet dinner and a* **prize drawing**.

'drawing board n [C] **1 (go) back to the drawing board** if you go back to the drawing board, you start again with a completely new plan or idea, after the one you tried before has failed: *The current system just isn't working – we need to go back to the drawing board and start afresh.* **2 on the drawing board** if a plan or product is on the drawing board, it is in the process of being planned or prepared: *Other car manufacturers have similar projects on the drawing board.* **3** a large flat board that artists and DESIGNERS work on

'drawing pin n [C] BrE a short metal pin with a round flat head, used especially for putting notices on boards or walls; ◪ **thumbtack** AmE

'drawing power n [U] an event's, performer's, place's etc ability to attract people to come and see them; ◪ **pulling power**

'drawing room n [C] formal a room, especially in a large house, where you can entertain guests or relax

drawl /drɔːl $ drɒːl/ v [I,T] to speak slowly, with vowel sounds that are longer than usual: *'Can't do that,' he drawled languidly.* —**drawl** n [singular]: *'What you got there?' he asked in a slow Texan drawl* .

drawn[1] /drɔːn $ drɒːn/ the past participle of DRAW

drawn[2] adj someone who looks drawn has a thin pale face, because they are ill, tired or worried

,drawn-'out adj taking more time than usual or more time than you would like: *The government wants to avoid a* **long drawn-out** *war against the rebel forces.*

draw·string /'drɔːstrɪŋ $ 'drɒː-/ n [C] a string through the top of a bag, piece of clothing etc that you can pull to make it tighter: *trousers with a drawstring waist*

dray /dreɪ/ n [C] a flat CART with four wheels that was used in the past for carrying heavy loads, especially BARRELS of beer

dread[1] /dred/ v [T] to feel anxious or worried about something that is going to happen or may happen: *I've got an interview tomorrow and I'm dreading it.* | **dread doing sth** *I'm dreading going back to work.* | **dread sb doing sth** *Tim dreaded his parents finding out.* | **dread (that)** *I'm dreading that I'll be asked to make a speech.* | **dread the thought/prospect of (doing) sth** *He dreaded the prospect of being all alone in that house.* | **I dread to think** *what will happen if they get elected* (=I think it will be very bad).

dread[2] n [singular, U] a strong fear of something that is going to happen or may happen: **dread of (doing) sth** *the dread of losing those we love* | **with dread** *Bernice looked with dread at the end of the passage.* | *The prospect of flying* **filled** *me* **with dread**. | *She* **lives in dread of** (=is continuously very afraid of) *the disease returning.*

dread·ed /'dredᵻd/ also **dread** literary adj [only before noun] making you feel afraid or anxious – often used humorously: *She couldn't put off the dreaded moment forever.*

dread·ful /'dredfəl/ adj **1** extremely unpleasant; ◪ **terrible**: *We've had some dreadful weather lately.* | *Michelle felt absolutely dreadful* (=very ill). **2** [only before noun] used to emphasize how bad something or someone is; ◪ **terrible**: *He soon realized he had made a dreadful mistake.*

dread·ful·ly /'dredfəli/ adv **1** extremely or very much: *They're dreadfully busy at the moment.* | *Would you mind dreadfully if I didn't come?* **2** very badly: *The team played dreadfully.*

dread·locks /'dredlɒks $ -lɑːks/ n [plural] a way of arranging your hair, popular with Rastafarians, in which it hangs in thick pieces that look like rope → see picture at **HAIRSTYLE**

dream[1] S2 W2 /driːm/ n [C]
1 WHILE SLEEPING a series of thoughts, images, and feelings that you experience when you are asleep; → **daydream**: **in a dream** *In my dream I flew to a forest of enormous trees.* | *I* **had** *a really weird* **dream** *last night.* | *Nick sleeps in my room because he has* **bad dreams** (=frightening dreams) *sometimes.* | [+about] *dreams about drowning* | **recurring dream** (=a dream you have again and again) | **be/seem like a dream** (=seem unreal) *Those few short months with Tony seemed like a dream to her.* | *Seeing him again was like* **a bad dream** (=so unpleasant that it seemed unreal).
2 WISH a wish to do, be, or have something – used especially when this seems unlikely: *Her dream is to make a movie.* | **dream of (doing) sth** *Sheila had dreams of university.* | **fulfil/realize a dream** *I fulfilled a childhood dream when I became champion in June.* | **the man/woman/dress/place etc of your dreams** (=the perfect man, woman etc) *I have just met the man of my dreams!* | **beyond your wildest dreams** (=better than anything you ever imagined or hoped for) | **not/never in your wildest dreams** (=used to emphasize that you think something is very strange or unlikely) *Never in my wildest dreams had I thought I would go to Hollywood.*
3 dream house/home/job etc something that seems perfect to someone: *I've finally found my dream house.* | *Win a dream holiday for two in San Francisco!*
4 in a dream having a state of mind in which you do not notice or pay attention to things around you: *Ruth went about her tasks in a dream.*
5 be a dream come true if something is a dream come true, it happens after you have wanted it to happen for a long time: *Marriage to her is a dream come true.*
6 like a dream extremely well or effectively: *The plan worked like a dream.*
7 be/live in a dream world to have ideas or hopes that are not correct or likely to happen: *If you think that all homeless people have it as easy as me, then you are living in dream world.*
8 be a dream be perfect or very desirable: *Her latest boyfriend is an absolute dream.* | *Some performers are a dream to work with; others are not.* | **sb's dream** (=something someone would really like) *She's every adolescent schoolboy's dream.*
9 in your dreams spoken used to say in a rude way that something is not likely to happen: *'I'm going to ask her to go out with me.' 'In your dreams!'*

dream[2] S3 v past tense and past participle **dreamed** or **dreamt** /dremt/
1 WISH [I,T] to think about something that you would like to happen or have: **dream of/about (doing) sth** *She dreamed of becoming a chef.* | *He's got the sort of money that you and I can* **only dream about**. | **dream (that)** *She dreamed that one day she would be famous.*
2 WHILE SLEEPING [I,T] to have a dream while you are asleep: [+about] *I dreamt about you last night.* | **dream (that)** *It's quite common to dream that you're falling.*
3 NOT PAY ATTENTION [I] to think about something else and not give your attention to what is happening around you; ◪ **daydream**: *She had been dreaming and had not followed the conversation.*
4 IMAGINE [I,T] to imagine that you have done, seen, or heard something that you have not: *I was sure I posted the letter but I* **must have dreamt** *it.*
5 never dreamed (that) used to say that you did not think that something would happen: *We never dreamed that we would get through to the next round.*
6 wouldn't dream of (doing) sth spoken used to say that you would never do something because you think it is bad or wrong: *I wouldn't dream of letting strangers look after my own grandmother!*
7 who would have dreamt that ...? spoken used to express surprise about something that has happened: *Who would have dreamed that this would happen?*
dream sth ⇔ **away** phr v
to waste time by thinking about what may happen: *She would just sit in her room dreaming away the hours.*
dream on phr v [only in imperative] spoken
used to tell someone that they are hoping for some-

thing that will not happen: *You think I'm going to help you move house? Dream on!*
  dream sth ⇔ **up** *phr v*
to think of a plan or idea, especially an unusual one: *He was continually dreaming up new schemes to promote and enlarge the business.*

dream·er /'dri:mə $ -ər/ *n* [C] **1** someone who has ideas or plans that are not practical: *She was a dreamer – not pragmatic.* **2** someone who dreams while they are asleep

dream·i·ly /'dri:mɪ̯li/ *adv* thinking about something pleasant and not about what is happening around you: *'I'm coming,' he replied dreamily, without moving.*

dream·land /'dri:mlænd/ *n* [U] **1** a happy place or situation that exists only in your imagination **2** *informal* sleep: *The kids are both far away in dreamland.*

dream·less /'dri:mləs/ *adj* dreamless sleep is very deep and peaceful

dream·like /'dri:mlaɪk/ *adj* as if happening in a dream; 🢒 **unreal**: *The film had a dreamlike quality.*

dreamt /dremt/ a past tense and past participle of DREAM

dream ˌticket *n* [singular] a combination of people who you think will be sure to win an election for a political party

dream·y /'dri:mi/ *adj* **1** looking as though you are thinking about something pleasant rather than what is happening around you: *a dreamy smile* **2** someone who is dreamy has a good imagination but is not very practical: *He was an artist, not particularly tidy, too dreamy to match her ways.* **3** pleasant, peaceful and relaxing: *The windows cast a dreamy light in the room.* **4** *informal* very attractive and desirable: *a book of dreamy chocolate recipes* —**dreaminess** *n* [U]

drear·i·ly /'drɪərɪ̯li $ 'drɪr-/ *adv* **1** sadly: *Laura stared drearily at herself in the mirror.* **2** dully: *a drearily predictable thriller*

drear·y /'drɪəri $ 'drɪri/ also **drear** /drɪə $ drɪr/ *literary adj* dull and making you feel sad or bored: *the same old dreary routine* | *a dreary winter's day* —**dreariness** *n* [U]

dreck /drek/ *n* [U] *AmE informal* something that is of very bad quality: *Readers for publishing houses see a lot of good stuff and a lot of dreck.*

dredge /dredʒ/ *v* **1** [I,T] to remove mud or sand from the bottom of a river, HARBOUR etc, or to search for something by doing this: *They were dredging for oysters.* **2** [T + with] to cover food lightly with flour, sugar etc
  dredge sth ⇔ **up** *phr v* **1** to start talking again about something that happened a long time ago, especially something unpleasant: *Newsweek magazine dredged up some remarks which he made last year.* **2** to manage to remember something, or to feel or express an emotion, with difficulty: *Robertson tried to dredge up an image of her in his mind.* | *From somewhere she dredged up a brilliant smile.* **3** to pull something up from the bottom of a river, lake etc

dredg·er /'dredʒə $ -ər/ also **dredge** *n* [C] a machine or ship used for digging or removing mud and sand from the bottom of a river, lake etc

dregs /dregz/ *n* **1** [plural] a small amount of a drink, sometimes with bits in, left at the bottom of a cup, glass, or bottle **2** **the dregs of society/humanity** *not polite* an offensive expression used to describe the people that you consider are the least important or useful in society

drei·del /'dreɪdl/ *n* [C] a TOP (=a toy that you spin) with a Hebrew letter on each of its four sides and a point at the bottom, used in a game played during Hanukkah

drench /drentʃ/ *v* [T] to make something or someone extremely wet: *In the early morning they had got drenched in the grass.* —**drenching** /'drentʃɪŋ/ *adj*: *drenching rain*

drenched /drentʃt/ *adj* **1** covered with a lot of a liquid: *Come on in – you're drenched!* | [+in/with] *I was*

drenched in sweat. | *chips drenched in vinegar* | **rain-drenched/sweat-drenched etc** *He changed out of his rain-drenched clothes.* **2** **drenched in/with light** *literary* something that is drenched with light has a lot of light shining on it

dress¹ [S2] [W2] /dres/ *n*
1 [C] a piece of clothing worn by a woman or girl that covers the top of her body and part or all of her legs; 🢒 **skirt**: *Sheila wore a long red dress.* | *a summer dress*
2 [U] clothes for men or women of a particular type or for a particular occasion: *a gentleman in **evening dress*** (=formal clothes worn especially at important social events) | *The play was performed in **modern dress*** (=clothes from the present time). | **dress code** (=a standard of what you should wear for a particular situation) *This restaurant has a strict dress code – no tie, no service.*

dress² [S2] [W2] *v*
1 **PUT ON CLOTHES** [I,T] to put clothes on yourself or someone else: *Aunt Margaret told her to dress herself in her nicest dress.* | *I dress the kids before I go to work.* | *I've got to go home to dress.* | *I dressed quickly.* | **dress sb in sth** *She dressed Louis in his best blue jersey.* ⚠ In spoken English, it is more usual to say **get dressed**.
2 **WEAR CLOTHES** [I] to wear a particular kind of clothes: *Dress warmly if you're going out for a walk.* | **dress casually/smartly** *I spend most of my time in the house with young children, so I dress casually.* | [+for] *How do you normally dress for work?* | *We usually **dress for dinner*** (=wear formal clothes for our evening meal).
3 **MAKE/CHOOSE CLOTHES** [T] to make or choose clothes for someone: *Versace dressed some of the most famous people in Hollywood.*
4 **WOUND/CUT ETC** [T] to clean, treat, and cover a wound
5 **MEAT/FISH** [T] to clean and prepare meat or fish so that it is ready to cook or eat: *dressed crab*
6 **SALAD** [T] to put oil, VINEGAR, salt etc onto a SALAD
7 **WINDOW** [T] to put an attractive arrangement in a shop window → WINDOW DRESSER
8 **SOLDIERS** [I,T] *technical* to stand in a straight line, or to make soldiers do this
9 **HAIR** [T] *formal* to arrange someone's hair into a special style
10 **WOOD/STONE ETC** [T] *technical* to prepare or put a special surface onto wood, stone, leather etc
  dress down *phr v*
1 to wear clothes that are more informal than the ones you would usually wear: *In many offices, people dress down on Fridays.*
2 **dress sb** ⇔ **down** to speak angrily to someone about something they have done wrong → DRESSING-DOWN
  dress up *phr v*
1 to wear special clothes for fun, or to put special clothes on someone: [+as] *He went to the party dressed up as a Chicago gangster.* | [+in] *I keep a box of old clothes for the children to dress up in.* | **dress sb** ⇔ **up** *We dressed him up as a gorilla.*
2 to wear clothes that are more formal than the ones you would usually wear: *It's a small informal party – you don't have to dress up.*
3 **dress** sth ⇔ **up** to make something more interesting or attractive: *It was the old offer dressed up as something new.*

dres·sage /'dresɑːʒ $ drɪ̯'sɑːʒ/ *n* [U] a competition in which a horse performs a complicated series of movements in answer to signals from its rider

ˈdress ˌcircle *n* [C] *BrE* the lowest of the curved rows of seats upstairs in a theatre; 🢒 **first balcony** *AmE*

dressed /drest/ *adj* **1** **get dressed** to put your clothes on: *Go and get dressed!* **2** having your clothes on or wearing a particular type of clothes: *Aren't you dressed yet?* | **half/fully dressed** *She lay down fully*

[1] 000, [2] 000, [3] 000, most frequent words in [S] poken and [W] ritten English

dressed on the bed. | **smartly/well-/elegantly etc dressed** *a very well-dressed young man* | [+**in**] *She was dressed in a two-piece suit.* | [+**as**] *The children came dressed as animals.* **3 dressed to kill** *informal* wearing very attractive clothes so that everyone notices and admires you **4 dressed (up) to the nines** *informal* wearing your best or most formal clothes

dress·er /'dresə $ -ər/ *n* [C] **1** *BrE* a large piece of furniture with open shelves for storing plates, dishes etc; ◨ **Welsh dresser 2** *AmE* a piece of furniture with drawers for storing clothes, sometimes with a mirror on top; ◨ **chest of drawers** *BrE*; → see picture at COMPARTMENT **3 a fashionable/stylish/sloppy etc dresser** someone who dresses in a fashionable etc way: *Stanley was an impeccable dresser.* **4** someone who takes care of someone's clothes, especially an actor's in the theatre, and helps them to dress

dress·ing /'dresɪŋ/ *n* **1** [C,U] a mixture of liquids, usually oil and VINEGAR, that you put on SALAD or raw vegetables: *a vinaigrette dressing* → FRENCH DRESSING, SALAD DRESSING **2** [C,U] *AmE* STUFFING (1) **3** [C] a special piece of material used to cover and protect a wound: *The nurse came to change his dressing.* → CROSS-DRESSING, POWER DRESSING, WINDOW DRESSING

dressing-'down *n* [singular] an occasion when you talk angrily to someone because they have done something wrong: **give sb/get a dressing-down** *The tobacco companies got a severe dressing-down.*

dressing gown *n* [C] *BrE, AmE formal* a piece of clothing like a long loose coat that you wear inside the house, usually over night clothes; ◨ **bathrobe, robe**

dressing room *n* [C] **1** a room where an actor or performer can get ready before going on stage, appearing on television etc **2** *AmE* a room or area in a store where you can try on clothes; ◨ **changing room** *BrE* **3** a small room next to a bedroom in some houses where you can get dressed

dressing ,table *n* [C] a piece of furniture like a table with a mirror on top, sometimes with drawers, that you use when you are doing your hair, putting on MAKE-UP etc

dressing-'up *BrE*; **dress-'up** *AmE n* [U] a children's game in which they put on special clothes and pretend that they are someone else

dress·mak·er /'dres,meɪkə $ -ər/ *n* [C] someone who makes their own clothes, or makes clothes for other people as a job —**dressmaking** *n* [U]

dress re,hearsal *n* [C] the final practice of a play, OPERA etc, using all the clothes, objects etc that will be used for the actual performance

dress sense *n* [U] the ability to choose clothes that make you look attractive

dress shirt *n* [C] a formal shirt, sometimes with a special decoration at the front, that a man wears under a DINNER JACKET

dress ,uniform *n* [C,U] a uniform that officers in the army, navy etc wear for formal occasions or ceremonies

dress·y /'dresi/ *adj* **1** dressy clothes are suitable for formal occasions: *Her outfit was smart but not too dressy.* **2** someone who is dressy likes to wear very fashionable or formal clothes

drew /druː/ the past tense of DRAW

drib·ble¹ /'drɪbəl/ *v* **1** [I,T] to let liquid come out of your mouth onto your face: *Watch out, the baby is dribbling on your shirt!* | *He was dribbling tea onto his tie.* **2** [I always + adv/prep] if a liquid dribbles somewhere, it flows in a thin irregular stream: *Blood from the wound dribbled down the side of his face.* **3** [I,T] to move the ball along with you by short kicks, BOUNCES, or hits in a game of football, BASKETBALL etc: *He was trying to dribble the ball past his opponents.* **4** [I always + adv/prep] if something such as money or news dribbles somewhere, it comes or goes in small irregular amounts: *Money is finally dribbling back into the coun-*

try now. **5** [T always + adv/prep] to pour something out slowly in an irregular way: *Dribble a few drops of olive oil over the pizza.*

dribble² *n* **1** [U] a small amount of liquid that has come out of your mouth: *He wiped the dribble from his chin.* **2 a dribble of sth** a small amount of liquid: *There was a dribble of brandy in the bottom of the bottle.* **3** [C] the act of moving the ball along with you by short kicks, BOUNCES or hits in a game of football, BASKETBALL etc

dribs and drabs /,drɪbz ən 'dræbz/ *n* **in dribs and drabs** in small irregular amounts or numbers over a period of time: *The guests arrived in dribs and drabs.*

dried /draɪd/ *adj* dried substances, such as food or flowers, have had the water removed: *dried herbs*

,dried 'fruit *n* [U] fruit, usually GRAPES, that has been dried and is often used in cooking

,dried 'milk *n* [U] milk that is made into a powder and can be used by adding water

dri·er /'draɪə $ -ər/ *n* another spelling of DRYER

drift¹ /drɪft/ *v* [I]
1 MOVE SLOWLY to move slowly on water or in the air: [+**out/towards etc**] *The rubber raft drifted out to sea.* | *Smoke drifted up from the jungle ahead of us.*
2 WITHOUT PLAN to move, change, or do something without any plan or purpose: [+**around/along etc**] *Jenni spent the year drifting around Europe.* | [+**into**] *I just drifted into teaching, really.* | [+**away**] *The others drifted away. Melanie stayed.* | **drift from sth to sth** *The conversation drifted from one topic to another.* | **let your gaze/eyes/thoughts/mind etc drift** *Idly she let her eyes drift over his desk.*
3 CHANGE to gradually change from being in one condition, situation etc into another without realizing it: [+**into**] *She was just drifting into sleep when the alarm went off.* | *He drifted in and out of consciousness.*
4 MONEY/PRICES if values, prices, SHARES etc drift, they gradually change: *The dollar drifted lower against the yen today.*
5 SNOW/SAND if snow, sand etc drifts, the wind blows it into large piles
6 let sth drift to allow something, especially something bad, to continue in the same way: *He couldn't let the matter drift for much longer.*
drift apart *phr v*
if people drift apart, their relationship gradually ends: *Over the years my college friends and I have drifted apart.*
drift off *phr v*
to gradually fall asleep: *I was just drifting off when the phone rang.* | *He felt himself **drifting off to sleep**.*

drift² *n*
1 SNOW/SAND [C] a large pile of snow or sand that has been blown by the wind: [+**of**] *The road is blocked with massive drifts of snow.* | *a snow drift*
2 CHANGE [singular] a slow change or development from one situation, opinion etc to another: [+**towards/ to**] *a drift towards longer working hours*
3 MOVEMENT OF PEOPLE [singular, U] a slow movement of large numbers of people that has not been planned: [+**from/to/into**] *the drift from the countryside to the cities*
4 the drift (of sth) the general meaning of what someone is saying: *So what's the drift of the argument?* | **follow/get/catch sb's drift** (=understand the general meaning of what someone is saying) *She didn't quite get my drift, did she?*
5 SHIPS/PLANES [U] the movement of a ship or plane from its original direction because of the movement of the wind or water
6 SLOW MOVEMENT [U] very slow movement, especially over water or through the air

drift·er /'drɪftə $ -ər/ *n* [C] **1** someone who is always moving from one job or place to another with no real purpose **2** a fishing boat that uses a floating net

drift·net /'drɪftnet/ n [C] a large fishing net that floats behind a boat

drift·wood /'drɪftwʊd/ n [U] wood floating in the sea or left on the shore

drill¹ /drɪl/ n **1** [C] a tool or machine used for making holes in something: *an electric drill* | *a whine like a dentist's drill* → PNEUMATIC DRILL **2** [C] a method of teaching students, sports players etc something by making them repeat the same lesson, exercise etc many times: *a pronunciation drill* **3 fire/emergency drill** an occasion when people practise what they should do in a dangerous situation such as a fire **4** [U] military training in which soldiers practise marching, using weapons etc: *rifle drill* **5 the drill** BrE old-fashioned the usual way that something is done: '*You know the drill?' 'Not really. Tell me again what to do.'* **6** [U] a type of strong cotton cloth **7** [C] **a)** a machine for planting seeds in rows **b)** a row of seeds planted by a machine

drill² v **1** [I,T] to make a hole in something using a drill: *Drill a hole in each corner.* | [+into/through] *He accidentally drilled into a water pipe.* | **drill for oil/water/gas etc** *BP has been licensed to drill for oil in the area.* **2** [T] to teach students, sports players etc by making them repeat the same lesson, exercise etc many times: **drill sb in sth** *She was drilling the class in the forms of the past tense.* | **drill sb to do sth** *I acted instinctively because I had been trained and drilled to do just that.* | *The team were well-drilled and organized.* **3** [T] to train soldiers to march or perform other military actions: *The sergeant was drilling the new recruits.* **4** [T] to plant seeds in rows using a machine

drill sth into sb phr v to keep telling someone something until they know it very well: *Mother had drilled it into me not to talk to strangers.*

'drilling ,platform n [C] a large structure in the sea used for drilling for oil, gas etc

dri·ly /'draɪli/ adv another spelling of DRYLY

drink

drink

sip

lap

suck

drink¹ S2 W2 /drɪŋk/ v past tense **drank** /dræŋk/ past participle **drunk** /drʌŋk/
1 [I,T] to take liquid into your mouth and swallow it: *You should drink plenty of water.* | *What would you like to drink?* | *Take a seat while I get you something to drink.* | *She filled the glass and drank.*
2 [I] to drink alcohol, especially regularly or too much: *He's been drinking heavily since his wife died.* | *I don't drink.* | *Don't drink and drive.* | *My flatmate Cherry drinks like a fish* (=regularly drinks a lot of alcohol).
3 drink yourself silly/into a stupor/to death etc to drink so much alcohol that you become very drunk or unconscious, or die: *If he goes on this way he'll drink himself to death.*
4 drink sb under the table to drink more alcohol than someone but not feel as ill as them: *He could drink nearly anyone under the table.*

5 What are you drinking? spoken used to offer to buy someone a drink, especially in a PUB
6 drink sb's health BrE to wish someone good health before having an alcoholic drink
drink sth ⇔ **in** phr v
to look at, listen to, feel, or smell something in order to enjoy it: *For a moment she just sat there, drinking in the atmosphere.*
drink to sth phr v
1 to wish someone success, good luck, good health etc before having an alcoholic drink: *Let's drink to your success in your new job.*
2 I'll drink to that! spoken used to agree with what someone has said
drink up phr v
to drink all of something: **drink sth ⇔ up** *Drink up your milk.*

drink² S1 W2 n
1 [C] an amount of liquid that you drink, or the act of drinking something: [+of] *Have a drink of water.* | *Do you want a drink of my tea?* | *He took a drink of his coffee.*
2 [C,U] liquid that you can drink: *They sell soft drinks* (=non-alcoholic drinks). | *food and drink companies*
3 [C,U] an alcoholic drink: *Have another drink.* | *After that news I need a stiff drink* (=strong alcohol).| **go for a drink** BrE (=go to a pub) *Let's go for a drink.*
4 [U] the habit of drinking too much alcohol, in a way that is very bad for your health: *The marriage ended because of her husband's drink problem* (=he drank too much alcohol). | *They had driven him to drink* (=made him start drinking too much alcohol regularly). | *After her retirement from the stage she took to drink* (=started drinking too much alcohol).
5 drinks [plural] BrE a social occasion when you have alcoholic drinks and sometimes food: **for drinks** *Don't forget we're invited to the Jones' for drinks on Sunday.*
6 the drink old-fashioned the sea, a lake, or another large area of water

drink·a·ble /'drɪŋkəbəl/ adj **1** water that is drinkable is safe to drink **2** wine, beer etc that is drinkable is of good quality and tastes pleasant

,drink-'driving n [U] BrE driving a car after having drunk too much alcohol; ⊟ **drunk-driving** AmE —**drink-driver** n [C]

drink·er /'drɪŋkə $ -ər/ n [C] **1** someone who regularly drinks alcohol: *Dave has always been a bit of a drinker.* | *He was a heavy drinker* (=he drank a lot). **2 coffee/wine/champagne etc drinker** someone who regularly drinks coffee, wine etc

drink·ing /'drɪŋkɪŋ/ n [U] the activity of drinking alcohol: *after a night of heavy drinking* (=drinking a lot of alcohol) | **drinking companion/buddy/partner etc**

'drinking ,fountain n [C] a piece of equipment in a public place that produces a stream of water for you to drink from

,drinking-'up time n [U] BrE the time when people are allowed to finish their drinks in a PUB, but cannot buy any more drinks

'drinking ,water n [U] water that is pure enough for you to drink

'drinks ma,chine n [C] BrE a machine that serves hot and cold drinks when you put money into it → see picture at SPORTS CENTRE

'drinks ,party n [C] BrE a party at which alcoholic drinks are served and where you mainly talk to people; ⊟ **cocktail party**

drip¹ /drɪp/ v **dripped, dripping** **1** [I,T] to let liquid fall in drops: *The tap's dripping.* | *Her boots were muddy and her hair was dripping.* | **drip blood/water/sweat etc** *John came in, his arm dripping blood.* | **be dripping with blood/sweat etc** *The hand that held the gun was dripping with sweat.* **2** [I] to fall in drops: [+down/from etc] *The rain dripped down his neck.* |

*Water was **dripping** through the ceiling.* **3 be drip-ping with sth** to contain or be covered in a lot of something: **be dripping with jewels/gems/pearls etc** *All the princes were dripping with gems.* | *His tone was now **dripping with sarcasm**.*

drip² *n* **1** [C] one of the drops of liquid that fall from something: *I put some plastic buckets on the floor to catch the drips.* **2** [singular, U] the sound or action of a liquid falling in drops: *The silence was broken only by a regular drip, drip, drip.* **3** [C] a piece of equipment used in hospitals for putting liquids directly into your blood; ▤ **IV**: **be/put sb on a drip** *At the hospital they put me on a drip.* **4** [C] *informal* someone who is boring and weak

drip-'dry *adj* drip-dry clothing does not need IRONING —**drip-dry** *v* [I,T]

drip·ping¹ /'drɪpɪŋ/ *n* [U] *BrE* the oily substance that comes out of meat when you cook it

dripping² *adj* extremely wet: *Take off that jacket – you're **dripping wet**.*

drip·py /'drɪpi/ *adj informal* very emotional in a silly way: *The movie is nothing but a drippy melodrama.*

drive¹ [S1] [W1] /draɪv/ *v past tense* **drove** /drəʊv $ droʊv/ *past participle* **driven** /'drɪvən/

1 VEHICLE a) [I,T] to make a car, truck, bus etc move along: [+to/down/off etc] *I am planning to drive to Morocco next year.* | *the man driving the car* | *Can you drive?* | *So when did you **learn to drive**?* | *Bye! Drive carefully!* | *He drives 12 miles to work.* | *He drives (=has) a BMW estate.* **b)** [I always + adv/prep] if a car, truck etc drives somewhere, it moves there: *After the accident, the other car just drove off.* **c)** [I] if people drive somewhere, they travel somewhere in a car: *Shall we drive or take the bus?* | [+to/down/off etc] *They drove back to Woodside.* **d)** [T always + adv/prep] to take someone somewhere in a car, truck etc: *She drove Anna to London.* | *I'll **drive** you **home**.* | **drive yourself** *I drove myself to hospital.*

2 MAKE SB MOVE [T] to force a person or animal to go somewhere: *Torrential rain drove the players off the course.* | *With a few loud whistles, they drove the donkeys out of the enclosure.*

3 MAKE SB DO STH [T] to strongly influence someone to do something: **drive sb to do sth** *The detective wondered what had driven Christine to phone her.* | **drive sb to/into sth** *The noises in my head have nearly driven me to suicide.* | *Phil, driven by jealousy, started spying on his wife.*

4 MAKE SB/STH BE IN A BAD STATE [T] to make someone or something get into a bad or extreme state, usually an emotional one: **drive sb crazy/mad/insane** (=make someone feel very annoyed) *This cough is driving me mad!* | **drive sb crazy/wild** (=make someone feel very sexually excited) | **drive sb up the wall/out of their mind** (=make someone feel very annoyed) | **drive sb to distraction/desperation** *The mosquitoes drive me to distraction.* | **drive sb/sth into sth** *The factory had been driven into bankruptcy.*

5 HIT/PUSH STH INTO STH [T] to hit or push something into something else: **drive sth into sth** *We watched Dad drive the posts into the ground.* | *She drove her heels into the sand.*

6 MAKE SB WORK [T] to make a person or animal work hard: **drive yourself** *Don't drive yourself too hard.*

7 SPORTS [I,T] **a)** to move a ball etc forward in a game of baseball, football, golf etc by hitting or kicking it hard and fast: *He drove the ball into the corner of the net.* **b)** to run with the ball towards the GOAL in sports such as BASKETBALL and American football

8 PROVIDE POWER [T] to provide the power for a vehicle or machine: **petrol-driven/electrically-driven/battery-driven etc** *a petrol-driven lawn mower*

9 RAIN/WIND ETC [I always + adv/prep] if rain, snow, wind etc drives somewhere, it moves very quickly in that direction: *The rain was driving down hard.*

10 drive a coach and horses through sth to destroy an argument, plan etc completely: *The new bill will drive a coach and horses through recent trade agreements.*

11 MAKE A HOLE [T always + adv/prep] to make a large hole in something using heavy equipment or machinery: *They're planning to drive a tunnel through the mountains.*

12 drive sth home to make something completely clear to someone: *He didn't have to **drive** the **point home**. The videotape had done that.*

13 drive a wedge between sb to do something that makes people disagree or start to dislike each other: *I don't want to drive a wedge between you and your father.* → **drive/strike a hard bargain** at HARD¹ (18)

drive at sth *phr v* what sb is driving at the thing someone is really trying to say; ▤ **get at**: *I still couldn't understand what Toby was driving at.*

drive sb ⇔ **away** *phr v* to behave in a way that makes someone leave: *He was cruel because he wanted to drive me away.*

drive sth ⇔ **down** *phr v* to make prices, costs etc fall quickly: *We have to drive down costs.*

drive sb/sth ⇔ **in** *phr v* to hit the ball so that another player can score a RUN in baseball

drive off *phr v*
1 to hit the ball to begin a game of golf
2 drive sb ⇔ **off** to force a person or animal to go away from you: *We keep dogs in the yard to drive off intruders.*

drive sb/sth ⇔ **out** *phr v*
1 to force someone or something to leave: *Downtown stores are being driven out by crime.*
2 *written* to make something stop existing: *As we went forward, our fear was driven out by horror.*

drive sth ⇔ **up** *phr v* to make prices, costs etc rise quickly: *The oil shortage drove gas prices up by 20 cents a gallon.*

drive² [S2] [W2] *n*

1 IN A CAR [C] a journey in a car: [+to/along etc] *Let's go for a drive along the coast.* | *Taylor took me for a drive through the town.* | **an hour's/a two hour etc drive** *It's a two hour drive from Calais to Thiepval.*

2 NATURAL NEED [C] a strong natural need or desire: *The treatment will not affect your sex drive.*

3 OUTSIDE YOUR HOUSE [C] the hard area or road between your house and the street; ▤ **driveway**: **in/on the drive** *He parked his car in the drive.*

4 EFFORT [C] an effort to achieve something, especially an effort by an organization for a particular purpose: *a recruitment drive for new members* | *economy drive* (=effort to reduce spending) | **drive to do sth** *a nationwide drive to crack down on crime*

5 DETERMINATION [U] determination and energy to succeed: *Brian has got tremendous drive.*

6 POWER [U] the power from an engine that makes the wheels of a vehicle go round: **front-wheel/rear-wheel/four-wheel drive**

7 COMPUTER [C] a piece of equipment in a computer that is used to get information from a DISK or to store information on it: **hard/floppy/A etc drive** → DISK DRIVE

8 SPORT [C] an act of hitting a ball hard, especially in tennis, baseball, or golf: *He hit a long, high drive to right field.*

9 MILITARY ATTACK [C] several military attacks: [+into] *a drive deep into enemy territory*

10 ANIMALS [C] when animals such as cows or sheep are brought together and made to move in a particular direction

11 Drive used in the names of roads: *They live at 141 Park Drive.*

'drive-by *adj* **drive-by shooting/killing** an occasion when someone is shot by someone in a moving car —**drive-by** *n* [C]

'drive-in *n* [C] **1** a restaurant where you are served and eat in your car **2** a place where you can watch films outdoors while sitting in your car

driv·el /'drɪvəl/ n [U] something that is said or written that is silly or does not mean anything: *Don't talk such drivel!* —**drivel** v [I]

driv·en¹ /'drɪvən/ the past participle of DRIVE

driven² adj trying extremely hard to achieve what you want: *He claims he is not a driven workaholic.* → **as pure as the driven snow** at PURE (11)

driv·er S1 W2 /'draɪvə $ -ər/ n [C]
1 someone who drives a car, bus etc; → **chauffeur**: *a taxi driver* I *Do you think you're a good driver?*
2 technical a piece of software that makes a computer work with another piece of equipment such as a printer or a mouse
3 a GOLF CLUB with a wooden head → **back seat driver** at BACK SEAT (2); → **Sunday driver** at SUNDAY (3)

‚driver's edu'cation also **‚driver's 'ed** n [U] AmE a course, usually taken in high school, that teaches you how to drive a car

'driver's ‚license n [C] AmE an official document or card that says that you are legally allowed to drive; ⊟ **driving licence** BrE

'drive shaft n [C] technical a part of a vehicle that takes power from the GEARBOX to the wheels

'drive-through also **drive-thru** n [C] a restaurant, bank etc where you can be served without getting out of your car

'drive·time, drive time /'draɪvtaɪm/ n [U] the time during the morning or afternoon when many people are driving to or from work; → **rush hour**: *a morning drivetime radio show*

drive·way /'draɪvweɪ/ n [C] the hard area or road between your house and the street; ⊟ **drive**

driv·ing¹ /'draɪvɪŋ/ n [U] the activity of driving a car, truck etc: *driving lessons* I *He was charged with causing death by dangerous driving.* I *hazardous driving conditions* (=weather that makes driving dangerous) → **in the driving seat** at SEAT¹ (11)

driving² adj **1 driving rain/snow** rain or snow that falls very hard and fast **2 driving force** someone or something that strongly influences people and makes them do something: [+**behind**] *Hawks was the driving force behind the project.* **3 driving ambition** a very great desire to do or achieve something

'driving ‚licence n [C] BrE an official document or card that says that you are legally allowed to drive; ⊟ **driver's license** AmE

'driving ‚range n [C] an open outdoor area where people practise hitting golf balls

'driving school n [C] a business that teaches people how to drive a car

'driving test n [C] the official test that you must pass in order to be legally allowed to drive on public roads

driz·zle¹ /'drɪzəl/ v **1 it is drizzling** if it is drizzling, light rain and mist come out of the sky: *The rain isn't too bad – it's only drizzling.* **2** [T always + adv/prep] to let a liquid fall on food in a small stream or in small drops: *Drizzle the soy sauce over the chicken.*

drizzle² n [singular, U] weather that is a combination of light rain and mist: *A light drizzle had started by the time we left.* —**driz·zly** /'drɪzli/ adj

droll /drəʊl $ droʊl/ adj amusing in an unusual way

drom·e·da·ry /'drɒmədəri $ 'drɑːməderi/ n plural **dromedaries** [C] a CAMEL with one HUMP on its back

drone¹ /drəʊn $ droʊn/ v [I] to make a continuous low dull sound: *An airplane droned overhead.*

    drone on phr v to speak in a boring way, usually for a long time: [+**about**] *Tom was droning on and on about work.*

drone² n **1** [singular] a continuous low dull sound: [+**of**] *the steady drone of traffic* **2** [C] a male BEE that does no work **3** [C] someone who has a good life but does not work to earn it or give anything back to society **4** [C] technical old-fashioned an aircraft that does not have a pilot, but is operated by radio

drool /druːl/ v **1** [I,T] BrE to let SALIVA (=the liquid in your mouth) come out of your mouth; → **slobber**: *The dog was drooling at the mouth.* **2** [I] to show in a silly way that you like someone or something a lot: [+**over**] *He was drooling over a Porsche.*

droop /druːp/ v **1** [I,T] to hang or bend down, or to make something do this: *The plant needs some water – it's starting to droop.* I *His eyelids began to droop* (=close, because he was sleepy). I *Jessie drooped her head.* **2** [I] to become sad or weak: *Our spirits drooped as we faced the long trip home.* —**droop** n [singular] —**droopy** adj: *a droopy moustache*

drop¹ S1 W2 /drɒp $ drɑːp/ v **dropped**, **dropping**
1 LET STH FALL [T] **a)** to stop holding or carrying something so that it falls: *He dropped his briefcase on a chair.* I *She screamed and dropped the torch.* **b)** to make something such as a bomb fall from a plane: *U.S. planes began dropping bombs on the city.* I *Supplies are being dropped for the refugees.*
2 FALL [I] to fall suddenly onto the ground or into something: [+**from/off**] *The apples are beginning to drop from the trees.* I *Your button has dropped off.*
3 MOVE YOUR BODY DOWN [I always + adv/prep, T] to lower yourself or part of your body suddenly: [+**down/onto/into**] *He dropped down onto the floor and hid under the table.* I *She dropped her head back against the cushion.*
4 BECOME LESS [I] to fall to a lower level or amount, especially a much lower level or amount: **drop suddenly/sharply/dramatically** *The number of deaths on the roads has dropped sharply.* I *Temperatures drop quite dramatically at night, so bring some warm clothing.* I [+**to**] *Their share of the market dropped to 50 percent this year.*
5 REDUCE [T] to reduce the level or amount of something: *You might be able to get them to drop the price.* I *As soon as she saw the police car she dropped her speed.*
6 NOT INCLUDE [T] to decide not to include someone or something: *His name was dropped from the list.* I **drop sb from a team/side** *Taylor was bitterly disappointed to be dropped from the England side.*
7 STOP DOING STH [T] to stop doing something, discussing something, or continuing with something: *The proposal was dropped after opposition from civil liberties groups.* I **drop charges/drop a case** *New evidence was presented to the court and the case was dropped.* I **drop a subject at school/university** (=stop studying it) *Students are allowed to drop history in Year 9.* I *You can't expect me to drop everything* (=completely stop doing whatever I am doing) *whenever you're in town.* I *Oh, drop the 'Senator'* (=stop calling me 'Senator') *- just call me Gordon.* I *Some time later, the matter was quietly dropped.*
8 STOP TALKING ABOUT STH [I,T] to stop talking about something: **drop the subject** *To her relief, Julius dropped the subject.* I **drop it** (=stop talking about a subject) *Just drop it, will you? I don't want to talk about it any more.* I *'What about the money?' 'We've agreed to let it drop* (=we have agreed not to talk about it any more).'
9 TAKE SB SOMEWHERE also **drop off** [T] to take someone by car to a place and leave them there, especially on your way to another place: *Just drop me here – I can walk the rest of the way.* I **drop sb at sth** *She dropped Johnny at the school gates at 8:30.*
10 TAKE STH SOMEWHERE [T] to take something to a place and leave it there: **drop sth round/in** *I've got your books – I'll drop them round to your place later.*
11 VISIT [I always + adv/prep] to visit someone you know, usually without arranging a particular time: [+**by/round**] *I just dropped by to see how you were getting on.* I *The kids drop round and see her from time to time.* I [+**into**] *Jan dropped into the office this morning to tell me her news.* I **drop in (on sb)** *Why don't you drop in for a drink one evening?*

⎧ 1 ⎭ 000, ⎧ 2 ⎭ 000, ⎧ 3 ⎭ 000, most frequent words in ⎧ S ⎭ poken and ⎧ W ⎭ ritten English

12 SLOPE DOWNWARDS [I always + adv/prep] if a path, land etc drops, it goes down suddenly, forming a steep slope: [+**down**] *The cliff dropped down over a hundred feet to the sea below.* | [+**away**] *On the left the ground drops away, giving a view over the rooftops.*

13 END A RELATIONSHIP [T] *informal* to suddenly stop having a relationship with someone, especially a romantic relationship: *She dropped him as soon as she found out he had been seeing another woman.*

14 until/till you drop until you are too tired to continue doing something: *We're going to shop till we drop!*

15 drop a hint to suggest or ask for something in an indirect way, hoping that the person you are talking to will understand what you mean: *He dropped some big hints about what he wanted for his birthday.*

16 drop sb a line/note *informal* to write a short letter to someone: *Drop us a line to let us know how you're getting on.*

17 drop dead **a)** *informal* to die suddenly **b)** *spoken informal* an impolite expression which you say to someone when you are extremely angry with them

18 sb's jaw dropped used to say that someone was very surprised

19 drop your eyes/gaze to stop looking at someone and look down, usually because you feel embarrassed or uncomfortable: *Ben looked at me in horror for a moment and then dropped his gaze.*

20 the wind drops the wind stops: *They waited for the wind to drop.*

21 drop a bombshell *informal* to suddenly tell someone a shocking piece of news: *Finally she dropped the bombshell. She was pregnant and I was the father.*

22 drop sb in it *informal* to say or do something that gets someone else into trouble: *You told her where we went on Friday night! You've really dropped me in it now!*

23 drop $50/£2000 etc [T] *informal* to lose money in a business deal, a game etc: *Phil dropped $200 playing poker yesterday.*

24 drop a catch to fail to catch a ball hit by a BATSMAN in CRICKET

25 drop a point to lose a point in a sports competition: *Real Madrid dropped a point at home yesterday.*

26 be dropping like flies *informal* if people are dropping like flies, they are getting ill or dying in large numbers

27 drop a clanger/brick *BrE* to say something embarrassing in a social situation

28 drop a stitch to let the wool fall off the needle when you are KNITTING

29 drop anchor to lower a boat's ANCHOR to the bottom of the sea, a lake etc so that the boat does not float away

30 drop acid *informal* to swallow LSD (=an illegal drug)

drop back also **drop behind** *phr v*
to move more slowly than other people so that they get ahead of you: *He started out with the leaders but at the first fence he dropped back.* | *Ellen dropped behind to tie her shoelace.*

drop off *phr v*
1 to begin to sleep: *She kept dropping off at her desk.* | *I must have dropped off to sleep.*
2 drop sb/sth ⇔ off to take someone or something to a place by car and leave them there on your way to another place: *I'll drop you off on my way home.*
3 to fall to a lower level or amount: *The number of graduates going into teaching has dropped off sharply.*

drop out *phr v*
1 to no longer do an activity or belong to a group: *The group gets smaller as members move away or drop out.*
2 to leave a school or university before your course has finished; → **dropout**: [+**of**] *Bill dropped out of college after his first year.*
3 to refuse to take part in ordinary society because you do not agree with its principles; → **dropout**: *In the 60s, Timothy Leary famously urged kids to 'Turn on, tune in and drop out.'*

drop² [S2] [W3] *n*

1 LIQUID [C] a very small amount of liquid that falls in a round shape: [+**of**] *As the first drops of rain began to fall, Michael started to run.* | *A single drop of blood splashed onto the floor.* | *A drop of sweat ran down her forehead and into her eye.* → RAIN DROP, TEARDROP

2 SMALL AMOUNT [usually singular] *informal* **a)** a small amount of liquid that you drink, especially alcohol: [+**of**] *She likes to add a drop of brandy to her tea.* | *George hasn't* **touched a drop** (=drunk any alcohol) *for years.* **b)** a small amount of something: [+**of**] *I haven't got a drop of sympathy for him.*

3 REDUCTION [singular] a reduction in the amount, level, or number of something, especially a large or sudden one; ◳ **fall**: [+**in**] *Manufacturers report a big drop in new orders.* | *a drop in temperature* | **a sharp/dramatic/marked drop in sth** *The results showed a sharp drop in profits.*

4 DISTANCE TO GROUND [singular] a distance from a higher point down to the ground or to a lower point: *There was a steep drop on one side of the track.* | *a 20-metre drop* | *There was an almost* **sheer** (=vertical) *drop to the valley below.*

5 at the drop of a hat immediately and without pausing to think about what you are going to do: *Some of these corporations threaten to sue at the drop of a hat.*

6 DELIVERY [C] an act of delivering something somewhere, for example by dropping it from a plane; ◳ **delivery**: *Air drops* (=from a plane) *of food aid were made to the region yesterday.* | *My first drop of the day is usually somewhere in north London.* → MAIL DROP

7 lemon/fruit/chocolate etc drop a sweet that tastes of LEMON etc

8 a drop in the ocean *BrE*, **a drop in the bucket** *AmE* a very small amount of something compared to what is needed or wanted: *5000 new schools are to be built, but this is just a drop in the ocean for such a vast country.*

9 eye/ear etc drops a type of medicine that you put in your eye, ear etc, one drop at a time

'drop cloth *n* [C] *AmE* a large cloth for covering furniture or floors in order to protect them from dust or paint; ◳ **dustsheet** *BrE*

,drop dead 'date *n* [C usually singular] *AmE informal* a date by which you must have completed something, because after this date it is no longer worth doing; → **deadline**

,drop-dead 'gorgeous *adj informal* very attractive

'drop-down ,menu *n* [C] a list of choices which appears on a computer screen when you CLICK on a place on the screen

'drop goal *n* [C] a GOAL in RUGBY football made with a dropkick

'drop-in *adj* [only before noun] a drop-in place is a place offering a service or support where you can go without having to make arrangements first: *a drop-in advice centre*

drop·kick /'drɒpkɪk $ 'drɑːp-/ *n* [C] a kick in a game such as RUGBY football, made by dropping the ball and kicking it immediately

drop·let /'drɒplɪ̩t $ 'drɑːp-/ *n* [C] a very small drop of liquid: [+**of**] *tiny* **droplets of water**

drop·out /'drɒpaʊt $ 'drɑːp-/ *n* [C] **1** someone who leaves school or college before they have finished: *a highschool dropout* **2** someone who refuses to take part in ordinary society because they do not agree with its social practices, moral standards etc

drop·per /'drɒpə $ 'drɑːpər/ *n* [C] a short glass tube with a hollow rubber part at one end, that you use to measure liquid one drop at a time

drop·pings /'drɒpɪŋz $ 'drɑː-/ *n* [plural] the solid waste that passes out of the bodies of animals or birds

'drop shot *n* [C] a shot in a game such as tennis in which the ball is hit softly and falls quickly to the ground

dross /drɒs $ drɑːs, drɔːs/ n [U]   **1** something that is of very low quality: *Most of the poems were pretentious dross.*   **2** waste or useless substances: *gold with impurities or dross*

drought /draʊt/ n [C,U] a long period of dry weather when there is not enough water for plants and animals to live

drove[1] /drəʊv $ droʊv/ the past tense of DRIVE

drove[2] n [C]   **1 droves** [plural] crowds of people: **in droves** *Tourists come in droves to see the White House.*   **2** a group of animals that are being moved together: [+of] *a drove of cattle*

drov·er /'drəʊvə $ 'droʊvər/ n [C] someone who moves cattle or sheep from one place to another in groups

drown /draʊn/ v   **1** [I,T] to die from being under water for too long, or to kill someone in this way: *Many people drowned when the boat overturned.* | *Jane was drowned in the river.* | **drown yourself** *Depressed, Peter tried to drown himself.*   **2** also **drown out** [T] if a loud noise drowns out another sound, it prevents it from being heard: *A train blew its whistle and drowned his voice.* | *The noise of the battle was drowned out by his aircraft's engine.*   **3** [T] to cover something, especially food, with more liquid than is necessary or nice: **drown sth in sth** *The fish was drowned in a rich sauce.*   **4** [I,T] to have a very strong feeling or a serious problem that is difficult to deal with: [+in] *Relief agencies are drowning in frustration.* | *The country is drowning in debt.*   **5 drown your sorrows** to drink a lot of alcohol in order to forget your problems

drowse /draʊz/ v [I] to be in a light sleep or to feel as though you are almost asleep: *I was drowsing in front of the television when you called.*

drow·sy /'draʊzi/ adj   **1** tired and almost asleep; ◘ **sleepy**: *The drug can make you drowsy.*   **2** so peaceful that you feel relaxed and almost asleep; ◘ **sleepy**: *a drowsy summer afternoon* —**drowsily** adv —**drowsiness** n [U]

drub·bing /'drʌbɪŋ/ n [C] an occasion when one team easily beats another team in sport: *Ireland gave England a drubbing at Twickenham.*

drudge /drʌdʒ/ n [C] someone who does hard boring work —**drudge** v [I]

drudg·e·ry /'drʌdʒəri/ n [U] hard boring work

drug[1] S2 W1 /drʌg/ n [C]
1 an illegal substance such as MARIJUANA or COCAINE, which some people take in order to feel happy, relaxed, or excited

> **take/use drugs**
> **do drugs** *informal* (=take drugs)
> **be on drugs** (=take drugs regularly)
> **experiment with drugs** (=try taking drugs)
> **come off drugs** (=stop taking drugs permanently)
> **high on drugs** (=experiencing the effects of a drug)
> **hard drugs** (=strong drugs such as HEROIN, COCAINE etc)
> **soft drugs** (=less strong drugs such as MARIJUANA)
> **recreational drugs** (=drugs people take for pleasure)
> **drug abuse**
> **drug overdose** (=when someone takes too much of a drug and becomes unconscious or dies)
> **drug trafficking/smuggling** (=bringing drugs into a country)

*A lot of young people start **taking drugs** at school.* | *One third of America's thirteen-year-olds **use drugs**.* | *I don't drink, and I don't **do drugs**.* | *She always looks as though she's **on drugs**.* | *All the band **experimented with drugs**, particularly LSD.* | *Parents should talk openly to their children about the dangers of **drug abuse**.* | *Jimi Hendrix died of a **drug overdose**.* | *After being returned to the USA he was convicted on **drug trafficking** charges.* | *the war on drugs*

2 a medicine, or a substance for making medicines: *a drug used in the treatment of cancer* | [+for] *new drugs for AIDS-related conditions* | *Drugs prescribed* (=ordered for people) *by doctors can be extremely hazardous if used in the wrong way* | *The big drug*

companies make huge profits.
3 a substance that people doing a sport sometimes take illegally to improve their performance: *She was banned from the Olympics after failing a **drug test** (=a test that shows if you have taken drugs).* | **performance-enhancing drugs**
4 [usually singular] a substance such as tobacco, coffee, or alcohol, that makes you want more and more of it
5 be (like) a drug if an activity is like a drug, you enjoy it so much that you want to do it more and more: *Athletics is like a drug, it keeps dragging you back for more.* → DESIGNER DRUG; → **miracle drug** at MIRACLE (3)

drug[2] v **drugged, drugging** [T]   **1** to give a person or animal a drug, especially in order to make them feel tired or go to sleep, or to make them perform well in a race: *Johnson drugged and attacked four women.* | *There was no evidence that the horse had been drugged.*   **2** to put drugs in someone's food or drink in order to make them feel tired or go to sleep; ◘ **spike**: *The wine had been drugged.*   **3 be drugged up to the eyeballs** *especially BrE* to have taken a lot of illegal drugs, or to have been given a lot of medicine: *She was in pain, despite being drugged up to the eyeballs.* —**drugged** adj

drug addict n [C] someone who cannot stop taking illegal drugs —**drug addiction** n [U]

drug baron n [C] someone who leads an organization that buys and sells large quantities of illegal drugs

drug czar n [C] an official employed by a government to try to stop the trade of illegal drugs

drug dealer n [C] someone who sells illegal drugs; ◘ **dealer**

drug·get /'drʌgɪt/ n [C,U] rough heavy cloth used especially as a floor covering, or a piece of this cloth

drug·gie /'drʌgi/ n [C] *informal* someone who often takes illegal drugs

drug·gist /'drʌgɪst/ n [C] *AmE old-fashioned* someone who is trained to prepare medicines, and works in a shop; ◘ **pharmacist**

drug rehabilitation also **drug rehab** n [U] the process of helping someone to live without illegal drugs after they have been ADDICTED to them

drug runner n [C] someone who brings illegal drugs from one country to another

drug·store /'drʌgstɔː $ -stɔːr/ n [C] *especially AmE* a shop where you can buy medicines, beauty products etc; ◘ **pharmacy** *AmE*; ◘ **chemist's** *BrE*

dru·id /'druːɪd/ n [C] a member of an ancient group of priests, in Britain, Ireland, and France, before the Christian religion

drums

drum — cymbal — bass drum — drum kit — conga drum — bongos — tambourine — snare drum

drum[1] /drʌm/ n [C]   **1** a musical instrument made of skin stretched over a circular frame, played by hitting it with your hand or a stick: *a big bass drum* | *1000 people marched, **beating drums** and carrying flags.* |

D

on drums *Trumpeter Red Rodney was playing with Kenny Clarke on drums* (=playing the drums). | *Jones **played the drums** in an all-girl band.* **2** a large round container for storing liquids such as oil, chemicals etc: *a 5 gallon oil drum* → see picture at CONTAINER **3** something that looks like a drum, especially part of a machine: *a brake drum* **4 bang/beat the drum for sb/sth** to speak eagerly in support of someone or something: *The company is banging the drum for their new software.* **5 the drum of sth** a sound like the sound a drum makes: *the steady drum of the rain on the window* → EARDRUM

drum² *v* **drummed, drumming 1** [I] to play a drum **2** [I,T] to make a sound similar to a drum by hitting a surface again and again: *I could hear the rain drumming against the windows.* | *Lisa **drummed** her **fingers** impatiently on the table.* **3 drum sth home** to use repeated arguments or messages in order to make sure that people understand something: *An information booklet will be available and press advertisements will drum home the message.*

drum sth **into** sb *phr v* to keep telling someone something until they cannot forget it: *'Don't talk to strangers' is a **message drummed into** children from an early age.*

drum sb **out of** sth *phr v* to force someone to leave an organization, place, or job: *He was drummed out of the army.*

drum sth ⇔ **up** *phr v* to get support, interest, attention etc from people by making an effort: *He travelled throughout Latin America **drumming up support** for the confederation.* | *The organization is using the event to **drum up business** (=get more work and sales).*

drum·beat /'drʌmbiːt/ *n* [C] the sound made when someone hits a drum

drum kit *n* [C] a set of drums, used especially by professional musicians → see picture at DRUM

drum ma,chine *n* [C] a piece of electronic equipment that makes patterns of sounds like drum music

drum 'major / $ '. ,../ *n* [C] the male leader of a MARCHING BAND

drum major'ette / $ '. ..,./ *n* [C] a MAJORETTE

drum·mer /'drʌmə $ -ər/ *n* [C] someone who plays drums

drum·ming /'drʌmɪŋ/ *n* [U] **1** when you play a drum, or the sound of a drum being played **2** the sound of something hitting a surface again and again: *the drumming of the horses' hooves*

drum 'n' bass /,drʌm ən 'beɪs/ *n* [U] a type of electronic dance music with a very hard fast beat

drum-roll *n* [C] A quick continuous beating of a drum, used especially to introduce an important event

drum·stick /'drʌm,stɪk/ *n* [C] **1** the lower part of the leg of a chicken or other bird, cooked as food **2** a stick that you use to hit a drum

drunk¹ /drʌŋk/ the past participle of DRINK

drunk² *adj* **1** [not before noun] unable to control your behaviour, speech etc because you have drunk too much alcohol; 🔒 **sober**: *You're drunk.* | *David would **get drunk** and I would have to take him home and put him to bed.* | [+on] *He was drunk on beer and whisky.* | **blind drunk** *BrE* (=very drunk) *All she wants to do is get blind drunk.* | **drunk as a lord** also **drunk as a skunk** (=very drunk) *He turned up one morning, drunk as a lord.* **2** being drunk and disorderly *law* the crime of behaving in a violent noisy way in a public place when you are drunk **3 drunk on/with sth** so excited by a feeling that you behave in a strange way: *drunk with happiness* → PUNCH-DRUNK; → roaring drunk at ROARING (5)

drunk³ also **drunk·ard** /'drʌŋkəd $ -ərd/ *n* [C] someone who is drunk or often gets drunk; → alcoholic

drunk 'driving *n* [U] *AmE* driving a car after having drunk too much alcohol; 🔒 **drink-driving** *BrE* —**drunk driver** *n* [C]

drunk·en /'drʌŋkən/ *adj* [only before noun] **1** drunk or showing that you are drunk: *McBride was a drunken bully.* | *She was lying **in a drunken stupor** (=nearly unconscious from being drunk) on the sidewalk.* **2** drunken party/orgy/brawl etc a party etc where people are drunk: *Tom got into a drunken brawl* (=fight) *in a bar.* —**drunkenly** *adv* —**drunkenness** *n* [U]

drunk tank *n* [C] *AmE informal* a cell in a prison for people who have drunk too much alcohol

dry¹ [S2] [W2] /draɪ/ *adj comparative* **drier**, *superlative* **driest**

1 NOT WET without water or liquid inside or on the surface; 🔒 **wet**: *I need to change into some dry clothes.* | *Make sure that the surface is clean and dry before you start to paint.* | *You should store disks in a cool, dry place.* | **shake/rub/wipe etc sth dry** *Jean rubbed her hair dry.* | *The path is **dry as a bone** (=very dry).* → BONE DRY

2 WEATHER having very little rain or MOISTURE; 🔒 **wet**; → **arid**: *The weather was hot and dry.* | *Eastern areas should stay dry tomorrow.* | *the **dry season** | These plants do not grow well in **dry conditions** (=when there is not much rain).* | *a prolonged **dry spell** (=period)*

3 dry mouth/skin/lips/hair etc without enough of the liquid or oil that is normally in your mouth, skin etc; → **parched**: *His heart was pounding and his mouth was dry.* | *Mary has dry, sensitive skin.* | *a shampoo for dry hair* | *She licked her dry lips.*

4 run/go dry if a lake, river etc runs dry, all the water gradually disappears, especially because there has been no rain: *The river ran dry last summer.*

5 HUMOUR someone with a dry sense of humour says funny and clever things while seeming to be serious: *He had a delightfully dry sense of humour.*

6 BORING boring, very serious, and without humour: *In schools, science is often presented in a dry and uninteresting manner.* | *a dry debate on policies*

7 dry cough a cough which does not produce any PHLEGM

8 dry wine/sherry etc wine etc that is not sweet: *a glass of dry white wine*

9 WITHOUT ALCOHOL not drinking alcohol, or not allowing any alcohol to be sold: *Paula had been dry for a year before she started drinking again.* | *Kuwait's a dry country.*

10 VOICE showing no emotion when you speak: *'Good evening gentlemen,' he said, in a dry voice.*

11 dry bread/toast bread etc eaten on its own without anything such as butter or JAM spread on it

12 THIRSTY *informal* thirsty

13 not a dry eye in the house used to say that everyone was crying because something was very sad – often used humorously —**dryness** *n* [U] → DRIP-DRY, DRY ROT; → **home and dry** at HOME² (6); → **leave sb high and dry** at HIGH² (5); → DRYLY

dry² [S2] [W3] *v* **dried, drying, dries** [I,T]

1 to make something dry, or to become dry: *Mrs Brown hung the washing on the line to dry.* | *He was **drying** his **hair** with a towel.* | *Mary **dried** her **hands**.* | *Leave the first coat of paint to dry before adding another.* | *She stood up and **dried** her **eyes** (=wiped away her tears).* | **dry yourself** *He quickly dried himself on the thin towel.*

2 also **dry up** *BrE* to rub plates, dishes etc dry with a cloth after they have been washed: *You wash and I'll dry.* | *Shall I dry up these glasses?* → CUT AND DRIED, DRIED

dry off *phr v*

to become dry or to make something dry, especially on the surface: *We swam in the sea, then stretched out on the sand to dry off.* | **dry sth ⇔ off** *He dried the camera off, hoping it would still work.*

dry out *phr v*

1 to become completely dry or to make something completely dry, especially after it has been very wet: *In* summer, water the plants regularly and never let the soil dry out. | **dry sth ⇔ out** The kitchen was flooded and it took ages to dry it out.

2 dry (sb) out to stop drinking alcohol after you have become an ALCOHOLIC, or to make someone do this: He's been drying out at a private clinic. | The hospital dried Michael out and sent him home.

dry up phr v

1 COME TO AN END if a supply of something dries up, it comes to an end and no more is available: Foreign investment may dry up. | The work soon dried up.

2 RIVER/LAKE ETC if something such as a river dries up, the water in it disappears: Across central and west Texas, waterholes and wells have dried up. | **dry sth ⇔ up** Taking too much water for household use is drying up the river.

3 STOP TALKING if someone dries up, they stop talking: 'It was -' She dried up again. | Everyone became embarrassed and conversation dried up.

4 PLATES/DISHES ETC BrE to rub plates, dishes etc dry with a cloth after they have been washed: **dry sth ⇔ up** I'll just dry up these mugs and we can have a coffee.

dry·ad /ˈdraɪæd/ n [C] a female spirit who lives in a tree, in ancient Greek stories

dry ˌbattery n [C] an electric BATTERY containing chemicals that are not in a liquid form

dry ˌcell n [C] the type of cell used in a dry battery

dry-ˈclean / $ '. ./ v [T] to clean clothes etc with chemicals instead of water —**dry ˈcleaning** n [U]

dry ˈcleaner's n plural dry cleaner's [C] a shop where you can take clothes etc to be dry-cleaned

dry dock n [C] a place where a ship can be taken out of the water for repairs

dry·er, **drier** /ˈdraɪə $ -ər/ n [C] a machine that dries things, especially clothes → HAIRDRYER, SPIN-DRYER, TUMBLE DRYER

dry-ˈeyed adj not crying

dry goods n [plural] **1** goods such as tobacco, tea, and coffee that do not contain liquid **2** AmE things that are made from cloth such as clothes, sheets, and curtains: a dry goods store

dry ˈice n [U] CARBON DIOXIDE in a solid form, which is used to make mist in a theatre or DISCO, or to keep food or other things cold

dry ˈland n [U] land rather than water: After three weeks at sea we were glad to be back on dry land again.

dry·ly, **drily** /ˈdraɪli/ adv if you say something dryly, you say something that is amusing but you appear to be completely serious: 'I hear you're a hero,' Philip said dryly.

dry-ˈroasted adj dry-roasted nuts have been cooked without any oil

dry ˈrot n [U] a disease in wood that turns it into powder

dry ˈrun n [C] an event that is a practice for a more important event: Both the parties are treating the local elections as a dry run.

dry-ˈshod adv without getting your feet wet

dry-stone ˈwall n [C] in Britain, a wall built with pieces of stone that are fitted closely together without using CEMENT to hold them in place

dry ˈwall n [U] AmE a type of board made of two large sheets of CARDBOARD with PLASTER between them, used to cover walls and ceilings —**dry-wall** v [I,T]

DSL /ˌdiː es ˈel/ n [C] technical digital subscriber line a telephone line that has special equipment which allows it to receive information from the Internet, or send information at very high speeds

DSS /ˌdiː es ˈes/ n the DSS the abbreviation of the Department of Social Security in Britain

DTI /ˌdiː tiː ˈaɪ/ n the DTI the abbreviation of the Department of Trade and Industry in Britain

DTP /ˌdiː tiː ˈpiː/ n [U] desktop publishing the work of arranging the writing and pictures for a magazine, small book etc, using a computer and special software

DT's BrE; **D.T.'s** AmE /ˌdiː ˈtiːz/ n the DT's a condition in which your body shakes and you see imaginary things, caused by drinking too much alcohol – used humorously

du·al /ˈdjuːəl $ ˈduːəl/ adj [only before noun] having two of something or two parts: **dual role/purpose/function** The bridge has a dual role, carrying both road and rail. | a **dual system** of education | **dual citizenship/ nationality** She has dual nationality, of Canada and Britain (=she is a citizen of Canada and Britain). —**duality** /djuˈæləti $ duː-/ n [U]

dual-band adj [only before noun] a dual-band MOBILE PHONE is able to work in at least two different countries because it can receive two different types of signals

dual ˈcarriageway n [C] BrE a main road that has two lines of traffic travelling in each direction, with a narrow part between them that has no traffic; ⊟ divided highway AmE

du·a·lis·m /ˈdjuːəlɪzəm $ ˈduː-/ n [U] technical the idea that there are two opposite parts or principles in everything, for example body and soul, or the state of having two parts or principles

dub¹ /dʌb/ v dubbed, dubbing [T] **1** [usually passive] to give something or someone a name that describes them in some way; → label, name: be dubbed sth The body, thousands of years old, was found in the Alps and dubbed 'The Iceman'. **2** to change the original spoken language of a film or television programme into another language: be dubbed into sth a British film dubbed into French **3** especially BrE to make a record out of two or more different pieces of music or sound mixed together **4** AmE to copy a recording from a tape or CD onto another tape **5** if a king or queen dubs someone, they give the title of KNIGHT to that person in a special ceremony

dub² n [U] a style of poetry or music from the West Indies with a strong regular beat

du·bi·ous /ˈdjuːbiəs $ ˈduː-/ adj **1** probably not honest, true, right etc: The firm was accused of dubious accounting practices. | Many critics regard this argument as dubious or, at best, misleading. | The assumption that growth in one country benefits the whole world is **highly dubious**. **2** [not before noun] not sure whether something is good or true; ⊟ doubtful: I can see you are dubious; take some time to think about it. | [+about] Some universities are dubious about accepting students over the age of 30. | 'Are you sure you know what you are doing?' Andy said, **looking dubious**. **3** the dubious honour/distinction/pleasure (of doing sth) a dubious honour etc is the opposite of an honour – used about something unpleasant that happens: The Stephensons **had the dubious honor** of being the 100th family to lose their home in the fire. **4** not good or not of good quality: The room was decorated in dubious taste. —**dubiously** adv —**dubiousness** n [U]

du·cal /ˈdjuːkəl $ ˈduː-/ adj like a DUKE or belonging to a duke

duc·at /ˈdʌkət/ n [C] a gold coin that was used in several European countries in the past

duch·ess /ˈdʌtʃɪs/ n [C] a woman with the highest social rank outside the royal family, or the wife of a DUKE: the Duchess of York

duch·y /ˈdʌtʃi/ n plural duchies [C] the land and property of a DUKE or DUCHESS; ⊟ dukedom

duck¹ S3 /dʌk/ n

1 [C] a very common water bird with short legs and a wide beak, used for its meat, eggs, and soft feathers

2 [C] a female duck; → drake

3 [U] the meat of a duck used as food: roast duck with orange sauce

1 000, 2 000, 3 000, most frequent words in S poken and W ritten English

4 take to something like a duck to water to learn how to do something very easily: *She took to dancing like a duck to water.*

5 also **ducks** *BrE spoken* used to speak to someone, especially a woman, in a friendly way: *What can I get you, ducks?*

6 [C] a SCORE of zero by a BATSMAN in a game of CRICKET → DEAD DUCK, LAME DUCK; → **like water off a duck's back** at WATER¹ (8); → DUCKS AND DRAKES, SITTING DUCK

duck² *v* **1** also **duck down** [I,T] to lower your head or body very quickly, especially to avoid being seen or hit: *If she hadn't ducked, the ball would have hit her.* | [+behind/under etc] *Jamie saw his father coming and ducked quickly behind the wall.* | *Tim ducked down to comb his hair in the mirror.* | *She **ducked** her **head** to look more closely at the inscription.* **2** [I always + adv/prep] to move somewhere very quickly, especially to avoid being seen or to get away from someone: [+into] *The two men ducked into a block of flats and disappeared.* | [+out of] *She ducked out of the door before he could stop her.* | [+back] *'Wait a minute', he called, ducking back inside.* **3** [T] *informal* to avoid something, especially a difficult or unpleasant duty; ◙ **dodge**: *The ruling body wanted to **duck** the **issue** of whether players had been cheating.* | *Glazer **ducked** a **question** about his involvement in the bank scandal.* **4** [T] to push someone under water for a short time as a joke: **duck sb under sth** *Tom grabbed him from behind to duck him under the surface.*

duck out of sth *phr v* to avoid doing something that you have to do or have promised to do: *I always ducked out of history lessons at school.*

duck·billed plat·y·pus /ˌdʌkbɪld ˈplætɪ̯pəs/ *n* [C] a PLATYPUS

duck·boards /ˈdʌkbɔːdz $ -bɔːrdz/ *n* [plural] long boards used to make a path over muddy ground

'ducking stool *n* [C] a seat on the end of a long pole, used in the past to put a person under water as a punishment

duck·ling /ˈdʌklɪŋ/ *n* [C] a young duck

ducks and 'drakes *n* [U] *BrE* a children's game in which you make flat stones jump across the surface of water

duck·weed /ˈdʌkwiːd/ *n* [U] a plant that grows on the surface of ponds

'duck·y¹ /ˈdʌki/ *n* *BrE spoken* used to speak to someone in a friendly way, especially a woman or child

ducky² *adj* *old-fashioned informal* **1** *AmE* perfect or satisfactory: *Well, that's **just ducky**.* **2** attractive in an amusing or interesting way; ◙ **cute**

duct /dʌkt/ *n* [C] **1** a pipe or tube that liquids, air, CABLES etc pass through: *Air is heated and then circulated through large ducts to all parts of the house.* **2** a narrow tube in your body or in a plant that liquid passes through: *a tear duct*

duc·tile /ˈdʌktaɪl $ -tl/ *adj* ductile metals can be pressed or pulled into shape without needing to be heated —**ductility** /dʌkˈtɪlɪ̯ti/ *n* [U]

duct·ing /ˈdʌktɪŋ/ *n* [U] a system of pipes or tubes that liquids, air, CABLES etc pass through

dud /dʌd/ *n* [C] **1** something that is useless, especially because it does not work correctly: *Several of the fireworks were duds.* **2 duds** [plural] *informal* clothes —**dud** *adj*: *a dud light bulb*

dude /djuːd $ duːd/ *n* [C] *AmE* **1** *informal* a man: *a real cool dude* **2** *old-fashioned* an American man from a city, who is living in or visiting a farm or RANCH

'dude ranch *n* [C] a holiday place in the US where you can ride horses and live like a COWBOY

dud·geon /ˈdʌdʒən/ *n* *formal* **in high dudgeon** in an angry or offended way – often used humorously

due¹ [S1] [W1] /djuː $ duː/ *adj*
1 [EXPECTED] [not before noun] expected to happen or arrive at a particular time: **due to do sth** *The team are*

due to fly to Italy next month.* | *His new book is due to be published next year.* | [+in/on/at] *She's pregnant and the baby's due in April.* | *The final results of the experiment are due on December 9.* | *I'm due at his office at 4.30.* | [+for] *The car is due for its annual service again.* | [+back] *When are the library books due back?* → DUE DATE

2 [OWED] owed to someone either as a debt or because they have a right to it: *Any money due you will be sent by cheque through the post.* | [+to] *Thanks are due to all those who took part.*

3 [MONEY] if an amount of money is due, it must be paid at a particular time: *The next income tax payment is due on 31 January.*

4 in due course at some time in the future when it is the right time, but not before: *Further details will be announced in due course.*

5 [PROPER] [only before noun] *formal* proper or suitable: *He was banned for six months for driving without due care and attention.* | **due regard/consideration** *We want the best for each individual child with due regard for the interests of the other children.*

6 with (all) due respect *spoken* used when you disagree with someone or criticize them in a polite way: *Dad, with all due respect, was not a very good husband.* → DULY, DUE TO

due² *n* **1 your due** your due is what you deserve, or something it is your right to have: *He accepted all the praise he received as his due.* | *Freddy, **to give** him his **due** (=to be fair to him), always tried to be honest.* **2 dues** [plural] regular payments you make to an organization of which you are a member; ◙ **fees**: *Robert failed to **pay** his **dues** last year.*

due³ *adv* **due north/south/east/west** directly to the north, south, east, or west

due 'date *n* [C usually singular] the date on which something is supposed to happen: *Fewer than five percent of women have their babies on their due date.*

du·el¹ /ˈdjuːəl $ ˈduːəl/ *n* [C] **1** a fight with weapons between two people, used in the past to settle a quarrel: *The officer **challenged** him **to** a **duel**.* **2** a situation in which two people or groups are involved in an angry disagreement: *a verbal duel*

duel² *v* **duelled, duelling** *BrE*, **dueled, dueling** *AmE* [I] to fight a duel

due 'process *n* [U] *AmE law* the correct process that should be followed in law and is designed to protect someone's legal rights

du·et¹ /djuˈet $ duˈet/ *n* [C] a piece of music for two singers or players; → **quartet, solo, trio**

duet² *v past tense* **duetted**, *past participle* **duetting** if one singer or musician duets with another, they sing or play together

'due to *prep* because of something: *The court of inquiry ruled that the crash was due to pilot error.* | *He has been absent from work due to illness.* | *The restaurant's success was **due largely to** its new manager.* | *Attendance at the meeting was small, **due in part to** (=partly because of) the absence of teachers.*

duff¹ /dʌf/ *n* [C] *AmE informal* the part of your body that you sit on; ◙ **bottom**: *Get off your duff (=stop sitting or stop being lazy) and help me!*

duff² *adj* *BrE informal* bad or useless

duff³ *v*

duff sb ⇔ **up** *phr v* *BrE informal* to fight someone and injure them

duf·fel bag, duffle bag /ˈdʌfəl bæg/ *n* [C] a bag made of strong cloth, with a round bottom and a string around the top

duffel coat, duffle coat /ˈdʌfəl kəʊt $ -koʊt/ *n* [C] a coat made of rough heavy cloth, usually with a HOOD and TOGGLES (=buttons shaped like tubes)

duf·fer /ˈdʌfə $ -ər/ *n* [C] *informal* someone who is stupid or not very good at something

dug /dʌɡ/ the past tense and past participle of DIG

dug·out /ˈdʌɡaʊt/ *n* [C] **1** a low shelter at the side of a sports field, where players and team officials sit **2** a shelter dug into the ground for soldiers to use; → **trench** **3** a small boat made by cutting out a hollow space in a tree trunk: *a dugout canoe*

duh /dʌ/ *interjection AmE* used to say that what some-one else has just said or asked is stupid

DUI /ˌdiː juː 'aɪ/ *n* [C,U] *law AmE* **driving under the influence** the crime of driving when you have had too much alcohol to drink; ◨ **DWI**: *There were a large number of DUI arrests on New Year's Eve.*

duke /djuːk $ duːk/ *n* [C] a man with the highest social rank outside the royal family; → **duchess**: *the Duke of Norfolk*

duke·dom /'djuːkdəm $ 'duːk-/ *n* [C] **1** the rank of a duke **2** the land and property belonging to a duke; ◨ **duchy**

dul·cet /'dʌlsɪt/ *adj* **sb's dulcet tones** someone's voice – used humorously: *Basil's dulcet tones could be heard in the corridor.*

dul·ci·mer /'dʌlsɪmə $ -ər/ *n* [C] **1** a musical instru-ment with up to 100 strings, played with light ham-mers **2** a small instrument with strings that is popular in American FOLK MUSIC, and is played across your knees

dull¹ ⟨S3⟩ /dʌl/ *adj comparative* **duller**, *superlative* **dullest**
1 BORING not interesting or exciting: *Life is never dull when Elizabeth is here.* | *a dull movie* | *It sounded pretty dull to me.* | *The weekly meeting tends to be deadly dull*(=very dull). | *Last week we had a hurricane.* **Never a dull moment** *running a hotel in the Caribbean* (=it's always interesting or exciting).
2 COLOUR/LIGHT not bright or shiny: *The bird is dull brown and gray in colour.* | *Her eyes were dull with dark shadows beneath them.* | *the dull afternoon light*
3 WEATHER not bright and with lots of clouds: *Out-side the weather was hazy and dull.* | *a dull sky*
4 PAIN a dull pain is not severe but does not stop; ◨ **sharp**: *a dull ache in her lower back* | *The pain was dull but persistent.*
5 SOUND not clear or loud: *The gates shut with a dull thud.*
6 KNIFE/BLADE not sharp; ◨ **blunt**
7 NOT INTELLIGENT *old-fashioned* not able to think quickly or understand things easily; ◨ **stupid**: *If you don't understand then you're duller than I thought.*
8 TRADE if business on the Stock Exchange is dull, few people are buying and selling —**dully** *adv*: *'Well Michael?' he said dully.* | *Her stomach ached dully.* —**dullness** *n* [U]

dull² *v* **1** [T] to make something become less sharp or clear: *He drank some alcohol to dull the pain.* | *Her fear and anxiety dulled her mind.* **2** [I,T] to become less bright or loud, or to make something become less bright or loud: *His eyes dulled a little.* | *The constant rain dulled all sound.*

dull·ard /'dʌləd $ -ərd/ *n* [C] someone who is stupid and has no imagination

du·ly /'djuːli $ 'duːli/ *adv* **1** in the proper or expected way: *Here are your travel documents, all duly signed.* **2** at the proper time or as expected: *The Queen duly appeared on the balcony to wave to the crowds.*

dumb¹ ⟨S3⟩ /dʌm/ *adj*
1 *informal* stupid: *What a dumb question.* | *a bunch of dumb kids* | *'What is it?' I asked, playing dumb* (=pre-tending to be stupid). | *She's no dumb blonde* (=a pretty woman with blonde hair who seems stupid).
2 unable to speak, because you are angry, surprised, shocked etc: *He stared at the burnt-out car in dumb disbelief.* | *She was struck dumb with terror.*
3 *old-fashioned* someone who is dumb is not able to speak at all. Many people think that this use is offen-sive; → **mute** → **deaf and dumb** at DEAF (1)
4 **dumb luck** *informal* something good that happens in an unexpected way, especially one that is not deserved: *It was just dumb luck that we found the place at all.*
5 **dumb animals/creatures** used to talk about animals

when you want to emphasize that humans often treat them badly and they cannot protect themselves —**dumbly** *adv*: *For a few seconds she gazed dumbly at him.* —**dumbness** *n* [U]

dumb² *v*
dumb *sth* ⇔ **down** to present news or information in a simple and attractive way without many details so that everyone can understand it – used to show disap-proval: *Have history textbooks been dumbed down over the past decade?* —**dumbing down** *n* [U]

dumb·bell /'dʌmbel/ *n* [C] **1** two weights connected by a short bar, that you can lift to strengthen your arms and shoulders; ◨ **weights** **2** *AmE informal* someone who is stupid

dumb·found·ed /dʌm'faʊndɪd/ *adj* extremely sur-prised: *He was completely dumbfounded by the incident.* —**dumbfound** *v* [T]

dum·bo /'dʌmbəʊ $ -boʊ/ *n plural* **dumbos** [C] *infor-mal* someone who is stupid

'**dumb show** *n* [C,U] the use of movements without words to express something; → **mime**

dumb·struck /'dʌmstrʌk/ *adj* so shocked or sur-prised that you cannot speak

ˌ**dumb 'waiter** *n* [C] a small LIFT used to move food, plates etc from one level to another in a restaurant, hotel etc to another

dum-dum /'dʌm dʌm/ *n* [C] a soft bullet that causes serious wounds because it breaks into pieces when it hits you

dum·my¹ /'dʌmi/ *n plural* **dummies** [C]
1 FOR CLOTHES a model that is the shape and size of a person, especially used in order to show clothes in a shop or when you are making clothes: *a shop-window dummy* | *a tailor's dummy*
2 COPY an object that is made to look like a tool, weapon, vehicle etc but which you cannot use: *During practice runs, the warheads in the missiles will be dummies.*
3 DOLL a small model of a person, with a mouth that can be moved so that it looks as though it is talking, used for entertainment: *a ventriloquist's dummy*
4 SPORTS *BrE* a move in a sport such as football in which a player pretends to pass the ball but does not, in order to deceive the other team's players
5 FOR BABIES *BrE* a specially shaped rubber object that you put in a baby's mouth for it to suck; ◨ **pacifier** *AmE*
6 STUPID PERSON *especially AmE informal* someone who is stupid: *No, you dummy. The other hand.*
7 CARD GAME cards that are placed on the table by one player for all the other players to see in a game of BRIDGE

dummy² *adj* [only before noun] a dummy tool, weapon, vehicle etc is made to look like a real one but you cannot use it; ◨ **replica**: *a dummy rifle*

ˌ**dummy 'run** *n* [C] an occasion when you practise doing something in complete detail to see if it works; ◨ **dry run**: *Do a dummy run to see how long it will take.*

dump¹ /dʌmp/ *v* [T]
1 PUT STH SOMEWHERE [always + adv/prep] to put something somewhere in a careless untidy way: *Mer-rill dumped her suitcase down in the hall.* | **dump sth on sth** *They dump tons of salt on icy road surfaces to make driving safer.* | **dump sth in/into sth** *He found a can of beef stew and dumped it in a saucepan to heat.*
2 GET RID OF STH **a)** to get rid of something that you do not want: *Ellie dumped all the photos of her ex-husband.* | *He dumped her body into the sea.* **b)** to get rid of waste material by taking it from people's houses and burying it under the soil: *Britain dumps more of its waste than any other European country.*
3 END RELATIONSHIP *informal* to end a relationship with someone: *Vicky dumped Neil yesterday.*
4 SELL GOODS to get rid of goods by selling them in a foreign country at a much lower price: [+in/on] *a*

D

campaign to stop cheap European beef being dumped in West Africa

5 COPY INFORMATION technical to copy information stored in a computer's memory on to something else such as a DISK or MAGNETIC TAPE → DUMPING

dump on sb phr v informal
1 dump sth on sb to unfairly give someone an unwanted job, duty, or problem to deal with: Don't just dump the extra work on me.
2 AmE to treat someone badly
3 AmE to criticize someone very strongly and often unfairly: politicians dumping on their opponents
4 dump (sth) on sb to tell someone all your problems and worries: We all dump our troubles on Mike.

dump² n [C]
1 WASTE a place where unwanted waste is taken and left: **rubbish dump** BrE/**garbage dump** AmE: The fire probably started in a rubbish dump. | Put the rest into a sack to take to **the dump**. | an underground nuclear waste dump | a dump site
2 WEAPONS a place where military supplies are stored, or the supplies themselves: There has been a series of explosions in an ammunition dump.
3 UNPLEASANT PLACE informal a place that is unpleasant to live in because it is dirty, ugly, untidy etc: ' What a dump,' she added as they entered the village. | Why are you living in a dump like this?
4 down in the dumps informal very sad and without much interest in life: She's feeling a bit down in the dumps.
5 COMPUTER technical the act of copying the information stored in a computer's memory onto something else, such as a DISK: a screen dump
6 take a dump informal not polite to pass solid waste from the BOWELS

dumper truck n [C] BrE a DUMP TRUCK

dump·ing /'dʌmpɪŋ/ n [U] the act of getting rid of dangerous waste material in a place that is not safe: The government has promised to stop dumping by the state-owned chemical plants.

dumping ground n [C] **1** a place where people get rid of waste material: [+for] Rivers have always been a dumping ground for man's unwanted waste. **2** a place where people are sent when no one knows how to deal with them: [+for] The prison has been the dumping ground for difficult prisoners for years.

dump·ling /'dʌmplɪŋ/ n [C] **1** a round lump of flour and fat mixed with water, cooked in boiling liquid and served with meat: chicken and dumplings **2** a sweet dish made of PASTRY filled with fruit: apple dumplings

Dump·ster /'dʌmpstə $ -ər/ n [C] trademark a large metal container used for waste in the US; ▪ **skip** BrE

dump truck AmE n [C] a vehicle with a large open container at the back that can move up to pour sand, soil etc onto the ground

dump·y /'dʌmpi/ adj someone who is dumpy is fat, short, and unattractive: a dumpy little man

dun /dʌn/ n [U] a brownish-grey colour —**dun** adj

dunce /dʌns/ n [C] old-fashioned someone who is slow at learning things: the dunce of the class

dunce's cap n [C] a tall pointed hat that a stupid student had to wear in school in the past

Dun·dee cake /dʌn'diː ˌkeɪk/ n [C,U] a British cake made with fruit and nuts

dun·der·head /'dʌndəhed $ -ər-/ n [C] old-fashioned someone who is stupid

dune /djuːn $ duːn/ n [C] a hill made of sand near the sea or in the desert; ▪ **sand dune**

dune buggy n [C] a car with big wheels and no roof that you can drive across sand; ▪ **beach buggy**

dung /dʌŋ/ n [U] solid waste from animals, especially cows

dun·ga·rees /ˌdʌŋɡə'riːz/ n [plural] **1** BrE loose trousers that have a square piece of cloth that covers

your chest, and long thin pieces that fasten over your shoulders; ▪ **overalls** AmE **2** AmE old-fashioned heavy cotton trousers used for working in; ▪ **jeans**

dun·geon /'dʌndʒən/ n [C] a dark underground prison, especially under a castle, that was used in the past

dunk /dʌŋk/ v **1** [T] to quickly put something into a liquid and take it out again, especially something you are eating: Jill dunked her ginger biscuit in her tea. | I dunked my head under the water and scrubbed at my hair. **2** [T] AmE to push someone under water for a short time as a joke; ▪ **duck** BrE **3** [I,T] to jump up by the basket and throw the ball down into it in BASKETBALL —**dunk** n [C] → dunk for apples at APPLE (3); → SLAM DUNK

dun·no /'dʌnəʊ $ -noʊ/ a way of saying 'I don't know'. Some people think that this use is not correct English: 'Do you want to come?' 'I dunno, I might.'

du·o /'djuːəʊ $ 'duːoʊ/ n plural **duos** [C] **1** two people who perform together or are often seen together: the comedy duo Reeves and Mortimer **2** a piece of music for two performers; ▪ **duet**

du·o·de·num /ˌdjuːə'diːnəm $ ˌduːə'diːnəm, duː'ɑːdn-əm/ n [C] the top part of your BOWEL, below your stomach —**duodenal** /ˌdjuːə'diːnl◂ $ ˌduːə'diːnl◂, duː'ɑːdn-əl/ adj: a duodenal ulcer

dupe¹ /djuːp $ duːp/ n [C] someone who is tricked, especially into becoming involved in something illegal

dupe² v [T usually passive] to trick or deceive someone: **dupe sb into doing sth** Consumers are being duped into buying faulty electronic goods.

du·plex /'djuːpleks $ 'duː-/ n [C] AmE a type of house that is divided into two parts, so that it has two separate homes in it

du·pli·cate¹ /'djuːplɪkeɪt $ 'duː-/ v [T] **1** to copy something exactly: New copies of the form can be duplicated from a master copy. | The video had been duplicated illegally. **2** to repeat something in exactly the same way: We don't want staff to duplicate each other's work. —**duplication** /ˌdjuːplɪ'keɪʃən $ ˌduː-/ n [U]

du·pli·cate² /'djuːplɪkət $ 'duː-/ adj [only before noun] exactly the same as something, or made as an exact copy of something: A **duplicate copy** should be made for the county record office. | a duplicate key

duplicate³ n [C] **1** an exact copy of something that you can use in the same way: [+of] Locksmiths can **make duplicates** of most keys. | She kept both the duplicate and the original. **2 in duplicate** if something is in duplicate, there are two copies of it: Copies of the proposal should be sent in duplicate.

du·plic·i·ty /djuː'plɪsɪti $ duː-/ n [U] dishonest behaviour that is intended to deceive someone —**duplicitous** adj

du·ra·ble /'djʊərəbəl $ 'dʊr-/ adj **1** staying in good condition for a long time, even if used a lot; ▪ **hardwearing**: Wood is a durable material. **2** continuing for a long time: His poetry has proved durable. —**durably** adv —**durability** /ˌdjʊərə'bɪlɪti $ ˌdʊr-/ n [U] → CONSUMER DURABLES

durable goods n [plural] AmE large things such as cars, televisions, and furniture, that you do not buy often; ▪ **consumer durables** BrE

du·ra·tion /djʊ'reɪʃən $ dʊ-/ n [U] the length of time that something continues: The course is of three years' duration. | **for the duration (of sth)** The package includes cycle hire for the duration of your holiday.

du·ress /djʊ'res $ dʊ-/ n [U] illegal or unfair threats: **under duress** The confession was obtained under duress.

Dur·ex /'djʊəreks $ 'dʊr-/ n trademark **1** [C] BrE a rubber CONTRACEPTIVE that a man wears over his PENIS during sex **2** [U] AusE clear narrow plastic that is sticky on one side and is used for fastening paper

dur·ing [S1] [W1] /'djʊərɪŋ $ 'dʊr-/ prep **1** from the beginning to the end of a period of time: During the summer she worked as a lifeguard. | He slept

calmly during the early part of the night. | *Foxes remain hidden during the day.*
2 at some point in a period of time: *My father was killed during the war.* | *I mentioned the subject during our discussions at her Washington office.*

WORD CHOICE: **during, while**

⚠ Do not say 'during doing something'. Say **while doing something**: *While travelling to work, I saw an accident* (NOT *During travelling to work, I saw an accident*).

⚠ Do not say 'during someone does something'. Say **while someone does something**: *He stole her money while she slept* (NOT *He stole her money during she slept*).

⚠ Do not say 'during someone is young/asleep etc'. Say **while someone is young/asleep etc**: *It's best to get your teeth fixed while you're still young* (NOT *during you're still young*). **during, for, or since?** See note at SINCE

---

durst /dɜːst $ dɜːrst/ *old use* the past tense of DARE

dusk /dʌsk/ *n* [U] the time before it gets dark when the sky is becoming less bright; ▪ **twilight**; → **dawn**: **at dusk** *The street lights go on at dusk.* → see picture at DAWN

dusk·y /ˈdʌski/ *adj* dark or not very bright in colour: *The room was filled with dusky shadows.* | **dusky pink/orange/blue etc** *a dusky pink room*

dust¹ S3 W3 /dʌst/ *n* [U]
1 dry powder consisting of extremely small bits of dirt that is in buildings on furniture, floors etc if they are not kept clean: *All the furniture was **covered in dust**.* | *a thick **layer of dust*** | *There's not a **speck of dust** in the kitchen.* | **gather/collect dust** (=become covered with dust) *Her old trophies were collecting dust on the shelves.* | ***Dust particles** floated in the sunlight.* | *A sudden breeze sent **motes of dust*** (=small bits of dust) *dancing in the air.*
2 dry powder consisting of extremely small bits of earth or sand: *The wind was blowing dust and leaves up from the ground.* | *A car sped past in a **cloud of dust**.*
3 powder consisting of extremely small bits of a particular substance: **coal/brick/chalk etc dust**
4 a dust *BrE* the act of dusting something: *I need to give the sitting room **a dust**.*
5 let the dust settle/wait for the dust to settle to allow or wait for a confused situation to become clear → **bite the dust** at BITE¹ (8); → DUSTY; → **leave sb in the dust** at LEAVE¹ (15); → **not see sb for dust** at SEE¹ (36)

dust² *v* **1** [I,T] to clean the dust from a surface by moving something such as a soft cloth across it: *Rachel dusted the books and the bookshelves.* | *I was dusting in the bedroom when the phone rang.* → see picture at CLEAN **2** also **dust down, dust off** [T] to remove something such as dirt or dust from your clothes by brushing them with your hands: *He got to his feet and dusted his knees.* | **dust yourself (down/off)** *Corbett dusted himself down and walked off.* **3** [T] to put a fine powder over something: **dust sth with sth** *Dust the biscuits with icing sugar.*
dust sth ⇔ **off** *phr v* **1** to remove something such as dust or dirt from your clothes by brushing them with your hands: *They were dusting off leaves and twigs.* | **dust yourself off** *He got to his feet and dusted himself off.* **2** to get something ready in order to use it again, after not using it for a long time: *The government is dusting off schemes for supporting creative industries.*

dust·bin S3 /ˈdʌstbɪn/ *n* [C] *BrE* a large container outside your house, used for holding waste until it is taken away; ▪ **garbage can** *AmE*; → see picture at BIN

'dustbin ˌman *n* [C] a DUSTMAN

'dust bowl *n* [C] an area of land that has DUST STORMS and very long periods without rain

'dust ˌbunny *n* [C] *AmE informal* a small ball of dust that forms in a place that is not cleaned regularly, such as under furniture

'dust cart *n* [C] *BrE* a large vehicle that goes from house to house to collect waste from dustbins; ▪ **garbage truck** *AmE*

'dust ˌcover *n* [C] *AmE* a paper cover of a book, which you can remove; ▪ **dust jacket**

dust·er /ˈdʌstə $ -ər/ *n* [C] **1** a cloth for removing dust from furniture **2** *AmE old-fashioned* a light coat that you wear to protect your clothes while you are cleaning the house **3** *AmE informal* a DUST STORM

'dust ˌjacket *n* [C] a paper cover of a book, which you can remove

dust·man /ˈdʌstmən/ *n plural* **dustmen** /-mən/ [C] *BrE* someone whose job is to remove waste from DUSTBINS; ▪ **garbage collector** *AmE*

dust·pan /ˈdʌstpæn/ *n* [C] a flat container with a handle that you use with a brush to remove dust and waste from the floor: *Have you got a dustpan and brush?* → see picture at BRUSH

dust·sheet /ˈdʌst-ʃiːt/ *n* [C] *especially BrE* a large sheet of cloth used to protect furniture from dust or paint; ▪ **drop cloth** *AmE*

'dust storm *n* [C] a storm with strong winds that carries large amounts of dust

dust-up /ˈdʌst-ʌp/ *n* [C] *BrE informal* a fight

dust·y /ˈdʌsti/ *adj* **1** covered with dust: *Adrian cycled along the dusty road.* | *Everything's really dusty.* **2 dusty blue/pink etc** blue etc that is not bright but is slightly grey: *The curtains had faded to a dusty pink.*

Dutch¹ /dʌtʃ/ *adj* **1** relating to the Netherlands, its people, or its language **2 go Dutch (with sb)** to share the cost of a meal in a restaurant **3 Dutch treat** *AmE* an occasion when you share the cost of something such as a meal in a restaurant

Dutch² *n* **1 the Dutch** [plural] people from the Netherlands **2** [U] the language used in the Netherlands → DOUBLE-DUTCH

ˌDutch 'auction *n* [C,U] a public sale at which the price of something is gradually reduced until someone will pay it

ˌDutch 'barn *n* [C] a farm building with a curved roof on a frame that has no walls, used for storing HAY

ˌDutch 'cap *n* [C] a round rubber CONTRACEPTIVE, that a woman wears inside her VAGINA during sex; ▪ **diaphragm, cap**

ˌDutch 'courage *n* [U] courage or confidence that you get when you drink alcohol

ˌDutch 'elm disˌease *n* [U] a disease that affects and kills ELM trees

Dutch·man /ˈdʌtʃmən/ *n plural* **Dutchmen** /-mən/ [C] **1** a man from the Netherlands **2 I'm a Dutchman** *BrE spoken* used to show that you do not believe something: *If that ball was out, then I'm a Dutchman.*

ˌDutch 'oven *n* [C] a large cooking pot with a lid

Dutch·wom·an /ˈdʌtʃˌwʊmən/ *n plural* **Dutchwomen** /-ˌwɪmɪn/ [C] a woman from the Netherlands

du·ti·a·ble /ˈdjuːtiəbəl $ ˈduː-/ *adj* dutiable goods are those that you must pay duty on

du·ti·ful /ˈdjuːtɪfəl $ ˈduː-/ *adj* doing what you are expected to do and behaving in a loyal and obedient way: *a dutiful son* | *Dutiful applause greeted his speech.*

dut·i·ful·ly /ˈdjuːtɪfəli $ ˈduː-/ *adv* if you do something dutifully, you do it because you think it is the correct way to behave: *I dutifully wrote down every word.*

du·ty ⟨S1⟩ ⟨W1⟩ /'djuːti $ 'duː-/ *n plural* **duties**
1 STH YOU MUST DO [C,U] something that you have to do because it is morally or legally right; ⊟ **obligation**

> do your duty
> it is sb's duty to do sth
> have a duty to do sth
> have a duty to sb/owe sb a duty
> sense of duty
> moral duty
> legal duty
> fail in your duty (=fail to do something that you should do for someone)
> be duty-bound to do sth *formal* (=have a duty to do something)

> *I promise I will **do my duty**. | We feel **it is our duty to** help her. | Local authorities **have a duty to** keep the streets clean. | You **have a duty to** your husband and to your children. | She has a strong **sense of moral duty**. | The unions have **failed in their duty** to female workers. | In the traditional Hindu family, the son is **duty-bound** to look after his mother.*

2 WORK [C usually plural, U] something you have to do as part of your job: **duties** *Martin's duties included cleaning the cars. | She works for her father doing part-time secretarial duties. | He will soon be fit enough to **carry out** his **duties** (=do his job). | He can only do **light duties**. | When Juliet **reported for duty** (=arrived and said she was ready to start work) she was sent to check on a new patient. | A teacher may be fired for **neglect of duty** (=failing to do their job properly). | He did three **tours of duty** in Vietnam (=three periods working in a foreign country as a soldier, government officer etc).*
3 be on/off duty to be working or not working at a particular time, especially when you are doing a job which people take turns to do, so that someone is always doing it: *He's **on night duty** next week. | Mary **goes on duty** (=starts working) tonight at half past ten. | What time do you **go off duty** (=finish work)?*
4 TAX [C,U] a tax you pay on something you buy: [+on] *the duty on cigarettes* | **customs duty** (=tax paid on goods coming into the country) → DEATH DUTIES, STAMP DUTY
5 do duty as sth to be used as something; ⊟ **serve as sth**: *The living room also does duty as a home office.* → DOUBLE DUTY, HEAVY-DUTY; → **jury duty** at JURY SERVICE; → **on active duty** at ACTIVE SERVICE

duty-'free[1] *adj* duty-free goods can be brought into a country without having to pay tax on them: *duty-free cigarettes* | *the duty-free shop* —**duty-free** *adv*

duty-free[2] *n* [C,U] alcohol, cigarettes etc that you can bring into a country without having to pay tax on them

du·vet /'duːveɪ, 'djuː- $ duː'veɪ/ *n* [C] *especially BrE* a large cloth bag filled with feathers or similar material that you use to cover yourself in bed; ⊟ **comforter** *AmE*; → see picture at BED

DVD /ˌdiː viː 'diː/ *n* [C,U] **digital video disc** or **digital versatile disc** a type of computer DISC that can store a large amount of information, sound, pictures, and video: *a DVD player* | *The film is now out on video and DVD.* → see picture at BEDROOM

DVT /ˌdiː viː 'tiː/ *n* [U] *medical* the abbreviation of **deep vein thrombosis**

dwarf[1] /dwɔːf $ dwɔːrf/ *n plural* **dwarfs** *or* **dwarves** [C] **1** an imaginary creature that looks like a small man: *Snow White and the Seven Dwarfs.* **2** a person who is a dwarf has not continued to grow to the normal height because of a medical condition. Many people think that this use is offensive. → WHITE DWARF

dwarf[2] *adj* [only before noun] a dwarf plant or animal is much smaller than the usual size: *a dwarf conifer*

dwarf[3] *v* [T usually passive] to be so big that other things are made to seem very small: *The cathedral is dwarfed by the surrounding skyscrapers.*

dweeb /dwiːb/ *n* [C] *AmE informal* someone who is weak, slightly strange, and not popular or fashionable

dwell /dwel/ *v past tense and past participle* **dwelt** /dwelt/ *or* **dwelled** [I always + adv/prep] *literary* to live in a particular place: *They dwelt in the middle of the forest.*
   dwell on/upon sth *phr v* to think or talk for too long about something, especially something unpleasant: *That is not a subject I want to dwell on.*

dwel·ler /'dwelə $ -ər/ *n* [C] **city/town/cave etc dweller** a person or animal that lives in a particular place: *City dwellers suffer higher pollution levels.*

dwell·ing ⟨S2⟩ /'dwelɪŋ/ *n* [C] *formal* a house, apartment etc where people live

'dwelling house *n* [C] *formal especially BrE* a house that people live in, not one that is being used as a shop, office etc

dwelt /dwelt/ a past tense and past participle of DWELL

DWI /ˌdiː dʌbəljuː 'aɪ/ *n* [C,U] *AmE law* **driving while intoxicated** the crime of driving when you have had too much alcohol to drink; ⊟ **DUI**

dwin·dle /'dwɪndl/ *v* [I] also **dwindle away** to gradually become less and less or smaller and smaller: *The elephant population is dwindling. | His money had dwindled away.* | [+to] *The stream has dwindled to a trickle.* —**dwindling** *adj*: *dwindling resources*

dye[1] /daɪ/ *n* [C,U] **1** a substance you use to change the colour of your clothes, hair etc: *hair dye* **2 dye job** *informal* someone who has had a dye job has used a substance to change the colour of their hair

dye[2] *v* [T] to give something a different colour using a dye: **dye sth black/blue/blonde etc** *Priscilla's hair was dyed jet black.* —**dyed** *adj*

dyed-in-the-'wool *adj* having strong beliefs, likes, or opinions that will never change: *Even dyed-in-the-wool traditionalists were impressed by the changes.*

dy·ing[1] /'daɪ-ɪŋ/ the present participle of DIE

dying[2] *adj* **1 dying moment/minutes/seconds** during the last minutes, seconds etc before something ends: *Chandler's goal was in the dying minutes of the game.* **2** [only before noun] happening just before someone dies: *It was her **dying wish** to have a simple burial.* **3 to your dying day** for the rest of your life: *He regretted the decision to his dying day.* **4** [only before noun] gradually decreasing until soon there will be none left: *Women who enjoy baking are a **dying breed**.* **5 the dying** [plural] people who are dying: *a hospice for the dying*

dyke, **dike** /daɪk/ *n* [C] **1** a wall or bank built to keep back water and prevent flooding **2** *taboo informal* an offensive word for a LESBIAN (=woman who is sexually attracted to women). Do not use this word. **3** *especially BrE* a narrow passage to carry water away; ⊟ **ditch**

dy·nam·ic[1] /daɪ'næmɪk/ *adj* **1** full of energy and new ideas, and determined to succeed: *dynamic and ambitious people* **2** continuously moving or changing: *a dynamic and unstable process* **3** *technical* relating to a force or power that causes movement —**dynamically** /-kli/ *adv*

dynamic[2] *n* **1 dynamics a)** [plural] the way in which things or people behave, react, and affect each other: [+of] *the dynamics of the family* | *He did research on **group dynamics** and leadership styles.* **b)** [U] the science relating to the movement of objects and the forces involved in movement **c)** [plural] changes in how loudly music is played or sung **2** [singular] *formal* something that causes action or change: [+of] *She regards class conflict as a central dynamic of historical change.*

dy·na·mis·m /'daɪnəmɪzəm/ *n* [U] energy and determination to succeed: *her entrepreneurial dynamism*

dy·na·mite[1] /'daɪnəmaɪt/ *n* [U] **1** a powerful explosive used especially for breaking rock: *a dynamite blast* **2** something or someone that is likely to cause a lot of trouble: *If the proposals became public they would be dynamite.* **3** *old-fashioned informal* someone or something that is very exciting or impressive: *The band is dynamite.*

dynamite² *v* [T] to damage or destroy something with dynamite

dy·na·mo /'daɪnəməʊ $ -moʊ/ *n plural* **dynamos** [C] **1** a machine that changes some other form of power directly into electricity: *bicycle lights powered by a dynamo* **2** someone who is excited about what they do and who puts a lot of energy into it: *the team's midfield dynamo* **3** something that has a strong effect on something else, and that makes things happen: *Oil is the dynamo of the country's economy.*

dyn·a·sty /'dɪnəsti $ 'daɪ-/ *n plural* **dynasties** [C] **1** a family of kings or other rulers whose parents, grandparents etc have ruled the country for many years: *The Habsburg dynasty ruled in Austria from 1278 to 1918.* **2** a period of time when a particular family ruled a country or area **3** *informal* a group or family that controls a particular business or organization for a long time: *the Rothschild banking dynasty*

d'you /djʊ, dʒə/ the short form of 'do you': *D'you know what I mean?*

dys·en·te·ry /'dɪsəntəri $ -teri/ *n* [U] a serious disease of your BOWELS that makes them BLEED and pass much more waste than usual

dys·func·tion·al /dɪs'fʌŋkʃənəl/ *adj* **1** not following the normal patterns of social behaviour, especially with the result that someone cannot behave in a normal way or have a satisfactory life: *dysfunctional family relationships* **2** not working properly or normally

dys·lex·i·a /dɪs'leksiə/ *n* [U] a condition that makes it difficult for someone to read and spell —**dyslexic** *adj*: *Two of the children in the class are dyslexic.*

dys·pep·si·a /dɪs'pepsiə, -'pepʃə/ *n* [U] a problem that your body has in dealing with the food you eat; ⊟ **indigestion**

dys·pep·tic /dɪs'peptɪk/ *adj* **1** suffering from dyspepsia **2** *old-fashioned* bad-tempered

dys·to·pi·a /dɪs'təʊpiə $ -'toʊ-/ *n* [C] an imaginary place where life is extremely difficult and a lot of unfair or immoral things happen; ⊟ **utopia**

dys·tro·phy /'dɪstrəfi/ → MUSCULAR DYSTROPHY

D

E, e

E, **e** /iː/ *plural* **E's** *or* **e's** *n* **1** [C,U] the fifth letter of the English alphabet **2** [C,U] the third note in the SCALE of C MAJOR or the musical KEY based on this note **3** [C] a mark given to a student's work to show that it is of very low quality **4** [C,U] ECSTASY (=an illegal drug)

E 1 *BrE technical* the written abbreviation of *earth* (=a connection between a piece of electrical equipment and the ground) **2** the abbreviation of *E number* **3** the written abbreviation of *east* or *eastern*

e-, **E-** /iː/ *prefix* **electronic** used before another word to mean something that is done on or involves the Internet: *e-shopping* | *e-commerce*

each S1 W1 /iːtʃ/ *determiner, pron, adv*
1 every one of two or more things or people, considered separately; → *every*: *She had a bottle in each hand.* | *Grill the fish for five minutes on each side.* | *Each member of the team is given a particular job to do.* | *We each have our own skills.* | *When the children arrive, you give them each a balloon.* | *There are four bedrooms, each with its own shower and WC.* | *The tickets cost £20 each* (=each ticket costs £20). | *You get two cookies each* (=every one of you gets two cookies). | [+of] *I'm going to ask each of you to speak for three minutes.* | *There are 250 blocks of stone, and each one weighs a ton.* | **each day/week/month etc** (=on each day, in each week etc) *a disease that affects about 10 million people each year*
2 each and every used to emphasize that you are talking about every person or thing in a group: *These are issues that affect each and every one of us.* | *Firemen face dangerous situations each and every day.*
3 each to his/their own used to say that we all have different ideas about how to do things, what we like etc, especially when you do not agree with someone else's choice: *I'd have chosen something more modern myself, but each to his own.*

WORD CHOICE: each, every
It is often correct to use either **each** or **every**, but they have slightly different meanings.
Use **each** when you are thinking about the people or things in a group separately, one by one: *Each student came forward to receive a medal* (emphasizes that they came forward one after another): *Each time you exercise, you get a little stronger.*
Use **every** when you are thinking about the whole group of people or things together, with no exceptions: *Every student was given a prize* (emphasizes that everyone in the group got a prize) | *Warm up every time you exercise.*
⚠ Do not use **each** with words such as 'almost', 'nearly', or 'not'. Use **every**: *Almost every window was broken.* | *Not every child enjoyed the party.*
⚠ Do not use **each** in negative clauses. Use **none**: *None of the answers were correct (NOT Each of the answers were not correct).*
each and **every** are followed by a singular verb: *Each item was thoroughly checked.* | *Every member wears a uniform.*
each and **every** are usually followed by a singular pronoun or determiner (he, she, it, him, himself etc): *Each component can be replaced separately if it breaks.* | *Every woman must decide for herself.*
But you can use 'they', 'them', 'their' etc when you do not want to say whether people are male or female: *Every child has their own room.*

each ˈother S1 W1 *pron* [not used as the subject of a sentence] used to show that each of two or more people does something to the other or others; → **one another**: *Susan and Robert kissed each other passionately.* | *The girls looked at each other.* | *They enjoy each other's company.* → **be at each other's throats** at THROAT (5)

each ˈway *adv BrE* if you BET (=try to win money by guessing the winner of a race) money each way, you will win if the horse or dog you choose comes first, second, or third —**each way** *adj*: *a £10 each way bet*

ea·ger /ˈiːgə $ -ər/ *adj* **1** very keen and excited about something that is going to happen or about something you want to do: **eager to do sth** *I was eager to get back to work as soon as possible.* | *He's a bright kid and eager to learn.* | *She's a very hard worker and very eager to please.* | *A crowd of eager young students were already waiting outside.* | [+for] *fans eager for a glimpse of the singer* **2 eager beaver** *informal* someone who is too keen and works harder than they should —**eagerly** *adv*: *They're eagerly awaiting the big day.* —**eagerness** *n* [U]: *People were pushing each other out of the way in their eagerness to get to the front.*

ea·gle¹ /ˈiːgəl/ *n* [C] **1** a very large strong bird with a beak like a hook that eats small animals, birds etc → see picture at BIRD OF PREY **2** two STROKES less than PAR (=(the usual number of strokes for a hole)) in a game of golf **3 eagle eye** used to say that someone is watching carefully or is likely to notice something: *They carried on working, under the eagle eye of the owner.*

eagle² *v* [T] to use two STROKES less than the usual number of strokes for a hole in a game of golf

eagle-ˈeyed *adj* [only before noun] very good at seeing or noticing things: *One eagle-eyed passerby noticed that the window was slightly open.*

ea·glet /ˈiːglɪt/ *n* [C] a young EAGLE

-ean /iən/ *suffix* [in adjectives and nouns] another form of the SUFFIX -AN: *Keynesean economics* (=according to the ideas of Keynes)

ear S2 W2 /ɪə $ ɪr/ *n*
1 PART OF YOUR BODY [C] one of the organs on either side of your head that you hear with: *She tucked her hair behind her ears.* | *She's had her ears pierced* (=small holes made in her ears in order to wear earrings). | **whisper/say (sth) in sb's ear** *Lou turned to Mark and whispered something in her ear.* | **long-eared/short-eared etc** *a long-eared rabbit* | **inner/middle ear** (=the parts inside your ear which you use to hear sounds)
2 HEARING [C] used to talk about hearing: **to sb's ears** | *It sounds odd to the ears of an ordinary English speaker.* | *I just wondered if the rumour had reached your ears* (=if you had heard it). → **prick (up) your ears** at PRICK¹ (5)
3 GRAIN [C] the top part of a plant such as wheat that produces grain: [+of] *an ear of corn*
4 smile/grin etc from ear to ear to show that you are very happy or pleased by smiling a lot: *She came out of his office, beaming from ear to ear.*
5 [singular] the ability to learn music, copy sounds etc: [+for] *She has no ear for languages at all.* | *a good ear for dialogue*
6 a sympathetic ear used to say that someone listens sympathetically to someone else saying: *He's always prepared to lend a sympathetic ear.*
7 close/shut your ears to sth to refuse to listen to bad or unpleasant news: *You can't just close your ears to their warnings.* → **turn a deaf ear** at DEAF (4); → **fall on deaf ears** at DEAF (5)
8 be all ears *informal* to be very keen to hear what someone is going to tell you: *As soon as I mentioned money, Karen was all ears.*
9 be out on your ear *informal* to be forced to leave a job, organization etc, especially because you have done something wrong: *You'd better start working harder, or you'll be out on your ear.*
10 be up to your ears in work/debt/problems etc to have a lot of work etc
11 have sth coming out (of) your ears *informal* to have too much of something: *We've got pumpkins coming out our ears this time of year.*
12 keep your/an ear to the ground to make sure that you always know what is happening in a situation
13 keep your ears open to always be listening in order to find out what is happening or to hear some useful

information: *I hope you'll all keep your eyes and ears open for anything unusual.*

14 go in (at) one ear and out (at) the other *informal* if information goes in one ear and out the other, you forget it as soon as you have heard it: *I don't know why I tell her anything. It just goes in one ear and out the other.*

15 give sb a thick ear *BrE informal* to hit someone on the ear: *Behave yourself or I'll give you a thick ear!*

16 have sb's ear to be trusted by someone so that they will listen to your advice, opinions etc: *He claimed to have the ear of several top ministers.*

17 play sth by ear to play music that you have heard without having to read written music → see also → **play it by ear** at PLAY¹ (11)

18 sb's ears are burning used to say that someone thinks that people are talking about them

19 sb's ears are flapping *BrE spoken* used to say that someone is trying to listen to your private conversation; → see also DOG-EARED; → **bend sb's ear** at BEND¹ (7); → **send sb off with a flea in their ear** at FLEA (2); → **make a pig's ear** of at PIG¹ (5); → **wet behind the ears** at WET¹ (7)

ear·ache /'ɪəreɪk $ 'ɪr-/ *n* [singular, U] a pain inside your ear: *I've got terrible earache and a sore throat.*

'**ear drops** *n* [plural] liquid medicine to put in your ear

ear·drum /'ɪədrʌm $ 'ɪr-/ *n* [C] a tight thin piece of skin over the inside of your ear which allows you to hear sound

ear·ful /'ɪəfʊl $ 'ɪr-/ **give sb an earful** *informal* to tell someone how angry you are about something they have done: *He gave me a real earful about being late so often.*

ear·hole /'ɪəhəʊl $ 'ɪrhoʊl/ *n* [C] *BrE informal* your ear → **clip round the earhole** at CLIP¹ (6)

earl /ɜːl $ ɜːrl/ *n* [C] a man with a high social rank: *the Earl of Warwick*

earl·dom /'ɜːldəm $ 'ɜːrl-/ *n* [C] **1** the rank of an earl **2** the land or property belonging to an earl

ear·li·est /'ɜːliəst $ 'ɜːr-/ **at the earliest** no earlier than the time or date mentioned: *Work will begin in October at the very earliest.*

'**ear lobe** *n* [C] the soft piece of flesh at the bottom of your ear

ear·ly¹ [S1] [W1] /'ɜːli $ 'ɜːrli/ *adj comparative* **earlier**, *superlative* **earliest**

1 FIRST PART in the first part of a period of time, event, or process

> early morning/afternoon/evening
> early spring/summer etc
> early August/January etc
> in the early days/months/years (=in the beginning)
> in your early twenties/forties/seventies etc (=aged 20–23, 40–43, 70–73 etc)
> the early 1920s/1980s/90s etc (=1920–1923, 1980–1983, 1990–1993 etc)
> as early as (=used for emphasizing an early time)
> the early stages/part (of sth)
> sb's early life/childhood/adolescence etc
> sb's early songs/books/work etc
> sb's early memories (=the things someone remembers from when they were very young)
> early signs/indications

the early morning sunshine | an afternoon in early spring | In the early days, the railways mainly carried goods. | She is in her early twenties. | the recession of the early 1980s | The money could be paid as early as next week. | He spent the early part of his career at St John's Hospital. | the experiences of early childhood | the early works of Shakespeare | My earliest memories are of fruit trees. | Early signs are encouraging.

2 BEFORE USUAL arriving or happening before the usual or expected time; ◧ late: **five minutes/three hours etc early** *The bus was ten minutes early.* | [+for] *I was a few minutes early for my appointment.* | *David decided to take early retirement* (=stop working before the normal age). | *She drank herself into an early grave* (=died younger than is normal).

3 BEGINNING used to emphasize that something has

just begun, especially when you do not know how it will develop: *It's too early to say whether the show will be a success.* | *It's early days yet. I don't want to make any predictions.*

4 NEW THING [only before noun] being one of the first people, events, machines etc: *Early motor cars had very poor brakes.* | *fossil evidence of early man*

5 the early hours the time between MIDNIGHT and morning: *I didn't finally get to bed until the early hours.* | **in the early hours of sth** *The attack happened in the early hours of Sunday morning.*

6 an early start a start made very early in the day because you have a lot to do, far to go etc: *We need to make an early start tomorrow.*

7 at/from an early age when you are very young, or starting when you were very young: *She's played tennis from a very early age.*

8 an early night if you have an early night, you go to bed earlier than usual; ◧ **a late night**: **have/get an early night** *I think I'll get an early night.*

9 early bird/early riser someone who always gets up very early in the morning

10 the early bird catches the worm used to say that if you do something early or before other people, you will be successful

11 early potatoes/lettuces etc potatoes etc that are ready to be picked before any others

early² [S1] [W1] *adv comparative* **earlier**, *superlative* **earliest**

1 before the usual, arranged, or expected time; ◧ late: *We arrived early.* | *They must have come home early.*

2 near the beginning of a period of time, event, process etc; ◧ late: [+in] *She went out early in the morning.* | *He was sent off early in the game.* | **early this/next/last year etc** *The building should be finished early next year.* | *The restaurant opened earlier this month.* | *We want to start as early as possible.* | *The disease is easy to treat if diagnosed early.*

3 early on at an early stage in a relationship, process etc: *I realized early on I'd never pass the exam.* | [+in] *We encountered problems early on in the project.*

,**early 'warning** *adj* **early warning system/device etc** a system or equipment which tells you that something bad, especially an enemy attack, is going to happen

ear·mark /'ɪəmɑːk $ 'ɪrmɑːrk/ *v* [T usually passive] to decide that something will be used for a particular purpose or have something done to it in the future: **earmark sb/sth for sth** *85% of foreign aid is earmarked by Congress for specific purposes.* | *schools earmarked for closure* | **earmark sb/sth as sth** *He had been earmarked as a potential leader.*

ear·muffs /'ɪəmʌfs $ 'ɪr-/ *n* [plural] two pieces of material joined by a band over the top of your head, which you wear to keep your ears warm

earn [S2] [W2] /ɜːn $ ɜːrn/ *v*

1 MONEY FOR WORK [I,T] to receive a particular amount of money for the work that you do

> earn money
> earn a wage/salary
> earn a living (=earn enough money for the things you need to live)
> earn a crust *BrE* (=earn enough money to live)
> be earning *BrE* (=to have a job)
> earn good money/earn well (=earn a lot of money)
> earn a fortune (=earn an extremely large amount of money)

He earns nearly £20,000 a year. | *You don't earn much money being a nurse.* | *He did all sorts of jobs to earn a living.* | *I was the only person in the house who was earning.* | *She was earning good money at the bank.* | *Chris will pay – he's earning a fortune.* → see box at GAIN¹

2 PROFIT [T] to make a profit from business or from putting money in a bank etc: *The movie earned £7*

E

million on its first day. | *You could* **earn** *a higher rate of* **interest** *elsewhere.*

3 STH DESERVED [T] **a)** to do something or have qualities that make you deserve something: *I think you've earned a rest.* | *He soon earned the respect of the players.* | *He hopes to* **earn** *a* **place** *in the Olympic team.* | *The company has* **earned** *a* **reputation** *for reliability.* **b)** if your actions or qualities earn you something, they make you deserve to have it: **earn sb sth** *That performance earned her an Oscar as Best Actress.*
4 **earn your/its keep a)** to do jobs in return for being given a home and food: *We older children were expected to earn our keep.* **b)** to be useful enough to be worth the time or money spent: *These aircraft are still earning their keep.*

earn·er /'ɜːnə $ 'ɜːrnər/ n [C] **1** someone who earns money for the job that they do: **high/low/average earner** *Private childcare is still too expensive for the average earner.* | *He is the only* **wage earner** *in the family.* **2** a business or activity which makes a profit: *the country's biggest export earner* **3** **a nice little earner** *BrE informal* something that earns you a lot of money

ear·nest¹ /'ɜːnɪst $ 'ɜːr-/ adj very serious and sincere: *a rather earnest young man* | *Matthews was in* **earnest conversation** *with a young girl.* | *an* **earnest desire** *to offer something useful to society* | **earnest expression/look/voice etc** | **earnest attempt/effort etc**
—**earnestly** adv: *earnestly discussing politics*
—**earnestness** n [U]

earnest² n **1** **in earnest** if something starts happening in earnest, it begins properly – used when it was happening in a small or informal way before: *On Monday your training* **begins in earnest!** **2** **be in earnest** to really mean what you are saying, especially when expressing an intention or wish: *She wasn't sure whether he was in earnest or not.* | **be in dead/deadly/ complete earnest** *Although he smiled, Ashley knew he was in deadly earnest.*

earn·ings /'ɜːnɪŋz $ 'ɜːr-/ n [plural] **1** the money that you receive for the work that you do; → **salary, pay** (2, 1): *an employee's average weekly earnings* | *He claimed compensation for* **loss of earnings.** **2** the profit that a company or country makes: *The company's earnings have dropped by 5% in the first quarter.* | *Oil provides 40% of Norway's* **export earnings.**

earnings-re·lated adj relating to the amount of money that you earn: *an earnings-related pension scheme*

ear·phone /'ɪəfəʊn $ 'ɪrfoʊn/ n [usually plural] a small piece of equipment connected by a wire to a radio, PERSONAL STEREO etc, which you put in or over your ears so that only you can listen to it; → see picture at PERSONAL STEREO

ear·piece /'ɪəpiːs $ 'ɪr-/ n [C] **1** a small piece of equipment that you put into your ear to hear a recording, message etc **2** [usually plural] one of the two pieces at the side of a pair of glasses that go round your ears **3** the part of a telephone that you listen through

ear·plug /'ɪəplʌg $ 'ɪr-/ n [C usually plural] a small piece of rubber that you put inside your ear to keep out noise or water

ear·ring /'ɪərɪŋ $ 'ɪr-/ n [C] a piece of jewellery that you wear on your ear: **gold/diamond/pearl etc earrings** | *She was wearing a* **pair of** *beautiful diamond* **earrings.** → see picture at JEWELLERY

ear·shot /'ɪəʃɒt $ 'ɪrʃɑːt/ n **1** **within earshot** near enough to hear what someone is saying: *Everyone within earshot soon knew her opinion of Reggie.* **2** **out of earshot** not near enough to hear what someone is saying: *I waited for her to get out of earshot before laughing.*

ear-splitting adj very loud: *There was an ear-splitting crack.*

earth¹ S2 W2 /ɜːθ $ ɜːrθ/ n
1 WORLD also **Earth** [singular, U] the PLANET that we live on: *the planet Earth* | **the earth** *The earth revolves around the sun.* | **the earth's surface/atmosphere/crust etc** *71% of the earth's surface is sea.* | **on earth** *the origin of life on Earth;* → see picture at GLOBE; → see picture at SOLAR SYSTEM
2 SOIL [U] the substance that plants grow in; ⊟ **soil**: **soft/bare/damp etc earth** *footprints in the wet earth* | *a lump of earth*
3 LAND [U] the hard surface of the world, as opposed to the sea or air; ⊟ **ground**: *The earth began to shake.* | *They watched the kite fall back to earth.* → see box at GROUND¹
4 **what/why/how etc on earth ...?** *spoken* used to ask a question when you are very surprised or angry: *What on earth did you do that for?*
5 **cost/pay/charge the earth** *informal* to cost etc a very large amount of money: *It must have cost the earth!*
6 **the biggest/tallest/most expensive etc ... on earth** the biggest etc example of something that exists: *the most powerful man on earth*
7 RELIGION [U] used in religion to refer to the time when people are alive as opposed to being in HEAVEN or HELL: *Jesus' time on earth* → **move heaven and earth** at HEAVEN (9); → **hell on earth** at HELL¹ (2)
8 **come back/down to earth (with a bump)** to stop behaving or living in a way that is not practical: *She soon brought him back down to earth.*
9 **no ... /nothing on earth** used to emphasize that you mean nothing at all: *Nothing on earth would have persuaded me to go.* | *There's no reason on earth why you should tell him.*
10 **look/feel etc like nothing on earth** *BrE* to look or feel very strange: *The next morning I felt like nothing on earth.*
11 ELECTRICITY [C usually singular] *BrE* a wire that makes a piece of electrical equipment safe by connecting it with the ground; ⊟ **ground** *AmE*
12 ANIMAL'S HOME [C] the hole where a wild animal such as a FOX lives; → **den, lair**
13 **go to earth** *BrE* to hide in order to escape from someone who is chasing you; ⊟ **go to ground**
14 **run sb/sth to earth** *BrE* to find someone, especially by looking in many places → DOWN-TO-EARTH; → **promise sb the moon/the earth** at PROMISE¹ (3); → **the salt of the earth** at SALT¹ (2)

earth² v [T] *BrE* to make electrical equipment safe by connecting it to the ground with a wire; ⊟ **ground** *AmE*: *Make sure that the machine is properly earthed.*

earth·bound /'ɜːθbaʊnd $ 'ɜːrθ-/ adj **1** unable to move away from the surface of the Earth **2** having very little imagination and thinking too much about practical things

earth·en /'ɜːθən, -ðən $ 'ɜːr-/ adj [only before noun] **1** an earthen floor or wall is made of soil **2** an earthen pot etc is made of baked clay

earth·en·ware /'ɜːθənweə, -ðən- $ 'ɜːrθənwer, -ðən-/ adj an earthenware pot, bowl etc is made of very hard baked clay —**earthenware** n [U]

earth·ling /'ɜːθlɪŋ $ 'ɜːrθ-/ n [C] a human – used in SCIENCE FICTION stories

earth·ly /'ɜːθli $ 'ɜːrθli/ adj **1** **no earthly reason/use etc** no reason, use etc at all: *I see no earthly reason why he shouldn't come.* **2** [only before noun] *literary* connected with life on Earth rather than in heaven: *our earthly pleasures* | *an earthly paradise*

earth mother n [C] a woman who has all the qualities expected of a mother and is especially interested in simple, natural ways of living

earth·quake /'ɜːθkweɪk $ 'ɜːrθ-/ n [C] a sudden shaking of the earth's surface that often causes a lot of damage: *An earthquake measuring 6.1 on the Richter scale struck southern California on June 28.* | *The city is in an earthquake zone.*

earth science n [C usually plural] a science, such as GEOLOGY, which involves the study of the physical world

earth-,shattering adj surprising or shocking and very important: an earth-shattering event

earth·wards /'ɜːθwədz $ 'ɜːrθwərdz/ also **earthward** /-wəd $ -wərd/ adv towards the earth's surface: The missile fell earthwards. —**earthward** adj

earth·work /'ɜːθwɜːk $ 'ɜːrθwɜːrk/ n [C usually plural] a large long pile of earth, used in the past to stop attacks

earth·worm /'ɜːθwɜːm $ 'ɜːrθwɜːrm/ n [C] a common type of long thin brown worm that lives in soil

earth·y /'ɜːθi $ 'ɜːrθi/ adj **1** tasting, smelling, or looking like earth or soil: earthy colours **2** talking about things that are often considered rude, especially sex and the human body, in a relaxed direct way: earthy language —**earthiness** n [U]

ear ,trumpet n [C] a type of tube that is wide at one end, used by old people in the past to help them hear

ear·wig /'ɪəˌwɪg $ 'ɪr-/ n [C] a long brown insect with two curved pointed parts at the back end of its body → see picture at INSECT

ease¹ /iːz/ n [U] **1 with ease** if you do something with ease, it is very easy for you to do it; ▤ **easily**: They won with ease. | The security codes could be broken with relative ease. | I was impressed by the ease with which the information could be retrieved. **2 at ease** feeling relaxed, especially in a situation in which people might feel a little nervous: [+with] She felt completely at ease with Bernard. | put/set sb at (their) ease (=make someone feel relaxed) She had an ability to put people at their ease. **3 ill at ease** not relaxed: You always look ill at ease in a suit. **4 ease of application/use etc** written how easy something is to use etc, or the quality of being easy to use etc: It emphasizes the software's convenience and ease of use. | for ease of sth The bowl is removable for ease of cleaning. **5** the ability to feel relaxed or behave in a natural relaxed way: He had a natural ease which made him very popular. **6 a life of ease** a comfortable life, without problems or worries **7 (stand) at ease** used to tell soldiers to stand in a relaxed way with their feet apart

ease² v

1 IMPROVE [I,T] if something unpleasant eases, or if you ease it, it gradually improves or becomes less: **ease the pain/stress/tension** He'll give you something to ease the pain. | **ease the pressure/burden** This should ease the burden on busy teachers. | measures to ease congestion in the city | Her breathing had eased.

2 MAKE EASIER [T] to make something, especially a process, happen more easily; ▤ **smooth**: The agreement will ease the way for other countries to join the EU.

3 MOVE [I,T always + adv/prep] to move yourself or something slowly and carefully into another place or position: She eased her shoes off. | **ease yourself into/through etc sth** Phil eased himself into an armchair. | **ease your way past/through etc sth** He eased his way through the crowd. | Jean eased back on the pillows and relaxed.

4 ease your grip to hold something less tightly

5 ease sb's mind to make someone feel less worried about something: It would ease my mind to know you had arrived safely.

ease (sb) into sth phr v
if you ease yourself or someone else into a new job etc, you start doing it gradually or help them to start: After the baby, she eased herself back into work.

ease off phr v
1 if something, especially something that you do not like, eases off, it improves or gets less; ▤ **ease up**: The rain had eased off a bit. | Why don't you wait until the traffic eases off a little?
2 ease off on sb to stop being unpleasant to someone or asking so much from them

ease out phr v
1 if a vehicle eases out, it slowly moves forward into the traffic
2 ease sb ⇔ out to make someone leave a job, a position

of authority etc, in a way that makes it seem as if they have chosen to leave

ease up phr v
1 to work less hard or do something with less energy than before: Just relax and ease up a little.
2 to start doing something less: [+on] You should ease up on the whisky.
3 to improve or get less; ▤ **ease off**: The snow was easing up.

ea·sel /'iːzəl/ n [C] a wooden frame that you put a painting on while you paint it → see picture at STAND

eas·i·ly [S1] [W1] /'iːzₗli/ adv
1 without problems or difficulties: They won quite easily. | We found the house easily enough. | **easily accessible/available etc** The castle is easily accessible by road. | **easily understood/identified etc** It's easily recognised by its bright blue tail feathers.
2 could/can/might easily used to say that something is possible or is very likely to happen: The first signs of the disease can easily be overlooked. | They could so easily have escaped. | Gambling can all too easily become an addiction (=used to say that something bad is very possible).
3 easily the best/biggest etc definitely the best etc: She is easily the most intelligent person in the class.
4 in a relaxed way: His son grinned easily back at him.

eas·i·ness /'iːzinₗs/ n [U] **1** a feeling of being relaxed and comfortable with someone **2** when something is not difficult

east¹ [S2] [W2] **East** /iːst/ written abbreviation **E** n [singular, U]
1 the direction from which the sun rises, and which is on the right if you are facing north: Which way is east? | **from/towards the east** He turned and walked away towards the east. | **to the east (of sth)** To the east of the pier were miles of sandy beaches.
2 the east the eastern part of a country or area: Housing in the east was as bad as ever. | [+of] the east of Scotland

east², **East** written abbreviation **E** adj **1** [only before noun] in the east or facing the east: I don't know the east coast well. | He was born in East Jerusalem. **2** an east wind comes from the east

east³ written abbreviation **E** adv **1** towards the east: We drove east along Brooklyn Avenue. | [+of] a small farming community 18 miles east of Paris | an east-facing bedroom **2 out east** to or in the countries in Asia, especially China and Japan: The drug is being used all the time out east.

East n **1 the East a)** the countries in Asia, especially China and Japan: Martial arts originated in the East. **b)** the countries in the eastern part of Europe and Central Asia: American relations with the East. **c)** AmE the part of the US east of the Mississippi River, especially the states north of Washington DC: She was born in the East but now lives in Atlanta. | I was born in Utah but went to college **back East**. **2 East-West relations/trade etc** political relations etc between countries in eastern Europe and those in western Europe and North America; → **Far East**, **Middle East**, **Near East**

east·bound /'iːstbaʊnd/ adj travelling or leading towards the east: A crash on the eastbound side of the freeway is blocking traffic.

East 'Coast n **the East Coast** the part of the US that is next to the Atlantic Ocean, especially those states north of Washington DC

East 'End n **the East End** the eastern part of London, north of the River Thames —**East Ender** n [C]

Eas·ter /'iːstə $ -ər/ n [C,U] **1** a Christian holy day in March or April when Christians remember the death of Christ and his return to life: on **Easter Sunday** → **GOOD FRIDAY** **2** the period of time just before and after Easter Day: **at Easter** We'll probably go away at Easter. | **Easter holiday/weekend/break** We spent the Easter holidays in Wales.

E

Easter 'Bunny n [singular] an imaginary rabbit that children believe brings chocolate eggs at Easter

'Easter egg n [C] **1** BrE a chocolate egg bought or given as a present at Easter **2** AmE an egg that has been coloured and decorated to celebrate Easter

eas·ter·ly¹ /'iːstəli $ -ərli/ adj **1** towards or in the east: We drove off **in an easterly direction**. **2** an easterly wind comes from the east

easterly² n plural **easterlies** [C] a wind that comes from the east

east·ern W2 , **Eastern** /'iːstən $ -ərn/ written abbreviation E adj
1 in or from the east of a country or area: the eastern shore of the island | farmers in eastern England
2 in or from the countries in Asia, especially China and Japan: Eastern religions
3 in or from the countries in the east part of Europe, especially the countries that used to have Communist governments: Eastern Europe

East·ern·er /'iːstənə $ -ərnər/ n [C] AmE someone from the eastern US, north of Washington DC

east·ern·most /'iːstənməʊst $ -ərnmoʊst/ adj furthest east: the easternmost part of the country

East 'Side n the East Side the southeastern part of Manhattan in New York, lived in mostly by poor people who have come to the US from other countries

east·wards /'iːstwədz $ -wərdz/ also **east·ward** /-wəd $ -wərd/ adv towards the east: The ship continued sailing eastwards. —**eastward** adj: We followed an eastward course up the river.

eas·y¹ S1 W1 /'iːzi/ adj comparative **easier**, superlative **easiest**
1 NOT DIFFICULT not difficult to do, and not needing much effort; ≠ **difficult**, **hard**: The test was easy. | Finishing the task will not be easy. | There must be an easier way to do that. | **easy to do sth** It's a great car, and very easy to drive. | instructions that are easy to follow | It would have been easy for the team to lose the game. | **make it easier (to do sth)** The software makes it easier to download music from the net. | Having you here does **make things** a lot **easier** for me. | **as easy as pie/ABC/falling off a log** (=very easy) | The station is **within easy reach** of (=close to) the town centre. | The park is **within easy** walking **distance** (=close enough to walk to).
2 COMFORTABLE comfortable or relaxed, and without problems; ≠ **hard**: On the whole, Dad has had an easy life. | **easy day/week etc** She had a nice easy day at home. | You can **have an easy time of it** now that the kids have all left home. | Why don't we **make life easy for ourselves** and finish it tomorrow?
3 NOT WORRIED not feeling worried or anxious; ≠ **uneasy**: We talk more openly when we feel easy and relaxed. | I can leave the children with my mother **with an easy mind**.
4 FRIENDLY friendly and pleasant with other people: She is gentle and **easy to be with**.
5 EASILY ATTACKED able to be hunted or attacked without difficulty: The soldiers on the streets are an **easy target** for terrorists. | Tourists are **easy prey** for thieves.
6 take the easy way out to end a situation in a way that seems easy, but is not the best or most sensible way: I just **took the easy way out** and gave him some cash.
7 have an easy time (of it) to have no problems or difficulties: She's not been having an easy time of it financially.
8 easy money money that you do not have to work hard to get: We can buy them for $10 and sell them for $25 – easy money.
9 easy on the eye/ear pleasant to look at or listen to: Soft colours are easy on the eye.
10 it's/that's easy for you to say spoken used when someone has given you some advice that would be difficult for you to follow
11 there are no easy answers used when saying that it is difficult to find a good way of dealing with a problem
12 I'm easy spoken used to say that you do not mind what choice is made: 'What would you like to do now?' 'I don't know, I'm easy.'
13 be (living) on easy street informal, especially AmE to be in a situation in which you have plenty of money: If I get this new job, we'll be living on easy street.
14 on easy terms if you buy something on easy terms, you pay for it with several small payments instead of paying the whole amount at once: New settlers in the west could buy land on relatively easy terms.
15 eggs over easy AmE eggs cooked on a hot surface and turned over quickly before serving
16 woman/lady/girl of easy virtue old-fashioned a woman who has sex with a lot of men
17 SEX informal someone, especially a woman, who is easy has a lot of sexual partners; → see also EASE, EASILY

WORD FOCUS: EASY
easy to do: simple, not difficult
very easy to do: be a piece of cake, be child's play, be a snap AmE, be a doddle BrE, anyone can do it, be like falling off a log informal
easy to use: user-friendly
easy job: cushy informal

easy² S2 adv
1 take it easy **a)** also **take things easy** to relax and not do very much: Take things easy for a few days and you should be all right. **b)** spoken used to tell someone to become less upset or angry: Just take it easy and tell us what happened. **c)** AmE spoken used to say goodbye
2 go easy on/with sth to not use too much of something: Go easy on salty foods such as bacon.
3 go easy on sb to be more gentle and less strict or angry with someone: Go easy on Peter for a while – he's having a hard time at school.
4 easier said than done especially spoken used to say that something would be very difficult to do: Finding the perfect house was easier said than done.
5 rest/breathe easy to stop worrying: We can rest easy now – we've got everything under control.
6 easy does it spoken used to tell someone to be more careful and slow, especially in moving
7 get off easy informal to escape severe punishment for something that you have done wrong: The rich could hire good lawyers and get off easy.
8 easy come, easy go spoken used when something, especially money, was easily obtained and is quickly used or spent
9 stand easy an order telling soldiers who are already standing at EASE to relax more

'easy chair n [C] a large comfortable chair; → **armchair**

easy-'going adj not easily upset, annoyed, or worried: Her easy-going nature made her popular.

easy 'listening n [U] music that is relaxing to listen to and has nice tunes, but is not very interesting

easy-pea·sy /ˌiːzi 'piːzi◂/ adj BrE a word meaning very easy, used especially by children

eat S1 W1 /iːt/ v past tense **ate** /et, eɪt $ eɪt/ past participle **eaten** /'iːtn/
1 FOOD [I,T] to put food in your mouth and chew and swallow it

eat well/healthily/sensibly (=eat food that will keep you healthy)
eat right AmE (=eat food that will keep you healthy)
eat properly BrE (=eat food that will keep you healthy)
eat hungrily
something to eat (=some food)
eat like a horse informal (=eat a very large amount)
eat like a bird informal (=eat very little)
a bite to eat informal (=some food)
eating habits
eating disorder (=a medical condition in which you do not eat normally)
ready-to-eat (=used to describe foods that you do not have to prepare)

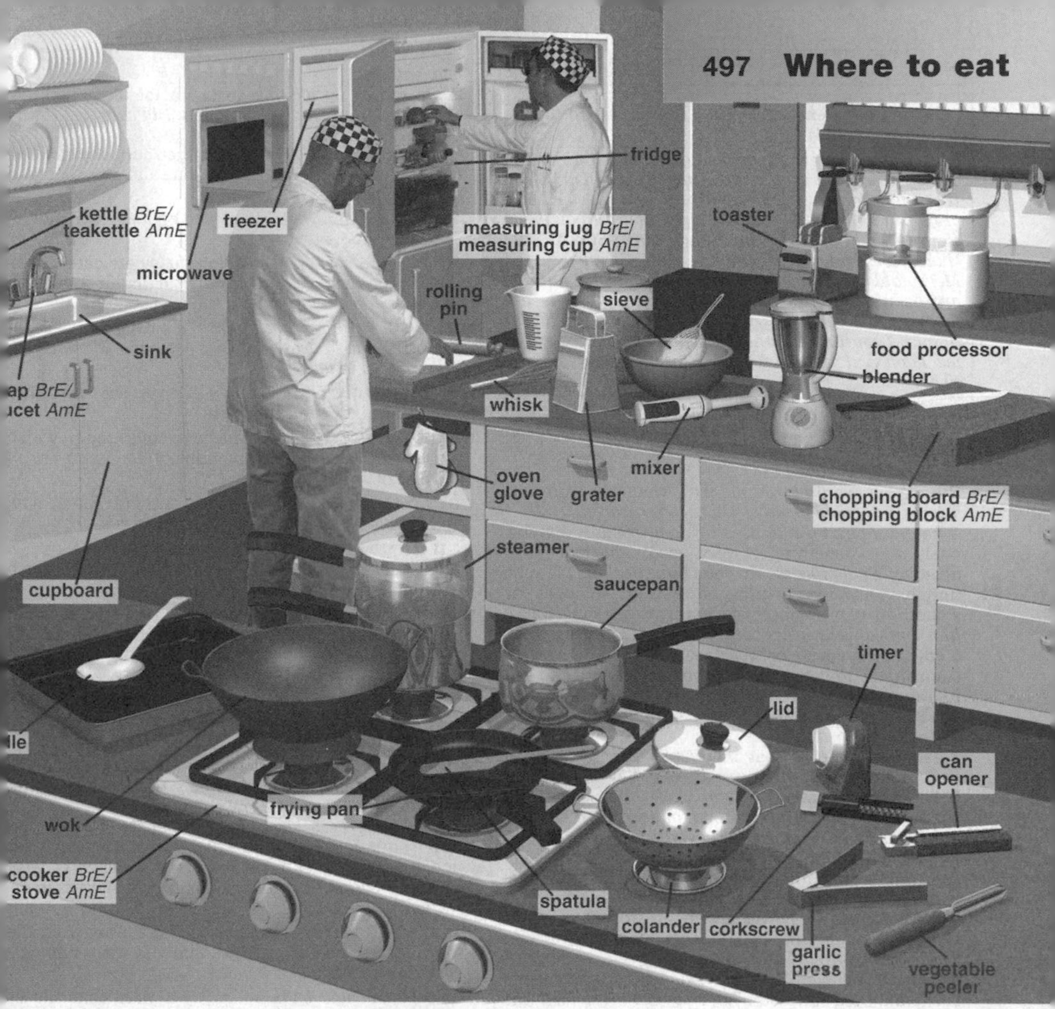

fridge
freezer
kettle BrE/
teakettle AmE
microwave
measuring jug BrE/
measuring cup AmE
toaster
rolling pin
sieve
sink
food processor
blender
ap BrE/
ucet AmE
whisk
mixer
oven glove
grater
chopping board BrE/
chopping block AmE
steamer
cupboard
saucepan
timer
lid
dle
can opener
frying pan
wok
cooker BrE/
stove AmE
spatula
colander
corkscrew
garlic press
vegetable peeler

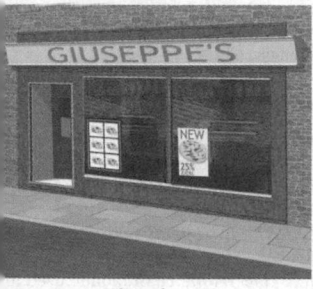

GIUSEPPE'S
NEW

pizzeria

Maison Rouge

restaurant

BIG D

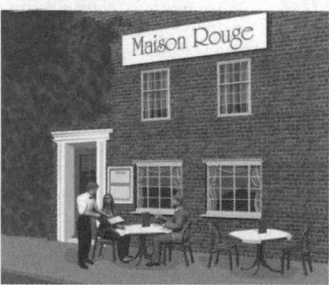

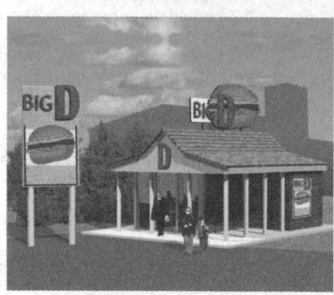

fast food restaurant

TOM'S PLAICE

fish and chip shop *BrE*

HONG KONG
CHINESE FOOD TO TAKE AWAY

takeaway *BrE*

SNACKS
MENU & PRICES

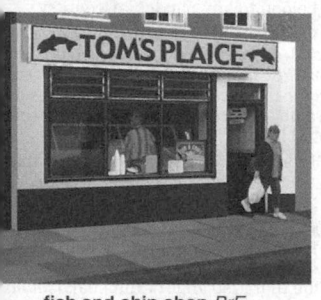

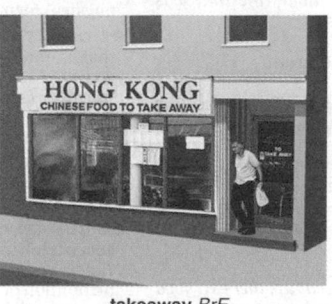

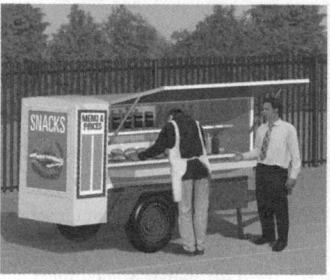

snack bar

I couldn't eat another thing/bite *spoken* (=used to say that you are full)

Felix chatted cheerfully as he ate. | *A small girl was eating an ice cream.* | *We had plenty to eat and drink.* | *It's important to* **eat** *healthily when you are pregnant.* | *I exercise and* **eat** *right and get plenty of sleep.* | *Would you like* **something to eat?** | *She can eat* **like a horse** *and never put on weight.* | *We stopped at McDonalds to get* **a bite to eat.** | *Good* **eating habits** *are the best way of preventing infection.* | **ready-to-eat** *foods such as deli meats and cheeses* | *'More cake?' 'No thanks,* **I couldn't eat another thing.'** | *No chicken for me. I don't eat meat* (=I never eat meat). | *Does Rob eat fish?*

2 **MEAL** [I,T] to have a meal: *Let's eat first and then go to a movie.* | *We had just started eating breakfast when the phone rang.* | [+at] *We could not afford to eat at Walker's very often.*

3 **eat your words** to admit that what you said was wrong: *I'm going to make you eat your words.*

4 **eat your heart out a)** used to say, especially humorously, that something is very good: *That's a great drawing. Pablo Picasso eat your heart out!* **b)** *BrE* to be unhappy about something or to want someone or something very much: *If you had any sense you'd forget him, but eat your heart out if you want to.*

5 **eat sb alive/eat sb for breakfast** to be very angry with someone or to defeat them completely: *You can't tell him that – he'll eat you alive!*

6 **USE** [T] to use a very large amount of something: *This car eats petrol.*

7 **eat humble pie** also **eat crow** *AmE* to admit that you were wrong and say that you are sorry

8 **I'll eat my hat** used to emphasize that you think something is not true or will not happen: *If the Democrats win the election, I'll eat my hat!*

9 **have sb eating out of your hand** to have made someone very willing to believe you or do what you want: *He soon had the client eating out of his hand.*

10 **eat sb out of house and home** to eat a lot of someone's supply of food, so that they have to buy more – used humorously

11 **what's eating sb?** *spoken* used to ask why someone seems annoyed or upset: *What's eating Sally today? She just yelled at me.*

12 **I could eat a horse** *spoken* used to say you are very hungry

13 **I/we won't eat you** *spoken* used to tell someone that you are not angry with them and they need not be frightened

14 **you are what you eat** used to say that you will be healthy if the food you eat is healthy → **EATS**; → **have your cake and eat it** at **CAKE**[1] (6)

eat sth ⇔ **away** *phr v*
to gradually remove or destroy something; **⊟ erode**: *The stones are being eaten away by pollution.*

eat away at sth/sb *phr v*
1 to gradually remove or reduce the amount of something: *His gambling was eating away at their income.*
2 to make someone feel very worried over a long period of time: *The thought of mother alone like that was eating away at her.*

eat in *phr v*
to eat at home instead of in a restaurant

eat into sth *phr v*
1 to gradually reduce the amount of time, money etc that is available: *John's university fees have been eating into our savings.*
2 to gradually damage or destroy something: *Acid eats into the metal, damaging its surface.*

eat out *phr v*
to eat in a restaurant instead of at home: *Do you eat out a lot?*

eat up *phr v*
1 to eat all of something: *Come on, eat up, there's a good girl.* | **eat** sth ⇔ **up** *She's made a cake and wants us to*

help eat it up.
2 **eat** sth ⇔ **up** *informal* to use a lot of something, especially until there is none left: *Big cars just eat up money.*
3 **be eaten up with/by jealousy/anger/curiosity etc** to be very jealous, angry etc, so that you cannot think about anything else

eat·a·ble /'iːtəbəl/ *adj* in a good enough condition to be eaten → **EDIBLE**

eat·er /'iːtə $ -ər/ *n* [C] **big/light/fussy etc eater** someone who eats a lot, not much, only particular things etc: *I've never been a big eater.*

eat·e·ry /'iːtəri/ *n plural* **eateries** [C] *informal* especially *AmE* a restaurant or other place to eat: *one of the best eateries in town*

'**eating ˌapple** *n* [C] an apple that you eat raw rather than cooked; → **cooking apple**

'**eating disˌorder** *n* [C] a medical condition in which you do not eat a normal amount of food and are ill because of this

eats /iːts/ *n* [plural] *informal* food, especially for a party: *You get the drink, and I'll organize the eats.*

eau de coˌlogne /ˌəʊ də kə'ləʊn $ ˌoʊ də kə'loʊn/ *n* [U] a sweet-smelling liquid used to make you feel fresh and smell nice

eaves /iːvz/ *n* [plural] the edges of a roof that stick out beyond the walls: *Birds had nested under the eaves.*

eaves·drop /'iːvzdrɒp $ -drɑːp/ *v* **eavesdropped**, **eavesdropping** [I] to deliberately listen secretly to other people's conversations; → **overhear**: *There was Helena eavesdropping outside the door.* —**eavesdropper** *n* [C]

ebb[1] /eb/ *n* **1** [singular] also **ebb tide** the flow of the sea away from the shore, when the TIDE goes out; **⊠ flood tide** **2** **be at a low ebb** to be in a bad state or condition: *His confidence is at a low ebb.* **3** **ebb and flow** a situation or state in which something increases and decreases in a kind of pattern: *the ebb and flow of the conversation* | *the ebb and flow of passengers in the station*

ebb[2] *v* [I] **1** if the TIDE ebbs, it flows away from the shore **2** also **ebb away** to gradually decrease: *Linda's enthusiasm began to ebb away.*

E·bo·la /ɪ'bəʊlə $ ɪ'boʊ-/ *n* [U] a VIRUS that causes bleeding from many parts of the body and usually causes death

eb·o·ny[1] /'ebəni/ *n* [U] a hard black wood

ebony[2] *adj literary* black: *her ebony hair*

e-book /'iː bʊk/ *n* [C] *electronic book* a book that you read on a computer screen or on a special small computer that you can hold in your hands, and that is not printed on paper

e·bul·li·ent /ɪ'bʌliənt, ɪ'bʊl-/ *adj formal* very happy and excited: *My father is a naturally ebullient personality.* —**ebullience** *n* [U]

EC /ˌiː 'siː/ *n* **the EC** *the European Community* the former name for the EU

e-cash /'iː kæʃ/ *n* [U] *electronic cash* money used to buy things on the Internet, but that does not exist in a physical form or belong to any particular country

ec·cen·tric[1] /ɪk'sentrɪk/ *adj* **1** behaving in a way that is unusual and different from most people: *His eccentric behaviour lost him his job.* | *Aunt Nessy was always a bit eccentric.* **2** *technical* eccentric circles do not have the same centre point; → **concentric** —**eccentrically** /-kli/ *adv*

eccentric[2] *n* [C] someone who behaves in a way that is different from what is usual or socially accepted: *I was regarded as something of an eccentric.*

ec·cen·tri·ci·ty /ˌeksen'trɪsɪti, -sən-/ *n plural* **eccentricities** **1** [U] strange or unusual behaviour: *Kate's mother had a reputation for eccentricity.* **2** [C] an opinion or action that is strange or unusual: *I found his eccentricities amusing rather than irritating.*

Ec·cles cake /ˈekəlz keɪk/ n [C] *BrE* a round cake filled with CURRANTS (=type of dried fruit)

ec·cle·si·as·tic /ɪˌkliːziˈæstɪk◂/ n [C] *formal* a priest, usually in the Christian church

ec·cle·si·as·ti·cal /ɪˌkliːziˈæstɪkəl/ also **ec·cle·sias·tic** /-ˈæstɪk/ adj relating to the Christian church or its priests: *ecclesiastical history*

ECG /ˌiː siː ˈdʒiː/ n [C] *especially BrE* **1** *electrocardiograph* a piece of equipment that records electrical changes in your heart **2** *electrocardiogram* a drawing produced by an ELECTROCARDIOGRAPH

ech·e·lon /ˈeʃəlɒn $ -lɑːn/ n [C] **1** also **echelons** a rank or level of authority in an organization, business etc, or the people at that level: **upper/higher/lower echelons** *the upper echelons of government* | *Their clients are drawn from the highest echelons of society.* **2** *technical* a line of ships, soldiers, planes etc arranged in a pattern that looks like a series of steps

ech·o¹ /ˈekəʊ $ ˈekoʊ/ v **1** [I] if a sound echoes, you hear it again because it was made near something such as a wall or hill: *The sound of an engine echoed back from the thick forest.* | [+through/round] *He could hear eerie noises echoing through the corridors.* **2** [I] if a place echoes, it is filled with sounds that are repeated or are similar to each other: [+with] *The house echoed with the sound of children's voices.* **3** [T] *literary* to repeat what someone else has just said: *'You bet,' she said, echoing his words.* **4** [T] to repeat an idea or opinion because you agree with it: *The article simply echoed the NRA's arguments against gun control.*

echo² n plural **echoes** [C] **1** a sound that you hear again after a loud noise, because it was made near something such as a wall: *Her scream was followed by a loud echo.* **2** something that is very similar to something that has happened or been said before: [+of] *The article contains echoes of an earlier report.* | *This idea finds an echo in many African countries.*

é·clair /ɪˈkleə, eɪ- $ ɪˈkler/ n [C] a long cake covered with chocolate and filled with cream

é·clat /eɪˈklɑː/ n [U] *literary* **1** praise and admiration: *Miller's new play has been greeted with great éclat.* **2** a way of doing something with a lot of style, especially in order to attract attention

e·clec·tic¹ /ɪˈklektɪk/ adj including a mixture of many different things or people, especially so that you can use the best of all of them: *galleries with an eclectic range of styles and artists* | *an eclectic mixture of 18th and 19th century furniture* —**eclectically** /-kli/ adv —**eclecticism** /-tɪsɪzəm/ n [U]

eclectic² n [C] *formal* someone who chooses the best or most useful parts from many different ideas, methods etc

e·clipse¹ /ɪˈklɪps/ n **1** [C] an occasion when the sun or the moon cannot be seen, because the Earth is passing directly between the moon and the sun, or because the moon is passing directly between the Earth and the sun: *an eclipse of the sun* | *a total eclipse* **2** [singular] a situation in which someone or something loses their power or fame, because someone or something else has become more powerful or famous: *Many people expected the growth of television to mean the eclipse of radio.* **3 in eclipse** *formal* less famous or powerful than you should be: *Mrs Bosanquet's novels are now in eclipse.*

eclipse² v [T] **1** if the moon eclipses the sun, the sun cannot be seen behind the moon, and if the Earth eclipses the moon, the moon cannot be seen because the Earth is between the sun and the moon **2** [often passive] to become more important, powerful, famous etc than someone or something else, so that they are no longer noticed; → **overshadow**: *The economy had eclipsed the environment as an election issue.*

e·clip·tic /ɪˈklɪptɪk/ n [singular] *technical* the path along which the sun seems to move

eco- /iːkəʊ $ iːkoʊ/ *prefix* relating to the environment: *eco-warriors* (=people who try to stop damage to the environment)

e·co-friend·ly /ˈiːkəʊ ˌfrendli $ ˈiːkoʊ-/ adj not harmful to the environment: *eco-friendly products*

E. co·li /ˌiː ˈkəʊlaɪ $ -ˈkoʊ-/ n [U] a type of BACTERIA that can make you very ill if it is in any food that you eat

e·co·log·i·cal /ˌiːkəˈlɒdʒɪkəl◂ $ -ˈlɑː-/ adj [only before noun] **1** connected with the way plants, animals, and people are related to each other and to their environment; → **environmental**: *an ecological disaster* **2** interested in preserving the environment; → **environment**: *ecological groups* —**ecologically** /-kli/ adv: *an ecologically-sound production process*

e·col·o·gist /ɪˈkɒlədʒɪst $ -ˈkɑː-/ n [C] a scientist who studies ecology

e·col·o·gy /ɪˈkɒlədʒi $ ɪˈkɑː-/ n [singular, U] the way in which plants, animals, and people are related to each other and to their environment, or the scientific study of this; → **environment**: *the natural ecology of the Earth* | *plant ecology*

e-comm /ˈiː kɒm $ -kɑːm/ n [U] *informal* the abbreviation of *e-commerce*

e-com·merce /ˈiː kɒmɜːs, $ -kɑːmɜːrs/ n [U] *electronic commerce* the activity of buying and selling goods and services and doing other business activities using a computer and the Internet: *e-commerce applications such as online ticketing and reservations*

ec·o·nom·ic [S3] [W1] /ˌekəˈnɒmɪk◂, ˌiː- $ -ˈnɑː-/ adj **1** [only before noun] relating to trade, industry, and the management of money; → **economy**: *Economic growth is slow.* | *the government's economic policy* | *Economic reform is needed.* | *In the current **economic climate*** (=conditions), *we must keep costs down.* **2** an economic process, activity etc produces enough profit for it to continue; [≠] **profitable**; [≠] **uneconomic**: *It is no longer economic for us to run the service.* ⚠ Do not confuse with **economical** (=cheap or not wasteful).

ec·o·nom·i·cal /ˌekəˈnɒmɪkəl, ˌiː- $ -ˈnɑː-/ adj **1** using money, time, goods etc carefully and without wasting any; → **economic**: *A small car is more economical to run.* | *good-quality clothes at economical prices* **2 economical with the truth** used humorously to say that someone is not telling the truth

ec·o·nom·i·cally /ˌekəˈnɒmɪkli, ˌiː- $ -ˈnɑː-/ adv **1** in a way that is related to systems of money, trade, or business: *In economically advanced countries, women marry later.* | [sentence adverb] *Economically, capitalism has transformed societies.* **2** in a way that uses money, goods, time etc without wasting any: *We produce food as economically as possible.* | *Small trees use space in the garden economically.*

ec·o·nom·ics [W3] /ˌekəˈnɒmɪks, ˌiː- $ -ˈnɑː-/ n **1** [U] the study of the way in which money and goods are produced and used; → **economic**: *a Harvard professor of economics* **2** [plural] the way in which money influences whether a plan, business etc will work effectively: *The economics of the scheme will have to be looked at very carefully.* → HOME ECONOMICS

e·con·o·mist /ɪˈkɒnəmɪst $ ɪˈkɑː-/ n [C] someone who studies the way in which money and goods are produced and used and the systems of business and trade

e·con·o·mize also **-ise** *BrE* /ɪˈkɒnəmaɪz $ ɪˈkɑː-/ v [I] to reduce the amount of money, time, goods etc that you use: [+on] *Higher taxes encourage people to economize on fuel.*

e·con·o·my¹ [S3] [W1] /ɪˈkɒnəmi $ ɪˈkɑː-/ n plural **economies** **1** [C] the system by which a country's money and goods are produced and used, or a country considered in this way: *a capitalist economy* | *the slowdown in the Japanese economy*

2 [C] something that you do in order to spend less money: *The council must **make economies** to meet government spending targets.* | *Not insuring your belongings is a **false economy** (=it is cheaper but could have bad results).*
3 [U] the careful use of money, time, goods etc so that nothing is wasted: *The gas fire was turned low for reasons of economy.* | *The company announced that it would cut 500 jobs as part of an **economy drive** (=a way to save money).*
4 economies of scale *technical* the financial advantages of producing something in very large quantities → BLACK ECONOMY, MARKET ECONOMY, MIXED ECONOMY

economy² *adj* **economy size/pack** a product that is cheaper because you are buying a larger amount

e'conomy ,class *n* [U] the cheapest type of seats in a plane —**economy class** *adv*: *We flew economy class.*

e'conomy class ,syndrome *n* [U] *BrE* a serious illness in which people get blood CLOTS because they have been sitting for a long time in a very small space on a plane; → DVT

e·co·sys·tem /'i:kəʊˌsɪstəm $ 'i:koʊ-/ *n* [C] all the animals and plants in a particular area, and the way in which they are related to each other and to their environment; → ecology

e·co·ter·ror·is·m /'i:kəʊˌterərɪzəm $ 'i:koʊ-/ *n* [U] when someone tries to stop or harm organizations or companies that do things that are bad for the environment —**ecoterrorist** *n* [C]

e·co·tour·is·m /'i:kəʊˌtʊərɪzəm $ 'i:koʊˌtʊr-/ *n* [U] the business of organizing holidays to natural areas, especially areas that are far away such as the RAIN FOREST, where people can visit and learn about the area in a way that will not hurt the environment —**ecotourist** *n* [C]

e·cru /'eɪkru:, 'ek-/ *n* [U] a pale brown colour —**ecru** *adj*

ec·sta·sy /'ekstəsi/ *n plural* **ecstasies** **1** [C,U] a feeling of extreme happiness: **in (an) ecstasy** *She was in an ecstasy of love.* | **go into ecstasies** (=become very happy and excited) **2** [U] an illegal drug that gives a feeling of happiness and energy. Ecstasy is especially used by people who go out to dance at clubs and parties.

ec·stat·ic /ɪk'stætɪk, ek-/ *adj* **1** feeling extremely happy and excited: *an ecstatic welcome from the thousands who lined the streets* **2 ecstatic review/praise/applause** a REVIEW (=an opinion about a film, play etc that appears in a newspaper or magazine), praise etc that say that something is very good: *The exhibition attracted thousands of visitors and ecstatic reviews.* —**ecstatically** /-kli/ *adv*

ECT /ˌiː siː 'tiː/ *n* [U] electro-convulsive therapy; another word for ELECTRIC SHOCK THERAPY

-ectomy /ˌektəmi/ *suffix* [in nouns] *technical* the removing of a particular part of someone's body by an operation: *an appendectomy* (=removing the appendix)

e·cu·men·i·cal /ˌiːkjʊˈmenɪkəl◂ $ ˌek-/ *adj* supporting the idea of uniting the different branches of the Christian religion —**ecumenically** /-kli/ *adv*

ec·ze·ma /'eksɪmə $ 'eksɪmə, 'egz-, ɪg'ziːmə/ *n* [U] a condition in which your skin becomes dry, red, and swollen

ed., Ed. /ed/ **1** the abbreviation of *education*: *Higher Ed.* **2** the written abbreviation of *edited*, *edition*, or *editor*

-ed /d, ᵻd, t/ *suffix* **1** forms the regular past tense and past participle of verbs. The past participle form is often used as an adjective: *I want, I wanted, I have wanted* | *I show, I showed, I have shown* | *He walked away.* | *a sound that echoed through the room* | *a wanted criminal* **2** [in adjectives] having a particular thing: *a bearded man* (=a man with a beard) | *a kind-hearted woman*

E·dam /'iːdæm, -dəm/ *n* [U] a type of yellow cheese from the Netherlands

ed·dy¹ /'edi/ *n plural* **eddies** [C] a circular movement of water, wind, dust etc: *the racing river caused swirling eddies*

eddy² *v* **eddied, eddying, eddies** [I] if water, wind, dust etc eddies, it moves around with a circular movement: *Mist eddied round the house.*

E·den /'iːdn/ also **the Garden of Eden** *n* [singular] in the Bible story, the garden where Adam and Eve, the first humans lived, often seen as a place of happiness and INNOCENCE

edge¹ S2 W2 /edʒ/ *n*
1 OUTSIDE PART [C] the part of an object that is furthest from its centre: *Put the lamb in the centre of the dish, with the vegetables and herbs around the edge.* | **the edge of sth** *the right hand edge of the page* | *Jennifer walked to the edge of the wood.* | *Billy sat on the edge of the bed.* | *He stood at the water's edge staring across the lake.* | *A leaf was on the ground, curling up at the edges.* → see picture at LIMIT
2 BLADE [C] the thin sharp part of a blade or tool that cuts: *a knife with a sharp edge*
3 ADVANTAGE [singular, U] something that gives you an advantage over others: *Companies are employing more research teams to give us an edge.* | *The next version of the software **will have** the **edge** over its competitors.*
4 on edge nervous, especially because you are expecting something unpleasant to happen: *Paul felt on edge about meeting Lisa.*
5 VOICE [singular] a quality in someone's voice that makes it sound slightly angry or impatient: *There was an edge of hostility in Jack's voice.* | *Desperation lent an edge to her voice.*
6 SLOPE [C] an area beside a very steep slope: *She walked almost to the edge of the cliff.*
7 on the edge of sth close to the point at which something different, especially something bad, will happen: *Their economy is on the edge of collapse.* | *She is on the edge of despair.*
8 QUALITY [singular] a special quality of excitement or danger: *The school's campaign has been given an extra edge by being filmed for television.*
9 take the edge off sth to make something less bad, good, strong etc: *Pascoe was drinking whisky to take the edge off the pain.*
10 on the edge of your seat giving all your attention to something exciting: *The film's ending had me on the edge of my seat.*
11 be on the edge *informal* to be behaving in a way that makes it seem as if you are going crazy → CUTTING EDGE → KNIFE-EDGE

edge² *v*
1 MOVE [I,T always + adv/prep] to move gradually with several small movements, or to make something do this: *Tim was edging away from the crowd.* | *She edged closer to get a better look.* | *He edged her towards the door.* | **edge your way into/round/through etc sth** *Christine edged her way round the back of the house.*
2 PUT AT EDGE [T usually passive] to put something on the edge or border of something: *The city square was edged by trees.* | **be edged with sth** *The tablecloth was edged with lace.*
3 CHANGE [I,T always + adv/prep] to change gradually, especially so as to get better or worse: [+up/down] *Profits have edged up.* | *The paper has **edged ahead** of (=been more successful than) its rivals.*
4 GRASS [T] to cut the edges of an area of grass so that they are tidy and straight

edge 'city *n* [C] *AmE* an area at the edge of a large city that has its own businesses, shops, offices etc, so that many of the people who used to live there while working in the large city now both live and work in the edge city

edge·ways /'edʒweɪz/ also **edge·wise** /-waɪz/ *adv* sideways → **get a word in edgeways** at WORD¹ (26)

edg·ing /'edʒɪŋ/ *n* [C,U] something that forms an edge or border: *a white handkerchief with blue edging*

edg·y /ˈedʒi/ adj **1** nervous and worried: *She's been edgy lately, waiting for the test results.* **2** aware of the newest ideas and styles and therefore considered very fashionable: *The band is trying to develop an edgy new image.*

EDI /ˌi: di: ˈaɪ/ n [U] technical the abbreviation of *electronic data interchange*

ed·i·ble /ˈedᵻbəl/ adj something that is edible can be eaten: *These berries are edible, but those are poisonous.*

e·dict /ˈiːdɪkt/ n [C] formal **1** an official public order made by someone in a position of power; **⬛ decree**: *The emperor issued an edict forbidding anyone to leave the city.* **2** any order – used humorously

ed·i·fice /ˈedᵻfᵻs/ n [C] formal a building, especially a large one: *Their head office was an imposing edifice.*

ed·i·fy /ˈedᵻfaɪ/ v **edified, edifying, edifies** [T] formal to improve someone's mind or character by teaching them something —**edification** /ˌedᵻfᵻˈkeɪʃən/ n [U]: *For our edification, the preacher reminded us what 'duty' meant.*

ed·i·fy·ing /ˈedᵻfaɪ-ɪŋ/ adj formal an edifying speech, book etc improves your mind or moral character by teaching you something – sometimes used humorously: *No-one would claim that the film is morally edifying.*

ed·it /ˈedᵻt/ v **1** [I,T] to prepare a book, piece of film etc for printing or broadcasting by removing mistakes or parts that are not acceptable: *The newspaper edits letters before printing them.* **2** [T] to prepare a book or article for printing by deciding what to include and in what order: *a collection of essays edited by John Gay* **3** [T] to prepare a film by deciding what to include and in what order **4** [T] to be responsible for the information that is included in a newspaper, magazine etc: *She used to edit the Observer.* —**edit** n [C]

edit sth ⇔ **out** phr v to remove something when you are preparing a book, piece of film etc for printing or broadcasting; **⬛ cut**: *The interviewer's questions have been edited out.*

e·di·tion W3 /ɪˈdɪʃən/ n [C]
1 the form that a book, newspaper, magazine etc is produced in: *a paperback edition* | *the US edition of Marie Claire magazine*
2 the copies of a book, newspaper etc that are produced and printed at the same time: *The textbook was first published in 1858 and is now in its 39th edition.* | *A limited edition of 2000 copies has been published.* | *first edition* (=the first copies of a particular book, that are often valuable)
3 a newspaper, magazine etc: *Martin was reading the early edition of the Evening News.*
4 a television or radio programme that is broadcast regularly or is part of a series: *the early evening edition of Scotland Today*

ed·i·tor W2 /ˈedᵻtə $ -ər/ n [C]
1 the person who is in charge of a newspaper or magazine, or part of a newspaper or magazine, and decides what should be included in it: [+of] *the editor of the Daily Telegraph* | *economics/sports/political etc editor*
2 someone who prepares a book or article for printing by deciding what to include and checking for any mistakes
3 someone who chooses what to include in a book on a particular subject: *the editor of a book of essays on modern poetry*
4 someone who prepares a film, television programme, or sound recording for broadcasting by deciding what to include and checking for any mistakes: *a TV script editor*
5 someone who reports on a particular subject for a radio or television news programme; → **correspondent**: *Here is John Simmonds, our Diplomatic Editor, with the latest news.*
6 technical a computer program that allows you to make changes to saved information → **COPY EDITOR, SUB-EDITOR**

ed·i·to·ri·al¹ /ˌedᵻˈtɔːriəl◄ / adj **1** relating to the preparation of a newspaper, book, television programme etc for printing or broadcasting: *an editorial assistant* **2** [usually before noun] expressing the opinion of a particular newspaper editor rather than just giving facts: *the paper's editorial column* —**editorially** adv: *The paper is editorially independent.*

ed·i·to·ri·al² n [C] a piece of writing in a newspaper that gives the editor's opinion about something, rather than reporting facts

ed·i·to·ri·a·lize also **-ise** BrE /ˌedᵻˈtɔːriəlaɪz/ v [I] to give your opinion and not just the facts about something, especially publicly: [+on/about/against etc] *The BBC is not supposed to editorialize about the news.*

ed·i·tor·ship /ˈedᵻtəʃɪp $ -tər-/ n [U] the position of being the editor of a newspaper or magazine, or the time during which someone is an editor

.edu /dɒt i: di: ˈjuː/ the abbreviation of *educational institution*, used in Internet addresses for schools, colleges etc

ed·u·ca·ble /ˈedjʊkəbəl $ ˈedʒə-/ adj able to learn or be educated: *At that time, deaf children were not considered educable.*

ed·u·cate /ˈedjʊkeɪt $ ˈedʒə-/ v [T] **1** [usually passive] to teach a child at a school, college, or university: *The Omerod School educates handicapped children.* | **be educated at sth** *He was educated at Bristol University.* **2** to give someone information about a particular subject, or to show them a better way to do something; → **teach**: **educate sb about/in/on sth** *a campaign to educate teenagers about HIV*

ed·u·cat·ed /ˈedjʊkeɪtᵻd $ ˈedʒə-/ adj **1** having been well taught and learned a lot: *a highly educated woman* **2** **university-educated/well-educated/ privately-educated etc** having had a particular type of education **3 educated guess** a guess that is likely to be correct because it is based on some knowledge: *Investors must make an educated guess as to the company's potential.*

ed·u·ca·tion S1 W1 /ˌedjʊˈkeɪʃən $ ˌedʒə-/ n
1 [singular, U] the process of teaching and learning, usually at school, college, or university: *the education system* | **get/receive an education** *She also hopes her children will get a good education.* | **university/college education** *I'm sure he has a college education.* | *efforts to increase access to* **higher education** (=education at college or university) → **formal education** at FORMAL¹ (6)
2 [U] the teaching of a particular subject: **health/sex education**
3 [U] the institutions and people involved with teaching: *the local education authority*
4 [singular] an interesting experience which has taught you something – often used humorously: *Having Jimmy to stay has been quite an education!* → **ADULT EDUCATION, FURTHER EDUCATION, HIGHER EDUCATION**

ed·u·ca·tion·al S2 W2 /ˌedjʊˈkeɪʃənəl◄ $ ˌedʒə-/ adj
1 relating to education: *the educational development of children*
2 teaching you something you did not know before: *educational games* —**educationally** adv

ed·u·ca·tion·al·ist /ˌedjʊˈkeɪʃənəlᵻst $ ˌedʒə-/ also **ed·u·ca·tion·ist** /-ʃənᵻst/ n [C] formal someone who knows a lot about ways of teaching and learning

ed·u·ca·tive /ˈedjʊkətɪv $ ˈedʒəkeɪ-/ adj something that is educative teaches you something: *The educative process needs to begin early in a child's life.*

ed·u·ca·tor /ˈedjʊkeɪtə $ ˈedʒəkeɪtər/ n [C] **1** formal a teacher or someone involved in the process of educating people **2** AmE an EDUCATIONALIST

ed·u·tain·ment /ˌedjʊˈteɪnmənt $ ˌedʒə-/ n [U] films, television programmes, or computer SOFTWARE that educate and entertain at the same time

Ed·ward·i·an /ed'wɔːdiən $ -'wɔːr-/ adj relating to the time of King Edward VII of Britain (1901-1910): an Edwardian house

-ee /iː/ suffix [in nouns] **1** someone who is being treated in a particular way: the payee (=someone who is paid) | a trainee | an employee **2** someone who is in a particular state or who is doing something: an absentee (=someone who is absent) | an escapee

EEC /ˌiː iː 'siː/ n the EEC the European Economic Community the former name for the EU

EEG /ˌiː iː 'dʒiː/ n [C] **1** electroencephalograph a piece of equipment that records the electrical activity of your brain **2** electroencephalogram a drawing made by an electroencephalograph

eek /iːk/ interjection an expression of sudden fear and surprise: Eek! A mouse!

eel /iːl/ n [C] a long thin fish that looks like a snake and can be eaten

e'en /iːn/ adv literary the short form of EVEN

e'er /eə $ er/ adv literary the short form of EVER

-eer /ɪə $ ɪr/ suffix [in nouns] someone who does or makes a particular thing: an auctioneer (=someone who runs auction sales) | a profiteer (=someone who makes unfair profits)

ee·rie /'ɪəri $ 'ɪri/ adj strange and frightening: the eerie sound of an owl hooting at night —**eerily** adv

e-fa·tigue /'iː fəˌtiːg/ also **electronic fatigue** n [U] problems that people have as a result of using computers too much or for too long, for example tiredness at work or a lack of communication

eff /ef/ v [I] BrE spoken informal **1 effing and blinding** swearing: Did you hear her effing and blinding at him? **2 eff off!** used to tell someone to go away instead of saying FUCK OFF → EFFING

ef·face /ɪ'feɪs/ v [T] formal **1** to destroy or remove something; ⚊ **erase**; → **deface**: Nothing can efface the last picture I have of them from my mind. **2 efface yourself** to behave in a quiet way so that people do not notice or look at you → SELF-EFFACING

ef·fect¹ S1 W1 /ɪ'fekt/ n

1 CHANGE/RESULT [C,U] the way in which an event, action, or person changes someone or something

have an effect (on sb/sth)
big/major/profound/significant/dramatic effect
bad/harmful/negative/damaging/detrimental/adverse effect
beneficial/positive effect
long-term effect
feel the effect (of sth)
knock-on-effect BrE (=an effect caused by the thing that happened before)
cumulative effect (=the effect of many things happening one after another)
the desired effect (=the effect you wanted)
cause and effect (=one thing directly causing the other)

[+on] My parents' divorce **had** a big **effect** on me. | [+of] the **harmful effects** of modern farming practices | the **long-term effects** of the drug | I could **feel the effects** of the thin mountain air. | This ingredient also **has the effect** of making your skin look younger. | A system failure has a **knock-on effect** throughout the whole hotel. | the **cumulative effect** of human activities on the global environment | A much lower dose of the painkiller can still produce **the desired effect**. | In mental illness, there is a complex relationship between **cause and effect**. → GREENHOUSE EFFECT, SIDE EFFECT

2 put/bring sth into effect to make a plan or idea happen: It won't be easy to put the changes into effect.
3 take effect to start to produce results: The morphine was starting to take effect and the pain eased.
4 LAW/RULE **a)** take effect/come into effect if a law, rule, or system takes effect or comes into effect, it officially starts **b)** be in effect if a law, rule, or system

is in effect, it is being used now
5 with immediate effect/with effect from formal starting to happen immediately, or from a particular date: Hoskins is appointed manager, with immediate effect.
6 in effect used when you are describing what you see as the real facts of a situation: In effect, we'll be earning less than we were last year.
7 to good/great/no etc effect used to show how successful an action is: We tried to wake him, but to no effect.
8 to this/that/the effect used when you are giving the general meaning of something, rather than the exact words: Jim told me to go away, or **words to that effect**. | The letter said something **to the effect that** she was no longer needed.
9 IDEA/FEELING [C usually singular] an idea or feeling that an artist, speaker, book etc tries to make you think of or to feel: [+of] Turner's paintings give an effect of light.
10 for effect if someone does something for effect, they do it in order to make people notice: She paused for effect, then carried on speaking.
11 PERSONAL POSSESSIONS effects [plural] formal the things that someone owns; ⚊ **belongings**: Don's few **personal effects** were in a suitcase under the bed.
12 FILM [C usually plural] an unusual or impressive sound or image that is artificially produced for a film, play, or radio programme → SOUND EFFECTS, SPECIAL EFFECT

effect² v [T] formal to make something happen: Many parents lack confidence in their ability to effect change in their children's behaviour. ⚠ Do not confuse with the verb **affect** (=to have an effect on something).

ef·fec·tive S2 W1 /ɪ'fektɪv/ adj
1 successful, and working in the way that was intended; ⚊ **ineffective**: The cheaper drugs are just as effective in treating arthritis. | the painting's **highly effective** use of colour | Training is often much less effective than expected. | the most effective ways of reducing inner city congestion
2 [no comparative, not before noun] if a law, agreement, or system becomes effective, it officially starts: [+from] The cut in interest rates is effective from Monday.
3 [no comparative, only before noun] real rather than what is officially intended or generally believed: The rebels are in effective control of the city. —**effectiveness** n [U]

ef·fec·tive·ly S2 W2 /ɪ'fektɪvli/ adv
1 in a way that produces the result that was intended: Children have to learn to communicate effectively.
2 used to describe what you see as the real facts of the situation: [sentence adverb]: Effectively, it has become impossible for us to help. | Most of the urban poor are effectively excluded from politics.

ef·fec·tu·al /ɪ'fektʃuəl/ adj formal producing the result that was wanted or intended; ⚊ **effective**; ⚊ **ineffectual**

ef·fem·i·nate /ɪ'femɪnət/ adj a man who is effeminate looks or behaves like a woman —**effeminately** adv —**effeminacy** n [U]

ef·fer·vesce /ˌefə'ves $ ˌefər-/ v [I] technical a liquid that effervesces produces small bubbles of gas

ef·fer·ves·cent /ˌefə'vesənt◂ $ ˌefər-/ adj **1** someone who is effervescent is very happy, excited, and active: an effervescent personality **2** a liquid that is effervescent produces small bubbles of gas; ⚊ **fizzy**, **sparkling** —**effervescence** n [U]

ef·fete /ɪ'fiːt $ e-/ adj formal **1** weak and powerless in a way that you dislike: an attack against effete intellectuals **2** an effete man looks or behaves like a woman

ef·fi·ca·cious /ˌefɪ'keɪʃəs◂/ adj formal working in the way you intended; ⚊ **effective**: an equally efficacious method of treatment

ef·fi·ca·cy /'efɪkəsi/ n [U + of] formal the ability of something to produce the right result; ⚊ **effectiveness**

ef·fi·cien·cy S3 W3 /ɪ'fɪʃənsi/ n
1 [U] the quality of doing something well and effectively, without wasting time, money, or energy;

⊞ inefficient: [+of] *the efficiency of the train service* | *considerable advancements in* **energy efficiency**
2 efficiencies [plural] the amounts of money, supplies etc that are saved by finding a better or cheaper way of doing something: *operating efficiencies*

ef·fi·cient [S2] [W3] /ɪˈfɪʃənt/ *adj* if someone or something is efficient, they work well without wasting time, money, or energy: **⊞ inefficient**: *a very efficient secretary* | *an efficient use of land* | *Lighting is now more* **energy efficient**. —**efficiently** *adv*

ef·fi·gy /ˈefɪdʒi/ *n plural* **effigies** **1** [C] a STATUE of a famous person: [+of] *an effigy of Saint Francis* **2** [U] a roughly made, usually ugly, model of someone you dislike: *a threat to* **burn** *the president* **in effigy**

ef·fing /ˈefɪŋ/ *adj* [only before noun] *BrE spoken* an offensive word used to emphasize that you are angry and to avoid saying the swear word 'FUCKING' directly: *She's gone to effing bingo again.* → **effing and blinding** at EFF

ef·flo·res·cence /ˌefləˈresəns/ *n* [U] *technical* the action of flowers, art etc forming and developing, or the period of time when this happens

ef·flu·ent /ˈefluənt/ *n* [C,U] *formal* liquid waste, especially chemicals or SEWAGE

ef·fort [S1] [W1] /ˈefət $ ˈefərt/ *n*
1 PHYSICAL/MENTAL ENERGY [U] the physical or mental energy that is needed to do something: *Lou lifted the box easily, without using much effort.* | **make the effort (to do sth)** *He made the effort to say something pleasant.* | **it takes effort (to do sth)** *It takes a lot of time and effort to get an exhibition ready.* | *An automatic car* **takes all the effort out of** *driving* (=it makes driving very easy). | *Frank* **put** *a lot of* **effort into** *the party.* | *Visit the cathedral when you're there. It's* **well worth the effort** (=it is definitely worth doing).
2 ATTEMPT [C,U] an attempt to do something, especially when this involves a lot of hard work or determination: **make an effort (to do sth)** *I know you don't like her, but please make an effort to be polite.* | *Jack has* **made a concerted effort** (=tried hard over a long time) *to improve his behaviour.* | *We* **make every effort to** *satisfy clients' wishes.* | *They* **made no effort** *to include us in the negotiations.* | **sb's effort(s) to do sth** *Tom's determined efforts to stop smoking haven't been very successful.* | *Church leaders are prepared to meet the terrorists* **in an effort to** (=in order to try to) *find peace.* | [+at] *Further efforts at negotiation have broken down.* | **through sb's efforts** (=because of their efforts) *The money was raised largely through the efforts of parents.* | *The meal was* **a joint effort** (=it was done by two people together).* | **despite sb's efforts** *Despite all our efforts we lost the game 1–0.* | *With* **a supreme effort** *of will Isabel forced back the tears.*
3 be an effort to be difficult or painful to do: *I was so weak that even standing up was an effort.*
4 PARTICULAR SITUATION [C] work that people do to achieve something in a particular situation: *the fundraising effort* | *the international* **relief effort** | *Everyone did what they could to support the* **war effort**.
5 good/bad/poor etc effort something that has been done well, badly etc: *Not a bad effort for a beginner!*

ef·fort·less /ˈefətləs $ ˈefərt-/ *adj* something that is effortless is done in a very skilful way that makes it seem easy: *Alexei rose to his feet with a single effortless movement.* —**effortlessly** *adv*: *He dived effortlessly into the turquoise water.*

ef·fron·te·ry /ɪˈfrʌntəri/ *n* [U] *formal* rude behaviour that shocks you because it is so confident: **have the effrontery to do sth** *She had the effrontery to ask me for more money.*

ef·ful·gent /ɪˈfʌldʒənt $ ɪˈfʊl-/ *adj literary* beautiful and bright —**effulgence** *n* [U]

ef·fu·sion /ɪˈfjuːʒən/ *n* [C,U] **1** *technical* a liquid or gas that flows out of something, or the act of flowing out: *a massive effusion of poisonous gas* **2** *formal* an uncontrolled expression of strong good feelings: *He greeted the guests with effusion.*

ef·fu·sive /ɪˈfjuːsɪv/ *adj* showing your good feelings in a very excited way: *Our host gave us an effusive welcome.* | [+in] *Dotty was effusive in her thanks.* —**effusively** *adv* —**effusiveness** *n* [U]

E-FIT /ˈiː fɪt/ *n* [C] *BrE trademark* a picture, made by using a computer, of a person who the police think was responsible for a crime, which they show on television or the Internet in order to try and catch the person

EFL /ˌiː ef ˈel/ *n* [U] **English as a Foreign Language** the teaching of English to people whose first language is not English, and who do not live in an English-speaking country

EFT /ˌiː ef ˈtiː/ *n* [C,U] *technical* the abbreviation of **electronic funds transfer**

e.g. /ˌiː ˈdʒiː/ the abbreviation of **for example**: *citrus fruits, e.g. oranges and grapefruit*

e·gal·i·tar·i·an /ɪˌɡælɪˈteəriən $ -ˈter-/ *adj* based on the belief that everyone is equal and should have equal rights: *an egalitarian society* —**egalitarianism** *n* [U]

---

egg   **E**

boiled eggs

poached eggs

fried egg

scrambled eggs

egg¹ [S1] [W2] /eg/ *n*
1 BIRD [C] a round object with a hard surface, that contains a baby bird, snake, insect etc and which is produced by a female bird, snake, insect etc: *Blackbirds* **lay** *their* **eggs** *in March.* | *an ostrich egg* | *The eggs* **hatch** (=break open to allow the baby out) *in 26 days.*
2 FOOD [C,U] an egg, especially one from a chicken, that is used for food: **fried/poached/boiled etc eggs** | *Joe always has* **bacon and egg** *for breakfast.* | *Whisk the* **egg white** (=the white part) *until stiff.* | *Beat in two of the* **egg yolks** (=the yellow part). → SCRAMBLED EGG
3 EGG SHAPE [C] something the same shape as an egg: *a chocolate Easter egg* → EASTER EGG
4 ANIMALS/PEOPLE [C] a cell produced by a woman or female animal that combines with SPERM (=male cell) to make a baby; **⊞ ovum**
5 (have) egg on your face if someone, especially someone in authority, has egg on their face, they have been made to look stupid by something embarrassing: *The Pentagon's been left with egg on its face.*
6 put all your eggs in one basket to depend completely on one thing or one course of action in order to get success, so that you have no other plans if this fails: *When planning your investments, it's unwise to put all your eggs in one basket.*
7 lay an egg *AmE informal* to fail or be unsuccessful at something that you are trying to do
8 good egg *old-fashioned* someone who you can depend on to be honest, kind etc → **kill the goose that lays the golden egg** at KILL¹ (14); → NEST EGG

egg² *v*
egg sb ⇔ on *phr v* to encourage someone to do something, especially something that they do not want

to do or should not do: *Bob didn't want to jump, but his friends kept egging him on.*

egg·cup /ˈeg-kʌp/ *n* [C] a small container that holds a boiled egg while you eat it → see picture at CUP

egg·head /ˈeghed/ *n* [C] *informal* someone who is very intelligent, and only interested in ideas and books

egg·nog /ˈegnɒg $ -nɑːg/ *n* [U] a drink made from eggs, sugar, milk, and alcohol, usually drunk at Christmas

egg·plant /ˈegplɑːnt $ -plænt/ *n* [C,U] *AmE* a large vegetable with smooth purple skin; ☒ **aubergine** *BrE*

,**egg 'roll** *n* [C] a SPRING ROLL

egg·shell /ˈegʃel/ *n* [C,U] **1** the hard outside part of a bird's egg **2** a type of paint, used especially on wood, that is not shiny when dry

'**egg-,timer** *n* [C] a small glass container with sand in it that runs from one part to the other in about three or five minutes, used for measuring the time it takes to boil an egg

e·go /ˈiːgəʊ, ˈegəʊ $ -goʊ/ *n plural* **egos** [C] **1** the opinion that you have about yourself: **big/enormous etc ego** *Richard has the biggest ego* (=thinks he is very clever and important) *of anyone I've ever met.* | *That promotion really boosted her ego* (=made her feel better about herself). | *I need someone to massage my* **bruised ego** (=when you feel less confident than before). | *a fragile ego* → ALTER EGO **2** *technical* the part of your mind with which you think and take action, according to Freudian PSYCHOLOGY; → ID, **superego**

e·go·cen·tric /ˌiːgəʊˈsentrɪk◂, ˌeg- $ -goʊ-/ *adj* thinking only about yourself and not about what other people might need or want; ☒ **self-centred** —**egocentricity** /ˌiːgəʊsenˈtrɪsᵻti, ˌeg- $ -goʊ-/ *n* [C,U]

e·go·is·m /ˈiːgəʊɪzəm, ˈeg- $ -goʊ-/ *n* [U] EGOTISM —**egoist** *n* [C] —**egoistic** /ˌiːgəʊˈɪstɪk◂, ˌeg- $ -goʊ-/ *adj*

e·go·ma·ni·ac /ˌiːgəʊˈmeɪniæk, ˌeg- $ -goʊ-/ *n* [C] someone who thinks that they are very important, and does not care whether they upset other people in order to get what they want

e·go·tis·m /ˈiːgətɪzəm, ˈeg-/ *n* [U] the belief that you are much better or more important than other people

e·go·tist /ˈiːgətᵻst, ˈeg-/ *n* [C] someone who likes to talk about how great and important they think they are —**egotistic** /ˌiːgəˈtɪstɪk◂, ˌeg-/ *adj*

e·go·tis·tic·al /ˌiːgəˈtɪstɪkəl◂, ˌeg-/ *adj* someone who is egotistical likes to talk about how great and important they think they are: *He's the most selfish, egotistical individual I have ever met!* —**egotistically** /-kli/ *adv*

'**ego ,trip** *n* [C] if someone is on an ego trip, they think that what they do makes them more important than other people – used to show disapproval: *Their singer's on a real ego trip.*

e·gre·gious /ɪˈgriːdʒəs/ *adj formal* an egregious mistake, failure, problem etc is extremely bad and noticeable —**egregiously** *adv*

e·gress /ˈiːgres/ *n* [U] *formal or law* the act of leaving a building or place, or the right to do this

e·gret /ˈiːgrᵻt, -et/ *n* [C] a bird that lives near water and has long legs and long white tail feathers

E·gyp·tian¹ /ɪˈdʒɪpʃən/ *adj* relating to Egypt or its people

Egyptian² *n* [C] someone from Egypt

eh /eɪ/ *interjection spoken* **1** *BrE* used when you want someone to repeat something because you did not hear it: *Eh? She's got how many children?* **2** used when you want someone to reply to you or agree with something you have said: *Maybe teenagers aren't as clueless as everyone thought, eh?* **3** *BrE* used when you are surprised by something that someone has said

Eid /iːd/ *n* [U] one of two important holidays in the Muslim religion

ei·der·down /ˈaɪdədaʊn $ -dər-/ *n* [C] a thick warm cover for a bed, filled with duck feathers; → **duvet**

eight /eɪt/ *number, n* **1** the number 8: *It's only eight days till Christmas.* | *They woke at eight* (=eight o'clock). | *My parents died when I was eight* (=eight years old). **2** [C] a team of eight people who row a racing boat, or the boat that they row

8 *written informal* a way of writing parts of words that sound like '-ate', '-eat', or '-ait', used especially in emails and TEXT MESSAGES: *gr8* (=great) | *I h8* (=hate) *homework!* | *It's 2 l8* (=too late)

eigh·teen /ˌeɪˈtiːn◂/ *number* the number 18: *At least eighteen bullets were fired.* | *Jim was eighteen* (=18 years old). —**eighteenth** *adj, pron: in the eighteenth century* | *her eighteenth birthday* | *I'm planning to leave on* **the eighteenth** (=the 18th day of the month).

eighth¹ /eɪtθ/ *adj* coming after seven other things in a series: *in the eighth century* | *her eighth birthday* —**eighth** *pron: I'm planning to leave on* **the eighth** (=the eighth day of the month).

eighth² *n* [C] one of eight equal parts of something

'**eighth note** *n* [C] *AmE technical* a musical note that continues for an eighth of the length of a WHOLE NOTE; ☒ **quaver** *BrE*

eigh·ty /ˈeɪti/ *number* **1** the number 80 **2 the eighties** [plural] also **the '80s, the 1980s** the years from 1980 to 1989: *The band was incredibly successful in the eighties.* | **the early/mid/late eighties** *Their troubles began in the mid eighties.* **3** be in your eighties to be aged between 80 and 89: **early/mid/late eighties** *Hilda Simpson was a woman in her early eighties.* **4** in the **eighties** if the temperature is in the eighties, it is between 80 degrees and 89 degrees: **in the low/mid/high eighties** *The temperature is expected to remain in the low eighties.* —**eightieth** *adj: her eightieth birthday*

ei·stedd·fod /aɪˈstedfəd $ -vɑːd/ *n* [C] an event in Wales at which there are competitions in singing, poetry, and music

ei·ther¹ S1 W1 /ˈaɪðə $ ˈiːðər/ *conjunction* **either ... or a)** used to begin a list of two or more possibilities: *You add either one or two cloves of garlic.* | *She's the kind of person you either love or hate.* → see box at ALSO **b)** used to say that if one thing does not happen then something else will have to: *It's your choice! Either she leaves or I will!* | *£75 seems a lot to pay for a starter motor, but it's either that or a new car!* **c)** an either-or situation a situation in which you cannot avoid having to make a decision or choice

either² S1 W1 *determiner, pron* **1** one or the other of two things or people; → **any**: *There's tea or coffee – you can have either.* | *We can offer a comfortable home to a young person of either sex.* | [+of] *Could either of you lend me five pounds?* **2** used to show that a negative statement is true about both of two things or people; → **neither**: *I've lived in New York and Chicago, but don't like either city very much.* | [+of] *There were two witnesses but I wouldn't trust either of them.* **3 either side/end/hand etc** both sides, ends, hands etc; ☒ **each**: *He sat in the back of the car with a policeman on either side.* | *There are shops at either end of the street.* **4 either way a)** used to say that something will be the same whichever of two things happens or is true: *You can get to Edinburgh by train or plane, but either way it's very expensive.* **b)** more or less than a certain amount or measurement: *A few marks either way can make the difference between a pass and a fail.* **c)** used to say that someone or something does not firmly support or want either one of two things: *'All right, let's do that,' said Camille, who didn't care either way.* **5 could go either way** if a situation could go either way, both possible results are equally likely: *The latest opinion poll suggests the vote could go either way.*

either³ adv **1** [in negatives] used to show that a negative statement is also true about another thing or person, or to add a different negative statement about something or someone; → **neither**: *I haven't seen the movie and my brother hasn't either* (=he also has not seen it). | *'I can't swim.' 'I can't, either.'* | *It's not an easy car to drive , and at $40,000 it's not cheap either.* **2 me either** *AmE* spoken used to say that a negative statement is also true about you: *'I don't have any money right now.' 'Me either.'*

e·jac·u·late /ɪˈdʒækjˈleɪt/ v [I,T] **1** when a man ejaculates, SEMEN comes out of his PENIS **2** *old-fashioned or literary* to suddenly shout or say something, especially because you are surprised —**ejaculation** /ɪˌdʒækjˈleɪʃən/ n [C,U]

e·ject /ɪˈdʒekt/ v **1** [T] to make someone leave a place or building by using force: **eject sb from sth** *The demonstrators were ejected from the hall.* **2** [T] to make someone leave a job or position very quickly: **eject sb from sth** *420 workers have been ejected from their jobs with no warning.* **3** [T] to suddenly send something out: *Two engines cut out and the plane started to eject fuel as it lost height.* **4** [I] if a pilot ejects, he or she escapes from a plane, using an ejector seat because it is going to crash **5** [I,T] if you eject a TAPE or DISK, or if it ejects, it comes out of a machine after you have pressed a particular button —**ejection** /ɪˈdʒekʃən/ n [C,U]

e'jector ,seat *BrE*; **e'jection ,seat** *AmE* n [C] a special seat that throws the pilot out of a plane when it is going to crash

eke /iːk/ v
  eke sth ⇔ **out** *phr v* **1 eke out a living/existence** to manage to live with very little money or food: *They eke out a miserable existence in cardboard shacks.* **2** to make a small supply of something such as food or money last longer by carefully using small amounts of it: *How did Mum manage to eke out the food when we were kids?*

EKG /ˌiː keɪ ˈdʒiː/ n [C] *AmE* **ECG**

e·lab·o·rate¹ /ɪˈlæbərˈt/ adj **1** having a lot of small parts or details put together in a complicated way: *pure silks embroidered with elaborate patterns* **2** carefully planned and organized in great detail: *a very elaborate telecommunications network* —**elaborately** adv: *an elaborately carved wooden statue.*

e·lab·o·rate² /ɪˈlæbəreɪt/ v [I,T] to give more details or new information about something: *He said he had new evidence, but refused to elaborate any further.* | [+on] *McDonald refused to elaborate on his reasons for resigning.* —**elaboration** /ɪˌlæbəˈreɪʃən/ n [C,U]

é·lan /ˈeɪlɒn $ eɪ'lɑːn/ n [U] *literary* a style that is full of energy and confidence: *The attack was planned and led with great élan.*

e·lapse /ɪˈlæps/ v [I not in progressive] *formal* if a particular period of time elapses, it passes: *Several months elapsed before his case was brought to trial.* | *The assignment must be completed within an overall* **elapsed time** *of one week.*

e·las·tic¹ /ɪˈlæstɪk/ n [U] a type of rubber material that can stretch and then return to its usual length or size: *The ball was attached to the bat with a* **piece of** *elastic.*

elastic² adj **1** made of elastic: *an elastic cord* **2** a material that is elastic can stretch and then go back to its usual length or size: *the horny elastic pad in a horse's hoof* **3** a system or plan that is elastic can change or be changed easily: *Demand for this type of holiday will probably be fairly elastic.* **4** *AmE* if a piece of clothing is elastic, it is made with material that can stretch: *children's pants with an elastic waist*

e·las·ti·cat·ed /ɪˈlæstˌkeɪtˌd/ adj *BrE* if a piece of clothing is elasticated, it is made with material that can stretch: *skirts with elasticated waists*

e,lastic 'band n [C] *BrE* a thin circular piece of rubber used for fastening things together; **⊟ rubber band**

e·las·tic·i·ty /ˌiːlæˈstɪsˌti/ n [U] **1** the ability of something to stretch and go back to its usual length or size: *the skin's natural elasticity* **2 elasticity of demand** *technical* the degree to which a change in the price of something leads to a change in the amount of it that is sold

E·las·to·plast /ɪˈlæstəplɑːst $ -plæst/ n [C,U] *trademark BrE* a piece of thin material that is stuck to the skin to cover cuts and other small wounds; **⊟ Band-Aid** *AmE*

e·lat·ed /ɪˈleɪtˌd/ adj extremely happy and excited, especially because of something that has happened or is going to happen: *He felt elated and mildly drunk.* | [+at/by] *She was elated at the prospect of a holiday.*

e·la·tion /ɪˈleɪʃən/ n [U] a feeling of great happiness and excitement

el·bow¹ /ˈelbəʊ $ -boʊ/ n [C] **1** the joint where your arm bends **2** the part of a shirt etc that covers your elbow **3 elbow grease** *informal* hard work and effort, especially when cleaning or polishing something **4 give sb the elbow** *BrE informal* to tell someone that you no longer like them or want them to work for you and that they should leave **5 elbow room** enough space in which to move easily: *There's more elbow room in the restaurant since they extended it.* **6** a curved part of a pipe → **rub elbows with sb** at RUB¹ (5)

elbow² v [T] to push someone with your elbows, especially in order to move past them: **elbow your way through/past/into etc sth** (=move through a group of people by pushing past them) *He elbowed his way to the bar and ordered a beer.* | *She pushed through the crowd, elbowing people out of the way.*

el·der¹ /ˈeldə $ -ər/ adj especially BrE the elder of two people, especially brothers and sisters, is the one who was born first: **elder brother/son/sister/daughter etc** *His elder son Liam became a lawyer.* | *Sarah is* **the elder** *of the two.* ⚠ It is more usual to say **older.**

elder² n [C] **1 be sb's elder** *formal* to be older than someone else: **be two/ten etc years sb's elder** *Janet's sister was eight years her elder.* **2 sb's elders (and betters)** people who are older than you and who you should respect **3** a member of a tribe or other social group who is important and respected because they are old: *a meeting of the village elders* **4** someone who has an official position of responsibility in some Christian churches **5 elder abuse** the crime of harming an old person **6** a small wild tree that has white flowers and black BERRIES

el·der·ber·ry /ˈeldəbəri $ -dərberi/ n plural **elderberries** [C] the fruit of the elder tree

el·der·ly [S2] [W2] /ˈeldəli $ ˈeldərli/ adj **1** used as a polite way of saying that someone is old or becoming old: *a well-dressed elderly woman* **2 the elderly** people who are old: *a retirement village for the elderly*

,elder 'statesman n [C] someone old and respected, especially a politician, who people ask for advice because of his or her knowledge and experience

el·dest /ˈeldˌst/ adj especially BrE the eldest of a group of people, especially brothers and sisters, is the one who was born first; → **old**: **eldest son/daughter/brother/child etc** *My eldest daughter is 17.* | *He was the* **eldest** *of six children.*

e·lect¹ [S2] [W3] /ɪˈlekt/ v [T usually passive] **1** to choose someone for an official position by voting: *the country's first* **democratically elected** *government* | *a new method for electing the leader of the party* | **elect sb to sth** *He was elected to a US state governorship.* | **elect sb (as) president/leader/mayor etc** *In 1768, John Wilkes was elected as their Member of Parliament.* **2 elect to do sth** *formal* to choose to do something: *You can elect to delete the message or save it.*

E

[1] 000, [2] 000, [3] 000, most frequent words in [S]poken and [W]ritten English

elect² *adj* **president-elect/governor-elect/prime
minister-elect etc** the person who has been elected as
president etc, but who has not yet officially started
their job

e·lec·tion S2 W1 /ɪˈlekʃən/ *n*
1 [C] when people vote to choose someone for an
official position: *The Labour Party won the 2001 elec-
tion by a huge majority.* | *Elections will be held on 14
February.* | **local/municipal/state/national election** *He
will be fighting local elections next May.* | **presidential/
mayoral/parliamentary etc election** *The next presiden-
tial election is due in two years.* | **stand for election** *BrE*:
*She was one of the first women to stand for election to
parliament.* | **run for election**
2 [singular] the fact of being elected to an official
position: *Within three months of his election he was
forced to resign.* | **sb's election to sth** *his election to
Parliament*; → see also GENERAL ELECTION

e·lec·tion·eer·ing /ɪˌlekʃəˈnɪərɪŋ $ -ˈnɪr-/ *n* [U]
speeches and other activities that are intended to
persuade people to vote for a particular person or
political party

e·lec·tive¹ /ɪˈlektɪv/ *adj formal* **1** an elective position or organization is one for which there is an
election: *the 34 elective seats in the National Assembly* **2** elective medical treatment is treatment that
you choose to have, although you do not have to:
elective surgery such as hip replacements **3** *AmE* an
elective course is one that students can choose to take,
although they do not have to take it in order to GRADUATE

elective² *n* [C] *AmE* a course that students can choose
to take, but they do not have to take it in order to
GRADUATE

e·lec·tor /ɪˈlektə $ -tər, -tɔːr/ *n* [C] someone who has
the right to vote in an election: *Over 36% of electors did
not vote at all.*

e·lec·to·ral /ɪˈlektərəl/ *adj* [only before noun] relating
to elections and voting: *Our electoral system strongly
favours two-party government.* | *a campaign for elec-
toral reform* —**electorally** *adv*

e,lectoral 'college *n* **the Electoral College** a group
of people chosen by the votes of the people in each US
state, who come together to elect the President, or a
similar group in other countries

e,lectoral 'register also **e,lectoral 'roll** *n* [C] an
official list of the people who are allowed to vote in an
election

e·lec·to·rate /ɪˈlektərɪt/ *n* [singular] all the people in
a country who have the right to vote: *A majority of the
electorate oppose the law.*

e·lec·tric S2 W3 /ɪˈlektrɪk/ *adj*
1 needing electricity to work, produced by electricity,
or used for carrying electricity: **electric light/kettle/
cooker etc** *the heat from a small electric fire* | **electric
current/power/charge** (=a flow of electricity) | *an elec-
tric blanket* (=one with electric wires in it, used for
making a bed warm) → see picture at FENCE
2 making people feel very excited: *The atmosphere in
the courtroom was electric.*

e·lec·tri·cal S3 /ɪˈlektrɪkəl/ *adj*
1 relating to electricity: *The fire was caused by an
electrical fault.* | *an electrical engineer* (=a person
who designs and makes electrical equipment)
2 using electricity: **electrical equipment/goods/appli-
ances etc** —**electrically** /-kli/ *adv*

e,lectrical 'storm also **e,lectric 'storm** *n* [C] a
violent storm with a lot of LIGHTNING

e,lectric ,blue *n* [U] a very bright blue colour
—**electric blue** *adj*

e,lectric 'chair *n* [C usually singular] a chair in which
criminals are killed using electricity, especially in the
US, in order to punish them for murder: *He faces death
by the electric chair in a Florida state prison.*

el·ec·tri·cian /ɪˌlekˈtrɪʃən, ˌelɪk-/ *n* [C] someone
whose job is to connect or repair electrical wires or
equipment

e·lec·tri·ci·ty S2 W3 /ɪˌlekˈtrɪsɨti, ˌelɪk-/ *n* [U]
1 the power that is carried by wires, CABLES etc, and is
used to provide light or heat, to make machines work
etc: *The farm was very isolated, but it had electricity.* |
the electricity supply | *the electricity bill*
2 a feeling of excitement

electric

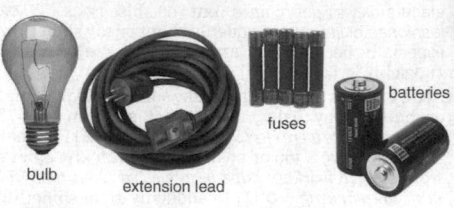

bulb

extension lead

batteries

fuses

e·lec·trics /ɪˈlektrɪks/ *n* [plural] *BrE* the parts of a
machine that use electrical power

e,lectric 'shock *n* [C] a sudden shock to your body,
caused by electricity

e,lectric 'shock ,therapy *n* [U] a method of
treatment for mental illness that involves sending
electricity through someone's brain; ▤ ECT

e·lec·tri·fy /ɪˈlektrɨfaɪ/ *v* **electrified, electrifying,
electrifies** [T] **1** if a performance or a speech electrifies people, it makes them feel very interested or
excited: *She would sit at the piano and sing, electrifying
us all.* **2** to change a railway so that it uses electrical
power, or to supply a building or area with electricity:
The west coast main line has been electrified.
—**electrifying** *adj* —**electrified** *adj: electrified fences*
—**electrification** /ɪˌlektrɨfɨˈkeɪʃən/ *n* [U]

electro- /ɪlektrəʊ, -trə $ -troʊ, -trə/ *prefix techni-
cal* **1** relating to electricity or made to work by electricity: *electrocute* (=to hurt or kill someone by
electricity) | *an electromagnet* **2** electric and some-
thing else: *electro-chemical*

e·lec·tro·car·di·o·gram /ɪˌlektrəʊˈkɑːdiəgræm
$ -troʊˈkɑːr-/ *n* [C] *technical* an ECG (2)

e·lec·tro·car·di·o·graph /ɪˌlektrəʊˈkɑːdiəgrɑːf
$ -troʊˈkɑːrdiəgræf/ *n* [C] *technical* an ECG (1)

e,lectro-con,vulsive 'therapy *n* [U] ELECTRIC
SHOCK THERAPY

e·lec·tro·cute /ɪˈlektrəkjuːt/ *v* [T usually pas-
sive] **1** *BrE* if someone is electrocuted, they are
injured or killed by electricity passing through their
body: *Last week a housewife was electrocuted by her
washing machine.* **2** to kill someone using electricity
—**electrocution** /ɪˌlektrəˈkjuːʃən/ *n* [U]

e·lec·trode /ɪˈlektrəʊd $ -troʊd/ *n* [C] a small piece of
metal or a wire that is used to send electricity through
a system or through a person's body: *The monkeys have
electrodes implanted into the brain to measure their
brain activity.*

e·lec·tro·en·ceph·a·lo·gram /ɪˌlektrəʊ-
ɪnˈsefələgræm, -trəʊen- $ -troʊ-/ *n* [C] *technical* an EEG
(2)

e·lec·tro·en·ceph·a·lo·graph /ɪˌlektrəʊ-
ɪnˈsefələgrɑːf, -trəʊen- $ -troʊɪnˈsefələgræf, -troʊen-/ *n*
[C] *technical* an EEG (1)

e·lec·trol·y·sis /ɪˌlekˈtrɒlɨsɨs, ˌelɪk- $ -ˈtrɑː-/ *n*
[U] **1** *technical* the process of separating a liquid into
its chemical parts by passing an electric current
through it **2** the process of using electricity to
destroy hair roots and to remove unwanted hairs from
your face etc

e·lec·tro·lyte /ɪˈlektrəlaɪt/ *n* [C] *technical* a liquid
that allows electricity to pass through it

e·lec·tro·mag·net /ɪˌlektrəʊˈmægnɨt $ -troʊ-/ *n* [C]
a piece of metal that becomes MAGNETIC (=able to attract
metal objects) when an electric current is turned on

e·lec·tro·mag·ne·tis·m /ɪˌlektrəʊˈmægnətɪzəm $ -troʊ-/ n [U] technical a force relating to electric and MAGNETIC FIELDS, or the study of this force —**electromagnetic** /ɪˌlektrəʊmægˈnetɪk◂ $ -troʊ-/ adj

e·lec·tron /ɪˈlektrɒn $ -trɑːn/ n [C] a very small piece of matter with a negative electrical CHARGE that moves around the NUCLEUS (=central part) of an atom; → **proton, neutron**

e·lec·tron·ic S3 W3 /ˌelɪkˈtrɒnɪk, ɪˌlek- $ -ˈtrɑː-/ adj
1 electronic equipment, such as computers and televisions, uses electricity that has passed through computer CHIPS TRANSISTORS, etc: electronic games | an electronic organizer (=a small piece of electronic equipment that you can use to record addresses, phone numbers etc)
2 using or produced by electronic equipment: electronic music | electronic banking | electronic publishing (=a system of producing books, magazines etc in a form that can be read on a computer) —**electronically** /-kli/ adv: electronically controlled gates | The information is recorded electronically.

e·lec·tron·i·ca /ˌelɪkˈtrɒnɪkə, ɪˌlek- $ -ˈtrɑː-/ n [U] a general word for various different types of electronic dance and listening music; → **drum 'n' bass, house music, techno, trance**

electronic ˈbanking n [U] a service provided by banks that allows people to pay money from one account to another, pay bills etc using the Internet; ⊟ **e-banking**

electronic ˈcash n [U] money that can be used to buy things on the Internet, but that does not exist in a physical form or belong to any particular country

electronic ˈdata ˌinterchange n [U] technical EDI a way for companies and banks to send information to each other by computer using an agreed FORMAT so that the company receiving the documents can easily read them on their computer and print them out on paper

electronic ˈfunds ˌtransfer n [C,U] EFT when money is moved from one bank account, business etc to another using only computer systems

electronic ˈmail n [U] EMAIL

electronic ˈmoney n [U] money that can be used to buy things on the Internet, but that does not exist in a physical form or belong to any particular country

electronic ˈorganizer n [C] a small piece of electronic equipment that you can use to record addresses, telephone numbers, dates of meetings etc

electronic ˈpublishing n [U] the business of producing books, magazines, or newspapers that are designed to be read using a computer

e·lec·tron·ics /ɪˌlekˈtrɒnɪks, ˌelɪk- $ -ˈtrɑː-/ n **1** [U] the study or industry of making equipment, such as computers and televisions, that work electronically: **electronics company/industry/firm etc** | an electronics engineer **2** [plural] electronic equipment: the market for consumer electronics

electronic ˈsignature n [C] a type of CODE that is used in an electronic document to prove who wrote it

electronic ˈtagging n [U] a system of attaching a small piece of electronic equipment to a criminal, which allows the police to know where he or she is

electronic ˈticketing n [U] a service provided by AIRLINES that allows people to buy their tickets on the Internet and usually does not give them tickets in the form of paper

e,lectron ˈmicroscope n [C] a very powerful MICROSCOPE (=scientific instrument used for looking at small objects) that uses ELECTRONS instead of light to make things look larger

e·lec·tro·plate /ɪˈlektrəʊpleɪt $ -troʊ-/ v [T usually passive] to put a very thin layer of metal onto the surface of an object, using ELECTROLYSIS

el·e·gant /ˈelɪɡənt/ adj **1** beautiful, attractive, or graceful: a tall, elegant young woman | You can dine in elegant surroundings. **2** an idea or a plan that is elegant is very intelligent yet simple: an elegant solution to the problem —**elegantly** adv —**elegance** n [U]: the style and elegance of the designs

el·e·gi·ac /ˌelɪˈdʒaɪək / adj literary showing that you feel sad about someone who has died or something that no longer exists: He spoke of his childhood in elegiac tones.

el·e·gy /ˈelɪdʒi/ n plural elegies [C] a sad poem or song, especially about someone who has died; → **eulogy**

el·e·ment S2 W1 /ˈelɪmənt/ n [C]
1 PART one part or feature of a whole system, plan, piece of work etc, especially one that is basic or important: Honesty is a vital element of her success. | [+of] the primary element in the country's economy | **important/key/essential/vital etc element** Besides ability, the other essential element in political success is luck. | Business and management elements are built into the course.
2 **element of surprise/truth/risk/doubt etc** an amount, usually small, of a quality or feeling: There is an element of truth in your argument.
3 CHEMISTRY a simple chemical substance such as CARBON or oxygen that consists of atoms of only one kind → COMPOUND¹ (1)
4 PEOPLE a group of people who form part of a larger group, especially when the rest of the group does not approve of them; → **faction**: the hard-line communist elements in the party
5 **the elements** [plural] the weather, especially bad weather: sailors battling against the elements
6 HEATING the part of a piece of electrical equipment that produces heat
7 **the elements of sth** the most simple things that you have to learn first about a subject: She doesn't even know the basic elements of politeness.
8 EARTH/AIR/FIRE/WATER one of the four substances (earth, air, fire, and water) from which people used to believe that everything was made
9 **be in your element** to be in a situation that you enjoy, because you are good at it: Graham was in his element, building a fire and cooking the steaks.
10 **be out of your element** to be in a situation that makes you uncomfortable or unhappy: She was out of her element in this dull little town.

el·e·men·tal /ˌelɪˈmentl / adj **1** simple, basic, and important: Love and fear are two of the most elemental human emotions. **2** technical existing as a simple chemical element that has not been combined with anything else: elemental sulphur

el·e·men·ta·ry /ˌelɪˈmentəri◂ / adj **1** simple or basic: the elementary principles of justice and democracy | You've made a very elementary mistake. **2** [only before noun] concerning the first and easiest part of a subject; → **intermediate, advanced**: I'm only familiar with the subject at an elementary level. | I know a little elementary science. **3** [only before noun] AmE relating to elementary school; ⊟ **primary** BrE: **elementary education**

elementary ˈparticle n [C] technical one of the types of pieces of matter including ELECTRONS, PROTONS, and NEUTRONS that make up atoms

eleˈmentary ˌschool n [C] a school in the US where basic subjects are taught for the first six years of a child's education

el·e·phant /ˈelɪfənt/ n [C] a very large grey animal with four legs, two TUSKS (=long curved teeth) and a TRUNK (=long nose) that it can use to pick things up → WHITE ELEPHANT

el·e·phan·tine /ˌelɪˈfæntaɪn◂ $ -tiːn◂ / adj formal slow, heavy, and awkward, like an elephant: elephantine footsteps

el·e·vate /ˈelɪveɪt/ v [T] **1** formal to move someone or something to a more important level or rank, or make them better than before: Language has elevated *humans above the other animals.* | **elevate sb/sth to sth** *Their purpose is to elevate AIDS to the top of government priorities.* **2** *technical* to lift someone or something to a higher position: *Gradually elevate the patient into an upright position.* **3** *technical* to increase the amount, temperature, pressure etc of something: *These drugs may elevate acid levels in the blood.*

el·e·vat·ed /ˈelɪ̩veɪt̩d/ *adj* **1** elevated thoughts, words etc seem to be intelligent or of high moral standard: *elevated philosophical language* **2** [only before noun] an elevated position or rank is very important and respected **3** raised off the ground or higher up than other things: *The train runs on an elevated track.* **4** *formal* elevated levels, temperatures etc are higher than normal: *elevated blood sugar levels*

,**elevated ˈrailway** *BrE*; ,**elevated ˈrailroad** *AmE n* [C] a railway that is above the streets in a town

el·e·vat·ing /ˈelɪ̩veɪtɪŋ/ *adj formal* making you feel interested in intelligent or moral subjects – sometimes used humorously: *The lecture was an exciting and elevating experience.*

el·e·va·tion /ˌelɪ̩ˈveɪʃən/ *n* **1** [singular] a height above the level of the sea: [+of] *The road climbs steadily to an elevation of 1400 feet.* **2** [U] *formal* an act of moving someone to a more important rank or position: [+to] *her sudden elevation to international stardom* **3** [C,U] *formal* an increase in the amount or level of something: *a sudden elevation of blood pressure* **4** [C] *technical* an upright side of a building, as shown in a drawing done by an ARCHITECT (=person who plans buildings): *the front elevation of a house* **5** [C] *technical* the angle made with the HORIZON by pointing a gun: *The cannon was fired at an elevation of 60 degrees.*

el·e·va·tor [S3] [W3] /ˈelɪ̩veɪtə $ -ər/ *n* [C] **1** *AmE* a machine that takes people and goods from one level to another in a building; ⊟ **lift** *BrE*: *We'll have to take the elevator.* → see picture at **STAY** **2** a machine with a moving belt and containers, used for lifting grain and liquids, or for taking things off ships

ˈ**elevator ˌmusic** *n* [U] *informal* the type of music that is played in shops and public places, and is usually thought to be boring

e·lev·en /ɪˈlevən/ *number, n* **1** the number 11: *She was sent to jail for eleven months.* | *I never go to bed before eleven* (=11 o'clock). | *James had worked every summer since he was eleven* (=11 years old). **2** [C] a team of 11 players in football or CRICKET: *He plays regularly in the first eleven* (=the best team of 11 players).

e,**leven-ˈplus** also **11-plus** *n* [singular] an examination that all children in Britain used to take at the age of 11 in order to decide what kind of SECONDARY SCHOOL they should go to. In some areas, children still take this examination.

e·lev·en·ses /ɪˈlevənzɪz/ *n* [U] *BrE old-fashioned* a cup of coffee or tea and a BISCUIT, that you have in the middle of the morning

e·lev·enth¹ /ɪˈlevənθ/ *adj* **1** coming after ten other things in a series: *in the eleventh century* | *her eleventh birthday* **2 the eleventh hour** the last moment before something important happens: *At the eleventh hour the government decided that something had to be done.* —**eleventh** *pron: I'm planning to leave on the eleventh* (=the 11th day of the month).

eleventh² *n* [C] one of eleven equal parts of something

elf /elf/ *n plural* **elves** /elvz/ [C] an imaginary creature like a small person with pointed ears and magical powers; → **fairy, pixie**

el·fin /ˈelfɪ̩n/ *adj* someone who looks elfin is small and delicate: *She had an elfin face and wide grey eyes.*

e·li·cit /ɪˈlɪsɪ̩t/ *v* [T] to succeed in getting information or a reaction from someone, especially when this is difficult: *When her knock elicited no response, she*

opened the door and peeped in. | **elicit sth from sb** *The test uses pictures to elicit words from the child.* —**elicitation** /ɪˌlɪsɪ̩ˈteɪʃən/ *n* [U]

e·lide /ɪˈlaɪd/ *v* [T] *technical* to leave out the sound of a letter or of a part of a word: *Most English speakers elide the first 'd' in 'Wednesday.'* —**elision** /ɪˈlɪʒən/ *n* [C,U]

el·i·gi·ble /ˈelɪdʒɪ̩bəl/ *adj* **1** someone who is eligible for something is able or allowed to do it, for example because they are the right age: [+for] *Students on a part-time course are not eligible for a loan.* | **eligible to do sth** *Over 500,000 18-year-olds will become eligible to vote this year.* **2** [only before noun] an eligible man or woman would be good to marry because they are rich, attractive, and not married: *Stephen was regarded as an eligible bachelor.* —**eligibility** /ˌelɪdʒɪ̩ˈbɪlɪ̩ti/ *n* [U]

e·lim·i·nate /ɪˈlɪmɪ̩neɪt/ *v* [T] **1** to completely get rid of something that is unnecessary or unwanted: **eliminate a need/possibility/risk/problem etc** *The credit card eliminates the need for cash or cheques.* | *The teacher should try to eliminate the possibility that the child has a hearing defect.* | **eliminate sth/sb from sth** *Fatty foods should be eliminated from the diet.* **2** [usually passive] to defeat a team or person in a competition, so that they no longer take part in it: *Our team was eliminated in the first round.* **3** to kill someone in order to prevent them from causing trouble: *a ruthless dictator who eliminated all his rivals* **4 eliminate sb from your enquiries** *BrE* if the police eliminate someone from their enquiries, they decide that that person did not commit a particular crime

e·lim·i·na·tion /ɪˌlɪmɪ̩ˈneɪʃən/ *n* [U] **1** ▮REMOVAL OF STH▮ the removal or destruction of something: [+of] *the elimination of lead in petrol* **2** ▮DEFEAT▮ the defeat of a team or player in a competition, so that they may no longer take part **3** ▮KILLING▮ the act of killing someone, especially to prevent them from causing trouble: [+of] *The killings are part of a campaign of elimination of the political opposition.* **4** ▮BODY PROCESS▮ *technical* the process of getting rid of substances that your body no longer needs: [+of] *the elimination of toxins from the body* → **process of elimination** at PROCESS¹ (6)

e·lite¹ /eɪˈliːt, ɪ-/ *n* [C] a group of people who have a lot of power and influence because they have money, knowledge, or special skills: **political/social/economic etc elite** *the domination of power by a small political elite* | *a struggle for power within the ruling elite*

elite² *adj* an elite group contains the best, most skilled or most experienced people or members of a larger group: *an elite group of artists* | *elite universities*

e·lit·ist /eɪˈliːtɪ̩st, ɪ-/ *adj* an elitist system, government etc is one in which a small group of people have more power and advantages than other people: *an elitist education system* —**elitism** *n* [U] —**elitist** *n* [C]

e·lix·ir /ɪˈlɪksə $ -ər/ *n* **1** [C] *literary* a magical liquid that is supposed to cure people of illness, make them younger etc: *the search for the elixir of life* **2** [C] something that is supposed to solve problems as if by magic: *The current new wave of technology should prove an economic elixir.*

E·liz·a·be·than /ɪˌlɪzəˈbiːθən◂/ *adj* relating to the period 1558–1603 when Elizabeth I was queen of England: *Elizabethan drama* —**Elizabethan** *n* [C]: *The Earl of Essex was a famous Elizabethan.*

elk /elk/ *n plural* **elk** [C] **1** *BrE* a very large brown North American, European, and Asian animal with wide flat horns; ⊟ **moose** *AmE* **2** *AmE* a large North American DEER

el·lipse /ɪˈlɪps/ *n* [C] a curved shape like a circle, but with two slightly longer and flatter sides; → **oval**

el·lip·sis /ɪˈlɪpsɪ̩s/ *n plural* **ellipses** /-siːz/ *technical* **1** [C,U] when words are deliberately left out of a sentence, though the meaning can still be understood. For example, you may say 'He's leaving but I'm not' instead of saying 'He's leaving but I'm not leaving.'   **2** [C] the sign (...) used in writing to show that some words have deliberately been left out of a sentence

el·lip·ti·cal /ɪˈlɪptɪkəl/ also **el·lip·tic** /-tɪk/ adj **1** having the shape of an ellipse: *Kepler published his discovery of the elliptical orbits of planets in 1609.* **2** elliptical speech or writing is difficult to understand because more is meant than is actually said: *The language is often elliptical and ambiguous.*

elm /elm/ n [C,U] a type of large tree with broad leaves, or the wood from this tree

el·o·cu·tion /ˌeləˈkjuːʃən/ n [U] good clear speaking in public, involving voice control, pronunciation etc: *elocution lessons* —**elocutionary** adj —**elocutionist** n [C]

e·lon·gate /ˈiːlɒŋɡeɪt $ ɪˈlɒːŋ-/ v [I,T] to become longer, or make something longer than normal: *Her legs were elongated by the very high heels which she wore.* —**elongation** /ˌiːlɒŋˈɡeɪʃən $ ɪˌlɒːŋ-/ n [C,U]

e·lon·gat·ed /ˈiːlɒŋɡeɪtɪd $ ɪˈlɒːŋ-/ adj longer than normal: *The picture shows two elongated figures dancing.*

e·lope /ɪˈləʊp $ ɪˈloʊp/ v [I] to leave your home secretly in order to get married: *My parents didn't approve of the marriage, so we eloped.* —**elopement** n [C,U]

el·o·quent /ˈeləkwənt/ adj **1** able to express your ideas and opinions well, especially in a way that influences people: *an eloquent appeal for support* **2** showing a feeling or meaning without using words: *The photographs are an eloquent reminder of the horrors of war.* —**eloquently** adv —**eloquence** n [U]

else S1 W1 /els/ adv
1 [used after words beginning with 'some-', 'every-', 'any-', and 'no-', and after question words] **a)** besides or in addition to someone or something: *There's something else I'd like to talk about as well.* | *I'd like you to come, and anyone else who's free.* | *He was awake now, as was everyone else.* | *Who else was at the party?* | 'Two coffees, please.' 'Anything else?' 'No, thanks.' | *Above all else* (=more than any other things) *she was seeking love.* **b)** used to talk about a different person, thing, place etc: *He went to live with another woman.* | *I'd like to live anywhere else but here.* | *If I can't trust you, who else can I trust?*
2 or else spoken **a)** used to say that there will be a bad result if someone does not do something: *Hurry up or else we'll miss the train.* **b)** used to say what another possibility might be: *The salesman will reduce the price or else include free insurance.* **c)** used to threaten someone: *Hand over the money, or else!* → see box at UNLESS
3 BrE spoken used after a question word to say that the thing, person, or place you have mentioned is the only one possible: *'What are you doing?' 'Waiting for you, what else?'*
4 what else can sb do/say? spoken used to say that it is impossible to do or say anything apart from what has been mentioned: *'Will you really sell the house?' ' 'What else can I do? I can't live here.';* → see also → **if nothing else** at NOTHING[1] (11); → **be something else** at SOMETHING (9)

else·where S2 W2 /elsˈweə, ˈelsweə $ ˈelswer/ adv in, at, or to another place: *She is becoming famous in Australia and elsewhere.* | *Kerala has less crime and alcoholism than elsewhere in India.*

ELT /ˌiː el ˈtiː/ n [U] especially BrE **English Language Teaching** the teaching of the English language to people whose first language is not English

e·lu·ci·date /ɪˈluːsɪdeɪt/ v [I,T] formal to explain something that is difficult to understand by providing more information: *The full picture has not yet been elucidated.* —**elucidation** /ɪˌluːsɪˈdeɪʃən/ n [C,U] —**elucidatory** /ɪˈluːsɪdətəri $ -dətɔːri/ adj

e·lude /ɪˈluːd/ v [T] **1** to escape from someone or something, especially by tricking them; ▪ **avoid**: *He managed to elude his pursuers by escaping into a river.* **2** if something that you want eludes you, you fail to find or achieve it: *She took the exam again, but*

again success eluded her. **3** if a fact or the answer to a problem eludes you, you cannot remember or solve it; ▪ **escape**: *The exact terminology eludes me for the moment.*

e·lu·sive /ɪˈluːsɪv/ adj **1** an elusive person or animal is difficult to find or not often seen: *She managed to get an interview with that elusive man.* **2** an elusive result is difficult to achieve: *She enjoys a firm reputation in this country but wider international success has been elusive.* **3** an elusive idea or quality is difficult to describe or understand: *For me, the poem has an elusive quality.* —**elusively** adv —**elusiveness** n [U]

elves /elvz/ n the plural of ELF

'em /əm/ pron spoken sometimes used as a short form of 'them': *Go on, Bill, you tell 'em!*

em- /ɪm, em/ prefix the form used for EN- before b, m, or p: *embittered* (=made to feel extremely disappointed) | *empowerment* (=when someone is given control of something)

e·ma·ci·at·ed /ɪˈmeɪʃieɪtɪd, -si-/ adj extremely thin from lack of food or illness: *The prisoners were ill and emaciated.* —**emaciation** /ɪˌmeɪʃiˈeɪʃən, -si-/ n [U]

e·mail¹, e-mail /ˈiː meɪl/ n **1** [U] a system that allows you to send and receive messages by computer; ▪ **electronic mail**: *contact someone by email* | *your email address* → see picture at OFFICE **2** [C,U] a message that is sent from one person to another using the email system: *Send me an e-mail when you have any news.* | *I haven't had time to check my email this morning.*

email², e-mail v [T] **1** to send someone an email: *Will you e-mail me about it?* **2** to send someone a document using email: *Can you email me the proposal by the end of today?*

em·a·nate /ˈeməneɪt/ v [T] formal to produce a smell, light etc, or to show a particular quality: *He emanates tranquility.* —**emanation** /ˌeməˈneɪʃən/ n [C,U]
emanate from sth phr v formal to come from or out of something: *Wonderful smells were emanating from the kitchen.*

e·man·ci·pate /ɪˈmænsɪpeɪt/ v [T] formal to give someone the political or legal rights that they did not have before: *Slaves were emancipated in 1834.* —**emancipation** /ɪˌmænsɪˈpeɪʃən/ n [U]

e·man·ci·pat·ed /ɪˈmænsɪpeɪtɪd/ adj **1** socially, politically, or legally free **2** old-fashioned an emancipated woman is not influenced by old-fashioned ideas about how women should behave

e·mas·cu·late /ɪˈmæskjʊleɪt/ v [T] **1** to make a man feel weaker and less male: *Some men feel emasculated if they work for a woman.* **2** to make someone or something weaker or less effective: *The bill has been emasculated by Congress.* **3** medical to remove all or part of a male's sex organs; ▪ **castrate** —**emasculation** /ɪˌmæskjʊˈleɪʃən/ n [U]

em·balm /ɪmˈbɑːm $ -ˈbɑːm, -ˈbɑːlm/ v [T] to treat a dead body with chemicals, oils etc to prevent it from decaying —**embalmer** n [C]

em·bank·ment /ɪmˈbæŋkmənt/ n [C] a wide wall of earth or stones built to stop water from flooding an area, or to support a road or railway

em·bar·go¹ /ɪmˈbɑːɡəʊ $ -ˈbɑːrɡoʊ/ n plural **embargoes** [C] an official order to stop trade with another country; ▪ **boycott, sanctions**: [+on/against] *an embargo on wheat exports* | *an embargo against the country* | **impose/lift an embargo** (=start or end one) *Many allies are pushing to lift the embargo.* | **trade/arms/oil etc embargo**

embargo² v [T] **1** to officially stop particular goods being traded with another country; ▪ **boycott**: *Several countries embargoed arms shipments to Yugoslavia.* **2** to stop information from being made public until a particular date or until permission is given; ▪ **censor**

E

em·bark /ɪmˈbɑːk $ -ɑːrk/ v [I,T] to go onto a ship or a plane, or to put or take something onto a ship or plane; ⊠ **disembark** —**embarkation** /ˌembɑːˈkeɪʃən $ -bɑːr-/ n [C,U]
  embark on/upon sth phr v to start something, especially something new, difficult, or exciting: He embarked on a new career as a teacher.

em·bar·rass /ɪmˈbærəs/ v [T] **1** to make someone feel ashamed, nervous, or uncomfortable, especially in front of other people: He didn't want to embarrass her by asking questions. **2** to do something that causes problems for a government, political organization, or politician, and makes them look bad: The revelations in the press have embarrassed the government.

em·bar·rassed /ɪmˈbærəst/ adj **1** feeling nervous and uncomfortable and worrying about what people think of you, for example because you have to talk or sing in public, or because you have made a silly mistake: Lori **gets embarrassed** if we ask her to sing. | He **looked embarrassed** when I asked him where he'd been. | **very/deeply/highly/acutely embarrassed** Michelle was **acutely embarrassed** (=very embarrassed) at having to ask for money. | **embarrassed smile/laugh/grin** etc Ken gave her an embarrassed grin. | There was an embarrassed silence. | **embarrassed to do sth** He was embarrassed to admit making a mistake. | [+about/at] I felt embarrassed about how untidy the house was. **2 financially embarrassed** having no money or having debts

WORD FOCUS: EMBARRASSED
similar words: **uncomfortable, awkward, sheepish, red-faced**
very embarrassed: **mortified**

em·bar·ras·sing /ɪmˈbærəsɪŋ/ adj making you feel ashamed, nervous, or uncomfortable: She asked a lot of **embarrassing questions**. | an **embarrassing situation** | [+for] This incident is deeply embarrassing for the government. —**embarrassingly** adv: an embarrassingly poor performance

em·bar·rass·ment /ɪmˈbærəsmənt/ n **1** [U] the feeling you have when you are embarrassed: [+at] She suffered extreme embarrassment at not knowing how to read. | He could not **hide** his **embarrassment** at his children's rudeness. | **to sb's embarrassment** To her embarrassment, she couldn't remember his name. **2** [C] an event that causes a government, political organization etc problems, and makes it look bad: [+to/for] The allegations have been an **acute embarrassment** (=serious and severe embarrassment) to the Prime Minister. | The scandal was a further **source of embarrassment** to the government. **3** [C] someone who behaves in a way that makes you feel ashamed, nervous, or uncomfortable: [+to] Tim's drinking has made him an embarrassment to the whole family. **4 financial embarrassment** debts or a lack of money that causes problems for you **5 an embarrassment of riches** so many good things that it is difficult to decide which one you want

em·bas·sy /ˈembəsi/ n plural **embassies** [C] a group of officials who represent their government in a foreign country, or the building they work in: the American Embassy in Paris

em·bat·tled /ɪmˈbætld/ adj formal **1** [only before noun] an embattled person, organization etc has many problems or difficulties: The embattled president had to resign. **2** surrounded by enemies, especially in war or fighting: The embattled army finally surrendered.

em·bed /ɪmˈbed/ v **embedded, embedding 1** [I,T usually passive] to put something firmly and deeply into something else, or to be put into something in this way: **be embedded in sth** A piece of glass was embedded in her hand. **2** [T usually passive] if ideas, attitudes, or feelings etc are embedded, you believe or feel them very strongly: Feelings of guilt are **deeply embedded** in

her personality. **3** [T] to put something such as a GRAPHIC into a computer program or page on the Internet

em·bel·lish /ɪmˈbelɪʃ/ v [T] **1** to make something more beautiful by adding decorations to it: **embellish sth with sth** The dress was embellished with gold threads. **2** to make a story or statement more interesting by adding details that are not true: She gave an embellished account of what had happened. —**embellishment** n [C,U]

em·ber /ˈembə $ -ər/ n [C usually plural] a piece of wood or coal that stays red and very hot after a fire has stopped burning: glowing embers

em·bez·zle /ɪmˈbezəl/ v [I,T] to steal money from the place where you work: Two managers were charged with embezzling $400,000. —**embezzlement** n [U] —**embezzler** n [C]

em·bit·tered /ɪmˈbɪtəd $ -ər/ adj angry, sad, or full of hate because of bad or unfair things that have happened to you; ⊠ **bitter**: a sick, embittered, and lonely old man —**embitter** v [T]

em·bla·zoned /ɪmˈbleɪzənd/ adj [not before noun] if something is emblazoned with a name, design etc, it has that design on it where it can easily be seen: [+with] a T-shirt emblazoned with a political slogan | [+on/across] The sponsor's name is emblazoned on the players' shirts. —**emblazon** v [T]

em·blem /ˈembləm/ n [C] **1** a picture, shape, or object that is used to represent a country, organization etc; → **logo**: [+of] The **national emblem** of Canada is a maple leaf. **2** something that represents an idea, principle, or situation: [+of] Expensive cars are seen as an emblem of success.

em·ble·mat·ic /ˌembləˈmætɪk◂/ adj formal seeming to represent or be a sign of something; ⊠ **representative**: [+of] The Vespa scooter became emblematic of sophisticated urban culture across Europe.

em·bod·i·ment /ɪmˈbɒdimənt $ ɪmˈbɑː-/ n **the embodiment of sth** someone or something that represents or is very typical of an idea or quality; ⊠ **epitome**: He is the embodiment of evil.

em·bod·y /ɪmˈbɒdi $ ɪmˈbɑːdi/ v **embodied, embodying, embodies** [T] **1** to be a very good example of an idea or quality; ⊠ **represent**: She embodies everything I admire in a teacher. **2** formal to include something: The latest model embodies many new improvements.

em·bold·en /ɪmˈbəʊldən $ -ˈboʊl-/ v [T] formal to give someone more courage: Emboldened by her smile, he asked her to dance.

em·bo·lis·m /ˈembəlɪzəm/ n [C] medical something such as a hard mass of blood or a small amount of air that blocks a tube carrying blood through the body

em·bos·sed /ɪmˈbɒs $ ɪmˈbɑːs, -ˈbɔːs/ adj having a surface that is decorated with a raised pattern: [+with] She was given a Bible embossed with her name. | embossed stationery —**emboss** v [T]

em·brace[1] /ɪmˈbreɪs/ v **1** [I,T] to put your arms around someone and hold them in a friendly or loving way; ⊠ **hug**: Jack warmly embraced his son. | Maggie and Laura embraced. **2** [T] formal to eagerly accept a new idea, opinion, religion etc: We hope these regions will embrace democratic reforms. | Most West European countries have embraced the concept of high-speed rail networks with enthusiasm. **3** [T] formal to include something as part of a subject, discussion etc: This course embraces several different aspects of psychology.

embrace[2] n [C] the act of holding someone close to you, especially as a sign of love: **in an embrace** They held each other in a tender embrace.

em·broi·der /ɪmˈbrɔɪdə $ -ər/ v **1** [I,T] to decorate cloth by sewing a pattern, picture, or words on it with coloured threads: **embroider sth with sth** The dress was embroidered with flowers. | **embroider sth on sth** A colourful design was embroidered on the sleeve of the shirt. | a richly embroidered jacket **2** [T] to make a story or report of events more interesting or exciting by adding details that are not true; ▤ **embellish**

em·broi·der·y /ɪmˈbrɔɪdəri/ *n plural* **embroideries 1** [C,U] a pattern sewn onto cloth, or cloth with patterns sewn onto it **2** [U] the act of sewing patterns onto cloth → see picture at HANDICRAFT **3** [U] imaginary details that are added to make a story seem more interesting or exciting; ▤ **embellishment**

em·broil /ɪmˈbrɔɪl/ *v* [T] to involve someone or something in a difficult situation: **embroil sb/sth in sth** *I became embroiled in an argument with the taxi driver.*

em·bry·o /ˈembriəʊ $ -brioʊ/ *n plural* **embryos** [C] **1** an animal or human that has not yet been born, and has just begun to develop; → **foetus 2** in embryo at a very early stage of development: *The system already exists in embryo.*

em·bry·ol·o·gy /ˌembriˈɒlədʒi $ -ˈɑːl-/ *n* [U] the scientific study of embryos —**embryologist** *n* [C]

em·bry·on·ic /ˌembriˈɒnɪk◂ $ -ˈɑːn-/ *adj* **1** at a very early stage of development: *The plans are still only in embryonic form.* **2** relating to an EMBRYO: *embryonic development* | *embryonic cells*

em·cee /ˌemˈsiː/ *n* [C] *AmE* **master of ceremonies** someone who introduces the performers on a television or radio programme or at a social event: *a game show emcee* —**emcee** *v* [I,T]

e·mend /ɪˈmend/ *v* [T] *formal* to remove the mistakes from something that has been written; → **amend** —**emendation** /ˌiːmenˈdeɪʃən/ *n* [C,U]

em·e·rald /ˈemərəld/ *n* **1** [C] a valuable bright green stone that is often used in jewellery **2** [U] a bright green colour —**emerald** *adj*

e·merge W2 /ɪˈmɜːdʒ $ -ɜːrdʒ/ *v* [I]
1 to appear or come out from somewhere: *The flowers emerge in the spring.* | [+**from**] *The sun emerged from behind the clouds.*
2 if facts emerge, they become known after being hidden or secret; → **come out**: *Eventually the* **truth** *emerged.* | *Later it emerged that the judge had employed an illegal immigrant.*
3 to come out of a difficult experience: [+**from**] *She emerged from the divorce a stronger person.*
4 to begin to be known or noticed: *a religious sect that emerged in the 1830s* | [+**as**] *Local government has recently emerged as a major issue.*

e·mer·gence /ɪˈmɜːdʒəns $ -ɜːr-/ *n* [U] **1** when something begins to be known or noticed: [+**of**] *the emergence of Japan as a world leader* **2** when someone or something comes out of a difficult experience: [+**from**] *the company's emergence from bankruptcy*

e·mer·gen·cy S2 W3 /ɪˈmɜːdʒənsi $ -ɜːr-/ *n plural* **emergencies** [C,U] an unexpected and dangerous situation that must be dealt with immediately; → **crisis**: *Lifeguards are trained to* **deal with emergencies**. | **in an emergency** *The staff need to know what to do in an emergency.* | **In case of emergency**, *press the alarm button.* | **emergency exit/supplies etc** (=used in an emergency) *$500,000 of* **emergency aid** *for the victims of the earthquake* | *The plane had to make an* **emergency landing**. | *The government called an emergency meeting to discuss the crisis.* → STATE OF EMERGENCY

eˈmergency ˌbrake *n* [C] *AmE* a piece of equipment in a car that you pull up with your hand to stop the car from moving; ▤ **handbrake**; → see picture at CAR

eˈmergency ˌcord *n* [C] *AmE* a chain that a passenger pulls to stop a train in an emergency; ▤ **communication cord** *BrE*

eˈmergency ˌroom *n* [C] *AmE* a part of a hospital that immediately helps people who have been hurt in an accident or who are extremely ill; ▤ **ER**; **casualty** *BrE*

eˈmergency ˌservices *n* [plural] *BrE* official organizations such as the police or the fire service, that deal with fires, crimes, and injuries

e·mer·gent /ɪˈmɜːdʒənt $ -ɜːr-/ *adj* [only before noun] in the early stages of existence or development: *the emergent nations of the world*

e·mer·ging /ɪˈmɜːdʒɪŋ $ -ɜːr-/ *adj* [only before noun] in an early state of development: *the country's emerging oil industry*

e·mer·i·tus /ɪˈmerɪtəs/ *adj* **emeritus professor/director etc** *or* **professor/director etc emeritus** a PROFESSOR, director etc who is no longer working but has kept his or her previous job title as an honour

em·e·ry /ˈeməri/ *n* [U] a very hard mineral that is used for polishing things and making them smooth

ˈemery board *n* [C] a narrow piece of stiff paper with emery on it, used for shaping your nails

e·met·ic /ɪˈmetɪk/ *n* [C] *medical* something that you eat or drink in order to make yourself VOMIT (=bring up food from your stomach) —**emetic** *adj*

em·i·grant /ˈemɪɡrənt/ *n* [C] someone who leaves their own country to live in another; → **immigrant**

em·i·grate /ˈemɪɡreɪt/ *v* [I] to leave your own country in order to live in another country; → IMMIGRATE: [+**to/from**] *He emigrated to Australia as a young man.* —**emigration** /ˌemɪˈɡreɪʃən/ *n* [C,U]

ém·i·gré /ˈemɪɡreɪ/ *n* [C] *formal* someone who leaves their own country to live in another, usually for political reasons: *Russian émigrés living in Paris*

em·i·nence /ˈemɪnəns/ *n* **1** [U] the quality of being famous and important: **of great/such etc eminence** *a scientist of great eminence* **2 Your/His Eminence** a title used when talking to or about a CARDINAL (=priest of high rank in the Roman Catholic Church) **3** [C] *literary* a hill or area of high ground

em·i·nence grise /ˌemɪnɒns ˈɡriːz $ -nɑːns-/ *n plural* **eminences grises** [C] someone who has unofficial power, often secretly, through someone else: *Borusa had no wish to become president, instead preferring to operate as an eminence grise behind the scenes.*

em·i·nent /ˈemɪnənt/ *adj* an eminent person is famous, important, and respected: *an eminent lawyer*

ˌeminent doˈmain *n* [U] *law* the right of the US government to take private land for public use

em·i·nent·ly /ˈemɪnəntli/ *adv formal* completely and without a doubt – use this to show approval: *Woods is* **eminently suitable** *for the job.*

e·mir /eˈmɪə $ eˈmɪr/ *n* [C] a Muslim ruler, especially in Asia and parts of Africa: *the Emir of Kuwait*

e·mir·ate /ˈemɪrət $ ɪˈmɪrət/ *n* [C] the country ruled by an emir, or his position

em·is·sa·ry /ˈemɪsəri $ -seri/ *n plural* **emissaries** [C] someone who is sent with an official message or to do official work; ▤ **envoy**: *Japan is sending two emissaries to Washington to discuss trade issues.*

e·mis·sion /ɪˈmɪʃən/ *n* **1** [C usually plural] a gas or other substance that is sent into the air: *Britain has agreed to cut emissions of nitrogen oxide from power stations.* **2** [U] the act of sending out light, heat, gas etc

e·mit /ɪˈmɪt/ *v* **emitted, emitting** [T] to send out gas, heat, light, sound etc: *The kettle emitted a shrill whistle.*

e·mol·li·ent /ɪˈmɒliənt $ ɪˈmɑː-/ *adj formal* **1** making something, especially your skin, softer and smoother: *Almond oil is renowned for its soothing, emollient properties.* **2** making someone feel calmer when they have been angry: *an emollient reply* —**emollient** *n* [C]

e·mol·u·ment /ɪˈmɒljᵿmənt $ ɪˈmɑːl-/ *n* [C,U] *formal* money or another form of payment for work you have done

e-mon·ey /ˈiː ˌmʌni/ also **e-cash** *n* [U] ELECTRONIC MONEY

e·mote /ɪˈməʊt $ ɪˈmoʊt/ *v* [I] to clearly show emotion, especially when you are acting: *Siskind encourages the children to emote to the music as they dance.*

e·mo·ti·con /ɪˈməʊtɪkɒn $ ɪˈmoʊtɪkɑːn/ *n* [C] a special sign that is used to show an emotion in EMAIL and on the Internet, often by making a picture. For example, the emoticon :-) looks like a smiling face and means that you have made a joke

e·mo·tion W3 /ɪˈməʊʃən $ ɪˈmoʊ-/ *n* [C,U] a strong human feeling such as love, hate, or anger: *Her voice was full of emotion.* | **conflicting/mixed emotions** *Sara listened with mixed emotions.* | *She was good at hiding her emotions.* | *Kim received the news without showing any visible sign of emotion.*

e·mo·tion·al S3 W3 /ɪˈməʊʃənəl $ ɪˈmoʊ-/ *adj*
1 [only before noun] relating to your feelings or how you control them: *She provided emotional support at a very distressing time for me.* | *Ann suffered from depression and a number of other emotional problems.* | *the physical and emotional state of the patient*
2 making people have strong feelings; ⬛ **emotive**: *Abortion is a very emotional issue.* | *The funeral was a very emotional experience for all of us.*
3 having strong feelings and showing them to other people, especially by crying: **get/become emotional** *He became very emotional when we had to leave.*
4 influenced by what you feel, rather than what you know: *an emotional response to the problem* —**emotionally** *adv*: *Nursing is an emotionally and physically demanding job.*

e·mo·tion·al·is·m /ɪˈməʊʃənəlɪzəm $ ɪˈmoʊ-/ *n* [U] a tendency to show or feel too much emotion

e·mo·tive /ɪˈməʊtɪv $ ɪˈmoʊ-/ *adj* making people have strong feelings; ⬛ **emotional**: *emotive issue/subject/word etc* *Child abuse is an emotive subject.* —**emotively** *adv*

em·pan·el /ɪmˈpænl/ **empanelled, empanelling** *BrE,* **empaneled, empaneling** *AmE v* [T] to choose the members of a JURY in a court of law

em·pa·thize also **-ise** *BrE* /ˈempəθaɪz/ *v* [I] to be able to understand someone else's feelings, problems etc, especially because you have had similar experiences; → **sympathize**: [+with] *My mother died last year so I can really empathize with what he's going through.*

em·pa·thy /ˈempəθi/ *n* [U] the ability to understand other people's feelings and problems; → **sympathy**: [+with/for] *She had great empathy with people.* —**empathetic** /ˌempəˈθetɪk◂/ also **empathic** *adj*

em·pe·ror /ˈempərə $ -ər/ *n* [C] the man who is the ruler of an EMPIRE

em·pha·sis S3 W2 /ˈemfəsɪs/ *n plural* **emphases** /-siːz/ [C,U]
1 special attention or importance: [+on] *In Japan there is a lot of emphasis on politeness.* | **put/place emphasis on sth** *The course places emphasis on practical work.* | *a change of emphasis in government policy*
2 special importance that is given to a word or phrase by saying it louder or higher, or by printing it in a special way: [+on] *The emphasis should be on the first syllable.* | *'And I can assure you,' she said with emphasis, 'that he is innocent.'*

em·pha·size S2 W2 also **-ise** *BrE* /ˈemfəsaɪz/ *v* [T]
1 to say something in a strong way: *The report emphasizes the importance of improving safety standards.* | *Logan made a speech emphasizing the need for more volunteers.* | **emphasize that/how** *The Prime Minister emphasized that there are no plans to raise taxes.*
2 to say a word or phrase louder or higher than others to give it more importance
3 to make something more noticeable: *The dress emphasized the shape of her body.*

em·phat·ic /ɪmˈfætɪk/ *adj* **1** expressing an opinion, idea etc in a clear, strong way to show its importance: *an emphatic denial* | **emphatic that** *Wilde was emphatic that the event should go ahead.* | [+about] *He was pretty emphatic about me leaving.* **2** **emphatic win/victory/defeat** a win etc in which one team or player wins by a large amount —**emphatically** /-kli/ *adv*

em·phy·se·ma /ˌemfɪˈsiːmə/ *n* [U] *medical* a serious disease that affects the lungs, making it difficult to breathe

em·pire W3 /ˈempaɪə $ -paɪr/ *n* [C]
1 a group of countries that are all controlled by one ruler or government: *the Roman empire*
2 a group of organizations controlled by one person: *a business empire*

ˈempire-ˌbuilding *n* [U] attempts to get more power within the organization you work for

em·pir·i·cal /ɪmˈpɪrɪkəl/ *adj* [only before noun] based on scientific testing or practical experience, not on ideas; ⬛ **theoretical, hypothetical**: *empirical evidence* —**empirically** /-kli/ *adv*

em·pir·i·cis·m /ɪmˈpɪrɪsɪzəm/ *n* [U] the belief in basing your ideas on practical experience —**empiricist** *n* [C]

em·place·ment /ɪmˈpleɪsmənt/ *n* [C] a place where a large gun is put and fired: *a gun emplacement*

em·ploy¹ S2 W2 /ɪmˈplɔɪ/ *v* [T]
1 to pay someone to work for you: *The factory employs over 2000 people.* | **employ sb as sth** *Kelly is employed as a mechanic.* | **employ sb to do sth** *We have been employed to look at ways of reducing waste.*
2 to use a particular object, method, skill etc in order to achieve something: **employ a method/technique/tactic etc** *The report examines teaching methods employed in the classroom.*
3 [usually passive] *formal* to spend your time doing a particular thing: **be employed in (doing) sth** *Her days are employed in gardening and voluntary work.*

em·ploy² *n* **in sb's employ** *old-fashioned* working for someone: *He had a number of servants in his employ.*

em·ploy·a·ble /ɪmˈplɔɪəbəl/ *adj* having skills or qualities that are necessary to get a job: *The training scheme aims to make people more employable.*

em·ploy·ee S2 W2 /ɪmˈplɔɪ-iː, ˌemplɔɪˈiː/ *n* [C] someone who is paid to work for someone else; ⬛ **worker**: *a government employee*

em·ploy·er S1 W2 /ɪmˈplɔɪə $ -ər/ *n* [C] a person, company, or organization that employs people: *The shoe factory is the largest employer in this area.*

em·ploy·ment S1 W1 /ɪmˈplɔɪmənt/ *n* [U]
1 the condition of having a paid job: *She was offered employment in the sales office.* | *terms and conditions of employment* | **employment opportunities/prospects** *The employment prospects for graduates in computer science are excellent.* | *Steve's still looking for full-time employment.* | *the needs of women who combine paid employment and care for their families* | **in employment** *21.7% of all those in employment were in part-time jobs.*
2 the act of paying someone to work for you: [+of] *Mexican law prohibits the employment of children under 14.*
3 the number of people who have jobs; ⬛ **unemployment**: *Nationwide employment now stands at 95%.* | **full employment** (=a situation in which everyone has a job) *Many economists consider full employment an unrealistic goal.*
4 *formal* the use of a particular object, method, skill etc to achieve something: [+of] *Was the employment of force justified?*

emˈployment ˌagency *n plural* **employment agencies** [C] a business that makes money by finding jobs for people; → **job centre**

em·po·ri·um /ɪmˈpɔːriəm/ *n plural* **emporiums** *or* **emporia** /-riə/ [C] *old-fashioned* a large shop

em·pow·er /ɪmˈpaʊə $ -ˈpaʊr/ *v* [T] **1** to give someone more control over their own life or situation: *The Voting Rights Act was needed to empower minority groups.* **2** *formal* to give a person or organization the legal right to do something: **be empowered to do sth** *The President is empowered to appoint judges to the Supreme Court.* —**empowerment** *n* [U]

em·press /'empr$\frac{1}{3}$s/ n [C] a female ruler of an EMPIRE, or the wife of an EMPEROR

emp·ties /'emptiz/ n [plural] bottles or glasses that are empty: *The barman collected the empties.*

emp·ti·ness /'emptin$\frac{1}{3}$s/ n [U]   **1** a feeling of great sadness and loneliness: *She felt an emptiness in her heart when he left.*   **2** when there is nothing or nobody in a place: [+of] *the silence and emptiness of the desert*

emp·ty¹ [S2] [W2] /'empti/ adj comparative **emptier**, superlative **emptiest**
1 CONTAINER having nothing inside: *an empty box* | *an empty bottle* | *an **empty space** behind the desk* | *The fuel tank's almost empty.*
2 PLACE an empty place does not have any people in it: *I hate coming home to an empty house.* | *The hall was **half-empty**.* | *The streets were empty.* | *The building stood empty for several years.*
3 NOT USED not being used by anyone: *I spotted an empty table in the corner.* | *He put his feet on an empty chair.*
4 PERSON/LIFE unhappy because nothing in your life seems interesting or important: *The divorce left him feeling empty and bitter.* | *Her life felt empty and meaningless.*
5 empty words/gestures/promises etc words etc that are not sincere, or have no effect: *His repeated promises to pay them back were just empty words.*
6 do sth on an empty stomach to do something without having eaten any food first: *I can't work properly on an empty stomach.*
7 empty nest also empty nest syndrome a situation in which parents become sad because their children have grown up and moved out of their house
8 empty of sth not containing a particular type of thing, or not having a particular quality: *The beach was almost empty of people.* —**emptily** adv

emp·ty² v **emptied**, **emptying**, **empties**   **1** also **empty out** [T] to remove everything that is inside something: *Did you empty the dishwasher?* | **empty sth onto/into sth** *Elinor emptied the contents of the envelope onto the table.* | *He emptied out the ashtray.*   **2** [I] if a place empties, everyone leaves it: *The stores were closing, and the streets began to empty.*
empty into sth phr v if a river empties into a larger area of water, it flows into it: *The Mississippi River empties into the Gulf of Mexico.*

,**empty-'handed** adj without getting what you hoped or expected to get: **return/come back etc empty-handed** *I spent all morning looking for a suitable present, but came home empty-handed.*

,**empty-'headed** adj informal silly and not intelligent

e·mu /'i:mju:/ n plural **emus** or **emu** [C] a large Australian bird that can run very fast but cannot fly

em·u·late /'emj$\frac{0}{3}$leɪt/ v [T] to do something or behave in the same way as someone else, especially because you admire them; ◻ **imitate**: *Young had hoped to **emulate the success** of Douglas Wilder.* —**emulation** /ˌemj$\frac{0}{3}$'leɪʃən/ n [U]

e·mul·si·fi·er /ɪ'mʌls$\frac{1}{3}$faɪə $ -ər/ n [C] a substance that is added, especially to food, to prevent liquids and solids from separating

e·mul·si·fy /ɪ'mʌls$\frac{1}{3}$faɪ/ v **emulsified**, **emulsifying**, **emulsifies** [I,T] to combine to become a smooth mixture, or to make two liquids do this

e·mul·sion /ɪ'mʌlʃən/ n [C,U]   **1** a mixture of liquids that do not completely combine, such as oil and water   **2** technical the substance on the surface of photographic film or paper that makes it react to light   **3** BrE also **emulsion paint** a type of paint used inside buildings on walls or ceilings that is not shiny when it dries; → **gloss, eggshell**

en- /ɪn, en/ prefix [in verbs]   **1** to make someone or something be in a particular state or have a particular quality: *enlarge* (=make something bigger) | *endanger* (=put someone in danger)   **2** to go completely around something, or include all of it: *encircle* (=surround everything)

-en /ən/ suffix   **1** [in adjectives] made of a particular material or substance: *a golden crown* | *wooden seats*   **2** [in verbs] to make something have a particular quality: *darken* (=make or become dark) | *strengthen* (=make or become stronger)

en·a·ble [S3] [W1] /ɪ'neɪbəl/ v [T] to make it possible for someone to do something, or for something to happen: **enable sb/sth to do sth** *The loan enabled Jan to buy the house.* | *There are plans to enlarge the runway to enable jumbo jets to land.* —**enabler** n [C]

-enabled /ɪneɪbəld/ suffix [in adjectives] **Internet-enabled/Java-enabled etc** a computer PROGRAM that is Internet-enabled, Java-enabled etc can be used with that program or includes it as one of its features: *Find out more about our free Internet-enabled software.*

en·a·bling /ɪ'neɪblɪŋ/ adj [only before noun] law an enabling law is one that makes something possible or gives someone special legal powers

en·act /ɪ'nækt/ v [T]   **1** formal to act in a play, story etc: *a drama enacted on a darkened stage*   **2** law to make a proposal into a law: *Congress refused to enact the bill.* —**enactment** n [C,U]

e·nam·el¹ /ɪ'næməl/ n [U]   **1** a hard shiny substance that is put onto metal, clay etc for decoration or protection   **2** the hard smooth outer surface of your teeth   **3** a type of paint that produces a shiny surface when it is dry —**enamel** adj

enamel² v **enamelled**, **enamelling** BrE, **enameled**, **enameling** AmE [T] to cover or decorate something with enamel

en·am·oured BrE; **enamored** AmE /ɪ'næməd $ -ərd/ adj   **1** [not before noun] liking something very much: [+of/with] *You don't seem very enamoured with your job.*   **2** formal in love with someone: [+of/with] *He was greatly enamoured of Elizabeth.*

en bloc /ɒn 'blɒk $ ɑːn 'blɑːk/ adv all together as a single unit, rather than separately: *You cannot dismiss these stories en bloc.*

en·camp /ɪn'kæmp/ v [I,T] formal to make a camp or put people, especially soldiers, in a camp: *The army was encamped near Damascus.*

en·camp·ment /ɪn'kæmpmənt/ n [C] a large temporary camp, especially of soldiers: *a military encampment*

en·cap·su·late /ɪn'kæpsj$\frac{0}{3}$leɪt $ -sə-/ v [T]   **1** to express or show something in a short way; ◻ **sum up**: *The words of the song neatly encapsulate the mood of the country at that time.* | **encapsulate sth in sth** *Her whole philosophy can be encapsulated in this one sentence.*   **2** to completely cover something with something else, especially in order to prevent a substance getting out: **encapsulate sth in sth** *The leaking fuel rods will be encapsulated in lead.* —**encapsulation** /ɪnˌkæpsj$\frac{0}{3}$'leɪʃən $ -sə-/ n [C,U]

en·case /ɪn'keɪs/ v [T] to cover or surround something completely: **encase sth in sth** *His broken leg was encased in plaster.*

-ence /əns/ suffix [in nouns] another form of the suffix -ANCE: *existence* | *occurrence*

en·ceph·a·li·tis /ɪnˌkefə'laɪt$\frac{1}{3}$s $ -ˌsef-/ n [U] medical swelling of the brain

en·chant /ɪn'tʃɑːnt $ ɪn'tʃænt/ v [T]   **1** formal if something that you see or hear enchants you, you like it very much: *I was enchanted by the way she smiled.* | *The garden enchanted her.*   **2** literary to use magic on something or someone

en·chant·ed /ɪn'tʃɑːnt$\frac{1}{3}$d $ ɪn'tʃæn-/ adj   **1** someone who is enchanted with someone or something likes them very much: [+with] *She was enchanted with the flowers you sent her.*   **2** an enchanted object or place has been changed by magic so that it has special powers; → **bewitched**: *an enchanted castle*

E

en·chant·er /ɪn'tʃɑːntə $ ɪn'tʃæntər/ n [C] literary someone who uses magic on people and things; → **wizard**

en·chant·ing /ɪn'tʃɑːntɪŋ $ ɪn'tʃæn-/ adj very pleasant or attractive: an enchanting place | an enchanting story | The child **looked enchanting** in a pale blue dress. —**enchantingly** adv

en·chant·ment /ɪn'tʃɑːntmənt $ ɪn'tʃænt-/ n **1** [U] the quality of being very pleasant or attractive: the enchantment of poetry **2** [C,U] literary a change caused by magic, or the state of being changed by magic

en·chant·ress /ɪn'tʃɑːntrɪ̆s $ ɪn'tʃæn-/ n [C] literary **1** a woman who uses magic on people and things; → **witch** **2** a woman who men think is very attractive and interesting

en·chi·la·da /ˌentʃɪ̆'lɑːdə/ n **1** [C] a Mexican food consisting of a TORTILLA (=flat piece of bread) that is rolled up and filled with meat or cheese, and covered with a spicy sauce **2** the big enchilada AmE informal something that is the most important or biggest of its type: We're aiming our products at the big enchilada – the home computer market. **3** the whole enchilada AmE informal all of something: Come on. Let's hear it – the whole enchilada.

en·cir·cle /ɪn'sɜːkəl $ -ɜːr-/ v [T] to surround someone or something completely: The island was encircled by a dusty road. —**encirclement** n [U]

en·clave /'enkleɪv, 'eŋ-/ n [C] a small area that is within a larger area where people of a different kind or nationality live: the former Portuguese enclave of East Timor

en·close /ɪn'kləʊz $ -'kloʊz/ v [T] **1** to put something inside an envelope as well as a letter: Please enclose a cheque with your order. | please find enclosed (=used in business letters to say that you are sending something with a letter) Please find enclosed an agenda for the meeting. **2** [usually passive] to surround something, especially with a fence or wall, in order to make it separate: The pool area is enclosed by a six-foot wall. | an enclosed area

en·clo·sure /ɪn'kləʊʒə $ -'kloʊʒər/ n **1** [C] an area surrounded by a wall or fence, and used for a particular purpose: the bear enclosure at the zoo **2** [U] the act of making an area separate by putting a wall or fence around it: the enclosure of arable land for pasture **3** [C] something that is put inside an envelope with a letter

en·code /ɪn'kəʊd $ -'koʊd/ v [T] to put a message or other information into CODE; **3** **decode, decipher**

encomium /ɪn'kəʊmiəm $ -'koʊ-/ n plural encomiums or encomia [C] formal the expression of a lot of praise

en·com·pass /ɪn'kʌmpəs/ v [T] formal **1** to include a wide range of ideas, subjects, etc: The study encompasses the social, political, and economic aspects of the situation. **2** to completely cover or surround something: The houses encompassed about 100 square metres.

en·core[1] /'ɒŋkɔː $ 'ɑːŋkɔːr/ n [C] an additional or repeated part of a performance, especially a musical one: The band came back onstage for an encore.

encore[2] interjection said when you have enjoyed a musical performance very much and want the performer to sing or play more

en·coun·ter[1] W3 /ɪn'kaʊntə $ -ər/ v [T] **1** to experience something, especially problems or opposition: **encounter problems/difficulties** They encountered serious problems when two members of the expedition were injured. | **encounter opposition/resistance** The government has encountered strong opposition to its plans to raise income tax. | The doctor had encountered several similar cases in the past. **2** formal to meet someone without planning to: I first encountered him when studying at Cambridge.

encounter[2] n [C] **1** an occasion when you meet someone, or do something with someone you do not know: She didn't remember our encounter last summer. | [+with] His **first encounter** with Wilson was back in 1989. | Bernstein began training the young musician after a **chance encounter** at a concert (=a meeting that happened by chance). | casual **sexual encounters** (=occasions when people have sex) | [+between] hostile encounters between supporters of rival football teams **2** an occasion when you meet or experience something: [+with] a child's first encounter with books | a **close encounter** with a snake (=a frightening situation in which you get too close to something)

en·cour·age S2 W1 /ɪn'kʌrɪdʒ $ ɪn'kɜːr-/ v [T] **1** to give someone the courage or confidence to do something; **3** **discourage**: I want to thank everyone who has encouraged and supported me. | **encourage sb to do sth** Cooder was encouraged to begin playing the guitar by his father. | **encourage sb in sth** Fleur encouraged Dana in her ambition to become a model. **2** to persuade someone to do something; **3** **discourage**: Cantor didn't mind if they worked late; in fact, he actively encouraged it. | **encourage sb to do sth** A 10p rise in cigarette prices is not enough to encourage smokers to stop. **3** to make something more likely to exist, happen, or develop: Violent TV programmes encourage anti-social behaviour. —**encouraged** adj [not before noun]: She felt encouraged by the many letters of support.

en·cour·age·ment /ɪn'kʌrɪdʒmənt $ ɪn'kɜː-/ n [U] when you encourage someone or something, or the things that encourage them: With encouragement, Sally is starting to play with the other children. | **words of encouragement** | **encouragement to do sth** She needed **no encouragement** to continue (=did not need any encouragement).

en·cour·ag·ing S3 /ɪn'kʌrɪ̆dʒɪŋ $ ɪn'kɜːr-/ adj giving you hope and confidence; **3** **reassuring**: The encouraging news is that typhoid is on the decrease. | The signs are encouraging — but there's a long way to go. —**encouragingly** adv

en·croach /ɪn'krəʊtʃ $ -'kroʊtʃ/ v [I always + adv/ prep] **1** to gradually take more of someone's time, possessions, rights etc than you should: [+on/upon] Bureaucratic power has encroached upon the freedom of the individual. **2** to gradually cover more and more land: [+into] The fighting encroached further east. —**encroachment** n [C,U]: foreign encroachment

en·crust·ed /ɪn'krʌstɪ̆d/ adj covered with a hard layer of something: [+with/in] a gold crown encrusted with diamonds | **mud-encrusted/jewel-encrusted etc** —**encrustation** /ˌɪnkrʌ'steɪʃən/ n [C,U]

en·crypt /ɪn'krɪpt/ v [T] to protect information by putting it into a special CODE that only some people can read, especially information that is on a computer; → **decrypt** —**encryption** /ɪn'krɪpʃən/ n [U]: secure encryption of data —**encrypted** adj: files stored in encrypted form

en·cum·ber /ɪn'kʌmbə $ -ər/ v [T usually passive] formal to make it difficult for you to do something or for something to happen; **3** **burden**: He died in 1874, **heavily encumbered** by debt. | [+with] The whole process was encumbered with bureaucracy. —**encumbrance** n [C]

en·cyc·li·cal /ɪn'sɪklɪ̆kəl/ n [C] a letter sent by the Pope to all Roman Catholic BISHOPS

en·cy·clo·pe·di·a also **encyclopaedia** BrE /ɪnˌsaɪklə'piːdiə/ n [C] a book or CD, or a set of these, containing facts about many different subjects, or containing detailed facts about one subject: the Encyclopedia of Music

en·cy·clo·pe·dic also **encyclopaedic** BrE /ɪnˌsaɪklə'piːdɪk◂/ adj having a lot of knowledge or information about a particular subject: an **encyclopedic knowledge** of medieval literature

end[1] S1 W1 /end/ n **1** LAST PART [singular] the last part of a period of time, event, activity, or story; **3** **beginning, start**: [+of] Costs are expected to double by the end of 2005. | at the end *What would she find at the end of her journey?* | *Hooker's death marked **the end of an era**.* | *I played the tape **from beginning to end**.*

2 FINISHED [singular] a situation in which something is finished or no longer exists: **put/bring an end to sth** *It's hoped the talks may bring an end to the violence.* | **call for/demand an end to sth** *The EU is demanding an end to the ivory trade.* | *At last it seemed the war might be **coming to an end**.* | *The spacecraft is nearing the **end of its useful life**.* | **be at an end** *He rose to indicate that the conversation was at an end.* | *Well, I hope that's the **end of the matter**.* | *Another year has passed, with **no end in sight** to the suffering.*

3 LONG OBJECT [C] the part of a place or long object that is furthest from its beginning or centre: [+of] *Jo joined the end of the line.* | *We sat at **opposite ends** of the table.* | **the far end** (=furthest from you) *of the room* | *The channel measures 20 feet **from end to end**.* | **stand/place sth on end** (=in an upright position) *Harry stood the box on end to open it.* | **lay/place sth end to end** (=in a line, with the ends touching) *bricks laid end to end*

4 TIP/POINT [C] the thin part of something long or narrow, that is furthest from you; ▤ **tip**: [+of] *The end of the pencil snapped.* | *He lost the end of his finger.* | *He wore spectacles perched on the **very end** of his nose.*

5 SCALE [C usually singular] one of the two points that begin or end a scale: **lower/cheaper etc end** *the cheaper end of the price range* | *At the **opposite end** of the political spectrum are the Marxist theories.* | *Some teenagers are just a nuisance, but **at the other end of the scale** there are kids who pose a real threat.*

6 CONNECTION [C usually singular] one of two places that are connected by a telephone call, journey etc: **the end of the phone/line** *Sometimes, all you need is a calm voice on the end of the phone.* | *We'll get a bus connection **at the other end**.* | *Any problems at your end* (=where you are)?

7 REMAINING PIECE [C] *especially BrE* a small piece of something that is left after you have finished with it: *cigarette ends*

8 AIM [usually plural] an aim or purpose, or the result you hope to achieve: **political/military etc ends** *40% of all research is undertaken for military ends.* | *She'll do anything to **achieve** her **own ends**.* | *Every task has a clear **end in view**.* | **to that end** *formal: He wants to cut costs, and to that end is looking at ways of cutting the company's operations.* | **an end in itself** (=something you do because you want to, not in order to get other advantages) *IT is a tool for learning, not merely an end in itself.* | **the end justifies the means** (=used to say that doing bad things is acceptable if they achieve an important result)

9 PART OF AN ACTIVITY [singular] *informal* part of a job, activity, or situation that involves or affects one person or group of people: *She works in the sales end of things.*

10 SPORT [C] one of the two halves of a sports field

11 DEATH [C usually singular] a word meaning death – used to avoid saying this directly: *He **met** his **end** (=died) in a car accident.*

12 at the end of the day *spoken* used to give your final opinion after considering all the possibilities: *At the end of the day, it's his decision.*

13 for days/weeks etc on end for many days, weeks etc without stopping: *He was beaten and denied sleep for days on end.*

14 in the end after a period of time, or after everything has been done: *What did you decide in the end?* → see box at LASTLY

15 end of story *spoken informal* used to avoid saying any more about a subject that is embarrassing or secret: *I tripped and hurt my arm. That's it – end of story.*

16 the end of your tether/rope the point at which you are so angry and tired of a situation that you can no longer deal with it: *Frustrated and bitter, Hogan had reached the end of his tether with politics.*

17 the end of the road/line the end of a process, activity,

or state: *Our marriage had **reached the end of the line**.*

18 make ends meet to have only just enough money to buy the things you need: *When Mike lost his job, we could barely make ends meet.*

19 it's not the end of the world *spoken* used to tell someone that a problem is not as bad as they think

20 hold/keep your end up *BrE informal* to stay brave and hopeful in a difficult situation

21 no end *spoken informal* very much: *Your letter cheered me up no end.*

22 no end of trouble/problems etc *spoken informal* a lot of trouble etc: *This will cause no end of trouble.*

23 the living end *AmE spoken* used as an expression of slight disapproval – often used humorously: *What will she do next? She's the living end!*

24 go to the ends of the earth *literary* to do everything possible to achieve something: *I'd go to the ends of the earth to be with him.*

25 to the end of time *literary* forever → DEAD END → ODDS AND ENDS; → be-all and end all at BE² (15); → to the bitter end at BITTER¹ (6); → burn the candle at both ends at BURN¹ (19); → jump/be thrown in at the deep end at DEEP¹ (17); → go off at the deep end at DEEP¹ (18); → be at a loose end at LOOSE¹ (14); → make sb's hair stand on end at HAIR (8); → be on/at the receiving end (of sth) at RECEIVE (5); → be on the sharp end of at SHARP¹ (19); → come to a sticky end at STICKY (6); → the tail end of sth at TAIL¹ (6); → at your wits' end at WIT (7); → get the wrong end of the stick at WRONG¹ (15)

end² S1 W1 *v*

1 [I,T] if a situation or activity ends, or if someone or something ends it, it finishes or stops; ◪ **start, begin**: *World War II ended in 1945.* | *talks aimed at ending the conflict* | **end by doing sth** *I'd like to end by inviting questions from the audience.* | [+with] *The festival will end with a spectacular laser show.*

2 [T] *literary* to spend the last part of your life in a particular place or doing a particular thing: *He **ended** his **days** in prison.* | *She seemed destined to end her days living alone.*

3 end your life/end it all to kill yourself

4 the ... to end all ... used to describe something that is the best, most important, or most exciting of its kind: *the movie with the car chase to end all car chases*

5 the year/week etc ending sth used to refer to the year etc that ends on a particular date: *the financial results for the year ending 31 Dec 2001*

  end in sth *phr v*

1 to finish in a particular way: *One in three marriages ends in divorce.*

2 it'll (all) end in tears *BrE spoken* used to say that something will have a bad result or not be successful

  end up *phr v*

to be in a particular situation, state, or place after a series of events, especially when you did not plan it: *He came round for a coffee and we ended up in bed together.* | *I wondered where the pictures would end up after the auction.* | **end up doing sth** *Most slimmers end up putting weight back on.* | [+with] *Anyone who swims in the river could end up with a nasty stomach upset.* | [+as] *He could end up as President.* | [+like] *I don't want to end up like my parents.*

en·dan·ger /ɪnˈdeɪndʒə $ -ər/ *v* [T] to put someone or something in danger of being hurt, damaged, or destroyed: *Smoking during pregnancy **endangers** your baby's life.* —**endangered** *adj: The lizards are classed as an **endangered species** (=one that soon may no longer exist).* —**endangerment** *n* [U] *legal: charges of child endangerment*

en·dear /ɪnˈdɪə $ ɪnˈdɪr/ *v*

  endear sb **to** sb *phr v* to make someone popular and liked: **endear yourself to sb** *The emperor saw an opportunity to endear himself to the Athenians.*

en·dear·ing /ɪnˈdɪərɪŋ $ ɪnˈdɪr-/ *adj* making someone love or like you: **endearing qualities/traits etc** *Shyness is* *one of her most endearing qualities.* | *an endearing smile* —**endearingly** *adv*

en·dear·ment /ɪn'dɪəmənt $ ɪn'dɪr-/ *n* [C,U] actions or words that express your love for someone: *nicknames and other* **terms of endearment**

en·deav·our[1] *BrE*; **endeavor** *AmE* /ɪn'devə $ -ər/ *v* [I] *formal* to try very hard: **endeavour to do sth** *We always endeavor to please our customers.*

endeavour[2] *BrE*; **endeavor** *AmE n* [C,U] *formal* an attempt to do something new or difficult: **scientific/creative etc endeavour** | *an outstanding example of* **human endeavor** | **endeavour to do sth** *They made every endeavour to find the two boys.* | *Despite our* **best endeavours***, we couldn't start the car.*

en·dem·ic /en'demɪk, ɪn-/ *adj* an endemic disease or problem is always present in a particular place, or among a particular group of people; → **epidemic, pandemic**: *Violent crime is now endemic in parts of Chicago.*

'end game, **end·game** /'endgeɪm/ *n* [C usually singular] the final stage of a war, disagreement etc when everyone is trying to gain an advantage for themselves

end·ing /'endɪŋ/ *n* **1** [C] the way that a story, film, activity etc finishes: **happy/perfect/surprise etc ending** *a story with a happy ending* | [+to] *Cookies and coffee are the perfect ending to a meal.* **2** [U] when a process stops or is finished, or when you finish it: [+of] *the first elections since the ending of the dictatorship* **3** [C] the last part of a word: *Verbal nouns have the ending -ing.*
→ **NEVER-ENDING**

en·dive /'endɪv $ 'endaɪv/ *n* [C,U] **1** *BrE* a vegetable with curly green leaves that you eat raw **2** *AmE* a vegetable with long white bitter-tasting leaves that you eat raw or cooked; ☰ **chicory** *BrE*

end·less /'endləs/ *adj* **1** very large in amount, size, or number: *an endless stream of visitors* | *The possibilities are endless.* | *He's been in a lot of trouble – drugs, guns, blackmail –* **the list is endless***.* **2** something that is endless seems to continue forever: *an endless round of boring meetings* —**endlessly** *adv*: *This city is endlessly fascinating.*

en·do·crine /'endəʊkrɪn $ -doʊ-/ *adj medical* relating to the system in your body that produces HORMONES: *the endocrine glands*

en·dor·phin /en'dɔːfɪn $ -'dɔːr-/ *n* [C usually plural] a chemical produced by your body that reduces pain and can make you feel happier

en·dorse /ɪn'dɔːs $ -ɔːrs/ *v* [T] **1** to express formal support or approval for someone or something: **endorse a proposal/an idea/a candidate etc** *The Prime Minister is unlikely to endorse this view.* **2** if a famous person endorses a product or service, they say in an advertisement that they use and like it **3** to sign your name on the back of a cheque to show that it is correct **4** [usually passive] *BrE* if your DRIVING LICENCE is endorsed for a driving offence, an official record is made on it to show that you are guilty of the offence —**endorsement** *n* [C,U]: *celebrity endorsements* | *the official endorsement of his candidacy*

en·do·scope /'endəskəʊp $ -skoʊp/ *n* [C] *medical* an instrument used by doctors who are performing a medical OPERATION on someone. It is a very small camera with a powerful LENS, which is pushed into the body through a very small hole and sends pictures back to the doctor.

en·dos·co·py /en'dɒskəpi $ -'dɑː-/ *n* [U] *medical* the medical examination of the inside of the body, using an endoscope

en·dow /ɪn'daʊ/ *v* [T] to give a college, hospital etc a large sum of money that provides it with an income
  endow sb/sth with sth *phr v formal* **1** to make someone or something have a particular quality, or to believe that they have it: *Her resistance to the Nationalists endowed her with legendary status.* **2** **be endowed with sth** to naturally have a good feature or quality: *She*

was endowed with both good looks and brains. **3** to give someone something; → see also **WELL-ENDOWED**

en·dow·ment /ɪn'daʊmənt/ *n* **1** [C,U] a sum of money given to a college, hospital etc to provide it with an income, or the act of giving this money **2** [C] a natural quality or ability that someone has

en'dowment ,policy *n* [C] *BrE technical* an insurance arrangement that pays you a sum of money after an agreed period of time

'end ,product *n* [C usually singular] something that is produced by a particular process or activity; → **by product**: *a high-quality end product* | *the end product of years of practice*

,end re'sult *n* [C usually singular] the final result of a process or activity: *If tasks are too challenging, the end result is that learners are discouraged.*

en·dur·a·ble /ɪn'djʊərəbəl $ ɪn'dʊr-/ *adj formal* if a bad situation is endurable, you can accept it, even though it is difficult or painful; ☰ **bearable**

en·dur·ance /ɪn'djʊərəns $ ɪn'dʊr-/ *n* [U] the ability to continue doing something difficult or painful over a long period of time: **physical/mental endurance** | *She was pushed* **beyond** *her* **powers of endurance***.* | *The marathon is a* **test of endurance***.* | **endurance sports/training** (=designed to test or improve your endurance)

en·dure /ɪn'djʊə $ ɪn'dʊr/ *v* **1** [T] to be in a difficult or painful situation for a long time without complaining: *It seemed impossible that anyone could endure such pain.* | **endure doing sth** *He can't endure being apart from me.* **2** [I] to remain alive or continue to exist for a long time: *friendships which endure over many years*

en·dur·ing /ɪn'djʊərɪŋ $ ɪn'dʊr-/ *adj* continuing for a very long time: *the* **enduring appeal** *of Shakespeare's plays* | *enduring hatred* —**enduringly** *adv*: *an enduringly popular performer*

'end ,user *n* [C] the person who uses a particular product, rather than the people who make or develop it

'end zone *n* [C] one of the areas at each end of an American football field that you touch with the ball to score

en·e·ma /'enɪmə/ *n* [C] a liquid that is put into someone's RECTUM to make their BOWELS empty

en·e·my W2 /'enəmi/ *n plural* **enemies** [C]
1 someone who hates you and wants to harm you: *She's a dangerous enemy to have.* | *Cats and dogs have always been* **natural enemies***.* | *an* **old enemy** *of her father* | **make an enemy (of sb)** *a ruthless businessman who made a lot of enemies* | *the unforgettable sight of the president shaking hands with his* **sworn enemy** (=an enemy you will always hate) | **sb's worst enemy** (=the person they hate most) *I* **wouldn't wish** *this* **on my worst enemy***.*
2 someone who opposes or competes against you: *political enemies* | *He was imprisoned for being 'an enemy of the revolution'.*
3 also **the enemy** the country against which your country is fighting in a war: *He was accused of collaboration with the enemy.* | **enemy forces/aircraft/territory etc** *a town behind* **enemy lines**
4 something that people think is harmful or damaging: *The usual enemies, cigarettes and alcohol, are targeted for tax rises.* | *The* **common enemy** *that united them was communism.*
5 **be your own worst enemy** to behave in a way that causes problems for yourself
6 **public enemy number one** *informal* someone famous who has done something bad and who a lot of people do not like: *His views made him public enemy number one in the eyes of the media.*
7 **the enemy within** people in a society etc that other people think are trying to secretly destroy or damage it: *efforts to label environmentalists as the enemy within*
8 if one thing is the enemy of another, the second thing cannot exist because the first thing destroys it: *Boredom is the enemy of learning.*

en·er·get·ic /ˌenə'dʒetɪk◂ $ -ər-/ *adj* having or needing a lot of energy or determination: *an energetic man* |

an energetic drive to get more customers | **energetic in doing sth** *We need to be more energetic in promoting ourselves abroad.* —**energetically** /-kli/ *adv: He fought energetically against apartheid.*

en·er·gize also **-ise** *BrE* /'enədʒaɪz $ -ər-/ *v* [T] **1** to make someone feel more determined and energetic: *The charity hopes the campaign will energise its volunteers.* **2** [usually passive] *technical* to make a machine work —**energizing** *adj*

energy

dam

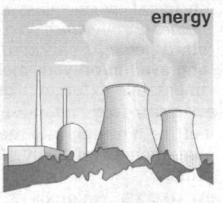
power station

oil rig/platform

coal mine

solar panels

wind turbine

en·er·gy S1 W1 /'enədʒi $ -ər-/ *n plural* **energies** [C,U]
1 the physical and mental strength that makes you able to do things: *Helping people takes time and energy.* | *Boy, where do those kids get their energy?* | *She was full of energy after her vacation.* | *a waste of energy* | **have the energy to do sth** *I don't have the energy to deal with it right now.* | *Try to put more energy into your defensive game.* | **nervous energy** (=too much energy that you have when you are nervous)
2 power that is used to provide heat, operate machines etc: **nuclear/solar etc energy** *research into renewable energy sources* | *the world's energy resources* | *energy consumption*
3 a special power that some people believe exists in their bodies and in some buildings: *There was a lot of energy in the room this morning – did you feel it?*
4 *technical* in physics, the ability that something has to work or move: *kinetic energy*
5 sb's energies the effort and interest that you use to do things: **apply/devote/channel your energies into/to sth** *She's devoting all her energies to the wedding plans.*

en·er·vate /'enəveɪt $ -ər-/ *v* [T] *formal* to make you feel tired and weak: *The hot sun enervated her to the point of collapse.* —**enervated** *adj* [not before noun]: *David felt too enervated to resist.* —**enervating** *adj*

en·fant ter·ri·ble /ˌɒnfɒn teˈriːblə $ ˌɑːnfɑːn-/ *n* [C] a young successful person who behaves in a way that is shocking but also amusing

en·fee·bled /ɪnˈfiːbəld/ *adj literary* very weak or ill —**enfeeble** *v* [T]

en·fold /ɪnˈfəʊld $ -ˈfoʊld/ *v* [T] *formal* to cover or surround someone or something completely: *The wizard screamed as the darkness enfolded him.* | *He reached out to enfold her in his arms.*

en·force /ɪnˈfɔːs $ -ɔːrs/ *v* [T] **1** to make people obey a rule or law: **enforce a law/ban etc** *Governments make laws and the police enforce them.* | *Parking restrictions will be strictly enforced.* **2** to make something happen or force someone to do something: **enforce sth on sb** *It is unlikely that a record company would enforce its views on an established artist.* —**enforceable** *adj: The recommendations are not legally enforceable.*

en·forced /ɪnˈfɔːst $ -ɔːrst/ *adj* made to happen, especially by things you cannot control: **enforced absence/separation etc** *a period of enforced isolation*

en·force·ment /ɪnˈfɔːsmənt $ -ɔːr-/ *n* [U] when people are made to obey a rule, law etc: *law enforcement*

en·forc·er /ɪnˈfɔːsə $ -ˈfɔːrsər/ *n* [C] someone whose job is to make sure people do the things they should: *a law enforcer* | *an enforcer for a drugs gang*

en·fran·chise /ɪnˈfræntʃaɪz/ *v* [T] to give a group of people the right to vote; ◆ **disenfranchise** —**enfranchisement** /-tʃɪz- $ -tʃaɪz-/ *n* [U]: *the enfranchisement of EU citizens* —**enfranchised** *adj: newly enfranchised shareholders*

en·gage W3 /ɪnˈgeɪdʒ/ *v formal*
1 [I always + prep] to be doing or to become involved in an activity: [+in/on/upon] *Only 10% of American adults engage in regular exercise.* | *The two parties engaged upon an escalating political struggle.* | *Mr Armstrong was engaged in prayer.* | **engage in doing sth** *Despite her illness, she remains actively engaged in shaping policy.*
2 [T] to attract someone's attention and keep them interested: **engage sb's interest/attention** *The toy didn't engage her interest for long.* | **engage sb in conversation** (=start talking to them)
3 engage with sb/sth to get involved with other people and their ideas in order to understand them: *Are you so tired you don't have the energy to engage with your kids?*
4 [T] *formal* to employ someone to do a particular job: **engage sb to do sth** *Her father engaged a tutor to improve her maths.* | **engage sb as sth** *We'd be able to engage local people as volunteers.*
5 [I,T] if you engage part of a machine, or if it engages, it moves so that it fits into another part of the machine; ◆ **disengage**: *She engaged the clutch and the car moved.* | [+with] *The wheel engages with the cog and turns it.*
6 [I,T] to begin to fight an enemy: *American forces did not directly engage.*

en·gaged /ɪnˈgeɪdʒd/ *adj* **1** if two people are engaged, they have agreed to marry: *Have you heard? Sally and Ray are getting engaged.* | *She is engaged to be married.* | [+to] *Kate's engaged to a guy from England.* **2** *BrE* if you call someone on the telephone and their line is engaged, they are already speaking to someone else; ◆ **busy** *AmE: She rang Mrs Tavett but the line was engaged.* | **engaged tone/signal** (=the sound you hear when the phone is engaged) **3** *BrE* a public toilet that is engaged is being used; ◆ **vacant 4 be otherwise engaged** *formal* to be unable to do something because you are doing something else

en·gage·ment /ɪnˈgeɪdʒmənt/ *n*
1 BEFORE MARRIAGE [C] an agreement between two people to marry, or the period of time they are engaged: [+of/to] *Their engagement was announced in the paper.* | *Tony was stunned when Lisa suddenly broke off their engagement* (=finished it). | **engagement ring** (=a ring that a man gives a woman to show that they are engaged)
2 ARRANGEMENT TO DO STH [C] an official arrangement to do something, especially one that is related to your work: **official/public/royal etc engagement** *The princess will continue to carry out royal engagements.* | *This is his only public speaking engagement on the tour.* | *His excuse of a prior*

engagement was accepted.

3 INVOLVEMENT [U] when you become involved with someone or something in order to understand them: [+with/in] *a strategy of engagement and cooperation with China | Many students pass without any real engagement in learning.*

4 FIGHTING [C,U] *technical* fighting between armies etc: *military **rules of engagement***

5 EMPLOYMENT [C,U] *formal* an official arrangement to employ or pay someone to do a particular job: *Please sign to indicate your acceptance of the **terms of engagement**.*

6 MACHINE PARTS [U] the fitting together of the working parts of a machine

en·gag·ing /ɪnˈɡeɪdʒɪŋ/ *adj* pleasant and attracting your interest: *an **engaging** smile* —**engagingly** *adv*

en·gen·der /ɪnˈdʒendə $ -ər/ *v* [T] *formal* to be the cause of a situation or feeling: *the changes in society engendered by the war | **engender** sth in sb relationships that engender trust in children*

en·gine S1 W2 /ˈendʒɪn/ *n* [C]
1 the part of a vehicle that produces power to make it move; → **motor**: *start/switch on an engine The engine won't start. | stop/turn off/switch off an engine He switched off the car's engine and waited. | Is the **engine running** smoothly? | diesel/petrol etc engine an old steam engine | We were stranded with **engine trouble** on a deserted highway.* → see picture at MOTORBIKE
2 a vehicle that pulls a railway train
3 [usually singular] *formal* something powerful that causes great changes in society: *engine of change/growth etc The Marshall Plan was the engine of postwar economic growth. | Rome's deadly **war engine** →*
FIRE ENGINE

en·gi·neer¹ S3 W3 /ˌendʒɪˈnɪə $ -ˈnɪr/ *n* [C]
1 someone whose job is to design or build roads, bridges, machines etc: **mechanical/electrical/software etc engineer** | *He trained as a **civil engineer** (=one who designs and builds roads, bridges etc).*
2 someone whose job is to take care of the engines on a ship or aircraft
3 *BrE* someone whose job is to repair electrical equipment or machines: **service/maintenance engineer**
4 *AmE* someone whose job is driving a train

engineer² *v* [T] **1** to make something happen by skilful secret planning: *powerful enemies who engineered his downfall | Perhaps she could engineer a meeting between them?* **2** to change the GENETIC structure of a plant, animal etc; ▣ **genetically modify**: *the dangers of engineering native plants | **genetically engineered** crops* **3** [often passive] *technical* to design and plan the building of roads, bridges, machines, etc

en·gi·neer·ing W2 /ˌendʒɪˈnɪərɪŋ $ -ˈnɪr-/ *n* [U] the work involved in designing and building roads, bridges, machines etc; → **civil engineering** → GENETIC ENGINEERING

En·glish¹ /ˈɪŋɡlɪʃ/ *n* **1** [U] the language used in Britain, the US, Australia, and some other countries: *Do you speak English? | leaflets written in **plain English** (=English that is easy to understand)* **2** the **English** [plural] people from England **3** [U] literature written in English, studied as a subject at school or university: *She decided to major in English.*

English² *adj* **1** relating to England or its people: *the English countryside | under English law* **2** relating to the language used in Britain, the US, Australia and some other countries: *English grammar*

English ˈbreakfast *n* [C usually singular] a large cooked breakfast consisting of BACON, eggs, TOAST etc; → **continental breakfast**

English ˈhorn *n* [C] *AmE* a long wooden musical instrument which is like an OBOE but with a lower sound; ▣ **cor anglais** *BrE*

En·glish·man /ˈɪŋɡlɪʃmən/ *n plural* **Englishmen** /-mən/ [C] **1** a man from England **2** an **Englishman's**

home is his castle *BrE* used to say that your home is a place where you can feel safe and do whatever you want

English ˈmuffin *n* [C] *AmE* a round thick flat piece of bread with small holes inside

En·glish·wom·an /ˈɪŋɡlɪʃˌwʊmən/ *n plural* **Englishwomen** /-ˌwɪmɪn/ [C] a woman from England

en·gorged /ɪnˈɡɔːdʒd $ -ɔːr-/ *adj formal* swollen and full of liquid

en·grave /ɪnˈɡreɪv/ *v* [T] **1** to cut words or designs on metal, wood, glass etc: *engrave sth on sth Their names are engraved on a stone tablet. | engrave sth with sth a pendant engraved with a simple design* **2** be engraved in/on your memory/mind/heart *literary* to be impossible to forget —**engraver** *n* [C]

en·grav·ing /ɪnˈɡreɪvɪŋ/ *n* **1** [C] a picture made by cutting a design into metal, putting ink on the metal, and then printing it **2** [U] the skill of engraving things

en·gross /ɪnˈɡrəʊs $ -ˈɡroʊs/ *v* [T] if something engrosses you, it interests you so much that you do not notice anything else: *The scene was stunning, and for a time engrossed all our attention. | engross yourself in sth Take your mind off it by engrossing yourself in a good book.* —**engrossed** *adj*: *Dad was engrossed in the paper. | Who's that guy Ally's been **engrossed in** conversation with all night?* —**engrossing** *adj*

en·gulf /ɪnˈɡʌlf/ *v* [T] **1** if an unpleasant feeling engulfs you, you feel it very strongly: *despair so great it threatened to engulf him* **2** to completely surround or cover something: *The building was engulfed in flames.*

en·hance W3 /ɪnˈhɑːns $ ɪnˈhæns/ *v* [T] to improve something: *Good lighting will enhance any room. | The publicity has done little to **enhance** his **reputation**.* —**enhancer** *n* [C]: *flavor enhancers* —**enhancement** *n* [C,U]

en·hanced /ɪnˈhɑːnst $ -ˈhænst/ *adj written* improved or better: *enhanced access to information*

e·nig·ma /ɪˈnɪɡmə/ *n* [C] someone or something that is strange and difficult to understand; ▣ **mystery**: *The neighbours regarded him as something of an enigma.*

en·ig·mat·ic /ˌenɪɡˈmætɪk◂/ *adj* mysterious and difficult to understand: **enigmatic smile/expression etc** —**enigmatically** /-kli/ *adv*: *'You'll see,' he replied enigmatically.*

en·join /ɪnˈdʒɔɪn/ *v* [T] **1** *formal* to order or try to persuade someone to do something: **enjoin sb to do sth** *The organisation has been enjoined to end all restrictions.* **2** *law* to legally prevent someone from doing something: **enjoin sb from doing sth** *The defendant was enjoined from using the patent.*

en·joy S1 W1 /ɪnˈdʒɔɪ/ *v* [T]
1 to get pleasure from something: *Sandra enjoys her job in the city. | I enjoyed **every minute** of it. | enjoy doing sth Young children enjoy helping around the house. | enjoy yourself (=be happy in a particular situation) Julia was just starting to enjoy herself.* ⚠ **Enjoy** is never followed by a preposition, and almost always has an object: *Did you enjoy it (NOT Did you enjoy)? | I enjoyed myself at Cal's (NOT I enjoyed at Cal's).*
2 *formal* to have a particular ability or advantage: *These workers enjoy a high level of job security.*
3 enjoy! *spoken* used to say that you hope someone gets pleasure from something you give them: *Here's your steak – enjoy!*

en·joy·a·ble S3 /ɪnˈdʒɔɪəbəl/ *adj* something enjoyable gives you pleasure: *Games can make learning more enjoyable. | an enjoyable experience* —**enjoyably** *adv*

en·joy·ment /ɪnˈdʒɔɪmənt/ *n* **1** [C,U] the feeling of pleasure you get from having or doing something, or something you enjoy doing: *Acting has **brought** me enormous enjoyment. | Unfortunately, a small minority want to **spoil** everyone else's enjoyment.* **2** [U] *formal* the fact of having something

en·large /ɪnˈlɑːdʒ $ -ɑːrdʒ/ *v* [I,T] if you enlarge something, or if it enlarges, it increases in size or scale: *an operation to enlarge her breasts* | *Police will have the pictures enlarged in an attempt to identify the thief.* | **enlarge sb's understanding/knowledge etc** *A good way to enlarge your vocabulary is to read a daily newspaper.*

    enlarge on/upon sth *phr v formal* to provide more information about something you have already mentioned: *Mrs Maughan did not enlarge on what she meant.*

en·large·ment /ɪn'lɑːdʒmənt $ -ɑːr-/ n **1** [C] a photograph that has been printed again in a bigger size **2** [C,U] an increase in size or amount: *enlargement of the EU*

en·lar·ger /ɪn'lɑːdʒə $ -'lɑːrdʒər/ n [C] a piece of equipment used to make photographs bigger

en·light·en /ɪn'laɪtn/ v [T] *formal* to explain something to someone: **enlighten sb as to/on/about sth** *Baldwin enlightened her as to the nature of the experiment.* —**enlightening** *adj*

en·light·ened /ɪn'laɪtnd/ *adj* **1** someone with enlightened attitudes has sensible, modern views and treats people fairly and kindly: **enlightened attitude/approach etc** | *'Empowerment' is the new buzz-word in enlightened management circles.* **2** showing a good understanding or knowledge of something: *We don't actually know, but I can make an enlightened guess.*

en·light·en·ment /ɪn'laɪtnmənt/ n [U] **1** *formal* when you understand something clearly, or when you help someone do this: *Isabel looked to Ron for enlightenment.* **2** the final stage reached in the Buddhist and Hindu religions when you no longer suffer or feel desire and you are at peace with the universe: *the quest for spiritual enlightenment*

en·list /ɪn'lɪst/ v **1** [T] to persuade someone to help you to do something: **enlist sb's help/services etc** *He has enlisted the help of a sports psychologist for the team.* | *The public are being enlisted to help.* **2** [I,T usually passive] to join the army, navy etc: [+as] *He enlisted as a private.* | [+in] *At the outbreak of war, he was enlisted in the army.* —**enlistment** n [C,U]

en·list·ed /ɪn'lɪstᵻd/ *adj* [usually before noun] having a rank below that of an officer in the army, navy etc: *officers and enlisted men*

en·liv·en /ɪn'laɪvən/ v [T] to make something more interesting: *Humour can help enliven a dull subject.*

en masse /ˌɒn 'mæs $ ˌɑːn-/ *adv* if people do something en masse, they do it together: *The management team resigned en masse.*

en·meshed /ɪn'meʃt/ *adj* [not before noun] very involved in an unpleasant or complicated situation: [+in/with] *Congress worried about becoming enmeshed in a foreign war.*

en·mi·ty /'enmᵻti/ n *plural* **enmities** [C,U] *formal* a feeling of hatred towards someone: [+between/towards] *the enmity between the two communities*

en·no·ble /ɪ'nəʊbəl $ ɪ'noʊ-/ v [T usually passive] *formal* **1** to improve your character: *art which ennobles the human race* **2** to make someone a member of the NOBILITY (=the people in society who have a high rank, such as princes etc) —**ennoblement** n [U] —**ennobling** *adj*

en·nui /ɒn'wiː $ ɑːn-/ n [U] *formal* a feeling of being tired, bored, and unsatisfied with your life

e·nor·mi·ty /ɪ'nɔːmᵻti $ -ɔːr-/ n *plural* **enormities** **1** [singular] the great size, seriousness, or difficulty of a situation, problem, event etc: [+of] *Even now, the full enormity of his crimes has not been exposed.* | *the enormity of the task* **2** [C usually plural] *formal* a very evil and cruel act; ◨ **atrocity**

e·nor·mous S2 W3 /ɪ'nɔːməs $ -ɔːr-/ *adj* very big in size or in amount; ◨ **huge**: *an enormous bunch of flowers* | *an enormous amount of money* | *The team made an enormous effort.*

e·nor·mous·ly /ɪ'nɔːməsli $ 'ɔːr-/ *adv* very or very much: *an enormously successful actor* | *The project has benefited enormously from Jan's knowledge.*

e·nough¹ S1 W1 /ɪ'nʌf/ *adv* [always after a verb, adjective, or adverb]
1 to the degree that is necessary or wanted: *Are the carrots cooked enough?* | *He just hadn't thought enough about the possible consequences.* | *You can go to school when you're old enough.* | [+for] *Is the water warm enough for you?* | **enough to do sth** *Will Evans be fit enough to play?* | *The rooms are all large enough to take a third bed.* | *Surely no one would be foolish enough to lend him the money?* | *You're late. It's just **not good enough** (=not satisfactory or acceptable).*
2 fairly but not very: *I was happy enough in Bordeaux, but I missed my family.* | *He's a nice enough young man.*
3 bad/difficult/hard etc enough used to say that a situation is already bad and you do not want it to get any worse: *Life's difficult enough without you interfering all the time.*
4 lucky/unfortunate etc enough to be/do sth used to say that someone is lucky or unlucky that something happens to them: *They were unlucky enough to be caught in the storm.*
5 would you be good/kind enough to do sth? *spoken* used to ask someone politely to do something for you: *Would you be good enough to hold the door open?*
6 strangely/oddly/curiously etc enough used to say that a fact or something that happens is strange or surprising: *Strangely enough, I didn't feel at all nervous when I faced the audience.*
7 near enough *BrE spoken* used when you are guessing a number, amount, time etc because you cannot be exact: *The full cost comes to £3000, near enough.* → **fair enough** at FAIR¹ (14); → **sure enough** at SURE² (1)

e·nough² S1 W2 *determiner, pron*
1 as many or as much as is needed or wanted: *Have I given you enough money?* | *Not enough is known about what happened.* | [+for] *There aren't enough chairs for everyone.* | **enough to do/eat etc** *Erica was worried that the children weren't getting enough to eat.* | **enough (sth) to do sth** *The police didn't have enough evidence to convict him.* | *He didn't even earn enough to pay the rent.* | *You've had **more than enough** time to make all the preparations.* | **enough to go round** (=enough of something for everyone to have some) *Do you think we've got enough pizza to go round?* | **not nearly/nowhere near enough** *informal* (=much less than you need) *We only had $500, and that was nowhere near enough to buy a new camcorder.* | **time/reason/trouble etc enough** *old-fashioned: Come on – there'll be time enough to chat later.*
2 used to say that a situation is already bad and you do not want it to get any worse: *She has enough problems without you two getting into fights.* | *I don't want to bother him – he has enough to worry about.*
3 have had enough (of sth) *spoken* used to say you are tired or angry about a situation and want it to stop: *When I got home I just sat down and cried. I'd had enough.* | *I've just about had enough of your stupid remarks.*
4 enough is enough *spoken* used to say that something that is happening should stop: *There comes a point when you say enough is enough.*
5 that's (quite) enough *spoken* used to tell someone to stop doing something: *Now, you two, that's quite enough. Sit down and be quiet.*
6 enough said *spoken* used to tell someone that they do not need to say any more because you understand the point they are making: *'He's the sort of man who wears a lot of jewellery.' 'Enough said.'*
7 can't get enough of sth/sb *informal* to enjoy something so much that you want more and more of it: *Her millions of fans can't get enough of her.*

GRAMMAR
enough comes after adjectives, never before: *This one is big enough (NOT enough big).* | *Is it warm enough for you?*
enough usually comes before nouns: *We haven't got*

enough time. | *Are there enough plates?*
Sometimes people use **enough** after nouns in particular expressions, but this is not very usual: *There will be time enough for that later.*
⚠ Nouns used with **enough** must be plural or uncountable, never singular: *There aren't enough books (NOT enough book).* | *She has enough money to live on.*

en·quire /ɪnˈkwaɪə $ -ˈkwaɪr/ v [I,T] *especially BrE* another spelling of INQUIRE

en·qui·ry [S3] [W3] /ɪnˈkwaɪəri $ ɪnˈkwaɪri, ˈɪŋkwəri/ n plural **enquiries** *especially BrE* another spelling of INQUIRY

en·rage /ɪnˈreɪdʒ/ v [T usually passive] to make someone very angry: *Many readers were enraged by his article.*

en·rap·tured /ɪnˈræptʃəd $ -ərd/ adj *formal* enjoying something so much that you can think of nothing else: *The orchestra played before an enraptured audience.*

en·rich /ɪnˈrɪtʃ/ v [T] **1** to improve the quality of something, especially by adding things to it: *Add fertilizer to enrich the soil.* | *Education can greatly enrich your life.* **2** to make someone richer **3** *technical* to increase the number of atoms in a NUCLEAR FUEL so that it produces more power —**enrichment** n [U]: *curriculum enrichment* —**enriched** adj: *enriched uranium*

en·rol *BrE*, **enroll** *AmE* /ɪnˈrəʊl $ -ˈroʊl/ v **enrolled, enrolling** [I,T] to officially arrange to join a school, university, or course, or to arrange for someone else to do this: [+on/for] *BrE: I decided to enrol for 'Art for Beginners'* | [+in] *especially AmE: Californians are rushing to enroll in special aerobics classes.*

enrolment *BrE*, **enrollment** *AmE* /ɪnˈrəʊlmənt $ ɪnˈroʊl-/ n **1** [U] the process of arranging to join a school, university, course etc: *Enrolment will take place in September.* **2** [C] the number of people who have arranged to join a school, university, course etc: *Student enrolments have more than doubled.*

en route /, ɒn ˈruːt $,ɑːn-/ adv on the way: [+from/to] *a flight en route from Tokyo to Sydney* | [+for] *BrE: We stayed there en route for London.* | *Why don't we stop for lunch en route?*

en·sconce /ɪnˈskɒns $ ɪnˈskɑːns/ v [T usually passive] to settle yourself in a place where you feel comfortable and safe: [+in/at/on etc] *Nick was comfortably ensconced in front of the TV set.* | **ensconce yourself** *Agnes had ensconced herself in the best bedroom.*

en·sem·ble /ɒnˈsɒmbəl $ ɑːnˈsɑːm-/ n **1** [C also + plural verb] *BrE* a small group of musicians, actors, or dancers who perform together regularly: **instrumental/string/brass etc ensemble** | [+of] *an ensemble of Mexican artistes* **2** [C usually singular] a set of things that go together to form a whole **3** [C usually singular] a set of clothes that are worn together: *an attractive ensemble*

en·shrine /ɪnˈʃraɪn/ v [T usually passive] *formal* if something such as a tradition or right is enshrined in something, it is preserved and protected so that people will remember and respect it: [+in] *The right of free speech is enshrined in the Constitution.*

en·shroud /ɪnˈʃraʊd/ v [T] *formal* to cover or surround something so that it is not possible to see, understand, or explain it: *hills enshrouded in mist* | *the mystery that enshrouds their disappearance*

en·sign /ˈensaɪn, -sən $ ˈensən/ n [C] **1** a flag on a ship that shows what country the ship belongs to: *the Russian ensign* **2** a low rank in the US navy, or an officer who has this rank

en·slave /ɪnˈsleɪv/ v [T usually passive] **1** to make someone a slave **2** *formal* if something enslaves you, it completely controls your life and your actions: *She seemed enslaved by hatred.* —**enslavement** n [U]

en·snare /ɪnˈsneə $ -ˈsner/ v [T] **1** *formal* to trap someone in an unpleasant or illegal situation, from

which they cannot escape: [+in] *Young girls were ensnared in prostitution rings.* **2** to catch an animal in a trap

en·sue /ɪnˈsjuː $ ɪnˈsuː/ v [I] *formal* to happen after or as a result of something: [+from] *problems that ensue from food and medical shortages*

en·su·ing /ɪnˈsjuːɪŋ $ -ˈsuː-/ adj [only before noun] happening after a particular action or event, especially as a result of it: **the ensuing battle/conflict/debate etc** *In the ensuing fighting, two students were killed.* | **the ensuing days/months/years etc** (=the days, months etc after an event) *The situation deteriorated over the ensuing weeks.*

en suite /ɒn ˈswiːt◂ $ ɑːn-/ adj, adv *BrE* **a)** an en suite bathroom is joined onto a bedroom: *Both bedrooms have en suite bathrooms.* **b)** an en suite bedroom has a bathroom joined onto it: *57 bedrooms, all en suite*

en·sure [S3] [W1] /ɪnˈʃʊə $ -ˈʃʊr/ *especially BrE* also **insure** *AmE* v [T] to make certain that something will happen properly; ▯ **make sure**: *facilities to ensure the safety of cyclists* | **ensure (that)** *The hospital tries to ensure that people are seen quickly.*

-ent /ənt/ suffix [in adjectives and nouns] someone or something that does something, or that has a particular quality: *local residents* → -ANT

en·tail /ɪnˈteɪl/ v [T] **1** to involve something as a necessary part or result: *A new computer system entails a lot of re-training.* | *Some foreign travel is entailed in the job.* | **entail doing sth** *The journey will entail changing trains twice.* **2** *old use* if you entail property, you arrange for it to be given to a specific person, usually your oldest son, when you die

en·tan·gle /ɪnˈtæŋɡəl/ v [T usually passive always + adv/prep] **1** to make something become twisted and caught in a rope, net etc: [+in/with] *Small animals can get entangled in the net.* **2** to involve someone in an argument, a relationship, or a situation that is difficult to escape from: **entangle sb in sth** *fears that the US could get entangled in another war* | **be entangled with sb** *I didn't want to become entangled with my best friend's wife.* —**entangled** adj

en·tan·gle·ment /ɪnˈtæŋɡəlmənt/ n **1** [C] a difficult situation or relationship that is hard to escape from: *She had always been afraid of any emotional entanglements.* **2** [U] when something becomes entangled in something **3** [C often plural] a fence made of BARBED WIRE that prevents enemy soldiers from getting too close

entendre n; → see DOUBLE ENTENDRE

en·tente /ɒnˈtɒnt $ ɑːnˈtɑːnt/ n [C,U] a situation in which two countries have friendly relations with each other; → **détente**: *the Anglo-Russian entente*

en·ter [S1] [W1] /ˈentə $ -ər/ v
1 GO INTO **a)** [I,T] to go or come into a place: *Silence fell as I entered the room.* | *Few reporters dared to enter the war zone.* **b)** [T] if an object enters part of something, it goes inside it: *The bullet had entered his brain.*
2 START WORKING [I,T] to start working in a particular profession or organization, or to start studying at a school or university: *Both the boys entered the army.* | *She entered politics in 1996.* | *He entered the Church* (=became a priest) *as a young man.*
3 START AN ACTIVITY [T] to start to take part in an activity, or become involved in a situation: *He entered the election as the clear favourite.* | *The rebels were prepared to enter negotiations* (=start discussing something).
4 COMPUTER **a)** [T] to put information into a computer by pressing the keys: *Press the return key to enter the information.* | **enter sth into sth** *The names are entered into a database.* **b)** [I,T] if you enter a computer system, you are given permission to use it by the computer: *It won't let you enter without a password.*
5 WRITE INFORMATION [T] to write information on a particular part of a form, document etc: *Don't forget to enter your postcode.* | [+in/into] *Enter your name in the space provided.*

6 COMPETITION/EXAMINATION [I,T] to arrange to take part in a race, competition, examination etc, or to arrange for someone else to take part: *At least 30 schools entered the competition.* | [+**for**] *Decisions about when he or she is entered for an examination should be taken very carefully.*

7 PERIOD OF TIME [T] to begin a period of time when something happens: *The economy entered a period of recession in the mid 1980s.* | **enter its third week/sixth day/second year etc** *The talks have now entered their third week.*

8 START TO EXIST [T] if a new idea, thought etc enters your head, or a new quality enters something, it suddenly starts to exist there: *A note of panic entered her voice.* | **it never entered sb's head/mind** (=used to say that someone never considered a particular idea, especially when this is surprising) *It never entered his head that she might be seeing someone else.*

9 enter sb's life if someone or something enters your life, you start to know them or be affected by them: *By the time Angie entered his life, he was almost 30.*

10 OFFICIAL STATEMENT [T] *formal* to make an official statement: *Wilson entered a plea of not guilty* (=said that he was not guilty at the beginning of a court case). | *Residents entered a number of objections to the scheme.*

enter into sth *phr v*
1 enter into an agreement/contract etc to make an official agreement to do something: [+**with**] *Some local authorities have entered into partnership with private companies.*
2 to start discussing or dealing with something: *It could be a problem, but we don't need to enter into that just yet.* | **enter into discussions/negotiations (with sb)** *The government refused to enter into discussions with the opposition.*
3 [usually in negatives] to affect a situation as something that you consider when you make a choice: *He always buys the best — money doesn't enter into it.*
4 enter into the spirit of it/things to take part in a game, party etc in an eager way

enter upon sth *phr v formal*
to start doing something or being involved in it: *countries newly entering upon industrialization*

en·te·ri·tis /ˌentəˈraɪtᵻs/ *n* [U] a painful infection in your INTESTINES

en·ter·prise W2 /ˈentəpraɪz $ -tər-/ *n*
1 [C] a company, organization, or business: *commercial enterprises such as banks and food manufacturers* | **state/public enterprise** *especially BrE* (=one owned by the government)
2 [U] the activity of starting and running businesses: *the management of state enterprise* (=done by the government) → FREE ENTERPRISE, PRIVATE ENTERPRISE
3 [C] a large and complicated project, especially one that is done with a group of other people; ◘ **initiative**: *The programme is a joint enterprise with the London Business School.*
4 [U] the ability to think of new activities or ideas and make them work: *We're looking for young people with enterprise and creativity.*

enterprise culture *n* [C,U] a society or attitude which encourages people to start new businesses and be successful

en·ter·pris·ing /ˈentəpraɪzɪŋ $ -tər-/ *adj* having the ability to think of new activities or ideas and make them work: *Some enterprising students are designing software.* | *an enterprising scheme to provide interest-free loans* —**enterprisingly** *adv*

en·ter·tain /ˌentəˈteɪn $ -tər-/ *v* **1** [I,T] to amuse or interest people in a way that gives them pleasure: **entertain sb with sth** *She entertained the children with stories, songs and drama.* | *A museum should aim to entertain as well as educate.* **2** [I,T] to invite people to your home for a meal, party etc, or to take your company's customers somewhere to have a meal, drinks etc: *Mark usually does the cooking when we entertain.* | *Do you get an allowance for entertaining*

clients? **3 entertain an idea/hope/thought etc** *formal* to consider an idea etc, or allow yourself to think that something might happen or be true: *She could never entertain the idea of living in the country.*

en·ter·tain·er /ˌentəˈteɪnə $ -tərˈteɪnər/ *n* [C] someone whose job is to tell jokes, sing etc in order to entertain people: *Sinatra remains one of the top entertainers of all time.* | *street entertainers*

en·ter·tain·ing¹ /ˌentəˈteɪnɪŋ◂ $ -tər-/ *adj* amusing and interesting: *Children's TV nowadays is much more entertaining.* | *an entertaining evening*

entertaining² *n* [U] when you invite people for meals or to parties, at home or for business reasons: *simple recipes for easy entertaining* | *The hotel is used for corporate entertaining* (=for business reasons).

en·ter·tain·ment S3 /ˌentəˈteɪnmənt $ -tər-/ *n*
1 [C,U] things such as films, television, performances etc that are intended to amuse or interest people: *The town provides a wide choice of entertainment.* | *There will be live entertainment* (=performed then, not recorded) *throughout the day.* | **light entertainment** (=comedy) | *The dolphins give good entertainment value* (=a lot of amusement and interest). | **the entertainment industry/business/world**
2 [U] *formal* when you entertain someone at home, or for business: *the entertainment of friends*

en·thral *BrE*; **enthrall** *AmE* /ɪnˈθrɔːl $ -ˈθrɒːl/ *v* **enthralled, enthralling** [T usually passive] to make someone very interested and excited, so that they listen or watch something very carefully: **be enthralled by/with sb/sth** *The children were enthralled by the story she was telling* —**enthralled** *adj*

en·thrall·ing /ɪnˈθrɔːlɪŋ $ -ˈθrɒːl-/ *adj* extremely interesting: *an enthralling experience*

en·throne /ɪnˈθrəʊn $ -ˈθroʊn/ *v* [T] if a king or queen is enthroned, there is a ceremony to show that they are starting to rule —**enthronement** *n* [C,U]

en·thuse /ɪnˈθjuːz $ ɪnˈθuːz/ *v* **1** [I] to talk about something in a very interested or excited way: [+**about/over**] *Rick was there, enthusing about life in Australia.*
2 [T usually passive] to make someone interested in something or excited by it: **be enthused by/with sth** *The owners were certainly enthused by the offer.*

en·thu·si·as·m W3 /ɪnˈθjuːziæzəm $ ɪnˈθuː-/ *n*
1 [U] a strong feeling of interest and enjoyment about something and an eagerness to be involved in it

with enthusiasm
great/much/considerable/enormous enthusiasm
little enthusiasm
lack of enthusiasm
full of enthusiasm (=very enthusiastic)
show (great/considerable/little) enthusiasm
lose enthusiasm
share sb's enthusiasm
fire sb with enthusiasm (=make them very enthusiastic)
generate enthusiasm (=make people enthusiastic)
dampen sb's enthusiasm (=make them less enthusiastic)
boundless/unbounded enthusiasm (=great enthusiasm)

*Gillian and Darren greeted the speakers **with great enthusiasm**.* | *We went along to the local diving club, **full of enthusiasm**.* | *They go about their tasks with **little enthusiasm**.* | [+**for**] *Britain's apparent **lack of enthusiasm** for such a scheme* | *Employers **showed little enthusiasm** for the new regulations.* | *He **shares** your **enthusiasm** for jazz.* | *I left university **fired with enthusiasm** for work.* | *A delay of two hours did not **dampen** their **enthusiasm**.*

2 [C] *formal* an activity or subject that someone is very interested in

E

en·thu·si·ast /ɪnˈθjuːziæst $ ɪnˈθuː-/ *n* [C] someone who is very interested in a particular activity or subject: **baseball/outdoors/sailing etc enthusiast** *a keep-fit enthusiast* | [+for] *an enthusiast for the latest management thinking*

en·thu·si·as·tic S3 /ɪnˌθjuːziˈæstɪk◂ $ ɪnˌθuː-/ *adj* feeling or showing a lot of interest and excitement about something: **enthusiastic about (doing) sth** *All the staff are enthusiastic about the project.* | *The singer got an enthusiastic reception.* | *an enthusiastic supporter of reform* —**enthusiastically** /-kli/ *adv*

en·tice /ɪnˈtaɪs/ *v* [T] to persuade someone to do something or go somewhere, usually by offering them something that they want: [+into/away/from etc] *The birds were enticed back into Britain 40 years ago.* | **entice sb/sth to do sth** *Our special offers are intended to entice people to buy.* —**enticement** *n* [C,U]

en·ti·cing /ɪnˈtaɪsɪŋ/ *adj* something that is enticing attracts or interests you a lot: *It was a hot day and the water looked enticing.* —**enticingly** *adv*

en·tire S3 W2 /ɪnˈtaɪə $ -ˈtaɪr/ *adj* [only before noun] used when you want to emphasize that you mean all of a group, period of time, amount etc; ➡ **whole**: *It was the worst day in my entire life.* | *The entire staff agreed.* | *Have you drunk the entire bottle?*

en·tire·ly S2 W2 /ɪnˈtaɪəli $ -ˈtaɪr-/ *adv* completely and in every possible way: *Our situation is entirely different.* | *The ridge consists entirely of volcanic rock.* | *Her reasons were not entirely clear.*

en·tir·e·ty /ɪnˈtaɪərᵻti $ -ˈtaɪr-/ *n formal* **1 in its/their entirety** including every part: *The film has been shown in its entirety for the first time.* **2 the entirety of sth** *formal* the whole of sth: *We stayed in the hotel throughout the entirety of the weekend.*

en·ti·tle S2 W2 /ɪnˈtaɪtl/ *v* [T often passive]
1 to give someone the official right to do or have something: **be entitled to (do) sth** *Full-time employees are entitled to receive health insurance.* | **entitle sb to sth** *Membership entitles you to the monthly journal.*
2 be entitled sth if a book, play etc is entitled something, that is its name: *a documentary entitled 'The Price of Perfection'*

en·ti·tle·ment /ɪnˈtaɪtlmənt/ *n* [C,U] the official right to have or do something, or the amount that you have a right to receive: [+to] *Do you need advice on your entitlement to state benefits?* | **benefit/holiday/pension etc entitlement** *The paid holiday entitlement is 25 days.*

en'titlement ˌprogram also **entitlement** *n* [C] a US government programme or system that gives money or help to people who need it

en·ti·ty /ˈentᵻti/ *n plural* **entities** [C] *formal* something that exists as a single and complete unit; ➡ **being**: *The mind exists as a separate entity.* | *Good design brings a house and garden together as a single entity.*

en·tomb /ɪnˈtuːm/ *v* [T usually passive] *formal* to bury or trap someone in something or under the ground

en·to·mol·o·gy /ˌentəˈmɒlədʒi $ -ˈmɑː-/ *n* [U] the scientific study of insects —**entomologist** *n* [C] —**entomological** /ˌentəməˈlɒdʒɪkəl◂ $ -ˈlɑː-/ *adj*

en·tou·rage /ˈɒntʊrɑːʒ $ ˈɑːn-/ *n* [C usually singular, also + plural verb] *BrE* a group of people who travel with an important person: *the president and his entourage*

en·trails /ˈentreɪlz/ *n* [plural] the inside parts of an animal or person's body, especially their INTESTINES

en·trance¹ S3 W3 /ˈentrəns/ *n*
1 [C] a door, gate etc that you go through to enter a place; ➡ **exit**: [+to/of] *the main entrance to the school* | **front/back/side entrance** | *the station entrance* | **entrance hall/foyer/gate etc**
2 [C usually singular] the act of entering a place or room, especially in a way that people notice: *Bridget made a dramatic entrance into the room.*
3 [U] the right or ability to go into a place: [+to] *Entrance to the museum is free.* | *Reporters even man-*

aged to **gain entrance** to her hotel. | *How much is the entrance fee* (=money you pay to get in somewhere)?
4 [U] permission to become a member of or become involved in a profession, university, society etc: *the initial interview for entrance to the Civil Service* | **entrance examinations**
5 [C] when a person, country, organization etc first becomes involved in a particular area of activity: [+into] *The referendum blocked Switzerland's entrance into the European Economic Area.*
6 make your/an entrance to come onto the stage in a play

en·trance² /ɪnˈtrɑːns $ -ˈtræns/ *v* [T usually passive] *literary* if someone or something entrances you, they make you give them all your attention because they are so beautiful, interesting etc: *I was entranced by the sweetness of her voice.* —**entranced** *adj* [not before noun]: *She stopped, entranced.* —**entrancing** *adj*: *entrancing stories*

en·trant /ˈentrənt/ *n* [C] **1** someone who takes part in a competition **2** *especially BrE* someone who has recently started studying at university, or working: [+to] *a fall in the number of new entrants to higher education*

en·trap /ɪnˈtræp/ *v* **entrapped, entrapping** [T] *formal* to trap someone or something, or make it impossible for them to escape from a situation, especially by tricking them: *He felt that she was trying to entrap him.*

en·trap·ment /ɪnˈtræpmənt/ *n* [U] the practice of trapping someone by tricking them, especially to show that they are guilty of a crime

en·treat /ɪnˈtriːt/ *v* [T] *formal* to ask someone, in a very emotional way, to do something for you; ➡ **beg**: **entreat sb to do sth** *His friends entreated him not to go.*

en·trea·ty /ɪnˈtriːti/ *n plural* **entreaties** [C,U] *formal* a serious request in which you ask someone to do something for you

en·trée /ˈɒntreɪ $ ˈɑːn-/ *n* **1** [C] the main dish of a meal, or a dish served before the main course – used in restaurants or on formal occasions: *an entrée of roast duck* **2** [C,U] *formal* the right or freedom to enter a place or to join a social group: [+to/into] *My family name gave me an entrée into upper class Boston society.*

en·trenched /ɪnˈtrentʃt/ *adj* strongly established and not likely to change – often used to show disapproval: [+in] *Ageism is entrenched in our society.* | **entrenched attitudes/positions/interests etc** *a deeply entrenched belief in male superiority* —**entrench** *v* [T]

en·trench·ment /ɪnˈtrentʃmənt/ *n* **1** [U] when an attitude, belief etc becomes firmly established **2** [C] a system of TRENCHES (=long deep holes) dug by soldiers for defence or protection

en·tre nous /ˌɒntrə ˈnuː $ ˌɑːn-/ *adv BrE spoken* used humorously to tell someone that what you are going to say is secret and they must not tell anyone else

en·tre·pre·neur /ˌɒntrəprəˈnɜː $ ˌɑːntrəprəˈnɜːr/ *n* [C] someone who starts a new business or arranges business deals in order to make money, often in a way that involves financial risks —**entrepreneurial** *adj*

en·tro·py /ˈentrəpi/ *n* [U] *technical* a lack of order in a system, including the idea that the lack of order increases over a period of time

en·trust /ɪnˈtrʌst/ *v* [T] to make someone responsible for doing something important, or for taking care of someone: **entrust sth/sb to sb** *She entrusted her son's education to a private tutor.* | **be entrusted with sth/sb** *I was entrusted with the task of looking after the money.*

en·try S2 W2 /ˈentri/ *n plural* **entries**
1 ACT OF ENTERING [C,U] the act of going into something; ➡ **exit**: [+into] *It was dark and their entry into the camp had gone unnoticed.* | *Harry made his entry into the village.* | *There was no sign of a forced entry.* | *How did the thieves gain entry* (=get in)?
2 BECOMING INVOLVED [U] when someone starts to take part in a system, a particular kind of work etc, or the permission they need in order to do this: [+into/to]

Britain's entry into the European Union | *the minimum height for entry into the police force* | *This enabled European banks to gain entry into new markets.* | *the entry requirements for a degree course*
3 RIGHT TO ENTER [U] the right to enter a place, building etc: [+to/into] *Entry to the gardens is included in the price of admission.* | *The refugees were repeatedly refused entry into* (=not allowed in) *the country.* | **no entry** (=written on signs to show that you are not allowed to go somewhere) | *an entry visa*
4 COMPETITION [C] **a)** something that you write, make, do etc in order to try and win a competition: *The winning entry will be published in our April issue.* | *What's the closing date for entries?* **b)** [usually singular] the number of people or things taking part in a competition: *We've attracted a record entry this year.*
5 STH WRITTEN [C] a piece of writing in a DIARY, or in a book containing information such as a dictionary: *a dictionary entry*
6 COMPUTER [U] the act of putting information into a computer: *data entry*
7 DOOR [C] also **entryway** *AmE* a door, gate, or passage that you go through to enter a place → ENTRANCE[1] (1)

entry ,level, **entry-level** *adj* entry level product/model/computer etc a product etc that is the most basic or simple of its kind, making it suitable for people who do not have much money to spend or who do not have experience using the product

En·try·phone /'entrifəʊn $ -foʊn/ *n* [C] *trademark* a type of telephone outside a building that allows visitors to ask someone inside to open the door

en·try·way /'entriweɪ/ *n* [C] *AmE* a door, gate, room, or passage that you go through to enter a place; ◨ **entry**

en·twine /ɪn'twaɪn/ *v* [I,T often passive] **1** to twist two things together or to wind one thing around another: *They walked together with their arms entwined.* **2 be entwined (with sth)** to be closely connected with something in a complicated way: *Our views of leadership are entwined with ideas of heroism.*

E num·ber /'iː ˌnʌmbə $ -ər/ *n* [C] *BrE* a number representing a chemical that has been added to a food, shown on the outside of a container

e·nu·me·rate /ɪ'njuːməreɪt $ ɪ'nuː-/ *v* [T] *formal* to name a list of things one by one

e·nun·ci·ate /ɪ'nʌnsieɪt/ *v* **1** [I,T] to pronounce words clearly and carefully **2** [T] *formal* to express an idea clearly and exactly: *ideas that Darwin was to enunciate decades later* —**enunciation** /ɪˌnʌnsi'eɪʃən/ *n* [U]

e·nure /ɪ'njʊə $ ɪ'njʊr/ *v* another spelling of INURE

en·vel·op /ɪn'veləp/ *v* [T] *formal* to cover or wrap something or someone up completely: [+in] *mountain peaks enveloped in mist* | *the enveloping darkness*

en·ve·lope S3 /'envələʊp $ -loʊp/ *n* [C]
1 a thin paper cover in which you put and send a letter: *envelopes and stamps* | *She tore open the envelope and frantically read the letter.* | *He got a job stuffing envelopes* (=filling them with letters) *at the campaign headquarters.* → SAE, SASE
2 a layer of something that surrounds something else: [+of] *an envelope of gases around the planet*
3 push the envelope *AmE* to try to go beyond the normal limits of something: *a musician who pushes the envelope of improvisation*

en·vi·a·ble /'enviəbəl/ *adj* an enviable quality, position, or possession is good and other people would like to have it: *Now he was in the enviable position of not having to work for a living.* —**enviably** *adv*

en·vi·ous /'enviəs/ *adj* wanting something that someone else has; → jealous: [+of] *Colleagues were envious of her success.* | *envious looks* —**enviously** *adv*

en·vi·ron·ment S1 W1 /ɪn'vaɪrənmənt/ *n* → see picture on next page
1 the environment the air, water, and land on Earth, which can be harmed by man's activities: *Some of these chemicals are very damaging to the environment.* |

legislation to protect the environment | *the effects of acid rain on the environment* | *the government minister for the environment*
2 [C,U] the people and things that are around you in your life, for example the buildings you use, the people you live or work with, and the general situation you are in: *Our first task was to improve the physical environment* (=buildings, furniture etc) *in the school.* | *Young children often feel happier in the home environment.* | *The company had failed to provide a safe environment for its workers.* | **working/learning environment** *a pleasant working environment* | **political/economic** environment *a stable economic environment*
3 [C] the natural features of a place, for example its weather, the type of land it has, and the type of plants that grow in it; → habitat: *a forest environment* | *a very adaptable creature that will eat different foods in different environments*

WORD FOCUS: **ENVIRONMENT**
good for the environment: **environmentally friendly, eco-friendly, sustainable, recyclable, biodegradable, renewable, organic**
people who want to protect the environment: **greens, eco-warriors**
things that cause harm to the environment: **pollution, greenhouse gases, global warming, acid rain, deforestation**
→ ozone layer, fossil fuel, cfc

en·vi·ron·men·tal S1 W2 /ɪnˌvaɪrən'mentl◂/ *adj*
1 concerning or affecting the air, land, or water on Earth: *the environmental damage caused by the chemical industry* | *an international meeting to discuss environmental issues* | *the environmental impact of pollution from cars* | *an environmental group* (=group of people who want to protect the environment)
2 concerning the people and things around you in your life, for example the buildings you use, the people you live or work with, and the general situation you are in: *This will reduce the environmental risks to employees' health.* —**environmentally** *adv*: *environmentally damaging projects*

en·vi·ron·men·tal·ist /ɪnˌvaɪrən'mentəlɪst/ *n* [C] someone who is concerned about protecting the environment

en,vironmentally 'friendly also **en,vironment 'friendly** *adj* products that are environmentally friendly do not harm the environment when they are made or when you use them; ◨ **eco-friendly**

en·vi·rons /ɪn'vaɪrənz/ *n* [plural] *formal* the area surrounding a place: *people living in Geneva and its environs* | *outside the environs of the college*

en·vis·age /ɪn'vɪzɪdʒ/ *v* [T] to think that something is likely to happen in the future: *The scheme cost a lot more than we had originally envisaged.* | **envisage doing sth** *I don't envisage working with him again.*

en·vi·sion /ɪn'vɪʒən/ *v* [T] to imagine something that you think might happen in the future, especially something that you think will be good; ◨ **envisage**: *As a young teacher, I envisioned a future of educational excellence.*

en·voy /'envɔɪ/ *n* [C] someone who is sent to another country as an official representative; ◨ **emissary**: *The United Nations is sending a special envoy to the area.*

en·vy¹ /'envi/ *v* **envied, envying, envies** [T] **1** to wish that you had someone else's possessions, abilities etc: *I really envy you and Ian, you seem so happy together.* | *She has a lifestyle which most people would envy.* | **envy sb sth** *He envied Rosalind her youth and strength.* **2 I don't envy you/her etc** *spoken* used to say that you are glad that you are not in the bad situation that someone else is in

envy² *n* [U] **1** the feeling of wanting something that someone else has; → jealousy: **with envy** *He watched the others with envy.* | [+of] *his envy of the young man's success* | **twinge/pang of envy** *I felt a twinge of envy*

fossil fuels and global warming

waste

air pollution

intensive farming

products harmful to the environment

acid rain

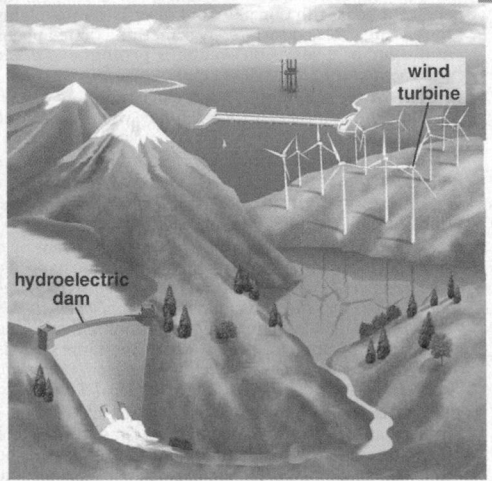

renewable/sustainable energy

recycling

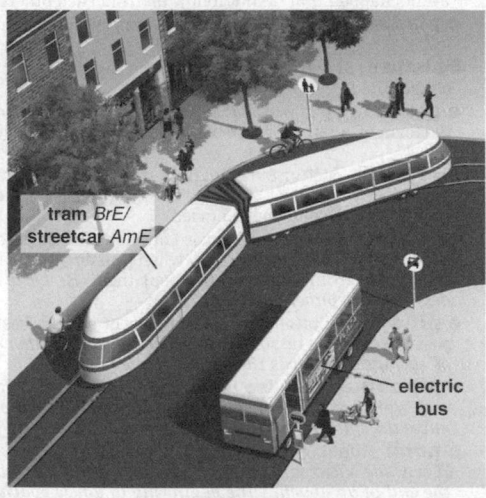

environmentally friendly transport *BrE*/transportation *AmE*

organic farming

ozone-friendly products

renewable resources

when I saw them together. | *She could see that all the other girls were* **green with envy** (=feeling a lot of envy). **2 be the envy of sb** to be something that other people admire and want to have very much: *an education system that is the envy of all European countries*

en·zyme /ˈenzaɪm/ *n* [C] a chemical substance that is produced in a plant or animal, and helps chemical changes to take place in the plant or animal

e·on /ˈiːən/ *n* [C] another spelling of AEON

ep·au·lette, epaulet /ˌepəˈlet/ *n* [C] a small piece of cloth attached to the shoulder of a coat or shirt, especially on a military uniform

é·pée /ˈeɪpeɪ, ˈep- $ eɪˈpeɪ, ˈepeɪ/ *n* [C] a narrow sword with a sharp point, used in the sport of FENCING

e·phem·e·ra /ɪˈfemərə/ *n* [plural] small cheap things that people use in their ordinary life: *a collection of sporting ephemera*

e·phem·e·ral /ɪˈfemərəl/ *adj* existing or popular for only a short time: *Fashion is by nature ephemeral.*

ep·ic¹ /ˈepɪk/ *n* [C] a book, poem, or film that tells a long story about brave actions and exciting events: *a Hollywood epic*

epic² *adj* **1** an epic book, poem, or film tells a long story about brave actions and exciting events: *an epic tale of mutiny on the high seas* | *epic poetry* **2** an epic event continues for a long time and involves brave or exciting actions: *his epic journey to South America* **3** very large and impressive: *He had produced a meal of epic proportions.*

ep·i·cen·tre *BrE*; **epicenter** *AmE* /ˈepɪˌsentə $ -ər/ *n* [C] **1** the place on the surface of the Earth that is right above the point where an EARTHQUAKE begins inside the Earth **2** the place where the most important things happen and important decisions are made: *London became the epicentre of the world fashion industry.*

ep·i·cure /ˈepɪkjʊə $ -kjʊr/ *n* [C] *formal* someone who enjoys good food and drink

ep·i·cu·re·an /ˌepɪkjʊˈriːən/ *adj formal* gaining pleasure from the senses, especially through good food and drink

ep·i·dem·ic /ˌepɪˈdemɪk◂/ *n* [C] **1** a large number of cases of a disease that happen at the same time; → **pandemic**: *Over 500 people died during last year's flu epidemic.* | [+of] *an epidemic of cholera* **2** a sudden increase in the number of times that something bad happens: [+of] *Britain is suffering an epidemic of petty crime.* —**epidemic** *adj* [only before noun]: *Violent crime is reaching epidemic proportions in some cities.*

ep·i·de·mi·ol·o·gy /ˌepɪˌdiːmiˈɒlədʒi $ -ˈɑːl-/ *n* [U] the study of the way diseases spread, and how to control them —**epidemiologist** *n* [C] —**epidemiological** /ˌepɪdiːmiəˈlɒdʒɪkəl $ -ˈlɑː-/ *adj*

ep·i·der·mis /ˌepɪˈdɜːmɪs $ -ɜːr-/ *n* [C,U] *technical* the outside layer of your skin

ep·i·dur·al /ˌepɪˈdjʊərəl◂ $ -ˈdʊr-/ *n* [C] a drug that is put into your back using a needle, done to prevent you feeling pain, especially when having a baby

ep·i·glot·tis /ˌepɪˈglɒtɪs $ -ˈglɑː-/ *n* [C] the piece of flesh that hangs down at the back of your throat

ep·i·gram /ˈepɪgræm/ *n* [C] a short sentence that expresses an idea in a clever or amusing way —**epigrammatic** /ˌepɪgrəˈmætɪk◂/ *adj*

epi·graph /ˈepɪgrɑːf $ -græf/ *n* [C] a short sentence written on a STATUE, or used as an introduction to a book

ep·i·lep·sy /ˈepɪlepsi/ *n* [U] a medical condition affecting your brain, that can make you suddenly become unconscious or unable to control your movements for a short time

ep·i·lep·tic¹ /ˌepɪˈleptɪk◂/ *adj* caused by epilepsy: *He had an epileptic fit.*

epileptic² *n* [C] someone who has epilepsy

ep·i·logue also **epilog** *AmE* /ˈepɪlɒg $ -lɔːg, -lɑːg/ *n* **1** [C] a speech or piece of writing that is added to the end of a book, film, or play and discusses or explains the ending **2** [singular] *literary* something that happens at the end of a series of events; → **prologue**: *a disastrous epilogue to his career*

E·piph·a·ny /ɪˈpɪfəni/ *n* [U] a Christian holy day on January 6th that celebrates the day when the Three Kings came to see the baby Jesus

e·pis·co·pal /ɪˈpɪskəpəl/ *adj* relating to a BISHOP: *his episcopal duties*

E,piscopal 'Church *n* [singular] a group of Christians in the US and Scotland

ep·i·sode /ˈepɪsəʊd $ -soʊd/ *n* [C] **1** an event or a short period of time during which something happens: *She decided she would try to forget the episode by the lake.* | *one of the most interesting episodes in his career* **2** a television or radio programme that is one of a series of programmes in which the same story is continued each week: *Watch next week's thrilling episode!* | [+of] *the first episode of a new drama series*

ep·i·sod·ic /ˌepɪˈsɒdɪk◂ $ -ˈsɑː-/ *adj formal* **1** something that is episodic happens from time to time and then stops for a while, rather than happening all the time: *his episodic involvement in politics* **2** an episodic story or memory is one in which a lot of different events happen that do not follow on from each other

e·pis·tle /ɪˈpɪsəl/ *n* [C] *formal* a long or important letter

Epistle *n* [C] one of the letters in the New Testament of the Bible

e·pis·to·la·ry /ɪˈpɪstələri $ -leri/ *adj formal* written in the form of a letter or a series of letters: *an epistolary novel*

ep·i·taph /ˈepɪtɑːf $ -tæf/ *n* [C] a short piece of writing on the stone over someone's GRAVE (=place in the ground where someone is buried)

ep·i·thet /ˈepɪθet/ *n* [C] a word or short phrase used to describe someone, especially when praising them or saying something unpleasant about them: *He hardly deserves the epithet 'fascist'.*

e·pit·o·me /ɪˈpɪtəmi/ *n* **the epitome of sth** the best possible example of something: *She looked the epitome of elegance.* | *He was the very epitome of evil.*

e·pit·o·mize also **-ise** *BrE* /ɪˈpɪtəmaɪz/ *v* [T] to be a very typical example of something: *This building epitomizes the spirit of the nineteenth century.*

e·poch /ˈiːpɒk $ ˈepək/ *n* [C] a period of history; ▪ **era**: *the Victorian epoch* | *The king's death marked the end of an epoch.* | *the beginning of a new epoch*

'epoch-,making *adj* very important in changing the way people live or the way a society is organized: *the epoch-making social changes of the 1960s*

e·pon·y·mous /ɪˈpɒnɪməs $ ɪˈpɑː-/ *adj* [only before noun] the eponymous character in a book, film, or play is the character whose name is in its title: *Hester, the book's eponymous heroine*

e·pox·y res·in /ɪˌpɒksi ˈrezɪn $ ɪˌpɑː-/ *n* [U] a type of glue

Ep·som salts /ˌepsəm ˈsɔːlts $ -ˈsɒlts/ *n* [plural] a white powder that can be mixed with water and used as a medicine

e·pub·lish·ing /ˈiː ˌpʌblɪʃɪŋ/ *n* [U] *electronic publishing* the business of producing books, magazines, or newspapers that are designed to be read using a computer —**e-publisher** *n* [C]

eq·ua·ble /ˈekwəbəl/ *adj* **1** *formal* someone who is equable remains calm and happy and does not often get annoyed: *a young man with a naturally equable temperament* **2** *technical* equable weather is neither too hot nor too cold: *a place with a pleasant, equable climate* —**equably** *adv*: *She smiled equably.*

e·qual¹ [S1] [W2] /ˈiːkwəl/ *adj*
1 [SAME] the same in size, number, amount, value etc as something else; → **equivalent**: **equal number/amount (of sth)** *Both candidates received an equal number of*

votes. | **(of) equal value/importance** *They believe that all work is of equal value.* | **equal in size/length/height etc** *The two towns are roughly equal in size.* | **of equal size/length/height etc** | [+**to**] *The rent was equal to half his monthly income.*

2 SAME RIGHTS/CHANCES having the same rights, opportunities etc as everyone else, whatever your race, religion, or sex: *Our constitution states that all men are equal.* | *Our education system should provide **equal opportunities** for all children.* | *The government is committed to achieving **equal rights** for women.*

3 be equal to sth a) to have the ability to deal with a problem, piece of work etc successfully; ⊟ **be up to**: *I'm not sure he's **equal to the task**.* | *Are you **equal to this challenge**?* **b)** to be as good as something else: *The architecture here is equal to any in the world.*

4 on equal terms/on an equal footing with neither side having any advantage over the other: *This law will help small businesses to compete on equal terms with large multinational corporations.*

5 all (other) things being equal *spoken* if things are as you normally expect them to be: *All things being equal, a small car will cost less than a larger one.*

equal² S2 v **equalled, equalling** *BrE*, **equaled, equaling** *AmE*

1 [linking verb] to be exactly the same in size, number, or amount as something else: *Two plus two equals four.* | *Prices should become more stable when supply equals demand.*

2 [T] to be as good as something else, or get to the same standard as someone or something else: *Thompson equalled the world record.*

3 be equalled (only) by sth used to say that two things are as strong or as important as each other: *Her distaste for books was equalled only by her dislike of people.*

4 [T] to produce a particular result or effect: *A highly-trained workforce equals high productivity.*

equal³ S3 n [C]

1 someone who is as important, intelligent etc as you are, or who has the same rights and opportunities as you do: *He treats all his staff as equals.* | *a friendship between equals* | [+**in**] *She wasn't his equal in intelligence.*

2 be the equal of sb/sth to be as good as someone or something else: *The company proved to be the equal of its US rivals.*

3 be without equal also **have no equal** *formal* to be better than everyone or everything else of the same type: *His paintings are without equal.*

e·qual·i·ty /ɪˈkwɒlɪti $ ɪˈkwɑː-/ n [U] a situation in which people have the same rights, advantages etc: [+**of**] *All people have the right to equality of opportunity.* | [+**with**] *Women have yet to achieve full equality with men in the workplace.* | [+**between**] *equality between men and women* | **racial/sexual equality** *The government must promote racial equality.*

e·qual·ize also **-ise** *BrE* /ˈiːkwəlaɪz/ v **1** [T] to make two or more things the same in size, value, amount etc: *We have tried to equalize the workload between the different teachers.* **2** [I] *BrE* to get a point in a game, so that you have the same number of points as your opponent: *England equalized ten minutes later.*

e·qual·iz·er also **-iser** *BrE* /ˈiːkwəlaɪzə $ -ər/ n [C] **1** *BrE* a point that you score in a game, that gives you the same number of points as your opponent: *England scored the equalizer with only ten minutes to go.* **2** something that makes all people equal because everyone experiences it in the same way: *Sport is a great equalizer in schools.*

e·qual·ly S2 W2 /ˈiːkwəli/ adv

1 [+ adj/adv] to the same degree or amount: *You must have a good education, but practical training is equally important.*

2 in equal parts or amounts: *We agreed to divide the money equally between everyone.*

3 [sentence adverb] used when introducing a second idea or statement that is as important as your first one: *We want the economy to grow, but equally we want low inflation.*

'equals sign *BrE*; **'equal sign** *AmE* n [C] the sign (=) that you use in mathematics to show that two things are the same size, number, or amount

eq·ua·nim·i·ty /ˌiːkwəˈnɪmɪ̥ti, ˌekwə-/ n [U] *formal* calmness in the way that you react to things, which means that you do not become upset or annoyed: *He received the news with surprising equanimity.*

e·quate /ɪˈkweɪt/ v [T] to consider that two things are similar or connected: **equate sth with sth** *Most people equate wealth with success.*

equate to sth *phr v* to be equal to something: *a rate of pay which equates to £6 per hour*

e·qua·tion W3 /ɪˈkweɪʒən/ n

1 [C] a statement in mathematics that shows that two amounts or totals are equal: *In the equation $2x + 1 = 7$, what is x?*

2 [C usually singular] the set of different facts, ideas, or people that all affect a situation and must be considered together: *The tourist industry forms a crucial **part of** the region's economic **equation**.* | *The question of cost has now **entered the equation**.*

3 [singular] when you consider that two things are similar or connected: *the equation of violence with power*

e·qua·tor, Equator /ɪˈkweɪtə $ -ər/ n **the equator** an imaginary line drawn around the middle of the Earth that is exactly the same distance from the North Pole and the South Pole: **on/at/near the equator** *a small village near the equator*; → see picture at GLOBE

eq·ua·to·ri·al /ˌekwəˈtɔːriəl◂/ adj **1** near the equator: *equatorial rainforests* **2** equatorial weather is very hot and wet: *an equatorial climate*

e·ques·tri·an /ɪˈkwestriən/ adj relating to horse-riding: *equestrian sports*

e·qui·dis·tant /ˌiːkwɪ̥ˈdɪstənt◂/ adj at an equal distance from two places: [+**from/between**] *The city is equidistant between London and Glasgow.*

e·qui·lat·e·ral tri·an·gle /ˌiːkwɪˈlætərəl ˈtraɪæŋɡəl/ n [C] *technical* a TRIANGLE (1) whose three sides are all the same length

e·qui·lib·ri·um /ˌiːkwɪ̥ˈlɪbriəm/ n [singular, U] **1** a balance between different people, groups, or forces that compete with each other, so that none is stronger than the others and a situation is not likely to change suddenly: *The government is anxious not to upset the economic equilibrium.* **2** a state in which you are calm and not angry or upset: *She struggled to recover her equilibrium.*

eq·uine /ˈekwaɪn, ˈiː-/ adj relating to horses, or looking like a horse

eq·ui·nox /ˈiːkwɪ̥nɒks, ˈe- $ -nɑːks/ n [C] one of the two times in a year when night and day are of equal length: *the spring equinox*

e·quip /ɪˈkwɪp/ v **equipped, equipping** [T] **1** to provide a person or place with the things that are needed for a particular kind of activity or work: **equip sb/sth with sth** *They spent a lot of money equipping the school with new computers.* | *He equipped himself with a hammer and nails.* | **be equipped with sth** *The rooms are equipped with video cameras.* | **be equipped to do sth** *The emergency services are equipped to deal with disasters of this kind.* | **well/poorly/fully etc equipped** *a well equipped hospital* **2** to give someone the information and skills that they need to do something: **equip sb with sth** *We equip students with the skills they will need once they leave college.* | **equip sb for sth** *training that will equip you for the job* | **equip sb to do sth** *We must equip young teachers to deal with difficult children.*

e·quip·ment S2 W2 /ɪˈkwɪpmənt/ n

1 [U] the tools, machines, clothes etc that you need to do a particular job or activity: *a shop selling camping equipment* | *some brand new computer equipment* |

E

piece/bit of equipment *a very useful piece of equipment* **2** [singular] the process of equipping someone or something: [+of] *A lot of money was spent on the equipment of the new hospital.*

eq·uit·a·ble /'ekwɨtəbəl/ *adj formal* treating all people in a fair and equal way; ☒ **inequitable**: *an equitable distribution of food supplies* —**equitably** *adv*: *The work should be shared more equitably.*

eq·ui·ty /'ekwɨti/ *n* **1** [U] *formal* a situation in which all people are treated equally and no one has an unfair advantage; ☒ **inequity**: *a society run on the principles of equity and justice* **2** [U] *technical* the amount of money that you would have left if you sold your house and paid off the money you borrowed to buy the house **3 equities** [plural] *technical* SHARES in a company from which the owner of the shares receives some of the company's profits rather than a fixed regular payment **4** [U] *law* the principle that a fair judgment must be made in a situation where the existing laws do not provide an answer

e·quiv·a·lent¹ W3 /ɪ'kwɪvələnt/ *adj* having the same value, purpose, job etc as a person or thing of a different kind: [+to] *a qualification which is equivalent to a degree* | *I had no dollars, but offered him an equivalent amount of sterling.* —**equivalence** *n* [U]

equivalent² *n* [C] something that has the same value, purpose, job etc as something else: *The word has no equivalent in English.* | [+of] *He had drunk the equivalent of 15 whiskies.*

e·quiv·o·cal /ɪ'kwɪvəkəl/ *adj* **1** if you are equivocal, you are deliberately unclear in the way that you give information or your opinion; ☒ **ambiguous**: *His answer was equivocal.* | *She was rather equivocal about her work.* **2** information that is equivocal is difficult to understand or explain because it contains different parts which suggest that different things are true: *The results of the police enquiry were equivocal.*

e·quiv·o·cate /ɪ'kwɪvəkeɪt/ *v* [I] *formal* to avoid giving a clear or direct answer to a question —**equivocation** /ɪ,kwɪvə'keɪʃən/ *n* [C,U]

er /ɜː, ə $ ɜːr, ər/ *interjection BrE* a sound you make when you do not know exactly what to say next: *Well, er – I'm not really sure.*

-er¹ /ə $ ər/ *suffix* forms the comparative of many short adjectives and adverbs: *hot, hotter* | *dry, drier* | *fast, faster* → -EST

-er² *suffix* [in nouns] **1** someone who does something or is doing something: *a dancer* | *a driver* **2** something that does something: *a scraper* (=a tool you use for scraping) → -AR, -OR

ER /,iː 'ɑː $ -'ɑːr/ *n* [C usually singular] *AmE informal* EMERGENCY ROOM

e·ra /'ɪərə $ 'ɪrə/ *n* [C] a period of time in history that is known for a particular event, or for particular qualities: [+of] *We live in an era of instant communication.* | *a new era of world peace* | *His death marked the end of an era.* | *the Victorian era*

e·rad·i·cate /ɪ'rædɨkeɪt/ *v* [T] to completely get rid of something such as a disease or a social problem: **eradicate sth from sth** *We can eradicate this disease from the world.* | *an attempt to eradicate inflation* | *This problem has now been completely eradicated.* —**eradication** /ɪ,rædɨ'keɪʃən/ *n* [U]

e·rase S3 /ɪ'reɪz $ ɪ'reɪs/ *v* [T]
1 to remove information from a computer memory or recorded sounds from a tape: *The computer crashed, and all our records were erased.*
2 to remove writing from paper: *Some of the names had been accidentally erased.*
3 to get rid of something so that it has gone completely and no longer exists: *Their dream is to erase poverty and injustice from the world.* | **erase sth from your mind/memory** *He couldn't erase the image from his mind.* | *She had tried to erase the memory of that day.*

e·ras·er /ɪ'reɪzə $ -sər/ *n* [C] a small piece of rubber that you use to remove pencil or pen marks from paper; ☒ **rubber** *BrE*; → see picture at STATIONERY

e·ra·sure /ɪ'reɪʒə $ -ʃər/ *n* [U] *formal* when you erase something, or when something is erased: *a way to avoid accidental erasure of data from your computer*

ere /eə $ er/ *prep, conjunction old use* or *literary* before

e·rect¹ /ɪ'rekt/ *adj* **1** in a straight upright position: *Martin stood erect on the platform.* **2** an erect PENIS or NIPPLE is stiff and bigger than it usually is because a person is sexually excited

erect² *v* [T] **1** *formal* to build something such as a building or wall: *an imposing town hall, erected in 1892* | *Police have erected barriers across the main roads into the town.* **2** to fix all the pieces of something together, and put it in an upright position; ☒ **put up**: *It took a couple of hours to erect the tent.* **3** to establish something such as a system or institution

e·rec·tion /ɪ'rekʃən/ *n* **1** [C] if a man has an erection, his PENIS increases in size and becomes stiff and upright because he is sexually excited: **have/get an erection** **2** [U] the act of building something or putting it in an upright position: [+of] *the erection of a new temple*

e·res·u·me also **e-résumé** /'iː ˌrezjʊmeɪ $ -re-zʊˌmeɪ/ *n* [C] *electronic resume* an electronic written record of your education and previous jobs that you send to an employer over the Internet when you are looking for a new job

er·ga·tive /'ɜːgətɪv $ 'ɜːr-/ *adj technical* an ergative verb can be either TRANSITIVE or INTRANSITIVE, with the same word used as the object of the transitive form and as the subject of the intransitive form, such as 'cooked' in the sentences 'He cooked the potatoes' and 'The potatoes cooked quickly'.

er·go /'ɜːgəʊ $ 'ɜːrgoʊ/ *adv formal* [sentence adverb] therefore

er·go·nom·ics /,ɜːgə'nɒmɪks $,ɜːrgə'nɑː-/ *n* [U] the way in which the careful design of equipment helps people to work better and more quickly: *We were very impressed with the machine's ergonomics.* —**ergonomic** *adj*: *a new ergonomic design* —**ergonomically** /-kli/ *adv* —**ergonomist** /ɜː'gɒnəmɨst $ ɜːr'gɑː-/ *n* [C]

ERM /,iː ɑːr 'em/ *n* [singular, U] the abbreviation of *exchange rate mechanism*

er·mine /'ɜːmɨn $ 'ɜːr-/ *n* **1** [U] an expensive white fur, used especially for the formal clothes of judges, kings, and queens **2** [C] a small animal whose fur is white in winter

e·rode /ɪ'rəʊd $ ɪ'roʊd/ *v* also **erode away** [I,T] **1** if the weather erodes rock or soil, or if rock or soil erodes, its surface is gradually destroyed: *The cliffs are being constantly eroded by heavy seas.* | *The rocks have gradually eroded away.* **2** to gradually reduce something such as someone's power or confidence: *Our personal freedom is being gradually eroded away.* | *Repeated exam failure had eroded her confidence.*

e·ro·ge·nous zone /ɪ,rɒdʒənəs 'zəʊn $ ɪ,rɑːdʒənəs 'zoʊn/ *n* [C] a part of your body that gives you sexual pleasure when it is touched

e·ro·sion /ɪ'rəʊʒən $ ɪ'roʊ-/ *n* [U] **1** the process by which rock or soil is gradually destroyed by wind, rain, or the sea: *the problem of soil erosion* | *the erosion of the coastline* **2** the process by which something is gradually reduced or destroyed: [+of] *the gradual erosion of our civil liberties*

e·rot·ic /ɪ'rɒtɪk $ ɪ'rɑː-/ *adj* **1** an erotic book, picture, or film shows people having sex, and is intended to make people reading or looking at it have feelings of sexual pleasure **2** erotic thoughts, feelings, or experiences involve sexual excitement: *an erotic dream* —**erotically** /-kli/ *adv*

e·rot·i·ca /ɪ'rɒtɪkə $ ɪ'rɑː-/ *n* [plural] erotic pictures, films, and writing; → **pornography**

e·rot·i·cis·m /ɪˈrɒtɪ̸sɪzəm $ ɪˈrɑː-/ n [U] a style or quality that expresses strong feelings of sexual love and desire, especially in works of art: *the eroticism of his early love poems*

err /ɜː $ ɜːr/ v [I] **1 err on the side of sth** to be more careful or safe than is necessary, in order to make sure that nothing bad happens: *It's always best to err on the side of caution.* **2** *old use* to make a mistake

er·rand /ˈerənd/ n [C] a short journey in order to do something for someone, for example delivering or collecting something for them: *I seemed to spend my life running errands for people.* | *She was always sending me on errands.* | **on an errand** *I couldn't stop because I was on an errand.* | *He quickly set out on his errand of mercy* (=journey to help someone in danger). → **(send sb on) a fool's errand** at FOOL[1] (11)

er·rant /ˈerənt/ adj [only before noun] *old-fashioned* behaving badly, usually by not obeying your parents or not being faithful to your husband or wife: *an errant wife* | *their errant son*

er·rat·ic /ɪˈrætɪk/ adj something that is erratic does not follow any pattern or plan but happens in a way that is not regular: *His breathing was becoming erratic.* | *She found it hard to cope with his erratic behaviour.* —**erratically** /-kli/ adv: *He always drives erratically.*

er·ra·tum /eˈrɑːtəm/ n plural **errata** /-tə/ [C] *technical* a mistake in a book, shown in a list added after the book is printed

er·ro·ne·ous /ɪˈrəʊniəs $ ɪˈroʊ-/ adj *formal* erroneous ideas or information are wrong and based on facts that are not correct: *His economic predictions are based on some erroneous assumptions.* —**erroneously** adv

er·ror [S2] [W2] /ˈerə $ ˈerər/ n
1 [C,U] a mistake: [+in] *There must be an error in our calculations.* | **make/commit an error** *The government has committed a serious error.* | **serious/grave/fatal error** *I realized I had made a fatal error.* | **computer/driver etc error** *The bill was sent to the wrong person because of a computer error.* | *The accident was caused by human error* (=a mistake by a person).
2 [C] a mistake when you are working on a computer, which means that the computer program cannot do what you want it to do: *An error message.*
3 error of judgment a mistake in the way that you examine a situation and decide what to do: *The decision to expand the company was an error of judgement.*
4 be in error to have made a mistake, especially when making an official decision: *The doctor has admitted that he was in error.*
5 do sth in error if you do something in error, you do it by mistake: *The wrong man was arrested in error.*
6 see the error of your ways *literary* to realize that you have been behaving badly and decide to stop; → **trial and error** at TRIAL[1] (4)

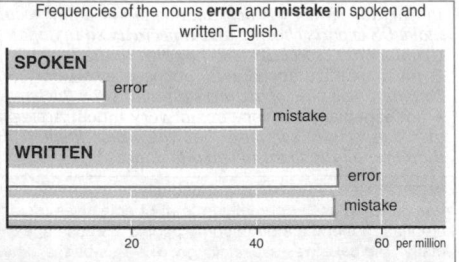

Frequencies of the nouns **error** and **mistake** in spoken and written English.

SPOKEN		
error		
	mistake	
WRITTEN		
	error	
	mistake	
20	40	60 per million

This graph shows that the word **mistake** is more common in spoken English than the word **error**. This is because error is not used in a very general way. It is used when describing particular types of mistake, for example in the expressions **computer error** or **error of judgement**, and sounds formal when used on its own. It is therefore more common in written English.

er·satz /ˈeəzæts $ ˈerzɑːts/ adj [usually before noun] artificial, and not as good as the real thing: *ersatz coffee*

erst·while /ˈɜːstwaɪl $ ˈɜːrst-/ adj [only before noun] *formal* former or in the past: *She found herself ostracized by erstwhile friends.* | *his erstwhile allies*

er·u·dite /ˈerʊ̸daɪt/ adj showing a lot of knowledge based on careful study; ⊟ **learned** —**eruditely** adv —**erudition** /ˌerʊ̸ˈdɪʃən/ n [U]

e·rupt /ɪˈrʌpt/ v [I] **1** if fighting, violence, noise etc erupts, it starts suddenly; ⊟ **break out:** *Violence erupted after police shot a student during the demonstration.* | *A political row erupted over the MP's comments.* **2** if a VOLCANO erupts, it explodes and sends smoke, fire, and rock into the sky → see picture at EXPLOSION **3** if a place or situation erupts, there is a sudden increase in activity or emotion: [+into] *They were angry to the point of erupting into riot.* | *Their conversations often erupted into minor squabbles.* **4 erupt into laughter/shouting etc** to suddenly start laughing, shouting etc: *He erupted into loud, desperate sobs.* **5** if spots erupt on your body, they suddenly appear on your skin —**eruption** /ɪˈrʌpʃən/ n [C,U]: *a volcanic eruption* | *the eruption of violence*

-ery /əri/ also **-ry** suffix (in nouns) **1** a quality or condition: *bravery* (=the quality of being brave) | *slavery* (=the condition of being a slave) **2** things of a particular kind: *machinery* (=different types of machines) | *all her finery* (=beautiful clothes) **3** a place where a particular activity happens: *a bakery* (=where bread is baked) | *an oil refinery*

es·ca·late /ˈeskəleɪt/ v [I,T] **1** if fighting, violence, or a bad situation escalates, or if someone escalates it, it becomes much worse: [+into] *Her fear was escalating into panic.* | *The fighting on the border is escalating.* | *We do not want to escalate the war.* **2** to become higher or increase, or to make something do this: *The costs were escalating alarmingly.* | *policies that escalate their own costs* | *escalating crime* —**escalation** /ˌeskəˈleɪʃən/ n [C,U]: *the escalation of fighting in June* | *a rapid escalation in value*

es·ca·la·tor /ˈeskəleɪtə $ -ər/ n [C] a set of moving stairs that take people to different levels in a building

es·ca·lope /ˈeskəlɒp $ ɪˈskæləp/ n [C] *BrE* a thin piece of meat with no bones in it, especially VEAL (=meat from a young cow), cooked in hot oil

es·ca·pade /ˈeskəpeɪd/ n [C] **1** an adventure or series of events that are exciting or contain some risk: *their dangerous escapades in the Great War* **2** *AmE* a sexual relationship that is exciting or risky, but that is not considered serious

es·cape¹ [S3] [W2] /ɪˈskeɪp/ v
1 PERSON/PLACE [I] to get away from a place or dangerous situation when someone is trying to catch you or stop you: *He broke down the door and escaped.* | [+from/through/over etc] *He escaped from prison in October.* | [+to] *She escaped to Britain in 1938.*
2 DANGER [I,T] to get away from a dangerous or bad situation: [+with] *He escaped with minor injuries.* | **escape unhurt/unscathed/unharmed etc** *A boy escaped unhurt when the fire in his room exploded.* | *They went to the hills to escape the summer heat.* | **escape sb's clutches** (=escape from someone) *The youth was trying to escape the clutches of two drunken female companions.*
3 AVOID [I,T] to avoid something bad or that you do not want to happen: *He narrowly escaped death in an avalanche.* | *The two passengers escaped serious injury.* | *They must not be allowed to escape justice.* | *It seemed impossible he would escape detection.*
4 GAS/LIQUID ETC [I] if gas, liquid, light, heat etc escapes from somewhere, it comes out: *Vents allow any steam to escape if the system overheats.*
5 SOUND [I,T] *literary* if a sound escapes from someone, they accidentally make that sound: *A small laugh escaped her.* | [+from] *Holman let a weary sigh escape from his lips.*
6 escape sb's attention/notice if something escapes your attention or notice, you do not see it or realize that it is there

[1] 000, [2] 000, [3] 000, most frequent words in [S]poken and [W]ritten English

E

7 the name/date/title etc escapes sb used to say that someone cannot remember something: *For some reason which escapes me, we had to take a taxi.*
8 there's no escaping (the fact) used to emphasize that something is definitely important or will definitely happen: *There's no escaping the fact that work has profound effects on emotions and health.*

escape² S3 *n*
1 [C,U] the act of getting away from a place, or a dangerous or bad situation: *The girl had no chance of escape.* | *Christina hoped it wouldn't be too long before she could **make** her escape.* | [+from] *the firm's **narrow escape** from bankruptcy* | *an **escape route*** | *They had a **lucky escape** (=were lucky not to be hurt or killed) when a car crashed into the front of their house.*
2 [singular, U] a way of forgetting about a bad or boring situation for a short time: [+from] *Travel can be an escape from the routine drudgery of life.*
3 [C,U] an amount of gas, liquid etc that accidentally comes out of the place where it is being kept, or an occasion when this happens: *The lid prevents the escape of poisonous gases.* → FIRE ESCAPE

es·caped /ɪ'skeɪpt/ *adj* [only before noun] an escaped person or animal has escaped from somewhere: *an escaped prisoner*

es·cap·ee /ˌeskeɪ'piː, ɪˌskeɪ'piː/ *n* [C] *literary* someone who has escaped from somewhere

es'cape ve,locity *n* [C,U] the speed at which a ROCKET must travel in order to get into space

es·cap·is·m /ɪ'skeɪpɪzəm/ *n* [U] activities or entertainment that help you forget about bad or boring things for a short time: *Books were **a form of escapism** from the real world.* —**escapist** *adj*: *pure escapist entertainment*

es·ca·pol·o·gist /ˌeskə'pɒlədʒɪst $ -'pɑː-/ *n* [C] *BrE* someone who escapes from ropes, chains, a cage etc to entertain people

e·scarp·ment /ɪ'skɑːpmənt $ -ɑːr-/ *n* [C] a high steep slope or cliff between two levels on a hill or mountain

es·cheat /ɪs'tʃiːt/ *n* [C] *AmE law* a legal process in which someone's money and property are given to the state after they die if they do not have a WILL, or if there is nobody else with a legal right to receive their money or property

es·chew /ɪs'tʃuː/ *v* [T] *formal* to deliberately avoid doing or using something: *I had eschewed politics in favour of a life practising law.*

e·scort¹ /ɪ'skɔːt $ -ɔːrt/ *v* [T] **1** to take someone somewhere, especially when you are protecting or guarding them: *The shipment was escorted by guards.* | **escort sb back/through/to etc (sth)** *Two Marines escorted Benny inside.* | *I escorted her to the door.* **2** to go with someone and show them a place: **escort sb around (sth)** *The company escorts prospective buyers around the property.* **3** *old-fashioned* to go with someone to a social event: *Bill escorted Ellie to the opera.*

es·cort² /'eskɔːt $ -ɔːrt/ *n* [C] **1** a person or a group of people or vehicles that go with someone in order to protect or guard them: *a **police escort*** | **under escort** *He was driven away to prison under armed escort* (=protected or guarded by an escort). **2** someone who goes with someone to a formal social event **3** someone who is paid to go out with someone socially: *an escort agency* **4** *AmE* a PROSTITUTE, especially one who goes to social events or on trips with the person who pays them

es·cri·toire /ˌeskrɪ'twɑː $ -'twɑːr/ *n* [C] *formal* a small writing desk

es·crow /'eskrəʊ $ -kroʊ/ *n* [U] *law* money, land, or a written contract, etc that is held by someone who is not directly involved in an agreement while the agreement is being achieved: *a property that is being **held in escrow***

es·cu·do /e'skuːdəʊ $ -doʊ/ *n plural* **escudos** [C] the standard unit of money used in Portugal before the EURO

e·scutch·eon /ɪ'skʌtʃən/ *n* [C] *formal* a SHIELD on which someone's COAT OF ARMS (=family sign) is painted

-ese /iːz/ *suffix* **1** [in nouns] the people or language of a particular country or place: *the Viennese* (=people from Vienna). | *I'm learning Japanese* (=the language of Japan). **2** [in adjectives] belonging to a particular country or place: *Chinese music* **3** [in nouns] *informal* language or words used by a particular group, especially when it sounds ugly or is difficult to understand: *journalese* (=language used in newspapers) | *officialese* (=language used in official or legal writing)

e·sig·na·ture /'iː ˌsɪgnətʃə $ -ər/ *n* [C] ELECTRONIC SIGNATURE

Es·ki·mo /'eskɪməʊ $ -moʊ/ *n plural* **Eskimo** or **Eskimos** [C] *old-fashioned* an INUIT (=someone who belongs to a race of people living in the very cold northern areas of North America). Many people now consider this word offensive.

ESL /ˌiː es 'el/ *n* [U] **English as a Second Language** the teaching of English to people, who are living in an English-speaking country, but whose first language is not English

ESOL /'iːsɒl $ -sɒːl/ *n* [U] the abbreviation of *English for Speakers of Other Languages*

e·soph·a·gus /ɪ'sɒfəgəs $ ɪ'sɑː-/ *n* [C] the American spelling of OESOPHAGUS

es·o·ter·ic /ˌesə'terɪk , ˌiːsə-/ *adj* known and understood by only a few people who have special knowledge about something: *the esoteric world of scientific supercomputing* —**esoterically** /-kli/ *adv*

ESP /ˌiː es 'piː/ *n* [U] **1 extra-sensory perception** the ability to know what will happen in the future, or to know what another person is thinking **2 English for Specific Purposes** or **English for Special Purposes** the teaching of English to business people, scientists etc whose first language is not English

esp. the written abbreviation of *especially*

es·pa·drille /ˌespə'drɪl $ 'espədrɪl/ *n* [C] a light shoe that is made of cloth and rope

es·pe·cial /ɪ'speʃəl/ *adj BrE formal* SPECIAL

es·pe·cial·ly S1 W1 /ɪ'speʃəli/ *adv*
1 [sentence adverb] used to emphasize that something is more important or happens more with one particular thing than with others; ▣ **particularly**: *I never liked long walks, especially in winter.* | *Art books are expensive to produce, especially if they contain colour illustrations.*
2 [+ adj/adv] to a particularly high degree or much more than usual; ▣ **particularly**: *I was especially fond of chocolate biscuits.* | *Feedback is especially important in learning skills.* | *A depreciation of the dollar would make US exports cheaper and especially so in Japan.* | *Graphics are especially well handled in the book.*
3 for a particular person, purpose etc: [+for] *She bought a new pair of trainers especially for the trip.*
4 not especially not very, or not very much: *Accidents aren't especially common, but you never know.* | *He didn't especially want to learn to dance.*

WORD CHOICE: especially, specially
It is better to use **especially** in front of adjectives to emphasize them, although some people also use **specially**: *The cake was especially good.* | *This part is especially interesting.*
Use **especially** to say that something applies more to one thing or situation than to others: *Everyone loved it, especially the children.* | *You should call first, especially if you're going to be late.*
Use **specially** to say that something is done or made for a particular purpose: *I got this specially for you.* | *specially designed equipment*
⚠ **Especially** never comes at the start of a sentence: *He loves fruit. He especially likes kiwis (NOT Especially he likes ...).*

Es·pe·ran·to /ˌespəˈræntəʊ $ -ˈrɑːntoʊ/ n [U] an artificial language invented in 1871 to help people from different countries in the world speak to each other

es·pi·o·nage /ˈespiənɑːʒ/ n [U] the activity of secretly finding out secret information and giving it to a country's enemies or a company's competitors; **⊟ spying**; → **spy**: *a campaign of industrial espionage against his main rival* → COUNTER-ESPIONAGE

es·pla·nade /ˌespləˈneɪd $ ˈesplənɑːd/ n [C] especially BrE a wide street next to the sea in a town

es·pouse /ɪˈspaʊz/ v [T] formal to support an idea, belief etc, especially a political one: **espouse a cause/policy etc** *He espoused a variety of scientific, social and political causes.* —**espousal** n [singular, U]: *her espousal of liberal reforms*

es·pres·so /eˈspresəʊ, ɪˈspre- $ -soʊ/ n plural **espressos** [C,U] strong black Italian coffee, or a cup of this coffee

es·prit de corps /eˌspriː də ˈkɔː $ -ˈkɔːr/ n [U] formal feelings of loyalty towards people who are all involved in the same activity as you; **⊟ team spirit**

es·py /ɪˈspaɪ/ v espied, espying, espies [T] literary to suddenly see someone or something; **⊟ spy**

Esq. 1 especially BrE **esquire** a title that is sometimes written after a man's name in the address on an official letter instead of using MR before the name **2** AmE a title of respect that is sometimes put after a lawyer's name: *Franklin Taylor Esq.*

-esque /esk/ suffix [in adjectives] **1** in the manner or style of a particular person, group, or place: *Kafkaesque* (=in the style of the writer Franz Kafka) **2** having a particular quality: *picturesque* (=pleasant to look at)

es·quire /ɪˈskwaɪə $ ˈeskwaɪr, ɪˈskwaɪr/ n [singular] a formal title that can be written after a man's name, especially in the address on an official letter

-ess /es, ɪs/ suffix [in nouns] a female: *an actress* (=a female actor) | *two lionesses*

es·say¹ S2 /ˈeseɪ/ n [C]
1 a short piece of writing about a particular subject by a student as part of a course of study: [+on/about] *an essay on Bernard Shaw*
2 a short piece of writing giving someone's ideas about politics, society etc: [+on] *Rousseau's Essay on the Origin of Languages*
3 formal an attempt to do something

es·say² /eˈseɪ/ v [T] formal to attempt to do something

es·say·ist /ˈeseɪ-ɪst/ n [C] someone who writes essays giving their ideas about politics, society etc

es·sence /ˈesəns/ n **1** [singular] the most basic and important quality of something: [+of] *The essence of Arsenal's style of football was speed.* | *She seems the very essence of kindness* (=she seems very kind). **2 in essence** used when talking about the most basic and important part of something, especially an idea, belief, or argument: *In essence his message was very simple.* **3** [C,U] a liquid obtained from a plant, flower etc that has a very strong smell or taste and is used especially in cooking: *vanilla essence* **4 sth is of the essence** used to say that something is very important: *Good communications are of the essence to remain competitive.* | **time/speed is of the essence** (=it is very important to do something quickly)

es·sen·tial¹ S2 W2 /ɪˈsenʃəl/ adj
1 extremely important and necessary: [+for/to] *A good diet is essential for everyone.* | **it is essential (that)** *It is essential that our pilots are given the best possible training.* | **it is essential to do sth** *It is essential to book in advance.* | *Window locks are fairly cheap and absolutely essential.* | *Even in small companies, computers are an essential tool.*
2 the essential part, quality, or feature of something is the most basic one: *The essential difference between Sam and me was the fact that I took life seriously.* | *The essential point of relay racing is that it is a team effort.*

essential² n **1** [C usually plural] something that is necessary to do something or in a particular situation: *She packed a few essentials.* | *We only had the bare essentials* (=the most necessary things). **2 the essentials** [plural] the basic and most important information or facts about a particular subject: [+of] *We have no reason to doubt the essentials of the girl's story.*

es·sen·tial·ly S2 W3 /ɪˈsenʃəli/ adv used when stating the most basic facts about something; **⊟ basically**: *Ballet is essentially a middle-class interest.* | *Suicide rates have remained essentially unchanged.* | [sentence adverb]: *Essentially, we are talking about the cold war period.*

es·sential ˈoil n [C] an oil from a plant that has a strong smell and is used for making PERFUME or in AROMATHERAPY

est. **1** the written abbreviation of *established*: *H. Perkins and Company, est. 1869* **2** the written abbreviation of *estimated*

-est /ɪst/ suffix forms the SUPERLATIVE of many short adjectives and adverbs: *cold, colder, coldest* | *early, earlier, earliest* → **-ER¹**

es·tab·lish S3 W1 /ɪˈstæblɪʃ/ v [T]
1 to start a company, organization, system, etc that is intended to exist or continue for a long time; **⊟ found**: *The city of Boerne was established by German settlers in the 1840s.* | *Our goal is to establish a new research centre in the North.*
2 to begin a relationship with someone or a situation that will continue: **establish relations/links/contact etc (with sb)** *Hungary established diplomatic relations with Chile in 1990.* | *I wondered why he should bother to try and establish contact with me.*
3 to find out facts that will prove that something is true: *The police must establish the facts of the case before proceeding.* | **establish that** *The autopsy established that he had been murdered.* | **establish whether/if** *I was never able to establish whether she was telling the truth.*
4 to make people accept that you can do something, or that you have a particular quality: **establish yourself (as/in)** *He had three years in which to establish himself as Prime Minister.* | *He'd already begun to establish quite a reputation as a journalist.*

es·tab·lished W3 /ɪˈstæblɪʃt/ adj [only before noun]
1 already in use or existing for a long period of time: *Competition from established businesses can be formidable.* | **well-established** *teaching methods* | *By 1969 the civil rights movement was already an established fact.* | *Every once in a while, the established order* (=people who rule) *is overthrown.*
2 known to do a particular job well, because you have done it for a long time: *an established professor of French literature*
3 established church/religion especially BrE the official church or religion in a particular country

es·tab·lish·ment S3 W2 /ɪˈstæblɪʃmənt/ n
1 [C] formal an organization or institution, especially a business, shop etc: *a top class training establishment*
2 the establishment the group of people in a society or profession who have a lot of power and influence and are often opposed to any kind of change or new ideas: *Young people are supposed to rebel against the Establishment.* | **the medical/legal/military etc establishment** *The public is treated with contempt by the art establishment.*
3 [U] the act of starting an organization, relationship, or system: [+of] *the establishment of NATO in 1949*

es·tate S2 W2 /ɪˈsteɪt/ n
1 [singular] law all of someone's property and money, especially everything that is left after they die: **sb's estate** *The property is part of the deceased's estate.*
2 [C] a large area of land in the country, usually with one large house on it and one owner: *a country estate*
3 [C] BrE an area where houses or buildings of a

E

similar type have all been built together in a planned way: **council/industrial/housing etc estate** → FOURTH ESTATE, REAL ESTATE

es'tate ˌagent n [C] *BrE* someone whose business is to buy and sell houses or land for people; ▤ **real estate agent**, **realtor** *AmE* —**estate agency** n [C]

es'tate car also **estate** n [C] *BrE* a car with a door at the back, folding back seats, and a lot of space at the back; ▤ **station wagon** *AmE*

es'tate tax n [C,U] a tax in the US on the money and possessions of a dead person; → **inheritance tax**

es·teem¹ /ɪˈstiːm/ n [U] a feeling of respect for someone, or a good opinion of someone: **hold sb in high/great esteem** *The critics held him in high esteem as an actor.* | **token/mark of sb's esteem** (=a sign of their respect) *Please accept the small gift we enclose as a mark of our esteem.* | [+for] *my father's complete lack of esteem for actors* → SELF-ESTEEM

esteem² v [T] *formal* to respect and admire someone or something: *Peden was greatly esteemed by the people of Ayrshire.* | *He was esteemed as a literary wit.*

es·teemed /ɪˈstiːmd/ adj [usually before noun] *formal* respected and admired: *the esteemed French critic Olivier Boissiere* | **highly esteemed** *scholars*

es·thete /ˈiːsθiːt $ ˈes-/ n [C] an American spelling of AESTHETE —**esthetic** /iːsˈθetɪk $ es-/ adj —**esthetical** adj —**esthetically** /-kli/ adv —**esthetics** n [U]

es·ti·ma·ble /ˈestɪ̞məbəl/ adj *formal* deserving respect and admiration; → **inestimable**

es·ti·mate¹ ▣S3 ▣W2 /ˈestɪ̞mɪ̞t/ n [C]
1 a calculation of the value, size, amount etc of something: **a rough estimate** (=not an exact calculation) *of how much time we'll need* | *A **conservative estimate** (=a deliberately low estimate) puts annual sales at around $100 million.* | *The figure will only be about two million, less than half the original estimate.* | *Some estimates put the number of deaths at several hundred.* → GUESSTIMATE
2 a statement of how much it will probably cost to build or repair something: [+for] *The garage said they'd send me an estimate for the work.*

es·ti·mate² ▣S3 ▣W3 /ˈestɪ̞meɪt/ v [T] to try to judge the value, size, speed, cost etc of something, without calculating it exactly: **be estimated to be/have/cost etc** *The tree is estimated to be at least 700 years old.* | **estimate sth at sth** *Organizers estimated the crowd at 50,000.* | **estimate that** *Scientists estimate that smoking reduces life expectancy by around 12 years on average.* | **estimate how many/what etc** *It is not easy to estimate how many people have the disease.* —**estimated** adj: *heroin with an estimated street value of £50,000* —**estimator** n [C]

es·ti·ma·tion /ˌestɪ̞ˈmeɪʃən/ n **1** [singular] a judgment or opinion about someone or something: **in sb's estimation** *In your estimation, who's going to win?* | **go up/come down in sb's estimation** (=be respected or admired more or less by someone) **2** [C] a calculation of the value, size, amount etc of something: *Estimations of their total world sales are around the 50 million mark.*

es·tranged /ɪˈstreɪndʒd/ adj **1** sb's **estranged husband/wife** someone's husband or wife whom they are no longer living with, used especially in newspaper reports **2** no longer seeing or talking to a relative or good friend, because of an argument: [+from] *Mill became estranged from his family after the marriage.* **3** no longer feeling any connection with something that used to be important in your life; ▤ **alienated**: [+from] *young adults who feel estranged from the church* —**estrangement** n [C,U]

es·tro·gen /ˈiːstrədʒən $ ˈes-/ n [U] the usual American spelling of OESTROGEN

es·tu·a·ry /ˈestʃuəri, -tʃəri $ -tʃueri/ n *plural* **estuaries** [C] the wide part of a river where it goes into the sea: *the Thames estuary* → see picture at RIVER

ˈestuary ˌEnglish n [U] a way of speaking English that is common in London and the southeast of England. In Estuary English /t/ is pronounced as a GLOTTAL STOP, and sometimes /l/ is pronounced like /w/.

ETA /ˌiː tiː ˈeɪ/ n [U] *estimated time of arrival* the time when a plane, ship etc is expected to arrive

e-tail·er /ˈiː ˌteɪlə $ -ər/ n [C] *electronic retailer* a business that sells products or services on the Internet, instead of in a shop —**e-tail** n [U]

et al /ˌet ˈæl/ adv written after a list of names to mean that other people are also involved in something: *Boers et al, 2001*

etc. also **etc** *BrE* /et ˈsetərə/ adv *et cetera* used in writing after a list to show that there are many other similar things or people that you could have added: *a shop which sells cards, calendars, wrapping paper etc* | **etc etc** (=used when you are rather bored or annoyed by the list you are giving) *The letter says pay at once, they've reminded us before etc etc.*

et cet·e·ra /et ˈsetərə/ adv the full form of etc

etch /etʃ/ v **1** [I,T] to cut lines on a metal plate, piece of glass, stone etc to form a picture or words: [+on] *a gravestone with three names etched on it* | *A laser is used to etch a pattern in the smooth surface of the disc.* **2** **be etched on/in your memory/mind** *literary* if an experience, name etc is etched on your memory or mind, you cannot forget it and you think of it often: *The island remained etched in my memory.* **3** [T usually passive] if someone's face is etched with pain, sadness etc, you can see these feelings from their expression: [+with] *Her face was etched with tiredness.* | *Craig saw lines of pain etched around her mouth.* **4** [T] to make lines or patterns appear on something very clearly: *etched glass*

etch·ing /ˈetʃɪŋ/ n [C] a picture made by printing from an etched metal plate

e·ter·nal /ɪˈtɜːnəl $ -ɜːr-/ adj **1** continuing for ever and having no end: *the Christian promise of eternal life* | *She's an **eternal optimist** (=she always expects that good things will happen).* **2** seeming to continue for ever, especially because of being boring or annoying; ▤ **never-ending**: *the eternal arguments between mother and son* **3** **eternal truths** principles that are always true

e·ter·nal·ly /ɪˈtɜːnəl-i $ -ɜːr-/ adv **1** for ever: *I'll be **eternally grateful** (=very grateful) to you for this.* **2** *informal* always or very often; ▤ **constantly**: *He's the sort of player who's eternally arguing with the referee.*

eˌternal ˈtriangle n [singular] *literary* the difficult situation that occurs when two people have a sexual relationship with the same person

e·ter·ni·ty /ɪˈtɜːnɪ̞ti $ -ɜːr-/ n **1** **an eternity** a period of time that seems very long because you are annoyed, anxious etc: *Here she waited for **what seemed like an eternity**.* | *That week was an eternity of solitude and boredom.* **2** [U] the whole of time without any end: *a little animal preserved for all eternity as a fossil* **3** [U] the state of existence after death that some people believe continues for ever

-eth /ɪ̞θ/ also **-th** suffix *old use* or *Biblical* forms the third person singular of verbs: *he giveth*

eth·a·nol /ˈeθənɒl, ˈiː- $ -noʊl/ n [U] *technical* ETHYL ALCOHOL

e·ther /ˈiːθə $ -ər/ n **1** [U] a clear liquid used in the past as an ANAESTHETIC to make people sleep before an operation **2** **the ether a)** the space through which radio waves or computer signals travel: *voices coming through the ether* **b)** also **aether** *BrE literary* the upper part of the sky

e·the·re·al /ɪˈθɪəriəl $ ɪˈθɪr-/ adj very delicate and light, in a way that does not seem real: *ethereal beauty* | *His music is ethereal.* —**ethereally** adv

E·ther·net /'iːθənet $ -ər-/ n [U] *trademark* a system used for connecting computer networks

eth·ic /'eθɪk/ n **1** [C] a general idea or belief that influences people's behaviour and attitudes: *The old ethic of hard work has given way to a new ethic of instant gratification.* → WORK ETHIC **2 ethics** [plural] moral rules or principles of behaviour for deciding what is right and wrong: *a report on the ethics of gene therapy* | **professional/business/medical ethics** (=the moral rules relating to a particular profession) *public concern about medical ethics* | *Televised news is based on a code of ethics.*

eth·i·cal /'eθɪkəl/ adj [no comparative] **1** relating to principles of what is right and wrong; ⊟ **moral: ethical issues/questions/problems** *The use of animals in scientific tests raises difficult ethical questions.* | *The president must have the highest **ethical standards.*** **2** morally good or correct; ⊠ **unethical**: *I don't think it's ethical for you to accept a job you know you can't do.* | **ethical investment** policies (=investing only in businesses that are considered morally acceptable) → UNETHICAL —**ethically** /-kli/ adv

eth·nic¹ [W3] /'eθnɪk/ adj
1 relating to a particular race, nation, or tribe and their customs and traditions: *The school teaches pupils from different ethnic groups.* | *ethnic Russians in Estonia* | **ethnic violence/divisions/strife etc** (=violence etc between people from different races or cultures) | **ethnic background/origin** *The students are from a variety of ethnic backgrounds.* | *plans to partition the republic **along ethnic lines*** (=in a way that keeps different ethnic groups apart)
2 ethnic cooking/fashion/design etc cooking, fashion etc from countries that are far away, which seems very different and unusual: *ethnic music* —**ethnically** /-kli/: *Surinam is culturally and ethnically diverse.*

ethnic² n [C] someone who comes from a group of people who are a different race, religion etc or who have a different background from most other people in that country: *In that neighborhood of New York, we were all ethnics.*

ethnic 'cleansing n [U] the action of forcing people to leave an area or country because of their RACIAL or national group

ethnic mi'nority n [C] a group of people of a different race from the main group in a country: *racial discrimination against doctors from ethnic minorities*

eth·no·cen·tric /ˌeθnəʊ'sentrɪk◂ $ -noʊ-/ adj based on the idea that your own race, nation, group etc is better than any other – used in order to show disapproval: *ethnocentric history textbooks* —**ethnocentrism** n [U] —**ethnocentricity** /ˌeθnəʊsen'trɪsʰti $ -noʊ-/ n [U]

eth·nog·ra·phy /eθ'nɒɡrəfi $ eθ'nɑː-/ n [U] the scientific description of different races of people —**ethnographer** n [C] —**ethnographic** /ˌeθnə'ɡræfɪk◂/ adj —**ethnographically** /-kli/ adv

eth·nol·o·gy /eθ'nɒlədʒi $ eθ'nɑː-/ n [U] the scientific study and comparison of different races of people; → anthropology, sociology —**ethnologist** n [C] —**ethnological** /ˌeθnə'lɒdʒɪkəl◂ $ -'lɑː-/ adj —**ethnologically** /-kli/ adv

e·thos /'iːθɒs $ 'iːθɑːs/ n [singular] the set of ideas and moral attitudes that are typical of a particular group: *a community in which people lived according to an ethos of sharing and caring*

eth·yl al·co·hol /ˌeθəl 'ælkəhɒl, ˌiːθaɪl- $ -hɔːl/ n [U] *technical* the type of alcohol in alcoholic drinks

E-tick·et /'iː ˌtɪkʰt/ n [C] *electronic ticket* a ticket, especially for a plane journey, that is stored in a computer and is not given to you in the form of paper

e·ti·o·lat·ed /'iːtiəleɪtʰd/ adj **1** *literary* pale and weak **2** *technical* a plant that is etiolated is weak and not very green because it has not received enough light —**etiolation** /ˌiːtiə'leɪʃən/ n [U]

et·i·ol·o·gy /ˌiːti'ɒlədʒi, $ -'ɑːlə-/ n [C,U] *technical* the cause of a disease or the scientific study of this —**etiological** /ˌiːtiə'lɒdʒɪkəl◂ $ -'lɑː-/ adj —**etiologically** /-kli/ adv

et·i·quette /'etɪket $ -kət/ n [U] the formal rules for polite behaviour in society or in a particular group: *strict rules of professional etiquette*

-ette /et/ suffix [in nouns] **1** a small thing of a particular type: *a kitchenette* (=small kitchen) | *a snackette* (=a very small meal) **2** a woman who is doing a particular job: *an usherette* (=female usher) **3** something that is not real, but is IMITATION (2): *flannelette* | *chairs covered with leatherette*

et·y·mol·o·gy /ˌetʰ'mɒlədʒi $ -'mɑː-/ n **1** [U] the study of the origins, history, and changing meanings of words **2** [C] a description of the history of a word —**etymologist** n [C] —**etymological** /ˌetʰmə'lɒdʒɪkəl◂ $ -'lɑː-/ adj —**etymologically** /-kli/ adv

EU /ˌiː 'juː/ n **the EU** the abbreviation of the *European Union*

eu·ca·lyp·tus /ˌjuːkə'lɪptəs/ n [C,U] a tall tree that produces an oil with a strong smell, used in medicines

Eu·cha·rist /'juːkərʰst/ n **the Eucharist** the holy bread and wine, representing Christ's body and blood, used during a Christian ceremony, or the ceremony itself; → **communion, mass** —**Eucharistic** /ˌjuːkə'rɪstɪk◂/ adj

eu·gen·ics /juː'dʒenɪks/ n [U] the study of methods to improve the mental and physical abilities of the human race by choosing who should become parents – used in order to show disapproval

eu·lo·gize also **-ise** BrE /'juːlədʒaɪz/ v [I,T] to praise someone or something very much: *The poem does not eulogize the dead soldiers.* | *Commentators are eulogizing about the 17-year-old left-hander.* —**eulogist** n [C] —**eulogistic** /ˌjuːlə'dʒɪstɪk◂/ adj

eu·lo·gy /'juːlədʒi/ n plural **eulogies** [C,U] a speech or piece of writing in which you praise someone or something very much, especially at a funeral: *The minister delivered a long eulogy.*

eu·nuch /'juːnək/ n [C] a man whose TESTICLES have been removed, especially someone who guarded a king's wives in some Eastern countries in the past

eu·phe·mis·m /'juːfʰmɪzəm/ n [C] a polite word or expression that you use instead of a more direct one to avoid shocking or upsetting someone: *'Pass away' is a euphemism for 'die'.*

eu·phe·mis·tic /ˌjuːfʰ'mɪstɪk◂/ adj euphemistic language uses polite words and expressions to avoid shocking or upsetting people —**euphemistically** /-kli/ adv

eu·pho·ri·a /juː'fɔːriə $ jʊ-/ n [U] an extremely strong feeling of happiness and excitement which usually only lasts for a short time: *There was a general atmosphere of pessimism after the euphoria of last year.*

eu·phor·ic /juː'fɒrɪk $ jʊ'fɔːrɪk, -'fɑː-/ adj feeling very happy and excited: *Scientists are euphoric at the success of the test.* —**euphorically** /-kli/ adv

Eu·ra·sian¹ /jʊ'reɪʒən, -ʃən/ adj **1** relating to both Europe and Asia **2** *old-fashioned* having one European parent and one Asian parent

Eurasian² n [C] *old-fashioned* someone who has one European parent and one Asian parent

eu·re·ka /jʊ'riːkə/ interjection *humorous* used to show how happy you are that you have discovered the answer to a problem, found something etc

eu·ro /'jʊərəʊ $ 'jʊroʊ/ n plural **euros** [C] a unit of money that can be used in most countries of the European Union: *the value of the euro against the dollar* | *Prices are given in pounds and euros.*

E

[1] 000, [2] 000, [3] 000, most frequent words in [S]poken and [W]ritten English

meet each other). | *one of the major* **sporting events** *of the year* | **charity/fund-raising etc event** *The school raises money by organizing fund-raising events.*
3 RACE/COMPETITION [C] one of the races or competitions that are part of a large sports competition: *The next event will be the 100 metres.* | *The 800 metres is not his best event.* → FIELD EVENT, THREE-DAY EVENT
4 in any/either event also **at all events** used to say that something will definitely happen or be true in spite of anything else that may happen; ◻ **in any case:** *I might see you tomorrow, but I'll phone in any event.*
5 in the event used to emphasize what actually happened in a situation as opposed to what you thought might happen; ◻ **as it happened:** *Extra police officers were brought in, although in the event the demonstration passed off peacefully.*
6 in the event of sth also **in the event that sth happens** used to tell people what they should do if something happens: *He left a letter for me to read in the event of his death.*
7 in the normal course of events if things happen in the normal way; ◻ **normally:** *In the normal course of events, the money should be released within about three months.*

,even-'tempered *adj* someone who is even-tempered is calm and does not easily become angry; ◻ **placid**
e·vent·ful /ɪ'ventfəl/ *adj* full of interesting or important events: *She's led quite an eventful life.* | *an eventful day*
e·ven·tide /'iːvəntaɪd/ *n* [U] *literary* evening
e·vent·ing /ɪ'ventɪŋ/ also **three-day eventing** *n* [U] a sport in which horses do three different sorts of competition, usually over three days
e·ven·tu·al /ɪ'ventʃuəl/ *adj* [only before noun] happening at the end of a long period of time or after a lot of other things have happened: *Sweden were the eventual winners of the tournament.* | *Both sides were happy with the eventual outcome of the talks.*
e·ven·tu·al·i·ty /ɪ,ventʃu'æləti/ *n plural* **eventualities** [C] *formal* something that might happen, especially something bad: **any/every eventuality** *We are prepared for any eventuality.* | *That is an unlikely eventuality.*
e·ven·tu·al·ly S1 W2 /ɪ'ventʃuəli, -tʃəli/ *adv* after a long time, or after a lot of things have happened: *He eventually escaped and made his way back to England.* | *Eventually, she got a job and moved to London.*; → see box at LASTLY
ev·er S1 W1 /'evə $ 'evər/ *adv*
1 a word meaning at any time; used mostly in questions, negatives, comparisons, or sentences with 'if': *Nothing ever seems to upset him.* | *Have you ever been to Paris?* | *I don't think I've ever been here before.* | *If you're ever in Seattle, come and see me.*
2 *formal* always: *Ever optimistic, I decided to take the exam again.*
3 hardly ever not very often: *We hardly ever go out.*
4 never ever *spoken* never: *You never ever offer to help!*
5 for ever for all time: *Nothing lasts for ever.*
6 as ever as always happens: *As ever, Joe was late.*
7 ever since continuously since: *My back has been bad ever since I fell and hurt it two years ago.*
8 ever after for all time after something: *I suppose they'll get married and live happily ever after.*
9 hotter/colder/better etc than ever even hotter etc than before: *Last night's show was better than ever.*
10 as friendly/cheerful/miserable etc as ever as friendly etc as someone or something usually is: *George was as miserable as ever.* | *The food was as bad as ever!*
11 ever so cold/wet/nice etc *BrE spoken* very cold, wet etc: *The assistant was ever so helpful.* | *Thanks ever so much.*
12 ever such a *BrE* used to emphasize what someone or something is like: *You'll like her, she's ever such a nice girl.*

13 ever-increasing/ever-present etc increasing, present etc all the time: *the ever-increasing problem of drugs in the inner cities*
14 Yours ever/Ever yours *informal* used at the end of a letter above the signature
15 if ever there was one *informal* used to say that someone or something is a typical example of something: *He's a natural comedian if ever there was one.*
ev·er·green¹ /'evəgriːn $ -ər-/ *adj* **1** an evergreen tree or bush does not lose its leaves in winter **2** an evergreen sportsman, singer etc is still good and popular even though they are fairly old: *the evergreen Cliff Richard*
evergreen² *n* [C] a tree or bush that does not lose its leaves in winter
ev·er·last·ing /,evə'lɑːstɪŋ◂ $,evər'læ-/ *adj formal* continuing for ever, even after someone has died; ◻ **eternal:** *everlasting fame* | *a symbol of God's everlasting love* | *a belief in life everlasting*
ev·er·more /,evə'mɔː $,evər'mɔːr/ *adv* **for evermore** *literary* for ever: *I will love you for evermore.*
ev·ery S1 W1 /'evri/ *determiner* [always followed by a singular countable noun]
1 used to refer to all the people or things in a particular group or all the parts of something: *We looked carefully at every car that drove past.* | *Every child will receive a certificate at the end of the course.* | *I enjoyed every minute of the film.* | *I listened carefully to every word he said.* | **every single** (=used to emphasize that you mean 'all') *He seems to know every single person in the school.* | **every last drop/bit/scrap etc** (=all of something, including even the smallest amount of it) *They made us pick up every last scrap of paper.* ⚠ **Each** or **every?** → see box at EACH
2 a) used to say how often something happens: **every day/week/month etc** (=at least once on each day, in each week etc) *They see each other every day.* | *Richard visits his mother every week.* | **every few seconds/ten days etc** *Re-apply your sunscreen every two hours.* | *Freda had to stop to rest every hundred metres or so* (=each time she had gone 100 metres). **b)** used to say how much distance there is between the things in a line: **every few feet/ten yards etc** *There were traffic lights every ten yards.*
3 every time whenever: *The roof leaks every time it rains.*
4 every now and then/again also **every so often** sometimes, but not often or regularly: *I still see her every now and then.*
5 every other the first, third, fifth etc or the second, fourth, sixth etc: *You only need to water plants every other day.* | *I visit my parents every other weekend.*
6 one in every three/two in every hundred etc used to show how common something is: *In Britain, one in every three marriages now ends in divorce.*
7 the strongest or greatest possible: *We wish you every happiness in your new home.* | *There is* **every chance** *that he will recover.* | *We have* **every reason** *to believe that the operation will be a success.* | *We have* **every intention** *of winning this competition.*
8 in every way in all ways: *The school's much better now in every way.*
9 every bit as good/important etc used to emphasize that something is equally as good, important etc as something else: *Taking regular exercise is every bit as important as having a healthy diet.* | *I loved him* **every bit as much** *as she did.*
10 every Tom, Dick, and Harry *spoken* used to mean 'everyone' or 'anyone', especially when you disapprove because there is no limit on who can be included: *I didn't want every Tom, Dick and Harry knowing about my private life.*
11 every which way *AmE informal* in every direction: *The kids ran off every which way.* → **every inch** at INCH¹ (3)
ev·ery·bod·y S1 W3 /'evribɒdi $ -bɑːdi/ *pron* everyone

ev·ery·day /ˈevrideɪ/ adj [only before noun] ordinary, usual, or happening every day: *the problems of every-day life* | *wearing everyday clothes* | *a simple, everyday object* | *Describe it in ordinary everyday language.* ⚠ Do not confuse with **every day** (=each day) *I see him every day.*

Ev·ery·man /ˈevrimæn/ n [singular] *literary* a typical, ordinary person who is not very rich and has the problems and difficulties that all people have

ev·ery·one [S1] [W1] /ˈevriwʌn/ pron every person; **everybody**: *If everyone is ready, I'll begin.* | *Send my best wishes to everyone in the family.* | *Of course every-one else thought it was hilarious!* | *Not everyone enjoys sport.* ⚠ Do not confuse with **every one** (=each one): *Every one of the CDs was damaged.*

ev·ery·place /ˈevripleɪs/ adv *AmE spoken* every-where

ev·ery·thing [S1] [W1] /ˈevriθɪŋ/ pron
1 each thing or all things: *Everything was covered in a thick layer of dust.* | *I decided to tell her everything.* | *Apart from the bus arriving late, everything else seemed to be going according to plan.*
2 all the things in your life, work etc: *Everything's fine at the moment.* | *I felt that everything was going wrong.*
3 **be/mean everything (to sb)** to be the most important thing in someone's life: *Money isn't everything.* | *His children mean everything to him.*
4 **have everything** to have all the things that people want in their lives: *What do you buy for the man who has everything?*
5 **and everything** *spoken* and a lot of other similar things: *Tina's worried about her work and everything.*
6 **have everything going for you** to have all the qualities that are likely to make you succeed: *You shouldn't worry so much – you've got everything going for you.*
7 **everything but the kitchen sink** *informal* all the equip-ment that you need and also a lot of things that you do not need – used humorously: *I think we've packed everything but the kitchen sink!*

ev·ery·where [S2] [W3] /ˈevriweə $ -wer/ also **every-place** *AmE spoken* adv
1 in or to every place: *I've looked everywhere but I can't find the map.* | *He's travelled everywhere in Europe.* | *The south should remain dry, but everywhere else will have heavy rain.*
2 **be everywhere** to be very common: *You must have seen the posters, they're everywhere.*

e·vict /ɪˈvɪkt/ v [T] to tell someone legally that they must leave the house they are living in: **evict sb from sth** *They were unable to pay the rent, and were evicted from their home.* | **be/get evicted** *They refused to leave and were forcibly evicted* (=evicted by force). | *attempts to have them evicted* —**eviction** /ɪˈvɪkʃən/ n [C,U]: *The family now faces eviction from their home.*

ev·i·dence¹ [S3] [W3] /ˈevɪdəns/ n
1 [U] facts or signs that show clearly that something exists or is true: [+of] *At present we have no evidence of life on other planets.* | [+for] *There is no evidence for these claims.* | **evidence that** *Do you have evidence that this treatment works?* | *They had failed to **provide evidence** of sufficient financial backing.* | **clear/strong/good evidence** *There is now clear evidence that these chemicals are damaging the environment.* | **medical/scientific etc evidence** *Medical evidence shows that men are more likely to have heart attacks than women.* | *The study produced one interesting **piece of evidence**.* | *There is **not a shred of evidence** to support the theory.*
2 [U] information that is given in a court of law in order to prove that someone is guilty or not guilty: *Murrow's evidence was enough to convict Hayes of murder.* | *He refused to **give evidence** at the trial.* | [+against] *There was very little evidence against the two men.* | **in evidence** *The documents may be used in evidence at the trial.*
3 **be in evidence** *formal* to be present and easily seen or noticed: *The police are always in evidence at football matches.* → KING'S EVIDENCE, QUEEN'S EVIDENCE, STATE'S EVIDENCE

evidence² v [T usually passive] *formal* to show that something exists or is true: *The volcano is still active, as evidenced by the recent eruption.*

ev·i·dent [W3] /ˈevɪdənt/ adj easy to see, notice, or understand; **obvious**, **clear**: **evident that** *It was evi-dent that she was unhappy.* | *It soon **became evident** that she was seriously ill.* | *It was **clearly evident** that the company was in serious financial difficulties.* | [+to] *It was evident to me that he was not telling the truth.* | [+in] *The growing popularity of the subject is evident in the numbers of students wanting to study it.* | *Bob began eating his lunch with evident enjoyment.* → SELF-EVIDENT

evidential /ˌevɪˈdenʃəl/ adj able to be used as evi-dence, or relating to evidence: *All jury members should have a copy of the evidential data.* —**evidentially** adv

ev·i·dent·ly /ˈevɪdəntli $ -dənt-, -dent-/ adv **1** used to say that something is true because you can see that it is true; **clearly**: *She was evidently a heavy smoker.* | *He was evidently in pain.* | *She was evidently upset by what she saw.* | [sentence adverb]: *Evidently, the build-ers had finished and gone home early.* **2** used to say that you have been told that something is true; **apparently**: *He was evidently a rude, unpleasant child.* | [sentence adverb]: *Evidently, the local authority are planning to close the school.*

e·vil¹ [W3] /ˈiːvəl/ adj
1 **BAD** someone who is evil deliberately does very cruel things to harm other people: *an evil dictator responsible for the deaths of millions* | *his evil deeds*
2 **WRONG** something that is evil is morally wrong because it harms people: *They condemned slavery as evil.*
3 **UNPLEASANT** very unpleasant: *an evil smell* | *a puddle of evil black liquid*
4 **DEVIL** connected with the Devil and having special powers to harm people: *evil spirits* | *an evil spell*
5 **the evil eye** the power, which some people believe exists, to harm people by looking at them: *He claimed to have the power of the evil eye.*
6 **the evil hour/day etc** a time when you expect some-thing unpleasant or difficult to happen: *Don't delay, you're only putting off the evil hour.* —**evilly** adv: *Jeff grinned evilly as he picked up the phone.*

evil² n **1** [C] something that is very bad or harmful: *She wanted to protect her children from the evils of the outside world.* | *Poverty is one of the greatest social evils of our time.* | *the evils of capitalism* **2** [U] cruel or morally bad behaviour in general: *There is too much evil in the world.* | *the eternal struggle between good and evil* → **the lesser of two evils** at LESSER (2); → **necessary evil** at NECESSARY¹ (3)

'evil-ˌdoer n [C] *old-fashioned* someone who commits crimes or does evil things

evil-minded adj immoral and cruel, and likely to cause a lot of harm or damage: *an evil-minded dictator*

e·vince /ɪˈvɪns/ v [T] *formal* to show a feeling or have a quality in a way that people can easily notice: *She evinced no surprise at seeing them together.*

e·vis·ce·rate /ɪˈvɪsəreɪt/ v [T] *formal* or *technical* to cut the organs out of a person's or animal's body

e·voc·a·tive /ɪˈvɒkətɪv $ ɪˈvɑː-/ adj making people remember something by producing a feeling or memory in them: [+of] *a picture that is wonderfully evocative of a hot, summer's day* | *beautiful, evocative music*

e·voke /ɪˈvəʊk $ ɪˈvoʊk/ v [T] to produce a strong feeling or memory in someone: *The photographs evoked strong memories of our holidays in France.* | *His appearance is bound to evoke sympathy.* | *Her speech evoked a hostile response.* —**evocation** /ˌevəˈkeɪʃən, ˌiːvəʊ- $ ˌevə-, ˌiːvoʊ-/ n [C,U]: *The poem is an evocation of lost love.*

ev·o·lu·tion W3 /ˌiːvəˈluːʃən, ˌevə- $ ˌevə-/ *n* [U]
1 the scientific idea that plants and animals develop and change gradually over a long period of time: [+of] *the evolution of mammals* | *the **theory of evolution*** **2** the gradual change and development of an idea, situation, or object: [+of] *the evolution of the computer*

ev·o·lu·tion·a·ry /ˌiːvəˈluːʃənəri, ˌevə- $ ˌevəˈluːʃəneri/ *adj* **1** relating to the way in which plants and animals develop and change gradually over a long period of time: *the evolutionary development of birds* | *Some scientists have rejected evolutionary theory.* **2** relating to the way in which ideas or situations gradually change and develop over a long period of time: *He is in favour of gradual, evolutionary social change.*

e·volve /ɪˈvɒlv $ ɪˈvɑːlv/ *v* [I,T] **1** if an animal or plant evolves, it changes gradually over a long period of time: [+from] *Fish evolved from prehistoric sea creatures.* | *Animals have evolved camouflage to protect themselves from predators.* **2** to develop and change gradually over a long period of time: *The school has evolved its own style of teaching.* | *Businesses need to evolve rapidly.* | [+out of] *The idea evolved out of work done by British scientists.* | [+into] *The group gradually evolved into a political party.*

ewe /juː/ *n* [C] a female sheep

ew·er /ˈjuːə $ ˈjuːər/ *n* [C] a large container for water, that was used in the past

ex /eks/ *n* [C usually singular] *informal* someone's former wife, husband, GIRLFRIEND, or BOYFRIEND: *I bumped into my ex in town.*

ex- /eks/ *prefix* former and still living: *his ex-wife* | *an ex-England cricketer*

ex·a·cer·bate /ɪgˈzæsəbeɪt $ -sər-/ *v* [T] to make a bad situation worse: *The recession has exacerbated this problem.* | *I don't want to exacerbate the situation.* —**exacerbation** /ɪgˌzæsəˈbeɪʃən $ -sər-/ *n* [U]

ex·act¹ S3 /ɪgˈzækt/ *adj*
1 completely correct in every detail: *Police are still investigating the exact cause of the accident.* | *What were his exact words?* | *The timing had to be exact.* | **exact location/position/spot etc** *The exact location of the hostages is unknown.* | **exact date/time/number/amount etc** *I know her birthday's in July, but I can't remember the exact date.* | **exact copy/replica** etc *It's not an exact copy, but most people wouldn't notice the difference.* | *Some concepts in Chinese medicine have no exact equivalent in Western medicine.*
2 to be exact *formal* used to emphasize that what you are saying is exact: *She has worked at the bank for many years, nine to be exact.*
3 the exact colour/moment/type etc used to emphasize that the same thing is involved: *the exact colour I was looking for* | *He came into the room at the exact moment I mentioned his name.* | *That's the **exact same** thing my dad said.*
4 the exact opposite (of sb/sth) someone or something that is as different as possible from another person or thing: *Gina's the exact opposite of her little sister.*
5 sth is not an exact science if you say that an activity is not an exact science, you mean that it involves opinions, guessing etc: *Predicting the weather is not an exact science.*
6 someone who is exact is very careful and thorough in what they do; ◻ **precise** —**exactness** *n* [U]

exact² *v* [T] **1** *formal* to demand and get something from someone by using threats, force etc: **exact sth from sb** *I exacted a promise from Ros that she wouldn't say a word.* **2 exact revenge (on sb)** if someone exacts revenge, they punish a person who has harmed them: *Leonard was determined to exact revenge on his wife's killer.* **3 exact a high/heavy price** if something exacts a high or a heavy price, it has a very bad effect on a person or on a situation: *The years of conflict have exacted a heavy price.*

ex·act·ing /ɪgˈzæktɪŋ/ *adj* demanding a lot of effort, careful work, or skill; ◻ **demanding**: *She was an exacting woman to work for.* | **exacting standards/demands/requirements etc** *He could never live up to his father's exacting standards.*

ex·act·i·tude /ɪgˈzæktɪˌtjuːd $ -tuːd/ *n* [U] *formal* the state of being exact

ex·act·ly S1 W2 /ɪgˈzæktli/ *adv*
1 used to emphasize that a number, amount, or piece of information is or should be completely correct in every detail: *It's exactly half past five.* | *The figures may not be exactly right, but they're close enough.* | **exactly where/what/when etc** *I can't remember exactly what she said.* | *It's a tragic situation and no one will ever know exactly what happened.* | **why/what/where etc exactly...?** *Where exactly did you stay in Portugal?*
2 used to emphasize that something is the same or different; ◻ **precisely**: *That's exactly what we've been trying to tell you.* | *It's exactly the kind of work I've been looking for.* | *She tries to be **exactly like** her older sister.* | *Kevin's teachers saw him as quiet and serious, but with his friends he was **exactly the opposite**.* | *The two candidates responded to the question in **exactly the same** way.*
3 not exactly *spoken* **a)** used as a reply to show that what someone has said is not completely correct or true: *'You hate Lee, don't you?' 'Not exactly. I just think he's a bit annoying, that's all.'* **b)** used to show that you mean the complete opposite, either humorously, or when you are annoyed; ◻ **hardly**: *I wouldn't bother asking Dave – he's not exactly Einstein (=he is stupid).*
4 *spoken* used as a reply to show that you think what someone has said is completely correct or true: *'So you think we should sell the house?' 'Exactly.'*

ex·ag·ge·rate /ɪgˈzædʒəreɪt/ *v* [I,T] to make something seem better, larger, worse etc than it really is: *I couldn't sleep for three days – I'm not exaggerating.* | **it's easy/difficult/impossible to exaggerate sth** *It's difficult to exaggerate the importance of sleep.*

ex·ag·ge·rat·ed /ɪgˈzædʒəreɪtd/ *adj* **1** if something is exaggerated, it is described as better, larger etc than it really is: *The revenue figures may be **slightly exaggerated**.* | **grossly/greatly/wildly exaggerated** *The danger had been greatly exaggerated.* **2** an exaggerated sound or movement is emphasized to make people notice: *an exaggerated sigh* | *He made an exaggerated bow.* | *He spoke with an exaggerated New York accent.* —**exaggeratedly** *adv*

ex·ag·ge·ra·tion /ɪgˌzædʒəˈreɪʃən/ *n* [C,U] a statement or way of saying something that makes something seem better, larger etc than it really is: *It would be an exaggeration to say that we were close friends.* | *It is **no exaggeration** to say that everyone will be affected by the new policy.* | *The situation can be described, without exaggeration, as disastrous.* | **slight/gross exaggeration** *That sounds like a slight exaggeration.*

ex·alt /ɪgˈzɔːlt $ -ˈzɒːlt/ *v* [T] *formal* **1** to put someone or something into a high rank or position **2** to praise someone, especially God: *Exalt ye the Lord.*

ex·al·ta·tion /ˌegzɔːlˈteɪʃən, ˌeksɔːl- $ -ɒːl-/ *n formal* **1** a very strong feeling of happiness **2** the state of being put into a high rank or position

ex·alt·ed /ɪgˈzɔːltd $ -ɒːl-/ *adj* **1** having a very high rank and highly respected: *I felt shy in such exalted company.* **2** *formal* filled with a great feeling of joy

ex·am S1 /ɪgˈzæm/ *n* [C]
1 a spoken or written test of knowledge, especially an important one: *At the end of each level, you **take an exam**.* | **pass/fail an exam** *Did you pass the exam?* | *He failed the school's **entrance exam**.* | **chemistry/French etc exam** *How did you do **in your exams**?* | *the stresses of **final exams*** | *The **exam results** will be posted up tomorrow.* | **oral/written exam** *Drivers have to take a written exam as part of their tests.* | **sit an exam** (=take an exam) *BrE formal: He'll sit his exams next summer.*
2 *AmE* the paper on which the questions for an exam

are written: *Do not open your exams until I tell you.*
3 *AmE* a set of medical tests: *an eye exam*

ex·am·i·na·tion S3 W2 /ɪɡˌzæmɪ̩'neɪʃən/ *n*
1 [C] *formal* a spoken or written test of knowledge, especially an important one; ▤ **exam**: *The examination results will be announced in September.* | *He's already taken the* **entrance examination**.
2 [C,U] the process of looking at something carefully in order to see what it is like: [+**of**] *a detailed examination of population statistics* | **under examination** *The proposals are still under examination.* | *The issues need* **further examination**. | **on examination** *On closer examination the vases were seen to be cracked.*
3 [C] a set of medical tests: *All patients had a complete physical examination.* | *A* **post-mortem examination** (=an examination on a dead body) *showed that he died from head injuries.*
4 [C,U] *law* the process of asking questions to get specific information, especially in a court of law → CROSS-EXAMINE

ex·am·ine S3 W2
/ɪɡ'zæmɪ̩n/ *v* [T]

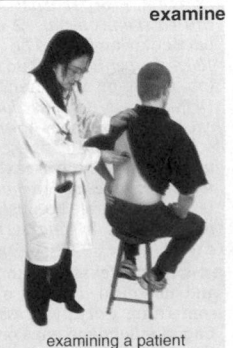
examine

1 to look at something carefully and thoroughly because you want to find out more about it: *A team of divers was sent down to examine the wreck.* | *Hegel's philosophy will be examined in detail in Chapter 4.* | **examine how/whether/what etc** *In the course, we will examine how and why Spain became a democracy in 1931.* | **examine sth for sth** *The police will have to examine the weapon for fingerprints.*; → see box at CONTROL²

examining a patient

2 if a doctor examines you, they look at your body to check that you are healthy
3 *formal* to ask someone questions to test their knowledge of a subject; ▤ **test**: **examine sb in/on sth** *You will be examined on American history.*
4 *law* to officially ask someone questions in a court of law → CROSS-EXAMINE

Frequencies of the verbs **examine, take/have a look at,** and **inspect** in spoken and written English.

SPOKEN
examine
take/have a look at
inspect

WRITTEN
examine
take/have a look at
inspect

100   200   300   400   500   per million

This graph shows that the expressions **have a look at** and **take a look at** are much more common in spoken English than the words **examine** or **inspect**. This is because **have a look at** and **take a look at** are much more general than **examine** or **inspect**, which mean to look at something carefully in order to find out about it or check if it is satisfactory. They are more common in written English.

ex·am·in·er /ɪɡ'zæmɪ̩nə $ -ər/ *n* [C] someone from a university, college, or professional institution who tests students' knowledge or ability

ex·am·ple S1 W1 /ɪɡ'zɑːmpəl $ ɪɡ'zæm-/ *n* [C]
1 a specific fact, idea, person, or thing that is used to explain or support a general idea, or to show what is typical of a larger group: [+**of**] *Can anyone give me an example of a transitive verb?* | **good/typical/prime/classic etc example** *This church is a good example of*

Gothic architecture. | *She* **cited** *a number of recent* **examples** *to support her theory.* | *Certain life events have to be registered by law. The most* **obvious examples** *are births, marriages and deaths.*
2 for example used before mentioning a specific thing, person, place etc in order to explain what you mean or to support an argument: *Many countries, for example Mexico and Japan, have a lot of earthquakes.* | *Car prices can vary a lot. For example, in Belgium the VW Golf costs $1000 less than in Britain.*
3 someone whose behaviour is very good and should be copied by others, or this type of behaviour: [+**to**] *Her courage is an example to us all.* | *Parents should* **set an example** *for their children.* | *I suggest you* **follow** *Rosie's* **example** (=copy her behaviour) *and start doing regular exercise.* | *The team captain* **leads by example**. | *She's a* **shining example** (=a very good example) *of what a mother should be.*
4 make an example of sb to punish someone so that other people are afraid to do the same thing

ex·as·pe·rate /ɪɡ'zɑːspəreɪt $ ɪɡ'zæ-/ *v* [T] to make someone very annoyed by continuing to do something that upsets them: *It exasperates me to hear comments like that.*

ex·as·pe·rat·ed /ɪɡ'zɑːspəreɪtɪ̩d $ -'zæs-/ *adj* very annoyed and upset: [+**with**] *He was becoming exasperated with the child.* | *an exasperated look.* —**exasperatedly** *adv*

ex·as·pe·rat·ing /ɪɡ'zɑːspəreɪtɪŋ $ -'zæs-/ *adj* extremely annoying: *You have this exasperating habit of never looking at me!* —**exasperatingly** *adv*

ex·as·pe·ra·tion /ɪɡˌzɑːspə'reɪʃən $ ɪɡˌzæs-/ *n* [U] when you feel annoyed because someone continues to do something that is upsetting you: *Carol sighed in exasperation.*

ex·ca·vate /'ekskəveɪt/ *v* [I,T] **1** if a scientist or ARCHAEOLOGIST excavates an area of land, they dig carefully to find ancient objects, bones etc: *Schliemann excavated the ancient city of Troy.* → see picture at DIG **2** *formal* to make a hole in the ground by digging up soil etc —**excavation** /ˌekskə'veɪʃən/ *n* [C,U]

ex·ca·va·tor /'ekskəveɪtə $ -ər/ *n* [C] **1** *BrE* a large machine that digs and moves earth and soil; ▤ **steam shovel** *AmE* **2** someone who digs to find things that have been buried under the ground for a long time

ex·ceed W3 /ɪk'siːd/ *v* [T] *formal*
1 to be more than a particular number or amount: *Working hours must not exceed 42 hours a week.* | *His performance* **exceeded** *our* **expectations**.
2 to go beyond what rules or laws say you are allowed to do: *He was fined for exceeding the speed limit.* | *The riot police had* **exceeded** *their* **authority**.

ex·ceed·ing·ly /ɪk'siːdɪŋli/ *adv formal* extremely: *Thank you. You've been exceedingly kind.*

ex·cel /ɪk'sel/ *v* **excelled, excelling** **1** [I, not in progressive] to do something very well, or much better than most people: [+**at/in**] *Rick has always excelled at foreign languages.* **2 excel yourself** *BrE* to do something better than you usually do: *Graham has excelled himself with the new exhibition.*

ex·cel·lence /'eksələns/ *n* [U] the quality of being excellent: [+**of**] *the excellence of the performance* | [+**in**] *the university's reputation for excellence.* | *centres of academic excellence* → PAR EXCELLENCE

Ex·cel·len·cy /'eksələnsi/ *n* **Your/His/Her Excellency** a way of talking to or about people who hold high positions in the state or the church: *His Excellency the Spanish ambassador*

ex·cel·lent S1 W2 /'eksələnt/ *adj*
1 extremely good or of very high quality: *What an excellent idea!* | *His car is in excellent condition.* | *Second-hand computers can be excellent value.*
2 *spoken* said when you approve of something; ▤ **great**: *'I'll bring the books over tonight.' 'Excellent.'* —**excellently** *adv*

E

ex·cept¹ S2 W2 /ɪkˈsept/ *conjunction, prep*
1 used to introduce the only person, thing, action, fact, or situation about which a statement is not true: *The office is open every day except Sundays.* | *You can have any of the cakes except this one.* | [+**for**] *Everyone went except for Scott and Dan.* | *She felt fine except for being a little tired.* | **except (that)** *Clarissa could think of nothing to say except that she was so sorry.* | [+**in/by/to** etc] *Staff are not permitted to make personal phone calls except in an emergency.* | **except when/where/if** *Benson kept the studio locked except when he was working there.* | **except do sth** *She had nothing to do except spend money.* | **except to do sth** *He wouldn't talk about work, except to say that he was busy.*
2 used to give the reason why something was not done or did not happen: **except (that)** *Liz would have run, except that she didn't want to appear to be in a hurry.*
3 *spoken* used to mention a fact that makes what you have just said seem less true: **except (that)** *I have earrings just like those, except they're blue* | *A date book would make a great gift, except that a lot of people already have one.*

WORD CHOICE: except, besides, apart from, unless
except means 'not including' or 'but not': *They invited everyone except Julie.*
besides means 'in addition to': *Besides Italy (NOT except Italy), I would like to visit France and Spain.*
apart from can be used with either meaning: *I ate everything apart from (OR except) the soup.* | *What do you like doing apart from (OR besides) swimming?*
except is not used to introduce another clause. Use **unless** or **except if, except when, except while, except that**: *We won't go unless you really want to (NOT except you really want to).* | *I cycle to work, except when it rains (NOT except it rains).*
In spoken English, people sometimes leave out 'that': *The play went well, except (that) a few people forgot their lines.*

---

ex·cept² *v* [T] *formal* to not include something: **except sth from sth** *High technology equipment would be excepted from any trade agreement.*

ex·cept·ed /ɪkˈseptɪd/ *adv* **sb/sth excepted** used to say that you are not including a particular person or thing in a statement about something: *History excepted, Peter has made good progress in all subjects this term.* → **present company excepted** at PRESENT¹ (7)

ex·cept·ing /ɪkˈseptɪŋ/ *prep formal* used to introduce the only thing or person in a group about which a statement is not true; ■ **except (for)**: *O'Rourke answered all the questions excepting the last one.*

ex·cep·tion S2 W2 /ɪkˈsepʃən/ *n* [C,U]
1 something or someone that is not included in a general statement or does not follow a rule or pattern: *It's been cold, but today's an exception.* | **with the exception of sb/sth** *We all laughed, with the exception of Maggie.* | **without exception** *Each plant, without exception, contains some kind of salt.* | **notable/important/ significant exception** *With one or two notable exceptions, there are few women conductors.* | **minor/ major exception** *With a few minor exceptions, the new edition is much like the previous one.* | *The law applies to all EU countries; Britain is no exception.* | *We don't usually accept checks, but for you we'll make an exception* (=not include you in this rule). | *The spelling of this word is an interesting exception to the rule.* | *Successful two-career couples are still the exception, not the rule* (=used to emphasize that something is unusual).
2 sb/sth is the exception that proves the rule *spoken* used to say that the fact that something is not true or does not exist in one situation emphasizes the fact that it is true or exists in general: *Most people here are very dedicated; I'm afraid Rhea's the exception that proves the rule.*

3 take exception to sth to be angry or upset because of something: *Tom took great exception to my remark about Americans.*

ex·cep·tion·al /ɪkˈsepʃənəl/ *adj* **1** unusually good; ■ **outstanding**: *Richard is an exceptional student.* | *exceptional bravery* **2** unusual and likely to happen often: *This is an exceptional case; I've never seen anything like it before.* | *Promotion in the first year is only given in exceptional circumstances.* → see box at UNUSUAL

ex·cep·tion·al·ly /ɪkˈsepʃənəli/ *adv* [+ adj/adv] extremely; ■ **outstandingly**: *She defended her position exceptionally well.* | *an exceptionally talented player*

ex·cerpt /ˈeksɜːpt $ -ɜːrpt/ *n* [C] a short piece taken from a book, poem, piece of music etc: [+**of/from**] *An excerpt of the speech appeared in the Sunday paper.*
—**excerpt** *v* [T usually passive]

ex·cess¹ /ɪkˈses, ˈekses/ *n* **1** [singular, U] a larger amount of something than is allowed or needed: *After you apply the oil, wait 20 minutes before wiping off any excess.* | [+**of**] *It was an excess of enthusiasm that caused the problem.* **2 in excess of sth** more than a particular amount: *The car reached speeds in excess of 100 miles per hour.* **3 do sth to excess** to do something too much or too often, so that it may harm you: *Drinking is OK as long as you don't do it to excess.* **4 excesses** [plural] harmful actions that are socially or morally unacceptable: [+**of**] *The government was unable to **curb** the excesses of the secret police.* | *the worst excesses of journalism* **5** [U] behaviour which is not acceptable because it is too extreme: *The minister preached a long sermon against the dangers of excess.*

ex·cess² /ˈekses/ *adj* [only before noun] **1** additional and not needed because there is already enough of something: *Cut any excess fat from the meat.* **2 excess baggage/luggage** bags or cases that weigh more than the legal limit that you can take on a plane

ex·ces·sive /ɪkˈsesɪv/ *adj* much more than is reasonable or necessary: *his excessive drinking* | *$15 for two beers seems a little excessive.* —**excessively** *adv*: *excessively high taxes*

ex·change¹ S2 W1 /ɪksˈtʃeɪndʒ/ *n*
1 GIVING/RECEIVING [C,U] the act of giving someone something and receiving something else from them: [+**of**] *an exchange of political prisoners* | **in exchange for sth** *I've offered to paint the kitchen in exchange for a week's accommodation.* | *Four of my cassettes for your Madonna CD is a fair exchange.* → PART EXCHANGE
2 ARGUMENT/DISCUSSION [C] a short conversation, usually between two people who are angry with each other: *a quiet exchange between the judge and the clerk* | *The DJ was fired after a heated exchange* (=a very angry conversation) *on air with a call-in listener.*
3 exchange of ideas/information etc when people discuss or share ideas, information etc: *The organization is dedicated to the free exchange of information.*
4 STH YOU BUY [C] the act of giving something you have bought back to the store where you bought it, for example because it does not work, fit etc, and taking something else instead: *The store's policy is not to allow returns or exchanges.*
5 MONEY [U] a process in which you change money from one CURRENCY to another: *Most capital cities have extensive exchange facilities.*
6 STUDENTS/TEACHERS [C] an arrangement in which a student, teacher etc visits another school or university to work or study: **on an exchange (with sb)** *I'm here for one term, on an exchange with Dr. Fisher.*
7 JOBS/HOMES ETC [C] an arrangement in which you stay in someone's home, do someone's job etc for a short time while that person stays in your home, does your job etc: *Kate's in New York on an employee exchange so she can get some more training.*
8 FIGHT [C] an event during a war or fight when two people, armies etc shoot or fire MISSILES at each other: **exchange of fire/gunfire**
9 BUILDING corn/wool/cotton etc exchange a larg

building in a town that was used in the past for buying and selling corn, wool etc → LABOUR EXCHANGE, STOCK EXCHANGE

exchange² v [T] **1 a)** to give someone something and receive the same kind of thing from them at the same time: *We still exchange gifts at Christmas.* | *At the end of the game players traditionally exchange shirts with each other.* | *We exchanged addresses and phone numbers.* **b)** to give someone something and receive something different from them; ◨ **change**: **exchange sth for sth** *Where can I exchange my dollars for pounds?* **2** to replace one thing with another; ◨ **swap**: **exchange sth for sth** *He exchanged the black jacket for a blue one.* **3 exchange words/looks etc (with sb)** if two people exchange words, looks etc, they talk to each other, look at each other etc: *Until this evening I had never so much as exchanged a word with him.* | *The two women exchanged glances and laughed.* | *I went over and exchanged greetings with everyone.* **4 exchange blows (with sb)** if two people exchange blows, they hit each other **5 exchange information/ideas etc** to discuss something or share information, ideas etc: *It's a place where people can chat and exchange ideas.* **6 exchange contracts** especially BrE to complete the final stage of buying a house by signing a contract with the person you are buying it from —**exchangeable** adj

ex'change rate n [C] the value of the money of one country compared to that of another country: *a more favourable exchange rate*

ex'change rate ,mechanism n [U] *ERM* a system for controlling the exchange rate between the money of one country and that of another

ex'change ,student n [C] a student who goes to a foreign country to study, usually as a part of a programme: *an 18-year-old exchange student from France*

Ex·cheq·uer /ɪksˈtʃekə $ ˈekstʃekər/ n the **Exchequer** the British government department that is responsible for collecting taxes and paying out public money; ◨ **treasury**

ex·cise¹ /ˈeksaɪz/ n [C,U] the government tax that is put on the goods that are produced and used inside a country: **excise officer** (=someone who collects excise) | **excise duty/tax** (=the money paid as excise) *excise duty on tobacco*; → see also CUSTOMS AND EXCISE

ex·cise² /ɪkˈsaɪz/ v [T] formal to remove or get rid of something, especially by cutting it out: *The tumour was excised.* —**excision** /ɪkˈsɪʒən/ n [C,U]

ex·cit·a·ble /ɪkˈsaɪtəbəl/ adj becoming excited too easily: *A puppy is naturally affectionate and excitable.* —**excitability** /ɪkˌsaɪtəˈbɪləti/ n [U]

ex·cite /ɪkˈsaɪt/ v [T] **1** [not in progressive] to make someone feel happy, interested, or eager: *His playing is technically brilliant, but it doesn't excite me.* **2** formal to cause a particular feeling or reaction; ◨ **arouse**: **excite interest/curiosity/sympathy etc** *The court case has excited a lot of public interest.* | *He tried not to do anything to excite the suspicion of the police.* | **excite comment/speculation/a reaction** *The book excited very little comment on this side of the Atlantic.* **3** to make someone feel sexual desire; ◨ **arouse 4** technical to make an organ, nerve etc in your body react or increase its activity

ex·cit·ed /ɪkˈsaɪtɪd/ adj **1** happy, interested, or hopeful because something good has happened or will happen: *Steve flies home tomorrow – we're all really excited.* | [+about] *Maria's starting to get pretty excited about the wedding.* | [+by/at] *We're all excited by the prospect of a party.* | **excited to do sth** *Michelle sounded excited to hear from him.* | **excited (that)** *I'm so excited that we're going to New York.* | *The food was nothing to get excited about* (=not very good or special). | *excited crowds of shoppers* **2** very nervous and upset about something so that you cannot relax: [+about] *There's no point getting excited about it. We can't change things.* **3** feeling sexual desire —**excitedly** adv: *People had gathered and were talking excitedly.*

ex·cite·ment S3 W3 /ɪkˈsaɪtmənt/ n **1** [U] the feeling of being excited: *The news caused great excitement among scientists.* | *sexual excitement* | [+of] *the excitement of becoming a parent* | [+at] *children filled with excitement at the thought of visiting Disneyland* | **wild/flushed/trembling etc with excitement** *She came in bubbling with excitement.* | **in sb's/the excitement** *In his excitement, he knocked over a lamp.* | *In the excitement of the moment, I forgot my camera.* **2** [C] an exciting event or situation: *We were both new to the excitements of life in the big city.*

ex·cit·ing S2 W3 /ɪkˈsaɪtɪŋ/ adj making you feel excited: *an exciting discovery* | *'Julia and Paul are getting married!' 'Oh, how exciting!'* | *I've got some very exciting news for you.* | *Let's do something exciting.* | *Melanie finds her work exciting and rewarding.* | **exciting opportunity/possibility/prospect etc** *exciting job opportunities* —**excitingly** adv: *the most excitingly original movie of the year*

ex·claim /ɪkˈskleɪm/ v [I,T] written to say something suddenly and loudly because you are surprised, angry, or excited: *'No!' she exclaimed in shock.*

ex·cla·ma·tion /ˌekskləˈmeɪʃən/ n [C] a sound, word, or short sentence that you say suddenly and loudly because you are surprised, angry, or excited: [+of] *horrified exclamations of disgust*

,excla'mation mark BrE; **,excla'mation point** AmE n the mark (!) that you write after a sentence or word that expresses surprise, anger, or excitement; → see picture at PUNCTUATION MARK

ex·clude S2 W3 /ɪkˈskluːd/ v [T] **1** to deliberately not include something; ◨ **include**: *a special diet that excludes dairy products* | *The judges decided to exclude evidence which had been unfairly attained.* | **exclude sth from sth** *Some of the data was specifically excluded from the report.* **2** to not allow someone to take part in something or not allow them to enter a place, especially in a way that seems wrong or unfair; ◨ **include**: *a mainstream exhibition that excluded women artists* | **exclude sb from (doing) sth** *The press had been deliberately excluded from the event.* | *Sarah heard the other girls talking and laughing and felt excluded.* **3** BrE to officially make a child leave their school because of their bad behaviour **4** to decide that something is not a possibility: *Social workers have excluded sexual abuse as a reason for the child's disappearance.* | *At this stage we cannot entirely exclude the possibility of staff cuts.*

ex·clud·ing /ɪkˈskluːdɪŋ/ prep not including – used especially when you are making a list or calculating a total: *Television is watched in 97 per cent of American homes (excluding Alaska and Hawaii).*

ex·clu·sion /ɪkˈskluːʒən/ n **1** [C,U] when someone is not allowed to take part in something or enter a place; ◨ **inclusion**: [+from] *the country's exclusion from the United Nations* **2** [C,U] BrE when a child is officially made to leave their school because of their bad behaviour **3 do sth to the exclusion of sth** to do something so much that you do not do, include, or have time for other things: *Your essays tend to concentrate on one theme to the exclusion of everything else.* **4** [C] something that is excluded from a contract; ◨ **inclusion**: *You will be sent full details of the exclusions of your insurance policy.* —**exclusionary** adj: *exclusionary business practices*

ex'clusion ,zone n [C] an area that people are not allowed to enter because it is dangerous or because secret things happen there: *the military exclusion zone*

ex·clu·sive¹ /ɪkˈskluːsɪv/ adj **1** available or belonging only to particular people, and not shared: **exclusive access/rights/use etc** *Our figure skating club has exclusive use of the rink on Mondays.* | **exclusive report/**

E

1 000, 2 000, 3 000, most frequent words in S poken and W ritten English

interview/coverage etc *Tune in to our exclusive coverage of Wimbledon.* | [+to] *This offer is exclusive to readers of The Sun.* **2** exclusive places, organizations, clothes etc are so expensive that not many people can afford to use or buy them: *Bel Air is an exclusive suburb of Los Angeles.* | *an exclusive girls' school* **3** deliberately not allowing someone to do something or be part of a group: *a racially exclusive hiring policy* **4 mutually exclusive** if two things are mutually exclusive, you cannot have or do both of them: *Lesbianism and motherhood are not mutually exclusive.* **5 exclusive of sth** not including something; **🔒 inclusive of sth**: *Our prices are exclusive of sales tax.* **6** concerned with only one thing: *The committee's exclusive focus will be to improve public transportation.* —**exclusivity** /ˌeksklu:ˈsɪvˌti/ also **exclusiveness** n [U]: *the exclusivity of private education*

exclusive² n [C] an important or exciting story that is printed in only one newspaper, because that newspaper was the first to find out about it: *a New York Post exclusive about the Kennedy marriage*

ex·clu·sive·ly /ɪkˈsklu:sɪvli/ adv only: *This offer is available exclusively to people who call now.*

ex·com·mu·ni·cate /ˌekskəˈmju:nˌkeɪt/ v [T] to punish someone by no longer allowing them to be a member of the Roman Catholic church —**excommunication** /ˌekskəmju:nˌˈkeɪʃən/ n [C,U]

,**ex-'con** n [C] *informal* a criminal who has been in prison but who is now free

ex·co·ri·ate /ɪkˈskɔ:rieɪt/ v [T] *formal* to express a very bad opinion of a book, play etc: *an excoriating review in the Times*

ex·cre·ment /ˈekskrɪˌmənt/ n [U] *formal* the solid waste material that you get rid of through your BOWELS

ex·cres·cence /ɪkˈskresəns/ n [C] *formal* **1** something that is bad, unnecessary, or ugly – used to show disapproval: *The new museum is nothing but an excrescence on the urban landscape.* **2** an ugly growth on an animal or plant

ex·cre·ta /ɪkˈskri:tə/ n [plural,U] *formal* the solid or liquid waste material that people and animals produce and get rid of from their bodies

ex·crete /ɪkˈskri:t/ v [I,T] *formal* to get rid of waste material from your body through your BOWELS, your skin etc; → **secrete**

ex·cre·tion /ɪkˈskri:ʃən/ n **1** [U] the process of getting rid of waste material from your body **2** [C,U] the waste material that people or animals get rid of from their bodies

ex·cru·ci·at·ing /ɪkˈskru:ʃieɪtɪŋ/ adj **1** extremely painful: *When I bend my arm, the pain is excruciating.* **2** if something is excruciating, it is extremely unpleasant, for example because it is boring or embarrassing: *Helen described the events of the night before in excruciating detail.* —**excruciatingly** adv: *His poetry is excruciatingly bad.*

ex·cul·pate /ˈekskʌlpeɪt/ v [T] *formal* to prove that someone is not guilty of something —**exculpation** /ˌekskʌlˈpeɪʃən/ n [U]

ex·cur·sion /ɪkˈskɜ:ʃən $ ɪkˈskɜ:rʒən/ n [C] **1** a short journey arranged so that a group of people can visit a place, especially while they are on holiday: [+to] *Included in the tour is an excursion to the Grand Canyon.* | **on an excursion** *We went on an excursion to the Pyramids.* **2** a short journey made for a particular purpose; **🔒 trip**: *a shopping excursion* **3 excursion into sth** *formal* an attempt to experience or learn about something that is new to you: *the company's excursion into new markets*

ex·cus·a·ble /ɪkˈskju:zəbəl/ adj behaviour that is excusable can be forgiven; **🔒 forgiveable**; **🔒 inexcusable**: *an excusable reaction of anger*

ex·cuse¹ [S2] /ɪkˈskju:z/ v [T]
1 excuse me *spoken* **a)** used when you want to get

someone's attention politely, especially when you want to ask a question: *Excuse me, can you tell me the way to the museum please?* **b)** used to say that you are sorry for doing something rude or embarrassing: *Oh, excuse me. I didn't know anyone was here.* **c)** used to ask someone politely to move so that you can walk past: *Excuse me, could I just squeeze past?* **d)** used to politely tell someone that you are leaving a place: *Excuse me a moment. I'll be right back.* **e)** used when you disagree with someone but want to be polite about it; **🔒 I'm sorry**: *Excuse me, but I don't think that's what he meant at all.* **f)** AmE used to show that you disagree with someone or are very surprised or upset by what they have just said: *'You're going to pay, right?' 'Excuse me?'* **g)** especially AmE used to ask someone to repeat something that they have just said; **🔒 pardon me**: *'What time is it?' 'Excuse me?' 'I asked you what time it is.'*
2 FORGIVE to forgive someone for doing something that is not seriously wrong, such as being rude or careless: *I'll excuse you this time, but don't be late again.* | *Please excuse my bad handwriting.* | **excuse sb for (doing) sth** *Please excuse me for being so late today.* | *Smith can be excused for his lack of interest in the course* (=his lack of interest is reasonable).
3 FROM A DUTY [usually passive] to allow someone not to do something that they are supposed to do: **excuse sb from (doing) sth** *Can I be excused from swimming today? I have a cold.*
4 EXPLAIN to be or give a good reason for someone's careless or offensive behaviour: *Nothing can excuse that kind of rudeness.*
5 FROM A PLACE to give someone permission to leave a place: *May I please be excused from the table?*
6 excuse yourself to say politely that you need to leave a place: *Richard excused himself and went to his room.*
7 excuse me (for living)! *spoken* used when someone has offended you or told you that you have done something wrong

---

WORD CHOICE: excuse me, pardon me, beg your pardon, sorry
excuse me and **pardon me** are polite expressions that you use when you do something that could be slightly embarrassing or rude, for example in the cases below. You usually use **sorry** to apologize after you have done something wrong.
→ see note at REGRET
Use **excuse me** when you want to interrupt someone, say something to a person you do not know, or get past someone: *Excuse me, do you know the time?* | *Excuse me, can I just reach across and get my bag?*
Use **excuse me** when you have to leave someone for a short time: *Excuse me for a moment while I make a call.*
excuse me can also be used, especially in American English, when you have not heard or understood what someone has said: *'You're late.' 'Excuse me?' 'I said you're late.' 'Oh, sorry.'* Speakers of British English usually use **pardon**: *'My name is Timothy.' 'Pardon?'*
In American English, it is also possible to use **pardon me** in these situations.
In British English, you usually say **pardon me** when you have done something slightly impolite such as burping or sneezing. In American English, you usually say **excuse me**.
I beg your pardon is a rather old-fashioned expression used to apologize for doing something embarrassing or for making a mistake in what you have said: *There are 65 – I beg your pardon – 56 students on the course.*
⚠ Do not confuse the verb **excuse** /ɪkˈskju:z/ with the noun **excuse** /ɪkˈskju:s/, which means a reason for doing something wrong, often an invented or false reason.

---

ex·cuse² [S3] /ɪkˈskju:s/ n [C]
1 a reason that you give to explain careless or offensive behaviour: **excuse for (doing) sth** *What's your excuse for being late this time?* | *I'm tired of listening to his excuses.* | *Fay's always making excuses for her husband's odd behavior.* | *I'm sure Mike has a good excuse*

for not coming. | **plausible/legitimate/valid etc excuse** | **lame/feeble/pathetic excuse** *That's a lame excuse.*
2 a reason that you invent to explain an action and to hide your real intentions: **excuse to do sth** *I need an excuse to call her.* | **[+for]** *The conference is an excellent excuse for a few days' holiday by the sea.* | *Illness was* **used as an excuse** *so the defendant could avoid trial.* | **look for/find an excuse** *They were looking for any excuse to start a fight.* | *I* **made** *an excuse at the first possible moment, and got up to leave.* | *The arrival of the doctor* **gave** *them an excuse to leave.*
3 there is no excuse for sth used to say that someone's behaviour is too bad to be explained or accepted: *There is no excuse for such rudeness.*
4 make your excuses to explain why you are not able to do something: *Please make my excuses at the meeting tomorrow.*
5 poor/rotten etc excuse for sth used when you think someone or something is very bad: *He's a rotten excuse for a lawyer. Why on earth did you hire him?*
6 *AmE* a note written by your doctor or one of your parents saying that you were ill on a particular day; **⊟ sick note** *BrE*

ex-di·rectory *adj BrE* a person or telephone number that is ex-directory is not in the public telephone book; **⊟ unlisted** *AmE*: *The number is ex-directory.* | *After several threatening calls, we decided to* **go ex-directory.**

ex·ec /ɪgˈzek/ *n* [C] an informal word for EXECUTIVE

ex·e·cra·ble /ˈeksɪ̈krəbəl/ *adj formal* extremely bad; **⊟ terrible**

ex·e·crate /ˈeksɪ̈kreɪt/ *v* [T] *literary* to express strong disapproval or hatred for someone or something

ex·e·cute /ˈeksɪ̈kjuːt/ *v* [T]
1 KILL SB to kill someone, especially legally as a punishment: **execute sb for sth** *Thousands have been executed for political crimes.* | *The report claims 13 people were* **summarily executed** *(=killed without any trial or legal process)* *by the guerrillas.* → see box at KILL[1]
2 DO STH *formal* to do something that has been carefully planned; **⊟ implement**: *The job involves drawing up and executing a plan of nursing care.*
3 PERFORM AN ACTION *formal* to perform a difficult action or movement: **beautifully/skilfully/poorly etc executed** *The skaters' routine was perfectly executed.*
4 COMPUTER *technical* if a computer executes a program or COMMAND (=instruction), it makes the program or command happen or work
5 LEGAL DOCUMENT *law* to make sure that the instructions in a legal document are followed
6 PRODUCE STH *formal* to produce a painting, book, film etc: *a boldly executed story*

ex·e·cu·tion /ˌeksɪ̈ˈkjuːʃən/ *n* **1** [C,U] when someone is killed, especially as a legal punishment: *their torture and* **summary execution** *(=execution without a trial or any legal process)* | *a public execution* | *He was granted* **a stay of execution** *(=delay in carrying out an execution).* **2** [U] *formal* a process in which you do something that has been carefully planned; **⊟ implementation**: **[+of]** *the formulation and execution of urban policy* **3** [U] *law* the process of making sure that the instructions in a legal document are followed: *the execution of a will* **4** [U] *formal* the performance of a difficult action or movement **5** [U] *formal* the process of producing something such as a painting, film, book etc, or the way it is produced: *art that is unusual in design and execution* **6** [C,U] *technical* when you make a computer program work, or a COMMAND (=instruction) happen

ex·e·cu·tion·er /ˌeksɪ̈ˈkjuːʃənə $ -ər/ *n* [C] someone whose job is to execute criminals

ex·ec·u·tive[1] S3 W2 /ɪgˈzekjɵtɪv/ *n* [C]
1 a manager in an organization or company who helps make important decisions: *a marketing executive* | **senior/top executive** *top executives on high salaries* → CHIEF EXECUTIVE
2 the executive the part of a government that makes

sure decisions and laws work well → JUDICIARY, LEGISLATURE
3 *BrE* a group of people who are in charge of an organization and make the rules: *the union's executive*

executive[2] *adj* [only before noun] **1** relating to the job of managing a business or organization and making decisions: *a commission with* **executive powers** | **executive body/committee etc** *(=a group of people who have the power to make decisions)* **2** for the use of people who have important jobs in a company: *the* **executive dining-room** **3** expensive and designed for people who earn a lot of money: **executive cars/homes etc** | **executive toys** *(=objects to play with at work)*

ex,ecutive 'privilege *n* [C] *AmE* the right of a president or other government leader to keep official records and papers secret

ex·ec·u·tor /ɪgˈzekjɵtə $ -ər/ *n* [C] someone who deals with the instructions in someone's WILL

ex·e·ge·sis /ˌeksɪ̈ˈdʒiːsɪ̈s/ *n plural* **exegeses** /-siːz/ [C,U] *formal* a detailed explanation of a piece of writing, especially a religious piece of writing

ex·em·plar /ɪgˈzemplə, -plɑː $ -plər, -plɑːr/ *n* [C] *formal* a good or typical example: **[+of]** *Milt's career is an exemplar of survival in difficult times.*

ex·em·pla·ry /ɪgˈzempləri/ *adj* **1** excellent and providing a good example for people to follow: *a company with an exemplary record on environmental issues* **2** [only before noun] an exemplary punishment is very severe and is intended to stop other people from committing the same crime

ex·em·pli·fy /ɪgˈzemplɪ̈faɪ/ *v* **exemplified, exemplifying, exemplifies** [T] *formal* **1** to be a very typical example of something: *The building exemplifies the style of architecture which was popular at the time.* **2** to give an example of something: *Problems are exemplified in the report.* —**exemplification** /ɪgˌzemplɪ̈fɪ̈ˈkeɪʃən/ *n* [C,U]

ex·empt[1] /ɪgˈzempt/ *adj* not affected by something, or not having to do it or pay it: **[+from]** *The interest is* **exempt from** *income tax.* | *Children are exempt from the charges.*

exempt[2] *v* [T] to give someone permission not to do or pay something: **exempt sb from sth** *Charities are* **exempted from** *paying the tax.* | *a document that exempts the owner from liability in case of accidents*

ex·emp·tion /ɪgˈzempʃən/ *n* **1** [C] an amount of money that you do not have to pay tax on: *You qualify for a* **tax exemption** *on the loan.* **2** [C,U] permission not to do or pay something that you would normally have to do or pay: **[+from]** *exemption from customs duties* | *The commission has the power to* **grant** *temporary* **exemptions.**

ex·er·cise[1] S1 W2 /ˈeksəsaɪz $ -ər-/ *n*
1 FOR HEALTH [U] physical activities that you do in order to stay healthy and become stronger: *Try to fit some regular exercise into your daily routine.* | *Working in an office, I don't* **get much exercise.** | **do/take exercise** *Most people need to do more exercise.* | **gentle/light exercise** *Gentle exercise can be beneficial for older people.* | **vigorous/strenuous exercise** *After the operation, you should avoid strenuous exercise.*
2 MOVEMENT [C] a movement or set of movements that you do regularly to keep your body healthy: *stretching exercises* | *You can* **do exercises** *to strengthen your stomach muscles.*
3 FOR A SKILL [C usually plural] an activity or process that helps you practise a particular skill: *relaxation exercises* | *role-playing exercises*
4 IN A BOOK [C] a set of questions in a book that test a student's knowledge or skill: *Do Exercises 3 and 4 on page 51 for homework.*
5 FOR A PARTICULAR RESULT [singular] an activity or situation that has a particular quality or result: *closing libraries as part of a cost-cutting exercise* | *It's a*

E

pointless exercise. | [+in] *Buying a house can be an exercise in frustration.*

6 ARMY/NAVY ETC [C,U] a set of activities for training soldiers etc: *a military exercise* | **on exercise** *Half the unit was away on exercise.*

7 the exercise of sth *formal* the use of a power or right: *the exercise of political leadership*

exercise² S3 W2 v

1 USE STH [T] *formal* to use a power, right, or quality that you have: *There are plans to encourage people to exercise their right to vote.* | *People who can* **exercise** *some* **control** *over their surroundings feel less anxious.*

2 DO PHYSICAL ACTIVITY [I] to do sports or physical activities in order to stay healthy and become stronger: *It's important to exercise regularly.*

3 USE PART OF YOUR BODY [T] to make a particular part of your body move in order to make it stronger: *Swimming exercises all the major muscle groups.*

4 ANIMAL [T] to make an animal walk or run in order to keep it healthy and strong: *people exercising their dogs in the park*

5 MAKE SB THINK [T] *formal* **a)** to make someone think about a subject or problem and consider how to deal with it: *It's an issue that's* **exercised** *the* **minds** *of scientists for a long time.* **b)** *BrE* if something exercises someone, they think about it all the time and are very anxious or worried – often used humorously: *It was clear that Flavia had been exercised by this thought.*

'**exercise ,bike** *n* [C] a bicycle that does not move and is used for exercising indoors → see picture at SPORTS CENTRE

'**exercise ,book** *n* [C] a book that students use for writing in

ex·ert /ɪɡˈzɜːt $ -ɜːrt/ *v* [T] **1** to use your power, influence etc in order to make something happen: *They exerted considerable influence within the school.* | *Environmental groups are* **exerting pressure on** *the government to tighten pollution laws.* **2 exert yourself** to work very hard and use a lot of physical or mental energy: *He has exerted himself tirelessly on behalf of the charity.*

ex·er·tion /ɪɡˈzɜːʃən $ -ɜːr-/ *n* [C,U] **1** a lot of physical or mental effort: *The afternoon's exertions had left us feeling exhausted.* | *mental exertion* **2** the use of power, influence etc to make something happen: *the exertion of authority*

ex·e·unt /ˈeksiʌnt/ *v* [I] a word written in the instructions of a play to tell two or more actors to leave the stage

ex·fo·li·ate /eksˈfəʊlieɪt $ -ˈfoʊ-/ *v* [I,T] to remove dead cells from your skin in order to make it smoother —**exfoliation** /eksˌfəʊliˈeɪʃən $ -ˌfoʊ-/ *n* [U]

ex gra·tia /ˌeks ˈɡreɪʃə/ *adj formal* an ex gratia payment is one that is made as a gift, and not as a legal duty: *an ex gratia payment of £15,000*

ex·hale /eksˈheɪl/ *v* [I,T] to breathe air, smoke etc out of your mouth; ☰ **inhale**: *Take a deep breath, then exhale slowly.* —**exhalation** /ˌekshəˈleɪʃən/ *n* [C,U]

ex·haust¹ /ɪɡˈzɔːst $ -ˈzɒːst/ *v* [T] **1** to make someone feel extremely tired: *A full day's teaching exhausts me.* | **exhaust yourself** *He'd exhausted himself carrying all the boxes upstairs.* **2** to use all of something; ☰ **use up**: *We are in danger of* **exhausting** *the world's oil* **supply.** | *Having exhausted all other possibilities, I asked Jan to look after the baby.* **3 exhaust a subject/ topic etc** to talk about something so much that you have nothing more to say about it: *Once we'd exhausted the subject of Jill's wedding, I didn't know what to say.*

exhaust² *n* **1** also **exhaust pipe** [C] a pipe on a car or machine that waste gases pass through **2** [U] the gas produced when an engine is working: *exhaust fumes* → see picture at CAR

ex·haust·ed /ɪɡˈzɔːstɪd $ -ˈzɒːs-/ *adj* **1** extremely tired; ☰ **worn out**: *You look absolutely exhausted.* | [+from/by] *I was exhausted by the journey.* **2** having or containing no more of a particular thing or substance: *an exhausted coal mine*

exhausted

ex·haust·ing /ɪɡˈzɔːstɪŋ $ -ˈzɒːs-/ *adj* making you feel extremely tired: *an exhausting process* | *It had been an exhausting day.*

ex·haus·tion /ɪɡˈzɔːstʃən $ -ˈzɒːs-/ *n* [U] **1** extreme tiredness: **with exhaustion** *He collapsed with exhaustion.* | **Sheer exhaustion** *forced him to give up.* | *Many runners were suffering from* **heat exhaustion** (=when you become tired and ill because you are too hot). | **nervous exhaustion** (=when you become ill because you have been working too hard or have been very worried) **2** when all of something has been used: [+of] *the exhaustion of oil supplies*

ex·haus·tive /ɪɡˈzɔːstɪv $ -ˈzɒːs-/ *adj* extremely thorough and complete: *an exhaustive investigation* | *The list is by no means exhaustive.* —**exhaustively** *adv*

ex·hib·it¹ /ɪɡˈzɪbɪt/ *v* **1** [I,T] to show something in a public place so that people can go to see it; ☰ **show**: *Her paintings have been exhibited all over the world.* **2** [T] *formal* to clearly show a particular quality, emotion, or ability: **exhibit signs/symptoms/behaviour etc** *a patient who is exhibiting classic symptoms of mental illness*

exhibit² *n* [C] **1** something, for example a painting, that is put in a public place so that people can go to see it: *The exhibits date from the 17th century.* **2** an object that is shown in court to prove whether someone is guilty or not: *Exhibit A is the hammer found next to the victim.* **3** *AmE* an exhibition: *a big exhibit in Milan*

ex·hi·bi·tion W2 /ˌeksɪˈbɪʃən/ *n* **1** [C] *especially BrE* a show of paintings, photographs, or other objects that people can go to see: [+of] *an exhibition of black and white photographs* | **stage/ mount/hold etc an exhibition** *The museum is staging an exhibition of Picasso's work.*; → see picture at GALLERY **2** [U] when something such as a painting is shown in a public place: [+of] *She never agreed to the public exhibition of her sculptures while she was still alive.* | **on exhibition** *A collection of paintings by David Hockney is on exhibition at the Museum of Art.*
3 exhibition of sth a situation in which someone shows a particular skill, feeling, or type of behaviour: *I've never seen such an exhibition of jealousy.*
4 make an exhibition of yourself to behave in a silly or embarrassing way; ☰ **make a fool of yourself**

ex·hi·bi·tion·is·m /ˌeksɪˈbɪʃənɪzəm/ *n* [U] **1** behaviour that is intended to make people notice or admire you – used to show disapproval **2** *medical* a medical condition that makes someone want to show their sexual organs in public places

ex·hi·bi·tion·ist /ˌeksɪˈbɪʃənɪst/ *n* [C] **1** someone who likes to make other people notice them – often used to show disapproval **2** *medical* someone who has a medical condition that makes them want to show their sexual organs in public places —**exhibitionist** *adj*

ex·hib·i·tor /ɪɡˈzɪbɪtə $ -ər/ *n* [C] a person or company who is showing their work or products to the public: *an exhibitor at a trade show*

ex·hil·a·rate /ɪɡˈzɪləreɪt/ *v* [T] to make someone feel very excited and happy

ex·hil·a·rat·ed /ɪɡˈzɪləreɪtɪd/ *adj* feeling extremely happy, excited, and full of energy: *Dan felt strangely exhilarated by the day's events.* —**exhilarate** *v* [T]

ex·hil·a·rat·ing /ɪɡˈzɪləreɪtɪŋ/ *adj* making you feel happy, excited, and full of energy: *an exhilarating experience* | *an exhilarating walk*

ex·hil·a·ra·tion /ɪɡˌzɪləˈreɪʃ*ə*n/ n [U] a feeling of being happy, excited, and full of energy: [+of] *She enjoyed the exhilaration of jet-skiing.*

ex·hort /ɪɡˈzɔːt $ -ɔːrt/ v [T] *formal* to try very hard to persuade someone to do something; ⊟ **urge: exhort sb to do sth** *Police exhorted the crowd to remain calm.* —**exhortation** /ˌeksɔːˈteɪʃ*ə*n $ -ɔːr-/ n [C,U]

ex·hume /ɪɡˈzjuːm, eksˈhjuːm $ ɪɡˈzuːm, ɪkˈsjuːm/ v [T] *formal* to remove a dead body from the ground, especially in order to check the cause of death; ⊟ **dig up** —**exhumation** /ˌekshjuˈmeɪʃ*ə*n $ ˌekshju-, ˌegzju-/ n [C,U]

ex·i·gen·cies /ˈeksᵻ̣dʒ*ə*nsiz, ɪɡˈzɪdʒ-/ n [plural] *formal* the things you must do in order to deal with a difficult or urgent situation; ⊟ **demands**: [+of] *the exigencies of war*

ex·i·gent /ˈeksᵻ̣dʒ*ə*nt, ˈegzᵻ-/ adj *formal*   **1** demanding a lot of attention from other people in a way that is unreasonable   **2** an exigent situation is urgent, so that you must deal with it very quickly

ex·ig·u·ous /ɪɡˈzɪɡuəs/ adj *formal* very small in amount: *exiguous earnings*

ex·ile¹ /ˈeksaɪl, ˈegzaɪl/ n   **1** [singular, U] a situation in which you are forced to leave your country and live in another country, especially for political reasons: **in exile** *a writer now living in exile* | *He **went into exile** to escape political imprisonment.* | **force/drive sb into exile** *The house was raided and the family was forced into exile.* | *He spent many years in **enforced exile**.* | **voluntary/self-imposed exile** *She had been in voluntary exile since 1990.*   **2** [C] someone who has been forced to live in exile: *political exiles;* → see also **TAX EXILE**

exile² v [T usually passive] to force someone to leave their country, especially for political reasons: **exile sb to sth** *Several of the leaders were arrested and exiled to France.* | **exile sb from sth** *a dictator who was exiled from his home country* | *the exiled former president*

ex·ist S3 W1 /ɪɡˈzɪst/ v [I not in progressive]
1 to happen or be present in a particular situation or place: *The custom of arranged marriages still exists in many countries.* | *Opportunities exist for students to gain sponsorship.* | *Stop pretending that the problem doesn't exist.* | *The club will **cease to exist** if financial help is not found.*
2 to be real or alive: *Do fairies really exist?* | *Tom acts as if I don't exist at times.*
3 to stay alive, especially in a difficult situation when you do not have enough money, food etc; ⊟ **survive**: [+on] *The hostages existed on bread and water for over five months.*

ex·ist·ence S3 W2 /ɪɡˈzɪst*ə*ns/ n
1 [U] the state of existing: [+of] *It is impossible to prove the existence of God.* | **in existence** *The organization has been in existence for 25 years.* | *Scientists have many theories about how the universe first **came into existence** (=started to exist).* | [+of] *The **very existence** of the museum is threatened by lack of funding.* | *the **continued existence** of economic inequalities*
2 [C usually singular] the type of life that someone has, especially when it is bad or unhappy: *Pablo led a miserable existence when he first moved to San Juan.* → **eke out a living/existence** at EKE

ex·ist·ent¹ /ɪɡˈzɪst*ə*nt/ adj *formal* existing now; 𝟋 **nonexistent**: *existent differences*

existent² n [C] *technical* something that is real and exists

ex·is·ten·tial /ˌegzɪˈstenʃ*ə*l◂/ adj [only before noun] *formal* relating to the existence of humans or to existentialism

ex·is·ten·tial·is·m /ˌegzɪˈstenʃ*ə*lɪz*ə*m/ n [U] *technical* the belief in PHILOSOPHY that people are responsible for their own actions and experiences, and that the world has no meaning —**existentialist** adj —**existentialist** n [C]

---

ex·ist·ing S3 W2 /ɪɡˈzɪstɪŋ/ adj [only before noun] present or being used now: *the existing laws* | *The service is available to all existing customers.*

ex·it¹ S3 /ˈegzᵻ̣t, ˈeksᵻ̣t/ n [C]
1 a door or space through which you can leave a public room, building etc: *We made for the nearest exit.* | *an exit door* | *Two men were blocking her exit.* | **emergency/fire exit** (=a special door used only when there is a fire etc); → see picture at STAY
2 [usually singular] when you leave a room or building: *They **made** a quick **exit** when they saw the police approaching.*
3 a place where vehicles can leave a road such as a MOTORWAY, and join another road: *Take the next exit for Lynchburg.*
4 [usually singular] when someone stops being involved in a competition or business, especially because they have not been successful; ⊟ **departure**: *France's early exit from the World Cup*

exit² v [I,T]   **1** *formal* to leave a place: [+from/through] *I exited through a side window.* | *He exited the courtroom in a fury.*   **2** to stop using a computer program: *Press F3 to exit.*   **3** used in the instructions of a play to tell an actor to leave the stage: *Exit Hamlet, bearing the body of Polonius.*

ˈexit ˌpoll n [C] the activity of asking people how they have voted in an election in order to discover the likely result

ex·o·dus /ˈeksədəs/ n [singular] a situation in which a lot of people leave a particular place at the same time: [+of] *A massive exodus of doctors is forcing the government to recruit from abroad.* | [+from/to] *the exodus from the countryside to the towns in the 19th century* | *I joined the **mass exodus** for drinks during the interval.*

ex·of·fi·ci·o /ˌeks əˈfɪʃiəʊ $ -ʃioʊ/ adj *formal* an ex-officio member of an organization is only a member because of their rank or position —**ex officio** adv

ex·on·e·rate /ɪɡˈzɒnəreɪt $ ɪɡˈzɑː-/ v [T] to state officially that someone who has been blamed for something is not guilty: **exonerate sb from/of sth** *He was totally exonerated of any blame.* —**exoneration** /ɪɡˌzɒnəˈreɪʃ*ə*n $ -ˌzɑː-/ n [U]

ex·or·bi·tant /ɪɡˈzɔːbᵻ̣t*ə*nt $ -ɔːr-/ adj an exorbitant price, amount of money etc is much higher than it should be; ⊟ **astronomical: exorbitant rent/prices etc** *exorbitant rates of interest* —**exorbitantly** adv

ex·or·cis·m /ˈeksɔːsɪz*ə*m $ -ɔːr-/ n [C,U]   **1** a process during which someone tries to make an evil SPIRIT leave a place by saying special words, or a ceremony when this is done   **2** *literary* the process of making yourself forget a bad memory or experience

ex·or·cist /ˈeksɔːsᵻ̣st $ -ɔːr-/ n [C] someone who tries to make evil SPIRITS leave a place

ex·or·cize also **-ise** BrE /ˈeksɔːsaɪz $ -ɔːr-/ v [T]   **1** to force evil SPIRITS to leave a place by using special words and ceremonies   **2** to make yourself forget a bad memory or experience: *trying to exorcise the past*

ex·ot·ic /ɪɡˈzɒtɪk $ ɪɡˈzɑː-/ adj something that is exotic seems unusual and interesting because it is related to a foreign country – used to show approval: *exotic birds* | *exotic places* —**exotically** /-kli/ adv

ex·ot·i·ca /ɪɡˈzɒtɪkə $ ɪɡˈzɑː-/ n [plural] things that are unusual and exciting, especially because they come from foreign countries

ex·ˌotic ˈdancer n [C] a dancer who takes off her clothes while dancing → STRIPTEASE

ex·pand S2 W3 /ɪkˈspænd/ v
1 [I,T] to become larger in size, number, or amount, or to make something become larger; ⊟ **expansion**; 𝟋 **contract**: *Water expands as it freezes.* | *Sydney's population **expanded rapidly** in the 1960s.* | *exercises that expand the chest muscles* | *his expanding waistline*

E

---

ex·ploit·a·tive /ɪkˈsplɔɪtətɪv/ adj taking as much as possible from someone or something and giving very little in return: *the exploitative nature of multinational companies*

ex·plo·ra·tion /ˌekspləˈreɪʃən/ n [C,U] **1** the act of travelling through a place in order to find out about it or find something such as oil or gold in it: *oil exploration facilities in the North Sea* | *You can then use this hut as a base for explorations into the mountains around.* | [+of] *the exploration of space* **2** when you try to find out more about something by discussing it, thinking about it etc: [+into/of] *an exploration into how an abused child becomes an abuser* | *the exploration of literary texts*

ex·plor·a·to·ry /ɪkˈsplɒrətəri $ ɪkˈsplɔːrətɔːri/ adj done in order to find out more about something: *He's going to have exploratory surgery on his knee.*

ex·plore S3 W2 /ɪkˈsplɔː $ -ˈsplɔːr/ v
1 [T] to discuss or think about something carefully; ▣ **look at**: *Management need to explore ways of improving office security.* | *I'm going to explore the possibility of a part-time job.*
2 [I,T] to travel around an area in order to find out about it: *Venice is a wonderful city to explore.*
3 explore (sth) for oil/minerals/gold etc to look for something such as oil, minerals etc
4 [T] written to feel something with your hand or another part of your body to find out what it is like: *Gingerly she explored the bump on her head with her fingers.*

ex·plo·rer /ɪkˈsplɔːrə $ -ər/ n [C] someone who travels through an unknown area to find out about it

---

explosions

burst

erupt

let off

blow up

ex·plo·sion /ɪkˈspləʊʒən $ -ˈsploʊ-/ n **1** [C] a loud sound and the energy produced by something such as a bomb bursting into small pieces; → **explode: bomb/gas/nuclear explosion** | *Several people were injured in a bomb explosion.* | *We heard a loud explosion.* | **huge/massive etc explosion** *A massive explosion ripped through the building.* **2** [C,U] a process in which something such as a bomb is deliberately made to explode: *Police carried out a controlled explosion of the device.* **3** [C] a sudden or quick increase in the number or amount of something: *the population explosion in India* | [+of] *the recent explosion of interest in Latin music and dance* **4** [C] a sudden expression of emotion, especially anger; ▣ **outburst 5** [C] a sudden very loud noise: [+of] *an explosion of laughter*

ex·plo·sive¹ /ɪkˈspləʊsɪv $ -ˈsploʊ-/ adj **1** able or likely to explode: *Because the gas is highly explosive, it needs to be kept in high-pressure containers.* | *A small explosive device (=bomb) was set off outside the UN headquarters today.* **2** [usually before noun] relating to or like an explosion: *the explosive force of volcanoes* **3** likely to become violent or to cause feelings of violence: *He's good at defusing potentially explosive*

situations. | *the explosive issue of uncontrolled immigration* **4** showing sudden strong or angry emotion: *Both men suddenly spoke in the same explosive tone of voice.* **5** [usually before noun] increasing suddenly or quickly in amount or number: *the explosive growth of microcomputers* **6** an explosive sound is sudden and loud —**explosively** adv —**explosiveness** n [U]

explosive² n [C,U] a substance that can cause an explosion → PLASTIC EXPLOSIVE

ex·po /ˈekspəʊ $ -poʊ/ n plural **expos** [C] informal an EXPOSITION (2)

ex·po·nent /ɪkˈspəʊnənt $ -ˈspoʊ-/ n [C] **1** an exponent of an idea, belief etc tries to explain it and persuade others that it is good or useful: [+of] *a leading exponent of desktop publishing* **2** an exponent of a particular skill, idea, or activity is someone who is good at it: [+of] *The most famous exponent of this approach to art was probably Charles Rennie Mackintosh.* **3** technical a sign written above and to the right of a number or letter to show how many times that quantity is to be multiplied by itself

ex·po·nen·tial /ˌekspəˈnenʃəl◂/ adj technical **1 exponential growth/increase etc** exponential growth, increase etc becomes faster as the amount of the thing that is growing increases: *an exponential increase in travel* **2** using a small number or letter slightly above and to the right of a number or letter that shows how many times a quantity is to be multiplied by itself —**exponentially** adv

ex·port¹ W2 /ˈekspɔːt $ -ɔːrt/ n
1 [U] the business of selling and sending goods to other countries; ▣ **import**: [+of] *a ban on the export of toxic waste* | **for export** *bales of cloth for export to the continent* | **export market/industry/earnings etc** | *Export licences (=official document allowing you to sell something abroad) for arms are strictly controlled.*
2 [C usually plural] a product that is sold to another country; ▣ **import**: *Wheat is one of the country's chief exports.* | *Selling insurance overseas is Britain's largest invisible export (=a service rather than a product).*

ex·port² /ɪkˈspɔːt $ -ɔːrt/ v **1** [I,T] to sell goods to another country; ▣ **import: export sth (from sb) to sb** *The company exports tuna to the US.* **2** [T] to introduce an activity, idea etc to another place or country: *Italian food has been exported all over the world.* **3** [T] technical to move computer information from one computer to another, from one computer document to another, or from one piece of software to another; ▣ import —**exportation** /ˌekspɔːˈteɪʃən $ -ɔːr-/ n [U]

ex·port·er /ɪkˈspɔːtə $ -ˈspɔːrtər/ n [C] a person, company, or country that sells goods to another country; ▣ **importer**: [+of] *With the expanded production of North Sea oil and gas, the UK has become a net exporter of fuel (=it exports more fuel than it imports).* | **major/leading exporter** *Japan is a leading exporter of textiles.*

ex·pose W3 /ɪkˈspəʊz $ -ˈspoʊz/ v [T]
1 SHOW to show something that is usually covered or hidden: *He lifted his T-shirt to expose a jagged scar across his chest.* | **expose sth to sth** *Potatoes turn green when exposed to light.*
2 TO STH DANGEROUS to put someone in a situation where they are not protected from something dangerous or unpleasant: **expose sb to sth** *The report revealed that workers had been exposed to high levels of radiation.* | **expose yourself to ridicule/criticism etc** (=say or do something that may make people laugh at you, criticize you etc)
3 TELL THE TRUTH to show the truth about someone or something, especially when it is bad: *The film exposes the utter horror of war.* | *The report exposes the weaknesses of modern medical practice.* | **expose sb as sth** *The baron was exposed as a liar and a cheat.*
4 SEE/EXPERIENCE to make it possible for someone to experience new ideas, ways of life etc: **expose sb to sth** *Some children are never exposed to classical music.*
5 expose yourself if a man exposes himself, he shows

his sexual organs to someone he does not know in a public place, usually because he is mentally ill

6 PHOTOGRAPH to allow light onto a piece of film in a camera in order to take a photograph

7 FEELINGS to show other people feelings that you usually hide, especially when this is not planned: *I'm afraid I might expose my real feelings for him.*

ex·po·sé /ek'spəʊzeɪ $ ˌekspə'zeɪ/ *n* [C] a story in a newspaper or on television that shows the truth about something, especially something dishonest or shocking: [+of] *an exposé of corrupt practices by lawyers*

ex·posed /ɪk'spəʊzd $ -'spoʊzd/ *adj* **1** not protected from the weather: *an exposed coastline* | *the side of the garden most exposed to wind* **2** not covered: *All exposed skin should be covered with protective cream.* **3** not protected from attack; ◨ **vulnerable**: *The old fort was very exposed.* | *These developments leave the British government in an exposed position.*

ex·po·si·tion /ˌekspə'zɪʃən/ *n* **1** [C,U] *formal* a clear and detailed explanation: [+of] *a lucid exposition of educational theories* **2** [C] a large public event at which you show or sell products, art etc

ex post fac·to law /ˌeks pəʊst 'fæktəʊ ˌlɔː $ -poʊst 'fæktoʊ ˌlɒː/ *n* [C] *law* a law that makes a particular action into a crime, and then punishes people who took that action before it had legally become a crime

ex·pos·tu·late /ɪk'spɒstʃʊleɪt $ -'spɑː-/ *v* [I] *formal* to express strong disapproval, disagreement, or annoyance with someone —**expostulation** /ɪkˌspɒstʃʊ'leɪʃən $ -ˌspɑː-/ *n* [C,U]

ex·po·sure W3 /ɪk'spəʊʒə $ -'spoʊʒər/ *n*

1 TO DANGER [U] when someone is in a situation where they are not protected from something dangerous or unpleasant: [+to] *Prolonged exposure to the sun can cause skin cancer.*

2 TRUTH [U] the action of showing the truth about someone or something, especially when it is bad: [+of] *the exposure of his underground political activity* | [+as] *her fear of exposure as a spy*

3 PUBLIC ATTENTION [U] the attention that someone or something gets from newspapers, television etc; ◨ **publicity**: *The failure of their marriage has got a lot of exposure recently.*

4 EXPERIENCE [singular, U] the chance to experience new ideas, ways of life etc: [+to] *The visit to Germany gave them exposure to the language.* | *her brief exposure to pop stardom*

5 BE VERY COLD [U] the harmful effects on your body of being outside in very cold weather without protection. *We nearly died of exposure on the mountainside.*

6 PHOTOGRAPHY [C] **a)** a length of film in a camera that is used to take a photograph: *I have three exposures left on this roll.* **b)** the amount of time that light is allowed to enter the camera when taking a photograph

7 SHOW [C] the act of showing something that is usually hidden

8 BUSINESS [C,U] the amount of financial risk that a company or person has

9 DIRECTION [singular] the direction in which a building, hill etc faces: *My bedroom has a southern exposure.*; → see also INDECENT EXPOSURE

ex·pound /ɪk'spaʊnd/ *v* [I,T] *formal* to explain or talk about something in detail: [+on] *She's always expounding on the latest dogmas of feminism.*

ex·press¹ S2 W1 /ɪk'spres/ *v* [T]

1 FEELING to tell or show what you are feeling or thinking by using words, looks, or actions: **express your views/opinions** *Bill's not afraid to express his opinions.* | *Parents have expressed their concerns about their children's safety.* | *She expressed an interest in seeing York.* | **express sth in/by/through sth** *Express your reasons for applying in simple terms.* | **express sympathy/fear/anger etc** *She doesn't express her emotions as much as he does.* | **express thanks/gratitude (for sth) (to sb)** (=thank someone in a speech or by writing a letter) *Finally, I'd like to express my sincere thanks to all those who have helped today.* |

express doubts/reservations *The USA expressed reservations before agreeing to sign the agreement.* | *Many people have expressed their opposition to the proposals for a new ring road.* | **express yourself** (=say what you think or feel) *Young children often have difficulty expressing themselves.* | *He first learnt to express himself through movement at his dance classes.* | *Words can't express* (=it is impossible to describe) *how angry we felt.*

2 PARTICULAR EMOTION to show or describe a particular feeling: *Many of Munch's paintings express a deep feeling of despair.*

3 sth expresses itself if something expresses itself, it becomes noticeable; ◨ **sth reveals itself**: *Religious faith expresses itself in a variety of ways.*

4 MATHEMATICS *technical* to change an amount or quantity into a different form, especially in mathematics: **express sth as/in sth** *Express three-quarters as a decimal.* | *The value of the coffee becomes significantly higher when expressed in foreign currency.*

5 FEEDING BABIES if a woman expresses milk, she presses milk out of her breast in order to feed it to her baby later

express² *adj* [only before noun] **1** deliberate and for a specific situation: *The school was founded with the express purpose of teaching deaf children.* **2** clear and definite: **express agreement/consent/authority etc** *He is not to leave without my express permission.* | *Matthew left express instructions to keep all doors locked.* **3 express train/coach/bus** a train or bus that does not stop at many places and can therefore travel more quickly **4 express post/mail** a system that delivers letters and packages very quickly **5** *AmE* designed to help you move through a place more quickly: *express lanes on the freeway* | *an express line at a supermarket* (=where people with only a few things to buy go to pay)

express³ *n* **1** [C usually singular] a train or bus that does not stop in many places and therefore travels quickly: **London – Gatwick Express/Orient Express** (=a fast train or bus which does a particular journey regularly) **2** [U] a post service that delivers letters and packages very quickly: *Send these books by express.*

express⁴ *adv* **send/deliver sth express** to send or deliver a letter, package etc quickly using a special post service

ex·pres·sion S2 W2 /ɪk'spreʃən/ *n*

1 STRONG FEELINGS/THOUGHTS [C,U] something you say, write, or do that shows what you think or feel: [+of] *I decided to go to the meeting as an expression of support.* | **expression of sympathy/thanks/regret etc** *The letter was a genuine expression of sympathy.* | *Student leaders are demanding greater* **freedom of expression** (=the right to say what you think without being punished). | **give (political/religious/artistic) expression to sth** *The Socialist Party was founded to give political expression to the working classes.* | *Another writer who seeks to give expression to popular oral culture is Jose Maria Arguedos.*

2 ON SB'S FACE [C,U] a look on someone's face that shows what they are thinking or feeling: [+of] *an expression of surprise* | *There was a* **blank expression on her face** (=no expression on her face). | *In the photograph he seemed* **devoid of facial expression** (=having no expression on his face). | *A* **pained** (=worried) *expression crossed her face.*

3 WORD/PHRASE [C] a word or group of words with a particular meaning: *The old-fashioned expression 'in the family way' means 'pregnant'.* | **pardon/forgive/excuse the expression** (=used when you think may offend someone by using particular words) *After the climb we were absolutely knackered, if you'll pardon the expression.*

4 MUSIC/ACTING [U] when you put feeling or emotion into the music that you are making or into your acting

5 MATHEMATICS [C] *technical* a sign or group of signs that represent a mathematical idea or quantity

ex·pres·sion·is·m /ɪk'spreʃənɪzəm/ *n* [U] a style of painting, writing, or music that expresses feelings rather than describing objects and experiences —**expressionist** *n* [C] —**expressionist** *adj* [only before noun]: *the expressionist movement*

ex·pres·sion·less /ɪk'spreʃənləs/ *adj* an expressionless face or voice does not show what someone thinks or feels; ❷ **expressive**: *a blank expressionless stare* —**expressionlessly** *adv*

ex·pres·sive /ɪk'spresɪv/ *adj* **1** showing very clearly what someone thinks or feels; ❷ **expressionless**: *her wonderfully expressive eyes* **2 be expressive of sth** *formal* showing a particular feeling or influence: *Her poem is expressive of calm days and peace of mind.* —**expressively** *adv* —**expressiveness** *n* [U]

ex·press·ly /ɪk'spresli/ *adv formal* **1** if you say something expressly, you say it very clearly and firmly: *He was expressly forbidden to speak to the girl.* **2** deliberately or for a specific purpose: *The building is expressly designed to conserve energy.*

ex'press ˌmail *n* [U] *AmE* a post service that delivers letters and packages very quickly

ex·press·way /ɪk'spreswei/ *n* [C] *AmE* a wide road in a city on which cars can travel very quickly without stopping; → see also FREEWAY, MOTORWAY

ex·pro·pri·ate /ɪk'sprəʊprieɪt $ -'sprəʊ-/ *v* [T] *formal* **1** if a government or someone in authority expropriates your private property, they take it away for public use **2** to take something from someone illegally in order to use it —**expropriation** /ɪkˌsprəʊpri'eɪʃən $ -ˌsprəʊ-/ *n* [C,U]

ex·pul·sion /ɪk'spʌlʃən/ *n* [C,U] **1** the act of forcing someone to leave a place; → **expel**: [+of] *the expulsion of the protesters* | [+from] *his expulsion from the Soviet Union in 1964* **2** the act of stopping someone from going to the school where they were studying or from being part of the organization where they worked: *The headmaster threatened the boys with expulsion.* | [+of] *the expulsion from the Communist Party of its former leader* **3** the act of forcing air, water, gas etc out of something

ex·punge /ɪk'spʌndʒ/ *v* [T] *formal* **1** to remove a name from a list, piece of information, or book **2** to make someone forget something unpleasant: **expunge sth from sth** *I wanted to expunge the memory of that first race from my mind.*

ex·pur·gat·ed /'ekspəgeɪtɪd $ -ər-/ *adj* an expurgated book, play etc has had some parts removed because they are considered harmful or offensive: *an expurgated version of her writings* —**expurgate** *v* [T]

ex·qui·site /ɪk'skwɪzɪt, 'ekskwɪ-/ *adj* **1** extremely beautiful and very delicately made: *the most exquisite craftsmanship* **2** very sensitive and delicate in the way you behave or do things: *She has exquisite taste in art.* **3** *literary* exquisite pain or pleasure is felt very strongly —**exquisitely** *adv* —**exquisiteness** *n* [U]

ˌex-'serviceman *n plural* **ex-servicemen** [C] *BrE* a man who used to be in the army, navy, or AIR FORCE

ˌex-'servicewoman *n plural* **ex-servicewomen** [C] *BrE* a woman who used to be in the army, navy, or AIR FORCE

ext. the written abbreviation of *extension* when you mean a particular telephone line

ex·tant /ɪk'stænt/ *adj formal* still existing in spite of being very old: *Few of the manuscripts are still extant.*

ex·tem·po·ra·ne·ous /ɪkˌstempə'reɪniəs◂/ *adj formal* spoken or done without any preparation or practice; ❸ **impromptu**: *an extemporaneous speech* —**extemporaneously** *adv*

ex·tem·po·re /ɪk'stempəri/ *adj formal* spoken or done without any preparation or practice; ❸ **impromptu**: *an extempore speech* —**extempore** *adv*

ex·tem·po·rize also **-ise** *BrE* /ɪk'stempəraɪz/ *v* [I] *formal* to speak or perform without preparation or practice —**extemporization** /ɪkˌstempəraɪ'zeɪʃən $ -rə-/ *n* [C,U]

ex·tend S3 W2 /ɪk'stend/ *v*
1 TIME [I + adv/prep,T] to continue for a longer period of time, or to make something last longer: *Management have agreed to extend the deadline.* | [+for/into/over etc] *Some of our courses extend over two years.* | **extend sth for/by/until sth** *The government has extended the ban on the import of beef until June.*
2 AREA/DISTANCE [I always + adv/prep] to continue for a particular distance or over a particular area: **+ across/over/through etc** *The River Nile extends as far south as Lake Victoria.* | **extend 100 km/30 yards etc (from sth)** *The shelf extends 20 cms from the bookcase.*
3 SIZE [T] to make a room, building, road etc bigger or longer: *We plan to extend the kitchen by six feet.*
4 INCLUDE/AFFECT **a)** [I always + adv/prep] to affect or include people, things, or places: [+to/beyond etc] *My duties at the school extend beyond just teaching.* | *The vote was extended to all women aged 21 and over in 1928.* **b)** [T] to make something affect more people, situations, areas etc than before: *British Coal is planning to extend its operations in Wales.* | **extend sth to sb/sth** *We can extend your insurance cover to travel abroad.*
5 OFFER HELP/THANKS [T] *formal* to officially offer someone help, sympathy, thanks etc: **extend sth to sb** *We'd like to extend a warm welcome to our French visitors.* | *I'd like to extend my thanks to all the catering staff.* | *The Coroner extended his sympathy to the victim's family.* | *The Headteacher has extended an invitation to the Prime Minister to visit the school.* | *The banks have decided to extend credit to the company* (=allow them to borrow more money).
6 ARMS/LEGS [T] to stretch out a hand or leg: *George extended his hand* (=offered to shake hands).
7 CONTINUE WINNING [T] to increase the number of points, games etc by which one person or team is ahead of other competitors: *Manchester United extended their lead at the top of the table to 10 points.*
8 FURNITURE [I,T] if a table or ladder extends, it can be made longer

ex·tend·ed /ɪk'stendɪd/ *adj* [only before noun] **1** made longer or bigger: *an extended business trip* | *The computer uses extended memory.* **2** long or longer than expected or planned: *If you are going abroad for an extended period of time, you should consider renting your house out.* **3** long and detailed: *an extended analysis of the film*

exˌtended 'family *n* [C] a family group that consists not only of parents and children but also of grandparents, AUNTS etc; → **nuclear family**

ex·ten·sion S2 W3 /ɪk'stenʃən/ *n*
1 MAKING STH BIGGER OR LONGER [C,U] the process of making a road, building etc bigger or longer, or the part that is added: [+of] *the extension of the Jubilee underground line*
2 EXTRA ROOMS [C] *BrE* another room or rooms which are added to a building: [+to] *the planned extension to the National Museum* | *a loft extension*
3 EXTRA TIME [C usually singular] an additional period of time allowed for something: *Donald's been given an extension to finish his thesis.* | *The pub's got an extension tonight* (=it will stay open longer than usual).
4 INCLUDE/AFFECT MORE THAN BEFORE [singular, U] the development of something in order to make it affect more people, situations, areas than before: [+of] *the extension of the copyright laws to cover online materials* | *an extension of the powers of the European Parliament*
5 TELEPHONE [C] **a)** one of many telephone lines connected to a central system in a large building, which all have different numbers: *Can I have extension 316, please?* | *Do you know Mr Brown's extension number?* **b)** one of the telephones in a house that all have the same number
6 by extension used when you want to mention some-

thing that is naturally related to something else: *My primary responsibility is to the pupils, and by extension to the teachers and parents.*
7 extensions [plural] long pieces of artificial hair that can be attached to your hair to make it look longer: **hair extensions**
8 COMPUTER [C] *technical* a set of three letters that follow the name of a computer FILE to show what it is. For example, the extension '.doc' shows that a file is a written document. → see picture at ELECTRIC
9 ELECTRIC WIRE [C] *BrE* an EXTENSION LEAD
10 STRETCH ARM/LEG [C,U] the position of a part of the body when it is stretched, or the process of stretching it
11 UNIVERSITY/COLLEGE [U] part of a university or college that offers courses to people who are not full time students

ex·ten·sion ˌlead *BrE*; **ex·ten·sion ˌcord** *AmE n* [C] an additional piece of electric wire that you attach to another wire to make a very long one; ▣ **extension**

ex·ten·sive W3 /ɪkˈstensɪv/ *adj*
1 large in size, amount, or degree: *The house stands in extensive grounds.* | *Fire has caused extensive damage to the island's forests.* | *the extensive use of pesticides*
2 containing or dealing with a lot of information and details: *Extensive research is being done into the connection between the disease and poor living conditions.* | *The exhibition has received extensive coverage in the national press.* —**extensively** *adv: As a student, he travelled extensively in the Middle East.*

ex·tent S2 W1 /ɪkˈstent/ *n*
1 to ... extent used to say how true something is or how great an effect or change is: **to a certain extent/to some extent/to an extent** (=partly) *We all to some extent remember the good times and forget the bad.* | *I do agree with him to an extent.* | **to a great/large extent** *Its success will depend to a large extent on local attitudes.* | **to a lesser/greater extent** (=less or more) *It will affect farmers in Spain and to a lesser extent in France.* | *They examined the* **extent to which** (=how much) *age affected language-learning ability.* | *To what extent* (=how much) *did she influence his decision?* | **to such an extent that/to the extent that** (=so much that) *Violence increased to the extent that residents were afraid to leave their homes.*
2 [U] how large, important, or serious something is, especially something such as a problem or injury: [+of] *Considering the extent of his injuries he's lucky to be alive.* | *It's too early to assess the full extent of the damage.*
3 [U] the length or size of something: *They opened out the nets to their full extent.* | **in extent** *The region is over 10,000 square kilometres in extent.*

ex·ten·u·at·ing /ɪkˈstenjuˌeɪtɪŋ/ *adj* **extenuating circumstances/factors etc** *formal* facts or reasons which make you feel that it was reasonable for someone to break the usual rules, or make you have sympathy for someone who did something wrong or illegal —**extenuation** /ɪkˌstenjuˈeɪʃən/ *n* [U]

ex·te·ri·or¹ /ɪkˈstɪəriə $ -ˈtɪriər/ *n* [C] **1** [usually singular] the outside of something, especially a building; ▣ **interior**: [+of] *the exterior of the factory* | *The dome is tiled* **on the exterior**. **2** calm/cool etc exterior behaviour that seems calm, unfriendly etc but which often hides a different feeling or attitude: *Beneath that calm exterior, he has a fierce will to win.*

exterior² *adj* [usually before noun] **1** on the outside of something; ▣ **interior**: *The exterior walls need a new coat of paint.* **2** exterior scenes in a film are filmed outdoors **3** coming from or relating to facts, situations etc other than the one you are considering: *information that is exterior to the text itself*

ex·ter·mi·nate /ɪkˈstɜːməˌneɪt $ -ɜːr-/ *v* [T] to kill large numbers of people or animals of a particular type so that they no longer exist: *Staff use the poison to exterminate moles and rabbits.* —**exterminator** *n* [C]

—**extermination** /ɪkˌstɜːmᵻˈneɪʃən $ -ɜːr-/ *n* [C,U]: *the extermination of the indigenous peoples*

ex·tern /ˈekstɜːn $ -ɜːrn/ *n* [C] *AmE* a university student who works in a particular type of job for a short time in order to gain experience of that type of work: *a finance major who was an extern with Merrill Lynch* —**extern** *v* [I]

ex·ter·nal W2 /ɪkˈstɜːnl $ -ɜːr-/ *adj*
1 OUTSIDE PART relating to the outside of something or of a person's body; ▣ **internal**: *the external appearance of the building* | **For external use only** (=written on medicines which must be put on your skin and not swallowed)
2 EFFECT relating to your environment or situation, rather than to your own qualities, ideas etc: *Low birth weight may be caused by* **external factors**, *such as smoking during pregnancy.* | *influences from the external environment*
3 ORGANIZATION coming from or happening outside a particular place or organization; ▣ **internal**: *information from external sources*
4 FOREIGN relating to foreign countries; ▣ **internal**: *China will not tolerate any external interference in its affairs.* | **external affairs/relations** *the Minister of External Affairs*
5 INDEPENDENT *BrE* coming from outside a particular school, university, or organization, and therefore independent; ▣ **internal**: **external examination/examiner** | **external auditors** (=someone from outside who looks at an organization's finances) —**externally** *adv: The job should be advertised internally and externally.*

ex·ter·nal·ize also **-ise** *BrE* /ɪkˈstɜːnəlaɪz $ -ɜːr-/ *v* [T] *formal* to express inner feelings; → **internalize** —**externalization** /ɪkˌstɜːnəlaɪˈzeɪʃən $ -ˌstɜːrnələ-/ *n* [C,U]

ex·ter·nals /ɪkˈstɜːnlz $ -ɜːr-/ *n* [plural] the outer appearance of a situation

ex·tern·ship /ˈekstɜːnʃɪp $ -tɜːrn-/ *n* [C] *AmE* a job that a university student does in order to gain experience in a particular area of work. Externships are usually not paid and usually last only a short time; → **extern**, **internship**: *an externship in a law firm*

ex·tinct /ɪkˈstɪŋkt/ *adj* **1** an extinct type of animal or plant does not exist any more: *Dinosaurs have been extinct for millions of years.* | *Pandas could* **become extinct in the wild**. | *an extinct species* **2** if a type of person, custom, skill etc is extinct, it does not exist in society any more **3** an extinct VOLCANO does not ERUPT any more; ▣ **active**

ex·tinc·tion /ɪkˈstɪŋkʃən/ *n* [U] **1** when a particular kind of animal or plant stops existing: *species* **in danger of extinction** | **on the verge/edge/brink of extinction** (=nearly extinct) *The breed was on the verge of extinction.* | *They were* **hunted** almost **to extinction**. | *Conservationists are trying to save the whale* **from extinction**. | **face extinction/be threatened with extinction** *Many endangered species now face extinction.* **2** when a type of person, custom, skill etc stops existing: *Their traditional way of life seems doomed to extinction.*

ex·tin·guish /ɪkˈstɪŋgwɪʃ/ *v* [T] *formal* **1** to make a fire or light stop burning or shining; ▣ **put out**: *Please extinguish all cigarettes.* | *Firemen were called to extinguish the blaze.* **2** to make an idea or feeling stop: *All hope was almost extinguished.*

ex·tin·guish·er /ɪkˈstɪŋgwɪʃə $ -ər/ *n* [C] a FIRE EXTINGUISHER

ex·tir·pate /ˈekstɜːpeɪt $ -ɜːr-/ *v* [T] *formal* to completely destroy something that is unpleasant or unwanted

ex·tol /ɪkˈstəʊl $ -ˈstoʊl/ v **extolled, extolling** [T] *formal* to praise something very much: **extol the virtues/ benefits etc of sth** *a speech extolling the merits of free enterprise*

ex·tort /ɪkˈstɔːt $ -ɔːrt/ v [T] to illegally force someone to give you something, especially money, by threatening them; → **blackmail: extort sth from sb** *Rebels extorted money from local villagers.* —**extortion** /ɪkˈstɔːʃən $ -ɔːr-/ n [U]: *He faces charges of kidnapping and extortion.* —**extortionist** n [C]

ex·tor·tion·ate /ɪkˈstɔːʃən ̣t $ -ɔːr-/ adj an extortionate price, demand etc is unreasonably high; ▣ **exorbitant**: *Many local taxi drivers charge extortionate rates.* —**extortionately** adv

ex·tra¹ S1 W2 /ˈekstrə/ adj
1 [only before noun] more of something, in addition to the usual or standard amount or number: *Could you get an extra loaf of bread?* | *Allow extra time for your journey.* | *Drivers are advised to take extra care.* | *Residents can use the gym at no extra cost.* | **an extra ten minutes/three metres etc** *I asked for an extra two weeks to finish the work.*
2 [not before noun] if something is extra, it is not included in the price of something and you have to pay more for it: *Dinner costs $15 but wine is extra.*

extra² pron an amount of something, especially money, in addition to the usual, basic, or necessary amount; ▣ **more: pay/charge/cost etc extra** *I earn extra for working on Sunday.*

extra³ adv **1** in addition to the usual things or the usual amount: *They need to offer something extra to attract customers.* | **one/a few etc extra** *I got a few extra in case anyone else decides to come.* | *I'll be making $400 extra a month.* **2** [+ adj/adv] used to emphasize an adjective or adverb: *You're going to have to work extra hard to pass the exam.* | *an extra special effort*

extra⁴ n [C] **1** something which is added to a basic product or service that improves it and often costs more: *Tinted windows and a sunroof are **optional extras** (=something that you can choose to have or not).* | *Be careful, there may be **hidden extras** (=additional charges which you are not told about).* | *It's got lots of useful **little extras**.* **2** an actor in a film who does not say anything but is part of a crowd: *He started his acting career as an extra.*

extra- /ekstrə/ prefix **1** outside or beyond: *extra-galactic* (=outside our galaxy) | *extracellular* (=outside a cell) **2** *informal* very or more than normal: *extra-large* | *extra-strong* | *extra-special*

ex·tract¹ /ɪkˈstrækt/ v [T] **1** *formal* to remove an object from somewhere, especially with difficulty: *You'll have to have that **tooth extracted**.* | **extract sth from sth** *He extracted an envelope from his inside pocket.* **2** to carefully remove a substance from something which contains it, using a machine, chemical process etc: **extract sth from sth** *Oils are extracted from the plants.* **3** to get something which you want from someone, such as information, money, help etc, especially when they do not want to give it to you: **extract sth from sb** *She had extracted a promise from him.* | *They used torture to **extract information** about their families.* **4** to take information or a short piece of writing from a book: *We need to extract the relevant financial data.* **5** to get an advantage or good thing from a situation: **extract sth from sth** *They aim to extract the maximum political benefit from the Games.*

ex·tract² /ˈekstrækt/ n **1** [C] a short piece of writing, music etc taken from a particular book, piece of music etc: [+**from**] *I've only seen short extracts from the film.* **2** [C,U] a substance obtained from something by using a special process: **vanilla/malt/plant etc extract** *Add one teaspoon of vanilla extract.*

ex·trac·tion /ɪkˈstrækʃən/ n **1** [C,U] the process of removing or obtaining something from something else: [+**of**] *the extraction of salt from seawater* | *the extrac-*

tion of information from appropriate reference sources | **mineral/oil etc extraction 2 be of French/Russian/ Italian etc extraction** to be from a French, Russian etc family even though you were not born in that country

ex·trac·tor /ɪkˈstræktə $ -ər/ also **ex·tractor ˌfan** n [C] a machine for removing air that is hot or smells unpleasant from a kitchen, factory etc

ex·tra·cur·ric·u·lar /ˌekstrəkəˈrɪkj ̣lə◂ $ -ər◂ / adj [only before noun] extracurricular activities are not part of the course that a student is doing at a school or college

ex·tra·dit·a·ble /ˈekstrədaɪtəbəl/ adj an extraditable crime is one for which someone can be extradited: *Possession of explosives is an extraditable offence.*

ex·tra·dite /ˈekstrədaɪt/ v [T] to use a legal process to send someone who may be guilty of a crime back to the country where the crime happened in order to judge them in a court of law: **extradite sb to/from Britain/the US etc** *They are expected to be extradited to Britain to face trial.* —**extradition** /ˌekstrəˈdɪʃən/ n [C,U]: *an extradition order*

ex·tra·ju·di·cial /ˌekstrədʒuːˈdɪʃəl◂ / adj [only before noun] beyond or outside the ordinary powers of the law

ex·tra·mar·i·tal /ˌekstrəˈmær ̣tl◂ / adj [only before noun] an extramarital sexual relationship is one that a married person has with a person who is not their husband or wife

ex·tra·mu·ral /ˌekstrəˈmjʊərəl◂ $ -ˈmjʊr-/ adj [only before noun] **1** relating to a place or organization but happening or done outside it: *extramural activities* **2** *especially BrE* extramural courses are for people who are not FULL-TIME students

ex·tra·ne·ous /ɪkˈstreɪniəs/ adj *formal* **1** not belonging to or directly related to a particular subject or problem; ▣ **irrelevant**: [+**to**] *Such details are extraneous to the matter in hand.* **2** coming from outside: *extraneous noises*

ex·tra·net /ˈekstrənet/ n [C] a computer system in a company that allows better communication between the company and its customers by combining Internet and INTRANET systems, so that some customers can view some of the company's private information that is not normally available on the Internet

ex·traor·di·naire /ɪkˌstrɔːdɪ ̣ˈneə $ -ˌstrɔːrdnˈer/ adj [only after noun] used, often humorously, to describe someone who is very good at doing something: **gardener/cakemaker/chef etc extraordinaire**

ex·traor·di·na·ri·ly /ɪkˈstrɔːdənər ̣li $ ɪkˌstrɔːrdnˈer ̣li, ˌekstrəˈɔːrdn-er ̣li/ adv *especially BrE* **1** [+ adj/adv] extremely: *We were extraordinarily lucky.* **2** in a way that seems strange: *Why had James behaved so extraordinarily?*

ex·traor·di·na·ry S3 W3 /ɪkˈstrɔːdənəri $ ɪkˈstrɔːrdnˌeri, ˌekstrəˈɔːr-/ adj
1 very unusual or surprising: *It took an extraordinary amount of work.* | *It's extraordinary that he should make exactly the same mistake again.* | **quite/most extraordinary** *BrE: Chris's behaviour that morning was quite extraordinary.* | **extraordinary thing to do/say/ happen** *What an extraordinary thing to do!* | **how extraordinary!** *BrE spoken* (=used to express surprise); → see box at UNUSUAL
2 very much greater or more impressive than usual; ▣ **incredible**: *a woman of extraordinary beauty* | *an extraordinary talent*
3 extraordinary meeting/session etc a meeting which takes place in addition to the usual ones
4 envoy/ambassador/minister extraordinary an official employed for a special purpose, in addition to the usual officials

ex·trap·o·late /ɪkˈstræpəleɪt/ v [I,T] to use facts about the present or about one thing or group to make a guess about the future or about other things or groups: **extrapolate (sth) from sth** *It is possible to extrapolate future developments from current trends.* | *You're extrapolating from your own feelings to mine.* |

extrapolate (sth) to sth *These results cannot, however, be extrapolated to other patient groups.* —**extrapolation** /ɪkˌstræpəˈleɪʃən/ *n* [C,U]

extra- sensory perˈception *n* [U] ESP

ex·tra·ter·res·tri·al¹ /ˌekstrətəˈrestriəl/ *n* [C] a creature that people think may exist on another PLANET

extraterrestrial² *adj* relating to things that exist outside the Earth

ex·tra·ter·ri·to·ri·al /ˌekstrəterɪˈtɔːriəl/ *adj formal* happening outside a particular country

extra ˈtime *n* [U] *especially BrE* a period of usually 30 minutes added to the end of a football game in some competitions if neither team has won after normal time; ▣ **overtime** *AmE*: **in extra time** *Beckham scored in extra time.* | *The match went into extra time.*

ex·trav·a·gant /ɪkˈstrævəgənt/ *adj* **1** spending or costing a lot of money, especially more than is necessary or more than you can afford: *Would it would be too extravagant to buy both?* | *an extravagant lifestyle* **2** doing or using something too much or more than is necessary: [+with] *Don't be too extravagant with the wine.* | *an extravagant display of loyalty* **3** if someone makes extravagant claims, promises etc, they make big claims or promises that are not true or real: *extravagant claims about the drug's effectiveness* **4** very impressive because of being very expensive, beautiful etc: *extravagant celebrations* —**extravagantly** *adv* —**extravagance** *n* [C,U]: *the extravagance of the Royal Palace* | *His only extravagance* (=the only expensive thing he bought) *was fine wine.*

ex·trav·a·gan·za /ɪkˌstrævəˈgænzə/ *n* [C] a very large and expensive entertainment: *a musical extravaganza*

ex·tra·vert /ˈekstrəvɜːt $ -ɜːrt/ *n* [C] another spelling of EXTROVERT

extra ˈvirgin *adj* extra virgin OLIVE OIL comes from OLIVES that are pressed for the first time, and is considered to be the best quality olive oil

ex·treme¹ [S3] [W3] /ɪkˈstriːm/ *adj*
1 [only before noun] very great in degree: *Extreme poverty still exists in many rural areas.* | **extreme care/caution** *It is necessary to use extreme caution with chemicals.* | *extreme cold* | *He had extreme difficulty getting hold of the ingredients.*
2 very unusual and severe or serious: **extreme example/case** *an extreme case of cruelty* | *Force is only justified* **in extreme circumstances.** | **extreme weather/conditions etc**
3 extreme west/end/left etc the part furthest to the west, nearest the end etc: *on the extreme edge of the cliff*
4 extreme opinions, beliefs, or organizations, especially political ones, are considered by most people to be unacceptable and unreasonable: *extreme right-wing nationalists*
5 [only before noun] **extreme sports/surfing/skiing etc** an extreme sport is one that is done in a way that has much more risk and so is more dangerous than an ordinary form of the sport
6 extreme athlete/surfer/skier etc someone who does extreme sports: *Extreme surfers will ride waves that reach heights of more than fifty feet.*

extreme² *n* [C] **1** a situation, quality etc which is as great as it can possibly be – used especially when talking about two opposites: [+of] *The bacteria can withstand extremes of heat and cold.* | *In fact, the truth lies* **between** *the two extremes.* | **at the other/opposite extreme** *At the other extreme is a country like Switzerland with almost no unemployment.* | *Advertisements seem to* **go from one extreme to the other** (=change from one extreme thing to something totally opposite). **2 in the extreme** to a very great degree: *This kind of experiment seems cruel in the extreme.* **3 to extremes** if someone does something to extremes, they do it to a point beyond what is normal or acceptable: **take/carry sth to extremes** *Problems only occur when this attitude is taken to extremes.* | *She had* **gone to extremes** *to avoid seeing him.*

ex,treme ˈfighting *n* [U] a competition, similar to BOXING, in which two people are allowed to hit or kick each other and in which there are almost no rules

ex·treme·ly [S1] [W2] /ɪkˈstriːmli/ *adv* [+ adj/adv] to a very great degree: *Earthquakes are extremely difficult to predict.* | *I'm extremely sorry to have troubled you.*

extremis *n* → IN EXTREMIS

ex·trem·is·m /ɪkˈstriːmɪzəm/ *n* [U] opinions, ideas, and actions, especially political or religious ones, that most people think are unreasonable and unacceptable

ex·trem·ist /ɪkˈstriːmɪst/ *n* [C] someone who has extreme political opinions and aims, and who is willing to do unusual or illegal things in order to achieve them: *The bomb was planted by right-wing extremists.* —**extremist** *adj*

ex·trem·i·ty /ɪkˈstreməti/ *n plural* **extremities** **1** [C usually plural] one of the parts of your body that is furthest away from the centre, for example your fingers and toes **2** [U] the degree to which something goes beyond what is usually thought to be acceptable: *The committee was uncomfortable about the extremity of the proposal.* **3** [C] the part that is furthest away from the centre of something: **eastern/southern etc extremity of sth** *an island at the southern extremity of New Zealand*

ex·tri·cate /ˈekstrɪkeɪt/ *v* [T] **1** to escape from a difficult or embarrassing situation, or to help someone escape: **extricate yourself/sb from sth** *How was he going to extricate himself from this situation?* **2** to remove someone from a place in which they are trapped: **extricate sb/yourself from sth** *Firemen had to extricate the driver from the wreckage.*

ex·trin·sic /ek'strɪnsɪk, -zɪk/ *adj formal* coming from outside or not directly relating to something; ▣ **intrinsic**: *Staff who complete extra qualifications receive no* **extrinsic rewards** (=no extra money etc). | *a combination of intrinsic and extrinsic factors*

ex·tro·vert, extravert /ˈekstrəvɜːt $ -ɜːrt/ *n* [C] someone who is active and confident, and who enjoys spending time with other people; ▣ **introvert**: *Her sister was always more of an extrovert.* —**extrovert** *adj*: *a friendly, extrovert young Australian*

ex·tro·vert·ed /ˈekstrəvɜːtɪd $ -vɜːr-/ *also* **extrovert** *adj* having a confident character and enjoying the company of other people; ▣ **introverted** —**extroversion** /ˌekstrəˈvɜːʃən $ -ˈvɜːrʒən/ *n* [U]

ex·trude /ɪkˈstruːd/ *v* [T] **1** *formal* to push or force something out through a hole **2** *technical* to force plastic or metal through a hole so that it has a particular shape —**extrusion** /ɪkˈstruːʒən/ *n* [C,U]

ex·u·be·rant /ɪgˈzjuːbərənt $ ɪgˈzuː-/ *adj* **1** happy and full of energy and excitement: *an exuberant personality* **2** exuberant decorations, patterns etc are exciting and complicated or colourful: *exuberant carvings* —**exuberance** *n* [U]: *She needs to try and control her natural exuberance.* —**exuberantly** *adv*

ex·ude /ɪgˈzjuːd $ ɪgˈzuːd/ *v* **1** [T] if you exude a particular quality, it is easy to see that you have a lot of it: *She exudes self-confidence.* | *He exuded an air of wealth and power* **2** [I,T] *formal* to flow out slowly and steadily, or to make something do this: *The plant exudes a sticky liquid.*

ex·ult /ɪgˈzʌlt/ *v* [I,T] *formal* to show that you are very happy and proud, especially because you have succeeded in doing something: [+at/in/over] *She exulted in her new discovery.* | *'We made the front page!' Jos exulted.* —**exultation** /ˌegzʌlˈteɪʃən/ *n* [U]: *a sense of exultation*

ex·ul·tant /ɪgˈzʌltənt/ *adj formal* very happy or proud, especially because you have succeeded in doing something: *an exultant mood* | *Ralph was exultant.* —**exultantly** *adv*

E

-ey /i/ *suffix* [in adjectives] the form used for -Y, especially after y: *clayey soil*

eye¹ S1 W1 /aɪ/ *n*
1 FOR SEEING WITH [C] one of the two parts of the body that you use to see with: *He's got brown eyes and a cheerful smile.* | *There were tears in her eyes as she listened to the story.* | *Ow! I've got something in my eye!* | *Jessica's eyes sparkled with excitement.* | **close/shut your eyes** *He yawned, closed his eyes again, and turned over.* | *Emily* **opened** *her eyes.* | **drop/lower your eyes** (=to look down) | **have/keep etc your eyes glued to sth** (=to be watching something with all your attention) *Winifred sat with her eyes glued to the television screen.* | *Clark's* **eyes narrowed** *as he saw the man approaching.* | *Louise's eyes widened.* | *All eyes were immediately turned* **on** (=everyone looked at) *Henry.* | *I've got an* **eye test** (=a test to check how well I can see) *tomorrow.* | **blue-eyed/one-eyed/bright-eyed** etc *a brown-eyed girl* → WIDE-EYED
2 WAY OF SEEING/UNDERSTANDING [C usually singular] a particular way of seeing, judging, or understanding something: *Go through your shopping list with* **a critical eye** *for foods with a high fat content.* | **with the eye of sb** *The magazine combines the accuracy of the scientist with the eye of the artist.* | **to sb's eye(s)** *The picture quality, to my eye, is excellent.* | **through the eyes of sb** (=from the point of view of a particular person) *The story is told through the eyes of a refugee child.* | **in the eyes of sb** (=according to a particular person or group) *Carl could do no wrong in the eyes of his parents.*
3 keep an eye on sth/sb to look after someone or something and make sure that they are safe: *Mary will keep an eye on the kids this afternoon.* | *We keep a watchful eye on our elderly neighbors.*
4 have/keep your eye on sb to carefully watch everything that someone does, especially because you do not trust them: *We want Taylor in jail where we can keep an eye on him.*
5 eye contact when you look directly at someone at the same time as they are looking at you: *People who are lying tend to avoid eye contact.* | *In a formal interview, try to maintain good eye contact with the interviewers.*
6 keep/have one eye/half an eye on sb/sth to be watching someone or something at the same time that you are doing something else: *Louise was stirring the soup with half an eye on the baby.*
7 have your eye on sth to want something that you think might become available: *He has his eye on the bigger apartment next door.*
8 the naked eye if you can see something with the naked eye, you can see it without using any artificial help such as a TELESCOPE or MICROSCOPE: **with the naked eye** *It's just about possible to see the planet with the naked eye on a clear night.* | **visible/invisible to the naked eye** *Dust mites are tiny creatures, invisible to the naked eye.*
9 before your very eyes also (right) in front of your eyes *especially spoken* if something happens before your very eyes, it happens where you can clearly see it: *The murder had apparently taken place before our very eyes.*
10 can't take your eyes off sb/sth to be unable to stop looking at someone or something, especially because they are extremely interesting or attractive: *She looked stunning. I couldn't take my eyes off her all evening.*
11 under the (watchful/stern etc) eye of sb while being watched by someone who is making sure that you behave properly or do something right: *We went to dances, but only under the watchful eye of our father.*
12 run/cast your eye over sth to look at something quickly: *She cast her eye over the front page of the paper.*
13 set/lay/clap eyes on sb/sth *spoken* to see something or meet someone, especially for the first time: *I loved that house from the moment I clapped eyes on it.*
14 keep an eye open/out (for sth) to watch carefully so that you will notice when someone or something appears: *Keep an eye out for rabbits in the field.*

15 with an eye to (doing) sth if you do something with an eye to doing something else, you do it in order to make the second thing more likely to happen: *Most novels are published with an eye to commercial success*
16 close/shut your eyes to sth to ignore something or pretend that you do not know it is happening: *Most governments know that we're heading for an environ mental catastrophe but they shut their eyes to it.*
17 have a (good) eye for sth to be good at noticing a particular type of thing, especially something attractive, valuable, or good quality etc: *Ernest has an eye for detail.* | *She's definitely got a good eye for a bargain.*
18 keep your eyes peeled/skinned *spoken* to watch carefully and continuously for something: [+for] *She stumbled along, keeping her eyes peeled for a phone box*
19 with your eyes open knowing fully what the problems, difficulties, results etc of a situation might be: *I've no-one to blame but myself – I went into this deal with my eyes open.*
20 can do sth with your eyes shut/closed to be able to do something very easily: *Believe me, you could run that place with your eyes closed.*
21 make eyes at sb/give sb the eye *informal* to look at someone in a way that shows you think they are sexually attractive: *Don't look now, but that guy over there is really giving you the eye.*
22 an eye for/on/to the main chance if you have an eye for the main chance, you will take advantage of any possible opportunity to get what you want – used to show disapproval
23 one in the eye for sb *BrE spoken* something that will annoy someone or give them a disadvantage – used especially when you think this is a good thing: *This latest judgement will definitely be one in the eye for the fast food corporations.*
24 an eye for an eye the idea that if someone does something wrong, you should punish them by doing the same thing to them: *An eye for an eye is no way to run a civilised justice system.*
25 for sb's eyes only used to say that something is secret and must only be seen by one particular person or group: *The information is for police eyes only.*
26 have eyes in the back of your head to know what is happening all around you, even when this seems impossible: *We'll have to be really careful – old Jonesey has eyes in the back of his head.*
27 get/keep your eye in *BrE informal* to practise or to continue practising an activity so that you become good at it
28 have eyes like a hawk to notice every small detail or everything that is happening, and therefore be very difficult to deceive: *We never got away with anything in Mrs. Podell's class – she had eyes like a hawk.*
29 have eyes popping (out of your head) *BrE especially spoken* to be very surprised, shocked, or excited by something you see
30 be up to your eyes in sth *BrE informal* to be very busy doing something: *He's up to his eyes in paperwork.*
31 have eyes bigger than your belly *spoken* used to say that you have taken more food than you are able to eat
32 only have eyes for sb if someone only has eyes for someone, they love and are interested in that person only
33 my eye! *old-fashioned spoken* used to say that you do not believe something
34 all eyes are on/watching/fixed on etc **a)** used to say that everyone is looking at someone or something: *All eyes were on the speaker, and nobody noticed me slip into the hall.* **b)** used to say that a lot of people are paying attention to a particular person or situation: *For the time being, all eyes are on the White House.*
35 in a pig's eye! *AmE spoken* used to show that you do not believe what someone is saying
36 CAMERA [singular] the eye of the camera is the way that you appear in photographs: *Fashion models are completely comfortable with the eye of the camera.*
37 NEEDLE [C] the hole in a needle that you put the thread through
38 FOR FASTENING CLOTHES [C] a small circle or

U-shaped piece of metal used together with a hook for fastening clothes
39 STORM [singular] the calm centre of a storm such as a HURRICANE
40 POTATO [C] a dark spot on a potato that a new plant can grow from → BIRD'S-EYE VIEW, BLACK EYE, CATSEYE, PRIVATE EYE, RED EYE; → **the apple of sb's eye** at APPLE (2); → **not bat an eye** at BAT² (2); → **turn a blind eye (to sth)** at BLIND¹ (3); → **see sth out of the corner of your eye** at CORNER¹ (8); → **the evil eye** at EVIL¹ (5); → **give sb the glad eye** at GLAD (6); → **look sb in the eye/face** at LOOK¹ (7); → **in your mind's eye** at MIND¹ (40); → **here's mud in your eye** at MUD; → **open sb's eyes (to)** at OPEN² (17); → **in the public eye** at PUBLIC¹ (4); → **make sheep's eyes at** at SHEEP (4); → **a sight for sore eyes** at SIGHT¹ (14); → **in the twinkling of an eye** at TWINKLING; → **keep a weather eye on** at WEATHER¹ (5); → **pull the wool over sb's eyes** at WOOL (4)

eye² v present participle **eyeing** or **eying** [T] to look at someone or something carefully, especially because you do not trust them or because you want something: *The man behind the desk eyed us suspiciously.* | *A crowd of local children gathered around, eying us in silence.*

  eye sb ⇔ **up** phr v informal to look at someone in a way that shows you think they are sexually attractive: *There was a group of lads at the bar, eyeing up every girl who walked in.*

eye·ball¹ /ˈaɪbɔːl $ -bɒːl/ n [C] **1** the round ball that forms the whole of your eye, including the part inside your head **2** eyeball to eyeball if two people are eyeball to eyeball, they are directly facing each other, especially in an angry or threatening way **3** up to the/your eyeballs in sth informal if someone is up to their eyeballs in something, they have more than they can deal with: *She's up to her eyeballs in debt.* **4** drugged/doped up to the eyeballs if someone is drugged up to the eyeballs, they have taken a lot of drugs so that their behaviour is severely affected

eyeball² v [T] informal to look directly and closely at something or someone: *They eyeballed each other suspiciously.*

eye·brow /ˈaɪbraʊ/ n [C] **1** the line of hair above your eye: *thick bushy eyebrows* **2** raise your eyebrows to move your eyebrows upwards in order to show surprise or disapproval: *'Really?' she said, raising her eyebrows.* | *This decision caused a few raised eyebrows* (=surprised some people). **3** be up to your eyebrows in sth spoken to have more of something than you can deal with: *I'm absolutely up to my eyebrows in work.*

eyebrow ,pencil n [C,U] a special pencil you can use to make your eyebrows darker

eye ,candy n [U] informal someone or something that is attractive to look at, but is not serious or important

eye-,catching adj something eye-catching is unusual or attractive in a way that makes you notice it: *an eye-catching design*

eye drops n [plural] special liquid which you put into your eyes because they are sore or dry, or as a medical treatment

eye·ful /ˈaɪfʊl/ n [C] **1 an eyeful** informal **a)** if you get an eyeful of something interesting or shocking, you see it **b)** old-fashioned something or someone, especially a woman, who is very attractive to look at **2** an amount of liquid, dust, or sand that has got into someone's eye

eye·glass /ˈaɪɡlɑːs $ -ɡlæs/ n **1** [C] a LENS for one eye, worn to help you see better with that eye; ◨ **monocle 2** **eyeglasses** [plural] old-fashioned or AmE a pair of GLASSES

eye·lash /ˈaɪlæʃ/ n [C] **1** one of the small hairs that grow along the edge of your EYELIDS **2 flutter your eyelashes** if a woman flutters her eyelashes, she moves them up and down very quickly, in order to look sexually attractive

eye·less /ˈaɪləs/ adj having no eyes

eye·let /ˈaɪḷt/ n [C] a hole surrounded by a metal ring that is put in leather or cloth so that a string can be passed through it

'eye ,level n [U] a height equal to the level of your eyes: **at/above/below eye level** *Your screen should be at eye level.* | *an eye-level grill*

eye·lid /ˈaɪlɪd/ n [C] a piece of skin that covers your eye when it is closed: *His eyelids began to droop* (=close, because he was sleepy). | *The room spun. Her eyelids fluttered* (=moved up and down quickly) *and she fainted.* → **not bat an eyelid** at BAT² (2)

eye·lin·er /ˈaɪˌlaɪnə $ -ər/ n [C,U] coloured MAKE-UP that you put along the edges of your eyelids to make your eyes look bigger or more noticeable: *She was wearing thick, black eyeliner.* | *an eyeliner pencil*

'eye-,opener n [C usually singular] an experience from which you learn something surprising or new: *The whole trip has been a real eye-opener.*

'eye patch n [C] a piece of material worn over one eye, usually because that eye has been damaged

eye·piece /ˈaɪpiːs/ n [C] the glass piece that you look through in a MICROSCOPE or TELESCOPE

'eye ,shadow n [C,U] coloured MAKE-UP that you put on your EYELIDS to make your eyes look more attractive → see picture at MAKE-UP

eye·sight /ˈaɪsaɪt/ n [U] your ability to see: **poor/ good/failing etc eyesight** *Eagles have very keen eyesight.* | *He had a problem with his eyesight.*

eye·sore /ˈaɪsɔː $ -sɔːr/ n [C] something that is very ugly, especially a building surrounded by other things that are not ugly: *The factory is an eyesore.*

'eye strain n [U] a pain you feel in your eyes, for example because you are tired or have been reading a lot

'eye tooth n [C] **1 sb would give their eye teeth for sth** spoken used to say that someone wants something very much: *I'd give my eye teeth to be able to play the piano like that.* **2** one of the long pointed teeth at the corner of your mouth; ◨ **canine tooth**

eye·wash /ˈaɪwɒʃ $ -wɒːʃ, -wɑːʃ/ n [U] BrE spoken old-fashioned something that you do not believe is true

eye·wear /ˈaɪweə $ -wer/ n [U] glasses, SUNGLASSES etc – used especially by companies who make them

eye·wit·ness /ˈaɪˌwɪtn̩s/ n [C] someone who has seen something such as a crime happen, and is able to describe it afterwards: **eyewitness account/report/testimony** *According to eyewitness accounts, soldiers opened fire on the crowd.* | *One eyewitness said he saw her talking to a man in a blue car.*

ey·ing /ˈaɪ-ɪŋ/ v a present participle of EYE²

eyot /eɪt, ˈeɪət/ n [C] BrE a small island in a river

ey·rie also **eyry** BrE /ˈɪəri, ˈeəri, ˈaɪəri $ ˈɪri, ˈeri, ˈaɪri/ n [C] **1** the NEST of a large bird, especially an EAGLE, that is usually built high up in rocks or trees **2** literary a room or building that is very high up

e-zine /ˈiː ziːn/ n [C] a magazine that can be read on the Internet

E

F, f

F, f /ef/ *plural* **F's, f's** *n* **1** [C,U] the sixth letter of the English alphabet **2** [C,U] the fourth note in the musical SCALE¹ (8) of C MAJOR or the musical KEY based on this note **3** [C] a mark given to a student's work to show that it is not good enough: *I got an F in chemistry.* → F-WORD

F **1** the written abbreviation of *Fahrenheit: Water boils at 212° F.* **2** the written abbreviation of *female*

f. also **f** *BrE* **1** the written abbreviation of *forte*, used in music to show that a part should be played or sung loudly **2** the written abbreviation of *female*

fa /faː/ *n* [U] the fourth note in a musical SCALE¹ (8) according to the SOL-FA system

FA /ˌef ˈeɪ‹/ *n* **1 the FA** *the Football Association* the organization that is in charge of professional football in England: *the FA Cup* **2 sweet FA** *BrE not polite* nothing

fab /fæb/ *adj BrE informal* extremely good: *a fab new car*

fa·ble /ˈfeɪbəl/ *n* **1** [C] a traditional short story that teaches a moral lesson, especially a story about animals: *the fable of the fox and the crow* **2** [U] fables or other traditional stories: *monsters of fable*

fa·bled /ˈfeɪbəld/ *adj literary* famous and often mentioned in traditional stories; ◨ **legendary**: *the fabled Fountain of Youth*

fab·ric W3 /ˈfæbrɪk/ *n*
1 [C,U] cloth used for making clothes, curtains etc; ◨ **material**: *our new range of fabrics and wallpapers* | **cotton/silk/synthetic etc fabric** *printed cotton fabric*
2 [singular] the fabric of a society is its basic structure, way of life, relationships, and traditions: [+of] *Drug abuse poses a major threat to the fabric of our society.* | *The country's social fabric is disintegrating.*
3 the fabric of sth the fabric of a building is its basic structure, including walls and the roof: *the need to preserve the fabric of the church*

fab·ri·cate /ˈfæbrɪkeɪt/ *v* [T] **1** to invent a story, piece of information etc in order to deceive someone: *The police were accused of fabricating evidence.* **2** *technical* to make or produce goods or equipment; ◨ **manufacture**: *The discs are expensive to fabricate.*

fab·ri·ca·tion /ˌfæbrɪˈkeɪʃən/ *n* **1** [C,U] a piece of information or story that someone has invented in order to deceive people: **complete/total/pure fabrication** *Of course, it might all be complete fabrication.* **2** [U] *technical* the process of making or producing something; ◨ **manufacture**

'fabric ˌsoftener; **'fabric conˌditioner** *BrE n* [C,U] a liquid that you put in water when washing clothes in order to make them feel softer

fab·u·lous /ˈfæbjʊləs/ *adj* **1** extremely good or impressive; ◨ **wonderful**: *You look fabulous!* | *a fabulous meal* | *The room has fabulous views across the lake.* **2** [only before noun] very large in amount or size; ◨ **huge**: *the Duke's fabulous wealth* **3** [only before noun] fabulous creatures, places etc are mentioned in traditional stories, but do not really exist

fab·u·lous·ly /ˈfæbjʊləsli/ *adv* **fabulously rich/expensive/successful etc** extremely rich, expensive etc

fa·cade, façade /fəˈsɑːd, fæ-/ *n* [C] **1** the front of a building, especially a large and important one: [+of] *the facade of the cathedral* | *an impressive building with a red brick facade* **2** [usually singular] a way of behaving that hides your real feelings: *Behind her*

cheerful *facade*, she's a really lonely person. | [+of] *She managed to maintain a facade of bravery.*

face¹ S1 W1 /feɪs/ *n* [C]
1 FRONT OF YOUR HEAD the front part of your head where your eyes, nose, and mouth are: *She had a beautiful face.* | *Her face was white with fear.* | *A big smile spread across his face.* | *I could see from the look on her face that something was wrong.* | *I felt like punching him in the face.* ⚠ Something is **on** someone's face, not in their face: *You've got a mark on your face.*
2 EXPRESSION an expression on someone's face

a long face (=an unhappy expression)
pull/make a face (=change your expression to make people laugh or to show you are angry, disappointed etc)
a blank face (=an expression that shows you do not know or recognize something)
a face like thunder (=a very angry expression)
sb's face lights up/brightens (=they start to look happy)
sb's face falls (=they start to look unhappy)
sb's face darkens (=they start to look angry or threatening)
see sth in sb's face
show in sb's face
sth is written all over sb's face (=something is obvious from someone's expression)
you should have seen his/her face *spoken* (=used to say that someone was very angry, surprised etc)
the look/expression on sb's face
a smile/grin/frown etc on sb's face

the children's happy faces	*I'll never forget my father's face – I'd never seen him so upset before.*	*What's the* **long face** *for?*	*Emma was* **making faces** *at me through the window.*	*Judging from her* **blank face***, I'd say she didn't know what we were talking about.*	*Mr Neeson came striding towards us with* **a face like thunder***.*	*David's* **face lit up** *when I mentioned her name.*	*Her* **face fell** *and I thought she might burst into tears.*	*Tom's* **face darkened** *and he turned angrily on Sam.*	*They were glad he was there. He could see it* **in** *their faces.*	*The disappointment was* **written all over** *his face.*	**You should have seen** *Gary's face when I told him I was resigning.*	*He had a surprised, slightly puzzled* **look on** *his face.*	*Sally watched him* **with a smile on** *her face.*

3 keep a straight face to not laugh or smile, even though something is funny
4 pale-faced/round-faced etc having a face that has a particular shape or colour: *a pale-faced youth* → RED-FACED
5 grim-faced/serious-faced etc showing a particular expression on your face: *Negotiators emerged grim-faced after the day's talks.* → BAREFACED, PO-FACED, POKER-FACED, STONY-FACED
6 PERSON a person: **new/different face** (=someone who you have not seen before) *There are a few new faces in class this year.* | *Gordon Bradley is a* **familiar face** (=someone who you know or have seen many times before) *at the Shrewsbury Flower Show.* | *It's* **the same old faces** (=people who you see often, especially too often) *at our meetings every week.* | **famous/well-known face** (=someone who is famous from television, magazines, films etc) | *She looked around at the* **sea of faces** (=lots of people seen together) *in the cafeteria.*
7 face to face a) if two people are standing face to face, they are very close and are looking at each other: **meet sb/talk to sb/explain sth etc face to face** (=to meet someone and talk to them, instead of just hearing about them, talking to them on the phone etc) *Actually, I've never met her face to face.* | *'You could have just phoned.' 'I wanted to explain things face to face.'* | **come face to face/find yourself face to face with sb** (=to meet someone, especially in a way that surprises or frightens you) *At that moment he came face to face with Sergeant Burke.* | *The two men stood face to face without a word.* **b)** if you come face to face with something difficult, you experience it and have to deal with it: *It*

was the first time he'd ever **come face to face with** *death.* | **bring sb face to face with sth** *Sometimes one is brought face to face with facts which cannot be ignored.* → FACE-TO-FACE

8 **say sth/tell sb sth to their face** if you say something unpleasant to someone's face, you say it to them directly, rather than to other people: *I told him to his face just what I thought of him.*

9 **face down/downwards** with the face or front towards the ground: *Keith was lying face down on the bed.*

10 **face up/upwards** with the face or front towards the sky: *The body was lying face up in the rain.*

11 **in the face of sth** in a situation where there are many problems, difficulties, or dangers: *It is amazing how Daniels has survived in the face of such strong opposition from within the party.*

12 **on the face of it** used to say that something seems true but that you think there may be other facts about it which are not yet clear: *It looks, on the face of it, like a minor change in the regulations.* | *On the face of it, his suggestion makes sense.*

13 **the face of sth** a) the nature or character of an organization, industry, system etc, and the way it appears to people: *technology that has changed the face of society* | *Is this the new face of the Tory party?* | **the ugly/unacceptable/acceptable face of sth** (=the qualities of an organization, industry etc which people find unacceptable or acceptable) *the unacceptable face of capitalism* b) the general appearance of a particular place: *the changing face of the landscape*

14 MOUNTAIN/CLIFF the face of a mountain, cliff etc is a steep vertical surface or side: [+of] *He fell and died while attempting to climb the north face of Mont Blanc.* | *The cliff face was starting to crumble into the sea.* | *a sheer* (=very steep) *rock face*

15 CLOCK the front part of a clock or watch, where the numbers and hands are → see colour picture at WATCH²

16 **lose face** if you lose face, you do something which makes you seem weak, stupid etc, and which makes people respect you less: *He doesn't want to back down* (=accept defeat in an argument) *and risk losing face.*

17 **save face** if you do something to save face, you do it so that people will not lose their respect for you: *Both countries saved face with the compromise.*

18 **disappear/vanish from/off the face of the earth** used to say that you have no idea where someone is and have not seen them in a very long time: *I haven't seen Paul in ages; he seems to have vanished off the face of the earth.*

19 **on the face of the earth** used when you are emphasizing a statement to mean 'in the whole world': *If she was the last woman on the face of the earth, I still wouldn't be interested!*

20 **sb's face doesn't fit** used to say that someone will not get or keep a particular job because they are not the kind of person that the employer wants

21 **set your face against sth** especially BrE to be very determined that something should not happen: *It is a shame that the local Labour Party has set its face against the scheme.*

22 MINE the part of a mine from which coal, stone etc is cut → COALFACE

23 OUTSIDE SURFACE one of the outside surfaces of an object or building: *A cube has six faces.*

24 SPORT the part of a RACKET or BAT etc that you use to hit the ball

25 **in your face**; **in yer face** BrE spoken informal behaviour, criticisms, remarks etc that are in your face are very direct and often shocking or surprising: *Bingham has a very 'in your face' writing style.*

26 **get in sb's face** spoken informal if someone gets in your face, they really annoy you

27 **get out of my face** spoken informal used to tell someone in an impolite way to go away because they are annoying you

28 **what's his face/what's her face** spoken informal used as a way of talking about someone when you cannot remember their name: *I saw old what's his face in school yesterday.*

29 **put your face on** informal to put MAKE-UP on: *I just need to run upstairs and put my face on.* → **blow up in sb's face** at BLOW UP (7); → **put on a brave face** at BRAVE¹ (3); → **do sth till you're blue in the face** at BLUE¹ (4); → **have egg on your face** at EGG¹ (5); → FACE-TO-FACE; → **fly in the face of** at FLY¹ (18); → **laugh in sb's face** at LAUGH¹ (11); → **long face** at LONG¹ (12); → **not just a pretty face** at PRETTY² (4); → **show your face** at SHOW¹ (15); → **shut your face** at SHUT¹ (2); → **a slap in the face** at SLAP² (2); → **be staring sb in the face** at STARE¹ (2); → **a straight face** at STRAIGHT² (8); → **wipe sth off the face of the earth** at WIPE¹ (8); → **wipe the smile/grin off sb's face** at WIPE¹ (7); → **have sth written all over your face** at WRITE (10)

face² S1 W1 *v* [T]

1 DIFFICULT SITUATION if you face or are faced with a difficult situation, or if a difficult situation faces you, it is going to affect you and you must deal with it: *Emergency services are facing additional problems this winter.* | *The President faces the difficult task of putting the economy back on its feet.* | *McManus is facing the biggest challenge of his career.* | *As the project comes to an end, many workers now face an uncertain future.* | *He must face the prospect of financial ruin.* | **be faced with sth** *I was faced with the awful job of breaking the news to the girl's family.* | *the difficulties faced by the police* | *If he is found guilty, he faces up to 12 years in jail.* | **face charges/prosecution** (=have legal charges brought against you) *He was the first member of the former government to face criminal charges.*

2 ADMIT A PROBLEM EXISTS also **face up to sth** to accept that a difficult situation or problem exists, even though you would prefer to ignore it

> **face the fact that**
> **face facts**
> **face the truth**
> **(let's) face it** spoken (=used when saying something that is hard for someone to accept)

> *Many couples refuse to face the fact that there are problems in their marriage.* | *You've got to face facts, Rachel. You can't survive on a salary that low.* | *He had to face the awful truth that she no longer loved him.* | *Face it, kid. You're never going to be a rock star.*

3 **can't face** if you can't face something, you feel unable to do it because it seems too unpleasant or difficult: *I don't want to go back to college – I just can't face it.* | *I can't face the thought of going into town when it's this hot.* | *She couldn't face the prospect of another divorce.* | **can't face doing sth** *He couldn't face driving all the way to Los Angeles.*

4 TALK/DEAL WITH SB to talk or deal with someone, when this is unpleasant or difficult for you: *You're going to have to face him sooner or later.* | *I don't know how I'm going to face her after what happened.* | *The accident left her feeling depressed and unable to face the world* (=be with people and live a normal life).

5 BE OPPOSITE to be opposite someone or something, or to be looking or pointing in a particular direction: *The two men stood facing each other, smiling.* | *When he turned to face her, he seemed annoyed.* | *Lunch is served on the terrace facing the sea.* | **south-facing/west-facing etc** *a south-facing garden* | **face north/east etc** *The dining room faces east.*; → see box at FRONT¹

6 OPPONENT/TEAM to play against an opponent or team in a game or competition: *Martinez will face Robertson in tomorrow's final.*

7 **face the music** informal to accept criticism or punishment for something you have done

8 BUILDING **be faced with stone/concrete etc** a building that is faced with stone, CONCRETE etc has a layer of that material on its outside surfaces

face sb ⇔ down phr v especially AmE to deal in a strong and confident way with someone who opposes you: *Harrison successfully faced down the mob of angry workers.*

face off phr v AmE to fight, argue, or compete with someone, or to get into

F

a position in which you are ready to do this: *The two candidates will face off in a televised debate on Friday.*
  face up to sth *phr v*
to accept and deal with a difficult fact or problem: *They'll never offer you another job; you might as well face up to it.* | *She had to face up to the fact that he was guilty.*

face card *n* [C] *AmE* the king, queen, or JACK in a set of playing cards; ◪ **court card** *BrE*

face-cloth /ˈfeɪsklɒθ $ -klɒːθ/ *n* [C] *BrE* a small square cloth used to wash your face or hands; ◪ **washcloth** *AmE*

face cream *n* [C,U] a thick cream used to keep the skin on your face soft and smooth

face-less /ˈfeɪsləs/ *adj* [usually before noun] a faceless person, organization, or building has nothing that makes them special, interesting, or different – used to show disapproval: *He had become just another faceless bureaucrat.* | *faceless modern office blocks*

face-lift /ˈfeɪslɪft/ *n* [C] **1** if you have a facelift, you have an operation in which doctors remove loose skin from your face in order to make you look younger **2** work or repairs that make a building or place look newer or better: *The new owner had given the pub a facelift.*

face-off *n* [C] **1** *informal especially AmE* a fight or argument: *a face-off between police and rioters* **2** the start of a game of ICE HOCKEY

face pack *n* [C] *BrE* a thick cream that you spread over your face and leave on for a short time, in order to clean and improve your skin

face powder *n* [U] powder that you put on your face in order to make it look less shiny

face saver *n* [C] an action or arrangement that prevents you from losing other people's respect

face-saving *adj* [only before noun] a face-saving action or arrangement prevents you from losing other people's respect: *a face-saving compromise*

fac-et /ˈfæsɪt/ *n* [C] **1** one of several parts of someone's character, a situation etc; ◪ **aspect**: [+of] *He has travelled extensively in China, recording every facet of life.* **2** **multi-faceted/many-faceted** consisting of many different parts: *The issues are complex and multi-faceted.* **3** one of the flat sides of a cut jewel

face time *n* [U] *AmE* **1** time that you spend at your job because you want other people, especially your manager, to see you there, whether or not you are actually doing good work: *Here we reward performance, not face time.* **2** time that you spend talking to someone when you are with them, rather than on the telephone: [+with] *In return for his donation, he wanted face time with the President.*

fa-ce-tious /fəˈsiːʃəs/ *adj* saying things that are intended to be clever and funny but are really silly and annoying: *Don't be so facetious!* | *facetious comments* **—facetiously** *adv* **—facetiousness** *n* [U]

face-to-face *adj* [only before noun] a face-to-face meeting, conversation etc is one where you are with another person and talking to them: *a face-to-face interview* → **face to face** at FACE¹ (7)

face value *n* **1** **take sth at face value** to accept a situation or accept what someone says, without thinking there may be a hidden meaning: *You shouldn't always take his remarks at face value.* **2** [singular, U] the value or cost shown on the front of something such as a stamp or coin

fa-cial¹ /ˈfeɪʃəl/ *adj* on your face or relating to your face: *Victor's facial expression didn't change.* | *facial hair* **—facially** *adv*: *Facially the boys are similar.*

facial² *n* [C] if you have a facial, you have a beauty treatment in which your face is cleaned and creams are rubbed into it

facial scrub *n* [C] a thick substance which you use to clean your face thoroughly

fa-cile /ˈfæsaɪl $ ˈfæsəl/ *adj* **1** a facile remark, argument etc is too simple and shows a lack of careful thought or understanding: *facile generalizations* **2** [only before noun] *formal* a facile achievement or success has been obtained too easily and has no value: *a facile victory* **—facilely** *adv* **—facileness** *n* [U]

fa-cil-i-tate /fəˈsɪlɪteɪt/ *v* [T] *formal* to make it easier for a process or activity to happen: *Computers can be used to facilitate language learning.* **—facilitation** /fəˌsɪlɪˈteɪʃən/ *n* [U]

fa-cil-i-tat-or /fəˈsɪlɪteɪtə $ -ər/ *n* [C] **1** someone who helps a group of people discuss things with each other or do something effectively **2** *technical* something that helps a process to take place

fa-cil-i-ty S3 W1 /fəˈsɪlɪti/ *n plural* **facilities**
1 **facilities** [plural] rooms, equipment, or services that are provided for a particular purpose: *All rooms have private facilities* (=private bathroom and toilet). | *The hotel has its own pool and leisure facilities.* | *toilet facilities* | *childcare facilities*
2 [C usually singular] a special part of a piece of equipment or a system which makes it possible to do something: *Is there a call-back facility on this phone?* | *a bank account with an overdraft facility*
3 [C] a place or building used for a particular activity or industry, or for providing a particular type of service: *a top-secret research facility* | *the finest indoor sports facility in the US*
4 [singular] a natural ability to do something easily and well; ◪ **talent**: [+for] *She has an amazing facility for languages.*
5 **the facilities** *AmE spoken* the toilet, used to be polite: *Excuse me, I have to use the facilities.*

fac-ing /ˈfeɪsɪŋ/ *n* [C,U] **1** an outer surface of a wall or building made of a different material from the rest in order to make it look attractive **2** material fastened to the inside of a piece of clothing to strengthen it **3** **facings** [plural] parts of a jacket, coat etc around the neck and wrists which have a different colour from the rest

fac-sim-i-le /fækˈsɪmɪli/ *n* [C] **1** an exact copy of a picture, piece of writing etc **2** *formal* a FAX

fact S1 W1 /fækt/ *n*
1 **TRUE INFORMATION** [C] a piece of information that is known to be true: *Newspapers have a duty to provide readers with the facts.* | [+about] *The book is full of interesting facts about the World Cup.* | [+of] *First of all, we need to establish the facts of the case.* | **it's a fact/that's a fact** (=used to emphasize that something is definitely true or that something definitely happened) *The divorce rate is twice as high as in the 1950s – that's a fact.* | **is that a fact?** (=used to reply to a statement that you find surprising, interesting, or difficult to believe) *'She used to be a professional singer.' 'Is that a fact?'* | **it's a (well-known/little-known etc) fact that** *It's a fact that most deaths from lung cancer are caused by smoking.* | *I know for a fact that* (=used to say that something is definitely true) *she earns more than I do.* | **get your facts right/straight** (=make sure you are right about something) *Mr Craig should get his facts straight before making false allegations.* | *Your ability to write and argue is of little use if you get your facts wrong* (=are wrong about something). | **stick to the facts** (=only say what you know is true) | **hard facts** (=information that is definitely true and can be proven) *We need hard facts not just interesting theories.* | **the bare facts** (=the basic details of a situation or story)
2 **the fact (that)** used when talking about a situation and saying that it is true: *Our decision to build the museum in Hartlepool was influenced by the fact that there were no national museums in the North East.* | *He refused to help me, despite the fact that I asked him several times.* | **given the fact (that)/in view of the fact (that)** (=used when saying that a particular fact influences your judgement about something or someone) *Given the fact that this is their first game, I think they did pretty well.* | **due to the fact (that)/owing to the fact (that)** (=because) *The school's poor exam record is*

largely due to the fact that it is chronically under-funded. | *The fact we didn't win when we were so close is very disappointing.*

3 in (actual) fact a) used when you are adding something, especially something surprising, to emphasize what you have just said: *I know the mayor really well. In fact, I had dinner with her last week.* **b)** used to emphasize that the truth about a situation is the opposite of what has been mentioned: *They told me it would be cheap but in fact it cost me nearly $500.* | *Her teachers said she was a slow learner, whereas in actual fact she was partially deaf.*

4 the fact (of the matter) is *spoken* used when you are telling someone what is actually true in a particular situation, especially when this may be difficult to accept, or different from what people believe: *The fact of the matter is that he's just not up to the job.*

5 the fact remains used to emphasize that what you are saying about a situation is true and people must realize this: *The fact remains that the number of homeless people is rising daily.*

6 REAL EVENTS/NOT A STORY [U] situations, events etc that really happened and have not been invented; **⟷ fiction**: *Much of the novel is based on fact.* | *It's a news reporter's job to separate fact from fiction.*

7 facts and figures [plural] the basic details, numbers etc concerning a particular situation or subject: *Here are a few facts and figures about the country.*

8 the facts speak for themselves used to say that the things that have happened or the things someone has done show clearly that something is true

9 after the fact after something has happened or been done, especially after a mistake has been made → **as a matter of fact** at MATTER¹ (4); → **face facts** at FACE² (2); → **in point of fact** at POINT¹ (17)

fact-,finding *adj* **fact-finding trip/visit/mission etc** an official trip, visit etc during which you try to find out facts and information about something for your organization, government etc

fac·tion /ˈfækʃən/ *n* **1** [C] a small group of people within a larger group, who have different ideas from the other members, and who try to get their own ideas accepted: *struggles between the different factions within the party* | *the leaders of the warring factions* **2** [U] *formal* disagreements and arguments between different groups within an organization: *jealousy and faction* —**factional** *adj*: *factional conflict*

fac·tion·al·is·m /ˈfækʃənəlizəm/ *n* [U] disagreements and arguments between different groups within an organization

fac·ti·tious /fækˈtɪʃəs/ *adj formal* made to happen artificially by people rather than happening naturally

fact of 'life *n plural* **facts of life** [C] **1** an unpleasant situation that exists and that must be accepted: *Mass unemployment seems to be a fact of life nowadays.* | *Persuading others to accept the hard financial facts of life is not a very popular job.* **2 the facts of life** the details about sex and how babies are born: *Mum told me the facts of life when I was twelve.*

fac·tor¹ S3 W1 /ˈfæktə $ -ər/ *n* [C]
1 CAUSE/INFLUENCE one of several things that influence or cause a situation: *The rise in crime is mainly due to social and economic factors.* | **[+in]** *The vaccina-*

tion program has been a major factor in the improvement of health standards. | **important/major/key/crucial factor** *The weather could be a crucial factor in tomorrow's game.* | **deciding/decisive/determining factor** (=the most important factor) *We liked both houses, but price was the deciding factor.*

2 LEVEL ON A SCALE a particular level on a scale that measures how strong or effective something is: *factor 15 suntan oil* | *Even in July the windchill factor* (=the degree to which the air feels colder because of the wind) *can be intense.*

3 by a factor of five/ten etc if something increases or decreases by a factor of five, ten etc, it increases or decreases by five times, ten times etc

4 MATHEMATICS *technical* a number that divides into another number exactly: *3 is a factor of 15.*

factor² *v* [T] *AmE technical* to divide a number into factors

factor sth ⟷ **in** also **factor sth into sth** *phr v technical* to include a particular thing in your calculations about how long something will take, how much it will cost etc

factor sth ⟷ **out** *phr v technical* to not include something in your calculations about how long something will take, how much it will cost etc

fac·to·ri·al /fækˈtɔːriəl/ *n* [C] *technical* the result when you multiply a whole number by all the numbers below it: *factorial 3 = 3 x 2 x 1*

fac·to·ry S2 W2 /ˈfæktəri/ *n plural* **factories** [C] a building or group of buildings in which goods are produced in large quantities, using machines: *a car factory* | *factory workers*

'factory ,farming *n* [U] a type of farming in which animals are kept inside, in small spaces or small CAGES, and made to grow or produce eggs very quickly —**factory farm** *n* [C]

,factory 'floor *n* **the factory floor a)** the area in a factory where goods are made **b)** the ordinary workers in a factory, rather than the managers: **on the factory floor** *There's been a lot of talk on the factory floor* (=among the ordinary workers) *about more layoffs in the spring.*

fac·to·tum /fækˈtəʊtəm $ -ˈtoʊ-/ *n* [C] *formal* a servant or worker who has to do many different kinds of jobs for someone

'fact sheet *n* [C] a piece of paper giving all the most important information about something

fac·tu·al /ˈfæktʃuəl/ *adj* based on facts or relating to facts: *Try to keep your account of events as factual as possible.* | **factual information/knowledge/statements etc** *Libraries are stores of factual information.* | *The report contained a number of factual errors.* —**factually** *adv*: *The document is factually correct.*

fac·ul·ty /ˈfækəlti/ *n plural* **faculties 1** [C] a department or group of related departments within a university: **[+of]** *the Faculty of Law* | *the Engineering Faculty* **2** [C,U] *AmE* all the teachers in a university: *Both faculty and students oppose the measures.* **3** [C usually plural] a natural ability, such as the ability to see, hear, or think clearly: *an assessment of the patient's mental faculties* | **in full possession of all your faculties** (=able to see, hear, think etc in the normal way) | **[+of]** *the faculty of sight* **4** [C] *formal* a particular skill that someone has: **[+for]** *She had a great faculty for absorbing information.*

fad /fæd/ *n* [C] something that people like or do for a short time, or that is fashionable for a short time: *Interest in organic food is not a fad, it's here to stay.* —**faddish** *adj* —**faddishness** *n* [U]

fad·dy /ˈfædi/ *adj* someone who is faddy dislikes many kinds of food – used to show disapproval: *Jackie's a terribly faddy eater.*

fade /feɪd/ v **1** also **fade away** [I] to gradually disappear: *Hopes of a peace settlement are beginning to fade.* | *Over the years her beauty had faded a little.* **2** [I,T] to lose colour and brightness, or to make something do this: *the fading evening light* | *a pair of faded jeans* | *The sun had faded the curtains.* **3** also **fade away** [I] to become weaker physically, especially so that you become very ill or die **4** [I] if a team fades, it stops playing as well as it did before

fade in *phr v* to appear slowly or become louder, or to make a picture or sound do this: **fade sth** ⇔ **in** *Additional background sound is faded in at the beginning of the shot.* —**'fade-in** *n* [C]

fade out *phr v* to disappear slowly or become quieter, or to make a picture or sound do this: **fade sth** ⇔ **out** *He slid a control to fade out the music.* —**'fade-out** *n* [C]

fae·ces also **feces** *AmE* /'fiːsiːz/ *n* [plural] *formal* solid waste material from the BOWELS —**faecal** /'fiːkəl/ *adj*

fae·ry, **faerie** /'feəri $ 'feri/ *n plural* **faeries** [C] *old use* a FAIRY

faff /fæf/ *v*
faff about/around *phr v BrE informal* to waste time doing unnecessary things: *Stop faffing around!*

fag /fæg/ *n* [C] **1** *BrE informal* a cigarette **2** *AmE taboo informal* a very offensive word for a HOMOSEXUAL man. Do not use this word. **3 be a fag** *BrE informal* to be a boring or difficult thing to do **4** a young student in some British PUBLIC SCHOOLS who has to do jobs for an older student

'fag end *n* [C] *BrE informal* the end of a cigarette that someone has finished smoking

fagged /fægd/ *adj BrE informal* **1** also **fagged out** [not before noun] extremely tired **2 I can't be fagged** *spoken* used to say that you are too tired or bored to do something; ▤ **I can't be bothered**

fag·got /'fægət/ *n* [C] **1** *BrE* a ball made of meat mixed with bread, which is cooked **2** *AmE taboo informal* a very offensive word for a HOMOSEXUAL man. Do not use this word. **3** *old-fashioned* small sticks that are tied together, used for burning on a fire

Fah·ren·heit /'færənhaɪt/ *n* [U] written abbreviation *F* a scale of temperature in which water freezes at 32° and boils at 212°: *72° Fahrenheit* (=72 degrees on the Fahrenheit scale) —**Fahrenheit** *adj*

fail¹ ⟨S2⟩ ⟨W1⟩ /feɪl/ *v*
1 ⟨NOT SUCCEED⟩ [I] to not succeed in achieving something: *It looks likely that the peace talks will fail.* | [+in] *He failed in his attempt to regain the world title.* | **fail to do sth** *Doctors failed to save the girl's life.* | *Millions of people have tried to quit smoking and failed miserably* (=been completely unsuccessful). | *his efforts to save his failing marriage* | *If all else fails, you may be advised to have an operation.*
2 ⟨NOT DO STH⟩ [I] to not do what is expected, needed, or wanted: **fail to do sth** *The letter failed to arrive.* | *Firms that fail to take advantage of the new technology will go out of business.* | *The government are failing in their duty to protect people.*
3 ⟨EXAM/TEST⟩ **a)** [I,T] to not pass a test or examination: *I failed my driving test the first time I took it.* | *Daniel failed maths but passed all his other subjects.* **b)** [T] to decide that someone has not passed a test or examination: *Her work was so bad that I had no choice but to fail her.*
4 I fail to see/understand *formal* used to show that you are annoyed by something that you do not accept or understand: *I fail to see why you find it so amusing.*
5 ⟨COMPANY/BUSINESS⟩ [I] if a company or business fails, it is unable to continue because of a lack of money
6 ⟨MACHINE/BODY PART⟩ [I] if a part of a machine or an organ in your body fails, it stops working: *The*

engine failed on take-off. | *The hospital said that his kidneys were failing.*
7 ⟨HEALTH⟩ [I] if your sight, memory, health etc is failing, it is gradually getting weaker or is not as good as it was: *Failing eyesight forced him to retire early.*
8 never fail to do sth to do something or happen so regularly that people expect it: *My grandson never fails to phone me on my birthday.*
9 your courage/will/nerve fails (you) if your courage etc fails, or if it fails you, you suddenly do not have it when you need it: *She had to leave immediately, before her courage failed her.*
10 fail sb to not do what someone has trusted you to do; ▤ **let sb down**: *I feel I've failed my children by not spending more time with them.*
11 ⟨CROPS⟩ [I] if crops fail, they do not grow or produce food, for example because of bad weather
12 ⟨RAINS⟩ [I] if the RAINS (=a lot of rain that falls at a particular time each year) fail, they do not come when expected or it does not rain enough → **words fail me** at **WORD¹** (28)

fail² *n* **1 without fail a)** if you do something without fail, you always do it: *Tim visits his mother every day without fail.* **b)** used to tell someone very firmly that they must do something: *I want that work finished by tomorrow, without fail!* **2** [C] an unsuccessful result in a test or examination; ▤ **pass**: *I got a fail in history.*

failed /feɪld/ *adj* **a failed actor/writer etc** someone who wanted to be an actor etc but was unsuccessful

fail·ing¹ /'feɪlɪŋ/ *n* [C] a fault or weakness: *I love him, despite his failings.*

failing² *prep* **failing that/this** used to say that if your first suggestion is not successful or possible, there is another possibility that you could try: *We will probably have the conference at the Hyatt Hotel or, failing that, at the Fairmont.*

'fail-safe *adj* **1** a fail-safe machine, piece of equipment etc contains a system that makes the machine stop working if one part of it fails **2** a fail-safe plan is certain to succeed

fail·ure ⟨S2⟩ ⟨W2⟩ /'feɪljə $ -ər/ *n*
1 ⟨LACK OF SUCCESS⟩ [C,U] a lack of success in achieving or doing something; ▤ **success**: *Winston is not someone who accepts failure easily.* | **failure to do sth** *the conference's failure to reach an agreement* | **end/result in failure** *Harry's plans ended in failure.*
2 ⟨UNSUCCESSFUL PERSON/THING⟩ [C] someone or something that is not successful; ▤ **success**: *I always felt a bit of a failure at school.* | **a total/complete failure** *The advertising campaign was a total failure.*
3 failure to do sth an act of not doing something which should be done or which people expect you to do: *Failure to produce proof of identity could result in prosecution.*
4 ⟨BUSINESS⟩ [C,U] a situation in which a business has to close because of a lack of money: *Business failures in Scotland rose 10% last year.*
5 ⟨MACHINE/BODY PART⟩ [C,U] an occasion when a machine or part of your body stops working properly: *The cause of the crash was engine failure.* | **heart/kidney/liver etc failure** *He died from kidney failure.* | [+in] *a failure in the computer system*
6 ⟨CROPS⟩ [C,U] an occasion when crops do not grow or produce food, for example because of bad weather: *a series of crop failures*

faint¹ /feɪnt/ *adj* **1** difficult to see, hear, smell etc: *She gave a faint smile.* | *a very faint noise* | *the faint light of dawn* **2 a faint hope/possibility/chance etc** a very small or slight hope etc: *There's still a faint hope that they might be alive.* **3 not have the faintest idea** to not know anything at all about something: *I don't have the faintest idea what you're talking about.* **4** feeling weak and as if you are about to become unconscious because you are very ill, tired, or hungry: *The heat* made him *feel quite faint.* | [+**with**] *I was faint with hunger.* —**faintly** *adv*: *Everyone looked faintly surprised.* | *The sun shone faintly through the clouds.* —**faintness** *n* [U] → **damn sb/sth with faint praise** at DAMN⁴ (6)

faint² *v* [I] **1** to suddenly become unconscious for a short time; ◼ **pass out**: *Several fans fainted in the blazing heat.* **2** *I nearly/almost fainted spoken* used to say that you were very surprised by something: *I nearly fainted when they told me the price.*

faint³ *n* [singular] an act of becoming unconscious: **in a (dead) faint** | *She fell down in a faint.*

faint-heart·ed /ˌfeɪnt ˈhɑːtɪd $ -ɑːr-/ *adj* **1** not trying very hard, because you do not want to do something, or you are not confident that you can succeed; ◼ **half-hearted**: *She made a rather faint-hearted attempt to stop him from leaving.* **2** sth is not for the **faint-hearted** used humorously to say that something is difficult and needs a lot of effort

fair¹ S1 W2 /feə $ fer/ *adj*
1 REASONABLE AND ACCEPTABLE a fair situation, system, way of treating people, or judgment seems reasonable, acceptable, and right; ◼ **unfair**: *All we are asking for is a fair wage.* | *£150 is a fair price.* | **fair trial/hearing** *the right to a fair trial* | *What do you think is the fairest solution?* | *The report is a fair summary of the issues facing us.* | **it is fair to do sth** *It seems fair to give them a second chance.* | **it's only fair (that)** (=used to say that it is right to do something) *It's only fair that we tell him what's happening.* | **it's fair to say (that)** (=used when you think what you are saying is correct or reasonable) *I think it's fair to say that by then he had lost the support of most of his staff.* | **it's not fair on sb** *I can't carry on working such long hours. It's not fair on my family.*
2 TREATING EVERYONE EQUALLY treating everyone in a way that is right or equal; ◼ **unfair**: *Why does Eric get to go and I don't?* ***It's not fair!*** | *Life isn't always fair.* | [+**to**] *The old law wasn't fair to women.* | **it's only fair (that)** *You pay him $10 an hour – it's only fair that I should get the same.* | *My boss expects a lot – but he's very fair.*
3 QUITE LARGE a fair size/amount/number/bit/distance etc *especially BrE* quite a large size, number etc: *I've still got a fair amount of work left to do.* | *We had travelled a fair way* (=quite a long distance) *by lunch time.* | **there's a fair chance (that)/of sth** (=it is quite likely that something will happen) *There's a fair chance we'll be coming over to England this summer.*
4 HAIR/SKIN someone who is fair, or who has fair hair or skin, has hair or skin that is very light in colour; ◼ **dark**
5 ACCORDING TO THE RULES a fair fight, game, or election is one that is played or done according to the rules; ◼ **unfair**
6 LEVEL OF ABILITY neither particularly good nor particularly bad; ◼ **average**: *Her written work is excellent but her practical work is only fair.*
7 WEATHER weather that is fair is pleasant and not windy, rainy etc; ◼ **fine**: *It should be generally fair and warm for the next few days.*
8 have had more than your fair share of sth to have had more of something, especially something unpleasant, than seems reasonable: *Poor old Alan! He's had more than his fair share of bad luck recently.*
9 give sb a fair crack of the whip *BrE informal* to give someone the opportunity to do something, especially so that they can show that they are able to do it
10 give sb/get a fair shake *AmE informal* to treat someone, or to be treated, in a way that gives everyone the same chances as everyone else: *Women don't always get a fair shake in business.*
11 by fair means or foul using any method to get what you want, including dishonest or illegal methods
12 all's fair in love and war used to say that in some situations any method of getting what you want is acceptable

13 PLEASANT/ATTRACTIVE *old use* or *literary* pleasant and attractive: *a fair maiden*

SPOKEN PHRASES
14 fair enough *especially BrE* used to say that you agree with someone's suggestion or that something seems reasonable; ◼ **OK**: *'I think we should split the bill.' 'Fair enough.'*
15 to be fair used when adding something after someone has been criticized, which helps to explain or excuse what they did; ◼ **in fairness**: *She should have phoned to tell us what her plans were although, to be fair, she's been very busy.*
16 be fair! *especially BrE* used to tell someone not to be unreasonable or criticize someone too much: *Now Pat, be fair, the poor girl's trying her hardest!*
17 fair's fair used when you think it is fair that someone should do something, especially because of something that has happened earlier: *Come on, fair's fair – I paid last time so it's your turn.*
18 fair comment *BrE* used to say that a remark or criticism seems reasonable
19 you can't say fairer than that *BrE* used to say that an offer you are making to someone is the best and fairest offer they can possibly get: *I'll give you £25 for it – you can't say fairer than that, can you?*
20 it's a fair cop *BrE* used humorously to admit that you should not be doing something that someone has caught you doing
21 with your own fair hands *BrE* if you do something with your own fair hands, you do it yourself without any help – used humorously

→ **have a fair idea of sth** at IDEA

fair² *n* [C] **1** also **funfair** *BrE* a form of outdoor entertainment, at which there are large machines to ride on and games in which you can win prizes; ◼ **carnival** *AmE* **2** *AmE* an outdoor event, at which there are large machines to ride on, games to play, and sometimes farm animals being judged and sold: **state/county fair** **3** **book/antiques/craft/trade etc fair** an event at which people or businesses show and sell their products: *the Frankfurt Book Fair* | *an antiques fair* | *a trade fair* (=where companies show their newest products) | *a craft fair* (=where people sell handmade products such as jewellery, paintings etc) **4** **job/careers fair** an event where people go to get information about different kinds of jobs **5** *BrE* an outdoor event with games and things to eat and drink, usually organized to get money for a school, club etc; ◼ **fête** **6** *BrE old-fashioned* a market where animals and farm products are sold: *a horse fair*

fair³ S2 W3 *adv*
1 win (sth)/beat sb fair and square to win a competition, sports match etc honestly and without cheating
2 play fair to do something in a fair and honest way: *In international trade, very few countries play fair.*

fair 'copy *n* [C] *BrE* a neat copy of a piece of writing

fair din·kum /ˌfeə ˈdɪŋkəm $ ˌfer-/ *adj AusE spoken* real or true

fair 'game *n* [U] if someone or something is fair game, it is acceptable, reasonable, or right to criticize them: *The young star's behavior made her fair game for the tabloid press.*

fair·ground /ˈfeəɡraʊnd $ ˈfer-/ *n* [C] an open space on which a FAIR² (1) takes place

fair-haired 'boy *n* [C] *AmE old-fashioned informal* someone who is likely to succeed because someone in authority likes them; ◼ **blue-eyed boy** *BrE*: *the boss's fair-haired boy*

fair·ly S1 W2 /ˈfeəli $ ˈferli/ *adv*
1 [+ adj/adv] more than a little, but much less than very; → **quite**: *The house had a fairly large garden.* | *She speaks English fairly well.* | *The instructions seem fairly straightforward.* → see box at RATHER
2 in a way that is fair, honest, and reasonable: *I felt I*

hadn't been treated fairly.
3 *BrE old-fashioned* used to emphasize the degree, force etc of an action: *He fairly raced past us on his bike.*

fair-'minded / $ '. ,../ *adj* able to understand and judge situations fairly and always considering other people's opinions: *He's a fair-minded man – I'm sure he'll listen to what you have to say.*

fair·ness /'feərnɪs $ 'fer-/ *n* [U] **1** the quality of being fair: *the basic fairness of the judicial system* **2 in fairness (to sb)** used after you have just criticized someone, in order to add something that explains their behaviour or performance; ▪ **to be fair**: *Tardelli had a poor match, although in fairness he was playing with a knee injury.*

fair 'play *n* [U] **1** playing according to the rules of a game without cheating: *rules designed to* **ensure fair play** **2** fair treatment of people without cheating or being dishonest: *the British tradition of fair play* | *This kind of behavior violates many people's* **sense of fair play**. → **turnabout is fair play** at TURNABOUT

fair 'sex *n* **the fair sex** also **the fairer sex** *old-fashioned* women

fair·way /'feəweɪ $ 'fer-/ *n* [C] the part of a GOLF COURSE that you hit the ball along towards the hole

fair-weather 'friend *n* [C] someone who only wants to be your friend when you are successful

fai·ry /'feəri $ 'feri/ *n plural* **fairies** [C] **1** a small imaginary creature with magic powers, which looks like a very small person **2** *old-fashioned not polite* an offensive word for a HOMOSEXUAL man

'fairy ,cake *n* [C] *BrE* a very small cake

fairy 'godmother *n* [C] **1** a woman with magic powers who saves someone from trouble, in a story **2** someone who helps people when they are in trouble

fai·ry·land /'feərilænd $ 'feri-/ *n* **1** [U] an imaginary place where fairies live **2** [singular] a place that looks very beautiful and special: *At night, the harbor is a fairyland.*

'fairy lights *n* [plural] *BrE* small coloured lights used especially to decorate a Christmas tree

fairy tale also **'fairy ,story** *n* [C] **1** a children's story in which magical things happen **2** a story that someone has invented and is difficult to believe

fai·ry·tale /'feəriteɪl $ 'feri-/ *adj* [only before noun] extremely happy, lucky etc in a way that usually only happens in children's stories: *a fairytale romance* | *The kiss was a fairytale ending to the evening.*

fait ac·com·pli /ˌfeɪt əˈkɒmpli $ -ˌækɑːmˈpliː/ *n* [singular] something that has already happened or been done and cannot be changed

faith W2 /feɪθ/ *n*
1 TRUST/CONFIDENCE IN SB/STH [U] a strong feeling of trust or confidence in someone or something: **have faith (in sb/sth)** *I still have faith in him.* | *'Have faith, Alexandra,' he said.* | **lose faith (in sb/sth)** *The public has lost faith in the government.* | **destroy/restore sb's faith (in sb/sth)** *It's really helped restore my faith in human nature.*
2 RELIGION **a)** [U] belief and trust in God: *deep religious faith* | [+in] *my faith in God* **b)** [C] one of the main religions in the world: *People from all faiths are welcome.* | **the Jewish/Muslim/Hindu etc faith** *members of the Jewish faith*
3 **break faith with sb/sth** to stop supporting or believing in a person, organization, or idea: *How could he tell them the truth without breaking faith with the Party?*
4 **keep faith with sb/sth** to continue to support or believe in a person, organization, or idea
5 **good faith** honest and sincere intentions: *He proposed a second meeting as a sign of his good faith.* | *The woman who sold me the car claimed she had* **acted in good faith** (=had not meant to deceive me).
6 **bad faith** intentions that are not honest or sincere

7 **an act of faith** something you do that shows you trust someone completely: *Allowing Ken to be in charge of the project was a total act of faith.*

'faith com,munity *n* [C] a group of people who share a particular set of religious beliefs: *In any faith community there are varying levels of commitment.*

faith·ful¹ /'feɪθfəl/ *adj* **1** [usually before noun] remaining loyal to a particular person, belief, political party etc and continuing to support them: *Hollis was a good and* **faithful friend**. | *years of* **faithful service** *to the company* | *our faithful family dog, Bogey* | *Eileen became a faithful member of the church.* | [+to] *He* **remained faithful** *to his principles to the last.* **2** [usually before noun] representing an event or an image in a way that is exactly true or that looks exactly the same: *a faithful account of what had happened* | *a faithful reproduction of the original picture* **3** if you are faithful to your wife, boyfriend etc, you do not have a sexual relationship with anyone else: [+to] *Do you think Bob's always been faithful to you?* **4** [only before noun] able to be trusted or depended on: *my faithful old Toyota* —**faithfulness** *n* [U]

faithful² *n* **1** **the faithful** [plural] **a)** the people who are very loyal to a leader, political party etc and continue to support them: *Hess still has the support of* **the party faithful**. **b)** the people who believe in a religion: *church bells calling the faithful to evening prayer* **2** [C] a loyal follower, supporter, or member: *A handful of* **old faithfuls** *came to the meeting.*

faith·ful·ly /'feɪθfəl-i/ *adv* **1** in a loyal way: *He had served the family faithfully for 40 years.* | *Ann faithfully promised never to tell my secret.* **2** in a regular way: *She wrote faithfully in her journal every day.* | *Every year, we faithfully make a trip up there to see him.* **3** **Yours faithfully** *BrE* the usual polite way of ending a formal letter, which you have begun with Dear Sir or Dear Madam → **Yours sincerely** at SINCERELY

'faith ,healing *n* [U] a method of treating illnesses by praying —**faith healer** *n* [C]

faith·less /'feɪθləs/ *adj formal* someone who is faithless cannot be trusted: *a faithless friend* —**faithlessness** *n* [U]

fake¹ /feɪk/ *n* [C] **1** a copy of a valuable object, painting etc that is intended to deceive people: *The painting was judged a fake.* | *Jones can spot a fake from 20 feet away.* **2** someone who is not what they claim to be or does not have the skills they say they have: *Her psychologist turned out to be a fake.*

fake² *adj* [usually before noun] **1** made to look like a real material or object in order to deceive people: *fake fur* | *a fake ID card* | *a fake $20 dollar bill* **2** not real and seeming to be something it is not, in order to deceive people: *I gave a fake name.* | *She was speaking with a fake German accent.* | *a fake smile of friendliness*

fake³ *v* **1** [T] to make something seem real in order to deceive people: *She faked her father's signature on the cheque.* | *The insurance company suspected that he had faked his own death.* | *The results of the experiments were faked.* **2** [I,T] to pretend to be ill, interested etc when you are not: *I thought he was really hurt but he was faking it.* **3** [I,T] to pretend to move in one direction, but then move in another, especially when playing sport: *He faked a pass and then handed the ball off to Perry.*

fake sb ⇔ **out** *phr v AmE* to deceive someone by making them think you are planning to do something when you are really planning to do something else

fa·kir /'feɪkɪə, 'fæ-, fæ'kɪə $ fə'kɪr, fæ-/ *n* [C] a travelling Hindu or Muslim holy man

fa·laf·el /fə'læfəl, -'lɑː- $ -'lɑː-/ *n* [C,U] fried balls of an Arabic food made with CHICKPEAS

fal·con /'fɔːlkən $ 'fæl-/ *n* [C] a bird that kills and eats other animals and can be trained to hunt → see picture at BIRD OF PREY

fal·con·er /'fɔːlkənə $ 'fælkənər/ *n* [C] someone who trains falcons to hunt

fal·con·ry /ˈfɔːlkənri $ ˈfæl-/ n [U] the skill or sport of using falcons to hunt

fall¹ [S1] [W1] /fɔːl $ fɒːl/ v past tense **fell** /fel/ past participle **fallen** /ˈfɔːlən $ ˈfɒːl-/
1 MOVE DOWNWARDS [I] to move or drop down from a higher position to a lower position: *The tree was about to fall.* | *The book fell from his hands.* | *Enough rain had fallen to flood the grounds.* | [+down] *Rob fell down the stairs.* | *She flushed and her eyes fell* (=she looked down).
2 STOP STANDING/WALKING ETC [I] to suddenly go down onto the ground after you have been standing, walking, or running, especially without intending to: *I fell and hit my head.* | **slip/stumble/trip etc and fall** *He slipped and fell on the ice.* | [+down] *Lizzie fell down and hurt her knee.* | *Peter was playing by the river when he fell in* (=fell into the water). | **fall to/on your knees** (=move down to the ground so that your body is resting on your knees) *She fell to her knees beside his body.*; → **fall flat on your face** at FLAT³ (5)
3 DECREASE [I] to go down to a lower level, amount, price etc, especially a much lower one; ≠ **rise**: *The rate of inflation was falling.* | *The island is warm all year round and winter temperatures never fall below 10 degrees.* | *He believes that educational standards are falling.* | [+from] *Advertising revenue fell from $98.5 million to $93.3 million.* | [+to] *The number of subscribers had fallen to 1000.* | **fall sharply/steeply** (=by a large amount) *London share prices fell sharply yesterday.*
4 BECOME [I, linking verb] to start to be in a new or different state: [+adj] *I'll stay with her until she falls asleep.* | *I think that I've fallen in love with Angela.* | *She fell ill with flu.* | *Albert fell silent and turned his attention to his food.* | [+into] *The house was empty for many years and fell into disrepair.* | *One false step can mean falling into debt.* | *He fell into despair.*
5 BELONG TO A GROUP [I always + prep] to belong to or be part of a particular group, area of responsibility, range of things, or type of things: [+into] *Many illnesses fall into the category of stress-related illnesses.* | *Leaders fall into two categories.* | [+within] *The judge said that this matter did not fall within the scope of the auditor's duties.* | [+under] *The job falls under the heading of 'sales and marketing'.* | *Meat and poultry production **fall under the control** of the Agriculture Department.*
6 fall short of sth to be less than the amount or standard that is needed or that you want: *This year's profit will fall short of 13%.* | *He would sack any of his staff who fell short of his high standards.*
7 fall victim/prey to sth/sb to get a very serious illness or be attacked or deceived by someone: *Breastfed babies are less likely to fall victim to stomach disorders.* | *Young men are more likely to fall victim to violence.*
8 night/darkness/dusk falls if night etc falls, it starts to become dark at the beginning of the night: *It grew colder as night fell.* | *Darkness had fallen by the time we reached home.*
9 silence/a hush/sadness etc falls *literary* used to say that a person, group, or place becomes quiet, sad etc: *A long silence fell between us.*
10 START DOING STH [I] to start doing something or being involved with something, often without intending to: *I fell into conversation with some guys from New York.* | *He had fallen into the habit of having a coffee every time he passed the coffee machine.*
11 fall into place a) if parts of a situation that you have been trying to understand fall into place, you start to understand how they are connected with each other: *Suddenly, all the details started falling into place.* **b)** if the parts of something that you want to happen fall into place, they start to happen in the way that you want: *I was lucky because everything fell into place at exactly the right time.*
12 fall to pieces/bits a) to break into many pieces; ≡ **fall apart**: *The book had been well used and finally fell to pieces.* **b)** if something such as a plan or a

relationship falls to pieces, it stops working properly; ≡ **fall apart**: *The family is falling to pieces.*
13 be falling to pieces/bits if something is falling to pieces, it is in very bad condition, especially because it is very old; ≡ **be falling apart**: *The house is falling to pieces.*
14 fall flat if a joke, remark, or performance falls flat, it fails to interest or amuse people: *Marlow's attempts at jokes fell flat.*
15 fall foul of sb/sth to do something which makes someone angry or which breaks a rule, with the result that you are punished: *He is worried that his teenage kids will **fall foul of the law**.*
16 fall by the wayside to fail, or to stop being done, used, or made: *Health reform was one of his goals that fell by the wayside.* | *Luxury items fall by the wayside during a recession.*
17 fall from grace/favour to stop being liked by people in authority: *He fell from grace for the first time when he was convicted of drink-driving.*
18 fall from a great height to be forced to leave an important job or position, or lose the respect that people had for you
19 fall into the hands/clutches of sb if something or someone falls into the hands of an enemy or dangerous person, the enemy etc gets control or possession of them: *He wants to prevent the business falling into the hands of a competitor.* | *We must not let these documents fall into the wrong hands.*
20 fall into a trap/pitfall to make a mistake that many people make: *Don't fall into the trap of feeling guilty.*
21 fall into step a) to start to walk next to someone else, at the same speed as them: [+beside/with] *Holly slowed her pace and fell into step with the old man.* **b)** to start doing something in the same way as the other members of a group: [+with] *The other countries on the Council are expected to fall into step with the US.*
22 fall into line to obey someone or do what other people want you to do, especially when you do not want to do it at first: *Most countries have signed the treaty but some are reluctant to fall into line.*
23 HANG DOWN [I always + adv/prep] to hang down loosely: [+over] *His dark hair fell over his face.*
24 LIGHT/SHADOW [I always + adv/prep] to shine on a surface or go onto a surface: *The last rays of sunlight were falling on the fields.* | *Arthur's shadow fell across the doorway.*
25 SPECIAL EVENT/CELEBRATION [I always + adv/prep] to happen on a particular day or at a particular time: *I'd like to dedicate this record to all whose anniversaries fall at this time of year.* | [+on] *Her birthday will fall on a Friday this year.*
26 LOSE POWER [I] if a leader or a government falls, they lose their position of power: *The previous government fell after only 6 months in office.*
27 BE TAKEN BY AN ENEMY [I] if a place falls in a war or an election, a group of soldiers or a political party takes control of it: [+to] *The city fell to the advancing Russian armies.*
28 BE KILLED [I] to be killed in a war; ≡ **die**
29 HIT [I always + adv/prep] to hit a particular place or a particular part of someone's body: [+on] *The first punch fell on his nose.*
30 it's as easy as falling off a log *spoken* used to say that something is very easy to do
31 VOICE/SOUND [I] if someone's voice or a sound falls, it becomes quieter or lower; ≠ **rise**
32 fall between two stools *BrE* to be neither one type of thing nor another, or be unable to choose between two ways of doing something
33 fall on stony ground *BrE* if a request, suggestion, joke etc falls on stony ground, it is ignored or people do not like it
34 fall from sb's lips *literary* if words fall from someone's lips, they say them

F

35 the stress/accent/beat falls on sth used to say that a particular part of a word, phrase, or piece of music is emphasized or is played more loudly than the rest: *In the word 'report', the stress falls on the second syllable.* → **be/fall under a spell** at SPELL[2] (3); → **fall on your feet** at FOOT[1] (19); → **sb's face fell** at FACE[1] (2); → **stand or fall by/on** at STAND[1] (33)

fall about *phr v BrE*
to laugh a lot about something: *It was so funny everyone just fell about laughing.*

fall apart *phr v*
1 if an organization, system, relationship etc falls apart, it stops being effective or successful: *Don't be reckless or your plans may fall apart.* | *The minister claimed that the health service was falling apart at the seams.*
2 be falling apart to be in very bad condition: *Tommy's old bicycle was rusty and falling apart.*
3 to break into pieces: *The book fell apart in my hands.*
4 to be unable to deal with your personal or emotional problems: *She had to get some rest or she was going to fall apart.*
5 sb's world/life falls apart if someone's world or life falls apart, something very bad and serious happens which changes their life: *When his wife left him, his world fell apart.*

fall away *phr v*
1 to slope down: *From where we stood, the ground fell away sharply to the valley floor.*
2 to become separated from something after being fixed to it: *The paint was falling away in patches.*
3 if a feeling falls away, you stop having it, usually suddenly: *The view from the top was wonderful and our tiredness fell away.*
4 *BrE* to decrease; **≡ fall**; **⧫ rise**: *Demand for our more theoretical courses has fallen away.*

fall back *phr v*
1 if soldiers fall back, they move back because they are being attacked; **≡ retreat**: *He yelled for his men to fall back.*
2 to move backwards because you are very surprised, frightened etc: *Scott fell back a pace in astonishment.*
3 *BrE* to decrease; **≡ fall**; **⧫ rise**: *When inflation started to rise, house prices fell back.*

fall back into sth *phr v*
to go back to doing something or behaving in a way which you did before: *I was amazed at how easily I fell back into the old routine.*

fall back on sb/sth *phr v*
to use something or depend on someone's help when dealing with a difficult situation, especially after other methods have failed: **have sb/sth to fall back on** *She has no relatives to fall back on.* | *Where negotiation fails, they must fall back on the law.* → **FALLBACK**

fall behind (sb/sth) *phr v*
1 to go more slowly than other people so that they gradually move further ahead of you: *His mother was chatting and didn't notice that he had fallen behind.* | *She hurt her ankle and had fallen behind the others.*
2 to become less successful than other people, companies, countries etc: *After her time in hospital, Jenny's parents are afraid she has fallen behind educationally.* | *Companies that are not market-driven risk falling behind the competition.*
3 to fail to finish a piece of work or pay someone money that you owe them at the right time: [+with/on] *After losing his job, he fell behind with his mortgage payments.* | *The project has fallen behind schedule.*

fall down *phr v*
1 be falling down if a building is falling down, it is in very bad condition: *The bridge is falling down and will need a million dollars to repair it.*
2 to fail because of a particular reason or in a particular way: *That's where the whole argument falls down.* | [+on] *He is falling down on the supervisory aspects of his job.* | *The local authority is falling down on the job of keeping the streets clean.*

fall for sb/sth *phr v informal*
1 to be tricked into believing something that is not true: *He is too smart to fall for that trick.*
2 to start to love someone: *That was the summer I worked at the fairground, and met and fell for Lucy.*
3 to like a place as soon as you see it

fall in *phr v*
1 if the roof, ceiling etc falls in, it falls onto the ground; **≡ collapse**
2 to start walking or forming a line of people behind someone else: [+behind] *His men fell in behind him and they left.*

fall into sth *phr v*
1 to move somewhere quickly by relaxing your body and letting it fall on something: *She turned and fell into his arms.* | *We fell into bed, exhausted.*
2 to start doing something by chance: *I fell into the job really.*

fall in with sb/sth *phr v*
1 to accept someone's ideas, decisions etc and not disagree with them: *Once she explained her problem, he was happy to fall in with her plans.*
2 to become friendly with a person or group of people after meeting them by chance; **≡ get in with**: *She fell in with the wrong crowd in her teens.*

fall off *phr v*
1 fall off (sth) if part of something falls off, it becomes separated from the main part: *The door handle keeps falling off.* | *A button had fallen off her jacket.*
2 if the amount, rate, or quality of something falls off, it decreases; **≡ fall**; **⧫ rise**: *Audience figures fell off during the second series of the programme.*
3 sb nearly/almost fell off their chair *spoken* used to say that someone was very surprised when something happened: *When I saw my brother on the stage I nearly fell off my chair.* → **fall off the back of a lorry** at LORRY

fall on/upon sb/sth *phr v*
1 if a duty or job falls on someone, they are responsible for doing it: *The responsibility usually falls on the mother.*
2 *literary* to eagerly start eating or using something: *She fell on the food as if she hadn't eaten for days.*
3 *literary* to suddenly attack or get hold of someone: *Some of the older boys fell on him and broke his glasses.*
4 sb's eyes/gaze/glance fall(s) on sth if your eyes etc fall on something, you notice it: *His eyes fell on her bag. 'Are you going somewhere?'*
5 fall on hard/bad times to experience difficulties and problems in your life such as not having enough money: *The aim is to raise money for workers who have fallen on hard times.* → **fall on deaf ears** at DEAF (5)

fall out *phr v*
1 to have a quarrel: [+with] *Carrie's always falling out with people.*
2 if a tooth or your hair falls out, it is then no longer attached to your body: *The drugs made her hair fall out.*
3 if soldiers fall out, they stop standing in a line and move away to different places

fall over *phr v*
1 to fall onto the ground or to fall from an upright position: *Tommy fell over and cut his knee badly.* | *Her bike fell over.*
2 fall over sth to hit your foot against something by mistake and fall to the ground; **≡ trip over**: *She fell over the dog and broke her front teeth.*
3 fall over yourself to do sth to be very eager to do something, especially something you do not usually do: *People were falling over themselves to help her.*

fall through *phr v*
if an agreement, plan, sale etc falls through, it is not completed successfully: *The studio planned to make a movie of the book but the deal fell through.*

fall to sb/sth *phr v*
1 if a duty or job falls to someone, they are responsible for doing it, especially when this is difficult or unpleasant: *It fell to me to give her the bad news.*
2 *written* to start doing something: *They fell to work with a will.* | **fall to doing sth** *He fell to thinking about how nice a warm bath would be.*

fall² S2 W2 *n*
1 MOVEMENT DOWN [C] movement down towards the ground or towards a lower position: *the first fall of autumn leaves* | *The rise and fall of the dancers' bodies create a pattern.* | *Mrs Evans had a fall* (=fell to the ground) *and broke her leg.* | *He stretched out his hands to break his fall* (=prevent himself from falling too quickly and hurting himself).
2 REDUCTION [C] a reduction in the amount, level, price etc of something; ◨ **rise**: [+in] *There has been a fall in oil prices.* | **sharp/steep fall** *the sharp fall in the birth rate in European countries* | [+of] *Their industrial output went down again in December, which meant a fall of 2.2% over the year.*
3 SEASON [singular] *AmE* the season between summer and winter, when leaves change colour and the weather becomes slightly colder; ◨ **autumn**: *Eleanor plans to go to Southwestern Community College this fall.* | *The area is beautiful in the fall.*
4 LOSS OF POWER/SUCCESS [singular] a situation in which someone or something loses their position of power or becomes unsuccessful: [+from] *The president lived on for twenty years after his fall from power.* | *the story of Napoleon's rise and fall* (=period of success followed by failure) | *Rumours are that the company is heading for a fall* (=is likely to fail soon).
5 fall from grace a situation in which someone stops being respected by other people or loses their position of authority, especially because they have done something wrong: *He was the head of the intelligence service until his fall from grace.*
6 DEFEAT [singular] a situation in which a country, city etc is defeated by an enemy: [+of] *the fall of Jerusalem in AD70*
7 falls also **Falls** [plural] a place where a river suddenly goes straight down over a cliff: *The spray from the falls is so dense that you can hardly see.* | *Niagara Falls*
8 SPORT [C] an act of forcing your opponent onto the ground in WRESTLING or JUDO
9 SNOW/ROCKS [C] an amount of snow, rocks etc that falls onto the ground: [+of] *Fresh falls of snow were forecast.* | *The road is blocked by a rock fall.*
10 the Fall also **the fall** the occasion in the Bible when God punished Adam and Eve by making them leave the Garden of Eden

fal·la·cious /fəˈleɪʃəs/ *adj formal* containing or based on false ideas: *Such an argument is misleading, if not wholly fallacious.* —**fallaciously** *adv*

fal·la·cy /ˈfæləsi/ *n plural* **fallacies**   **1** [C] a false idea or belief, especially one that a lot of people believe is true; ◨ **misconception**: *It's a common fallacy that a neutered dog will become fat and lazy.* **2** [C,U] *formal* a weakness in someone's argument or ideas which is caused by a mistake in their thinking → **PATHETIC FALLACY**

fall·back /ˈfɔːlbæk $ ˈfɒːl-/ *n* [C] something that can be used or done if a supply, method etc fails: *It's wise to have an extra video player as a fallback.* | *Do you have a fallback option?* → **fall back on sb/sth** at **FALL¹**

fall·en¹ /ˈfɔːlən $ ˈfɒːl-/ *v* the past participle of FALL

fallen² *adj* **1** [only before noun] on the ground after falling down: *The road was blocked by a fallen tree.* | *fallen leaves* **2** a **fallen woman** *old-fashioned* a woman who has had a sexual relationship with someone she is not married to **3** the **fallen** [plural] *formal* soldiers who have been killed in a war

fall guy *n* [C] *informal especially AmE* **1** someone who is punished for someone else's crime or mistake; ◨ **scapegoat**: *Browne claims that the company was simply looking for a fall guy.* **2** someone who is easily tricked or made to seem stupid

fal·li·ble /ˈfæləbəl/ *adj formal* able to make mistakes or be wrong; ◨ **infallible**: *Humans are fallible.* | *These surveys are often a rather fallible guide to public opinion.* —**fallibility** /ˌfæləˈbɪləti/ *n* [U]

falling-'out *n* **have a falling-out (with sb)** *informal* to have a bad quarrel with someone

falling 'star *n* [C] a SHOOTING STAR

'fall-off also **ˌfalling-'off** *BrE n* [singular] a decrease in the level, amount, or number of something; ◨ **fall**; ◨ **rise**: [+in] *a fall-off in profits*

fal·lo·pi·an tube /fəˌləʊpiən ˈtjuːb $ fəˈloʊpiən tuːb/ *n* [C] *medical* one of the two tubes in a female through which eggs move to the UTERUS

fall·out /ˈfɔːlaʊt $ ˈfɒːl-/ *n* [U] **1** the dangerous RADIOACTIVE dust which is left in the air after a NUCLEAR explosion and which slowly falls to earth: *protection against radioactive fallout* **2** the results of a particular event, especially when they are unexpected: *The political fallout of the affair cost him his job.*

'fallout ˌshelter *n* [C] a building under the ground in which people can shelter from a NUCLEAR attack

fal·low /ˈfæləʊ $ -loʊ/ *adj* **1** fallow land is dug or PLOUGHED but is not used for growing crops: *They let the land lie fallow for a year.* **2** **fallow period** a time when nothing is done or achieved: *The band went through a fallow period in the late 90s.*

'fallow deer *n* [C] a small European DEER which is yellowish brown with white spots

false S3 W3 /fɔːls $ fɒːls/ *adj*
1 UNTRUE a statement, story etc that is false is completely untrue: *Please decide whether the following statements are true or false.* | *false accusations*
2 WRONG based on incorrect information or ideas: *I don't want to give you any false hopes.* | *The statement gives us a false impression that we understand something when we do not.* | *We often make false assumptions about people of other cultures.* | **a false sense of security** (=a feeling of being safe when you are not really safe)
3 NOT REAL a) not real, but intended to seem real and deceive people: *The drugs were hidden in a suitcase with a false bottom.* | *The man had given a false name and address.* **b)** artificial: **false teeth/hair/eyelashes etc**
4 NOT SINCERE not sincere or honest, and pretending to have feelings that you do not really have: *She's so false.* | *a false laugh* | *'You played brilliantly.' 'Not really,' Ian replied with false modesty.*
5 false economy something that you think will save you money but which will really cost you more: *It's a false economy not to have travel insurance.*
6 under false pretences if you get something under false pretences, you get it by deceiving people: *He was accused of obtaining money under false pretences.*
7 false move/step a small movement or action that will result in harm: *One false move and you're dead.*
8 false imprisonment/arrest the illegal act of putting someone in prison or ARRESTING them for a crime they have not committed

ˌfalse aˈlarm *n* [C] a situation in which people wrongly think that something bad is going to happen: *Fire fighters responded to a false alarm at one of the college dormitories.* | *The patient was okay – it was a false alarm.*

ˌfalse ˈdawn *n* [C] *formal* a situation in which something good seems likely to happen, but it does not: *The ceasefire turned out to be another false dawn.*

ˌfalse ˈfriend *n* [C] **1** a word in a foreign language that is similar to one in your own, so that you wrongly think they both mean the same thing **2** someone who seems to be your friend but is not

false·hood /ˈfɔːlshʊd $ ˈfɒːls-/ *n formal* **1** [C] a statement that is untrue; ◨ **lie**: *Saunders is deliberately telling a falsehood.* **2** [U] the practice of telling lies; ◨ **lying**: *No one had accused me of falsehood before.* **3** [U] the state of not being true: *Most people believe in right and wrong, truth and falsehood.*

ˌfalse ˈpositive *n* [C] something that is wrongly thought or shown to be a particular thing, especially after a scientific test or RESEARCH: *50% of the 170 compounds were judged to be carcinogenic, but some of these might be false positives.* | *Many substances give false positive reactions in allergy skin testing.*

false 'start n [C]   **1** an unsuccessful attempt to begin a process or event: *After several false starts, the concert finally began.*   **2** a situation at the beginning of a race when one competitor starts too soon and the race has to start again

false 'teeth n [plural] a set of artificial teeth worn by someone who has lost their natural teeth; ▪ **dentures**

fal·set·to /fɔːlˈsetəʊ $ fɒːlˈsetoʊ/ n plural **falsettos** [C] a very high male voice —**falsetto** adv

fals·ies /ˈfɔːlsiz $ ˈfɒːl-/ n [plural] informal pieces of material inside a BRA used to make a woman's breasts look larger

fal·si·fy /ˈfɔːlsɨfaɪ $ ˈfɒːl-/ v **falsified, falsifying, falsifies** [T] to change figures, records etc so that they contain false information: *The file was altered to falsify the evidence.* —**falsification** /ˌfɔːlsɨfɨˈkeɪʃən $ ˌfɒːl-/ n [C,U]: *the falsification of records*

fal·si·ty /ˈfɔːlsɨti $ ˈfɒːl-/ n [U] formal the quality of being false or not true; ▪ **truth**

fal·ter /ˈfɔːltə $ ˈfɒːltər/ v   **1** [I] to become weaker and unable to continue in an effective way: *The economy is showing signs of faltering.* | *My mother's grip upon the household never faltered.*   **2** [I,T] to speak in a voice that sounds weak and uncertain, and keeps stopping: *Laurie's voice faltered as she tried to thank him.* | *'I can't,' she faltered.*   **3** [I] to become less certain and determined that you want to do something: *We must not falter in our resolve.*   **4** [I] to stop walking or to walk in an unsteady way because you suddenly feel weak or afraid: *She faltered for a moment.*

fal·ter·ing /ˈfɔːltərɪŋ $ ˈfɒːl-/ adj   **1** nervous and uncertain or unsteady: *a baby's first faltering steps*   **2** becoming less effective or successful: *the faltering Mideast peace talks* —**falteringly** adv

fame /feɪm/ n [U] the state of being known about by a lot of people because of your achievements: **win/achieve/gain/find fame** *Streisand won fame as a singer before she became an actress.* | **rise/shoot to fame** *Plant shot to fame in the seventies as the lead singer of Led Zeppelin.* | **international/worldwide/national fame** | *At that time, the Beatles were at the height of their fame.* | *The town's only* **claim to fame** (=the only reason why it is well known) *is that Queen Elizabeth I once visited it.* | *He set off to find* **fame and fortune.** | **of ... fame** (=used to show what someone is famous for) *Hugh Grant, of 'Notting Hill' fame*

famed /feɪmd/ adj written well-known; ▪ **famous**: *the famed literary critic Nathan Hall* | [+**for**] *the island of Lontar, famed for its nutmeg and cloves*

fa·mil·i·al /fəˈmɪliəl/ adj [only before noun] formal connected with a family or typical of a family; ▪ **family**: *familial obligations* | *familial relationships*

fa·mil·i·ar¹ S2 W2 /fəˈmɪliə $ -ər/ adj   **1** someone or something that is familiar is well-known to you and easy to recognize: *a familiar tune* | **look/sound familiar** *The voice on the phone sounded familiar.* | [+**to**] *The signs of drug addiction are familiar to most doctors.* | *It was a relief to be back in* **familiar surroundings.** | *Beggars on the street are becoming a* **familiar sight.** | *This kind of situation was* **all too familiar** (=very familiar) *to John.* | *Her face seems* **vaguely familiar,** *but I can't quite place her.*   **2** be familiar with sth to have a good knowledge or understanding of something: *Are you familiar with this type of machine?* | *I'm not really familiar with her poetry, sorry to say.*   **3** be on familiar terms with sb to know someone well and be able to talk to them in an informal way: *He's on familiar terms with all the teachers.*   **4** talking to someone as if you know them well although you do not: [+**with**] *I thought he was being a bit familiar with my wife.*   **5** informal and friendly in speech, writing etc: *The novel is written in an easy, familiar style.* → **FAMILIARLY**

familiar² n [C] a cat or other animal that lives with a WITCH and has magical powers

fa·mil·iar·ise /fəˈmɪliəraɪz/ v a British spelling of FAMILIARIZE

fa·mil·i·ar·i·ty /fəˌmɪliˈærɨti/ n [U]   **1** a good knowledge of a particular subject or place: [+**with**] *In fact his familiarity with the Bronx was pretty limited.*   **2** the quality of being well-known to you: *I miss the familiarity of home.*   **3** a relaxed way of speaking to someone or behaving with someone: *He treated her with the easy familiarity of an equal.*   **4 familiarity breeds contempt** an expression meaning that if you know someone too well, you find out their faults and respect them less

fa·mil·i·ar·ize also **-ise** BrE /fəˈmɪliəraɪz/ v **familiarize yourself/sb with sth** to learn about something so that you understand it, or to teach someone else about something so that they understand it: *Employees must familiarize themselves with the health and safety manual.* —**familiarization** /fəˌmɪliəraɪˈzeɪʃən $ -rə-/ n [U]: *a one-day familiarization course*

fa·mil·i·ar·ly /fəˈmɪliəli $ -liərli/ adv in an informal or friendly way: *Charles, familiarly known as Charlie*

fam·i·ly S1 W1 /ˈfæməli/ n plural **families**   **1** CLOSELY RELATED GROUP [C] a group of people who are related to each other, especially a mother, a father, and their children

the whole family/all the family
member of a family/family member
a family of three/four/five etc
a close/close-knit family (=a family whose members have a close relationship)
immediate family (=closest relations)
nuclear family (=a family consisting of a mother, a father, and their children)
family background (=the sort of family someone comes from)
one-parent family/single-parent family
the Royal Family (=the King or Queen and their family)
family home/car/holiday etc
a family film/show etc (=that is suitable for children as well as adults)
family life
family resemblance (=when members of the same family look like each other)
family gathering (=when members of a family who do not live together arrange to meet)
family unit

Do you know the family next door? | *The Webb family still has its farm over there.* | [also + plural verb] BrE: *The family now live in London.* | **The whole family** *had caught colds.* | *For younger* **members of the family,** *there is an outdoor play area.* | *This house isn't big enough for* **a family of seven.** | *My family has always been* **close.** | *Is there a history of heart disease in your* **immediate family?** | *He lost contact with his* **extended family.** | *the traditional* **nuclear family** | *children living in a* **one-parent family** | *The Royal Family must now rethink its attitude to marriage.* | *the break-up of the* **family unit**

2 ALL YOUR RELATIONS [C,U also + plural verb BrE] all the people you are related to, including those who are now dead: *I'm moving to Detroit because I have some family there.* | *My family come from Scotland originally.* | **in sb's family** *That painting has been in our family* (=been owned by our family) *for 200 years.* | *Asthma* **runs in the family** (=is common in the family).   **3** CHILDREN [C] children: *Couples with* **young families** *wouldn't want to live here.* | *They're getting married next year, and hope to* **start a family** (=have children) *straight away.* | **bring up/raise a family** *the problems of bringing up a family on a very low income*   **4 family size/pack etc** a container or package containing a large amount of a product   **5** GROUP OF ANIMALS/THINGS [C] technical a group of related animals, plants, languages etc: **the cat/parrot/squirrel etc family** *The cat family includes lions*

F

and tigers. | *Spanish and Italian are part of the Romance language family.*
6 she's/he's family *informal* used to emphasize your connection with someone who is related to you
7 in the family way *old-fashioned* PREGNANT

family ˈcircle n [C usually singular] a group of people who are closely related to each other – used especially when emphasizing that someone does or does not belong to this group

family ˈcredit n [U] money given by the government in Britain to parents who do not earn much money

family ˈdoctor n [C] a doctor trained to treat the general health problems of people of all ages; ⊟ **GP**

family ˌman n [C] **1** a man who enjoys being at home with his wife or partner and children **2** a man with a wife or partner and children

family ˌname n [C] the name someone shares with all the members of their family; ⊟ **surname**, **last name**

family ˈplanning n [U] the practice of controlling the number of children that are born by using CONTRACEPTION: *a family planning clinic*

family ˈpractice n [U] a part of medical practice in the US in which doctors learn to treat general health problems of people of all ages

family pracˈtitioner n [C] *especially BrE* a GP

family ˌroom n [C] **1** a room in a house where the family can play games, watch television etc **2** a hotel room which has enough space for several people, especially parents and children, to sleep **3** a room in a PUB in Britain where children are allowed to sit

family ˈtree n [C] a drawing that gives the names of all the members of a family over a long period of time, and shows how they are related to each other

family ˈvalues n [plural] traditional ideas about what a family should be like, which emphasize the importance of marriage – used especially when talking about politics: *The party places great emphasis on family values.*

fam·ine /ˈfæmɪn/ n [C,U] a situation in which a large number of people have little or no food for a long time and many people die: *the great potato famine in Ireland* | **severe/widespread famine** *Widespread famine had triggered a number of violent protests.* | *A million people are facing famine.*

fam·ished /ˈfæmɪʃt/ adj [not before noun] *informal* extremely hungry; ⊟ **starving**: *What's for supper? I'm famished.*

fa·mous S2 W2 /ˈfeɪməs/ adj
1 a) known about by many people in many places: *a famous actor* | *Many famous people have stayed in the hotel.* | *The Eiffel Tower is a famous landmark* (=famous place or building that is easy to recognize). | [+for] *France is famous for its wine.* | [+as] *Virginia is famous as the birthplace of several US presidents.* | *Da Vinci's world-famous portrait of the Mona Lisa* **b)** the **famous** [plural] people who are famous: *a nightclub used by the rich and famous*
2 famous last words *spoken* used when someone has said too confidently that they can do something or that something will happen

fa·mous·ly /ˈfeɪməsli/ adv **1 get on/along famously** *old-fashioned* to have a friendly relationship with someone **2** in a way that is famous: *The trouble with common sense, as Voltaire famously observed, is that it is not very common.*

fan¹ S2 W2 /fæn/ n [C]
1 someone who likes a particular sport or performing art very much, or who admires a famous person: *Hundreds of football fans began rioting in the streets.* | [+of] *He's a big fan of Elvis Presley.* | **fan mail/letters** (=letters sent to famous people by their fans)
2 a) a machine with turning blades that is used to cool the air in a room by moving it around: *a ceiling fan* **b)** a flat object that you wave with your hand which makes the air cooler; → see picture at STAY

fans

fan

electric fan

fan² v [T] **fanned**, **fanning 1** to make air move around by waving a fan, piece of paper etc so that you feel cooler: **fan yourself** *People in the audience were fanning themselves with their programmes.* **2** *literary* to make someone feel an emotion more strongly; ⊟ **fuel**: *Her resistance only fanned his desire.* | **fan the flames (of sth)** *The book will serve to fan the flames of debate like no other.* **3 fan a fire/flame etc** to make a fire burn more strongly by blowing or moving the air near it: *Then the wind rose, fanning a few sparks in the brush.*
fan out *phr v* **1** if a group of people fan out, they walk forwards while spreading over a wide area **2 fan sth ⇔ out** to spread out a group of things that you are holding so that they make a half-circle: *Fan the cards out, then pick one.* **3** if something such as hair or clothing fans out, it spreads out in many directions

fa·nat·ic /fəˈnætɪk/ n [C] **1** someone who has extreme political or religious ideas and is often dangerous; ⊟ **extremist**: *fanatics who represent a real danger to democracy* | *a religious fanatic* **2** someone who likes a particular thing or activity very much; ⊟ **enthusiast**: *a health food fanatic* | *a fitness fanatic* **fanatical** adj. *a fanatical sportsman* | *He was fanatical about tidiness.* —**fanatically** /-kli/ adv

fa·nat·i·cis·m /fəˈnætɪsɪzəm/ n [U] extreme political or religious beliefs – used to show disapproval; ⊟ **extremism**: *The bombing symbolizes the worst of religious fanaticism.*

fan belt n [C] the belt that operates a FAN which keeps a car engine cool

fan·ci·a·ble /ˈfænsiəbəl/ adj *BrE* sexually attractive

fan·ci·er /ˈfænsiə $ -ər/ n [C] **pigeon/horse etc fancier** someone who breeds or is interested in a particular kind of animal or plant

fan·ci·ful /ˈfænsɪfəl/ adj **1** imagined rather than based on facts – often used to show disapproval: *a fanciful story* | *The suggestion that there was a conspiracy is not entirely fanciful.* **2** full of unusual and very detailed shapes or complicated designs: *fanciful decorations* —**fancifully** adv

fan club n [C] an organization for FANS of a particular team, famous person etc

fan·cy¹ S3 /ˈfænsi/ v **fancied**, **fancying**, **fancies** [T]
1 LIKE/WANT *BrE informal* to like or want something, or want to do something; ⊟ **feel like**: *Fancy a quick drink, Emma?* | **fancy doing sth** *Sorry, but I don't fancy going out tonight.*
2 SEXUAL ATTRACTION *BrE informal* to feel sexually attracted to someone: *All the girls fancied him.*
3 fancy yourself *BrE informal* to behave in a way that shows you think you are very attractive or clever: *That bloke on the dance floor really fancies himself.*
4 fancy yourself (as) sth *BrE* to believe, usually wrongly, that you have particular skills or are a particular type

of person: *He fancies himself an artist.* | *She fancies herself as another Madonna.*
5 THINK STH WILL BE SUCCESSFUL *BrE* to think someone or something is likely to be successful in something: *Which team do you fancy this year?* | *I don't fancy our chances of getting a ticket this late.*
6 *fancy!/fancy that! BrE spoken* used to express your surprise or shock about something: *'The Petersons are getting divorced.' 'Fancy that!'* | *Fancy seeing you here!*
7 THINK/BELIEVE *literary* to think or believe something without being certain: **fancy (that)** *She fancied she heard a noise downstairs.*

fancy² *n plural* **fancies**
1 LIKING/WISH [singular] *especially BrE* **a)** a feeling, especially one that is not particularly strong or urgent, that you like someone or want to have something: **take a fancy to sb/sth** (=decide that you like someone or want to have something) *Mr Hill took a real fancy to Clara.* | *Wanting to go to Mexico was just a **passing fancy*** (=the feeling did not last long). | *Because of its high cost, a carpet is not an item that you change **as the fancy takes you*** (=whenever you want). **b)** **take/catch your fancy** if something takes or catches your fancy, you like it or want to have it: *Did you see anything that took your fancy?*
2 **tickle sb's fancy** *informal* to seem attractive or amusing to someone: *The idea of playing a joke on her tickled his fancy.*
3 IDEA [C] *old-fashioned* an idea or opinion that is not based on fact: *Oh, that was just a fancy of his.*
4 IMAGINATION [U] *literary* imagination or something that you imagine → **flight of fancy** at FLIGHT (6)

fancy³ S3 *adj comparative* **fancier**, *superlative* **fanciest**
1 fancy hotels, restaurants, cars etc are expensive and fashionable; ▤ **swanky**: *Harry took me to a fancy restaurant for our anniversary.* | **fancy prices** *BrE* (=very high and often unreasonable prices)
2 having a lot of decoration or bright colours, or made in a complicated way: *fancy soaps in seashell shapes* | *I just want a basic sports coat – **nothing fancy**.*
3 complicated and needing a lot of skill; ▤ **straightforward**: *I can't do all that fancy stuff on the computer.* | *Negotiating a deal can take some **fancy footwork*** (=skill at making deals).
4 [only before noun] *AmE* fancy food is of a high quality

fancy dress *n* [U] *BrE* clothes that you wear, especially to parties, that make you look like a famous person, a character from a story etc: *an invitation to a fancy-dress party*

fancy-free *adj* able to do anything you like because you do not have a family or other responsibilities: *Ten years ago I was **footloose and fancy-free**.*

fancy man *n* [C] *old-fashioned* a man that a married woman has a sexual relationship with, who is not her husband

fancy woman *n* [C] *old-fashioned* a woman that a married man has a sexual relationship with, who is not his wife

fan·cy·work /ˈfænsiwɜːk $ -wɜːrk/ *n* [U] decorative sewing; ▤ **embroidery**

fan·dan·go /fænˈdæŋɡəʊ $ -ɡoʊ/ *n plural* **fandangos** [C] a fast Spanish or South American dance, or the music for this dance

fan·fare /ˈfænfeə $ -fer/ *n* **1** [C] a short loud piece of music played on a TRUMPET to introduce an important person or event **2** [U] a lot of activity, advertising, or discussion relating to an event: *The deal was announced with much fanfare.*

fang /fæŋ/ *n* [C] a long sharp tooth of an animal such as a snake or wild dog

fan·light /ˈfænlaɪt/ *n* [C] **1** *especially BrE* a small window above a door or a larger window; ▤ **transom** *AmE* **2** *AmE* a window shaped like a half-circle

fan·ny /ˈfæni/ *n plural* **fannies** [C] *informal* **1** *AmE* the part of your body that you sit on; ▤ **bottom** **2** *BrE taboo informal* a very offensive word for a woman's outer sex organs. Do not use this word; ▤ **genitals**

fan·ta·si·a /fænˈteɪziə, ˌfæntəˈziːə $ fænˈteɪʒə/ *n* [C] a piece of music that does not have a regular form or style

fan·ta·size also **-ise** *BrE* /ˈfæntəsaɪz/ *v* [I,T] to imagine that you are doing something which is very pleasant or exciting, but which is very unlikely to happen: [+about] *Sometimes she fantasized about buying a boat and sailing around the world.* | **fantasize that** *I used to fantasize that my real parents were famous movie stars.*

fan·tas·tic S3 /fænˈtæstɪk/ *adj*
1 extremely good, attractive, enjoyable etc: *You look fantastic!* | *It's a fantastic place, really beautiful!*
2 *spoken* used when someone has just told you something good; ▤ **excellent**, **wonderful**: *'I've passed my driving test.' 'Fantastic!'* | *That's fantastic news!*
3 a fantastic amount is extremely large; ▤ **huge**: *Kids spend fantastic amounts of money on CDs.*
4 a fantastic plan, suggestion etc is not likely to be possible: *a fantastic scheme*
5 [only before noun] a fantastic story, creature, or place is imaginary and is very strange and magical; ▤ **fantastical**: *fantastic tales of dragons and fairy queens* —**fantastically** /-kli/ *adv*

fan·tas·ti·cal /fænˈtæstɪkəl/ *adj* strange, unreal, and magical; ▤ **fantastic**: *fantastical creatures with golden wings and lions' faces*

fan·ta·sy /ˈfæntəsi/ *n plural* **fantasies** **1** [C,U] an exciting and unusual experience or situation you imagine happening to you, but which will probably never happen: *I used to **have fantasies about** living in Paris with an artist.* | *sexual fantasies* | *Young children sometimes can't distinguish between fantasy and reality.* | *He **lived in a fantasy world** of his own, even as a small boy.* **2** [singular, U] an idea or belief that is based only on imagination, not on real facts: *Memories can sometimes be pure fantasy, rather than actual recollections.* **3** [C] a story, film etc that is based on imagination and not facts: *a surrealist fantasy set in a South American village*

fantasy football *n* [U] a game in which lots of people make imaginary football teams by choosing real players. They get points according to how well the players do in real games, and the winner is the person whose team gets the most points

fan·zine /ˈfænziːn/ *n* [C] a magazine written by and for people who admire and support a popular musician, a sports team etc

FAQ /fæk, ˌef eɪ ˈkjuː/ *n* [C usually plural] a frequently asked question

far¹ S1 W1 /fɑː $ fɑːr/ *adv comparative* **farther** /ˈfɑːðə $ ˈfɑːrðər/ *or* **further** /ˈfɜːðə $ ˈfɜːrðər/, *superlative* **farthest** /ˈfɑːðɪst $ ˈfɑːr-/ *or* **furthest** /ˈfɜːðɪst $ ˈfɜːr-/
1 DISTANCE **a)** a long distance; → **a long way**: *Have you driven far?* | *Since I changed jobs, I have to travel further to get to work.* | *Let's see who can jump the furthest!* | [+from] *The children don't go far from home.* | [+away] *She wants to move as far away from here as possible.* | *They could hear the sound of water not far away.* | [+down] *He lives further down the street.* | **further afield** (=further away from where you are now) *If you want to go further afield, there are bicycles for hire.* | **further north/south etc** *Many birds fly further south in the autumn.* | *The plains stretched for **as far as the eye could see*** (=all the distance you could see). | *The lake is about 4 miles away, but we probably **won't get that far*** (=won't go as far as that place). **b)** **how far** used when asking the distance between two places, or when talking about the distance between two places: *How far is it to the station?* | *The man didn't say how far it was to the next town.* **c)** **as far as sth** to a place or point, but not beyond it: *They managed to get as far as the Spanish border.* △ **Far** is used mainly in questions

and negative sentences. In other kinds of sentences use **a long way away** *The airport is quite a long way away (NOT is quite far).*
2 **A LOT/VERY MUCH** very much, or to a great degree: **far better/easier etc** *The new system is far better than the old one.* | *There are a far greater number of women working in television than twenty years ago.* | **far more/less** *I enjoyed it far more than I expected.* | **far too much/long/busy etc** *That's far too much to pay.* | *It would take me far too long to explain.* | [+**above/below/beyond**] *He bought it for a price that was far beyond* (=much more than) *its real value.* | *The teacher said that her writing skills were far below average.* | *We've kept the original features of the house **as far as possible*** (=as much as possible). | ***How far** do those old, outdated laws affect today's legislation?* | *His style was **far removed*** (=very different) *from that of Picasso.* | **not far off/out/wrong** (=close to being correct) *I guessed it would cost $100 and it was $110, so I was not far out.*
3 **PROGRESS** used to talk about how much progress someone makes, or how much effect something has: *He started to explain, but he didn't **get far*** (=he did not succeed in saying very much) *before Mary interrupted him.* | **get as far as doing sth** *They had got as far as painting the kitchen.* | *Many people felt that the new law did not **go far enough*** (=did not have a big enough effect, so that more needed to be done).
4 **TIME** a long time in the past or the future, or a long time into a particular period: [+**into**] *We talked far into the night.* | [+**ahead**] *They want to plan much further ahead than the next two or three years.* | *The first petrol-driven car was produced **as far back as** 1883.* → FAR-OFF
5 **go too far** also **take/carry sth too far** to do something too extreme: *One day she will go too far.* | *Some people thought he had gone too far in his criticism of the police.*
6 **go so far/as far as to do sth** *spoken* to do or say something extreme: *The government went so far as to try to arrest opposition leaders.* | *I wouldn't go so far as to say that we agreed on the subject.*
7 **so far** also **thus far** *formal* until now: *So far we have not had to borrow any money.* | *They're delighted with the replies they've received from the public thus far.*
8 **so far so good** *spoken* used to say that things have been happening successfully until now: *We've reached the semi-finals. So far so good.*
9 **far from sth** used to say that something very different is true or happens: *Conditions are still far from ideal.* | **far from doing/being sth** *Far from helping the situation, you've just made it worse.*
10 **far from it** *spoken* used to say that the opposite of what has just been said is true: *'Are you bored?' 'Far from it. I could listen all night.'* | *Local people aren't objecting – far from it.*
11 **far and wide** over a large area: *His fame spread far and wide.* | *People **came from far and wide*** (=came from many places) *to see the concert.*
12 **by far/far and away** used to say that something is much better, worse etc than anything else: *Watching sport was by far the most popular activity on Saturday afternoons.* | *Spring is far and away the best time to visit the islands.*
13 **sb will/would/should etc go far** used to say that you think someone will be successful in the future: *He was the best student in his year, and everyone was sure he would go far.*
14 **as/so far as I'm concerned** *spoken* used when giving your opinion about something: *As far as I'm concerned she can come home whenever she likes.*
15 **as/so far as sth is concerned** *spoken* used when you want to talk about a particular thing: *As far as money's concerned, there shouldn't be a problem.*
16 **as/so far as I know/I can remember/I can tell/I can see etc** *spoken* used to say that you think something is true, although it is possible that you do not know all the facts or cannot remember completely: *There weren't any buildings there at all, as far as I can remember.* | *As far as I can see, there's nothing else to discuss.*

17 **far be it from me to do sth** *spoken* used when saying that you do not want to criticize someone or say what they should do, especially when this is what you are really about to do: *Far be it from me to try and teach you your job, but don't you think you should have been more careful?*
18 **as far as it goes** used to say that an idea, suggestion, plan etc is satisfactory, but only to a limited degree: *His theories are fine, as far as they go.*
19 **not go far** **a)** if money does not go far, you cannot buy very much with it: *My salary doesn't go very far these days.* **b)** if a supply of something does not go far, it is not enough: *The coffee won't go far if everyone wants a cup.*
20 **in so far as/insofar as/in as far as** *formal* to the degree that: *The research suggests that the drug will be successful, in so far as one can draw conclusions from such a small sample size.*

far² S1 W1 *adj comparative* **farther** *or* **further**, *superlative* **farthest** *or* **furthest**
1 a long distance away; ⊟ **near**: *We can walk to my house from here. It isn't far.* | *You could see the mountains in the far distance.*
2 **the far side/end/corner etc** the side, end etc that is furthest from you; ⊟ **near**: *They crossed the bridge and walked along the far side of the stream.* | *There was a piano in the far corner of the room.*
3 **the far north/south etc** the part of a country or area that is furthest in the direction of north, south etc: *It will become windy in the far north and west.*
4 **the far left/right** people who have views LEFT-WING or RIGHT-WING political opinions: *The candidate for the far right got ten percent of the vote.*
5 **be a far cry from sth** to be very different from something: *The company lost £3 million, which is a far cry from last year's £60 million profit.*

far·a·way /'fɑːrəweɪ/ *adj* **1** [only before noun] *literary* a long distance away; ⊟ **distant**: *She dreamed of flying away to exotic faraway places.* | *faraway noises* **2** **a faraway look** an expression on your face which shows that you are not paying attention but thinking about something very different: *His eyes had a distant faraway look, like a sailor staring out to sea.*

farce /fɑːs $ fɑːrs/ *n* **1** [singular] an event or a situation that is very badly organized or does not happen properly, in a way that is silly and unreasonable: *She admitted that the interview had been a complete farce from start to finish.* **2** [C,U] a humorous play or film in which the characters are involved in complicated and silly situations, or the style of writing or acting that is used

far·ci·cal /'fɑːsɪkəl $ 'fɑːr-/ *adj* **1** a situation or event that is farcical is very silly and badly organized: *Opposition leaders described the government's plans as 'farcical'.* **2** a farcical play or film is a humorous one in which the characters become involved in silly and complicated situations —**farcically** /-kli/ *adv*

fare¹ /feə $ fer/ *n* **1** [C] the price you pay to travel somewhere by bus, train, plane etc: **bus/train/air/cab fare** *Air fares have shot up by 20%.* | **half-fare/full-fare** *Children under 14 travel half-fare.*; → see box at COST¹ **2** [U] *written* food, especially food served in a restaurant or eaten on a special occasion: *traditional Christmas fare* **3** [C] a passenger in a taxi **4** [U] something that is offered to the public, especially as entertainment: *The movie is suitable family fare.*

fare² *v* **fare well/badly/better etc** to be successful, unsuccessful etc: *Although Chicago has fared better than some cities, unemployment remains a problem.* | *He wondered how Ed had fared in the interview.*

Far ˈEast *n* **the Far East** the countries in the east of Asia, such as China, Japan, Korea etc —**Far Eastern** *adj* → MIDDLE EAST, NEAR EAST

fare·well[1] /ˌfeəˈwel ◂ $ ˌfer-/ n **1** [C,U] *old-fashioned* the action of saying goodbye: *Mourners gathered to bid farewell to the victims of the plane tragedy.* | *a farewell speech* **2** farewell party/dinner/drink etc a party or dinner that you have because someone is leaving a job, city etc: *40 of her colleagues gathered for her farewell presentation.*

farewell[2] *interjection old use* goodbye

far-ˈfetched *adj* extremely unlikely to be true or to happen: *All this may sound a bit far-fetched, but companies are already developing 'intelligent' homes.*

far-ˈflung *adj* **1** very distant: **far-flung corners/places/regions etc** *expeditions to far-flung corners of the globe* | *people flying to far-flung destinations* **2** spread out over a very large area: *Email enables far-flung friends to keep in touch.*

far ˈgone *adj* [not before noun] *informal* very sick, drunk, crazy etc: *She's pretty far gone – can you drive her home?*

farm[1] S3 W2 /fɑːm $ fɑːrm/ n [C] **1** an area of land, used for growing crops or keeping animals: *a 300-hectare farm* | *farm workers* | *farm animals* | *Joe had worked on the farm all his life.* | **a pig/dairy/cattle etc farm** *He runs a pig farm in Lincolnshire.* ⚠ Say **on** a/the **farm,** not 'in a/the farm'. **2** the main house on a farm where the farmer lives → **factory farm** at FACTORY FARMING; → FISH FARM, FUNNY FARM

farm[2] *v* [I,T] **1** to use land for growing crops or keeping animals: *The family has farmed here for generations.* | *The land has been farmed organically since 1995.* **2** farmed salmon/fish/rabbits etc fish and animals that have been raised on farms, and not caught from the wild

farm sb/sth ⇔ out *phr v* **1** to send work to other people instead of doing it yourself: [+to] *The processing will be farmed out to people in local villages.* **2** to send someone to a different place where they will be looked after – used to show disapproval: [+to] *At the age of 16 she was farmed out to family friends.*

farm·er S3 W2 /ˈfɑːmə $ ˈfɑːrmər/ n [C] someone who owns or manages a farm

ˈfarmers' ˌmarket n [C] a place where farmers bring their fruit, vegetables, meat, and other products to sell directly to people in a town or city

farm·hand /ˈfɑːmhænd $ ˈfɑːrm-/ n [C] someone who works on a farm

farm·house /ˈfɑːmhaʊs $ ˈfɑːrm-/ n [C] the main house on a farm, where the farmer lives → see picture at COUNTRY

farm·ing /ˈfɑːmɪŋ $ ˈfɑːr-/ n [U] the practice or business of growing crops or keeping animals on a farm: **sheep/dairy/livestock etc farming** | **organic/intensive farming** | *the farming industry*

farm·land /ˈfɑːmlænd, -lənd $ ˈfɑːrmlænd/ n [U] land used for farming

farm·stead /ˈfɑːmsted $ ˈfɑːrm-/ n [C] a farmhouse and the buildings around it

farm·yard /ˈfɑːmjɑːd $ ˈfɑːrmjɑːrd/ n [C] an area surrounded by farm buildings

far-ˈoff *adj literary* **1** a long way from where you are; ⊟ **distant: a far-off land/country/place etc** *visitors from a far-off land* | *far-off galaxies* **2** a long time ago: *in those far-off days when we were young*

far-ˈout *adj* very strange or unusual; ⊟ **weird:** *Tim's designs were just far-out.*

far-ˈreaching *adj* having a great influence or effect: **far-reaching reforms/proposals/changes** *These countries need to carry out far-reaching reforms to modernize their economies.* | **far-reaching implications/impact/effects** *Tourism has had far-reaching effects on the island's culture.*

far·ri·er /ˈfæriə $ -ər/ n [C] someone who makes shoes for horses' feet; → **blacksmith**

Far·si /ˈfɑːsi $ ˈfɑːr-/ n [U] the language of Iran; ⊟ **Persian**

far-ˈsighted / $ ˈ. ,../ *adj* **1** far-sighted people, ideas, or plans are wise because they show an understanding of what will happen in the future: *far-sighted investments* | *a far-sighted politician* **2** *especially AmE* able to see or read things clearly only when they are far away from you; ⊟ **short-sighted;** ⊟ **long-sighted** *BrE* —**far-sightedness** n [U]

fart[1] /fɑːt $ fɑːrt/ v [I] *not polite* to make air come out of your BOWELS; ⊟ **break wind**

fart about/around *phr v informal* to waste time not doing very much: *Stop farting around and get on with your work!*

fart[2] n **1** [C] *not polite* an act of making air come out of your BOWELS **2 old fart** *informal* a stupid and uninteresting older person

far·ther[1] /ˈfɑːðə $ ˈfɑːrðər-/ *adv* **1** a greater distance than before or than something else; a COMPARATIVE form of 'far'; ⊟ **further:** *We decided not to go any farther.* | **farther away/apart/down/along etc** *The boats were drifting farther and farther apart.* | *a resort town farther up the coast* | **farther south/north etc** *Two miles farther south is the village of Santa Catarina.* | *Most of them were locals, but some had come from **farther afield** (=a greater distance away).* **2** if you do something farther, you do it more or to a greater degree; ⊟ **further:** *We'd better investigate farther.* | *The police decided not to **take** the matter any **farther** (=do more about it).* ⚠ In spoken English it is more usual to use **further.**

farther[2] *adj* [only before noun] more distant; a COMPARATIVE form of 'far'; ⊟ **further:** *A table stood at the farther end of the kitchen.*

far·thest[1] /ˈfɑːðɪst $ ˈfɑːr-/ *adv* at or to the greatest distance away; the SUPERLATIVE form of 'far': *My sister was the one who travelled farthest.* | **farthest away/apart etc** *She lived farthest away from school of all of us.* ⚠ In spoken English it is more usual to use **furthest.**

farthest[2] also **furthest** *adj* the most distant; the SUPERLATIVE form of 'far': *the farthest corners of the globe*

far·thing /ˈfɑːðɪŋ $ ˈfɑːr-/ n [C] an old British coin that was worth one quarter of a PENNY

fas·cia /ˈfeɪʃə/ n [C] *BrE* **1** a DASHBOARD **2** a long board above a shop with the shop's name on it

fas·ci·nate /ˈfæsɪneɪt/ v [T not in progressive] if someone or something fascinates you, you are attracted to them and think they are extremely interesting: *The idea of travelling through time fascinates me.*

fas·ci·nat·ed /ˈfæsɪneɪtɪd/ *adj* [not before noun] extremely interested by something or someone: *I was fascinated by her voice.* | **fascinated to see/hear/learn etc** *Ed was fascinated to see gorillas in the wild.*

fas·ci·nat·ing S3 /ˈfæsɪneɪtɪŋ/ *adj* extremely interesting: *a fascinating book* | *That sounds **absolutely fascinating.*** | **find sb/sth fascinating** *I found him quite fascinating.* —**fascinatingly** *adv*

fas·ci·na·tion /ˌfæsɪˈneɪʃən/ n **1** [singular, U] the state of being very interested in something, so that you want to look at it, learn about it etc; → **obsession:** [+for/with] *Police knew of his fascination with guns.* | **fascination** *The children watched in fascination.* **2** [C,U] something that interests you very much, or the quality of being very interesting: **hold/have a fascination for sb** *India will always hold a great fascination for me.* | *The fascination lay in the mystery of what was inside the box.*

fas·cis·m /ˈfæʃɪzəm/ n [U] a RIGHT-WING political system in which people's lives are completely controlled by the state and no political opposition is allowed

fas·cist /ˈfæʃɪst/ n [C] **1** someone who supports fascism: *The fascists came to power in 1933.* **2** *informal* someone who is cruel and unfair and does not like people to argue with them: *My last boss was a real fascist.* **3** *informal* someone who has extreme RIGHT-WING opinions —**fascist** *adj: Mussolini's fascist regime*

fash·ion¹ S2 W2 /'fæʃən/ n
1 [singular, U] something that is popular or thought to be good at a particular time: [+**for**] *the fashion for so-called 'discovery methods' of learning* | [+**in**] *The emerging science of photography was already changing fashions in art.* | *Eastern religions used to be the fashion in the 60s.* | *His ideas are coming back into fashion* (=they are becoming popular again). | *Their music will never go out of fashion* (=stop being fashionable). | *Self-help books are now all the fashion* (=they are very fashionable).
2 [C, U] a style of clothes, hair etc that is popular at a particular time: *They sold the latest fashions from Europe* (=the most recent fashions). | *The 1960s space-age look has influenced both men's and women's fashions.* | *Hats are in fashion again this year* (=they are fashionable). | *Grey is out of fashion now* (=it is no longer fashionable). | *extreme designs which will go out of fashion as quickly as they came in* (=stop being fashionable). | *Fur coats were considered to be the height of fashion and sophistication* (=were thought to be very fashionable). | *Teenage girls are very fashion conscious* (=they are very concerned about wearing the latest fashions).
3 [U] the business or study of making and selling clothes, shoes etc in new and changing styles: *a leading men's fashion magazine* | *the fall fashion shows in New York, Milan, and Paris* | *She used to be one of the world's top fashion models.* | *fashion photographer Richard Avedon* | *The dark-eyed Italian is set to take the fashion world by storm* (=become very successful in the world of fashion). | *She hopes to find work in the fashion industry* (=all the companies and people who are involved in fashion). | *a 22-year-old student at the London College of Fashion*
4 **in a ... fashion** in a particular way: *Please leave the building in an orderly fashion.* | *Perhaps they could sit down and discuss things in a civilised fashion.* | *She will be working out her problems in her own fashion* (=in the way that she usually does this) *and should be allowed to do so.*
5 **after a fashion** not very much, not very well, or not very effectively: *'Can you speak Russian?' 'After a fashion.'*
6 **after the fashion of sb** in a style that is typical of a particular person: *Her early work is very much after the fashion of Picasso and Braque.*
7 **like it's going out of fashion** *informal* use this to emphasize that someone does something a lot or uses a lot of something: *Danny's been spending money like it's going out of fashion.* → **parrot fashion** at PARROT¹ (2)

fashion² v [T] **1** to shape or make something, using your hands or only a few tools: **fashion sth from sth** *He fashioned a box from a few old pieces of wood.* | **fashion sth into sth** *Jamie could take a piece of wood and fashion it into a wonderful work of art.* **2** [usually passive] to influence and form someone's ideas and opinions: *We are all unique human beings, fashioned by life experiences.*

-fashion /fæʃən/ *suffix* [in adverbs] like something, or in the way that a particular group of people does something: *They ate Indian-fashion, using their fingers.*

fash·ion·a·ble /'fæʃənəbəl/ *adj* **1** popular, especially for a short period of time; ⬛ **unfashionable**: *Strong colours are very fashionable at the moment.* | **it is fashionable (for sb) to do sth** | *It suddenly became fashionable for politicians to talk about green issues.* **2** popular with, or used by, rich people; ⬛ **unfashionable**: **a fashionable resort/area/address etc** *He runs a very fashionable restaurant near the Harbor.* —**fashionably** *adv: fashionably dressed young ladies*

'**fashion house** n [C] a company that produces new and expensive styles of clothes

fash·ion·ist·a /ˌfæʃə'niːstə/ n [C] *informal* someone who is very interested in fashion and who likes the very newest styles

'**fashion plate** n [C] *informal* someone who likes to wear very fashionable clothes

'**fashion show** n [C] an event at which new styles of clothes are shown to the public

'**fashion ˌstatement** n [C] something that you own or wear that is considered new or different, and that is intended to make other people notice you: *Mobile phones make a big fashion statement.*

'**fashion ˌvictim** n [C] *informal* someone who always wears what is fashionable, even if it makes them look bad

fast¹ S2 W3 /fɑːst $ fæst/ *adv*
1 MOVING QUICKLY moving quickly: *Slow down – you're driving too fast.* | *a fast-moving river* | *Johnny ran off as fast as his legs could carry him* (=running as quickly as he could).
2 IN A SHORT TIME happening in a short time: *Kids grow up fast these days.* | *The survivors needed help fast.* | *How fast can you get the job done?* | **fast becoming/disappearing/approaching etc** *Access to the Internet is fast becoming a necessity.* | *It all happened so fast I didn't even notice I was bleeding.*
3 **fast asleep** sleeping very deeply: *Nick was lying on the sofa, fast asleep.*
4 **be stuck/held fast** to become or be firmly fixed and unable to move: *The boat was stuck fast in the mud.* | *She tried to pull her hand free, but it was held fast.*
5 **be getting/be going nowhere fast** *informal* to not succeed in making progress or achieving something: *I kept asking her the same question, but I was getting nowhere fast.*
6 **not so fast** *spoken* used to tell someone not to be too eager to do or believe something: *Not so fast. We've got to prove it first, haven't we?*
7 **fast by sth** *literary* very close to something: *fast by the river* → **play fast and loose with sb** at PLAY¹ (30); → **stand fast** at STAND¹ (25); → **thick and fast** at THICK² (2)

> **WORD FOCUS: FAST**
> *moving very quickly*: **at high speed, like lightning, at top speed, flat out**
> *doing something quickly*: **quick, rapid, swift, prompt, speedy**
> *happening quickly*: **rapid, speedy, meteoric, at an alarming rate, in no time**

fast² S2 W2 *adj*
1 MOVING QUICKLY moving or able to move quickly: *a fast car* | *He's one of the fastest runners in the world.*
2 IN A SHORT TIME doing something or happening in a short time: *The subway is the fastest way to get downtown.* | *The company must give a faster response to clients' requests.* | *The rainforests are being chopped down at an alarmingly fast rate.* | *I'm a fast learner.*
3 CLOCK [not before noun] a clock that is fast shows a later time than the real time: *That can't be the time – my watch must be fast.* | **five minutes/an hour etc fast** *I always keep my watch 15 minutes fast.*
4 **fast track** a way of achieving something more quickly than is normally done: **on the fast track** | *a young actress on the fast track to fame and success*
5 **fast road** a road on which vehicles can travel very quickly
6 **fast film/lens** a film or LENS (2) that can be used when there is little light, or when photographing something that is moving very quickly
7 COLOUR a colour that is fast will not change when clothes are washed → COLOURFAST
8 SPORTS a fast surface is one on which a ball moves very quickly

F

9 fast and furious done very quickly with a lot of effort and energy, or happening very quickly with a lot of sudden changes: *Arsenal's opening attack was fast and furious.*

10 sb is a fast worker *informal* used to say that someone can get what they want very quickly, especially in starting a sexual relationship with another person

11 fast talker someone who talks quickly and easily but is often not honest or sincere

12 WOMAN *old-fashioned* becoming involved quickly in sexual relationships with men: *fast cars and fast women*

13 make sth fast to tie something such as a boat or tent firmly to something else

14 fast friends *literary* two people who are very friendly for a long time → FAST FOOD, FAST-FORWARD, FAST LANE; → **make a fast buck** at BUCK¹ (1); → **pull a fast one** at PULL¹ (10)

fast³ *v* [I] to eat little or no food for a period of time, especially for religious reasons: *Muslims fast during Ramadan.*

fast⁴ *n* [C] a period during which someone does not eat, especially for religious reasons: *Gandhi drank some orange juice to break* (=end) *his three-week fast.*

fast·ball /'fɑːstbɔːl $ 'fæstbɒːl/ *n* [C] a ball that is thrown very hard and quickly towards the BATTER in a game of BASEBALL

'fast ,day *n* [C] a day when you do not eat any food, especially for religious reasons

fas·ten /'fɑːsən $ 'fæ-/ *v*

1 CLOTHES/BAG ETC also **fasten up a)** [T] to join together the two sides of a coat, shirt, bag etc so that it is closed; ▤ **do up**; ▣ **unfasten**: *'I'm going now,' she said, fastening her coat.* | *Fasten your seat belt.* **b)** to become joined together with buttons, hooks etc; ▤ **do up**: *I was so fat that my skirt wouldn't fasten.*

2 WINDOW/GATE ETC [I,T] to firmly close a window, gate etc so that it will not open, or to become firmly closed; ▣ **unfasten**: *Make sure all the windows are securely fastened before you leave.*

3 ATTACH STH TO STH [T] to attach something firmly to another object or surface: **fasten sth with sth** *Fasten the edges of the cloth together with pins.* | **fasten sth to sth** *They fastened the rope to a tree.*

4 HOLD STH TIGHTLY [I,T] to hold something firmly with your hands, legs, arms, or teeth: **fasten sth around/round sth** *She fastened her arms around his neck.* | **[+around/round]** *A strong hand fastened round her wrist.* | **[+on/onto]** *Their long claws allow them to fasten onto the rocks and hold firm.*

5 fasten your eyes/gaze on sb/sth to look at someone or something for a long time: *He rose, his eyes still fastened on the piece of paper.*

6 fasten your attention on sb/sth to think a lot about one particular thing or person *He was working quietly, all his attention fastened on the task.*

fasten on/upon sth *phr v*

to give particular attention to something because you think it is important or interesting: *My mother fastened on the word "unsafe".*

fasten onto sb/sth also **fasten on to sb/sth** *phr v*

1 to give particular attention to something because you think it is important or interesting

2 to follow someone and stay with them, especially when they do not want you to; ▤ **latch onto sb** *The dog seemed lost and fastened onto us.*

fas·ten·er /'fɑːsənə $ 'fæsənər/ also **fas·ten·ing** /'fɑːsənɪŋ $ 'fæ-/ *n* [C] **1** something that you use to join something together, such as a button on a piece of clothing: *shoes with velcro fasteners* **2** something that is used to keep a door, window etc firmly shut

fast food

takeaway pizza

chips *BrE*/ French fries *AmE*

glass of cola

hot dog

hamburger   toasted sandwich

'fast food *n* [U] food such as HAMBURGERS which is prepared quickly and that you can take away with you → see picture at EAT

,fast-'forward *v* [I,T] **1** to wind a tape or video forwards quickly without playing it **2** to move quickly to a later point in a story: **[+to]** *Fast-forward to America at the turn of the century.* —**fast-forward** *n* [U]

fas·tid·i·ous /fæˈstɪdiəs/ *adj* very careful about small details in your appearance, work etc; ▤ **meticulous**: *people who are fastidious about personal hygiene and appearance* —**fastidiously** *adv* —**fastidiousness** *n* [U]

'fast lane *n* **1 the fast lane** *informal* an exciting way of life that involves dangerous and expensive activities: *Brenda is a lady who loves life in the fast lane.* **2** [C usually singular] the part of a big road where people drive fastest: *I broke down in the fast lane of the M6.*

fast·ness /'fɑːstn̩s $ 'fæst-/ *n* [C] *literary* a place that is safe because it is difficult to reach; ▤ **stronghold**: *mountain fastnesses*

'fast track *n* [singular] the fast track to something is the fastest way of achieving it: *Many saw independence as the fast track to democracy.*

'fast-track *adj* [only before noun] happening or making progress more quickly than is usual: *a fast-track procedure for adoption*

fat¹ S2 W3 /fæt/ *adj comparative* **fatter**, *superlative* **fattest**

1 FLESH weighing too much because you have too much flesh on your body; ▣ **thin**: *Are you suggesting I'm too fat?* | *a short fat man in his early fifties* | *You'll get fat if you eat all that chocolate.* | *He looks much fatter than in his photo.*

2 OBJECT thick or wide; ▣ **thin**: *Dobbs was smoking a fat cigar.* | *a big fat book* → see picture at THICK

3 MONEY [only before noun] *informal* containing or worth a large amount of money: *a fat cheque* | *Of course the supermarkets' aim is to make fat profits.*

4 fat chance *informal* used to say that something is very unlikely to happen: **[+of]** *'You can go to bed now and sleep easy.' 'Fat chance of that!'*

5 (a) fat lot of good/use *spoken* not at all useful or helpful: *Fat lot of use you are in the kitchen.*

6 fat cat *informal* someone who has too much money, especially someone who is paid too much for their job – used in order to show disapproval: *the fat cats at the top who have recently been given obscene pay increases*

7 in fat city *AmE old-fashioned* having plenty of money

8 grow fat on sth to become rich because of something used to show disapproval: *The finance men had grown*

fat on managing other people's money.
9 a fat lip *informal* a lip that is swollen because it has been hit: *My friend was badly injured with bruised ribs and a fat lip.*
10 APPROVAL *informal* another spelling of PHAT; used to show approval, especially of someone or something that is fashionable, interesting, or attractive: **fat/phat beats** (=music that sounds good) *Check out these fat beats.* —**fatness** *n* [U]: *a rise in fatness in children*

WORD CHOICE: fat, overweight, obese, chubby, plump, big, well-built

fat is a very direct word. You might use it about yourself but it will usually cause offence if you use it about someone else: *I'm so fat at the moment!*

overweight is a more polite way to say that someone is fatter than they usually are or than they should be: *She is a little overweight.*

obese is a word used especially by doctors to describe people who are very fat, in a way that is bad for their health.

chubby is a more informal word and is used especially of children or of rounded body parts such as cheeks or knees.

plump means fat and rounded in a pleasant way: *a plump, motherly woman*

big and **well-built** are fairly polite ways to describe someone with a large, strong, or fat body: *For big men like him, air travel can be uncomfortable.*

---

fat² *n* **1** [U] a substance that is stored under the skin of people and animals, that helps to keep them warm: *Rolls of fat bulged over his collar.* | *I didn't like the meat – there was too much fat on it.* **2** [C,U] an oily substance contained in certain foods: *Cream has a high fat content.* | **high/low in fat** *This cheese is relatively low in fat.* | *You should think about reducing your fat intake* (=the amount of fat you eat). | **high-fat/low-fat** *a low-fat diet* → SATURATED FAT **3** [C,U] an oily substance taken from animals or plants and used in cooking: *Place the chicken in the hot fat.* **4 the fat is in the fire** used to say that there will be trouble because of something that has happened **5 live off the fat of the land** to get enough money to live comfortably without doing much work **6 run to fat** to start to become fat, especially because you are getting older or do not do much exercise → **chew the fat** at CHEW¹ (4); → PUPPY FAT

fa·tal /ˈfeɪtl/ *adj* **1** resulting in someone's death: *potentially fatal diseases* | **fatal accident/illness/injury** etc *a fatal climbing accident* | *If it is not treated correctly, the condition can* **prove fatal** (=be fatal). **2** having a very bad effect, especially making someone fail or stop what they are doing: [+to] *Disunity finally* **proved fatal** *to the rebels' cause.* | *There was one* **fatal flaw** (=serious weakness) *in his argument.* | *His presidential hopes suffered a* **fatal blow** *in New Hampshire.* | **fatal mistake/error** *Telling your employees they're unimportant is a fatal error.*

fa·tal·is·m /ˈfeɪtl-ɪzəm/ *n* [U] the belief that there is nothing you can do to prevent events from happening —**fatalist** *n* [C]

fa·tal·is·tic /ˌfeɪtlˈɪstɪk◂/ *adj* believing that there is nothing you can do to prevent events from happening: *a fatalistic approach to life* —**fatalistically** /-kli-/ *adv*

fa·tal·i·ty /fəˈtæləti/ *n plural* **fatalities 1** [C] a death in an accident or a violent attack: *a 50% increase in the number of traffic fatalities* **2** [U] *formal* the fact that a disease is certain to cause death: *The most serious form of skin cancer has a 30 percent fatality rate.* **3** [U] *formal* the feeling that you cannot control what happens to you

fa·tal·ly /ˈfeɪtl-i/ *adv* **1** in a way that causes death: **fatally injured/wounded** *Two officers were fatally injured in the explosion.* **2** in a way that will make something fail or be unable to continue: **fatally flawed/weakened/damaged** etc *Bolton's idea was fatally flawed.* | *He has been fatally undermined by his own finance minister.*

ˈfat camp *n* [C] *informal* a place where children who are fat go to lose weight and to exercise, especially in the summer

fate /feɪt/ *n*
1 [C usually singular] the things that will happen to someone, especially unpleasant events

---

suffer a fate
seal/decide/settle sb's fate (=make it certain that something will happen to someone)
meet the same/a similar fate
leave/abandon sb to their fate (=leave someone when something terrible could happen to them)
the fate awaiting sb (=what will happen to someone)
accept a fate
resign yourself to your fate (=accept it)
a fate befalls sb (=they suffer a particular fate)
sb's ultimate fate (=the final things that happen)

I wouldn't wish such a fate on my worst enemy. | [+of] *No one knows what the fate of the hostages will be.* | *The rest of Europe was to* **suffer** *the same* **fate.** | *A meeting to* **decide the fate** *of the factory is to be held today.* | *She wanted to prevent other children from* **meeting the same fate.** | *They had abandoned him and left him to his fate.* | *Spencer's father had died young, and he feared that the same* **fate awaited** *him.* | *They would rather starve to death than* **accept** *the* **fate** *of slavery.* | *She seemed placidly* **resigned to her fate.** | *the fate that* **befell** *a captured rebel general* | *Nothing is known of Green's origins or* **ultimate fate,** *only that he was involved in building the church.*

2 [U] a power that is believed to control what happens in people's lives: *Fate plays cruel tricks sometimes.* | **a twist/quirk of fate** (=something unexpected that happens) *By a* **strange twist of fate** *Smith's first match is against the team that gave him the sack last season.*
3 a fate worse than death something terrible that might happen to you – often used humorously: *He had rescued an innocent young girl from a fate worse than death.*
4 the Fates the three goddesses who, according to the ancient Greeks, controlled what happened to people → **tempt fate** at TEMPT (3)

fat·ed /ˈfeɪtɪd/ *adj* certain to happen or to do something because a mysterious force is controlling events; **■ destined: be fated to do sth** *I'm fated to spend my last years in an old folks' home.* → ILL-FATED

fate·ful /ˈfeɪtfəl/ *adj* [usually before noun] having an important, especially bad, effect on future events: **fateful day/night/year** etc *The goalkeeper on that fateful day in 1954 was Fred Martin of Aberdeen.* | *When his rent was raised, he made the fateful decision to move north.* —**fatefully** *adv*

ˈfat farm *n* [C] *AmE informal* a place where people who are fat can go to lose weight and improve their health → HEALTH FARM

ˌfat-ˈfree *adj* containing no fat: *fat-free yoghurt*

fat·head /ˈfæthed/ *n* [C] *informal* a stupid person; **■ idiot** —**fat-ˈheaded** *adj*

fa·ther¹ S1 W1 /ˈfɑːðə $ -ər/ *n* [C]
1 PARENT a male parent: *Ask your father to help you.* | *Andrew was very excited about becoming a father.* | *He's been like a father to me.* | **a father of two/three/four** etc (=a man with two, three etc children) *The driver, a father of four, escaped uninjured.* | *Steve recently became the proud father of a 7lb 12oz baby girl.*
2 PRIEST **Father** a priest, especially in the Roman Catholic church: *I have sinned, Father.* | *Father Devlin* → HOLY FATHER
3 fathers [plural] people related to you who lived a long time ago; **■ ancestors**: *Our fathers were exiles from their native land.* → FOREFATHER
4 GOD **Father** a way of talking to or talking about God, used in the Christian religion: *our* **Heavenly Father**
5 the father of sth the man who was respon-

sible for starting something: *Freud is the father of psychoanalysis.*
6 from father to son if property or skill passes from father to son, children receive it or learn it from their parents: *This is a district where old crafts are handed down from father to son.*
7 like father like son used to say that a boy behaves like his father, especially when this behaviour is bad
8 a bit of how's your father BrE informal the act of having sex – used humorously → CITY FATHERS, FOUNDING FATHER

father² v [T] **1** to become the father of a child by making a woman PREGNANT: *Hodgkins fathered seven children.* **2** formal to start an important new idea or system: *Bevan fathered the concept of the National Health Service.*
father sth on sb phr v BrE formal to claim that someone is responsible for something when they are not: *A collection of Irish stories was fathered on him.*

Father 'Christmas n [singular] BrE an imaginary man who wears red clothes, has a long white beard, and is said to bring presents to children at Christmas; ⊟ **Santa Claus**

'father figure n [C] an older man who you trust and respect: [+to/for] *Ken was a father figure to all of us.*

fa·ther·hood /'fɑːðəhʊd $ -ðər-/ n [U] the state of being a father: *The idea of fatherhood frightens me.*

fa·ther·ing /'fɑːðərɪŋ/ n [U] the skills and activities involved in being a father: *Don't get me wrong, fathering certainly has changed.*

'father-in-,law n plural **fathers-in-law** [C] the father of your husband or wife

fa·ther·land /'fɑːðəlænd $ -ðər-/ n [singular] the place where someone or their family was born → MOTHER COUNTRY, MOTHERLAND

fa·ther·ly /'fɑːðəli $ -ðər-/ adj [only before noun] kind and gentle in a way that is considered typical of a good father: *He took my arm in a fatherly way.* | *fatherly advice*

'Father's Day n [C] a day on which people give cards and presents to their father

fath·om¹ /'fæðəm/ n [C] a unit for measuring the depth of water, equal to six feet or about 1.8 metres

fathom² v also **fathom out** [T] to understand what something means after thinking about it carefully; ⊟ **work out**: *I still can't fathom out what she meant.* | [+how/why/where etc] *Mark couldn't fathom why she resented him so much.*

fath·om·less /'fæðəmləs/ adj literary impossible to measure or understand: *the fathomless depths of the sea*

fa·tigue /fə'tiːg/ n **1** [U] very great tiredness; ⊟ **exhaustion**: with fatigue *Sam's face was grey with fatigue.* | from fatigue *He's suffering from physical and mental fatigue.* **2** [U] technical a weakness in metal or wood, caused when it is bent or stretched many times, which is likely to make it break: *metal fatigue* **3 fatigues** [plural] loose-fitting army clothes

fa·tigued /fə'tiːgd/ adj formal extremely tired; ⊟ **exhausted**: *Sara looked white and fatigued.*

fa·tigu·ing /fə'tiːgɪŋ/ adj formal extremely tiring; ⊟ **exhausting**

fat·so /'fætsəʊ $ -soʊ/ n plural **fatsoes** [C] informal an insulting word for someone who is fat

fat·ted /'fætɪd/ adj → **kill the fatted calf** at KILL¹ (15)

fat·ten /'fætn/ v **1** [I,T] to make an animal become fatter so that it is ready to eat, or to become fat and ready to eat **2** [T] to make an amount larger: *These projects simply serve to fatten the pockets of developers.*
fatten sb/sth ⇔ up phr v to make a person or animal fatter: *My parents are always trying to fatten me up.*

fat·ten·ing /'fætn-ɪŋ/ adj likely to make you fat: *Fats are the most fattening foods of all.*

fat·tist /'fætɪst/ adj informal having or showing unkind attitudes towards people who are fat: *fattist jokes*

fat·ty¹ /'fæti/ adj containing a lot of fat: *Avoid fatty foods.*

fatty² n plural **fatties** [C] informal an insulting word for someone who is fat

,fatty 'acid n [C] technical an acid that the cells in your body need to use food effectively

fat·u·ous /'fætʃuəs/ adj very silly or stupid; ⊟ **idiotic**: *fatuous questions* —**fatuously** adv —**fatuousness** n [U]

fat·wa /'fætwɑː/ n [C] an official order made by an important Islamic religious leader

fau·cet /'fɔːsɪt $ 'fɒː-/ n [C] AmE the thing that you turn on and off to control the flow of water from a pipe; ⊟ **tap** BrE; → see picture at MATERIAL

fault¹ S2 W3 /fɔːlt $ fɒːlt/ n [C]
1 RESPONSIBLE FOR MISTAKE if something bad that has happened is your fault, you should be blamed for it, because you made a mistake or failed to do something: *I'm really sorry – it's all my fault.* | be sb's fault (that) *It's your fault we're late.* | *I didn't sleep well that night, but it was my own fault.* | be sb's fault for doing sth *It's my fault for not making your new job clearer.*
2 at fault if someone is at fault, they are responsible for something bad that has happened: *The police said that the other driver was at fault.* | *Some people claim that it is the UN that is at fault.*
3 STH WRONG WITH STH a) something that is wrong with a machine, system, design etc, which prevents it from working properly: *a design fault* | [+in] *It sounds as if there's a fault in one of the loudspeakers.* **b)** something that is wrong with something, which could be improved; ⊟ **flaw**: *There are two serious faults in Hobsbawm's discussion of nationalism.* | For all its *faults* (=in spite of its faults) *we love this city.* **c)** a mistake in the way that something was made, which spoils its appearance: [+in] *The sweater had a fault in it and I had to take it back.*
4 SB'S CHARACTER a bad or weak part of someone's character: *His worst fault is his arrogance.* | I may have my *faults*, but ingratitude is not one of them. | For all his *faults* (=in spite of his faults) *he was a good father.*
5 through no fault of her/my etc own used to say that something bad that happened to someone was not caused by them: *Through no fault of our own we are currently two players short.*
6 CRACK a large crack in the rocks that form the Earth's surface: *the San Andreas fault in Northern California*
7 generous/loyal/honest etc to a fault extremely generous, kind etc: *Barry's kind, caring and generous to a fault.*
8 TENNIS a mistake made when a player is SERVING the ball in tennis → DOUBLE FAULT; → find fault with sb/sth FIND¹ (14)

WORD CHOICE: fault, blame, mistake
If someone causes something bad, you can say that it is **their fault** or that they are **to blame**: *The accident was my fault.* | *Nobody is to blame for what happened.*
⚠ Do not say that someone 'has the/a etc fault': *We didn't think that it was our fault OR that we were to blame (NOT that we had any fault).*
⚠ Do not say that something is 'someone's blame'.
Use **fault** to mean something that is wrong with a machine or system, or something that you could criticize about a person or thing: *The car engine had developed a fault.* | *The book's only fault is that it is too long.*
Use **mistake** to mean something that is wrong in someone's grammar, spelling, calculations, decisions etc: *Please correct any mistakes (NOT faults) in my letter.*

fault² v [T usually passive] to criticize someone or something for a mistake: *The judge cannot be faulted on his decision.* | it is hard/difficult to fault sb/sth *You* might not like *O'Donnel's arrogance, but it's hard to fault what he does on the field.*

fault·less /'fɔːltləs $ 'fɒlt-/ *adj* having no mistakes; ☰ **perfect**: *a faultless performance* —**faultlessly** *adv*

fault-,tolerant *adj* fault-tolerant computer/machine a computer that continues working even if it has a fault or when there is a fault in a program

fault·y /'fɔːlti $ 'fɒlti/ *adj* **1** not working properly, or not made correctly: *Customers may ask for a refund if the goods are faulty.* | *a faulty gene that causes breast cancer* **2** a faulty way of thinking about something contains a mistake, so that you make a wrong decision: *an idea based on a faulty understanding of biology*

faun /fɔːn $ fɒːn/ *n* [C] an ancient Roman god with the body of a man and the legs and horns of a goat

fau·na /'fɔːnə $ 'fɒː-/ *n* [C,U] *technical* all the animals living in a particular area or period in history → FLORA

fauv·is·m /'fəʊvɪzəm $ 'foʊ-/ *n* [U] a style of painting that uses pure bright colours, which was developed in the early 20th century

faux /fəʊ $ foʊ/ *adj* [only before noun] *especially AmE* artificial, but made to look real: *faux pearls*

faux pas /,fəʊ 'pɑː, 'fəʊ pɑː $,foʊ 'pɑː/ *n plural* **faux pas** /-'pɑːz/ [C] an embarrassing mistake in a social situation

fa·va bean /'fɑːvə biːn/ *n* [C] *AmE* a large flat pale green bean; ☰ **broad bean** *BrE*

fave /feɪv/ *n* [C] *informal* a favourite person or thing: *a band that's a college fave* —**fave** *adj*

fa·vor /'feɪvə $ -ər/ *n, v* the American spelling of FAVOUR

fa·vor·a·ble /'feɪvərəbəl/ *adj* the American spelling of FAVOURABLE

fa·vored /'feɪvəd $ -vərd/ *adj* the American spelling of FAVOURED

fa·vo·rite /'feɪvərɪt/ *adj, n* the American spelling of FAVOURITE

fa·vo·rit·is·m /'feɪvərɪtɪzəm/ *n* [U] the American spelling of FAVOURITISM

fa·vour[1] [S1] [W2] *BrE*; **favor** *AmE* /'feɪvə $ -ər/ *n*
1 [HELP] [C] something that you do for someone in order to help them or be kind to them

do sb a favour (=do something for someone)
as a favour (to sb) (=because you want to be kind, not because you have to)
ask sb a favour/ask a favour of sb (=ask someone to do something for you)
owe sb a favour (=feel that you should do something for someone because they have done something for you)
return a favour (=do something for someone because they have done something for you)
be doing sb a favour (=used to say that something that seems bad will benefit someone)
do yourself a favour (=do something good for yourself)
a personal favour
a political favour

Could you do me a favour and tell Kelly I can't make it? | *He hired John as a favour to his father.* | *Paul, can I ask you a favor?* | *I owed him a favour so I couldn't say no.* | *She helps me out when I have too much to do, and I return the favour when I can.* | *Do yourself a favour and make sure you get some time to yourself.*

2 [SUPPORT/APPROVAL] [U] support, approval, or agreement for something such as a plan, idea, or system: **in favour of sth** *Senior ministers spoke in favour of the proposal.* | *I talked to Susie about it, and she's **all in favor** (=completely approves) of going.* | **find/gain/win favour** *The idea may find favor with older people.* | **in sb/sth's favour** *The vote was 60–59 in the government's favor.* | *In Sweden and other countries, nuclear power has **lost favor**.* | **look on/view/regard sth with favour** *formal* (=support something, and want to help it succeed) *Employers are more likely to look with favour on experienced candidates.* | **All in favour** (=used when asking people to vote on something by raising a

hand)? | **vote/decide in favour of sth** (=vote or decide to support something) *288 members voted in favor of the ban.* | **find/rule in favour of sb** *formal* (=make a legal decision that supports someone)
3 [POPULAR/UNPOPULAR] [U] when someone or something is liked or approved of by people, or not liked or approved of: **be in favour (with sb)** *The island is very much in favour as a holiday destination.* | **be out of favour (with sb)** *The stock is currently out of favor with investors.* | **find/gain/win favour** *Radcliffe's books began to find favour with the reading public.* | **come/be back in favour** (=become popular again) *Fountain pens have come back in favour.* | **fall/go out of favour** (=stop being approved of) *Grammar-based teaching methods went out of favour in the 60s and 70s.*
4 [ADVANTAGE] [U] if something is in someone's favour, it gives them an advantage over someone else: *Conditions on court are very much in Williams' favour.* | *The new rules should actually **work in your favor**.* | *Duncan **had** his height and weight **in his favour** during the fight.* | **the odds are (stacked) in sb's favour** (=someone has a big advantage)
5 [CHOOSE STH INSTEAD] do sth in favour of sth if you decide not to use one thing in favour of another, you choose the other one because you think it is better: *Plans for a tunnel were rejected in favour of a bridge.*
6 do sb/sth no favours, not do sb/sth any favours to do something that makes someone or something look worse than they are, or that does not help at all: *Low interest rates don't do savers any favours.*
7 [UNFAIR SUPPORT] [U] support that is given to one person or group and not to others, in a way that does not seem fair: *Teachers should not **show favour to** any pupil.*
8 do me/us a favour! *BrE spoken* used when you are annoyed because someone has asked a silly question or done something to upset people: *Do us a favour, Mike, and shut up!* | *'Did you like it?' 'Do me a favour!'*
9 [GIFT] [C] *AmE* a PARTY FAVOR
10 [SEX] favours [plural] *old-fashioned* when you allow someone to have sex with you: *She shared her sexual favors with many men.* → curry favour (with sb) at CURRY[2]; → without fear or favour at FEAR[1] (6); → be thankful/grateful for small favours at SMALL[1] (13)

favour[2] [W3] *BrE*; **favor** *AmE v* [T]
1 [PREFER] to prefer someone or something to other things or people, especially when there are several to choose from: *Both countries seem to favour the agreement.* | *I loose clothing of the type favoured in Arab countries* | **favour sb/sth over sb/sth** *Florida voters favored Bush over Gore by a very small margin.*
2 [GIVE AN ADVANTAGE] to treat someone much better than someone else, in a way that is not fair: *a tax cut that favours rich people* | **favour sb over sb** *a judicial system that favours men over women*
3 [HELP] to provide suitable conditions for something to happen: *The current economy does not favour the development of small businesses.*
4 [LOOK LIKE] *old-fashioned* to look like one of your parents or grandparents
favour sb with sth *phr v formal*
to give someone something such as a look or reply: *McIntosh favoured her with a smile.*

fa·vour·a·ble *BrE*; **favorable** *AmE* /'feɪvərəbəl/ *adj* **1** a favourable report, opinion, or reaction shows that you think that someone or something is good or that you agree with them: *favourable film reviews* | *The response has been overwhelmingly favourable.* **2** suitable and likely to make something happen or succeed: *The disease spreads quickly under favourable conditions.* | [+for/to] *a financial environment that is favourable to job creation* **3** if a LOAN, agreement, rate etc is favourable, the conditions are reasonable and not too expensive or difficult: *a favourable interest rate* | *the favorable terms of the settlement* **4** making

F

people like or approve of someone or something: *A smart appearance makes a **favourable impression** at an interview.* —**favourably** adv

fa·voured BrE; **favored** AmE /'feɪvəd $ -ərd/ adj [only before noun] **1** receiving special attention, help, or treatment, sometimes in an unfair way: *a list of favoured customers* | *China's **most-favored-nation** trading status with the US* **2** chosen or preferred by many people: *Brittany is a favoured holiday destination for families.* **3** a favoured team, player etc is one that is expected to win: **be favoured to do sth** *Silva is favoured to win a medal in the marathon.* **4** having desirable qualities: *a house in a favoured position on a hill*

fa·vou·rite¹ [S3] [W3] BrE; **favorite** AmE /'feɪvər̯t/ adj [only before noun]
1 your favourite person or thing is the one that you like the most: *a child's favourite toy* | *What's your favourite colour?* | *a favorite spot for picnickers*
2 favourite son a politician, sports player etc who is popular with people in the place that they come from

favourite² BrE; **favorite** AmE n [C] **1** something that you like more than other things of the same kind: *Can we have strawberries? They're my favourite.* | an **old/firm/particular favourite** *a sweater that's an old favorite* | [+with] *Roald Dahl's books are firm favourites with children.* **2** someone who is liked and treated better than others by a teacher or parent: *You always were Dad's favourite.* | **play favorites** AmE (=treat one person better than others) *The manager insisted he doesn't play favorites.* → FAVOURITISM **3** the team, player etc that is expected to win a race or competition: **favourite to do sth** *Italy were the favourites to win the World Cup.* | *Atwood was the **hot favourite** for the Booker Prize.*

fa·vou·ri·tis·m BrE; **favoritism** AmE /'feɪvər̯-tɪzəm/ n when you treat one person or group better than others, in an unfair way: *their favouritism towards their first son*

fawn¹ /fɔːn $ fɒːn/ n **1** [C] a young DEER **2** [U] a pale yellow-brown colour

fawn² adj having a pale yellow-brown colour

fawn³ v [I] to praise someone and be friendly to them in an insincere way, because you want them to like you or give you something: [+on/over] *I refused to fawn over her or flatter her.* —**fawning** adj

fax¹ /fæks/ n **1** [C] a letter or message that is sent in electronic form down a telephone line and then printed using a special machine: *Did you get my fax?* **2** [C] also **fax machine** a machine used for sending and receiving faxes: *What's your fax number?* **3** [U] the system of sending letters and messages using a fax machine: **by fax** *You can book tickets by fax or on-line.*

fax² v [T] to send someone a letter or message using a fax machine: **fax sb sth** *She asked me to fax her the details.* | **fax sth (through/on) to sb** *The contract should be faxed to him today.*

fay /feɪ/ n [C] literary a FAIRY (1) - used especially in poetry

faze /feɪz/ v [T] informal if a new or difficult situation fazes you, it makes you feel confused or shocked, so that you do not know what to do: *John was embarrassed, but it didn't faze Mike a bit.*

FBI /ˌef biː 'aɪ/ n the FBI *the Federal Bureau of Investigation* the police department in the US that is controlled by the central government, and that deals with crimes that break national laws rather than state laws; → CIA

FC /ˌef 'siː/ BrE the abbreviation of *football club*, used in the names of teams: *Liverpool FC*

FE /ˌef 'iː/ n [U] BrE the abbreviation of FURTHER EDUCATION

fe·al·ty /'fiːəlti/ n [U] old-fashioned loyalty to a king, queen etc

fear¹ [S3] [W1] /fɪə $ fɪr/ n
1 [C,U] the feeling you get when you are afraid or worried that something bad is going to happen

fear that
your deepest/worst/greatest fear
irrational fear (=a fear that is not reasonable or based on logic)
groundless fear (=a fear that you need not have because what you are afraid of does not happen)
deep-seated fear (=a very strong fear that is difficult to change)
in fear (of sth)
be in fear of/for your life (=afraid that you may be killed)
be/live in fear (of sth) (=be always afraid of something)
without fear (of sth)
trembling/shivering/shaking with fear
paralysed with fear (=so afraid that you cannot move)
confirm sb's fears (=show that what you are afraid of has happened)
allay/dispel sb's fears (=stop someone from being afraid)
sb's hopes and fears

The boy's eyes were full of fear. | [+of] *a fear of flying* | *There are fears that share prices could decrease still further.* | [+for] *The girl's parents expressed fears for her safety.* | *Their **worst fears** became a reality.* | *an **irrational fear** of spiders* | *As it turned out, their **fears** were **groundless**.* | *They looked at one another **in fear**.* | *Thousands of people are **in fear of their lives** following the shootings.* | *Ordinary people **lived in fear** of being arrested by the secret police.* | *People must be able to express their views **without fear**.* | *Rachel was **shaking with fear**.* | *She wept as the policeman **confirmed** her worst **fears**.* | *What **hopes and fears** do you have for the future?*

2 for fear (that), for fear of sth because you are worried that you will make something happen: *She finally ran away for fear that he would kill her.* | **for fear of doing sth** *He got to the station early, for fear of missing her.*
3 no fear! BrE informal used humorously to say that you are definitely not going to do something: *'Are you going to Bill's party tonight?' 'No fear!'*
4 [U] the possibility or danger that something bad might happen: *There's no fear of revolt now.*
5 put the fear of God into sb informal to make someone feel that they must do something, by making sure they know what will happen if they do not do it: *The Italian manager must have put the fear of God into his team.*
6 without fear or favour BrE formal in a fair way: *The law must be enforced without fear or favour.*

WORD CHOICE: fear, afraid, frightened
fear (noun) is the feeling of being afraid. Do not say that you 'have fear'. Use **be afraid** or **be frightened**: *My whole body was paralysed with fear.*	*She was suddenly very afraid.*	*We were too frightened to speak.*
The verb **to fear** is used mainly in literature or newspapers, and not usually in speech: *She feared that he would not be found alive.*	*Fearing more riots, the government made concessions.*
It is more usual to say that someone **is afraid** or **is frightened**: *My parents are afraid that I'll get involved with drugs.*	*People were frightened of being mugged.*

fear² [W2] v
1 [I,T] to feel afraid or worried that something bad may happen: *Fearing violence, the group asked for police protection.* | **fear (that)** *Police fear that there may be further terrorist attacks.* | **fear to do sth** formal: *Women feared to go out at night.* | **fear for sb** *His wife seemed depressed, and he feared for his children.* | **fear for sb's safety/life** *a terrifying ordeal in which she feared for her life* | *Hundreds of people are **feared dead** in the ferry disaster.*
2 fear the worst to think that the worst possible thing has happened or might happen: *When Tom heard about the accident he immediately feared the worst.*

3 [T] to be afraid of someone and what they might do: *As a leader, he was distrusted and even feared.*
4 I fear *formal* used when telling someone that you think that something bad has happened or is true: **I fear (that)** *I fear that there is little more we can do.* | **I fear so/I fear not** *'Were they satisfied?' 'I fear not.'*
5 fear not/never fear *formal* used to tell someone not to worry: *Never fear, he'll be with us soon.* → GOD-FEARING

fear·ful /'fɪəfəl $ 'fɪr-/ *adj* **1** *formal* frightened that something might happen: *a shy and fearful child* | [+of] *People are fearful of rising crime in the area.* | **fearful that** *Officials are fearful that the demonstrations will cause new violence.* **2** *BrE* extremely bad; ⏛ **awful, terrible:** *The room was in a fearful mess.* **3** [only before noun] *written* very frightening; ⏛ **terrifying:** *a fearful creature* —**fearfulness** *n* [U]

fear·ful·ly /'fɪəfəli $ 'fɪr-/ *adv* **1** in a way that shows you are afraid: *She glanced fearfully over her shoulder.* **2** [+ adj/adv] *BrE old-fashioned* extremely: *She's fearfully clever.*

fear·less /'fɪələs $ 'fɪr-/ *adj* not afraid of anything: *These dogs are absolutely fearless.* | *a fearless explorer* —**fearlessly** *adv* —**fearlessness** *n* [U]

fear·some /'fɪəsəm $ 'fɪr-/ *adj* very frightening: *a fearsome weapon*

fea·si·ble /'fiːzɪbəl/ *adj* a plan, idea, or method that is feasible is possible and is likely to work: *a feasible solution* | **economically/technically/politically etc feasible** *It was no longer financially feasible to keep the community centre open.* —**feasibly** *adv* —**feasibility** /ˌfiːzɪˈbɪləti/ *n* [U]: *a feasibility study*

feast¹ /fiːst/ *n* [C] **1** a large meal where a lot of people celebrate a special occasion; → **banquet:** *a wedding feast* | *The king promised to hold a great feast for all his people.* **2** a very good large meal: *all the ingredients for a spaghetti feast* | **midnight feast** (=a meal eaten secretly at night by children) **3** an occasion when there are a lot of enjoyable things to see or do: [+for] *Next week's film festival should be a real feast for cinema-goers.* | *The play is also a visual feast.* **4** a day or period when there is a religious celebration: *the feast day of St. Francis* → MOVABLE FEAST

feast² *v* **1 feast on/upon sth** to eat a lot of a particular food with great enjoyment: *We feasted on chicken and roast potatoes.* **2 feast your eyes on sb/sth** to look at someone or something with great pleasure: *If you like luxury cars, feast your eyes on these.* **3** [I] to eat and drink a lot to celebrate something

feat /fiːt/ *n* [C] something that is an impressive achievement, because it needs a lot of skill, strength etc to do: **remarkable/considerable/incredible etc feat** *They climbed the mountain in 28 days, a remarkable feat.* | [+of] *an incredible feat of engineering* | **perform/ accomplish/achieve a feat** *the woman who performed the feat of sailing around the world alone* | **no mean feat** (=something that is difficult to do) *It is no mean feat to perform such a difficult piece.*

feath·er¹ S3 /'feðə $ -ər/ *n* [C]
1 one of the light soft things that cover a bird's body: *an ostrich feather* | **feather bed/pillow etc** (=a bed etc that is filled with feathers)
2 a feather in your cap something you have done that you should be proud of → **light as a feather** at LIGHT² (4); → **birds of a feather** at BIRD (5); → **ruffle sb's feathers** at RUFFLE¹ (2)

feather² *v* [T] **1 feather your nest** to get money by dishonest methods **2** to put feathers on an ARROW → **tar and feather sb** at TAR² (3)

feather bedding *n* [U] the practice of letting workers keep their jobs even if they are not needed or do not work well

feather boa *n* [C] a long SCARF made of feathers and worn around a woman's neck

feath·er·brained /'feðəbreɪnd $ -ər-/ *adj* extremely silly

feather duster *n* [C] a stick with feathers on the end that you use to remove dust

feath·ered /'feðəd $ -ərd/ *adj* **1** having feathers, or made from feathers **2 feathered friend** *informal* a bird – used humorously

feath·er·weight /'feðəweɪt $ -ər-/ *n* [C] a BOXER who weighs less than 57.15 kilograms, and who is heavier than a BANTAMWEIGHT but lighter than a LIGHTWEIGHT

feath·er·y /'feðəri/ *adj* looking or feeling light and soft, like a feather: *The plant has feathery leaves.*

fea·ture¹ S2 W1 /'fiːtʃə $ -ər/ *n* [C]
1 a part of something that you notice because it seems important, interesting, or typical: *Air bags are a standard feature in most new cars.* | [+of] *An important feature of Van Gogh's paintings is their bright colours.* | **common feature** *Striped tails are a common feature of many animals.* | *The room's only redeeming feature (=thing that makes it acceptable) was that it was cheap.* | **main/important/significant etc feature** *The most distinctive feature of the dinosaurs was their size.* | *One of the distinguishing features (=features that are different from other things of the same sort) of modern banking is its dependence on computers.*
2 a piece of writing about a subject in a newspaper or a magazine, or a special report on television or on the radio: [+on] *a special feature on holidaying with your dog*
3 [usually plural] a part of someone's face, such as their eyes, nose etc: *He had fine delicate features.* | *Her eyes were her best feature.*
4 a part of the land, especially a part that you can see: *Hedges are an important feature of the landscape in Britain.*
5 a film being shown at a cinema: *There were a couple of short cartoons before the main feature.* | **double feature** (=when two films are shown together)

feature² W3 *v*
1 [I,T] to include or show something as a special or important part of something, or to be included as an important part: *The exhibition features paintings by contemporary artists.* | *a cruise ship featuring extensive spa facilities* | [+in] *A study of language should feature in an English literature course.* | **be featured in sth** *Pupils visited some of the websites featured in the article.* | **feature prominently/strongly/heavily etc** *Violence seems to feature heavily in all of his books.* | **feature sb as sth** *The film featured Marlon Brando as the Godfather.*
2 [T] to show a film, play etc: *The Retro Theatre is featuring films by Frank Capra this week.*

feature film *n* [C] a full-length film that has a story and is acted by professional actors, and which is usually shown in a cinema

fea·ture·less /'fiːtʃələs $ -tʃər-/ *adj* a featureless place has no interesting parts to notice: *featureless plains*

Feb. also **Feb** *BrE* the written abbreviation of *February*

fe·brile /'fiːbraɪl $ 'febrəl/ *adj* **1** *literary* full of nervous excitement or activity: *a febrile imagination* **2** *medical* relating to or caused by a fever

Feb·ru·a·ry /'februəri, 'febjʊri $ 'febjueri/ *n* [C,U] written abbreviation **Feb.** the second month of the year, between January and March: **next/last February** *Mum died last February.* | **in February** *We can do it in February.* | **on February 6th** *She was allowed home on February 6th.* | **on 6th February** *BrE: Francis was born on 6th February 1928.* | **February 6** *AmE: I finally arrived February 6.*

fe·ces /'fiːsiːz/ *n* the American spelling of FAECES —**fecal** /'fiːkəl/ *adj*

feck·less /'fekləs/ *adj* lacking determination, and not achieving anything in your life: *Alice's feckless younger brother* —**fecklessly** *adv* —**fecklessness** *n* [U]

fec·und /'fekənd, 'fiːkənd/ *adj formal* able to produce many children, young animals, or crops; ◨ **fertile** —**fecundity** /fɪ'kʌndᵻti/ *n* [U]

fed¹ /fed/ *v* the past tense and past participle of FEED¹ →
FED UP

fed² *n* [C] *AmE informal* a police officer in the FBI

fed·e·ral W3 /'fedərəl/ *adj*
1 a federal country or system of government consists of a group of states which control their own affairs, but which are also controlled by a single national government which makes decisions on foreign affairs, defence etc: *Switzerland is a federal republic.*
2 relating to the central government of a country such as the US, rather than the government of one of its states: *federal law | federal taxes*

,**Federal ,Bureau of Investi'gation** *n* [singular] the FBI

fed·e·ral·is·m /'fedərəlɪzəm/ *n* [U] belief in or support for a federal system of government

fed·e·rate /'fedəreɪt/ *v* [I + with] if a group of states federate, they join together to form a federation

fed·e·ra·tion /,fedə'reɪʃən/ *n* **1** [C] a group of organizations, clubs, or people that have joined together to form a single group: *the National Federation of Women's Institutes* **2** [C] a group of states that have joined together to form a single group: *the Russian Federation* **3** [U] when groups of people, states etc join together to form a larger group

fe·do·ra /fɪ'dɔːrə/ *n* [C] a soft hat with a BRIM that curls upwards slightly

,**fed 'up** *adj informal* annoyed or bored, and wanting something to change: *She felt tired and a bit fed up.* | [+with] *I'm really fed up with this constant rain.* | *Anna got fed up with waiting.*

fee S2 W2 /fiː/ *n* [C] an amount of money that you pay to do something or that you pay to a professional person for their work: *school fees | The health club* **charges** *an annual membership fee.* | *Cable TV subscribers* **pay** *monthly fees.* | **entrance/entry fee** (=fee to enter a place) *Park entrance fees have gone up to $15.* | *The run, to raise money for breast cancer, has a £10* **entry** *fee* (=fee to enter a competition). | **doctor's/lawyer's/accountant's etc fees** | **legal/medical fee** *The insurance company paid all my medical fees.* | *My solicitor charges a* **flat** *fee* (=an amount that does not change) *for handling the sale of a house.*; → see box at COST¹; → see box at PAY²

fee·ble /'fiːbəl/ *adj* **1** extremely weak: *His voice sounded feeble and far away.* | *She was too feeble to leave her room.* **2** not very good or effective: *a feeble excuse | a rather feeble committee*

,**feeble-'minded** *adj* **1** stupid or not sensible: *a feeble-minded policy* **2** *old use* having much less than average intelligence —**feeble-mindedness** *n* [U]

feed¹ S1 W2 /fiːd/ *v past tense and past participle* **fed** /fed/
1 GIVE FOOD [T] **a)** to give food to a person or animal: *Have you fed the cat?* | **feed yourself** *She was too weak to feed herself.* | **feed sth to sb** *Several children were feeding bread to the ducks.* | **feed sb on/with sth** *They were fed well on her mother's home cooking.* **b)** to provide enough food for a group of people: *groceries to feed a family of five | The prison is required to feed and clothe the prisoners.*
2 PLANT [T] to give a special substance to a plant, which helps it grow: *Feed the tomatoes once a week.* |

feeding a baby

feeding a parrot

feed

feed sth with sth *Feed houseplants with a liquid fertiliser.*
3 ANIMAL/BABY [I] if a baby or an animal feeds, they eat: *Frogs generally feed at night.* | *Let your baby feed as long as she wants.*
4 **well-fed/under-fed/poorly-fed** having plenty of food or not enough food: *a well-dressed, well-fed woman*
5 COMPUTER [T always + adv/prep] to put information into a computer over a period of time: **feed sth into sth** *Figures are fed into the computer, which then predicts the likely profit.*
6 SUPPLY STH [T] to supply something, especially a liquid, gas, or electricity: *The public baths are fed by natural springs.* | **feed sth to sth** *The sound is fed directly to the headphones.* | **feed sth with sth** *Laura crouched by the fire, feeding it with dry sticks.*
7 PUT STH INTO STH [T] to put something into something else, especially gradually and through a small hole: **feed sth into/through sth** *A tube was fed down the patient's throat into her stomach.* | **feed sth into sth** *She fed her last two coins into the machine for a cup of coffee.* | *Shelton* **fed** *the electricity* **meter**.
8 INCREASE EMOTION [T] to increase the strength of an emotion, desire etc: *Her depression grew, fed by her bitter experiences.*
9 **feed an addiction/need etc** to satisfy a strong need, such as a need for a drug: *He committed both crimes to feed his addiction to heroin.*
10 INFORMATION [T] to give someone information or ideas over a period time: **feed sb with sth** *She feeds the media with stories, which is a way of getting free advertising.* | **feed sth to sb** *US intelligence had been feeding false information to a KGB agent.*
11 SPORT [T] to throw or hit a ball to someone else on your team, especially so that they can make a point: **feed sth to sb** *Johnson fed the ball to Kyman, who scored.*
12 **feed lines/jokes to sb** to say things to another performer so that they can make jokes
13 **feed your face** *informal* to eat a lot of food; ◨ **stuff yourself**
14 TV/RADIO [T] to send a television or radio programme somewhere so that it can be broadcast
15 **feed sb a line** *informal* to tell someone something which is not true, so that they will do what you want → BREAST-FEED, FORCE-FEED, SPOON-FEED; → **mouth to feed** at MOUTH¹ (10)

feed back *phr v*
to give advice or criticism to someone about something they have done: [+on] *We're just waiting for the manager to feed back on it.* | **feed sth ⇔ back (to sb)** *I am grateful to all those who fed back their comments.* | *They feed back to the government the reactions of the people affected.*

feed into sth *phr v*
to have an effect on something or help to make it happen: *The influence of Italian designer fashion feeds into sports fashion.*

feed off sth *phr v*
1 if an animal feeds off something, it gets food from it: *birds that feed off the seeds from trees*
2 to use something to increase, become stronger, or succeed – sometimes used to show disapproval: *fad diets that feed off our desire to be thin*

feed on sth *phr v*
1 if an animal feeds on a particular food, it usually eats that food: *Owls feed on mice and other small animals.*
2 if a feeling or process feeds on something, it becomes stronger because of it: *Prejudice feeds on ignorance.*

feed sb **up** *phr v BrE*
to give someone a lot of food to make them more healthy; ◨ **fatten up** *AmE*

feed² *n*
1 BABY [C] *BrE* one of the times when you give milk to a small baby: *the two a.m. feed*
2 ANIMAL FOOD [U] food for animals: *fish feed*
3 SUPPLY [C] a tube or piece of equipment which supplies a machine with something, especially FUEL

4 TV/RADIO/COMPUTER [C,U] when a television or radio signal, computer information etc is sent somewhere, or the connection that is used to do this: *a live satellite feed from the space station*
5 MEAL [C] *old-fashioned* a big meal

feed·back S4 /'fiːdbæk/ *n* [U]
1 advice, criticism etc about how successful or useful something is: *How can I provide feedback without making someone angry?* | [+on] *Try to give each student some feedback on the task.*
2 a very unpleasant high noise, caused when a MICROPHONE is too close to an AMPLIFIER

feed·bag /'fiːdbæg/ *n* [C] *AmE* a bag put around a horse's head containing food; ⊟ **nosebag**

feed·er /'fiːdə $ -ər/ *n* [C]   **1** a container with food for animals or birds: *a bird feeder*   **2** something that provides supplies for something else: *The Shyok River is a major feeder of the Indus River.* | *The length of the feeder pipe is 50m.*   **3** a piece of equipment that supplies something to a machine: *the printer's paper feeder*   **4** a person or animal that eats in a particular way: *Catfish are bottom feeders.* (=they feed at the bottom of rivers)   **5** a small road, railway line, or AIRLINE service that takes traffic to a main road, line, or service

feeder ,school *n* [C] a school from which many students go to a SECONDARY SCHOOL in the same area

feeding-,bottle *n* [C] a plastic bottle used for giving milk to a baby or young animal

feeding ground *n* [C] a place where a group of animals or birds find food to eat

feel¹ S1 W1 /fiːl/ *v past tense and past participle felt* /felt/
1 FEELING/EMOTION [linking verb, T] to experience a particular physical feeling or emotion: *Do you still feel hungry?* | *You can never tell what he's feeling.* | *Stop exercising if you feel any pain.* | **feel fine/good/comfortable etc** *I'm feeling a little better today.* | *Marie immediately felt guilty.* | **feel as if/as though** *When his dad left, he felt as though his world had turned upside-down.* | *I felt like I'd really achieved something.*
2 NOTICE [T not in progressive] to notice something that is happening to you, especially something that is touching you: *She felt his warm breath on her cheek.* | *The earthquake was felt as far south as San Diego.* | **feel sb/sth do sth** *She felt his arms go round her.* | **feel yourself doing sth** *I felt myself blushing.*
3 FEEL SMOOTH/DRY ETC [linking verb] to give you a particular physical feeling, especially when you touch or hold something: **feel smooth/cold/damp etc** *Her hands felt rough.* | *The house felt hot and stuffy.* | **feel as if/as though** *My leg feels as if it's broken.* | *It's nice fabric – it feels like velvet.*
4 FEEL GOOD/STRANGE/EXCITING ETC [linking verb] if a situation, event etc feels good, strange etc, that is the emotion or feeling that it gives you: *After twenty years, seeing him again felt very strange.* | **feel ... to be/do sth** *It felt wonderful to be wearing clean clothes again.* | *How does it feel to be 40?* | *It's been a year since her daughter died, but to her, it still feels like yesterday.*
5 HAVE AN OPINION [T not usually in progressive] to have a particular opinion, especially one that is based on your feelings, not on facts: **feel (that)** *Some of the parents felt the school wasn't doing enough about bullying.* | [+about] *How would you feel about working with Nicole for a while?* | *The experience of rape can change how a woman feels about her body.* | **feel sure/certain** (=think that something is definitely true) *She felt sure she'd made the right decision.*
6 feel like (doing) sth *spoken* to want to have something or do something: *He didn't feel like going to work.* | *Do you feel like another drink?*
7 TOUCH [T] to touch something with your fingers to find out about it: *She felt his forehead. Perhaps he had a temperature.* | *Mum, feel this stone. Isn't it smooth?* | **feel how hard/soft/rough etc sth is** *He could feel how damp his shirt was against his chest.*

8 feel around/on/in etc sth (for sth) to search for something with your fingers: *She felt in her bag for a pencil.*
9 feel the force/effects/benefits etc of sth to experience the good or bad results of something: *The local economy is beginning to feel the effects of the recession.*
10 feel the need to do sth to believe that you need to do something: *Children who can talk to their parents feel less need to try drugs.*
11 feel your way a) to move carefully, with your hands out in front of you, because you cannot see properly: *Silently, she felt her way across the room.* **b)** to do things slowly and carefully, because you are not completely sure about a new situation: [+towards] *The European Union is still feeling its way towards common policies.*
12 feel free *spoken* used to tell someone that they can do something if they want to: *'Could I use your phone for a minute?' 'Feel free.'* | **feel free to do sth** *Please feel free to make suggestions.*
13 I know (just/exactly) how you feel *spoken* used to express sympathy with someone or with a remark they have just made: *I know how you feel, Mark, but maybe it's better not to confront him.*
14 not feel yourself *spoken* to not feel as healthy or happy as usual: *I don't know what's wrong. I just don't feel quite myself.*
15 feel your age to realize that you are not as young or active as you used to be: *Looking at his grandson made him really feel his age.*
16 feel the cold/heat to suffer because of cold or hot weather: *Old people tend to feel the cold more.*
17 feel a death/a loss etc to react very strongly to a bad event, especially someone's death: *Susan felt her grandmother's death more than the others.*

feel for sb *phr v*
to feel sympathy for someone: *At the Center, the other mothers know what it's like, and they really feel for you.*
feel sb ⇔ out *phr v AmE informal*
to find out what someone's opinions or feelings are, without asking them directly: *I thought I'd feel out some of my colleagues before the meeting.*
feel sb ⇔ up *phr v informal*
to touch someone sexually, without their permission
feel up to sth *phr v* [usually in questions and negatives] *informal*
to have the strength, energy etc to do something: *I just didn't feel up to going.*

feel² S3 *n*
1 [singular] a quality that something has that makes you feel or think a particular way about it: *Despite their age, the photographs have a modern feel.* | [+about] *The restaurant has a nice relaxed feel about it.*
2 [singular] the way that something feels when you touch it: [+of] *I like the feel of this cloth.* | *a soft feathery feel*
3 have/get/give a feel for sth *informal* to have or develop an understanding of something and skill in doing it: *exercises that give a child a feel for numbers and measurements*
4 [U] when you use your hands, body etc to feel something; ⊟ **touch: by feel** *She found the light switch by feel.*

feel·er /'fiːlə $ -ər/ *n* [C usually plural]   **1** one of the two long things on an insect's head that it uses to feel or touch things. Some sea animals also have feelers.   **2 put out feelers** to carefully try to discover what people think about something that you want to do: *They seem interested in a peace settlement and have begun putting out feelers.*

feel-good *adj*   **1 feel-good film/programme/music etc** a film etc whose main purpose is to make you feel happy   **2 feel-good factor** *especially BrE* a feeling among ordinary people that everything is going well, and that they do not need to worry about losing their jobs or spending money

1 000, 2 000, 3 000, most frequent words in S poken and W ritten English

feel·ing¹ S1 W1 /ˈfiːlɪŋ/ n

1 ANGER/SADNESS/JOY ETC [C] an emotion that you feel, such as anger, sadness, or happiness: [+of] *terrible feelings of guilt* | *It's a great feeling when a wild animal shows you affection.* | *It was the last game of the season, and feelings were running high* (=people were very angry or excited).

2 WAY SB THINKS/FEELS **feelings** [plural] someone's feelings are their thoughts, emotions, and attitudes: *He's considerate of other people's feelings.* | *Don't worry. It won't hurt my feelings if you change your mind.* | *Children only slowly develop the ability to put their feelings into words* (=describe what they are thinking and feeling). | *My parents had mixed feelings* (=had both good and bad feelings) *about all the changes.*

3 OPINION [C] a belief or opinion about something, especially one that is influenced by your emotions: *My personal feeling is that not enough has been done.* | [+on] *She has strong feelings on the issue of abortion.* | [+about] *a survey on people's feelings about the candidates* | *His gut feeling* (=opinion based on emotion) *was that Burns was probably guilty.*

4 have/get a feeling (that) to think that something is probably true, or will probably happen: [+(that)] *Leslie suddenly got the feeling that somebody was watching her.* | *He had a sneaking feeling* (=a slight feeling that something is true, without being sure) *that they were laughing at him.* | *Garry had a sinking feeling* (=had a sudden bad feeling that something is true) *that he was making a mistake.* | [+about] *I have a good feeling about this. I think it's going to work.*

5 GENERAL ATTITUDE [U] a general attitude among a group of people about a subject: *the anti-American feeling in the region* | [+against/in favour of] *Johnson underestimated the strength of public feeling against the war in Vietnam.* | *the depth of feeling against nuclear weapons*

6 HEAT/COLD/PAIN ETC [C] something that you feel in your body, such as heat, cold, tiredness etc: *I keep getting this funny feeling* (=a strange feeling) *in my neck.* | [+of] *feelings of dizziness*

7 ABILITY TO FEEL [U] the ability to feel pain, heat etc in part of your body: *Harry had lost all feeling in his toes.*

8 EFFECT OF A PLACE/BOOK ETC [singular] the effect that a place, book, film etc has on people and the way it makes them feel: [+of] *the town's strong feeling of history* | *It gives a feeling of eating outdoors, without having to worry about being rained on.*

9 I know the feeling *spoken* said when you understand how someone feels because you have had the same experience: *'It's so embarrassing when you can't remember someone's name.' 'I know the feeling.'*

10 the feeling is mutual *spoken* said when you have the same feeling about someone as they have towards you: *My dad hated my boyfriend, and the feeling was mutual.*

11 bad/ill feeling anger, lack of trust etc between people, especially after an argument or unfair decision: *The changes have caused a lot of ill feeling among the workforce.*

12 with feeling in a way that shows you feel very angry, happy etc: *Chang spoke with great feeling about the injustices of the regime.*

13 a feeling for sth **a)** an ability to do something or understand a subject, which you get from experience: *It's an orchestra that has always shown a special feeling for Brahms' music.* **b)** a natural ability to do something; ▣ talent: *She has a natural feeling for mathematical ideas.*

14 EMOTIONS NOT THOUGHT [U] a way of reacting to things using your emotions, instead of thinking about them carefully: *The Romantic writers valued feeling above all else.* → no hard feelings at HARD¹ (19); → hurt sb's feelings at HURT¹ (4)

feeling² *adj* showing strong feelings: *a feeling look*
—**feelingly** *adv*

'fee-ˌpaying *adj BrE* **1** fee-paying school a school which you have to pay to go to **2** fee-paying student/patient a student or PATIENT who pays for their education or medical treatment

feet /fiːt/ *n* the plural of FOOT → get/have cold feet at COLD¹ (6); → feet of clay at FOOT¹ (26); → have itchy feet at ITCHY (3)

feign /feɪn/ *v* [T] *formal* to pretend to have a particular feeling or to be ill, asleep etc: *Feigning a headache, I went upstairs to my room.*

feint¹ /feɪnt/ *n* [C] a movement or an attack that is intended to deceive an opponent, especially in BOXING

feint² *v* [I,T] to pretend to hit someone in BOXING

feist·y /ˈfaɪsti/ *adj* having a strong determined character and being willing to argue with people – use this to show approval: *DiFranco charmed the audience with her feisty spirit.*

fe·laf·el /fəˈlæfəl, -ˈlɑː- $ -ˈlɑː-/ *n* another spelling of FALAFEL

feld·spar /ˈfeldspɑː $ -ɑːr/ *n* [U] a type of grey or white mineral

fe·li·ci·ta·tions /fɪˌlɪsɪˈteɪʃənz/ *interjection formal* said to wish someone happiness

fe·li·ci·tous /fɪˈlɪsɪtəs/ *adj formal* or *literary* well-chosen and suitable: *a felicitous choice of candidate*

fe·li·ci·ty /fɪˈlɪsɪti/ *n formal* **1** [U] happiness: *domestic felicity* **2** [U] the quality of being well-chosen or suitable: *a felicity of language* **3** felicities [plural] *BrE formal* suitable or well-chosen remarks or details

fe·line¹ /ˈfiːlaɪn/ *adj* **1** relating to cats or other members of the cat family, such as lions **2** looking like or moving like a cat: *She moves with feline grace.*

feline² *n* [C] *technical* a cat or a member of the cat family, such as a tiger

fell¹ /fel/ *v* the past tense of FALL

fell² *n* [C usually plural] a mountain or hill in the north of England

fell³ *v* [T usually passive] **1** to cut down a tree: *More than 100 trees were felled in just over an hour.* **2** *written* to knock someone down with great force: *The goalkeeper was felled by a coin thrown from the crowd.*

fell⁴ *adj* in one fell swoop also at one fell swoop *BrE* doing a lot of things at the same time, using only one action: *A single company can close a factory, eliminating 74,000 jobs in one fell swoop.*

fel·la S3 /ˈfelə/ *n* [C] *spoken informal* **1** a man: *There's a fella outside who wants to see you.* **2** *especially BrE* a BOYFRIEND: *What do you think of Janet's new fella?*

fel·la·ti·o /fəˈleɪʃiəʊ $ -ʃioʊ/ *n* [U] the practice of touching a man's PENIS with the lips and tongue to give sexual pleasure; → cunnilingus

fel·ler /ˈfelə $ -ər/ *n* [C] *spoken old-fashioned* a man

fel·low¹ /ˈfeləʊ $ -loʊ/ *n* [C] **1** *old-fashioned* a man: *Paul's an easy-going sort of fellow.* **2** sb's fellows *BrE old-fashioned* people that you work with, study with, or who are in the same situation as you: *Wooderson's courage earned him the respect of his fellows.* **3** *AmE* a GRADUATE student who has a fellowship in a university **4** *especially BrE* a member of an important society or a college: *She is a Fellow of the Royal College of Surgeons.* → BEDFELLOW

fellow² W3 *adj*
1 fellow workers/students/countrymen etc people that you work with, study with, or who are in the same situation as you
2 our fellow man/men other people in general: *We all have obligations to our fellow men.*

ˌfellow ˈfeeling *n* [U] *literary* a feeling of sympathy and friendship towards someone because they are like you: *As an only child myself, I had a fellow feeling for Laura.*

fel·low·ship /ˈfeləʊʃɪp $ -loʊ-/ *n* **1** [U] a feeling of friendship resulting from shared interests or experiences: *Regular outings contribute to a sense of fellow-*

ship among co-workers. **2** [C] a group of people who share an interest or belief, especially Christians who have religious ceremonies together **3** [C] *BrE* a job at a university which involves making a detailed study of a particular subject **4** [C] **a)** *especially AmE* money given to a student to allow them to continue their studies at an advanced level; → **scholarship**: *Florian came to the United States on a Fulbright fellowship.* **b)** *AmE* a group of officials who decide which students will receive this money: *He received a gold medal from the Artists' Fellowship in New York.*

fellow 'traveller *BrE*; **fellow traveler** *AmE n* [C] someone who supports and agrees with the beliefs of an organization, such as the Communist Party, but does not belong to it – used to show disapproval

fel·on /'felən/ *n* [C] *law* someone who is guilty of a serious crime: *By law,* **convicted felons** (=criminals who are sent to prison) *may not own or use guns.*

fel·o·ny /'feləni/ *n plural* **felonies** [C,U] *law* a serious crime such as murder; → **misdemeanour**

felt¹ /felt/ *v* the past tense and past participle of FEEL

felt² *n* [U] a thick soft material made of wool, hair, or fur that has been pressed flat

felt-tip 'pen also **,felt-tipped 'pen**; **'felt-tip** *BrE n* [C] a pen that has a hard piece of felt at the end that the ink comes through → see picture at STATIONERY

fem. **1** the written abbreviation of *female* **2** the written abbreviation of *feminine*

fe·male¹ [S3] [W2] /'fi:meɪl/ *adj*
1 relating to women or girls; ◧ **male**; → **feminine**: *female voters* | *Over half of the staff is female.*
2 belonging to the sex that can have babies or produce eggs; ◧ **male**: *a female spider*
3 a female plant or flower produces fruit; ◧ **male**
4 *technical* a female part of a piece of equipment has holes into which the male part can be fitted; ◧ **male**

female² [W3] *n* [C]
1 an animal that belongs to the sex that can have babies or produce eggs; ◧ **male**
2 a woman or girl; ◧ **male**: *As a group, females performed better on the test than males.*
3 a plant that produces flowers or fruit; ◧ **male**

female 'condom *n* [C] a loose rubber tube with one end closed, that fits inside a woman's VAGINA when she is having sex, so that she will not have a baby

fem·i·nine /'femɪnɪn/ *adj* **1** having qualities that are considered to be typical of women, especially by being gentle, delicate, and pretty: *Dianne loved pretty feminine things.* **2** relating to being female; ◫ **female**: *traditional feminine roles* | *Amelia's report describes the experience from a feminine point of view.* **3** a feminine noun, PRONOUN etc belongs to a class of words that have different INFLECTIONS from MASCULINE or NEUTER words; **masculine**

fem·i·nin·i·ty /ˌfemɪˈnɪnɪti/ *n* [U] qualities that are considered to be typical of women, especially qualities that are gentle, delicate, and pretty; → **masculinity**: *You don't have to lose your femininity to be an independent, successful woman.*

fem·i·nis·m /'femɪnɪzəm/ *n* [U] the belief that women should have the same rights and opportunities as men

fem·i·nist [W3] /'femɪnɪst/ *n* [C] someone who supports the idea that women should have the same rights and opportunities as men: *She's been an outspoken feminist for over twenty years.* —**feminist** *adj* [only before noun]: *feminist literature*

fem·i·nize also **-ise** *BrE* /'femɪnaɪz/ *v* [T] to change something so that it includes women, is suitable for women, or is considered typical of women: *women who resist cultural attempts to feminize them*

femme fa·tale /ˌfæm fəˈtɑːl $ ˌfem-/ *n plural* **femmes fatales** [C] a beautiful woman who men find very attractive, even though she may make them unhappy

fe·mur /'fiːmə $ -ər/ *n* [C] *medical* the THIGH bone —**femoral** /'femərəl/ *adj* [only before noun]

fen /fen/ also **fenland** *n* [C,U] an area of low flat wet land, especially in Eastern England

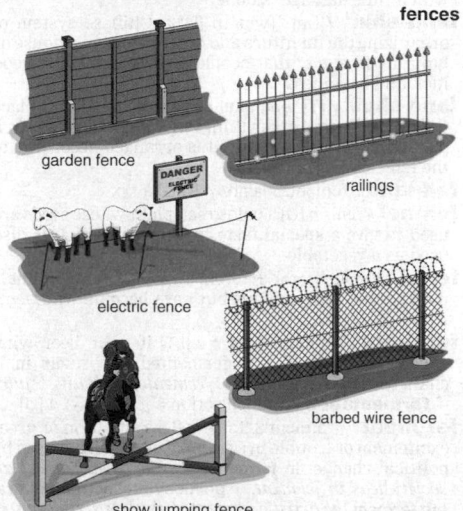

fences

garden fence

railings

DANGER

electric fence

barbed wire fence

show jumping fence

fence¹ [S3] /fens/ *n* [C]
1 a structure made of wood, metal etc that surrounds a piece of land
2 a wall or other structure that horses jump over in a race or competition
3 *informal* someone who buys and sells stolen goods
4 **sit/be on the fence** to avoid saying which side of an argument you support → **mend (your) fences** at MEND¹ (4)

fence² *v* **1** [T] to put a fence around something: *old farmhouses and fenced gardens* **2** [I] to fight with a long thin sword as a sport **3** [I + with] to answer someone's questions in a clever way in order to get an advantage in an argument
fence sb/sth ⇔ **in** *phr v* **1** to surround a place with a fence: *The yard was fenced in to keep out wolves.* **2** to make someone feel that they cannot leave a place or do what they want: *Young mothers often feel fenced in at home.*
fence sth ⇔ **off** *phr v* to separate one area from another area with a fence: *a planting area fenced off from the main garden*

'fence-,mending *adj* [only before noun] **fence-mending measures/talks/trip etc** fence-mending trips, talks etc are between countries who have a disagreement about something, and are meant to try to improve relations between them —**fence-mending** *n* [U]

fenc·er /'fensə $ -ər/ *n* [C] someone who fights with a long thin sword as a sport

fenc·ing /'fensɪŋ/ *n* [U] **1** the sport of fighting with a long thin sword **2** fences or the pieces of wood, metal etc used to make them

fend /fend/ *v* **fend for yourself** to look after yourself without needing help from other people: *The kids had to fend for themselves while their parents were away.*
fend sb/sth **off** *phr v* **1** to defend yourself against someone who is attacking you; ◫ **fight sb** ⇔ **off**: *Tabitha threw up an arm to fend her attacker off.* **2** to defend yourself from something such as difficult questions, competition, or a situation you do not want to deal with: *She uses her secretary to fend off unwanted phone calls.* | *The company managed to fend off the hostile takeover bid.*

fend·er /'fendə $ -ər/ *n* [C] **1** *AmE* the side part of a car that covers the wheels; ◧ **wing** *BrE*; → see picture at CAR **2** a low metal wall around a FIREPLACE that prevents burning wood or coal from falling out **3** *AmE* a curved piece of metal over the wheel of a bicycle that prevents water and mud from flying up; ▤ **mudguard** *BrE*

'fender-,bender *n* [C] *AmE informal* a car accident in which little damage is done

feng shui[1] /ˌfʌŋ ˈʃweɪ/ *n* [U] a Chinese system of organizing the furniture and other things in a house or building in a way that people believe will bring good luck and happiness

feng shui[2] *v* [T] **feng shui a room/house etc** to place the furniture and other things in a room or house in a particular position so that it is arranged according to the feng shui system

fen·land /ˈfenlənd, -lænd/ *n* [C,U] a FEN

fen·nel /ˈfenl/ *n* [U] a pale green plant whose seeds are used to give a special taste to food and which is also used as a vegetable

fer·al /ˈferəl, ˈfɪərəl $ ˈferəl, ˈfɪrəl/ *adj* feral animals used to live with humans but have become wild: *feral cats*

fer·ment[1] /fəˈment $ fər-/ *v* [I,T] if fruit, beer, wine etc ferments, or if it is fermented, the sugar in it changes to alcohol: *fermented fruit juice* —**fermentation** /ˌfɜːmenˈteɪʃən $ ˌfɜːrmən-/ *n* [U]

fer·ment[2] /ˈfɜːment $ ˈfɜːr-/ *n* [U] a situation of great excitement or trouble in a country, especially caused by political change: **in ferment** | *In the 1960s, American society was in ferment.* | **political/intellectual/cultural etc ferment** *the artistic ferment of the late sixth century*

fern /fɜːn $ fɜːrn/ *n* [C] a type of plant with green leaves shaped like large feathers, but no flowers —**ferny** *adj*; → see picture at FLOWER

fe·ro·cious /fəˈrəʊʃəs $ -ˈroʊ-/ *adj* **1** violent, dangerous, and frightening: *a ferocious, hungry lion* | *a ferocious battle* | *The storm grew more and more ferocious with each second.* **2** very strong, severe, and unpleasant: *The congressman is one of the President's most ferocious critics.* | *The heat was ferocious.* | *Butler is famous for his ferocious temper.* **3** relating to an emotion that is felt very strongly: *Parker was driven by a ferocious determination to succeed.* —**ferociously** *adv*

fe·ro·ci·ty /fəˈrɒsəti $ fəˈrɑː-/ *n* [U] the state of being extremely violent and severe: [+of] *Detectives were shocked by the ferocity of the attack.*

fer·ret[1] /ˈferət/ *n* [C] a small animal with a pointed nose, used to hunt rats and rabbits

ferret[2] *v* [I] **1** [always + adv/prep] *informal* to search for something that is lost or hidden among a lot of things or inside a drawer, box etc: [+**around/round/about**] *He started ferreting around in his desk.* | [+**for**] *She ferreted in her bag for a pen.* **2** to hunt rats and rabbits using a ferret

 ferret sth ⇔ **out** *phr v* **1** to succeed in finding something such as a piece of information, that is difficult to find: *It's been difficult for reporters to ferret out the facts in this case.* | *Uncle Vernon ferreted out the laundry box from under the stairs.* **2** *AmE* to find and usually get rid of someone who is causing a problem: *The new program is meant to ferret out problem cops.*

Fer·ris wheel /ˈferəs ˌwiːl/ *n* [C] *especially AmE* a very large upright wheel with seats on it for people to ride on in an AMUSEMENT PARK; ▤ **big wheel** *BrE*

fer·rous /ˈferəs/ *adj technical* containing or related to iron: *ferrous metals*

fer·rule /ˈferuːl, ˈferəl $ ˈferəl/ *n* [C] *technical* a piece of metal or rubber put on the end of a stick to make it stronger

fer·ry[1] /ˈferi/ *n plural* **ferries** [C] a boat that carries people or goods across a river or a narrow area of water

ferry[2] *v* **ferried, ferrying, ferries** [T always + adv/prep] to carry people or things a short distance from one place to another in a boat or other vehicle: **ferry**

sb/sth (from sth) to sth *The ship was used to ferry supplies to Russia during the war.* | **ferry sb/sth across sth** *ferrying passengers across the Channel*

fer·ry·boat /ˈferibəʊt $ -boʊt/ *n* [C] a ferry

fer·tile /ˈfɜːtaɪl $ ˈfɜːrtl/ *adj* **1** fertile land or soil is able to produce good crops: *800 acres of fertile cropland* **2** able to produce babies, young animals, or new plants; ▤ **infertile**: *Most men remain fertile into old age.* **3 a fertile imagination/mind/brain** an imagination, mind etc that is able to produce a lot of interesting and unusual ideas **4** [only before noun] a fertile situation is one in which something can easily develop and succeed: *the fertile Philadelphia music scene of the 1960s*

fer·til·i·ty /fɜːˈtɪləti $ fɜːr-/ *n* [U] **1** the ability of the land or soil to produce good crops **2** the ability of a person, animal, or plant to produce babies, young animals, or seeds; ▤ **infertility**

fer'tility ,drug *n* [C] a drug given to a woman to help her have a baby

fer·ti·lize also **-ise** *BrE* /ˈfɜːtəlaɪz $ ˈfɜːrtl-aɪz/ *v* [T] **1** to make new animal or plant life develop: *After the egg has been fertilized, it will hatch in about six weeks.* **2** to put fertilizer on the soil to make plants grow —**fertilization** /ˌfɜːtəlaɪˈzeɪʃən $ ˌfɜːrtl-əˈzeɪ-/ *n* [U]

fer·ti·liz·er S3 /ˈfɜːtəlaɪzə $ ˈfɜːrtl-aɪzər/ *n* [C,U] a substance that is put on the soil to make plants grow

fer·vent /ˈfɜːvənt $ ˈfɜːr-/ *adj* believing or feeling something very strongly and sincerely: *a fervent appeal for peace* | *fervent admirer/believer etc a fervent supporter of human rights* —**fervently** *adv*

fer·vid /ˈfɜːvɪd $ ˈfɜːr-/ *adj formal* believing or feeling something too strongly —**fervidly** *adv*

fer·vour *BrE*; **fervor** *AmE* /ˈfɜːvə $ ˈfɜːrvər/ *n* [U] very strong belief or feeling: *religious fervour* | *revolutionary fervour* | *patriotic fervor*

fess /fes/ *v*

 fess up *AmE informal* to admit that you have done something wrong, although it is not very serious; ▤ **own up**: *Come on, fess up! Who ate that last cookie?*

fest /fest/ *n* a **beer/song/food etc fest** an informal occasion when a lot of people do a fun activity together, such as drinking beer, singing songs, or eating food → SLUGFEST

fes·ter /ˈfestə $ -ər/ *v* [I] **1** if an unpleasant feeling or problem festers, it gets worse because it has not been dealt with: *The dispute can be traced back to resentments which have festered for centuries.* **2** if a wound festers, it becomes infected: *festering sores* **3** if rubbish or dirty objects fester, they decay and smell bad

fes·ti·val S3 W3 /ˈfestɪvəl/ *n* [C]
1 an occasion when there are performances of many films, plays, pieces of music etc, usually happening in the same place every year: *the Newport Jazz festival* | [+**of**] *the Swansea Festival of Music and the Arts*
2 a special occasion when people celebrate something such as a religious event, and there is often a public holiday: *Christmas is one of the main festivals in the Christian Calendar.* | *religious festivals*

fes·tive /ˈfestɪv/ *adj* **1** looking or feeling bright and cheerful in a way that seems suitable for celebrating something: *The atmosphere was festive and jolly.* | *John was obviously in a festive mood.* **2 festive occasion** a day when you celebrate something special such as a birthday **3 the festive season/period/holiday** the period around CHRISTMAS **4** [only before noun] relating to Christmas: *festive cheer* | *festive gifts*

fes·tiv·i·ty /feˈstɪvəti/ *n* **1 festivities** [plural] things such as drinking, eating, or dancing that are done to celebrate a special occasion: *The festivities started with a procession through the town.* **2** [U] a happy feeling that exists when people celebrate something: *There was an air of festivity in the village.*

fes·toon¹ /feˈstuːn/ v [T usually passive] to cover something with flowers, long pieces of material etc, especially for decoration: **be festooned with/in sth** *Malaga was festooned with banners and flags in honour of the king's visit.*

festoon² n [C] *formal* a long thin piece of material, flowers etc, used especially for decoration

fet·a cheese /ˌfetə ˈtʃiːz/ also **feta** n [U] a white cheese from Greece made from SHEEP'S milk or GOAT'S milk

fe·tal /ˈfiːtl/ adj the usual American spelling of FOETAL

fetch¹ [S2] /fetʃ/ v [T]
1 especially BrE to go and get something or someone and bring them back: *Quick! Go and fetch a doctor.* | *Shannon went upstairs to fetch some blankets.* | **fetch sb/sth from sth** *Would you mind going to fetch the kids from school?* | **fetch sb sth/fetch sth for sb** *Fetch me some coffee while you're up.* ⚠ **Fetch** or **bring?** → see box at BRING
2 to be sold for a particular amount of money, especially at a public sale – used especially in news reports: *The painting is expected to fetch at least $20 million.*
3 fetch and carry to do simple and boring jobs for someone as if you were their servant: *Am I supposed to fetch and carry for him all day?*
4 BrE to make people react in a particular way: *This announcement fetched a huge cheer from the audience.*
  fetch up phr v BrE informal
[always + adv/prep] to arrive somewhere without intending to: *I fell asleep on the train and fetched up in Glasgow.*

fetch² n **play fetch** if you play fetch with a dog, you throw something for the dog to bring back to you

fetch·ing /ˈfetʃɪŋ/ adj attractive, especially because the clothes you are wearing suit you: *Your sister looks very fetching in that dress.*

fête¹ /feɪt/ n [C] **1** BrE an outdoor event where there are competitions and things to eat and drink, usually organized to get money: *the church fête* **2** AmE a special occasion to celebrate something: *a farewell fête in honor of the mayor*

fête² v [T usually passive] to honour someone by holding public celebrations for them: *The team was fêted from coast to coast.*

fet·id /ˈfetɪd/ adj formal having a strong bad smell; 🔲 **stinking**: *the black fetid water of the lake* | *the dog's fetid breath*

fet·ish /ˈfetɪʃ/ n [C] **1** a desire for sex that comes from seeing a particular type of object or doing a particular activity, especially when the object or activity is considered unusual: *a leather fetish* **2** something you are always thinking about or spending too much time doing; → **obsession**: [+for/about] *Sue has a real fetish about keeping everything tidy.*

fet·ish·ist /ˈfetɪʃɪ̊st/ n [C] someone who gets sexual pleasure from unusual objects or activities —**fetishism** n [U]

fet·lock /ˈfetlɒk $ -lɑːk/ n [C] the back part of a horse's leg, just above the HOOF

fet·ter /ˈfetə $ -ər/ v [T usually passive] literary **1** to restrict someone's freedom and prevent them from doing what they want: *fettered by family responsibilities* **2** to put chains on a prisoner's hands or feet; 🔲 **chain**

fet·ters /ˈfetəz $ -ərz/ n [plural] literary **1** the things that prevent someone from being free; 🔲 **constraints**: [+of] *breaking the fetters of convention* **2** chains that were put around a prisoner's feet in past times

fet·tle /ˈfetl/ n **in fine/good fettle** old-fashioned healthy or working properly

fe·tus /ˈfiːtəs/ n the usual American spelling of FOETUS

feud¹ /fjuːd/ n [C] an angry and often violent quarrel between two people or groups that continues for a long time: [+over] *a bitter feud over territory* | [+with/between] *a feud between rival drug organizations*

feud² v [I] to continue quarrelling for a long time, often in a violent way: **feud (with sb) over sth** *The neighboring states are feuding over the rights to the river.*

feud·al /ˈfjuːdl/ adj [only before noun] relating to feudalism: *the feudal system* | *feudal society*

feu·dal·is·m /ˈfjuːdl-ɪzəm/ n [U] a system which existed in the Middle Ages, in which people received land and protection from a lord when they worked and fought for him

feu·dal·is·tic /ˌfjuːdlˈɪstɪk◂/ adj based on a system in which only a few people have all the power in a way that seems very old-fashioned

fe·ver /ˈfiːvə $ -ər/ n **1** [C,U] an illness or a medical condition in which you have a very high temperature: *Andy has a fever and won't be coming into work today.* | *I woke up this morning with a fever and an upset stomach.* | *She's running a fever* (=has a fever). | *a high/low/slight fever The usual symptoms are a pink rash with a slight fever.* → HAY FEVER, SCARLET FEVER, YELLOW FEVER, GLANDULAR FEVER, RHEUMATIC FEVER **2** [singular] a situation in which many people feel very excited or feel very strongly about something: [+of] *a fever of excitement on Wall Street* | **election/carnival etc fever** (=great interest or excitement about a particular activity or event) *Soccer fever has been sweeping the nation as they prepare for the World Cup.* **3 (at) fever pitch** BrE if people's feelings are at fever pitch, they are extremely excited: *The nation was at fever pitch in the days leading up to the election.* | *After a second night of rioting, tensions in the city reached fever pitch.* → CABIN FEVER

fever blister n [C] AmE a COLD SORE

fe·vered /ˈfiːvəd $ -ərd/ adj [only before noun] literary **1** extremely excited or worried; 🔲 **feverish**: *the child's fevered cries* **2** suffering from a fever; 🔲 **feverish**: *She wiped his fevered brow* (=a hot forehead caused by a fever). **3 a fevered imagination/mind/brain** a mind that imagines strange things that are not real: *These stories are merely a product of her fevered imagination.*

fe·ver·ish /ˈfiːvərɪʃ/ adj **1** suffering from a fever: *She lay in bed, too feverish to sleep.* | *There was a feverish blush to his cheeks.* **2** very excited or worried about something: *They waited in a state of feverish anxiety for their mother to come home.* | *The show was about to begin and backstage there were signs of feverish activity* (=activity that is done very quickly because there is not much time). —**feverishly** adv: *Congress is working feverishly to pass the bill.*

few [S1] [W1] /fjuː/ determiner, pron, adj comparative **fewer**, superlative **fewest**
1 [no comparative] a small number of things or people: **a few** *I have to buy a few things at the supermarket.* | *Pam called to say she's going to be a few minutes late.* | *There were a few people sitting at the back of the hall.* | *There are a few more things I'd like to discuss.* | [+of] *I've read a few of her books.* | *I could suggest many different methods, but anyway, here are just a few.* | *There are only a very few* (=not many) *exceptions.* | **the last/next few** *The office has been closed for the last few days.* | **every few days/weeks etc** *The plants need to be watered every few days.* | **the/sb's few days/weeks etc** *She had enjoyed her few days in Monaco.*
2 quite a few/a good few/not a few a fairly large number of things or people: *She must have cooked a good few dinners over the years.* | [+of] *There were hundreds of protesters, not a few of whom were women.*
3 not many or hardly any people or things; 🔲 **many**: *low-paid jobs that few people want* | *Many people expressed concern, but few were willing to help.* | *The team that makes the fewest mistakes usually wins.* | [+of] *Very few of the staff come from the local area.* | *Mr Wingate was full of explanations, but precious few* (=hardly any) *of them made sense.* | **the few** *The cathedral was one of the few buildings not destroyed in*

F

the war. | *This hospital is one of the few that are equipped to provide transplant surgery.* | **sb's few belongings/friends etc** *I gathered together my few possessions.*

4 no fewer than used to emphasize that a number is large: *I tried to contact him no fewer than ten times.*

5 as few as 5/10 etc used to emphasize how surprisingly small a number is: *Sometimes as few as 20 out of 500 or more candidates succeed in passing all the tests.*

6 to name/mention but a few used when you are mentioning only a small number of people or things as examples of a large group: *This is a feature of languages such as Arabic, Spanish and Portuguese, to name but a few.*

7 the (privileged/chosen) few the small number of people who are treated better than others and have special advantages: *Such information is made available only to the chosen few.* | *The needs of the many have been ignored — instead, the priority has been to bring benefits only to the few.*

8 be few and far between to be rare: *Jobs are few and far between at the moment.*

9 have had a few (too many) *informal* to have drunk too much alcohol: *He looks as if he's had a few!*

WORD CHOICE: a few, few, a little, little, a bit, fewer, less

a few and **few** are used before plural nouns.
a few means 'a small number': *It will take a few minutes.* | *I've got a few friends who live nearby.*
few means 'not many'. It emphasizes how small the number is. It is mainly used in writing or formal speech: *Few people would deny her talent.* | *He has few interests outside his work.*
In spoken English or informal writing it is more usual to say **not many**: *Not many people saw what happened.*
a little and **little** are used before uncountable nouns.
a little means 'some, but not a lot': *We still have a little time left.*
In spoken British English, it is more usual to say **a bit**: *'Are you tired?' 'A bit.'* | *I've got a bit of money left.*
little means 'not much'. It emphasizes how small the amount is. It is mainly used in writing or formal speech: *There is now little hope of success.*
In spoken English or informal writing it is more usual to say **not much**: *There was not much milk left.*
The comparative of **few** is **fewer**: *Few people have read the book, and even fewer understand it.*
The comparative of **little** is **less**: *We know little about his adult life, and less about his childhood.*
⚠ Sometimes people use **less** before a plural noun, but many people think that this is incorrect, so it is better to use **fewer**: *a village of fewer (NOT less) than 200 inhabitants*

---

fey /feɪ/ *adj* very sensitive and behaving or talking in a strange way: *a fey and delicate child*

fez /fez/ *n* [C] a round red hat with a flat top and no BRIM

ff *and following* used in writing to refer to the pages after the one you have mentioned: *pages 17ff*

fi·an·cé /fi'ɒnseɪ $,fiːɑːn'seɪ/ *n* [C] the man whom a woman is going to marry

fi·an·cée /fi'ɒnseɪ $,fiːɑːn'seɪ/ *n* [C] the woman whom a man is going to marry

fi·as·co /fi'æskəʊ $ -koʊ/ *n plural* **fiascoes** *or* **fiascos** [C] an event that is completely unsuccessful, in a way that is very embarrassing or disappointing; ▣ **disaster**: *The first lecture I ever gave was a complete fiasco.*

fi·at /ˈfiːæt, ˈfaɪæt/ *n* [C] *formal* an official order given by someone in a position of authority, without considering what other people want: **by fiat** *The matter was settled by presidential fiat.*

fib¹ /fɪb/ *n* [C] *spoken* a small unimportant lie; → **white lie**: *He's been known to tell fibs.*

fib² *v* **fibbed, fibbing** [I] *spoken* to tell a small unimportant lie: *I think you're fibbing.* —**fibber** *n* [C]

---

fi·ber /ˈfaɪbə $ -ər/ *n* the American spelling of FIBRE

fi·ber·board /ˈfaɪbəbɔːd $ -bərbɔːrd/ *n* the American spelling of FIBREBOARD

fi·ber·glass /ˈfaɪbəɡlɑːs $ -bərɡlæs/ *n* the American spelling of FIBREGLASS

fi·bre *BrE*; **fiber** *AmE* /ˈfaɪbə $ -ər/ *n* **1** [U] the parts of plants that you eat but cannot DIGEST. Fibre helps to keep you healthy by moving food quickly through your body: *Fruit and vegetables are high in fibre content.* | *food that is high in dietary fibre* **2** [C,U] a mass of threads used to make rope, cloth etc: **natural/synthetic/man-made etc fibre** *Nylon is a man-made fibre.* **3** [C] a thin thread, or one of the thin parts like threads that form natural materials such as wood or CARBON **4 nerve/muscle fibres** the thin pieces of flesh that form the nerves or muscles in your body **5 with every fibre of your being** *literary* if you feel something with every fibre of your being, you feel it very strongly: *He wanted her with every fibre of his being.* → **moral fibre** at MORAL¹ (2); → OPTICAL FIBRE

fi·bre·board *BrE*; **fiberboard** *AmE* /ˈfaɪbəbɔːd $ -bərbɔːrd/ *n* [U] board made from wood fibres pressed together

fi·bre·glass *BrE*; **fiberglass** *AmE* /ˈfaɪbəɡlɑːs $ -bərɡlæs/ *n* [U] a light material made from small glass threads pressed together, used for making sports cars, small boats etc

fibre 'optics *n* [U] the process of using very thin threads of glass or plastic to carry information in the form of light, especially on telephone lines: *fibre-optic cables*

fi·brous /ˈfaɪbrəs/ *adj* consisting of many fibres or looking like fibres: *The coconut has a fibrous outer covering.*

fib·u·la /ˈfɪbjʊlə/ *n* [C] *medical* the outer bone of the two bones in your leg below your knee

fick·le /ˈfɪkəl/ *adj* **1** someone who is fickle is always changing their mind about people or things that they like, so that you cannot depend on them – used to show disapproval: *an unpredictable and fickle lover* **2** something such as weather that is fickle often changes suddenly —**fickleness** *n* [U]: *the fickleness of fame*

fic·tion /ˈfɪkʃən/ *n* **1** [U] books and stories about imaginary people and events; ▣ **non-fiction**: *romantic fiction* | *historical fiction* **2** [C] something that people want you to believe is true but which is not true: *preserving the fiction of his happy childhood*

fic·tion·al /ˈfɪkʃənəl/ *adj* fictional people, events etc are imaginary and from a book or story: *fictional characters* | *The novel is set in the fictional German town of Kreiswald.*

fic·tion·al·ize also **-ise** *BrE* /ˈfɪkʃənəlaɪz/ *v* [T] to make a film or story about a real event, changing some details and adding some imaginary characters: *a fictionalized account of his life in Berlin*

fic·ti·tious /fɪk'tɪʃəs/ *adj* not true, or not real: *a fictitious address* | *The author fills this real town with fictitious characters.*

fic·tive /ˈfɪktɪv/ *adj AmE* imaginary and not real: *the fictive world of James Bond*

fid·dle¹ /ˈfɪdl/ *n* [C] *informal* **1** a VIOLIN **2** *BrE* a dishonest way of getting money: *an insurance fiddle* | **on the fiddle** | *They suspected he was on the fiddle* (=getting money dishonestly or illegally) *all along.* **3 be a fiddle** to be difficult to do and involve complicated movements of your hands: *This blouse is a bit of a fiddle to do up.* → **fit as a fiddle** at FIT² (1); → **play second fiddle (to sb)** at PLAY¹ (22)

fiddle² *v* **1** [I] to keep moving and touching something, especially because you are bored or nervous: *Stop fiddling, will you!* | *I sat and fiddled at the computer for a while.* | [+with] *She was at her desk in the living room, fiddling with a deck of cards.* **2** [T] *BrE informal* to give false information about something, in order to avoid paying money or to get extra money: *Bert had been fiddling his income tax for years.* | **fiddle**

the books (=give false figures in a company's financial records) **3** [I] to play a VIOLIN

fiddle around also **fiddle about** BrE phr v to waste time doing unimportant things

fiddle around with sth also **fiddle about with sth** BrE phr v **1** to move the parts of a machine in order to try to make it work or repair it: *I've been fiddling around with this old car for months but I still can't get it to work.* **2** to make small unnecessary changes to something – used to show disapproval: ◪ **mess around with:** *Why did you let her fiddle about with the remote control?* | *The bus company is always fiddling around with the schedules.*

fiddle with sth phr v **1** to move part of a machine in order to make it work, without knowing exactly what you should do: *After fiddling with the tuning I finally got JFM.* **2** to move or touch something that does not belong to you, in an annoying way: *Don't let him fiddle with my bag.*

fid·dler /'fɪdlə $ -ər/ n [C] **1** someone who plays the VIOLIN, especially if they play FOLK MUSIC **2** someone who gives false information, especially on official documents, in order to pay less money or get more than they should: *tax fiddlers* —**fiddling** n [U]

fid·dle·sticks /'fɪdl̩stɪks/ interjection old-fashioned said when you disagree with someone, or are slightly annoyed about something

fid·dling /'fɪdlɪŋ/ adj [only before noun] unimportant, and annoying: *fiddling little jobs around the house*

fid·dly /'fɪdli/ adj BrE informal difficult to do, especially because you have to deal with very small objects: *Fixing the TV was a fiddly job.*

fi·del·i·ty /fɪ'deləti/ n [U] formal **1** when you are loyal to your husband, girlfriend etc, by not having sex with anyone else; ◪ **loyalty;** ◪ **infidelity:** *the importance of marital fidelity* (=in marriage) **2** when you are loyal to a person, an organization, or something that you believe in; ◪ **loyalty:** [+to] *his fidelity to the company over 25 years* **3** formal how much a film, a piece of written work etc remains unchanged from an earlier piece of work, or the facts that are known: [+to] *the movie's fidelity to the original book* → HIGH FIDELITY

fid·get¹ /'fɪdʒət/ v [I] to keep moving your hands or feet, especially because you are bored or nervous: *The kids had started to fidget.* | [+with] *Stop fidgeting with your pens!*

fidget² n [C] informal someone who is unable to sit or stand still

fid·get·y /'fɪdʒəti/ adj informal unable to stay still, especially because of being bored or nervous: *The boys get fidgety if they can't play outside.*

fie /faɪ/ interjection old use **fie on sb** used to express anger or disapproval towards someone

field¹ [S1] [W1] /fiːld/ n [C]
1 FARM an area of land in the country, especially one where crops are grown or animals feed on grass: *a view of green fields and rolling hills* | [+of] *a field of wheat* | **corn/rice/wheat etc field** *working in the cotton fields*; → see picture at COUNTRY
2 SUBJECT a subject that people study or an area of activity that they are involved in as part of their work: [+of] *her work in the field of human rights* | *Peter's an expert in his field.* | *He's the best-known American outside the field of* (=not connected with) *politics.*
3 SPORT an area of ground where sports are played: **a baseball/football/cricket etc field** *the local soccer field* | **on/off the field** *The team have had a bad year, both on and off the field.* | *Fans cheered as the players took the field* (=went onto the field).
4 PRACTICAL WORK work or study that is done in the field is done in the real world rather than in a class or LABORATORY: **in the field** *His theories have not yet been tested in the field.* | **field trials/testing/research etc** → FIELD TRIP, FIELDWORK
5 COMPETITORS a) all the people, companies, products etc that are competing against each other: *the field of candidates for the presidential election* | **be ahead**

of/lead the field (=be doing better than the others) *Germany was leading the field with a figure of 53%.* **b)** all the horses or runners in a race: *Prince led the field* (=was ahead of the others) *as they came around the final bend.*
6 magnetic/gravitational/force field the area in which a natural force is felt or has an effect: *the Earth's magnetic field*
7 coal/oil/gas field a large area of land where coal, oil, or gas is found: *North Sea oil fields*
8 the field (of battle) the time or place where there is fighting in a war: *The new tank has yet to be tested in the field.* | *medals won* **on the field of battle**
9 field of vision/view the whole area that you are able to see without turning your head
10 snow/ice field a large area of land covered with snow or ice
11 field of fire the area that you can hit when you shoot from a particular position
12 leave the field clear for sb to make it possible for someone to do something or to be successful at something, by not competing with them: *Josh left the company, leaving the field clear for me.*
13 COMPUTERS in a computer document, an amount of space made available for a particular type of information: *an empty field* (=not yet written in) → **have a field day** at FIELD DAY; → **play the field** at PLAY¹ (29)

field² v [T] **1** if you field a team, an army etc, they represent you or fight for you in a competition, election, or war: *The Ecology Party fielded 109 candidates.* | *We fielded a team of highly talented basketball players.* **2** to answer questions, telephone calls etc, especially when there are a lot of them or the questions are difficult: *The Minister fielded questions on the Middle East and other issues.* | *The press office fielded numerous calls from the media.* **3 be fielding** the team that is fielding in a game of CRICKET or baseball is the one that is throwing and catching the ball, rather than the one hitting it; ◪ **be batting 4** if you field the ball in a game of CRICKET or baseball, you stop it after it has been hit

'field corn n [U] AmE a type of corn grown to feed to animals, rather than to be eaten by people → SWEETCORN

'field day n [C] **1 have a field day** informal to have a chance to do a lot of something you want, especially the chance to criticize someone: *The newspapers had a field day when the trial finished.* **2** AmE a day when students at a school have sports competitions and parents watch; ◪ **sports day** BrE

field·er /'fiːldə $ -ər/ also **fieldsman** BrE n [C] one of the players who tries to catch the ball in a game of CRICKET or baseball

'field e,vent n [C] a sport such as jumping or throwing the JAVELIN in an outdoor competition → TRACK EVENT

'field ,glasses n [plural] BINOCULARS

'field ,goal n [C] **1** the act of kicking the ball over the GOAL in American football **2** the act of putting the ball through the net to get points in BASKETBALL

'field ,hockey n [U] AmE HOCKEY played on grass

'field ,hospital n [C] a temporary hospital for soldiers that is near where the fighting is

'field ,marshal n [C] an officer of the highest rank in the British army

field·mouse /'fiːldmaʊs/ n plural **fieldmice** /-maɪs/ [C] a mouse that has a long tail and lives in fields

'field ,officer n [C] **1** BrE someone who works for an organization whose job involves practical outdoor work, especially work connected with the countryside **2** an officer of high rank in the British army

fields·man /'fiːldzmən/ n plural **fieldsmen** /-mən/ [C] BrE FIELDER

'field ,sports n [plural] BrE sports that happen in the countryside, such as hunting, shooting, and fishing

F

'field test n [C] a test of a new piece of equipment, done in the place where it will be used rather than in a LABORATORY —**field-test** v [T]

'field trip n [C] an occasion when students go somewhere to learn about a particular subject, especially one connected with nature or science: *a geography field trip*

field·work /'fiːldwɜːk $ -wɜːrk/ n [U] the study of scientific or social subjects, done outside the class or LABORATORY —**fieldworker** n [C]

fiend /fiːnd/ n [C] **1** a very cruel, evil, or violent person: *a heartless fiend* | *Both of them were fighting like fiends.* | **a sex/rape fiend** (=one who commits very unpleasant sex attacks) **2** **television/sports/fresh-air etc fiend** someone who likes watching television, doing sports etc a lot, or more than is normal; ⬛ **fanatic** **3** **drug/dope/cocaine etc fiend** someone who takes a lot of illegal drugs **4** an evil spirit

fiend·ish /'fiːndɪʃ/ adj **1** cruel and unpleasant: *a particularly fiendish practical joke* **2** very clever in an unpleasant way: *a fiendish plan* **3** extremely difficult or complicated: *several fiendish exam questions* —**fiendishly** adv —**fiendishness** n [U]

fierce /fɪəs $ fɪrs/ adj **1** done with a lot of energy and strong feelings, and sometimes violent: *There was fierce fighting in the city.* | **fierce attack/opposition/criticism etc** *The government's policies came under fierce attack.* | *The plan has evoked a fierce debate.* | **fierce competition** *between the companies* **2** a fierce person or animal is angry or ready to attack, and looks very frightening: *fierce guard dogs* | *She turned round, looking fierce.* **3** fierce emotions are very strong and often angry: *These people take fierce pride in their independence.* **4** fierce cold, heat, or weather is much colder, hotter etc than usual: *a fierce wind* **5** **something fierce** AmE spoken more loudly, strongly etc than usual: *It was snowing something fierce.* —**fiercely** adv —**fierceness** n [U]

fierce

fi·er·y /'faɪəri $ 'faɪri/ adj **1** very red or orange, and looking like fire: *a fiery sunset* | *leaves that turn fiery red in autumn* **2** becoming angry or excited very quickly: *He has a fiery temper.* **3** showing or encouraging anger or excitement: *a fiery speech* **4** fiery food or drink tastes very strong, making part of your body feel hot

fi·es·ta /fi'estə/ n [C] a religious holiday with dancing, music etc, especially in Spain and South America

fife /faɪf/ n [C] a musical instrument like a small FLUTE, often played in military bands

fif·teen /ˌfɪf'tiːn◂/ number, n **1** the number 15: *a coastal village fifteen miles south of Tourane* | *They met when she was fifteen* (=15 years old). **2** [C] a team of 15 players in RUGBY UNION —**fifteenth** adj, pron: *in the fifteenth century* | *her fifteenth birthday* | *I'm planning to leave on the fifteenth* (=the 15th day of the month).

fifth¹ /fɪfθ/ adj **1** coming after four other things in a series: *in the fifth century* | *her fifth birthday* **2** **fifth wheel** AmE informal someone who is not wanted in a particular group of people: *They'd made her feel like a fifth wheel.* —**fifth** pron: *I'm planning to leave on the fifth* (=the fifth day of the month). —**fifthly** adv

fifth² n [C] **1** one of five equal parts of something **2** AmE an amount of alcohol equal to 1/5 of an American GALLON (2), sold in bottles: *a fifth of bourbon*

fifth 'column n [C] a group of people who work secretly to help the enemies of the country where they live or the organization in which they work —**fifth columnist** n [C]

fif·ty /'fɪfti/ number, n **1** the number 50 **2** **the fifties** [plural] also **the '50s**, **the 1950s** the years between 1950 and 1959: *Standards of living rose in the fifties.* | **the early/mid/late fifties** *The play was written in the late fifties.* **3** **be in your fifties** to be aged between 50 and 59: **early/mid/late fifties** *He must be in his early fifties by now.* **4** **in the fifties** if the temperature is in the fifties, it is between 50 degrees and 59 degrees: **in the low/mid/high fifties** *sunny, with temperatures in the mid fifties* **5** [C] a piece of paper money that is worth 50 dollars or 50 pounds: *I can give you five tens for that fifty if you want.* —**fiftieth** adj: *her fiftieth birthday*

ˌfifty-'fifty adv, adj spoken **1** if you divide something fifty-fifty, you divide it equally between two people, companies etc: **divide/split/share sth fifty-fifty** *The companies split the profits fifty-fifty.* | *We'll share it on a **fifty-fifty basis**.* | **go fifty-fifty (on sth)** (=share the cost of something equally) *We went fifty-fifty on a new TV set.* **2** if there is a fifty-fifty chance of something happening, it is equally likely to happen as not to happen: **a fifty-fifty chance** *of winning*

fig /fɪg/ n [C] **1** a soft sweet fruit with a lot of small seeds, often eaten dried, or the tree on which this fruit grows → see picture at FRUIT **2** **not give a fig/not care a fig (about/for sth/sb)** old-fashioned informal to not be at all concerned about or interested in something or someone

fig. **1** the written abbreviation of *figure* **2** the written abbreviation of *figurative*

fight¹ [S1] [W1] /faɪt/ v past tense and past participle **fought** /fɔːt $ fɒːt/
1 **WAR** [I,T] to take part in a war or battle: [+in] *the families of those who fought in the war* | [+against/with] *rebel forces fighting against the Russians* | [+about/over/for] *They fought for control of the islands.* | *Neither country is capable of **fighting** a long war.* | *Later the Indians fought the Anglo settlers.*
2 **HIT PEOPLE** [I,T] if someone fights another person, or if two people fight, they hit and kick the other person in order to hurt them: [+with] *Two guys were fighting with each other in the street.* | [+about/over/for] *They were fighting over a girl.* | *She fought him desperately, kicking and biting.*
3 **TRY TO DO STH** [I,T] to try hard to do or get something: [+for] *The men were fighting for higher wages.* | *Stockley is **fighting for** his **life** (=trying to stay alive), with serious head injuries.* | *She **fought** her **way** back into the first team.* | **fight to do sth** *The president was fighting to survive.*
4 **PREVENT STH** [I,T] to try very hard to prevent something or to get rid of something unpleasant that already exists: [+against] *People are fighting against repression and injustice.* | *We will fight terrorism, wherever it exists.*
5 **COMPETE** [I,T] to take part in an election or compete strongly for something, especially a job or political position: **fight an election/a campaign** *The prime minister decided to fight an early general election.* | **fight (sb) for sth** *He had to fight several other applicants for the job.* | *Both men were used to fighting for power.*
6 **ARGUE** [I] to argue about something: [+with] *I heard her fighting with the boss.* | [+about/over] *They're fighting about who should do the dishes.*
7 **SPORT** [I,T] to take part in a BOXING match: *Ali fought Foreman for the heavyweight title.*
8 **EMOTION** [I,T] to try very hard not to have or show a feeling: *She fought her fear.* | [+with] *She was clearly fighting with her emotions.*
9 **LAW** [T] to try to get something or prevent something in a court of law: *The insurance company are fighting the claims in court.*
10 **fight your way (through/past etc sb/sth)** to move somewhere with difficulty, for example because there

are so many people around you: *We fought our way through the crowd.*
11 fight a losing battle to try to do something that you probably cannot succeed in doing: *I'm fighting a losing battle on this diet.*
12 have a fighting chance to have a chance to do something or achieve something if you try very hard: *Lewis has a fighting chance to win the gold medal.*
13 fight tooth and nail (for sth)/fight sth tooth and nail to try very hard to do or achieve something, or to prevent something: *He's rich now, but he had to fight tooth and nail for it.*
14 fight to the death/finish to fight until one person or group is dead or completely defeated
15 fight your own battles fight for what you want, without needing help from other people: *Mum, I can fight my own battles now.*
16 fighting spirit the desire to fight or win: *In the second half the team showed their true fighting spirit.*
17 fighting words/talk something you say that shows that you want to fight hard for something
18 fight fire with fire to use the same methods as your opponents in an argument, competition etc
19 fight like cat and dog if two people fight like cat and dog, they argue a lot because they dislike each other or disagree: *I didn't get on with her at work either – we fought like cat and dog.*
20 fighting fit *BrE* extremely fit and healthy
21 fight your corner *BrE* to try to persuade people that your ideas about something are right and should be accepted: *The Prime Minister made it clear that Britain would fight its corner on Europe.*
22 fight shy of (doing) sth *BrE* to try to avoid doing something or being involved in something: *Many women fight shy of motherhood.*

fight back *phr v*
1 to work hard to achieve or oppose something, especially in a situation where you are losing: *United fought back and scored a last-minute goal.* | [+against] *She was fighting back against the cancer.*
2 to use violence or arguments against someone who has attacked you or argued with you: *The rebels are fighting back.*
3 fight sth ⇔ back to try hard not to have or show a feeling: *She looked away, fighting back her tears.* | *He fought back the impulse to slap her.*

fight sth ⇔ **down** *phr v*
to try hard not to have or show a feeling: *Doug fought down a feeling of panic.*

fight sb/sth ⇔ **off** *phr v*
1 to keep someone away, or stop them doing something to you, by fighting or opposing them: *Bodyguards had to fight off the crowds.* | *The company managed to fight off a takeover attempt.*
2 to succeed in stopping other people getting something, and to get it for yourself: *Allan fought off stiff competition from throughout the UK to win one of only four places at the college.*
3 to try hard to get rid of something, especially an illness or a feeling: *Elaine's fighting off a cold.*

fight sth **out** *phr v*
to argue or fight until a disagreement is settled: *We left them to fight it out.*

fight² S2 W3 *n*
1 HIT [C] a situation in which two people or groups hit, push etc each other: *Sam's always getting into fights at school.* | [+with] *He got drunk and had a fight with Jim.* | [+between] *A fight broke out between the two gangs.* | [+over/about] *fights over territory* | **pick/start a fight** *The big guy was trying to pick a fight.* | a **street fight**
2 ACHIEVE/PREVENT STH [singular] the process of trying to achieve something or prevent something: [+for] *the fight for justice and democracy* | *The little girl lost her fight for life* (=fight to stay alive) *last night.* | [+against] *the fight against crime* | **fight to do sth** *the fight to get financial aid* | *You'll* **have a fight on your hands** (=it will be difficult) *to convince the committee.*

3 ARGUMENT [C] an argument: [+with] *They've had a fight with the neighbours.* | [+over/about] *fights over money*
4 SPORT [C] a BOXING match: *Are you going to watch the big fight tonight?*
5 BATTLE [C] a battle between two armies: [+for] *the fight for Bunker Hill*
6 ENERGY [U] energy or the desire to keep fighting for something you want: *There's plenty of fight left in your grandmother.*
7 put up a good fight to work very hard to fight or compete in a difficult situation: *Our team put up a good fight.*
8 a fight to the death/finish a fight that continues until one side is completely defeated

fight·back /'faɪtbæk/ *n* [C] *BrE* an attempt by someone to get back to a position of strength after they have lost it, especially in sport: *Arsenal staged a spirited fightback in the second half.*

fight·er /'faɪtə $ -ər/ *n* [C] **1** also **'fighter plane/aircraft/jet** a small fast military plane that can destroy other planes: *He was shot down by enemy fighters.* | a **fighter pilot** **2** someone who fights, especially as a sport **3** someone who keeps trying to achieve something in difficult situations: *James is a fighter – he never gives up.* → FIREFIGHTER, FREEDOM FIGHTER

fight·ing /'faɪtɪŋ/ *n* [U] when people or groups fight each other in a war, in the street etc: [+between] *heavy fighting between government and rebel forces* | *Fighting broke out in the crowds.*

'fig leaf *n* [C] the large leaf of the fig tree, sometimes shown in paintings as covering people's sex organs

fig·ment /'fɪgmənt/ *n* **a figment of sb's imagination** something that you imagine is real, but which does not exist

fig·u·ra·tive /'fɪgjərətɪv, -gə-/ *adj* **1** a figurative word or phrase is used in a different way from its usual meaning, to give you a particular idea or picture in your mind; → **literal**: *He's my son,* **in the figurative sense** *of the word.* **2** technical figurative art shows objects, people, or the countryside as they really look; → **abstract** —**figuratively** *adv*: *They have a taste – figuratively speaking – for excitement.*

fig·ure¹ S1 W1 /'fɪgə $ 'fɪgjər/ *n* [C]
1 NUMBER **a)** [usually plural] a number representing an amount, especially an official number: **unemployment/sales/trade figures** *Ohio's employment figures for December* | *Government figures underestimate the problem.* | *It's about 30,000* **in round figures** (=to the nearest 10, 20, 100 etc). **b)** a number from 0 to 10, written as a sign rather than a word: *the figure '2'* | *executives with salaries* **in six figures** (=more than £99,000) | a **four/five/six figure number** (=a number in the thousands, ten thousands, hundred thousands etc) → DOUBLE FIGURES, SINGLE FIGURES
2 AMOUNT OF MONEY a particular amount of money: [+of] *an estimated figure of $200 million*
3 PERSON **a)** someone who is important or famous in some way: **a leading/key/central figure** *Several leading figures resigned from the party.* | *the outstanding political figure of his time* **b)** someone with a particular type of appearance or character, especially when they are far away or difficult to see: *a tall figure in a hat* | *Through the window I could see the commanding figure of Mrs Bradshaw.* → **cult figure** at CULT²
4 WOMAN'S BODY the shape of a woman's body: *She has a good figure.* | **keep/lose your figure** (=stay thin or become fat) | *Most women have to* **watch their figure** (=be careful not to get fat).
5 father/mother/authority figure someone who is considered to be like a father etc, or to represent authority, because of their character or behaviour
6 figures [plural] *BrE* the activity of adding, multiplying etc numbers; ⬛ **arithmetic**: *a natural ability with*

F

figure 590

figures | have a head for figures (=be good at arithmetic)

7 MATHEMATICAL SHAPE a GEOMETRIC shape: *A hexagon is a six-sided figure.*

8 PAINTING/MODEL a person in a painting or a model of a person: *the figure in the background* → FIGURINE

9 DRAWING written abbreviation *fig.* a numbered drawing or a DIAGRAM in a book

10 put a figure on it/give an exact figure to say exactly how much something is worth, or how much or how many of something you are talking about: *It's worth a lot but I couldn't put a figure on it.*

11 a fine figure of a man/woman someone who is tall and has a good body

12 a figure of fun someone who people laugh at

13 ON ICE a pattern or movement in FIGURE SKATING

figure² S2 W3 *v*

1 [I] to be an important part of a process, event, or situation, or to be included in something: [+in/among] *Environmental issues figured prominently in the talks.* | *My wishes didn't figure among his considerations.* | *Reform now figures high on the agenda.*

2 [T] *informal* to form a particular opinion after thinking about a situation: **figure (that)** *From the way he behaved, I figured that he was drunk.* | *It was worth the trouble, I figured.*

3 that figures/(it) figures *spoken especially AmE* **a)** used to say that something that happens is expected or typical, especially something bad: *'It rained the whole weekend.' 'Oh, that figures.'* **b)** used to say that something is reasonable or makes sense: *It figures that she'd be mad at you, after what you did.*

4 go figure *AmE spoken* said to show that you think something is strange or difficult to explain: *'He didn't even leave a message.' 'Go figure.'*

5 [T] *AmE* to calculate an amount: *I'm just figuring my expenses.*

figure on sth *phr v informal especially AmE*
to expect something or include it in your plans: *She was younger than any of us had figured on.*

figure sb/sth ⇔ **out** *phr v*
1 to think about a problem or situation until you find the answer or understand what has happened: **figure out how/what/why etc** *Can you figure out how to do it?* | *If I have a map, I can figure it out.* | *Don't worry, we'll figure something out* (=find a way to solve the problem).
2 to understand why someone behaves in the way they do: *Women. I just can't figure them out.*

fig·ured /ˈfɪɡəd $ ˈfɪɡjərd/ *adj* [only before noun] *formal* decorated with a small pattern

fig·ure·head /ˈfɪɡəhed $ ˈfɪɡjər-/ *n* [C] **1** someone who seems to be the leader of a country or organization but who has no real power; → **puppet**: *The Queen is merely a figurehead.* **2** a wooden model of a woman that used to be placed on the front of ships

figure of 'eight *BrE*; **figure 'eight** *AmE n* [C] the pattern or shape of a number eight, as seen in a knot, dance etc

figure of 'speech *n* [C] a word or expression that is used in a different way from the normal meaning, to give you a picture in your mind

figure ˌskating *n* [C] a kind of SKATING in which you move in patterns on the ice —**figure skater** *n* [C]

fig·u·rine /ˌfɪɡjʊˈriːn, ˈfɪɡjʊriːn $ ˌfɪɡjʊˈriːn/ *n* [C] a small model of a person or animal used as a decoration

fil·a·ment /ˈfɪləmənt/ *n* [C] a very thin thread or wire: *an electric filament*

fil·bert /ˈfɪlbət $ -bərt/ *n* [C] *especially AmE* a HAZELNUT

filch /fɪltʃ/ *v* [T] *informal* to steal something small or not very valuable; ◪ **pinch, nick** *BrE*: *He filched a bottle of wine from the cellar.*

file¹ S1 W2 /faɪl/ *n* [C]
1 a set of papers, records etc that contain information about a particular person or subject: [+on] *Mendoza*

---

read over the file on the murders. | *The FBI keeps files on former White House employees.* | *We will keep your details on file* (=store them for later use). | *police/case/ medical etc file a copy of the court file*

2 a box or piece of folded card in which you store loose papers: *She pulled a blue file from the shelf.*

3 information on a computer that you store under a particular name

open a file
close a file
save a file
create a file
delete a file
copy a file
access a file
edit a file (=make changes to it)
download a file (=make a copy of a file on the hard disk of your computer)
text/data/graphics file (=containing text etc)

Click on the icon to open the file. | *You can always save the file into another directory.* | *files downloaded from the Internet* | *a plain text file*

4 a metal tool with a rough surface that you rub on something to make it smooth → NAIL FILE

5 a line of people who are standing or walking one behind the other: [+of] *a file of soldiers marching in step* | **in file** *It was dark as we set off in file.* → SINGLE FILE, RANK AND FILE

file² S3 *v*

1 [T] to keep papers, documents etc in a particular place so that you can find them easily: *The contracts are filed alphabetically.* | *file sth under sth I looked to see if anything was filed under my name.* | **file sth away** *The handbooks are filed away for future reference.*

2 [T] to give or send an official report or news story to your employer: *The officer left the scene without filing a report.*

3 [I always + adv/prep, T] *law* to give a document to a court or organization so that it can be officially recorded and dealt with: **file a complaint/lawsuit/petition etc (against sb)** *Mr Genoa filed a formal complaint against the department.* | [+for] *The Morrisons have filed for divorce.* | *Today is the deadline for Americans to file their tax returns.*

4 [I always + adv/prep] if people file somewhere, they walk there in a line: *We began to file out into the car park.* | *The mourners filed past the coffin.*

5 [I always + adv/prep, T] to use a metal or wooden tool to rub something in order to make it smooth: *File down the sharp edges.* | *She sat filing her nails.*

'file ˌcabinet *n* [C] *AmE* a piece of office furniture with drawers for storing letters, reports etc; ◪ **filing cabinet** *BrE*

file·name /ˈfaɪlneɪm/ *n* [C] the name you give to a particular computer file

fil·et /ˈfɪlɪt $ ˈfɪlɪt, -leɪ, fɪˈleɪ/ *n,v* an American spelling of FILLET

fil·i·al /ˈfɪliəl/ *adj formal* relating to the relationship of a son or daughter to their parents: *her filial duty*

fil·i·bus·ter /ˈfɪlɪbʌstə $ -ər/ *v* [I,T] to try to delay action in Congress or another law-making group by making very long speeches: *Opponents of the bill threatened to filibuster its final stages.* —**filibuster** *n* [C]

fil·i·gree /ˈfɪlɪgriː/ *n* [U] delicate designs or decorations made of gold or silver wire: *silver filigree jewellery*

fil·ing /ˈfaɪlɪŋ/ *n* **1** [U] the work of arranging documents in the correct FILES **2** filings [plural] small sharp bits that come off when a piece of metal is cut or FILED: *iron filings* **3** [C] a document, report etc that is officially recorded: *a bankruptcy filing*

'filing ˌcabinet *n* [C] *BrE* a piece of office furniture with drawers for storing letters, reports etc; ◪ **file cabinet** *AmE*; → see picture at OFFICE

fill¹ S1 W1 /fɪl/ v

1 BECOME/MAKE FULL also **fill up** [I,T] if a container or place fills, or if you fill it, enough of something goes into it to make it full: *He poured her a drink, then filled his own glass.* | *My job was filling the flour sacks.* | *Take a deep breath and allow your lungs to fill.* | **fill (sth) with sth** *Her eyes filled with tears.* | **fill sth to the brim/to overflowing** (=fill something completely) *a bucket filled to the brim with ice* | *There was just enough wind to fill the sails.* | *Miller's band was filling dancehalls* (=attracting a lot of people) *all over the country.*
2 LARGE THING/NUMBER [T] if a thing or group fills something, there is no space left: *Crowds of well-wishers filled the streets.* | *His wartime experiences would fill a book!* | *All the seats were filled and a number of people were standing.* | *Numerous pictures fill every available space.*
3 SOUND/SMELL/LIGHT [T] if a sound, smell, or light fills a place, you notice it because it is very loud or strong: *The smell of freshly baked bread filled the room.* | **be filled with sth** *The air was filled with the sound of children's laughter.*
4 EMOTIONS [T] if you are filled with an emotion, or if it fills you, you feel it very strongly: **be filled with admiration/joy/happiness etc** *I was filled with admiration for her.* | **be filled with horror/fear/anger/doubt/remorse** *Their faces were suddenly filled with fear.* | **fill sb with sth** *The prospect filled him with horror.*
5 PROVIDE STH [T] to provide something that is needed or wanted but which has not been available or present before: **fill a need/demand** *Volunteers fill a real need for teachers in the Somali Republic.* | **fill a gap/hole/niche etc** *I spent most of the summer filling the gaps in my education.* | *The company has moved quickly to fill the niche in the overnight travel market.*
6 SPEND TIME [T] if you fill a period of time with a particular activity, you spend that time doing it: **fill your time/the days etc (with sth)** *I have no trouble filling my time.*
7 PERFORM A JOB [T] to perform a particular job, activity, or purpose in an organization, or to find someone or something to do this: **fill a post/position/vacancy etc** *Women fill 35% of senior management positions.* | *Thank you for your letter. Unfortunately, the vacancy has already been filled.* | *The UK should find another weapon to fill the same role.*
8 CRACK/HOLE also **fill in** [T] to put a substance into a hole, crack etc to make a surface level: *Fill in any cracks before starting to paint.* | *materials developed to fill tooth cavities*
9 **fill yourself (up)/fill your face** *informal* to eat so much food that you cannot eat any more
10 **fill an order** to supply the goods that a customer has ordered: *The company is struggling to fill $11 million in back orders.*
11 **fill the bill** *AmE* to have exactly the right qualities; ▪ **fit the bill** *BrE*: *We needed an experienced reporter and Willis fills the bill.*
12 **fill sb's shoes** to do the work that someone else normally does, especially when this is difficult because they have set a high standard

fill in *phr v*
1 DOCUMENT **fill sth ⇔ in** to write all the necessary information on an official document, form etc: *Don't forget to fill in your boarding cards.*
2 TELL SB NEWS **fill sb ⇔ in** to tell someone about recent events, especially because they have been away from a place: [+on] *I think you'd better fill me in on what's been happening.*
3 CRACK/HOLE **fill sth ⇔ in** to put a substance into a hole, crack etc so it is completely full and level
4 **fill in time** to spend time doing something unimportant while you are waiting for something to happen: *She flipped through a magazine to fill in the time.*
5 SPACE **fill sth ⇔ in** to paint or draw over the space inside a shape
6 DO SB'S JOB to do someone's job because they are not there: [+for] *I'm filling in for Joe for a few days.*

fill out *phr v*
1 **fill sth ⇔ out** to write all the necessary information on an official document, form etc
2 if you fill out, or your body fills out, you become slightly fatter: *Eric is starting to fill out around the waist.*
3 if a young person fills out, their body becomes more like an adult's body, for example by having bigger muscles, developing breasts etc: *At puberty, a girl's body begins to fill out.*
4 **fill sth ⇔ out** to add more details to a description or story

fill up *phr v*
1 if a container or place fills up, or if you fill it up, it becomes full: **fill sth ⇔ up** *Shall I fill the car up* (=with petrol)*?* | [+with] *Her eyes filled up with tears.*
2 **fill (yourself) up** *informal* to eat so much food that you cannot eat any more: [+with/on] *Don't fill yourself up with cookies.* | *He filled up on pecan pie.*
3 **fill sb up** *informal* food that fills you up makes you feel as though you have eaten a lot when you have only eaten a small amount

fill² *n* **1** **have had your fill of sth** *informal* to have done something or experienced something, especially something unpleasant, so that you do not want any more: *I've had my fill of screaming kids for one day.* **2** **eat/drink your fill** *old-fashioned* to eat or drink as much as you want or need

fill·er /ˈfɪlə $ -ər/ *n* [C,U] **1** *BrE* a substance used to fill cracks in wood, walls etc, especially before you paint them **2** stories, information, pictures etc that are not important but are used to fill a page in a newspaper or magazine

filler cap *n* [C] *BrE* the lid that fits over the hole in a car that you pour a liquid into, especially oil or petrol

fil·let¹; **filet** *AmE* /ˈfɪlɪt $ ˈfɪlət, -leɪ, fɪˈleɪ/ *n* [C] a piece of meat or fish without bones: [+of] *a fillet of sole*

fillet²; **filet** *AmE* v [T] to remove the bones from a piece of meat or fish: *filleted fish*

fill-in *n* [singular] *BrE informal* someone who does someone else's job because that person is not there: *I'm here as a fill-in while Robert's away.*

fill·ing¹ /ˈfɪlɪŋ/ *adj* food that is filling makes your stomach feel full: *Pasta and rice are both very filling.*

filling² *n* **1** [C] a small amount of metal that is put into your tooth to cover a hole: *gold fillings* **2** [C,U] the food that you put inside a PIE, sandwich etc: *cherry filling* **3** [C,U] the soft material inside a CUSHION, PILLOW etc

filling station *n* [C] a place where you can buy petrol for your car; ▪ **petrol station** *BrE*

fil·lip /ˈfɪlɪp/ *n* [singular] something that improves a situation or adds excitement or interest to something; ▪ **boost**: *A cut in lending rates would give a fillip to the housing market.* | *British athletics received a tremendous fillip when Wells won the Gold.*

fil·ly /ˈfɪli/ *n plural* **fillies** [C] a young female horse; → **colt, foal**

film¹ S2 W1 /fɪlm/ *n*
1 [C] a story that is told using sound and moving pictures, shown at a cinema or on television; ▪ **movie** *AmE*

watch/see a film
appear/star in a film
show/screen a film
make/shoot a film
film premiere (=the first time when a film is shown)

*Have you **seen** any good **films** recently?* | *We stayed in to **watch** the late-night film.* | [+about] *a film about a young dancer* | *a special **screening** of the **film** for critics* | *a Hollywood **film premiere*** | *Poitier starred in the classic film 'In the Heat of the Night'.*

2 [U] moving pictures of real events that are shown on television or at a cinema: *newsreel film* | *the race to be*

first with film footage (=pictures) *of news events*
3 [U] the work of making films, considered as an art or a business: *I'm interested in photography and film.* | *the film industry* | *a background in film and animation*
4 [C,U] the thin plastic used in a camera for taking photographs or recording moving pictures: *I shot five rolls of film on vacation.* | **record/capture/preserve sth on film** *The whole incident was recorded on film.*; → see picture at REEL
5 [singular] a very thin layer of liquid, powder etc on the surface of something: [+of] *a film of oil on the surface of the water* → CLINGFILM

F

film² *v* [I,T] to use a camera to record a story or real events so that it can be shown in the cinema or on television: *The love scenes are sensitively filmed.* | *She's in Zimbabwe filming a documentary for the BBC.* | *a thriller filmed entirely on location in Washington* —**filming** *n* [U]: *Filming starts in October.*
film over *phr v* if your eyes film over, they become covered with a thin layer of liquid

film·go·er /ˈfɪlmɡəʊə $ -ɡoʊər/ *n* [C] *BrE* someone who goes to see films, especially regularly; → **theatregoer**; ▣ **moviegoer** *AmE*

film·ic /ˈfɪlmɪk/ *adj formal* relating to films or the art of making films: *a new filmic style*

film-,maker, film·mak·er /ˈfɪlmˌmeɪkə $ -ər/ *n* [C] someone who makes films, especially a DIRECTOR or PRODUCER —**film-making** *n* [U]

film noir /ˌfɪlm ˈnwɑː $ -ˈnwɑːr/ *n plural* **films noirs** *(same pronunciation)* [C,U] a film that deals with subjects such as evil, moral problems etc, often using a story about people involved in a crime and filmed in a way that seems dark or filled with shadows

film star *n* [C] *BrE* a famous actor or actress in cinema films; ▣ **movie star** *AmE*

film·strip /ˈfɪlmˌstrɪp/ *n* [C] a photographic film that shows photographs, pictures etc one at a time, not as moving pictures: *an educational filmstrip*

film·y /ˈfɪlmi/ *adj* very thin, so that you can almost see through it: *a filmy nightdress*

fi·lo /ˈfiːləʊ $ -oʊ/ *also* **filo ,pastry** *n* [U] a type of very thin PASTRY which is used by placing many layers together

Fi·lo·fax /ˈfaɪləfæks/ *n* [C] *trademark* a small book for writing addresses, things you must do etc, which has pages you can add or remove → personal organizer

personal organizer

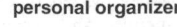

fil·ter¹ /ˈfɪltə $ -ər/ *n* [C] **1** something that you pass water, air etc through in order to remove unwanted substances and make it clean or suitable to use: **water/air/oil etc filter** *a pond filter* | *coffee filter papers* | *filter cigarettes* (=with a filter at the end) **2** a piece of equipment or computer program

that only allows certain sounds, images, signals, types of information etc to pass through it: *a UVA light filter* | *The firm uses electronic filters to prevent workers from accessing the Internet.* **3** *BrE* a traffic light that shows car drivers when they can turn right or left

filter² *v* **1** [T] to remove unwanted substances from water, air etc by passing it through a special substance or piece of equipment: *The water in the tank is constantly filtered.* | *The ozone layer filters harmful UV rays from the sun.* **2** [I always + adv/prep] if people filter somewhere, they move gradually to that place: *Chattering noisily, the crowd began to filter into the auditorium.* **3** [I always + adv/prep] if news, information etc filters somewhere, people gradually hear about it from each other: *The news gradually filtered through from Bombay last night.* **4** [I always + adv/prep] if light or sound filters into a place, it can be seen or heard only slightly: *Moonlight filtered in through the frosted window.* | *The familiar notes of Beethoven's 'Für Elise' filtered from the bar.* **5** [I,T] *BrE* if traffic filters, or if a system filters it, cars can turn left or right while other vehicles going straight ahead must wait
filter sth⇔out *phr v* **1** to remove something, using a filter: *The pump filters out mud.* **2** to remove words, information etc that you do not need or want: *Net users can filter out unwanted emails with software.*

filter tip *n* [C] a filter at one end of a cigarette that removes some of the harmful substances from the smoke —**filter-tipped** *adj*

filth /fɪlθ/ *n* **1** [U] very offensive language, stories, or pictures about sex: *I don't know how you can watch that filth!* **2** [U] dirt, especially a lot of it: *a mound of filth and rubbish* | *people living in filth* | *Passing cars covered his shoes with filth.* **3 the filth** *BrE informal* an offensive word for the police

filth·y¹ ⟨S3⟩ /ˈfɪlθi/ *adj comparative* **filthier**, *superlative* **filthiest**
1 very dirty: *The house was filthy, with clothes and newspapers strewn everywhere.*
2 showing or describing sexual acts in a very rude or offensive way: **filthy language/story/joke etc** | *Your problem is you've got a filthy mind* (=you are always thinking about sex).
3 showing anger or annoyance: **filthy mood/temper** *Simon had been drinking and was in a filthy temper.* | *She gave him a filthy look.*
4 filthy weather/night/day the weather, a night etc that is very cold and wet: *It's a filthy night to be out.*

filthy² *adv informal* **1 filthy dirty** very dirty **2 filthy rich** very rich – usually used to say you think someone has too much money

fil·trate /ˈfɪltreɪt/ *n* [C,U] *technical* a liquid from which a substance has been removed using a FILTER

fil·tra·tion /fɪlˈtreɪʃən/ *n* [U] the process of cleaning a liquid by passing it through a FILTER

fin /fɪn/ *n* [C] **1** one of the thin body parts that a fish uses to swim → see picture at FRESHWATER **2** part of a plane that sticks up at the back and helps it to fly smoothly → AIRCRAFT **3** *also* **tail fin** a thin piece of metal that sticks out from a car or bomb at the back **4** a FLIPPER

fi·na·gle /fɪˈneɪɡəl/ *v* [T] *AmE informal* to obtain something that is difficult to get by using unusual or unfair methods: *How he finagled four front row seats to the game I'll never know.* —**finagling** *n* [U]

fi·nal¹ ⟨S1⟩ ⟨W1⟩ /ˈfaɪnəl/ *adj*
1 [only before noun] last in a series of actions, events, parts of a story etc: *The final episode will be shown tonight.* | *students preparing for their final examinations* | *Stone is filming the final instalment of his Vietnam trilogy.* | *the final stages in their relationship* | *They scored in the final minutes of the game.* | *The final whistle* (=blown at the end of a game) *was only seconds away when Redknapp equalised.* | **final demand** *BrE* (=the last bill you receive for money you owe before court action is taken against you)

2 [only before noun] being the result at the end of a process: *the quality of the final product* | *Does anyone know the final score?* | **final result/outcome** *I do not know what the final outcome will be.*
3 if a decision, offer, answer etc is final, it cannot or will not be changed: *The judge's decision is final.* | **final decision/say/approval etc** *We can advise the client, but in the end it is he who has the final say.* | *Is that your final answer?* | **and that's final!** (=used to say forcefully that you will not change your decision) *She's not coming with us, and that's final!*
4 [only before noun] happening at or near the end of an event or process: *In the final years of his life, Hervey achieved high office in the church.*
5 used to emphasize that the last thing in a series of events is very severe or damaging; ■ **ultimate**: **final indignity/humiliation** *The vote of no confidence was the final humiliation for a government that had been clinging to office.* → **in the final analysis** at ANALYSIS (4)

final² n [C]　**1** the last and most important game, race, or set of games in a competition: **be through to/reach the final** *He's through to the men's tennis final for the first time.* | **the finals** (=the last few games or races in a competition) *the NBA finals*　**2 finals** [plural] *BrE* the set of examinations that students take at the end of their time at university; ■ **final exams**: **sit/take your finals** *Anna sat her finals last summer.*　**3** *AmE* an important test that you take at the end of a particular class in high school or college

fi·na·le /fɪ'nɑːli $ fɪ'næli/ n [C] the last part of a piece of music or of a show, event etc: *the finale of a Broadway show* | *a game with a dramatic finale* | **grand finale** (=very impressive end to a show) *The fireworks were the grand finale of the ceremonies.*

fi·nal·ist /'faɪnəl-ɪ̣st/ n [C] one of the people or teams that reaches the final game in a competition

fi·nal·i·ty /faɪ'nælɪ̣ti/ n [U] the quality something has when it is finished or complete and cannot be changed: **a sense/air of finality** *The word 'retirement' has a terrible air of finality about it.*

fi·nal·ize also **-ise** *BrE* /'faɪnəl-aɪz/ v [T] to finish the last part of a plan, business deal etc: *Jo flew out to Thailand to finalize the details of the deal.* —**finalization** /ˌfaɪnəlaɪ'zeɪʃən $ -nl-ə-/ n [U]

fi·nal·ly S2 W1 /'faɪnəl-i/ adv
1 after a long time; ■ **eventually**: *After several delays we finally took off at six o'clock.* | *Finally, Karpov cracked under the pressure.* → see box at LASTLY
2 [sentence adverb] used to introduce the last in a series of things; ■ **lastly**; → **firstly**: *And finally, I'd like to thank the crew.*
3 used when talking about the last in a series of actions: *She drove off at great speed, hit several parked cars, and finally crashed into a lamp-post.*
4 in a way that does not allow changes: *The matter was not finally settled until 1475.*

fi·nance¹ S3 W2 /'faɪnæns, fɪ̣'næns $ fɪ̣'næns, 'faɪnæns/ n
1 [U] the management of money by governments, large organizations etc: *leasing and other forms of business finance* | *Russia's finance minister* | *the world of high finance* (=financial activities involving very large amounts of money)
2 finances [plural] the money that an organization or person has, and the way that they manage it: *concerns about the company's finances* | *She refused to answer questions about her personal finances.*
3 [U] money provided by a bank or other institution to help buy or do something: [+for] *We need to raise finance for further research.*

finance² W3 v [T] to provide money, especially a lot of money, to pay for something; ■ **fund**: *The concerts are financed by the Arts Council.* —**financing** n [U]: *The financing for the deal has been approved in principle.*

finance company *AmE* / $.'. ,.../ **'finance house** /.'. ./ *BrE* n [C] a company that lends money, especially to businesses

fi·nan·cial S3 W1 /fɪ̣'nænʃəl, faɪ-/ adj [usually before noun] relating to money or the management of money: *financial transactions* | *financial assistance* | *a financial advisor* | *Organic farmers should be encouraged with financial incentives.* | *It was a wonderful film, but not exactly a financial success* (=something that makes a profit). | **financial difficulties/problems/crisis** —**financially** adv: *He was successful and financially secure.* | *Is the project financially viable?*

fi,nancial 'aid n [U] *AmE* money given or lent to students at college or university to pay for their education

fi,nancial insti'tution n [C] *technical* a business organization that lends and borrows money, for example a bank: *All the big financial institutions cut their interest rates today.*

fi,nancial 'year n [singular] *especially BrE* the 12-month period over which a company's accounts are calculated; ■ **fiscal year** *AmE*

fi·nan·cier /fɪ̣'nænsɪə, faɪ'næn- $ ˌfɪnən'sɪr/ n [C] someone who controls or lends large sums of money

finch /fɪntʃ/ n [C] a small bird with a short beak

find¹ S1 W1 /faɪnd/ v past tense and past participle **found** /faʊnd/ [T]
1 GET BY SEARCHING to discover, see, or get something that you have been searching for: *I can't find the car keys.* | *Hold on while I find a pen.* | *Her body was later found hidden in the bushes.* | *I have to find somewhere else to live.* | *She had almost given up hope of finding a husband.* | **find sb sth** *Tony asked us to find him office facilities in New York.* | *Her mother went to the shops, and on her return, Kathleen was **nowhere to be found*** (=could not be found).
2 SEE BY CHANCE to discover something by chance, especially something useful or interesting: *I found a purse in the street.* | *We found a really good bar near the hotel.*
3 DISCOVER STATE OF SB/STH to discover that someone or something is in a particular condition or doing a particular thing when you see or touch them: *I'm sure we'll find her hard at work when we get home.* | *He tried the door and found it unlocked.* | *She woke to find a man by her bed.* | **find sb/sth doing sth** *Often he found her quietly weeping alone.* | **find (that)** *She looked at her glass and was amazed to find it was empty.*
4 DO STH WITHOUT MEANING TO to be in a particular state or do a particular thing, or to realize that this is happening, especially when you did not expect or intend it: *After wandering around, we found ourselves back at the hotel.* | **find yourself/your mind etc doing sth** *When he left, Karen found herself heaving a huge sigh of relief.* | *She tried to concentrate, but found her mind drifting back to Alex.* | **find (that)** *He found he was shivering.*
5 LEARN STH BY STUDY to discover or learn something by study, tests, sums etc: *The federal government isn't doing enough to find a cure.* | *How do you find the square root of 20?* | **be found to do sth** *The liquid was found to contain 7.4g of phenylamine.* | **find that** *His study found that married men and women had similar spending patterns.*
6 THINK/FEEL to have a particular feeling or opinion, or to have a particular feeling or opinion about someone or something: *Will Gary and Gail find happiness together?* | **find sth/sb easy/useful/interesting etc** *She found the work very dull.* | *Lots of women I know find him attractive.* | *I found them quite easy to use.* | **find it hard/easy/difficult etc (to do sth)** *Hyperactive children find it difficult to concentrate.*
7 EXPERIENCE to have the experience of discovering that something happens or is true: **find (that)** *You might find that his work improves now he's at a new school.* | *I find people are often surprised at how little it costs.* | **find sb/sth doing sth** *I think you'll find more women*

F

entering the film business now. | **find sb/sth to be sth** *I found the people to be charming and very friendly.*

8 EXIST IN A PLACE be found somewhere if something is found somewhere, it lives or exists there naturally: *This species is only found in West Africa.*

9 GET ENOUGH MONEY/TIME ETC to succeed in getting enough of something, especially money, time, or energy, to be able to do something: *He's struggling to find the money for the trip.* | *Where are we going to find the time, the support, and the resources to do all this?*

10 IN A COURT OF LAW to make an official decision in a court of law: **find sb guilty/not guilty (of sth)** *Both men were found guilty of illegally entering the country.* | **find in sb's favour** *The tribunal found in favour of the defendant.*

11 find your way (somewhere) to reach a place by discovering the right way to get there: *Will you be able to find your way back?*

12 find its way somewhere *informal* if something finds its way somewhere, it arrives or gets there after some time: *Only one of her inventions has found its way into the shops.*

13 find comfort/pleasure/fulfilment etc in sth to experience a good feeling because of something: *He eventually found solace in religion.*

14 find fault with sb/sth to criticize someone or something, often unfairly and frequently: *He could always find fault with something, either in my writing or in my personality.*

15 find it in your heart/yourself to do sth *literary* to feel able or willing to do something: *Seb could not find it in his heart to tell Nahum.*

16 find yourself *informal* to discover what you are really like and what you want to do – often used humorously: *She went to India to find herself.*

17 find favour (with sb/sth) *formal* be liked or approved of by someone: *The recipes rapidly found favour with restaurant owners.*

18 find your feet to become confident in a new situation, especially one that is difficult at first: *Rob is still finding his feet as a coach.*

19 find its mark/target **a)** if a bullet, ARROW etc finds its mark etc, it hits what it is supposed to hit **b)** if a remark, criticism etc finds its mark etc, it has the effect that you intended to have: *She soon saw that her accusation had found its mark.*

20 find your voice **a)** also **find your tongue** to manage to say something after being too nervous to talk **b)** if a writer, musician etc finds their voice, they are able to express their views, ideas, art etc in the way they want to: *a young film-maker who has finally found his voice*

21 be found wanting *formal* to not be good enough: *Their defence was found wanting.*

find against sb *phr v law*
to judge that someone is wrong or guilty: *The inspectors are likely to find against the company.*

find for sb *phr v law*
to judge that someone is right or not guilty: *The judge found for the plaintiff.*

find out *phr v*
1 to get information, after trying to discover it or by chance: **find out who/what/how etc** *Has anyone bothered to find out how much all this is going to cost?* | **find out if/whether** *Did you find out whether there are any seats left?* | **find out (that)** *I found out that my parents had never been married.* | **find sth ⇔ out** *To find out more, visit our website.* | **find out (sth) about sth** *I need to find out more about these night courses.* | [+**from**] *We could find out from the local council.* | *I thought it best to let you find out for yourself.* → see box at KNOW[1]
2 find sb out [usually passive] if you are found out, someone discovers that you have been doing something dishonest or illegal; → catch: *What happens if we get found out?*

find² *n* [C] **1** a find something very good or useful that you discover by chance: *That restaurant was a real*

find! **2** something that someone finds, especially by digging or by searching under water: *important archaeological finds*

find·er /'faɪndə $ -ər/ *n* [C] **1** someone who finds something that was lost or stolen: *The finder usually receives a reward.* **2** finders keepers (losers weepers) *spoken* used to say that if someone finds something they have the right to keep it

fin de siè·cle /ˌfæn də 'sjeklə/ *adj* [only before noun] typical of the end of the 19th century, especially its art literature, and attitudes

find·ing W2 /'faɪndɪŋ/ *n* [C]
1 [usually plural] the information that someone has discovered as a result of their study, work etc: *Surveys conducted in other countries reported similar findings.*
2 *law* a decision made by a judge or JURY

fine¹ S1 W1 /faɪn/ *adj*
1 ACCEPTABLE [not before noun] *especially spoken* satisfactory or acceptable; ⊟ OK: *'We're meeting a 8.30.' 'Okay, fine.'* | **looks/seems/sounds fine** *In theory the scheme sounds fine.* | *If you want to use cheese instead of chicken, that's fine.* | *'Do you want chili sauce on it?' 'No, it's fine as it is, thanks.'* | **I'm fine (thanks, thank you)** *spoken* (=used when telling someone that you do not want any more when they offer you something) *'More coffee?' 'No, I'm fine, thanks.'* | **that's fine by me/that's fine with me etc** *spoken* (=used when saying that you do not mind about something) *If Scott wanted to keep his life secret, that was fine by her.*
2 HEALTHY in good health; ⊟ OK: *'How are you?' 'Fine, thanks, how are you?'* | *I feel fine, really.*
3 VERY GOOD [usually before noun] very good or of a very high standard: *Many people regard Beethoven's fifth symphony as his finest work.* | *He's a very fine player.* | *It's a fine idea.* | *Hatfield House is a fine example of Jacobean architecture.* | *The restaurant was chosen for its good food and fine wines.*
4 WEATHER bright and not raining: *If it's fine tomorrow we'll go out.* | **a fine day/morning/evening** | *I hope it stays fine for you.*
5 NARROW very thin or narrow: *Fine needles are inserted in the arm.* | *a fine thread* | *very fine hairs* → see picture at THIN
6 DELICATE [usually before noun] attractive, neat, and delicate: *fine china* | *Her dark hair accentuates her fine features* (=nose, eyes, cheeks etc).
7 SMALL **a)** fine details, changes, differences etc are very small and therefore difficult to understand or notice: *We stayed up discussing the finer points of Marxist theory.* **b)** in small grains, pieces, or drops: *A fine drizzle started falling.* | *a mixture of fine and coarse breadcrumbs* **c)** fine material is made so that the spaces between the threads are very small: *fine netting* | *scarlet cloth with a very fine weave*
8 BAD [only before noun] *especially spoken* used humorously to say that someone or something is bad in some way: *That's another fine mess* (=bad situation) *he's got himself into.* | *You're a fine one to talk* (=you are criticizing someone for something you do yourself).
9 SPEECH/WORDS sounding important and impressive, but probably not true or honest: *Only time will tell whether these fine sentiments will translate into action.*
10 a fine man/woman etc a good person that you respect: *Your father is a fine man, a real gentleman.*
11 a fine line between sth and sth if you say that there is a fine line between two different things, you mean that they are so similar that one can easily become the other: *There's a fine line between bravery and recklessness.*
12 get sth down to a fine art to practise something so often that you become very skilled at it: *Mike had got the breakfast routine down to a fine art.*
13 not to put too fine a point on it *informal* used when you are criticizing something in a plain and direct way: *That's a real 'pub, not to put too fine a point on it.*
14 finer feelings someone's finer feelings are the moral values they have, such as love, honour, loyalty etc: *You*

can hardly expect such finer feelings in a thief.
15 a fine figure of a man/woman *literary* someone who looks big, strong, and physically attractive: *In his portrait, Donlevy is a fine figure of a man.*
16 sb's finest hour a time when someone is very successful, brave etc: *The tournament proved to be Gascoigne's finest hour.* → **chance would be a fine thing** at CHANCE¹ (12)

fine² *adv* **1** *especially spoken* in a way that is satisfactory or acceptable: *'How's it going?' 'Fine, thanks.'* | *The dress fitted me fine.* | *If I had a good job and my boyfriend stayed at home, that'd* **suit me fine** (=be very acceptable to me). **2 do fine** *spoken* **a)** to be satisfactory or acceptable: *'Something very light,' he ordered. 'An omelette will do fine.'* **b)** to do something well or in a satisfactory way: *Don't worry, you're doing fine. Keep at it.* **c)** to be healthy and well: *'How's your husband?' 'He's doing fine, thank you.'* **3** if you cut something fine, you cut it into very small or very thin pieces; ◨ **finely** **4 cut it/things fine** *informal* to leave yourself only just enough time to do something

fine³ *v* [T] to make someone pay money as a punishment: *She was fined for speeding.* | **fine sb for (doing) sth** *The club was fined £50,000 for financial irregularities.* | **fine sb £200/$500 etc**

fine⁴ *n* [C] money that you have to pay as a punishment: *a £40 fine* | **pay a fine/pay £100/$50 etc in fines** *She was ordered to pay £150 in parking fines, plus court costs.* | *Councils will get sweeping powers to* **impose fines** *on drivers who park illegally.* | **heavy/hefty fine** (=a large fine) *If convicted, the men face heavy fines.*

fine 'art *n* [U] **the fine arts** forms of art, especially paintings or SCULPTURE, that are produced and admired for their beauty and high quality: *Can photography be considered fine art?* | *the faculty of fine arts*

fine·ly /'faɪnli/ *adv* **1** into very thin or very small pieces: *finely chopped onion* **2** in a very careful, delicate, or exact way: *Saunders' finely crafted drawings* | *These instruments are very finely tuned.* **3** beautifully or impressively: *He wore a silk cloak over a finely embroidered robe.* | *high-quality, finely carved statues*

fine 'print *n* [U] SMALL PRINT

fi·ne·ry /'faɪnəri/ *n* [U] *literary* clothes and jewellery that are beautiful or very expensive, and are worn for a special occasion: *The guests arrived in all their finery.*

fi·nesse¹ /fɪ'nes/ *n* [U] if you do something with finesse, you do it with a lot of skill and style: *Dario played the sonata with great finesse.*

finesse² *v* [T] **1** to handle a situation well, but in a way that is slightly deceitful **2** *AmE* to do something with a lot of skill and style

fine-tooth 'comb *n* [C] **go through/over sth with a fine-tooth comb** to examine something very carefully and thoroughly: *The police went over the scene of the crime with a fine-tooth comb.*

fine-'tune *v* [T] to make very small changes to something such as a machine, system, or plan, so that it works as well as possible: *Over the next few days, we fine-tuned the scheme and made some useful improvements.* —**fine tuning** *n* [U]

fin·ger¹ [S2] [W2] /'fɪŋgə $ -ər/ *n* [C]
1 PART OF YOUR HAND one of the four long thin parts on your hand, not including your thumb: *The woman had a ring on her finger, so I assumed she was married.* | *We ate with our fingers.* | **run your fingers through/over/along etc sth** *She ran her fingers through his hair.* → INDEX FINGER, LITTLE FINGER, FOREFINGER, MIDDLE FINGER, RING FINGER; → see picture at HAND
2 cross your fingers a) to hope that something will happen the way you want: *We're* **keeping our fingers crossed** *that she's going to be OK.* **b)** to secretly put one finger over another finger, because you are telling a lie – done especially by children: *'He's nice,' said Laura, crossing her fingers under the table.*
3 not lift/raise a finger to not make any effort to help someone with their work: *I do all the work around the house – Frank never lifts a finger.*

4 put your finger on sth to know or be able to explain exactly what is wrong, different, or unusual about a situation: *There was something about the man that worried Wycliffe, but he couldn't put his finger on it.*
5 not lay a finger on sb to not hurt someone at all, especially not to hit them: *If you so much as lay a finger on me, I'll call the police!*
6 have/keep your finger on the pulse (of sth) to always know about the most recent changes or developments in a particular situation or activity: *people with their finger on the pulse of fashion and pop culture*
7 have a finger in every pie/in many pies to be involved in many activities and to have influence over a lot of people, used especially when you think someone has too much influence
8 twist/wrap/wind sb around your little finger to be able to persuade someone to do anything that you want: *Ed could wrap his mother around his little finger.*
9 the finger of blame/suspicion: *The* **finger of suspicion** *immediately fell on Broderick.*
10 OF A GLOVE the part of a GLOVE that covers your finger
11 SHAPED LIKE A FINGER anything that is long and thin, like the shape of a finger, especially a piece of land, an area of water, or a piece of food: *fish fingers* | *chocolate fingers* | [+of] *the long finger of Chile*
12 pull/get your finger out *BrE informal* used to tell someone to work harder
13 put two fingers up at sb *BrE informal* to show someone you are angry with them in a very offensive way by holding up your first two fingers with the back of your hand facing them
14 give sb the finger *AmE informal* to show someone you are angry with them in a very offensive way by holding up your middle finger with the back of your hand facing them
15 be all fingers and thumbs *BrE* to use your hands in an awkward or careless way, so that you drop or break things
16 long-fingered/slim-fingered etc having long fingers, slim fingers etc: *lovely long-fingered hands*
17 DRINK an amount of an alcoholic drink that is as high in the glass as the width of someone's finger: *two fingers of whiskey* → BUTTERFINGERS, FISH FINGER; → **have your hands/fingers in the till** at TILL² (3); → **count sth on the fingers of one hand** at COUNT¹ (7); → **have green fingers** at GREEN¹ (10); → **burn your fingers/get your fingers burnt** at BURN¹ (16); → **point the/a finger at sb** at POINT² (9); → **let sth slip through your fingers** at SLIP¹ (15); → **snap your fingers** at SNAP¹ (7); → **have sticky fingers** at STICKY (6); → **work your fingers to the bone** at WORK¹ (29)

finger² *v* [T] **1** to touch or handle something with your fingers: *She fingered the beautiful cloth with envy.* **2** *informal* if someone, especially a criminal, fingers another criminal, they tell the police what they have done

fin·ger·board /'fɪŋgəbɔːd $ -gərbɔːrd/ *n* [C] the long part of a STRINGED INSTRUMENT which the player presses the strings onto

'finger bowl *n* [C] a small bowl in which you wash your fingers during a meal

fin·ger·ing /'fɪŋgərɪŋ/ *n* [U] the positions in which a musician puts his or her fingers to play a piece of music, or the order in which he or she uses the fingers

fin·ger·mark /'fɪŋgəmɑːk $ -gərmɑːrk/ *n* [C] a mark made by dirty fingers on something clean

fin·ger·nail /'fɪŋgəneɪl $ -gər-/ *n* [C] the hard flat part that covers the top end of your finger; ◨ **nail**; → see picture at HAND

'finger-paints *n* [plural] special paints that children use to paint with, using their fingers —**finger painting** *n* [U]

'finger-,pointing *n* [U] when people blame other people for something that has gone wrong, instead of trying to solve the problem: *There followed months of name-calling and finger-pointing.*

fin·ger·print /'fɪŋgə,prɪnt $ -gər-/ *n* [C] a mark made by the pattern of lines at the end of a person's finger, which is used by the police to find out who has committed a crime: *His fingerprints were all over the gun.* | *He was careful not to **leave** any **fingerprints**.* | *The police questioned Beresford and **took** his **fingerprints*** (=made a record of them). —**fingerprint** *v* [T]

fin·ger·print·ing /'fɪŋgə,prɪntɪŋ $ -gər-/ *n* [U] the practice of making a record of people's fingerprints, and using them to try and find out who has committed a crime → GENETIC FINGERPRINTING

fin·ger·spell·ing /'fɪŋgə,spelɪŋ $ -gər-/ *n* [U] a system of speaking to people who are DEAF by touching their hand with your fingers and making the shapes of letters

fin·ger·tip /'fɪŋgə,tɪp $ -gər-/ *n* [C]   **1** the end of your finger, that is furthest away from your hand: *She touched his cheek gently with her fingertips.* → see picture at HAND   **2 have sth at your/their fingertips** to have knowledge or information ready and available to use very easily: *We have all the facts and figures at our fingertips.*   **3 to his/her fingertips** *BrE* in all ways; completely: *She's British to her fingertips.*

fin·i·cky /'fɪnɪki/ *adj*   **1** too concerned with unimportant details and small things that you like or dislike; ▣ **fussy**: *She's very finicky about what she eats.*   **2** needing to be done very carefully, while paying attention to small details; ▣ **fiddly**: *a finicky job*

fin·ish¹ S1 W2 /'fɪnɪʃ/ *v*
   1 STOP DOING STH also **finish off** [I,T] to complete the last part of something that you are doing: *You can't go anywhere until you've finished your homework.* | *Have you finished that book yet?* | **finish doing sth** *I finished typing the report just minutes before it was due.* | *'How's the decorating going?' 'We've nearly finished.'*
   2 END [I] *especially BrE* when an event, activity, or period of time finishes, it ends, especially at a particular time: *The football season finishes in May.* | *What time does school finish?*
   3 EAT/DRINK also **finish up/off** [T] to eat or drink all the rest of something, so there is none left: *I'll just finish my coffee.*
   4 END STH BY DOING STH also **finish off** [I,T] to complete an event, performance, piece of work etc by doing one final thing: [+with] *The party finished with a sing-song.* | **finish (sth) by doing sth** *I would like to finish by thanking you all for your help.*
   5 RACE [I,T] to be in a particular position at the end of a race, competition etc: **finish first/second/third etc** *He finished second in the 100 metres, behind Ben Johnson.*
   6 TAKE AWAY SB'S STRENGTH also **finish off** [T] to take away all of someone's strength, energy etc; ▣ **do sb in**: *Another run like that would just about finish me.*
   7 USE ALL OF STH [I,T] *BrE* to completely use up the supply of something, especially food: *The ice cream's finished – can you get some more?*
   8 put/add the finishing touches (to sth) to add the final details that make your work complete: *The band are currently putting the finishing touches to their new album.*
   9 SURFACE [T] to give the surface of something, especially wood, a smooth appearance by painting, polishing, or covering it: *The furniture had been attractively finished in a walnut veneer.*

finish off *phr v*
   1 finish sth ⇔ off to complete the last part of something that you are doing: *It'll take me a couple of hours to finish this job off.*
   2 finish sth ⇔ off to use or eat all of something, so there is none left: *Who finished off the cake?*
   3 to complete an event, performance, piece of work etc by doing one final thing: [+with] *We'll finish off with a track from Adam's new album.* | **finish sth ⇔ off** *She finished off her speech by thanking her sponsors.* | **finish**

off/finish sth ⇔ off by doing sth *Finish off by cleaning the monitor and the keyboard.*
   4 finish sb/sth ⇔ off to kill a person or animal when they are already weak or wounded
   5 finish sb ⇔ off to take away all of someone's strength, energy etc

finish up *phr v*
   1 *BrE informal* to arrive at a particular place, after going to other places first; ▣ **end up**: *I took a long holiday in Italy and finished up in Rome.*
   2 *BrE informal* to get into a particular state or situation as the result of what you have done, especially without planning or expecting it; ▣ **end up**: *One of the guys tried to bribe a police officer and finished up in jail.* | [+with] *Brett got into a fight and finished up with a broken wrist.*
   3 finish sth ⇔ up to eat or drink all the rest of something, so there is none left: *Come on, finish up your drinks.*

finish with sth/sb *phr v*
   1 have/be finished with sth to no longer need to use something: *Have you finished with the scissors?*
   2 have/be finished with sb to have finished talking to someone or dealing with them, especially when you are angry with them or want to punish them: *Don't go. I haven't finished with you yet.* | *'When I'm finished with you,' he said, 'you'll be lucky if you're still alive.'*
   3 to end a romantic or sexual relationship with someone: *So I told him I wanted to finish with him.*

finish² S3 *n*
   1 [C] the end or last part of something: *I was watching the race but I didn't get to see the finish.* | *The day was a disaster **from start to finish*** (=from the beginning until the end). | *I won't walk out – I like to see things **through to the finish**.* | **a close finish** (=an end of a race where two competitors are very close to each other)
   2 a fight to the finish a fight or game in which the teams or competitors struggle until one is completely defeated
   3 [C,U] the appearance of the surface of an object after it has been painted, polished etc: *That table has a beautiful finish.*

fin·ished /'fɪnɪʃt/ *adj*   **1** [not before noun] no longer doing, dealing with, or using something; ▣ **done**: *I'm almost finished.* | [+with] *Are you finished with my tools yet?*   **2** [only before noun] fully and properly made or completed: *It took a long time to do, but the **finished product** was worth it.* | **finished article** *BrE*: *The painting began to look like the finished article.*   **3** [not before noun] no longer successful, effective, or able to continue: *If the bank refuses to increase our loan, we're finished!*

'finishing ˌline also **'finish line** *AmE n* the finishing line the line at which a race ends: *James crossed the finish line in just under four minutes.* → STARTING LINE

'finishing ˌschool *n* [C] a private school where rich girls go to learn social skills

fi·nite /'faɪnaɪt/ *adj*   **1** having an end or a limit; ⊞ **infinite**: *the earth's **finite resources***   **2** *technical* a finite verb form shows a particular time. 'Am' , 'was', and 'are' are examples of finite verb forms, but 'being' and 'been' are not; ⊞ **non-finite**

fink¹ /fɪŋk/ *n* [C] *AmE informal old-fashioned*   **1** someone who tells the police, a teacher, or a parent when someone else breaks a rule or a law   **2** a person who you do not like or respect

fink² *v* [I +on] *AmE informal old-fashioned* to tell the police, a teacher, or a parent that someone has broken a rule or a law; ▣ **squeal on sb**

fi·ord /'fiːɔːd, fjɔːd $ fiːˈɔːrd, fjɔːrd/ *n* another spelling of FJORD

fir /fɜː $ fɜːr/ *n* [C] a tree with leaves shaped like needles that do not fall off in winter: *a fir tree*

'fir cone *n* [C] the hard brown fruit that contains the seeds of a fir tree

fire engine

fire extinguisher

fire escape

fireworks

fire hydrant

fireman/firefighter

fire¹ [S1] [W1] /faɪə $ faɪr/ *n*

1 FLAMES THAT DESTROY THINGS [C,U] uncontrolled flames, light, and heat that destroy and damage things

> **start a fire** (=deliberately make a fire start burning)
> **set fire to sth/set sth on fire** (=deliberately make something start burning)
> **be on fire** (=be burning)
> **put out a fire** (=stop a fire burning)
> **fight a fire** (=try to make a fire stop burning)
> **a fire breaks out** (=a fire starts suddenly)
> **sth catches fire** (=something starts burning)
> **a fire burns**
> **a fire goes out** (=a fire stops burning)
> **a fire rages/blazes** (=a fire burns strongly for a long time over a large area)
> **a fire smoulders** (=a little smoke comes from a fire, when it has almost gone out)
> **forest fire** (=a very large fire in a forest)
> **brush fire** (=a very large fire in an area of grass)
> **house fire**

> *The warehouse was completely destroyed by fire.* | *Thirty people died in a fire in downtown Chicago.* | *Police think that the fire was started deliberately.* | *Rioters set fire to a whole row of stores.* | *Sparks from the fireplace could easily set the curtains on fire.* | *The house is on fire!* | *It took firefighters several hours to put out the fire.* | *Residents were evacuated when fire broke out in a block of flats yesterday.* | *One of the plane's engines had caught fire.* | *People were throwing water on the flames, but the fire was burning more strongly every minute.* | *smoke from smouldering fires* | *A massive forest fire is still raging in western Java.*

2 FLAMES FOR HEATING/COOKING ETC [C] burning material used to heat a room, cook food etc, or get rid of things you do not want: *Can you put another log on the fire?* | **by the fire/in front of the fire** *Come and sit in front of the fire.* | *a log fire* | *a coal fire* | *a camp fire* (=when you are camping) | **make/build/start/light a fire** *You put up the tent and I'll make a fire.* | **An open fire** (=a fire that burns wood or coal in a FIREPLACE) *was burning in the front room.* | *Mr Trotter sat by the roaring fire.* | *the dying embers of the fire* (=pieces of wood, coal etc that have almost been completely burned)

3 HEATING EQUIPMENT [C] *BrE* a machine that produces heat to warm a room, using gas or electricity as power: *a gas fire* | *an electric fire* | **turn the fire on/off** *Turn on the fire, I'm cold.* | **turn the fire up/down** (=make it hotter or colder)

4 SHOOTING [U] shots fired from a gun, especially many guns at the same time: *Troops opened fire on* (=started shooting at) *the demonstrators.* | *These women did vital work, often under enemy fire.* | *The rebels agreed to hold their fire* (=not shoot). → **be in the line of fire** at LINE¹ (35)

5 BE ATTACKED be/come under fire **a)** to be severely

criticized for something you have done – used in news reports: *Rail chiefs came under fire after raising train fares for the second time this year.* **b)** to be shot at: [+from] *Our patrol came under fire from rooftop gunmen.*

6 EMOTION [U] a very strong emotion that makes you want to think about nothing else: [+of] *the fire of religious fanaticism*

7 fire in your belly a strong desire to achieve something: *Three years later, Ali returned to boxing with a new fire in his belly.*

8 SICK/INJURED be on fire *literary* a part of your body that is on fire feels very painful

9 light a fire under sb *AmE spoken* to do something that makes someone who is being lazy start doing their work

10 go through fire (and water) (for sb) *old-fashioned* to do something very difficult and dangerous for someone

11 fire and brimstone a phrase describing Hell, used by some religious people → CEASEFIRE; → **add fuel to the fire/flames** at ADD (9); → **fight fire with fire** at FIGHT¹ (18); → **get on like a house on fire** at HOUSE¹ (13); → **hang fire** at HANG¹ (12); → **play with fire** at PLAY¹ (26); → **set the world on fire** at WORLD¹ (22); → **there's no smoke without fire** at SMOKE¹ (5)

> **WORD FOCUS: FIRE**
> *a big fire that causes a lot of damage:* **blaze, inferno, conflagration** *literary*
> *someone whose job is to put out fires:* **firefighter, fireman, the fire department** *AmE,* **the fire brigade** *BrE*
> → flame

fire² [S3] [W3] *v*

1 SHOOT [I,T] to shoot bullets or bombs: [+at/on/into] *Soldiers fired on the crowd.* | **fire sth at sb** *The police fired two shots at the suspects before they surrendered.* | **fire a gun/weapon/rifle etc** (=make it shoot) *the sound of a gun being fired* | **fire bullets/missiles/rockets etc** *Guerrillas fired five rockets at the capital yesterday, killing 23 people.*

2 JOB [T] to force someone to leave their job; ◨ **sack** *BrE:* **be/get fired** *She didn't want to get fired.* | **fire sb from sth** *I've just been fired from my job, and I don't know what to do.* | **fire sb for sth** *The airline fired him for being drunk.*

3 EXCITE [T] to make someone feel interested in something and excited about it; ◨ **inspire: be fired with enthusiasm** *I was fired with enthusiasm to go traveling in Asia.* | **fire sb's enthusiasm/imagination** *stories of magic and adventure that fire children's imaginations*

4 QUESTIONS fire questions at sb to ask someone a lot of questions quickly, often in order to criticize them

5 wood/gas-fired/coal-fired using wood, gas, or coal as FUEL: *a gas-fired stove* | *a coal-fired boiler*

6 CLAY [T] to bake bricks, clay pots etc in a KILN: *fired earthenware*

7 ENGINE [I] if a vehicle's engine fires, the petrol is lit to make the engine work

8 be firing on all cylinders *informal* to be thinking or doing something well, using all your mental abilities and energy: *When the team's firing on all cylinders, they can beat the best in the league.*

fire away *phr v*

[only in imperative] *spoken* used to tell someone that you are ready to answer questions: *'Do you mind if I ask you something, Woody?' 'Fire away.'*

fire back *phr v*

to quickly and angrily answer a question or remark: [+at] *President Bush has fired back at his critics.*

fire sth ⇔ off *phr v*

1 to shoot a bullet, bomb etc into the air: *Chuck reloaded and fired off both barrels.* | *Mexicans have a tradition of firing off guns to welcome in the new year.*

---

[1] 000, [2] 000, [3] 000, most frequent words in [S] poken and [W] ritten English

2 to quickly send an angry letter to someone: *I fired off a furious letter to the editor.*

fire sb ⇔ **up** *phr v* [usually passive]
to make someone become very excited, interested, or angry: *It was alarming the way she got so fired up about small things.*

'fire a,larm *n* [C] a piece of equipment that makes a loud noise to warn people of a fire in a building: *We were in the middle of an exam when the fire alarm went off.* | *Someone set off the fire alarm.*

'fire ant *n* [C] a type of insect that lives in groups. They build large piles of earth to live in, and can give a very painful bite.

fire·arm /ˈfaɪrɑːm $ ˈfaɪrɑːrm/ *n* [C] *formal* a gun: *He was charged with illegal possession of a firearm.*

fire·ball /ˈfaɪəbɔːl $ ˈfaɪrbɒːl/ *n* [C] a ball of fire, especially one caused by an explosion: *The jet exploded in midair and turned into a fireball.*

fire·bomb¹ /ˈfaɪəbɒm $ ˈfaɪrbɑːm/ *n* [C] a bomb that makes a fire start burning when it explodes

firebomb² *v* [T] to attack a place with firebombs: *His home was firebombed by animal rights activists.*
—**firebombing** *n* [U]

fire·brand /ˈfaɪəbrænd $ ˈfaɪr-/ *n* [C] someone who tries to make people angry about a law, government etc so that they will try to change it: *an idealistic young firebrand from the valleys*

fire·break /ˈfaɪəbreɪk $ ˈfaɪr-/ *n* [C] a narrow piece of land where all the plants and trees have been removed, made to prevent fires from spreading

fire·brick /ˈfaɪəˌbrɪk $ ˈfaɪr-/ *n* [C] a brick that is not damaged by heat, used in chimneys

fire bri,gade *n* [C] **1** *BrE* the FIRE SERVICE; ◨ **fire department** *AmE* **2** *AmE* a group of people who work together to stop fires burning, but are not paid to do this

fire·bug /ˈfaɪəbʌg $ ˈfaɪr-/ *n* [C] *informal* someone who deliberately starts fires to destroy property; ◨ **arsonist**

'fire ,chief *n* [C] someone who is in charge of all the FIRE STATIONS in a city or area

fire·crack·er /ˈfaɪəˌkrækə $ ˈfaɪrˌkrækər/ *n* [C] a small FIREWORK that explodes loudly

'fire de,partment *n* [C] *AmE* the organization that works to prevent fires and stop them burning; ◨ **fire service** *BrE*

'fire ,door *n* [C] a heavy door in a building that is kept closed to help to prevent a fire from spreading

'fire drill *n* [C,U] an occasion when people pretend that a building is burning and practise leaving it, so that they learn what to do if there is a real fire

'fire-,eater *n* [C] an entertainer who puts burning sticks into his mouth —**fire-eating** *n* [U]

'fire ,engine *n* [C] a special large vehicle that carries equipment and the people that stop fires burning, especially the equipment that shoots water at a fire; ◨ **fire truck** *AmE*; → see picture at FIRE

'fire es,cape *n* [C] metal stairs or a metal LADDER on the outside of a tall building, that people can use to escape if there is a fire → see picture at FIRE

'fire ,exit *n* [C] a door that is used to let people out of a building such as a cinema, hotel, restaurant etc when there is a fire

'fire ex,tinguisher *n* [C] a metal container with water or chemicals in it, used for stopping small fires → see picture at FIRE

'fire fight *n* [C] *technical* a short gun battle, involving soldiers or the police

fire·fight·er also **fire fighter** /ˈfaɪəˌfaɪtə $ ˈfaɪrˌfaɪtər/ *n* [C] someone whose job is to stop fires burning; → **fireman**

'fire ,fighting *n* [U] **1** the work of stopping fires burning **2** *BrE* the actions that are taken to find out what has caused a sudden problem in an organization, machine etc, and to correct it

fire·fly /ˈfaɪəflaɪ $ ˈfaɪr-/ *n plural* **fireflies** [C] an insect with a tail that shines in the dark

fire·guard /ˈfaɪəgɑːd $ ˈfaɪrgɑːrd/ *n* [C] *BrE* a large wire or metal screen that is put in front of a FIREPLACE to protect people; ◨ **firescreen** *AmE*; → see picture at FIREPLACE

fire·house /ˈfaɪəhaʊs $ ˈfaɪr-/ *n* [C] *AmE* a small FIRE STATION, especially in a small town

'fire ,hydrant *n* [C] a water pipe in a street used to get water to stop fires burning → see picture at FIRE

'fire ,iron *n* [C] a metal tool used to move or put coal or wood on a fire in a FIREPLACE

fire·light /ˈfaɪəlaɪt $ ˈfaɪr-/ *n* [U] the light produced by a small fire: *The room glowed in the firelight.*

fire·light·er /ˈfaɪəˌlaɪtə $ ˈfaɪrˌlaɪtər/ *n* [C] *BrE* a piece of a substance that burns easily and helps to light a coal fire

fire·man /ˈfaɪəmən $ ˈfaɪr-/ *n plural* **firemen** /-mən/ [C] a man whose job is to stop fires burning; ◨ **firefighter**; → see picture at FIRE

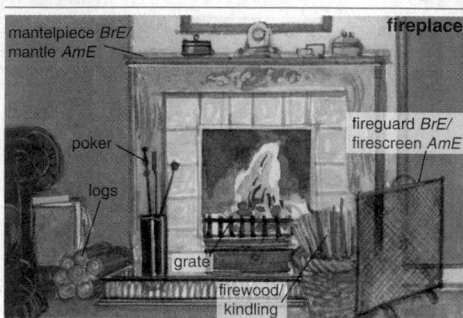

mantelpiece *BrE*/ mantle *AmE*

fireguard *BrE*/ firescreen *AmE*

poker

logs

grate

firewood/ kindling

fireplace

fire·place /ˈfaɪəpleɪs $ ˈfaɪr-/ *n* [C] a special place in the wall of a room, where you can make a fire

fire·pow·er /ˈfaɪəˌpaʊə $ ˈfaɪrˌpaʊr/ *n* [U] **1** *technical* the number of weapons that an army, military vehicle etc has available **2** the amount of something important or necessary that is available: *There is no shortage of financial firepower to fund atomic research.*

fire·proof /ˈfaɪəpruːf $ ˈfaɪr-/ *adj* a building, piece of cloth etc that is fireproof cannot be badly damaged by flames: *fireproof clothing* —**fireproof** *v* [T]

'fire-,raising *n* [U] *BrE* the crime of starting a fire deliberately; ◨ **arson** —**fire-raiser** *n* [C]

'fire re,tardant also **fire-retardant** *adj* fire retardant materials or substances do not burn easily and are put on things to stop them from burning quickly: *furniture treated with fire-retardant chemicals*

'fire sale *n* [C] a sale of goods at a lower price because they have been slightly damaged by a fire, or of goods that cannot be stored because of a fire

fire·screen /ˈfaɪəskriːn $ ˈfaɪr-/ *n* [C] *AmE* a large wire or metal screen that is put in front of a FIREPLACE to protect people; ◨ **fireguard** *BrE*

'fire ,service also **fire brigade** *n* [C usually singular] *BrE* the organization that works to prevent fires and stop them burning; ◨ **fire department** *AmE*

fire·side /ˈfaɪəsaɪd $ ˈfaɪr-/ *n* [C usually singular] the area close to or around a small fire, especially in a home: *a cat dozing by the fireside*

'fire ,station *n* [C] a building where the equipment used to stop fires burning is kept, and where FIREFIGHTERS stay until they are needed

fire·storm /ˈfaɪəstɔːm $ ˈfaɪrstɔːrm/ *n* [C] **1** a very large fire that is kept burning by the high winds that it causes **2** a lot of protests, complaints, or arguments that happen suddenly and all at once; ◨ **storm**: [+of] *Green's proposal provoked a firestorm of protests.*

fire·trap /ˈfaɪətræp $ ˈfaɪr-/ *n* [C] a building that would be very difficult to escape from if a fire started there

fire truck *n* [C] *AmE* a FIRE ENGINE

fire·wall /ˈfaɪəwɔːl $ ˈfaɪrwɒl/ *n* [C] **1** a special wall that prevents fires from spreading to other parts of a building **2** a system that protects a computer NETWORK from being used or looked at by people who do not have permission to do so **3** a system that is used by large financial or law companies to stop secret information from being passed from one department to another

fire·wa·ter /ˈfaɪəˌwɔːtə $ ˈfaɪrˌwɔːtər, -ˌwɑː-/ *n* [U] *informal* a strong alcoholic drink, such as WHISKY

fire·wood /ˈfaɪəwʊd $ ˈfaɪr-/ *n* [U] wood that has been cut or collected in order to be burned in a fire → see picture at FIREPLACE

fire·work /ˈfaɪəwɜːk $ ˈfaɪrwɜːrk/ *n* [C usually plural] **1** a small container filled with powder that burns or explodes to produce coloured lights and noise in the sky: *a New Year's Eve* ***fireworks display*** | *Jeff and David were in the back yard* ***setting off fireworks.*** → see picture at FIRE **2** *spoken* used to say that someone will be angry: ***There'll be fireworks*** *if I get home late again.* **3** something that is exciting or impressive: *The real fireworks are provided by Shakespeare's poetry.*

firing line *n* **(be) in the firing line** to be in a position or situation in which you can be attacked or blamed for something, often unfairly

firing squad *n* [C] a group of soldiers whose duty is to punish prisoners by shooting and killing them

firm¹ S1 W1 /fɜːm $ fɜːrm/ *n* [C] a business or company, especially a small one: **electronics/advertising/law etc firm** *She works for an electronics firm.* | **a firm of accountants/solicitors/builders etc** *Kevin is with a firm of accountants in Birmingham.*

firm² S2 W2 *adj*
1 not completely hard, but not soft, and not easy to bend into a different shape: *The sofa cushions are fairly firm.* | *a firm green apple* | *Most doctors recommend sleeping on a firm mattress.*
2 strongly fixed in position, and not likely to move; ◨ **secure**: *Make sure the ladder feels firm before you climb up.* | *A concrete foundation was poured after digging down to firm ground.* | *Mount the tanks side by side on* ***a firm base.***
3 not likely to change: **firm conviction/commitment/belief etc** *Our client hasn't reached a firm decision on the matter yet.* | *Blackpool remains a* ***firm favourite*** *with holiday makers from Northern Ireland.* | *Corey was always a* ***firm believer*** *in prayer.* | *They made a* ***firm offer*** *(=offered to pay a particular amount) on the house over the weekend.* | *Diana and Laura have been* ***firm friends*** *(=close friends) since their early teens.*
4 showing in the way that you behave or speak that you are the person in control and that you are not likely to change your answer, belief etc: *Cal replied with a polite but firm 'no'.* | *What this country needs is firm leadership.* | **be firm with sb** *You need to be firm with her or she'll try to take advantage of you.*
5 HAND **a firm grip/hold/grasp etc** if you have something in a firm grip etc, you are holding it tightly and strongly: *He took a firm grip of my arm and marched me towards the door.* | *a firm handshake*
6 **take a firm stand/line** to state your opinion clearly and not be persuaded to change it
7 **stand/hold firm** to not change your actions or opinions: [+against] *Jones is urging Christians to stand firm against abortion.*
8 **firm hand** a strict way of dealing with someone: *These children need a firm hand.*
9 MONEY [not before noun] if the value of a particular country's money is firm, it does not fall in value: [+against] *The pound is still firm against the dollar.*
—**firmly** *adv* —**firmness** *n* [U]

firm³ W3 *v* [T]
to press down on soil to make it harder or more solid

firm sth ⇔ **up** *phr v*
1 to make arrangements, ideas etc more definite and exact: *We're hoping to firm up the deal later this month.*
2 to make a part of your body have more muscle and less fat by exercising

fir·ma·ment /ˈfɜːməmənt $ ˈfɜːr-/ *n* **the firmament** *literary* the sky or heaven

firm·ware /ˈfɜːmweə $ ˈfɜːrmwer/ *n* [U] *technical* instructions to computers that are stored on CHIPS rather than in programs → HARDWARE (1), SOFTWARE

first¹ S1 W1 /fɜːst $ fɜːrst/ *adj*
1 IN A SERIES coming before all the other things or people in a series: *Ella was his first girlfriend.* | **the first thing/time/day etc** *The first time I flew on a plane I was really nervous.* | *In the first year, all students take five courses.* | *John said the first thing that came into his head.* | *This was the first step towards achieving a peace agreement.* | *There's a meeting on the first Monday of every month.* | **the first two/three/few etc** *I only read the first two chapters of the book.* | *It rained during the first few days of the trip.* | *The* ***first and last*** *mountain I climbed was Mount Rundle in Banff* (=it was the only mountain I ever climbed).
2 **for the first time** used to say that something has never happened or been done before: *For the first time in his life he felt truly happy.* | *The survey revealed that, for the first time, there are more women in the workplace than men.* | *Not for the first time she wondered how he coped with so many children.*
3 MAIN most important: *Our first priority is to maintain the standard of work.* | *As I see it, my first responsibility is to my family.*
4 **in the first place a)** used to talk about the beginning of a situation, or the situation before something happened: *Why did you agree to meet her in the first place?* | *He wouldn't have given you the job in the first place if he didn't think you could do it.* **b)** *written* used to give the first in a list of reasons or points: *Her success was secured by two factors. In the first place, she had the support of managers.*
5 **in the first instance** *formal* at the start of a situation or series of actions: *The appointment of research officer will be for two years in the first instance.* | *Enquiries should be made in the first instance to the Human Resources Director.*
6 **at first glance/sight** the first time that you look at someone or something, before you notice any details: *At first glance the twins look identical.* | *At first sight, there didn't appear to be much damage.* → **love at first sight** at LOVE² (2)
7 **first things first** used to say that something should be done or dealt with first because it is the most important
8 **(at) first hand** if you see, experience, hear etc something at first hand, you see, experience etc it yourself, not through other people: *Many people have seen the horrors of war at first hand.* → FIRST-HAND
9 **first prize/place** the prize that is given to the best person or thing in a competition: **win/take first prize** *She won first prize in a painting competition.* | [+of] *There is a first prize of £10,000.*
10 **first choice** the thing or person you like best: *John was our first choice as a name for the baby.*
11 **first thing** as soon as you get up in the morning, or as soon as you start work: *I'll call you first thing tomorrow.* | *We're leaving first thing.*
12 **at first light** *literary* very early in the morning: *The search will resume at first light tomorrow.*
13 **make the first move** to be the person who starts to do something when someone else is too nervous, embarrassed etc to do it: *He was glad she had made the first move and kissed him.*
14 **not have the first idea about sth** *also* **not know/understand the first thing about sth** to not know anything about a subject, or not know how to do something: *I wouldn't have the first idea about what to*

F

do in that situation. | *I don't know the first thing about cars.*

15 the first flush of sth the beginning of a good period of time when you are young, successful etc: **be in the first flush of passion/youth etc** *He was no longer in the first flush of youth.* | *The first flush of enthusiasm had passed.*

16 JOB TITLE used in the title of someone's job or position to show that they have a high rank: *the first officer* | *the First Lord of the Admiralty*

17 first among equals someone who is officially on the same level as other people but really has more power

18 of the first water *old-fashioned* of the highest quality

first² adv 1 before anything or anyone else: *Cindy and Joe arrived first.* | *An extra five points will be given to the team that finishes first.* | *First of all we'd better make sure we've got everything we need.* **2** before doing anything else, or before anything else happens: *I'll join you in a minute but I need to make a phone call first.* **3** done for the first time: *The book was first published in 2000.* **4** at the beginning of a situation or activity: *When we were first married we lived in Toronto.* | *We first became friends when we worked together.* **5** [sentence adverb] also **first of all** used before saying the first of several things you want to say; ■ **firstly:** *First, I'd like to thank everyone for coming.* **6 first off** *informal* **a)** before doing anything else: *First off I'd like you all to fill in an evaluation sheet.* **b)** used before saying the first of several things you want to say, especially when you are annoyed: *First off I didn't agree with the comments in your email.* **7 first up** *BrE spoken informal* used to introduce the first thing you are going to talk about, or the first thing that is going to happen: *First up is the Blues song 'Mississippi Lad'.* **8 put sb/sth first** to consider someone or something as the most important person or thing: *We need to choose energy policies that put the environment first.* | *Businesses should always put the customer first.* **9 come first a)** to be the most important person or thing to someone: *The care and well-being of patients should always come first.* | *As far as I'm concerned, the children come first.* | [+with] *Business always came first with Luke.* **b)** to win a competition: [+in] *The choir came first in all sections of the competition.* **10 first and foremost** used to emphasize the most important quality, purpose, reason etc: *Dublin is thought of first and foremost for its literary heritage.* **11 first and last** used to emphasize that something is the most important thing or quality: *She regarded herself as a teacher first and last, not a writer.* **12 first come, first served** used to say that something will be given to the people who ask for it first, when there is not enough for everyone: *Tickets will be allocated on a first come, first served basis.*

> **WORD CHOICE: first, first of all, firstly, at first**
> Use **first**, **first of all**, or **firstly** to introduce the first item in a list of two or more points, instructions etc: *First, make sure the screws are securely fixed in position. Then attach the wire.* | *The plan was not practical, firstly because of the cost, and secondly because local people did not support it.*
> Use **first** or **first of all** to say what happens first in a series of actions: *First I fed the baby. Then I made myself a sandwich.*
> Use **at first** to say what happened at the beginning of a period of time, when this changed later: *At first I was nervous, but I soon started to relax.*

first³ n 1 at first used to talk about the beginning of a situation, especially when it is different now: *At first, Gregory was shy and hardly spoke.* | *I felt quite disappointed at first.* **2** [C usually singular] something that has never happened or been done before: [+for] *The 3–0 defeat was a first for the team.* | *These results*

are firsts in the history of women's athletics. | *'I think he'll agree to it.' 'That will be a first.'* **3 from the (very) first** from the beginning of a situation: *I was against the idea from the first.* | *I should have known from the first that the relationship would never work.* **4** [C] the highest mark you can get in a university DEGREE in Britain: *Helen got a first in Law.* **5** [U] the lowest GEAR in a car or other vehicle, that you use when moving slowly; ■ **first gear: in first** *You should be in first on a hill like this.* | *He put the car into first and roared away.*

first⁴ pron 1 the first the first person to do something, or the first thing to happen: *There are now many similar housing projects but this was the first.* | *We hope this year's festival will be the first of many.* | **the first to do sth** *I always thought my sister would be the first to get married.* | *James was the first to arrive.* **2 the first I knew/heard** used when you have just discovered something that other people already know, and you are slightly annoyed: *The first I knew he was in Chicago was when I got an email from him.* | [+of/about] *The first I knew about it was when Tony called me this morning.* **3 the First** *spoken* used after the name of a king, queen, or Pope when other later ones have the same name: *Queen Elizabeth the First* (=written as Queen Elizabeth I)

first 'aid *n* [U] simple medical treatment that is given as soon as possible to someone who is injured or who suddenly becomes ill: *Being given first aid at the scene of the accident probably saved his life.*

first 'aider *n* [C] *BrE* someone who is trained to give first aid

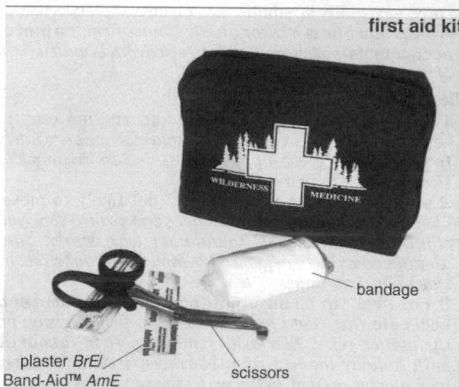

first aid kit

plaster *BrE*/
Band-Aid™ *AmE*

scissors

bandage

first 'aid kit *n* [C] a special bag or box containing BANDAGES and medicines to treat people who are injured or become ill suddenly

first 'base *n* [C] **1 a)** the first of the four places in a game of baseball that a player must touch before gaining a point **b)** the position of a defending player near this place: *He plays first base for the Red Sox.* **2 get to/reach first base** *AmE informal* **a)** to reach the first stage of success in an attempt to achieve something: *You've gotten to first base if you've landed an interview.* **b)** *old-fashioned informal* to kiss someone in a sexual way, used especially by young men to talk about the first stage in a sexual relationship

first·born /ˈfɜːstbɔːn $ ˈfɜːrstbɔːrn/ *n* [singular] your first child —**firstborn** *adj: her firstborn son*

first 'class *n* **1** [U] the best and most expensive seats on a plane or train, or rooms in a hotel: *We prefer to travel in first class.* → BUSINESS CLASS, CABIN CLASS, ECONOMY CLASS, TOURIST CLASS **2** [U] **a)** a class of post used in Britain for letters and parcels, that is quicker and more expensive than second-class post; → **second class b)** the class of post used in the US for ordinary business and personal letters **3** [C] the highest class of degree from a British university

first-class adj **1** of very good quality, and much better than other things of the same type: *This is a first-class wine.* | *His writing is first-class.* **2** relating to the class of post that is the most expensive and quickest to arrive: **first-class stamp/mail/post etc 3** relating to the best and most expensive class of seats on a plane or train, or rooms in a hotel: **first-class passenger/seat/compartment etc —first class** adv: *If I send the letter first class it should arrive tomorrow.* | *travel first class*

first ˈcousin n [C] a child of your AUNT or UNCLE; ▤ **cousin**

first deˈgree n **1** [C usually singular] BrE used to talk about a university degree such as a BA or a BSc, obtained by people who do not already have a degree **2 murder in the first degree** AmE first-degree murder

first-deˈgree adj [only before noun] **1 first-degree burn** a burn that is not very serious **2 first-degree murder** AmE murder of the most serious type, in which someone deliberately kills someone else; → **manslaughter**

first eˈdition n [C] one of the first copies of a book, which is often valuable: *an impressive collection of 19th century first editions*

first-ˈever adj [only before noun] happening for the first time: *the novelist's first-ever television interview* | *It was the first-ever visit to China by an American president.*

first ˈfamily, First Family n the first family the family of the President of the US

first ˈfloor n **1 the first floor** BrE the floor of a building just above the one at the bottom level; → **ground floor**: *a flat on the first floor* **2 the first floor** AmE the floor of a building at the bottom level: *Fire broke out on the first floor of the apartment building.*

first ˈfruits n [plural] BrE the first good result of something: [+of] *the first fruits of the government's privatization policy*

first ˈgear n [U] the lowest GEAR in a car or other motor vehicle, used when starting to move or when going up or down a very steep hill

first geneˈration n [singular] **1** people who have moved to live in a new country, or the children of these people **2** the first type of a machine to be developed: [+of] *the first generation of hand-held computers* **3** the first people to do something: [+of] *the first generation of radical feminists in the US* —**first-generation** adj: *first-generation Americans*

first ˈhalf n [C] the first of two equal periods of time that a sports match is divided into

first-ˈhand also **first·hand** /ˌfɜːstˈhænd $ ˌfɜːrst-/ adj [only before noun] **first-hand experience/knowledge/account etc** experience etc that has been learned or gained by doing something yourself or by talking to someone yourself; → **second-hand**: *journalists with first-hand experience of working in war zones* —**first-hand** adv: *experience gained first-hand* → (at) **first hand** at FIRST¹ (8)

first ˈlady n **1 the first lady** the wife of the President of the US, or of the GOVERNOR of a US state **2** [C usually singular] a woman who is considered to be the very best at a particular thing: [+of] *the first lady of jazz, Billie Holiday*

first ˈlanguage n [C] the language that you first learn as a child; ▤ **native language/tongue, mother tongue**; → **second language**

first lieuˈtenant n [C] a middle rank in the US army, Marines, or Air Force, or someone who has this rank

first ˈlight n [U] the time at the beginning of day when light first appears; ▤ **dawn, daybreak**

first·ly S2 /ˈfɜːstli $ -ɜːr-/ adv [sentence adverb] used to say that the fact or reason that you are going to mention is the first one and will be followed by others; → **finally, lastly**: *Firstly, I would like to thank everyone who has contributed to this success.*; → see box at FIRST²

first ˈmate also **first officer** n [C] an officer who has the rank just below captain on a ship that is not a military ship

first name n [C] **1** the name or names that come before your family name; ▤ **Christian name;** → **surname, last name**: *Her first name's Helen, but I don't know her surname.* **2 be on first name terms (with sb)** BrE; **be on a first name basis** AmE to know someone well enough to call them by their first name

first ˈnight n [C] the evening when the first public performance of a show, play etc is given

first ofˈfender n [C] someone who is guilty of breaking the law for the first time

first ˈofficer n [C] FIRST MATE

first-past-the-ˈpost adj [only before noun] BrE a first-past-the-post system of electing a politician, a government etc is one in which the person or party who gets the most votes wins: *Britain's first-past-the-post electoral system* | **first-past-the-post voting**

first ˈperson n **1 the first person** technical a form of a verb or a pronoun that is used to show that you are the speaker. For example, 'I', 'me', and 'us' are first person pronouns, and 'I am' is the first person singular of the verb 'to be'; → **second person, third person 2** [singular] a way of telling a story in which the writer or speaker tells it as though they were involved in the story; → **third person**: *a first person narrative* | **in the first person** *The 'Great Gatsby' is written in the first person.*

first-ˈrate adj of the very best quality; ▤ **excellent**: *He's a first-rate surgeon*

first reˈfusal n BrE **have/give sb first refusal on sth** to let someone decide whether to buy something before you offer to sell it to other people: *I'll let you have first refusal on the car.*

first ˈstrike n [C] an attack made on your enemy before they attack you, especially an attack made using NUCLEAR weapons

first-ˈstring adj [only before noun] a first-string player in a team plays when the game begins because they are the most skilled; → **second-string**

first-time ˈbuyer n [C] someone who is buying a house or an apartment for the first time

First ˈWorld n **the First World** the rich industrial countries of the world; → **Third World** —**first world** adj [always before noun]: *first world economies*

First World ˈWar n **the First World War** the big war fought in Europe between 1914 and 1918, which involved many different countries; ▤ **World War I**

firth /fɜːθ $ fɜːrθ/ n [C] a narrow area of sea between two areas of land, or the place where a river flows into the sea – used especially in Scotland: *the Firth of Forth*

fis·cal /ˈfɪskəl/ adj formal relating to money, taxes, debts etc that are owned and managed by the government: *a fiscal crisis* | **fiscal policy/measure** *sound* (=good) *fiscal policy* | *a fiscal matter* —**fiscally** adv: *fiscally conservative*

fiscal ˈyear n [C] **1** the 12 month period used by governments to calculate spending and how much tax a person or business must pay: **last/current/coming/next fiscal year 2** AmE the 12 month period over which a company calculates its profits or losses; ▤ **financial year** BrE

fish¹ S2 W1 /fɪʃ/ n plural **fish** or **fishes 1** [C] an animal that lives in water, and uses its FINS and tail to swim: *Ronny **caught** three huge **fish** this afternoon.* | *Over 1,500 different species of fish inhabit the waters around the reef.* | *The stonefish is the most deadly of all fishes.* | *The lake is well stocked with fish* (=fish have been put into the lake). | **freshwater/ saltwater/tropical fish** | **a shoal/school of fish** (=a large group of fish swimming together)

2 [U] the flesh of a fish used as food; → **seafood**: *One usually drinks white wine with fish.*
3 (be/feel) like a fish out of water to feel uncomfortable because you feel you do not belong in a place or situation: *I felt like a fish out of water in my new school.*
4 there are plenty more fish in the sea used to tell someone whose relationship has ended that there are other people they can have a relationship with
5 neither fish nor fowl neither one thing nor another
6 have other/bigger fish to fry *informal* to have other things to do, especially more important things
7 odd fish/queer fish *BrE old-fashioned* someone who is slightly strange or crazy
8 cold fish an unfriendly person who seems to have no strong feelings
9 a big fish in a little/small pond someone who is important in or who has influence over a very small area → **drink like a fish** at DRINK¹ (2); → **another/a different kettle of fish** at KETTLE (3)

fish² *v*   **1** [I] to try to catch fish; → **fishing**: *Dad really loves to fish.* | [+for] *a Japanese vessel fishing for tuna in the Eastern Pacific*   **2** [I always +adv/prep] *informal* to search for something in a bag, pocket etc: [+about/around] *She fished around in her purse and pulled out a photo.* | [+for] *Chris fished in his pocket for a coin.*   **3** [T] to try to catch fish in a particular area of water; → **fishing**: *Other nations are forbidden to fish the waters within 200 miles of the coast.*   **4 fish for compliments** to try to make someone say something nice about you, usually by first criticizing yourself – used to show disapproval: *It's sickening the way he's always fishing for compliments.*   **5** [I] to try to find out information, without asking directly: *'Are you here with your wife?' she asked, fishing.*
   fish sb/sth ⇔ out a) to pull someone or something out of water: [+of] *The body was fished out of the East River a week later.* **b)** to find something after searching through a bag, pocket etc, and take it out: [+of] *Eric fished a peppermint out of the bag.*

fish and 'chips *n* [U] a meal consisting of fish covered with BATTER (=a mixture of flour and milk) and cooked in oil, served with long thin pieces of potato also cooked in oil: *Get some fish and chips on your way home.* | *a fish and chip shop* → see picture at EAT

fish·bowl /'fɪʃbəʊl $ -boʊl/ *n* [C]   **1** a glass bowl that you can keep fish in   **2** a place or situation in which you cannot do anything in private: *Being in a small town like this is like living in a fishbowl.*

fish·cake /'fɪʃkeɪk/ *n* [C] a small round flat food consisting of cooked fish mixed with cooked potato

fish·er·man /'fɪʃəmən $ -ʃər-/ *n plural* **fishermen** /-mən/ [C] someone who catches fish as a sport or as a job → ANGLER

fish·e·ry /'fɪʃəri/ *n plural* **fisheries** [C]   **1** a part of the sea where fish are caught in large numbers   **2** a FISH FARM

fish-eye 'lens *n* [C] a type of curved LENS (=piece of glass on the front of a camera) that allows you to take photographs of a wide area

fish 'farm also **fishery** *n* [C] an area of water used for breeding fish as a business —**fish farming** *n* [U]

fish 'finger *n* [C] *BrE* a long piece of fish covered with BREADCRUMBS or BATTER and cooked; **☐ fish stick** *AmE*

fish fry *n plural* **fish fries** [C] *AmE* an outdoor event held to raise money for an organization, at which fish is cooked and eaten

fish·hook /'fɪʃhʊk/ *n* [C] a small hook with a sharp point at one end, that is fastened to the end of a long string in order to catch fish

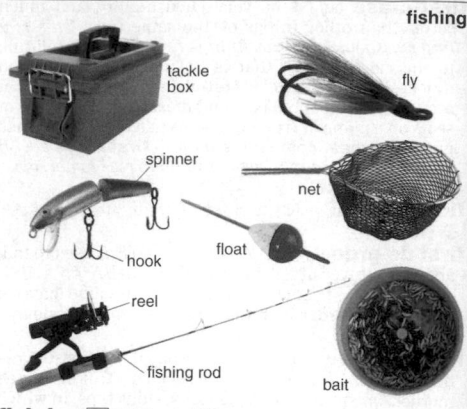
fishing

tackle box
fly
spinner
net
hook
float
reel
fishing rod
bait

fish·ing S3 /'fɪʃɪŋ/ *n* [U]
   1 the sport or business of catching fish: *Fishing is one of his hobbies.* | *Terry's going fishing at Lake Arrowhead next weekend.* | **deep sea/freshwater/saltwater fishing** | **salmon/trout/bass etc fishing** → FLYFISHING
   2 be on a fishing expedition *AmE informal* to try to find out secret information by asking a lot of questions about different things

'fishing line *n* [U] very long string made of strong material and used to catch fish

'fishing rod also **'fishing pole** *n* [C] a long thin pole with a long string and a hook attached to it, used for catching fish

'fishing ,tackle *n* [U] equipment used for fishing

'fish ,kettle *n* [C] *BrE* a long deep dish used for cooking whole fish

'fish meal *n* [U] dried fish crushed into a powder and put on the land to help plants grow

fish·mon·ger /'fɪʃmʌŋɡə $ -maːŋɡər, -mʌn-/ *n* [C] *BrE*   **1** someone who sells fish   **2** also **fishmonger's** a shop that sells fish

fish·net stock·ings /ˌfɪʃnet 'stɒkɪŋz $ -'staː-/ also **,fishnet 'tights** or **fish-nets** /'fɪʃnets/ *BrE* *n* [plural] STOCKINGS with a pattern of small holes that make them look like a net

'fish slice *n* [C] *BrE* a kitchen tool used especially for turning food when cooking, with a wide flat part and a handle; **☐ spatula**

'fish stick *n* [C] *AmE* a FISH FINGER

fish·tail /'fɪʃteɪl/ *v* [I] *AmE* if a vehicle or aircraft fishtails, the back end of it slides from side to side, usually because the tyres are sliding on water or ice

fish·wife /'fɪʃwaɪf/ *n plural* **fishwives** /-waɪvz/ [C] *especially BrE* an insulting word for a woman who shouts a lot and is often in a bad temper

fish·y /'fɪʃi/ *adj*   **1** *informal* seeming bad or dishonest; **☐ suspicious**: *There's something very fishy about him.*   **2** tasting or smelling of fish: *a fishy smell*

fis·sile /'fɪsaɪl $ -səl/ *adj technical* able to be split by atomic fission

fis·sion /'fɪʃən/ *n* [U] *technical*   **1** the process of splitting an atom to produce large amounts of energy or an explosion; → **fusion**   **2** the process of dividing a cell into two or more parts

fis·sure /'fɪʃə $ -ər/ *n* [C] a deep crack, especially in rock or earth

fist /fɪst/ *n* [C]   **1** the hand when it is tightly closed, so that the fingers are curled in towards the PALM. People close their hand in a fist when they are angry or are going to hit someone: *She held the money tightly in her fist.* | *Malcolm clenched his fist (=held his fist very tightly closed) angrily.* | *Dooley stood up and shook his fist in her face.* | *Varney slammed his fist down onto the table so hard the dishes jumped.* → HAM-FISTED, TIGHT-FISTED;

→ **hand over fist** at HAND¹ (35) **2 make a good/bad fist of sth** *BrE informal* to make a successful or unsuccessful attempt to do something

fist fight *n* [C] a fight in which people hit each other with their BARE fists

fist·ful /ˈfɪstfʊl/ *n* [C] an amount that is as much as you can hold in your hand: [+**of**] *a child clutching a fistful of toffees*

fis·ti·cuffs /ˈfɪstɪkʌfs/ *n* [plural] *old-fashioned* a fight in which you use your BARE hands to hit someone – often used humorously

fit¹ S1 W2 /fɪt/ *v past tense and past participle* **fitted** *also AmE present participle* **fitting**

1 CLOTHES a) [I,T not in progressive] if a piece of clothing fits you, it is the right size for your body: *His clothes did not fit him very well.* | *The uniform fitted her perfectly.* | *The jacket's fine, but the trousers don't fit.* | *I know this dress is going to fit you like a glove* (=fit you very well). ⚠ Use **fit** to say that clothes are not too big or too small. Use **suit** to say that clothes look attractive on someone *The dress fits, but it doesn't suit me.* **b)** [T usually passive] to try a piece of clothing on someone to see if it is the right size for them, or to make sure a special piece of equipment is right for them: **fit sb for sth** *I'm being fitted for a new suit tomorrow.* | **fit sb with sth** *He may need to be fitted with a hearing aid.*

2 RIGHT SIZE/SHAPE a) [I,T] if something fits in a place, it is the right size or shape to go there: *I couldn't find a key which fitted the lock.* | *Most cookers are designed to fit level with your worktops.* | [+**in/into/under etc**] *The plastic cover fits neatly over the frame.* | [+**together**] *All these bits of tubing are supposed to fit together.* **b)** [T always + adv/prep] to put something carefully into a place that is the right size or shape for it: *She fitted the last piece into the jigsaw puzzle.*

3 ENOUGH SPACE [I,T] if something fits into a place, there is enough space for it: *I wanted to put the wardrobe behind the door, but I don't think it'll fit.* | *You might be able to fit some small flowering plants between the larger bushes.* | **fit sth in/into sth** *I don't think we'll be able to fit any more people into the car.* | *We should be able to fit one more in.*

4 EQUIPMENT/PART [T] to put a piece of equipment into a place, or a new part onto a machine, so that it is ready to be used: **fit sth on/to etc sth** *I need to fit a lock on the bathroom door.* | *Anti-theft devices are fitted to all our cars.* | **be fitted with sth** *The windows and doors are all fitted with security locks.*

5 MATCH/BE SUITABLE [I,T] if something fits another thing, it is similar to it or suitable for it: *The punishment should fit the crime.* | *Police said the car fits the description of the stolen vehicle.* | *Scientists often select facts to fit their theories.* | *He didn't fit the conventional image of a banker.* | [+**with**] *The rhythm should fit with the meaning of a poem.*

6 fit sb for sth *formal* to make someone suitable for something or able to do something: *His natural authority fitted him for a senior position.*

7 fit the bill to be the type of person or thing that you want: *We wanted an experienced sportscaster, and Waggoner fit the bill.*

8 if the cap fits (, wear it) *BrE*, **if the shoe fits (, wear it)** *AmE spoken* used to tell someone that you think a criticism of them is true: *'So you think I'm a liar.' 'Well, if the cap fits...'* → **sb's face doesn't fit** at FACE¹ (20)

fit in *phr v*
1 if someone fits in, they are accepted by the other people in a group: *I never really fitted in at school.* | [+**with**] *I wasn't sure if she would fit in with my friends.*
2 fit sth/sb ⇔ **in** to manage to do something or see someone, even though you have a lot of other things to do; ◨ **squeeze sth/sb** ⇔ **in**: *The doctor said he can fit me in at 4:30.* | *I wanted to fit in a swim before breakfast.*
3 if something fits in with other things, it is similar to them or goes well with them: *I don't know quite how this new course will fit in.* | [+**with**] *A new building must fit in with its surroundings.* | *You can't expect a baby to fit in with your existing routine.*

fit into sth *phr v*
1 to be part of a group or system: *Some of the patients we see do not fit neatly into any of the existing categories.* | *How does this fit into the company's overall marketing strategy?*
2 to be accepted by the people in a group or organization: *She fitted into the team very well.*

fit sb/sth ⇔ **out** *phr v BrE*
to provide a person or place with the equipment, furniture, or clothes that they need: *The office had been fitted out in style.* | [+**with**] *The new recruits were fitted out with uniforms and weapons.*

fit together *phr v*
1 if something fits together or you fit it together, different pieces can be joined to make something: *Look, the tubes fit together like this.* | **fit sth together** *The pictures show you how to fit it together.*
2 if a story, set of facts, set of ideas etc fit together, they make sense when considered together: *Telecom and computer businesses fit together well.*

fit sb/sth ⇔ **up** *phr v BrE*
1 to provide a place with the furniture or equipment that it needs; ◨ **fit sth** ⇔ **out**: [+**with**] *The rooms are now fitted up with electric lights.*
2 *informal* to make someone seem guilty of a crime when they are really not guilty: *I knew that I had been fitted up.*

fit² S2 W3 *adj comparative* **fitter**, *superlative* **fittest**
1 STRONG someone who is fit is strong and healthy, especially because they exercise regularly; ◧ **unfit**: *You must be very fit if you do so much running.* | *He was young, good-looking, and physically fit.* | *I swim twice a week to try and keep fit.* | [+**for**] *He may not be fit for Saturday's match.* | **fit to do sth** *I don't know if I'll be fit enough to take part in the race.* | *Psychiatrists said he was fit to stand trial* (=he was mentally healthy enough). | *She's over eighty now, but still as fit as a fiddle* (=very fit). | **fighting fit** (=very fit) *BrE: I had just come back from holiday and was fighting fit.*
2 SUITABLE suitable or good enough for something; ◧ **unfit**: [+**for**] *We had to make sure the land was fit for drilling.* | *Some of the food was not fit for human consumption.* | *This book is not fit for publication!* | **fit to do sth** *He is not fit to govern this country!* | *This room is not fit to be seen!*
3 see/think fit (to do sth) to decide that something is the best thing to do, especially when other people do not agree with you: *The government saw fit to ignore our advice.* | *Sort out the problem in any way you think fit.*
4 in a fit state (to do sth) *especially BrE* healthy enough or in good enough condition for something: *I was still very shocked and in no fit state to work.* | *We'll have to make sure the house is in a fit state to receive visitors.*
5 fit for a king of very good quality: *The meal they provided was fit for a king.*
6 ATTRACTIVE *BrE* sexually attractive
7 fit to drop *BrE informal* extremely tired; ◧ **exhausted**: *It was getting late and most of us were fit to drop.*
8 fit to burst *BrE informal* if you are laughing, shouting etc fit to burst, you are doing it a lot: *The girls were laughing fit to burst.*
9 fit to be tied *AmE* very angry, anxious, or upset: *I was fit to be tied when she didn't come home until 2 a.m.*

fit³ *n*
1 EMOTION [C] a time when you feel an emotion very strongly and cannot control your behaviour: [+**of**] *She killed him in a fit of temper.* | *He quit his job in a fit of drunken depression.*
2 LOSE CONSCIOUSNESS [C] a short period of time when someone loses consciousness and cannot control their body because their brain is not working properly: *She used to have fits as a baby.* | *people who suffer from epileptic fits*
3 LAUGH/COUGH [C] a short time during which you laugh or cough a lot in a way that you cannot control: *He had a violent coughing fit.* | [+**of**] *The girls collapsed*

F

into a fit of the giggles. | *We were all **in fits of laughter** trying to clear up the mess.* | *Carl **had** us all **in fits** (=made us laugh a lot) with his stories.*
4 have/throw a fit *informal* to be very angry or shocked: *If your mother finds out about this, she'll have a fit.*
5 RIGHT SIZE [singular] the way in which something fits on your body or fits into a space: *The dress was a perfect fit.* | *I managed to get everything into the suitcase, but it was a **tight fit**.*
6 SUITABLE [singular] *formal* if there is a fit between two things, they are similar to each other or are suitable for each other: [+**between**] *We must be sure that there's a fit between the needs of the children and the education they receive.*
7 in/by fits and starts if something happens in fits and starts, it does not happen smoothly, but keeps starting and then stopping again: *Technology advances by fits and starts.* | *He spoke in fits and starts.*

fit⁴ *v* **fitted, fitting** [I] *BrE* to have a SEIZURE (=a sudden condition in which someone cannot control the movements of their body): *The patient was still fitting.* —**fitting** *n* [U]: *Fitting continued for more than 5 minutes.*

fit·ful /'fɪtfəl/ *adj* not regular, and starting and stopping often: *John awoke from a fitful sleep.* | *The peace talks only seem to be making fitful progress.* —**fitfully** *adv*: *She slept fitfully.*

fit·ment /'fɪtmənt/ *n* [C usually plural] *BrE* a piece of furniture or equipment that is made especially for a particular space in a room: *bathroom fitments*

fit·ness /'fɪtnɪs/ *n* [U] **1** when you are healthy and strong enough to do hard work or play sports: *an exercise programme to improve your fitness* | *Running marathons requires a high level of **physical fitness**.* **2** the degree to which someone or something is suitable or good enough for a particular situation or purpose: [+**for**] *He questioned McNeil's fitness for high office.* | **fitness to do sth** *The doctor will first determine your fitness to receive the anaesthetic.*

fit·ted /'fɪtɪd/ *adj* **1 be fitted with sth** to have or include something as a permanent part: *Is your car fitted with an alarm?* **2** [only before noun] *BrE* built, made, or cut to fit a particular space: *a fitted wardrobe* | *a fitted kitchen* | *fitted carpets* **3** [only before noun] fitted clothes are designed so that they fit closely to someone's body; **☒ loose**: *a fitted black jacket* **4** [not before noun] *BrE* having the right qualities or experience for a particular job: *Elinor is **well fitted** to be the sales manager.*

fit·ter /'fɪtə $ -ər/ *n* [C] *BrE* someone who puts together or repairs machines or equipment: *a gas fitter*

fit·ting¹ /'fɪtɪŋ/ *n* [C] **1** [usually plural] *BrE* a piece of equipment in a house, for example a COOKER or a FRIDGE, that can be moved or taken with you when you sell the house → **fixtures and fittings** at FIXTURE (2) **2** [usually plural] an outside part of a piece of equipment that makes it possible to use or handle it: *a sink with chrome fittings* (=handle and taps) | *new light fittings* **3** an occasion when you put on a piece of clothing that is being made for you, to see if it fits properly

fitting² *adj formal* right for a particular situation or occasion; **☒ appropriate**: *I thought the memorial was a fitting tribute to the President.* | *a **fitting end** to what was a memorable trip* | **it is only fitting (that)** *It is only fitting that Simon propose the first toast tonight.*

fitting room *n* [C] an area in a shop where you can put on clothes to see how they look; **☒ dressing room** *AmE*

five /faɪv/ *number, n* **1** the number 5: *There is also a golf course five miles away.* | *I'll be back by five* (=five o'clock). | *The family moved to Canada when he was five* (=five years old). **2** [C] a piece of paper money that is worth five dollars or five pounds; → **fiver**: *Do you have two fives for a ten?* **3 give sb (a) five** *informal* to hit the inside of someone's hand with your hand to show that

you are very pleased about something **4 take five** *spoken* used to tell people to stop working for a few minutes **5 fives** [U] a British ball game in which the ball is hit with the hand against any of three walls; → **handball** → HIGH FIVE, NINE TO FIVE

five-and-'ten also **five-and-'dime** *n* [C] *AmE old-fashioned* a shop that sells many different types of inexpensive goods, especially for the house; **☒ dime store**

five-a-'side *adj* [only before noun] *BrE* five-a-side football is played with five players on each side, usually indoors → see picture at SPORTS CENTRE

five o'clock 'shadow *n* [singular] the dark colour on a man's chin where the hair has grown during the day

fiv·er /'faɪvə $ -ər/ *n* [C] *BrE informal* a piece of paper money worth five pounds: *Lend me a fiver, mate?*

'five-spot *n* [C] *AmE old-fashioned* a piece of paper money worth five dollars: *It only costs a five-spot.*

'five-star *adj* [only before noun] a five-star hotel, restaurant etc has been judged to be of the highest standard

five star 'general *n* [C] *AmE* a GENERAL of the highest rank, who controls an army

fix¹ S2 W2 /fɪks/ *v*
1 REPAIR [T] to repair something that is broken or not working properly: *He's outside fixing the brakes on the car.* | *Ellis was able to quickly find and fix the problem.* → see picture at REPAIR; → see box at REPAIR¹
2 LIMIT [T] **a)** to decide on a limit for something, especially prices, costs etc, so that they do not change; **☒ set**: **fix sth at sth** *The interest rate has been fixed at 6.5%.* | *Rent was fixed at $1,750 per month.* **b)** if two or more companies fix the price for a particular product or service, they secretly agree on the price they will charge for it, in order to keep the price high and make more profit. This practice is illegal: *The government accused the two companies of fixing petrol prices.*
3 fix a time/date/place etc to decide on a particular time etc when something will happen: *Have you fixed a date for the wedding yet?*
4 ARRANGE also **fix up** [I,T] *spoken* to make arrangements for something: *'So when do I get to meet them?' 'Tomorrow, if I can fix it.'* | **fix (it) for sb to do sth** *I've fixed for you to see him this afternoon or four.*
5 ATTACH [T] to attach something firmly to something else, so that it stays there permanently: **fix sth to/on sth** *The shelves should be fixed to the wall with screws.*
6 PREPARE FOOD [T] *informal especially AmE* to prepare a meal or drinks; **☒ get**: *I'll watch the kids and you fix dinner.* | **fix sb sth** *Can I fix you a snack?* | *Terry fixed herself a cold drink and sat out on the balcony.*
7 SOLVE [T] to find a solution to a problem or bad situation: *The government seems confident that environmental problems can be fixed.*
8 fix your attention/eyes/mind etc on sb/sth to think about or look at someone or something carefully: *Aziz tried to fix his mind on the job at hand.* | *Every eye was fixed on the new girl.*
9 fix sb with a stare/glare/look etc *literary* to look directly at someone for a long time: *Rachel fixed him with an icy stare.*
10 HAIR/FACE [T] *especially AmE* to make your hair or MAKE-UP look neat and attractive: *Who fixed your hair for the wedding?* | *Hold on. Let me just fix my face* (=put on make-up) *before we go out.*
11 CAT/DOG [T] *AmE informal* to do a medical operation on a cat or dog so that it cannot have babies; **☒ neuter**
12 RESULT [T] to arrange an election, game etc dishonestly, so that you get the result you want: *Many suspected that the deal had been fixed in advance.*
13 PAINTINGS/PHOTOGRAPHS [T] *technical* to use a chemical process on paintings, photographs etc that makes the colours or images permanent
14 PUNISH [T] *informal* used to say that you will

punish someone you are angry with: *If anybody did that to me, I'd fix him good.*

15 be fixing to do sth *AmE spoken* to be preparing to do something – used in some parts of the US: *I'm fixing to go to the store. Do you need anything?*

fix on sb/sth *phr v*
to choose a suitable thing or person, especially after thinking about it carefully: *We've finally fixed on a place to have the concert.*

fix sb/sth ⇔ **up** *phr v*
1 to arrange a meeting, event etc: *I fixed up an interview with him.* | *We'll have to fix up a time to meet.*
2 to decorate or repair a room or building; ▣ **do up**: *We fixed up the guest bedroom before my parents came to stay.*
3 to provide someone with something they want: [+with] *Can you fix me up with a bed for the night?*
4 to find a suitable romantic partner for someone: [+with] *I asked my best friend to fix me up with someone.*

fix² *n* **1** [C] something that solves a problem: *Robinson called the proposal a **quick fix** (=a temporary or easy solution) of limited value.* **2 (be) in a fix** to have a problem that is difficult to solve; ▣ **(be) in a mess**: *We're going to be in a real fix if we miss that bus.* | *That's put us in a fix.* **3** [singular] an amount of something, especially an illegal drug such as HEROIN, that you often use and badly want: *addicts looking for a fix* | *I need my fix of caffeine in the morning or I can't think.* **4 get a fix on sb/sth a)** to find out exactly where someone or something is: *He peered out, trying to get a fix on the enemy's position.* **b)** to understand what someone or something is really like: *I couldn't seem to get a fix on the situation.* **5** [singular] something that has been dishonestly arranged: *People think the election was a fix.*

fix·a·ted /fɪkˈseɪtˌd/ *adj* always thinking or talking about one particular thing: [+on] *He never used to be so fixated on losing weight.*

fix·a·tion /fɪkˈseɪʃən/ *n* [C] **1** a very strong interest in or love for someone or something, that is not natural or healthy: [+on/with/about] *Carlo has an absolute fixation with the royal family.* | *a mother fixation* **2** *technical* a kind of mental illness in which someone's mind or emotions stop developing

fix·a·tive /ˈfɪksətɪv/ *n* [C,U] **1** a substance used to stick things together or to hold things such as false teeth in place **2** a chemical used on a painting or photograph so that the colours do not change

fixed [S3] [W3] /fɪkst/ *adj*
1 [not before noun] firmly fastened to a particular position: [+to/in/on] *a mirror fixed to the bathroom wall* **2** fixed times, amounts, meanings etc cannot be changed; ▣ **set**: *The classes begin and end at fixed times.* | *fixed prices* | *My contract was for a fixed term of five years.* | *interest at 10%, fixed for 5 years*
3 have fixed ideas/opinions to have very definite ideas or opinions that you will not change – often used to show disapproval: [+about/on] *He has very fixed ideas about how a wife should behave.*
4 how are you fixed for sth? *spoken* used to ask someone how much of something they have, or to ask about an arrangement: *How are you fixed for cash?* | *How are we fixed for Monday?*
5 a fixed smile, expression etc does not show any emotion or does not show how someone really feels
6 be of/have no fixed abode/address *BrE law* to not have a permanent place to live

ˌfixed ˈassets *n* [plural] *technical* land, buildings, or equipment that a business owns and uses

ˌfixed ˈcapital *n* [U] *technical* buildings or machines that a business owns and that can be used for a long time to produce goods

ˌfixed ˈcosts *n* [plural] *technical* costs, such as rent, that a business has to pay even when it is not producing anything; → **variable costs**

ˌfixed ˈincome *n* [C] an amount of money that you receive to live on that does not change: *pensioners living on a fixed income*

fix·ed·ly /ˈfɪksˌdli/ *adv* without looking at or thinking about anything else: **stare/gaze/look fixedly at sth** *Ann stared fixedly at the screen.*

fix·er /ˈfɪksə $ -ər/ *n* [C] someone who is good at arranging things and solving problems for other people, sometimes by using dishonest methods: *a political fixer*

fix·ings /ˈfɪksɪŋz/ *n* **1 the fixings** *AmE* the vegetables, bread etc that are eaten with meat at a large meal; ▣ **the trimmings** *BrE*: *turkey with all the fixings* **2** [plural] *BrE* things that are used to hold other things together, for example SCREWS

fix·i·ty /ˈfɪksˌti/ *n* [U] *formal* when something does not change: [+of] *fixity of purpose*

fix·ture /ˈfɪkstʃə $ -ər/ *n* [C] **1** *BrE* a sports match that has been arranged for a particular time and place: *a list of this season's fixtures* **2** [usually plural] a piece of equipment that is fixed inside a house or building and is sold as part of the house: *light fixtures* | **fixtures and fittings** *BrE* (=all the equipment that is normally included as part of a house or building when it is sold) **3 be a (permanent) fixture** to be always present and not likely to move or go away: *Gerrard soon became a permanent fixture in the Liverpool team.*

fizz¹ /fɪz/ *v* [I] if a liquid fizzes, it produces a lot of bubbles and makes a continuous sound: *champagne fizzing out of the bottle*

fizz² *n* [singular, U] **1** the bubbles of gas in some kinds of drinks, or the sound that they make **2** *BrE informal* CHAMPAGNE

fiz·zle /ˈfɪzəl/ *v*
fizzle out *phr v informal* to gradually stop happening, especially because people become less interested: *Their romance just fizzled out.*

fiz·zy /ˈfɪzi/ *adj* **1** a fizzy liquid contains bubbles of gas; → **sparkling, flat**: *fizzy water* → see picture at STILL **2 fizzy drink** *BrE* a sweet non-alcoholic drink with bubbles of gas

fjord, fiord /ˈfiːɔːd, fjɔːd $ fiːˈɔːrd, fjɔːrd/ *n* [C] a narrow area of sea between high cliffs, especially in Norway

flab /flæb/ *n* [U] *informal* soft loose flesh on a person's body – used to show disapproval: *simple advice to help you **fight the flab** (=lose weight)*

flab·ber·gas·ted /ˈflæbəgɑːstˌd $ -bərgæs-/ *adj informal* extremely surprised or shocked: *When I heard how much money we'd made, I was absolutely flabbergasted.*

flab·by /ˈflæbi/ *adj informal* **1** having unattractive soft loose flesh rather than strong muscles: *a flabby stomach* **2** used to describe something that is weak or not effective; ▣ **powerful**: *intellectually flabby arguments* | *The band's performance was tired and flabby.* —**flabbiness** *n* [U]

flac·cid /ˈflæsˌd, ˈflæksˌd/ *adj technical* soft and weak instead of firm: *a flaccid penis* —**flaccidity** /flæˈsɪdˌti, flæk-/ *n* [U]

flack /flæk/ *n* **1** another spelling of FLAK **2** [C] *AmE informal* someone whose job is to represent an organization and answer questions about it, especially when something bad has happened: *They spent millions on lobbyists and flacks to improve their image.*

flag¹ /flæg/ *n* [C] **1** a piece of cloth with a coloured pattern or picture on it that represents a country or organization: *Children **waving flags** greeted the Russian leader.* | *the flag of Kenya* | *the Spanish flag* | **a flag is flying** (=a flag is shown on a pole) *Flags were **flying at half-mast** because of the death of the Premier.* **2** a coloured piece of cloth used in some sports as a signal or as a sign showing the position of something: *The*

F

flag went down, and the race began. | *a free kick near the* ***corner flag*** (=flag on a football pitch) → see picture at GOLF **3 the flag** an expression meaning a country or organization and its beliefs, values, and people: *loyalty to the flag* **4 keep the flag flying** to achieve success on behalf of your country in a competition: *Bristol kept the flag flying for English rugby with this win.* **5** a FLAGSTONE → **fly the flag** at FLY¹ (13)

flag² *v* **flagged, flagging 1** [T] to make a mark against some information to show that it is important: *I've flagged the parts I want to comment on.* **2** [I] to become tired or weak: *By the end of the meeting we had begun to flag.*

flag sb/sth ⇔ **down** *phr v* to make the driver of a vehicle stop by waving at them: *I flagged down a taxi.*

fla·gel·lant /'flædʒɨlənt, flə'dʒelənt/ *n* [C] *formal* someone who whips themselves, especially as a religious punishment

fla·gel·late /'flædʒɨleɪt/ *v* [T] *formal* to whip yourself or someone else, especially as a religious punishment —**flagellation** /ˌflædʒɨ'leɪʃən/ *n* [U]

flag football *n* [U] *AmE* a game like American football in which players tear off small pieces of cloth called flags from around other players' waists instead of knocking them down; → **touch football**

flagged /flægd/ *adj* covered with FLAGSTONES

flag·ging /'flægɪŋ/ *adj* becoming tired or losing strength: **flagging spirits/energy/morale** *By now the wine had lifted her flagging spirits.* | *He presents himself as the man to revive the party's **flagging** fortunes.* | *concern for the country's **flagging** economy*

flag·on /'flægən/ *n* [C] a large container for liquids, especially beer or wine

flag·pole /'flægpəʊl $ -poʊl/ *n* [C] a tall pole on which a flag hangs; ⊟ **flagstaff**

fla·grant /'fleɪgrənt/ *adj* a flagrant action is shocking because it is done in a way that is easily noticed and shows no respect for laws, truth etc: **flagrant abuse/violation/breach etc** *flagrant violations of human rights* | *a **flagrant disregard** for the law* —**flagrantly** *adv*

flag·ship /'flægʃɪp/ *n* [C] **1** the most important ship in a group of ships belonging to the navy **2** [usually singular] the best and most important product, building etc that a company owns or produces: *the flagship of the new Ford range* | *The firm has just opened a **flagship** store in Las Vegas.* | *the company's **flagship** product*

flag·staff /'flægstɑːf $ -stæf/ *n* [C] a tall pole on which a flag hangs; ⊟ **flagpole**

flag·stone /'flægstəʊn $ -stoʊn/ *n* [C] a smooth flat piece of stone used for floors, paths etc

flag-waving *n* [U] the expression of strong national feelings, especially when these feelings seem too extreme

flail¹ /fleɪl/ *v* **1** [I,T] to wave your arms or legs in an uncontrolled way: *He flailed wildly as she tried to hold him down.* | [+**around/about**] *James flailed about in the shallow water.* **2** [T] to beat someone or something violently, usually with a stick **3** [I,T] to beat grain with a flail

flail² *n* [C] a tool consisting of a stick that swings from a long handle, used in the past to separate grain from wheat by beating it

flair /fleə $ fler/ *n* **1** [singular] a natural ability to do something very well; ⊟ **talent**: *Jo has a flair for languages.* **2** [U] a way of doing things that is interesting and shows imagination: **artistic/creative flair** *a job for which artistic flair is essential* | *Irwin has real entrepreneurial flair.*

flak, flack /flæk/ *n* [U] **1** *informal* strong criticism: *Lilley has **taken** a lot of **flak** for his views on drugs.* **2** bullets or SHELLS that are shot from the ground at enemy aircraft → FLAK JACKET

flake¹ /fleɪk/ *n* [C] **1** a small thin piece that breaks away easily from something else: [+**of**] *flakes of snow* | *chocolate flakes* → SNOWFLAKE **2** *AmE informal* someone who seems strange or who often forgets things; ⊟ **space cadet**

flake² *v* **1** also **flake off** [I] to break off in small thin pieces: *The paint is beginning to flake off.* | *Use a moisturising cream to stop your skin flaking.* **2** [I,T] to break fish or another food into small thin pieces, or to break in this way: *Poach the fish until it flakes easily.* | *Remove the skin and flake the flesh.*

flake out *phr v informal* **1** *BrE* to fall asleep because you are extremely tired: *Phil's flaked out on the sofa.* **2** *AmE* to do something strange, or to not do what you said you would do: [+**on**] *Kathy said she'd help but she flaked out on us.*

flak jacket *n* [C] a special coat made of strong, heavy material to protect soldiers and policemen from bullets

flak·y /'fleɪki/ *adj* **1** tending to break into small thin pieces: *flaky pastry* | *flaky skin* **2** *informal especially AmE* a flaky person is slightly strange or often forgets things: *Carrie's pretty flaky but she's fun to be with.* —**flakiness** *n* [U]

flam·bé /'flɒmbeɪ $ flɑːm'beɪ/ also **flam·béed** /'flɒmbeɪd $ flɑːm'beɪd/ *adj* food that is flambéed has an alcoholic drink such as BRANDY poured over it to produce flames

flam·boy·ant /flæm'bɔɪənt/ *adj* **1** behaving in a confident or exciting way that makes people notice you: **flamboyant style/character/personality** *Randall's flamboyant style of play* | *Spencer lifted his arms in a **flamboyant** gesture.* **2** brightly coloured and easily noticed: *flamboyant clothes* | *Penny has red hair and a rather flamboyant appearance.* —**flamboyantly** *adv* —**flamboyance** *n* [U]

flame¹ /fleɪm/ *n*
1 [C,U] hot bright burning gas that you see when something is on fire

> **douse flames** (=pour water on them to make them stop burning)
> **fan flames** (=make them burn more by waving something in front of them)
> **smother flames** (=put something over them to make them stop burning)
> **flames flicker/dance** (=they move)
> **flames engulf sth** (=they surround and burn something)
> **flames lick sth** (=they touch something lightly)
> **flames leap** (=they go high into the air)
> **candle/coal/gas flame**
> **naked flame** (=one that is not enclosed)

Flames poured out of the windows of the building. | *They rushed past us with buckets of water and tried to **douse** the **flames**.* | *They sat around the campfire, watching the **flickering flames**.* | *A home video showed how quickly **flames engulfed** the building.* | *a candle flame*

2 in flames burning in a way that is difficult to control: *When we reached Mandalay it was in flames.* | *They escaped just as the house was **engulfed in flames**.*
3 go up in flames/burst into flames to suddenly begin burning in a way that is difficult to control: *The helicopter burst into flames after hitting a power line.*
4 a flame of anger/desire/passion etc *literary* a strong feeling: *Flames of desire shot through her.*
5 [C] an angry or rude email → **old flame** at OLD (4); → **naked flame** at NAKED (5); → **fan the flames** at FAN² (2); → **add fuel to the fire/flames** at ADD (9)

flame² *v* [I] **1** *literary* to become suddenly bright with light or colour, especially red or orange: *Erica's cheeks flamed with anger.* **2** *literary* to burn brightly: *A great fire flamed in an open fireplace.* **3** to send someone an angry or rude message in an email or on a BULLETIN BOARD

fla·men·co /flə'meŋkəʊ $ -koʊ/ *n plural* **flamencos** [C,U] a fast exciting Spanish dance, or the music that is played for this dance

flame·proof /ˈfleɪmpruːf/ also **ˈflame reˌsistant**
adj **1** made of or covered with substances that will not burn easily **2** flameproof cooking dishes can be used in very hot places, such as in an OVEN

ˈflame ˌthrower *n* [C] a machine like a gun that shoots flames or burning liquid, used as a weapon or for clearing plants

flam·ing /ˈfleɪmɪŋ/ *adj* [only before noun] **1 a flaming row/temper** a very angry argument or temper: *They seem to have a flaming row at least once a week.* **2** covered with flames: *Residents panicked as flaming petrol poured down the street.* **3** *BrE informal* used to emphasize what you are saying, especially when you feel annoyed: *You flaming idiot!* **4** orange or bright red in colour: *flaming red hair*

fla·min·go /fləˈmɪŋɡəʊ $ -ɡoʊ/ *n plural* **flamingos** *or* **flamingoes** [C] a large pink tropical bird with very long thin legs and a long neck

flam·ma·ble /ˈflæməbəl/ *adj* something that is flammable burns easily; → **inflammable**, **nonflammable**: *Caution! Highly flammable liquid.*

flan /flæn/ *n* [C] *especially BrE* **1** a round PIE or cake that is filled with fruit, cheese etc **2** *AmE* a sweet baked food made with eggs, milk, and sugar; → **pie**, **quiche**

flange /flændʒ/ *n* [C] the flat edge that stands out from an object such as a railway wheel, to keep it in the right position or strengthen it

flank¹ /flæŋk/ *n* [C] **1** the side of an animal's or person's body, between the RIBS and the HIP **2** the side of an army in a battle, or a sports team when playing: *We were attacked on our left flank.* **3** the side of a hill, mountain, or very large building

flank² *v* [T] to be on both sides of someone or something: *Lewis entered flanked by two bodyguards.* | *mountains flanking the road*

flan·nel¹ /ˈflænl/ *n* **1** [U] soft cloth, usually made of cotton or wool, used for making clothes: *a flannel shirt* **2** [C] *BrE* a piece of cloth you use to wash yourself; ▣ **facecloth**; ▣ **washcloth** *AmE* **3** [U] *BrE informal* something that someone says that has no real meaning or does not tell you what you want to know **4** flannels [plural] *BrE* men's trousers made of flannel

flannel² *v* **flannelled**, **flannelling** [I,T] *BrE* to say things that have no real meaning in order to avoid answering a question directly or to hide your lack of knowledge

flan·nel·ette /ˌflænəlˈet/ *n* [U] soft cotton cloth used especially for making night clothes and sheets

flap¹ /flæp/ *n*
1 FLAT PIECE OF SOMETHING [C] a thin flat piece of cloth, paper, skin etc that is fixed by one edge to a surface, which you can lift up easily: *Open the tent flap, will you?* | *A loose flap of skin covered the wound.* → CAT FLAP
2 MOVEMENT [singular] the noisy movement of something such as cloth in the air: *the flap of the sails*
3 EXCITEMENT/WORRY **a flap** *informal* a situation in which people feel very excited or worried about something: **be in a flap** *Rafi's in a bit of a flap over the wedding plans.* → UNFLAPPABLE
4 PART OF AIRCRAFT [C] a part of the wing of an aircraft that can be raised or lowered to help the aircraft go up or down

flap² *v* **flapped**, **flapping** **1** [I,T] if a bird flaps its wings, it moves them up and down in order to fly **2** [I,T] to move quickly up and down or from side to side, often making a noise: *The flags were flapping in the breeze.* | *Flap your arms to keep warm.* **3** [I] *BrE informal* to behave in an excited or nervous way: *There's no need to flap!*

flap·jack /ˈflæpdʒæk/ *n* [C] **1** *BrE* a cake made of OATS, sugar, SYRUP, and butter **2** *AmE* a PANCAKE

flap·per /ˈflæpə $ -ər/ *n* [C] a fashionable young woman in the late 1920s

flare¹ /fleə $ fler/ *v* **1** also **flare up** [I] to suddenly begin to burn, or to burn more brightly for a short time: *The fire flared up again.* **2** also **flare up** [I] if strong feelings flare or flare up, people suddenly become angry, violent etc: *Rioting has flared up in several northern towns.* | *Tempers flared during the debate.* **3** also **flare up** [I] if a disease or illness flares up, it suddenly becomes worse: *The injury has flared up again, keeping him out of today's game.* **4** [I,T] if a person or animal flares their NOSTRILS (=the openings at the end of the nose), or if their nostrils flare, their nostrils become wider because they are angry: *The bull flared its nostrils and charged.* **5** [I always + adv/prep] if a piece of clothing flares out, it becomes wider at one end: [+out] *The dress flares out from the hips.* —**flared** *adj*: *flared jeans*

flare² *n* **1** [C] a piece of equipment that produces a bright flame, or the flame itself, used outdoors as a signal: *The distress flares were spotted by another ship.* **2** [C usually singular] a sudden bright flame: *There was a brief flare as the match was lit.* **3** flares [plural] trousers that become wide below the knee

ˈflare-up *n* [C] **1** a situation in which someone suddenly becomes angry or violent: *Apart from one or two flare-ups the match went fairly smoothly.* **2** a situation in which someone suddenly has problems because of a disease or illness after not having any problems for a long time: *a flare-up of her arthritis*

flash¹ ⑤ /flæʃ/ *v*
1 SHINE [I,T] to shine suddenly and brightly for a short time, or to make something shine in this way: *Lightning flashed overhead.* | **flash sth into/at/towards sb/sth** *Why is that guy flashing his headlights at me?* | *Red warning lights* **flashed on and off** (=shone for a short time and then stopped shining).
2 PICTURES [I always + adv/prep] to be shown quickly on television, on a computer, or on a film: [+across/ onto/past etc] *Images of the war flashed across the screen.*
3 flash through sb's mind/head/brain if thoughts, images, memories etc flash through your mind, you suddenly think of them or remember them: *The possibility that Frank was lying flashed through my mind.*
4 flash a smile/glance/look etc (at sb) to smile or look at someone quickly and for a short time: *'I love this city,' he said, flashing a big smile.*
5 SHOW STH QUICKLY [T] to show something to someone for only a short time: *He flashed his identification card.*
6 NEWS/INFORMATION [T always + adv/prep] to send news or information somewhere quickly by radio, computer, or SATELLITE: **flash sth across/to sth** *Reporters at the scene flashed the news to their offices.*
7 MOVE QUICKLY [I always + adv/prep] to move very quickly: [+by/past/through] *A meteor flashed through the sky.*
8 EYES [I] *literary* if your eyes flash, they look very bright for a moment, especially because of a sudden emotion: [+with] *Janet's blue eyes flashed with anger.*
9 SEX ORGANS [I,T] if a man flashes, or if he flashes someone, he shows his sexual organs in public; → **flasher**
10 sb's life flashes before their eyes if someone's life flashes before their eyes, they suddenly remember many events from their life because they are in great danger and might die
11 TIME PASSING QUICKLY [I always + adv/prep] if a period of time or an event flashes by or flashes past, it seems to end very quickly: [+by/past] *Our vacation seemed to just flash by.*
  flash sth ⇔ **around** *phr v*
to use or show something in a way that will make people notice you and think you have a lot of money: *He's always flashing his money around.*
  flash back *phr v*
to suddenly think about or show something that hap-

F

pened in the past, especially in a film, book etc: [+to] *From here the movie flashes back to Billy's first meeting with Schultz.* → FLASHBACK

flash forward *phr v*
if a film, book etc flashes forward, it shows what happens in the future: [+to] *The movie then flashes forward to their daughter's fifth birthday.*

flash² *n*
1 LIGHT [C] a bright light that shines for a short time and then stops shining: *Two flashes mean danger.* | [+of] *A flash of lightning lit up the night sky.* | **brilliant/blinding flash** *a brilliant flash of light*
2 CAMERA [C,U] a special bright light used when taking photographs indoors or when there is not much light: *Did the flash go off?*
3 in/like a flash also **quick as a flash** very quickly: *Just wait here. I'll be back in a flash.*
4 flash of inspiration/brilliance/insight/anger etc if someone has a flash of BRILLIANCE, anger etc, they suddenly have a clever idea or a particular feeling
5 a flash in the pan a sudden success that ends quickly and is unlikely to happen again: *Beene's new novel proves he isn't just a flash in the pan.*
6 BRIGHT COLOUR/STH SHINY [C] if there is a flash of something brightly coloured or shiny, it appears suddenly for a short time: [+of] *The bird vanished in a flash of blue.*
7 COMPUTER [U] *trademark* a system of instructions for a computer that is used especially to make pictures on a website appear to move: *Flash animation*
8 LOOK [C] *BrE* a quick look used humorously; ◧ **glimpse**
9 MILITARY [C] *BrE* a small piece of coloured cloth worn on the shoulder of a military uniform → NEWSFLASH

flash³ *adj* **1 flash flood/fire** a flood or fire that happens very quickly or suddenly, and continues for only a short time **2** *BrE informal* looking very new, bright, and expensive – used to show disapproval: *a big flash car* **3** *BrE informal* liking to have expensive clothes and possessions so that other people notice you – used to show disapproval: *Chris didn't want to seem flash in front of his mates.*

flash·back /ˈflæʃbæk/ *n* **1** [C,U] a scene in a film, play, book etc that shows something that happened before that point in the story: *The events of the hero's childhood are shown as a series of flashbacks.* **2** [C] a sudden very clear memory of something that happened to you in the past: *Eaton still has flashbacks of the crash.* **3** [C] an occasion when someone has the same bad feeling that they had when they took an illegal drug in the past: *Many users of this drug experience flashbacks.* **4** [C] *technical* a burning gas or liquid that moves back into a tube or container

flash bulb *n* [C] a small object that produces a bright light, used when taking photographs indoors or when there is not much light

flash·card /ˈflæʃkɑːd $ -kɑːrd/ *n* [C] a card with a word or picture on it, used in teaching

flash·er /ˈflæʃə $ -ər/ *n* [C] a man who shows his sexual organs to women in public; → **flash**

flash·gun /ˈflæʃɡʌn/ *n* [C] a piece of equipment that lights a special bright light when you press the button on a camera to take a photograph

flash·light /ˈflæʃlaɪt/ *n* [C] *AmE* a small electric light that you can carry in your hand; ◧ **torch** *BrE*

flash·point /ˈflæʃpɔɪnt/ *n* [C] **1** a place where trouble or violence might easily develop suddenly and be hard to control: *Hebron has been a flashpoint for years.* **2** [usually singular] *technical* the lowest temperature at which a liquid such as oil will produce enough gas to burn if a flame is put near it

flash·y /ˈflæʃi/ *adj informal* **1** big, bright, or expensive, and intended to be impressive – used to show disapproval: *large flashy cars* **2** someone who is flashy

wears expensive clothes, JEWELLERY etc in a way that is intended to be impressive – used to show disapproval: *a flashy dresser*

flask /flɑːsk $ flæsk/ *n* [C] **1** *BrE* a special type of bottle that you use to keep liquids either hot or cold, for example when travelling; ◧ **Thermos 2** a HIP FLASK **3** a glass bottle with a narrow top, used in a LABORATORY

flat¹ [S2] [W2] /flæt/ *adj comparative* **flatter**, *superlative* **flattest**
1 SURFACE smooth and level, without raised or hollow areas, and not sloping or curving: *houses with flat roofs* | *a perfectly flat sandy beach* | *The countryside near there is flat as a pancake* (=very flat). | *Work on a clean, flat surface.* → see picture at LANDSCAPE
2 MONEY a flat rate, amount of money etc is fixed and does not change or have anything added to it: *Clients are charged a flat rate of £250 annually.* | *We charge a flat fee for car hire.*
3 TYRE/BALL a flat tyre or ball has no air or not enough air in it
4 NOT DEEP not very deep, thick, or high, especially in comparison to its width or length: *The cake came out of the oven flat, not fluffy.*
5 DRINK a drink that is flat does not taste fresh because it has no more bubbles of gas in it; ◧ **fizzy**
6 NOT INTERESTING [not before noun] a performance, book etc that is flat lacks interest, excitement, or energy: *Arsenal looked flat for large parts of the game.*
7 BATTERY *BrE* a flat BATTERY has lost its electrical power; ◧ **dead** *AmE*: *Have you checked that the batteries haven't gone flat* (=become flat)?
8 BUSINESS/TRADE if prices, economic conditions, trade etc are flat, they have not increased or improved over a period of time: *Analysts are expecting flat sales in the coming months.*
9 E flat/B flat/A flat etc a musical note that is one SEMITONE lower than the note E, B, A etc; → **sharp**, **natural**
10 MUSICAL SOUND if a musical note is flat, it is played or sung slightly lower than it should be; ◧ **sharp**
11 VOICE not showing much emotion, or not changing much in sound as you speak: *'He's dead,' she said in a flat voice.*
12 a flat refusal/denial etc a refusal etc that is definite and which someone will not change: *Our requests were met with a flat refusal.*
13 be flat on your back a) to be lying down so that all of your back is touching the floor **b)** to be very ill so that you have to stay in bed for a period of time: *I've been flat on my back with the flu all week.*
14 SHOES flat shoes have very low heels
15 LIGHT having little variety of light and dark: *Flat lighting is typical of Avedon's portraits.*
16 and that's flat! *BrE spoken old-fashioned* used to say that you will definitely not change what you have just said; ◧ **and that's that**: *I won't go, and that's flat!*
—**flatness** *n* [U] → **in/into a flat spin** at SPIN² (6); → FLAT FEET

flat² [S2] [W3] *n* [C]
1 PLACE TO LIVE *especially BrE* a place for people to live that consists of a set of rooms that are part of a larger building; ◧ **apartment**: *They have a flat in Crouch End.* | *a two-bedroom flat* | *The building was knocked down to make way for a block of flats* (=a large building with many flats in it). → GRANNY FLAT
2 TYRE *especially AmE* a tyre that does not have enough air inside; ◧ **flat tyre**: *Damn, the car has a flat.* | *He stopped to change a flat.*
3 MUSIC **a)** a musical note that is one SEMITONE lower than a particular note **b)** the sign (♭) in written music that shows that a note is one SEMITONE lower than a particular note; → **sharp**, **natural**
4 LAND flats [plural] an area of land that is at a low level, especially near water: *mud flats*
5 SHOES flats [plural] *AmE* a pair of women's shoes with very low heels

6 the flat of sb's hand/a knife/a sword etc the flat part or flat side of something
7 on the flat *BrE* on ground that is level and does not slope

flat³ *adv*
1 FLAT POSITION in a position in which the surface of something is against another surface without curving or sloping: *The bed can be folded flat for storage.* | *He lay flat on the floor.* | *That night I lay flat on my back and stared up at the ceiling.*
2 three minutes/10 seconds etc flat *informal* in exactly three minutes, ten seconds etc – used to emphasize that something happens or is done very quickly: *I was dressed in five minutes flat.*
3 fall flat *informal* if a joke, story etc falls flat, it does not achieve the effect that is intended: *Unfortunately, what could have been a powerful drama fell flat.*
4 MUSIC if you sing or play music flat, you sing or play slightly lower than the correct note so that the sound is unpleasant; ◨ **sharp**
5 fall flat on your face a) to fall so that you are lying on your chest on the ground: *Babe slipped and fell flat on her face.* **b)** *informal* to not have the result you want or expect, especially when this is embarrassing: *The theory falls flat on its face when put into practice.*
6 flat out *informal* **a)** as fast as possible: *Everyone's working flat out to finish on time.* **b)** *AmE* in a direct and complete way; ◨ **straight out**: **ask/tell sb flat out** *She asked him flat out if he was seeing another woman.*
7 tell sb flat *BrE spoken* to tell someone something directly and definitely; ◨ **straight out**: *I told him flat that I didn't want to see him again.* → **flat broke** at BROKE² (1)

flat·bed /'flætbed/ *adj* [only before noun] having a flat surface to put something on: *a flatbed scanner* | *a flatbed truck* —**flatbed** *n* [C]

,flat 'cap *n* [C] *BrE* a cap made of cloth, with a stiff piece that sticks out at the front

flat·car /'flætkɑː $ -kɑːr/ *n* [C] *AmE* a railway carriage without a roof or sides, used for carrying goods

,flat-'chested *adj* a woman who is flat-chested has small breasts

,flat 'feet *n* [plural] a medical condition in which someone's feet rest flat on the ground because the middle of each foot is not as curved as it should be

flat·fish /'flæt,fɪʃ/ *n plural* **flatfish** [C] a type of sea fish with a thin flat body, such as COD or PLAICE

,flat-'footed *adj* **1** having flat feet **2** *informal* moving in an awkward way; ◨ **clumsy**: *The defence looked flat-footed as Sutton scored easily.* **3 catch sb flat-footed** *AmE* to surprise someone so that they cannot do something in the way they ought to; ◨ **catch sb off guard**: *The President's announcement seemed to catch Democrats flat-footed.*

flat·let /'flætlət/ *n* [C] *BrE* a small apartment

flat·line /'flætlaɪn/ *v* **be flatlining** to be at a low level or standard that is neither increasing nor decreasing: *The Tories have been flatlining in the polls for the last three months.*

flat·ly /'flætli/ *adv* **1 flatly refuse/deny/oppose etc sth** to say something in a direct and definite way that is not likely to change: *He flatly denied ever having met the woman.* **2** without showing any emotion: *'Aunt Alicia has changed her will,' she said flatly.*

flat·mate /'flætmeɪt/ *n* [C] *BrE* someone who shares a flat with one or more other people; ◨ **roommate** *AmE*

,flat-pack also ,flat pack *n* [C] *BrE* furniture that is sold as parts in a box and has to be put together: *flat-pack furniture*

,flat ,racing *n* [U] *BrE* horse racing without any fences on flat ground; → **steeplechase**

flat·ten /'flætn/ *v* **1** also **flatten out** [I,T] to make something flat or flatter, or to become flat or flatter: *Use a rolling pin to flatten the dough.* | *The land flattened out as we neared the coast.* **2** [T] to destroy a building or town by knocking it down, bombing it etc; ◨ **level**:

Hundreds of homes were flattened by the tornado. **3 flatten yourself against sth** to press your body against something: *I flattened myself against the wall.* **4** [T] *informal* to defeat someone completely and easily in a game, argument etc: *We flattened them 6–0.* **5** [T] *informal* to hit someone very hard

flat·ter /'flætə $ -ər/ *v* [T] **1** to praise someone in order to please them or get something from them, even though you do not mean it: *Perry would always flatter Mrs. Mitchell by praising her cooking.* **2** to make someone look as attractive as they can; ◨ **suit**: *That dress really flatters your figure.* **3** to make something look or seem more important or better than it is: *Lewis's novel doesn't flatter Midwestern attitudes and morals.* **4 flatter yourself** if you flatter yourself that something is true about your abilities or achievements, you make yourself believe it is true, although it is not: **flatter yourself that** *She flatters herself that she could have been a model.* —**flatterer** *n* [C]

flat·tered /'flætəd $ -ərd/ *adj* [not before noun] pleased because someone has shown you that they like or admire you: *We were flattered by all the attention.*

flat·ter·ing /'flætərɪŋ/ *adj* clothes, pictures etc that are flattering make someone look as attractive as they can or make something as good as possible, even if it is not really very good: *That colour is very flattering.*

flat·ter·y /'flætəri/ *n* [U] **1** praise that you do not really mean **2 flattery will get you nowhere/everywhere** used humorously when someone has praised you and you want to say that you will help them or not help them

flat·top /'flættɒp $ -tɑːp/ *n* [C] a type of hair style that is very short and looks flat on top → see picture at HAIRSTYLE

flat·u·lence /'flætjʊləns $ -tʃə-/ *n* [U] the condition of having too much gas in the stomach —**flatulent** *adj*

flat·ware /'flæt,weə $ -,wer/ *n* [U] *AmE* knives, forks, and spoons; ◨ **cutlery**

flaunt /flɔːnt $ flɒːnt, flɑːnt/ *v* [T] **1** to show your money, success, beauty etc so that other people notice it – used to show disapproval: *The rich flaunted their wealth while the poor starved on the streets.* **2 if you've got it, flaunt it** *spoken* used humorously to tell someone not to hide their beauty, wealth, or abilities

flau·tist /'flɔːtɪst $ 'flɒː-/ *n* [C] *BrE* someone who plays the FLUTE; ◨ **flutist** *AmE*

fla·va /'fleɪvʌ/ *n* [U] *informal* a quality that something has that makes you feel or think a particular way about it; ◨ **flavour**: *music with a little bit of Caribbean flava*

fla·vour¹ *BrE*; **flavor** *AmE* /'fleɪvə $ -ər/ *n* **1** [C] the particular taste of a food or drink: *Which flavor do you want – chocolate or vanilla?* | [+of] *a dry wine with flavors of honey and apricot* | **a nutty/smoky/bitter etc flavour** *White poppy seeds have a distinctive nutty flavour.* | **a delicate/strong/rich etc flavour** *The cheese is firm in texture and has a strong flavour.* **2** [U] the quality of tasting good: **add/give flavour (to sth)** *A pinch of herbs will add flavour to any dish.* **3** [C,U] a substance used to give something a particular taste; ◨ **flavouring**: *artificial flavours* **4** [singular] a quality or feature that makes something have a particular style or character: *The stories have a strong regional flavour.* | [+of] *Critics claim the building would destroy the flavor of the neighborhood.* **5** [singular] an idea of what the typical qualities of something are: [+of] *Marston's book gives you a flavour of life in the 16th century.* **6 flavour of the month** an idea, person, style etc that is very popular at a particular time

flavour² *BrE*; **flavor** *AmE v* [T] to give something a particular taste or more taste

fla·voured *BrE*; **flavored** *AmE* /'fleɪvəd $ -vərd/ *adj* **1** **strawberry-flavoured/chocolate-flavoured etc**

1 000, 2 000, 3 000, most frequent words in S poken and W ritten English

tasting of STRAWBERRIES, chocolate etc   **2** having had a flavour added: *flavored coffees*

fla·vour·ful *BrE*; **flavorful** *AmE* /'fleɪvəful $ -vər-/ *adj* having a strong pleasant taste: *flavourful cheese*

fla·vour·ing *BrE*; **flavoring** *AmE* /'fleɪvərɪŋ/ *n* [C,U] a substance used to give something a particular flavour or increase its flavour: *This yoghurt contains no artificial flavourings.*

fla·vour·some /'fleɪvəsəm $ -vər-/ *BrE*; **flavorful** *AmE adj* having a strong pleasant taste; ⊟ **bland**: *a flavorful Mexican dish*

flaw /flɔː $ flɒː/ *n* [C]   **1** a mistake, mark, or weakness that makes something imperfect; ⊟ **defect**: [+in] *a flaw in the software* | **serious/major/basic/minor etc flaw** *a slight flaw in the glass* | *A **design flaw** (=a mistake or weakness in the way something was made) caused the engine to explode.*   **2** a mistake or problem in an argument, plan, set of ideas etc: [+of] *Beautiful scenery does not make up for the flaws of this film.* | [+in] *There is a **fundamental flaw** in Walton's argument.* | **fatal flaw** (=a weakness that makes something certain to fail)   **3** a fault in someone's character: *Jealousy is Othello's major flaw.* | *the former President's character flaws*

flawed /flɔːd $ flɒːd/ *adj* spoiled by having mistakes, weaknesses, or by being damaged: *a flawed concept* | **fatally/fundamentally/deeply etc flawed** *The research behind this report is seriously flawed.*

flaw·less /'flɔːləs $ 'flɒː-/ *adj* having no mistakes or marks, or not lacking anything; ⊟ **perfect**: *Adrian's flawless French* —**flawlessly** *adv*

flax /flæks/ *n* [U]   **1** a plant with blue flowers, used for making cloth and oil   **2** the thread made from this plant, used for making LINEN

flax·en /'flæksən/ *adj literary* flaxen hair is light yellow in colour; ⊟ **blond**

flay /fleɪ/ *v* [T]   **1** *formal* to criticize someone very severely: *She was well-known for flaying public officials in her daily column.*   **2** *literary* to whip or beat someone very severely   **3** *formal* to remove the skin from an animal or person, especially one that is dead

flea /fliː/ *n* [C]   **1** a very small insect without wings that jumps and bites animals and people to eat their blood: *Are you sure the dog has fleas?*   **2** **send sb off with a flea in their ear** *BrE* to talk angrily to someone, especially because they have done something you disapprove of

flea·bag /'fliːbæg/ *n* [C] *informal*   **1** *BrE* a dirty animal or person that you dislike   **2** *AmE* also **fleabag hotel** a cheap dirty hotel

flea collar *n* [C] a special collar, worn by a dog or cat, that contains chemicals to keep fleas away from them

flea market *n* [C] a market where old or used goods are sold

flea·pit /'fliː‚pɪt/ *n* [C] *old-fashioned* a cheap dirty cinema or theatre – used humorously

fleck /flek/ *n* [C]   **1** a small mark or spot: [+of] *a black beard with flecks of gray*   **2** a small piece of something: [+of] *flecks of sawdust*

flecked /flekt/ *adj* [not before noun] having small marks or spots, or small pieces of something, covering a surface: [+**with**] *red cloth flecked with white*

fledged /fledʒd/ *adj* → FULLY-FLEDGED

fledg·ling¹, **fledgeling** /'fledʒlɪŋ/ *n* [C] a young bird that is learning to fly

fledgling², **fledgeling** *adj* [only before noun] a fledgling state or organization has only recently been formed and is still developing; → **infant**: *a fledgling republic*

flee /fliː/ *v past tense and past participle* **fled** /fled/ [I,T] *written* to leave somewhere very quickly, in order to escape from danger: *His attackers turned and fled.* | *Masaari spent six months in prison before fleeing the*

country. | [+to/from/into] *Many German artists fled to America at the beginning of World War II.*

fleece¹ /fliːs/ *n*   **1** [C] the woolly coat of a sheep, especially the wool and skin of a sheep when it has been made into a piece of clothing   **2** [U] an artificial soft material used to make warm jackets   **3** [C] *BrE* a jacket made of this artificial material

fleece² *v* [T] *informal* to charge someone too much money for something, especially by tricking them

fleec·y /'fliːsi/ *adj* soft and woolly, or looking soft and woolly: *fleecy white towels*

fleet¹ /fliːt/ *n* [C]   **1** a group of ships, or all the ships in a navy: *the US seventh fleet*   **2** a group of vehicles that are controlled by one company: [+of] *a fleet of taxis*

fleet² *adj literary* fast or quick: *Atalanta was **fleet of foot** (=able to run quickly).*

fleet ‚admiral *n* [C] the highest rank in the US navy, or someone who holds this rank

fleet·ing /'fliːtɪŋ/ *adj* [usually before noun] lasting for only a short time; ⊟ **brief**: *a fleeting smile* | *For one **fleeting moment**, Paula allowed herself to forget her troubles.* | *I caught a **fleeting glimpse** of them as they drove past.* | *Carol was paying a **fleeting visit** to Paris.* —**fleetingly** *adv*

Fleet Street *n* [singular] a street in London where many important newspaper offices used to be, often used as a name for the British newspaper industry

Flem·ish /'flemɪʃ/ *n* [U] a language like German spoken in northern Belgium; → **Dutch**

flesh¹ W3 /fleʃ/ *n* [U]
1 the soft part of the body of a person or animal that is between the skin and the bones: *a freshwater fish with firm white flesh*
2 the skin of the human body: *His flesh was red and covered in sores.*
3 the soft part of a fruit or vegetable that can be eaten: *Cut the melon in half and scoop out the flesh.* → see picture at FRUIT
4 **in the flesh** if you see someone in the flesh, you see someone who you previously had only seen in pictures, films etc: *He looked much shorter in the flesh than on television.*
5 **make sb's flesh creep/crawl** to make someone feel frightened, nervous, or uncomfortable: *The way he stared at her made her flesh creep.*
6 **your own flesh and blood** someone who is part of your family: *How can he treat his own flesh and blood that way?*
7 **the flesh** *literary* the physical human body, as opposed to the mind or spirit: **the pleasures/desires/temptations of the flesh** (=things such as drinking, eating a lot, or having sex)
8 **put flesh on sth** *BrE* to give more details about something to make it clear, more interesting etc; ⊟ **flesh sth ⇔ out**: *I'll try to put some flesh on the plan Margaret has outlined.*
9 **go the way of all flesh** *literary* to die → **get your pound of flesh** at POUND¹ (5); → **press the flesh** at PRESS² (14); → **the spirit is willing but the flesh is weak** at SPIRIT¹ (16)

flesh² *v*
flesh sth ⇔ out *phr v* to add more details to something in order to make it clear, more interesting etc; ⊟ **put flesh on sth**: *You need to flesh out your argument with a few more examples.*

flesh-coloured *BrE*; **flesh-colored** *AmE adj* having a pinkish colour like the colour of white people's skin: *flesh-coloured tights*

flesh·pots /'fleʃpɒts $ -pɑːts/ *n* [plural] areas in a city or town where there are many places that people go to for pleasure, especially sexual pleasure – used humorously

flesh wound *n* [C] a wound that cuts the skin but does not injure the organs and bones inside the body

flesh·y /'fleʃi/ adj **1** having a lot of flesh: *the fleshy part of your hand* **2** having a soft thick inner part: *a plant with fleshy leaves*

flew /fluː/ v the past tense of FLY

flex¹ /fleks/ v [T] **1** to tighten your muscles or bend part of your body **2 flex your muscles** to show your ability to do something, especially your skill or power: *The new role will allow Delaney to flex her acting muscles.*

flex² n [C] *BrE* an electrical wire covered with plastic, used to connect electrical equipment to an electricity supply; ▤ **cord** *AmE*; → **lead**

flex·i·bil·i·ty /ˌfleksᵻˈbɪlᵻti/ n [U] **1** the ability to change or be changed easily to suit a different situation: *Employees expect flexibility in the workplace.* **2** the ability to bend or be bent easily: *Stretching exercises will help your flexibility.*

flex·i·ble /'fleksᵻbəl/ adj **1** a person, plan etc that is flexible can change or be changed easily to suit any new situation; ▨ **inflexible**: *We can be flexible about your starting date.* | **extremely/highly/fairly etc flexible** *Our new computer software is extremely flexible.* | *The government needs a more flexible approach to education.* **2** something that is flexible can bend or be bent easily: *shoes with flexible rubber soles* —**flexibly** adv

flex·i·time /'fleksitaɪm/ *BrE*; **flex·time** /'flekstaɪm/ *AmE* n [U] a system in which people work a particular number of hours each week or month, but can change the times at which they start and finish each day

flick¹ /flɪk/ v **1** [T usually + adv/prep] to make something move away by hitting or pushing it suddenly or quickly, especially with your thumb and finger: *Papa flicked the ash from his cigar.* **2** [I,T always + adv/prep] to move with a sudden quick movement, or to make something move in this way: [+**from/up/down**] *The cow's tail flicked from side to side.* | **flick sth up/down etc** *Jackie flicked her long hair back.* **3** [T] to move a switch so that a machine or piece of electrical equipment starts or stops; ▤ **flip**: *I felt inside the doorway and flicked the light switch.* | **flick sth on/off** *Sandra flicked the TV on.* **4 flick a glance/look at sb/sth** *BrE* to look very quickly at someone or something: *Leith flicked a glance at her watch.* **5** [T] if you flick something such as a TOWEL or rope, you move it so that the end moves quickly away from you: *The old man flicked his whip and the horses moved off.*

  flick through sth *phr v* to look at a book, magazine, set of photographs etc quickly: *Will flicked through Carla's photo album.*

flick² n **1** [C] a short quick sudden movement or hit with a part of your body, whip etc: *With a flick of the wrist, Frye sent the ball into the opposite court.* **2 flick of a switch** used to emphasize how easy it is to start a machine and use it: *I can shut off all the power in the building at the flick of a switch.* **3** [C usually singular] especially *AmE* a film: *an action flick* **4 the flicks** *BrE* old-fashioned the cinema **5 have a flick through sth** *BrE* to look at a book, magazine, set of pictures etc very quickly: *I had a quick flick through your report.*

flick·er¹ /'flɪkə $ -ər/ v [I] **1** to burn or shine with an unsteady light that goes on and off quickly: *The overhead lights flickered momentarily.* **2** [always + adv/prep] if an emotion or expression flickers on someone's face or through their mind, it exists or is shown for only a short time: [+**across/through/on etc**] *A puzzled smile flickered across the woman's face.* **3** to quickly make a sudden small movement or series of movements: *Polly's eyelids flickered, then she slept.*

flicker² n [C] **1** an unsteady light that goes on and off quickly: [+**of**] *the flicker of the firelight* **2 a flicker of emotion/uncertainty/excitement etc** a feeling or expression that continues for a very short time: *She saw a flicker of doubt in his eyes.* **3** a quick sudden movement or series of movements

flick knife n [C] *BrE* a knife with a blade inside the handle that moves quickly into position when you press a button; ▤ **switchblade** *AmE*

fli·er /'flaɪə $ -ər/ n another spelling of FLYER

flies /flaɪz/ a FLY³ (2)

flight ⓢ₃ ⓦ₂ /flaɪt/ n

1 TRAVEL [C] a journey in a plane or space vehicle, or the plane or vehicle that is making the journey

> **book a flight**
> **catch a flight** (=get on a plane to go somewhere)
> **miss a flight** (=arrive too late to get on a plane)
> **cancel a flight**
> **a long/short flight**
> **a domestic flight** (=to another place in the same country)
> **an international flight** (=to another country)
> **a non-stop/direct flight**
> **a connecting flight** (=a flight to continue a journey, after a previous flight)

*He immediately **booked a flight** to Toulouse.* | *Bernstein **caught** the first **flight** out of Washington.* | *We need to hurry or we'll **miss** our **flight**.* | *All **flights** out of Chicago were **cancelled**.* | *Many people have trouble sleeping after a **long flight**.* | *a **short flight** in a hot air balloon* | *Soon smoking will be banned on all **domestic flights**.* | *The number of **international flights** fell last year.* | *British Airways offers **non-stop flights** from London to Tehran.* | *We only had 20 minutes to make our **connecting flight**.*

2 FLYING [U] when something flies through the air: **in flight** *pelicans in flight* | *In 1968, the first supersonic airliner took flight* (=began flying).

3 MOVEMENT THROUGH AIR [U] an object's or bird's movement through the air: *During its flight, the weapon twists and turns.*

4 STAIRS [C] a set of stairs between one floor and the next: *Bert lives two flights down from here.* | **a flight of stairs/steps** *She fell down a whole flight of stairs.*

5 ESCAPE [U] when you leave a place in order to try and escape from a person or a dangerous situation: [+**from**] *Donald Wood's hasty flight from South Africa early in 1978* | **take flight** also **take to flight** *BrE*: *When the alarm sounded, the whole gang took flight.* | **put sb to flight** (=make someone run away especially by fighting or threatening them)

6 flight of fancy/imagination/fantasy thoughts, ideas etc that are full of imagination but that are not practical or sensible

7 BIRDS [C] a group of birds all flying together: [+**of**] *a flight of swallows* → IN-FLIGHT, TOP-FLIGHT

flight at·tendant n [C] someone who serves food and drinks to passengers on a plane, and looks after their comfort and safety

flight crew n [C] the people, such as the pilot and flight attendants, who work on a plane during a flight

flight deck n [C] **1** the room in a plane where the pilot sits to control the plane **2** the flat surface of a ship which military aircraft use to fly into the air from

flight·less /'flaɪtləs/ adj unable to fly: *a flightless bird*

flight lieu·ten·ant n [C] a middle rank in the British air force, or someone who holds this rank

flight path n [C] the course that a plane or space vehicle travels along

flight re·cord·er n [C] a piece of equipment in an aircraft that records details such as the plane's speed and direction; ▤ **black box**

flight ser·geant n [C] a middle rank in the British air force, or someone who holds this rank

flight sim·u·la·tor n [C] a machine used to train pilots that copies closely the movements and conditions that exist when flying an aircraft

flight·y /'flaɪti/ adj a woman who is flighty changes her ideas and opinions often, and only remains interested in people or things for a short time

flim·flam /'flɪmflæm/ n [U] *old-fashioned informal* information or ideas that are not true or seem very stupid: *I was sick of his intellectual flimflam.*

flim·sy /'flɪmzi/ adj **1** flimsy cloth or clothing is light and thin: *a flimsy cotton dress* **2** something that is flimsy is not strong or well-made, and will break easily: *a flimsy wooden building* **3** a flimsy agreement is weak and can easily be damaged or broken: *a flimsy alliance between the two tribal groups* **4** a flimsy argument or excuse does not seem very likely and people do not believe it; **◪ convincing**: *The evidence against him is extremely flimsy.* | *a flimsy excuse* —**flimsily** adv —**flimsiness** n [U]

flinch /flɪntʃ/ also **flinch away** v [I] **1** to move your face or body away from someone or something because you are in pain, frightened, or upset: [+at] *She flinched at the touch of his hand.* | [+from] *The boy flinched away from him.* **2** to feel embarrassed or upset: [+at] *Jo flinched at her sister's insensitivity.* **3 not flinch from (doing) sth** to be willing to do something even though it is difficult or unpleasant: *He never flinched from doing his duty.*; → **unflinching**

fling¹ /flɪŋ/ v past tense and past participle **flung** /flʌŋ/ [T always + adv/prep]
1 THROW STH to throw something somewhere using a lot of force: **fling sth into sth** *He flung the box into the river.* | *People cheered and flung their hats into the air.* **2 MOVE STH** to throw or move something roughly and carelessly: *He flung his coat over the back of a chair.* | *She flung back the covers and got up.* | *He flung the books aside angrily.* **3 PUSH SB** to push someone roughly, especially so that they fall to the ground; **◪ throw**: *He grabbed her arm and flung her to the ground.* **4 MOVE YOUR BODY** to move yourself or part of your body quickly, using a lot of force; **◪ throw**: *He flung himself down on the bed.* | *She flung her arms round Louise.* **5 SAY STH** to say something to someone in an angry way; **◪ throw**: *fling sth at sb People were flinging all sorts of accusations at her.* | *His own words were flung back at him.* **6 fling sth open** to open a door or window roughly, using a lot of force: *The door was flung open and Selkirk entered.* **7 fling sb in prison/jail** to put someone in prison, often without having a good reason: *Opposition leaders were flung into jail.* **8 fling yourself into sth** to start doing something with a lot of energy: *After the divorce he flung himself into his work to forget her.* **9 fling yourself at sb a)** to move suddenly towards someone in order to attack them or hold them: *He flung himself at her and snatched the bag.* | *The children flung themselves at him, squealing with joy.* **b)** *informal* to show in a very clear, open way that you want to have a sexual relationship with someone – used to show disapproval

fling sth ⇔ **off** phr v
to quickly remove a piece of clothing; **◪ tear off**: *He flung off his coat.*

fling sb/sth ⇔ **out** phr v BrE informal
1 to make someone leave a place when they do not want to; **◪ throw out**: [+of] *He was flung out of school for swearing at a teacher.*
2 to get rid of something you no longer want or need; **◪ throw out**: *If it doesn't work, just fling it out.*

fling² n [C usually singular] **1** a short and not very serious sexual relationship: *They had a brief fling a few years ago.* **2** a short period of time during which you enjoy yourself without worrying about anything: *He sees this as his final fling before he retires.*

flint /flɪnt/ n **1** [U] a type of smooth hard stone that makes a small flame when you hit it with steel **2** [C] a piece of this stone or a small piece of metal that makes a small flame when you hit it with steel

flint·y /'flɪnti/ adj **1** *literary* not showing any emotions; **◪ hard, icy**: *flinty look/stare Duvall gave him a flinty stare.* **2** like flint or containing flint

flip¹ /flɪp/ v **flipped, flipping**
1 MOVE [I,T always + adv/prep] to move something with a quick sudden movement so that it is in a different position: *He flipped the top off the bottle and poured himself a drink.* | *She flipped the lid of the box open and looked inside.* | [+over] *He flipped the paper over and started writing on the back.*
2 TURN IN THE AIR [T] to make a flat object such as a coin go upwards and turn over in the air; **◪ toss**: *We flipped a coin to see who would go first.* | *There's quite an art to flipping pancakes.*
3 ANGRY [I] *informal* to suddenly become very angry or upset; **◪ lose it**: *I just flipped and started shouting.*
4 TURN A SWITCH [T] to move a switch so that a machine or piece of electrical equipment starts or stops; **◪ flick**: *Anna flipped the switch that opened the front gate.* | **flip sth on/off** *Josie flipped on the radio.*
5 TURN PAGES [I,T] to turn the pages of a book or newspaper quickly, especially because you are looking for something: *He picked up the newspaper and flipped straight to the sports pages.* | [+through] *I flipped through my address book but couldn't find her phone number.*
6 flip your lid *informal* to suddenly become very angry; **◪ go crazy**: *Mom flipped her lid when she found out I was pregnant.*

flip sb ⇔ **off** phr v AmE informal
also **flip sb the bird** to make a rude sign at someone by lifting up your middle finger and keeping your other fingers down

flip² n [C] **1** an action in which you make a flat object such as a coin go upwards and turn over in the air; **◪ toss**: *In the end the decision was made by the flip of a coin.* **2** a movement in which you jump up and turn over in the air, so that your feet go over your head; **◪ somersault**: *I tripped and almost did a backward flip down the stairs.* **3** an action in which you turn the pages of a book or newspaper quickly, especially because you are looking for something; **◪ flick**: [+through] *I had a quick flip through my cookery books and found a recipe that sounded quite nice.*

flip³ adj informal not said or meant seriously; **◪ flippant**: *I was fed up with his flip comments.*

flip chart n [C] a set of large pieces of paper that are connected at the top so that you can turn the pages over to present information to people → see picture at OFFICE

flip-flop v **flip-flopped, flip-flopping** [I] AmE informal to change your opinion about something —**flip-flop** n [C]: *an incredible political flip-flop*

flip-flops n [plural] open summer shoes, usually made of rubber, with a V-shaped band across the front to hold your feet; **◪ thongs** AmE

flip·pant /'flɪpənt/ adj not being serious about something that other people think you should be serious about: *a rather flippant remark* | [+about] *You shouldn't be flippant about such things.* —**flippantly** adv —**flippancy** n [U]: *This is no time for flippancy.*

flip·per /'flɪpə $ -ər/ n [C] **1** a flat part on the body of some large sea animals such as SEALS, that they use for swimming **2** a large flat rubber shoe that you wear to help you swim faster

flip phone n [C] a MOBILE PHONE that has a cover which opens upwards

flip·ping /'flɪpɪŋ/ adj, adv BrE spoken used to show that you are slightly annoyed about something: *It's too flipping cold to go outside!* | *This flipping pen doesn't work!*

flip side n [singular] **1** the bad effects of something that also has good effects: *The flip side of the treatment is that it can make patients feel very tired.* **2** old-fashioned the side of a record that does not have the main song on

flirt¹ /flɜːt $ flɜːrt/ v [I] to behave towards someone in a way that shows that you are sexually attracted to them, although you do not really want a relationship with them: [+with] *She accused him of flirting with* *other women.* | *She was flirting outrageously* (=a lot) *with some of the managers.*

flirt with sth *phr v* **1** to consider doing something, but not be very serious about it: *He had flirted with the idea of emigrating.* **2** to do something that is dangerous or could cause problems for you: *Climbers enjoy flirting with danger.*

flirt² *n* [C] someone who flirts with people: **a terrible/ dreadful etc flirt** (=someone who flirts a lot) *She's an incorrigible flirt!*

flir·ta·tion /flɜːˈteɪʃən $ flɜːr-/ *n* **1** [C] a short period of time during which you are interested in something: [+with] *He started his own business last year, after a brief flirtation with political life.* **2** [U] behaviour that shows you are attracted to someone sexually: *She had no objection to a little mild flirtation.* **3** [C] a short sexual relationship which is not serious: ◻ **fling**: [+with] *She had a brief flirtation with one of the maths students.*

flir·ta·tious /flɜːˈteɪʃəs $ flɜːr-/ *adj* behaving in a way that deliberately tries to attract sexual attention: *She gave him a flirtatious smile.* | *a flirtatious giggle* —**flirtatiously** *adv* —**flirtatiousness** *n* [U]

flit /flɪt/ *v* **flitted, flitting** [I always + adv/prep] to move lightly or quickly and not stay in one place for very long: *Birds flitted about in the trees above them.* | *She seemed to spend her life flitting from one country to another.* | *His eyes flitted to his watch.*

float¹ /fləʊt $ floʊt/ *v*
1 ON WATER **a)** [I] to stay or move on the surface of a liquid without sinking: *I wasn't sure if the raft would float.* | *She spent the afternoon floating on her back in the pool.* | [+along/down/past etc] *A couple of broken branches floated past us.* **b)** [T] to put something on the surface of a liquid so that it does not sink: *The logs are trimmed and then floated down the river.*
2 IN THE AIR [I always + adv/prep] if something floats, it moves slowly through the air or stays up in the air: *I looked up at the clouds floating in the sky.* | *Leaves floated gently down from the trees.*
3 MUSIC/SOUNDS/SMELLS ETC [I always + adv/prep] if sounds or smells float somewhere, people in another place can hear or smell them: *The sound of her voice came floating down from an upstairs window.*
4 WALK GRACEFULLY [I] to walk in a slow light graceful way: ◻ **glide**: *Rachel floated around the bedroom in a lace nightgown.*
5 IDEAS [T] to suggest an idea or plan in order to see if people like it: *We first floated the idea back in 1992.*
6 MONEY [T] *technical* if the government of a country floats its money, the value of the money is allowed to change freely in relation to money from other countries: *Russia decided to float the rouble on the foreign exchange market.*
7 COMPANY [T] to sell SHARES in a company or business to the public for the first time: **float sth on sth** *The company will be floated on the stockmarket next year.* → FLOTATION (1)
8 CHEQUE [T] *AmE* to write a cheque when you do not have enough money in the bank to pay it
float around *phr v informal*
to be present in a place: *There's a lot of cash floating around in the economy at the moment.*

float² *n* [C]
1 VEHICLE a large vehicle that is decorated to drive through the streets as part of a special event: *We stood and watched the Carnival floats drive past.*
2 DRINK *AmE* a sweet drink that has ice cream floating in it
3 FOR FISHING a small light object that floats on the surface of the water, used by people to catch fish to show where their line is → see picture at FISHING
4 FOR SWIMMING a flat light object that you can rest part of your body on in water to help you learn to swim
5 MONEY a small amount of money that someone in a shop keeps so that they have enough money to give change to people

6 RELAXATION a time when you sit in a FLOTATION TANK in order to treat illness or injury, or to relax

floa·ta·tion /fləʊˈteɪʃən $ floʊ-/ *n* a British spelling of FLOTATION

float·ing¹ /ˈfləʊtɪŋ $ ˈfloʊ-/ *adj* [only before noun] often changing, and not staying the same: *You can choose either a fixed or floating interest rate for the loan.* | *The area has a large floating population.*

floating² *n* [U] the activity of sitting in a FLOTATION TANK in order to relax, or to treat illness or injury

floating voter *n* [C] someone who does not always vote for the same political party at elections

flock¹ /flɒk $ flɑːk/ *n* **1** [C] a group of sheep, goats, or birds: [+of] *a flock of small birds* **2** [C usually singular] a large group of people; ◻ **crowd**: [+of] *a flock of children* **3** [C usually singular] a priest's flock is the group of people who regularly attend his or her church **4** [U] small pieces of wool or cotton that are used for filling CUSHIONS **5** also **flocking** /ˈflɒkɪŋ $ ˈflɑː-/ *AmE* [U] a soft substance that is used to make patterns on the surface of WALLPAPER, curtains etc

flock² *v* [I always +adv/prep] if people flock to a place, they go there in large numbers because something interesting or exciting is happening there: [+to/into/ down etc] *People have been flocking to the exhibition.* | **flock to do sth** *Tourists flock to see the town's medieval churches and buildings.*

floe /fləʊ $ floʊ/ *n* [C] an ICE FLOE

flog /flɒg $ flɑːg/ *v* **flogged, flogging** [T] **1** to beat a person or animal with a whip or stick: *He was publicly flogged and humiliated.* **2** *informal* to sell something: *I'm going to flog all my old video tapes.* **3 be flogging a dead horse** *spoken* to be wasting time or effort by trying to do something that is impossible **4 flog sth to death** *BrE informal* to repeat a story or use an idea etc so often that people become bored with it: *They take a good idea and flog it to death.*

flog·ging /ˈflɒgɪŋ $ ˈflɑːgɪŋ/ *n* [C] a punishment in which someone is severely beaten with a whip or stick

flood¹ [S3] /flʌd/ *v*
1 COVER WITH WATER [I,T] to cover a place with water, or to become covered with water: *Towns and cities all over the country have been flooded.* | *The houses down by the river flood quite regularly.*
2 RIVER [I,T] if a river floods, it is too full, and spreads water over the land around it: *There are now fears that the river could flood.*
3 GO/ARRIVE IN LARGE NUMBERS [I always + adv/ prep] to arrive or go somewhere in large numbers; ◻ **pour, flow**: *Refugees are still flooding across the border.* | *Donations have been flooding in since we launched the appeal.*
4 flood sth with sth to send a very large number of things to a place or organization: *a plan to flood the country with forged banknotes*
5 be flooded with sth to receive so many letters, complaints, or inquiries that you cannot deal with them all easily: *We've been flooded with offers of help.*
6 flood the market to produce and sell a very large number of one type of thing, so that the price goes down: [+with] *Car manufacturers have been accused of flooding the market with cheap cars.*
7 LIGHT [I,T] if light floods a place or floods into it, it makes it very light and bright: [+into] *Light flooded into the kitchen.* | **flood sth with sth** *The morning sun flooded the room with a gentle light.*
8 FEELING [I always + adv/prep,T] if a feeling or memory floods over you or floods back, you feel or remember it very strongly: [+over/back] *I felt happiness and relief flooding over me.* | *Memories of my time in Paris flooded back.*
9 ENGINE [I,T] if an engine floods or if you flood it, it has too much petrol in it, so that it will not start

F

be flooded out phr v

to be forced to leave your home because of floods

flood² S3 n

1 [C,U] a very large amount of water that covers an area that is usually dry: *The village was cut off by floods.* | *the worst floods for over fifty years*

2 [C] a very large number of things or people that arrive at the same time: [+of] *The UN appealed for help with the **flood of refugees** crossing the border.*

3 in **floods of tears** crying a lot: *She came downstairs in floods of tears.*

4 in **flood** a river that is in flood has much more water in it than usual → **flash flood** at FLASH³ (1)

flood·gate /'flʌdgeɪt/ n [C] **1 open the floodgates a)** if something opens the floodgates, or if the floodgates open, it suddenly becomes possible for a lot of things to happen which were prevented from happening before: *If this case is successful it could open the floodgates for thousands of similar claims.* | *There are fears that the floodgates will open and large numbers of parents will take their children out of school.* **b)** if the floodgates open, or if something opens the floodgates, someone begins to cry and show their emotions after keeping them hidden: *His display of kindness to her opened the floodgates again, and she began to sob loudly.* **2** a gate that is used to control the flow of water from a large lake or river

flood·ing /'flʌdɪŋ/ n [U] a situation in which an area of land becomes covered with water, for example because of heavy rain: *The heavy rain has led to **serious flooding** in some areas.* | *The river banks have been built up to prevent flooding.*

flood·light /'flʌdlaɪt/ n [C] a very bright light that is used to light the outside of a building or sports ground at night: *The church was lit up by floodlights.* | **under floodlights** *The game will be played under floodlights.*

flood·lit /'flʌdlɪt/ adj surrounded by floodlights so that people can see at night: *a floodlit football pitch*

flood·plain n [C] the large area of flat land on either side of a river that is sometimes covered with water when the river becomes too full

flood tide n [C] the flow of the sea in towards the land; → **ebb tide**

flood·wa·ter /'flʌdwɔːtə $ -wɒːtər, -wɑː-/ n [plural, U] water that covers an area during a flood

floor¹ S1 W1 /flɔː $ flɔːr/ n [C]

1 IN A BUILDING the flat surface that you stand on inside a building: *a polished wooden floor* | *There was a puddle of water on the kitchen floor.* | *a warehouse that has 410,000 square feet of **floor space*** → see box at GROUND¹

2 IN A CAR BrE the part of a car that forms its inside floor; **▤ floorboard** AmE

3 LEVEL IN BUILDING one of the levels in a building: *a ground floor flat* | **on the top/first/tenth etc floor** *Our office is on the top floor.* | [+of] *We are located on the seventh floor of the building.*; → see box at STOREY

4 OCEAN/FOREST/CAVE FLOOR ETC the ground at the bottom of the ocean, the forest etc: *creatures that live on the ocean floor* → see box at GROUND¹

5 FOR DANCING an area in a room where people can dance: *There were two or three couples already on the **dance floor**.* | **take (to) the floor** (=begin dancing) *Everyone took to the floor for the last waltz.*

6 WHERE PEOPLE WORK a large area in a building where a lot of people do their jobs: *The stock market floor was wildly busy.* | *He wasn't keen on the idea of working on the **shop floor*** (=the part of a factory where people make things using machines).

7 LIMIT an officially agreed limit below which something cannot go; → ceiling: *Manufacturers have tried to **put a floor under** the price of their products.*

8 the floor a) the people attending a public meeting: *Are there any questions from the floor?* **b)** the part of a parliament, public meeting place etc where people sit:

The delegates crowded the floor of the House.

9 take the floor to begin speaking at an important public meeting: *The chairman then took the floor.*

10 have the floor to be speaking or have the right to speak at an important public meeting: *He stepped aside to allow other speakers to have the floor.*

11 go through the floor if a price, amount etc goes through the floor, it becomes very low; **▤ go through the roof**: *In the past few years share prices have gone through the floor.*

floor² v [T] **1** to surprise or shock someone so much that they do not know what to say or do: *A couple of the questions completely floored me.* **2** to hit someone so hard that they fall down: *He was floored in the first round of the fight.* **3** AmE informal to make a car go as fast as possible: *I got into the car and **floored it**.*

floor·board /'flɔːbɔːd $ 'flɔːrbɔːrd/ n [C] **1** a board in a wooden floor: *I lifted the carpet to check the floorboards for damp and woodworm.* **2** AmE the floor in a car

floor·ing /'flɔːrɪŋ/ n [U] any material that is used to make or cover floors: *We've chosen wood flooring for the hall.* | *vinyl flooring*

floor lamp n [C] AmE a tall lamp that stands on the floor; **▤ standard lamp** BrE

floor-length adj [only before noun] long enough to reach the floor: *floor-length curtains* | *a floor-length skirt*

floor plan n [C] a drawing of the shape of a room or building and the position of things in it, as seen from above; **▤ ground plan**

floor show n [C] a performance by singers, dancers etc at a NIGHTCLUB

floo·zy, floozie /'fluːzi/ n plural **floozies** [C] old-fashioned a woman who has sexual relationships with a lot of different men, in a way that you disapprove of

flop¹ /flɒp $ flɑːp/ v **flopped, flopping** [I] **1** [always + adv/prep] to sit or lie down in a relaxed way, by letting all your weight fall heavily onto a chair etc: *He flopped down onto the bed.* | *I got home and flopped in front of the TV.* **2** [always + adv/prep] to hang or fall loosely, in an uncontrolled way: *His head flopped back pathetically.* **3** informal if something such as a product, play, or idea flops, it is not successful because people do not like it

flop² n **1** [C] informal a film, play, product etc that is not successful; **▤ hit: disastrous/spectacular etc flop** *The film was a complete flop.* **2** [singular] the movement or noise that something makes when it falls heavily: *He fell with a flop into the water.* → BELLY FLOP

flop·house /'flɒphaʊs $ 'flɑːp-/ n [C] AmE informal a very cheap hotel where people can stay when they have very little money and nowhere to live; **▤ doss house** BrE

flop·py /'flɒpi $ 'flɑːpi/ adj something that is floppy is soft and hangs down loosely rather than being stiff: *a floppy hat* | *a dog with long floppy ears*

floppy disk also **floppy** n [C] a square piece of plastic that you can store computer information on, and which you can remove from and put into a computer; → **hard disk**

flo·ra /'flɔːrə/ n [U] all the plants that grow in a particular place or country: *Tourism is damaging the **flora and fauna*** (=plants and animals) *of the island.*

flo·ral /'flɔːrəl/ adj made of flowers or decorated with flowers or pictures of flowers: *a scarf with a bold floral* pattern | *a pretty floral dress* | *a light floral fragrance* | *There were **floral tributes*** (=flowers sent as a sign of respect after someone has died) *from friends and colleagues.*

flor·id /'flɒrɪd $ 'flɔː-, 'flɑː-/ *adj literary* **1** a florid face is red in colour: *a middle-aged man with a florid complexion* **2** florid language, music, or art has a lot of extra unnecessary details or decorations: *a book written in a very florid style*

flor·in /'flɒrɪn $ 'flɔː-, 'flɑː-/ *n* [C] a coin that was used in Britain before 1971, worth about 10p

flor·ist /'flɒrɪst $ 'flɔː-/ *n* [C] **1** someone who owns or works in a shop that sells flowers and indoor plants for the home → see picture at OCCUPATION **2** also **florist's** a shop that sells flowers and indoor plants for the home

floss¹ /flɒs $ flaːs, flɔːs/ *n* [U] **1** a type of thin thread that you use for cleaning between your teeth; ☐ **dental floss** **2** a type of thin thread that you use for sewing

floss² *v* [T] to clean between your teeth using floss

flo·ta·tion /fləʊˈteɪʃən $ floʊ-/ *n* [C,U] **1** a time when SHARES in a company are made available for people to buy for the first time: *The company has decided to postpone its flotation on the stock market until next year.* **2** **flotation chamber/compartment etc** a container filled with air or gas, fixed to something to make it float

floˈtation ˌtank *n* [C] a large container full of warm salty water, often with a cover on it to make it dark inside, that you float in so that you can relax, or to treat illness or injury

flo·til·la /fləˈtɪlə $ floʊ-/ *n* [C] a group of small ships

flot·sam /'flɒtsəm $ 'flɑː-/ *n* [U] **1** broken pieces of wood and other things from a wrecked ship, floating in the sea or scattered on the shore: *He would walk along the beach collecting the **flotsam and jetsam** that had been washed ashore.* **2** things that people no longer want and so throw away: *works of art made from the **flotsam and jetsam** of everyday life* **3** people who are very poor and do not have jobs or homes: *Camps were set up to shelter the **flotsam and jetsam** of the war.*

flounce¹ /flaʊns/ *v* [I always + adv/prep] to walk in a quick determined way without looking at people because you are angry: *She flounced out of the room.*

flounce² *n* **1** [C] a band of cloth that is stitched onto a curtain or a piece of clothing in folds as a decoration: *a group of local girls dressed in frills and flounces* **2** [singular] a way of walking in a quick determined way without looking at people, because you are angry: *She walked off with a flounce.*

flounced /flaʊnst/ *adj* decorated with flounces: *a flounced skirt*

floun·der¹ /'flaʊndə $ -ər/ *v* [I] **1** to not know what to say or do because you feel confused or upset: *I found myself floundering as I tried to answer her questions.* | *'I'm sorry,' she **floundered** helplessly.* **2** to have a lot of problems and be likely to fail completely: *More and more firms are floundering because of the recession.* **3** [always + adv/prep] to be unable to move easily because you are in deep water or mud, or cannot see very well: *They were floundering chest-deep in the freezing water.* | [+around] *I could hear them floundering around in the dark.*

flounder² *n plural* **flounder** *or* **flounders** [C,U] a type of small fish that you can eat

flour¹ /flaʊə $ flaʊr/ *n* [U] a powder that is made by crushing wheat or other grain and is used for making bread, cakes etc: **white/wholemeal/rice/wheat etc flour** → PLAIN FLOUR, SELF-RAISING FLOUR

flour² *v* [T] to cover a surface with flour when you are cooking: *Roll the pastry out on a lightly floured board.*

flour·ish¹ /'flʌrɪʃ $ 'flɜːrɪʃ/ *v* **1** [I] to develop well and be successful; ☐ **thrive**: *The economy is booming and small businesses are flourishing.* **2** [I] to grow well and be very healthy; → **thrive**: *Most plants will flourish in the rich deep soils here.* **3** [T] to wave something in

your hand in order to make people notice it: *She walked quickly to the desk, flourishing her cheque book.*

flour·ish² *n* **1** **with a flourish** with a large confident movement that makes people notice you: *He opened his wallet with a flourish and took out a handful of notes.* **2** [usually singular] a special or impressive part of something: *There's nothing like a luxurious dessert to give a menu a **final flourish**.* | **with a flourish** *They finished the season with a flourish, winning their last three matches.* **3** [C] a loud part of a piece of music, played especially when an important person enters: *a flourish of trumpets* **4** [C] a curved line that you use to decorate writing

flour·y /'flaʊəri $ 'flaʊri/ *adj* **1** covered with flour or tasting of flour: *She wiped her floury hands on her apron.* **2** floury potatoes become very soft and break easily when they are cooked

flout /flaʊt/ *v* [T] to deliberately disobey a law, rule etc, without trying to hide what you are doing: *Some companies flout the rules and employ children as young as seven.* | **deliberately/openly flout sth** *The union had openly flouted the law.*

flow¹ S2 W2 /fləʊ $ floʊ/ *n*

1 **LIQUID/GAS/ELECTRICITY** [C usually singular] a smooth steady movement of liquid, gas, or electricity: [+of] *He struggled to swim against the flow of the water.* | *I tied a towel round his leg to try to **stem the flow** of blood.*

2 **TRAFFIC** [C usually singular, U] the steady movement of traffic: *a new road system to improve traffic flow through the city centre*

3 **GOODS/PEOPLE/INFORMATION** [C usually singular] the movement of goods, people, or information from one place to another: [+of] *the flow of funds from the US to Europe* | *There has been a **steady flow** of people leaving the area.* | *They have accused the government of trying to block the **free flow** of information.* | *an attempt to **stem the flow** of refugees across the border*

4 **SPEECH/WRITING** [U] the continuous stream of words or ideas when someone is speaking, writing, or thinking about something: *I didn't want to **interrupt** her flow, so I said nothing.*

5 **OF THE SEA** [singular] the regular movement of the sea towards the land: *the **ebb and flow** of the tide*

6 **in full flow** *informal* if someone is in full flow, they are busy talking about something and seem likely to continue for a long time

7 **go with the flow** to agree that you will do the thing that most people want to do: *I don't mind, I'll just go with the flow.*

8 **go against the flow** to do something very different from what other people are doing → CASH FLOW; → **ebb and flow** at EBB¹ (3)

flow² S3 *v* [I]

1 **LIQUID/GAS/ELECTRICITY** when a liquid, gas, or electricity flows, it moves in a steady continuous stream: [+over/down/through etc] *These gates regulate the amount of water flowing into the canal.* | *If the windows are shut, air cannot **flow freely** through the building.*

2 **GOODS/PEOPLE/INFORMATION** [always + adv/prep] if goods, people, or information flow from one place to another, they move there in large numbers or amounts; ☐ **pour, flood**: *Money has been flowing into the country from Western aid agencies.* | *The number of refugees flowing into the area is still increasing.*

3 **TRAFFIC** if traffic flows, it moves easily from one place to another: *The new one-way system should help the traffic to flow better.*

4 **ALCOHOL** if alcohol flows at a party, people drink a lot and there is a lot available: *Beer and whisky flowed freely as the evening wore on.*

5 **WORDS/IDEAS** if conversation or ideas flow, people talk or have ideas steadily and continuously, without anything stopping or interrupting them: *Everyone was relaxed and the conversation flowed freely.*

F

F

6 SEA when the sea flows, it moves towards the land: *We watched the tide **ebb and flow**.*

7 FEELINGS if a feeling flows through you or over you, you feel it strongly: [+**through/over**] *She felt hot rage flowing through her.*

8 CLOTHES/HAIR if clothing or hair flows, it falls or hangs loosely and gracefully: *Her long hair flowed down her back.*

9 flow from sth to happen as a result of something: *the political consequences that flowed from this decision*

flow chart also **'flow ,diagram** n [C] a drawing that uses shapes and lines to show how the different stages in a process are connected to each other → see picture at CHART

flow·er¹ S2 W2 /'flaʊə $ -ər/ n [C]
1 a coloured or white part that a plant or tree produces before fruit or seeds: *a lovely rose bush with delicate pink flowers* | *fields full of beautiful **wild flowers***
2 a small plant that produces beautiful flowers: *He wasn't interested in growing flowers in the garden.* | *She bent down and **picked** a **flower**.* | **bunch/bouquet of flowers** *The first night we met he gave me a bunch of flowers.* | *a beautiful **flower arrangement*** (=flowers arranged together in an attractive way)
3 in flower a plant or tree that is in flower has flowers on it: *It was May, and the apple trees were all in flower.* | *Roses start to **come into flower** in June.*
4 the flower of sth literary the best part of something: *young men killed in the flower of their youth*

flower² v [I] **1** to produce flowers: *Bulbs that you plant in the autumn should flower the following spring.* **2** literary to develop in a very successful way: *the economic and social conditions that will allow democracy to flower*

'flower ar,ranging n [U] the skill of arranging flowers in an attractive way

flow·er·bed /'flaʊəbed $ -ər-/ n [C] an area of ground, for example in a garden, in which flowers are grown

'flower child n plural **flower children** [C] a young person in the 1960s and 70s who was against war and wanted peace and love in society

flow·ered /'flaʊəd $ -ərd/ adj decorated with a pattern of flowers; ☐ **floral, flowery**: *a flowered silk dress*

'flower girl n [C] AmE a young girl who carries flowers at a wedding ceremony

flow·er·ing /'flaʊərɪŋ/ n **the flowering of sth** formal when something develops in a very successful way: *The nineteenth century saw a flowering of science and technology.*

flow·er·pot /'flaʊəpɒt $ -ərpɑːt/ n [C] a plastic or clay pot in which you grow plants → see picture at POT

'flower ,power n [U] the ideas of young people in the 1960s and 70s who believed that peace and love were the most important things in life

flow·er·y /'flaʊəri/ adj **1** decorated with a pattern of flowers; ☐ **floral, flowered**: *a flowery cotton dress* **2** a flowery place has a lot of flowers growing in it: *a flowery meadow* **3** a flowery smell or taste is strong and sweet, like flowers: *her flowery perfume* **4** flowery speech or writing uses complicated and rare words instead of simple clear language: *flowery language*

flow·ing /'flaʊɪŋ $ 'floʊ-/ adj **1** hanging or moving in a smooth graceful way: *She had pale skin and dark, flowing hair.* | *long, flowing robes* **2** continuing in a smooth, graceful way, with no sudden changes: *a flowing melody* | *flowing curves*

flown /fləʊn $ floʊn/ v the past participle of FLY¹

fl oz BrE; **fl. oz.** AmE the written abbreviation of **fluid ounce** or fluid ounces

flu /fluː/ n [U] a common illness that makes you feel very tired and weak, gives you a sore throat, and makes you cough and have to clear your nose a lot; ☐ **influenza**: *Steven's still **in bed with flu**.* | *She's got the flu.* | *I couldn't go because I **had flu**.* | **a flu virus/bug** *the spread of the flu virus* | *Doctors now fear a **flu epidemic**.*

flub /flʌb/ v **flubbed, flubbing** [T] AmE informal to make a mistake or do something badly; ☐ **fluff, mess sth ⇔ up**: *Several of the actors flubbed their lines.*

fluc·tu·ate /'flʌktʃueɪt/ v [I] if a price or amount fluctuates, it keeps changing and becoming higher and lower; ☐ **vary**: [+**between**] *Prices were volatile, fluctuating between $20 and $40.* | [+**around**] *The number of children in the school fluctuates around 100.* | *Insect populations **fluctuate wildly** from year to year.*

fluc·tu·a·tion /,flʌktʃu'eɪʃən/ n [C,U] a change in a price, amount, level etc; ☐ **variation**: [+**in**] *the fluctuation in interest rates* | *Prices are subject to fluctuation.*

flue /fluː/ n [C] a metal pipe or tube that lets smoke or heat from a fire out of a building

flu·ent /'fluːənt/ adj **1** able to speak a language very well: [+**in**] *She was fluent in English, French, and German.* **2** fluent French/Japanese etc someone who speaks fluent French etc speaks it like a person from that country: *He spoke in fluent Italian.* **3** fluent speech or writing is smooth and confident, with no mistakes: *He was a fluent and rapid prose writer.* **4** fluent movements are smooth and gentle, not sudden and sharp: *She rose with the fluent movement of an athlete.* —**fluently** adv: *He spoke French fluently.* —**fluency** n [U]

flowers and plants

rose
violets
narcissus
chrysanthemums
thistle
clover
rushes
fern
ivy
tulips
lily
orchid
holly
daisy
carnations

fluff¹ /flʌf/ n [U]   **1** soft light bits of thread that have come from wool, cotton, or other materials: *He was picking bits of fluff off his trousers.* | *a ball of carpet fluff*   **2** soft light hair or feathers, especially on a young bird or animal: *The chicks were just balls of yellow fluff.*   **3** news, music, writing, work etc that is not serious or important: *a magazine full of pop and fashion fluff*

fluff² v [T]   **1** *informal* to make a mistake or do something badly; ▣ **mess sth** ⇔ **up**: *He fluffed his shot and missed the goal.* | *She fluffed her lines in the first scene.*   **2** also **fluff sth** ⇔ **up/out** to make something soft become larger by shaking it: *She fluffed up the pillows for me.*   **3** also **fluff sth** ⇔ **up/out** if a bird fluffs its feathers, it raises them and makes itself look bigger

fluff·y /flʌfi/ adj   **1** very light and soft to touch: *a fluffy little kitten* | *fluffy towels* → see picture at SURFACE   **2** food that is fluffy is made soft and light by mixing it quickly so that a lot of air is mixed into it: *Cream the butter and sugar until the mixture is light and fluffy.*   **3** fluffy clouds look light and soft

flu·id¹ /fluːɪd/ n [C,U] *technical* a liquid; → **gas**, **solid**: *He is not allowed solid food yet, only fluids.* | *a powerful cleaning fluid*

fluid² adj   **1** a situation that is fluid is likely to change   **2** fluid movements are smooth, relaxed, and graceful: *a loose, fluid style of dancing*   **3** a fluid substance is a liquid; → **gaseous**, **solid** —**fluidity** /fluːɪdt̬i/ n [U]

fluid ˈounce n [C] written abbreviation **fl oz** a unit for measuring liquid, equal to 1/20 PINT or 0.028 litres in Britain, and 1/16 pint or 0.030 litres in the US

fluke /fluːk/ n [C] *informal* something good that happens because of luck: *He agreed that the second goal was a fluke.* —**fluky**, **flukey** adj: *a fluky win*

flume /fluːm/ n [C] a long narrow structure built for water to slide down, which is used to move water or wood, or which people slide down for fun: *a log flume* → see picture at SPORTS CENTRE

flum·moxed /flʌməkst/ adj completely confused by something; ▣ **bewildered**: *I was completely flummoxed by the whole thing.* —**flummox** v [T]

flung /flʌŋ/ v the past tense and past participle of FLING¹

flunk /flʌŋk/ v *informal especially AmE*   **1** [I,T] to fail a test: *Tony flunked chemistry last semester.*   **2** [T] to give someone low marks on a test so that they fail it; ▣ **fail**: *She hadn't done the work so I flunked her.*

   flunk out phr v *informal especially AmE* to be forced to leave a school or college because your work is not good enough: [+of] *Ben messed around and flunked out of college.*

flun·key, **flunky** /flʌŋki/ n [C] *informal* someone who does small jobs for an important person, especially someone who does this because they are trying to please the person – used to show disapproval: *One of his flunkeys let me in.*

flu·o·res·cent /fluəˈresnt $ flu-, flɔː-/ adj   **1** fluorescent colours are very bright and easy to see, even in the dark: *a fluorescent pink T-shirt*   **2** a fluorescent light contains a tube filled with gas, which shines with a bright light when electricity is passed through it —**fluorescence** n [U]

flu·o·ri·date /fluərɪdeɪt $ flʊr-, flɔːr-/ v [T] to add fluoride to the water supply —**fluoridation** /ˌfluərɪˈdeɪʃən $ ˌflʊr-, ˌflɔːr-/ n [U]

flu·o·ride /fluəraɪd $ -flʊr-/ n [U] a chemical which is believed to help protect teeth against decay

flu·o·rine /fluəriːn $ flʊr-/ n [U] a chemical substance that is usually in the form of a poisonous pale yellow gas. It is a chemical ELEMENT: symbol F

fluo·ro·car·bon /ˌfluərəʊˈkɑːbən $ ˌflʊrəʊˈkɑːr-/ n [C] any chemical that contains fluorine and CARBON: *the problem of pollution from fluorocarbons* → CFC

flur·ried /flʌrid $ flɜːrid/ adj confused and nervous or excited; ▣ **flustered**: *Jack never seemed to be flurried, even when they were very busy.*

flur·ry /flʌri $ flɜːri/ n plural **flurries**   **1** [singular] a time when there is suddenly a lot of activity and people are very busy: [+of] *After a quiet spell there was a sudden flurry of phone calls.* | *The day started with a flurry of activity.*   **2** [C] a small amount of snow or rain that is blown by the wind: [+of] *He opens the door and a flurry of snow blows in.* | *Snow flurries are expected overnight.*

flush¹ /flʌʃ/ n

   1 REDNESS ON FACE [singular] a red colour that appears on your face when you are angry or embarrassed; ▣ **blush**: *His words brought a warm flush to her face.* → HOT FLUSH

   2 FEELINGS **a flush of anger/embarrassment/excitement** etc a sudden feeling of anger, embarrassment etc; ▣ **surge**: *She felt a sudden flush of anger.*

   3 TOILET [C] **a)** the part of a toilet that cleans it with a sudden flow of water: *The flush isn't working properly.* **b)** the act of cleaning a toilet by forcing water through it

   4 CARDS [C] a set of cards that someone has in a card game that are all of the same SUIT

   5 **the first flush of youth/manhood** the beginning of a period of time when you are young etc: *a group of adolescent boys in the first flush of manhood*

   6 **a flush of sth** a large number of things that happen or arrive at the same time: *The spring brings a flush of young animals to the farm.*

flush² v

   1 BECOME RED [I] to become red in the face, for example when you are angry or embarrassed; ▣ **blush**: *Susan flushed deeply and looked away.* | *He flushed angrily.* | **flush red/crimson/scarlet** *Robyn felt her cheeks flush scarlet.* | [+with] *Mrs Cooper flushed with indignation.*

   2 TOILET [I,T] if you flush a toilet, or if it flushes, you make water go through it to clean it: *Why do children never remember to flush the loo?* | *She flushed the rest of her drink down the toilet.*

   3 CLEAN STH [T] to force water through a pipe in order to clean it: **flush sth through sth** *They flush clean water through the pipes once a day.*

   flush sb/sth ⇔ **out** phr v
   1 to make someone leave a place where they are hiding: *The government is determined to flush out the terrorists.*   **2** to clean something by forcing water through it: *The heating system needs to be flushed out once a year.* | *Drinking water helps flush out toxins from the body.*

flush³ adj   **1** if two surfaces are flush, they are at exactly the same level, so that the place where they meet is flat: [+with] *Make sure that the cupboard is flush with the wall.*   **2** [not before noun] *informal* if someone is flush, they have plenty of money to spend: *I'm feeling flush at the moment.*

flushed /flʌʃt/ adj   **1** red in the face: *He looked hot and rather flushed.* | *Her cheeks were flushed, her expression angry.* | [+with] *He leaned forward, his face flushed with anger.*   **2** **flushed with success/excitement/pleasure** etc excited because you have achieved something: *The team are still flushed with success after their weekend victory.*

flus·ter¹ /flʌstə $ -ər/ v [T] to make someone nervous and confused by making them hurry or interrupting them: *Don't fluster me, or I'll never be ready on time.*

fluster² n BrE **in a fluster** nervous and confused because you are trying to do things quickly

flus·tered /flʌstəd $ -ərd/ adj confused and nervous: *Paul was looking flustered and embarrassed.* | *I always get flustered in interviews.*

flute /fluːt/ n [C]   **1** a musical instrument like a thin pipe, that you play by holding it across your lips, blowing over a hole, and pressing down buttons with your fingers; → **flautist**   **2** a tall narrow glass, used especially for drinking CHAMPAGNE

F

1 000, 2 000, 3 000, most frequent words in S spoken and W written English

flut·ed /'fluːtɨd/ *adj* something that is fluted has hollow or rounded lines down it: *fluted stone columns*

flut·ist /'fluːtɨst/ *n* [C] *AmE* someone who plays the flute; ◼ **flautist** *BrE*

flut·ter¹ /'flʌtə $ -ər/ *v* **1** [I,T] if a bird or insect flutters, or if it flutters its wings, it flies by moving its wings lightly up and down: *A small bird fluttered past the window.* **2** [I] to make small gentle movements in the air: *Dead leaves fluttered slowly to the ground.* | *The flag fluttered in the light breeze.* **3** [I] if your heart or your stomach flutters, you feel very excited or nervous **4** [I] if your eyelids flutter, they move slightly when you are asleep: *Her eyelids fluttered but did not open.* **5 flutter your eyelashes (at sb)** if a woman flutters her eyelashes at a man, she looks at him and moves her eyes to make herself attractive to him

flut·ter² *n* [singular] **1** a feeling of being nervous, confused, or excited: **in a flutter** *She was all in a flutter.* | *His sudden resignation caused quite a flutter.* **2 a flutter of sth** a sudden feeling that is not very strong: *She felt a flutter of curiosity.* **3** a light gentle movement: **[+ of]** *a flutter of wings* **4 have a flutter** *BrE informal* to risk a small amount of money on the result of something such as a horse race; ◼ **have a bet**

flu·vi·al /'fluːviəl/ *adj technical* relating to rivers or caused by rivers

flux /flʌks/ *n* [U] a situation in which things are changing a lot and you cannot be sure what will happen: *Everything is in flux at the moment.* | *The education system is still in a state of flux.*

fly¹ S2 W2 /flaɪ/ *v past tense* **flew** /fluː/, *past participle* **flown** /fləʊn $ floʊn/

1 TRAVEL BY PLANE [I] to travel by plane: *She's flying back to the States tomorrow.* | *Will you take the train there or fly?* | *Maurice is nervous about flying, so he usually travels overland.* | **[+to]** *The prime minister will be flying to Delhi later today for a three-day visit.* | **[+from/out of/in etc]** *He was arrested at Heathrow after flying from Brussels airport.* | *Lewis stopped off in Jamaica before flying on to Toronto.*

2 MOVE THROUGH THE AIR [I] if a plane, spacecraft etc flies, it moves through the air: *The plane was attacked as it flew over restricted airspace.*

3 CONTROL A PLANE [I,T] to be at the controls of a plane and direct it as it flies: *She was the first woman to fly Concorde.* | *The pilot was instructed to fly the plane to Montreal airport.* | *Sonny learnt to fly when he was 15.*

4 SEND SB/STH BY PLANE [T] to take goods or people somewhere by plane: *The injured boy was flown by air ambulance to the Royal London Hospital.* | **fly sth into/out of etc sth** *US planes have been flying food and medical supplies into the area.*

5 USE AIR COMPANY/SERVICE [I,T] to use a particular AIRLINE or use a particular type of ticket when you travel by plane: *We usually fly economy class.* | *Millions of passengers fly British Airways every year.*

6 CROSS SEA BY PLANE [T] to cross a particular ocean or area of sea in a plane: *Who was the first person to fly the Atlantic?*

7 BIRDS/INSECTS [I] to move through the air using wings: *The mother bird will feed her chicks until they are able to fly.* | *The evening air was clouded with mosquitoes and other flying insects.* | **[+away/off/in etc]** *At that moment, a wasp flew in through the open window.* | *The little robin shook its feathers and flew away.*

8 MOVE SOMEWHERE QUICKLY [I] **a)** to move somewhere quickly and suddenly: **[+down/across/out of etc]** *Ellen flew across the room and greeted her uncle with a kiss.* | *Rachel's hand flew to her mouth.* | **[+open/shut]** *The door flew open and a child rushed out.* **b)** to move quickly and suddenly through the air: *There was a loud explosion, and suddenly there was glass flying everywhere.* | *William hit Jack on the head and sent his glasses flying.* | *The ball bounced off the wall and went flying into the garden next door.*

9 KITE [T] to make a KITE fly in the air: *In the park people were walking their dogs or flying their kites.*

10 (I) **must fly** *spoken* used to say that you must leave quickly

11 MOVE FREELY [I] to move freely and loosely in the air: *Harriet ran after him, her hair flying behind her.*

12 FLAG [I,T] if a flag flies, or if you fly it, it is fixed to the top of a tall pole so that it can be easily seen: *After the invasion, people were forbidden to fly their national flag.* | *The flags were flying cheerfully in the breeze.* | *The government ordered that all flags should be flown at half mast* (=halfway down the pole, in order to express public sadness at someone's death).

13 fly the flag to behave in a way that shows that you are proud of your country, organization etc

14 time flies also **the hours/the days etc fly** used to say that a period of time seems to pass very quickly: *'Is it midnight already?' 'Well, you know what they say – time flies when you're having fun!'* | **[+by]** *The following weeks flew by, and soon it was time to leave.*

15 fly into a rage/temper/panic etc to suddenly get extremely angry, extremely worried etc: *Rebecca flew into a rage when she realized no-one had been listening to her.*

16 fly off the handle *informal* to suddenly get very angry: *Calm down, Terry – there's no need to fly off the handle.*

17 let fly (sth) a) to suddenly start shouting angrily at someone; ◼ **let loose:** *The prisoner let fly with a torrent of abuse.* **b)** to suddenly attack someone, especially with bullets or a weapon that is thrown: **[+with]** *The soldiers let fly with a hail of machine-gun fire.*

18 fly in the face of sth to be the opposite of what most people think is reasonable, sensible, or normal: *He likes to fly in the face of convention.*

19 ESCAPE [T] *formal* to leave somewhere in order to escape; ◼ **flee:** *By the time the police arrived, the men had flown.*

20 be flying high to be having a lot of success: *The architectural firm has been flying high recently.*

21 fly the nest a) if a young bird flies the nest, it has grown old enough to look after itself and is no longer dependent on its parents **b)** if a young person flies the nest, he or she moves out of their parents' home in order to live independently: *Now that the kids have flown the nest, I'm thinking about taking a job abroad.*

22 PLAN [I] *AmE* a plan that will fly will be successful and useful: *News is that the plan for the new hotel isn't going to fly.*

23 fly a kite to tell people about an idea, plan etc in order to get their opinion: *In my latest book, I wanted to fly the kite for an unfashionable theory.* → KITE-FLYING (2)

24 go fly a kite *AmE spoken* used to tell someone to go away, stop saying something, or stop annoying you

25 rumours/accusations etc are flying when a lot of people are talking about something, saying someone has done something wrong etc: *Rumours were flying as to how the fire started.*

26 fly the coop *AmE informal* to leave or escape: *All my children have flown the coop now.*

27 fly by the seat of your pants *informal* to have to deal with a situation by guessing what to do, because you know very little about it; ◼ **wing it:** *Sometimes you'll get back and find that things have changed, so you'll be flying by the seat of your pants for a while.* → **the bird has flown** at BIRD (8); → **as the crow flies** at CROW¹ (3); → **sparks fly** at SPARK¹ (6)

fly at sb also **fly into sb** *AmE phr v*
to suddenly rush towards someone and try to hit them because you are very angry with them

fly² *v* **flied, flying, flies** [I] to hit a ball in baseball high into the air

fly³ *n plural* **flies** [C]
1 INSECT a small flying insect with two wings: *There were flies buzzing all around us.* → see picture at INSECT
2 TROUSERS *especially AmE* also **flies** [plural] *BrE* the part at the front of a pair of trousers which you can open: *He quickly did up his fly.* | *Your flies are undone.*

3 sb wouldn't hurt/harm a fly *informal* used to say that someone is very gentle and is not likely to hurt anyone
4 be dying/dropping etc like flies *informal* used to say that a lot of people are dying or becoming ill
5 a fly in the ointment *informal* the only thing that spoils something and prevents it from being successful: *The only fly in the ointment was Jacky.*
6 be a fly on the wall to be able to watch what happens without other people knowing that you are there: *I wish I'd been a fly on the wall during that conversation.*
→ FLY-ON-THE-WALL
7 there are no flies on sb *BrE spoken* used to say that someone is not stupid and cannot be tricked
8 on the fly **a)** *technical* while a computer program is actually running: *The code is translated on the fly.* **b)** while dealing with a situation, rather than before dealing with it: *So far, policy is being made on the fly.*
9 FISHING a hook that is made to look like a fly and is used for catching fish → see picture at FISHING
10 BASEBALL a fly ball

fly⁴ *adj* **1** *informal* very fashionable and attractive: *Wear something really fly for your Friday date.* **2** *BrE old-fashioned* clever and not easily tricked: *He's a bit of a fly character.*

fly·a·way /'flaɪəweɪ/ *adj* **flyaway hair** hair that is soft and thin and becomes untidy easily

fly ball *n* [C] a ball that has been hit high into the air in a game of BASEBALL

fly·blown /'flaɪbləʊn $ -bloʊn/ *adj BrE* **1** old, dirty, and in bad condition **2** meat that is flyblown has flies' eggs in it and is not suitable for eating

fly·boy /'flaɪbɔɪ/ *n* [C] *AmE informal* someone who flies a plane, especially in the US ARMED FORCES; → **pilot**

fly·by /'flaɪbaɪ/ *n plural* **fly-bys** [C] an occasion when a spacecraft flies close to a PLANET etc in order to gather information about it

fly-by-ˌnight *adj* [only before noun] *informal* a fly-by-night company or businessman is one that you cannot trust because they have only been in business for a short time and are only interested in making quick profits

fly·catch·er /'flaɪˌkætʃə $ -ər/ *n* [C] a type of small bird that catches flies and other insects in the air

fly-drive ˈholiday *n* [C] a holiday arranged at a fixed price that includes your flight to a place, a car to drive while you are there, and a place to stay

fly·er, flier /'flaɪə $ -ər/ *n* [C] **1** a small sheet of paper advertising something: *People were giving out flyers advertising the event.* **2** *informal* a pilot: *She was one of the first solo flyers.* **3** someone who travels in an aircraft: *Delays are familiar to all regular flyers.*

fly·fish·ing /'flaɪˌfɪʃɪŋ/ *n* [U] the sport of fishing in a river or lake with special hooks that are made to look like flies

fly ˈhalf *n* [C] a player in a game of RUGBY. A fly half has to be able to run quickly.

fly·ing¹ /'flaɪ-ɪŋ/ *adj* **1** [only before noun] able to fly; ⊟ **winged**: *a story about a flying horse* **2** with flying colours if you pass a test with flying colours, you are very successful in it **3** a flying visit a quick visit because you do not have much time **4** a flying start a very good or successful start: *The appeal has got off to a flying start, with over £200,000 raised in the first week.* **5** a flying jump/leap a long high jump made while you are running: *He took a flying leap and just managed to clear the stream.*

flying² *n* [U] the activity of travelling by plane: *Quite a lot of people are still nervous about flying.*

flying ˈbuttress *n* [C] a curved line of stones or bricks that are joined to the outside wall of a large building such as a church, and help to support it

flying ˈdoctor *n* [C] a doctor, especially in Australia, who goes by plane to visit sick people who live a long way from the nearest town

flying ˈfish *n* [C] a type of sea fish that can jump out of the water and move along in the air for a short way

flying ˈfox *n* [C] a type of BAT that lives in hot countries and eats fruit

flying ˌofficer *n* [C] an officer in the British airforce

flying ˈpicket *n* [C] someone who travels to different factories during a STRIKE and tries to persuade workers to stop working

flying ˈsaucer *n* [C] a large round spacecraft from somewhere else in space, that some people believe they have seen in the sky; → UFO

flying ˈsquad *n* [C] a special group of police officers in Britain whose job is to travel quickly to the place where there has been a serious crime: *the head of Scotland Yard's Flying Squad*

flying ˈtackle *n* [C] a way of stopping someone from running by putting your arms around their legs and making them fall over

fly leaf *n* [C] a page at the beginning or end of a book, on which there is no printing

fly-on-the-ˈwall *adj* [only before noun] a fly-on-the-wall television programme shows people's daily lives in a very natural way, because they forget that they are being filmed → be a fly on the wall at FLY³ (6)

fly·o·ver /'flaɪ-əʊvə $ -oʊvər/ *n* [C] **1** *BrE* a bridge that takes one road over another road; ⊟ **overpass** *AmE* **2** *AmE* a flight by a group of planes on a special occasion for people to watch; ⊟ **flypast** *BrE*

fly·pa·per /'flaɪˌpeɪpə $ -ər/ *n* [C,U] paper covered with a sticky substance that is hung up in a room in order to catch flies

fly·past /'flaɪpɑːst $ -pæst/ *n* [C] *BrE* a flight by a group of planes on a special occasion for people to watch; ⊟ **flyover** *AmE*

fly·sheet /'flaɪʃiːt/ *also* **fly** *n* [C] a sheet of material that is put over a tent to protect it from the rain

fly·swat·ter /'flaɪˌswɒtə $ -ˌswɑːtər/ *n* [C] a piece of plastic that you use for hitting and killing flies

fly·weight /'flaɪweɪt/ *n* [C] a BOXER who weighs less than 50.80 kilograms, and who is heavier than a STRAW-WEIGHT but lighter than a BANTAMWEIGHT

fly·wheel /'flaɪwiːl/ *n* [C] a heavy wheel that keeps a machine working at a steady speed

FM /ˌef 'em◂/ *n* [U] *frequency modulation* a system used for broadcasting radio programmes; → AM

foal¹ /fəʊl $ foʊl/ *n* [C] a young horse; → colt, filly

foal² *v* [I] to give birth to a foal

foam¹ /fəʊm $ foʊm/ *n* [U] **1** *also* **foam rubber** a type of soft rubber with a lot of air in it, used in furniture: *a foam mattress* **2** a mass of very small bubbles on the surface of a liquid; ⊟ **froth**: *She scraped the foam off her coffee.* **3** a substance which is like a very thick soft liquid with a lot of bubbles in it: *Firefighters using water and foam are still tackling the blaze.* | shaving foam —**foamy** *adj*

foam² *v* [I] **1** to produce foam: *The green water splashed and foamed over the rocks.* **2** be foaming at the mouth **a)** to have bubbles coming out of your mouth because you are very ill **b)** *informal* to be very angry

fob¹ /fɒb $ fɑːb/ *v* fobbed, fobbing *informal*
fob sb ⇔ **off** *phr v* **1** to tell someone something that is not true in order to stop them from complaining: [+with] *She fobbed him off with a promise to pay him the money next week.* **2** to give someone something that is not very good instead of the thing they really want: [+with] *They tried to fob me off with a cheap camera.*

fob² *n* [C] a small object that is fixed to a key ring as a decoration

fob watch *n* [C] a watch that fits into a pocket, or is pinned to a woman's dress

fo·cac·ci·a /fəʊˈkætʃiə $ foʊˈkɑːtʃə/ *n* [U] a type of Italian bread

fo·cal /'fəʊkəl $ 'foʊ-/ *adj* [only before noun] the focal thing is the one that people pay most attention to: *This issue has now become the focal centre of interest.*

F

'**focal length** n [C] technical the distance between the centre of a lens and the focal point

'**focal point** n [C] **1** the person or thing that you pay most attention to: [+of] The swimming pool is the focal point of the hotel. | [+for] The new tax has been the focal point for much discussion. **2** technical the point at which beams of light meet after they have been through a LENS

fo'c'sle /'fəʊksəl $ 'foʊ-/ n [C] BrE the front part of a ship, where the sailors live; ▣ **forecastle** AmE

fo·cus[1] W2 /'fəʊkəs $ 'foʊ-/ v **focused** or **focussed**, **focusing** or **focussing**
  1 GIVE ATTENTION TO STH [I,T] to give special attention to one particular person or thing, or to make people do this: [+on] He felt he needed to focus more on his career. | **focus your attention/mind/efforts on sth** She tried to focus her mind on her work. | **focus (sb's) mind/attention (on sth)** (=make people give their attention to something) We need to focus public attention on this issue.
  2 CAMERA/TELESCOPE [I,T] to point a camera or TELE-SCOPE at something, and change the controls slightly so that you can see that thing clearly: [+on] She turned the camera and focussed on Martin's face. | **focus sth on sth** He focused his binoculars on the building opposite.
  3 EYES [I,T] if your eyes focus, or if you focus your eyes, you look at something and can see it clearly: [+on] All eyes focussed on her. | His eyes were focussed straight ahead.
  4 LIGHT [T] if you focus beams of light, you aim them onto a particular place

focus[2] W2 n
  1 [singular] the thing, person, situation etc that people pay special attention to

the focus is on sth
the focus of attention/concern/interest
the focus of debate
the main/central/primary focus (of sth)
become the focus (of/for sth)
provide a focus (for sth)
shift the focus (of sth)
the focus shifts (from sth) (to sth)

The **focus** of recent research has **been on** environmental issues. | [+of] The war in Bosnia had become **the focus of** media **attention**. | **The focus of interest** in the series is what goes on in everyday life. | Another **focus of** feminist **debate** has been the film industry. | I shall now turn to the **main focus** of this essay. | Eggs **became the focus for** the food poisoning scare. | **The focus** of the conference **shifted from** population growth to the education of women.

  2 [U] if your focus is on something, that is the thing you are giving most attention to: [+on] Our main focus is on helping people get back into work. | a **shift of focus**
  3 **come into focus/bring sth into focus** if something comes into focus, or you bring it into focus, people start to talk about it and pay attention to it: These issues have recently come into **sharp focus** (=people have started to talk about them a lot).
  4 **in focus/out of focus** if a photograph or an instrument such as a camera is in focus, you can see the picture clearly. If it is out of focus, you cannot see the picture clearly.
  5 [U] the clearness of the picture seen through an instrument such as a camera: He raised his binoculars and adjusted the focus.

'**focus group** n [C] a small group of people that a company, political party etc asks questions in order to find out what they think of their products, actions etc

fo·cussed BrE; **focused** AmE /'fəʊkəst $ 'foʊ-/ adj paying careful attention to what you are doing, in a way that shows you are determined to succeed: I've got to stay focussed if I want to win this competition.

fod·der /'fɒdə $ 'fɑːdər/ n [U] **1** food for farm animals **2** something or someone that is useful only for a particular purpose – used in order to show disapproval: [+for] The murders made prime fodder for newspapers. → CANNON FODDER

foe /fəʊ $ foʊ/ n [C] literary an enemy: Britain's friends and foes

foe·tal, fetal /'fiːtl/ adj [only before noun] belonging or related to a foetus: a test to detect foetal abnormalities

'**foetal po·sition** n [C] the body position of an unborn child inside its mother, in which the body is curled and the legs are pulled up against the chest

foe·tus, fetus /'fiːtəs/ n [C] a baby or young animal before it is born; → embryo

fog[1] /fɒg $ fɑːg, fɔːg/ n **1** [C,U] cloudy air near the ground which is difficult to see through; ▣ **mist**: **thick/dense/freezing fog** We got lost in the thick fog. | It will be a cold night, and there may be **fog patches**. | A **blanket of fog** covered the fields. | The **fog lifted** (=disappeared) in the afternoon. **2** [singular] informal a state in which you feel confused and cannot think clearly: My mind was **in a fog**. | [+of] the fog of tiredness

fog[2] v **fogged, fogging 1** also **fog up** [I,T] if something made of glass fogs or becomes fogged, it becomes covered in small drops of water that make it difficult to see through; ▣ **mist up, steamed up**: The windscreen had fogged up. **2** [T] to make something less clear; ▣ **cloud**

fog·bound /'fɒgbaʊnd $ 'fɑːg-, 'fɔːg-/ adj unable to travel or work normally because of fog: The airport was fogbound.

fo·gey, fogy /'fəʊgi $ 'foʊ-/ n plural **fogeys** or **fogies** [C] someone who has old-fashioned ideas and does not like change: You're turning into a real **old fogey**!

fog·gy /'fɒgi $ 'fɑːgi, 'fɔːgi/ adj **1** if the weather is foggy, there is fog: a foggy day in November | driving in foggy conditions **2 not have the foggiest (idea)** spoken to not know at all: None of us had the foggiest idea about how to put the tent up. **3** if your mind is foggy, you cannot think or remember things clearly

fog·horn /'fɒghɔːn $ 'fɑːghɔːrn, 'fɔːg-/ n [C] **1** a loud horn on a ship, used in fog to warn other ships of its position **2 a voice like a foghorn** informal a very loud unpleasant voice

'**fog lamp** BrE; '**fog light** AmE n [C] a strong light on the front of a car that helps drivers to see when there is FOG → see picture at CAR

foi·ble /'fɔɪbəl/ n [C] a small weakness or strange habit that someone has, which does not harm anyone else; ▣ **peculiarity**: We all have our little foibles.

foie gras /ˌfwɑː 'grɑː/ n [U] a smooth food made from the LIVER of a GOOSE

foil[1] /fɔɪl/ n **1** [U] metal sheets that are as thin as paper, used for wrapping food: **silver/aluminium/kitchen foil** Cover the chicken with silver foil and bake. → TINFOIL **2** [U] paper that is covered with very thin sheets of metal: chocolates in foil wrappers **3 be a foil to/for sb/sth** to emphasize the good qualities of another person or thing, by being very different from them: The simple stone floor is the **perfect foil** for the brightly coloured furnishings. **4** [C] a light narrow sword used in FENCING

foil[2] v [T often passive] to prevent something bad that someone is planning to do: A massive arms-smuggling plan has been foiled by the CIA.

foist /fɔɪst/ v
  foist sth on/upon sb phr v to force someone to accept or have to deal with something that they do not want: I keep getting work foisted on me at the last minute.

fold

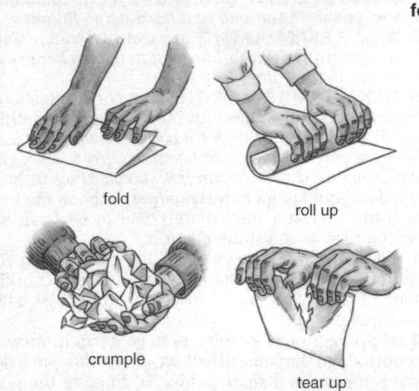

fold

roll up

crumple

tear up

fold¹ /fəʊld $ foʊld/ v

1 BEND [T] to bend a piece of paper, cloth etc by laying or pressing one part over another: *Fold the paper along the dotted line.* | *It'll fit in if you fold it in half.* | **fold sth over/under/down etc** *Spoon the filling onto the dough, fold it over, and press down the edges.*

2 SMALLER/NEATER also **fold up** [T] to fold something several times so that it makes a small neat shape; → **unfold**: *I wish you kids would fold up your clothes!* | *He folded the map neatly.*

3 FURNITURE ETC [I,T] if something such as a piece of furniture folds, or you fold it, you make it smaller or move it to a different position by bending it: *The chairs fold flat for storage.* | **fold (sth) away/up/down etc** *a useful little bed that folds away when you don't need it* | *Can you fold the shutters back?* → FOLDING

4 **fold your arms** to bend your arms so that they rest together against your body: *George stood silently with his arms folded.*

5 BUSINESS also **fold up** [I] if an organization folds, it closes because it does not have enough money to continue

6 COVER [T always + adv/prep] to cover something, especially by wrapping it in material or putting your hand over it: **fold sth in sth** *a silver dagger folded in a piece of white cloth*

7 **fold sb in your arms** *literary* to hold someone closely by putting your arms around them

fold sth ⇔ **in** also **fold sth into sth** *phr v*
to gently mix another substance into a mixture when you are preparing food: *Next, fold in the sugar.*

fold² *n* [C]

1 LINE a line made in paper or material when you fold one part of it over another: *Bend back the card and cut along the fold.*

2 SKIN/MATERIAL [usually plural] the folds in material, skin etc are the loose parts that hang over other parts of it: *Her dress hung in soft folds.*

3 **the fold** the group of people that you belong to and share the same beliefs and ideas as: **return/come back to the fold** *The Church will welcome him back into the fold.* | **stray from/leave the fold** *a former advocate of free market economics who had strayed from the fold*

4 SHEEP a small area of a field surrounded by a wall or fence where sheep are kept for safety; ▤ **pen**; → **corral**

5 ROCK *technical* a bend in layers of rock, caused by movements underground in the earth

-fold /fəʊld $ foʊld/ *suffix* **1** [in adjectives] of a particular number of kinds: *The government's role in healthcare is twofold: first, to provide the resources and, second, to make their work better for patients.* **2** [in adverbs] a particular number of times: *The value of the house has increased fourfold* (=it is now worth four times as much as before).

fold·a·way /'fəʊldəweɪ $ 'foʊld-/ *adj* [only before noun] a foldaway bed, table etc can be folded up so it uses less space; → **folding**

fold·er /'fəʊldə $ 'foʊldər/ *n* [C] **1** a container for keeping loose papers in, made of folded card or plastic → see picture at OFFICE **2** a group of related documents that you store together on a computer

fold·ing /'fəʊldɪŋ $ 'foʊl-/ *adj* [only before noun] a folding bicycle, bed, chair etc has parts that you can bend or fold together to make it easier to carry or store; → **foldaway**; → see picture at CHAIR

fo·li·age /'fəʊli-ɪdʒ $ 'foʊ-/ *n* [U] the leaves of a plant: *dark green foliage*

fo·lic acid /ˌfəʊlɪk 'æsɪ̯d, ˌfɒ- $ ˌfoʊ-, ˌfɑː-/ *n* [U] a VITAMIN found especially in green vegetables, used by the body to produce red blood cells

fo·li·o /'fəʊliəʊ $ 'foʊlioʊ/ *n* [C] *plural* **folios** *technical* **1** a book made with very large sheets of paper **2** a single numbered sheet of paper from a book

folk¹ S2 /fəʊk $ foʊk/ *n*

1 [plural] also **folks** *especially AmE* people: *I'm sure there are some folk who would rather they weren't here.* | *Thanks to the folks at NBC.* | *Wait till the folks back home hear about this!* | **young/old folk** *BrE old-fashioned*: *Young folk these days don't know the meaning of work.*

2 **folks** [plural] **a)** *especially AmE* your parents and family: *Is it OK if I call my folks?* **b)** used when talking to a group of people in a friendly way: *That's all for now, folks.*

3 country/farming etc folk [plural] also **country folk** *AmE literary* people who live in a particular area or do a particular kind of work: *simple country folk*

4 [U] FOLK MUSIC: *a folk singer*

folk² *adj* [only before noun] **1** folk art, stories, customs etc are traditional and typical of the ordinary people who live in a particular area: *folk tales* | *an Irish folk song* **2** folk science/psychology/wisdom etc science etc that is based on the ideas or beliefs that ordinary people have, and does not involve a high level of technical knowledge **3** folk medicine/remedy a traditional type of medical treatment that uses plants or simple treatments rather than scientific methods

folk dance *n* [C] a traditional dance from a particular area, or a piece of music for this dance —**folk dancer** *n* [C]

folk hero *n* [C] someone who people in a particular place admire very much because of something they have done: *Casey Jones is a well-known American folk hero.*

folk·lore /'fəʊklɔː $ 'foʊklɔːr/ *n* [U] the traditional stories, customs etc of a particular area or country

folk music also **folk** *n* [U] **1** traditional music that has been played by ordinary people in a particular area for a long time **2** a style of popular music in which people sing and play GUITARS, without any electronic equipment

folk·sy /'fəʊksi $ 'foʊ-/ *adj informal* **1** *especially AmE* friendly and informal: *The town had a certain folksy charm.* **2** in a style that is typical of traditional countryside styles or customs

fol·li·cle /'fɒlɪkəl $ 'fɑː-/ *n* [C] one of the small holes in the skin that hairs grow from

fol·low S1 W1 /'fɒləʊ $ 'fɑːloʊ/ *v*

1 GO AFTER [I,T] to go, walk, drive etc behind or after someone else: *Are those men following us?* | *The patrol car followed the BMW for a few miles and then lost it.* | *Tom's already gone out to Rome and his wife and children will follow shortly.* | **follow sb into/to etc sth** *Peggy followed her out onto the landing.*

2 HAPPEN AFTER [I,T] to happen or do something after something else: *The agreement followed months of*

F

negotiation. | *The assassination of Martin Luther King in 1968 was followed by that of Robert Kennedy.* | **there follows sth** *After weeks of intense fighting, there followed a brief period of calm.* | *Most EU countries have signed the agreement and the US is expected to follow shortly* (=soon). → FOLLOWING³

3 COME AFTER [I,T] to come directly after something else in a series, list, or order: *The chapters that follow deal mainly with mathematics.* | *In English, the letter Q is always followed by U.* | *We had vegetable casserole with a fruit salad to follow* (=as part of a meal). | **there follows sth** *There followed several pages of incomprehensible statistics.*

4 **as follows** used to introduce a list of things that you will mention next: *The winners are as follows: in third place, Mandy Johnson; in second place ...*

5 DO WHAT SB SAYS [T] to do something in the way that someone has told or advised you to do it: *He followed the doctor's advice and had no further trouble.* | *Follow the instructions very carefully when filling in the form.* | *They followed the plan that Elizabeth had worked out.*

6 **follow the signs/sb's directions** to go somewhere by a particular way according to road signs or to what someone has told you: *Just follow the signs for the airport.* | *I followed Brown's directions and found the farm quite easily.*

7 DO THE SAME THING [I,T] to do the same thing as someone else: *Some state schools follow the example of private schools in asking parents to donate money.* | *Environmentalists are urging the government to follow the lead of Scandinavian countries in this matter.* | *She's just like any young woman who enjoys following the latest fashions* (=wearing fashionable clothes). | **follow sb into sth** (=do the same job as someone else) *He does not want to follow his father into a scientific career.*

8 BELIEVE IN STH [T] to believe in and obey a particular set of religious or political ideas

9 GO IN PARTICULAR DIRECTION [T] **a)** to continue along a particular road, river etc: *I followed the main road up the mountain.* | *Tom followed the track that leads to the old Roman road.* **b)** to go in the same direction as something else, or to go parallel to something else: *The road follows the line of the river for several miles.*

10 UNDERSTAND [I,T] to understand something such as an explanation or story; ▪ **grasp**: *I didn't quite follow what he was saying.* | **easy/difficult/hard etc to follow** *The plot is a little difficult to follow.*

11 BE A RESULT [I] to be true as a result of something else that is true: [+from] *The conclusion that follows from these findings is that inner city schools need more investment, not less.* | *It doesn't necessarily follow that you're going to do well academically even if you're highly intelligent.*

12 BE INTERESTED [T] to be interested in something and in the way it develops: *Have you been following that crime series on TV?* | *I've been following his progress very closely.* | *She just doesn't understand people who follow football or any other kind of sport.*

13 follow a pattern/course/trend etc to continue to happen or develop in a particular way, especially in a way that is expected: *In Australia, the weather follows a fairly predictable pattern.*

14 follow suit to do the same as someone else has done: *Budget companies have been so successful that other airlines have had to follow suit and lower their fares.*

15 follow in sb's footsteps to do the same job or to work or live in the same way as someone else before you, especially someone in your family: *He is a doctor and expects his son to follow in his footsteps.*

16 BE ABOUT [T] to show or describe someone's life or a series of events, for example in a film or book: *The book follows the plight of an orphaned Irish girl who marries into New York society.*

17 be a hard act to follow to be so good or successful at something that it will be difficult for the next person,

team etc to be as good: *We're looking for a replacement for Sue, but she's going to be a hard act to follow.*

18 WATCH CAREFULLY [T] to carefully watch someone do something: *She followed Simon with her eyes as he walked to the gate.*

19 THINK ABOUT/STUDY [T] to study or think about a particular idea or subject and try to learn something from it: *It turned out we were both following the same line of research.* | *If you follow that idea to its logical conclusion, we'd have to ban free speech altogether.*

20 follow your instincts/feelings/gut reaction etc to do the thing that you immediately feel is best without needing to stop and think about it

21 follow the herd/crowd to do the same thing that most other people are doing, without really thinking about it for yourself – used in order to show disapproval

22 follow your nose *informal* **a)** to go straight forward or continue in the same direction: *Just follow your nose until you come to a small bridge.* **b)** to go to the place from where there is a particular smell coming: *I followed my nose to the kitchen, where Marcie was making coffee.* **c)** to do something in the way that you feel is right: *After a few years in the detective game, you learn to follow your nose.*

23 follow a profession/trade/way of life etc to do a particular job or have a particular way of life

follow sb **around** also **follow sb about** *BrE phr v* to follow someone everywhere they go, especially when this is annoying: *She told him to go away and stop following her around.*

follow on *phr v*
1 to happen after something else and be connected with it; → **follow-on**: [+from] *The discussion sessions are supposed to follow on from this morning's lecture.*
2 to go to the same place as someone else at a later time: *You go ahead – I'll follow on later.*

follow through *phr v*
1 to do what needs to be done to complete something or make it successful: *The project went wrong when the staff failed to follow through.* | **follow sth ⇔ through** *If you have followed through all the exercises in this book, you should be ready for the second year course.*
2 to continue moving your arm after you have hit the ball in tennis, GOLF etc; → **follow-through**

follow sth ⇔ **up** *phr v*
1 to find out more information about something and take action if necessary: *The police take people's statements and then follow them up.*
2 to do something in addition to what you have already done in order to make it more likely to succeed: [+with] *If there is no response to your press release, follow it up with a phone call.* | *This experiment was quickly followed up by others using different forms of the drug.* → FOLLOW-UP

fol·low·er /ˈfɒləʊə $ ˈfɑːloʊər/ *n* [C] someone who believes in a particular system of ideas, or who supports a leader who teaches these ideas; → **disciple**, **supporter**: *Marx and his followers were convinced that capitalism would destroy itself.* | [+of] *followers of Sun Myung Moon, better known as Moonies* → CAMP FOLLOWER

fol·low·ing¹ S2 W1 /ˈfɒləʊɪŋ $ ˈfɑːloʊ-/ *adj*
1 the following afternoon/month/page/chapter etc the next afternoon, month etc; ▪ **preceding**: *He was sick in the evening, but the following day he was better.*
2 the following example/way etc the example, way etc that will be mentioned next: *Payment may be made in any of the following ways: cheque, cash, or credit card.*
3 a following wind a wind that is blowing in the same direction as a ship, and helps it to move faster

following² *n* [C] **1** [usually singular] a group of people who support or admire someone: *The band has a big following in Europe.* **2** the following the people or things that you are going to mention: *The following have been selected to play in tomorrow's game: Louise Carus, Fiona Douglas...*

following³ *prep* after an event or as a result of it; ▪ **before**: *Following the president's speech, there will be* a few minutes for questions. | Thousands of refugees left the country following the outbreak of civil war.

follow-my-'leader BrE; **follow-the-'leader** AmE n [U] a children's game in which one of the players does actions which all the other players must copy

follow-on n [C] something that is done or made in addition to something else, or done to continue something that was done before; → **follow on**: [+to/from] The inspection was a follow-on from the review process. | a follow-on product

follow-through n [singular] **1** the continued movement of your arm after you have hit the ball in tennis, golf etc; → **follow through 2** the things that someone does in order to complete a plan; → **follow through**: The budget has to cover not only the main project but the follow-through.

follow-up¹ adj [only before noun] done in order to find out more or do more about something; → **follow up**: a follow-up study on children and poverty

follow-up² n **1** [C,U] something that is done to make sure that earlier actions have been successful or effective; → **follow up**: preventative treatment and follow-up several weeks later **2** [C] a book, film, article etc that comes after another one that has the same subject or characters: Spielberg says he's planning to do a follow-up to their hit album

fol·ly /ˈfɒli $ ˈfɑːli/ n plural **follies 1** [C,U] formal a very stupid thing to do, especially one that is likely to have serious results: Somerville bitterly regretted his folly at becoming involved. | **it would be folly to do sth** It would be sheer folly to reduce spending on health education. | the follies of aristocratic society **2** [C] an unusual building that was built in the past as a decoration, not to be used or lived in

fo·ment /fəʊˈment $ foʊ-/ v **foment revolution/trouble/discord etc** formal to cause trouble and make people start fighting each other or opposing the government; ▣ **stir up**: They were accused of fomenting rebellion. —**fomentation** /ˌfəʊmenˈteɪʃən, -mən- $ ˌfoʊ-/ n [U]

fond /fɒnd $ fɑːnd/ adj **1 be fond of sb** to like someone very much, especially when you have known them for a long time and almost feel love for them: Joe's quite fond of her, isn't he? | Over the years we've **grown** very **fond of** each other. **2 be fond of (doing) sth** to like something, especially something you have liked for a long time: I'm not overly fond of cooking. | I'd **grown fond of** the place and it was difficult to leave. **3 be fond of doing sth** to do something often, especially something that annoys other people: My grandfather was very fond of handing out advice to all my friends. **4** [only before noun] a fond look, smile, action etc shows you like someone very much; ▣ **affectionate**: He gave her a fond look. | As we parted we said a fond farewell. **5 have fond memories of sth/sb** to remember someone or something with great pleasure: Marie still had fond memories of their time together. **6 a fond hope/belief** a belief or hope that something will happen, which seems silly because it is very unlikely to happen: **in the fond hope/belief that** They sent him to another school in the fond hope that his behaviour would improve. —**fondness** n [U]: a fondness for expensive clothes → FONDLY

fon·dant /ˈfɒndənt $ ˈfɑːn-/ n **1** [U] a soft mixture made from sugar and water, used for covering cakes: a cake decorated with **fondant icing 2** [C] a soft sweet made of fondant

fon·dle /ˈfɒndl $ ˈfɑːndl/ v [T] to gently touch and move your fingers over part of someone's body in a way that shows love or sexual desire: She fondled his neck.

fond·ly /ˈfɒndli $ ˈfɑːndli/ adv **1 fondly imagine/believe/hope etc** to believe something that is untrue, hope for something that will probably not happen etc: Some people still fondly believe that modern science can solve all the world's problems. **2** in a way that shows you like someone very much; ▣ **lovingly**: He turned to see her smiling fondly at him.

fon·due /ˈfɒndjuː $ fɑːnˈduː/ n [C,U] a dish made of melted cheese or chocolate into which you put small pieces of meat, fruit etc using a long fork → see picture at POT

font /fɒnt $ fɑːnt/ n [C] **1** technical a set of letters of a particular size and style, used for printing books, newspapers etc or on a computer screen **2** a large stone container in a church, that holds the water used for the ceremony of BAPTISM

food S1 W1 /fuːd/ n
1 [C,U] things that people and animals eat, such as vegetables or meat

---

good food
hot/cold/spicy/fatty/starchy food
Italian/French/Chinese etc food
fresh food
frozen food
processed food (=food that has chemicals in it to make it last a long time)
canned food also **tinned food** BrE (=sold in cans)
junk food (=food that is full of sugar or fat and is bad for your health)
fast food (=hamburgers and other foods that are made to be eaten quickly)
health food (=food that is thought to be good for your health)
organic food (=food that is produced without using harmful chemicals)
baby food
dog/pet/cat food
be off your food BrE (=not want to eat your food)
food shortage
food scare (=when people are afraid to eat a particular kind of food)
the food industry
food colouring/additives

The restaurant serves good food at affordable prices. | Try not to eat too much spicy food. | I love Italian food, especially pasta. | He eats a lot of junk food and doesn't get enough exercise. | a fast food restaurant | People are willing to pay more for organic food. | Her little boy has a fever and he's been off his food. | Severe food shortages have led to rioting against the military government. | The recent series of food scares has made people more wary of eating meat. | Consumer pressure is being put upon the food industry to cut down on factory farming methods.

2 food for thought something that makes you think carefully: The teacher's advice certainly gave me food for thought.

food bank n [C] AmE a place that gives food to poor people

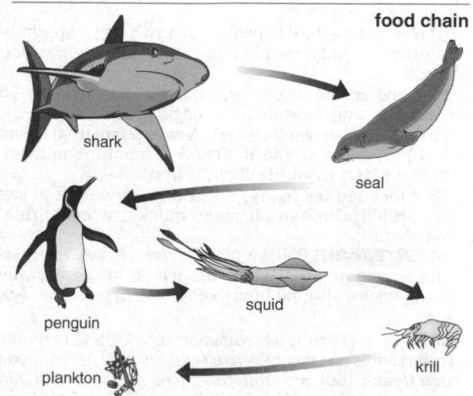

food chain

shark
seal
penguin
squid
plankton
krill

food chain n **the food chain** all animals and plants considered as a group in which a plant is eaten by an

F

insect or animal, which is then eaten by another animal and so on: *Pollution is affecting many creatures lower down the food chain.*

'food ,coupon n [C] *AmE* a FOOD STAMP

'food court n [C] the area in a shopping centre where there are many small restaurants

'food group n [C] one of the groups that types of food are divided into, such as meat, vegetables, or milk products

food·ie /'fuːdi/ n [C] *informal* someone who is very interested in cooking and eating food; → **gourmet**

'food ,poisoning n [U] a stomach illness caused by eating food that contains harmful BACTERIA, so that you VOMIT

'food ,processor n [C] a piece of electrical equipment used to prepare food by cutting and mixing it → see picture at EAT

'food stamp also **food coupon** n [C] an official piece of paper that the US government gives to poor people so they can buy food

food·stuff /'fuːdstʌf/ n [C usually plural, U] food – used especially when talking about the business of producing or selling food: *a shortage of basic foodstuffs*

fool¹ /fuːl/ n

1 STUPID PERSON [C] a stupid person or someone who has done something stupid; ◨ **idiot**: *What a fool she had been to think that he would stay.* | *Like a fool, I accepted straight away.* | *You silly old fool!*

2 make a fool of yourself to do something stupid that you feel embarrassed about afterwards and that makes you seem silly: *Sorry I made such a fool of myself last night. I must have been drunk.*

3 make a fool of sb to deliberately do something to make someone else seem stupid: *I suddenly realised that I was being made a fool of.*

4 any fool can do sth *spoken* used to say that it is very easy to do something or to see that something is true: *Any fool could have seen what would happen.*

5 be no/nobody's fool to be difficult to trick or deceive, because you have a lot of experience and knowledge about something: *Katherine was nobody's fool when it came to money.*

6 gooseberry/strawberry etc fool *BrE* a sweet food made of soft cooked fruit mixed with cream

7 more fool you/him etc *BrE spoken* used to say that you think someone was stupid to do something, and it is their own fault if this causes trouble: *'Jim smashed up my car.' ' More fool you for letting him borrow it!'*

8 not suffer fools gladly if you say that someone doesn't suffer fools gladly, they do not have any patience with people who they think are stupid

9 be living in a fool's paradise to feel happy and satisfied, and believe there are no problems, when in fact this is not true

10 play/act the fool to behave in a silly way, especially in order to make people laugh: *Stop playing the fool! You'll fall.*

11 (send sb on) a fool's errand to make someone go somewhere or do something for no good reason

12 fools rush in (where angels fear to tread) used to say that people are stupid if they do something immediately without thinking about it first

13 a fool and his money are soon parted used to say that stupid people spend money quickly without thinking about it

14 ENTERTAINER [C] a man whose job was to entertain a king or other powerful person in the past, by doing tricks, singing funny songs etc; ◨ **jester** → APRIL FOOL

fool² v **1** [T] to trick someone into believing something that is not true: *Even art experts were fooled.* | **you don't/can't fool me** *You can't fool me with that old excuse.* | **be fooled by sth** *Don't be fooled by appearances.* | **fool sb into doing sth** *I was fooled into believing their promises.* **2** fool yourself to try to make

yourself believe something that you know is not really true: *It's no good fooling yourself. He's not coming back.* **3** you could have fooled me *spoken* used to show that you do not believe what someone has told you: *'Look, we're doing our best to fix it.' 'Well, you could have fooled me.'* **4** sb is just fooling *spoken* used to say that someone is not serious and is only pretending that something is true; ◨ **sb is just kidding**: *Don't pay any attention to Henry. He's just fooling.*

fool around also **fool about** *BrE phr v* **1** to waste time behaving in a silly way or doing things that are not important; ◨ **mess around**: *He always used to fool around in class.* **2** to behave in a way which is careless and not responsible; ◨ **mess around**: [+with] *Some idiot's been fooling around with the electricity supply!* **3** *AmE* to spend time doing something that you enjoy, but that does not have a particular purpose; ◨ **mess around**: *The boys were out in the yard, just fooling around.* **4** to have a sexual relationship with someone else's wife, boyfriend etc; ◨ **mess around**: *She found out that he'd been fooling around behind her back.*

fool with sth *phr v AmE informal* **1** to touch or play with something, especially when you should not; ◨ **mess with sth**: *Who's been fooling with the radio dial?* **2** to become involved in something which could cause damage or be dangerous; ◨ **mess with sth**

fool³ *adj* [only before noun] *AmE informal* silly or stupid; ◨ **foolish**: *What did you say a fool thing like that for?*

fool·e·ry /'fuːləri/ n [U] *BrE old-fashioned* silly or stupid behaviour

fool·har·dy /'fuːlhɑːdi $ -ɑːr-/ adj taking stupid and unnecessary risks; ◨ **reckless**: *a foolhardy attempt to capture more territory* —**foolhardiness** n [U]

fool·ish /'fuːlɪʃ/ adj **1** a foolish action, remark etc is stupid and shows that someone is not thinking sensibly; ◨ **silly**: *I've never heard anything so foolish in all my life.* | *It would be foolish to ignore his advice.* | **be foolish enough to do sth** *I was foolish enough to believe him.* **2** a foolish person behaves in a silly way or looks silly; ◨ **stupid**: *I was young and foolish at the time.* | *a foolish grin* | **look/feel foolish** *He'd been made to look foolish.* —**foolishly** adv: *She foolishly agreed to go with them.* —**foolishness** n [U]

fool·proof /'fuːlpruːf/ adj a foolproof method, plan, system etc is certain to be successful; ◨ **infallible**: *a foolproof way of preventing credit card fraud*

fools·cap /'fuːlskæp/ n [U] a large size of paper, especially paper for writing on

,fool's 'gold n [U] **1** a kind of yellow metal that exists in some rocks and looks like gold **2** something that you think will be very exciting, very attractive etc but in fact is not

foos·ball /'fuːzbɔːl $ -bɒːl/ also **foos** /fuːs/ n [U] *informal* TABLE FOOTBALL, especially played as a sport rather than a game

foos·er /'fuːzə $ -ər/ n [C] *informal* someone who plays foosball

foot¹ S1 W1 /fʊt/ n *plural* **feet** /fiːt/ [C]

1 BODY PART the part of your body that you stand on and walk on

the sole of your foot (=the base of your foot)
bare feet (=without any socks or shoes)
front/back/hind feet (=of an animal)
wipe your feet (=wipe them on a mat to remove dirt)
stamp your feet (=bang them noisily on the ground)
tap your feet (=bang them gently on the ground)
shuffle your feet (=move from one foot to the other)
at sb's feet (=on the ground near your feet)

My foot hurts. | *I had blisters on the soles of my feet.* | *I dropped a glass earlier, so don't walk around in bare feet.* | *The vet examined the horse's hind feet.* | *Don't wipe your feet on the carpet!* | *She stood on the platform, her suitcase at her feet.*

2 MEASUREMENT *plural* **feet** or **foot** written abbreviation *ft* a unit for measuring length, equal to 12 INCHES or about 30 centimetres: *He's six feet tall, with blonde hair.* | *Mark was standing just a few feet away from me.* | *I'd say she's about five foot three* (=five feet and three inches). | **a one/two/three etc foot sth** *a four foot wall* | **square feet/cubic feet** *15,000 square feet of office space*

3 BOTTOM PART **the foot of sth** the lowest or bottom part of something: **the foot of the stairs/ladder etc** *He walked to the foot of the stairs.* | **the foot of a mountain/cliff etc** *a small cottage at the foot of the hill* | **at the foot of sth** *a large wooden trunk at the foot of his bed* | *The date is shown* **at the foot of the page.**

4 on foot if you go somewhere on foot, you walk there: *It takes about 30 minutes on foot, or 10 minutes by car.*

5 get/jump/rise etc to your feet to stand up after you have been sitting: *Mike leapt to his feet and ran towards the window.*

6 be on your feet a) to be standing for a long time without having time to sit down: *The worst thing about working in the shop is that you're on your feet all day.* → **dead on your feet** at DEAD[1] (8) **b)** to be standing up: *As soon as the bell rang the class were on their feet and out of the door.* **c)** to feel better again after being ill and in bed: *We'll soon have you on your feet again.*

7 be/get back on your feet to have enough money again, or to be successful again after having problems: *I need to get back on my feet again and forget all this.*

8 off your feet sitting or lying down, rather than standing or walking: *The doctor told me to stay off my feet for a few days.*

9 knock/lift etc sb off their feet to make someone fall over: *They were blown off their feet by the force of the explosion.*

10 be rushed/run off your feet to be very busy: *Before Christmas, most salespeople are rushed off their feet.*

11 set foot in sth to go to or enter a place: *She swore she would never set foot in his house again.*

12 be/get under your feet to annoy you by always being in the same place as you and preventing you from doing what you want: *I hate summer vacation. The kids are under my feet all day long.*

13 put your foot down a) to say very firmly that someone must do something or must stop doing something: *You'll just have to put your foot down and tell him he can't stay out on school nights.* **b)** *informal* to make a car go faster

14 put your feet up *informal* to relax, especially by sitting with your feet supported on something

15 put your foot in it *especially BrE*; **put your foot in your mouth** *especially AmE* to say something without thinking carefully, so that you embarrass or upset someone: *I've really put my foot in it this time. I didn't realize that was her husband!*

16 start/get off on the wrong/right foot to start a relationship badly or well: *Simon and I got off on the wrong foot but we're good friends now.*

17 not put a foot wrong *BrE* to do everything right and make no mistakes, especially in your job

18 have/keep both feet on the ground to think in a sensible and practical way and not have ideas or aims that will be impossible to achieve: *It was a great result, but we have to keep our feet firmly on the ground.*

19 fall/land on your feet to get into a good situation because you are lucky, especially after being in a difficult situation: *Don't worry about Nina, she always falls on her feet.*

20 get/have/keep your foot in the door to get your first opportunity to work in a particular organization or industry

21 have a foot in both camps to be involved with or connected with two opposing groups of people

22 have sb/sth at your feet used to say that people admire or respect someone very much: *All Paris was at his feet.* → **have the world at your feet** at WORLD[1] (24)

23 have two left feet *informal* to be very CLUMSY

24 have one foot in the grave to be very old or very ill – used humorously

25 ...my foot! *BrE old-fashioned* used to show that you do not believe something that someone has just said:

£50 *my foot! It'll cost £200 at least.*

26 leave feet first to die before you leave a place or job – used humorously: *If you keep fooling around with that gun you'll be leaving this camp feet first.*

27 feet of clay someone that you admire who has feet of clay has faults and weaknesses that you did not realize they had

28 foot soldier/patrol a soldier or group of soldiers that walks and does not use a horse or a vehicle

29 foot passenger a passenger on a ship who has not brought a car with them

30 a) left-footed/right-footed using your left foot or right foot when you kick a ball **b) flat-footed/four-footed** having a particular type or number of feet

31 foot pedal/brake/pump etc a machine or control that you operate using your feet

32 SOCK **the foot** the part of a sock that covers your foot

33 POETRY *technical* a part of a line of poetry in which there is one strong BEAT and one or two weaker ones → **the boot is on the other foot** at BOOT[1] (6); → **get/have cold feet** at COLD[1] (6); → UNDERFOOT; → **drag your feet/heels** at DRAG[1] (8); → **find your feet** at FIND[1] (18); → **from head to foot** at HEAD[1] (1); → **stand on your own (two) feet** at STAND[1] (31); → **sweep sb off their feet** at SWEEP[1] (14); → **have itchy feet** at ITCHY (3); → **not let the grass grow under your feet** at GRASS[1] (6); → **vote with your feet** at VOTE[1] (8)

foot² *v* **foot the bill** to pay for something, especially something expensive that you do not want to pay for: *He ordered drinks and then left me to foot the bill!*

foot·age /'fʊtɪdʒ/ *n* [U] cinema film showing a particular event: *old footage from the First World War*

foot and 'mouth dis,ease *n* [U] a serious disease that kills cows and sheep

foot·ball S1 W2 /'fʊtbɔːl $ -bɒːl/ *n*
1 [U] *BrE* a game played by two teams of eleven players who try to kick a round ball into the other team's GOAL; ◨ **soccer**: *Which football team do you support?* | *kids playing football in the street* | *My Dad took me to watch my first football match.* | *a football club* | **football fan/supporter** *a group of Scottish football fans* | **foot-ball boots/kit/shirt** (=clothes worn to play football) | **football pitch/ground/stadium**; → see picture at FOOTWEAR
2 [U] *AmE* a game played by two teams of eleven players who try to carry or kick an OVAL ball into the other team's GOAL; ◨ **American football** *BrE*: *college football games* | *a football field* | *He* **played football** *in high school.*
3 football hooligan *BrE* someone who behaves in a noisy or violent way at a football match
4 [C] a ball used in these games → FLAG FOOTBALL; → **political football** at POLITICAL (4)

foot·bal·ler /'fʊtbɔːlə $ -bɒːlər/ *n* [C] *BrE* someone who plays football, especially a professional player; ◨ **soccer player** *AmE*

football ,pools *n* [plural] another word for the POOLS

foot·bridge /'fʊt,brɪdʒ/ *n* [C] a narrow bridge used by people who are walking → see picture at BRIDGE

foot-dragging *n* [U] when someone is deliberately being slow to do something; → **drag your feet**

foot·er /'fʊtə $ -ər/ *n* **1 six-footer/eighteen-footer etc** someone or something that measures six feet tall, eighteen feet long etc **2** [C] a line of writing which appears at the bottom of each page of a document which is printed by a computer; → **header**

foot·fall /'fʊtfɔːl $ -fɒːl/ *n* [C,U] *literary* the sound of each step when someone is walking; ◨ **footstep**: *heavy footfalls*

'foot fault *n* [C] a mistake in tennis when the person who SERVES is not standing behind the line

1 000, **2** 000, **3** 000, most frequent words in **S** poken and **W** ritten English

foot·hill /'fʊt‚hɪl/ n [C usually plural] one of the smaller hills below a group of high mountains: *the foothills of the Himalayas*

foot·hold /'fʊthəʊld $ -hoʊld/ n [C] **1** a position from which you can start to make progress and achieve your aims: **gain/establish a foothold** *Extreme right-wing parties gained a foothold in the latest European elections.* **2** a small hole or crack where you can safely put your foot when you are climbing a steep rock

foot·ie /'fʊti/ n [U] *BrE informal* football

foot·ing /'fʊtɪŋ/ n **1** [singular] the conditions or arrangements on which something is based: **put/place sth on a ... footing** *He wanted to put their relationship on a permanent footing.* | **a financial/commercial/legal etc footing** *The city started the new year on a stronger financial footing.* | **on an equal footing (with sb/sth)/on the same footing (as sb/sth)** (=in the same state or condition as other people or things) *The new law puts women on an equal legal footing with men.* | *Many of the old polytechnics are now on the same footing as universities.* | **a sound/firm/secure footing** *They managed to get the business onto a more secure footing.* | *The whole country was on a war footing* (=ready to go to war at any time). **2** [singular] a firm hold with your feet when you are standing on a dangerous surface: *Seb struggled to keep his footing on the slippery path.* | **lose/miss your footing** (=be unable to keep standing or balancing) *The girl lost her footing and fell about 150 feet.* **3** [C usually plural] the solid base of bricks, stone etc that is under a building to support it and fasten it to the ground; **⊟ foundation**

foot·lights /'fʊtlaɪts/ n [plural] a row of lights along the front of the stage in a theatre; **→ spotlight**

'foot ‚locker n [C] *AmE* a large strong box that you keep your things in, used especially by soldiers

foot·loose /'fʊtluːs/ adj free to do exactly what you want because you have no responsibilities, for example when you are not married or do not have children: *footloose students traveling around Europe* | *When the kids leave home, you'll be* **footloose and fancy-free** (=free and without worries).

foot·man /'fʊtmən/ n plural **footmen** /-mən/ [C] a male servant in the past who opened the front door, announced the names of visitors etc

foot·note /'fʊtnəʊt $ -noʊt/ n [C] **1** a note at the bottom of the page in a book, which gives more information about something **2** a piece of additional information that is not very important but is interesting or helps you understand something: [+to] *There was an interesting footnote to the story.*

foot·path /'fʊtpɑːθ $ -pæθ/ n [C] especially BrE a narrow path for people to walk along, especially in the country; **⊟ trail** *AmE*

foot·plate /'fʊtpleɪt/ n [C] *BrE* the place on a steam train where the driver stood

foot·print /'fʊt‚prɪnt/ n [C] **1** also **footmark** a mark made by a foot or shoe: *We followed the footprints of a deer in the snow.* **2** technical the amount of space on a desk that a computer uses: *PCs with a 50% smaller footprint than other models*

foot·rest /'fʊt-rest/ n [C] something that supports your feet when you are sitting, for example a small piece of furniture or the part of a MOTORCYCLE where you put your feet

foot·sie /'fʊtsi/ n **play footsie (with sb)** informal **a)** to secretly touch someone's feet with your feet under a table to show that you think they are sexually attractive **b)** *AmE* to work together and help each other in a dishonest way: *politicians playing footsie with each other*

foot·sore /'fʊtsɔː $ -sɔːr/ adj having feet that hurt because you have walked a long distance

foot·step /'fʊtstep/ n [C] the sound each step makes when someone is walking: *He* **heard** *someone's* **foot-steps** *in the hall.* **→ follow (in) sb's footsteps** at **FOLLOW** (15)

foot·stool /'fʊtstuːl/ n [C] a low piece of furniture used to support your feet when you are sitting down

footwear

lace — tongue — lining — upper — heel — sole — sandals — shoes — toe — shoes

football boots *BrE*/ cleats *AmE*

bowling shoes

hiking boots

ballet shoes

clogs

boots

stilettos

slippers

foot·wear /'fʊtweə $ -wer/ n [U] things that people wear on their feet, such as shoes or boots: *outdoor footwear*

foot·work /'fʊtwɜːk $ -wɜːrk/ n [U] **1** skilful use of your feet when dancing or playing a sport: **good/neat/ fancy etc footwork** *The England keeper revealed some fancy footwork in the victory over Nottingham Forest.* **2** skilful methods that you use to achieve something: **fancy/deft/nifty etc footwork** *It took a bit of deft footwork to get them to agree.*

foot·y /'fʊti/ n [U] *BrE informal* football: *footy fans*

fop /fɒp $ fɑːp/ n [C] old-fashioned a man who is very interested in his clothes and appearance – used to show disapproval —**foppish** adj —**foppishness** n [U]

for¹ [S1] [W1] /fə; *strong* fɔː $ fər; *strong* fɔːr/ prep **1** used to say who is intended to get or use something, or where something is intended to be used: *I've got a present for you.* | *Someone left a message for Vicky.* | *English Language course for foreign students* | *We need a new battery for the radio.* | *These chairs are for the main office.* **2** in order to help someone or something: *I looked after the kids for them.* | *Let me carry that bag for you.* | *The doctor knew that there was nothing he could do for her.* | *Charles died fighting for his country.* | *What can I do for you* (=used to ask a customer if you can help them)? **3** used to say what the purpose of an object, action etc is: **for doing sth** *a knife for cutting bread* | *What did you do that for?* | *I've bought him a watch for his birthday.* | *the documents prepared for his defence* **4** in order to have, do, get, or obtain something: *Are you waiting for the bus?* | *the qualifications necessary for a career in broadcasting* | *Mother was too ill to get up for dinner.* | *I paid $3 for a ticket.* | *For further details, write to this address.* | *Let's go for a walk.* **5** used to say how long an action or situation continues for: *Bake the cake for 40 minutes.* | *We had been talking for a good half hour.* | *He's been off work for a while.*

⚠ **Since, during,** or **for?** → see box at SINCE

6 used to talk about distance: *We walked for miles.* | *Factories stretch for quite a way along the canal.*

7 if something is arranged for a particular time, it is planned that it should happen then: *I've invited them for 9 o'clock.* | *A special meeting has been arranged for 18th October.*

8 used to say where a person, vehicle etc is going: *I set off for work.* | *the train for Manchester* | *A few days later she would be leaving for New York.*

9 used to say what the price or value of something is: *a cheque for a hundred pounds* | *The diamond was insured for two thousand dollars.*

10 because of or as a result of something: *If, for any reason, you cannot attend, please inform us.* | *We could hardly see for the mist.* | *You'll feel better for a break.* | **for doing sth** *a reward for making good progress* | *Campbell was arrested for dangerous driving.*

11 used to say which thing or person your statement or question is related to: *I'm sure she's the ideal person for the job.* | *The questions on this paper are too difficult for 10-year-olds.* | *Are you all right for money?* | *Fortunately for him, he can swim.*

12 used to say which person or thing your feelings are directed towards: *I came away feeling sorry for poor old George.* | *My deep love for him still remains.* | *They show no respect for authority.*

13 used to say at which meal you eat something: *We had pasta for lunch.*

14 used to say which company, team etc you belong to: *I've worked for the BBC ever since I left university.* | *Deborah used to play for the A team.* | *He writes for a weekly paper.*

15 supporting or in agreement with something or someone: *We have studied the arguments for and against nuclear energy.* | *How many people voted for the proposal?* | *Three cheers for the captain.* | **be all for (doing) sth** (=support something very much) *I'm all for giving people more freedom.*

16 used to say what a word or sign means: *What's the French word for 'happy'?* | *Red is for danger.*

17 used to say that a particular quality of someone or something is surprising when you consider what they are: *She looks young for her age.* | *It's cold for July.*

18 as a representative of other people: *Paisley claims to speak for the majority of local people.*

19 used to say what is possible, difficult, necessary, unusual etc: **for sb/sth to do sth** *It's unusual for Donald to be so bad-tempered.* | *There is an urgent need for someone to tackle this problem.* | *Here is a chance for everyone to learn new skills.* | *There's nothing worse than for a parent to ill-treat a child.* | *It was too far for her to walk in high-heeled shoes.*

20 for each/every used to say that there is a relationship between one amount and another: *For each mistake, you'll lose half a point.* | *For every three people who agree, you'll find five who don't.*

21 sth is not for sb used to say that something is not the kind of thing that someone likes or will enjoy: *City life is not for me.* | *This book is not for everyone.*

22 it is (not) for sb to do sth used to say whether it is someone's right or duty to do something: *It's not for me to tell you what to do.* | *It will be for you to decide what action you should take.*

23 if it wasn't/weren't for sb/sth also **if it hadn't been for sb/sth** used to say who or what prevents or prevented something from happening: *If it hadn't been for you, I should have drowned.*

24 that's/there's sb/sth for you! *spoken* **a)** used to say that a particular kind of behaviour or situation is typical of someone or something, especially when you do not expect anything better from that person or thing: *I know it's outrageous, but that's Melissa for you.* **b)** used when you are annoyed or disappointed to say that something is the opposite of the quality you are mentioning: *Well, there's gratitude for you! Here am I trying to help and you tell me not to interfere!*

25 be (in) for it *spoken* to be likely to be blamed or punished: *You'll be in for it if she finds out what you've done!*; → see box at SINCE

for² S2 W1 *conjunction formal* used to introduce the reason for something; ⬛ **because:** *I cannot tell whether she is old or young, for I have never seen her.* | *He found it increasingly difficult to read, for his eyesight was beginning to fail.*

for·age¹ /'fɒrɪdʒ $ 'fɑː-, 'fɔː-/ *v* [I] **1** to go around searching for food or other supplies: [+for] *People are being forced to forage for food and fuel.* | *In the summer, the goats forage freely* (=in any place they want to go). **2** to search for something with your hands in a bag, drawer etc; ⬛ **ferret around:** [+around/through/among etc] *She foraged around in her purse and produced her ticket.* —**forager** *n* [C]

forage² *n* **1** [U] food supplies for horses and cattle **2** [singular] *BrE* an act of searching for something

for·ay /'fɒreɪ $ 'fɔː-, 'fɑː-/ *n* [C] **1** a short attempt at doing a particular job or activity, especially one that is very different from what you usually do: [+into] *It will be my first foray into local government.* | *Wright is about to make his first foray into the music business.* **2** a short sudden attack by a group of soldiers, especially in order to get food or supplies; → **raid:** [+into] *their nightly forays into enemy territory* **3** a short journey somewhere in order to get something or do something; ⬛ **trip:** [+into/to] *We make regular forays to France to buy wine.* —**foray** *v* [I]

for·bade /fə'bæd, -'beɪd $ fər/ *v* the past tense of FORBID

for·bear¹ /fɔː'beə, fə- $ fɔːr'ber, fər-/ *v past tense* **forbore** /-'bɔː $ -'bɔːr/, *past participle* **forborne** /-'bɔːn $ -'bɔːrn/ [I] *literary* to not do something you could or would like to do because you think it is wiser not to: [+from] *He decided to forbear from interfering.* | **forbear to do sth** *Clara forbore to mention his name.*

for·bear² /'fɔːbeə $ 'fɔːrber/ *n* [C] a FOREBEAR

for·bear·ance /fɔː'beərəns $ fɔːr'ber-/ *n* [U] *formal* the quality of being patient, able to control your emotions, and willing to forgive someone who has upset you

for·bear·ing /fɔː'beərɪŋ $ fɔːr'ber-/ *adj formal* patient and willing to forgive

for·bid /fə'bɪd $ fər-/ *v past tense* **forbade** /-'bæd, -'beɪd/ *past participle* **forbidden** /-'bɪdn/ *present participle* **forbidding** [T] **1** to tell someone that they are not allowed to do something, or that something is not allowed; ⬛ **permit: forbid sb to do sth** *He was forbidden to leave the house, as a punishment.* | **forbid sb from doing sth** *Women are forbidden from going out without a veil.* | **strictly/expressly/explicitly etc forbid** *The law strictly forbids racial or sexual discrimination.* ⚠ It is more usual to say that someone is **not allowed** to do something, rather than **forbidden** to do it: *I'm not allowed to stay out after midnight.* **2 God/Heaven forbid** *spoken* used to emphasize that you hope that something will not happen: *'Supposing I had an accident.' 'God forbid!'* **3** *formal* to make it impossible for someone to do something; ⬛ **prevent:** *Lack of space forbids listing the names of all those who contributed.*

for·bid·den /fə'bɪdn $ fər-/ *adj* **1** not allowed, especially because of an official rule; → **banned: it is forbidden (to do sth)** *It is forbidden to smoke at school.* | **be strictly/expressly/absolutely etc forbidden** *Alcohol is strictly forbidden in Saudi Arabia.* **2** a forbidden place is one that you are not allowed to go to: [+to] *The Great Mosque is forbidden to Christians.* **3** a forbidden activity, subject etc is one that people think that you should not do, talk about etc: *Sex was always a forbidden topic.* | **forbidden fruit** (=something that you should not have, but that you want) *Forbidden fruit is always more attractive.*

F

for·bid·ding /fəˈbɪdɪŋ $ fər-/ *adj* having a frightening or unfriendly appearance: **forbidding place/land/landscape etc** *We sailed past the island's rather dark and forbidding cliffs.* | *His face was forbidding, even hostile.*
—**forbiddingly** *adv*

for·bore /fɔːˈbɔː, fə- $ fɔːrˈbɔːr, fər-/ *v* the past tense of FORBEAR

for·borne /fɔːˈbɔːn, fə- $ fɔːrˈbɔːrn, fər-/ *v* the past participle of FORBEAR

force¹ S3 W1 /fɔːs $ fɔːrs/ *n*
1 MILITARY a) [C usually plural] a group of people who have been trained to do military work for a government or other organization: **government/military/defence etc forces** *The riots had to be suppressed by government forces.* | *He strengthened American forces in the Gulf.* | *a plan to disarm the rebel forces* (=those fighting against the government) **b) the forces** *BrE* the army, navy, and AIR FORCE: **in the forces** *Both her sons are in the forces.* **c) nuclear/conventional forces** NUCLEAR weapons or ordinary weapons: *short-range nuclear forces* → AIR FORCE, ARMED FORCES, GROUND FORCES; → **peacekeeping force** at PEACEKEEPING; → **security forces** at SECURITY (1); → TASK FORCE (2)
2 MILITARY ACTION [U] military action used as a way of achieving your aims: *Peace cannot be imposed by force.* | *The UN will allow the use of force against aircraft violating the zone.*
3 VIOLENCE [U] violent physical action used to get what you want: *The police used force to overpower the demonstrators.* | **by force** *In the end he had to be thrown out of the house by force.* | *They kicked the door down using sheer brute force.*
4 PHYSICAL POWER [U] the amount of physical power with which something moves or hits another thing; → **strength**: [+of] *The force of the explosion blew out all the windows.* | **with great/considerable/increasing etc force** *He raised his hand and struck her with terrifying force.*
5 NATURAL POWER [C,U] a natural power or event: *the force of gravity* | *powerful natural forces such as earthquakes, floods, and drought* | *the forces of nature*
6 ORGANIZED GROUP [C usually singular] a group of people who have been trained and organized to do a particular job: *the company's sales force* | *the quality of the teaching force* → POLICE FORCE
7 STRONG INFLUENCE [C] something or someone who is powerful and has a lot of influence on the way things happen: **the driving force (behind sth/sb)** (=the person or thing that makes something happen) *Betty Coward was the driving force behind the project.* | **a force for change/peace/democracy etc** (=someone or something that makes change, peace etc more likely to happen) *Healthy competition is a force for innovation.* | *He's a quick and decisive player – a force to be reckoned with* (=a person, team, company etc that influences what happens). | *The fall in prices was due to forces beyond their control.* → MARKET FORCES
8 POWERFUL EFFECT [U] the powerful effect that something has on you: *Even after 30 years, the play has lost none of its force.* | *She was aware of the force of his personality.*
9 join/combine forces (with sb/sth) to work together so that you can deal with a problem, be more powerful etc: **join forces to do sth** *Local schools have joined forces with each other to share facilities.*
10 in force **a)** if a law, rule etc is in force, it already exists: *The trade embargo has been in force for a year.* **b)** in a large group, especially in order to protest about something; ▣ **in large numbers**: *Villagers turned out in force to protest about the new road.*
11 come into force/bring sth into force if a new law, rule, change etc comes or is brought into force, it starts to exist: *Parking restrictions in the town centre came into force last month.*
12 by/through/out of force of habit because you have always done a particular thing and it is difficult to

change: *I get up at 6 o'clock every day from force of habit.*
13 by/through force of circumstance(s) *BrE* if something happens by force of circumstance, events outside your control make it happen
14 WIND a) force 8/9/10 etc a unit for measuring the strength of the wind **b)** gale/hurricane force wind extremely strong wind that does a lot of damage
15 POLICE the force a word meaning the POLICE FORCE, used especially by police officers
16 the forces of good/evil *literary* people or things that increase the amount of good or bad in the world: *the battle against the forces of evil* → LABOUR FORCE, TOUR DE FORCE, WORKFORCE

force² S2 W1 *v* [T]
1 MAKE SB DO STH to make someone do something they do not want to do; → **persuade**: **force sb/yourself to do sth** *Government troops have forced the rebels to surrender.* | *Due to the high cost of borrowing, many companies have been forced to close.* | *I had to force myself to get up this morning.* | **force sb/sth into (doing) sth** *women who are forced into arranged marriages* | *Bad health forced him into taking early retirement.*
2 MAKE SB/STH MOVE [always + adv/prep] to make someone or something move in a particular direction or into a different position, especially through or using great strength; ▣ **push**: *Westerly gales forced the ship off course.* | *Firemen entering the building were forced back by flames.* | *She tried to keep the door shut but the man forced it open.*
3 force your way through/into etc sth also **force your way in/out/past etc** to push very hard in order to get somewhere: *The doctor forced his way through the crowd.* | *Demonstrators forced their way past.*
4 MAKE STH HAPPEN to make something happen or change, especially more quickly than planned or expected: *the unfortunate events that forced his resignation* | *We need to force the pace on alternative energy policies.* | **force prices/interest rates etc down/up** *The effect will be to increase unemployment and force down wages.*
5 force a door/lock/window to open a door etc using physical strength, often causing damage: *I forced the lock on the cupboard to see what was inside.*
6 force the issue to do something that makes it necessary for someone to make decisions or take action, instead of waiting to see what happens: *Polly decided to force the issue by demanding an explanation.*
7 force sb's hand to make someone do something unwillingly or earlier than they had intended: *They're reluctant to sell the house yet but the right offer could force their hand.*
8 force a smile/laugh etc to make yourself smile, laugh etc even though you feel upset or annoyed
　force sth ⇔ **back** *phr v*
to stop yourself from showing that you are upset or frightened, especially with difficulty: *Janet forced back her tears.*
　force sth ⇔ **down** *phr v*
1 to make yourself eat or drink something, although you do not want it: *I managed to force down a piece of stale bread.*
2 to make a plane land by threatening to attack it: *The hijacked plane was forced down by military jets.*
　force sth **on/upon** sb *phr v*
to make someone do or accept something even though they do not want to: *It's no good trying to force a diet on someone.* | *people who try to force their own views on you*
　force sth ⇔ **out of** sb *phr v*
to make someone tell you something by asking them many times, threatening etc: *I wasn't going to tell Matt but he forced it out of me.*

forced /fɔːst $ fɔːrst/ *adj* **1** a forced smile, laugh etc is not natural or sincere: *'Oh, hello,' said Eileen, with forced brightness.* **2** [only before noun] done suddenly and quickly because the situation makes it necessary, not because it was planned or wanted: *The plane had to* *make a forced landing in a field.* | *the forced repatriation of thousands of refugees*

forced 'entry *n* [C,U] an occasion when someone gets into a building illegally by breaking a door, window etc: *The police found no signs of forced entry.*

forced 'labour *BrE*; **forced labor** *AmE n* [U] when prisoners or SLAVES are forced to do very hard physical work, or a system in which this happens: *Two million suffered imprisonment or forced labour.*

force-feed *v past tense and past participle* **force-fed** [T] to force someone to eat by putting food down their throat

force·ful /'fɔːsfəl $ 'fɔːrs-/ *adj* **1** a forceful person expresses their opinions very strongly and clearly and people are easily persuaded by them; ▪ **strong**: *a forceful personality/character/opponent etc He gained a reputation as a forceful member of the party.* **2** forceful arguments, reasons etc are strongly and clearly expressed; ▪ **powerful**: *a forceful attack on government policy* **3** having a powerful effect that is likely to change a situation: *The President hasn't been forceful enough in changing the judicial system.* | *Governments should adopt a more forceful approach to improve the environment.* **4** using physical force —**forcefully** *adv* —**forcefulness** *n* [U]

force ma·jeure /ˌfɔːs mæˈʒɜː $ ˌfɔːrs mɑːˈʒɜːr/ *n* [U] *law* unexpected events, for example a war, that prevent someone from doing what they had officially planned or agreed to do. An event like this can legally allow an agreement or contract to be changed or ended.

for·ceps /'fɔːseps, -səps $ 'fɔːr-/ *n* [plural] a medical instrument used for picking up and holding things: *a pair of forceps* → see picture at TOOL

for·ci·ble /'fɔːsɪ̬bəl $ 'fɔːr-/ *adj* done using physical force: *the forcible overthrow of the government* | *signs of forcible entry into the building*

for·ci·bly /'fɔːsɪ̬bli $ 'fɔːrs-/ *adv* **1** using physical force: *The police threatened to have protestors forcibly removed.* **2** in a way that has a strong clear effect; ▪ **powerfully**: *The case was forcibly put by the speaker.*

ford /fɔːd $ fɔːrd/ *n* [C] a place where a river is not deep, so that you can walk or drive across it —**ford** *v* [T]

fore¹ /fɔː $ fɔːr/ *n* **to the fore** to or in a position of importance or influence: *Environmental issues came to the fore in the 1980s.* | *The case brought to the fore a lot of racial tensions.*

fore² *adj* [only before noun] *technical* the fore parts of a ship, plane, or animal are the parts at the front —**fore** *adv*

fore- /fɔː $ fɔːr/ *prefix* **1** before: *The enemy had been forewarned.* → **forewarned is forearmed** at FOREWARN (2) **2** placed at the front: *her forenames* | *a horse's forelegs* **3** the front part of something: *his forehead*

fore·arm /'fɔːrɑːm $ -ɑːrm/ *n* [C] the lower part of the arm, between the hand and the elbow

fore·bear /'fɔːbeə $ 'fɔːrber/ *n* [C usually plural] *formal* someone who was a member of your family a long time in the past; ▪ **ancestor**

fore·bod·ing /fɔːˈbəʊdɪŋ $ fɔːrˈboʊ-/ *n* [U] a strong feeling that something bad is going to happen soon: *She waited for news with a grim sense of foreboding.*

fore·cast¹ /'fɔːkɑːst $ 'fɔːrkæst/ *n* [C] a description of what is likely to happen in the future, based on the information that you have now; → **prediction**: *The weather forecast is good for tomorrow.* | **profit/sales/ growth forecast** *the company's annual sales forecast*

forecast² *v past tense and past participle* **forecast** *or* **forecasted** [T] to make a statement saying what is likely to happen in the future, based on the information that you have now; ▪ **predict**: *Rain has been forecast for the weekend.* | **forecast (that)** *The Federal Reserve Bank forecasts that the economy will grow by 2% this year.*

fore·cast·er /'fɔːkɑːstə $ 'fɔːrkæstər/ *n* [C] someone whose job is to say what is likely to happen in the future, especially what kind of weather is expected: *the*

weather forecaster | *Economic forecasters think that the stock market is set to fall.*

fore·castle /'fəʊksəl $ 'foʊk-/ *n* [C] *AmE technical* the front part of a ship, where the sailors live; ▪ **fo'c'sle** *BrE*

fore·close /fɔːˈkləʊz $ fɔːrˈkloʊz/ *v* [I] *technical* if a bank forecloses, it takes away someone's property because they have failed to pay back the money that they borrowed from the bank to buy it: [+**on**] *Building societies may foreclose on a mortgage if payments are not kept up.* —**foreclosure** /-ˈkləʊʒə $ -ˈkloʊʒər/ *n* [C,U]: *housing foreclosures*

fore·court /'fɔːkɔːt $ 'fɔːrkɔːrt/ *n* [C] *BrE* a large open area in front of a building such as a garage or hotel

fore·doomed /fɔːˈduːmd $ fɔːr-/ *adj formal* intended by FATE (=the power that is believed to control people's lives) to be unsuccessful or unhappy; ▪ **doomed**

fore·fa·ther /'fɔːˌfɑːðə $ 'fɔːrˌfɑːðər/ *n* [C usually plural] **1** the people, especially men, who were part of your family a long time ago in the past; ▪ **ancestor**: *sb's forefathers What would our forefathers have thought?* **2** someone in the past who did something important that influences your life today: *Two hundred years ago our forefathers established this nation.*

fore·fin·ger /'fɔːˌfɪŋgə $ 'fɔːrˌfɪŋgər/ *n* [C] the finger next to your thumb; ▪ **index finger**

fore·foot /'fɔːfʊt $ 'fɔːr-/ *n plural* **forefeet** /-fiːt/ [C] *BrE* one of the two front feet of an animal with four legs

fore·front /'fɔːfrʌnt $ 'fɔːr-/ *n* **1 be at/in/to the forefront (of sth)** to be in a leading position in an important activity that is trying to achieve something or develop new ideas: *The company has always been at the forefront of science and technology.* | *Prison conditions have been pushed to the forefront of public debate.* **2 be in/at/to the forefront of sb's mind/attention etc** to be what someone is thinking about most, because it is very important to them; → **at the back of sb's mind**: *Fear of unemployment was at the forefront of everyone's minds.*

fore·gath·er, forgather /fɔːˈgæðə $ fɔːrˈgæðər/ *v* [I] *formal* to meet in a group; ▪ **gather**

fore·go /fɔːˈgəʊ $ fɔːrˈgoʊ/ *v* another spelling of FORGO

fore·go·ing /fɔːˈgəʊɪŋ $ fɔːrˈgoʊ-/ *adj, n formal* **the foregoing (sth)** something that has just been mentioned, read, dealt with etc; ▪ **following**: *The foregoing examples illustrate this point.* | *The foregoing helps to explain these results.*

foregone con'clusion *n* **be a foregone conclusion** if something is a foregone conclusion, its result is certain, even though it has not happened yet: *The election result was a foregone conclusion.*

fore·ground /'fɔːgraʊnd $ 'fɔːr-/ *n* **1** the foreground the part of the view in a picture or a photograph that is closest to you when you are looking at it; ▪ **background**: *There were three figures in the foreground.* **2 be in the foreground** to be regarded as important and receive a lot of attention: *Education has been very much in the foreground recently.*

fore·hand /'fɔːhænd $ 'fɔːr-/ *n* [singular] a way of hitting the ball in tennis and some other games, with the flat part of your hand facing the direction of the ball; → **backhand** —**forehand** *adj*; → see picture at BACKHAND

fore·head /'fɒrɪ̬d, 'fɔːhed $ 'fɔːrɪ̬d, 'fɑː-, 'fɔːrhed/ *n* [C] the part of your face above your eyes and below your hair

for·eign S3 W1 /'fɒrɪ̬n $ 'fɔː-, 'fɑː-/ *adj* **1** from or relating to a country that is not your own: *foreign students* | *Can you speak any foreign languages?* | *the success of foreign companies in various industries* | *I thought she sounded foreign.* | *transactions in foreign currencies* **2** [only before noun] involving or dealing with other

countries; ◪ **domestic**: *America's foreign policy* | **foreign investment/trade etc** *Foreign competition provides consumers with a greater variety of goods.* | *our budget for foreign aid* (=financial help to countries in need) | *the Chinese Foreign Minister*
3 be foreign to sb *formal* **a)** to seem strange to someone as the result of not being known or understood; ◪ **be alien to sb**: *The language of finance and economics is quite foreign to me.* **b)** to be not typical of someone's usual character: *Aggression is completely foreign to his nature.*
4 foreign body/matter/object *formal* a piece of dirt, glass, or other material that has got inside something, especially someone's body, and that should not be there: *cells that are designed to attack and destroy foreign bodies* —**foreignness** *n* [U]

foreign af·fairs *n* [plural] politics, business matters etc that affect or concern the relationship between your country and other countries

Foreign and Commonwealth Office *n* another name for the Foreign Office

for·eign·er /'fɒrɪnə $ 'fɔːrɪ̯nər, 'fɑː-/ *n* [C] someone who comes from a different country: *Some of the local people are suspicious of foreigners.*

foreign ex·change *n* **1** [U] used to talk about buying and selling foreign money: **foreign exchange markets/rates/transactions etc** *The dollar is expected to fall in the foreign exchange markets.* **2** [U] foreign money, especially money obtained by selling goods to a foreign country: *foreign exchange earned through exports* **3** also **exchange** [C] an arrangement through which a student exchanges homes, schools etc with a student from another country for a particular length of time, especially in order to learn a language: *The school organizes a foreign exchange to France.*

Foreign Office also **Foreign and Commonwealth Office** *n* the Foreign Office the British government department that is responsible for dealing with matters concerning other countries

Foreign Secretary *n* [C] the British Government minister who is in charge of the Foreign Office

fore·knowl·edge /fɔːˈnɒlɪdʒ $ fɔːrˈnɑːl-/ *n* [U] *formal* knowledge that something is going to happen before it actually does

fore·leg /'fɔːleg $ 'fɔːr-/ *n* [C] one of the two front legs of an animal with four legs

fore·lock /'fɔːlɒk $ 'fɔːrlɑːk/ *n* [C] **1** a piece of hair that falls over someone's forehead **2** the hair on a horse's head that grows between its ears and hangs forward on its face **3 tug/touch your forelock** *BrE* to show too much respect towards someone in authority – used to show disapproval

fore·man /'fɔːmən $ 'fɔːr-/ *n plural* **foremen** /-mən/ [C] **1** a worker who is in charge of a group of other workers, for example in a factory **2** the leader of a JURY, who announces their decision in court

fore·most /'fɔːməʊst $ 'fɔːrmoʊst/ *adj* **1** the best or most important; ◪ **leading**, **top**: *one of the country's foremost authorities on chemical warfare* | *Rostropovich was long considered the world's foremost cellist.* **2** in a leading position among a group of people or things: [+among/amongst] *Sharpton was foremost among the protestors.* | *Economic concerns are foremost on many voters' minds.* → **first and foremost** at FIRST² (10)

fore·name /'fɔːneɪm $ 'fɔːr-/ *n* [C] *BrE formal* someone's FIRST NAME; ◪ **Christian name**; → **surname**

fo·ren·sic /fəˈrensɪk, -zɪk/ *adj* [only before noun] relating to the scientific methods used for finding out about a crime: *forensic evidence/science/medicine etc Forensic experts found traces of blood in the car.* | *a career in forensic science* | *a forensic pathologist*

fo·ren·sics /fəˈrensɪks, -zɪks/ *n* [U] the use of scientfic tests to solve crimes

fore·play /'fɔːpleɪ $ 'fɔːr-/ *n* [U] sexual activity, such as kissing and touching the sexual organs, that happens before having sex

fore·run·ner /'fɔːˌrʌnə $ -ər/ *n* [C] **1** someone or something that existed before something similar that developed or came later: [+of] *Babbage's engine was later seen as the forerunner of the modern computer.* **2** a sign or warning that something is going to happen

fore·see /fɔːˈsiː $ fɔːr-/ *v past tense* **foresaw** /-ˈsɔː $ -ˈsɒː/, *past participle* **foreseen** /-ˈsiːn/ [T] to think or know that something is going to happen in the future; → **predict**: *I've put your name on the list and I don't foresee any problems.* | *The disaster could not have been foreseen.* | **foresee that** *Few analysts foresaw that oil prices would rise so steeply.* | **foresee what/how etc** *No one foresaw what he was planning.*

fore·see·a·ble /fɔːˈsiːəbəl $ fɔːr-/ *adj* **1 for/in the foreseeable future** for as long as it is possible to know what is likely to happen: *The situation is likely to continue for the foreseeable future.* **2 in the foreseeable future** fairly soon: *There is a possibility of water shortages in the foreseeable future.* **3** foreseeable difficulties, events etc should be planned for because they are very likely to happen in the future: *The judge found that it was not foreseeable that the fuel would catch fire.* | *foreseeable risk*

fore·shad·ow /fɔːˈʃædəʊ $ fɔːrˈʃædoʊ/ *v* [T] to show or say that something will happen in the future: *The revolution foreshadowed an entirely new social order.*

fore·shore /'fɔːʃɔː $ 'fɔːrʃɔːr/ *n* [C usually singular, U] *BrE* **1** the part of the shore between the highest and lowest levels that the sea reaches **2** the part of the shore between the edge of the sea and the part of the land that has houses, grass etc

fore·short·ened /fɔːˈʃɔːtnd $ fɔːrˈʃɔːrtnd/ *adj formal* **1** objects, places etc that are foreshortened appear to be smaller, shorter, or closer together than they really are: *Viewed from high up, their bodies were oddly foreshortened.* **2** ended before the usual or expected time: *a foreshortened career* —**foreshorten** *v* [T]

fore·sight /'fɔːsaɪt $ 'fɔːr-/ *n* [U] the ability to imagine what is likely to happen in the future; → **forethought**: *It was an example of the authorities' lack of foresight.* | **foresight to do sth** *Luckily I'd had the foresight to get in plenty of food.*

fore·skin /'fɔːˌskɪn $ 'fɔːr-/ *n* [C] a loose fold of skin covering the end of a man's PENIS

for·est S2 W2 /'fɒrɪst $ 'fɔː-, 'fɑː-/ *n* [C] a large area of land that is covered with trees; → **wood**: **thick/dense forest** *Much of Scandinavia is covered in dense forest.* | *a tropical forest* | *the danger of forest fires* → RAIN FOREST; → **not see the forest for the trees** at SEE¹ (41)

fore·stall /fɔːˈstɔːl $ fɔːrˈstɒːl/ *v* [T] *formal* to prevent something from happening or prevent someone from doing something by doing something first: *a measure intended to forestall further attacks*

for·est·ed /'fɒrɪ̯stɪd $ 'fɔː-, 'fɑː-/ *adj* forested areas are covered in forests: **thickly/heavily/densely etc forested** *heavily forested terrain*

for·est·er /'fɒrɪstə $ 'fɔːrɪ̯stər, 'fɑː-/ *n* [C] someone who works in a forest taking care of, planting, and cutting down the trees

for·est·ry /'fɒrɪ̯stri $ 'fɔː-, 'fɑː-/ *n* [U] the science or skill of looking after large areas of trees

fore·taste /'fɔːteɪst $ 'fɔːr-/ *n* **be a foretaste of sth** to be a sign of something more important, more impressive etc that will happen in the future: *Two spectacular wins at the start of the season were a foretaste of things to come.*

fore·tell /fɔːˈtel $ fɔːr-/ *v past tense and past participle* **foretold** /-ˈtəʊld $ -ˈtoʊld/ [T] *formal* to say what will happen in the future, especially by using special magical powers; ◼ **predict**: *the birth of Christ, foretold by prophets*

fore·thought /ˈfɔːθɔːt $ ˈfɔːrθɒːt/ *n* [U] careful thought or planning before you do something; → **foresight**: **the forethought to do sth** *No one had the forethought to bring a map.*

fore·told /fɔːˈtəʊld $ fɔːrˈtoʊld/ *v* the past tense and past participle of FORETELL

for·ev·er S3 also **for ever** *BrE* /fərˈevə $ -ər/ *adv*
1 for all future time: *I wanted that moment to last forever.* | *Many valuable works of art were lost forever.*
2 especially spoken for a very long time: *Once built, stone walls last forever.* | *It took forever to clean up after the party.* | *The meeting seemed to go on forever and a day.*
3 be forever doing sth *spoken* to do something often, especially in a way that annoys people; ◼ **be always doing sth**: *He's forever making comments about my weight.*
4 forever and ever a phrase meaning forever, used especially in stories
5 go on forever *AmE* to be extremely long or large: *The road just went on forever.*

fore·warn /fɔːˈwɔːn $ fɔːrˈwɔːrn/ *v* [T often passive] **1** to warn someone about something dangerous, unpleasant, or unexpected before it happens: **forewarn sb of/about sth** *We'd been forewarned of the dangers of travelling at night.* **2 forewarned is forearmed** used to say that it is better to know about something before it happens, so that you can be prepared for it — **forewarning** *n* [C,U]

fore·wom·an /ˈfɔːˌwʊmən $ ˈfɔːr-/ *n plural* **forewomen** /-ˌwɪmɪn/ [C] **1** a female worker who is in charge of a group of other workers, especially in a factory **2** a woman who is the leader of a JURY and announces their decision in court

fore·word /ˈfɔːwɜːd $ ˈfɔːrwɜːrd/ *n* [C] a short piece of writing at the beginning of a book that introduces the book or its writer

for·feit¹ /ˈfɔːfɪt $ ˈfɔːr-/ *v* [T] to lose a right, position, possession etc or have it taken away from you because you have broken a law or rule: *By being absent from the trial, he forfeited the right to appeal.* | *She was fined £3,000 and ordered to forfeit her car.*

forfeit² *n* [C] something that is taken away from you or something that you have to pay, because you have broken a rule or made a mistake

forfeit³ *adj* **be forfeit** *formal* to be legally or officially taken away from you as a punishment: *The company's property may even be forfeit.*

for·feit·ure /ˈfɔːfɪtʃə $ ˈfɔːrfɪtʃər/ *n* [C,U] *formal* when someone has their property or money officially taken away because they have broken a law or rule: *Refusal to sign meant forfeiture of property and exile.*

for·gath·er /fɔːˈgæðə $ fɔːrˈgæðər/ *v* another spelling of FOREGATHER

for·gave /fəˈɡeɪv $ fər-/ *v* the past tense of FORGIVE

forge¹ /fɔːdʒ $ fɔːrdʒ/ *v* **1** [T] to develop something new, especially a strong relationship with other people, groups, or countries; ◼ **form**: **forge a relationship/alliance/link etc (with sb)** *In 1776 the United States forged an alliance with France.* | *The two women had forged a close bond.* | *Back in the 1980s, they were attempting to forge a new kind of rock music.* **2** [T] to illegally copy something, especially something printed or written, to make people think that it is real; → **counterfeit**: *Someone stole my credit card and forged my signature.* | *a forged passport* **3** [I always + adv/prep] *written* to move somewhere or continue doing something in a steady determined way: [+into/through] *Crowds of people forged through the streets towards the embassy.* | *He forged into the lead in the fourth set.* | [+on] *Her speech wasn't going down too well, but she forged on.* **4** [T] to make something from a piece of metal by heating the metal and shaping it

forge ahead *phr v* to make progress, especially quickly: [+with] *Jo's forging ahead with her plans to write a film script.*

forge² *n* [C] **1** a place where metal is heated and shaped into objects **2** a large piece of equipment that produces high temperatures, used for heating and shaping metal objects

forg·er /ˈfɔːdʒə $ ˈfɔːrdʒər/ *n* [C] someone who illegally copies documents, money, paintings etc and tries to make people think they are real

for·ge·ry /ˈfɔːdʒəri $ ˈfɔːr-/ *n plural* **forgeries 1** [C] a document, painting, or piece of paper money that has been copied illegally; ◼ **fake**: *The painting was a very clever forgery.* **2** [U] the crime of copying official documents, money etc

for·get S1 W1 /fəˈɡet $ fər-/ *v past tense* **forgot** /-ˈɡɒt $ -ˈɡɑːt/, *past participle* **forgotten** /-ˈɡɒtn $ -ˈɡɑːtn/ *v*
1 FACTS/INFORMATION [I,T] to not remember facts, information, or people or things from the past: *I'm sorry, I've forgotten your name.* | *I know you told me, but I forgot.* | *What happened that day will never be forgotten.* | [+about] *Karl says he forgot about our date.* | *She forgot all about their anniversary.* | **forget (that)** *I forgot that there's a speed limit here.* | **forget how/what/when/why etc** *How can you forget where you've parked the car?* | *He's someone who never forgets a face* (=forgets who someone is). | **I was forgetting ...** (=said when you have just remembered or been reminded about something) *spoken*: *Oh yes, I was forgetting she was pregnant.*
2 STH YOU MUST DO [I,T] to not remember to do something that you should do: *'Did you remember to post that letter?' 'Oh, sorry, I forgot.'* | *Give me your phone number before I forget* (=forget to get it). | **forget to do sth** *Someone's forgotten to turn off their headlights.* | **clean forget** *AmE* (=completely forget) *He meant to invite Monica, but he clean forgot.*
3 LEAVE STH SOMEWHERE [T] to not remember to bring something that you need with you: **forget your keys/money/cigarettes etc** *Oh no, I've forgotten my wallet.*
4 STOP THINKING ABOUT [I,T] to stop thinking or worrying about someone or something: *Forget him, he's not worth it.* | *At my age, I think I can forget fashion.* | **forget (that)** *After a while you'll forget you're wearing contact lenses.* | [+about] *I'll never be able to forget about the accident.*
5 NOT CARE ABOUT [I,T] to not care about or give attention to someone or something any longer: [+about] *Don't forget about your old friends when you go off to college, okay?* | *You can't afford to forget your relationship with your husband.*
6 STOP A PLAN [I,T] to stop planning to do something because it is no longer possible or sensible: [+about] *We'll have to forget about going on holiday.* | *If we can't get any funding we might as well forget the whole thing.*
7 not forgetting sth *BrE* used to add something to a list of things you have mentioned: *You'll have to pay for the packaging and transportation costs, not forgetting airport taxes.*
8 forget yourself a) to do something stupid or embarrassing, especially by losing control of your emotions: *Lisa forgot herself and reached out to touch his knee.* **b)** *BrE* to become so involved in something that you do not think about or notice anything else; ◼ **lose yourself**: **forget yourself in sth** *Often he would forget himself in his work for hours.*

9 don't forget a) used to remind someone to do something: *We need bread, milk, and eggs – don't forget.* | **don't forget to do sth** *Don't forget to lock up when you leave.* **b)** used to remind someone about an important fact or detail that they should consider: **don't forget (that)** *But don't forget that you have to pay interest on the loan.* | *Don't forget, I'll be home late*

tonight... **c)** used to remind someone to take something with them: *Don't forget your sandwiches.*
10 forget it *spoken* **a)** used to tell someone that something is not important and they do not need to worry about it: *'Sorry I didn't phone.' 'Forget it.'* **b)** used to tell someone to stop asking or talking about something, because it is annoying you: *I'm not coming with you, so forget it.* **c)** also **forget that!** *AmE* used to tell someone that you refuse to do something or that it will be impossible to do something: *'Can you lend me $10.' 'Forget it, no way.'* | *If you're thinking of getting Roy to help, you can forget it.* **d)** used when someone asks you what you just said and you do not want to repeat it: *'What did you say?' 'Nothing, just forget it.'*
11 I'll never forget sth used to say that you will always remember something from the past, because it was sad, funny, enjoyable etc: *I'll never forget the look on his face when he opened the door.*
12 aren't you forgetting...?/haven't you forgotten...? used to remind someone about something, often humorously: *Aren't you forgetting that you're already married?*
13 I forget used to say that you cannot remember a particular detail about something: **I forget what/where/how etc** *I forget what he said exactly but it was very rude.* | **I forget the name/details etc** *I forget the name of the street, but it's the first on the left.*
14 and don't you forget it used to remind someone angrily about an important fact that should make them behave differently: *I'm the boss around here, and don't you forget it!*

for·get·ful /fə'getfəl $ fər-/ *adj* often forgetting things —**forgetfully** *adv* —**forgetfulness** *n* [U]

for'get-me-ˌnot *n* [C] a small plant with pale blue flowers

for·get·ta·ble /fə'getəbəl $ fər-/ *adj* not very interesting or good – often used humorously: ■ **unforgettable**: *He'd had a role in one or two forgettable movies.*

for·giv·a·ble /fə'gɪvəbəl $ fər-/ *adj* if something bad is forgivable, you can understand how it happened and you can easily forgive it; ■ **unforgivable**: *It was an easily forgivable mistake.*

for·give S3 /fə'gɪv $ fər-/ *v past tense* **forgave** /-'geɪv/, *past participle* **forgiven** /-'gɪvən/ [I,T]
1 to stop being angry with someone and stop blaming them, although they have done something wrong: **forgive sb for (doing) sth** *I've tried to forgive him for what he said.* | *He never forgave her for walking out on him.* | **forgive myself/yourself etc** *If anything happened to the kids I'd never forgive myself.* | **you're forgiven** *spoken* (=used to tell someone that you are not angry with them) *'I'm really sorry.' 'It's okay, you're forgiven.'* | **forgive sb sth** *God forgives us our sins.* | *He didn't look the sort of man to forgive and forget* (=forgive someone and no longer think about it).
2 forgive me *spoken* used when you are going to say or do something that might seem rude or offensive and you want it to seem more polite: *Forgive me, but I don't think that is relevant.* | **forgive me for asking/saying etc sth** also **forgive my asking/saying etc** *Forgive me for saying so, but that's nonsense.* | *Forgive my phoning you so late.*
3 sb can be forgiven for thinking/believing/feeling etc sth used to say that it is easy to understand why someone might think or do something: *You could be forgiven for thinking football is a religion here.*
4 forgive a debt/loan *formal* if a country or organization forgives a debt, it says that the money does not have to be paid back; ■ **write off**: *Saudi Arabia's decision to forgive the debt owed by the poorest Islamic countries*

for·give·ness /fə'gɪvnɪs $ fər-/ *n* [U] when someone forgives another person: **ask/beg/pray etc for (sb's) forgiveness** *He never admitted his guilt or asked for forgiveness.*

for·giv·ing /fə'gɪvɪŋ $ fər-/ *adj* willing to forgive: *My father was a kind and forgiving man.*

for·go /fɔː'gəʊ $ fɔːr'goʊ/ *v past tense* **forwent** /-'went/ *past participle* **forgone** /-'gɒn $ -'gɔːn/ *present participle* **forgoing** [T] to not do or have something pleasant or enjoyable: *I had to forgo lunch.*

for·got /fə'gɒt $ fər'gɑːt/ *v* the past tense of FORGET

for·got·ten[1] /fə'gɒtn $ fər'gɑːtn/ *v* the past participle of FORGET

forgotten[2] *adj* [usually before noun] that people have forgotten about or do not pay much attention to: *a forgotten corner of the churchyard*

fork[1] /fɔːk $ fɔːrk/ *n* [C] **1** a tool you use for picking up and eating food, with a handle and three or four points: *Put the knives and forks on the table.* → see picture at MULTIPURPOSE **2** a garden tool used for digging, with a handle and three or four points → PITCHFORK[1]; → see picture at GARDENING **3** a place where a road, river, or tree divides into two parts, or one of the parts it divides into: *the north fork of the Sacramento river* | *Take the left fork then go straight on.* **4 fork of lightning** a sudden flash of LIGHTNING with two or more lines of light **5** one of the two metal bars between which the front wheel of a bicycle or MOTORCYCLE is fixed → see picture at BICYCLE → TUNING FORK

fork[2] *v* **1** also **fork off** [I] if a road, river etc forks, it divides into two parts; → **divide**, **split**: *The path forked off in two directions.* **2 fork (off) left/right** to go left or right when a road divides into two parts; ⊟ **turn**: *Fork left at the bottom of the hill.* **3** [T always + adv/prep] to put food into your mouth or onto a plate using a fork: **fork sth into/onto etc sth** *He forked some bacon into his mouth.* **4** [T always + adv/prep] to put MANURE into soil or to move soil around using a large garden fork: **fork sth in/over etc** *In November, the soil should be forked over.*

fork out (sth) *phr v informal* to spend a lot of money on something, not because you want to but because you have to: [+for/on] *I had to fork out £600 on my car when I had it serviced.* | *We don't want to have to fork out for an expensive meal.*

fork sth ⇔ **over** *phr v informal especially AmE* to give money to someone or something, or spend money on something: *The arena won't be finished until private donors fork over more money.*

forked /fɔːkt $ fɔːrkt/ *adj* having one end divided into two or more parts: *Snakes have forked tongues.*

ˌforked 'lightning *n* [U] lightning that looks like a line of light that divides into several smaller lines near the bottom; → **sheet lightning**

fork·ful /'fɔːkfʊl $ 'fɔːrk-/ *n* [C] an amount of food on a fork: [+of] *huge forkfuls of food*

ˌfork-lift 'truck also **ˌfork-lift** *n* [C] a vehicle with special equipment on the front for lifting and moving heavy things

for·lorn /fə'lɔːn $ fər'lɔːrn/ *adj* **1** seeming lonely and unhappy: *a forlorn figure sitting all by herself* | *Ana sat with a bowed head and spoke in a forlorn voice.* **2** a place that is forlorn seems empty and sad, and is often in bad condition: *The house looked old and forlorn.* **3** [only before noun] a forlorn hope, attempt, struggle etc is not going to be successful: *We continued negotiating in the forlorn hope of finding a peace formula.* —**forlornly** *adv*

form[1] S1 W1 /fɔːm $ fɔːrm/ *n*
1 TYPE [C] a particular type of something that exists in many different varieties: [+of] *a severe form of cancer* | *The bicycle is an environment-friendly form of transport.* | *the art forms of the twentieth century*
2 WAY STH IS/APPEARS [C] the way something is or appears to be: *We oppose racism in all its forms.* | **in the form of sth** *People are bombarded with information in the form of TV advertising.* | *Vitamin C can be taken in capsule or tablet form.* | *A typical training programme takes the form of a series of workshops.*
3 SHAPE [C] a shape: [+of] *the shadowy forms of the divers swimming below the boat* | **in the form of sth** *The*

main staircase was in the form of a big 'S'. | *The female form* is a thing of beauty.

633

formally

4 DOCUMENT [C] an official document with spaces where you write information, especially about yourself: *Application forms are available from the college.* | *Just complete the entry form* (=write the answers to the questions on a form) *and return it.* | **fill in/out a form** (=write the answers to the questions on a form) *Fill in the form and send it back with your cheque.*

5 ART/LITERATURE [U] the structure of a work of art or piece of writing, rather than the ideas it expresses, events it describes etc: *the distinction between form and content*

6 PERFORMANCE [U] how well a sports person, team, musician etc is performing, or has performed recently: *I have been greatly encouraged by the team's recent form.* | **on present/current/past etc form** *On current form he's one of the top three players in the country.* | **in good/fine/great form** *He's been in good form all this season.* | *He had no qualms about dropping players he thought were off form* (=not performing well).

7 SCHOOL [C] *BrE* a class in a school: **first/second/sixth etc form** *examinations taken in the fourth form* → FORM TEACHER

8 GRAMMAR [C] a way of writing or saying a word that shows its number, tense etc. For example, 'was' is a past form of the verb 'to be'.

9 CRIMINAL RECORD [U] *BrE informal* if someone has form, they are known to the police because they have committed crimes in the past

10 bad form *old-fashioned* behaviour that is considered to be socially unacceptable; ☐ **bad manners**: *It used to be considered bad form to talk about money.*

11 form of words a way of expressing something official; ☐ **wording**: *The precise form of words has been agreed by the 12 heads of government.*

12 be in good/fine/great form also **be on good/fine/great etc form** *BrE* to be full of confidence and energy, so that you do something well or talk in an interesting or amusing way: *Michelle was in great form at last week's conference.*

13 take form **a)** to begin to exist or develop: *The womb represents the very first place in which life takes form*. **b)** to start to become a particular shape: *As the men worked, I watched the ship's hull take form.* → **true to form** at TRUE¹ (7)

form² S1 W1 *v*

1 ESTABLISH [T] to establish an organization, committee, government etc: *The winning party will form the government.* | *CARE was formed in 1946 and helps the poor in 38 countries.*

2 BE PART OF STH [linking verb] to be the thing, or one of the things, that is part of something else, often having a particular use: *Love and trust should form the basis of a marriage.* | *The project forms part of a larger project investigating the history of the cinema.* | *The river formed a natural boundary between the two countries.*

3 START TO EXIST [I,T] to start to exist, or make something start to exist, especially as the result of a natural process: *The rocks were formed more than 4000 million years ago.* | *By midnight ice was already forming on the roads.* | *Sulphur dioxide and nitrogen oxide combine to form acid rain.*

4 MAKE/PRODUCE [T] to make something by combining two or more parts: *In English the past tense of a verb is usually formed by adding 'ed'.*

5 SHAPE/LINE [I,T] to come together in a particular shape or line, or to make something have a particular shape; ☐ **make**: *Film-goers began to form a line outside the cinema.* | *Cut off the corners of the square to form a diamond.*

6 RELATIONSHIP [T] to establish and develop a relationship with someone: *She seemed incapable of forming any relationships.* | *On returning to Boston, she formed a close friendship with her aunt.*

7 form an opinion/impression/idea to use available information to develop or reach an opinion or idea: *She formed the opinion that one of the pupils was bullying the other.*

8 INFLUENCE [T] to have a strong influence on how someone's character develops and the type of person they become; ☐ **mould**: *Events in early childhood often help to form our personalities in later life.*

form·al¹ S2 W2 /ˈfɔːməl $ ˈfɔːr-/ *adj*

1 OFFICIAL [usually before noun] made or done officially or publicly; ☐ **informal**: *formal recognition of the reformed church* | *a formal agreement between the countries* | *The staff say there is no formal structure for negotiating pay increases.* | **make/lodge a formal complaint** *Mr Kelly has lodged a formal complaint against the police.*

2 BEHAVIOUR formal behaviour is very polite, and is used in official or important situations, or with people you do not know well; ☐ **informal**: *Over the years, teaching methods have changed and become less formal.*

3 LANGUAGE formal language is used in official or serious situations; ☐ **informal**: *'Yours sincerely' is a formal way of ending a letter.*

4 EVENT/OCCASION a formal event is important, and people who go to it wear special clothes and behave very politely; ☐ **informal**: *I've met her twice but only on formal occasions.* | *a formal dinner*

5 CLOTHES formal dress is clothing such as a TUXEDO for men or a long dress for women, that is worn to formal events; ☐ **casual, informal**: *We insist on formal dress for dinner.*

6 formal education/training/qualifications education etc in a subject or skill, that you receive in a school, college etc rather than practical experience of it: *knowledge and wisdom gained from experience rather than from formal education*

7 ORGANIZED done in a very organized way; ☐ **informal**: *The course includes formal lectures and more informal seminars.*

8 GARDEN/PARK a formal garden, park, or room is arranged in a very organized way; ☐ **informal**: *the palace's beautifully restored formal gardens* → FORMALLY

formal² *n* [C] *AmE* **1** a dance at which you have to wear formal clothes **2** an expensive and usually long dress that women wear on formal occasions

for·mal·de·hyde /fɔːˈmældɪhaɪd $ fɔːr-/ *n* [U] a strong-smelling gas that can be mixed with water and used for preserving things such as dead animals to be used in science etc: *frogs preserved in formaldehyde*

for·mal·ise /ˈfɔːməlaɪz $ ˈfɔːr-/ *v* a British spelling of FORMALIZE

form·al·is·m /ˈfɔːməlɪzəm $ ˈfɔːr-/ *n* [U] a style or method in art, religion, or science that pays a lot of attention to the rules and correct forms of something, rather than to inner meanings —**formalist** *n* [C] *adj* —**formalistic** *adj* /ˌfɔːməˈlɪstɪk◄ $ ˌfɔːr-/

for·mal·i·ty /fɔːˈmælɪti $ fɔːr-/ *n plural* **formalities** **1** [C usually plural] something that you must do as a formal or official part of an activity or process: *the formalities necessary for a valid marriage* **2** [C usually singular] something you must do even though it has no practical importance or effects: **just/only/merely etc a formality** *Getting a gun licence here seems to be just a formality.* **3** [U] careful attention to polite behaviour and language in formal situations: *There is always some degree of formality when one speaks to a stranger.* | *The loan was arranged with little formality.*

for·mal·ize also **-ise** *BrE* /ˈfɔːməlaɪz $ ˈfɔːr-/ *v* [T] to make a plan, decision, or idea official, especially by deciding and clearly describing all the details: *Final arrangements for the takeover have yet to be formalized.* —**formalization** /ˌfɔːməlaɪˈzeɪʃən $ ˌfɔːrmələ-/ *n* [U]

for·mal·ly /ˈfɔːməli $ ˈfɔːr-/ *adv* **1** officially; ☐ **informally**: *We announced a decision formally recognizing the new government.* **2** in a polite way;

F

◧ informally: *He put his hand out formally, and Liza took it.* | *'I apologize, Captain,' she said formally.*

for·mat¹ W3 /'fɔːmæt $ 'fɔːr-/ *n* [C]
1 the way in which something such as a television show or meeting is organized or arranged: *The courses were run to a consistent format.*
2 the size, shape, design etc, in which something such as a book or magazine is produced: *a large-format book for the partially-sighted*
3 used to talk about video, CD, tape etc when saying what type of equipment it can be played on

for·mat² *v* **formatted, formatting** [T] **1** *technical* to organize the space on a computer DISK so that information can be stored on it **2** to arrange the pages of a book or the information on a computer etc into a particular design: *better ways to format your spreadsheets* —**formatting** *n* [U] —**formatted** *adj*

for·ma·tion W2 /fɔːˈmeɪʃən $ fɔːr-/ *n*
1 [U] the process of starting a new organization or group; ◧ **creation**: [+of] *the formation of a new government*
2 [U] the process by which something develops into a particular thing or shape: [+of] *the substances which lead to the formation of ozone* | *We now know a lot more about the early stages of planetary formation.*
3 [C] the way in which a group of things are arranged to form a pattern or shape: *troop formations*
4 in formation if a group of planes, ships, soldiers etc are moving in formation, they are flying, marching etc in a particular order or pattern: *a squadron of aircraft, flying in formation*
5 [C,U] rock or cloud that is formed in a particular shape, or the shape in which it is formed: **rock/cloud formation** *the canyon's impressive rock formations*
6 [C,U] *technical* society, politics etc seen as a system of practices and beliefs: **social/political/cultural etc formation** *Marx founded a new science: the science of the history of social formations.*

for·ma·tive /'fɔːmətɪv $ 'fɔːr-/ *adj* [only before noun] having an important influence on the way someone or something develops: **formative years/period/stages etc** (=the period when someone's character develops) *He exposed his children to music throughout their formative years.* | **formative influence/effect etc** *International politics were a formative influence on the British labour movement.*

for·mer¹ S2 W1 /'fɔːmə $ 'fɔːrmər/ *adj* [only before noun]
1 happening or existing before, but not now; → **present, previous**: *the former Soviet Union* | *Their farm has been reduced to half its former size.*
2 having a particular position in the past; ◧ **ex-**; → **present**: *my former husband* | *former president Clinton*
3 in former times/years in the past
4 sb/sth's **former self** what someone or something was like before they were changed by age, illness, trouble etc: *She seems more like her former self.* | **be a shadow/ghost of your former self** (=be much less confident, healthy, energetic etc than you used to be) *The team's a shadow of its former self.*

former² *n* **1 the former** *formal* the first of two people or things that you have just mentioned; ◧ **the latter**: *Of the two possibilities, the former seems more likely.* **2 first/second/sixth etc former** *BrE* used in some schools to show which class a student is in, according to how many years they have been in school

for·mer·ly /'fɔːməli $ 'fɔːrmərli/ *adv* in earlier times; ◧ **previously**: *Kiribati, formerly known as the Gilbert Islands* | *This elegant hotel was formerly a castle.*

For·mi·ca /fɔːˈmaɪkə $ fɔːr-/ *n* [U] *trademark* strong plastic made in thin sheets, used especially for covering the surfaces of tables and kitchen COUNTERS

for·mi·da·ble /'fɔːmɪdəbəl, fəˈmɪd- $ 'fɔːr-/ *adj* **1** very powerful or impressive, and often frightening: *The building is grey, formidable, not at all*

picturesque.* | *The new range of computers have formidable processing power.* **2** difficult to deal with and needing a lot of effort or skill: **formidable task/challenge** *the formidable task of local government reorganization* —**formidably** *adv*

form·less /'fɔːmləs $ 'fɔːrm-/ *adj* without a definite shape: *To the listener, this music is incoherent and formless.* | *formless horrors that await you in the fog* —**formlessly** *adv* —**formlessness** *n* [U]

'form ,letter *n* [C] a standard letter that is sent to a number of people

'form ,teacher *n* [C] *BrE* the teacher who is responsible for all the students in the same class at a school

for·mu·la W3 /'fɔːmjᵿlə $ 'fɔːr-/ *n plural* **formulas** *or* **formulae** /-liː/
1 [singular] a method or set of principles that you use to solve a problem or to make sure that something is successful: *We're still searching for a peace formula.* | [+for] *a formula for the withdrawal of US forces from the area* | *There is no **magic formula** (=a method that is certain to be successful) that will transform sorrow into happiness.* | *With viewing figures up a million, the programme has a **winning formula**.*
2 [C] a series of numbers or letters that represent a mathematical or scientific rule: *the formula for calculating distance* | *Sugar is represented by the simple formula CHO.*
3 [C] a list of the substances used to make a medicine, FUEL, drink etc, showing the amounts of each substance that should be used: *Our products are handmade from traditional formulas.*
4 Formula One/Two/Three etc a type of car racing, in which the different types are based on the size of the cars' engines: *a Formula One car*
5 [U] a type of liquid food for babies that is similar to a woman's breast milk
6 [C] a fixed and familiar series of words that seems meaningless or insincere: *a speech full of the usual formulas and clichés*

for·mu·la·ic /ˌfɔːmjᵿˈleɪ-ɪk◂ $ ˌfɔːr-/ *adj formal* containing or made from ideas or expressions that have been used many times before and are therefore not very new or interesting: *Children love jokes and riddles that are heavily formulaic.*

for·mu·late /'fɔːmjᵿleɪt $ 'fɔːr-/ *v* [T] **1** to develop something such as a plan or a set of rules, and decide all the details of how it will be done: **formulate a policy/plan/strategy etc** *Tawney formulated Labour Party education policy in 1922.* | **formulate an idea/theory** *Charles Darwin formulated the theory of natural selection.* **2** to think carefully about what to say, and say it clearly: *We are studying the situation but have not formulated any response yet.* —**formulation** /ˌfɔːmjᵿˈleɪʃən $ ˌfɔːr-/ *n* [C,U]: *the formulation of clear objectives*

for·ni·cate /'fɔːnᵻkeɪt $ 'fɔːr-/ *v* [I] a word meaning to have sex with someone who you are not married to – used to show strong disapproval —**fornication** /ˌfɔːnᵻˈkeɪʃən $ ˌfɔːr-/ *n* [U]

for·sake /fəˈseɪk $ fər-/ *v past tense* **forsook** /-ˈsʊk/, *past participle* **forsaken** /-ˈseɪkən/ [T] *formal* **1** to leave someone, especially when you should stay because they need you; ◧ **abandon**: *children forsaken by their parents* **2** to stop doing, using, or having something that you enjoy; ◧ **give up**: *She will never forsake her vegetarian principles.* **3** to leave a place, especially when you do not want to: *He has forsaken his native Finland to live in Britain.* → **GODFORSAKEN**

for·sooth /fəˈsuːθ $ fər-/ *adv old use* certainly

for·swear /fɔːˈsweə $ fɔːrˈswer/ *v past tense* **forswore** /-ˈswɔː $ -ˈswɔːr/, *past participle* **forsworn** /-ˈswɔːn $ -ˈswɔːrn/ [T] *formal* to stop doing something or promise that you will stop doing something; ◧ **renounce**: *We are forswearing the use of chemical weapons for any reason.*

fort /fɔːt $ fɔːrt/ n [C] a strong building or group of buildings used by soldiers or an army for defending an important place → **hold the fort** at HOLD¹ (33)

for·te¹ /ˈfɔːteɪ $ fɔːrt/ n **1 be sb's forte** to be something that you do well or are skilled at: *He found that running long distances was **not** his forte.* | *As a writer, her forte is comedy.* **2** [C] a note or line of music played or sung loudly

for·te² /ˈfɔːteɪ $ ˈfɔːr-/ adj, adv technical played or sung loudly; **◨ piano**

forth S2 /fɔːθ $ fɔːrθ/ adv
1 and so forth used to refer to other things of the type you have already mentioned, without actually naming them; **◨ et cetera:** *She started telling me about her bad back, her migraines, and so forth.*
2 [only after verb] *formal* going out from a place or point, and moving forwards or outwards: *The house was still burning, pouring forth thick black smoke.* → **back and forth** at BACK¹ (11); → **hold forth** at HOLD¹; → **put forth** at PUT; → **sally forth** at SALLY²; → **set forth** at SET¹

forth·com·ing /ˌfɔːˈkʌmɪŋ◂ $ ˌfɔːrθ-/ adj **1** [only before noun] a forthcoming event, meeting etc is one that has been planned to happen soon: *the forthcoming elections* | *Keep an eye on the noticeboards for forthcoming events.* **2** willing to give information about something; **◨ unforthcoming:** [+about] *IBM is usually pretty forthcoming about the markets for its products.* **3** [not before noun] if something is forthcoming, it is given or offered when needed – often used to say that this does not happen: *When no reply was forthcoming, she wrote again.*

forth·right /ˈfɔːθraɪt $ ˈfɔːrθ-/ adj direct and honest – used in order to show approval: *She answered in her usual forthright manner.*

forth·with /fɔːˈθwɪθ, -ˈwɪθ $ fɔːrθ-/ adv formal immediately: *He was fined £40, with 28 days' imprisonment if the money was not produced forthwith.*

for·ti·fi·ca·tion /ˌfɔːtɪfɪ̣ˈkeɪʃən $ ˌfɔːr-/ n **1** [U] the process of making something stronger or more effective **2 fortifications** [plural] towers, walls etc built around a place in order to protect it or defend it: *a site of ancient fortifications dating from about 500 B.C.*

fortified wine n [C,U] wine such as SHERRY or PORT that has strong alcohol added

for·ti·fy /ˈfɔːtɪfaɪ $ ˈfɔːr-/ v **fortified, fortifying, fortifies** [T] **1** to build towers, walls etc around an area or city in order to defend it: *The town was heavily fortified.* **2** to encourage an attitude or feeling and make it stronger; **◨ strengthen:** *Her position was fortified by election successes and economic recovery.* **3** *written* to make someone feel physically or mentally stronger: **fortify yourself (with sth)** *We fortified ourselves with a breakfast of bacon and eggs.* **4** [usually passive] to make food or drinks more healthy by adding VITAMINS to them: *fortified breakfast cereals* | **fortify sth with sth** *foods fortified with vitamin B*

for·tis·si·mo /fɔːˈtɪsɪ̣məʊ $ fɔːrˈtɪsɪ̣moʊ/ adj, adv music that is fortissimo is played or sung very loudly; **◨ pianissimo;** → **forte**

for·ti·tude /ˈfɔːtɪtjuːd $ ˈfɔːrtɪtuːd/ n [U] formal courage shown when you are in great pain or experiencing a lot of trouble; **◨ strength:** *Winnie is a woman of quiet fortitude who has endured a lot of suffering.*

fort·night S3 /ˈfɔːtnaɪt $ ˈfɔːrt-/ n [C usually singular] BrE two weeks: *a fortnight's holiday* | *in a fortnight's time* | *a fortnight ago*

fort·night·ly /ˈfɔːtnaɪtli $ ˈfɔːrt-/ adj, adv BrE happening every fortnight or once a fortnight: *We used to dread my uncle's fortnightly visits.*

for·tress /ˈfɔːtrɪ̣s $ ˈfɔːr-/ n [C] a large strong building used for defending an important place

for·tu·i·tous /fɔːˈtjuːɪ̣təs $ fɔːrˈtuː-/ adj formal happening by chance, especially in a way that has a good result: *The meeting with Jack was fortuitous.* —**fortuitously** adv

for·tu·nate S3 /ˈfɔːtʃənət $ ˈfɔːr-/ adj
1 someone who is fortunate has something good happen to them, or is in a good situation; **◨ lucky: fortunate to do sth** *I've been fortunate to find a career that I love.* | *I was **fortunate enough** to obtain a research studentship at Stanford.* | **fortunate in doing sth** *She felt fortunate in being able to please herself where she lived.* | **fortunate that** *I'm fortunate that I have such an understanding wife.* | **more/less fortunate than sb** *We've been more fortunate than a lot of farmers.*
2 a fortunate event is one in which something good happens by chance, especially when this saves you from trouble or danger; **◨ lucky:** *By a fortunate coincidence, a passer-by heard her cries for help.*
3 the less fortunate people who are poor: *We should all consider the plight of the less fortunate.*

for·tu·nate·ly /ˈfɔːtʃənətli $ ˈfɔːr-/ adv [sentence adverb] happening because of good luck; **◨ luckily:** *Fortunately, everything worked out all right in the end.*

for·tune S3 W3 /ˈfɔːtʃən $ ˈfɔːr-/ n
1 MONEY [C] a very large amount of money: *He made a fortune selling property in Spain.* | *My first painting sold for £25, **a small fortune** then for an art student.* | *Bill Traylor died in poverty in 1947, but his art is **worth a fortune**.* | *The carpet must have **cost a fortune**.* | *It is quite easy to decorate your house without **spending a fortune**.* | *Her **personal fortune** was recently estimated at £37 million.*
2 CHANCE [U] chance or luck, and the effect that it has on your life: *I had the good fortune to work with a brilliant head of department.* | *Sickness or ill fortune could reduce you to a needy situation.* | *I felt it was useless to struggle against fortune.*
3 WHAT HAPPENS TO YOU [C usually plural] the good or bad things that happen in life: *a downturn in the company's fortunes* | *This defeat marked a change in the team's fortunes.* | *The geographical position of the frontier fluctuated with **the fortunes of war** (=the things that can happen during a war).*
4 tell sb's fortune to tell someone what will happen to them in the future by looking at their hands, using cards etc → **soldier of fortune;** → **fame and fortune** at FAME; → **a hostage to fortune** at HOSTAGE (3); → **seek your fortune** at SEEK (4)

fortune cookie n [C] a BISCUIT served in Chinese restaurants, containing a piece of paper that says what is supposed to happen to you in the future

fortune-teller n [C] someone who uses cards or looks at people's hands in order to tell them what is supposed to happen to them in the future —**fortune telling** n [U]

for·ty /ˈfɔːti $ ˈfɔːrti/ number **1** the number 40 **2 the forties** [plural] also **the '40s, the 1940s** the years from 1940 to 1949: *The place was built as a casino in the forties.* | **the early/mid/late forties** *He spent several years in Paris in the late forties.* **3 be in your forties** to be aged between 40 and 49: **early/mid/late forties** *The woman was probably in her mid forties.* **4 in the forties** if the temperature is in the forties, it is between 40 degrees and 49 degrees: **in the low/mid/high forties** *The temperature was up in the high forties.* —**fortieth** adj: *her fortieth birthday*

forty-five n **1** [number] 45 **2** also **45** [C] a small record with one song on each side **3** also **.45, Colt 45** [C] trademark a small gun

forty winks n [U] informal a very short sleep: *I felt a lot better after I had forty winks.*

for·um /ˈfɔːrəm/ n [C] **1** an organization, meeting, TV programme etc where people have a chance to publicly discuss an important subject: [+for] *The journal aims to provide a forum for discussion and debate.* | [+on] *the new national forum on the environment* **2** a group of computer users who are interested in a particular subject and discuss it using EMAIL or the Inter-

F

net **3** a large outdoor public place in ancient Rome used for business and discussion

for·ward¹ [S1] [W1] /'fɔːwəd $ 'fɔːrwərd/ also **forwards** /-wədz $ -wərdz/ *adv*
1 towards a place or position that is in front of you; ◪ **backwards**: *He leaned forward, his elbows resting on the table.* | *The crowd surged forwards.* | *She took another small step forward.*
2 towards greater progress, improvement, or development: *We agreed that the sensible way forward was for a new company to be formed.* | *After the Labour Party conference, he stated that we could now go forward as a united party.* | *'Britain is now ready to move forward' he said.*
3 towards the future in a way that is hopeful; ◪ **backwards**: *I felt that at last I could begin to look forward.*
4 from that/this day/time/moment etc forward beginning on that day or at that time: *They never met again from that day forward.*
5 go forward to/into to successfully complete one stage of a competition so that you are able to compete in the next stage: *South Korea went forward into the next round of the World Cup.*
6 if you put a clock or a watch forward, you change it so that it shows a later time, for example when the time changes to BRITISH SUMMER TIME; ◪ **back**: *We put our watches forward by 2 hours.* | *The clocks go forward this weekend.*
7 in or towards the front part of a ship → FAST-FORWARD; → **look forward to sth** at LOOK¹; → **backwards and forwards** at BACKWARDS (5)

forward² [S2] [W3] *adj*
1 [only before noun] closer to a person, place, or position that is in front of you; ◪ **backward**: *Army roadblocks prevented any further forward movement.* | *Always enter or leave a helicopter from a forward direction.*
2 forward planning/thinking plans, ideas etc that are helpful in a way that prepares you for the future: *With a bit of forward planning we make sure your budget goes as far as possible.*
3 no further forward not having made much progress, especially compared to what was expected: *We are no further forward in solving the crime.*
4 [only before noun] at or near the front of a ship, vehicle, building etc; ◪ **rear**: *We sat in one of the forward sections of the train.*
5 *formal* too confident and friendly in dealing with people you do not know very well: *My father thinks she's far too forward for a young girl.*

forward³ *v* [T] **1** to send letters, goods etc to someone when they have moved to a different address; ◪ **send on**: *Would you make sure that you forward my mail promptly?* **2** to send letters, information etc to someone: **forward sth to sb** *Flight times will be forwarded to you with your travel documentation.* **3** *formal* to help something to develop so that it becomes successful; ◪ **further**: *I see this new responsibility as a good chance to forward my career.*

forward⁴ *n* [C] an attacking player on a team in sports such as football and BASKETBALL; → **back**, **defender**

forwarding ad,dress / $ '... ,.../ *n* [C] an address that you leave for someone when you move to a new place so that they can send your letters etc to you: *Did she leave a forwarding address?*

forward-,looking *adj* planning for and thinking about the future in a positive way, especially by being willing to use modern methods or ideas; → **backward-looking**: *a forward-looking Russian statesman*

for·ward·ness /'fɔːwədnəs $ 'fɔːrwərd-/ *n* [U] behaviour that is too confident or friendly

forward 'roll *n* [C] *BrE* a movement in GYMNASTICS in which you roll over forwards onto your back so that your feet go over your head

for·wards /'fɔːwədz $ 'fɔːrwərdz/ *adv* FORWARD

forward slash *n* [C] *BrE* a line (/) used in writing, to separate words, numbers, or letters; ◪ **slash**

fos·sil /'fɒsəl $ 'fɑː-/ *n* [C] **1** an animal or plant that lived many thousands of years ago and that has been preserved, or the shape of one of these animals or plants that has been preserved in rock: *fossils of early reptiles* | *Marine sponges have a long fossil record* (=their development has been recorded over a long period). → see picture at STONE → LIVING FOSSIL **2** *informal* an insulting word for an old person

fossil ,fuel *n* [C,U] a FUEL such as coal or oil that is produced by the very gradual decaying of animals or plants over millions of years: *Environmentalists would like to see fossil fuels replaced by renewable energy sources.* → see picture at ENVIRONMENT

fos·sil·ize also **-ise** *BrE* /'fɒsɪlaɪz $ 'fɑː-/ *v* **1** [usually passive] if people, ideas, systems etc fossilize or are fossilized, they never change or develop, even when there are good reasons why they should change: *Most couples, however fossilized their relationship, have some interests in common.* **2** [I,T] to become or form a FOSSIL by being preserved in rock: *fossilized dinosaur bones* —**fossilization** /,fɒsɪlaɪ'zeɪʃən $,fɑːsɪlə-/ *n* [U]

fos·ter¹ /'fɒstə $ 'fɑːstər/ *v* **1** [T] to help a skill, feeling, idea etc develop over a period of time; ◪ **encourage**, **promote**: *The bishop helped foster the sense of a community embracing all classes.* **2** [I,T] to take someone else's child into your family for a period of time but without becoming their legal parent; → **adopt**: *The couple wanted to adopt a black child they had been fostering.*

foster² *adj* **1 foster mother/father/parents** the people who foster a child: *It is sometimes difficult to find suitable foster parents.* **2 foster child/son/daughter** a child who is fostered **3 foster brother/sister** someone who has different parents from you, but who is being brought up in the same family **4 foster home** a private home where a child is fostered

fought /fɔːt $ fɒːt/ *v* the past tense and past participle of FIGHT

foul¹ /faʊl/ *adj*
1 SMELL/TASTE a foul smell or taste is very unpleasant; ◪ **disgusting**: *He woke up with a foul taste in his mouth.* | *a pile of foul-smelling garbage* | *He put down his mug of foul-tasting coffee.*
2 in a foul mood/temper *BrE* in a very bad temper and likely to get angry: *The argument with his mother left Putt in a foul mood.*
3 AIR/WATER very dirty: *Refugees in the camps are short of food and at risk from foul water.* | *extractor fans to remove foul air from the tunnel*
4 foul language rude and offensive words: *She claimed she had been subjected to abuse and foul language.*
5 WEATHER especially *BrE* foul weather is stormy and windy, with a lot of rain or snow: *Always carry foul weather gear when you go out walking.* —**foully** *adv* —**foulness** *n* [U] → **by fair means or foul** at FAIR¹ (11); → **fall foul of sb/sth** at FALL¹ (15)

foul² *v* **1 a)** [T] if a sports player fouls another player, they do something that is not allowed by the rules **b)** [I,T] to hit a ball outside the limit of the playing area in baseball **2** also **foul up** [T] *formal* to make something very dirty, especially with waste: *rivers and lakes fouled almost beyond recovery by pollutants*
foul up *phr v informal* **1** to do something wrong or spoil something by making mistakes; → **foul-up**: *We can't afford to foul up this time.* | **foul sth ⇔ up** *Glen completely fouled up the seating arrangements.* **2 foul sth ⇔ up** to make something very dirty, especially with waste: *He lit a cigarette and started to foul up the air with stinging yellow smoke.*

foul³ *n* [C] **1** an action in a sport that is against the rules: *Wright was booked for a foul on the goalkeeper.* **2** a hit in baseball which goes outside the limits of the playing area

foul line *n* [C] a line marked on a sports field outside of which a ball cannot be legally played

foul-'mouthed *adj* swearing too much: *Harry was a nasty foul-mouthed old devil.* —**'foul mouth** *n* [C]

foul 'play *n* [U] **1** if the police think someone's death was caused by foul play, they think that person was murdered: *The police said they had no reason to* **suspect foul play**. | *Detectives have not* **ruled out foul play**. **2** an action that is dishonest, unfair, or illegal, especially one that happens during a sports game

'foul-up *n* [C] *informal* a problem caused by a stupid or careless mistake; → **foul up**: *a computer system foul-up*

found¹ /faʊnd/ *v* the past tense and past participle of FIND

found² W3 *v* [T]
1 to start something such as an organization, company, school, or city, often by providing the necessary money; **⬛ establish**: *Founded in 1935 in Ohio, Alcoholics Anonymous is now a world-wide organization.* | *Eton College was founded by Henry VI in 1440.*
2 be founded on/upon sth a) to be the main idea, belief etc that something else develops from; **⬛ be based on sth**: *The British parliamentary system is founded on debate and opposition.* **b)** to be the solid layer of CEMENT, stones etc that a building is built on: *The castle is founded on solid rock.*
3 *technical* to melt metal and pour it into a MOULD (=a hollow shape), to make things such as tools and parts for machines —**founding** *n* [U]: *the founding of the University of Chicago* → WELL-FOUNDED

foun·da·tion W2 /faʊnˈdeɪʃən/ *n*
1 BUILDING [C] the solid layer of CEMENT, bricks, stones etc that is put under a building to support it: *It took the builders three weeks to* **lay the foundations**. | *The earthquake* **shook the foundations** *of the house.*
2 BASIC IDEA [C] a basic idea, principle, situation etc that something develops from: [+of] *All theories should be built on a foundation of factual knowledge.* | **solid/ firm foundation** *The course gives students a solid foundation in the basics of computing.*
3 ORGANIZATION [C] an organization that gives or collects money to be used for special purposes, especially for CHARITY or for medical RESEARCH: *the British Heart Foundation*
4 ESTABLISHMENT [U] the establishment of an organization, business, school etc; **⬛ founding**: *The school has served the community since its foundation in 1835.*
5 be without foundation also **have no foundation** *formal* if a statement, idea etc is without foundation, there is no proof that it is true; **⬛ be groundless**: *Davis dismissed the allegations as being without foundation.*
6 lay/provide the foundation(s) for sth to provide the conditions that will make it possible for something to be successful: *Careful planning laid the foundations for the nation's economic miracle.*
7 SKIN [U] a cream in the same colour as your skin that you put on before the rest of your MAKE-UP
8 shake/rock the foundations of sth also **shake/rock sth to its foundations** to completely change the way something is done or the way people think by having a completely new idea: *Darwin's theory rocked the scientific establishment to its foundations.*

foun'dation ,course *n* [C] *BrE* a general course of study that introduces students to a subject, and is taught in the first year at some universities in Britain

foun'dation ,stone *n* [C] **1** a large stone that is placed at the base of a new building, usually by an important person as part of a ceremony **2** the facts, ideas, principles etc that form the base from which something else develops: *Greek and Latin were once viewed as the foundation stones of a good education.*

found·er¹ /ˈfaʊndə $ -ər/ *n* [C] someone who establishes a business, organization, school etc

founder² *v* [I] *formal* **1** to fail after a period of time because something has gone wrong: *Their marriage began to founder soon after the honeymoon.* | [+on] *The talks foundered on disagreements between the two parties.* **2** if a ship or boat founders, it fills with water and sinks: [+on] *The ship foundered on the rocks.*

founder 'member *n* [C] *BrE* someone who has helped to establish a new organization, club etc and is one of its first members; **⬛ charter member** *AmE*

found·ing /ˈfaʊndɪŋ/ *n* [singular] the establishment of an organization, business, school etc; **⬛ foundation**: *the founding of the African National Congress in 1912*

founding 'father *n* [C] someone who begins something such as a new way of thinking, or a new organization: [+of] *Saint Basil, one of the founding fathers of the Greek Orthodox Church*

found·ling /ˈfaʊndlɪŋ/ *n* [C] *old use* a baby who has been left by its parents, and is found and looked after by other people

foun·dry /ˈfaʊndri/ *n plural* **foundries** [C] a place where metals are melted and poured into MOULDS (=hollow shapes) to make parts for machines, tools etc: *an iron foundry*

fount /faʊnt/ *n* **the fount of all knowledge/wisdom etc** *literary* the place, person, idea etc that all knowledge, WISDOM etc comes from

foun·tain /ˈfaʊntən $ ˈfaʊntn/ *n* [C] **1** a structure from which water is pushed up into the air, used for example as decoration in a garden or park **2** a flow of liquid, or of something bright and colourful that goes straight up into the air: [+of] *A fountain of blood was pouring from his chest.* | *A fountain of sparks shot high into the night sky.* **3 fountain of sth** *written* a SOURCE or supply of something: *Sir Robert was a fountain of information on Asian affairs.* → DRINKING FOUNTAIN, SODA FOUNTAIN

foun·tain·head /ˈfaʊntənhed $ ˈfaʊntn-/ *n* [singular] the origin of something; **⬛ source**

'fountain pen *n* [C] a pen that you fill with ink; → **ballpoint**; → see picture at STATIONERY

four /fɔː $ fɔːr/ *number, n* **1** the number 4: *She is married with four children.* | *They arrived just after four* (=four o'clock). | *Luke will soon be four* (=four years old). **2 on all fours** supporting your body with your hands and knees: *He was down on all fours playing with the puppy.* **3 in fours** in groups of four people or things: *The boxes were stacked in fours.* → FOURSOME **4** [C] a hit in CRICKET that scores four RUNS because it goes over the edge of the playing area **5** [C] a team of four people who row a racing boat, or the boat that they row **6 the four corners of the Earth/world** *literary* places or countries that are very far away from each other: *People from the four corners of the world have come to Ontario to make it their home.* → **four ply** at PLY²

4 *written informal* a way of writing "for", used especially in emails and TEXT MESSAGES: *a message 4 U* (=for you)

four-by-'four, 4x4 *n* [C] a vehicle that has four wheels and a FOUR-WHEEL DRIVE

four·fold /ˈfɔːfəʊld $ ˈfɔːrfoʊld/ *adj, adv* four times as much or as many: *a fourfold increase in price* | *Profits rose fourfold.*

four-leaf 'clover also **four-leaved 'clover** *BrE n* [C] a CLOVER plant that has four leaves instead of the usual three, and is considered to be lucky

four-letter 'word *n* [C] a word that is considered very rude and offensive, especially one relating to sex or body waste; **⬛ swearword**

four-poster 'bed also **four-'poster** *n* [C] a bed with four tall posts at the corners, a cover fixed at the top of the posts, and curtains around the sides → see picture at BED

four·some /ˈfɔːsəm $ ˈfɔːr-/ *n* [C] a group of four people, especially two men and two women, who come together for a social activity or sport: *Jim and Tina made up a foursome with Jean and Bruce.*

F

1 000, 2 000, 3 000, most frequent words in S poken and W ritten English

'four-square¹ also **foursquare** /ˈfɔːskweə $ ˈfɔːr-skwer/ adj **1** a building that is four-square is strongly built and square in shape **2** BrE old use firm and determined

four-square² also **foursquare** adv **1** if you stand four-square behind someone, you support them completely: *He stood four-square behind the Prime Minister in the dispute.* **2** firmly and solidly: *The hut stood four-square in a corner of the garden.*

'four-star¹ adj [only before noun] a four-star hotel, restaurant etc has been judged to be of a very high standard

'four-star² n [U] BrE a type of petrol with LEAD in it

four-star 'general n [C] AmE a GENERAL of a high rank in the US army

four-stroke 'engine n [C] an engine that works with two up and down movements of a PISTON

four-teen /ˌfɔːˈtiːn◂ $ ˌfɔːr-/ number the number 14: *He used to work fourteen hours a day.* | *I started playing the guitar when I was fourteen* (=14 years old). **—fourteenth** adj, pron: *in the fourteenth century* | *my fourteenth birthday* | *I'm planning to leave on the fourteenth* (=the 14th day of the month).

fourth¹ /fɔːθ $ fɔːrθ/ adj coming after three other things in a series: *in the fourth century* | *her fourth birthday* **—fourth** pron **—fourthly** adv

fourth² pron the fourth thing in a series: *the fourth of July*

fourth³ n [C] ¼; one of four equal parts: **one-fourth/ three-fourths** → QUARTER¹ (1)

fourth di'mension n **the fourth dimension** an expression meaning 'time', used especially by scientists and writers of SCIENCE FICTION

fourth es'tate n **the fourth estate** newspapers, news magazines, television and radio news, the people who work for them, and the political influence that they have; ◻ **press**

four-wheel 'drive n [C,U] a system in a vehicle which gives the power of the engine to all four wheels to make it easier to drive, or a vehicle that has this type of system

fowl /faʊl/ n plural **fowl** or **fowls** [C,U] **1** a bird, such as a chicken, that is kept for its meat and eggs, or the meat of this type of bird **2** old use any bird

fox¹ /fɒks $ faːks/ n **1** [C] a wild animal like a dog with reddish-brown fur, a pointed face, and a thick tail **2** [C] informal someone who is clever and good at deceiving people: *He was a sly old fox.* **3** [U] the skin and fur of a fox, used to make clothes **4** [C] AmE informal someone who is sexually attractive

fox² v [T] BrE informal **1** to be too difficult for someone to do or understand: *We were foxed by the problem.* **2** to confuse or deceive someone in a clever way

fox-glove /ˈfɒksɡlʌv $ ˈfaːks-/ n [C] a tall plant with many bell-shaped flowers

fox-hole /ˈfɒkshəʊl $ ˈfaːkshoʊl/ n [C] **1** a hole in the ground that soldiers use to fire from or hide from the enemy **2** a hole in the ground where a fox lives

fox-hound /ˈfɒkshaʊnd $ ˈfaːks-/ n [C] a dog with a very good sense of smell, trained to hunt and kill foxes

fox-hunt-ing /ˈfɒksˌhʌntɪŋ $ ˈfaːks-/ n [U] the sport of hunting FOXES with dogs while riding on a horse **—foxhunt** n [C]

fox 'terrier n [C] a small dog with short hair

fox-trot /ˈfɒkstrɒt $ ˈfaːkstraːt/ n [C] a formal dance which combines short quick steps with long slow steps, or a piece of music for this dance **—foxtrot** v [I]

fox-y /ˈfɒksi $ ˈfaːksi/ adj **1** informal especially AmE sexually attractive; ◻ **sexy**: *a foxy lady* **2** like a FOX in appearance: *a foxy face* **3** skilful at deceiving people; ◻ **cunning**

foy-er /ˈfɔɪeɪ $ ˈfɔɪər/ n [C] **1** a room or hall at the entrance to a public building; ◻ **lobby: hotel/theatre/ cinema etc foyer;** → see picture at STAY **2** AmE a small room or hall at the entrance to a house or apartment

FPO /ˌef piː ˈəʊ $ -ˈoʊ/ the written abbreviation of *field post office* or *fleet post office*, used as part of the address of someone in the American navy or army

Fr BrE; **Fr.** AmE **1** a written abbreviation of *Father*, used before the name of a priest **2** a written abbreviation of *franc* **3** the written abbreviation of *French* **4** the written abbreviation of *France*

frac-as /ˈfrækaː $ ˈfreɪkəs/ n [singular] a short noisy fight involving several people: *Eight people were injured in the fracas.*

frac-tal /ˈfræktəl/ n [C] technical a pattern, usually produced by a computer, that is made by repeating the same shape many times in smaller and smaller sizes

frac-tion /ˈfrækʃən/ n [C] **1** a very small amount of something: [+of] *I got these shoes at a fraction of the original price.* | *She paused for a fraction of a second.* **2** a part of a whole number in mathematics, such as ½ or ¾

frac-tion-al /ˈfrækʃənəl/ adj **1** very small in amount; ◻ **tiny**: *a fractional increase* | *There was a fractional hesitation before he said yes.* **2** technical happening or done in a series of steps **3** technical relating to fractions, in mathematics **—fractionally** adv

frac-tious /ˈfrækʃəs/ adj someone who is fractious becomes angry very easily; ◻ **irritable**: *Children become fractious when they are tired.* | **fractious baby/ child etc —fractiousness** n [U]

frac-ture¹ /ˈfræktʃə $ -ər/ v [I,T] **1** if a bone or other hard substance fractures, or if it is fractured, it breaks or cracks: *The immense pressure causes the rock to fracture.* | **fracture your leg/arm/hip etc** *He fractured his right leg during training.* **2** if a group, country etc fractures, or if it is fractured, it divides into parts in an unfriendly way because of disagreement; ◻ **split**: *The opposition has been fractured by bitter disputes.*

fracture² n [C] a crack or broken part in a bone or other hard substance: *a stress fracture in his left knee* | *a hairline fracture* (=very thin crack) | *a fractured shoulder* → COMPOUND FRACTURE, SIMPLE FRACTURE

frac-tured /ˈfræktʃəd $ -ərd/ adj broken or cracked: **fractured skull/jaw/rib etc** *She suffered a fractured skull in the accident.*

frag-ile /ˈfrædʒaɪl $ -dʒəl/ adj **1** easily broken or damaged; ◻ **delicate**; ▣ **strong**: *fragile bones* | *Be careful with that vase – it's very fragile.* **2** a fragile situation is one that is weak or uncertain, and likely to become worse under pressure; ▣ **strong**: *the country's fragile economy* | *Relations between the two countries are in a fragile state.* | *the party's fragile unity* **3** **fragile health** a weak physical condition because of illness **4** thin and delicate: *fragile beauty* **5** BrE if someone feels fragile they feel ill, especially because they have drunk too much alcohol **—fragility** /frəˈdʒɪləti/ n [U]

frag-ment¹ W3 /ˈfrægmənt/ n [C] a small piece of something that has broken off or that comes from something larger: *glass fragments* | [+of] *fragments of broken pottery*

frag-ment² /fræɡˈment $ ˈfræɡment, fræɡˈment/ v [I,T] to break something, or be broken into a lot of small separate parts – used to show disapproval: *the dangers of fragmenting the Health Service* **—fragmented** adj: *a fragmented society* **—fragmentation** /ˌfræɡmənˈteɪʃən, -men-/ n [U]

frag-ment-a-ry /ˈfræɡməntəri $ -teri/ adj consisting of many different small parts: *a fragmentary account of the incident*

fra-grance /ˈfreɪɡrəns/ n **1** [C,U] a pleasant smell; ▣ **scent**: [+of] *the rich fragrance of a garden flower* **2** [C] a liquid that you put on your body to make it smell pleasant; ◻ **perfume, scent**

fra-grant /ˈfreɪɡrənt/ adj having a pleasant smell: *fragrant flowers* **—fragrantly** adv

frail /freɪl/ adj **1** someone who is frail is weak and thin because they are old or ill: *frail elderly people* | *her frail health* | frail body/physique | mentally/physically frail **2** something that is frail is easily damaged or broken; ◙ **fragile**: *It seemed impossible that these frail boats could survive in such a storm.* | *the country's frail economy*

frail·ty /'freɪlti/ n plural **frailties 1** [U] the lack of strength or health; ◙ **weakness**: [+of] *the frailty of her thin body* **2** [C,U] something bad or weak in your character; ◙ **weakness**: *human frailties*

frame¹ [S3] [W3] /freɪm/ n
1 BORDER [C] a structure made of wood, metal, plastic etc that surrounds something such as a picture or window, and holds it in place: *They removed the picture from its wooden frame.* | door/window/picture frame; → see picture at LIMIT
2 STRUCTURE [C] the structure or main supporting parts of a piece of furniture, vehicle, or other object: *a bicycle frame* | *the frame of the chair*
3 BODY [C] the general shape formed by the bones of someone's body: large/thin/slight etc frame
4 GLASSES [C usually plural] the metal or plastic part of a pair of GLASSES that holds the LENSES
5 MAIN FACTS/IDEAS [C usually singular] the main ideas, facts etc that something is based on: *A clear explanation of the subject provides a frame on which a deeper understanding can be built.* | *Some comments may or may not be understood as harassment, depending on your frame of reference* (=knowledge and beliefs that influence the way you think).
6 be in/out of the frame (for sth) to have or not have the chance to take part in something; ◙ **be in/out of the running (for sth)**: *Liverpool are in the frame for a place in the Cup Final.*
7 FILM [C] an area of film that contains one photograph, or one of the series of separate photographs that make up a film or video
8 SPORT [C] a complete part in the games of SNOOKER or BOWLING: *I won the next three frames.*
9 INTERNET [C] one of the areas into which a WEBPAGE is divided → CLIMBING FRAME, COLD FRAME; → frame of mind at MIND¹ (15)

frame² v [T] **1** to surround something with something else so that it looks attractive or can be seen clearly: *Sarah's face was framed by her long dark hair.* | *She stood there, framed against the doorway.* **2** to put a picture in a structure that will hold it firmly: *I'm going to get the picture framed.* | *a framed photograph* **3** to deliberately make someone seem guilty of a crime when they are not guilty, by lying to the police or in a court of law; ◙ **set up**: *Needham's lawyers claimed that he had been framed by the police.* | frame sb for sth *The two men were framed for murder.* **4** formal to carefully plan the way you are going to ask a question, make a statement etc: *She wondered how she was going frame the question.* **5** formal to organize and develop a plan, system etc: *Newman played a central role in framing the new law.* **6** gilt-framed/wood-framed etc having a frame or frames of a particular colour or material: *wire-framed spectacles*

frame-up n [C] a plan to make someone seem guilty of a crime which they did not do; ◙ **set-up**

frame·work [W3] /'freɪmwɜːk $ -wɜːrk/ n [C]
1 [usually singular] a set of ideas, rules, or beliefs from which something is developed, or on which decisions are based: [+of/for] *This paper provides a framework for future research.*
2 social/legal/political etc framework the structure of a society, a legal or political system etc: *We have to act within the existing legal framework.*
3 the main supporting parts of a building, vehicle, or object: *the metal framework of the roof*

franc /fræŋk/ n [C] the standard unit of money in various countries, and used in France and Belgium before the EURO

fran·chise¹ /'fræntʃaɪz/ n **1 a)** [C,U] permission given by a company to someone who wants to sell its goods or services: *a franchise holder* | *a franchise agreement* | under franchise *The beer is brewed in Britain under franchise.* **b)** [C] a business that operates as a franchise **2** [C] *AmE* a professional sports team **3** [U] *formal* the legal right to vote in your country's elections

franchise² v [T] to give or sell a franchise to someone

fran·chi·see /ˌfræntʃaɪˈziː/ n [C] someone who is given or sold a franchise to sell a company's goods or services

fran·chi·sor, franchiser /'fræntʃaɪzə $ -ər/ n [C] a company that sells a franchise

Franco- /ˈfræŋkəʊ $ -koʊ/ prefix [in nouns and adjectives] **1** relating to France: *a Francophile* (=someone who loves France) **2** French and something else: *the Franco-Belgian border*

Fran·co·phone, francophone /'fræŋkəʊˌfəʊn $ -koʊˌfoʊn/ adj having French as a first or main language: Francophone countries/nations/communities —**Francophone** n [C]

Fran·glais /ˈfrɒŋɡleɪ $ ˌfrɑːŋˈɡleɪ/ n [U] *informal* a mixture of the French and English languages

frank¹ /fræŋk/ adj **1** honest and truthful: be frank with sb *He was completely frank with her about what happened.* | be frank about sth *She was quite frank about the whole thing.* | frank discussion/interview/exchange of views etc **2** to be frank *spoken* used when you are going to say something that is true, but which other people may not like: *To be perfectly frank, I think it's a bad idea.* —**frankness** n [U]

frank² v [T] to print a sign on an envelope showing that the cost of sending it has been paid; → franking machine

frank³ n [C] *AmE* a frankfurter

frank·en·food /ˈfræŋkənfuːd/ also **Frank-en·stein foods** /ˈfræŋkənstaɪn ˌfuːdz/ n [C usually plural] *informal* a food that has been produced by plants that were GENETICALLY MODIFIED – used when you disapprove of this process

frank·fur·ter /ˈfræŋkfɜːtə $ -fɜːrtər/ also **frank** *AmE* n [C] a long reddish smoked SAUSAGE

frank·in·cense /ˈfræŋkɪnsens/ n [U] a substance that is burnt to give a sweet smell, especially at religious ceremonies

franking ma·chine n [C] *BrE* a machine used by businesses that puts a mark on letters and packages to show that POSTAGE has been paid; ◙ **postage meter** *AmE*; → frank

frank·ly [S3] /ˈfræŋkli/ adv
1 used to show that you are saying what you really think about something: *Frankly, I think the Internet is overrated.* | *His behaviour was frankly disgraceful.*
2 honestly and directly: *She answered all our questions frankly.* | *Nicholas frankly admitted that the report was a pack of lies.*

fran·tic /ˈfræntɪk/ adj **1** extremely worried and frightened about a situation, so that you cannot control your feelings: get/become frantic *There was still no news of Jill, and her parents were getting frantic.* | [+with] *Your mother's been frantic with worry wondering where you've been.* **2** extremely hurried and using a lot of energy, but not very organized; ◙ **hectic**: *I spent three frantic days trying to get everything ready.* | frantic effort/attempt *Despite our frantic efforts, we were unable to save the boy's life.* | frantic pace/rush/haste etc *There was a frantic rush to escape from the building.* | *a day of frantic activity* | *a frantic search for her father* —**frantically** /-kli/ adv: *He frantically searched for the key.*

frat /fræt/ n [C] *AmE informal* a FRATERNITY: *a frat boy* (=member of a fraternity)

fra·ter·nal /frə'tɜːnl $ -ɜːr-/ *adj formal* **1** showing a special friendliness to other people because you share interests or ideas with them: *fraternal solidarity amongst union members* | **fraternal association/organization/society** **2** relating to brothers: *fraternal loyalty* —**fraternally** *adv*

fra·ter·ni·ty /frə'tɜːnəti $ -ɜːr-/ *n plural* **fraternities** **1** **the teaching/scientific/criminal etc fraternity** all the people who work in a particular profession or share a particular interest **2** [C] a club at an American college or university that has only male members; → **sorority** **3** [U] *formal* a feeling of friendship between members of a group: *fraternity between nations*

frat·er·nize also **-ise** *BrE* /'frætənaɪz $ -ər-/ *v* [I] to be friendly with someone, especially if you have been ordered not to be friendly with them: [**+with**] *The troops were forbidden to fraternize with the enemy.* —**fraternization** /ˌfrætənaɪ'zeɪʃən $ -tərnə-/ *n* [U]

frat·ri·cid·al /ˌfrætrɪ'saɪdl◂/ *adj* [only before noun] a fratricidal war or struggle is one in which people kill members of their own society or group

frat·ri·cide /'frætrɪsaɪd/ *n* [C,U] the crime of murdering your brother or sister

fraud /frɔːd $ frɒːd/ *n* **1** [C,U] the crime of deceiving people in order to gain something such as money or goods: **tax/insurance/credit card etc fraud** *He's been charged with tax fraud.* | *electoral fraud* | *She was found guilty of fraud.* **2** [C] someone or something that is not what it is claimed to be: *I felt like a fraud.* | *The police exposed the letter as a fraud.*

fraud·ster /'frɔːdstə $ 'frɒːdstər/ *n* [C] someone who has committed a fraud

fraud·u·lent /'frɔːdjʊlənt $ 'frɒːdʒə-/ *adj* intended to deceive people in an illegal way, in order to gain money, power etc: *a fraudulent insurance claim* | *a fraudulent statement* | *fraudulent activity/behaviour/conduct* —**fraudulently** *adv*: *He was accused of fraudulently using a stolen credit card.* —**fraudulence** *n* [U]

fraught /frɔːt $ frɒːt/ *adj* **1** **fraught with problems/difficulties/danger etc** full of problems etc: *Their marriage has been fraught with difficulties.* **2** full of anxiety or worry; ▤ **tense**: *a fraught atmosphere* | *a fraught situation* | *Julie sounded rather fraught when I spoke to her.*

fray¹ /freɪ/ *v* [I,T] **1** if cloth or other material frays, or if something frays it, the threads become loose because the material is old: *The collar had started to fray on Jack's raincoat.* | *He had frayed the bottom of his jeans.* **2** if someone's temper or nerves fray, or something frays them, they become annoyed: *Tempers soon began to fray.* —**frayed** *adj*: *The carpet was badly frayed.*

fray² *n* **the fray** an argument or fight: *Three civilians were injured during the fray.* | **into the fray** *He launched himself into the fray.* | **join/enter the fray** *The other soldiers quickly joined the fray, launching missile attacks in the city.*

fraz·zle /'fræzəl/ *n BrE informal* **1** **be burnt to a frazzle** to be completely burnt **2** **be worn to a frazzle** to feel very tired and anxious

fraz·zled /'fræzəld/ *adj informal* feeling tired and anxious, for example after a journey or because you are very busy: *The meeting left me feeling completely frazzled.*

freak¹ /friːk/ *n* [C] **1** *informal* someone who is extremely interested in a particular subject so that other people think they are strange or unusual: *a fitness freak* | *a religious freak* | *a computer freak* **2** someone who is considered to be very strange because of the way they look, behave, or think; ▤ **weirdo**: *These glasses make me look like a freak.* | *Women who studied engineering used to be considered freaks.* **3** **a control freak** someone who always wants to control situations and other people **4** also **freak of**

nature something in nature that is very unusual: *Due to some freak of nature, it snowed in June.* **5** an unexpected and very unusual event: *By some freak of fate, he walked away from the crash completely unhurt.* | *April's sales figures were a freak.*

freak² *adj* [only before noun] unexpected and very unusual: *a freak result* | *He was crushed to death in a freak accident.* | **freak wind/wave/storm etc** *The men drowned when a freak wave sank their boat.*

freak³ *v* [I] *informal* to become suddenly angry or afraid, especially so that you cannot control your behaviour; ▤ **flip**: *When Ben heard about the accident, he just freaked.*

freak out *phr v informal* to become very anxious, upset or afraid, or make someone very anxious, upset or afraid: *People just freaked out when they heard the news.* | **freak sb ⇔ out** *The whole idea freaked me out.*

freak·ish /'friːkɪʃ/ *adj* very unusual and strange, and sometimes frightening; ▤ **weird**: *freakish weather* —**freakishly** *adv* —**freakishness** *n* [U]

freak·y /'friːki/ *adj spoken* strange or unusual and a bit frightening; ▤ **weird**: *The movie was kind of freaky.*

freck·le /'frekəl/ *n* [C usually plural] freckles are small brown spots on someone's skin, especially on their face, which the sun can cause to increase in number and become darker; → **mole**

freck·led /'frekəld/ *adj* having freckles: **freckled face/skin**

free¹ [S1] [W1] /friː/ *adj*
1 **NO COST** something that is free does not cost you any money: *Admission is free for children under 9.* | *All students are offered free accommodation.* | *Send for our free information pack for more details.* | *There's a special free gift with this month's magazine.*
2 **NOT A PRISONER** not held, tied up, or kept somewhere as a prisoner: *He knew he could be free in as little as three years.* | *With one leap he was free!* | *He walked out of the courtroom a free man.* | *They have called on the government to set all political prisoners free.* | *He was found not guilty and walked free from the court.* | *The animals are allowed to run free in the park.* | *Hundreds of dogs roam free on the streets.* | **break/pull/struggle free** *She managed to break free from her attacker.*
3 **NOT CONTROLLED** allowed to do or say whatever you want, or allowed to happen, without being controlled or restricted by anyone or anything: *We had a free and open discussion about religion.* | **free to do sth** *Remember, you are free to say no.* | [**+from**] *Newspapers today are entirely free from government control.* | *Women are struggling to break free from tradition.* | [**+of**] *I longed to be free of my family.* | *He became president following the country's first free elections last year.* | *We would all support the principle of free speech.* | *For the first time in its history, the country has a free press.* | *Patients are now allowed free access to their medical records.* | *The legislation will allow the free movement of goods through all the countries in Europe.*
4 **NOT BUSY** if you are free, or have some free time, you have no work, and nothing else that you must do; → **available**: *I'm free next weekend.* | [**+for**] *Are you free for lunch tomorrow?* | **free to do sth** *At last I was free to concentrate on my own research.* | **a free day/morning/half-hour etc** *I haven't got a free day this week.* | *Children these days have very little free time.*
5 **NOT BEING USED** something that is free is available to use because it is not already being used: *Is this seat free?* | *I'm afraid we don't have any free tables this evening.* | *He used his free hand to unlock the door and open it.*
6 **NOT SUFFERING** not suffering from something: [**+of**] *At last she was free of pain.* | [**+from**] *A lot of the patients are now free from symptoms.* | **pain-free/trouble-free etc** *a stress-free life*
7 **NOT CONTAINING STH** not containing something: [**+from/of**] *All our drinks are free from artificial colour-*

ings and flavourings. | **fat-free/dairy-free etc** *a fat-free yoghurt*

8 TAX if something is free of tax, you do not have to pay tax on it: [+of] *This income should be free of tax.* | **tax-free/duty-free etc** *tax-free earnings* | *an opportunity to buy duty-free goods*

9 feel free *spoken* used to tell someone that they can do something: *Feel free to ask questions.* | *'Can I use your bathroom?' 'Yes, feel free.'*

10 free and easy relaxed, friendly, and without many rules: *I knew that life wasn't going to be so free and easy now.* | *the free and easy atmosphere of university life*

11 free spirit someone who lives as they want to rather than in the way that society considers normal

12 give sb a free hand/rein to let someone do whatever they want or need to do in a particular situation: *The producer was given a free rein with the script.*

13 it's no free lunch also **there's no such thing as a free lunch** used to say that you should not expect to get something good without having to pay for it or make any effort

14 it's a free country *BrE* used, usually humorously, to say that you are or should be allowed to do something, after someone has said that you should not do it: *It's a free country. You can't stop me.*

15 get/take a free ride *informal* to get something without paying for it or working for it, because other people are paying or working for it: *They are encouraging all workers to join the union rather than just taking a free ride on those who do join.*

16 be free with sth to be very generous with something: *He seems to be very free with other people's money.* | *She is always free with her advice.*

17 make free with sth *informal* to use something that belongs to someone else when you should not: *I knew that they had been making free with our food.*

18 NOT RESTRICTED something that is free is not held, blocked, or restricted: *We opened both doors to allow a free flow of air through the building.*

19 CHEMICALS *technical* a free chemical substance is not combined with any other substance: *the amount of free oxygen in the atmosphere*

free² W3 *v* **freed, freeing** [T]

1 RELEASE to allow someone to leave prison or somewhere they have been kept as a prisoner; ⊟ **release**: *He expects to be freed quite soon.* | *The terrorists have at last agreed to free the hostages.* | **free sb from sth** *She was freed from prison last week.*

2 NOT CONTROL to allow someone to say and do what they want, after controlling or restricting them in the past: **free sb from/of sth** *The press has now been freed from political control.* | *She longed to be freed of her responsibilities.* | *Art frees the imagination.*

3 ALLOW SB/STH TO MOVE to move someone or something so that they are no longer held, fixed, or trapped; ⊟ **release**: *He struggled to free himself, but the ropes were too tight.* | *I couldn't free the safety catch.* | **free sb/sth from sth** *All the victims have now been freed from the wreckage.*

4 STOP SB SUFFERING to stop someone suffering from something by removing it: **free sb from sth** *new drugs that can free people from pain* | *At last the country has been freed from its enormous debts.*

5 MAKE AVAILABLE also **free sth ⇔ up** to make something available so that it can be used: *I need to free up some of the disk space on my computer.* | *This should free some money for investment.*

6 GIVE SB MORE TIME also **free sb ⇔ up** to give someone time to do something by taking away other jobs that they have to do: **free sb (up) from sth** *Taking away the burden of administration will free teachers to concentrate on teaching.* | *We have freed up some staff to deal with the backlog of work.*

free³ *adv* **1** without payment: *Children under four can travel free.* | *You can get advice free from your local library.* | **for free** *He offered to do the work for free.* | *All these services are available to the public free of charge.* **2** not fixed or held in a particular place or

position: *The ropes were now hanging free.* | *A gold chain swung free around his neck.* → **FREELY, SCOT-FREE**

-free /friː/ *suffix* [in adjectives and adverbs] without something that you do not want: *a trouble-free journey* | *duty-free cigarettes* | *a salt-free diet* | *They live in the house rent-free.*

free 'agent *n* [C] someone who is not responsible to anyone else and can do what they want

free and 'easy; **free-and-easy** *BrE adj* very informal and relaxed: *the free-and-easy atmosphere of the local pub*

free·bie /'friːbi/ *n* [C] *informal* something that you are given free, usually by a company: **on a freebie** *The company paid for the minister to fly out to Australia on a freebie.* | **freebie holiday/hotel/flight etc** *A waiter was handing round freebie glasses of wine.*

free·boot·er /'friːbuːtə $ -ər/ *n* [C] someone who joins in a war in order to steal other people's goods and money

free·born /ˌfriːˈbɔːn◂ $ -ˈbɔːrn◂/ *adj old use* not born as a slave

free col,lective 'bargaining *n* [U] *BrE* talks between TRADE UNIONS and employers about pay or working conditions that are not controlled by law

free·dom S2 W2 /'friːdəm/ *n*

1 [C,U] the right to do what you want without being controlled or restricted by anyone; → **liberty**: *People here like their freedom and privacy.* | *the rights and freedoms of citizens* | **freedom to do sth** *We do not have the freedom to do just what we like.* | *the freedom to vote* | **freedom of speech/expression/choice etc** (=the legal right to say what you want, choose your own religion etc) *The First Amendment guarantees freedom of expression.* | **individual/personal freedom** *The government was accused of using the law to restrict individual freedom* | **press/academic/political etc freedom**

2 [U] the state of being free and allowed to do what you want: *Kids have too much freedom these days.* | *The teachers are given* **complete freedom** *in their choice of teaching methods.* | **freedom to do sth** *The wheelchair gives him the freedom to go out on his own.* | *Tracksuits are designed to give you* **freedom of movement**.

3 [U] the state of being free because you are not in prison; ⊟ **captivity, imprisonment**: *The prisoner was recaptured after only 48 hours of freedom.*

4 freedom from sth the state of not being affected by something that makes you worried, unhappy, afraid etc: **freedom from fear/pain/worry etc** *The contraceptive pill gave women freedom from the fear of pregnancy.*

5 freedom of choice the right or ability to choose whatever you want to do or have: *The new satellite TV channels offer viewers greater freedom of choice.*

6 freedom of information the legal right of people in some countries to see information which the government has about people and organizations

7 freedom of the city in Britain, an honour given by a city to someone who has done something special

'freedom ,fighter *n* [C] someone who fights in a war against an unfair or dishonest government, army etc; → **guerrilla, terrorist**

free 'enterprise *n* [U] the principle and practice of allowing private business to operate without much government control; → **private enterprise**

'free fall, free-fall *n* [singular, U] **1** the movement of someone or something through the air without engine power, for example before a PARACHUTE opens after someone has jumped out of a plane: **in/into free fall** *The spacecraft is now in free fall towards the Earth.* **2** a very fast and uncontrolled fall in the value of something: *the free-fall in housing prices* | **in/into free fall** *The economy is in free fall.* —**free-falling** *adj*

F

1 000, 2 000, 3 000, most frequent words in S poken and W ritten English

ˈfree-ˌfloating adj not connected to or influenced by anything: *a free-floating exchange rate* | *a free-floating currency*

Free·fone /ˈfriːfəʊn $ -foʊn/ n trademark another spelling of FREEPHONE

ˌfree-for-ˈall n [singular] informal **1** a situation in which there is total freedom and anything can happen – used to show disapproval: *the free-for-all of sexual activity in the 1970s* **2** a noisy quarrel or fight involving a lot of people: *A controversial penalty decision sparked a free-for-all at the end of the match.*

free·form /ˈfriːfɔːm $ -fɔːrm/ adj [only before noun] freeform music or art does not have a standard structure or form, and uses new ideas or methods

free·hand /ˈfriːhænd/ adj [only before noun] drawn by hand without using any special tools: **freehand drawing/sketch** —**freehand** adv

free·hold /ˈfriːhəʊld $ -hoʊld/ n [C,U] BrE law when you completely own a building or piece of land for an unlimited time; → **leasehold**: *They bought the freehold of their house.* —**freehold** adj: *a freehold property* —**freehold** adv: *The property will be sold freehold.*

free·hold·er /ˈfriːhəʊldə $ -hoʊldər/ n [C] BrE an owner of freehold land or property; → **leaseholder**

ˌfree ˈhouse n [C] in Britain, a PUB that can buy beer from different BREWERIES (=a company that makes beer etc), rather than being controlled by one brewery

ˌfree ˈkick n [C] a chance for a player on one football team to kick the ball freely from a position shown by the REFEREE, given because the other team has done something wrong

free·lance /ˈfriːlɑːns $ -læns/ adj, adv working independently for different companies rather than being employed by one particular company: *She works freelance from home.* | **freelance journalist/writer/photographer etc** —**freelance** v [I]: *He's freelancing for several translation agencies.* —**freelance** also **freelancer** n [C]

free·load·er /ˈfriːləʊdə $ -loʊdər/ n [C] informal someone who takes food, drink, or other things from other people, without giving anything in return – used to show disapproval —**freeload** v [I]

ˌfree ˈlove n [U] old-fashioned the practice or principle of having sex with people without being faithful to one person or without being married

free·ly /ˈfriːli/ adv **1** without anyone stopping or limiting something: *the country's first freely elected president* | *EU members are allowed to travel freely between member states.* | **talk/speak/write etc freely** *In France he could write freely, without fear of arrest.* | *We went outside so that we could talk freely without being overheard.* **2** if something moves freely, it moves smoothly and nothing prevents it from doing this: *She was breathing freely.* | *If your muscles are tense, blood cannot circulate freely.* | *The leg injury was preventing him from moving freely.* **3 freely available** very easy to obtain: *Information is freely available on the Internet.* **4 freely admit/acknowledge sth** to agree that something is true, even though telling the truth is difficult or embarrassing: *They freely admitted using the drug.* **5** generously and willingly: *She gave freely to charity.*

free·man /ˈfriːmən/ n plural **freemen** /-mən/ [C] someone who is not a slave

ˌfree ˈmarket n [C] an economic system in which prices are not controlled by the government: *a free market economy*

ˌfree marketˈeer n [C] someone who thinks that prices should be allowed to rise and fall naturally and should not be fixed by the government

Free·ma·son /ˈfriːˌmeɪsən, ˌfriːˈmeɪsən/ also **Mason** n [C] a man who belongs to a secret society in which each member helps the other members to become successful

Free·ma·son·ry, **freemasonry** /ˈfriːmeɪsənri, ˌfriːˈmeɪ-/ n [U] the system and practices of Freemasons

ˌfree ˈpardon n [C] BrE law the official act of forgiving someone for a crime

ˌfree ˈperiod n [C] BrE a period of time in a school day when a student does not have a class

free·phone, **Freefone** /ˈfriːfəʊn $ -foʊn/ n [U] trademark BrE an arrangement by which a company or organization pays the cost of telephone calls made to it; → **toll-free**

ˌfree ˈport n [C] a port or airport in one country where goods from other countries can be brought in and taken out without being taxed

Free·post /ˈfriːpəʊst $ -poʊst/ n [U] trademark BrE an arrangement by which a company or organization pays the cost of letters that you send to it by post

ˌfree ˈradical n [C] technical an atom or group of atoms with at least one free ELECTRON, which combines with other atoms very easily: *It is thought that free radicals can damage cells.*

ˌfree-ˈrange adj relating to a type of farming which allows animals such as chickens and pigs to move around and eat naturally, rather than being kept in a restricted space; → **battery**: *free-range eggs*

free·si·a /ˈfriːziə $ -ʒə/ n [C] a plant with pleasant-smelling yellow, white, pink, or purple flowers

free·stand·ing /ˌfriːˈstændɪŋ◂/ adj **1** not fixed to a frame, wall, or other support: *a freestanding bookcase* **2** able to exist on its own and not as part of something bigger: *The modules can be offered as free-standing courses.*

free·style /ˈfriːstaɪl/ n **1** [U] a swimming race in which swimmers can use any style they choose, usually CRAWL: *the 100m freestyle* **2** [U] a sports competition in which competitors can use any movements they choose: *freestyle wrestling* **3** [C] a RAP song in which the singer says words directly from their imagination, without planning or writing them first

free·think·er /ˌfriːˈθɪŋkə $ -ər/ n [C] someone who has their own opinions, ideas, and beliefs, rather than accepting other people's – used to show approval —**freethinking** adj

ˌfree-to-ˈair adj BrE free-to-air television or television programmes do not cost extra money to watch: *free-to-air television coverage of rugby league matches*

ˌfree ˈtrade n [U] a situation in which the goods coming into or going out of a country are not controlled or taxed

ˌfree ˈverse n [U] poetry that does not have a fixed structure and does not RHYME; → **blank verse**

ˌfree ˈvote n [C] BrE a situation in which members of the British parliament can choose how to vote rather than following the choice of their political party

free·ware /ˈfriːweə $ -wer/ n [U] free computer software, often available on the Internet; → **shareware**

free·way S2 W3 /ˈfriːweɪ/ n [C] AmE a very wide road in the US, built for fast travel; → **motorway**, **expressway**, **highway**: *the Central Freeway*

free·wheel /ˌfriːˈwiːl/ v [I] to ride a bicycle or drive a vehicle down a hill, without using power from your legs or the engine

free·wheel·ing /ˌfriːˈwiːlɪŋ◂/ adj [only before noun] informal not worried about rules or what will happen in the future: *A lot of the girls envied me my independent, freewheeling life.*

ˌfree ˈwill n [U] **1 do sth of your own free will** to do something because you want to, not because someone else has forced you to: *He came of his own free will.* **2** the ability to make your own decisions about what to do, rather than being controlled by God or Fate

freeze¹ /friːz/ v past tense **froze** /frəʊz $ froʊz/, past participle **frozen** /ˈfrəʊzən $ ˈfroʊ-/
1 LIQUID [I,T] if a liquid or something wet freezes or is

frozen, it becomes hard and solid because the temperature is very cold; → **melt, thaw**: *The lake had frozen overnight.*
2 FOOD [I,T] to preserve food for a long time by keeping it at a very low temperature, or to be preserved in this way: *I think I'll freeze that extra meat.* | *Tomatoes don't freeze well.*
3 MACHINE/ENGINE [I] if a machine, engine, pipe etc freezes, the liquid inside it becomes solid with cold, so that it does not work properly: *The water pipes have frozen.*
4 WEATHER **it freezes** if it freezes outside, the temperature falls to or below FREEZING POINT: *Do you think it'll freeze tonight?*
5 FEEL COLD [I] to feel very cold: *I nearly froze to death watching that football match.*
6 WAGES/PRICES [T] if a government or company freezes wages, prices etc, they do not increase them for a period of time: *The government has been forced to cut spending and freeze public-sector wages.*
7 MONEY/PROPERTY [T] to legally prevent money in a bank from being spent, property from being sold etc: *The court froze their assets.*
8 STOP MOVING [I] to stop moving suddenly and stay completely still and quiet: *I froze and listened; someone was in my apartment.* | [+with] *She froze with horror.*
9 FILM [T] to stop a film or video in order to be able to look at a particular part of it; → **freeze-frame**: *He froze the picture on the screen.*
10 sb's blood freezes used to say that someone is very frightened or shocked: *I heard his scream and felt my blood freeze.*

freeze sb ⇔ **out** *phr v*
to deliberately prevent someone from being involved in something, by making it difficult for them, being unkind to them etc: *Why did you freeze me out?*

freeze over *phr v*
if an area or pool of water freezes over, its surface turns into ice: *We'll go skating if the lake has frozen over.*

freeze up *phr v*
1 if a machine, engine, or pipe freezes up, the liquid inside becomes solid with cold so that it does not work properly; ◻ **freeze**
2 to suddenly be unable to speak or act normally: *I wouldn't know what to say. I'd just freeze up.*

freeze² *n* **1** [C] a time when people are not allowed to increase prices or pay: **a price/pay/wage freeze** | [+on] *a freeze on pay rises* **2** [C] the stopping of some activity or process: [+on] *The government have imposed a freeze on civil service appointments.* **3** [singular] *BrE* a period of extremely cold weather **4** [C usually singular] *AmE* a short period of time, especially at night, when the temperature is extremely low → DEEP FREEZE

freeze-'dried / $ '. ./ *adj* freeze-dried food has been frozen and dried very quickly in order to preserve it

freeze-frame *n* [U] when you stop the action on a video at one particular place; → **freeze**: *Press the freeze-frame button.* —**freeze-frame** *v* [T]

freez·er /'friːzə $ -ər/ *n* [C] **1** a large piece of electrical kitchen equipment in which food can be stored at very low temperatures for a long time; ◻ **deep freeze**; → **fridge**; → see picture at EAT **2** *AmE* a part of a FRIDGE in which food can be stored at very low temperatures for a long time; ◻ **freezer compartment** *BrE*

freezer com,partment *n* [C] *BrE* a part of a FRIDGE in which food can be stored at very low temperatures for a long time; ◻ **freezer** *AmE*

freez·ing¹ /'friːzɪŋ/ *n* [U] **above/below freezing** above or below the temperature at which water freezes: *It was well below freezing last night.*

freezing² *adj, adv* **1** extremely cold: *It's freezing in this house. Can't I turn on the heating?* | *We were freezing cold in the tent last night.* **2** below the temperature at which water turns to ice: *freezing fog*

freezing ,point *n* **1** [U] the temperature at which water turns into ice; → **boiling point** **2** [C usually singular] the temperature at which a particular liquid freezes: *Alcohol has a lower freezing point than water.*

freight¹ /freɪt/ *n* **1** [U] goods that are carried by ship, train, or aircraft, and the system of moving these goods: *freight services* | *We'll send your personal belongings by **air freight** and your furniture by **sea freight**.* **2** [C] *AmE* a FREIGHT TRAIN

freight² *v* [T] to send goods by air, sea, or train

freight car *n* [C] part of a train which carries goods

freight·er /'freɪtə $ -ər/ *n* [C] a ship or aircraft that carries goods

freight train *n* [C] a train that carries goods

French¹ /frentʃ/ *adj* relating to France, its people, or its language: *an excellent French wine*

French² *n* **1 the French** [plural] people from France **2** [U] the language used in France, and some other countries: *How do you ask for directions in French?* **3 pardon/excuse my French** *spoken* used to say sorry for swearing

French 'bean *n* [C] *BrE* a long thin green vegetable that is usually cooked and eaten whole; ◻ **green bean**

French 'bread *n* [U] a long thin LOAF of white bread

French 'doors *n* [plural] *especially AmE* FRENCH WINDOWS

French 'dressing *n* [U] a mixture of oil and VINEGAR that is put on SALADS

French 'fry also **fry** *n plural* **French fries** [C usually plural] *especially AmE* a long thin piece of potato that has been cooked in hot oil; ◻ **chip** *BrE*; → see picture at FAST FOOD

French 'horn also **horn** *especially BrE n* [C] a musical instrument made of BRASS, that is curved round into a circle with a wide opening at one end

French 'kiss *n* [C] a kiss made with your mouths open and with your tongues touching

French 'letter *n* [C] *BrE old-fashioned informal* a CONDOM

French 'loaf *n* [C] *BrE* a long thin LOAF of white bread; ◻ **baguette**

French·man /'frentʃmən/ *n plural* **Frenchmen** /-mən/ [C] a man from France

French 'plait *n* [C] a hairstyle in which the hair is put into a PLAIT that starts from the top of the head at the back

French 'pleat *n* [C] a hairstyle in which the hair is combed across at the back of the head, rolled under, and pinned

French 'polish *n* [U] a clear liquid put on wooden furniture to protect it and make it shine

French 'stick *n* [C] a long thin LOAF of white bread; ◻ **baguette**

French 'toast *n* [U] pieces of bread put into a mixture of egg and milk and then cooked in hot oil

French 'windows *n* [plural] a pair of doors made mostly of glass, usually opening onto a garden or BALCONY

French·wom·an /'frentʃ,wʊmən/ *n plural* **Frenchwomen** /-,wɪmɪn/ [C] a woman from France

fre·net·ic /frɪ'netɪk/ *adj* frenetic activity is fast and not very organized; ◻ **frantic**: *She rushes from job to job at a frenetic pace.*

fren·zied /'frenzid/ *adj* frenzied activity is fast and uncontrolled, usually because it is done by someone feeling very anxious or excited: *A woman was stabbed to death in a **frenzied attack** on her home tonight.* | *frenzied efforts to find a solution* —**frenziedly** *adv*

fren·zy /'frenzi/ *n plural* **frenzies 1** [C,U] a state of great anxiety or excitement, in which you cannot control your behaviour: [+of] *a frenzy of religious feeling* | **in a frenzy** *The women were screaming and in a frenzy to get home.* | *Doreen had **worked** herself **into***

F

a frenzy. **2** [C] a time when people do a lot of things very quickly: [+of] *There had been a frenzy of activity in my absence.* | *a selling frenzy* **3 a feeding frenzy a)** an occasion when a lot of people get involved in an activity in an uncontrolled way: *The film put America's moviegoers into a feeding frenzy.* **b)** an occasion when a lot of wild animals, especially SHARKS, eat something in a very excited way

fre·quen·cy W3 /ˈfriːkwənsi/ *n plural* **frequencies**
1 [U] the number of times that something happens within a particular period of time or within a particular group of people: [+of] *the frequency of serious road accidents* | **the high/low frequency (of sth)** *the higher frequency of diabetes in older people* | *Side effects from prescribed drugs are being reported **with increasing frequency*** (=more and more often). | *The relative frequency of fraternal twins has halved since 1950.*
2 [U] the fact that something happens a lot; ☒ **regularity**: *Businesses come and go **with alarming frequency**.*
3 [C,U] *technical* the number of radio waves, sound waves etc that pass any point per second: *This station broadcasts on three different frequencies.* | **high/low frequency** *Dolphins produce a high frequency sound.* | *the **frequency range** of the human ear*

fre·quent¹ W3 /ˈfriːkwənt/ *adj* happening or doing something often; ☒ **infrequent: more/less frequent** *Her headaches are becoming less frequent.* | *Trains rushed past at **frequent intervals**.* | *She was a **frequent visitor** to the house.*

fre·quent² /frɪˈkwent $ frɪˈkwent, ˈfriːkwənt/ *v* [T] *formal* to go to a particular place often: *The bar was frequented by actors from the nearby theatre.*

fre·quent·ly S3 W2 /ˈfriːkwəntli/ *adv* very often or many times: *Limestone was frequently used as a building material.*

fres·co /ˈfreskəʊ $ -koʊ/ *n plural* **frescoes** *or* **frescos** [C] a painting made on a wall while the PLASTER is still wet; → **mural**

fresh S2 W2 /freʃ/ *adj*
1 NEW adding to or replacing something: *I'll just make some fresh coffee.* | *The report provides fresh evidence about the way the business was run.* | *You'll have to start again on a fresh sheet of paper.*
2 NEW AND INTERESTING good or interesting because it has not been done, seen etc before: *Ryan will bring a **fresh approach** to the job.* | *We need some fresh ideas.* | *Let's take a **fresh look** at the problem.*
3 RECENT done, experienced, or having happened recently: *There were fresh fox tracks around the hen huts.* | *The accident was still **fresh in her mind**.*
4 a fresh start when you start something again in a completely new and different way after being unsuccessful: *I hope Jim and I can get back together and **make a fresh start**.*
5 FOOD/FLOWERS **a)** fresh food has recently been picked or prepared, and is not frozen or preserved: **fresh fruit/vegetables/fish/bread etc** | *The beans are fresh from the garden.* **b)** fresh flowers have recently been picked
6 fresh air air from outside, especially clean air: *Let's open the windows and have some fresh air in here!* → **breath of fresh air** at BREATH (2)
7 fresh water fresh water contains no salt and comes from rivers and lakes; → **saltwater**
8 TASTE/SMELL ETC [usually before noun] pleasantly clean or cool: *a fresh minty taste* | *It's a light, fresh wine.*
9 APPEARANCE pleasant, bright, and clean; ☒ **dull**: *The kitchen is decorated in fresh blues and greens.* | *She has brown hair, hazel eyes and a **fresh complexion**.*
10 WEATHER if the wind is fresh, it is quite cold and strong: *a fresh breeze*
11 NOT TIRED [not usually before noun] full of energy because you are not tired: *She always seems fresh and lively, even at the end of the day.* | *Despite his busy day he arrived looking **as fresh as a daisy*** (=not tired and ready to do things).

12 fresh from sth a) also **fresh out of sth** *AmE* having just finished your education or training, and not having a lot of experience: *He's fresh out of law school.* **b)** having just come from a particular place or experience: *The team is fresh from their victory over the French.*
13 be fresh out of sth *AmE spoken* to have just used your last supplies of something: *I'm fresh out of beer. Will you take a cola instead?*
14 fresh-made/fresh-cut/fresh-grated etc *AmE* having just been made, cut etc: *fresh-ground coffee*
15 get/be fresh with sb *old-fashioned* to behave rudely in a way which shows sexual interest, or lack of respect —**freshness** *n* [U + of]: *the freshness of the early morning* | *the freshness and vitality of youth*

fresh·en /ˈfreʃən/ *v* **1** also **freshen up** [T] to make something look or feel clean, new, attractive, cool etc; ☒ **brighten (up):** *I'm going to buy some white paint to freshen up the bathroom walls.* **2** [I] if the wind freshens, it gets colder and stronger **3** also **freshen up** [T] to add more liquid to a drink: *The waitress freshened our coffee.*
freshen up *phr v* to wash your hands and face in order to feel clean and comfortable: **freshen yourself up** *Fiona's gone to freshen herself up.*

fresh·er /ˈfreʃə $ -ər/ *n* [C] *BrE* a student who has just started at a college or university

fresh-faced *adj* fresh-faced people have a face that looks young and healthy: *a fresh-faced youth*

fresh·ly /ˈfreʃli/ *adv* **freshly ground/picked/made etc** recently ground, picked etc: *freshly ground pepper*

fresh·man /ˈfreʃmən/ *n plural* **freshmen** /-mən/ [C] *AmE* a student in the first year of HIGH SCHOOL or university

freshwater fish

fin | gills
trout | perch
pike | salmon

fresh·wa·ter /ˈfreʃwɔːtə $ -wɔːtər, -wɑː-/ *adj* [only before noun] **1** having water that contains no salt; → **saltwater**: *freshwater lakes* **2** living in water that contains no salt; → **saltwater**: *freshwater crabs*

fret¹ /fret/ *v* **fretted, fretting** [I] to worry about something, especially when there is no need: *Don't fret – everything will be all right.* | [+about/over] *She's always fretting about the children.* | **fret that** *men of fifty fretting that they're no longer young*

fret² *n* [C] one of the raised lines on the fretboard of a GUITAR etc

fret·board /ˈfretbɔːd $ -bɔːrd/ *n* [C] the long piece of wood on the NECK (=straight part) of a GUITAR against which the fingers press the strings to change the note

fret·ful /ˈfretfəl/ *adj* anxious and complaining, and unable to relax: *The child was tired and fretful.* —**fretfully** *adv* —**fretfulness** *n* [U]

fret·saw /ˈfretsɔː $ -sɔː/ *n* [C] a tool for cutting patterns in wood

fret·ted /ˈfretɪd/ *adj* cut or shaped into complicated patterns as decoration

fret·work /ˈfretwɜːk $ -wɜːrk/ *n* [U] patterns cut into thin wood, metal etc or the activity of making these patterns

Freud·i·an /ˈfrɔɪdiən/ *adj* **1** relating to Sigmund Freud's ideas about the way the mind works, and the way it can be studied **2** a Freudian remark or action is connected with the ideas about sex that people have in their minds but do not usually talk about

Freudian 'slip n [C] something you say that is different from what you intended to say, and shows your true thoughts

Fri. also **Fri** BrE the written abbreviation of **Friday**

fri·a·ble /ˈfraɪəbəl/ adj technical friable rocks or soil are easily broken into very small pieces or into powder

fri·ar /ˈfraɪə $ -ər/ n [C] a member of a religious group of Catholic men, who travelled around in the past teaching about Christianity and who were very poor; → **monk**

fri·a·ry /ˈfraɪəri/ n plural **friaries** [C] a place where friars live; → **monastery**

fric·as·see /ˈfrɪkəseɪ $ ˌfrɪkəˈsiː/ n [C,U] food consisting of small pieces of meat in a thick white sauce: chicken fricassee

fric·a·tive /ˈfrɪkətɪv/ n [C] technical a sound, such as /f/ or /z/, made by forcing your breath through a narrow opening between your lips and teeth, or your tongue and teeth

fric·tion /ˈfrɪkʃən/ n **1** [C,U] disagreement, angry feelings, or unfriendliness between people; ◨ **tension**: **cause/create friction** Having my mother living with us causes friction at home. | [+between] the usual frictions between parents and their teenage children | [+with] His independent attitude was a constant **source of friction** with his boss. **2** [U] technical the natural force that prevents one surface from sliding easily over another surface: Putting oil on both surfaces reduces friction. **3** [U] when one surface rubs against another: Check your rope frequently, as friction against the rock can wear it away.

Fri·day /ˈfraɪdi, -deɪ/ n [C,U] written abbreviation **Fri.** the day between Thursday and Saturday: **on Friday** It's Kate's birthday on Friday. | Diane won't be here Friday. AmE | **Friday morning/afternoon etc** Can you meet me Friday morning? | **last Friday** I had a terrible time last Friday. | **this Friday** We're flying to Vienna this Friday. | **next Friday** (=Friday of next week) Her appointment is next Friday. | **a Friday** (=one of the Fridays in the year) We got married on a Friday.

fridge [S2] /frɪdʒ/ n [C] a large piece of electrical kitchen equipment, used for keeping food and drinks cool; ◨ **refrigerator**, → **freezer**; → see picture at EAT

fridge-'freezer n [C] BrE a large piece of electrical kitchen equipment, of which one part is a fridge and one part is a FREEZER

'fridge ˌmagnet n [C] a MAGNET with a picture on it or in an interesting shape, used for decorating the outside of a FRIDGE

fried /fraɪd/ adj **1** having been cooked in hot oil: fried chicken **2** AmE informal unable to think clearly, because you are tired, anxious etc: My brain is just totally fried.

friend [S1] [W1] /frend/ n [C]

1 **PERSON YOU LIKE** someone who you know and like very much and enjoy spending time with

> a friend of mine/yours/Billy's etc
> best friend (=the friend you like the most)
> good/close friend (=one of the friends you like the most)
> old friend (=a friend you have known for a long time)
> trusted friend
> lifelong friend (=someone who is your friend for the whole of your life)
> friend of a friend
> circle of friends (=all the friends someone has)
> a mutual friend (=someone who is a friend of both you and someone else)
> a childhood/boyhood/girlhood friend

> Jerry, this is my friend Lucinda. | Is this man **a friend of yours?** | Julia was the wife of his **best friend.** | One of her **closest friends** died at the weekend. | I didn't expect this treatment from my father's **oldest friend.** | She told this to only a few **trusted friends.** | I met Stephano through **a friend of a friend.** | Few people

smoke in my **circle of friends.** | Jill is **a mutual friend** of ours.

2 **be friends (with sb)** to be someone's friend: I've been friends with the Murkets for twenty years.

3 a) **make friends** to become friendly with people: Jenny has always found it easy to make friends at school. **b)** **make friends with sb** to become friendly with someone: He made friends with an old fisherman.

4 **be just (good) friends** used to say that you are not having a romantic relationship with someone: I'm not going out with Nathan – we're just good friends.

5 **SUPPORTER** someone who supports an organization such as a theatre, ART GALLERY, CHARITY etc by giving money or help: [+of] the Friends of the Tate

6 **NOT AN ENEMY** someone who has the same beliefs, wants to achieve the same things etc as you, and will support you: our friends and allies around the world | She shot him a quick glance as if unsure whether he was friend or foe. | Don't worry, you're among friends.

7 **PARLIAMENT/COURT OF LAW** BrE **a)** **my honourable friend** used by a member of parliament when speaking about another member of parliament **b)** **my learned friend** used by a lawyer when speaking about another lawyer in a court of law

8 **be no friend of sth** to not like or be a supporter of something: I'm no friend of socialism, as you know.

9 **Friend** a member of the Society of Friends; ◨ **quaker**

10 **our/your friend** spoken used humorously to talk about someone you do not know, who is doing something annoying: Our friend with the loud voice is back.

11 **have friends in high places** to have important people who can help you

12 **a friend in need** someone who helps you when you need it

friend·less /ˈfrendləs/ adj literary having no friends and no one to help you

friend·ly [S2] [W3] /ˈfrendli/ adj comparative **friendlier**, superlative **friendliest**

1 behaving towards someone in a way that shows you like them and are ready to talk to them or help them; ◨ **unfriendly**: a friendly smile | I've found a great pub – good beer and a friendly atmosphere. | [+to/towards] Why is he suddenly so friendly towards you, Charlotte?

2 **be friendly with sb** to be friends with someone: Betty's very friendly with the Jacksons.

3 not at war with your own country, or not opposing you; ◨ **hostile**: friendly nations

4 BrE a friendly game is played for pleasure or practice, and not because it is important to win: a friendly match against AC Milan

5 **user-friendly/customer-friendly etc** not difficult for particular people to understand or use: a user-friendly computer program | a customer-friendly shopping mall

6 **environmentally-friendly/ozone-friendly/eco-friendly etc** not harmful to the environment, OZONE LAYER etc: eco-friendly washing powder

7 **friendly fire** bombs, bullets etc that accidentally kill people who are fighting on the same side —**friendliness** n [U]

friendly² n plural **friendlies** [C] BrE a game played for pleasure or practice, and not because it is important to win

'friendly so,ciety n [C] an association in Britain that people regularly pay small amounts of money to, which then provides them with money when they become old or ill

friend·ship [W3] /ˈfrendʃɪp/ n

1 [C] a relationship between friends: [+between] The friendship between father and youth deepened. | [+with]

F

his friendship with King Edward VII | her **close friendship** *with her aunt | a* **lifelong friendship** *| The two boys* **formed** *a deep and lasting* **friendship**. *| He and Matthew* **struck up a friendship** (=began to be friends).
2 [U] the feelings and behaviour that exist between friends: *I could always rely on Gary for friendship and support. | The Indians have* **extended the hand of friendship** (=shown that they want to be friends with another country).

fri·er /'fraɪə $ -ər/ *n* another spelling of FRYER

fries /fraɪz/ *n* [plural] long thin pieces of potato that have been cooked in hot oil; ▣ **chips** *BrE*

Frie·si·an /'friːziən $ -ʒən/ *n* [C] *especially BrE* a type of cow that is black and white

frieze /friːz/ *n* [C] a decoration that goes along the top of the walls of a room or a building

frig·ate /'frɪɡət/ *n* [C] a small fast ship used especially for protecting other ships in wars

frig·ging /'frɪɡɪŋ/ *adj* [only before noun] *spoken not polite* used to emphasize something you are saying when you are angry, annoyed etc: *I can't open the frigging door!*

fright /fraɪt/ *n* **1** [singular, U] a sudden feeling of fear: *You gave me such* **a fright** *creeping up on me like that! |* **get/have a fright** *I got an awful fright when I realised how much money I owed. |* **with fright** *He was shaking with fright. |* **in fright** *Several of the children cried out in fright.* **2** **take fright** to be very afraid of something, especially so that you run away from it or do not do something that you were going to do: *The bird took fright and flew away. | She had promised to marry him, but took fright at the last moment.* **3 look a fright** *old-fashioned* to look untidy or unattractive → STAGE FRIGHT

fright·en /'fraɪtn/ *v* [T] to make someone feel afraid; ▣ **scare**: *Don't stand so near the edge! You're frightening me. | She was frightened by the anger in his eyes. | Computers used to frighten me, but not now. |* **frighten sb to death/frighten the life out of sb** (=make someone feel extremely afraid) *He drove at a speed which frightened Lara to death.*
   frighten sb ⇔ **away** *phr v* to make a person or animal go away by making them feel afraid: *Terrorist activity in the area has frightened most tourists away.*
   frighten sb **into** sth *phr v* to force someone to do something by making them afraid: **frighten sb into doing sth** *He frightened me into staying silent.*
   frighten sb/sth ⇔ **off** *phr v* to make a person or animal so nervous or afraid that they go away or do not do something they were going to do: *The investors were frightened off by the company's low profits that year.*

fright·ened ⟨S2⟩ /'fraɪtnd/ *adj* feeling afraid; ▣ **scared**: *Don't be frightened. We're not going to hurt you. |* [+of] *I was frightened of being left by myself in the house. | Her father had an awful temper and she was always frightened of him. |* **frightened to do sth** *The boy was frightened to speak. |* **frightened that** *She's frightened that her ex-husband will find her. | To tell the truth, I was* **frightened to death** (=very frightened). *| a frightened horse* ⚠ Do not confuse **frightened,** which describes a feeling, and **frightening,** which describes something that makes you feel frightened: *a frightened child | a frightening experience;* → see box at FEAR[1]

fright·en·ers /'fraɪtn-əz $ -ərz/ *n* [plural] *BrE informal* **put the frighteners on sb** to make someone do what you want by threatening them

fright·en·ing /'fraɪtn-ɪŋ/ *adj* making you feel afraid or nervous; ▣ **scary**: *That's a frightening thought. | Going into hospital can be very frightening for a child. | It was the most frightening experience of my life. |* **it is frightening (to do sth)** *It's frightening to think how easily children can be hurt.* —**frighteningly** *adv: The ice seemed frighteningly thin.*

fright·ful /'fraɪtfəl/ *adj old-fashioned especially BrE* **1** unpleasant or bad; ▣ **awful, terrible**: *There's been a frightful accident.* **2** used to emphasize how bad something is; ▣ **awful, terrible**: *Her hair was a frightful mess.*

fright·ful·ly /'fraɪtfəli/ *adv BrE old-fashioned* very: *I'm frightfully sorry about the delay.*

fri·gid /'frɪdʒɪd/ *adj* **1** a woman who is frigid does not like having sex **2** *literary* not friendly or kind; ▣ **cold, icy, frosty**: *The guard looked at us with a frigid stare.* **3** *formal* very cold; ▣ **icy**: *His breath steamed in the frigid air.* —**frigidly** *adv* —**frigidity** /frɪ'dʒɪdəti/ *n* [U]

frill /frɪl/ *n* [C] **1** a narrow piece of cloth that has many small folds in it, and that is attached to something as a decoration: *She was wearing a white blouse with frills at the cuffs.* **2 frills** [plural] attractive but unnecessary features: **without/with no frills** *It was just a comfortable flat with no frills. | We supply basic,* **no-frills** *tractors at low prices.*

frill·y /'frɪli/ *adj* decorated with lots of frills: *a frilly skirt*

fringe¹ /frɪndʒ/ *n* [C] **1** *BrE* if you have a fringe, your hair is cut so that it hangs down over your forehead; ▣ **bangs** *AmE*: *a tall girl with straight brown hair and a fringe* → see picture at LIMIT **2** a decorative edge of hanging threads on a curtain, piece of clothing etc **3** **on the fringes (of sth) a)** not completely belonging to or accepted by a group of people who share the same job, activities etc: *a small group on the fringes of the art world* **b)** also **on the fringe** at the part of something that is farthest from the centre; ▣ **on the edge of sth**: *Nina remained on the fringe of the crowd.* → **the lunatic fringe** at LUNATIC (3)

fringe² *adj* [only before noun] **fringe group/event/issue etc** a group, event etc that is less important or popular than the main group etc, or whose opinions are not accepted by most other people involved in the same activity; ▣ **mainstream**: *He used a party conference fringe meeting to defend terrorism. | The environment is no longer a fringe issue. | a fringe religious sect*

fringe³ *v* [T] to be around the edge of something: *A line of trees fringed the pool.*

ˈfringe ˌbenefit *n* [C usually plural] an additional service or advantage given with a job besides wages: *A competitive salary with fringe benefits will be offered.*

ˌfringe ˈtheatre *n* [U] *BrE* plays by new writers, often on difficult subjects or written in unusual ways, that are not performed in the main theatres

frip·pe·ry /'frɪpəri/ *n plural* **fripperies** [C usually plural] an unnecessary and useless object or decoration

Fris·bee /'frɪzbi/ *n* [C,U] *trademark* a piece of plastic shaped like a plate that you throw to someone else to catch as a game. The game is also called Frisbee.

frisk /frɪsk/ *v* **1** [T] to search someone for hidden weapons, drugs etc by feeling their body with your hands: *We were frisked at the airport – can you believe it?* **2** [I] if a young animal frisks, it runs and jumps playfully; ▣ **skip**: *The lambs were frisking around the pen.*

frisk·y /'frɪski/ *adj* **1** full of energy and fun: *a frisky horse* **2** *informal* feeling sexually excited; ▣ **horny** —**friskily** *adv* —**friskiness** *n* [U]

fris·son /'friːsɒn $ friː'soʊn/ *n* [C usually singular] a sudden feeling of excitement or fear; ▣ **shiver**: [+of] *A frisson of alarm went through her.*

frit·ter¹ /'frɪtə $ -ər/
   fritter sth ⇔ **away** *phr v* to waste time, money, or effort on something small or unimportant: [+on] *He frittered away a fortune on fast cars and gambling.*

fritter² *n* [C] a thin piece of fruit, vegetable, or meat covered with a mixture of eggs and flour and cooked in hot fat: **apple/corn/banana etc fritter**

fritz /frɪts/ *n AmE informal* **be/go on the fritz** if something is or goes on the fritz, it is not working correctly; ▣ **be/go on the blink**: *My TV is on the fritz.*

fri·vol·i·ty /frɪˈvɒlɨti $ -ˈvɑː-/ *n plural* **frivolities** **1** [C,U] behaviour or activities that are not serious or sensible, especially when you should be serious or sensible: *I don't think such frivolity helps the organization's public image.* **2** [C] something that is silly and unimportant: *Try not to be distracted by the frivolities of the world.*

friv·o·lous /ˈfrɪvələs/ *adj* **1** not serious or sensible, especially in a way that is not suitable for a particular occasion: *The court discourages frivolous law suits.* **2** a frivolous person likes having fun rather than doing serious or sensible things – used to show disapproval: 🔁 **serious** —**frivolously** *adv*

frizz /frɪz/ *v* [I,T] *informal* if your hair frizzes, or if you frizz it, it curls very tightly —**frizz** *n* [U]: *how to give your hair more shape and less frizz*

frizz·y /ˈfrɪzi/ *adj* frizzy hair is very tightly curled

fro /frəʊ $ froʊ/ *adv* → TO AND FRO

frock /frɒk $ frɑːk/ *n* [C] **1** *old-fashioned* a woman's or girl's dress: *a party frock* **2** a long loose piece of clothing worn by some Christian MONKS

frock 'coat / $ '. ./ *n* [C] a knee-length coat for men, worn in the 19th century

frog /frɒg $ frɑːg, frɔːg/ *n* [C] **1** a small green animal that lives near water and has long legs for jumping; → **toad** **2 have a frog in your throat** *informal* to have difficulty in speaking, especially because of a sore throat **3 Frog** *taboo* a very offensive word for someone from France. Do not use this word.

frog·man /ˈfrɒgmən $ ˈfrɑːg-, ˈfrɔːg-/ *n plural* **frogmen** /-mən/ [C] *BrE* someone who swims under water using special equipment to help them breathe, especially as a job; 🔁 **diver**: *Police frogmen have been searching the lake looking for a weapon.*

frog·march /ˈfrɒgmɑːtʃ $ ˈfrɑːgmɑːrtʃ, ˈfrɔːg-/ *v* [T always + adv/prep] *BrE* to force someone to walk somewhere by holding their arms very tightly by their side or behind their back

frog·spawn /ˈfrɒgspɔːn $ ˈfrɑːgspɒːn, ˈfrɔːg-/ *n* [U] *BrE* frog's eggs

frol·ic¹ /ˈfrɒlɪk $ ˈfrɑː-/ *v* **frolicked**, **frolicking** [I] *written* to play in an active happy way: *Lambs frolicked in the next field.*

frolic² *n* [C,U] *written* a fun enjoyable game or activity: *Everyone joined in the Saturday night frolics.*

from [S1] [W1] /frəm; *strong* frɒm $ frəm; *strong* frʌm, frɑːm/ *prep*
1 WHERE SB/STH STARTS starting at a particular place or position: *How do you get from here to Colchester?* | *an empire stretching from Syria to Spain* | *The hotel is on the main road from Newport.* | *Ernest twice ran away from home.*
2 DISTANCE AWAY used when talking about the distance between places or people to mention one of the places or people: *We live about five miles from Boston.* | *a large Victorian house only fifty yards from my workplace* | *He was standing only a few feet away from me.*
3 WHEN STH STARTS starting at a particular time: *He'll be here tomorrow from about seven o'clock onwards.* | *We're going to tell her on her birthday – that's two weeks from today.* | *From now on, I will only be working in the mornings.* | *housewives who work from morning to night* (=without stopping)
4 ORIGINAL CONDITION used to say what condition or situation something is in before it changes: *translating from French into English* | *When she arrived, things just went from bad to worse* (=got even worse)!
5 from place to place/house to house etc to a number of places: *She went from house to house asking if anyone had seen the child.*
6 from day to day/from minute to minute etc used to say that something continues or keeps changing: *My health is improving from day to day.*
7 vary/change etc from sth to sth to change or be different according to the person, situation, time etc

involved: *The treatment will vary from patient to patient.*
8 RANGE used to mention the two ends of a range: **from sth to sth** *Prices range from £10,000 to over £100,000.* | *a place where you can buy anything from a handgun to a rocket launcher*
9 POSITION WHEN WATCHING used to say where someone is when they see or watch something: *From the top of the hill, you can see for miles.* | *There's a man watching us from behind that fence.*
10 BEING REMOVED used to say where something is before it is removed: *She pulled her chair away from her desk.* | *Philip snatched the book from my hand.* | *He took a knife from his pocket.* | *Subtract three from fifteen.*
11 ABSENT used to say where someone would normally be, when they are not there: *The boy's absence from class has been noted.* | *I have a brother, but he's away from home at present.*
12 ORIGIN used to say where something was or who had it before you obtained it: *I got the idea from Colin.* | *Do you know where the information came from?* | *Gray caught smallpox from his nephew.* | *I'll show you a short extract from one of our training videos.* | *We usually buy our cheese from a shop in the market.* | *You have to choose the right answer from a list.*
13 SENT/GIVEN BY SB used to say who sends or gives something: *He had received a bill for nineteen dollars from St Peter's hospital.* | *I had a phone call from John.* | *You need to get permission from the owner.* | *with lots of love from Elaine* (=used at the end of a letter or on a card)
14 PLACE OF BIRTH/WORK used to say where someone was born, where they live, or where they work: *We invited speakers from all the regions.* | *Students from all faculties will have access to the machines.* | *There's a man from the tax office on the phone.* | *I'm from Yorkshire* (=I was born in Yorkshire).
15 CAUSE used to state the cause of something: *mothers who are exhausted from all the sleepless nights* | *Death rates from accidents have been on the increase.* | *a patient suffering from stomach pains* | *The community benefits from having an excellent health service.*
16 FORMING OPINIONS **a)** used to say what made you form a particular opinion: *From what I've read, the company seems to be in difficulties.* | *It's obvious from a quick glance that the plan has changed dramatically.* **b)** used to say how a subject is being considered: *These changes are ideal from my point of view.* | *We have spent a lot of time looking at the problem from all angles.*
17 MADE OF STH used to say what substance is used to make something: *Bread is made from flour, water, and yeast.* | *a cabinet constructed from chipboard*
18 PREVENTED used to say what is prevented or forbidden: **from doing sth** *These problems have prevented me from completing the work.* | *people who have been disqualified from driving* | *Tourist coaches will be banned from entering the city centre.*
19 HARM used to mention something bad that you do not want to affect someone or something: *ways of protecting yourself from attack* | *I will keep you safe from harm.*
20 DIFFERENCE used when you are comparing things or people to mention one of the things or people: *She's quite different from her sister.* | *Our two cats are so alike, I can never tell one from the other.*

from·age frais /ˌfrɒmɑːʒ ˈfreɪ $ frəˌmɑːʒ-/ *n* [U] *BrE* a thick creamy food made from milk and similar to YOGHURT

frond /frɒnd $ frɑːnd/ *n* [C] a leaf of a FERN or PALM¹ (2)

front¹ [S1] [W1] /frʌnt/ *n*
1 PART THAT IS FURTHEST FORWARD the front the part of something that is furthest forward in the direction that it is facing or moving; 🔁 **back**: [+of] *Ricky stepped forward to the front of the stage and began to sing.* | **the front of the line/queue** *It took ages*

F

to get to the front of the queue. | **at/in the front (of sth)** She always sits at the front of the class. | I found a good place on the bus, on the top deck, right at the front.
2 SIDE THAT FACES FORWARD the front the front of something is the side or surface that faces forward; 🔁 **back**: [+of] Harvey ran quickly round the front of the car to try and open the other door. | the control panel on the front of the machine | He wore an old sweater with a coffee stain down the front.
3 MOST IMPORTANT SIDE the front the most important side or surface of something, that you look at first; 🔁 **back**: **on the front** Dean sent me a lovely postcard with a picture of Bolton Abbey on the front. | | [+of] She's on the front (=a picture of her is on the front) of this month's magazine. | There's an introduction at the front of the book (=in the first pages).
4 BUILDING the front the most important side of a building, where you go in; 🔁 **back**: [+of] Ben had just finished painting the front of the house.
5 in front of sb/sth a) further forward than someone or something; 🔁 **behind**: He was standing in front of her in the lunch queue, and they just got talking. | He walked along in front of me, holding the lantern. | Suddenly, something ran across the road in front of the car. | An old wooden desk stood in front of the window. **b)** facing someone or something: The door opened and Harriet stood in front of him. | She sat down in front of the mirror and brushed her hair carefully. | Billy crouched in front of the fire to warm his hands. **c)** outside a building, near its entrance: There was a small garden in front of the house. | It was raining as we parked in front of the hotel. **d)** if you say or do something in front of someone, you do it where they can see or hear you: Don't swear in front of the children! | The match was played in front of a crowd of 8000. **e)** if you have problems or difficulties in front of you, you will soon need to deal with them ➔ **in front of your eyes** at EYE[1] (9)
6 in front a) ahead of something or someone; 🔁 **behind**: He drove straight into the car in front. **b)** winning something such as a sports match or competition; ⬛ **ahead**; 🔁 **behind**: His 20th-minute goal put Leeds back in front. **c)** in the area nearest the most forward part of something, or nearest the entrance to a building
7 on a ... front in a particular area of activity: **on the economic/political etc front** On the technical front, there have been a number of important developments. | Excellent teamwork from our staff has brought improvement **on all fronts**. | **on the domestic/international front** On the domestic front, de Gaulle's priority was to secure his government's authority. | **on a wide/broad/limited front** Schemes of this kind enjoyed success only on a limited front.
8 out front also **out the front/out in front** BrE the area near the entrance to a building: Hurry up! The taxi is out front.
9 in (the) front/up front in the front part of a car, next to the driver or where the driver sits: Mom, can I sit in the front?
10 in front of the television/TV/computer etc watching a television or using a computer: The average child spends three to four hours in front of the TV. | I spend most of my time **sitting in front of** a computer.
11 up front informal **a)** money that is paid up front is paid before work is done, or before goods are supplied: We need two hundred pounds up front. **b)** directly and clearly from the start: It's important to tell potential clients this up front. ➔ UPFRONT
12 WEATHER [C] technical the place where two areas of air of different temperatures meet, often shown as a line on weather maps: **warm/cold front** (=an area of warm or cold air)
13 SEA the front BrE a wide road next to the beach where people can walk for pleasure: We could always go for a stroll along the front.
14 BODY your front your chest, or the part of your

body that faces forward: You've spilled juice all down your front! | He was asleep, lying on his front with his head turned to one side.
15 ILLEGAL ACTIVITIES [C] a legal business that someone operates in order to hide the illegal activities that they are involved in: [+for] The casino was used as a front for cross-border smuggling operations.
16 HIDE FEELINGS [singular] if you put on a front, you behave in a way that is happier, braver etc than you really feel: **put on/show a front** Jenny didn't want Adam to see how worried she was. So she put on a **brave front**. | His arrogance is just a front. Deep down he's really insecure. | When disciplining children, it is important that parents **present a united front** (=show that they both feel the same about a situation).
17 ORGANIZATION [singular] used in the name of a political party or unofficial military organization: the People's Liberation Front
18 WAR [C] the area where fighting happens in a war; ⬛ **front line**: He joined the army, and was immediately sent to the front. | Her husband was shot down over the Western Front. ➔ HOME FRONT
19 CHURCH [C] a side of a large important church building: the west front of Rouen cathedral

---

WORD CHOICE: in front, opposite, face
If something or someone is **in front of** a building, they are directly outside the front of it: Meet me in front of the station.
If something or someone is **opposite** a building, they are outside the front of it on the other side of a street, area of land etc: the fields opposite the school
Use the verb **face** to say that a building has something outside the front of it: My apartment block faces (NOT is in front of) the sea. | a house facing the square
WORD CHOICE: in front of, before
⚠ Use **in front of** not 'before', to talk about doing something so that people can see or hear you: I had to explain myself in front of (NOT before) the whole class.
⚠ Use **before**, not 'in front of',to talk about the order in which things happen: Before starting (NOT In front of starting), let's list what we have to do.

---

front² S1 W2 adj [only before noun]
1 at, on, or in the front of something; 🔁 **back**: Two of his front teeth had been knocked out. | the front cover of 'Hello!' magazine | the front wheel of his bicycle | the dog's front legs | **front door/garden/porch** (=at the front of a house) We walked up the front steps and into the reception area. | **front seat/row** We got there an hour early in order to get seats in the front row.
2 a front organization is a legal one that is run in order to hide a secret or illegal activity: a front organization for importing heroin ➔ FRONT MAN (1)
3 technical a front vowel sound is made by raising your tongue at the front of your mouth, such as the vowel sound in 'see'; ➔ **back**

front³ v **1** [T] especially BrE if someone fronts something such as a musical group or a television programme, they lead it and are the person that the public sees most: Fronted by Alan Hull, the band had a number of memorable hits. **2** [T usually passive] also **front onto sth** BrE if a building or area of land is fronted by something or fronts onto it, it faces that thing: The house was fronted by a large ornamental lake. | The hotel entrance fronted onto a busy road. **3 be fronted by/with sth** to be covered or decorated at the front with something: a large building fronted with marble

front·age /ˈfrʌntɪdʒ/ n [U] the part of a building or piece of land that is along a road, river etc

front·al /ˈfrʌntl/ adj [only before noun] formal **1** at or relating to the front part of something: the frontal armour of the new tanks **2 frontal attack/assault a)** a direct attack on the front of an army: The minefields make an all-out frontal attack almost impossible. **b)** an attack or criticism that is very strong and direct: After the election, the party launched into a frontal assault on the British media. **3** *medical* relating to the front part of the head: *tissues in the **frontal lobes** of the brain* → FULL FRONTAL

frontal system *n* [C] *technical* a weather FRONT[1] (12)

front and center *adj, adv AmE* in a very important position, where it will receive attention: *Prayer in schools has become a front-and-center issue.*

front bench *n* [C] the front row of seats on each side of the British parliament, on which the leaders of the political parties sit; → **back bench**

front·bench·er /ˌfrʌntˈbentʃə $ -ər/ *n* [C] someone who sits on a front bench in the British parliament; → **backbencher**

front desk *n* [U] the desk where visitors go when they arrive at a hotel or organization

front door *n* [C usually singular] the main entrance door to a house, at the front; → **back door**

fron·tier /ˈfrʌntɪə $ frʌnˈtɪr/ *n* **1** [C] *especially BrE* the border of a country: [+between/with] *Lille is close to the frontier between France and Belgium.* | *on/at the frontier Troops established a road block on the frontier.* | **frontier town/area/post etc** (=a town etc on a frontier) **2 the frontier** an area where people have never lived before, that not much is known about, especially in the western US before the 20th century: *a novel about a family's struggle on the American frontier* | *space, the final frontier* **3 the frontiers of knowledge/ physics etc** the limits of what is known about something: **push back the frontiers** (=discover new things)

fron·tiers·man /ˈfrʌntɪəzmən $ frʌnˈtɪrz-/ *n plural* **frontiersmen** /-mən/ [C] a man who lived on the American frontier, especially in the 19th century

fron·tis·piece /ˈfrʌntɪspiːs/ *n* [C] a picture or photograph at the beginning of a book, usually opposite the page with the title on it

front line *n* **1** [C usually singular] the place where fighting happens in a war; **3 front: in/on the front line** *troops who had served in the front line at Magdeburg* | *three miles behind the front line* **2 in the front line a)** doing something that has not been done before: *in the front line of the fight against cancer* **b)** likely to be blamed for an organization's mistakes —**front-line** *adj* [only before noun]: *front-line troops*

front man *n* [C usually singular] **1** a person who speaks for an organization, for example an illegal one, but is not the leader of it **2** *also* **frontman** the leader, and usually the singer, of a musical group

front matter *n* [U] all the pages at the very beginning of a book, including the page with the title on it

front office *n* [singular] the people in a business who manage things or who deal directly with the public; → **back office**

front of house *n* [U] *BrE* the areas in a theatre or hotel which are used by the public —**front-of-house** *adj: the front-of-house manager*

front-page *adj* [only before noun] **front-page news/ article/story etc** something that is printed on the first page of a newspaper because it is very important or exciting

front room *n* [C] the main room in a house where you usually sit; **3 living room**

front-runner *n* [C] the person or thing that is most likely to succeed in a competition: *the front-runner in June's presidential election*

frost[1] /frɒst $ frɒːst/ *n* **1** [C,U] very cold weather, when water freezes: **late/early/first frost** *Even in May we can sometimes get a late frost.* | **hard/heavy/sharp/ severe frost** (=extremely cold weather) *three continuous nights of hard frost* | **the risk of frost damage to crops** **2** [U] ice that looks white and powdery and covers things that are outside when the temperature is very cold: *The grass and trees were white with frost.*

frost[2] *v* [T] *especially AmE* to cover a cake with a mixture of powdery sugar and liquid; **3 ice** *BrE*

frost over/up *phr v* to become covered in frost: *Overnight all the windowpanes had frosted over.*

---

frost·bite /ˈfrɒstbaɪt $ ˈfrɒːst-/ *n* [U] a condition caused by extreme cold, that makes your fingers and toes swell, become darker, and sometimes fall off: *I nearly got frostbite.* —**frostbitten** /-bɪtn/ *adj*

frost·ed /ˈfrɒstɪd $ ˈfrɒːstɪd/ *adj*
1 GLASS frosted glass/window etc frosted glass has been given a rough surface, so that it is not transparent: *the frosted glass of the bathroom window*
2 COLD WEATHER *literary* covered with frost; **3 frosty**: *the frosted garden*
3 CAKE *especially AmE* covered with frosting; **3 iced** *BrE*: *chocolate frosted cupcakes*
4 HAIR *AmE* frosted hair has parts that have been made much lighter than others by using chemicals

frost·ing /ˈfrɒstɪŋ $ ˈfrɒːstɪŋ/ *n* [U] *especially AmE* a sweet substance put on cakes and made from powdery sugar and butter; **3 icing** *BrE*

frost·y /ˈfrɒsti $ ˈfrɒːsti/ *adj* **1 a)** extremely cold: *a beautiful frosty morning* | *frosty air* **b)** covered with FROST: *the frosty ground* **2** unfriendly; **3 icy: frosty stare/look/tone** *He gave me a frosty stare.* | *the frosty silence that followed her announcement* | *My words got a frosty reception.* —**frostily** *adv*

froth[1] /frɒθ $ frɒːθ/ *n* **1** [singular, U] a mass of small BUBBLES on the top of a liquid; **3 foam**: *'Excellent beer,' he said, wiping the froth from his mouth.* **2** [singular, U] small white BUBBLES of SALIVA around a person's or animal's mouth **3** [U] talk or ideas that are attractive but have no real value or meaning: *The book has too much froth and not enough fact.*

froth[2] *v* [I] **1** *also* **froth up** if a liquid froths, it produces or contains a lot of small BUBBLES on top. *When you first open the bottle the beer will froth for a few seconds.* **2** if someone's mouth froths, SALIVA comes out as small white BUBBLES **3 froth at the mouth a)** to have SALIVA coming out of your mouth as small white BUBBLES **b)** *informal* to be extremely angry

froth·y /ˈfrɒθi $ ˈfrɒːθi/ *adj* **1** a liquid that is frothy has lots of small BUBBLES on top: *a mug of frothy coffee* **2** a frothy book, film etc is enjoyable but not serious or important —**frothily** *adv*

frown[1] /fraʊn/ *v* [I] to make an angry, unhappy, or confused expression, moving your EYEBROWS together: *She frowned as she read the letter.* | [+at] *Mattie frowned at him disapprovingly.*

frown on/upon sb/sth *phr v* to disapprove of someone or something, especially someone's behaviour: *Even though divorce is legal, it is still frowned upon.*

frown[2] *n* [C usually singular] the expression on your face when you move your EYEBROWS together because you are angry, unhappy, or confused: **with a frown** *He looked at her with a puzzled frown.*

froze /frəʊz $ froʊz/ *v* the past tense of FREEZE[1]

fro·zen[1] /ˈfrəʊzən $ ˈfroʊ-/ *v* the past participle of FREEZE[1]

frozen[2] *adj*
1 FOOD frozen food has been stored at a very low temperature in order to preserve it; → **freeze**: *You can use fresh or frozen fish.* | *frozen peas*
2 be frozen (stiff) *spoken* to feel very cold: *You must be frozen! Come and sit by the fire.*
3 EARTH earth that is frozen is so cold it has become very hard: *The ground is frozen for most of the year.* | *the frozen wastes of Siberia*
4 AREA OF WATER a river, lake etc that is frozen has a layer of ice on the surface
5 be frozen with fear/terror/fright to be so afraid, shocked etc that you cannot move

fruc·tose /ˈfrʌktəʊs $ -oʊs/ *n* [U] a type of natural sugar in fruit juices and HONEY

fru·gal /ˈfruːɡəl/ *adj* **1** careful to buy only what is necessary; **3 extravagant**: *As children we were taught to be frugal and hard-working.* | *He led a remarkably* *frugal existence.* **2** a frugal meal is a small meal of plain food; ☐ **simple**; ☐ **extravagant**: *a frugal break-fast* —**frugally** *adv* —**frugality** /fruː'ɡælⁱti/ *n* [U]

fruit¹ S2 W2 /fruːt/ *n plural* **fruit** *or* **fruits**

1 [C,U] something that grows on a plant, tree, or bush, can be eaten as a food, contains seeds or a stone, and is usually sweet: *Try to eat plenty of fresh fruit.* | *fruit and vegetables* | *a glass of fruit juice* | *a large garden with fruit trees* → DRIED FRUIT, SOFT FRUIT

2 [C,U] *technical* the part of a plant, bush, or tree that contains the seeds

3 the fruit(s) of sth the good results that you have from something, after you have worked very hard: *I'm look-ing forward to retirement and having time to enjoy the fruits of my labour* (=the results of my hard work).

4 in fruit *technical* trees, plants etc that are in fruit are producing their fruit

5 the fruits of the earth *literary* all the natural things that the earth produces, such as fruit, vegetables, or minerals → **bear fruit** at BEAR¹ (9)

fruit² *v* [I] *technical* if a tree or a plant fruits, it produces fruit

fruit bat *n* [C] a large BAT (=small animal like a flying mouse) that lives in hot countries and eats fruit

fruit·cake /'fruːtkeɪk/ *n* **1** [C,U] a cake that has dried fruit in it **2** [C] *informal* someone who is men-tally ill or behaves in a strange way: *He's an absolute fruitcake.* | *You really are nutty as a fruitcake* (=crazy).

fruit·er·er /'fruːtərə $ -tərər/ *n* [C] *BrE old-fashioned* someone who sells fruit

fruit fly *n* [C] a small fly that eats fruit or decaying plants

fruit·ful /'fruːtfəl/ *adj* **1** producing good results; ☐ **fruitless**: *Today's meeting proved more fruitful than last week's.* | *a busy and fruitful time* | *Annual business*

reports were a fruitful source of information. **2** *literary* land that is fruitful produces a lot of crops —**fruitfully** *adv* —**fruitfulness** *n* [U]

fru·i·tion /fruˈɪʃən/ *n* [U] *formal* if a plan, project etc comes to fruition, it is successfully put into action and completed, often after a long process: **come to/bring to/reach fruition** *His proposals only came to fruition after the war.* | *Many people have worked together to bring this scheme to fruition.*

fruit·less /'fruːtləs/ *adj* failing to achieve what was wanted, especially after a lot of effort; ☐ **fruitful**: **fruitless attempt/exercise** *a fruitless attempt to settle the dispute* | *So far, their search has been fruitless.* —**fruitlessly** *adv*

fruit ma,chine *n* [C] *BrE* a machine which you put money into, and which gives you more money back if three of the same pictures appear on a screen; ☐ **slot machine**

fruit 'salad *n* [C,U] a dish of many different types of fruit cut into small pieces

fruit·y /'fruːti/ *adj* **1** tasting or smelling strongly of fruit: *a very fruity wine* **2** *BrE* a voice or laugh that is fruity sounds deep and pleasant

frump /frʌmp/ *n* [C] a woman who is frumpy

frump·y /'frʌmpi/ also **frump·ish** /'frʌmpɪʃ/ *adj* a woman who is frumpy looks unattractive because she dresses in old-fashioned clothes

frus·trate /frʌˈstreɪt $ 'frʌstreɪt/ *v* [T] **1** if some-thing frustrates you, it makes you feel annoyed or angry because you are unable to do what you want: *The fact that he's working with amateurs really frustrates him.* **2** [usually passive] to prevent someone's plans, efforts, or attempts from succeeding: *Their attempts to speak to him were frustrated by the guards.*

frus·trat·ed /frʌˈstreɪtⁱd $ 'frʌstreɪtⁱd/ *adj* **1** feel-ing annoyed, upset, and impatient, because you cannot control or change a situation, or achieve something: *He*

F

fruit

pith — segment
oranges
bananas
grapes
lemons
pineapple

pip
apples
watermelon
seeds
core
cherries
stone
peaches

pear
stalk
flesh
avocado
coconuts

raspberries
kiwi fruit
figs
melon

plums
lime
strawberries
mango
grapefruits

gets frustrated *when people don't understand what he's trying to say.* | [+**with/at**] *She had become increasingly frustrated with her life.* | **sexually frustrated** (=feeling dissatisfied because you do not have any opportunity to have sex) **2 a frustrated artist/actor/poet etc** someone who wants to develop a particular skill but has not been able to do this

frus·trat·ing /frʌ'streɪtɪŋ $ 'frʌstreɪtɪŋ/ *adj* making you feel annoyed, upset, or impatient because you cannot do what you want to do: *My job can be very frustrating sometimes.* | *This is an immensely frustrating experience for the student.*

frus·tra·tion /frʌ'streɪʃən/ *n* **1** [C,U] the feeling of being annoyed, upset, or impatient, because you cannot control or change a situation, or achieve something: *People often feel a **sense of frustration** that they are not being promoted quickly enough.* | **in/with frustration** *I was practically screaming with frustration.* | *In spite of his frustrations, he fell in love with the country.* **2** [U] the fact of being prevented from achieving what you are trying to achieve: [+**of**] *The frustration of his ambitions made him a bitter man.*

fry¹ S3 /fraɪ/ *v* **fried, frying, fries**
1 [I,T] to cook something in hot fat or oil, or to be cooked in hot fat or oil: *Fry the potatoes, covered, for about 20 minutes.* | *I could smell onions frying.* → DEEP FRY, STIR-FRY¹; → see picture at EGG
2 [I,T] *AmE informal* to kill someone in an ELECTRIC CHAIR, or to be killed in an electric chair, as a punishment

fry² also **french fry** *plural* **fries** *n* [C usually plural] *especially AmE* a long thin piece of potato that has been cooked in fat; 🔲 **chip** *BrE*

fry³ *n* [plural] very young fish → SMALL FRY

fry·er, frier /'fraɪə $ -ər/ *n* [C] **1 deep (fat) fryer** a big deep pan for frying food **2** *AmE* a chicken that has been specially bred to be fried

frying ,pan *n* [C] **1** a round flat pan with a long handle, used for frying food → see picture at PAN; → see picture at EAT **2 out of the frying pan and into the fire** to go from a bad situation to one that is even worse

fry-up *n* [C] *BrE informal* a meal of fried food such as eggs, BACON, potatoes etc

ft *BrE*; **ft.** *AmE* the written abbreviation of *foot* or *feet*: *a board 6ft x 4ft*

Ft. the written abbreviation of *fort*, used in the names of places: *Ft. Lauderdale*

FT, F/T the written abbreviation of *full-time*; → PT

FTSE In·dex /'fʊtsi ,ɪndeks/ also **FT 100 Share Index** /,ef tiː wʌn hʌndr̩d 'ʃeər ,ɪndeks $ -'ʃer-/, **FTSE 100** *n* the FTSE Index *the Financial Times Stock Exchange Index* a daily list of prices of shares on the London Stock Exchange, based on the daily average prices of shares in the top 100 companies; → **the Dow Jones Index**

fuch·sia /'fjuːʃə/ *n* **1** [C,U] a garden bush with hanging bell-shaped flowers that are red, pink, or white **2** [U] a bright pink colour

ftp also **FTP** /,ef tiː 'piː/ *n* [U] file transfer protocol; a set of rules that allow you to send documents from one computer to another —**ftp** *v* [T]

fuck¹ S3 /fʌk/ *v taboo spoken*
1 fuck you/it/them etc used to show that you are very angry at something or someone, or that you do not care about them at all: *Well, fuck you then. I'll go on my own.*
2 [I,T] to have sex with someone
3 fuck me *especially BrE* used when you think something is surprising or impressive
4 go fuck yourself/himself/themselves etc used to show you are very angry with someone: *Why don't you go fuck yourself!*
    fuck around *phr v*
1 to waste time or behave in a silly or careless way: *Will you two stop fucking around!*
2 fuck sb around/about *BrE* to make someone angry or annoyed by wasting their time: *Don't fuck me around, OK?*

    fuck off *phr v*
to go away – used especially to tell someone to go away in an extremely rude way
    fuck sb ⇔ **over** *phr v AmE*
to treat someone very badly: *They'll just fuck you over if you let them.*
    fuck up *phr v*
1 fuck sb ⇔ **up** to make someone very unhappy and confused so that they cannot live normally or have normal relationships; → **mess sb up**: *Heroin fucks you up.*
2 to make a mistake or do something badly; → **mess up**: *You really fucked up this time.* | **fuck** sth ⇔ **up** *I'm scared of fucking things up.*
    fuck with sb *phr v*
to annoy someone or make them angry; → **mess with** sb: *I wouldn't fuck with Alfie if I were you.*

fuck² *interjection taboo* used when you are very annoyed about something: *Fuck! I've forgotten my keys!*

fuck³ *n taboo spoken* **1 the fuck** used when you are angry or surprised to emphasize what you are saying: *Get the fuck off my property!* | *Shut the fuck up!* | **what/how/who etc the fuck** *What the fuck do you think you're doing?* **2** [C usually singular] the act of having sex **3 not give a fuck** also **not give a flying fuck** *AmE* to not care at all what happens

,fuck 'all *n* [U] *BrE taboo spoken* nothing: *Most of the time he sat around doing fuck all.*

fucked /fʌkt/ *adj taboo spoken* **1** also **fucked up** completely broken or in a very bad condition: *The engine's completely fucked.* **2** in a very bad situation which will not improve: *If she can't lend me the money, I'm fucked.*

,fucked 'up *adj taboo spoken* **1** very unhappy and confused, so that you cannot control your life properly; → **messed up**: *After three years with Johnny, I was completely fucked up.* **2** also **fucked** completely broken or in a very bad condition: *These speakers are fucked up.* **3** *AmE* having drunk too much alcohol or taken illegal drugs

fuck·er /'fʌkə $ -ər/ also **fuck** *n* [C] *taboo spoken* someone who you dislike very much or think is stupid

fuck·head /'fʌkhed/ *n* [C] *AmE taboo spoken* someone who you dislike very much or think is stupid

fuck·ing S1 /'fʌkɪŋ/ *adj* [only before noun] *adv taboo spoken*
1 used to emphasize that you are angry or annoyed: *It's none of your fucking business!* | *I know fucking well you're lying to me.* | *What the fucking hell are you staring at?*
2 used to emphasize your opinion of something: *That's fucking good coffee.* | *What a fucking idiot!*

fuck·wit /'fʌkwɪt/ *n* [C] *taboo spoken* someone you dislike very much or think is stupid. Do not use this word.

fud·dle /'fʌdl/ *v* [T] *BrE informal* if something, especially alcohol or drugs, fuddles you or your mind, it makes you unable to think clearly —**fuddled** *adj*: *her fuddled mind*

fud·dy-dud·dy /'fʌdi ,dʌdi/ *n plural* **fuddy-duddies** [C] someone who has old-fashioned ideas and attitudes: *You're such an **old fuddy-duddy**!* —**fuddy-duddy** *adj*

fudge¹ /fʌdʒ/ *n* **1** [U] a soft creamy brown sweet food **2 a fudge** *BrE* an attempt to deal with a situation that does not solve its problems completely, or only makes it seem better

fudge² *v* **1** [I,T] to avoid giving exact details or a clear answer about something: *He tried to **fudge the issue** by saying that he did not want to specify periods.* **2** [T] to change important figures or facts to deceive people: *Sibley has been fudging his data for years now.*

fu·el¹ S2 W2 /'fjuːəl/ *n* [C,U] a substance such as coal, gas, or oil that can be burned to produce heat or energy: *The plane was running low on fuel.* | *Coal is one of the cheapest fuels.* | *the car's performance and **fuel***

consumption (=how much fuel it uses to travel a particular distance) | *an empty fuel tank* → **add fuel to the fire/flames** at ADD (9)

fuel² v **fuelled, fuelling** BrE, **fueled, fueling** AmE **1** [T] to make something, especially something bad, increase or become stronger: *His words fuelled her anger still more.* | **fuel speculation/rumours/controversy etc** *Progress was slow, fueling concerns that the stadium would not be finished on time.* **2** also **fuel up** [I,T] if you fuel a vehicle or if it fuels up, fuel is put into it: *We'd better fuel up at the next town.* | *The van was fuelled and waiting in the basement car park.*

'**fuel cell** n [C] a piece of equipment that combines two different ELEMENTS, such as OXYGEN and HYDROGEN, to produce electricity in order to supply power to a vehicle or machine

'**fuel-ef,ficient** adj a fuel-efficient engine or vehicle burns fuel in a more effective way than usual, so that it loses less fuel

'**fuel in,jection** n [U] a method of putting liquid fuel directly into an engine, which allows a car to ACCELERATE more quickly

fug /fʌg/ n [singular] BrE informal air inside a room that feels heavy and unpleasant because of smoke, heat, or too many people: *the fug of the bar*

fu·gi·tive¹ /'fjuːdʒᵻtɪv/ n [C] someone who is trying to avoid being caught by the police: [+**from**] *a fugitive from US justice*

fugitive² adj [only before noun] **1** trying to avoid being caught by the police **2** literary lasting for a very short time: *rare and fugitive visits*

fugue /fjuːg/ n [C,U] a piece of music with a tune that is repeated regularly in different KEYS by different voices or instruments

-ful¹ /fəl/ suffix [in adjectives] **1** full of something: *an eventful day* **2** having the quality of something or causing something: *restful colours* | *Is it painful?* —**fully** /fəli/ suffix [in adverbs]: *shouting cheerfully*

-ful² /fʊl/ suffix [in nouns] **1** the amount of a substance needed to fill a particular container: *two cupfuls of milk* **2** as much as can be carried by or contained in a particular part of the body: *an armful of flowers*

ful·crum /'fʊlkrəm, 'fʌl-/ n plural **fulcrums** or **fulcra** /-krəə/ [C] the point on which a LEVER (=bar) turns, balances, or is supported in turning or lifting something

ful·fil S3 W3 BrE; **fulfill** AmE /fʊl'fɪl/ v **fulfilled, fulfilling** [T] **1** if you fulfil a hope, wish, or aim, you achieve the thing that you hoped for, wished for etc: *Visiting Disneyland has fulfilled a boyhood dream.* | *Being deaf hasn't stopped Karen fulfilling her ambition to be a hairdresser.* | *It was then that the organization finally began to fulfill the hopes of its founders.* | **fulfil an aim/a goal/an objective** *an analysis of how different countries are attempting to fulfill their political goals* **2** to do or provide what is necessary or needed: **fulfil a role/duty/function etc** *A good police officer is not fulfilling his role if he neglects this vital aspect.* | **fulfil a requirement/condition/obligation etc** *Britain was accused of failing to fulfil its obligations under the EU Treaty.* | *Much of the electrical equipment failed to fulfill safety requirements.* | *There is little doubt that the scheme fulfils a need for our community.* **3** **fulfil a promise/pledge etc** formal to do what you said you would do; ◱ **keep**; ◱ **break**: *I'd like to see him fulfil his promise to reorganize the army.* **4** **fulfil your potential/promise** to be as successful as you possibly can be: *We want to make sure that all children are able to fulfil their potential.* **5** if your work fulfils you, it makes you feel satisfied because you are using all your skills, qualities etc **6** **fulfil yourself** to feel satisfied because you are using all your skills, qualities etc: *She succeeded in fulfilling herself both as an actress and as a mother.*

7 **fulfil a prophesy** if a PROPHESY is fulfilled, something happens that someone said would happen

ful·filled /fʊl'fɪld/ adj happy and satisfied because your life is interesting and you are doing useful or important things: *Adult education helps people achieve more fulfilled lives.*

ful·fil·ling /fʊl'fɪlɪŋ/ adj making you feel happy and satisfied because you are doing interesting, useful, or important things: *Nursing is still one of the most fulfilling careers.*

ful·fil·ment BrE; **fulfillment** AmE /fʊl'fɪlmənt/ n. [U] **1** the feeling of being happy and satisfied with your life because you are doing interesting, useful, or important things: *Are you looking for greater fulfillment and satisfaction in your work?* | *a deep sense of fulfilment that makes life worthwhile* | **seek/find fulfilment** *The real joy of the priesthood is helping people find personal fulfilment.* **2** when something you wanted happens or is given to you; ◱ **achievement**: [+**of**] *the fulfillment of a long-held dream* **3** the act of doing something that you promised or agreed to do: **fulfilment of a promise/duty/condition etc** *People are wondering if they will ever see the fulfillment of the government's campaign pledges.*

full¹ S1 W1 /fʊl/ adj
1 NO SPACE containing as much or as many things or people as possible, so there is no space left; → **empty**: *The train was completely full.* | *Don't talk with your mouth full.* | *The class is full, but you can register for next term.* | [+**of**] *The kitchen was full of smoke.* | **be crammed/stuffed/packed etc full of sth** *Ted's workshop was crammed full of old engines.* | **half-full/three-quarters full etc** *McQuaid filled his glass until it was three-quarters full.* | *The bath was full to the brim* (=completely full) *with hot water.* | **full (up) to bursting** (=completely full) BrE informal: *The filing cabinet was full to bursting.*
2 INCLUDING EVERYTHING [only before noun] complete and including all parts or details: *Please write your full name and address on the form.* | *The Health Centre offers a full range of services.* | *Lotus will not reveal full details until the Motor Show.* | *The BBC promised a full investigation.* | *I don't think he's telling us the full story* (=everything he knows about the matter).
3 HIGHEST AMOUNT/LEVEL [only before noun] the highest level or greatest amount of something that is possible; ◱ **maximum**: *rising prosperity and full employment* | *The charity helps disabled children reach their full potential.* | *Few customers take full advantage of off-peak fares.* | *Parker was driving at full speed when he hit the wall.* | **in full leaf/bloom** *The roses were now in full bloom.*
4 HAVING A LOT OF STH **be full of sth a)** to contain many things of the same kind: *a garden full of flowers* | *His essay was full of mistakes.* | *The music papers were full of gossip about the band.* | *Life's full of surprises, isn't it?* **b)** to feel, express, or show a lot of a particular emotion or quality: **full of excitement/energy/hope etc** *Lucy was a happy child, always full of life.* | *He was full of praise for the work of the unit.* **c)** to talk or think a lot about a particular thing: *She was full of plans for the wedding.*
5 FOOD also **full up** BrE [not before noun] having eaten so much food that you cannot eat any more: *No more, thanks. I'm full.*
6 EMPHASIS [only before noun] used to emphasize an amount, quantity, or rate: **three/six etc full days/years/pages etc** *We devote five full days a month to training.* | *His pants rose a full three inches off his shoes.*
7 BUSY busy and involving lots of different activities: *Before her illness, Rose enjoyed a full life.* | *Go to bed. You've a full day tomorrow.*
8 RANK having or giving all the rights, duties etc that belong to a particular rank or position: **full professor/member/colonel etc** *Only full members have the right to vote.* | *a full driving licence*
9 **be full of yourself** to have a high opinion of yourself

– used to show disapproval: *My first impression was that he was a bit full of himself.*
10 be full of crap/shit/it *not polite* a rude expression used to say that someone often says things that are wrong or stupid: *Don't listen to Jerry. He's full of it.*
11 CLOTHES made using a lot of material and fitting loosely: *a dress with a full skirt*
12 BODY large and rounded in an attractive way: **full figure/face/breasts** etc *clothes for the fuller figure*
13 TASTE having a strong satisfying taste: *Now you can enjoy Nescafé's **fuller flavour** in a decaffeinated form.* → FULL-BODIED
14 SOUND pleasantly loud and deep: *the rich full sound of the cello*
15 full price not a reduced price: *If you're over 14, you have to pay full price.*
16 in full view of sb so that all the people in a place can see, especially when this is embarrassing or shocking: *The argument happened on stage in full view of the audience.*
17 be in full swing if an event or process is in full swing, it has reached its highest level of activity: *By 8.30, the party was in full swing.*
18 full speed/steam ahead doing something with as much energy and effort as possible: *With last season's misery behind them, it's full steam ahead for the Bears.*
19 be full of beans to be excited and have lots of energy
20 (at) full blast *informal* as strongly, loudly, or quickly as possible: *The heater was on full blast but I was still cold.* | *a car stereo playing Wagner at full blast*
21 (at) full tilt/pelt moving as fast as possible: *She ran full tilt into his arms.*
22 be in full cry if a group of people are in full cry, they are criticizing someone very strongly: *Anyone who's seen the world's press in full cry can understand how Diana felt.*
23 to the full; to the fullest *AmE* in the best or most complete way: *Ed believes in **living life to the full**.*
24 come/go/turn full circle to be in the same situation in which you began, even though there have been changes during the time in between: *Fashion has come full circle and denim is back.* → FULLY; → have your hands full at HAND[1] (29); → draw yourself up to your full height at DRAW UP (4)

full[2] *n* in full including the whole of something: *The debt must be **paid in full**.* | *His statement on the handling of prisoners is worth quoting in full.*

full[3] *adv* directly: [+on/in] *She looked him full in the face as she spoke.*

full·back /ˈfʊlbæk/ *n* [C] a player in a football team who plays in defence, stopping opponents from getting the ball; ⊟ **defender**

full 'beam *n BrE* on full beam car HEADLIGHTS (=the main lights at the front) that are on full beam are switched to a position that makes them shine very brightly and straight ahead; ⊟ **high beam** *AmE*; → **dipped**

full-'blooded *adj* [only before noun] **1** done with a lot of energy or in a complete way: *The conflict could escalate into a full-blooded war.* **2** having parents, grandparents etc from only one race of people: *Her father is a full-blooded Cherokee.*

full-blown *adj* [only before noun] having all the qualities of something that is at its most complete or advanced stage: *The drop in shares could develop into a full-blown crisis.* | *full-blown AIDS*

full 'board *n* [U] a hotel offering full board provides guests with all their meals; → **half board**: *A two-night break costs £125 full board.*

full-'bodied *adj* **1** a full-bodied wine or other drink has a pleasantly strong taste; → **light** **2** a full-bodied sound is complicated and interesting

full 'bore *adv AmE* fast and with a lot of energy: *Kate took a huge slice and was going at it full bore.*

full-'colour *BrE*; **full-color** *AmE adj* [only before noun] printed using coloured inks rather than only black and white: *a full-colour brochure*

full-court 'press *n* [singular] **1** a method of defending in a strong way in BASKETBALL **2** *AmE informal* the use of pressure or influence by several groups on someone: *The DEA and the Justice Department put a full-court press on the drug barons.*

full-'cream *adj BrE* full-cream milk is ordinary milk without any of the fat removed; → **skimmed**, **semi-skimmed**

full 'dress *n* [U] special clothes worn for official occasions: *officers in full dress uniform*

ful·ler's earth /ˌfʊləz ˈɜːθ $ -ərz ˈɜːrθ/ *n* [U] dried clay made into a powder that is used to clean cloth or oil

full 'face *adj* **1** showing the whole of someone's face; → **profile**: *In portraits, chiefs were invariably shown full face.* **2** covering or protecting your whole face: *a fullface helmet*

full-'fat *adj BrE* full-fat milk, cheese etc contains all the fat that is naturally in it; → **low fat**, **reduced fat**

full-'fledged *AmE*; **fully 'fledged** *BrE adj* [only before noun] completely developed, trained, or established: *India has the potential to become a full-fledged major power.*

full 'frontal *adj* [only before noun] **1** showing the whole of the front of someone's body without clothes on: *scenes of full frontal nudity* **2** done in a direct and strong way: *a full frontal attack on the government*

full-'grown *AmE*; **fully-grown** *BrE adj* a full-grown animal, plant, or person has developed to their full size and will not grow any bigger: *A full-grown elephant may weigh 2,000 pounds.*

full 'house *n* [C usually singular] **1** an occasion at a cinema, concert hall, sports field etc when there are no empty seats: *Billy Graham is a speaker who can be sure of playing to a full house.* **2** three cards of one kind and a pair of another kind in a game of POKER

full-'length[1] *adj* **1** full-length mirror/photograph/portrait etc a mirror etc that shows all of a person, from their head to their feet **2** full-length skirt/dress/coat etc a skirt etc that reaches the ground, or is the longest possible for that particular type of clothing: *a full-length evening dress* **3** full-length play/book/film etc a play etc that is the normal length: *Stravinsky's only full-length opera*

full-length[2] *adv* someone who is lying full-length is lying flat with their legs straight out: *Ali was stretched out full-length on the couch.*

full 'lock *n* [U] *BrE* if you turn the STEERING WHEEL of a car to full lock, you turn it as far as it can be turned

full 'marks *n* [plural] **1** if you give someone full marks, you praise them for doing something well: **full marks to sb (for sth)** *Not the most stylish mobile, but full marks to Marconi for originality.* **2** *BrE* the highest number of points you can get for school work

full 'monty *n* the full monty *informal* the whole amount of something that people want and expect: *The ice cream was covered in sauce, nuts, chocolate – the full monty.*

full 'moon *n* [singular] the moon when you can see all of it as a complete circle; → **new moon**, **half moon**, **crescent moon**

ful·lness /ˈfʊlnəs/ *n* [U] **1** in the fullness of time *formal* after a period of time, when a situation has developed; ⊟ **in due course**: *I'm sure he'll tell us what's bothering him in the fullness of time.* **2** the quality of being large and round in an attractive way: *Use a red gloss on your bottom lip to give it fullness.* **3** the quality of being complete **4** the quality of having a pleasantly strong taste or deep sound: *This recording has a fullness and warmth that brings out the brilliance of the piece.* **5** the condition of being full: *Do you have a feeling of fullness after even a small meal?*

F

full-'on adj [only before noun] extreme: *If you're going for full-on glamour, add some sparkly jewellery.*

full-'page adj [only before noun] covering all of one page in a newspaper or magazine: *a full-page advert*

full-'scale adj [only before noun] **1** as complete or thorough as possible: **full-scale attack/war/riot etc** | **full-scale study/review etc** *The government will conduct a full-scale inquiry into the crash.* **2** a full-scale drawing, model etc is the same size as the thing it represents

full-'size adj of the largest possible size: *The battery can run a full-size laptop for 12 hours.* | *a full-size basketball court*

full 'stop¹ n [C] *BrE* a point (.) that marks the end of a sentence or the short form of a word; ▣ **period** *AmE*: *Put a full stop at the end of the sentence.*

full stop² interjection *BrE informal* used at the end of a sentence to emphasize that you do not want to say any more about a subject; ▣ **period** *AmE*: *I don't have a reason. I just don't want to go, full stop.*

full-'term adj [only before noun] a full-term baby is born after a PREGNANCY of the normal length; → **premature**

full 'time n [U] *BrE* the end of the normal period of playing time in a sports game; → **half time**: *As the ball went in, the referee blew his whistle for full time.*

full-'time S3 adj, adv
1 for all the hours of a week during which it is usual for people to work, study etc; → **part-time**: **work/study etc full-time** *She works full-time and has two kids.* | *The success of the series enabled her to concentrate full-time on writing.* | **full-time staff/student etc** *They're looking for full-time staff at the library.* | **full-time job/education etc** *We aim to double the number of young people in full-time study.* **2** **be a full-time job** to be very hard work and take a lot of time: *Keeping pace with changes is a full-time job.*

ful·ly S2 W2 /'fʊli/ adv completely: *The restaurant is fully booked this evening.* | *Elisa has not fully recovered from the incident.* | *I am fully aware of your problems.* | *The changes in policy are fully described in the review.* | *I fully accept that what he says is true.* | *This concept is discussed more fully in Chapter 9.*

fully 'dressed adj [not before noun] wearing clothes, including things such as shoes: *She collapsed fully dressed on the bed.*

fully-'fledged *BrE*; **full-fledged** *AmE* adj [only before noun] completely developed, trained, or established: *After seven years of training she's now a fully-fledged doctor.*

fully-'grown *BrE*; **full-grown** *AmE* adj a fully-grown animal, plant, or person has developed to their full size and will not grow any bigger: *After six weeks, the larva emerges as a fully-grown beetle.*

ful·mi·nate /'fʊlmɪneɪt, 'fʌl-/ v [I] formal to criticize someone or something angrily: [+at/against/about] *Mick was fulminating against the unfairness of it all.* —**fulmination** /ˌfʊlmɪ'neɪʃən, ˌfʌl-/ n [C,U]

ful·some /'fʊlsəm/ adj formal a fulsome speech or piece of writing sounds insincere because it contains too much praise, expressions of thanks etc: **fulsome gratitude/praise/tribute etc** *The book contains a fulsome dedication to his wife.* —**fulsomely** adv: *a fulsomely congratulatory message* —**fulsomeness** n [U]

fum·ble /'fʌmbəl/ v **1** also **fumble around** [I,T] to try to hold, move, or find something with your hands in an awkward way: [+at/in/with] *She dressed, her cold fingers fumbling with the buttons.* | [+for] *I fumbled around in my bag for a cigarette.* | *She reached round to fumble the light on.* **2** [I,T] if you fumble with your words when you are speaking, you have difficulty saying something: [+for] *Asked for an explanation, Mike had fumbled for words.* | *The second candidate fumbled her*

lines. **3** [I,T] to drop a ball after catching it: *Quarterback Rattay was hit and fumbled the ball.* —**fumble** r [C] —**fumbling** n [C]

fume /fjuːm/ v **1** [I,T] to be angry about something [+at/over/about] *She sat in the car, silently fuming about what he said.* | *'You've no right to be here,' he fumed.* **2** [I] to give off smoke or gases

fumes S3 /fjuːmz/ n [plural] strong-smelling gas or smoke that is unpleasant to breathe in: *paint fumes*

fu·mi·gate /'fjuːmɪɡeɪt/ v [T] to remove disease, BACTERIA, insects etc from somewhere using chemicals, smoke, or gas —**fumigation** /ˌfjuːmɪ'ɡeɪʃən/ n [U]

fun¹ S2 /fʌn/ n [U]
1 an experience or activity that is very enjoyable and exciting

> **have fun** (=have an enjoyable time)
> **good/great fun** especially *BrE*
> **a lot of fun** especially *AmE*
> **harmless fun** (=enjoyable activities that do not have a bad effect on anyone)
> **good clean fun** (=enjoyable activities that do not involve anything bad or immoral)
> **sound like fun**
> **join in the fun**
> **it's no fun**

There's plenty of fun for all the family. | *The children were having so much fun, I hated to call them inside.* | *Why don't you come with us? It'll be great fun.* | *Basketball games are a lot of fun to watch.* | *It was a little bit of harmless fun, that's all.* | *Snowboarding – that sounds like fun.* | *Several Internet sites are inviting people to join in the fun for free.* | *It's no fun eating on your own.*

2 **for fun** also **just for the fun of it** if you do something for fun, you do it because you enjoy it and not for any other reason: *I simply believe that killing animals for fun is wrong.* | *Like most people her age, Deborah struck up relationships just for the fun of it.*
3 **sb is (great/good) fun** *BrE* used to say that someone is enjoyable to be with because they are happy and amusing: *You'll like her, darling, she's great fun.*
4 behaviour that is not serious and shows happiness and enjoyment: *Jan's always so cheerful and full of fun.* | *Her sense of fun made her very popular at college.* | *Evelyn would tease her, but only in fun.*
5 **fun and games** activities, behaviour etc that are not serious – often used to show disapproval
6 **make fun of sb/sth** to make unkind, insulting remarks about someone or something: *I'm not making fun of you. I admire what you did.*
7 **like fun** *AmE spoken old-fashioned* used to say that something is not true or will not happen: *'I'm going to Barbara's house.' 'Like fun you are! Come and finish your chores first.'* → **figure of fun** at FIGURE¹ (12); → **poke fun at** at POKE¹ (6)

fun² S2 W3 adj [only before noun]
1 enjoyable and amusing: *Try snowboarding – it's a really fun sport.* | **a fun day/evening etc**
2 a fun person is enjoyable to be with because they are happy and amusing: *She's a really fun person to be around.*

func·tion¹ S3 W1 /'fʌŋkʃən/ n
1 [C,U] the purpose that something has, or the job that someone or something does: **perform/fulfil a function** *In your new job you will perform a variety of functions.* | *The church fulfils a valuable social function.* | *The nervous system regulates our bodily functions* (=eating, breathing, going to the toilet etc). | *Bauhaus architects thought that function was more important than form.*
2 [C] a large party or official event: *This room may be hired for weddings and other functions.*
3 [C usually singular] technical a quantity or quality whose value changes according to another quantity or quality that is related to it: *The degree of drought is largely a function of temperature and drainage.*
4 [C] one of the basic operations performed by a computer

function² v [I] **1** to work in the correct or intended way: **function normally/correctly/properly etc** *Flights in and out of Taipei are functioning normally again.* | *Her legs have now ceased to function.* | *You know I can't function* (=cannot perform normal activities) *without a coffee in the morning.* **2** if something functions in a particular way, it works in that way: *an understanding of how the economy functions*

function as sth *phr v* if something functions as a particular thing, it does what that type of thing normally does, or is used as that thing: *A library is functioning as a temporary hospital to cope with casualties.*

func·tion·al /ˈfʌŋkʃənəl/ adj **1** designed to be useful rather than beautiful or attractive; **F** **decorative**: *buildings that are sensitively designed, not purely functional* **2** something that is functional is working correctly; **F** **operational**: *By 2004, the Supertram is expected to be fully functional.* **3** relating to the purpose of something: *The two departments have slight functional differences.* —**functionally** adv

functional food n [C,U] food that is designed to improve health and lower the risk of disease, for example by increasing the amount of VITAMINS in it, or removing some of the FAT; **F** **nutraceuticals**

func·tion·al·is·m /ˈfʌŋkʃənəlɪzəm/ n [U] the idea that the most important thing about a building, piece of furniture etc is that it is useful —**functionalist** n [C] —**functionalist** adj

func·tion·al·i·ty /ˌfʌŋkʃəˈnælɪ̩ti/ n plural **functionalities** [C,U] one or all of the operations that a computer, software program, or piece of equipment is able to perform

func·tion·a·ry /ˈfʌŋkʃənəri $ -neri/ n plural **functionaries** [C] someone who has a job doing unimportant or boring official duties: *a meeting of Party functionaries*

function key n [C] technical a key on a computer KEYBOARD that tells the computer to do something

function word n [C] a word that does not mean anything on its own, but shows the relationship between other words in a sentence, for example words such as 'but' or 'if'

fund¹ S3 W1 /fʌnd/ n
1 [C] an amount of money that is collected and kept for a particular purpose: *The house fell into disrepair until a restoration fund was set up.* | **pension/hardship/compensation etc fund** → **FUNDING, TRUST FUND**
2 funds [plural] money that an organization needs or has: *A sale is being held to raise funds for the school.* | **government/public funds** *claims that ministers had misused public funds* | *The park remains unfinished due to lack of funds.* | *The Museum is so short of funds* (=has so little money) *it may have to sell the painting.*
3 [singular] an organization that collects money, for example to help people who are ill, old etc; → **charity**: *We give to the Children's Fund every Christmas.*
4 a fund of sth a large supply of something: *He had a fund of stories about his boyhood.*
5 in funds formal having enough money to do something

fund² S3 W3 v [T] to provide money for an activity, organization, event etc: *The project is jointly funded by several local companies.* | *government-funded research*

fun·da·men·tal S2 W2 /ˌfʌndəˈmentl◂/ adj
1 relating to the most basic and important parts of something: *We have to tackle the fundamental cause of the problem.* | **fundamental change/difference/distinction/shift etc** *a fundamental difference in opinion* | **fundamental mistake/error** *Novice programmers sometimes make fundamental errors.* | *the fundamental principles of liberty and equality*
2 very necessary and important: *fundamental human rights* | [+to] *Water is fundamental to survival.*

fun·da·men·tal·ist /ˌfʌndəˈmentəlɪ̩st/ n [C]
1 someone who follows religious laws very strictly: *Muslim fundamentalists* **2** a Christian who believes that everything in the Bible is completely and actually true —**fundamentalism** n [U] —**fundamentalist** adj: *a fundamentalist doctrine*

fun·da·men·tal·ly /ˌfʌndəˈmentəli/ adv in every way that is important or basic: *The conclusions of the report are fundamentally wrong.* | *The political culture of the US is fundamentally different.*

fun·da·men·tals /ˌfʌndəˈmentlz/ n **the fundamentals (of** sth**)** the most important ideas, rules etc that something is based on: *an introduction to the fundamentals of design and print production*

fund·ing /ˈfʌndɪŋ/ n [U] money that is provided by an organization for a particular purpose: *College directors have called for more government funding.*

fund·rais·er /ˈfʌnd ˌreizə $ -ər/ n [C] **1** someone who collects money for a CHARITY, political party etc, for example by arranging social events that people pay to attend **2** an event that is organized to collect money for a CHARITY, political party etc

fund·rais·ing /ˈfʌndˌreizɪŋ/ n [U] the activity of collecting money for a specific purpose, especially in order to help people who are ill, old etc: *an Action Pack full of fundraising ideas*

fu·ne·ral /ˈfjuːnərəl/ n [C] **1** a religious ceremony for burying or CREMATING (=burning) someone who has died; → **burial, cremation**: *The funeral will be held at St. Martin's Church.* | *Hundreds of mourners attended the funeral of the two boys.* | *the minister who conducted the funeral service* | *Nelson's funeral procession down the Thames* | *Ramdas, the third son of the Mahatma, set fire to the funeral pyre.* | **funeral expenses/costs** **2** it's your funeral spoken used to warn someone that they, and no one else, must deal with the results of their actions

funeral di,rector n [C] someone who is paid to organize a funeral; **F** **undertaker** BrE

funeral home also **funeral ,parlour** n [C] the place where a body is kept before a funeral

fu·ne·ra·ry /ˈfjuːnərəri $ -nəreri/ adj [only before noun] relating to a funeral or the place where someone is buried: *a funerary monument*

fu·ne·re·al /fjuˈnɪəriəl $ -ˈnɪr-/ adj sad, slow, and suitable for a funeral: *funereal music* | *moving at a funereal pace*

fun·fair /ˈfʌnfeə $ -fer/ n [C] BrE a noisy outdoor event where you can ride on machines, play games to win prizes etc; **F** **fair**

fun·gal /ˈfʌŋgəl/ adj connected with or caused by a FUNGUS: *a fungal infection*

fun·gi·cide /ˈfʌndʒɪ̩said, ˈfʌŋgɪ̩-/ n [C,U] a chemical used for destroying fungus

fun·gus /ˈfʌŋgəs/ n plural **fungi** /-dʒai, -gai/ or **funguses** [C,U] a simple type of plant that has no leaves or flowers and that grows on plants or other surfaces. MUSHROOMS and MOULD are both fungi.

fu·nic·u·lar /fjuˈnɪkjᵿlə $ -ər/ n [C] a small railway that carries people up and down a steep hill or mountain, pulled by a thick metal rope

funk¹ /fʌŋk/ n [U] **1** a style of music with a strong RHYTHM that is based on JAZZ and African music **2 in a (blue) funk** AmE informal very unhappy, worried, or afraid: *She's in a funk about giving her talk on Sunday.* **3** AmE informal a strong smell that comes from someone's body

funk² v [T] BrE old-fashioned to avoid doing something because it is difficult, or because you are afraid

funk·y /ˈfʌŋki/ adj informal **1** modern, fashionable, and interesting: *Add a touch of style with these functional yet funky wall lights.* **2** funky music is simple with a strong RHYTHM that is easy to dance to **3** AmE having a bad smell or a dirty appearance

fun·nel¹ /ˈfʌnl/ n [C] **1** a thin tube with a wide top that you use for pouring liquid into a container with a narrow opening, such as a bottle **2** BrE a metal CHIMNEY that allows smoke from a steam engine or steamship to get out

funnel² v **funnelled, funnelling** BrE, **funneled, funneling** AmE **1** [I,T always + adv/prep] if you funnel something somewhere, or if it funnels there, it goes there by passing through a narrow opening: *Police at the barriers funnelled the crowd into the arena.* | *Incoming tides funnel up the channel with enormous power.* **2** [T always + adv/prep] to send money, information etc from various places to someone; ⊟ **channel**: *His office funneled millions of dollars in secret contributions to the re-election campaign.*

fun·nies /ˈfʌniz/ n **the funnies** AmE informal a number of different CARTOONS in a newspaper or magazine

fun·ni·ly /ˈfʌnₗli/ adv **1 funnily enough** spoken used to say that something is unexpected or strange: *Funnily enough, I was just about to call you when you called me.* **2** in an amusing or strange way

fun·ny S1 W3 /ˈfʌni/ adj comparative **funnier**, superlative **funniest**

1 AMUSING making you laugh: **funny story/joke/film etc** *Do you remember any funny stories about work?* | **hilariously/hysterically/wickedly funny** *a wickedly funny scene from the film* | *a search for the funniest man in Britain* | *If this is your idea of a joke, I don't **find** it at all **funny**.* | *Luckily, when I explained the situation, he **saw the funny side** (=recognized that it was partly funny).* | *His laughter stopped her mid-sentence. 'What's so funny?' she demanded.* | *It's not funny (=don't laugh), Paul; poor Teresa was nearly in tears.* ⚠ Do not use **funny** to mean 'enjoyable'. Use **fun**: *The picnic was really fun.*

2 STRANGE unusual, strange, or difficult to explain: *I had a **funny feeling** something was going to happen.* | *What's that funny smell?* | *It's **funny how** you remember the words of songs, even ones you don't really like.* | **It's funny (that)** *It's funny that the kids are so quiet.* | **That's funny.** *I was sure I had $5 in my purse, but it's not there now.* | *People tell me I ran the greatest race of my life, but **the funny thing is** I can't remember much about it.* | *It's **a funny old world** (=strange or unusual things happen in life).*

3 DISHONEST appearing to be illegal, dishonest, or wrong: *There's **something funny going on** here.* | *Remember, Marvin, no **funny business** while we're out.*

4 a funny look if you give someone a funny look, you look at them in a way that shows you think they are behaving strangely: *I hunkered down, ignoring the funny looks from passers-by.*

5 ILL feeling slightly ill: *I always **feel funny** after a long car ride.*

6 CRAZY BrE informal slightly crazy: *After his wife died he **went** a bit **funny**.*

7 go funny informal if a machine, piece of equipment etc goes funny, it stops working properly: *I just turned it on and the screen went all funny.*

8 very funny! spoken used when someone is laughing at you or playing a trick and you do not think it is amusing: *Very funny! Who's hidden my car keys?*

9 I'm not being funny (but) BrE spoken used when you are serious or do not want to offend someone: *I'm not being funny, but we haven't got much time.*

10 funny little sth used to describe something you like because it is small, unusual, or interesting: *The town centre is crammed with funny little shops.* | *his funny little grin*

11 funny peculiar or funny ha-ha? BrE; **funny weird/strange or funny ha-ha?** AmE used when someone has described something as funny and you want to know whether they mean it is strange or amusing: *'Tim's a funny guy.' 'Funny weird or funny ha-ha?'*

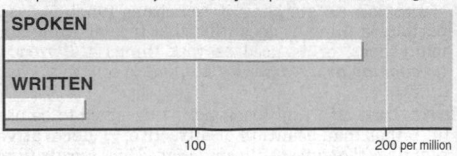

WORD FOCUS: FUNNY
similar words: **amusing, humorous, witty, comical**
very funny: **hilarious, hysterical**
something that someone says that is intended to make people laugh: **joke, pun, play on words**
→ comedy, irony, satire, comedian

Frequencies of the adjective **funny** in spoken and written English.

SPOKEN	
WRITTEN	
	100	200 per million

This graph shows that the adjective **funny** is much more common in spoken English than in written English. This is because it is used in a lot of common spoken phrases.

ˈ**funny bone** n [singular] the soft part of your elbow that particularly hurts when you hit it

ˈ**funny farm** n [C] informal an expression meaning a PSYCHIATRIC hospital that some people consider offensive – used humorously

fun·ny·man /ˈfʌnimæn/ n plural **funnymen** /-men/ [C] a man who works as a COMEDIAN - used in newspapers etc: *the nation's best-loved funnyman*

ˈ**funny ˌmoney** n [U] informal money that has been printed illegally; → **counterfeit**

ˈ**funny ˌpapers** n [plural] AmE informal another expression for the FUNNIES

fun·ny·wom·an /ˈfʌniˌwʊmən/ n plural **funnywomen** /-ˌwɪmɪn/ [C] a woman who works as a COMEDIAN - used in newspapers etc

ˈ**fun ˌrun** n [C] an event in which people run a long distance in order to collect money for CHARITY

fur¹ /fɜː $ fɜːr/ n **1** [U] the thick soft hair that covers the bodies of some animals, such as cats, dogs, and rabbits → FURRY (1) **2** [C,U] the skin of a dead animal with the fur still attached: *a fur coat* | *a fur-lined jacket* | *a ban on **fur farming** (=keeping and killing animals for their fur)* → see picture at MATERIAL **3** [C] a coat or piece of clothing made of fur: *Lady Yolanda was swathed in elegant furs.* **4** [U] a material that looks and feels like fur: **imitation/fake/artificial etc fur** *a pair of gloves trimmed with fake fur* **5** [U] a harmful or unpleasant substance that sometimes forms on surfaces that are always wet, such as water pipes; ⊟ **scale 6 the fur flies** used to say that an angry argument or fight starts: *If you're both feeling frustrated, the fur may fly.*

fur² v **furred, furring** also **fur up** BrE [I] to become covered with an unwanted substance —**furred** adj: *Symptoms include dry lips and a furred tongue.*

fu·ri·ous /ˈfjʊəriəs $ ˈfjʊr-/ adj **1** very angry: [+**at/about**] *Residents in the area are furious at the decision.* | [+**with**] *She was furious with herself for letting things get out of hand.* | **furious that** *Her family are furious that her name has been published by the press.* | *She was **absolutely furious**.* **2** [usually before noun] done with a lot of energy, effort, or speed: *Neil set off at a **furious** pace.* | **furious debate/argument etc** *There was a furious row over the proposals.* | *The action is **fast and furious**.* → **fury** —**furiously** adv

furled /fɜːld $ fɜːrld/ adj a furled newspaper, flag etc has been rolled or folded neatly: *He held a furled umbrella in one hand.* —**furl** v [T]

fur·long /ˈfɜːlɒŋ $ ˈfɜːrlɒːŋ/ n [C] a unit for measuring length, equal to about 201 metres, which is used in horse racing. There are eight furlongs in a mile.

fur·lough /ˈfɜːləʊ $ ˈfɜːrloʊ/ n [C,U] **1** a period of time when a soldier or someone working in another country can return to their own country; ⊟ **leave**: *a young soldier home **on furlough*** **2** AmE a period of time when workers are told not to work, especially because there is not enough money to pay them; →

layoff: *workers forced to take a long, unpaid furlough* **3** *AmE* a short period of time during which a prisoner is allowed to leave prison before returning: *Morton stabbed the man while on furlough.* —**furlough** *v* [T] *AmE: 280,000 federal workers have been furloughed.*

fur·nace /ˈfɜːnɪs $ ˈfɜːr-/ *n* [C] **1** a large container for a very hot fire, used to produce power, heat, or liquid metal **2** a piece of equipment used to heat a building

fur·nish /ˈfɜːnɪʃ $ ˈfɜːr-/ *v* [T] **1** to put furniture and other things into a house or room: *Having bought the house, they couldn't afford to furnish it.* | **furnish sth with sth** *a room furnished with a desk and swivel chair* **2** *formal* to supply or provide something: *Will these finds furnish more information on prehistoric man?* | **furnish sb/sth with sth** *John was furnished with a list of local solicitors.* —**furnished** *adj*: *The bedrooms are elegantly furnished.* | *a fully furnished flat*

fur·nish·ings /ˈfɜːnɪʃɪŋz $ ˈfɜːr-/ *n* [plural] the furniture and other things, such as curtains, in a room: *a home furnishings store*

fur·ni·ture [S2] [W3] /ˈfɜːnɪtʃə $ ˈfɜːrnɪtʃər/ *n* [U] large objects such as chairs, tables, beds, and cupboards: *I helped him choose the furniture for his house.* | *I can't think of a single piece of furniture in my house that I bought new.* | *office furniture*

fu·ro·re /fjʊˈrɔːri, ˈfjʊərɔː $ ˈfjʊrɔːr/ *BrE*; **fu·ror** /ˈfjʊərɔː $ ˈfjʊrɔːr/ *AmE n* [singular] a sudden expression of anger among a large group of people about something that has happened; ▪ **row**: **cause/create a furore** *The security leaks have caused a widespread furore.* | **[+over/about]** *the furor over the oil embargo*

fur·ri·er /ˈfʌriə $ ˈfɜːriər/ *n* [C] someone who makes or sells fur clothing

fur·row¹ /ˈfʌrəʊ $ ˈfɜːroʊ/ *n* [C] **1** a deep line or fold in the skin of someone's face, especially on the forehead; → **wrinkle**: *A deep furrow appeared between his brows.* **2** a wide deep line made in the surface of something, especially the ground: *the regular furrows of a plowed field* | *The river cuts a long straight furrow between the hills.*

furrow² *v* **1** [I,T] to make the skin on your face form deep lines or folds, especially because you are worried or thinking hard: *Quin's brow furrowed in concentration.* **2** [T] to make a wide, deep line in the surface of something —**furrowed** *adj*: *a furrowed brow*

fur·ry /ˈfɜːri/ *adj* **1** covered with fur or short threads; → **fluffy**: *furry kittens* | *pink furry slippers* | *furry leaves* **2** **furry friends** *informal* used humorously to talk about animals in general; → **feathered friend**

fur·ther¹ [S1] [W1] /ˈfɜːðə $ ˈfɜːrðər/ *adv* **1** [MORE] more, or to a greater degree: *A spokesman declined to comment until the evidence could be studied further.* | *The flavour of the wine is further improved during the aging period.* | *Whaling in Australia was stopped. But the Australian government went further* (=said or did something more extreme) *and proposed a global ban.* | **[+into/away etc]** *Marcus sank further and further into debt.*
2 **take sth further** to take action at a more serious or higher level, especially in order to get the result you want: *The police do not propose to take the matter further.* | **take sth a stage/step further** *Critics want the government to take this one stage further and ban the film altogether.*
3 [DISTANCE] also **farther** a greater distance, or beyond a particular place: *They walked a little further.* | **[+up/away/along etc]** *His farm is located further away from Riobamba than his brother's.* | *His hands moved further down her back.* | *They've never been further south than San Diego.*
4 [TIME] into the past or the future: **[+back/on/ahead etc]** *Five years further on, a cure has still not been found.* | *The records don't go any further back than 1960.* | *It might be a sign, much further down the road* (=in the future), *of a change in policy.*

5 [IN ADDITION] [sentence adverb] *formal* used to introduce something additional that you want to talk about; ▪ **furthermore**: *Butter sales have fallen because margarine has improved in flavor. Further, butter consumption has decreased because of links to heart disease.*
6 **further to sth** *written formal* used in letters to mention a previous letter, conversation etc about the same matter: *Further to your letter of February 5th, we can confirm your order.*
7 **nothing could be further from the truth** used when you want to say that something is completely untrue: *People often described him as a bitter academic, but nothing could be further from the truth.*
8 **nothing could be/is further from sb's mind/thoughts** used to emphasize that someone is not thinking about or intending something
9 **sth must not go any further** used to say that something you are telling someone is secret or private

further² *adj* [only before noun] **1** more or additional: *Are there any further questions?* | *We have decided to take no further action.* | **further details/information etc** *Visit our website for further details.* | **a further 10 miles/5 minutes etc** *Cook gently for a further 10 minutes.* **2** **until further notice** until you are told that something has changed: *Lacunza ordered the suspension of the elections until further notice.*

further³ *v* [T] to help something progress or be successful; → **promote**: *He dedicated his life to furthering the cause of world peace.* | *Alan had been using her to further his career.*

fur·ther·ance /ˈfɜːðərəns $ ˈfɜːr-/ *n* [U] *formal* the act or process of helping something progress or be done. **[+of]** *the furtherance of science* | **in furtherance of sth** *Staff are encouraged to use information resources in furtherance of their own professional interests.*

further edu·cation *n* [U] *BrE abbreviation* **FE** education for adults after leaving school, that is not at a university; → **higher education**

fur·ther·more [W3] /ˌfɜːðəˈmɔː $ ˈfɜːrðərmɔːr/ *adv* [sentence adverb] *formal* in addition to what has already been said: *He is old and unpopular. Furthermore, he has at best only two years of political life ahead of him.*

fur·ther·most /ˈfɜːðəməʊst $ ˈfɜːrðərmoʊst/ *adj formal* most distant; ▪ **furthest**: *In the furthermost corner sat a tall thin man.*

fur·thest /ˈfɜːðɪst $ ˈfɜːr-/ *adj, adv* **1** at the greatest distance from a place or point in time; ▪ **farthest**: *There was a huge tapestry on the furthest wall.* | **[+away/from]** *He walked slowly toward the end of the jury box furthest from the judge.* **2** more or to a greater degree than other people or things, or than before: *Maltby's book has probably gone furthest in explaining these events.*

fur·tive /ˈfɜːtɪv $ ˈfɜːr-/ *adj* behaving as if you want to keep something secret; ▪ **secretive**: *There was something furtive about his actions.* | *furtive glances/looks* *Chris kept stealing furtive glances at me.* —**furtively** *adv*: *She opened the door and looked furtively down the hall.* —**furtiveness** *n* [U]

fu·ry /ˈfjʊəri $ ˈfjʊri/ *n* **1** [U] extreme, often uncontrolled anger; ▪ **rage**: *I was shaking with fury.* | *Jenny stepped forward, her eyes blazing with fury.* | *The report was leaked to the press, much to the president's fury.* **2** [singular] a feeling of extreme anger: *'Go on then!' shouted Jamie in a fury.* 'See if I care!' **3** **a fury of sth** a state of very busy activity or strong feeling: *She was listening with such a fury of concentration that she did not notice Arthur had left.* | *In a fury of frustration and fear Nina bit his hand.* **4** **like fury** *informal* with great effort or energy: *We went out and played like fury.* **5** [U] *literary* used to describe very bad weather conditions: *At last the fury of the storm*

F

lessened. **6 Fury** one of the three snake-haired goddesses in ancient Greek stories who punished crime; → **furious**

furze /fɜːz $ fɜːrz/ *n* [U] a wild bush with sharp stems and bright yellow flowers

fuse¹ /fjuːz/ *n* [C] **1** a short thin piece of wire inside electrical equipment which prevents damage by melting and stopping the electricity when there is too much power: *two 13 amp fuses* | *I taught him how to change a fuse.* | **blow a fuse** (=make it melt by putting too much electricity through it); → see picture at ELECTRIC **2** also **fuze** *AmE* a thing that makes a bomb, FIREWORK etc from exploding until you are a safe distance away, or makes it explode at a particular time **3 a short fuse** if someone has a short fuse, they get angry very easily → **blow a fuse** at BLOW¹ (16)

fuse² *v* [I,T] **1** to join together physically, or to make things join together, and become a single thing: **fuse (sth) together** *The egg and sperm fuse together as one cell.* **2** to combine different qualities, ideas, or things, or to be combined; ◨ **merge**: *Their music fuses elements as diverse as Cajun, bebop and Cuban waltzes.* | **fuse (sth) with sth** *Leonard takes Carver-style dirty realism and fuses it with the pace of a detective story.* | **fuse (sth) into sth** *We intend to fuse the companies into a single organization.* **3** *BrE* if electrical equipment fuses, or if you fuse it, it stops working because a fuse has melted: *The lights have fused again.* **4** *technical* if a rock or metal fuses, or if you fuse it, it becomes liquid by being heated: *Lead fuses at quite a low temperature.* → FUSION

'fuse box *n* [C] a box that contains the fuses of the electrical system of a house or other building

fused /fjuːzd/ *adj BrE* if a piece of electrical equipment is fused, it is fitted with a fuse

fu·se·lage /ˈfjuːzəlɑːʒ $ -sə-/ *n* [C] the main part of a plane, in which people sit or goods are carried

fu·si·lier /ˌfjuːzɪ¦ˈlɪə $ -ˈlɪr/ *n* [C] a soldier in the past who carried a light gun called a MUSKET

fu·sil·lade /ˌfjuːzɪ¦ˈleɪd $ -sɪ-/ *n* [C usually singular] **1** a quick series of shots fired from a gun, or a quick series of other objects that are thrown: [+of] *a fusillade of bullets* **2** a quick series of questions or remarks

fu·sion /ˈfjuːʒən/ *n* [C,U] **1** a combination of separate qualities or ideas: *Her work is a fusion of several different styles.* | *the best fusion cuisine in the whole of Vancouver* **2** a physical combination of separate things; → **fission**: *the energy that comes from the fusion of hydrogen atoms* → NUCLEAR FUSION **3** a type of music which mixes JAZZ with other types of music, especially ROCK → FUSE²

'fusion ,bomb *n* [C] another word for a HYDROGEN BOMB

fuss¹ S3 /fʌs/ *n* [singular, U]
1 anxious behaviour or activity that is usually about unimportant things: *James said he'd better be getting back or there'd be a fuss.* | *The Steamatic enables you to clean any carpet with the minimum of fuss.*
2 attention or excitement that is usually unnecessary or unwelcome: *They wanted a quiet wedding without any fuss.* | *Until I heard her sing I couldn't see what all the fuss was about* (=why people liked it so much).
3 make a fuss/kick up a fuss (about sth) to complain or become angry about something, especially when this is not necessary: *Josie kicked up a fuss because the soup was too salty.* | *I don't know why you're making such a fuss about it.*
4 make a fuss of sb/sth *BrE*; **make a fuss over sb/sth** *AmE* to pay a lot of attention to someone or something, to show that you are pleased with them or like them: *Make a fuss of your dog when he behaves properly.*

fuss² *v* [I] **1** to worry a lot about things that may not be very important: *I wish you'd stop fussing – I'll be perfectly all right.* **2** to pay too much attention to small unimportant details: [+with/around/about] *Paul*

was fussing with his clothes, trying to get his tie straight. **3** *AmE* to behave in an unhappy or angry way: *The baby woke up and started to fuss.*

fuss over sb/sth *phr v* to pay a lot of attention or too much attention to someone or something, especially to show that you are pleased with them or like them: *His aunts fussed over him all the time.*

fussed /fʌst/ *adj* **not be fussed (about sth)** *BrE spoken* to not mind what happens or is done; ◨ **bothered**: *'Where do you want to go?' 'I'm not fussed.'*

fuss·pot /ˈfʌsˌpɒt $ -ˌpɑːt/ *BrE*; **fuss·bud·get** /ˈfʌsˌbʌdʒɪt/ *AmE old-fashioned n* [C] *informal* someone who worries about unimportant things

fuss·y /ˈfʌsi/ *comparative* **fussier**, *superlative* **fussiest** *adj* **1** very concerned about small, usually unimportant details, and difficult to please: [+about] *Leonora was fussy about her looks.* | *A lot of small children are fussy eaters* (=they dislike many types of food). | *'Do you want to go out or just rent a movie?' 'I'm not fussy.'* (=I don't mind) **2** fussy clothes, objects, buildings etc are very detailed and decorated – used to show disapproval; ◨ **plain**, **simple**: *The furniture looked comfortable, nothing fussy or too elaborate.* **3** with small, exact, and careful actions, sometimes showing nervousness: *She patted her hair with small fussy movements.* —**fussily** *adv* —**fussiness** *n* [U]

fus·ti·an /ˈfʌstiən $ -tʃən/ *n* [U] **1** a type of rough heavy cotton cloth, worn especially in the past **2** *literary* words that sound important but have very little meaning —**fustian** *adj*

fus·ty /ˈfʌsti/ *adj* **1** if rooms, clothes, buildings etc are fusty, they have an unpleasant smell, because they have not been used for a long time; ◨ **musty** **2** *informal* ideas or people that are fusty are old-fashioned: *fusty old academics* —**fustiness** *n* [U]

fu·tile /ˈfjuːtaɪl $ -tl/ *adj* actions that are futile are useless because they have no chance of being successful; ◨ **pointless**: *a futile attempt/effort a futile attempt to save the paintings from the flames* | *My efforts to go back to sleep proved futile.* | **it is futile to do sth** | *It was futile to continue the negotiations.* —**futility** /fjuːˈtɪləti/ *n* [U]: *This sums up Owen's thoughts on the futility of war.*

fu·ton /ˈfuːtɒn $ -tɑːn/ *n* [C] a MATTRESS used for sleeping on, especially in Japan → see picture at BED

fu·ture¹ S1 W1 /ˈfjuːtʃə $ -ər/ *adj* [only before noun]
1 likely to happen or exist at a time after the present: *We are now more able to predict future patterns of climate change.* | *We've been able to save this land from development and preserve it for future generations.* | *the debate over the future development of the European Union* | **future wife/husband/son-in-law etc** (=someone who will be your wife, husband, son-in-law etc)
2 *technical* the form of a verb used for talking about things that are going to happen: *the future tense*
3 for future reference something kept for future reference is kept in order to be used or looked at in the future

future² S1 W2 *n*
1 the future a) the time after the present: *What are your plans for the future?* | *It may be useful at some time in the future.* | **in the near/immediate future** (=soon) *The recession shows no signs of easing in the immediate future.* | **in/for the foreseeable future** (=for as long as you can imagine or plan for) *We will not be hiring anyone else in the foreseeable future.* | *We hope to create more jobs in the not too distant future* (=fairly soon). | *Our firm must look to the future* (=plan for what will happen). **b)** *technical* the form of a verb that shows that something will happen or exist at a later time. In the sentence, 'I will leave tomorrow,' the verb is in the future.
2 in future *BrE* from now on: *In future, staff must wear identity badges at all times.*

F

3 [C] what someone or something will do or what will happen to them in the future

what the future holds (=what will happen)
have a great/bright/promising future (ahead of you) (=have a good chance of being successful in the future)
sb's/sth's future lies in/with sth (=someone or something will be involved with something in the future)
the future looks good/bright/bleak etc
face an uncertain/bleak/dark future
fears/hopes/plans for the future
shape the future (=help to decide what will happen in the future)
foretell/predict the future
a brighter future

The islands should have the right to decide their own future. | *[+of] Ferguson is optimistic about the future of the business.* | *I've decided to return to Mitford and stay there, no matter* **what the future holds**. | *She's only 17, and* **has a great future ahead** *of her in tennis.* | *Let us hope our* **future lies in** *peace, not war.* | *For small companies, the* **future looks bleak**. | *The film-makers asked children about their* **hopes for the future**. | *a leader who will* **shape** *the organization's* **future**

4 have a/no future to have a chance or no chance of being successful or continuing: *Does this school have a future?*
5 there's a/no future in sth used to say that something is likely or not likely to be successful: *He felt there was no future in farming.*
6 futures [plural] *technical* goods, money, land etc that will be supplied or exchanged in the future at a time and price that has already been agreed

future ˈperfect *n technical* the future perfect the form of a verb that shows that the action described will be complete before a particular time in the future, formed in English by 'will have' or 'shall have', as in 'I will have finished by 5 o'clock.' —**future perfect** *adj*

future-proof¹,   **fu·ture·proof**   /ˈfjuːtʃəpruːf $ -tʃər-/ *v* [T] to make or plan something in such a way that it will not become ineffective or unsuitable for use in the future: *plans to future-proof the company's network*

future-proof² *adj* if something is future-proof, it will not become ineffective or unsuitable for use in the future: *future-proof software*

futures ˌmarket *n* [C] *technical* a market where FUTURES are bought and sold

fu·tur·is·m /ˈfjuːtʃərɪzəm/ *n* [U] a style of art, music, and literature in the early 20th century which emphasized the importance of modern things, especially technology and machines —**futurist** *n* [C]

fu·tur·is·tic /ˌfjuːtʃəˈrɪstɪk◂/ *adj* **1** something which is futuristic looks unusual and modern, as if it belongs in the future instead of the present: *The futuristic sports stadium is the pride of the city.* **2** futuristic ideas, books, films etc imagine what may happen in the future, especially through scientific developments: *Orwell's disturbing futuristic novel, '1984'*

fu·tu·ri·ty /fjuˈtjʊərᵻti $ -ˈtʊr-/ *n* [U] *formal* the time after the present; ⟷ **future**

fu·tu·rol·o·gy /ˌfjuːtʃəˈrɒlədʒi $ -ˈrɑː-/ *n* [U] the activity of trying to say correctly what will happen in the future —**futurologist** *n* [C]

futz /fʌts/ *v*
futz around *phr v AmE informal* to waste time, especially by doing small, unimportant jobs slowly: *I spent the entire day just futzing around.*

fuze /fjuːz/ *n* an American spelling of FUSE

fuzz /fʌz/ *n* **1** [singular, U] thin soft hair or a substance like hair that covers something: *When Jack was born he had a fuzz of black hair on his head.* **2** [U] *AmE* a small amount of soft material that has come from clothing etc; ⟷ **fluff** **3 the fuzz** *informal* an insulting way of talking to or about the police, used especially in the 1960s and 1970s

fuzz·y /ˈfʌzi/ *adj* **1** if a sound or picture is fuzzy, it is unclear; → **blurred**: *Some of the photos were so fuzzy it was hard to tell who was who.* **2** unclear or confused; ⟷ **clear**: *There's a fuzzy line between parents' and schools' responsibilities.* **3** covered with soft short hair or fur: *I stroked the kitten's fuzzy back.* **4** fuzzy hair is very curly and sticks straight up —**fuzzily** *adv* **fuzziness** *n* [U]

ˌfuzzy ˈlogic *n* [U] *technical* a type of LOGIC which is used to try to make computers think like humans

fwd the written abbreviation of *forward*

FWIW for what it is worth; an abbreviation used in emails, to say that you are not sure if what you are writing is very useful

f-word /ˈef wɜːd $ -wɜːrd/ *n* [C] used when you are talking about the word FUCK but do not want to say it because it is offensive: *Mommy, Billy said the f-word.*

fwy. *AmE* the written abbreviation of *freeway*

FX /ˌef ˈeks/ **1** the abbreviation of *foreign exchange* **2** the abbreviation of *special effect*s

-fy /faɪ/ *suffix* [in verbs] another form of the suffix -IFY

FY *AmE* the abbreviation of *fiscal year*

FYI, **fyi** *for your information* used especially in short business notes and emails, when you are telling someone something they need to know

F

G, g

G, g /dʒiː/ *plural* **G's, g's** *n* **1** [C,U] the seventh letter of the English alphabet **2** [C,U] the fifth note in the musical SCALE of C MAJOR or the musical KEY based on this note **3** [singular,U] *AmE* used to describe a film that has been officially approved as suitable for people of any age; → **PG**; ⊟ **U** *BrE* **4** [C] *technical* a unit for measuring the force caused by GRAVITY on an object as it starts to move faster and faster: *Astronauts endure a force of several G's during take-off.* | *high g-forces* **5** [U] *AmE* a GRAND (=$1000)

g a written abbreviation of ***gram*** or grams

gab /gæb/ *v* **gabbed, gabbing** [I + about] *informal* to talk continuously, usually about things that are not important: *You two were gabbing so much you didn't even see me!* — **gabby** *adj* → **the gift of the gab** at GIFT (5)

gab·ar·dine, gaberdine /'gæbədiːn, ˌgæbə'diːn $ 'gæbərdiːn/ *n* **1** [U] a strong material which does not allow water to go through and is often used for making coats **2** [C] a coat made from gabardine

gab·ble¹ /'gæbəl/ *v* **gabbled, gabbling** [I,T] to say something so quickly that people cannot hear you clearly or understand you properly: *Just calm down, stop gabbling, and tell me what has happened.* | *Gina tends to gabble away when she's excited.*

gabble² *n* [singular,U] a lot of talking that is difficult to understand, especially when several people are talking at the same time; ⊟ **babble**: *a gabble of voices*

gab·er·dine /'gæbədiːn, ˌgæbə'diːn $ 'gæbərdiːn/ *n* another spelling of GABARDINE

gab·fest /'gæbfest/ *n* [C] *especially AmE informal* an occasion when people talk to each other after a lot

ga·ble /'geibəl/ *n* [C] the upper end of a house wall where it joins with a sloping roof and makes a shape like a TRIANGLE: *the gable end of the barn* → see picture at ROOF

ga·bled /'geibəld/ *adj* having one or more gables: *a gabled cottage* | *gabled roofs*

gad /gæd/ *v* **gadded, gadding**
gad about/around *phr v informal* to go out and enjoy yourself, going to many different places, especially when you should be doing something else: *While I'm at home cooking, he's gadding about with his friends.*

gad·a·bout /'gædəbaʊt/ *n* [C] *informal* someone who goes out a lot or travels a lot in order to enjoy themselves

gad·fly /'gædflaɪ/ *n plural* **gadflies** [C] **1** someone who annoys other people by criticizing them **2** a fly that bites cattle and horses

gad·get /'gædʒɪt/ *n* [C] a small, useful, and cleverly-designed machine or tool: *a neat gadget for sharpening knives*; → see box at MACHINE¹

gad·get·ry /'gædʒɪtri/ *n* [U] modern gadgets in general – sometimes used in order to show disapproval: *I don't understand how all this electronic gadgetry works.*

Gae·lic /'geilɪk, 'gælɪk/ *n* [U] one of the Celtic languages, especially spoken in parts of Scotland and in Ireland — **Gaelic** *adj*: *Gaelic poetry*

Gaelic 'football *n* [U] a game played in Ireland between two teams of 15 players, using a round ball that can be kicked or hit with the hands

gaff /gæf/ *n* [C] **1** *BrE informal* the place where someone lives: *a wretched dirty gaff* **2** a stick with a hook at the end, used to pull big fish out of the water

gaffe /gæf/ *n* [C] an embarrassing mistake made in a social situation or in public; ⊟ **faux pas**: *The consul's comments were a major diplomatic gaffe.*

gaf·fer /'gæfə $ -ər/ *n* [C] **1** the person who is in charge of the lighting in making a cinema film **2** *BrE informal* an old man – used humorously **3** *BrE informal* a man who is in charge of people, especially in a factory; ⊟ **boss**

gag¹ /gæg/ *v* **gagged, gagging** **1** [I] to be unable to swallow and feel as if you are about to bring up food from your stomach: *The foul smell made her gag.* | [+on] *He almost gagged on his first mouthful of food.* **2** [T] to put a piece of cloth over someone's mouth to stop them making a noise: *Thugs gagged her and tied her to a chair.* | *He left his victim bound and gagged* (=tied up and with something over their mouth that stops them speaking). **3** [T] to stop people saying what they want to say and expressing their opinions: *an attempt to gag political activists* → **GAG ORDER, GAG RULE** **4 be gagging to do sth/be gagging for sth** *BrE informal* to be very eager to do or have something: *They were gagging to sign the contract.* **5 be gagging for it** *BrE informal* to be very eager to have sex

gag² *n* [C] **1** *informal* a joke or funny story: *He told a few gags.* | *It was a bit of a running gag* (=a joke which is repeated) *in the show.* **2** a piece of cloth put over someone's mouth to stop them making a noise

ga·ga /'gɑːgɑː/ *adj* [not before noun] *informal* **1** an insulting word used to describe someone who is confused because they are old: *Sid keeps forgetting my name. I think he's going a bit gaga.* **2** having a strong but often temporary feeling of love for someone; ⊟ **infatuated**: [+about/over] *I can't imagine why Susan is so gaga about him.*

gage /geɪdʒ/ *n* an American spelling of GAUGE

gag·gle /'gægəl/ *n* **1 a gaggle of tourists/children etc** a noisy group of people: *a gaggle of teenage girls* **2 a gaggle of geese** a group of GEESE

gag ,order *n* [C] an order made by the court to prevent any public reporting of a case which is still being considered by a court of law

gag rule *n* [C] a rule or law that stops people from talking about a subject during a particular time or in a particular place

gai·e·ty /'geiəti/ *n old-fashioned* **1** [U] when someone or something is cheerful and fun: *Lars enjoyed the warmth and gaiety of these occasions.* → GAY¹ (3) **2 gaieties** [plural] enjoyable events or activities: *Elaine missed the gaieties of life in Paris.*

gai·ly /'geili/ *adv* **1** in a happy way; ⊟ **cheerfully**: *'Morning, Albert,' she called gaily.* **2** in a way that shows you do not care about, or do not realize, the effects of your actions: *They gaily went on talking after the film had started.* **3 gaily coloured/painted/decorated etc** having bright cheerful colours: *gaily coloured tropical birds*

gain¹ S2 W2 /gein/ *v*
1 **GET STH** [T] to obtain or achieve something you want or need: **gain control/power** | *Radical left-wing parties gained control of local authorities.* | *After gaining independence in 1957, it was renamed 'Ghana'.* | **gain a degree/qualification etc** *He gained a doctorate in Chemical Engineering.*
2 **GET GRADUALLY** [I,T] to gradually get more and more of a quality, feeling etc, especially a useful or valuable one: *She has **gained a reputation** as a good communicator.* | *Many of his ideas have **gained popular support**.* | *an opportunity to **gain experience** in a work environment* | *The youngsters gradually **gain confidence** in their abilities.* | [+in] *The sport has **gained in popularity** in recent years.*
3 **ADVANTAGE** [I,T] to get an advantage from a situation, opportunity, or event: **gain (sth) from (doing) sth** *There is much to be **gained** from seeking expert advice early.* | *an attempt to gain a competitive advantage over their rivals* | *Who really **stands to gain** (=is likely to get an advantage) from these tax cuts?* | *There's **nothing to be gained** (=it will not help you) by losing your temper.*
4 **INCREASE** [T] to increase in weight, speed, height,

or value: *Carrie's **gained** a lot of **weight** recently.* | *The dollar has gained 8% against the yen.*

5 gain access/entry/admittance etc (to sth) to manage to enter a place, building, or organization: *New ramps will help the disabled gain better access.* | *methods used by burglars to gain entry to houses*

6 gain an understanding/insight/impression etc to learn or find out about something: [+of] *We are hoping to gain a better understanding of the underlying process.* | *This enabled me to gain an overall impression of the school.*

7 gain ground to make steady progress and become more popular, more successful etc: *The anti-smoking lobby has steadily gained ground in the last decade.*

8 gain time to deliberately do something to give yourself more time to think; **⊟ lose time**

9 CLOCK [I,T] if a clock or watch gains, or if it gains time, it goes too fast; **⊟ lose**

10 ARRIVE [T] *literary* to reach a place after a lot of effort or difficulty: *The swimmer finally gained the river bank.* → **nothing ventured, nothing gained** at VENTURE[2] (3)

  gain on sb/sth *phr v*
  to gradually get closer to a person, car etc that you are chasing: *Quick – they're gaining on us!*

gain² W3 *n*

1 ADVANTAGE [C] an advantage or improvement, especially one achieved by planning or effort: *The party made considerable gains at local elections.* | [+in] *substantial gains in efficiency* | [+from] *the potential gains from improved marketing* | [+to/for] *There are obvious gains for the student.*

2 INCREASE [C,U] an increase in the amount or level of something; **⊟ loss**: [+in] *a gain in weekly output* | [+of] *Retail sales showed a gain of 0.4%.* | *The Democratic Party needed a **net gain** of only 20 votes.* | *Eating too many fatty goods could cause **weight gain**.*

3 PROFIT [U] financial profit, especially when this seems to be the only thing someone is interested in; **⊟ loss**: *financial/economic/capital etc gain They are seeking to realize the maximum financial gain.* | [+of] *a pre-tax gain of $20 million* | **for gain** *Such research should not be for personal gain.* → CAPITAL GAINS

4 ill-gotten gains money or advantages obtained dishonestly – used humorously

gain·ful /ˈgeɪnfəl/ *adj* **gainful employment/work/activity** *formal* work or activity for which you are paid —**gainfully** *adv*: *gainfully employed*

gain·say /ˌgeɪnˈseɪ/ *v* past tense and past participle **gainsaid** /-ˈsed/ [T usually in negatives] *formal* to say that something is not true, or to disagree with someone; **⊟ contradict**: *No one dared to gainsay him.*

gait /geɪt/ *n* [singular] the way someone walks: *a slow shuffling gait*

gai·ter /ˈgeɪtə $ -ər/ *n* [C usually plural] a cloth or leather covering worn below the knee by men in the past, or now by walkers to keep their legs dry

gal¹ /gæl/ *n* [C] *AmE informal* a girl or woman – used especially by older people: *She's a great gal.*

gal² *BrE*; **gal.** *AmE* the written abbreviation of **gallon** or **gallons**

ga·la /ˈgɑːlə $ ˈgeɪlə, ˈgælə/ *n* [C] **1** a public entertainment or performance to celebrate a special occasion: **gala dinner/performance/night etc** *the Society's Gala Dinner* | *a charity gala evening* **2** *BrE* a sports competition, especially in swimming

ga·lac·tic /ɡəˈlæktɪk/ *adj* relating to a galaxy

gal·ax·y /ˈɡæləksi/ *n plural* **galaxies 1** [C] one of the large groups of stars that make up the universe **2 the Galaxy** the large group of stars which our sun and its PLANETS belong to **3** [singular] a large number of things that are similar: [+of] *a galaxy of British artistic talent*

gale /geɪl/ *n* [C] **1** a very strong wind: *a severe gale* | *it's blowing a gale BrE* (=it's very windy) **2 a gale/gales of laughter** a sudden loud sound of laughter: *The bar erupted into gales of laughter.*

'**gale force** also **gale-force** *adj* a gale force wind is strong enough to be dangerous or cause damage —**gale-force** *adv*: *blowing gale-force*

gall¹ /ɡɔːl $ ɡɒːl/ *n* **1 have the gall to do sth** to do something rude and unreasonable that most people would be too embarrassed to do: *He even had the gall to blame Lucy for it.* **2** [U] *old-fashioned* anger and hate that will not go away; **⊟ resentment 3** [U] *old-fashioned* BILE **4** [C] a swelling on a tree or plant caused by damage from insects or infection **5** [C] a painful place on an animal's skin, caused by something rubbing against it

gall² *v* [T] to make someone feel upset and angry because of something that is unfair: *It really galled him to see Anita doing so well now.* → GALLING

gal·lant¹ /ˈɡælənt/ *adj old-fashioned* **1** a man who is gallant is kind and polite towards women: *a gallant young gentleman* **2** brave: *a gallant attempt to save lives*

gal·lant² /ɡəˈlænt, ˈɡælənt $ ɡəˈlænt, ɡəˈlɑːnt/ *n* [C] *old-fashioned* a well-dressed young man who is kind and polite towards women

gal·lan·try /ˈɡæləntri/ *n* [U] *formal* **1** courage, especially in a battle: *a medal for gallantry* **2** polite attention given by men to women

'**gall ˌbladder** *n* [C] the organ in your body in which BILE is stored

gal·le·on /ˈɡæliən/ *n* [C] a sailing ship used mainly by the Spanish from the 15th to the 17th century

gallery

exhibition in an art gallery

gal·le·ry W3 /ˈɡæləri/ *n plural* **galleries** [C]
1 a) a large building where people can see famous pieces of art: *an exhibition of African art at the Hayward Gallery* | *details of museums and **art galleries** in the city* **b)** a small privately owned shop or STUDIO where you can see and buy pieces of art

2 a) an upper floor or BALCONY built on an inner wall of a hall, theatre, or church, from which people can watch a performance, discussion etc: *the **public gallery** in Congress* | **in the gallery** *We could only afford seats up in the gallery.* **b) the gallery** the people sitting in a gallery **3 play to the gallery** to do or say something just because you think it will please people and make you popular **4** a level passage under the ground in a mine or CAVE → PRESS GALLERY, SHOOTING GALLERY

G

gal·ley /'gæli/ *n* [C] **1** a kitchen on a ship: *The fire extinguishers are stored in the galley.* **2** a long low Greek or Roman ship with sails which was rowed by SLAVES in the past **3** *technical* **a)** a TRAY used in the process of printing books etc which holds TYPE **b)** also **galley proof** a sheet of paper on which a new book is printed, so that mistakes can be put right before it is divided into pages

Gal·lic /'gælɪk/ *adj* relating to or typical of France or French people: *Gallic charm*

gal·ling /'gɔːlɪŋ $ 'gɒː-/ *adj* making you feel upset and angry because of something that is unfair; ◨ **annoying**: *The most galling thing is that the guy who got promoted is less qualified than me.*

gal·li·vant /'gælɪˌvænt/ *v* [I] *informal* to spend time enjoying yourself and going from place to place for pleasure – used humorously in order to show disapproval: [+about/around] *She should be home with the children, not gallivanting around.*

gal·lon /'gælən/ *n* [C] **1** written abbreviation **gal** a unit for measuring liquids, equal to eight PINTS. In Britain this is 4.55 litres, and in the US it is 3.79 litres: *a 20 gallon fish tank* | *The car does about 50 **miles per gallon**.* **2** *informal* a lot of a liquid: *We drank gallons of coffee to keep ourselves awake.*

gal·lop¹ /'gæləp/ *v* **1** [I] if a horse gallops, it moves very fast with all its feet leaving the ground together; → canter, trot: *A neighbour's horse came galloping down the road, riderless.* | *a galloping horse* → see picture at MOVEMENT **2** [I,T] if you gallop, you ride very fast on a horse or you make it go very fast: [+along/off/towards etc] *I watched as Jan galloped away.* **3** [I always + adv/prep] to move very quickly; ◨ **run**: *Ian came galloping down the stairs.*

gallop² *n* **1 a)** [singular] the movement of a horse at its fastest speed, when all four feet leave the ground together; → canter, trot: *The horses broke into a gallop* (=begin to go very fast). | **at a/full gallop** *Mounted police charged at full gallop.* **b)** [C] a ride on a horse when it is galloping **2** [singular] a very fast speed: **at a/full gallop** *The project began at full gallop.*

gal·lop·ing /'gæləpɪŋ/ *adj* [only before noun] increasing or developing very quickly: **galloping inflation/ consumption etc** *galloping inflation of 20 to 30%*

gal·lows /'gæləʊz $ -loʊz/ *n plural* **gallows** [C] a structure used for killing criminals by hanging them from a rope

gallows humour *BrE*; **gallows humor** *AmE n* [U] humour which makes very unpleasant or dangerous things seem funny

gall·stone /'gɔːlstəʊn $ 'gɒːlstoʊn-/ *n* [C] a hard stone which can form in your GALL BLADDER

ga·loot /gə'luːt/ *n* [C] *AmE old-fashioned* someone who is not at all graceful and does not dress neatly: *You clumsy galoot!*

ga·lore /gə'lɔː $ -'lɔːr/ *adj* [only after noun] in large amounts or numbers: *bargains galore in the sales*

ga·losh·es /gə'lɒʃɪz $ -'lɑː-/ *n* [plural] *old-fashioned* rubber shoes worn over ordinary shoes when it rains or snows

ga·lumph /gə'lʌmf/ *v* [I always + adv/prep] *informal* to move in a noisy, heavy, and awkward way

gal·van·ic /gæl'vænɪk/ *adj* **1** *formal* making people react suddenly with strong feelings or actions: *The bomb warning had a galvanic effect.* **2** *technical* relating to the production of electricity by the action of acid on metal

gal·va·nise /'gælvənaɪz/ *v* a British spelling of GALVANIZE

gal·va·nis·m /'gælvənɪzəm/ *n* [U] *technical* the production of electricity by the use of chemicals, especially as in a BATTERY

gal·va·nize also **-ise** *BrE* /'gælvənaɪz/ *v* [T] to shock or surprise someone so that they do something to solve

a problem, improve a situation etc: **galvanize sb into (doing) sth** *The possibility of defeat finally galvanized us into action.* | *The report galvanized world opinion.*

gal·va·nized also **-ised** *BrE* /'gælvənaɪzd/ *adj* **galvanised iron/metal etc** metal that has had a covering of ZINC put on it so that it does not RUST

gam·bit /'gæmbɪt/ *n* [C] **1** something that you do or say which is intended to give you an advantage in an argument: *a clever debating gambit* | *These questions are often an **opening gambit** (=the thing you say first) for a negotiation.* **2** a planned series of moves at the beginning of a game of CHESS

gam·ble¹ /'gæmbəl/ *v* [I,T] **1** to risk money or possessions on the result of something such as a card game or a race, when you do not know for certain what the result will be; → **bet**: *Their religion forbids them to drink or gamble.* | [+on] *Jack loves gambling on the horses.* **2** to do something that involves a lot of risk, and that will not succeed unless things happen the way you would like them to: [+on] *They're gambling on Johnson being fit for Saturday's game.* | **gamble sth on sth** *Potter gambled everything on his new play being a hit.* | **gamble that** *She was gambling that he wouldn't read it too carefully.* | [+with] *We can't relax our safety standards – we'd be gambling with people's lives.* —**gambler** *n* [C]: *Stevens was a **compulsive gambler**.*
gamble sth ⇔ away *phr v* to lose the whole of an amount of money by gambling: *Nielsen gambled his inheritance away.*

gamble² *n* [singular] an action or plan that involves a risk but that you hope will succeed: *It was a big gamble for her to leave the band and go solo.* | [+on] *The gamble on the harvest had paid off* (=succeeded). | *Ellen had to admit the gamble had paid off* (=succeeded). | *In a depressed market, we cannot afford to **take a gamble** on a new product.*

gam·bling /'gæmblɪŋ/ *n* [U] when people risk money or possessions on the result of something which is not certain, such as a card game or a horse race; → **betting**: *The lottery is probably the most popular form of gambling.* | *gambling debts* | *The police raided a number of illegal **gambling dens** (=places for illegal gambling).*

gam·bol /'gæmbəl/ *v* **gambolled, gambolling** *BrE*, **gamboled, gamboling** *AmE* [I] *literary* to jump or run around in a lively active way; ◨ **frolic**: *lambs gambolling in a field* —**gambol** *n* [C]

game¹ S1 W1 /geɪm/ *n*
1 ACTIVITY OR SPORT [C] **a)** an activity or sport in which people compete with each other according to agreed rules: **computer/card/ball etc game** *Dan's never liked card games.* | *We used to **play games** like draughts or chess.* | *You'll have to explain **the rules of the game**.* **b)** an occasion when a game is played; → **match**: *Did you see the game on TV last night?* | [+against/with] *England's World Cup game against Holland* | **game of cards/tennis etc** *How about a game of chess?* | **win/lose a game** *They've won their last three games.* | **home game** (=played at a team's own sports field) | **away game** (=played at an opposing team's sports field) → BALL GAME, BOARD GAME, VIDEO GAME, WAR GAME
2 games [plural] **a)** a large organized sports event: *the Olympic Games* **b)** *BrE* organized sports as a school subject or lesson; ◨ **P.E.**: *We have games on Thursdays.* | *a games lesson*
3 PART OF A MATCH [C] one of the parts into which a single match is divided, for example in tennis or BRIDGE¹ (4): *Graf leads, two games to one.*
4 CHILDREN [C] a children's activity in which they play with toys, pretend to be someone else etc: [+of] *a game of hide-and-seek* | *The boys were **playing** a game in the backyard.*
5 SKILL sb's game how well someone plays a particular game or sport: **improve/raise your game** *Liam's taking lessons to improve his game.* | *the strongest aspect of his game*
6 give the game away to spoil a surprise or secret by doing or saying something that lets someone guess

what the secret is: *Lynn gave the game away by laughing when Kim walked in.*

7 beat sb at their own game also **play sb at their own game** *BrE* to beat someone or fight back against them by using the same methods that they use

8 NOT SERIOUS **be a game** to be something that you do to enjoy yourself rather than for a serious purpose: *It's just a game to them. They don't really care what happens.*

9 play games (with sb) a) to behave in a dishonest or unfair way in order to get what you want: *Are you sure he's really interested, and not just playing silly games with you?* **b)** to not be serious about doing something: *We want a deal. We're not interested in playing games.*

10 ANIMALS/BIRDS [U] wild animals, birds, and fish that are hunted for food, especially as a sport: *game birds* → BIG GAME

11 the only game in town used to say that something is the only possible choice in a situation: *The Church of England is no longer the only game in town.*

12 BUSINESS [singular] *informal* an area of work or business: *We're new to the game and we've still got a lot to learn.* | *I've been in this game for over 10 years.*

13 what's her/your etc game? *BrE spoken* used to ask what the true reason for someone's behaviour is: *Reg is being very nice all of a sudden. What's his game?*

14 the game's up *spoken* used to tell someone that something wrong or dishonest that they have done has been discovered: *Come out, Don. The game's up.*

15 a game of chance a game in which you risk money on the result: *Poker is a game of chance.*

16 sb got game *AmE informal* used to say that someone is very skilful at doing something, especially playing a sport

17 be on the game *BrE informal* to be a PROSTITUTE

18 make someone's game of sb *old-fashioned* to make fun of someone → FAIR GAME; → **fun and games** at FUN[1] (5); → **the name of the game** at NAME[1] (10); → **a mug's game** at MUG[1] (5)

game[2] *adj* **1** willing to try something dangerous, new, or difficult: *Okay. I'm game if you are.* | [+for] *He's always game for a laugh.* | **game to do sth** *'Who's game to have a try?'* **2 game leg** *old-fashioned* an injured or painful leg —**gamely** *adv*

game[3] *v AmE* **game the system** to use rules or laws to get what you want in an unfair but legal way

game·keep·er /'geɪmkiːpə $ -ər/ *n* [C] someone whose job is to look after wild animals and birds that are kept to be hunted on private land

game park *n* [C] a GAME RESERVE

game plan *n* [C] a plan for achieving success, especially in business or sports: *He has his game plan all worked out.*

game·play /'geɪmpleɪ/ *n* [U] the way that a computer game is designed and the skills that you need to play it: *This is packed with brilliant graphics and gameplay.*

game point *n* [C,U] the situation in a game such as tennis in which one player will win the game if they win the next point; → **match point**

gam·er /'geɪmə $ -ər/ *n* [C] *informal* **1** someone who plays computer games **2** *AmE* a person who is very good at a sport and helps their team to win games

game re·serve also **game pre·serve** *AmE n* [C] a large area of land that is designed for wild animals to live in safely

game show *n* [C] a television programme in which people play games or answer questions to win prizes: *a game show contestant*

games·man·ship /'geɪmzmənʃɪp/ *n* [U] the ability to succeed by using the rules of a game or activity to your own advantage

gam·ete /'gæmiːt/ *n* [C] *technical* a type of cell which joins with another cell, starting the development of a baby or other young creature

game warden *n* [C] someone whose job is to look after wild animals in a GAME RESERVE

gam·ey, gamy /'geɪmi/ *adj* having the strong taste of wild animals that are hunted for food

ga·mine /'gæmiːn/ *n* [C] *literary* a small thin girl or woman who looks like a boy —**gamine** *adj: a gamine hairstyle*

gam·ing /'geɪmɪŋ/ *n* [U] **1** *informal* the activity of playing computer games: *online gaming* **2** *old-fashioned* the activity of playing cards or other games of chance for money; ◻ **gambling**: *gaming tables*

gam·ma /'gæmə/ *n* [C] the third letter of the Greek alphabet

gamma ray *n* [C usually plural] a beam of light with a short WAVELENGTH, that can pass through solid objects —**gamma radi·ation** *n* [U]

gam·mon /'gæmən/ *n* [U] *BrE* meat from a pig's leg which has been preserved using salt; → **bacon**: *gammon steak*

gam·my /'gæmi/ *adj BrE old-fashioned* a gammy leg or knee is injured or painful

gam·ut /'gæmət/ *n* [singular] the complete range of possibilities: [+of] *College life opened up a whole gamut of new experiences.* | *Her feelings that day ran the gamut of emotions* (=included all the possibilities between two extremes).

gam·y /'geɪmi/ *adj* another spelling of GAMEY

gan·der /'gændə $ -ər/ *n* [C] **1** a male GOOSE[1] **2 have/take a gander at sth** *spoken* to look at something

G & T /ˌdʒiː ən 'tiː/ *n* [C,U] **gin and tonic** a popular alcoholic drink served with ice and a thin piece of LEMON

gang[1] S3 /gæŋ/ *n* [C]

1 a) a group of young people who spend time together, and who are often involved in crime or drugs and who often fight against other groups: *two rival street gangs* | **gang member/member of a gang** *The parents have denied that their son is a gang member.* | *the problem of inner-city gang violence* **b)** a group of young people together in one place, especially young people who might cause trouble: [+of] *There were always gangs of kids hanging around the mall.* | *a victim of gang warfare*

2 a group of criminals who work together: *Several gangs were operating in the area.* | *Armed gangs have hijacked lorries.* | [+of] *a gang of smugglers*

3 *informal* a group of friends, especially young people: *The whole gang will be there next weekend.*

4 a group of workers or prisoners doing physical work together → CHAIN GANG

gang[2] *v*

gang up on/against sb *phr v* if people gang up on someone, they join together to attack, criticize, or oppose them, especially in a way that seems unfair: *Schoolchildren are quick to gang up on anyone who looks or behaves differently.*

gang together *phr v* if people gang together, they form a group in order to do something together, especially to oppose something: *The smaller shopkeepers ganged together to beat off competition from the supermarkets.*

gang-bang *n* [C] **1** *informal* an occasion when several people have sex with each other at the same time **2** a GANG RAPE —**gang-bang** *v* [I,T]

gang·bust·ers /'gæŋˌbʌstəz $ -ərz/ *n* **like gang-busters** *AmE informal* very eagerly and with a lot of energy, or very quickly: *They were going like gangbusters, then all of a sudden everything went wrong.*

gang·land /'gæŋlænd, -lənd/ *adj* **a gangland killing/murder/shooting etc** a killing etc relating to the world of organized and violent crime: *Sharp may have been the victim of a gangland revenge killing.*

gan·gling /'gæŋglɪŋ/ *adj* unusually tall and thin, and not able to move gracefully; ◻ **lanky**: *an awkward gangling teenager*

G

gan·gli·on /ˈɡæŋɡliən/ n [C] technical **1** a painful raised area of skin that is full of liquid, often on the back of your wrist **2** a mass of nerve cells

gan·gly /ˈɡæŋɡli/ adj another form of GANGLING

gang·plank /ˈɡæŋplæŋk/ n [C] a board for walking on between a boat and the shore, or between two boats

gang ˌrape n [C] an occasion when several men attack a woman and force her to have sex with them

gan·grene /ˈɡæŋɡriːn/ n [U] a condition in which your flesh decays in part of your body, because blood has stopped flowing there as a result of illness or injury —**gangrenous** /-ɡrɪnəs/ adj

gang·sta /ˈɡæŋstʌ/ n [C] AmE informal someone who is a member of a GANG: gangstas in South Central L.A.

gangsta ˌrap n [U] a type of RAP music with words about drugs, violence, and life in poor areas of cities —**gangsta rapper** n [C]

gang·ster /ˈɡæŋstə $ -ər/ n [C] a member of a violent group of criminals

gang·way /ˈɡæŋweɪ/ n [C] **1** a space between two rows of seats in a theatre, bus, or train; ◨ **aisle 2** a large board or steps between a boat and the shore for people to walk down **3 gangway!** spoken used to tell people in a crowd to let someone go through

gan·ja /ˈɡændʒə/ n [U] informal MARIJUANA

gan·net /ˈɡænɪt/ n [C] **1** a large sea bird that lives in large groups on cliffs **2** BrE informal someone who eats a lot

gan·try /ˈɡæntri/ n plural **gantries** [C] a large metal frame which is used to support heavy machinery or railway signals

gaol /dʒeɪl/ n, v a British spelling of JAIL

gaol·bird /ˈdʒeɪlbɜːd $ -bɜːrd/ n a British spelling of JAILBIRD

gaol·er /ˈdʒeɪlə $ -ər/ n a British spelling of JAILER

gap S2 W2 /ɡæp/ n [C]
1 A SPACE a space between two objects or two parts of an object, especially because something is missing: [+in] The neighbors' dog got in through a gap in the hedge. | a gap in the traffic | [+between] the gap between the two rows of seats; → see picture at HOLE
2 DIFFERENCE a big difference between two situations, amounts, groups of people etc; → gulf: [+between] the widening gap between the rich and the poor | **bridge/close/narrow the gap** (=reduce the amount or importance of a difference) His films attempt to bridge the gap between tradition and modernity. | The gap has narrowed to just 12 points now. | It seems that the **trade gap** is widening (=the difference between the amount a country imports and exports). → GENERATION GAP
3 STH MISSING something missing that stops something else from being good or complete: [+in] There are huge gaps in my knowledge of history. | Frank's death has left a big gap in my life. | **fill/plug the gap** He filled the gap left by Hirst's retirement.
4 IN TIME a period of time when nothing is happening, that exists between two other periods of time when something is happening: [+in] an awkward gap in the conversation | [+between] The gaps between his visits got longer and longer. → GAP YEAR
5 IN A MOUNTAIN a low place between two higher parts of a mountain
6 gap in the market a product or service that does not exist, so that there is an opportunity to develop that product or service and sell it

gape /ɡeɪp/ v [I] **1** to look at something for a long time, especially with your mouth open, because you are very surprised or shocked; ◨ **stare**: [+at] What are all these people gaping at? **2** also **gape open** to open widely or be wide open: Dan stood at the door, his shirt gaping open.

gap·ing /ˈɡeɪpɪŋ/ adj [only before noun] a gaping hole, wound, or mouth is very wide and open

gap-ˈtoothed adj [usually before noun] having wide spaces between your teeth: **gap-toothed smile/grin**

gap year n [C] BrE a year between leaving school and going to university, which some young people use as an opportunity to travel, earn money, or get experience of working: Some students choose to work in high-tech industries during their gap year.

gar·age¹ S2 /ˈɡærɪdʒ, -ɑːʒ $ ɡəˈrɑːʒ/ n
1 [C] a building for keeping a car in, usually next to or attached to a house; → **carport**: I'll just go and put the car in the garage. | **a double/single/two-car/one-car garage** Their house had a **double garage**. | an automatic garage door
2 [C] also **parking garage** especially AmE a building in a public place where cars can be parked: We parked in an **underground garage** near the hotel.
3 [C] a place where motor vehicles are repaired: My car's at the garage.
4 [C] BrE a place where you buy petrol; ◨ **petrol station**; ◨ **gas station** AmE
5 [U] a type of popular music played on electronic instruments, with a strong fast beat and singing: a collection of the latest dance and garage hits

garage² v [T] to put or keep a vehicle in a garage

garage ˌband n /$.ˈ. ˌ./ n [C] a group of musicians who play ROCK music and practise in a garage

garage ˌsale n /$.ˈ. ˌ./ n [C] AmE a sale of used furniture, clothes etc from people's houses, usually held in or near someone's garage

ga·ram ma·sa·la /ˌɡɑːrəm məˈsɑːlə, -mɑː-/ n [U] a mixture of SPICES which gives a hot taste to food, used especially in Indian cooking

garb /ɡɑːb $ ɡɑːrb/ n [U] formal a particular style of clothing, especially clothes that show your type of work or look unusual: priestly garb

gar·bage S3 /ˈɡɑːbɪdʒ $ ˈɡɑːr-/ n [U]
1 especially AmE waste material, such as paper, empty containers, and food thrown away; ◨ **rubbish** BrE: Can you take out the garbage when you go?
2 stupid words, ideas etc; ◨ **rubbish** BrE: You're talking garbage.
3 garbage in, garbage out used to say that if the DATA (=information) you put into a computer is bad, the results you get back will be bad, even if the computer program you use works properly

garbage ˌcan n [C] AmE a container with a lid for holding waste until it can be taken away; ◨ **dustbin** BrE

garbage colˌlector n [C] AmE someone whose job is to remove waste from garbage cans; ◨ **dustman** BrE

garbage disˌposal n [C] AmE a small machine in the kitchen SINK which breaks vegetable waste into small pieces so that it washes down the DRAIN of the sink; ◨ **waste disposal** BrE

garbage man n [C] AmE a garbage collector

garbage ˌtruck n [C] AmE a large vehicle which goes from house to house to collect the contents of garbage cans; ◨ **dust cart** BrE

gar·ban·zo /ɡɑːˈbænzəʊ $ ɡɑːrˈbɑːnzoʊ/ also **gar·banzo ˌbean** n plural **garbanzos** [C] AmE CHICKPEA

garbed /ɡɑːbd $ ɡɑːrbd/ adj be garbed in sth literary to be dressed in a particular type of clothing: singers garbed in costumes of gold

gar·bled /ˈɡɑːbəld $ ˈɡɑːr-/ adj a garbled statement or report is very unclear and confusing; ◨ **confused**: The papers had some garbled version of the story. | a garbled phone message —**garble** v [T] —**garble** n [U]

gar·çon /ˈɡɑːsɒn $ ɡɑːrˈsoʊn/ n [C] BrE a waiter in a French restaurant

gar·den¹ S1 W1 /ˈɡɑːdn $ ˈɡɑːr-/ n
1 [C] BrE the area of land next to a house, where there are flowers, grass, and other plants, and often a place for people to sit; ◨ **yard** AmE: He's outside in the garden. | Grace brought us some flowers from her garden. | Our house has a small garden. | a **garden**

shed | **back/front garden** (=at the back or the front of the house)
2 [C] *AmE* a part of the area next to a house, which has plants and flowers in it: **vegetable/herb/rose garden** *The house has a beautiful herb garden.*
3 gardens [plural] a large area of land where plants and flowers are grown so that the public can go and see them: *the **Botanical Gardens** at Kew*
4 Gardens *BrE* used in the name of streets: *211 Roland Gardens* → KITCHEN GARDEN, MARKET GARDEN; → **lead sb up the garden path** at LEAD¹ (12)

WORD FOCUS: GARDEN
parts of a garden: **lawn, flowerbed, hedge, patio, rockery, pond, greenhouse, compost heap, kitchen garden**
things you do in the garden: **cut the grass/mow the lawn, weed** the flowerbeds, **sow** seeds, **plant** flowers/bushes/trees, **water** the plants, **cut back/prune** roses and other bushes, **trim** the hedge

---

garden² *v* [I] to work in a garden, keeping it clean, growing plants etc

garden ,centre *n* [C] *BrE* a place that sells plants, flowers, and equipment for gardens; ☐ **nursery** *AmE*

garden 'city *n* [C] *BrE* a town that has been designed to have a lot of trees, areas of grass, and open spaces

gar·den·er /'gɑːdnə $ 'gɑːrdnər/ *n* [C] **1** someone whose job is to work in gardens → see picture at OCCUPATION **2** someone who enjoys growing flowers and plants: *Mom has always been a good gardener.*

gar·de·ni·a /gɑːˈdiːniə $ gɑːr-/ *n* [C] a large white pleasant-smelling flower that grows on a bush

garden equipment

wheelbarrow
rake
watering can
lawn mower
spade
fork
trowel
gardening gloves
shears
sprinkler
flowerpot

gar·den·ing /'gɑːdnɪŋ $ 'gɑːr-/ *n* [U] the activity of working in a garden, growing plants, cutting a LAWN etc: *I might **do** a bit of **gardening** this afternoon.* | **gardening gloves/tools/equipment etc**

Garden of 'Eden *n* → EDEN

garden ,party *n* [C] *BrE* a formal party for a lot of people which is held in a large garden in the afternoon

garden-va,riety *adj* [only before noun] *especially AmE* very ordinary and not very interesting: *This is not one of your garden-variety cases of fraud.*

---

gar·gan·tu·an /gɑːˈgæntʃuən $ gɑːr-/ *adj written* extremely large; ☐ **gigantic**: *a meal of gargantuan proportions* | *gargantuan task*

gar·gle¹ /'gɑːgəl $ 'gɑːr-/ *v* [I] to clean the inside of your mouth and throat by blowing air through water or medicine in the back of your throat: [+with] *Gargling with salt water may help your sore throat.*

gargle² *n* **1** [C,U] liquid that you gargle with; ☐ **mouthwash 2** a gargle the act of gargling

gar·goyle /'gɑːgɔɪl $ 'gɑːr-/ *n* [C] a stone figure of a strange and ugly creature, that carries rain water from the roof of an old building, especially a church

gar·ish /'geərɪʃ $ 'ger-/ *adj* very brightly coloured in a way that is unpleasant to look at; ☐ **brash**; ☐ **subtle**: *Many of the rugs are too garish for my taste.* | *garish colors* —**garishly** *adv*: *a garishly painted house* —**garishness** *n* [U]

gar·land¹ /'gɑːlənd $ 'gɑːr-/ *n* [C] a ring of flowers or leaves, worn on your head or around your neck for decoration or for a special ceremony; → **wreath**: [+of] *garlands of flowers*

garland² *v* [T usually passive] *literary* to decorate someone or something, especially with flowers: **be garlanded with sth** *The tree was garlanded with strings of coloured lights.*

gar·lic ⬛ /'gɑːlɪk $ 'gɑːr-/ *n* [U] a plant like a small onion, used in cooking to give a strong taste: *Add a crushed **clove of garlic** (=single section of it).* → see picture at VEGETABLE —**garlicky** *adj*: *his garlicky breath*

'garlic ,press *n* [C] a tool used to crush garlic → see picture at EAT

gar·ment /'gɑːmənt $ 'gɑːr-/ *n* [C] *formal* a piece of clothing: *She pulled the garment on and zipped it up.* | **garment industry/factory/district etc** *She works in the garment district of Manhattan.* | *a beautiful range of hand knitted garments* | **outer/upper garment** *The outer garment was a loose-fitting robe.* → UNDERGARMENT; → see box at CLOTHES

'garment ,bag *n* [C] a special bag used to carry clothes such as suits and dresses: *I packed the dresses in a black garment bag.*

gar·ner /'gɑːnə $ 'gɑːrnər/ *v* [T] *formal* to take or collect something, especially information or support; → **glean**: *The party garnered 70 percent of the vote.*

gar·net /'gɑːnɪt $ 'gɑːr-/ *n* **1** [C] a dark red stone used as a jewel **2** [U] a dark red colour

gar·nish¹ /'gɑːnɪʃ $ 'gɑːr-/ *n* [C] a small amount of food such as SALAD or fruit that you place on food to decorate it

garnish² *v* [T] to add something to food in order to decorate it: **garnish sth with sth** *Garnish each dish with a slice of lemon.*

gar·ret /'gærɪt/ *n* [C] a small uncomfortable room at the top of a house, just under the roof; → **attic**

gar·ri·son¹ /'gærɪsən/ *n* [C] **1** a group of soldiers living in a town or FORT and defending it: *The garrison was called out when news of the enemy's advance was received.* | *a garrison town* **2** the buildings where a garrison of soldiers live

garrison² *v* [T] to send a group of soldiers to defend or guard a place: *Our regiment will garrison the town.*

gar·rotte /gəˈrɒt $ gəˈrɑːt/ *v* [T] to kill someone by pulling a metal collar or wire tightly around their neck; → **strangle** —**garrotte** *n* [C]

gar·ru·lous /'gærələs/ *adj* always talking a lot; ☐ **talkative**: *Ian isn't normally this garrulous!* —**garrulously** *adv* —**garrulousness** *n* [U]

gar·ter /'gɑːtə $ 'gɑːrtər/ *n* [C] **1** a band of ELASTIC (=material that stretches) worn around your leg to keep a sock or STOCKING up **2** *AmE* one of four pieces of elastic fixed to a woman's underwear and to her stockings to hold them up; ☐ **suspender** *BrE*

'garter ,belt n [C] AmE a piece of women's underwear with garters hanging down from it which fasten onto STOCKINGS and hold them up; ■ **suspender belt** BrE

'garter ,snake n [C] a harmless American snake with lines of colour along its back

gas[1] S1 W2 /gæs/ n plural **gases** or **gasses**
1 [C,U] a substance such as air, which is not solid or liquid, and usually cannot be seen: hydrogen gas | toxic/poisonous/noxious gases a cloud of toxic gas | a gas cylinder/bottle (=for storing gas) → GREENHOUSE GAS
2 [U] a clear substance like air that is burned for heating or cooking: **gas cooker/stove/oven** | Can you light the gas for me? | The explosion was caused by a **gas leak** from the water heater.
3 gas mark 4/5/6 etc BrE a measurement of the temperature of a gas OVEN
4 [U] AmE also **gasoline** a liquid made from PETROLEUM, used mainly for producing power in the engines of cars, trucks etc; ■ **petrol** BrE: I probably spend over $200 a month on gas. | The mechanic found a hole in the **gas tank**.
5 the gas AmE the gas PEDAL of a car; ■ **accelerator**: We stepped on the gas (=pushed down the gas pedal and made the car go faster) and sped away.
6 [U] a clear substance like air that is used for medical reasons, for example to make people feel less pain or make them sleep during an operation: an anaesthetic gas → LAUGHING GAS
7 [U] a type of gas used as a weapon, because it harms or kills people when they breathe it in: mustard gas → NERVE GAS, POISON GAS, TEAR GAS
8 [U] AmE informal the condition of having a lot of air in your stomach; ■ **wind** BrE
9 a gas AmE old-fashioned spoken something that is fun and makes you laugh a lot

gas[2] v past tense **gassed**, past participle **gassing** **1** [T] to poison or kill someone with gas **2** [I] BrE informal to talk for a long time about unimportant or boring things; ■ **chat**: They were just standing there gassing away.
gas up phr v AmE to put petrol in a car: We'd better gas up before we go. | **gas sth ⇔ up** George gassed up the car.

gas·bag /'gæsbæg/ n [C] informal someone who talks too much; ■ **windbag**

'gas ,chamber n [C] a large room in which people or animals are killed with poisonous gas

gas·e·ous /'gæsiəs $ 'gæsiəs, -ʃəs/ adj like gas or in the form of gas

'gas-fired adj especially BrE using gas as a fuel: a gas-fired central heating system

'gas-,guzzler n [C] AmE informal a car that uses a lot of petrol —**gas-guzzling** adj

gash /gæʃ/ n [C] a large deep cut or hole in something, for example in a person's skin: Blood poured from a deep gash in her forehead. —**gash** v [T]: One day Frank gashed his hand on a bit of broken glass.

gas·hold·er /'gæs,həʊldə $ -,hoʊldər/ n [C] BrE a very large round metal container or building from which gas is carried in pipes to buildings

gas·ket /'gæskɪt/ n [C] **1** a flat piece of material, often rubber, placed between two surfaces so that steam, oil, gas etc cannot escape **2 blow a gasket a)** if a vehicle blows a gasket, steam or gas escapes from the engine **b)** informal to become very angry

gas·light /'gæs-laɪt/ n **1** [U] the light produced from burning gas **2** [C] also **gas lamp** a lamp in a house or on the street which gives light from burning gas → see picture at LAMP

gas·man /'gæsmæn/ n plural **gasmen** /-men/ [C] BrE informal someone whose job is to come to your home to see how much gas you have used or to repair your gas system

'gas mask n [C] a piece of equipment worn over your face to protect you from poisonous gases

'gas ,meter n [C] a piece of equipment that measures how much gas is used in a building

gas·o·hol /'gæsəhɒl $ -hɔːl/ n [U] AmE petrol with a small amount of alcohol in it, which can be used in cars and is cheaper than petrol

gas·o·line /'gæsəliːn/ n [U] AmE a liquid obtained from PETROLEUM, used mainly for producing power in the engines of cars, trucks etc; ■ **petrol** BrE

gas·om·e·ter /gæ'sɒmɪtə $ -'sɑːmɪtər/ n [C] BrE a GASHOLDER

gasp[1] /gɑːsp $ gæsp/ v **1** [I,T] to breathe in suddenly in a way that can be heard, especially because you are surprised or in pain: [+in/with] Ollie gasped with pain and slumped forward. | [+at] The audience gasped at the splendour of the costumes. | 'My leg!' he gasped. 'I think it's broken!' **2** [I] to breathe quickly in a way that can be heard because you are having difficulty breathing; → pant: **gasp for air/breath** Brendan climbed slowly, gasping for breath. **3 be gasping (for sth)** BrE spoken to feel that you urgently need something such as a drink or cigarette: I'm gasping for a pint!

gasp[2] n [C] **1** when you take in a breath suddenly in a way that can be heard, especially because you are surprised or in pain: [+of] With a gasp of pure horror, Lewis jumped up and ran. | She **gave a little gasp** and clutched George's hand. **2** when you breathe in quickly because you are having difficulty breathing: Her breath came in shallow gasps. **3 sb's/sth's last gasp** the time when someone is about to die, or when something is about to stop happening or existing: the last gasp of an industry in decline

'gas ,pedal n [C] AmE the thing that you press with your foot to make a car go faster; ■ **accelerator**; → see picture at CAR

'gas ring n [C] BrE a metal ring that gets hot when gas passes through it, used for cooking food; ■ **burner** AmE

'gas ,station n [C] AmE a place where you can buy petrol and oil for motor vehicles; ■ **petrol station** BrE

gas·sy /'gæsi/ adj BrE a gassy drink has too much gas in it; → **fizzy**: This beer is really gassy.

gas·tric /'gæstrɪk/ adj [only before noun] technical **1** relating to your stomach: gastric ulcers **2 gastric juices** the acids in your stomach that break food into smaller parts **3 gastric flu** an illness that makes you VOMIT and gives you DIARRHOEA

gas·tri·tis /gæ'straɪtɪs/ n [U] medical an illness which makes the inside of your stomach become swollen, so that you feel a burning pain

gas·tro·en·te·ri·tis /,gæstrəʊentə'raɪtɪs $ -troʊ-/ n [U] medical a painful illness which makes your stomach and INTESTINE become swollen

gas·tro·in·tes·tin·al /,gæstrəʊɪn'testɪnəl $ -troʊ-/ adj medical of or relating to the stomach and INTESTINES

gas·tro·nom·ic /,gæstrə'nɒmɪk◂ $ -'nɑː-/ adj [only before noun] formal relating to the art of cooking good food or the pleasure of eating it: the gastronomic delights of Thailand —**gastronomically** /-kli/ adv

gas·tron·o·my /gæ'strɒnəmi $ gæ'strɑː-/ n [U] formal the art and science of cooking and eating good food

,gas 'turbine n [C] an engine in which a wheel of special blades is driven round at high speed by hot gases, producing a lot of power: the ship's four gas turbine engines

gas·works /'gæswɜːks $ -wɜːrks/ n plural **gasworks** [C] a place where gas is made from coal so that it can be used to produce heat and energy

gate[1] S2 W2 /geɪt/ n
1 [C] the part of a fence or outside wall that you can

open and close so that you can enter or leave a place; → **door**: *We went through the gate into the orchard.* | *the wrought-iron gates of the palace* | **open/close/shut a gate** *I left the engine running and ran back to close the gate.* | **front/back/main gate** *Make sure that the back gate is locked, please.* | **garden/farm/school gate** *The children poured out of the school gates.*
2 [C] the place where you leave an airport building to get on a plane: *Air France flight 76 leaves from gate 6A.*
3 -gate used with the name of a place or a person to give a name to an event involving dishonest behaviour by a politician or other public official: *Irangate*
4 a) [C] *BrE* the number of people who go in to see a sports event, especially a football match **b)** [U] *BrE* also **gate money** the amount of money that these people pay

gate² *v* [T] *BrE* to prevent a student from leaving a school as a punishment for behaving badly

gâ·teau /'gætəʊ $ gɑ:'toʊ/ *n plural* **gâteaux** /-təʊz $ -'toʊz/ [C,U] *BrE* a large sweet cake, often filled and decorated with cream, fruit, chocolate etc → see picture at DESSERT

gate·crash /'geɪtkræʃ/ *v* [I,T] to go to a party that you have not been invited to —**gatecrasher** *n* [C]

gated com'munity *n* [C] *AmE* an area of houses and sometimes also shops, tennis courts etc, where a fence or wall surrounds the area and the entrance is guarded

gate·house /'geɪthaʊs/ *n* [C] a small building next to the gate of a park or at the entrance to the land surrounding a big house

gate·keep·er /'geɪtˌki:pə $ -ər/ *n* [C] **1** someone whose job is to open and close a gate, and to allow or not allow people to go through it **2** someone in an organization who has a lot of influence over what products the organization buys, who it buys them from etc **3** someone in an organization who tells customers or people with questions which people in the organization should be able to help them

gate·post /'geɪtpəʊst $ -poʊst/ *n* [C] **1** one of two strong upright poles set in the ground to support a gate **2 between you, me, and the gatepost** *BrE spoken* used to say that you are going to tell someone your opinion, but you want it to be a secret

gate·way /'geɪt-weɪ/ *n* **1** [C] the opening in a fence, wall etc that can be closed by a gate **2 gateway to sth a)** a place, especially a city, that you can go through in order to reach another much bigger place: *St. Louis is the gateway to the West.* **b)** a way of achieving something: *To me a way in the country is a gateway to happiness.* **3** [C] a way of connecting two computer NETWORKS

gateway ˌdrug *n* [C] a drug such as CANNABIS which is not a very dangerous drug, but which some people believe leads to the use of more dangerous drugs such as HEROIN

gath·er¹ S2 W2 /'gæðə $ -ər/ *v*
1 COME TOGETHER [I,T] to come together and form a group, or to make people do this: *A crowd gathered to watch the fight.* | *Thousands of people gathered outside the embassy.* | [+**around/round**] *Gather round, everyone, so that you can see the screen.* | *During the air raids, we gathered the children around us and sang songs.* | [+**together**] *Could the bride's family all gather together for a photo?* | **be gathered** *Dozens of photographers were gathered outside Jagger's villa.*
2 KNOW/THINK [I,T not in progressive] to believe that something is true because of what you have seen or heard; ◫ **understand**: *You two know each other, I gather.* | **gather (that)** *I gather you've had some problems with our sales department.* | **from what I can gather/as far as I can gather** (=this is what I believe to be true) *She's his niece, from what I can gather.*
3 COLLECT [I,T] to get things from different places and put them together in one place: *The researcher's job is to gather information about people.* | *They had gathered 440,000 signatures to support their demand.* | [+**up/together**] *Debbie gathered up the clothes.*
4 gather speed/force/momentum etc to move faster,

become stronger, get more support etc: *The cart gathered speed as it coasted down the hill.* | *The international relief effort appears to be gathering momentum.*
5 gather dust if something gathers dust, it is not being used: *You may as well take these books – they're just gathering dust on the shelf.*
6 CLOTH [T] **a)** to pull material into small folds: *The skirt is gathered at the waist.* **b)** to pull material or a piece of clothing closer to you: *Moira gathered her skirts round her and climbed the steps.*
7 gather yourself/your strength/your thoughts to prepare yourself for something you are going to do, especially something difficult: *I took a few moments to gather my thoughts before going into the meeting.*
8 CLOUDS/DARKNESS [I] *literary* to gradually become more cloudy or get darker: *Storm clouds were gathering so we hurried home.* | **the gathering darkness/dusk/shadows etc** *the evening's gathering shadows*
9 gather sb to you/gather sb up *literary* to take someone into your arms and hold them in order to protect them or show them love

gather² *n* [C] a small fold produced by pulling cloth together

gath·er·er /'gæðərə $ -ər/ *n* [C] someone who gathers something: *information gatherers* | *Groups of hunters and gatherers* (=people who found plant food) *used to roam Europe.*

gath·er·ing /'gæðərɪŋ/ *n* [C] **1** a meeting of a group of people: *a select gathering of 20 or 30 people* **2 intelligence/information etc gathering** the process of collecting information from many different places **3** a fold or group of folds in cloth

ga·tor /'geɪtə $ -ər/ *n* [C] *AmE informal* an ALLIGATOR

gauche /gəʊʃ $ goʊʃ/ *adj* doing or saying wrong or impolite things, especially because you do not know the right way to behave: *It would be gauche to mention the price.* —**gaucheness** *n* [U]

gau·cho /'gaʊtʃəʊ $ -tʃoʊ/ *n plural* **gauchos** [C] a South American COWBOY

gau·dy /'gɔːdi $ 'gɒːdi/ *adj* clothes, colours etc that are gaudy are too bright and look cheap – used to show disapproval: *gaudy jewelry* —**gaudily** *adv* —**gaudiness** *n* [U]

gauge¹ also **gage** *AmE* /geɪdʒ/ *n* [C]
1 INSTRUMENT an instrument for measuring the size or amount of something: **fuel/temperature/pressure etc gauge** *The petrol gauge is still on full.*
2 WIDTH/THICKNESS a measurement of the width or thickness of something such as wire or metal: *a 27 gauge needle* | *heavy gauge black polythene*
3 a gauge of sth something that helps you make a judgment about a person or situation: *Retail sales are a gauge of consumer spending.* | *The tests will give parents a gauge of how their children are doing.*
4 RAILWAY the distance between the lines of a railway or between the wheels of a train: *a standard gauge railway* | **broad/narrow gauge** (=with more/less than the standard distance between the rails)
5 GUN the width of the BARREL of a gun: *a 12-gauge shotgun*

gauge² *v* [T] **1** to judge how people feel about something or what they are likely to do: [+**whether/what/ how etc**] *It is difficult to gauge what the other party's next move will be.* | *I looked at Chris, trying to gauge his reaction.* **2** to measure or calculate something by using a particular instrument or method: *The thermostat will gauge the temperature and control the heat.*

gaunt /gɔːnt $ gɒːnt/ *adj* **1** very thin and pale, especially because of illness or continued worry; ◫ **drawn**: *the old man's gaunt face* **2** *literary* a building, mountain etc that is gaunt looks very plain and unpleasant: *a gaunt cathedral* —**gauntness** *n* [U]

gaunt·let /'gɔːntlɪt $ 'gɒːnt-/ *n* **1 throw down the gauntlet** to invite someone to fight or compete over a disagreement **2 pick up/take up the gauntlet** to accept

G

the invitation to fight or compete over a disagreement **3 run the gauntlet** to be criticized or attacked by a lot of people: *The foreign secretary ran the gauntlet of demonstrators.* **4** [C] a long GLOVE that covers someone's wrist and protects their hand, for example in a factory **5** [C] a GLOVE covered in metal, used for protection by soldiers in the past

gauze /gɔːz $ gɒːz/ *n* [U] **1** very thin transparent material with very small holes in it **2** also **gauze bandage** *AmE* thin cotton with very small holes in it that is used for tying around a wound: *His hands were wrapped in gauze bandages.* **3** a material made of thin threads of metal or plastic: *They covered the tubes with wire gauze.* —**gauzy** *adj*: *a gauzy white dress*

gave /geɪv/ the past tense of GIVE

gav·el /'gævəl/ *n* [C] a small hammer that the person in charge of a meeting, court of law, AUCTION etc hits on a table in order to get people's attention

gawd /gɔːd $ gɒːd/ *interjection informal* used in writing to represent the word 'God' when it is said in this way as an expression of surprise, fear etc

gawk /gɔːk $ gɒːk/ *v* [I] *informal* to look at something for a long time, in a way that looks stupid; ≠ **stare**: [+at] *Don't just stand there gawking at those girls!*

gaw·ky /'gɔːki $ 'gɒːki/ *adj* someone who is gawky moves or behaves in an awkward way; ≠ **clumsy**: *a gawky, long-legged teenager* —**gawkiness** *n* [U]

gawp /gɔːp $ gɒːp/ *v* [I] *BrE informal* to look at something for a long time, especially with your mouth open because you are surprised; ≠ **gape**: [+at] *I was carried out on a stretcher, with everyone gawping at me.* | *He felt their gawping eyes on him.*

gay¹ [S3] /geɪ/ *adj*
1 if someone, especially a man, is gay, they are sexually attracted to people of the same sex; ≠ **homosexual**; → **straight, lesbian**: *the gay community in London* | *gay men and lesbians* | *a gay bar* | *a campaigner for gay rights* (=equal treatment for gay people)
2 *old-fashioned* bright or attractive: *gay colours*
3 *old-fashioned* cheerful and excited: *She felt excited and quite gay.*
4 with gay abandon in a careless way, without careful thought —**gayness** *n* [U] → GAILY, GAIETY

gay² *n* [C] someone who is HOMOSEXUAL, especially a man

gay 'pride *n* [U] a political and social movement that encourages HOMOSEXUAL people not to keep the fact that they are homosexual a secret, and to be proud of themselves: *a gay pride march*

gaze¹ /geɪz/ *v* [I always + adv/prep] to look at someone or something for a long time, giving it all your attention, often without realizing you are doing so; ≠ **stare**: [+into/at etc] *Nell was still gazing out of the window.* | *Patrick sat gazing into space* (=looking straight in front, not at any particular person or thing).

gaze² *n* [singular] a long steady look: *She felt embarrassed under his steady gaze.* | **lower/drop your gaze** *Ellen smiled uncomfortably and lowered her gaze.* | **meet sb's gaze** (=look directly at someone who is looking at you) *He didn't dare to meet her gaze.*

ga·ze·bo /gəˈziːbəʊ $ -ˈzeɪboʊ, -ˈziː-/ *n plural* **gazebos** [C] a small building with open sides in a garden, where you can sit and look at the view

ga·zelle /gəˈzel/ *n* [C] a type of small DEER, which jumps very gracefully and has large beautiful eyes

ga·zette /gəˈzet/ *n* [C] **1** *BrE* an official newspaper, especially one from the government giving important lists of people who have been employed by them etc **2** used in the names of some newspapers: *the Phoenix Gazette*

gaz·et·teer /ˌgæzɪ'tɪə $ -'tɪr/ *n* [C] a list of names of places, printed as a dictionary or as a list at the end of a book of maps

ga·zil·lion /gəˈzɪljən/ *quantifier informal* an extremely large number; ≠ **a lot**: *I have a gazillion things to do.* —**gazillion** *n* [C]: *gazillions of dollars*

ga·zump /gəˈzʌmp/ *v* [T usually passive] *BrE informal* if you are gazumped, the person who is selling you a house sells it to another person who offers them more money: *We were gazumped at the last minute.* —**gazumping** *n* [U]

ga·zun·der /gəˈzʌndə $ -ər/ *v* [T] *BrE informal* **be gazundered** if you are gazundered, someone who has agreed to buy your house says that they will only buy it for less than the amount originally agreed

GB 1 the written abbreviation of *Great Britain* **2** also **Gb** the written abbreviation of *gigabyte* or gigabytes

GBH /ˌdʒiː biː 'eɪtʃ/ *n* [U] *BrE law* **grievous bodily harm** the serious crime of attacking someone and injuring them

GCE /ˌdʒiː siː 'iː/ *n* [C,U] *General Certificate of Education* an examination in a range of subjects, done by students in schools in England and Wales at O LEVEL and A LEVEL. In 1988, GCE O levels were replaced by GCSEs: *two GCE A level passes*

GCSE /ˌdʒiː siː es 'iː/ *n* [C,U] *General Certificate of Secondary Education* an examination in a range of subjects, done by students in schools in England and Wales, usually at the age of 15 or 16; → O level, A level, GNVQ: **do/take (your) GCSEs** | *Adam took his GCSEs last year.* | **GCSE exam/course/coursework/results etc**

GDP /ˌdʒiː diː 'piː/ *n* [singular] *gross domestic product* the total value of all goods and services produced in a country, in one year, except for income received from abroad; → GNP

gear¹ [S3] /gɪə $ gɪr/ *n*
1 IN CARS ETC [C,U] the machinery in a vehicle such as a car, truck, or bicycle that you use to go comfortably at different speeds

in/into ... gear
first/second/third etc gear
high/low gear
top/bottom gear *BrE*
reverse gear (=for driving backwards)
change gear *BrE*
change/switch/shift gears *AmE* (=change to a different gear)
crunch/grind the gears (=change gear in a way that makes an unpleasant noise)
in/into gear (=with a gear connecting the engine to the wheels)
out of gear (=with the engine not connected to the wheels)

His mountain bike had 18 gears. | *Andy drove cautiously along in third gear.* | *Does this thing have a reverse gear?* | *Any cyclist can climb a difficult hill; you just change gear.* | *Don't turn off the engine while you're still in gear.* | *It's a good habit to take the car out of gear while you're at a stoplight.*

2 [C,U] used to talk about the amount of effort and energy that someone is using in a situation: *During this period, Japan's export industries were in top gear* (=were as active as they could be). | *The Republican's propaganda machine moved into high gear.* | **step up a gear** *BrE* (=increase the level of effort) *United stepped up a gear in the second half.*

3 change gear *BrE*; **change/switch/shift gears** *AmE* to start doing something in a different way, especially using more or less energy or effort: *The boss expects us to be able to change gear just like that.*

4 EQUIPMENT [U] a set of equipment or tools you need for a particular activity: *He's crazy about photography – he's got all the gear.* | *We'll need camping gear when we go away.*

5 CLOTHES [U] a set of clothes that you wear for a particular occasion or activity: *Bring your rain gear.* | *police in riot gear*

6 MACHINERY [U] a piece of machinery that performs a particular job: *the landing gear of a plane* | *heavy lifting gear*

7 DRUGS [U] *BrE informal* a word meaning illegal drugs, used by people who take drugs

8 get your ass in gear *AmE informal* used to tell someone to hurry; ◾ **move your ass**: *You'd better get your ass in gear – you're late.*

gear² *v* [T] **be geared to sb/sth** to be organized in a way that is suitable for a particular purpose or situation: *The typical career pattern was geared to men whose wives didn't work.* | **be geared to do sth** *The course curriculum is geared to span three years.*

gear up *phr v* to prepare for something: [+for] *The organization is gearing up for a convention in May.* | **gear up/be geared up to do sth** *Fast food restaurants are geared up to serve thousands of people daily.*

gear·box /ˈɡɪəbɒks $ ˈɡɪrbɑːks/ *n* [C] the system of gears in a vehicle

gear·ing /ˈɡɪərɪŋ $ ˈɡɪr-/ *n* [U] *technical* the relationship between the amount of money that a company is worth and the amount that it owes in debts

'gear ˌlever *n* [C] a metal rod that you move in order to control the gears of a vehicle → see picture at BICYCLE

'gear shift *n* [C] *AmE* a gear lever → see picture at CAR

'gear stick *n* [C] *BrE* a gear lever → see picture at CAR

geck·o /ˈɡekəʊ $ -koʊ/ *n plural* **geckos** *or* **geckoes** [C] a type of small LIZARD

gee¹ /dʒiː/ *interjection especially AmE* used to show that you are surprised or annoyed; → **wow**: *Aw, gee, Mom, do we have to go?*

gee² *v*

gee up *phr v BrE* **1 gee sb** ⇔ **up** *informal* to encourage someone to try harder: *The team needs a captain who can gee them up a bit.* **2 gee up!** used to tell a horse to go faster

'gee-gee *n* [C] *BrE* a horse – used especially by children or when you are talking to children

geek /ɡiːk/ *n* [C] *informal* someone who is not popular because they wear unfashionable clothes, do not know how to behave in social situations, or do strange things; ◾ **nerd**: *a computer geek* —**geeky** *adj*

geese /ɡiːs/ the plural of GOOSE

ˌgee 'whiz *interjection AmE old-fashioned* used to show that you are surprised or annoyed

gee-whiz *adj AmE informal* very good, in a way that is impressive and exciting: *gee-whiz graphics*

geez /dʒiːz/ *interjection* another spelling of JEEZ

gee·zer /ˈɡiːzə $ -ər/ *n* [C] *informal* **1** *BrE* a man: *I know this geezer.* **2** *AmE* an old man

Gei·ger count·er /ˈɡaɪɡə ˌkaʊntə $ -gər ˌkaʊntər/ *n* [C] an instrument that finds and measures RADIOACTIVITY

G8 /dʒiː ˈeɪt/ *n* **the G8** eight of the most important industrial nations in the world (Britain, Canada, France, Germany, Italy, Japan, Russia, and the US) who meet regularly to discuss the world economic situation

gei·sha /ˈɡeɪʃə/ *also* **'geisha girl** *n* [C] a Japanese woman who is trained in the art of dancing, singing, and providing entertainment, especially for men

gel¹ /dʒel/ *n* [C,U] a thick wet substance that is used in beauty or cleaning products: *hair gel* | *shower gel*

gel² *v* **gelled, gelling** **1** *also* **jell** *especially AmE* [I] if a thought, plan etc gels, it becomes clearer or more definite: *Don't start writing until the idea has gelled in your mind.* **2** *also* **jell** *especially AmE* [I] if two or more people gel, they start working well together as a group: [+with] *He did not gel with Chapman.* | *After two days, the group gelled into a team.* **3** *also* **jell** *especially AmE* [I] if a liquid gels, it becomes firmer or thicker **4** [T] to put gel into your hair: *gelled hair*

gel³ /ɡel/ *n* [C] *BrE old-fashioned* used to represent the word 'girl', when it is said in this way

gel·a·tin, **gelatine** /ˈdʒelətɪn $ -tn/ *n* [U] a clear substance obtained from boiled animal bones, used for making JELLY

ge·lat·i·nous /dʒɪˈlætɪnəs $ -ˈlætn-əs/ *adj* in a state between solid and liquid, like a gel

geld /ɡeld/ *v* [T] to remove the TESTICLES of a horse

geld·ing /ˈɡeldɪŋ/ *n* [C] a horse that has been gelded

gel·id /ˈdʒeləd/ *adj written* very cold

gel·ig·nite /ˈdʒelɪɡnaɪt/ *n* [U] a powerful explosive

gem /dʒem/ *n* [C] **1** *also* **'gem stone** a beautiful stone that has been cut into a special shape; ◾ **jewel**: *precious gems* → see picture at STONE **2** something that is very special or beautiful: *Every single ad in the campaign has been a gem.* | *The Fortune is a tiny gem of a theatre.* | [+of] *little gems of advice* **3** a very helpful or special person: *Ben, you're a real gem!*

Gem·i·ni /ˈdʒemɪnaɪ $ -ni/ *n* **1** [U] the third sign of the ZODIAC, represented by TWINS, which some people believe affects the character and life of people born between May 22 and June 21 **2** [C] someone who was born between May 22 and June 21

gen¹ /dʒen/ *n* [U] *BrE informal* information: [+on] *She has all the gen on cheap flights.*

gen² *v* **genned, genning**

gen up *phr v BrE informal* to learn a lot of information about something for a particular purpose: [+on] *It's a good idea to gen up on the company's product before the interview.*

Gen. *also* **Gen** *BrE* the written abbreviation of *General*: *Gen. Philippe Morillon*

gen·darme /ˈʒɒndɑːm $ ˈʒɑːndɑːrm/ *n* [C] a French police officer

gen·der /ˈdʒendə $ -ər/ *n*
1 [C,U] the fact of being male or female

gender differences/distinctions (=differences between men and women)
gender roles
gender inequality/bias (=when one gender is treated more fairly than another)
gender relations
gender stereotype (=a fixed idea of what men or women are like)
gender politics (=the way that men and women compete with each other for power)
gender issues (=ideas and problems related to being male or female in society)
gender identity (=whether someone is male or female)

people of the same gender | *Discrimination on grounds of race or gender is forbidden.* | *There may be* **gender differences** *in attitudes to paid work.* | *traditional* **gender roles** | **gender biases** *in books* | *toys that do not reinforce* **gender stereotypes** | *a science fiction story dealing with* **gender issues**

2 [C] males or females, considered as a group: *differences between the genders*
3 a) [U] the system in some languages of marking words such as nouns, adjectives, and PRONOUNS as being MASCULINE, FEMININE, or NEUTER **b)** [C] a group such as FEMININE into which words are divided in this system

'gender ˌbender *n* [C] *informal* someone who behaves or dresses in a way typical of the opposite sex

'gender ˌbias *n* [C,U] when men and women are treated differently, in a way that is unfair

ˌgender-spe'cific *adj* relating only to males or only to females: *gender-specific language*

gene S2 W2 /dʒiːn/ *n* [C] a part of a cell in a living thing that controls what it looks like, how it grows, and how it develops. People get their genes from their parents: *human genes* | *the genes that regulate cell division*

ge·ne·al·o·gy /ˌdʒiːniˈælədʒi/ *n plural* **genealogies** **1** [U] the study of the history of families **2** [C] a drawing or description that explains how each person in a family is related to the others —**genealogist** *n* [C] —**genealogical** /ˌdʒiːniəˈlɒdʒɪkəl $ -ˈlɑː-/ *adj*: *a useful source of genealogical information*

'gene pool *n* [C] all of the genes available to a particular SPECIES

gen·e·ra /ˈdʒenərə/ the plural of GENUS

G

gen·e·ral¹ [S1] [W1] /'dʒenərəl/ adj [usually before noun]
1 [NOT DETAILED] describing or relating to only the main features or parts of something, not the details: *a general introduction to computing* | *I skimmed through it to get a general impression of the text.* | *I have a general idea of what I want to express.* | *He spoke in general terms about greater competitiveness.*
2 [RELATING TO WHOLE] involving the whole of a situation, group, or thing, rather than specific parts of it: *There has been a general decline in standards.* | *ways to improve your general health*
3 [ORDINARY] ordinary or usual: *general cooking and cleaning* | *I hate paperwork as a general rule.*
4 [MOST PEOPLE] shared by or affecting most people, or most of the people in a group: *These courses are based around topics of general interest.* | *How soon can the drug be made available for general use?*
5 [NOT LIMITED] not limited to one use, activity, subject etc: *The next ten minutes passed in general conversation.* | *It's a good general fertilizer.* | *Watford General Hospital* | *This type of microphone is suitable for general use.*
6 [APPROXIMATE] used to talk about an approximate area or direction: *Pat and his friend were in the general area of the crime when it happened.* | *They started walking in the general direction of the pub.*
7 [JOB] used in the name of a job to show that the person who does it has complete responsibility: *the general manager* | *the Attorney General* → GENERALLY

general² n **1** [C] an officer of very high rank in the army or air force **2 in general a)** usually or in most situations: *In general, about 10% of the candidates are eventually offered positions.* **b)** used when talking about the whole of a situation, group, or thing, rather than specific parts of it: *a feeling of dissatisfaction with life in general* | *These policies are unpopular with politicians and people in general.* | *We're trying to raise awareness about the environment in general and air pollution in particular.*

,general anaes'thetic *BrE*; general anesthetic *AmE* n [C,U] a medicine that makes you unconscious during an operation so that you do not feel any pain; → local anaesthetic: *I had the operation done under general anaesthetic.*

,general 'counsel n [C] **1** the legal officer of a US company with the highest rank **2** a firm of US lawyers that gives general legal advice

,general de'livery n [U] *AmE* a post office department that keeps someone's letters until that person comes to get them; ▣ poste restante *BrE*

,general e'lection n [C] an election in which all the people in a country who can vote elect a government: *during the 1987 general election campaign* | *an attempt to persuade the government to hold a general election* (=have a general election)

,general 'headquarters n [plural] the place from which the actions of an organization, especially a military one, are controlled

gen·e·ral·ise /'dʒenərəlaɪz/ v a British spelling of GENERALIZE

gen·e·ral·ist /'dʒenərəlɪst/ n [C] a person who knows about many different things and can do many things well; ▣ specialist —generalist adj

gen·e·ral·i·ty /,dʒenə'rælɪti/ n plural generalities **1** [C usually plural] a very general statement that avoids mentioning details or specific cases: *The Secretary of State has given us nothing today but bland generalities.* **2** the generality of sth *BrE formal* most of a group of people or things: *Temporary workers are considerably younger than the generality of workers.* **3** [U] *formal* the quality of being true or useful in most situations

gen·e·ral·i·za·tion also **-isation** *BrE* /,dʒenərəlaɪ'zeɪʃən $ -lə-/ n **1** [C] a statement about all the members of a group that may be true in some or

many situations but is not true in every case: *You can't make generalizations about what men and women are like.* | broad/sweeping/gross generalization *a sweeping generalization based on speculation* **2** [U] the act of making generalizations

gen·e·ral·ize also **-ise** *BrE* /'dʒenərəlaɪz/ v **1** [I] to form a general principle or opinion after considering only a small number of facts or examples: [+from] *She has a tendency to generalize from her husband to all men.* **2** [I] to make a general statement about the whole of a group or thing: [+about] *It is difficult to generalise about the kind of people who come on these courses.* **3** [T] *formal* to say that an idea, result etc is related to a larger group: *Can we generalise this principle?* | generalize sth to sth *the issue of whether the research findings can be generalized to a wider population*

gen·e·ral·ized also **-ised** *BrE* /'dʒenərəlaɪzd/ adj [usually before noun] involving or relating to many things, people, or parts: *generalized statements* | *generalized anxiety*

,general 'knowledge n [U] knowledge of facts about many different subjects: *a general knowledge quiz*

gen·er·al·ly [S1] [W1] /'dʒenərəli/ adv **1** considering or relating to the whole of a thing or group, rather than to details or specific cases or parts; ▣ broadly: *It was generally a positive conversation.* | *She's not really ill, just generally run-down.* | [sentence adverb]: *Generally, part-timers work in low-status, low-wage occupations.* | *The second survey was concerned with working-class culture more generally.* **2** by or to most people; ▣ widely: generally regarded/accepted/known etc *The plants are generally regarded as weeds.* | *a generally accepted view* | *It could be five years before the drug is generally available.* **3** usually or most of the time; ▣ usually: *I generally get in to work by 8.00.* **4** generally speaking used to introduce a statement that is true in most cases but not always: *Generally speaking, the more expensive the stereo, the better it is.*

,general 'practice n **1** [U] the work of a doctor or lawyer who deals with all the ordinary types of illnesses or legal cases, rather than one specific type **2** [C] a group of lawyers or doctors who do all types of work

,general prac'titioner n [C] a doctor who is trained in general medicine; ▣ GP

,general 'public n the general public [also + plural verb *BrE*] the ordinary people in a country, rather than people belonging to a particular group: *health education aimed at the general public*

,general-'purpose adj [only before noun] suitable for most situations or jobs, or having a wide range of uses: *a general-purpose computer*

gen·er·al·ship /'dʒenərəlʃɪp/ n [U] the skill or position of being a general

,general 'staff n the general staff the group of military officers who work for a military leader

,general 'store n [C] a shop that sells a wide variety of goods, especially one in a small town

,general 'strike n [C] a situation when most of the workers in a country refuse to work in order to protest about working conditions, wages etc

gen·e·rate [W2] /'dʒenəreɪt/ v [T] **1** to produce or cause something; ▣ create: *a useful technique for generating new ideas* | *The program would generate a lot of new jobs.* | generate revenue/profits/income etc *Tourism generates income for local communities.* | generate excitement/interest/support etc *The project generated enormous interest.* **2** to produce heat, electricity, or another form of energy: *Wind turbines generate electricity for the local community.*

gen·e·ra·tion [S2] [W2] /,dʒenə'reɪʃən/ n **1** [C also + plural verb *BrE*] all people of about the same

age: *Like most of my generation, I had never known a war.* | *In my generation the divorce rate is very high.* | *the need to preserve the planet for future generations* | [+of] *the post-war generation of writers* | **the younger/ older generation** (=the younger or older people in society) *The younger generation don't know what hard work is.* | *The story has been handed down from generation to generation.*
2 [C] all the members of a family of about the same age: *Friction is common when three generations live together.* | **first-generation/second-generation etc** (=being a member of the first, second etc generation to live or be born in a country) *first-generation immigrants* | *a third-generation American*
3 [C] the average period of time between the birth of a person and the birth of that person's children: **for generations** *Some families have lived here for generations.* | *The country's attitude toward government is harsher than it was a generation ago.*
4 [C] a group of things that were developed from something else, or from which better things were developed: [+of] *the new generation of mobile phones* | *the first generation of nuclear power stations* | **first-generation/second-generation etc** *second-generation computers*
5 [U] the process of producing something or making something happen; ≡ **production**: [+of] *the generation of electricity*

gen·e·ra·tion·al /ˌdʒenəˈreɪʃənəl/ *adj* [usually before noun] connected with a particular generation or the relationship between different generations: *generational conflict* | *generational divisions*

gene'ration ,gap *n* [singular] the lack of understanding or the differences between older people and younger people

Generation X /ˌdʒenəreɪʃən 'eks/ *n* [U] the group of people who were born during the late 1960s and the 1970s in the US

gen·e·ra·tive /ˈdʒenərətɪv/ *adj formal* **1** able to produce something: *the generative power of the life force* **2** **generative grammar/linguistics/phonology** the description of a language using rules that produce all the possible correct sentences of the language

gen·e·ra·tor /ˈdʒenəreɪtə $ ər/ *n* [C] **1** a machine that produces electricity: *an emergency generator* **2** a company that produces electricity **3** something that produces something else: [+of] *good generators of income*

ge·ner·ic /dʒɪˈnerɪk/ *adj* [usually before noun] **1** relating to a whole group of things rather than to one thing: **generic term/name (for sth)** *Fine Arts is a generic term for subjects such as painting, music and sculpture.* **2** a generic product does not have a special name to show that it is made by a particular company: **generic drugs** —**generically** /-kli/ *adv*

gen·e·ros·i·ty /ˌdʒenəˈrɒsəti $ -ˈrɑː-/ *n* [U] a generous attitude, or generous behaviour: *an act of great generosity* | [+to/towards] *his generosity to the poor* | *I shall never forget the generosity shown by the people of Bastaisk.* | *acts of generosity*

gen·e·rous /ˈdʒenərəs/ *adj* **1** someone who is generous is willing to give money, spend time etc, in order to help people or give them pleasure; ≡ **mean**: [+to] *She's always very generous to the kids.* | [+with] *Jim is very generous with his time.* | **it/that is generous (of sb)** *It was generous of them to ask Anna along.* | **generous offer/support/donation etc** *my employer's generous offer to pay the bill* **2** larger or more than the usual size or amount; ≡ **measly**: *a generous glass of wine* | **generous amount/helping/measure etc** *a generous helping of pasta* | *He had a well-shaped, generous mouth.* **3** sympathetic in the way you deal with people, and tending to see the good qualities in someone or something; ≡ **mean**: *She was generous enough to overlook my little mistake.* —**generously** *adv*: *Please give generously to the refugee fund.* | *Spread each slice generously with butter.*

gen·e·sis /ˈdʒenəsɪs/ *n* [singular] *formal* the beginning or origin of something: [+of] *the genesis of the myth*

'gene ,therapy *n* [U] a way of treating certain diseases by using GENETIC ENGINEERING

ge·net·ic /dʒɪˈnetɪk/ *adj* relating to GENES or GENETICS: *genetic defects* | *each person's genetic make-up* | *genetic research* —**genetically** /-kli/ *adv*: *genetically determined characteristics*

ge,netically 'modified also **ge,netically engin'eered** *adj* **GM** genetically modified foods or plants have had their genetic structure changed so that they are not affected by particular diseases or harmful insects

ge,netic 'code *n* [C] the arrangement of GENES that controls the way a living thing develops

ge,netic engin'eering *n* [U] the science of changing the genetic structure of an animal, plant, or human, usually to make them stronger or healthier —**genetic engineer** *n* [C]

ge,netic 'fingerprinting *n* [U] the process of examining the pattern of someone's GENES, especially in order to find out if they are guilty of a crime

ge·net·ics /dʒɪˈnetɪks/ *n* [U] the study of how the qualities of living things are passed on in their GENES —**geneticist** /-tɪsɪst/ *n* [C]

ge·ni·al /ˈdʒiːniəl/ *adj* friendly and happy: *a genial smile* —**genially** *adv* —**geniality** /ˌdʒiːniˈæləti/ *n* [U]

ge·nie /ˈdʒiːni/ *n* [C] a magical creature in old Arabian stories that will do what you want when you call it

gen·i·tal /ˈdʒenɪtl/ *adj* [only before noun] relating to or affecting the outer sex organs: *the genital area* | *genital mutilation*

gen·i·tals /ˈdʒenɪtlz/ also **gen·i·ta·li·a** /ˌdʒenɪˈteɪliə/ *n* [plural] *formal* or *technical* the outer sex organs

gen·i·tive /ˈdʒenɪtɪv/ *n* [C] *technical* a form of a noun in some languages which shows a relationship of possession or origin between one thing and another —**genitive** *adj*

ge·ni·us /ˈdʒiːniəs/ *n* **1** [U] a very high level of intelligence, mental skill, or ability, which only a few people have: *The film reveals Fellini's genius.* | **work/ writer/man etc of genius** *Wynford was an architect of genius.* | **a stroke of genius** (=a very clever idea) *At the time, his appointment seemed a stroke of genius.* | *a work of pure genius* **2** [C] someone who has an unusually high level of intelligence, mental skill, or ability: *Freud was a genius.* | **musical/comic/mathematical etc genius** | **a genius at (doing) sth** *My father was a genius at storytelling.* **3** **a genius for (doing) sth** special skill at doing something: *That woman has a genius for organization.* | *Warhol's genius for publicity*

gen·o·cide /ˈdʒenəsaɪd/ *n* [U] the deliberate murder of a whole group or race of people; → **ethnic cleansing**: *The military leaders were accused of genocide.* —**genocidal** /ˌdʒenəˈsaɪdl/ *adj*: *a genocidal regime*

ge·nome /ˈdʒiːnəʊm $ -noʊm/ *n* [C] *technical* all the GENES in one cell of living thing: *the human genome*

ge·no·mic /dʒiːˈnəʊmɪk $ -ˈnɑː-/ *adj technical* relating to all the GENES that are found in one type of living thing

gen·o·type /ˈdʒenətaɪp, ˈdʒiː-/ *n* [C] *technical* the GENETIC nature of one type of living thing

gen·re /ˈʒɒnrə $ ˈʒɑːnrə/ *n* [C] *formal* a particular type of art, writing, music etc, which has certain features that all examples of this type share: [+of] *a new genre of filmmaking* | *a literary genre*

gent /dʒent/ *n* [C] **1** *informal especially BrE* a GENTLEMAN: *a well-dressed elderly gent* | *I've always prided myself on being a perfect gent.* **2** **the gents** *BrE* a public toilet for men; ≡ **men's room** *AmE*

gen·teel /dʒenˈtiːl/ *adj* **1** polite, gentle, or graceful: *She broke into a genteel run.* **2** old-fashioned from or relating to a good social class —**genteelly** *adv*

gen·tian /'dʒenʃən/ n [C] a small plant with blue or purple flowers that grows in mountain areas

gen·tile, Gentile /'dʒentaɪl/ n [C] someone who is not Jewish —**gentile** adj [only before noun]

gen·til·i·ty /dʒen'tɪləti/ n [U] formal the quality of being polite, gentle, or graceful, and of seeming to belong to a high social class: The hotel had an air of discreet gentility.

gen·tle S3 W3 /'dʒentl/ adj
1 kind and careful in the way you behave or do things, so that you do not hurt or damage anyone or anything; ≠ **rough**: Arthur was a very gentle, caring person. | **gentle voice/smile/touch** 'Where does it hurt?' she asked in a gentle voice. | [+with] Be gentle with the baby.
2 not extreme, strong, or violent: **gentle exercise/walk/stroll etc** a program of regular gentle exercise | the **gentle pressure** of Jill's hand | After a little **gentle persuasion**, she agreed to go back to her family. | Melt the butter over a **gentle heat** (=low heat).
3 a gentle wind or rain is soft and light: a **gentle breeze**
4 a gentle hill or slope is not steep or sharp: the gentle slopes of Mt Pelee —**gentleness** n [U] → GENTLY

gen·tle·folk /'dʒentlfəʊk $ -foʊk/ n [plural] old use people belonging to the higher social classes

gen·tle·man S3 W2 /'dʒentlmən/ n plural gentle-men /-mən/ [C]
1 a polite word for a man, used especially when talking to or about a man you do not know; → **lady**: Could you serve this gentleman please, Miss Bath? | Good morning, **ladies and gentlemen**. | An elderly gentleman was asleep next to the fire.
2 a man who is always polite, has good manners, and treats other people well; → **lady**: Martin – always the **perfect gentleman** – got to his feet when my mother walked in. | Mr Field was a **real gentleman**.
3 old-fashioned a man from a high social class, especially one whose family owns a lot of property; → **lady**: an English **country gentleman**

gentleman 'farmer n [C] especially BrE a man belonging to a high social class who owns and runs a farm, but who usually hires people to do the work

gen·tle·man·ly /'dʒentlmənli/ adj a man who is gentlemanly speaks and behaves politely, and treats other people with respect

gentleman's a'greement n [C] an agreement that is not written down, made between people who trust each other

gen·tle·wom·an /'dʒentl,wʊmən/ n plural gentle-women /-,wɪmɪn/ [C] old use a woman who belongs to a high social class

gent·ly W3 /'dʒentli/ adv
1 in a gentle way: 'You go back to bed now,' he said gently. | She kissed me gently on the cheek. | Gently cook the peppers for 10–15 minutes. | Rain pattered gently on the roof above. | The road curved gently upwards.
2 **gently/gently does it!** BrE spoken used to tell someone to be careful when they are handling something, moving something etc: Gently, Sammy, you don't want to break it.

gen·tri·fi·ca·tion /,dʒentrɪfɪ'keɪʃən/ n [U] a gradual process in which an area in bad condition where poor people live is changed by people with more money coming to live there and improving it —**gentrify** /'dʒentrɪfaɪ/ v [T usually passive]

gen·try /'dʒentri/ n [plural] old-fashioned people who belong to a high social class: a member of the **landed gentry** (=gentry who own land)

gen·u·flect /'dʒenjʊflekt/ v [I] formal **1** to bend one or both knees when in church or a holy place as a sign of respect **2** to show too much respect towards someone or something – used to show disapproval; ≈ **kow-tow**: [+to] He was a man of principle, refusing to genuflect to the party leadership. —**genuflection** /,dʒenjʊ'flekʃən/ n [C,U]

gen·u·ine S3 W3 /'dʒenjuɪn/ adj
1 a genuine feeling, desire etc is one that you really feel, not one you pretend to feel; ≈ **sincere**: **genuine interest/concern/desire etc** The reforms are motivated by a genuine concern for the disabled. | a genuine fear of invasion | 'Did he really?' Her surprise seemed genuine.
2 something genuine really is what it seems to be; ≈ **real**: We need laws that will protect genuine refugees. | The strap is genuine leather.
3 someone who is genuine is honest and friendly and you feel you can trust them; ≈ **false**: She is the most genuine person I've ever met.
4 the genuine article a) informal a person or thing that is a true example of their type: If you want to meet a real Southerner, Jake is the genuine article. **b)** something that is real and is not a copy intended to deceive people: Some fake designer clothes are so good that people have no idea they're not buying the genuine article. —**genuinely** adv: The boy seemed genuinely interested. —**genuineness** n [U]

ge·nus /'dʒiːnəs, 'dʒen-/ n plural genera /'dʒenərə/ [C] technical one of the groups into which scientists divide animals or plants, in which the animals or plants are closely related but cannot produce babies together. A genus includes fewer members than a FAMILY and more members than a SPECIES.

ge·o- /dʒiːəʊ, dʒɪə $ dʒiːoʊ, dʒɪə/ prefix technical relating to the Earth or its surface: geophysics | geopolitical

ge·o·des·ic /,dʒiːəʊ'desɪk◂, -'diː- $,dʒiːoʊ-/ adj [only before noun] having a shape or structure made from small flat pieces, usually TRIANGLES or PENTAGONS, that are put together to form curves: a geodesic dome

ge·og·ra·pher /dʒiːˈɒɡrəfə, 'dʒɒɡ- $ dʒiːˈɑːɡrəfər/ n [C] someone who has studied geography to a high level

ge·o·graph·i·cal /,dʒiːəˈɡræfɪkəl◂/ also **ge·o·graph·ic** /-ˈɡræfɪk◂/ adj **1** relating to the place in an area, country etc where something or someone is: **geographical area/location/position** a large geographical area | their geographical proximity to Japan (=nearness to Japan) **2** relating to geography: geographical research work —**geographically** /-kli/ adv

ge·og·ra·phy /dʒiːˈɒɡrəfi, 'dʒɒɡ- $ dʒiːˈɑːɡ-/ n [U] **1** the study of the countries, oceans, rivers, mountains, cities etc of the world: a geography lesson → PHYSICAL GEOGRAPHY, POLITICAL GEOGRAPHY **2** the geography of a building, city etc is the way all its parts are arranged: [+of] The geography of the flats made it hard to get to know our neighbours.

ge·ol·o·gy /dʒiˈɒlədʒi $ -ˈɑːlə-/ n [U] the study of the rocks, soil etc that make up the Earth, and of the way they have changed since the Earth was formed —**geologist** n [C] —**geological** /,dʒiːəˈlɒdʒɪkəl $ -ˈlɑː-/ adj: geological periods —**geologically** /-kli/ adv

ge·o·man·cer /'dʒiːəmænsə $ -ər/ n [C] an expert in geomancy

ge·o·man·cy /'dʒiːəmænsi/ n [U] the belief that arranging your home, house, office etc in a particular way will bring you good or bad luck; → **feng shui**

ge·o·met·ric /,dʒiːəˈmetrɪk◂/ also **ge·o·met·ri·cal** /-trɪkəl/ adj **1** having or using the shapes and lines in GEOMETRY, such as circles or squares, especially when these are arranged in regular patterns: a geometric design **2** relating to GEOMETRY —**geometrically** /-kli/ adv

geo,metric pro'gression n [C] a set of numbers in order, in which each is multiplied by a specific number to produce the next number in the series (as in 1, 2, 4, 8, 16,...); → **arithmetic progression**

ge·om·e·try /dʒiˈɒmɪtri $ -ˈɑːm-/ n [U] the study in MATHEMATICS of the angles and shapes formed by the relationships of lines, surfaces, and solid objects in space

ge·o·phys·ics /,dʒiːəʊ'fɪzɪks $,dʒiːoʊ-/ n [U] the study of the movements of parts of the Earth, and the forces involved with this, including the weather, the oceans etc —**geophysical** adj —**geophysicist** /-z'ɔ-sᵻst/ n [C]

ge·o·pol·i·tics /ˌdʒiːəʊˈpɒlᵻtɪks $ ˌdʒiːoʊˈpɑː-/ n [U] ideas and activities relating to the way that a country's position, population etc affect its political development and its relationship with other countries, or the study of this —**geopolitical** /ˌdʒiːəʊpəˈlɪtɪkəl◂ $ ˌdʒiːoʊ-/ adj

Geor·die /ˈdʒɔːdi $ ˈdʒɔːr-/ n BrE informal **1** [C] someone from Tyneside in North East England **2** [U] a way of speaking that is typical of people from Tyneside

Geor·gian /ˈdʒɔːdʒən, -dʒiən $ ˈdʒɔːrdʒən/ adj Georgian buildings, furniture etc come from the 18th century, when Britain was ruled by the Kings George the First, Second, and Third: *Georgian townhouse*

ge·o·ther·mal /ˌdʒiːəʊˈθɜːməl◂ $ -oʊˈθɜːr-/ adj relating to or coming from the heat inside the earth: *a geothermal energy plant*

ge·ra·ni·um /dʒəˈreɪniəm/ n [C] a plant with red, pink, or white flowers and round leaves

ger·bil /ˈdʒɜːbəl $ ˈdʒɜːr-/ n [C] a small animal with fur, a tail, and long back legs, that is often kept as a pet

ge·ri·at·ric /ˌdʒeriˈætrɪk◂/ adj **1** [only before noun] relating to the medical care and treatment of old people: *a specialist in geriatric medicine* **2** informal too old to work well: *a geriatric rock star*

ge·ri·at·rics /ˌdʒeriˈætrɪks/ n [U] the medical treatment and care of old people; → **gerontology** —**geriatrician** /ˌdʒeriəˈtrɪʃən/ n [C]

germ /dʒɜːm $ dʒɜːrm/ n [C] **1** a very small living thing that can make you ill → BACTERIA: *Put disinfectant down the toilet to kill any germs.* **2 the germ of an idea/theory/feeling etc** the early stage of an idea, feeling etc that may develop into something bigger and more important: *The germ of a story began to form in his mind.* **3** technical the part of a plant or animal that can develop into a new plant or animal: *germ cells containing DNA* → WHEATGERM, GERM WARFARE

Ger·man¹ /ˈdʒɜːmən $ ˈdʒɜːr-/ adj relating to Germany, its people, or its language: *German history* | *a young German couple*

German² n **1** [C] someone from Germany **2** [U] the language used in Germany, Austria, and parts of Switzerland

ger·mane /dʒɜːˈmeɪn $ dʒɜːr-/ adj formal an idea, remark etc that is germane to something is related to it in an important and suitable way; ◼ **relevant**: [+to] *an article which is germane to the subject being discussed*

Ger·man·ic /dʒɜːˈmænɪk $ dʒɜːr-/ adj **1** relating to the language family that includes German, Dutch, Swedish, and English **2** relating to or typical of Germany or German people

,German 'measles n [U] an infectious disease that causes red spots on your body, and can damage an unborn child; ◼ **rubella**

,German 'shepherd n [C] a large dog rather like a WOLF that is often used by the police, for guarding property etc; ◼ **Alsatian** BrE

ger·mi·nate /ˈdʒɜːmᵻneɪt $ ˈdʒɜːr-/ v **1** [I,T] if a seed germinates, or if it is germinated, it begins to grow; ◼ **sprout** **2** [I] if an idea, feeling etc germinates, it begins to develop: *The idea of setting up his own company began to germinate in his mind.* —**germination** /ˌdʒɜːmᵻˈneɪʃən $ ˌdʒɜːr-/ n [U]

germ 'warfare n [U] the use of harmful BACTERIA in war to cause illness and death among the enemy

ger·on·tol·o·gy /ˌdʒerɒnˈtɒlədʒi $ ˌdʒerənˈtɑː-/ n [U] the scientific study of old age and its effects on the body; → **geriatrics** —**gerontologist** n [C] —**gerontological** /dʒəˌrɒntəˈlɒdʒɪkəl◂ $ -ˌrɑːntəˈlɑː-/ adj

ger·ry·man·der·ing /ˈdʒerimændərɪŋ/ n [U] when politicians change the size and borders of an area

before an election, so that one person, group, or party has an unfair advantage —**gerrymander** v [I,T]

ger·und /ˈdʒerənd/ n [C] technical a noun in the form of the PRESENT PARTICIPLE of a verb, for example 'shopping' in the sentence 'I like shopping'

ge·stalt /gəˈʃtɑːlt/ n [C] technical a whole thing that is different from all its parts, and has qualities that are not present in any of its parts by themselves: *gestalt psychology*

Ge·sta·po /geˈstɑːpəʊ $ -poʊ/ n **the Gestapo** the secret police force used by the state in Germany during the Nazi period

ges·ta·tion /dʒeˈsteɪʃən/ n [singular, U] **1** medical the process by which a child or young animal develops inside its mother's body before birth, or the period of time when this happens; → **pregnancy**: *The gestation period of a horse is about 11 months.* **2** formal the process by which a new idea, piece of work etc is developed, or the period of time when this happens; ◼ **development**: **in gestation** *The report was a very long time in gestation.*

ges·tic·u·late /dʒeˈstɪkjᵿleɪt/ v [I] to make movements with your arms and hands, usually while speaking, because you are excited, angry, or cannot think of the right words to use; ◼ **gesture**: *Jane gesticulated wildly and shouted 'Stop! Stop!'* —**gesticulation** /dʒeˌstɪkjᵿˈleɪʃən/ n [C,U]

ges·ture¹ W3 /ˈdʒestʃə $ -ər/ n **1** [C,U] a movement of part of your body, especially your hands or head, to show what you mean or how you feel: **in a ... gesture (of sth)** *Jim raised his hands in a despairing gesture.* | *Luke made an obscene gesture with his finger.* | [+of] *She shook her head with a gesture of impatience.* **2** [C] something that you say or do, often something small, to show how you feel about someone or something

---

nice gesture
symbolic gesture (=something you do to show people how you feel)
grand gesture (=something you do to make people notice you)
gesture of goodwill/friendship
gesture of solidarity/support
gesture of defiance
make a gesture (towards sb/sth) (=do something to show that you have some respect for someone or something)

*They decided it would be a **nice gesture** to send her a card.* | *Tearing up the price list was simply a **symbolic gesture.*** | [+of] *As a **gesture of goodwill**, we have decided to waive the charges on this occasion.* | [+towards] *The Queen has now **made a gesture** towards public opinion.*

—**gestural** adj

gesture² v [I] to move your hand, arm, or head to tell someone something, or show them what you mean: [+to/towards/at] *Brad gestured towards the door. 'Get out.'* | **gesture for sb to do sth** *He gestured for her to take a seat.*

ge·sund·heit /gəˈzʊndhaɪt/ interjection AmE used to wish someone good health when they have just SNEEZED; ◼ **bless you**

get S1 W1 /get/ v past tense **got** /gɒt $ gɑːt/, past participle **got** BrE, **gotten** /ˈgɒtn $ ˈgɑːtn/ AmE, present participle **getting**

1 RECEIVE [T not in passive] to receive something that someone gives you or sends you: *She got loads of presents.* | *What did you get for Christmas?* | *We get a lot of junk mail.* | **get sth from sb** *We got a letter from Pam this morning.* | **get sth off sb** spoken informal: *I got it off*

G

my Dad. | *I **got** a few games **free** when I bought my computer.* → see box at GAIN[1]

2 OBTAIN [T] to obtain something by finding it, asking for it, or paying for it: *We need to get help quickly!* | *It would be a good idea to get professional advice.* | *You may be able to get a grant from the local authority.* | *He cleared his throat to get our attention.* | **get sth for sb** *I want you to get some information for me.* | **get sb sth** *His father managed to get him a job at the local factory.*

3 BRING [T] to bring someone or something back from somewhere: *Run upstairs and get a pillow.* | *I went back into the office to get a pen.* | *Shall I **go and get** the phone book?* | **get sb/sth from sth** *She's just gone to get the kids from school.* | **get sth for sb** *I'll get a towel for you.* | **get sb sth** *I'll get you a chair.*; → see box at BRING

4 BUY [T] **a)** to buy something: *Where did you get that jacket?* | **get sth for sb** *Joe's going to get tickets for all of us.* | **get sb sth** *While you're out, could you get me some batteries?* | **get yourself sth** *He's just got himself a new van.* | **get sth from sth** *I usually get vegetables from the supermarket.* | **get sth for $20/£100/50p etc** *You can get a decent PC for about £500 now.* | *It's a lovely coat, and I managed to **get it cheap** in the sales.* **b)** spoken to pay for something for someone else: *I'll get these drinks.* **c)** to buy a newspaper regularly: *My parents always used to get the Daily Telegraph.*

5 MONEY [T] **a)** to receive money for doing work: *Hospital doctors get a minimum of £50,000 a year.* | **get £2000/$4000 etc for doing sth** *He gets £4 an hour for stacking shelves at the local supermarket.* **b)** to receive money when you sell something: **get £100/$200 etc for sth** *You should get a couple of hundred pounds for your old car.* | *Did you **get a good price for** it?* → see box at GAIN[1]

6 HAVE A FEELING/IDEA [T] to start to have a feeling or an idea: *She began to get an uncomfortable feeling that she was being watched.* | *I got a terrible shock when I saw how ill he looked.* | *I got the impression that everyone was fed up with us.* | **get pleasure from/out of sth** *She gets a lot of pleasure from her garden.*

7 HAVE/EXPERIENCE [T] to have, do, or experience something: *You don't get enough exercise.* | *I never get time to read these days.* | *The west of the country gets quite a lot of rain.* | *We might get the chance to go to America this year.*

8 ILLNESS [T not in passive] to catch an illness: *I got flu last winter and was in bed for three weeks.* | *She was worried she might get food poisoning.*

9 ACHIEVE [T] to achieve something: *I got 98% in my last maths test.* | *the person who gets the highest score*

10 RECEIVE A PUNISHMENT [T] to receive something as a punishment: *He got ten years in prison for his part in the robbery.*

11 ARRIVE [I always + adv/prep] to arrive somewhere: *What time will we get there?* | *We didn't get home until midnight.* | [+to] *We got to Paris that evening.*

12 REACH A POINT [I always + adv/prep] to reach a particular point or stage of something: *I've got as far as chapter 5.* | *I couldn't wait to get to the end of the book.* | *Where have you got up to in the story?* | *It was disappointing to lose, having got this far in the competition.*

13 get (sb) somewhere/anywhere/nowhere if you get somewhere, or if an action gets you somewhere, you make progress: *I think we're getting somewhere at last.* | *We didn't seem to be getting anywhere.* | *I've tried arguing, but it got me nowhere.*

14 MOVE [I always +adv/prep] to move or go somewhere: *Get out of my house!* | *We managed to get past the guards.* | *They shouted at us to get back.* | *Peter **got to** his feet* (=stood up).

15 MAKE STH MOVE [T always + adv/prep] to make something or someone move to a different place or position, especially with some difficulty: *I couldn't get the disk out of the computer.* | *Could you help me get the wardrobe up the stairs?* | *We must get food and emergency aid into the area as quickly as possible.*

16 TRAVEL [T] to travel somewhere on a train, bus etc:

You can get a bus to the station. | *I got the 9:15 from London to Edinburgh.*

17 BECOME [linking verb] to change to a new feeling, situation, or state; **▣ become**: *Don't get upset.* | *She soon got bored with the job.* | *He calmed down as he got older.* | *Eat your dinner before it gets cold.* | *This is getting silly.* | **get to be sth** informal: *It's getting to be a problem.* | *How did you get to be so smart?*; → see box at BECOME

18 MAKE SB/STH BECOME STH [T] to make someone or something change to a new feeling, situation, or state: *Sometimes she gets me so angry!* | *Don't get the children too excited.* | *He was terrified of getting her pregnant.* | *It took them fifteen minutes to get the boat ready.*

19 BE HURT/BROKEN ETC [linking verb, T] used to say that something, especially something bad, happens to someone or something: **get hurt/broken/stolen etc** *You might get hurt if you stand there.* | *Mind the camera doesn't get broken.* | *My dad got killed in a car crash.* | *I knew I would get shouted at if I was late home.* | *This is a question we very often get asked.* | **get sth caught/stuck etc** *She got her foot caught in the wire.*

20 MAKE STH HAPPEN TO SB/STH [T] **a)** to accidentally make someone or something experience something: *You're going to get us all killed!* | *Mind you don't get yourself burned.* **b)** to do something, or arrange for it to be done: *I need to get the washing machine fixed.* | *We must get this work finished on time.*

21 MAKE STH DO STH [T not in passive] to make something do a particular thing: **get sth to do sth** *I couldn't get the engine to start.* | **get sth doing sth** *We got the lawn mower working again eventually.*

22 MAKE SB DO STH [T not in passive] to persuade or force someone to do something: **get sb to do sth** *I'll get Terry to check the wiring for me.* | *We couldn't get him to sign the agreement.* | **get sb doing sth** *In the end, we got the children clearing the playground.*

23 UNDERSTAND [T not in passive or progressive] informal to understand something: *I don't think she got the joke.* | *I don't **get it** - it doesn't make sense.* | **get what/how/who etc** *I still don't get how she knew about the meeting.*

24 COOK [T not in passive] to prepare food or a meal: *She's just getting lunch.* | **get sb sth** *Shall I get you a sandwich?*

25 RADIO/TELEVISION [T not in passive or progressive] to be able to receive a particular radio signal, television station etc: *Can you get satellite TV here?*

26 ANSWER THE DOOR/TELEPHONE [T] informal to answer the door or telephone: *Can you get the phone for me?*

27 CATCH SB [T] to catch someone: *The police got him in the end.*

28 HURT/KILL SB [T] informal to attack, hurt, or kill someone: *The other gang members threatened to get him if he went to the police.* | *I'll get you for this!*

29 TRICK SB [T] informal to deceive or trick someone: *I got you that time!*

30 ON THE TELEPHONE [T] if you get someone on the telephone, they answer the telephone when you have made a call, and so you talk to them: *I tried phoning him at work, but I just got his secretary.*

31 get doing sth to begin doing something: *We got talking about the old days.* | *I think we should get going quite soon.* | *What are we all waiting for? Let's get moving!*

32 get to do sth informal to have the opportunity to do something: *We got to meet all the stars after the show.* | *She gets to travel all over the place with her job.*

33 get to like/know/understand sb/sth to gradually begin to like, know, or understand someone or something: *It'll take a while for you to get to know everyone.* | *After a while, I got to like him.*

SPOKEN PHRASES
34 you get sth used to say that something happens or exists: *I didn't know you got tigers in Europe.*

35 you've got me (there) used to say you do not know the answer to something

36 it/what gets me used to say that something really annoys you: *It really gets me the way he leaves wet towels on the bathroom floor.* | *What gets me is their attitude.*

37 get this *especially AmE* used to draw attention to something surprising or interesting that you are about to mention: *And the whole thing only cost – get this – $12.95.*

→ **have got** at HAVE²

get about *BrE phr v*
1 to go or travel to different places: *She's eighty now, and doesn't get about much any more.* | *He's got an old van which he uses for getting about.*
2 if news or information gets about, it is told to a lot of people: *I don't really want this to get about.*

get across *phr v*
to succeed in communicating an idea or piece of information to someone, or to be communicated successfully: **get sth ⇔ across** *It took him ages to get his point across.* | *We must get across the simple fact that drugs are dangerous.* | *The message isn't getting across.* | [+to] *It is important that we get this message across to voters.*

get ahead *phr v*
to be successful and do better than other people in a job or work: *She soon found that it wasn't easy to get ahead in the movie business.*

get along *phr v*
1 if two or more people get along, they have a friendly relationship: *We've always got along quite well.* | [+with] *They seem to get along with each other.*
2 to deal with a job or situation or to make progress: *How's Sam getting along at university?* | [+without] *Don't worry, we'll get along without you.*
3 *spoken* I must/I'd better be getting along used to say that it is time for you to leave, for example because you have something else to do

get around *phr v*
1 get around (sth) to go or travel to different places: *We had to use public transport to get around.* | *It's quite easy to get around London.*
2 if news or information gets around, it is told to a lot of people: *News of the accident soon got around.* | *Word got around that the department might be closed.*
3 get around sth to avoid something that is difficult or causes problems for you: *I think we should be able to get around most of these problems.* | *She was always very clever at getting around the rules.*

get around to sth *phr v*
to do something that you have been intending to do for some time: *I meant to phone her yesterday, but I never got around to it.* | **get around to doing sth** *We finally got around to clearing out the garage.*

get at sb/sth *phr v*
1 CRITICIZE to keep criticizing someone in an unkind way: *Why is he always getting at me?* | *He felt he was being got at by the other students.*
2 be getting at sth to be trying to say something in a way that is difficult for other people to understand: *What are you getting at, Helen?* | *Do you see the point I'm getting at?*
3 REACH to be able to reach something: *We had to move the washing machine out to get at the wiring behind it.*
4 INFORMATION to discover information, especially the truth about a situation: *I was determined to get at the truth.*
5 THREATEN *informal* to use threats to influence the decision of people who are involved in a court case: *Do you think some of the jury have been got at?*

get away *phr v*
1 LEAVE to leave a place, especially when this is not easy: *The meeting dragged on, and I didn't get away until seven.* | [+from] *I like to get away from London at the weekend.*
2 ON HOLIDAY *informal* to take a holiday away from the place you normally live: *Will you manage to get away this summer?* | [+to] *We're hoping to get away to Scotland for a few days.*
3 ESCAPE to escape from someone who is chasing you or trying to catch you: *The three men got away in a stolen car.* | [+from] *We knew it wouldn't be easy to get away from the police.* | [+with] *The thieves got away with jewellery worth over £50,000.*
4 get away! *BrE spoken* used to say you are very surprised by something or do not believe it
5 the one that got away something good that you nearly had or that nearly happened

get away from sb/sth *phr v*
1 to avoid something that is difficult or unpleasant for you, or that limits what you can do in some way: *I needed to get away from the pressures of work for a while.* | *She wanted to get away from the traditional ideas of what theatre is about.* | **There is no getting away from** this fact (=you cannot avoid or deny this fact).
2 to begin to talk about other things rather than the subject you are supposed to be discussing: *I think we're getting away from the main issue.*
3 get away from it all to have a relaxing holiday: *You need to get away from it all for a couple of weeks.*

get away with sth *phr v*
1 to not be caught or punished when you have done something wrong: *Watch Frank – he'll cheat if he thinks he can get away with it.* | *No one insults my family and gets away with it!*
2 get away with murder *informal* to not be punished for doing something wrong: *Some of those children get away with murder!*
3 to receive only a small punishment for something: *The charge was reduced to manslaughter, and she got away with three years in prison.*
4 to do something without experiencing any problems or difficulties, even though it is not the best thing to do: *At school he had always got away with doing the bare minimum amount of work.* | *The colour's not quite right, but I think you'll get away with it.*

get back *phr v*
1 RETURN to return to a place: *I'll talk to you when I get back.* | [+to] *He got back to the office just before lunchtime.*
2 DO STH AGAIN to start doing something again or talking about something again: [+to] *Let's get back to the main point of the discussion.* | *Well, I must get back to work.* | [+into] *Have you ever thought about getting back into teaching?*
3 BE IN STATE AGAIN to change to a previous state or condition again: [+to] *Life was beginning to get back to normal.* | *I couldn't get back to sleep.* | [+together] *Do you think they'll get back together* (=start having a relationship again)?
4 GET STH AGAIN get sth ⇔ back to get something again after you have lost it or someone else has taken it: *Did you get your books back?*
5 PUNISH SB get sb back *informal* to do something to hurt or harm someone who has hurt or harmed you: [+for] *I'll get you back for this!*

get back at sb *phr v*
to do something to hurt or harm someone who has hurt or harmed you: *He'll probably go out with her just to get back at me.*

get back to sb *phr v informal*
to talk to someone or telephone them later in order to answer a question or give them information: *I'll find out the prices and get back to you.*

get behind *phr v*
1 if you get behind with a job, payments, rent etc, you do not do or pay as much of it as you should have by a particular time: [+with] *I don't want to get behind with my work.* | *You can always catch up later if you get behind.*
2 get behind sb *informal* to support someone: *The crowd really got behind them and cheered them on.*

G

get by phr v

to have enough money to buy the things you need, but no more: *I don't earn a huge salary, but we get by.* | [+on] *Sometimes they had to get by on very little.*

get down phr v

1 MAKE SB SAD get sb down to make someone feel unhappy and tired: *His lack of social life was beginning to get him down.*

2 WRITE STH DOWN get sth ⇔ down to write something, especially something that someone is saying: *He was followed by a group of reporters trying to get down every word he said.* | *It's important to get things down on paper.*

3 EAT/DRINK get sth down (sb) to eat or drink something, or persuade someone else to eat or drink something: *I knew I'd feel better once I'd got some food down.* | *Get that tea down you.* | *He still says he's not hungry, and I can't get anything down him.*

4 AFTER A MEAL BrE to leave the table after a meal – used by children or when you are talking to children: *Please may I get down?*

get down to sth phr v

to start doing something that is difficult or needs a lot of time or energy: *It's time we got down to work.* | *We need to get down to some serious talking.* | **get down to doing sth** *I always find it hard to get down to revising.*

get in phr v

1 ENTER to enter a place, especially when this is difficult: *We managed to get in through a window.* | *The theatre was already full, and we couldn't get in.*

2 ARRIVE if a train, plane etc gets in at a particular time, it arrives at that time: *What time does the bus get in?* | [+to] *We get in to Heathrow at ten o'clock.*

3 GET HOME to arrive home: *We didn't get in until late.* | *What time do the boys get in from school?*

4 BE ELECTED to be elected to a position of political power: *The Conservatives have promised to increase spending on health and education if they get in.*

5 COLLEGE/UNIVERSITY to be allowed to be a student at a university, college etc: *I applied to Bristol University, but I didn't get in.*

6 BUY A SUPPLY get sth ⇔ in to buy a supply of something: *I must remember to get some food in for the weekend.*

7 CROPS get sth ⇔ in to gather a crop and bring it to a sheltered place: *The whole village was involved with getting the harvest in.*

8 ASK FOR WORKER get sb ⇔ in to ask someone to come to your home to do a job, especially to repair something: *We'll have to get a plumber in.*

9 GIVE STH TO SB get sth in to send something to a particular place or give it to a particular person: *Please can you get your essays in by Thursday.* | *It's best to get your insurance claim in as quickly as possible.*

10 DO STH get sth ⇔ in to manage to do something even though you do not have much time: *We're hoping to get in a game of golf over the weekend.*

get in on sth phr v informal

to become involved in something that other people are doing or planning: *Quite a few companies would like to get in on the project.* | *The scheme has proved very successful, and now other local authorities are keen to get in on the act* (=become involved in something exciting or interesting).

get in with sb phr v informal

to become friendly with someone: *He got in with a bad crowd and started getting into trouble.*

get into sth

1 ENTER to enter a place, especially when this is difficult: *The door was locked and we couldn't get into the house.*

2 ARRIVE to arrive at a place: *What time do we get into New York?*

3 BE ELECTED to be elected to a parliament: *He first got into parliament in 1982.*

4 COLLEGE/UNIVERSITY to be allowed to be a student at a university, college etc: *She got into Edinburgh University.*

5 TEAM to be made a member of a team: *Do you think you might get into the Olympic team this year?*

6 START DOING STH to start doing or feeling something, or being in a particular situation: *He's started getting into trouble at school.* | *My parents were always terrified of getting into debt.* | *She got into the habit of going for long walks by herself.* | *He got into a terrible temper and started throwing things around.*

7 BECOME INVOLVED to begin to be involved in doing something: *How did you first get into script writing?* | *She was starting to get into politics.*

8 ENJOY informal to begin to enjoy something or be interested in it: *I first got into jazz when I was at college.*

9 CLOTHING informal to put on a piece of clothing, especially when this is difficult because the piece of clothing is too small for you: *I don't know how she managed to get into those trousers.*

10 what's got into sb? spoken used to express surprise that someone is behaving very differently from the way they usually behave: *I don't know what's got into Sally recently.*

get off phr v

1 LEAVE to leave a place, or to help someone to leave a place: *We'll try and get off straight after lunch.* | **get off sth** *Get off my land!* | **get sb off** *I'll phone you as soon as I've got the children off to school.*

2 FINISH WORK get off (sth) to finish work and leave the place where you work at the end of the day: *I usually get off at six o'clock.* | *What time do you get off work?*

3 SEND STH get sth off to send a letter or package by post: *I'll have to get this letter off by tonight.* | [+to] *I'll get the forms off to you today.*

4 CLOTHING get sth off to remove a piece of clothing: *Why don't you get those wet clothes off?*

5 NOT BE PUNISHED if someone gets off, they are not punished for doing something wrong, or they receive only a small punishment: *In the end he got off because there wasn't enough evidence against him.* | *The police felt he had got off very lightly.* | [+with] *If you're lucky, you'll get off with a fine.*

6 HELP SB NOT BE PUNISHED get sb off to help someone avoid being punished for a crime: *Her lawyers were confident that they could get her off.*

7 SLEEP get (sb) off to go to sleep, or to help a child go to sleep: *I went to bed but couldn't get off to sleep.* | *It took us ages to get the baby off.*

8 get off to a good/bad etc start to start in a particular way: *The day had got off to a bad start.*

9 STOP TALKING ABOUT STH get off sth to stop talking about a subject: *Can we get off the subject of death, please?*

10 STOP TOUCHING STH get off (sth/sb) informal used to tell someone to stop touching something or someone: *Get off me!* | *Get off those cakes, or there'll be trouble.* | *Get off* (=stop touching me)!

11 tell sb where to get off informal to tell someone that they are asking you for too much or are behaving in a way you will not accept: *He wanted £50, but I told him where to get off.*

12 get off your butt/ass AmE spoken not polite used to tell someone that they should stop being lazy and start doing something useful

get off on sth phr v informal

to become excited by something, especially sexually excited

get off with sb phr v informal

to start a sexual relationship with someone: *She spent the whole evening trying to get off with Phil.*

get on phr v

1 LIKE SB especially BrE if people get on, they like each other and have a friendly relationship with each other: [+with] *I've always got on well with Henry.* | *The two boys get on well most of the time.*

2 PROGRESS to deal with a job or situation or to make progress: *How is George getting on at school?* | [+with] *How are you getting on with your essay?* | [+without] *I* *don't know how we'll get on without Michael.*

3 CONTINUE DOING STH to continue doing something: [+**with**] *Be quiet and get on with your work!*

4 BE SUCCESSFUL to be successful in your job: *You'll have to work hard if you want to get on.*

5 CLOTHING get sth on to put a piece of clothing on: *I can't get my boots on!*

6 be getting on a) if time is getting on, it is quite late: *Come on, it's getting on and we ought to go home.* | *I realized that time was getting on and we would have to hurry.* **b)** *informal* if someone is getting on, they are quite old

7 getting on for 90/10 o'clock/2000 etc almost a particular age, time, number etc: *Mrs McIntyre must be getting on for 90 by now.* | *The total cost was getting on for $100,000.*

8 get it on *AmE informal* to have sex

9 get on with it! *spoken* used to tell someone to hurry: *Will you lot stop messing around and get on with it!*

10 let sb get on with it *informal* to let someone do something on their own, and not help them or tell them what to do: *She wanted to decorate her room, so I just let her get on with it.*

get onto sb/sth *phr v*

1 SPEAK/WRITE TO SB *informal* to speak or write to someone: *I'll get onto my lawyer about this.*

2 LEARN ABOUT SB *informal* to find out about someone who has been doing something wrong: *How did the police get onto him?*

3 BE ELECTED to be elected as a member of a committee, a political organization etc: *She was quite keen to get onto the management committee.*

4 TALK ABOUT STH to begin to talk about a subject after you have been discussing something else: *After a few minutes they got onto the subject of the election.*

5 DO STH *informal* to start dealing with something: *Right, I'll get onto it straight away.*

get out *phr v*

1 LEAVE to leave a room or building: *You ought to get out into the fresh air.* | *Mary screamed at me to get out.* | [+**of**] *Get out of the kitchen!*

2 ESCAPE to escape from a place: *Some of the animals had got out.* | [+**of**] *He was determined to get out of prison.*

3 HELP SB ESCAPE get sb out to help someone leave a place or escape from a place: *It's important to get these people out as soon as possible.* | [+**of**] *We knew it was going to be difficult to get him out of the country.*

4 TAKE STH FROM A PLACE get sth ⇔ out to take something from the place where it is kept: *She got out her violin and started to play.*

5 INFORMATION if information gets out, a lot of people then know it although it is meant to be secret: *We have to make absolutely certain that none of this gets out.* | *It's bound to get out that he's retiring soon.*

6 PRODUCE STH get sth ⇔ out to produce a book or other product that can be sold to people: *We're hoping to get the new catalogue out next week.*

7 SAY STH get sth ⇔ out to succeed in saying something, especially when this is very difficult: *I wanted to tell him I loved him, but couldn't get the words out.*

get out of sth *phr v*

1 AVOID DOING STH to avoid doing something you have promised to do or are supposed to do: *See if you can get out of that meeting tomorrow.* | **get out of doing sth** *He's trying to get out of tidying his room.*

2 STOP DOING STH to stop doing something or being involved in something: *I wanted to get out of teaching.*

3 MAKE SB GIVE/TELL YOU STH get sth out of sb to force or persuade someone to tell you something or give you something: *I was determined to get the truth out of her.*

4 ENJOY STH get sth out of sth to enjoy something you do or experience, or to learn something as a result: *I hope he got something out of his visit.* | **get sth out of doing sth** *Children can get a lot out of being involved in community projects.*

get over

1 ILLNESS get over sth to become well again after an

lot of pressure at work, and sometimes it gets to me a bit. | *Don't let things get to you.*
2 get to thinking/wondering sth *informal* to start thinking something: *He got to thinking how disappointed his parents would be.*
  get together *phr v*
1 if people get together, they meet in order to spend time with each other: *We must get together some time for a drink.*
2 if two people get together, they start a romantic or sexual relationship
3 get sth ⇔ **together** to collect things together: *I need to get some paperwork together for the meeting.*
4 get sb ⇔ **together** to bring people together to make a group: *He got together a group of local businessmen to discuss the problem.*
5 get sth ⇔ **together** to succeed in getting enough money to do or buy something: *We're trying to get together enough money to buy a flat.*
6 get sth together *informal* to change your life so that it is organized and you are in control of it: *He's just trying to get his life together at the moment.* | **get yourself together** *I'm staying with my parents for a while, until I've got myself together a bit.*
7 get it together *spoken* to be organized and successful in your life, job etc: *The government can't seem to get it together on the environment.*
  get up *phr v*
1 get (sb) up to get out of your bed after sleeping, or to make someone get out of their bed: *We didn't get up until lunch time.* | *Get me up at seven, would you?*
2 to stand up: *He got up and walked over to the window.*
3 if a wind or storm gets up, it starts and gets stronger
4 be got up as/in sth *BrE informal* to be dressed in particular clothes: *He arrived at the party got up as Count Dracula.* | *The men were all got up in suits.*
5 get it up *informal* to get an ERECTION (1)
  get up to sth *phr v*
to do something, especially something slightly bad: *Go upstairs and see what the kids are getting up to.* | *What did you get up to at the weekend?*

get·a·way /ˈgetəweɪ/ *n* [C] **1** an escape from a place or unpleasant situation, especially after committing a crime: *The gunmen made a getaway on foot.* | **getaway car/vehicle/van** (=a car etc used by criminals to escape after a crime) **2** *especially AmE* a short holiday away from home, or a place where people go for a short holiday: *Big Bear Lake is a popular weekend getaway*.

'get-go *n* **from the get-go** *AmE informal* from the beginning: *From the get-go, I knew these tapes were special.*

'get-to,gether *n* [C] a friendly informal meeting or party: *a family get-together*

get·up /ˈgetʌp/ *n* [C] *informal* a set of clothes, especially strange or unusual clothes: *I hardly recognized him in that getup!*

,get-up-and-'go *n* [U] *informal* energy and determination to do things: *He was the only candidate who had any get-up-and-go.*

gey·ser /ˈgiːzə $ ˈgaɪzər/ *n* [C] **1** a natural spring that sends hot water and steam suddenly into the air from a hole in the ground **2** *BrE* a machine fixed to a wall over a bath or SINK and used for heating water

ghast·ly /ˈgɑːstli $ ˈgæstli/ *adj* **1** very bad or unpleasant; ▣ **horrible**: *a ghastly little hotel* | *The whole thing was a ghastly mistake.* | *The weather was ghastly.* **2** making you very frightened, upset, or shocked: *a ghastly accident* **3 look/feel ghastly** to look or feel ill, upset, or unhappy: *Are you all right? You look ghastly!* —**ghastliness** *n* [U]

ghee /giː/ *n* [U] melted butter made from the milk of a cow or BUFFALO, used in Indian cooking

gher·kin /ˈgɜːkɪn $ ˈgɜːr-/ *n* [C] a small type of CUCUMBER that has been preserved in VINEGAR to make a type of PICKLE

ghet·to /ˈgetəʊ $ -toʊ/ *n plural* **ghettos** *or* **ghettoes** [C] **1** a part of a city where people of a particular race or class, especially people who are poor, live separately from the rest of the people in the city. This word is sometimes considered offensive; ➔ **slum**: *unemployment in the ghetto* **2** a part of a city where Jews were forced to live in the past: *the Warsaw ghetto*

'ghetto ,blaster *n* [C] *informal* a large radio and TAPE RECORDER that can be carried around, and is often played very loudly in public places. This word is sometimes considered offensive in American English; ▣ **boom box** *AmE*

ghet·to·ize also **-ise** *BrE* /ˈgetəʊaɪz $ -toʊ-/ *v* [T] **1** to force people to live in a ghetto **2** to make part of a town become a ghetto

ghost¹ /gəʊst $ goʊst/ *n* [C]
1 SPIRIT the spirit of a dead person that some people think they can feel or see in a place: [+of] *the ghost of Old Tom Morris* | *They say the young girl's ghost still haunts* (=often appears in) *the house.* | *He looked as if he'd seen a ghost* (=he looked very frightened). ➔ HOLY GHOST
2 MEMORY/EFFECT the memory or effect of someone or something bad that lived, existed, or happened in the past: [+of] *The ghost of Stalinism still affects life in Russia today.*
3 the ghost of a smile/sound etc a smile etc that is so slight you are not sure it happened: *The ghost of a smile flitted across her sad features.*
4 TELEVISION/COMPUTER a second image that is not clear on a television or computer screen
5 give up the ghost a) if a machine gives up the ghost, it does not work any more and cannot be repaired – used humorously: *Unfortunately, my car's just given up the ghost.* **b)** to die
6 (not) a ghost of a chance not even a slight chance of doing something, or of something happening: *They don't stand a ghost of a chance of winning.*

ghost² *v* [T] to write something as a GHOST WRITER

ghost·ly /ˈgəʊstli $ ˈgoʊst-/ *adj* slightly frightening and seeming to be related to ghosts or spirits: *a ghostly figure in a white dress*

'ghost ,story *n* [C] a story about ghosts that is intended to frighten people

'ghost town *n* [C] a town that used to have a lot of people living and working in it, but now has very few or none

'ghost train *n* [C] a small train ride at a FUNFAIR, that is designed to frighten you by taking you through a dark place full of SKELETONS and things that jump out at you

'ghost ,writer *n* [C] someone who is paid to write a book or story for another person, who then says it is their own work —**ghost-write** *v* [T]

ghoul /guːl/ *n* [C] **1** an evil spirit in stories that takes bodies from GRAVES (=place in the ground where dead people are buried) and eats them **2** someone who gets pleasure from unpleasant things such as accidents that shock other people —**ghoulish** *adj*

GHQ /ˌdʒiː eɪtʃ ˈkjuː/ *n* [U] *general headquarters* the place that a large military operation is controlled from

GI /ˌdʒiː ˈaɪ/ *n* [C] a soldier in the US army, especially during the Second World War

gi·ant¹ /ˈdʒaɪənt/ *adj* [only before noun] extremely big, and much bigger than other things of the same type: *a giant electronics company* | *a giant tortoise*

giant² *n* [C] **1** an extremely tall strong man, who is often bad and cruel, in children's stories **2** a very large successful company: *the German chemicals giant, BASF* **3** a very big man, animal, or plant **4** someone who is very good at doing something: [+of] *Miles Davis, truly one of the giants of jazz*

gi·ant·ess /ˈdʒaɪəntes/ *n* [C] an extremely tall strong woman, who is often bad and cruel, in children's stories

'giant ,killer *n* [C] *BrE* a person, sports team etc that defeats a much stronger opponent

giant 'panda n [C] a PANDA (1)

gib·ber /'dʒɪbə $ -ər/ v [I] to speak quickly in a way that is difficult to understand, especially because you are very frightened or shocked; → **jabber**: [+with] '*It was her,*' *said Ruth, gibbering with fear.* —**gibbering** adj BrE: *a gibbering wreck* (=someone who is very shocked or frightened)

gib·ber·ish /'dʒɪbərɪʃ/ n [U] something you write or say that has no meaning, or is very difficult to understand; ⊟ **nonsense**: *You're talking gibberish!*

gib·bet /'dʒɪbɪt/ n [C] a wooden frame on which criminals were HANGED in the past with a rope around their neck; ⊟ **gallows**

gib·bon /'ɡɪbən/ n [C] a small animal like a monkey, with long arms and no tail, that lives in trees in Asia

gibe /dʒaɪb/ n another spelling of JIBE

gib·lets /'dʒɪblɪts/ n [plural] organs such as the heart and LIVER, that you remove from a chicken or other bird before you cook it

gid·dy /'ɡɪdi/ adj **1** feeling slightly sick and unable to balance, because everything seems to be moving; ⊟ **dizzy**: *Greg stared down from the seventh floor and began to feel giddy.* **2** feeling silly, happy, and excited, or showing this feeling: [+with] *Sheila felt giddy with excitement.* **3 giddy heights** a situation in which you have a lot of success: *Although she had been quite a successful model, she had never reached the giddy heights of the Paris fashion world.* **4** old-fashioned silly and not interested in serious things: *Fiona's very pretty but a bit giddy.* —**giddily** adv —**giddiness** n [U]

GIF /ɡɪf/ n [C] technical **graphics interchange format** a type of computer FILE that contains images and is used on the Internet

gift S2 W2 /ɡɪft/ n [C]
1 something that you give someone, for example to thank them or because you like them, especially on a special occasion; ⊟ **present**

> give sb a gift
> receive a gift
> make sb a gift of sth formal (=give someone something as a gift)
> birthday/wedding/Christmas etc gift
> free gift (=something that a shop or business gives you)
> make a good/ideal gift (=be a good gift)
> gift ideas (=ideas of things you could give someone)

The earrings were a gift from my aunt. | [+of] *a generous gift of £50* | *The clock was given as a retirement gift when he left the police.* | *expensive wedding gifts* | *Enjoy a free gift with any purchase of $20 or more.* | *This excellent cookbook would make an ideal gift for anyone just going away to college.*

2 a) a natural ability; ⊟ **talent**: [+for] *a gift for languages* | *He was a kind man, with a gift for forming lasting friendships.* | [+of] *She has the rare gift of being able to laugh at herself.* **b)** an ability that is given to you by God: [+of] *He was said to have possessed the gift of prophecy.* | *the use of spiritual gifts* → **GIFTED**
3 a gift BrE informal something that is easier or cheaper than you expected: *The third goal was an absolute gift.*
4 gift (from God) something good you receive or something good that happens to you, even though you might not deserve it: *This opportunity was a gift from God.*
5 the gift of the gab BrE, the gift of gab AmE informal an ability to speak confidently and to persuade people to do what you want: *Jo has always had the gift of the gab.*
6 be in sb's gift BrE formal if something is in your gift, you have the power to decide who it should be given to: *All appointments to military and administrative posts were in the gift of the king.*
7 never/don't look a gift horse in the mouth spoken used to tell someone to be grateful for something that has been given to them, instead of asking questions about it or finding something wrong with it → **God's gift to sb/sth** at GOD (3)

'gift cer,tificate n [C] AmE a special piece of paper that is worth a particular amount of money when it is exchanged for goods in a shop, often given as a present; ⊟ **gift token** BrE

gift·ed /'ɡɪftᵻd/ adj having a natural ability to do one or more things extremely well; → **talented**: **gifted musician/artist/teacher etc** *She was an extremely gifted poet.* | **academically/musically/athletically etc gifted** *his musically gifted son* | **gifted child** (=one who is extremely intelligent) | [+with] *Gifted with a superb voice, she became the Opera's leading soprano.*

'gift shop n [C] a shop that sells small things that are suitable for giving as presents

'gift ,token also **'gift ,voucher** n [C] BrE a special piece of paper that is worth a particular amount of money when it is exchanged for goods in a shop, often given as a present; ⊟ **gift certificate** AmE

'gift wrap, **'gift ,wrapping** n [U] attractive coloured paper used for wrapping presents in

'gift-wrap also **gift wrap** v gift-wrapped, gift-wrapping [T] to wrap a present with gift wrap, especially in a shop: *Would you like that gift-wrapped, sir?*

gig¹ /ɡɪɡ/ n [C] **1** a performance by a musician or a group of musicians playing modern popular music or JAZZ, or a performance by a COMEDIAN: **do/play/have a gig** *The band are doing a gig in Sheffield on Nov 12.* **2** AmE informal a job, especially one that does not last for a long time **3** informal a gigabyte

gig² v gigged, gigging [I] to give a performance of modern popular music or JAZZ

giga- /ɡɪɡə/ prefix [in nouns] a BILLION - used with units of measurement

gig·a·byte /'ɡɪɡəbaɪt/ n [C] written abbreviation **GB** or **Gb** a unit for measuring computer information, equal to 1,024 MEGABYTES, and used less exactly to mean a BILLION bytes.

gi·gan·tic /dʒaɪˈɡæntɪk/ adj extremely big; ⊟ **huge**: *a gigantic skyscraper* —**gigantically** /-kli/ adv

gig·gle¹ /'ɡɪɡəl/ giggled, giggling v [I] to laugh quickly, quietly, and in a high voice, because something is funny or because you are nervous or embarrassed: *If you can't stop giggling you'll have to leave the room.*

giggle² n **1** [C] a quick, quiet, high-sounding laugh: '*Catch me if you can,*' *she said with a giggle.* | *Vicky suppressed a nervous giggle.* | *He looked so ridiculous I got the giggles* (=started to giggle). | *Soon the whole group had the giggles.* | *Margaret was seized by a fit of the giggles* (=she could not stop giggling). | **give sb the giggles** (=make someone start giggling) **2 a giggle** BrE informal something that you think is fun to do that will not hurt anyone or anything: *Go on, it'll be a giggle!*

gig·gly /'ɡɪɡli/ adj giggling a lot: *a giggly schoolgirl*

gig·o·lo /'ʒɪɡələʊ, 'dʒɪ- $ -loʊ/ n plural gigolos [C] a man who is paid by a rich woman, especially an older woman, to have sex with her

gild /ɡɪld/ v [T] **1** to cover something with a thin layer of gold or with something that looks like gold: *a gilded frame* **2** literary to make something look as if it is covered in gold: *The autumn sun gilded the lake.* **3 gild the lily** to spoil something by trying to improve it when it is already good enough

gill¹ /ɡɪl/ n [C] **1** one of the organs on the sides of a fish through which it breathes **2 full/packed/stuffed etc to the gills** informal completely full: *The bar was packed to the gills on Monday night.* → see picture at FRESHWATER

gill² /dʒɪl/ n [C] a unit for measuring liquid, equal to ¼ PINT. In Britain this is 0.14 litres, and in the US it is 0.12 litres.

gilt¹ /ɡɪlt/ n **1** [U] a thin shiny material, such as gold or something similar, used to cover objects for decoration **2** [C] a STOCK or SHARE that is GILT-EDGED

G

for someone to do something, or for something to happen: *I've asked him to give me a couple more days to finish my essay.* | *Flexible working hours could give working parents more time to spend with their children.*

22 I give it six weeks/a month etc *spoken* used to say that you do not think something will continue successfully for very long: *I give the project six months at the most before it all falls apart.*

23 not give sth a second thought/another thought to not think or worry about something at all: *The matter didn't seem important, and I hardly gave it a second thought.*

24 BE LESS STRICT [I] to be willing to change what you think or do according to what else happens: *I think that both sides need to give a little.*

25 STATE A DECISION [T] *BrE* to state what your official decision or judgement is, for example in a game: *The referee has given a penalty.* | *The jury will be giving its verdict within the next couple of days.*

26 GIVE A MARK/SCORE [T] to decide that someone should have a particular score or mark for something that they have done: *She only gave me a B for my last essay.* | *The judges have given him top marks for this performance.*

27 BEND/STRETCH [I] if a material gives, it bends or stretches when you put pressure on it: *New shoes often feel tight, but the leather should give a little after a few days.*

28 BREAK/MOVE [I] if something gives, it breaks or moves away suddenly because of weight or pressure on it: *The branch suddenly gave beneath him.* | *I pushed against the door with all my might, but it still wouldn't give.*

29 give me sth (any day/time) *spoken* used to say that you like something much more than something else: *Give me good old-fashioned rock 'n' roll any day!*

30 would give anything/a lot/your right arm etc for sth *spoken* used when you would like something very much: *I'd give my right arm for a figure like that.*

31 not give a damn/shit etc *spoken not polite* used to say that you do not care at all about something: *I don't give a damn what you think.*

32 don't give me that *spoken* used to say that you do not believe someone's excuse or explanation: *Don't give me that! I know exactly where you've been!*

33 give sb what for *spoken* to tell someone angrily that you are annoyed with them: *I'll give that boy what for when I see him!*

34 give as good as you get to fight or argue with someone using the same amount of skill or force that they are using: *I don't worry about Emma because I know she can give as good as she gets.*

35 give and take *informal* to help other people and do things for them as well as expecting them to do things for you: *You have to learn to give and take in any relationship.*

36 give or take a few minutes/a penny/a mile etc *spoken* used to say that the amount or figure that you have just mentioned is nearly correct, but not exactly: *It'll be a couple of thousand pounds, give or take fifty or so.*

37 I'll give you that *spoken* used to admit that someone is right about something: *I was wrong to trust him, I'll give you that.*

38 give sb to understand/think/believe sth *formal* to make someone think that a particular thing is true: *I was given to understand that I would be offered a permanent job.*

39 give it to sb straight *informal* to tell someone something in a clear direct way: *There's no point in beating about the bush, so I'll give it to you straight.*

40 I give you the chairman/prime minister/groom etc *BrE spoken* used at the end of a formal speech to invite people to welcome a special guest

41 SEX [T] *old-fashioned* if a woman gives herself to a man, she has sex with him

put something in someone's hand: **hand, pass**
officially give something to someone: **award, present, grant, confer, allocate**
give something to people in a group: **hand out, pass around, distribute**
give to a charity: **donate**
give something to people after you die: **leave, pass on, bequeath**

give sb/sth **away** *phr v*
1 to give something to someone because you do not want or need it for yourself: *I gave most of my books away when I left college.* | [+to] *Give your old clothes away to a thrift shop.*
2 to give something to someone without asking for any money, rather than selling it to them: *We're giving away a free diary with tomorrow's newspaper.* | [+to] *We have 1,000 CDs to give away to our readers.*
3 to show where someone is or what they are doing or thinking when they are trying to keep this a secret: *Don't worry, I won't give you away.* | *Sue tried to smile, but her voice gave her away.* | **give yourself away** *I knew that if I moved I would give myself away.* | *The look on his face **gave the game away** (=showed something that he was trying to keep secret).*
4 to tell someone something that you should keep secret: *He gave away as little information as possible.* | *I don't want to give away exactly how the system works.* | *I don't want to **give the game away** (=give information that should be secret) by saying too much.*
5 to lose in a game or competition by doing something badly or making mistakes: *We gave away two goals in the first half.* | *The Democrats are now in danger of giving the whole election away.*
6 to give formal permission for a woman to marry a man as part of a traditional wedding ceremony

give sth ⇔ **back** *phr v*
1 to give something to the person it belongs to or the person who gave it to you: *This isn't your money and you must give it back.* | *Of course you can have a look at it, as long as you give it back.* | **give sth back to sb** *I'll give the keys back to you tomorrow morning.* | **give sb sth** ⇔ **back** *Her ex-husband refused to give her back any of her old photos and letters.*
2 to make it possible for someone to have or do something again; ▤ **restore**: **give sb sth** ⇔ **back** *He underwent an expensive operation to give him back his sight.* | *The company finally agreed to give the women their old jobs back.* | **give sth back to sb** *This legislation will give more power back to local authorities.*

give in *phr v*
1 to finally agree to do or accept something that you had at first opposed, especially because someone has forced or persuaded you to: *Eventually I gave in and accepted the job on their terms.* | *Bob's wife went on at him so much that eventually he gave in.* | [+to] *The government refused to give in to their demands.*
2 to accept that you are defeated in a game, fight, competition etc; → **surrender**: *The rebels were eventually forced to give in.* | *We will carry on fighting to the end. We will never give in.*
3 give sth ⇔ in *BrE* to give a piece of work or something you have written to someone in authority; ▤ **hand in**: *You were supposed to give this work in four days ago.* | *Rose decided to **give in her notice** (=officially say she was going to leave her job).* | [+to] *All assignments must be given in to your teacher by Friday.*

give in to sth *phr v*
to no longer try to stop yourself from doing something you want to do: *Don't give in to the temptation to argue back.* | *If you feel the urge for a cigarette, try not to give in to it.*

give of sth *phr v formal*
if you give of yourself, your time, your money etc, you do things for other people without expecting anything in return: *Retired people are often willing to give of their time to help with community projects.*

give off sth *phr v*
to produce a smell, light, heat, a sound etc: *The wood*

gave off a sweet, perfumed smell as it burned. | *Try not to breathe in the fumes given off by the paint.*

give onto sth *phr v*
if a window, door, or building gives onto a particular place, it leads to that place or you can see that place from it: *the garden gate that gives onto the main road* | *a small balcony giving onto fields*

give out *phr v*
1 give sth ⇔ out to give something to each person in a group; **☐ hand out**: *Can you give the drinks out, please?* | [+to] *Students were giving out leaflets to everyone on the street.*
2 if part of your body gives out, it stops working properly or becomes much weaker: *Just as I approached the town, my legs finally gave out.*
3 if a supply of something gives out, there is none left: *My money was beginning to give out and there were no jobs to be found.* | *After two hours her patience gave out.*
4 give out sth to produce something such as light, heat, or a signal; **☐ emit**: *A gas lamp gave out a pale yellowish light.*
5 give sth ⇔ out *BrE formal* to announce something, especially officially: *It was given out that the government was to enter into negotiations with the rebels.*

give over *phr v BrE spoken informal*
to stop doing or saying something that is annoying other people: *I wish you lot would just give over!* | **give over doing sth** *Oh, give over complaining, we're nearly there.*

give sth **over to** sb/sth *phr v*
1 be given over to sth to be used for a particular purpose: *The land surrounding the village was given over to vineyards.* | *The whole day was given over to cooking and preparing for the celebrations.*
2 give yourself over to sth to spend all your time doing something: *In his youth he had given himself over to pleasure.*
3 to give responsibility for or control over something to a particular person, organization etc: *The running of internal affairs was given over to the Chancellor.*

give up *phr v*
1 give sth ⇔ up to stop doing something, especially something that you do regularly: *Darren has decided to give up football at the end of this season.* | *She gave up her job and started writing poetry.* | **give up doing sth** *I gave up going to the theatre when I moved out of London.* | *Why don't you give up smoking?*
2 to stop trying to do something: *We spent half an hour looking for the keys, but eventually gave up and went home.* | *I give up. What's the answer?* | *You shouldn't give up so easily.* | **give up doing sth** *I gave up trying to persuade him to continue with his studies.* | **give sth ⇔ up** *She has still not given up the search.*
3 give yourself/sb up to allow yourself or someone else to be caught by the police or enemy soldiers: *The siege ended peacefully after the gunman gave himself up.* | [+to] *In the end, his family gave him up to the police.*
4 give up sth to use some of your time to do a particular thing: *I don't mind giving up a couple of hours a week to deal with correspondence.*
5 give sth/sb ⇔ up to give something that is yours to someone else: *The family refused to give up any of their land.* | *She was put under tremendous pressure to give the baby up.* | [+to] *I would always give my seat up to an elderly person on the bus.*
6 give sb ⇔ up to end a romantic relationship with someone, even though you do not really want to: *I knew deep down that I should give him up.*
7 give sb up for dead/lost etc to believe that someone is dead and stop looking for them: *The ship sank and the crew were given up for dead.* → **give up the ghost** at GHOST[1] (5)

give up on sb/sth *phr v*
to stop hoping that someone or something will change or improve: *He'd been in a coma for six months, and doctors had almost given up on him.* | *At that point, I hadn't completely given up on the marriage.*

give yourself up to sth *phr v*
to allow yourself to feel an emotion completely, without trying to control it: *He gave himself up to despair.*

give² *n* [U] the ability of a material or substance to bend or stretch when put under pressure: *The rope **has** quite a bit of **give** in it.*

give-and-take *n* [U] a willingness between two people or groups to understand each other, and to let each other have or do some of the things they want: *In any relationship there has to be some give-and-take.*

give·a·way¹ /ˈɡɪvəweɪ/ *n* **1** [singular] something that makes it easy for you to guess something: **be a clear/dead giveaway** (=make it very easy to guess something) *He'd been smoking dope; his glazed eyes were a dead giveaway.* **2** [C] something that is given away free, especially something that a shop gives you when you buy a product

giveaway² *adj* [only before noun] giveaway prices are extremely cheap

giv·en¹ /ˈɡɪvən/ the past participle of GIVE

given² *adj* [only before noun] **1** any/a given... any particular time, situation, amount etc that is being used as an example: *On any given day in the Houston area, half the hospital beds are empty.* | *The rules are to be followed in any given situation.* | **at any given time/moment** *There are thought to be around 10,000 young homeless Scots in London at any given time.* **2** previously arranged: *The wrapping machine was pre-set to wrap a given number of biscuits.* | *Candidates will have to give a presentation on a given topic.* | *a game in which, at a given signal, everyone has to stand still* **3 be given to (doing) sth** *formal* to tend to do something, especially something that you should not do: *He was a quiet man, not usually given to complaining.* **4 take sth as given** to accept that something is true or exists, especially when you are developing an idea or argument: *The fact that people find change difficult is taken as given.*

given³ *prep* taking something into account: *Given the circumstances, you've done really well.* | **given that** *Given that the patients have some disabilities, we still try to enable them to be as independent as possible.*

given⁴ *n* [C] a basic fact that you accept as being true: *Sandra will be at least 15 minutes late – that's a given.* | *The concept is **taken as a given** in social studies.*

given name *n* [C] *AmE* your FIRST NAME

giv·ing /ˈɡɪvɪŋ/ *adj* kind, caring, and generous; **☐ mean**: *She's a very giving person.*

giz·mo /ˈɡɪzməʊ $ -moʊ/ *n plural* **gizmos** [C] *informal* a small piece of equipment – used when you cannot remember or do not know its correct name

giz·zard /ˈɡɪzəd $ -ərd/ *n* [C] a part of a bird's stomach that breaks down food into smaller pieces

gla·cé /ˈɡlæseɪ $ ɡlæˈseɪ/ *adj* [only before noun] *BrE* glacé fruits, especially CHERRIES, have been covered in sugary liquid; **☐ candied**

glacé icing /$.,. ˈ../ *n* [U] *BrE* a type of ICING used to decorate cakes

gla·cial /ˈɡleɪʃəl/ *adj* **1** relating to ice and glaciers, or formed by glaciers: *a glacial valley* | *glacial deposits* **2** a glacial look or expression is extremely unfriendly; **☐ icy** **3** extremely slow: *Change was coming, but at a glacial pace.* **4** extremely cold; **☐ icy**: *a glacial wind* —**glacially** *adv*

gla·ci·a·tion /ˌɡleɪsiˈeɪʃən/ *n* [U] *technical* the process in which land is covered by glaciers, or the effect this process has

gla·ci·er /ˈɡlæsiə $ ˈɡleɪʃər/ *n* [C] a large mass of ice which moves slowly down a mountain valley

glad [S2] [W3] /ɡlæd/ *adj* [no comparative]
1 [not before noun] pleased and happy about something **glad (that)** *I'm really glad I don't have to go back there again.* | *We're so glad you came.* | **glad to do sth** *I am glad to be back home.* | **glad to see/hear etc** *I'm glad to*

see you looking so well. | **glad when** *I'll be glad when the war is over.* | *'I've decided to accept the job.' 'I'm glad.'* | [+**about**] *She wasn't leaving after all. He was glad about that.* | [+**for**] *'Jamie's been accepted for medical school!' 'I'm so glad for him.'* → GLADLY
2 be glad of sth to be grateful for something: *Thanks Marge, I'll be glad of the help.* | **be glad of an opportunity/chance/excuse to do sth** *They were glad of the chance to finally get some sleep.* | *It was cold outside, and she was glad of her coat.*
3 be glad to (do sth) to be very willing and eager to do something: *We will be glad to send you any information you may need.* | *I'm sure he'd be **only too glad to** (=extremely willing to) help you.* | *'Would you give me a hand?' ' **I'd be glad to.** '*
4 I would be glad if *formal* used in formal situations or letters to ask someone to do something for you: *I'd be glad if you'd let me know when the funeral is.*
5 glad tidings/news *old-fashioned* good news
6 give sb the glad eye *BrE old-fashioned* to look at someone in a way that shows you are sexually attracted to them
7 glad rags *old-fashioned informal* your best clothes that you wear for special occasions —**gladness** *n* [U] → GLAD-HAND

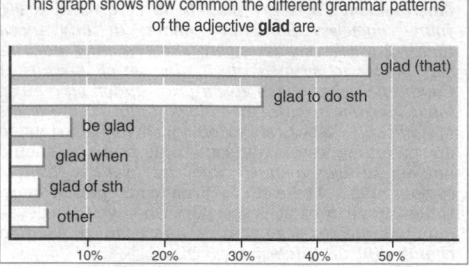
This graph shows how common the different grammar patterns of the adjective **glad** are.

glad (that) | glad to do sth | be glad | glad when | glad of sth | other
10% 20% 30% 40% 50%

glad·den /'glædn/ *v* [T] *old-fashioned* to make someone feel pleased and happy: *It will **gladden** the **hearts** of my friends to see you.*
glade /gleɪd/ *n* [C] *literary* a small open space in a wood or forest
glad-'hand *v* [I,T] to talk to or welcome people in a very friendly way, especially when this is not sincere: *He moved among the guests, glad-handing well-wishers.*
glad·i·a·tor /'glædieɪtə $ -ər/ *n* [C] a soldier who fought against other men or wild animals as an entertainment in ancient Rome —**gladiatorial** /ˌglædiə'tɔːriəl◂/ *adj*: *gladiatorial combat*
glad·i·o·lus /ˌglædi'əʊləs $ -'oʊ-/ *n plural* **gladioli** /-laɪ/ [C] a tall garden plant with long leaves and large brightly-coloured flowers
glad·ly /'glædli/ *adv* **1** willingly or eagerly: *I would gladly have done it for him.* **2** happily: *'Here's Michelle!' he said gladly.* → **not suffer fools gladly** at SUFFER (4)
glam /glæm/ *adj informal* attractive, exciting, and connected with wealth and success; ▤ **glamorous**: *glam young film directors*
glam·or /'glæmə $ -ər/ *n* an American spelling of GLAMOUR
glam·o·rize *also* **-ise** *BrE* /'glæməraɪz/ *v* [T] to make something seem more attractive than it really is: *TV has been accused of glamorizing crime.* —**glamorization** /ˌglæməraɪ'zeɪʃən $ -rə-/ *n* [U]
glam·or·ous /'glæmərəs/ *adj* attractive, exciting, and related to wealth and success: *She led an exciting and glamorous life.* | *the most glamorous neighbourhood in the city* | *a glamorous actress* | *On television, she looks so glamorous.*
glam·our *usually* **glamor** *AmE* /'glæmə $ -ər/ *n* [U] **1** the attractive and exciting quality of being connected with wealth and success: [+**of**] *Forget all you*

read about the glamour of television. **2** a style of attractiveness that suggests wealth: *Designer clothes are not a passport to instant glamour.* **3 glamour girl/boy** a performer who is more noticeable for their attractiveness than for their skill or ability
glance¹ [W3] /glɑːns $ glæns/ *v* [I always + adv/prep]
1 to quickly look at someone or something: [+**at/up/down** etc] *The man glanced nervously at his watch.* | *Wyatt glanced around the restaurant.* | *Emily glanced over her shoulder.*
2 to read something very quickly: [+**at/through** etc] *Can you glance through these figures for me?*
glance off (sth) *phr v*
1 to hit a surface at an angle and then move away from it in another direction: *The bullet had crushed his helmet and glanced off.*
2 *literary* if light glances off a surface, it flashes or shines back from it: *The sun was glancing off the icy tips of gleaming rock.*

> **WORD CHOICE: glance, glimpse**
> **glance** (verb) means 'to look quickly and deliberately' and a **glance** is the act of quickly looking at someone or something: *I glanced at my watch.* | *She gave me an amused glance.*
> **glimpse** (verb) means 'to see something or someone by chance for a very short time' and a **glimpse** is a sight that you see by chance for a very short time: *I glimpsed someone behind the curtain.* | *We got a glimpse of her face as she hurried past.*

glance² [W3] *n* [C]
1 a quick look: *He gave her a quick glance and smiled.* | **sidelong/sideways glance** *She couldn't resist a sidelong glance* (=a look that is not direct) *at him.* | **take/shoot/throw/cast a glance (at sb)** (=look at someone or something quickly) *The couple at the next table cast quick glances in our direction.* | *The brothers **exchanged glances** (=looked at each other quickly).*
2 at a glance a) if you know something at a glance, you know it as soon as you see it: *He saw at a glance what had happened.* **b)** in a short form that is easy to read and understand: *Here are our top ten ski resorts at a glance.*
3 at first glance/sight when you first look at something: *At first glance, the place seemed deserted.*
glanc·ing /'glɑːnsɪŋ $ 'glæn-/ *adj* **1 a glancing blow** a hit that partly misses so that it does not have its full force **2 a glancing reference/mention** a short or indirect reference to something or someone —**glancingly** *adv*
gland /glænd/ *n* [C] an organ of the body which produces a substance that the body needs, such as HORMONES, SWEAT, or SALIVA: *the pituitary gland*
glan·du·lar /'glændjʊlə $ -dʒələr/ *adj* related to the glands, or produced by the glands
glandular 'fever *n* [U] *BrE* an infectious disease which makes your LYMPH NODES swell up and makes you feel weak for a long time afterwards
glare¹ /gleə $ gler/ *v* [I] **1** to look angrily at someone for a long time; → **stare**: [+**at**] *She glared at him accusingly.* | [+**into/across/round** etc] *He glared round the room as if expecting a challenge.* **2** [always + adv/prep] to shine with a very strong bright light which hurts your eyes: *The sun glared down on us.*
glare² *n* **1** [singular, U] a bright unpleasant light which hurts your eyes: **the glare of sth** *the harsh glare of the desert sun* | *a special screen to reduce glare* **2** [C] a long angry look; → **stare**: *She gave him a hostile glare.* **3 the glare of publicity/the media/public scrutiny etc** the full attention of newspapers, television etc, especially when you do not want it
glar·ing /'gleərɪŋ $ 'gler-/ *adj* **1** very bad and very noticeable; ▤ **obvious**: *The book's most **glaring omission** is the lack of an index.* | *a **glaring example** of political corruption* **2** too bright and difficult to look at: *the **glaring light** of high noon*

in a way that is very clear and easy to notice: *Some of the clues were glaringly obvious.*

glas·nost /ˈɡlæznɒst $ ˈɡlɑːsnoʊst/ *n* [U] the POLICY begun by Mikhail Gorbachev in the USSR in the 1980s of allowing discussion of the country's problems

---

glasses

wine glass

brandy glass *BrE*/ snifter *AmE*

long glass

beer glass

shot glass

---

glass¹ S1 W1 /ɡlɑːs $ ɡlæs/ *n*

1 TRANSPARENT MATERIAL [U] a transparent solid substance used for making windows, bottles etc: *a glass bowl* | *a piece of broken glass* | **pane/sheet of glass** (=a flat piece of glass with straight edges) | *the cathedral's stained glass windows* → see picture at MATERIAL

2 FOR DRINKING [C] a container used for drinking made of glass; → **cup: wine/brandy/champagne etc glass** | *Nigel raised his glass in a toast to his son.*

3 AMOUNT OF LIQUID [C] the amount of a drink contained in a glass: [+of] *She poured us a glass of wine each.*

4 FOR EYES **glasses** [plural] two pieces of specially cut glass or plastic in a frame, which you wear in order to see more clearly; ◻ **spectacles**: *He was clean-shaven and wore glasses.* | *I need a new pair of glasses.* | **distance/reading glasses** ⚠ Do not say 'a glasses': *She's got nice (NOT a nice) glasses.* → DARK GLASSES, FIELD GLASSES

5 GLASS OBJECTS [U] objects which are made of glass, especially ones used for drinking and eating: *a priceless collection of Venetian glass*

6 people in glass houses shouldn't throw stones used to say that you should not criticize someone for having a fault if you have the same fault yourself

7 under glass plants that are grown under glass are protected from the cold by a glass cover

8 MIRROR [C] *old-fashioned* a mirror

9 the glass *old-fashioned* a BAROMETER → CUT GLASS, GROUND GLASS, LOOKING GLASS, MAGNIFYING GLASS, PLATE GLASS; → **raise your glass** at RAISE¹ (16); → SAFETY GLASS, STAINED GLASS

glass² *v*

glass sth ⇔ **in** *phr v BrE* to cover something with glass, or to build a glass structure around something

glass ceiling *n* [singular] the attitudes and practices that prevent women or particular groups from getting high level jobs, even though there are no actual laws or rules to stop them: *Goodhue shattered the glass ceiling as the first female publisher at Time Inc.*

glassed-in *adj* surrounded by a glass structure: *a glassed-in porch*

glass fibre *n* [U] FIBREGLASS

glass·ful /ˈɡlɑːsful $ ˈɡlæs-/ *n* [C] the amount of liquid a glass will hold

glass·house /ˈɡlɑːshaʊs $ ˈɡlæs-/ *n* [C] *BrE* **1** a building made mainly of glass which is used for growing plants; ◻ **greenhouse 2 the glasshouse** *informal* a military prison

glass·ware /ˈɡlɑːsweə $ ˈɡlæswer/ *n* [U] glass objects, especially ones used for drinking and eating

---

glass·y /ˈɡlɑːsi $ ˈɡlæsi/ *adj* **1** smooth and shining, like glass: *the glassy surface of the lake* **2** glassy eyes show no feeling or understanding, and do not move

glassy-eyed *adj* having eyes that do not move or show any expression

glau·co·ma /ɡlɔːˈkəʊmə $ ɡlɔːˈkoʊ-/ *n* [U] an eye disease in which increased pressure inside your eye gradually makes you lose your sight

glaze¹ /ɡleɪz/ *v* **1** [I] also **glaze over** if your eyes glaze over, they show no expression, usually because you are very bored or tired: *Sometimes his eyes would glaze over for a second or two.* **2** [T] to cover plates, cups etc made of clay with a thin liquid that gives them a shiny surface **3** [T] to cover food with a liquid which gives it an attractive shiny surface: *Glaze the rolls with egg-white.* **4** [T] to fit glass into window frames in a house, door etc

glaze² *n* [C,U] **1** a liquid that is used to cover plates, cups etc made of clay to give them a shiny surface **2** a liquid which is put onto food to give it an attractive shiny surface **3** a transparent covering of oil paint spread over a painting

glazed /ɡleɪzd/ *adj* **glazed look/eyes/expression etc** if you have a glazed look, your eyes show no expression, usually because you are very bored or tired

gla·zi·er /ˈɡleɪziə $ -ʒər/ *n* [C] someone whose job is to fit glass into window frames

glaz·ing /ˈɡleɪzɪŋ/ *n* [U] glass that has been used to fill windows → DOUBLE GLAZING

gleam¹ /ɡliːm/ *v* [I] **1** to shine softly; ◻ **glimmer**: *His teeth gleamed under his moustache.* | [+with] *The wooden panelling was gleaming with wax polish.* **2** if your eyes or face gleam with a feeling, they show it; ◻ **glint**: [+with] *He laughed, his eyes gleaming with amusement.* —**gleaming** *adj*: *gleaming white walls*

> **WORD CHOICE: gleam, glint, glisten, glitter, glow**
> **gleam** is used especially of smooth clean surfaces that shine: *She polished the car until it gleamed.* | *gleaming white teeth*
> **glint** means to shine brightly with a small flash of light. It is used especially of shiny metals: *Her jewellery glinted in the sun.*
> **glisten** is used of wet or oily surfaces that shine: *The wet streets glistened.*
> **glitter** means to shine brightly with many small flashes of light: *the glittering frost*
> **glow** means to shine with a warm soft steady light. It is often used of things that give off heat: *The coal in the fireplace was still glowing.*

gleam² *n* [C] **1** a small pale light, especially one that shines for a short time; ◻ **glimmer**: [+of] *They saw a sudden gleam of light.* **2** the brightness of something that shines; ◻ **glint**: [+of] *the gleam of gold and diamonds* **3** an emotion or expression that appears for a moment on someone's face: [+of] *She saw a gleam of amusement in his eyes.* | *Rose looked at me with a furious gleam in her eyes.* **4 sth is a gleam in sb's eye** used to say that something is being planned or thought about, but does not yet exist: *In those days, CD-ROMs were still just a gleam in the eye of some young engineer.*

glean /ɡliːn/ *v* **1** [T] to find out information slowly and with difficulty: **glean sth from sb/sth** *Additional information was gleaned from other sources.* **2** [I,T] to collect grain that has been left behind after the crops have been cut

glean·ings /ˈɡliːnɪŋz/ *n* [plural] small pieces of information that you have found out with difficulty

glee /ɡliː/ *n* [U] a feeling of satisfaction and excitement, often because something bad has happened to

G

someone else; ◰ **delight**: *Manufacturers are **rubbing** their **hands** with glee as they prepare to cash in.*

glee club *n* [C] *AmE* a group of people who sing together for enjoyment

glee·ful /ˈgliːfəl/ *adj* very excited and satisfied: *a gleeful laugh* —**gleefully** *adv*

glen /glen/ *n* [C] a deep narrow valley in Scotland or Ireland

glib /glɪb/ *adj* **1** said easily and without thinking about all the problems involved – used to show disapproval: *glib generalizations* **2** speaking easily but without thinking carefully – used to show disapproval: *glib politicians* —**glibly** *adv* —**glibness** *n* [U]

glide¹ /glaɪd/ *v* [I] **1** [always + adv/prep] to move smoothly and quietly, as if without effort: [+**across/ over/down** etc] *couples gliding over the dance-floor* **2 a)** if a bird glides, it flies without moving its wings **b)** if a plane glides, it flies without using an engine **3** [always + adv/prep] to do or achieve things easily: [+**through**] *Kennedy seemed to glide through life.*

glide² *n* [C] **1** a smooth quiet movement that seems to take no effort **2** *technical* the act of moving from one musical note to another without a break in sound **3** *technical* a vowel which is made by moving your tongue from one position to another; → **diphthong**

glid·er /ˈglaɪdə $ -ər/ *n* [C] a light plane that flies without an engine

glid·ing /ˈglaɪdɪŋ/ *n* [U] the sport of flying in a glider → HANG-GLIDING

glim·mer¹ /ˈglɪmə $ -ər/ *n* [C] **1** a small sign of something such as hope or understanding: [+**of**] *a glimmer of hope for the future* **2** a light that is not very bright; ◰ **gleam**: [+**of**] *the first glimmer of dawn*

glimmer² *v* [I] to shine with a light that is not very bright; ◰ **gleam**: *a weak, glimmering light*

glim·mer·ing /ˈglɪmərɪŋ/ *n* [C often plural] a small sign of thought or feeling: *The glimmerings of an idea began to come to him.*

glimpse¹ /glɪmps/ *n* [C] **1** a quick look at someone or something that does not allow you to see them clearly: [+**of**] *They caught a glimpse of a dark green car.* | **brief/fleeting/quick glimpse** (=a very short look) *We only had a fleeting glimpse of the river.* **2** a short experience of something that helps you begin to understand it: [+**of/into/at**] *a glimpse of what life might be like in the future*

glimpse² *v* [T] **1** to see someone or something for a moment without getting a complete view of them; ◰ **catch sight of**: *I glimpsed a figure at the window.* → see box at GLANCE¹ **2** to begin to understand something for a moment: *For the first time she glimpsed the truth about her sister.*

glint¹ /glɪnt/ *v* [I] **1** if a shiny surface glints, it gives out small flashes of light; ◰ **sparkle**: *The gold rims of his spectacles glinted in the sun.* → see box at GLEAM¹ **2** if light glints off a surface, it shines back off it: *Sunlight glinted off the windows of a tall apartment building.* **3** if your eyes glint, they shine and show an unfriendly feeling

glint² *n* [C] **1** a look in someone's eyes which shows a particular feeling; ◰ **gleam**: *a humorous glint in her eyes* **2** a flash of light from a shiny surface

glis·ten /ˈglɪsən/ *v* [I] to shine and look wet or oily: [+**with**] *The boy's back was glistening with sweat.* | *glistening black hair*; → see box at GLEAM¹

glitch /glɪtʃ/ *n* [C] a small fault in a machine or piece of equipment, that stops it working: *a software glitch*

glit·ter¹ /ˈglɪtə $ -ər/ *v* [I] **1** to shine brightly with flashing points of light; ◰ **sparkle**: *The river glittered in the sunlight.* → see box at GLEAM¹ **2** if someone's eyes glitter, they shine very brightly and show a particular strong emotion: [+**with**] *His blue eyes glittered with anger.*

glitter² *n* [U] **1** brightness consisting of many flashing points of light: *the glitter of his gold cigarette case* **2** *literary* a bright shining expression in someone's eyes that shows a particular emotion; ◰ **gleam**: *There was no mistaking the mocking glitter in his eyes.* **3** the exciting attractive quality of a place or a way of life which is connected with rich or famous people: *The glamour and glitter of London was not for him.* **4** very small pieces of shiny paper that are used for decoration —**glittery** *adj*: *glittery earrings*

glit·te·ra·ti /ˌglɪtəˈrɑːti/ *n* [plural] people who are rich, famous, and fashionable

glit·ter·ing /ˈglɪtərɪŋ/ *adj* [usually before noun] **1** giving off many small flashes of light; ◰ **sparkling**: *glittering jewels* **2** very successful: *a glittering career* **3** connected with rich, famous and fashionable people: *a glittering Hollywood premiere*

glitz /glɪts/ *n* [U] the exciting, attractive quality which is connected with rich, famous and fashionable people; ◰ **glamour**: *show business glitz*

glitz·y /ˈglɪtsi/ *adj* exciting and attractive because of being connected with rich, famous, and fashionable people; ◰ **glamorous**: *glitzy London parties*

gloam·ing /ˈgləʊmɪŋ $ ˈgloʊ-/ *n* **the gloaming** *literary* the time in the early evening when it is becoming dark; ◰ **dusk**

gloat /gləʊt $ gloʊt/ *v* [I] to show in an annoying way that you are proud of your own success or happy about someone else's failure: [+**over**] *The fans are still gloating over Scotland's victory.* —**gloat** *n* [singular]

glob /glɒb/ *n* [C] *informal* a small amount of something soft or liquid that has a round shape; ◰ **dollop**: *globs of paint*

glo·bal W3 /ˈgləʊbəl $ ˈgloʊ-/ *adj*
1 affecting or including the whole world; → **universal**: *global climate change* | *a slowdown in the global economy*
2 considering all the parts of a problem or situation together: *We are taking a global view of our business.*
3 affecting a whole computer system, program, or FILE —**globally** *adv*

glo·bal·i·za·tion also **-isation** *BrE* /ˌgləʊbəlaɪˈzeɪʃən $ ˌgloʊbələ-/ *n* [U] the process of making something such as a business operate in a lot of different countries all around the world, or the result of this: *the increasing globalization of world trade*

glo·bal·ize also **-ise** *BrE* /ˈgləʊbəlaɪz $ ˈgloʊ-/ *v* [I,T] if a company, industry, or ECONOMY globalizes or is globalized, it has business activities all over the world

global ˈvillage *n* [singular] a name for the world, used to emphasize the degree to which everything is connected and each part depends on the others

global ˈwarming *n* [U] a general increase in world temperatures caused by increased amounts of CARBON DIOXIDE around the Earth → see picture at ENVIRONMENT

globe /gləʊb $ gloʊb/ *n* [C] **1** a round object with a map of the Earth drawn on it **2 the globe** the world: *We export our goods all over the globe.* **3** an object shaped like a ball; ◰ **sphere**

globe ˈartichoke *n* [C] *BrE* an ARTICHOKE

globe·trot·ter /ˈgləʊbtrɒtə $ ˈgloʊbtrɑːtər/ *n* [C] *informal* someone who spends a lot of their time travelling to many different countries —**globe-trotting** *adj* —**globe-trotting** *n* [U]

glob·u·lar /ˈglɒbjʊlə $ ˈglɑːbjələr/ *adj* in the shape of a globule or a globe

glob·ule /ˈglɒbjuːl $ ˈglɑː-/ *n* [C] a small drop of a liquid, or of a solid that has been melted: *globules of fat*

glock·en·spiel /ˈglɒkənspiːl $ ˈglɑː-/ *n* [C] a musical instrument consisting of many flat metal bars of different lengths, that you play with special hammers; → **xylophone**

glom /glɒm $ glɑːm/ *v* **glommed, glomming**
glom onto sth *phr v* *AmE informal* **1** to become

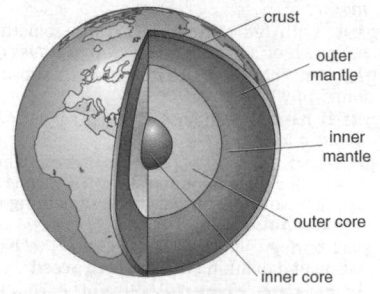

globe

axis
North Pole
Arctic Circle
line of latitude
line of longitude
Tropic of Cancer
northern hemisphere
southern hemisphere
equator
Tropic of Capricorn
South Pole
Antarctic Circle

crust
outer mantle
inner mantle
outer core
inner core

attached to someone or something so strongly that it is difficult to break the attachment: *The antibodies glom onto the virus and destroy it.* **2** to be very attracted to an idea, opinion, style etc: *College students have glommed onto the new African styles.*

gloom /gluːm/ *n* [singular, U] **1** *literary* almost complete darkness: *He peered into the gathering* (=increasing) *gloom.* **2** a feeling of great sadness and lack of hope: *a time of high unemployment and economic gloom* → **doom and gloom** at **DOOM²**

gloom·y /ˈgluːmi/ *comparative* **gloomier**, *superlative* **gloomiest** *adj* **1** making you feel that things will not improve; ▣ **depressing**: *The report paints a gloomy picture of the economy.* **2** sad because you think the situation will not improve; ▣ **depressed**: *Anne dismissed these gloomy thoughts from her mind.* **3** dark, especially in a way that makes you feel sad: *It was a gloomy room with one small window.* —**gloomily** *adv*

glop /glɒp $ glɑːp/ *AmE;* **gloop** /gluːp/ *BrE n* [U] *informal* a thick soft wet mass of something —**gloppy** *adj*

glo·ri·fied /ˈglɔːrɨfaɪd/ *adj* [only before noun] made to seem like something more important: *Many bosses view secretaries as no more than glorified typists.*

glo·ri·fy /ˈglɔːrɨfaɪ/ *v* **glorified, glorifying, glorifies** [T] **1** to make someone or something seem more important or better than they really are: *films which glorify violence* **2** to praise someone or something, especially God —**glorification** /ˌglɔːrɨfɨˈkeɪʃən/ *n* [U]: *the glorification of war*

glo·ri·ous /ˈglɔːriəs/ *adj* **1** having or deserving great fame, praise, and honour: *We have in our grasp a truly glorious future.* | *a glorious victory* **2** very beautiful or impressive: *glorious views of the rocky coast* | *a glorious red sky* **3** glorious weather is sunny and hot: *glorious sunshine* **4** extremely enjoyable; ▣ **wonderful**: *We had a glorious afternoon of sailing.* —**gloriously** *adv*

glo·ry¹ /ˈglɔːri/ *n plural* **glories 1** [U] the importance, honour, and praise that people give someone they admire a lot: *She dreamt of future glory as an Olympic champion.* | *Goran's **moment of glory** came*

when he defeated Rafter. | *He began the season in a **blaze of glory**, scoring seven goals in as many games.* **2** [C] an achievement that is greatly admired or respected, or makes you very proud: [+of] *one of the finest artistic glories of Florence* | *monuments to **past glories*** | *Becoming a Supreme Court judge was the **crowning glory*** (=most successful part) *of her career.* **3** [U] when something is beautiful and impressive in appearance: *They spent $10 million restoring the theatre to its former glory.* | **in all its/their etc glory** *The sun emerged from behind the clouds in all its glory.* **4 bask/bathe in sb's/sth's (reflected) glory** to share some of the importance and praise that belongs to someone close to you **5 glory days** a time in the past when someone was admired: *the team's glory days in the late '80s* **6 to the (greater) glory of sb/sth** *formal* in order to increase the honour that is given to someone or something: *The cathedral was built to the greater glory of God.* **7 Glory (be) to God/Jesus etc** *spoken* used to say that God deserves praise, honour, and thanks

glory² *v* **gloried, glorying, glories**
glory in sth *phr v* to enjoy or be proud of something: *She didn't like to glory in her past victories.*

gloss¹ /glɒs $ glɔːs, glɑːs/ *n* **1** [singular,U] a bright shine on a surface: *This gel will add gloss to even the dullest hair.* | **polish/shine to a high gloss** *The silverware had been polished to a high gloss.* **2** [singular,U] an attractive appearance on the surface of something that may hide something less pleasant: *Beneath the gloss of success was a tragic private life.* | *The injury to Keane **took the gloss off** Manchester United's victory.* **3** [C] a note in a piece of writing that explains a difficult word, phrase, or idea **4** [singular] a description or explanation that makes something seem more attractive or acceptable than it really is: *The minister was accused of **putting a gloss on** the government's poor performance.* **5 gloss finish/print** a surface or photograph that has been made shiny **6** also **gloss paint** [U] paint that looks shiny after it dries; → **matt**

gloss² *v* [T] to provide a note in a piece of writing, explaining a difficult word, phrase, or idea
gloss over sth *phr v* to avoid talking about something unpleasant, or to say as little as possible about it: *She glossed over the details of her divorce.*

glos·sa·ry /ˈglɒsəri $ ˈglɔː-, ˈglɑː-/ *n plural* **glossaries** [C] a list of special words and explanations of their meanings, often at the end of a book

gloss·y¹ /ˈglɒsi $ ˈglɔːsi, ˈglɑːsi/ *adj* **1** shiny and smooth: *her glossy black hair* | *the glossy surface of the leaves* → see picture at **SURFACE** **2 glossy magazine/brochure etc** a magazine etc that is printed on good quality shiny paper, usually with lots of colour pictures **3** something that is glossy has an attractive appearance on the surface that may hide something less pleasant: *a glossy election campaign* —**glossiness** *n* [U]

glossy² *n plural* **glossies** [C usually plural] **1** *BrE* also **glossy magazine** a magazine that is printed on good quality shiny paper, usually with lots of colour pictures **2** a photograph printed on shiny paper

glottal 'stop *n* [C] *technical* a speech sound made by completely closing and then opening your glottis, which in some forms of spoken English may take the place of a /t/ between vowel sounds or may be used before a vowel sound

glot·tis /ˈglɒtɨs $ ˈglɑː-/ *n* [C] *technical* the space between your VOCAL CORDS which helps to make the sound of your voice. When this space is opened and closed, the movement produces a sound —**glottal** *adj*

glove /glʌv/ *n* [C] **1** a piece of clothing that you wear on your hand in order to protect it or keep it warm; → **mitten**: *a pair of gloves* | *boxing gloves* | *rubber/leather etc gloves* **2 the gloves are off** used to say that people are ready to begin a fight or argument → **fit (sb) like a glove** at **FIT¹ (1)**; → **hand in glove** at **HAND¹ (34)**

G

gloves

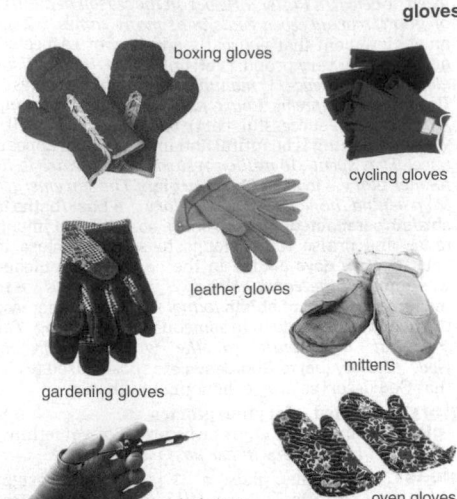

boxing gloves

cycling gloves

leather gloves

mittens

gardening gloves

surgical gloves

oven gloves

'glove com·partment also **'glove box** n [C] a small cupboard in a car in front of the passenger seat, where small things such as maps can be kept → see picture at CAR

gloved /glʌvd/ adj wearing a glove

'glove ˌpuppet n [C] BrE a PUPPET that you put over your hand; ▪ **hand puppet** AmE

glow¹ /gləʊ $ gloʊ/ n [singular] **1** a soft steady light: [+from] the glow from the dying fire | [+of] the dim glow of the lightbulb | the warm glow of the setting sun | the green glow of the computer monitor **2** the pink colour in your face or body that you have when you are healthy, have been doing exercise, or are excited: She had a **healthy glow** in her cheeks. **3** a glow of pleasure/satisfaction/happiness etc a strong feeling of pleasure etc: Sophie felt a glow of pride.

glow² v [I] **1** to produce or REFLECT a soft steady light; ▪ **shine**: The bedside lamp glowed dimly. | The fireplace was still glowing with the remains of last night's fire. | The red tip of his cigarette was glowing in the dark. → see box at GLEAM¹ **2** if your face or body glows, it is pink or hot because you are healthy, have been doing exercise, or are feeling a strong emotion: [+with] She looked exceptionally well, **glowing with health**. **3** glow with pride/joy/pleasure etc to look very happy because you feel proud etc: She gazed up at him, glowing with happiness. **4** if something glows with a quality or colour, it is attractive and has strong colours: [+with] The interior of the house glowed with colour, warmth, and life.

glow·er /'glaʊə $ -ər/ v [I] to look at someone in an angry way; ▪ **glare**: [+at] She glowered at him disapprovingly. —**glower** n [C]

glow·ing /'gləʊɪŋ $ 'gloʊ-/ adj **1** glowing report/account/description etc a report etc that is full of praise: I've had glowing reports from Neil about your work. **2** in glowing terms using a lot of praise: He speaks of you in glowing terms. —**glowingly** adv

'glow-worm n [C] an insect that produces a small amount of light from its body

glu·cose /'gluːkəʊs $ -koʊs/ n [U] a natural form of sugar that exists in fruit

glue¹ S3 /gluː/ n [C,U] a sticky substance used for joining things together

glue² v present participle **gluing** or **glueing** [T] **1** to join two things together using glue; ▪ **stick**: glue sth (back) together The sheets are glued together with strong adhesive. | glue sth in place/position Check that you have glued everything in place properly. **2** be

glued to sth informal **a)** to look at something with all your attention: He was glued to the TV when the Olympics were on. **b)** to not move because you are very interested, surprised, frightened etc: We were glued to our chairs, listening intently to every word. | be glued to the spot BrE: Sarah was glued to the spot, terrified by the scene in front of her.

'glue-ˌsniffing n [U] the habit of breathing in gases from glues in order to produce a state of pleasure —**glue sniffer** n [C]

glue·y /'gluːi/ adj **1** sticky like glue **2** covered with glue

glum /glʌm/ adj comparative **glummer**, superlative **glummest** if someone is glum, they feel unhappy and do not talk a lot; ▪ **gloomy**: Anna looked glum. | After dinner, Kate lapsed into a glum silence. —**glumly** adv She stared glumly at her plate. —**glumness** n [U]

glut¹ /glʌt/ n [C usually singular] a supply of something especially a product or crop, that is more than is needed; ▪ **shortage**: [+of] a glut of oil on the world market

glut² v **glutted, glutting** [T] to cause something to have too much of something: the glutted property market

glu·ten /'gluːtn/ n [U] a sticky PROTEIN substance that is found in wheat flour

glu·ti·nous /'gluːtˈnəs $ -tn-əs/ adj very sticky: glutinous mud

glut·ton /'glʌtn/ n [C] **1** someone who eats too much **2** a glutton for punishment someone who seems to enjoy working hard or doing something unpleasant —**gluttonous** adj

glut·ton·y /'glʌtəni/ n [U] formal the bad habit of eating and drinking too much; ▪ **greed**

gly·ce·rine, glycerin /'glɪsərɪn/ n [U] a thick sweet transparent liquid made from fats and used in medicines, explosives, and foods

gm plural **gm** or **gms** the written abbreviation of **gram** or grams

GM /ˌdʒiː 'em/ adj BrE **genetically modified** GM foods or plants have had their GENETIC structure changed so that they are not affected by particular diseases or harmful insects

GMO /ˌdʒiː em 'əʊ $ -'oʊ/ n [C] **genetically modified organism** a plant or other living thing whose GENES have been changed by scientists, especially in order to make it less likely to get diseases or be harmed by insects etc —**GMO** adj [only before noun]: GMO crops

GMT /ˌdʒiː em 'tiː/ n [U] BrE the abbreviation of **Greenwich Mean Time**, the time as measured at Greenwich in London, that is used as an international standard for measuring time

gnarled /nɑːld $ nɑːrld/ adj **1** a gnarled tree or branch is rough and twisted with hard lumps **2** gnarled hands or fingers are twisted, rough, and difficult to move, usually because they are old

gnarl·y /'nɑːli $ 'nɑːr-/ adj **1** a gnarly tree or branch is rough and twisted with hard lumps ▪ **gnarled 2** gnarly hands or fingers are twisted, rough, and difficult to move, usually because they are old; ▪ **gnarled 3** AmE spoken a word meaning very good or excellent, used by young people: 'Look at the size of that wave.' 'Gnarly!' **4** AmE spoken a word meaning very bad, used by young people: a gnarly car wreck

gnash /næʃ/ v gnash your teeth to be very angry or unhappy about something, or to move your teeth against each other so that they make a noise, especially because you are unhappy or angry

gnash·ers /'næʃəz $ -ərz/ n [plural] BrE informal teeth

gnat /næt/ n [C] a small flying insect that bites

gnaw /nɔː $ nɒː/ v [I,T always + adv/prep] to keep biting something hard; ▪ **chew**: Dexter gnawed his pen thoughtfully. | A rat had gnawed a hole in the box. | [+at/on] The puppy was gnawing on a bone.

gnaw (away) at sb/sth phr v to make someone feel worried or frightened, over a period of time: Some thing was gnawing at the back of his mind. | Doubt was gnawing away at her confidence.

gnaw·ing /ˈnɔːɪŋ $ ˈnɒː-/ adj [only before noun] worrying or painful, especially for a long time: gnawing doubts

gnome /nəʊm $ noʊm/ n [C] **1** a creature in children's stories who looks like a little old man. Gnomes have pointed hats, live under the ground, and guard gold, jewels etc. **2** a stone or plastic figure representing one of these creatures: a **garden gnome**

gno·mic /ˈnəʊmɪk $ ˈnoʊ-/ adj written gnomic remarks are short, clever, and difficult to understand

GNP /ˌdʒiː en ˈpiː/ n [singular] **gross national product** the total value of all the goods and services produced in a country, usually in a single year; → **GDP**

gnu /nuː/ n plural **gnu** or **gnus** [C] a large African animal with a tail and curved horns; ⊟ **wildebeest**

GNVQ /ˌdʒiː en viː ˈkjuː/ n [C,U] **General National Vocational Qualification** a course of study and examination in practical subjects such as business, information technology, ENGINEERING etc, done by some students in schools in England and Wales, usually at the age of 16; → **BTEC, A level, GCSE**

go¹ [S1] [W1] /ɡəʊ $ ɡoʊ/ v past tense **went** /went/ past participle **gone** /ɡɒn $ ɡɔːn/ third person singular **goes** /ɡəʊz $ ɡoʊz/
1 MOVE/TRAVEL a) [I always + adv/prep] also **been** to travel or move to a place that is away from where you are or where you live; → **come**: There's nothing more we can do here. Let's **go home**. | Have you ever been to Japan? | I have been to (=have travelled to) Germany several times. | Where are you going? | We're going to Canada in the summer. | Dinah went into the kitchen. | She went over and put her arm around him. | I'm going round to her house to find out what's wrong. | I'll just go up (=go upstairs) and ask him what he wants. **b)** [I,T] to move or travel in a particular way or for a particular distance: It took us over an hour to go ten miles. | The car was going much too fast. | We went a different way from usual that day. | **go by bus/train/car** etc It'll be quicker to go by train. **c) go and do sth** also **go do sth** AmE [not in past tenses] to move to a particular place in order to do something: Go wash your hands before lunch. | I went and spoke to the manager. ⚠ **Come** or **go?**; → see box at DEEN; → see box at COME¹
2 go flying/laughing/rushing etc to move in a particular way, or to do something as you are moving: The plate went crashing to the floor. | The bullet went flying over my head. | John went rushing off down the corridor.
3 ATTEND a) [I] to be at a concert, party, meeting etc: [+to] Are you going to Manuela's party? | I first went to a rock concert when I was 15. **b) go to school/church/work** etc to regularly attend school, a church etc: He doesn't go to the synagogue these days.
4 LEAVE [I] to leave a place: What time does the last train go? | Right, let's go! | She turned to go. | **be/get going** It's late! I must get going.
5 DO PARTICULAR ACTIVITY [I,T] to leave the place where you are, in order to do something: **go for a walk/swim** etc Let's go for a walk. | **go shopping/swimming/skiing** etc I need to go shopping this afternoon. | **go on a trip/tour/cruise** etc My parents are going on a cruise.
6 be going to do sth a) to intend to do something: I'm going to tell Dad what you said. **b)** used to talk about what will happen in the future: He looked as if he was going to cry. | It's going to rain later. → **GONNA**
7 REACH [I always + adv/prep, not in progressive] to reach as far as a particular place or to lead to a particular place: The road goes through the middle of the forest. | The belt won't go around my waist.
8 CHANGE [linking verb] to change in some way, especially by becoming worse than before: The company went bankrupt last year. | **go bad/sour** etc The bread's gone mouldy. | **go grey/white** etc Her hair is starting to go grey. | **go mad/deaf/bald** etc He went crazy and tried

to kill her. | **go wild/mad/white** etc **with sth** The crowd was going wild with excitement.; → see box at BECOME
9 HAPPEN [I always + adv/prep] to happen or develop in a particular way: How did your French test go? | **go well/smoothly/fine** etc The party went well. | Everything's going fine at the moment. | I feel very encouraged by **the way things are going**. | Many industries have been forced to cut jobs and it looks like the electronics industry is **going the same way**.
10 how are things going?/how's it going?/how goes it? spoken used to ask someone what is happening in their life, especially used as a greeting: 'Hi Jane. How's it going?' 'Fine, thanks.'
11 USUAL POSITION [I always + adv/prep, not in progressive] if something goes somewhere, that is its usual position: Where do the plates go? | The book goes on the top shelf.
12 FIT [I not in progressive] to be the right size, shape, or amount for a particular space: [+in/under/inside etc] I don't think all that will go in the suitcase.
13 BE SENT [I] to be sent or passed on: [+by/through/to etc] The email went to everyone in the company. | That letter should go by special delivery. | Complaints must go through the proper channels.
14 BE IN A PARTICULAR STATE/CONDITION [linking verb] to be in a particular state or condition, especially a bad one: Many families are forced to **go hungry**.
15 go unanswered/unnoticed/unrewarded etc to not be answered, noticed etc: All my letters went unanswered. | He hoped that his nervousness would go unnoticed.
16 START [I] to start doing something: The preparations have been completed and we're ready to go. | Generally the action doesn't **get going** (=start) until after midnight. | I'm going to **get going on** (=start doing) the decorating next week.
17 WORK WELL [I] if a clock, watch, or machine goes, it moves and works as it should do: My watch isn't going. | I couldn't **get the pump going** (=make it work).
18 MAKE MOVEMENT [I always + adv/prep] used when you are telling someone about what movement someone or something made: She went like this with her hand.
19 SAY [T] spoken informal to say something: I asked her what she meant and she just went, 'Don't ask!'
20 MAKE A SOUND [T] to make a particular sound: The balloon suddenly went bang.
21 don't go doing sth spoken used to tell someone not to do something, especially something that is wrong or bad: It's a secret, so don't go telling everyone.
22 have gone and done sth spoken used when you are surprised or annoyed by what someone has done: Kay's gone and lost the car keys!
23 to go a) still remaining before something happens: Only ten days to go to Christmas! **b)** still having to be done or dealt with before you have finished: Laura's sat six exams and has two more to go. **c)** still to travel before you reach the place you are going to: only another five miles left to go **d)** used for saying that you want to take food away from a restaurant and eat it somewhere else: Two chicken dinners with corn to go.
24 don't go there spoken informal used to say that you do not want to think or talk about something: 'John and Clare having children?' 'Don't go there!' | 'What if the two of them...' **Don't even go there!**
25 STORY/DISCUSSION/SONG ETC [I always + adv/prep, T not in progressive] used to talk about what something such as a story or song consists of: The argument goes like this. | We need to 'spread a little happiness', as the song goes. | **The story goes that** my grandfather saved his captain's life in battle.
26 WHISTLE/BELL ETC [I] to make a noise as a warning or signal: A bell goes to mark the end of each class.
27 here/there sb goes again spoken used when someone has annoyed you by doing something they know

G

you do not like: *There you go again, jumping to conclusions.*

28 DISAPPEAR [I] to no longer exist or no longer be in the same place; ▣ **disappear**: *Has your headache gone yet?* | *The door was open and all his things had gone.*

29 GET INTO WORSE CONDITION [I] if one of your senses such as sight, hearing etc is going, it is getting worse: *Dad's eyesight is starting to go.* | *I'd forgotten that. My mind must be going.*

30 TO BE OBEYED [I] if what someone says goes, that person is in authority and what they say should be obeyed: *Phil's in charge around here, and what he says goes.*

31 BE DAMAGED [I] to become weak, damaged etc, or stop working properly: *The bulb's gone in the bathroom.* | *My jeans are starting to go at the knee.*

32 DIE [I] to die – use this when you want to avoid saying the word 'die': *Now that his wife's gone, he's all on his own.* | *When I go, I'd like to have my ashes scattered at sea.* → **dead and gone** at DEAD¹ (1)

33 BE SPENT [I] to be spent: *I don't know where all my money goes!* | [+on] *Half her salary goes on the rent.*

34 BE SOLD [I] to be sold: [+for/at] *A house like this would go for £250,000.* | [+to] *The jewels will go to the highest bidder.* | *He bought me some CDs which were going cheap* (=were being sold at a low price).

35 PAY MONEY [I] to offer a particular amount of money for something: *I'll give you $500 for it but I can't go any higher than that.* | [+to] *I think we could probably go to £15,000.*

36 going, going, gone! *spoken* used to say that something has been sold at an AUCTION

37 TIME [I always + adv/prep] used to say how quickly or slowly time passes: *The day seemed to go so slowly.*

38 there/bang goes sth *spoken* used to say that you are disappointed because something has stopped you doing or getting what you wanted: *Well, there goes my chance of fame!*

39 go to show/prove/indicate etc sth to help to prove something: *It just goes to show how much people judge each other by appearances.*

40 be going *informal* to be available: *Are there any jobs going at the café?* | *I'll take that if it's going spare.*

41 COLOURS/STYLES/TASTES [I] if colours, tastes, styles etc go, they look, taste etc good together: *I don't think pink and yellow really go.* | [+with] *Do you think this shirt will go with the skirt I bought?* | [+together] *Pork and apple go especially well together.*

42 as sb/sth goes used for comparing someone or something with the average person or thing of that type: *As marriages go, it certainly wasn't dull.*

43 go all out to try very hard to do or get something: [+for] *We're going all out for victory in this afternoon's game.* | go all out to do sth *The company will be going all out to improve on last year's sales.*

44 have nothing/not much/a lot etc going for sb/sth used to talk about how many advantages and good qualities someone or something has: *It's a town that's got a lot going for it.*

45 where does sb/sth go from here? *spoken* used to ask what should be done next, especially when there is a problem: *So where do you think we should go from here?*

46 LEAVE A JOB [I] to leave your job, especially because you are forced to: *He was becoming an embarrassment to the government and had to go.* | *If Jill goes, who will take her place?*

47 GET RID OF STH [I] if something goes, someone gets rid of it: *The policies will have to go if the party is to win the next election.* | *A hundred jobs are expected to go following the merger.*

48 TOILET [I] *informal* to make waste come out of your body

go about *phr v*
1 go about sth to start to do something: *I want to learn German but I don't know the best way to go about it.* | go about doing sth *The leaflet tells you how to go about making a will.*

2 go about sth to do something in the way that you usually do: *The villagers were going about their business as usual.* | *She went about her preparations in a quiet businesslike way.*

3 *BrE* if a ship goes about, it turns to go in the opposite direction

go after sth/sb *phr v*
1 to follow or chase someone or something because you want to catch them: *Joe went after her to make sure she was unhurt.*

2 to try to get something: *I can't decide whether to go after the job or not.*

go against sb/sth *phr v*
1 if something goes against your beliefs, principles etc, it is opposite to them: *This goes against everything I've been brought up to believe in.* | *I often have to make decisions that go against the grain* (=are not what I would normally choose to do).

2 to do the opposite of what someone wants or advises you to do: *She was scared to go against her father's wishes.*

3 if a decision, judgment etc goes against you, you do not get the result you want: *His lawyer hinted that the case might go against him.* | *The vote went against the government.*

go ahead *phr v*
1 to start to do something, especially after planning it or asking permission to do it: [+with] *They've decided to go ahead with plans to build 50 new houses on the site.* | go ahead and do sth *I went ahead and arranged the trip anyway.*

2 if an event or process goes ahead, it happens: *A judge has ruled that the music festival can go ahead.*

3 *spoken* used to give someone permission to do something, or let them speak before you: *'Do you mind if I open the window?' 'No, go ahead.'* | *If you want to leave, go right ahead.*

4 also **go on ahead** to go somewhere before the other people in your group: *You go ahead and we'll catch you up later.* | [+of] *He stood back to let Sue go ahead of him.*

5 to start to be winning a game or competition: *Dulwich went ahead after 22 minutes.* → **GO-AHEAD¹**

go along *phr v*
1 if you do something as you go along, you do it without planning or preparing it: *He was making the story up as he went along.* | *I never had formal training, I just learned the job as I went along.*

2 to go to an event or a place where something is happening: [+to] *I might go along to the meeting tonight.*

3 to happen or develop in a particular way: *Things seem to be going along nicely.*

go along with sb/sth *phr v*
1 to agree with or support someone or something: *I would be happy to go along with the idea.* | *Often it was easier to go along with her rather than risk an argument.*

2 go along with you! *BrE spoken old-fashioned* used to tell someone that you do not believe what they are saying

go around also **go round** *BrE phr v*
1 DRESS/BEHAVE also **go about** *BrE* to behave or dress in a particular way: go around doing sth *You can't go around accusing people like that.* | *He goes around in a T-shirt even in winter.*

2 ILLNESS go around (sth) also **go about (sth)** *BrE* if an illness is going around, a lot of people get it: *He had a bad dose of the flu virus that was going around.* | *There are a lot of nasty bugs going around.*

3 NEWS/STORY go around (sth) also **go about (sth)** *BrE* if news, a story, a joke etc is going around, a lot of people hear it and are talking about it: *A rumour was going around that I was having an affair with my boss.* | *There was a lot of gossip going around the village.*

4 go around with sb/go around together also **go around with sb** *BrE* to meet someone often and spend a lot of time with them: *I used to go around with a bad crowd.*

5 enough/plenty to go around enough for each person

Is there enough ice-cream to go around? | *There were never enough textbooks to go around.*

6 what goes around comes around used to say that if someone does bad things now, bad things will happen to them in the future

7 go around in your head if words, sounds etc go around in your head, you keep remembering them for a long time: *That stupid song kept going around in my head.* → **go around/round in circles** at CIRCLE¹ (5)

go at sth/sb *phr v* [not in passive] *informal*

1 to attack someone or argue with someone in a noisy way: *The two dogs went at each other as soon as I opened the gate.*

2 to do something, or start to do something, with a lot of energy: *Mary went at the task with great enthusiasm.*

go away *phr v*

1 to leave a place or person: *Go away and leave me alone!* | *I went away wondering if I'd said the wrong thing.*

2 to travel to a place and spend some time there, for example for a holiday: *Are you going away this year?* | [+for] *We're going away for the weekend.* | [+to] *He's going away to college next year.* | [+on] *I'm going away on a business trip next week.*

3 if a problem, unpleasant feeling etc goes away, it disappears: *Ignoring the crime problem won't make it go away.*

go back *phr v*

1 to return to a place that you have just come from: *I think we ought to go back now.* | [+to/into/inside etc] *I felt so sick I just wanted to go back to bed.* | [+for] *I had to go back for my passport* (=to get my passport).

2 there's no going back *spoken* used to say that you cannot make a situation the same as it was before: *I realized that once the baby was born there would be no going back.*

3 [always + adv/prep] to have been made, built, or started at some time in the past: *It's a tradition that goes back at least 100 years.* | [+to] *The building goes back to Roman times.*

4 if people go back a particular length of time, they have known each other for that length of time: *Peter and I go back 25 years.* | We **go back a long way** (=we have been friends for a long time).

5 to think about a particular time in the past or something that someone said before: *If you go back 20 years, most people didn't own a computer.* | [+to] *I'd like to go back to the point that was made earlier.*

go back on sth *phr v*

to not do something that you promised or agreed to do: **go back on your word/promise/decision** *Delors claimed that the President had gone back on his word.*

go back to sth *phr v*

to start doing something again after you have stopped for a period of time: *He went back to sleep.* | **go back to doing sth** *She went back to watching TV.*

go before *phr v*

1 to happen or exist before something else: *In some ways this program improves on what has gone before.*

2 go before sb/sth if something goes before a judge, group of people in authority etc, they consider it before making a decision: *The case will go before the court.* | *The proposal is likely to go before the committee.*

go beyond sth *phr v*

to be much better, worse, more serious etc than something else: *Their relationship had gone beyond friendship.* | *This goes beyond all limits of acceptable behaviour.*

go by *phr v*

1 if time goes by, it passes: *Things will get easier as time goes by.* | as the days/weeks/years go by *As the weeks went by, I became more and more worried.* | hardly a day/week/month etc goes by *Hardly a week goes by without some food scare being reported in the media.* | in days/times/years etc gone by (=in the past) *These herbs would have been grown for medicinal purposes in days gone by.*

2 go by sth to form an opinion about someone or something from the information or experience that

you have: *You can't always go by appearances.* | *If his past plays are anything to go by, this should be a play worth watching.*

3 go by sth to do things according to a set of rules or laws: *Only a fool goes by the rules all the time.* | *There was no doubt that the referee had gone by the book* (=had obeyed all the rules). → **go by the board** at BOARD¹ (8); → **go by the name of sth** at NAME¹ (1)

go down *phr v*

1 GET LOWER to become lower in level, amount etc: *His income went down last year.* | *Computers have gone down in price.* | go down by 10%/250/\$900 etc *Spending has gone down by 2%.*

2 STANDARD if something goes down, its quality or standard gets worse: *This neighbourhood has really gone down in the last few years.*

3 go down well/badly/a treat etc **a)** to get a particular reaction from someone: *His suggestion did not go down very well.* | *The movie went down very well in America.* | *The speech went down a treat* with members (=members liked it very much). | *The idea went down like a lead balloon* (=was not popular or successful). **b)** if food or drink goes down well, you enjoy it: *I'm not that hungry so a salad would go down nicely.*

4 GO FROM ONE PLACE TO ANOTHER to go from one place to another, especially to a place that is further south: [+to] *We're going down to Bournemouth for the weekend.* | *He's gone down to the store to get some milk.*

5 go down the shops/club/park etc *BrE spoken informal* to go to the shops, a club etc: *Does anyone want to go down the pub tonight?*

6 SHIP if a ship goes down, it sinks: *Ten men died when the ship went down.*

7 PLANE if a plane goes down, it suddenly falls to the ground: *An emergency call was received shortly before the plane went down.*

8 BECOME LESS SWOLLEN to become less swollen: *The swelling will go down if you rest your foot.*

9 LOSE AIR if something that is filled with air goes down, air comes out and it becomes smaller and softer: *Your tyre's gone down.*

10 BE REMEMBERED [always + adv/prep] to be recorded or remembered in a particular way: [+as] *The talks went down as a landmark in the peace process.* | *The carnival will go down in history* (=be remembered for many years) *as one of the best ever.*

11 COMPETITION/SPORT **a)** to lose a game, competition, or election: *The Hawkers went down 5–9.* | [+by] *The government went down by 71 votes.* | [+to] *Liverpool went down to Juventus.* **b)** to move down to a lower position in an official list of teams or players: [+to] *United went down to the second division.*

12 COMPUTER if a computer goes down, it stops working for a short time: *If one of the file servers goes down, you lose the whole network.*

13 LIGHTS if lights go down, they become less bright: *The lights went down and the curtain rose on an empty stage.*

14 SUN when the sun goes down, it appears to move down until you cannot see it any more

15 WIND if the wind goes down, it becomes less strong: *The wind had gone down but the night had turned chilly.*

16 PRISON *informal* to be sent to prison: *He went down for five years.*

17 HAPPEN *spoken informal* to happen: *the type of guy who knows what's going down* | *What's going down?*

18 LEAVE UNIVERSITY *BrE formal old-fashioned* to leave Oxford or Cambridge University at the end of a period of study

go down on sb *phr v*

to touch someone's sexual organs with the lips and tongue in order to give them sexual pleasure

go down with sth *phr v BrE informal*

to become ill, especially with an infectious disease: *Half the team had gone down with flu.*

G

go for sb/sth *phr v*

1 ATTACK *BrE* to attack or criticize someone: *The dog suddenly went for me.*

2 TRY TO GET STH to try to get or win something: *Jackson is going for his second gold medal here.* | **go for it** *spoken* (=used to encourage someone to try to achieve something) *If you really want the job, go for it!*; → **go for broke** at BROKE² (3)

3 CHOOSE *BrE* to choose something: *I think I'll go for the chocolate cake.*

4 I could/would go for sth *spoken* used to say that you would like to do or have something: *A full meal for less than five bucks! I could go for that!*

5 LIKE *informal* to like a particular type of person or thing: *Annie tends to go for older men.*

6 the same goes for sb/sth/sth also that goes for sb/sth too *spoken* used to say that a statement you have just made is true about someone or something else too: *Close all doors and lock them when you go out. The same goes for windows.*

go in *phr v*

when the sun or the moon goes in, cloud moves in front of it so that it cannot be seen

go in for sth *phr v*

1 to do an examination or take part in a competition: *I go in for all the competitions.*

2 to do or use something often because you enjoy it or like it: *I never really went in for sports.*

3 to choose something as your job: *I suppose I could go in for advertising.*

go in with sb *phr v*

to join with someone else to start a business or organization: *Ellie's going in with a friend who's just started a café.*

go into sth *phr v*

1 JOB [not in passive] to start to do a particular type of job: *I always wanted to go into nursing.* | *She's thinking of going into business* (=starting a business).

2 TIME/MONEY/EFFORT [not in passive] to be spent or used to get, make, or do something: *Years of research have gone into this book.* | **go into doing sth** *A great deal of time and effort has gone into ensuring that the event runs smoothly.*

3 EXPLAIN to explain, describe, or examine something in detail: *I don't want to go into the matter now.* | *I don't want to go into details now.*

4 COMPUTER [not in passive] to open a particular computer program, WINDOW, or FILE: *Go into your D drive.*

5 BE IN A PARTICULAR STATE [not in passive] to start to be in a particular state or condition: *She went into labour at midnight and the baby was born at 8 am.* | *The company went into liquidation.*

6 HIT [not in passive] if a vehicle goes into a tree, wall, or another vehicle, it hits it: *His car went into a lamppost in the high street.*

7 DIVIDE [not in passive] if a number goes into another number, the second number can be divided by the first: *12 goes into 60 five times.*

8 BEGIN TO MOVE IN PARTICULAR WAY [not in passive] if a vehicle goes into a particular movement, it starts to do it: *The plane had gone into a steep descent.*

go off *phr v*

1 LEAVE to leave a place, especially in order to do something: *He went off in search of something to eat.* | *John decided to go off on his own.* | [+to] *He went off to work as usual.* | **go off to do sth** *Geoff went off to play golf.*

2 EXPLODE to explode or fire: *The bomb went off at 6.30 this morning.* | *Fireworks were going off all over the city.* | *The gun went off and the bullet went flying over his head.*

3 MAKE A NOISE if an ALARM goes off, it makes a noise to warn you about something: *The thieves ran away when the alarm went off.* | *I've set the alarm clock to go off at 7 am.*

4 STOP LIKING **go off sb/sth** *BrE informal* to stop liking something or someone: *Many women go off coffee*

during pregnancy. | **go off doing sth** *I've gone off cooking lately.*

5 STOP WORKING if a machine or piece of equipment goes off, it stops working: *The central heating goes off at 9 o'clock.* | *Suddenly, all the lights went off.*

6 go off well/badly etc to happen in a particular way: *The party went off very well.*

7 HAPPEN *BrE spoken informal* to happen; ▣ **go on** *There was a blazing row going off next door.*

8 DECAY *BrE* if food goes off, it becomes too bad to eat: *The milk's gone off.*

9 SLEEP to go to sleep: *I'd just gone off to sleep when the phone rang.*

10 GET WORSE *BrE informal* to get worse: *He's a singer whose talent has gone off in recent years.*

go off on sb *phr v AmE informal*

to criticize or speak to someone in a very angry way

go off with sth/sb *phr v informal*

1 to leave your usual sexual partner in order to have a relationship with someone else: *She's gone off with her husband's best friend.*

2 to take something away from a place without having permission: *Who's gone off with my pen?*

go on *phr v*

1 CONTINUE **a)** to continue doing something or being in a situation: **go on doing sth** *He went on working until he was 91.* | [+with] *One of the actors was unwell and couldn't go on with the performance.* | *I can't go on like this for much longer.* **b)** to continue without stopping: *The noise goes on 24 hours a day.* | *The screaming went on and on* (=continued for a long time). → ONGOING

2 HAPPEN to happen: *I don't know what's going on. What were the children doing while all this was going on?* | *Like all good resorts, there is plenty going on.* → GOINGS-ON

3 DO STH NEXT to do something after you have finished doing something else: **go on to do sth** *She went on to become a successful surgeon.* | [+to] *Go on to the next question when you've finished.*

4 CONTINUE TALKING to continue talking, especially after stopping or changing to a different subject: *Go on, I'm listening.* | *'But,' he went on, 'we have to deal with the problems we're facing.'* | [+with] *After a short pause, Maria went on with her story.*

5 go on *spoken* **a)** used to encourage someone to do something: *Go on, have another piece of cake.* **b)** used when you are agreeing to do something or giving permission for something: *'Are you sure you won't have another drink?' 'Oh, go on then.'* | *'Can I go outside, Dad?' 'Yeah, go on then.'* **c)** also **go on with you** *BrE old-fashioned* used to tell someone that you do not believe them

6 USE AS PROOF **go on sth** to base an opinion or judgment on something: *Police haven't much to go on in their hunt for the killer.*

7 START TO WORK if a machine or piece of equipment goes on, it starts to work: *The heat goes on automatically at 6 o'clock.*

8 TIME to pass: *As time went on, I grew fond of him.*

9 BEHAVE *BrE informal* the way someone goes on is the way they behave: *The way she's going on, she'll have a nervous breakdown.*

10 be going on (for) 5 o'clock/60/25 etc to be nearly a particular time, age, number etc: *Nancy must be going on for 60.* | *She's one of those wise teenagers who's 16 going on 70* (=she behaves as though she is older than she is).

11 GO IN FRONT also **go on ahead** to go somewhere before the other people you are with: *Bill went on in the car and I followed on foot.*

12 TALK TOO MUCH *informal* to talk too much: *I really like Clare but she does go on.* | [+about] *I got tired of him going on about all his problems.* | *He just went on and on about his new girlfriend.*

13 CRITICIZE *BrE informal* to continue to criticize someone or ask them to do something in a way that annoys them: *The way she went on, you would have thought it was all my fault.* | [+at] *Stop going on at me!* | **go on at sb to do sth** *My wife's always going on at me to*

14 **DEVELOP** *BrE spoken informal* to develop or make progress
15 **to be going on with/to go on with** *BrE informal* if you have enough of something to be going on with, you have enough for now: *Have you got enough money to be going on with?*

go out *phr v*
1 **LEAVE YOUR HOUSE** to leave your house, especially in order to enjoy yourself: *Are you going out tonight?* | [+**for**] *We went out for a meal and then on to a movie.* | **go out doing sth** *Liam goes out drinking every Friday.* | **go out to do sth** *Can I go out to play now?* | **go out and do sth** *You should go out and get some fresh air.*
2 **RELATIONSHIP** to have a romantic relationship with someone: *They've been going out for two years now.* | [+**with**] *Tina used to go out with my brother.* | [+**together**] *How long have you been going out together?*
3 **FIRE/LIGHT** to stop burning or shining: *Suddenly the candle went out.*
4 **TV/RADIO** *BrE* to be broadcast on television or radio: *The programme goes out live at 5 o'clock on Mondays.*
5 **BE SENT** to be sent: *A copy of the instructions should go out with the equipment.* | *The magazine goes out to all members at the end of the month.*
6 **GAME/SPORT** to stop playing in a competition because you have lost a game: *He went out in the first round.*
7 **MOVE ABROAD** to travel to another country in order to live and work there: [+**to**] *They are looking for nurses to go out to Saudi Arabia.*
8 **NO LONGER FASHIONABLE** to stop being fashionable or used: *Hats like that went out years ago.* | *This kind of entertainment **went out with the ark** (=is very old-fashioned).*
9 **SEA** when the TIDE goes out, the sea moves away from the land; **🔁** **come in**
10 **MAKE PUBLIC** if news or a message goes out, it is officially announced to everyone: *The appeal went out for food and medicines.*
11 **your heart/thoughts go out to sb** used to say that you feel sympathy for someone and you are thinking about them: *Our hearts go out to the victim's family.*
12 **TIME** [always + adv/prep] *literary* to end: *March went out with high winds and rain.*

go over *phr v*
1 **THINK ABOUT** go over sth to think very carefully about something: *I had gone over and over what happened in my mind.*
2 **EXAMINE** go over sth to search or examine something very carefully: *In the competition, the judge goes over each dog and assesses it.*
3 **REPEAT** go over sth to repeat something in order to explain it or make sure it is correct: *Once again I went over exactly what I needed to say.*
4 **CLEAN** go over sth to clean something
5 **go over well** also **go over big** *AmE* if something goes over well, people like it: *That kind of salesman talk doesn't go over very well with the scientists.*

go over to sth *phr v*
1 to change to a different place or person for the next part of a television or radio programme: *We're going over to the White House for an important announcement.*
2 to change to a different way of doing things: *They went over to a computerized records system.*
3 to change to a different political party or religion: *the Labour MP who went over to the Conservatives last year*

go round *phr v BrE*
→ GO AROUND

go through *phr v*
1 **DIFFICULT/UNPLEASANT SITUATION** go through sth to experience a difficult or unpleasant situation, feeling etc: *When you're going through a crisis, it often helps to talk to someone.* | *He's going through a divorce at the moment.* | *It is devastating for a parent to watch a child go through misery.*
2 **PROCESS** go through sth to experience a particular

process: *Candidates must go through a process of selection.* | *Caterpillars go through several stages of growth.*
3 **USE** go through sth to use up money or a supply of something: *We went through five pints of milk last week.*
4 **LAW** go through (sth) if a law goes through, or goes through Parliament, it is officially accepted
5 **DEAL/AGREEMENT** if a deal or agreement goes through, it is officially accepted and agreed: *He accepted the offer and the deal went through.* | *The sale of the land went through.*
6 **PRACTISE** go through sth to practise something, for example a performance: *Let's go through the whole thing again, from the beginning.*
7 **SEARCH** go through sth to search something in order to find something in particular: *Dave went through his pockets looking for the keys.* | *Customs officers went through all my bags.*
8 **READ/DISCUSS** go through sth to read or discuss something in order to make sure it is correct: *We'll go through the details later on.* | *Do you want me to go through this and check your spellings?*

go through with sth *phr v*
to do something you had promised or planned to do, even though it causes problems or you are no longer sure you want to do it: *He bravely went through with the wedding ceremony even though he was in a lot of pain.* | *I had no choice but to go through with it.*

go to sb/sth *phr v* [not in passive]
1 to begin to experience or do something, or begin to be in a particular state: *I lay down and went to sleep.* | *Britain and Germany went to war in 1939.*
2 to be given to someone or something: *All the money raised will go to local charities.* | *The house will go to his daughter when he dies.*

go together *phr v*
1 [not in progressive] if two things go together, they exist together or are connected in some way: *Alcohol abuse and eating disorders often go together.*
2 *old-fashioned* if two people are going together, they are having a romantic relationship

go towards sth *phr v* [not in passive]
if money goes towards something, it is used to pay part of the cost of that thing: *The money will go towards a new hospice.* | **go towards doing sth** *All money raised will go towards renovating the building.*

go under *phr v*
1 if a business goes under, it has to stop operating because of financial problems: *More than 7000 businesses have gone under in the last three months.*
2 to sink beneath the surface of water: *The Titanic finally went under.* | *She went under, coughing and spluttering.*

go up *phr v*
1 **INCREASE** to increase in price, amount, level etc: *Train fares have gone up.* | *Blood-sugar levels go up as you digest food.* | **go up by 10%/250/£900 etc** *Unemployment in the country has gone up by a million.* | **go up from sth to sth** *Spending on research went up from $426 million to $461 million.*
2 **BUILDING/SIGN** if a building or sign goes up, it is built or fixed into place: *It was a lovely place before all these new houses went up.*
3 **EXPLODE/BURN** to explode, or be destroyed in a fire: *He had left the gas on and the whole kitchen went up.* | *The whole building **went up in flames**.* → **go up in smoke** at SMOKE¹ (3)
4 **SHOUT** if a shout or a CHEER goes up, people start to shout or cheer: [+**from**] *A great cheer went up from the audience.*
5 **TO ANOTHER PLACE** *BrE* to go from one place to another, especially to a place that is further north, or to a town or city from a smaller place: [+**to**] *We're going*

up to Scotland next weekend. | *He went up to the farm to get some eggs.*

6 LIGHTS if lights go up, they become brighter: *when the lights went up at the end of the performance*

7 UNIVERSITY *BrE formal old-fashioned* to begin studying at a university, especially Oxford or Cambridge University

go with sb/sth *phr v* [not in passive]

1 BE PART OF to be included as part of something: *The house goes with the job.* | *He had fame, money, and everything that goes with it.* | **go with doing sth** *Responsibility goes with becoming a father.*

2 EXIST TOGETHER to often exist with something else or be related to something else: *Ill-health often goes with poverty.*

3 RELATIONSHIP *old-fashioned* to have a romantic relationship with someone

4 HAVE SEX *informal* to have sex with someone

5 AGREE to accept someone's idea or plan: *Let's go with John's original proposal.*

go without *phr v*

1 go without (sth) to not have something that you usually have: *I like to give the children what they want even if I have to go without.* | *It is possible to go without food for a few days.*

2 it goes without saying (that) used to say that something is so clearly true that it does not need to be said: *The Internet, too, it goes without saying, is a good source of information.*

go² [S1] *n plural* **goes**

1 [C] an attempt to do something: *'I can't open this drawer.' 'Here, let me **have a go.**'* | *On the tour, everyone can **have a go at** making a pot.* | *I'd thought about it for some time and decided to **give it a go** (=try to do something).* | *I **had a good go** (=tried hard) at cleaning the silver.* | **at/in one go** *Ruby blew out all her candles at one go.* | *I'm not sure it will work but **it's worth a go.***

2 YOUR TURN [C] someone's turn in a game or someone's turn to use something: *Whose go is it?* | *It's your go.* | *Can I **have a go on** your guitar?* | *Don't I **get a go?***

3 make a go of sth *informal* to make something succeed, especially a business or marriage: *Nikki was determined to **make a go of the business.*** | *Many businesses are struggling hard to **make a go of it.***

4 £3/$50 etc a go *informal* used for saying how much it costs to do something or buy something: *At £3 a go, the cards are not cheap.*

5 on the go *informal* **a)** if you have something on the go, you have started it and are busy doing it: *Even with three top films on the go, Michelle is reluctant to talk about herself.* | *He **has** at least two other projects **on the go.*** **b)** very busy doing a lot of things: *Children are always on the go.*

6 sth is a go *AmE spoken* used to say that things are working correctly or that you have permission to do something: *The trip to London is a go.*

7 sth is (a) no go *spoken* used to say that something is not allowed or will not happen: *The hotel is no go for dogs.* → **NO-GO AREA**

8 it's all go *BrE spoken* it is very busy: *It's all go around here.* | *It's all go in the commercial property market.*

9 have a go *spoken, especially BrE* **a)** to criticize someone: *You're always having a go.* | *[+at] Will you stop having a go at me!* | *I **have a go at sb for/about sth** Mum had a go at me for not doing my homework.* **b)** to attack someone: *A whole gang of yobs were standing around, just waiting to have a go.* **c)** to try to catch someone who you see doing something wrong, rather than waiting for the police: *The public should not be encouraged to have a go.*

10 ENERGY [U] *BrE* energy and a desire to do things: *There's plenty of go in him yet.*

11 all the go *old-fashioned* very fashionable

goad¹ /ɡəʊd $ ɡoʊd/ *v* [T] **1** to make someone do something by annoying or encouraging them until they do it; → **provoke**: **goad sb into (doing) sth** *Kathy*

goaded him into telling her what he had done. | **goad sb on** *They goaded him on with insults.* **2** to push animals ahead of you with a sharp stick

goad² *n* [C] **1** something that forces someone to do something: *The offer of economic aid was a goad to political change.* **2** a sharp stick for making animals move forward

'go-ahead¹ *n* **give (sb) the go-ahead/get the go-ahead** to give or be given permission to start doing something: *The company has been given the go-ahead to build a new supermarket.*

go-ahead² *adj* [only before noun] *BrE* using new methods or ideas and therefore likely to succeed: *a go-ahead company*

goal [S2] [W1] /ɡəʊl $ ɡoʊl/ *n* [C]

1 something that you hope to achieve in the future; ⊟ **aim**: *His **ultimate goal** was to set up his own business.* | **achieve/reach a goal** *They achieved their goal of increasing sales by five percent.* | **set (yourself/sb) a goal** (=decide what you or someone else should try to achieve) | **long-term goal/short-term goal** (=that you hope to achieve after a long or short time)

2 the area between two posts where the ball must go in order to score in games such as football or HOCKEY: **be in goal/keep goal** *BrE* (=be the goalkeeper)

3 the action of making the ball go into a goal, or the score gained by doing this: *I scored the first **goal.***

goal·ie /'ɡəʊli $ 'ɡoʊ-/ *n* [C] *informal* a goalkeeper

goal·keep·er /'ɡəʊl,kiːpə $ 'ɡoʊl,kiːpər/ *n* [C] the player in a sports team whose job is to try to stop the ball going into the goal; ⊟ **goaltender** *AmE*

goal·kick /'ɡəʊlkɪk $ 'ɡoʊl-/ *n* [C] a kick in football taken by a goalkeeper after the attacking team has kicked the ball over the goal line

goal·less /'ɡəʊl-ləs $ 'ɡoʊl-/ *adj* a goalless match is one in which no goals are scored

'goal line *n* [C] a line at either end of the playing area in sports such as football or HOCKEY, along which the goal is placed

goal·mouth /'ɡəʊlmaʊθ $ 'ɡoʊl-/ *n* [C] the area directly in front of a GOAL

goal·post /'ɡəʊlpəʊst $ 'ɡoʊlpoʊst/ *n* [C usually plural] **1** one of the two posts, with a bar along the top or across the middle, that form the GOAL in games such as football and HOCKEY; ⊟ **post**; → see picture at SPORTS CENTRE **2 move/shift the goalposts** *BrE informal* to change the rules, limits etc for something while someone is trying to do something, making it more difficult for them – used to show disapproval

goal·ten·der /'ɡəʊl,tendə $ 'ɡoʊl,tendər/ *n* [C] *AmE* GOALKEEPER

goat /ɡəʊt $ ɡoʊt/ *n* [C] **1** an animal that has horns on top of its head and long hair under its chin, and can climb steep hills and rocks. Goats live wild in the mountains or are kept as farm animals. **2 get sb's goat** *spoken informal* to make someone extremely annoyed **3 old goat** *informal* an unpleasant old man, especially one who annoys women in a sexual way **4 act/play the goat** *BrE informal* to behave in a silly way → **BILLY GOAT, NANNY GOAT**

goa·tee /ɡəʊ'tiː $ ɡoʊ-/ *n* [C] a small pointed BEARD on the end of a man's chin

goat·herd /'ɡəʊthɜːd $ 'ɡoʊthɜːrd/ *n* [C] someone who looks after a group of goats

gob¹ /ɡɒb $ ɡɑːb/ *n* [C] *informal* **1** *BrE* an impolite word for someone's mouth: *Jean told him to shut his gob.* | *She's always stuffing her gob with food.* **2** a mass of something wet and sticky: *[+of] There's a gob of gum on my chair.* **3 gobs** *AmE* a large amount of something: *[+of] gobs of money*

gob² *v* **gobbed, gobbing** [I] *BrE informal* to blow a small amount of liquid out of your mouth; ⊟ **spit**

gob·bet /'ɡɒbɪt $ 'ɡɑː-/ *n* [C] *old use* a small piece of something, especially food

gob·ble /'ɡɒbəl $ 'ɡɑː-/ *v* *informal* **1** also **gobble up/down** [I,T] to eat something very quickly, especially in an impolite or GREEDY way; ▣ **wolf**: *Don't gobble your food!* | *She gobbled down her lunch.* **2** [I] to make a sound like a TURKEY —**gobble** n [C]

gobble sth ⇔ **up** phr v informal **1** if one company gobbles up a smaller company, it buys it and takes control of it: *Air France gobbled up its main French rivals, Air Inter and UTA.* **2** to quickly use a lot of a supply of something such as money or land: *Inflation has gobbled up our wage increases.* **3** to eat something very quickly, especially in an impolite or GREEDY way: *We gobbled up all of the cake in one evening.*

gob·ble·dy·gook also **gobbledegook** BrE /ˈɡɒbəldiɡuːk $ ˈɡɑːbəldiɡʊk, -ɡuːk/ n [U] informal complicated language, especially in an official or technical document, that is impossible or difficult to understand – used to show disapproval

gob·bler /ˈɡɒblə $ ˈɡɑːblər/ n [C] AmE informal a male TURKEY

go-between n [C] someone who takes messages from one person or group to another because the two sides cannot meet or do not want to meet: **act/serve as a go-between** *A UN representative will act as a go-between for leaders of the two countries.*

gob·let /ˈɡɒblɪt $ ˈɡɑːb-/ n [C] a cup made of glass or metal, with a base and a stem but no handle

gob·lin /ˈɡɒblɪn $ ˈɡɑːb-/ n [C] a small ugly creature in children's stories that likes to trick people

gob·smacked /ˈɡɒbsmækt $ ˈɡɑːb-/ adj BrE spoken informal very surprised or shocked

go-cart n another spelling of GO-KART

god /ɡɒd $ ɡɑːd/ n
1 God the spirit or BEING who Christians, Jews, Muslims etc pray to, and who they believe created the universe

believe in God
worship God
pray to God
belief/faith in God
God's will/the will of God (=what God wants to happen)
the word of God (=what God says)
gift from/of God
Almighty God/God Almighty (=used in prayers and HYMNS)

Most Americans still believe in God. | *Nothing could shake his belief in God.* | *He thought it was the will of God that he should suffer.* | *We believe that the Bible is the word of God.* | *Every day is a gift from God.*

⚠ In this sense, **God** is written with a capital letter and without 'the': *We asked God (NOT the God) to help us.* Expressions containing the word God such as **oh my God** are common in spoken English but can offend religious people.
2 [C] a male spirit or BEING who is believed by some religions to control the world or part of it, or who represents a particular quality; → **goddess**: [+of] *Mars, the god of war* | **Roman/Greek etc god**
3 God's gift to sb/sth someone who thinks they are perfect or extremely attractive – used to show disapproval: *Paul thinks he's God's gift to women.*
4 [C] someone who is admired very much: *To his fans he is a god.*
5 [C] something which you give too much importance or respect to: *Money became his god.*
6 the gods a) the force that some people believe controls their lives, bringing them good or bad luck: *The gods are against us.* **b)** BrE informal old-fashioned the seats high up and at the back of a theatre
7 God/oh (my) God/good God/God almighty spoken used to emphasize what you are saying, when you are surprised, annoyed, or amused: *Oh God, how embarrassing!*
8 for God's sake spoken used to emphasize something you are saying or when you are annoyed: *For God's sake, shut up!*
9 I swear/hope/wish/pray to God spoken used to emphasize that you promise, hope etc that something is true: *I hope to God nothing goes wrong.*
10 God forbid (that) spoken used to say that you very

much hope that something will not happen: *God forbid that this should ever happen again.*
11 God (only) knows spoken **a)** used to show that you are annoyed because you do not know something, or because you think that something is unreasonable: **God (only) knows who/what/how etc** *God knows what she's doing in there.* | *It'll cost God only knows how much.* **b)** used to emphasize what you are saying: *God knows, it hasn't been easy.*
12 what/how/where/who in God's name spoken used to emphasize a question when you are angry or surprised: *Where in God's name have you been?*
13 God help you/him etc spoken used to warn someone that something bad will happen: *God help you if you spill anything on the carpet.*
14 God help us spoken said humorously when you think that something bad is going to happen: *'Simon's doing the cooking.' 'God help us!'*
15 honest to God spoken used to emphasize that you are not lying or joking: *Honest to God, I didn't tell her!*
16 God willing spoken used to say that you hope there will be no problems: *We'll be moving next month, God willing.*
17 God bless spoken used to say that you hope someone will be safe and happy, especially when you are saying goodbye: *Good night and God bless.*
18 God give me strength! spoken used when you are becoming annoyed
19 there is a God! spoken said when someone is explaining that something very good happened to them at a time when they thought that their situation was very bad: *In walked four gorgeous, blond Swedish boys, and I thought, 'There is a God!'*
20 God rest his/her soul also **God rest him/her** spoken old use used to show respect when speaking about someone who is dead
21 by God spoken old use used to emphasize how determined or surprised you are → **there but for the grace of God** at GRACE[1] (6); → **in the lap of the gods** at LAP[1] (6); → **play God** at PLAY[1] (8); → **thank God/goodness/heavens** at THANK (2)

WORD FOCUS: GOD
places where people worship God: **church** (Christians)	**temple** (Buddhists and Hindus)	**mosque** (Muslims)	**synagogue** (Jews)
treated with great respect because of being connected with God: **holy, sacred**
having strong beliefs in God: **devout, pious**
someone who does not believe in God: **atheist**
someone who is not sure if God exists: **agnostic**
→ **spiritual**

god-awful, God-awful, god·aw·ful /ˈɡɒdɔːfəl $ ˈɡɑːdɔː-/ adj [only before noun] informal very bad or unpleasant. Some Christian people find this word offensive: *What's that god-awful smell?*

god·child /ˈɡɒdtʃaɪld $ ˈɡɑːd-/ n plural **godchildren** /-tʃɪldrən/ [C] the child that a GODPARENT promises to help and to teach Christian values to. This promise is made at a BAPTISM ceremony.

god·dam·mit also **God 'damn it** /ɡɒˈdæmɪt $ ˌɡɑːdˈdæm-/ interjection a word used to express annoyance, anger etc. Some Christian people consider this word offensive.

god·damn, goddam /ˈɡɒdæm $ ˌɡɑːdˈdæm/ also **god·damned** /-dæmd/ adj [only before noun] spoken a word used to show that you are angry or annoyed, considered offensive by some Christians: *Where's the goddamn key?* —**goddamn, goddam, goddamned** adv: *I just did something so goddamned stupid.*

god·daugh·ter /ˈɡɒdˌdɔːtə $ ˈɡɑːdˌdɔːtər/ n [C] a female godchild

god·dess, Goddess /ˈɡɒdəs $ ˈɡɑː-/ n [C] **1** a female BEING who is believed to control the world or part

G

of it, or represents a particular quality: *Aphrodite, goddess of love* **2 screen goddess** an attractive female film star

god·fa·ther /'gɒd,fɑːðə $ 'gɑːd,fɑːðər/ *n* [C] **1** a male GODPARENT **2** *informal* the head of a criminal organization such as the MAFIA **3 the godfather of sth** someone who began or developed something such as a type of music: *Afrika Bambaataa, the Godfather of hip hop*

God-,fearing *adj old use* leading a good life and following the rules of the Christian religion: *God-fearing people*

god·for·sak·en, **Godforsaken** /'gɒdfəseɪkən $ 'gɑːdfər-/ *adj* [only before noun] a godforsaken place is far away from where people live and contains nothing interesting, attractive, or cheerful: *How can you stand living in this godforsaken town?*

God-given *adj* [usually before noun] received from God: *She has a God-given talent for singing.* | **a God-given right** (=the right to do something without asking anyone else's opinion) *The protesters have no God-given right to disrupt the life of the city.*

God·head /'gɒdhed $ 'gɑːd-/ *n* **the Godhead** *formal* a word that Christians use to mean the Father, the Son, and the Holy Spirit, who they consider to be one God in three people

god·less /'gɒdləs $ 'gɑːd-/ *adj old use* not respecting God or not believing in a god —**godlessness** *n* [U]

god·like /'gɒdlaɪk $ 'gɑːd-/ *adj* having a quality like God or a god; ◨ **divine**: *godlike powers*

god·ly /'gɒdli $ 'gɑːdli/ *adj old use* obeying God and leading a good life —**godliness** *n* [U]

god·moth·er /'gɒd,mʌðə $ 'gɑːd,mʌðər/ *n* [C] a female GODPARENT

god·pa·rent /'gɒd,peərənt $ 'gɑːd,per-/ *n* [C] someone who promises at a BAPTISM ceremony to help a child, and to teach him or her Christian values

god·send /'gɒdsend $ 'gɑːd-/ *n* [singular] something good that happens to you when you really need it: [+for/to] *The hot weather has been a godsend for ice-cream sellers.*

god·son /'gɒdsʌn $ 'gɑːd-/ *n* [C] a male GODCHILD

god·speed, **Godspeed** /,gɒd'spiːd $ 'gɑːdspiːd, ,gɑːd'spiːd/ *n* [U] *spoken old use* used to wish someone good luck, especially before a journey

God squad *n* **the God squad** an insulting way of describing Christians who try to persuade other people to become Christians

go·er /'gəʊə $ 'gəʊər/ *n* [C] **1** *BrE spoken old use* a woman who has sex with different men: *She's a bit of a goer.* **2** also **-goer** used after words such as party, church, and theatre to form nouns that refer to people who regularly go to parties, church etc: *cinema-goers*

go·fer /'gəʊfə $ 'gəʊfər/ *n* [C] *informal* someone who carries messages etc for their employer

go-'getter / $ '. ,.../ *n* [C] someone who is likely to be successful because they are very determined and have a lot of energy —**go-getting** *adj*

gog·gle /'gɒgəl $ 'gɑː-/ *v* [I] *old-fashioned* to look at something with your eyes wide open in surprise or shock; ◨ **gape**: [+at] *They were goggling at us as if we were freaks.*

goggle-'eyed *adj* with your eyes wide open and looking directly at something, especially in surprise or shock

gog·gles /'gɒgəlz $ 'gɑː-/ *n* [plural] a pair of GLASSES made of glass or plastic with a rubber or plastic edge that fit against your skin and protect your eyes → see picture at SAFETY

go-go *adj AmE informal* **1** a go-go period of time is one in which prices and the amount workers are paid increase very quickly: *the go-go 1980s* **2** go-go STOCKS increase in value very quickly in a short period of time, but involve a lot of risk

go-go ,dancer *n* [C] a woman who dances with sexy movements in a bar or NIGHTCLUB —**go-go dancing** [U]

go·ing¹ /'gəʊɪŋ $ 'gəʊ-/ *n* [U] **1** the difficulty or speed with which something is done: **hard/rough/slow** etc **going** *I'm getting the work done, but it's slow going.* **good going/not bad going** *We climbed the mountain in three hours, which wasn't bad going.* **2** the act of leaving a place; ◨ **departure**: *His going will be no great loss to the company.* **3 heavy going** if a book, play etc is heavy going, it is boring and difficult to understand **4 while the going's good** *spoken* if you suggest doing something while the going's good, you think it should be done before it becomes difficult or impossible: *Let's leave while the going's good.* **5 when the going gets tough, the tough get going** when the conditions become difficult, strong people begin to do something in a determined way **6 the going** *BrE* the condition of the ground, especially for a horse race → **comings and goings** at COMING¹ (2)

going² *adj* **1 the going rate/price/salary** etc the usual amount you pay or receive as payment for something [+for] *Thirty dollars an hour is the going rate for a math tutor.* **2 the biggest/best/nicest** etc **sth going** the biggest, best etc of a particular thing: *It's some of the best beer going.* **3** [not before noun] *BrE informal* available: *Are there any jobs going where you work?* **4 have a lot going for you** to have many advantages and good qualities that will bring success: *Stop being so depressed. You have a lot going for you.* **5 a going concern** a business which is making a profit and is expected to continue to do so **6** also **-going** used after words such as cinema and theatre to form adjectives that describe people who regularly go to the cinema, theatre etc: *the cinema-going public*

,going-'over *n* [singular] *informal* **1** a thorough examination of something to make sure it is all right; → **once-over**: *The media gave his personal life a pretty firm going-over.* **2 give sth a going-over** to improve the condition of something, for example by cleaning it thoroughly: *You ought to give the place a going-over with the Hoover once in a while.* **3 give sb a going-over** *BrE* to hit someone and hurt them

,goings-'on *n* [plural] activities or events that are strange or interesting, and often illegal: *She was shocked by some of the goings-on at the school.*

go-kart, **go-cart** *n* [C] a small car made of an open frame on four wheels, and used in races —**go-karting** *n* [U]

gold¹ S2 W2 /gəʊld $ goʊld/ *n* **1** [U] a valuable soft yellow metal that is used to make coins, jewellery etc. It is a chemical ELEMENT: symbol Au: *a gold ring* | **pure/solid gold** *solid gold watches* | **9/18/22/24 carat gold** (=a measurement used to show how pure gold is); → **strike gold** at STRIKE¹ (14); → see picture at MATERIAL **2** [U] coins, jewellery etc made of gold: *She came to the party* **dripping with gold** (=wearing a lot of gold). **3** [C,U] the colour of gold: *The room was decorated in golds and blues.* | *Gold looks good on people with dark hair.* **4** [C] *informal* a GOLD MEDAL → **have a heart of gold** at HEART (2)

gold² *adj* **1** made of gold: **gold watch/chain/ring** etc **2** having the colour of gold: *a gold jacket*; → **golden**

gold·brick /'gəʊldbrɪk $ 'goʊld-/ also **gold·brick·er** /-brɪkə $ -ər/ *n* [C] *AmE informal* someone who stays away from their work, especially by pretending that they are ill —**goldbrick** *v* [I]

,gold 'card *n* [C] *BrE* a type of CREDIT CARD that gives you special advantages such as a high spending limit

gold ,digger *n* [C] *informal* an attractive woman who uses her looks to get money from rich men

gold dust n [U] **1** gold in the form of a fine powder **2 be like gold dust** BrE to be very valuable and difficult to find: *Cup final tickets are like gold dust.*

gold·en W3 /'gəʊldən $ 'goʊl-/ adj
1 having a bright yellow colour like gold: *golden hair | golden sand*
2 a golden opportunity a good chance to get something valuable or to be very successful: *He wasted a golden opportunity when he missed from the penalty spot.*
3 golden boy/girl someone who is popular and successful: *Hollywood's golden girl, Julia Roberts*
4 [only before noun] a golden period of time is one of great happiness or success: **golden years/days etc** *the golden years of childhood* | *the **golden age** of radio*
5 sb is golden AmE spoken informal used to say that someone is in a very good situation and is likely to be successful: *If the right editor looks at your article, you're golden.*
6 literary made of gold: *a golden crown*

golden anni'versary n plural **golden anniversaries** [C] especially AmE the date that is exactly 50 years after the beginning of something, especially a wedding; → **diamond anniversary**, **silver anniversary**; 🔲 **golden wedding** BrE, **golden jubilee** BrE

golden 'eagle n [C] a large light brown bird that lives in northern parts of the world

golden 'handcuffs n [plural] informal things such as a large SALARY or a good PENSION that make important workers want to continue working for an organization, rather than leave to work for a competing organization

golden 'handshake n [C] BrE a large amount of money given to someone when they leave their job

golden hel'lo n [C] BrE informal a large amount of money that is given to a new employee, in order to persuade them not to go to work for another organization: *New teachers are given golden hellos.*

golden 'jubilee n [C] BrE the date that is exactly 50 years after an important event, such as the occasion when someone became king or queen; → **diamond jubilee**, **silver jubilee**; 🔲 **golden anniversary** AmE: *the Queen's golden jubilee celebrations*

golden 'oldie n [C] informal a song, film etc that is old, but which many people still like

golden 'parachute n [C] informal part of a business person's contract which states that they will be paid a large amount of money if they lose their job, for example if the company is sold

golden 'raisin n [C] AmE a small pale RAISIN (=dried fruit) used in baking; 🔲 **sultana** BrE

golden re'triever n [C] a large dog with light brown fur

golden 'rule n [C] a very important principle, way of behaving etc that should be remembered: *The golden rule of cooking is to use fresh ingredients.*

golden 'syrup n [U] BrE a sweet thick liquid made from sugar that is used in cooking

golden 'wedding BrE n [C] the date that is exactly 50 years after a wedding; 🔲 **golden anniversary**; → **diamond wedding**, **silver wedding**

gold·field /'gəʊldfiːld $ 'goʊld-/ n [C] an area of land where gold can be found

gold·finch /'gəʊldfɪntʃ $ 'goʊld-/ n [C] a small singing bird with yellow feathers on its wings

gold·fish /'gəʊldfɪʃ $ 'goʊld-/ n plural **goldfish** [C] a small shiny orange fish often kept as a pet

'goldfish ˌbowl n **1** [C] a round glass bowl in which fish are kept as pets **2** [singular] a situation in which people know about everything that happens in your life: *Popstars have to live their life in a goldfish bowl.*

gold 'leaf n [U] gold which has been beaten into extremely thin sheets and is used to cover things such as picture frames for decoration

gold 'medal n [C] a prize made of gold that is given to someone for winning a race or competition; → **bronze medal**, **silver medal** —**gold medallist** BrE; **gold medalist** AmE

gold·mine, **gold mine** /'gəʊldmaɪn $ 'goʊld-/ n [C] **1** informal a business or activity that produces large profits: *The nightclub turned out to be a real goldmine.* **2** a place where gold is dug out from a hole in the ground **3 be sitting on a goldmine** to own something very valuable, especially without realizing it

gold-'plated adj something that is gold-plated has a layer of gold on top of another metal —**gold plate** n [U]

gold-'rimmed adj having a gold edge or border: *gold-rimmed glasses*

gold rush n [C] a situation when a lot of people hurry to a place where gold has just been discovered

gold·smith /'gəʊld,smɪθ $ 'goʊld-/ n [C] someone who makes or sells things made from gold

'gold ˌstandard n **the gold standard** technical the use of the value of gold as a fixed standard on which to base the value of money

golf

flag

green   hole

woods

putter

bunker

irons

golf S2 W3 /gɒlf $ gɑːlf, gɔːlf/ n [U] a game in which the players hit a small white ball into holes in the ground with a set of golf clubs, using as few hits as possible: *He plays golf on Sundays.* | *a **round of golf*** (=complete game of golf) —**golfer** n [C] —**golfing** n [U]

'golf ball n [C] a small hard white ball used in the game of golf

'golf club n [C] **1** a long wooden or metal stick used for hitting the ball in the game of golf **2** an organization of people who play golf, or the land and buildings they use

'golf course n [C] an area of land where golf is played

'golf links n plural **golf links** [C] a golf course, especially by the sea

gol·li·wog /'gɒliwɒg $ 'gɑːliwɑːg/ n [C] a child's DOLL made of cloth, like a man with a black face, white eyes, and short black hair. Golliwogs are considered offensive to black people.

gol·ly¹ /'gɒli $ 'gɑːli/ interjection spoken old use used to express surprise; 🔲 **gosh**

golly² n plural **gollies** [C] informal a golliwog

go·nad /'gəʊnæd $ 'goʊ-/ n [C] technical the male or female sex organ in which the SPERM or eggs are produced

gon·do·la /'gɒndələ $ 'gɑːn-, gɑːn'doʊlə/ n [C] **1** a long narrow boat with a flat bottom and high points at each end, used on the CANALS in Venice in Italy **2** the place where passengers sit that hangs beneath an AIRSHIP or BALLOON[1] (2)   **3** the enclosed part of a CABLE CAR where the passengers sit

gon·do·lier /ˌɡɒndə'lɪə $ ˌɡɑːndə'lɪr/ n [C] someone whose job is to take people for rides in a gondola

gone[1] /ɡɒn $ ɡɒːn/ the past participle of GO

gone[2] adj **1 be gone a)** to be no longer in a particular place: *The door slammed and he was gone.* | *I turned round for my bag and it was gone.* **b)** to be dead or to no longer exist: *His wife's been gone for several years.* | *Many of the old houses are gone now.* → **dead and gone** at DEAD[1] (1)   **2 be gone on sb** BrE informal to be very attracted to someone of the opposite sex: *Kate's really gone on that boy next door.* **3 be five/six/seven etc months gone** BrE informal to have been PREGNANT for five, six etc months → **going, going, gone** at GO[1] (36)

gone[3] prep BrE informal later than a particular time or older than a particular age; ■ **past**: *When we got home it was gone midnight.*

gon·er /'ɡɒnə $ 'ɡɒːnər/ n informal **be a goner** if someone is a goner, they are soon going to die, to fall, be caught etc: *Someone hit me from behind and I thought I was a goner.*

gong /ɡɒŋ $ ɡɒːŋ, ɡɑːŋ/ n [C] **1** a round piece of metal that hangs in a frame and which you hit with a stick to give a deep ringing sound. It is used as a musical instrument or to announce that a meal is ready **2** BrE informal a MEDAL, title, or prize that someone is given

gon·na /'ɡɒnə, ɡənə $ 'ɡɒːnə, ɡənə/ spoken informal a way of saying 'going to': *This isn't gonna be easy.*

gon·or·rhe·a, gonorrhoea /ˌɡɒnə'rɪːə $ ˌɡɑː-/ n [U] a disease of the sex organs that is passed on during sex

gon·zo jour·nal·is·m /'ɡɒnzəʊ ˌdʒɜːnəlɪzəm $ 'ɡɑːnzoʊ ˌdʒɜːr-/ n [U] AmE informal newspaper reporting that is concerned with shocking or exciting the reader and not with giving serious news —**gonzo journalist** n [C]

goo /ɡuː/ n [U] informal an unpleasantly sticky substance; → **gooey**: *My washbag's covered in goo.*

good[1] S1 W1 /ɡʊd/ adj comparative **better** /'betə $ -ər/ superlative **best** /best/
1 OF A HIGH STANDARD of a high standard or quality; ■ **bad, poor**: *a good hotel* | *good quality cloth* | *The train service is not very good.* | *My French is better than my Spanish.* | *You'll receive the best medical treatment.* | *His qualifications aren't good enough.* → see box at WELL[1]
2 SKILFUL able to do something well: *She's a very good player.* | *Do you know a good builder?* | **good at (doing) sth** *Alex is very good at languages.* | *She's good at making things .* | **[+with]** *As a politician, you need to be good with words* (=skilful at using words). | *He's very good with people* (=skilful at dealing with people). | **do/make a good job (of doing sth)** (=do something well) *Mike's done a good job of painting the windows.*
3 WHAT YOU WANT used about something that is what you want or happens in the way that you want; ■ **bad**: *That's good news!* | *I need a bit of good luck.*
4 PLEASANT/ENJOYABLE pleasant and enjoyable: **it's good to do sth** *It's good to see you again.* | **have a good time/day/weekend etc** *Did you have a good vacation?* | *That was good fun.*
5 SUCCESSFUL/CORRECT likely to be successful or correct: *She's full of good ideas.* | *Well, can you think of a better plan?* | *What's the best way to deal with this?* | *The police have a pretty good idea who did it.* | *I'm not sure, but I could make a good guess.*
6 SUITABLE suitable or convenient: *Is this a good time to talk to you?* | *It was a good place to rest.* | **good for (doing) sth** *It's a good day for going to the beach.* | **be good for sb** especially AmE: *Ten o'clock is good for me.*
7 USEFUL useful or helpful; ■ **bad**: *Do you want some good advice?* | *The best thing you can do is wait here.* | *You should make good use of your time.*

8 BEHAVING WELL behaving well and not causing any trouble – used especially about a child; ■ **well-behaved**; ■ **naughty**: *She's such a good baby.* | *The kids were as good as gold* (=very good). → **be on your best behaviour** at BEHAVIOUR (2)
9 MAKES YOU HEALTHY likely to make you healthy either physically or mentally; ■ **bad**: **[+for]** *Fresh fruit and vegetables are good for you.* | *Watching too much TV isn't good for you.* | **good to eat/drink** *They have to learn which wild foods are good to eat.*
10 KEEPS STH IN GOOD CONDITION be good for sth likely to improve the condition of something: *products that are good for the environment* | *The publicity has been good for business.*
11 PHYSICALLY WELL [used especially in negatives and comparatives] healthy or well: *'How are you?' 'Better thanks.'* | *Lyn's not feeling too good today.*
12 NOT DAMAGED OR WEAK if the condition of something is good, it is not damaged or weak: **in good condition/shape** *It's in pretty good condition for an old car.* | *Boris had always kept his body in good shape.* | *The Chancellor announced that the economy is in good shape.* | *Once the boat's repaired, it'll be as good as new* (=in perfect condition). | **sb's good eye/arm/leg etc** (=the one that is not damaged) *He sat up, supporting himself on his good arm.*
13 KIND kind and understanding about what other people need or want: **[+about]** *Dad lent me the money. He was very good about it.* | **it/that/this is good of sb** *It was good of him to offer you a lift.* | *The company's always been very good to me.*
14 MORALLY RIGHT behaving correctly or being right according to accepted moral standards; ■ **bad**: *a good man* | *I try to be good, but it isn't always easy.* | *Well, that's my good deed for the day* (=something good you try to do for someone else every day). | *I'm on the side of the good guys* (=people who behave in a morally right way, for example in a film).
15 LARGE large in amount, size, range etc; → **goodish**: *We've had a good crop of apples.* | *There's a good range of leisure facilities.* | *I'd been waiting a good while* (=a fairly long time). | *Our team has a good chance of winning* (=is fairly likely to win).
16 REASONABLE PRICE a good price is reasonable and not expensive: *$30 sounds like a good price to me.*
17 COMPLETELY/THOROUGHLY [only before noun] doing something for a long time, so that you do it completely and thoroughly: *You need a good rest.* | *Take a good look at it.* | *She sat down and had a good cry.* | *This time he waited until he was good and ready* (=completely ready).
18 a good deal a lot: *It cost a good deal, I can tell you.* | **a good deal of trouble/time/work etc** *I went to a good deal of trouble to get this ticket.* | **a good deal bigger/better etc** *He was a good deal older than her.*
19 good value (for money) BrE something that is good value is not expensive, or is worth what you pay for it: *The three-course menu is varied and good value for money.*
20 good for sth a) able to be used for a particular period of time; ■ **valid**: **good for one month/a year etc** *Your passport is good for another three years.* **b)** likely to continue living or being useful for a particular time or distance, even though old or not in good condition: **good for some time/a hundred miles etc** *This old truck is good for another 100,000 miles.* **c)** informal likely to give you something or provide something: *Dad should be good for a few bucks.*
21 a good three miles/ten years etc at least three miles, ten years etc, and probably more: *It's a good mile away.* | *He's a good ten years younger than her.*
22 as good as almost: **as good as done/finished etc** *The summer's as good as over.* | **as good as dead/ruined/useless etc** *This carpet's as good as ruined.*
23 a good few/many a fairly large number of things or people: *I've done this a good few times now.* | *A good many people were upset about the new tax.*
24 too good to be true/to last informal so good that you cannot believe it is real, or you expect something bad to

happen: *Their relationship had always seemed too good to be true.*

25 **sb's too good for sb** used to say that you think the second person does not deserve to have a relationship with the first: *George is a good lad, too good for you!*
26 **in your own good time** *informal* if you do something in your own good time, you do it only when you are ready to do it, rather than when other people want you to: *I'll tell him in my own good time.*
27 **in good time (for sth/to do sth)** *BrE* if you do something in good time, you do it early enough to be ready for a particular time or event: *Ben arrived in good time for dinner.*
28 **hanging/shooting etc is too good for sb** *spoken* used to say that someone has done something so bad that they deserve the most severe punishment available
29 **as good a time/place etc as any** used to say that although a time etc is not perfect, there will probably not be a better one: *I suppose this is as good a place as any to stay.*
30 **be as good as your word** to do something that you promised to do
31 **a good word for sb/sth** something good that you say about someone or something: *Dan put in a good word for you at the meeting.* | *have/find a good word (to say) No one had a good word to say for her.*
32 **be in sb's good books** *informal* if you are in someone's good books, they are pleased with you or your work: *I'll ask my boss for the day off – I'm in her good books just now.*
33 **have a good thing going** to have or be doing something that is successful: *They've got a good thing going with that little shop of theirs.*
34 **be onto a good thing** *BrE informal* to have found an easy way of being successful or getting what you want: *Andrew knew when he was onto a good thing.*
35 **make good** also **make it good** to become successful and rich after being poor – used especially in newspapers: *a country boy who made good in New York*
36 **make good** a debt/loss etc to pay someone money that you owe, or to provide money to replace what has been lost – used especially in business: *The loss to the company was made good by contributions from its subsidiaries.*
37 **make good your escape** *literary* to succeed in escaping
38 **the good life** an expensive way of living with good food, fast cars etc: *his weakness for women and the good life*
39 **the good old days** the good times in the past: *We talked for hours about the good old days.*
40 **sb's good offices** *formal* help that someone provides, especially someone in a position of power
41 **good Samaritan** someone who gives help to people in trouble
42 **the good book** *old-fashioned* the Bible → **so far so good** at FAR¹ (8); → **give as good as you get** at GIVE¹ (34); → **while the going's good** at GOING¹ (4); → **hold good** at HOLD¹ (14); → **for good measure** at MEASURE² (8); → **pay good money for sth** at MONEY (5); → **bad/good sailor** at SAILOR (2); → **that's/it's all well and good** at WELL³ (4)

SPOKEN PHRASES
43 **good a)** used to say that you are pleased about something: *Good. I'm glad that's finished.* | *'I got an A in Biology, Mum.' ' Oh, good.'* **b)** used to tell someone that you think their work or what they are doing is good: *'Is the answer five?' 'Yes, good.'*
44 **that's good** used to say that you approve of something: *'I've booked a table.' 'Oh, that's good.'*
45 **(that's a) good idea/point/question** used to say that someone has just said or suggested something interesting or important that you had not thought of before: *'But it's Sunday, the bank will be closed.' 'Good point.'*
46 **good luck** used to say that you hope that someone is successful or that something good happens to them: *Good luck in your exams.*
47 **good luck to him/them etc** used to say that you

---

hope someone is successful, even if you think this is unlikely: *'They're hoping to finish it by November.' 'Good luck to them.'*
48 **good for sb** used to say that you approve of something that someone has done: *'I've decided to accept the job.' 'Good for you.'*
49 **it's a good thing** also **it's a good job** *BrE* used to say that you are glad something happened, because there would have been problems if it had not happened: *It's a good thing you're at home. I've lost my keys.* | **and a good thing/job too** *BrE*: *She's gone, and a good thing too.*
50 **that's/it's not good enough** used to say that you are not satisfied with something and that you are annoyed about it: *It's just not good enough. I've been waiting an hour!*
51 **be good and ready** to be completely ready: *We'll go when I'm good and ready and not before.*
52 **that's a good one** used to tell someone that you do not believe something they have said and think it is a joke or a trick: *You won $50,000? That's a good one!*
53 **be good for a laugh** also **be a good laugh** *BrE* to be enjoyable or amusing: *It's Hazel's party tomorrow. Should be good for a laugh.*
54 **good old John/Karen etc** used to praise someone, especially because they have behaved in the way that you expect them to: *Good old Ed! I knew he wouldn't let us down.*
55 **good grief/God/Lord/heavens/gracious!** used to express surprise or anger: *'It's going to cost us £500.' 'Good grief!'*
56 **good girl/boy/dog etc** used to tell a child or animal that they have behaved well or done something well: *Sit! Good dog.*
57 **if you know what's good for you** used in a threatening way to tell someone to do something or something bad will happen to them: *Do as he says, if you know what's good for you!*
58 **would you be good enough to do sth** also **would you be so good as to do sth** *formal* used to ask someone very politely to do something: *Would you be good enough to help me with my bags?*
59 **all in good time** *BrE* used when someone wants to do something soon but you want to wait a little: *'When can we open our presents, Mom?' 'All in good time, Billy.'*
60 **have a good one** *AmE* used to say goodbye and to wish someone a nice day
61 **be good to go** *AmE informal* to be ready to do something: *I've got my shoes and I'm good to go.*
62 **be as good as it gets** *spoken* if a situation is as good as it gets, it is not going to improve: *Enjoy yourself while you can. This is as good as it gets.*
63 **it's all good** *especially AmE informal* used to say that a situation is good or acceptable, or that there is not a problem: *Don't worry about it, man – it's all good.*
64 **very good** *BrE old-fashioned* used to tell someone in a position of authority that you will do what they have asked: *'Tell the men to come in.' 'Very good, sir.'*
65 **(jolly) good show** *BrE old-fashioned* used to say that you approve of something someone has done

---

WORD FOCUS: GOOD
very good: excellent, fantastic, wonderful, great, terrific, neat *AmE*, superb, amazing, outstanding, brilliant, impressive, fine, first-class, out of this world
of good quality: high quality, top quality, superior, deluxe, classy
morally good: decent, virtuous, respectable, honourable *BrE*/honorable *AmE*, upright, beyond reproach

good² *n* **1** **no good/not much good/not any good a)** not useful or suitable: *One lesson's not much good – you need five or six.* | *'I could come next week.' 'That's no good. I'll be away.'* | [+for] *The land here isn't any good for agricultural crops.* | [+to] *You're no good to me if you can't drive a car.* **b)** of a low standard or level of ability: *The movie wasn't much good.* | *Is the new*

G

headteacher any good? | **no good at (doing) sth** *I'm no good at speaking in public.* **c)** morally bad: *Stay away from Jerry – he's no good.* **2 it's no good (doing sth)** used to say that an action will not achieve what it is intended to achieve: *It's no good telling him – he won't listen.* **3 do some good/do sb good** to have a useful effect: *She works for a small charity where she feels she can do some good.* | *I'll talk to him but I don't think it will do any good.* | *A bit more exercise would do you good.* → **do more harm than good** at HARM[1] (1) **4 what's the good of...?/what good is...?** used to say that it is not worth doing or having something in a particular situation: *What's the good of buying a boat if you're too busy to use it?* | *What good is money when you haven't any friends?* **5 for good** permanently: *The injury may keep him out of football for good.* **6 for the good of sb/sth** in order to help someone or improve a situation: *We must work together for the good of the community.* | *Take the medicine – it's for your own good!* **7** [U] behaviour, attitudes, forces etc that are morally right: *She is definitely an influence for good on those boys.* | *There's a lot of good in him, in spite of his rudeness.* | *the struggle between good and evil* → DO-GOODER **8 be up to no good** *informal* to be doing or planning something wrong or dishonest: *Those guys look like they're up to no good.* **9 the common/general good** *formal* the advantage of everyone in society or in a group: *countries united for the common good* **10 be (all) to the good** used to say that something that happens is good, especially when it is in addition to or as the result of something else: *If further improvements can be made, that would be all to the good.*

good[3] *adv AmE spoken informal* well. Many teachers think this is not correct English: *The business is **doing good** now.* | *Listen to me good!*

good ,after'noon *formal* used to say hello when you are greeting someone in the afternoon, especially someone you do not know; → **good evening**, **good morning**

good·bye /gʊd'baɪ/ used when you are leaving someone, or when they are leaving; → **hello**: *Goodbye, John, see you tomorrow.* | *I just have to **say goodbye** to Jane.* | **say your goodbyes** (=say goodbye to several people or everyone) *We said our goodbyes and left.*

good 'day *old-fashioned especially BrE* used to say hello or goodbye, especially in the morning or afternoon: *I must get back. Good day to you.*

good 'evening *formal* used to say hello when you are greeting someone in the evening, especially someone you do not know; → **good afternoon**, **good morning**, **good night**

,good 'faith *n* [U] when a person, country etc intends to be honest and sincere and does not intend to deceive anyone: **in good faith** *The report claimed that the company had **acted in good faith**.* | **sign/show/gesture etc of good faith** *A ceasefire was declared as a sign of good faith.*

good-for-'nothing *adj* a good-for-nothing person is lazy and useless: *an idle good-for-nothing drunk* —**'good-for-nothing** *n* [C]: *Ian's a stupid good-for-nothing.*

,Good 'Friday *n* [C,U] the Friday before the Christian holiday of Easter, that Christians remember as the day Jesus Christ was CRUCIFIED

,good-heart·ed /,gʊd 'hɑːtɪd $ -'hɑːr-/ *adj* kind and generous

,good 'humour *BrE*; **good humor** *AmE n* [U] a happy, friendly character or attitude to life: *At eighty her eyes still sparkled with good humour.* —**good-humoured** *adj*: *He was patient and good-humoured.* —**good-humouredly** *adv*

good·ie, goody /'gʊdi/ *n* [C] *BrE informal* someone in a book or film who is good and does things you approve of; **baddie**: *the goodies and the baddies*

good·ish /'gʊdɪʃ/ *adj BrE informal* **1** fairly good but not very good: *'Is the pay good?' 'Goodish.'* **2 a goodish distance/number etc** a fairly long way, a fairly large number etc

,good-'looking *adj* someone who is good-looking is attractive —**good-looker** *n* [C]; → see box at BEAUTIFUL

good 'looks *n* [plural] the attractive appearance of someone's face: *his natural good looks*

good·ly /'gʊdli/ *adj* [only before noun] **1 a goodly number/sum/amount etc** *old-fashioned* a large amount: *£1500 is still a goodly sum.* **2** *old use* pleasant in appearance or good in quality

good 'morning [S2] *interjection formal* used to say hello when you are greeting someone in the morning; → **good afternoon**, **good evening**

,good 'name *n* [singular] the good opinion that people have of someone or something; **reputation**: [+of] *It threatened to damage the good name of the firm.*

,good 'nature *n* [U] a naturally kind and helpful character or attitude to people: *He had his father's good looks and his mother's good nature.*

good-na·tured /gʊd 'neɪtʃəd $ -ərd/ *adj* naturally kind and helpful and not easily made angry —**good-naturedly** *adv*

,good 'neighbourliness *n* [U] *BrE* when countries or people try to have friendly and helpful relationships with others that are near them

good·ness [S2] /'gʊdnɪs/ *n* [U]
1 my goodness!/goodness (gracious) me! *spoken* said when you are surprised or sometimes angry: *My goodness, you have spent a lot!*
2 for goodness' sake *spoken* said when you are annoyed or surprised, especially when telling someone to do something: *For goodness' sake stop arguing!*
3 goodness (only) knows *spoken* used to emphasize that you are not sure about something, or to make a statement stronger: *That bar's been closed for goodness knows how long.* | *Goodness knows, I tried to help him!*
4 BEING GOOD the quality of being good: *the desire to see goodness and justice in the world*
5 BEST PART the part of food which is good for your health: *All the goodness of an egg is in the yolk.*
6 have the goodness to do sth *old-fashioned formal* used when asking someone to do something in an extremely polite way: *Please have the goodness to wait.*
7 out of the goodness of sb's heart used when someone has done something in order to be kind or helpful to other people: *He did it out of the goodness of his heart.*

good 'night [S3] used to say goodbye when you are leaving someone or they are leaving at night, or before going to sleep; → **good evening**: *Good night. Sleep well.*

goods [S2] [W2] /gʊdz/ *n* [plural]
1 things that are produced in order to be sold: **electrical/industrial/agricultural etc goods** *furniture, carpets and other household goods* | *the large market for **consumer goods** (=televisions, washing machines etc)* | *Britain's leading exporter of **manufactured goods** (=things that are made not grown)* | *There will be tax increases on a wide range of **goods and services**.* → DRY GOODS
2 things that someone owns and that can be moved: *They were charged with handling **stolen goods**.* | *We collected up our goods and left.*
3 *BrE* things which are carried by road, train etc; **freight**: *a goods train*
4 come up with the goods/deliver the goods *informal* to do what is needed or expected: *He's a great player. He always comes up with the goods on the day.*
5 have/get the goods on sb *AmE* to have or find proof that someone is guilty of a crime: *Face it, Bukowski, we got the goods on you!*
6 damaged goods someone whose actions mean that they no longer have a good effect or influence on something: *After the scandal, he was considered damaged goods by the party.* → **worldly goods** at WORLDLY (1)

,goods and 'chattels *n* [plural] *BrE law* personal possessions

good 'sense *n* [U] the quality someone has when they are able to make sensible decisions about what to do: *Mrs Booth showed a lot of good sense.* | **have the good sense to do sth** *Mark had the good sense not to argue.* | *It **makes good sense** (=is sensible) to do some research before buying.*

good-'tempered *adj* pleasant, kind, and not easily made angry; ⊟ **bad-tempered**

good·will /ˌgʊdˈwɪl◂/ *n* [U] **1** kind feelings towards or between people and a willingness to be helpful: *A fund was set up as a **goodwill gesture** to survivors and their families.* | **the season of goodwill** (=Christmas) **2** the value that a company has because it has a good relationship with its customers: *The sale price also covers the goodwill of the business.*

good·y¹ /ˈgʊdi/ *n plural* **goodies** [C usually plural] *informal* **1** something that is nice to eat: *We bought lots of goodies for the picnic.* **2** something attractive, pleasant, or desirable: *The competition gives you the chance to win all sorts of goodies.* **3** *BrE* a GOODIE

goody² *interjection* a word used by children to express pleasure or excitement

goody-goody *n plural* goody-goodies also **goody-two-shoes** *AmE* [C] someone who tries hard to be very good and helpful in order to please their parents, teachers etc – used especially by children to show disapproval

goo·ey /ˈguːi/ *adj comparative* **gooier,** *superlative* **gooiest** *informal* **1** sticky and soft: *gooey cakes* | *gooey mud* **2** showing your love for someone in a way that other people think is silly; ⊟ **soppy**: *Babies make her **go all gooey**.*

goof¹ /guːf/ also **goof up** *v* [I,T] *informal especially AmE* to make a silly mistake: *Somebody goofed and entered the wrong amount.* | *The restaurant totally goofed up our reservations.*

goof around *phr v AmE informal* to spend time doing silly things or not doing very much; ⊟ **mess about** *BrE*: *We spent the afternoon just goofing around on our bikes.*

goof off *phr v AmE informal* to waste time or avoid doing any work: *He's been goofing off at school.*

goof² *n* [C] *informal especially AmE* **1** also **goof up** a silly mistake: *The goof could cost the city $5 million.* **2** also **goofball** someone who is silly

goof·ball /ˈguːfbɔːl $ -bɒːl/ *n* [C] *AmE* someone who is silly or stupid

goof·y /ˈguːfi/ *adj informal* stupid or silly: *A goofy grin spread across her face when she saw the card.*

goo·gly /ˈguːgli/ *n plural* **googlies** [C] **1** a ball in the game of CRICKET that is thrown to an opponent so that it looks as if it will go in one direction but goes in the other **2 bowl sb a googly** *BrE informal* to ask someone a question that is intended to trick them

goo·lie, gooly /ˈguːli/ *n* [C usually plural] *BrE informal* a rude or humorous word meaning a TESTICLE

goon /guːn/ *n* [C] *informal* **1** *especially BrE* a silly or stupid person **2** *especially AmE* a violent criminal who is paid to frighten or attack people

goop /guːp/ *n* [U] *AmE informal* a thick slightly sticky substance

goose¹ /guːs/ *n plural* **geese** /giːs/ **1 a)** [C] a bird that is like a duck but is larger and makes loud noises **b)** [C] a female goose; → **gander 2** [U] the cooked meat of this bird **3** [singular] *old-fashioned informal* a silly person → WILD GOOSE CHASE; → **wouldn't say boo to a goose** at BOO² (3); → **kill the goose that lays the golden egg** at KILL¹ (14); → **what's sauce for the goose is sauce for the gander** at SAUCE (3)

goose² *v* [T] *AmE informal* to touch or press someone on their bottom as a joke

goose·ber·ry /ˈgʊzbəri, ˈguːz-, ˈguːs- $ ˈguːsberi/ *n plural* **gooseberries** [C] **1** a small round green fruit that grows on a bush and has a sour taste **2 be a gooseberry** also **play gooseberry** *BrE informal* to be with

two people who are having a romantic relationship and who want to be alone together

goose ,pimples also **goose·bumps** /ˈguːsbʌmps/ *especially AmE n* [plural] also **goose·flesh** /ˈguːsfleʃ/ [U] small raised spots on your skin that you get when you are cold or frightened

goose·step /ˈguːs-step/ *n* **the goosestep** a way of marching by soldiers, in which they lift their legs quite high and do not bend their knees —**goosestep** *v* [I]

GOP /ˌdʒiː əʊ ˈpiː $ -oʊ-/ *n AmE* **the GOP** **the Grand Old Party** another name for the Republican Party in US politics

go·pher /ˈgəʊfə $ ˈgoʊfər/ *n* [C] **1** a North and Central American animal like a large rat that lives in holes in the ground **2** also **Gopher** *trademark* a computer program that helps people find and use information quickly on the Internet

Gor·di·an knot /ˌgɔːdiən ˈnɒt $ ˌgɔːrdiən ˈnɑːt/ *n* **cut/untie the Gordian knot** to quickly solve a difficult problem by determined action: *In recent years, governments have tried to cut the Gordian knot by imposing cuts in state support to the railways.*

gore¹ /gɔː $ gɔːr/ *v* [T usually passive] if an animal gores someone, it wounds them with its horns or TUSKS: *He was attacked and gored by a bull.*

gore² *n* [U] *literary* thick dark blood that has flowed from a wound; → **gory**: *He likes movies with plenty of **blood and gore** (=violence).*

gorge¹ /gɔːdʒ $ gɔːrdʒ/ *n* [C] **1** a deep narrow valley with steep sides **2 feel your gorge rise** *BrE* to feel very sick or angry, especially when you see or smell something very unpleasant

gorge² *v* **1 gorge yourself (on sth)** to eat until you are too full to eat any more; ⊟ **stuff yourself**: *We gorged ourselves on ripe plums.* **2 be gorged with sth** to be completely full of something: *The insect sucks until it is gorged with blood.*

gorge³ *adj BrE spoken informal* extremely beautiful or attractive

gor·geous S3 /ˈgɔːdʒəs $ ˈgɔːr-/ *adj informal* **1** extremely beautiful or attractive: *'What do you think of my new flatmate?' 'He's **absolutely gorgeous!'* | *You look gorgeous, Maria.* → see box at BEAUTIFUL **2** extremely pleasant or enjoyable; ⊟ **lovely**: *a gorgeous cake* | *The hotel room had a gorgeous view.* —**gorgeously** *adv*

gor·gon /ˈgɔːgən $ ˈgɔːr-/ *n* [C] **1 Gorgon** one of the three sisters in ancient Greek stories who had snakes on their heads that made anyone who looked at them change into stone **2** *BrE informal* an ugly frightening woman

go·ril·la /gəˈrɪlə/ *n* [C] **1** a very large African monkey that is the largest of the APES **2** a man who is very large and who looks as if he might become violent

gorm·less /ˈgɔːmləs $ ˈgɔːrm-/ *adj BrE informal* very stupid: *a gormless grin* | *a gormless boy* —**gormlessly** *adv*

gorse /gɔːs $ gɔːrs/ *n* [U] a PRICKLY bush with bright yellow flowers, which grows in the countryside in Europe

gor·y /ˈgɔːri/ *adj* **1** *informal* clearly describing or showing violence, blood, and killing: *a gory horror movie* | *gory tales of murder* **2 (all) the gory details** all the details about an unpleasant or interesting event – often used humorously: *Come on, I want to hear all the gory details.* **3** *literary* covered in blood

gosh S2 /gɒʃ $ gɑːʃ/ *interjection informal* used to express surprise: *Gosh, it's cold.*

gos·ling /ˈgɒzlɪŋ $ ˈgɑːz-, ˈgɔːz-/ *n* [C] a young GOOSE

go-'slow *n* [C] *BrE* a protest against an employer in which the workers work as slowly as possible; → **work-to-rule, strike**; ⊟ **slowdown** *AmE*

G

gos·pel /'gɒspəl $ 'gɑːs-/ n **1** Gospel [C] one of the four books in the Bible about Christ's life: *the Gospel according to St Luke* **2** also **Gospel** [singular] the life of Christ and the ideas that he taught: **preach/spread the gospel** (=tell people about it) *Missionaries were sent to preach the Gospel.* | *gospel stories* **3** [C usually singular] a set of ideas that someone believes in very strongly and tries to persuade other people to accept: **spread/preach the gospel** *spreading the gospel of science* **4** also **gospel truth** [U] something that is completely true: *Don't take everything she says as gospel* (=don't believe everything she says). **5** also **gospel music** [U] a type of Christian music in which religious songs are sung very loudly: *a gospel choir*

gos·sa·mer /'gɒsəmə $ 'gɑːsəmər/ n [U] **1** *literary* a very light thin material **2** the light silky thread which SPIDERS leave on grass and bushes

gos·sip¹ /'gɒsɪp $ 'gɑː-/ n
1 [U] information that is passed from one person to another about other people's behaviour and private lives, often including unkind or untrue remarks

> **piece of gossip**
> **the latest gossip**
> **juicy/hot gossip** (=interesting gossip)
> **idle gossip** (=gossip not based on facts)
> **common gossip** (=something that everyone knows and is talking about)
> **office gossip**
> **village gossip** *BrE*
> **exchange gossip** (=talk about other people's private lives with someone)

[+about] *Here's an interesting **piece of gossip** about Mrs Smith.* | *What's the **latest gossip**?* | *Do you want to hear some **juicy gossip**?* | *She had no time for **idle gossip**.* | *It was **common gossip** how he felt about her.* | *You miss a lot of **office gossip** when you have a day off work.* | *On Sundays all the men gather in the square to **exchange** local gossip.*

2 [C usually singular] a conversation in which you exchange information with someone about other people's lives and things that have happened: *Phil's in there, having a gossip with Maggie.*
3 [C] someone who likes talking about other people's private lives – used to show disapproval: *Rick's a terrible gossip.*

gossip² v [I] to talk about other people's behaviour and private lives, often including remarks that are unkind or untrue: [+about] *The whole town was gossiping about them.*

'gossip ,column n [C] a regular article in a newspaper or magazine about the behaviour and private lives of famous people —**gossip columnist** n [C]

gos·sip·y /'gɒsɪpi $ 'gɑː-/ adj informal **1** a gossipy conversation, letter etc is informal and full of gossip **2** a gossipy person likes to gossip: *gossipy secretaries*

got /gɒt $ gɑːt/ the past tense and a participle of GET ⚠ You cannot say 'I/he/she etc got' in the present tense. Say you **have** something or **have got** something: *I've got (NOT I got) a new bike.*

got·cha /'gɒtʃə $ 'gɑː-/ interjection **1** a word meaning 'I've got you' used when you catch someone or trick them in some way **2** a word meaning 'I understand': *'Yeah, 5 o'clock, gotcha.'*

goth /gɒθ $ gɑːθ/ n **1** [U] a type of slow sad popular music that is played on electric GUITARS and KEY-BOARDS **2** [C] someone who likes goth music —**goth** also **gothic** adj

Goth·ic /'gɒθɪk $ 'gɑː-/ adj **1** the Gothic style of building was common in Western Europe between the 12th and 16th centuries and included tall pointed ARCHES and windows and tall PILLARS: *a Gothic church* **2** a Gothic story, film etc is about frightening things that happen in mysterious old buildings and lonely places,

in a style that was popular in the early 19th century **3** Gothic writing, printing etc has thick decorated letters

got·ta /'gɒtə $ 'gɑːtə/ spoken informal a short form of 'have got to', 'has got to', 'have got a', or 'has got a', which most people think is incorrect: *We gotta go now.*

got·ten /'gɒtn $ 'gɑːtn/ AmE the past participle of GET → ILL-GOTTEN GAINS

US/UK DIFFERENCE
In American English, **gotten** is the usual past participle of **get**: *I'd gotten an A on the test.* | *It has gotten really warm.* | *I heard they had gotten divorced.*
gotten is not used as the past participle for **got to** meaning 'must'. Speakers of American English say **had to** rather than **had got to**: *We had to be there on time.*
In British English, **gotten** is not used. The past participle of **get** in British English is **got**: *I had got a letter from my sister in Australia.*

gou·ache /guˈɑːʃ, gwɑːʃ/ n **1** [U] a method of painting using colours that are mixed with water and made thicker with a type of glue **2** [C] a picture painted in this way

gouge¹ /gaʊdʒ/ v [T] to make a deep hole or cut in the surface of something: *He took a knife and gouged a hole in the bottom of the boat.*
gouge sth ⇔ out phr v **1** to form a hole, space etc by digging into a surface and removing material, or to remove material by digging: [+of] *A rough road had been gouged out of the rock.* | *30,000 tonnes of slate are gouged out of the mountains every week.* **2 gouge sb's eyes out** to remove someone's eyes with a pointed weapon

gouge² n [C] a hole or cut made in something, usually by a sharp tool or weapon

gou·lash /'guːlæʃ $ -lɑːʃ, -læʃ/ n [C,U] a dish of meat cooked in liquid with a hot-tasting pepper, originally from Hungary

gourd /gʊəd $ gɔːrd, gʊrd/ n [C] a round fruit whose outer shell can be used as a container, or the container made from this fruit

gour·mand /'gʊəmənd $ 'gʊr-/ n [C] someone who likes to eat and drink a lot

gour·met¹ /'gʊəmeɪ $ 'gʊr-, gʊrˈmeɪ/ adj [only before noun] producing or relating to very good food and drink: *a gourmet cook* | *gourmet dinners*

gourmet² n [C] someone who knows a lot about food and wine and who enjoys good food and wine

gout /gaʊt/ n [U] a disease that makes your toes, fingers, and knees swollen and painful

gov 1 Gov. the written abbreviation of *governor* **2** .gov used in Internet addresses for government websites

gov·ern W3 /'gʌvən $ -ərn/ v
1 [I,T] to officially and legally control a country and make all the decisions about taxes, laws, public services etc; ◨ **rule**: *the military leaders who govern the country* | *a country governed by a military élite* | *The party had been governing for seven months.*
2 [T] if rules, principles etc govern the way a system or situation works, they control how it happens: *legislation governing the export of live animals* | *The universe is governed by the laws of physics.*

gov·ern·ess /'gʌvənɪs $ -ər-/ n [C] a female teacher in the past, who lived with a rich family and taught their children at home

gov·ern·ing /'gʌvənɪŋ $ -ər-/ adj **1** [only before noun] having the power and authority to control an organization, country etc; ◨ **ruling**: *FIFA is the governing body of world soccer* (=the group of people who control it). | *The Democrats are now the governing party* (=the party in power) *in the country.* | *the governing class of ancient Rome* **2 governing principle** a principle that has the most important influence on something: *Freedom of speech is one of the governing principles in a democracy.*; → self-governing

gov·ern·ment [S2] [W1] /'gʌvəmənt, 'gʌvənmənt $ 'gʌvərn-/ n
1 also **Government** [C usually singular also + plural verb BrE] the group of people who govern a country or state: *The Government are planning further cuts in public spending.* | *The US government has tightened restrictions on firearms.* | *Neither party had the majority necessary to* **form a government** (=become the government after an election). | **democratic/totalitarian etc government** *The country now has a democratic government for the first time.* | *A* **coalition government** (=government made up of members of several political parties) *will now be established.* | **under a government** (=during the period of a government) *Structural reforms are unlikely under the present government.* | *a meeting with government officials* | *the restructuring of government departments* | *Government spending on health care totals about $60 billion a year.*
2 [U] a form or system of government: *Most people in the country support the return to democratic government.* → LOCAL GOVERNMENT, CENTRAL GOVERNMENT
3 [U] the process or way of governing: **in government** *What would the opposition do if they were in government* (=governing the country)? | *the importance of good government in developing countries*
4 [U] AmE the degree to which the government controls economic and social activities: *The protest march was really about* **big government** (=when the government controls many activities).

gov·ern·men·tal /,gʌvə'mentl◂, ,gʌvən-$,gʌvərn-/ adj of a government, or relating to government: *an attempt to restrict governmental power* | **governmental body** (=organization controlled by the government)

government 'health 'warning n [C] BrE a notice that must be put on products such as cigarettes, to warn people that they are dangerous to their health

gov·er·nor [W3], **Governor** /'gʌvənə $ -vərnər/ n [C]
1 a) the person in charge of governing a state in the US **b)** the person in charge of governing a country that is under the political control of another country
2 BrE a member of a committee that controls an organization or institution: *a school governor* | *the hospital's* **board of governors**
3 BrE the person in charge of an institution: *the prison governor* | [+of] *the governor of the central bank*
4 BrE a GUVNOR

Governor-'General n [C] someone who represents the King or Queen of Britain in other Commonwealth countries which are not REPUBLICS: *the Governor-General of Australia*

gov·ern·or·ship /'gʌvənəʃɪp $ -vərnər-/ n [U] the position of being governor, or the period during which someone is governor

govt. the written abbreviation of *government*

gown /gaʊn/ n [C] **1** a long dress that a woman wears on formal occasions: **wedding/evening/ball gown** *a white silk wedding gown* **2** a long loose piece of clothing worn for special ceremonies by judges, teachers, lawyers, and members of universities; **robe** **3** a long loose piece of clothing worn in a hospital by someone doing or having an operation: *a hospital gown* → DRESSING GOWN

GP BrE; **G.P.** AmE /,dʒiː 'piː/ n [C] **general practitioner** a doctor who is trained in general medicine and treats people in a particular area or town: *I've got an appointment with my GP at five o'clock.*

GPA /,dʒiː piː 'eɪ/ n [C] **grade point average** the average of a student's marks over a period of time in the US education system

GPS /,dʒiː piː 'es/ n [U] **Global Positioning System** a system that uses radio signals from SATELLITES to show your exact position on the Earth on a special piece of equipment

grab¹ [S3] [W3] /græb/ v grabbed, grabbing [T]
1 WITH YOUR HAND to take hold of someone or something with a sudden or violent movement; **snatch**: *I grabbed my bag and ran off.* | *Two men grabbed her and pushed her to the ground.* | *Kay* **grabbed hold of** *my arm to stop herself falling.* | **grab sth from sb/sth** *I managed to grab the gun from Bowen.*
2 FOOD/SLEEP informal to get some food or sleep quickly because you are busy; **snatch**: *Why don't you go and grab some sleep?* | *Hang on while I grab a cup of coffee.* | *Let's grab a bite to eat before we go.*
3 GET STH FOR YOURSELF to get something for yourself, sometimes in an unfair way: *Try to get there early and grab good seats.* | *Bob tried to grab all the profit.*
4 CHANCE/OPPORTUNITY informal also **grab at sth** to take an opportunity, accept an invitation etc immediately: *I think you should* **grab** *your* **chance** *to travel while you're young.* | *She* **grabbed** *the* **opportunity** *to go to America.* | *Melanie grabbed at the invitation to go.* | *This is our chance to grab a slice of this new market.*
5 GET ATTENTION to get someone's attention: *The book is full of good ideas to grab your students' attention.* | *The plight of the refugees immediately* **grabbed the headlines** (=was the most important story in the newspapers).
6 how does sth grab you? spoken used to ask someone if they would be interested in doing a particular thing: *How does the idea of a trip to Spain grab you?*

grab at/for sth phr v
to quickly and suddenly put out your hand to try and catch or get something: *I grabbed at the glass just before it fell.* | *Lucy grabbed for the money.*

grab² n **1 make a grab for/at sth** to suddenly try to take hold of something: *As soon as he turned his back, I made a grab for the revolver.* **2 be up for grabs** informal if a job, prize, opportunity etc is up for grabs, it is available for anyone who wants to try to have it **3** [C] the act of getting something quickly, especially in a dishonest way: *a shameless power grab to eliminate opposition* | *Officials denounced the settlers' land grab.*

'grab ,bag n AmE **1** [C] a container filled with small presents that you put your hand in to pick one out; **lucky dip** BrE **2** [singular] a mixture of different things or styles: [+of] *The treaty covers a grab bag of issues.* **3** [singular] informal a situation in which things are decided by chance

grace¹ /greɪs/ n
1 WAY OF MOVING [U] a smooth way of moving that looks natural, relaxed, and attractive; **gracefulness**: *Lena moved with the grace of a dancer.*
2 BEHAVIOUR **a)** [U] polite and pleasant behaviour: *The hotel maintains traditional standards of elegance, style, and grace.* | **have the grace to do sth** *He didn't even have the grace to apologize* (=he was not polite enough to apologize). **b)** **graces** [plural] the skills needed to behave in a way that is considered polite and socially acceptable: *Max definitely lacked* **social graces.**
3 MORE TIME [U] also **grace period** AmE more time that is allowed to someone to finish a piece of work, pay a debt etc: **a day's/week's etc grace** *I got a few days' grace to finish my essay.*
4 with (a) good/bad grace in a willing and pleasant way, or an unwilling and angry way: *Kevin smiled and accepted his defeat with good grace.* | *With typical bad grace, they refused to come to the party.*
5 GOD'S KINDNESS formal [U] God's kindness that is shown to people: *We are saved by God's grace.*
6 there but for the grace of God (go I) used to say that you feel lucky not to be in the same bad situation as someone else
7 PRAYER [U] a prayer thanking God, said before a meal: *My father* **said grace.**
8 SOUL [U] the state of someone's soul when it is free from evil, according to Christian belief: *He died* **in a state of grace** (=when God has forgiven you for the wrong things you have done).

G

9 Your/His etc Grace used as a title when talking to or about a DUKE, DUCHESS, or ARCHBISHOP
10 the Graces three beautiful Greek goddesses who often appear in art → **airs and graces** at AIR¹ (9); → **fall from grace** at FALL¹ (17); → **saving grace** at SAVE¹ (14)

grace² v [T] **1** grace sth/sb with your presence to bring honour to an occasion or group of people by coming to something – said humorously when someone comes late or does not often come to meetings etc: *Ah so you've decided to grace us with your presence!* **2** formal to make a place or an object look more attractive: *His portrait graces the wall of the drawing room.*

grace·ful /ˈgreɪsfəl/ adj **1** moving in a smooth and attractive way, or having an attractive shape or form: *Her movements were graceful and elegant.* | *The branches formed a graceful curve.* **2** behaving in a polite and pleasant way: *Her father was a quiet man with graceful manners.* —**gracefully** adv: *She rose gracefully to her feet and went to the door.* —**gracefulness** n [U]

grace·less /ˈgreɪsləs/ adj **1** not being polite, especially when someone has been kind to you: *He was bad-tempered and graceless in defeat.* **2** moving or doing something in a way that seems awkward; ⊟ **graceful**: *The soldiers were graceless with their heavy packs and helmets.* **3** something that is graceless is unattractive and unpleasant to look at; ⊟ **graceful**: *graceless architecture* —**gracelessly** adv

gra·cious /ˈgreɪʃəs/ adj **1** behaving in a polite, kind, and generous way, especially to people of a lower rank: *Sibyl was the most gracious, helpful, and generous person to work with.* | *a gracious apology* **2** having the kind of expensive style, comfort, and beauty that only rich people can afford: *a gracious manor house* | *a magazine about gracious living* **3** **gracious (me)!/good gracious!/goodness gracious!** old-fashioned used to express surprise or to emphasize 'yes' or 'no': *Good gracious! What on earth has happened to your feet?* | *'Did you ever go back?' 'Good gracious, no.'* **4** a gracious act by or gift from God is kind and forgiving **5** [only before noun] used as a polite way of describing a royal person: *our gracious Queen* —**graciously** adv —**graciousness** n [U]

grad /græd/ n [C] AmE informal a GRADUATE

grad·a·ble /ˈgreɪdəbəl/ adj an adjective which is gradable can be used in the COMPARATIVE or SUPERLATIVE forms, or with words such as 'very' or 'fairly' —**gradability** /ˌgreɪdəˈbɪləti/ n [U]

gra·da·tion /grəˈdeɪʃən/ n [C] formal a small change or difference between points on a scale: *There are many gradations of colour between light and dark blue.*

grade¹ [S3] [W3] /greɪd/ n [C]
1 STANDARD a particular level of quality that a product, material etc has: *The best grades of tea are expensive.* | *industrial grade diamonds* | **high/low grade** *low grade products*
2 RANK a particular level of job: *There are lots of jobs in junior grades.*
3 MARK IN SCHOOL a mark that a student is given for their work or for an examination: *He got a grade A in maths.* | *Tim worked hard and got good grades.*
4 make the grade to succeed or reach the necessary standard: *What does it take to make the grade as a top golfer?*
5 SCHOOL YEAR one of the 12 years that students are at school in the American school system, or the students in a particular year: **second/eleventh etc grade** *My brother is in the sixth grade.* | *a fifth-grade teacher*
6 SLOPE AmE a slope or a degree of slope, especially in a road or railway; ⊟ **gradient** BrE

grade² v [T] **1** to say what level of a quality something has, or what standard it is: **grade sth according to sth** *Pencils are graded according to softness.* | *All the parks are regularly checked and graded by tourist board inspectors.* **2** especially AmE to give a mark to an examination paper or to a piece of school work; ⊟ **mark**: *Ted is grading papers in his office.* **3** to give a particular rank and level of pay to a job

grade ˌcrossing n [C] AmE a place where a road and railway cross each other, usually with gates that shut the road while the train passes; ⊟ **level crossing** BrE

grad·ed /ˈgreɪdɪd/ adj designed to suit different levels of learning: *graded coursebooks*

grade point ˌaverage n [C] AmE GPA

-grader /ˈgreɪdə $ -ər/ suffix [in nouns] **first-grader/fourth-grader etc** a student in one of the 12 years in an American school

grade ˌschool n [C,U] AmE an ELEMENTARY SCHOOL

gra·di·ent /ˈgreɪdiənt/ n [C] a slope or a degree of slope, especially in a road or railway; ⊟ **grade** AmE: *a steep gradient*

grad school n [C,U] AmE informal a GRADUATE SCHOOL

grad·u·al /ˈgrædʒuəl/ adj **1** happening slowly over a long period of time; ⊟ **sudden**: *There has been a gradual change in climate.* | *the gradual decline in manufacturing industry* | *Education is a gradual process.* **2** a gradual slope is not steep

grad·u·al·ly [S2] [W3] /ˈgrædʒuəli/ adv slowly, over a long period of time; ⊟ **suddenly**: *Jill gradually became aware of an awful smell.* | *Gradually, my ankle got better.*

grad·u·ate¹ /ˈgrædʒuᵻt/ n [C] **1** someone who has completed a university degree, especially a first degree; → **undergraduate**: *a Harvard graduate* | **[+of]** *a graduate of Edinburgh University* | *university graduates* | *a history graduate* | **[+in]** *He's a graduate in philosophy.* **2** AmE someone who has completed a course at a college, school etc: *a high-school graduate*

grad·u·ate² /ˈgrædʒueɪt/ v **1** [I] to obtain a degree, especially a first degree, from a college or university: **[+from]** *Kate graduated from medical school last year.* | **[+in]** *He graduated in physics from Cambridge University.* **2** [I] AmE to complete your education at HIGH SCHOOL: **[+from]** *Jerry graduated from high school last year.* **3** **graduate (from sth) to sth** to start doing something that is bigger, better, or more important: *As an actress she has graduated from small roles to more substantial parts.* **4** [T] especially AmE to give a degree or DIPLOMA to someone who has completed a course

grad·u·ate³ /ˈgrædʒuᵻt/ adj [only before noun] especially AmE relating to or involved in studies done at a university after completing a first degree; ⊟ **postgraduate** BrE: *a graduate student*

grad·u·at·ed /ˈgrædʒueɪtᵻd/ adj **1** divided into different levels: *graduated rates of taxation* **2** a tool or container that is graduated has small marks on it showing measurements

graduate ˌschool n [C,U] AmE a college or university where you can study for a MASTER'S DEGREE or a DOCTORATE after receiving your first degree, or the period of time when you study for these degrees

grad·u·a·tion /ˌgrædʒuˈeɪʃən/ n **1** [U] the time when you complete a university degree course or your education at an American HIGH SCHOOL: *After graduation Neil returned to Ohio.* | *On graduation* (=after completing a first degree), *Nancy became an art teacher.* **2** [C] a ceremony at which you receive a university degree or a DIPLOMA from an American HIGH SCHOOL: *graduation day* **3** [C] a mark on an instrument or container used for measuring

Graeco- /griːkəʊ, grekəʊ $ -koʊ/ prefix another spelling of GRECO-

graf·fi·ti /græˈfiːti, grə-/ n [U] rude, humorous, or political writing and pictures on the walls of buildings, trains etc: *The walls are daubed with graffiti.*

graft¹ /grɑːft $ græft/ n **1** [C] a piece of healthy skin or bone taken from someone's body and put in or on another part of their body that has been damaged: *Martha had to have several skin grafts.* **2** [C] a piece cut from one plant and tied to or put inside a cut in another, so that it grows there **3** [U] informal especially

BrE hard work: *Our success has been due to sheer **hard graft**.* **4** [U] *especially AmE* the practice of obtaining money or advantage by the dishonest use of influence or power: *He promised to end graft in public life.*

graft² *v* **1** [T] to remove a piece of skin, bone etc from part of someone's body and put it onto or into a part of their body that has been damaged: **graft sth onto/to sth** *The technique involves grafting a very thin slice of bone onto the damaged knee.* **2** [T + on/onto] to join a part of a plant or tree onto another plant or tree **3** [T] to add something very different to something, so that it becomes part of it: **graft sth onto sth** *New elements are being grafted onto our traditional form of government.* | **graft sth on** *It is a seventeenth century farmhouse with some Victorian additions grafted on.* **4** [I] *informal especially BrE* to work hard

  graft off sb *phr v AmE* to get money or advantages from someone by the dishonest use of influence, especially political influence

Grail /greɪl/ *n* → HOLY GRAIL

grain /greɪn/ *n*

1 FOOD **a)** [U] the seeds of crops such as corn, wheat, or rice that are gathered for use as food, or these crops themselves: *big sacks of grain* | *Last year's grain harvest was the biggest ever.* **b)** [C] a single seed of corn, wheat etc: *grains of rice*
2 LINES IN WOOD ETC [singular] the natural lines you can see in a substance such as wood, which are the result of its structure: **along the grain** (=in the same direction as the grain) *Cut along the grain of the wood.* | **across the grain** (=at 90 degrees to the grain)
3 SMALL PIECE [C] a single very small piece of a substance such as sand or salt: [+of] *a grain of sand* | *There were crumbs and grains of sugar on the table.*
4 **a grain of sth** a very small amount of something: *The story was so silly it wouldn't have fooled anyone with a grain of sense.* | *There is a **grain of truth** in all folklore and legend.*
5 **against the grain** if something goes against the grain, it is not what you would naturally or normally do: *Mary is always honest and **it went against the grain** to tell lies.*
6 MEASURE [C] the smallest unit for measuring weight, equal to about 0.06 grams. It is used for weighing medicines → **take sth with a pinch/grain of salt** at SALT¹ (3)

grain·y /ˈgreɪni/ *adj* a photograph that is grainy has a rough appearance, as if the images are made up of spots

gram S3 also **gramme** *BrE* /græm/ *n* [C] written abbreviation **g** or **gm** the basic unit for measuring weight in the METRIC SYSTEM

-gram /græm/ *suffix* [in nouns] a message delivered as an amusing surprise: *On his birthday we sent him a kissagram* (=a woman who was paid to give him a message and kiss him).

gram·mar S3 W3 /ˈgræmə $ -ər/ *n*
1 [U] the rules by which words change their forms and are combined into sentences, or the study or use of these rules: *Check your spelling and grammar.* | *the rules of English grammar*
2 [C] a particular description of grammar or a book that describes grammar rules: *A dictionary lists the words, a grammar states the rules.*

gram·mar·i·an /grəˈmeəriən $ -ˈmer-/ *n* [C] someone who studies and knows about grammar

'grammar ˌschool *n* [C,U] **1** a school in Britain for children over the age of 11 who have to pass a special examination to go there; → **comprehensive school 2** *AmE old-fashioned* an ELEMENTARY SCHOOL

gram·mat·i·cal /grəˈmætɪkəl/ *adj* **1** [only before noun] concerning grammar: *grammatical rules* **2** correct according to the rules of grammar: ▪ **ungrammatical —grammatically** /-kli/ *adv*

gramme /græm/ *n* a British spelling of GRAM

gram·o·phone /ˈgræməfəʊn $ -foʊn/ *n* [C] *old-fashioned* a RECORD PLAYER

gran /græn/ *n* [C] *BrE informal* grandmother

gran·a·ry /ˈgrænəri $ ˈgreɪ-, ˈgræ-/ *n plural* **granaries** [C] a place where grain, especially wheat, is stored

Granary *adj* [only before noun] *trademark BrE* Granary bread is bread which contains whole grains of wheat

grand¹ S2 W3 /grænd/ *adj*
1 big and very impressive; ▪ **humble**: *a grand country house* | *The party was a grand affair.* | *New Yorkers build on a grand scale.*
2 aiming or intended to achieve something impressive: *Henry Luce had a grand design for America's future.* | *The company's grand ambition was to become the first and biggest global airline.*
3 important and rich: *He looked very grand in his ceremonial uniform.* | *the grand end of West Avenue*
4 Grand a) used in the titles of buildings or places that are big and impressive: *the Grand Hotel* | *Grand Central Station* **b)** used in the titles of some people who belong to the highest social class: *the Grand Duke of Baden*
5 *informal* excellent: *We all had a grand time.* | *Thank you, Shirley, that's grand.*
6 **a grand total** the final total you get when you add up several numbers or amounts: [+of] *You could add the £15,000 Bonus to the First Prize and win a grand total of £125,000!*
7 **grand (old) age** an age when someone is quite old: *She had reached the grand old age of 80.*
8 **the Grand Old Man of sth** a man who has been involved in an activity or a profession for a long time and is highly respected: *the Grand Old Man of British theatre* **—grandly** *adv*: *'I am training her to cook for royalty,' Auguste said grandly.*

grand² *n* [C] *informal* **1** *plural* **grand** a thousand pounds or dollars: *The car cost him fifteen grand.* **2** a GRAND PIANO

gran·dad S2 *especially BrE* also **granddad** /ˈgrændæd/ *n informal* [C] grandfather

gran·dad·dy, **granddaddy** /ˈgrændædi/ *n plural* **grandaddies** [C] *AmE informal* **1** grandfather **2 the grandaddy of sth** the first or greatest example of something: *Louis Armstrong, the grandaddy of all jazz trumpeters*

grand·child S3 /ˈgræntʃaɪld/ *n plural* **grandchildren** /-ˌtʃɪldrən/ [C] the child of your son or daughter

grand·dad /ˈgrændæd/ *n* the usual American spelling of GRANDAD

grand·dad·dy /ˈgrændædi/ *n AmE* another spelling of GRANDADDY

grand·daugh·ter /ˈgræn,dɔːtə $ -,dɔːtər/ *n* [C] the daughter of your son or daughter

gran·dee /grænˈdiː/ *n* [C] **1** a politician of the highest social class who has a lot of influence **2** a Spanish or Portuguese NOBLEMAN of the highest rank, in the past

gran·deur /ˈgrændʒə $ -ər/ *n* [U] impressive beauty, power, or size: *the grandeur of the mountains* → **delusions of grandeur** at DELUSION (2)

grand·fa·ther S3 /ˈgrænd,fɑːðə $ -ər/ *n* [C] the father of your father or mother

'grandfather ˌclock *n* [C] an old-fashioned tall clock which stands on the floor → see picture at CLOCK

ˌgrand fi'nale *n* [C] the last and most impressive or exciting part of a show or performance

gran·dil·o·quent /grænˈdɪləkwənt/ *adj formal* using words that are too long and formal in order to sound important; ▪ **pompous —grandiloquence** *n* [U]

gran·di·ose /ˈgrændiəʊs $ -oʊs/ *adj* grandiose plans sound very important or impressive, but are not practical: **grandiose scheme/plan/idea etc** *grandiose schemes of urban renewal*

G

1 000, 2 000, 3 000, most frequent words in S poken and W ritten English

,**grand 'jury** n [C] *law* a group of people in the US who decide whether someone charged with a crime should be judged in a court of law —**grand juror** n [C]

,**grand 'larceny** n [U] *AmE law* the crime of stealing very valuable goods

grand·ma S1 /'grænmɑː/ n [C] *informal* grandmother

grand mal /ˌgrɒn 'mæl $ ˌgrɑːn-/ n [U] *technical* a serious form of EPILEPSY; → **petit mal**

,**grand 'master** n [C] a CHESS player of a very high standard

grand·moth·er S3 /'græn,mʌðə $ -ər/ n [C] the mother of your mother or father

,**grand 'opera** n [C,U] an OPERA with a serious subject in which all the words are sung

grand·pa S1 /'grænpɑː/ n [C] *informal* grandfather

grand·par·ent /'græn,peərənt $ -,per-/ n [C usually plural] one of the parents of your mother or father: *My grandparents live in Sussex.*

,**grand pi'ano** also **grand** n [C] the type of large piano often used in concerts, with strings in a horizontal position; → **upright piano**

Grand Prix /ˌgrɒn 'priː $ ˌgrɑːn-/ n plural **Grands Prix** /-'priː, -priːz/ [C] one of a set of international races, especially a car race

,**grand 'slam** n [C] **1** also **Grand Slam** the winning of all of a set of important sports competitions in the same year: *Wales won the Grand Slam.* **2** a hit in BASEBALL which gets four points because it is a HOME RUN and there are players on all the bases **3** the winning of all of the TRICKS possible in one game of cards, especially in BRIDGE

,**Grand 'Slam** adj [only before noun] a Grand Slam sports event is one of the set of most important competitions in a particular sport: *She won three Grand Slam titles.*

grand·son /'grænsʌn/ n [C] the son of your son or daughter

grand·stand /'grændstænd/ n [C] a large structure that has many rows of seats where people sit and watch sports competitions, games, or races

grand·stand·ing /'grændstændɪŋ/ n [U] *AmE* an action that is intended to make people notice and admire you: *His opening the new school is just a piece of political grandstanding.*

,**grand 'tour** n [C] **1 the grand tour** a trip round Europe made in the past by young British or American people from rich families as part of their education **2** an occasion when someone takes you around a building to show it to you – used humorously: *They took us on a grand tour of their new house.*

grange /greɪndʒ/ n [C] a large country house with farm buildings

gran·ite /'grænɪt/ n [U] a very hard grey rock, often used in building

gran·ny¹ S3 /'græni/ n plural **grannies** [C] *informal* grandmother

granny², **grannie** adj [only before noun] *BrE* of a style typically used by old women: *granny shoes*

'**granny ,flat** n [C] *BrE* a separate place inside or next to someone's house that is designed for an old relative to live in

'**granny ,knot** n [C] a knot that is like a REEF KNOT but is tied wrongly so that it is not firm

gra·no·la /grə'nəʊlə $ -'noʊ-/ n [U] *AmE* breakfast food made from mixed nuts, grains, and seeds

grant¹ S2 W2 /grɑːnt $ grænt/ v [T]
1 *formal* to give someone something or allow them to have something that they have asked for: *Britain could grant Spain's request.* | *I would love to be able to grant her wish.* | **grant sb sth** *The council have granted him permission to build on the site.* | **grant sth to sb** *A licence to sell alcohol was granted to the club.* | **grant**

that (=used in prayers) *Grant that we may know your presence and love.*
2 to admit that something is true although it does not make much difference to your opinion; → **concede**: *He's got talent, I grant you, but he doesn't work hard enough.*
3 take it for granted (that) to believe that something is true without making sure: *He just took it for granted that he would pass the exam.*
4 take sb/sth for granted to expect that someone or something will always be there when you need them and never think how important or useful they are: *Bridget was careful not to take him for granted.*

grant² S1 W2 n [C] an amount of money given to someone, especially by the government, for a particular purpose: *The university gets a government grant.* | *Anyone wishing to **apply for a grant** should write to the Treasurer.* | [+of] *a grant of £50,000* | [+from] *These studios are funded by a grant from the Kress Foundation.*

grant·ed /'grɑːntɪd $ 'græn-/ adv [sentence adverb] used when you admit that something is true: *Granted, the music is not perfect, but the flaws are outweighed by the sheer joy of the piece.*

,**grant-main'tained** adj a grant-maintained school in Britain receives its money directly from the central government rather than from the local government

gran·u·lar /'grænjʊlə $ -ər/ adj consisting of granules

gran·u·lat·ed /'grænjʊleɪtɪd/ adj granulated sugar is in the form of small white grains

gran·ule /'grænjuːl/ n [C] a small hard piece of something: *coffee granules*

grape /greɪp/ n [C] one of a number of small round green or purple fruits that grow together on a VINE. Grapes are often used for making wine: *a **bunch of grapes*** | *grape juice* → **sour grapes** at SOUR¹ (5); → see picture at FRUIT

grape·fruit /'greɪpfruːt/ n [C,U] a round yellow CITRUS fruit with a thick skin, like a large orange → see picture at FRUIT

grape·vine /'greɪpvaɪn/ n [C] **1 hear sth on the grapevine** to hear about something because the information has been passed from one person to another in conversation: *I heard about his resignation on the grapevine.* **2** a climbing plant on which grapes grow; → **vine**

graph /grɑːf $ græf/ n [C] a drawing that uses a line or lines to show how two or more sets of measurements are related to each other; → **chart**: *Martin showed me a graph of their recent sales.* → see picture at CHART

graph·ic /'græfɪk/ adj **1** a graphic account or description of an event is very clear and gives a lot of details, especially unpleasant ones; → **vivid**: *a graphic account of her unhappy childhood* | *His illness is described **in graphic detail**.* **2** [only before noun] connected with or including drawing, printing, or designing: *a graphic artist* | *the graphic arts*

graph·i·cal /'græfɪkəl/ adj [usually before noun] relating to or containing graphics, especially on a computer: *a simple graphical representation of the problem*

graph·i·cally /'græfɪkli/ adv **1** if you describe something graphically, you describe it very clearly with a lot of detail; → **vividly** **2** *formal* using a graph: *statistics represented graphically*

,**graphical 'user ,interface** n [C] *GUI* a way of showing and organizing information on a computer screen that is easy to use and understand

,**graphic de'sign** n [U] the art of combining pictures, words, and decoration in the production of books, magazines etc —**graphic designer** n [C]

graph·ics /'græfɪks/ n [plural] pictures or images that are designed to represent objects or facts, especially in a computer program

graphics ,card also **graphics a,dapter** n [C] a CIRCUIT BOARD that connects to a computer and allows the computer to show images, such as video images, on its screen

graph·ite /ˈɡræfaɪt/ n [U] a soft black substance that is a kind of CARBON, used in pencils, paints, and electrical equipment

gra·phol·o·gy /ɡræˈfɒlədʒi $ -ˈfɑː-/ n [U] the study of HANDWRITING in order to understand people's characters —**graphologist** n [C]

graph ,paper n [U] paper with many squares printed on it, used for drawing GRAPHS

-graphy /ɡrəfi/ suffix used in nouns to mean a way of making pictures or of writing: radiography | photography | calligraphy

grap·ple /ˈɡræpəl/ v [I] to fight or struggle with someone, holding them tightly; ▪ **wrestle**: [+with] Two men grappled with a guard at the door.

grapple with sth phr v to try hard to deal with or understand something difficult: The Government has to grapple with the problem of unemployment. | Molly's upstairs grappling with her maths homework.

grappling ,iron also **grappling ,hook** n [C] an iron tool with several hooks that you tie to a rope and use to hold a boat still, look for objects on the bottom of a river etc

grasp¹ /ɡrɑːsp $ ɡræsp/ v [T] **1** to take and hold something firmly; ▪ **grip**: I grasped his arm firmly and led him away. | Alan grasped the handle and pulled it. **2** [not in progressive] to completely understand a fact or an idea, especially a complicated one: At that time, we did not fully grasp the significance of what had happened. | Some people find the idea of relativity difficult to grasp. | **grasp what/how etc** A short opening paragraph enables the reader to quickly grasp what the article is about. | **grasp that** Nick had grasped that something was wrong. **3 grasp an opportunity** to eagerly and quickly use an opportunity to do something: She is ready to grasp any opportunity to expand the business. **4 grasp the nettle** BrE to deal with an unpleasant situation firmly and without delay: We need to grasp the nettle of prison reform.

grasp at sth phr v to try to hold on to something: His foot slipped and he grasped at the top of the wall.

grasp² n [singular] **1** the way you hold something or your ability to hold it; ▪ **grip**: Luke took her arm in a firm grasp and led her through the gate. | He had allowed the ball to slip from his grasp. **2** your ability to understand a complicated idea, situation, or subject; ▪ **understanding**: [+of] Her grasp of the issues was impressive. | **a good/firm/thorough etc grasp of sth** Steve has a good grasp of the European legal system. | [+on] After two months, his grasp on the subject was improving. **3** your ability to achieve or gain something: **within sb's grasp** An agreement to end the war seemed within their grasp. | **beyond sb's grasp** Many families with children are finding suitable housing beyond their grasp. **4** literary control or power: The king was determined not to let Scotland slip from his grasp.

grasp·ing /ˈɡrɑːspɪŋ $ ˈɡræs-/ adj too eager to get money and unwilling to give any of it away or spend it: Hanson was a hard, grasping man.

grass¹ [S2] [W2] /ɡrɑːs $ ɡræs/ n
 1 IN FIELDS AND GARDENS a) [U] a very common plant with thin leaves that covers the ground in fields and gardens and is often eaten by animals: She enjoyed the feel of grass beneath her feet. | **a blade of grass** (=single leaf) **b)** [C] a particular kind of grass: All grasses need light to grow well.
 2 the grass an area of grass, especially an area where the grass is kept cut short: I walked across the grass. | Keep off the grass.
 3 DRUG [U] informal MARIJUANA
 4 CRIMINAL [C] BrE informal someone, usually a criminal, who gives information about other criminals to the police – used to show disapproval; ▪ **informer**;

▪ **stoolpigeon** AmE → SUPERGRASS
 5 the grass is greener (on the other side) used to say that other places or situations seem better than yours, although they may not really be better
 6 not let the grass grow under your feet to not waste time or delay starting something
 7 put sb out to grass informal to make someone leave their job because they are too old to do it effectively → GRASS ROOTS; → **snake in the grass** at SNAKE¹ (2)

grass² v [I] also **grass sb up** BrE informal to tell the police about a criminal's activities: [+on] Burton grassed on other prisoners.

grass sth ⇔ **over** phr v to cover land with grass

grass ,court n [C] a tennis court which has a grass surface for the players to play on; → **hard court**

grass·hop·per /ˈɡrɑːsˌhɒpə $ ˈɡræs,hɑːpər/ n [C] an insect that has long back legs for jumping and that makes short loud noises → **knee-high to a grasshopper** at KNEE-HIGH (2); → see picture at INSECT

grass·land /ˈɡrɑːslænd $ ˈɡræs-/ n [U] also **grasslands** [plural] a large area of land covered with wild grass; ▪ **prairie**

grass ,roots n **the grass roots** the ordinary people in an organization, rather than the leaders —**grass roots** adj: We are hoping for full participation at grass roots level.

grass snake n [C] a common snake that is not poisonous

gras·sy /ˈɡrɑːsi $ ˈɡræsi/ adj covered with grass: a grassy bank

grate¹ /ɡreɪt/ n [C] the metal bars and frame that hold the wood, coal etc in a FIREPLACE → see picture at FIREPLACE

grate² v **1** [T] to rub cheese, vegetables etc against a rough or sharp surface in order to break them into small pieces: grated cheese | Peel and grate the potatoes. **2** [T] written to talk in a low rough voice; → **hiss**: 'Let me go,' he grated harshly. **3** [I] to annoy someone: [+on] Mr Fen had a loud voice that grated on her ears. **4** [I,T] to make an unpleasant sound by rubbing, or to make something do this: The stones beneath her shoes grated harshly.

grate·ful [W3] /ˈɡreɪtfəl/ adj
 1 feeling that you want to thank someone because of something kind that they have done, or showing this feeling; ▪ **ungrateful**: [+for] I'm so grateful for all your help. | [+to] I am very grateful to all those who took the trouble to write to me. | **grateful (that)** She should be grateful that he was making things easier for her. | **extremely/deeply/eternally etc grateful** I am extremely grateful for the assistance your staff have provided. | Our **grateful thanks** go to all who participated. | She gave me a grateful look.
 2 I would be grateful if you could/would ... formal used to make a request: I would be most grateful if you could send me an invoice in due course. —**gratefully** adv: All contributions will **be gratefully received**. | The authors gratefully acknowledge your financial support.

grat·er /ˈɡreɪtə $ -ər/ n [C] a tool used for grating food: a cheese grater → see picture at EAT

grat·i·fy /ˈɡrætɪfaɪ/ v **gratified, gratifying, gratifies** [T] formal **1** [usually passive] to make someone feel pleased and satisfied: He was gratified by Lucy's response. | **be gratified to see/hear/learn etc** John was gratified to see the improvement in his mother's health since she had come home. **2** to satisfy a desire, need etc: She did not propose to gratify Gloria's curiosity any further. —**gratification** /ˌɡrætɪfɪˈkeɪʃən/ n [C,U]: sexual gratification

grat·i·fy·ing /ˈɡrætɪfaɪ-ɪŋ/ adj pleasing and satisfying: **it's gratifying to do sth** | It's gratifying to note that already much has been achieved. | The support was considerable and very gratifying. —**gratifyingly** adv

grat·in /ˈɡrætæn $ ˈɡrɑːtn/ n [C,U] a dish containing vegetables or fish, covered in cheese or cheese sauce and cooked in an OVEN

grat·ing¹ /ˈɡreɪtɪŋ/ n [C] a metal frame with bars across it, used to cover a window or hole: *Leaves clogged the grating over the drain.*

grating² adj a grating sound is hard and unpleasant: *a harsh grating voice* —**gratingly** adv

grat·is /ˈɡrætɪ̱s, ˈɡreɪ-/ adj, adv done or given without payment; ▤ **free**: *Medical advice was provided gratis.*

grat·i·tude /ˈɡrætɪ̱tjuːd $ -tuːd/ n [U] the feeling of being grateful; ▣ **ingratitude**: *Tears of gratitude filled her eyes.* | [+to/towards] *She had a deep gratitude towards David, but she did not love him.* | [+for] *The committee expressed its gratitude for the contribution he had made.* | **in gratitude for sth** *Will you let me take you out to dinner tomorrow in gratitude for what you've done?* | **with gratitude** *She accepted his offer with gratitude.* → **debt of gratitude** at DEBT (4)

gra·tu·i·tous /ɡrəˈtjuːɪ̱təs $ -tuː-/ adj said or done without a good reason, in a way that offends someone; ▣ **unnecessary**: *children's books which include gratuitous violence* —**gratuitously** adv: *There is no point in gratuitously antagonizing people.*

gra·tu·i·ty /ɡrəˈtjuːɪ̱ti $ -tuː-/ n plural **gratuities** [C] formal **1** a small gift of money given to someone for a service they provided; ▣ **tip 2** especially BrE a large gift of money given to someone when they leave their job, especially in the army, navy etc

grave¹ /ɡreɪv/ n [C] **1** the place in the ground where a dead body is buried; → **tomb**: *At the head of the grave there was a small wooden cross.* **2 the grave** literary death: *He took that secret to the grave.* **3 sb would turn in their grave** used to say that someone who is dead would strongly disapprove of something happening now: *The way Bill plays that piece would have Mozart turning in his grave.* → **dig your own grave** at DIG¹ (8); → **from (the) cradle to (the) grave** at CRADLE¹ (3); → **have one foot in the grave** at FOOT¹ (24); → **silent as the grave** at SILENT (3); → **a watery grave** at WATERY (4)

grave² adj **1** grave problems, situations, or worries are very great or bad; → **serious**: *Matthew's life is in grave danger.* | *The report expressed grave concern over the technicians' lack of training.* | *I have grave doubts about his ability.* | *The situation is becoming very grave.* **2** looking or sounding quiet and serious, especially because something important or worrying has happened; ▣ **sombre**: *Turnbull's face was grave as he told them about the accident.* —**gravely** adv: *Adam nodded gravely.* | *We are gravely concerned (=very concerned) about these developments.* → GRAVITY

grave³ /ɡrɑːv/ adj a grave ACCENT is a mark put above a letter in some languages such as French to show the pronunciation, for example è; → **acute**, **circumflex**

grave·dig·ger /ˈɡreɪvˌdɪɡə $ -ər/ n [C] someone whose job is to dig graves

grav·el /ˈɡrævəl/ n [U] small stones, used to make a surface for paths, roads etc: *a gravel path* | **gravel pit** (=a place where gravel is dug out of the ground)

grav·elled /ˈɡrævəld/ adj a gravelled path or road has a surface made of gravel

grav·el·ly /ˈɡrævəli/ adj **1** a gravelly voice has a low rough sound **2** covered with or mixed with gravel: *gravelly soil*

grave·side /ˈɡreɪvsaɪd/ n **at the graveside** beside a GRAVE, especially when someone is being buried there —**graveside** adj [only before noun]

grave·stone /ˈɡreɪvstəʊn $ -stoʊn/ n [C] a stone above a GRAVE showing details of the person buried there; ▣ **tombstone**

grave·yard /ˈɡreɪvjɑːd $ -jɑːrd/ n [C] **1** an area of ground where people are buried, often next to a church; → **cemetery**, **churchyard 2** a place where things that are no longer wanted are left: *a graveyard for old cars* **3** a place where people or things fail

'graveyard ˌshift n [C] especially AmE a regular period of working time that begins late at night and continues until the early morning, or the people who work during this time

grav·i·tas /ˈɡrævɪtæs/ n [U] formal a seriousness of manner that people respect

grav·i·tate /ˈɡrævɪ̱teɪt/ v [I always + adv/prep] formal to be attracted to something and therefore move towards it or become involved with it: [+to/towards] *Most visitors to London gravitate to Piccadilly Circus and Leicester Square.*

grav·i·ta·tion /ˌɡrævɪ̱ˈteɪʃən/ n [U] technical the force that causes two objects such as PLANETS to move towards each other because of their MASS; → **gravity**: *Newton's law of gravitation*

grav·i·ta·tion·al /ˌɡrævɪ̱ˈteɪʃənəl◂/ adj [usually before noun] technical related to or resulting from the force of gravity: *the Moon's gravitational field* | *the gravitational pull of the moon*

grav·i·ty /ˈɡrævɪ̱ti/ n [U] **1** technical the force that causes something to fall to the ground or to be attracted to another PLANET; → **gravitation**: *the force of gravity* **2** formal the extreme and worrying seriousness of a situation: [+of] *I could not hide from her the gravity of the situation.* | *The penalties should be proportionate to the gravity of the offence.* **3** an extremely serious way of behaving or speaking: *The Consul spoke slowly and with great gravity.* → CENTRE OF GRAVITY

gra·vy /ˈɡreɪvi/ n [U] **1** a sauce made from the juice that comes from meat as it cooks, mixed with flour and water **2** informal AmE something good that is more than you expected to get

'gravy ˌboat n [C] a long JUG that you pour gravy from

'gravy ˌtrain n **the gravy train** informal an organization, activity, or business from which many people can make money or profit without much effort: *Privatization is not always the gravy train that governments promise.*

gray /ɡreɪ/ adj, n, v the usual American spelling of GREY

graze¹ /ɡreɪz/ v **1** [I,T] if an animal grazes, or if you graze it, it eats grass that is growing: [+on] *Groups of cattle were grazing on the rich grass.* | *fields where they used to graze their sheep* **2** [T] to accidentally break the surface of your skin by rubbing it against something: *I fell on the gravel, severely grazing my knee.* **3** [T] to touch something lightly while passing it, sometimes damaging it: *A bullet grazed his arm.* **4** [I] informal to eat small amounts of food all through the day instead of having regular meals

graze² n [C] a wound caused by rubbing that slightly breaks the surface of your skin: *Adam walked away from the crash with just a graze on his left shoulder.* | *minor cuts and grazes*

GRE /ˌdʒiː ɑːr ˈiː/ n [C] trademark **Graduate Record Examination** an examination that is done by students in the US who have completed a first DEGREE and want to go to GRADUATE SCHOOL

grease¹ /ɡriːs/ n [U] **1** a fatty or oily substance that comes off meat when it is cooked, or off food made using butter or oil **2** a thick oily substance that is put on the moving parts of a car, machine etc to make it run or move smoothly **3** an oily substance that is produced by your skin → **elbow grease** at ELBOW¹ (3)

grease² v [T] **1** to put butter, grease etc on a pan etc to prevent food from sticking to it: *Grease the pan before you pour the batter in.* | *a greased baking tray* **2 grease sb's palm** to give someone money in a secret or dishonest way in order to persuade them to do something: *Joseph was able to grease a few palms, thus helping his brother to escape.* **3 like greased lightning** informal extremely fast

grease·paint /ˈɡriːs-peɪnt/ n [U] a thick soft kind of paint that actors use on their face or body

grease·proof pa·per /ˌgriːs-pruːf ˈpeɪpə $ -ər/ *n*
[U] *BrE* a kind of paper that butter, GREASE, etc cannot
pass through, used in cooking and for wrapping food;
◨ **waxed paper** *AmE*

greas·er /ˈgriːsə, -zə $ -ər/ *n* [C] *old-fashioned* a young
man who is very interested in MOTORCYCLES and cars, and
who behaves in a rough way

greas·y /ˈgriːsi, -zi/ *adj* **1** covered in grease or oil;
◨ **oily**: *a shampoo for greasy hair* | *The food was heavy
and greasy.* → see picture at SURFACE **2** slippery: *Police
say the rain's making the roads greasy.* **3** too polite
and friendly in a way that seems insincere or unpleasant; ◨ **smarmy** —**greasily** *adv* —**greasiness** *n* [U]

ˌgreasy ˈspoon *n* [C] a small cheap restaurant that
mainly serves FRIED food

great¹ S1 W1 /greɪt/ *adj comparative* **greater**, *superlative* **greatest**
1 LARGE [usually before noun] very large in amount or
degree: *The movie was a great success.* | *The news came
as possibly the greatest shock of my life.* | *The paintings
cost **a great deal** (=a lot) of money.* | *John always takes
great care over his work.* | *It gives me great pleasure*
(=I am very pleased) *to introduce tonight's speaker.* |
*It's **a great pity that** none of his poems survive.* | *The
temptation was too great to resist.* △ **Big, large,** or
great?; → see box at BIG¹
2 EXCELLENT *especially spoken* very good; ◨ **won-
derful, fantastic**: *The weather here is great.* | *It's great
to be home.* | *a great day out for all the family* |
sound/taste/smell/feel etc great *I worked out this
morning and I feel great.* | *You look great in that dress.* |
great for doing sth *Email's great for keeping in touch.* |
the great thing about sb/sth (=the very good thing
about someone or something) *The great thing about
Alex is that he's always willing to explain things to you.*
3 IMPORTANT **a)** [usually before noun] important or
having a lot of influence: *one of the greatest scientific
achievements of our time* | *What makes a novel **truly
great**?* | *great historical events* **b)** used in the title of a
person or event that was very important in the past:
Peter/Catherine etc the Great *I'm reading a biography
of Alexander the Great.* | *the Great Depression* | **the
Great War** *old-fashioned* (=World War One)
4 GENEROUS very good or generous in a way that
people admire: *a great humanitarian gesture*
5 EXTREMELY SKILFUL famous for being able to do
something extremely well: *Ali was undoubtedly one of
the greatest boxers of all time.* | *a book about the lives of
the great composers*
6 BIG *written* very big; ◨ **huge**: *A great crowd had
gathered.* | *A great iron stove filled half the room.*
7 DOING STH A LOT used to emphasize that someone
does something a lot: **a great talker/reader/admirer etc**
*Anthony's a great talker – sometimes you just can't get a
word in.* | *Len was **a great believer in** the power of
positive thinking.* | **be a great one for doing sth** *She's a
great one for telling stories about her schooldays.*
8 **great big** *spoken* very big: *Get your great big feet off
my table!*
9 **to a greater or lesser extent** used to emphasize that
something is always true, even though it is more true
or noticeable in some situations than others: *Most
companies operate in conditions that are to a greater or
lesser extent competitive.*
10 **be no great shakes** *informal* to not be very good,
interesting, or skilful: *The work's no great shakes, but
at least I'm earning.*
11 **be going great guns** *informal* to be doing something
extremely well: *After a slow start, the Tigers are going
great guns.*
12 BAD *spoken informal* used when you are disappointed or annoyed about something: *'Daniel's cancelled the party.' 'Oh great!'*
13 ANIMAL/BIRD/PLANT ETC used in the names of
some animals or plants, especially when they are
bigger than other animals or plants of the same type:
the Great Crested Grebe
14 **the great outdoors** *informal* the countryside, consid-

ered as enjoyable and healthy: *He had a taste for
adventure and the great outdoors.*
15 **great minds (think alike)** *spoken* used humorously
when you and another person have had the same idea
16 **the greater good** a general advantage that you can
only gain by losing or harming something that is
considered less important: *Some wars are fought for the
greater good.*
17 **the great and the good** people who are considered
important – used humorously
18 **the great apes** the different types of animals that
are similar to large monkeys, considered as a group:
*Alone of the great apes, the gorilla is not very efficient at
using tools.*
19 **the great divide** a situation in which there is a big
difference between groups in society, areas of a country etc, for example a big difference between their
wealth or attitudes: *The great divide between north and
south seems to be as unbridgeable as ever.*
20 **Greater London/Los Angeles/Manchester etc** London, Los Angeles etc and its outer areas
21 **huge/enormous great** *BrE spoken* used to emphasize how big something is
22 **Great Scott!/Great Heavens!** *spoken old-fashioned*
used to express shock or surprise
23 **great with child** *literary* very soon to have a baby
—**greatness** *n* [U]: *a symbol of national greatness* |
She was destined for greatness.

great² *n* [C usually plural] a very successful and famous
person in a particular sport, profession etc: *Jack Nick-
laus is one of golf's **all-time greats**.* | *I think his show's
OK, but I wouldn't call him one of the greats.*

great- /greɪt/ *prefix* **1** **great-grandfather/great-
grandmother/great-aunt/great-uncle** the GRANDFATHER,
GRANDMOTHER etc of your parents **2** **great-grandchild/
great-granddaughter etc** the GRANDCHILDREN of your
child

great·coat /ˈgreɪtkəʊt $ -koʊt/ *n* [C] a long heavy coat

ˌGreat ˈDane *n* [C] a very large short-haired dog

great·ly W3 /ˈgreɪtli/ *adv formal* extremely or very
much: **greatly increased/reduced** *The cost of repairs
has greatly increased in recent years.* | *All offers of help
will be **greatly appreciated**.* | *The quality of health care
varies greatly.*

grebe /griːb/ *n* [C] a water bird similar to a duck

Gre·cian /ˈgriːʃən/ *adj literary* from ancient Greece, or
having a style or appearance that is considered typical
of ancient Greece: *a Grecian urn*

Greco-, Graeco- /ˈgriːkəʊ, ˈgrekəʊ $ -koʊ/ *prefix* [in
nouns and adjectives] ancient Greek and something
else: *Greco-Roman art*

greed /griːd/ *n* [U] a strong desire for more food,
money, power, possessions etc than you need: *people
motivated by jealousy and greed*

greed·y /ˈgriːdi/ *comparative* **greedier**, *superlative*
greediest *adj* always wanting more food, money, power,
possessions etc than you need: *a greedy and selfish
society* | *He looked at the gold with greedy eyes.* | *Have
you eaten them all, you greedy pig?* | [+for] *They are
greedy for profits.* —**greedily** *adv*: *He grabbed the bottle
and drank greedily.* —**greediness** *n* [U]

Greek¹ /griːk/ *adj* relating to Greece, its people, or its
language: *Greek yoghurt*

Greek² *n* **1** [C] someone from Greece **2** [U] the
language used in modern or ancient Greece **3** [C]
AmE a member of a SORORITY or FRATERNITY at an American college or university **4** **it's all Greek to me** *informal*
used to say that you cannot understand something

green¹ S1 W2 /griːn/ *adj*
1 COLOUR having the colour of grass or leaves: *beau-
tiful green eyes* | *Raw coffee beans are green in colour.* |
dark/light/pale/bright green *a dark green dress* → BOTTLE
GREEN, LIME GREEN; → **olive green** at OLIVE (3); → PEA GREEN

G

2 GRASSY covered with grass, trees, bushes etc: *green fields*

3 FRUIT/PLANT not yet ready to be eaten, or very young: *The bananas are still green.* | *tiny green shoots of new grass*

4 ENVIRONMENT a) also **Green** [only before noun] connected with the environment or its protection: *green issues such as the greenhouse effect and global warming* | *He was an early champion of green politics.* b) harming the environment as little as possible: *We need to develop greener cleaning products.*

5 WITHOUT EXPERIENCE *informal* young and lacking experience; ⊟ **naive**: *I was pretty green then; I had a lot of things to learn.*

6 ILL *informal* looking pale and unhealthy because you are ill: *George looked a bit green the next morning.* | **look green about/around the gills** (=look pale and ill)

7 green with envy wishing very much that you had something that someone else has

8 the green-eyed monster *literary* JEALOUSY - often used humorously

9 have green fingers *BrE*; **have a green thumb** *AmE* to be good at making plants grow

10 the green stuff *AmE informal* money —**greenness** n [U]

green² [S2] [W3] n

1 [C,U] the colour of grass and leaves: *a room decorated in pale blues and greens* | *different shades of green*

2 greens [plural] *informal* vegetables with large green leaves: *Eat your greens.*

3 [C] a level area of grass, especially in the middle of a village: *I walked home across the green.* → VILLAGE GREEN

4 [C] a smooth flat area of grass around each hole on a GOLF COURSE: *the 18th green* → see picture at GOLF

5 Green [C] someone who belongs to or supports a political party which thinks the protection of the environment is very important: *The Greens have 254 candidates in the election.*

green³ v [T] **1** to fill an area with growing plants in order to make it more attractive: *Existing derelict land is needed for greening the cities.* **2** to make a person or organization realize the importance of environmental problems

green·back /'gri:nbæk/ n [C] *AmE informal* an American BANKNOTE

green 'bean n [C] a long thin green vegetable which is picked before the beans inside it grow; ⊟ **French bean** *BrE*; → see picture at VEGETABLE

green 'belt n [C,U] an area of land around a city where building is not allowed, in order to protect fields and woods

green 'card n [C] **1** a document that a foreigner must have in order to work legally in the US **2** a British motor insurance document that you need when you drive abroad

green·e·ry /'gri:nəri/ n [U] green leaves and plants: *the rich greenery of grass and trees*

green·field site /'gri:nfi:ld ˌsaɪt/ n [C] a piece of land that has never been built on before; → **brownfield site**

green·fly /'gri:nflaɪ/ n plural **greenflies** or **greenfly** [C] a very small green insect that feeds on and damages young plants; ⊟ **aphid**

green·gage /'gri:ngeɪdʒ/ n [C] a juicy greenish-yellow PLUM

green·gro·cer /'gri:nˌgrəʊsə $ -ˌgroʊsər/ n [C] *especially BrE* **1** someone who owns or works in a shop selling fruit and vegetables **2 greengrocer's** a greengrocer's shop

green·horn /'gri:nhɔ:n $ -hɔ:rn/ n [C] *informal especially AmE* someone who lacks experience of something

green·house /'gri:nhaʊs/ n [C] a glass building used for growing plants that need warmth, light, and protection

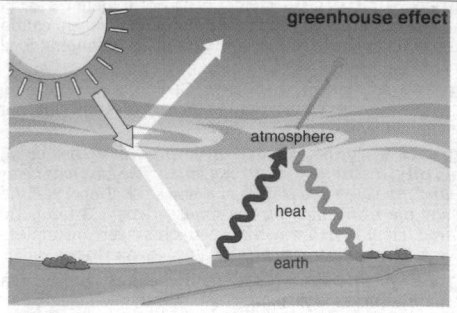
greenhouse effect

'greenhouse ef,fect n [singular] the gradual warming of the air surrounding the Earth as a result of heat being trapped by POLLUTION; → **global warming**

'greenhouse ,gas n [C] a gas, especially CARBON DIOXIDE or METHANE, that is thought to trap heat above the Earth and cause the greenhouse effect

green·ing /'gri:nɪŋ/ n **the greening of sb/sth** when a person or organization starts to think and know more about environmental problems

green·ish /'gri:nɪʃ/ adj slightly green

green 'light n [C] **1** a TRAFFIC LIGHT that shows cars they can go forward **2 give sb/sth the green light** to allow a project, plan etc to begin: *The government has given the green light to Sunday trading.*

green 'onion n [C] *AmE* an onion with a small white round part and a long green stem, usually eaten raw; ⊟ **spring onion** *BrE*

green 'paper n [C] a document produced by the British government containing proposals to be discussed, which may later be used in making laws; → **white paper, bill**

green 'pepper n [C] a hollow green vegetable that you can cook or eat raw in SALADS

green revo'lution n [singular] **1** a large increase in the amount of crops, such as wheat or rice, that are produced because of improved scientific methods of farming **2** the interest in protecting the environment that has developed in many parts of the world

'green room n **the green room** the room in a theatre, television STUDIO etc in which performers wait when they are not on stage performing

green 'salad n [C] a SALAD made with LETTUCE and other raw green vegetables

green 'tea n [U] light-coloured tea made from leaves that have been heated with steam, especially popular in eastern Asia

Green·wich Mean Time /ˌgrenɪtʃ 'mi:n taɪm, ˌgrɪ-, -nɪdʒ-/ abbreviation **GMT** n [U] the time as measured at Greenwich in London

greet /gri:t/ v [T] **1** to say hello to someone or welcome them: *Belinda greeted her warmly.* | **greet sb with sth** *Bill opened the door to Harold and greeted him with cries of welcome.* **2** [usually passive] to react to something in a particular way: **be greeted with/by sth** *His statement was greeted with cries of astonishment and indignation.* **3** to be the first thing you see or hear when you arrive somewhere: *Complete silence greeted us as we entered the room.*

greet·er /'gri:tə $ -ər/ n [C] someone who greets people politely as they enter a place, especially someone who does this as a job

greet·ing /'gri:tɪŋ/ n [C,U] **1** something you say or do when you meet someone: **in greeting** *She raised her hand in greeting.* | *I smiled a polite greeting, but the woman hardly acknowledged me.* | *The two cousins* **exchanged greetings** (=greeted each other). **2** *birthday/Christmas etc greetings* a message saying that you hope someone will be happy and healthy on their BIRTHDAY, at Christmas etc **3 greetings!** *old use* used to say hello to someone

greetings ,**card** BrE; '**greeting card** AmE n [C] a card that you send to someone on their BIRTHDAY, at Christmas etc

gre·gar·i·ous /grɪ'geəriəs $ -'ger-/ adj **1** friendly and preferring to be with other people; ▤ **sociable**; ▨ **solitary 2** technical gregarious animals tend to live in a group; ▨ **solitary** —**gregariously** adv —**gregariousness** n [U]

Gre·go·ri·an cal·en·dar /grɪ,gɔːriən 'kælɪ̯ndə $ -dər/ n [singular] the system of arranging the 365 days of the year in months and giving numbers to the years from the birth of Christ, used in the West since 1582

Gregorian chant /grɪ,gɔːriən 'tʃɑːnt $ -'tʃænt/ n [C,U] a kind of church music for voices alone

grem·lin /'gremlɪ̯n/ n [C] an imaginary evil spirit that is blamed for problems in machinery

gre·nade /grɪ̯'neɪd/ n [C] a small bomb that can be thrown by hand or fired from a gun: a hand grenade

gren·a·dier /,grenə'dɪə◂ $ -'dɪr◂/ n [C] a soldier in a famous REGIMENT of the British army

gren·a·dine /'grenədiːn, ,grenə'diːn/ n [U] a sweet liquid made from POMEGRANATES that is used in drinks

grew /gruː/ the past tense of GROW

grey[1] BrE S2 W2 **gray** AmE /greɪ/ adj
1 COLOUR having the colour of dark clouds, neither black nor white: an old lady with grey hair | a grey sky | **dark/light grey** dark grey trousers → BATTLESHIP GREY, IRON-GREY; → **slate grey** at SLATE[1] (3)
2 HAIR having grey hair: **go/turn grey** She was a tall thin woman who had gone grey early.
3 FACE looking pale because you are tired, frightened, or ill: [+with] As he listened, his face went grey with shock.
4 BORING boring and unattractive; ▨ **colourful**: the grey anonymous men in government offices | visions of a grey and empty world
5 WEATHER if the weather is grey, the sky is full of clouds and the sun is not bright; ▨ **bright**: a grey day
6 OF OLD PEOPLE [only before noun] BrE connected with old people: the grey vote
7 grey area used to talk about a situation in which something is not clearly a particular thing, so that people are not sure how to deal with it: people in the grey area between loyalty and opposition to the government —**greyness** n [U]

grey[2] BrE; **gray** AmE n [C,U] the colour of dark clouds, neither black nor white: Do you have these skirts in grey? | dull greys and browns

grey[3] BrE; **gray** AmE v [I] if someone greys, their hair becomes grey: Jim was greying a little at the temples. | a full head of greying hair

grey·hound /'greɪhaʊnd/ n [C] a type of thin dog that can run very fast and is used in races

grey·ing BrE; **graying** AmE /'greɪ-ɪŋ/ n **the greying of sth** the situation in which the average age of a population increases, so that there are more old people than there were in the past: the graying of classical music audiences

grey·ish BrE; **grayish** AmE /'greɪ-ɪʃ/ adj slightly grey: The stone was a greyish colour.

'**grey ,market** BrE; **gray market** AmE n [C] **1** the system by which people buy and sell goods that are hard to find, in a way that is legal but not morally good or correct; → **black market 2** technical a situation in which people are buying and selling SHARES just before they are officially made available to be sold for the first time

'**grey ,matter** BrE; **gray matter** AmE n [U] informal your intelligence, or your brain

,**grey 'pound** n BrE **the grey pound** the money that older people have available to spend, especially after their children have grown up and left home: the power of the grey pound

grid /grɪd/ n [C] **1** a metal frame with bars across it → CATTLE GRID **2** a pattern of straight lines that cross each other and form squares: Its streets were laid out in a

grid pattern. **3** a set of numbered lines printed on a map so that the exact position of any place can be referred to: The pilots were just given a **grid reference** (=number referring to a point on a map) of the target. **4** the network of electricity supply wires that connects POWER STATIONS and provides electricity to buildings in an area: the **national grid** (=the electricity supply in a country) **5** also **starting grid** a set of starting positions for all the cars in a motor race

'**grid com,puting** n [U] a system of running a computer program using a lot of small computers that are connected together in order to do very complicated jobs

grid·dle /'grɪdl/ n [C] a round iron plate that is used for cooking flat cakes on top of a STOVE or over a fire

grid·dle·cake /'grɪdl,keɪk/ n [C] AmE a PANCAKE

grid·i·ron /'grɪdaɪən $ -ərn/ n [C] **1** an open frame of metal bars for cooking meat or fish over a very hot fire **2** AmE a field marked in white lines for American football

grid·lock /'grɪdlɒk $ -lɑːk/ n [U] especially AmE **1** a situation in which streets in a city are so full of cars that they cannot move **2** a situation in which nothing can happen, usually because people disagree strongly: The battle over spending led to gridlock. —**gridlocked** adj

grief /griːf/ n **1** [U] extreme sadness, especially because someone you love has died: [+over/at] The grief she felt over Helen's death was almost unbearable. | **with grief** Charles was overcome with grief. **2** [C] something that makes you feel extremely sad: Every change in our lives brings with it griefs. **3 good grief!** spoken used when you are slightly surprised or annoyed: Good grief! What a mess! **4 come to grief** to fail, or to be harmed or destroyed in an accident: candidates who come to grief in exams **5 give sb grief** informal to criticize someone in an annoying way **6** [U] informal trouble or problems: You'll save yourself a lot of grief if you check the measurements first.

'**grief-,stricken** adj feeling very sad because of something that has happened: The grief-stricken widow refused to leave her dead husband's side.

griev·ance /'griːvəns/ n [C,U] a belief that you have been treated unfairly, or an unfair situation or event that affects and upsets you

> **have a grievance (against sb)**
> **legitimate/genuine grievance** (=when you really have been treated unfairly)
> **air your grievances** (=tell people you think you have been treated unfairly)
> **nurse a grievance** (=think continuously about the fact that you have been treated unfairly)
> **file a grievance** AmE (=officially complain)
> **settle a grievance** (=solve one)
> **grievance procedure** (=a system for dealing with employees' grievances)
> **sense of grievance**

anyone who **has a** legitimate **grievance against** the company | a means of overcoming **genuine grievances** | There must be an opportunity for both sides to **air** their **grievances**. | The teachers' contract established a **grievance procedure**. | the **sense of grievance** which characterized him as a young man

grieve /griːv/ v **1** [I,T] to feel extremely sad, especially because someone you love has died: [+over/for] He died, and every day since then I have grieved for him. | People need time to grieve after the death of a loved one. | She grieved the loss of her only son. **2** [T] if something grieves you, it makes you feel very unhappy; ▨ **upset**: My aunt, **it grieves** me to say, gets things confused.

grieved /griːvd/ adj literary very sad and upset: [+at] King George V had been very grieved at the outbreak of the Great War.

G

grog /grɒg $ grɑːg/ n [U] **1** a strong alcoholic drink, especially RUM mixed with water **2** *informal* any alcoholic drink

grog·gy /'grɒgi $ 'grɑːgi/ *adj* weak and unable to move well or think clearly because you are ill or very tired: *I felt really groggy after 15 hours on the plane.*

groin /grɔɪn/ n [C] **1** the place where the tops of your legs meet the front of your body **2** a GROYNE

grom·met /'grɒmɪt $ 'grɑː-/ n [C] **1** a small metal ring that is used around a hole in cloth or leather to make it stronger **2** *BrE* a small piece of plastic that a doctor puts into a child's ear in order to remove liquid from it

groom[1] /gruːm, grʊm/ v **1** [T] to clean and brush an animal, especially a horse **2** [T] to prepare someone for an important job or position in society by training them over a long period: **groom sb for sth** *Tim was being groomed for a managerial position.* | **groom sb to do sth** *Clare's been groomed to take her father's place when he retires.* **3** [T] to take care of your own appearance by keeping your hair and clothes clean and tidy: *Her hair is always perfectly groomed.* → **WELL-GROOMED** **4** [I,T] if an animal grooms itself or another animal, it cleans its own fur and skin or that of the other animal —**grooming** n [U]: *Long-haired dogs need a lot of grooming.*

groom[2] n [C] **1** a BRIDEGROOM **2** someone whose job is to feed, clean, and take care of horses

grooms·man /'gruːmzmən, 'grʊms-/ n *plural* **groomsmen** /-mən/ [C] *AmE* a friend of a BRIDEGROOM who has special duties at a wedding; ▤ **best man** *BrE*

groove /gruːv/ n [C] **1** a thin line cut into a hard surface: *The bolt slid easily into the groove.* | *a shallow groove cut into the cliff* **2** **be stuck in a groove** to do something in the same way for a long time so that it becomes boring: *Our product range was stuck in a groove.* **3** *informal* the beat of a piece of popular music: *a hypnotic dub groove*

grooved /gruːvd/ *adj* having a groove or several grooves: *a slightly grooved surface*

groov·y /'gruːvi/ *adj* old-fashioned *informal* a word meaning fashionable, modern, and fun, used especially in the 1960s

grope[1] /grəʊp $ groʊp/ v **1** [I] to try to find something that you cannot see by feeling with your hands: [+for] *Ginny groped for her glasses on the bedside table.* | [+around] *We groped around in the darkness.* **2** [I,T] to go somewhere by feeling the way with your hands because you cannot see: **grope your way along/across etc** *I was groping my way blindly through the trees.* | *Ally groped steadily towards the door.* **3** **grope for sth** to try hard to find the right words to say or the right solution to a problem but without any real idea of how to do this: *She hesitated, seeming to grope for words.* **4** [T] *informal* to move your hands over someone's body to get sexual pleasure, especially when they do not want you to do this

grope[2] n [C usually singular] *informal* touching someone's body to get sexual pleasure, especially when they do not want you to do this

gross[1] [S3] /grəʊs $ groʊs/ *adj*
1 [TOTAL] [only before noun] **a)** a gross sum of money is the total amount before any tax or costs have been taken away; → **net**: *a gross profit of $5 million* | **gross income/salary/pay etc** *a family with gross earnings of just £75 per week* **b)** a gross weight is the total weight of something, including its wrapping
2 [VERY BAD] [only before noun] clearly wrong and unacceptable: **gross negligence/misconduct etc** *soldiers accused of gross violations of human rights* | *The company described reports of environmental disaster as gross exaggeration.* | **gross indecency** (=the crime of doing something that is sexually offensive)
3 [NASTY] *spoken* very unpleasant to look at or think about; ▤ **disgusting**: *Ooh, gross! I hate spinach!*

4 [FAT] *informal* extremely fat and unattractive —**grossly** *adv* [+ adj/adv]: *Lambert was grossly overweight.* | *Medical records were found to be grossly inadequate.* —**grossness** n [U]

gross[2] *adv* **earn £20,000/$30,000 etc gross** to earn £20,000 etc before tax has been taken away; → **net**: *a junior executive earning $50,000 gross*

gross[3] v [T] to gain an amount as a total profit, or earn it as a total amount, before tax has been taken away; → **net**: *The movie has already grossed over $10 million.*

gross sb ⇔ **out** *phr v AmE spoken* to make someone wish they had not seen or been told about something because it is so unpleasant; ▤ **disgust**: *His dirty fingernails really gross me out.*

gross[4] n *plural* **gross** [C] a quantity of 144 things: [+of] *two gross of candles*

gross do·mestic 'product n [singular] GDP

gross 'margin n [C] *technical* the difference between what something costs to produce and what it is sold for

gross ,national 'product n [singular] GNP

gross 'profit n [C] GROSS MARGIN

gro·tesque[1] /grəʊ'tesk $ groʊ-/ *adj* **1** unpleasant, shocking, and offensive: *It's grotesque to portray peace campaigners as unpatriotic.* | *By modern standards, the treatment of prisoners was grotesque.* **2** extremely ugly in a strange or unnatural way: *a grotesque figure with a huge head* —**grotesquely** *adv*

grotesque[2] n **1** [C] a picture, SCULPTURE etc of someone who is strangely ugly **2** **the grotesque** a grotesque style in art

grot·to /'grɒtəʊ $ 'grɑːtoʊ/ n *plural* **grottos** or **grottoes** [C] a small attractive CAVE

grot·ty /'grɒti $ 'grɑːti/ *adj BrE informal* **1** nasty, dirty, or unpleasant; ▤ **manky**: *a grotty little bar* **2** ill: *The next day I felt a bit grotty.*

grouch[1] /graʊtʃ/ n *informal* **1** [C] someone who is always complaining: *an old grouch* **2** [C] something unimportant that you complain about

grouch[2] v [I] *informal* to complain in a slightly angry way; ▤ **moan**: [+about] *He's always grouching about something!*

grouch·y /'graʊtʃi/ *adj informal* in a bad temper, especially because you are tired; ▤ **bad-tempered** —**grouchiness** n [U]

ground[1] [S1] [W1] /graʊnd/ n

ground
sweeping the floor
digging the ground

1 [EARTH] [U] **a)** the surface of the earth: **the ground** *The leaves were slowly fluttering to the ground.* | *He lay on the ground and stared up at the sky.* | *The ground was frozen solid.* | **above/below/under ground** *At night, badgers feed above ground.* | *These youngsters work 70 metres below ground level.* | *A raised platform stood 2 metres off the ground.* | *The air raids were followed by military action* **on the ground** (=on land). | **ground troops** (=soldiers who fight on land) **b)** the soil on and under the surface of the earth: *Dig the ground over in the autumn.* | *Plant the seeds 2 cm deep in the ground.* | *The ground was dry, far too dry for growing corn.*
2 [AREA OF LAND] **a)** [U] an area of land without buildings, fences, woods etc: *The landscape is a mixture of* **open ground** *and woodland.* | *They were standing on the* **waste ground** (=land in a town that is not being used) *behind the car park.* **b)** [C] *BrE* also **grounds** [plural] *especially AmE* an area of land or sea that is used for a particular purpose: *fishing grounds* | **parade/hunting/burial etc ground** *These fields served as a hunting ground for the local people.* | *The rivers are*

used as **dumping grounds** for industrial waste. | He is buried in sacred ground. → PLAYGROUND (1) **c)** grounds [plural] the land or gardens surrounding a large building: We decided to take a stroll in the hotel grounds.
3 REASON grounds [plural] a good reason for doing, believing, or saying something: **grounds for (doing) sth** Mental cruelty can be **grounds for divorce**. | There are **strong grounds** for believing his statement. | **have grounds to do sth** Did the police have **reasonable grounds** to arrest him? | **on moral/legal/medical etc grounds** The proposal was rejected on environmental grounds. | **on (the) grounds of sth** Flying was ruled out on grounds of cost. | 'You're under arrest.' 'On what grounds?' | **on the grounds that** We oppose the bill, on the grounds that it discriminates against women.
4 SUBJECT [U] a subject or area of knowledge: At meetings, we just keep **going over the same ground** (=talking about the same things). | His latest movie looks set to **break new ground** (=introduce new and exciting ideas). | **familiar/home ground** (=a subject etc that you know something about) In his latest book, McManus returns to more familiar ground.
5 OPINION [U] a general opinion or set of attitudes: Often parents and teenagers find they have little **common ground** (=they do not share the same attitudes etc). | **the middle/centre ground** (=opinions that are not extreme that most people would agree with) Both parties are battling to **occupy the centre ground**. | Careful, Laura. You could be **treading on dangerous ground** (=expressing opinions etc that might offend someone). | Each side was unwilling to **give ground** (=change their opinion).
6 SPORT [C] BrE the place where a particular sport is played; → **stadium**: a new football ground | It's their first defeat at their **home ground** (−the ground that belongs to a particular team) all season.
7 hold/stand your ground a) to stay where you are when someone threatens you, in order to show them that you are not afraid: The men threatened him, but he stood his ground and they fled. **b)** to refuse to change your mind about something, even though people are opposing you: Jason vowed to stand his ground, even if it meant losing his job.
8 get off the ground to start to be successful: Her show never really got off the ground in the UK.
9 gain ground a) to become more successful: It was feared that the extreme right might be gaining considerable ground in the election campaign. **b)** if an idea, belief etc gains ground, more people start to accept it: His theories gradually gained ground among academics. **c)** to get closer to someone or something that you are competing with
10 lose ground to become less successful compared with someone or something you are competing with: The Indian team seem determined to regain the ground they lost in the last game.
11 breeding/fertile/proving ground a situation in which something develops quickly or successfully: The region, with its widespread poverty, provided fertile ground for revolutionary activitists. | **prepare/lay the ground** (=to provide the situation or conditions in which something can develop successfully) | **[+for]** My task was to prepare the ground for the recruitment of support workers.
12 burn/raze sth to the ground to destroy a city, building etc completely by fire, bombs etc: The city of Tortona was burnt to the ground.
13 work/drive/run yourself into the ground to work so hard that you become very tired or ill: Kay's working herself into the ground trying to meet her deadlines.
14 on the ground in the place or situation where something important is happening, rather than somewhere else – used especially in news reports: While the politicians talk of peace, the situation on the ground remains tense.
15 stamping ground BrE; **stomping ground** AmE informal someone's stamping ground is an area where they are known or have a lot of influence: I guess he'll try to reach his **old stomping ground** to drum up support.

16 ELECTRICAL [singular] AmE a wire that connects a piece of electrical equipment to the ground for safety; ⊟ **earth** BrE
17 grounds [plural] small pieces of solid material that sink to the bottom of a liquid: coffee grounds
18 go to ground BrE to make it hard for people to find you: The man has gone to ground since his photograph was published in a national newspaper.
19 run sb/sth to ground BrE to succeed in finding someone or something after a long search
20 BACKGROUND [C] technical the colour used as the background for a design → **cut the ground from under sb's feet** at CUT[1] (37); → **have/keep both feet on the ground** at FOOT[1] (18); → **suit sb down to the ground** at SUIT[2] (1); → **be thin on the ground** at THIN[1] (12); → **hit the ground running** at HIT[1] (24)

ground² v
1 AIRCRAFT [T usually passive] to stop an aircraft or pilot from flying: All planes are grounded until the fog clears.
2 BOAT [I,T] if you ground a boat or if it grounds, it hits the bottom of the sea so that it cannot move: Both boats grounded on a mud bank.
3 be grounded in/on sth to be based on something: Lewis' ideas were grounded in his strong Christian faith.
4 CHILD [T] informal to stop a child going out with their friends as a punishment for behaving badly: I got home at 2 am and Dad grounded me on the spot.
5 ELECTRICITY [T] AmE to make a piece of electrical equipment safe by connecting it to the ground with a wire; ⊟ **earth** BrE → WELL-GROUNDED
ground sb in sth phr v
to teach someone the basic things they should know in order to be able to do something: Most seven-year-olds are grounded in the basics of reading and writing.

ground³ adj [only before noun] ground coffee or nuts have been broken up into powder or very small pieces, using a special machine

ground⁴ the past tense and past participle of GRIND[1]

ground bait n [U] food that you throw onto a river, lake etc when you are fishing in order to attract fish

ground beef n [U] AmE BEEF that has been cut up into very small pieces, often used to make HAMBURGERS; ⊟ **mince** BrE

ground·break·ing /'graʊndˌbreɪkɪŋ/ adj groundbreaking work involves making new discoveries, using new methods etc: groundbreaking research

ground cloth n [C] AmE a piece of material that water cannot pass through, which people sleep on when they are camping; ⊟ **groundsheet** BrE

ground con·trol n [U] the people on the ground who are responsible for guiding the flight of spacecraft or aircraft

ground crew n [C] the group of people who work at an airport looking after the aircraft; ⊟ **ground staff** BrE

ground·ed /'graʊndᵻd/ adj **1** reasonable and in control of your emotions, even when this is difficult **2** someone who is grounded understands their own character and knows what is really important: *Simmons says that her family* **keeps** *her* **grounded. 3** someone, especially a child, who is grounded is kept indoors as a punishment

ground·er /'graʊndə $ -ər/ *n* [C] a ball that is hit along the ground in a game of BASEBALL

ˌground 'floor *n* **1** [C] *especially BrE* the floor of a building that is at ground level; ☐ **first floor** *AmE*: *a ground floor flat* | *The dining room is on the ground floor.* → FLOOR¹ (3) **2 be/get in on the ground floor** to become involved in a plan, business activity etc from the beginning

ˈground ˌforces also **ˈground ˌtroops** *n* [plural] soldiers that fight on the ground rather than at sea or in the air

ˌground 'glass *n* [U] **1** glass that has been made into a powder **2** glass that has been rubbed on its surface so that you cannot see through it, but light passes through it – used for example on a camera

ground·hog /'graʊndhɒg $ -hɑːg, -hɒːg/ *n* [C] a small North American animal that has thick brown fur

ground·ing /'graʊndɪŋ/ *n* **1** [singular] a training in the basic parts of a subject or skill: [+in] *A basic grounding in math is essential for the economics course.* | **get/have a grounding in sth** *Applicants must have a good grounding in human resources management.* | **a good/thorough/solid etc grounding** *The aim of the course is to give students a thorough grounding in English pronunciation.* **2** [C] *AmE* a punishment for a child's bad behaviour in which they are not allowed to go out with their friends for a period of time **3** [C,U] the process of officially stopping an aircraft from flying, especially because it is not safe to fly **4** [U] when someone knows what their own character is like and understands what is really important and what is not: *a sense of grounding*

ground·less /'graʊndləs/ *adj* not based on facts or reason; ☐ **well-founded**: *Fortunately my suspicions* **proved groundless.** | *Mr Kay's lawyer said the accusations were groundless.*

ˈground ˌlevel *n* [singular] the same level as the surface of the earth, rather than above it or below it: *The flats are set around a courtyard with shops at ground level.*

ground·nut /'graʊndnʌt/ *n* [C] *BrE technical* a PEANUT or peanut plant

ˈground plan *n* [C] **1** a drawing of how a building is arranged at ground level, showing the size, position, and shape of walls, rooms etc; ☐ **floor plan 2** a plan for doing something in the future: *documents which formed the ground plan for the welfare state*

ˈground rent *n* [C,U] rent that you pay to the person who owns the land that your house, office etc is built on

ˈground rules *n* [plural] the basic rules or principles on which future actions or behaviour should be based: **lay down/establish ground rules for sth** *Our book lays down the ground rules for building a patio successfully.*

ground·sheet /'graʊndʃiːt/ *n* [C] *BrE* a piece of material that water cannot pass through which people sleep on when they are camping; ☐ **ground cloth** *AmE*; → see picture at TENT

grounds·man /'graʊndzmən/ *n plural* **groundsmen** /-mən/ [C] *especially BrE* a man whose job is to take care of a large garden or sports field; ☐ **groundskeeper** *AmE*

ˈground ˌsquirrel *n* [C] a GOPHER

ˈground staff *n* [C] *BrE* **1** the people who take care of the grass and equipment at a sports ground **2** the group of people who work at an airport looking after the aircraft; ☐ **ground crew**

ˈground ˌstroke *n* [C] a way of hitting the ball after it has hit the ground in tennis and similar games

ground·swell /'graʊndswel/ *n* [singular] a sudden increase in a particular feeling among people: [+of] *There is a* **groundswell of opinion** *that tougher laws are needed.* | *a* **groundswell of support** *for the Prime Minister*

ground·wa·ter /'graʊnd,wɔːtə $ -,wɒːtər, -,wɑː-/ *n* [U] water that is below the ground: *There are fears that groundwater might become contaminated.*

ground·work /'graʊndwɜːk $ -wɜːrk/ *n* [U] something that has to happen before an activity or plan can be successful: *His speech* **laid** *the* **groundwork** *for independence.* | *Much of* **the groundwork has** *already* **been done.**

ˌground 'zero *n* [U] the exact place where a bomb explodes: *Buildings within 25 km of ground zero would be flattened.*

group¹ S1 W1 /gruːp/ *n* [C]
1 [also + plural verb *BrE*] several people or things that are all together in the same place: [+of] *a group of children* | *a small group of islands* | *Get into groups of four.* | *He was surrounded by a group of admirers.* | **in groups** *Dolphins travel in small groups.* | *A group of us are going to London.*
2 several people or things that are connected with each other: *a left-wing terrorist group* | [+of] *She is one of a group of women who have suffered severe side-effects from the drug.* | **age/ethnic/income etc group** (=people of the same age, race etc) *Minority groups are encouraged to apply.*
3 several companies that all have the same owner; → **chain**: *a giant textiles group* | [+of] *He owns a group of hotels in southern England.*
4 a number of musicians or singers who perform together, playing popular music; ☐ **band** → BLOOD GROUP, FOCUS GROUP, INTEREST GROUP, PLAYGROUP, PRESSURE GROUP, WORKING GROUP

group² *v* **1** [I,T] to come together and form a group, or to arrange things or people together in a group: **group (sth) together/round/into etc** *The photo shows four men grouped round a jeep.* | *Different flowers can be grouped together to make a colourful display.* | *small producers who group together to sell their produce* **2** [T always + adv/prep] to divide people or things into groups according to a system: *We were grouped into six age bands.* | *We've grouped the questions under three headings.*

ˌgroup 'captain *n* [C] a fairly high rank in the British air force, or someone who has this rank

ˌgroup dy'namics *n* [plural] the way in which people in a group behave towards each other when they are working together or doing an activity together

group·ie /'gruːpi/ *n* [C] a young woman who follows popular musicians or other famous people around, hoping to meet them

group·ing /'gruːpɪŋ/ *n* **1** [C] a number of people, things, or organizations that do something together or have the same interests, qualities, or features: [+of] *a grouping of eight opposition parties* | **political/social/ economic etc grouping** *During this period the family unit becomes the natural social grouping.* | *a loose grouping* (=informal and not well organized) *of anti-capitalist protesters* **2** [U] the act of putting people or things into groups: *the grouping of students by ability*

ˌgroup 'practice *n* [C,U] a group of several doctors who all work in the same building

ˌgroup 'therapy *n* [U] a method of treating people with emotional problems by getting them to meet and talk as a group

grouse¹ /graʊs/ *n* **1** [C,U] *plural* **grouse** a small bird that is hunted and shot for food and sport, or the flesh of this bird: *the grouse shooting season* | *roast grouse* **2** [C] *informal* a complaint: *His main grouse is that he isn't paid enough.*

grouse² *v* [I] *informal* to complain about something; ☐ **moan**: [+about] *I haven't really got much to grouse about.*

grout /graʊt/ n [U] a mixture of sand and water that you spread between TILES when you fix them to a wall —**grout** v [I,T]

grove /grəʊv $ groʊv/ n **1** [C] a piece of land with trees growing on it: [+of] *a small grove of beech trees* | *olive/lemon/palm etc grove He owns an orange grove near Tel Aviv.* **2** Grove used in the names of roads: *Lisson Grove*

grov·el /ˈɡrɒvəl $ ˈɡrɑː-, ˈɡrʌ-/ v grovelled, grovelling BrE, groveled, groveling AmE **1** [I] to praise someone a lot or behave with a lot of respect towards them because you think that they are important and will be able to help you in some way – used to show disapproval; ▣ **crawl**: [+to] *I had to really grovel to the bank manager to get a loan.* **2** [I always + adv/prep] to move along the ground on your hands and knees: *I saw him grovelling in the road for his hat.* —**grovelling** adj: *a grovelling apology*

grow S1 W1 /grəʊ $ groʊ/ v past tense **grew** /gruː/ past participle **grown** /grəʊn $ groʊn/
1 INCREASE **a)** [I] to increase in amount, size, number, or strength; ▣ **shrink**: *Support for Mr Thompson is growing.* | [+by] *Sales of new cars grew by 10% last year.* | [+from/to] *The number of students at the college has grown from 200 to over 500.* | *A growing number of people are taking part-time jobs.* | **grow rapidly/slowly/steadily** *The economy has grown steadily over the last ten years.* | *Fears are growing for the crew's safety.* | [+in] *a city that is still growing in size* | *Skiing has really grown in popularity.* | *There is growing concern about climate change.* | *my growing interest in China* **b)** [T] to make a business or part of a business bigger and more successful: *We want to grow the export side of the business.*
2 PERSON/ANIMAL [I] to become bigger, taller etc over a period of time in the process of becoming an adult; ▣ **shrink**: *You've really grown since I last saw you.* | *Victor seemed to grow taller every day.* | **grow 2 inches/5cm etc** *Stan grew two inches in six months.*
3 PLANTS **a)** [I] if plants grow, they exist and develop in a natural way: *a tree which will grow well in most types of soil* | *The plants grow wild* (=grow without anyone looking after them) *by the river.* **b)** [T] to make plants or crops develop and produce fruit or flowers; → **raise**: *Many families own plots of land to grow food.* | *Britain grows 6,000,000 tonnes of potatoes a year.* | *The growing season is from April to September.*
4 HAIR/NAILS **a)** [T] if you grow your hair or nails, you do not cut them: *I've decided to grow my hair long.* | **grow a beard/moustache b)** [I] when hair or nails grow, they become longer
5 BECOME **a)** [I always + adj] to change and become different quite slowly: *The sound was growing louder.* | *Her tastes have changed as she's grown older.* | *Donna has grown tired of being a model.* | *Gradually, Fiona's eyes grew used to the darkness* (=she gradually became able to see a little better). **b)** [I] to gradually change your opinions and have a feeling that you did not have before: **grow to like/hate/respect etc** *After a while the kids grew to like Mr Cox.* | *the city he had grown to love*; → box at BECOME
6 IMPROVE [I] to gradually become better, bigger etc: [+as] *She's grown tremendously as a musician.*
7 it/money doesn't grow on trees spoken used to say that you should not waste money

grow apart phr v
if two people grow apart, their relationship becomes less close: *The couple had been growing apart for years.*

grow into sb/sth phr v
1 to develop over time and become a particular kind of person or thing: *Sue grew into a lovely young woman.* | *The first show has grown into a full-fledged series.*
2 to gradually learn how to do a job or deal with a situation successfully: *She will grow into her new role over the next few months.*
3 if a child grows into clothes, he or she becomes big enough to wear them

grow on sb phr v
if something grows on you, you gradually like it more and more: *I hated his music at first, but it grows on you.*
grow out phr v
if you grow out a hair style, or if it grows out, you gradually grow your hair until the style disappears: **grow sth ⇔ out** *I'm growing my fringe out.*
grow out of sth phr v
1 if a child grows out of clothes, he or she becomes too big to wear them; ▣ **outgrow**
2 if someone grows out of something, they stop doing it as they get older; ▣ **outgrow**: *Mike finally seems to be growing out of his rebelliousness.*
3 to develop or happen as a result of something else that happened or existed: *His art grew out of his love of nature.* | *legislation which grew out of concern over the increasing crime rate*

grow up phr v
1 to develop from being a child to being an adult: *What do you want to be when you grow up?* | *I grew up in Chicago.*
2 grow up! spoken used to tell someone to behave in a more responsible way, like an adult
3 to start to exist or develop gradually: *Trading settlements grew up by the river.*

grow·bag /ˈgrəʊbæg $ ˈgroʊ-/ n another spelling of GRO-BAG

grow·er /ˈɡrəʊə $ ˈɡroʊər/ n [C] **1** a person or company that grows fruit or vegetables in order to sell them: **fruit/vegetable/tobacco etc grower** *apple growers* **2** a plant that grows and develops in a particular way: **fast/slow etc grower** *Bamboo is a very vigorous grower.*

growing pains n [plural] **1** problems and difficulties that happen when an organization or system is new: *the growing pains of a new republic* **2** pain that children who are growing feel in their arms and legs

growl /graʊl/ v **1** [I] if an animal growls, it makes a long deep angry sound; → **bark, snarl**: [+at] *The dog growled at me.* **2** [I,T] to say something in a low angry voice; ▣ **snarl**: *'Get out of my way,' he growled.* | [+at] *'Who are you?' he growled at me.* —**growl** n [C]: *He heard a low growl behind him.*

grown¹ /grəʊn $ groʊn/ adj [only before noun] **1** grown man/woman an adult man or woman, used especially when you think someone is not behaving as an adult should: *Who ever heard of a grown man being scared of the dark?* **2** grown children/daughter/son children etc who are now adults: *I've got two grown daughters and a son.*

grown² the past participle of GROW

grown-up¹ adj **1** fully developed as an adult: *Before you know it, the children will be grown-up and leaving home.* | *I've got two grown-up sons.* **2** behaving in a responsible way, like an adult; ▣ **mature**; → **childish**: *I expect more grown-up behaviour of you.*

grown-up² n [C] an adult – used by or to children: *If you're frightened, tell one of the grown-ups.* ⚠ This word is mostly used by young children. Otherwise it is more usual to say **adult**.

growth W2 /grəʊθ $ groʊθ/ n
1 INCREASE [singular,U] an increase in amount, number, or size; ▣ **decline**: [+in/of] *We've seen an enormous growth in the number of businesses using the Web.* | *the rapid growth of world population* | *the recent growth of interest in African music*
2 BUSINESS/ECONOMY [singular,U] an increase in the value of goods or services produced and sold by a business or a country; ▣ **decline**: *measures to stimulate economic growth* | *strong/rapid/slow etc growth a period of rapid growth in the economy* | *The company is preparing for zero growth* (=no growth) *this year.* | *growth area/industry Debt collection is a huge growth industry.*

3 SIZE/STRENGTH [singular,U] the development of the physical size, strength etc of a person, animal, or plant over a period of time: *Vitamins are essential for healthy growth.* | *a means of stimulating **plant growth*** | *a **growth hormone*** (=substance in the body that causes you to grow)

4 IMPORTANCE [singular,U] a gradual increase in the importance or influence that something has: [+of] *Cinemas declined with the growth of television.*

5 PERSONAL DEVELOPMENT [U] the development of someone's character, intelligence, or emotions: *A loving home is essential for a child's **personal growth**.* | *emotional/intellectual/spiritual etc growth the journey toward spiritual growth*

6 DISEASE [C] a swelling on or inside a person, animal, or plant, caused by disease; → **tumour**: *a cancerous growth* | [+on] *a growth on his lung*

7 GROWING THING [C,U] something that has grown: *Feed the plants to encourage new growth.* | *His chin bore a thick growth of stubble.*

groyne, **groin** /grɔɪn/ n [C] a low wall built out into the sea to prevent the sea from removing sand and stones from the shore

grub¹ /grʌb/ n **1** [U] *informal* food: *Let's get some grub.* **2** [C] an insect when it is in the form of a small soft white worm

grub² v **grubbed**, **grubbing** [I always + adv/prep] *informal* to look for something on the ground or just under the ground, especially by moving things around: *Jake got on the floor and grubbed about under the desk.* | [+for] *chickens grubbing for worms*
grub sth ⇔ **up/out** phr v to dig plants out of the ground: *Farmers were encouraged to grub up hedgerows.*

grub·by /ˈgrʌbi/ adj **1** fairly dirty: *a grubby handkerchief* | *a gang of grubby kids* **2** grubby behaviour or activity is morally unpleasant: *the grubby details of his financial dealings* **3** **grubby hands/paws/mitts** *informal* used to talk about someone touching something or becoming involved in it when you do not want them to: *Keep your grubby paws to yourself!* | *I bet he can't wait to get his grubby hands on my money!* —**grubbiness** n [U]

grub·stake /ˈgrʌbˌsteɪk/ n [U] *AmE informal* an amount of money that is provided to develop a new business in return for a share of the profits

grudge¹ /grʌdʒ/ n [C]
1 a feeling of dislike for someone because you cannot forget that they harmed you in the past

> have/bear/hold a grudge
> harbour/nurse a grudge (=try to continue feeling dislike for a long time)
> someone/an employee etc with a grudge
> personal grudge

[+against] *Is there anyone who might have had a grudge against her?* | *Mr Gillis was not normally a man to bear grudges.* | *I'm not harbouring some secret grudge against you.* | *It could be the work of someone with a grudge against the company.* | *You let nasty little personal grudges creep in.*

2 **grudge fight/match** a fight or sports competition between two people who dislike each other a lot

grudge² v [T] to do or give something very unwillingly: **grudge doing sth** *I really grudge paying for poor service.* | **grudge sb sth** *I don't grudge him his success.* —**grudging** adj [usually before noun]: *a grudging apology* | *He looked at Nick with grudging respect.* —**grudgingly** adv: *He grudgingly admitted he'd been wrong.*

gru·el /ˈgruːəl/ n [U] a food made of OATS cooked in water or milk, which poor people ate in the past

gru·el·ling BrE; **grueling** AmE /ˈgruːəlɪŋ/ adj very difficult and tiring: *The cast took a break from their gruelling schedule.* | *a grueling journey*

grue·some /ˈgruːsəm/ adj very unpleasant or shocking, and involving someone being killed or badly injured: *Police described it as a particularly gruesome attack.* | *Spare me the gruesome details.* —**gruesomely** adv

gruff /grʌf/ adj speaking in a rough, unfriendly voice: *His manner can be rather gruff.* | *a gruff reply* | *His voice became gruff.* —**gruffly** adv —**gruffness** n [U]

grum·ble /ˈgrʌmbəl/ v **1** [I,T] to keep complaining in an unhappy way; ◨ **moan**: [+about/at] *Farmers are always grumbling about the weather.* | **grumble that** *A few passengers grumbled that their cabins were too small.* | *'This is boring,' Kathleen grumbled.* **2** [I] to make a low continuous sound; ◨ **rumble**: *Thunder grumbled overhead.* **3** **mustn't/can't grumble** BrE spoken used to say that you are fairly healthy and happy: *'How are you today?' 'Mustn't grumble.'* —**grumble** n [C]: *the usual grumbles about pay*

grum·bling /ˈgrʌmblɪŋ/ n **1** [U] also **grumblings** [plural] a complaint about something: *She paid up, with some grumbling.* | *Soon, the grumblings turned to open discontent.* **2** [U] a low continuous sound: *the grumbling of distant thunder*

grump·y /ˈgrʌmpi/ adj bad-tempered and easily annoyed: *Mina's always a bit grumpy first thing in the morning.* —**grumpily** adv —**grumpiness** n [U]

grunge /grʌndʒ/ n [U] **1** a style of fashion and music popular with young people in the 1990s, involving loud electric music and dirty clothes, hair etc: *grunge rock* **2** AmE informal unpleasant dirt: *What's all that grunge in the bathtub?* —**grungy** adj: *a pair of grungy trainers*

grunt¹ /grʌnt/ v **1** [I,T] to make short sounds or say a few words in a rough voice, when you do not want to talk: *He just grunted and carried on reading his book.* **2** [I] if a person or animal grunts, they make short low sounds in their throat: *Grunting with effort, she lifted me up.*

grunt² n [C] **1** a short low sound that a person or animal makes in their throat: *Chris gave a grunt and went back to sleep.* **2** AmE informal someone who does hard physical work for low pay: *We get the grunts to move the crates.* **3** AmE informal a soldier in the INFANTRY

grunt work n [U] AmE informal the difficult and uninteresting part of a job: *These guys do the grunt work in preparing tax returns.*

gryph·on /ˈgrɪfən/ n another spelling of GRIFFIN

G-spot /ˈdʒiː spɒt $ -spɑːt/ n [C] informal the place in a woman's VAGINA where she is thought to feel the most sexual pleasure

G-string /ˈdʒiː strɪŋ/ n [C] a very small piece of underwear that covers only the sexual organs

Gt. also **Gt** BrE adj [only before noun] the written abbreviation of **Great**, used in names: *Gt Britain*

gua·ca·mo·le /ˌgwɑːkəˈməʊli $ -ˈmoʊ-/ n [U] a cold Mexican dish made with crushed AVOCADO

gua·no /ˈgwɑːnəʊ $ -noʊ/ n [U] solid waste from sea birds, put on soil to help plants grow

guar·an·tee¹ S2 W3 /ˌgærənˈtiː/ v [T]
1 a) to promise to do something or to promise that something will happen: **guarantee (that)** *I guarantee you'll love this film.* | **guarantee sb sth** *If you send the application form in straight away, I can guarantee you an interview.* | **guarantee to do sth** *I cannot guarantee to work for more than a year.* | *The law guarantees equal rights for men and women.* **b)** to make a formal written promise to repair or replace a product if it breaks within a specific period of time: *All our products are **fully guaranteed**.* | **guarantee sth against sth** *The stereo is guaranteed against failure for a year.*
2 LEGALLY RESPONSIBLE to promise that you will pay back money that someone else has borrowed, if they do not pay it back themselves: *The bank will only lend me money if my parents guarantee the loan.*
3 CERTAIN to make it certain that something will

happen: *In movies, talent by no means guarantees success.* | **guarantee that** *The built-in thermostat guarantees that the water remains at the same temperature all the time.* | **be guaranteed to do sth** *This latest incident is guaranteed to make the situation worse.* | **be guaranteed sth** *Even if you complete your training, you aren't guaranteed a job.*

guarantee² [S2] *n* [C]
1 a formal written promise to repair or replace a product if it breaks within a specific period of time; ◘ **warranty**: *They offer a two-year guarantee on all their electrical goods.* | **come with/carry a guarantee** *Our computers come with a one year guarantee.* | **under guarantee** *Is your TV under guarantee* (=protected by a guarantee)? | *a **money-back guarantee***
2 a formal promise that something will be done: [+of] *I'm afraid there's no guarantee of success.* | **guarantee that** *I cannot give a **guarantee** that there will be no redundancies.*
3 a) a promise that you will pay back money that someone else has used or borrowed, if they do not pay it themselves **b)** something valuable that you give to someone to keep until you have done something you promised to do: *The bank is holding the airline's assets as guarantees.*

guar·an·tor /ˌgærənˈtɔː $ -ˈtɔːr/ *n* [C] *law* someone who promises to pay a debt if the person who should pay it does not

guard¹ [S3] [W3] /gɑːd $ gɑːrd/ *n*
1 PERSON [C] **a)** someone whose job is to protect a place or person: *There were two **security guards** on duty outside the building.* | *We were stopped by **border guards**.* | **Armed guards** *were posted by the exit.* **b)** someone whose job is to prevent prisoners from escaping: *The **prison guards** were reasonably friendly.*
2 PROTECTION [U] the act or duty of protecting places or people, or of preventing prisoners from escaping: **be on guard** *Who was on guard the night the fire broke out?* | **keep/stand guard (over sb/sth)** *Gunmen stood guard at the camp entrance.* | **be under (police/armed etc) guard** (=to be guarded by a group of people) *He was taken to hospital, where he is now under police guard.*
3 SOLDIERS a) [singular] a group of soldiers who guard someone or something: *The President has called in the National Guard.* **b) the Guards** *BrE* a group of soldiers who protect the king or queen
4 EQUIPMENT [C] something that is used to protect someone or something from damage or injury: *a face guard* | *a fire guard*
5 ON A TRAIN [C] *BrE* a person whose job is to be in charge of a train; ◘ **conductor** *AmE*
6 on your guard to be paying attention to what is happening in order to avoid danger, being tricked etc: *These men are dangerous so you'll need to **be on your guard**.* | *Something in his tone **put** her **on her guard**.*
7 catch/throw sb off guard to surprise someone by doing something that they are not ready to deal with: *Senator O'Hare was caught off guard by the question.*
8 guard of honour a group of people who walk or stand together at a special occasion in order to show respect: *Police colleagues formed a guard of honour at her funeral.*
9 the old guard a group of people in an organization who want to do things in the way they were done in the past: *the Communist old guard*
10 FIGHTING [singular] the position of holding your arms or hands up in a fight in order to defend yourself: *He swung at me and I brought my guard up.*
11 SPORT [C] **a)** one of two players on a BASKETBALL team who is responsible for moving the ball to help their team gain points **b)** one of two players on an American football team who plays either side of the centre

guard² *v* [T] **1** to protect a person, place, or object by staying near them and watching them: *The Sergeant told Swift to guard the entrance.* | *a lioness guarding her cubs* | **guard sb/sth against sth** *There is no one to*

guard these isolated farms against attack. **2** to watch a prisoner to prevent them from escaping **3** to protect something such as a right or a secret by preventing other people from taking it away, discovering it etc: *chiefs who **jealously guarded** their independence* | *a **closely guarded secret*** **4** to prevent another sports player from gaining points, getting the ball etc

guard against *sth phr v* to prevent something from happening: *Exercise can guard against a number of illnesses.* | **guard against doing sth** *Nurses should guard against becoming too attached to their patients.*

guard dog *n* [C] a dog that is trained to guard a place → see picture at GUIDE DOG

guard·ed /ˈgɑːdɪd $ ˈgɑːr-/ *adj* not giving very much information or showing your feelings about something; ◘ **cautious**: *The minister was quite guarded in his comments.* | *He gave the proposal a guarded welcome.* —**guardedly** *adv*

guard·house /ˈgɑːdhaʊs $ ˈgɑːrd-/ *n* [C] a building for soldiers who are guarding the entrance to a military camp

guard·i·an /ˈgɑːdiən $ ˈgɑːr-/ *n* [C] **1** someone who is legally responsible for looking after someone else's child, especially after the child's parents have died: **sb's guardian** *His aunt is his **legal guardian**.* **2** *formal* someone who guards or protects something: [+of] *The US sees itself as the guardian of democracy.*

guardian 'angel *n* [C] **1** a good SPIRIT who is believed to protect a person or place **2** someone who helps or protects someone else when they are in trouble

guard·i·an·ship /ˈgɑːdiənʃɪp $ ˈgɑːr-/ *n* [U] *law* the position of being legally responsible for someone else's child

guard·rail /ˈgɑːd-reɪl $ ˈgɑːrd-/ *n* [C] **1** a bar that is intended to prevent people from falling from a bridge, cliff etc **2** *AmE* a bar that is intended to prevent cars from going off the road in an accident; ◘ **crash barrier** *BrE*

guard·room /ˈgɑːd-rʊm, -ruːm $ ˈgɑːrd-/ *n* [C] a room for soldiers who are guarding a military camp

guards·man /ˈgɑːdzmən $ ˈgɑːr-/ *n plural* **guardsmen** /-mən/ [C] a soldier who is a member of a GUARD

'guard's van *n* [C] *BrE* the part of a train where the person in charge of it travels; ◘ **caboose** *AmE*

gua·va /ˈgwɑːvə/ *n* [C] a tropical fruit with pink flesh and a lot of seeds

gu·ber·na·to·ri·al /ˌguːbənəˈtɔːriəl◂ $ -bər-/ *adj formal* relating to the position of being a GOVERNOR: *gubernatorial elections*

guer·ril·la /gəˈrɪlə/ *n* [C] a member of a small unofficial military group that fights in small groups: **guerrilla war/warfare** *American troops found themselves fighting a guerrilla war.* | *left-wing guerrillas* | *a guerrilla leader*

guess¹ [S1] [W3] /ges/ *v*
1 [I,T] to try to answer a question or form an opinion when you are not sure whether you will be correct: *I'd say he's around 50, but I'm only guessing.* | **guess right/correctly/wrong** *If you guess correctly, you have another turn.* | **guess what/who/how etc** *You can guess what happened next.* | [+at] *We can only guess at the cause of the crash.* | *What star sign are you? No, **let me guess**.* | **difficult/hard/easy etc to guess** *It's hard to guess his age because he dyes his hair.*
2 [I,T] to realize that something is true even though you do not know for certain: **guess (that)** *I guessed that you must be related because you look so similar.* | [+from] *I guessed from his expression that he already knew about the accident.* | *Can you guess the identity of this week's special guest?*
3 keep sb guessing to make someone feel excited or not sure about what will happen next: *a thriller that keeps audiences guessing*
4 I guess *spoken* **a)** used to say that you think something is true or likely, although you are not sure: *His*

light's on, so I guess he's still up. **b)** used to say that you will do something even though you do not really want to: *I'm tired, so I guess I'll stay home tonight.*
5 I guess so/not *spoken* used to agree or disagree with a statement or question: *'You're one lucky guy.' 'I guess so.'* | *'I don't really have any choice, do I?' 'I guess not.'*
6 guess what/you'll never guess who/what etc *spoken* used before you tell someone something that will surprise them: *Guess what! Bradley's resigned.* | *You'll never guess who I saw today.* → SECOND-GUESS

guess² S2 n [C]
1 an attempt to answer a question or make a judgement when you are not sure whether you will be correct

> **make a guess (at sth)**
> **have a guess (at sth)** *BrE*
> **take a guess (at sth)** *AmE*
> **hazard a guess** (=guess something, when you feel very uncertain)
> **give sb three guesses** (=allow someone to guess three times)
> **lucky guess**
> **good guess**
> **best guess**
> **educated/informed guess** (=one that is likely to be correct because you have enough information)
> **rough guess** (=one that is not exact)
> **wild guess** (=one made without much thought)
> **my guess is (that)**
> **at a guess** (=used to show that what you are saying is just a guess)

*If I had to **make a guess**, I'd say Sam was the youngest.* | *Does anyone want to **take a guess** at what all this has to do with grammar?* | *I can only **hazard a guess** at what it must have been like.* | *I'll **give you three guesses** who I'm going out with tonight.* | *It had been a **lucky guess**, that was all.* | *It's a **good guess**, but wrong nonetheless.* | *Our **best guess** is that the forests will not recover for a long time.* | *People started making **educated guesses** about the outcome of the election.* | *I'd say she's about 35, but that's only a **rough guess**.* | *My **guess is that** there won't be many people there today.* | *At a **guess**, she'd had an argument with her boyfriend.* → see box at SUPPOSE

2 be anybody's guess to be something that no one knows: *What she's going to do with her life now is anybody's guess.*
3 your guess is as good as mine *spoken* used to tell someone that you do not know any more than they do about something

guess·ti·mate /'gestǝmɪt/ *n [C] informal* an attempt to judge a quantity by guessing it; → **estimate**: *Could you give us a guesstimate of the numbers involved?* —**guesstimate** /-tǝmeɪt/ *v [I,T]*

guess·work /'gesw3ːk $ -w3ːrk/ *n [U]* the method of trying to find the answer to something by guessing: *There's a lot of guesswork in these calculations.*

guest¹ S2 W2 /gest/ *n [C]*
1 AT AN EVENT someone who is invited to an event or special occasion: *a banquet for 250 distinguished guests* | **as sb's guest** *You are here as my guests.* | **dinner/wedding etc guests** *Most of the wedding guests had left.* | *Among the invited guests were Jerry Brown and Elihu Harris.* | *The actress was **guest of honour** (=the most important guest) at the launch.* | *I've nearly finished the **guest list** for the wedding.*
2 IN A HOUSE someone you have invited to stay in your home for a short time: *We have guests staying right now.* → HOUSE GUEST
3 IN A HOTEL someone who is paying to stay in a hotel: *Use of the sauna is free to guests.*
4 ON A SHOW someone famous who is invited to take part in a show, concert etc, in addition to those who usually take part: *We have some great guests for you tonight.* | *Fontaine **appeared as a guest** on the show.*
5 be my guest *spoken* used to give someone permission

to do what they have asked to do: *'Do you mind if I look at your notes?' 'Be my guest.'*

guest² *adj* [only before noun] **1** for guests to use: *He was still asleep in the guest bedroom.* **2** a guest star, speaker etc is someone famous or important who is invited to take part in an event, in addition to the people who usually take part: *Camfield was lucky in getting Cage and Rampling as guest stars.* | *He will **make a special guest appearance** on next week's show.*

guest³ *v* [I] to take part in a show, concert etc as a guest: [+on] *She guested on a comedy show last year.*

guest book *n [C]* a book in which everyone who comes to a formal occasion or stays at a hotel signs their name

guest·house /'gesthaʊs/ *n [C]* a private house where people can pay to stay and have meals

guest room *n [C]* a bedroom for a visitor or visitors to use

guest worker *n [C]* a worker from one country who works in another country for a short time

guff /gʌf/ *n [U] informal* remarks that are stupid and untrue; ▣ **nonsense**: *I don't believe any of that guff!*

guf·faw /gǝ'fɔː $ -'fɒː/ *v* [I] to laugh loudly: *We guffawed at what Graham had written.* —**guffaw** *n [C]:* *The announcement was greeted with loud guffaws.*

GUI /'guːi/ *n [C] technical* **graphical user interface** a way of showing and organizing information on a computer screen that is easy to use and understand

guid·ance W3 /'gaɪdəns/ *n [U]*
1 help and advice that is given to someone about their work, education, or personal life: [+on/about] *I went to a counselor for guidance on my career.* | **under sb's expert guidance** *I was looking forward to working under her expert guidance.* | **parental/spiritual etc guidance** *Children need moral guidance to make their way in the world.*
2 the process of directing a MISSILE while it is flying through the air: *a missile with a sophisticated electronic guidance system*

guide¹ S2 W2 /gaɪd/ *n [C]*
1 FOR DECIDING/JUDGING something that provides information and helps you to form an opinion or make a decision: *The polls are not a reliable guide of how people will vote.* | *The figures are only a **rough guide**.*
2 PERSON **a)** someone whose job is to take tourists to a place and show them around: *a tour guide* | *an experienced **mountain guide*** **b)** someone who advises you and influences the way you live: *my spiritual guide*
3 INSTRUCTIONS **a)** a book or piece of writing that provides information on a particular subject or explains how to do something: [+to] *a guide to North American birds* | *Follow our **step-by-step guide**.* | *Details of how to use the various programs are in the user guide.* **b)** a guidebook
4 GIRL *BrE* **a) the Guides** the Guides Association, which teaches girls practical skills; → **scout b)** a member of the Guides Association

guide² *v* [T] **1** to take someone to a place; ▣ **lead**: **guide sb along/through etc** *He guided us through the narrow streets to the central mosque.*; → see box at DIRECT² **2** to help someone or something to move in a particular direction: **guide sb/sth into/towards etc** *He guided her firmly towards the sofa.* | *Searchlights were used to guide the ship into the harbour.* **3** to influence someone's behaviour or ideas: *Teenagers need adults to guide them.* **4** to show someone the right way to do something, especially something difficult or complicated: **guide sb through sth** *Guide your students through the program one section at a time.*

guide·book /'gaɪdbʊk/ *n [C]* a book about a city, country etc: *travel guidebooks*

guided missile *n [C]* a MISSILE that is controlled electronically while it is flying

guide dog *BrE/*
seeing eye dog *AmE*

guard dog

guide dog *n* [C] a dog trained to guide a blind person; ⊟ **seeing eye dog** *AmE*

guided 'tour *n* [C] if someone takes you on a guided tour, they show you around a place of interest and tell you all about it: [+of/around/round] *You will be taken on a guided tour of the palace.*

guide·line /'gaɪdlaɪn/ *n* [C usually plural] **1** rules or instructions about the best way to do something: [+for] *a new set of guidelines for teachers* | [+on] *guidelines on the employment of children* | **draw up/issue guidelines** *The hospital has issued new guidelines on the treatment of mentally ill patients.* | *This chapter* **gives** *you some* **guidelines** *to help you in your work.* | **clear/strict guidelines** *Today most planning authorities enforce fairly strict guidelines on new houses.* **2** something that helps you form an opinion or make a decision: *When starting a new business, try to follow these general guidelines.* | **within ... guidelines** *Teachers can choose books within certain broad guidelines.*

guid·ing /'gaɪdɪŋ/ *adj* **1** guiding principle something that helps you decide what to do in a difficult situation: *Fairness, rather than efficiency, is the guiding principle.* **2** guiding light/hand/star someone whose ideas and advice people follow: *Eddie was his hero – his guiding light.* | *He really needed a guiding hand.*

guild /gɪld/ *n* [C] an organization of people who do the same job or have the same interests: *the Women's Guild*

guil·der /'gɪldə $ -ər/ *n* [C] the standard unit of money used in the Netherlands before the EURO

guild·hall /ˌgɪld'hɔːl, 'gɪldhɔːl $ 'gɪldhɒːl/ *n* [C] a large building in which members of a guild met in the past

guile /gaɪl/ *n* [U] *formal* the use of clever but dishonest methods to deceive someone; ⊟ **cunning**: *With a little guile she might get what she wanted.* —**guileful** *adj*

guile·less /'gaɪl-ləs/ *adj* behaving in an honest way, without trying to hide anything or deceive people; ⊟ **open**

guil·le·mot /'gɪlɪˌmɒt $ -maːt/ *n* [C] a black and white sea bird with a narrow beak

guil·lo·tine¹ /'gɪlətiːn/ *n* [C] **1** a piece of equipment used to cut off the heads of criminals, especially in France in the past **2** *BrE* a piece of equipment used to cut large sheets of paper **3** *BrE* the setting of a time limit on a discussion in the British parliament: *Opposition leaders accused the government of introducing a guillotine motion to stifle debate.*

guillotine² *v* [T] **1** to cut off someone's head using a guillotine **2** *BrE* to limit the period of time allowed for the discussion of a possible new law in the British parliament

guilt¹ /gɪlt/ *n* [U]
1 a strong feeling of shame and sadness because you know that you have done something wrong

feeling/sense of guilt
consumed/overwhelmed/racked with/by guilt (=feeling very guilty)
pang/twinge/stab of guilt (=a sudden feeling of guilt)
guilt complex (=when you cannot stop feeling very guilty)
burden of guilt (=a strong feeling of guilt)

He used to buy them expensive presents, out of guilt. |

[+about/at/over] *Don't you have any feelings of guilt about leaving David?* | *He felt an enormous sense of guilt when he thought about how he'd treated her.* | *I was racked with guilt at my part in making her this unhappy.* | *Sometimes I felt little pangs of guilt.*

2 the fact that you have broken an official law or moral rule; 🔁 **innocence**: *He made no attempt to deny his guilt.*

3 responsibility and blame for something bad that has happened: [+for] *Guilt for poorly behaved children usually lies with the parents.*

4 be on a guilt trip *informal* to have a feeling of guilt about something when it is unreasonable

5 lay a guilt trip on sb *AmE informal* to make someone feel bad about something: *I wish my parents would stop laying a guilt trip on me for not going to college.*

guilt² *v*
guilt sb into sth *phr v AmE informal* to make someone feel guilty, so they will do what you want: **guilt sb into doing sth** *Her parents guilted her into not going to the concert.*

guilt·less /'gɪltləs/ *adj formal* not responsible for a crime or for having done something wrong; 🔁 **innocent**

guilt-ridden *adj* feeling so guilty about something that you cannot think about anything else

guilt·y S2 W3 /'gɪlti/ *adj*
1 ASHAMED feeling very ashamed and sad because you know that you have done something wrong: [**about/at**] *I feel really guilty at forgetting her birthday again.* | *She looked self-conscious and guilty.* | *It was his guilty conscience that made him offer to help.*
2 OF A CRIME having done something that is a crime; 🔁 **innocent**: [+of] *The jury found her guilty of murder.* | *He was found not guilty of the death of PC Jones.* | *He pleaded guilty to two charges of theft.*
3 responsible for behaviour that is morally or socially unacceptable: **be guilty of doing sth** *Some journalists are guilty of reporting scandal in order to sell papers.*
4 the guilty party *formal* the person who has done something illegal or wrong —**guiltily** *adv*

guin·ea /'gɪni/ *n* [C] a British gold coin or unit of money used in the past, worth one pound and one SHILLING (£1.05). Prices are sometimes still given in guineas when buying or selling RACEHORSES.

guinea fowl *n* [C] a grey bird that is often eaten as food

guinea pig *n* [C] **1** a small furry animal with short ears and no tail, which is often kept as a pet **2** someone who is used in a scientific test to see how successful or safe a new product, system etc is

guise /gaɪz/ *n* [C] *formal* the way someone or something appears to be, which hides the truth or is only temporary: **in/under the guise of sth** *They operated a drug-smuggling business under the guise of an employment agency.* | *It's the same ideas in a different guise.*

gui·tar W3 /gɪ'taː $ -'taːr/ *n* [C] a musical instrument with six strings that you play by pulling the strings with your fingers or with a PLECTRUM (=small piece of plastic, metal etc): **an acoustic/an electric/a classical guitar** → BASS GUITAR, STEEL GUITAR; → see picture at STRINGED INSTRUMENT

gui·tar·ist /gɪ'taːrɪst/ *n* [C] someone who plays the guitar

gu·lag /'guːlæg $ -laːg/ *n* [C] one of a group of prison camps in the former USSR, where conditions were very bad

gulch /gʌltʃ/ *n* [C] *AmE* a narrow deep valley formed in the past by flowing water, but usually dry now

gulf W3 /gʌlf/ *n* [C]
1 a large area of sea partly enclosed by land: *the Gulf of Mexico*
2 the Gulf the Arabian Gulf, or the countries next to it: *the smaller Gulf states*

G

3 a great difference and lack of understanding between two groups of people, especially in their beliefs, opinions, and way of life; ◨ **gap**: [+**between**] *the huge gulf between management and unions | a growing gulf between old and young*

Gulf Stream *n* the Gulf Stream a current of warm water that flows across the Atlantic Ocean from the Gulf of Mexico towards Europe

gull /gʌl/ *n* [C] a large common black and white sea bird that lives near the sea; ◨ **seagull**

gul·let /ˈgʌlɪ̯t/ *n* [C] the tube at the back of your mouth through which food goes down your throat

gul·ley /ˈgʌli/ *n* another spelling of gully

gul·li·ble /ˈgʌlɪ̯bəl/ *adj* too ready to believe what other people tell you, so that you are easily tricked: *Plastic replicas of the Greek pottery are sold to gullible tourists.* —**gullibility** /ˌgʌlɪ̯ˈbɪlɪ̯ti/ *n* [U]

gul·ly /ˈgʌli/ *n plural* **gullies** [C] **1** a small narrow valley, usually formed by a lot of rain flowing down the side of a hill **2** a deep DITCH

gulp¹ /gʌlp/ *v* **1** also **gulp down** [T] to swallow large quantities of food or drink quickly; ◨ **bolt**: *She gulped down her breakfast and ran for the bus.* **2** [I] to swallow suddenly because you are surprised or nervous: *I gulped when I saw the bill.* **3** also **gulp in** [T] to breathe in large amounts of air quickly: *We rushed outside and gulped in the sweet fresh air.* **4** be gulping for air to breathe in large amounts of air quickly because you do not have enough air in your body

 gulp sth ⇔ **back** *phr v* to stop yourself from expressing your feelings: *Sandra tried to gulp back her tears.*

gulp² *n* [C] **1** a large amount of something that you swallow quickly, or the action of swallowing: [+**of**] *He took a huge gulp of brandy.* | **in one gulp/at a gulp** *Charlie drank the whisky in one gulp.* **2** a large amount of air that you breathe in quickly: *gulps of fresh air*

gum¹ /gʌm/ *n* **1** [C usually plural] your gums are the two areas of firm pink flesh at the top and bottom of your mouth, in which your teeth are fixed **2** [U] CHEWING GUM **3** [U] *BrE* a type of glue used to stick light things such as paper together **4** [U] a sticky substance found in the stems of some trees **5** [C] a GUM TREE **6 by gum!** *spoken old-fashioned* used to express surprise

gum² *v* **gummed**, **gumming** [T always + adv/prep] *BrE old-fashioned* to stick things together using glue; ◨ **glue**: **gum sth to sth** *A large label had been gummed to the back of the photograph.*

 gum sth ⇔ **up** *phr v informal* to prevent a machine from moving and working properly: *Dirt had got inside the watch and gummed up the works.*

gum·ball /ˈgʌmbɔːl $ -bɒːl/ *n* [C] *AmE* CHEWING GUM in the form of a small round brightly coloured sweet

gum·bo /ˈgʌmbəʊ $ -boʊ/ *n* [U] **1** a thick soup made with meat, fish, and OKRA (=a small green vegetable) **2** a word used in some parts of the US for OKRA

gum·boot /ˈgʌmbuːt/ *n* [C] *BrE old-fashioned* a tall boot made of rubber that you wear to keep your feet dry; ◨ **wellington boot**

gum·drop /ˈgʌmdrɒp $ -draːp/ *n* [C] a small sweet that you chew

gum·my /ˈgʌmi/ *adj* **1** sticky or covered in glue **2** a gummy smile shows the GUMS in someone's mouth when they have no teeth

gump·tion /ˈgʌmpʃən/ *n* [U] the ability and determination to decide what needs to be done and to do it: *At least she had the gumption to phone me.*

gum·shoe /ˈgʌmʃuː/ *n* [C] *AmE old-fashioned* a DETECTIVE

gum·shoe·ing /ˈgʌmˌʃuːɪŋ/ *n* [U] *AmE informal* when you try to find out information about something; ◨ **detective work**

gum tree *n* [C] **1** a tall tree which produces a strong-smelling oil that is used in medicine; ◨ **eucalyptus 2 be up a gum tree** *BrE informal* to be in a very difficult situation

gun¹ [S2] [W2] /gʌn/ *n* [C]

1 a metal weapon which shoots bullets or SHELLS: **have/hold/carry a gun** *I could see he was carrying a gun.* | *I've never fired a gun in my life.* | *Jake was pointing a gun at the door.* | *Two policemen were killed in a gun battle last night.*

2 put/hold a gun to sb's head a) to put a gun very close to someone's head to shoot them or to force them to do something: *He put a gun to her head and told the cashier to hand over the money.* **b)** to force someone to do something they do not want to do: *You chose to live here. Nobody put a gun to your head.*

3 a tool that forces out small objects or a liquid by pressure: *a paint gun | a nail gun* → FLASHGUN, SPRAY GUN

4 also **starting pistol** a gun which is fired into the air at the start of a race

5 *AmE informal* **big/top gun** someone who is very important within an organization: *Jed wanted to impress a Harvard professor and some other big guns.*

6 hired gun *AmE informal* someone who is paid to shoot someone else

7 with all guns blazing if you do something with all guns blazing, you do it with a lot of energy, determination, and noise → SON OF A GUN; → **stick to your guns** at STICK¹; → **jump the gun** at JUMP¹ (11); → **be going great guns** at GREAT¹ (11); → **spike sb's guns** at SPIKE¹ (6)

gun² *v* **gunned**, **gunning 1 be gunning for sb** *informal* to be trying to find an opportunity to criticize or harm someone: *Why is he gunning for me?* **2 be gunning for sth** *informal* to be trying very hard to obtain something: *He's gunning for your job.* **3** [T] *AmE informal* to make the engine of a car go very fast by pressing the ACCELERATOR very hard

 gun sb ⇔ **down** *phr v* [usually passive] to shoot someone and badly injure or kill them, especially someone who cannot defend themselves: *A policeman was gunned down as he left his house this morning.*

gun·boat /ˈgʌnbəʊt $ -boʊt/ *n* [C] **1** a small ship that carries several large guns **2 gunboat diplomacy** the practice of threatening to use force against another country to make them agree to your demands

gun carriage *n* [C] a frame with wheels on which a large heavy gun is moved around

gun con·trol *n* [U] *law* laws that limit the ways in which guns can be sold, owned, and used

gun dog *n* [C] a dog that is trained to find and bring back dead birds that have been shot for sport; ◨ **bird dog** *AmE*

gun·fight /ˈgʌnfaɪt/ *n* [C] a fight between people using guns —**gunfighter** *n* [C]

gun·fire /ˈgʌnfaɪə $ -faɪr/ *n* [U] the repeated shooting of guns, or the noise made by this: *I heard a burst of distant gunfire.* | *Two men were shot in an exchange of gunfire with the police.*

gunge¹ /gʌndʒ/ *n* [U] *BrE informal* any substance that is dirty, sticky, or unpleasant; ◨ **gunk** *AmE* —**gungy** *adj*

gunge² *v* **be gunged up with sth** *BrE informal* to be blocked with a dirty sticky substance: *The waste pipe is all gunged up.*

gung-ho /ˌgʌŋ ˈhəʊ $ -ˈhoʊ/ *adj informal* very eager to do something dangerous or violent: *The sporting opportunities here should suit the most gung-ho of tourists.*

gunk¹ /gʌŋk/ *n* [U] *AmE informal* any substance that is dirty, sticky, or unpleasant; ◨ **gunge** *BrE* —**gunky** *adj*

gunk² *v* **be gunked up (with sth)** *AmE informal* to be blocked with a dirty sticky substance: *Here's your problem. The fuel line's all gunked up.*

gun·man /ˈgʌnmən/ *n plural* **gunmen** /-mən/ [C] a criminal who uses a gun

gun·met·al /ˈgʌnˌmetl/ *n* [U] **1** a dull grey-coloured metal which is a mixture of COPPER, TIN, and ZINC **2** a dull blue-grey colour

G

gun·nel /'gʌnl/ n [C] a GUNWALE

gun·ner /'gʌnə $ -ər/ n [C] **1** a soldier, sailor etc whose job is to aim or shoot a large gun **2** a soldier in the British ARTILLERY (=part of the army which uses heavy guns): *Gunner Smith*

gun·ner·y /'gʌnəri/ n [U] the skill of shooting with large heavy guns: *a gunnery officer*

gun·ny·sack /'gʌnisæk/ n [C] AmE a large bag made from rough material and used for storing grain, coal, potatoes etc

gun·point /'gʌnpɔɪnt/ n **at gunpoint** while threatening someone or being threatened with a gun: *She was held at gunpoint for 37 hours.*

gun·pow·der /'gʌn,paʊdə $ -ər/ n [U] an explosive substance used in bombs and FIREWORKS

gun-·running n [U] the activity of taking guns into a country secretly and illegally, especially so that they can be used by people who want to fight against their government —**gun-runner** n [C]

gun·ship /'gʌnʃɪp/ n [C] a military HELICOPTER used to protect other helicopters and to destroy enemy guns

gun·shot /'gʌnʃɒt $ -ʃɑːt/ n **1** [C] the action of shooting a gun, or the sound that this makes: *She says she heard a gunshot at about midnight.* **2** [U] the bullets fired from a gun: **gunshot wounds**

gun·sling·er /'gʌn,slɪŋə $ -ər/ n [C] AmE informal someone who is very skilful at using guns, especially a criminal

gun·smith /'gʌn,smɪθ/ n [C] someone who makes and repairs guns

gun-·toting adj [only before noun] carrying a gun: *gun-toting gangs on the street*

gun·wale /'gʌnl/ n [C] the upper edge of the side of a boat or small ship

gup·py /'gʌpi/ n plural **guppies** [C] a small brightly-coloured tropical fish

gur·gle¹ /'gɜːgəl $ 'gɜːr-/ v [I] **1** if water gurgles, it flows along gently with a pleasant low sound; ◨ **burble**: *We could hear the stream gurgling down in the valley.* **2** if a baby gurgles, it makes a happy low sound in its throat

gurgle² n [C] **1** the happy low sound that someone makes in their throat: *a gurgle of laughter* **2** the pleasant low sound of water moving along gently

gur·ney /'gɜːni $ 'gɜːr-/ n [C] AmE a long narrow table with wheels used for moving sick people in a hospital

gu·ru /'ɡoruː/ n [C] **1** informal someone who knows a lot about a particular subject, and gives advice to other people: *a management guru* | *a fashion guru* **2** a Hindu religious teacher or leader

gush¹ /gʌʃ/ v **1 a)** [I always + adv/prep] if a liquid gushes, it flows or pours out quickly and in large quantities; ◨ **spurt**: [+out/from/down etc] *Water gushed from the broken pipe.* | *He opened the door and smoke gushed out.* **b)** [T] if something gushes a liquid, the liquid pours out quickly and in large quantities; ◨ **spurt**: *The wound gushed blood.* **2** [I,T] to express your praise, pleasure etc in a way that other people think is too strong: *'I simply loved your book,' she gushed.* **3** also **gush out** [I] if words or emotions gush out, you suddenly express them very strongly: *All that pent up frustration gushed out in a torrent of abuse.*

gush² n **1** [C usually singular] a large quantity of something, usually a liquid, that suddenly pours out of something; ◨ **spurt**: *a gush of ice-cold water* **2 a gush of relief/self pity etc** a sudden feeling or expression of emotion

gush·er /'gʌʃə $ -ər/ n [C] a place in the ground where oil or water comes out very forcefully, so that a pump is not needed

gush·ing /'gʌʃɪŋ/ also **gush·y** /'gʌʃi/ adj informal expressing praise, pleasure etc in a way that other people think is too strong: *the gushing praise of the New York critics* —**gushingly** adv

gus·set /'gʌsɪt/ n [C] a piece of material that is stitched into a piece of clothing to make it stronger, wider, or more comfortable in a particular place

gus·sy /'gʌsi/ v **gussied, gussying, gussies**
  gussy sb/sth ⇔ **up** phr v AmE informal to make someone look attractive by dressing them in their best clothes, or to make something look attractive by decorating it: *All the girls will be gussied up for the party.*

gust¹ /gʌst/ n [C] **1** a sudden strong movement of wind, air, rain etc: [+of] *A sudden gust of wind blew the door shut.* | *Gusts of up to 200 kph may be experienced.* **2 gust of laughter** a sound of loud laughter: *Gusts of laughter came from the nextdoor room.*

gust² v [I] if the wind gusts, it blows strongly with sudden short movements: *winds gusting at up to 45 miles per hour*

gus·to /'gʌstəʊ $ -toʊ/ n [U] **with gusto** if you do something with gusto, you do it with a lot of eagerness and energy: *They sang hymns with great gusto.*

gust·y /'gʌsti/ adj with wind blowing in strong sudden movements: *a cold, gusty October night*

gut¹ /gʌt/ n
  1 gut reaction/feeling/instinct informal a reaction or feeling that you are sure is right, although you cannot give a reason for it: *He had a gut feeling that Sarah was lying.*
  2 COURAGE guts [plural] informal the courage and determination you need to do something difficult or unpleasant: *It **takes guts** to start a new business on your own.* | **have the guts (to do sth)** *No-one had the guts to tell Paul what a mistake he was making.*
  3 INSIDE YOUR BODY a) guts [plural] all the organs in someone's body, especially when they have come out of their body: *There were blood and guts all over the place.* **b)** [C] the tube through which food passes from your stomach; ◨ **intestine**: *It can take 72 hours for food to pass through the gut.*
  4 STOMACH [C] informal someone's stomach, especially when it is large; ◨ **belly**: *He felt as if someone had just kicked him in the gut.* | *Phil has a huge **beer gut** (=unattractive fat stomach caused by drinking too much beer).*
  5 STRING [U] a type of strong string made from the INTESTINE of an animal, and used for musical instruments such as VIOLINS → CATGUT
  6 MACHINE/EQUIPMENT guts [plural] informal the parts inside a machine or piece of equipment
  7 MOST IMPORTANT PARTS guts [plural] informal the most important or basic parts of something: [+of] *the guts of the problem*
  8 at gut level if you know something at gut level, you feel sure about it, though you could not give a reason for it: *She knew at gut level that he was guilty.*
  9 I'll have sb's guts for garters BrE informal used to say that you would like to punish someone severely for something they have done → BLOOD-AND-GUTS; → **bust a gut** at BUST¹ (3); → **hate sb's guts** at HATE¹ (2); → **spill your guts** at SPILL¹ (4)

gut² v **gutted, gutting** [T] **1** [usually passive] to completely destroy the inside of a building, especially by fire: *The building was completely gutted by fire.* **2** to remove the organs from inside a fish or animal in order to prepare it for cooking **3** to change something by removing some of the most important or central parts → GUTTED

gut·less /'gʌtləs/ adj informal lacking courage or determination; ◨ **spineless**: *I should have had the support of my team, but they were really gutless.*

guts·y /'gʌtsi/ adj informal **1** if someone's behaviour is gutsy, it is brave and determined: *It was a gutsy performance by McTaggart.* **2** if something is gutsy, it is strong and interesting: *a gutsy, full-bodied wine*

gut·ted /'gʌtɪd/ adj **1** seriously damaged or completely destroyed: *We drove slowly past the gutted buildings.* **2** BrE spoken very shocked or disappointed; ◨ **devastated**: *I was gutted when I lost my job.*

gut·ter¹ /'gʌtə $ -ər/ n **1** [C] the low part at the edge of a road where water collects and flows away: *The gutters were blocked and overflowing.* **2** [C] an open pipe fixed to the edge of a roof to collect and carry away rain water → see picture at ROOF **3 the gutter** the bad social conditions of the lowest and poorest level of society: *Men like him usually ended up in jail – or the gutter.* **4 the gutter press** *BrE* the newspapers that print shocking stories about people's personal lives – used to show disapproval; → **tabloid**

gutter² *v* [I] *literary* if a CANDLE gutters, it burns with an unsteady flame

gut·ter·ing /'gʌtərɪŋ/ *n* [U] *BrE* the open pipes that are fixed to the edge of the roof of a house to collect and carry away rain water

gut·ter·snipe /'gʌtəsnaɪp $ -ər-/ *n* [C] *old-fashioned* a dirty untidy badly-behaved child from a poor home

gut·tur·al /'gʌtərəl/ *adj* a guttural voice or sound is or seems to be produced deep in someone's throat; ▣ **throaty**

guv /gʌv/ *n BrE spoken* used by men, as a way of talking to a male customer in a shop, taxi etc: *Where to, guv?*

guv·nor, **guv'nor** /'gʌvnə $ -ər/ *n BrE spoken old-fashioned informal* **1** [C] a man who is in a position of authority over you, usually your employer: *You'll have to speak to the guvnor about that.* **2** used as a way of talking to a man of a higher social class than you

guy [S1] [W3] /gaɪ/ *n* [C]
1 *informal* a man; ▣ **bloke**: *Dave's a nice guy when you get to know him.* | *Jake's a real tough guy.*
2 *BrE* a model of a man burnt every year on Guy Fawkes' Night, in Britain
3 also **guy rope** a rope that stretches from the top or side of a tent or pole to the ground to keep it in the right position
4 guys [plural] *AmE spoken* used when talking to or about a group of people, male or female: *Hey you guys! Where are you going?*
5 no more Mr Nice Guy! *spoken* used to say that you will stop trying to behave honestly and fairly → **wise guy** at WISE¹ (5)

Guy Fawkes' Night /ˌgaɪ ˈfɔːks naɪt $ -ˈfɔːks-/ *n BrE* November 5th, when people in Britain light FIRE-WORKS and burn a GUY on a fire; ▣ **bonfire night**

guz·zle /'gʌzəl/ *v* [I,T] *informal* **1** to eat or drink a lot of something, eagerly and quickly – usually showing disapproval; → **scoff**: *They've been guzzling beer all evening.* **2** if a vehicle guzzles petrol, it uses a lot of it in a wasteful way → GAS-GUZZLER

gym /dʒɪm/ *n* **1** [C] a special building or room that has equipment for doing physical exercise; ▣ **gymnasium: at/in a gym** *I try and work out at the local gym once a week.* | *I go to the gym as often as I can.* **2** [U] exercises that people do indoors for physical development and as a sport, especially at school: *We've got gym this afternoon.* | *Where's my gym kit?*

gym·kha·na /dʒɪm'kɑːnə/ *n* [C] *BrE* a sporting even at which people on horses compete in races and jump ing competitions

gym·na·si·um /dʒɪm'neɪziəm/ *n* [C] *formal* a GYM → see picture at SPORTS CENTRE

gym·nast /'dʒɪmnæst, -nəst/ *n* [C] someone who i: good at gymnastics and competes against other people in gymnastic competitions

gym·nas·tics /dʒɪm'næstɪks/ *n* [U] **1** a spor involving physical exercises and movements that nee skill, strength, and control, and that are often per formed in competitions: *a gymnastics display* | *W don't do gymnastics at school.* **2 mental/intellectual moral gymnastics** very clever thinking **3 verbal/lin guistic gymnastics** using words in a very clever wa —**gymnastic** *adj*: *The girls went through their gymnas tic routine.*

'**gym shoe** *n* [C] a light shoe with a cloth top and a fla rubber bottom that children wear for games and spor at school; ▣ **plimsoll** *BrE*

gym·slip /'dʒɪmˌslɪp/ *n* [C] *BrE* a type of dress withou sleeves that girls wore in the past over a shirt as a par of their school uniform

gy·nae·col·o·gy *BrE*; **gynecology** *AmE* /ˌgaɪnɪˈkɒlədʒi $ -ˈkɑː-/ *n* [U] the study and treatmen of medical conditions and illnesses that affect only women, and usually relating to a woman's ability to have babies —**gynaecologist** *n* [C —**gynaecological** /ˌgaɪnɪkəˈlɒdʒɪkəl $ -ˈlɑː-/ *adj*

gyp¹ /dʒɪp/ *n informal* **1 give sb gyp** *BrE* **a)** to be painful: *My bad leg is really giving me gyp today.* **b)** to punish someone or be angry with them because of something they have done **2** [singular] *AmE* **a)** some thing that you were tricked into buying **b)** a situation in which you feel you have been cheated: *What a gyp.*

gyp² *v* **gypped**, **gypping** [T] *AmE informal* to chea someone: *Ten bucks? You've been gypped!*

gyp·sum /'dʒɪpsəm/ *n* [U] a soft white substance tha is used to make PLASTER OF PARIS

gyp·sy also **gipsy** /'dʒɪpsi/ *n plural* **gypsies** [C] **1** a member of a group of people originally from India, who traditionally live and travel around in CARAVANS, and who now live all over the world. Most gypsies prefer to be called ROMANIES; → **traveller** **2** someone who does not like to stay in the same place for a long time

gy·rate /dʒaɪˈreɪt $ ˈdʒaɪreɪt/ *v* **1** [I,T] to turn around fast in circles; ▣ **spin**: *The dancers gyrated wildly to the beat of the music.* **2** [I] if the value of money in business gyrates, it moves up and down a lot; → **fluctuate**: *Stock and bond markets have gyrated in recent weeks.* —**gyration** /dʒaɪˈreɪʃən/ *n* [C,U]

gy·ro·scope /'dʒaɪrəskəʊp $ -skoʊp/ *n* [C] a wheel that spins inside a frame and is used for keeping ships and aircraft steady. It can also be a child's toy. —**gyroscopic** /ˌdʒaɪrəˈskɒpɪk $ -ˈskɑː-/ *adj*

H, h

H, h /eɪtʃ/ *plural* **H's, h's** *n* [C,U] the eighth letter of the English alphabet → AITCH → H-BOMB

ha /hɑː/ *interjection* used when you are surprised or have discovered something interesting: *Ha! I thought it might be you hiding there!*

ha·be·as cor·pus /ˌheɪbiəs ˈkɔːpəs $ -ˈkɔːr- / *n* [U] *law* a law which says that a person can only be kept in prison following a court's decision

hab·er·dash·er /ˈhæbədæʃə $ -bərdæʃər/ *n* [C] *old-fashioned* a shopkeeper who sells haberdashery

hab·er·dash·er·y /ˈhæbədæʃəri $ -bər-/ *n plural* **haberdasheries** **1** [C] *BrE* a shop or part of a large store where things used for making clothes are sold **2** [C] *AmE old-fashioned* a shop or part of a large store where men's clothes, especially hats, are sold **3** [U] the goods sold in these shops

hab·it S3 W3 /ˈhæbɪt/ *n*
1 USUAL/REGULAR [C,U] something that you do regularly or usually, often without thinking about it because you have done it so many times before

> **good/bad habit**
> **become a habit**
> **be in the habit of doing sth** also
> **have a/the habit of doing sth** (=do something regularly)
> **get into/in the habit (of doing sth)** (=start doing something regularly)
> **get out of the habit (of doing sth)** (=stop doing something regularly)
> **develop/form a habit**
> **change a habit**
> **break/kick a habit** (=stop doing something which is bad for you)
> **change/break the habit(s) of a lifetime** (=stop doing what you have done for many years)
> **out of habit/from habit** (=because it is a habit)
> **(by/from) force of habit** (=because it is a habit which is difficult to change)
> **eating/drinking habits** (=the kinds of things you eat or drink regularly)
> **buying/spending habits** (=the kinds of things you buy regularly)
> **viewing habits** (=the kind of television shows you regularly watch)
> **social habits**
>
> *Regular exercise is a **good habit** for kids to develop.* | *Thinking negatively can **become a habit**.* | *Jeff **was in the habit of** taking a walk after dinner.* | *She **has a habit of** playing with her hair when she's nervous.* | *Since I stopped taking lessons, I've **got out of the habit** of practising my saxophone.* | *Try to **break** the **habit** of adding salt to your food at the table.* | *Why **break the habit of a lifetime** and start being cautious now?* | *Some people drink alcohol as much **from habit** as from desire.* | *'Hello, Miss Smith.' – 'I'm Mrs Jones now.' – 'Sorry, **force of habit**.'* | *the **spending habits** of the average British woman*

2 DRUGS [C] a strong physical need to keep taking a drug regularly: *A lot of drug addicts get into petty crime to support their habit.* | **heroin/cocaine etc habit** *His cocaine habit ruined him physically and financially.*
3 not make a habit of (doing) sth *spoken* used to say that someone does not usually do something bad or wrong, or should not do it again: *I don't make a habit of this*

sort of thing.* | *You're ten minutes late. I hope you're not going to make a habit of this.*
4 I'm not in the habit of doing sth *spoken* used when you are annoyed, to say that you would not do something: *I'm not in the habit of lying to my friends.*
5 have a habit of doing sth if something has a habit of doing something, it usually or often does – used humorously: *Life has a habit of springing surprises.*
6 old habits die hard used to say that it is difficult to make people change their attitudes or behaviour: *She knew it probably wasn't necessary any more, but old habits die hard.*
7 habit of thought/mind the way someone usually thinks about something, or their usual attitudes
8 CLOTHING [C] a long loose piece of clothing worn by people in some religious groups: *a nun's habit* → **a creature of habit** at CREATURE (3)

> **WORD CHOICE: habit, custom, tradition, practice**
> A **habit** is something that you do often, because you have done it many times before.
> Do not use **habit** when you are talking about actions or ways of doing things that have existed among a group of people for a very long time. Use **tradition** or **custom**. Use **tradition** when the thing you are referring to has existed for many years, especially when it has been passed down from parents to children: *It is a tradition in his family for all first-born males to be called Peter.* Use **custom** to refer to something that is considered normal or polite, especially when you are talking about other countries or other times: *the Japanese custom of taking off your shoes when you enter someone's house* Use **practice** to talk about the usual way of doing something in a particular area of life: *the practice of killing animals for their fur*

hab·it·a·ble /ˈhæbɪtəbəl/ *adj* good enough for people to live in: *It would cost a fortune to make the place habitable.*

hab·i·tat /ˈhæbɪtæt/ *n* [C,U] the natural home of a plant or animal: *watching monkeys in their **natural habitat*** | *The grassland is an important habitat for many wild flowers.*

hab·i·ta·tion /ˌhæbɪˈteɪʃən/ *n formal* **1** unfit for human habitation a building that is unfit for human habitation is not safe or healthy for people to live in **2** [U] the act of living in a place: *There was no sign of habitation as far as the eye could see.* **3** [C] a house or place to live in

'habit-forming *adj* a drug or activity that is habit-forming makes you want to keep taking it, keep doing it etc

ha·bit·u·al /həˈbɪtʃuəl/ *adj* **1** [only before noun] doing something from habit, and unable to stop doing it: **habitual criminal/offender/felon etc** | **habitual drinker/gambler etc** **2** done as a habit that you cannot stop: *His drinking had become habitual.* **3** [only before noun] usual or typical of someone: *James took his habitual morning walk around the garden.* **—habitually** *adv*: *men who are habitually violent*

ha·bit·u·ate /həˈbɪtʃueɪt/ *v* be/become habituated to (doing) sth *formal* to be used to something or gradually become used to it: *Over the centuries, these animals have become habituated to living in a dry environment.*

ha·bit·u·é /həˈbɪtʃueɪ/ *n* [C +of] *formal* someone who regularly goes to a particular place or event; ≠ regular

ha·ci·en·da /ˌhæsiˈendə/ *n* [C] a large farm in Spanish-speaking countries

hack¹ /hæk/ *v* **1** [I,T] to cut something roughly or violently: **hack (away) at sth** *She hacked away at the ice, trying to make a hole.* | **hack sth off/down etc** *Whole forests have been hacked down.* | **hack your way through/into sth** *He hacked his way through the undergrowth.* | *Both men had been **hacked to death***

(=killed using large knives). **2** [I,T] to secretly find a way of getting information from someone else's computer or changing information on it: [+**into**] *Somebody hacked into the company's central database.* | *He managed to hack the code.* → **HACKER** **3 can't hack sth** *informal* to feel that you cannot continue to do something that is difficult or boring: *I've been doing this job for years, but I just can't hack it anymore.* **4** [I always + adv/prep] *BrE* to ride a horse along roads or through the country **5** [I] to cough in a loud unpleasant way

hack sb **off** *phr v BrE informal* to annoy someone: *His attitude really hacks me off!*

hack² /hæk/ *n* [C] **1** a writer who does a lot of low quality work, especially writing newspaper articles: *A Sunday newspaper hack uncovered the story.* **2** an unimportant politician: *The meeting was attended by the usual old party hacks.* **3** a way of using a computer to get into someone else's computer system without their permission **4** *AmE informal* a taxi, or a taxi driver **5** an act of hitting something roughly with a cutting tool: *One more hack and the branch was off.* **6** an old tired horse **7** a horse you can pay money to ride on **8** *BrE* a ride on a horse: *a long hack across the fields*

hacked 'off *adj BrE informal* extremely annoyed: *I'm getting really hacked off about the whole thing.*

hack·er /'hækə $ -ər/ *n* [C] *informal* someone who secretly uses or changes the information in other people's computer systems: *A hacker had managed to get into the system.* —**hacking** *n* [U]: *Companies are increasingly worried by the threat of hacking and computer viruses.*

hacking 'cough *n* [usually singular] a repeated painful cough with an unpleasant sound

hack·les /'hækəlz/ *n* [plural] **1 sb's hackles rise** if someone's hackles rise, they begin to feel very angry, because someone's behaviour or attitude offends them: *Laura heard his remark, and felt her hackles rising.* | **raise sb's hackles** (=make someone angry) *His tactless remarks were enough to raise anyone's hackles.* **2** the long feathers or hairs on the back of the neck of some animals and birds, which stand up straight when they are in danger

hack·ney car·riage /'hækni ˌkærɪdʒ/ *n* [C] *BrE* **1** a carriage pulled by a horse, used in the past like a taxi **2** also **hackney cab** *formal* a taxi

hack·neyed /'hæknid/ *adj* a hackneyed phrase is boring and does not have much meaning because it has been used so often

hack·saw /'hæksɔ $ -sɒː/ *n* [C] a cutting tool with small teeth on its blade, used especially for cutting metal → see picture at **SAW**

had /d, əd, həd; *strong* hæd/ the past tense and past participle of HAVE

had·dock /'hædək/ *n plural* **haddock** [C,U] a common fish that lives in northern seas and is often used as food

Ha·des /'heɪdiːz/ *n* [U] the land of the dead in the stories of ancient Greece; ▣ **hell**

had·n't /'hædnt/ short for 'had not': *If I hadn't seen it myself, I'd never have believed it.*

hae·ma·tol·o·gy *BrE*; **hematology** *AmE* /ˌhiːmə'tɒlədʒi $ -'tɑː-/ *n* [U] the scientific study of blood

hae·mo·glo·bin *BrE*; **hemoglobin** *AmE* /ˌhiːmə'gləʊbɪn $ -'gloʊ-/ *n* [U] a red substance in the blood that contains iron and carries oxygen

hae·mo·phil·i·a *BrE*; **hemophilia** *AmE* /ˌhiːmə'fɪliə/ *n* [U] a serious disease that prevents a person's blood from becoming thick, so that they lose a lot of blood easily if they are injured

hae·mo·phil·i·ac *BrE*; **hemophiliac** *AmE* /ˌhiːmə'fɪliæk/ *n* [C] a person who suffers from haemophilia

hae·mor·rhage¹ *BrE*; **hemorrhage** *AmE* /'hemərɪdʒ/ *n* [C,U] **1** a serious medical condition in which a person BLEEDS a lot, sometimes inside their body: *He died of a massive brain haemorrhage.* **2** when a company or country loses a lot of money or people very quickly: [+**of**] *We have seen a haemorrhage of jobs from the region.*

haemorrhage² *BrE*; **hemorrhage** *AmE v* **1** [I] to lose a lot of blood in a very short time **2** [T] to lose a lot of something over a short period of time, such as money or jobs: *The once prosperous town has hemorrhaged manufacturing jobs over the last 15 years.*

hae·mor·rhoids *BrE*; **hemorrhoids** *AmE* /'hemərɔɪdz/ *n* [plural] painfully swollen BLOOD VESSELS near a person's ANUS

haft /hɑːft $ hæft/ *n* [C] *technical* a long handle on an AXE¹ or other weapon

hag /hæg/ *n* [C] *old-fashioned* an ugly or unpleasant woman, especially one who is old or looks like a WITCH

hag·gard /'hægəd $ -ərd/ *adj* someone who looks haggard has lines on their face and dark marks around their eyes, especially because they are ill, worried, or tired: *Sam looked tired and haggard.* | *a haggard face*

hag·gis /'hægɪs/ *n* [C,U] a food eaten in Scotland, made from the heart and other organs of a sheep, cut up and boiled in a skin made from the sheep's stomach

hag·gle /'hægəl/ *v* [I] to argue when you are trying to agree about the price of something: [+**over**] *tourists haggling over the price of souvenirs* | [+**with**] *Ted was haggling with the street vendors.* —**haggling** *n* [U]

hag·i·og·ra·phy /ˌhægi'ɒgrəfi $ -'ɑːg-/ *n plural* **hagiographies** [C,U] **1** a book about the lives of SAINTS **2** a book about someone that praises them too much

hah /hɑː/ *interjection* another spelling of HA

ha-'ha *interjection* **1** used in writing to represent a shout of laughter **2** *spoken* used, sometimes angrily, to show that you do not think something is funny: *Oh, very funny, John, ha ha.*

hai·ku /'haɪkuː/ *n plural* **haiku** *or* **haikus** [C] a type of Japanese poem with three lines consisting of five, seven, and five SYLLABLES

hail¹ /heɪl/ *n* **1** [U] frozen rain drops which fall as hard balls of ice: *heavy showers of rain and hail* **2 a hail of bullets/stones etc** a large number of bullets, stones etc that are thrown or fired at someone: *The aircraft were met by a hail of gunfire.* **3 a hail of criticism/abuse etc** a lot of criticism etc: *The proposals met with a hail of criticism.*

hail² *v* **1** [T] to describe someone or something as being very good: **hail sb/sth as sth** *Lang's first film was immediately hailed as a masterpiece.* | **be hailed sth** *The new service has been hailed a success.* | *A young man is being **hailed a hero** tonight after rescuing two children.* **2** [T] to call to someone in order to greet them or try to attract their attention: *She leaned out of the window and hailed a passerby.* | **hail a cab/taxi** *The hotel doorman will hail a cab for you.* **3 it hails** if it hails, small balls of ice fall like rain: *It's windy and hailing outside.*

hail from sth *phr v old-fashioned* to have been born in a particular place: *And where do you hail from?*

Hail Ma·ry /ˌheɪl 'meəri $ -'meri/ *n* [C] a special Roman Catholic prayer to Mary, the mother of Jesus

hail·stone, **hail stone** /'heɪlstəʊn $ -stoʊn/ *n* [C] a small ball of frozen rain

hail·storm /'heɪlstɔːm $ -ɔːrm/ *n* [C] a storm when a lot of HAIL falls

hair ⟨S1⟩ ⟨W1⟩ /heə $ her/ *n* **1** [U] the mass of things like fine threads that grows on your head

brush/comb your hair
do your hair (=arrange it in a style)
have/get your hair cut/done (=by a hairdresser)
short/long hair
shoulder-length hair
fair/blonde hair (=hair that is yellowish-white in colour)
dark hair
red/auburn hair also
ginger hair BrE (=hair that is orangey-brown in colour)
straight/curly hair
frizzy hair (=hair that is tightly curled)
wavy hair (=hair with loose curls)
fine/thick hair
lank hair (=hair that is thin, straight, and unattractive)
dark-haired/fair-haired/long-haired etc
strand of hair (=a thin piece of hair)
lock of hair (=a fairly thick piece of hair)
mop of hair (=a large amount of thick untidy hair)
be losing your hair (=be going bald)
run your fingers through your/sb's hair
ruffle/tousle sb's hair (=make it untidy by rubbing your hand through it)

She put on her lipstick and **brushed her hair**. | *I must get my* **hair cut** – *it's getting very long.* | *You've* **had your hair done** *differently.* | *His* **hair was short** *and dark.* | *a young woman with short* **blonde hair** | *Her long* **wavy hair** *was tied back with a bow.* | *He's a tall,* **fair-haired** *guy.* | *He had a* **mop of** *curly black* **hair**. | *Men are always worrying about* **losing their hair**. | *She kissed him on the cheek and* **ruffled his hair**.

⚠ When you mean 'all the hair on a person's head', **hair** is an uncountable noun: *He has black hair* (NOT *He has black hairs*).

2 [C] one of the long fine things like thread that grows on people's heads and on other parts of their bodies, or similar things that grow on animals: *The cat has left white hairs all over the sofa.* | *I'm starting to get a few grey hairs.* | *I found a hair in my meal.* | **long-haired/short-haired** *long-haired cats*
3 be tearing/pulling your hair out to be very worried or angry about something, especially because you do not know what to do: *Anyone else would have been tearing their hair out trying to work it out.*
4 let your hair down *informal* to enjoy yourself and start to relax, especially after working very hard: *The party gave us all a chance to really let our hair down.*
5 bad hair day a day when your hair does not look tidy or neat even when you try to arrange it carefully – used humorously: *I'm having a bit of a bad hair day.*
6 keep your hair on BrE *spoken* used to tell someone to keep calm and not get annoyed: *All right, all right, keep your hair on! I'm sorry.*
7 get in sb's hair *informal* to annoy someone, especially by always being near them
8 make sb's hair stand on end to make someone very frightened
9 make sb's hair curl if a story, experience etc makes your hair curl, it is very surprising, frightening, or shocking: *tales that would make your hair curl*
10 not have a hair out of place to have a very neat appearance
11 not turn a hair to remain completely calm when something bad or surprising suddenly happens
12 not harm/touch a hair of/on sb's head to not harm someone in any way
13 the hair of the dog (that bit you) alcohol that you drink to cure a headache caused by drinking too much alcohol the night before – used humorously → **have a good/fine/thick etc head of hair** at HEAD¹ (14); → **not see hide nor hair of** at HIDE² (5); → **split hairs** at SPLIT¹ (8)

hair·brush /ˈheəbrʌʃ $ ˈher-/ n [C] a brush you use on your hair to make it smooth → see picture at BRUSH

hair·care, **hair care** /ˈheəkeə $ ˈherker/ n [U] the act of washing and drying your hair and shaping it into a style: *advice on makeup and hair care* —**haircare** *adj* [only before noun]: *haircare products*

hair·cloth /ˈheəklɒθ $ ˈherklɒːθ/ n [U] a type of rough material made from animal hair

hair·cut /ˈheəkʌt $ ˈher-/ n [C] **1** when you have a haircut, someone cuts your hair for you: **have/get a haircut** *I haven't had a haircut for months!* | *You need a haircut!* **2** the style your hair is cut in: *Do you like my new haircut?*

hair·do /ˈheədu $ ˈher-/ n plural **hairdos** [C] informal the style in which someone's hair is cut or shaped; ⊟ **hairstyle**

hair·dress·er /ˈheəˌdresə $ ˈherˌdresər/ n [C] **1** a person who cuts, washes, and arranges people's hair in particular styles; → **barber 2 the hairdresser's** BrE the hairdresser's shop; ⊟ **salon**; → **barber's**: *an appointment at the hairdresser's* —**hairdressing** *n* [U]

hair·dry·er, **hairdrier** /ˈheəˌdraɪə $ ˈherˌdraɪər/ n [C] a machine that blows out hot air for drying hair; → **blow-dryer**

hair·grip /ˈheəgrɪp $ ˈher-/ n [C] BrE a small thin piece of metal that a woman uses to hold her hair in place; ⊟ **bobby pin** AmE

hair·less /ˈheələs $ ˈher-/ adj with no hair: *Young rabbits are born blind and hairless.*

hair·line /ˈheəlaɪn $ ˈher-/ n [C] **1** the line around your head, especially at the front, where your hair starts growing: *He had put on weight, and his hairline was beginning to recede.* **2 a hairline crack/fracture** a very thin crack: *a hairline fracture in a bone*

hair·net /ˈheənet $ ˈher-/ n [C] a very thin net that stretches over your hair to keep it in place

hair·piece /ˈheəpiːs $ ˈher-/ n [C] a piece of false hair that you wear on your head to make your own hair look thicker; → **wig**, **toupée**

hair·pin /ˈheəˌpɪn $ ˈher-/ n [C] a pin made of wire bent into a U-shape to hold long hair in position

hairpin 'bend also **hairpin 'turn** AmE n [C] a very sharp U-shaped curve in a road

'hair-raising adj frightening and dangerous in a way that is exciting: *a hair-raising car chase*

hair's breadth n [singular] a very small amount or distance: *The bullet missed me by a hair's breadth.*

hair 'shirt n [C] a shirt made of rough uncomfortable cloth containing hair, worn in the past by some religious people to punish themselves

'hair slide n [C] BrE a small attractive metal or plastic object that a woman uses to fasten her hair in place; ⊟ **barrette** AmE

'hair-splitting n [U] when people pay too much attention to small differences and unimportant details, especially in an argument → **split hairs** at SPLIT¹ (8)

hair·spray /ˈheəspreɪ $ ˈher-/ n [U] a sticky liquid that you SPRAY on your hair to keep it in place

hair·style /ˈheəstaɪl $ ˈher-/ n [C] the style in which someone's hair has been cut or shaped: *Do you like my new hairstyle?*

hair 'trigger n [C] a TRIGGER¹ on a gun that needs very little pressure to fire the gun

'hair-trigger adj [only before noun] easily made angry: *his hair-trigger temperament*

hair·y /ˈheəri $ ˈheri/ adj comparative **hairier**, superlative **hairiest 1** a hairy person or animal has a lot of hair on their body: *a skinny guy with hairy legs* | *a hairy caterpillar* **2** informal dangerous or frightening, often in a way that is exciting: *It was pretty hairy climbing down the cliff.* | *We had a few hairy moments when I thought the boat was going to sink.* —**hairiness** *n* [U]

haj, **hajj** /hædʒ/ n [C] a journey to Mecca for religious reasons, that all Muslims try to make at least once in their life

haj·ji /ˈhædʒi/ n [C] used as a title for a Muslim who has made a haj

hake /heɪk/ n plural **hake** [C,U] a sea fish, used as food

H

hairstyles

bob

braid

flattop

crew cut

dreadlocks

ponytail

bun

pigtails

mohican

mullet

quiff

perm

ha·kim /hɑːˈkiːm/ *n* [C] a Muslim doctor

ha·lal, **hallal** /hɑːˈlɑːl/ *adj* [only before noun] halal meat is meat from an animal that has been killed in a way that is approved by Muslim law

hal·berd /ˈhælbəd $ -ərd/ *n* [C] a type of sword that was used as a weapon in the past

hal·cy·on /ˈhælsiən/ *adj* **halcyon days** *literary* a time in the past when you were very happy: *She often recalled the halcyon days of her youth.*

hale /heɪl/ *adj* **hale and hearty** someone, especially an old person, who is hale and hearty is very healthy and active: *She's still hale and hearty at 74.*

half¹ S1 W1 /hɑːf $ hæf/ *predeterminer, pron, adj* [only before noun]
1 50% exactly or about 50% (½) of an amount, time, distance, number etc: [+of] *Over half of the children live in one-parent families.* | *Only half the guests had arrived by seven o'clock.* | *If you look at our members, at least half are women.* | **half a mile/pound/hour etc** *half a pound of butter* | *It's about half a mile down the road.* | *She drank half a bottle of wine.* | **half a million dollars** | **a half hour/mile etc** *You can't just waltz in a half hour late.* | *It's about a half mile down the road.* | *a half day excursion to the island* | *He demanded a half share of the money.* | **half the price/size/length etc** *It's*
only half the size of a normal violin. | *They offered to pay half the cost of repairs.*
2 MOST OF the largest part of something: [+of] *We missed half of what he said because someone was talking.* | *She seems to be asleep half the time.* | *Getting covered in mud is half the fun.*
3 TIME half (past) one/two/three etc *BrE* thirty minutes after the hour mentioned: *I rang at about half six.* | *I got home at about half past one.* | *We'll be there by seven or half past.*
4 COMBINATION if something is half one thing and half something else, it is a combination of those two things: *He's half English, half Swiss.*
5 half a dozen a) six: *half a dozen eggs* **b)** a small number of people or things: *There were half a dozen other people in front of me.*
6 half a/the chance a small opportunity to do something, especially one which someone would take eagerly: *I'd go to university if I got half the chance.* | *Many kids would sleep till noon given half a chance.*
7 half an eye/ear if you have half an eye on something or if you are listening with half an ear, you are giving only part of your attention to it: *He listened with only half an ear and his thoughts wandered.* | *The teacher kept half an eye on them all through the lesson.*
8 be half the battle *spoken* used to say that when you have done the most difficult part of an activity, the rest is easy: *Getting the audience to like you is half the battle.*
9 half a minute/moment/second etc *spoken* a very short time: *Hold on, this will only take half a second.*
10 only half the story an explanation that is not complete, used especially to say that someone is trying to keep something secret: *Journalists are convinced that she was only telling them half the story.*
11 have half a mind to do sth *spoken* used to say that you would like to do something but you probably will not do it: *He had half a mind to ask for his money back.* | *I have half a mind to tell your mother about this.*
12 half measures actions or methods that are not strong enough, and so are not effective in dealing with a difficult problem: *This is no time for half measures.*

GRAMMAR
⚠ You do not usually say 'the half': *I've only read half of the story* (NOT *I've only read the half of the story*). The only time you say 'the half' is when you are referring to a particular half: *the first half of the book*
⚠ Do not say 'one and half', 'two and half' etc. Say **one and a half**, **two and a half** etc: *She is two and a half years old.* These numbers are followed by a plural noun, not a singular one: *one and a half days* (NOT *one and a half day*)
⚠ Do not say 'half of hour'. Say **half an hour** or, especially in spoken American English, **a half hour**.

half² S1 W2 *n plural* **halves** /hɑːvz $ hævz/ [C]
1 50% one of two equal parts of something: *Two halves make a whole.* | **one/two etc and a half** (=1½, 2½ etc) *My son's three and a half now.* | *an hour and a half later* | *two and a half thousand people* | **first/second/other half (of sth)** *in the first half of the nineteenth century* | *He kept the other half of the cake for himself.* | **top/bottom/northern etc half (of sth)** *A veil covered the lower half of her face.* | *the southern half of the country* | **break/cut/tear etc sth in half** (=into two equal parts) *She tore the piece of paper in half.* | **reduce/cut sth by half** (=make something 50% smaller) *a plan to cut European forces by half*
2 SPORT one of the two parts into which a sports event is divided: **first/second half** *France played very well in the first half.*
3 PLAYER a player who plays in the middle part of the field in sports like football, RUGBY etc: *the 23-year-old Newcastle* **centre half**
4 BEER *BrE* a half of a PINT of beer: [+of] *Can I have a half of lager, please?*
5 TICKET *BrE* a child's ticket, for example on a bus or train, that is cheaper than an adult's ticket: *One and a*

half to Waterloo, please.

6 a ... and a half *informal* used when you think that something is very unusual or surprising, or very good: *That was a meal and a half!*

7 the half of it *spoken* used to emphasize that a situation is more difficult, complicated, or unpleasant than people realize: *Everyone knows she's a difficult girl, but they don't know the half of it.*

8 your better half/other half *old-fashioned* used humorously to mean your husband or wife: *Let me introduce you to my better half.*

9 not do sth by halves to do something very eagerly and using a lot of care and effort: *I'm sure it will be a fantastic wedding. Eva never does anything by halves.*

10 go halves (on sth) to share something, especially the cost of something, equally between two people: *Do you want to go halves on a pizza?*

11 too clever/rich/good etc by half *BrE informal* very clever, rich etc in an annoying way: *That boy's too arrogant by half.*

12 how the other half lives how people who are much richer or much poorer than you manage their lives, work, money etc

half³ S2 *adv*
1 partly, but not completely: *He was half in the water and half out.* | *She was standing there half dressed, putting on her makeup.* | *The door was only half closed.* | *The jug was still half full.* | *a half-empty wine bottle* | *I was only half awake.* | *He looked half asleep.* | *I was half expecting her to say 'no'.* | *I half hoped that they wouldn't come,* | *I said it half jokingly.*
2 used to emphasize something bad, to say that it is almost an extremely bad thing: *The kitten looked half starved.* | *He was half dead with exhaustion.* | *I had been driven half out of my mind with worry.*
3 a) half as much/big etc half the size, amount etc of something else: *The new machine has all the same functions, but is only half as large.* **b) half as much/big etc again** larger by an amount that is equal to half the original size: *A flat in London costs almost half as much again as a flat in Glasgow.*
4 not half as/so good/interesting etc (as sb/sth) much less good, less interesting etc than something or something else: *The movie wasn't half as entertaining as the book.* | *She can't love you half as much as I do.*
5 not half *BrE spoken* used when you want to emphasize an opinion or statement: *She doesn't half talk once she gets started.*
6 not half bad *spoken* an expression meaning good, used especially when you are rather surprised that something is good: *Actually, the party wasn't half bad.*
7 half and half partly one thing and partly another: *The group was about half and half, complete beginners and people with some experience.*

half-and-'half *n* [U] *AmE* a mixture that is half milk and half cream, used in coffee or tea

half-arsed /ˌhɑːf ˈɑːst◂ $ ˈhæf ɑːrst/ *BrE*; **half-assed** /ˌhɑːf ˈæst $ ˈhæf æst/ *AmE adj* [only before noun] *informal* **1** doing something without making much effort: *He made a half-arsed attempt to clean up after the party.* **2** completely stupid: *What a half-assed idea!*

half·back /ˈhɑːfbæk $ ˈhæf-/ *n* [C] **1** a player in a game of football, RUGBY, HOCKEY etc who plays in the middle part of the field **2** a player in American football who, at the start of play, is behind the front line of players and next to the FULLBACK

half-'baked *adj informal* a half-baked idea, suggestion, plan etc has not been properly planned: *He's always coming out with these half-baked ideas which will never work.*

half 'board, half-board *n* [U] *BrE* the price of a room in a hotel that includes breakfast and dinner: *half board accommodation* → FULL BOARD

half-breed *n* [C] *taboo* a very offensive word for someone whose parents are of different races, espe-

cially one white parent and one Native American parent. Do not use this word; → **mixed race** —**half-breed** *adj*

half-'brother *n* [C] a brother who is the son of only one of your parents; → **half-sister**

half-caste *n* [C] *taboo* a very offensive word for someone whose parents are of different races. Do not use this word; → **mixed race** —**half-caste** *adj*

half 'cocked also **half 'cock** *BrE* **go off half cocked; go off at half cock** *BrE* to do something without enough thought or preparation, so that it is not successful

half-'crazed *adj* behaving in a slightly crazy, uncontrolled way: [+with] *She was half-crazed with pain.*

half 'crown *n* [C] a coin used in Britain before 1971. There were eight half crowns in a pound.

half-'cut *adj BrE old-fashioned* drunk

half 'day, half-day *n* [C] a day when you work or go to school either in the morning or the afternoon, but not all day: *Friday is my half day off.*

half-day *adj* [only before noun] a half-day event takes place in either the morning or the afternoon: *half-day courses on study skills*

half 'dollar *n* [C] an American or Canadian coin worth 50 cents

half-heart·ed /ˌhɑːf ˈhɑːtd◂ $ ˌhæf ˈhɑːr-/ *adj* done without much effort and without much interest in the result: *Congress has made half-hearted attempts at finance reform.* —**half-heartedly** *adv*

half-'holiday *n* [C] *BrE old-fashioned* an afternoon in which children do not have to go school; ▪ **half day**

half-'hour, half hour *n* [C] a period of time that is 30 minutes long: *Fay had been in her room for a good half-hour.* —**half-hour** *adj: a half-hour TV show*

half-'hourly *adj, adv BrE* done or happening every half hour: *Trains depart at half-hourly intervals from 10.30 am until 4.00 pm.*

half-'length *adj* a half-length painting or picture shows the top half of someone's body → FULL-LENGTH¹ (1)

half-'life *n* [C] the length of time it takes a RADIOACTIVE substance to lose half of its RADIOACTIVITY

half-'light *n* [U] the dull grey light you see when it is almost dark but not completely dark: *the cold half-light of the early morning*

half-'mast *n* **at half-mast a)** if a flag is flying at half-mast, it has been raised to the middle of the pole in order to show respect and sadness for someone who has died **b)** *BrE humorous* if a piece of clothing is at half-mast, it is lower down the body than is usual

half 'measures, half-measures *n* [plural] *BrE* actions or methods that are not effective in dealing with the whole of a difficult problem: *Half measures will not fix the health care system.*

half 'moon *n* [C] the shape of the moon when only half of it is showing → FULL MOON, NEW MOON (1)

half nel·son /ˌhɑːf ˈnelsən $ ˌhæf-/ *n* [C] a way of holding your opponent's arm behind their back in the sport of WRESTLING

half 'note *n* [C] *AmE* a musical note which continues for half the length of a WHOLE NOTE; ▪ **minim** *BrE*

half·penny /ˈheɪpni/ *n plural* **halfpennies** [C] a small coin worth half of one PENNY, used in Britain in the past

half 'pipe, half·pipe /ˈhɑːfpaɪp $ ˈhæf-/ *n* [C] **1** a CONCRETE structure which has a rounded bottom and sides and is used for SKATEBOARDING **2** a structure which has a rounded bottom and sides, is made from snow, and is used for SNOWBOARDING

half 'price *n* [U] half the usual price; → **full price: at half price** *Many shoes are at half price or less.* —**half-price** *adj: Half-price tickets will be sold on the day.* —**half price** *adv: Children aged 2–14 go half price.*

ˈhalf-ˌsister n [C] a sister who is the daughter of only one of your parents; → **half-brother**

ˈhalf step n [C] AmE the difference in PITCH between any two notes that are next to each other on a piano; ◻ **semitone**

ˌhalf-ˈterm n [C] BrE a short holiday from school in the middle of a TERM

half-tim·bered /ˌhɑːf ˈtɪmbəd◂ $ ˌhæf ˈtɪmbərd◂/ adj a half-timbered house is usually old and shows the wooden structure of the building on the outside walls

ˌhalf-ˈtime, half time n [U] a short period of rest between two parts of a game, such as football or BASKET-BALL: **at half-time** The score at half-time was 34–7. | Another penalty from Roberts gave Gloucester a half-time lead. → **FULL TIME**

half·tone /ˌhɑːfˈtəʊn◂ $ ˈhæftoʊn/ n **1** [U] a method of printing black and white photographs that shows different shades of grey by changing the number of black DOTS in an area of the photograph **2** [C] a photograph printed by this method

ˈhalf-truth n [C] a statement that is only partly true, especially one that is intended to keep something secret: His replies were full of evasions and half-truths.

half·way /ˌhɑːfˈweɪ◂ $ ˌhæf-/ adj, adv **1** at a middle point in space or time between two things; ◻ **partway**: [+through/up/down/between etc] He chased Kevin halfway up the stairs. | It was a terrible film – I left halfway through. | traffic queues stretching back halfway to London | **the halfway stage/mark/point** They've just reached the halfway stage of the project. **2** be halfway there to have done something that will allow you to achieve something else: Establish the right relationships at work and you're halfway there. **3** be/come/go halfway to doing sth to achieve something partly but not completely: We're still only halfway to finishing the job. **4** halfway decent/normal/successful etc informal reasonably good, normal, successful etc: the only halfway decent hotel around here → **meet sb halfway** at MEET¹ (19)

ˌhalfway ˈhouse n **1** [singular] BrE something which is a combination of the qualities of two different things: Belief is a kind of halfway house between non-belief and absolute proof. **2** [C] a place for former prisoners or people who have had problems such as mental illness, where they can live until they are ready to live on their own

ˈhalf-wit n [C] informal a stupid person —**ˌhalf-ˈwitted** adj: I'm not half-witted, you know.

ˌhalf-ˈyearly adj, adv done or happening every six months: half-yearly meetings | The interest you earn will be paid half-yearly in June and December.

hal·i·but /ˈhælɪbət/ n plural **halibut** [C] a large flat sea fish used as food

hal·i·to·sis /ˌhælɪˈtəʊsɪs $ -ˈtoʊ-/ n [U] technical a condition in which someone's breath smells very bad; ◻ **bad breath**

hall S1 W2 /hɔːl $ hɒːl/ n [C]
1 ENTRANCE the area just inside the door of a house or other building, that leads to other rooms; ◻ **hallway: in the hall** We hung our coats in a cupboard in the hall. | a huge tiled **entrance hall**
2 CORRIDOR a passage in a building or house that leads to many of the rooms; ◻ **corridor, hallway**: Each floor had ten rooms on both sides of the hall.
3 PUBLIC BUILDING a building or large room for public events such as meetings or dances: **sports/exhibition/banqueting etc hall** The school has a new sports hall. | Five hundred people filled the lecture hall. | **church/village hall** (=used by people who live in a place) A coffee morning is to be held in the village hall. | a concert at Carnegie Hall → **CITY HALL** (2), CONCERT HALL, DANCE HALL, MUSIC HALL (2), TOWN HALL
4 FOR STUDENTS especially BrE a college or univer-

sity building where students live; ◻ **hall of residence**; ◻ **dorm** AmE: **in hall** For a brief time they had shared a room in hall.

hal·lal /hɑːˈlɑːl/ adj another spelling of HALAL

hal·le·lu·jah /ˌhælɪˈluːjə/ interjection used to express thanks, JOY, or praise to God —**hallelujah** n [C]

hall·mark¹ /ˈhɔːlmɑːk $ ˈhɒːlmɑːrk/ n [C] **1** an idea, method, or quality that is typical of a particular person or thing: [+of] These hotels still offer the sort of service which were the hallmarks of the grand days of travel. | The explosion **had all the hallmarks of** a terrorist attack. | Their performance did not **bear the hallmark** of European champions. **2** a mark put on silver, gold, or PLATINUM that shows the quality of the metal, and where and when it was made

hallmark² v [T] to put a hallmark on silver, gold, or PLATINUM

hal·lo /həˈləʊ, hæ- $ -ˈloʊ/ interjection an old-fashioned British spelling of HELLO

ˌHall of ˈFame n [C] in the US, a list of famous sports players or a building where their uniforms, equipment and information about them are shown

ˌhall of ˈresidence n [C] BrE a college or university building where students live; ◻ **dorm** AmE

hal·lowed /ˈhæləʊd $ -loʊd/ adj **1** holy or made holy by religious practices; → **sacred**: The bones will be buried in **hallowed ground**. **2** important and respected by a lot of people: the **hallowed halls** of government | hallowed traditions

Hal·low·een, Hallowe'en /ˌhæləʊˈiːn◂ $ -loʊ-/ n [U] the night of October 31st, which is now celebrated by children, who dress in COSTUMES and go from house to house asking for sweets, especially in the US and Canada. In the past, people believed the souls of dead people appeared on Halloween.

hal·lu·ci·nate /həˈluːsɪneɪt/ v [I] to see or hear things that are not really there

hal·lu·ci·na·tion /həˌluːsɪˈneɪʃən/ n [C,U] something which you imagine you can see or hear, but which is not really there, or the experience of this: The patients suffered hallucinations caused by the drug.

hal·lu·ci·na·to·ry /həˈluːsɪnətəri $ -tɔːri/ adj formal **1** causing hallucinations or resulting from hallucinations: hallucinatory drugs **2** using strange images, sounds etc like those experienced in a hallucination: hallucinatory poetry

hal·lu·cin·o·gen /həˈluːsɪnədʒən/ n [C] a substance that causes hallucinations

hal·lu·cin·o·gen·ic /həˌluːsɪnəˈdʒenɪk◂/ adj hallucinogenic drugs make people experience hallucinations

hall·way /ˈhɔːlweɪ $ ˈhɒːl-/ n [C] **1** the area just inside the door of a house or other building, that leads to other rooms; ◻ **hall 2** a passage in a building or house that leads to many of the rooms; ◻ **hall, corridor**

ha·lo /ˈheɪləʊ $ -loʊ/ n plural **halos** [C] **1** a bright circle that is often shown above or around the heads of holy people in religious art **2** a circle of light or something bright: [+of] a halo of sunlight | a halo of blonde curls

hal·o·gen /ˈhælədʒən/ n [U] **1** a halogen light uses halogen gas to produce light: **halogen bulb/lamp/light etc 2** one of a group of five simple chemical substances that make COMPOUNDS easily

ha·lon /ˈheɪlɒn $ -lɑːn/ n [U] technical a COMPOUND gas that damages the OZONE LAYER

halt¹ /hɔːlt $ hɒːlt/ n **1** [singular] a stop or pause: Heavy snowfalls **brought** traffic **to a halt** (=made it stop moving). | The World Championship was **brought to a temporary halt** (=was stopped from continuing). | **come/grind/screech etc to a halt** (=stop moving or continuing) The whole process seems to have ground to a halt. | Joe slammed on the brakes and the car skidded to a halt. | The President has **called for a halt** to the wave of emigration. ⚠ Do not say 'get to a halt'. Say 'come to a halt'. **2 call a halt (to sth)** to stop an activity from continuing: *I urge those responsible to call a halt to the violence.* **3** [C] *BrE* a place in the countryside where a train stops to let passengers get off, but where there is no station

halt² v **1** [T] to prevent someone or something from continuing – used especially in news reports; ⬛ **stop**: *The government has failed to halt economic decline.* | *Safety concerns have led them to halt work on the dam.* **2** [I] to stop moving: *The parade halted by a busy corner.* **3 halt!** used as a military order to tell someone to stop moving or soldiers to stop marching: *Company halt!* | *Halt! Who goes there?*

hal·ter /ˈhɔːltə $ ˈhɔːltər/ n [C] **1** a rope or leather band that fastens around a horse's head, usually used to lead the horse **2** also **halter top, halterneck** a type of clothing for women that ties behind the neck and across the back, so that the arms and back are not covered: *Jen was wearing black shorts and a halter.*

halt·ing /ˈhɔːltɪŋ $ ˈhɔːl-/ adj if your speech or movements are halting, you stop for a moment between words or movements, especially because you are not confident; ⬛ **hesitant**: *We carried on a rather halting conversation.* —**haltingly** adv

halve /hɑːv $ hæv/ v [T] **1** to reduce something by a half: *Cash cuts have halved the number of places available on training courses.* **2** to cut or divide something into two equal pieces: *Halve the potatoes lengthwise.*

halves /hɑːvz $ hævz/ **1** the plural of HALF **2 go halves (with sb)** *BrE* if you go halves with someone, you divide something equally between you, especially money

hal·yard /ˈhæljəd $ -ərd/ n [C] *technical* a rope used to raise or lower a flag or sail

ham¹ /hæm/ n **1** [C,U] the upper part of a pig's leg, or the meat from this that has been preserved with salt or smoke; → **gammon**: *a ham sandwich* | *a seven-pound ham* **2** [C] someone who receives and sends radio messages for fun rather than as their job **3** [C] *informal* an actor who performs with too much false emotion

ham² v **hammed, hamming ham it up** *informal* to perform with too much false emotion when acting

ham·burg·er /ˈhæmbɜːgə $ -bɜːrgər/ n **1** [C] a flat round piece of finely cut BEEF (=meat from a cow) which is cooked and eaten in a bread BUN → see picture at **FAST FOOD 2** [U] *AmE* beef that has been cut into very small pieces; ⬛ **mince** *BrE*

ham-fist·ed /ˌhæm ˈfɪstɪd◂/ also **ham-ˈhanded** adj *informal* **1** not at all skilful or careful in the way that you deal with people; ⬛ **inept**: *They made several ham-fisted attempts to spy on her.* **2** not at all skilful with your hands; ⬛ **clumsy**

ham·let /ˈhæmlɪt/ n [C] a very small village

ham·mer¹ /ˈhæmə $ -ər/ n [C]
1 TOOL a) a tool with a heavy metal part on a long handle, used for hitting nails into wood **b)** a tool like this with a wooden head used to make something flat, make a noise etc: *an auctioneer's hammer* → see picture at TOOL
2 come/go under the hammer to be offered for sale at an AUCTION
3 hammer blow *BrE* an event that damages something very seriously: [+**for**] *The decision is a hammer blow for the coal industry.*
4 hammer and tongs *informal* **a)** if people go at each other hammer and tongs, they fight or argue very loudly **b)** if someone does something hammer and tongs, they do it with all their energy
5 GUN the part of a gun that hits the explosive CHARGE that fires a bullet
6 SPORT a heavy metal ball on a wire with a handle at the end, which you throw as far as possible as a sport
7 PIANO a wooden part of a PIANO that hits the strings inside to make a musical sound

hammer² v
1 HIT WITH A HAMMER [I,T] to hit something with a

hammer in order to force it into a particular position or shape: **hammer sth in/into sth** *Hammer the nails into the back of the frame.* | **hammer away (at sth)** *All afternoon, Martin had been hammering away in the conservatory.* | *the sound of hammering and sawing*
2 HIT REPEATEDLY [I] to hit something many times, especially making a loud noise; ⬛ **pound, bang**: [+**at**] *Daniella hammered at the door.* | *The rain was hammering against the window.*
3 HURT WITH PROBLEMS [T] to hurt someone or something by causing them a lot of problems: *British industry was being hammered by the recession.*
4 HIT HARD [T] *informal* to hit or kick something very hard: *Robinson hammered the ball into the goal.*
5 CRITICIZE [T] to strongly criticize or attack someone for something they have said or done: *The president has been hammered for his lack of leadership.*
6 hammer sth home to make sure that people understand something by repeating it many times: *The message must be hammered home that crime doesn't pay.*
7 HEART [I] if your heart hammers, you feel it beating strongly and quickly; ⬛ **pound**: *She stood outside the door, her heart hammering.*
8 DEFEAT [T] *informal* to defeat someone completely at a sport: *Arsenal hammered Manchester United 5–0.*
hammer away phr v
1 to keep saying something because you want people to understand or accept it: [+**at**] *I keep hammering away at this point because it's important.*
2 to work hard and continuously at something: [**at**] *You need to keep on hammering away at achieving your goals.*
hammer sth ⇔ in also **hammer sth into sb** phr v to keep saying something until people completely understand it: *The coach hammered his message into the team.*
hammer sth ⇔ out phr v to decide on an agreement, contract etc after a lot of discussion and disagreement: *Leading oil producers tried to hammer out a deal.*

hammer and ˈsickle n [singular] **1** the sign of a hammer crossing a SICKLE on a red background, used as a sign of COMMUNISM **2** the flag of the former Soviet Union

ham·mered /ˈhæməd $ -ərd/ adj [not before noun] *informal* very drunk

ham·mer·ing /ˈhæmərɪŋ/ n [singular, U] **1 take a hammering/be given a hammering** to be attacked or defeated very severely: *The city took a real hammering during the war.* **2** the sound of someone hitting something with a hammer or with their hands: *There was a loud hammering at the door.*

ham·mock /ˈhæmək/ n [C] a large piece of cloth that is hung between two trees or posts so that you can sleep in it → see picture at BED

ham·my /ˈhæmi/ adj if a performance by an actor is hammy, it is done with too much false emotion

ham·per¹ /ˈhæmpə $ -ər/ v [T] to make it difficult for someone to do something: *She tried to run, but was hampered by her heavy suitcase.* | *An attempt to rescue the men has been hampered by bad weather.*

hamper² n [C] **1** *BrE* a basket with a lid, which is used for carrying food or sending it to someone as a present: *a picnic hamper* | *They sent us a lovely Christmas hamper.* → see picture at BASKET **2** *AmE* a large basket that you put dirty clothes in until they can be washed; ⬛ **laundry basket** *BrE*

ham·ster /ˈhæmstə $ -ər/ n [C] a small animal that looks like a mouse with no tail

ham·string¹ /ˈhæmˌstrɪŋ/ n [C] a TENDON behind your knee, which sometimes gets injured when you do sport: *He pulled a hamstring in training.* | **hamstring injury/problem/strain etc**

hamstring² *v past tense and past participle* **hamstrung** /-strʌŋ/ [T] to make someone unable to take the action they want or need to take, especially by restricting them: *The President feels he is hamstrung by Congress.*

---

hand

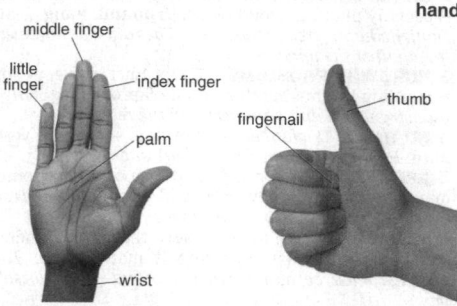

middle finger

little finger   index finger

     thumb

fingernail

palm

wrist

hand¹ [S1] [W1] /hænd/ *n*

1 PART OF BODY [C] the part of your body at the end of your arm, including your fingers and thumb, that you use to hold things

> **sb's left/right hand**
> **in sb's hand**
> **the palm of your hand** (=the inside surface of your hand)
> **the back of your hand** (=the outside surface of your hand)
> **wave your hand**
> **clap your hands**
> **hold hands (with sb)**
> **shake sb's hand** also
> **shake hands (with sb)** (=as a greeting)
> **take sb by the hand** (=hold someone's hand in order to take them somewhere)
> **join hands** (=take hold of someone's hand, for example in a dance)
> **clasp your hands** (=hold them together tightly)
> **fold your hands** (=put them together and rest them on something)
> **raise your hand** also
> **put your hand up** *BrE* (=lift your hand in the air, especially to show that you want to answer or ask a question)
> **on (your) hands and knees** (=in a crawling position)
> **with your bare hands** (=without using a tool, weapon, machine etc)

> *Go wash your hands.* | *Steve gripped the steering wheel tightly with both hands.* | *He held the pencil in his* **right hand**. | *In her hand was a tattered old photograph.* | *a small book, no bigger than the* **palm of** *my hand* | *She* **waved** *her* **hand** *to the crowd.* | *They were laughing and cheering and* **clapping** *their* **hands**. | *The young couple were* **holding hands**. | *The two leaders* **shook hands**. | *Marika* **took** *the child* **by the hand** *and led her away.* | *They all* **joined hands** *in a big circle.* | *Sally sat with her* **hands folded** *in her lap.* | **Raise** *your* **hand** *if you know the answer.* | *I had to get down* **on my hands and knees** *and look under the settee.* | *He was capable of killing a man* **with his bare hands**.

2 HELP a hand help with something – used in the following phrases: **need/want a hand** *Do you need a hand packing?* | **give/lend (sb) a hand** *Can you give me a hand to lift this?* | *If you get stuck, Denise is always willing to lend a hand.* | **I could do with a hand/use a hand** (=it would be useful to have some help) *We could certainly do with a hand.* → A HELPING HAND at HELP¹ (9); → see box at **HELP¹**

3 CONTROL [singular, U] control, power, or influence that someone has: *The President has* **strengthened the hand** *of the gun lobby.* | *This matter is too important to be left* **in the hands of** (=in the control of) *an inexperi-*

enced lawyer. | *a manager with* **a firm hand** (=who controls things strictly)

4 get out of hand if a situation or person gets out of hand, they become impossible to control any longer: *The previously peaceful demonstration seemed to be getting out of hand.*

5 on the other hand also **on the one hand . . . on the other hand** used to give another opinion or fact that should be considered as well as the one you have just given: *I'd like to eat out, but on the other hand I should be trying to save money.* ⚠ Do not say 'on one hand'. Say **on the one hand.**

6 hands off *spoken* used to say that someone cannot have, take, or touch something: *Hey! Hands off that CD! It's mine!* | *Tell your little brother to* **keep** *his* **hands off** *my car.* → HANDS-OFF

7 in hand a) if something is in hand, it is being done or dealt with: *Plans are in hand to perform 'Oz' next semester.* | *Lisa seemed to* **have** *things* **in hand** *by the time he returned.* | **job/task/matter etc in hand** *Our officers have to concentrate 100 per cent on the task in hand.* | **take sb in hand** (=begin to deal with someone's problems etc) **b)** *BrE* if you work a week, a month etc in hand, you do not get paid until after you have worked two weeks, two months etc **c)** *BrE* if you have time, money etc in hand, you have it available: *I usually have a few days' leave in hand at the end of the year.* **d)** *BrE* if a team or player has a game in hand in a competition, they still have another game to play in which they could gain more points

8 in the hands of sb/in sb's hands being dealt with or cared for by someone: *The matter is in the hands of the police.* | **in good/safe/capable etc hands** *You can be sure your children are in good hands.* | *The fear is that nuclear secrets could* **fall into the wrong hands**. ⚠ Do not say 'in the hands of' someone. Say **in the hands of someone.** → A SAFE PAIR OF HANDS at SAFE¹ (11)

9 hands up a) with your arms straight up in the air – used especially to tell someone to do this as a sign that they will not attack you: *Hands up! You're under arrest!* | *The men emerged from the building with their hands up.* **b)** used to tell people to put their arm straight up in the air if they know the answer to a question or want to say something: *Hands up if you agree with what Eric was saying.*

10 at hand *formal* **a)** likely to happen soon: *Recent economic performance suggests that a major crisis is at hand.* **b)** close to you and available to be used: *Don't worry,* **help is at hand**! **c)** needing to be dealt with now: *Peter turned his attention to the task at hand.*

11 to hand *BrE* something that is to hand is close to you, so that you can reach it easily

12 on hand close by and ready when needed: *Our staff are always on hand to help.*

13 by hand a) done or made by a person rather than a machine: *We had to wash our clothes by hand.* **b)** delivered by someone personally, rather than being sent through the post, emailed etc

14 (at) first hand if you know or experience something first hand, you have personal experience of it: *an opportunity to view at first hand the workings of the court*

15 (at) second/third/fourth hand if you know something second, third etc hand, someone tells you about it, but you have no personal experience of it: *Until now, information has been second or third hand, but this news comes from someone who was there.*

16 at the hands of sb caused or done by a particular person – used about something bad or unpleasant that someone does: *Anyone who* **suffered at the hands of** *care workers will be entitled to compensation.* | *This is their third defeat at the hands of the world champions.*

17 get your hands on sth *informal* to succeed in getting something: *She's only marrying him to get her hands on his money.*

18 lay your hands on sth to find or get something: *I would read any book I could lay my hands on.*

19 come to hand if something comes to hand, it is there for you to use – used especially about something that is there by chance: *They ran, picking up whatever weapons came to hand.*

20 get your hands on sb *spoken* to catch someone you are angry with: *Just wait till I get my hands on you!*

21 have a hand in sth to influence or be involved in something: *He had a hand in both goals.*

22 hand in hand **a)** (go) hand in hand if two things go hand in hand, they are closely connected: *Wealth and power go hand in hand in most societies.* | [+with] *They say that genius often goes hand in hand with madness.* **b)** if two people walk, stand etc hand in hand, they walk, stand etc while they are holding each other's hand: *They walked hand in hand in silence up the path.*

23 have sth/sb on your hands to have a difficult job, problem, situation etc to deal with: *I'm afraid we have a murder on our hands, Inspector.*

24 be off your hands if something or someone is off your hands, you are not responsible for them any more: *Once this problem is off our hands we can relax for a while.* | take sb/sth off sb's hands *She wants someone to take the kids off her hands occasionally.*

25 try your hand at (doing) sth to try to do something you have not tried before: *John dreamed of being a writer and had tried his hand at poetry.*

26 turn your hand to (doing) sth to do something well, even if it is the first time you have tried: *Larry's one of those men who can turn their hand to anything.*

27 out of hand without even stopping to consider what someone has suggested, asked for etc: **reject/dismiss/refuse etc sth out of hand** *Aromatherapy was dismissed out of hand by traditional doctors.*

28 hands down easily: **win (sth)/beat sb hands down** *Nigel always won hands down in any argument.*

29 have your hands full to be very busy or too busy: *Can't it wait? I already have my hands full.*

30 good with your hands skilful at making things

31 on either/every hand *written* on both sides or in every direction: *Thick forest stood on either hand.*

32 get your hands dirty **a)** *informal* to do hard or dirty physical work – usually used in questions or negative statements: *It's not that the jobs aren't there, it's just that she doesn't want to get her hands dirty.* **b)** to get involved in the difficult, dishonest, or unpleasant side of something: *He never talked to the media or got his hands dirty in any way.*

33 keep your hand in to do something that you used to do a lot, so you do not forget how to do it: *You should at least work part-time, just to keep your hand in.*

34 hand in glove closely connected with someone, especially in an illegal activity: *Far from being independent, the government and media work hand in glove.*

35 hand over fist *informal* if you gain or lose something hand over fist, you gain or lose it very quickly: *Five years ago, the company was losing money hand over fist.*

36 a big hand *spoken* used to tell the people who are watching a performance to CLAP or CHEER loudly: *Let's all give the girls a big hand.*

37 all hands on deck also **all hands to the pumps** *BrE informal* used to say that everyone is needed to help in a particular situation: *With only half an hour to get everything ready, it was all hands on deck.*

38 the left hand does not know what the right hand is doing used to say that two parts of an organization that should be doing the same thing are each doing different things without the other knowing.

39 WORKER [C] someone who does physical work on a farm, factory, ship etc: *The farm hands slept in a narrow hut next to the barn.*

40 CARDS [C] **a)** the playing cards given to one person in a game: *a winning hand* **b)** a single game of cards

41 CLOCK [C] a long thin piece of metal that points at the numbers on a clock: **hour/minute/second hand**; → see picture at WATCH

42 WRITING [singular] *old-fashioned* someone's HANDWRITING

43 sb's hands are tied if someone's hands are tied, they cannot help in a particular situation because of rules, laws etc: *The bank claims its hands are tied by federal regulators.*

44 tie/bind sb hand and foot **a)** to tie up someone's hands and feet **b)** to make it very difficult or impossible for someone to do what they think is best

45 can do sth with one hand (tied) behind your back *spoken* used to say that you can do something very easily

46 not do a hand's turn *BrE old-fashioned informal* to do no work at all

47 sb's hand (in marriage) *old-fashioned* permission for a man to marry a particular woman: *He asked for her hand in marriage.*

48 HORSE [C] a unit for measuring the height of a horse, equal to about 10 centimetres → CASH-IN-HAND, FREEHAND, HANDS-ON, LEFT-HAND, RIGHT-HAND; → be an old hand (at sth) at OLD (17); → bite the hand that feeds you at BITE[1] (15); → have blood on your hands at BLOOD[1] (2); → have your hands/fingers in the till at TILL[2] (3); → force sb's hand at FORCE[2] (7); → overplay your hand at OVERPLAY (2); → shake sb's hand/shake hands with sb at SHAKE[1] (4); → wash your hands of sth at WASH[1] (5)

hand[2] [S2] [W2] v [T]

1 to give something to someone else with your hand: **hand sb sth** *He handed the teacher a slip of paper.* | **hand sth to sb** *He lit a cigarette and handed it to her.* | *This form must be handed to all employees.*

2 you have to hand it to sb *spoken* used to say that you admire someone: *You have to hand it to her. She's really made a success of that company.*

hand sth ⇔ **around** also **hand sth round** *BrE phr v* to offer something to each person in a group: *Willie helped hand the mugs around.*

hand sth ⇔ **back** *phr v*

1 to give something back to the person who gave it to you, with your hand: [+to] *Kurt examined the document and handed it back to her.* | **hand sb sth** ⇔ **back** *She handed him his pen back.*

2 to give something back to the person who used to own it: [+to] *The land was handed back to its original owner.* | **hand sb sth** ⇔ **back** *The government has promised to hand investors back their money.*

hand sth ⇔ **down** *phr v*

1 to give or leave something to people who will live after you: [+to] *The ring was handed down to her from her grandmother.* | *stories handed down by word of mouth* → HAND-ME-DOWN

2 hand down a decision/ruling/sentence etc to officially announce a decision, punishment etc

hand sth ⇔ **in** *phr v* to give something to someone in authority: *Tom has handed in his resignation.* | *Did you hand your homework in on time?*

hand sth ⇔ **on** *phr v* to give something to someone: *The clock was handed on from Kevin's father.* | *He was accused of handing on government secrets.*

hand sth ⇔ **out** *phr v* to give something to each person in a group; **☐ distribute:** *Could you start handing these books out please?* | [+to] *He was handing out leaflets to members of the audience.* → HANDOUT

hand over *phr v*

1 hand sth ⇔ over to give something to someone with your hand, especially because they have asked for it or should have it: *The soldiers were ordered to hand over their guns.* | [+to] *He handed the phone over to me.*

2 to give someone power or responsibility over something which you used to be in charge of: **hand sth** ⇔ **over (to sb)** *On his retirement, he handed the business over to his son.* | *Political control has been handed over to religious leaders.* | [+to] *Now she feels the time has come to hand over to someone else.*

hand·bag [S3] /ˈhændbæg/ *n* [C] a small bag in which a woman carries money and personal things; **☐ purse** *AmE*; → see picture at BAG

[1] 000, [2] 000, [3] 000, most frequent words in [S]poken and [W]ritten English

hand·ball /'hændbɔːl $ -bɒːl/ *n* **1** [U] a game in which two teams try to score points by throwing or hitting a ball with their hands **2** [U] a game in which players hit a ball against a wall with their hand **3** [C] a ball that is used to play handball **4** [C,U] the act of touching the ball with your hands in a game of football, which is not allowed: *The referee gave a free kick for handball.*

hand·bill /'hænd,bɪl/ *n* [C] a small printed notice or advertisement that is given to people: *Students distributed handbills calling for better funding for schools.*

hand·book /'hændbʊk/ *n* [C] a short book that gives information or instructions about something: *the Fiction Writer's Handbook*

hand·brake /'hændbreɪk/ *n* [C] *BrE* a BRAKE in a car that you pull up with your hand to stop the car from moving when it is parked; ⊟ **emergency brake** *AmE*; → see picture at CAR

hand·car /'hændkɑ $ -kɑːr/ *n* [C] *AmE* a small railway vehicle that people move along by pushing large handles up and down

hand·cart /'hændkɑːt $ -kɑːrt/ *n* [C] a small vehicle that you push or pull by hand and use for carrying goods

hand·clap /'hændklæp/ *n* *BrE* **slow handclap** if people give someone a slow handclap, they hit their hands together slowly to show that they disapprove of them

hand·craft·ed /'hænd,krɑːftɪ̣d $ -,kræft-/ *adj* skilfully made by hand, not by machine; ⊟ **handmade**: *a handcrafted rocking chair*

hand·cuff /'hændkʌf/ *v* [T] to put handcuffs on someone

hand·cuffs /'hændkʌfs/ *n* [plural] a pair of metal rings joined by a chain. Handcuffs are used for holding a prisoner's wrists together: *They put handcuffs on the two men and led them away.* | *in handcuffs He was brought into the court in handcuffs.* | *a pair of handcuffs* → see picture at LOCK

hand-eye co-ordi'nation *n* [U] the way in which your hands and eyes work together, especially in sport, so that you can throw, hit, and catch a ball

hand·ful /'hændfʊl/ *n* **1** [C] an amount that you can hold in your hand: [+of] *The boy picked up a handful of stones and started throwing them at us.* **2 a handful of sth** a very small number of people or things: *There were only a handful of people there.* **3 be a handful** *informal* someone, especially a child, who is difficult to control: *She's a lovely child, but she can be a bit of a handful sometimes.*

hand gre,nade *n* [C] a small bomb that you throw

hand·gun /'hændgʌn/ *n* [C] a small gun that you hold in one hand when you fire it

hand-'held *adj* a hand-held machine is small enough to hold in your hand when you use it: *a hand-held camera* | *hand-held video games*

hand·held /'hændheld/ *n* [C] a PDA

hand·hold /'hændhəʊld $ -hoʊld/ *n* [C] a part of something that you can hold onto when climbing it

hand·i·cap¹ /'hændikæp/ *n* [C] **1** *old-fashioned* if someone has a handicap, a part of their body or their mind has been permanently injured or damaged. Many people think that this word is offensive. **2** a situation that makes it difficult for someone to do what they want: *Not speaking the language is a real handicap.* **3** an advantage that is given to a weaker player in a game of GOLF: *He's improved a lot, and his handicap has come down from 18 to 12.* **4** a race for horses in which the best horses carry extra weight so that all the horses have an equal chance of winning

handicap² *v* **handicapped**, **handicapping** [T] to make it difficult for someone to do something that they want or need to do: *The charity is handicapped by lack of funds.*

hand·i·capped /'hændikæpt/ *adj old-fashioned* **1** if someone is handicapped, a part of their body or their mind has been permanently injured or damaged. Some people think that this word is offensive: *a special school for mentally handicapped children* **2 the handicapped** [plural] people who are handicapped. Some people think that this expression is offensive; → DISABLED

handicrafts

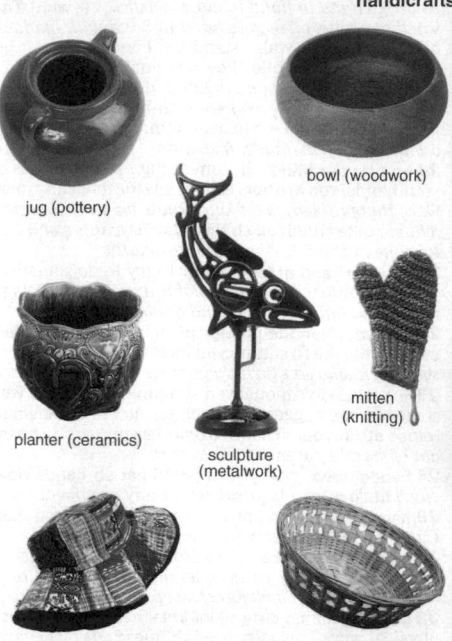

jug (pottery)

bowl (woodwork)

planter (ceramics)

sculpture (metalwork)

mitten (knitting)

hat (patchwork)

basket (weaving)

hand·i·craft /'hændikrɑːft $ -kræft/ also **craft** *n* [C usually plural] **1** an activity such as sewing or making baskets, in which you use your hands in a skilful way to make things **2** something that someone has made in a skilful way using their hands: *a shop selling pottery and traditional handicrafts*

hand·i·ly /'hændɪ̣li/ *adv* **1** something that is handily placed is in a position where it can easily be reached or used: *She kept the key handily by the back door.* **2** *AmE* if you win something handily, you win easily

hand·i·work /'hændiwɜːk $ -wɜːrk/ *n* [U] **sb's handiwork a)** something that someone has made or done using their hands in a skilful way: *She stood back and admired her handiwork.* **b)** something that someone has done or caused: *The explosion looks like the handiwork of terrorists.*

hand job *n* [C] *informal* the act of touching or rubbing a man's sex organs to give him sexual pleasure

hand·ker·chief /'hæŋkətʃɪf $ -kər-/ *n* [C] a piece of cloth that you use for drying your nose or eyes; ⊟ **hankie**

han·dle¹ ⟦S2⟧ ⟦W2⟧ /'hændl/ *v*
1 ⟦DO WORK⟧ [T] to do the things that are necessary to complete a job: *I handled most of the paperwork.* | *The case is being handled by a top lawyer.* | *The finance department handles all the accounts.* | *Computers can handle huge amounts of data.*
2 ⟦DEAL WITH A SITUATION⟧ [T] to deal with a situation or problem by behaving in a particular way and making particular decisions: *The headmaster handled the situation very well.* | *I knew I had handled the matter badly.* | *Leave it to me. I can handle it.* | *Most customers were satisfied with the way their complaints were handled.* | *Opposition leaders will be watching carefully to see how the Prime Minister handles the crisis.*
3 ⟦DEAL WITH A PERSON⟧ [T] to deal with a person or behave towards them in a particular way, especially in

order to keep them happy: *Martin might be useful to us, but he would have to be handled carefully.* | *Some customers are quite difficult to handle.*

4 NOT BECOME UPSET [T] to not become upset in a difficult situation: *She can't handle it when people criticize her.* | *He doesn't handle stress very well.*

5 HOLD [T] to touch something or pick it up and hold it in your hands: *He had never handled a weapon before.* | *We teach the children to handle the animals gently.* | *He was roughly handled by the mob.*

6 CONTROL A VEHICLE a) [T] to control the movement of a vehicle or an animal: *I didn't know if I'd be able to handle such a large vehicle.* **b)** [I] the way a vehicle handles is how easy it is to control: **handles well/badly** *The car handles well, even on wet roads.*

7 MOVE GOODS [T] to move goods from one place to another: *The Post Office handles nearly 2 billion letters and parcels over the Christmas period.*

8 BUY/SELL GOODS [T] to buy or sell goods: *Bennet was charged with* **handling stolen goods.**

handle² [S3] *n* [C]
1 the part of a door that you use for opening it: *Then he turned the handle and went in.*
2 the part of an object that you use for holding it: *a knife with a carved wooden handle* | *the handle of his cup* | *a broom handle*
3 get a handle on sth to start to understand a situation, subject etc: *It's difficult to get a handle on how widespread this problem is.* → **fly off the handle** at FLY¹ (16)

han·dle·bar mous·tache /ˌhændlbɑː məˈstɑːʃ $ -bɑːr ˈmʌstæʃ/ *n* [C] a long thick MOUSTACHE which curves upwards at both ends

han·dle·bars /ˈhændlbɑːz $ -bɑːrz/ *n* [plural] also **handlebar** the bar above the front wheel of a bicycle or MOTORCYCLE that you turn to control its direction → see picture at BICYCLE¹

han·dler /ˈhændlə $ -ər/ *n* [C] **1** someone who trains an animal, especially a dog: *a police dog handler* **2** someone who touches, carries, or moves things as their job: *All food handlers should be properly trained.* | *baggage handlers at the airport* **3** someone who helps and advises an important person: *She is kept well away from the press by her handlers.*

hand·ling /ˈhændlɪŋ/ *n* [U] **1** the way in which someone does a job or deals with a situation, problem, or person: [+of] *The President has been much criticized for his handling of the crisis.* | *Such a situation needs very careful handling.* **2** the act of touching something: *The equipment should be able to withstand a certain amount of rough handling.* **3** the act of buying, selling, or moving goods: *cargo handling* | *A special licence is required for the manufacture or handling of any dangerous chemical.* **4** the way in which a vehicle can be controlled, especially how easy it is for a driver to control it: *It's a lovely little car – the ride is comfortable and the handling excellent.*

handling ˌcharge *n* [C] the amount that someone charges for dealing with goods or moving them from one place to another

hand·loom /ˈhændluːm/ *n* [C] a small machine for weaving by hand

hand ˌluggage *n* [U] the small bags that you carry with you when you are travelling on a plane

hand·made /ˌhændˈmeɪd◂/ *adj* made by people using their hands, not by a machine: *a pair of expensive handmade shoes* → see picture at HOMEMADE

hand·maid·en /ˈhændˌmeɪdn/ also **hand·maid** /ˈhændmeɪd/ *n* [C] **1** *old-fashioned* a female servant **2** *formal* something that supports an idea, system, or way of life: [+of] *Science must not become the handmaiden of the state.*

hand-me-down *n* [C] a piece of clothing which has been used by someone and then given to another person: *She refused to wear hand-me-downs.* | *hand-me-down clothes*

hand·out /ˈhændaʊt/ *n* [C] **1** money or goods that are given to someone, for example because they are

poor: *people who have to live on handouts from the state* | *a cash handout* **2** a piece of paper with information, which is given to people who are attending a lesson, meeting etc: *Please read the handout.*

hand·o·ver /ˈhændəʊvə $ -oʊvər/ *n* [singular] **1** the act of giving someone else control of a place or business: *The president will remain in office until the official handover in April.* | [+of] *United Nations troops will be in the country to ensure a smooth handover of power.* | *the handover of the business* | [+to] *The handover to civilian government has been delayed.* **2** the act of giving something to someone: [+of] *They demanded the immediate handover of all relevant documents.* → **hand over** at HAND²

hand·picked /ˌhændˈpɪkt◂/ *adj* someone who is handpicked has been carefully chosen for a special purpose: *one of his handpicked advisers*

hand·rail /ˈhænd-reɪl/ *n* [C] a long bar that is fixed to the side of a set of stairs for people to hold while they walk up or down

hand·saw /ˈhændsɔː $ -sɒː/ *n* [C] a small tool for cutting wood, which has a flat metal blade with a lot of sharp V-shaped teeth

hand·set /ˈhændset/ *n* [C] **1** the part of a telephone that you hold near your ear and mouth **2** the part of a MOBILE PHONE that you hold in your hand

hands·free /ˈhændzfriː/ *adj* [only before noun] a handsfree machine is one that you can use without using your hands: *a handsfree phone*

hand·shake /ˈhændʃeɪk/ *n* [C] **1** the act of taking someone's right hand and shaking it, which people do when they meet or leave each other or when they have made an agreement: *He greeted me with a handshake and a glass of wine.* | *Her handshake was warm and firm.* **2** a special signal sent between two computers, FAX machines etc when they begin to exchange information —**handshaking** *n* [U] → GOLDEN HANDSHAKE

hands-off *adj* [only before noun] a hands-off way of organizing something involves letting people do what they want and make their own decisions, without telling them what to do: *a hands-off style of management* | *The government has a hands-off approach to the industry.*

hand·some /ˈhænsəm/ *adj* **1 a)** a man who is handsome looks attractive; ◨ **good-looking**: *an extremely handsome young man* | *Sam was tall, dark and handsome.* | *his handsome face* → see box at BEAUTIFUL **b)** a woman who is handsome looks attractive in a strong healthy way **2** an animal, object, or building that is handsome looks attractive in an impressive way: *a row of handsome Georgian houses* **3** [only before noun] a handsome amount of money is large: *He managed to make a handsome profit out of the deal.* | *a handsome fee* **4** [only before noun] a handsome gift or prize is worth a lot of money: *There are some handsome prizes to be won.* **5** [only before noun] a handsome victory is important and impressive: *They won a handsome victory in the elections.* —**handsomely** *adv*: *He was handsomely rewarded by the king.*

hands-on *adj* [usually before noun] doing something yourself rather than just talking about it or telling other people to do it: *a chance to get some hands-on experience of the job* | *He has a very hands-on approach to management.*

hand·spring /ˈhændsprɪŋ/ *n* [C] a quick movement in which you put your hands on the ground, move your feet over your head, and stand up again

hand·stand /ˈhændstænd/ *n* [C] a movement in which you put your hands on the ground and your legs in the air

hand-to-hand *adj* [only before noun] hand-to-hand fighting is a way of fighting in which people use their hands and knives rather than guns: *hand-to-hand*

H

fighting/combat etc *There was fierce hand-to-hand fighting in the streets of the city.* | *They were defeated in hand-to-hand combat.*

hand-to-'mouth *adj* if you have a hand-to-mouth existence, you have only just enough money and food to live

'hand tool *n* [C] a tool that does not use electricity

'hand ,towel *n* [C] a small piece of cloth that you use for drying your hands

hand·wash /'hændwɒʃ $ -wɒːʃ, -waːʃ/ *v* [T] if you handwash a piece of clothing, you wash it by hand, not in a washing machine

hand·writ·ing /'hænd,raɪtɪŋ/ *n* [U] the style of someone's writing: *I recognised her handwriting on the envelope.* | *My handwriting has never been very neat.*

hand·writ·ten /,hænd'rɪtn◂/ *adj* written by hand, not printed: *a handwritten letter*

hand·y [S3] /'hændi/ *comparative* **handier**, *superlative* **handiest** *adj*
1 useful: *It's quite a handy little tool.* | *It's very handy having a light above your desk.* | *Take your swimming trunks with you – they might come in handy* (=be useful).
2 *informal* near and easy to reach: *I always keep my gun handy just in case.* | *Do you have a piece of paper handy?* | [+for] *BrE: The house was in Drury Lane, very handy for the theatre.*
3 good at using something, especially a tool: [+with] *He's very handy with a screwdriver.*

hand·y·man /'hændimæn/ *n plural* **handymen** /-men/ [C] someone who is good at doing repairs and practical jobs in the house

hang¹ [S1] [W2] /hæŋ/ *v past tense and past participle* **hung** /hʌŋ/
1 [TOP PART FASTENED] **a)** also **hang up** [T always + adv/prep] to put something in a position so that the top part is fixed or supported, and the bottom part is free to move and does not touch the ground: *Philip hung his coat on a hook behind the door.* | *She hung the sheets on the washing line.* **b)** [I always + adv/prep] to be in a position where the top part is fixed or supported, and the bottom part is free to move and does not touch the ground: *An old-fashioned gas lamp hung from the ceiling.* | *Her long hair hung loose about her shoulders.* | *The shirt hung down almost to his ankles.*
2 [PICTURE ETC] **a)** [T] to fix a picture, photograph etc to a wall: *I wanted to hang the picture in the hall, by the front door.* **b)** [I always + adv/prep] if a picture, photograph etc is hanging somewhere, it is fixed to a wall: *There was a large family photograph hanging on the wall.* **c)** **be hung with sth** if the walls of a room are hung with pictures or decorations, the pictures etc are on the walls: *The entrance hall was hung with rich tapestries.*
3 [KILL/BE KILLED] *past tense and past participle* **hanged** [I,T] to kill someone by dropping them with a rope around their neck, or to die in this way, especially as a punishment for a serious crime: **be hanged for sth** *He was hanged for murder.* | **hang yourself** *Corey hanged himself in his prison cell.* | *If he is found guilty, he will almost certainly hang.*
4 [PAPER] [T] to fasten attractive paper to a wall in order to decorate a room: *We spent the afternoon hanging wallpaper.*
5 [DOOR] [T] to fasten a door in position: *Hanging a door is quite a tricky job.*
6 [MIST/SMOKE/SMELL] [I + adv/prep] if something such as smoke hangs in the air, it stays in the air for a long time: *The smoke from the bonfires hung in the air.* | *A thick mist hung over the town.*
7 hang open if a door, someone's mouth etc hangs open, it is open
8 hang in the balance if something hangs in the balance, it is not certain what will happen to it: *The future of the company hangs in the balance.*

9 hang by a thread if something is hanging by a thread, it is in a very dangerous situation and may not continue: *He is still in hospital, his life hanging by a thread.*
10 hang (on) in there also **hang tough** *spoken especially AmE* to remain brave and determined when you are in a difficult situation: *Don't worry. Just hang on in there.*
11 hang your head to look ashamed and embarrassed: *She hung her head, not sure how to reply.* | *Daphne had hung her head in shame.*
12 hang fire to wait for a short while before you do something: *I think we should hang fire for a week.*
13 leave sth hanging in the air to leave something in a situation where it has not been explained, completed, or dealt with: *His resignation has left some important questions hanging in the air.*
14 hang a right/left *AmE spoken* to turn right or left when driving: *Go straight on for two blocks, then hang a left.*
15 [I] *AmE spoken* to spend time somewhere, relaxing and enjoying yourself: [+with] *We were just hanging with the dudes at Mike's house.*
16 I'll be hanged if *BrE old-fashioned* used to express annoyance or to say that you will not allow something to happen: *I'll be hanged if I'll give them any money!*
17 hang it (all) *BrE old-fashioned* used to say that you are disappointed or annoyed about something
18 hang sth *BrE old-fashioned* used to say that you are not going to do something: *Oh hang the report, let's go for a drink.*

hang about *phr v BrE*
1 *spoken* to move slowly or take too long doing something: *Come on, we haven't got time to hang about!*
2 hang about (sth) to spend time somewhere without any real purpose: *There were always groups of boys hanging about in the square.* | *He normally hung about the house all day.*
3 hang about! *spoken* **a)** used to ask someone to wait or stop what they are doing **b)** used when you have just noticed or thought of something that is interesting or wrong: *Hang about – that can't be right.*

hang about with sb *phr v BrE informal* to spend a lot of time with someone

hang around/round (sth) *phr v informal* to wait or spend time somewhere, doing nothing: *I hung around the station for an hour but he never came.*

hang around with sb *phr v* to spend a lot of time with someone: *The people I used to hang around with were much older than me.*

hang back *phr v*
1 to stay a short distance away from someone or something, and not go too near them: *Instinctively he hung back in the shelter of a rock.*
2 to not say or do something because you are shy or afraid

hang on *phr v*
1 to hold something tightly: [+to] *She hung on to the side of the cart as it rattled over the stones.* | *Hang on tight!*
2 hang on! *BrE spoken* **a)** used to ask or tell someone to wait: ▪ **hold on**: *Hang on! I'll be back in a minute.* **b)** used when you have just noticed or thought of something that is interesting or wrong
3 hang on sth to depend on something: *Everything hangs on the outcome of this meeting.*
4 hang on sb's words/every word to pay close attention to everything someone is saying: *She was watching his face, hanging on his every word.*

hang on to sth also **hang onto sth** *phr v* to keep something: *I think I'll hang on to the documents for a bit longer.*

hang out *phr v*
1 *informal* to spend a lot of time in a particular place or with particular people: [+with] *I don't really know who she hangs out with.* | *Where do the youngsters hang out?*
→ HANGOUT
2 hang sth ⇔ out to hang clothes outside in order to dry them: *My job was to hang out the washing.* | *Hang the wet things out to dry.*
3 let it all hang out *informal* to relax and do what you like

hang over sth/sb *phr v*
if something bad is hanging over you, you are worried or anxious about it: *The threat of redundancy was still hanging over us.* | *It's not very nice to have huge debts hanging over your head.*
hang together *phr v*
1 if a plan, story, set of ideas etc hangs together, it is well organized and its different parts go well together: *Her story just doesn't hang together.*
2 if people hang together, they help each other
hang up *phr v*
1 to finish a telephone conversation: *I said goodbye and hung up.* | [+on] *Don't hang up on me – I need to talk to you.*
2 hang sth ⇔ up to hang clothes on a hook etc: *She took her coat off and hung it up.*
3 hang up your hat/football boots/briefcase etc *informal* to stop doing a particular kind of work → HANG-UP, HUNG-UP

hang² *n* **get the hang of sth** *informal* to learn how to do something or use something: *It seems difficult at first, but you'll soon get the hang of it.*

hang·ar /'hæŋə $ -ər/ *n* [C] a very large building in which aircraft are kept

hang·dog /'hæŋdɒg $ -dɔːg/ *adj* **hangdog expression/ look** an expression that shows you feel sorry or ashamed about something: *I could tell from his hangdog look that things had gone badly.*

hang·er /'hæŋə $ -ər/ also **coat hanger, clothes hanger** *n* [C] a curved piece of wood or metal with a hook on top, used for hanging clothes on: *She took off her jacket and hung it on a hanger.*

hanger-'on *n plural* **hangers-on** [C] someone who spends a lot of time with a rich or important person, because they hope to get some advantage for themselves: *He was surrounded by a crowd of friends and hangers-on.*

'hang-glider *n* [C] **1** a large frame covered with cloth that you hold on to and fly slowly through the air on, without an engine **2** someone who flies using a hang-glider

'hang-gliding *n* [U] the sport of flying using a hang-glider → see picture at AERIAL

hang·ing /'hæŋɪŋ/ *n* **1** [C,U] the act of killing someone by putting a rope around their neck and hanging them, used as a punishment: *public hangings* | *people who believe that bringing back hanging will reduce the amount of crime* **2** [C] a large piece of cloth that is hung on a wall as a decoration: *a colourful wall hanging*

hanging 'basket *n* [C] a basket with plants growing in it that is hung on the outside of a building as decoration

hang·man /'hæŋmən/ *n plural* **hangmen** /-mən/ [C] someone whose job is to kill criminals by hanging them

hang·nail /'hæŋneɪl/ *n* [C] a piece of skin that has become loose near the bottom of your FINGERNAIL

hang·out /'hæŋaʊt/ *n* [C] *informal* a place someone likes to go to often: *The bar is a favourite hangout for students.*

hang·o·ver /'hæŋəʊvə $ -oʊvər/ *n* [C] **1** a pain in your head and a feeling of sickness that you get the day after you have drunk too much alcohol: *I had a terrible hangover the next day.* **2** a hangover from sth something from the past that still exists or happens but is no longer necessary or useful: *This feeling was a hangover from her schooldays.* | *an institution which is a hangover from Victorian times*

'hang-up, hang·up /'hæŋʌp/ *n* [C] *informal* a feeling of worry or embarrassment about something that you have although there is no real reason to feel this way: *She had cured him of all his hang-ups.* | [+about] *She's got a real hang-up about her body.* → hang up at HANG¹

hank /hæŋk/ *n* [C] an amount of wool or thread that has been wound into a loose ball

han·ker /'hæŋkə $ -ər/ *v*
hanker after/for sth *phr v* to feel strongly that you want something: *She hankered for a new life in a different country.* | *holidaymakers who hanker after the sun*

han·ker·ing /'hæŋkərɪŋ/ *n* [singular] a strong wish to have or do something: [+for/after] *his hankering for adventure* | **a hankering to do sth** *I've always had a hankering to be a doctor.*

han·kie, hanky /'hæŋki/ *n* [C] *informal* a HANDKERCHIEF

hank·y-pank·y /ˌhæŋki 'pæŋki/ *n* [U] *informal* sexual activity – used humorously

han·som /'hænsəm/ also **'hansom ˌcab** *n* [C] a small vehicle pulled by a horse which was used in the past as a taxi

Ha·nuk·kah, Chanukah /'hɑːnʊkə $ 'kɑːnəkə, 'hɑː-/ *n* [C,U] an eight-day Jewish holiday in November or December

ha'penny /'heɪpni/ *n* another spelling of HALFPENNY

hap·haz·ard /ˌhæp'hæzəd◂ $ -ərd◂/ *adj* happening or done in a way that is not planned or organized: **a haphazard way/manner/fashion** *I continued my studies in a rather haphazard way.* | *Educational provision in the country is haphazard.* —**haphazardly** *adv*: *bushes growing haphazardly here and there*

hap·less /'hæpləs/ *adj* [only before noun] *literary* unlucky: *The hapless passengers were stranded at the airport for three days.*

hap·pen S1 W1 /'hæpən/ *v* [I]
1 when something happens, there is an event, especially one that is not planned; ▪ occur: *When did the accident happen?* | *It's impossible to predict what will happen next.* | **something/nothing/anything happens** *Something terrible has happened.* | *She carried on as if nothing had happened.* | *This was bound to happen sooner or later.* | *This kind of thing happens all the time.* | *We'll still be friends, whatever happens.*
2 something/anything/what happens to sb/sth if something happens to someone or something, they are affected by an event: *He should be here by now – something must have happened to him.* | *The same thing happened to me last year.* | *What's happened to your coat? It's all ripped.* | *What will happen to the collection now?*
3 happen to do sth if you happen to do something, you do it by chance: *I happened to see James in town.*
4 sb/sth happens to be sth used when telling someone something in an angry way: *This happens to be my house!*
5 as it happens/it just so happens used to tell someone something that is surprising, interesting, or useful: *As it happens, I know someone who might be able to help you.*
6 these things happen used to tell someone not to worry about a mistake they have made, an accident they have caused etc: *It's not your fault – these things happen.*
7 whatever happened to sb/sth? used to ask where a person or thing is now: *Whatever happened to Steve? I haven't seen him for years.* → **accidents (will) happen** at ACCIDENT (5)
happen on/upon sb/sth *phr v literary* or *old-fashioned*
to find something or meet someone by chance: *I happened on the restaurant by chance.*

hap·pen·ing¹ S2 /'hæpənɪŋ/ *n* [C usually plural] something that happens, especially a strange event: **strange/ unusual/mysterious etc happenings** *There have been reports of strange happenings in the town.*

happening² *adj informal* fashionable and exciting: *Brighton is definitely a happening place.*

hap·pen·stance /'hæpənstæns/ *n* [C,U] *literary* chance, or something that happens by chance

H

1 000, 2 000, 3 000, most frequent words in S poken and W ritten English

hap·pi·ly /ˈhæpɪ̯li/ adv **1** in a happy way: *Michelle smiled happily.* | *I'm a happily married man.* | *So she married the prince, and they lived happily ever after* (=used at the end of children's stories to say that someone was happy for the rest of their life). **2** [sentence adverb] fortunately: *Happily, his injuries were not serious.* **3** very willingly: *I'd happily go for you.* | *Most restaurants will happily accept payment by cheque.*

hap·pi·ness /ˈhæpɪnɪ̯s/ n [U] the state of being happy: *Juliet's eyes shone with happiness.* | *We want our children to have the best possible chance of happiness.*

hap·py **S1** **W1** /ˈhæpi/ adj comparative **happier**, superlative **happiest**
1 having feelings of pleasure, for example because something good has happened to you or you are very satisfied with your life; **F** sad: *It's a lovely house and we've been very happy here.* | *I've never felt happier in my life.* | *He was a happy child who rarely cried.* | *the happy faces of the children* | *I loved her and thought I could make her happy.* | **happy to do sth** *John will be so happy to see you.* | **happy (that)** *I'm happy that everything worked out well in the end.* | **be/feel happy for sb** *What a wonderful opportunity! I'm so happy for you.* | **happy in your work/job etc** | **happy to be doing sth** *We're very happy to be taking part.* | **the happy couple** (=a couple that have just got married or will soon get married)
2 [usually before noun] a happy time, relationship, event etc is a good one that makes you feel happy: *This has been the happiest day of my life.* | *They had a very happy marriage.* | *I have lots of happy memories of the place.* | *The story has a happy ending, however.* | *When's the happy event* (=the birth of your child)?
3 [not before noun] satisfied or not worried: [+with] *On the whole, I'm happy with the way I look.* | *People living nearby are not happy with the decision.* | [+about] *Mom wasn't happy about Tess going off travelling on her own.* | *I pretended to agree with her, just to keep him happy.* | **happy doing sth** *I'm quite happy doing what I'm doing.*
4 be happy to do sth to be very willing to do something, especially to help someone: *Our team will be happy to help.* | *I'd be happy to take you in my car.*
5 Happy Birthday/New Year/Christmas etc used to wish someone happiness on a special occasion: *Happy Birthday, Michael!* | *Happy Thanksgiving, everyone!*
6 many happy returns used to wish someone happiness on their BIRTHDAY
7 [only before noun] fortunate or lucky: *By a happy coincidence, James was also in town that weekend.* | *I'm in the happy position of not having to work.*
8 a happy medium (between sth and sth) a way of doing something that is not extreme but is somewhere between two possible choices: *I always tried to strike a happy medium between having a home that looked like a bomb had hit it and becoming obsessively tidy.*
9 [only before noun] formal suitable: *His choice of words was not a very happy one.*

WORD FOCUS: words meaning HAPPY
cheerful behaving in a way that shows you are happy | **in a good mood** happy at a particular time, and therefore friendly to other people | **pleased/glad** happy because something good has happened | **delighted/thrilled/overjoyed/ecstatic** very happy because something good has happened | **contented** happy with your life | **optimistic/positive** believing that good things will happen in the future | **gleeful/gloating** smug happy because something bad has happened to someone else

happy-clap·py /ˌhæpi ˈklæpi◂/ adj BrE informal relating to a Christian church where people sing, shout, show their emotions, and encourage other people to join their church – used to show disapproval: *happy-clappy Christians* —**happy clappy** n [C]

happy-go-ˈlucky adj enjoying life and not worrying about things: *a happy-go-lucky kind of person*

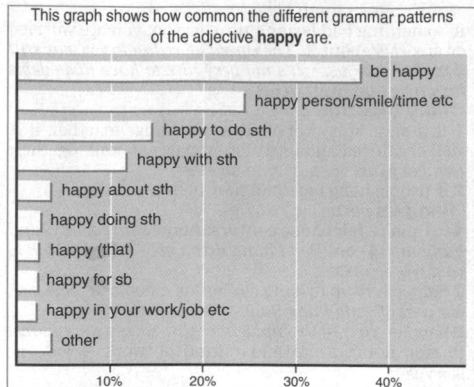

This graph shows how common the different grammar patterns of the adjective **happy** are.

- be happy
- happy person/smile/time etc
- happy to do sth
- happy with sth
- happy about sth
- happy doing sth
- happy (that)
- happy for sb
- happy in your work/job etc
- other

10% 20% 30% 40%

ˈhappy hour n [C,U] a special time in a bar when alcoholic drinks are sold at lower prices

har·a·kir·i /ˌhærəˈkɪri/ n [U] a way of killing yourself by cutting open your stomach, used in the past in Japan to avoid losing honour

ha·rangue /həˈræŋ/ v [T] to speak in a loud angry way, often for a long time, in order to criticize someone or to persuade them that you are right: **harangue sb about sth** *He stood on the street corner, haranguing passers-by about the stupidity of the forthcoming war.* —**harangue** n [C]

har·ass /ˈhærəs, həˈræs/ v [T] **1** to make someone's life unpleasant, for example by frequently saying offensive things to them or threatening them: *A number of black youths have complained of being harassed by the police.* | **sexually/racially harass sb** (=harass someone because of their sex or race) *One woman engineer claimed that she had been sexually harassed by a male manager.* **2** to keep attacking an enemy again and again

har·assed /ˈhærəst, həˈræst/ adj BrE anxious and tired because you have too many problems or things to do: *He looked pale and harassed.*

har·ass·ment /ˈhærəsmənt, həˈræsmənt/ n [U] when someone behaves in an unpleasant or threatening way towards you: *African-Americans have been complaining about police harassment for years.* | [+of] *Political parties are banned, and harassment of dissidents is commonplace.* | **sexual/racial harassment** (=because of someone's sex or race) *We need effective strategies to combat sexual harassment in the workplace.*

har·bin·ger /ˈhɑːbɪndʒə $ ˈhɑːrbɪndʒər/ n [C] literary or formal a sign that something is going to happen soon: [+of] *These birds are considered to be harbingers of doom.*

har·bour¹ BrE; **harbor** AmE /ˈhɑːbə $ ˈhɑːrbər/ n [C] an area of water next to the land where the water is calm, so that ships are safe when they are inside it: *as they sailed into Portsmouth Harbour*

harbour BrE/ harbor AmE

har·bour² BrE; **harbor** AmE v [T] **1** to keep bad thoughts, fears, or hopes in your mind for a long time: *I think he's harbouring some sort of grudge against me.* | *She began to harbour doubts over the wisdom of their journey.* **2** to contain something, especially something hidden and dangerous: *Sinks and draining boards can harbour germs.* **3** to protect and hide criminals that the police are searching for

ˈharbour ˌmaster n [C] the official who is in charge of a harbour

H

hard¹ S1 W1 /hɑːd $ hɑːrd/ *adj comparative* **harder**, *superlative* **hardest**

1 FIRM TO TOUCH firm, stiff, and difficult to press down, break, or cut; **◼ soft**: *a hard wooden chair* | *the hardest substance known to man* | *After months without rain, the ground was too hard to plough.*

2 DIFFICULT difficult to do or understand; **◼ difficult**; **◼ easy**: *This year's exam was much harder than last year's.* | *You'll have to make some hard decisions.* | *They're a hard team to beat.* | **it is hard to believe/imagine/see/know** etc *It was hard to see what else we could have done.* | *It's hard to believe that anyone would say something like that.* | **find it hard to do sth** *I was finding it hard to concentrate.* | *Permanent jobs are* **hard to come by** (=difficult to find or get). | **be hard for sb** *It must be hard for her, bringing up three kids on her own.* | *Telling my parents is going to be* **the hardest thing** *about it.* | **have a hard time doing sth** (=be difficult for someone to do something) *You'll have a hard time proving that.* | *I had a hard time persuading him to accept the offer.* | *Such criticism was* **hard to take** (=difficult to accept).

3 WORK/EFFORT [usually before noun] using or involving a lot of mental or physical effort: *To be successful in sport requires* **hard work** *and a great deal of determination.* | *After* **a hard day** *at work, I just want to come home and put my feet up.* | **a hard day's work/walking/skiing** etc *There's a sauna where you can relax after a hard day's skiing.* | *Becoming a doctor never interested him. It was* **too much like hard work** (=it would involve too much work).

4 FULL OF PROBLEMS a situation or time that is hard is one in which you have a lot of problems, especially when you do not have enough money: *She's had* **a hard life**. | **Times were hard** *and they were forced to sell their house.* | *He had clearly* **fallen on hard times** (=did not have much money).

5 be hard on sb a) to criticize someone in a way that is unfair, or to be too strict with them: *Perhaps I'm too hard on her.* **b)** to have a bad effect on someone: *Divorce can be very hard on children.*

6 be hard on sth to have a bad effect on something: *Standing all day is very hard on the feet.*

7 do sth the hard way to learn, achieve, or do something after a bad experience or by making mistakes: *He learned the hard way about the harsh reality of the boxing world.* | *Make sure you put the baby's diaper on before you start feeding her. I learned this lesson the hard way.* | *He earned his promotion the hard way.*

8 USING FORCE using a lot of force: *Jane gave the door a good hard push.* | *She gave him a hard slap.*

9 hard evidence/facts/information etc facts that are definitely true and can be proved: *There is no hard evidence to support this theory.*

10 UNKIND showing no sympathetic or gentle feelings: *a hard face* | *Her voice was hard and cold.* | *You're a hard man, John.*

11 hard going a) difficult to do and needing a lot of effort: *A strong wind made the race very hard going.* **b)** boring, or difficult to deal with, talk to etc: *I find some of his friends pretty hard going.*

12 make hard work of sth to make something you are doing seem more difficult than it really is: *Juventus were making hard work of what should have been an easy game.*

13 be hard at it/work *informal* to be very busy doing something: *Sarah was hard at it on her computer.*

14 WATER hard water contains a lot of minerals, and does not mix easily with soap; **◼ soft**

15 hard luck a) *BrE spoken* used to tell someone that you feel sorry for them because they have not succeeded in what they were trying to do: *'I failed my driving test.' 'Oh, hard luck!'* **b)** when bad things happen to you that are not your fault: *You've had your share of hard luck.* | [+on] *It was hard luck on you.* **c)** *spoken* also **hard cheese** *BrE* used to say that you do not care if someone is having problems, does not like something etc: *If you don't like the idea then hard luck!* | *'He doesn't know what to do.' 'Well that's his hard luck!'*

16 give sb a hard time *informal* **a)** to treat someone badly or cause problems for them: *Giving you a hard time, is she?* | *They reached the border where officials gave them a hard time.* **b)** to criticize someone a lot: *Hostile critics have given Hartman a hard time.*

17 have a hard time to have a lot of problems or bad experiences: *I'm glad she's happy at last – she's had such a hard time.* | *Vegetarians still often have a hard time of it when it comes to eating out.*

18 drive/strike a hard bargain to demand a lot or refuse to give too much when you are making an agreement: *The company is believed to have struck a hard bargain.*

19 hard feelings a) anger between people because of something that has happened: *We'd known each other too long for hard feelings.* | *I have no hard feelings towards Steve.* **b) no hard feelings** *spoken* used to tell someone that you do not want to be angry with them or for them to be angry with you: *I'm sorry it didn't work out, but no hard feelings, eh?*

20 take a (long) hard look at sth/sb to think carefully about something, especially with the result that you change your opinions or behaviour: *You should take a long hard look at the issues before committing yourself.* | *Newspaper editors should take a long hard look at themselves and clean up their act.*

21 hard line a strict way of dealing with someone or something: *The president should abandon his hard line in the region.* | **take/adopt a hard line (on sth)** *The school takes a very hard line on drugs.*

22 hard news news stories that are about serious subjects or events: *TV news programs seem to be more interested in gossip than in hard news.*

23 NOT FRIGHTENED *BrE spoken* strong, ready to fight, and not afraid of anyone or anything: *He thinks he's really hard.* | *Jones was known as soccer's* **hard man**.

24 (as) hard as nails someone who is hard as nails seems to have no feelings such as fear or sympathy

25 a hard taskmaster/master someone who makes people work too hard

26 a hard winter/frost a very cold winter or FROST; **◼ mild**

27 the hard left/right people who have extreme LEFT-WING or RIGHT-WING political aims and ideas; **◼ far left/right**: *concerns about the re-emergence of the hard right in some areas*

28 LIGHT *especially literary* hard light is bright and unpleasant; **◼ harsh**: *the hard brilliance of the moonlight*

29 ALCOHOL [only before noun] *informal* very strong: *hard liquor* | *I never touch* **the hard stuff** (=strong alcohol). → **HARD DRUGS**

30 a hard left/right a big turn to the left or right, for example when you are driving; **◼ sharp**

31 PRONUNCIATION a hard 'c' is pronounced /k/ rather than /s/; a hard 'g' is pronounced /g/ rather than /dʒ/; → **soft** —**hardness** *n* [U]: *a material that would combine the flexibility of rubber with the hardness of glass*

WORD FOCUS: HARD

hard and not bending: **solid, firm, stiff, rigid**
meat that is too hard: **tough**
skin that is old and hard: **leathery, calloused**
hard and easily broken: **brittle**

hard² S1 W2 *adv comparative* **harder**, *superlative* **hardest**

1 USING ENERGY/EFFORT using a lot of effort, energy, or attention: *She has* **worked hard** *all her life.* | *He had* **thought long and hard** *before getting involved with the project.* | *She* **tried her hardest** *to ignore what he'd said.* | *Ella was concentrating very hard.* | *I couldn't convince him no matter how hard I tried.* | *Sam stared hard at the floor.*

2 WITH FORCE with a lot of force: *You need to hit the ball hard.* | *He slammed the door hard behind him.* | *It was raining very hard.*

H

3 BECOME SOLID becoming solid, stiff, or firm: *By now the cement had set hard.*

4 be hard hit/be hit hard to be badly affected by something that has happened: *Sales were hard hit by high interest rates.*

5 be hard put/pressed/pushed to do sth *informal* to have difficulty doing something: *You'd be hard pressed to find anyone better for the job.* → HARD-PRESSED

6 be/feel hard done by *informal* to be or feel unfairly treated: *As a child I felt hard done by, living so far away from my friends.*

7 take sth hard to be very upset about something, especially bad news: *Alan took his mother's death particularly hard.*

8 hard upon/on sth *BrE formal* soon after something: *His second major contract followed hard upon the first.*

9 laugh/cry hard to laugh, cry etc a lot: *He laughed so hard he had tears in his eyes* → HARD BY, HARD UP; → **(hard/hot/close) on sb's heels** at HEEL¹ (7b); → **(hard/hot/close) on the heels of sth** at HEEL¹ (7a); → **play hard to get** at PLAY¹ (23)

,**hard-and-'fast** *adj* [only before noun] clear, definite, and always able to be used: *It is impossible to give **hard-and-fast rules**, but here are some points to consider.*

hard·back /'hɑːdbæk $ 'hɑːrd/ also **hardcover** *n* [C] a book that has a strong stiff cover: **in hardback** *His first novel sold over 40,000 copies in hardback.* —**hardback** *adj*: *a hardback edition of 'The Joy of Cooking'* → PAPERBACK

hard·ball /'hɑːdbɔːl $ 'hɑːrbɒːl/ *n* [U] *AmE* **play hardball** *informal* to be very determined to get what you want, especially in business or politics

,**hard-'bitten** *adj* not easily shocked or upset, because you have had a lot of experience: *a hard-bitten cop*

hard·board /'hɑːdbɔːd $ 'hɑːrdbɔːrd/ *n* [U] a material made from small pieces of wood pressed together

,**hard-'boiled** *adj* **1** a hard-boiled egg has been boiled until it becomes solid → SOFT-BOILED **2** *informal* **a)** not showing your emotions and not influenced by your feelings; ▣ **tough**: *a hard-boiled marketing executive* **b)** **hard-boiled film/thriller/fiction etc** a film etc that deals with people who do not show their emotions

,**hard 'by** *adv, prep BrE old use* very near: *in a house hard by the city gate*

,**hard 'cash** *n* [U] paper money and coins, not cheques or CREDIT CARDS

'**hard ,copy** *n* [C,U] information from a computer that is printed out onto paper, or the printed papers themselves

'**hard core** *n* [singular] *BrE* **a)** the small group of people that are most active within a group or organization: *the hard core of the Communist party* **b)** a group of people who cannot be persuaded to change their behaviour or beliefs: *There is still a small hard core of football supporters who cause trouble whenever they can.*

'**hard-core, hard·core** /'hɑːdkɔː $ 'hɑːrdkɔːr/ *adj* **1** [only before noun] having an extreme way of life or an extreme belief that is very unlikely to change: *a hard-core drug addict* | *hard-core racists* **2 hard-core pornography** magazines, films etc that show the details of sexual behaviour, often in an unpleasant way

,**hard 'court** *n* [C] an area for playing tennis which has a hard surface, not grass

hard·cov·er /'hɑːdkʌvə $ 'hɑːrdkʌvər/ also **hardback** *n* [C] a book that has a strong stiff cover —**hardcover** *adj* → PAPERBACK

,**hard 'currency** *n* [C,U] money that is from a country that has a strong ECONOMY and is therefore unlikely to lose its value

,**hard 'disk** *n* [C] a stiff DISK inside a computer that is used for storing information → FLOPPY DISK

'**hard-,drinking** *adj* [only before noun] a hard-drinking person drinks a lot of alcohol

'**hard drive** *n* [C] the part of a computer where information and programs are stored, consisting of HARD DISKS and the electronic equipment that reads what is stored on them

,**hard 'drugs** *n* [plural] very strong illegal drugs such as HEROIN and COCAINE → SOFT DRUG

,**hard-'earned** *adj* [only before noun] earned or achieved after a lot of effort: **hard-earned money/cash etc** *Don't be too quick to part with your hard-earned cash.* | *a hard-earned victory*

,**hard-'edged** *adj* dealing with difficult subjects or criticizing someone severely in a way that may offend some people: *a hard-edged collection of songs*

hard·en /'hɑːdn $ 'hɑːrdn/ *v* [I,T] **1** to become firm or stiff, or to make something firm or stiff; ▣ **soften**: *It will take about 24 hours for the glue to harden.* **2** if your attitude hardens, or if something hardens it, you become more strict and determined and less sympathetic; ▣ **soften**: *Attitudes towards the terrorists have hardened even more since the attack.* **3** *written* if your face or voice hardens, or if something hardens it, you look or sound less sympathetic or happy; ▣ **soften**: *His face hardened momentarily, then he looked away.* **4 harden your heart** to make yourself not feel pity or sympathy for someone

hard·ened /'hɑːdnd $ 'hɑːr-/ *adj* **1 hardened criminal/police officer etc** a criminal, police officer etc who has had a lot of experience of things that are shocking and is therefore less affected by them **2 become hardened (to sth)** to become used to something shocking because you have seen it many times

,**hard-'fought** *adj* a hard-fought game, competition etc involves two opposing sides who are trying very hard to defeat each other: **a hard-fought battle/contest/game etc** *one of the most hard-fought games this season* | *a hard-fought battle for the presidency*

,**hard 'hat** *n* [C] a protective hat, worn especially by workers in places where buildings are being built → see picture at HAT

,**hard-'headed** *adj* practical and able to make difficult decisions without letting your emotions affect your judgment: *a hard-headed business tycoon*

,**hard-'heart·ed** /,hɑːd 'hɑːtɪd $,hɑːrd 'hɑːr-/ *adj* not caring about other people's feelings

,**hard-'hitting** *adj* criticizing someone or something in a strong and effective way: *a hard-hitting report*

,**hard 'labour** *BrE*; **hard labor** *AmE n* [U] punishment in prison which consists of hard physical work

,**hard-'line** *adj* having extreme political beliefs, and refusing to change them: *a hard-line Marxist* → **hard line** at HARD¹ (21)

hard·lin·er /,hɑːd'laɪnə‹, 'hɑːdlaɪnə $,hɑːrd'laɪnər‹/ *n* [C] a politician who wants political problems to be dealt with in a strong and extreme way

,**hard-'luck ,story** *n plural* **hard-luck stories** [C] a story you tell someone about bad things that have happened to you, in order to get their sympathy or help

hard·ly S2 W2 /'hɑːdli $ 'hɑːrdli/ *adv* **1** almost not: *My parents divorced when I was six, and I hardly knew my father.* | *The children were so excited they could hardly speak.* | *I can hardly believe it.* | **Hardly anyone** (=almost no one) *writes to me these days.* | *Dad ate hardly anything* (=almost nothing). | *There was hardly any* (=very little) *traffic.* | *She lives in Spain, so we hardly ever* (=almost never) *see her.* | **hardly a day/week/month etc goes by without/when** (=used to say that something happens almost every day, week etc) *Hardly a month goes by without another factory closing down.*; → see box at RARELY **2** used to mean 'not', when you are suggesting that the person you are speaking to will agree with you: *It's hardly surprising that she won't answer his calls after the way he's treated her.* | *You can hardly blame Tom for not waiting.* | *My boss could hardly be described as handsome.* | **hardly the time/place/person etc** (=a very unsuitable time, place, person) *This is hardly the place*

to discuss the matter.
3 used to say that something has only just happened: *The serious building work has hardly begun.* | **hardly ... when/before** *She had hardly sat down when the phone rang.*

GRAMMAR

Do not use **hardly** with a negative word: *I can hardly believe he said that (NOT I can't hardly believe he said that).* | *There's hardly any milk left (NOT There's hardly no milk left).*

Use **hardly** just before the main verb: *He could hardly speak (NOT He hardly could speak).*

Do not use **hardly** at the beginning of a sentence, except in very formal writing: *I had hardly got in the house when the phone rang* is the usual way to say this. It is possible to say: *Hardly had I got in the house when the phone rang* but this is very formal

⚠ Do not use **hardly** as the adverb of **hard**. The adverb of **hard** is **hard**: *I tried hard to remember (NOT I tried hardly to remember).* | *Students have to study very hard (NOT Students have to study very hardly).*

---

hard-'nosed *adj* [usually before noun] not affected by emotions, and determined to get what you want: *a hard-nosed businessman*

hard of 'hearing *adj* [not before noun] **1** unable to hear very well; → **deaf** **2** **the hard of hearing** [plural] people who are unable to hear very well

hard-on *n* [C] *informal not polite* an ERECTION (1)

hard 'porn *n* [U] magazines, films etc that show sexual behaviour in an unacceptable, sometimes violent way → **SOFT PORN**

hard-'pressed *adj* having a lot of problems and not enough money or time: *The new exams will only add to the workload of already hard-pressed teachers.* → **be hard pressed to do sth** at **HARD²** (5)

hard 'rock *n* [U] a type of ROCK MUSIC that is played loudly, has a strong beat, and uses electric instruments

hard 'sell *n* [singular] **1** a way of selling something in which there is a lot of pressure on you to buy; **₤** **soft sell** **2** *AmE* if an idea is a hard sell, it is difficult to get people to accept it

hard·ship /'hɑːdʃɪp $ 'hɑːrd-/ *n* [C,U] something that makes your life difficult or unpleasant, especially a lack of money, or the condition of having a difficult life: *an economic policy that caused great hardship for many people* | *Many students are suffering severe financial hardship.* | [+of] *the hardships of war*

hard 'shoulder *n* [singular] *BrE* the area at the side of a big road where you are allowed to stop if you have a problem with your car; **₤** **shoulder** *AmE*

hard 'up *adj* **1** if you are hard up, you do not have much money: *I'm a bit hard up at the moment.* **2** not having something that you want or need: *'How about a date with Tom?' 'No, thanks, I'm not that hard up.'* | [+for] *The media are obviously hard up for stories.*

hard·ware /'hɑːdweə $ 'hɑːrdwer/ *n* [U] **1** computer machinery and equipment, as opposed to the programs that make computers work → **SOFTWARE** **2** equipment and tools for your home and garden **3** the machinery and equipment that is needed to do something: *tanks and other military hardware*

hard-'wearing *adj BrE* products that are hard-wearing will remain in good condition for a long time even when they are used a lot; **₤** **long-wearing** *AmE*

hard-'wired *adj technical* computer systems that are hard-wired are controlled by HARDWARE rather than SOFTWARE and cannot be easily changed by the user

hard-'won *adj* achieved only after a lot of effort and difficulty: *The people were not prepared to give up their hard-won independence.*

hard·wood /'hɑːdwʊd $ 'hɑːrd-/ *n* [C,U] strong heavy wood from trees such as OAK, used for making furniture → **SOFTWOOD**

hard-'working *adj* working with a lot of effort: *a hard-working teacher*

---

har·dy /'hɑːdi $ 'hɑːrdi/ *adj* **1** strong and healthy and able to bear difficult living conditions: *hardy mountain goats* **2** a hardy plant is able to live through the winter —**hardiness** *n* [U]

hardy pe'rennial *n* [C] **1** a hardy plant that produces flowers for several years **2** *BrE* an idea that is often suggested or discussed

hare¹ /heə $ her/ *n plural* **hare** *or* **hares** [C] an animal like a rabbit but larger, which can run very quickly

hare² *v* [I always + adv/prep] *BrE informal* to run or go very fast: [+off] *He hared off down the road.*

'hare-brained *adj* a hare-brained plan or idea is very silly or unlikely to succeed: *his latest hare-brained scheme*

hare·lip /ˌheə'lɪp $ ˌher-/ *n* [singular] *old-fashioned* an offensive word for the condition of having your top lip divided into two parts because it did not develop correctly before birth

har·em /'hɑːrim, hɑː'riːm $ 'hɑːrəm, 'her-/ *n* [C] **1** the group of wives or women who lived with a rich or powerful man in some Muslim societies in the past **2** part of a Muslim house that is separate from the rest of the house, where only women live

har·i·cot /'hærɪkəʊ $ -koʊ/ *also* **haricot 'bean** *n* [C] *BrE* a small white bean; **₤** **navy bean** *AmE*

hark /hɑːk $ hɑːrk/ *v* **1** **hark at him/her/you!** *BrE old-fashioned spoken* used when you think someone is saying something stupid or acting as if they are more important than they really are: *Hark at him! I bet he couldn't do any better.* **2** **hark!** *old use* used to tell someone to listen
hark back *phr v* to remember and talk about things that happened in the past: [+to] *It's useless to continually hark back to the past.*
hark back to sth *phr v* to be similar to something in the past: *music that harks back to the early age of jazz*

har·ken /'hɑːkən $ 'hɑːr-/ *v* another spelling of HEARKEN

har·le·quin¹ /'hɑːlɪ̩kwɪn $ 'hɑːr-/ *n* [C] a character in some traditional plays who wears brightly coloured clothes and plays tricks

harlequin² *adj* [only before noun] a harlequin pattern is made up of DIAMOND shapes in many different colours

har·lot /'hɑːlət $ 'hɑːr-/ *n* [C] *old use* a PROSTITUTE

harm¹ S3 /hɑːm $ hɑːrm/ *n* [U]
1 damage, injury, or trouble caused by someone's actions or by an event

---

do harm (to sth)/do sth harm
cause (sb/sth) harm
suffer harm
do more harm than good (=cause more problems rather than improving the situation)
serious harm
physical harm
psychological/emotional harm
there is no harm in (doing) sth (=used to say that something seems reasonable)
where's the harm in that? *spoken* (=used when you think that something seems reasonable, although other people may not)
no harm done *spoken* (=used to tell someone not to worry about something they have done)

Modern farming methods have done considerable harm to the countryside. | *Socks that are too tight can cause as much harm as badly fitting shoes.* | *It is a parent's responsibility to ensure that their children do not suffer any harm.* | *Criticizing people's work often does more harm than good.* | *This won't do his career serious harm.* | *protection from physical harm* | *There's no great harm in taking something to relieve a headache.* | *I'm only trying to earn a bit of money. Where's the harm in that?* | *It was a silly thing to do, but don't worry. No harm done.* → **GRIEVOUS BODILY HARM**

---

2 come to no harm/not come to any harm to not be hurt or damaged: *She was relieved to see the children had come to no harm.*
3 mean no harm/not mean any harm to have no intention of hurting or upsetting anyone: *She's a terrible gossip but she means no harm.*
4 there's no harm in doing sth/it does no harm to do sth *spoken* used to suggest something to someone: *There's no harm in trying.* | *It does no harm to ask.*
5 it wouldn't do sb any harm to do sth *spoken* used to suggest that someone should do something that may be helpful or useful to them: *It wouldn't do you any harm to get some experience first.*
6 out of harm's way a) if someone or something is out of harm's way, they are in a place where they cannot be hurt or damaged: *Copies of your documents should be kept in a safe place, well out of harm's way.* **b)** if something dangerous is out of harm's way, it is in a place where it cannot hurt anyone or damage anything: *If you have small children, make sure that you store all medicines out of harm's way.*

harm² v [T] **1** to damage something: *chemicals that harm the environment* **2** to physically hurt a person or animal: *The kidnappers didn't harm him, thank God.* **3 harm sb's image/reputation** to make people have a worse opinion of a person or group

harm·ful /'hɑːmfəl $ 'hɑːrm-/ *adj* causing or likely to cause harm: *the harmful effects of smoking* | *harmful bacteria* | **[+to]** *chemicals that are harmful to the environment*

harm·less /'hɑːmləs $ 'hɑːrm-/ *adj* **1** unable or unlikely to hurt anyone or cause damage: *Her brother's a bit simple, but he's quite harmless.* **2** not likely to upset or offend anyone: *It was just a bit of harmless fun.* —**harmlessly** *adv*: *The spear whistled harmlessly over his head.* —**harmlessness** *n* [U]

har·mon·ic /hɑː'mɒnɪk $ hɑːr'mɑː-/ *adj technical* relating to the way notes are played or sung together to give a pleasing sound: *harmonic scales*

har·mon·i·ca /hɑː'mɒnɪkə $ hɑːr'mɑː-/ *n* [C] a small musical instrument that you play by blowing or sucking and moving it from side to side near your mouth

har·mo·ni·ous /hɑː'məʊniəs $ hɑːr'moʊ-/ *adj* **1** harmonious relationships are ones in which people are friendly and helpful to one another **2** sounds that are harmonious are very pleasant **3** parts, colours etc that are harmonious look good or work well together: *The decor is a harmonious blend of traditional and modern.* —**harmoniously** *adv*

har·mo·ni·um /hɑː'məʊniəm $ hɑːr'moʊ-/ *n* [C] a musical instrument with a KEYBOARD and metal pipes like a small ORGAN

har·mo·nize also **-ise** BrE /'hɑːmənaɪz $ 'hɑːr-/ *v* **1** [I] if two or more things harmonize, they work well together or look good together: **[+with]** *We want to make sure that the new offices harmonize with the other buildings in the area.* **2** [T] to make two or more sets of rules, taxes etc the same: *the proposal to harmonize tax levels throughout the EU* **3** [I] to sing or play music in HARMONY

har·mo·ny /'hɑːməni $ 'hɑːr-/ *n plural* **harmonies** **1** [C usually plural, U] notes of music combined together in a pleasant way: **in harmony** *a choir singing in perfect harmony* | *the gorgeous vocal harmonies on 'Mexicali Rose'* | *three-part harmonies* **2** [U] when people live or work together without fighting or disagreeing with each other: *I do believe it is possible for different ethnic groups to live together in harmony.* | **peace and harmony** *an era of peace and harmony* | **live/work etc in harmony** *formal* to agree with another idea, feeling etc, or look good with other things: *Your suggestions are not in harmony with the aims of this project.* **4** [U] the

pleasant effect made by different things that form an attractive whole: *the harmony of sea and sky* → DISCORD

har·ness¹ /'hɑːnɪ̯s $ 'hɑːr-/ *n* [C,U] **1** a set of leather bands used to control a horse or to attach it to a vehicle it is pulling **2** a set of bands used to hold someone in a place or to stop them from falling: *a safety harness* → see picture at SAFETY **3 in harness** BrE doing your usual work: *I felt glad to be back in harness.* **4 in harness (with sb)** BrE working closely with another person or group

harness² v [T] **1** to control and use the natural force or power of something: *We can harness the power of the wind to generate electricity.* **2** to fasten two animals together, or to fasten an animal to something using a harness **3** to put a harness on a horse

harp¹ /hɑːp $ hɑːrp/ *n* [C] a large musical instrument with strings that are stretched across a vertical frame with three corners, and that you play with your fingers —**harpist** *n* [C]; → see picture at STRINGED INSTRUMENT

harp² v

harp on about sth BrE; **harp on sth** AmE *phr v informal* to talk about something continuously, especially in a way that is annoying or boring: *My grandfather harps on about the war all the time.*

har·poon /hɑː'puːn $ hɑːr-/ *n* [C] a weapon used for hunting WHALES —**harpoon** v [T]

harp·si·chord /'hɑːpsɪkɔːd $ 'hɑːrpsɪkɔːrd/ *n* [C] a musical instrument like a PIANO, used especially in the past —**harpsichordist** *n* [C]

har·py /'hɑːpi $ 'hɑːrpi/ *n plural* **harpies** [C] **1** *literary* a cruel woman **2 Harpy** a cruel creature in ancient Greek stories, with the head and upper body of a woman and the wings and feet of a bird

har·ri·dan /'hærɪdən/ *n* [C] *old-fashioned* a bad-tempered unpleasant woman

har·row /'hærəʊ $ -roʊ/ *n* [C] a farming machine with sharp metal blades, used to break up the earth before planting crops —**harrow** v [I,T]

har·row·ing /'hærəʊɪŋ $ -roʊ-/ *adj* very frightening or shocking and making you feel very upset: *a harrowing experience* | *a harrowing story*

har·ry /'hæri/ v **harried, harrying, harries** [T] **1** to keep attacking an enemy **2** to keep asking someone for something in a way that is upsetting or annoying

harsh /hɑːʃ $ hɑːrʃ/ *adj*
1 CONDITIONS harsh conditions are difficult to live in and very uncomfortable; **▤ severe**: *The hostages are being held in extremely harsh conditions.* | **harsh winter/weather/climate** *the harsh Canadian winters* | *a vulnerable young girl suddenly exposed to the harsh realities of life*
2 TREATMENT/CRITICISM severe, cruel, or unkind: **harsh criticism/treatment/punishment etc** *His theory met with harsh criticism from colleagues.* | *the harsh measures taken against the protestors* | *'She's an idiot!' 'Aren't you being a bit harsh?'* | *a harsh, authoritarian regime* | *He had harsh words (=severe criticism) for the Government.*
3 SOUND unpleasantly loud and rough; **▤ soft**: **harsh voice/laugh/tone etc** *His voice was harsh and menacing.*
4 LIGHT/COLOUR unpleasantly bright; **▤ soft**: *She stood outside, blinking in the harsh sunlight.*
5 LINES/SHAPES ETC ugly and unpleasant to look at: *the harsh outline of the factories against the sky*
6 CLEANING SUBSTANCE too strong and likely to damage the thing you are cleaning: *My skin is quite sensitive and I find some soaps too harsh.* —**harshly** *adv*: *'Shut up,' Boris said harshly.* —**harshness** *n* [U]

hart /hɑːt $ hɑːrt/ *n* [C] *old use* a male DEER

har·vest¹ /'hɑːvɪ̯st $ 'hɑːr-/ *n* **1** [C,U] the time when crops are gathered from the fields, or the act of gathering them: **at harvest/at harvest time** *every year at harvest time* | **wheat/rice/grape etc harvest** *It rained for the potato harvest.* **2** [C] the crops that have been gathered, or the amount and quality of the crops gathered: **good/bumper harvest** (=a lot of crops) *Plum growers are expecting a bumper harvest this year.* | **poor/bad harvest** (=few crops) **3 reap a harvest** to get good or bad results from your actions: *The company is now reaping the harvest of careful planning.*

harvest² *v* [I,T] to gather crops from the fields

har·vest·er /ˈhɑːvɪstə $ ˈhɑːrvɪstər/ *n* [C] someone who gathers crops → **combine harvester** at COMBINE² (1)

harvest ˈfestival *n* [C] *especially BrE* a church service held in the autumn to thank God for the harvest → THANKSGIVING

has /z, əz, həz; *strong* hæz/ the third person singular of the present tense of HAVE

ˈhas-been *n* [C] *informal* someone who was important or popular but who has now been forgotten

hash¹ /hæʃ/ *n* **1 make a hash of sth** *informal* to do something very badly: *I made a real hash of my exams.* **2** [U] *informal* HASHISH **3** [C,U] a dish made with cooked meat and potatoes: *corned beef hash* **4** [C,U] *BrE* the symbol #

hash² *v*

hash sth ⇔ **out** *phr v AmE informal* to discuss something very thoroughly and carefully, especially until you reach an agreement: *The reorganization plan was hashed out September 16.*

ˌhash ˈbrowns *n* [plural] potatoes that are cut into very small pieces, pressed together, and cooked in oil

hash·ish /ˈhæʃɪʃ, -iːʃ/ *n* [U] the strongest form of the drug CANNABIS

has·n't /ˈhæzənt/ the short form of 'has not': *Hasn't she finished yet?*

hasp /hɑːsp $ hæsp/ *n* [C] a flat piece of metal used to fasten a door, lid etc

has·sle¹ /ˈhæsəl/ *n* **1** [C,U] *spoken* something that is annoying, because it causes problems or is difficult to do: *I don't feel like cooking tonight, it's too much hassle.* | *It's such a hassle not having a washing machine.* **2** [C] *AmE informal* an argument between two people or groups: *hassles with the management*

hassle² *v* **hassled**, **hassling** [T] *informal* to annoy someone, especially by asking them many times to do something: *Stop hassling me! I said I'll call them tomorrow.*

has·sock /ˈhæsək/ *n* [C] **1** a small CUSHION for kneeling on in a church **2** *AmE* a soft round piece of furniture used as a seat or for resting your feet on; ☐ **pouf** *BrE*

hast /hæst/ **thou hast** *old use* a way of saying 'you have'

haste /heɪst/ *n* [U] **1** great speed in doing something, especially because you do not have enough time; ☐ **hurry**: *I soon regretted my haste.* | **in your haste to do sth** *In his haste to leave, he forgot his briefcase.* **2 in haste** *written or formal* quickly or in a hurry: *They left in haste, without even saying goodbye.* **3 make haste** *old use* to hurry or do something quickly **4 more haste less speed** *BrE*; **haste makes waste** *AmE* used to say that it is better to do something slowly, because if you do it too quickly you will make mistakes

has·ten /ˈheɪsən/ *v formal* **1** [T] to make something happen faster or sooner: *Their departure was hastened by an abnormally cold winter.* **2** [I] to do or say something quickly or without delay; ☐ **hurry**: **hasten to do sth** *I hastened to assure her that there was no danger.* **3 I hasten to add** used when you realize that what you have said may not have been understood correctly: *an exhausting course, which, I hasten to add, was also great fun* **4** [I always + adv/prep] *literary* to go somewhere quickly

hast·i·ly /ˈheɪstɪli/ *adv written* quickly, perhaps too quickly; ☐ **hurriedly**: *a hastily arranged news conference* | *'Don't worry,' Jenny added hastily.* 'I checked with Lizzie first.' | *I may have acted hastily.*

hast·y /ˈheɪsti/ *adj* **1** done in a hurry, especially with bad results; ☐ **hurried**: *He soon regretted his hasty decision.* | *a hasty breakfast* **2 be hasty** to do something too soon, without careful enough thought: *Let's not be hasty – sit down for a moment.*

hats and headwear

top hat

bonnet

hard hat

peaked cap

sun hat

bobble hat *BrE*

bowler hat *BrE/*
derby *AmE*

baseball cap   sombrero   beret

hat [S1] [W3] /hæt/ *n* [C]

1 a piece of clothing that you wear on your head: *Maria was wearing a beautiful new hat.* | **straw/cowboy/bowler etc hat** | **in a hat** *a man in a fur hat* | **bowler-hatted/top-hatted etc** (=wearing a bowler hat, top hat etc) *a bowler-hatted gentleman*

2 keep sth under your hat *informal* to keep something secret

3 be wearing your teacher's/salesman's etc hat also **have your teacher's/salesman's etc hat on** *informal* to be performing the duties of a teacher etc, which are not your only duties: *I'm a manager now and only put my salesman's hat on when one of our sales reps is having real problems.*

4 I take my hat off to sb also **hats off to sb** *informal* used to say you admire someone very much because of what they have done: *I take my hat off to Ian – without him we'd have never finished this project on time.*

5 be drawn/pulled/picked out of the/a hat if someone's name is drawn out of a hat, they are chosen, for example as the winner of a competition, because their name is the first one that is taken out of a container containing the names of all the people involved: *The first correct entry out of the hat on September 2nd will win a prize.*

6 pass the hat around to collect money from a group of people, especially in order to buy someone a present → HARD HAT; → **OLD HAT**; → **at the drop of a hat** at DROP² (5); → **I'll eat my hat** at EAT (8); → **hang up your hat** at HANG UP (3); → **be talking through your hat** at TALK¹ (29)

hat·band /ˈhætbænd/ *n* [C] a band of cloth or leather fastened around a hat as a decoration

ˈhat box *n* [C] a special box used for carrying a hat in

hatch¹ /hætʃ/ *v* **1** also **hatch out** [I,T] if an egg hatches, or if it is hatched, it breaks, letting the young bird, insect etc come out: *The eggs take three days to hatch.* **2** also **hatch out** [I,T] if a young bird, insect etc hatches, or if it is hatched, it comes out of its egg: *All the chicks have hatched out.* **3 hatch a plot/plan/deal etc** to form a plan etc in secret

H

hatch² n [C] **1** a hole in a ship or aircraft, usually used for loading goods, or the door that covers it: **escape hatch** (=a hole in an aircraft etc through which you can escape) **2** also **hatchway** a small hole in the wall or floor between two rooms, or the door that covers it **3 down the hatch** *spoken informal* something you say before drinking an alcoholic drink quickly

hatch·back /'hætʃbæk/ n [C] a car with a door at the back that opens upwards

hatch·er·y /'hætʃəri/ n *plural* **hatcheries** [C] a place for hatching eggs, especially fish eggs

hatch·et /'hætʃɪt/ n [C] a small AXE with a short handle → **bury the hatchet** at BURY (9)

hatchet-faced adj having an unpleasantly thin face with sharp features

hatchet ,job n [C] *BrE informal* a newspaper article, television programme etc that criticizes someone severely and unfairly: [+on] *They were afraid I was going to* **do a hatchet job** *on them.*

hatchet ,man n [C] *informal* someone who is employed to make unpopular changes in an organization

hatch·ing /'hætʃɪŋ/ n [U] fine lines drawn on or cut into a surface

hatch·way /'hætʃweɪ/ n [C] a HATCH² (2)

hate¹ S1 W3 /heɪt/ v [T not in progressive]
1 to dislike something very much; ◧ **love**: *It's the kind of movie you either love or hate.* | *He hates his job.* | *I hate the way I sound on tape.* | **hate doing sth** *Paul hates having his picture taken.* | **hate to do sth** *I hate to see you unhappy.* | **hate it when** *Pam hates it when Lee calls her at work.* | **hate sb doing sth** *Jenny's mother hates her staying out late.*
2 to dislike someone very much and feel angry towards them; ◧ **love**: *Why do you hate me so much?* | **hate sb for (doing) sth** *She hated him for being so happy.* | **hate yourself** *I hated myself for feeling jealous of her.* | **hate sb's guts** *informal* (=hate someone very much)
3 **I'd hate (for) sb/sth to do sth** *spoken* used to emphasize that you do not want something to happen: *I'd hate you to go.* | *I'd hate for him to think I wasn't interested.*
4 I hate to think what/how/where etc *spoken* used when you feel sure that something would have a bad result, or when an idea is unpleasant to think about: *I hate to think what would have happened if you hadn't called the police.* | *I hate to think how many women he has assaulted since then.*
5 I hate to say it, but.../I hate to tell you this, but... *spoken* used when saying something that you do not want to say, for example because it is embarrassing: *I hate to say it, but I was glad when he went home.*
6 I hate to ask/interrupt/disturb etc *spoken* used to say that you are sorry that you have to ask etc: *I hate to ask you this, but would you mind giving me a lift home?* | *I hate to interrupt, but it's urgent.* —**hated** adj: *the hated security police* —**hater** n [C]: *I'm not a man hater.*

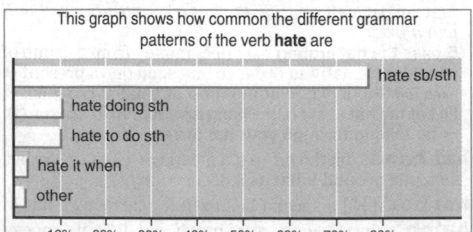

This graph shows how common the different grammar patterns of the verb **hate** are

		hate sb/sth
	hate doing sth	
	hate to do sth	
hate it when		
other		

10% 20% 30% 40% 50% 60% 70% 80%

hate² n [U] an angry unpleasant feeling that someone has when they hate someone and want to harm them; ◧ **hatred**; ◧ **love**: *Her eyes were full of hate.* | [+for] *Mrs Williams has spoken of her hate for her husband's killers.* → **pet hate** at PET³ (2)

hate cam,paign n [C] a series of things that a person or group does in order to upset or harm someone they hate

hate crime n [C,U] a crime that is committed against someone only because they belong to a particular race, religion etc

hate·ful /'heɪtfəl/ adj *old-fashioned* very bad, unpleasant, or unkind: *It was all the fault of that hateful man!*

hate mail n [U] letters that express a lot of hatred towards the person to whom they are sent: *She complained to the police after receiving threatening phone calls and hate mail.*

hath /hæθ/ *old use* has

hat·pin /'hæt,pɪn/ n [C] a long pin that is used to make a woman's hat stay on her head

ha·tred /'heɪtrɪd/ n [C,U] an angry feeling of extreme dislike for someone or something; ◧ **love**: *A look of pure hatred flashed across her face.* | [+of/for/towards] *his intense hatred of all foreigners* | *Abby made no secret of her hatred for her father.* | **passionate/intense/deep etc hatred** *Ellis was a sick young man with a deep hatred of women.* | *the old hatreds and prejudices that simmered below the surface*

hat stand n [C] a tall pole with hooks at the top used to hang coats and hats on

hat·ter /'hætə $ -ər/ n [C] *old-fashioned* someone who makes or sells hats → **as mad as a hatter** at MAD (2)

hat trick n [C] a series of three successes, especially in sports such as football when the same person scores three times: *Saunders* **scored a hat trick** *in the final game of the series.* | [+of] *a hat trick of victories*

haugh·ty /'hɔːti $ 'hɒː-/ adj behaving in a proud unfriendly way; → **stuck up**: *a haughty laugh* —**haughtily** adv —**haughtiness** n [U]

haul¹ /hɔːl $ hɒːl/ v [T] **1** to pull something heavy with a continuous steady movement: **haul sth off/onto/out of etc sth** *She hauled her backpack onto her back.* | *the steam locomotive which hauled the train* | *I hauled the door shut behind me.* **2 haul yourself up/out of sth etc a)** to move somewhere with a lot of effort, especially because you are injured or tired: *Patrick hauled himself painfully up the stairs.* **b)** to succeed in achieving a higher position in society, in a competition etc: *He is confident that the club can haul themselves further up the league.* **3 haul sb over the coals** *BrE* to criticize someone severely because they have done something wrong; ◧ **rake sb over the coals** *AmE* **4 haul off and hit/punch/kick sb** *AmE informal* to try to hit someone very hard **5 haul ass** *AmE spoken not polite* to hurry
haul sb off *phr v* to force someone to go somewhere that they do not want to go, especially to prison: *Police handcuffed him and hauled him off to jail.*
haul sb up *phr v informal* to officially bring someone to a court of law to be judged: [+before/in front of] *Campbell was hauled up in front of the magistrate.*

haul² n [C] **1** a large amount of illegal or stolen goods: *The gang escaped with a haul worth hundreds of pounds.* | [+of] *A haul of stolen cars has been seized by police officers.* **2 long/slow haul** something that takes a lot of time and effort: *At last we've won our freedom but* **it's been a long bitter haul.** **3** the amount of fish caught when fishing with a net → LONG-HAUL, SHORT-HAUL

haul·age /'hɔːlɪdʒ $ 'hɒːl-/ n [U] the business of carrying goods in trucks or trains for other companies: *the road haulage industry*

haul·i·er /'hɔːliə $ 'hɒːliər/ *BrE*, **haul·er** / $ 'hɒːlər/ *AmE* n [C] a company that carries goods in trucks or trains for other companies

haunch /hɔːntʃ $ hɒːntʃ/ n [C] **1 haunches** [plural] the part of your body that includes your bottom, your HIPS, and the tops of your legs: **on your haunches** *They squatted on their haunches playing dice.* **2** one of the back legs of a four-legged animal, especially when it is used as meat → see picture at BIG CAT

haunt¹ /hɔːnt $ hɒːnt/ v [T not in progressive] **1** if the soul of a dead person haunts a place, it appears there often: *The pub is said to be haunted by the ghost of a former landlord.* **2** to make someone worry or make them sad: *Clare was haunted by the fear that her husband was having an affair.* **3** to cause problems for someone over a long period of time: *an error that would come back to haunt them for years to come*

haunt[2] *n* [C] a place that someone likes to go to often: [+of] *The Café Vienna was a favourite haunt of journalists and actors.*

haunt·ed /ˈhɔːntɪd $ ˈhɒːn-/ *adj* **1** a haunted building is believed to be visited regularly by the soul of a dead person: *a haunted house* **2** **haunted expression/look** a very worried or frightened expression

haunt·ing /ˈhɔːntɪŋ $ ˈhɒːn-/ *adj* sad but also beautiful and staying in your thoughts for a long time: *a haunting melody* —**hauntingly** *adv*

haute cou·ture /ˌəʊt kuːˈtjʊə $ ˌoʊt kuːˈtʊr/ *n* [U] the business of making and selling expensive and fashionable clothes for women —**haute couturier** *n* [C]

haute cui·sine /ˌəʊt kwɪˈziːn $ ˌoʊt-/ *n* [U] cooking of a very high standard, especially French cooking

hau·teur /əʊˈtɜː $ hɒːˈtɜːr/ *n* [U] *formal* a proud, very unfriendly manner

have[1] [S1] [W1] /v, əv, əv, həv; *strong* hæv/ *auxiliary verb past tense and past participle* **had** /d, əd, həd; *strong* hæd/ *third person singular* **has** /z, əz, həz; *strong* hæz/
1 used with past participles to form PERFECT tenses: *Our guests have arrived.* | *Has anyone phoned?* | *We've been spending too much money.* | *I hadn't seen him for fifteen years.* | 'I hope you've read the instructions.' 'Yes, of course I have.' | *You haven't done much, have you?*
2 **sb had better/best do sth** used to say that someone should do something: *You'd better phone to say you'll be late.* | *We'd better not tell Jim about our plans just yet.*
3 **had sb done sth** *formal* if someone had done something: *Had we known about it earlier, we could have warned people of the danger.*

have[2] [S1] /hæv/ *v* [T]
1 QUALITY/FEATURE also **have got** [not in progressive] *especially BrE* used to say what someone or something looks like, what qualities or features they possess etc: *She has dark hair and brown eyes.* | *Sullivan's music does have a certain charm.* | *You need to have a lot of patience to be a teacher.* | *Wild rice has a very nutty flavour.* | *He didn't even have the courtesy to answer my letter.* | **have it in you** (=have the skill or special quality needed to do something) *You should have seen the way Dad was dancing – I didn't know he had it in him!*
2 INCLUDE/CONTAIN also **have got** [not in progressive] *especially BrE* to include or contain something or a particular number of things or people: *Japan has a population of over 120 million.* | *How many pages has it got?* | **have sth in it/them** *Check that the tank still has water in it.*
3 OWN also **have got** [not in progressive] *spoken especially BrE* used to say that someone owns something or that it is available for them to use: *They used to have a Mercedes Benz.* | *Has your secretary got a fax machine?* | *Have you ever had your own business?* | *He's a lovely dog – how long have you had him?* | *Can I have the car tonight, Dad?*
4 CARRY/HOLD also **have got** [not in progressive] *especially BrE* to be holding something or carrying it with you: *Have you got a match?* | *Look out! He's got a gun.* | **have sth on/with you** *Have you got any money on you?* | *I'm afraid I don't have my address book with me.*
5 DO STH *BrE* to do something: **have a look/walk/sleep/talk/think etc** *We were just having a look around.* | *Are you going to have a swim?*
6 EAT/DRINK/SMOKE to eat, drink, or smoke something: *She sat down and had another drink.* | *Someone had been having a cigarette in the toilet.* | **have lunch/a meal etc** *I usually have breakfast at about seven o'clock.*
7 EXPERIENCE to experience something or be affected by something: *We've been having a lot of difficulties with our new computer system.* | *I'm afraid your son has had a serious accident.* | *He is in hospital having treatment for a knee injury.* | *I hope you have a*

good holiday. | **have a good/terrible etc time** *Thanks for everything – we had a great time.* | **have sb doing sth** *He found it quite natural to have people fussing over him.*
8 IDEA/FEELING also **have got** [not in progressive] *especially BrE* to think of something or to experience a particular feeling: *If you have any good ideas for presents, let me know.* | *I have lots of happy memories of my time in Japan.* | *He had an awful feeling of guilt.*
9 DISEASE/INJURY/PAIN also **have got** [not in progressive] *especially BrE* to suffer from a disease, injury, or pain: *Sarah's got a cold.* | *One of the victims had a broken leg.*
10 RECEIVE also **have got** *especially BrE* to receive something: *I had lots of phone calls.* | **have sth from sb** *Have you had any news yet from Graham?* | *I expect he had some help from his father.*
11 AMOUNT OF TIME also **have got** [not in progressive] *especially BrE* if you have a particular amount of time, it is available for you to do something: *You have just 30 seconds to answer the question.* | **have time (to do sth)** *I haven't time to stop and talk just now.*
12 **have your hair cut/your house painted etc** to pay a professional person to cut your hair etc for you: *Where do you normally have your hair done?* | *We'd only just had a new engine put in.*
13 **have sth stolen/broken/taken etc** if you have something stolen, broken etc, someone steals, breaks etc something that belongs to you: *She had all her jewellery stolen.* | *Mullins had his nose broken in a fight.*
14 **have sth ready/done/finished etc** to have made something ready to be used, or have finished doing something: *I should have the car ready by Monday.*
15 IN A POSITION OR STATE also **have got** [not in progressive] *especially BrE* used to say that your body or something else is in a particular position or state, because you moved or did something: **have sth open/closed/on etc** *I had my eyes half-closed.* | *Janice likes to have the window open.* | *She had her back to the door.* | **have sth doing sth** *He's always got the stereo playing full blast.*
16 FAMILY/FRIENDS also **have got** [not in progressive] *especially BrE* used to say that there is someone who is your relation or friend: *She has an uncle who lives in Wisconsin.* | *It was very nice for Alice to have friends of her own age.*
17 JOB/DUTY also **have got** [not in progressive] *especially BrE* to be employed in a particular job or to be responsible for doing something: *Her boyfriend has a well-paid job.* | *The headteacher has responsibility for the management of the school.* | **have sth to do** *I can't stand here talking – I have work to do* (=there is work that I must do).
18 EMPLOY/BE IN CHARGE OF also **have got** [not in progressive] *especially BrE* to employ or be in charge of a group of workers: *Margaret Gillies currently has a team of 20 volunteers working for her.*
19 GOODS/ROOMS AVAILABLE also **have got** [not in progressive] *especially BrE* if a shop or a hotel has goods or rooms, they are available for you to buy or use: *Do you have any single rooms?* | *They didn't have any sweaters in my size.*
20 **have (got) sb with you** if you have someone with you, they are present with you: *Luckily I had a friend with me who spoke German.*
21 HOLD SB also **have got** [not in progressive] *especially BrE* to hold someone violently by a part of their body: *They had him by the throat.*
22 VISITORS/GUESTS if you have visitors or guests, they have come to your home, office etc: *Sorry, I didn't realize you had visitors.* | *We had friends to stay over the weekend.*
23 EVENT if you have an event such as a meeting, party, or concert, it happens because you have organized it: *We're having a party on Saturday – you're very welcome to come.*

H

24 EFFECT to cause a particular result: *a mistake that could have disastrous results* | *Cardew was having a bad influence on the other students.*

25 OPPORTUNITY used to say that an opportunity or choice is available for you: *If you have the chance, you should go and see it – it's a really good film.* | *Women managers have a choice as to whether they wear trousers or a skirt.* | *Last year I had the honour of meeting the Duke of Edinburgh.*

26 BABY if a woman has a baby, it is born from her body: *Anna insisted on having the baby at home.*

27 MAKE SB DO STH [not in progressive] **a)** to affect someone in a way that makes them start doing something: **have sb laughing/crying etc** *Within minutes he had the whole audience laughing and clapping.* **b)** to persuade or order someone to do something: **have sb doing sth** *She had me doing all kinds of jobs for her.* | **have sb do sth** especially AmE: *I'll have Hudson show you to your room.*

28 have done with sth to finish or settle an argument or a difficult situation: *I should throw you out now and have done with it.*

29 rumour/legend/word has it used when you are reporting what people say or what a story says: *Rumour has it that Kim is not his child.*

30 have (got) sth/sb (all) to yourself if you have a place, time, or person all to yourself, you do not have to share them with anyone else: *He couldn't wait to have Beth all to himself.* | *It was the first time I'd had a room to myself.*

31 SEX informal to have sex with someone: *I expect she's had lots of men.*

32 have it off/away with sb BrE informal to have sex with someone

SPOKEN PHRASES

33 can/could/may I have say this to politely ask someone to give you something: *Can I have the bill, please?* | *Could we have our ball back?*

34 I'll have/we'll have say this to ask for something that you have chosen in a restaurant or shop: *I'll have a T-bone steak and chips, please.*

35 OFFERING SB STH used to offer something to someone: *Have another sandwich.* | *Won't you have a drink before you go?* | *Please have a seat, and the doctor will be right with you.*

36 NOT ALLOW won't/can't have sth used to say that someone will not allow something to happen: *They're trying to play tricks on me again, but I won't have it.* | **won't/can't have sb doing sth** *I won't have you walking home all by yourself.* | *We can't have people wandering about on private land.*

37 have (got) it coming used to say that you are not sorry that something bad has happened to someone, because they deserved it: *I'm not surprised his wife left him – he's had it coming for years.*

38 I've got it used to say you have suddenly thought of the solution to a problem or that you suddenly understand a situation

39 you have me there also you've got me there used to say that you do not know the answer to a question: *'What makes you think women can't do that kind of work?' He scratched his head. 'Well, now, you've got me there.'*

40 I'll have you know used to start to tell someone something when you are annoyed with them: *I'll have you know you're insulting the woman I love.*

41 have (got) it in for sb to want to make life difficult for someone because you dislike them: *Dean thinks his teachers have it in for him.*

42 sb/sth has had it **a)** if someone has had it, they are going to fail or die, or be in serious trouble: *Press the wrong button and you've had it.* **b)** if someone has had it, they are very tired or annoyed and cannot continue with something: *I can't believe he's done it again. I've had it with him!* **c)** BrE if something has had it, it no longer works and cannot be repaired: *The engine's had it.*

43 be not having any (of that) to refuse to agree to something, listen to someone etc: *I tried to explain to her, but she just wasn't having any of it.*

44 sb has been had used to say that someone has been deceived, for example by being tricked into paying too much: *You paid £200? You've been had!*

have (got) sth against sb/sth *phr v*
to dislike or be opposed to someone or something for a particular reason: *I don't know what it is, but Roger seems to have something against women.* | *I can't see what you've got against the idea.* | *I have nothing against foreigners* (=have no reason to dislike them).

have (got) sb in *phr v BrE*
if you have someone in, they are doing some work in your home, for example building work: *We've had the builders in all week, so everything's in a mess.*

have on
1 have (got) sth on to be wearing a piece of clothing or type of clothing: *He had his best suit on.* | *Jimmy had nothing on but his socks.*
2 have (got) the TV/radio/washing machine etc on if you have your television, radio etc on, you have switched it on and it is working: *Billie has the radio on all day long.*
3 be having sb on especially BrE to be trying to make someone believe something that is not true, especially as a joke: *Don't believe a word he says. He's having you on!*
4 have (got) sth on BrE to have arranged to do something, go somewhere etc, especially when this means you cannot do something else: *Sorry, I can't help you this weekend – I've got too much on already.*
5 have (got) sth on sb to know about something bad that someone has done: *What do the police have on him?*
6 have (got) nothing on sb/sth informal to not be nearly as good as someone or something else: *Rock 'n' roll has got nothing on these African rhythms.*

have sth out *phr v*
1 to have a tooth etc removed by a medical operation
2 have it out (with sb) informal to settle a disagreement or difficult situation by talking to the person involved, especially when you are angry with them: *I'm going round to his house to have it out with him.*

have sb over also **have sb round** especially BrE *phr v*
if you have someone over, they come to your house for a meal, drink etc because you have invited them: *We must have you over for dinner before we leave.*

have sb up *phr v* [usually passive] BrE informal
to make someone go to a court of law because you think they have committed a crime: **have sb up for sth** *Last year he was had up for drunken driving.*

have³ S1 *v,* **have got to do sth** especially BrE
1 if you have to do something, you must do it because it is necessary or because someone makes you do it: *We don't have to rush – there's plenty of time.* | *I hate having to get up early in the morning.* | *If you earn more than £5000, you will have to pay tax.* | *I've got to be at the hospital at 4 o'clock.* | *It'll have to be on a Sunday. I'll be working every other day.*
2 used to say that it is important that something happens, or that something must happen if something else is to happen: *There has to be an end to the violence.* | *You've got to believe me!* | *There will have to be a complete ceasefire before the Government will agree to talks.* | *You have to be good to succeed in this game.*
3 used to tell someone how to do something: *First of all you have to mix the flour and the butter.*
4 used to say that you are sure that something will happen or something is true: *House prices have to go up sooner or later.* | *This has to be a mistake.* | *You have got to be joking!* | *No one else could have done it – it had to be Neville.*
5 used to suggest that someone should do something because you think it would be enjoyable or useful: *You'll have to come and meet my wife some time – she'd love to meet you.*

6 *spoken* used when something annoying happens in a way that things always seem to happen: *Of course it had to happen on today, when all the shops are shut.*
7 *spoken* used to say that only one thing or person is good enough or right for someone: *For Francesca it has to be the Ritz – nowhere else will do.*
8 do you have to do sth? *spoken* used to ask someone to stop doing something that annoys you: *Lieutenant, do you have to keep repeating everything I've just said?*
9 I have to say/admit/confess *spoken* used to show that you are making an honest statement even though it may be embarrassing for you: *I have to say I don't know the first thing about computers.* → MUST¹

ha·ven /ˈheɪvən/ n [C] a place where people or animals can live peacefully or go to in order to be safe: [+for] *The riverbanks are a haven for wildlife.* | *St Ives, a haven for artists and hippies* | **a haven of peace/ tranquillity/calm** *In the middle of the city, this garden is a haven of tranquillity.* → SAFE HAVEN, TAX HAVEN

have-'nots n **the have-nots** the poor people in a country or society: *a country where the have-nots far outnumber the haves* → HAVES

have·n't /ˈhævənt/ the short form of 'have not'

hav·er·sack /ˈhævəsæk $ -ər-/ n [C] *BrE old-fashioned* a bag that you carry on your back; 🔲 **back- pack, rucksack**

haves /hævz/ n **the haves** the rich people in a country or society: *the widening gap between the haves and the have-nots* → HAVE-NOTS

hav·oc /ˈhævək/ n [U] a situation in which there is a lot of damage or a lack of order, especially so that it is difficult for something to continue in the normal way: **cause/create havoc** *A strike will cause havoc for commuters.* | *policies that would wreak havoc on the country's economy* | *Rain has continued to play havoc with sporting events.*

haw /hɔː $ hɒː/ v another spelling of HA (1) → **hum and haw** at HUM¹ (4)

hawk¹ /hɔːk $ hɒːk/ n [C] **1** a large bird that hunts and eats small birds and animals **2** a politician who believes in using military force; 🔲 **dove 3 watch sb like a hawk** to watch someone very carefully **4 have eyes like a hawk** to be quick to notice things, especially small details

hawk² v **1** [T] to try to sell goods, usually by going from place to place and trying to persuade people to buy them **2** [I,T] to cough up PHLEGM

hawk·er /ˈhɔːkə $ ˈhɒːkər/ n [C] someone who carries goods from place to place and tries to sell them

hawk-eyed *adj* quick to notice small details

hawk·ish /ˈhɔːkɪʃ $ ˈhɒːk-/ *adj* supporting the use of military force in order to deal with political problems —**hawkishness** n [U]

haw·ser /ˈhɔːzə $ ˈhɒːzər/ n [C] *technical* a thick rope or steel CABLE used on a ship

haw·thorn /ˈhɔːθɔːn $ ˈhɒːθɔːrn/ n [C,U] a small tree with small white flowers, red berries, and sharp points

hay /heɪ/ n [U] **1** long grass that has been cut and dried, often used as food for cattle **2 make hay (while the sun shines)** to take the opportunity to do something now, because you may not be able to do it later **3 hit the hay** *informal* to go to bed → **a roll in the hay** at ROLL² (10)

hay ,fever n [U] a medical condition, like a bad COLD that is caused by breathing in POLLEN (=dust from plants)

hay·loft /ˈheɪlɒft $ -lɒːft/ n [C] the top part of a farm building where hay is stored

hay·mak·ing /ˈheɪˌmeɪkɪŋ/ n [U] the process of cut-ting and drying long grass to make hay

hay·rick /ˈheɪrɪk/ n [C] a HAYSTACK

hay·ride /ˈheɪraɪd/ n [C] *AmE* a ride in a CART filled with hay, usually as part of a social event

hay·stack /ˈheɪstæk/ also **hayrick** n [C] a large, firmly built pile of hay → **like looking for a needle in a haystack** at NEEDLE¹ (7)

hay·wire /ˈheɪwaɪə $ -waɪr/ *adj* **go haywire** *informal* to start working in completely the wrong way: *My com-puter's gone haywire.*

haz·ard¹ /ˈhæzəd $ -ərd/ n [C] **1** something that may be dangerous, or cause accidents or problems: [+to/for] *Polluted water sources are a hazard to wildlife.* | *That pile of rubbish is a **fire hazard** (=something that is likely to cause a fire).* | **health/safety hazard** *the health hazard posed by lead in petrol* **2** a risk that cannot be avoided: **the hazards of sth** *the economic hazards of running a small farm* | **occupational hazard** (=a danger that exists in a job) *Divorce seems to be an occupational hazard for politicians.*

haz·ard² v [T] **1** to say something that is only a suggestion or guess and that might not be correct: *$50,000? I don't know. I'm only **hazarding a guess.*** **2** *formal* to risk losing your money, property etc in an attempt to gain something

'hazard ,lights n [plural] special lights on a vehicle that flash to warn other drivers of danger

haz·ard·ous /ˈhæzədəs $ -zər-/ *adj* dangerous, espe-cially to people's health or safety: [+to] *The chemicals in paint can be **hazardous to health**.* | *the disposal of hazardous waste*

haze¹ /heɪz/ n [singular, U] **1** smoke, dust, or mist in the air which is difficult to see through: [+of] *a haze of cigarette smoke* | *The sun was surrounded by a golden haze.* **2** the feeling of being very confused and unable to think clearly: *in a drunken haze*

haze² v [T] *AmE* to play tricks on a new student or to make them do silly or dangerous things, as part of joining the school or a club at the school —**hazing** n [U]: *bizarre hazing rituals*

haze over *phr v* to become HAZY: *The sky hazed over.*

ha·zel¹ /ˈheɪzəl/ n **1** [C,U] a small tree that produces nuts **2** [U] the green-brown colour of some people's eyes

hazel² *adj* hazel eyes are a green-brown colour

ha·zel·nut /ˈheɪzəlnʌt/ n [C] the nut of the HAZEL¹ tree → see picture at NUT

haz·mat, HazMat /ˈhæzmæt/ n [U] *hazardous mate-rials* substances that are dangerous to people's health: *Paint and other chemicals can be taken to a HazMat center for disposal.*

haz·y /ˈheɪzi/ *adj* **1** air that is hazy is not clear because there is a lot of smoke, dust, or mist in it: *hazy sunshine* **2** an idea, memory etc that is hazy is not clear or exact: *My memories of the holiday are rather hazy.* | [+about] *She was a little hazy about the details.* —**hazily** *adv* —**haziness** n [U]

H-bomb /ˈeɪtʃ bɒm $ -bɑːm/ n [C] *informal* HYDROGEN BOMB

HCF /ˌeɪtʃ siː ˈef/ *technical* the abbreviation of **highest common factor**

he¹ S1 W1 /i, hi; *strong* hiː/ *pron* [used as the subject of a verb]
1 used to refer to a man, boy, or male animal that has already been mentioned or is already known about: *'Where's Paul?' 'He's gone to the cinema.'* | *It was he who first suggested the idea.*
2 used when talking about someone who may be male or female. Some people think this use is old-fashioned: *Everyone should do what he considers best.* ⚠ → see note at THEY
3 He used when writing about God

he² /hiː/ n [singular] *informal* a male person or animal: *I discovered that Mel wasn't a he, but a she.*

he- /hiː/ *prefix* a male animal: *a he-goat*

H.E. the written abbreviation of *His/Her Excellency*, used in the title of an AMBASSADOR

head¹ S1 W1 /hed/ n
1 TOP OF BODY [C] the top part of your body that has your face at the front and is supported by your neck

H

turn your head
shake your head (=move it from side to side, especially to show disagreement)
nod your head (=move it up and down, especially to show agreement)
raise/lift your head (=look up)
bow/bend/lower your head (=look downwards)
hang your head (=look downwards, especially because you are ashamed)
cock your head (=hold your head at an angle)
scratch your head
sb's head aches
sb's head throbs (=it aches badly)
from head to foot/toe (=over your whole body)
bald head (=one with no hair on it)
the crown of your head (=the top of the back of your head)
head injury

He kissed the top of her head. | *He **turned** his **head** and looked at me.* | *The men were whispering and **shaking** their **heads**.* | *'You're pregnant?' She **nodded** her **head**.* | *Let us all **bow** our **heads** in prayer.* | *I had no reason to **hang** my **head**. I had nothing to be ashamed of.* | *Her **head** was **cocked** to one side.* | *Tommy **scratched** his **head** thoughtfully.* | *My **head's throbbing**. I'm going to bed.* | *He was shaking **from head to foot**.* | *Brian's **bald head** glistened in the blazing sun.* | *Wearing a helmet reduces the risk of **head injury**.*

2 MIND [C] your mind or mental ability: *The problem only exists inside his head.* | **do sth in your head** (=calculate something mentally) *I can't do those figures in my head.* | **Use your head** *to work out the answer.* | **come into/pop into your head** *Jackie said the first thing that came into her head.* | **get sth into your head** (=understand something) *'It's over, Jake,' she said. 'Try and get that into your head.'* | **take/get it into your head (to do sth)** (=decide to do something, especially something stupid) *At about two in the morning, Alan took it into his head to go for a swim.* | **get/put sth out of your head** (=stop thinking or worrying about something) *Try to put it out of your head for the time being.* | **put sth into sb's head** (=make someone think or believe something) *What's put that idea into her head?'* | **get your head round sth** *BrE* (=be able to understand something) *I just can't get my head round what's been going on here.*
3 CALM/SENSIBLE **a)** keep your head to remain calm and sensible in a difficult or frightening situation: *We need a candidate who can keep his or her head even when clients get aggressive.* | **keep a clear/cool/calm head** *Get to sleep early tonight – you'll need to keep a clear head tomorrow at the trial.* **b)** lose your head to become unable to behave calmly or sensibly in a difficult or frightening situation: *You'll be OK as long as you don't lose your head and forget he's the real enemy.* **c)** have your head screwed on (straight/right) *informal* to be sensible and able to deal with difficult situations: *He wondered what Gemma thought about it all. She seemed to have her head screwed on.*
4 PERSON IN CHARGE [C] **a)** a leader or person in charge of a group or organization: [+of] *You should discuss the matter with your head of department.* | *A meeting of Commonwealth **heads of state** will be held next month.* | **head waiter/chef/gardener etc** (=the person in charge of a group of waiters etc) **b)** also **head teacher** *BrE* the person in charge of a school; ▤ **principal** *AmE*: *From now on all violent incidents should be reported directly to the head.* → CROWNED HEAD, HEAD BOY, HEAD GIRL, HEADMASTER, HEADMISTRESS
5 FRONT/LEADING POSITION [singular] the front or the most important position: **(at) the head of sth** *Jenny marched proudly at the head of the procession.* | **At the head of the table** (=the place where the most important person sits) *sat the senior partners.* | **at sth's/sb's head** *The band of soldiers marched into the yard, their defeated captain at their head.*
6 CRAZY [C] usually singular] used in particular

phrases to talk about someone being crazy or very stupid: *People going out in conditions like this **need** their **heads examined**.* | **be off your head** *BrE: You must be off your head if you think that.* | *If I walk in looking like that, they'll think I'm **not right in the head**.*
7 a head/per head for each person: *Dinner works out at $30 a head.* | *average incomes per head*
8 RIVER/VALLEY [C usually singular] the place where a river, valley etc begins
9 come to a head also bring sth to a head if a problem or difficult situation comes to a head, or something brings it to a head, it suddenly becomes worse and has to be dealt with quickly: *Things came to a head in the summer of 1997.*
10 FLOWER/PLANT [C] the top of a plant where its flowers or leaves grow: *She was outside cutting the dead heads off the roses.* | [+of] *a head of lettuce*
11 HEIGHT/DISTANCE [singular] the length of a head, used to measure height or distance: *She saw her father, a head above the rest of the crowd.* | **by a (short) head** (=used to say that a horse won or lost a race but only by a small amount)
12 COIN heads the side of a coin that has a picture of a person's head on it: **heads or tails?** *BrE spoken* (=used to decide something, by asking someone which side of a coin they guess will be showing when you throw it in the air and it lands); → **tails** at TAIL[1] (5b)
13 laugh/shout/scream etc your head off *informal* to laugh, shout etc very loudly: *Fans were screaming their heads off.*
14 have a good/fine/thick etc head of hair to have a lot of hair on your head
15 get/put your head down *informal* **a)** to start working in a quiet determined way: *It's time you got your head down and did some revision.* **b)** *BrE* to sleep
16 keep your head down to try to avoid being noticed or getting involved in something: *Do what you're told and keep your head down.*
17 as soon as your head hits the pillow if you fall asleep as soon as your head hits the pillow, you fall asleep as soon as you lie down
18 be out of/off your head *informal* to not know what you are doing because you have taken drugs or drunk too much alcohol: *He was off his head on various drugs.*
19 go to sb's head *informal* **a)** if alcohol goes to your head, it quickly makes you feel drunk **b)** if success goes to someone's head, it makes them feel more important than they really are: *She never let fame go to her head.*
20 TOOL [C usually singular] the wide end of a long narrow tool or piece of equipment
21 put your heads together to discuss a difficult problem together: *The next morning, we all put our heads together to decide what should be done.*
22 go over sb's head **a)** to be too difficult for someone to understand: *The explanation went completely over my head.* **b)** to do something without discussing it with a particular person or organization first, especially when you should have discussed it with them: *The President went over the head of Congress and called a referendum.*
23 can't make head or/nor tail of sth *informal* to be completely unable to understand something
24 have your head in the clouds to think about something in a way that is not practical or sensible, especially when you think things are much better than they really are
25 have a (good) head for figures/facts/business etc to be naturally good at doing calculations, remembering facts etc
26 head for heights the ability to look down from high places without feeling ill or nervous
27 a big head *informal* the opinion that you are much better, more important, more skilful etc than you really are: *I suppose I did do OK, but I'd be silly to get a big head about it.*
28 keep your head above water to manage to continue to live on your income or keep your business working when this is difficult because of financial problems: *For years they struggled to keep their heads above water.*

29 be/stand head and shoulders above sb to be much better than other people: *One contestant stood head and shoulders above the rest.*

30 hold up your head also **hold your head high** to show pride or confidence, especially in a difficult situation: *If you do this, you'll never be able to hold your head up again.*

31 be (like) banging/bashing etc your head against a brick wall *spoken* used to say that you are making no progress at all in what you are trying hard to do: *I've tried to talk some sense into them, but it's like banging my head against a brick wall.*

32 bang/knock sb's heads together *spoken* used to say that two people or groups should be forced to stop arguing and start to behave sensibly

33 bite/snap sb's head off to talk to someone very angrily with no good reason: *I offered to help her, but she just bit my head off.*

34 turn/stand sth on its head to make people think about something in the opposite way to the way it was originally intended: *The attorney quickly turned his main defense argument on its head.*

35 give sb their head to give someone the freedom to do what they want to do

36 be/fall head over heels in love to love or suddenly start to love someone very much: *Sam was head over heels in love with his new bride.*

37 heads will roll *spoken* used to say that someone will be punished severely for something that has happened: *Heads will roll for this!*

38 on your own head be it *spoken* used to tell someone that they will be blamed if the thing they are planning to do goes wrong

39 do your head in *BrE spoken informal* to make you feel confused and annoyed: *Turn that noise down – it's doing my head in!*

40 be/get in over your head to be or get involved in something that is too difficult for you to deal with: *In business, start small and don't get in over your head.*

41 be over your head in debt *AmE* to owe so much money that there is no possibility of paying it all back

42 go head to head with sb to deal with or oppose someone in a very direct and determined way: *Rather than go head to head with their main rivals, they decided to try a more subtle approach.*

43 heads up! *AmE spoken* used to warn people that something is falling from above

44 BEER [C] the layer of small white BUBBLES on the top of a glass of beer

45 ELECTRONICS [C] a piece of equipment that changes information on a recording tape, a computer HARD DISK etc into electrical messages that electronic equipment can use

46 head of cattle/sheep etc [plural] a particular number of cows, sheep etc: *a farm with 20 head of cattle*

47 head of water/steam pressure that is made when water or steam is kept in an enclosed space

48 get/build up a head of steam to become very active after starting something slowly

49 LAND [singular] *BrE* a high area of land that sticks out into the sea – used in names: *Beachy Head*

50 INFECTION [C] the centre of a swollen spot on your skin

51 give (sb) head *informal* to perform ORAL SEX on someone → **bury your head in the sand** at BURY (8); → **knock sth on the head** at KNOCK¹ (16) ; → **off the top of your head** at TOP¹ (18); → **sb can do sth standing on their head** at STAND¹ (40); → **turn sb's head** at TURN¹ (18); → **two heads are better than one** at TWO (8)

head² S2 W2 *v*

1 GO TOWARDS also **be headed** [I always + adv/prep] to go or travel towards a particular place, especially in a deliberate way: [+for/towards/back etc] *The ship was heading for Cuba.* | *It's about time we were heading home.* | **head north/south etc** *We headed south towards the capital.* | *Where are you guys headed?*

2 FUTURE be heading also **be headed** [I always + adv/prep] if you are heading for a particular situation,

especially a bad one, it seems likely to happen: [+for] *Forecasters predict the region's economy is heading for disaster.* | *Where is your life heading?*

3 BE IN CHARGE also **head up** [T] to be in charge of a team, government, organization etc: *David was asked to head up the technical team.* | *an interim government headed by the former Prime Minister*

4 AT TOP [T] **a)** to be at the top of a list or group of people or things: *The movie heads the list of Oscar nominations.* **b)** be headed if a page is headed with a particular name, title, image etc, it has it on the top: *The page was headed 'Expenses'.* | *officially-headed writing paper*

5 AT FRONT [T] to be at the front of a line of people: *A procession headed by the Queen was due to set off at four o'clock.*

6 FOOTBALL [I,T always + adv/prep] to hit the ball with your head, especially in football

    head off *phr v*

1 to leave or to go to another place: *I'm heading off now.*

2 head sth ⇔ off to prevent something from happening, especially something bad: *The President intervened to head off the conflict.*

3 head sb ⇔ off to stop someone going somewhere by moving in front of them: *Soldiers headed them off at the border.*

-head /hed/ *suffix* [in nouns] **1** the top of something: *the pithead* (=the top of a coalmine) | *a letterhead* (=a name and address printed at the top of a letter) **2** the place where something begins: *a fountainhead*

head·ache /'hedeɪk/ *n* [C] **1** a pain in your head: *I had a really bad headache, and couldn't go to work.* | **a splitting/pounding headache** (=a very bad headache) ⚠ Do not say that you 'have headache'. Say that you **have a headache**. **2** *informal* a problem that is annoying or difficult to deal with —**headachy** *adj*: *a headachy feeling*

head·band /'hedbænd/ *n* [C] a band that you wear around your head to keep your hair off your face or as a decoration

head·bang·er /'hedbæŋə $ -ər/ *n* [C] *informal* someone who enjoys HEAVY METAL music and moves their head around violently to the beat of the music —**headbanging** *n* [U] —**headbang** *v* [I]

head·board /'hedbɔːd $ -bɔːrd/ *n* [C] the upright board at the end of a bed where your head is

head 'boy *n* [C] the boy who is chosen in a British school each year to represent the school

head·butt /'hedbʌt/ *v* [T] to deliberately hit someone with your head

head·case /'hedkeɪs/ *n* [C] *informal* a crazy person

head ,cold a cold that makes it difficult for you to breathe

head count *n* **1** [C] the act of counting how many people are present in a particular place at one time: *The teachers did a head count to check that none of the kids were missing.* **2** [C,U] *technical* the number of people working for a company

head·dress /'hed-dres/ *n* [C] something that someone wears on their head, especially for decoration on a special occasion: *The bride wore white with a pearl headdress.*

head·ed /'hedɪd/ *adj* **1** red-headed/curly-headed etc having red hair, curly hair etc: *a bald-headed man* (=having no hair) *in a shiny suit* **2** two-headed/three-headed etc having two heads etc: *a two-headed monster* **3** headed notepaper/paper *BrE* paper for writing letters that has your name and address printed at the top

head·er /'hedə $ -ər/ *n* [C] **1** an action in football in which you hit the ball with your head **2** information at the top of a page, especially things such as numbers that appear on each page of a document **3** informa-

H

tion at the beginning of an email message that shows when it was sent, who wrote it etc → DOUBLE-HEADER

head-first, **head-first** /ˌhedˈfɜːst◂ $ -ˈfɜːrst◂/ *adv* **1** if you fall headfirst, your head goes down first, and the rest of your body follows afterwards: **dive/fall/jump/plunge head-first** *I fell head-first down the stairs.* **2** if you do something head-first, you become involved in it too quickly, without having time to think about it carefully: *a remark that sent him tumbling head-first into another controversy*

'**head game** *n* [C usually plural] *AmE informal* if you play head games with someone, especially someone you are in a romantic relationship with, you deceive them or try to get them to behave as you want them to: *He's obviously* **playing head games** *with you.*

head-gear /ˈhedɡɪə $ -ɡɪr/ *n* [U] *informal* hats and other things that you wear on your head

ˌ**head** '**girl** *n* [C] the girl who is chosen in a British school each year to represent the school

head-hunt-er /ˈhedˌhʌntə $ -ər/ *n* [C] someone who finds people with the right skills and experience to do particular jobs, and who tries to persuade them to leave their present jobs —**headhunt** *v* [T]

head-ing /ˈhedɪŋ/ *n* [C] **1** the title written at the beginning of a piece of writing, or at the beginning of part of a book: *chapter headings* **2** a name that is given to a group of things or people, that helps to describe them as a group: *writers who might* **come under the heading of** *postmodern fiction writers*

head-lamp /ˈhedlæmp/ *n* [C usually plural] a HEADLIGHT

head-land /ˈhedlənd/ *n* [C] an area of land that sticks out from the coast into the sea

head-less /ˈhedləs/ *adj* **1** without a head: *a headless corpse* **2** **run around like a headless chicken** *informal* to be going from one place to another in a way that is not organized at all

head-light /ˈhedlaɪt/ also **headlamp** *n* [C usually plural] **1** one of the large lights at the front of a vehicle, or the beam of light produced by this: *Suddenly, a figure appeared* **in my headlights.** → see picture at CAR **2** **like a rabbit/deer caught in headlights** so frightened or confused that you do not know what to do

head-line¹ S3 /ˈhedlaɪn/ *n* [C]
1 the title of a newspaper report, which is printed in large letters above the report: *a paper carrying the front-page headline: 'Space Aliens meet with President'* **2** **the headlines** the important points of the main news stories that are read at the beginning of a news programme on radio or television
3 **make/grab (the) headlines** also **be in/hit the headlines** to be reported in many newspapers and on radio and television: *a scandal that grabbed the headlines for weeks* | *The former MP found himself back in the headlines again.*

headline² *v* **1** [I,T] to appear as the main performer or band in a show: *Eminem is headlining at the festival this year.* **2** [T usually passive] to give a headline to an article or story

'**headline-grabbing** *adj* headline-grabbing news is important and reported in many newspapers and on radio and television: *The story was headline-grabbing material in the nationals.*

head-lin-er /ˈhedlaɪnə $ -ər/ *n* [C] the main performer or band in a concert

head-lock /ˈhedlɒk $ -lɑːk/ *n* [C] a way of holding someone around their neck so that they cannot move: *His opponent* **had him in a headlock.**

head-long /ˈhedlɒŋ $ -lɒːŋ/ *adv* **1** **rush/plunge headlong into sth** if you rush headlong into something, you start doing it too quickly without thinking carefully **2** with your head first and the rest of your body following; 🔲 **headfirst**: *I fell headlong into a pool of icy water.* **3** very quickly, without looking

where you are going: *Mortimer almost* **ran headlong into** *a patrol.* —**headlong** *adj*

head-man /ˈhedmæn/ *n plural* **headmen** /-men/ [C] the most important man in a village where a tribe lives; 🔲 **chief**

head-mas-ter /ˌhedˈmɑːstə $ ˈhed,mæstər/ *n* [C] *BrE* a male teacher who is in charge of a school; 🔲 **head teacher**; 🔲 **principal** *AmE*

head-mis-tress /ˌhedˈmɪstrɪ̩s $ ˈhed,mɪs-/ *n* [C] *BrE* a female teacher who is in charge of a school; 🔲 **head teacher**; 🔲 **principal** *AmE*

ˌ**head** '**office** *n* [C] the main office of a company

ˌ**head of** '**state** *n plural* **heads of state** [C] the main representative of a country, such as a queen, king, or president, who may not have duties in the country's government

ˌ**head-'on** *adv* **1** **crash/collide/smash etc head-on** if two vehicles crash etc head-on, the front part of one vehicle hits the front part of the other **2** if someone deals with a problem head-on, they do not try to avoid it, but deal with it in a direct and determined way: **face/tackle/meet sth head-on** *The police are trying to tackle car crime head-on.* **3** if two people or teams meet head-on in an argument, competition etc, they compete against each other and try to win in a very determined way —**head-on** *adj*: *a head-on collision*

head-phones /ˈhedfəʊnz $ -foʊnz/ *n* [plural] a piece of equipment that you wear over your ears to listen to the radio, music etc without other people hearing it

head-piece /ˈhedpiːs/ *n* [C] something you wear on your head, usually for decoration

head-quar-tered /ˈhed,kwɔːtəd, ˈhedˈkwɔːtəd $ -ɔːrtərd/ *adj* **be headquartered** to have your headquarters at a particular place: *Many top companies are headquartered in northern California.*

head-quar-ters /ˈhed,kwɔːtəz, ˌhedˈkwɔːtəz $ -ɔːrtərz/ *abbreviation* **HQ** *n plural* **headquarters** [C] **1** the main building or offices used by a large company or organization: *the headquarters of the United Nations* **2** the place from which military operations are controlled

head-rest /ˈhed-rest/ *n* [C] the top part of a chair or of a seat in a car, plane etc that supports the back of your head → see picture at CAR

head-room /ˈhed-rʊm, -ruːm/ *n* [U] **1** the amount of space above your head, especially when you are in a car **2** *BrE* the amount of space above a vehicle when it is under a bridge

head-rush /ˈhedrʌʃ/ *n* [C] a sudden feeling of extreme pleasure and excitement, especially one that you get soon after using an illegal drug such as ECSTASY or COCAINE

head-scarf /ˈhedskɑːf $ -skɑːrf/ *n plural* **headscarves** /-skɑːvz $ -skɑːrvz/ [C] a square piece of cloth that women wear on their heads and tie under their chins

head-set /ˈhedset/ *n* [C] a set of HEADPHONES, often with a MICROPHONE attached

head-ship /ˈhedʃɪp/ *n* [C] **1** the position of being in charge of an organization **2** *BrE* the job of being in charge of a school

head-stand /ˈhedstænd/ *n* [C] a position in which you turn your body UPSIDE DOWN, with your head and hands on the floor and your legs and feet in the air: *Can you do a headstand?*

ˌ**head** '**start** *n* [C] **1** an advantage that helps you to be successful: **give sb/get/have a head start** *Give your children a head start by sending them to nursery school.* **2** a start in a race in which you begin earlier or further ahead than someone else

head-stone /ˈhedstəʊn $ -stoʊn/ *n* [C] a piece of stone on a GRAVE, with the name of the dead person written on it; 🔲 **gravestone, tombstone**

head-strong /ˈhedstrɒŋ $ -strɒːŋ/ *adj* very determined to do what you want, even when other people advise you not to do it

head 'table n [C] a table at a formal meal where the most important people sit, or the people who are giving speeches

head 'teacher n [C] BrE the teacher who is in charge of a school; ⊟ **principal** AmE

head-to-'head adv competing directly with another person or group: Courier companies are **going head-to-head** with the Post Office. —**head-to-head** adj: a head-to-head contest —**head-to-head** n [C]

head·wa·ters /'hedwɔːtəz $ -wɔːtərz, -wɑː-/ n [plural] the streams that form a river

head·way /'hedweɪ/ n **make headway a)** to make progress towards achieving something – used especially when this is difficult: [+towards/in/with etc] Foreign firms have made little headway in the U.S. market. **b)** to move forwards – used especially when this is slow or difficult: Stormy weather stopped the ship from making headway.

head·wind /'hed,wɪnd/ n [C,U] a wind that blows directly towards you when you are moving

head·word /'hedwɜːd $ -wɜːrd/ n [C] technical one of the words whose meaning is explained in a dictionary

head·y /'hedi/ adj [usually before noun] **1** a heady smell, drink etc is pleasantly strong and seems to affect you strongly: a heady combination of wine and brandy **2** very exciting in a way that makes you feel as if you can do anything you want to: the heady atmosphere of the early sixties

heal /hiːl/ v [I,T] **1** also **heal up** if a wound or a broken bone heals or is healed, the flesh, skin, or bone grows back together and becomes healthy again: It took three months for my arm to heal properly. **2** to make someone who is ill become healthy again, especially by using natural powers or prayer; → **cure**: a preacher who claims that he can heal the sick **3** to become mentally or emotionally strong again after a bad experience, or to help someone to do this: Ann says the only way to heal after rape is to talk about it. | The trauma of divorce can often be healed by successful remarriage. **4** if an argument or disagreement between people heals or you heal it, the people stop arguing or disagreeing: **heal the wounds/breach/division/rift** Our main goal must be to heal the divisions in our society. | The rift between the two younger men never healed.

heal over phr v if a wound or an area of broken skin heals over, new skin grows over it and it becomes healthy again

heal·er /'hiːlə $ -ər/ n [C] **1** someone who is believed to be able to cure people using natural powers, rather than by using medicine → **faith healer** at FAITH HEALING **2** something that makes a bad experience seem less painful: Time is a great healer.

heal·ing /'hiːlɪŋ/ n [U] **1** the treatment of illness using natural powers or prayer rather than medicine: The medical establishment is taking healing increasingly seriously. → FAITH HEALING **2** the process of becoming healthy and strong again: the healing process

health S1 W1 /helθ/ n [U]
1 the general condition of your body and how healthy you are

damage your health
improve your health
good/excellent health
poor/ill health
failing health (=when someone is becoming more ill)
be in good/excellent/the best of health
be in poor health
be good/bad for your health
sb's state of health
mental health
health care
health problem
health benefits (of sth)
health risk/hazard (=something that could damage your health)
health warning (=a warning printed on a product that can harm you)

I'm worried about my husband's **health**. | Smoking can seriously **damage** your **health**. | things that can be done to **improve** the **health** of older people | I have always enjoyed **good health**. | Sara had to leave her job due to **ill health**. | He is 75 and **in poor health**. | A low-fat diet is **better** for your **health**. | The type of vitamin needed depends on **the state of health** of the individual. | a young man with **mental health problems** | the **health benefits** of doing yoga | Air pollution is a serious **health hazard**.

⚠ Do not say that something is 'good for health' or 'bad for health'. Say that it is **good for your health** or **bad for your health**.

2 the work of providing medical services to keep people healthy: The government has promised to spend more on health and education. | health insurance | nurses and other health workers → PUBLIC HEALTH
3 when you have no illness or disease: Even if you haven't got much money, at least you've got your health. | When we last met, he was **glowing with health** (=was clearly very healthy).
4 how successful something such as a business, an organization, or a country's ECONOMY is: The monthly trade figures are seen as an indicator of the health of the economy. → **a clean bill of health** at CLEAN[1] (13)

,health and 'safety n [U] an area of government and law concerned with people's health and safety, especially at work: health and safety regulations

'health care n [U] the service that is responsible for looking after the health of all the people in a country or an area: The government has promised wide-ranging health care for all. | health care workers

'health ,centre BrE; **health center** AmE n [C] a building where several doctors work, and where people can go for medical treatment

'health club n [C] a place where people who have paid to become members can go to do physical exercise

'health farm n [C] BrE a place where people pay to stay so that they can do physical exercise, eat healthy food, and have beauty treatments; ⊟ **health spa** AmE

'health food n [C,U] food that contains only natural substances, and that is good for your health

health·ful /'helθfəl/ adj formal likely to make you healthy: healthful mountain air

'health pro,fessional n [C] someone such as a doctor, nurse, DENTIST etc, whose job involves people's health

'health ,service n [C] a public service that is responsible for providing people with medical care: reforms to the health service → NATIONAL HEALTH SERVICE

'health ,spa n [C] AmE a place where people pay to stay so that they can do physical exercise, eat healthy food, and have beauty treatments; ⊟ **health farm** BrE

'health ,visitor n [C] a nurse in Britain who visits people in their homes

health·y S3 W3 /'helθi/ adj comparative **healthier**, superlative **healthiest**
1 PERSON/ANIMAL/PLANT physically strong and not likely to become ill or weak: a healthy baby boy | I've always been perfectly healthy until now.
2 GOOD FOR YOUR BODY good for your body: a healthy lifestyle | a healthy diet | the importance of healthy eating
3 SHOWING GOOD HEALTH showing that you are healthy: Her face had a healthy glow. | All of our kids have healthy appetites (=they like to eat a lot).
4 BEHAVIOUR/ATTITUDE used to describe an attitude, feeling, or behaviour that is natural, normal, and sensible: I don't think it's healthy for her to spend so much time alone. | healthy respect/disrespect/scepticism etc a healthy disrespect for silly regulations
5 COMPANY/RELATIONSHIP ETC a healthy company, society, relationship, ECONOMY etc is working effectively

and successfully: *a healthy economy with a well-trained workforce*
6 AMOUNT large and showing that someone is successful – used about amounts of money: *a healthy profit* | *a healthy bank balance* —**healthily** *adv* —**healthiness** *n* [U]

heap¹ /hiːp/ *n* [C] **1** a large untidy pile of things: *a rubbish heap* | [+of] *There was a heap of stones where the building used to be.* | **in a heap** *The envelopes for posting lay in a heap on her desk.* | *We piled the branches into heaps for burning.* → see picture at BUNDLE **2 heaps** *informal* a lot of something: [+of] *The children have heaps of energy.* | **heaps better/bigger etc** (=much better, bigger etc) **3 fall/collapse etc in a heap** to fall down and lie without moving: *They finally collapsed in a heap on the grass.* **4** *humorous* an old car that is in bad condition **5 at the top/bottom of the heap** high up and successful or low down and unsuccessful in an organization or in society: *The very poor are at the bottom of the heap.* **6 be struck all of a heap** *BrE old-fashioned informal* to be suddenly very surprised or confused

heap² *v* [T] **1** also **heap up** to put a lot of things on top of each other in an untidy way; ◻ **pile**: [+on] *Jean heaped logs on the fire.* **2 heap sth with sth** to put a lot of something on a surface; ◻ **pile**: *She gave him a glass of whisky and heaped his plate with food.* **3 heap praise/insults etc on sb** to praise, insult etc someone a lot: *He heaped all the blame on his secretary.*

heaped /hiːpt/ *adj BrE* **heaped teaspoon/tablespoon etc** an amount of something that is as much as a spoon can hold: *Add three heaped teaspoons of sugar.*

hear S1 W1 /hɪə $ hɪr/ *v past tense and past participle* **heard** /hɜːd $ hɜːrd/
1 HEAR SOUNDS/WORDS ETC [I,T not in progressive] to know that a sound is being made, using your ears: *Blanche heard a crash as the back door was flung open.* | *Did anyone see or hear anything last night?* | *Old Zeke doesn't hear too well any more.* | **hear sb/sth doing sth** *Jenny could hear them arguing outside.* | **hear sb do sth** *She heard Tom go upstairs.* | **hear what/who etc** *I couldn't hear what they were saying most of the time.* | **be heard to do sth** *She didn't want to be heard to criticize him.* ⚠ Do not confuse **hear** with **listen to**, which means 'hear and pay attention to': *You should listen to my advice (NOT You should hear my advice).*
2 LISTEN TO SB/STH [T not in progressive] to listen to what someone is saying, the music they are playing etc: *Maggie did not wait to hear an answer.* | *Did you hear that programme on whales the other night?* | **hear what** *I want to hear what the doctor has to say.* | **I hear what you say/what you're saying** *spoken* (=used to tell someone that you have listened to their opinion, but do not agree with it) *I hear what you say, but I don't think we should rush this decision.*
3 BE TOLD STH [I,T not usually in progressive] to be told or find out a piece of information: *I heard a rumor that he was getting married soon.* | **hear (that)** *I'm so sorry to hear he died.* | *She'll be pleased to hear that she can leave hospital tomorrow.* | [+about] *Teresa heard about the decision later.* | [+of] *I've heard of a job which would be just right for you.* | *This was the first I'd heard of any trouble in the area* (=I had just heard news of trouble for the first time). | *He was last heard of in Washington* (=he was in Washington the last time someone had information about him). | **hear anything/much of sb/sth** *We don't hear anything of him these days.* | **so I hear/so I've heard** *spoken* (=used to say that you have been told something or know it already) *There's a nasty infection going round, so I hear.* | **hear what/how/who etc** *Did you hear what happened to Julia?* | *I've heard it said that they met in Italy.*
4 IN COURT [T] to listen to all the facts in a case in a court of law in order to make a legal decision: *The Supreme Court heard the case on Tuesday.*
5 have heard of sb/sth to know that someone or

something exists because they have been mentioned to you before: *'Do you know Jill Marshall?' 'No, I've never heard of her.'*
6 not hear the last of sb used to say that someone will continue to complain about something or cause problems: *I'll sue him. He hasn't heard the last of me yet.*
7 you could hear a pin drop used to emphasize how quiet a place is: *You could have heard a pin drop in there.*

8 won't/wouldn't hear of it used to say that you refuse to agree with a suggestion or proposal: *I said we should go back, but Dennis wouldn't hear of it.*
9 I/he etc will never hear the end of it used to say that someone will continue to talk about something for a long time: *If my Mum finds out, I'll never hear the end of it.*
10 be hearing things to imagine you can hear a sound when really there is no sound: *There's no one there. I must be hearing things.*
11 (do) you hear? used to emphasize that you are giving someone an order and they must obey you: *I want you to leave right now. Do you hear?*
12 you can't hear yourself think used to emphasize how noisy a place is: *Just shut up, Tom. I can't hear myself think.*
13 now hear this! *AmE old use* used to introduce an important official announcement
14 hear! hear! used in a discussion or meeting to say that you agree with what the speaker is saying
15 have you heard the one about... used when asking someone if they know a joke
16 I've heard that one before used when you do not believe someone's excuse or explanation

→ UNHEARD OF
hear from sb *phr v* [not in progressive]
1 to receive news or information from someone: *Do you ever hear from Jack?* | *Police want to hear from anyone who has any information about the attack.* | *I look forward to hearing from you* (=hope to receive news from you).
2 to listen to someone giving their opinion in a radio or television discussion programme: *a chance to hear from some of the victims of violent crime*
hear sb **out** *phr v* [not in passive]
to listen to all of what someone wants to tell you without interrupting them: *Just hear me out, will you?*

hear·er /ˈhɪərə $ ˈhɪrər/ *n* [C] someone who hears something; ◻ **listener**

hear·ing S3 W2 /ˈhɪərɪŋ $ ˈhɪr-/ *n*
1 [U] the sense which you use to hear sounds: **have good/bad etc hearing** *She has remarkable hearing for a lady of her age.* | *a child with a hearing disability* → HARD OF HEARING
2 [C] a meeting of a court or special committee to find out the facts about a case: *a court hearing* | *a disciplinary hearing*
3 [C usually singular] an opportunity for someone to explain their actions, ideas, or opinions: *Let's give both sides a fair hearing.*
4 in/within sb's hearing if you say something in someone's hearing, you say it where they can hear you: *There are some words we don't use in the children's hearing.*

'hearing aid *n* [C] a small object which fits into or behind your ear to make sounds louder, worn by people who cannot hear well

'hearing-im,paired *adj* **a)** not able to hear well; ◻ **hard of hearing;** → **deaf b) the hearing-impaired** people who are not able to hear well

hear·ken, harken /ˈhɑːkən $ ˈhɑːr-/ *v* [I + to] *literary* to listen

hear·say /ˈhɪəseɪ $ ˈhɪr-/ *n* [U] something that you have heard about from other people but do not know to be definitely true or correct: *I wouldn't take any notice of it – it's just hearsay.*

hearse /hɜːs $ hɜːrs/ *n* [C] a large car used to carry a dead body in a COFFIN at a funeral

heart [S1] [W1] /hɑːt $ hɑːrt/ *n*

1 BODY ORGAN [C] the organ in your chest which pumps blood through your body

> sb's **heart** beats
> sb's **heart** pounds/thuds/thumps (=it beats very strongly)
> sb's **heart** races (=it beats very fast)
> a weak **heart** (=an unhealthy heart)
> **heart** trouble/problems
> a **heart** condition (=something wrong with your heart)
> sb's **heart** rate (=the number of times their heart beats per minute)

*Regular exercise is good for the **heart**. | Can you **hear** my **heart** beating? | Her cheeks were hot and her **heart** was pounding. | My **heart** raced. Were we going to land safely? | Daniel had no history of **heart** problems. | She suffers from a rare **heart** condition. | His breathing and **heart** rate were now normal.* → see picture at HUMAN

2 EMOTIONS/LOVE [C] the part of you that feels strong emotions and feelings: *His **heart** was full of anger and grief. | The plight of the refugees had tugged at the nation's **heart**. | The doctor had an extremely kind **heart**. | She could hardly speak for the **ache** in her **heart**. | It would break Kate's **heart** (=make her extremely sad) to leave the lovely old house. | He left the country **with a heavy heart** (=great sadness). | Edith loved her boy with all her **heart and soul**. | I was still pretty innocent then when it came to **affairs of the heart** (=matters relating to love and sex). | a woman with a **heart of gold** (=very kind character) | Sometimes I think he's got a **heart of stone** (=very cruel character). | I'm glad I **followed** my **heart** rather than my head for once. | **kind-hearted/cold-hearted/hard-hearted etc** (=having a kind, unkind, cruel etc character) He thinks of himself as a warm-hearted and caring human being.*

3 YOUR CHEST [C usually singular] the part of your chest near your heart: *He put his hand on his **heart**.*

4 SHAPE [C] a shape used to represent a heart

5 from the (bottom of your) heart with great sincerity and strength of feeling: *Leonard spoke from the **heart**. | I want to thank you from the bottom of my **heart**. | She sang the songs **straight from the heart**.*

6 in your heart (of hearts) if you know, feel, or believe something in your heart, you are secretly sure about it although you may not admit it: *In her **heart** she knew she would never go. | **Deep in his heart**, he wanted Laura back.*

7 IMPORTANT PART OF STH [singular] the most important or central part of a problem, question etc: **the heart of sth** *difficult issues **at the heart of** science policy | We must **get to the heart of** the problem.*

8 ENCOURAGEMENT [U] confidence and courage: *This inspiring service **gave us new heart**. | We mustn't **lose heart** when people complain. | We've got to **take a** bit of **heart** from the fact that we won.*

9 at heart if you are a particular kind of person at heart, that is the kind of person that you really are even though you may appear or behave differently: *He may be a working class boy at **heart**, but his lifestyle has been transformed. | Let's face it, we're all romantics at **heart**.* → **have sb's (best) interests at heart** at INTEREST[1] (5); → **young at heart** at YOUNG[1] (5)

10 THE CENTRE OF AN AREA [C] the middle part of an area furthest from the edge: **in the heart of sth** *You're lucky to live in a house like this in the **heart** of London. | **at the heart of sth** an old house at the heart of an ancient forest*

11 close/dear to sb's heart very important to someone: *The President liked to go to Williamsburg, a place close to his **heart**. | Money is dear to Kathleen's **heart**.*

12 by heart when you know something by heart, you remember all of it exactly: *After a few days of phoning Stephanie, he knew her number by **heart**. | Actors have to learn their lines by **heart**.*

13 sb's heart sinks used to say that someone suddenly lost hope and began to feel unhappy: *Her **heart** sank when she saw the number of books she had to read.*

14 with all your heart with all your strength, energy, or emotion: *He hates Los Angeles with all his **heart**. | We sang the hymn with all our **hearts**.*

15 take sth to heart to consider what someone says to you very seriously, often because it upsets you: *Anne took his criticisms very much to **heart**. | We took Stephen's warnings to **heart**.*

16 sb's heart goes out to sb used to say that someone feels a lot of sympathy towards another person: *My **heart** goes out to the families of the victims.*

17 CARD GAMES **a)** [C] a heart shape printed in red on a playing card **b) hearts** [plural] the SUIT (=set) of playing cards that have these shapes on them: *the ace of **hearts*** **c)** [C] one of the cards in this set: *Have you got any **hearts**?*

18 do sth to your heart's content to do something as much as you want: *She had lazed around the pool to her **heart's** content. | The dog can run to its **heart's** content out there.*

19 sb's heart misses/skips a beat used to say that someone suddenly feels a moment of fear or excitement: *His **heart** missed a beat as he saw the body of a small child at the water's edge.*

20 set your heart on sth to want something very much: *His father bought him the bike he had set his **heart** on. | She had set her **heart** on becoming a hairdresser.*

21 a man/woman etc after my own heart someone who likes the same things or behaves in the same way that you do: *Geoff really is a man after my own **heart**.*

22 cry/sing etc your heart out if you cry, sing etc your heart out, you do it with all your energy or emotion: *He found me crying my **heart** out and was so kind.* → **eat your heart out** at EAT (4); → **pour your heart out** at POUR

23 your heart's desire/everything your heart could desire the one thing you want most, or everything that you could possibly want: *To have a baby was her **heart's** desire.*

24 not have the heart to do something to be unable to do something because it will make someone unhappy: *I didn't have the **heart** to tell her that her beautiful vase was broken.*

25 sb's heart isn't in it used to say that someone does not really want to do something: *She's getting bored with the job and her **heart's** not in it.*

26 do sth out of the goodness of your heart to do something out of kindness, not because you have been asked or expect a reward: *All these people were helping us out of the goodness of their **hearts**.*

27 take sb to your heart if people take someone to their hearts, they like them very much: *The fans have taken Hudson to their **hearts**.*

28 VEGETABLE [C] the firm middle part of some vegetables: *artichoke **hearts***

29 give/lose your heart to sb to start to love someone very much

30 my heart was in my mouth used to say that you suddenly felt very afraid

31 sb's heart is in the right place *informal* used to say that someone is really a kind person and has the right feelings about something important: *I don't think his idea will work, though his **heart's** in the right place.*

32 it does your heart good to see/hear sth used to say that something makes you feel happy

33 sb's heart leaps *literary* used to say that someone suddenly feels happy and full of hope: *'I couldn't live without you,' he said and Jane's **heart** leapt.*

34 be in good heart *formal* to feel happy and confident: *The team are in good **heart** and ready for the season's matches.*

35 have a heart! used to tell someone not to be too strict or unkind – used humorously

36 know the way to sb's heart to know the way to

H

please someone – used humorously
37 my heart bleeds (for sb) used to say that you do not really feel any sympathy towards someone → **a broken heart** at BROKEN[2] (9); → **cross my heart** at CROSS[1] (11); → **have a change of heart** at CHANGE[2] (1); → **sick at heart** at SICK[1] (9); → **strike at the heart of sth** at STRIKE[1] (7); → **wear your heart on your sleeve** at WEAR[1] (8); → **win sb's heart** at WIN[1] (3)

heart·ache /ˈhɑːteɪk $ ˈhɑːrt-/ n [U] a strong feeling of great sadness and anxiety

heart at·tack n [C] **1** a sudden serious medical condition in which someone's heart stops working normally, causing them great pain: **have/suffer a heart attack 2 give sb/have a heart attack** informal to make someone suddenly feel frightened, surprised, or shocked, or to suddenly feel this way: *You almost gave me a heart attack there!*

heart·beat /ˈhɑːtbiːt $ ˈhɑːrt-/ n [C,U] **1** the action or sound of your heart as it pumps blood through your body **2 be a heartbeat away from sth** to be very close to a situation or position **3 in a heartbeat** AmE very quickly, without delay: *Things can change in a heartbeat.* **4 the heartbeat of sth** AmE the main origin of activity or excitement in a place or organization

heart·break /ˈhɑːtbreɪk $ ˈhɑːrt-/ n [U] great sadness or disappointment

heart·break·ing /ˈhɑːtˌbreɪkɪŋ $ ˈhɑːrt-/ adj making you feel extremely sad or disappointed —**heartbreakingly** adv

heart·brok·en /ˈhɑːtˌbrəʊkən $ ˈhɑːrtˌbroʊ-/ adj extremely sad because of something that has happened

heart·burn /ˈhɑːtbɜːn $ ˈhɑːrtbɜːrn/ n [U] an unpleasant burning feeling in your stomach or chest caused by acid from your stomach; → **indigestion**

heart dis·ease n [C,U] an illness which prevents your heart from working normally

heart·en /ˈhɑːtn $ ˈhɑːr-/ v [T usually passive] to make someone feel happier and more hopeful; ◼ **dishearten** —**heartening** adj —**hearteningly** adv

heart fail·ure n [U] a serious medical condition in which someone's heart stops working properly, often resulting in death; ◼ **heart attack**

heart·felt /ˈhɑːtfelt $ ˈhɑːrt-/ adj very strongly felt and sincere: *a heartfelt apology*

hearth /hɑːθ $ hɑːrθ/ n [C] **1** the area of floor around a FIREPLACE in a house → see picture at FIREPLACE **2 hearth and home** literary your home and family

heart·i·ly /ˈhɑːtɪ̈li $ ˈhɑːr-/ adv **1** with energy and enjoyment: *'Great to see you,' she said heartily.* | *Hugh laughed heartily at the joke.* **2** completely or very much: *This is a book I heartily recommend to all hill walkers.* | *Madge had become heartily sick of the city* **3** eat heartily to eat a large amount

heart·land /ˈhɑːtlənd $ ˈhɑːrt-/ n [C] **1 the heartland** the central part of a country or area of land **2** the most important part of a country or area for a particular activity, or the part where a political group has most support: *the Democratic heartlands of the Deep South*

heart·less /ˈhɑːtləs $ ˈhɑːrt-/ adj cruel and not feeling any pity: *How can you be so heartless?* —**heartlessly** adv —**heartlessness** n [U]

heart-lung ma·chine n [C] a machine that pumps blood and oxygen around someone's body during a medical operation

heart·rend·ing /ˈhɑːtˌrendɪŋ $ ˈhɑːrt-/ adj making you feel great pity; ◼ **heartbreaking**: *heartrending stories of children being taken from their parents*

heart-searching n [U] the process of examining very carefully your feelings about something or your reasons for doing something

heart-stopping adj very exciting or frightening

heart·strings /ˈhɑːtˌstrɪŋz $ ˈhɑːrt-/ n [plural] **tug/ tear/pull at sb's heartstrings** to make someone feel strong love or sympathy

heart·throb /ˈhɑːtθrɒb $ ˈhɑːrtθrɑːb/ n [C] a famous actor, singer etc who is very attractive to women

heart-to-'heart n [C] a conversation in which two people say honestly and sincerely what they really feel about something: *Why don't you have a heart-to-heart with him and sort out your problems?* —**heart-to-heart** adj: *a heart-to-heart talk*

heart·warm·ing /ˈhɑːtˌwɔːmɪŋ $ ˈhɑːrtˌwɔːr-/ adj making you feel happy because you see other people being happy or kind to each other: *a heartwarming sight* —**heartwarmingly** adv

heart·y /ˈhɑːti $ ˈhɑːrti/ adj **1** happy and friendly and usually loud: *a hearty laugh* **2** old-fashioned strong and healthy → **hale and hearty** at HALE **3** a hearty meal is very large **4** especially BrE with a friendly, noisy, and happy manner that is not sincere —**heartiness** n [U] → HEARTILY

heat[1] S2 W2 /hiːt/ n
1 WARMTH [U] warmth or the quality of being hot: *Ice needs heat to melt.* | *Insulating the attic is a good way to reduce heat loss.*
2 the heat very hot weather or a high temperature: *The heat was making them tired.* | *Angela liked to rest during the heat of the day* (=the hottest part of the day). | *Firefighters were beaten back by the intense heat and smoke.*
3 IN COOKING [C usually singular, U] the level of temperature used when cooking or heating something: **(a) low/medium/high heat** *Cook the chicken portions over a high heat.* | **turn off/down/up the heat** *When the milk comes to the boil, turn off the heat.* | *Now reduce the heat and cover the pan.*
4 STRONG FEELINGS [U] strong feelings, especially anger or excitement: *Reconciliation services can take the heat out of* (=reduce the anger in) *the dispute.* | **in the heat of sth** *Quick decisions had to be made in the heat of the negotiations.* | **In the heat of the moment** (=when feelings were very strong) *Nick threatened to resign.*
5 PRESSURE [U] strong pressure on someone: **The heat is on** (=there is a lot of pressure) *as schools struggle to finish their entries by the deadline.* | *The team* **turned up the heat** (=used more effort against their opponents) *in the last few minutes to score two more goals.* | *There was a lot of heat, and it affected our relationship.*
6 SYSTEM TO HEAT BUILDING [U] AmE the system in a house or other building that keeps it warm in the winter, or the warmth from this system; ◼ **heating** BrE: *Can you turn up the heat?*
7 IN A RACE [C] a part of a race or competition whose winners then compete against each other in the next part: *Bill finished second in his heat.*
8 on heat BrE; **in heat** AmE if a female animal is on heat, her body is ready to have sex with a male → DEAD HEAT, WHITE HEAT; → **if you can't stand the heat, get out of the kitchen** at STAND[1] (16)

heat[2] v [T] to make something become warm or hot; ◼ **warm up**: *Heat the milk until it boils.*
heat up phr v **1** to become warm or hot, or to make something become warm or hot: *The stove takes a while to heat up.* | **heat sth ⇔ up** *I heated up the remains of last night's supper.* **2** if a situation heats up, it becomes dangerous or full of problems
heat sth through phr v to heat food thoroughly

heat·ed /ˈhiːtɪ̈d/ adj **1** a heated SWIMMING POOL, room etc is made warm using a heater **2 heated argument/ debate/discussion** etc an argument etc that is full of angry and excited feelings —**heatedly** adv

heat·er /ˈhiːtə $ -ər/ n [C] a machine for making air or water hotter: *Did you turn the heater off?*

heat ex·haustion n [U] weakness and sickness caused by doing too much work, exercise etc in hot weather

heath /hiːθ/ n [C] an area of open land where grass, bushes, and other small plants grow, especially in Britain

hea·then[1] /'hiːðən/ adj old-fashioned not connected with or belonging to the Christian religion or any of the large established religions

heathen[2] n plural **heathen** [C] old-fashioned **1** someone who is not connected with the Christian religion or any of the large established religions – used to show disapproval; → **pagan 2** someone who refuses to believe in something – often used humorously

heath·er /'heðə $ -ər/ n [U] a low plant with small purple, pink, or white flowers which grows on hills

Heath Rob·in·son /ˌhiːθ 'rɒbʲnsən $ -'rɑː-/ adj BrE a Heath Robinson machine, system etc is very complicated in an amusing way but not at all practical

heat·ing S2 /'hiːtɪŋ/ n [U] especially BrE a system for making a room or building warm; ▤ **heat** AmE → CENTRAL HEATING

heat·proof /'hiːtpruːf/ adj heatproof material cannot be damaged by heat

heat pump n [C] part of a machine that takes heat from one place to another

heat rash n [C,U] painful or ITCHY red spots on someone's skin caused by heat

heat-re·sistant adj not easily damaged by heat

heat-·seeking adj a heat-seeking weapon is able to find and move towards the hot gases from an aircraft or ROCKET and destroy it

heat·stroke /'hiːtstrəʊk $ -stroʊk/ n [U] fever and weakness caused by being outside in the heat of the sun for too long → SUNSTROKE

heat wave n [C] a period of unusually hot weather, especially one that continues for a long time; ▤ **cold spell**

heave[1] /hiːv/ v
1 PULL/LIFT [I,T] to pull or lift something very heavy with one great effort: **heave sb/sth out of/into/onto etc sth** Alan heaved his suitcase onto his bed. | Mary heaved herself out of bed. | [+on/at] BrE: He heaved on the steering wheel and swung the car into a side street.
2 THROW [T] to throw something heavy using a lot of effort: John heaved the metal bar over the fence.
3 heave a sigh to breathe in and then breathe out noisily and slowly once: Rebecca **heaved a sigh of relief**.
4 MOVE UP AND DOWN [I] to move up and down with very strong movements: Michael's shoulders heaved with silent laughter. | The sea heaved up and down beneath the boat.
5 VOMIT [I] informal to VOMIT
6 past tense and past participle **hove** heave in sight/into view literary to appear, especially by getting closer from a distance: A few moments later a large ship hove into view. → HEAVING

heave to phr v past tense and past participle **hove to** /ˌhəʊv 'tuː $ ˌhoʊv-/ technical if a ship heaves to, it stops moving

heave[2] n **1** [C] a strong pulling, pushing, or lifting movement: He gave the door a good heave. **2** [U] literary a strong rising or falling movement

heave-·ho interjection, n **1** old-fashioned used as an encouragement to a person or group of people who are pulling something, especially on ships **2** give someone the (old) heave-ho informal to end a relationship with someone, or to make someone leave their job

heav·en S3 /'hevən/ n
1 also **Heaven** PLACE OF GOD [singular] the place where God is believed to live and where good people are believed to go when they die; → **paradise**: **in heaven** He believed that he and his wife would one day be together again in heaven.
2 ENJOYABLE SITUATION [U] informal an extremely enjoyable situation or place; ▤ **paradise**: Sitting by the pool with a good book is my idea of heaven. | **in heaven** Put a baseball in his hand and he's in heaven. | Living on the farm for Jim was **heaven on earth**. | a **match/marriage made in heaven** (=a happy and successful marriage)

SPOKEN PHRASES
3 for heaven's sake a) used to show that you are annoyed or angry: Oh, for heaven's sake, Mark, do you have to make everything into a joke? b) used to emphasize a question, request, order, or opinion: For heaven's sake, let's all get to sleep.
4 heaven (only) knows a) used to emphasize that you do not know something: He won't tell me what he thinks. Heaven knows why. b) used to emphasize what you are saying: Sue can't take a holiday yet, though heaven knows she needs a rest.
5 heaven help sb a) used to express sympathy for someone who is in a dangerous or difficult situation: 'The two boys are going to the dentist on Thursday.' 'Heaven help the dentist.' b) used to say that you will be very angry with someone if they do something: Heaven help him if he ever comes back here again!
6 heaven forbid used to say that you very much hope something will not happen: What would you do financially if, heaven forbid, your husband died?
7 what/how/why etc in heaven's name used when asking a surprised and angry question: Where in heaven's name have you been?

8 the heavens literary the sky: He looked up towards the heavens. | Just then, **the heavens opened** (=it started to rain heavily).
9 move heaven and earth to try very hard to achieve something: I would move heaven and earth to help her. → be in seventh heaven at SEVENTH[1] (2); → thank heaven(s) at THANK (2)

heav·en·ly /'hevənli/ adj **1** old-fashioned extremely pleasant, enjoyable, or beautiful: That smells heavenly. | We found a tiny hotel in a heavenly spot with a beautiful bay. **2** [only before noun] biblical existing in or belonging to heaven: God's heavenly kingdom | **heavenly Father** (=God) | **the Heavenly Host** (=all the angels) **3** literary existing in or relating to the sky or stars: **heavenly bodies** (=the moon, PLANETS and stars)

Heav·ens! /'hevənz/ also **Good Heavens!**, **Heav·ens a·bove!** interjection used to express surprise, especially when you are annoyed: Good Heavens, what a mess!

heaven-·sent /ˈ ··· ·/ adj literary happening fortunately at exactly the right time: a heaven-sent opportunity

heav·en·ward /'hevənwəd $ -wərd/ also **heav·en·wards** /-wədz $ -wərdz/ adv literary towards the sky

heav·ily W3 /'hevʲli/ adv
1 in large amounts, to a high degree, or with great severity; ▤ **very**: I became heavily involved in politics. | The report was heavily criticized in the press. | a heavily populated area | thousands of **heavily armed** troops | His wife was **heavily pregnant** at the time. | it **rains/snows heavily** It's been raining heavily all day. | **drink/smoke heavily** Paul was drinking heavily by then. | **heavily dependent/reliant/influenced** Britain is heavily dependent on imports for its raw materials.
2 sleep heavily if you sleep heavily, you cannot be woken easily
3 breathe heavily to breathe slowly and loudly: Breathing heavily, I stopped and sat down to rest.
4 heavily built having a large broad body that looks strong
5 if you do or say something heavily, you do it slowly and with a lot of effort, especially because you are sad or bored: He was walking heavily, his head down. | Emily sighed heavily. | 'I suppose so,' she said heavily.
6 be heavily into sth informal to do something a lot or be very interested in it: Sid was heavily into drugs by the time he left school.

heav·ing /'hiːvɪŋ/ adj BrE informal very busy or full of people: [+with] The city was heaving with shoppers.

heav·y¹ S1 W1 /'hevi/ *adj comparative* **heavier**, *superlative* **heaviest**

1 WEIGHT weighing a lot; **☒ light**: *The wardrobe was too heavy for me to move on my own.* | *a heavy suitcase* | *The males are seven times heavier than the females on average.* | *How heavy is the parcel* (=how much does it weigh?)*?*

2 AMOUNT/DEGREE/SEVERITY great in amount, degree, or severity

heavy traffic
heavy rain/snow
heavy fighting
heavy drinking also
heavy drinker
heavy smoking also
heavy smoker
heavy burden/demands/pressure
heavy fine
heavy casualties (=a lot of deaths or injuries)
heavy losses
heavy defeat
heavy cold
heavy use of sth
The traffic going into London was very heavy. | *Heavy rain has caused flooding in many areas.* | *Heavy fighting was reported near the border.* | *Heavy drinking during pregnancy can damage your baby.* | *I used to be a heavy smoker.* | *the heavy burden of taxation* | *If found guilty, they face heavy fines or even prison.* | *There were heavy casualties on both sides.* | *England's heavy defeat in yesterday's match* | *She's in bed with a heavy cold.* | *the film's heavy use of special effects*

3 NEEDING PHYSICAL EFFORT needing a lot of physical strength and effort: *My son does most of the heavy outdoor work.* | *She has a bad back and can't do any heavy lifting.*

4 NEEDING MENTAL EFFORT not easy or entertaining and needing a lot of mental effort: *I want something to read on holiday – nothing too heavy.*

5 heavy going difficult to understand or deal with: *I found his latest novel a bit heavy going.*

6 be heavy on sth *informal* to use a lot or too much of something: *The car's rather heavy on oil.*

7 heavy with sth *literary* full of something: *The apple trees were heavy with fruit.* | *The garden was heavy with the scent of summer.* | *'Of course,' she said, her voice heavy with sarcasm.*

8 heavy schedule/timetable/day etc a time in which you have a lot to do: *Let's go to bed. We've got a heavy day tomorrow.*

9 heavy breathing breathing that is slow and loud → HEAVY BREATHER

10 make heavy weather of sth *BrE* to make something that you are doing seem more difficult or complicated than it really is – used to show disapproval: *Why does he need to make such heavy weather of a simple task?*

11 WEAPONS/MACHINES [only before noun] large and powerful: *tanks and other heavy weapons* | *heavy artillery* (=large powerful guns) | *a company which manufactures heavy machinery*

12 MATERIALS/CLOTHES ETC heavy materials, clothes, shoes, or objects are thick or solidly made: *a heavy winter coat* | *the sound of heavy boots* | *Melt the butter in a heavy pan over a medium heat.* | *heavy velvet curtains*

13 FOOD solid and making your stomach feel full and uncomfortable; **☒ light**: *a heavy meal* | *heavy fruitcake*

14 EYES if your eyes are heavy, it is difficult to keep them open, usually because you are tired: *His eyes felt heavy with fatigue.*

15 BODY/FACE a) large, broad, and solid: *his heavy features* | *Kyle is a tall man with a heavy build* (=a large broad body). b) *AmE* used to politely describe someone who is fat; **☒ large**

16 WITH FORCE hitting something or falling with a lot of force or weight: *the sound of heavy footsteps in the hall* | *Ali caught him with a heavy blow to the jaw.*

17 GROUND a) soil that is heavy is thick and solid b) a sports ground or race track that is heavy is muddy: *a very heavy pitch* | *The going was heavy* (=it was muddy for the horse races) *at Cheltenham yesterday.*

18 SMELL strong and usually sweet: **heavy scent/perfume etc** *the heavy scent of the lilies*

19 AIR too warm and not at all fresh because there is no wind: *Even at dusk the air was still heavy.*

20 EMOTIONS *informal* a relationship or situation that is heavy involves serious or strong feelings: *She didn't want things to get too heavy at such an early stage in their relationship.*

21 get heavy (with sb) *informal* to start behaving in a threatening or strict way: *He came round and started getting heavy about the money I owed him.*

22 heavy silence/atmosphere a situation in which people do not speak and feel sad, anxious, or embarrassed: *A heavy silence fell upon the room.*

23 heavy sky/clouds clouds that look dark and grey as though it will soon rain

24 heavy sleeper someone who does not wake easily

25 heavy irony/sarcasm remarks that very clearly say the opposite of what you really feel

26 heavy seas sea with big waves: *The ship went down in heavy seas off the coast of Scotland.*

27 with a heavy heart *literary* feeling very sad: *It was with a heavy heart that Kate said goodbye.*

28 heavy date *AmE* a very important DATE (=an occasion when you meet someone you like in a romantic way) with a BOYFRIEND or GIRLFRIEND – usually used humorously —**heaviness** *n* [U]

heavy² *adv* **1** time hangs/lies heavy on your hands if time hangs or lies heavy on your hands, it seems to pass slowly because you are bored or have nothing to do **2** be heavy into sth *AmE spoken informal* to be very involved in an activity, especially one that is not good for you: *Eric was real heavy into drugs for a while.*

heavy³ *n plural* **heavies** [C] *informal* a large strong man who is paid to protect someone or to threaten other people

heavy 'breather *n* [C] a man who telephones a woman and does not speak, but breathes loudly, in order to get sexual pleasure —**heavy breathing** *n* [U]

heavy 'cream *n* [U] *AmE* thick cream; **☒ double cream** *BrE*

heavy-'duty *adj* **1** heavy-duty materials are strong and thick and not easily damaged: *heavy-duty canvas* **2** heavy-duty machines or equipment are designed to be used for very hard work **3** *informal especially AmE* very complicated, serious, or extreme: *Today, she was going to do some heavy-duty cleaning.*

heavy 'goods .vehicle *n* [C] an HGV

heavy-'handed *adj* taking too much action or extreme action, especially without thinking about other people's feelings: *a heavy-handed style of management* —**heavy-handedness** *n* [U]

heavy-heart·ed /ˌhevi 'hɑːtˑ‍ɪd $ -'hɑːr-/ *adj literary* very sad

heavy 'hitter *n* [C] *AmE* **1** a person or company that has a lot of power, especially in business or politics **2** a BASEBALL player who hits the ball very hard

heavy 'industry *n* [U] industry that produces large goods such as cars and machines, or materials such as coal, steel, or chemicals → LIGHT INDUSTRY

heavy 'metal *n* **1** [U] a type of ROCK music with a strong beat, played very loudly on electric GUITARS **2** [C] *technical* a metal that has a high DENSITY, such as gold, MERCURY, or LEAD. Many heavy metals are poisonous.

heavy 'petting *n* [U] *old-fashioned* sexual activities that do not involve actually having sex

heavy-'set *adj* someone who is heavy-set is large and looks strong or fat

heav·y·weight /'heviweɪt/ *n* [C] **1** someone or something that is very important or has a lot of influence: *one of the heavyweights of the movie indus-*

try **2** a BOXER who weighs more than 86.18 kilograms, and who belongs to the heaviest weight class of boxers

He·bra·ic /hɪˈbreɪ-ɪk/ *adj formal* connected with the Hebrew language or people: *Hebraic literature*

He·brew /ˈhiːbruː/ *n* **1** [U] the language traditionally used by the Jewish people **2** [C] a member of the Jewish people in ancient times —**Hebrew** *adj*

heck¹ /hek/ *interjection informal* **1** used to show that you are annoyed or to emphasize what you are saying: *Oh heck! I've lost my keys!* | *'Do you believe him?' 'Heck, no.'* **2 did he heck/will it heck etc** *BrE* used to say in a strong way that someone did not do something, something will not happen etc: *'Did he offer to pay for it?' 'Did he heck.'*

heck² *n* [singular, U] *spoken informal* **1** used like 'hell' to emphasize what you are saying: *It cost a heck of a lot of money.* | **where/how/who etc the heck** *Where the heck are we?* | *He sure as heck didn't tell me.* **2 what the heck** used to say that you will do something even though you really should not do it: *It's rather expensive, but what the heck.* **3 for the heck of it** for fun, or for no particular reason

heck·le /ˈhekəl/ *v* [I,T] to interrupt and try to embarrass someone who is speaking or performing in public —**heckler** *n* [C] —**heckling** *n* [U]

hec·tare /ˈhektɑː, -teə $ -ter/ *n* [C] written abbreviation *ha* a unit for measuring area, equal to 10,000 square metres; → **acre**

hec·tic /ˈhektɪk/ *adj* **1** very busy or full of activity: *I've had a pretty hectic day.* | *a hectic social life* **2** *written* if your face is a hectic colour, it is very pink: *the hectic flush on her cheeks*

hec·tor /ˈhektə $ -ər/ *v* [I,T] to speak to someone in an angry threatening way: *a hectoring tone of voice*

he'd /id, hid; *strong* hiːd/ **1** the short form of 'he had': *By the time I got there he'd gone.* **2** the short form for 'he would': *I'm sure he'd help if he could.*

hedge¹ /hedʒ/ *n* [C] **1** a row of small bushes or trees growing close together, usually dividing one field or garden from another **2** something that protects you against possible problems, especially financial loss: [+against] *Buying a house will be a hedge against inflation.* → **look as if you've been dragged through a hedge backwards** at DRAG¹ (13)

hedge² *v* hedged, hedging [I,T] **1** to avoid giving a direct answer to a question: *You're hedging again – have you got the money or haven't you?* | *'That depends on my partner,' she hedged.* **2 hedge your bets** to reduce your chances of failure or loss by trying several different possibilities instead of one: *It's a good idea to hedge your bets by applying to more than one college.*

hedge against sth *phr v* to try to protect yourself against possible problems, especially financial loss: *Smart managers will hedge against price increases.*

be hedged in *phr v* **1** to be surrounded or enclosed by something: *The building was hedged in by trees.* **2** if you feel hedged in by something, you feel that your freedom is restricted by it

hedge·hog /ˈhedʒhɒg $ -hɑːg, -hɔːg/ *n* [C] a small brown European animal whose body is round and covered with sharp needle-like SPINES

hedge·row /ˈhedʒrəʊ $ -roʊ/ *n* [C] *BrE* a line of bushes growing along the edge of a field or road

he·don·ist /ˈhiːdən-ɪst/ *n* [C] someone who believes that pleasure is the most important thing in life —**hedonism** *n* [U] —**hedonistic** /ˌhiːdənˈɪstɪk◂/ *adj*

heed¹ /hiːd/ *v* [T] *formal* to pay attention to someone's advice or warning: *If she had only heeded my warnings, none of this would have happened.*

heed² *n* **pay heed to sth/take heed of sth** *formal* to pay attention to something, especially something someone says, and seriously consider it: *The government was taking little heed of these threats.* | *Tom paid no heed to her warning.*

heed·less /ˈhiːdləs/ *adj* **heedless of sth** *literary* not paying attention to something: *O'Hara rode on, heedless of danger.* —**heedlessly** *adv*

heel¹ /hiːl/ *n* [C]
1 OF YOUR FOOT the curved back part of your foot; → **toe**
2 OF A SHOE the raised part on the bottom of a shoe that makes the shoe higher at the back: *black boots with high heels* | **high-heeled/low-heeled/flat-heeled etc** *her low-heeled blue shoes*; → see picture at FOOTWEAR
3 OF A SOCK the part of a sock that covers your heel
4 OF YOUR HAND the part of your hand between the bottom of your thumb and your wrist: *Using the heel of your hand, press the dough firmly into shape.*
5 heels [plural] a pair of women's shoes with high heels: *Whenever she wore heels she was taller than the men she worked with.*
6 at sb's heels if a person or animal is at your heels, they are following closely behind you: *He could hear the dog trotting at his heels.* | *Omar hurried inside with the boy at his heels.*
7 a) (hard/hot/close) **on the heels of sth** very soon after something: *The decision to buy Peters came hard on the heels of the club's promotion to Division One.* **b)** (hard/hot/close) **on sb's heels** following closely behind someone, especially in order to catch or attack them: *With the enemy army hard on his heels, he crossed the Somme at Blanche-Taque.*
8 bring sb to heel to force someone to behave in the way that you want them to
9 come to heel *BrE* **a)** if a dog comes to heel, it comes back to its owner when the owner calls it **b)** if someone comes to heel, they start to behave in the way that you want them to
10 take to your heels *written* to start running away: *As soon as he saw me he took to his heels.*
11 turn/spin on your heel *written* to suddenly turn away from someone, especially in an angry or rude way: *Before anyone could say a word, he turned on his heel and walked out of the room.*
12 under the heel of sb/sth completely controlled by a government or group: *a people under the heel of an increasingly dictatorial regime*
13 BAD MAN *old-fashioned* a man who behaves badly towards other people → ACHILLES' HEEL, DOWN-AT-HEEL, WELL-HEELED; → **click your heels** at CLICK¹ (1); → **cool your heels** at COOL² (4); → **dig your heels in** at DIG¹ (4); → **drag your heels** at DRAG¹ (8); → **be/fall head over heels in love** at HEAD¹ (36); → **kick your heels** at KICK¹ (9)

heel² *v* **1 heel!** *spoken* used to tell your dog to walk next to you **2** [T] to put a heel on a shoe
heel over *phr v* if something heels over, it leans to one side as if it is going to fall: *The ship was heeling over in the wind.*

heft /heft/ *v* [T] **1** to lift something heavy: **heft sth onto/into etc sth** *He hefted his bag into the car.* **2** to lift or hold something in order to judge how heavy it is: *Quinn hefted the package in his hands.*

hef·ty /ˈhefti/ *adj* [usually before noun] **1** big and heavy: *a tall, hefty man* | *a hefty tome* (=large thick book) | *hefty camera equipment* **2** a hefty amount of something, especially money, is very large: *a hefty fine* **3** *BrE* a hefty blow, kick etc is done using a lot of force: *He aimed a hefty kick at the door.* | *a hefty shove*

he·gem·o·ny /hɪˈgeməni, ˈhedʒɪməni $ hɪˈdʒeməni, ˈhedʒɪmoʊni/ *n* [U] *formal* a situation in which one state or country controls others

heif·er /ˈhefə $ -ər/ *n* [C] a young cow that has not yet given birth to a CALF; → **bullock, ox, steer**

height S2 W2 /haɪt/ *n*
1 HOW TALL [C,U] how tall someone or something is: *Sam's about the same height as his sister now.* | *State your age, height, and weight.* | *buildings of different heights* | **6 feet/10 metres etc in height** *None of these sculptures was less than three metres in height.* | **a height of 6 feet/10 metres etc** *Sunflowers can grow to a height of fifteen feet.*

H

2 DISTANCE ABOVE THE GROUND [C,U] the distance something is above the ground: *It's a miracle she didn't break her neck falling from that height.* | **a height of 2500 feet/10,000 metres etc** *The aircraft was flying at a height of 10,000 metres.* | **gain/lose height** (=move higher or lower in the sky) *The plane was rapidly losing height.*

3 HIGH PLACE **a)** [C] a place or position that is a long way above the ground: **from a height** *a bird that opens shellfish by dropping them from a height onto rocks* | *Rachel had always been **scared of heights**.* | **have a head for heights** (=not be afraid of heights) **b) heights** [plural] a particular high place – used especially in place names: *the Golan Heights*

4 new/great/dizzy etc heights **a)** a very high level of achievement or success: **rise to/reach etc ... heights** *He reached the dizzy heights of the national finals.* | *They took ice dancing **to new heights**.* **b)** a very great level or degree: *War fever had reached new heights.*

5 the height of sth the busiest or most extreme part of a period or activity; ◘ **peak**: *the height of the tourist season*

6 be at the height of your success/fame/powers etc to be more successful, famous etc than at any other time: *The Beatles were at the height of their fame.*

7 be the height of fashion/stupidity/luxury etc to be extremely fashionable, stupid etc: *Flared trousers were considered to be the height of fashion in those days.*

height·en /ˈhaɪtn/ v [I,T] if something heightens a feeling, effect etc, or if a feeling etc heightens, it becomes stronger or increases; ◘ **intensify**; → **strengthen**: *There are fears that the march will heighten racial tension.* | *Increased levels of fat in the diet could heighten the risk of cancer.* | **heighten (sb's) awareness (of sth)** (=make people realize something more clearly) *The case has heightened public awareness of the problem of sexual harassment.*

hei·nous /ˈheɪnəs/ adj formal **1** very shocking and immoral: *a heinous crime* **2** AmE spoken informal extremely bad: *The food in the cafeteria is pretty heinous.* —**heinousness** n [U]

heir /eə $ er/ n [C] **1** the person who has the legal right to receive the property or title of another person when they die: [+to] *John was the sole heir to a vast estate.* | **heir to the throne** (=the person who will become king or queen) **2** the person who will take over a position or job after you, or who does things or thinks in a similar way to you: *Jonson was his political heir as leader of the Nationalist Party.*

heir ap·parent n plural **heirs apparent** [C] **1** an heir whose right to receive the family property, money, or title cannot be taken away **2** someone who seems very likely to take over a person's job, position etc when that person leaves

heir·ess /ˈeərɪs, ˈeəres $ ˈer-/ n [C] a woman who will receive or has received a lot of money or property when an older member of her family dies

heir·loom /ˈeəluːm $ ˈer-/ n [C] a valuable object that has been owned by a family for many years and that is passed from the older members to the younger members: *a family heirloom*

heist /haɪst/ n [C] AmE informal an act of stealing something very valuable from a shop, bank etc; ◘ **robbery**: *a jewelry heist* —**heist** v [T]

held /held/ the past tense and past participle of HOLD

hel·i·cop·ter /ˈhelɪkɒptə $ -kɑːptər/ n [C] a type of aircraft with large metal blades on top which turn around very quickly to make it fly; ◘ **chopper**

helicopter ˌpad also **hel·i·pad** /ˈhelɪpæd/ n [C] an area where helicopters can land

he·li·o·trope /ˈhiːliətrəup, ˈhe- $ ˈhiːliətroup/ n [C] a garden plant with nice-smelling pale purple flowers

hel·i·port /ˈhelipɔːt $ -pɔːrt/ n [C] a small airport for HELICOPTERS

he·li-ski·ing /ˈheliˌskiːɪŋ/ n [U] the sport of flying a HELICOPTER to a place in the mountains where you can SKI on deep snow that no one else has skied on

he·li·um /ˈhiːliəm/ n [U] a gas that is lighter than air and is used to make BALLOONS float. It is a chemical ELEMENT: symbol He

he·lix /ˈhiːlɪks/ n plural **helices** /-lɪsiːz/ [C] technical a line that curves and rises around a central line; ◘ **spiral** → DOUBLE HELIX

he'll /il, hil; strong hiːl/ the short form of 'he will' or 'he shall': *Don't worry, he'll be there.*

hell[1] S1 W3 /hel/ n

1 WHEN YOU DIE also **Hell** [U] the place where the souls of bad people are believed to be punished after death, especially in the Christian and Muslim religions

2 SUFFERING [singular, U] a place or situation in which people suffer very much, either physically or emotionally: *War is hell.* | *My mother **made** my **life hell**.* | *These past few days have been a **living hell**.* | *She must have **gone through hell** every day, the way we teased her about her weight.* | **pure/absolute/sheer etc hell** *They described the war zone as sheer hell.* | *He says his time in jail was **hell on earth**.*

3 UNPLEASANT SITUATION [singular, U] informal a situation, experience, or place that is very unpleasant: *The traffic was hell this morning.* | **pure/absolute/sheer etc hell** | *'How was your exam?' 'Sheer hell!'*

4 what/how/why/where etc the hell spoken not polite used to show that you are very surprised or angry: *What the hell are you doing, wasting my time?* | *How the hell are we going to do that?*

5 a/one hell of a sth spoken not polite used to emphasize the idea that something is very big, very good, very bad etc: *I've come one hell of a long way to get here.* | *Envy like yours is a hell of a good motive for murder.*

6 go to hell! spoken not polite used when you are very angry with someone: *If John doesn't like it, he can go to hell!*

7 feel/look like hell spoken not polite to feel or look very ill or tired: *I've been feeling like hell all week.*

8 beat/surprise/scare the hell out of sb informal not polite to beat, surprise etc someone very much: *We have only one aim: to beat the hell out of the opposition.*

9 (just) for the hell of it spoken not polite for no serious reason, or only for fun: *They shot people just for the hell of it.*

10 what the hell! spoken not polite used to say that you will do something and not worry about any problems it causes: *Elaine poured herself a large glass of whisky – what the hell, it was Christmas.*

11 to hell with sb/sth spoken not polite used to say that you do not care about someone or something any more: *I want to live for the present, and to hell with the consequences.*

12 run/hurt/fight etc like hell informal not polite to run, fight etc very quickly or very much: *My new shoes hurt like hell.*

13 like hell/the hell spoken not polite used to say that you do not agree with what someone has said: *'You keep out of this, Ma.' 'Like hell I will.'*

14 the sth/sb from hell informal not polite something or someone that is the worst you can imagine: *She was the flatmate from hell.* | *It was the holiday from hell.*

15 guilty/shy/mad/angry etc as hell spoken not polite very guilty,shy etc: *If I had your problems, I'd be mad as hell.*

16 sure as hell spoken not polite used to emphasize that something is true: *I don't scare easily, but I was sure as hell scared.*

17 give sb hell informal not polite to treat someone in an unpleasant or angry way: *She didn't like him, and gave him hell at the slightest opportunity.*

18 get the hell out (of somewhere) informal not polite to leave a place quickly and suddenly: *Let's get the hell out of here!*

19 there'll be hell to pay spoken not polite used to say that people will be very angry: *If they find us there'll be hell to pay.*

20 go to hell and back to go through a very difficult situation: *I'd go to hell and back for that boy.*
21 all hell broke loose *informal not polite* used to say that people suddenly become very noisy or angry: *Journalists woke him with the news and all hell broke loose.*
22 come hell or high water *informal not polite* in spite of any problems or difficulties: *I decided I would get the job done by Friday, come hell or high water.*
23 go to hell in a handbasket *AmE informal not polite* if a system or organization has gone to hell in a handbasket, it has stopped working well and is now working very badly: *The education system in this country has gone to hell in a handbasket.*
24 hell's bells *spoken old-fashioned* also **hell's teeth** *BrE* used to express great annoyance or surprise
25 play (merry) hell with sth *BrE informal* to make something stop working or happening as it should: *The cold weather played hell with the weekend sports schedule.*
26 raise hell *informal not polite* to protest strongly and angrily about a situation
27 run/go hell for leather *informal not polite* to run as fast as possible
28 hell on wheels *AmE informal not polite* someone who does exactly what they want and does not care what happens as a result.
29 when hell freezes over *informal not polite* used to say that something will never happen
30 catch hell *AmE spoken not polite* to be blamed or punished: *You'll catch hell when your Mom comes home!* → **not a hope in hell (of doing sth)** at HOPE² (3)

hell² *interjection not polite* **1** used to express anger or annoyance: *Oh hell! I've left my purse at home.* **2** used to emphasize a statement: *Well, hell, I don't know!*

hell-'bent *adj* [not before noun] very determined to do something, especially something that other people do not approve of: **hell-bent on (doing) sth** *young people who are hell-bent on having a good time*

Hel·lene /'heliːn/ *n* [C] *formal* a Greek, especially an ancient Greek

Hel·len·ic /heˈlenɪk/ *adj* connected with the history, society, or art of the ancient Greeks

'hell-hole *n* [C] a very dirty, ugly, and unpleasant place: *His son ran away from school, calling it a hell-hole.*

hell·ish /'helɪʃ/ *adj informal* extremely bad or difficult: *I've had a hellish day at work.* —**hellishly** *adv*: *a hellishly difficult exam*

hel·lo S1 /həˈləʊ, he- $ -ˈloʊ/ also **hallo, hullo** *BrE interjection, n* [C]
1 used as a greeting when you see or meet someone: *Hello, John! How are you?* | *Stanley, come and say hello to your nephew.* | *Well, hello there! I haven't seen you for ages.*
2 used when answering the telephone or starting a telephone conversation: *Hello – may I speak to Anne?*
3 used when calling to get someone's attention: *Hello! Is there anybody home?*
4 used when you think someone is not acting sensibly or has said something stupid: *You didn't remember her birthday? Hello!*
5 *BrE* used to show that you are surprised or confused by something: *Hello! What's happened here?*
6 say hello to have a quick conversation with someone: *Promise you'll look in and say hello when you have time.*

hell·uv·a /'heləvə/ *adj, adv spoken* used to emphasize that someone or something is very good, bad, big etc: *He's got a helluva temper.* | *He's a helluva nice guy.*

helm /helm/ *n* **1** [C] the wheel or control which guides a ship or boat **2 at the helm a)** in charge of something: *We have a new prime minister at the helm.* **b)** guiding a ship or boat **3 take the helm a)** to start being in charge of something such as a business or organization: *Wright took the helm at the food retailer in December 2001.* **b)** to start guiding a ship or boat.

hel·met /'helmɪt/ *n* [C] a strong hard hat that soldiers, MOTORCYCLE riders, the police etc wear to protect their heads → CRASH HELMET, PITH HELMET; → see picture at ACCIDENT

hel·met·ed /'helmɪtɪd/ *adj* wearing a helmet

helms·man /'helmzmən/ *n plural* **helmsmen** /-mən/ [C] someone who guides a ship or boat

help¹ S1 W1 /help/ *v*
1 [I,T] to make it possible or easier for someone to do something by doing part of their work or by giving them something they need: *If there's anything I can do to help, just give me a call.* | *I helped her to carry her cases up the stairs.* | *She helped him choose some new clothes.* | *herbal products that help you to relax and sleep* | **help (to) do sth** *She was coming to help clean the machines.* | **help sb with sth** *Can I help you with the washing up?* | *My father said he's going to help me with the fees.* | **help sb on/off with sth** (=help someone put on or take off a piece of clothing) *Here, let me help you on with your coat.* | **help sb somewhere** (=help someone get to a particular place, especially because they are old, ill, or hurt) *She helped the old man across the road.*
2 [I,T] to make a situation better, easier, or less painful: *Crying won't help.* | *If you get rid of your car you could be helping the environment.* | *It helps my concentration if I listen to music while I'm working.* | *It helped a lot to know that someone understood how I felt.* | *Eight hours of deep sleep helped enormously.*
3 help yourself (to sth) a) to take some of what you want, without asking permission – used especially when offering food to someone: *Please help yourself to some cake.* **b)** *informal* to steal something: *Obviously he had been helping himself to the money.*
4 Help! *spoken* used to call people and ask them to help you when you are in danger
5 sb can't help (doing) sth also **sb can't help but do sth** used to say that someone is unable to change their behaviour or feelings, or to prevent themselves from doing something: *She couldn't help it if she was being irrational.* | *'Stop biting your nails.' 'I can't help it.'* | *I can't help the way I feel about you.* | *Lee could not help but agree with her.* | **sb can't help feeling/thinking/wondering etc sth** *I can't help feeling that there has been a mistake.* | *I couldn't help thinking about the past.*
6 I couldn't help myself/she couldn't help herself etc to be unable to stop yourself from doing something you should not do: *She knew she sounded just like her mother but she couldn't help herself.*
7 it can't be helped *spoken* used to say that there is nothing you can do to change a bad situation: *She said she had to leave him for a while; it couldn't be helped.*
8 sb is helping the police with their enquiries *BrE* the police are interviewing someone about a crime, especially because they believe that this person may have committed the crime
9 a helping hand help and support: **give/lend/offer etc sb a helping hand** *She's been giving me a helping hand with the children.*
10 not if I can help it *spoken* used to say that you are not going to do something: *'Are you going to watch the school play?' 'Not if I can help it.'*
11 God help him/them etc *spoken* used to say that something bad may happen to someone: *'Good luck.' 'God help me. I think I'm going to need it.'*
12 so help me (God) used when making a serious promise, especially in a court of law

help sth ⇔ **along** *phr v*
to make a process or activity happen more quickly or easily: *She asked a few questions to help the conversation along.*

help out *phr v*
to help someone because they are busy or have problems: *Do you need anyone to help out in the shop?* | **help sb** ⇔ **out (with sth)** *I helped her out when Stella became ill.* | *She was helping him out with his mortgage repayments.*

H

WORD CHOICE: help, assist, give sb a hand, lend a hand, help out
Help is the most general verb meaning 'to make it possible or easier for someone to do something'.: Note that in the patterns **help to do something**
or **help someone to do something** you can leave out the 'to' and say **help do something** or **help someone do something**: *Cleaner water will help prevent disease. | money to help people build new homes.*
Assist is a formal word, and means to help someone by doing part of the work for them, especially the things that are not very important: *Would you be kind enough to assist me in a small experiment?*
⚠ Do not say 'assist someone to do something'. Say **assist someone with something** or **assist someone in doing something.**
Give sb a hand, lend a hand, and **help out** are used in more informal English. **Give sb a hand** means to help someone, especially by carrying or lifting things: *Can you give me a hand stacking up these boxes?* **Lend a hand** and **help out** mean to help someone, especially when there are not enough people to do something: *Police came from other areas to lend a hand. | Their friends helped out with the fundraising.*

help² [S1] [W1] *n*
1 [U] things you do to make it easier or possible for someone to do something: *Thank you for all your help. |* [+with] *Do you want any help with the washing-up? | Old people may need help decorating their homes. | Ask for help if necessary. |* **with the help of sb/with sb's help** *We manage, with the help of a nurse who comes daily. | I get a lot of help and I'm really grateful. | She screamed at them to go and get help.*
2 [singular, U] if someone or something is a help to you, they are useful and make it easier for you to do something: *That map isn't much help. |* **with the help of sth** *I managed to make myself understood with the help of a phrase book. |* **be of great/little/no/some etc help (to sb)** *Let me know if I can be of any help to you. |* **be a (great/big/tremendous/real etc) help (to sb)** *Any information would be a great help. | You've been a real help to me, Carrie.*
3 [U] advice, treatment, information, or money which is given to people who need it: *A lot of these children need professional help. |* [+with] *You may be able to ask for help with the rent. | We received no help from the police.*
4 [U] a part of a computer program that helps someone using it by giving additional information
5 the help *AmE* someone's servant or servants

help desk *n* [C] a department of a company that people call for help, especially with computer problems

help·er /'helpə $ -ər/ *n* [C] **1** someone who helps another person; ⯀ **assistant**: *I was a classroom helper at the local primary school.* **2** *AmE* someone who is employed to do some of the work in someone else's home

help·ful [S2] [W3] /'helpfəl/ *adj*
1 providing useful help in making a situation better or easier: *Thank you for your advice; it's been very helpful. |* **it is helpful (for sb) to do sth** *It is helpful to discuss your problems with your friends. | It is helpful for family members to gain a basic understanding of the illness. |* **It is helpful if** *we address a few key questions here. |* **helpful in doing sth** *We hope this leaflet has been helpful in answering your questions. |* **helpful advice/hints/suggestions etc** *Our sales staff are there to give you helpful advice.*
2 always willing to help people: *She's a helpful child. | I'm only trying to be helpful.* —**helpfully** *adv* —**helpfulness** *n* [U]

help·ing /'helpɪŋ/ *n* [C] the amount of food that someone gives you or that you take; ⯀ **serving**: *a double helping of pie*

help·less /'helpləs/ *adj* **1** unable to look after yourself or to do anything to help yourself: *He began to feel depressed and helpless. | a vicious attack on a helpless victim | Newman threw out a hand in a helpless gesture.* **2** unable to control a strong feeling that you have: [+with] *He was near to death, and I was helpless with fear. | helpless laughter/rage/tears etc We both collapsed into helpless giggles.* —**helplessly** *adv* —**helplessness** *n* [U]

help·line /'helplaɪn/ *n* [C] a telephone number that you can ring if you need advice or information

help·mate /'helpmeɪt/ also **help·meet** /-miːt/ *n* [C] *literary* a helpful partner, usually a wife

help screen *n* [C] a screen that appears when you ask for help in using a computer program, showing extra information or advice

hel·ter-skel·ter¹ /ˌheltə ˈskeltə $ ˌheltər ˈskeltər/ *adv* done quickly, in a disorganized way: *He ran helter-skelter down the slope.*

helter-skelter² *n* [C] *BrE* a tall structure in a FAIRGROUND which you sit on at the top and slide round and round to the bottom

hem¹ /hem/ *n* [C] the edge of a piece of cloth that is turned under and stitched down, especially the lower edge of a skirt, trousers etc → see picture at LIMIT

hem² *v* **hemmed, hemming** **1** [T] to turn under the edge of a piece of material or clothing and stitch it in place **2 hem and haw** *AmE* to keep pausing before saying something, and avoid saying it directly
hem sb/sth ⇔ **in** *phr v* **1** to surround someone or something closely: *They were hemmed in on all sides by the soldiers and the dogs. | The market place is hemmed in by shops and banks.* **2** to make someone feel that they are not free to do what they want to do: *They hem in the child with endless rules and restrictions.*

he-man *n plural* **he-men** [C] *humorous* a strong man with powerful muscles

hem·i·sphere /'hemɪsfɪə $ -fɪr/ *n* [C] **1** a half of the earth, especially one of the halves above and below the EQUATOR: *the Northern hemisphere* → see picture at GLOBE **2** one of the two halves of your brain **3** half of a SPHERE (=an object which is round like a ball) —**hemispherical** /ˌhemɪˈsferɪkəl/ *adj*

hem·line /'hemlaɪn/ *n* [C] the length of a dress, skirt etc: *Short hemlines are in this spring.*

hem·lock /'hemlɒk $ -lɑːk/ *n* [C,U] a very poisonous plant, or the poison that is made from it

he·mo·glo·bin /ˌhiːməˈɡləʊbɪn $ ˈhiːməˌɡloʊbɪn/ *n* [U] the American spelling of HAEMOGLOBIN

he·mo·phil·i·a /ˌhiːməˈfɪliə/ *n* [U] the American spelling of HAEMOPHILIA

he·mo·phil·i·ac /ˌhiːməˈfɪliæk/ *n* [C] the American spelling of HAEMOPHILIAC

hem·or·rhage /'hemərɪdʒ/ *n* [C,U] the American spelling of HAEMORRHAGE

hem·or·rhoids /'hemərɔɪdz/ *n* [plural] the American spelling of HAEMORRHOIDS

hemp /hemp/ *n* [U] a type of plant that is used to make rope and sometimes to produce the drug CANNABIS

hen /hen/ *n* [C] **1** an adult female chicken **2** a fully grown female bird

hence [W2] /hens/ *adv formal*
1 [sentence adverb] for this reason: *The cost of transport is a major expense for an industry. Hence factory location is an important consideration.*
2 **ten days hence/five months hence etc** ten days from now, five months from now etc

hence·forth /ˌhensˈfɔːθ, ˈhensfɔːθ $ -ɔːrθ/ also **hence·for·ward** /ˌhensˈfɔːwəd $ -ˈfɔːrwərd/ *adv formal* from this time on: *Multiple Sclerosis (henceforth referred to as MS)*

hench·man /'hentʃmən/ *n plural* **henchmen** /-mən/ [C] a faithful supporter of a political leader or a criminal, who is willing to do illegal things or use violence

hen house *n* [C] a small building where chickens are kept

hen·na /ˈhenə/ *n* [U] a reddish-brown substance used to change the colour of hair or skin —**henna** *v* [T]

ˈhen ˌparty *n* [C] *BrE informal* a party for women only, that happens just before one of them gets married → STAG PARTY

hen·pecked /ˈhenpekt/ *adj* a man who is henpecked is always being told what to do by his wife, and is afraid to disagree with her: *a henpecked husband*

he·pat·ic /hɪˈpætɪk/ *adj* [only before noun] *medical* relating to your LIVER

hep·a·ti·tis /ˌhepəˈtaɪtəs◂/ *n* [U] a disease of the LIVER that causes fever and makes your skin yellow. There are several types of hepatitis: hepatitis A, which is less severe, and hepatitis B and C which are much more serious

hep·ta·gon /ˈheptəgən $ -gɑːn/ *n* [C] a shape with seven straight sides —**heptagonal** /hepˈtægənəl/ *adj*

hep·tath·lon /hepˈtæθlən/ *n* [singular] a women's sports competition involving seven running, jumping, and throwing events

her¹ S1 W1 /ə, hə; *strong* hɜː $ ər, hər; *strong* hɜːr/ *determiner* [possessive form of 'she']
1 belonging to or connected with a woman, girl, or female animal that has already been mentioned: *She looked at her watch.* | *Her room was pleasant and airy.* | *She makes* ***her own*** *clothes.*
2 *old-fashioned* connected with a country, ship, car etc that has already been mentioned: *Her top speed is about 110 miles an hour.*

her² S1 W1 *pron* [object form of 'she']
1 used to refer to a woman, girl, or female animal that has already been mentioned or is already known about: *Jane? I don't really know her.* | *Margaret wants me to go with her.* | *Give her the keys.* | *I think it was her, but I'm not sure.*
2 *old-fashioned* used to refer to a country, ship, car etc that has already been mentioned: *God bless this ship and all who sail in her.*

her·ald¹ /ˈherəld/ *v* [T] **1** to be a sign of something that is going to come or happen soon: *A flash of lightning and a peal of thunder heralded torrential rain.* | *Flashing blue lights heralded the arrival of the police.* **2** to say publicly that someone or something will be good or important: **be heralded as sth** *When it opened, the hospital was heralded as a new way forward in nursing care.*

herald² *n* **1** [C] someone who carried messages from a ruler in the past **2 herald of sth** a sign that something is soon going to happen: *a bowl of daffodils, the first bright heralds of spring*

her·ald·ry /ˈherəldri/ *n* [U] the study of COATS OF ARMS —**heraldic** /heˈrældɪk/ *adj*

herb /hɜːb $ ɜːrb, hɜːrb/ *n* [C] a small plant that is used to improve the taste of food, or to make medicine: *Sprinkle the dish with chopped fresh herbs.*

her·ba·ceous /həˈbeɪʃəs $ hɜːrˈbeɪ-, ɜːr-/ *adj technical* plants that are herbaceous have soft stems rather than hard stems made of wood

herˌbaceous ˈborder *n* [C] part of a garden where people grow plants that live for many years and do not need to be replaced

herb·al /ˈhɜːbəl $ ˈɜːr-, ˈhɜːr-/ *adj* [only before noun] made of herbs: *herbal remedies* | *herbal tea*

herb·al·ist /ˈhɜːbələst $ ˈɜːr-, ˈhɜːr-/ *n* [C] someone who grows, sells, or uses HERBS, especially to treat illness

ˌherbal ˈmedicine *n* **1** [U] the practice of treating illness using plants **2** [C,U] medicine made from plants

herb·i·cide /ˈhɜːbəsaɪd $ ˈhɜːr-, ˈɜːr-/ *n* [C,U] *technical* a substance used to kill unwanted plants

her·bi·vore /ˈhɜːbəvɔː $ ˈhɜːrbəvɔːr, ˈɜːr-/ *n* [C] an animal that only eats plants; → **carnivore, omnivore** —**herbivorous** /hɜːˈbɪvərəs $ hɜːr-, ɜːr-/ *adj*

her·cu·le·an /ˌhɜːkjʊˈliːən◂, hɜːˈkjuːliən $ -ɜːr-/ *adj* needing great strength or determination: *a herculean task*

herd¹ /hɜːd $ hɜːrd/ *n* **1** [C] a group of animals of one kind that live and feed together; → **flock**: [+of] *a herd of cattle* | *herds of elephants* **2 the herd** people generally, especially when thought of as being easily influenced by others: *You have to be an individual; it's no use running with the herd.* | *the* ***herd instinct*** (=the need to behave in the same way as everyone else does)

herd² *v* **1** [T always + adv/prep] to bring people together in a large group, especially roughly: *The prisoners were* ***herded together****.* | *I don't want to be herded around with a lot of tourists.* | **herd sb into sth** *The visitors were herded into two large halls.* **2** [T] to make animals move together in a group: *It was Thomas's duty to herd the cows.*

herds·man /ˈhɜːdzmən/ *n plural* **herdsmen** /-mən/ [C] a man who looks after a herd of animals

here S1 W1 /hɪə $ hɪr/ *adv*
1 in this place: *What are you doing here?* | *Shall we eat here?* | *Come here for a minute.* | *This switch here controls the lights.* | *My friend here will show you the way.* | **up/down/in/out here** *What was she doing up here in the woods?* | *Would you close the window? It's cold in here.* | *Come on. I'm* ***over here****.* | *Will you be* ***back here*** *tonight?* | *There are no good pubs* ***round here****.* | *I'm resigning* ***here and now****.*
2 at this point in time: *Spring is here at last.* | *Here is your chance to change your life.* | *Here is where the trouble starts.*
3 here and there scattered around or happening in several different places: *The house just needs a bit of paint here and there.*

SPOKEN PHRASES

4 here is/are sth also **here it is/here they are a)** used when you are giving something to someone, or showing something to them: *Here's the money you lent me.* | *Here are some pictures of John when he was little.* **b)** used when you have found something you were looking for: *Have you seen my pen? Oh, here it is.*
5 used when you are giving or offering something to someone: *Here, have my chair. I don't mind standing.*
6 here you are/here you go used when you are giving something to someone: *Here you are, a boxful of tools.* | *'Here you go.' Callum handed her a glass of orange juice.*
7 at this point in a discussion: *Here I'd like to add a note of caution.* | *There is no space to discuss this issue here.* | *I'm not sure what you mean here.*
8 here goes! also **here we go** used when you are going to try to do something difficult or dangerous, and you do not know what will happen: *I've never ridden a motorbike before, so here goes!*
9 here we go used when you are starting to do something or when something is starting to happen: *Right, here we go, the game's starting.*
10 here's to sb/sth used when you are going to drink something to wish someone good luck, show your respect for them etc: *Here's to the happy couple.* | *Here's to your new job.*
11 here he/she etc is also **sb/sth is here** used to say that someone or something has arrived: *Here they are, late as usual.* | *Ah, look – here's the postman.* | *Tony's here for his messages.*
12 here we are used when you have finally arrived somewhere you were travelling to: *Here we are – home at last.*
13 here comes sb/sth used when you can see something or someone arriving: *Here comes lunch.*
14 *BrE* used to get someone's attention or to show that you are annoyed: *Here! Just what do you think you're doing?*

H

15 here we go again *informal* used when something unpleasant is beginning to happen again: *Most of us are peaceful and decent, but here we go again, in our fifth war of this century.*
16 here to stay if something is here to stay, it has become a part of life and will continue to be so: *Mobile phones are definitely here to stay.*
17 here, there, and everywhere *informal* in many different places: *I spent the weekend driving the kids here, there, and everywhere.*
18 neither here nor there not important: *You never liked him much, did you?' 'What I think about him is neither here nor there. He's your friend.'*
19 the here and now the present time: **in the here and now** *To be able to live fully in the here and now, one must first learn how to honour the past.*
20 sb/sth is here to do sth used to say what someone or something's duty or purpose is: *We're here to serve you.*
21 here he/she etc is (doing sth) used to describe the present situation, especially one you did not expect to happen: *I didn't think I'd ever be able to afford it, but here I am sitting in my own little fitted kitchen.*

here·a·bouts /ˌhɪərəˈbaʊts, ˈhɪərəbaʊts $ ˌhɪr-, ˈhɪr-/ *adv* somewhere near the place where you are: *There must be a pub hereabouts.*

here·af·ter¹ /ˌhɪərˈɑːftə $ ˌhɪrˈæftər/ *adv* **1** [sentence adverb] *formal* from this time **2** *formal* after death: *his belief in God and a life hereafter* **3** *law* in a later part of an official or legal document: *the Ulster Democratic Unionist Party (hereafter DUP)*

hereafter² *n* **the hereafter** a life after death: *Do you believe in the hereafter?*

here·by /ˌhɪəˈbaɪ, ˈhɪəbaɪ $ ˌhɪr-, ˈhɪr-/ *adv law* as a result of this statement – used in official situations: *I hereby agree to the conditions of this contract.*

he·red·i·ta·ry /hɪˈredɪ̱təri $ -teri/ *adj* **1** a quality or illness that is hereditary is passed from a parent to a child before the child is born; → **genetic 2** *BrE* a hereditary position, rank, or title can be passed from an older to a younger person in the same family, usually when the older one dies: *a hereditary peer*

he·red·i·ty /hɪˈredɪ̱ti/ *n* [U] the process by which mental and physical qualities are passed from a parent to a child before the child is born; → **genetics**

here·in /ˌhɪərˈɪn $ ˌhɪr-/ *adv formal* in this place, situation, document etc: *the conditions stated herein* | *Herein lies a problem.* → **THEREIN**

here·in·af·ter /ˌhɪərɪnˈɑːftə $ ˌhɪrɪnˈæftər/ *adv law* later in this official statement, document etc: *the Council of the Law Society (hereinafter called the Council)*

here·of /ˌhɪərˈɒv $ hɪrˈʌv, -ˈɑːv/ *adv formal* or *law* relating to or belonging to this document: *This Agreement commences on the date of signature hereof.* → **THEREOF**

her·e·sy /ˈherɪ̱si/ *n plural* **heresies** [C,U] **1** a belief that disagrees with the official principles of a particular religion: *He was executed for heresy.* **2** a belief, statement etc that disagrees with what a group of people believe to be right: *To come to work without a shirt and tie was considered heresy.*

her·e·tic /ˈherɪ̱tɪk/ *n* [C] someone who is guilty of heresy: *Cranmer was put to death as a heretic.* —**heretical** /hɪ̱ˈretɪkəl/ *adj*

here·to /ˌhɪəˈtuː $ ˌhɪrˈtuː/ *adv formal* to this: *A copy of the document is hereto appended.*

here·to·fore /ˌhɪətʊˈfɔː $ ˈhɪrtʊfɔːr/ *adv formal* before this time: *In recent years we have seen greater emphasis than heretofore on the voice of the consumer.*

here·up·on /ˌhɪərəˈpɒn $ ˌhɪrəˈpɑːn/ *adv formal* at or after this moment

here·with /ˌhɪəˈwɪð, -ˈwɪθ $ ˌhɪr-/ *adv formal* with this letter or document: *I enclose a copy of this report herewith for your information.*

her·i·ta·ble /ˈherɪ̱təbəl/ *adj law* property that is heritable can be passed from the older members of a family to the younger ones

her·i·tage /ˈherɪ̱tɪdʒ/ *n* [singular, U] the traditional beliefs, values, customs etc of a family, country, or society; → **inheritance**: *the importance of preserving the national heritage* | *beautiful old buildings which are part of our heritage* | **cultural/architectural/literary etc heritage** *the cultural heritage of Italy*

her·maph·ro·dite /hɜːˈmæfrədaɪt $ hɜːr-/ *n* [C] a living thing that has both male and female sexual organs —**hermaphrodite** *adj*

her·met·ic·ally /hɜːˈmetɪkli $ hər-/ *adv technical* **hermetically sealed** very tightly closed so that air cannot get in or out; ▣ **airtight** —**hermetic** *adj*

her·mit /ˈhɜːmɪ̱t $ ˈhɜːr-/ *n* [C] someone who lives alone and has a simple way of life, usually for religious reasons → **RECLUSE**

her·mit·age /ˈhɜːmɪ̱tɪdʒ $ ˈhɜːr-/ *n* [C] a place where a hermit lives or has lived in the past

'hermit ˌcrab *n* [C] a kind of CRAB that lives in the empty shells of other sea creatures

her·ni·a /ˈhɜːniə $ ˈhɜːr-/ *n* [C,U] a medical condition in which an organ pushes through the muscles that are supposed to contain it; ▣ **rupture**

he·ro W3 /ˈhɪərəʊ $ ˈhɪroʊ/ *n plural* **heroes** [C]
1 a man who is admired for doing something extremely brave; → **heroine**

national hero (=a hero in a particular country)
local hero
war hero (=a soldier who was very brave in a war)
unsung hero (=someone whose bravery was not noticed or recognized)
folk hero (=an ordinary person who does something brave and becomes a hero in a particular place)
accidental hero (=someone who becomes a hero by chance)
be hailed as a hero (=be said to be a hero)

*He had dared to speak out against injustice, and overnight he became a **national hero**. | His father was a **war hero**, a former fighter pilot. | the **unsung heroes** who drove convoys of aid to Bosnia | [+of] a hero of the Great War | A man **hailed as a hero** for fifty years has been unmasked as a traitor.*

2 the man or boy who is the main character in a book, film, play etc; → **heroine**: [+of] *Phileas Fogg, hero of Jules Verne's Around the World in Eighty Days*
3 a man who is admired very much for a particular skill or quality; → **heroine**: **sb's hero** *When I was small, Uncle Fred was my hero.* | [+of] *Einstein is the hero of those who explore science at its deepest level.*
4 *AmE* a long thin SANDWICH filled with meat, cheese etc

he·ro·ic /hɪˈrəʊɪk $ -ˈroʊ-/ *adj* **1** extremely brave or determined, and admired by many people; ▣ **courageous**: *her heroic efforts to save her family* | *Lawrence's heroic struggle against his destiny.* | *She portrayed him as a heroic figure.* **2** a heroic story, poem etc has a hero in it, usually from ancient LEGENDS **3** **on a heroic scale/of heroic proportions** very large or great: *a battle on a heroic scale* —**heroically** /-kli/ *adv*

he,roic 'couplet *n* [C] a pair of lines in poetry which end with the same sound and that have five beats in each line

he·ro·ics /hɪˈrəʊɪks $ -ˈroʊ-/ *n* [plural] brave actions or words, often ones that are meant to seem impressive to other people: *America's present need is not heroics, but calm diplomacy.*

her·o·in /ˈherəʊɪn $ -roʊ-/ *n* [U] a powerful and illegal drug made from MORPHINE: **be on/use/take heroin** | *a heroin addict*

her·o·ine /'herəʊɪn $ -roʊ-/ *n* [C]   **1** a woman who is admired for doing something extremely brave; → **hero**: [+**of**] *a heroine of the French Resistance*   **2** the woman or girl who is the main character in a book, film, play etc; → **hero**: [+**of**] *Myra, the fictional heroine of The Women's Room*   **3** a woman who is admired very much for a particular skill or quality; → **hero**, **idol**: **sb's heroine** *Oprah is my heroine.*

her·o·is·m /'herəʊɪzəm $ -roʊ-/ *n* [U] very great courage: *stories of heroism and self-sacrifice*

her·on /'herən/ *n* [C] a large bird with very long legs and a long beak, that lives near water

ˈhero ˌworship *n* [U] great admiration for someone who is thought to be very brave, good, skilful etc – often used to show disapproval —**hero-worship** *v* [T]

her·pes /'hɜːpiːz $ 'hɜːr-/ *n* [U] a very infectious disease that causes spots on the skin, for example on the sexual organs or face

her·ring /'herɪŋ/ *n plural* **herrings** *or* **herring** [C] a long thin silver sea fish that can be eaten → **RED HERRING**

her·ring·bone /'herɪŋbəʊn $ -boʊn/ *n* [U] a pattern consisting of a continuous line of V shapes, used in cloth etc

hers [S3] /hɜːz $ hɜːrz/ *pron* [possessive form of 'she'] used to refer to something that belongs to or is connected with a woman, girl, or female animal that has already been mentioned: *He bent and touched his mouth to hers.* | *These are my gloves. Hers are in the drawer.* | *The idea was hers.* | *of hers Paul's a friend of hers.*

her·self [S2] [W1] /ə'self, hə-; *strong* hɜː- $ ər-, hɔr-; *strong* hɜːr-/ *pron* [reflexive form of 'she']
1 used to show that the woman or girl who does something is affected by her own action: *She cut herself on some broken glass.* | *She made herself a cup of coffee.*
2 a) used to emphasize that you are talking about one particular woman or girl: *It must be true that she's leaving because she told me so herself.* | *The ornate Town Hall was opened by Queen Victoria herself.* **b)** used after 'like', 'as', or 'except' instead of 'her': *She met other mothers in the same situation as herself.*
3 (all) by herself a) alone: *Miss Bennet lives by herself.* **b)** without help from anyone else: *The little girl wrote the letter all by herself.*
4 not be/feel/seem herself *informal* if a woman or girl is not herself, she does not feel or behave as she usually does, for example because she is upset or ill: *You must forgive her – she's not herself at present.*
5 have sth (all) to herself if a woman or girl has something to herself, she does not have to share it with anyone else: *Alice had the house to herself while her parents were away.*

hertz /hɜːts $ hɜːrts/ *n plural* **hertz** [C] written abbreviation *Hz* a unit for measuring the FREQUENCY of SOUND WAVES

he's /iz, hiz; *strong* hiːz/   **1** the short form of 'he is': *He's a writer.* | *He's reading.*   **2** the short form of 'he has': *He's bought a new car.*

hes·i·tan·cy /'hezɪtənsi/ also **hes·i·tance** /-təns/ *n* [U] when someone is uncertain or slow in doing or saying something

hes·i·tant /'hezɪtənt/ *adj* uncertain about what to do or say because you are nervous or unwilling: *Gail gave me a hesitant little smile.* | **hesitant about (doing) sth** *They seemed hesitant about coming in.* | **hesitant to do sth** *She is hesitant to draw conclusions until the study is over.* —**hesitantly** *adv*

hes·i·tate /'hezɪteɪt/ *v*   **1** [I] to pause before saying or doing something because you are nervous or not sure: *Kay hesitated for a moment and then said 'yes'.* | [+**about/over**] *He was still hesitating over whether to leave or not.*   **2 don't hesitate to do sth** used to tell someone that it is correct or right for them to do something and they do not have to worry about offending anyone: *Don't hesitate to contact me if you need any more information.* —**hesitatingly** *adv*

hes·i·ta·tion /ˌhezɪ'teɪʃən/ *n* [C,U] when someone hesitates: *After some hesitation one of them began to speak.* | **without hesitation** *He agreed without hesitation.* | **have no hesitation in doing sth** *I would have no hesitation in recommending Philip for the position.* | **a slight/brief/momentary etc hesitation** *There was a slight hesitation in Jamie's voice.*

hes·si·an /'hesiən $ 'heʃən/ *n* [U] *BrE* thick rough cloth sometimes used for making SACKS; ⊟ **burlap** *AmE*

hetero- /hetərəʊ, -rə $ -roʊ, -rə/ *prefix* other; opposite; different: **heterosexual** (=attracted to the opposite sex)

het·e·ro·dox /'hetərədɒks $ -dɑːks/ *adj formal* heterodox beliefs, practices etc are not approved of by a particular group, especially a religious one

het·e·ro·ge·ne·ous /ˌhetərəʊ'dʒiːniəs $ -roʊ-/ also **het·e·rog·e·nous** /ˌhetə'rɒdʒənəs◂ $ -'rɑː-/ *adj formal* consisting of parts or members that are very different from each other; ⊟ **homogeneous**: *a heterogeneous collection of buildings* —**heterogeneously** *adv* —**heterogeneity** /ˌhetərəʊdʒɪ'niːɪti $ -roʊ-/ *n* [U]

het·e·ro·sex·u·al /ˌhetərə'sekʃuəl◂/ *adj* sexually attracted to people of the opposite sex; ⊟ **straight**; → **bisexual**, **homosexual**

het up /ˌhet 'ʌp/ *adj* [not before noun] *BrE informal* anxious, upset, or slightly angry: [+**about/over**] *Mike tends to get het up about silly things.*

heu·ris·tic /hjʊ'rɪstɪk/ *adj formal*   **1** heuristic education is based on discovering and experiencing things for yourself   **2** helping you in the process of learning or discovery —**heuristically** /-kli/ *adv*

heu·ris·tics /hjʊ'rɪstɪks/ *n* [U] *formal* the study of how people use their experience to find answers to questions or to improve performance

hew /hjuː/ *v past tense* **hewed**, *past participle* **hewed** also **hewn** /hjuːn/ *literary* [I,T] to cut something with a cutting tool: *hewn stone* → **ROUGH-HEWN**

hex /heks/ *n* [C] *AmE* an evil CURSE that brings trouble: *I think he's trying to put a hex on me.* —**hex** *v* [T]

hex·a·dec·i·mal /ˌheksə'desɪməl◂/ also **hex** *adj technical* hexadecimal numbers are based on the number 16 and are mainly used on computers

hex·a·gon /'heksəgən $ -gɑːn/ *n* [C] a shape with six sides —**hexagonal** /hek'sægənəl/ *adj*

hex·am·e·ter /hek'sæmɪtə $ -ər/ *n* [C] *technical* a line of poetry with six main beats

hey /heɪ/ *interjection*   **1** a shout used to get someone's attention or to show surprise, interest, or annoyance: *Hey, wait a minute!*   **2** *informal* hello: *Hey, what's up?*

hey·day /'heɪdeɪ/ *n* [C usually singular] the time when someone or something was most popular, successful, or powerful: **in sb's heyday** *a picture of Greta Garbo in her heyday*

hey pres·to /ˌheɪ 'prestəʊ $ -toʊ/ *interjection BrE* used to say that something happens so easily that it seems to be magic; ⊟ **presto** *AmE*

HGV /ˌeɪtʃ dʒiː 'viː/ *n* [C] *BrE heavy goods vehicle* a large road vehicle used for moving goods; ⊟ **truck**

hi [S1] /haɪ/ *interjection informal* hello: *Hi! How are you?* | *Hi there! I haven't seen you for ages.*

hi·a·tus /haɪ'eɪtəs/ *n* [C usually singular]   **1** *formal* a break or INTERRUPTION in an activity: *Talks between the two countries have resumed after a six-year hiatus.* | [+**in**] *a hiatus in research* | **a brief/short/long hiatus** *There was a brief hiatus in the war.*   **2** *technical* a space where something is missing, especially in a piece of writing

hi·ber·nate /'haɪbəneɪt $ -ər-/ *v* [I] if an animal hibernates, it sleeps for the whole winter —**hibernation** /ˌhaɪbə'neɪʃən $ -bər-/ *n* [U]

hi·bis·cus /haɪ'bɪskəs/ *n* [C,U] a tropical plant with large brightly coloured flowers

H

hic·cup[1], **hiccough** /ˈhɪkʌp, -kəp/ n [C] **1** [usually plural] a sudden repeated stopping of the breath, usually caused by eating or drinking too fast: **get/have hiccups** BrE; **get/have the hiccups** AmE: Don't drink so fast – you'll get hiccups. **2** a small problem or delay: [+in] a hiccup in the negotiations

hiccup[2] v hiccupped, hiccupping [I] to have hiccups

hick /hɪk/ n [C] AmE informal someone who lives in the countryside, and is thought to be uneducated or stupid —**hick** adj: hick towns

hick·ey /ˈhɪki/ n [C] AmE a red mark on someone's skin caused by someone else sucking it as a sexual act; ⊟ **lovebite** BrE

hick·o·ry /ˈhɪkəri/ n plural **hickories** [C,U] a North American tree that produces nuts, or the wood that comes from this tree

hid /hɪd/ the past tense of HIDE

hid·den[1] /ˈhɪdn/ the past participle of HIDE

hidden[2] adj **1** difficult to see or find: the use of hidden cameras | Some areas can hold hidden dangers for dogs. | the hidden meaning behind his words | Be on the lookout for hidden costs in hotel bills. **2** not easy to notice or realize: He wants each pupil to have the chance to discover **hidden talents**. **3** **hidden agenda** the secret purpose behind a plan or activity that you do not tell other people about – used to show disapproval: Voters suspected a hidden political agenda. | Was there a hidden agenda behind this decision?

hide[1] S2 W2 /haɪd/ v past tense **hid** /hɪd/ past participle **hidden** /ˈhɪdn/
1 [T] to deliberately put or keep something or someone in a place where they cannot easily be seen or found: **hide sth in/under/behind etc** Marcia hid the pictures in her desk drawer. | She **keeps** a bottle of gin **hidden** behind a stack of books. | **hide sth/sb from sb** He was accused of trying to hide evidence from the police.
2 [T] to cover something so that it cannot be seen clearly: The church roof was half hidden by trees. | Her tangled hair hid her face.
3 [I] to go or stay in a place where no one will see or find you: Quick, he's coming! We'd better hide. | [+in/under/ behind etc] Harry hid under the bed. | **hide from sb** Weiss spent two years hiding from the Nazis.
4 [T] to keep someone in a place where other people will not find them: The old woman hid him in her cellar for three days. | **hide sb from sb** We'll have to hide him from the soldiers.
5 [T] to keep your real feelings, plans, or the truth secret, so that they cannot be known by other people: **hide your disappointment/embarrassment/confusion etc** She laughed to hide her nervousness. | He took off his ring to **hide the fact** that he was married. | He told the jury that he is innocent and has nothing to hide. | **hide sth from sb** Don't try to hide anything from me. → **hide your light under a bushel** at BUSHEL

hide[2] n [C] **1** BrE a place from which you can watch animals or birds without being seen by them; ⊟ **blind** AmE **2** an animal's skin, especially when it has been removed to be used for leather: ox hide gloves **3** **have/ tan sb's hide** spoken to punish someone severely – used humorously **4** **sb's hide** spoken used to talk about someone when they are in a difficult situation: He would say anything in court to try and **save** his own **hide** (=save himself). **5 not see hide nor hair of sb** spoken to not see someone anywhere for a fairly long time: I haven't seen hide nor hair of him for ages.

hide-and-ˈseek also **hide-and-go-ˈseek** AmE n [U] a children's game in which one player shuts their eyes while the others hide, and then goes to look for them

hide·a·way /ˈhaɪdəweɪ/ n [C] a place where you can go when you want to be alone

hide·bound /ˈhaɪdbaʊnd/ adj having old-fashioned attitudes and ideas – used to show disapproval: hidebound reactionaries

hid·e·ous /ˈhɪdiəs/ adj extremely unpleasant or ugly: a hideous dress | hideous crimes | Dinnertime that day was hideous. —**hideously** adv: Her face was hideously scarred. —**hideousness** n [U]

hide·out /ˈhaɪdaʊt/ n [C] a place where someone goes because they do not want anyone to find them

hid·ing /ˈhaɪdɪŋ/ n **1** [U] when someone stays somewhere in secret, especially because they have done something illegal or are in danger: **be in/go into/come out of hiding** He went into hiding in 1973. **2** [singular] spoken informal **a)** a severe physical punishment; ⊟ **beating**: You'll **get a good hiding** when you come home! | You're not too big for a hiding, you know. **b)** an occasion when you defeat someone in a sports game **3 be on a hiding to nothing** BrE informal to be completely wasting your time trying to do something

ˈhiding ˌplace n [C] a place where you can hide or where you can hide something

hier·ar·chi·cal /haɪˈrɑːkɪkəl $ -ɑːr-/ adj if a system, organization etc is hierarchical, people or things are divided into levels of importance: **hierarchical structure/organization/system etc** a hierarchical society —**hierarchically** /-kli/ adv

hier·ar·chy /ˈhaɪrɑːki $ -ɑːr-/ n plural **hierarchies** **1** [C,U] a system of organization in which people or things are divided into levels of importance: a rigid social hierarchy | She worked her way up through the corporate hierarchy to become president. **2** [C] the most important and powerful members of an organization: the church hierarchy

hier·o·glyph·ics /ˌhaɪrəˈglɪfɪks/ n [U] a system of writing that uses pictures to represent words —**hieroglyphic** adj: hieroglyphic script

hi-fi /ˈhaɪ faɪ, ˌhaɪ ˈfaɪ/ n plural **hi-fis** [C] old-fashioned a piece of high quality electronic equipment for playing recorded music; ⊟ **stereo** —**hi-fi** adj: hi-fi speakers

hig·gle·dy-pig·gle·dy /ˌhɪgəldi ˈpɪgəldi/ adj things that are higgledy-piggledy are mixed together in an untidy way —**higgledy-piggledy** adv

high[1] S1 W1 /haɪ/ adj comparative **higher**, superlative **highest**
1 FROM BOTTOM TO TOP measuring a long distance from the bottom to the top; ⊟ **low**: This is the highest mountain in Japan. | The camp was surrounded by a high fence. | **100 feet/30 metres etc high** Waves of up to 40 metres high were recorded. | a ten-foot high statue | **How high** is the Eiffel Tower? | **chest/waist/knee etc high** (=as high as your chest etc) The grass was knee-high. ⚠ Do not use **high** to describe people, animals, trees, plants, and narrow things of above average height. Use **tall**: You're getting very tall (NOT You're getting very high) | tall buildings (NOT high buildings); → see box at BIG[1]
2 ABOVE GROUND in a position that is a long way, or a longer way than usual, above the ground, floor etc; ⊟ **low**: The apartment had spacious rooms with high ceilings. | a high shelf | high altitudes | The sun was already high in the sky. | **High up** among the clouds, we saw the summit of Everest.
3 LARGE NUMBER a high amount, number, or level is large, or larger than usual; ⊟ **low**: Temperatures remained high for the rest of the week. | Lower-paid workers often cannot afford the high cost of living in the capital. | **high level/degree/rate etc (of sth)** High levels of car use mean our streets are more congested than ever. | high crime rates | high interest rates | **high price/charge/tax etc** If you want better public services, you'll have to pay higher taxes – it's as simple as that. | The train was approaching **at high speed**. | **high proportion/percentage etc (of sth)** (=a very large part of a number) A high proportion of women with children under five work full-time.
4 GOOD STANDARD a high standard, quality etc is very good; ⊟ **low**: a high performance computer | **high quality** a range of high quality goods at low prices | Our aim is to provide the highest quality service to all our customers. | **high standard** (=very good levels of work,

achievement, behaviour etc) *The general standard of the entries was very high.* | *Our guests expect us to* **maintain high standards**.

5 CONTAINING A LOT containing a lot of a particular substance or quality; **⊟ low: high in sth** *Choose foods that are high in fiber and low in calories.* | **a high sugar/salt/fibre etc content** *Red meat tends to have a high fat content.*

6 RANK/POSITION having an important position in society or within an organization; **⊟ low:** *a high rank in the US Navy* | *the City's highest honour* | **high up** (=in a powerful position) *someone high up in the CIA* | **high office** (=an important position) *Both of them held high office in the Anglican Church.* | **high society** (=rich people of the highest social class) → HIGH-CLASS, HIGH-RANKING, HIGH-UP; → **friends in high places** at FRIEND (11)

7 ADVANCED [only before noun] advanced and often complicated: *We can offer all the benefits of the latest* **high technology**. | *the world of* **high finance** | **the higher animals/mammals/organisms etc** (=animals etc that are more intelligent or advanced than others)

8 high opinion/regard/praise etc strong approval of someone or something, or an expression of strong approval: *I've always had a high opinion of her work.* | **hold sb/sth in high esteem/regard** (=respect them very much) *As an educationalist, he was held in very high esteem.* | *Romsey earned high praise from his boss.*

9 high priority also **high on the list/agenda** important and needing to be done or dealt with quickly: *Most people feel that education needs to be given higher priority.* | *Arms control is high on the agenda.*

10 high hopes/expectations when someone hopes or expects that something will be very good or successful: *My expectations of the place were never very high, but I didn't think it would be this bad.* | **have high hopes/expectations** *Like many young actors, I had high hopes when I first started out.*

11 SOUND near or above the top of the range of sounds that humans can hear; **⊟ low:** *I always had difficulty reaching the high notes* (=when singing). | *a high squeaky voice* → HIGH-PITCHED

12 high point also **high spot** *BrE* an especially good part of an activity or event: *The visit to the ancient capital city was one of the high points of the tour.*

13 high ground a) an area of land that is higher than the area surrounding it: *Villagers herded the livestock to high ground to keep them safe during the floods.* **b)** a better, more moral, or more powerful position in an argument or competition: *Neither side in this conflict can claim the moral high ground.*

14 high spirits feelings of happiness and energy, especially when you are having fun: *It was a bright sunny day and we set off in high spirits.* | *I don't think they intended any harm – it was just high spirits.*

15 HAPPY/EXCITED [not before noun] happy and excited: *I was still high from the applause they'd given me.*

16 DRUGS [not before noun] behaving in a strange and excited way as the result of taking drugs: [+on] *Most people there were high on cocaine.* | **get high** (=take a drug to make yourself high) *Steve was as high as a kite* (=strongly affected by drugs or alcohol).

17 SEA/RIVER having risen to a high level; **⊟ low:** *The river is at its highest in spring.* → HIGH TIDE

18 it is **high time sb did sth** used to say that something should be done now: *It's high time you got a job.*

19 TIME the middle or the most important part of a particular period of time: **high summer** | **high noon** (=12 o'clock in the middle of the day) → HIGH SEASON

20 high wind a strong wind

21 high alert a situation in which people are told to be ready because there is a strong possibility of an attack or of something dangerous happening: **put/place sb on high alert** *Troops were put on high alert.*

22 high life/living the enjoyable life that rich and fashionable people have: *We're all stuck here, while he's off living the high life in New York.*

23 high drama/adventure very exciting events or situations: *a life with moments of high drama*

24 end/finish/begin etc (sth) on a high note to end, finish something etc in a successful way: *The team finished their tour on a high note in Barbados.*

25 high principles/ideals ideas about personal behaviour based on the belief that people should always behave in an honest and morally good way: *a man of high moral principles*

26 high and mighty talking or behaving as if you think you are better or more important than other people: *Don't get high and mighty with me.*

27 be/get on your high horse to give your opinion about something in a way that shows you think you are definitely right and that other people are wrong: *If she'd get down off her high horse for a moment, she might realize there's more than one point of view here.*

28 FOOD *BrE* cheese, meat etc that is high is not fresh and has a strong smell or taste

29 high days and holidays *BrE* special occasions

30 high complexion/colouring *BrE* a naturally pink or red face

31 in high dudgeon *formal* in an angry or offended way – often used humorously

32 LANGUAGE a) **high style/register** *BrE* a very formal style of language, especially used in literature **b)** **high German/Dutch etc** a form of a language used for formal purposes that is often different from the ordinary form used by most people → HIGHLY; → **stink to high heaven** at STINK[1] (1)

high² *adv*

1 ABOVE THE GROUND at or to a level high above the ground, the floor etc; **⊟ low:** *He kicked the ball high into the air, over the heads of the crowd.* | [+**above/into etc**] *Hotel Miramar is situated high above the bay.* | *A ski lift whisks you high into the mountains.*

2 VALUE/COST/AMOUNT at or to a high value, cost, amount etc; **⊟ low:** *If prices shoot up any higher, no-one be able to afford to live in the area.* | *Tom scored higher than anyone else in the class.*

3 SOUND with a high sound: *A strange cry rang high into the night.*

4 ACHIEVEMENT at or to a high rank or level of achievement, especially within a company; **⊟ low:** *It seems that the higher you rise, the less time you have to actually do your job.* | *My parents always encouraged me to aim high.*

5 (leave sb/sth) high and dry a) if someone is left high and dry, they are left without any help or without the things that they need **b)** if a boat, area etc is left high and dry, it is left on land because the water that surrounded it has gone down: *The once-thriving port of Rye was left high and dry as sea levels retreated.*

6 look/search high and low to try to find someone or something by looking everywhere: *We looked high and low for Sandy but couldn't find her.* → **hold your head high** at HOLD[1] (16); → **live high on the hog** at LIVE[1] (26); → **be riding high** at RIDE[1] (6); → **run high** at RUN[1] (28)

high³ *n* [C]

1 NUMBER/AMOUNT the highest price, number, temperature etc that has ever been recorded, or that has been recorded within a particular period of time: *Highs of 40°C were recorded in the region last summer.* | **a new/record/ten-year etc high** *The price of oil reached a new high this week.*

2 EXCITEMENT *informal* a feeling of great happiness or excitement: *They're bound to be on a high after such an incredible victory.* | *the emotional highs and lows of a new romance*

3 DRUGS a feeling of pleasure or excitement produced by some drugs

4 WEATHER an area of high PRESSURE that affects the weather

5 SCHOOL a short form of HIGH SCHOOL, used in the name of a school: *Benjamin Franklin High*

H

6 from on high from someone in a position of authority – used humorously: *An order came from on high.*

7 on high *formal* **a)** at a high temperature as measured by an electric OVEN etc: *Microwave on high for 8 minutes.* **b)** *formal* in a high place or heaven: *An angel came from on high.*

-high /haɪ/ *suffix* [in adjectives] of a particular height: *The wall was about chest-high* (=as high as your chest). | *a 7000 metre-high mountain*

high·ball /'haɪbɔːl $ -bɔːl/ *n* [C] *especially AmE* an alcoholic drink, especially WHISKY or BRANDY mixed with water or SODA

'high ˌbeams *n* [plural] *AmE* lights at the front of a car that are on as brightly as possible

high-'born *adj formal* born into the highest social class; ◨ **low-born**

high·boy /'haɪbɔɪ/ *n* [C] *AmE* a piece of tall wooden furniture with many drawers; ◨ **tallboy** *BrE*

high·brow /'haɪbraʊ/ *adj* **1** a highbrow book, film etc is very serious and may be difficult to understand **2** someone who is highbrow is interested in serious or complicated ideas and subjects; ◨ **intellectual** —**highbrow** *n* [C] → LOWBROW, MIDDLEBROW

high·chair /ˌhaɪˈtʃeə $ 'haɪtʃer/ *n* [C] a special tall chair that a young child sits in to eat → see picture at CHAIR

High 'Church *n* [singular] the part of the Church of England that is closest in its beliefs to the Roman Catholic Church —**High Church** *adj* → LOW CHURCH

high-'class *adj* [usually before noun] of good quality and style, and usually expensive; ◨ **low-class**: *a high-class restaurant*

high com'mand *n* [singular] the most important leaders of a country's army, navy etc: *the German High Command*

high com'mission *n* [C] **1** a group of people working for a government or an international organization to deal with a specific problem **2** a group of people with official duties concerning the relationship of one Commonwealth country with another —**High Commissioner** *n* [C]

High 'Court *n* [C usually singular] a court of law that is at a higher level than ordinary courts and that can be asked to change the decisions of a lower court

high-defi'nition *adj* [only before noun] a high-definition television or computer shows images very clearly

high-'end *adj* [usually before noun] *AmE* relating to products or services that are more expensive and of better quality than other products of the same type: *high-end computer memory chips* → LOW-END

higher edu'cation *n* [U] college or university education as opposed to school or HIGH SCHOOL

higher mathe'matics *n* [U] different types of advanced mathematics that are studied and taught at universities

higher-'up *n* [C] *informal* someone who has a high rank in an organization: *Rumour has it that the higher-ups want to push the schedule forward.*

high ex'plosive *n* [C,U] a substance that explodes with great power and violence

high·fa·lu·tin /ˌhaɪfəˈluːtɪn◂ $ -tn◂/ *adj informal* highfalutin language or behaviour seems silly although it is intended to be impressive – used to show disapproval

high fi'delity *adj* [usually before noun] high fidelity recording equipment produces sound that is very clear → HI-FI

high 'five *n* [C] *especially AmE* the action of hitting someone's open hand with your own above your heads to show that you are pleased about something

high-'flier, high flyer *n* [C] someone who is extremely successful in their job or in school: *a young businessman considered a highflyer by the media* —**high-flying** *adj*

high-'flown *adj* high-flown language sounds impressive but does not have much real meaning

high-'grade *adj* [only before noun] of the best quality: *high-grade beef*

high-'handed *adj* using your authority in an unreasonable way: *She resented his high-handed manner.* | *high-handed and insensitive management decisions* —**high-handedly** *adv* —**high-handedness** *n* [U]

high 'heels *n* [plural] women's shoes with high heels

high jinks also **hi·jinks** *AmE* /'haɪdʒɪŋks/ *n* [plural] old-fashioned noisy or excited behaviour when people are having fun: *youthful high jinks*

high jump *n* **1 the high jump** a sports event in which someone runs and jumps over a bar that is raised higher each time they jump **2 be (in) for the high jump** *BrE informal* if someone is for the high jump, they will be punished for something they have done wrong —**high jumper** *n* [C]

high·land /'haɪlənd/ *adj* [only before noun] **1** also **Highland** relating to the Scottish Highlands or its people: *Highland pipers* **2** in or relating to an area with a lot of mountains; → **lowland**: *the highland capital of Quito*

High·land·er /'haɪləndə $ -ər/ *n* [C] someone from the Scottish Highlands

high·lands /'haɪləndz/ *n* [plural] **1 the Highlands** an area in the north of Scotland where there are a lot of mountains **2** an area of a country where there are a lot of mountains: *forested highlands* → LOWLANDS

high-'level *adj* [only before noun] **1** in a powerful position or job, or involving people who are in powerful positions or jobs: *high-level executives* | **high-level meetings/talks/negotiations etc** *a high-level conference on arms control* **2** at a high degree or strength: *The virus has shown high-level resistance to penicillin* **3** involving very technical or complicated ideas **4** a high-level computer language is similar to human language rather than machine language → LOW-LEVEL

high·light¹ W3 /'haɪlaɪt/ *v* [T] **1** to make a problem or subject easy to notice so that people pay attention to it: *Your resume should highlight your skills and achievements.* **2** to mark written words with a special coloured pen, or in a different colour on a computer: *Use the cursor to highlight the name of the document you want to print.* **3** to make some parts of your hair a lighter colour than the rest —**highlighting** *n* [U]

highlight² *n* **1** [C] the most important, interesting, or enjoyable part of something such as a holiday, performance, or sports competition: [+of] *That weekend in Venice was definitely the highlight of our trip.* | [+from] *At 11.30 we'll be showing highlights from the Third Round of the FA Cup.* **2 highlights** [plural] areas of hair that have been made a lighter colour than the rest **3** [C] *technical* a light bright area on a painting or photograph

high·light·er /'haɪlaɪtə $ -ər/ *n* [C] a special light-coloured pen used for marking words in a book, article etc → see picture at OFFICE

high·ly S2 W2 /'haɪli/ *adv* **1** [+ adj, adv] very: **highly successful/effective/efficient** *a highly successful politician* | *Tom's mother was highly critical of the school's approach.* | *highly competitive industries* | *a highly desirable neighborhood* | **highly unlikely/likely/improbable/probable** *It's highly unlikely that the project will be finished on time.* | *T.S. Eliot's highly influential poem, 'The Waste Land'* | *a highly controversial issue* **2** [+ adj, adv] to a high level or standard: **highly skilled/**

trained/educated *She is a highly educated woman.* | *highly paid experts* | *a highly developed economy*
3 highly placed in an important or powerful position: *a highly placed government official*
4 highly strung *especially BrE*; **high-strung** *AmE* nervous and easily upset or excited: *a highly strung child*
5 if you think highly of someone or something, you think they are very good and you admire them: **think/ speak highly of sb** *I've always thought very highly of Michael.* | *a highly regarded author*

High 'Mass *n* [C,U] a very formal church ceremony in the Roman Catholic Church

high-'minded *adj* having very high moral standards or principles: *a high-minded sermon on charity* —**high-mindedly** *adv* —**high-mindedness** *n* [U]

High·ness /'haɪnᵻs/ *n* [C] **Your/Her/His Highness** used to speak to or about a king, queen, prince etc

high-'octane *adj* high-octane petrol is of a very high quality

high-per'formance *adj* **high-performance cars/ computers/tyres etc** cars, computers etc that are able to go faster, do more work etc than normal ones

high-'pitched *adj* a high-pitched voice or sound is very high; ▣ **low-pitched**

high-'powered *adj* [usually before noun] **1** a high-powered machine, vehicle, or piece of equipment is very powerful: *a high-powered automobile* **2** very important or successful: *a high-powered publisher*

high-'pressure *adj* [only before noun] **1** a high-pressure job or situation is one in which you need to work very hard; ▣ **stressful 2 high-pressure sales/ selling methods etc** very direct and often successful ways of persuading people to buy something: *high-pressure sales techniques* **3** containing or using a very high pressure or force of water, gas, air etc: *high-pressure hoses*

high-'priced *adj* costing a lot of money; ▣ **low-priced, inexpensive**: *high-priced apartments* | *high-priced lawyers*

high 'priest *n* [C] **1** *informal* someone who is famous for being the best at a type of art, music etc, and whose ideas or work change the way that other people think about and make art, music etc: [+of] *the high priest of modern jazz* **2** the most important PRIEST in some religions

high 'priestess *n* [C] **1** *informal* a woman who is famous for being the best at a type of art, music etc, and whose ideas or work change the way that other people think about and make art, music etc **2** the most important PRIESTESS in some religions

high-'principled *adj* having high moral standards

high-'profile *adj* [only before noun] attracting a lot of public attention, usually deliberately; ▣ **low profile**: *a high-profile public figure* —**high profile** *n* [singular]

high-'ranking *adj* [only before noun] having a high position in a government or other organization; ▣ **low-ranking**: *high-ranking officials*

high re'lief *n* [U] **1** a form of art in which figures cut in stone or wood stand out from the surface → BAS-RELIEF **2 throw sth into high relief** to make something very clear and easy to notice

high-rise *adj* [only before noun] high-rise buildings are tall buildings with many levels —**high rise** *n* [C]: *They live in a high rise on the East Side.* → LOW-RISE

high-'risk *adj* [only before noun] involving a risk of death, injury, failure etc; ▣ **low-risk**: *high-risk investments* | **high-risk patients/groups etc** *cancer screening for women over 55 and other high-risk groups*

high road *n* [C] **1** *old-fashioned* a main road **2 take the (moral) high road** *AmE* to do what you believe is right according to your beliefs: *Daley has taken the high road in his campaign.*

high 'roller *n* [C] *AmE informal* someone who spends a lot of money carelessly or risks a lot of money on games, races etc

high school *n* **1** [C,U] a school in the US and Canada for children of 14 or 15 to 18 years old; → **junior high school**: **in high school** *We were friends in high school.* | *high school students* | *high school graduates* **2** [singular] used in the names of some schools in Britain for children from 11 to 18 years old: *Leytonstone High School for Girls* → SECONDARY SCHOOL

high 'seas *n* **the high seas** *literary* the areas of ocean around the world that do not belong to any particular country

high 'season *n* [singular, U] *especially BrE* the time of year when businesses make a lot of money and prices are high, especially in the tourist industry; ▣ **peak season** → LOW SEASON

high-'sounding *adj* [only before noun] high-sounding statements, principles etc seem very impressive but are often insincere

high-'speed *adj* [only before noun] **1** designed to travel or operate very fast: *a high-speed train* | **high-speed computer/network/modem etc** *high-speed Internet access* **2 high-speed chase** a situation when the police drive very fast to try to catch someone in a car

high-'spirited *adj* **1** someone who is high-spirited has a lot of energy and enjoys fun and adventure **2** a high-spirited horse is nervous and hard to control

high street *n* *BrE* **1** [C] the main street of a town where most of the shops and businesses are: *Camden High Street* | **in/on the high street** *A new bookshop had opened in the high street.* | **high street banks/shops/ stores etc 2 the high street** used to talk about shops and the money people spend in them: *This year was exceptionally difficult on the high street.*

high 'table *n* [singular, U] *BrE* the table where the most important people at a formal occasion sit; ▣ **head table**

high·tail /'haɪteɪl/ *v* **hightail it** *informal* to leave a place quickly: *kids hightailing it down the street on their bikes*

high 'tea *n* [C,U] *BrE* a meal of cold food, cakes etc eaten in the early evening

high-tech /ˌhaɪ 'tek◂/ *adj* [usually before noun] **1** using high technology: *high-tech industries* | *a £1 million high-tech security system* | *high-tech weapons* → LOW-TECH **2** high-tech furniture, designs etc are made in a very modern style —**high tech** *n* [U]

high tech'nology *n* [U] the use of the most modern machines and methods in industry, business etc

high-'tension *adj* **high-tension wires/cables etc** wires etc that have a powerful electric current going through them

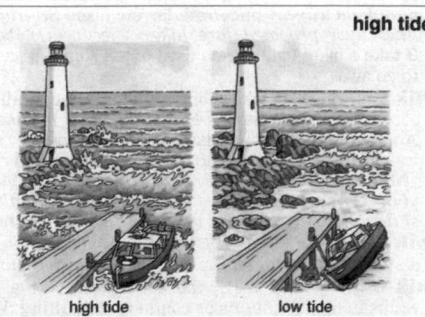

high tide

high tide   low tide

high 'tide *n* **1** [C,U] the point or time at which the sea reaches its highest level; ▣ **low tide**: *High tide is at seven in the morning.* | **at high tide** *The waves became much more powerful at high tide.* **2** [singular] the time when something is at its best or most successful: *the high tide in the party's fortunes*

high-tops *n* [plural] *AmE informal* sports shoes that cover your ANKLES —**high-top** *adj*: *high-top basketball shoes*

H

high 'treason n [U] the crime of putting your country in great danger, for example by giving military secrets to the enemy

high-up n [C] BrE informal someone who has a high rank in an organization; ☐ **higher-up**

high 'water n [U] the period of time during which the water in a river or the sea is at its highest level because of the TIDE → **come hell or high water** at HELL¹ (22)

high 'water mark n [singular] **1** the mark that shows the highest level that the sea or a river reaches **2** the time when someone or something is most successful: [+of] the high water mark of Herrera's presidency

high·way S2 /'haɪweɪ/ n [C]
1 especially AmE a wide main road that joins one town to another: Interstate Highway 75 → FREEWAY, EXPRESSWAY, MOTORWAY
2 the public highway BrE law a road or roads that the public has the right to use
3 highway robbery AmE informal a situation in which something costs you a lot more than it should: It's highway robbery, charging that much for gas!

Highway 'Code n [singular] the set of official rules and laws about driving and using roads in Britain

high·way·man /'haɪweɪmən/ n plural **highwaymen** /-mən/ [C] someone who stopped people and carriages on the roads and robbed them, especially in the 17th and 18th centuries

highway pa·trol n [singular] the police who make sure that people obey the law on main roads in the US

high wire n [C usually singular] a tightly stretched rope or wire high above the ground that someone walks along as part of a CIRCUS performance; ☐ **tightrope**

hi·jack¹ /'haɪdʒæk/ v [T] **1** to use violence or threats to take control of a plane, vehicle, or ship; → **carjack**: The airliner was hijacked by a group of terrorists. **2** to take control of something and use it for your own purposes: Some people think the party has been hijacked by right-wing extremists. —**hijacker** n [C]

hijack² n [C] BrE when a plane, vehicle etc is hijacked

hi·jack·ing /'haɪdʒækɪŋ/ n **1** [C,U] the use of violence or threats to take control of a plane: the recent series of airplane hijackings **2** [U] the act of stealing goods from vehicles

hi·jinks /'haɪdʒɪŋks/ n [plural] an American spelling of HIGH JINKS

hike¹ /haɪk/ n [C] **1** a long walk in the mountains or countryside: a hike in the woods **2** especially AmE informal a large increase in prices, wages, taxes etc; ☐ rise: [+in] The president has proposed a hike in the minimum wage. | **price/rate/tax etc hikes** Several airlines have proposed fare hikes, effective October 1. **3 take a hike** AmE spoken used to tell someone rudely to go away

hike² v **1** [I,T] to take a long walk in the mountains or countryside: **hike sth** AmE: His dream is to hike the Appalachian Trail. **2** also **hike up** [T] especially AmE to increase a price, tax etc by a large amount; ☐ **raise**
hike sth ⇔ up especially AmE **1** to lift up a piece of your clothing: She hiked her skirt up to climb the stairs. **2** to increase a price, tax etc by a large amount

hik·er /'haɪkə $ -ər/ n [C] someone who walks long distances in the mountains or country for pleasure

hik·ing /'haɪkɪŋ/ n [U] the activity of taking long walks in the mountains or country; → **walking**: We're going to do some hiking this summer. | Utah is a great place to go hiking. → see picture at FOOTWEAR

hi·lar·i·ous /hɪ'leəriəs $ -'ler-/ adj extremely funny: a hilarious story —**hilariously** adv

hi·lar·i·ty /hɪ'lærɪti/ n [U] laughter, or a feeling of fun: Eva joined in the hilarity as much as anyone.

hill S2 W2 /hɪl/ n [C]
1 an area of land that is higher than the land around it, like a mountain but smaller; → **uphill, downhill**

steep hill
rolling hills (=hills with long gentle slopes)
wooded hill (=one covered with trees)
green hill (=one covered with grass)
climb a hill (=walk or drive up a hill)
brow/crest of a hill (=the top part of a hill)
hills and valleys
hill farm/town
hill country (=a rural area where there are a lot of hills)

Their house is on a hill overlooking the sea. | the top of Sidbury Hill | A cart was making its way up the **steep hill** on which the village stood. | In the spring, **rolling hills** around Yakima Valley turn white with blossom. | the **hill towns** of central Italy → see picture at COUNTRY

2 a slope on a road: There's a steep hill ahead. → DOWNHILL, UPHILL
3 the Hill AmE CAPITOL HILL
4 over the hill no longer young, and therefore no longer attractive or good at doing things: Kathleen thinks she's over the hill, but she's only 32.
5 it doesn't amount to a hill of beans AmE spoken it is not important

hill·bil·ly /'hɪlbɪli/ n plural **hillbillies** [C] AmE an insulting word meaning an uneducated poor person who lives in the mountains

hill·ock /'hɪlək/ n [C] especially BrE a little hill

hill·side /'hɪlsaɪd/ n [C] the sloping side of a hill

hill station n [C] a town in the hills in South Asia

hill·top /'hɪltɒp $ -tɑːp/ n [C] the top of a hill

hill·walk·ing /'hɪlˌwɔːkɪŋ $ -ˌwɒːk-/ n [U] BrE the activity of walking on hills for pleasure —**hillwalker** n [C]; → see picture at OUTDOOR

hill·y /'hɪli/ comparative **hillier**, superlative **hilliest** adj having a lot of hills: **hilly region/area/terrain etc**; → see picture at LANDSCAPE

hilt /hɪlt/ n [C] **1** the handle of a sword or knife, where the blade is attached **2 to the hilt** completely: **support/defend/back sb to the hilt** I'm backing the PM to the hilt on this.

him S1 W1 /ɪm; strong hɪm/ pron [object form of 'he']
1 used to refer to a man, boy, or male animal that has already been mentioned or is already known about: Are you in love with him? | Why don't you ask him yourself? | He repeated what she had told him. | I knew it was him as soon as I heard his voice.
2 used when talking about someone who may be male or female. Some people think this use is old-fashioned: If you can convince a child you love him, you can teach him anything. ⚠ → see note at THEY

him·self S1 W1 /ɪm'self; strong hɪm'self/ pron [reflexive form of 'he']
1 a) used to show that the man or boy who does something is affected by his own action: In despair, the young boy had hanged himself. | His name is James but he calls himself Jim. | He poured himself a glass of orange juice. **b)** used after words such as 'everyone', 'anyone', and 'someone' to talk about people in general being affected by their own actions: Everyone should learn to respect himself.
2 a) used to emphasize that you are talking about one particular man or boy: It was the President himself who opened the door. | It must be true – he said so himself. **b)** used after 'like', 'as', or 'except' instead of 'him': The other passengers were all refugees like himself.
3 (all) by himself a) alone: He's lived by himself since his wife died. | Winston was sitting all by himself. **b)** without help from anyone else: It was the first time he felt he had achieved something by himself.
4 not be/feel/seem himself informal if a man or boy is not himself, he does not feel or behave as he usually does, for example because he is upset or ill: Rick hasn't seemed himself lately.
5 have sth (all) to himself if a man or boy has something

to himself, he does not have to share it with anyone else: *John at last had a bedroom all to himself.*

hind¹ /haɪnd/ *adj* [only before noun] relating to the back part of an animal with four legs: **hind legs/feet/quarters/limbs → talk the hind legs off a donkey** at TALK¹ (10)

hind² *n* [C] *BrE* a female DEER

hin·der /'hɪndə $ -ər/ *v* [T] to make it difficult for something to develop or succeed: *His career has been hindered by injury.* | *policies that will hinder rather than help families* ⚠ Do not confuse **hinder** and **prevent** even though they have similar meanings. **Hinder** means to make the progress or development of something slow down or stop. **Prevent** means to make it impossible for someone to do something: *His poor health prevented him from going to work* (NOT *His poor health hindered him from going to work*).

Hin·di /'hɪndi/ *n* [U] an official language in India

hind·most /'haɪndməʊst $ -moʊst/ *adj* → **devil take the hindmost** at DEVIL (13)

hind·quar·ters /'haɪnd,kwɔːtəz $ -,kwɔːrtərz/ *n* [plural] the back part of an animal with four legs

hin·drance /'hɪndrəns/ *n* **1** [C] something or someone that makes it difficult for you to do something: [+to] *The floods have been a major hindrance to relief efforts.* | *A degree is more of a hindrance than a help in British industry.* **2** [U] *formal* the act of making it difficult for someone to do something: *Visitors are allowed to wander without hindrance.* → **without let or hindrance** at LET² (2)

hind·sight /'haɪndsaɪt/ *n* [U] the ability to understand a situation only after it has happened; → **foresight. with/in hindsight** *With hindsight, I should have seen the warning signs.* | **the benefit/wisdom of hindsight** *With the benefit of hindsight, it's easy to criticize.*

Hin·du /'hɪnduː, ,hɪn'duː◂/ *n plural* **Hindus** [C] someone whose religion is Hinduism —**Hindu** *adj*: *a Hindu temple*

Hin·du·is·m /'hɪndu-ɪzəm/ *n* [U] the main religion in India, which includes belief in REINCARNATION

hinge¹ /hɪndʒ/ *n* [C] a piece of metal fastened to a door, lid etc that allows it to swing open and shut

hinge² *v* [T usually passive] to attach something, using a hinge —**hinged**: *a hinged lid*
  hinge on/upon sth *phr v* if a result hinges on something, it depends on it completely: *His political future hinges on the outcome of this election.* | *The case against him hinged on Lewis' evidence.*

hint¹ /hɪnt/ *n* [C]
1 something that you say or do to suggest something to someone, without telling them directly

hint that
give (sb) a hint
drop a hint (=give a hint)
take/get a hint also
take/get the hint (=understand someone's hint)
broad/strong/heavy hint (=one that is very easy to understand)
subtle/vague/gentle hint (=one that is not very easy to understand)
*There have been **hints that** he may take up coaching.* | *'Look, I can't tell you.' 'Oh, come on, **give me a hint.**'* | [+about/as to] *Miles had been **dropping** heavy **hints** about the cost of petrol.* | *I made it clear I wasn't interested in him, but he didn't **take the hint.****

2 a very small amount or sign of something: [+of] *'What time do we have to leave?' he asked with a hint of impatience.* | *We shall have to turn back if there's the slightest hint of fog.*
3 a useful piece of advice about how to do something; 🔲 **tip: helpful/handy hints** | [+on/about] *helpful hints on looking after house plants*

hint² *v* [I,T] to suggest something in an indirect way, but so that someone can guess your meaning: [+at] *What are you hinting at?* | **hint (that)** *He hinted strongly that he might be prepared to send troops in.*

hin·ter·land /'hɪntəlænd $ -ər-/ *n* [singular] an area of land that is far from the coast, large rivers, or the places where people live: *the rural hinterland*

hip¹ /hɪp/ *n* [C] **1** one of the two parts on each side of your body between the top of your leg and your waist: *She stood there with her hands on her hips glaring at him.* | *The old lady had fallen and broken her hip.* → see picture at SKELETON **2** the red fruit of some kinds of ROSES; 🔲 **rose hip**

hip² *adj informal* **1** doing things or done according to the latest fashion; 🔲 **cool**: *McMillan's novel gets my vote for hippest book of the year.* **2 be/get hip to sth** to learn about a new product, idea etc: *More and more people are getting hip to e-banking.*

hip³ *interjection* **hip, hip, hooray!** used as a shout of approval

hip flask *n* [C] a small container for alcoholic drinks, that fits into your pocket → see picture at BOTTLE

hip hop *n* [U] a kind of popular dance music with a regular heavy BEAT and spoken words; → **rap**

hip-hop *n* [U] a type of popular CULTURE among young people in big cities, especially African Americans, which includes RAP music, dancing, and GRAFFITI art

hip·pie, hippy /'hɪpi/ *n* [C] someone, especially in the 1960s, who opposed violence peacefully and often wore unusual clothes, had long hair, and took drugs for pleasure

hip·po /'hɪpəʊ $ -poʊ/ *n plural* **hippos** [C] *informal* a hippopotamus

hip pocket *n* [C] a back pocket in a pair of trousers or a skirt

Hip·po·crat·ic oath /,hɪpəkrætɪk 'əʊθ $ -'oʊθ/ *n* [singular] the promise made by doctors that they will obey the principles of the medical profession

hip·po·pot·a·mus /,hɪpə'pɒtəməs $ -'pɑː-/ *n plural* **hippopotamuses** *or* **hippopotami** /-maɪ/ [C] a large grey African animal with a big head and mouth that lives near water; → **rhinoceros**

hip·py /'hɪpi/ *n plural* **hippies** [C] another spelling of HIPPIE

hip·ster /'hɪpstə $ -ər/ *n* **1** [C] *informal* someone who is considered fashionable: *Legendary hipsters Stomp bring street theater to Boston this week.* **2 hipsters** [plural] *BrE* trousers that fit tightly over your HIPS and do not cover your waist

hire¹ [S3] /haɪə $ haɪr/ *v* [T]
1 *BrE* to pay money to borrow something for a short period of time; 🔲 **rent** *AmE*: *The best way to explore the island is to hire a car.* | *What does it cost to hire a boat for a week?* ⚠ **Hire, lease, or rent?** → see box at RENT¹
2 a) to employ someone for a short time to do a particular job: *Employers hire skilled people on fixed-term contracts.* | **hire sb to do sth** *A City lawyer has been hired to handle the case.* **b)** *AmE* to employ someone: *Businesses may only hire foreign workers where an American cannot be found.* | **the power to hire and fire** (=employ and dismiss people)
  hire sth ⇔ **out** *phr v BrE*
1 to allow someone to borrow something for a short time in exchange for money: [+to] *a little company that hires out boats to tourists*
2 hire yourself out to arrange to work for someone: *They were so poor they had to hire themselves out on the farms.*

hire² *n* [U] *BrE* an arrangement in which you pay a sum of money to borrow something for a short time: *a car hire company* | **for hire** *boats for hire* | **on hire** *The crane is on hire from a local firm.* → **ply for hire** at PLY¹ (3)

hired hand *n* [C] someone who is employed to help on a farm

1️⃣ 000, 2️⃣ 000, 3️⃣ 000, most frequent words in 🆂 poken and 🆆 ritten English

hire·ling /'haɪəlɪŋ $ 'haɪr-/ n [C] old-fashioned someone who will work for anyone who will pay them – used to show disapproval

,**hire 'purchase** n [U] BrE **HP** a way of buying expensive goods by regularly paying small amounts over a period of time; **▤ installment plan** AmE

hir·sute /'hɜːsjuːt, hɜː'sjuːt $ 'hɜːrsuːt, hɜːr'suːt/ adj literary humorous having a lot of hair on your body and face; → **hairy**

his [S1] [W1] /ɪz; strong hɪz/ determiner, pron [possessive form of 'he']
1 used to refer to something that belongs to or is connected with a man, boy, or male animal that has already been mentioned: Leo took off his coat and sat down. | I love his sense of humour, don't you? | Even **his own** mother would not have recognized him. | My eyesight is better than his. | Lewis denies that the child is his. | My relatives all live in the States – his are in France. | **of his** Garry introduced us to some **friends of his**. | Perhaps he's ashamed of that car of his.
2 used to refer to something that belongs to or is connected with someone who may be male or female. Some people think this use is old-fashioned: Everyone had his own work to do. | the obligations of a doctor to his patients ⚠ → see note at THEY

Hi·span·ic¹ /hɪ'spænɪk/ adj from or relating to countries where Spanish or Portuguese are spoken, especially ones in Latin America; → **Latino**: Miami's Hispanic community | Hispanic Studies

Hispanic² n [C] someone who comes from a country where Spanish or Portuguese is spoken, especially one in Latin America; → **Latino, Latina**: In California, Hispanics make up 19.2 percent of the population.

hiss /hɪs/ v **1** [I,T] to say something in a loud whisper: 'Get out!' she hissed furiously. | [+at] She hissed at me to be quiet. **2** [I] to make a noise which sounds like 'ssss': The cat backed away, hissing. | Snakes only hiss when they are afraid. **3** [I,T] if a crowd hisses a speaker, they interrupt them with angry sounds to show that they do not like them: He was booed and hissed during a stormy meeting. —**hiss** n [C]: She heard a faint hiss as the metal struck the water.

,**hissy 'fit** n [C] informal a sudden moment of unreasonable anger and annoyance; **▤ tantrum: throw/have a hissy fit** Williams threw a hissy fit when she decided her hotel room wasn't big enough.

his·ta·mine /'hɪstəmiːn/ n [C,U] medical a chemical substance produced by your body during an ALLERGIC reaction; → **antihistamine**

his·to·gram /'hɪstəgræm/ n [C] technical a BAR CHART

his·to·ri·an [W3] /hɪ'stɔːriən/ n [C] someone who studies history, or the history of a particular thing: art/literary/military etc historian

his·tor·ic /hɪ'stɒrɪk $ -'stɔː-, -'stɑː-/ adj [usually before noun] **1** a historic place or building is very old: the restoration of historic buildings | ancient historic sites | our historic monuments **2** a historic event or act is very important and will be recorded as part of history: a historic meeting of world leaders | 'It is a **historic moment**,' he told journalists. **3** formal having taken place or existed in the past: It's unlikely that the share price will exceed historic levels. **4** historic times are the periods of time whose history has been recorded; → **prehistoric**: Extinct volcanoes are those that have not erupted in historic times.

his·tor·i·cal [W2] /hɪ'stɒrɪkəl $ -'stɔː-, -'stɑː-/ adj [usually before noun]
1 relating to the past: places **of historical interest** | It is important to look at the novel in its **historical context**.
2 connected to the study of history: historical evidence/research etc
3 historical events, facts, people etc happened or existed in the past: Was King Arthur a real historical figure?

4 describing or based on events in the past: a historical novel —**historically** /-kli/ adv: How historically significant is this discovery?

his,toric 'present n [singular] technical the present tense, used in some languages to describe events in the past to make them seem more real

his·to·ry [S2] [W1] /'hɪstəri/ n plural histories
1 **PAST EVENTS** [U] all the things that happened in the past, especially the political, social, or economic development of a nation

throughout history
recent/modern history
early/ancient history
recorded history (=history since people wrote facts down)
local history
American/British etc history
human history
period in/of history
the first time in history (=the first time that something has ever happened)
change the course of history (=do something that has a lot of important effects)
steeped in history (=closely connected with important events in history)
history shows/tells (that)

Throughout history the achievements of women have been largely ignored. | [+of] *the post-war history of Europe* | *No man in **recent history** has done more to rebuild the Democratic Party.* | *the **early history** of Scotland* | *Other meteor storms have occurred in **recorded history**.* | *a museum devoted to **local history*** | *one of the darkest episodes in **American history*** | *an interesting **period in** Egyptian **history*** | *a decision that **changed the course of history*** | *a college **steeped in history**.* | ***History shows that** the usual response to violent protest is repression.*

2 **DEVELOPMENT OF STH** [singular, U] the events that took place from the beginning and during the development of a particular place, activity, institution etc: [+of] the worst disaster in the history of space travel | **long/brief/75-year etc history** The 1970s were the most successful in the theater's long history.
3 **SUBJECT** [U] the study of past events as a subject in school or university: European/art/economic etc history a degree in European history | ancient/modern history | a history lesson
4 **ACCOUNT** [C] an account of past events: [+of] a history of World War II | a **potted history** (=very short) of Gielgud's life BrE
5 **PAST LIFE** [C,U] a record of something that has affected someone or been done by them in the past: medical/employment/career etc history Your doctor will ask for your medical history. | [+of] Is there any history of heart disease in your family? | The defendant **had a history of** violent assaults on women.
6 **make history** to do something important that will be recorded and remembered: Lindbergh made history when he flew across the Atlantic.
7 **sth will go down in history** used to say that something is important enough to be remembered and recorded: This day will go down in history as the start of a new era in South Africa.
8 **history repeats itself** used to say that things often happen in the same way as they did before
9 **the history books** the record of past events: Mozart's genius earned him a place in the history books.
10 **... and the rest is history** informal used to say that everyone knows the rest of a story you have been telling
11 **that's (past/ancient) history** spoken informal used to say that something is not important any more → NATURAL HISTORY, CASE HISTORY

his·tri·on·ics /ˌhɪstri'ɒnɪks $ -'ɑːn-/ n [plural] very loud and emotional behaviour that is intended to get sympathy and attention – used to show disapproval —**histrionic** adj

hit¹ S1 W2 /hɪt/ *v past tense and past participle* **hit**, *present participle* **hitting**

1 **TOUCH SB/STH HARD** [T] to touch someone or something quickly and hard with your hand, a stick etc: *He raised the hammer and hit the bell.* | **hit sb/sth with sth** *The robbers hit him over the head with a baseball bat.*

2 **CRASH INTO STH** [T] to move into something or someone quickly and with force: *The tanks exploded as the plane hit the ground.* | *He was taken to hospital after being hit by a car.*

3 **HURT YOURSELF** [T] to move a part of your body quickly against something accidentally, causing pain; ◫ **bang**: *The ceiling's low, so be careful you don't hit your head.* | **hit sth on/against sth** *She slipped and hit her head on the sidewalk.*

4 **SPORT** [T] **a)** if you hit a ball or other object, you make it move forward quickly by hitting it with a BAT, stick etc; ◫ **strike**: *Hit the ball as hard as you can.* **b)** to get points by hitting a ball in a game such as BASEBALL or CRICKET: *Last year, Griffey hit 49 home runs.*

5 **PRESS** [T] *informal* to press a part in a machine, car, etc to make it work: *Maria hit the brakes just in time.*

6 **ATTACK** [T] to attack something or wound someone with a bomb, bullet etc: *Our ship was **badly hit** and sank within minutes.* | *A second shot hit her in the back.* | *The bomb failed to **hit** its **target**.*

7 **AFFECT BADLY** [I,T] if something bad hits a place or a person, it suddenly happens and affects people badly: *The village has been hit by a devastating drought.* | *Hurricane Louis is expected to hit at the weekend.* | **be badly/severely/hard hit** *The company has been hard hit by the drop in consumer confidence.* | *The south of the country is **the worst hit** by the recession.*

8 **HAVE PROBLEMS** [I] to experience trouble, problems etc: **hit a snag/problems/a bad patch etc** *My father hit a bad patch, he had to sell the house.*

9 **REACH A LEVEL/NUMBER** [T] to reach a particular level or number: *Sales have **hit the 1 million mark**.* | **hit a peak/an all-time high etc** | *Earnings hit a peak in the early 1980s.* | **hit rock-bottom/an all-time low etc** *Oil prices have hit rock-bottom.*

10 **REALIZE** [T] if a fact hits you, you suddenly realize its importance and feel surprised or shocked: *It's impossible to pinpoint a moment when **it hit me** that I was 'a success'.* | *He was gone before they **knew what had hit** them* (=realized what had happened).

11 **SMELL/SIGHT ETC** [T] if a smell or sight hits you, you suddenly smell or see it: *The smell of stale smoke hit him as he entered.*

12 **ARRIVE** [T] *informal* to arrive at a place: *They hit the main road two kilometres further on.* | **hit town** *AmE: I'll look for work as soon as I hit town.*

13 **hit the road/trail** *informal* to begin a journey

14 **hit the shops/streets** if a product hits the shops, it becomes available to buy: *I managed to get a copy of the book before it hit the shops.*

15 **hit the headlines** to be reported widely on television, in newspapers etc: *The couple hit the headlines last year when their relationship broke down.*

16 **hit the bottle** *informal* to start drinking too much alcohol regularly: *After his marriage failed, he hit the bottle big time.*

17 **hit the dirt/the deck** *informal* to fall to the ground in order to avoid something dangerous: *My first instinct was to hit the dirt.*

18 **hit a (brick) wall** *informal* to suddenly not be able to make any progress: *I felt I'd hit a wall with my playing.*

19 **hit the buffers/skids** *informal* if a plan, project etc hits the buffers, it fails: *Croft's comeback hit the skids yesterday when she lost in the quarter-finals.*

20 **hit sb when they are down** *informal* to upset or harm someone when they are already defeated

21 **hit sb where it hurts** *informal* to do something that you know will upset someone in the most damaging way: *You should hit your husband where it hurts – in his wallet!*

22 **hit it off (with sb)** *informal* if two people hit it off, they like each other as soon as they meet: *I knew you'd hit it off with Mike.*

23 **hit the big time**; **hit it big** *AmE informal* to suddenly become very famous, successful, and rich: *The 25-year-old painter hopes to hit it big in New York.*

24 **hit the ground running** to start doing something successfully without any delay: *Law graduates are expected to hit the ground running.*

25 **hit the jackpot a)** to win a lot of money **b)** to have a big success: *Owens hit the jackpot in his first professional game with the Cowboys.*

26 **hit the nail on the head** *informal* used to say that what someone has said is exactly right: *You've hit the nail on the head there, David.*

27 **hit home a)** if a remark, criticism etc about you hits home, you realize that it is true: *Graham didn't reply, but she could see her words had hit home.* **b)** if a blow or kick hits home, it hits the thing it is aimed at

28 **hit the spot** *informal* to have exactly the good effect that you wanted, especially when you are hungry or thirsty

29 **hit the roof/ceiling** *informal* to be very angry: *Ranieri returned, saw the mess, and hit the roof.*

30 **hit the sack**; **hit the hay** *AmE informal* to go to bed → **the shit hits the fan** at SHIT² (17); → **hit/strike paydirt** at PAYDIRT

> **WORD FOCUS: HIT**
> *with your fist*: **punch, thump, bash**
> *with your open hand as a punishment*: **smack, spank, slap**
> *with a hammer*: **bang, hammer**
> *in order to get attention*: **bang, knock, tap, hammer**
> *accidentally*: **bump into, crash into, strike, bang, knock, collide (with)**

hit back *phr v*
to attack or criticize a person or group that has attacked or criticized you; ◫ **retaliate**: [+at] *The actress hit back at claims that she had threatened a member of staff.* | [+with] *United were a goal down, but hit back with an equalizer.* | **hit back by doing sth** *He hit back by calling his critics 'lazy'.*

hit on sb/sth *phr v*
1 also **hit upon sth** to have an idea or discover something suddenly or unexpectedly; ◫ **come up with**: *Then we **hit on the idea** of asking viewers to donate money over the Net.*
2 *AmE informal* to talk to someone in a way that shows you are sexually attracted to them: *Dave has hit on most of the women in the department.*

hit out *phr v*
to try to hit someone: *When he felt someone grab him, he hit out wildly.*

hit out at sb/sth *phr v*
also **hit out against sb/sth** to express strong disapproval of someone or something; ◫ **attack**: *The bishop hit out at the government's policy on the homeless.*

hit sb **with** sth *phr v informal*
1 to tell someone something interesting, exciting, or shocking: *The next morning, Steve hit me with the truth.*
2 *AmE* to punish or try to harm someone by doing something that will cause problems for them: *The next day, we found they'd hit us with a lawsuit.*

hit sb **up for** sth *phr v AmE spoken*
to ask someone for money: *Did he hit you up for cash again?*

hit² S3 *n* [C]
1 **SUCCESSFUL** something such as a film, play, song etc that is very popular and successful: **a hit single/show/record etc** *the hit musical 'Phantom of the Opera'* | **a big/smash/number 1 etc hit** *the Beatles' greatest hits* | *Which band **had a hit** with 'Bohemian Rhapsody'?* | **be a hit with sb** (=be liked by them) *It's hoped the new museum will be a big hit with families.*
2 **HIT STH** an occasion when something that is aimed at something else touches it, reaches it, or damages it: *Our ship took a **direct hit** and sank.*
3 **COMPUTER a)** an occasion when someone visits a website: *The site had 2,000 hits in the first week.* **b)** a

result of a computer search, especially on the Internet: *thousands of irrelevant hits*
4 *informal* a feeling of pleasure obtained from taking an illegal drug
5 *informal* a murder that has been arranged to happen → HIT MAN

,hit-and-'miss also **,hit-or-'miss** *adj* done in a way that is not planned or organized; → **random**: *The campaign was rather a hit-and-miss affair.*

,hit-and-'run *adj* [only before noun] a hit-and-run accident is one in which a car driver hits someone and does not stop to help: **hit-and-run driver**

hitch¹ /hɪtʃ/ *v* **1** [I,T] *informal* to get free rides from the drivers of passing cars by standing at the side of the road and putting a hand out with the thumb raised; ▤ **hitchhike**: [+across/around/to] *He plans to hitch right round the coast of Ireland.* | **hitch a ride/lift (with sb)** *We hitched a ride with a trucker.* **2** [T] also **hitch up** to move a piece of clothing you are wearing so that it is higher than it was before: *She hitched her skirt above her knees and knelt down.* **3 get hitched** *informal* to get married: *They got hitched without telling their parents.* **4** [T] also **hitch up** to lift yourself into a higher position by pushing with your hands: **hitch yourself (up) onto/on sth** *Gail hitched herself up onto the high stool.* **5 a)** [T always + adv/prep] to fasten something to something else, using a rope, chain etc: **hitch sth to sth** *He hitched our pickup to his trailer.* | *a goat hitched to a rickety fence* **b)** [T] also **hitch up** to fasten an animal to something with wheels so that the animal can pull it forwards: *I hitched up the horse and drove out into the fields.*

hitch² *n* [C] **1** a small problem that makes something difficult or delays it for a short time: **technical/slight/last-minute hitch** *In spite of some technical hitches, the first program was a success.* | *The whole show went without a hitch.* **2** a type of knot: *a half hitch*

hitch·hike /'hɪtʃhaɪk/ also **hitch** *v* [I] to travel to places by getting free rides from drivers of passing cars: [+around/to/across etc] *She spent her gap year hitchhiking around the world.* —**hitchhiker** *n* [C]: *I picked up a hitchhiker on our way back.*

hi-tech /ˌhaɪˈtek◂/ *informal* another spelling of HIGH-TECH

hith·er /'hɪðə $ -ər/ *adv old use* here: *Coloured fish darted **hither and thither** (=backwards and forwards).*

hith·er·to /ˌhɪðəˈtuː◂ $ -ər-/ *adv formal* up to this time: *a species of fish hitherto unknown in the West*

'hit list *n* [C] *informal* the names of people, organizations etc that a person or group plans to harm: **on sb's hit list** *He was on a terrorist's hit list.* | [+of] *The company drew up a hit list of shops it expects to close.*

'hit man *n* [C] a criminal who is employed to kill someone

'hit pa,rade *n* **the hit parade** *old-fashioned* a list that shows which popular records have sold the most copies

'hit squad *n* [C] a group of criminals who are employed to kill someone

HIV /ˌeɪtʃ aɪ ˈviː◂/ *n* [U] a type of VIRUS (=a very small living thing that causes disease) that enters the body through blood or sexual activity, and can develop into AIDS: **HIV positive/negative** (=having or not having HIV in your body)

hive¹ /haɪv/ *n* **1** [C] also **beehive** a small box where BEES are kept, or the bees that live in this box → see picture at HOME **2 a hive of industry/activity etc** *BrE* a place that is full of people who are very busy: *This marketplace was once a hive of activity.* **3 hives** [U] a skin disease in which a person's skin becomes red and sore

hive² *v*
hive sth ⇔ **off** *phr v BrE* to sell one part of a business: *the trend for television companies to hive off their advertising departments*

hi·ya /'haɪjə/ *interjection informal* used to say hello

hm, hmm /m, hm/ *interjection* a sound that you make to express doubt, a pause, or disagreement

H.M. also **HM** *BrE* /ˌeɪtʃ ˈem/ the abbreviation of *His/Her Majesty*: *HM the Queen*

HMS /ˌeɪtʃ em ˈes/ *His/Her Majesty's Ship* used before the name of a ship in the British navy: *HMS Belfast*

HNC /ˌeɪtʃ en ˈsiː/ *n* [C] *Higher National Certificate* a British college or university examination, usually in a technical or business subject. HNCs are lower in level than HNDs

HND /ˌeɪtʃ en ˈdiː/ *n* [C] *Higher National Diploma* a British college or university examination, usually in a technical or business subject

ho /həʊ $ hoʊ/ *n* [C] *AmE spoken informal* **1** a PROSTITUTE **2** *not polite* an offensive word for a woman or girl who you do not respect because she is too willing to have sex with many different people; ▤ **slut**

hoard¹ /hɔːd $ hɔːrd/ *n* [C] a collection of things that someone hides somewhere, especially so they can use them later: [+of] *the discovery of a hoard of gold coins*

hoard² *v* also **hoard up** [T] to collect and save large amounts of food, money etc, especially when it is not necessary to do so: *families who hoarded food during the strike* —**hoarder** *n* [C]: *I'm a hoarder when it comes to clothes.*

hoard·ing /'hɔːdɪŋ $ 'hɔːr-/ *n* [C] *BrE* **1** a large board fixed high on a wall outside on which large advertisements are shown; ▤ **billboard** *AmE*: *advertising hoardings* → see picture at TOWN **2** a high fence around a piece of land where something is being built

hoar·frost /'hɔːfrɒst $ 'hɔːrfrɒːst/ *n* [U] *formal* a thin layer of ice that forms on objects outside when it is very cold; ▤ **frost**: *A light hoarfrost covered the fields.*

hoarse /hɔːs $ hɔːrs/ *adj* if you are hoarse, or if your voice is hoarse, you speak in a low rough voice, for example because your throat is sore: *He was hoarse from laughing.* | **hoarse voice/whisper/groan etc** —**hoarsely** *adv* —**hoarseness** *n* [U]

hoar·y /'hɔːri/ *adj* **1** [usually before noun] a hoary joke, remark etc is so well-known that people no longer find it amusing or interesting: *Not that **hoary old chestnut** (=old idea, joke, remark etc) again.* **2** *old-fashioned* grey or white in colour, especially through age

hoax /həʊks $ hoʊks/ *n* [C] **1** a false warning about something dangerous: *a bomb hoax* | **hoax calls** (=telephone calls giving false information) *to the police* **2** an attempt to make people believe something that is not true: *an elaborate hoax*

hob /hɒb $ hɑːb/ *n* [C] *BrE* the flat top of a COOKER

hob·ble /'hɒbəl $ 'hɑː-/ *v* **1** [I always + adv/prep] to walk with difficulty, especially because your legs or feet hurt; → **limp**: *He hobbled into the room on crutches.* **2** [T usually passive] to deliberately make sure that a plan, system etc cannot work successfully: *Many start-ups are hobbled by a lack of sufficient capital.* **3** [T] to loosely fasten two of an animal's legs together, to stop it from running away

hob·by S3 /'hɒbi $ 'hɑː-/ *n plural* **hobbies** [C] an activity that you enjoy doing in your free time; → **interest, pastime**: *What are your hobbies?* | *Susan's hobbies include reading, cooking, and drama.* | *Retirement gave him the time to pursue his hobbies.* —**hobbyist** *n* [C]: *keen wine hobbyists*

hob·by·horse /'hɒbihɔːs $ 'hɑːbihɔːrs/ *n* [C] **1** a subject that someone has strong opinions about and that they talk about too much: *I'm afraid safe driving isn't Jaqui's only hobbyhorse.* | **be on your hobbyhorse** *Vicky was on her hobbyhorse again.* **2** an old-fashioned toy made of a horse's head on a stick

hob·gob·lin /hɒbˈɡɒblᵻn, ˈhɒbɡɒb- $ ˈhɑːbɡɑːb-/ *n* [C] a GOBLIN

hob·nailed /'hɒbneɪld $ 'hɑːb-/ also **hob·nail** /-neɪl/ *adj* [only before noun] *especially BrE old-fashioned* hobnailed boots have large nails fastened to the bottom to make them last longer

hob·nob /'hɒbnɒb $ 'hɑːbnɑːb/ *v* **hobnobbed, hobnobbing** [I] *informal* to spend time talking to people who are in a higher social position than you: [+with] *He spent the first day hobnobbing with the management.*

ho·bo /'həʊbəʊ $ 'hoʊboʊ/ *n plural* **hobos** [C] *AmE* someone who travels around and has no home or regular job; ☐ **tramp** *BrE*

Hob·son's choice /ˌhɒbsənz 'tʃɔɪs $ ˌhɑːb-/ *n* [U] a situation in which there is only one thing you can do, so you do not really have any choice at all

hock¹ /hɒk $ hɑːk/ *n* **1** [U] *BrE* a German white wine: *a glass of hock* **2 in hock** *informal* **a)** in debt: **be in hock to sb** *The fashion chain is still in hock to the banks.* **b)** something that is in hock has been sold temporarily because its owner needs some money: *He's a musician, but his guitar is in hock.* **3** [C] a piece of meat from above the foot of a pig: *pork hocks* **4** [C] the middle joint of an animal's back leg

hock² *v* [T] *informal* to sell something temporarily because you need some money; ☐ **pawn**

hock·ey /'hɒki $ 'hɑːki/ *n* [U] **1** *BrE* a game played on grass by two teams of 11 players, with sticks and a ball; ☐ **field hockey** *AmE* **2** *AmE* a game similar to hockey, but played on ice; ☐ **ice hockey** *BrE*

ho·cus-po·cus /ˌhəʊkəs 'pəʊkəs $ ˌhoʊkəs 'poʊ-/ *n* [U] a method or belief that you think is based on false ideas: *He thinks psychology is a load of hocus-pocus.*

hod /hɒd $ hɑːd/ *n* [C] *BrE* a box with a long handle, used for carrying bricks

hodge-podge /'hɒdʒ pɒdʒ $ 'hɑːdʒ pɑːdʒ/ *n* [singular] *AmE informal* a lot of things mixed up together in no order; ☐ **jumble**; ☐ **hotch-potch** *BrE*

hoe /həʊ $ hoʊ/ *n* [C] a garden tool with a long handle, used for removing WEEDS (=unwanted plants) from the surface of the soil —**hoe** *v* [I,T]: *Hoe the ground in spring.*

hog¹ /hɒg $ hɑːg, hɔːg/ *n* [C] **1** *especially AmE* a large pig that is kept for its meat; → **boar, sow 2 go the whole hog** *informal* to do something thoroughly: *Let's go the whole hog and order champagne.* **3 go hog wild** *AmE informal* to suddenly do an activity in an uncontrolled way **4** *informal* someone who takes too much of something that should be shared; ☐ **pig:** *You greedy hog!* → ROAD HOG

hog² *v* **hogged, hogging** [T] *informal* to keep, use, or have all of something that should be shared: *How much longer are you going to hog the bathroom?* | *He's been hogging the limelight (=having all the attention, praise etc).*

Hog·ma·nay /'hɒgmənei $ ˌhɑːgmə'nei/ *n* [U] *BrE* New Year's Eve and the parties that take place at that time in Scotland

hogs·head /'hɒgzhed $ 'hɑːgz-, 'hɔːgz-/ *n* [C] *BrE* a large container for holding beer, or the amount that it holds

hog·wash /'hɒgwɒʃ $ 'hɑːgwɑːʃ, 'hɔːg-, -wɒʃ/ *n* [U] *informal* stupid or untrue talk; ☐ **nonsense, rubbish:** *That's a load of hogwash!*

ˌho 'ho *interjection* used to represent the sound of laughter

ˌho-'hum *interjection informal* used to say that you are bored

hoick /hɔɪk/ also **hoick up** *v* [T] *BrE informal* to lift or pull something up with a sudden movement: *She hoicked her skirt up and began to dance.*

hoi pol·loi /ˌhɔɪ pə'lɔɪ/ *n* [U] an insulting word for ordinary people

hoist¹ /hɔɪst/ also **hoist up** *v* [T] **1** to raise, lift, or pull up something, especially using ropes: *The crew hurried to hoist the flag.* **2 be hoist with/by your own**

petard *formal* to be harmed or embarrassed by the plans you had made to hurt other people – often used humorously

hoist² *n* **1** [C] a piece of equipment used for lifting heavy objects with ropes; → **crane:** *a boat hoist* **2** [usually singular] a movement that lifts something up: *Give me a hoist onto your shoulders.*

ho·key /'həʊki $ 'hoʊ-/ *adj AmE* expressing emotions in an old-fashioned or silly way: *a hokey song*

ho·kum /'həʊkəm $ 'hoʊ-/ *n* [U] *informal* something that seems true or impressive but that is wrong or not sincere: *All that talk is just a bunch of hokum.*

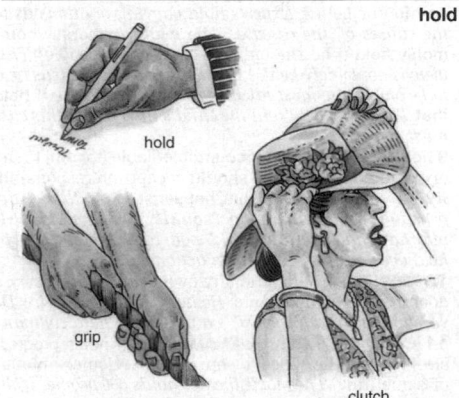

hold

hold

grip

clutch

hold¹ S1 W1 /həʊld $ hoʊld/ *v past tense and past participle* **held** /held/

1 IN YOUR HAND/ARMS **a)** [T] to have something in your hand, hands, or arms: *Could you hold my bag for me?* | **hold sth in your hand/arms** *He was holding a knife in one hand.* | *I held the baby in my arms.* | **hold hands** (=hold each other's hands) *They sat holding hands under a tree.* | **hold sb close/tightly** (=with your arms around someone) *Max held her close and wiped away her tears.* **b)** [T always + adv/prep] to move your hand or something in your hand in a particular direction: **hold sth out/up etc** *He held out his hand to help her to her feet.* | *Hold the picture up so we can see it.*

2 EVENT [T] to have a meeting, party, election etc in a particular place or at a particular time: *This year's conference will be held at the Hilton Hotel.* | *A thanksgiving ceremony was held to mark the occasion.* | *The funeral was held on a grey day in November.* | *In April, the President held talks with Chinese leaders.*

3 KEEP STH IN POSITION [T] to make something stay in a particular position: **hold sth open/up etc** *We used rolled-up newspapers to hold the windows open.* | *Remember to hold your head up and keep your back straight.* | **hold sth in place/position** *A couple of screws should hold it in place.* | *Lift your head off the floor and hold this position for five seconds.*

4 JOB/TITLE **a)** to have a particular job or position, especially an important one: *Do you really think he's capable of holding such a responsible position?* | **hold the post/position/office etc (of sth)** *She was the first woman to hold the office of Australian state premier.* | *The governor had held the post since 1989.* | *Whoever is elected will hold office* (=have an important political position) *for four years.* **b)** to have a particular title or record, because you have won a competition, are the best at something etc: *The programme still holds the record for the longest running TV series.* | *The last Briton to hold the title was Bert Nicholson.*

5 KEEP/STORE [T] to keep something to be used when it is needed: *Further copies of the book are held in the library.* | *Weapons were held at various sites.*

1 000, 2 000, 3 000, most frequent words in S poken and W ritten English

6 KEEP STH AVAILABLE FOR SB [T] to agree not to give something such as a ticket, a place at a restaurant, a job etc to anyone except a particular person: *We can hold the reservation for you until next Friday.* | **hold sth open** *You can't expect them to hold the job open for much longer – you'll have to decide whether you want it or not.*

7 KEEP SB SOMEWHERE [T] to keep someone somewhere, and not allow them to leave: *Police are holding two men in connection with the robbery.* | **hold sb prisoner/hostage/captive** *A senior army officer was held hostage for four months.* | **hold sb incommunicado** (=keep someone somewhere and not allow them to communicate with anyone)

8 OPINION [T not in progressive] to have a particular opinion or belief: *Experts hold varying opinions as to the causes of the disease.* | **be widely/generally/commonly held** (=be the opinion of a lot of people) *This view is not widely held.* | **be held to be sth** *She was held to be one of the most talented actors of her time.* | **hold that** *The judge held that the child's interests in this case must come first.*

9 **hold sb responsible/accountable/liable (for sth)** to say or decide that someone should accept the responsibility for something bad that happens: *If anything happens to her, I'll hold you personally responsible.* | *He may have had a terrible childhood, but he should still be held accountable for his own actions.*

10 OWN STH [T] to officially own or possess money, a document, a company etc: *He holds shares in ICI.* | *Do you hold a valid passport?* | *a privately held company*

11 CONTAIN PARTICULAR AMOUNT [T not in progressive] to have the space to contain a particular amount of something: *The movie theater holds 500 people.* | *The tank should hold enough to last us a few days.*

12 SUPPORT [I,T] to be strong enough to support the weight of something or someone: *Careful! I'm not sure that branch will hold you.* | *The bridge didn't look as though it would hold.*

13 STAY AT SAME LEVEL [I,T] to stay at a particular amount, level, or rate, or to make something do this: *The bank is holding interest rates at 4%.* | *Since then, the pound has held steady against the dollar.* | **hold sb's interest/attention** (=make someone stay interested) *Colourful pictures help hold the students' interest.*

14 NOT CHANGE [I] to continue to be true, good, available etc: *What I said yesterday holds.* | *Does your invitation still hold?* | **hold true/good** *Twenty years on, his advice still holds good.* | **weather/luck holds (out)** (=continues to be good) *If our luck holds, we could reach the final.*

15 STOP/DELAY [T] *spoken* used in particular phrases to tell someone to wait or not to do something: *I'll have a tuna fish sandwich please – and hold the mayo.* (=do not give me any) | **Hold it!** *We're not quite ready.* | **hold your horses!** (=used to tell someone to do something more slowly or carefully)

16 hold your head up also **hold your head high** to behave as if you are proud of yourself or respect yourself: *They may have lost the game, but I still think they've earned the right to hold their heads high today.*

17 hold your breath **a)** to deliberately not breathe out for a short time: *Hold your breath and count to ten.* **b)** to not breathe out and try not to make a sound because you do not want to be noticed: *Julie shrank back against the wall and held her breath.* **c)** not hold your breath *spoken* used to say that you do not expect something to happen, even though someone has said it will: *He promised he'd phone, but I'm not holding my breath.*

18 hold (your) fire **a)** to not shoot at someone when you were going to **b)** to not criticize, attack, or oppose someone when you were going to: *The president urged his party to hold fire on the issue a few days longer.*

19 TELEPHONE [I] also hold the line *spoken* to wait until the person you have telephoned is ready to answer: *Mr Stevens is busy at the moment – would you like to hold?* | *Please hold the line while I transfer you.*

20 ARMY [T] if an army holds a place, it controls it or defends it from attack: *The French army held the town for three days.*

21 MUSICAL NOTE [T] to make a musical note continue for a particular length of time

22 FUTURE [T] *formal* if the future holds something, that is what may happen: *Thousand of workers are waiting to see what the future holds.*

23 HAVE A QUALITY [T] *formal* to have a particular quality: **hold (little) interest/appeal/promise etc** *Many church services hold little appeal for modern tastes.*

24 hold your own (against sb) to successfully defend yourself or succeed in a difficult situation, competition etc: *He was a good enough player to hold his own against the Americans.*

25 not hold a candle to sb/sth to be much worse than someone or something else

26 be left holding the baby *BrE*, **be left holding the bag** *AmE* to be left as the only person responsible for dealing with a difficult situation, especially something someone else started: *He was left holding the financial baby when his musical partner joined another band.*

27 hold sway to have a lot of influence or power: *Among people here, traditional values still hold sway.*

28 hold court to get the attention of everyone while you are talking, especially when you are trying to entertain people: *Joey would walk into the bar and hold court all night.*

29 hold your tongue *spoken* used to tell someone to stop talking or to not tell someone about something: *I reckon you've just got to learn to hold your tongue.*

30 hold all the cards to have all the advantages in a situation in which people are competing or arguing: *'There's not much we can do. They seem to hold all the cards,' said Dan gloomily.*

31 hold fast (to sth) to keep believing strongly in something

32 hold a conversation to have a conversation

33 hold the fort to be responsible for something while the person usually responsible for it is not there: *She's holding the fort while the manager's on holiday.*

34 hold the lead/advantage to be winning in a competition, game etc: *Celtic held the lead in the first half.*

35 there's no holding sb (back) *spoken* used to say that someone is so determined to do something that you cannot prevent them from doing it

36 can hold your drink/liquor/alcohol etc to be able to drink a lot of alcohol without getting drunk or ill

37 not hold water if an excuse, a statement etc does not hold water, it does not seem to be true or reasonable: *His explanation of where the money came from just doesn't hold water.*

38 hold sth/sb dear *formal* to care about something or someone a lot: *We were facing the loss of everything we held dear.*

39 hold the road if a car holds the road well you can drive it quickly around bends without losing control → **hold a course** at COURSE[1] (8)

hold sth against sb *phr v*
to continue to dislike someone or not forgive them because of something bad they have done in the past: *You can't still hold that against him, surely?*

hold back *phr v*
1 hold sb/sth ⇔ back to make someone or something stop moving forward: *Police in riot gear held back the demonstrators.*
2 hold sth ⇔ back to stop yourself from feeling or showing a particular emotion: *She struggled to hold back her tears.* | *Anger flooded through her. She couldn't hold it back.*
3 hold sb/sth ⇔ back to prevent someone or something from making progress: *They felt the British economy was being held back by excessive government controls.*
4 hold (sb) back to be unwilling to do something, especially because you are being careful, or to make someone unwilling to do something: *In the current situation many investors are holding back.* | *She wanted to tell him but pride held her back.*

5 hold sth ⇔ **back** to keep something secret: *Tell me all about it – don't hold anything back!*

hold sb/sth ⇔ **down** *phr v*
1 to make someone or something stay on something, and stop them from moving away or escaping: *We had to hold the tent down with rocks to stop it blowing away.* | *It took three strong men to hold him down.*
2 to prevent the level of something such as prices from rising: *We will aim to hold down prices.*
3 hold down a job to succeed in keeping a job for a period of time: *He's never held down a job for longer than a few weeks.*
4 to keep people under control or limit their freedom: *The people were held down for centuries by their conquerors.*

hold forth *phr v*
to give your opinion on a subject, especially for a long time: [+on] *The speaker was holding forth on the collapse of modern society.*

hold off *phr v*
1 to delay doing something: *Buyers have been holding off until the price falls.* | **hold off (on) doing sth** *Hold off making your decision until Monday.*
2 hold sb ⇔ **off a)** to prevent someone who is trying to attack or defeat you from succeeding: *Not even a gun could hold him off forever.* **b)** to prevent someone from coming towards you or succeeding in speaking to you: *There's already a crowd of reporters outside – I'll try to hold them off for a while.*
3 if rain or bad weather holds off, it does not start, although it looked as if it would: *The rain held off until after the game.*

hold on *phr v*
1 *spoken* **a)** to wait for a short time: *Hold on, I'll just get my coat.* **b)** used when you have just noticed, heard, or remembered something interesting or wrong: *Hold on a minute! Isn't that your brother's car over there?* **c)** used to ask someone on the telephone to wait until the person they want to talk to is available: *Can you hold on? I'll try to find her.*
2 to have your hands or arms tightly around something: *Hold on tight!* | [+to] *Hold on to my arm.*
3 to continue doing something that is very difficult to do: *San Francisco held on to win 4–2.*

hold on to sb/sth *phr v*
to keep something rather than losing it, selling it, or giving it to someone else: *The soldiers held on to the bridge for three more days.* | *I think I'll hold on to these old records for now.*

hold out *phr v*
1 hold out sth to think or say that something is possible or likely to happen, especially something good: **not hold out much hope/hold out little hope** *Negotiators aren't holding out much hope of a peaceful settlement.* | **hold out the prospect/promise of sth** *alternative methods which hold out the promise of improved health*
2 if a supply of something holds out, there is still some left: *Water supplies won't hold out much longer.*
3 to continue to successfully defend a place that is being attacked: *The rebels held out for another night but then fresh forces arrived.*
4 to try to prevent yourself from doing something that someone is trying to force you to do: [+against] *I didn't know how much longer I could hold out against their relentless questioning.*

hold out for sth *phr v*
to not accept anything less than you have asked for: *Transport workers are holding out for a 20% pay rise.*

hold out on sb *phr v informal*
to not tell someone about something important: *She must have been holding out on him all these years.*

hold sth **over** *phr v*
1 [usually passive] *formal* to do or deal with something at a later time: *The matter was held over for further review.* → **HOLDOVER**
2 hold sth over sb to use something bad that you know about someone to make them do what you want: *He knows I've been in prison and is holding it over me.*
3 be held over *especially AmE* if a play, film, concert etc is held over, it is shown for longer than planned because it is very popular

hold to sth *phr v*
1 if you hold to a belief, principle, promise etc, you believe it or behave according to it: *He admitted he did not hold to the traditional view of God.* | *The Secretary of State must hold to his policy.*
2 hold sb **to sth** to make someone do what they have promised: *'I'll ask him tomorrow.' 'OK, but I'm going to hold you to that.'*
3 hold sb **to sth** *BrE* to prevent your opponent in a sports game from getting more than a particular number of points: *Norway held Holland to a 2–2 draw.*

hold together *phr v*
1 if a group or organization holds together, or if something holds it together, it stays strong and does not separate into different parts or groups: *Against all expectations, the coalition held together well.* | **hold sth** ⇔ **together** *In those days the Church held the community together.*
2 to remain whole and good enough to use, or to make something do this: *Incredibly, the raft held together till we reached the opposite shore.* | **hold sth** ⇔ **together** *I wondered how the structure was held together.*

hold up *phr v*
1 hold sth ⇔ **up** to support something and prevent it from falling down: *The roof is held up by massive stone pillars.*
2 hold sb/sth ⇔ **up** [usually passive] to delay someone or something: *Sorry I'm late – I was held up at work.*
3 hold up sth to rob or try to rob a place or person by using violence: *Two armed men held up a downtown liquor store last night.* → **HOLD-UP**
4 to not become weaker: *His physical condition has held up well.*

hold sb/sth **up as** sth *phr v*
to use someone or something as a good example or as proof of something: *The school is held up as a model for others.* | *This incident will be held up as proof that tougher controls are needed.*

hold with sth *phr v*
not hold with sth *BrE* used to say that someone does not approve of something: *He says he doesn't hold with all this politically correct stuff.* | **not hold with doing sth** *I don't hold with hitting children in any circumstances.*

WORD CHOICE: hold, take/get hold of, pick up
Hold means to have something in your hand, hands, or arms: *He was holding a piece of paper.*
If you want to talk about someone putting their hands or fingers around something and starting to hold it, use **take/get hold of**: *She got hold of the knife and stabbed him.*
If you want to talk about someone putting their fingers around something and taking it, especially from the floor, use **pick up**: *I picked up all the toys from the floor.*
⚠ Use **pick** not **pick up** when you are talking about pulling flowers off a plant: *She was in the garden picking flowers* (NOT *She was in the garden picking up flowers*).

---

hold² S2 W3 *n*
1 HOLDING STH [singular] the action of holding something with your hands; ◨ **grip**

tight/firm hold (on sth)
tighten your hold (on sth)
loosen/release your hold (on sth)
have/keep hold of sth (=be holding something)
get/take hold of sth (=start holding something)
catch/grab/seize hold of sth (=take hold of something quickly and firmly)
lose your hold (on sth) (=accidentally let go of something)

[+on] *She released her **tight hold** on the dog.* | *He **tightened** his hold, refusing to let her go.* | *Make sure you **keep hold of** my hand when we cross the road.* | *I **took hold of** her hand and gently led her away.* | ***Grab hold of** the rope and pull yourself up.*

2 get hold of sth also **get a hold of sth** *AmE* to find or borrow something so that you can use it: *I need to get hold of a car.* | *She managed to get a hold of a copy.*
3 get hold of sb also **get a hold of sb** *AmE* to find and speak to someone about something: *I must get hold of Vanessa to see if she can babysit.*
4 CONTROL/POWER [singular] control, power, or influence over something or someone: **get/keep a hold on/of sth** *He struggled to get a hold of his emotions.* | *I've always kept a tight hold on our finances.* | *I realized that the woman had a hold over my father.*
5 on hold a) if something is on hold, it is going to be done or dealt with at a later date rather than now: *The plans are on hold until after the election.* | *Since having the kids, my career has been put on hold.* **b)** if you are on hold, you are waiting to talk to someone on the telephone: *We try not to keep people on hold for more than a couple of minutes.* | *The agent put me on hold while she consulted a colleague.*
6 take (a) hold to start to have a definite effect: *The fever was beginning to take hold.*
7 get hold of an idea/an impression/a story etc to learn or begin to believe something: *Where on earth did you get hold of that idea?*
8 FIGHT [C] a particular position that you hold an opponent in, in a fight or a sport such as WRESTLING
9 CLIMBING [C] somewhere you can put your hands or feet to help you climb something: *The cliff was steep and it was difficult to find a hold.*
10 SHIP [C] the part of a ship below the DECK[1] (1) where goods are stored
11 no holds barred when there are no rules or limits on what you are allowed to do: *It seems there are no holds barred when it comes to making a profit.*

hold·all /ˈhɔʊld-ɔːl $ ˈhoʊld-ɒːl/ *n* [C] *BrE* a large bag used for carrying clothes and other things when you are travelling → see picture at BAG

hold·er S3 W2 /ˈhɔʊldə $ ˈhoʊldər/ *n* [C]
1 someone who owns or controls something: *the 800m world record holder* | *Season-ticket holders are furious at the rise in rail fares.* | *British passport holders* | [+of] *holders of ordinary shares*
2 something that is used to hold an object: **candle/cigarette/test-tube etc holder**

hold·ing W3 /ˈhɔʊldɪŋ $ ˈhoʊl-/ *n* [C] something which a person owns, especially land or SHARES in a company: [+in] *The government has decided to sell its 21% holding in the firm.* | **land/property/currency etc holding** *companies with large property holdings*

holding company *n* [C] a company that completely or partly owns other companies, as well as doing business itself

holding pattern *n* [C usually singular] **1** the path that an aircraft flies along while it is waiting for permission to land **2** a situation in which you cannot act because you are waiting for the result of something: **in a holding pattern** | *My career is in a holding pattern right now.*

hold·o·ver /ˈhɔʊld,əʊvə $ ˈhoʊld,oʊvər/ *n* [C] *AmE* an action, feeling, or idea that has continued from the past into the present; ➡ **hangover**: [+from] *Her terrible fear of dogs is a holdover from her childhood.* → **hold over** at HOLD[1]

hold-up *n* [C] **1** a situation that stops something from happening or making progress; ➡ **delay**: *traffic hold-ups on the highway* | *Despite the odd hold-up, we finished on time.* **2** *informal* an attempt to rob a place or person by threatening them with a weapon: *a bank hold-up* → **hold up** at HOLD[1]

hole[1] S1 W2 /hɔʊl $ hoʊl/ *n* [C]
1 SPACE IN STH SOLID an empty space in something solid: [+in] *There was a huge hole in the road.* | *I began digging a hole for the plant.* ⚠ Do not say there is a hole *on* something. Say there is a hole *in* something.

hole
gap
canyon
crater
crack

2 SPACE STH CAN GO THROUGH a space in something solid that allows light or things to pass through: [+in] *They climbed through a hole in the fence.* | *These socks are full of holes.* | *bullet holes* (=made by bullets)
3 EMPTY PLACE a place where someone or something should be, but is missing: [+in] *Their departure will leave a gaping hole in Grand Prix racing.*
4 WEAK PART a weak part or fault in something such as an idea or plan: *The theory is full of holes.* | [+in] *If you have holes in your game, work on them.*
5 ANIMAL'S HOME the home of a small animal: *a rabbit hole*
6 UNPLEASANT PLACE *informal* an unpleasant place: *I've got to get out of this hole.*
7 GOLF a) a hole in the ground that you try to get the ball into in the game of golf **b)** one part of a GOLF COURSE with this kind of hole at one end → see picture at GOLF
8 hole in one when someone hits the ball in golf from the starting place into the hole with only one hit
9 make a hole in sth *informal* to use a large part of an amount of money, food etc: *Holidays can make a big hole in your savings.*
10 be in a hole *informal* to be in a difficult situation
11 be in the hole *AmE spoken* to owe money: *I was something like $16,000 in the hole already.*
12 need/want sth like a hole in the head *spoken* used to say that you definitely do not need or want something: *I need this conversation like a hole in the head.* → **ace in the hole** at ACE[1] (7); → **BLACK HOLE**; → **square peg in a round hole** at SQUARE[1] (12); → **WATERING HOLE**

hole[2] *v* **1** [I,T] to hit the ball into a hole in golf: *He holed the putt with ease.* **2 be holed** if a ship is holed, something makes a hole in it
hole out *phr v* to hit the ball into a hole in golf
hole up also **be holed up** *phr v informal* to hide somewhere for a period of time: [+in/with/at] *The gunmen are still holed up in the town.*

hole-in-the-'wall *n* [C] **1** *BrE informal* a machine in or outside a bank from which you can obtain money using a special card; ➡ **ATM, cash machine** **2** *AmE* a small dark shop or restaurant

hol·ey /ˈhɔʊli $ ˈhoʊ-/ *adj* full of holes: *holey sweaters*

hol·i·day[1] S2 W2 /ˈhɒlɪdi, -deɪ $ ˈhɑːlɪ̈deɪ/ *n*
1 [C,U] *BrE* also **holidays** a time of rest from work, school etc; ➡ **vacation** *AmE*: *The school holidays start tomorrow.* | **on holiday** *I'm away on holiday until the 1st of June.* | *Won't your business suffer if you take a holiday?*
2 [C,U] *BrE* also **holidays** a period of time when you travel to another place for pleasure; ➡ **vacation** *AmE*

on holiday
go on holiday also
go on your holidays
have/take a holiday
holiday abroad
summer holiday
family holiday
skiing/camping/walking etc holiday
holiday resort (=a place with many hotels where a lot of people go on their holidays)
holiday brochure (=a magazine that advertises holidays)
holiday snaps *informal* (=photographs taken while on holiday)
holiday romance

We're going to Spain for our holidays. | He caught malaria while on holiday in Africa. | When are you going on holiday? | I didn't have a proper holiday this year. | This was his first holiday abroad. | her annual summer holiday | a popular Spanish holiday resort | It was just a harmless holiday romance.

3 [C] a day fixed by law on which people do not have to go to work or school: *The 4th of July is a national holiday in the US.*
4 the holiday season, the holidays a) *AmE* the period between Thanksgiving and New Year **b)** *BrE* the period in the summer when most people take a holiday → **BANK HOLIDAY, PUBLIC HOLIDAY**

GRAMMAR
British English speakers say **holiday**, not **holidays**, in the structures **be on holiday, go on holiday** and **return/come back from holiday**: *something to read when you are on holiday* (NOT *when you are on holidays*) | *When you come back from holiday, it's hard to work* (NOT *When you come back from holidays*).
Holidays is usually used after **the, my, your** etc: *Soon it will be the holidays. | Where do you want to go for your holidays?*
⚠ Do not say 'be in (your) holidays' or 'go in (your) holidays'. Say **go on holiday** or **go on your holidays** or **be on holiday** or **be on your holidays**.
⚠ Do not say 'make a holiday'. Say **have a holiday**.

holiday² *v* [I] *BrE* to spend your holiday in a place – used especially in news reports; **目 vacation** *AmE*: [+in/at] *They're holidaying in Majorca.*
holiday camp *n* [C] *BrE* a place where people go for their holidays and where activities are organized for them
holiday home *n* [C] *BrE* a house that someone owns where they go during their holidays
hol·i·day·mak·er /ˈhɒlɨdiˌmeɪkə $ ˈhɑːlɨˌdeɪˌmeɪkər/ *n* [C] *BrE* someone who has travelled to a place on holiday; → **tourist**; **目 vacationer** *AmE*
holier-than-ˈthou *adj* showing that you think you are morally better than other people – used to show disapproval; **目 self-righteous**
hol·i·ness /ˈhəʊlinɨs $ ˈhoʊ-/ *n* **1** [U] the quality of being pure and good in a religious way **2 Your/His Holiness** used as a title for talking to or about the Pope
ho·lis·tic /həʊˈlɪstɪk $ hoʊ-/ *adj* **1** considering a person or thing as a whole, rather than as separate parts: *a holistic approach to design* **2 holistic medicine/treatment/healing etc** medical treatment based on the belief that the whole person must be treated, not just the part of their body that has a disease; → **alternative medicine** —**holistically** /-kli/ *adv*
hol·lan·daise /ˌhɒlənˈdeɪz◂ $ ˈhɑːləndeɪz/ *also* **hol·landaise ˈsauce** *n* [U] a creamy sauce made with butter, eggs, and LEMON
hol·ler /ˈhɒlə $ ˈhɑːlər/ *v* [I,T] *informal especially AmE* to shout loudly; **目 yell**: [+at] *I heard someone hollering at me.* —**holler** *n* [C]
hol·low¹ /ˈhɒləʊ $ ˈhɑː-/ *adj*
1 EMPTY INSIDE having an empty space inside: *a hollow tree*

2 hollow eyes/cheeks etc eyes etc where the skin sinks inwards: *He was short and thin, with a sharp nose and hollow eyes.*
3 SOUND a hollow sound is low and clear like the sound made when you hit something empty: *There was a hollow thump as the cars collided.*
4 NO VALUE words, events, or people that are hollow have no real worth or value: *They won, but it was a hollow victory. | Even as he spoke, Ivan was well aware of the **hollow ring** to his words.*
5 hollow laugh/voice etc a hollow laugh or voice makes a weak sound and is without emotion —**hollowly** *adv*: *Sam laughed hollowly.* —**hollowness** *n* [U]
hollow² *n* [C] a place in something that is at a slightly lower level than its surface; **目 dip**: *Make a slight hollow in the middle of each cake.*
hollow³ *v* [T usually passive] to make the surface of something curve inwards: *The steps were hollowed by centuries of use.*
hollow sth ⇔ out *phr v* to make a hole or empty space by removing the inside part of something
hol·ly /ˈhɒli $ ˈhɑːli/ *n plural* **hollies** [C,U] a small tree with sharp dark green leaves and red berries (BERRY), or the leaves and berries of this tree used as a decoration at Christmas → see picture at **FLOWER**
hol·ly·hock /ˈhɒlihɒk $ ˈhɑːlihɑːk/ *n* [C] a tall thin garden plant with many flowers growing together
Hol·ly·wood /ˈhɒliwʊd $ ˈhɑː-/ *n* a part of Los Angeles in California where films are made, often used to refer to the film industry in general: *one of Hollywood's major stars*
hol·o·caust /ˈhɒləkɔːst $ ˈhɑːləkɒːst/ *n* [C] **1** a situation in which there is great destruction and a lot of people die: *a nuclear holocaust* **2 the Holocaust** the killing of millions of Jews and other people by the Nazis during the Second World War
hol·o·gram /ˈhɒləgræm $ ˈhoʊl-,ˈhɑːl-/ *n* [C] a kind of photograph made with a LASER that looks as if it is not flat when you look at it from an angle —**holographic** /ˌhɒləˈgræfɪk◂ $ ˌhoʊl-, ˌhɑːl-/ *adj* —**holography** /hɒˈlɒɡrəfi $ hoʊ-, hɑː-/ *n* [U]
hols /hɒlz $ hɑːlz/ *n* [plural] *BrE old-fashioned* holidays
Hol·stein /ˈhɒlstaɪn $ ˈhoʊl-/ *n* [C] *AmE* a black and white cow; **目 Friesian** *BrE*
hol·ster /ˈhəʊlstə $ ˈhoʊlstər/ *n* [C] a leather object for carrying a small gun, that is worn on a belt
ho·ly W3 /ˈhəʊli $ ˈhoʊ-/ *adj comparative* **holier,** *superlative* **holiest**
1 connected with God and religion; → **sacred**: *the holy city of Benares*
2 very religious: *a holy man*
3 holy cow/mackerel etc *spoken* used to express feelings such as surprise or fear
4 a holy terror *informal* someone, especially a child, who causes problems for other people → **take (holy) orders** at **ORDER¹** (18)
Holy ˈBible *n* **the Holy Bible** the holy book of the Christian religion; **目 the Bible**
Holy Comˈmunion *n* [U] the Christian ceremony in which people eat bread and drink wine as signs of Christ's body and blood; **目 Communion**
Holy ˈFamily *n* **the Holy Family** Jesus, his mother Mary, and her husband Joseph
Holy ˈFather *n* [singular] used when speaking to or about the Pope
Holy ˈGhost *n* **the Holy Ghost** God in the form of a SPIRIT according to the Christian religion; **目 Holy Spirit**
Holy ˈGrail *n* **1** [singular] something that people want very much, but which is very difficult or impossible to achieve: [+of] *Nuclear fusion is the Holy Grail of*

H

1 000, 2 000, 3 000, most frequent words in S poken and W ritten English

energy production. **2 the Holy Grail** the cup believed to have been used by Christ before his death

'Holy Land *n* **the Holy Land** the parts of the Middle East where most of the events mentioned in the Bible happened

,holy of 'holies *n* [singular] **1** *humorous* a special place where only a few people are allowed to go **2 the Holy of Holies** the most holy part of a Jewish temple

,Holy 'See *n* **the Holy See** *formal* the authority of the Pope, and everything he is responsible for

,Holy 'Spirit *n* [singular] God in the form of a SPIRIT according to the Christian religion; ▤ **Holy Ghost**

'holy ,war *n* [C] a war that is fought to defend the beliefs of a religion; → **crusade, jihad**

,holy 'water *n* [U] water that has been BLESSED by a priest

'Holy Week *n* [singular] the week before Easter in the Christian church

,Holy 'Writ *n* [U] **1** writing or instructions that people treat as if it were completely true in every detail: *Lenin's word was by no means accepted as holy writ.* **2** *old-fashioned* the Bible

hom·age /'hɒmɪdʒ $ 'hɑː-/ *n* [singular] *formal* something you do to show respect for someone or something you think is important: *The film pays homage to Martin Scorsese's 'Mean Streets'.*

hom·bre /'ɒmbreɪ $ 'ɑːm-/ *n* [C] *AmE informal* a man, especially one who is strong

hom·burg /'hɒmbɜːɡ $ 'hɑːmbɜːrɡ/ *n* [C] a soft hat for men, with a wide BRIM (=edge)

homes (animals)

stable
hutch
kennel
barn
pigsty
hive

home¹ [S1] [W1] /həʊm $ hoʊm/ *n*

1 PLACE WHERE YOU LIVE [C,U] the house, apartment, or place where you live: *They have a beautiful home in California.* | *Good luck in your new home!* | **at home** *Last night we stayed at home and watched TV.* | **away from home** *He was spending more and more time away from home.* | **work from/at home** (=do your work at home instead of at a company office) | *A family of birds **made** their **home** (=started living) under the roof.*

2 FAMILY [C,U] the place where a child lived with his or her family: *Jack **left home** when he was 16.* | *Were you still **living at home** (=with your parents)?* | *Carrie moved out of the **family home** a year ago.*

3 WHERE YOU CAME FROM/BELONG [C,U] the place where you came from or where you usually live, especially when this is the place where you feel happy and comfortable: *She was born in Italy, but she's **made** Charleston her **home**.* | **back home** *The folks back home*

don't really understand what life is like here.

4 YOUR COUNTRY [U] the country where you live, as opposed to foreign countries: **at home** *auto sales at home and abroad* | **back home** *Even though he's been travelling around the world, he's kept up with what's going on back home.*

5 be/feel at home a) to feel comfortable in a place or with a person: [+in/with] *I'm already feeling at home in the new apartment.* | *After a while we began to feel at home with each other.* **b)** to feel happy or confident about doing or using something: [+with/in] *Practise using the video until you feel quite at home with it.*

6 PROPERTY [C] a house, apartment etc considered as property which you can buy or sell: *Attractive, modern homes for sale.*

7 FOR TAKING CARE OF SB [C] a place where people who are very old or sick, or children who have no family are looked after: *an old people's home* | *I could never **put** Dad **into** a **home**.* → **CHILDREN'S HOME, NURSING HOME, REST HOME**

8 make yourself at home *spoken* used to tell someone who is visiting you that they should relax: *Sit down and make yourself at home.*

9 make sb feel at home to make someone feel relaxed by being friendly towards them: *We like to make our customers feel at home.*

10 the home of sth a) the place where something was first discovered, made, or developed: *America is the home of baseball.* **b)** the place where a plant or animal grows or lives: *India is the home of elephants and tigers.*

11 SPORTS TEAM at home if a sports team plays at home, they play at their own sports field; ▤ **away**: [+to] *Birmingham Bullets are at home to Kingston.*

12 home from home *BrE*; **home away from home** *AmE* a place that you think is as pleasant and comfortable as your own house

13 home sweet home used to say how nice it is to be in your own home

14 dogs'/cats' home *BrE* a place where animals with no owners are looked after

15 find a home for sth *BrE* to find a place where something can be kept: *Can you find a home for the piano?*

16 what's that when it's at home? *BrE spoken* used humorously to ask what a long or unusual word means

17 GAMES [U] a place in some games or sports which a player must try to reach in order to win a point → **HOME PLATE, HOME RUN**

home² [S1] [W1] *adv*

1 to or at the place where you live: *Is Sue home from work yet?* | **bring/take sb/sth home** *They brought the baby home from the hospital on Friday.* | *We **stayed home** last night.* | *I'm **going home** now. See you tomorrow.* | **come/get/reach etc home** (=arrive at your home) *It was midnight by the time we got home.* | *What time are you coming home?* ⚠ Do not use a preposition (a word such as 'at' or 'to') before **home** when it is an adverb: *I travel home by bus* (NOT *I travel at home by bus*). *He returned home* (NOT *He returned to home*).

2 take home £120 per week/$600 a month etc to earn a certain amount of money after tax has been taken off: *The average worker takes home around $300 a week.*

3 hit/drive/hammer etc sth home a) to make sure that someone understands what you mean by saying it in an extremely direct and determined way: *We really need to drive this message home.* **b)** to hit or push something firmly into the correct position

4 bring sth home to sb/come home to sb to make you realize how serious, difficult, or dangerous something is: *The episode has brought home to me the pointlessness of this war.*

5 hit/strike home if a remark, situation, or experience hits home, it makes you realize how serious, difficult, or dangerous something is: *She could see that her remark had hit home.*

6 be home and dry *BrE informal* to have succeeded in doing something

7 be home free *AmE informal* to have succeeded in doing the most difficult part of something: *If I last five years with no symptoms, I'll be home free.* → **close to home** at CLOSE² (19)

home³ *adj* [only before noun] **1** relating to or belonging to your home or family: **home address/number** (=the address or telephone number of your house) | *These children need a proper **home life**. **2** done at home or intended for use in a home: *good old-fashioned **home cooking*** | *a home computer* **3** played or playing at a team's own sports field, rather than an opponent's field: **home team/game/crowd/club etc** *The home team took the lead after 25 minutes.* **4** relating to a particular country, as opposed to foreign countries; ⊟ **domestic**: *The meat was destined for the home market.*

home⁴ *v*

home in on sth *phr v* **1** to aim exactly at an object or place and move directly to it: *The bat can home in on insects using a kind of 'radar'.* **2** to direct your efforts or attention towards a particular fault or problem: *He homed in on the one weak link in the argument.*

'home base *n* **1** [C, usually singular] the place that someone returns to in order to rest, learn new things, or exchange information: *The band's home base is Seattle.* **2** [C, usually singular] the main office of a company; ⊟ **headquarters** **3** [singular] *AmE* the place where you stand to hit the ball in baseball; ⊟ **home plate**

home·bod·y /ˈhəʊmˌbɒdi $ ˈhoʊmˌbɑːdi/ *n plural* **homebodies** [C] *informal* someone who enjoys being at home

home·boy /ˈhəʊmbɔɪ $ ˈhoʊm-/ *n* [C] *AmE informal* a friend or someone from the same area or GANG as you – used especially by young people

home 'brew *n* [U] *informal* beer made at home —**home brewed** *adj*

home·buy·er /ˈhəʊmˌbaɪə $ ˈhoʊmˌbaɪər/ *n* [C] someone who is buying a home

home·com·ing /ˈhəʊmˌkʌmɪŋ $ ˈhoʊm-/ *n* **1** [C] an occasion when someone comes back to their home after a long absence **2** [C,U] *AmE* an occasion when former students return to their high school or college

home eco'nomics *n* [U] the study of cooking, sewing, and other skills used at home, taught as a subject at school

home 'front *n* [singular] the people who stay and work in their own country while others go abroad to fight in a war: **on the home front** | *The film is set on the home front in 1943.*

home·girl /ˈhəʊmgɜːl $ ˈhoʊmgɜːrl/ *n* [C] a female HOMEY

home·grown /ˌhəʊmˈgrəʊn◂ $ ˌhoʊmˈgroʊn◂/ *adj* **1** made or produced in your own country, town etc: *homegrown rock stars* **2** homegrown vegetables and fruit are grown in your own garden

home 'help *n* [C] *BrE* someone who helps ill or old people in their homes with cleaning, cooking etc

home·land /ˈhəʊmlænd, -lənd $ ˈhoʊm-/ *n* [C] **1** the country where someone was born **2** a large area of land where a particular group of people can live

home·less /ˈhəʊmləs $ ˈhoʊm-/ *adj* **1** without a home: *Thousands of people have been **made home-less**.* **2 the homeless** [plural] people who have nowhere to live, and who often live on the streets —**homelessness** *n* [U]

home 'loan *n* [C] *informal* an amount of money that you borrow in order to buy a home; ⊟ **mortgage**

home·ly /ˈhəʊmli $ ˈhoʊm-/ *adj* **1** *BrE* simple in a way that makes you feel comfortable: *a modern hotel with a homely atmosphere* **2** *BrE* a homely person is warm and friendly and enjoys home life: *Mrs Keane is a comfortable, homely person.* **3** *AmE* not very attractive; ⊟ **plain** *BrE*

home·made /ˌhəʊmˈmeɪd◂ $ ˌhoʊm-/ *adj* made at home and not bought from a shop; ⊟ **shop-bought**: *homemade cake*

homemade

homemade bread

handmade shoes

home·mak·er /ˈhəʊmˌmeɪkə $ ˈhoʊmˌmeɪkər/ *n* [C] *especially AmE* a woman who works at home cleaning and cooking etc and does not have another job; ⊟ **housewife**

home 'movie *n* [C] a film you make, often of a family occasion, that is intended to be shown at home; ⊟ **home video**

home 'office *n* [C] a room in someone's home where that person works, which usually has equipment such as a computer, FAX machine etc; → **study**

'Home ,Office *n* **the Home Office** the British government department which deals with keeping order in the country, controlling who enters the country etc

ho·me·op·a·thy /ˌhəʊmiˈɒpəθi $ ˌhoʊmiˈɑːp-/ *n* [U] a system of medicine in which a disease is treated by giving extremely small amounts of a substance that causes the disease —**homeopathic** /ˌhəʊmiəˈpæθɪk◂ $ ˌhoʊ-/ *adj* —**homeopath** /ˈhəʊmiəˌpæθ $ ˈhoʊ-/ *n*

home·own·er /ˈhəʊmˌəʊnə $ ˈhoʊmˌoʊnər/ *n* [C] someone who owns their home

home·page, home page /ˈhəʊmpeɪdʒ $ ˈhoʊm-/ *n* [C] the first page of a website, which often contains LINKS to other pages on that website

home plate *n* [singular] the place where you stand to hit the ball in baseball and the last place the player who is running must touch in order to get a point; → **home base**

hom·er /ˈhəʊmə $ ˈhoʊmər/ *n* [C] *AmE informal* a home run in baseball —**homer** *v* [I]

'home room *n* [C] *AmE* a classroom where students have to go to at the beginning of every school day

home 'rule *n* [U] the right of a country or area to have its own government and laws

home 'run *n* [C] a long hit in BASEBALL which allows the player who hits the ball to run around all the BASES and get a point: *I didn't think I could **hit a home run**.*

home·school /ˈhəʊmskuːl $ ˈhoʊm-/ *v* [I,T] to teach children at home instead of sending them to school: *She and her husband homeschool their three kids.* | *Why did you decide to homeschool?* | *homeschooled students* —**homeschooling** *n* [U]: *information about home-schooling* —**homeschool** *adj* [only before noun]: *home-school programs* | *a group of homeschool families*

'Home ,Secretary *n* [C] the British Government minister who is in charge of the Home Office

home·sick /ˈhəʊmˌsɪk $ ˈhoʊm-/ *adj* feeling unhappy because you are a long way from your home —**homesickness** *n* [U]

home·spun /ˈhəʊmspʌn $ ˈhoʊm-/ *adj* **1** homespun ideas are simple and ordinary **2** homespun cloth is woven at home

home·stead¹ /ˈhəʊmsted, -stɪd $ ˈhoʊm-/ *n* [C] **1** a farm and the area of land around it **2** *AmE* a piece of land, usually for farming, given to people in the past by the US government

homestead² *v* [I,T] *AmE* to live and work on a homestead —**homesteader** *n* [C]

H

home 'stretch n [singular] **1** also **home straight** BrE the last part of a race where there is a straight line to the finish **2** the last part of an activity or journey: **in/into the home stretch** as the election campaign headed into the home stretch

home 'town especially BrE also **home·town** especially AmE /ˌhəʊmˈtaʊn $ ˌhoʊm-/ n [C] the place where you were born and spent your childhood: **sb's home town** He hired a car and drove up to his home town. | She's written for her hometown newspaper.

home 'truth n [C usually plural] a true but unpleasant fact that someone tells you about yourself: It's time someone **told** him **a few home truths**.

home 'video n [C] BrE a film you make, often of a family occasion, that is intended to be shown at home; ▣ **home movie** AmE

home·ward /ˈhəʊmwəd $ ˈhoʊmwərd/ adv **1** also **homewards** BrE towards home: She turned and made her way homeward. **2 homeward bound** literary going towards home —**homeward** adj: his homeward trip

home·work ▣2️⃣ /ˈhəʊmwɜːk $ ˈhoʊmwɜːrk/ n [U] **1** work that a student at school is asked to do at home; → **classwork**: **do/start/finish your homework** Fiona was lying on the floor doing her homework. | **biology/history/German etc homework** I need to help Sam with his music homework. ⚠ Do not say 'write your homework' or 'make your homework'. Say **do your homework**. **2** if you do your homework, you prepare for an important activity by finding out information you need; → **research**: It's worth **doing** a bit of **homework** before buying a computer.

home·work·er /ˈhəʊmˌwɜːkə $ ˈhoʊmˌwɜːrkər/ n [C] someone who does their job in their home —**homeworking** n [U]

hom·ey¹ /ˈhəʊmi $ ˈhoʊ-/ adj especially AmE pleasant, like home; ▣ **homely** BrE: The restaurant has a relaxed, homey atmosphere.

homey² n [C] AmE informal a friend or someone who comes from your area or GANG

hom·i·cid·al /ˌhɒmɪˈsaɪdl◂ $ ˌhɑː-/ adj likely to murder someone: a homicidal maniac

hom·i·cide /ˈhɒmɪsaɪd $ ˈhɑː-/ n **1** [C,U] especially AmE the crime of murder; → **manslaughter 2** [U] AmE the police department that deals with murders

hom·i·ly /ˈhɒmɪli $ ˈhɑː-/ n plural **homilies** [C] **1** formal advice about how to behave that is often unwanted **2** literary a speech given as part of a Christian church ceremony

hom·ing /ˈhəʊmɪŋ $ ˈhoʊm-/ adj a bird or animal that has a homing instinct has a special ability that helps it find its way home over long distances

'homing de·vice n [C usually singular] a special part of a weapon that helps it to find its target

'homing ˌpigeon n [C] a PIGEON that is able to find its way home over long distances

hom·i·ny /ˈhɒmɪni $ ˈhɑː-/ n [U] a food made from crushed dried CORN (2)

ho·mo /ˈhəʊməʊ $ ˈhoʊmoʊ/ n plural **homos** [C] informal not polite a very offensive word for a HOMOSEXUAL

homo- /həʊməʊ, -mə, hɒmə hoʊmoʊ, -mə, hɑːmə/ prefix formal or technical same: **homosexual** (=sexually attracted to people of the same sex) | **homographs** (=words spelt the same way)

ho·moe·o·path /ˈhəʊmiəˌpæθ $ ˈhoʊ-/ n [C] a British spelling of HOMEOPATH

ho·moe·op·athy /ˌhəʊmiˈɒpəθi $ ˌhoʊmiˈɑːp-/ n [U] a British spelling of HOMEOPATHY

ho·mo·ge·ne·ous /ˌhəʊməd̩ʒiːniəs◂ $ ˌhoʊ-/ **ho·mog·e·nous** /hɒˈmɒdʒ̩nəs $ -ˈmɑː-/ adj consisting of people or things that are all of the same type; → **heterogeneous**: a homogeneous society —**homogeneously** adv

ho·mo·ge·nize also **-ise** BrE /həˈmɒdʒənaɪz $ -ˈmɑː-/ v [T] to change something so that its parts become similar or the same: plans to homogenize the various school systems

ho·mo·ge·nized also **-ised** BrE /həˈmɒdʒ̩naɪzd $ -ˈmɑː-/ adj homogenized milk has had the cream on top mixed with the milk

hom·o·graph /ˈhɒməɡrɑːf, ˈhəʊ- $ ˈhɑːməɡræf, ˈhoʊ-/ n [C] technical a word that is spelled the same as another, but is different in meaning, origin, grammar, or pronunciation. For example, the noun 'record' is a homograph of the verb 'record'; → **homonym**, **homophone**

hom·o·nym /ˈhɒmənɪm, ˈhəʊ- $ ˈhɑː-, ˈhoʊ-/ n [C] technical a word that is spelt the same and sounds the same as another, but is different in meaning or origin. For example, the noun 'bear' and the verb 'bear' are homonyms; → **homograph**, **homophone**

ho·mo·pho·bi·a /ˌhəʊməˈfəʊbiə $ ˌhoʊməˈfoʊ-/ n [U] hatred and fear of HOMOSEXUALS —**homophobic** adj

hom·o·phone /ˈhɒməfəʊn, ˈhəʊ- $ ˈhɑːməfoʊn, ˈhoʊ-/ n [C] technical a word that sounds the same as another but is different in spelling, meaning, or origin. For example, 'knew' and 'new' are homophones.; → **homograph**, **homonym**

Ho·mo sa·pi·ens /ˌhəʊməʊ ˈsæpienz $ ˌhoʊmoʊ ˈseɪpiənz/ n technical [U] the type of human being that exists now

ho·mo·sex·u·al /ˌhəʊməˈsekʃuəl, ˌhɒmə- $ ˌhoʊ-/ adj formal if someone, especially a man, is homosexual, they are sexually attracted to people of the same sex; ▣ **gay**: One of Ruth's brothers was homosexual. | homosexual men | a homosexual relationship; → **bisexual**, **heterosexual** —**homosexual** n [C] —**homosexuality** /ˌhəʊməsekʃuˈæli̩ti, ˌhɒ- $ ˌhoʊ-/ n [U]

hon /hʌn/ pron AmE spoken a short form of HONEY, used to address someone you love: I'm sorry, hon.

Hon. also **Hon** BrE **1** the written abbreviation of **honourable**: the Hon George Borwick **2** BrE the written abbreviation of **honorary**, used in official job titles: the Hon. Treasurer

hon·cho /ˈhɒntʃəʊ $ ˈhɑːntʃoʊ/ n plural **honchos** [C] informal an important person who controls something, especially a business; ▣ **boss**: the **head honcho**

hone /həʊn $ hoʊn/ v [T] **1** to improve your skill at doing something, especially when you are already very good at it: He set about **honing his skills** as a draughtsman. | **finely honed** (=extremely well-developed) intuition **2** formal to make knives, swords etc sharp; ▣ **sharpen**

hon·est ▣1️⃣ ▣3️⃣ /ˈɒnɪst $ ˈɑːn-/ adj
1 CHARACTER someone who is honest always tells the truth and does not cheat or steal; ▣ **dishonest**: He was a hard-working, honest man. | Ann had an honest face.
2 STATEMENT/ANSWER ETC not hiding the truth or the facts about something; ▣ **frank**: Do you want my honest opinion? | **an honest answer** | **Let's be honest**: the only reason she married him was for his money. | [+with] At least he was honest with you. | [+about] She was always very honest about her feelings.
3 to be honest (with you) spoken used when you tell someone what you really think: To be honest, I don't like him very much.
4 honest! spoken used to try to make someone believe you: I didn't mean to hurt him, honest!
5 honest to God spoken used to emphasize that something you say is true: Honest to God, I wasn't there.
6 WORK honest work is done using your own efforts and without cheating: I bet he's never **done an honest day's work** in his life! | I'm just trying to **earn an honest living**.
7 ORDINARY GOOD PEOPLE honest people are not famous or special, but behave in a good, socially acceptable way: She came from a good, honest, working-class background.

8 make an honest woman (out) of sb *old-fashioned* to marry a woman because you have had a sexual relationship with her

hon·est·ly S2 /ˈɒnᵻstli $ ˈɑːn-/ *adv*
1 used to emphasize that what you are saying is true, even though it may seem surprising: *I honestly don't know how old my parents are.* | *I can honestly say that I never worry about him now.*
2 *spoken* used when you are shocked or annoyed by something someone has said or done; ◧ **really**: *Honestly! Do you ever listen?*
3 *spoken* used to try to make someone believe that what you have just said is true: *It wasn't me, honestly!*
4 in an honest way; ◧ **truthfully**: *Tell me honestly, Kate, what do you think of John?* | *We talked openly and honestly.* | *'No, I don't,' she answered honestly.*

honest-to-ˈgoodness *adj* [only before noun] simple and good: *plain honest-to-goodness home cooking*

hon·es·ty /ˈɒnᵻsti $ ˈɑːn-/ *n* [U] **1** the quality of being honest; ◧ **dishonesty**: *a politician of rare honesty and courage* **2 in all honesty** used when telling someone that what you are saying is what you really think: *It was not, in all honesty, a very good start.*

hon·ey /ˈhʌni/ *n* [U] **1** a sweet sticky substance produced by BEES, used as food **2** *especially AmE spoken* used to address someone you love; ◧ **love**: *Hi, honey.*

hon·ey·bee /ˈhʌnibiː/ *n* [C] a BEE that makes honey

hon·ey·comb /ˈhʌnikəʊm $ -koʊm/ *n* [C] **1** a structure made by BEES, which consists of many six-sided cells in which honey is stored **2** something that is arranged or shaped in this pattern

hon·ey·combed /ˈhʌnikəʊmd $ -koʊmd/ *adj* [+with] filled with many holes, hollow passages etc

hon·ey·dew /ˈhʌnidjuː $ -duː/ *n* **1** [U] a sticky substance that some insects leave on plants **2** also **honeydew melon** [C] a type of MELON with yellow skin and green flesh

hon·eyed /ˈhʌnid/ *adj* **1** *literary* honeyed words or honeyed voices sound soft and pleasant, but are often insincere **2** tasting like HONEY or covered in honey

hon·ey·moon¹ /ˈhʌnimuːn/ *n* [C] **1** a holiday taken by two people who have just got married: **on your honeymoon** *We went to Italy on our honeymoon.* **2** also **honeymoon period** the period of time when a new government, leader etc has just started and no one criticizes them: *By 1987, the honeymoon was over.*

honeymoon² *v* [I always + adv/prep] to go somewhere for your honeymoon —**honeymooner** *n* [C]

hon·ey·pot /ˈhʌnipɒt $ -paːt/ *n* [C] something that is attractive to a lot of people; ◧ **magnet**

hon·ey·suck·le /ˈhʌniˌsʌkəl/ *n* [C,U] a climbing plant with pleasant-smelling yellow or pink flowers

honk¹ /hɒŋk $ haːŋk, hɔːŋk/ *n* [C] **1** a loud noise made by a car horn **2** a loud noise made by a GOOSE

honk² *v* [I,T] if a car horn or a GOOSE honks, it makes a loud noise: *Several drivers honked their horns and waved.*

hon·ky, honkie /ˈhɒŋki $ ˈhaːŋ-, ˈhɔːŋ-/ *n plural* **honkies** [C] *AmE taboo* a very offensive word for a white person, used by black people. Do not use this word.

honky-tonk¹ /ˈhɒŋki tɒŋk $ ˈhaːŋki taːŋk, ˈhɔːŋki tɔːŋk/ *n* [C] *AmE* a cheap bar where COUNTRY MUSIC is played

honky-tonk² *adj* **honky-tonk music/piano** a type of piano music which is played in a loud cheerful way

hon·or /ˈɒnə $ ˈaːnər/ *n* [C,U] the American spelling of HONOUR

hon·or·a·ble /ˈɒnərəbəl $ ˈaːn-/ *adj* the American spelling of HONOURABLE

ˌhonorable ˈdischarge *n* [C] *AmE* if you leave the army with an honorable discharge, your behaviour and work have been very good; ◧ **dishonorable discharge**

hon·o·rar·i·um /ˌɒnəˈreəriəm $ ˌaːnəˈrer-/ *n plural* **honoraria** /-riə/ [C] *formal* a sum of money offered to a professional for a piece of advice, a speech etc

hon·or·ar·y /ˈɒnərəri $ ˈaːnəreri/ *adj* **1** an honorary title, rank, or university degree is given to someone as an honour: *Brown received an honorary doctorate from Seoul University.* **2** an honorary position in an organization is held without receiving any payment **3** an honorary member of a group is treated like a member of that group but does not belong to it

hon·o·ree /ˌɒnəˈriː $ ˌaːn-/ *n* [C] someone who receives an honour or AWARD: *Guests clapped and cheered for the honorees.*

hon·or·if·ic /ˌɒnəˈrɪfɪk◂ $ ˌaːnə-/ *n* [C] an expression or title that is used to show respect for the person you are speaking to

ˈhonor roll *n* [C] *AmE* a list of the best students in a school or college

ˈhonor ˌsystem *n* [singular] *AmE* an agreement between members of a group to obey rules, although no one checks to make sure that they are being followed

hon·our¹ W3 *BrE*; **honor** *AmE* /ˈɒnə $ ˈaːnər/ *n*
1 STH THAT MAKES YOU PROUD [singular] *formal* something that makes you feel very proud

> **great honour**
> **rare honour** (=a very special honour)
> **dubious honour** (=something that you are not sure that you should be proud of)
> **the honour of doing sth**
> **have the honour of doing sth**
> **it is an honour to do sth** (=used as a polite way of saying that you are pleased to do something)
> **do sb the honour of doing sth** (=make someone proud and happy by doing something for them)

> *It is a great honour, something I never expected.* | *Over 100 players competed for the honour of representing the county in the National Finals.* | *Earlier this year, I had the honor of meeting the President.* | *It is an honour to have you here.* | *Will you do me the honour of becoming my wife?*

2 RESPECT [U] the respect that you, your family, your country etc receive from other people, which makes you feel proud: [+of] *He was prepared even to die in order to defend the honour of his family.* | **national/family/personal etc honour** *For the French team, winning tomorrow's game is a matter of national honour.*
3 in honour of sb/sth a) in order to show how much you admire and respect someone: *The stadium was named in honour of the club's first chairman.* | **in sb's honour** *A special dinner will be held in her honour.* **b)** to celebrate an event: *An oak tree was planted in honour of the occasion.*
4 GIVEN TO SB [C] something such as a special title or MEDAL given to someone to show how much people respect them for what they have achieved: *Reverend Peters was nominated for the honour by colleagues at Walworth Methodist Church.* | **highest honour** (=most important honour) *The medal is the highest honour the association can bestow* (=give).
5 MORAL PRINCIPLES [U] strong moral beliefs and standards of behaviour that make people respect and trust you: *My father was a man of honour and great integrity.* | *Her actions were always guided by a deep sense of honour* (=strong desire to do what is morally right). | **matter/point/question of honour** (=something that you feel you must do because of your moral principles) *It had become a point of honour not to tell him about Lori.*
6 AT UNIVERSITY/SCHOOL a) **with honours** *BrE* if you pass a university degree with honours, you pass it at a level that is higher than the most basic level **b)** **with honors** *AmE* if you finish high school or college with honors, you get one of the highest grades **c)** **First**

H

| 1 | 000, | 2 | 000, | 3 | 000, most frequent words in | S | spoken and | W | ritten English |

Class/Second Class Honours *BrE* the highest or second highest level of degree at a British university

7 Your/His/Her Honour used when speaking to or about a judge: *No, Your Honour.*

8 place of honour the seat or place which is given to the most important guest or object: *The vase she gave me occupies the place of honor in my living room.*

9 with full military honours if someone is buried with full military honours, there is a military ceremony at their funeral

10 do the honours *spoken* to pour the drinks, serve food etc at a social occasion: *Liz, would you do the honors?*

11 your word of honour a very serious promise that what you are saying is true: *I won't try to see you again. I give you my word of honour.*

12 be an honour to sb/sth to bring admiration and respect to your country, school, family etc because of your behaviour or achievements: *He's an honour to his family and his country.*

13 be/feel honour bound to do sth *formal* to feel that it is your moral duty to do something: *We felt honor bound to attend their wedding.*

14 on your honour a) if you swear on your honour to do something, you promise very seriously to do it **b)** *old-fashioned* if you are on your honour to do something, you are being trusted to do it

15 SEX [U] *old use* if a woman loses her honour, she has sex with a man she is not married to → **guest of honour** at GUEST[1] (1); → MAID OF HONOUR

honour[2] *BrE*; **honor** *AmE v* [T] **1 be/feel honoured (to do sth)** to feel very proud and pleased! *I felt very honoured to be included in the team.* **2** *formal* to show publicly that someone is respected and admired, especially by praising them or giving them a special title: **honour sb with sth** *He was honored with an award for excellence in teaching.* | **honour sb for sth** *Two firefighters have been honoured for their courage.* **3 honour a promise/contract/agreement etc** to do what you have agreed to do: *Once again the government has failed to honour its promises.* | *We pray that both sides will continue to honour their commitment to the peace agreement.* **4** to treat someone with special respect: *In a marriage, you need to honour one another.* | *I was treated like an honored guest.* **5 honour a cheque** if your bank honours a cheque that you have given someone, it pays the money to that person **6 sb has decided to honour us with their presence** used humorously when someone arrives late, or to someone who rarely comes to a meeting, class etc

honourable *BrE*; **honorable** *AmE adj* **1** an honourable action or activity deserves respect and admiration: *My father didn't think acting was an honorable profession.* **2** behaving in a way that is morally correct and shows you have high moral standards: *a principled and honourable man* **3** an honourable arrangement or agreement is fair to everyone who is involved in it —**honourably** *adv*

Hon·our·a·ble *BrE*; **Honorable** *AmE* /'ɒnərəbəl $ 'ɑːn-/ *adj* **1** written abbreviation **Hon.** used in Britain in the titles of children whose father is a lord and in the titles of judges and members of parliament **2** written abbreviation **Hon.** used in the US when writing to or about a judge or important person in the government **3 the Honourable Gentleman/the Honourable Lady/my Honourable Friend/the Honourable Member** used by British members of parliament when talking to or about each other in the House of Commons → RIGHT HONOURABLE

honourable mention *BrE*; **honorable mention** *AmE n* [C] a special honour in a competition for work that was of high quality but did not get a prize

honours degree *n* [C] a British university degree that is above the basic level in one or two particular subjects: **first/second/third class honours degree** | **joint honours degree** (=a degree in two main subjects)

honours list *n* [C] a list of important people in Britain to whom titles are given as a sign of respect

hooch, hootch /huːtʃ/ *n* [U] *especially AmE informal* strong alcohol, especially alcohol that has been made illegally

hood /hʊd/ *n* [C] **1 a)** a part of a coat, jacket etc that you can pull up to cover your head: *Why don't you put your hood up if you're cold?* **b)** a cloth bag that goes over someone's face and head so that they cannot be recognized or cannot see; → **balaclava**: *He was abducted by four men wearing hoods.* **2** *AmE* the metal covering over the engine on a car; ⊟ **bonnet** *BrE*: **under the hood** *Check under the hood and see what that noise is.* → see picture at CAR **3** a cover fitted above a COOKER to remove the smell of cooking; → **extractor (fan)** **4** *BrE* a folding cover on a car or PRAM, which gives protection from the rain **5** also '**hood** *AmE informal* a NEIGHBOURHOOD **6** *AmE informal* a HOODLUM

-hood /hʊd/ *suffix* [in nouns] **1** used to refer to a period of time or a state: *during his childhood* (=when he was a child) | *parenthood* (=the state of being a parent) **2** the people who belong to a particular group: *the priesthood* (=all the people who are priests)

hood·ed /'hʊdɪd/ *adj* having or wearing a hood: *a hooded cape*

hood·ie /'hʊdi/ *n* [C] *informal* a type of jacket with a HOOD

hood·lum /'huːdləm/ *n* [C] a criminal, often a young person, who does violent or illegal things; ⊟ **gangster**

hood·wink /'hʊdˌwɪŋk/ *v* [T + into] to trick someone in a clever way so that you can get an advantage for yourself

hoo·ey /'huːi/ *n* [U] *AmE informal* stupid talk; ⊟ **nonsense**

hoof[1] /huːf $ hʊf, huːf/ *n plural* **hoofs** or **hooves** /huːvz $ hʊvz, huːvz/ [C] **1** the hard foot of an animal such as a horse, cow etc **2 on the hoof** *BrE* if you do something on the hoof, you do it quickly while doing something else at the same time

hoof[2] *v* **hoof it** *informal* to run or walk quickly

hoof·er /'huːfə $ 'hʊfər, 'huː-/ *n* [C] *informal* a dancer, especially one who works in the theatre

hoo-ha /'huː haː/ *n* [singular, U] *BrE* noisy talk or excitement about something unimportant; ⊟ **fuss**: *What's all the hoo-ha about?*

hook[1] S3 /hʊk/ *n* [C]

1 HANGING THINGS a curved piece of metal or plastic that you use for hanging things on; → **peg**: *Tom hung his coat on the hook behind the door.*

2 CATCHING FISH a curved piece of thin metal with a sharp point for catching fish → see picture at FISHING

3 let/get sb off the hook to allow someone or help someone to get out of a difficult situation: *I wasn't prepared to let her off the hook that easily.*

4 leave/take the phone off the hook to leave or take the telephone RECEIVER (=the part you speak into) off the part where it is usually placed so that no one can call you

5 be ringing off the hook *AmE* if your telephone is ringing off the hook, a lot of people are calling you

6 INTEREST something that is attractive and gets people's interest and attention; ⊟ **draw**: *You always need a bit of a hook to get people to go to the theatre.*

7 by hook or by crook if you are going to do something by hook or by crook, you are determined to do it, whatever methods you have to use: *The police are going to get these guys, by hook or by crook.*

8 HITTING SB a way of hitting your opponent in BOXING, in which your elbow is bent; → **punch, jab**

9 hook, line, and sinker if someone believes something hook, line, and sinker, they believe a lie completely → BOAT HOOK, CURTAIN HOOK; → **sling your hook** at SLING[1] (4)

hook[2] *v* [T]

1 FISH to catch a fish with a hook: *I hooked a 20-pound salmon last week.*

2 FASTEN [always + adv/prep] to fasten or hang some-

thing onto something else: **hook sth onto/to sth** *Just hook the bucket onto the rope and lower it down.*
3 BEND YOUR FINGER/ARM ETC [always + adv/prep] to bend your finger, arm, or leg, especially so that you can pull or hold something else: *Ruth hooked her arm through Tony's.* | *He tried to hook his leg over the branch.*
4 INTEREST/ATTRACT *informal* to succeed in making someone interested in something or attracted to something: *cigarette ads designed to hook young people*
5 ELECTRONIC EQUIPMENT [always + adv/prep] also **hook up** to connect a piece of electronic equipment to another piece of equipment or to an electricity supply; → **hook-up**: *We've got a CD player, but it's not hooked up yet.* | **hook sth together** *Computers from different manufacturers can often be hooked together.*
6 BALL to throw or kick a ball so that it moves in a curve
  hook up with sb/sth *phr v informal especially AmE*
1 a) to start having a sexual relationship with someone **b)** to meet someone and become friendly with them; ◨ **meet up with**: *Did you ever hook up with Maisy while you were there?* **c)** to agree to work together with another organization for a particular purpose
2 hook sb up with sth to help someone get something that they need or want; ◨ **fix up with**: *Do you think you can hook me up with some tickets for tonight?*

hook·ah /ˈhʊkə/ n [C] a pipe for smoking drugs, that consists of a long tube and a container of water

hook and 'eye n [U] a small metal hook and ring used for fastening clothes

hooked /hʊkt/ adj **1** curved outwards or shaped like a hook: *a hooked nose* **2** [not before noun] *informal* if you are hooked on a drug, you feel a strong need for it and you cannot stop taking it; ◨ **addicted**: [+on] *I know a girl who **got hooked** on cocaine.* **3** [not before noun] *informal* if you are hooked on something, you enjoy it very much and you want to do it as often as possible: [+on] *I **got hooked** on TV when I was sick.* **4** having one or more hooks

hook·er /ˈhʊkə $ -ər/ n [C] *informal* a woman who has sex with men for money; ◨ **prostitute**

'hook-up n [C] a temporary connection between two pieces of equipment such as computers, or between a piece of equipment and an electricity or water supply

hook·y /ˈhʊki/ n **play hooky** *AmE old-fashioned* to stay away from school without permission; ◨ **truant** *BrE*

hoo·li·gan /ˈhuːlɪɡən/ n [C] a noisy violent person who causes trouble by fighting etc: *football hooligans* —**hooliganism** n [U]

hoop /huːp $ hʊp, huːp/ n [C] **1** a large ring made of wood, metal, plastic etc **2** a large ring that children used to play with in the past, or that CIRCUS animals are made to jump through **3 a)** the ring that you have to throw the ball through to score points in BASKETBALL **b)** **hoops** [plural] *AmE informal* the game of BASKETBALL **4** jump/go through hoops if someone makes you jump through hoops, they make you do lots of difficult or boring things before you are allowed to do what you want to do **5** also **hoop earrings** an EARRING that is shaped like a ring → COCK-A-HOOP, HULA HOOP

hooped /huːpt/ adj BrE in the shape of a hoop, or containing something in the shape of a hoop: *hooped earrings*

hoop·la /ˈhuːplɑː $ ˈhuːp-, ˈhʊp-/ n [U] **1** especially AmE excitement about something which attracts a lot of public attention: *all the hoopla that surrounded the trial* **2** BrE a game in which prizes can be won by throwing a ring over an object from a distance

hoo·ray /hʊˈreɪ, ˌhuːˈreɪ◂/ interjection shouted when you are very glad about something —**hooray** n [C] → **hip hip hooray** at HIP³

hoot¹ /huːt/ n [C] **1** a shout or laugh that shows you think something is funny or stupid: **hoot of laughter/derision etc** *Hoots of laughter rose from the audience.* **2** a sound that an OWL makes **3** a short clear sound made by a vehicle or ship, as a warning **4 be a**

hoot *spoken* to be very funny or amusing **5 don't give a hoot/don't care two hoots** *spoken* to not care at all about someone or something: [+about] *It was clear that Owen didn't care two hoots about her.*

hoot² v **1** [I,T] if a vehicle or ship hoots, it makes a loud clear noise as a warning: [+at] *The car behind was hooting at me.* **2** [I] if an OWL hoots, it makes a long 'oo' sound **3** [I,T] to laugh loudly because you think something is funny: **hoot with laughter/glee/mirth etc** *He had the audience hooting with laughter.*

hoot·er /ˈhuːtə $ -ər/ n [C] **1** BrE a piece of equipment that makes a loud noise and is used on cars, ships, or in factories; ◨ **horn 2** BrE informal a nose **3** **hooters** [plural] AmE informal not polite an offensive word for a woman's breasts

Hoo·ver /ˈhuːvə $ -ər/ n [C] trademark BrE a VACUUM CLEANER

hoover v [I,T] BrE to clean a floor, CARPET etc using a VACUUM CLEANER (=a machine that sucks up dirt); ◨ **vacuum**; → see picture at CLEAN

hooves /huːvz $ hʊvz, huːvz/ the plural of HOOF

hop¹ /hɒp $ hɑːp/ v **hopped, hopping**
1 JUMP [I] to move by jumping on one foot: *The little girl ran off, hopping and skipping as she went.* → see picture at JUMP
2 [I] if a bird, an insect, or a small animal hops, it moves by making quick short jumps
3 [I always + adv/prep] *informal* to move somewhere quickly or suddenly: *Hop in – I'll drive you home.* | *Patrick hopped out of bed and quickly got dressed.*
4 hop a plane/bus/train etc AmE informal to get on a plane, bus, train etc, especially after suddenly deciding to do so: *So we hopped a bus to Phoenix that night.*
5 hop it! BrE old-fashioned used to rudely tell someone to go away
6 hopping mad *informal* very angry; ◨ **furious**

hop² n [C]
1 catch sb on the hop to do something when someone is not expecting it and is not ready
2 JUMP a short jump
3 PLANT **a)** **hops** [plural] parts of dried flowers used for making beer, which give the beer a bitter taste **b)** the tall plant on which these flowers grow
4 FLIGHT a single short journey by plane: *It's just a short hop from Cleveland to Detroit.*
5 DANCE old-fashioned a social event at which people dance → HIP-HOP

hope¹ S1 W1 /həʊp $ hoʊp/ v [I,T]
1 to want something to happen or be true and to believe that it is possible or likely: **hope (that)** *We hope that more women will decide to join the course.* | *I do hope everything goes well.* | *It was hoped that the job would be filled by a local person.* | *Let's just hope someone finds her bag.* | *I hope to God I haven't left the car window open.* | **hope to do sth** *Joan's hoping to study law at Harvard.* | [+for] *We were hoping for good weather.* | *Liam decided to ignore the warning and just hope for the best* (=hope that a situation will end well when there is a risk of things going wrong). | *I rang my parents, hoping against hope* (=hoping for something that is very unlikely to happen or be true) *that they hadn't left yet.* ⚠ Do not say that you 'hope something would happen'. Say that you **hope something will happen**: *I hope the weather will be nice* (NOT *I hope the weather would be nice*).
2 I hope so *spoken* used to say that you hope something that has been mentioned happens or is true: '*Do we get paid this week?*' '*I certainly hope so!*'
3 I hope not *spoken* used to say that you hope something that has been mentioned does not happen or is not true: *I don't think I'm busy that day, or at least I hope not.*
4 I'm hoping *spoken* used to say that you hope something will happen, especially because you are depending on it: **I'm hoping (that)** *I'm hoping the car will be*

fixed by Friday. | **I'm hoping to do sth** *We were hoping to see you today.*
5 I hope (that) *spoken* used when you want to be polite and to make sure that you are not interrupting or offending someone: *I hope I'm not interrupting you.* | *I **hope you don't mind** me asking, but why are you moving?*
6 I should hope so (too)/I should hope not *BrE spoken* used to say that you feel very strongly that something should or should not happen: *'They'll get their money back.' 'I should hope so too, after being treated like that.'* → see box at **WISH**[1]

hope² [W2] n

1 FEELING [C,U] a feeling of wanting something to happen or be true and believing that it is possible or likely

---

hope that
(have) hopes of (doing) sth
be full of hope
give/offer hope to sb (=make it possible for people to have hope)
lose/give up/abandon hope (of sth) (=stop hoping)
live in hope (=keep hoping for something)
not hold out any/much hope (=have very little hope)
in the hope that (=because you hope that something will happen)
in the hope of doing sth (=because you hope that you will do it)
a vain/forlorn hope also **false hope** (=when what you hope for will not happen)
glimmer/ray of hope (=a little hope, or something that gives you a little hope)
a symbol/beacon of hope (=something that makes people have hope)

*The President has expressed the **hope that** relations will improve.* | *[+for] She hadn't told Julie about her hopes for a reconciliation with Ross.* | *Rita **has hopes of** eventually studying to be a nurse.* | *The people **are full of hope** for the future.* | *This new treatment **offers hope to** thousands of cancer patients.* | *Michael's parents had almost **given up hope of** ever seeing him again.* | *We haven't had any success yet, but we **live in hope**.* | *We could try asking them, but I **don't hold out much hope**.* | *Should they sell now or hang on **in the hope that** the shares will soon be worth serious money?* | *We came to the island **in the hope of** finding a simpler way of life.* | *Such a lie is unkind because it keeps **false hope** alive.* | *She said the unemployment figures were a **glimmer of hope**.*

---

2 STH YOU HOPE FOR [C] something that you hope will happen: **sb's hope** *She told him all her secret hopes and fears.* | *My hope is that by next summer I'll have saved enough money to go travelling.*
3 CHANCE [C,U] a chance of succeeding or of something good happening: *[+of] It was rush hour, and there was no hope of getting a seat.* | *It was a desperate plan, with little hope of success.* | **hope (that)** *There's still a **faint hope** (=small hope) that the two sides will reach an agreement.* | **not a hope!** *spoken* (=used to say that there is no chance of something happening) | **not a hope in hell (of doing sth)** *spoken* (=not even the smallest chance of success) *They don't have a hope in hell of winning.* | **some hope/what a hope!** *BrE spoken* (=used humorously to say that there is no chance that something will happen) *'Your dad might lend you the car.' 'Some hope!'*
4 have high/great hopes to be confident that someone or something will be successful: *[+of] We have great hopes of her – she's very talented.* | *[+for] Parents often have such high hopes for their children.*
5 raise (sb's) hopes to make someone feel that it is likely that what they want to happen will happen: *It wouldn't be fair to raise her hopes of success.*
6 dash/shatter (sb's) hopes to disappoint someone by making something that they want to happen seem impossible: *The report dashes hopes of an early*

improvement in the economy.
7 get/build sb's hopes up to allow someone to believe that what they want to happen is likely to happen: ***Don't get your hopes up**. There'll be a lot of people applying for the job.*
8 be sb's last/only/best hope to be someone's last, only etc chance of getting the result they want: *Please help me. You're my last hope.* | *[+of] Joshua's only hope of survival was a heart transplant.*
9 be beyond hope if a situation is beyond hope, it is so bad that there is no chance of any improvement: *[+of] Some of the houses were beyond hope of repair.* → **pin your hopes on sb/sth** at **PIN**²

'hoped-for *adj* [only before noun] *written* used to describe something that you want to happen and think is possible or likely: *I was at home when the desperately hoped-for call came through.*

hope·ful¹ /'həʊpfəl $ 'hoʊp-/ *adj* **1** believing that what you hope for is likely to happen; ▤ optimistic: *[+about] Everyone's feeling pretty hopeful about the future.* | **hopeful (that)** *I'm hopeful that we can find a solution.* | **be hopeful of (doing) sth** *BrE: He is still hopeful of playing in Saturday's game.* **2** making you feel that what you hope for is likely to happen; ▤ promising: *The vote is a **hopeful sign** that attitudes in the church are changing.* | *Things might get better, but it doesn't look very hopeful right now.*
—**hopefulness** *n* [U]

hopeful² *n* [C] *written* someone who is hoping to be successful, especially in acting, sports, politics etc: *Thousands of **young hopefuls** were auditioned for the role.* | *Republican presidential hopefuls*

hope·ful·ly [S1] /'həʊpfəli $ 'hoʊp-/ *adv*
1 [sentence adverb] a way of saying what you hope will happen, which some people think is incorrect: *Hopefully, I'll be back home by ten o'clock.* | *By then the problem will hopefully have been solved.*
2 in a way that shows that you are hopeful: *'Will there be any food left over?' he asked hopefully.*

hope·less [S3] /'həʊpləs $ 'hoʊp-/ *adj*
1 if something that you try to do is hopeless, there is no possibility of it being successful: *We tried to stop the flames from spreading, but we knew it was hopeless.* | *Getting your work published often seems a **hopeless task**.* | *I kept on struggling forward, even though I knew it was hopeless.*
2 a hopeless situation is so bad that there is no chance of success or improvement: *The situation is not as hopeless as it might seem.* | *the millions who live in hopeless poverty*
3 *especially BrE informal* very bad; ▤ terrible: *I'm a hopeless cook.* | **hopeless at (doing) sth** *My brother was always pretty hopeless at ball games.* | *[+with] I'm hopeless with machinery.* | *I've got a hopeless memory.* | *The public transport system was absolutely hopeless.*
4 feeling no hope: *I began to feel lonely and hopeless.*
5 used, often humorously, to say that someone's bad behaviour cannot be changed: *Oh, James, you really are a **hopeless case** (=it seems impossible to change your behaviour)!* | **hopeless romantic/materialist/drunk etc** *She was a hopeless romantic, always convinced that one day she would meet the man of her dreams.*
—**hopelessness** *n* [U]

hope·less·ly /'həʊpləsli $ 'hoʊp-/ *adv* **1** used when emphasizing how bad a situation is, and saying that it will not get better: *We found ourselves hopelessly outnumbered by the enemy.* | *She felt hopelessly confused.* | *I was trying to find the museum, but I got hopelessly lost.* **2 be/fall hopelessly in love (with sb)** to have or develop very strong feelings of love for someone **3** feeling that you have no hope: *'When will I see you again?' he asked hopelessly.*

,hopped-'up *adj AmE informal* **1** happy and excited, especially after taking drugs **2** a hopped-up car, engine etc has been made much more powerful

hop·per /'hɒpə $ 'hɑːpər/ *n* [C] a large FUNNEL¹ (1)

hop·scotch /ˈhɒpskɒtʃ $ ˈhɑːpskɑːtʃ/ n [U] a children's game in which each child has to jump from one square drawn on the ground to another

horde /hɔːd $ hɔːrd/ n [C] a large crowd moving in a noisy uncontrolled way: [+of] *There were hordes of people inside the station.*

ho·ri·zon /həˈraɪzən/ n **1 the horizon** the line far away where the land or sea seems to meet the sky: **on the horizon** *We could see a ship on the horizon.* ⚠ Do not say 'in the horizon'. Say **on the horizon**. **2 horizons** [plural] the limit of your ideas, knowledge, and experience: **broaden/expand sb's horizons** *a course of study that will broaden your horizons* **3 on the horizon** to seem likely to happen in the future: *Business is good now, but there are a few problems on the horizon.*

hor·i·zon·tal¹ /ˌhɒrɪˈzɒntl◂ $ ˌhɑːrɪˈzɑːntl◂ / adj flat and level: *a horizontal surface* —**horizontally** adv; → **diagonal, vertical**

horizontal² n **1** [C] a horizontal line or surface **2 the horizontal** a horizontal position: *eleven degrees below the horizontal*

hor·mone /ˈhɔːməʊn $ ˈhɔːrmoʊn/ n [C] a chemical substance produced by your body that influences its growth, development, and condition —**hormonal** /hɔːˈməʊnəl $ hɔːrˈmoʊ-/ adj: *hormonal changes*

hormone re·placement ther·a·py n [U] HRT

horn¹ /hɔːn $ hɔːrn/ n
1 ANIMAL a) [C] the hard pointed thing that grows, usually in pairs, on the heads of animals such as cows and goats; → **antlers b)** [U] the substance that animals' horns are made of: *a knife with a horn handle* **c)** [C] a part of an animal's head that sticks out like a horn, for example on a SNAIL
2 ON A CAR [C] the thing in a vehicle that you use to make a loud sound as a signal or warning: **sound/toot/honk/blow your horn** (=make a noise with your horn); → see picture at CAR
3 MUSICAL INSTRUMENT [C] **a)** a musical instrument like a long metal tube that is wide at one end, that you play by blowing **b)** informal a TRUMPET **c)** a FRENCH HORN **d)** a musical instrument made from an animal's horn → ENGLISH HORN
4 drinking horn/powder horn etc a container in the shape of an animal's horn, used in the past for drinking from, carrying GUNPOWDER etc
5 draw/pull in your horns to reduce the amount of money you spend
6 be on the horns of a dilemma to be in a situation in which you have to choose between two equally unpleasant or difficult situations → blow your own trumpet/horn at BLOW¹ (21); → lock horns at LOCK¹ (6); → take the bull by the horns at BULL¹ (3)

horn² v
horn in phr v AmE informal to interrupt or try to take part in something when you are not wanted; **butt in**: [+on] *Don't try and horn in on our fun.*

horn·bill /ˈhɔːnbɪl $ ˈhɔːrn-/ n [C] a tropical bird with a very large beak

horned /hɔːnd $ hɔːrnd/ adj [only before noun] having horns or something that looks like horns: *horned cattle* | *a horned toad*

hor·net /ˈhɔːnɪt $ ˈhɔːr-/ n [C] **1** a large black and yellow flying insect that can sting; → **wasp 2 hornets' nest** a situation in which there is a lot of trouble and quarrelling: *The new production targets have stirred up a hornet's nest.*

horn·pipe /ˈhɔːnpaɪp $ ˈhɔːrn-/ n [C] a traditional dance performed by SAILORS or the music for this dance

horn-rimmed /ˌhɔːn ˈrɪmd◂ $ ˌhɔːrn-/ adj horn-rimmed glasses/spectacles glasses with frames made of plastic that looks like horn

horn·y /ˈhɔːni $ ˈhɔːrni/ adj **1** informal sexually excited: *feeling horny* **2** informal sexually attractive: *I think he's horny.* **3** skin that is horny is hard and rough **4** made of a hard substance like horn: *the bird's horny beak*

hor·o·scope /ˈhɒrəskəʊp $ ˈhɑːrəskoʊp, ˈhɔː-/ n [C] a description of your character and the things that will happen to you, based on the position of the stars and PLANETS at the time of your birth; → **zodiac**

hor·ren·dous /hɒˈrendəs, hə- $ hɑː-, hɔː-/ adj **1** frightening and terrible; **horrific**: *a horrendous experience* | *She suffered horrendous injuries.* **2** informal extremely unreasonable or unpleasant: *horrendous debts* | *The traffic was horrendous.* —**horrendously** adv

hor·ri·ble S2 /ˈhɒrɪbəl $ ˈhɔː-, ˈhɑː-/ adj
1 very bad – used for example about things you see, taste, or smell, or about the weather: *The weather has been really horrible all week.* | *a horrible smell* | *The food looked horrible, but it tasted OK.*
2 very unpleasant and often frightening, worrying, or upsetting: *a horrible dream* | **I have a horrible feeling** *that we're going to miss the plane.*
3 rude and unfriendly: *She's a horrible person.* | *What a horrible thing to say!* | **be horrible to sb** *Why are you being so horrible to me?* —**horribly** adv: *Her face was horribly scarred.* | *The whole plan had gone horribly wrong.*

WORD FOCUS: HORRIBLE
taste or smell: **nasty, not very nice, revolting, disgusting, foul, unpleasant, gross** informal
experience, situation, or feeling: **nasty, not very nice, terrible, unpleasant**
person: **nasty, not very nice, obnoxious, mean** AmE, **unpleasant, objectionable**

hor·rid /ˈhɒrɪd $ ˈhɔː-, ˈhɑː-/ adj especially BrE **1** informal very unpleasant; **nasty**: *a horrid smell* **2** old-fashioned behaving in a nasty unkind way: *Don't be so horrid!*

hor·rif·ic /hɒˈrɪfɪk, hə- $ hɔː-, hɑː-/ adj extremely bad, in a way that is frightening or upsetting; **horrifying**: horrific crash/accident/attack etc *a horrific plane crash* | *His injuries were horrific.* —**horrifically** /-kli/ adv

hor·ri·fy /ˈhɒrɪfaɪ $ ˈhɔː-, ˈhɑː-/ v horrified, horrifying, horrifies [T] to make someone feel very shocked and upset or afraid: *Henry was horrified by what had happened.* | horrified to see/hear/find etc *She was horrified to discover that he loved Rose.*

hor·ri·fy·ing /ˈhɒrɪfaɪ-ɪŋ $ ˈhɔː-, ˈhɑː-/ adj extremely bad, especially in a way that is frightening or upsetting; **horrific**: *murder, rape and other horrifying crimes* | *It's horrifying to see how much poverty there is here.* —**horrifyingly** adv

hor·ror W3 /ˈhɒrə $ ˈhɔːrər, ˈhɑː-/ n
1 [U] a strong feeling of shock and fear: **in horror** *Staff watched in horror as he set himself alight.* | **with horror** *Many people recoil with horror when they see a big spider like this.* | **to sb's horror** (=making someone shocked or afraid) *To my horror, I realised my shirt was wet with blood.* | *You should have seen the look of horror on his face.*
2 [C usually plural] something that is very terrible, shocking, or frightening: [+of] *the horrors of war*
3 the horror of something when a situation or event is very unpleasant or shocking: *Dense smoke surrounded them, adding to the horror of the situation.* | *Only when the vehicle was lifted did the full horror of the accident become clear.*
4 have a horror of sth to be afraid of something or dislike it very much: *He has a horror of snakes.*
5 little horror BrE a young child who behaves badly
6 give sb the horrors to make someone feel unreasonably frightened or nervous
7 horror of horrors BrE used to say how bad something is – often used humorously when you think something is not really very bad

1 000, 2 000, 3 000, most frequent words in S poken and W ritten English

'horror ,movie *especially AmE* also **'horror ,film** *BrE* n [C] a film in which strange and frightening things happen

'horror ,story n [C] **1** *informal* a report about bad experiences, bad conditions etc: *horror stories about patients being given the wrong drugs* **2** a story in which strange and frightening things happen

'horror-,struck also **'horror-,stricken** adj suddenly very shocked and frightened

hors d'oeu·vre /ɔː 'dɜːv $,ɔːr 'dɜːrv/ *plural* **hors d'oeuvres** /-'dɜːvz $ -'dɜːrvz/ n [C] food that is served in small amounts before the main part of the meal; → **entrée, main course**

horse¹ S3 W1 /hɔːs $ hɔːrs/ n
1 [C] a large strong animal that people ride and use for pulling heavy things; → **pony, equine, equestrian**: *a horse and cart | Lee had never ridden a horse before.*
2 the horses *BrE informal* horse races: *Jim likes a bet on the horses.*
3 [C] a piece of sports equipment in a GYMNASIUM that people jump over
4 (straight/right) from the horse's mouth if you hear or get information straight from the horse's mouth, you are told it by someone who has direct knowledge of it
5 horses for courses *BrE* the process of matching people with suitable jobs or activities
6 a two/three/four etc horse race a competition or an election that only two etc competitors can win
7 a horse of a different color, a horse of another color *AmE* something that is completely different from another thing
8 horse sense *old-fashioned* sensible judgement gained from experience; ▣ **common sense**
9 [U] *old-fashioned informal* HEROIN → DARK HORSE; → **never/don't look a gift horse in the mouth** at GIFT (7); → **be flogging a dead horse** at FLOG (3); → **hold your horses** at HOLD¹ (15); → **put the cart before the horse** at CART¹ (4); → STALKING HORSE, WHITE HORSES

horse² v
horse around/about phr v informal to play roughly; → **horseplay**: *Stop horsing around – you'll break something!*

horse·back /'hɔːsbæk $ 'hɔːrs-/ n **on horseback** riding a horse —**horseback** adj [only before noun]

horse·box /'hɔːsbɒks $ 'hɔːrsbɑːks/ n [C] *BrE* a large vehicle for carrying horses, often pulled by another vehicle; ▣ **horse trailer** *AmE*

,horse 'chestnut / $ '. ,../ n [C] **1** a large tree which produces shiny brown nuts and has white or pink flowers **2** a nut from this tree; ▣ **conker**

'horse-drawn adj [only before noun] horse-drawn vehicles are pulled by a horse

horse·fly /'hɔːsflaɪ $ 'hɔːrs-/ n plural **horseflies** [C] a large fly that bites horses and cattle

horse·hair /'hɔːsheə $ 'hɔːrsher/ n [U] the hair from a horse's MANE and tail, sometimes used to fill the inside of furniture

horse·man /,hɔːsmən $ 'hɔːrs-/ n plural **horsemen** /-mən/ [C] someone who rides horses

horse·man·ship /'hɔːsmənʃɪp $ 'hɔːrs-/ n [U] the skill involved in riding horses

horse·play /'hɔːspleɪ $ 'hɔːrs-/ n [U] *old-fashioned* rough noisy play in which people push or hit each other for fun

horse·pow·er /'hɔːs,paʊə $ 'hɔːrs,paʊr/ n plural **horsepower** [C,U] written abbreviation **hp** a unit for measuring the power of an engine, or the power of an engine measured like this: *a two-hundred horsepower engine | the superior horsepower of Volkswagen*

'horse ,racing n [U] a sport in which horses with riders race against each other; → **flat racing, steeplechase, jockey**

horse·rad·ish /'hɔːs,rædɪʃ $ 'hɔːrs-/ n [C,U] a plant whose root has a very strong hot taste

'horse-riding n [U] *BrE* the activity of riding horses; ▣ **riding**

horse·shit /'hɔːʃ-ʃɪt $ 'hɔːrʃ-/ n [U] *AmE informal not polite* nonsense; ▣ **bullshit**

horse·shoe /'hɔːʃ-ʃuː, 'hɔːs- $ 'hɔːr-/ n [C] **1** a U-shaped piece of iron that is fixed onto the bottom of a horse's foot → see picture at MATERIAL **2** an object in the shape of a horseshoe that is a sign of good luck

'horse show n [C] a sports event in which people compete to show their skill in riding horses

'horse-,trading n [U] when the people, especially business people or politicians, who are involved in a discussion try hard to gain an advantage for their own side – used to show disapproval: *There will be no horse-trading and no electoral pacts.*

'horse ,trailer n [C] *AmE* a large vehicle for carrying horses, pulled by another vehicle; ▣ **horsebox** *BrE*

horse·wom·an /'hɔːs,wʊmən $ 'hɔːrs-/ n plural **horsewomen** /-,wɪmɪn/ [C] a woman who rides horses

hors·ey, horsy /'hɔːsi $ 'hɔːrsi/ adj **1** *informal* very interested in horses and riding **2 horsey face/smell etc** a face etc that is like a horse's

hor·ti·cul·ture /'hɔːtɨ,kʌltʃə $ 'hɔːrtɨ,kʌltʃər/ n [U] the practice or science of growing flowers, fruit and vegetables; → **gardening, agriculture** —**horticultural** /,hɔːtɨ'kʌltʃərəl◂ $,hɔːr-/ adj —**horticulturalist** n [C]

hose¹ /həʊz $ hoʊz/ n **1** [C] *BrE* a long rubber or plastic tube which can be moved and bent to put water onto fires, gardens etc; ▣ **hosepipe** *BrE* **2** [U] TIGHTS, STOCKINGS, or socks – used especially in shops; ▣ **hosiery**

hose² v [T] **1** to wash or pour water over something or someone, using a hose: **hose sth/sb down** *Would you hose down the car for me?* **2** *AmE informal* to cheat or deceive someone

hose·pipe /'həʊzpaɪp $ 'hoʊz-/ n [C] *BrE* a long hose

ho·sier·y /'həʊzjəri $ 'hoʊʒəri/ also **hose** n [U] a general word for TIGHTS, STOCKINGS, or socks, used in shops and in the clothing industry

hos·pice /'hɒspɨs $ 'hɑː-/ n [C] a special hospital for people who are dying

hos·pi·ta·ble /'hɒspɪtəbəl, hɒ'spɪ- $ hɑː'spɪ-, 'hɑːspɪ-/ adj **1** friendly, welcoming, and generous to visitors; ▣ **inhospitable**: *The local people were very kind and hospitable.* **2** used for describing an environment in which things can grow; ▣ **inhospitable**: *The Sahara is one of the world's least hospitable regions.* —**hospitably** adv

hos·pi·tal S2 W1 /'hɒspɪtl $ 'hɑː-/ n [C,U] a large building where sick or injured people receive medical treatment

in hospital *BrE*
in the hospital *AmE*
go to hospital *BrE*
go to the hospital *AmE*
come/be out of hospital *BrE*
come/be out of the hospital *AmE*
leave hospital *BrE*
leave the hospital *AmE*
be taken to hospital *BrE*
be taken to the hospital *AmE*
be rushed to hospital *BrE*
be rushed to the hospital *AmE*
be airlifted/flown to hospital *BrE* **be airlifted/flown to the hospital** *AmE* (=be taken to hospital in a plane)
be admitted to hospital *BrE* **be admitted to the hospital** *AmE* (=be brought into a hospital for treatment)
be discharged/released from hospital *BrE* **be discharged/released from the hospital** *AmE* (=be allowed to leave a hospital because you are better)
psychiatric hospital (=a hospital for people with mental illness)
maternity hospital (=a hospital where women have their babies)
hospital treatment/care
hospital stay (=the period that someone spends in hospital)

*He's **in hospital** recovering from an operation. | By the time she **went to the hospital**, the pain was really* *bad.* | *Your mother should be out of hospital within three days.* | *She was treated by paramedics at the scene before being rushed to hospital.* | *A man has been admitted to hospital with gunshot wounds.* | *He is likely to be discharged from the hospital later today.* | *a top-security psychiatric hospital* | *More than 20 officers needed hospital treatment.* | *surgical techniques which avoid the need for a hospital stay* → see picture at TOWN

WORD FOCUS: HOSPITAL

types of hospital: **medical center** *AmE* (a big hospital) | **maternity hospital** (for women who are having a baby) | **mental hospital/psychiatric hospital** (for people who are mentally ill) | **clinic** (for people receiving a particular kind of treatment) | **hospice** (for people who are dying) | **nursing home** (for old people)

parts of a hospital: **A&E** *also* **casualty** *BrE*, **emergency room** *AmE*, **operating theatre** *BrE*/**operating room** *AmE*, **ward**, **unit**

people in a hospital: **doctor**, **nurse**, **surgeon**, **patient**, **orderly**

---

hos·pi·tal·i·ty /ˌhɒspɔˈtælᵻti $ ˌhɑː-/ n [U] **1** friendly behaviour towards visitors: *Thanks for your hospitality over the past few weeks.* **2** services such as food and drink that an organization provides for guests at a special event: *the use of a yacht for corporate hospitality* | *There was a reception in the hospitality suite before the game.* → corporate hospitality at CORPORATE (1)

hos·pi·tal·ize *also* **-ise** *BrE* /ˈhɒspɪtl-aɪz $ ˈhɑː-/ v [T usually passive] if someone is hospitalized, they are taken into a hospital for treatment —**hospitalization** /ˌhɒspɪtl-aɪˈzeɪʃən $ ˌhɑːspɪtl-əˈzeɪ-/ n [U]

host¹ W3 /həʊst $ hoʊst/ n [C]
1 AT A PARTY someone at a party, meal etc who has invited the guests and who provides the food, drink etc; → **hostess**: *Our host greeted us at the door.*
2 ON TELEVISION/RADIO someone who introduces and talks to the guests on a television or radio programme; ▤ **compère** *BrE*: *a game show host*
3 COUNTRY/CITY a country, city, or organization that provides the necessary space, equipment etc for a special event: *host country/government/city etc the host city for the next Olympic Games* | **play host (to sth)** (=provide the place, food etc for a special meeting or event) *The gallery is playing host to an exhibition of sculpture.*
4 a (whole) host of people/things a large number of people or things: *A host of showbusiness celebrities have pledged their support.*
5 IN CHURCH the Host *technical* the bread that is used in the Christian ceremony of Communion
6 ANIMAL/PLANT *technical* an animal or plant on which a smaller animal or plant is living as a PARASITE

host² v [T] **1** to provide the place and everything that is needed for an organized event: *Which country is going to host the next World Cup?* **2** to introduce a radio or television programme: *Next week's show will be hosted by Sarah Cox.*

hos·tage /ˈhɒstɪdʒ $ ˈhɑː-/ n [C] **1** someone who is kept as a prisoner by an enemy so that the other side will do what the enemy demands; → **kidnap**: *The group are holding two western tourists hostage* (=keeping them as hostages). | *a family taken hostage at gunpoint yesterday* **2 be (a) hostage to sth** to be influenced and controlled by something, so that you are not free to do what you want: *Our country must not be held hostage to our past.* **3 a hostage to fortune** something that you have promised to do which may cause you problems in the future

hos·tel /ˈhɒstl $ ˈhɑː-/ n [C] **1** a place where people can stay and eat fairly cheaply **2** a YOUTH HOSTEL **3** a place where people who have no homes can stay

hos·tel·ry /ˈhɒstəlri $ ˈhɑː-/ n plural **hostelries** [C] *old use* a PUB or hotel

host·ess /ˈhəʊstᵻs $ ˈhoʊ-/ n [C] **1** a woman at a party, meal etc who has invited all the guests and provides them with food, drink etc; → **host 2** a woman who introduces and talks to the guests on a television or radio show; → **host 3** a woman who shows people to seats in a restaurant in the US **4** a woman whose job is to entertain men at a NIGHTCLUB

hos·tile /ˈhɒstaɪl $ ˈhɑːstl, ˈhɑːstaɪl/ adj **1** angry and deliberately unfriendly towards someone and ready to argue with them: *Southampton fans gave their former coach a hostile reception.* | *Carr wouldn't meet Feng's stare, which was openly hostile.* | *his hostile attitude* | [+to/towards] *The boy feels hostile towards his father.* **2** opposing a plan or idea very strongly: [+to/towards] *Senator Lydon was hostile to our proposals.* **3** belonging to an enemy: *hostile territory* **4** used to describe conditions that are difficult to live in, or that make it difficult to achieve something: *hostile environment/climate/terrain etc a guide to surviving in even the most hostile terrain* | *Sales increased last year despite the hostile economic environment.* **5 hostile takeover/bid** a situation in which a company tries to buy another company which does not want to be bought

hos·til·i·ty /hɒˈstɪlᵻti $ hɑː-/ n **1** [U] when someone is unfriendly and full of anger towards another person: [+towards/between] *hostility towards foreigners* | [+toward] *AmE: hostility toward Jews* | **open/outright hostility** (=hostility that is clearly shown) *They eyed each other with open hostility* . **2** [U] strong or angry opposition to something: *The reform program was greeted with hostility by conservatives.* | [+to/towards] *There is a lot of public hostility to the tax.* | *Pictures of refugees aroused popular hostility* (=felt by a lot of people) *towards the war.* | [+toward] *AmE: Republican hostility toward slavery* **3 hostilities** [plural] *formal* fighting in a war: *a cessation of hostilities*

hos·tler /ˈɒslə $ ˈhɑːstlər, ˈɑːs-/ n [C] the usual American spelling of OSTLER

hot¹ S1 W2 /hɒt $ hɑːt/ adj comparative **hotter**, superlative **hottest**
1 HIGH TEMPERATURE a) something that is hot has a high temperature – used about weather, places, food, drink, or objects; ▤ **cold**: *a hot day in July* | *It's so hot in here. Can I open the window?* | *Be careful, the water's very hot.* | *The bar serves hot and cold food.* | *people who live in hot countries* (=where the weather is usually hot) | **boiling/broiling** *AmE* **scorching/baking/roasting hot** (=used about weather that is very hot) *a scorching hot week in August* | **stifling/sweltering/unbearably hot** (=used about weather that is very hot and uncomfortable) *The office gets unbearably hot in summer.* | **boiling/scalding/steaming hot** (=used about liquid that is extremely hot) *The coffee was scalding hot.* | **piping hot** (=used about food that is nice and hot) *Serve the soup piping hot.* | **red hot** (=used to describe an object or surface that is very hot) *The handle was red hot.* | **white hot** (=used to describe metal that is extremely hot) *He held the metal in the flame until it became white hot.* **b)** if you feel hot, your body feels hot in a way that is uncomfortable: *I was hot and tired after the journey.* | *The wine made her feel hot.* **c)** if clothes are hot, they make you feel too hot in a way that is uncomfortable: *This sweater's too hot to wear inside.*
2 SPICY food that tastes hot has a burning taste because it contains strong spices; ▤ **mild**: *a hot curry*
3 VERY POPULAR/FASHIONABLE *informal* something or someone that is hot is very popular or fashionable, and everyone wants to use them, see them, buy them etc: *one of the hottest young directors in Hollywood* | *Michael Owen is already one of soccer's hottest properties* (=actors or sports players who are very popular). | *The movie is going to be this summer's hot ticket* (=an event that is very popular or fashionable, and that everyone wants to go and see). | **be the hottest thing since (sliced bread)** (=used about someone or something that is very good and popular, so that everyone

H

wants them) *Her new book is supposed to be the hottest thing since Harry Potter.*
4 GOOD *informal* very good, especially in a way that is exciting: *a hot young guitar player* | *a hot piece of software* | *His new film is* **hot stuff** (=very good). | **be hot at doing sth** *She's pretty hot at swimming too.* | **not so hot/not very hot** *informal* (=not very good) *Some of the tracks on the record are great, but others are not so hot.* | **be hot shit** *AmE informal not polite* (=used about someone or something that people think is very good)
5 SEXY a) *informal* someone who is hot is very attractive sexually: *The girls all think he's* **hot stuff.** **b)** *informal* a film, book, photograph etc that is hot is sexually exciting: *his hot and steamy first novel* **c)** **a hot date** *informal* a meeting with someone who you feel very attracted to sexually: *She has a hot date with Michel.* **d) be hot on/for sb** *informal* to be sexually attracted to someone
6 DIFFICULT/DANGEROUS [not before noun] *informal* difficult or dangerous to deal with: *If* **things get too hot** (=a situation becomes too difficult or dangerous to deal with), *I can always leave.* | *Wilkinson found his opponent a little* **too hot to handle** (=too difficult to deal with or beat). | *The climate was too hot politically to make such radical changes.*
7 a **hot issue/topic** etc a subject that a lot of people are discussing, especially one that causes a lot of disagreement: *The affair was a hot topic of conversation.* | *one of the hottest issues facing medical science*
8 in the **hot seat** in an important position and responsible for making difficult decisions
9 in **hot water** if someone is in hot water, they are in trouble because they have done something wrong: *The finance minister found himself in hot water over his business interests.* | **land/get yourself in hot water** *She got herself in hot water with the authorities.*
10 ANGRY a) get hot under the collar *spoken* to become angry – used especially when people get angry in an unreasonable way about something that is not important: *I don't understand why people are getting so hot under the collar about it.* **b) have a hot temper** someone who has a hot temper becomes angry very easily → HOT-TEMPERED
11 hot and bothered *informal* upset and confused because you have too much to think about or because you are in a hurry: *People were struggling with bags and cases, looking hot and bothered.*
12 have/hold sth in your hot little hand *informal* used to emphasize that you have something: *You'll have the report in your hot little hands by Monday.*
13 RECENT/EXCITING NEWS hot news is about very recent events and therefore interesting or exciting: *Do you want to hear about all the latest* **hot gossip?**
14 be hot off the press if news or a newspaper is hot off the press, it has just recently been printed
15 CHASING SB/STH CLOSELY a) in **hot pursuit** following someone quickly and closely because you want to catch them: *The car sped away with the police in hot pursuit.* **b) hot on sb's trail/tail** close to and likely to catch someone you have been chasing: *The other car was hot on his tail.* **c) hot on sb's heels** following very close behind someone: *Mrs Bass's dog was already hot on his heels.*
16 come/follow hot on the heels of sth to happen or be done very soon after something else: *The news came hot on the heels of another plane crash.*
17 hot on the trail of sth very close to finding something: *journalists hot on the trail of a news story*
18 blow/go hot and cold to keep changing your mind about whether you like or want to do something: *She keeps blowing hot and cold about the wedding.*
19 go hot and cold to experience a strange feeling in which your body temperature suddenly changes, because you are very frightened, worried, or shocked
20 I don't feel **too hot/so hot/very hot** *spoken informal* I feel slightly ill: *I'm not feeling too hot today.*
21 be hot on sth *informal* **a)** to know a lot about

something: *He's pretty hot on aircraft.* **b)** *BrE* to be very strict about something; ▣ **tight:** *The company is very hot on security.*
22 be hot for sth *informal* to be ready for something and want it very much: *Europe is hot for a product like this.* | *He was hot for revenge.*
23 be hot to trot *informal* **a)** to be ready to do something or be involved with something **b)** to feel sexually excited and want to have sex with someone
24 hot competition if the competition between people or companies is hot, they are all trying very hard to win or succeed: *Competition for the best jobs is getting hotter all the time.*
25 hot favourite the person, team, horse etc that people think is most likely to win: *United are hot favourites to win the championship.*
26 hot tip a good piece of advice about the likely result of a race, business deal etc: *a hot tip on the stockmarket*
27 STOLEN GOODS *informal* goods that are hot have been stolen
28 MUSIC *informal* music that is hot has a strong exciting RHYTHM
29 more sth than you've had hot dinners *BrE spoken humorous* used to say that someone has had a lot of experience of something and has done it many times: *She's delivered more babies than you've had hot dinners.*
30 hot money money that is frequently moved from one country to another in order to make a profit → HOTLY, HOTS

hot² *v* **hotted, hotting**
hot up *phr v BrE informal* **1** if something hots up, there is more activity or excitement: *Things generally hot up a few days before the race.* **2 the pace hots up** used to say that the speed of something increases

ˌhot ˈair *n* [U] things that someone says which are intended to sound impressive, but do not really mean anything or are not true: *The theory was dismissed as a lot of hot air.*

hot-ˈair balˌloon *n* [C] a large BALLOON filled with hot air used for carrying people up into the sky → see picture at BALLOON

hot·bed /ˈhɒtbed $ ˈhɑːt-/ *n* **be a hotbed of sth** a place where a lot of a particular type of activity, especially bad or violent activity, happens: *the university was a hotbed of radical protest*

ˌhot-ˈblooded *adj* having very strong emotions such as anger or love, that are difficult to control; ▣ **passionate**

ˌhot ˈcake *BrE*; hot·cake *AmE* /ˈhɒtkeɪk $ ˈhɑːt-/ *n* [C] **1 be selling/going like hot cakes** if things are selling like hot cakes, they are very popular and people are buying a lot of them very quickly: *Copies of the book are selling like hot cakes.* **2** *AmE* a PANCAKE

ˌhot ˈchocolate *n* [C,U] a hot drink made with chocolate powder and milk or water

hotch·potch /ˈhɒtʃpɒtʃ $ ˈhɑːtʃpɑːtʃ/ *BrE*, **hodgepodge** *AmE n* [singular] *informal* a number of things mixed up without sensible order or arrangement

ˌhot-cross ˈbun *n* [C] a round sweet bread roll with a mark in the shape of a cross on top, that is traditionally eaten just before Easter

ˌhot ˈdesk *n* [C] *BrE* a desk which is used by different workers on different days, instead of by the same worker every day —**hot-desking** *n* [U]

ˈhot dish *n* [C,U] *AmE* hot food cooked and served in a deep covered dish

ˈhot dog¹ / $ ˈ../ *n* [C] a cooked SAUSAGE in a long piece of bread → see picture at FAST FOOD

ˈhot dog² *v* **hot dogged, hot dogging** [I] *AmE informal* to do dangerous and exciting tricks or movements in sports such as SKIING or SURFING

ho·tel [S2] [W1] /həʊˈtel $ hoʊ-/ *n* [C] a building where people pay to stay and eat meals: **stay at/in a hotel** *We'll be staying at the Hotel Ibis.* | *She watched TV in her* **hotel room** *and waited for him to call.* | **hotel bar/**

restaurant/lobby/foyer etc *The hotel bar was closed.* | **check into a hotel** also **book into a hotel** *BrE: They checked into a cheap hotel.* | **check out of a hotel** *You must check out of the hotel by 10 a.m.*

ho·tel·i·er /həʊˈteliei, -liə $ oʊtəlˈjei, hoʊ-/ n [C] someone who owns or manages a hotel

hot ˈflush *BrE*; **hot ˈflash** *AmE* /$ ˈ. ./ n [C] a sudden hot feeling, especially one which women have during their MENOPAUSE

hot·foot /ˌhɒtˈfʊt $ ˈhɑːtfʊt/ v **hotfoot it** *informal* to walk or run quickly: *I hotfooted it out of there as soon as possible.* —**hot-foot** adv: *Karl arrived hot-foot from the airport.*

hot·head /ˈhɒthed $ ˈhɑːt-/ n [C] someone who does things too quickly without thinking —**hotheaded** /ˌhɒtˈhed�‚d‚ $ ˌhɑːt-/ adj

hot·house /ˈhɒthaʊs $ ˈhɑːt-/ n [C] **1** a heated building, usually made of glass, where delicate plants can grow → GREENHOUSE **2** **hothouse atmosphere/environment etc** a situation or place where there is a lot of activity and ideas

ˈhot key n [C] one or more keys that you can press on a computer KEYBOARD to make the computer quickly do a particular set of actions

hot·line, ˈhot line /ˈhɒtlaɪn $ ˈhɑːt-/ n [C] a special telephone line for people to find out about or talk about something: *Call our crime hotline today.*

ˈhot link n [C] a HYPERLINK which allows you to move from one place in a computer document to another, or to a particular place in a different document, especially on the Internet

hot·ly /ˈhɒtli $ ˈhɑːtli/ adv **1** in an excited or angry way: **hotly debated/disputed/denied etc** *The rumor has been hotly denied.* **2** done with a lot of energy and effort: *one of the most **hotly contested** congressional elections* | *The man ran out of the store, **hotly pursued** (=chased closely) by security guards.*

ˈhot pants n [plural] very short tight women's SHORTS

hot·plate /ˈhɒtpleɪt $ ˈhɑːt-/ n [C] a metal surface, usually on a COOKER, that can be heated so that you can cook a pan of food on it

hot·pot /ˈhɒtpɒt $ ˈhɑːtpɑːt/ n [C,U] **1** *BrE* a mixture of meat, potatoes, and onions, cooked slowly together; → stew **2** *AmE* a piece of electrical equipment with a small container, used to boil water

hot po·ta·to n [C] a subject or problem that no one wants to deal with, because it is difficult and any decision might make people angry: *The issue has become a **political hot potato**.*

ˈhot rod n [C] *AmE informal* an old car that has been fitted with a powerful engine to make it go faster

hots /hɒts $ hɑːts/ n **have/get the hots for sb** *informal* to be sexually attracted to someone

hot·shot /ˈhɒtʃɒt $ ˈhɑːtʃɑːt/ n [C] *informal* someone who is very successful and confident: *a hotshot lawyer*

hot spot, hot·spot /ˈhɒtspɒt $ ˈhɑːtspɑːt/ n [C] **1** a place where there is a lot of heat or RADIATION: *Many microwaves heat unevenly, leading to hot spots in the milk.* | *Hot spots of radioactivity were found near the*

power station. **2** a place that is popular for entertainment or a particular activity: *They played regularly at legendary hot spots such as the UFO Club.* **3** a place where there is likely to be fighting or a particular problem: *The report identified eight pollution hot spots.* **4** a part of a computer image on the screen that you can CLICK on to make other pictures, words etc appear **5** *especially AmE* a place where a fire can spread from

ˌhot ˈspring n [C] a place where hot water comes up naturally from the ground

hot-ˈtempered adj having a tendency to become angry easily: *a hot-tempered young man* → **hot temper** at HOT¹ (10b)

hot ˈtie /ˈhɒti $ ˈhɑːti/ n [C] *informal* someone who is very sexually attractive

ˌhot ˈtub n [C] a heated bath that several people can sit in together; → **jacuzzi** → JACUZZI

hot-ˈwater ˌbottle n [C] a rubber container full of hot water, used to make a bed warm → see picture at BOTTLE

ˈhot-wire v [T] *informal* to start the engine of a vehicle using the wires of the IGNITION system, instead of a key

hou·mous, houmus /ˈhuːməs, ˈhʊ-/ n [U] other spellings of HUMMUS

hound¹ /haʊnd/ n [C] **1** a dog which is fast and has a good sense of smell, used for hunting **2** *informal* a dog

hound² v [T] **1** to keep following someone and asking them questions in an annoying or threatening way; → **harass**: *After the court case Lee was hounded relentlessly by the press.* **2** **hound sb out (of/from sth)** to make things so unpleasant for someone that they are forced to leave a place, job etc; ◪ **drive out**: *The family were hounded out of their home by 18 months of abuse.*

hour S1 W1 /aʊə $ aʊr/ n [C]

1 60 MINUTES written abbreviation **hr** a unit for measuring time. There are 60 minutes in one hour, and 24 hours in one day.

> **for an hour/two hours/three hours etc**
> **in an hour/in an hour's time** (=when an hour has passed)
> **an hour/two hours etc later**
> **an hour/two hours etc ago/earlier**
> **within hours (of sth)** (=only a few hours after something)
> **half an hour** also
> **a half hour** *AmE*
> **(a) quarter of an hour**
> **three quarters of an hour**
> **an hour's work** (=work that it took you an hour to do)
> **an hour's walk/drive**
> **miles/kilometres per hour** (=used in speeds)
> **£10/$5.50 etc an hour** (=used to say how much someone is paid or how much you pay to use something)
> **pay/charge by the hour** (=pay or charge someone according to the number of hours it takes to do something)

> *The interview will last about two hours.* | *I study **for an hour** every night.* | *I'll be back **in three hours**.* | ***Three hours later** he was back.* | *Her bag was stolen **within hours** of her arrival.* | *You weren't interested in my story **a half hour** ago.* | *It takes about a **quarter of an hour** to walk into town.* | *[+of] After four hours of talks, an agreement was reached.* | *The hotel is only an **hour's drive** from the airport.* | *a top speed of 120 **miles an hour*** | *This was freelance work, **paid by the hour**.* | *a five- hour delay*

2 BUSINESS/WORK ETC **hours** [plural] a fixed period of time in the day when a particular activity, business etc happens: *hours of business 9.00–5.00* | **office/opening hours** *Please call during office hours.* | **working hours/hours of work** *the advantages of flexible working hours* | **visiting hours** (=the time when you can visit someone in hospital) | **after hours** (=after the time when a business, especially a bar, is supposed to close) **3** (work) **long/regular etc hours** if you work long, regular etc hours, the period that you work is longer than usual, always the same etc: *the long hours worked by hospital doctors* | *Many hospital staff have to work **unsocial hours*** (=work in the evenings so that you cannot spend time with family or friends). | **work all the hours God sends** (=work all the time that you can) **4** TIME OF DAY a particular period or point of time during the day or night: **in the early/small hours (of the morning)** (=between around midnight and two or three o'clock in the morning) *There was a knock on the door in the early hours of the morning.* | *Who can be calling **at this** late **hour**?* (=used when you are surprised or annoyed by how late at night or early in the morning something is) | **daylight/daytime hours** *The park is open during daylight hours.* | **the hours of darkness/daylight** *literary*: *Few people dared to venture out during the hours of darkness.* | **unearthly/ungodly hour** (=used when you are complaining about how early or late something is) *We had to get up at some ungodly hour to catch a plane.* | **at all hours/at any hour (of the day or night)** (=at any time) *If you have a problem, you know you can call at any hour of the day or night.* | *She's up studying **till all hours*** (=until unreasonably late at night). → **waking hours/life/day etc** at WAKING **5** LONG TIME [usually plural] *informal* a long time or a time that seems long: *We had to spend hours filling in forms.* | **for hours (on end)** *It'll keep the children amused for hours on end.* | *a really boring lecture that went on for hours and hours* | *She lay awake for **hour after hour*** (=for many hours, continuously). **6** O'CLOCK the time of the day when a new hour starts, for example one o'clock, two o'clock etc: **strike/chime the hour** (=if a clock strikes the hour, it rings, to show that it is one o'clock, seven o'clock etc) | **(every hour) on the hour** (=every hour at six o'clock, seven o'clock etc) *There are flights to Boston every hour on the hour.* | **10/20 etc minutes before/after the hour** *AmE* (=used on national radio or television in order to give the time without saying which hour it is, because the broadcast may be coming from a different time zone) *It's twelve minutes before the hour, and you're listening to the Morning Edition on NPR.* **7** 1300/1530/1805 etc hours used to give the time in official or military reports and orders: *The helicopters lifted off at 0600 hours.* **8** by the hour/from hour to hour if a situation is changing by the hour or from hour to hour, it is changing very quickly and very often: *This financial crisis is growing more serious by the hour.* **9** lunch/dinner hour the period in the middle of the day when people stop work for a meal: *I usually do the crossword in my lunch hour.* **10** IMPORTANT TIME [usually singular] an important moment or period in history or in your life: **sb's finest/greatest/darkest hour** *This was our country's finest hour.* | **sb's hour of need/glory etc** (=a time when someone needs help, is very successful etc) *Don't desert me in my hour of need.* **11** of the hour important at a particular time, especially the present time: *one of the burning questions of the hour* | **the hero/man of the hour** (=someone who does something very brave, is very successful etc at a particular time) → **the eleventh hour** at ELEVENTH[1] (2); → HOURLY, HAPPY HOUR, RUSH HOUR, ZERO HOUR

hour·glass /'aʊəglɑːs $ 'aʊrglæs/ *n* [C] **1** a glass container for measuring time in which sand moves slowly from the top half to the bottom in exactly one hour; → **egg-timer 2 hourglass figure** a woman who has an hourglass figure has a narrow waist in comparison with her chest and HIPS

'hour ,hand *n* [C] the shorter of the two pieces on a clock or watch that show you the time; → **minute hand**

hour·ly /'aʊəli $ 'aʊrli/ *adj* [only before noun] **1** happening or done every hour: *hourly news broadcasts* | *Buses run at hourly intervals.* **2 hourly pay/earnings/fees etc** the amount you earn or charge for every hour you work: *They are paid an hourly rate.* —**hourly** *adv*: *The database is updated hourly.*

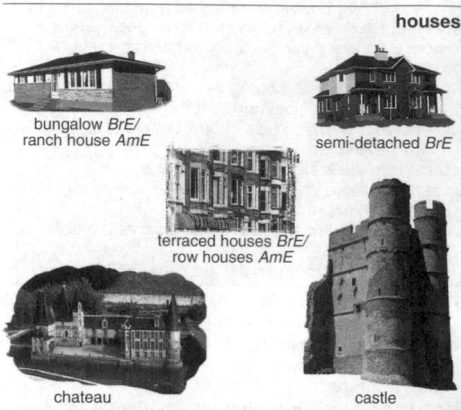

houses

bungalow *BrE*/ ranch house *AmE*

semi-detached *BrE*

terraced houses *BrE*/ row houses *AmE*

chateau

castle

house[1] S1 W1 /haʊs/ *plural* **houses** /'haʊzɪz/ *n* **1** WHERE SOMEONE LIVES [C] **a)** a building that someone lives in, especially one that has more than one level and is intended to be used by one family: *a four bedroom house* | **in a house** *every room in the house* | **at sb's house** *We met at Alison's house.* | *Why don't you all come over to our house for coffee?* | **move house** *BrE* (=leave your house and go to live in another one) **b)** the house all the people who live in a house; ▪ **household**: *He gets up at six and disturbs the whole house.* **2** BUILDING **a)** opera/court/movie etc house a large public building used for a particular purpose **b)** House *BrE* used in the names of large buildings, especially offices: *the BBC television studios at Broadcasting House* **c)** hen house/coach house/storehouse etc a building used for a particular purpose **3** GOVERNMENT [C] a group of people who make the laws of a country: *The President will address both houses of Congress.* | **the House of Commons/Lords/Representatives/Assembly** | *the speaker of the house* → LOWER HOUSE, UPPER HOUSE **4** COMPANY [C] a company, especially one involved in a particular area of business: *America's oldest **publishing house*** | *a small independent **software house*** | *an **auction house*** | *a famous Italian **fashion house*** **5** THEATRE [C] **a)** the part of a theatre, cinema etc where people sit; ▪ **backstage**: *The show has been playing to **full houses**.* | *The house was half empty.* | *The **house lights** went down and the music started.* **b)** the people who have come to watch a performance; ▪ **audience**: **full/packed/empty house** (=a large or small audience) *The show has been playing to packed houses since it opened.* | *A cheer went round the house* (=everyone cheered). **6** in house if you work in house, you work at the offices of a company or organization, not at home → IN-HOUSE **7** put/set/get your (own) house in order used to say that someone should improve the way they behave before criticizing other people **8** bring the house down to make a lot of people laugh, especially when you are acting in a theatre **9** be on the house if drinks or meals are on the house, you do not have to pay for them because they are provided free by the owner of the bar, restaurant etc **10** house wine also house red/white ordinary wine that is provided by a restaurant to be drunk with meals: *A glass of house red, please.* **11** get on/along like a house on fire *BrE informal* to quickly have a very friendly relationship **12** set up house to start to live in a house, especially with another person: *The two of them set up house in Brighton.*

13 keep house to regularly do all the cleaning, cooking etc in a house: *His daughter keeps house for him.*
14 SCHOOL [C] *BrE* in some schools, one of the groups that children of different ages are divided into to compete against each other, for example in sports competitions
15 ROYAL FAMILY [C] an important family, especially a royal family: *the House of Windsor*
16 MUSIC [U] HOUSE MUSIC
17 house of God/worship *literary* a church
18 this house *formal* used to mean the people who are voting in a formal DEBATE when you are stating the proposal that is being discussed → DOLL'S HOUSE; → **eat sb out of house and home** at EAT (10); → OPEN HOUSE, PUBLIC HOUSE; → **(as) safe as houses** at SAFE¹ (5)

WORD FOCUS: HOUSE
types of house: **terraced house** *BrE*/**row house** *AmE* one of several houses that are joined together |
detached house *BrE* a house that is not joined to another house | **semi-detached house** *BrE* a house that is attached to another house on one side | **cottage** a small house in the country | **bungalow** *BrE* a small house with one floor | **duplex** *AmE* a house that is divided into two separate homes | **apartment** *also* **flat** *BrE* a set of rooms where someone lives, which is part of a larger building | **condominium/condo** *AmE* an apartment in a large building, which is owned by the people who live there | **studio apartment/studio** *also* **bedsit** *BrE* an apartment with one main room and no separate bedroom
a very large house: **mansion, palace, country house** *BrE,* **stately home** *BrE*
someone who sells houses and land: **estate agent** *BrE,* **real estate agent** *AmE,* **realtor** *AmE*
someone who rents a house from another person: **tenant**
someone who owns a house and rents it to people: **landlord, landlady**
→ residence, property, dwelling, abode, lease, lessee

house² /haʊz/ *v* [T] **1** to provide someone with a place to live: [+in] *The refugees are being housed in temporary accommodation.* **2** if a building, place, or container houses something, it is kept there: [+in] *The collection is currently housed in the British Museum.* | *the plastic case which houses the batteries*

'**house ar,rest** *n* **be under house arrest** to be kept as a prisoner by a government, staying inside your house rather than in a prison
house·boat /'haʊsbəʊt $ -boʊt/ *n* [C] a river boat that you can live in
house·bound /'haʊsbaʊnd/ *adj* not able to leave your house, especially because you are ill or old
house·boy /'haʊsbɔɪ/ *n* [C] *old-fashioned not polite* a man who is employed to do general work at someone's house
house·break·er /'haʊs,breɪkə $ -ər/ *n* [C] a thief who enters someone else's house by breaking locks, windows etc; ▣ **burglar** —**housebreaking** *n* [U]
house·bro·ken /'haʊs,brəʊkən $ -,broʊ-/ *adj AmE* a pet animal that is housebroken has been trained not to make the house dirty with its URINE and FAECES; ▣ **house-trained** *BrE*
'**house call** *n* [C] a visit that someone, especially a doctor, makes to a person in that person's home as part of their job
house·coat /'haʊs-kəʊt $ -koʊt/ *n* [C] a long loose coat worn at home to protect clothes while cleaning etc
house·fly /'haʊsflaɪ/ *n plural* **houseflies** [C] a common type of fly that lives in people's houses
house·ful /'haʊsfʊl/ *n* **a houseful of sth** a large number of people or things in your house: *He grew up in the houseful of women.*
'**house ,guest** *n* [C] a friend or relative who is staying in your house for a short time
house·hold¹ S2 W2 /'haʊshəʊld $ -hoʊld/ *n* [C] all the people who live together in one house; ▣ **house:** *A*

791   **houseroom**

growing number of households have at least one computer. | *Families are classified by the occupation of* **the head of the household** (=the person who earns the most money and is most respected in a house).
household² *adj* [only before noun] **1** relating to looking after a house and the people in it; ▣ **domestic:** **household goods/products/items etc** *washing powder and other household products* | *household chores* **2 be a household name/word** to be very well known: *Coca Cola is a household name around the world.*
house·hold·er /'haʊs,həʊldə $ -,hoʊldər/ *n* [C] *formal* someone who owns or is in charge of a house
'**house ,husband** *n* [C] a husband who stays at home and does the cooking, cleaning etc; → **housewife**
house·keep·er /'haʊs,kiːpə $ -ər/ *n* [C] someone who is employed to manage the cleaning, cooking etc in a house or hotel ⚠ Do not confuse **housekeeper** and **housewife.** A housekeeper is someone who is paid by the owners of a house to do cooking and cleaning. A housewife is a woman who looks after her house rather than going out to work.
house·keep·ing /'haʊs,kiːpɪŋ/ *n* [U] **1** the work and organization of things that need to be done in a house, hotel etc, for example cooking and buying food: *the company in charge of the catering and housekeeping at the college* **2** *BrE* also **housekeeping money** an amount of money that is kept and used to pay for food and other things needed in the home **3** jobs that need to be done to keep a system working properly
house·maid /'haʊsmeɪd/ *n* [C] *old-fashioned* a female servant who cleans someone's house
house·man /'haʊsmən/ *n plural* **housemen** /-mən/ [C] *BrE* someone who has nearly finished training as a doctor and is working in a hospital; ▣ **intern** *AmE*
'**house ,martin** *n* [C] a small black and white European bird of the SWALLOW family
house·mas·ter /'haʊs,mɑːstə $ -,mæstər/ *n* [C] *especially BrE* a male teacher who is in charge of one of the houses (=groups of children of different ages) in a school; → **housemistress**
house·mate /'haʊsmeɪt/ *n* [C] *BrE* a person who you share a house with but who is not a member of your family; → **flatmate**; ▣ **roommate** *AmE*
house·mis·tress /'haʊs,mɪstrɪs/ *n* [C] *especially BrE* a female teacher who is in charge of one of the houses (=groups of children of different ages) in a school; → **housemaster**
'**house ,music** *also* **house** *n* [U] a type of popular dance music
,**house of 'cards** *n* [singular] a plan that is so badly arranged that it is likely to fail
,**House of 'Commons** *n* **the House of Commons** the part of the British or Canadian parliament whose members are elected by the people
,**House of 'Lords** *n* **the House of Lords** the part of the British parliament whose members are not elected but have positions because of their rank or title
,**House of Repre'sentatives** *n* **the House of Representatives** the larger of the two parts of the US Congress or of the parliament of Australia or New Zealand; → **Senate**
'**house ,party** *n* [C] a group of people who stay as guests in someone's house and have a party there
house·phone /'haʊsfəʊn $ -foʊn/ *n* [C] a telephone that can only be used to make calls within a building, especially a hotel
house·plant /'haʊsplɑːnt $ -plænt/ *n* [C] a plant that you grow inside your house for decoration; ▣ **pot plant** *BrE*
house·proud /'haʊspraʊd/ *adj BrE* spending a lot of time on keeping your house clean and tidy
house·room /'haʊsruːm, -rʊm/ *n* [U] *BrE* **1** space in a house for a person or thing **2 not give sth house-**

room *informal* used to emphasize that you do not like something and do not want it

Houses of 'Parliament *n* the Houses of Parliament the buildings where the British parliament meets, or the parliament itself; → House of Commons, House of Lords

'house-sit *v past tense and past participle* **house-sat**, *present participle* **house-sitting** [I] to look after someone's house while they are away —**housesitter** *n* [C]

house-to-'house *adj* house-to-house inquiries/ search/collection etc inquiries etc that are made by visiting each house in a particular area; → **door-to-door**: *The abduction sparked a house-to-house search in the Willenhall area.*

house·top /'haustɒp $ -tɑːp/ *n* [C] the top part of a house; ▤ **rooftop**: *a view over the housetops*

'house-trained *adj BrE* a pet animal that is housetrained has been trained not to make the house dirty with its URINE and FAECES; ▤ **housebroken** *AmE* —**housetrain** *v* [T]

house·wares /'hauswaɜz $ -werz/ *n* [plural] *AmE* small things used in the home, for example plates, lamps etc, or the department of a large shop that sells these things

'house-,warming *n* [C usually singular] a party that you give to celebrate moving into a new house: *Are you coming to Jo's house-warming on Friday?* | *a house-warming party*

house·wife /'hauswaɪf/ *n plural* **housewives** /-waɪvz/ [C] a married woman who works at home doing the cooking, cleaning etc, but does not have a job outside the house; ▤ **homemaker**; → **house husband**

house·work /'hauswɜːk $ -wɜːrk/ *n* [U] work that you do to take care of a house, for example washing, cleaning etc; → **chore**: **do (the) housework** *I spent all morning doing the housework.* | *I don't like doing housework.* ⚠ Do not say 'houseworks'. **Housework** is an uncountable noun.

hous·ing W2 /'hauzɪŋ/ *n*
1 [U] the houses or conditions that people live in: *health problems caused by bad housing* | *a scheme to provide affordable housing for local people*
2 [U] the work of providing houses for people to live in: *government housing policy* | *public services such as education, housing and transport*
3 [C] a protective cover for a machine: *the engine housing*

'housing associ,ation *n* [C] an organization in Britain, formed by a group of people working together to build or buy homes for themselves

'housing es,tate *BrE*; **'housing de,velopment** *AmE n* [C] a large number of houses that have been built together in a planned way; → **council house**

'housing ,project *n* [C] *AmE* a group of houses or apartments, usually built with government money, for poor families

hove /həuv $ houv/ [I] a past tense and past participle of HEAVE

hov·el /'hɒvəl $ 'hʌ-, 'hɑː-/ *n* [C] a small dirty place where someone lives, especially a very poor person

hov·er /'hɒvə $ 'hʌvər, 'hɑː-/ *v* [I] **1** if a bird, insect, or HELICOPTER hovers, it stays in one place in the air: [+over/above] *flies hovering above the surface of the water*; → see picture at MOVEMENT **2** to stay nervously in the same place, especially because you are waiting for something or are not certain what to do: *Her younger brother hovered in the background watching us.* | [+around/about] *I noticed several reporters hovering around outside the courtroom.* **3** [always + adv/prep] if a level, price etc hovers around a certain amount, it stays close to that amount, only changing slightly up or down: [+around/between etc] *The dollar has been hovering around the 110 yen level.*

hov·er·craft /'hɒvəkrɑːft $ 'hʌvərkræft, 'hɑː-/ *plural* **hovercraft** *or* **hovercrafts** *n* [C] a vehicle that travels just above the surface of land or water, travelling on a strong current of air that the engines produce beneath it; → **hydrofoil**

HOV lane /,eɪtʃ əu 'viː leɪn $ -ou-/ *n* [C] **high-occupancy vehicle lane** a LANE on main roads that can only be used by vehicles carrying three or more passengers when there is a lot of traffic

how S1 W1 /hau/ *adv, conjunction*
1 used to ask or talk about the way in which something happens or is done: *How do you spell your name?* | *How can I help you?* | *I'd like to help in some way, but I'm not sure how.* | *He explained how the system worked.* | *We both used to work at the airport – that's how we met.* | **how to do sth** *I don't know how to get to your house.* | *Alan showed me how to load the gun.* | *advice on how best* (=the best way) *to invest your money* | *They had a number of suggestions as to how the service could be improved.* | *This still leaves the question of how local services should be funded.* | **how on earth/in the world etc** (=used for emphasis when you are surprised, angry etc) *How on earth did you find out?*
2 used to ask or talk about the amount, size, degree etc of something: *How big is the state of Louisiana?* | *How many kids do they have now?* | *How long have you been learning English?* | *Do you know how old it is?* | *They couldn't tell exactly how far away the bridge was.* | *She wondered how much Angela already knew.* | **how much?** (=used to ask the price of something) *How much are the tickets?* | *Can you tell me how much the repairs will cost?*
3 *spoken* **a)** used to ask about someone's health, especially when you meet them: *'Hi Laurie, how are you?' 'Fine, thanks. How are you?'* | *Has Ros had the baby yet? How is she?* | *'How's your ankle this morning?' 'Better, thanks.'* **b)** used when you meet someone to ask for news about their life, work etc: *So how's it going at work these days? Still enjoying it?* | *'How are things with you?' 'Fine.'* | *How are you doing?*
4 used to ask someone about their opinion or experience of something: *How was the film?* | *'How's your steak?' 'Mmm, it's good.'* | *How did your exams go?* | *How do you feel about seeing Peter again?* | *How's that? Does that feel comfortable?*
5 used after certain adjectives or verbs to refer to an event or situation: *It's amazing how they've managed to get everything finished so quickly.* | *I remember how she always used to have fresh flowers in the house.*
6 [+ adj/adv] used to emphasize the quality you are mentioning: *How lovely to see you!* | *'John's been in an accident.' 'Oh, how awful!'* | *I didn't realize how difficult it was to get tickets.* | *He was impressed at how well she could read.*
7 *old-fashioned or written* used to say that something happens to a very great degree: *How the crowd loved it!*

SPOKEN PHRASES
8 how about...? **a)** used to make a suggestion about what to do; ▤ **what about**: *No, I'm busy on Monday. How about Tuesday at seven?* | **how about doing sth** *How about putting the sofa closer to the window?* | *How about we have that game when we get back?* | *How about if we tell the police where Newley is hiding?* | **how's about** *AmE*: *How's about going to the beach this afternoon?* **b)** used to ask about another person or thing: *'Mary and Ken are still away.' 'And how about Billy?'* | *I need a long cold drink. How about you?*
9 how do you mean? used to ask someone to explain something they have just said: *'What's your family situation?' 'How do you mean?' 'Are you married?'*
10 how come? *informal* used to ask why something has happened or why a particular situation exists, especially when you are surprised by it: *How come Dave's home? Isn't he feeling well?*
11 how do you do? *formal* used as a polite greeting when you meet someone for the first time
12 how can/could sb do sth? used when you are very surprised by something or disapprove strongly of

something: *William! How can you say such a thing?* | *How could anyone be so cruel?*

13 how you like/want *BrE informal* in whatever way you like or want: *Then you can arrange it how you like.*

14 how about that!/how do you like that! used when you think something is surprising, rude, impressive etc: *He scored two goals! How about that!*

15 how's that for sth? used to say that you think something is very impressive: *I've already arranged everything. How's that for efficiency?*

16 how ... is that? *informal* **a)** used to say that an action or event has a particular quality to a great degree: *He sent himself a card for Valentine's Day. How sad is that?* **b)** used to say that an action or event does not have a particular quality: *They say they're not going to leave, but how likely is that?*

17 how so? used to ask someone to explain an opinion they have given: *'Rick's parents are a little strange, I think.' 'How so?'*

18 how about if...? *informal* used to mention something that may happen, and ask what should be done if it does happen: *How about if we quit now?*

19 and how! *old-fashioned* used to say 'yes' strongly in reply to a question: *'Was Matt drunk?' 'And how!'*

→ **how dare you** at DARE¹ (2)

how·dah /ˈhaʊdə/ *n* [C] a covered seat used for riding an ELEPHANT

how·dy /ˈhaʊdi/ *interjection AmE informal* hello

how·ev·er¹ [S2] [W1] /haʊˈevə $ -ər/ *adv*
1 used when you are adding a fact or piece of information that seems surprising, or seems very different from what you have just said; ◻ **nevertheless**: *This is a cheap and simple process. However there are dangers.* | *an extremely unpleasant disease which is, however, easy to treat*
2 used to say that it does not matter how big, good, serious etc something is because it will not change a situation in any way; ◻ **no matter how**: *You should report any incident, however serious or minor it is.* | *We'll have to finish the job, however long it takes.* | **however much/many** *I really want the car, however much it costs.*
3 *especially BrE* used to show surprise when you ask how something happens or how someone does something: *However did he get that job?*

however² *conjunction* in whatever way: *You can do it however you like.* | *If we win the match we'll be delighted, however it happens.* | *However you look at it, it was a wicked thing to do.*

how·it·zer /ˈhaʊɪtsə $ -ər/ *n* [C] a heavy gun that fires SHELLS high into the air

howl¹ /haʊl/ *v* **1** [I] if a dog, WOLF, or other animal howls, it makes a long loud sound; → **bark**: *The dogs howled all night.* **2** [I] to make a long loud cry because you are unhappy, angry, or in pain, or because you are amused or excited: *Upstairs, one of the twins began to howl* (=cry). | [+in/with] *Somewhere, someone was howling in pain.* | *He makes audiences* **howl with laughter.** **3** [I,T] to shout or demand something angrily: [+for] *Republicans have been howling for military intervention.* **4** [I] if the wind howls, it makes a loud high sound as it blows: *wind howling in the trees*

howl sb/sth ⇔ down *phr v* to prevent someone or something from being heard by shouting loudly and angrily; ◻ **shout down**

howl² *n* [C] **1** a long loud sound made by a dog, WOLF, or other animal; → **bark** **2** a loud cry or shout showing pain, anger, happiness: [+of] *He let out a howl of anguish.* | *There were howls of protest.* | *This suggestion was greeted with* **howls of laughter.** **3** a loud high sound made by the wind blowing

howl·er /ˈhaʊlə $ -ər/ *n* [C] *informal* a stupid mistake that makes people laugh; ◻ **blunder**

howl·ing /ˈhaʊlɪŋ/ *adj* [only before noun] **be a howling success** something that is a howling success is extremely successful

hp /ˌeɪtʃ ˈpiː/ the abbreviation of *horsepower*

HP /ˌeɪtʃ ˈpiː/ *n* [U] *BrE* the abbreviation of *hire purchase*: *We bought the carpets on HP.*

HQ /ˌeɪtʃ ˈkjuː/ *n* [U] the abbreviation of *headquarters*

hr *BrE*; **hr.** *AmE plural* **hrs** the written abbreviation of *hour* or hours

HRH the written abbreviation of *His/Her Royal Highness*

HRT /ˌeɪtʃ ɑː ˈtiː $ -ɑːr-/ *n* [U] *hormone replacement therapy* treatment for women during and after the MENOPAUSE, in which they are given HORMONES to replace those which are lacking

ht. also **ht** *BrE* the written abbreviation of *height*

HTML /ˌeɪtʃ tiː em ˈel/ *n* [U] *technical hypertext markup language* a computer language used for producing pages of writing and pictures that can be put on the Internet: *HTML documents*

http /ˌeɪtʃ tiː tiː ˈpiː/ *technical hypertext transfer protocol* a set of standards that control how computer documents that are written in HTML connect to each other

H₂O /ˌeɪtʃ tuː ˈəʊ $ -oʊ/ *n* [U] the chemical sign for water

hub /hʌb/ *n* [C] **1** the central and most important part of an area, system, activity etc, which all the other parts are connected to; ◻ **centre**: [+of] *Birmingham is at the hub of Britain's motorway network.* | *the commercial hub of the region* **2** the central part of a wheel to which the AXLE is joined → see picture at BICYCLE

hub·bub /ˈhʌbʌb/ *n* [singular, U] **1** a mixture of loud noises, especially the noise of a lot of people talking at the same time **2** a situation in which there is a lot of activity, excitement, or argument; → **commotion**

hub·by /ˈhʌbi/ *n plural* **hubbies** [C] *informal* husband

hub·cap /ˈhʌbkæp/ *n* [C] a round metal cover for the centre of a wheel on a vehicle

hu·bris /ˈhjuːbrɪs/ *n* [U] *literary* too much pride

huck·le·ber·ry /ˈhʌkəlbəri $ -beri/ *n plural* **huckleberries** a small dark-blue North American fruit that grows on a bush

huck·ster /ˈhʌkstə $ -ər/ *n* [C] *AmE* someone who tries to sell things in a way that is too forceful and not honest – used to show disapproval —**hucksterism** *n* [U]

hud·dle¹ /ˈhʌdl/ *v* **1** [I,T] also **huddle together/up** if a group of people huddle together, they stay very close to each other, especially because they are cold or frightened: *We lay huddled together for warmth.* | [+around] *People huddled around the radio, waiting for news.* **2** [I always + adv/prep] to lie or sit with your arms and legs close to your body because you are cold or frightened: *She huddled under the blankets.* | *The snow blew against his huddled body.* **3** [I] *AmE* to sit or stand with a small group of people in order to discuss something privately: *The executive board huddled to discuss the issue.* **4** [I] if American football players huddle, they gather around one player who tells them the plan for the next part of the game

huddle² *n* [C] **1** a group of people or things that are close together, but not arranged in any particular order, pattern, or system: [+of] *a huddle of straw huts* | *Huddles of men stood around talking.* **2** a group of players in American football who gather around one player who tells them the plan for the next part of the game **3** **get/go into a huddle** to form a small group away from other people in order to discuss something

hue /hjuː/ *n* [C] *literary* **1** a colour or type of colour; → **tint, shade**: *a golden hue* **2** a type of opinion, belief etc: **of every hue/of all hues** (=of many kinds) *political opinions of every hue*

hue and cry *n* [singular] *written* angry protests about something, usually from a group of people

huff¹ /hʌf/ *v informal* **1** **huff and puff a)** to breathe out in a noisy way, especially when you do something that

---

H

involves a lot of physical effort: *He was huffing and puffing by the time he got to the top.* **b)** to show clearly that you strongly disagree with or are annoyed about something: *After a lot of huffing and puffing, he eventually gave in to our request.* **2** [T] to say something in a way that shows you are annoyed, often because someone has offended you: *'I haven't got time for that now,' huffed Sam irritably.*

huff² *n* **in a huff** feeling angry or bad-tempered, especially because someone has offended you: **go off/walk off/leave etc in a huff** *She stormed out in a huff.*

huff·y /ˈhʌfi/ *adj informal* in a bad MOOD (=the way that you feel), especially because someone has offended you: *Some customers get huffy when you ask them for their ID.* —**huffily** *adv*

hug¹ /hʌɡ/ *v* **hugged, hugging** [T] **1** to put your arms around someone and hold them tightly to show love or friendship; ▤ **embrace**: *We stood there crying and hugging each other.* | *She went to her daughter and hugged her tightly.* **2** to put your arms around yourself: **hug your knees/arms/legs etc** *Sarah sat on the floor, hugging her knees.* | **hug yourself** *She stood close to the wall, hugging herself against the cold.* **3** to move along the side, edge, top etc of something, staying very close to it: *The small boats hugged the coast.* **4** if clothes hug your body, they fit closely; → **close-fitting**: **body-/figure-hugging** *a figure-hugging dress* **5** to hold something in your arms close to your chest: *He was hugging a big pile of books.* **6 hug yourself with joy/delight etc** *BrE* to feel very pleased with yourself: *Kate hugged herself with pleasure after receiving the award.*

hug² *n* [C] the action of putting your arms around someone and holding them tightly to show love or friendship: *Paul gave me a big hug.* | *Nesta greeted the visitors with hugs and kisses.* → BEAR HUG

huge |S2| |W2| /hjuːdʒ/ *adj*
1 extremely large in size, amount, or degree; ▤ **enormous**: *a huge dog* | *huge crowds* | *Your room's huge compared to mine.* | *These shoes make my feet look huge.* | **a huge amount/sum/quantity etc** *huge sums of money* | *the huge scale of the problem* | **a huge loss/profit/increase etc** *a huge increase in cost* | **a huge range/variety/selection etc** *a huge range of issues* | **a huge success/disappointment etc** *The play was a huge success.* | **a huge difference/gap etc** *The new system has made a huge difference.*
2 *informal* very popular or famous: *David Hasselhoff is huge in Germany.* —**hugely** *adv*: *hugely successful* —**hugeness** *n* [U]

huh /hʌh, hʌ/ *interjection* **1** used to show that you have not heard or understood a question: *'Carly, are you listening to me?' 'Huh?'* **2** *especially AmE* used at the end of a question, often to ask for agreement: *Not a bad little place, huh?* **3** used to show disagreement or surprise, or to show that you do not find something impressive: *'She looks nice.' 'Huh! Too much make-up, if you ask me.'*

hu·la /ˈhuːlə/ *n* [singular] a Polynesian dance done by women using gentle movements of the HIPS

'hula hoop *n* [C] a large plastic ring which you swing around your waist by moving your HIPS

hulk /hʌlk/ *n* [C] **1** a large heavy person or thing: *a hulk of a man* **2** the main part of an old ship, vehicle etc that has decayed or been destroyed

hulk·ing /ˈhʌlkɪŋ/ *adj* [only before noun] very big and often awkward: *Two hulking figures guarded the entrance of the club.*

hull¹ /hʌl/ *n* [C] **1** the main part of a ship that goes in the water: **wooden-hulled/steel-hulled etc** (=having a wood, steel etc hull) **2** the outer covering of seeds, rice, grain etc

hull² *v* [T] to take off the outer part of vegetables, rice, grain etc

hul·la·ba·loo /ˌhʌləbəˈluː, ˈhʌləbəluː/ *n* [singular] *informal* **1** excited talk, newspaper stories etc, especially when something surprising or shocking is happening; ▤ **fuss**: *There was a huge hullabaloo when the book was first published.* **2** a lot of noise, especially made by people shouting; ▤ **commotion**: *She looked up to see what all the hullabaloo was about.*

hul·lo /hʌˈləʊ $ -loʊ/ *interjection especially BrE* another spelling of HELLO

hum¹ /hʌm/ *v* **hummed, humming 1** [I,T] to sing a tune by making a continuous sound with your lips closed: **hum to yourself** *Tony was humming to himself as he drove along.* | *He began to hum a tune.* **2** [I] to make a low continuous sound: *Machines hummed on the factory floor.* **3** [I] if a place hums, it is full of activity – use this to show approval; → **busy**: *By nine o'clock, the restaurant was humming.* | [+with] *The streets were humming with life.* **4 hum and haw** *BrE* to take a long time deciding what to say or do; → **hesitate**: ▤ **hem and haw** *AmE*

hum² *n* [singular] **1** a low continuous sound: [+of] *the distant hum of traffic* **2 hum of excitement/approval etc** the sound of people talking because they are excited etc

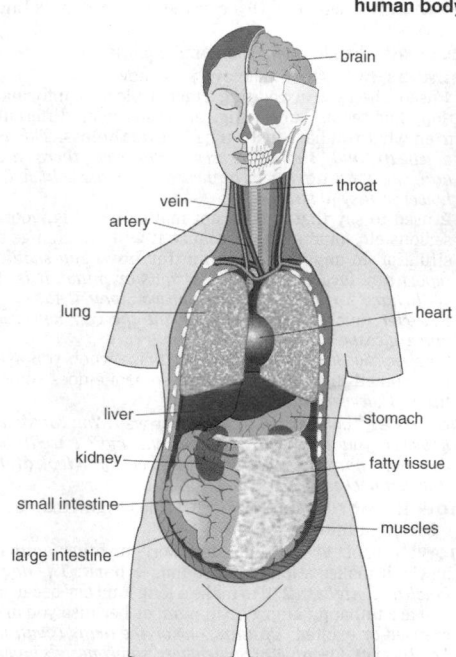

human body

brain
throat
vein
artery
lung
heart
liver
stomach
kidney
fatty tissue
small intestine
muscles
large intestine

hu·man¹ |W1| /ˈhjuːmən/ *adj*
1 belonging to or relating to people, especially as opposed to machines or animals

the human body
the human brain/mind
the human spirit
the human eye (=used especially when talking about how difficult something is to see)
human behaviour/activity/relationships
human experience
human life
human society
human error
for human consumption (=to be eaten by people)

*There are many different cell types in **the human body**. | the power of **the human mind** | The desire for joy lies deep within **the human spirit**. | Infra-red light is invisible to **the human eye**. | theories of **human behaviour** | different areas of **human experience** | respect for the absolute value of **human life** | The* *accident was the result of **human error**. | The meat was declared unfit **for human consumption**.*

2 human weaknesses, emotions etc are those which are typical of people: *He was also a person with very obvious human failings.*
3 sb is only human used to say that someone should not be blamed for what they have done
4 having the same feelings and emotions as ordinary people: *He's really not so bad. When you get to know him he seems quite human.*
5 a/the human touch someone, especially someone in authority, who has the human touch deals with people in a kind friendly way and is able to understand their feelings and problems: *The President has been accused of lacking the human touch.*
6 human interest a quality that makes a story interesting because it is about people's feelings, lives, relationships etc: *As a trainee reporter, she covered human interest stories.*
7 the human condition the experiences, emotions, needs etc that all people share, especially considered as a situation from which it is impossible to escape
8 human chain a line of people: *Firefighters formed a **human chain** to carry the brothers to safety.*
9 put a human face on sth also **give sth a human face** to make an important event or principle understandable to ordinary people by directing their attention to the way it affects a particular person: *Anne Frank was the girl whose diary put a human face on the Holocaust.*
10 capitalism/communism/socialism etc with a human face a capitalist etc economic and political system that does not ignore people's needs

human² W3 also **human 'being** *n* [C] a person

hu·mane /hjuːˈmeɪn/ *adj* treating people or animals in a way that is not cruel and causes them as little suffering as possible; ⏸ **inhumane**: *the campaign for the humane treatment of criminals | a better, more humane world* —**humanely** *adv*

hu·man·is·m /ˈhjuːmənɪzəm/ *n* [U] **1** the belief that human problems can by solved through science rather than religion **2 Humanism** the study during the Renaissance of the ideas of the ancient Greeks and Romans —**humanist** *n* [C] —**humanistic** /ˌhjuːməˈnɪstɪk‹/ *adj*

hu·man·i·tar·i·an /hjuːˌmænɪˈteəriən $ -ˈter-/ *adj* [only before noun] concerned with improving bad living conditions and preventing unfair treatment of people: **humanitarian aid/assistance/relief** *Humanitarian aid is being sent to the refugees.* | **humanitarian grounds/ reasons/purposes** *He was released from prison on humanitarian grounds.* —**humanitarian** *n* [C] —**humanitarianism** *n* [U]

hu·man·i·ty /hjuːˈmænɪti/ *n* **1** [U] people in general: *We want a clean healthy environment for all humanity. | crimes against humanity* **2** [U] kindness, respect, and sympathy towards others; ⏸ **inhumanity**: *a man of deep humanity* **3** [U] the state of being human rather than an animal or machine: **common/ shared humanity** *We must never forget our common humanity.* **4 (the) humanities** [plural] subjects of study such as literature, history, or art, rather than science or mathematics; ⏸ **(the) arts**

hu·man·ize also **-ise** *BrE* /ˈhjuːmənaɪz/ *v* [T] to make a place or system more pleasant or more suitable for people: *an attempt to humanize prison conditions*

hu·man·kind /ˌhjuːmənˈkaɪnd/ *n* [U] people in general; ⏸ **mankind**

hu·man·ly /ˈhjuːmənli/ *adv* **humanly possible a)** used to emphasize that something is possible: *She wanted to put as much distance as was humanly possible between herself and Adrian.* **b)** used to emphasize that someone did all they could: *The doctors did everything humanly possible to save the child's life.*

human 'nature *n* [U] **1** the qualities or ways of behaving that are natural and common to most

people **2 it's (only/just) human nature** *spoken* used to say that a particular feeling or way of behaving is normal and natural

hu·man·oid /ˈhjuːmənɔɪd/ *adj* having a human shape and qualities: *The robot was humanoid in appearance.* —**humanoid** *n* [C]

human 'race *n* **the human race** all people, considered together as a group; ⏸ **mankind**

human re'sources / $ ˌ.. '.../ *n* [U] **HR** the department in a company that deals with employing, training, and helping people

human 'right *n* [C usually plural] one of the basic rights which many societies think every person should have to be treated in a fair equal way without cruelty, for example by their government, or the right to vote: *human rights violations*

human 'shield *n* [C] someone who is taken and kept as a prisoner by a criminal in order to protect the criminal from being killed, injured, or caught

hum·ble¹ /ˈhʌmbəl/ *adj* **1** not considering yourself or your ideas to be as important as other people's; ⏸ **proud**; → **humility**: *a modest and humble man* **2** having a low social class or position: *He started his career as a humble peanut farmer. |* **humble background/origins** etc *Iacocca rose from humble beginnings to become boss of Ford.* **3 in my humble opinion** *spoken* used humorously to give your opinion about something **4 my humble apologies** *BrE spoken* used humorously to say you are sorry **5** [only before noun] simple and ordinary, but useful or effective: *The humble potato may be the key to feeding the world's population.* **6 eat humble pie** to admit that you were wrong about something **7 your humble servant** *BrE old use* a formal way of ending a letter **8 sb's humble abode** someone's house or apartment - used humorously: *Welcome to our humble abode.* —**humbly** *adv*

humble² *v* **1 be humbled** if you are humbled, you realize that you are not as important, good, kind etc as you thought you were: *You can't help but be humbled when you enter this cathedral.* **2** [T] to easily defeat someone who is much stronger than you are: *The mighty U.S. army was humbled by a small South East Asian country.* **3 humble yourself** to show that you are not too proud to ask for something, admit you are wrong etc: *I knew he had humbled himself to ask for my help.* —**humbling** *adj*: *a humbling experience*

hum·bug /ˈhʌmbʌg/ *n* **1** [U] insincere or dishonest words or behaviour: *He dismissed the Prime Minister's comments as 'pure humbug'.* **2** [C] *BrE* a hard sweet made from boiled sugar, usually with a PEPPERMINT taste **3** [C] *old-fashioned* someone who behaves in a dishonest or insincere way, for example by pretending to be someone they are not; ⏸ **imposter**

hum·ding·er /ˌhʌmˈdɪŋə $ -ər/ *n* **a humdinger** *informal* a very exciting or impressive game, performance, or event: *a real humdinger of a match*

hum·drum /ˈhʌmdrʌm/ *adj* boring and ordinary, and having no variety or interest; ⏸ **tedious**: **humdrum existence/job/life etc** *the prisoners' humdrum routine*

hu·me·rus /ˈhjuːmərəs/ *n plural* **humeri** /-raɪ/ [C] *technical* the bone between your shoulder and elbow

hu·mid /ˈhjuːmɪd/ *adj* if the weather is humid, you feel uncomfortable because the air is very wet and usually hot: *Tokyo is extremely humid in mid-summer. |* **humid air/climate/atmosphere etc** ⚠ **Humid, moist,** or **damp?** → see box at DAMP¹

hu·mid·i·fi·er /hjuːˈmɪdɪfaɪə $ -ər/ *n* [C] a machine that makes the air in a room less dry

hu·mid·i·fy /hjuːˈmɪdɪfaɪ/ *v* **humidified, humidifying, humidifies** [T] to add very small drops of water to the air in a room etc because the air is too dry

hu·mid·i·ty /hjuːˈmɪdɪti/ *n* [U] **1** the amount of water contained in the air: *The room is kept at 72* *degrees and 50% relative humidity.* **2** when the air is very warm and wet: *a day of hot sunshine and humidity*

hu·mil·i·ate /hjuːˈmɪlieɪt/ v [T] to make someone feel ashamed or stupid, especially when other people are present; ▣ **embarrass**: *Her boss humiliated her in front of all her colleagues.* —**humiliated** adj: *I've never felt so humiliated in all my life.*

hu·mil·i·at·ing /hjuːˈmɪlieɪtɪŋ/ adj making you feel ashamed, embarrassed, and angry because you have been made to look weak or stupid; ▣ **embarrassing**: *a humiliating defeat* —**humiliatingly** adv

hu·mil·i·a·tion /hjuːˌmɪliˈeɪʃən/ n **1** [U] a feeling of shame and great embarrassment, because you have been made to look stupid or weak: *the humiliation of having to ask her parents for money* **2** [C] a situation that makes you feel humiliated: *The government suffered a series of political humiliations.*

hu·mil·i·ty /hjuːˈmɪləti/ n [U] the quality of not being too proud about yourself – use this to show approval; ▣ **modesty**; → **humble**

humming bird n [C] a very small brightly-coloured tropical bird whose wings move very quickly

hum·mock /ˈhʌmək/ n [C] BrE a very small hill

hum·mus /ˈhuːməs, ˈhʊ-/ another spelling of HUMUS

hu·mon·gous also **humungous** BrE /hjuːˈmʌŋɡəs/ adj informal very big; ▣ **enormous**: *rich people living in humongous houses*

hu·mor·ist /ˈhjuːmərᵻst $ ˈhjuː-, ˈjuː-/ n [C] someone, especially a writer, who tells funny stories; → **comedian**

hu·mor·ous /ˈhjuːmərəs $ ˈhjuː-, ˈjuː-/ adj funny and enjoyable: *humorous stories* | *The film has some mildly humorous moments.* —**humorously** adv

hu·mour¹ BrE; **humor** AmE /ˈhjuːmə $ ˈhjuːmər, ˈjuː-/ n [U]
1 the ability or tendency to think that things are funny, or funny things you say that show you have this ability

> sense of humour
> sb's brand of humour
> **black humour** (=jokes, funny stories etc about the unpleasant parts of life)
> **schoolboy humour** (=jokes, funny stories etc that are silly and rude but not offensive)
> **dry/deadpan humour** (=when someone pretends to be serious when they are really joking)
> **wry humour** (=when someone jokes about something bad or difficult)
> **a flash/trace/touch of humour** (=a small amount of humour)

> *his humour and charm* | *Greg's feeble attempt at humour* | *English humour* | *It's vital to have a **sense of humor** in this job.* | *The host puts the contestants at ease with his own **brand of humour**.* | *He showed **flashes of humor** that delighted the audience.*

2 the quality in something that makes it funny and makes people laugh: *He failed to see the humour of the situation.*
3 in a good/an ill/a bad humour formal in a good or bad mood: *He was in a good humour this morning.* → **GOOD HUMOUR**
4 out of humour BrE old-fashioned in a bad mood

humour² BrE; **humor** AmE v [T] to do what someone wants or to pretend to agree with them so that they do not become upset: *'Of course,' he said, humouring her.*

hu·mour·less BrE; **humorless** AmE /ˈhjuːmələs $ ˈhjuːmər-, ˈjuː-/ adj too serious and not able to laugh at things that other people think are funny —**humourlessly** adv

hump¹ /hʌmp/ n **1** [C] a large round shape that rises above the surface of something: *the hump of a hill* **2 speed/traffic humps** BrE a series of humps in the road, designed to make traffic slow down **3** [C] A raised part on the back of a CAMEL **4** [C] a raised part on someone's back that is caused by an unusually

curved SPINE; → **hunchback 5 be over the hump** to have finished the most difficult part of something **6 give sb the hump/get the hump** BrE spoken to make someone feel angry or upset, or to feel angry or upset

hump² v informal **1** [T] BrE to carry something heavy from one place to another with difficulty; ▣ **heave**, **lug**; → **drag**: **hump sth down/along/across etc** *I managed to hump the suitcases upstairs.* **2** [I,T] not polite to have sex with someone

hump·back /ˈhʌmpbæk/ n [C] **1** a HUMPBACK WHALE **2** a HUNCHBACK

hump-backed 'bridge also **humpback 'bridge** n [C] BrE a short bridge with a steep slope on each side → see picture at BRIDGE

humpback 'whale also **humpback** n [C] a large WHALE

humph /hʌmf, hmh, hm/ interjection used to show that you do not believe something or do not approve of something

humus¹, hummus /ˈhuːməs, ˈhʊ-/ n [U] a Greek food made from a soft mixture of CHICKPEAS, oil, and GARLIC

hu·mus² /ˈhjuːməs/ n [U] soil made of decayed plants, leaves etc which is good for growing plants; → **compost**

hunch¹ /hʌntʃ/ n [C] if you have a hunch that something is true or will happen, you feel that it is true or will happen; → **suspicion**: **have a hunch (that)** *I had a hunch that something like this would happen.* | **sb's hunch** *My hunch is that she's his mother.*

hunch² v **1** [I always + adv/prep] to bend down and forwards so that your back forms a curve: [+over] *He had to hunch over the steering wheel to see anything.* **2 hunch your shoulders** to raise your shoulders into a rounded shape because you are cold, anxious etc —**hunched** adj: *a hunched figure sitting by the fire*

hunch·back /ˈhʌntʃbæk/ n [C] not polite an offensive word for someone who has a large raised part on their back because their SPINE curves in an unusual way

hun·dred /ˈhʌndrᵻd/ number, n plural **hundred** or **hundreds 1** the number 100: *The tree was probably a hundred years old.* | **two/three/four etc hundred** *I make nine hundred dollars a week.* | *a journey of 15 hundred miles* | **hundreds of people/years/pounds etc** *Hundreds of people were reported killed or wounded.* **2** a very large number of things or people: **a hundred** *They've had this argument a hundred times before.* | **hundreds of sth** *He's had hundreds of girlfriends.* **3 a/one hundred percent** spoken **a)** completely: *I'm not a hundred percent sure where she lives.* **b)** BrE completely well: *I'm still not really feeling a hundred per cent.* **4 give a hundred percent** also **give a hundred and ten percent** to do everything you can in order to achieve something: *Everyone on the team gave a hundred per cent.* **5** [C] a piece of paper money that is worth 100 dollars or 100 pounds: *Can you change a hundred for five twenties?* —**hundredth** adj: *her hundredth birthday* —**hundredth** n [C]

hun·dred·weight /ˈhʌndrᵻdweɪt/ n plural **hundredweight** [C] written abbreviation **cwt** a unit for measuring weight, equal to 112 pounds or 50.8 kilograms in Britain, and 100 pounds or 45.3 kilograms in the US

hung /hʌŋ/ past tense and past participle of HANG

hun·ger¹ /ˈhʌŋɡə $ -ər/ n **1** [U] lack of food, especially for a long period of time, that can cause illness or death; ▣ **starvation**: **die of/from hunger** *Thousands of people are dying from hunger every day.* **2** [U] the feeling that you need to eat; → **thirst**: *Try to satisfy your hunger by eating some fruit.* | **hunger pangs** (=sudden feelings of being hungry) **3** [singular, U] a strong need or desire for something: [+for] *her hunger for knowledge* | *a hunger for success*

hunger² v

hunger for/after sth phr v literary to want something very much: *The nation was hungering for change.*

'**hunger strike** n [C,U] a situation in which someone refuses to eat for a long time in order to protest about something: *300 students occupied the building and over 50 went on hunger strike.* —**hunger striker** n [C]

,**hung** '**jury** n [singular] a JURY (1) that cannot agree whether someone is guilty of a crime

hung·o·ver /hʌŋ'əʊvə $ -'oʊvər/ adj if someone is hungover, they feel ill because they drank too much alcohol the previous evening → HANGOVER

,**hung** '**parliament** n [C] BrE a parliament in which no political party has more elected representatives than the others added together

hun·gri·ly /'hʌŋgrɪli/ adv **1** in a way that shows you want to eat something very much; → **greedily**: *She hungrily ate a slice of bread.* **2** literary in a way that shows you want something very much: *He hungrily kissed her mouth.*

hun·gry S3 /'hʌŋgri/ adj comparative **hungrier**, superlative **hungriest**
1 wanting to eat something; → **thirsty**: *I was cold, tired and hungry.* | *If you get hungry, there's some cold chicken in the fridge.* | *Do you still feel hungry?*
2 ill or weak as a result of not having enough to eat for a long time: *We can't justify wasting food when half the world is hungry.*
3 go hungry to not have enough to eat: *Thousands of families go hungry every day .*
4 wanting or needing something very much; ◘ **eager**: [+for] *She is hungry for success.* | **hungry to do sth** *Stan was hungry to learn.*
5 the hungry people who do not have enough food to eat
6 power-hungry/news-hungry etc wanting power, news etc very much: *a power-hungry politician*

,**hung-'up** be hung-up about/on sth informal to be thinking or worrying too much about someone or something → HANG-UP

hunk /hʌŋk/ n [C] **1** a thick piece of something, especially food, that has been taken from a bigger piece: [+of] *a hunk of bread* **2** informal a sexually attractive man with a big strong body

hun·ker /'hʌŋkə $ -ər/ v
hunker down phr v AmE **1** to bend your knees so that you are sitting on your heels very close to the ground; ◘ **squat** **2** to make yourself comfortable in a safe place, especially for a long time **3** informal to prepare yourself for a difficult situation

hunk·y /'hʌŋki/ adj a man who is hunky is sexually attractive and has a big strong body; → **macho**

hun·ky-dor·y /,hʌŋki 'dɔːri/ adj [not before noun] informal if a situation is hunky-dory, everyone feels happy and there are no problems; ◘ **OK**

hunt¹ /hʌnt/ v **1** [I,T] to chase animals and birds in order to kill or catch them: *the slopes where I hunted deer as a kid* | *Wolves tend to hunt in packs* (=hunt in groups). **2** [I] to look for someone or something very carefully; ◘ **search**: [+for] *The kids were hunting for shells on the beach.* | *Detectives are busy hunting for clues.* **3** [I,T] to search for and try to catch a criminal or someone who is your enemy: *The police are still hunting the killer.* | [+for] *The FBI were called in to hunt for the spy.* **4** [I,T] BrE to hunt FOXES as a sport, riding on horses and using dogs
hunt sb/sth ⇔ down phr v to search for a person or animal until you catch them, especially in order to punish or kill them: *The government agency was created to hunt down war criminals.*
hunt sb/sth ⇔ out phr v **1** to search for someone or something in order to catch, kill, or destroy them: *The plane was on a mission to hunt out enemy submarines.* **2** to search for and find something that you need or want, but which is difficult to find: *In the school library he hunted out books on politics.*

hunt² n [C] **1** an occasion when people chase animals in order to kill or catch them: **lion/rhino/stag etc hunt** **2** [usually singular] a search for someone or something that is difficult to find: [+for] *the hunt for the missing child* | **the hunt is on** (=used to say that people

have started looking for someone or something) | **murder hunt** (=a search for a person who has killed someone) | **have a hunt around for sth** BrE informal (=look for something) *I'll have a hunt around for it in my desk.* → TREASURE HUNT, WITCH-HUNT **3** a sporting event in Britain in which people ride on horses and hunt FOXES using dogs **4** in Britain, a group of people who regularly hunt FOXES together

hunt·er /'hʌntə $ -ər/ n **1** [C] a person who hunts wild animals, or an animal that hunts other animals for food **2 souvenir/autograph/bargain etc hunter** someone who looks for or collects a particular type of thing → BOUNTY HUNTER

,**hunter-'gatherer** n [C] a member of group of people that lives by hunting and looking for plants that can be eaten, rather than by keeping animals for food or by growing crops

hunt·ing /'hʌntɪŋ/ n [U] **1** chasing and killing animals for food or sport **2** in Britain, the sport of hunting FOXES; ◘ **foxhunting** **3 job-hunting/house-hunting/flat-hunting** the activity of looking for a job, house, or flat **4 go hunting** to hunt for animals, especially as a sport —**hunting** adj: *a hunting rifle*

'**hunting ,ground** n [C] **1** a place where animals are hunted **2 a happy/good hunting ground (for sth)** a place where people who are interested in a particular thing can easily find what they want: *Madeira used to be a happy hunting ground for antique collectors.*

hunt·ress /'hʌntrɪs/ n [C] literary a female hunter

,**hunt sabo'teur** n [C] BrE member of a group that tries to stop people from hunting FOXES

hunts·man /'hʌntsmən/ n plural **huntsmen** /-mən/ [C] literary **1** a man who hunts animals **2** BrE someone who hunts FOXES for sport

hur·dle¹ /'hɜːdl $ 'hɜːr-/ n **1** [C] a problem or difficulty that you must deal with before you can achieve something; ◘ **obstacle**: *Finding enough money for the project was the first hurdle.* | **overcome/clear/get over etc a hurdle** (=deal successfully with a problem) **2** [C] one of a series of small fences that a person or horse has to jump over during a race: **clear a hurdle** (=successfully jump over a hurdle) **3 the 100 metres/400 metres hurdles** a race in which the runners have to jump over hurdles

hurdle² v **1** [I,T] to jump over something while you are running: *He hurdled the fence and ran off down the street.* **2** [I] to run in hurdle races —**hurdler** n [C] —**hurdling** n [U]

hur·dy-gur·dy /'hɜːdi ,ɡɜːdi $,hɜːrdi 'ɡɜːrdi/ n plural **hurdy-gurdies** [C] a small musical instrument that you play by turning a handle; → **barrel organ**

hurl /hɜːl $ hɜːrl/ v **1** [T always + adv/prep] to throw something with a lot of force, especially because you are angry: *Demonstrators were hurling bricks through the windows.* | *He hurled a chair across the set, smashing lamps and vases.* **2 hurl abuse/insults/accusations etc (at sb)** to shout at someone in a loud and angry way: *He was accused of hurling abuse at the referee.* **3 hurl yourself at/against etc sb/sth** also **hurl yourself down** to throw yourself at someone or something with a lot of force: *She wanted to hurl herself into his arms.* **4** [I,T] AmE informal to VOMIT

hurl·ing /'hɜːlɪŋ $ 'hɜːr-/ n [U] an Irish ball game played with sticks by two teams of 15 players —**hurler** n [C]

hur·ly-bur·ly /'hɜːli ,bɜːli $,hɜːrli 'bɜːrli/ n [U] a lot of busy noisy activity: *the hurly-burly of city life*

hur·ray /hʊ'reɪ/, also **hur·rah** /hʊ'rɑː/ interjection HOORAY → **hip, hip, hurray!** at HIP³

hur·ri·cane /'hʌrɪkən $ 'hɜːrɪkeɪn/ n [C] a storm that has very strong fast winds and that moves over water; → **cyclone, typhoon, tornado**

1 000, 2 000, 3 000, most frequent words in S poken and W ritten English

hyped 'up *adj informal* very excited or nervous and unable to keep still: *Wayne was so hyped up that we thought he was drunk.*

hy·per /'haɪpə $ -ər/ *adj informal* extremely excited or nervous about something: *No, don't give Luke any candy – it'll make him hyper.*

hyper- /haɪpə $ -pər/ *prefix* **1** more than usual, especially too much: *hypersensitive* (=too sensitive) | *hyper-inflation* | *a hyper-extended knee* **2** beyond the usual size or limits: *a hyperlink* (=from one website to another)

hy·per·ac·tive /ˌhaɪpərˈæktɪv◂/ *adj* someone, especially a child, who is hyperactive is too active, and is not able to keep still or be quiet for very long; → **attention deficit disorder** —**hyperactivity** /ˌhaɪpəræk'tɪvₔti/ *n* [U]

hy·per·bo·le /haɪ'pɜːbəli $ -ɜːr-/ *n* [C,U] a way of describing something by saying it is much bigger, smaller, worse etc than it actually is; ◼ **exaggeration**: *It was not hyperbole to call it the worst storm in twenty years.* —**hyperbolic** /ˌhaɪpə'bɒlɪk◂ $ -pər'bɑː-/ *adj*

hy·per·crit·i·cal /ˌhaɪpə'krɪtɪkəl◂ $ -pər-/ *adj* too eager to criticize other people and things, especially about small details —**hypercritically** /-kli/ *adv*

hy·per·in·fla·tion /ˌhaɪpərɪn'fleɪʃən/ *n* [U] a very fast rise in prices that seriously damages a country's ECONOMY

hy·per·link /'haɪpəlɪŋk $ -pər-/ *n* [C] a word or picture in a WEBSITE or computer document that will take you to another page or document if you CLICK on it: *We should encourage hyperlinks to each other's webpages.*

hy·per·mar·ket /'haɪpəˌmɑːkₔt $ -pərˌmɑːr-/ *n* [C] *BrE* a very large SUPERMARKET

hy·per·sen·si·tive /ˌhaɪpə'sensₔtɪv◂ $ -pər-/ *adj* **1** if someone is hypersensitive to a drug, substance etc, their body reacts very badly to it; ◼ **allergic**: [+to] *I discovered I was hypersensitive to caffeine.* **2** very easily offended or upset: [+to] *She's hypersensitive to any form of criticism.* —**hypersensitivity** /ˌhaɪpəsensₔ'tɪvₔti $ -pər-/ *n* [U]

hy·per·ten·sion /ˌhaɪpə'tenʃən $ -pər-/ *n* [U] *technical* a medical condition in which your BLOOD PRESSURE is too high

hy·per·text /'haɪpəˌtekst $ -pər-/ *n* [U] *technical* a way of writing computer documents that makes it possible to move from one document to another by CLICKING on words or pictures, especially on the Internet

hy·per·ven·ti·late /ˌhaɪpə'ventₔleɪt $ -pər'ventl-eɪt/ *v* [I] to breathe too quickly or too deeply, so that you get too much OXYGEN and feel DIZZY —**hyperventilation** /ˌhaɪpəventₔ'leɪʃən $ -pərventl'eɪ-/ *n* [U]

hy·phen /'haɪfən/ *n* [C] a short written or printed line (-) that joins words or SYLLABLES; → **dash**

hy·phen·ate /'haɪfəneɪt/ *v* [T] to join words or SYLLABLES with a HYPHEN —**hyphenated** *adj* —**hyphenation** /ˌhaɪfə'neɪʃən/ *n* [U]

hyp·no·sis /hɪp'nəʊsₔs $ -'noʊ-/ *n* [U] **1** a state similar to sleep, in which someone's thoughts and actions can be influenced by someone else: **under hypnosis** *While under hypnosis, the victim was able to describe her attacker.* **2** the act of producing this state

hyp·no·ther·a·py /ˌhɪpnəʊ'θerəpi $ -noʊ-/ *n* [U] the use of hypnosis to treat emotional or physical problems —**hypnotherapist** *n* [C]

hyp·not·ic[1] /hɪp'nɒtɪk $ -'nɑː-/ *adj* **1** making you feel tired or unable to pay attention to anything else, especially because of a regularly repeated sound or movement: *His voice had a smooth hypnotic effect.* | *the hypnotic beat of the drum* **2** [only before noun] relating to HYPNOSIS: *a hypnotic trance* —**hypnotically** /-kli/ *adv*

hypnotic[2] *n* [C] *technical* a drug that helps you to sleep; ◼ **sleeping pill**

hyp·no·tise /'hɪpnətaɪz/ *v* [T] a British spelling of hypnotize

hyp·no·tis·m /'hɪpnətɪzəm/ *n* [U] the practice of hypnotizing people

hyp·no·tist /'hɪpnətₔst/ *n* [C] someone who hypnotizes people

hyp·no·tize also **-ise** *BrE* /'hɪpnətaɪz/ *v* [T] **1** to produce a sleep-like state in someone so that you can influence their thoughts and actions **2** [usually passive] to be so interesting or exciting that people cannot think of anything else; ◼ **mesmerized**: *We were completely hypnotized by her performance of the Haydn.*

hy·po /'haɪpəʊ $ -poʊ/ *n plural* **hypos** [C] *informal* a HYPODERMIC

hypo- /haɪpəʊ, -pə $ -poʊ, -pə/ *prefix technical* less than usual, especially too little: *hypothermia* (=condition in which your body temperature is too low) | *a hypodermic injection* (=given under the skin)

hy·po·chon·dri·a /ˌhaɪpə'kɒndriə $ -'kɑːn-/ *n* [U] when someone continuously worries that there is something wrong with their health, even when they are not ill

hy·po·chon·dri·ac /ˌhaɪpə'kɒndriæk $ -'kɑːn-/ *n* [C] someone who always worries about their health and thinks they may be ill, even when they are really not ill —**hypochondriac** *adj*

hy·poc·ri·sy /hɪ'pɒkrₔsi $ -'pɑː-/ *n* [U] when someone pretends to have certain beliefs or opinions that they do not really have – used to show disapproval; ◼ **sincerity**: *It would be sheer hypocrisy to pray for success, since I've never believed in God.*

hyp·o·crite /'hɪpəkrɪt/ *n* [C] someone who pretends to have certain beliefs or opinions that they do not really have – used to show disapproval

hyp·o·crit·i·cal /ˌhɪpə'krɪtɪkəl◂/ *adj* behaving in a way that is different from what you claim to believe – used to show disapproval; ◼ **sincere**: **it's hypocritical (of sb) to do sth** *It's hypocritical of these universities to call their football players student-athletes.*

hy·po·der·mic[1] /ˌhaɪpə'dɜːmɪk◂ $ -ɜːr-/ *n* [C] an instrument with a very thin hollow needle used for putting drugs directly into the body through the skin; ◼ **syringe**

hypodermic[2] *adj* used to give an INJECTION beneath the skin: *a hypodermic needle*

hy·pot·e·nuse /haɪ'pɒtₔnjuːz $ -'pɑːtənuːs, -nuːz/ *n* [C] *technical* the longest side of a TRIANGLE that has a RIGHT ANGLE

hy·po·ther·mi·a /ˌhaɪpəʊ'θɜːmiə $ -poʊ'θɜːr-/ *n* [U] a serious medical condition caused by extreme cold

hy·poth·e·sis /haɪ'pɒθəsₔs $ -'pɑː-/ *n plural* **hypotheses** /-siːz/ **1** [C] an idea that is suggested as an explanation for something, but that has not yet been proved to be true; ◼ **theory**: *One hypothesis is that the victim fell asleep while driving.* | **prove/test/support etc a hypothesis** *We hope that further research will confirm our hypothesis.* | [+about] *The authors reject the hypothesis about unemployment contributing to crime.* **2** [U] ideas or guesses rather than facts; ◼ **speculation**: *All this is mere hypothesis.*

hy·poth·e·size also **- ise** *BrE* /haɪ'pɒθəsaɪz $ -'pɑː-/ *v* [I,T] to suggest a possible explanation that has not yet been proved to be true: **hypothesize that** *Scientists hypothesize that the dinosaurs were killed by a giant meteor.*

hy·po·thet·i·cal /ˌhaɪpə'θetɪkəl◂/ *adj* based on a situation that is not real, but that might happen: **hypothetical situation/example/question** *Brennan brought up a hypothetical case to make his point.* | *The question is purely hypothetical.*; → **imaginary** —**hypothetically** /-kli/ *adv*

hys·ter·ec·to·my /ˌhɪstə'rektəmi/ *n plural* **hysterectomies** [C,U] a medical operation to remove a woman's UTERUS

hys·te·ri·a /hɪ'stɪəriə $ -'steriə/ *n* [U] **1** extreme excitement that makes people cry, laugh, shout etc in a way that is out of control: *In a fit of hysteria, Silvia*

H

blamed me for causing her father's death. **2** a situation in which a lot of people feel fear, anger, or excitement, which makes them behave in an unreasonable way: *Since the General's death, the population has been gripped by* **mass hysteria**. **3** *medical* a medical condition which upsets someone's emotions and makes them suddenly feel very nervous, excited, anxious etc

hys·ter·i·cal /hɪˈsterɪkəl/ *adj* **1** unable to control your behaviour or emotions because you are very upset, afraid, excited etc: *Janet became hysterical and began screaming.* | *Everyone in the studio burst into* **hysterical laughter**. **2** *informal* extremely funny; ⮑ **hilarious**: *It was absolutely hysterical! I've never*

laughed so much. —**hysterically** /-kli/ *adv*

hys·ter·ics /hɪˈsterɪks/ *n* [plural] *spoken* **1** when you are unable to control your behaviour or emotions because you are very upset, afraid, excited etc: *She* **went into hysterics** *when she heard about her husband.* | **have hysterics** (=be extremely upset or angry) *BrE: Mum'd have hysterics if she knew what you'd done.* **2 in hysterics** if someone is in hysterics, they are laughing and not able to stop: *The audience was in hysterics.*

Hz the written abbreviation of *hertz*

H

I, i

ice cream

block of ice ice bucket

ice cube tray

I¹ ⟨S1⟩ ⟨W1⟩ /aɪ/ *pron* [used as the subject of a verb] used by the person speaking or writing to refer to himself or herself: *I moved to this city six years ago.* | *I'm not late again, am I?* | *My husband and I enjoy going to the theatre.* ⚠ Do not say 'taller than I', 'younger than I', 'better than I' etc. Say **taller than me, younger than me, better than me** or **taller than I am, younger than I am, better than I am** etc.

I², **i** /aɪ/ *plural* **I's**, **i's** *n* **1** [C,U] the ninth letter of the English alphabet **2** [C] the number one in the system of ROMAN NUMERALS **3** I-25, I-40 etc the name of an INTERSTATE (=important road between states in the US)

-i /-i/ *plural* **-is** *suffix* **1** [in nouns] a person from a particular country or place, or their language: *two Pakistanis* | *speakers of Hindi* **2** [in adjectives] of a particular place or country: *Bengali food* | *the Israeli army*

i·amb /ˈaɪæm $ ˈaɪæm, ˈaɪæmb/ also **i·am·bus** /aɪˈæmbəs/ *n* [C] *technical* a unit of RHYTHM in poetry, that has one short or weak beat followed by a long or strong beat, as in the word 'alive' —**iambic** /aɪˈæmbɪk/ *adj*

i·ambic pen·tameter *n* [C,U] a common pattern of beats in English poetry, in which each line consists of five iambs

-ian /iən/ *suffix* [in adjectives and nouns] another form of the suffix -AN: *Dickensian characters* (=like those in Dickens' books) | *a librarian* (=someone who works in a library)

-iana /iɑːnə $ iænə/ *suffix* also **-ana** [in nouns] a group or collection of objects, papers, etc that are related to someone or something: *Victoriana* | *Shakespeariana*

I·be·ri·an /aɪˈbɪəriən $ -ˈbɪr-/ *adj* relating to Spain or Portugal, or its people: *the Iberian peninsula*

i·bex /ˈaɪbeks/ *n plural* **ibexes** *or* **ibex** [C] a wild goat that lives in the mountains of Europe, Asia, and North Africa

ib·id /ˈɪbɪd/ also **ib·i·dem** /ˈɪbɪdem, ɪˈbaɪdem/ *adv* used in formal writing to mean from the same book, writer, or article as the one that has just been mentioned

-ibility /ˌbɪləti/ *suffix* [in nouns] another form of the suffix -ABILITY: *invincibility* | *flexibility*

ibis /ˈaɪbɪs/ *n plural* **ibises** [C] a large bird with a long beak and long legs that is related to the STORK

-ible /ˌbəl/ *suffix* [in adjectives] another form of the suffix -ABLE: *irresistible* | *visible*

i·bu·pro·fen /ˌaɪbjuːˈprəʊfen $ -ˈproʊfən/ *n* [U] a medicine that reduces pain, INFLAMMATION, and fever

-ic /ɪk/ *suffix* **1** [in adjectives] of, like, or related to a particular thing: *photographic* (=of photography) | *an alcoholic drink* (=containing alcohol) | *polysyllabic* (=containing several SYLLABLES) | *pelvic* (=of the pelvis) | *Byronic* (=like or connected with the poet Byron) **2** [in nouns] someone who is affected by a particular unusual condition, a mental illness for example: *an alcoholic* (=someone who cannot stop drinking alcohol) —**ically** /ɪkli/ [in adverbs]: *photographically*

-ical /ɪkəl/ *suffix* [in adjectives] another form of the suffix -IC (1): *historical* (=of history) | *satirical* —**ically** /ɪkli/ [in adverbs]: *historically*

ICBM /ˌaɪ siː biː ˈem/ *n* [C] *Intercontinental Ballistic Missile;* a MISSILE that can travel very long distances

ice¹ ⟨S2⟩ ⟨W3⟩ /aɪs/ *n*
1 [U] water that has frozen into a solid state; → **icy**: *Would you like some ice in your drink?* | *Her hands were as cold as ice.* | *Spring flowers pushed through the slowly melting ice.* | *The city spent $7 million to remove snow and ice from the roads.* | *a cup full of* **crushed ice** | *Linda's hair sparkled with tiny* **ice crystals**.
2 keep/put something on ice to do nothing about a plan or suggestion for a period of time: *I'm putting my plans for a new car on ice until I finish college.*
3 be (skating) on thin ice to be in a situation in which you are likely to upset someone or cause trouble: *You'd better not be late for work again, Hugo – you're skating on thin ice.*
4 the ice a specially prepared surface of ice where you can ICE SKATE or play ICE HOCKEY: *The two teams are ready to take to the ice.*
5 [C] **a)** a frozen sweet food made with fruit juice; ▣ **sorbet b)** *old-fashioned especially BrE* an ICE CREAM
6 [U] *AmE* diamonds → **BLACK ICE**, **DRY ICE**; → **break the ice** at **BREAK¹** (29); → **cut no ice** at **CUT¹** (39)

ice² *v* [T] *especially BrE* to cover a cake with ICING (=a mixture made of liquid and very fine sugar); ▣ **frost** *AmE*

ice sth ⇔ down *phr v AmE* to cover an injured part of the body in ice to stop it from swelling: *Make sure you ice that ankle down as soon as you get inside.*

ice over/up also **be iced over/up** *phr v* to become covered with ice: *Schools were closed when the roads iced over.* | *The plane's engines had iced up.*

Ice Age *n* [C] one of the long periods of time, thousands of years ago, when ice covered many northern countries

ice·berg /ˈaɪsbɜːg $ -bɜːrg/ *n* [C] a very large mass of ice floating in the sea, most of which is under the surface of the water → **the tip of the iceberg** at **TIP¹** (4)

iceberg lettuce *n* [C,U] a firm round pale green LETTUCE

ice-'blue *adj* very pale blue: *his ice-blue eyes* —**ice-blue** *n* [U]

ice·bound /ˈaɪsbaʊnd/ *adj* surrounded by ice, especially so that it is impossible to move

ice·box /ˈaɪsbɒks $ -baːks/ *n* [C] *AmE old-fashioned* **1** a REFRIGERATOR **2** a special cupboard into which people in the past put ice in order to keep food cold

ice·break·er /ˈaɪsˌbreɪkə $ -ər/ *n* [C] **1** something that you say or do to make people less nervous when they first meet: *This game is an effective icebreaker at the beginning of a semester.* → **break the ice** at **BREAK¹** (29) **2** a ship that cuts a passage through floating ice

ice bucket *n* [C] **1** a container filled with ice to keep bottles of wine cold → see picture at **ICE** **2** a container in which pieces of ice are kept for putting in drinks

ice cap *n* [C] an area of thick ice that permanently covers the North and South Poles

ice-'cold *adj* extremely cold: *ice-cold drinks* | *Her hands were ice-cold.*

ice 'cream ⟨S2⟩ / $ '. ./ *n*
1 [U] a frozen sweet food made of milk, cream, and

sugar, with fruit, nuts, chocolate etc sometimes added to it: *vanilla ice cream* → see picture at DESSERT **2** [C] a small amount of this food for one person: *Mummy, can I have an ice cream?*

ˈice cream ˌcone *n* [C] a hard thin cooked cake shaped like a CONE, that you put ice cream in, or one of these with ice cream in it

ˈice cream ˌparlor *n* [C] *AmE* a restaurant that only sells ice cream

ˌice-cream ˈsoda *n* [C] a mixture of ice cream, sweet SYRUP, and SODA WATER, served in a tall glass

ˈice cube *n* [C] a small block of ice used to make drinks cold → see picture at ICE

iced /aɪst/ *adj* **1** iced drinks are made very cold or served with ice: *iced water* | *iced tea* | *iced coffee* **2** an iced cake has ICING on the top

ˈice ˌfishing *n* [U] the sport of catching fish through a hole in the ice on a lake or river

ˈice floe *n* [C] an area of ice floating in the sea, that has broken off from a larger mass

ˈice ˌhockey *n* [U] *BrE* a sport played on ice, in which players try to hit a hard flat round object into the other team's GOAL with special sticks; **◳ hockey** *AmE*

ˈice ˌlolly *n plural* **ice lollies** [C] *BrE* a piece of sweet-tasting ice on a stick, that you suck; **◳ popsicle** *AmE*

ice·man /ˈaɪsmæn/ *n plural* **icemen** /-men/ [C] *AmE* a man who delivered ice to people's houses in the past, so that they could keep food cold

ˈice pack *n* [C] **1** a bag containing ice that is put on injured or painful parts of your body to keep them cold **2** a large area of crushed ice floating in the sea → PACK ICE

ˈice pick *n* [C] a sharp tool used for cutting or breaking ice

ˈice rink *n* [C] a specially prepared surface of ice where you can ICE-SKATE

ˈice sheet *n* [C] an ICE CAP

ˈice skate *n* [C usually plural] a special boot with thin metal blades on the bottom, that allows you to move quickly on ice → ROLLER SKATE; → see picture at SKATE

ice-skate *v* [I] to slide on ice wearing ice skates **—ice-skater** *n* [C] **—ice-skating** *n* [U]

ˈice ˌwater *n* [C,U] very cold water with pieces of ice in it, or a glass of this

-ician /ɪʃən/ *suffix* [in nouns] a skilled worker who deals with a particular thing: *a beautician* (=someone who gives beauty treatments) | *a technician* (=someone with technical or scientific skills)

i·ci·cle /ˈaɪsɪkəl/ *n* [C] a long thin pointed piece of ice hanging from a roof or other surface

-icide /ɪsaɪd/ *suffix* also **-cide** [in nouns] someone or something that kills a particular person or thing, or the act of killing: *insecticide* (=chemical substance for killing insects) | *suicide* (=the act of killing yourself) **—-icidal** /ɪsaɪdl/ *suffix* [in adjectives] **—-icidally** /ɪsaɪdl-i/ *suffix* [in adverbs]

i·ci·ly /ˈaɪsˌli/ *adv* if you say something icily, or look at someone icily, you do it in an angry or very unfriendly way: *'I want you to leave now,' she said icily.*

ic·ing /ˈaɪsɪŋ/ *n* [U] **1** a mixture made from very fine light sugar and liquid, used to cover cakes ; **◳ frosting** *AmE* **2** **the icing on the cake** something that makes a very good experience even better: *It was a great day, but meeting her there was just the icing on the cake!*

ˈicing ˌsugar *n* [U] *BrE* very fine light sugar that is mixed with liquid to make icing; **◳ powdered sugar** *AmE*

ick·y /ˈɪki/ *adj spoken* very unpleasant, especially to look at, taste, or feel; **◳ yucky**: *There was some icky black stuff between the tiles.*

i·con /ˈaɪkɒn $ -kɑːn/ *n* [C] **1** a small sign or picture on a computer screen that is used to start a particular operation: *To open a new file, click on the icon at the top of the screen.* **2** someone famous who is admired by

many people and is thought to represent an important idea: *a 60s cultural icon* **3** also **ikon** a picture or figure of a holy person that is used in worship in the Greek or Russian Orthodox Church **—iconic** /aɪˈkɒnɪk $ -ˈkɑː-/ *adj*

i·con·o·clast /aɪˈkɒnəklæst $ -ˈkɑː-/ *n* [C] *formal* someone who attacks established ideas and customs

i·con·o·clas·tic /aɪˌkɒnəˈklæstɪk◂ $ -ˌkɑːn-/ *adj formal* iconoclastic ideas, opinions, writings etc attack established beliefs and customs: *Wolfe's theories were revolutionary and iconoclastic.* **—iconoclasm** /aɪˈkɒnəklæzəm $ -ˈkɑː-/ *n* [U]

i·co·nog·ra·phy /ˌaɪkəˈnɒɡrəfi $ -ˈnɑː-/ *n* [U] the way that a particular people, religious or political group etc represent ideas in pictures or images: *Native American iconography*

-ics /ɪks/ *suffix* [in nouns] **1** the scientific study or use of something: *linguistics* (=the study of language) | *electronics* (=the study or making of electronic equipment) **2** the actions typically done by someone with particular skills: *athletics* (=running, jumping, throwing, etc) | *acrobatics* **3** used to make nouns out of words ending in -ICAL or -IC: *the acoustics* (=sound qualities) *of the hall*

ICU /ˌaɪ siː ˈjuː/ *n* [C] *intensive care unit* a department in a hospital that gives special attention and treatment to people who are very sick or badly injured

ic·y /ˈaɪsi/ *adj* **1** extremely cold; **◳ frosty**: *an icy wind* | *The bath water was icy cold.* **2** covered in ice: *an icy mountain road* **3** an icy remark, look etc shows that you feel annoyed with or unfriendly towards someone: *an icy stare* → ICILY **—iciness** /ɪ/ [U]

id /ɪd/ *n* [U] *technical* according to Freudian PSYCHOLOGY, the part of your mind that is completely unconscious but has hidden needs and desires → EGO (2), SUPEREGO

I'd /aɪd/ **1** the short form of 'I had': *I wish I'd said that.* **2** the short form of 'I would': *I'd leave now if I were you.*

ID¹ /ˌaɪ ˈdiː/ *n* [C,U] a document that shows your name and date of birth, usually with a photograph; **◳ identification**: *I'll need to see some ID before I can let you in.* | *a fake ID*

ID² *v* [T] *spoken* to IDENTIFY a criminal or dead body: *Police are still looking for someone who can ID the body.*

ID card /ˌaɪ ˈdiː kɑːd $ -kɑːrd/ *n* [C] an IDENTITY CARD

-ide /aɪd/ *suffix* [in nouns] *technical* a chemical substance made up of two or more ELEMENTS: *cyanide* | *sulphide*

i·dea [S1] [W1] /aɪˈdɪə/ *n*
1 **PLAN/SUGGESTION** [C] a plan or suggestion for a possible course of action, especially one that you think of suddenly

> have an idea
> get an idea
> give sb an idea
> come up with/hit on an idea (=think of a new idea)
> the idea of (doing) sth
> good/great/brilliant idea
> bad/stupid/crazy idea
> it is a good/bad idea to do sth
> be full of ideas also
> be bursting with ideas (=have a lot of ideas)
> toy with an idea (=think about a plan, but not very seriously)
> exchange/share ideas also
> an exchange of ideas
> fire ideas off each other (=discuss each other's ideas and think of good new ones)

I've had an idea. Why don't we walk into town? | *She got the idea from an article in a fashion magazine.* | *What gave you the idea of using a male actor for the part?* | *Mike's always good at coming up with new ideas.* | *It was my wife's idea to move house.* | [+for] *The idea for the book came from an old war movie.* |

What a great idea! | *I knew it was a bad idea to leave him on his own.* | *She was always very enthusiastic and bursting with ideas.* | *an exchange of ideas between academic and business communities* | *Lately I've been toying with the idea of going back to school.*

⚠️ Do not say 'the idea to do something'. Say **the idea of doing something**. However, you can say it is **a good idea to do something** and **it was your idea to do something**.

2 KNOWLEDGE [C,U] a general understanding of something, based on some knowledge about it: *Could you give me an idea of how bad his injuries are?* | *You must have some idea* (=have at least a little knowledge) *of what happened to the money.* | *Don't worry if you don't understand it right now – you'll get the idea* (=begin to understand or be able to do something). | **have no idea/not have any idea** *She doesn't have any idea where they've gone.* | **a general/rough idea** (=a not very exact idea) *Can you give me a rough idea of how much the repairs will cost?* | **not have the faintest/ slightest/foggiest idea** *spoken: I don't have the faintest idea what to get Rachel for her birthday.*

3 AIM/INTENTION [C,U] the aim, intention, or purpose of doing something: *The idea is to teach children to save money.* | [+of/behind] *The idea behind the outing is to encourage employees to get to know each other.* | *They wanted Mike to go to law school, but he had other ideas* (=had different plans).

4 HOW YOU IMAGINE SOMETHING TO BE [C,U] an image in your mind of what something is like or should be like: [+of] *Chefs differ in their idea of what makes a good dessert.* | *I only have a vague idea of the kind of work I'll be doing.* | *It helps if you have a clear idea of what you want.* | **not my idea of sth** *Chocolate milk and a piece of cake is not my idea of dinner.* | *The very idea of kissing him made her feel physically sick.*

5 BELIEF/OPINION [C usually plural] someone's opinions or beliefs about something: [+about] *She had some rather unusual ideas about raising children.* | **where did you get that idea?** (=used to say that what someone thinks is completely wrong) *No, I'm not seeing Jane. Where did you get that idea?*

6 PRINCIPLE [C] a principle or belief about how something is or should be: [+of] *The whole idea of democracy was something strange and new to most people.* | **idea that** *It's based on the idea that all people are created equal.*

7 have an idea (that) to be fairly sure that something is true, without being completely sure: *I'm not sure where my necklace is, but I have a pretty good idea who took it.*

8 get the wrong idea to think that something is true when it is not: *Don't get the wrong idea about Dan and Helen – they're just friends.*

9 have the right idea to act or think in a way that will probably lead to the correct result: *He still makes a few mistakes but I reckon he's got the right idea.*

10 that's/there's an idea *spoken* used to say that you like what someone has just suggested: *'Why don't you invite Paula to come with us?' 'There's an idea.'*

11 that's the idea *spoken* **a)** used to tell someone who is learning to do something that they are doing it in the right way, in order to encourage them: *Keep your knees bent and lean forward slightly. That's the idea!* **b)** used to emphasize what the main point of something is, or to say that someone understands that point: *'You're thinking of getting a new job?' 'Yeah, that's the idea.'*

12 bright idea a very clever idea, often used in a joking way to mean a very stupid idea or action: *Whose bright idea was it to leave the back door wide open?*

13 give sb ideas/put ideas into sb's head to make someone think of doing something that they had not thought of doing before, especially something that they should not do: *Nick tells me he wants a motorbike. Have you been putting ideas into his head?*

14 is it sb's idea of a joke? used when you are surprised

and often rather annoyed by what someone has said or done: *'She wants you to do it by tomorrow.' 'Is that your idea of a joke?'*

15 what's the big idea? *spoken* used when you cannot understand why someone has done something

16 you have no idea (how/what etc) *spoken* used when you are telling someone that something is extremely good, bad etc: *You have no idea how worried I was.*

17 the idea! *old-fashioned spoken* used to express surprise or disapproval when someone has said something stupid or strange → **buck your ideas up** at BUCK UP (4)

i·deal¹ S2 W2 /aɪˈdɪəl◂/ *adj*
1 the best or most suitable that something could possibly be: *advice on how to reach your ideal weight* | *The scheme offers an ideal opportunity for youngsters to get training.* | *With so much rain, conditions are far from ideal.* | [+for] *An elastic waist makes these jeans ideal for the larger woman.* | *an ideal place for a pleasant walk*
2 [only before noun] an ideal world, job, system etc is one that you imagine to be perfect, but that is not likely to really exist: *In an ideal world there would be no need for a police force.*

ideal² *n* [C] **1** a principle about what is morally right or a perfect standard that you hope to achieve: [+of] *the ideal of a free and democratic society* | *the long-vanished ideals of the 1950s* **2** a perfect example of what something should be like: [+of] *Are our ideals of beauty changing?*

i·deal·ise /aɪˈdɪəlaɪz/ *v* [T] a British spelling of IDEALIZE

i·deal·is·m /aɪˈdɪəlɪzəm/ *n* [U] **1** the belief that you should live your life according to high standards and principles, even when they are very difficult to achieve; → **realism**: *the idealism of the younger generation* | *moral and religious idealism* **2** *technical* a way of using art or literature to show the world as a perfect place, even though it is not; → **realism, naturalism**

i·deal·ist /aɪˈdɪəlɪst/ *n* [C] someone who tries to live according to high standards or principles, especially in a way that is not practical or possible; → **realist**

i·deal·is·tic /ˌaɪdɪəˈlɪstɪk◂/ *adj* believing that you should live according to high standards and principles, even if they cannot really be achieved, or showing this belief; → **realistic**: *idealistic young doctors* | *the idealistic values of the 1960s* —**idealistically** /-kli/ *adv*

i·deal·ize also **-ise** *BrE* /aɪˈdɪəlaɪz/ *v* [T] to imagine or represent something or someone as being perfect or better than they really are: *Society continues to idealize the two-parent family.* | *an idealized view of marriage* —**idealization** /aɪˌdɪəlaɪˈzeɪʃən $ -lə-/ *n* [C,U]

i·deal·ly S3 /aɪˈdɪəli/ *adv*
1 used to describe the way you would like things to be, even though this may not be possible: [sentence adverb] *Ideally, your car should have high security locks.* | *Fruit and vegetables should ideally be organically grown.*
2 ideally suited/placed/situated etc having the best qualities, experience, knowledge etc for a particular situation: *He was ideally suited for the job.* | *The hotel is ideally located for enjoying the beauty of Yorkshire.*

id·em /ˈɪdem, ˈaɪdem/ *written* from the same book, writer etc as the one that has just been mentioned

i·den·ti·cal /aɪˈdentɪkəl/ *adj* exactly the same, or very similar: *four identical houses* | [+to/with] *Nutritionally, infant formulas are almost identical to breast milk.* | *The ingredients are identical with those of competing products.* | [+in] *The sisters were identical in appearance and character.* —**identically** /-kli/ *adv*; → see picture at TWIN

i,dentical 'twin *n* [C usually plural] one of a pair of brothers or sisters born at the same time, who develop from the same egg and look almost exactly alike; → **fraternal twin**

i·den·ti·fi·a·ble /aɪˈdentɪfaɪəbəl/ *adj* able to be recognized: [+as] *She looked young, and was immediately identifiable as a trainee.* | [+by] *The police were identifiable by their uniform.*

i·den·ti·fi·ca·tion /aɪˌdentɪfɪˈkeɪʃən/ n [U] **1** *ID* official papers or cards, such as your PASSPORT, that prove who you are: *Do you have any identification?* | **form/ proof of identification** *Bring some form of identification, preferably a passport.* | *fingerprinting as a **means of identification**.* **2** when someone says officially that they know who someone else is, especially a criminal or a dead person: *His body was taken to Brighton mortuary for identification.* **3** when you recognize something or discover exactly what it is: [+of] *the identification of customer needs* | *the identification of children who need professional help* **4** the act of saying that two things are very closely related: **identification of sth with sth** *the identification of sexism with women's oppression* **5** a strong feeling of sympathy with someone that makes you able to share their feelings: [+with] *my identification with the heroine of the book*

i‚dentifiˈcation paˌrade also **identity parade** n [C] *BrE* a process in which someone who has seen a crime take place looks at a group of people to see if they can recognize the criminal; ◧ **line-up** *AmE*

i·den·ti·fy W1 /aɪˈdentɪfaɪ/ v **identified, identifying, identifies** [T]
1 to recognize and correctly name someone or something: *He was too far away to be able to identify faces.* | *The police took fingerprints and **identified the body**.* | **identify sb/sth as sb/sth** *Eye witnesses identified the gunman as an army sergeant.* | *The aircraft were identified as American.*
2 to recognize something or discover exactly what it is, what its nature or origin is etc: *Scientists have identified the gene that causes abnormal growth.* | *They identified a number of problem areas.*
3 if a particular thing identifies someone or something, it makes them easy to recognize: **identify sb as sb** *His accent identified him as a Frenchman.*

identify with *phr v*
1 **identify with sb/sth** to feel sympathy with someone or be able to share their feelings: *Humans can easily identify with the emotional expressions of chimpanzees.* | *He identified with our distress and despair.*
2 **identify sb with sth** to think that someone is very closely related to or involved with something such as a political group: *She has always been identified with the radical left.*
3 **identify sth with sb/sth** to think that something is the same as, or closely related to, something else: *the attempt to identify crime with poverty and social problems*

I·den·ti·kit /aɪˈdentɪˌkɪt/ n [C] *BrE trademark* **1** a method used by the police in which a picture of a criminal is produced from descriptions given by people who have seen the crime take place; ◧ **composite** *AmE*: *an identikit picture* **2** used to describe things that are all exactly the same, with no interesting or unusual features: *new identikit cities*

i·den·ti·ty W2 /aɪˈdentɪti/ n *plural* **identities**
1 [C,U] someone's identity is their name or who they are

sb's identity/the identity of sb
know sb's identity
disclose/reveal sb's identity
hide/conceal sb's identity
discover sb's identity
protect sb's identity (=make sure no one finds out who someone is)
false identity (=when someone pretends to be another person)
(a case of) mistaken identity (=when you think someone is a different person)
sb's true identity (=who someone really is)
proof of identity (=something that proves you are who you say you are)
identity papers/documents (=documents that show you are who you say you are)

The identity of the killer is still unknown. | *He maintained he did not **know** the **identity** of the*

woman. | *Why did she need to **conceal** her **identity**?* | *Police are trying to **discover** the **identity** of a baby found by the side of a road.* | *They will testify behind a screen in order to **protect** their **identities**.* | *She applied for a teaching job under a **false identity**.* | *One theory was that the attack was a **case of mistaken identity**.* | *Journalists should have to produce **proof of identity**.*

2 [U] the qualities and attitudes that a person or group of people have, that make them different from other people: *Children need continuity, security, and a **sense of identity**.* | *Travelling alone can lead to a **loss of identity**.* | **national/cultural/social etc identity** (=a strong feeling of belonging to a particular group, race etc) *Our strong sense of national identity has been shaped by our history.* | **identity crisis/crisis of identity** (=a feeling of uncertainty about who you really are and what your purpose is) *My father experienced an identity crisis in middle age.*
3 [U] *formal* exact SIMILARITY between two things

iˈdentity ˌcard n [C] a card with your name, date of birth, and photograph on it, that proves who you are; ◧ **ID card**

iˈdentity paˌrade n [C] *BrE* an IDENTIFICATION PARADE

id·e·o·gram /ˈɪdiəgræm/ also **id·e·o·graph** /-grɑːf $ -græf/ n [C] a written sign, for example in Chinese, that represents an idea or thing rather than the sound of a word

i·de·o·log·ic·al /ˌaɪdiəˈlɒdʒɪkəl◂ $ -ˈlɑː-/ *adj* based on strong beliefs or ideas, especially political or economic ideas: *The party is split by ideological differences.*
—**ideologically** /-kli/ *adv*

i·de·o·logue /ˈaɪdiəˌlɒg $ -ˌlɔːg, -ˌlɑːg/ also **i·de·ol·o·gist** /ˌaɪdiˈɒlədʒɪst $ -ˈɑːl-/ n [C] someone whose actions are very much influenced by an ideology

i·de·ol·o·gy W3 /ˌaɪdiˈɒlədʒi $ -ˈɑːl-/ n *plural* **ideologies** [C,U] a set of beliefs on which a political or economic system is based, or which strongly influence the way people behave: *the ideologies of fascism and communism* | *a new ideology based on individualism*

id·i·o·cy /ˈɪdiəsi/ n *plural* **idiocies** [C,U] something that you think is extremely silly or stupid; ◧ **stupidity**: *The idiocy of his behaviour appalled her.* | *He smiled calmly at the idiocies of mankind.*

id·i·o·lect /ˈɪdiəlekt/ n [C,U] *technical* the way in which a particular person uses language → DIALECT

id·i·om /ˈɪdiəm/ n **1** [C] a group of words that has a special meaning that is different from the ordinary meaning of each separate word. For example, 'under the weather' is an idiom meaning 'ill'. **2** [C,U] *formal* or *technical* a style of expression in writing, speech, or music that is typical of a particular group of people: *the new musical idiom*

id·i·o·mat·ic /ˌɪdiəˈmætɪk◂/ *adj* **1** **idiomatic expression/phrase** an idiom **2** typical of the natural way in which someone speaks or writes when they are using their own language: *He had the ability to write fluent, accurate, and idiomatic English.* | *the idiomatic richness of the Spanish language* —**idiomatically** /-kli/ *adv*

id·i·o·syn·cra·sy /ˌɪdiəˈsɪŋkrəsi/ n *plural* **idiosyncrasies** [C] **1** an unusual habit or way of behaving that someone has: *my uncle's idiosyncrasies* **2** an unusual or unexpected feature that something has: *one of the many idiosyncrasies of English spelling* —**idiosyncratic** /ˌɪdiəsɪnˈkrætɪk◂/ *adj*

id·i·ot /ˈɪdiət/ n [C] **1** a stupid person or someone who has done something stupid: *It was all your fault, you idiot.* **2** *old use* someone who is mentally ill or has a very low level of intelligence —**idiotic** /ˌɪdiˈɒtɪk◂ $ -ˈɑːt-/ *adj*: *Stop asking such idiotic questions.* —**idiotically** /-kli/ *adv*

[1] 000, [2] 000, [3] 000, most frequent words in [S]poken and [W]ritten English

'idiot-ˌproof adj something that is idiot-proof is so easy to use or do that even stupid people will not break it or make a mistake: idiot-proof instructions

i·dle¹ /'aɪdl/ adj **1** not working or producing anything; 🔁 **busy**: I cannot afford to leave the land lying idle. | The whole team stood idle, waiting for the mechanic. | The workers have been idle for the last six months. **2** not serious, or not done with any definite intention: She was not a woman to make idle threats. | idle chatter/talk/gossip etc | It was only from idle curiosity that she went into the barn. **3** lazy: Go and wake up that idle brother of yours. **4 it is idle to do sth** it is not worth doing something, because nothing will be achieved: It would be idle to deny that great progress was made. **5 the idle rich** rich people who do not have to work —**idleness** n [U] —**idly** adv: They sat around, chatting idly. | I cannot **stand idly by** and let him take the blame.

idle² v **1** [I] if an engine idles, it runs slowly while the vehicle, machine etc is not moving: He flicked a switch and let the boat idle. **2** [I] to spend time doing nothing: Sometimes he went for a walk; sometimes he just idled. **3** [T] AmE to stop using a factory or stop providing work for your workers, especially temporarily; 🔁 **shut down**: The company has reduced its workforce and indefinitely idled a number of its US plants.

idle sth ⇔ **away** phr v to spend time in a relaxed way, doing nothing: They idled their time away in the pub.

id·ler /'aɪdlə $ -ər/ n [C] old-fashioned someone who is lazy and does not work

i·dol /'aɪdl/ n [C] **1** someone or something that you love or admire very much; 🔁 **hero**: [+of] She is the idol of countless teenagers. | She had made an idol of her husband. | a **pop idol 2** a picture or STATUE that is worshipped as a god

i·dol·a·try /aɪ'dɒlətri $ -'dɑː-/ n [U] **1** the practice of worshipping idols **2** when you admire someone or something too much —**idolatrous** adj

i·dol·ize also **-ise** BrE /'aɪdəl-aɪz/ v [T] to admire and love someone so much that you think they are perfect: They had one child, a girl whom they idolized.

id·yll /'ɪdəl,'ɪdɪl $ 'aɪdl/ n [singular] literary a place or experience in which everything is peaceful and everyone is perfectly happy: a **rural idyll**

i·dyl·lic /ɪ'dɪlɪk, aɪ- $ aɪ-/ adj an idyllic place or time is very beautiful, happy, and peaceful, with no problems or dangers: **idyllic setting/surroundings/scene etc** If you want old-world tradition in an idyllic setting, this is the hotel for you. —**idyllically** /-kli/ adv: idyllically happy

-ie /i/ suffix [in nouns] informal another form of the suffix ·y: dearie

i.e. /ˌaɪ 'iː/ written before a word or phrase that gives the exact meaning of something you have just written or said: The film is only open to adults, i.e. people over 18.

if¹ [S1] [W1] /ɪf/ conjunction **1** used when talking about something that might happen or be true, or might have happened: We'll stay at home if it rains. | If you need money, I can lend you some. | If I didn't apologize I'd feel guilty. | If you had worked harder, you would have passed your exams. | What would happen to your family if you were to die in an accident? | If Dad were here, he would know what to do. | Taste the soup and add salt and pepper if necessary. | I want to get back by five o'clock if possible. | I think I can fix it tomorrow. If not, you'll have to wait till Friday. | Is the book available, and if so where? | The missiles can be fired only if the operator types in a six-digit code. | We'll face that problem if and when it comes along (=if it happens or when it happens). | If by any chance you can't manage dinner tonight, perhaps we can at least have a drink together. → see box at UNLESS **2** used to mention a fact, situation, or event that

someone asks about, or is not certain about: He stopped to ask me if I was all right. | I don't know if what I am saying makes any sense. | I doubt if anyone will remember me. | I'm not sure **if** this is the right road **or not**. **3** used to mention a type of event or situation when talking about what happens on occasions of that type: If I go to bed late I feel dreadful in the morning. | Plastic will melt if it gets too hot. **4** used when saying what someone's feelings are about a possible situation: You don't seem to care if I'm tired. | I'm sorry if I upset you. | It would be nice if we could spend more time together. **5** spoken used when making a polite request: I wonder if you could help me. | I'd be grateful if you would send me further details. | Would you mind if I open a window? | If you would just wait for a moment, I'll try to find your papers. **6** used when you are adding that something may be even more, less, better, worse etc than you have just said: Brian rarely, if ever, goes to bed before 3 am. | Their policies have changed little, if at all, since the last election. | Her needs are just as important as yours, if not more so. | The snow was now two feet deep, making it difficult, if not impossible, to get the car out. **7 even if** used to emphasize that, although something may happen or may be true, it will not change a situation: I wouldn't tell you even if I knew. | Even if she survives, she'll never fully recover. **8 if anything** used when adding a remark that changes what you have just said or makes it stronger: It's warm enough here in London. A little too warm, if anything. **9** spoken used during a conversation when you are trying to make a suggestion, change the subject, or interrupt someone else: If I might just make a suggestion, I think that the matter could be easily settled with a little practical demonstration. | If I could just take one example to illustrate this. **10 if I were you** spoken used when giving advice and telling someone what you think they should do: I wouldn't worry about it if I were you. **11 if only a)** used to express a strong wish, especially when you know that what you want cannot happen: If only he had talked to her sooner! | If only I weren't so tired! **b)** used to give a reason for something, though you think it is not a good one: Media studies is regarded as a more exciting subject, if only because it's new. **12** used to say that although something may be true, it is not important: If he has a fault at all, it is that he is too generous. | Her only problem, if you can call it a problem, is that she expects to be successful all the time. **13** used when adding one criticism of a person or thing that you generally like: The eldest son was highly intelligent, if somewhat lazy. | Lunch was a grand if rather noisy affair. → **as if** at AS² (9); → **if ever there was one** at EVER (15); → **what if...?** at WHAT¹ (18)

GRAMMAR
When you are using **if** to talk about something that might happen in the future, use the present simple tense, not **will** or **shall**: if I fail the test (NOT if I will fail the test).
To refer to the present or the future after **if** when you are talking about something unlikely or untrue, use the past tense, not 'would' or 'should': If someone gave me the money, I'd buy a car tomorrow (NOT If someone would give me the money...)
⚠ In formal English or in writing, use **were** not **was** when the subject of the clause is **I, he, she, it, there** or a singular noun: If I were in that position, I'd get legal advice. | Imagine how you would feel if your child were killed.
In normal conversation, you can also use **was**: If I was ten years younger, I'd go out with him.
⚠ The expression **if I were you** is fixed. Do not say 'if I was you', even in normal conversation: If I were you, I'd have a talk with your parents.
To refer to the past when you are talking about something that did not happen, use the past perfect tense: If he had married Laura, he would have been unhappy (NOT If he would have married Laura...).

if² n [C] informal **1 ifs and buts** BrE, **ifs, ands, or buts** AmE if you do not want any ifs and buts, you want someone to do something quickly without arguing: *No ifs and buts – just make sure the job is done by tomorrow!* **2 and it's a big if** used to say that something is not likely to happen: *The team will go racing next year if – and it's a very big if – they can raise six million pounds.* **3** something that may or may not happen: *There are too many ifs in this plan of yours.*

if·fy /'ɪfi/ adj informal **1** BrE not very good: *That meat smells a bit iffy to me.* **2** not certain to happen; ▣ **doubtful**: *The July date is still rather iffy.*

-iform /ˌfɔːm $ ˌfɔːrm/ suffix [in adjectives] technical having a particular shape: *cruciform* (=cross-shaped)

-ify /ˌfaɪ/ suffix [in verbs] also **-fy 1** to make something be in a particular state or condition: *to purify* (=make or become pure) | *to clarify the situation* (=make it clear) **2** to fill someone with a particular feeling: *Spiders terrify me* (=make me very afraid). **3** informal to do something in a silly or annoying way: *to speechify* (=make speeches, using important sounding words) **4** to make something or someone be like or typical of a person or group: *Frenchified* (=like the French).

ig·loo /'ɪgluː/ n [C] a house made from blocks of hard snow or ice

ig·ne·ous /'ɪgniəs/ adj technical igneous rocks are formed from LAVA (=hot liquid rock)

ig·nite /ɪg'naɪt/ v **1** [I,T] formal to start burning, or to make something start burning: *The petrol tank suddenly ignited.* | *The candle ignited the plastic and started a small fire.* **2** [T] to start a dangerous situation, angry argument etc: *events which ignited the war in Europe*

ig·ni·tion /ɪg'nɪʃən/ n **1** [singular] the electrical part of a vehicle's engine that makes it start working → see picture at CAR **2** [C usually singular] the place in a car where you put in a key to start the engine **3** [U] formal the act of starting to burn or of making something start to burn

ig·no·ble /ɪg'nəʊbəl $ -'noʊ-/ adj formal ignoble thoughts, feelings, or actions are ones that you should feel ashamed or embarrassed about: *ignoble feelings of intense jealousy*

ig·no·min·i·ous /ˌɪgnə'mɪniəs/ adj formal making you feel ashamed or embarrassed; ▣ **humiliating**: *ignominious defeat/failure/retreat etc* | *an ignominious end to his career* —**ignominiously** adv

ig·no·mi·ny /'ɪgnəmɪni/ n [U] formal an event or situation that makes you feel ashamed or embarrassed, especially in public; ▣ **humiliation**: [+of] *He feared the ignominy of being exposed as a spy.*

ig·no·ra·mus /ˌɪgnə'reɪməs/ n plural **ignoramuses** [C] old-fashioned someone who does not know about things that most people know about

ig·no·rance /'ɪgnərəns/ n [U] **1** lack of knowledge or information about something: *Excuse my ignorance, but how does it actually work?* | [+of] *our ignorance of the true situation* | **in ignorance** *I would have remained in ignorance if Shaun hadn't mentioned it.* | [+about] *public fear and ignorance about AIDS* **2 ignorance is bliss** used to say that if you do not know about a problem, you cannot worry about it

ig·no·rant /'ɪgnərənt/ adj **1** not knowing facts or information that you ought to know: *an ignorant and uneducated man* | [+of] *Political historians are often rather ignorant of economics.* | [+about] *Many school-leavers are ignorant about the range of job opportunities.* | *Many people remain blissfully ignorant about the dangers of too much sun* (=happy because they do not know about the dangers).; → see box at IGNORE **2** caused by a lack of knowledge and understanding: *an ignorant remark* | *ignorant opinions* **3** BrE spoken rude or impolite: *ignorant behaviour* —**ignorantly** adv

ig·nore S2 W2 /ɪg'nɔː $ -'nɔːr/ v [T] **1** to deliberately pay no attention to something that you have been told or that you know about: *You can't ignore the fact that many criminals never go to prison.* | *problems which we can't afford to ignore* **2** to behave as if you had not heard or seen someone or something: *The phone rang, but she ignored it.* | *Sam rudely ignored the question.* | **completely/totally ignore sb/sth** *He had completely ignored her remark, preferring his own theory.*

> **WORD CHOICE: ignore, be ignorant of, not know**
> If you ignore something, you know about it or have seen or heard it, but deliberately do not take notice of it: *We cannot ignore the problem.*
> ⚠ Do not use **ignore** to mean 'not know about something'. Use **not know** instead: *We don't know how famous people live their lives (NOT We ignore how famous people live their lives).*
> You can say that you **are ignorant of** something, especially when you should know about it: *They seem to be ignorant of the dangers involved.*

i·gua·na /ɪ'gwɑːnə/ n [C] a large tropical American LIZARD → see picture at REPTILE

i·kon /'aɪkɒn $ -kɑːn/ n another spelling of ICON

il- /ɪ/ prefix the form used for IN- before l: *illogical* (=not logical)

ilk /ɪlk/ n [singular] a particular type; ▣ **kind**: **of that/his/their etc ilk** *Irving Berlin and composers of his ilk* | **sb and that/his/their etc ilk** *Mrs Taylor and her ilk talk absolute rubbish.*

ill¹ S3 W3 /ɪl/ adj
1 especially BrE suffering from a disease or not feeling well; ▣ **sick** AmE

> feel ill
> become/fall/get ill also
> be taken ill
> make sb ill
> seriously/critically/gravely ill (=very ill)
> chronically ill (=always ill)
> mentally ill
> terminally ill (=with an illness you will die from)

Bridget can't come – she's ill. | *I was feeling ill that day and decided to stay at home.* | *She was suddenly taken ill at school.* | *All these diets are making you ill.* | [+with] *Her husband has been ill with bladder trouble.* | *A number of these patients are seriously ill.* | *caring for mentally ill people* | *a hospice for the terminally ill* → see box at SICK¹

2 [only before noun] bad or harmful: *Many people consumed the poisoned oil without ill effects.* | *the neglect and ill treatment of children* | *He was unable to join the army because of ill health.*
3 ill at ease nervous, uncomfortable, or embarrassed: *He always felt shy and ill at ease at parties.*
4 it's an ill wind (that blows nobody any good) spoken used to say that every problem brings an advantage for someone → ILL FEELING, ILL WILL

ill² adv **1 sb can ill afford (to do) sth** to be unable to do or have something without making the situation you are in very difficult: *I was losing weight which I could ill afford to lose.* | *Most gamblers can ill afford their habit.* **2 think/speak ill of sb** formal to think or say unpleasant things about someone: *She really believes you should never speak ill of the dead.* **3 bode ill** formal to give you a reason to think that something bad will happen: *The look on his face boded ill for somebody.*

ill³ n **1 ills** [plural] problems and difficulties: *He wants to cure all the ills of the world.* **2** [U] formal harm, evil, or bad luck: *She did not like Matthew but she would never wish him ill.*

ill- /ɪl/ prefix badly or not enough: *ill-concealed boredom* | *ill-formed sentences*

This graph shows how common the adjectives **ill** and **sick** are in British and American English.

ill

| BrE |
| AmE |

20 40 60 per million

sick

| BrE |
| AmE |

20 40 60 per million

In British English the word **ill** means not healthy. Americans usually use **sick** for this meaning. In British English **sick** can be used in this way, but is more commonly used in expressions such as **be sick** or **feel sick** meaning to vomit or feel that you are going to vomit.

I'll /aɪl/ the short form of 'I will' or 'I shall': *I'll see you tomorrow.*

ill-ad'vised *adj* not sensible or not wise and likely to cause problems in the future: **ill-advised to do sth** *You would be ill-advised to go out alone at night.* | *ill-advised remarks* —**ill-advisedly** /-əd'vaɪzᵈli/ *adv*

ill-as'sorted *adj* an ill-assorted group of people or things do not seem to belong together in a group

ill-'bred *adj* rude or behaving badly, especially because your parents did not teach you to behave well

ill-con'ceived *adj* not planned well and not having an aim that is likely to be achieved: *The policy was ill-conceived and wrong-headed.*

ill-con'sidered *adj* decisions, actions, ideas etc that are ill-considered have not been carefully thought about: *The tax reforms are ill-considered.*

ill-de'fined *adj* **1** not described clearly enough: *Some jobs in the company are pretty ill-defined.* **2** not clearly marked, or not having a clear shape; ☐ **indistinct**: *The borders were vague and ill-defined.*

ill-dis'posed *adj formal* unfriendly or unsympathetic: *an ill-disposed character*

il·le·gal¹ /ɪ'liːgəl/ *adj* not allowed by the law; ☐ **unlawful**; ☐ **legal**: *illegal drugs* | *illegal activities* such as prostitution and gambling | **it is illegal to do sth** *It is illegal to sell tobacco to someone under 16.* —**illegally** *adv*: *They entered the country illegally.* —**illegality** /ˌɪlɪ'gælᵻti/ *n* [U]

illegal² *n* [C] *AmE* spoken an illegal immigrant: *Illegals are still slipping through in unacceptable numbers.*

il·legal 'immigrant also **il·legal 'alien** *AmE n* [C] someone who comes to live in another country without official permission

il·le·gi·ble /ɪ'ledʒᵻbəl/ *adj* difficult or impossible to read; ☐ **legible**: *His handwriting is totally illegible.* —**illegibly** *adv* —**illegibility** /ɪˌledʒᵻ'bɪlᵻti/ *n* [U]

il·le·git·i·mate /ˌɪlᵻ'dʒɪtᵻmᵻt◂/ *adj* **1** born to parents who are not married; ☐ **legitimate**: *his illegitimate son* **2** not allowed or acceptable according to rules or agreements; ☐ **legitimate**: *a distinction between legitimate and illegitimate trade* —**illegitimately** *adv* —**illegitimacy** *n* [U]

ill-e'quipped *adj* not having the necessary equipment or skills for a particular situation or activity: **ill-equipped to do sth** *The rebels were ill-equipped to cope with Western weapons and forces.* | [+for] *Their army is ill-equipped for modern warfare.*

ill-'fated *adj literary* unlucky and leading to serious problems or death: *an ill-fated venture*

ill 'feeling *n* [U] angry feelings towards someone: *'I'm sorry. No ill feeling?' 'None,' she replied.*

ill-'fitting *adj* ill-fitting clothes do not fit the person who is wearing them; ☐ **well-fitting**: *Many children have problems with their feet, caused by ill-fitting shoes.*

ill-'founded *adj formal* based on something that is untrue: *His fears proved ill-founded.*

ill-gotten 'gains *adj* money that was obtained in an unfair or dishonest way – used humorously: *Well, I hope you enjoy your ill-gotten gains.*

il·lib·e·ral /ɪ'lɪbərəl/ *adj formal* **1** not supporting people's rights to say or do what they want; ☐ **liberal**: *illiberal and undemocratic policies* **2** not generous —**illiberally** *adv* —**illiberality** /ɪˌlɪbə'rælᵻti/ *n* [U]

il·li·cit /ɪ'lɪsᵻt/ *adj* not allowed by laws or rules, or strongly disapproved of by society; → **illegal**: *illicit drugs* | *the illicit trade in stolen cattle* —**illicitly** *adv*

ill-in'formed *adj* knowing less than you should about a particular subject: [+about] *Some employers are ill-informed about education.*

il·lit·e·rate¹ /ɪ'lɪtərᵻt/ *adj* **1** someone who is illiterate has not learned to read or write **2** badly written, in an uneducated way: *It was an illiterate letter, full of mistakes.* **3 economically/politically/scientifically etc illiterate** knowing very little about economics, politics etc —**illiteracy** *n* [U]

illiterate² *n* [C] someone who has not learned to read or write

ill-'judged *adj formal* an action that is ill-judged has not been thought about carefully enough; ☐ **well-judged**: *an ill-judged choice of words*

ill-'mannered *adj formal* not polite and behaving badly in social situations; ☐ **well-mannered**: *The fellow is an ill-mannered brute.*

ill·ness S2 W3 /'ɪlnᵻs/ *n* [C,U] a disease of the body or mind, or the condition of being ill → DISEASE

have an illness/suffer from an illness
recover from an illness
serious illness
minor illness
short/long illness
childhood illness
acute illness (=an illness that becomes serious very quickly)
chronic illness (=an illness that lasts a long time and cannot be cured)
fatal illness (=an illness which causes death)
terminal illness (=an illness which cannot be cured and that causes death, often slowly)
mental illness
the symptoms of an illness (=the things that show that someone has it)
through illness (=because of illness)

*She **had** all the normal childhood **illnesses**.* | *I'd been told I'd been **suffering from** various illnesses.* | *Her mother was just **recovering from** an illness.* | *Have you ever had any **serious illnesses**?* | *He died in hospital yesterday after a **short illness**.* | *patients with **chronic illnesses*** | *Her husband was diagnosed with a **terminal illness**. (=doctors found that her husband had a terminal illness)* | *Stress can cause **mental illness**.* | *I've never missed a day's work **through illness** in my life.* | *ways to improve your health and reduce the risk of illness*

Illness and **disease** are often used in the same way and are equally common in spoken English.
However, **illness** is more often used to refer to the length of time or state of being unwell: *He died after a long illness.* | *if you are off school because of illness*
⚠ Do not use **illness** to talk about less serious problems such as headaches or colds.
Disease is a particular kind of illness, especially one that spreads from one person to another or affects a particular part of your body: *infectious diseases* | *heart disease*
⚠ **Disease** can also be used to mean a lot of different diseases: *Cigarette smoking causes death and disease.*

il·lo·gi·cal /ɪ'lɒdʒɪkəl $ ɪ'lɑː-/ *adj* not sensible or reasonable; ☐ **logical**: *illogical and unreasonable fear* | **it is illogical to do sth** *It is illogical to assume you can do* *the work of three people.* —**illogically** /-kli/ *adv* —**illogicality** /ɪˌlɒdʒɜ̩'kælɨti $ ɪˌlɑː-/ *n* [U]

,**ill-pre'pared** *adj* not ready for something: [+for] *The country was ill-prepared for war.*

,**ill-'served** *adj* [not before noun] not helped by something or not represented well: *The north-east of the country is ill-served by the rail network.*

,**ill-'starred** *adj literary* unlucky and likely to cause or experience a lot of problems or unhappiness: *an ill-starred love affair*

,**ill-'suited** *adj* not useful for a particular purpose: [+to] *a country ill-suited to wheat farming*

,**ill-'tempered** *adj formal* **1** easily made angry or impatient; ⊟ **bad-tempered** **2** an ill-tempered meeting, argument etc is one in which people are angry and often rude to each other: *Six players were sent off in an ill-tempered game.*

,**ill-'timed** *adj* happening, done, or said at the wrong time; ⊞ **well-timed**: *His remarks were ill-timed.*

,**ill-'treat** *v* [T] to be cruel to someone, especially to a child or animal: *a rescue centre for ill-treated horses* —**ill-treatment** *n* [U]

il·lu·mi·nate /ɪ'luːmɨ̩neɪt, ɪ'ljuː- $ ɪ'luː-/ also **illumine** *v* [T] **1** to make a light shine on something, or to fill a place with light: *A single candle illuminated his face.* | *At night the canals are beautifully illuminated.* **2** *formal* to make something much clearer and easier to understand: *The report illuminated the difficult issues at the heart of science policy.*

il·lu·mi·nat·ed /ɪ'luːmɨ̩neɪt ɨ̩d, -'ljuː- $ -'luː-/ *adj* **1** lit up by lights: *An illuminated sign flashed on and off.* **2 illuminated manuscript/book** a book of a type produced by hand in the Middle Ages, whose pages are decorated with gold paint and other bright colours

il·lu·mi·nat·ing /ɪ'luːmɨ̩neɪtɪŋ, ɪ'ljuː- $ ɪ'luː-/ *adj* making things much clearer and easier to understand: *a very illuminating book*

il·lu·mi·na·tion /ɪˌluːmɨ̩'neɪʃən, ɪˌljuː- $ ɪˌluː-/ *n formal* **1** [U] lighting provided by a lamp, light etc: *White candles, the only illumination, burned on the table.* | *The rooms were flooded with soft illumination.* **2** [C usually plural] a picture or pattern painted on a page of a book, especially in the past: *the illuminations in a medieval manuscript* **3 illuminations** *BrE* a show of coloured lights used to make a town bright and colourful: *the Blackpool illuminations* **4** [C,U] *formal* a clear explanation or understanding of a particular subject

il·lu·mine /ɪ'luːmɨ̩n, ɪ'ljuː- $ ɪ'luː-/ *v* [T] to illuminate

il·lu·sion /ɪ'luːʒən/ *n* [C] **1** an idea or opinion that is wrong, especially about yourself; → **delusion**: **illusion that** *They suffer from the illusion that they cannot solve their problems.* | *She was under no illusion that he loved her.* | *It is an illusion that the Arctic is dark in winter.* | *She had no illusions about her physical attractions.* | *'I hate to shatter your illusions,' he said.* **2** something that seems to be different from the way it really is: [+of] *He was unlikely to be satisfied with the illusion of power.* | **give/create an illusion** *The mirrors in the room gave an illusion of greater space.* | *Credit creates the illusion that you can own things without paying for them.* → **OPTICAL ILLUSION**

il·lu·sion·ist /ɪ'luːʒənɨ̩st/ *n* [C] someone who does surprising tricks that make things seem to appear or happen; ⊟ **magician**

il·lu·so·ry /ɪ'luːsəri/ also **il·lu·sive** /ɪ'luːsɪv/ *adj formal* false but seeming to be real or true: *First impressions can often prove illusory.*

il·lus·trate [W2] /'ɪləstreɪt/ *v* [T]
1 to make the meaning of something clearer by giving examples: *Let me give an example to illustrate the point.* | *She illustrated her discussion with diagrams.* **2** to be an example which shows that something is true or that a fact exists: **illustrate that** *This dispute illustrates that the regime is deeply divided.* | **illustrate how** *The following examples illustrate how this operates in*

practice. | *This illustrates a fundamental weakness in the system.* **3** to put pictures in a book, article etc: *Over a hundred diagrams, tables and pictures illustrate the book.*

il·lus·tra·tion /ˌɪlə'streɪʃən/ *n* **1** [C] a picture in a book, article etc, especially one that helps you to understand it: *The book contains 62 pages of illustrations.* **2** [C,U] a story, event, action etc that shows the truth or existence of something very clearly: [+of] *a striking illustration of 19th century attitudes to women* | *For the purposes of illustration, some of the more important symptoms are listed below.* **3** [U] the act or process of illustrating something

il·lus·tra·tive /'ɪləstreɪtɪv, -strət- $ ɪ'lʌstrətɪv/ *adj* **1** helping to explain the meaning of something: [+of] *The case is illustrative of a common pattern.* | *For illustrative purposes, only a simple example is given here.* **2** having pictures, especially to help you understand something: *graphics and other illustrative material* → **ILLUSTRATE**

il·lus·tra·tor /'ɪləstreɪtə $ -ər/ *n* [C] someone who draws pictures, especially for books

il·lus·tri·ous /ɪ'lʌstriəs/ *adj formal* famous and admired because of what you have achieved: *She has had an illustrious career.* | *Wagner was just one of many illustrious visitors to the town.*

,**ill 'will** *n* [U] unfriendly or unkind feelings towards someone: *He said the accusation had been made from hatred and ill will.*

im- /ɪm, ɪ/ *prefix* the form used for IN- before b, m, or p: *immobilize* | *impossible*

I'm /aɪm/ the short form of 'I am': *I'm a student.*

IM /ˌaɪ 'em/ *n* [U] *instant messaging* a type of service available on the Internet that allows you to quickly exchange written messages with people that you know

im·age [S3] [W1] /'ɪmɪdʒ/ *n* [C]
1 PUBLIC OPINION the opinion people have of a person, organization, product etc, or the way a person, organization etc seems to be to the public: *The hotel and casino industry is working hard on improving its image.* | *The party has to project the right image.* | [+of] *Attempts were made to improve the public image of the police.*
2 IDEA IN MIND a picture that you have in your mind, especially about what someone or something is like or the way they look: [+of] *He had no visual image of her, only her name.* | *He had the clearest image in his mind of his mother and father.*
3 PICTURE/WHAT YOU SEE a) a picture of an object in a mirror or of a camera: *She peered closely at her image in the mirror.* **b)** a picture on the screen of a television, cinema, or computer: *Jill Sharpe was little more than a name, a glossy image on a television screen.* **c)** a picture or shape of a person or thing that is copied onto paper or is cut in wood or stone: *carved images*
4 DESCRIPTION a word, phrase, or picture that describes an idea in a poem, book, film etc: *He paints a very romantic image of working-class communities.*
5 be the (very/living/spitting) image of sb to look exactly like someone or something else: *He's the spitting image of his mother.*
6 in the image of sb/sth *literary* in the same form or shape as someone or something else: *According to the Bible, man was made in the image of God.* → **MIRROR IMAGE**

im·ag·e·ry /'ɪmɪdʒəri/ *n* [U] the use of words or pictures to describe ideas or actions in poems, books, films etc: [+of] *the imagery of love* | *Their dreams commonly involved complex stories with visual imagery.*

i·ma·gi·na·ble /ɪ'mædʒɨ̩nəbəl/ *adj* **1** used to emphasize that something is the best, worst etc that can be imagined: *The travel brochure is full of the most wonderful resorts imaginable.* **2** used to emphasize

im·mi·grant /'ɪmɪ̰grənt/ n [C] someone who enters another country to live there permanently; → **emigrant**: *an illegal immigrant* | *a new wave of immigrants from the Middle East*

im·mi·grate /'ɪmɪ̰greɪt/ v [I] to come into a country in order to live there permanently; → **emigrate**: *His father and mother immigrated when he was two.*

im·mi·gra·tion /ˌɪmɪ̰'greɪʃən/ n [U] **1** the process of entering another country in order to live there permanently; → **emigration**: *He called for a common European policy on immigration.* **2** the total number of people who immigrate: *Immigration fell in the 1980s.* **3** also **immigration control** the place at an airport, sea port etc where officials check the documents of everyone entering the country

im·mi·nent /'ɪmɪ̰nənt/ adj an event that is imminent, especially an unpleasant one, will happen very soon: **imminent danger/threat/death/disaster etc** *He was in imminent danger of dying.* | *He smiled in anticipation of her imminent arrival.* | *A new trade agreement is imminent.* —**imminence** n [U]: *the imminence of the General Election* —**imminently** adv

im·mo·bile /ɪ'məʊbaɪl $ ɪ'moʊbəl/ adj **1** not moving at all; ▤ **motionless**: *She could see a figure sitting immobile, facing the sea.* **2** unable to move or walk normally: *Kim's illness had rendered her completely immobile.* —**immobility** /ˌɪmə'bɪlɪ̰ti/ n [U]

im·mo·bi·lize also **-ise** BrE /ɪ'məʊbɪ̰laɪz $ ɪ'moʊ-/ v [T] **1** to prevent someone or something from moving: *The broken limb must be immobilized immediately.* | *She was immobilized with a broken leg.* **2** to stop something from working: *The car's security device will immobilize the ignition system.* —**immobilization** /ɪˌməʊbɪ̰laɪ'zeɪʃən $ ɪˌmoʊbələ-/ n [U]

im·mo·bi·liz·er /ɪ'məʊbɪ̰laɪzə $ ɪ'moʊbɪ̰laɪzər/ n [C] BrE a piece of equipment that is fitted to a car to stop it moving if someone tries to steal it

im·mod·e·rate /ɪ'mɒdərɪ̰t $ ɪ'mɑː-/ adj formal not within reasonable and sensible limits; ▤ **excessive**: *immoderate drinking* —**immoderately** adv

im·mod·est /ɪ'mɒdɪst $ ɪ'mɑː-/ adj **1** having a very high opinion of yourself and your abilities, and not embarrassed about telling people how clever you are; ▤ **modest**: *Webb was an immodest publicist of his own achievements.* **2** clothes that are immodest show too much of someone's body; ▤ **revealing**; ▤ **modest 3** old-fashioned behaviour that is immodest shocks or embarrasses people: *They thought it was immodest for both sexes to swim together.* —**immodestly** adv —**immodesty** n [U]

im·mo·late /'ɪmələɪt/ v [T] formal to kill someone or destroy something by burning them —**immolation** /ˌɪmə'leɪʃən/ n [U]

im·mor·al /ɪ'mɒrəl $ ɪ'mɔː-/ adj **1** morally wrong; → **amoral**: *Deliberately making people suffer is immoral.* | *It's immoral to be rich while people are starving and homeless.* **2** not following accepted standards of sexual behaviour —**immorally** adv —**immorality** /ˌɪmə'rælɪ̰ti/ n [U]: *the immorality of bombing civilians*

im·mor·tal /ɪ'mɔːtl $ -ɔːr-/ adj **1** living or continuing for ever; ▤ **mortal**: *Plato believed that the soul is immortal.* **2** an immortal line, play, song etc is so famous that it will never be forgotten: *In the immortal words of Henry Ford, 'If it ain't broke, don't fix it.'* —**immortal** n [C]

im·mor·tal·i·ty /ˌɪmɔː'tælɪ̰ti $ -ɔːr-/ n [U] the state of living for ever or being remembered for ever: *the immortality of the soul*

im·mor·tal·ize also **-ise** BrE /ɪ'mɔːtəlaɪz $ -ɔːr-/ v [T usually passive] to make someone or something famous for a long time, especially by writing about them, painting a picture of them etc: *Dickens' father was immortalized as Mr Micawber in 'David Copperfield'.*

im·mo·va·ble /ɪ'muːvəbəl/ adj **1** impossible to move: *Lock your bike to something immovable like a railing or lamp-post.* **2** impossible to change or persuade: *The president is immovable on this issue.* —**immovably** adv

im·mune /ɪ'mjuːn/ adj **1** [not before noun] someone who is immune to a particular disease cannot catch it: *Once we've had the disease, we're immune for life.* **2 immune response/reaction** the reaction of the body's immune system to something that is harmful: *HIV is a progressive disease which the immune response ultimately fails to control.* **3** [not before noun] not affected by something that happens or is done: [+to] *The Labour Party is not immune to new ideas.* **4** [not before noun] specially protected from something unpleasant: [+from] *The senior members of the group appeared to be immune from arrest.*

im'mune ˌsystem n [C] the system by which your body protects itself against disease: *This flu is a warning to me that my immune system is not as strong as it ought to be.*

im·mu·nise /'ɪmjɪ̰naɪz/ v a British spelling of IMMUNIZE

im·mu·ni·ty /ɪ'mjuːnɪ̰ti/ n [U] **1** the state or right of being protected from particular laws or from unpleasant things: [+from] *They were granted immunity from prosecution.* **2** the state of being immune to a disease: [+to] *immunity to infection* | [+from] *immunity from smallpox*

im·mu·nize also **-ise** BrE /'ɪmjɪ̰naɪz/ v [T] to protect someone from a particular illness by giving them a VACCINE; ▤ **vaccinate**, **inoculate**: **immunize sb against sth** *There is still no vaccine to immunize people against the virus.* —**immunization** /ˌɪmjɪ̰nai'zeɪʃən $ -nə-/ n [C,U]

im·mu·nol·o·gy /ˌɪmjɪ̰'nɒlədʒi $ -'nɑː-/ n [U] the scientific study of the prevention of disease and how the body reacts to disease

im·mure /ɪ'mjʊə $ ɪ'mjʊr/ v [T] formal or literary to shut someone in a place so that they cannot get out

im·mu·ta·ble /ɪ'mjuːtəbəl/ adj formal never changing or impossible to change: *This decision should not be seen as immutable.* —**immutably** adv —**immutability** /ˌɪmjuːtə'bɪlɪ̰ti/ n [U]

I-mode phone /'aɪ məʊd ˌfəʊn $ -moʊd ˌfoʊn/ n [C] trademark a MOBILE PHONE that has a small screen which you can use for Internet and e-mail services

imp /ɪmp/ n [C] **1** a child who behaves badly, but in a way that is funny **2** a small creature in stories who has magic powers and behaves very badly → **IMPISH**

im·pact¹ W2 /'ɪmpækt/ n

1 [C] the effect or influence that an event, situation etc has on someone or something: [+on/upon] *We need to assess the impact on climate change.* | **major/significant/ profound etc impact** | *Higher mortgage rates have already had a major impact on spending.* | [+of] *an international meeting to consider the environmental impacts of global warming* ⚠ Do not say 'cause an impact' on something. Say **have an impact** on something. **2** [C,U] the force of one object hitting another: *The force of the impact knocked the breath out of her.* **3 on impact** at the moment when one thing hits another: *The plane's wing was damaged on impact.*

im·pact² /ɪm'pækt/ v [I,T] especially AmE to have an important or noticeable effect on someone or something: [+on/upon] *The Food Safety Act will progressively impact on the way food businesses operate.*

im·pact·ed /ɪm'pæktɪd/ adj a tooth that is impacted is growing under another tooth so that it cannot develop properly

im·pair /ɪm'peə $ -'per/ v [T] to damage something or make it not as good as it should be: *The illness had impaired his ability to think and concentrate.* —**impairment** n [U]

im·paired /ɪm'peəd $ -'perd/ adj damaged, less strong, or not as good as before: *impaired vision* |

(=used to describe someone who cannot see, hear etc well)

im·pair·ment /ɪmˈpeəmənt $ ɪmˈper-/ *n* [C,U] **mental/visual/cognitive/hearing** etc **impairment** a condition in which a part of a person's mind or body is damaged or does not work well

im·pa·la /ɪmˈpɑːlə/ *n plural* **impala** [C] a large African ANTELOPE

im·pale /ɪmˈpeɪl/ *v* [T often passive] if someone or something is impaled, a sharp pointed object goes through them: **be impaled on sth** *Their heads were impaled on Charles Bridge as a warning to others.* —**impalement** *n* [C,U]

im·pal·pa·ble /ɪmˈpælpəbəl/ *adj formal* **1** impossible to touch or feel physically; **➡ palpable** **2** very difficult to understand

im·pan·el /ɪmˈpænl/ *v* another spelling of EMPANEL

im·part /ɪmˈpɑːt $ -ɑːrt/ *v* [T] *formal* **1** to give a particular quality to something: **impart sth to sth** *Use a piece of fresh ginger to impart a Far-Eastern flavour to simple ingredients.* **2** to give information, knowledge, wisdom etc to someone: *She had information that she couldn't wait to impart.*

im·par·tial /ɪmˈpɑːʃəl $ -ɑːr-/ *adj* not involved in a particular situation, and therefore able to give a fair opinion or piece of advice; **➡ fair**; **➡ biased**: *We offer **impartial advice** on tax and insurance.* | *an **impartial inquiry** into the deaths* | *an impartial observer* —**impartially** *adv* —**impartiality** /ˌɪmˌpɑːʃiˈæləti $ -ɑːr-/ *n* [U]

im·pass·a·ble /ɪmˈpɑːsəbəl $ ɪmˈpæ-/ *adj* a road, path, or area that is impassable is impossible to travel along or through: *The mountains are impassable.*

im·passe /æmˈpɑːs $ ˈɪmpæs/ *n* [singular] a situation in which it is impossible to continue with a discussion or plan because the people involved cannot agree: **at an impasse** *The political process is at an impasse.* | *Negotiations seemed to have **reached an impasse.***

im·pas·sioned /ɪmˈpæʃənd/ *adj* full of strong feeling and emotion: *She appeared on television to make an **impassioned plea** for help.* | *an impassioned speech*

im·pas·sive /ɪmˈpæsɪv/ *adj* not showing any emotion: *Her **impassive face** showed no reaction at all.* —**impassively** *adv*: *The children studied him impassively.* —**impassivity** /ˌɪmpæˈsɪvəti/ *n* [U]

im·pa·tience /ɪmˈpeɪʃəns/ *n* [U] **1** annoyance at having to accept delays, other people's weaknesses etc; **➡ patience**: [+with] *his impatience with the slowness of bureaucratic procedures* | *A note of impatience had entered his voice.* **2** great eagerness for something to happen, especially something that is going to happen soon: **impatience to do sth** *She was bursting with impatience to tell Natalia what had happened.*

im·pa·tient /ɪmˈpeɪʃənt/ *adj* **1** annoyed because of delays, someone else's mistakes etc; **➡ patient**: **become/grow impatient (with sb/sth)** *We are growing impatient with the lack of results.* | *He turned away with an impatient gesture.* **2** [not before noun] very eager for something to happen and not wanting to wait: **impatient to do sth** *Alec strode down the street, impatient to be home.* | **impatient for sb to do sth** *He was eager to talk to Shildon and impatient for him to return from lunch.* —**impatiently** *adv*

im·peach /ɪmˈpiːtʃ/ *v* [T] *law* if a government official is impeached, they are formally charged with a serious crime in a special government court: *The governor was impeached for using state funds improperly.* —**impeachment** *n* [C,U]

im·pec·ca·ble /ɪmˈpekəbəl/ *adj* without any faults and impossible to criticize; **➡ perfect**: *She has taught her children **impeccable manners.*** | *a bar with impeccable service* —**impeccably** *adv*: *impeccably dressed*

im·pe·cu·ni·ous /ˌɪmpɪˈkjuːniəs◂/ *adj formal* having very little money, especially over a long period – sometimes used humorously: *He came from a respectable if*

impecunious family. —**impecuniously** *adv* —**impecuniousness** *n* [U]

im·ped·ance /ɪmˈpiːdəns/ *n* [singular,U] *technical* a measure of the power of a piece of electrical equipment to stop the flow of an ALTERNATING CURRENT

im·pede /ɪmˈpiːd/ *v* [T] to make it difficult for someone or something to move forward or make progress: *Storms at sea **impeded** our **progress.***

im·ped·i·ment /ɪmˈpedəmənt/ *n* [C] **1** a physical problem that makes speaking, hearing, or moving difficult: *a **speech impediment*** **2** a situation or event that makes it difficult or impossible for someone or something to succeed or make progress: [+to] *War is one of the greatest impediments to human progress.*

im·ped·i·men·ta /ɪmˌpedɪˈmentə/ *n* [plural] things that you think you need to have or do, but which can slow your progress – often used humourously

im·pel /ɪmˈpel/ *v* **impelled, impelling** [T] *formal* if something impels you to do something, it makes you feel very strongly that you must do it; → **compel**: **impel sb to do sth** *The lack of democracy and equality impelled the oppressed to fight for independence.*

im·pend·ing /ɪmˈpendɪŋ/ *adj* an impending event or situation, especially an unpleasant one, is going to happen very soon: **impending danger/doom/death/disaster** etc *She had a sense of impending disaster.* | *impending changes in government legislation*

im·pen·e·tra·ble /ɪmˈpenɪtrəbəl/ *adj* **1** impossible to get through, see through, or get into: *The trees formed a dark and **impenetrable barrier.*** | *the impenetrable blackness of the night* **2** very difficult or impossible to understand: *impenetrable legal jargon* —**impenetrably** *adv* —**impenetrability** /ɪmˌpenɪtrəˈbɪləti/ *n* [U]

im·per·a·tive¹ /ɪmˈperətɪv/ *adj* **1** extremely important and needing to be done or dealt with immediately: *It is imperative that politicians should be good communicators.* | **it is imperative (for sb) to do sth** *It is imperative to meet face to face with the client.* | *It is imperative for us to remain on good terms.* **2** *technical* an imperative verb is one that expresses an order, such as 'stand up' —**imperatively** *adv*

imperative² *n* [C] **1** something that must be done urgently: *A broad and balanced education is an imperative for raising standards.* **2** *formal* an idea or belief that has a strong influence on people, making them behave in a particular way: *Sharing food is the most important **moral imperative** in Semai society.* **3** *technical* the form of a verb that expresses an order. For example, in the order 'come here', 'come' is in the imperative

im·per·cep·ti·ble /ˌɪmpəˈseptɪbəl $ -pər-/ *adj* almost impossible to see or notice: *Such changes are imperceptible to even the best-trained eye.* —**imperceptibly** *adv*: *The daylight faded almost imperceptibly into night.* —**imperceptibility** /ˌɪmpəseptɪˈbɪləti $ -pər-/ *n* [U]

im·per·fect¹ /ɪmˈpɜːfɪkt $ -ɜːr-/ *adj* not completely correct or perfect; **➡ flawed**: *the imperfect world we live in* | *I got it cheap because it's slightly imperfect.* —**imperfectly** *adv* —**imperfection** /ˌɪmpəˈfekʃən $ -pər-/ *n* [C,U]

imperfect² *n* **the imperfect** *technical* the form of a verb which is used when talking about an action in the past that is not complete. For example, 'I was eating.'

im·pe·ri·al /ɪmˈpɪəriəl $ -ˈpɪr-/ *adj* [only before noun] **1** relating to an EMPIRE or to the person who rules it: *Britain's **imperial expansion** in the 19th century* | *a major **imperial power*** **2** relating to the system of weights and measurements based on pounds, INCHES, miles etc

im·pe·ri·al·is·m /ɪmˈpɪəriəlɪzəm $ -ˈpɪr-/ *n* [U] **1** a political system in which one country rules a lot of other countries; → **colonialism**: *a book on the history of British imperialism* **2** the way in which a rich or powerful country's way of life, culture, businesses etc influence and change a poorer country's way of life etc: **cultural/economic/social etc imperialism** *Small nations resent Western cultural imperialism.* —**imperialist** *n* [C] —**imperialist** *adj*

im·per·il /ɪmˈperəl/ *v* **imperilled, imperilling** BrE, **imperiled, imperiling** AmE [T] *formal* to put something or someone in danger; **≡ endanger**: *Tax increases now might imperil economic recovery.*

im·pe·ri·ous /ɪmˈpɪəriəs $ -ˈpɪr-/ *adj* giving orders and expecting to be obeyed, in a way that seems too proud: *She raised her hand in an imperious gesture.* —**imperiously** *adv* —**imperiousness** *n* [U]

im·per·ish·a·ble /ɪmˈperɪʃəbəl/ *adj formal* existing or continuing for a long time or for ever: *a set of imperishable truths*

im·per·ma·nent /ɪmˈpɜːmənənt $ -ɜːr-/ *adj formal* not staying the same for ever; **≡ temporary**; **⊟ permanent**: *single-storey structures, built from cheap and impermanent materials* —**impermanence** *n* [U]: *His philosophy stressed the impermanence of the world.*

im·per·me·a·ble /ɪmˈpɜːmiəbəl $ -ɜːr-/ *adj technical* not allowing liquids or gases to pass through; **⊟ permeable**: *No paint is impermeable to water vapour.*

im·per·mis·si·ble /ˌɪmpɜːˈmɪsɪbəl $ -ɜːr-/ *adj formal* something that is impermissible cannot be allowed; **⊟ permissible**

im·per·son·al /ɪmˈpɜːsənəl $ -ɜːr-/ *adj* **1** not showing any feelings of sympathy, friendliness etc: *Business letters do not have to be impersonal and formal.* | *Sometimes she seems a very impersonal, even unkind, mother.* **2** a place or situation that is impersonal does not make people feel that they are important: *I hate staying in hotels; they're so impersonal.* | *a formal and impersonal style of management* **3** *technical* in grammar, an impersonal sentence or verb is one where the subject is represented by 'it' or 'there', as in the sentence 'It rained all day' —**impersonally** *adv*

im·per·son·ate /ɪmˈpɜːsəneɪt $ -ɜːr-/ *v* [T] **1** to pretend to be someone else by copying their appearance, voice, and behaviour, especially in order to deceive people: *Do you know it is a very serious offence to impersonate a police officer?* **2** to copy someone's voice and behaviour, especially in order to make people laugh: *In the film he amusingly impersonates a woman.* —**impersonation** /ɪmˌpɜːsəˈneɪʃən $ -ɜːr-/ *n* [C,U]: *He's renowned for his Elvis impersonation.*

im·per·son·a·tor /ɪmˈpɜːsəneɪtə $ -ˈpɜːrsəneɪtər/ *n* [C] someone who copies the way that other people look, speak, and behave, as part of a performance: *a female impersonator*

im·per·ti·nent /ɪmˈpɜːtɪnənt $ -ɜːr-/ *adj* rude and not respectful, especially to someone who is older or more important; **≡ cheeky**: *He was always asking impertinent questions.* | *You are an impertinent young woman.* —**impertinently** *adv* —**impertinence** *n* [U]

im·per·tur·ba·ble /ˌɪmpəˈtɜːbəbəl $ -pərˈtɜːr-/ *adj* remaining calm and unworried in spite of problems or difficulties —**imperturbably** *adv* —**imperturbability** /ˌɪmpətɜːbəˈbɪlɪti $ -pərtɜːr-/ *n* [U]

im·per·vi·ous /ɪmˈpɜːviəs $ -ɜːr-/ *adj* [not before noun] **1** *formal* not affected or influenced by something and seeming not to notice it: [+to] *His ego was impervious to self-doubt.* **2** *technical* not allowing anything to enter or pass through: *impervious volcanic rock* | [+to] *materials that are impervious to water*

im·pe·ti·go /ˌɪmpɪˈtaɪɡəʊ $ -ɡoʊ/ *n* [U] an infectious skin disease

im·pet·u·ous /ɪmˈpetʃuəs/ *adj* tending to do things very quickly, without thinking carefully first, or showing this quality; **≡ impulsive**: *He was high-spirited*

and impetuous. | *She might live to regret this impetuous decision.* —**impetuously** *adv* —**impetuousness** *n* [U] —**impetuosity** /ɪmˌpetʃuˈɒsɪti $ -ˈɑː-/ *n* [U]

im·pe·tus /ˈɪmpɪtəs/ *n* [U] **1** an influence that makes something happen or makes it happen more quickly: [+for] *The report may provide further impetus for reform.* | *The discovery gave fresh impetus to the research.* **2** *technical* the force that makes an object start moving, or keeps it moving

im·pi·e·ty /ɪmˈpaɪəti/ *n plural* **impieties** *formal* [C,U] lack of respect for religion or God, or an action that shows this; → **impious**

im·pinge /ɪmˈpɪndʒ/ *v*
  impinge on/upon sb/sth *phr v formal* to have a harmful effect on someone or something: *Personal problems experienced by students may impinge on their work.* —**impingement** *n* [C,U]

im·pi·ous /ˈɪmpiəs/ *adj formal* lacking respect for religion or God; → **impiety**: *an impious crime* —**impiously** *adv* —**impiousness** *n* [U]

imp·ish /ˈɪmpɪʃ/ *adj* showing a lack of respect or seriousness in a way that is amusing rather than bad; **≡ mischievous**: *a little girl with dark hair and an impish grin* —**impishly** *adv*

im·plac·a·ble /ɪmˈplækəbəl/ *adj* very determined to continue opposing someone or something: *implacable enemies* | *The government faces implacable opposition on the issue of nuclear waste.* —**implacably** *adv*: *He remained implacably opposed to Stalin's regime.* —**implacability** /ɪmˌplækəˈbɪlɪti/ *n* [U]

im·plant¹ /ɪmˈplɑːnt $ ɪmˈplænt/ *v* **1** [T] to strongly fix an idea, feeling, attitude etc in someone's mind or character: **implant sth in sth** *A deep sense of patriotism had been implanted in him by his father.* **2** [T] to put something into someone's body by performing a medical operation: *Surgeons successfully implanted an artificial hip.* | **implant sth in/into sth** *A donor egg fertilised by her husband's sperm will be implanted in her womb.* **3** [I] *medical* if an egg or EMBRYO implants, it begins to develop normally: *The fertilized egg implants and becomes a foetus.* —**implantation** /ˌɪmplɑːnˈteɪʃən $ -plæn-/ *n* [U]

im·plant² /ˈɪmplɑːnt $ -plænt/ *n* [C] something artificial that is put into someone's body in a medical operation; → **transplant**: *silicone breast implants*

im·plau·si·ble /ɪmˈplɔːzəbəl $ -ˈplɒː-/ *adj* difficult to believe and therefore unlikely to be true; **⊟ plausible**: **implausible theory/idea/explanation etc** *Margaret found his excuse somewhat implausible.* | *It's not entirely implausible that a galaxy could be identical to our own.* —**implausibly** *adv* —**implausibility** /ɪmˌplɔːzəˈbɪlɪti $ -ˌplɒː-/ *n* [U]

im·ple·ment¹ W3 /ˈɪmpləment/ *v* [T] to take action or make changes that you have officially decided should happen: **implement a policy/plan/decision etc** *We have decided to implement the committee's recommendations in full.* —**implementation** /ˌɪmpləmenˈteɪʃən/ *n* [U]: *the implementation of the peace plan*

im·ple·ment² /ˈɪmpləmənt/ *n* [C] a tool, especially one used for outdoor physical work: *farming implements*

im·pli·cate /ˈɪmplɪkeɪt/ *v* [T] **1** to show or suggest that someone is involved in a crime or dishonest act: *The allegations implicated Abe to such an extent he was forced to resign.* | **implicate sb in sth** *Three police officers are implicated in the cover-up.* **2** [usually passive] *formal* if something is implicated in something bad or harmful, it is shown to be its cause: **be implicated in sth** *Viruses are known to be implicated in the development of some cancers.*

im·pli·ca·tion W2 /ˌɪmplɪˈkeɪʃən/ *n* **1** [C usually plural] a possible future effect or result of an action, event, decision etc: [+of] *What are the implications of these proposals?* | *This election has profound implications for the future of U.S. democracy.* | **consider/discuss/examine the implications** *His talk will examine the wider implications of the Internet*

2 [U] a situation in which it is shown or suggested that someone or something is involved in a crime or a dishonest act; → **implicate: the implication of sb (in sth)** *the implication of the former Chief of Staff in a major scandal*
3 [C,U] a suggestion that is not made directly but that people are expected to understand or accept; → **imply:** *They are called 'Supertrams', the implication being that* (=which is meant to suggest that) *they are more advanced than earlier models.* | **by implication** | *The law bans organized protests and, by implication, any form of opposition.*

im·pli·cit /ɪmˈplɪsɪt/ adj **1** suggested or understood without being stated directly; ◻ **explicit: implicit criticism/threat/assumption** *Her words contained an implicit threat.* | *His statement is being seen as implicit criticism of the work of research laboratories.* **2** formal forming a central part of something, but without being openly stated: [+in] *Confidentiality is implicit in your relationship with a counselor.* **3** complete and containing no doubts: **implicit faith/trust/belief** *They had implicit faith in his powers.* —**implicitly** adv: *They believed implicitly in their own superiority.*

im·plode /ɪmˈpləʊd $ -ˈploʊd/ v [I] **1** technical to explode inwards; ◻ **explode:** *The windows on both sides of the room had imploded.* **2** written if an organization or system implodes, it fails suddenly, often because of faults that it has; ◻ **collapse:** *Most nations learned their lesson during the 1930s when trade imploded and incomes plunged.* —**implosion** /ɪmˈpləʊʒən $ -ˈploʊ-/ n [C,U]

im·plore /ɪmˈplɔː $ -ɔːr/ v [I,T] formal to ask for something in an emotional way; ◻ **beg:** *'Don't go,' I implored her.* | **implore sb to do sth** *She implored the soldiers to save her child.* —**imploring** adj: *a ragged child with imploring eyes*

im·ply W2 /ɪmˈplaɪ/ v **implied, implying, implies** [T] **1** to suggest that something is true, without saying this directly; → **infer, implication: imply (that)** *Cleo blushed. She had not meant to imply that he was lying.* | *an implied threat*
2 if a fact, event etc implies something, it shows that it is likely to be true; ◻ **suggest: imply (that)** *The high level of radiation in the rocks implies that they are volcanic in origin.*
3 if one thing implies another, it proves that the second thing exists: *Democracy implies a respect for individual liberties.* | *High profits do not necessarily imply efficiency.*

im·po·lite /ˌɪmpəˈlaɪt◂/ adj not polite; ◻ **rude:** *an impolite remark* | **it is impolite (of sb) (to do sth)** *Would it be impolite of me to ask exactly where you've been?* —**impolitely** adv

im·pol·i·tic /ɪmˈpɒlɪtɪk $ -ˈpɑː-/ adj formal behaving in a way that is not careful and that could make people think you are not sensible; ◻ **unwise:** *It was considered impolitic of him to spend too much time with the party radicals.*

im·pon·der·a·ble /ɪmˈpɒndərəbəl $ -ˈpɑːn-/ n [C usually plural] formal something that cannot be exactly measured, judged, or calculated: *There are too many imponderables to make an accurate prediction.* —**imponderable** adj: *an imponderable question*

im·port¹ /ˈɪmpɔːt $ -ɔːrt/ n **1** [C,U] a product that is brought from one country into another so that it can be sold there, or the business of doing this; ◻ **export:** *a ban on beef imports* | *the abolition of import duties* (=taxes) | [+from] *cheap imports from Asia* | *American demand for Japanese imports* (=goods from Japan) | *the import of electrical goods* | *an application for an import licence* **2** [C] something new or different that is brought to a place where it did not previously exist: *The beetle is thought to be a European import.* **3** [U] formal importance or meaning: *a matter of no great import*

im·port² /ɪmˈpɔːt $ -ɔːrt/ v [T] **1** to bring a product from one country into another so that it can be sold there; ◻ **export:** *In 2001, Britain exported more cars than it imported.* | **import sth from sth** *All the meat is imported from France.* **2** to introduce something new or different in a place where it did not previously exist: *The unusual designs were probably imported from Iran.* | **import sth to/into sth** *The US comedy format was gradually imported to UK screens.* **3** to move information from one computer to another; ◻ **export: import sth from/into sth** *You can now import graphics from other applications.* —**imported** adj: *imported autos* | *imported data*

im·por·tance S2 W1 /ɪmˈpɔːtəns $ -ɔːr-/ n [singular, U] the quality of being important: **the importance of sth** *the importance of regular exercise* | *The fur trade now exceeded timber in importance.* | *Hindus* **attach great importance to** *food preparation.* (=it is very important to them) | **great/growing/paramount etc importance** *The men were on a mission of* **vital importance** *to their country.* | **of primary/secondary/equal importance** *Sometimes we forget that the media coverage of a sport is actually of secondary importance to the event itself.* | *I agree about the importance of these proposals* (=the reasons why they are important). | *Just being in the studio gave her a* **sense of importance** (=she felt important).

im·por·tant S1 W1 /ɪmˈpɔːtənt $ -ɔːr-/ adj
1 an important event, decision, problem etc has a big effect or influence on people's lives or on events in the future: *a very important meeting* | *The accident taught him an important lesson.* | *Happiness is more important than money.* | *'What did you say?' 'Oh, nothing important.'* | **it is important (to do sth)** *It's important to explain the procedure to the patient.* | **It's vitally important that** *you understand the danger.* | [+for] *It was important for the president to continue his schedule, regardless of the bomb threat.* | [+to] *Nothing could be more important to me than my family.* ⚠ When you mean that you care or think about something a lot, say that it is **important to** you, not that it is 'important for' you.
2 people who are important have a lot of power or influence: *a very important customer* | *They carry guns because it makes them feel important.*

> **WORD FOCUS: IMPORTANT**
> similar words: **main, key, chief, principal, leading, vital, crucial, essential, significant**
> not important: **unimportant, trivial, minor, irrelevant, insignificant**

im·por·tant·ly /ɪmˈpɔːtəntli $ -ɔːr-/ adv **1** [sentence adverb] used to show that your next statement or question is more, equally etc important than what you said before: **more/most/less/equally importantly** *Most importantly, you must keep a record of everything you do.* **2** in a way that shows you think that what you are saying or doing is important: *He strode importantly into the room.*

im·por·ta·tion /ˌɪmpɔːˈteɪʃən $ -ɔːr-/ n **1** [C,U] formal the act of bringing something new or different to a place where it did not previously exist, or something that arrives in this way: [+of] *restrictions on the importation of American movies* **2** [U] technical the business of bringing things into a country from other countries in order to sell them; ◻ **import:** [+of] *a law prohibiting the importation of tuna*

im·port·er /ɪmˈpɔːtə $ -ˈpɔːrtər/ n [C] a person, company, or country that buys goods from other countries so they can be sold in their own country; ◻ **exporter**

im·por·tu·nate /ɪmˈpɔːtʃɒnət $ -ɔːr-/ adj formal continuously asking for things in an annoying or unreasonable way: *importunate demands* —**importunity** /ˌɪmpəˈtjuːnɪti $ -pərˈtuː-/ n [U]

im·por·tune /ˌɪmpəˈtjuːn $ ˌɪmpərˈtuːn/ v [T] formal to ask someone for something continuously in an annoying or unreasonable way; → **beg**

im·pose W2 /ɪmˈpəʊz $ -ˈpoʊz/ v
1 [T] if someone in authority imposes a rule, punishment, tax etc, they force people to accept it: *The court can impose a fine or a prison sentence.* | **impose sth on sth/sb** *The government imposed a ban on the sale of ivory.*
2 [T] to force someone to have the same ideas, beliefs etc as you: **impose sth on sb** *parents who impose their own moral values on their children*
3 [I] *formal* to expect or ask someone to do something for you when this is not convenient for them: [+on/upon] *We could ask to stay the night, but I don't want to impose on them.*
4 [T] to have a bad effect on something or someone and to cause problems for them: **impose a burden/hardship etc (on sb/sth)** *Military spending imposes a huge strain on the economy.*

im·pos·ing /ɪmˈpəʊzɪŋ $ -ˈpoʊ-/ adj large, impressive, and appearing important: *an imposing building* | *He's a tall, quietly spoken, but imposing figure.*

im·po·si·tion /ˌɪmpəˈzɪʃən/ n **1** [U] the introduction of something such as a rule, punishment, tax etc: [+of] *the imposition of martial law* **2** [C usually singular] *formal* something that someone expects or asks you to do for them, which is not convenient for you: *I know it's an imposition, but could I use your bathroom?*

im·pos·si·ble¹ S2 W2 /ɪmˈpɒsəbəl $ ɪmˈpɑː-/ adj
1 CAN'T BE DONE something that is impossible cannot happen or be done; ☒ **possible**

> it is impossible (for sb) to do sth
> make sth impossible
> find it impossible to do sth
> prove impossible (=be impossible, because you have tried but not succeeded)
> virtually/almost/practically/nearly impossible
> well-nigh impossible (=almost impossible)
> absolutely/utterly impossible
> seemingly impossible (=seeming to be impossible)
> physically impossible
> impossible task
> impossible feat (=something that is impossible to do)
> impossible dream (=something you want but that will never happen)
> difficult, if not impossible (=difficult, and perhaps impossible)

'I want to speak to Mr Franks.' 'I'm afraid that's impossible.' | *It's impossible to be accurate about these things.* | *The noise made sleep impossible.* | *Members with young children often found it impossible to attend evening meetings.* | *It is difficult to find work these days, but for blind people it is virtually impossible.* | *He was faced with a seemingly impossible task.* | *It was physically impossible to get the fridge through the door.* | *Six months ago, peace seemed an impossible dream.* | *Such mental attitudes are difficult, if not impossible, to change.*

2 SITUATION a situation that is impossible is one that you cannot deal with: *We were in an impossible situation. Whatever we decided to do would upset someone.* | *Helen's refusal to cooperate put me in an impossible position.* | *His attitude is making life impossible for the rest of the team.* | *He was facing impossible odds.*
3 PERSON behaving in a very unreasonable and annoying way: *Oh, you're just impossible!*
—**impossibly** adv: *Some sales managers think selling abroad is impossibly difficult.* | *He looked impossibly handsome in his formal suit.* —**impossibility** /ɪmˌpɒsəˈbɪləti $ -ˌpɑː-/ n [C,U]: *100 percent airline security is a practical impossibility.*

impossible² n **the impossible** something that cannot be done: **attempt/do/ask etc the impossible** *I just want to be able to buy healthy food at a reasonable price. Is that asking the impossible?*

im·pos·tor also **imposter** *AmE* /ɪmˈpɒstə $ ɪmˈpɑːstər/ n [C] someone who pretends to be someone else in order to trick people: *The nurse was soon discovered to be an impostor.*

im·po·tent /ˈɪmpətənt/ adj **1** unable to take effective action because you do not have enough power, strength, or control: *Emergency services seem impotent in the face of such a disaster.* | *impotent rage* **2** a man who is impotent is unable to have sex because he cannot get an ERECTION —**impotently** adv —**impotence** n [U]: *political impotence*

im·pound /ɪmˈpaʊnd/ v [T] *law* if the police or law courts impound something you have or own, they keep it until it has been decided that you can have it back; ☒ **confiscate**: *He sued the police after they impounded his car.*

im·pov·e·rish /ɪmˈpɒvərɪʃ $ ɪmˈpɑː-/ v [T] **1** to make someone very poor: *Falling coffee prices have impoverished many Third World economies.* | *families impoverished by debt* **2** to make something worse in quality: *Fast-growing trees remove nutrients and impoverish the soil.* —**impoverished** adj: *an impoverished student* —**impoverishment** n [U]: *spiritual impoverishment*

im·prac·ti·ca·ble /ɪmˈpræktɪkəbəl/ adj *formal* impossible or very difficult to do for practical reasons: *It was an appealing plan but quite impracticable.* —**impracticably** adv —**impracticability** /ɪmˌpræktɪkəˈbɪləti/ n [U]

im·prac·ti·cal /ɪmˈpræktɪkəl/ adj **1** not sensible or possible for practical reasons: *The road toll scheme was dismissed as impractical.* | *James was a foolish man, full of impractical plans.* **2** not good at dealing with ordinary practical matters, such as making or repairing things: *Sandra was hopelessly impractical around the house.* —**impractically** /-kli/ adv —**impracticality** /ɪmˌpræktɪˈkæləti/ n [U]: *the sheer impracticality of collecting DNA from such a large population*

im·pre·ca·tion /ˌɪmprɪˈkeɪʃən/ n [C] *literary* an offensive word or phrase, used when someone is very angry

im·pre·cise /ˌɪmprɪˈsaɪs◂/ adj not clear or exact; ☒ **precise**, **exact**: *vague, imprecise estimates* | *Alcohol affects the brain, making speech slurred and imprecise.* —**imprecisely** adv —**imprecision** /-ˈsɪʒən/ n [U]: *an imprecision in the terminology*

im·preg·na·ble /ɪmˈpregnəbəl/ adj *formal* **1** a building that is impregnable is so strong that it cannot be entered by force: *an impregnable fortress* **2** strong and impossible to change or influence: *her impregnable obstinacy*

im·preg·nate /ˈɪmpregneɪt $ ɪmˈpreg-/ v [T] **1** to make a substance spread completely through something, or to spread completely through something: **impregnate sth with sth** *The mats have to be impregnated with disinfectant.* **2** *technical* to make a woman or female animal PREGNANT

im·pre·sa·ri·o /ˌɪmprɪˈsɑːriəʊ $ -rioʊ/ n plural **impresarios** [C] someone who organizes performances in theatres, concert halls etc

im·press W3 /ɪmˈpres/ v
1 [not in progressive] to make someone feel admiration and respect: *Steve borrowed his dad's sports car to impress his girlfriend.* | **impress sb/with/by sth** *We were very impressed by the standard of work.* | *One candidate in particular impressed us with her knowledge.* | *She was a simple girl, easily impressed by Tom's sophistication.* | *I think the chief exec was favourably impressed by your presentation.* | *'He's a lawyer?' Mum looked suitably impressed* (=as impressed as you would expect).
2 to make the importance of something clear to someone: **impress sth on sb** *Father impressed on me the value of hard work.*
3 to press something into a soft surface so that a mark or pattern appears on it: *patterns impressed in the clay*

im·pres·sion S3 W2 /ɪmˈpreʃən/ n
1 [C,U] the opinion or feeling you have about someone or something because of the way they seem

give/create/convey an impression
leave sb with an impression
leave an impression (on sb)
have/get the impression (that)
make an impression (on sb) (=make someone admire
  or remember you)
first/initial impression (=the impression you get when
  you see someone or something for the first time)
good/favourable impression
bad impression
false/wrong/misleading impression
lasting/indelible impression
overall/general impression
the distinct impression (that)

> *Arriving late won't **create a** very favourable
> **impression**. | We were **left with the impression that**
> the contract was ours if we wanted it. | I **get the** distinct
> **impression** that we're not wanted here. | It was their
> first meeting and Richard was determined to **make an
> impression**. | When it comes to job interviews, **first
> impressions** are important. | Canceling the conference
> will make a very **bad impression**. | The final score
> gives a **false impression** of the game. | How you greet
> a customer can leave a **lasting impression**. | The
> **overall impression** was one of chaos.*

2 be under the impression (that) to believe that something is true when it is not: *I'm sorry, I was under the
impression that you were the manager.*
3 [C] when someone copies the speech or behaviour of
a famous person in order to make people laugh; ▤ imitation: *Jean does a great **impression** of Madonna.*
4 [C] a picture or drawing of what someone or something might look like, or what something will look like
in the future: **+of** *an **artist's impression** of the new
building*
5 [C] a mark left by pressing something into a soft
surface: *Some of the fallen trees had **left** a clear **impression** in the hardened mud.*
6 [C] all the copies of a book printed at one time; →
edition

im·pres·sion·a·ble /ɪmˈpreʃənəbəl/ *adj* someone
who is impressionable is easily influenced, especially
because they are young: *The kids are at an **impressionable** age.*

im·pres·sion·is·m,   **Impressionism**
/ɪmˈpreʃənɪzəm/ *n* [U] **1** a style of painting used
especially in France in the 19th century which uses
colour instead of details of form to produce effects of
light or feeling; → realism   **2** a style of music from the
late 19th and early 20th centuries that produces feelings and images by the quality of sounds rather than
by a pattern of notes

im·pres·sion·ist /ɪmˈpreʃənɪst/ *n* [C] **1** someone
who copies the speech or behaviour of famous people
in order to entertain other people   **2** someone who
uses impressionism in the paintings or music that they
produce: *impressionist painters*

im·pres·sion·is·tic /ɪmˌpreʃəˈnɪstɪk◂/ *adj* based
on a general feeling of what something is like,
rather than on specific facts or details: *The officers
seemed to make only an impressionistic assessment.*
—**impressionistically** /-kli/ *adv*

im·pres·sive [W3] /ɪmˈpresɪv/ *adj* something that is
impressive makes you admire it because it is very
good, large, important etc: *Among the guests was an
impressive array of authors and critics. | the remains
of an impressive Roman villa* —**impressively** *adv*: *The
latest version has an impressively user-friendly interface.* —**impressiveness** *n* [U]

im·pri·ma·tur /ˌɪmprɪˈmeɪtə, -ˈmɑː- $ -ər/ *n* [singu-
lar] **1** *formal* approval of something, especially from
an important person: *His actions have the imprimatur
of the Secretary of State.*   **2** *technical* official permission to print a book, given by the Roman Catholic
Church

im·print¹ /ˈɪmprɪnt/ *n* [C] **1** the mark left by an
object being pressed into or onto something: **[+of]** *the
imprint of her hand on the soft sand*   **2** *technical* the
name of a PUBLISHER as it appears on a book

im·print² /ɪmˈprɪnt/ *v* **1** [T] to print or press the
mark of an object on something: **imprint sth with/on/
in/onto sth** *One snowy morning footprints and tyre
marks were imprinted in the snow.*   **2** *literary* to become
fixed in your mind or memory so that you never forget:
imprint sth on your mind/memory/brain etc *The sight of
Joe's dead body was imprinted on his mind forever.*

im·pris·on /ɪmˈprɪzən/ *v* [T] **1** to put someone in
prison or to keep them somewhere and prevent them
from leaving: *The government imprisoned all opposi-
tion leaders. | She was imprisoned within his strong
arms.*   **2** if a situation or feeling imprisons people, it
restricts what they can do: *Many elderly people feel
imprisoned in their own homes.*

im·pris·on·ment /ɪmˈprɪzənmənt/ *n* [U] the state of
being in prison, or the time someone spends there:
They were sentenced to 6 years' imprisonment. | **life
imprisonment**

im·prob·a·ble /ɪmˈprɒbəbəl $ -ˈprɑː-/ *adj* **1** not
likely to happen or to be true; ▤ **unlikely**; ◱ **prob-
able**: *a film with an improbable plot | It seems **highly
improbable** that he had no knowledge of the
affair.*   **2** surprising and slightly strange: *improbable
combinations of colours* —**improbably** *adv*
—**improbability** /ɪmˌprɒbəˈbɪləti $ -ˌprɑː-/ *n* [C,U]

im·promp·tu /ɪmˈprɒmptjuː $ ɪmˈprɑːmptuː/ *adj*
done or said without any preparation or planning:
impromptu speech/party/meeting etc *The band gave an
impromptu concert on the roof of the studio.*
—**impromptu** *adv*

im·prop·er /ɪmˈprɒpə $ -ˈprɑːpər/ *adj* **1** dishonest,
illegal, or morally wrong: **it is improper (for sb) to do
sth** *He realised that it was improper for a police officer to
accept gifts.* | **improper behaviour/conduct/dealings etc**
*allegations of improper banking practices | improper
sexual conduct*   **2** not sensible, right, or fair in a
particular situation; ▤ **inappropriate**: **it is improper
to do sth** *It would be improper of me to comment before
the election outcome is known.*   **3** wrong or not correct
—**improperly** *adv*: *If you are improperly dressed, you
will not be admitted.*

im,proper 'fraction *n* [C] *technical* a FRACTION such
as 107/8 in which the top number is larger than the
bottom number; ◱ **proper fraction**

im·pro·pri·e·ty /ˌɪmprəˈpraɪəti/ *n plural* **impropri-
eties** [C,U] *formal* behaviour or an action that is wrong
or unacceptable according to moral, social, or professional standards: *Accusations of impropriety were
made against the company's directors.*

im·prov /ˈɪmprɒv $ -prɑːv/ *n* [U] *informal* **improvisa-
tion** acting, singing, performing etc without preparing
what you will say first: *comedy improv*

im·prove [S2] [W1] /ɪmˈpruːv/ *v*
[I,T] to make something better, or to become better: *a
course for students wishing to improve their English |
The doctors say she is improving (=after being ill). | You
could use the money for improving your home. | Many
wines **improve with age** (=get better as they get older).*
  improve on/upon sth *phr v*
to do something better than before or make something
better than before: *Bertorelli has scored 165 points, and
I don't think anyone will improve on that.*

im·proved /ɪmˈpruːvd/ *adj* [usually before noun] better
than before: *improved performance | Our washing pow-
der now has a **new improved** formula.*

im·prove·ment [W2] /ɪmˈpruːvmənt/ *n*
1 [C,U] the act of improving something or the state of
being improved: **[+in/on/to]** *There's been a big improve-
ment in the children's behaviour. | an improvement on*

[1] 000, [2] 000, [3] 000, most frequent words in [S] poken and [W] ritten English

earlier models | *We need to carry out some improvements to the system.* | **dramatic/major/significant/substantial etc improvement** *a marked improvement in her condition* | *It could be quite some time before we* ***see*** *any* ***improvement***. | *This month's sales figures* ***show*** *some* ***improvement***. | *Your English is much better, but there's still* ***room for improvement*** (=it could be even better). **2** [C] a change or addition that improves something: *Are you thinking of making some improvements to your home?*

im·prov·i·dent /ɪmˈprɒvɪdənt $ -ˈprɑː-/ *adj formal* too careless to save any money or to plan for the future —**improvidence** *n* [U] —**improvidently** *adv*

im·pro·vise /ˈɪmprəvaɪz/ *v* [I,T] **1** to do something without any preparation, because you are forced to do this by unexpected events: *I forgot to bring my notes, so I had to improvise.* **2** to make something by using whatever you can find because you do not have the equipment or materials that you need: *There were no spare nappies, so we had to improvise with what we could find.* | *Annie improvised a sandpit for the children to play in.* **3** to invent music, words, a statement etc from your imagination, rather than planning or preparing it first: *I just started playing, and the other guys started improvising around me.* | *an improvised sketch* —**improvisation** /ˌɪmprəvaɪˈzeɪʃən $ ɪmˌprɑːvə-/ *n* [C,U]

im·pru·dent /ɪmˈpruːdənt/ *adj formal* not sensible or wise: *The banks made hundreds of imprudent loans in the 1970s.* —**imprudently** *adv* —**imprudence** *n* [C,U]

im·pu·dent /ˈɪmpjʊdənt/ *adj formal* or *old-fashioned* rude and showing no respect to other people; ≡ **cheeky** —**impudence** *n* [U]: *He stared at me with a mixture of impudence and hostility.*

im·pugn /ɪmˈpjuːn/ *v* [T] *formal* to express doubts about someone's honesty, courage, ability etc: *I did not mean to impugn her professional abilities.*

I

im·pulse /ˈɪmpʌls/ *n* **1** [C,U] a sudden strong desire to do something without thinking about whether it is a sensible thing to do; ≡ **urge**: **impulse to do sth** *a sudden impulse to laugh* | *Marge's first impulse was to run.* | *Gerry couldn't* ***resist the impulse*** *to kiss her.* | **on impulse** *On impulse, I picked up the phone and rang her.* | *Most beginners* ***buy*** *plants* ***on impulse*** *and then hope for the best.* | **impulse buying/shopping** (=when you buy things that you had not planned to buy) **2** [C] *technical* a short electrical signal that travels in one direction along a nerve or wire: *The eye converts light signals to nerve impulses.* **3** [C] a reason or aim that causes a particular kind of activity or behaviour: *It is the passions which provide the main impulse of music.*

im·pul·sion /ɪmˈpʌlʃən/ *n* [singular,U] *formal* a strong force or desire that causes something to happen or exist

im·pul·sive /ɪmˈpʌlsɪv/ *adj* someone who is impulsive does things without considering the possible dangers or problems first: *Rosa was impulsive and sometimes regretted things she'd done.* | *In a burst of impulsive generosity, I offered to pay.* —**impulsively** *adv*: *'Oh, Anne, I do love you!' he said impulsively.* —**impulsiveness** *n* [U]

im·pu·ni·ty /ɪmˈpjuːnɪti/ *n* **do sth with impunity** if someone does something bad with impunity, there is no risk that they will be punished for it: *It's astonishing that these criminals are free to walk the streets with impunity.*

im·pure /ɪmˈpjʊə $ -ˈpjʊr/ *adj* **1** not pure or clean, and often consisting of a mixture of things instead of just one; ≠ **pure**: *drug dealers selling impure heroin* **2** *old-fashioned* impure thoughts, feelings etc are morally bad because they are about sex – sometimes used humorously: *He tried, without success, to rid his mind of any impure thoughts about Julia.*

im·pu·ri·ty /ɪmˈpjʊərɪti $ -ˈpjʊr-/ *n plural* **impurities** **1** [C usually plural] a substance of a low quality that is contained in or mixed with something else, making it less pure: *All natural minerals contain impurities.* | *Our oatmeal face mask absorbs impurities from your skin.* **2** [U] the state of being impure

im·pute /ɪmˈpjuːt/ *v*
impute sth **to** sb *phr v formal* to say, often unfairly, that someone is responsible for something bad or has bad intentions: *The police were not guilty of the violence imputed to them.* —**imputation** /ˌɪmpjʊˈteɪʃən/ *n* [C,U]

in[1] S1 W1 /ɪn/ *prep*

1 used with the name of a container, place, or area to say where someone or something is: *There's some sugar in the cupboard.* | *My mother was in the kitchen.* | *He took us for a drive in his new car.* | *I found her sitting up in bed.* | *Manson spent fifteen years in prison.* | *a hole in the ground* | *Mr Fisher is in Boston this week.* | *My parents live in New Zealand now.* → see box at **AT**

2 into a container, place etc: *I never went in pubs.* | *He almost drowned when he fell in the river.* | *You can put your pyjamas in the bottom drawer.* | *Get in the car.* | *She looked in her handbag, but her keys were not there.*

3 used to say how something is done or happens: *a room furnished in the modern style* | *Her parents always talk to her in German.* | *She shouted my name in a harsh voice.* | *a short note scribbled in pencil* | *The title was printed in capital letters.* | *We waited in silence.*

4 used with the names of months, years, seasons etc to say when something happens: *Shaw first visited Russia in 1927.* | *Bright yellow flowers appear in late summer.* | *He retired in October.*

5 during a period of time: *It was amazing how much we managed to do in a day.* | *the hardest decision I ever made in my life*

6 at the end of a period of time: *I'll be with you in a minute.* | *The results will be announced in two weeks' time.* → see box at **AFTER**[1]; → see box at **BY**[1]

7 used with negatives or with 'first' to say how much time has passed since the last time something happened: *I haven't enjoyed myself so much in years.* | *It was the team's first win in eighteen months.*

8 used to name the book, document, film etc where something or someone appears: *You shouldn't believe everything you read in the newspapers.* | *Which actress starred in the film 'Cleopatra'?* | *There are a few mistakes in your essay.* | *In his speech Professor Leary praised the work of the volunteers.*

9 making up the whole of something or included as part of something: *There are twelve programmes in the series.* | *How many minutes are there in an hour?* | *Think of a word with eight letters in it meaning 'cold'.* | *Owen will be playing in the England team tomorrow.*

10 doing or affecting a particular kind of job: *a career in industry* | *He's been in politics for fifteen years.* | *reforms in education*

11 wearing something: *He looked very handsome in his uniform.* | *She was dressed in a blue linen suit.*

12 used to talk about the state or situation of something or someone: *I hear that their marriage is in trouble.* | *The engine appears to be in good condition.* | *His life was in danger.* | *The castle now lies in ruins.*

13 used to say what activity a group of people do: *About 4000 students took part in the protest.* | *his role in the negotiations*

14 used to talk about the shape, arrangement, or course of something or someone: *I want you all to stand in a circle.* | *She slept curled up in a ball.* | *Can you walk in a straight line?*

15 used between a smaller number and a larger number to say how common or how likely something is: *One in 10 homes now has cable TV.* | *Smokers have a one in three chance of dying from their habit.*

16 used before a plural number or amount to say how many people or things are involved, or how many there are in each group: *Eggs are still sold in half dozens.* | *The children work in pairs.* | **in their hundreds/thousands etc** (=in very large numbers) *People flocked in their thousands to greet their new princess.*

17 used between a smaller number or amount and a

larger one to say what a rate is: *Income tax stands at 23 pence in the pound.* | *a hill with a gradient of one in six* **18** used to say what colour something is or what it is made of: *Do you have the same pattern in blue?* | *a sculpture in white marble*
19 used to say what specific thing your statement is related to: *Milk is very rich in calcium.* | *Clark had become more extreme in his opinions.* | *an increase in fuel prices* | *The street is about a mile in length.*
20 used to refer to the weather or the physical conditions somewhere: *I've been standing in the rain for over an hour.* | *Would you prefer to sit in the shade?*
21 used to say what feeling you have when you do something: *She looked at me in horror.* | *It was all done purely in fun.*
22 used before the name of someone or something when you are saying how they are regarded: *You have a very good friend in Pat.* | *In Dwight D. Eisenhower the Republicans had found the ideal candidate.*
23 used to say what person or thing has the quality you are mentioning: *There was a hint of spring in the air.* | *I don't think Freddy had it in him to be a killer.* | *She's everything I'd want in a wife* (=she has every quality I would want a wife to have).
24 used to name the substance, food, drink etc that contains something: *Vitamin D is found in butter.*
25 used to say how many parts something is divided into: *a radio serial in four parts* | **in two/halves/pieces etc** *I tore the letter in two and threw the pieces in the fire.*
26 while doing something or while something is happening, and as a result of this: *In all the confusion, it is quite possible that some people got tickets without paying.* | *In my excitement, I forgot all about the message.* | **in doing sth** *In trying to protect the queen, Howard had put his own life in danger.*
27 in that used after a statement to begin to explain in what way it is true: *I've been lucky in that I have never had to worry about money.*
28 be in your 20s/30s/40s etc to be between the ages of 20 and 29, 30 and 39 etc: *Matthews was already in his mid 40s.* → **in all** at ALL¹ (11)

in² [S1] [W1] *adv*
1 in or inside a container, place, vehicle etc; ◧ **out**: *Eric held the boat steady while the children got in.* | *He went to the ticket machine and put a coin in.* | *She dived in and swam out to the yacht.*
2 inside or into a building, especially your home or the place where you work; ◧ **out**: *Come in and sit down.* | *I'm afraid Mr Stewart won't be in until tomorrow morning.* | *We're staying in this evening.*
3 if a train, boat, or plane is in, it has arrived at a station, airport etc: *Our train's not in yet.* | *When's her flight due in?*
4 given or sent to a person or organization to be dealt with by them: *All entries must be in by next week.* | *Letters have been pouring in from all over the country.* | *Have you handed your essay in yet?*
5 if you write, paint, or draw something in, you add it in the correct place: *Fill in your name and address on the form provided.* | *The information is typed in by trained keyboarders.*
6 if a player or team is in during a game of CRICKET (2), they are BATTING
7 if a ball is in during a game, it is inside the area where the game is being played; ◧ **out**: *Agassi's second serve was just in.*
8 if a politician or a political party is in, they have been elected: *Labour recorded its highest vote ever, but the Tories got in again.*
9 towards the centre; ◨ **inward(s)**: *The map had started to curl in at the edges.*
10 when the TIDE is in, the sea by the shore is at its highest level; ◧ **out**: *The tide was in, and the sea lapped against the harbour wall.*
11 be in for sth if someone is in for something unpleasant, it is going to happen to them: *I'm afraid he's in for a bit of a disappointment.*
12 be in for it *informal* if someone is in for it, they are

going to be punished: *If they find out what I've done, I'll be in for it, won't I?*
13 be/get in on sth to be or become involved in something that is happening: *I think you ought to be in on this discussion, Ted.*
14 be in with sb *informal* to have a friendly relationship with someone: *She's in with the theatrical crowd.* | *You have to* **be well in with** *the directors* (=be very friendly with them) *if you want to get promotion here.*
15 be in at the beginning/start (of sth) to be present or involved when something starts: *I was lucky enough to be in at the start of the project.* → **have (got) it in for sb** at HAVE² (41)

in³ *BrE*; **in.** *AmE plural* **in** or **ins** the written abbreviation of *inch* or inches

in⁴ *adj informal* fashionable; ◧ **out**: *Red is definitely the in colour this year.* | *Long skirts are in at the moment.* | *I joined the club because it seemed the in thing to do.*

in⁵ *n* **the ins and outs of sth** all the facts and details of something: *The book guides you through the ins and outs of choosing and growing garden flowers.*

in- /ɪn/ *prefix* the opposite or lack of something; ◧ **not**; → **un-, il-, im-, ir-**: *insensitive* (=not sensitive) | *incautious* (=not cautious) | *inattention* (=lack of attention)

in·a·bil·i·ty /ˌɪnəˈbɪləti/ *n* [singular, U] the fact of being unable to do something: **inability to do sth** *Alcoholism can result in an inability to cope.* | *the government's inability to enforce the ceasefire*

in ab·sen·ti·a /ˌɪn æbˈsentiə $ -ˈsenʃə/ *adv law* without being present: *He was tried and convicted in absentia.*

in·ac·ces·si·ble /ˌɪnəkˈsesəbəl◂/ *adj* **1** difficult or impossible to reach; ◧ **accessible**: *In winter, the villages are inaccessible by road.* | [+to] *A long flight of stairs made the center inaccessible to disabled visitors.* **2** difficult or impossible to understand or afford; ◧ **accessible**: *Stockhausen's music is thought to be difficult and inaccessible.* —**inaccessibly** *adv* —**inaccessibility** /ˌɪnəksesəˈbɪləti/ *n* [U]

in·ac·cu·ra·cy /ɪnˈækjʊrəsi/ *n plural* **inaccuracies** **1** [C] a statement that is not completely correct: *Jansen's review contained several inaccuracies.* **2** [U] a lack of correctness: *As a journalist you simply cannot tolerate inaccuracy.*

in·ac·cu·rate /ɪnˈækjʊrət/ *adj* not completely correct; ◧ **accurate**: *A lot of what has been written about him is inaccurate.* | **inaccurate information/data etc** *He was fined $300,000 for making inaccurate statements to Congress.* —**inaccurately** *adv*

in·ac·tion /ɪnˈækʃən/ *n* [U] the fact that someone is not doing anything: *Several newspapers have criticized the President for inaction.*

in·ac·tive /ɪnˈæktɪv/ *adj* **1** not doing anything, not working, or not moving; ◧ **active**: *The brain cells are inactive during sleep.* | *Young people are becoming politically inactive.* **2** not taking part in something that normally you would take part in: *Graham's knee injury means he will be inactive for Sunday's game.* **3** *technical* an inactive substance does not react chemically with other substances

in·ac·tiv·i·ty /ˌɪnækˈtɪvəti/ *n* [U] the state of not doing anything, not moving, or not working: *Don't suddenly take up violent exercise after years of inactivity.* | *The time spent between jobs should not be a* **period of inactivity**.

in·ad·e·qua·cy /ɪnˈædɪkwəsi/ *n plural* **inadequacies** **1** [U] a feeling that you are not as good, clever, skilled etc as other people: *Unemployment can cause* **feelings of inadequacy** *and low self-esteem.* **2** [U] the fact of not being good enough in quality, ability, size etc for a particular purpose: [+of] *the inadequacy of local health care* **3** [C usually plural] a fault or weakness: *I'm quite aware of my own inadequacies.*

in·ad·e·quate /ɪnˈædɪkwət/ *adj* **1** not good enough, big enough, skilled enough etc for a particular purpose; ◪ **adequate**: *inadequate resources* | [+for] *The parking facilities are inadequate for a busy shopping centre.* | **totally/wholly/woefully/hopelessly etc inadequate** *The building's electrical system was completely inadequate.* | *The new air conditioning system* ***proved inadequate***. **2** someone who feels inadequate thinks other people are better, more skilful, more intelligent etc than they are: *The teacher made us* ***feel inadequate*** *and stupid if we made mistakes.* —**inadequately** *adv*: *Colleges have been inadequately funded for years.*

in·ad·mis·si·ble /ˌɪnədˈmɪsɪbəl◂/ *adj law* inadmissible information is not allowed to be used in a court of law: *The* ***evidence*** *issued on 12 February was ruled* ***inadmissible***. —**inadmissibly** *adj* —**inadmissibility** /ˌɪnədmɪsɪˈbɪlɪti/ *n* [U]

in·ad·vert·ent·ly /ˌɪnədˈvɜːtəntli $ -ɜːr-/ *adv* without realizing what you are doing; ◪ **accidentally**: *Viruses can be spread inadvertently by email users.* | *Robinson's name was inadvertently omitted from the list.* —**inadvertent** *adj*: *inadvertent exposure to chemicals* —**inadvertence** *n* [U]

in·ad·vis·a·ble /ˌɪnədˈvaɪzəbəl◂/ *adj* [not before noun] an action that is inadvisable is not sensible; ◪ **unwise**: *Changes in the patient's condition may make surgery inadvisable.* | **it is inadvisable to do sth** *It is inadvisable to involve more than one contractor on a project.*

in·a·li·en·a·ble /ɪnˈeɪliənəbəl/ *adj* [usually before noun] *formal* an inalienable right, power etc cannot be taken from you: *inalienable human rights*

i·nam·o·ra·ta /ɪˌnæməˈrɑːtə/ *n* [C] *literary* the woman that a man loves – sometimes used humorously

i·nane /ɪˈneɪn/ *adj* very stupid or without much meaning: *Most pop lyrics are pretty inane.* | *an inane remark* —**inanely** *adv*: *Dave smiled inanely.* —**inanity** /ɪˈnænɪti/ *n* [C,U]

in·an·i·mate /ɪnˈænɪmət/ *adj* not living: *an inanimate object*

in·ap·pli·ca·ble /ˌɪnəˈplɪkəbəl, ɪnˈæplɪkəbəl $ ɪnˈæplɪk-/ *adj* rules, statements, questions etc that are inapplicable are not suitable, correct, or able to be used in a particular situation; ◪ **applicable**: [+to] *Most of the new regulations are inapplicable to us.*

in·ap·pro·pri·ate /ˌɪnəˈprəʊpri-ət $ -ˈproʊ-/ *adj* not suitable or right for a particular purpose or in a particular situation; ◪ **appropriate**: **wholly/totally/completely etc inappropriate** *His comments were wholly inappropriate on such a solemn occasion.* | **it is inappropriate (for sb) to do sth** *It would be inappropriate for me to comment until we know more of the facts.* | [+for] *an inappropriate gift for a child* | [+to] *marketing techniques that are totally inappropriate to education* | **inappropriate behaviour/response/language etc** —**inappropriately** *adv*: *inappropriately dressed* —**inappropriateness** also **inappropriacy** *n* [U]

in·apt /ɪnˈæpt/ *adj formal* an inapt phrase, statement etc is not right for a particular situation; ➔ **inept**: *a very inapt comment* —**inaptly** *adv* —**inaptness** *n* [U]

in·ar·tic·u·late /ˌɪnɑːˈtɪkjʊlɪt◂ $ -ɑːr-/ *adj* **1** not able to express your feelings clearly or easily; ◪ **articulate**: *My meetings with him left me inarticulate with rage.* **2** speech that is inarticulate is not clearly expressed or pronounced; ◪ **articulate**: *Making an inarticulate sound, he turned away.* —**inarticulately** *adv* —**inarticulateness** also **inarticulacy** *n* [C,U]

in·as·much as /ˌɪnəzˈmʌtʃ əz/ *conjunction formal* used to explain the way in which, what you are saying is true: *Ann is guilty, inasmuch as she knew what the others were planning.*

in·at·ten·tion /ˌɪnəˈtenʃən/ *n* [U] lack of attention: *a moment of inattention* | [+to] *inattention to detail*

in·at·ten·tive /ˌɪnəˈtentɪv◂/ *adj* not giving enough attention to someone or something; ◪ **attentive**: *accidents caused by inattentive or reckless drivers* —**inattentively** *adv* —**inattentiveness** *n* [U]

in·au·di·ble /ɪnˈɔːdɪbəl $ -ˈɒː-/ *adj* too quiet to be heard; ◪ **audible**: *The noise of the wind made her cries inaudible.* —**inaudibly** *adv*: *'No,' she whispered, almost inaudibly.* —**inaudibility** /ɪnˌɔːdɪˈbɪlɪti $ -ˌɒː-/ *n* [U]

in·au·gu·ral /ɪˈnɔːɡjʊrəl $ ɪˈnɒː-/ *adj* [only before noun] **1** an inaugural speech is the first given by someone who is starting an important job: *the President's televsied inaugural address* | *the inaugural lecture of the new Professor of American Literature* **2** an inaugural event is the first in a planned series of similar events: *Concorde's inaugural flight* | *the inaugural match of Major League Soccer* —**inaugural** *n* [C] *AmE*: *More than 200,000 people attended Carter's inaugural.*

in·au·gu·rate /ɪˈnɔːɡjʊreɪt $ ɪˈnɒː-/ *v* [T] **1** to hold an official ceremony when someone starts doing an important job in government: **inaugurate sb as sth** *On 8 January 1959 De Gaulle was inaugurated as First President of the Republic.* **2** to open a building or start an organization, event etc for the first time: *The Turner Prize was inaugurated in 1984.* **3** *formal* if an event inaugurates an important change or period of time, it comes at the beginning of it: *The International Trade Agreement inaugurated a period of high economic growth.* —**inauguration** /ɪˌnɔːɡjʊˈreɪʃən $ ɪˌnɒː-/ *n* [C,U]: *President Hoover's inauguration*

in·aus·pi·cious /ˌɪnɔːˈspɪʃəs◂ $ ˌɪnɒː-/ *adj formal* seeming to show that success in the future is unlikely; ◪ **auspicious**: *an* ***inauspicious start*** —**inauspiciously** *adv*

in-'between *adj* in the middle between two points, sizes, periods of time etc: *She was at that in-between age, neither a girl nor a woman.*

in·board /ˈɪnbɔːd $ -bɔːrd/ *adj* inside a boat: **inboard motor/engine** ➔ OUTBOARD MOTOR

in·born /ˌɪnˈbɔːn◂ $ -ɔːrn◂/ *adj* an inborn quality or ability is one you have had naturally since birth: *Mammals have an inborn fear of snakes.* | *Good taste is inborn and cannot be learned.*

in·bound /ˈɪnbaʊnd/ *adj AmE* an inbound flight or train is arriving at a place; ◪ **outbound**; ◪ **incoming** *BrE*

in-'bounds *adv AmE* if the ball is in-bounds in a sport, it is in the playing area

in·box, in box /ˈɪnbɒks $ -bɑːks/ *n* [C] **1** the place in a computer email program where new messages arrive: *I had 130 emails in my inbox this morning.* **2** *AmE* a container on an office desk that is used to hold letters, documents etc that you must deal with; ◪ **in tray** *BrE* ➔ OUTBOX; ➔ see picture at TRAY

in·bred /ˌɪnˈbred◂/ *adj* **1** produced by inbreeding **2** having developed as a natural part of your character: *inbred ambition*

in·breed·ing /ˈɪnbriːdɪŋ/ *n* [U] when children, animals, or plants are produced from closely related members of the same family: *He was born with a rare bone disease, probably the result of aristocratic inbreeding.*

in·built /ˈɪnbɪlt/ *adj* [only before noun] *BrE* an inbuilt quality, feature etc is part of the nature of someone or something: *plants with inbuilt resistance to disease* | *History has an inbuilt tendency to repeat itself.*

Inc. /ɪŋk/ the written abbreviation of *incorporated*; ➔ **Ltd, plc**: *General Motors Inc.*

in·cal·cu·la·ble /ɪnˈkælkjʊləbəl/ *adj formal* too great to be calculated: *Her contribution to our work is incalculable.* | **incalculable importance/value/worth etc** *treasures of incalculable value* | **incalculable harm/damage/suffering etc** *The outbreak of hostilities will cause incalculable misery.*

in·can·des·cent /ˌɪnkænˈdesənt◂ $ -kən-/ *adj* **1** very angry: *The Prince was said to be* ***incandescent with rage***. **2** *technical* producing a bright light

when heated: *the invention of the incandescent lamp* **3** *literary* very bright: *incandescent flowers*
—**incandescence** *n* [U]

in·can·ta·tion /ˌɪnkænˈteɪʃən/ *n* [C,U] special words that someone uses in magic, or the act of saying these words: *a book of spells and incantations*

in·ca·pa·ble /ɪnˈkeɪpəbəl/ *adj* [not before noun] not able to do something; **☒ capable**: [+of] *He seemed incapable of understanding how she felt.* | *75% of the electorate believe his party is incapable of government.* | *The stroke rendered her* **incapable** *of speech.* ⚠ Do not say 'incapable to do something'. Say **incapable of doing something.** —**incapability** /ɪnˌkeɪpəˈbɪlɪti/ *n* [U]

in·ca·pa·ci·tate /ˌɪnkəˈpæsɪteɪt/ *v* [T] *formal* **1** to make you too ill or weak to live and work normally: *Her mother has been incapacitated by a fall.* | *an incapacitating injury* **2** to stop a system, piece of equipment etc from working properly: *A successful attack would incapacitate military training camps.* —**incapacitation** /ˌɪnkəpæsɪˈteɪʃən/ *n* [U]

in·ca·pa·ci·ty /ˌɪnkəˈpæsɪti/ *n* [singular, U] *formal* lack of the ability to do things or to do something: *temporary incapacity through illness* | **mental/physical/intellectual etc incapacity** *Evidence of his mental incapacity was never produced in court.* | **incapacity to do sth** *The main problem is the author's incapacity to convey his ideas.*

in·car·ce·rate /ɪnˈkɑːsəreɪt/ *v* [T usually passive] *formal* to put or keep someone in prison; **☒ imprison**: *He spent nearly half his life incarcerated in prison.* —**incarceration** /ɪnˌkɑːsəˈreɪʃən $ -ˌkɑːr-/ *n* [U]

in·car·nate¹ /ɪnˈkɑːnɪt $ -ɑːr-/ *adj* **1 be evil/beauty/greed etc incarnate** to have an extreme amount of a particular quality: *He is now respectability incarnate.* **2** having taken human form: *Jesus, the incarnate son of God* | *The media cast him as* **the devil incarnate** (=someone very evil).

in·car·nate² /ˈɪnkɑːneɪt $ -ɑːr-/ *v* [T] *formal* **1** to represent a particular quality in a physical or human form: *The crown incarnates national power.* **2** to make something appear in a human form

in·car·na·tion /ˌɪnkɑːˈneɪʃən $ -ɑːr-/ *n* **1** [C,U] the state of living in the form of a particular person or animal. According to some religions, people have several different incarnations; → **reincarnation**: *She believes she was an Egyptian queen* **in a previous incarnation.** **2** [C] a period of time when someone or something has a particular job, use etc: *The building has gone through several incarnations, as a station, cafe, and most recently a club.* **3 the/an incarnation of sth** someone who has a lot of a particular quality, or represents it: *She was the incarnation of wisdom.* **4** [singular] the act of God coming to Earth in the human form of Christ, according to the Christian religion

in·cau·tious /ɪnˈkɔːʃəs $ -ˈkɒː-/ *adj* if you are incautious, you do not think about the possible bad results of your actions: *incautious remarks* | *The wine had made her incautious.* —**incautiously** *adv*

in·cen·di·a·ry¹ /ɪnˈsendiəri $ -dieri/ *adj* **1** [only before noun] designed to cause a fire: **incendiary bomb/device** *The explosion seems to have been caused by an incendiary device.* **2** an incendiary speech, piece of writing etc is intended to make people angry: *a hip-hop album with incendiary lyrics*

incendiary² *n plural* **incendiaries** [C] a bomb designed to cause a fire

in·cense¹ /ˈɪnsens/ *n* [U] a substance which has a pleasant smell when you burn it: *a church filled with the smell of incense* | *lighted incense sticks*

in·cense² /ɪnˈsens/ *v* [T] to make someone very angry: *Spectators were incensed by the referee's decision.*

in·censed /ɪnˈsenst/ *adj* [not before noun] very angry; **☒ furious**: *Pat was so incensed he got up and hit Jack.* | [+at] *Fans were incensed at the decision to ban the*

song. | **incensed that** *Passengers are incensed that rail companies make huge profits while service remains poor.*

in·cen·tive [S3] /ɪnˈsentɪv/ *n* [C,U] something that encourages you to work harder, start a new activity etc: *As an* **added incentive**, *there's a bottle of champagne for the best team.* | **create/provide/give sb an incentive** *Awards provide an incentive for young people to improve their skills.* | **incentive to do sth** *Farmers lack any incentive to manage their land organically.* | **economic/financial/tax etc incentives** *a recycling drive backed with financial incentives*

in·cep·tion /ɪnˈsepʃən/ *n* [singular] *formal* the start of an organization or institution: *a CD collection covering the band from its inception in 1994*

in·ces·sant /ɪnˈsesənt/ *adj* [usually before noun] continuing without stopping; **☒ constant**: *The child's incessant talking started to irritate her.* | *incessant rain* —**incessantly** *adv*: *They quarrelled incessantly.*

in·cest /ˈɪnsest/ *n* [U] sex between people who are closely related in a family: *Abortions would only be allowed in cases of rape or incest.*

in·ces·tu·ous /ɪnˈsestʃuəs/ *adj* **1** involving sexual activity between people who are closely related in a family: *an incestuous relationship* **2** involving a small group of people who only spend time with or help each other, not people outside the group – used to show disapproval: *an incestuous political community*

inch¹ [S2] [W3] /ɪntʃ/ *n* [C]
1 written abbreviation *in* a unit for measuring length, equal to 2.54 centimetres. There are 12 inches in a foot.: *The curtains were an inch too short.* | *Rainfall here is under 15 inches a year.* | **a one/two/three etc inch sth** *a six inch nail*
2 a very small distance: *Derek leaned closer, his face* **only inches from** *hers.* | *The bus missed us* **by inches.** | *On several occasions they came* **within inches of** *death.*
3 every inch a) completely or in every way: *With her designer clothes and elegant hair, she* **looks every inch** *the celebrity.* **b)** the whole of an area or distance: [+of] *Every inch of space in the tiny shop was crammed with goods.* | *Italy deserved to win, though Greece made them fight* **every inch of the way.**
4 give sb an inch and they'll take a yard/mile used to say that if you allow someone a little freedom or power, they will try to take more
5 inch by inch moving very gradually and slowly: *Inch by inch, he lowered himself from the roof.*
6 not give/budge an inch to refuse to change your decision or opinion, even though people are trying to persuade you to do this: *Neither side is prepared to give an inch in the negotiations.*
7 beat/thrash etc sb to within an inch of their life to beat someone very hard and thoroughly: *Another word out of you and I'll beat you to within an inch of your life.*

inch² *v* [I,T always + adv/prep] to move very slowly in a particular direction, or to make something do this: *I inched forward along the ground.*

in·cho·ate /ɪnˈkəʊɪt $ -koʊ-/ *adj formal* inchoate ideas, plans, attitudes etc are only just starting to develop

in·ci·dence /ˈɪnsɪdəns/ *n* [C usually singular] *formal* the number of times something happens, especially crime, disease etc; → **rate**: [+of] *Why did the incidence of heroin use continue to climb?* | **high/low etc incidence** *Smokers had the highest incidence of colds.*

in·ci·dent [W2] /ˈɪnsɪdənt/ *n* [C]
1 an event, especially one that is unusual, important, or violent: *A spokesman said it was an* **isolated incident.** | *Am I at risk because of some incident in my sexual past?* | **shooting/stabbing incident** *Many shooting incidents go unreported.* | **without incident** *The plane landed without incident.*
2 a serious disagreement between two countries: *You could have caused a major* **diplomatic incident.**

[1] 000, [2] 000, [3] 000, most frequent words in [S]poken and [W]ritten English

in·ci·den·tal[1] /ˌɪnsɪ'dentl◂/ *adj* **1** happening or existing in connection with something else that is more important: *Increased motivation is more than an* ***incidental benefit*** *of reward schemes.* | [+to] *companies that carry out investment business that is incidental to their main activity* **2** [not before noun] naturally happening as a result of something: [+to] *Drinking too much is almost incidental to bartending.*

incidental[2] *n* [C usually plural] something that you have to do, buy etc which you had not planned to: *Carry extra cash for taxis, tips and other incidentals.*

in·ci·den·tal·ly S3 /ˌɪnsɪ'dentəli/ *adv* **1** [sentence adverb] used to add more information to what you have just said, or to introduce a new subject that you have just thought of; ▤ **by the way**: *Incidentally, where were you born?* | *The wine, incidentally, goes very well with a mature cheese.* **2** in a way that was not planned, but as a result of something else: *Quite incidentally, I got some useful information at the party.*

incidental 'music *n* [U] music played during a play, film etc that helps produce a particular feeling

'incident ˌroom *n* [C] *BrE* a room in a police station or other place where police work on solving a particular serious crime

in·cin·e·rate /ɪn'sɪnəreɪt/ *v* [T usually passive] *formal* to burn something completely in order to destroy it: *All the infected clothing was incinerated.* —**incineration** /ɪnˌsɪnə'reɪʃən/ *n* [U]: *an incineration plant*

in·cin·e·ra·tor /ɪn'sɪnəreɪtə $ -ər/ *n* [C] a machine designed to burn things in order to destroy them

in·cip·i·ent /ɪn'sɪpiənt/ *adj* [only before noun] *formal* starting to happen or exist: *a sign of incipient madness*

in·cise /ɪn'saɪz/ *v* [T always + prep] *formal* to cut a pattern, word etc into something, using a sharp instrument: *an inscription incised in stone*

in·ci·sion /ɪn'sɪʒən/ *n* [C] a neat cut made into something, especially during a medical operation

in·ci·sive /ɪn'saɪsɪv/ *adj* showing intelligence and a clear understanding of something: **incisive remarks/criticism etc** *Her questions were well-formulated and incisive.* | *The error was obvious to an incisive mind like his.* —**incisively** *adv* —**incisiveness** *n* [U]

in·ci·sor /ɪn'saɪzə $ -ər/ *n* [C] one of the eight flat teeth at the front of your mouth → CANINE[2] (1), MOLAR

in·cite /ɪn'saɪt/ *v* [T] to deliberately encourage people to fight, argue etc: *They were charged with inciting racial hatred.* | **incite sb to do sth** *a person who incites others to commit an offence* | **incite sb to sth** *There was no evidence that he had incited members of the group to violence.* —**incitement** *n* [C,U]: *incitement to murder*

in·ci·vil·i·ty /ˌɪnsɪ'vɪlɪti/ *n plural* **incivilities** [C,U] *formal* impolite behaviour, remarks etc

in·clem·ent /ɪn'klemənt/ *adj formal* inclement weather is unpleasantly cold, wet etc

in·cli·na·tion /ˌɪŋklɪ'neɪʃən/ *n* **1** [C,U] a feeling that makes you want to do something: *My natural inclination was to say no.* | **inclination to do sth** *Neither of my children* **showed** *the slightest* **inclination** *to follow me into journalism.* | *Teachers simply do not have* **the time or the inclination** *to investigate these matters.* **2** [C,U] a tendency to think or behave in a particular way: **inclination to do sth** *an inclination to see everything in political terms* | [+to/towards] *She's troubled by her son's inclination toward atheism.* | **by inclination** *Bart was a romantic by inclination.* **3** [C] a movement made down towards the ground: *She greeted Maggie with an inclination of the head.* **4** [C,U] *formal* a slope or the angle at which something slopes

in·cline[1] /ɪn'klaɪn/ *v* [not in progressive] **1** [T] *formal* if a situation, fact etc inclines you to do or think something, it influences you towards a particular action or opinion: **incline sb to do sth** *The accident inclined him to reconsider his career.* **2** [I] *formal* to

think that a particular belief or opinion is most likely to be correct: **incline to do sth** *I incline to accept the official version of events.* | [+to/towards] *I incline to the opinion that this principle extends to cases of religious discrimination.* **3** [I,T] to slope at a particular angle, or to make something do this: *The telescope is inclined at an angle of 43 degrees.* **4** **incline your head** to bend your neck so that your head is lowered

in·cline[2] /'ɪnklaɪn/ *n* [C] a slope: *a steep incline*

in·clined S3 /ɪn'klaɪnd/ *adj*
1 **be inclined to agree/think/believe etc** to hold a particular opinion, but not very strongly: *Arthur has some strange ideas, but on this occasion I'm inclined to agree with him.*
2 **be inclined to do sth/inclined to sth** to be likely to do something or behave in a particular way: *Commandos are inclined to shoot first and ask questions later.* | *He was inclined to self-pity.*
3 **be/feel inclined (to do sth)** to want to do something, but without having a strong desire: *It was Sunday morning, and she was not inclined to get up yet.* | *You can visit our chatrooms, if you* **feel so inclined***.*
4 **artistically/musically/mathematically etc inclined** naturally interested in or good at art, music etc: *For the artistically inclined, the street markets are full of interest.*
5 sloping or leaning in a particular direction

in·close /ɪn'kləʊz $ -'kloʊz/ *v* another spelling of ENCLOSE

in·clos·ure /ɪn'kləʊʒə $ -'kloʊʒər/ *n* another spelling of ENCLOSURE

in·clude S2 W1 /ɪn'kluːd/ *v* [T]
1 [not in progressive] if one thing includes another, the second thing is part of the first: *Does the price include postage?* | *His job includes looking after under-21 teams.* | *The curriculum includes courses in computing.*
2 to make someone or something part of a larger group or set; ▤ **exclude**: *The team is stronger now they've included Roscoe.* | **include sth in/on sth** *Service is included in the bill.* | *Would you include a Walkman on your list of essentials?*

WORD CHOICE: include, consist of, comprise, be composed of, be made up of
Use **include** to mention only some of the things that something has as its parts: *The price includes lunch.*
If you want to mention all the parts that something has in it, use **consist of, comprise, be composed of,** or **be made up of**: *The Romance family of languages consists of French, Spanish, Italian, and several other languages.* | *The house comprises two bedrooms, a kitchen and a living room.* | *The jury was composed of nine whites, one Hispanic, and two Asian Americans.* | *an organization made up of 600,000 small business owners*
⚠ Do not say that something 'is consisted of' certain things or that it 'consists' them. Say it **consists of** them.
⚠ Do not say that something 'comprises of' certain things, even though you might hear English speakers say this. Most careful users consider this to be incorrect so you should avoid using it.
⚠ Do not say that something 'is composed by' or 'is composed with' certain things. Say it **is composed of** them.

---

in·clud·ed /ɪn'kluːdɪd/ *adj* [only after noun] including someone or something: *Everyone has to go to the dentist, you included.*

in·clud·ing S2 W1 /ɪn'kluːdɪŋ/ *prep* used to introduce something or someone that is part of a larger group or amount you have just mentioned; ▤ **excluding**: *The price is £25.50, including postage and packing.* | *You'll need a variety of skills, including leadership and negotiating.*

in·clu·sion /ɪn'kluːʒən/ *n* **1** [U] the act of including someone or something in a larger group or set, or the fact of being included in one: [+in] *His inclusion in the team has caused controversy.* | *photos chosen for*

inclusion in the magazine | [+of] The inclusion of early recordings on the CD is a bonus. **2** [C] someone or something that has been included in a larger group: With the recent inclusions there will be 28 delegates in all.

in·clu·sive /ɪnˈkluːsɪv/ adj **1** an inclusive price or cost includes everything; ◨ **exclusive: all-inclusive/ fully inclusive** The fully inclusive fare for the trip is £22. | [+of] The rent is £120 a week, inclusive of heating. **2** including a wide variety of people, things etc; ◨ **exclusive:** Not everyone shares his vision of an inclusive America. **3 (from)** April to June **inclusive/15 to 20 inclusive** etc used to refer to a range of months, numbers etc, including the ones that start and end the range ⚠ In American English, it is more usual to use the word 'through': Monday through Friday

in·cog·ni·to /ˌɪnkɒɡˈniːtəʊ $ ˌɪnkɑːɡˈniːtoʊ/ adv if a famous person does something incognito, they do it without letting people know who they are: That night, Lenin travelled incognito to the party headquarters.

in·co·her·ent /ˌɪnkəʊˈhɪərənt◂ $ -koʊˈhɪr-/ adj **1** not expressed or organized clearly, and therefore difficult to understand: an incoherent, over-long action movie | He called the policy 'incoherent and ill-thought out'. **2** speaking in a way that cannot be understood, because you are drunk, feeling a strong emotion etc: Ben, drunk and incoherent, slumped in a chair. —**incoherently** adv: She began to mutter incoherently. —**incoherence** n [U]

in·come [S2] [W1] /ˈɪŋkʌm, ˈɪn-/ n [C,U] the money that you earn from your work or that you receive from INVESTMENTS, the government etc ; → see box at PAY[2]

on a ... income (=earning a particular amount)
high/low income
high-income/low-income
annual income
family/household income
disposable income (=your income after tax and necessary bills have been paid)
taxable income (=the part of your income on which you pay tax)
net income (=your income after you have paid taxes)
gross income (=your income before you have paid taxes)
investment income (=income from investments)
source of income
loss of income
supplement your income (with sth) (=increase your income by doing something)

People **on a high income** should pay more tax. | **low-income** families | His **annual income** is £250,000. | workers with a **family income** of less than $30,000 | Older people may have more **disposable income** because their houses are paid for. | [+from] income from savings and pensions | Welfare is their only **source of income**. | You should be insured against **loss of income**. | He **supplements** his income with a part-time bar job.

in·com·er /ˈɪnkʌmə $ -ər/ n [C] BrE someone who comes to live in a place: We've lived here for 17 years, but they still see us as incomers.

income sup·port n [U] money that is given by the government in Britain to people who have no income or a very low income

income tax n [U] tax paid on the money that you earn

in·com·ing /ˈɪnkʌmɪŋ/ adj [only before noun] **1** arriving or coming to a place; ◨ **outgoing:** incoming flights | Incoming calls were monitored. | the incoming tide **2** an incoming president, government etc has just been elected or chosen; ◨ **outgoing:** It is hoped that the incoming administration will inject some life into Capitol Hill.

in·com·mu·ni·ca·do /ˌɪnkəmjuːnɪˈkɑːdəʊ $ -doʊ/ adv, adj if you are incommunicado, you are in a place where other people cannot speak to you: He is reportedly being **held incommunicado** at a military prison.

in·com·pa·ra·ble /ɪnˈkɒmpərəbəl $ -ˈkɑːm-/ adj extremely good, beautiful etc, and much better than others: an incomparable view of San Marco | a wine of incomparable flavour —**incomparably** adv

in·com·pat·i·ble /ˌɪnkəmˈpætəbəl◂/ adj **1** two people who are incompatible have such different characters, beliefs etc that they cannot have a friendly relationship; ◨ **compatible:** I don't know why they ever got married. They're totally incompatible. **2** two things that are incompatible cannot exist or be accepted together: [+with] Business interests are incompatible with public office. | Politeness and truth are often **mutually incompatible**. **3** two things that are incompatible are of different types and so cannot be used together; ◨ **compatible:** [+with] The laser printer is incompatible with the new computer. | incompatible blood groups —**incompatibility** /ˌɪnkəmpætəˈbɪləti/ n [U]: sexual incompatibility

in·com·pe·tence /ɪnˈkɒmpətəns $ -ˈkɑːm-/ n [U] lack of the ability or skill to do a job properly; ◨ **competence: managerial/professional etc incompetence** allegations of professional incompetence | The report blamed police incompetence for the tragedy.

in·com·pe·tent /ɪnˈkɒmpətənt $ -ˈkɑːm-/ adj not having the ability or skill to do a job properly; ◨ **competent:** an incompetent teacher | weak, incompetent leadership | **incompetent to do sth** The Prime Minister is incompetent to govern the country. —**incompetent** n [C] —**incompetently** adv

in·com·plete[1] /ˌɪnkəmˈpliːt◂/ adj not having everything that should be there, or not completely finished; ◨ **complete:** Unfortunately I do not have the information because our records are incomplete. | an incomplete process | TV ads implied that a woman was **incomplete without a man**. —**incompletely** adv —**incompleteness** n [U]

incomplete[2] n [C] AmE a GRADE given to school or college students when they have not completed all the work for a course

in·com·pre·hen·si·ble /ˌɪnkɒmprɪˈhensəbəl $ -ˌkɑːm-/ adj difficult or impossible to understand: legal documents full of incomprehensible jargon | I find your attitude quite incomprehensible. | [+to] His accent made his speech incomprehensible to me. —**incomprehensibly** adv —**incomprehensibility** /ˌɪnkɒmprɪhensəˈbɪləti $ -ˌkɑːm-/ n [U]

in·com·pre·hen·sion /ˌɪnkɒmprɪˈhenʃən $ -ˌkɑːm-/ n [U] the state of not being able to understand something: He spread his hands in a gesture of incomprehension.

in·con·ceiv·a·ble /ˌɪnkənˈsiːvəbəl/ adj too strange or unusual to be thought real or possible: A few years ago a car fuelled by solar energy would have been inconceivable. | **It is inconceivable that** a man in such a powerful position could act so unwisely. —**inconceivably** adv

in·con·clu·sive /ˌɪnkənˈkluːsɪv◂/ adj not leading to a clear decision or result; ◨ **conclusive:** The evidence against the two men was inconclusive. | A coalition government was formed after inconclusive elections. —**inconclusively** adv —**inconclusiveness** n [U]

in·con·gru·i·ty /ˌɪnkənˈɡruːəti/ n plural **incongruities** [C,U] the fact that something is strange, unusual, or unsuitable in a particular situation: The incongruity of her situation struck Gina with unpleasant force. | [+between] He didn't see the slightest incongruity between the idealism of his plays and his own morals.

in·con·gru·ous /ɪnˈkɒŋɡruəs $ -ˈkɑːŋ-/ adj strange, unexpected, or unsuitable in a particular situation: The new theatre looks utterly incongruous in its setting. —**incongruously** adv

in·con·se·quen·tial /ˌɪnkɒnsɪˈkwenʃəl◂ $ - kɑːn-/ adj not important; ◨ **insignificant:** inconsequential but amusing chatter —**inconsequentially** adv

in·con·sid·er·a·ble /ˌɪnkənˈsɪdərəbəl◂/ *adj* **not inconsiderable** *formal* used to emphasize that something is large or important; ◰ **considerable**: *He has built up a not inconsiderable business empire.*

in·con·sid·er·ate /ˌɪnkənˈsɪdərₔ̱t◂/ *adj* not caring about the feelings, needs, or comfort of other people; ◰ **thoughtless**; ◰ **considerate**: *inconsiderate motorists* | **it was inconsiderate (of sb) to do sth** *It was very inconsiderate of you to keep us waiting.* —**inconsiderately** *adv*

in·con·sis·ten·cy /ˌɪnkənˈsɪstənsi/ *n plural* **inconsistencies 1** [U] when someone keeps changing their behaviour, reactions etc so that other people become confused; ◰ **consistency 2** [C,U] a situation in which two statements are different and cannot both be true; ◰ **contradiction**: *There were several glaring inconsistencies (=very noticeable differences) in his report.* | [+**between**] *Defence counsel looks for inconsistency between witness statements.*

in·con·sis·tent /ˌɪnkənˈsɪstənt◂/ *adj* **1** two statements that are inconsistent cannot both be true; ◰ **contradictory**; ◰ **consistent**: *The accounts of the witnesses are inconsistent.* | [+**with**] *His results are inconsistent with the data we produced.* **2** not right according to a particular set of principles or standards; ◰ **consistent**: [+**with**] *His conduct was inconsistent with what is expected of a Congressman.* **3** inconsistent behaviour, work etc changes too often from good to bad; ◰ **consistent**: *The team's performance has been highly inconsistent this season.*

in·con·so·la·ble /ˌɪnkənˈsəʊləbəl◂/ *adj* so sad that it is impossible for anyone to comfort you: *The boy was inconsolable after the death of his dog.* —**inconsolably** *adv*: *She wept inconsolably.*

in·con·spic·u·ous /ˌɪnkənˈspɪkjuəs◂/ *adj* not easily seen or noticed; ◰ **conspicuous**: *an inconspicuous little restaurant* | *She stood by the wall, trying to **look** inconspicuous.* —**inconspicuously** *adv*

in·con·stant /ɪnˈkɒnstənt $ -ˈkɑːn-/ *adj literary* unfaithful in love or friendship —**inconstancy** *n* [U]

in·con·test·a·ble /ˌɪnkənˈtestəbəl◂/ *adj* clearly true and impossible to disagree with; ◰ **indisputable**: *We had incontestable proof of her innocence.*

in·con·ti·nent /ɪnˈkɒntₔ̱nənt $ -ˈkɑːn-/ *adj* unable to control the passing of liquid or solid waste from your body —**incontinence** *n* [U]

in·con·tro·ver·ti·ble /ˌɪnˌkɒntrəˈvɜːtₔ̱bəl $ ˌkɑːntrəˈvɜːr-/ *adj* definitely true and impossible to be proved false; ◰ **indisputable**: *CCTV provided incontrovertible evidence that he was at the scene of the crime.* —**incontrovertibly** *adv*

in·con·ve·ni·ence¹ /ˌɪnkənˈviːniəns/ *n* **1** [U] problems caused by something which annoy or affect you: *We apologise for the delay and any inconvenience caused.* | **the inconvenience of (doing) sth** *the inconvenience of having to find another buyer* **2** [C] someone or something that causes problems for you: *a minor inconvenience* | [+**to**] *His early arrival was clearly an inconvenience to his host.*

inconvenience² *v* [T] to cause problems for someone: *I don't want to inconvenience you any further.*

in·con·ve·ni·ent /ˌɪnkənˈviːniənt◂/ *adj* causing problems, often in a way that is annoying; ◰ **convenient**: *Monday's a bit inconvenient for me. How about Wednesday?* | *Am I calling at an inconvenient time?* —**inconveniently** *adv*

in·cor·po·rate [W3] /ɪnˈkɔːpəreɪt $ -ɔːr-/ *v* [T] to include something as part of a group, system, plan etc: **incorporate sth into/in sth** *We've incorporated many environmentally-friendly features into the design of the building.* | *Our original proposals were not incorporated in the new legislation.* —**incorporation** /ɪnˌkɔːpəˈreɪʃən $ -ɔːr-/ *n* [U]: *the incorporation of the college into the university*

in·cor·po·rat·ed /ɪnˈkɔːpəreɪtₔ̱d $ -ɔːr-/ *Inc adj* used after the name of a company in the US to show that it has become a CORPORATION; → **limited**

in·cor·po·re·al /ˌɪnkɔːˈpɔːriəl $ -kɔːr-/ *adj formal* not existing in any physical form: *Plato demonstrated the incorporeal nature of the soul.*

in·cor·rect /ˌɪnkəˈrekt◂/ *adj* **1** not correct or true: *The information you gave us was incorrect.* **2** not following the rules of polite or fair behaviour; ◰ **impolite**: *It would be incorrect of me to comment.* —**incorrectly** *adv*: *Sorry, you answered incorrectly.*

in·cor·ri·gi·ble /ɪnˈkɒrₔ̱dʒₔ̱bəl $ -ˈkɔː-/ *adj* someone who is incorrigible is bad in a way that cannot be changed or improved – often used humorously: **an incorrigible liar/rogue** | *Peter, you are an incorrigible flirt!* —**incorrigibly** *adv*

in·cor·rup·ti·ble /ˌɪnkəˈrʌptₔ̱bəl◂/ *adj* **1** someone who is incorruptible cannot be persuaded to do wrong or illegal things: *A good judge must be incorruptible.* **2** *formal* material that is incorruptible will never decay and cannot be destroyed —**incorruptibility** /ˌɪnkərʌptₔ̱ˈbɪlₔ̱ti/ *n* [U]

in·crease¹ [S2] [W1] /ɪnˈkriːs/ *v* [I,T] if you increase something, or if it increases, it becomes bigger in amount, number, or degree; ◰ **decrease, reduce**: *The population increased dramatically in the first half of the century.* | *political tensions that might increase the likelihood of war* | *Visits to the site have increased threefold since May.* | **increase in value/price/importance etc** *Investments are certain to increase in value.* | **increase (sth) by sth** *Food prices increased by 10% in less than a year.* | **increase (sth) from/to sth** *The salary is £18,600 a year, increasing to £23,000.* —**increasing** *adj*: *the increasing difficulty of finding trained staff* | *European leaders watched events unfold with increasing alarm.* —**increased** *adj*: *Quality improvements produced increased demand for our goods.* | *an increased incidence of childhood leukaemia*

in·crease² [S3] [W1] /ˈɪnkriːs/ *n* [C,U] a rise in amount, number, or degree; ◰ **decrease**

tax increase
wage/pay/salary increase
price increase
fare increase
substantial/large increase
huge/massive increase (=a very large increase)
dramatic/sharp increase (=a sudden large increase)
significant/marked increase (=a definite and noticeable increase)
slight/small/modest increase
gradual increase
threefold/fourfold/fivefold etc increase (=an increase by three, four etc times)
be on the increase (=be increasing)

[+**in**] *an increase in the crime rate* | *Recent **tax increases** have affected the poor more than the rich.* | *the **dramatic increase** in the population aged over 65* | *There has been a **marked increase** in the use of firearms.* | *Cases of tuberculosis are **on the increase**.*

in·creas·ing·ly [W2] /ɪnˈkriːsɪŋli/ *adv* more and more all the time: *Marketing techniques are becoming increasingly sophisticated.* | *Increasingly, young people distrust all forms of government.*

in·cred·i·ble /ɪnˈkredₔ̱bəl/ *adj* **1** extremely good, large, or great; ◰ **unbelievable**: *The view is just incredible.* | *There was blood everywhere and the pain was incredible.* **2** too strange to be believed or very difficult to believe; ◰ **unbelievable**: *It's incredible that he survived the fall.* | *It's incredible how much Tom has changed since he met Sally.* | *I find it almost incredible that no-one noticed these errors.*

in·cred·i·bly [S3] /ɪnˈkredₔ̱bli/ *adv*
1 [+adj/adv] *informal* extremely: *Nicotine is incredibly addictive.*
2 [sentence adverb] in a way that is hard to believe: *The knife had pierced his heart, but incredibly he was still alive.*

in·cre·du·li·ty /ˌɪnkrɪ̩'djuːlɪ̩ti $ -'duː-/ n [U] a feeling that you cannot believe something; **☐ disbelief**: *When she told her family she was gay, they reacted with a mixture of shock and incredulity.*

in·cred·u·lous /ɪn'kredjɪ̩ləs, -dʒə-/ adj unable or unwilling to believe something: *'You sold the car?' she asked, incredulous.* | **incredulous look/expression/voice etc** *She shot him an incredulous look.* —**incredulously** adv

in·cre·ment /'ɪŋkrɪ̩mənt/ n [C] **1** a regular increase in the amount of money someone is paid: *a salary of £18,000, with annual increments of 2.5%* **2** formal the amount by which a number, value, or amount increases

in·cre·men·tal /ˌɪŋkrɪ̩'mentl◂/ adj formal **1** [usually before noun] increasing in amount or value gradually and by a regular amount: *incremental pay scales* **2** happening gradually over time: *Mr Kennedy said that progress on reforms would be incremental.* | *a process of incremental change* —**incrementally** adv: *You need to make changes in your diet incrementally.*

in·crim·i·nate /ɪn'krɪmɪ̩neɪt/ v [T] to make someone seem guilty of a crime: **incriminate yourself** *He refused to answer questions for fear he might incriminate himself.* —**incriminating** adj: *incriminating evidence* —**incrimination** /ɪnˌkrɪmɪ̩'neɪʃən/ n [U]

'in-crowd n the **in-crowd** a small group of people in an organization who are fashionable, popular, or powerful, but who do not let many other people join them: *I was never one of the in-crowd at school.*

in·cu·bate /'ɪŋkjɪ̩beɪt/ v [I,T] **1** if a bird incubates its eggs, or if the eggs incubate, they are kept warm until they HATCH (=the birds inside are born) **2** technical if a disease incubates, or if you incubate it, it develops in your body until you show physical signs of it —**incubation** /ˌɪŋkjɪ̩'beɪʃən/ n [U]: *Hepatitis has a long incubation period.*

in·cu·ba·tor /'ɪŋkjɪ̩-beɪtə $ -ər/ n [C] **1** a piece of hospital equipment into which very small or weak babies are put to keep them alive and warm **2** a heated container for keeping eggs warm until they HATCH (=the young birds are born) **3** an organization which helps new businesses to develop by giving them office space, services, and equipment, and providing them with business and technical advice: *a high-tech incubator on the East coast*

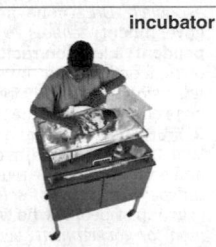

incubator

in·cu·bus /'ɪŋkjɪ̩bəs/ n plural **incubuses** or **incubi** /-baɪ/ [C] **1** someone or something that causes a lot of worries or problems: *Joyce regarded his US citizenship as a moral and political incubus.* **2** a male DEVIL that in the past was believed to have sex with a sleeping woman → **SUCCUBUS**

in·cul·cate /'ɪŋkʌlkeɪt $ ɪn'kʌl-/ v [T] formal to fix ideas, principles etc in someone's mind: **inculcate sth in/into sb** *I try to inculcate a sense of responsibility in my children.* | *Not all schools manage to successfully inculcate a love of learning.* —**inculcation** /ˌɪŋkʌl'keɪʃən/ n [U]

in·cum·ben·cy /ɪn'kʌmbənsi/ n plural **incumbencies** [C usually singular, U] formal the state of holding an official position, especially in politics, or the time when someone holds an official position

in·cum·bent[1] /ɪn'kʌmbənt/ n [C] formal someone who has been elected to an official position, especially in politics, and who is doing that job at the present time: *In the June elections, Morris easily defeated the incumbent, Tom Smith.*

incumbent[2] adj formal **1 it is incumbent upon/on sb to do sth** if it is incumbent upon you to do something, it is your duty or responsibility to do it: *It is incumbent*

upon parents to control what their children watch on TV. **2** the incumbent president/priest/government etc the president etc at the present time

in·cur /ɪn'kɜː $ -'kɜːr/ v **incurred, incurring** [T] formal **1** if you incur a cost, debt, or a fine, you have to pay money because of something you have done, or you do not make money: **incur expenses/costs/losses/debts etc** *If the council loses the appeal, it will incur all the legal costs.* | *The heavy losses incurred by airlines since September 11th* **2** if you incur something unpleasant, it happens to you because of something you have done: **incur sb's displeasure/wrath/disapproval etc** *She wondered what she'd done to incur his displeasure this time.*

in·cur·a·ble /ɪn'kjʊərəbəl $ -'kjʊr-/ adj **1** impossible to cure; **☐ curable**: **incurable disease/illness/condition** *She has a rare, incurable disease.* **2** impossible to change: *My mother is an incurable optimist.* —**incurably** adv: *incurably romantic*

in·cur·sion /ɪn'kɜːʃən, -ʒən $ ɪn'kɜːrʒən/ n [C] formal **1** a sudden attack into an area that belongs to other people: [+into] *a combined British and French incursion into China in 1857* **2** the sudden arrival of something or someone into a place or activity where they do not belong or have not been before, used especially to say that they are not welcome: [+into] *The media was criticized for its thoughtless incursion into the domestic grief of the family.* | *The Japanese incursion into the U.S. domestic electronics market*

in·debt·ed /ɪn'detɪ̩d/ adj **1 be (deeply/greatly) indebted to sb** to be very grateful to someone for the help they have given you: *We are deeply indebted to Dr Allen and the rest of the hospital staff.* **2** owing money to someone: *the 17 most heavily indebted nations* —**indebtedness** n [U]

in·de·cen·cy /ɪn'diːsənsi/ n plural **indecencies 1** [U] law behaviour that is sexually offensive, especially INDECENT EXPOSURE **2** [C] formal an action that is shocking or offensive

in·de·cent /ɪn'diːsənt/ adj **1** something that is indecent is shocking and offensive, usually because it involves sex or shows parts of the body that are usually covered: *He was found guilty of possessing indecent photographs of young boys.* | *You can't go out in that dress – it's positively indecent!* **2** completely unacceptable: *The funeral formalities were performed with almost indecent haste.* —**indecently** adv: *an indecently short skirt*

in·decent as·sault n [C,U] law the crime of making a sexual attack on someone, touching or threatening to touch them, but not RAPING them (=forcing them to have sex)

in·decent ex·po·sure n [U] law the criminal offence of deliberately showing your sex organs in a place where this is likely to offend people

in·de·ci·pher·a·ble /ˌɪndɪ'saɪfərəbəl◂/ adj impossible to read or understand: *an indecipherable signature*

in·de·ci·sion /ˌɪndɪ'sɪʒən/ n [U] the state of being unable to decide what to do: *There were weeks of indecision about who would go and when.*

in·de·ci·sive /ˌɪndɪ'saɪsɪv◂/ adj **1** unable to make clear decisions or choices; **☐ decisive**: *a weak and indecisive leader* **2** not having a clear result; **☐ inconclusive**: *a confused, indecisive battle* —**indecisively** adv —**indecisiveness** n [U]

in·deed S3 W1 /ɪn'diːd/ adv **1** [sentence adverb] used to emphasize a statement or answer: *The blood tests prove that Vince is indeed the father.* | *'Would it help if you had an assistant?' 'It would indeed.'*

2 [sentence adverb] *formal* used to introduce an additional statement that emphasizes or supports what you have just said: *I didn't mind at all. Indeed, I was pleased.*
3 *especially BrE* used with 'very' and an adjective or adverb to emphasize a statement or description: *Most of the essays were very good indeed.* | *Thank you very much indeed.*
4 *spoken especially BrE* used to show that you are surprised or annoyed by something that someone has just told you: *'He said he was too busy to see you.' 'Did he, indeed?'*
5 why/how/who etc indeed? *spoken* used when someone has asked you a question, to show that you do not know the answer and you do not think there can be a satisfactory answer: *'Why would John have left without saying a word?' 'Why indeed?'* | *'How can anyone justify such shameful behaviour?' 'How indeed?'*

in·de·fat·i·ga·ble /ˌɪndɪˈfætɪɡəbəl/ *adj formal* determined and never giving up: *an indefatigable campaigner for human rights* —**indefatigably** *adv*
in·de·fen·si·ble /ˌɪndɪˈfensɪbəl/ *adj* **1** too bad to be excused or defended: *The law is morally indefensible and in need of reform.* **2** impossible or very difficult to defend from military attack —**indefensibly** *adv*
in·de·fi·na·ble /ˌɪndɪˈfaɪnəbəl/ *adj* an indefinable feeling, quality etc is difficult to describe or explain: *She felt an indefinable sadness.* —**indefinably** *adv*
in·def·i·nite /ɪnˈdefənɪt/ *adj* **1** an indefinite action or period of time has no definite end arranged for it: *The next day the union voted to begin an indefinite strike.* | *The picture has been loaned for an indefinite period to the National Gallery.* **2** not clear or exact; ☐ **vague**: *Teachers find the report's terminology so indefinite that it is confusing.*
in,definite 'article *n* [C] *technical* the word 'a' or 'an'; → **definite article**
in·def·i·nit·ely /ɪnˈdefənɪtli/ *adv* **1** for a period of time for which no definite end has been arranged: *The project has been postponed indefinitely.* **2** without giving clear or exact details
in,definite 'pronoun *n* [C] *technical* a word such as 'some', 'any', or 'either' that is used instead of a noun, but does not say exactly which person or thing is meant
in·del·i·ble /ɪnˈdelɪbəl/ *adj* **1** impossible to remove or forget; ☐ **permanent**: *Her words left an indelible impression on me for years to come.* **2** indelible ink/pencil/marker etc ink etc that makes a permanent mark which cannot be removed —**indelibly** *adv*: *a moment indelibly imprinted on my mind*
in·del·i·cate /ɪnˈdelɪkət/ *adj formal* likely to embarrass or shock people; ☐ **rude**: *an indelicate comment* —**indelicacy** *n* [U]
in·dem·ni·fy /ɪnˈdemnɪfaɪ/ *v* **indemnified, indemnifying, indemnifies** [T] *law* **1** [+ against/for] to promise to pay someone if something they own is damaged or lost **2** [+ for] to pay someone money because of loss, injury, or damage that they have suffered —**indemnification** /ɪnˌdemnɪfɪˈkeɪʃən/ *n* [C,U]
in·dem·ni·ty /ɪnˈdemnɪti/ *n plural* **indemnities** *law* **1** [U] protection against loss or damage, especially in the form of a promise to pay for any losses or damage: *insurance providing indemnity against future liabilities* **2** [C] a payment for the loss of money, goods etc
in·dent[1] /ɪnˈdent/ *v* [T] to start a line of writing further towards the middle of the page than other lines: *Use the Tab key to indent the first line of a paragraph.*
in·dent[2] /ˈɪndent/ *n* [C] *especially BrE* **1** an official order for goods or equipment: [+for] *He cancelled the indent for silk scarves.* **2** an indentation
in·den·ta·tion /ˌɪndenˈteɪʃən/ *n* [C] **1** also **indent** a space at the beginning of a line of writing **2** also

indent a cut into the surface or edge of something: *Gently make a small indentation in the center of each cookie.*
in·dent·ed /ɪnˈdentɪd/ *adj* an indented edge or face has cuts or marks in it: *our deeply indented coastline*
in·den·ture /ɪnˈdentʃə $ -ər/ *n plural* **indentures** [C,U] a formal contract, especially in the past, between an APPRENTICE and his MASTER (=employer), or the act of arranging this —**indentured** *adj*: *indentured servants*
in·de·pen·dence [W2] /ˌɪndɪˈpendəns/ *n* [U]
1 political freedom from control by the government of another country: [+from] *Nigeria gained independence from Britain in 1960.* | *Lithuania was the first of the Soviet republics to declare independence* (=officially state its independence).
2 the time when a country becomes politically independent: *The country has made great advances since independence.*
3 the freedom and ability to make your own decisions in life, without having to ask other people for permission, help, or money: *ways of helping old people maintain their independence* | *Having a job gives you financial independence.*
Inde'pendence ,Day *n* [C,U] **1** the day every year on which a country celebrates its independence from another country that controlled it in the past **2** this day in the U.S., celebrated on 4th July
in·de·pen·dent [W2] /ˌɪndɪˈpendənt/ *adj*
1 NOT OWNED/CONTROLLED BY STH [usually before noun] an independent organization is not owned or controlled by, or does not receive money from, another organization or the government: *There are plans to split the corporation into a number of smaller independent companies.* | *an independent charity* | *small independent bookshops* | [+of] *We need a central bank that is independent of the government.* | **independent school** *especially BrE* (=one not owned or paid for by the government) *schools in the independent sector* | **independent television/radio/broadcasting etc** *BrE* (=not owned or paid for by the government) *independent television companies* | **independent film** (=one not made or produced by a large film production company)
2 FAIR [usually before noun] an independent organization or person is not involved in a particular situation, and can therefore be trusted to be fair in judging it: *an independent panel of scientists* | *An independent body* (=group of people who work together) *has been set up to monitor government spending.* | *There were no independent witnesses to the shooting.* | **independent inquiry/advice/opinion etc** (=carried out by or given by an independent person or organization) *Human rights groups have called for an independent inquiry into the killings.* | *the results of an independent study*
3 COUNTRY an independent country is not governed or controlled by another country: *India became independent in 1947.*
4 PERSON a) confident and able to do things by yourself in your own way, without needing help or advice from other people; ☐ **dependent**: *Now that my sons are becoming more independent, I have more time for myself.* | *a strong-willed, independent young woman* | *He's now helping other people with spinal injuries to lead an independent life.* | [+of] *By this age, the child becomes relatively independent of his mother.* **b)** having enough money to live without having to ask for help from other people: *It was always very important to me to be financially independent.* | [+of] *Robert aimed to be independent of his parents by the time he was twenty.*
5 independent study/learning when you study on your own rather than being taught by a teacher: *The tapes can be used in class or for independent study.*
6 woman/man etc of independent means someone who has their own income from property, INVESTMENTS etc, so that they do not have to work or depend on anyone else
7 SEPARATE if one thing is independent of another, the two are not connected, or the second thing does not influence the first: [+of] *reports from two separate*

sources entirely independent of one another | *Three independent studies all arrived at the same conclusion.*
8 POLITICIAN [usually before noun] an independent politician does not belong to a particular party: *Independent candidates won three seats.* **—independently** *adv*: *The two departments operate independently of each other.* | *She had elderly parents who could no longer live independently.*

Independent *n* [C] a politician who does not belong to a political party

independent 'clause *n* [C] *technical* a CLAUSE which can make a sentence by itself, for example 'she went home' in the sentence 'She went home because she was tired.'; ◙ **main clause**

in-depth *adj* [only before noun] thorough, complete, and considering all the details: **in-depth study/research/analysis etc** *an in-depth study of patients' needs* | *a series of in-depth interviews*

in·de·scri·ba·ble /ˌɪndɪˈskraɪbəbəl / *adj* something that is indescribable is so terrible, so good, so strange etc that you cannot describe it, or it is too difficult to describe: *a feeling of indescribable joy* **—indescribably** *adv*: *an indescribably awful smell*

in·de·struc·ti·ble /ˌɪndɪˈstrʌktʃbəl / *adj* too strong to be destroyed: *her indestructible optimism* | *Gold is virtually indestructible.* **—indestructibility** /ˌɪndɪstrʌktʃˈbɪlʒti/ *n* [U]

in·de·ter·mi·na·ble /ˌɪndɪˈtɜːmʒnəbəl $ -ɜːr-/ *adj* impossible to find out or calculate exactly: *water of indeterminable depth* **—indeterminably** *adv*

in·de·ter·mi·nate /ˌɪndɪˈtɜːmʒnʒt $ -ɜːr-/ *adj* impossible to know about definitely or exactly: *a girl of indeterminate age* **—indeterminately** *adv* **—indeterminacy** *n* [U]

in·dex¹ [W3] /ˈɪndeks/ *n* [C]
1 *plural* **indexes** an alphabetical list of names, subjects etc at the back of a book, with the numbers of the pages where they can be found
2 *plural* **indexes** a set of cards or a DATABASE containing information, usually arranged in alphabetical order and used especially in a library
3 *plural* **indices** /ˈɪndʒsiːz/ a standard by which the level of something can be judged or measured: [+of] *The changing size of an infant's head is considered an index of brain growth.*
4 *plural* **indices** /ˈɪndʒsiːz/ *or* **indexes** *technical* a system by which prices, costs etc can be compared to those of a previous date

index² *v* [T] [usually passive] **1** if documents, information etc are indexed, an index is made for them: *The reports are indexed by subject and location.* **2** to arrange for the level of wages, PENSIONS etc to increase or decrease according to the level of prices: [+to] *BrE*: *demands that wages be indexed to the rise in prices* [+for] *AmE*: *an amount indexed for inflation* **—indexation** /ˌɪndekˈseɪʃən/ *n* [C,U]

index card *n* [C] a small card for writing on, used especially in an INDEX¹ (2)

index ,finger *n* [C] the finger next to your thumb; ◙ **forefinger** → **see picture at** HAND¹

index-'linked *adj* *BrE technical* index-linked wages, PENSIONS etc, increase or decrease according to the rise or fall of prices

In·di·an¹ /ˈɪndiən/ *n* **1** [C] someone from India **2** [C] a member of one of the races that lived in North, South, and Central America before the Europeans arrived; ◙ **Native American 3** [singular] *BrE informal* a meal of Indian food, or a restaurant that sells Indian food: *Do you fancy going out for an Indian?*

Indian² *adj* **1** relating to India or its people **2** relating to the Indians of North, South, and Central America

Indian 'summer *n* [C] **1** a period of warm weather in autumn **2** a happy or successful time, especially near the end of your life or CAREER

in·di·cate [W1] /ˈɪndʒkeɪt/ *v*
1 [T] to show that a particular situation exists, or that something is likely to be true: **indicate (that)** *Research indicates that over 81% of teachers are dissatisfied with their salary.* | *Long skid marks on the pavement indicated the driver had attempted to brake.* | *The study indicates a strong connection between poverty and crime.*
2 [T] to say or do something to make your wishes, intentions etc clear: *The Russians have already indicated their willingness to cooperate.* | *Professor Johnson has indicated his intention to retire at the end of next year.* | **indicate (that)** *Ralph patted the sofa to indicate that she should join him.* | *Please indicate your preference on the booking form.*
3 [T] to direct someone's attention to something or someone, for example by pointing: *'That's her,' said Toby, indicating a girl on the other side of the room.*
4 [T] to represent something: *Sales targets are indicated on the graph by a vertical dotted line.*
5 [I,T] *BrE* to show the direction in which you intend to turn in a vehicle, using lights or your hands; ◙ **signal**: *Don't forget to indicate before you pull out.*

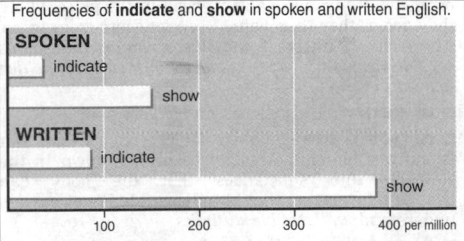

Frequencies of **indicate** and **show** in spoken and written English.

This graph shows that **show** is much more common than **indicate** in both spoken and written English. This is because **show** is much more general in meaning and is more commonly used in informal English than **indicate**.

in·di·ca·tion [W3] /ˌɪndʒˈkeɪʃən/ *n* [C,U] a sign, remark, event etc that shows what is happening, what someone is thinking or feeling, or what is true: [+of] *Dark green leaves are a good indication of healthy roots.* | *He gave no indication of his own feelings at all.* | *Could you give me some indication as to when I am likely to receive a reply?* | **indication (that)** *Taking a career history along with you will be a clear indication that you are well organized.* | *Indications are that the situation hasn't improved much.* | *There is every indication* (=there are very clear signs) *that it is true.*

in·dic·a·tive¹ /ɪnˈdɪkətɪv/ *n* [C,U] *technical* the form of a verb that is used to make statements. For example, in the sentences 'Penny passed her test', and 'Michael likes cake', the verbs 'passed' and 'like' are in the indicative.

in·dic·a·tive² *adj* **1 be indicative of sth** to be a clear sign that a particular situation exists or that something is likely to be true: *This behaviour is indicative of her whole attitude, I'm afraid.* **2** *technical* an indicative verb form is used for making statements

in·di·ca·tor /ˈɪndʒkeɪtə $ -ər/ *n* [C] **1** something that can be regarded as a sign of something else: *All the main economic indicators suggest that trade is improving.* **2** *BrE* one of the lights on a car that flash to show which way the car is turning; ◙ **turn signal** *AmE* **3** a POINTER on a machine that shows the temperature, pressure, speed etc → **see picture at** CAR

in·di·ces /ˈɪndʒsiːz/ a plural of INDEX

in·dict /ɪnˈdaɪt/ *v* [I,T] *law especially AmE* to officially charge someone with a criminal offence: **indict sb for sth** *He was indicted for vehicular homicide in 1987.*

in·dict·a·ble /ɪnˈdaɪtəbəl/ *adj* *law especially AmE* an indictable offence is one for which you can be indicted

in·dict·ment /ɪnˈdaɪtmənt/ *n* **1 be an indictment of sth** to be a very clear sign that a system, method etc is very bad or very wrong: *The fact that these children cannot read is a damning indictment of our education system.* **2** [C] *law especially AmE* an official written statement charging someone with a criminal offence **3** [U] *law especially AmE* the act of officially charging someone with a criminal offence

in·die¹ /ˈɪndi/ *adj* [only before noun] used to refer to popular music that is performed by new bands or singers, and produced by small independent companies: *indie music* | *an indie band*

indie² *n* [C] a small independent company, especially one that produces popular music

in·dif·fer·ence /ɪnˈdɪfərəns/ *n* [U] lack of interest or concern: [+to] *his apparent indifference to material luxuries* | *Whether you stay or leave is **a matter of** total **indifference to** me* (=I do not care).

in·dif·fer·ent /ɪnˈdɪfərənt/ *adj* **1** not at all interested in someone or something: [+to] *Sarah was absolutely indifferent to him, and it hurt.* **2** not particularly good; 🔁 **mediocre**: *an indifferent cook* —**indifferently** *adv*

in·di·ge·nous /ɪnˈdɪdʒənəs/ *adj formal* indigenous people or things have always been in the place where they are, rather than being brought there from somewhere else; 🔁 **native**: [+to] *Blueberries are indigenous to America.* | *the many indigenous cultures which existed in Siberia*

in·di·gent /ˈɪndɪdʒənt/ *adj formal* very poor

in·di·ges·ti·ble /ˌɪndɪˈdʒestɪbəl/ *adj* **1** food that is indigestible cannot easily be broken down in the stomach into substances that the body can use **2** information that is indigestible is not easy to understand: *indigestible statistics*

in·di·ges·tion /ˌɪndɪˈdʒestʃən/ *n* [U] pain that you get when your stomach cannot break down food that you have eaten; → **heartburn**: *Spicy food always gives me indigestion.*

in·dig·nant /ɪnˈdɪgnənt/ *adj* angry and surprised because you feel insulted or unfairly treated: [+at/about] *Liz was indignant at the way her child had been treated.* | *I got an indignant reply from Mr Norris.* —**indignantly** *adv*: *'Of course I didn't tell her!' Sasha said indignantly.*

in·dig·na·tion /ˌɪndɪgˈneɪʃən/ *n* [U] feelings of anger and surprise because you feel insulted or unfairly treated: *To his indignation, Charles found that his name was not on the list.* | **with/in indignation** *Lou's voice quivered with indignation.* | [+at/about/over] *Her indignation at such rough treatment was understandable.* | *He stormed into her office, full of **righteous indignation**.*

in·dig·ni·ty /ɪnˈdɪgnəti/ *n plural* **indignities** [C,U] a situation that makes you feel very ashamed and not respected: *The prisoners were subjected to all sorts of indignities.* | **the indignity of (doing) sth** *Two of the diplomats **suffered the indignity of** being arrested.* | **the final/ultimate/crowning etc indignity**

in·di·go /ˈɪndɪgəʊ $ -goʊ/ *n* [U] a dark purple-blue colour —**indigo** *adj*

in·di·rect /ˌɪndɪˈrekt/ *adj* **1** not directly caused by something; 🔁 **direct**: *Losing weight is an **indirect result** of smoking cigarettes.* | *The **indirect effects** of climate change may be profound.* **2** an indirect way to a place is not the straightest way; 🔁 **direct**: *They took an indirect route, avoiding the town centre.* **3** not saying or showing something in a clear definite way; 🔁 **direct**: *George's comments were an indirect way of blaming me.* —**indirectly** *adv*: *Perhaps I was indirectly responsible for the misunderstanding.*

indirect 'cost *n* [C usually plural] *technical* money that a business must spend, not directly on its products or services, but on other things such as buildings or wages

indirect 'discourse *n* [U] *AmE technical* INDIRECT SPEECH

indirect 'object *n* [C] *technical* an OBJECT of a verb that refers to the person that something is given to, said to, made for etc. For example, in the sentence 'I asked him a question', the indirect object is 'him'.

indirect 'speech *BrE*; **indirect discourse** *AmE* also, **reported speech** *n* [U] *technical* a way of reporting what someone said without repeating their exact words. For example, in the sentence 'Julia said that she didn't want to go', the clause 'that she didn't want to go' is indirect speech. Her actual words were 'I don't want to go'.

indirect 'tax *n* [C] a tax which is added to the cost of goods and services; → **direct tax** —**indirect tax'ation** *n* [U]

in·dis·cer·ni·ble /ˌɪndɪˈsɜːnɪbəl $ -ɜːr-/ *adj* very difficult to see, hear, or notice: *The path was almost indiscernible in the mist.*

in·dis·ci·pline /ɪnˈdɪsəplɪn/ *n* [U] *formal* a lack of control in the behaviour of a group of people, with the result that they behave badly; 🔁 **discipline**: *Indiscipline among the troops eventually led to a riot.*

in·dis·creet /ˌɪndɪˈskriːt/ *adj* careless about what you say or do, especially by talking about things which should be kept secret; 🔁 **discreet**: *It was very indiscreet of Colin to tell them about our plan.*

in·dis·cre·tion /ˌɪndɪˈskreʃən/ *n* [C,U] an action or remark that shows a lack of good judgment, especially one that is morally unacceptable: *Earl describes his past links with the racist group as a **youthful indiscretion**.* | *rumours of the former president's sexual indiscretions*

in·dis·crim·i·nate /ˌɪndɪˈskrɪmənət/ *adj* an indiscriminate action is done without thinking about what harm it might cause: **indiscriminate attacks/killing/violence/bombing etc** *terrorists responsible for indiscriminate killing* | *the **indiscriminate use** of chemical fertilizers* | *Even so-called 'tactical' nuclear weapons are indiscriminate in their effect.* —**indiscriminately** *adv*: *Soldiers fired indiscriminately into the crowd.*

in·dis·pen·sa·ble /ˌɪndɪˈspensəbəl/ *adj* someone or something that is indispensable is so important or useful that it is impossible to manage without them; 🔁 **essential**: [+to] *This book is indispensable to anyone interested in space exploration.* | **indispensable for/in (doing) sth** *Meat is not indispensable for maintaining a healthy diet.* | *Mobile phones have become an **indispensable part** of our lives.*

in·dis·posed /ˌɪndɪˈspəʊzd $ -ˈspoʊzd/ *adj* [not before noun] *formal* **1** ill and therefore unable to be present: *Mrs Rawlins is temporarily indisposed.* **2 indisposed to do sth** not willing to do something

in·dis·po·si·tion /ɪnˌdɪspəˈzɪʃən/ *n formal* [C,U] a slight illness

in·dis·pu·ta·ble /ˌɪndɪˈspjuːtəbəl/ *adj* an indisputable fact must be accepted because it is definitely true: *The evidence was indisputable.* —**indisputably** *adv*: *This novel is indisputably his finest work.*

in·dis·so·lu·ble /ˌɪndɪˈsɒljʊbəl $ -ˈsɑː-/ *adj formal* an indissoluble relationship cannot be destroyed: *the indissoluble link between language and culture* —**indissolubly** *adv*

in·dis·tinct /ˌɪndɪˈstɪŋkt/ *adj* an indistinct sound, image, or memory cannot be seen, heard, or remembered clearly; 🔁 **distinct**: *She muttered something indistinct.* | *My memory of what happened next is indistinct.* —**indistinctly** *adv*

in·dis·tin·guish·a·ble /ˌɪndɪˈstɪŋgwɪʃəbəl/ *adj* things that are indistinguishable are so similar that you cannot see any difference between them: [+from] *an artificial material that is almost indistinguishable from real silk*

in·di·vid·u·al¹ S3 W1 /ˌɪndɪˈvɪdʒuəl/ *adj* **1** [only before noun] considered separately from other people or things in the same group: *Each individual* *leaf on the tree is different.* | *the needs of the individual customer*

2 [only before noun] belonging to or intended for one person rather than a group: *Children get more individual attention in small classes.* | *You can have the bathroom designed to suit your individual needs.* | *individual portions of jam*

3 an individual style, way of doing things etc is different from anyone else's – usually used to show approval; ⊟ **distinctive**: *a tennis player with a highly individual style* | *a very individual way of dressing*

individual² W1 n [C]
1 a person, considered separately from the rest of the group or society that they live in: *the rights of the individual* | *Each individual receives two genes, one inherited from each parent.* | *Most churches were built with donations from private individuals* (=ordinary people, rather than the government or companies).
2 a person of a particular kind, especially one who is unusual in some way: *a strange-looking individual*

in·di·vid·u·al·is·m /ˌɪndɪˈvɪdʒuəlɪzəm/ n [U] **1** the belief that the rights and freedom of individual people are the most important rights in a society: *Capitalism encourages competition and individualism.* **2** the behaviour or attitude of someone who does things in their own way without being influenced by other people

in·di·vid·u·al·ist /ˌɪndɪˈvɪdʒuəlɪst/ n [C] someone who does things in their own way and has different opinions from most other people: *Geoff was too much of an individualist to be team captain.* —**individualistic** /ˌɪndɪˌvɪdʒuəˈlɪstɪk◄/ also **individualist** adj: *She has a highly individualistic approach to painting.*

in·di·vid·u·al·i·ty /ˌɪndɪˌvɪdʒuˈæləti/ n [U] the qualities that make someone or something different from other things or people: *We like our staff to show their individuality rather than wear a uniform.*

in·di·vid·u·al·ized also **-ised** BrE /ˌɪndɪˈvɪdʒuəlaɪzd/ adj designed to fit the special needs of a particular person or thing: *an individualized training program* —**individualize** v [T]

in·di·vid·u·al·ly /ˌɪndɪˈvɪdʒuəli/ adv separately, not together in a group: *The bridegroom thanked them all individually.* | *individually wrapped portions of cheese*

in·di·vid·u·ate /ˌɪndɪˈvɪdʒueɪt/ v formal **1** [T] to make someone or something clearly different from others of the same kind: *The characters in the play are beautifully individuated.* **2** [I] AmE to have an idea of yourself as an independent person, separate from other people

in·di·vis·i·ble /ˌɪndɪˈvɪzəbəl◄/ adj something that is indivisible cannot be separated or divided into parts; ⊟ **divisible** —**indivisibly** adv

Indo- /ɪndəʊ $ -doʊ/ prefix [in nouns and adjectives] Indian and something else: *Indo-European languages*

in·doc·tri·nate /ɪnˈdɒktrɪneɪt $ ɪnˈdɑːk-/ v [T] to train someone to accept a particular set of beliefs, especially political or religious ones, and not consider any others: *People were indoctrinated not to question their leaders.* —**indoctrination** /ɪnˌdɒktrɪˈneɪʃən $ ɪnˌdɑːk-/ n [U]: *The military in particular were subjected to intense political indoctrination.*

Indo-'European adj the Indo-European group of languages includes English, French, Hindi, Russian, and most of the other languages of Europe and northern India

in·do·lent /ˈɪndələnt/ adj formal lazy —**indolence** n [U]

in·dom·i·ta·ble /ɪnˈdɒmɪtəbəl $ ɪnˈdɑː-/ adj formal having great determination or courage: *an indomitable old lady* | **indomitable spirit/will/courage etc** *Alice was a woman of indomitable spirit.*

in·door /ˈɪndɔː $ -ɔːr/ adj [only before noun] used or happening inside a building; ⊟ **outdoor**: *an indoor swimming pool* | *the world indoor athletics championship* | *Too much central heating can harm indoor plants.* ⚠ Do not confuse **indoor** and **indoors**.

Indoor is an adjective and **indoors** is an adverb: *I stayed indoors* (NOT *I stayed indoor*). | *indoor sports* (NOT *indoors sports*)

in·doors /ˌɪnˈdɔːz◄ $ -ɔːrz◄/ adv into or inside a building; ⊟ **outdoors**: *Let's go indoors and have something to eat.* | *It rained all day so we had to stay indoors.*

in·dorse /ɪnˈdɔːs $ -ɔːrs/ v another spelling of ENDORSE

in·drawn /ˈɪndrɔːn $ -drɒːn/ adj **indrawn breath** *written* air that someone breathes in a way that can be heard, especially because they are shocked: *She heard Mitch's swiftly indrawn breath.*

in·du·bi·ta·bly /ɪnˈdjuːbɪtəbli $ ɪnˈduː-/ adv formal certainly or without doubt: *Mr Sachs is indubitably charming.* —**indubitable** adj

in·duce /ɪnˈdjuːs $ ɪnˈduːs/ v [T] **1** formal to persuade someone to do something, especially something that does not seem wise: **induce sb to do sth** *Nothing would induce me to vote for him again.* **2** medical to make a woman give birth to her baby, by giving her a special drug: *She had to be induced because the baby was four weeks late.* | *The doctor decided to* **induce labour**. **3** formal to cause a particular physical condition: *Patients with eating disorders may use drugs to induce vomiting.* | **drug-induced/stress-induced etc** *a drug-induced coma*

in·duce·ment /ɪnˈdjuːsmənt $ ɪnˈduːs-/ n [C,U] a reason for doing something, especially something that you will get as a result: **inducement to do sth** *Businesses were offered inducements to move to the area.* | **financial inducements** *to attract good job candidates*

in·duct /ɪnˈdʌkt/ v [T usually passive] formal **1** to officially give someone a job or position of authority, especially at a special ceremony: **induct sb to/into sth** *18 new junior ministers were inducted into the government.* **2** AmE to officially introduce someone into a group or organization, especially the army **3** to officially introduce someone into an important place of honour at a special ceremony: **induct sb into sth** *Barry was inducted into the Basketball Hall of Fame in 1987.*

in·duc·tee /ˌɪndʌkˈtiː/ n [C] AmE someone who is joining a special group, especially the army

in·duc·tion /ɪnˈdʌkʃən/ n **1** [C,U] the introduction of someone into a new job, company, official position etc, or the ceremony at which this is done: **induction course/programme/period etc** *a two-day induction course* | *Mrs Simpson is responsible for the induction of new library staff.* **2** [C,U] medical the process of making a woman give birth to her baby by giving her a special drug **3** [U] technical the production of electricity in one object by another that already has electrical or MAGNETIC power **4** [U] technical a process of thought that uses known facts to produce general rules or principles → DEDUCTION

in'duction ,coil n [C] technical a piece of electrical equipment that changes a low VOLTAGE to a higher one

in·duc·tive /ɪnˈdʌktɪv/ adj technical **1** using known facts to produce general principles: *inductive reasoning* **2** connected with electrical or MAGNETIC induction

in·dulge /ɪnˈdʌldʒ/ v **1** [I,T] to let yourself do or have something that you enjoy, especially something that is considered bad for you: [+in] *Most of us were too busy to indulge in heavy lunchtime drinking.* | *Eva had never been one to indulge in self-pity.* | **indulge yourself** *Even if you're dieting, you can indulge yourself* (=eat what you want) *once in a while.* | *Ray has enough money to indulge his taste for expensive wines.* **2** [T] to let someone have or do whatever they want, even if it is bad for them: *His mother spoiled him, indulging his every whim.* **3** [I] to take part in an activity, especially an illegal one: [+in] *Women do not indulge in crime to the same extent as men.*

in·dul·gence /ɪnˈdʌldʒəns/ n **1** [U] the habit of allowing yourself to do or have whatever you want, or allowing someone else to do or have whatever they want → **self-indulgence** at SELF-INDULGENT **2** [C] something that you do or have for pleasure, not because you need it: *An occasional glass of wine was his only indulgence.* **3** [U] *formal* willingness to ignore someone's faults or weaknesses: *a spirit of indulgence and forgiveness* **4** [C] a promise of freedom from punishment by God, sold by priests in the Middle Ages

in·dul·gent /ɪnˈdʌldʒənt/ *adj* willing to allow someone, especially a child, to do or have whatever they want, even if this is not good for them: *expensive toys bought by their indulgent grandparents* —**indulgently** *adv*

in·dus·tri·al W1 /ɪnˈdʌstriəl/ *adj*
1 relating to industry or the people working in it: **industrial production/output** *Industrial production has risen by 0.5% since November.* | **industrial development/growth** *rapid post-war industrial development* | **industrial conflict/dispute/unrest** (=disagreement between workers and their employers) *Last year 1.3 million workers took part in industrial disputes.* | **industrial accident/injury** (=happening at work)
2 having many industries: **industrial countries/nations/states** *a meeting of the world's major industrial nations* | **industrial area/zone** *pollution in industrial areas* | *By 1900 Britain was a mainly **industrial society**.*
3 of the type used in industry: *cleaning products that are for **industrial use** only* (=not to be used at home) —**industrially** *adv*

in,dustrial 'action *n* [U] *BrE* an action such as a STRIKE (=stopping work) taken by workers involved in a disagreement with their employer

in,dustrial archae'ology *n* [U] the study of old factories, machines etc

in,dustrial 'arts *n* [U] *AmE* a subject taught in school about how to use tools, machinery etc

in,dustrial 'espionage *n* [U] stealing secret information from one company in order to help another company

in,dustrial es'tate *BrE*; **in,dustrial 'park** *AmE* a piece of land, often on the edge of a town, where there are factories and businesses

in·dus·tri·al·is·m /ɪnˈdʌstriəlɪzəm/ *n* [U] the system by which a society gets its wealth through industries and machinery

in·dus·tri·al·ist /ɪnˈdʌstriəlɪst/ *n* [C] a person who owns or runs a factory or industrial company

in·dus·tri·al·i·za·tion also **-isation** *BrE* /ɪnˌdʌstriəlaɪˈzeɪʃən $ -ələ-/ *n* [U] when a country or place develops a lot of industry —**industrialize** /ɪnˈdʌstriəlaɪz/ *v* [I,T]

in·dus·tri·al·ized /ɪnˈdʌstriəlaɪzd/ *adj* an industrialized country or place has a lot of factories, mines etc

in,dustrial re'lations *n* [plural] the relationship between workers and employers

In,dustrial Revo'lution *n* **the Industrial Revolution** the period in the 18th and 19th centuries in Europe and the USA when machines were invented and the first factories were established

in'dustrial-,strength *adj* an industrial-strength substance is very strong – often used humorously: *They served us industrial-strength coffee.*

in,dustrial tri'bunal *n* [C] *BrE* a court which judges disagreements between workers and their employers

in·dus·tri·ous /ɪnˈdʌstriəs/ *adj* someone who is industrious works hard; ⚘ **hard-working** —**industriously** *adv*

in·dus·try S3 W1 /ˈɪndəstri/ *n plural* **industries**
1 [U] **a)** the large-scale production of goods or of substances such as coal and steel: *a decline in **manufacturing industry*** | **heavy/light industry** (=the production of large or small goods) *Heavy industry was concentrated in the north of the country.* | *This type of*

software is widely used in industry. **b)** the people who work in industry: *an agreement that will be welcomed by both sides of industry* (=employers and workers)
2 [C] businesses that produce a particular type of thing or provide a particular service: **coal/car/textile etc industry** *I work in the oil industry.* | **tourist/travel/leisure/catering etc industry** *Italy's thriving tourist industry* | *new jobs in **service industries*** (=businesses such as banking and tourism)
3 [U] *formal* the fact of working hard: *Gould is a man of great industry.*
4 [singular] an area of work which has grown too large – used to show disapproval: *another book from the Shakespeare industry*

i·ne·bri·a·ted /ɪˈniːbrieɪtɪd/ *adj formal* drunk

in·ed·i·ble /ɪnˈedɪbəl/ *adj* if something is inedible, you cannot eat it because it tastes bad or is poisonous; ⚘ **edible**: *The meat was so burnt that it was inedible.*

in·ed·u·ca·ble /ɪnˈedjʊkəbəl $ -dʒə-/ *adj formal* impossible or very difficult to educate

in·ef·fa·ble /ɪnˈefəbəl/ *adj formal* too great to be described in words: *ineffable joy* —**ineffably** *adv*

in·ef·fec·tive /ˌɪnɪˈfektɪv◂/ *adj* something that is ineffective does not achieve what it is intended to achieve; ⚘ **effective**: **ineffective in doing sth** *The chemical was almost totally ineffective in killing the weeds.* | [+against] *Various drugs have proved ineffective against the virus.* | *an ineffective marketing campaign* —**ineffectively** *adv* —**ineffectiveness** *n* [U]: *the ineffectiveness of most diets*

in·ef·fec·tu·al /ˌɪnɪˈfektʃuəl◂/ *adj* not having the ability, confidence, or personal authority to get things done: *an ineffectual leader* | *She remembered her ineffectual efforts to comfort him.* —**ineffectually** *adv*

in·ef·fi·cient /ˌɪnɪˈfɪʃənt◂/ *adj* not using time, money, energy etc in the best way; ⚘ **efficient**: *an inefficient use of resources* | *Local government was inefficient.* —**inefficiently** *adv* —**inefficiency** *n* [C,U]: *problems due to the inefficiency of management*

in·el·e·gant /ɪnˈelɪgənt/ *adj* not graceful or attractive; ⚘ **elegant**: *an inelegant expression* —**inelegantly** *adv* —**inelegance** *n* [U]

in·el·i·gi·ble /ɪnˈelɪdʒɪbəl/ *adj* not allowed to have or do something because of a law or rule; ⚘ **eligible**: [+for] *Temporary workers are ineligible for the pension scheme.* | **ineligible to do sth** *People under 18 are ineligible to vote.* —**ineligibility** /ɪnˌelɪdʒɪˈbɪlɪti/ *n* [U]

in·e·luc·ta·ble /ˌɪnɪˈlʌktəbəl◂/ *adj formal* impossible to avoid —**ineluctably** *adv*

in·ept /ɪˈnept/ *adj* not good at doing something; ⚘ **capable, skilful**: *inept leadership* | *He was criticized for his inept handling of the problem.* | **politically/socially inept** *Blake was intellectually able but politically inept.* —**ineptly** *adv* → INAPT

in·ept·i·tude /ɪˈneptɪtjuːd $ -tuːd/ *n* [U] *formal* lack of skill: *the ineptitude of the people in charge*

in·e·qual·i·ty /ˌɪnɪˈkwɒlɪti $ -ˈkwɑː-/ *n plural* **inequalities** [C,U] an unfair situation, in which some groups in society have more money, opportunities, power etc than others; ⚘ **equality**: [+in] *There are inequalities in wealth distribution.* | [+of] *inequality of opportunity* | [+between] *inequalities between men and women* | **social/gender/racial etc inequality** *a policy that aims to redress racial inequalities*

in·eq·ui·ta·ble /ɪnˈekwɪtəbəl/ *adj formal* not equally fair to everyone: *an inequitable distribution of wealth* —**inequitably** *adv*

in·eq·ui·ty /ɪnˈekwɪti/ *n plural* **inequities** [C,U] *formal* lack of fairness, or something that is unfair; ⚘ **equity**: [+of] *the inequities of the legal system* | [+in] *There are huge inequities in the distribution of research funding.* | **racial/social inequity** *a report on racial inequity in the UK*

in·e·rad·i·ca·ble /ˌɪnɪˈrædɪkəbəl◂/ *adj formal* impossible to change or remove: *ineradicable hostility* —**ineradicably** *adv*

in·ert /ɪˈnɜːt $ -ɜːrt/ *adj* **1** *technical* not producing a chemical reaction when combined with other substances: *inert gases* **2** *literary* not moving, or not having the strength or power to move: *He lay, inert, in his bed.* **3** not willing to do anything: *The government was perceived to be inert and inefficient.* —**inertness** *n* [U]

in·er·tia /ɪˈnɜːʃə $ -ɜːr-/ *n* [U] **1** when no one wants to do anything to change a situation: *political inertia* **2** *technical* the force that keeps an object in the same position or keeps it moving until it is moved or stopped by another force **3** a lack of energy and a feeling that you do not want to do anything —**inertial** *adj*

in·es·ca·pa·ble /ˌɪnɪˈskeɪpəbəl◂/ *adj* an inescapable fact or situation is one that you cannot avoid or ignore: *She didn't want to confront the inescapable fact that she would have to sell the house.* | *The inescapable conclusion is that he was murdered by someone in his own family.* —**inescapably** *adv*

in·es·sen·tial /ˌɪnɪˈsenʃəl◂/ *adj formal* not needed; ▤ **unnecessary**; ▤ **essential**: *inessential details* —**inessentials** *n* [plural]

in·es·ti·ma·ble /ɪnˈestɪməbəl/ *adj formal* too much or too great to be calculated: *a painting of inestimable value*

in·ev·i·ta·bil·i·ty /ɪˌnevɪtəˈbɪlɪti/ *n* [singular, U] the fact that something is certain to happen, or something that is certain to happen: [+of] *the inevitability of death*

in·ev·i·ta·ble W3 /ɪˈnevɪtəbəl/ *adj*
1 certain to happen and impossible to avoid: *A further escalation of the crisis now seems inevitable.* | **it is inevitable (that)** *It's inevitable that doctors will make the occasional mistake.* | **inevitable consequence/result** *Disease was an inevitable consequence of poor living conditions.*
2 the inevitable a situation that is certain to happen: *One day the inevitable happened and I got a speeding ticket.*

in·ev·i·ta·bly W3 /ɪˈnevɪtəbli/ *adv* used for saying that something is certain to happen and cannot be avoided: *The decision will inevitably lead to political tensions.* | [sentence adverb] *Inevitably, the situation did not please everyone.*

in·ex·act /ˌɪnɪɡˈzækt◂/ *adj* not exact: *Earthquake prediction is an inexact science.*

in·ex·cu·sa·ble /ˌɪnɪkˈskjuːzəbəl◂/ *adj* inexcusable behaviour is too bad to be excused: *an inexcusable act of aggression* —**inexcusably** *adv*

in·ex·haus·ti·ble /ˌɪnɪɡˈzɔːstɪbəl $ -ˈzɒːs-/ *adj* something that is inexhaustible exists in such large amounts that it can never be finished or used up: *She has an inexhaustible supply of funny stories.* | *a man of inexhaustible energy*

in·ex·o·ra·ble /ɪnˈeksərəbəl/ *adj formal* an inexorable process cannot be stopped: *the inexorable decline of Britain's manufacturing industry* | *the seemingly inexorable rise in crime* —**inexorably** *adv* —**inexorability** /ɪnˌeksərəˈbɪlɪti/ *n* [U]

in·ex·pen·sive /ˌɪnɪkˈspensɪv◂/ *adj* cheap – use this to show approval; ▤ **expensive**: *a good selection of inexpensive wines* | *Painting is a relatively inexpensive way to enhance your home.* —**inexpensively** *adv*

in·ex·pe·ri·ence /ˌɪnɪkˈspɪəriəns $ -ˈspɪr-/ *n* [U] lack of experience: *youthful inexperience*

in·ex·pe·ri·enced /ˌɪnɪkˈspɪəriənst◂ $ -ˈspɪr-/ *adj* not having had much experience: *inexperienced pilots*

in·ex·pert /ɪnˈekspɜːt $ -ɜːrt/ *adj formal* not having the skill to do something; ▤ **expert**: *an inexperienced and inexpert teacher* —**inexpertly** *adv*

in·ex·plic·a·ble /ˌɪnɪkˈsplɪkəbəl◂ $ ɪnˈeksplɪkəbəl, ˌɪnɪkˈsplɪk-/ *adj* too unusual or strange to be explained or understood; ▤ **incomprehensible**, **strange**: *inexplicable behaviour* | *For some inexplicable reason, he felt depressed.* —**inexplicably** *adv*

in·ex·pres·si·ble /ˌɪnɪkˈspresəbəl◂/ *adj formal* an inexpressible feeling is too strong to be described in words: *inexpressible gratitude* —**inexpressibly** *adv*

in·ex·press·ive /ˌɪnɪkˈspresɪv◂/ *adj* a face that is inexpressive shows no emotion

in ex·tre·mis /ˌɪn ɪkˈstriːmɪs/ *adv formal* **1** in a very difficult situation when you need to do something very extreme **2** at the moment of death

in·ex·tric·a·ble /ˌɪnɪkˈstrɪkəbəl◂, ɪnˈekstrɪk-/ *adj formal* two or more things that are inextricable are closely related and affect each other: *the inextricable connection between language and culture*

in·ex·tric·a·bly /ˌɪnɪkˈstrɪkəbli, ɪnˈekstrɪk-/ *adv* **be inextricably linked/bound up/mixed etc** if two or more things are inextricably linked etc, they are very closely related and affect each other: *Physical health is inextricably linked to mental health.* | *Economic and social history are inextricably bound up with each other.*

in·fal·li·ble /ɪnˈfæləbəl/ *adj* **1** always right and never making mistakes; ▤ **fallible**: *No expert is infallible.* | *an infallible memory* **2** something that is infallible always works or has the intended effect: *He had an infallible cure for a hangover.* —**infallibly** *adv* —**infallibility** /ɪnˌfæləˈbɪlɪti/ *n* [U]

in·fa·mous /ˈɪnfəməs/ *adj* well known for being bad or evil: *an infamous killer* | *Los Angeles' infamous smog* | [+for] *This area is infamous for drugs and prostitution.* —**infamously** *adv*

in·fa·my /ˈɪnfəmi/ *n* [U] the state of being evil or well known for evil things

in·fan·cy /ˈɪnfənsi/ *n* [U] **1** the period of a child's life before they can walk or talk: **in infancy** *In the past, many children died in infancy.* **2** the time when something is just starting to be developed: *The research stretched from the infancy of radio broadcasting through to today.* | *Genetic engineering is still in its infancy.*

in·fant¹ W3 /ˈɪnfənt/ *n*
1 [C] *formal* a baby or very young child: *An infant's skin is very sensitive.* → SUDDEN INFANT DEATH SYNDROME
2 infants [plural] children in school in Britain between the ages of four and eight

infant² *adj* [only before noun] **1 infant school/teacher/class etc** a school, teacher etc for children aged between four and eight in Britain **2** intended for babies or very young children: *infant formula milk* **3** an infant company, organization etc has just started to exist or be developed: *infant industries*

in·fan·ti·cide /ɪnˈfæntɪsaɪd/ *n* [U] the crime of killing a child

in·fan·tile /ˈɪnfəntaɪl/ *adj* **1** infantile behaviour seems silly in an adult because it is typical of a child; ▤ **childish**: *infantile jokes* **2** [only before noun] *technical* relating to or affecting babies and very young children: *infantile development*

infantile pa'ralysis *n* [U] *old-fashioned* POLIO

infant mor'tality rate *n* [C] the number of deaths of babies under one year old, expressed as the number out of every 1000 babies born alive in a year

in·fan·try /ˈɪnfəntri/ *n* [U] soldiers who fight on foot: *an infantry regiment* → CAVALRY

in·fan·try·man /ˈɪnfəntrimən/ *n plural* **infantrymen** /-mən/ [C] a soldier who fights on foot

in·fat·u·at·ed /ɪnˈfætʃueɪtɪd/ *adj* having strong feelings of love for someone or a strong interest in something that makes you unable to think in a sensible way: [+with] *John had become infatuated with the French teacher.* | *My mother's infatuated with dieting.*

in·fat·u·a·tion /ɪnˌfætʃuˈeɪʃən/ *n* [C,U] a strong feeling of love for someone or interest in something, especially a feeling that is unreasonable and does not continue for a long time: [+with] *the current infatuation with '70s style* | *Shaw's infatuation with the actress is evident in his writing.*

in·fect /ɪnˈfekt/ v [T] **1** to give someone a disease: *People with the virus may feel perfectly well, but they can still infect others.* | [+with] *the number of people infected with HIV* **2** [usually passive] to make something contain something harmful that gives people a disease: [+with] *Eggs known to be infected with salmonella were allowed to go on sale.* **3** if a feeling or interest that you have infects other people, it makes them begin to feel the same way or have the same interest: *Lucy's enthusiasm soon infected the rest of the class.* **4** if a VIRUS infects your computer or DISKS, it changes or destroys the information in them

in·fect·ed /ɪnˈfektɪd/ adj **1** a part of your body or a wound that is infected has harmful BACTERIA in it which prevent it from HEALING; → **disinfect**: *an infected finger* | *Clean the wound so it doesn't get infected.* **2** food, water etc that is infected contains BACTERIA that spread disease **3** if a computer or DISK is infected, the information in or on it has been changed or destroyed by a computer VIRUS

in·fec·tion W3 /ɪnˈfekʃən/ n
1 [C] a disease that affects a particular part of your body and is caused by BACTERIA or a VIRUS: *an ear infection* | **mild/slight/severe infection** *a slight infection in the bladder*
2 [U] when someone is infected by a disease: *Always sterilize the needle to prevent infection.*

in·fec·tious /ɪnˈfekʃəs/ adj **1** an infectious illness can be passed from one person to another, especially through the air you breathe: *infectious diseases* | *Flu is highly infectious.* **2** someone who is infectious has an illness and could pass it to other people **3** infectious feelings or laughter spread quickly from one person to another: *an infectious smile* | *infectious enthusiasm* —**infectiously** adv

in·fer /ɪnˈfɜː $ -ɜːr/ v inferred, inferring [T] to form an opinion that something is probably true because of information that you have: **infer sth from sth** *A lot can be inferred from these statistics.* | **infer that** *From the evidence we can infer that the victim knew her killer.*

in·fer·ence /ˈɪnfərəns/ n **1** [C] something that you think is true, based on information that you have: **draw/make inferences (about/from sth)** *What inferences have you drawn from this evidence?* **2** [U] when someone infers something: **by inference** *He was portrayed as a hero and, by inference, Thompson as the villain.* —**inferential** /ˌɪnfəˈrenʃəl◂/ adj: *inferential evidence* —**inferentially** adv

in·fe·ri·or¹ /ɪnˈfɪəriə $ -ˈfɪriər/ adj **1** not good, or not as good as someone or something else; ✗ **superior**: *I felt very inferior among all those academics.* | *wine of inferior quality* | *inferior goods* | [+to] *I always felt slightly inferior to her.* | *Their performance was inferior to that of other teams.* ⚠ Do not say 'inferior than' something. Say **inferior to** something. **2** formal lower in rank; ✗ **superior**: *an inferior court of law* | *He refused to accept a job of inferior status.*

inferior² n [C] someone who has a lower position or rank than you in an organization; ✗ **superior**

in·fe·ri·or·i·ty /ɪnˌfɪəriˈɒrɪti $ -ˌfɪriˈɔːr-/ n [U] when someone or something is not good or not as good as someone or something else; ✗ **superiority**: *moral inferiority* | **sense/feeling of inferiority** *He had a deep-rooted feeling of inferiority.*

in,feri'ority ,complex n [C usually singular] a continuous feeling that you are much less important, clever etc than other people

in·fer·nal /ɪnˈfɜːnl $ -ɜːr-/ adj **1** [only before noun] old-fashioned used to express anger or annoyance about something: *I wish the children would stop that infernal noise.* **2** literary relating to HELL and evil —**infernally** adv

in·fer·no /ɪnˈfɜːnəʊ $ -ɜːrnoʊ/ n plural infernos [C] **1** an extremely large and dangerous fire – used especially in news reports: **raging/blazing inferno** *Within minutes the house had become a raging inferno.* **2** literary when someone has very strong feelings that are difficult to control: *She was desperately trying to calm the inferno raging within her.*

in·fer·tile /ɪnˈfɜːtaɪl $ -ˈfɜːrtl/ adj **1** unable to have babies: *infertile couples* **2** infertile land or soil is not good enough to grow plants in

in·fer·til·i·ty /ˌɪnfəˈtɪlɪti $ -fər-/ n [U] when someone is unable to have a baby: *There are many possible causes of infertility in women.* | *infertility treatments*

in·fest /ɪnˈfest/ v [T usually passive] **1** if insects, rats etc infest a place, there are a lot of them and they usually cause damage: **be infested with sth** *The kitchen was infested with cockroaches.* | **shark-infested/rat-infested etc** *shark-infested waters* **2** if things or people you do not want infest a place, there are too many of them: *an area infested with holiday homes* —**infestation** /ˌɪnfeˈsteɪʃən/ n [C,U]

in·fi·del /ˈɪnfɪdəl/ n [C] literary not polite an offensive word for someone who has a different religion from you

in·fi·del·i·ty /ˌɪnfɪˈdelɪti/ n plural infidelities [C,U] when someone has sex with a person who is not their wife, husband, or partner: *marital infidelity*

in·field /ˈɪnfiːld/ n [singular] **1** the part of a CRICKET field nearest to the player who hits the ball; ⬛ **outfield** **2** the part of a baseball field inside the four bases; ⬛ **outfield** **3** the group of players in this part of the CRICKET or baseball field —**infielder** n [C]

in·fight·ing /ˈɪnfaɪtɪŋ/ n [U] when members of the same group or organization argue, or compete with each other in an unfriendly way: *political infighting*

in·fill /ˈɪnfɪl/ n [U] especially BrE **1** something that is used to fill a space: *infill panels* **2** the process of filling a space, especially by building new houses: *infill developments* —**infill** v [I,T]

in·fil·trate /ˈɪnfɪltreɪt $ ɪnˈfɪltreɪt, ˈɪnfɪl-/ v **1** [I always + adv/prep,T] to secretly join an organization or enter a place in order to find out information about it or harm it: *Police attempts to infiltrate neo-Nazi groups were largely unsuccessful.* | [+into] *Rebel forces have been infiltrating into the country.* **2** [T] to secretly put people into an organization or place in order to find out information or to harm it: **infiltrate sb into sth** *They repeatedly tried to infiltrate assassins into the palace.* **3** [T] to become a part of something – used especially to show disapproval: *Commercialism has been infiltrating universities for the past decade.* —**infiltrator** n [C] —**infiltration** /ˌɪnfɪlˈtreɪʃən/ n [U]

in·fi·nite /ˈɪnfɪnɪt/ adj **1** very great in amount or degree: *a woman of infinite patience* | **an infinite number/variety of sth** *There was an infinite variety of drinks to choose from.* **2** without limits in space or time; ⬛ **finite**: *The universe is infinite.* → **in sb's (infinite) wisdom** at WISDOM (4); → NON-FINITE

in·fi·nite·ly /ˈɪnfɪnɪtli/ adv [+ adj/adv] very much – used especially when comparing things: *This school is infinitely better than the last one I went to.* | *Being on your own is infinitely preferable to being in an unhappy relationship.* | *someone with infinitely more experience*

in·fin·i·tes·i·mal /ˌɪnfɪnɪˈtesɪməl◂/ adj extremely small: *infinitesimal changes in temperature* —**infinitesimally** adv: *infinitesimally small*

in·fin·i·tive /ɪnˈfɪnɪtɪv/ n [C] technical in grammar, the basic form of a verb, used with 'to' in English. In the sentence 'I want to watch television.' 'to watch' is an infinitive → SPLIT INFINITIVE

in·fin·i·tude /ɪnˈfɪnɪtjuːd $ -tuːd/ n [singular, U] formal a number or amount without limit: *the vast infinitude of space*

in·fin·i·ty /ɪnˈfɪnɪti/ n **1** [U] a space or distance without limits or an end: *the infinity of space* **2** [singular, U] a number that is too large to be calculated: *In the equation below, as E goes to zero, n approaches infinity.* | [+of] *There is an infinity of possible solutions.*

in·firm /ɪnˈfɜːm $ -ɜːrm/ adj **1** weak or ill for a long time, especially because you are old: *Her grandmother* *is elderly and infirm.* **2 the infirm** people who are weak or ill for a long time, especially because they are old: *The hotel is on a hill, which is not ideal for the infirm.*

in·fir·ma·ry /ɪnˈfɜːməri $ -ɜːr-/ *n plural* **infirmaries** [C] **1** a hospital – often used in the names of hospitals in Britain **2** a room in a school or other institution where people can get medical treatment

in·fir·mi·ty /ɪnˈfɜːmɪ̥ti $ -ɜːr-/ *n plural* **infirmities** [C,U] *formal* bad health or a particular illness

in fla·gran·te /ˌɪn fləˈɡrænteɪ, -ti/ *adv formal* during the act of having sex, especially with someone else's husband or wife – sometimes used humorously: *They were caught in flagrante by Donna's husband.*

in·flame /ɪnˈfleɪm/ *v* [T] to make someone's feelings of anger, excitement etc much stronger: *The shooting inflamed ethnic tensions.*

in·flamed /ɪnˈfleɪmd/ *adj* a part of your body that is inflamed is red and swollen, because it is injured or infected: *an inflamed eye*

in·flam·ma·ble /ɪnˈflæməbəl/ *adj* **1** *formal* inflammable materials or substances will start to burn very easily; ▣ **flammable**; ▣ **nonflammable**: *Petrol is highly inflammable.* **2** easily becoming angry or violent, or making people angry or violent: *inflammable language*

in·flam·ma·tion /ˌɪnfləˈmeɪʃən/ *n* [C,U] swelling and pain in part of your body, which is often red and feels hot: [+of] *inflammation of the colon*

in·flam·ma·to·ry /ɪnˈflæmətəri $ -tɔːri/ *adj* **1** an inflammatory speech, piece of writing etc is likely to make people feel angry: *inflammatory remarks* **2** *technical* an inflammatory disease or medical condition causes inflammation: *inflammatory bowel disease*

in·fla·ta·ble¹ /ɪnˈfleɪtəbəl/ *adj* an inflatable object has to be filled with air before you can use it: *an inflatable mattress*

inflatable² *n* [C] an object that has to be filled with air before you can use it, especially a boat or toy

in·flate /ɪnˈfleɪt/ *v* **1** [I,T] to fill something with air or gas so it becomes larger, or to become filled with air or gas: *It took us half an hour to inflate the dinghy.* | *Her life jacket failed to inflate.* **2** [I] to make something seem more important or impressive than it really is: *The success further inflated his self-confidence.* | **be grossly/vastly/hugely inflated** *The numbers of people involved have been grossly inflated by the media.* **3** [I,T] *technical* to increase in price or make something increase in price: *Hotels often inflate prices at particular times of the year.* | *Costs were inflating.*

in·flat·ed /ɪnˈfleɪtɪ̥d/ *adj* **1** inflated prices, amounts etc are high and unreasonable; **grossly/vastly/hugely inflated** *company directors on grossly inflated salaries* **2** inflated ideas, opinions etc about someone or something make them seem better, more important etc than they really are: *He has a very inflated opinion of himself.* **3** filled with air or gas

in·fla·tion S2 W2 /ɪnˈfleɪʃən/ *n* [U] **1** a continuing increase in prices, or the rate at which prices increase: **inflation rate/rate of inflation** *The annual rate of inflation fell.* | *Inflation is now running at over 16%.* | *countries with high inflation* **2** the process of filling something with air

in·fla·tion·a·ry /ɪnˈfleɪʃənəri $ -ʃəneri/ *adj* relating to or causing price increases: *inflationary pressures in the economy* | *A new round of wage increases could trigger an inflationary spiral* (=a continuing rise in both wages and prices).

in·flect /ɪnˈflekt/ *v* [I] *technical* if a word inflects, its form changes according to its meaning or use

in·flect·ed /ɪnˈflektɪ̥d/ *adj technical* an inflected language contains many words which change their form according to their meaning or use

in·flec·tion, inflexion /ɪnˈflekʃən/ *n* **1** [U] *technical* the way in which a word changes its form to show a

difference in its meaning or use **2** [C] *technical* one of the forms of a word that changes in this way, or one of the parts that is added to it **3** [C,U] the way the sound of your voice goes up and down when you are speaking —**inflectional** *adj*

in·flex·i·ble /ɪnˈfleksɪ̥bəl/ *adj* **1** unwilling to make even the slightest change in your attitudes, plans etc; ▣ **flexible**: *inflexible attitudes towards change* **2** inflexible rules, arrangements etc are impossible to change; ▣ **flexible**: *This approach is too inflexible and too costly.* **3** inflexible material is stiff and will not bend; ▣ **flexible** —**inflexibly** *adv* —**inflexibility** /ɪnˌfleksɪ̥ˈbɪlɪ̥ti/ *n* [U]

in·flex·ion /ɪnˈflekʃən/ *n* [C,U] another spelling of INFLECTION

in·flict /ɪnˈflɪkt/ *v* **1** [T] to make someone suffer something unpleasant: **inflict sth on/upon sb** *The strikes inflicted serious damage on the economy.* | *Detectives warned that the men could inflict serious injury.* **2 inflict yourself/sb on sb** to visit or be with someone when they do not want you – used humorously: *Was it really fair to her friends to inflict her nephew on them?* —**infliction** /ɪnˈflɪkʃən/ *n* [U]: *the deliberate infliction of pain*

'in·flight *adj* [only before noun] provided during a plane journey: *in-flight entertainment*

in·flow /ˈɪnfləʊ $ -floʊ/ *n* **1** [C] the movement of people, money, goods etc into a place; ▣ **outflow**: [+of] *an inflow of funds from abroad* **2** [singular, U] the flow of water into a place; ▣ **outflow**

in·flu·ence¹ S2 W1 /ˈɪnfluəns/ *n*
1 [C,U] the power to affect the way someone or something develops, behaves, or thinks without using direct force or orders: *There is no doubt that Bohr's influence was immense.* | [+on/over] *the unions' influence over local politics* | **under sb's influence/under the influence of sb/sth** *They had come under the influence of a strange religious sect.* | **have/exert/exercise influence** *The Council had considerable influence over many government decisions.* | *They were accused of interfering with voters or exerting **undue influence*** (=too much influence).
2 [C] someone or something that has an influence on other people or things: **bad/good/positive etc influence (on sb)** *Gayle's mother said I was a bad influence on her daughter.* | *For centuries the country remained untouched by **outside influences**.*
3 under the influence (of alcohol/drink/drugs etc) drunk or feeling the effects of a drug

influence² S2 W2 *v* [T] to affect the way someone or something develops, behaves, thinks etc without directly forcing or ordering them: *Marx was **strongly influenced** by the historian Niebuhr.* | **influence a decision/outcome/choice etc** *Several factors are likely to influence this decision.* | **influence sb to do sth** *What influenced you to take up nursing?*

in·flu·en·tial /ˌɪnfluˈenʃəl◂/ *adj* having a lot of influence and therefore changing the way people think and behave: *He had influential friends.* | [+in] *Dewey was influential in shaping economic policy.* | *a **highly influential** art magazine*

in·flu·en·za /ˌɪnfluˈenzə/ *n* [U] *medical* an infectious disease that is like a very bad cold; ▣ **flu**

in·flux /ˈɪnflʌks/ *n* [C] the arrival of large numbers of people or large amounts of money, goods etc, especially suddenly: [+of] *a sudden influx of cash* | **massive/great/huge etc influx** *a large influx of tourists in the summer*

in·fo /ˈɪnfəʊ $ -foʊ/ *n* [U] *informal* information

in·fo·mer·cial /ˈɪnfəʊmɜːʃəl $ -foʊmɜːr-/ *n* [C] a long television advertisement that provides a lot of information and seems like a normal programme

in·form S2 W2 /ɪnˈfɔːm $ -ɔːrm/ *v* [T] *formal*
1 to formally or officially tell someone about some-

thing or give them information: **inform sb about/of sth** *Please inform us of any change of address as soon as possible.* | **inform sb (that)** *We regret to inform you that your application has been rejected.* | *They decided to inform the police.*
2 *formal* to influence someone's attitude or opinion: *Her experience as a refugee informs the content of her latest novel.*

inform on/against sb *phr v*
to tell the police or an enemy information about someone that will harm them: *He denied that he had ever informed on his neighbours.*

in·for·mal W3 /ɪnˈfɔːməl $ -ɔːr-/ *adj*
1 relaxed and friendly without being restricted by rules of correct behaviour; ☒ **formal**: *The atmosphere at work is fairly informal.* | *The two groups met for informal talks.*
2 an informal style of writing or speaking is suitable for ordinary conversations or letters to friends; ☒ **formal**
3 informal clothes are suitable for wearing at home or in ordinary situations; ☒ **casual**; ☒ **formal** —**informally** *adv* —**informality** /ˌɪnfɔːˈmælɪ̣ti $ -fɔːr-/ *n* [U]

in·for·mant /ɪnˈfɔːmənt $ -ɔːr-/ *n* [C] **1** someone who secretly gives the police, the army etc information about someone else; ☒ **informer**: *One of the witnesses was a paid informant for the FBI.* **2** *technical* someone who gives information about their language, social customs etc to someone who is studying them

in·for·ma·tion S1 W1 /ˌɪnfəˈmeɪʃən $ -fər-/ *n* [U]
1 facts or details that tell you something about a situation, person, event etc: *I need more information.* | [+that] *We have received information that Grant may have left the country.* | [+about/on] *The book contains information about a wide variety of subjects.* | *The guide will* **provide** *you with* **information** *about the area.* | **further/additional/more etc information** *For further information, call the number below.* | **gather/collect information** *The survey didn't collect any information about temporary workers.* | *The book is packed with* **useful information.** | *She sent me* **detailed information** *about the project.* | *I've one or two useful* **pieces of information** *to pass on to you.* | **my/our etc information is** (=used to say what you know about a situation) *My information is that Gary wants to stay with the club.* ⚠ Information is an uncountable noun. Do not say 'informations' or 'an information'.
2 *AmE* the telephone service which provides telephone numbers to people who ask for them; ☒ **directory enquiries** *BrE*
3 for your information *spoken* used when you are telling someone that they are wrong about a particular fact: *For your information, I've worked as a journalist for six years.*
4 for information only written on copies of letters and documents that are sent to someone who needs to know about them but does not have to deal with them → **inside information** at ɪɴsɪᴅᴇ³ (2) —**informational** *adj*

This graph shows some of the words most commonly used with the noun **information**.

	5	10	15	20 per million
information about				
information on				
provide information				
further/additional information				
gather/collect information				
relevant/useful/necessary information				
detailed information				
piece of information				

infor'mation ˌcentre *n* [C] a place where you can get information about an area, event etc

ˌinformation 'overload *n* [U] when someone gets too much information at one time, for example on the Internet, and becomes tired and unable to think very carefully about any of it: *The greater the amount of data, the greater the risk of information overload.*

infor'mation reˌtrieval *n* [U] the process of finding stored information, especially on a computer

ˌinforˌmation 'science *n* [U] the science of collecting, arranging, storing, and sending out information

information suˌperˈhighˌway /ˌɪnfəmeɪʃən ˌsuːpəˈhaɪweɪ, -sjuː- $ -fərmeɪʃən ˌsuːpər-/ *n* **the information superhighway** the Internet

information techˌnology *n* [U] *IT* the study or use of electronic processes for gathering and storing information and making it available using computers

infor'mation ˌtheory *n* [U] *technical* the mathematical principles related to sending and storing information

in·for·ma·tive /ɪnˈfɔːmətɪv $ -ɔːr-/ *adj* providing many useful facts or ideas: *an informative and entertaining book* —**informatively** *adv*

in·formed /ɪnˈfɔːmd $ -ɔːr-/ *adj* **1** having a lot of knowledge or information about a particular subject or situation: *Informed sources said it was likely that the President would make a televised statement.* | **well-informed/ill-informed** *I became reasonably well-informed about the subject.* **2 informed decision/choice/judgement etc** a decision etc that is based on knowledge of a subject or situation: *Good information is essential if people are to make informed choices about services.* **3 keep sb informed** to give someone the latest news and details about a situation: *Please keep me* **fully informed** *of any developments.*

in·form·er /ɪnˈfɔːmə $ -ɔːrmər/ *n* [C] someone who secretly tells the police, the army etc about criminal activities, especially for money

in·fo·tain·ment /ˌɪnfəʊˈteɪnmənt $ -foʊ-/ *n* [U] television programmes that deal with important subjects in a way that people can enjoy

infra- /ɪnfrə/ *prefix technical* below something in a range: *the infra-red end of the spectrum* → ᴜʟᴛʀᴀ- (2)

in·frac·tion /ɪnˈfrækʃən/ *n* [C,U] *formal* an act of breaking a rule or law: [+of] *minor infractions of the rules*

inf·ra-red /ˌɪnfrə ˈredˎ/ *adj* infra-red light gives out heat but cannot be seen → ᴜʟᴛʀᴀᴠɪᴏʟᴇᴛ

in·fra·struc·ture /ˈɪnfrəˌstrʌktʃə $ -ər/ *n* [C,U] the basic systems and structures that a country or organization needs in order to work properly, for example roads, railways, banks etc: *Some countries lack a suitable economic infrastructure.* | *a $65 billion investment package in education, health care and infrastructure* —**infrastructural** *adj*

in·fre·quent /ɪnˈfriːkwənt/ *adj* not happening often; ☒ **rare**; ☒ **frequent**: *They would make infrequent visits to the house.* —**infrequency** *n* [U]

in·fre·quent·ly /ɪnˈfriːkwəntli/ *adv* **1** not often; ☒ **rarely**; ☒ **frequently**: *Jeremy does play cricket, but very infrequently.* **2 not infrequently** *formal* fairly often: *The censors changed some names and dialogue and, not infrequently, banned controversial films completely.*

in·fringe /ɪnˈfrɪndʒ/ *v* [T] to do something that is against a law or someone's legal rights: *A backup copy of a computer program does not infringe copyright.* —**infringement** *n* [C,U]: *the infringement of human rights*

infringe on/upon sth *phr v* to limit someone's freedom in some way: *Some students argued that the rule infringed on their right to free speech.*

in·fu·ri·ate /ɪnˈfjʊərieɪt $ -ˈfjʊr-/ *v* [T] to make someone extremely angry: *Her actions infuriated her mother.* | *It* **infuriated** *him* **that** *Beth was with another man.*

in·fu·ri·a·ting /ɪnˈfjʊərieɪtɪŋ $ -ˈfjʊr-/ adj very annoying: *The infuriating thing is that he is always right.* —**infuriatingly** adv: *an infuriatingly tricky crossword puzzle*

in·fuse /ɪnˈfjuːz/ v **1** [T] formal to fill something or someone with a particular feeling or quality: **be infused with sth** *Her books are infused with humour and wisdom.* | **infuse sth into sth** *These new designers are infusing fresh interest into the New York fashion scene.* **2** [I,T] if you infuse tea or HERBS, or if they infuse, you leave them in very hot water while their taste passes into the water

in·fu·sion /ɪnˈfjuːʒən/ n **1** [C,U] the act of putting a new feeling or quality into something: [+of] *Further education badly needs the infusion of more resources.* **2** [C,U] medical the act of putting medicine slowly into someone's body, or the medicines themselves: *intravenous infusions of cardiac drugs* **3** [C] a drink made with HERBS in hot water that is usually taken as a medicine

-ing /ɪŋ/ suffix **1** forms the present participle of verbs: *They're dancing.* | *to go dancing* | *a dancing bear* **2** [in U nouns] the action or process of doing something: *She hates swimming.* | *No parking.* **3** [in C nouns] **a)** an example of doing something: *to hold a meeting* **b)** a product or result of doing something: *a beautiful painting* **4** [in nouns] something used to do something or used for making something: *a silk lining* | *ten metres of curtaining* (=cloth for curtains)

in·ge·ni·ous /ɪnˈdʒiːniəs/ adj **1** an ingenious plan, idea, or object works well and is the result of clever thinking and new ideas: *Many fish have ingenious ways of protecting their eggs from predators.* | *an ingenious device* **2** someone who is ingenious is very good at inventing things or at thinking of new ideas —**ingeniously** adv

in·ge·nu·i·ty /ˌɪndʒəˈnjuːɪti $ -ˈnuː-/ n [U] skill at inventing things and thinking of new ideas

in·gé·nue /ˈænʒeɪnjuː $ ˈændʒənuː/ n [C] a young girl, especially in a film or play, who has not had much experience of life

in·gen·u·ous /ɪnˈdʒenjuəs/ adj an ingenuous person is simple, trusting, and honest, especially because they have not had much experience of life; → **disingenuous** —**ingenuously** adv —**ingenuousness** n [U]

in·gest /ɪnˈdʒest/ v [T] technical to take food or other substances into your body; → **digest** —**ingestion** /ɪnˈdʒestʃən/ n [U] → DIGEST¹ (1)

in·gle·nook /ˈɪŋɡəlnʊk/ n [C] BrE a seat by the side of a large open FIREPLACE, or the space that it is in

in·glo·ri·ous /ɪnˈɡlɔːriəs/ adj literary causing shame and dishonour: *an inglorious defeat* —**ingloriously** adv

in·got /ˈɪŋɡət/ n [C] a piece of pure metal, especially gold, usually shaped like a brick

in·grained /ɪnˈɡreɪnd/ adj **1** ingrained attitudes or behaviour are firmly established and therefore difficult to change: [+in] *The idea of doing our duty is deeply ingrained in most people.* **2** ingrained dirt is under the surface of something and very difficult to remove

in·grate /ɪnˈɡreɪt, ˈɪŋɡreɪt $ ˈɪŋɡreɪt/ n [C] formal an ungrateful person

in·gra·ti·ate /ɪnˈɡreɪʃieɪt/ v **ingratiate yourself (with sb)** to try very hard to get someone's approval – used to show disapproval: *His policy is to ingratiate himself with anyone who might be useful to him.*

in·gra·ti·at·ing /ɪnˈɡreɪʃieɪtɪŋ/ adj trying too hard to get someone's approval – used to show disapproval: *an ingratiating smile* —**ingratiatingly** adv

in·grat·i·tude /ɪnˈɡrætɪtjuːd $ -tuːd/ n [U] the quality of not being grateful: *I've never seen such ingratitude!*

in·gre·di·ent /ɪnˈɡriːdiənt/ n [C] **1** one of the foods that you use to make a particular food or dish: *Combine all the ingredients in a large bowl.* | *The food is home-cooked using fresh ingredients.* **2** a quality you need to achieve something: *John has all the ingredients of a*

great player. | *Investment in new product development is an essential ingredient of corporate success.* **3** active ingredient the substance in a product such as a medicine that causes the product's intended result: *Acetic acid is the chief active ingredient in vinegar.*

in·gress /ˈɪnɡres/ n [U] literary the right to enter a place, or the act of entering it

in-group n [C] a small group of people involved in an organization or activity who like the same things and are friendly with each other, but do not want other people to join them; ☒ **clique**

in·grow·ing /ˌɪnˈɡrəʊɪŋ $ -ˈɡroʊ-/ BrE; **in·grown** /-ˈɡrəʊn $ -ˈɡroʊn/ AmE adj [no comparative] an ingrowing TOENAIL grows inwards, cutting into the surrounding skin

in·hab·it /ɪnˈhæbɪt/ v [T] if animals or people inhabit an area or place, they live there: *The woods are inhabited by many wild animals.* | *I have no idea what sort of people inhabit the area.* | *inhabited islands* —**inhabitable** adj

in·hab·i·tant /ɪnˈhæbɪtənt/ n [C] one of the people who live in a particular place: *a city of six million inhabitants*

in·ha·lant /ɪnˈheɪlənt/ n [C,U] a medicine or drug that you breathe in, for example when you have a cold

in·hale /ɪnˈheɪl/ v [I,T] to breathe in air, smoke, or gas; ☒ **exhale**: *It is dangerous to inhale ammonia fumes.* | *Myra lit another cigarette and inhaled deeply* (=breathed in a lot of smoke). —**inhalation** /ˌɪnhəˈleɪʃən/ n [U]: *One man was treated for smoke inhalation* (=when you breathe smoke from a fire).

in·hal·er /ɪnˈheɪlə $ -ər/ n [C] a small plastic tube containing medicine that you breathe in, in order to make breathing easier

in·here /ɪnˈhɪə $ -ˈhɪr/ v
inhere in sth phr v technical to be a natural part of something

in·her·ent /ɪnˈhɪərənt, -ˈher- $ -ˈhɪr-, -ˈher-/ adj formal a quality that is inherent in something is a natural part of it and cannot be separated from it: [+in] *I'm afraid the problems you mention are inherent in the system.* | *Every business has its own inherent risks.* —**inherently** adv: *Firefighting is an inherently dangerous occupation.*

in·her·it /ɪnˈherɪt/ v **1** [I,T] to receive money, property etc from someone after they have died: **inherit sth from sb** *He inherited a fortune from his grandmother.* | *inherited wealth* **2** [T] if you inherit a situation, especially one in which problems have been caused by other people, you have to deal with it: *The present government inherited a closed, state-dominated economy.* **3** [T] to have the same character or appearance as your parents: **inherit sth from sb** *Mr. Grass inherited his work ethic from his father.* | *I inherited my mother's curly hair.* **4** [T] to get something that someone else does not want any more: **inherit sth from sb** *We inherited the furniture from the previous tenants.*

in·her·i·tance /ɪnˈherɪtəns/ n **1** [C,U] money, property etc that you receive from someone who has died: *Lucinda has to fight for her life and her inheritance in this gripping novel.* **2** [U] physical or mental qualities that you inherit from your family: *Our genetic inheritance cannot be changed.* **3** [U] ideas, skills, literature etc from the past that influence people in the present: *ideas that have become part of our cultural inheritance*

in'heritance ˌtax n [U] a tax that you have to pay when you receive money or property from someone who has died

in·her·i·tor /ɪnˈherɪtə $ -ər/ n [C] **1** someone who receives money, property etc from someone who has just died **2** someone who follows in an established way of life or thinking: [+of] *These writers are inheritors of his work.*

in·hib·it /ɪnˈhɪbət/ v [T]   **1** to prevent something from growing or developing well: *An unhappy family life may inhibit children's learning.*   **2** to make someone feel embarrassed or nervous so that they cannot do or say what they want to: **inhibit sb from doing sth** *Recording the meeting may inhibit people from expressing their real views.*

in·hib·it·ed /ɪnˈhɪbətəd/ adj too embarrassed or nervous to do or say what you want: [+about] *Many people are inhibited about discussing sexual matters.*

in·hi·bi·tion /ˌɪnhəˈbɪʃən/ n   **1** [C,U] a feeling of shyness or embarrassment that stops you doing or saying what you really want: *She had no inhibitions about saying what she felt.* | *People tend to **lose** their **inhibitions** when they've drunk a lot of alcohol.*   **2** [U] technical when something is restricted or prevented from happening or developing: *a marked inhibition of cell growth*

in·hos·pi·ta·ble /ˌɪnhɒˈspɪtəbəl $ -hɑː-/ adj   **1** an inhospitable place is difficult to live or stay in because the weather conditions are unpleasant or there is no shelter: *an inhospitable climate* | *He trekked across some of the most inhospitable terrain in the world.*   **2** an inhospitable person does not welcome visitors in a friendly way: [+to] *Some governments are inhospitable to aid workers.*

in-'house adj, adv working within a company or organization: *We have an in-house training unit.* | *The keyboarding is done in-house.*

in·hu·man /ɪnˈhjuːmən/   **1** very cruel or without any normal feelings of pity: *The refugees had suffered degrading and inhuman treatment.*   **2** lacking any human qualities in a way that seems strange or frightening: *a strange inhuman sound* —**inhumanly** adv

in·hu·mane /ˌɪnhjuːˈmeɪn/ adj extremely cruel and causing unacceptable suffering: *the inhumane treatment of political prisoners* | *I was shocked by the inhumane conditions.* —**inhumanely** adv

in·hu·man·i·ty /ˌɪnhjuːˈmænəti/ n [U] very cruel behaviour or actions: *the inhumanity of some political systems*

in·im·i·cal /ɪˈnɪmɪkəl/ adj formal making it difficult for something to exist or happen: *a cold, inimical climate* | [+to] *conditions inimical to development*

in·im·i·ta·ble /ɪˈnɪmətəbəl/ adj too good or skilful for anyone else to copy with the same high standard; ▣ **unique**: *the inimitable Billie Holliday* | **your own inimitable way/style etc** *He entertained us in his own inimitable style.* —**inimitably** adv → IMITATE

in·iq·ui·tous /ɪˈnɪkwətəs/ adj formal very unfair and morally wrong: *an iniquitous system of taxation*

in·iq·ui·ty /ɪˈnɪkwəti/ n plural **iniquities** [C,U] formal the quality of being very unfair or evil, or something that is very unfair: [+of] *He went on and on about the iniquities of bourgeois oppression.* | *They were trying to protect their son from iniquity.* → **den of iniquity** at DEN (6)

i·ni·tial¹ W2 /ɪˈnɪʃəl/ adj [only before noun] happening at the beginning; ▣ **first**: *an initial investment of £5000* | **initial stage/phase/period** *the initial stages of the disease* | *The initial response has been encouraging.*

initial² n [C]   **1** the first letter of someone's first name: *'Can I have your initial, Mr Davies?' 'It's G, Mr G Davies.'*   **2 initials** [plural] the first letters of all your names in order: *His initials are DPH: they stand for David Perry Hallworth.*

initial³ v **initialled, initialling** BrE, **initialed, initialing** AmE [T] to write your initials on a document to make it official or to show that you agree with something; → **sign**: *The two countries have initialled a new defence co-operation agreement.*

i·ni·tial·ly W3 /ɪˈnɪʃəli/ adv at the beginning: *Stan initially wanted to go to medical school.* | *Initially, I thought I would only stay there a year.*

i·ni·ti·ate¹ /ɪˈnɪʃieɪt/ v [T]   **1** formal to arrange for something important to start, such as an official process or a new plan: *They have decided to initiate legal proceedings against the newspaper.* | *Intellectuals have initiated a debate on terrorism.*   **2** to tell someone about something or show them how to do something: **initiate sb into sth** *Those kids were initiated into heroin use at a young age.*   **3** to introduce someone into an organization, club, group etc, usually with a special ceremony: **initiate sb into sth** *At the age of thirteen the boys in the tribe are initiated into manhood.*

i·ni·ti·ate² /ɪˈnɪʃiət/ n [C] someone who has been allowed to join a particular organization, club, or group and has been taught its secrets

i·ni·ti·a·tion /ɪˌnɪʃiˈeɪʃən/ n [C,U]   **1** the process of officially introducing someone into a club or group, or of introducing a young person to adult life, often with a special ceremony: *The club has an **initiation ceremony** for new members.* | **initiation rite/ritual** *initiation rituals for young boys at puberty* | [+into] *rites of initiation into their religion*   **2** the act of starting something such as an official process, a new plan etc: [+of] *the initiation of criminal proceedings*

i·ni·tia·tive W2 /ɪˈnɪʃətɪv/ n
1 DECISIONS [U] the ability to make decisions and take action without waiting for someone to tell you what to do: *I wish my son would **show** more **initiative**.* | *Don't keep asking me for advice. **Use** your **initiative**.* | *Lt. Carlos was not obeying orders. He **acted on** his **own initiative** (=he was not told what to do).*
2 PLAN [C] an important new plan or process to achieve a particular aim or to solve a particular problem: *a government initiative to help exporters* | *an education initiative* | [+for] *a new initiative for peace in the Middle East*
3 CONTROL **the initiative** if you have or take the initiative, you are in a position to control a situation and decide what to do next: *Why don't you **take the initiative** and ask him out?* | *Politicians need to **seize the initiative** from the terrorists.* | *The government must not **lose the initiative** in the fight against terrorism.*
4 LAW [C] law a process by which ordinary citizens can officially suggest a change in the law by signing a PETITION

i·ni·ti·a·tor /ɪˈnɪʃieɪtə $ -ər/ n [C] someone who thinks of and starts a new plan or process: [+of] *the initiator of the proposal*

in·ject /ɪnˈdʒekt/ v [T]   **1** to put liquid, especially a drug, into someone's body by using a special needle: **inject sth into sb/sth** *The drug is injected directly into the base of the spine.* | **inject sb with sth** *I have to inject myself with insulin.*   **2** to improve something by adding excitement, interest etc to it: **inject sth into sth** *Traditional handbag makers are injecting more fun into their designs.* | *A market building can inject new life into an area.*   **3** to provide more money, equipment etc for something: **inject sth into sth** *They need to inject more money into sports facilities.*

in·jec·tion S3 /ɪnˈdʒekʃən/ n
1 [C,U] an act of putting a drug into someone's body using a special needle; → **shot**: *The nurse **gave** me a tetanus injection.* | [+of] *an injection of insulin* | *The children hate **having injections**.* | *The only sure treatment is antibiotics, preferably by injection.*
2 [C] an addition of money to something in order to improve it: [+of] *a massive injection of public funds* | *Our local football club may fold unless it **gets** a **cash injection**.*
3 [C,U] the act of forcing a liquid into something: *a fuel injection system*

'in-joke n [C] a joke that is only understood by a particular group of people

in·ju·di·cious /ˌɪndʒuːˈdɪʃəs◂/ adj formal an injudicious action, remark etc is not sensible and is likely to have bad results: *He has apologized for his injudicious remarks.* —**injudiciously** adv

in·junc·tion /ɪnˈdʒʌŋkʃən/ *n* [C] **1** *law* an order given by a court which tells someone not to do something: [+against] *The family is **seeking** an injunction against the book's publication.* | *The judge refused to **grant** an injunction.* | *They failed to **obtain** an injunction.* **2** *formal* a piece of advice or an order from someone in authority

in·jure /ˈɪndʒə $ -ər/ *v* [T] **1** to hurt yourself or someone else, for example in an accident or an attack; → **wound**: *Angus injured his leg playing rugby yesterday.* | **be badly/seriously/critically injured** *Two people have been critically injured in a road accident.* **2** **injure sb's pride/feelings etc** to say unfair or unpleasant things that hurt someone's pride, feelings etc ⚠ **injure, wound, hurt**, or **damage**; → see box at DAMAGE²

injured

injured   wounded

in·jured /ˈɪndʒəd $ -ərd/ *adj* **1** having a wound or damage to part of your body; → **wounded**: *an injured bird* | *Chelsea have three injured players.* | *Grandpa was **badly injured** in the war.* | *The car accident **left him seriously injured**.* **2** **the injured** the people who have been hurt; → **the wounded**: *Many of the injured are still in a serious condition.* **3** **injured look/expression etc** a look that shows you feel you have been treated unfairly **4** **injured pride/feelings etc** a feeling of being upset or offended because you think you have been unfairly treated **5** **the injured party** *formal* the person who has been unfairly treated in a particular situation

in·ju·ri·ous /ɪnˈdʒʊəriəs $ -ˈdʒʊr-/ *adj formal* causing injury, harm, or damage: [+to] *Smoking is injurious to health.*

in·ju·ry W2 /ˈɪndʒəri/ *n plural* **injuries**
1 [C,U] a wound or damage to part of your body caused by an accident or attack

---

serious injury
minor injury
suffer an injury
sustain an injury (=suffer an injury – used especially in newspaper reports)
escape/avoid injury (=not be injured)
through injury (=because of injury)
head/leg/shoulder etc injury
an injury to the head/the chest etc
internal injuries (=injuries inside your body)
multiple injuries (=a large number of injuries at the same time)
do yourself an injury *BrE spoken* (=accidentally hurt yourself – used especially when warning someone to be careful)
personal injury claim (=a legal claim made against the person or company that caused your injury)

*She was taken to hospital with **serious head injuries**.* | *He **suffered** horrific **injuries** in the attack.* | *The driver of the truck **sustained** only **minor injuries** to his legs and arms.* | *Luckily she **escaped injury**.* | *Beckham has missed several games **through injury**.* | *The pilot was treated for suspected **internal injuries**.* | *Don't lift that toolbox – you'll **do yourself an injury**!* | *He's a lawyer who specializes in **personal injury claims**.*

---

2 [U] *law* damage to someone's feelings: [+to] *He claimed serious injury to his reputation.* → **add insult to injury** at ADD (8)

'injury ,time *n* [U] *BrE* playing time added on to a game such as football because of time lost when players are injured; → **extra time**

in·jus·tice /ɪnˈdʒʌstɪs/ *n* **1** [C,U] a situation in which people are treated very unfairly and not given their rights: [+of] *the injustice of slavery* | [+against] *innumerable injustices against the black population* | *The movie deals with injustices suffered by Native Americans.* | *He had developed a deep **sense of** social injustice.* **2** **do sb an injustice** to judge someone's character or abilities unfairly: *To say that you are a poor cook is to do yourself an injustice.*

ink¹ /ɪŋk/ *n* **1** [C,U] a coloured liquid that you use for writing, printing or drawing: *Please write in black ink.* **2** [U] the black liquid in sea creatures such as OCTOPUSES and SQUID

ink² *v* [T] **1** to put ink on something **2** to make a document, agreement etc official and legal by writing your SIGNATURE on it: *The two companies have inked a deal.*
     ink sth ⇔ in *phr v* to complete something done in pencil by drawing over it in ink

'ink·jet ,print·er /ˈɪŋkdʒet ,prɪntə $ -ər/ *n* [C] an electronic PRINTER, usually connected to a small computer; → **dot-matrix printer**, **laser printer**

ink·ling /ˈɪŋklɪŋ/ *n* [C usually singular] a slight idea about something; → **suspicion**: *I had an inkling that she was pregnant.* | [+of] *She had absolutely no inkling of what was going on.*

'ink pad *n* [C] a small box containing ink on a thick piece of cloth, used for putting ink onto a STAMP that is then pressed onto paper

ink·well /ˈɪŋk-wel/ *n* [C] a container for ink which fits into a hole in a desk

ink·y /ˈɪŋki/ *adj* **1** *literary* very dark – used especially in poetry: *I stared out into the inky blackness of the night.* **2** marked with ink: *inky fingers*

in·laid /ˌɪnˈleɪd◂/ *adj* **1** an inlaid box, table, floor etc has little pieces of another material set into its surface for decoration: [+with] *a wooden jewellery box inlaid with ivory* **2** [+ in/into] metal, stone etc that is inlaid into the surface of another material is set into its surface as decoration

in·land¹ /ˈɪnlənd/ *adj* [only before noun] an inland area, city etc is not near the coast: *the largest area of inland water in the south east*

in·land² /ɪnˈlænd/ *adv* in a direction away from the coast and towards the centre of a country: *The mountains are five miles inland.* | *We set off inland.*

,Inland 'Revenue *n* **the Inland Revenue** the government department which collects national taxes in Britain

'in-laws *n* [plural] *informal* your relatives by marriage, especially the father and mother of your husband or wife; → **mother-in-law**, **father-in-law**: *We have to spend Christmas with the in-laws.*

in·lay /ˈɪnleɪ/ *n* **1** [C,U] a material which has been set into the surface of furniture, floors etc for decoration, or the pattern made by this: *a cedarwood casket with gold inlay* **2** [C] a substance used by a DENTIST to fill a hole in a decayed tooth

in·let /ˈɪnlet, ˈɪnlət/ *n* [C] **1** a narrow area of water that reaches from the sea or a lake into the land: *There are several sheltered inlets along the coast.* **2** the part of a machine through which liquid or gas flows in; ▪ **outlet**: *a fuel inlet*

,in-line 'skate *n* [C] a special boot for ROLLER SKATING with a single row of wheels attached under it; ▪ **Rollerblade**; → see picture at SKATE

---

in·lo·co pa·ren·tis /ɪn ˌləʊkəʊ pəˈrentɪs $ -ˌloʊkoʊ-/ adv formal or law having the responsibilities of a parent for someone else's child: *As a teacher, you should regard yourself as being in loco parentis.*

in·mate /ˈɪnmeɪt/ n [C] someone who is being kept in a prison

in me·mo·ri·am /ɪn mᵻˈmɔːriəm/ prep an expression meaning 'in memory of', used especially on the stone above the place where a dead person is buried

in·most /ˈɪnməʊst $ -moʊst/ adj [only before noun] **1** your inmost feelings, desires etc are your most personal and secret ones: *In his inmost heart, he knew he didn't love me.* **2** formal furthest inside a place, and so difficult to see or find: *Apparently there are bats in the inmost caves.*

inn /ɪn/ n [C] **1** a small hotel or PUB, especially an old one in the countryside → see picture at **STAY** **2** a word used in the names of some PUBS and hotels: *We're staying at the Holiday Inn.*

in·nards /ˈɪnədz $ -ərdz/ n [plural] informal **1** the parts inside your body, especially your stomach; ⧉ **guts** **2** the parts inside a machine

in·nate /ˌɪˈneɪt◂/ adj **1** an innate quality or ability is something you are born with: *Children have an innate ability to learn language.* **2** an innate belief is something you feel strongly about and are unlikely to change: *the innate conservatism of the farming community* —**innately** adv: *the army's innately conservative values*

in·ner W2 /ˈɪnə $ -ər/ adj [only before noun] **1** on the inside or close to the centre of something; ⧉ **outer**: *an inner room* | *inner London* | *the inner ear* **2** inner thoughts or feelings are ones that you feel strongly but do not always show to other people: *Yoga gives me a sense of inner calm.* | *She'll need great inner strength to get over the tragedy.* | *She never shared her inner thoughts with anyone.* **3** relating to things which happen or exist but are not easy to see: *I'll never understand the inner workings of the film industry.* | *The inner life of a political party must be fascinating.* **4 inner circle** the few people in an organization, political party etc who control it or share power with its leader: *members of the President's inner circle* **5 sb's inner voice** thoughts or feelings inside your head which seem to warn or advise you: *My inner voice told me to be cautious.*

,inner 'city n plural **inner cities** [C] the part near the middle of a city, especially where the buildings are in a bad condition and the people are poor: *the problems of our inner cities* —**inner city** adj: *inner-city schools*

in·ner·most /ˈɪnəməʊst $ -nərmoʊst/ adj [only before noun] **1** your innermost feelings, desires etc are your most personal and secret ones: *a man who would never share his innermost thoughts with anyone* **2** formal furthest inside or nearest to the centre; ⧉ **outermost**: *the innermost depths of the cave*

'inner tube n [C] a rubber tube filled with air that is inside a tyre

in·ning /ˈɪnɪŋ/ n [C] one of the nine playing periods in a game of baseball or SOFTBALL

in·nings /ˈɪnɪŋz/ n plural **innings 1** [C] the period of time in a game of CRICKET when a team or player BATS **2 he/she had a good innings** BrE informal used about someone who has died to say that they had a long life

in·nit /ˈɪnɪt/ BrE spoken used at the end of a statement or in reply to a statement, often to emphasize what has just been said: *'Did you see the way Schumacher went past him?' 'Innit.'*

inn·keep·er /ˈɪnˌkiːpə $ -ər/ n [C] old use someone who owns or manages an INN

in·no·cence /ˈɪnəsəns/ n [U] **1** the fact of being not guilty of a crime; ⧉ **guilt**: *Can you prove your innocence?* | **protest/maintain your innocence** (=say repeatedly that you are not guilty) *The prisoners continued to protest their innocence.* **2** lack of experience of life or knowledge of the bad things in the world: *In our innocence we believed everything we were told.* | *the innocence of childhood* **3 in all innocence** if you do or say something in all innocence, you have no intention of doing harm or of offending anyone

in·no·cent¹ /ˈɪnəsənt/ adj **1** not guilty of a crime; ⧉ **guilty**: *Nobody would believe that I was innocent.* | [+of] *He's innocent of murder.* | *The court found him innocent and he was released.* **2** innocent victims/bystanders/people etc people who get hurt or killed in a war or crime although they are not directly involved in it: *Many innocent civilians are among the casualties.* **3** done or said without intending to harm or offend anyone: *He was startled by their angry reaction to his innocent remark.* **4** not having much experience of the bad things in the world, so that you are easily deceived; ⧉ **naive**: *I was thirteen years old and very innocent.* —**innocently** adv

innocent² n [C] someone who does not have much experience of the bad things in life

in·noc·u·ous /ɪˈnɒkjuəs $ ɪˈnɑːk-/ adj not offensive, dangerous, or harmful: *an innocuous remark* | *He's a perfectly innocuous young man.* —**innocuously** adv

in·no·vate /ˈɪnəveɪt/ v [I,T] to start to use new ideas, methods, or inventions: *the need for large businesses to innovate* | *The company has successfully innovated new products and services.*

in·no·va·tion W3 /ˌɪnəˈveɪʃən/ n **1** [C] a new idea, method, or invention: [+in] *recent innovations in English teaching* **2** [U] the introduction of new ideas or methods: *We must encourage innovation if the company is to remain competitive.* | [+in] *We need to encourage innovation in industry.* | *Many people feel bewildered by the speed of technological innovation.*

in·nov·at·ive /ˈɪnəvtɪv $ ˈɪnəˌveɪtɪv/ also **innova·tory** adj **1** an innovative idea or way of doing something is new, different, and better than those that existed before: *an innovative approach to language teaching* | *innovative schemes for recycling waste materials* **2** using clever new ideas and methods: *an innovative design team*

in·no·va·tor /ˈɪnəveɪtə $ -ər/ n [C] someone who introduces changes and new ideas

in·no·va·to·ry /ˈɪnəveɪtəri $ ˈɪnəvətɔːri/ adj INNOVATIVE

in·nu·en·do /ˌɪnjuˈendəʊ $ -doʊ/ n plural **innuendoes** or **innuendos** [C,U] a remark that suggests something sexual or unpleasant without saying it directly, or these remarks in general; → **double entendre**: *His writing is full of sexual innuendoes.* | *a campaign based on rumour, innuendo, and gossip*

in·nu·me·ra·ble /ɪˈnjuːmərəbəl $ ɪˈnuː-/ adj very many, or too many to be counted; ⧉ **countless**: *She's served on innumerable committees.*

in·nu·mer·ate /ɪˈnjuːmərᵻt $ ɪˈnuː-/ adj unable to do simple calculations or understand basic mathematics —**innumeracy** n [U]

i·noc·u·late /ɪˈnɒkjᵿleɪt $ ɪˈnɑː-/ v [T] to protect someone against a disease by putting a weak form of the disease into their body using a needle; → **immunize, vaccinate: inoculate sb against sth** *All the children had been inoculated against hepatitis.* —**inoculation** /ɪˌnɒkjᵿˈleɪʃən $ -ˌnɑːk-/ n [C,U]

in·of·fen·sive /ˌɪnəˈfensɪv◂/ adj unlikely to offend or upset anyone: *Her husband was a small, inoffensive-looking man.*

in·op·e·ra·ble /ɪnˈɒpərəbəl $ ɪnˈɑː-/ adj **1** an inoperable illness or medical condition cannot be treated by an operation: *an inoperable brain tumour* **2** something that is inoperable cannot be used: *The bombing rendered the airfield inoperable.*

in·op·e·ra·tive /ɪn'ɒpərətɪv $ ɪn'ɑː-/ adj formal **1** a machine that is inoperative is not working, or is not in working condition **2** a system or a law that is inoperative does not work any more or cannot be made to work

in·op·por·tune /ɪn'ɒpətjuːn $ ˌɪnɑːpər'tuːn/ adj formal **1** an inopportune moment or time is not suitable or good for something; **≠ opportune**: I'm afraid you've called at rather an **inopportune moment**. **2** happening at an unsuitable or bad time: an inopportune visit

in·or·di·nate /ɪn'nɔːdənət $ -ɔːr-/ adj far more than you would reasonably or normally expect; **≠ excessive**: Testing is taking up an **inordinate amount** of teachers' time. —**inordinately** adv: She's inordinately fond of her parrot.

in·or·gan·ic /ˌɪnɔː'gænɪk $ -ɔːr-/ adj not consisting of anything that is living: inorganic matter —**inorganically** /-kli/ adv

inorganic 'chemistry n [U] technical the part of chemistry concerning the study of substances that do not contain CARBON; **→ organic chemistry**

in·pa·tient /'ɪnˌpeɪʃənt/ n [C] someone who stays in a hospital while they receive treatment **→ OUTPATIENT**

in·put¹ W3 /'ɪnpʊt/ n
1 [U] information that is put into a computer; **≠ output**: If the input data specified it, the file will close and the process terminates.
2 [C,U] ideas, advice, money, or effort that you put into a job or activity in order to help it succeed: [+into/to] Farmers contributed most of the input into the survey. | [+from] We'll need input from community nurses.
3 [C,U] technical electrical power that is put into a machine for it to use

input² v past tense and past participle **inputted** or **input**, present participle **inputting** [T] to put information into a computer; **≠ output**: **be input to sth** The information is input to our computer system.

in·quest /'ɪŋkwest/ n [C] **1** a legal process to find out the cause of someone's death: [+into] The coroner will **hold** an **inquest** into the deaths. | The inquest heard that she died from multiple injuries. **2** an unofficial discussion about the reasons for someone's defeat or failure to do something: [+into] The Tories will **hold** a private **inquest** into why they were defeated.

in·qui·e·tude /ɪn'kwaɪətjuːd $ -tuːd/ n [U] literary a feeling of anxiety

in·quire, enquire /ɪn'kwaɪə $ -'kwaɪr/ v [I,T] formal to ask someone for information: 'Why are you doing that?' the boy inquired. | [+about] I am writing to inquire about your advertisement in The Times. | **inquire whether/why/how etc** The waiter inquired whether we would like to sit near the window. | **inquire sth of sb** 'Where's the station?' she inquired of a passer-by. | Toby would have liked to **inquire further** (=ask more questions). | I did not inquire the reason for his lateness. —**inquirer** n [C]
inquire after sb/sth phr v to ask about someone's health, what they are doing etc: He called me aside to inquire after my daughter.
inquire into sth phr v to ask questions in order to get more information about something: The investigation will inquire into the company's financial dealings.

in·quir·ing, enquiring /ɪn'kwaɪərɪŋ $ -'kwaɪr-/ adj [only before noun] **1** an inquiring look or expression shows that you want to ask about something: She raised an inquiring eyebrow towards Murray. **2** an inquiring mind someone who has an inquiring mind is very interested in finding out more about everything: As a child he had a lively inquiring mind. —**inquiringly** adv: Victor looked at her inquiringly.

in·quir·y W3 **enquiry** /ɪn'kwaɪəri $ ɪn'kwaɪri, 'ɪŋkwəri/ n plural **inquiries**
1 [C] a question you ask in order to get information: [+about] We're getting a lot of inquiries about our new London-Rio service. | [+from] inquiries from potential applicants | I don't know who sent the gift, but I'll **make** some **inquiries**. | **help the police with their inquiries** BrE

(=to answer questions about a crime)
2 [U] the act or process of asking questions in order to get information: On further inquiry, it emerged that Malcolm had not been involved in the incident. | The local council set up a committee of inquiry to look into policing arrangements. | **scientific/intellectual inquiry**
3 [C] an official process to find out about something: [+into] a judicial inquiry into the deaths | **launch/set up/hold an inquiry (into sth)** The Civil Aviation Authority has agreed to hold an inquiry into the accident. | The police have launched a **murder inquiry**. | Parents have called for an **independent inquiry** into the accident. **→ line of inquiry** at LINE¹ (12)

in·qui·si·tion /ˌɪŋkwɪ'zɪʃən/ n **1 the Inquisition** a Roman Catholic organization in the past whose aim was to find and punish people who had unacceptable religious beliefs **2** [C usually singular] a series of questions that someone asks you in a threatening or unpleasant way: I had to face a two-hour inquisition from my parents about where I'd been.

in·quis·i·tive /ɪn'kwɪzətɪv/ adj **1** asking too many questions and trying to find out too many details about something or someone: I'd have asked more questions, but I didn't want to seem inquisitive. **2** interested in a lot of different things and wanting to find out more about them: a cheerful, inquisitive little boy | an inquisitive mind; **→ curious** —**inquisitively** adv: He peeped inquisitively into the drawer. —**inquisitiveness** n [U]

in·quis·i·tor /ɪn'kwɪzətə $ -ər/ n [C] **1** someone who is asking you a lot of difficult questions and making you feel very uncomfortable **2** an official of the INQUISITION —**inquisitorial** /ɪnˌkwɪzɪ'tɔːriəl/ adj —**inquisitorially** adv

in·road /'ɪnrəʊd $ -roʊd/ n [usually plural] **make inroads into/on sth a)** to have an important effect or influence on something, especially by taking something away from it: Video is making huge inroads into attendance figures at movie theaters (=taking away its customers). | They have made significant inroads into the European market. | The administrative workload is making massive inroads into our working day (=taking away time). **b)** to make some progress towards achieving something difficult: We haven't made much of an inroad into the backlog of work.

in·rush /'ɪnrʌʃ/ n [C usually singular] a sudden flow of something that enters a place: The inrush of fresh air filled the room.

ins and 'outs n [plural] all the exact details of a complicated situation, problem, system etc: [+of] I don't really know all **the ins and outs** of the matter.

in·sane /ɪn'seɪn/ adj **1** informal completely stupid or crazy, often in a way that is dangerous: That's an insane risk. | The whole idea sounds absolutely insane to me. | Why did you do that? Have you **gone insane**? **2** someone who is insane is permanently and seriously mentally ill so that they cannot live in normal society: The killer was declared criminally insane. **3 the insane** people who are mentally ill: a hospital for the insane **4 drive sb insane** informal to make someone feel more and more annoyed or angry, usually over a long period of time; **≠ drive sb mad**: My little brother's been driving me insane all weekend. —**insanely** adv: insanely jealous | She giggled insanely.

in·san·i·ta·ry /ɪn'sænətəri $ -teri/ adj insanitary conditions or places are very dirty and likely to cause disease; **≠ unsanitary** AmE

in·san·i·ty /ɪn'sænəti/ n [U] **1** the state of being seriously mentally ill, so that you cannot live normally in society; **≠ madness**: The court acquitted Campbell on the grounds of temporary insanity. **2** very stupid actions that may cause you serious harm; **≠ lunacy**: Can't they see the insanity of dumping radioactive waste in the sea?

in·sa·tia·ble /ɪnˈseɪʃəbəl/ *adj* always wanting more and more of something: **insatiable appetite/desire/demand etc (for sth)** *his insatiable appetite for power* | *our insatiable thirst for knowledge* —**insatiably** *adv*

in·scribe /ɪnˈskraɪb/ *v* [T] to carefully cut, print, or write words on something, especially on the surface of a stone or coin: *Inside the cover someone had inscribed the words 'To Thomas, with love'.* | **be inscribed in/on sth** *The team's name is inscribed on the base of the trophy.* | **be inscribed with sth** *The tomb was inscribed with a short poem.*

in·scrip·tion /ɪnˈskrɪpʃən/ *n* [C] a piece of writing inscribed on a stone, in the front of a book etc: *a Latin inscription on the memorial stone*

in·scru·ta·ble /ɪnˈskruːtəbəl/ *adj* someone who is inscrutable shows no emotion or reaction in the expression on their face so that it is impossible to know what they are feeling or thinking: *He stood silent and inscrutable.* —**inscrutably** *adv* —**inscrutability** /ɪnˌskruːtəˈbɪlɪti/ *n* [U]

insects

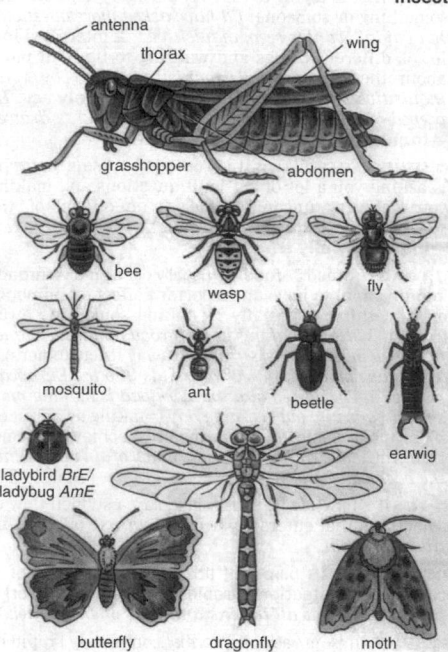

antenna
thorax
wing
grasshopper
abdomen
bee
wasp
fly
mosquito
ant
beetle
ladybird *BrE*/
ladybug *AmE*
earwig
butterfly
dragonfly
moth

in·sect /ˈɪnsekt/ *n* [C] a small creature such as a fly or ANT, that has six legs, and sometimes wings: *an insect bite* | *mosquitoes and other flying insects* | *Don't forget to bring* **insect repellant** (=a chemical to keep insects away).

in·sec·ti·cide /ɪnˈsektɪˌsaɪd/ *n* [U] a chemical substance used for killing insects → PESTICIDE —**insecticidal** /ɪnˌsektɪˈsaɪdl◂/ *adj*

in·sec·ti·vore /ɪnˈsektɪˌvɔː $ -vɔːr/ *n* [C] a creature that eats insects for food; → **carnivore, herbivore, omnivore** —**insectivorous** /ˌɪnsekˈtɪvərəs◂/ *adj*

in·se·cure /ˌɪnsɪˈkjʊə◂ $ -ˈkjʊr◂/ *adj* **1** not feeling at all confident about yourself, your abilities, or your relationships with people: *She's very insecure about her appearance.* | *She felt lonely and insecure away from her family.* **2** a job, INVESTMENT etc that is insecure does not give you a feeling of safety, because it might be taken away or lost at any time: *Many of them work in low-paid, insecure jobs.* **3** a building or structure that is insecure is not safe, because it could fall down —**insecurity** *n* [C,U]: *Student teachers often*

suffer from a great sense of insecurity. | *her deepest fears and insecurities* —**insecurely** *adv*

in·sem·i·nate /ɪnˈsemɪˌneɪt/ *v* [T] to put SPERM into a woman or female animal in order to make her have a baby —**insemination** /ɪnˌsemɪˈneɪʃən/ *n* [U] → ARTIFICIAL INSEMINATION

in·sen·sate /ɪnˈsenseɪt/ *adj formal* **1** not able to feel things **2** unreasonable and crazy: *an insensate hatred of America*

in·sen·si·bil·i·ty /ɪnˌsensɪˈbɪlɪti/ *n* [U] **1** *formal* the state of being unconscious **2** *old-fashioned* inability to experience feelings such as love, sympathy, anger etc

in·sen·si·ble /ɪnˈsensɪbəl/ *adj formal* **1** not knowing about something that could happen to you; 🔲 **unaware**: [+of] *She remained insensible of the dangers that lay ahead.* **2** unable to feel something or be affected by it: [+to/of] *insensible to the cold* **3** *literary* not conscious: *He fell to the ground, insensible.* —**insensibly** *adv*

in·sen·si·tive /ɪnˈsensɪtɪv/ *adj* **1** not noticing, or not taking the care to notice, other people's feelings, and not realizing when they are upset or when something that you do will upset them: *One insensitive official insisted on seeing her husband's death certificate.* | *an insensitive remark* | [+to] *She's totally insensitive to Jack's feelings.* **2** [not before noun] not paying attention to what is happening or to what people are saying, and therefore not changing your behaviour because of it: [+to] *Companies that are insensitive to global changes will lose sales.* | *The service is insensitive to the needs of local people.* **3** [not before noun] not affected by physical effects or changes: [+to] *insensitive to pain* —**insensitively** *adv* —**insensitivity** /ɪnˌsensɪˈtɪvɪti/ *n* [U]

in·sep·a·ra·ble /ɪnˈsepərəbəl/ *adj* **1** people who are inseparable are always together and are very friendly with each other: *Jane and Sarah soon became inseparable companions.* | [+from] *Tom was inseparable from his dog, Snowy.* **2** things that are inseparable cannot be separated or cannot be considered separately: [+from] *Britain's economic fortunes are inseparable from the world situation.* —**inseparably** *adv* —**inseparability** /ɪnˌsepərəˈbɪlɪti/ *n* [U]

in·sert¹ /ɪnˈsɜːt $ -ɜːrt/ *v* [T] **1** to put something inside or into something else: **insert sth in/into/between sth** *His hand shook slightly as he inserted the key into the lock.* **2** to add something to the middle of a document or piece of writing: **insert sth in/into/between sth** *His manager inserted a new clause into his contract.* | *Insert your comments in the space below.*

in·sert² /ˈɪnsɜːt $ -ɜːrt/ *n* [C] **1** printed pages that are put inside a newspaper or magazine in order to advertise something: *a six-page insert on computer software* **2** something that is designed to be put inside something else: *He wore special inserts in his shoes to make him look taller.*

in·ser·tion /ɪnˈsɜːʃən $ -ɜːr-/ *n* **1** [U] the act of putting something inside something else **2** [C] something that is added to the middle of a document or piece of writing

in-'service *adj* **in-service training/courses etc** training etc that you do while you are working in a job

in·set¹ /ˈɪnset/ *n* [C] **1** a small picture, map etc in the corner of a page or larger picture etc, which shows more detail or information: *The venture earned Mr Taylor (inset) millions of dollars.* **2** something which is fixed into or onto the surface of something else: *a pendant with a diamond inset*

in·set² /ɪnˈset/ *v past tense and past participle* **inset**, *present participle* **insetting** [T] **1** if something is inset with decorations or jewels, they are fixed into or on its surface: **inset sth with sth** *a wooden box inset with ivory* | **inset sth into sth** *spotlights inset into the ceiling* **2** to put a small picture, map etc on a printed page

in·shore /ˌɪnˈʃɔː◂ $ -ˈʃɔːr◂/ *adv* near, towards, or to the shore; 🔲 **offshore**: *The fishing boats usually stay close inshore.* —**inshore** *adj*: *inshore waters*

in·side¹ S2 W2 /ɪnˈsaɪd/ adv, prep
1 CONTAINER in or into a container or other closed space so as to be completely covered or surrounded; ⬛ **outside**: *The jewels were locked away inside the safe.* | *I sent the money inside an envelope addressed to Ann.* | *Carl picked up the book and stuffed it inside his jacket.* | *Her car was locked and the keys were inside.*
2 BUILDING/ROOM in or into a building or room; ⬛ **outside**: *It's raining. We'll have to go inside.* | *She could hear voices inside, but no-one came to the door.* | *Mail was piled up just inside the doorway.* | *The sound seemed to be coming from inside the house.* | [+of] *AmE: There were more than 20 people packed inside of her dorm room.*
3 COUNTRY/AREA in a country or area – used when you want to emphasize that something is happening there and not in other places; ⬛ **outside**: *Very little is known of events inside this mysterious country.* | *The guerrillas were said to be operating from bases inside the war zone.*
4 ORGANIZATION if someone is inside a group or organization, they are part of it; ⬛ **outside**: *women's influence inside the Party* | *The information comes from sources inside the company.* | *Discussions should involve local people both inside and outside the school.*
5 HEAD/MIND if something happens inside you, or inside your head or mind, it is part of what you think and feel, especially when you do not express it: *You just don't understand how I feel inside!* | *Steve's a strange guy – you never know what's going on inside his head.* | *Anger bubbled up deep inside her.* | [+of] *AmE: Something inside of me told me not to trust him.*
6 BODY in your body: *She could feel the baby kicking inside her.* | *You'll feel better once you've got a good meal inside you* (=after you have eaten something).
7 TIME **a)** in less than a particular amount of time: *A full report is expected inside three months.* | **inside the hour/month etc** (=before an hour, month etc has passed) *We'll be back inside the hour.* | [+of] *especially AmE: Our aim is to get the whole job finished inside of a week.* **b)** less than a particular amount of time; ⬛ **outside**: *Jonson's time of 9.3 seconds was just inside the world record.*
8 PRISON informal in prison: *My boyfriend's been inside for a year.*

in·side² /ɪnˈsaɪd, ˈɪnsaɪd/ n **1 the inside** the inner part of something, which is surrounded or hidden by the outer part; ⬛ **the outside**: *on the inside The apple's rotten on the inside.* | [+of] *condensation on the inside of the window* | *The door had been locked from the inside.* **2 inside out** with the usual outside parts on the inside: *You've got that jumper inside out.* | *Her umbrella blew inside out.* | *I always **turn** my jeans **inside out** to wash them.* **3 turn a room/building etc inside out** to search a place very thoroughly by moving everything that is in it: *The drug squad turned the apartment inside out.* **4 know sth inside out** *BrE,* **know sth inside and out** *AmE* to know something in great detail: *She knows her subject inside out.* **5 on the inside** someone who is on the inside is a member of a group or an organization: *Someone on the inside must have helped with the robbery.* **6 on the inside** *BrE* if a car passes another car on the inside, it passes on the side that is away from the driver **7 sb's inside/insides** informal someone's stomach: *My insides are beginning to complain about the lack of food.*

in·side³ /ˈɪnsaɪd/ adj **1** in or facing the inner part of something: *the inside pages of the newspaper* | *the inside pocket of his jacket* **2 inside information/the inside story etc** information that is available only to people who are part of a particular group or organization: *Police believe the robbers may have had inside information.* **3 the inside lane** *BrE* the LANE that is furthest away from the middle of the road

in·sid·er /ɪnˈsaɪdə $ -ər/ n [C] someone who has a special knowledge of a particular organization because they are part of it; ⬛ **outsider**: *an insider's view of the way that a Japanese company works*

in·sid·er ˈtrading also **in·sider ˈdealing** n [U] the crime of using secret information that you have about a company or knowledge of a situation to buy or sell SHARES at a profit

inside ˈtrack n [C] **1** the part of a circular track for racing that is nearest to the centre of the circle and is therefore shorter **2** *AmE* a position that gives someone an advantage over the people they are competing against: *the inside track to success in business*

in·sid·i·ous /ɪnˈsɪdiəs/ adj formal an insidious change or problem spreads gradually without being noticed, and causes serious harm: *an insidious trend towards censorship of the press* **—insidiously** adv **—insidiousness** n [U]

in·sight /ˈɪnsaɪt/ n **1** [C] a sudden clear understanding of something or part of something, especially a complicated situation or idea: [+into] *The article gives us a real **insight** into the causes of the present economic crisis.* | *The research **provides** new **insights** into the way we process language.* **2** [U] the ability to understand and realize what people or situations are really like: *a woman of great insight*

in·sight·ful /ˈɪnsaɪtfəl/ adj able to understand or showing that you understand what a situation or person is really like; ⬛ **perceptive**: *an insightful analysis*

in·sig·ni·a /ɪnˈsɪɡniə/ n plural **insignia** [C] a BADGE or sign that shows what official or military rank someone has, or which group or organization they belong to; → **emblem**: *the royal insignia* | *military insignia*

in·sig·nif·i·cant /ˌɪnsɪɡˈnɪfɪkənt◀/ adj too small or unimportant to consider or worry about; ⬛ **trivial**: *You realize that your problems are insignificant in comparison.* | **insignificant** number/amount **—insignificantly** adv **—insignificance** n [U]

in·sin·cere /ˌɪnsɪnˈsɪə $ -ˈsɪr◀/ adj pretending to be pleased, sympathetic etc, especially by saying nice things, but not really meaning what you say: *an insincere smile* | *an offer which she knew to be impractical and insincere* **—insincerely** adv **—insincerity** /ˌɪnsɪnˈserəti/ n [U]

in·sin·u·ate /ɪnˈsɪnjueɪt/ v [T] **1** to say something which seems to mean something unpleasant without saying it openly, especially suggesting that someone is being dishonest; ⬛ **imply**: **insinuate that** *Are you insinuating that the money was stolen?* | *What are you trying to insinuate?* **2** formal to gradually gain someone's love, trust etc by pretending to be friendly and sincere: *He managed to insinuate his way into her affections.* | **insinuate yourself into sth** *He insinuated himself into Mehmet's confidence.* **3** formal to move yourself or a part of body into a place: *a large cat insinuated itself through the gap*

in·sin·u·a·tion /ɪnˌsɪnjuˈeɪʃən/ n **1** [C] something that someone says which seems to mean something unpleasant, but does not say this openly: *She rejected the insinuation that she was partly to blame.* **2** [U] when someone says something insinuating

in·sip·id /ɪnˈsɪpɪd/ adj **1** food or drink that is insipid does not have much taste; ⬛ **bland**: *an insipid pasta dish* **2** not interesting, exciting, or attractive: *insipid colours* **—insipidly** adv **—insipidness, insipidity** /ˌɪnsɪˈpɪdəti/ n [U]

in·sist S3 W2 /ɪnˈsɪst/ v [I]
1 to say firmly and often that something is true, especially when other people think it may not be true: **insist (that)** *Mike insisted that he was right.* | *His friends insisted he had no connection with drugs.* | [+on] *She kept insisting on her innocence.*
2 to demand that something should happen: *Stay for supper – I insist!* | **insist (that)** *They insisted that everyone should come to the party.* | *He insisted I should take a taxi and offered to pay for it.* | *We insist on the highest standards of cleanliness in the hotel.* | *insist*

1 000, 2 000, 3 000, most frequent words in S spoken and W written English

on/upon doing sth *He insisted upon checking everything himself.*
3 if you insist *spoken* used when agreeing to do something that you do not really want to do: *'Why don't you call them up today?' 'Oh, if you insist!'*
4 insist on doing sth to keep doing something, especially something that is inconvenient or annoying: *She will insist on washing her hair just when I want to have a bath.*

in·sis·tence /ɪnˈsɪstəns/ *n* [U] when you demand that something should happen and refuse to let anyone say no: **insistence that** *his insistence that they discuss the problem* | [+on] *an insistence on punctuality* | **at sb's insistence** (=because someone insisted) *At her father's insistence, she joined them for a drink.*

in·sis·tent /ɪnˈsɪstənt/ *adj* **1** demanding firmly and repeatedly that something should happen: **insistent that** *She was insistent that they should all meet for dinner.* | [+on] *They were insistent on good manners.* **2** making a continuous pattern of sounds that is difficult to ignore: *the music's insistent rhythm* —**insistently** *adv: The bell rang again insistently.*

in si·tu /ɪn ˈsɪtjuː $ ɪn ˈsaɪtuː/ *adv* if something remains in situ, it remains in its usual place

in·so·far /ˌɪnsəˈfɑː $ -ˈfɑːr/ *adv* → **in so far as** at FAR¹ (20)

in·sole /ˈɪnsəʊl $ -soʊl/ *n* [C] the inside part of a shoe, or a piece of cloth, leather etc which is the same shape as your foot that you put inside your shoe

in·so·lent /ˈɪnsələnt/ *adj* rude and not showing any respect: *an insolent tone of voice* | *You insolent child!* —**insolently** *adv* —**insolence** *n* [U]

in·sol·u·ble /ɪnˈsɒljɵbəl $ ɪnˈsɑːl-/ *adj* **1** an insoluble problem is or seems impossible to solve: *insoluble conflicts within the department* **2** an insoluble substance does not become a liquid when you put it into a liquid; ▣ **soluble**; → **dissolve**

in·sol·va·ble /ɪnˈsɒlvəbəl $ ɪnˈsɑːl-/ *adj especially AmE* an insolvable problem is or seems impossible to solve; ▣ **insoluble** —**insolvably** *adv*

in·sol·vent /ɪnˈsɒlvənt $ ɪnˈsɑːl-/ *adj* not having enough money to pay what you owe; ▣ **bankrupt**: *The company was later declared insolvent* (=officially said to be insolvent). —**insolvency** *n* [C,U]

in·som·ni·a /ɪnˈsɒmniə $ ɪnˈsɑːm-/ *n* [U] if you suffer from insomnia, you are not able to sleep

in·som·ni·ac /ɪnˈsɒmniæk $ ɪnˈsɑːm-/ *n* [C] someone who cannot sleep easily —**insomniac** *adj*

in·so·much /ˌɪnsəʊˈmʌtʃ $ -soʊ-/ *adv formal* **1 insomuch that** *especially AmE* to such a degree that **2** another form of the word INASMUCH

in·sou·ci·ance /ɪnˈsuːsiəns/ *n* [U] *formal* a cheerful feeling of not caring or worrying about anything; ▣ **nonchalance**: *an air of insouciance* —**insouciant** *adj* —**insouciantly** *adv*

in·spect /ɪnˈspekt/ *v* [T] **1** to examine something carefully in order to find out more about it or to find out what is wrong with it: *I got out of the car to inspect the damage.* | *Police inspected the scene and interviewed all the staff.* | **inspect sth for sth** *The police will inspect the venue for safety.*; → see box at CONTROL² **2** to make an official visit to a building, organization etc to check that everything is satisfactory and that rules are being obeyed: *The building is regularly inspected by the fire-safety officer.* | *General Allenby arrived to inspect the troops.*

in·spec·tion ⑤³ /ɪnˈspekʃən/ *n* [C,U]
1 an official visit to a building or organization to check that everything is satisfactory and that rules are being obeyed: [+of] *regular inspections of the prison* | *An inspection was carried out at the school.* | **tour of inspection** (=an official visit to inspect something)
2 a careful examination of something to find out more about it or to check for anything wrong: **for inspection**

Copies of the documents are available for inspection (=people can look at them) *at local libraries.* | **(on) close/closer inspection** (=when looked at in detail) *However, on closer inspection, a number of problems emerged.* | *Close inspection of the plane's engines revealed several small defects.*

in·spec·tor /ɪnˈspektə $ -ər/ *n* [C] **1** an official whose job is to check that something is satisfactory and that rules are being obeyed: *ticket inspectors* | *a Health and Safety inspector* | *Standards of discipline at the school were strongly criticized in the inspector's report.* **2** a police officer of middle rank: *Inspector Blake* → CHIEF INSPECTOR

in·spec·tor·ate /ɪnˈspektərɪt/ *n* [C] *BrE* the group of INSPECTORS who officially inspect schools, factories etc

in·spector of 'taxes *n* [C] *BrE* a government official who calculates what tax each person should pay; ▣ **tax inspector**

in·spi·ra·tion /ˌɪnspɪˈreɪʃən/ *n* [C,U]
1 a good idea about what you should do, write, say etc, especially one which you get suddenly

---

provide inspiration (for sth)
seek/look for inspiration
draw/take inspiration (from sb/sth) (=get inspiration from someone or something)
inspiration comes from sb/sth
have an inspiration
flash of inspiration
source of inspiration (for/to sb)
divine inspiration (=inspiration from God)
creative/poetic/artistic inspiration

---

*The Malvern Hills have **provided inspiration** for many artists and musicians over the decades.* | *He raised his eyes to the altar as if **seeking inspiration**.* | *He **draws inspiration from** ordinary scenes.* | *Mary Quant's **inspiration comes from** the glam style of the 70s.* | *He had a sudden **flash of inspiration**.* | *He has always been a **source of inspiration** for me.*

2 a person, experience, place etc that gives you new ideas for something you do: *The seascapes of Cape Cod were her inspiration.* | [+for/behind] *He was the inspiration for Wordsworth's poem 'The Old Huntsman'.*
3 be an inspiration to sb to make someone feel encouraged to be as good, successful etc as possible: *People like Tara are an inspiration to us all.*
4 under the inspiration of sb used to say who made a person or group want to do something: *the spread of improved nursing under the inspiration of Florence Nightingale*

in·spi·ra·tion·al /ˌɪnspɪˈreɪʃənəl◂/ *adj* providing encouragement or new ideas for what you should do: *Jones proved an inspirational figure in Welsh rugby.*

in·spire /ɪnˈspaɪə $ -ˈspaɪr/ *v* [T] **1** to encourage someone by making them feel confident and eager to do something: *We need someone who can inspire the team.* | **inspire sb to do sth** *He inspired many young people to take up the sport.* | **inspire sb to sth** *I hope this success will inspire you to greater efforts.* | *Inspired by the sunny weather, I decided to explore the woods.* **2** to make someone have a particular feeling or react in a particular way: *Gandhi's quiet dignity inspired great respect.* | **inspire confidence** (=make people feel confident because they trust your ability) *His driving hardly inspires confidence.* | *The hospital's record does not inspire confidence.* **3** to give someone the idea for something, especially a story, painting, poem etc: *The story was inspired by a chance meeting with an old Russian duke.* | *a range of designs inspired by wild flowers* **4** technical to breathe in

in·spired /ɪnˈspaɪəd $ -ˈspaɪrd/ *adj* **1** having very exciting special qualities that are better than anyone or anything else: *an inspired leader* | *Wordsworth's most inspired poems* | *an inspired performance* **2 inspired guess/choice etc** a good or successful choice, guess etc that is based on inspiration not facts: *In an inspired move, they took on the young and relatively inexperienced Ray Unwin as director.*

3 politically/religiously etc inspired started for political, religious etc reasons: *We suspect that the violence was politically inspired.*

in·spir·ing /ɪnˈspaɪərɪŋ $ -ˈspaɪr-/ *adj* giving people a feeling of excitement and a desire to do something great; 🔄 **uninspiring**: *inspiring music* | *King was a great orator and an inspiring leader.*

in·sta·bil·i·ty /ˌɪnstəˈbɪləti/ *n plural* **instabilities** [C,U] **1** when a situation is not certain because there is the possibility of sudden change; 🔄 **stability**: *the instability of the market* | *political instability in the region* **2** mental problems that are likely to cause sudden changes of behaviour; → **unstable**: *nervous instability*

in·stall W3 /ɪnˈstɔːl $ -ˈstɒːl/ *v* [T] **1** to put a piece of equipment somewhere and connect it so that it is ready to be used: *They've installed the new computer network at last.* | *Security cameras have been installed in the city centre.* **2** to add new software to a computer so that it is ready to be used; 🔄 **uninstall**: *We've installed new anti-virus software.* **3** to put someone in an important job or position, especially with a ceremony: *Churchill was installed as Chancellor of the university.* **4 install yourself in/at etc** to settle somewhere as if you are going to stay for a long time

in·stal·la·tion /ˌɪnstəˈleɪʃən/ *n* **1** [U] when someone fits a piece of equipment somewhere: *the installation and maintenance of alarm systems* **2** [C] a piece of equipment that has been fitted in its place: *The whole computer installation was nearly new.* **3** [C] a place where industrial or military equipment, machinery etc has been put: *nuclear installations* **4** [C] a piece of modern art which can include objects, light, sound etc **5** [U] *formal* the ceremony of putting someone in an important job or position: *the installation of the new bishop*

in'stallment ˌplan *n* [singular, U] *AmE* a system of paying for goods by a series of small regular payments; 🔄 **hire purchase** *BrE*

in·stal·ment also **installment** *AmE* /ɪnˈstɔːlmənt $ ɪnˈstɒːl-/ *n* [C] **1** one of a series of regular payments that you make until you have paid all the money you owe: *the second instalment of a loan* | *They're letting me pay for the washing machine by monthly instalments.* **2** one of the parts of a story that appears as a series of parts, especially in a magazine, newspaper etc: *the first instalment of a science fiction trilogy*

in·stance¹ S3 W2 /ˈɪnstəns/ *n* **1 for instance** for example: *We need to rethink the way we consume energy. Take, for instance, our approach to transport.* **2** [C] an example of a particular kind of situation: [+of] *They came across many instances of discrimination.* | **instance where/when** *instances where safety regulations have been breached* | *In this instance I think she was mistaken.* **3 in the first instance** at the beginning of a series of actions: *Anyone wishing to join the society should apply in the first instance to the secretary.* **4 at sb's instance** *formal* because of someone's wish or request

instance² *v* [T] *formal* to give something as an example: *She instanced the first chapter as proof of his skill in constructing scenes.*

in·stant¹ S3 /ˈɪnstənt/ *adj* **1** [usually before noun] happening or produced immediately; 🔄 **immediate**: *an instant success* | *a system that provides instant access to client information* | *The women took an instant dislike to one another.* | *The programme brought an instant response.* **2** [only before noun] instant food, coffee etc is in the form of powder and prepared by adding hot water: *instant coffee* | *instant soup*

instant² *n* [C] **1** [usually singular] a moment: *She caught his eye for an instant.* | *When the rain started,* *the crowd vanished in an instant* (=immediately). | [+of] *an instant of panic* | *She stepped towards the door and in that very same instant, the doorbell rang.* **2 the instant (that)** as soon as something happens: *The instant I saw him, I knew he was the man from the restaurant.* | *Jen burst out laughing the instant she walked in.* **3 this instant** *spoken* used when telling someone, especially a child, to do something immediately; 🔄 **now**: *Come here this instant!*

in·stan·ta·ne·ous /ˌɪnstənˈteɪniəs◂/ *adj* happening immediately: *modern methods of instantaneous communication* —**instantaneously** *adv*

in·stant·ly /ˈɪnstəntli/ *adv* immediately: *All four victims died instantly.* | *The information was instantly available.*

ˌinstant ˈmessaging *n* [U] a type of service available on the Internet that allows you to quickly exchange written messages with people that you know: *instant messaging services* —**instant message** *n* [C]

ˌinstant ˈreplay *n* [C] *AmE* an important moment in a sports game on television that is shown again immediately after it happens; 🔄 **action replay** *BrE*

in·stead S1 W1 /ɪnˈsted/ *adv* **1 instead of sb/sth** used to say what is not used, does not happen etc, when something else is used, happens etc: *You probably picked up my keys instead of yours.* | *Could I have tuna instead of ham?* | *Instead of being annoyed, he seemed quite pleased.* **2** used to say what is done, when you have just said that a particular thing is not done: *Geoff didn't study law. Instead, he decided to become an actor.* | *If Jo can't attend the meeting, I could go instead.*

in·step /ˈɪnstep/ *n* [C] **1** the raised part of your foot between your toes and your ANKLE **2** the part of a shoe that covers your instep

in·sti·gate /ˈɪnstəɡeɪt/ *v* [T] **1** to make a process start, especially one relating to law or politics: *Charles instigated a programme of reforms.* **2** to persuade someone do something bad or violent: *He accused union leaders of instigating the disturbances.* —**instigator** *n* [C]

in·sti·ga·tion /ˌɪnstəˈɡeɪʃən/ *n* [U] **1 at sb's instigation** also **at the instigation of sb** *formal* because of someone's suggestion, request, or demand: *an inquiry set up at the instigation of the White House* **2** the act of starting something

in·stil *BrE*; **instill** *AmE* /ɪnˈstɪl/ *v* **instilled**, **instilling** [T] to teach someone to think, behave, or feel in a particular way over a period of time: **instil confidence/fear/discipline etc into sb** *A manager's job is to instil determination into his players.*

in·stinct /ˈɪnstɪŋkt/ *n* [C,U] a natural tendency to behave in a particular way or a natural ability to know something, which is not learned; → **intuition**: [+for] *Animals have a natural instinct for survival.* | **instinct to do sth** *the human instinct to form relationships* | **by instinct** *Birds build nests by instinct.* | **sexual/maternal/survival instinct** | *Her instinct told her that something was wrong.* | **sb's first instinct** (=what someone feels like doing first when something happens) *His first instinct was to rush back to Isobel.*

in·stinc·tive /ɪnˈstɪŋktɪv/ *adj* based on instinct and not involving thought: *a mother's instinctive love* —**instinctively** *adv*: *He knew instinctively that she would not forgive him.*

in·stinc·tu·al /ɪnˈstɪŋktʃuəl/ *adj technical* instinctive

in·sti·tute¹ W2 /ˈɪnstəˌtjuːt $ -tuːt/ *n* [C] an organization that has a particular purpose such as scientific or educational work, or the building where this organization is based; → **academy**: *research institutes* | [+of/for] *the Institute for Space Studies*

institute² *v* [T] *formal* to introduce or start a system, rule, legal process etc: *We had no choice but to institute court proceedings against the airline.*

in·sti·tu·tion W1 /ˌɪnstɪ̍'tjuːʃən $ -'tuː-/ n
1 [C] a large organization that has a particular kind of work or purpose: **financial/educational/research etc institution** *the Government and other political institutions* | *powerful institutions such as world banks* | *the Institution of Electrical Engineers*
2 [C] an important system of organization in society that has existed for a long time: *social institutions such as the family and religion* | **the institution of marriage/monarchy etc** *The scandal threatened to undermine the institution of the Presidency.*
3 [C] a building that people are sent to when they need to be looked after, for example old people or children with no parents – often used to show disapproval: *I was determined not to put my mother in an institution.* | *a mental institution* (=for the mentally ill)
4 [U] when something is started or introduced, especially something relating to the law or politics: [+of] *the institution of divorce proceedings*
5 be an institution if a person, place, event etc is an institution, they have been an important part of a place for a very long time – often used humorously: *The British pub isn't just somewhere to drink – it's an institution.*

in·sti·tu·tion·al /ˌɪnstɪ̍'tjuːʃənəl $ -'tuː-/ adj [usually before noun] **1** relating to an institution: *children in institutional care* **2** institutional attitudes and behaviour have existed for a long time in an organization and have become accepted as normal even though they are bad: *accusations of institutional racism in the police force*

in·sti·tu·tion·al·ize also **-ise** BrE /ˌɪnstɪ̍'tjuːʃənəlaɪz $ -'tuː-/ v [T] **1** old-fashioned to put someone in an institution for old people, a mental hospital etc **2** to make something a normal, accepted part of a social system or organization: *the struggle to institutionalize equality for women*

in·sti·tu·tion·al·ized also **-ised** BrE /ˌɪnstɪ̍'tjuːʃənəlaɪzd $ -'tuː-/ adj **1** institutionalized attitudes and behaviour have existed for a long time in an organization and have become accepted as normal even though they are bad: **institutionalized racism/sexism etc** *institutionalized corruption within the state* **2** someone who has become institutionalized has lived for a long time in a prison, mental hospital etc and now cannot easily live outside one **3** forming part of a society or system: *institutionalised democracy*

in-'store adj [only before noun] happening within a large shop or store: *an in-store bakery*

in·struct /ɪn'strʌkt/ v [T] **1** to officially tell someone what to do; → **order**: **instruct sb to do sth** *His secretary was instructed to cancel all his engagements.* | **instruct (sb) that** *The judge immediately instructed that Beattie be released.* | *Eva went straight to the hotel, as instructed* (=as she had been told). | **instruct sb what to do** *He had instructed the slaves what to say when questioned.* **2** formal to teach someone something, or show them how to do something: **instruct sb in sth** *Greater effort is needed to instruct children in road safety.* | **instruct sb how to do sth** *Employees are instructed how to make a complaint.* **3** [usually passive] BrE formal to officially tell someone about something: **instruct sb that** *I was instructed that £20,000 had been paid into my account.* **4** BrE law to employ a lawyer to represent you in court

in·struc·tion S3 W2 /ɪn'strʌkʃən/ n
1 instructions [plural] the written information that tells you how to do or use something; → **directions**: *Install the machine according to the manufacturer's instructions.* | *Press enter and follow the on-screen instructions.* | [+for] *Both products come with detailed instructions for use.* | **instructions on (how to do) sth** *Are there any instructions on how to plant the trees?* | **instruction book/manual/leaflet etc** *Read the instruction book carefully.* ⚠ Do not say 'instructions how to do something' or 'instructions to do something'. Say **instruc-**tions on how to do something.
2 [C usually plural] a statement telling someone what they must do; → **orders**: **instructions to do sth** *He had specific instructions to check everyone's identity cards.* | **instructions that** *Mrs Edwards gave instructions that she was not to be disturbed.* | **on sb's instructions** (=having been told by someone to do something) *On the landlord's instructions, the barmaid refused to serve him.* | **My instructions are** (=I have been told) *to give the package to him personally.* | *Make sure you carry out the doctor's instructions.* | **be under instruction to do sth** (=have been told to do something) *The police were under instruction to fire if necessary.*
3 [U] formal teaching that you are given in a particular skill or subject: *religious instruction* | *driving instruction* | [+in] *The school gives instruction in First Aid.* | **under instruction** (=being taught) *This group of trainees is still under instruction.*

in·struc·tion·al /ɪn'strʌkʃənəl/ adj formal providing instruction: **instructional programmes/materials/techniques etc** *a free instructional video.*

in·struc·tive /ɪn'strʌktɪv/ adj providing a lot of useful information: *Thank you, that was very instructive.* | *an instructive comparison*

in·struc·tor /ɪn'strʌktə $ -ər/ n [C] **1** someone who teaches a sport or practical skill: *a driving instructor* | *ski instructors* **2** AmE someone who teaches in an American college or university and who has a rank below ASSISTANT PROFESSOR: *a social studies instructor*; → see box at TEACHER

in·stru·ment W2 /'ɪnstrʊmənt/ n [C]
1 TOOL a small tool used in work such as science or medicine: *surgical instruments*
2 MUSIC an object used for producing music, such as a piano or VIOLIN; ⬛ **musical instrument**; → **instrumental**, **instrumentalist**: *electronic instruments* | **brass/wind/percussion/stringed etc instrument**
3 FOR MEASURING a piece of equipment for measuring and showing distance, speed, temperature etc: *a failure of the flight instruments* | *sensitive earthquake-detecting instruments*
4 METHOD [usually singular] something or someone that is used to get a particular result: [+of] *Interest rates are an important instrument of economic policy.* | **instrument for (doing) sth** *Good management should be an instrument for innovation.*
5 FOR HURTING something that is used to hit or hurt someone: *Death was due to a blow on the head with a blunt instrument.* | **instrument of torture** (=an object used to make people suffer pain until they give information)
6 instrument of fate/God literary someone or something that is used by a power beyond our control

in·stru·men·tal¹ /ˌɪnstrʊ'mentl◂/ adj **1 be instrumental in (doing) sth** formal to be important in making something happen: *He was instrumental in developing links with European organizations.* **2** instrumental music is for instruments, not for voices —**instrumentally** adv

instrumental² n [C] a piece of music in which no voices are used, only instruments

in·stru·men·tal·ist /ˌɪnstrʊ'mentəlɪst/ n [C] someone who plays a musical instrument → **VOCALIST**

in·stru·men·ta·tion /ˌɪnstrʊmen'teɪʃən/ n [U]
1 the way in which a piece of music is arranged to be played by several different instruments **2** the set of instruments used to help in controlling a machine: *aircraft instrumentation*

'instrument ˌpanel n [C] the board in front of the pilot of an aircraft, where all the instruments are; → **dashboard**

in·sub·or·di·na·tion /ˌɪnsəbɔːdɪ̍'neɪʃən $ -ˌbɔːrdn'eɪ-/ n [U] formal when someone refuses to obey a person who has more authority than them; ⬛ **disobedience**: *Howell was fired for gross insubordination.* —**insubordinate** /ˌɪnsə'bɔːdɪnɪt $ -ɔːr-/ adj

in·sub·stan·tial /ˌɪnsəbˈstænʃəl◂/ *adj* **1** *formal* not solid, large, strong, or definite: *The evidence seemed very insubstantial.* | *an insubstantial meal* | *In the distance was the insubstantial outline of a ship.* **2** *literary* not existing as a real object or person: *insubstantial ghosts*

in·suf·fe·ra·ble /ɪnˈsʌfərəbəl/ *adj* extremely annoying or unpleasant; ⊟ **unbearable**: *an insufferable bully* | *The heat was insufferable.* —**insufferably** *adv*

in·suf·fi·cient /ˌɪnsəˈfɪʃənt◂/ *adj formal* not enough, or not great enough: *Insufficient resources have been devoted to the health service.* | [+for] *His salary was insufficient for their needs.* | **insufficient (sth) to do sth** *The heating is insufficient to kill the bacteria.* | *At the moment, there's insufficient evidence to arrest anyone.* —**insufficiently** *adv* —**insufficiency** *n* [singular, U]

in·su·lar /ˈɪnsjʊlə $ ˈɪnsələr, ˈɪnʃə-/ *adj* **1** interested in your own group, country, way of life etc and no others – used to show disapproval; → **parochial**: *an insular community* | *the insular world of the law* **2** *formal* relating to or like an island —**insularity** /ˌɪnsjʊˈlærəti $ -sə-, -ʃə-/ *n* [U]

in·su·late /ˈɪnsjʊleɪt $ ˈɪnsə-, ˈɪnʃə-/ *v* [T] **1** to cover or protect something with a material that stops electricity, sound, heat etc from getting in or out: **insulate sth from/against sth** *Pipes may need insulating against the cold.* | *an insulated attic* **2** to keep someone apart from particular experiences or influences, especially unpleasant ones: **insulate sb from sth** *The royal family tried to insulate him from the prying eyes of the media.*

insulating tape *n* [U] a type of sticky tape used for wrapping around electric wires to insulate them

in·su·la·tion /ˌɪnsjʊˈleɪʃən $ ˌɪnsə-/ *n* [U] **1** when something is insulated or someone insulates something: *Good insulation can save you money on heating bills.* **2** material used to insulate something, especially a building: *glass-fibre insulation*

in·su·la·tor /ˈɪnsjʊleɪtə $ ˈɪnsəleɪtər/ *n* [C] a material or object which does not allow electricity, heat, or sound to pass through it; ⊟ **conductor**: *Wood is an excellent insulator.*

in·su·lin /ˈɪnsjʊlɪn $ ˈɪnsə-/ *n* [U] a substance produced naturally by your body which allows sugar to be used for energy: *diabetic patients requiring insulin*

in·sult¹ /ɪnˈsʌlt/ *v* [T] **1** to offend someone by saying or doing something they think is rude: *Nobody insults my family and gets away with it!* | *I hope Andy won't be insulted if I don't come.* | **insult sb by doing sth** *They insult us by ignoring our complaints.* **2 insult sb's intelligence** to say or do something that suggests you think someone is stupid: *I won't insult your intelligence by lying. Yes, I told him.*

in·sult² /ˈɪnsʌlt/ *n* [C] **1** a remark or action that is offensive or deliberately rude: *She was shouting insults at her boyfriend.* | *$200 for all that work? It's an insult.* | *Their offer was so low I took it as an insult* (=thought it was meant to be an insult). **2 be an insult to sb's intelligence** to offend someone by being too simple or stupid: *Some advertising is an insult to our intelligence.* → **add insult to injury** at ADD (8)

in·sult·ing /ɪnˈsʌltɪŋ/ *adj* very rude and offensive to someone: *insulting remarks* | [+to] *Sexist language is insulting to women.* —**insultingly** *adv*

in·su·pe·ra·ble /ɪnˈsjuːpərəbəl◂ $ ɪnˈsuː-/ *adj formal* an insuperable difficulty or problem is impossible to deal with: *There were insuperable obstacles, and the plan was abandoned.* | *As usual, the hero was facing insuperable odds.*

in·sup·port·a·ble /ˌɪnsəˈpɔːtəbəl $ -ˈpɔːr-/ *adj formal* extremely bad or annoying; ⊟ **unbearable**: *insupportable pain* | *Her behaviour was insupportable.*

in·sur·ance [S3] [W2] /ɪnˈʃʊərəns $ -ˈʃʊr-/ *n* **1** [U] an arrangement with a company in which you pay them money, especially regularly, and they pay the costs if something bad happens, for example if you become ill or your car is damaged; → **assurance, third**

party insurance: *Your father took out insurance to cover the mortgage.* | **health/car/travel etc insurance** | [+against] *insurance against loss of income due to unemployment* | [+on/for] *Do you have insurance on your house and its contents?* | **claim (for) sth on your insurance** (=get an insurance company to pay for something) *We can probably claim the damage on our insurance.* → LIFE INSURANCE **2** [U] the business of providing insurance: *My brother works in insurance.* | **insurance company/group etc** *the insurance industry* **3** [U] *BrE* the money that you pay regularly to an insurance company; ⊟ **insurance premium**: [+on] *How much is the insurance on your car?* **4** [singular, U] protection against something bad happening: [+against] *An extra lock on the door is an added insurance against burglars.* → NATIONAL INSURANCE

in'surance ad,juster *n* [C] *AmE* someone who is employed by an insurance company to decide how much to pay people who have had an accident, had something stolen etc; ⊟ **loss adjuster** *BrE*

in'surance ,broker also **in'surance ,agent** *n* [C] someone who arranges and sells insurance as their job

in'surance ,policy *n plural* **insurance policies** [C] a written agreement for insurance with an insurance company

in'surance ,premium *n* [C] the money that you pay regularly to an insurance company

in·sure /ɪnˈʃʊə $ -ˈʃʊr/ *v* **1** [I,T] to buy insurance so that you will receive money if something bad happens to you, your family, your possessions etc: *Have you insured the contents of your home?* | **insure (sth/sb) against loss/damage/theft/sickness etc** *It is wise to insure your property against storm damage.* | **insure sth for £1000/$2000 etc** *You should insure the painting for at least £100,000.* **2** [T] to provide insurance for something or someone: *Many companies won't insure young drivers.* **3** an American spelling of ENSURE

insure (yourself) against sth *phr v* to protect yourself against the risk of something bad happening by planning or preparing: *Take advice to insure yourself against being misled.*

in·sured /ɪnˈʃʊəd $ -ˈʃʊrd/ *adj* **1** if someone or something is insured, there is insurance relating to them: *Apparently the jewellery wasn't insured.* | **insured to do sth** *I'm not insured to drive Anne's car.* **2 the insured** *law* the person or people who are insured

in·sur·er /ɪnˈʃʊərə $ -ˈʃʊrər/ *n* [C] a person or company that provides insurance

in·sur·gen·cy /ɪnˈsɜːdʒənsi $ -ɜːr-/ *n plural* **insurgencies** [C,U] *formal* an attempt by a group of people to take control of their government using force and violence; ⊟ **rebellion**; → **counterinsurgency**

in·sur·gent /ɪnˈsɜːdʒənt $ -ɜːr-/ *n* [C usually plural] *formal* one of a group of people fighting against the government of their own country, or against authority; ⊟ **rebel**: *communist insurgents* —**insurgent** *adj*

in·sur·mount·a·ble /ˌɪnsəˈmaʊntəbəl◂ $ -sər-/ *adj formal* an insurmountable difficulty or problem is too large or difficult to deal with: *The language difference proved an insurmountable barrier.*

in·sur·rec·tion /ˌɪnsəˈrekʃən/ *n* [C,U] *formal* an attempt by a large group of people within a country to take control using force and violence; ⊟ **rebellion**: [+against] *an armed insurrection against the party in power* —**insurrectionist** *n* [C]

in·tact /ɪnˈtækt/ *adj* [not before noun] not broken, damaged, or spoiled: *Only the medieval tower had remained intact.* | *His reputation survived intact.*

in·ta·gli·o /ɪnˈtɑːliəʊ $ -lioʊ/ *n plural* **intaglios** [C,U] the art of cutting patterns into a hard substance, or the pattern that you get by doing this

in·ter a·li·a /ˌɪntər ˈeɪliə, -ˈɑːliə/ adv formal among other things: The paper discussed, inter alia, political, economic, and social issues.

in·ter·breed /ˌɪntəˈbriːd $ -ər-/ v past tense and past participle **interbred** /-ˈbred/ [I + with, T] to produce young animals from parents of different breeds or groups; → **crossbreed, inbreeding**

in·ter·cede /ˌɪntəˈsiːd $ -ər-/ v [I] formal to speak in support of someone, especially in order to try to prevent them from being punished; → **intercession**: [+with] My good friend, Senator Bowie, interceded with the authorities on my behalf.

in·ter·cept /ˌɪntəˈsept $ -ər-/ v [T] to stop something or someone that is going from one place to another before they get there: an attempt to intercept drugs being smuggled over the border | Harker's phone calls had been intercepted. —**interception** /-ˈsepʃən/ n [C,U]

in·ter·ces·sion /ˌɪntəˈseʃən $ -tər-/ n formal **1** [U] when someone talks to a person in authority in order to prevent something bad happening to someone else; → **intercede 2** [C,U] a prayer asking for someone to be helped or cured

in·ter·change¹ /ˈɪntətʃeɪndʒ $ -ər-/ n **1** [C,U] an exchange, especially of ideas or thoughts: [+of] the interchange of ideas between students and staff **2** [C] a point where two or more MOTORWAYS or main roads meet

in·ter·change² /ˌɪntəˈtʃeɪndʒ $ -ər-/ v [I,T] to put each of two things in the place of the other, or to be exchanged in this way

in·ter·change·a·ble /ˌɪntəˈtʃeɪndʒəbəl $ -tər-/ adj things that are interchangeable can be used instead of each other: These two words are almost interchangeable. | a camera with interchangeable lenses —**interchangeably** adv —**interchangeability** /ˌɪntətʃeɪndʒəˈbɪl₃ti $ -tər-/ n [U]

in·ter·cit·y /ˌɪntəˈsɪti $ -tər-/ adj [only before noun] happening between two or more cities, or going from one city to another: intercity rivalry | intercity trains

in·ter·col·le·giate /ˌɪntəkəˈliːdʒₐt $ -tər-/ adj [only before noun] intercollegiate competitions, especially sports competitions, happen between teams from different colleges: intercollegiate athletics/sports etc

in·ter·com /ˈɪntəkɒm $ ˈɪntərkɑːm/ n [C] a communication system by which people in different parts of a building, aircraft etc can speak to each other: The pilot's voice came over the intercom.

in·ter·con·nect /ˌɪntəkəˈnekt $ -tər-/ v [I] **1** if two systems, places etc are interconnected, or if they interconnect, they are joined together: a series of interconnected lakes | interconnecting rooms | Our operating system can now interconnect with other networks. **2** if two facts, ideas, events etc are interconnected, or if they interconnect, they are related and one is affected by or caused by the other: In Freud's theory, the two areas of sexuality and violence are interconnected. | a number of separate but interconnected issues —**interconnection** /-ˈnekʃən/ n [C,U]: the interconnection between rich and poor countries

in·ter·con·ti·nen·tal /ˌɪntəkɒntₐˈnentl $ -tərkɑːn-/ adj going from one CONTINENT to another, or happening between two continents: an intercontinental flight | intercontinental trade

in·ter·course /ˈɪntəkɔːs $ ˈɪntərkɔːrs/ n [U] formal **1** also **sexual intercourse** the act of having sex **2** an exchange of ideas, feelings etc which make people or groups understand each other better: social intercourse

in·ter·cut /ˌɪntəˈkʌt $ -ər-/ past tense and past participle **intercut**, present participle **intercutting** v [T usually passive] if a film is intercut with particular pictures, sounds, or music, they appear in different places during the film

in·ter·de·nom·i·na·tio·nal /ˌɪntədₐˈnɒmₐˈneɪʃənəl $ ˌɪntərdₐˈnɑː-/ adj between or involving Christians from different groups

in·ter·de·part·men·tal /ˌɪntəˌdiːpɑːˈmentl $ ˌɪntərdₐˌpɑːrtˈmentl/ adj [usually before noun] between or involving different departments of a company, government etc: intense interdepartmental rivalry

in·ter·de·pen·dence /ˌɪntədₐˈpendəns $ -tər-/ also **in·ter·de·pen·den·cy** /-dənsi/ n [C usually singular, U] a situation in which people or things depend on each other: [+of] the interdependence of our body's immune and nervous systems

in·ter·de·pen·dent /ˌɪntədₐˈpendənt‹ $ -tər-/ adj depending on or necessary to each other: countries with interdependent economies —**interdependently** adv

in·ter·dict /ˈɪntədɪkt $ -ər-/ n [C] **1** law an official order from a court telling someone not to do something **2** technical a punishment in the Roman Catholic Church, by which someone is not allowed to take part in church ceremonies —**interdict** /ˌɪntəˈdɪkt $ -ər-/ v [T] —**interdiction** /-ˈdɪkʃən/ n [C,U]

in·ter·dis·ci·plin·ary /ˌɪntəˌdɪsₐˈplɪnəri $ ˌɪntər ˈdɪsəpləneri/ adj involving ideas, information, or people from different subjects or areas of study: an interdisciplinary research centre

in·terest¹ S2 W1 /ˈɪntr₃st/ n

1 [singular, U] if you have an interest in something or someone, you want to know or learn more about them

have an interest in sth
show interest (in sth)
express (an) interest (in sth) (=say that you are interested in something or want to buy it)
take an interest (in sth) (=be interested in something)
have no interest in sth
lose interest (in sth) (=stop being interested)
arouse/generate/attract interest (=make people interested)
pique sb's interest AmE (=make someone interested)
great/keen interest
abiding interest (=an interest you have had for a long time)
lack of interest
with interest

[+in] My parents encouraged my interest in science. | I'd recommend this book to anyone who **has an interest in** jazz. | Ben has **shown an interest in** learning French. | My mother had never **expressed** any interest in the garden. | Babies soon begin to **take an interest** in the world around them. | John appeared to **have no interest in** girls. | I watched the first few episodes, but soon **lost interest**. | The last round of bidding **aroused** considerable **interest**. | Our survey reveals a disturbing **lack of interest** in teacher training. | I read your article **with** great **interest**.

2 [C usually plural] an activity that you enjoy doing or a subject that you enjoy studying: His interests include walking and golf. | As a biologist, my main interest has been human genetics. | Her **outside interests** (=interests that are not part of her work) were numerous.

3 [U] a quality or feature of something that attracts your attention or makes you want to know more about it: A Persian rug will **add** colour and **interest** to your hallway. | be of (no) interest (to sb) (=be interesting or not interesting to someone) It's a book that will be of interest to a wide range of readers. | What you do in your private life is of no interest to me. | art galleries, museums and other **places of interest** | topics of general interest (=that everyone wants to know about)

4 [U] **a)** the extra money that you must pay back when you borrow money: [+on] The interest on the loan is 16% per year. | How much are the monthly interest payments? **b)** money paid to you by a bank or financial institution when you keep money in an account there: an account that **pays** higher interest | The more you save, the more interest you'll **earn**. → COMPOUND INTEREST, INTEREST RATE, SIMPLE INTEREST

5 [C usually plural, U] the things that bring advantages to someone or something: **protect/look after/safeguard sb's interests** *The regulations were introduced in order to safeguard the interests of local fishing communities.* | **be in sb's (best) interest(s) (to do sth)** (=be the best thing for someone) *The court decided that it was in the girl's best interests to remain with her grandparents.* | **have sb's (best) interests at heart** (=care about someone and want to do what is best for them) *He has your best interests at heart, you know.* | *We've got to balance economic interests and environmental interests.*

6 be in the national/public interest to be good or necessary for the safety or success of a country and its people: *I believe it is in the public interest that these facts are made known.*

7 in the interest(s) of justice/safety/efficiency etc in order to make a situation or system fair, safe etc: *The race was postponed in the interests of safety.*

8 (just) out of interest/as a matter of interest *spoken* used to say that you are asking a question only because you are interested and not because you need to know: *Just out of interest, how much did they offer you?*

9 [C] if you have an interest in a particular company or industry, you own shares in it: *The company is believed to be keen to sell its extensive brewing interests.* | *His business interests are spread throughout Europe.* | **controlling interest** (=enough shares to control what decisions are taken) *In 1986 GM acquired a controlling interest in the sports car maker Lotus.*

10 [C usually plural] a group of people in the same business who share aims or ideas: *Farming interests now dominate many of the National Park committees.* | *The majority of Brazil's huge commercial interests support the measure.* | *the need to reform the political system and reduce the influence of* **special interests** (=groups who are concerned about particular subjects)

11 have no interest in doing sth to not want to do something: *I have no interest in continuing this conversation.*

12 declare an interest (in sth) to officially state that you are connected with something or someone, and so cannot be completely fair and independent when making a decision involving them

13 human interest/love interest the part of a story, film, or event which is interesting because it shows things about people's lives or romantic relationships: *As a trainee reporter, she spent most of her time on* **human interest stories.** → **conflict of interest** at CONFLICT¹ (6); → SELF-INTEREST; → **vested interest** at VESTED (1)

interest² *v* [T] **1** to make someone want to pay attention to something and find out more about it: *Here's an article which might interest you.* | **What interests me is** *all the history of these places.* | **It may interest you to know that** *a number of scholarships are available.* **2 interest yourself in sth** *formal* to give something a lot of attention because you want to find out more about it: *He had always interested himself in foreign affairs.* **3** to try to persuade someone to buy, do, or eat something: **interest sb in sth** *The salesman tried to interest me in the higher-priced model.* | **Could I interest you in a drink/dessert etc?** (=used as a polite way of offering someone a drink etc)

in·terest·ed [S1] [W2] /'ɪntrɪ̩stɪ̩d/ *adj*
1 giving a lot of attention to something because you want to find out more about it or because you enjoy it; ☒ **uninterested, bored:** [+in] *I've always been interested in music.* | *All she's interested in is clothes.* | *I wasn't sure if he was really interested or if he was just being polite.* | **interested to hear/know/see etc** *I'd be very interested to hear your opinion.*
2 if you are interested in doing or having something, you want to do it or have it: *I've got a spare ticket for the opera if you're interested.* | **interested in (doing) sth** *Sheila's interested in starting her own business.* | *Would you be interested in a second-hand car?*
3 interested party/group a person or group that is directly or personally concerned with a situation and

---

is likely to be affected by its results; ☒ **disinterested:** *All interested parties are invited to attend the meeting.* —**interestedly** *adv*

similar words: **intrigued, curious, absorbed**
very interested: **fascinated, engrossed, enthralled, spellbound**

interest-free *adj* an interest-free LOAN has no interest charged on it: *interest-free credit*

interest group *n* [C] a group of people who join together to try to influence the government in order to protect their own particular rights, advantages etc

in·terest·ing [S1] [W2] /'ɪntrɪ̩stɪŋ/ *adj* if something is interesting, you give it your attention because it seems unusual or exciting or provides information that you did not know about; ☒ **uninteresting, boring:** *That's an interesting question.* | *a really interesting TV programme* | **find sth interesting** *I found his talk very interesting.* | *Did you meet any interesting people?* | **it is interesting to see/know etc** *It will be interesting to see what happens when he gets a bit older.* | **It's interesting that** *no one remembers seeing the car.*

similar words: **absorbing, intriguing**
very interesting: **fascinating, gripping, riveting, engrossing, enthralling, spellbinding**

⚠ Do not confuse **interested**, which describes a feeling, and **interesting**, which describes something that makes you feel interested: *Are you interested in ballet?* | *an interesting talk on photography*

in·terest·ing·ly /'ɪntrɪ̩stɪŋli/ *adv* **1** [sentence adverb] used to introduce a fact that you think is interesting: *Interestingly, none of their three children ever married.* | **Interestingly enough,** *Pearson made no attempt to deny the rumour.* **2** in an interesting way: *His essay was clearly and interestingly written.*

interest rate *n* [C] the PERCENTAGE amount charged by a bank etc when you borrow money or paid to you by a bank when you keep money in an account there

in·ter·face¹ /'ɪntəfeɪs $ -ər-/ *n* [C] **1** the way in which you see the information from a computer program on a screen, or how you type information into the program; → **GUI** **2** *technical* the part of a computer system that connects two different machines **3** the way in which two subjects, events etc affect each other: [+between] *The book deals with the interface between accountancy and law.* **4** *technical* the surface where two things touch each other

interface² *v* **1** [I,T + with] *technical* if you interface two parts of a computer system, or if they interface, you connect them **2** [I + with] if two people or groups interface with each other, they communicate with each other and work together

in·ter·faith /'ɪntəfeɪθ $ -ər-/ *adj* [only before noun] between or involving people of different religions: *an interfaith Thanksgiving service*

in·ter·fere /ˌɪntə'fɪə $ -tər'fɪr/ *v* [I] to deliberately get involved in a situation where you are not wanted or needed; ☒ **meddle:** *My daughter-in-law said that I was interfering, but I was only trying to help.* | [+in] *It's not the church's job to interfere in politics.*

interfere with sth/sb *phr v* **1** to prevent something from succeeding or from happening in the way that was planned: *Anxiety can interfere with children's performance at school.* **2** if something interferes with a radio or television broadcast, it spoils the sound or picture that you receive **3** *BrE* to touch a child sexually: *He was arrested for interfering with young boys.*

in·ter·fer·ence /ˌɪntə'fɪərəns $ -tər'fɪr-/ *n* [U] **1** an act of interfering: [+in] *I resent his interference in my work.* | *Industrial relations should be free from state interference.* **2** unwanted noise on the radio, television, or on the telephone, or faults in the television

[1] 000, [2] 000, [3] 000, most frequent words in [S]poken and [W]ritten English

picture **3** *especially AmE* the act of blocking or touching another player in a sports game, for example by standing in front of them or holding on to them, when you are not supposed to; ▤ **obstruction** *BrE* **4 run interference** *AmE* **a)** to protect a player who has the ball in American football by blocking players from the opposing team **b)** to help someone to achieve something by dealing with people or problems that might cause them trouble

in·ter·fer·on /ˌɪntəˈfɪərɒn $ ˌɪntərˈfɪrɑːn/ *n* [U] a chemical substance that is produced by your body to fight against VIRUSES that cause disease

in·ter·ga·lac·tic /ˌɪntəɡəˈlæktɪk◂ $ -tər-/ *adj* between the large groups of stars in space

in·ter·gen·e·ra·tion·al /ˌɪntədʒenəˈreɪʃənəl $ -tər-/ *adj* between or involving people from different age groups: *intergenerational communication*

in·ter·gov·ern·men·tal /ˌɪntəɡʌvəˈmentl, -vən- $ ˌɪntərɡʌvərn-/ *adj* [only before noun] between or involving governments of different countries: *an intergovernmental conference*

in·ter·im¹ /ˈɪntərɪm/ *adj* [only before noun] **1** intended to be used or accepted for a short time only, until something or someone final can be made or found: *an interim report* | *He received an interim payment of £10,000.* | *He was appointed president until an interim government was established.* **2 interim period** the period of time between two events: *During the interim period, air quality has deteriorated.*

interim² *n* **in the interim** in the period of time between two events; ▤ **meanwhile**: *The child will be adopted but a relative is looking after him in the interim.*

in·te·ri·or¹ /ɪnˈtɪəriə $ -ˈtɪriər/ *n* **1** [C usually singular] the inner part or inside of something; ▣ **exterior**: *The interior of the church was dark.* | *the car's warm interior* **2 the interior** the part of a country that is farthest away from the coast: *The interior of the country is mainly desert.* **3 Minister/Department of the Interior** the government minister or department that deals with matters within a country rather than abroad

interior² *adj* [only before noun] inside or indoors; ▣ **exterior**: *The interior walls are all painted white.*

in·terior 'decorator *n* [C] an interior designer —**interior decorating** also **interior decoration** *n* [U]

in·terior de'signer *n* [C] someone whose job is to plan and choose the colours, materials, furniture etc for the inside of buildings, especially people's houses —**interior design** *n* [U]

in·ter·ject /ˌɪntəˈdʒekt $ -ər-/ *v* [I,T] *formal* to interrupt what someone else is saying with a sudden remark: *'That's absolute rubbish!' he interjected.*

in·ter·jec·tion /ˌɪntəˈdʒekʃən $ -ər-/ *n* **1** [C] *technical* a word or phrase used to express a strong feeling such as shock, pain, or pleasure; ▤ **exclamation 2** [C,U] *formal* an interruption or the act of interrupting

in·ter·laced /ˌɪntəˈleɪst◂ $ -ər-/ *adj* things that are interlaced are joined together, with parts of the one thing going over or around parts of the other: *patterns of interlaced squares* —**interlace** *v* [I,T]

in·ter·link /ˌɪntəˈlɪŋk $ -ər-/ *v* [I,T] to connect or be connected with something else: *a chain of interlinking loops*

in·ter·lock /ˌɪntəˈlɒk $ ˌɪntərˈlɑːk/ *v* [I,T] if two or more things interlock, or if they are interlocked, they fit firmly together: *a puzzle with 500 interlocking pieces*

in·ter·loc·u·tor /ˌɪntəˈlɒkjʊtə $ ˌɪntərˈlɑːkjʊtər/ *n* [C] *formal* your interlocutor is the person you are speaking to

in·ter·lop·er /ˈɪntələupə $ -tərloupər/ *n* [C] someone who enters a place or group where they should not be

in·ter·lude /ˈɪntəluːd $ -ər-/ *n* [C] **1** a period of time between two events or situations, during which something different happens: *a brief interlude of peace before a return to the battlefield* **2** a short period of time between the parts of a play, concert etc; ▤ **intermission 3** a short piece of music, talk etc used to fill such a period **4** a short romantic or sexual meeting or relationship: *a romantic interlude*

in·ter·mar·ry /ˌɪntəˈmæri $ -ər-/ *v* **intermarried, intermarrying, intermarries** [I] **1** if people from two social, racial, or religious groups intermarry, people from one group marry people from the other: [+**with**] *Over the centuries these Greeks intermarried with the natives.* **2** to marry someone within your own group or family: *It is not unusual for royal cousins to intermarry.* —**intermarriage** /-ˈmærɪdʒ/ *n* [C,U]: *intermarriage between ethnic groups*

in·ter·me·di·a·ry /ˌɪntəˈmiːdiəri $ ˌɪntərˈmiːdieri/ *n* plural **intermediaries** [C] a person or organization that tries to help two other people or groups to agree with each other; → **go-between**: *Jackson acted as an intermediary between the two parties.* —**intermediary** *adj* [only before noun]: *an intermediary role in the talks*

in·ter·me·di·ate¹ /ˌɪntəˈmiːdiət◂ $ -tər-/ *adj* **1 a)** an intermediate class, course etc is at a level of knowledge or skill that is between the basic level and the advanced level: *a book aimed at students at the intermediate level and above* **b)** intermediate students, sports players etc have reached a level of knowledge or skill that is between the basic level and the advanced level: *intermediate learners of English* **2** an intermediate stage in a process of development is between two other stages: *an intermediate stage during which the disease is dormant*

intermediate² *n* [C] a student, sports player etc who has reached a level of knowledge or skill that is between the basic level and the advanced level: *a ski resort particularly suited to beginners and intermediates*

inter'mediate ˌschool *n* [C] *AmE* a JUNIOR HIGH SCHOOL or MIDDLE SCHOOL

in·ter·ment /ɪnˈtɜːmənt $ -ɜːr-/ *n* [C,U] *formal* the act of burying a dead body; ▤ **burial**; → **inter**

in·ter·mi·na·ble /ɪnˈtɜːmɪnəbəl $ -ɜːr-/ *adj* very long and boring; ▤ **endless**: *interminable delays* —**interminably** *adv*: *an interminably long speech*

in·ter·min·gle /ˌɪntəˈmɪŋɡəl $ -tər-/ *v* [I,T usually passive] to mix together or mix something with something else: *The pain and the anger were intermingled.*

in·ter·mis·sion /ˌɪntəˈmɪʃən $ -tər-/ *n* [C] *especially AmE* a short period of time between the parts of a play, concert etc; ▤ **interlude**; ▤ **interval** *BrE*

in·ter·mit·tent /ˌɪntəˈmɪtənt◂ $ -tər-/ *adj* stopping and starting often and for short periods; ▤ **sporadic**: *The weather forecast is for sun, with intermittent showers.* —**intermittently** *adv*

in·ter·mix /ˌɪntəˈmɪks $ -ər-/ *v* [I,T] to mix together, or mix things together

in·tern¹ /ɪnˈtɜːn $ -ɜːrn/ *v* [T] to put someone in prison without charging them with a crime, for political reasons or during a war; → **internee, internment**

in·tern² /ˈɪntɜːn $ -ɜːrn/ *n* [C] *AmE* **1** someone who has nearly finished training as a doctor and is working in a hospital; ▤ **houseman** *BrE*; → **internship 2** someone, especially a student, who works for a short time in a particular job in order to gain experience; → **internship**

in·ter·nal /ɪnˈtɜːnl $ -ɜːr-/ *adj* [usually before noun] **1** within a particular country; ▤ **domestic**; ▣ **external**: *We have no interest in interfering in the internal affairs of other countries.* | *the threat to internal security* | *internal markets* **2** within a company or organization rather than outside it; ▣ **external**: *There's to be an internal inquiry into the whole affair.* | *the internal mail*

3 inside your body; ◨ **external**: internal organs/injuries
4 inside something rather than outside; ◨ **external**: *They've knocked down a couple of internal walls.*
5 existing in your mind; ◧ **inner**: *internal doubts* —**internally** *adv*: *The matter will be dealt with internally.* | *This medicine must not be taken internally.*

in,ternal com'bustion ,engine *n* [C] an engine that produces power by burning petrol, used in most cars

in·ter·nal·ize also **-ise** *BrE* /ɪnˈtɜːnəlaɪz $ -ɜːr-/ *v* [T] if you internalize a particular belief, attitude, behaviour etc, it becomes part of your character —**internalization** /ɪnˌtɜːnəlaɪˈzeɪʃən $ ɪnˌtɜːrnələ-/ [U]

in,ternal 'medicine *n* [U] *AmE* a type of medical work in which doctors treat illnesses that do not need operations

In,ternal 'Revenue ,Service also **In,ternal 'Revenue** *n* the IRS

in·ter·na·tion·al¹ S3 W1 /ˌɪntəˈnæʃənəl $ -tər-/ *adj* relating to or involving more than one nation; → **national**: *international trade/market/competition* | *the response of the international community* | *the UN and other international organizations* → INTERNATIONAL RELATIONS, INTERNATIONALLY

international² *n* [C] **1** an international sports game **2** *BrE* someone who plays for one of their country's sports teams; → **national**

International 'Date Line *n* [singular] an imaginary line that goes from the NORTH POLE to the SOUTH POLE, to the east of which the date is one day later than it is to the west

in·ter·na·tion·al·is·m /ˌɪntəˈnæʃənəlɪzəm $ -tər-/ *n* [U] the belief that nations should work together and help each other —**internationalist** *n* [C] —**internationalist** *adj*

in·ter·na·tion·al·ize also **-ise** *BrE* /ˌɪntəˈnæʃənəlaɪz $ -tər-/ *v* [T] to make something international or bring it under international control —**internationalization** /ˌɪntənæʃənəlaɪˈzeɪʃən $ ˌɪntərnæʃənələ-/ *n* [U]

in·ter·na·tion·al·ly /ˌɪntəˈnæʃənəli $ -tər-/ *adv* in many different parts of the world, → **international**: *These days businesses have to be able to compete internationally.* | **internationally** *famous/recognized/known* etc *an internationally famous sculptor*

International 'Monetary ,Fund *n* the IMF

international re'lations *n* [plural] the political relationships between countries, or the study of this

in·ter·ne·cine /ˌɪntəˈniːsaɪn $ ˌɪntərˈniːsən◂, -ˈnesiːn◂/ *adj* [only before noun] *formal* internecine fighting or struggles happen between members of the same group or nation: *internecine warfare*

in·tern·ee /ˌɪntɜːˈniː $ -ɜːr-/ *n* [C] someone who is put into prison during a war or for political reasons, without having had a TRIAL; → **intern**

Internet, in·ter·net /ˈɪntənet $ -tər-/ *n* the Internet a computer system that allows millions of computer users around the world to exchange information: **on the Internet** *You can find all kinds of information on the internet.* | *More and more companies are using the internet to conduct their business.* | *Do you have* **access to the Internet***?* | *an internet café* (=a café with computers where people can pay to use the Internet)

WORD FOCUS: INTERNET
places on the Internet: **website/site, webpage, chatroom**
things you do on the Internet: **surf the net** (spend time looking at websites for fun) | **visit websites** and **chatrooms, download files** from the Internet, **email** people or **chat** with them, **shop online** or **work online**. You can also **bookmark** sites that you want to go back to regularly, or put them on your list of **favourites**.
→ see also email, intranet, extranet, cyberspace, virtual, search engine, isp, browser

'Internet ,banking also **online banking** *n* [U] a service provided by banks so that people can find out information about their bank account, pay bills etc using the Internet

in·tern·ist /ˈɪntɜːnɪst $ -ɜːr-/ *n* [C] *AmE* a doctor who has a general knowledge about all illnesses and medical conditions of organs inside your body, and who treats illnesses that do not need operations

in·tern·ment /ɪnˈtɜːnmənt $ -ɜːr-/ *n* [U] the practice of keeping people in prison during a war or for political reasons, without charging them with a crime; → **intern**: *an internment camp*

in·tern·ship /ˈɪntɜːnʃɪp $ -ɜːrn-/ *n* [C] *AmE* **1** a job that lasts for a short time, that someone, especially a student, does in order to gain experience; → **intern 2** a job that someone who has nearly finished training as a doctor does in a hospital; → **intern**

in·ter·pen·e·trate /ˌɪntəˈpenɪtreɪt $ -tər-/ *v* [I,T] *formal* to spread through something or spread through each other —**interpenetration** /ˌɪntəpenɪˈtreɪʃən $ -tər-/ *n* [C,U]

in·ter·per·son·al /ˌɪntəˈpɜːsənəl $ -tərˈpɜːr-/ *adj* relating to relationships between people: *interpersonal skills* | *interpersonal communication*

in·ter·plan·e·ta·ry /ˌɪntəˈplænɪtəri◂ $ ˌɪntərˈplænɪteri◂/ *adj* [only before noun] between the PLANETS: *interplanetary space missions*

in·ter·play /ˈɪntəpleɪ $ -ər-/ *n* [U] the way in which two people or things affect each other: [+of] *the interplay of ideas* | [+between] *the interplay between military and civilian populations*

In·ter·pol /ˈɪntəppɒl $ -tərpoʊl/ *n* an international police organization that helps national police forces to catch criminals

in·ter·po·late /ɪnˈtɜːpəleɪt $ -ɜːr-/ *v* [T] *formal* **1** to put additional words into a piece of writing; ◧ **insert 2** to interrupt someone by saying something —**interpolation** /ɪnˌtɜːpəˈleɪʃən $ -ˌtɜːr-/ *n* [C,U]

in·ter·pose /ˌɪntəˈpəʊz $ -tərˈpoʊz/ *v* [T] *formal* **1** to put yourself or something else between two other things: *She interposed herself between the general and his wife.* **2** to say something when other people are having a conversation or argument, interrupting them: *'That might be difficult,' interposed Regina.*

in·ter·pret W3 /ɪnˈtɜːprɪt $ -ɜːr-/ *v*
1 [I,T] to translate spoken words from one language into another: *They spoke good Spanish, and promised to interpret for me.*
2 [T] to believe that something someone does or something that happens has a particular meaning: **interpret sth as sth** *His refusal to work late was interpreted as a lack of commitment to the company.*
3 [T] to explain the meaning of something: *Freud's attempts to interpret the meaning of dreams*
4 [T] to perform a part in a play, a piece of music etc in a way that shows your feelings about it or what you think it means

in·ter·pre·ta·tion W2 /ɪnˌtɜːprɪˈteɪʃən $ -ɜːr-/ *n* [C,U]
1 the way in which someone explains or understands an event, information, someone's actions etc: *One possible interpretation is that they want you to resign.* | *It's difficult to* **put** *an accurate* **interpretation on** (=explain) *the survey results.* | *What exactly the author meant by that statement is* **open to interpretation** (=able to be understood or explained in different ways).
2 the way in which someone performs a play, a piece of music etc and shows what they think and feel about it: *Laurence Olivier's brilliant interpretation of Henry V*

in·ter·pre·ta·tive /ɪnˈtɜːprɪtətɪv $ ɪnˈtɜːrprəteɪtɪv/ also **interpretive** *adj* **1** relating to, explaining, or understanding the meaning of something: *Reading is an interpretative process.* **2** relating to how feelings are expressed through music, dance, art etc: *interpretive dance*

in·ter·pret·er /ɪnˈtɜːprɪ̩tə $ -ˈtɜːrprə̩tər/ n [C] **1** someone who changes spoken words from one language into another, especially as their job; → **translator**: *Speaking through an interpreter* (=using an interpreter), *Ahmed said, 'I'm very worried about my wife and children'.* **2** a computer program that changes an instruction into a form that can be understood directly by the computer

in·ter·pre·tive /ɪnˈtɜːprɪ̩tɪv $ -ɜːr-/ adj interpretative

in·ter·ra·cial /ˌɪntəˈreɪʃəl◄/ adj between different races of people; → **multiracial**: *interracial marriage*

in·ter·reg·num /ˌɪntəˈregnəm/ n plural **interregnums** or **interregna** /-nə/ n [C] formal a period of time when a country or organization has no ruler or leader, and they are waiting for a new one

in·ter·re·late /ˌɪntərɪˈleɪt/ v [I] if two things interrelate, they are connected and have an effect on each other: *We will be discussing how the interests of state, parent and child interrelate.* | [+with] *Each part of the course interrelates with all the others.*

in·ter·re·lat·ed /ˌɪntərɪˈleɪtɪ̩d◄/ adj things that are interrelated are connected and have an effect on each other: *Unemployment and inflation are interrelated.* | *Many interrelated factors are at work here.*

in·ter·re·la·tionship /ˌɪntərɪˈleɪʃənʃɪp/ also **in·ter·re·la·tion** /-rɪˈleɪʃən/ n [C,U] a connection between two things that makes them affect each other

in·ter·ro·gate /ɪnˈterəgeɪt/ v [T] to ask someone a lot of questions for a long time in order to get information, sometimes using threats: *The police interrogated the suspect for several hours.* —**interrogator** n [C]: *He refused to tell his interrogators anything.* —**interrogation** /ɪn̩terəˈgeɪʃən/ n [C,U]

in·ter·rog·a·tive[1] /ˌɪntəˈrɒgətɪv◄ $ -ˈrɑː-/ adj **1** technical an interrogative sentence, PRONOUN etc asks a question or has the form of a question. For example, 'who' and 'what' are interrogative pronouns. **2** written if someone gives you an interrogative look or uses an interrogative voice, they want to know the answer to a question; ☐ **questioning** —**interrogatively** adv

interrogative[2] n technical **1** the interrogative the form of a sentence or verb that is used for asking questions; → **indicative**: *Put this statement into the interrogative.* **2** [C] a word such as 'who' or 'what' that is used in asking questions

in·ter·rupt /ˌɪntəˈrʌpt/ v **1** [I,T] to stop someone from continuing what they are saying or doing by suddenly speaking to them, making a noise etc: *Will you stop interrupting me when I'm talking!* | *Sorry to interrupt, but I need to ask you to come downstairs.* **2** [T] to make a process or activity stop temporarily: *My studies were interrupted by the war.* **3** [T] if something interrupts a line, surface, view etc it stops it from being continuous —**interruption** /-ˈrʌpʃən/ n [C,U]: *Let's go somewhere where we can talk without interruption.* ⚠ Do not use **interruption** to mean a short period when students or workers can stop working and relax. Use **break** instead: *Between the two classes there is a 15 minute break.*

in·ter·sect /ˌɪntəˈsekt $ -ər-/ v **1** [I,T] if two lines or roads intersect, they meet or go across each other **2** [T usually passive] to divide an area with several lines, roads etc: *The plain is intersected by a network of canals.*

in·ter·sec·tion /ˌɪntəˈsekʃən, ˈɪntəsekʃən $ -tər-/ n **1** [C] a place where roads, lines etc cross each other, especially where two roads meet; ☐ **junction** BrE **2** [U] the act of intersecting something

in·ter·sperse /ˌɪntəˈspɜːs $ -tərˈspɜːrs/ v [T usually passive] **1** be interspersed with sth if something is interspersed with a particular kind of thing, it has a lot of them in it: *sunny periods interspersed with show-*ers **2** intersperse sth with sth to put something in between pieces of speech or writing, parts of a film etc

in·ter·state[1] /ˈɪntəsteɪt $ -tər-/ n [C] AmE a wide road that goes between states, on which cars can travel very fast

interstate[2] adj [only before noun] involving different states, especially in the US: *interstate commerce*

in·ter·stel·lar /ˌɪntəˈstelə◄ $ -tərˈstelər/ adj [only before noun] happening or existing between the stars

in·ter·stice /ɪnˈtɜːstɪ̩s $ -ɜːr-/ n [C usually plural] formal a small space or crack in something or between things

in·ter·twine /ˌɪntəˈtwaɪn $ -tər-/ v [I,T] **1** if two situations, ideas etc are intertwined, they are closely related to each other: *be closely/inextricably intertwined The problems of crime and unemployment are closely intertwined.* **2** if two things intertwine, or if they are intertwined, they are twisted together: [+with] | *a necklace of rubies intertwined with pearls*

in·ter·val W3 /ˈɪntəvəl $ -tər-/ n [C] **1** the period of time between two events, activities etc: *He left the room, returning after a short interval with a message.* | [+between] *The interval between arrest and trial can be up to six months.* **2** sunny/bright intervals short periods of fine weather between cloudy, rainy weather etc **3** at weekly/20 minute etc intervals every week, 20 minutes etc: *The trains run at half-hourly intervals.* **4** at regular intervals a) something that happens at regular intervals happens often: *The phone rang at regular intervals all afternoon.* b) objects that are placed at regular intervals have all been placed at the same distance from each other: *Trees had been planted at regular intervals.* **5** BrE a short period of time between the parts of a play, concert etc; ☐ **intermission** AmE: *We can get some drinks in the interval.* **6** technical the amount of difference in PITCH between two musical notes

in·ter·vene /ˌɪntəˈviːn $ -tər-/ v **1** [I] to become involved in an argument, fight, or other difficult situation in order to change what happens: [+in] *The police don't usually like to intervene in disputes between husbands and wives.* | *The army will have to intervene to prevent further fighting.* **2** [I,T] to interrupt someone when they are speaking: *'Stop shouting, Emily,' John intervened.* **3** [I] if an event intervenes, it delays or interrupts something else: *He was just establishing his career when the war intervened.* **4** [I] if a period of time intervenes, it comes between two events: *In the six years that intervened I saw them once.*

in·ter·ven·ing /ˌɪntəˈviːnɪŋ $ -tər-/ adj the intervening years/months/period etc time that passes between two events: *I hadn't seen him since 1980, and he had aged a lot in the intervening years.*

in·ter·ven·tion W3 /ˌɪntəˈvenʃən $ -tər-/ n [C,U] the act of becoming involved in an argument, fight, or other difficult situation in order to change what happens: *government intervention to regulate prices*

in·ter·ven·tion·ist /ˌɪntəˈvenʃən̩ɪst $ -tər-/ adj based on the belief of a government or organization that it should take action or spend money to influence the ECONOMY (=financial system) or what happens in other countries: *interventionist approach/role/policy The UN adopted a more interventionist approach in the region.* —**interventionism** n [U]

in·ter·view[1] S3 W2 /ˈɪntəvjuː $ -ər-/ n **1** [C,U] a formal meeting at which someone is asked questions in order to find out whether they are suitable for a job, course of study etc

interview

have an interview
go for an interview
be called/invited for (an) interview
conduct an interview (=interview someone)
at interview *BrE*
job interview
first interview
second interview (=a more detailed interview after
you have been successful in a previous interview)

[+for] *He **has an interview** next Thursday for a job on
the Los Angeles Times.* | *I got a letter asking me to **go
for an interview** the next day.* | *Remember to take the
phone off the hook while you are **conducting** the
interview.* | *a portfolio of work presented **at
interview*** | *I've got another **job interview** tomorrow.*

2 [C] an occasion when a famous person is asked
questions about their life, experiences, or opinions for
a newspaper, magazine, television programme etc:
[+with] *an interview with the President* | **newspaper/
radio/television interview** | *Elton John gave an **inter-
view** to Barbara Walters* (=he answered her
questions). | *an **exclusive interview** (=one that is
given to only one newspaper, programme etc)
3 [C] an official meeting with someone who asks you
questions: *a police interview*

interview² S2 *v* [T] to ask someone questions during
an interview: **interview sb for sth** *We're interviewing six
candidates for the job.* | **interview sb about sth** *The
police want to interview you about the accident.*
—**interviewing** *n* [U]: *interviewing skills*

in·ter·view·ee /ˌɪntəvjuˈiː $ -tər-/ *n* [C] the person
who answers the questions in an interview

in·ter·view·er /ˈɪntəvjuːə $ -tərvjuːər/ *n* [C] the per-
son who asks the questions in an interview

in·ter·war /ˌɪntəˈwɔː◂ $ -tərˈwɔːr◂/ *adj* [only before
noun] happening or relating to the period between the
First and the Second World Wars: *the interwar years*

in·ter·weave /ˌɪntəˈwiːv $ -ər-/ *v past tense* **inter-
wove** /-ˈwəʊv $ -ˈwoʊv/ *past participle* **interwoven**
/-ˈwəʊvən $ -ˈwoʊ-/ [T usually passive] **1** if two things
are interwoven, they are closely related or combined in
a complicated way: **closely/inextricably/tightly etc interwoven** *The two themes are inextricably interwoven in
the book.* | **be interwoven with sth** *practical help for the
bereaved interwoven with emotional support* **2** to
weave two or more things together: **be interwoven with
sth** *silk interwoven with gold and silver threads*

in·tes·tate /ɪnˈtesteɪt, -stɪt/ *adj law* **die intestate** to
die without having made a WILL (=a statement about
who you want to have your property after you die)

in·tes·tine /ɪnˈtestɪn/ *n* [C] the long tube in your
body through which food passes after it leaves your
stomach; ◻ **gut** —**intestinal** *adj* → **LARGE INTESTINE, SMALL
INTESTINE**

in-ˈthing *n* **be the in-thing** *informal* to be very fashionable at the moment

in·ti·ma·cy /ˈɪntɪməsi/ *n* **1** [U] a state of having a
close personal relationship with someone: [+of] *the
intimacy of marriage* | [+between] *a close sense of
intimacy between parent and child* **2 intimacies** [plu-
ral] things you say or do to someone you have a close
personal relationship with: *She thought back over the
intimacies they'd shared and the plans they'd
made.* **3** [U] a situation in which you feel you are in
private with someone: *the cosy intimacy of the
cafe* **4** [U] *formal* sex – used especially by lawyers and
police when they want to avoid using the word 'sex'

in·ti·mate¹ /ˈɪntɪmɪt/ *adj*
1 RESTAURANT/MEAL/PLACE private and friendly so
that you feel comfortable: *the intimate atmosphere of a
country pub* | *an intimate meal for two* | *The collection
has been moved from its **intimate setting** to the British
Museum.*

2 FRIENDS having an extremely close friendship: *an
intimate friend of Picasso's* | *an intimate relationship* |
*She's **on intimate terms with** important people in the
government.*
3 intimate knowledge of sth very detailed knowledge of
something as a result of careful study or a lot of
experience: *his intimate knowledge of the coal industry*
4 PRIVATE relating to very private or personal matters: *the publication of **intimate details** of their affair*
5 SEX *formal* **a)** relating to sex: *The virus can only be
transmitted through intimate contact.* **b) be intimate
with sb** to have sex with someone
6 intimate link/connection etc a very close connection
between two things: *the intimate connection between
physical and mental health* —**intimately** *adv*: *The two
aspects are intimately connected.* | *I am intimately
acquainted with the state of my bank account.*

in·ti·mate² /ˈɪntɪmeɪt/ *v* [T] *formal* to make people
understand what you mean without saying it directly:
intimate that *He intimated, politely but firmly, that we
were not welcome.* | **intimate sth to sb** *She had already
intimated to me her wish to leave.*

in·ti·mate³ /ˈɪntɪmɪt/ *n* [C] *formal* a close personal
friend

in·ti·ma·tion /ˌɪntɪˈmeɪʃən/ *n* [C,U] *formal* **1** an
indirect or unclear sign that something may happen:
the first intimations of the approaching conflict **2** the
act of officially telling someone about something:
*Without early intimation of the dates of the training
sessions, enthusiasm for training could decrease.*

in·tim·i·date /ɪnˈtɪmɪdeɪt/ *v* [T] **1** to frighten or
threaten someone into making them do what you want:
intimidate sb into doing sth *They tried to intimidate the
young people into voting for them.* | *Attempts to intimi-
date her failed.* **2** to make someone feel worried and
not confident: *The whole idea of going to Oxford intimidated me.* —**intimidation** /ɪnˌtɪmɪˈdeɪʃən/ *n* [U]: *She
had endured years of intimidation and violence.* | *the
intimidation of voters*

in·tim·i·dat·ed /ɪnˈtɪmɪdeɪtɪd/ *adj* [not before noun]
feeling worried and lacking confidence because of the
situation you are in or the people you are with: *I was
shy, and felt intimidated by the older students.*

in·tim·i·dat·ing /ɪˈtɪmɪdeɪtɪŋ/ *adj* making you feel
worried and not confident: *Some people find interview
situations very intimidating.*

in·to S1 W1 /ˈɪntə; *before vowels* ˈɪntu; *strong* ˈɪntuː/
prep
1 TO THE INSIDE OF STH to the inside or inner part of
a container, place, area etc: *Come into the office.* | *He
thrust his hand into his coat pocket.* | *There must be
another way into the cave.* | *Sue got back into bed and
pulled the quilt over her head.* | *I've got to go into town
this morning and do some shopping.* | *We dived into the
sea and swam to the shore.*
2 BECOMING INVOLVED used to say that someone
becomes involved in a situation or activity, or becomes
part of a group: *At the age of 16, I went into the printing
trade as an apprentice.* | *They tried to drag me into their
quarrel.* | *a player who deserves to get back into the
England team*
3 CHANGING used to say that someone or something
starts being in a different state or form: *She fell into a
deep sleep.* | *The whole banking system was thrown into
confusion.* | *I screwed my wet handkerchief into a ball.* |
Cut the cake into pieces. | *Neruda's poems have been
translated into English.*
4 HITTING STH used to say that a person or vehicle

hits someone or something after moving towards them: *He almost bumped into me as he rushed past.* | *The car swerved and crashed into the wall.*
5 DIRECTION in a particular direction: *They rode off into the sunset.* | *Make sure you're speaking directly into the microphone.*
6 TIME at or until a certain time: *Andy and I talked well into the night.* | *John was well into his forties before he got married.*
7 FINDING OUT used to say what someone is trying to find out information about: *an investigation into the events leading up to his death* | *I've been doing some research into this.*
8 DIVIDING NUMBERS *spoken* used when you are dividing one number by another: *Eight into twenty-four is three.*
9 be into sth *spoken* to like and be interested in something: *I'm really into folk music.*
10 be into sb *AmE informal* to owe someone money: *He's into me for $50.*

in·tol·e·ra·ble /ɪnˈtɒlərəbəl $ -ˈtɑː-/ *adj* too difficult, bad, annoying etc for you to accept or deal with; **🔁 tolerable**: *'This is intolerable!' exclaimed Sir Rufus.* | *The pain had become intolerable.* | **intolerable burden/strain/pressure** *Caring for an elderly relative can become an intolerable burden.* —**intolerably** *adv*

in·tol·e·rance /ɪnˈtɒlərəns $ -ˈtɑː-/ *n* **1** [U] unwillingness to accept ways of thinking and behaving that are different from your own; **🔁 tolerance: racial/religious intolerance 2** [C,U] an inability to take particular medicines or eat particular foods without suffering bad effects; → **allergic**: [+of] *an intolerance of alcohol* | **food/glucose/lactose intolerance**

in·tol·e·rant /ɪnˈtɒlərənt $ -ˈtɑː-/ *adj* **1** not willing to accept ways of thinking and behaving that are different from your own; **🔁 tolerant**: [+of] *people who are intolerant of other people's political beliefs* **2** not able to take particular medicines or eat particular foods without suffering bad effects: [+of] *A number of patients were intolerant of the diet.* | *She's lactose-intolerant* (=unable to drink particular types of milk).

in·to·na·tion /ˌɪntəˈneɪʃən/ *n* **1** [C,U] the way in which the level of your voice changes in order to add meaning to what you are saying, for example by going up at the end of a question: *intonation patterns* **2** [U] *technical* the playing or singing of correct musical notes

in·tone /ɪnˈtəʊn $ -ˈtoʊn/ *v* [T] *formal* to say something slowly and clearly without making your voice rise and fall much as you speak: *The priest intoned the blessing.*

in to·to /ˌɪn ˈtəʊtəʊ $ -ˈtoʊtoʊ/ *adv* as a whole; **🔁 totally**: *They accepted the plan in toto.*

in·tox·i·cant /ɪnˈtɒksɪkənt $ -ˈtɑːk-/ *n* [C] *technical* something that makes you drunk

in·tox·i·cat·ed /ɪnˈtɒksɪkeɪtɪd $ -ˈtɑːk-/ *adj* **1** *formal* drunk; **🔁 sober**: *The driver was clearly intoxicated.* **2** happy, excited, and unable to think clearly, especially as a result of love, success, power etc: [+by/with] *He rapidly became intoxicated with his own power.* —**intoxicate** *v* [T] —**intoxication** /ɪnˌtɒksɪˈkeɪʃən $ -ˌtɑːk-/ *n* [U]

in·tox·i·cat·ing /ɪnˈtɒksɪkeɪtɪŋ $ -ˈtɑːk-/ *adj* **1** *formal* intoxicating drinks can make you drunk **2** making you feel happy, excited, and unable to think clearly: *the intoxicating combination of her beauty and wit*

intra- /ɪntrə/ *prefix formal* or *technical* **1** inside; **🔁 within**: *intra-departmental* (=within a department) **2** into: *an intravenous injection* (=into a vein)

in·trac·ta·ble /ɪnˈtræktəbəl/ *adj formal* **1** an intractable problem is very difficult to deal with or solve: *the seemingly intractable problem of human greed* **2** having a strong will and difficult to control —**intractability** /ɪnˌtræktəˈbɪləti/ *n* [U]

in·tra·mu·ral /ˌɪntrəˈmjʊərəl◂ $ -ˈmjʊr-/ *adj AmE* happening within one school, or intended for the students of one school: *an intramural softball competition* → EXTRAMURAL

in·tra·net /ˈɪntrənet/ *n* [C] a computer network used for exchanging or seeing information within a company; → **Internet, extranet**

in·tran·si·gent /ɪnˈtrænsɪdʒənt/ *adj formal* unwilling to change your ideas or behaviour, in a way that seems unreasonable; **🔁 stubborn**: *an intransigent attitude* —**intransigence** *n* [U]: *He accused the government of intransigence.*

in·tran·si·tive /ɪnˈtrænsɪtɪv/ *adj technical* an intransitive verb has a subject but no object. For example, in the sentence 'they arrived', 'arrived' is intransitive. Intransitive verbs are marked [I] in this dictionary; **🔁 transitive** —**intransitively** *adv*

in·tra·pre·neur /ˌɪntrəprəˈnɜː $ -ˈnɜːr/ *n* [C] someone who works for a large company and whose job is to develop new ideas or ways of doing business for that company; → **entrepreneur** —**intrapreneuring** *n* [U]

in·tra·state /ˈɪntrəsteɪt/ *adj* [only before noun] *AmE* within one US state; → **interstate**: *intrastate commerce*

in·tra·ve·nous /ˌɪntrəˈviːnəs◂/ *adj* [only before noun] through or into a VEIN (=tube in the body taking blood back to the heart): *an intravenous injection* | *intravenous drug users* —**intravenously** *adv*: *The drug was given intravenously.*

in tray *n* [C] a container on your desk for work and letters that need to be dealt with; **🔁 out tray**; → see picture at TRAY

in·trep·id /ɪnˈtrepɪd/ *adj* willing to do dangerous things or go to dangerous places – often used humorously: *intrepid explorers*

in·tri·ca·cy /ˈɪntrɪkəsi/ *n plural* **intricacies 1 the intricacies of sth** the complicated details of something: *the intricacies of private banking* **2** [U] the state of containing a large number of parts or details: *designs of amazing intricacy and sophistication*

in·tri·cate /ˈɪntrɪkət/ *adj* containing many small parts or details that all work or fit together: *intricate patterns* —**intricately** *adv*: *intricately woven fabric*

in·trigue¹ /ɪnˈtriːg/ *v* **1** [T] if something intrigues you, it interests you a lot because it seems strange or mysterious: *Other people's houses always intrigued her.* **2** [I] *formal* to make secret plans to harm someone or make them lose their position of power: [+against] *While King Richard was abroad, the barons had been intriguing against him.*

in·trigue² /ˈɪntriːg/ *n* [C,U] the making of secret plans to harm someone or make them lose their position of power, or a plan of this kind: *It's an exciting story of political intrigue and murder.* | *a web of intrigue* (=complicated set of secret plans) | [+of] *political intrigues of the capital*

in·trigued /ɪnˈtriːgd/ *adj* very interested in something because it seems strange or mysterious: [+by/with] *He was intrigued by her reaction.* | **intrigued to know/learn etc** *She was intrigued to know what he planned to do next.*

in·tri·guing /ɪnˈtriːgɪŋ/ *adj* something that is intriguing is very interesting because it is strange, mysterious, or unexpected: *The magazine carries an intriguing mixture of high fashion, gossip and racing.* —**intriguingly** *adv*

in·trin·sic /ɪnˈtrɪnsɪk, -zɪk/ *adj* being part of the nature or character of someone or something: *the intrinsic interest of the subject* | **intrinsic nature/quality/value/property of sth** *There is nothing in the intrinsic nature of the work that makes it more suitable for women.* | [+to] *Flexibility is intrinsic to creative management.* —**intrinsically** /-kli/ *adv*: *Science is seen as intrinsically good.*

in·tro /ˈɪntrəʊ $ -troʊ/ *n plural* **intros** [C] *informal* a short part at the beginning of a song, piece of writing etc; → **introduction**

intro- /ˈɪntrə/ *prefix* into, especially into the inside: *introspection* (=examining your own feelings)

in·tro·duce S3 W1 /ˌɪntrəˈdjuːs $ -ˈduːs/ *v* [T]
1 WHEN PEOPLE MEET if you introduce someone to another person, you tell them each other's names for the first time: *Have you two been introduced? Tom, this is Greg.* | **introduce sb to sb** *June, let me introduce you to Bob.* | **introduce yourself** (=formally tell someone who you are) *May I introduce myself? My name is Meg Johnson.*
2 NEW SYSTEM/PRODUCT to bring a plan, system, or product into use for the first time: *They want to introduce a system of identity cards.* | *The store have introduced a new range of food for children.*
3 BRING STH TO A PLACE to bring a type of thing somewhere for the first time: **introduce sth to/into sth** *The grey squirrel was introduced into Britain from North America.*
4 NEW EXPERIENCE to show someone something or tell them about it for the first time: **introduce sb to sth/introduce sth to sb** *Malcolm introduced me to the joys of wine-tasting.*
5 PROGRAMME/PUBLIC EVENT to speak at the beginning of and sometimes during a television or radio programme, or at the beginning of a public event: *Jim Adams will introduce tonight's programme.*
6 START A CHANGE to make something new start to happen or exist in a situation: *The peace agreement has introduced a feeling of optimism here.*
7 LAW to formally present a possible new law to be discussed: *Several senators introduced legislation aimed at sexual harassment.*
8 PUT STH INTO STH *technical* to put something carefully into something else: **introduce sth into sth** *Fuel was introduced into the jet pipe.*

in·tro·duc·tion W2 /ˌɪntrəˈdʌkʃən/ *n*
1 NEW SYSTEM/PRODUCT [U] the act of bringing something into use for the first time: [+of] *the introduction of a range of new products* | *With the introduction of independent taxation, a married woman's position is much clearer.*
2 BRING STH TO A PLACE **a)** [U] the act of bringing something somewhere for the first time: [+of] *the introduction of Buddhism to China nearly 2000 years ago* **b)** [C] a type of thing that is brought somewhere for the first time: *The potato was a sixteenth century introduction.*
3 WHEN MEETING SB [C] the act of formally telling two people each other's names when they first meet: *Pete, are you going to make the introductions?* | *Our first contestant needs no introduction* (=everyone already knows the person).
4 BOOK/SPEECH [C] a written or spoken explanation at the beginning of a book, speech etc: *In the introduction he explains why he wrote the book.* | *Mr Brown gave a brief introduction to the course.*
5 MUSIC [C] a short part at the beginning of a song or piece of music
6 EXPLANATION [C] something that explains the basic facts of a subject: [+to] *The book is a useful introduction to British geology.*
7 NEW EXPERIENCE [C] someone's first experience of something: [+to] *an introduction to water sports*
8 LETTER [C] a letter by someone else that explains who you are, which you can give to a person you have not met before

in·tro·duc·to·ry /ˌɪntrəˈdʌktəri/ *adj* [only before noun] **1** said or written at the beginning of a book, speech etc in order to explain what it is about: **introductory chapter/paragraph** *the objectives described in the introductory chapter* | *as the chairman said in his introductory remarks* **2** intended for people who have never done a particular activity before: *an introductory course in data processing* **3** **introductory offer/price etc** a special low price that is charged for a new product for a limited period of time: *Don't miss our introductory offer!*

---

inure *(running head)*

in·tro·spec·tion /ˌɪntrəˈspekʃən/ *n* [U] the process of thinking deeply about your own thoughts, feelings, or behaviour

in·tro·spec·tive /ˌɪntrəˈspektɪv◂/ *adj* tending to think deeply about your own thoughts, feelings, or behaviour: *a shy and introspective person* —**introspectively** *adv*

in·tro·vert /ˈɪntrəvɜːt $ -ɜːrt/ *n* [C] someone who is quiet and shy, and does not enjoy being with other people; → **extrovert**

in·tro·vert·ed /ˈɪntrəvɜːtɪd $ -ɜːr-/ *adj* someone who is introverted is quiet and shy and does not enjoy being with other people; → **extrovert, extroverted** —**introversion** /ˌɪntrəˈvɜːʃən $ -ˈvɜːrʒən/ *n* [U]

in·trude /ɪnˈtruːd/ *v* [I] **1** to interrupt someone or become involved in their private affairs in an annoying and unwanted way: *Would I be intruding if I came with you?* | [+into/on/upon] *Employers should not intrude into the private lives of their employees.* **2** to come into a place or situation, and have an unwanted effect: [+on] *It is to be hoped that TV cameras never intrude on this peaceful place.*

in·trud·er /ɪnˈtruːdə $ -ər/ *n* [C] **1** someone who illegally enters a building or area, usually in order to steal something: *The police think the intruder got in through an unlocked window.* **2** someone who is in a place where they are not wanted: *At first I felt like an intruder in their family.*

in·tru·sion /ɪnˈtruːʒən/ *n* [C,U] **1** when someone does something or something happens that affects your private life or activities in an unwanted way: [+into/on/upon] *I resented this intrusion into my domestic affairs.* | *the unwelcome intrusion of the press* **2** when something comes into a place or situation and has an unwanted effect: *the intrusion of badly designed new buildings in the historic high street*

in·tru·sive /ɪnˈtruːsɪv/ *adj* affecting someone's private life or interrupting them in an unwanted and annoying way: *They found the television cameras too intrusive.*

in·tu·it /ɪnˈtjuːɪt $ -ˈtuː-, -ˈtjuː-/ *v* [T] *formal* to know or guess something because of a feeling you have, rather than because of facts you know

in·tu·i·tion /ˌɪntjuˈɪʃən $ -tu-, -tju-/ *n* **1** [U] the ability to understand or know something because of a feeling rather than by considering the facts; → **instinct**: *feminine intuition* | *Intuition told her it was unwise to argue.* **2** [C] an idea about what is true in a particular situation based on a feeling rather than facts: **intuition (that)** *He had an intuition there was trouble brewing.* | *We should trust our intuitions.*

in·tu·i·tive /ɪnˈtjuːɪtɪv $ -ˈtuː-, -ˈtjuː-/ *adj* **1** an intuitive idea is based on a feeling rather than on knowledge or facts; → **instinctive**: *He seemed to have an intuitive awareness of how I felt.* **2** someone who is intuitive is able to understand situations without being told or having any proof about them —**intuitively** *adv*

In·u·it[1] /ˈɪnjuɪt, ˈɪnuɪt $ ˈɪnuɪt/ *adj* relating to the Inuit

Inuit[2] *n* [C] **1** someone who belongs to a race of people who live in the very cold northern areas of North America; → **Eskimo 2 the Inuit** [plural] the people who belong to this race

I·nuk /ˈɪnʊk $ ɪˈnʌk/ *n* another word for an Inuit

in·un·date /ˈɪnəndeɪt/ *v* [T] **1 be inundated (with/by sth)** to receive so much of something that you cannot easily deal with it all; → **swamp**: *After the broadcast, we were inundated with requests for more information.* **2** *formal* to cover an area with a large amount of water; → **flood**: *The tidal wave inundated vast areas of cropland.* —**inundation** /ˌɪnənˈdeɪʃən/ *n* [C,U]

in·ure /ɪˈnjʊə $ ɪˈnjʊr/ *v*
inure sb to sth *phr v* [usually passive] to make some-

one become used to something unpleasant, so that they are no longer upset by it: *Nurses soon become inured to the sight of suffering.*

in·vade /ɪnˈveɪd/ v **1** [I,T] to enter a country, town, or area using military force, in order to take control of it: *The Romans invaded Britain 2000 years ago.* **2** [T] to go into a place in large numbers, especially when you are not wanted: *Every summer the town is invaded by tourists.* | *Fans invaded the pitch at half-time.* **3** [T] to get involved in something in an unwanted and annoying way: *What right does he have to invade my privacy?* | *Patients are given the feeling that they mustn't try to invade medical territory* (=try to deal with things that are not their responsibility). → INVASION

in·vad·er /ɪnˈveɪdə $ -ər/ n [C] a soldier or a group of soldiers that enters a country or town by force in order to take control of it: *Invaders from the south ransacked the town.*

in·val·id¹ /ɪnˈvælɪd/ adj **1** a contract, ticket, claim etc that is invalid is not legally or officially acceptable; 🔒 **valid**: *Without the right date stamped on it, your ticket will be invalid.* **2** an argument, reason etc that is invalid is not based on true facts or clear ideas, and lacks good judgment; 🔒 **valid** **3** if something you type into a computer is invalid, the computer does not recognize or accept it: *Filename in invalid format.*

in·va·lid² /ˈɪnvəliːd, -lɪd $ -lɪd/ n [C] someone who cannot look after themselves because of illness, old age, or injury: *I resented being treated as an invalid.*
—**invalid** adj [only before noun]

in·va·lid³ v
be invalided out also **be invalided home** phr v BrE to have to leave the army, navy etc because you are ill or injured

in·val·i·date /ɪnˈvælɪdeɪt/ v [T] **1** to make a document, ticket, claim etc no longer legally or officially acceptable: *Failure to disclose all relevant changes may invalidate your policy.* **2** to show that something such as a belief or explanation is wrong: *Later findings invalidated the theory.*

in·va·lid·i·ty /ˌɪnvəˈlɪdəti/ n [U] formal **1** the state of being too ill, old, or injured to work: *invalidity benefit* **2** the state of being not legally or officially acceptable

in·val·u·a·ble /ɪnˈvæljuəbəl, -jʊbəl $ -ˈvæljʊbəl/ adj extremely useful; [+to/for] *Your advice has been invaluable to us.* | **invaluable in/for (doing) sth** *This help was invaluable in focusing my ideas.* | *The internet is an invaluable source of information.*

in·var·i·a·ble /ɪnˈveəriəbəl $ -ˈver-/ adj **1** always happening in the same way, at the same time etc: *His invariable answer was 'Wait and see.'* **2** technical never changing; 🔒 **variable**: *Mass, unlike weight, is invariable.*

in·var·i·a·bly /ɪnˈveəriəbli $ -ˈver-/ adv if something invariably happens or is invariably true, it always happens or is true: *It invariably rains when I go there.* | *The security guards were invariably ex-servicemen.*

in·va·sion /ɪnˈveɪʒən/ n **1** [C,U] when the army of one country enters another country by force, in order to take control of it: [+of] *the invasion of Normandy* **2** [C] the arrival in a place of a lot of people or things, often where they are not wanted: *the annual invasion of teenagers for the Glastonbury Festival* **3** **invasion of privacy** a situation in which someone tries to find out details about another person's private affairs in a way that is upsetting and often illegal

in·va·sive /ɪnˈveɪsɪv/ adj **1** invasive medical treatment involves cutting into someone's body: *invasive surgery* **2** an invasive disease spreads quickly and is difficult to stop: *invasive bladder cancers*

in·vec·tive /ɪnˈvektɪv/ n [U] formal rude and insulting words that someone says when they are very angry: *He let out a stream of invective.*

in·veigh /ɪnˈveɪ/ v
inveigh against sb/sth phr v formal to criticize someone or something strongly

in·vei·gle /ɪnˈveɪɡəl, ɪnˈviː- $ ɪnˈveɪ-/ v
inveigle sb **into** sth phr v formal to persuade someone to do what you want, especially in a dishonest way: **inveigle sb into doing sth** *She had inveigled me into taking messages to her lover.*

in·vent /ɪnˈvent/ v [T] **1** to make, design, or think of a new type of thing: *Alexander Graham Bell invented the telephone in 1876.* ⚠ Do not confuse **invent** and **discover.** To discover something means to be the first person to find it or to know that it exists: *Scientists have discovered a new type of bacteria.* **2** to think of an idea, story etc that is not true, usually in order to deceive people: *They invented a very convincing alibi.*

in·ven·tion /ɪnˈvenʃən/ n **1** [C] a useful machine, tool, instrument etc that has been invented: *The dishwasher is a wonderful invention.* **2** [U] the act of inventing something: *The invention of the computer has revolutionized the business world.* **3** [C,U] a story, explanation etc that is not true: *They subsequently admitted that the story was pure invention.* **4** [U] the ability to think of new and clever ideas: *With such powers of invention he should get a job easily.*

in·ven·tive /ɪnˈventɪv/ adj able to think of new, different, or interesting ideas; 🔒 **creative**: *one of the most talented and inventive drummers in modern music*
—**inventively** adv —**inventiveness** n [U]

in·ven·tor /ɪnˈventə $ -ər/ n [C] someone who has invented something, or whose job is to invent things: *the inventor of the vacuum cleaner*

in·ven·tory /ˈɪnvəntri $ -tɔːri/ n plural **inventories** **1** [C] a list of all the things in a place: [+of] *We made an inventory of everything in the apartment.* **2** [C,U] AmE all the goods in a shop; 🔒 **stock**

in·verse¹ /ˌɪnˈvɜːs◂ $ -ˈvɜːrs◂/ adj [only before noun] **1** if there is an inverse relationship between two amounts, one gets bigger at the same rate as the other gets smaller: *Clearly, the amount of money people save increases in inverse proportion to the amount they spend.* | *the inverse relationship between prices and interest rates* **2** technical exactly opposite —**inversely** adv

inverse² n [singular] technical the complete opposite of something; → **reverse**

in·ver·sion /ɪnˈvɜːʃən $ -ˈvɜːrʒən/ n [C,U] **1** formal the act of changing something so that it is the opposite of what it was before, or of turning something upside down (=the bottom is on the top and the top is on the bottom) **2** technical a type of weather condition in which the air nearest the ground is cooler than the air above it

in·vert /ɪnˈvɜːt $ -ɜːrt/ v [T] formal to put something in the opposite position to the one it was in before, especially by turning it upside down (=the bottom is on the top and the top is on the bottom)

in·ver·te·brate /ɪnˈvɜːtɪbrət, -breɪt $ -ɜːr-/ n [C] a living creature that does not have a BACKBONE → VERTEBRATE —**invertebrate** adj

in·verted 'comma n [C usually plural] BrE **1** one of a pair of marks (") or (") that are put at the beginning and end of a written word, sentence etc to show that someone said it or wrote it, or when writing the title of a book, song etc; 🔒 **quotation mark** → PUNCTUATION MARK **2** **in inverted commas** spoken used to show that a word you are using to describe something is only what it is usually called, and not what you think it really is: *Her friends, in inverted commas, all disappeared when she was in trouble.*

in·verted 'snobbery n [U] BrE the idea that everything that is typical of the upper classes must be bad

in·vest W3 /ɪnˈvest/ v
1 [I,T] to buy shares, property, or goods because you hope that the value will increase and you can make a profit: *I've got a few thousand dollars I'm looking to*

invest. | **invest (sth) in sth** *Oliver made a fortune by investing in antique furniture.* | *Williams invested a large sum of money in Swiss stocks.* | *He had invested heavily* (=invested a lot of money) *in the bond market.*
2 [I,T] if a government, business, or organization invests in something, they spend a large amount of money to improve it or help it succeed: **invest (sth) in sth** *The city has invested millions of dollars in the museum.* | *The factory plans to invest in new computers.*
3 [T] to use a lot of time, effort etc or spend money in order to make something succeed: **invest sth in sth** *It was very difficult to leave a home we had invested so much in.*
  invest (sth) **in** sth *phr v*
to buy something or spend money or time on something, because it will be useful for you: *It's about time you invested in a new shirt.* | *Everyone here has a lot invested in their careers.*
  invest sb/sth **with** sth *phr v formal*
1 to officially give someone power to do something: *Jody has invested Alan with great power over her career.*
2 to make someone or something seem to have a particular quality or character: *Richard's heavy-rimmed glasses invested him with an air of intelligence.*
in·ves·ti·gate W2 /ɪnˈvestɪgeɪt/ v
1 [I,T] to try to find out the truth about or the cause of something such as a crime, accident, or scientific problem: *The state police are investigating the incident.* | *The study investigates the impact of violent TV programming on children.* | *I heard a noise and went downstairs to investigate.*
2 [T] to try to find out more about someone's character, actions etc, because you think they may have been involved in a crime: *Penney was already being investigated by the police on suspicion of murder.*
in·ves·ti·ga·tion W2 /ɪnˌvestɪˈgeɪʃən/ n
1 [C] an official attempt to find out the truth about or the causes of something such as a crime, accident, or scientific problem: *The investigation continued for nearly three years.* | [+into] *The authorities are planning to launch a full-scale investigation into the crash.* | [+of] *Baker demanded an investigation of the district attorney's office.* | *a criminal investigation* | *A private detective was hired to conduct the investigation.*
2 [U] the act of investigating something: [+of] *the investigation of computer fraud* | **under investigation** (=being investigated) *The whole issue is still under investigation.*
in·ves·ti·ga·tive /ɪnˈvestɪgətɪv $ -geɪtɪv/ adj **investigative journalism/report/work** work or activities that involve investigating something
in·ves·ti·ga·tor /ɪnˈvestɪgeɪtə $ -ər/ n [C] someone who investigates things, especially crimes: *police investigators* → PRIVATE INVESTIGATOR
in·ves·ti·ga·to·ry /ɪnˈvestɪgətəri $ -gətɔːri/ adj [only before noun] relating to investigating something: *the investigatory powers of the Office of Fair Trading*
in·ves·ti·ture /ɪnˈvestɪtʃə $ -tʃʊr/ n [C] formal a ceremony at which someone is given an official title: [+of] *the investiture of the Prince of Wales*
in·vest·ment W1 /ɪnˈvestmənt/ n
1 [C,U] the use of money to get a profit or to make a business activity successful, or the money that is used

make an investment (in sth)
return on an investment (=profit from an investment)
short-term/long-term investment (=one that will give you profit in a short time, or only after a long time)
stimulate/encourage/attract investment
investment income

Foreign investment in Taiwan rose by 79% last year. | *A Certificate of Deposit remains one of the safest investments.* | *We plan to buy some property as an investment.* | [+in] *That year, Japanese investment in American real estate totaled $13.06 billion.* | [+of] *Each of us was required to put up a minimum investment of $5,000.* | *The Postal Service has made a large investment in new technology.* | *Shareholders want to see a*

better return on their investment. | *tax cuts aimed at stimulating investment and expanding the economy*
2 [C] something that you buy or do because it will be useful later: **a good/sound investment** *The lessons cost me over $500, but I consider them a good investment.*
3 [singular,U] when you spend a large amount of time, energy, emotion etc on something: *a huge investment of time and effort*
in·vestment ˌbank n [C] a bank that buys and sells SECURITIES, STOCKS, or BONDS —**investment banker** n [C] —**investment banking** n [U]
in·vestment ˌclub n [C] a group of people who meet regularly to decide which invesments to buy and sell together, with money that they all put into the group: *O'Hara belongs to an investment club in Detroit.*
in·vest·or W3 /ɪnˈvestə $ -ər/ n [C] someone who gives money to a company, business, or bank in order to get a profit
in·vet·e·rate /ɪnˈvetərət/ adj [only before noun] *written* **1 inveterate liar/smoker/womanizer etc** someone who lies a lot, smokes a lot etc and cannot stop **2 inveterate fondness/distrust/hatred etc** an attitude or feeling that you have had for a long time and cannot change
in·vid·i·ous /ɪnˈvɪdiəs/ adj *written* unpleasant, especially because it is likely to offend people or make you unpopular: *By innocently lying to detectives, she'd put herself in an invidious position.*
in·vi·gi·late /ɪnˈvɪdʒəleɪt/ v [I,T] *BrE* to watch people who are taking an examination and make sure that they do not cheat; ▤ **proctor** *AmE* —**invigilator** n [C]
in·vig·o·rate /ɪnˈvɪgəreɪt/ v [T] **1** if something invigorates you, it makes you feel healthier, stronger and have more energy: *At my age, the walk into town is enough to invigorate me.* | *He felt invigorated after a day in the country.* **2** [usually passive] to make the people in an organization or group feel excited again, so that they want to make something successful: *Carey's hope was that the church would be renewed and invigorated.*
in·vig·o·ra·ting /ɪnˈvɪgəreɪtɪŋ/ adj making you feel healthy and giving you a lot of energy: *an invigorating swim before breakfast*
in·vin·ci·ble /ɪnˈvɪnsɪbəl/ adj **1** too strong to be destroyed or defeated: *an invincible army* | *Young athletes think of themselves as invincible.* **2** an invincible belief, attitude etc is extremely strong and cannot be changed —**invincibility** /ɪnˌvɪnsɪˈbɪlɪti/ n [U]
in·vi·o·la·ble /ɪnˈvaɪələbəl/ adj *formal* an inviolable right, law, principle etc is extremely important and should be treated with respect and not broken or removed —**inviolability** /ɪnˌvaɪələˈbɪlɪti/ n [U]: *the inviolability of the country's borders*
in·vi·o·late /ɪnˈvaɪələt/ adj *formal* something that is inviolate cannot be attacked, changed, or destroyed
in·vis·i·ble /ɪnˈvɪzɪbəl/ adj **1** something that is invisible cannot be seen; ▤ **visible**: *The house was surrounded by trees and invisible from the road.* | [+to] *The Stealth bomber is meant to be invisible to radar.* | *Using a telescope, Galileo discovered stars that were invisible to the naked eye.* | **virtually/practically/almost etc invisible 2** not noticed, or not talked about: *There's an invisible barrier that keeps women out of top jobs.* **3 invisible earnings/exports/trade etc** money that is made from services and TOURISM rather than from products —**invisibly** adv —**invisibility** /ɪnˌvɪzɪˈbɪlɪti/ n [U]
in·visible ˈink n [U] ink that cannot be seen on paper until it is heated, treated with chemicals etc, and is used for writing secret messages
in·vi·ta·tion /ˌɪnvɪˈteɪʃən/ n
1 [C] a written or spoken request to someone, inviting them to go somewhere or do something

invitation to do sth
receive/get an invitation
accept an invitation (=say yes)
refuse/turn down/decline an invitation (=say no)
issue/extend an invitation *formal* (=invite someone)
open/standing invitation (=an invitation to do something at any time you like)
dinner/lunch invitation
formal invitation

Shortly afterwards, Dawson received an invitation to speak at a scientific conference. | *She accepted his invitation to join him for lunch.* | [+to] *Roger never turns down an invitation to dinner.* | *I extend an invitation to the minister to visit this area.* | *We've got a standing invitation. Maybe we should go tonight.*

2 [U] the act of being invited or of inviting someone to go somewhere or do something: **by invitation** *Attendance at the seminars is by invitation only* (=only those people who have been invited can attend). | *They were always dropping by, usually without invitation.* | **at sb's invitation/at the invitation of sb** *Kegl traveled to Nicaragua at the invitation of the education minister.*
3 [C] a card inviting someone to attend a party, wedding etc: **party/wedding invitation** *We sent out more than 300 wedding invitations.* | [+to] *Did you get an invitation to Jason's party?*
4 [singular, U] encouragement to do something: **take sth as an invitation to do sth** *He seemed to take my silence as an invitation to talk.*
5 be an open invitation for/to sb to make it very easy for someone to rob you or harm you: *Leaving the car unlocked is just an open invitation to thieves.*

in·vite¹ S2 W2 /ɪnˈvaɪt/ v [T]
1 to ask someone to come to a party, wedding, meal etc: **invite sb to sth** *Who should we invite to the party?* | **invite sb to do sth** *Gail invited me to stay with her while her husband was out of town.* | **invite sb for sth** *Why don't you invite her for a drink at the club one evening?* | *I'm afraid I wasn't invited.*
2 to politely ask someone to do something: **invite sb to do sth** *Anyone interested in contributing articles is invited to contact the editor.*
3 to encourage something bad to happen, especially without intending to: *Any government that sells arms to dictators is inviting trouble.*
invite sb **along** *phr v*
to ask someone if they would like to come with you when you are going somewhere: *Why don't you invite Barbara along?*
invite sb **back** *phr v*
1 to ask someone to come to your home, hotel etc after you have been out somewhere together: [+for] *Richard often used to invite me back for coffee after the show.*
2 to ask someone to come to your home, your office etc again: *If you keep arguing with Gerry, they won't invite us back.*
invite sb **in** *phr v*
to ask someone to come into your home: *After a few seconds, the door opened and Mrs Barnes invited me in.*
invite sb **out** *phr v*
to ask someone to go somewhere with you, especially to a restaurant or film: [+for] *We invited Clarissa out for ice cream.*
invite sb **over** also **invite sb round** *BrE phr v*
to ask someone to come to your home, usually for a drink or a meal: [+for] *Max has invited me over for dinner.*
in·vite² /ˈɪnvaɪt/ *n* [C] *informal* an invitation to a party, meal etc
in·vit·ing /ɪnˈvaɪtɪŋ/ *adj* something that is inviting is very attractive and makes you want to be near it, try it, taste it etc: *The log fire looked warm and inviting.* —**invitingly** *adv*: *She smiled invitingly.*

in vi·tro fer·ti·li·za·tion /ɪn ˌviːtrəʊ fɜːtᵻlaɪˈzeɪʃən $ -troʊ fɜːrtələ-/ *n* [U] *technical* a process in which a human egg is FERTILIZED outside a woman's body
in vivo /ɪn ˈviːvəʊ $ -voʊ/ *adj technical* taking place in the body —**in vivo** *adv*
in·vo·ca·tion /ˌɪnvəˈkeɪʃən/ *n* **1 the invocation** *AmE* a speech or prayer at the beginning of a ceremony or meeting **2** [C,U] *literary* a request for help, especially from a god
in·voice¹ /ˈɪnvɔɪs/ *n* [C] a list of goods that have been supplied or work that has been done, showing how much you owe for them; → **bill**
invoice² *v* [T] to send someone an invoice
in·voke /ɪnˈvəʊk $ -ˈvoʊk/ *v* [T] *formal* **1** if you invoke a law, rule etc, you say that you are doing something because the law allows or forces you to: *The UN threatened to invoke economic sanctions if the talks were broken off.* **2** to make a particular idea, image, or feeling appear in people's minds by describing an event or situation, or by talking about a person; → **evoke**: *a painting that invokes images of the Rocky Mountains* | *During his speech, he invoked the memory of Harry Truman.* **3** to use a law, principle, or THEORY to support your views **4** to operate a computer program **5** to ask for help from someone more powerful than you, especially a god: *St. Genevieve is often invoked against plagues.* **6** to make spirits appear by using magic: *invoking the spirits of their ancestors*
in·vol·un·ta·ry /ɪnˈvɒləntəri $ ɪnˈvɑːlənteri/ *adj* **1** an involuntary movement, sound, reaction etc is one that you make suddenly and without intending to because you cannot control yourself: *When Willie tapped on a window, Miguel gave an involuntary jump.* **2** happening to you although you do not want it to: *involuntary part-time workers* —**involuntarily** *adv*
in·volve S2 W1 /ɪnˈvɒlv $ ɪnˈvɑːlv/ *v* [T]
1 if an activity or situation involves something, that thing is part of it or a result of it: *What will the job involve?* | *I didn't realize putting on a play involved so much work.* | **involve doing sth** *Running your own business usually involves working long hours.*
2 to include or affect someone or something: *These changes will involve everyone on the staff.* | *There have been four accidents involving Forest Service planes.*
3 to ask or allow someone to take part in something: **involve sb in (doing) sth** *Try to involve as many children as possible in the game.* | *We want to involve the workforce at all stages of the decision-making process.*
4 involve yourself to take part actively in a particular activity: [+in] *Reilly involves himself in every aspect of his company's business.*
in·volved S2 W3 /ɪnˈvɒlvd $ ɪnˈvɑːlvd/ *adj*
1 be/get involved to take part in an activity or event, or be connected with it in some way: [+in] *More than 30 software firms were involved in the project.* | *I don't want to get involved in some lengthy argument about who is to blame.* | *I'm afraid your son's been involved in an accident* (=he is one of the people in an accident). | [+with] *Landel has been involved with the Hercules project for years.* | **actively/deeply/heavily involved** (=involved very much) *Mrs. Cummings has been actively involved with the church for years.*
2 work/effort etc involved in doing sth [not before noun] the amount of work, money, effort etc that is needed in order to make something succeed: *Most people don't realize the amount of effort involved in writing a novel.*
3 be involved with sb a) to be having a romantic relationship with someone, especially a sexual one: *The senator denied that he was romantically involved with a member of his staff.* **b)** to spend time with someone that you have a relationship with: *Fathers are encouraged to be more involved with their families.*
4 having so many different parts that it is difficult to understand; ■ **complicated**: *The plot was so involved that very few people knew what was going on.*
in·volve·ment W3 /ɪnˈvɒlvmənt $ -ˈvɑːlv-/ *n*
1 [U] the act of taking part in an activity or event, or

the way in which you take part in it; ◨ **participation**: *School officials say they welcome parental involvement.* | [+**in**] *His new book examines the United States' involvement in World War II.* | [+**with**] *The police have been looking into Harris's possible involvement with a series of robberies.*
2 [C] something that you take part in or spend time doing: *sporting involvements* | *her political involvements*
3 [U] the feeling of excitement and satisfaction that you get from an activity: [+**in**] *Weaver admitted a strong emotional involvement in her client's case.*
4 [C,U] a romantic relationship between two people, especially when they are not married to each other: [+**with**] *Donna knew nothing of her husband's involvement with another woman.*

in·vul·ne·ra·ble /ɪnˈvʌlnərəbəl/ *adj* someone or something that is invulnerable cannot be harmed or damaged if you attack or criticize them; ◨ **vulnerable**: *Gerry's confidence made him feel invulnerable.* | [+**to**] *We will not be satisfied until this city is safe and invulnerable to attack.* —**invulnerability** /ɪnˌvʌlnərəˈbɪlɪti/ *n* [U]

in·ward /ˈɪnwəd $ -wərd/ *adj written* **1** [only before noun] felt or experienced in your own mind but not expressed to other people; ◨ **outward**: *a feeling of inward satisfaction* | *inward panic* **2** towards the inside or centre of something —**inwardly** *adv*: *I managed to smile, but inwardly I was furious.*

'inward-ˌlooking *adj* an inward-looking person or group is more interested in themselves than in other people – used to show disapproval

in·wards /ˈɪnwədz $ -wərdz/ *especially BrE*; **inward** *AmE adv* towards the inside of something; ◨ **outwards**: *A breeze blew the curtains inwards.*

'in-word *n* [C] a word that is popular at a particular time, or among a particular group of people, but that does not usually continue to be popular for long: *the latest in-word amongst teenagers*

ˌin-your-ˈface also **in-yer-face** *adj BrE informal* in-your-face behaviour is intended to be noticed and to shock or upset people

i·o·dine /ˈaɪədiːn $ -daɪn/ *n* [U] a dark blue chemical substance that is used on wounds to prevent infection. It is a chemical ELEMENT: symbol I

i·on /ˈaɪən $ ˈaɪən, ˈaɪɑːn/ *n* [C] *technical* an atom which has been given a positive or negative force by adding or taking away an ELECTRON

-ion /ən/ *suffix* [in nouns] the act, state, or result of doing something: *the completion of the task* (=act of finishing it) | *his election* (=he was elected) *to the post* | *Young children demand a lot of attention.*

I·on·ic /aɪˈɒnɪk $ aɪˈɑː-/ *adj* made in the simply decorated style of ancient Greek buildings: *an Ionic column*

i·on·ize also **-ise** *BrE* /ˈaɪənaɪz/ *v* [I,T] to form ions or make them form —**ionization** /ˌaɪənaɪˈzeɪʃən $ -nə-/ *n* [U]

i·on·iz·er also **-iser** *BrE* /ˈaɪənaɪzə $ -ər/ *n* [C] a machine used to make the air in a room more healthy by producing negative IONS

i·on·o·sphere /aɪˈɒnəsfɪə $ aɪˈɑːnəsfɪr/ *n* the ionosphere the part of the ATMOSPHERE which is used to help send radio waves around the Earth

i·o·ta /aɪˈəʊtə $ -ˈoʊtə/ *n* not one/an iota not even a small amount: *It won't make an iota of difference.*

IOU /ˌaɪ əʊ ˈjuː $ -oʊ-/ *n* [C] *informal* a note that you sign to say that you owe someone some money

IPA /ˌaɪ piː ˈeɪ/ *n* [U] *International Phonetic Alphabet* a system of special signs, used to represent the sounds made in speech

IPO /ˌaɪ piː ˈəʊ $ -ˈoʊ/ *n* [C] *initial public offering*; the first time that STOCK in a company is available for the public to buy on the STOCK MARKET

ip·so fac·to /ˌɪpsəʊ ˈfæktəʊ $ -soʊ ˈfæktoʊ/ *adv formal* used to show that something is known from or proved by the facts

IQ /ˌaɪ ˈkjuː/ *n* [C] *intelligence quotient* your level of intelligence, measured by a special test, with 100 being the average result: *an IQ of 130*

ir- /ɪ/ *prefix* used instead of IN- before the letter r; ◨ **not**: *irregular* (=not regular)

IRA /ˌaɪ ɑːr ˈeɪ/ *n* **1** the IRA *the Irish Republican Army* an illegal organization that wants to unite Northern Ireland and the Republic of Ireland; → **Sinn Fein** **2** /ˈaɪrə/ *AmE individual retirement account* a special bank account in which you can save money for your RETIREMENT without paying tax on it until later

i·ras·ci·ble /ɪˈræsɪbəl/ *adj written* easily becoming angry: *an irascible old man*

i·rate /ˌaɪˈreɪt◂/ *adj* extremely angry, especially because you think you have been treated unfairly: *an irate customer*

ire /aɪə $ aɪr/ *n* [U] *written* anger: **raise/arouse/draw sb's ire** (=make someone angry) *The proposal has drawn the ire of local residents.*

ir·i·des·cent /ˌɪrɪˈdesənt◂/ *adj formal* showing colours that seem to change in different lights: *small iridescent blue flies* —**iridescence** *n* [U]

i·rid·i·um /ɪˈrɪdiəm/ *n* [U] a hard and very heavy metal that is combined with PLATINUM to make jewellery and is used in scientific instruments. It is a chemical ELEMENT: symbol Ir

i·ris /ˈaɪrɪs $ ˈaɪrɪs/ *n* [C] **1** a tall plant with long, thin leaves and large purple, yellow, or white flowers **2** the round coloured part of your eye, that surrounds the black PUPIL

I·rish[1] /ˈaɪrɪʃ $ ˈaɪrɪʃ/ *adj* relating to Ireland or its people

Irish[2] *n* the Irish [plural] people from Ireland

ˌIrish ˈcoffee *n* [C,U] coffee with cream and WHISKY

I·rish·man /ˈaɪrɪʃmən $ ˈaɪr-/ *n plural* **Irishmen** /-mən/ [C] a man from Ireland

ˌIrish ˈstew *n* [C,U] a dish of meat, potatoes, and onions boiled together

I·rish·wom·an /ˈaɪrɪʃˌwʊmən $ ˈaɪr-/ *n plural* **Irishwomen** /-ˌwɪmɪn/ [C] a woman from Ireland

irk /ɜːk $ ɜːrk/ *v* [T] if something irks you, it makes you feel annoyed: *Luna never told me what irked her that Sunday morning.*

irk·some /ˈɜːksəm $ ˈɜːrk-/ *adj formal* annoying: *an irksome journey*

i·ron[1] ⒮⒊ ⒲⒉ /ˈaɪən $ ˈaɪərn/ *n*
1 METAL [U] a common hard metal that is used to make steel, is MAGNETIC, and is found in very small quantities in food and blood. It is a chemical ELEMENT: symbol Fe: *the iron and steel industry* | *a driveway with large iron gates* | *iron ore* (=rock that contains iron) | *the absorption of iron from food* → WROUGHT IRON, CAST IRON; → see picture at MATERIAL
2 FOR CLOTHES [C] a thing used for making clothes smooth, which has a heated flat metal base

iron
iron
ironing board

3 have several irons in the fire to be involved in several different activities or have several plans all happening at the same time: *He has several economic irons in the fire, including gold and diamond mines.*
4 SPORT [C] a GOLF CLUB made of metal rather than wood: *a 5-iron* → see picture at GOLF
5 CHAINS irons [plural] *especially literary* a chain used to prevent a prisoner from moving: *leg irons* → **a will of iron/an iron will** at WILL[2] (1); → **pump iron** at PUMP[2] (8); → **rule sb/sth with a rod of iron** at RULE[2] (5); → **strike while the iron's hot** at STRIKE[1] (27)

iron² S3 *v* [T]
to make clothes smooth using an iron; ⊟ **press**: *Have you ironed my shirt?* → IRONING
iron sth ⇔ **out** *phr v*
to solve or get rid of problems or difficulties, especially small ones: *We need to iron out a few problems first.*

iron³ *adj* [only before noun] very firm and strong or determined: *He runs the company with an iron fist.*

'Iron Age *n* **the Iron Age** the period of time about 3000 years ago when iron was first used for making tools, weapons etc → BRONZE AGE, STONE AGE

i·ron·clad /ˈaɪənˌklæd $ -ərn-/ *adj* **1** an ironclad agreement, proof, defence etc is so strong and sure that it cannot be changed or argued against: *an ironclad guarantee* **2** old-fashioned covered with iron: *an ironclad battleship*

,Iron 'Curtain *n* **the Iron Curtain** the name that was used for the border between the Communist countries of Eastern Europe and the rest of Europe

,iron-'grey *BrE*; **iron-gray** *AmE adj* iron-grey hair is dark grey

i·ron·ic /aɪˈrɒnɪk $ aɪˈrɑː-/ also **i·ron·i·cal** /-ɪkəl/ *adj* **1** an ironic situation is one that is unusual or amusing because something strange happens or the opposite of what is expected happens or is true: *Your car was stolen at the police station! How ironic!* | *It's ironic that her husband smoked for thirty years, and yet she's the one who died of lung cancer.* | *In an ironic twist, the most trustworthy character in the film turned out to be the thief.* **2** using words that are the opposite of what you really mean, often in a joking way: *ironic comments* | *When I told Lucy I loved her book, she thought I was being ironic.* → SARCASTIC

i·ron·i·cally /aɪˈrɒnɪkli $ aɪˈrɑː-/ *adv* **1** [sentence adverb] used when talking about a situation in which the opposite of what you expected happens or is true: *Ironically, his cold got better on the last day of his holiday.* **2** in a way that shows you really mean the opposite of what you are saying: *'Oh, no problem!' said Terry, ironically.*

i·ron·ing /ˈaɪənɪŋ $ -ər-/ *n* [U] **1** the activity of making clothes smooth with an iron: *I hate doing the ironing.* **2** clothes that are waiting to be ironed or have just been ironed: *I'm tired and there's still a pile of ironing to do.*

'ironing ,board *n* [C] a small narrow table used for ironing clothes → see picture at IRON

,iron 'lung *n* [C] a large machine with a metal case used to help people to breathe

i·ron·mon·ger /ˈaɪənˌmʌŋɡə $ ˈaɪərnˌmʌŋɡər, -ˌmɑːŋ-/ *n* [C] *BrE old-fashioned* **1** someone who works in or owns a shop that sells tools and equipment for your home and garden **2 ironmonger's** a shop that sells this equipment —**ironmongery** *n* [U]

,iron 'rations *n* [plural] small amounts of high energy food, carried by soldiers, mountain climbers etc

i·ron·ware /ˈaɪənweə $ ˈaɪərnwer/ *n* [U] articles made of iron

i·ron·work /ˈaɪənwɜːk $ ˈaɪərnwɜːrk/ *n* [U] fences, gates etc made of iron bent into attractive shapes

i·ron·y /ˈaɪərəni $ ˈaɪrə-/ *n plural* **ironies 1** [C,U] a situation that is unusual or amusing because something strange happens, or the opposite of what is expected happens or is true: *Life is full of little ironies.* | **tragic/cruel/bitter etc irony** *The tragic irony is that the drug was supposed to save lives.* **2** [U] when you use words that are the opposite of what you really mean, often in order to be amusing: **trace/hint/touch of irony** *Wagner calls his program 'the worst talk show in America,' without a hint of irony.* | **heavy irony** *BrE* (=a lot of irony) *'Of course Michael won't be late; you know how punctual he always is,' she said with heavy irony.* → SARCASM → DRAMATIC IRONY

ir·ra·di·ate /ɪˈreɪdieɪt/ *v* [T usually passive] **1** technical if someone or something is irradiated, X-RAYS or RADIOACTIVE beams are passed through them **2** technical if food is irradiated, it is treated with RADIATION in order to kill BACTERIA and make it last longer: *irradiated food* **3** literary to make something look bright as if a light is shining onto it —**irradiation** /ɪˌreɪdiˈeɪʃən/ *n* [U]

ir·ra·tion·al /ɪˈræʃənəl/ *adj* not based on clear thought or reason; ⊟ **unreasonable**; ⊟ **rational, reasonable**: *an irrational fear of flying* | *He's becoming increasingly irrational.* —**irrationally** *adv* —**irrationality** /ɪˌræʃəˈnæləti/ *n* [U]

ir·rec·on·ci·la·ble /ɪˌrekənˈsaɪləbəl◂/ *adj* **1** irreconcilable positions etc are so strongly opposed to each other that it is not possible for them to reach an agreement: **irreconcilable differences/conflicts** *The differences between the landowners and the conservationists were irreconcilable from the start.* **2** if two beliefs or ideas are irreconcilable, it is not possible to believe both of them: [+with] *This belief was irreconcilable with the Church's doctrine of salvation.* **3 irreconcilable differences** strong disagreements between two people who are married, given as a legal reason for getting a DIVORCE

ir·re·cov·er·a·ble /ˌɪrɪˈkʌvərəbəl◂/ *adj formal* something that is irrecoverable is lost or has gone and you cannot get it back: *irrecoverable loss of sight* | *The insurance premium is wholly irrecoverable.*

ir·re·deem·a·ble /ˌɪrɪˈdiːməbəl◂/ *adj* **1** formal too bad to be corrected, repaired, or saved: *Very few children are irredeemable.* **2** technical irredeemable BONDS pay interest to the person who is lending money but do not have a set date saying when the money being lent must be paid back —**irredeemably** *adv*

ir·re·duc·i·ble /ˌɪrɪˈdjuːsᵻbəl◂ $ -ˈduː-/ *adj* written an irreducible sum, level etc cannot be made smaller or simpler —**irreducibly** *adv*

ir·re·fu·ta·ble /ˌɪrɪˈfjuːtəbəl◂ $ ɪˈrefjᵿtəbəl, ˌɪrɪˈfjuː-/ *adj* an irrefutable statement, argument etc cannot be proved to be wrong, and must be accepted: **irrefutable evidence/proof/facts** *irrefutable proof of his innocence* —**irrefutably** *adv*

ir·reg·u·lar¹ /ɪˈreɡjᵿlə $ -ər/ *adj* **1** having a shape, surface, pattern etc that is not even, smooth, or balanced; ⊟ **uneven**; ⊟ **regular**: *a jagged, irregular coastline* | *It has a highly irregular shape, covered in bumps and indentations.* **2** not happening at times that are an equal distance from each other; ⊟ **regular**: *He's receiving medication for an irregular heartbeat.* | *Beamish only returned to Britain at irregular intervals.* **3** not happening or done at the normal time for doing something; ⊟ **regular**: *Funeral directors often work long, irregular hours.* **4** formal not obeying the usually accepted legal or moral rules: *It would be highly irregular* (=extremely irregular) *for a minister to accept payments of this kind.* **5 irregular verb/plural etc** a verb or a form of a word that does not follow the usual pattern of grammar, such as the verb 'catch' or the plural 'fish'; ⊟ **regular 6** *AmE* a word meaning CONSTIPATED (=unable to easily pass food waste from your body), used in order to be polite —**irregularly** *adv* —**irregularity** /ɪˌreɡjᵿˈlærᵻti/ *n* [C,U]: *The club were found guilty of financial irregularities.*

irregular² *n* [C] a soldier who is not an official member of a country's army

ir·rel·e·vance /ɪˈreləvəns/ also **ir·rel·e·van·cy** /-vənsi/ *n* **1** [U] a lack of importance in a particular situation **2** [C] someone or something that is not important in a particular situation: [+of] *debates on the irrelevance of the education system*

ir·rel·e·vant /ɪˈreləvənt/ *adj* not useful or not relating to a particular situation, and therefore not important; ⊟ **relevant**: *We're focusing too much on irrelevant details.* | *Students viewed Latin as boring and irrelevant.* | **largely/totally/completely etc irrelevant** *His age is completely irrelevant if he can do the job.* |

[+to] *The defendant's lawyer argued that his past offenses were irrelevant to this case.* —**irrelevantly** *adv*

ir·re·li·gious /ˌɪrɪˈlɪdʒəs◂ / *adj formal* opposed to religion, or not having any religious feeling

ir·re·me·di·a·ble /ˌɪrɪˈmiːdiəbəl◂ / *adj formal* so bad that it is impossible to make it better

ir·rep·a·ra·ble /ɪˈrepərəbəl/ *adj written* irreparable damage, harm etc is so bad that it can never be repaired or made better: *Extensive mining will cause irreparable damage to the area.* —**irreparably** *adv*

ir·re·place·a·ble /ˌɪrɪˈpleɪsəbəl / *adj* too special, valuable, or unusual to be replaced by anything else: *Works of art were lost, many of them irreplaceable.*

ir·re·pres·si·ble /ˌɪrɪˈpresɨbəl◂ / *adj written* full of energy, confidence, and happiness so that you never seem unhappy: *an irrepressible optimist* —**irrepressibly** *adv*

ir·re·proach·a·ble /ˌɪrɪˈprəʊtʃəbəl◂ $ -ˈprəʊtʃ-/ *adj formal* something, such as someone's behaviour, that is irreproachable is so good that you cannot criticize it

ir·re·sis·ti·ble /ˌɪrɪˈzɪstɨbəl◂ / *adj* **1** so attractive, desirable etc that you cannot prevent yourself from wanting it: [+to] *It's difficult to find Natalie irresistible.* | *Men find Natalie irresistible.* **2** too strong or powerful to be stopped or prevented: *I was overcome by an irresistible urge to cry.* —**irresistibly** *adv*

ir·res·o·lute /ɪˈrezəluːt/ *adj formal* unable to decide what to do; ▣ **uncertain**; ▣ **resolute** —**irresolution** /ˌrezəˈluːʃən/ *n* [U]

ir·re·spec·tive /ˌɪrɪˈspektɪv/ *adv formal* **irrespective of sth** used when saying that a particular fact has no effect on a situation and is not important: *The course is open to anyone, irrespective of age.*

ir·re·spon·si·ble /ˌɪrɪˈspɒnsɨbəl◂ $ -ˈspɑːn-/ *adj* doing careless things without thinking or worrying about the possible bad results; ▣ **responsible**: **totally/ highly/completely etc irresponsible** *When it comes to money, Dan is completely irresponsible.* | **it is irresponsible (for sb) to do sth** *It would be irresponsible not to turn up for work without calling.* | *It was highly irresponsible of him to leave the children on their own in the pool.* —**irresponsibly** *adv*: *He was acting totally irresponsibly.* —**irresponsibility** /ˌɪrɪspɒnsɨˈbɪlɨti $ -spɑːn-/ *n* [U]

ir·re·triev·a·ble /ˌɪrɪˈtriːvəbəl◂ / *adj formal* **1** an irretrievable situation cannot be made right again: *the irretrievable breakdown of their marriage* **2 irretrievable loss** the loss of something that you can never get back —**irretrievably** *adv*: *irretrievably lost*

ir·rev·e·rent /ɪˈrevərənt/ *adj* someone that is irreverent, does not show respect for organizations, customs, beliefs etc that most other people respect – often used to show approval: *his irreverent sense of humour* | *She has an irreverent attitude towards marriage.* —**irreverently** *adv* —**irreverence** *n* [U]

ir·re·ver·si·ble /ˌɪrɪˈvɜːsɨbəl◂ $ -ɜːr-/ *adj* **1** irreversible damage, change etc is so serious or so great that you cannot change something back to how it was before; ▣ **reversible**: *Fossil fuels have caused irreversible damage to the environment.* **2** if an illness or bad physical condition is irreversible, it will continue to exist and cannot be cured: *Miller is in an irreversible coma.* | *irreversible blindness* —**irreversibly** *adv His reputation was irreversibly damaged by the affair.*

ir·rev·o·ca·ble /ɪˈrevəkəbəl/ *adj* an irrevocable decision, action etc cannot be changed or stopped: *Think about the situation carefully before you take an irrevocable step.* —**irrevocably** *adv*: *machines that irrevocably changed the pattern of rural life*

ir·ri·gate /ˈɪrɨgeɪt/ *v* [T] **1** to supply land or crops with water: *The water in Lake Powell is used to irrigate the area.* | **irrigated land/farms/crops** **2** *technical* to wash a wound with a flow of liquid —**irrigation** /ˌɪrɨˈgeɪʃən/ *n* [U]: *major irrigation projects*

ir·ri·ta·ble /ˈɪrɨtəbəl/ *adj* getting annoyed quickly or easily; ▣ **crabby**: *Jo was tired, irritable, and depressed.* —**irritably** *adv* —**irritability** /ˌɪrɨtəˈbɪlɨti/ *n* [U]

ir·ri·tant /ˈɪrɨtənt/ *n* [C] **1** *formal* something that keeps annoying you over a period of time: *Low flying aircraft are a constant irritant in this area.* **2** a substance that can make a part of your body painful and sore: *a skin irritant*

ir·ri·tate /ˈɪrɨteɪt/ *v* [T] **1** to make someone feel annoyed or impatient, especially by doing something many times or for a long period of time: *It really irritates me when he doesn't help around the house.* **2** to make a part of your body painful and sore: *This cream may irritate sensitive skin.*

ir·ri·tat·ed /ˈɪrɨteɪtɨd/ *adj* **1** feeling annoyed and impatient about something: [+about/at/with/by] *John was getting irritated by all her questions.*; → see box at **NERVOUS** **2** painful and sore: *Her throat and eyes were irritated.*

ir·ri·tat·ing /ˈɪrɨteɪtɪŋ/ *adj* an irritating habit, situation etc keeps annoying you: *He's the most irritating man I've ever met.* | *He was smiling in a way I found very irritating.* | **irritating habit/characteristics/mannerisms** *She has an irritating habit of interrupting everything you say.* | *a dry irritating cough* —**irritatingly** *adv*

ir·ri·ta·tion /ˌɪrɨˈteɪʃən/ *n* **1** [U] the feeling of being annoyed about something, especially something that happens repeatedly or for a long time: *The heavy traffic is a constant source of irritation.* | [+at/with] *The doctor's irritation at being interrupted showed.* **2** [C] something that makes you annoyed: *The children are just an irritation for him when he's trying to work.* **3** [U] a painful, sore feeling on a part of your body: *The astringent can cause irritation to sensitive skin.* | *a throat irritation*

ir·rup·tion /ɪˈrʌpʃən/ *n* [C] *formal* a sudden rush of people or things into a place

IRS /ˌaɪ ɑːr ˈes/ *n* **the IRS** *the Internal Revenue Service* the department of the US government that collects national taxes

is /s, z, əz; *strong* ɪz/ the third person singular of the present tense of BE

-isation /aɪzeɪʃən $ əzeɪ-/ *suffix* a British spelling of -IZATION

ISBN /ˌaɪ es biː ˈen/ *n* *International Standard Book Number* a number that is given to every book that is PUBLISHED

ISDN /ˌaɪ es diː ˈen/ *n* [U] *Integrated Services Digital Network* a system that is used to send computer information at very high speed along an electronic wire similar to a telephone line

-ise /aɪz/ *suffix* [in verbs] a British spelling of -IZE

-ish /ɪʃ/ *suffix* **1** [in nouns] the people or language of a particular country or place: *Are the British unfriendly?* | *learning to speak Turkish* | *She's Swedish.* **2** [in adjectives] of a particular place: *Spanish food* (=from Spain) **3** [in adjectives] typical of or like a particular type of person: *foolish behaviour* (=typical of a fool) | *Don't be so childish!* (=do not behave like a child) | *snobbish* **4** [in adjectives] the ending of some adjectives that show disapproval: *selfish* **5** [in adjectives] rather; ▣ **quite**: *youngish* (=not very young, but not old either) | *tallish* | *reddish hair* **6** [in adjectives] *spoken* APPROXIMATELY: *We'll expect you eightish* (=at about 8 o'clock). | *He's fortyish* (=about 40 years old).

Is·lam /ˈɪslɑːm, ˈɪz-, ɪsˈlɑːm/ *n* [U] **1** the Muslim religion, which was started by Muhammad and whose holy book is the Koran **2** the people and countries that follow this religion —**Islamist** *n* [C] —**Islamic** /ɪzˈlæmɪk, ɪs-/ *adj*

is·land [W2] /ˈaɪlənd/ *n* [C] a piece of land completely surrounded by water: *The Cayman Islands* | *the Greek* *island of Crete* | **on an island** *No cars are allowed on the island.* → DESERT ISLAND; → see picture at COUNTRY

is·land·er /ˈaɪləndə $ -ər/ *n* [C] someone who lives on an island

is·let /ˈaɪlɪ̯t/ *n* [C] *literary* a very small island

-ism /ɪzəm/ *suffix* [in nouns] **1** a political belief or religion based on a particular principle or the ideas and beliefs of a particular person: *socialism* | *Buddhism* **2** the action or process of doing something: *his criticism of my work* **3** an action or remark that has a particular quality: *her witticisms* (=funny remarks) **4** the state of being like something or someone, or having a particular quality: *heroism* (=being a HERO; bravery) | *magnetism* (=being MAGNETIC) **5** illness caused by too much of something: *alcoholism* **6** the practice of treating people unfairly because of something: *sexism* (=making unfair differences between men and women) | *racism*

is·m /ˈɪzəm/ *n* [C] *informal* used to describe a set of ideas or beliefs whose name ends in 'ism', especially when you think that they are not sensible or practical

isle /aɪl/ *n* [C] a word for an island, used in poetry or in names of islands: *the British Isles*

is·n't /ˈɪzənt/ the short form of 'is not'

iso- /aɪsəʊ, -sə $ -soʊ, -sə/ *prefix technical* the same all through or in every part; ▤ **equal**: *an isotherm* (=line joining places of equal temperature)

i·so·bar /ˈaɪsəbɑː $ -bɑːr/ *n* [C] *technical* a line on a weather map joining places where the air pressure is the same

i·so·late /ˈaɪsəleɪt/ *v* [T] **1** to separate one person, group, or thing from other people or things: *The town was isolated by the floods.* | *The US has sought to isolate Cuba both economically and politically.* | **isolate sb from sb** *Presley's phenomenal early success isolated him from his friends.* | **isolate sb from sth** *New-born babies must be isolated from possible contamination.* **2** if you isolate an idea, problem etc, you consider it separately from other things that are connected with it: **isolate sth from sth** *It is impossible to isolate political responsibility from moral responsibility.* **3** *technical* to separate a substance, disease etc from other substances so that it can be studied: **isolate sth from sth** *The hepatitis B virus has been isolated from breast milk.*

i·so·lat·ed W3 /ˈaɪsəleɪtɪ̯d/ *adj*
1 an isolated building, village etc is far away from any others; ▤ **remote**: *small isolated communities* | *Not many people visit this isolated spot.*
2 feeling alone and unable to meet or speak to other people: *Young mothers often feel isolated.*
3 an isolated action, event, example etc happens only once, and is not likely to happen again: **isolated incident/case/event** *Police say that last week's protest was an isolated incident.*

i·so·la·tion /ˌaɪsəˈleɪʃən/ *n* [U] **1** when one group, person, or thing is separate from others: *Because of its geographical isolation, the area developed its own unique culture.* | **[+of]** *the isolation of rural areas* | **international/diplomatic/political isolation** *the country's continuing political isolation* | **in isolation** *The political prisoner had been held in complete isolation.* | *The mansion sits in splendid isolation on top of the hill* (=it is far from everything and looks impressive). | **isolation hospital/ward** *BrE: Scarlet fever victims had to go to the isolation hospital.* | *a patient's isolation period* **2** when someone feels alone and unable to meet or speak to other people: *Retirement can often cause feelings of isolation.* | *elderly people living in social isolation* **3 in isolation (from sth)** if something exists or is considered in isolation, it exists or is considered separately from other things that are connected with it: *The future of health care cannot be considered in isolation from economic factors.*

i·so·la·tion·is·m /ˌaɪsəˈleɪʃ(ə)nɪzəm/ *n* [U] beliefs or actions that are based on the political principle that

your country should not be involved in the affairs of other countries —**isolationist** *adj: isolationist policies* —**isolationist** *n* [C]

i·so·met·rics /ˌaɪsəˈmetrɪks/ *n* [plural] exercises that make your muscles stronger by pushing against each other

i·sos·ce·les tri·an·gle /aɪˌsɒsəliːz ˈtraɪæŋɡəl $ -ˌsɑː-/ *n* [C] a three-sided shape in which two of the sides are the same length → EQUILATERAL TRIANGLE

i·so·therm /ˈaɪsəθɜːm $ -ɜːrm/ *n* [C] *technical* a line on a weather map joining places where the temperature is the same

i·so·tope /ˈaɪsətəʊp $ -toʊp/ *n* [C] *technical* one of the possible different forms of an atom of a particular ELEMENT (=simple chemical substance)

ISP /ˌaɪ es ˈpiː/ *n* [C] **Internet service provider** a business that provides a connection to the Internet for people's computers

Is·rae·li¹ /ɪzˈreɪli/ *adj* relating to Israel or its people: *the Israeli government*

Israeli² *n* [C] someone from Israel

Is·rael·ite /ˈɪzrəlaɪt $ ˈɪzriə-/ *n, adj biblical* someone who lived in Israel in the past when it was ruled by kings, or relating to this country or its people

is·sue¹ /ˈɪʃuː, ˈɪsju $ ˈɪʃuː/ *n*
1 SUBJECT/PROBLEM [C] a subject or problem that is often discussed or argued about, especially a social or political matter that affects the interests of a lot of people

the issue of sth
raise an issue (=say that an issue should be discussed)
address an issue (=discuss or deal with an issue)
resolve an issue
avoid/dodge/duck/evade an issue (=avoid discussing an issue)
confuse/cloud an issue (=make an issue more difficult by talking about things not related to it)
important/key/major/big issue
thorny/vexed issue (=difficult issue)
complex issue
sensitive issue
political/social/economic/environmental issues
sth is not the issue spoken (=used to say that something is not the important part of what you are discussing)

Abortion is a highly controversial issue. | *We should **raise the issue** of discrimination with the council.* | *Dillon **addressed the issue of** child abuse in his speech.* | *How the **issue is resolved** is crucial.* | *When asked about the bill, the senator tried to **duck the issue**.* | *They're **clouding the issue** with uninformed judgements.* | *The **key issue** is whether workers should be classified as 'employees'.* | *the **thorny issue** of creating a single European currency* | *Economic issues should get more attention.* | *Unemployment **is not the issue** - the real problem is the decline in public morality.*

2 MAGAZINE [C] a magazine or newspaper printed for a particular day, week, or month: **[+of]** *the January issue of Newsweek* | **the current/latest issue** *Have you seen the latest issue?*
3 take issue with sb/sth to disagree or argue with someone about something: *It is difficult to take issue with his analysis.* | **take issue with sb over sth** *I must take issue with you over what you said yesterday.*
4 make an issue (out) of sth to argue about something, especially in a way that annoys other people because they do not think it is important: *I was upset by Eleanor's remarks, but didn't make an issue of it.*
5 have issues (with sb/sth) *informal* **a)** to have problems dealing with something because of something that happened in the past: *There's a self-help group for people who have issues with money.* **b)** if you have issues with someone or something, you do not agree with or approve of them: *I have a few issues with Marc.*
6 at issue *formal* the problem or subject at issue is the most important part of what you are discussing or

considering: *At issue here is the extent to which exam results reflect a student's ability.*

7 ACT OF GIVING STH [singular] the act of officially giving people something to use: *the issue of identity cards to all non-residents*

8 SET OF THINGS FOR SALE [C] a new set of something such as SHARES or stamps, made available for people to buy: *We launched the **share issue** on March 1. | a new issue of bonds*

9 die without issue *old use* to die without having any children

issue² W2 *v* [T]

1 to officially make a statement, give an order, warning etc: *Silva **issued** a **statement** denying all knowledge of the affair. | a warning issued by the Surgeon General*

2 if an organization or someone in an official position issues something such as documents or equipment, they give these things to people who need them: **issue a passport/permit/visa etc** *The US State department issues millions of passports each year.* | **issue sb with sth** *All the workers were issued with protective clothing.* | **issue sth to sb** *The policy document will be issued to all employees.*

3 to officially produce something such as new stamps, coins, or SHARES and make them available to buy

issue forth *phr v literary*
if something issues forth, it comes out of a place or thing: [+**from**] *A low grunt issued forth from his throat.*

issue from sth *phr v literary*
if something issues from a place or thing, it comes out of it: *Smoke issued from the factory chimneys.*

-ist /ɪ̈st/ *suffix* **1** [in nouns] someone who believes in a particular religion or set of principles or ideas: *a Buddhist | an atheist | a Scottish Nationalist* **2** [in adjectives] relating to or showing a particular political or religious belief: *her socialist views | rightist parties* (=political parties with RIGHT-WING opinions) **3** [in nouns] someone who studies a particular subject, plays a particular instrument, or does a particular type of work: *a linguist* (=someone who studies or learns languages) | *a novelist* (=someone who writes NOVELS) | *a guitarist* (=someone who plays the GUITAR) | *a machinist* (=someone who operates a machine) → **-OLO-GIST** **4** [in adjectives] treating people unfairly because of something: *a very sexist remark* (=making unfair differences between men and women) **5** [in nouns] someone who treats people unfairly because of something: *They're a bunch of racists.*

isth·mus /ˈɪsməs/ *n* [C] a narrow piece of land with water on both sides, that connects two larger areas of land: *the Isthmus of Panama*

it S1 W1 /ɪt/ *pron* [used as subject or object]

1 used to refer to a thing, animal, situation, idea etc that has already been mentioned or is already known about: *'Where's your office?' 'It's on the third floor.' | I love the spring – it's a wonderful time of the year. | There were people crying, buildings on fire. It was terrible! | Don't blame me. It wasn't my idea. | This little beast is a lemur and it lives in Madagascar.*

2 used to refer to the situation that someone is in now, or what is happening now: *I can't stand it any longer. I'm resigning. | How's it going, Bob? I haven't seen you for ages. | And the worst of it is the car isn't even paid for yet. | Stop it, you two. You're just being silly.*

3 used as the subject or object of a verb when the real subject or object is later in the sentence: *It worries me the way he keeps changing his mind. | What's it like being a sailor? | Apparently it's cheaper to fly than to go by train. | It's a pity you couldn't come. | It seems that we are not welcome here. | I found it hard to concentrate.*

4 used as the subject of a sentence when you are talking about the weather, the time, a distance etc: *Is it still raining? | It was 4 o'clock and the mail still hadn't come. | It's my birthday today. | It's over 200 miles from London to Manchester. | It gets dark very early in the winter. | It's three years since I last saw her.*

5 used with the verb 'be' to emphasize that you are talking about one particular thing, person, group etc

and not any other: *It's Lawrence you should be talking to. | It was malaria that killed him. | It was in New Zealand that Elizabeth first met Mr Cronje.*

6 used to refer to a baby when you do not know what sex the baby is: *What will you call it if it's a boy?*

7 a) used to say who a person is: *'Who's that over there?' 'It's Robert Morley.'* **b)** *spoken* used to say who is speaking, especially on the telephone: *Hello, it's Frank here. | It's all right, it's only me.*

8 *informal* used to refer to sex: *Have you done it with him yet?*

9 if it wasn't/weren't for sb/sth also **if it hadn't been for sb/sth** used to say who or what prevents or prevented something from happening: *We would have arrived much earlier if it hadn't been for the snow.*

10 *informal* a particular ability or quality that is needed in order to do something: *In a job like advertising, you've either got it or you haven't!*

11 this is it *spoken* used to say that something you expected to happen is actually going to happen: *This is it, boys, the moment we've been waiting for.*

12 that's it *spoken* **a)** used to say that something is completely finished or that a situation cannot be changed: *That's it then. There's nothing more we can do.* **b)** used to tell someone that they are doing something correctly: *Slowly...slowly. Yeah, that's it.* **c)** also **that does it** used when you are angry about a situation and you do not want it to continue: *That's it. I'm leaving.*

13 think you're it *informal* to think you are more important than you are: *Just because he got a higher mark he really thinks he's it.*

IT /ˌaɪ ˈtiː/ *n* [U] *information technology* the study or use of electronic processes and equipment for storing information and making it available

I·tal·i·an¹ /ɪˈtæliən/ *adj* relating to Italy, its people, or its language

Italian² *n* **1** [C] someone from Italy **2** [U] the language used in Italy

I·tal·i·a·nate /ɪˈtæliəneɪt/ *adj* with an Italian style or appearance: *an Italianate villa*

i·tal·i·cize also **-ise** *BrE* /ɪˈtælɪˌsaɪz/ *v* [T] to put or print something in italics —**italicized** *adj*

i·tal·ics /ɪˈtælɪks/ *n* [plural] a type of printed letters that lean to the right, often used to emphasize particular words: **in italics** *This example is written in italics.* → ROMAN —**italic** *adj*: *italic script*

Italo- /ɪtæləʊ $ -loʊ/ *prefix* [in nouns and adjectives] Italian and something else: *a joint Italo-German proposal*

itch¹ /ɪtʃ/ *v* **1** [I,T] if part of your body or your clothes itch, you have an unpleasant feeling on your skin that makes you want to rub it with your nails; → **scratch**: *My feet were itching terribly. | The label on this shirt itches me.* **2 be itching to do sth, be itching for sth** *informal* to want to do something very much and as soon as possible: *He was itching for a fight.*

itch² *n* **1** [singular] an uncomfortable feeling on your skin that makes you want to rub it with your nails: *Scratch my back – I **have an itch**.* **2** *informal* a strong desire to do or have something: [+**for**] *an itch for adventure*

itch·y /ˈɪtʃi/ *adj comparative* **itchier**, *superlative* **itchiest** **1** if part of your body is itchy, it feels slightly unpleasant and you want to rub it with your nails: *My eyes sometimes get red and itchy in the summer. | an itchy rash* **2** if clothes are itchy, they make your skin feel slightly unpleasant, so that you want to rub your skin with your nails; ■ **scratchy**: *These tights are all itchy.* **3** wanting to go somewhere new or do something different: *He's had that job now for about eight years, and he's starting to **get itchy**. | I've only been back home for a few months and I've already got **itchy feet** (=the desire to go somewhere new).* **4 itchy fingers** *informal* someone with itchy fingers is likely to steal things: *I tucked the bills deep into my pocket, away from ttchy fingers.* – **itchiness** *n* [U]

it'd /'ɪtəd/ *usually spoken* the short form of 'it would' or 'it had': *I'd do it if I thought it'd help.*

-ite /aɪt/ *suffix* **1** [in nouns] a follower or supporter of a particular idea or person – often used in order to show disapproval: *a group of Trotskyites* (=followers of Trotsky's political ideas) | *the Pre-Raphaelites* **2** [in adjectives] relating to a particular set of religious or political ideas, or with the ideas of a particular person: *his Reaganite opinions* **3** someone who lives in a particular place or belongs to a particular group: *a Brooklynite* (=someone from Brooklyn) | *the Israelites* (=in the Bible)

i·tem W1 /'aɪtəm/ *n*
1 [C] a single thing, especially one thing in a list, group, or set of things: *He opened the cardboard box and took out each item.* | *The store is having a sale on furniture and household items.* | **item on the agenda/list/menu** *We went on to the next item on the agenda.* | **item of clothing/furniture/jewellery etc** (=a single piece of clothing, furniture, jewellery etc) | *luxury items such as exotic spices and perfumes* | *The original 1965 bottle is now a collector's item* (=one of a set of objects people like to collect because they are interesting or valuable).
2 [C] a single, usually short, piece of news in a newspaper or magazine, or on television: *I also saw that news item in the Sunday Times.*
3 be an item *informal* if two people are an item, they are having a romantic or sexual relationship

i·tem·ize also **-ise** *BrE* /'aɪtəmaɪz/ *v* [T] to make a list and give details about each thing on the list: *an itemized bill*

it·e·rate /'ɪtəreɪt/ *v* [T] **1** if a computer iterates, it goes through a set of instructions before going through them for a second time **2** *formal* to say or do something again —**iteration** /ˌɪtəˈreɪʃən/ *n* [C,U] —**iterative** /'ɪtərətɪv/ *adj* [only before noun]: *iterative processes*

i·tin·e·rant /aɪˈtɪnərənt/ *adj* [only before noun] *formal* travelling from place to place, especially to work: *itinerant labourers* —**itinerant** *n* C

i·tin·e·ra·ry /aɪˈtɪnərəri $ -nəreri/ *n plural* **itineraries** [C] a plan or list of the places you will visit on a journey: *His itinerary would take him from Bordeaux to Budapest.*

-itis /aɪtɪs/ *suffix* [in nouns] **1** an illness or infection that effects a particular part of your body: *tonsillitis* (=infection of the TONSILS) **2** *humorous* the condition of having too much of something or liking something too much: *televisionitis* (=watching too much television)

it'll /'ɪtl/ *usually spoken* the short form of 'it will': *It'll be dark before they get back.*

it's /ɪts/ **1** the short form of 'it is': *It's raining.* **2** a short form of 'it has': *It's been cloudy all day.* ⚠ Do not confuse **it's** and **its**. **Its** (without an apostrophe) is a possessive form like **my**, **his**, **their** etc.

its S1 W1 /ɪts/ *determiner* [possessive form of 'it'] used to refer to something that belongs to or is connected with a thing, animal, baby etc that has already been mentioned: *Salzburg is famous for its beautiful buildings.* | *The hotel has its own pool.* ⚠ Do not confuse **its** and **it's**. **It's** (with an apostrophe) means 'it is' or 'it has'.

it·self S1 W1 /ɪt'self/ *pron* [reflexive form of 'it']
1 used to show that a thing, organization, animal, or baby that does something is affected by its own action: *The cat lay on the sofa, washing itself.* | *The machine switches itself off when the process is complete.* | *a small local enterprise that has transformed itself into a highly successful company*
2 used to emphasize that you are talking about one particular thing, organization etc: *We've checked the wiring so the problem may be the television itself.*

3 in/of itself considered separately from any other facts: *There is a slight infection in the lung which in itself is not serious.*
4 (all) by itself a) alone: *Will the dog be safe left in the car by itself?* **b)** without help or without a person making it work: *The door seemed to open all by itself.*
5 (all) to itself not shared with other things: *This idea deserves a chapter to itself.*

it·sy-bit·sy /ˌɪtsi 'bɪtsi◂/ also **it·ty-bit·ty** /ˌɪti 'bɪti◂/ *adj* [only before noun] *spoken* very small – used humorously

iTV /ˌaɪ ti: 'vi:/ *n* [U] *interactive television* a type of television programme that allows people who are watching at home to answer questions or find out more information by using a computer or special equipment

ITV /ˌaɪ ti: 'vi:/ *n Independent Television* a group of British television companies that are paid for by advertising

-ity /ɪti/ also **-ty** *suffix* [in nouns] the state of having a particular quality, or something that has that quality: *with great regularity* (=regularly) | *such stupidities* (=stupid actions or remarks)

IUD /ˌaɪ ju: 'di:/ *n* [C] *intra-uterine device* a small plastic or metal object used inside a woman's UTERUS (=place where a baby develops) to prevent a baby being born; ⊟ **coil**

IV /ˌaɪ 'vi:/ *n* [C] *AmE intravenous* medical equipment that is used to put liquid directly into your blood; ⊟ **drip** *BrE*

I've /aɪv/ *usually spoken* the short form of 'I have': *I've never been here before.*

-ive /ɪv/ *suffix* [in nouns and adjectives] someone or something that does something or can do something: *an explosive* (=substance that can explode) | *a detective* (=someone who tries to discover facts about crimes) | *the adoptive parents* (=who ADOPT a child)

IVF /ˌaɪ vi: 'ef/ *n* [U] *in vitro fertilization* a process in which a human egg is FERTILIZED outside the woman's body

i·vied /'aɪvid/ *adj literary* covered with ivy

i·vo·ry /'aɪvəri/ *n plural* **ivories 1** [U] the hard smooth yellowish-white substance from the TUSKS (=long teeth) of an ELEPHANT: *an ivory chess set* **2** [U] a yellowish white colour: *an ivory silk wedding gown* **3** [C often plural] something made of ivory, especially a small figure of a person or animal: *a collection of Chinese ivories*

ivory 'tower *n* [C] a place or situation where you are separated from the difficulties of ordinary life and so are unable to understand them, used especially to describe a college or university: *an academic in an ivory tower*

i·vy /'aɪvi/ *n plural* **ivies** [C,U] a climbing plant with dark green shiny leaves → POISON IVY; → see picture at FLOWER

Ivy League *n* the Ivy League a group of eight old and respected universities in the northeastern US —**Ivy League** *adj*: *an Ivy League college*

-ization also **-isation** *BrE* /aɪzeɪʃən $ əzeɪ-/ *suffix* makes nouns from verbs ending in -IZE: *civilization* | *crystallization*

-ize also **-ise** *BrE* /aɪz/ *suffix* [in verbs] **1** to make something have more of a particular quality: *We need to modernize our procedures.* (=make them more modern) | *Americanized spelling* (=spelling made more American) | *privatized transport* (=bus or train services that are owned and operated by private companies) **2** to change something to something else, or be changed to something else: *The liquid crystallized.* (=turned into CRYSTALS) **3** to speak or think in the way mentioned: *to soliloquize* (=speak a SOLILOQUY, to yourself) | *I sat and listened to him sermonizing.* (=speaking solemnly, as if in a SERMON) **4** to put into a particular place: *She was hospitalized after the accident.*

J, j

J, j /dʒeɪ/ *plural* **J's, j's** *n* [C,U] the tenth letter of the English alphabet

J the written abbreviation of *joule* or joules

jab¹ /dʒæb/ *v* **jabbed, jabbing** [I,T] to push something into or towards something else with short quick movements: [+**at**] *She jabbed at the elevator buttons.* | *When I didn't respond, he* **jabbed** *a finger at me.* | **jab sb with sth** *Stop jabbing me with your elbow!* | **jab sth into sth** *The soldier jabbed a rifle into his ribs.*

jab² *n* [C] **1** a sudden hard hit, especially with a pointed object or your FIST (=closed hand): *a boxer with a good* **left jab** **2** something you say to criticize someone or something else: *White House officials* **took** *a sharp jab at the Democrats' plan.* **3** *BrE informal* an INJECTION given to prevent you from catching a disease; ▣ **shot**: *a typhoid jab*

jab·ber /'dʒæbə $ -ər/ *v* [I,T] to talk quickly in an excited and unclear way – used to show disapproval: *The tourists were jabbering away on the bus.* —**jabber** *n* [singular, U]

jack¹ /dʒæk/ *n* [C] **1** a piece of equipment used to lift a heavy weight off the ground, such as a car, and support it while it is in the air: *a hydraulic jack* **2** a card used in card games that has a man's picture on it and is worth less than a queen and more than a ten: **jack of hearts/clubs etc** | *a pair of jacks* **3** an electronic connection for a telephone or other electric machine: *a phone jack* **4 a) jacks** [plural] a children's game in which the players try to pick up small objects called jacks while BOUNCING and catching a ball **b)** a small metal or plastic object that has six points, used in this game **5** a small white ball at which players aim larger balls in the game of BOWLS **6 jack (shit)** *AmE* spoken not polite a rude expression meaning nothing at all: *He doesn't know jack shit about cars.* → JUMPING JACK, UNION JACK

jack² *v*

jack sb around *phr v AmE spoken* to waste someone's time by deliberately making things difficult for them: *Stop jacking me around and make up your mind!*

jack sth ⇔ in *phr v BrE informal* to stop doing something: *I'd love to jack in my job and go and live in the Bahamas.*

jack off *phr v AmE informal not polite* to MASTURBATE

jack sth ⇔ up *phr v* **1** to lift something heavy off the ground using a jack: *Jack the car up higher – I can't get the tire off.* **2** *informal* to increase prices, sales etc by a large amount: *They're just interested in jacking up their profit margins.*

jack·al /'dʒækɔ:l, -kəl $ -kəl/ *n* [C] a wild animal like a dog that lives in Asia and Africa and eats the remaining parts of dead animals

jack·ass /'dʒæk-æs/ *n* [C] *AmE spoken not polite* an offensive word for an annoying stupid person

jack·boot /'dʒækbu:t/ *n* [C] a boot worn by soldiers that covers their leg up to the knee —**jackbooted** *adj*

jack·daw /'dʒækdɔː $ -dɒː/ *n* [C] a black bird like a CROW that sometimes steals small, bright objects

jack·et ▣S2▣ ▣W3▣ /'dʒækɪt/ *n* [C]

1 a short, light coat: **a leather/denim/linen etc jacket** *a suede jacket* → BOMBER JACKET, DINNER JACKET, LIFE JACKET, STRAITJACKET (1)

2 the part of a suit that covers the top part of your body: *Gene has to wear a jacket and tie to work.* | *tweed jackets* → SPORTS JACKET

3 a stiff piece of folded paper that fits over the cover of a book to protect it; ▣ **dust jacket**

4 *AmE* a stiff paper cover that protects a record; ▣ **sleeve** *BrE*

5 a cover that surrounds and protects some types of machines

jacket po·ta·to *n* [C] *BrE* a potato baked with its skin on; ▣ **baked potato**

Jack Frost *n* [singular] a way of describing FROST as a person – used especially when talking to children

jack·ham·mer /'dʒæk,hæmə $ -ər/ *n* [C] *AmE* a large powerful tool used to break hard materials such as the surface of a road; ▣ **pneumatic drill** *BrE*

jack-in-the-box *n* [C] a children's toy shaped like a box with a figure inside that springs out when the box is opened

jack·knife¹ *n plural* **jack-knives** [C] **1** a knife with a blade that folds into its handle **2** a DIVE in which you bend at the waist when you are in the air

jack·knife² *v* [I] if a large vehicle with two parts jack-knifes, it slides out of control and the back part swings towards the front part: *The truck skidded on the ice and jack-knifed.*

jack-of-all-trades *n* [singular] someone who can do many different types of work, but who often is not very skilled at any of them

jack-o'-lan·tern /,dʒæk ə 'læntən $ -ərn/ *n* [C] a PUMPKIN (1) that has a face cut into it and a CANDLE put inside to shine through the holes

jack·pot /'dʒækpɒt $ -pɑːt/ *n* [C] a large amount of money that you can win in a game that is decided by chance: *a £50,000 jackpot* | *jackpot winners* → **hit the jackpot** at HIT¹ (25)

jack·rab·bit /'dʒæk,ræbɪt/ *n* [C] a large North American HARE (=animal like a large rabbit) with very long ears

Jack Rob·in·son /,dʒæk 'rɒbɪnsən $ -'rɑː-/ *n* **before you can say Jack Robinson** *old-fashioned* very quickly or suddenly

Jack the Lad *n* [singular] *BrE spoken* a young man who enjoys drinking alcohol and going out with his male friends, and who thinks he is sexually attractive

Jac·o·be·an /,dʒækə'biːən / *adj* belonging to or typical of the period between 1603 and 1623 in Britain, when James I was king of England: *Jacobean drama*

Jac·o·bite /'dʒækəbaɪt/ *n* [C] someone who in the 17th or 18th centuries who supported King James II of England and wanted one of his DESCENDANTS to rule England —**Jacobite** *adj*

Ja·cuz·zi /dʒə'kuːzi/ *n* [C] *trademark* a large indoor bath that makes hot water move in strong currents around your body → HOT TUB, SPA (2); → see picture at SPORTS CENTRE

jade /dʒeɪd/ *n* [U] **1** a hard, usually green stone often used to make jewellery: *a jade necklace* **2** also **jade green** the light green colour of jade

ja·ded /'dʒeɪdɪd/ *adj* someone who is jaded is no longer interested in or excited by something, usually because they have experienced too much of it: *The concert should satisfy even the most jaded critic.*

jag /dʒæg/ *n* [C] *informal* **crying/shopping/talking etc jag** a short period of time when you suddenly cry etc without controlling how much you do it

jag·ged /'dʒægɪd/ *adj* having a rough or pointed edge or surface: *the broken bottle's jagged edge* | *the jagged rocks of St. Saviour's Point* —**jaggedly** *adv*; → see picture at SURFACE

jag·u·ar /'dʒægjuə $ 'dʒægwɑːr/ *n* [C] a large South American wild cat with brown and yellow fur with black spots → see picture at BIG CAT

jail¹ also **gaol** *BrE* /dʒeɪl/ *n* [C,U] a place where criminals are kept as part of their punishment, or

J

Jek·yll and Hyde /ˌdʒekᵻl ənd 'haɪd/ n [C] someone who is sometimes nice but at other times is unpleasant

jell /dʒel/ v another spelling of GEL

jel·lied /'dʒelid/ adj [only before noun] especially BrE cooked or served in jelly: *jellied eels*

Jell-O, jello /'dʒeləʊ $ -loʊ/ n [U] AmE trademark a soft sweet food made from fruit juice and GELATIN; ⊟ **jelly** BrE

jel·ly /'dʒeli/ n plural **jellies** **1** [C,U] BrE a soft sweet food made from fruit juice and GELATIN; ⊟ **Jell-O** AmE: *raspberry jelly* **2** [C,U] a thick sweet substance made from boiled fruit and sugar with no pieces of fruit in it, eaten especially on bread; → **jam**: *a peanut butter and jelly sandwich* | *damson jelly* **3** [U] especially BrE a soft solid substance made from meat juices and GELA-TIN **4** [U] a substance that is solid but very soft, and moves easily when you touch it: *frogs' eggs floating in a protective jelly* **5 feel like/turn to jelly** if your legs or knees feel like jelly, they start to shake because you are frightened or nervous **6 jellies** [plural] BrE informal a drug that makes you feel relaxed and sleepy, which some people use illegally **7 jellies** [plural] shoes made of clear coloured plastic

'**jelly ,baby** n [C] BrE trademark a small soft sweet made in the shape of a baby in a variety of colours

'**jelly bean** n [C] a small soft sweet with different tastes and colours that is shaped like a bean

jel·ly·fish /'dʒelifɪʃ/ n plural **jellyfish** [C] a sea animal that has a round transparent body and can sting you

'**jelly ,roll** n [C] AmE a long thin cake that is rolled up with JAM or cream inside; ⊟ **swiss roll** BrE

jem·my /'dʒemi/ BrE; **jimmy** AmE n plural **jemmies** [C] a short strong metal bar used especially by thieves to break open locked doors, windows etc —**jemmy** v [T]

je ne sais quoi /ˌʒə nə seɪ 'kwɑː/ n [singular] a good quality that you cannot easily describe – often humorous: *the je ne sais quoi that makes the village magical*

jeop·ar·dize also **-ise** BrE /'dʒepədaɪz $ -ər-/ v [T] to risk losing or spoiling something important: *large-scale military offensives which could jeopardize the UN peace process*

jeop·ar·dy /'dʒepədi $ -ər-/ n **in jeopardy** in danger of being lost or harmed: *Thousands of jobs are in jeopardy.* | **put/place sth in jeopardy** *The killings could put the whole peace process in jeopardy.*

jer·e·mi·ad /ˌdʒerᵻ'maɪəd/ n [C] formal a long speech or piece of writing that complains about a situation, or says that bad things will happen

jerk¹ /dʒɜːk $ dʒɜːrk/ v **1** [I,T] to move with a quick sudden movement, or to make part of your body move in this way: *Wilcox jerked his head to indicate that they should move on.* | *'Is that the only way out of here?' he asked, jerking a thumb at the door.* | [+back/up/for-wards etc] *Suddenly he jerked back in his chair.* | *The sound of the phone jerked me awake.* **2** [I,T] to pull something suddenly and roughly: [+at] *Doyle jerked at the girl's hair, to make her sit down.* | *She jerked open the car door and got out.*

jerk sb **around** phr v AmE informal to waste someone's time or deliberately make things difficult for them

jerk off phr v informal not polite especially AmE to MASTURBATE

jerk out sth phr v written to say something quickly and nervously: *'Don't lie,' she jerked out.*

jerk² n [C] **1** a sudden quick movement: *He gave a sudden jerk of his head.* | **with a jerk** *She started the car with a jerk and hit the bumper of the car in front.* **2** informal someone, especially a man, who is stupid or who does things that annoy or hurt other people: *I swore at him for being such a jerk.*

jer·kin /'dʒɜːkᵻn $ -ɜːr-/ n [C] a short jacket that covers your body but not your arms, worn in the past

jerk·y¹ /'dʒɜːki $ -ɜːr-/ adj jerky movements are rough, with many starts and stops; **⊟ smooth**: *His skin was dry and hot, his breathing rapid and jerky.* | *The bus came to a jerky halt.* —**jerkily** adv —**jerkiness** n [U]

jerky² n [U] AmE meat that has been cut into thin pieces and dried in the sun or with smoke

jer·ry-built /'dʒeri ˌbɪlt/ adj built cheaply, quickly, and badly

jer·sey /'dʒɜːzi $ -ɜːr-/ n **1** [C] a shirt made of soft material, worn by players of sports such as football and RUGBY **2** [C] BrE a piece of clothing made of wool that covers the upper part of your body and your arms; **⊟ sweater** **3** [U] a soft material made of cotton or wool

Jersey n [C] a light brown cow that gives high quality milk

Je·ru·sa·lem ar·ti·choke /dʒəˌruːsələm 'ɑːtᵻtʃəʊk $ -'ɑːrtᵻtʃoʊk/ n [C] an ARTICHOKE

jest¹ /dʒest/ n [C] formal something you say that is intended to be funny, not serious; **⊟ joke**: *I wasn't sure whether to treat her words as a jest.* | **in jest** *His serious face told me that he was not speaking in jest.*

jest² v [I] formal or old use to say things that you do not really mean in order to amuse people: *"Do I look as if I am jesting?" she asked, her face pale and tense.* —**jestingly** adv

jest·er /'dʒestə $ -ər/ n [C] a man employed in the past by a ruler to entertain people with jokes, stories etc

Je·su·it /'dʒezjuᵻt $ 'dʒeʒuᵻt, 'dʒezuᵻt/ n [C] a man who is a member of the Roman Catholic Society of Jesus

Je·sus¹ /'dʒiːzəs/ also ˌ**Jesus** '**Christ** n the man who Christians believe was the son of God, and on whose life and ideas Christianity is based

Jesus² interjection not polite used to express anger, surprise, or shock: *Jesus! That was close!* ⚠ Be careful about using **Jesus** in this way because Christians find it offensive.

jet¹ /dʒet/ n **1** [C] a fast plane with a jet engine: **jet fighter/aircraft/airliner** *a squadron of F-6 jet fighter aircraft* | *He owns a private jet.* → **JUMBO JET** **2** [C] a narrow stream of liquid or gas that comes quickly out of a small hole, or the hole itself: [+of] *She soaped herself beneath the refreshing jets of water.* **3** [U] a hard black stone that is used for making jewellery

jet² v **jetted, jetting** [I always + adv/prep] **1** informal to travel by plane, especially to many different places: [+off] *We're jetting off for a sunshine holiday in the Caribbean.* | *business executives jetting around the world* **2** if a liquid or gas jets out from somewhere, it comes quickly out of a small hole

ˌ**jet-'black** adj very dark black: *jet-black hair* —**jet black** n [U]

'**jet ,engine** n [C] an engine that pushes out a stream of hot air and gases behind it, used in aircraft

'**jet lag** n [U] the tired and confused feeling that you can get after flying a very long distance, especially because of the difference in time between the place you left and the place you arrived at: *I'm suffering from jet lag but I'll feel better after a good night's sleep.* —**jet-lagged** adj

jet·lin·er /'dʒetlaɪnə $ -ər/ n [C] AmE a large aircraft, especially one that carries passengers

ˌ**jet-'propelled** adj using a jet engine for power

ˌ**jet pro'pulsion** n [U] the use of a jet engine for power

jet·sam /'dʒetsəm/ n [U] things that are thrown from a ship and float on the sea towards the shore → **flotsam and jetsam** at **FLOTSAM**

'**jet set** n **the jet set** old-fashioned rich and fashionable people who travel a lot —**jet-setter** n [C]

'**Jet Ski** n [C] trademark a small fast vehicle on which one or two people can ride over water for fun

'**jet stream** n [singular] a current of very strong winds high above the Earth's surface

jet·ti·son /ˈdʒetɪsən, -zən/ v [T]   **1** to get rid of something or decide not to do something any longer: *The scheme was jettisoned when the government found it too costly.*   **2** to throw things away, especially from a moving plane or ship

jet·ty /ˈdʒeti/ n plural **jetties** [C] a wide wall or flat area built out into the water, used for getting on and off boats; → **pier**

Jew /dʒuː/ n [C] someone whose religion is Judaism, or who is a member of a group whose traditional religion is Judaism

jew·el /ˈdʒuːəl/ n [C]   **1** a valuable stone, such as a diamond; ▤ **gem**   **2 jewels** [plural] jewellery or other objects made with valuable stones and used for decoration: *She loved dressing up and wearing priceless jewels.*   **3** a very small stone used in the machinery of a watch   **4** something or someone that is very valuable, attractive, or important: *He introduced her to Budapest, a jewel of a city.*   **5 the jewel in the crown** the best or most valuable part of something: *Puddings are the jewel in the crown of British cookery.* → CROWN JEWEL

'jewel ˌcase n [C] a plastic box for holding a CD

jew·elled BrE; **jeweled** AmE /ˈdʒuːəld/ adj decorated with jewels: *the famous jewelled eggs of Fabergé*

jew·el·ler BrE; **jeweler** AmE /ˈdʒuːələ $ -ər/ n [C]   **1** someone who buys, sells, makes, or repairs jewellery   **2 jeweller's** a shop selling jewellery and watches

jewellery *BrE*/**jewelry** *AmE*

ring

necklace

earrings

brooch

bangle

bracelet

jew·el·lery ⒮₃ BrE; **jewelry** AmE /ˈdʒuːəlri/ n [U] small things that you wear for decoration, such as rings or NECKLACES | *a piece of jewellery* | *She wears a lot of gold jewelry.* → COSTUME JEWELLERY

Jew·ish /ˈdʒuːɪʃ/ adj relating to Jews or Judaism: *the Jewish religion* | *My husband is Jewish.*

Jew·ry /ˈdʒuːri/ n [U] old use the Jewish people

Jez·e·bel /ˈdʒezəbel, -bəl/ n [C] old use a sexually immoral woman

jib¹ /dʒɪb/ n [C]   **1** a small sail in front of the large sail on a boat; → **mainsail**   **2** the long part of a CRANE

jib² v **jibbed, jibbing** [I] especially BrE to be unwilling to do or accept something: [+at] *He jibbed at the price I asked for.*

jibe¹, gibe /dʒaɪb/ n [C] an unkind remark intended to make someone seem silly: *She was tired of his cheap jibes.*

jibe² v   **1** [I] AmE informal if two statements, reports etc jibe with each other, the information in them matches: [+with] *His report did not jibe with the facts.*   **2** [I + at] to say something that is intended to make someone seem silly

jif·fy /ˈdʒɪfi/ also **jiff** /dʒɪf/ n spoken **in a jiffy** very soon: *I'll be with you in a jiffy.*

'Jiffy bag n [C] BrE trademark a thick soft envelope, used for posting things that might break

jig¹ /dʒɪg/ n [C]   **1** a type of quick dance, or a piece of music for this dance   **2** a piece of equipment for holding a tool, a piece of wood etc in position

jig² v **jigged, jigging** [I always + adv/prep] to dance or move up and down with quick short movements

jig·ger /ˈdʒɪgə $ -ər/ n [C] a unit for measuring alcohol, equal to 1.5 OUNCES, or the small glass this is measured with

jig·ger·y-po·ker·y /ˌdʒɪgəri ˈpəʊkəri $ -ˈpoʊ-/ n [U] BrE informal secret dishonest activity to make something seem what it is not: *There's been some jiggery-pokery with the figures.*

jig·gle /ˈdʒɪgəl/ v [I,T] to make something move from side to side or up and down with short quick movements, or to move like this: *She jiggled the handle of the pram to make the baby stop crying.* | *'Wake up,' he said, jiggling up and down on the bed.*

jig·gy /ˈdʒɪgi/ adj **get jiggy** AmE informal **a)** to dance with a lot of energy to popular music **b)** to have sex

jig·saw /ˈdʒɪgsɔː $ -sɒː/ n [C]   **1** also **'jigsaw ˌpuzzle** a picture cut up into many pieces that you try to fit together   **2** [usually singular] a very complicated situation, especially one that you are trying to understand: *As he explained, another piece of the jigsaw fell into place.*   **3** a tool for cutting out shapes in thin pieces of wood

ji·had /dʒɪˈhɑːd, dʒɪˈhæd/ n [C] a holy war fought by Muslims

jilt /dʒɪlt/ v [T] to suddenly end a close romantic relationship with someone: *She jilted her fiance just before the wedding.*

jim·my /ˈdʒɪmi/ n plural **jimmies** [C] the American form of the word JEMMY —**jimmy** v [T]

jin·gle¹ /ˈdʒɪŋgəl/ v [I,T] to shake small metal things together so that they make a sound, or to make this sound: *He jingled his car keys.*

jingle² n   **1** [C] a short song used in advertisements   **2** [singular] the sound of small metal objects being shaken together

jin·go·is·m /ˈdʒɪŋgəʊɪzəm $ -goʊ-/ n [U] a strong belief that your own country is better than others – used to show disapproval: *a mood of warlike jingoism* —**jingoistic** /ˌdʒɪŋgəʊˈɪstɪk◂ $ -goʊ-/ adj

jink /dʒɪŋk/ v [I] to change direction suddenly: *He jinked left, then right, throwing the plane into steep and sudden turns.*

jinks /dʒɪŋks/ n → HIGH JINKS

jinn /dʒɪn/ n [C] a GENIE

jinx /dʒɪŋks/ n [singular] someone or something that brings bad luck, or a period of bad luck that results from this: *The company had suffered so many disasters that some employees feared a jinx.*

jinxed /dʒɪŋkst/ adj often having bad luck, or making people have bad luck: *They seem to be jinxed when it comes to playing in the UK.*

jit·ter·bug /ˈdʒɪtəbʌg $ -ər-/ n [singular] a fast JAZZ dance popular in the 1940s

jit·ters /ˈdʒɪtəz $ -ərz/ n [plural] informal a nervous, worried feeling, especially before an important event: *The jitters are worst in the capital, where 61% of people are fearful of a terrorist attack.*

jit·ter·y /ˈdʒɪtəri/ adj informal anxious or nervous: *It was probably the tension that made him jittery.*

jive¹ /dʒaɪv/ n   **1** [C,U] a very fast dance, popular especially in the 1930s and 1940s, performed to fast JAZZ music   **2** [U] AmE informal statements that you do not believe are true: *Don't give me any of that jive!*

jive² v   **1** [I] to dance a jive   **2** [T] AmE informal to try to make someone believe something that is not true

Jnr adj BrE the written abbreviation of **junior**, used after the name of a man who has the same name as his father: *Sammy Davis Jnr*

job ⒮₁ ⒲₁ /dʒɒb $ dʒɑːb/ n
  1 WORK [C] the regular paid work that you do for an employer

J

shared by them: *The two ministers have issued a joint statement.* | *Both companies are involved in the joint development of a new medium-sized car.* | *Both parties must sign the form if the account is to be in joint names* (=belong to two named people). | *The meal was a joint effort* (=two or more people worked on it together).
2 joint venture a business activity begun by two or more people or companies working together
3 joint resolution *law* a decision or law agreed by both houses of the US Congress and signed by the President
—**jointly** *adv: tenants who are jointly responsible for their rent*

joint² *n* [C] **1** a part of your body that can bend because two bones meet there: **knee/neck/hip/elbow etc joint** *a permanently damaged knee joint* **2** *BrE* a large piece of meat, usually containing a bone: [+of] *a joint of beef* **3** a place where two things or parts of an object are joined together: *What should I use to seal the joint between a carport roof and the house wall?* **4 out of joint a)** if a bone in your body is out of joint, it has been pushed out of its correct position **b)** if a system, group etc is out of joint, it is not working properly: *Something is out of joint in our society.* → **put sb's nose out of joint** at NOSE¹ (15) **5** *informal* a cheap bar, club, or restaurant: *a hamburger joint* → CLIP JOINT **6** *informal* a cigarette containing CANNABIS; **⊟ spliff** → **case the joint** at CASE² (2)

joint³ *v* [T] to cut meat into joints

joint·ed /'dʒɔɪntɪd/ *adj* having joints and able to move and bend: *a jointed puppet*

joint 'honours *n* [U] a university degree course in Britain in which two main subjects are studied; → **single honours**

joint-'stock ,company *n* [C] *AmE* a company that is owned by all the people with SHARES in it

joist /dʒɔɪst/ *n* [C] one of the beams that support a floor or ceiling

joke¹ S2 W3 /dʒəʊk $ dʒoʊk/ *n* [C]
1 something that you say or do to make people laugh, especially a funny story or trick

> **crack/make a joke** (=say something funny)
> **tell a joke** (=tell a funny story)
> **get a joke** (=understand why something is funny)
> **play a joke (on sb)** (=trick someone)
> **as a joke/for a joke** *BrE* (=to make people laugh)
> **private joke** (=a joke only a few people understand)
> **inside joke** *AmE* (=a joke that only a few people with knowledge about a particular subject or event will understand)
> **practical joke** (=a trick)
> **dirty joke** (=a joke about sex)
> **sick joke** (=an unpleasant joke)

> *Do you know any good jokes?* | [+about] *a joke about absent-minded professors* | *There's no need to make silly jokes, David.* | *He was always telling jokes and making people laugh.* | *She never gets my jokes.* | *She wondered if the others were playing a joke on her.* | *I couldn't go out with someone for a joke, could you?* | *They seemed to be sharing a private joke.* | *What the workers think is a practical joke, management might regard as sabotage.*

> ⚠ Do not say 'say a joke'. Say **tell a joke** or **tell someone a joke.**

2 be a joke *informal* to be completely useless, stupid, or unreasonable: *The whole meeting was a joke.*
3 go/get/be beyond a joke a situation that has got beyond a joke has become serious and worrying: *This rain's getting beyond a joke – let's go inside.*
4 sth is no joke used to emphasize that a situation is serious or that someone really means what they say: *The risk he's taking is no joke.* | *It's no joke bringing up a child on your own.*

5 sb can take a joke used to say that someone is able to laugh at jokes about themselves: *Your problem is you just can't take a joke.*
6 make a joke (out) of sth to treat something serious as if it was intended to be funny: *He could not bring himself to apologise. Instead, he tried to make a joke of it.*
7 sb's idea of a joke *spoken* a situation that someone else thinks is funny but you do not: *Look, if this is your idea of a joke, I don't find it at all funny.*
8 the joke's on sb used to say that something has happened to make someone seem stupid, especially when they were trying to make other people seem stupid → IN-JOKE, PRACTICAL JOKE; → **standing joke** at STAND-ING¹ (3)

joke² S3 *v* [I]
1 to say things that are intended to be funny and that you do not really mean: [+about] *I never joke about money.* | [+with] *As we left the hospital he joked with the staff.* | **joke that** *His father joked that his son was trying to put him out of business.* | *Calm down, Jo, I was only joking.*
2 you're joking/you must be joking also **you've got to be joking** *spoken* used to tell someone that what they are suggesting is so strange or silly that you cannot believe that they are serious: *'Tell him.' 'You must be joking – he'd never believe me.'*
3 joking apart/aside *BrE* used before you say something serious after you have been joking —**jokingly** *adv*

jok·er /'dʒəʊkə $ 'dʒoʊkər/ *n* [C] **1** *informal* someone who behaves in a way you think is stupid: *Look at that joker – he's doing 25 miles an hour at the most.* **2** a PLAYING CARD that has no fixed value and is only used in some card games **3** someone who makes a lot of jokes **4 the joker in the pack** something or someone whose effect on future events cannot be known

jok·ey, joky /'dʒəʊki $ 'dʒoʊ-/ *adj informal* not serious and tending to make people laugh: *Dave was a sweet man, very jokey about everything.* —**jokily** *adv* —**jokiness** *n* [U]

jol·lies /'dʒɒliz $ 'dʒɑː-/ *n* **get your jollies** *AmE spoken* to get pleasure from a particular experience or activity, especially a strange activity

jol·li·fi·ca·tion /,dʒɒlɪfɪ'keɪʃən $,dʒɑː-/ *n* [C,U] *old-fashioned* fun and enjoyment

jol·li·ty /'dʒɒlɪti $ 'dʒɑː-/ also **jollities** *n* [U] *formal* when people are happy and enjoying themselves: *a night of riotous jollity*

jol·ly¹ /'dʒɒli $ 'dʒɑːli/ *adj especially BrE* **1** happy and enjoying yourself: *Everybody was in a very relaxed and jolly mood.* **2** *old-fashioned* very pleasant and enjoyable: *We had a jolly time with the family.*

jolly² *adv BrE old-fashioned informal* **1** very: *Sounds like a jolly good idea to me.* | *It was all jolly good fun.* **2 jolly well** used to emphasize an opinion or to show that you are annoyed: *Right, I'm going to clear up, and you can jolly well help me.* **3 jolly good!** *spoken* used to say that you are pleased by what someone has just said

jolly³ *v BrE*
jolly sb along *phr v* to try to make someone do something faster by encouraging them: *He jollied people along and got useful information out of them.*
jolly sb into sth *phr v informal* to gently persuade someone to do something: *She jollied the children into going for a walk.*
jolly sth ⇔ up *phr v* to make an event or place more pleasant or exciting

Jolly 'Roger *n* [singular] a black flag with a picture of bones on it, used in the past by PIRATES; **⊟ skull and crossbones**

jolt¹ /dʒəʊlt $ dʒoʊlt/ *v* **1** [I,T] to move suddenly and roughly, or to make someone or something move in this way; **⊟ jerk**: *We jolted along rough wet roads through* *an endless banana plantation.* **2** [T] to give someone a sudden shock or surprise: *The phone jolted him awake.* | **jolt sb into/out of sth** *It jolted me into making the decision to quit.* | *Her sharp words seemed to jolt him out of his depression.*

jolt² *n* [C usually singular] **1** a sudden shock: [+of] *Melanie experienced a jolt of surprise.* | **with a jolt** *Henry sat up with a jolt.* | *The oil crisis has given the government quite a jolt.* **2** a sudden rough shaking movement: *People felt the first jolt of the earthquake at about 8 a.m.*

Jones·es /'dʒəʊnzɪz $ 'dʒoʊn-/ *n* → **keep up with the Joneses** at KEEP UP (4)

josh /dʒɒʃ $ dʒɑːʃ/ *v* [I,T] *old-fashioned* to talk to someone or laugh at them in a gentle joking way: *The guys josh him and call him an egghead.*

joss stick /'dʒɒs ˌstɪk $ 'dʒɑːs-/ *n* [C] a stick of INCENSE

jos·tle /'dʒɒsəl $ 'dʒɑː-/ *v* **1** [I,T] to push or knock against someone in a crowd, especially so that you can get somewhere or do something before other people: [+for] *Followers of the president jostled for position in front of the TV cameras.* **2** [I] to compete for something such as attention or a reward: *A thousand thoughts were jostling around inside my mind.*

jot¹ /dʒɒt $ dʒɑːt/ *v* **jotted, jotting**
jot sth ⇔ down *phr v* to write a short piece of information quickly: *Let me jot down your number and I'll call you tomorrow.*

jot² *n* **not a jot** *old-fashioned* not at all or none at all: *There was not a jot of humour in the man.*

jot·ter /'dʒɒtə $ 'dʒɑːtər/ *n* [C] *BrE* a small book for writing notes in

jot·tings /'dʒɒtɪŋz $ 'dʒɑː-/ *n* [plural] *informal* short notes, usually written to remind yourself about something: *her private jottings*

joule /dʒuːl $ dʒuːl, dʒaʊl/ written abbreviation *J n* [C] a unit for measuring energy or work

jour·nal /'dʒɜːnl $ -ɜːr-/ *n* [C] **1** a serious magazine produced for professional people or those with a particular interest: *the British Medical Journal* **2** a written record that you make of the things that happen to you each day; ▪ **diary**: *He decided to keep a journal.*

jour·nal·ese /ˌdʒɜːnəlˈiːz $ -ɜːr-/ *n* [U] language that is typical of newspapers

jour·nal·is·m /'dʒɜːnəl-ɪzəm $ -ɜːr-/ *n* [U] the job or activity of writing news reports for newspapers, magazines, television, or radio: *a career in journalism* | *The hospital has been the target of investigative journalism* (=journalism that examines an event or situation in order to find out the truth).

jour·nal·ist W3 /'dʒɜːnəl-ɪ̈st $ -ɜːr-/ *n* [C] someone who writes news reports for newspapers, magazines, television, or radio; → **reporter**: *a well-known journalist and broadcaster* —**journalistic** /ˌdʒɜːnəlˈɪstɪk◂ $ -ɜːr-/ *adj* [only before noun]: *journalistic skills*

jour·ney¹ S3 W2 /'dʒɜːni $ -ɜːr-/ *n* [C]
1 *especially BrE* a time spent travelling from one place to another, especially over a long distance; ▪ **trip** *AmE*

make a journey
go on a journey (=make a long journey)
break a journey *BrE* (=make a short stop in a journey)
car/train/bus journey
outward journey (=a journey to a place)
return journey (=a journey home from a place)
safe journey (=used especially to wish someone a good journey)
wasted journey (=one that did not achieve the result you wanted)
leg of a journey (=one part of a journey)

[+to/from/between] *my journey to China* | *a long slow journey from Odessa* | [+through/across etc] *our journey across Europe* | *the friends they made on the journey* | *I still use my car, but now I make fewer journeys.* | *We are going on a journey to a strange country.* | *We broke our journey to have a picnic.* | *the*

six-hour train journey home from London | *The return journey was uneventful.* | *Have a safe journey.* | *To avoid a wasted journey, ring the number below to check that the event is still on.* | *On Thursday we set off on the final leg of our journey.* → see box at TRAVEL²

2 *literary* a long and often difficult process by which someone or something changes and develops: *our journey through life* | *The novel is an account of his spiritual journey.*

journey² *v* [I always + adv/prep] *literary* to travel: *They left the town and journeyed south.*

jour·ney·man /'dʒɜːnimən $ -ɜːr-/ *n plural* **journeymen** /-mən/ [C] *old-fashioned* **1** a trained worker who works for someone else **2** an experienced worker whose work is acceptable but not excellent

jour·no /'dʒɜːnəʊ $ 'dʒɜːrnoʊ/ *n plural* **journos** [C] *BrE informal* a JOURNALIST

joust /dʒaʊst/ *v* [I] **1** to fight with LANCES (=long sticks) while riding horses, as part of a formal competition in the past **2** to compete or argue with someone: [+with] *The minister and I have often jousted with each other.* —**joust** *n* [C]

Jove /dʒəʊv $ dʒoʊv/ *n* **by Jove!** *BrE old-fashioned* used to express surprise or to emphasize something: *By Jove, you're right!*

jo·vi·al /'dʒəʊviəl $ 'dʒoʊ-/ *adj* friendly and happy: *He addressed me in a jovial manner.* —**jovially** *adv* —**joviality** /ˌdʒəʊviˈælɪ̈ti $ ˌdʒoʊ-/ *n* [U]

jowl /dʒaʊl/ *n* [C usually plural] the skin that covers your lower jaw on either side of your face: *a man with heavy jowls* (=jowls that hang down slightly) → **cheek by jowl** at CHEEK¹ (3)

joy¹ W3 /dʒɔɪ/ *n*
1 [U] great happiness and pleasure: *the look of joy on her face* | **with/for joy** *I leaped into the air with joy.* | *She wept for joy.* | *I didn't exactly jump for joy* (=I was not very pleased) *when I heard the news.*
2 [C] something or someone that gives you happiness and pleasure: [+of] *one of the joys of travelling alone* | *The garden was his pride and joy.* | **be a joy to watch/drive/use etc** *The children's singing was a joy to listen to.*
3 no joy/not any joy *BrE spoken* if you have no joy, you do not succeed in getting something: *I phoned the pub, but no joy. The landlord didn't know where she was.*

joy² *v* [I] *literary* to be happy because of something

joy·ful /'dʒɔɪfəl/ *adj* very happy, or likely to make people very happy: *Christmas is a joyful occasion for children.* | *the joyful news* —**joyfully** *adv* —**joyfulness** *n* [U]

joy·less /'dʒɔɪləs/ *adj* without any happiness at all: *a joyless marriage* —**joylessly** *adv*

joy·ous /'dʒɔɪəs/ *adj literary* very happy, or likely to make people very happy: *a joyous occasion* | *Our music is a joyous celebration of life.* —**joyously** *adv* —**joyousness** *n* [U]

joy·rid·ing /'dʒɔɪˌraɪdɪŋ/ *n* [U] the crime of stealing a car and driving it in a fast and dangerous way for fun —**joyride** *v* [I] —**joyrider** *n* [C]

joy·stick /'dʒɔɪˌstɪk/ *n* [C] an upright handle that you use to control something such as an aircraft or a computer game

JP /ˌdʒeɪ ˈpiː/ *n* [C] the abbreviation of *Justice of the Peace*; ▪ **magistrate**

JPEG also **JPG** /'dʒeɪ peg/ *n* [C] *technical* **Joint Photographic Experts Group** a type of computer FILE used on the Internet that contains pictures, photographs, or other images

J

1 000, 2 000, 3 000, most frequent words in S poken and W ritten English

Jr. *AmE* the written abbreviation of *junior*, used after the name of a man who has the same name as his father: *Alan Parks, Jr.*

jub·i·lant /ˈdʒuːbˈlənt/ *adj* extremely happy and pleased because of a success: *Radicals were jubilant at getting rid of him.* | *The fans were in jubilant mood as they left the stadium.* —**jubilantly** *adv*

ju·bi·la·tion /ˌdʒuːbˈleɪʃən/ *n* [U] *formal* happiness and pleasure because you have been successful: *There was jubilation that a local team had come first.*

ju·bi·lee /ˈdʒuːbˈliː, ˌdʒuːbˈliː/ *n* [C] a date that is celebrated because it is exactly 25 years, 50 years etc after an important event → DIAMOND JUBILEE, GOLDEN JUBILEE, SILVER JUBILEE

Ju·da·is·m /ˈdʒuːdeɪ-ɪzəm, ˈdʒuːdə- $ ˈdʒuːdə-, ˈdʒuːdi-/ *n* [U] the Jewish religion based on the sacred books known as the Hebrew Scriptures. These writings contain many of the books that are also in the Old Testament of the Christian BIBLE. —**Judaic** /dʒuːˈdeɪ-ɪk/ *adj*

Ju·das /ˈdʒuːdəs/ *n* [C] someone who is not loyal to a friend; ☐ traitor

jud·der /ˈdʒʌdə $ -ər/ *v* [I] if a vehicle or machine judders, it shakes violently: *The engine juddered to life.* —**judder** *n* [C]

judge¹ W2 /dʒʌdʒ/ *n* [C]
1 the official in control of a court who decides how criminals should be punished: *The trial judge specifies the number of years to be spent in prison.* | **federal judge/high court judge etc** (=a judge in a particular court)
2 someone who decides on the result of a competition: *The panel of judges included several well-known writers.* → see picture at UMPIRE
3 **a good/bad judge of sth** someone whose opinion on something is usually right or wrong: *Sandra's a very good judge of character.*
4 **be the judge (of sth)** to be the person whose opinion on something matters or is accepted: *No-one else can say what its value to you is – only you can be the judge of that.*
5 **let me be the judge of that** *spoken* used to tell someone angrily that you do not need their advice
6 **as sober as a judge** someone who is as sober as a judge is not drunk at all

judge² S2 W3 *v* **judged, judging**
1 OPINION [I,T] to form or give an opinion about someone or something after thinking carefully about all the information you know about them

judge sb/sth by sth
judge that
judge sb/sth (to be) sth
judge whether/how/what etc
difficult/hard to judge
impossible to judge
judge the success/quality/merits of sth
judge sth objectively
judge it best/right/proper etc to do sth
judge sb harshly
judge it safe to do sth

You should never judge a person by their looks. | *Judge us on the improvements we make in the economy.* | *The therapist judged that Margaret had made a serious attempt to kill herself.* | *pollutants that were judged hazardous to human health* | *I am in no position to judge whether what she is doing is right or wrong.* | *The economic results of the reforms are very difficult to judge.* | *The likelihood of future bombs was impossible to judge.* | *We judge the success of a product by the number of sales it brings in.* | *His conduct, judged objectively by what he has done, is dishonest.* | *Robert wanted to go and help him, but judged it best to stay where he was.* | *Do not judge her too harshly, as she was very young at the time.*

2 **judging by/from sth** used to say that you are making a guess based on what you have just seen, heard, or learned: *Judging by his jovial manner he must have enjoyed his meal.* | *Judging from what you say in your letter, you don't sound well.*
3 COMPETITION [I,T] to decide on the result of a competition: *I had the difficult task of judging the competition.* | **judge sb on sth** *Competitors will be judged on speed and accuracy.*
4 CRITICIZE [I,T] to form an opinion about someone, especially in an unfair or criticizing way: *He just accepts people for what they are and he doesn't judge them.*
5 LAW [T] to decide whether someone is guilty of a crime in court
6 **it's not for sb to judge** used to say that you do not think someone has the right to give their opinion about something: *Was it the right decision? It's not for us to judge.*
7 **as far as I can judge** used to say that you think what you are saying is true, but you are not sure
8 **don't judge a book by its cover** used to say that you should not form an opinion based only on the way something looks

judg·ment W2 also **judgement** *BrE* /ˈdʒʌdʒmənt/ *n*
1 OPINION [C,U] an opinion that you form, especially after thinking carefully about something: *It's too soon to make a judgment about what the outcome will be.* | *In my judgment, we should accept his offer.* | **pass judgment (on sth)** (=give your opinion, especially a negative one) *Our aim is to help him, not to pass judgment on what he has done.* | *I'd advise you to reserve judgment* (=not decide your opinion before you have all the facts). | **against your better judgment** (=even though you do not think it is a sensible thing to do) *I lent him the money, against my better judgment.*
2 ABILITY TO DECIDE [U] the ability to make sensible decisions about what to do and when to do it: *I've known him for years and I trust his judgment.* | **professional/personal etc judgment** *The minister showed a lack of political judgment.* | *a decision based on sound judgment* (=good judgment) *Watch carefully and use your judgment.* → **error of judgment** at ERROR (3)
3 LAW [C,U] an official decision given by a judge or a court of law: *The company were fined £6 million, following a recent court judgment.*
4 **a judgment (on sb/sth)** *formal* something bad that happens to someone and seems like a punishment for the things they have done wrong
5 **judgment call** *AmE informal* a decision you have to make yourself because there are no fixed rules in a situation → LAST JUDGMENT, VALUE JUDGMENT; → **sit in judgment** at SIT (10)

judg·ment·al, **judgemental** *BrE* /dʒʌdʒˈmentl/ *adj* criticizing people very quickly – used to show disapproval

judgment day, **Judgement Day** *n* [singular, not with the] also **the day of judgment** the last day of the world when all people will be judged by God for what they have done, according to Christianity and some other religions

ju·di·ca·ture /ˈdʒuːdɪkətʃə $ -ər/ *n* **the judicature** *formal* judges as a group and the organization, power etc of the law

ju·di·cial /dʒuːˈdɪʃəl/ *adj* relating to the law, judges, or their decisions; → **legislative**: *the judicial system* —**judicially** *adv*

ju·di·cia·ry /dʒuːˈdɪʃəri $ -ʃieri, -ʃəri/ *n* **the judiciary** *formal* all the judges in a country who, as a group, form part of the system of government

ju·di·cious /dʒuːˈdɪʃəs/ *adj formal* done in a sensible and careful way: *a judicious choice* —**judiciously** *adv*

ju·do /ˈdʒuːdəʊ $ -doʊ/ *n* [U] a Japanese sport or method of defence in which you try to throw your opponent onto the ground

J

jug

vase

pitcher

jug /dʒʌg/ n [C] **1** BrE a container with a wide curved opening at the top and a handle, used especially at meals for pouring liquids; **≣ pitcher** AmE: a milk jug **2** AmE a deep round container with a very narrow opening at the top and a handle, used for holding liquids; **≣ pitcher** BrE **3** also **jugful** /'dʒʌgfʊl/ the amount of liquid that a jug will hold: [+of] a jug of water **4** **jugs** not polite a woman's breasts

jug·ger·naut /'dʒʌgənɔːt $ -ərnɒːt/ n [C] **1** BrE a very large vehicle that carries goods over long distances; **≣ semi** AmE **2** a very powerful force, organization etc whose effect or influence cannot be stopped: the juggernaut of industrialization

jug·gle /'dʒʌgəl/ v **1** [I,T] to keep three or more objects moving through the air by throwing and catching them very quickly: [+with] One guy was juggling with five balls. **2** [I,T] to try to fit two or more jobs, activities etc into your life, especially with difficulty: **juggle sth (with sth)** It's hard trying to juggle a job with kids and the housework. **3** [T] to change things or arrange them in the way you want, or in a way that makes it possible for you to do something: **juggle sth around** If I juggle these appointments around, I can fit you in. → **balancing/juggling act** at ACT¹ (12)

juggle

juggling

jug·gler /'dʒʌglə $ -ər/ n [C] someone who juggles objects in the air, especially to entertain people

jug·u·lar /'dʒʌgjʊlə $ -ər/ n [C usually singular] **1** jugular vein the large VEIN in your neck that takes blood from your head back to your heart **2** go for the jugular informal to criticize or attack someone very strongly, especially in order to harm them

juice¹ /dʒuːs/ n **1** [C,U] the liquid that comes from fruit and vegetables, or a drink that is made from this: a carton of orange juice | A coke and a tomato juice, please. **2** [C usually plural] the liquid that comes out of meat when it is cooked **3** gastric/digestive juice(s) the liquid inside your stomach that helps you to DIGEST food **4** [U] informal something that produces power, such as petrol or electricity: Okay, turn on the juice. → stew in your own juice at STEW² (2)

juice² v [T] to get the juice out of fruit or vegetables **juice sth ⇔ up** phr v AmE informal to make something more interesting or exciting

juiced /dʒuːst/ adj [not before noun] AmE **1** also **juiced up** informal excited **2** old-fashioned drunk

juic·er /'dʒuːsə $ -ər/ n [C] a kitchen tool used for getting juice out of fruit

juic·y /'dʒuːsi/ adj comparative **juicier**, superlative **juiciest 1** containing a lot of juice: a juicy lemon **2** juicy gossip/details/stories etc informal interesting or shocking information, especially about peo-

ple's sexual behaviour: Want to hear a juicy bit of news? **3** informal involving work that is enjoyable and satisfying: She's been trying to get a really juicy role for years. **4** informal involving a lot of money: a big juicy cheque —**juiciness** n [U]

ju·jit·su /dʒuː'dʒɪtsuː/ n [U] a type of fighting from Japan, in which you hold, throw, and hit your opponent

juke·box /'dʒuːkbɒks $ -bɑːks/ n [C] a machine in bars, restaurants etc that plays music when you put money in it

jukebox

Ju·ly /dʒʊ'laɪ/ n plural **Julies** [C,U] written abbreviation **Jul.** the seventh month of the year, between June and August: next/last July Laura came over to England last July. | in July I plan to graduate in July. | on July 6th Two months later, on July 6th, he fired Owens. | on 6th July BrE: 'When's the concert?' 'On 6th July.' | July 6 AmE: The competition ends July 6.

jum·ble¹ /'dʒʌmbəl/ n **1** [singular] a lot of different things mixed together in an untidy way, without any order: [+of] a jumble of old toys | Inside she was a jumble of emotions. **2** [U] BrE things to be sold at a jumble sale; **≣ rummage** AmE

jumble² also **jumble up** v [T often passive] to mix things together in an untidy way, without any order: The photographs were all jumbled up. | Ben's words became jumbled.

jumble sale n [C] BrE a sale of used clothes, books etc in order to get money for a local church, school etc; **≣ rummage sale** AmE

jum·bo /'dʒʌmbəʊ $ -boʊ/ adj [only before noun] informal larger than other things of the same type: jumbo-sized hot dogs

jumbo jet also **jumbo** n [C] a very large plane for carrying passengers

jump¹ S2 W3 /dʒʌmp/ v
1 UPWARDS **a)** [I] to push yourself up into the air, or over or away from something etc using your legs: How high can you jump? | jump over/across/onto etc sth He jumped over the wall and ran off. | Fans were **jumping up and down** (=jumping repeatedly) and cheering. | jump clear (of sth) (=jump out of danger) We managed to jump clear of the car before it hit the wall. **b)** [T] to go over or across something by jumping: He jumped the gate, landing on the concrete.
2 DOWNWARDS [I] to let yourself drop from a place that is above the ground: The cats **jumped down** and came to meet us. | jump from/out of/onto etc sth Three people saved themselves by jumping from the window.
3 MOVE FAST [I always + adv/prep] to move quickly or suddenly in a particular direction; **≣ leap**: [+up/back/in etc] Matt jumped up to answer the phone. | We all jumped in a taxi. | She **jumped to** her feet and left.
4 IN FEAR/SURPRISE [I] to make a quick sudden movement because you are surprised or frightened: Marcia jumped. 'What's that noise?' | Sorry, I didn't mean to **make you jump** (=surprise or frighten you). | Don't shout. I nearly **jumped out of my skin** (=was very shocked or frightened)!
5 INCREASE [I] to increase or improve suddenly and by a large amount: jump (from ...) to sth Profits jumped to £2.6 million last year. | Norway jumped from ninth to third place. ⚠ Do not say that an amount, level, price etc 'jumps up'. Say it jumps.
6 KEEP CHANGING [I,T] to change quickly and often from one idea, place, position etc to another – used to show disapproval: jump from sth to sth Cathy kept jumping from one topic to another. | jump about/around (sth) I've been jumping about the file instead of working straight through it.

J

7 MISS A STAGE [I,T] to move suddenly to a further part of a book, discussion, leaving out the part in between: *I'm afraid I jumped a couple of chapters.* | [+to] *The movie suddenly jumped ahead to the future.*

8 MACHINE [I] if a machine or piece of equipment jumps, it moves suddenly because something is wrong with it: *Why does the video keep jumping like this?*

9 ATTACK [T] *informal* to attack someone suddenly: *Somebody jumped him in the park last night.*

10 jump to conclusions to form an opinion about something before you have all the facts: *There may be a simple explanation. Let's not jump to conclusions.*

11 jump the gun to start doing something too soon, especially without thinking about it carefully

12 jump for joy to be extremely happy and pleased

13 jump down sb's throat *informal* to suddenly speak angrily to someone

14 jump the queue *BrE* to go in front of others who are already waiting in a line – used to show disapproval → QUEUE-JUMPING

15 jump through hoops to do a series of things that are difficult or annoying, but that are necessary in order to achieve something: *We had to jump through hoops to get our visas in time.*

16 jump ship **a)** to leave an organization that you are working for, especially in order to join another: *The best employees jumped ship at the first opportunity.* **b)** to leave a ship on which you are working as a sailor, without permission

17 jump bail to leave a town, city, or country where a court of law has ordered you to stay until your TRIAL¹ (1)

18 jump to it! *spoken* used to order someone to do something immediately

19 (go) jump in a lake! *spoken* used to rudely tell someone to go away

20 jump the rails *BrE*; jump the tracks *AmE* if a train jumps the rails, it suddenly goes off the metal tracks it is moving along

21 jump a light also jump the lights to drive through red TRAFFIC LIGHTS without stopping

22 jump a train *especially AmE* to travel on a train, especially a FREIGHT TRAIN, without paying

23 CAR [T] *AmE* to JUMP-START a car

24 SEX [T] *spoken not polite* to have sex with someone

jump at sth *phr v*
to eagerly accept the chance to do something: *I jumped at the chance of a trip to Hong Kong.*

jump in *phr v*
to interrupt someone or suddenly join a conversation: *Lena quickly jumped in with a diverting remark.*

jump on sb *phr v informal*
to criticize or punish someone, especially unfairly: [+for] *He used to jump on me for every little mistake.*

jump out at sb *phr v*
if something jumps out at you, it is extremely noticeable, often in a way you do not like: *I don't like jewellery that jumps out at you.*

jump

leap

jump

hop

skip

jump² *n* [C]

1 UP an act of pushing yourself suddenly up into the air using your legs; ◨ leap: *the best jump of the competition* | *a dancer famous for his impressive jumps*

2 DOWN an act of letting yourself drop from a place that is above the ground: do/make a jump *Douglas made his first 10,000 foot parachute jump yesterday.*

3 INCREASE a sudden large increase in an amount or value: [+in] *a jump in inflation rates*

4 PROGRESS *especially BrE* a large or sudden change, especially one that improves things: *The new law is a great jump forward for human rights.*

5 with a jump *BrE* if you wake, sit up etc with a jump, you do it very suddenly because you are surprised or shocked: *She woke with a jump, hearing a noise downstairs.*

6 keep/stay one jump ahead (of sb) *BrE informal* to keep your advantage over the people you are competing with by always being the first to do or know something new

7 STH YOU JUMP OVER a fence, gate, or wall that a person or horse has to jump over in a race or competition: *Her horse cleared all the jumps in the first round.*

8 get a jump on sb/sth *AmE informal* to gain an advantage, especially by doing something earlier than usual or earlier than someone else: *I want to get a jump on my Christmas shopping.* → HIGH JUMP, LONG JUMP; → take a running jump at RUNNING² (8); → SKI JUMP, TRIPLE JUMP

jump ball *n* [C] the act of throwing the ball up in a game of BASKETBALL, so that one player from each team can try to gain control of it

jumped-up *adj* [only before noun] *BrE informal* a jumped-up person thinks they are more important than they really are, because they have improved their social position: *a jumped-up little bureaucrat*

jump·er S3 /'dʒʌmpə $ -ər/ *n* [C]

1 *BrE* a piece of clothing made of wool that covers the upper part of your body and arms; ◨ sweater, pullover

2 *AmE* a dress without SLEEVES usually worn over a shirt; ◨ pinafore *BrE*

3 a person or animal that jumps

jumper cables *n* [plural] *AmE* thick wires used to connect the BATTERIES of two cars in order to start the car that has lost power

jumping jack *n* [C] *AmE* a jump that is done from a standing position with your arms and legs pointing out to the side

jumping-off point *n* [C] a place to start from, especially at the beginning of a journey

jump jet *n* [C] an aircraft that can take off and land by going straight up and down

jump leads *n* [plural] *BrE* thick wires used to connect the BATTERIES of two cars in order to start the car that has lost power

jump rope *n* [C] *AmE* a long piece of rope that children use for jumping over; ◨ skipping rope *BrE* —**jump rope** *v* [I]

jump shot *n* [C] an action in BASKETBALL in which you throw the ball towards the basket as you jump in the air

jump-start *v* [T] **1** also jump *AmE* to start a car whose BATTERY has lost power by connecting it to the battery of another car **2** to help a process or activity to start or become more successful: *Congress hopes the tax cut will jump-start the economy.* —**jump start** *n* [C]

jump·suit /'dʒʌmpsuːt, -sjuːt $ -suːt/ *n* [C] a piece of clothing like a shirt and a pair of trousers joined together, worn especially by women

jump-up *n* [U] a type of popular music from the Caribbean with a strong, regular beat, or a party, event etc where this music is played: *jump-up kids* (=young people who like this type of music)

jump·y /'dʒʌmpi/ *adj* worried or nervous especially because you are expecting something bad to happen; ◨ anxious

Jun. also **Jun** *BrE* the written abbreviation of *June*

junc·tion S3 /'dʒʌŋkʃən/ *n* [C] a place where one road, track etc joins another; ◨ intersection: *the junction of Abbot Road and Mill Street* | *Junction 5 on the M40*

junc·ture /'dʒʌŋktʃə $ -ər/ *n* [C usually singular] *formal* a particular point in an activity or period of time: *At* *this juncture*, I suggest we take a short break. | *The talks are at a **critical juncture** (=very important point).*

June /dʒuːn/ n [C,U] written abbreviation **Jun.** the sixth month of the year, between May and July: *next/last June I finished school last June.* | *in June My birthday is in June.* | *on June 6th We met on June 6th.* | *on 6th June BrE: He resigned on 6th June.* | *June 6 AmE: The first round will be held June 6.*

jun·gle /ˈdʒʌŋɡəl/ n **1** [C,U] a thick tropical forest with many large plants growing very close together: *the Amazon jungle* **2** [singular] a situation in which it is difficult to become successful or get what you want, especially because a lot of people are competing with each other: *the media jungle* **3** [singular] something that is very untidy, complicated, or confusing: [+of] *a jungle of freeways and highways* **4** [U] a type of very fast dance music → CONCRETE JUNGLE; → **law of the jungle** at LAW (8)

jungle ˌgym n [C] AmE a large frame made of metal bars for children to climb on; ◨ **climbing frame** BrE

Ju·ni·or /ˈdʒuːniə $ -ər/ written abbreviation **Jr.** AmE, **Jnr** BrE used after the name of a man or boy who has the same name as his father: *John F. Kennedy, Jr.*

junior¹ W3 adj [only before noun]
1 having a low rank in an organization or profession; ◨ **senior**: *a junior doctor* | [+to] *There are several people junior to me* (=with a lower rank than me).
2 relating to sport for young people below a particular age: *the junior football club*
3 BrE relating to a school for children below the age of 11: *the junior classrooms*
4 AmE relating to the year before the final year of HIGH SCHOOL or college: *the second semester of my junior year* → SENIOR¹

junior² n **1** be two/five/ten etc years sb's junior also be sb's junior by two/five/ten etc years *written* to be two, five, ten etc years younger than someone: *She married a man seven years her junior.* **2** [C] a young person who takes part in sport for people below a particular age: *The juniors use the courts on Tuesday night.* **3** [C] especially BrE someone who has a low rank in an organization or profession: *an office junior* **4** [C] BrE a child who goes to a JUNIOR SCHOOL **5** [C] AmE a student in the year before the final year of HIGH SCHOOL or college → FRESHMAN, SENIOR² (1), SOPHOMORE **6** Junior AmE spoken a name used humorously when speaking to or about a boy or a younger man, especially your son: *Where's Junior?*

junior ˈcollege n [C,U] a college in the US or Canada where students take a course of study that continues for two years; ◨ **community college**

junior ˈhigh school also **junior ˈhigh** n [C,U] a school in the US and Canada for children aged between 12 and 14 or 15 → MIDDLE SCHOOL (2), SENIOR HIGH SCHOOL

junior ˌschool n [C,U] a school in Britain for children aged 7 to 11

junior ˈvarsity n [C,U] AmE JV a team of younger or less experienced sports players who represent a school or university; → varsity

ju·ni·per /ˈdʒuːnɪpə $ -ər/ n [C,U] a small bush that produces purple BERRIES that can be used in cooking

junk¹ /dʒʌŋk/ n **1** [U] old or unwanted objects that have no use or value: *This cupboard's full of junk.* ⚠ Do not use **junk** when you are talking about things such as empty packets, cans, and bottles that are left in a public place. Use **litter**: *Don't drop litter in the street.* **2** [U] JUNK FOOD **3** [C] a Chinese sailing boat

junk² v [T] to get rid of something because it is old or useless

junk bond n [C] a BOND which has a high risk and is often sold to pay for a TAKEOVER

jun·ket /ˈdʒʌŋkɪt/ n [C] informal especially AmE an expensive trip paid for by government money or by a business for people they employ – used to show disapproval

junk food also **junk** n [U] informal food that is not healthy, for example because it contains a lot of fat, sugar etc

junk·ie, junky /ˈdʒʌŋki/ n [C] informal **1** someone who takes dangerous drugs and is dependent on them **2** a TV/sports etc junkie someone who likes something so much that they seem to be dependent on it – used humorously: *a technology junkie*

junk mail n [U] letters, especially advertisements, that are sent by organizations to large numbers of people – used to show disapproval

junk shop n [C] a shop that buys and sells old furniture, clothes etc

junk·y /ˈdʒʌŋki/ n plural **junkies** [C] another spelling of JUNKIE

junk yard n [C] AmE a place where old or broken furniture, cars etc can be left, or bought and sold

jun·ta /ˈdʒʌntə, ˈhʊntə/ n [C] a military government that has gained power by using force

Ju·pi·ter /ˈdʒuːpɪtə $ -ər/ n the PLANET that is fifth in order from the sun and is the largest in the SOLAR SYSTEM: *a space probe on its way to Jupiter* → see picture at SOLAR SYSTEM

ju·rid·i·cal /dʒʊˈrɪdɪkəl/ adj formal relating to judges or the law

jur·is·dic·tion /ˌdʒʊərɪsˈdɪkʃən $ ˌdʒʊr-/ n [U] the right to use an official power to make legal decisions, or the area where this right exists: [+over sb/sth] *The committee **has jurisdiction** over all tax measures.*

ju·ris·pru·dence /ˌdʒʊərɪsˈpruːdəns $ ˌdʒʊr-/ n [U] formal the science or study of law

ju·rist /ˈdʒʊərɪst $ ˈdʒʊr-/ n [C] formal someone who has a very detailed knowledge of law

ju·ror /ˈdʒʊərə $ ˈdʒʊrər/ n [C] a member of a jury

ju·ry /ˈdʒʊəri $ ˈdʒʊri/ n plural **juries** [C] **1** a group of 12 ordinary people who listen to the details of a case in court and decide whether someone is guilty or not: *the members of the jury* | *The jury found him not guilty.* | *the right to **trial by jury** | **sit/serve on a jury** (=be part of a jury)* **2** a group of people chosen to judge a competition **3 the jury is (still) out on sth** used to say that something has not been finally decided: *Is it good value? The jury is still out on that.* → GRAND JURY

jury box n [C usually singular] the place where the jury sits in a court

jury ˌservice BrE; **jury ˌduty** AmE n [U] a period of time during which you must be part of a jury

just¹ S1 W1 /dʒəst; strong dʒʌst/ adv
1 exactly: *A good strong cup of coffee is just what I need right now.* | *The house was large and roomy; just right for us.* | *She looks just like her mother.* | *Just what do you think you're trying to do?* | **just on** BrE: *It's just on three o'clock.* | **Just then** (=exactly at that moment) *Mrs Robovitch appeared at the bedroom door.* | **Just as** (=at the exact moment when) *I opened the door, the telephone started to ring.* | *A nice hot bath – **just the thing** (=exactly the right thing) to relax sore muscles.*
2 nothing more than the thing, amount, action etc that you are mentioning; ◨ **only**: *It's nothing serious – just a small cut.* | *Don't be too hard on him – he's just a kid.* | *Can you wait just a few minutes?* | *It's not just me – there are other people involved as well.*
3 only a short time ago: *John's just told me that he's getting married.* | *I've just been out shopping.*
4 at this moment or at that moment: *Wait a minute, I'm just coming.* | *He was just leaving when the phone rang.* | *I'm just finishing my homework – it won't take long.* | *The concert was just about to start.*
5 used to emphasize what you are saying: *It just isn't true.* | *I just love being in the mountains.* | *It was just wonderful to see Joyce again.* | *I just wish I could believe you.*
6 only by a small amount, time, distance etc: **just**

everything else: [+of] *Unprecedented change has been the keynote of the electronic revolution.*

keynote² *adj* [only before noun] relating to the most important part of a formal meeting, report etc: **keynote speech/address/lecture** etc *He is scheduled to deliver the keynote address at an awards ceremony.* | *Bill Gates is booked as the **keynote speaker**.*

keynote³ *v* [I,T] to give the keynote speech at a formal meeting, ceremony etc: *The event is usually keynoted by the prime minister.*

key·pad /'ki:pæd/ *n* [C] a small box with buttons on it, used to put information into a computer, telephone etc

key·pal /'ki:pæl/ *n* [C] someone with whom you regularly exchange e-mail; → **penpal**: *If your daughter is interested in having a keypal next year, please have her get in touch.*

key ring *n* [C] a metal ring that you keep keys on

key signature *n* [C] a set of marks at the beginning of a line of written music to show which KEY it is in

key·stone /'ki:stəʊn $ -stoʊn/ *n* **1** [C] the large central stone in an ARCH that keeps the other stones in position **2** [singular] *formal* the most important part of an idea, belief, or process that influences how it develops: [+of] *The keystone of any personal injury case is medical evidence.*

key·stroke /'ki:strəʊk $ -stroʊk/ *n* [C] the action of pressing a key on a computer or other machine

key·word /'ki:wɜːd $ -wɜːrd/ *n* [C] a word that you type into a computer so that it will search for that word on the Internet: *You can find the site by entering the keyword 'Quark'.*

kg *plural* **kg** *or* **kgs** the written abbreviation of *kilogram* or kilograms

kha·ki /'kɑːki $ 'kæki, 'kɑːki/ *n* [U] **1** a dull green-brown or yellow-brown colour **2** cloth of this colour, especially when worn by soldiers —**khaki** *adj*: *a khaki uniform*

kha·kis /'kɑːkiz $ 'kækiz, 'kɑː-/ *n* [plural] trousers made of khaki cloth

kha·lif /'keɪlɪf, kɑː'liːf/ *n* [C] another spelling of CALIPH

khan /kɑːn/ *n* [C] a ruler or official in India or central Asia, or their title

kHz the written abbreviation of *kilohertz*

kib·ble /'kɪbəl/ *n* [U] small round pieces of dried dog or cat food

kib·butz /kɪ'bʊts/ *n plural* **kibbutzim** /-sɪm/ [C] a type of farm in Israel where many people live and work together

kib·itz /'kɪbɪts/ *v* [I] *AmE informal* **1** to make unhelpful remarks while someone is doing something **2** to talk about things that everyone already knows in a boring way: *incessant philosophical kibbitzing* —**kibitzer** *n* [C]: *the usual crowd of kibitzers*

kib·lah, **qiblah** /'kɪblə/ *n* [singular] the direction towards which Muslims turn when they pray

ki·bosh /'kaɪbɒʃ $ -bɑːʃ/ *n* **put the kibosh on sth** *old-fashioned informal* to stop a plan, idea etc from developing; ▣ **ruin**

kick¹ [S2] [W3] /kɪk/ *v* [I,T]

1 to hit something with your foot: **kick sth down/over/around** etc *Billy was kicking a ball around the yard.* | *The police kicked the door down.* | **kick sb in the stomach/face/shin** etc *There was a scuffle and he kicked me in the stomach.*

2 to move your legs as if you were kicking something: *He kicked off his shoes and lay back on the bed.* | *a row of dancers kicking their legs in the air* | *A horse trotted past, kicking up dust from the road.*

3 kick yourself *spoken* used to say that you are annoyed with yourself because you have done something silly, made a mistake etc: *You'll kick yourself when I tell you the answer.* | *United will be kicking themselves for*

missing several chances.

4 kick the habit to stop doing something that is a harmful habit, such as smoking, taking drugs etc: *The scheme has already helped hundreds of smokers to kick the habit.*

5 kick sb when they are down to criticize or attack someone who is already in a weak or difficult position: *The media can't resist kicking a man when he's down.*

6 kick sb in the teeth; **kick sb in the stomach/pants** *AmE informal* to disappoint someone or treat them badly at a time when they need help: *We all have times when life kicks us in the teeth.*

7 kick sb's ass/butt *AmE informal not polite* to punish or defeat someone: *We're gonna kick San Francisco's ass good tonight.*

8 kick ass *AmE informal not polite* used to say that someone or something is very good or impressive: *Tucson pop band Shoebomb kick some serious ass.*

9 kick your heels *BrE* to waste time waiting for something: *We were left kicking our heels for half the day.*

10 kick up your heels to enjoy yourself a lot at a party, event etc: *The charity ball is a chance to kick up your heels and help a good cause.*

11 kick sth into touch *BrE informal* to stop a plan or project before it is completed: *A hitch resulted in the deal being kicked firmly into touch.*

12 kick up a fuss/stink/row *informal* to complain loudly about something: *Won't he kick up a fuss when he discovers they're missing?*

13 kicking and screaming protesting violently or being very unwilling to do something: *The London Stock Exchange **was dragged kicking and screaming** into the 20th century.*

14 kick the shit out of sb *informal not polite* to hurt someone very badly by kicking them many times

15 kick against the pricks *BrE informal* to hurt or damage yourself by trying to change something that cannot be changed

16 kick sb upstairs to move someone to a new job that seems to be more important than their last one, but that actually gives them less influence

17 be kicking (it) *AmE spoken* to be relaxing and having a good time: *I was just kicking with my buddies.*

18 be kicking it *AmE spoken* to be having a romantic or sexual relationship with someone: [+with] *My sources say that she was kicking it with Thomas while she was on tour.*

19 kick over the traces *BrE old-fashioned* to start behaving badly by refusing to accept any control or rules

20 kick the bucket *old-fashioned* to die – used humorously

kick (out) against sth *phr v*
to react strongly against something: *She has kicked out against authority all her life.*

kick around *phr v*
1 kick sth around to think about or discuss an idea before making a decision: *We kicked that suggestion around and in the end decided to go ahead.*

2 kick sb around to treat someone badly and unfairly: *I have my pride, you know. They can't kick me around.*

3 kick around (sth) to be in a place doing things but without any firm plans; ▣ **knock around**: *He kicked around India for a few months.*

4 to be left in a place untidily or forgotten: *There's a copy of the report kicking around somewhere.*

kick back *phr v AmE*
to relax: *Your waitress will take your order while you kick back and enjoy the game.*

kick in *phr v*
1 *informal* to start or to begin to have an effect: *The storm is expected to kick in shortly after sunrise.* | *The painkillers kicked in and he became sleepy.*

2 kick in (sth) to join with others in giving money or help; ▣ **chip in**: *Bill never wants to kick in.* | *We were each asked to kick in 50 cents toward the cost.*

3 kick sb's head/face/teeth in to injure someone badly by kicking them: *He threatened to come round and kick my head in.*

4 kick a door in to kick a locked door so hard that it breaks open: *We had to get the police to kick the door in.*

kick off *phr v*

1 if a meeting, event, or a football game kicks off, it starts: *What time does the laser show kick off?* | *The match kicks off at noon.* | [+with] *The series kicked off with an interview with Brando.*

2 *informal* if you kick off a discussion, meeting, event etc, you start it: *OK Marion, would you care to kick off?* | **kick sth ⇔ off (with sth)** *I'm going to kick off today's meeting with a few remarks about the budget.*

3 kick sb off sth *informal* to remove someone from a team or group: *Joe was kicked off the committee for stealing funds.*

4 *AmE informal* to die

kick sb ⇔ **out** *phr v*

to make someone leave a place, job etc; ▤ **throw out**: *Bernard's wife kicked him out.* | [+of] *He was kicked out of the golf club.*

kick² *n* [C] **1** a movement of your foot or leg, usually to hit something with your foot: *Brazil scored with the last kick of the match.* | *Rory aimed a kick at her leg and missed.* | *kung fu kicks* | *If the door won't open just give it a good kick.* **2** the act of kicking the ball in a sports game such as football, or the ball that is kicked and the direction it goes in: *Benjamin struck a post with an overhead kick.* | **free/penalty kick** (=an opportunity, allowed by the rules, for a player in one team to kick the ball without being stopped by the other team) *Pearce came forward to take the free kick.* **3** something that you enjoy because it is exciting; ▤ **thrill: get a kick out of/from (doing) sth** *Gerald gets a kick out of dressing as a woman.* | **give sb a kick** *It gives her a kick to get you into trouble.* | **do sth (just) for kicks** *She used to steal from shops for kicks.* **4 a kick up the arse/backside/pants etc** *informal* criticism or strong encouragement to make someone do something they should have done: *What Phil needs is a good kick up the arse.* **5 a kick in the teeth** *informal* something that is very disappointing or upsetting that happens when you need support: *This broken promise is a real kick in the teeth for our fans.* **6 a kick** *informal* used to talk about the strong effect of a drink or drug or the strong taste that some food has: *The wine had a real kick.*

kick

kick-ass *adj AmE informal* strong, powerful, and sometimes violent: *a kick-ass attitude*

kick·back /ˈkɪkbæk/ *n* [C] *informal* money that someone pays secretly and dishonestly in return for someone's help; ▤ **bribe**

kick·ball /ˈkɪkbɔːl $ -bɒːl/ *n* [U] an American game for children, similar to baseball, in which you kick the ball

kick·box·ing /ˈkɪkˌbɒksɪŋ $ -ˌbɑːks-/ *n* [U] a form of BOXING in which you kick someone as well as hitting them —**kickboxer** *n* [C]

kick·er /ˈkɪkə $ -ər/ *n* **1** [C] a player in a sports team who kicks the ball to score points **2** [singular] *AmE* a surprising or unexpected end to an event: *The kicker came when the reporter asked the 22-mile runner whether she was tired.*

kick·off /ˈkɪk-ɒf $ -ɒːf/ *n* [C usually singular] **1** the time when a football game starts, or the first kick of the game: *Kickoff is at 3.00.* **2** *informal* the beginning of a new activity

kick·stand /ˈkɪkstænd/ *n* [C] a thin piece of metal on the bottom of a bicycle or MOTORCYCLE that supports it in an upright position when it is not moving → see picture at MOTORBIKE

kick-start¹ *v* [T] **1** to do something to help a process or activity start or develop more quickly: *He urged further interest rate cuts in a bid to kick-start the economy.* **2** to start a MOTORCYCLE using your foot

kick-start² *n* **1** [C] also **kick-starter** the part of a MOTORCYCLE that you press with your foot to start it **2** [singular] action taken to make a plan, project etc start or develop more quickly: *Motivation is the kick-start you need to succeed at work.*

kid¹ S1 W2 /kɪd/ *n*

1 [C] *informal* a child: *She'd always loved animals since she was a little kid.* | *He's married with three kids.* | *A neighbor volunteered to keep an eye on* **the kids** (=their children or the children they are responsible for).

2 [C] *informal* a young person: *college kids*

3 [C usually singular] used by adults to address a person who is younger than them: *Hey kid, come here.*

4 kid's stuff also; **kid stuff** *AmE* something that is too easy or boring: *Pokemon? Oh boy, that is kid stuff!*

5 a) a young goat **b)** [U] very soft leather made from the skin of a young goat: *a pair of white kid boots*

6 kid gloves a way of treating someone kindly and carefully because they easily become upset: **treat/ handle sb with kid gloves** *I want you to treat Hayley with kid gloves today. She's still upset about her father.*

kid² *v* **kidded, kidding** *informal* **1** [I,T] to say something that is not true, especially as a joke; ▤ **joke: just/only kidding** *Don't get mad, I was only kidding.* **2** [T] to make jokes or say funny things about someone in a friendly way; ▤ **tease: kid sb about sth** *We were kidding Mom about being a grandmother.* | **kid sb (that)** *My friends kidded me that my gear would fill the car.* **3 no kidding?/are you kidding?** *spoken* used when you are so surprised by what someone has told you that you do not completely believe them: *Carlotta's 39? No kidding?* **4 no kidding** *spoken* **a)** used to say that you understand and agree with what someone has just said: *'That girl has some major problems.' 'Yeah, no kidding.'* **b)** used to emphasize a threat or that you are telling the truth: *If you break that thing, you'll be grounded for a week – no kidding.* | *And then he saw us and – no kidding – he asked us if we wanted a ride.* **5** [T] to let yourself believe something that is untrue or unlikely: **kid yourself (that)** *Don't kid yourself he'll ever change.* | *We thought we could change the world. Just who were we trying to kid?* **6 I kid you not** *spoken* used to emphasize that you are telling the truth —**kidding** *n* [U]

kid around *phr v* to behave in a silly way: *Stop kidding around and listen.*

kid³ *adj* **kid sister/brother** *especially AmE informal* your kid sister or brother is younger than you are; ▤ **little sister/brother** *BrE*

kid·die¹, kiddy /ˈkɪdi/ *n* [C] *informal especially BrE* a young child: *a sandpit for the kiddies*

kiddie², kiddy *adj* [only before noun] made, involving, or intended for young children: *a kiddie seat*

kiddie-cam *n* [C] a camera that allows parents to see their children when the parents are somewhere else

kid·do /ˈkɪdəʊ $ -doʊ/ *n plural* **kiddos** [C usually singular] *especially AmE spoken informal* used by adults to address a young person: *Come on kiddo, let's go.*

kid·nap /ˈkɪdnæp/ *v* **kidnapped, kidnapping** also, **kidnaped, kidnaping** *AmE* [T] to take someone somewhere illegally by force, often in order to get money for returning them; → **ransom:** *Police appealed for witnesses after a woman was kidnapped at gunpoint and assaulted.* —**kidnapper** *n* [C]: *the hunt for the kidnapper* —**kidnapping** also **kidnap** *n* [C,U]: *a series of kidnappings*

kid·ney S3 /ˈkɪdni/ *n*

1 [C] one of the two organs in your lower back that separate waste products from your blood and make

K

URINE: *a kidney transplant* → see picture at HUMAN[1]
2 [C,U] one or more of these organs from an animal, used as food: *steak and kidney pie*

kidney bean *n* [C] a dark red bean that is shaped like the letter C

kid·ult /ˈkɪdʌlt/ *n* [C] an adult who likes to play games or buy things that most people consider more suitable for children

kike /kaɪk/ *n* [C] *taboo* a very offensive word for someone who is Jewish. Do not use this word.

kill¹ S1 W1 /kɪl/ *v*
1 MAKE SB/STH DIE [I,T] to make a person or animal die: *Why did she kill her husband?* | *Murray held a gun to his head and threatened to kill him.* | *Four people were killed when a train plunged into a flooded river.* | **be killed instantly/outright** (=immediately) *The driver was killed instantly.* | *Bleach kills household germs.* | *Smoking kills.*
2 kill yourself a) to cause your own death: *You're going to kill yourself on that bike.* | *After her husband died, Mary tried to kill herself.* **b)** to work very hard to achieve something in a way that makes you ill or tired: *It's not worth killing yourself over it.* | **kill yourself to do sth** *He about killed himself to make the business go.*
3 MAKE STH STOP/FAIL [T] to make something stop operating or fail: *Joe pulled in and killed the engine.* | *The out-of-town shopping centre will kill local trade.* | **kill your speed** (=drive slowly)
4 BE ANGRY WITH SB [T] *informal* to be very angry with someone: *Mom will kill me if I'm late.*
5 ANNOYED/SAD [T] to make someone feel annoyed, sad, concerned etc: **it kills sb to do sth** *It kills me to see him working so hard.* | *What happened next? The suspense is killing me.*
6 would/could kill for sth also **would kill to do sth** to want something so much that you will do almost anything to get it or do it: *I could kill for a smoke right now.* | *In those days, actors would kill to break into film.*
7 my head/back etc is killing me *spoken* used to say that a part of your body is hurting a lot: *I've walked miles and my feet are killing me.*
8 kill time/an hour etc to spend time doing something which is not important while you are waiting to do something important or waiting for something else to happen: *With time to kill, he took a cab to the centre.*
9 kill a beer/bottle of wine etc *spoken* to drink or finish drinking a beer etc quickly: *Let's kill these beers and go.*
10 MAKE SB LAUGH [T] to make someone laugh a lot: **kill yourself laughing** *They weren't bothered — in fact they were killing themselves laughing.*
11 it won't/wouldn't kill sb (to do something) *spoken* used to say that someone could easily do something, and ought to do it: *It wouldn't kill you to help out once in a while.*
12 (even) if it kills me *spoken* used to emphasize that you are determined to do something even though it is very difficult: *I'm completing this course, even if it kills me.*
13 kill two birds with one stone to achieve two things with one action
14 kill the goose that lays the golden egg to destroy the thing that brings you profit or success
15 kill the fatted calf to welcome someone home with a big meal etc after they have been away for a long time
16 kill sb with kindness to be too kind to someone, in a way that actually harms them
17 kill or cure used to say that something you are going to do will be either successful or fail completely → **dressed to kill** at DRESSED (3)
kill sth ⇔ off *phr v*
1 to cause the death of a lot of living things; ◨ **destroy**: *Pollution is rapidly killing off plant life.*
2 to stop or remove something completely; ◨ **destroy**: *These figures kill off any hope that the economy is poised for recovery.*

WORD CHOICE: **kill, murder, execute, put to death, kill yourself, commit suicide, slaughter, massacre, assassinate**
There are many different words meaning to kill someone.
Kill is the most general: *He says he did not mean to kill his wife.* | *Thousands of Russian soldiers were killed in the war.*
Use **murder** to talk about deliberately killing someone, especially after planning to do it: *He is charged with murdering a policeman.*
When you are talking about killing someone as a punishment for a crime, use **execute** or **put** someone **to death**: *He was executed by a firing squad.* | *the first person to be put to death in San Quentin jail*
If someone deliberately causes their own death, say that they **commit suicide** or that someone **kills himself** or **herself**: *the feeling of hopelessness that led him to commit suicide,* | *It was not the first time she had tried to kill herself.*
Slaughter and **massacre** mean to violently kill a large number of people who cannot defend themselves. These words are used mainly in writing or journalism: *Hundreds of innocent civilians were slaughtered.* | *Soldiers massacred 900 men, women, and children in the village.*
Use **assassinate** to talk about killing an important person, especially a politician: *J.F.Kennedy was assassinated in Dallas in 1963.*

kill² *n* **1** [C usually singular] the act of killing a hunted animal: *He raised his knife for the kill.* **2 move in/close in for the kill** to come closer to something in order to kill, defeat, or destroy it: *Enemy submarines were moving in for the kill.* **3** [singular] an animal that is killed by another animal: *The cubs will share the remains of the kill.*

kill·er¹ /ˈkɪlə $ -ər/ *n* [C] **1** a person, animal, or thing that kills: *Heart disease is America's number one killer.* | *the hunt for her killers* | *weed killer* → **serial killer** at SERIAL² (1) **2** *informal* something or someone that is very difficult, tiring, or boring: *The new project is a killer.* **3** *informal* something that is very exciting or impressive: *I'm not saying the film is a killer, but it's cool.*

killer² *adj* [only before noun] **1** very harmful or dangerous: *a killer hurricane* | *a swarm of killer bees* **2** *informal* very attractive, good, impressive etc: *a book called 'How to Build a Killer Website'* **3 killer instinct** a very strong desire to succeed in a situation or activity etc that is very competitive: *Young players these days lack the killer instinct.*

killer whale *n* [C] a black and white WHALE that eats meat

kill·ing /ˈkɪlɪŋ/ *n* [C] **1** the act of killing someone deliberately; ◨ **murder**: *a series of gangland killings* | *They murdered fifteen boys in a killing spree* (=an occasion when someone murders many people in a short period of time) *across southern California.* **2 make a killing** *informal* to make a lot of money in a short time: *He made a killing on the stock exchange.*

kill·joy /ˈkɪldʒɔɪ/ *n* [C] someone who spoils other people's pleasure

kiln /kɪln/ *n* [C] a special OVEN for baking clay pots, bricks etc

ki·lo /ˈkiːləʊ $ -loʊ/ *n plural* **kilos** [C] a kilogram

kilo- /kɪlə/ *prefix* [in nouns] a thousand – used with units of measurement

kil·o·byte /ˈkɪləbaɪt/ *n* [C] *K* or *KB* a unit for measuring computer information, equal to 1024 BYTES

kil·o·gram also **kilogramme** *BrE* /ˈkɪləɡræm/ *n* [C] written abbreviation *kg* a unit for measuring weight, equal to 1000 grams

kil·o·hertz /ˈkɪləhɜːts $ -ɜːr-/ *n plural* **kilohertz** [C] written abbreviation *kHz* a unit for measuring the FREQUENCY of SOUND WAVES, especially radio signals, equal to 1000 HERTZ

K

kil·o·me·tre [S3] *BrE*; **kilometer** *AmE* /ˈkɪləˌmiːtə, kɪˈlɒmɪ̯tə $ kɪˈlɑːmɪ̯tər/ *n* [C] written abbreviation *km* a unit for measuring distance, equal to 1000 metres

kil·o·watt /ˈkɪləwɒt $ -wɑːt/ *n* [C] written abbreviation *kW* a unit for measuring electrical power, equal to 1000 WATTS

kilowatt 'hour *n* [C] written abbreviation *kWh* a unit for measuring electrical power, equal to the amount of work produced by one kilowatt in one hour

kilt /kɪlt/ *n* [C] a type of thick skirt made of TARTAN (=material with a pattern of lines and squares) that is traditionally worn by Scottish men —**kilted** *adj*

kil·ter /ˈkɪltə $ -ər/ *n* **out of kilter/off kilter** not working as well as usual: *Pollution has **thrown** the Earth's chemistry **out of kilter**.*

kim·chi /ˈkɪmtʃi/ *n* [U] a Korean hot-tasting dish made of PICKLED cabbage and other vegetables

ki·mo·no /kɪˈməʊnəʊ $ -ˈmoʊnoʊ/ *n plural* **kimonos** [C] a traditional piece of Japanese clothing like a long loose coat, worn at special ceremonies

kin /kɪn/ *n* [plural] **1** *informal* also **kinsfolk, kinfolk** your family **2 next of kin** *formal* your most closely related family: *We'll have to notify the next of kin of his death.*; → **kindred** → KITH AND KIN

kind¹ [S1] [W1] /kaɪnd/ *n*
1 [C,U] one of the different types of a person or thing that belong to the same group; ⧉ **sort, type**

> all kinds/every kind
> different/various kinds
> a certain/particular kind
> some kind
> any kind
> the same kind
> the right kind
> the worst kind
> of its/their kind
> of this kind
> what kind (of sth)?
> that kind of thing
> precisely/exactly the kind (that)

> [+of] *They sell **all kinds** of things.* | *The flowers attract several **different kinds** of insects.* | *Certain kinds of medical care are more expensive than others.* | *Greg was working on **some kind** of deal in Italy.* | *Get me a sandwich – **any kind** will do.* | *You can't get in unless you're wearing **the right kind** of clothes.* | *This is hypocrisy of **the worst kind**.* | *It is the biggest centre of its kind.* | *What kind of food do you want?* | *I like yoga, aerobics, and **that kind of thing**.* | *This is precisely **the kind** of sensational attitude I most deplore.* → see box at TYPE¹

2 the kind used to describe a person with a particular character, feelings, opinions etc: *Ted just isn't the marrying kind.* | *Rob isn't the kind of person to worry.*
3 kind of; kinda *AmE spoken* slightly but not exactly, or in some ways; ⧉ **sort of**: *I'm kind of glad I didn't win.* | *He's kinda dumb, isn't he?*
4 a kind of (a) sth *spoken* used to say that your description of something is not exact: *a kind of reddish-brown color*
5 two/three etc of a kind two, three etc people or things that are very similar: *You and your brother are two of a kind.*
6 one of a kind the only one of a particular type of thing: *Each unique plate is handpainted and one of a kind.*
7 something of the/that kind *spoken* something similar to what was expected or talked about: *Rosa was shocked by the news, although she had suspected something of the kind might happen.*
8 nothing/anything of the kind *spoken* used to emphasize that what has been said is not true: *I never said anything of the kind!*
9 of a kind used to say that something is not as good as it should be: *Elections of a kind are held, but there is only one party to vote for.*

10 in kind reacting to something someone has done by doing the same thing: *After recent bombings, counter-terrorist forces could retaliate in kind.* → **payment in kind** at PAYMENT (3)

kind² [S3] *adj comparative* **kinder**, *superlative* **kindest**
1 saying or doing things that show that you care about other people and want to help them or make them happy; ⧉ **unkind**; → **kindly, kindness**: [+to] *They've been very kind to me.* | *It wasn't a very kind thing to say.* | *She's a very kind and generous person.* | **it's kind of sb (to do sth)** *It's kind of you to say that.* | *It's really kind of them to let us use their pool.* | *We thanked the priest for his **kind** words.* | *Thank you for your help. You've been **most kind** (=said when thanking someone very politely).* | **thank you for your kind invitation/offer** (=said when thanking someone very politely for their invitation or offer) | *Ms Jarvis is unable to accept your **kind invitation**.* | *Thank you for your **kind offer**.*
2 not causing harm or suffering: [+to] *Life has been very kind to me.* | *I need a soap that's kinder to my skin.* | *Let's hope the weather's kind tomorrow.*
3 would you be kind enough to do sth/be so kind as to do sth *formal* used to make a polite request: *Would you be kind enough to close the door, please?* ⚠ If you use these expressions in informal English, they can sound rude or unfriendly. Use **please could you...?** or **would you mind...?** instead.
4 kind regards *written* used to end a formal but fairly friendly letter

WORD FOCUS: KIND
similar words: nice, considerate, thoughtful, sympathetic, benevolent, compassionate, gentle

kin·der·gar·ten /ˈkɪndəgɑːtn $ -dərgɑːrtn/ *n* [C,U] **1** *AmE* a school or class for children aged five **2** *BrE* a school for children aged two to five; ⧉ **nursery school**

kind-heart·ed /ˌkaɪnd ˈhɑːtɪd◂ $ -ɑːr-/ *adj* kind and generous: *a kind-hearted gesture* —**kind-heartedly** *adv* —**kind-heartedness** *n* [U]

kin·dle /ˈkɪndl/ *v* [I,T] **1** if you kindle a fire, or if it kindles, it starts to burn **2** to make someone feel interested, excited, hopeful etc: **kindle sth in sb** *A love of poetry was kindled in him by his mother.*

kin·dling /ˈkɪndlɪŋ/ *n* [U] small sticks, leaves etc that you use to start a fire → see picture at FIREPLACE

kind·ly¹ /ˈkaɪndli/ *adv* **1** in a kind way; ⧉ **generously**: **kindly offer/agree/give etc** *Mr Nunn has kindly agreed to let us use his barn for the dance.* **2 not take kindly to sth** to be unwilling to accept a situation because it annoys you: *She does not take kindly to criticism.* **3 look kindly on sb/sth** to approve of someone or something: *Jimmy would probably not look too kindly on our request.* **4** *spoken formal* a word meaning 'please', which is often used when you are annoyed: *Will you kindly put that book back?*

kindly² *adj old-fashioned* kind and caring for other people: *Mrs Gardiner was a kindly old soul.* ⚠ It is more usual to say **kind**. —**kindliness** *n* [C]

kind·ness /ˈkaɪndnɪ̯s/ *n* **1** [U] kind behaviour towards someone: *I can't thank you enough for your kindness.* **2** [C] a kind action: **do sb a kindness** *It would be doing him a kindness to tell him the truth.* → **kill sb with kindness** at KILL¹ (16)

kin·dred¹ /ˈkɪndrɪ̯d/ *n* [U] *old use* your whole family; → **kin**

kindred² *adj* [only before noun] **1 a kindred spirit** someone who thinks and feels the way you do **2** *formal* belonging to the same group or family: *The protest included members of Free the Streets and kindred organisations.*

ki·net·ic /kɪˈnetɪk, kaɪ-/ *adj technical* relating to movement: *kinetic energy*

ki·net·ics /kɪˈnetɪks, kaɪ-/ *n* [U] the science that studies movement

K

kin·folk /'kɪnfəʊk $ -foʊk/ n [plural] AmE old-fashioned
KINSFOLK

king W1 /kɪŋ/ n [C]
1 RULER a man who rules a country because he is from a royal family; → **queen**: [+of] Henry VIII, King of England | On 2 December Henry VI was **crowned king** (=made the king at an official ceremony).
2 THE BEST the king of sth someone or something that people think is the most important or best of a particular type of person or thing: the King of Rock 'n' Roll | the king of Swiss cheeses | The lion is **the king of the jungle**.
3 SUCCESSFUL if you live like a king, feel like a king etc, you are very successful, happy, rich etc: With her at my side, I felt like a king.
4 CHESS the most important piece in CHESS → see picture at CHESS
5 CARDS a playing card with a picture of a king on it
6 IMPORTANT be king if something is king at a particular time, it has a big influence on people: back in the days when jazz was king
7 a king's ransom a very large amount of money

king·dom W3 /'kɪŋdəm/ n [C]
1 a country ruled by a king or queen: the United Kingdom | [+of] the kingdom of Thailand
2 the animal/plant/mineral kingdom one of the three parts into which the natural world is divided
3 the kingdom of heaven/God also God's kingdom heaven
4 kingdom come informal a phrase used to describe the end of the world, death, or the end of time: He left the gas on and nearly **blew** us all **to kingdom come**.

king·fish·er /'kɪŋ,fɪʃə $ -ər/ n [C] a small brightly-coloured bird with a blue body that catches fish in rivers

king·ly /'kɪŋli/ adj formal good enough for a king, or typical of a king: a kingly feast

king·mak·er /'kɪŋ,meɪkə $ -ər/ n [C] someone who influences the choice of people for important jobs: Her death thrust Newman into the position of kingmaker.

king·pin /'kɪŋ,pɪn/ n [C usually singular] **1** the person or thing in a group that is the most important or that has the most power – used especially in news reports: **crime/drug etc kingpin** a mafia kingpin **2** technical a thin strong piece of metal used in HINGES

K **,King's 'Counsel** n a KC

,King's 'English also **Queen's English** n the King's English old-fashioned correct English, as it is spoken in Britain

,king's 'evidence n turn King's evidence BrE to give information about other criminals in order to get a less severe punishment; → queen's evidence; ▤ state's evidence AmE

king·ship /'kɪŋʃɪp/ n [U] the official position or condition of being a king: the responsibilities of kingship

'king-size also **'king-sized** adj **1** very large, and usually the largest size of something: a king-size bed | king-sized cigarettes **2** informal very big, strong, or extreme: a king-size headache

kink¹ /kɪŋk/ n [C] **1** a twist in something that is normally straight: [+in] The water hose had a kink in it. **2** a small problem in a plan, system etc: Given the size of the task a few kinks are inevitable. **3** something strange or dangerous in someone's character

kink² v [I,T] to have or get a kink: Take care to avoid kinking the wire.

kink·y /'kɪŋki/ adj **1** informal having or showing unusual ways of getting sexual excitement: kinky sex videos **2** kinky hair has a lot of small curves —**kinkiness** n [U] —**kinkily** adv

kins·folk /'kɪnzfəʊk $ -foʊk/ also **kinfolk** AmE n [plural] old-fashioned your family

kin·ship /'kɪnʃɪp/ n **1** [U + with] literary a family relationship: the ties of kinship **2** [singular, U] a strong connection between people; → **rapport**: [+between] The sense of kinship between the two men is surprising. | He felt a **kinship** with the only other American on the base.

kins·man /'kɪnzmən/ n plural kinsmen /-mən/ [C] old use a male relative

kins·wom·an /'kɪnz,wʊmən/ n plural kinswomen /-,wɪmɪn/ [C] old use a female relative

ki·osk /'kiːɒsk $ -ɑːsk/ n [C] **1** a small building in the street where newspapers, sweets etc are sold **2** BrE old-fashioned a public telephone box

kiosk

telephone kiosk/box

kip¹ /kɪp/ n [singular, U] BrE informal a period of sleep: I've only had an hour's kip. | We ought to get some kip.

kip² v kipped, kipping [I] BrE informal to sleep somewhere, especially somewhere that is not your home: [+down] There are rooms for drivers to kip down for the night. | [+on] Mum says you can kip on the sofa tonight.

kip·per /'kɪpə $ -ər/ n [C] a HERRING (=type of fish) that has been preserved using smoke and salt —**kippered** adj: kippered herring

kirk /kɜːk $ kɜːrk/ n **1** [C] a church – used in Scotland and Northern England **2** the Kirk the Church of Scotland

kirsch /kɪəʃ $ kɪrʃ/ n [U] a strong alcoholic drink made from CHERRY juice

kis·met /'kɪzmet, 'kɪs-/ n [U] literary the things that will happen to you in your life; ▤ fate

kiss¹ S3 W3 /kɪs/ v
1 [I,T] to touch someone with your lips as a greeting, to show them love, or as part of a sexual relationship: Maggie leaned forward and kissed her cheek. | Georgina took him in her arms and kissed him on the lips. | As they parted, Jim and Mary kissed (=they kissed each other). | **kiss sb gently/lightly** He kissed her gently and stroked her hair. | **kiss sb goodbye/goodnight etc** Kiss Daddy goodnight.
2 [T] to touch something with your lips as a sign of respect: She raised the crucifix to her lips and kissed it.
3 kiss goodbye to sth/kiss sth goodbye informal to accept that you will lose something or lose an opportunity to do something: She knew if she concentrated on her marriage she could kiss her career goodbye.
4 kiss sth better spoken used, especially to a child, to say that you will take away the pain of something by kissing them: Here, let Mommy kiss it better.
5 kiss my ass AmE informal not polite an insulting expression used to show that you do not respect someone
6 kiss (sb's) ass AmE informal not polite to be too nice to someone who can give you something you want – used to show disapproval
7 [T] literary if the wind, sun etc kisses something, it gently moves or touches it
kiss up to sb phr v AmE informal
to try to please someone in order to get them to do something for you – used to show disapproval; ▤ **suck up to** BrE: If you say that, it'll look like you're kissing up to me.

kiss² n [C] **1** an act of kissing: Do you remember your first kiss? | Come and **give** your girl **a kiss**. | a big/long/quick etc kiss a passionate kiss **2** give sb the kiss of life especially BrE to make someone start breathing again by blowing air into their lungs when they have almost DROWNED etc **3 the kiss of death** *informal* something that spoils or ruins a plan, activity etc → FRENCH KISS; → **blow sb a kiss** at BLOW¹ (9)

kiss·a·gram /ˈkɪsəgræm/ *n* [C] another spelling of KISSOGRAM

ˌkiss-and-ˈtell *n* [C usually singular] a story, article, book etc in which someone tells the public the secret details of a romantic relationship that they had with a famous person

kis·ser /ˈkɪsə $ -ər/ *n* [C] *informal* **1** [usually singular] your mouth: *She slapped me right in the kisser.* **2** a person who is kissing: **a good/bad etc kisser**

ˌkissing ˈcousin *n* [C] *AmE old-fashioned* someone you are not closely related to, but whom you know well

kiss·o·gram, **kissagram** /ˈkɪsəgræm/ *n* [C] a humorous greeting for your BIRTHDAY etc that is delivered by someone in a special COSTUME who delivers it and kisses you

kit¹ /kɪt/ *n* **1** [C] a set of tools, equipment etc that you use for a particular purpose or activity: *Sally keeps her make-up kit in her bag.* | *a bike repair kit* | *a shaving kit* | *a drum kit* **2** [C] something that you buy in parts and put together yourself: *model kits for making boats* | *kit cars* **3** [U] electronic equipment, especially computers and computer software: *The new kit includes a CD-ROM and DAT drive.* **4** [C,U] *BrE* a set of clothes and equipment that you use for a particular purpose such as playing a sport: *sports kit* | *football kits* **5** [U] a set of clothes and equipment used by soldiers, SAILORS, etc: *The soldiers are trained to jump from the planes with full kit on.* **6 get your kit off** *BrE informal* to take your clothes off **7 the whole kit and caboodle** *old-fashioned* everything → DRUM KIT, FIRST AID KIT, TOOL KIT

kit² *v* **kitted**, **kitting**

  kit sb/sth ⇔ **out/up** *phr v* [usually passive] *BrE* if someone or something is kitted out with clothes or equipment, they are provided with the clothes or equipment needed for an activity: [+with/in] *The studio is lavishly kitted out with camera equipment.* | *Mark was kitted up in mountaineering skis, boots, and equipment.*

kit bag, **kit·bag** /ˈkɪtbæg/ *n* [C] *especially BrE* a long narrow bag used by soldiers, SAILORS etc, for carrying their clothes and other possessions

kitch·en S1 W2 /ˈkɪtʃən/ *n* [C]

1 the room where you prepare and cook food: *Sam went into the kitchen to make a pot of tea.* | *She is in the kitchen making a meal.* → see picture at STAY

2 everything but the kitchen sink *humorous* used when someone has brought too many things with them

ˌkitchen ˈcabinet *n* [C] a group of people who give advice informally to the leader of the government, not officially

kitch·en·ette /ˌkɪtʃɪˈnet/ *n* [C] a small room or area where you can prepare and eat food, especially in an office or FLAT

ˌkitchen ˈgarden *n* [C] *BrE* a part of a garden where you grow your own fruit and vegetables: ☐ **vegetable patch/plot**

ˈkitchen ˌroll *BrE* also **ˌkitchen ˈtowel** *n* [U] thick paper used for cleaning up small amounts of liquid, food etc

ˌkitchen ˈsink ˌdrama *n* [C] *BrE* a serious play or film about problems that families have at home

kitch·en·ware /ˈkɪtʃənweə $ -wer/ *n* [U] pots, pans, and other things used for cooking

kite¹ /kaɪt/ *n* [C] **1** a light frame covered in coloured paper or plastic that you let fly in the air on the end of one or two long strings **2** a type of HAWK (=bird that eats small animals) **3** *AmE informal* an illegal cheque **4 fly a kite** to make a suggestion to see what people will think of it → **go fly a kite** at FLY¹ (24); → **high as a kite** at HIGH¹ (24)

kite² *v* [I,T] *AmE informal* **1** also **kite up** to raise the cost of something; ☐ **hike up**: *Soaring medical costs keep kiting up insurance premiums.* **2** to obtain money using an illegal cheque

ˈkite-ˌflying *n* [U] **1** the game or sport of flying a kite **2** *BrE* when you tell people about an idea, plan etc in order to get their opinion

Kite·mark /ˈkaɪtmɑːk $ -mɑːrk/ *n* [C] *trademark* a mark in the shape of a KITE which is officially put on goods in Britain to show that their quality is of a good standard

ˈkite ˌsurfing *n* [U] the activity of moving across water on a SURFBOARD while holding a large KITE which is attached to strong strings

kith and kin /ˌkɪθ ən ˈkɪn/ *n* [plural] *old-fashioned* family and friends

kitsch /kɪtʃ/ *n* [U] objects, films etc that are cheap and unfashionable, and which often amuse people because of this —**kitsch**, **kitschy** *adj*

kit·ten /ˈkɪtn/ *n* [C] **1** a young cat **2 have kittens** *BrE spoken informal* to be very anxious or upset about something

ˈkitten ˌheels *n* [plural] shoes or boots worn by women, with very thin high heels that curve under the shoes —**kitten-heel** *adj* [only before noun]: *kitten-heel ankle boots*

kit·ten·ish /ˈkɪtn-ɪʃ/ *adj old-fashioned* a kittenish woman behaves in a silly way in order to attract men

kit·ty /ˈkɪti/ *n plural* **kitties** [C] **1** [usually singular] the money that people have collected for a particular purpose: *How much money is there left in the kitty?* **2** [usually singular] the money that the winner of a game of cards receives **3** a word for a cat, used especially by children

ˈkitty-ˌcorner *adv AmE informal* on the opposite corner of a street from a particular place: [+from/to] *The drugstore is kitty-corner from the bank.*

ki·wi /ˈkiːwiː/ *n* [C] **1** a New Zealand bird that has very short wings and cannot fly **2** *informal* someone from New Zealand

ˈkiwi fruit *n* [C] a small sweet fruit with a brown skin, which is green inside → see picture at FRUIT¹

klans·man /ˈklænzmən/ *n plural* **klansmen** /-mən/ [C] *AmE* a member of the Ku Klux Klan

Klax·on /ˈklæksən/ *n* [C] *trademark* a loud horn that was fixed onto police cars and other official vehicles in the past

Kleen·ex /ˈkliːneks/ *n plural* **Kleenex** [C,U] *trademark* a TISSUE: *a box of Kleenex*

klep·to·ma·ni·a /ˌkleptəˈmeɪniə/ *n* [U] a mental illness in which you have a desire to steal things

klep·to·ma·ni·ac /ˌkleptəˈmeɪniæk/ also **klep·to** /ˈkleptəʊ $ -toʊ/ *informal n* [C] someone suffering from kleptomania

kludge /kluːdʒ, klʌdʒ/ *n* [C] a computer system or program that is made or written very quickly and not very well —**kludge** *v* [T]

klutz, **clutz** /klʌts/ *n* [C] *AmE* someone who drops things and falls easily —**klutzy** *adj*

km *plural* **km** *or* **kms** the written abbreviation of *kilometre* or kilometres

knack /næk/ *n informal* **1** [singular] a natural skill or ability; → **talent**: **knack for doing sth** *Some people seem to have a knack for making money.* | **knack of doing sth** *Thomson's knack of scoring vital goals makes him important to the team.* **2 have a knack of doing sth** *BrE* to have a tendency to do something: *He has a knack of saying the wrong thing.*

knack·er /ˈnækə $ -ər/ *v* [T] *BrE spoken informal* **1** to become extremely tired; ☐ **exhaust**: **knacker yourself**

K

(out) *Slow down – you'll knacker yourself out!* **2 knacker your elbow/hand** etc to hurt your elbow etc so that you cannot use it

knack·ered /'nækəd $ -ərd/ *adj BrE spoken informal* **1** extremely tired; ▪ **exhausted 2** too old or broken to use; ▪ **clapped-out** *BrE: a knackered old bike*

'knackers' yard also **knacker's** *n [C] BrE* **1** a place where horses are killed **2 ready/fit for the knacker's yard** too old to be useful or to work properly

knap·sack /'næpsæk/ *n [C] AmE* a bag that you carry on your shoulders; ▪ **backpack, rucksack**

knave /neɪv/ *n [C]* **1** *BrE* the playing card with a value between the ten and queen; ▪ **jack**: *the knave of hearts* → **CARD**[1] (7) **2** *old-fashioned* a dishonest boy or man —**knavish** *adj: cunning, knavish tricks* —**knavishly** *adv*

knav·e·ry /'neɪvəri/ *n [U] old use* dishonest behaviour

knead /niːd/ *v [T]* **1** to press a mixture of flour and water many times with your hands: *Knead the dough for three minutes.* **2** to press someone's muscles many times to help cure pain or to help someone relax

knee¹ S2 W2 /niː/ *n [C]*
1 the joint that bends in the middle of your leg: *Lucy had a bandage round her knee.* | **on your knees** *She was on her knees* (=kneeling) *weeding the garden.* | **sink/fall/drop to your knees** (=move so that you are kneeling) *Tim fell to his knees and started to pray.* | *a painful knee injury*
2 the part of your clothes that covers your knee: *His jeans had holes in both knees.*
3 on sb's knee on the top part of your legs when you are sitting down: *Daddy, can I sit on your knee?*
4 knees knocking (together) if your knees are knocking, you are feeling very afraid or very cold
5 on your knees in a way that shows you have no power but want or need something very much: *Unemployment was so bad in the 1930s that they went on their knees nearly to get jobs.*
6 bring sb/sth to their knees a) to defeat a country or group of people in a war: *The bombing was supposed to bring the country to its knees.* **b)** to have such a bad effect on an organization, activity etc that it cannot continue; ▪ **cripple**: *The recession has brought many companies to their knees.*
7 put/take sb over your knee *old-fashioned* to punish a child by hitting them
8 on bended knee(s) *old-fashioned* in a way that shows great respect for someone → **knee/elbow pad** at **PAD**[1] (1); → **learn/be taught sth at your mother's knee** at **MOTHER**[1] (4); → **the bee's knees** at **BEE** (5); → **weak at the knees** at **WEAK** (13)

knee² *v [T + in]* to hit someone with your knee: *I kneed him in the groin.*

'knee ,breeches *n [plural]* tight trousers that end at your knee, worn especially in the past

'knee cap *n [C]* the bone at the front of your knee → see picture at **SKELETON**

knee·cap /'niːkæp/ *v* **kneecapped, kneecapping** [T] to shoot someone's knee caps as an unofficial punishment

,knee-'deep *adj* **1** deep enough to reach your knees: [+in] *knee deep in mud* | *knee-deep in snow* **2** [not before noun] *informal* having a lot of something: [+in] *knee deep in work*

,knee-'high *adj* **1** tall enough to reach your knees: *knee-high grass* **2 knee-high to a grasshopper** *old-fashioned* used when talking about the past to say that someone was a young child then

'knee-jerk *adj* [only before noun] a knee-jerk reaction, answer etc is what you feel or say about a situation from habit, without thinking about it; ▪ **automatic**: *A victim's knee-jerk reaction to the crime is often revenge.*

kneel /niːl/ also **kneel down** *v past tense and past participle* **knelt** /nelt/ also **kneeled** *AmE* [I] to be in or move into a position where your body is resting on your knees: *Tom knelt down and patted the dog.* | [+on] *She knelt on the floor and put more wood on the fire.*

'knee-length *adj* long or tall enough to reach your knees: *a knee-length skirt*

'knees-up *n [C] BrE informal* a noisy party: *After the wedding there was a bit of a knees-up.*

knell /nel/ *n [C] literary* the sound of a bell being rung slowly because someone has died → **DEATH KNELL**

knelt /nelt/ the past tense and past participle of **KNEEL**

knew /njuː $ nuː/ the past tense of **KNOW**[1]

knick·er·bock·ers /'nɪkə,bɒkəz $ 'nɪkər,baːkərz/ *n* [plural] short loose trousers that fit tightly at your knees, worn especially in the past

knick·ers /'nɪkəz $ -ərz/ *n* [plural] **1** *BrE* a piece of women's underwear worn between the waist and the top of the legs; ▪ **panties**: *a pair of frilly knickers* → see picture at **UNDERWEAR 2** *AmE* **KNICKERBOCKERS 3 (don't) get your knickers in a twist** *BrE spoken* used to say that someone is upset, or to tell someone not to get upset

knick-knack /'nɪk næk/ *n [C]* a small object used as a decoration; ▪ **ornament**: *They had various knick-knacks on the top of the bookcase.*

knife¹ S3 W3 /naɪf/ *n plural* **knives** /naɪvz/ *[C]*
1 a metal blade fixed into a handle, used for cutting or as a weapon; → **scalpel**: *a knife and fork* | *Some young people are carrying knives to defend themselves.* | *a kitchen knife* | *Use a sharp knife to cut the melon into sections.* → **CARVING KNIFE, FLICK KNIFE, PALETTE KNIFE, PAPER KNIFE, PENKNIFE**; → see picture at **MULTIPURPOSE**
2 the knives are out (for sb) *informal* used to say that people are being extremely unfriendly in criticizing someone: *The knives are out for the vice president.*
3 twist/turn the knife (in the wound) to say something that makes someone more upset about a subject they are already unhappy about
4 stick/put etc the knife in/into someone *BrE informal* to dislike someone and be very unfriendly towards them
5 under the knife *informal* having a medical operation
6 you could cut the atmosphere/air/tension with a knife used to say that you felt the people in a room were angry with each other
7 like a (hot) knife through butter *informal* used to say that something happens or is done very easily, without any problems

knife² *v [T]* to put a knife into someone's body; ▪ **stab**: *She had been knifed to death.* —**knifing** *n [C]*

'knife-edge *n* [singular] **1** a situation in which the result is extremely uncertain: **on a knife-edge** *His future in the job is balanced on a knife-edge.* | *a knife-edge vote* **2** a situation which makes someone very anxious: **on a knife-edge** *Living with him, she is constantly on a knife-edge.* | *the knife-edge of insecurity* **3** something that is narrow or sharp

knife·point /'naɪfpɔɪnt/ *n* **at knifepoint** using a knife to threaten someone: *An eighty-year-old man was robbed at knifepoint in his home.*

knight¹ /naɪt/ *n [C]* **1** a man with a high rank in the past who was trained to fight while riding a horse: *knights in armour* → **WHITE KNIGHT 2** a man who has received a **KNIGHTHOOD** and has the title 'SIR' before his name **3** the **CHESS** piece with a horse's head on it → see picture at **CHESS 4 a knight in shining armour** a brave man who saves someone, especially a woman, from a dangerous situation

knight² *v [T]* to give someone the rank of knight

,knight 'errant *n [C]* a knight in the past who travelled looking for adventure

knight·hood /'naɪthʊd/ *n [C,U]* a British rank and title which is given to a man as an honour for achievement or for doing good things; → **Dame**

K

knight·ly /ˈnaɪtli/ *adj literary* relating to knights or typical of a knight, especially behaving with courage and honour: *knightly deeds of chivalry*

knit /nɪt/ *v present participle* **knitting** [I,T] **1** *past tense and past participle* **knitted** to make clothing out of wool, using two KNITTING NEEDLES; → **crochet**: *My grandmother taught me how to knit.* | *She's knitting a sweater.* | **knit sb sth** *Emily knitted him some socks.* **2** *past tense and past participle* **knitted** to use a PLAIN (=basic) knitting stitch: *Knit one, purl one.* **3** *past tense and past participle* **knit** to join people, things, or ideas more closely together, or to be joined closely together: [+**together**] *In a good report, individual sentences knit together in a clear way that readers can follow.* | **closely/tightly etc knit** (=with all the members having close relationships) *a closely knit community* | *Harold is part of a tightly knit team.* **4** *past tense and past participle* **knit** a bone that knits after being broken grows into one piece again: [+**together**] *The pin holds the bones in place while they knit together.* **5 knit your brows** to show you are worried, especially by moving your EYEBROWS together —**knitter** *n* [C] → **CLOSE-KNIT, TIGHT-KNIT**

knit·ting /ˈnɪtɪŋ/ *n* [U] **1** something that is being knitted **2** the activity or action of knitting clothes → see picture at HANDICRAFT

'knitting ˌneedle *n* [C] one of the two long sticks with round ends that you use to knit something → see picture at SEWING

knit·wear /ˈnɪt-weə $ -wer/ *n* [U] knitted clothing: *a knitwear shop*

knives /naɪvz/ the plural of KNIFE[1]

knob /nɒb $ nɑːb/ *n* [C] **1** a round handle or thing that you turn to open a door, turn on a television etc: *He thought the door was locked, but he **turned the knob** and the door opened.* | *a brass **door knob*** | *I adjusted the volume knob and sat down.* **2 a knob of sth** a small piece of something; ▤ **lump**: *Melt a knob of butter in the pan.* **3** *BrE spoken not polite* a PENIS **4 with (brass) knobs on** *BrE spoken old-fashioned* used especially by children to reply to an insult: *'You're fat and lazy.' 'Fat and lazy to you with brass knobs on!'*

knob·bly /ˈnɒbli $ ˈnɑːbli/ *also* **knob by** /ˈnɒbi $ ˈnɑːbi/ *AmE adj* with hard parts that stick out from under the surface of something: *knobbly knees*

knock[1] S1 W3 /nɒk $ nɑːk/ *v*
1 DOOR [I] to hit a door or window with your closed hand to attract the attention of the people inside: *I knocked and knocked but nobody answered.* | [+**at/on**] *We knocked at the door but there was no one there.* | *Wilson went up and knocked on the door.*
2 HIT AND MOVE STH [T always + adv/prep] to hit something with a short quick action so that it moves or falls: **knock sth out of/from sth** *As I got up, I knocked a pencil out of its holder.* | *He knocked the knife from my hand.* | **knock sth over** *At that moment, Sally knocked over her glass of wine.* | **knock sth aside** *She tried to knock the gun aside but she was not fast enough.*
3 HIT SB HARD [T always + adv/prep] to hit someone very hard: *He **knocked** her **to the** ground and kicked her.* | **knock sb unconscious/cold/senseless** (=hit someone so hard that they fall unconscious) *Simon could knock a man unconscious with one punch to the jaw.* | *Garry answered the door only to be **knocked flying** as two policemen came rushing in.*
4 HIT PART OF YOUR BODY [T] to hit something with part of your body: **knock sth against sth** *Morse knocked his shin against a large suitcase standing just inside the door.* | **knock sth on sth** *She knocked her head on a stone.*
5 knock on doors to go to every house or apartment in an area asking the people who live there for information or support: *Gathering that information means knocking on doors and asking people questions.*
6 be knocking on the door to be wanting to join a group or team – used in news reports: *Five countries have permanent seats on the UN Security Council but Ger-*

many and Japan, among others, are knocking on the door.
7 REMOVE WALL [T] to remove a wall or part of a building in order to make a bigger room or space: **knock sth into sth** *We could make a bigger living space by knocking two rooms into one.* | **knock sth through** *The wall between the kitchen and the dining room has been partially knocked through.*
8 knock a hole in/through sth to make a hole in something, especially a wall: *We could knock a hole through the wall into the cupboard.*
9 CRITICIZE [T] to criticize someone or their work, especially in an unfair or annoying way: *The British press always knock British winners at any sport.* | *'Designer fashion is silly.' '**Don't knock it**, it's an important industry.'*
10 BALL [T always + adv/prep] to kick or hit a ball somewhere: *The aim is to knock the ball into the opposing goal.*
11 knock sb for six *BrE informal* to shock or upset someone very much or make them physically weak: *This flu has really knocked me for six.*
12 knock the stuffing out of sb *informal* to make someone lose their confidence: *Suzanne was very upset when her mother left home. It knocked the stuffing out of her.*
13 knock sb sideways *BrE* to upset someone so much that it is difficult for them to deal with something: *His daughter's death knocked Tom sideways.*
14 knock some sense into sb/into sb's head *informal* to make someone learn to behave in a more sensible way: *The struggle to build up her own business had knocked some sense into her.*
15 knock (sb's) heads together *informal* to tell people who are arguing that they must stop and behave more sensibly: *None of them can agree and it needs someone to knock heads together.*
16 knock sth on the head *BrE informal* to stop something happening: *We wanted to go for a picnic, but the rain's knocked that on the head.*
17 knock sb's socks off *also* **knock sb dead** *spoken* to surprise and please someone by being very impressive: *With that dress and your new haircut, you'll knock him dead.*
18 knock sb off their pedestal/perch to stop admiring someone that you previously thought was perfect: *The press were determined to knock the princess off the pedestal that they had put her on.*
19 knock spots off sb/sth *BrE spoken* to be much better than someone or something: *The new computer system knocks spots off the old one.*
20 knock on wood *AmE* used to say that you hope your good luck so far will not change; ▤ **touch wood** *BrE*
21 knock it off *spoken* used to tell someone to stop doing something, because it is annoying you
22 MAKE A NOISE [I] if an engine or pipes etc are knocking, they make a noise like something hard being hit, usually because something is wrong with them
23 HEART [I] if your heart is knocking, it is beating hard, especially because you are afraid; ▤ **pound**
24 I'll knock your head/block off *spoken* used when threatening to hit someone very hard: *If you say that again, I'll knock your head off!*
25 knock the bottom out of sth *informal* to make something such as a market or industry fail suddenly: *A sudden drop in supplies of certain chemicals could knock the bottom out of the engineering industry.* → **knock/beat sb/sth into a cocked hat** at COCKED HAT (1); → **knock sb into shape** at SHAPE[1] (3); → **knees knocking (together)** at KNEE[1] (4)

knock around *also* **knock about** *BrE phr v informal*
1 HIT SB **knock sb around** to hit someone several times: *My father used to knock me and my brother around.*
2 RELAX **knock around (sth)** to spend time somewhere, without doing anything very serious or important;

hang-around: *On Saturdays I knock around with my friends.* | *We spent the day just knocking around the house.*
3 TRAVEL knock around sth to travel to different places; **kick around**: *For a couple of years we knocked around the Mediterranean.*
4 IDEAS knock sth ⟺ around to discuss and think about an idea, plan etc with other people: *We've been knocking around a few ideas.*
5 BALL knock sth around *BrE* to play a game with a ball, but not in a serious way; **kick about**
6 BE SOMEWHERE *BrE* if something or someone is knocking around, it is somewhere but you are not sure exactly where: *Is there a screwdriver knocking about anywhere?*

knock sb/sth **back** phr v informal
1 knock sth ⟺ back to quickly drink large quantities of a drink, especially an alcoholic drink: *Brenda knocked the brandy back quickly.*
2 knock sb back sth to cost you a lot of money: *His new car knocked him back several thousand dollars.*
3 knock sb back *BrE* to make someone feel upset, shocked, or physically weak

knock sb/sth **down** phr v
1 HIT/PUSH SB knock sb ⟺ down to hit or push someone so that they fall to the ground: *Something hit him from behind and knocked him down.* → KNOCKDOWN[2]
2 HIT SB WITH A VEHICLE knock sb ⟺ down to hit someone with a vehicle while you are driving, so that they are hurt or killed: *A child was in hospital last night after being knocked down by a car.*
3 DESTROY knock sth ⟺ down to destroy a building or part of a building; **demolish**: *They want to knock the house down and rebuild it.*
4 REDUCE PRICE knock sth ⟺ down informal to reduce the price of something by a large amount: *The new stove we bought was knocked down from $800 to $550.* → KNOCKDOWN[1]
5 ASK SB TO REDUCE PRICE knock sb down to sth informal to persuade someone to reduce the price of something they are selling you: *She's asking for £150 but I'll try to knock her down to £100.*

knock sth **into** sb phr v
to make someone learn something: *Parsons must knock these lessons into the team before Saturday.*

knock off phr v informal
1 STOP WORK knock off (sth) to stop working and go somewhere else: *There was no one in the office because they'd all knocked off for lunch.* | *Do you want to knock off early today?* | *We usually knock off work at about twelve on Saturday.*
2 REDUCE A PRICE knock sth ⟺ off to reduce the price of something by a particular amount: *I'll knock off £10.* | knock sth off sth *Travel agents are knocking £50 and sometimes £100 off the price of holidays.*
3 REDUCE AMOUNT knock sth ⟺ off to reduce a total by a particular amount: knock sth off sth *Moving house will knock an hour off Ray's journey to work.*
4 PRODUCE knock sth ⟺ off to produce something quickly and easily: *Roland makes a lot of money knocking off copies of famous paintings.*
5 MURDER knock sb ⟺ off to murder someone
6 STEAL knock sth ⟺ off *BrE* to steal something

knock out phr v
1 UNCONSCIOUS knock sb ⟺ out to make someone become unconscious or go to sleep: *The champion knocked Biggs out in the seventh round.* | knock yourself out *His head hit a table as he fell and he knocked himself out.* | *The nurse gave me some medicine which totally knocked me out.* → KNOCKOUT[1] (1)
2 DEFEAT knock sb/sth ⟺ out to defeat a person or team in a competition so that they can no longer take part: *The German team were knocked out in the first round.* | knock sb/sth out of sth *He first hit the headlines when he knocked Becker out of the French Open Tournament.* → KNOCKOUT[1] (3)
3 DESTROY knock sth ⟺ out to damage something so

that it does not work: *The air raids were planned to knock out communications on the ground.*
4 ADMIRE knock sb out informal if something knocks you out, it is very impressive and surprises you because it is so good: *She loved the movie. It knocked her out.* → KNOCKOUT[1] (2)
5 PRODUCE knock sth ⟺ out informal to produce something easily and quickly: *Paul has been knocking out new songs for the album.*
6 knock yourself out informal to work very hard in order to do something well

knock sb/sth ⟺ **over** phr v
1 to hit someone with a vehicle while you are driving, so that they are hurt or killed: *A woman was knocked over by a bus last year.*
2 *AmE* informal to rob a place such as a shop or bank and threaten or attack the people who work there

knock sth ⟺ **together** phr v informal
to make something quickly, using whatever you have available: *We should be able to knock something together with what's in the fridge* (=make a meal from items of food in the fridge).

knock sb/sth ⟺ **up** phr v informal
1 to make something quickly and without using much effort: *Michael knocked up a shed in the back garden.*
2 *BrE* to wake someone up by knocking on their door: *What time do you want me to knock you up in the morning?*
3 informal not polite to make a woman PREGNANT

knock[2] n **1** [C] the sound of something hard hitting a hard surface: *a loud knock at the door* | *a knock in the engine* **2** [C] the action of something hard hitting your body: *He got a knock on the head when he fell.* **3** take a knock informal to have some bad luck or trouble: *Clive's taken quite a few hard knocks lately.*

knock·a·bout /ˈnɒkəbaʊt $ ˈnɑːk-/ adj [only before noun] *BrE* knockabout humour involves making fun of someone or something in a rough way, or behaving in a silly way

knock·back /ˈnɒkbæk $ ˈnɑːk-/ n [C] a refusal or REJECTION that you receive

knock·down[1] /ˈnɒkdaʊn $ ˈnɑːk-/ adj [only before noun] informal a knockdown price is very cheap

knockdown[2] n [C] when a BOXER falls down when he is hit

knock-down-'drag-out adj [only before noun] *AmE* informal a knock-down-drag-out argument or fight is an extremely angry or violent one

knock·er /ˈnɒkə $ ˈnɑːkər/ n [C] **1** a piece of metal on an outside door of a house that you hit against the door to attract the attention of the people inside → DOORKNOCKER **2** knockers [plural] spoken not polite an offensive word meaning a woman's breasts

knock-'kneed adj having knees that point slightly inwards; → bow-legged

knock·off /ˈnɒkɒf $ ˈnɑːkɒːf/ n [C] *AmE* informal a cheap copy of something expensive

'knock-on adj *BrE* have a knock-on effect (on sth) to start a process in which everything that happens causes something else to happen: *These price rises will have a knock-on effect on the economy.*

knock·out[1] /ˈnɒk-aʊt $ ˈnɑːk-/ n [C] **1** when a BOXER hits his opponent so hard that he falls down and cannot get up again: *The fight ended in a knockout.* **2** informal someone or something that is very attractive or successful: *Her dress was a knockout.* **3** a type of competition in which only the winning players or teams at each stage continue to play until there is only one winner

knockout[2] adj informal **1** knockout punch/blow a) a hard hit that knocks someone down so that they cannot get up again b) an action or event that causes defeat or failure: *High interest rates have been a knockout blow to the business.* **2** relating to a type of competition in which only the winning players or teams at each stage continue to play: *Scotland's failure to get through the* knockout stage of the competition **3 knockout pills/ drops etc** PILLS etc that make someone unconscious

knock-up n [C] BrE the time before a tennis match officially starts when the players hit the ball to each other for practice; → **warm-up**

knoll /nəʊl $ noʊl/ n [C] a small round hill

knot¹ /nɒt $ nɑːt/ n [C]

1 STRING/ROPE ETC a) a part where one or more pieces of string, rope, cloth etc have been tied or twisted together

tie a knot
tie sth in a knot
undo a knot (=unfasten it)
loosen a knot
a tight knot

Are you any good at **tying knots**? | Thread the string through the hoop and **tie** it **in a knot**. **b)** a part where hair, a thread etc has become accidentally twisted together: I can't get the knots out of my hair. | [+in] There's a knot in my shoelace.

2 HAIR STYLE a hair style in which your hair is arranged in a tight round shape on top of your head
3 WOOD a hard round place in a piece of wood where a branch once joined the tree
4 SHIP'S SPEED a unit for measuring the speed of ships and aircraft, equal to about 1853 metres per hour
5 PEOPLE a small group of people standing close together: [+of] Knots of delegates stood around outside the conference centre.
6 FEELING a tight uncomfortable feeling caused by a strong emotion such as fear or anger: [+of] a knot of anxiety in her stomach | Her stomach **was in knots**.
7 HARD MASS a tight painful place in a muscle → GORDIAN KNOT; → **at a rate of knots** at RATE¹ (7); → **tie the knot** at TIE² (5); → **tie yourself (up) in knots** at TIE¹ (6)

knot² v knotted, knotting **1** [T] to tie together two ends or pieces of string, rope, cloth etc: A pretty scarf was loosely knotted around her neck. **2** [I] if hair, a thread etc knots, it becomes twisted together **3** [I,T] if a muscle or other part of your body knots, or is knotted, it feels tight and uncomfortable: Fear and anxiety knotted her stomach.

knot·ted /'nɒtɪd $ 'nɑː-/ adj
1 TIED tied in a knot or in several knots: a knotted handkerchief on his head
2 MUSCLE if a muscle or other part of your body is knotted, it feels tight and uncomfortable: knotted shoulder muscles
3 get knotted! BrE spoken used to tell someone rudely to go away or that you do not agree with them
4 HANDS knotted hands or fingers are twisted because of old age or too much work

knot·ty /'nɒti $ 'nɑːti/ adj **1** difficult to solve: a knotty problem **2** knotty wood contains a lot of hard round places where branches once joined the tree

know¹ S1 W1 /nəʊ $ noʊ/ v past tense **knew** /njuː $ nuː/ past participle **known** /nəʊn $ noʊn/
1 HAVE INFORMATION [I,T not in progressive] to have information about something: Who knows the answer? | There are instructions telling you everything you need to know. | Didn't you know that? | **know what/how/where etc** Do you know what time it is? | I don't know where to go. | **know (something/nothing etc) about sth** I need to know more about the job before I decide whether to apply for it. | Little is known about the author's childhood. | I **know all about** David and what he's been up to! | **know (something/nothing etc) of sth** I wonder if he knew of the plan? | Do you know of any good restaurants in the area? | You know nothing of this business. | **know (that)** We know that greenhouse gases can affect the climate. | **Let me know** (=tell me) what time you're planning to arrive. | I thought you'd **want to know** immediately. | **If you must know**, I was with James last night (=used when you are angry because someone wants to know something). | **without sb/sb's knowing** | He slipped out of the house without his parents

knowing (=secretly). | **How did** he **know** (=how did he find information about) our names? | **as you/we know** 'I'm divorced, as you know,' she said briefly. | **be known to do sth** Smoking is known to increase a person's risk of developing lung cancer.; → see box at IGNORE

2 BE SURE [I,T not in progressive] to be sure about something: 'Are you seeing Jim tomorrow?' 'I don't know yet.' | **know (that)** I know I won't get the job. | Ruth knew that she couldn't continue in the relationship for much longer. | **know what/why/how etc** I know exactly what you need! | **know if/whether** The boy stared at him uncertainly, not knowing whether to believe him. | I don't know if I'll be able to come. | **knowing (that)** She forced herself to go out, knowing that she would feel more depressed if she stayed at home. | **How do you know** (=what makes you sure) he won't do it again? | **know sb/sth to be sth** It's a story that I know to be true. | I think he's still living in Chicago, but I don't **know for sure**. | **As far as I know**, they're arriving on Saturday (=used when you think something is true but are not sure). | I doubt I'll win, but **you never know** (=used when you cannot be sure about something, but something good might happen).

3 BE FAMILIAR WITH SB/STH [T not in progressive] to be familiar with a person, place etc: I've known her for twenty years. | Are you really thinking of leaving Kevin for a guy you barely know? | Do you know the nightclub on the corner of Maine Street? | I don't **know** him very well. | We're still **getting to know** each other really. | **know sb from sth** I know her from school. | **know sb as sth** Many people knew him as a local businessman. | Hepburn **is best known for** (=people are most likely to be familiar with) her roles in classic films such as 'My Fair Lady'. | The museum outlines the development of the city **as we know it** today. | Does he **know the way** to your house (=know how to get there)? | I grew up here; I **know** the place **like the back of my hand** (=I know it very well). | I only **know** her **by sight** (=I often see her but have not really spoken to her). | She didn't **know me from Adam**, but she was really helpful (=she did not know me at all). | **knowing sb/if I know sb** (=used to say that you expect someone to behave in a particular way because you know them well) Knowing Sumi, my note's probably still in her pocket. | He'll be chatting up the women, if I know Ron!

4 REALIZE [I,T] to realize, find out about, or understand something: Hardly knowing what he was doing, Nick pulled out a cigarette. | She knew the risks involved. | **know (that)** Suddenly she knew that something was terribly wrong. | **know how/what/why etc** I didn't know how difficult it would be. | **know to do sth** She knows not to tell anyone. | **(do/if) you know what I mean?** (=used to ask if someone has understood you) It's nice to have a change sometimes. Know what I mean? | 'I just felt so tired.' 'Yeah, **I know what you mean**.' (=I understand, because I have had the same experience) | I **should have known** it wouldn't be easy. | I **might have known** (=I am annoyed but not surprised) you would take that attitude. | **know exactly/precisely** I know exactly how you feel. | **know perfectly well/full well/only too well** He knew full well that what he was doing was dangerous. | **sb will never know/no one will ever know** Just take it, no one will ever know. | 'That's not what I mean, **and you know it**,' Cara protested. | **if I had known/if I'd have known** I wouldn't have come if I'd known you were so busy. | **Little did** she **know** (=she did not know) that years later she would have her own pool and luxury apartment in Florida. | She **knew nothing of** what had happened earlier that day.

5 SKILL/EXPERIENCE [T not in progressive] to have learned a lot about something or be skilful and experienced at doing something: I don't know enough history to make a comparison. | I taught him everything he

K

knowl·edge·a·ble /'nɒlɪdʒəbəl $ 'nɑː-/ adj knowing a lot: [+about] *Graham's very knowledgeable about wines.* —**knowledgeably** adv

known¹ /nəʊn $ noʊn/ the past participle of KNOW¹

known² W3 adj
1 [only before noun] used about something that people know about or have discovered: *a study of all the known facts* | *her last known address* | *Apart from vaccines, there is no known way to protect against meningitis.*
2 [only before noun] a known criminal, drug dealer etc is someone who people know to be regularly involved in criminal activities or to do other things that are disapproved of: *He was found with several other known sex offenders.* | *a known liar*
3 be known for sth to be famous or known about by a lot of people because of something: *He's known for his stunning good looks.* | *The region is known for its fine wines*
4 well-known/little-known/lesser-known used when saying how famous someone is: *works by lesser-known French artists*

knuck·le¹ /'nʌkəl/ n [C] **1** your knuckles are the joints in your fingers, including the ones where your fingers join your hands: *Her knuckles whitened as she gripped the gun.* **2** a piece of meat around the lowest leg joint of a pig: *a knuckle of pork* **3 near the knuckle** BrE informal rude, or likely to give offence: *Some of his jokes are a bit near the knuckle.* → **a rap on/over the knuckles** at RAP¹ (6); → **rap sb on/over the knuckles** at RAP² (5)

knuckle² v
knuckle down phr v informal to suddenly start working or studying hard; ⊟ **get down to:** *If he doesn't knuckle down soon, he'll never get through those exams.* | [+to] *He is clearly ready to knuckle down to the task.*
knuckle under phr v informal to accept someone's authority or orders although you do not want to

'knuckle-,dragger n [C] informal a man who is stupid

'knuckle-,duster n [C] a piece of metal that covers all the knuckles of the hand, used as a weapon

knuck·le·head /'nʌkəlhed/ n [C] AmE spoken someone stupid – used when you are not very angry with them; ⊟ **blockhead** BrE

KO¹ /,keɪ 'əʊ $ -'oʊ/ n [C,U] the abbreviation of *knockout*

KO² v past tense and past participle **KO'd**, third person singular **KO's** [T] informal to hit someone so hard that they become unconscious

ko·a·la /kəʊ'ɑːlə $ koʊ-/ also **ko,ala 'bear** / $.'.. ,./ n [C] an Australian animal like a small grey bear with no tail that climbs trees and eats leaves

kohl /kəʊl $ koʊl/ n [U] a black pencil used around women's eyes to make them more attractive

kohl·ra·bi /kəʊl'rɑːbi $ koʊl-/ n [U] a vegetable of the CABBAGE family

kook /kuːk/ n [C] AmE informal someone who is silly or crazy —**kooky** adj

kook·a·bur·ra /'kʊkəbʌrə/ n [C] an Australian bird whose song sounds like laughter

Ko·ran, Qur'an /kɔː'rɑːn, kə- $ kə'ræn, -'rɑːn/ n the Koran the holy book of the Muslims —**Koranic** /kə'rænɪk/ adj

kor·ma /'kɔːmə $ 'kɔːr-/ n [C,U] an Indian dish made with meat and cream: *chicken korma*

ko·sher /'kəʊʃə $ 'koʊʃər/ adj **1 a)** kosher food is prepared according to Jewish law **b)** kosher restaurants or shops sell food prepared in this way **2** informal something that is kosher is honest, legal, or really what it is claimed to be: *Are you sure this offer is kosher?*

kow·tow /,kaʊ'taʊ/ v [I] informal to be too eager to obey or be polite to someone in authority: [+to] *We will not kowtow to the government.*

KP /,keɪ 'piː/ n [U] AmE work that soldiers or children at a camp have to do in a kitchen

kph *kilometres per hour* used to describe the speed of something, especially a vehicle or the wind

kraal /krɑːl/ n [C] a village in South Africa with a fence around it

kraut /kraʊt/ n [C] taboo a very offensive word for someone from Germany. Do not use this word.

Krem·lin /'kremlɪn/ n **the Kremlin** the government of Russia and the former USSR, or its buildings in Moscow

krill /krɪl/ n [U] small SHELLFISH → see picture at FOOD CHAIN

Kriss Krin·gle /,krɪs 'krɪŋgəl/ n AmE another name for SANTA CLAUS

kro·na /'krəʊnə $ 'kroʊ-/ n plural **kronor** /-nɔː $ -nɔːr/ [C] the standard unit of money in Sweden and Iceland

kro·ne /'krəʊnə $ 'kroʊ-/ n plural **kroner** /-nə $ -nər/ [C] the standard unit of money in Denmark and Norway

Kru·ger·rand /'kruːgə,rænd/ n [C] a South African gold coin

kryp·ton /'krɪptɒn $ -tɑːn/ n [U] a colourless gas that is found in very small quantities in the air and is used in FLUORESCENT lights and LASERS. It is a chemical ELEMENT: symbol Kr

kt the written abbreviation of *knot*

Kt the written abbreviation of *knight*

ku·dos /'kjuːdɒs $ 'kuːdɑːs/ n [U] the state of being admired and respected for being important or for doing something important: *He acquired kudos just by appearing on television.*

Ku Klux Klan /,kuː klʌks 'klæn/ n **the Ku Klux Klan** a secret American political organization of Protestant white men who oppose people of other races or religions

kum·quat /'kʌmkwɒt $ -kwɑːt/ n [C] a fruit that looks like a very small orange

kung fu /,kʌŋ 'fuː/ n [U] an ancient Chinese fighting art in which you attack people with your hands and feet

Kurd /kɜːd $ kɜːrd/ n [C] a member of a people living in Iran, Iraq, and Turkey

kvetch /kvetʃ/ v [I] AmE informal to keep complaining —**kvetch** n [C]

kW the written abbreviation of *kilowatt* or kilowatts

kWh the written abbreviation of *kilowatt hour* or kilowatt hours

K

L, l

L, l /el/ *plural* **L's, l's** *n* **1** [C,U] the 12th letter of the English alphabet **2** [C] the number 50 in the system of ROMAN NUMERALS

L **1** the written abbreviation of *large*, used on clothes to show the size **2** the written abbreviation of *lake*, used on maps **3** the written abbreviation of *learner*, used on cars to show that the driver is a learner → L-PLATE

l 1 the written abbreviation of *litre* or litres **2** the written abbreviation of *line*

la /lɑː/ *n* [U] the sixth note in a musical SCALE, according to the SOL-FA system

lab /læb/ *n* [C] *informal* a LABORATORY: *the school science lab*

Lab the written abbreviation of *Labour*, in British politics

la·bel¹ W3 /'leɪbəl/ *n* [C]
1 a piece of paper or another material that is attached to something and gives information about it: *a luggage label* | **on the label** *It says 'Dry clean' on the label.*
2 a word or phrase which is used to describe a person, group, or thing, but which is unfair or not correct: *Men these days have to avoid attracting the 'sexist' label.*
3 a record company: *their new release on the Ace Sounds label*
4 designer label clothes made by fashionable companies: *Fancy designer labels tend to come with fancy price tags to match.* → OWN LABEL

label² *v* **labelled, labelling** *BrE*, **labeled, labeling** *AmE* [T] **1** to attach a label onto something or write information on something: *Label the diagram clearly.* | **label sth sth** *The file was labelled 'Top Secret'.* | **label sth with sth** *Each bag of seeds is labelled with the grower's name.* **2** to use a word or phrase to describe someone or something, but often unfairly or incorrectly: **label sb/sth (as) sth** *The newspapers had unjustly labelled him a troublemaker.* | *The regime was inevitably labelled as 'communist'.*

la·bi·a /'leɪbiə/ *n* [plural] *technical* the outer parts of the female sex organ

la·bi·al /'leɪbiəl/ *n* [C] *technical* a speech sound made using one or both lips; → **bilabial** —**labial** *adj*

la·bor /'leɪbə $ -ər/ *n, v* the American spelling of LABOUR

la·bor·a·tory W3 /lə'bɒrətri $ 'læbrətɔːri/ *n plural* **laboratories** [C] a special room or building in which a scientist does research or prepares substances: *a research laboratory* | *laboratory tests/experiments/studies* | *tests on laboratory animals* → LANGUAGE LABORATORY

Labor Day *n* [U] *AmE* a public holiday in the US on the first Monday in September

la·bored /'leɪbəd $ -bərd/ *adj* the American spelling of LABOURED

la·bor·er /'leɪbərə $ -bərər/ *n* the American spelling of LABOURER

la·bo·ri·ous /lə'bɔːriəs/ *adj* taking a lot of time and effort: *laborious process/task/business etc Collecting the raw materials proved a long and laborious task.* | *the laborious business of drying the crops* —**laboriously** *adv*: *A beetle began to crawl laboriously up his leg.*

'labor ,union *n* [C] *AmE* an organization that represents the ordinary workers in a particular trade or profession, especially in meetings with employers; **☐ trade union** *BrE*

La·bour /'leɪbə $ -ər/ *n* the British LABOUR PARTY: **under Labour** *Most people will pay higher taxes under Labour.* | *They always vote Labour.* | *a Labour government* | **Labour MP/candidate**

labour¹ S3 W1 *BrE*; **labor** *AmE n*
1 WORK [U] work, especially physical work: *The garage charges £30 an hour for labour.* | *Many women do hard manual labour* (=work with their hands). | *Workers withdrew their labour* (=protested by stopping work) *for twenty-four hours.* → HARD LABOUR
2 WORKERS [U] all the people who work for a company or in a country

> skilled labour (=workers who have special skills)
> unskilled labour (=workers who have no special skills)
> casual labour (=workers who do jobs that are not permanent)
> cheap labour
> child labour
> slave labour
> labour costs
> labour shortage
> labour market (=all the people available to work)

> *a shortage of* **skilled labor** | *Wages for* **unskilled labour** *are very low.* | *small commercial farmers who depend on a* **casual labour** *supply* | *These countries are a source of* **cheap labour**. | *the use of* **child labour** | *produce grown by* **slave labor** | *We need to reduce our* **labour costs**. | **Labour shortages** *have forced the Japanese into making heavy use of industrial robots.* | *the changing role of mothers in the* **labour market** → LABOUR FORCE, LABOUR MARKET

3 BABY [singular, U] the process of giving birth to a baby: **in labour** *Meg was in labour for ten hours.* | **went into labour** *Diane went into labour at 2 o'clock.* | **a long/short/difficult labour** | *The labour pains were unbearable.* | **labour ward/room** (=a room in a hospital where women give birth)
4 **a labour of love** something that is hard work but that you do because you want to
5 **sb's labours** *formal* a period of hard work: *After several hours gardening we sat down to admire the results of our labours.*

labour² *BrE*; **labor** *AmE v* [I] **1** to work hard: *They laboured all day in the mills.* | **[+over]** *I've been labouring over this report all morning.* | **labour to do sth** *Ray had little talent but laboured to acquire the skills of a writer.* **2** **labour under a delusion/misconception/misapprehension etc** to believe something that is not true: *She had laboured under the misconception that Bella liked her.* **3** **labour the point** to describe or explain something in too much detail or when people have already understood it **4** [always + adv/prep] to move slowly and with difficulty: *I could see the bus labouring up the steep, windy road.*

'labour camp *BrE*; **'labor camp** *AmE n* [C] a prison camp where prisoners have to do hard physical work

la·boured *BrE*; **labored** *AmE* /'leɪbəd $ -bərd/ *adj* **1** if someone's breathing is laboured, it is difficult for them to breathe **2** if writing or speaking is laboured, it takes a lot of effort and is not good: *Some of the episodes are very laboured.*

la·bour·er *BrE*; **laborer** *AmE* /'leɪbərə $ -ər/ *n* [C] someone whose work needs physical strength, for example building work; → **worker**: *a farm labourer*

'labour ex,change *n* [C] *old-fashioned* a British government office where people went to find jobs in the past; → **job centre**

'labour force *BrE*; **labor force** *AmE n* [C usually singular] all the people who work for a company or in a country

la·bour·ing / *BrE*; **laboring** *AmE* 'leɪbərɪŋ/ *adj* [only before noun] **1** **labouring class/family etc** *old-*

L

1 000, 2 000, 3 000, most frequent words in S poken and W ritten English

fashioned people who do hard physical work and who do not have a lot of money or power, considered as a group: _They wanted to provide education for the labouring classes._ **2** involving hard physical work: _a labouring job_

labour-'intensive _BrE_; **labor-intensive** _AmE adj_
an industry or type of work that is labour-intensive needs a lot of workers; → **capital intensive**: _labour-intensive farming methods_

'labour ,market _BrE_; **labor market** _AmE n_ [C] the people looking for work and the jobs that are available at that time: _married women re-entering the labour market_

'labour ,movement _BrE_; **labor movement** _AmE n_
the labour movement the organizations, political parties etc that represent working people

'Labour ,Party _n_ [also + plural verb _BrE_] **the Labour Party** a political party in Britain and some other countries that aims to improve social conditions for ordinary working people and poorer people; → **Conservative Party**

'labour ,relations _BrE_; **labor relations** _AmE n_ [plural] the relationship between employers and workers: _a company with good labour relations_

'labour-,saving _BrE_; **labor-saving** _AmE adj_ [only before noun] making it easier for you to do a particular job: _labour-saving device/gadget/equipment etc_

Lab·ra·dor /'læbrədɔː $ -ɔːr/ _n_ [C] a large dog with fairly short yellow or black hair

la·bur·num /lə'bɜːnəm $ -ɜːr-/ _n_ [C,U] a small tree with long hanging stems of yellow flowers and poisonous seeds

lab·y·rinth /'læbərɪnθ/ _n_ [C] **1** a large network of paths or passages which cross each other, making it very difficult to find your way; **⊟** **maze**: [+of] _a labyrinth of underground tunnels_ **2** something that is very complicated and difficult to understand: [+of] _Decisions are frequently delayed in the labyrinth of Whitehall committees._ —**labyrinthine** /ˌlæbə'rɪnθaɪn/ _adj_: _labyrinthine corridors_

lace¹ /leɪs/ _n_ **1** [U] a fine cloth made with patterns of many very small holes: _a handkerchief trimmed with lace_ | _lace curtains_ **2** [C usually plural] a string that is pulled through special holes in shoes or clothing to pull the edges together and fasten them → see picture at FOOTWEAR

lace² _v_ [T] **1** also **lace up** to fasten something by tying a lace; **⊟** **tie**: _Lace up your shoes or you'll trip over._ | **lace sth to sth** _The canvas was laced to a steel frame._ **2** to add a small amount of alcohol or a drug to a drink: **lace sth with sth** _coffee laced with Irish whiskey_ **3** _written_ to weave or twist several things together: **lace sth together** _Hannah laced her fingers together._
 lace sth with sth _phr v_ **1** to include something all through something you write or say: _He laces his narrative with a great deal of irrelevant information._ **2** **be laced with sth** _written_ to have some of a quality: _Iris's voice was heavily laced with irony._

la·ce·rate /'læsəreɪt/ _v_ [T] **1** to cut skin deeply with something sharp: _His fingers were badly lacerated by the broken glass._ **2** to criticize someone very strongly; **⊟** **slate**

la·ce·ra·tion /ˌlæsə'reɪʃən/ _n_ [C,U] _technical_ a cut in your skin: [+to] _multiple lacerations to the upper arms_

'lace-up _n_ [C usually plural] _especially BrE_ a shoe that is fastened with a lace —**lace-up** _adj_: _shiny black lace-up shoes_

lace·work /'leɪswɜːk $ -wɜːrk/ _n_ [U] lace, or something that looks like lace

lach·ry·mose /'lækrɪməʊs $ -moʊs/ _adj formal_ often crying; **⊟** **tearful**

lack¹ S3 W2 /læk/ _n_ [singular, U] when there is not enough of something, or none of it; **⊟** **shortage**

a complete/total lack of sth
an apparent lack of sth
for lack of sth (=because something is not present or does not exist)
a distinct/marked lack of sth
no lack of sth (=plenty of something)
a relative/comparative lack of sth
no lack of sth (=plenty of something)

[+of] _new parents suffering from lack of sleep_ | _Too many teachers are treated with a lack of respect._ | _comments based on a **total lack of** information_ | _Does their **apparent lack of** progress mean they are not doing their job properly?_ | _tours that are cancelled **for lack of** bookings_ | _There was **no lack of** willing helpers._ | _health problems linked to poor diet and a **relative lack of** exercise_

lack² W3 _v_
1 [T] to not have something that you need, or not have enough of it: _Alex's real problem is that he lacks confidence._ **⚠** Do not use the verb **lack** before 'in' or 'of': _We lack ideas (NOT We lack in/of ideas)._ However, you can use the phrases **be lacking in** and **a lack**: _We are lacking in ideas_ OR _We have a lack of ideas._
2 **not lack for sth** _formal_ to have a lot of something: _He does not lack for critics._

lack·a·dai·si·cal /ˌlækə'deɪzɪkəl◂/ _adj_ not showing enough interest in something or not putting enough effort into it: _David has a rather lackadaisical approach to his work._

lack·ey /'læki/ _n_ [C] someone who always does what a particular person tells them to do – used to show disapproval

lack·ing /'lækɪŋ/ _adj_ [not before noun] **1** not having enough of something or any of it: [+in] _He was **lacking in confidence.**_ | _She seems to be entirely lacking in intelligence._ | _The new designs have all been **found lacking** in some important way._ **2** if something that you need or want is lacking, it does not exist: _Financial backing for the project is still lacking._ | _These qualities are **sadly lacking** today._

lack·lus·tre _BrE_; **lackluster** _AmE_ /'læk,lʌstə $ -ər/ _adj_ **1** not exciting, impressive etc; **⊟** **dull**: _a lacklustre performance_ **2** not shining; **⊟** **dull**: _lacklustre hair_

la·con·ic /lə'kɒnɪk $ -'kɑː-/ _adj_ using only a few words to say something —**laconically** /-kli/ _adv_: _'She left,' said Pascoe laconically._

lac·quer¹ /'lækə $ -ər/ _n_ [U] **1** a liquid painted onto metal or wood to form a hard shiny surface; → **varnish** **2** _old-fashioned_ HAIRSPRAY

lacquer² _v_ [T] **1** to cover something with lacquer: _a black lacquered box_ **2** _old-fashioned_ to use lacquer on your hair

la·crosse /lə'krɒs $ lə'krɔːs/ _n_ [U] a game played on a field by two teams of ten players, in which each player has a long stick with a net on the end of it and uses this to throw, catch, and carry a small ball

lac·tate /læk'teɪt $ 'lækteɪt/ _v_ [I] if a woman or female animal lactates, she produces milk to feed her baby or babies with

lac·ta·tion /læk'teɪʃən/ _n_ [U] _technical_ the production of milk by a woman or female animal

lac·tic ac·id /ˌlæktɪk 'æsɪd/ _n_ [U] an acid produced by muscles after exercising and found in sour milk

lac·tose /'læktəʊs $ -toʊs/ _n_ [U] a type of sugar found in milk, sometimes used as a food for babies and sick people

la·cu·na /lə'kuːnə/ _n plural_ **lacunae** /-niː/ _or_ **lacunas** [C] _formal_ a place where something is missing in a piece of writing

lac·y /'leɪsi/ _adj_ made of LACE or looking like lace: _lacy underwear_ | _a plant with delicate, lacy leaves_

lad S3 W3 /læd/ _n_ [C] _BrE_
1 _old-fashioned or informal_ a boy or young man; → **lass**: _a young lad_ | _Things were different when I was a lad._
2 **the lads** _spoken_ a group of male friends that a man

works with or spends his free time with: *a night out with the lads* | **one of the lads** (=a member of your group of friends)
3 a bit of a lad *spoken* a man that people like even though he behaves rather badly: *That Chris is a bit of a lad, isn't he?*
4 lad culture *informal* the way in which some young men behave, involving typically male activities such as drinking a lot of alcohol, driving fast cars, and watching football – used to show disapproval
5 also **stable lad** a boy or man who works with horses; ▤ **stable boy** → JACK THE LAD

lad·der¹ S3 /'lædə $ -ər/
n [C]
1 a piece of equipment
used for climbing up to or
down from high places. A
ladder has two bars that
are connected by RUNGS
(=short bars that you use
as steps): *She climbed up
the ladder.* | *He hurt himself falling off a ladder.*
→ ROPE LADDER, STEPLADDER
2 a series of levels which
someone moves up and
down within an organization, profession, or society: **career/corporate
ladder** *Stevens slowly
worked his way up the corporate ladder.* | *Becoming a doctor would be a step up the **social ladder**.* | *the first step on the ladder of success*
3 *BrE* a long thin hole in STOCKINGS or TIGHTS where some stitches have broken; ▤ **run** *AmE*: *Yes, I know I've got a ladder in my tights.* → SNAKES AND LADDERS

ladder² *v* [I,T] *BrE* if STOCKINGS or TIGHTS ladder, or if you ladder them, a long thin hole is made in them because some stitches have broken; ▤ **run** *AmE*

lad·die, laddy /'lædi/ *n* [C] *BrE informal* a boy

lad·dish /'lædɪʃ/ *adj BrE* a young man who is laddish likes spending time with other men, drinking alcohol and enjoying things like sport, sex, and music; → **lad**

lad·dis·m /'lædɪzəm/ *n* [U] *BrE* the attitudes and behaviour of some young men in Britain, who drink a lot of alcohol, and are mainly interested in sport, sex, and music; → **lad**: *the culture of laddism*

la·den /'leɪdn/ *adj* **1** *literary* heavily loaded with something, or containing a lot of something: [+with] *The tables were laden with food.* | **fully/heavily laden** *The lorry was fully laden.* | **snow-laden branches** **2** having a lot of a particular quality, thing etc: [+with] *She was laden with doubts about the affair.* | *trucks laden with equipment* | *a **debt-laden** company*

lad·ette /læ'det/ *n* [C] *BrE* a young woman who likes to do some things that young men typically do, such as drinking a lot of alcohol and talking about sex and sports; → **lad**

la-di-da, la-di-dah /ˌlɑː diː 'dɑː/ *adj informal* used to describe someone's behaviour when you think they are talking and behaving as if they consider themselves better than other people; ▤ **snobbish**: *a la-di-da attitude*

'ladies' man also **lady's man** *n* [singular] *old-fashioned* a man who likes to spend time with women, and thinks they enjoy being with him

'ladies' room *n* [C] *AmE* a women's toilet; ▤ **ladies** *BrE*

lad·ing /'leɪdɪŋ/ *n* [U] BILL OF LADING

la·dle¹ /'leɪdl/ *n* [C] a large deep spoon with a long handle, used for lifting liquid food, especially soup, out of a container → see picture at EAT

ladle² *v* [T] also **ladle out** to put soup or other liquid food onto plates or into bowls, especially using a ladle

la·dy S2 W2 /'leɪdi/ *n plural* **ladies** [C]
1 a) a woman of a particular type or age: **young/old/**

elderly etc lady b) a word meaning woman, used especially to describe women's sports or products made for women: **ladies' team/champion/championship etc** *the ladies' darts team* | *ladies' fashion/clothing/shoes etc* | *ladies' underwear* **c)** *old-fashioned* a word meaning woman, used in order to be polite; → **gentleman**: *The young lady at reception sent me up here.* | *Give your coat to the lady over there.* | **lady doctor/lawyer etc** (=a polite word, which many women find offensive, for a woman doctor, lawyer, etc)
2 a woman who is polite and behaves very well; → **gentleman**: *She knows how to behave like a lady.*
3 Lady used as the title of the wife or daughter of a British NOBLEMAN or the wife of a KNIGHT: *Lady Spencer*
4 the ladies a) *BrE* a women's toilet; ▤ **ladies' room** *AmE*; → **the gents' b)** a word meaning women, often used humorously: *His boyish good looks made him a favourite with the ladies.* → LADIES' MAN
5 ladies *spoken formal* used to speak to a group of women: *Ladies and gentlemen, may I have your attention please?*
6 a woman, especially one with a strong character – used to show approval: *She can be a tough lady to negotiate with.*
7 lady friend a woman that a man is having a romantic relationship with – often used humorously; ▤ **girlfriend**: *I saw Chris with his new lady friend.*
8 lady of leisure a woman who does not work and has a lot of free time – used humorously: *So you're a lady of leisure now that the kids are at school?*
9 *AmE spoken* used when talking directly to a woman you do not know, when you are angry with her: *Hey lady, would you mind getting out of my way?*
10 Our Lady an expression used to mean Mary, the mother of Jesus Christ
11 the lady of the house *old-fashioned* the most important woman in a house, usually the mother of a family
12 *old-fashioned* a woman born into a high social class in Britain: *I could see the Queen, surrounded by her lords and ladies.*
13 *old-fashioned* a man's wife: *the captain and his lady* → BAG LADY; → **cleaning lady** at CLEANING; → FIRST LADY; → **leading lady** at LEADING¹; → LOLLIPOP LADY, OLD LADY; → **young lady** at YOUNG¹ (3)

la·dy·bird /'leɪdibɜːd $ -bɜːrd/ *BrE*; **la·dy·bug** /'leɪdibʌg/ *AmE n* [C] a small round BEETLE (=a type of insect) that is usually red with black spots → see picture at INSECT

,lady-in-'waiting *n plural* **ladies-in-waiting** [C] a woman who looks after and serves a queen or PRINCESS

la·dy·like /'leɪdilaɪk/ *adj old-fashioned* if a woman or girl is ladylike, she behaves in a polite and quiet way that was once believed to be typical of or suitable for women: *ladylike behaviour*

la·dy·ship /'leɪdiʃɪp/ *n* **your/her ladyship a)** used as a way of speaking to or talking about a woman with the title of Lady; → **lordship b)** *BrE spoken* use this to talk about a woman who thinks she is very important – used humorously: *Do you think her ladyship will be joining us?*

'lady's man *n* [singular] another spelling of LADIES' MAN

lag¹ /læg/ *v* **lagged, lagging 1** [I,T] to move or develop more slowly than others: [+behind] *She stopped to wait for Ian who was lagging behind.* | *Britain is lagging behind the rest of Europe.* **2** [T] *BrE* to cover water pipes etc with a special material to prevent the water inside them from freezing or the heat from being lost: *We've had the hot-water tank lagged.*

lag² *n* [C] a delay or period of waiting between one event and a second event: *a **time lag*** → JET LAG, OLD LAG

la·ger S3 /'lɑːgə $ -ər/ *n BrE* [C,U] a light-coloured beer, or a glass of this type of beer: **can/bottle/glass etc of lager** *a pint of lager*

'lager lout *n* [C] *BrE informal* a young man who drinks too much and then behaves violently or rudely

lag·gard /ˈlægəd $ -ərd/ *n* [C] *old-fashioned* someone or something that is very slow or late —**laggardly** *adj*

lag·ging /ˈlægɪŋ/ *n* [U] *BrE* special material used to protect a water pipe or container from heat or cold

la·goon /ləˈguːn/ *n* [C]   **1** a lake of sea water that is partly separated from the sea by rocks, sand, or CORAL: *a coastal lagoon*   **2** *AmE* a small lake which is not very deep, near a larger lake or river

lah-di-dah /ˌlɑː diː ˈdɑː/ *adj* another spelling of LA-DI-DA

laid /leɪd/ *v* past tense and past participle of LAY

laid-ˈback *adj* relaxed and seeming not to be worried about anything: *I don't know how you can be so laid-back about your exams.* | **laid-back attitude/manner/approach** *He is famed for his laid-back attitude.*

lain /leɪn/ *v* the past participle of LIE¹

lair /leə $ ler/ *n* [C]   **1** the place where a wild animal hides and sleeps; ▣ **den**   **2** a place where you go to hide or to be alone; ▣ **den**: *a smuggler's lair*

laird /leəd $ lerd/ *n* [C] *BrE* a person who owns a very large area of land in Scotland; → **squire 1**

lai·ry /ˈleəri $ ˈleri/ *adj BrE informal* behaving in a way that is very loud, or with too much confidence: *He's a bit lairy, your friend Mick.*

lais·sez-faire, **laisser-faire** /ˌleseɪ ˈfeə, ˌleɪ- $ -ˈfer/ *n* [U]   **1** the principle that the government should allow the ECONOMY or private businesses to develop without any state control or influence: *the policy of laissez-faire* | **laissez-faire economics/capitalism**   **2** **laissez-faire attitude/approach etc** when you do not become involved in other people's personal affairs

la·i·ty /ˈleɪˌti/ *n* the laity all the members of a religious group apart from the priests; → **layman**

lake ⑤③ ⓦ③ /leɪk/ *n*
  1 [C] a large area of water surrounded by land: *Lake Michigan* → see picture at COUNTRY
  2 **wine/milk etc lake** *BrE* a very large amount of wine, milk etc that has been produced but is not needed or used; → **mountain 3**

lake·side /ˈleɪksaɪd/ *adj* [only before noun] beside a lake: *a lakeside restaurant* —**lakeside** *n* [singular]

ˈla-la land *n* **be/live in la-la land** to think that a situation is much better than it really is, in a way that seems slightly stupid

lam /læm/ *n* **on the lam** *AmE informal* escaping or hiding from someone, especially the police: *Brenner was recaptured after three weeks on the lam.*

la·ma /ˈlɑːmə/ *n* [C] a Buddhist priest in Tibet or Mongolia

lamb¹ /læm/ *n*   **1** [C] a young sheep   **2** [U] the meat of a young sheep; → **mutton**: *roast lamb* | *a leg of lamb* | **lamb chop/cutlet/stew etc**   **3** [C] *spoken* used to talk to or talk about someone who is gentle and lovable, especially a child: *Ben's asleep now, the little lamb.*   **4** **like a lamb to the slaughter** used when someone is going to do something dangerous, but they do not realize it or have no choice   **5** **like a lamb** quietly and without any argument: *Suzie went off to school like a lamb today.* → **mutton dressed as lamb** at MUTTON (2)

lamb² *v* [I] to give birth to lambs: *The ewes are lambing this week.* —**lambing** *n* [U]: *the lambing season*

lam·ba·da /læmˈbɑːdə $ lɑːm-, ləm-/ *n* [singular, U] a sexy modern dance from Brazil in which two people hold each other closely and move their bodies at the same time

lam·bast, **lambaste** /ˈlæmbæst/ *v* [T] *formal* to criticize someone or something very strongly, usually in public; ▣ **slate**: *Democrats lambasted the President's budget plan for being 'inadequate'.*

lambs·wool /ˈlæmzwʊl/ *n* [U] soft wool from LAMBS, used for making clothes: **lambswool jumper/sweater/blanket etc**

lame¹ /leɪm/ *adj*   **1 a)** unable to walk properly because your leg or foot is injured or weak: *a lame dog* |

go lame (=become lame)   **b) the lame** [plural] people who are lame   **2** a lame explanation or excuse is weak and difficult to believe: **lame excuse/explanation** *She gave some lame excuse about missing the bus.* | *a lame attempt to deflect criticism* → LAMELY   **3** *informal* boring or not very good; ▣ **poor**: *A lot of the songs on this album are a bit lame.* | *the company's lame performance* —**lameness** *n* [U]

lame² *v* [T usually passive] to make a person or animal unable to walk properly; ▣ **cripple**: *The fall left him badly lamed.*

la·mé /ˈlɑːmeɪ $ lɑːˈmeɪ/ *n* [U] cloth containing gold or silver threads: *a gold lamé dress*

ˌlame ˈduck *n* [C]   **1** a person, business etc that is having problems and needs help   **2** **lame duck president/governor/legislature etc** *informal* a president, GOVERNOR etc with no real power because his or her period in office will soon end

lame·ly /ˈleɪmli/ *adv written* if you say something lamely, you do not sound confident and other people find it difficult to believe you; ▣ **weakly**: *'It wasn't my responsibility,' he lamely explained.*

la·ment¹ /ləˈment/ *v written*   **1** [I,T] to express feelings of great sadness about something: *The nation lamented the death of its great war leader.*   **2** [T] to express annoyance or disappointment about something you think is unsatisfactory or unfair: **lament that** *He lamented that people had expected too much of him too soon.* | *She lamented the fact that manufacturers did not produce small packs for single-person households.* | **lament the lack/absence/decline etc of sth** *Steiner lamented the lack of public interest in the issue.*

lament² *n* [C] a song, piece of music, or something that you say, that expresses a feeling of sadness: *A lone piper played a lament.* | **[+for]** *a lament for the dead*

lam·ent·a·ble /ˈlæməntəbəl, ləˈmentəbəl/ *adj formal* very unsatisfactory or disappointing; ▣ **terrible**: *a lamentable state of affairs* | *a lamentable lack of support for the idea* | *It is lamentable that the officer failed to deal with the situation.* —**lamentably** *adv*

lam·en·ta·tion /ˌlæmənˈteɪʃən/ *n* [C,U] *formal* deep sadness or something that expresses it: *There was lamentation throughout the land at news of the defeat.*

lam·i·nate /ˈlæmɪˌnət/ *n* [C,U] laminated material

lam·i·nated /ˈlæmɪˌneɪtɪd/ *adj*   **1** laminated material is made by joining several thin layers on top of each other: *laminated glass*   **2** covered with a thin layer of plastic for protection: *a laminated ID card* —**laminate** *v* [T]

lamps

table lamp
gaslight
oil lamp
desk lamp

lamp ⑤③ /læmp/ *n* [C]
  1 an object that produces light by using electricity, oil, or gas: **table/desk/bedside lamp** | **oil/electric/fluorescent lamp** → FOG LAMP, HEADLAMP, HURRICANE LAMP, SAFETY LAMP, STANDARD LAMP
  2 a piece of electrical equipment used to provide a special kind of heat, especially as a medical treatment: **infrared/ultraviolet lamp** → SUNLAMP, BLOWLAMP

lamp·light /ˈlæmp-laɪt/ *n* [U] the soft light produced by a lamp: *Her eyes shone in the lamplight.*

lamp·light·er /ˈlæmp‚laɪtə $ -ər/ *n* [C] someone whose job was to light lamps in the street in the past

lam·poon /læmˈpuːn/ *v* [T] to criticize someone or something in a humorous way that makes them seem stupid: *The Prime Minister was frequently lampooned in political cartoons.* —**lampoon** n [C]

lamp-post, **lamp post**, **lamp·post** /'læmp-pəʊst $ -poʊst/ n [C] a tall pole that supports a light over a street or public area

lamp·shade /'læmpʃeɪd/ n [C] a cover fixed over a LIGHT BULB for decoration and in order to reduce or direct its light → see picture at BEDROOM

LAN /læn/ n [C] technical *local area network* a system that connects computers to each other within a building or organization so that people can use and work on the same information

lance¹ /lɑːns $ læns/ n [C] a long thin pointed weapon that was used in the past by soldiers riding on horses

lance² v [T] to cut a small hole in someone's flesh with a sharp instrument to let out PUS (=yellow liquid produced by infection)

lance corporal n [C] a low level rank in the Marines or the British army, or someone who has this rank

lan·cet /'lɑːnsɪt $ 'læn-/ n [C]　**1** a small very sharp pointed knife with two cutting edges, used by doctors to cut skin and flesh; **scalpel**　**2** lancet window/arch *technical* a tall narrow window or ARCH that is pointed at the top

land¹ S1 W1 /lænd/ n
1 GROUND [U] an area of ground, especially when used for farming or building: *500 acres of land | a piece of open land* (=land which has not been built on) | *fertile/arid/dry land | agricultural/arable land | waste/vacant/derelict land | housing/industrial etc land a shortage of housing land | land prices* → DOCKLAND, FARMLAND; → see box at GROUND¹
2 NOT SEA [U] the solid dry part of the Earth's surface: *After 21 days at sea, we sighted land.* | **by land** *Troops began an assault on the city by land and sea.* | **on land** *The crocodile lays its eggs on land.* | **land bird/animal** *The white stork is one of the biggest land birds of the region.* → DRY LAND
3 COUNTRY [C] *literary* a country or area: *Their journey took them to many foreign lands.* | **native land** (=the land where you were born) *He's fiercely proud of his native land.* | *Australia represented a real land of opportunity for thousands of people.*
4 NOT CITY the land the countryside thought of as a place where people grow food: **live off the land** (=grow or catch all the food you need) *A third of the region's population still lives off the land.* | **work/farm the land** (=grow crops) *Many people were forced to give up working the land.*
5 PROPERTY [U] the area of land that someone owns: *He ordered us to get off his land.* | *private/public/common land*
6 see/find out how the land lies *spoken* to try to discover what the situation really is before you make a decision
7 (in) the land of the living *spoken* awake – used humorously
8 the land of milk and honey an imaginary place where life is easy and pleasant
9 in the land of nod *old-fashioned* asleep → be/live in cloud-cuckoo-land at CLOUD¹ (7); → DRY LAND, DREAMLAND, FAIRYLAND; → the lie of the land at LIE³ (3) → NEVER-NEVER LAND → PROMISED LAND → WASTELAND → WONDERLAND

land² S2 W3 v
1 PLANE/BIRD/INSECT **a)** [I] if a plane, bird, or insect lands, it moves safely down onto the ground; **take off**: *Flight 846 landed five minutes ago.* | *The bird landed gracefully on the water.* **b)** [T] to make a plane move safely down onto the ground at the end of a journey: *The pilot managed to land the aircraft safely.*
2 ARRIVE BY BOAT/PLANE [I] to arrive somewhere in a plane, boat etc: [+on/in/at etc] *We expect to be landing in Oslo in about fifty minutes.* | *In 1969, the first men landed on the moon.*
3 FALL/COME DOWN [I always + adv/prep] to come down through the air onto something; **drop**: [+in/on/under etc] *A large branch landed on the hood of my car.* | *Louis fell out of the tree and landed in a holly*

---

bush. | *She fell and **landed heavily** on the floor.* | *A couple of bombs landed quite near to the village.*
4 GOODS/PEOPLE [T] if a boat or aircraft lands people or goods, it brings them to a place, and the people get out or the goods are carried out: *The troops were landed by helicopter.*
5 JOB/CONTRACT ETC [T] *informal* to succeed in getting a job, contract etc that was difficult to get: *He landed a job with a law firm.* | **land yourself sth** *Bill's just landed himself a part in a Broadway show.*
6 land sb in trouble/hospital/court etc to cause someone to have serious problems or be in a difficult situation: *Connie's going to land herself in big trouble if she keeps arriving late for work.* | *She developed pneumonia which landed her in hospital.*
7 land sb in it *BrE spoken informal* to get someone into trouble by telling other people that they did something wrong; **drop sb in it**: *Geoff landed me in it by saying I should have checked that the door was locked.*
8 PROBLEMS [I always + adv/prep] to arrive unexpectedly, and cause problems: [+in/on/under etc] *Just when I thought my problems were over, this letter landed on my desk.*
9 land a punch/blow etc to succeed in hitting someone
10 land on your feet to get into a good situation again, after having problems: *She certainly landed on her feet when she got that job.*
11 CATCH FISH [T] to catch a fish
land up *phr v BrE informal*
to be in a particular place, situation, or position after a lot of things have happened to you; **end up**: [+in] *We landed up in a bar at 3 am.* | *Be careful that you don't land up in serious debt.* | [+with] *I landed up with five broken ribs.*
land sb with sth *phr v* [usually passive] *informal*
to give someone something unpleasant to do, because no one else wants to do it: *Maria's been landed with all the tidying up as usual.*

land agent n [C] *BrE* someone whose job is to look after land, cattle, farms etc that belong to someone else

lan·dau /'lændɔː $ -daʊ/ n [C] a four-wheeled carriage that is pulled by horses and has a top that folds back

land-based *adj* placed on or living on the land: *land-based missiles | land-based animals*

land·ed /'lændɪd/ *adj* [only before noun]　**1** landed gentry/family/nobility a family or group that has owned a lot of land for a long time　**2** including a lot of land: *landed estates*

land·fall /'lændfɔːl $ -fɒːl/ n　**1** [C] a LANDSLIDE (2)　**2** [C,U] *literary* the land that you see or arrive at after a long journey by sea or air, or the act of arriving there

land·fill /'lændfɪl/ n　**1** [U] the practice of burying waste under the ground, or the waste buried in this way　**2** [C] a place where waste is buried under the ground

land·hold·ing, **land-holding** /'lænd,həʊldɪŋ $ -,hoʊl-/ n [C,U] the land that is owned by someone

land·ing /'lændɪŋ/ n　**1** [C,U] the action of bringing an aircraft down to the ground after being in the air; **take-off**: *take-off and landing procedures* | *crash/emergency landing* (=a sudden landing caused by a problem with the engine etc) | *the Apollo moon landings* → SOFT LANDING　**2** [C] the floor at the top of a set of stairs or between two sets of stairs: *the first-floor landing*　**3** [C] the action of bringing soldiers onto land that is controlled by the enemy: *the first landings of American Marines at Da Nang*　**4** [C] a LANDING STAGE

landing craft n *plural* landing craft [C] a flat-bottomed boat that opens at one end so that soldiers and equipment can be moved directly onto the shore

landing gear n [U] an aircraft's wheels and other parts that support them; **undercarriage**

L

'landing net n [C] *BrE* a net on a long handle used for lifting a fish out of the water after you have caught it

'landing stage n [C] *BrE* a wooden structure for moving passengers and goods to and from boats

'landing strip n [C] a flat piece of ground that has been prepared for aircraft to use; ⊟ **airstrip**

land·la·dy /'lænd,leɪdi/ n plural **landladies** [C] **1** a woman who rents a room, building, or piece of land to someone; → **landlord** **2** *BrE* a woman who owns or manages a PUB; → **landlord**

land·less /'lændləs/ adj owning no land

land·locked /'lændlɒkt $ -lɑːkt/ adj a landlocked country, state etc is surrounded by other countries, states etc and has no coast

land·lord W3 /'lændlɔːd $ -lɔːrd/ n [C]
1 a man who rents a room, building, or piece of land to someone; → **landlady**
2 *BrE* a man who owns or manages a PUB; → **landlady**

land·lub·ber /'lænd,lʌbə $ -ər/ n [C] *old-fashioned* someone who does not have much experience of the sea or ships

land·mark /'lændmɑːk $ -mɑːrk/ n [C] **1** something that is easy to recognize, such as a tall tree or building, and that helps you know where you are: *One of Belfast's most famous landmarks, the Grosvenor Hall, has been demolished.* **2** one of the most important events, changes, or discoveries that influences someone or something: *The discovery of penicillin was a landmark in the history of medicine.* | **landmark decision/case/ruling** *The Supreme Court issued a landmark decision in January 2001.*

land·mass /'lændmæs/ n [C] *technical* a large area of land such as a CONTINENT

land·mine /'lændmaɪn/ n [C] a bomb hidden in the ground that explodes when someone walks or drives over it

'land ,office n [C] a government office in Britain that keeps records about the sale of land and who buys and sells it; ⊟ **land registry** *BrE*

land·own·er /'lænd,əʊnə $ -,oʊnər/ n [C] someone who owns land, especially a large amount of it: *wealthy landowners* —**landowning** adj: *Britain's landowning aristocracy* —**landownership** n [U]

'land re,form n [C,U] the political principle of sharing farm land so that more people own some of it

'land ,registry n plural **land registries** [C] a government office in Britain that keeps records about the sale of land and who owns it; ⊟ **land office** *AmE*

land·scape¹ W3 /'lændskeɪp/ n
1 [C] an area of countryside or land of a particular type, used especially when talking about its appearance: *the beauty of the New England landscape* | **rural/industrial/urban etc landscape**
2 [C] a picture showing an area of countryside or land: *English landscape artists* → see picture at PAINTING
3 the political/social landscape the general situation in which a particular activity takes place: *Recent electoral shocks have shaken the European political landscape.*
4 [U] a way of printing a document in which the long sides are horizontal and the short sides are vertical; → **portrait** → **a blot on the landscape** at BLOT² (2)

landscape² v [T often passive] to make a park, garden etc look attractive and interesting by changing its design, and by planting trees and bushes etc: *The area around the mill pond has also been landscaped.* —**landscaping** n [U]

,landscape 'architect n [C] someone whose job is to plan the way an area of land looks, including roads, buildings, and planted areas —**landscape architecture** n [U]

,landscape 'gardening n [U] the profession or art of arranging gardens and parks so that they look attractive and interesting —**landscape gardener** n [C]

landscapes

flat

mountainous

hilly

rolling

land·slide /'lændslaɪd/ n [C] **1** [usually singular] a victory in an election in which one person or party gets a lot more votes than all the others: *a landslide election victory* | **by a landslide** *The SNP candidate won by a landslide.* **2** a sudden fall of a lot of earth or rocks down a hill, cliff etc

land·slip /'lændslɪp/ n [C] *BrE* a small fall of earth or rocks down a hill, cliff etc, that is smaller than a landslide

land·ward /'lændwəd $ -wərd/ adj facing towards the land and away from the sea; → **seaward**: *the landward side of the hill* —**landwards** adv

lane S3 W3 /leɪn/ n [C]
1 a narrow road in the countryside; → **path**: *a quiet country lane*
2 a road in a city, often used in road names: *the Hilton Hotel in Park Lane* | *a network of alleys and back lanes* (=narrow unimportant roads, often behind a row of houses)
3 one of the two or three parallel areas on a road which are divided by painted lines to keep traffic apart: *That idiot changed lanes without signalling.* | **the inside/middle/outside lane** *Use the outside lane for overtaking only.* | **the fast/slow lane** *Cars in the fast lane were travelling at over 80 miles an hour.* | **three-lane motorway/highway/road** → BUS LANE, CYCLE LANE
4 one of the narrow parallel areas marked for each competitor in a running or swimming race
5 a line or course along which ships or aircraft regularly travel between ports or airports: *busy shipping lanes* → life in the fast lane at FAST LANE (1); → walk/trip down memory lane at MEMORY (7)

lan·guage S2 W1 /'læŋgwɪdʒ/ n
1 ENGLISH/FRENCH/ARABIC ETC [C,U] a system of communication by written or spoken words, which is used by the people of a particular country or area

speak a language
master a language (=succeed in learning a language)
language teacher/student/learner
foreign language
sb's first language/native language (=the first language someone learned)
sb's second language
sb's command of a language (=someone's ability to speak a language)
the language barrier (=the problem of communicating with people who speak a different language)
the English/Japanese/German etc language
the official language
modern languages (=languages that are still spoken)
dead language (=a language that is no longer spoken)

L

How many languages do you speak? | *It took him several years to master the language.* | *common problems for foreign language learners* | *a book intended for language teachers* | *Andrea's native language is German.* | *For the majority of Tanzanians, Swahili is their second language.* | *She had lived in Italy for years, and her command of the language was excellent.* | *I didn't speak much Japanese, and I was worried that the language barrier might be a problem.* | *one of the best known poems in the English language* | *The official language of Ghana is English.* | *a degree in modern languages* | *a dead language such as Latin*

2 COMMUNICATION [U] the use of written or spoken words to communicate: *the origins of language* | spoken/written language

3 STYLE/TYPE OF WORDS [U] **a)** the words and style of writing used in poetry or writing: *literary language* | *poetic language* **b)** the words used in a particular activity or job: [+of] *the language of science*: legal/medical/technical etc language | ordinary/everyday language

4 COMPUTERS [C,U] *technical* a system of instructions for operating a computer: *a programming language for the web*

5 SWEARING [U] *informal* words that most people think are offensive: mind/watch your language *spoken* (=stop swearing) | bad/foul/abusive language

6 strong language **a)** angry words used to tell people exactly what you mean **b)** words that most people think are offensive; ⊟ **swearing**

7 SOUNDS/SIGNS/ACTIONS [C,U] signs, movements, or sounds that express ideas or feelings: [+of] *the language of bees* | *the language of dolphins* → BODY LANGUAGE, SIGN LANGUAGE, speak the same language at SPEAK (11)

WORD FOCUS: LANGUAGE

dialect the form of a language that is spoken in a particular area | **slang** informal words used by people who belong to a particular group, for example young people, criminals etc | **jargon** words used by people who do a particular job or are interested in a particular subject, which ordinary people cannot easily understand | **terminology** words used in a particular subject such as science or medicine | **journalese** language often used in newspapers | **legalese** *disapproving* language used by lawyers or in legal documents, which is difficult for ordinary people to understand

---

language la·bor·a·tory /ˈ.. ˌ..../ *n plural* **language laboratories** [C] a room in a school or college where you can learn to speak a foreign language by listening to tapes and recording your own voice

lan·guid /ˈlæŋgwɪd/ *adj literary* **1** slow or lazy and involving very little energy or activity: *He greeted Charles with a languid wave of his hand.* | *We spent a languid afternoon by the pool.* **2** lazy and involving very little activity —**languidly** *adv*

lan·guish /ˈlæŋgwɪʃ/ *v* [I] **1** if someone languishes somewhere, they are forced to remain in a place where they are unhappy: [+in] *Shaw languished in jail for fifteen years.* **2** if something languishes, it fails to improve and develop or become successful; → **founder**; ❷ **flourish**: *The housing market continues to languish.* | *The shares are languishing at just 46p after yesterday's fall.* | *West Ham United are currently languishing at the bottom of the league.*

lan·guor /ˈlæŋgə $ -ər/ *n* [U] *literary* **1** a pleasant feeling of laziness: *Lying there beside her, he was filled with an agreeable languor.* **2** when the air is heavy and there is no wind: *the languor of a hot afternoon* —**languorous** *adj* —**languorously** *adv*

lank /læŋk/ *adj* lank hair is thin, straight, and unattractive

lank·y /ˈlæŋki/ *adj* someone who is lanky is tall and thin, and moves awkwardly; ⊟ **gangling**: *a lanky young man* —**lankiness** *n* [U]

lan·o·lin /ˈlænəl-ˌn/ *n* [U] an oil that is obtained from sheep's wool, and is used in skin creams

lan·tern /ˈlæntən $ -ərn/ *n* [C] a lamp that you can carry, consisting of a metal container with glass sides that surrounds a flame or light → CHINESE LANTERN, MAGIC LANTERN

lap¹ /læp/ *n* [C]
1 the upper part of your legs when you are sitting down; ⊟ **knee**: on sb's lap *Shannon sat on her mother's lap.* | in sb's lap *His hands were folded in his lap.*
2 a single journey around a race track: *Rubens Barrichello finished a lap ahead of his team-mate.* | lap of honour *BrE*/victory lap *AmE* (=a lap to celebrate winning) *The entire team took a victory lap in front of their cheering fans.*
3 *AmE* a single journey from one end of a swimming pool to another: do/run/swim a lap *Every morning she swims 50 laps in the pool.*
4 PART OF JOURNEY a part of a long journey; ⊟ **leg**: [+of] *The last lap of their journey was by ship.*
5 in the lap of luxury having an easy and comfortable life with a lot of money, possessions etc: *She wasn't used to living in the lap of luxury.*
6 in the lap of the gods *BrE* if the result of something is in the lap of the gods, you do not know what will happen because it depends on things you cannot control

lap² *v* **lapped, lapping** **1** [I,T] if water laps something or laps against something such as the shore or a boat, it moves against it or hits it in small waves: [+against/over etc] *The waves lapped gently against the rocks.* | *The tide was lapping the harbour wall.* **2** also **lap up** [T] if an animal laps water, milk etc, it drinks it by putting its tongue into it → see picture at DRINK¹ **3** [T] to pass a competitor in a race who is one complete lap behind you: *Erik Gomas spun off the track when trying to lap Andrew Scott.* —**lapping** *n* [U]: *She could hear the soft lapping of the sea.*

lap sth ⇔ up *phr v* **1** to enjoy something without worrying about whether it is good, true etc: *She's lapping up all the attention she's getting.* | *The humour was lapped up by an appreciative crowd.* **2** if an animal laps up water, milk etc, it drinks it by putting its tongue into it: *The cat began to lap up the milk.*

ˈlap ˌdancing *n* [U] a type of dancing in which a young woman uses sexy movements and removes her clothes while sitting on a customer's LAP in a NIGHTCLUB —**lap dancer** *n* [C]

ˈlap dog, lap·dog /ˈlæpdɒg $ -dɒːg/ *n* [C] **1** a small pet dog **2** someone who is completely under the control of someone else and will do anything they say – used to show disapproval

la·pel /ləˈpel/ *n* [C] the part of the front of a coat or JACKET that is joined to the collar and folded back on each side

lap·i·da·ry /ˈlæpɪˌdəri $ -deri/ *adj* [only before noun] **1** *formal* well-written and accurate: *the lapidary style of the poem* **2** *technical* relating to the cutting or polishing of valuable stones or jewels

lap·is laz·u·li /ˌlæpɪs ˈlæzjuli $ -ˈlæzəli/ *n* [C,U] a valuable bright blue stone, used especially in jewellery

lapse¹ /læps/ *n* [C] **1** a short period of time during which you fail to do something well or properly, often caused by not being careful: momentary/temporary/occasional etc lapse *Despite the occasional lapse, this was a fine performance by the young saxophonist.* | *A defensive lapse by Keown allowed Tottenham to score.* | [+in] lapses in security | [+of] *A single lapse of concentration cost Sampras the game.* | *a lapse of judgement* | *After taking the drug, several patients suffered memory lapses* (=when you cannot remember something for a short time). **2** a failure to do something you should do, especially to behave correctly: *He forgot to offer Darren a drink, but Marie did not appear to notice the lapse.* **3** [usually singular] a period of time between two

L

events: *The usual **time lapse** between request and delivery is two days.* | [+of] *a lapse of about ten seconds*

lapse² v [I] **1** to gradually. come to an end or to stop for a period of time: *The conversation lapsed.* **2** if a contract, agreement etc lapses, it comes to an end, usually because an agreed time limit has passed: *Your booking will automatically lapse unless you confirm it.* **3** to stop believing in or following a religion: *those people who have lapsed from the practice of their religion* **4** *formal* if a period of time lapses, it passes: *Many years had lapsed since her first visit to Wexford.*

lapse into sth *phr v* **1** lapse into unconsciousness/silence/sleep etc to go into a quiet or less active state: *He lapsed into a coma and died two days later.* | *Alison lapsed into puzzled silence.* **2** to begin to behave or speak in a way that you did before: *She lapsed back into her old ways.* | *Occasionally he lapsed into his native German.* **3** to get into a worse state or become worse: *Following his death, the Empire lapsed into chaos.* | *His poetry often lapses into sentimentality.*

lapsed /læpst/ *adj* [only before noun] no longer having the beliefs you used to have, especially religious beliefs; **🔲 practising**: *a lapsed Catholic*

lap·top /ˈlæptɒp $ -tɑːp/ also **laptop computer** *n* [C] a small computer that you can carry with you; → **desktop**

lap·wing /ˈlæp,wɪŋ/ *n* [C] a small black and white European bird with raised feathers on its head; **🔲 peewit**

laptop

laptop
computer

lar·ce·ny /ˈlɑːsəni $ ˈlɑːr-/ *n plural* **larce·nies** [C,U] *law* the act or crime of stealing → **PETTY LARCENY**

larch /lɑːtʃ $ lɑːrtʃ/ *n* [C,U] a tree that looks like a PINE tree but drops its leaves in winter

lard¹ /lɑːd $ lɑːrd/ *n* [U] white fat from pigs that is used in cooking

lard² v [T] to put small pieces of BACON onto meat before cooking it

lard sth **with** sth *phr v* to include a lot of something, especially something that is not necessary, in a speech, piece of writing, plan etc: *a speech larded with Biblical quotations*

lard-ass *n* [C] *AmE spoken not polite* an offensive word for someone who is fat

lar·der /ˈlɑːdə $ ˈlɑːrdər/ *n* [C] a small room or large cupboard for storing food in a house; → **pantry**

large¹ [S1] [W1] /lɑːdʒ $ lɑːrdʒ/ *adj comparative* **larger**, *superlative* **largest**

1 big in size, amount, or number; **🔲 small**: *Los Angeles is the second largest city in the US.* | *The T-shirt comes in Small, Medium and Large.* | *a large ovenproof pan* | *large sums of money* | *those who drink large amounts of coffee* | *A **large number** of students have signed up for the course.* → see box at **BIG¹**

2 a large person is tall and often fat; **🔲 small**

3 be at large if a dangerous person or animal is at large, they have escaped from somewhere or have not been caught: *The escaped prisoners are still at large.*

4 the population/public/society/world etc at large people in general: *The chemical pollution poses a threat to the population at large.*

5 the larger issues/question/problem/picture more general facts, situations, or questions related to something: *The book helps to explain the larger picture in the Middle East.*

6 in large part/measure *formal* mostly: *Their success was due in large part to their ability to speak Spanish.*

7 (as) large as life *BrE spoken* used when someone has appeared or is present in a place where you did not

expect to see them: *I turned a corner and there was Joe, as large as life.*

8 larger than life someone who is larger than life is very amusing or exciting in an attractive way

9 by and large used when talking generally about someone or something: *Charities, by and large, do not pay tax.* → **loom large** at **LOOM¹** (3); → **writ large** at **WRIT²**

large² v **large it (up)** *BrE informal* to enjoy yourself, especially in a way that involves drinking alcohol, dancing etc: *Here's a picture of us larging it up in Brighton last summer.*

large in·testine *n* [C] the lower part of your BOWELS, where food is changed into solid waste matter; → **small intestine**; → see picture at **HUMAN¹**

large·ly [S3] [W2] /ˈlɑːdʒli $ ˈlɑːr-/ *adv* mostly or mainly: *The state of Nevada is largely desert.* | *It had been a tiring day, largely because of all the tedious waiting.*

large-scale *adj* [only before noun] **1** using or involving a lot of effort, people, supplies etc; **🔲 small-scale**: *a large-scale rescue operation* **2** a large-scale map, model etc is drawn or made bigger than usual, so that more details can be shown

lar·gesse, largess /lɑːˈʒes $ lɑːrˈdʒes/ *n* [U] *formal* when someone gives money or gifts to people who have less than they do, or the money or gifts that they give; **🔲 generosity**

larg·ish /ˈlɑːdʒɪʃ $ ˈlɑːr-/ *adj informal* fairly big

lar·go /ˈlɑːɡəʊ $ ˈlɑːrɡoʊ/ *adj, adv technical* played or sung slowly and seriously —**largo** *n* [C]

lar·i·at /ˈlæriət/ *n* [C] *AmE* a LASSO

lark¹ /lɑːk $ lɑːrk/ *n* [C] **1** a small brown singing bird with long pointed wings; **🔲 skylark** **2** *informal* something that you do to amuse yourself or as a joke: **as/for a lark** *I only went along for a lark.* **3 blow/sod/bugger etc that for a lark** *BrE spoken not polite* used when you stop doing something or refuse to do something because it needs too much effort: *Paint the whole room? Sod that for a lark!* **4** *BrE spoken* used to describe an activity that you think is silly or difficult: *Salad again? How long are you going to keep up this healthy eating lark?* **5 be up with the lark** to get up very early

lark² v

lark about/around *phr v BrE informal* to have fun by behaving in a silly way; **🔲 mess about**: *A couple of boys were larking about in the pool.*

lar·va /ˈlɑːvə $ ˈlɑːrvə/ *n plural* **larvae** /-viː/ [C] a young insect with a soft tube-shaped body, which will later become an insect with wings; **🔲 grub** —**larval** *adj*; → see picture at **METAMORPHOSIS**

lar·yn·gi·tis /ˌlærɪnˈdʒaɪtɪs/ *n* [U] an illness which makes talking difficult because your larynx and throat are swollen

lar·ynx /ˈlærɪŋks/ *n plural* **larynges** /ləˈrɪndʒiːz/ **larynxes** [C] the part in your throat where your voice is produced

la·sa·gne *BrE*; **lasagna** *AmE* /ləˈsænjə, -ˈzæn- $ -ˈzɑːn-/ *n* [C,U] a type of Italian food made with flat pieces of PASTA, meat, or vegetables, and cheese

las·civ·i·ous /ləˈsɪviəs/ *adj* showing strong sexual desire, or making someone feel this way: *a lascivious wink* —**lasciviously** *adv* —**lasciviousness** *n* [U]

la·ser /ˈleɪzə $ -ər/ *n* [C] **1** a piece of equipment that produces a powerful narrow beam of light that can be used in medical operations, to cut metals, or to make patterns of light for entertainment: *laser surgery* **2** a beam of light produced by a laser

laser disk *n* [C] a DISK like a CD which can be read by laser light and used in computers or to watch films

laser pointer *n* [C] a small piece of equipment that produces a LASER beam, used by teachers and people who are giving talks in order to point at things on a map, board etc

laser printer *n* [C] a machine connected to a computer system which prints by using laser light

lash¹ /læʃ/ v

1 TIE [T always + adv/prep] to tie something tightly to

something else with a rope; ▤ **bind**: **lash sth to sth** *The oars were lashed to the sides of the boat.*
2 WIND/RAIN/SEA [I always + adv/prep, T] if the wind, sea etc lashes something, it hits it with violent force: *Giant waves lashed the sea wall.* | [+**against/down/across**] *The wind lashed violently against the door.*
3 HIT [T] to hit a person or animal very hard with a whip, stick etc: *Oliver lashed the horses to go faster.*
4 TAIL [I,T] if an animal lashes its tail or its tail lashes, it moves it from side to side quickly and strongly, especially because it is angry
5 CRITICIZE [I,T] to criticize someone angrily – used especially in newspapers: *Democrats lashed Republican plans, calling them extreme.* | [+**back**] *Gallins lashed back at those who accused him of corruption.*
lash out *phr v*
1 to suddenly speak angrily to someone or criticize someone angrily: [+**at**] *Olson lashed out at the media.*
2 to try to hit someone, with a series of violent, uncontrolled movements: [+**at**] *She would suddenly lash out at other children.*

lash² *n* [C] **1** a hit with a whip, especially as a punishment: *They were each given fifty lashes.* **2** [usually plural] one of the hairs that grow around the edge of your eyes; ▤ **eyelash** **3** a sudden or violent movement like that of a whip: *With a lash of its tail, the lion sprang at its prey.* **4** the thin piece of leather at the end of a whip

lash·ing /ˈlæʃɪŋ/ *n* [C] **1** a punishment in which someone is hit with a whip; ▤ **whipping** **2** a rope that fastens something tightly to something else **3 lashings of sth** *BrE old-fashioned* a large amount of food or drink: *apple pie with lashings of cream*

lass /læs/ also **las·sie** /ˈlæsi/ *n* [C] a girl or young woman – used especially in Scotland and the north of England; → **lad**

las·si·tude /ˈlæsɪ̩tjuːd $ ˈlæsətjuːd, -tuːd/ *n* [U] *formal* tiredness and lack of energy or interest; ▤ **weariness**

las·so¹ /ləˈsuː, ˈlæsəʊ $ -soʊ/ *n plural* **lassos** *or* **lassoes** [C] a rope with one end tied in a circle, used to catch cattle and horses, especially in the western US

lasso² *v* [T] to catch an animal using a lasso

last¹ [S1] [W1] /lɑːst $ læst/ *determiner, adj*
1 most recent or nearest to the present time; → **next**(12) : *I hadn't seen him since the last meeting.* | **last night/week/year etc** *Did you see the game on TV last night?* | *The law was passed last August.* | *Interest in golf has grown rapidly in the last ten years.* | *Things have changed since **the last time** (=the most recent occasion) you were here.*
2 happening or existing at the end, with no others after; ▣ **first**: *I didn't read the last chapter of the book.* | *The next meeting will be held in the last week in June.* | **the last person/thing etc to do sth** *Anna was the last person to see him alive.* | **last but one/two etc** (=last except for one other, two others etc) *on the last but one day of his trial*
3 remaining after all others have gone, been used etc: *Can I have the last piece of cake?* | **every last** (=used to emphasize that you mean all of something) *All the money was gone; every last penny of it.*
4 the last minute/moment the latest possible time before something happens: *Travelers will find it hard to get a hotel room at the last minute.* | *He never makes a decision until almost the last moment.*
5 the last person/thing used to make a strong negative statement about someone or something: *She's the last person I'd expect to meet in a disco* (=I would not expect to meet her in a disco at all). | *Money was the last thing I cared about right now.* | **the last thing sb needs/wants** *The last thing she needed was for me to start crying too.*
6 be the last straw to be the final thing in a series of annoying things that makes someone very angry: *He'd broken his promise again, and it was the last straw.*
7 last thing (at night) at the very end of the day: *Take a*

couple of these pills last thing at night to help you sleep.
8 on your last legs *informal* **a)** very tired: *Sarah looks as if she's on her last legs.* **b)** very ill and likely to die soon
9 on its last legs *informal* old or in bad condition, and likely to stop working soon: *The car's on its last legs.*
10 be the last word in sth to be the best, most modern, or most comfortable example of something: *It's the last word in luxury holidays.* → **last resort** at **RESORT¹** (2); → **with your last/dying breath** at **BREATH** (9) → **LAST HURRAH**; → **have the last laugh** at **LAUGH²** (6); → **the last/final word** at **WORD¹** (14)

last² [S1] [W1] *adv*
1 most recently before now; → **next**: *When I last saw her, she was working in New York.*
2 after everything or everyone else; ▣ **first**: *Who is speaking last?* | *Add the flour last.* | **last of all** (=used when giving a final point or piece of information) *Last of all, I'd like to thank everyone for coming*
3 last but not least used when mentioning the last person or thing in a list, to emphasize that they are still important: *Last but not least, let me introduce Jane, our new secretary.*

last³ [S1] [W1] *n, pron*
1 the last the person or thing that comes after all the others; ▣ **first**: *I think this box is the last.* | **the last to do sth** *He was the first to arrive and the last to leave.*
2 at (long) last if something happens at last, it happens after you have been hoping, waiting, or working for it a long time: *At last it was time to leave.* | *We reached the summit at last.* → see box at **LASTLY**
3 the day/week/year etc before last the day, week etc before the one that has just finished: *I sent the letter off the week before last.*
4 the last of sth the remaining parts of something: *John ate the last of the bread at lunchtime.*
5 sb hasn't heard the last of sb/sth if you have not heard the last of someone or something, they may return and cause problems for you in the future: *We haven't heard the last of football violence.*
6 sb will never hear the last of sth if you will never hear the last of something, someone will be angry with you about it for a long time: *If my mother sees me, I'll never hear the last of this.*
7 the last I heard *spoken* used to tell someone the most recent news that you know about a person or situation: *The last I heard, she was at college studying law.*
8 to the last *formal* until the end of an event or the end of someone's life: *He died in 1987, insisting to the last he was innocent.*

last⁴ [S1] [W2] *v*
1 [I always + adv/prep] to continue for a particular length of time: [+**for/until/through etc**] *The hot weather lasted for the whole month of June.* | **last an hour/ten minutes etc** *Each lesson lasts an hour.* | *The ceasefire didn't last long.*
2 [I,T] to continue to exist, be effective, or remain in good condition for a long time: *This good weather won't last.* | **last (sb) two days/three weeks etc** *A good coat will last you ten years.* | *Cut flowers will last longer if you put flower food in the water.*
3 last out (sth) *BrE* [I always + adv/prep] to manage to remain in the same situation, even when this is difficult: *They won't be able to last much longer without fresh supplies.* | *If you go into the job with that attitude, you won't last long.* | *She feared she might not be able to last out the afternoon in court without fainting.*
4 [I,T always + adv/prep] to be enough for someone for a period of time; ▤ **do**: **last (sb) two days/three weeks etc** *The water supply should last another 48 hours.* | *We only had $50 to last us the rest of the month.*

last⁵ *n* [C] a piece of wood or metal shaped like a human foot, used by someone who makes and repairs shoes

L

[1] 000, [2] 000, [3] 000, most frequent words in [S]poken and [W]ritten English

last 'call n [U] *AmE* the time when customers in a bar can order one more drink before the bar closes; ▬ **last orders** *BrE*

last-'ditch adj **a last-ditch attempt/effort etc** a final attempt to achieve something before it is too late: *The negotiators made a last-ditch effort to reach an agreement.*

last hur'rah n [C usually singular] *AmE* a final effort, event etc at the end of a long period of work, a life etc: *He's made it clear that this Olympics, his third, will be his last hurrah.*

last·ing /'lɑːstɪŋ $ 'læs-/ adj [usually before noun] strong enough, well enough planned etc to continue for a very long time; ▬ **long-lasting**: *The reforms will bring **lasting benefits**.* | *Their generosity made a **lasting impression** on me.* | *a solution that would bring **lasting peace***

last 'judgment n **the last judgment** the time after death when everyone is judged by God for what they have done in life, according to Christianity and some other religions; ▬ **judgment day**

last·ly /'lɑːstli $ 'læst-/ adv [sentence adverb] used when telling someone the last thing at the end of a list or a series of statements; ▣ **firstly**: *Lastly, could I ask all of you to keep this information secret.*

WORD CHOICE: lastly, finally, eventually, in the end, at last
⚠ Do not use **lastly** to say what happened at the end of a period of time or after several other things happened. Use one of the following expressions:
Use **finally** or **eventually** to say that something happens after a long time: *Finally we managed to get the car to start.* | *When she eventually turned up, the food was cold.*
Use **eventually** or **in the end** to say what the result or outcome of something was: *They eventually got bored and went home.* | *In the end we decided to cancel the trip.*
Use **at last** to say that something happens after a long period of waiting or trying, when you are glad about this: *It's good to be home at last.* | *At last, the pizza's here!*
Use **lastly** or **finally** to introduce the last point you want to make, the last action in a series of actions, or the last item in a list: *Lastly, I would like to remind you that smoking is not allowed.* | *Load the paper, select the number of copies, and lastly press 'Print'.* | *You add flour, salt, and finally milk.*

---

last-'minute adj [only before noun] happening or done as late as possible before something else happens: *a few last-minute changes to the script*

last name n [C] *especially AmE* a SURNAME

last 'orders n [plural] *BrE* the time when customers in a bar or PUB can order one more drink before the bar closes; ▬ **last call** *AmE*

last 'post n **the last post** the tune played on a BUGLE at British military funerals, or to call soldiers back to camp for the night

last 'rites n [plural] **the last rites** the ceremony performed in some religions, especially the Catholic religion, for people who are dying

lat. also **lat** *BrE* the written abbreviation of *latitude*

latch¹ /lætʃ/ n [C] **1** a small metal or plastic object used to keep a door, gate, or window closed: *Gwen lifted the latch and opened the gate.* → see picture at LOCK² **2** *especially BrE* a type of lock for a door that you can open from the inside by turning a handle, but that you need a key to open from the outside: **on the latch** (=shut but not locked) *Ray went out, leaving the door on the latch.*

latch² v [T] to fasten a door, gate, or window with a latch
latch on phr v *BrE informal* to understand: *He's so thick it took him ages to latch on.*

latch onto sb/sth also **latch on to sb/sth** phr v *informal* **1** to become very interested in something: *Don't just latch on to the latest management fads.* **2** to follow someone and keep trying to talk to them, get their attention etc, especially when they would prefer to be left alone: *He latched onto Sandy at the party and wouldn't go away.* **3** to hold tightly to something with your hand, mouth etc: *a baby latching on to its mother's breast*

latch·key /'lætʃkiː/ n [C] **1** a key that opens a lock on an outside door of a house or apartment **2 latch-key kid** *old-fashioned* a child whose parents both work and who spends time alone in the house after school

late¹ S1 W1 /leɪt/ adj comparative **later**, superlative **latest**
1 AFTER EXPECTED TIME arriving, happening, or done after the time that was expected, agreed, or arranged; ▣ **early**: *Sorry I'm late – I overslept.* | **ten minutes/two hours etc late** *You're half an hour late.* | *The train was even later than usual.* | *We apologize for the late departure of flight AZ709.* | *There are penalties if loan repayments are late.* | [+**for**] *Cheryl was late for school.* | [+**with**] *We've never been late with the rent.*
2 NEAR THE END [only before noun] used to refer to the part near the end of a period of time; ▣ **early**: *a late eighteenth century building* | *Paul's in his late forties.* | *in the late 1980s* | *By late afternoon, she had done 10 drawings.*
3 be too late to arrive or do something after the time when something could or should have been done: *He shouted a warning but it was too late.* | **too late to do sth** *Are we too late to get tickets?* | *It was too late to turn back.*
4 AFTER USUAL TIME happening or done after the usual or normal time: *a late breakfast* | *The harvest was late this year because of the rain.* | *She looked tired – too many **late nights*** (=nights when she went to bed after the normal time).
5 EVENING near the end of a day: *the late movie* | *It's late - I'd better go home.*
6 DEAD [only before noun] dead: **late husband/wife** *Mrs. Moore's late husband*
7 late developer/bloomer a) a child who develops socially, emotionally, or physically at a later age than other children **b)** someone who does not become successful until they are older
8 it's (a little/bit) late in the day (to do sth) used to show disapproval because someone has done something too late: *It's a bit late in the day to start having objections.*
9 late of sth *formal* used about someone who has died fairly recently: *Billy Hicks, late of this parish*
—**lateness** n [U]: *penalties for lateness at work* | *despite the lateness of the hour*

late² S2 W3 adv comparative **later**, superlative **no superlative**
1 after the usual time: *The stores are open later on Thursdays.* | *Ellen has to **work late** tonight.* | *Can you stay late?*
2 after the arranged or expected time; ▣ **early**: **ten minutes/two hours etc late** *The bus came ten minutes late.*
3 too late after the time when something could or should have been done: *The advice came too late.*
4 near to the end of a period of time or an event: [+**in**] *The wedding took place late in May.* | *It was not a place to walk in **late at night**.*
5 as late as sth used to express surprise that something considered old-fashioned was still happening so recently: *Capital punishment was still used in Britain as late as the 1950s.*
6 of late *formal* recently: *Birth rates have gone down of late.*
7 late in life if you do something late in life, you do it at an older age than most people do
8 better late than never used to say that you are glad someone has done something, or to say that they should do something even though they are late → **run late** at RUN¹ (39)

'late-,breaking adj late-breaking news concerns events that happen just before a news broadcast or just before a newspaper is printed

late·com·er /'leɪt,kʌmə $ -ər/ n [C] someone who arrives late

late·ly /'leɪtli/ adv recently: What have you been doing lately? | Lately, I've had trouble sleeping.

'late-night adj [only before noun] happening late at night: late-night television | late-night shopping

la·tent /'leɪtənt/ adj something that is latent is present but hidden, and may develop or become more noticeable in the future; → **dormant**: [+in] The virus remains latent in the body for many years. | latent aggression —**latency** n [U]

lat·er¹ [S1] [W1] /'leɪtə $ -ər/ adv
1 after the time you are talking about or after the present time: I'm going out for a bit – I'll see you later. | **two years/three weeks etc later** He became Senator two years later. | later that day/morning/week etc The baby died later that night. | **later in the day/week/year** The dentist could fit you in later in the week.
2 later on at some time after the present time: I can't eat all of this – I'll finish it later on.
3 not later than sth used to say that something must be done by a particular time in the future: Completed entry forms should arrive not later than 31st July.

later² adj [only before noun] **1** coming in the future or after something else; **≢** earlier: The role of marketing is dealt with in a later chapter. | The launch was postponed to a later date. **2** more recent; **≢** earlier: The engine has been greatly improved in later models. **3** in later years/life when someone is older: Using a sunscreen when you are young helps you to have healthy skin in later years.

lat·e·ral /'lætərəl/ adj formal **1** relating to the sides of something, or movement to the side: The wall is weak and requires lateral support. **2** relating to positions, jobs, relationships etc that are at the same level or rank: Employees can expect lateral moves to different departments, to gain experience. —**laterally** adv

,lateral 'thinking n [U] a way of thinking in which you use your imagination to see relationships between things that are not normally thought of together

lat·est¹ /'leɪt‚st/ adj [only before noun] the most recent or the newest: all the latest gossip | His latest film is one of the funniest he's ever made.

latest² n **1** the latest informal the most recent or newest thing: [+in] Wednesday's session was the latest in a series of planning meetings. | **the latest in ... technology/equipment** (=the most modern equipment) using the latest in medical technology **2** at the latest no later than the time mentioned: I should be back by 11 o'clock at the latest.

la·tex /'leɪteks/ n [U] **1** a thick white liquid produced by some plants, especially the rubber tree, and used in making rubber, paint, glue etc: a doctor's latex gloves **2** an artificial substance similar to latex

lath /lɑːθ, læθ $ læθ/ n [C] a long flat narrow piece of wood used in building to support PLASTER (=material used to cover walls)

lathe /leɪð/ n [C] a machine that shapes wood or metal, by turning it around and around against a sharp tool

la·ther¹ /'lɑːðə $ 'læðər/ n [singular, U] **1** a white mass of bubbles produced by mixing soap in water **2** a white mass that forms on a horse's skin when it has been SWEATING; **≢** foam **3** get in a lather also **work yourself into a lather** informal to get very anxious or upset about something: By the time Alan called, Jody had worked herself into a lather. **4** in a lather very worried, upset, or excited: He was in a lather of anticipation.

lather² v **1** [I] to produce a lather: This soap lathers really well. **2** [T] to cover something with lather

Lat·in¹ /'lætɪn $ 'lætn/ n **1** [U] the language used in ancient Rome **2** [C] someone from Latin America **3** [C] someone from a Southern European

country whose language developed from Latin, for example Spain, Portugal, or Italy

Latin² adj **1** relating to the Latin language: a Latin inscription **2** from or relating to South America: Latin music **3** from or relating to Southern European countries whose languages developed from Latin, for example Spain, Portugal, or Italy

La·ti·na /læ'tiːnə/ n [C] AmE a woman in the US whose family comes from Latin America; → **Hispanic**

,Latin A'merican adj relating to South or Central America, or its people

La·ti·no /læ'tiːnəʊ $ -noʊ/ n plural **Latinos** [C] AmE a man in the US whose family comes from Latin America. The plural 'Latinos' can mean a group of men and women, or just men; → **Hispanic** —**Latino** adj: Latino culture

lat·i·tude /'læt‚tjuːd $ -tuːd/ n **1** [C,U] the distance north or south of the EQUATOR (=the imaginary line around the middle of the world), measured in degrees; → **longitude**; → see picture at GLOBE **2** latitudes [plural] an area at a particular latitude: The birds breed in northern latitudes. | the oceans of the lower latitude **3** [U] formal freedom to choose what you do or say: **considerable/greater latitude** (=a lot of freedom to choose) Pupils enjoy considerable latitude in deciding what they want to study. | [+in/for] Employees should have some latitude in organizing their work. —**latitudinal** /,læt‚'tjuːd‚nəl $ -'tuːdn-əl/ adj

la·trine /lə'triːn/ n [C] a toilet that is outdoors in a camp or military area

lat·te /'læteɪ $ 'lɑː-/ n [C,U] very strong coffee with a lot of STEAMED milk in it, or a cup of this type of coffee

lat·ter¹ [W2] /'lætə $ -ər/ n the latter formal the second of two people or things just mentioned; **≢** former: Where unemployment and crime are high, it can be assumed that the latter is due to the former.

latter² adj [only before noun] formal **1** being the second of two people or things, or the last in a list just mentioned; **≢** former: In the latter case, buyers pay a 15% commission. **2** the latter part of a period of time is nearest to the end of it: Celebrations are planned for the latter part of November.

'latter-day adj [only before noun] **1** a latter-day Versailles/Tsar/Robin Hood etc something or someone that exists now but is like a famous thing or person that existed in the past: He ruled his business empire like a latter-day Tsar. **2** relating to a recent period of time, rather than an earlier one: Latter-day students could never meet the college entrance standards required in the 1940s.

lat·ter·ly /'lætəli $ -ər-/ adv BrE formal **1** recently: Scientists have studied the moon through telescopes, and, latterly, from satellites. **2** towards the end of a period of time; → **formerly**: O'Rourke retired after a 15-year career with Bisons, latterly as chief executive.

lat·tice /'læt‚s/ n [C] **1** also **lat·tice·work** /'læt‚swɜːk $ -wɜːrk/ a pattern or structure made of long pieces of wood, plastic etc that cross each other so that the spaces between them are shaped like DIAMONDS **2** technical a regular arrangement of objects

,lattice 'window also **,latticed 'window** n [C] BrE a type of window made of many small pieces of glass shaped like DIAMONDS

laud /lɔːd $ lɒːd/ v [T] formal to praise someone or something

laud·a·ble /'lɔːdəbəl $ 'lɒːd-/ adj formal deserving praise, even if not completely successful; **≢** praiseworthy: a laudable attempt —**laudably** adv

lau·da·num /'lɔːdənəm $ 'lɒː-/ n [U] a substance containing the drug OPIUM, used in the past to control pain and help people to sleep

laud·a·to·ry /'lɔːdətəri $ 'lɒːdətɔːri/ adj formal expressing praise: a laudatory biography

L

laugh[1] [S2] [W2] /lɑːf $ læf/ v

1 [I] to make sounds with your voice, usually while you are smiling, because you think something is funny: *Maria looked at him and laughed.* | [+at/about] *'I didn't know what I was doing,' she said, laughing at the memory.* | *Tony was laughing so hard he had to steady himself on the table.* | *Nora laughed so much that she nearly cried.* | **laugh heartily/uproariously/hysterically etc** (=laugh a lot) *The kids tumbled around on the floor, laughing hysterically.* | *He couldn't help it; he burst out laughing* (=suddenly started laughing). | **laugh your head off** | *He's one of the few writers who can make me laugh out loud.*

2 [T] to say something in a voice that shows you are amused: *'You look ridiculous!' Nick laughed.*

3 not know whether to laugh or cry to feel upset or annoyed about something bad that has happened, but also able to see that there is something funny about it: *And when I couldn't find the passports – honestly, I didn't know whether to laugh or cry!*

4 don't make me laugh *spoken* used when someone has just told you something that is completely untrue, asked for something impossible etc: *'Can you finish this by tomorrow?' 'Don't make me laugh.'*

5 no laughing matter *informal* something serious that should not be joked about: *It's no laughing matter having to walk by a group of rowdy drunks every night just to get home.*

6 be laughed out of court also **be laughed out of town/business etc** *AmE* if a person or idea is laughed out of court etc, the idea is not accepted because people think it is completely stupid: *We can't propose that! We'd be laughed out of court!*

7 you have to laugh *spoken* used to say that, even though a situation is annoying or disappointing, you can also see that there is something funny about it

8 be laughing all the way to the bank *informal* to make a lot of money without making much effort

9 sb will be laughing on the other side of their face *spoken* used to say that although someone is happy or confident now, they will be in trouble later

10 be laughing *BrE spoken informal* to be happy or in a good situation, for example because something has had a successful result for you: *Well they paid me, didn't they, so I'm laughing.*

11 laugh in sb's face to behave towards someone in a way that shows that you do not respect them: *I told my sister what I thought, and she just laughed in my face.*

12 laugh up your sleeve to be secretly happy, especially because you have played a trick on someone or criticized them without them knowing

---

WORD FOCUS: words meaning LAUGH

giggle to laugh repeatedly in a silly way because you are amused, embarrassed, or nervous | **snigger** to laugh unkindly and quietly, especially at something that is not meant to be funny | **chuckle** to laugh quietly, especially because you are thinking about something funny | **roar/howl with laughter** to laugh very loudly because you think something is very funny | **be in hysterics** to laugh uncontrollably | **crack up** *informal* to suddenly start laughing a lot

---

laugh at sb/sth *phr v*
1 to make unkind or funny remarks about someone, because they have done or said something you think is stupid; ◉ **tease**: *I'm afraid the other kids will laugh at me because I don't understand.*
2 to seem not to care about something that most people would worry about: *Young offenders just laugh at this sort of sentence.*

laugh sth ⇔ **off** *phr v*
to pretend that something is less serious than it really is by laughing or joking about it: *Knox laughed off rumors that he would be running for mayor.*

laugh[2] [S3] n
1 [C] the act of laughing or the sound you make when you laugh: *a nervous laugh* | **with a laugh** *'What a mess!'*

she said, with a laugh. | *At first she was silent, then she gave a nervous laugh.* | *It was a nightmare at the time, but afterwards we all had a good laugh* (=laughed a lot) *about it.* | *This scene gets one of the biggest laughs in the movie.* | *Tell me – I could use a laugh* (=I am upset or sad and would like to hear something funny).

2 [C] if something is a laugh, you have fun and enjoy yourself when you are doing it: *We all went to the beach last night – it was a really good laugh.* | *The other campers were nice, and we had a great laugh together.* | *It was a great holiday with lots of laughs.*

3 sb is a (good) laugh *BrE* to be amusing and fun to be with: *I like Peter – he's a good laugh.*

4 for laughs also **for a laugh** *BrE* for fun: *We took the hot-air balloon ride, just for laughs.*

5 that's a laugh *spoken* used to say that something is silly or unlikely: *Me? Star in a film? That's a laugh.*

6 have the last laugh to finally be successful, win an argument etc, after other people have earlier criticized you, defeated you etc: *Men make jokes about women drivers, but women have the last laugh – their insurance rates are cheaper.*

7 be a laugh a minute *informal* to be very funny – sometimes used humorously to mean that someone or something is not at all funny

laugh·a·ble /ˈlɑːfəbəl $ ˈlæ-/ *adj* something that is laughable is impossible to believe or be serious about, because it is so silly or bad; ◉ **ridiculous**: *The promises are so far from reality that they are laughable.* —**laughably** *adv*

'laughing gas *n* [U] *informal* a gas that is sometimes used to stop you feeling pain during an operation

laugh·ing·ly /ˈlɑːfɪŋli $ ˈlæ-/ *adv* **1** if something is laughingly called something, the name is a joke, or is not suitable: *The news network was laughingly referred to as the 'Disaster Channel.'* **2** if you do something laughingly, you are laughing while you do it

'laughing stock also **laugh·ing·stock** *AmE* /ˈlɑːfɪŋstɒk $ ˈlæfɪŋstɑːk/ *n* [C] someone who is a laughing stock has done something so silly that people have no respect for them: *The programme has made the U.S. a laughingstock.*

'laugh lines *n* [plural] the American form of LAUGHTER LINES

laugh·ter /ˈlɑːftə $ ˈlæftər/ *n* [U] when people laugh, or the sound of people laughing: *Foster joined in the laughter.* | *He looked shocked, then burst into laughter* (=started laughing). | **roar/scream/shriek with laughter** (=laugh very loudly) *Audiences roared with laughter.* | *He shook with laughter.* | **peals/gales/howls etc of laughter** (=loud laughs) *The comment brought peals of laughter from her classmates.*

'laughter lines *n* [plural] *BrE* lines on your skin around your eyes, which can be seen when you laugh; ◉ **laugh lines** *AmE*

'laugh track *n* [C] recorded laughter that is used during a television show to make it sound as if people are laughing during the performance

launch[1] [W2] /lɔːntʃ $ lɒːntʃ/ v [T]
1 **START STH** to start something, usually something big or important: *The organization has launched a campaign to raise $150,000.* | *The Canadian police plan to launch an investigation into the deal.* | **launch an attack/assault/offensive** *The press launched a vicious attack on the President.* | *The book launched his career as a novelist.*

2 **PRODUCT** to make a new product, book etc available for sale for the first time: *The company hopes to launch the new drug by next October.*

3 **BOAT** to put a boat or ship into the water

4 **SKY/SPACE** to send a weapon or spacecraft into the sky or into space: *A test satellite was launched from Cape Canaveral.*

5 **COMPUTER** to make a computer program start; ◉ **open**: *Double-click on an icon to launch an application.*

6 launch yourself forwards/up/from etc to jump up and

forwards into the air with a lot of energy
launch into sth phr v
1 to suddenly start a description or story, or suddenly start criticizing something: *Nelson launched into a blistering criticism of greedy lawyers.*
2 to suddenly start doing something: *Don't just launch into exercise without warming up first.*
launch out phr v BrE
to start something new, especially something that involves risk

launch² n [C] **1** when a new product, book etc is made available or made known: [+of] *the launch of a new women's magazine* | *a new product launch* **2** a large boat with a motor **3** when a weapon or spacecraft is sent into the sky or into space

launch·er /ˈlɔːntʃə $ ˈlɒːntʃər/ n [C] an object that is used to send a weapon or spacecraft into the sky: *a rocket launcher*

launch pad also **launching pad** n [C] **1** a base from which a weapon or spacecraft is sent up into the sky **2** an event, group, or activity that helps someone start something: [+for] *Ellington's band was a launching pad for many gifted jazz musicians.*

launch·pad /ˈlɔːntʃpæd $ ˈlɒːntʃ-/ n [C] a place on the Internet that helps you start to find information about a particular subject: *Their website is a good launchpad to other sites.*

laun·der /ˈlɔːndə $ ˈlɒːndər/ v [T] **1** to put money which has been obtained illegally into legal businesses and bank accounts, so that you can hide it or use it: *a law designed to prevent money laundering* **2** formal to wash and IRON clothes, sheets etc

laun·der·ette /ˌlɔːndəˈret $ ˌlɒːn-/ also **laundrette** /lɔːnˈdret $ lɒːn-/ BrE; **Laun·dro·mat** /ˈlɔːndrəmæt $ ˈlɒːn-/ AmE n [C] trademark a place where you can go to wash your clothes in machines that work when you put coins in them

laun·dry /ˈlɔːndri $ ˈlɒːn-/ n plural **laundries** **1** [U] clothes, sheets etc that need to be washed or have just been washed: *She did the laundry* (=washed the clothes etc) *and hung it out to dry.* | *Ben was folding laundry.* | **clean/dirty laundry** *a pile of dirty laundry* **2** [C] a place or business where clothes etc are washed and IRONED → see picture at STAY → **air/wash your dirty laundry** at DIRTY¹ (7)

laundry basket n [C] **1** BrE a large basket that you put dirty clothes in until you wash them; ▯ **hamper** AmE; → see picture at BASKET **2** a basket used for carrying clothes that have been or need to be washed

laundry list n [C] informal a list of a lot of different things: *a laundry list of criticisms*

lau·re·ate /ˈlɔːriɑt/ n [C] someone who has been given an important prize or honour, especially the NOBEL PRIZE: *Nigeria's Nobel laureate, Wole Soyinka* → POET LAUREATE

laur·el /ˈlɒrəl $ ˈlɔː-, ˈlɑː-/ n **1** [C,U] a small tree with smooth shiny dark green leaves that do not fall in winter **2** **rest/sit on your laurels** to be satisfied with what you have achieved and therefore stop trying to achieve anything new **3** **look to your laurels** to work hard in order not to lose the success that you have achieved **4** **laurels** [plural] honours that you receive for something you have achieved: *academic laurels*

lav /læv/ n [C] BrE spoken a LAVATORY

la·va /ˈlɑːvə/ n [U] hot liquid rock that flows from a VOLCANO, or this rock when it has become solid → see picture at VOLCANO

lava lamp n [C] a lamp that has a coloured liquid substance inside it that moves up and down

lav·a·to·ri·al /ˌlævəˈtɔːriəl/ adj BrE lavatorial jokes are about going to the toilet

lav·a·to·ry /ˈlævətəri $ -tɔːri/ n plural **lavatories** [C] formal a toilet or the room a toilet is in

lav·en·der /ˈlævəndə $ -ər/ n **1** [C,U] a plant that has grey-green leaves and purple flowers with a strong pleasant smell **2** [U] a pale purple colour

lav·ish¹ /ˈlævɪʃ/ adj **1** large, impressive, or expensive: *a royal palace on a lavish scale* | *a lavish lifestyle* | *The food was lavish.* **2** very generous: [+with/in] *We were always lavish with financial aid in times of crisis.* | *He was always lavish in his praise of my efforts.* —**lavishly** adv: *their lavishly illustrated catalogue* —**lavishness** n [U]

lavish² v [T] to give someone or something a lot of love, praise, money etc: **lavish sth on/upon sb** *He lavished attention on her.* | **lavish sb with sth** *Hug your children and lavish them with love.*

law S1 W1 /lɔː $ lɒː/ n
1 **SYSTEM OF RULES** also **the law** [U] the whole system of rules that people in a particular country or area must obey

break the law (=do something illegal)
obey the law
become law (=officially be made a law)
enforce the law (=make people obey the law)
by law (=according to the law)
be against the law (=be illegal)
within the law (=legal or legally)
tax/copyright/divorce etc law (=all the laws about tax etc)
criminal law
civil law
international law
federal law AmE (=the law of the US, not of a particular state)

Should people do what they think is right even when it means breaking the law? | *Elected officials ought to obey the law.* | *The Suicide Act became law in 1961.* | *By law, seatbelts must be worn by all passengers.* | *In Sweden it is against the law to hit a child.* | *They were fully convinced they were performing their duties within the law.* | *an interesting area of criminal law* | *the principles of international law* | *Federal law protects workers who are disabled.*

2 A RULE [C] a rule that people in a particular country or area must obey: **immigration/labour/libel etc law** | **under a law** *Five people arrested under anti-terrorism laws were released without charge.* | [+on] *European laws on equal opportunities* | [+against] *The laws against drug use were very severe.* | **laws passed by Parliament**
3 **law and order** a situation in which people respect the law, and crime is controlled by the police, the prison system etc: *We are concerned about the breakdown of law and order in the country.*
4 POLICE **the law** the police: *I think she may be in trouble with the law.*
5 WHAT ALWAYS HAPPENS [C] something that always happens in nature or society, or a statement that describes this: [+of] *the law of supply and demand* | *the laws of nature* | *the law of gravity*
6 STUDY/PROFESSION also **the law** [U] law as a subject of study, or the profession of being a lawyer: *She's studying law in London.*
7 SPORT/ACTIVITY [C] one of the rules which controls a sport or activity: *the laws of football*
8 **the law of the jungle a)** the idea that people should only look after themselves and not care about other people if they want to succeed **b)** the principle that only the strongest creatures will stay alive
9 **the law of averages** the PROBABILITY that one result will happen as often as another if you try something often enough: *The law of averages says we'll win at least once.*
10 **be a law unto himself/herself etc** to behave in an independent way and not worry about the usual rules of behaviour or what other people do or think: *Boys his age are a law unto themselves.*
11 **take the law into your own hands** to do something illegal in order to put right something that you think is

L

not fair, for example by violently punishing someone instead of telling the police: *vigilantes who take the law into their own hands*

12 go to law to go to court in order to settle a problem: *the right of consumers to go to law if they need to*

13 be above the law someone who is above the law does not have to obey the law: *Many ministers seem to regard themselves as above the law.*

14 there's no law against sth *spoken* used to tell someone who is criticizing you that you are not doing anything wrong

15 there ought to be a law against sth *spoken* used to say that you do not think something should be accepted or allowed: *There ought to be a law against cutting off power supplies in the middle of February.*

16 sb's word is law used to say that someone is always obeyed without argument → CIVIL LAW, COMMON LAW, CRIMINAL LAW, ROMAN LAW, SOD'S LAW; → **lay down the law** at LAY DOWN (3); → **unwritten law** at UNWRITTEN

'law-a,biding *adj* respectful of the law and obeying it: *a law-abiding citizen*

'law-,breaker *n* [C] someone who does something illegal; **◻ criminal** —**law-breaking** *n* [U]

'law court *n* [C] a room or building where legal cases are judged

'law en,forcement *n* [U] the job of making sure that the law is obeyed: *law enforcement agencies*

'law enforcement ,agent *n* [C] *AmE* a police officer

'law firm *n* [C] a company that provides legal services and employs many lawyers

law·ful /'lɔːfəl $ 'lɒː-/ *adj formal* or *law* allowed or recognized by law; **◻ legal**: *It is not lawful to kill or injure a pet animal.* | *a lawful arrest* | *his lawful wife* —**lawfully** *adv* —**lawfulness** *n* [U]

law·less /'lɔːləs $ 'lɒː-/ *adj* not obeying the law, or not controlled by the law; **▣ law-abiding**: *this increasingly lawless society* | *These border areas are among the most lawless regions in the world.* —**lawlessness** *n* [U]

'Law Lords *n* the Law Lords members of the British House of Lords who hold high positions in the legal profession, and form the highest court in the British legal system

law·mak·er /'lɔːmeɪkə $ 'lɒːmeɪkər/ *n* [C] *especially AmE* any elected official responsible for making laws; **◻ legislator**

law·man /'lɔːmæn $ 'lɒː-/ *n plural* **lawmen** /-men/ [C] *AmE informal* any officer who is responsible for making sure that the law is obeyed

lawn /lɔːn $ lɒːn/ *n* **1** [C,U] an area of ground in a garden or park that is covered with short grass: *I spent all morning mowing the lawn* (=cutting the grass). | *a carefully tended lawn* **2** [U] a fine cloth made from cotton or LINEN

'lawn ,bowling *n* [U] *AmE* a game played on grass in which you try to roll a big ball as near as possible to a smaller ball; **◻ bowls** *BrE*

'lawn chair *n* [C] *AmE* a light chair that you use outside, especially one that folds up

'lawn ,mower *n* [C] a machine that you use to cut grass → see picture at GARDENING

'lawn ,party *n* [C] *AmE* a formal party held outside in the afternoon, especially in a large garden; **◻ garden party** *BrE*

,lawn 'tennis *n* [U] *formal* TENNIS

'law school *n* [C,U] a part of a university or a special school in the US where you study to become a lawyer after you get your BACHELOR'S DEGREE

law·suit /'lɔːsuːt, -sjuːt $ 'lɒːsuːt/ *n* [C] a problem or complaint that a person or organization brings to a court of law to be settled; **◻ suit**: [+**against**] *His lawyer filed a lawsuit against the city.*

law·yer S3 W2 /'lɔːjə $ 'lɒːjər/ *n* [C] someone whose job is to advise people about laws, write formal agreements, or represent people in court

lax /læks/ *adj* not strict or careful enough about standards of behaviour, work, safety etc; **◻ slack**: *lax in (doing) sth The company has been lax in carrying out its duties.* | *lax security* —**laxity** also **laxness** *n* [U]

lax·a·tive /'læksətɪv/ *n* [C] a medicine or something that you eat which makes your BOWELS empty easily —**laxative** *adj*

lay¹ S1 W2 /leɪ/ *v* the past tense of LIE¹

lay² *v past tense and past participle* **laid** /leɪd/

1 PUT SB/STH DOWN [T always + adv/prep] to put someone or something down carefully into a flat position; **◻ place**: *He laid his hand on my shoulder.* | *They laid a wreath at the place where so many people died.* | *Lay the material flat on the table.*

2 lay bricks/carpet/concrete/cables etc to put or fasten bricks, a CARPET etc in the correct place, especially on the ground or floor: *The carpet was laid last week.* | *The project involved laying an oil pipeline across the desert.*

3 BIRD/INSECT ETC [I,T] if a bird, insect etc lays eggs, it produces them from its body: *The flies lay their eggs on decaying meat.* | *A cuckoo is able to lay in a range of different nests.*

4 TABLE [T] *BrE* to put the cloth, plates, knives, forks etc on a table, ready for a meal; **◻ set**: *John was laying the table.* | *As she spoke, she was laying him a place at the table.*

5 lay the foundations/groundwork/base to provide the conditions that will make it possible for something to happen or be successful: [+**for**] *Mandela helped lay the foundations for a new democratic South Africa.* | *It was an invention which laid the foundations of modern radio technology.*

6 GIVE INFORMATION [T] *formal* to make a statement, give information etc in an official or public way; **◻ put**: *Several proposals have been laid before the committee.*

7 lay emphasis/stress on sth *formal* to emphasize something because you believe it is very important: *a political philosophy that lays great stress on individual responsibility*

8 lay a hand/finger on sb [usually in negatives] to touch someone with the intention of hurting them: *I swear I didn't lay a finger on him.* | *If you lay one hand on me, I'll scream.*

9 lay bare/open sth also lay sth bare/open a) to show what something is really like, or stop hiding facts, feelings etc: *Every aspect of their private life has been laid bare.* b) to remove the thing that is covering or hiding something else: *When the tide goes out, vast stretches of sand are laid bare.*

10 lay sb/sth open to sth to do something that makes it possible for other people to blame you, criticize you etc: lay yourself open to sth *By doing that, he laid himself open to ridicule.* | *Not to have taken action would have laid the department open to charges of negligence.*

11 lay waste sth also lay waste to sth *formal* to destroy or damage something, especially in a war: *The island was laid waste and abandoned.* | *an attack which laid waste to hundreds of villages*

L

12 lay plans/a trap etc to carefully prepare all the details of something: *We are laying plans now in order to be successful in the future.* | **the best-laid plans** (=plans that have been made carefully) *Bad weather can upset even the best-laid travel plans.*
13 lay claim to (doing) sth to say that something belongs to you or say that you deserve something: *The town can lay claim to having the oldest theatre in Britain.* | *No one has laid claim to the property.*
14 lay siege to sb/sth **a)** if a group of people lay siege to a place, they try to get control by surrounding it: *The armies laid siege to Vienna in 1529.* **b)** to do everything you can to get someone to talk to you or notice you: *A group of young men were always at the stage door, trying to lay siege to the girls.*
15 HAVE SEX get laid [T] *informal* to have sex with someone: *All he wants to do is go out and get laid.*
16 LIE [I] *spoken* to be in a position in which you are flat – some people consider this use to be incorrect; ⊟ lie
17 RISK MONEY [T] *especially BrE* to risk an amount of money on the result of a race, sports game etc; ⊟ bet: lay sth on sth *She laid £50 on the favourite, Golden Boy.* | lay money (that) *I'd lay money that he will go on to play for England.*
18 lay sb/sth on the line **a)** to state something, especially a threat, demand, or criticism, in a very clear way: *Lay it on the line and tell them what's really been happening.* **b)** also put sb/sth on the line to risk losing your life, your job etc, especially in order to help someone: *I've laid myself on the line for him once already.*
19 lay sth at the door of sb/sth also lay sth at sb's door to blame something or someone for something: *The continued divisions within the party cannot be laid entirely at his door.* | *Many illnesses are being laid at the door of stress.*
20 lay sb low **a)** [usually passive] if an illness lays someone low, they are unable to do their normal activities for a period of time: [+with] *She's been laid low with flu for a week.* **b)** *literary* to make someone fall down, or injure them seriously
21 lay sb to rest *formal* to bury someone after they have died: *She was laid to rest beside her husband.* → lay/put sth to rest at REST¹ (10)
22 lay the ghost (of sth) to finally stop being worried or upset by something from the past → lay your hands on sth at HAND¹ (18); → lay the blame on sb/sth at BLAME²; → put/lay your cards on the table at CARD¹ (13)

lay about sb *phr v literary or old-fashioned*
to attack someone violently; ⊟ set about: [+with] *He laid about his attackers with a stick.*

lay sth ⇔ aside *phr v*
1 to stop using something and put it down, especially so you can do something else; ⊟ put aside: *Richard had laid aside his book to watch what was happening.*
2 to stop behaving in a particular way, or stop having particular feelings, especially so you can achieve something; ⊟ put aside: *On the day of the wedding, all arguments between the families were laid aside.* | *As a doctor, you often need to lay aside your personal feelings.*
3 also lay sth ⇔ by to keep something, especially money, so you can use it in the future; ⊟ put by: *She'd laid aside a few pounds each week from her wages.*

lay sth ⇔ down *phr v*
1 OFFICIALLY STATE to officially state something or say that rules, principles etc must be obeyed: *He had already clearly laid down his view in his opening speech.* | lay down that *The contract laid down that the work must be completed before 2025.*
2 WEAPONS if people lay down their weapons, they stop fighting: *The terrorists were urged to lay down their arms.*
3 lay down the law to tell other people what to do, how they should think etc, in a very strong or impolite way: *I could hear him laying down the law.*
4 lay down your life *formal* to die in order to help other people: [+for] *He was even prepared to lay down his life for his friends.*

lay sth ⇔ in *phr v formal especially BrE*
to get and store a supply of something to use in the future: *He likes to lay in a few special drinks for the festive season.*

lay into sb/sth *phr v*
to attack or criticize someone or something: *Outside the club, two men were laying into each other.*

lay off *phr v*
1 lay sb ⇔ off to stop employing someone because there is no work for them to do; → layoff: *The company laid off 250 workers in December.* | *Millions of people have been laid off in the steel industry.*
2 lay off (sth) *informal* to stop using or doing something: *I think you'd better lay off alcohol for a while.* | lay off doing sth *I had to lay off running for several months.*
3 lay off (sb) *informal* to stop annoying someone or hurting them: *Just lay off, will you!* | *I wish he'd lay off me!*
4 lay sth ⇔ off to pass the ball to someone in your team in a game such as football – used in sports reports: lay sth off to sb *Murphy has the ball and then lays it off to Owen.*

lay sth on *phr v*
1 lay sth ⇔ on *especially BrE* to provide something such as food, entertainment, or transport for a group of people: *They laid on a buffet for his farewell party.* | *A bus has been laid on to take you home.*
2 lay sth on sb to ask someone to do something, especially something that is difficult or something they will not want to do: *Sorry to lay this on you, but we need someone to give a talk at the conference next week.*
3 lay it on (thick) *informal* **a)** to praise someone or something too much, especially in order to get what you want **b)** to talk about something in a way that makes it seem more important, serious etc than it really is; ⊟ exaggerate

lay sb/sth ⇔ out *phr v*
1 SPREAD to spread something out: *Lay out the map on the table and let's have a look.*
2 ARRANGE to arrange or plan a building, town, garden etc; ⊟ set out: *The garden is laid out in a formal pattern.*
3 EXPLAIN to describe or explain something clearly; ⊟ set out: *The financial considerations are laid out in a booklet called 'How to Borrow Money'.*
4 SPEND *informal* to spend money, especially a lot of money; → outlay: lay out sth on sth *What's the point in laying out money on something you'll only wear once?*
5 HIT *informal* to hit someone so hard that they fall down and become unconscious: *One of the guards had been laid out and the other was missing.*
6 BODY to prepare a dead body so that it can be buried

lay over *phr v AmE*
to stay somewhere for a short time before continuing your trip; → layover

lay up *phr v*
1 be laid up (with sth) to have to stay in bed because you are ill or injured: *I was laid up for a week with flu.*
2 to stop using a boat or vehicle, especially while it is being repaired: lay sth ⇔ up *Most of the yachts were laid up for the winter.*
3 lay sth ⇔ up *old-fashioned* to collect and store something to use in the future: *We started laying up firewood for the winter.*

WORD CHOICE lay, lie
The verb **lay** must have an object. It is a slightly literary way to say 'put something somewhere': *She lays a silk cloth over the table.*
The verb **lie** does not have an object. It means 'be or get into a horizontal position somewhere': *Let's lie on the grass.* | *Lie down here for a while.*
⚠ **lay** is also the past tense of **lie**: *I lay on the couch and tried to relax.* The past tense of **lay** is **laid**: *He laid his hand on my shoulder.*

L

lay³ adj [only before noun] **a)** not trained or not knowing much about a particular profession or subject; → **layman**: lay witnesses **b)** not in an official position in the church: a lay preacher

lay⁴ n [C] **1 the lay of the land a)** the situation that exists at a particular time: Get the lay of the land before you make any decisions. **b)** the appearance of an area of land, for example the way it slopes **2 the lay of sth** the appearance of something and where each part of it is: Mr. Lowe will give you the lay of the camp and tell you what we're going to be doing. **3 be a good/quick/easy etc lay** informal to be a good, quick etc person to have sex with **4** literary a poem or song

lay·a·bout /ˈleɪəbaʊt/ n [C] BrE informal a lazy person who avoids work

lay·a·way /ˈleɪəweɪ/ n [U] AmE a method of buying goods in which you give the seller of the goods a small amount of money to keep the goods until you can pay the full price: I put the dress on layaway. —**layaway** adj

'lay-by n plural **lay-bys** [C] BrE a space next to a road where vehicles can stop

lay·er¹ S3 W3 /ˈleɪə $ -ər/ n [C]
1 an amount or piece of a material or substance that covers a surface or that is between two other things: [+of] A **thick layer** of dust lay on the furniture. | The moon was shining through a **thin layer** of cloud. | He pulled off **layer upon layer** of clothing (=many layers of clothing). | **in layers** Arrange the peppers, garlic and tomatoes in layers. → OZONE LAYER
2 one of several different levels in a complicated organization, system, set of ideas etc: [+of] We are operating with fewer layers of management. | There are multiple layers of meaning in the story. | the **multi-layered** nature of organizations (=they have many layers)

layer² v [T] **1** to make a layer of something or put something down in layers: Layer the raw sliced vegetables in a shallow baking dish. **2** to cut someone's hair so that the hair on top is in shorter lengths than the lower hair: I have layered, shoulder-length brown hair.

lay·ette /leɪˈet/ n [C] a complete set of clothing and other things that a new baby needs

lay·man /ˈleɪmən/ n plural **laymen** /-mən/ [C] **1** someone who is not trained in a particular subject or type of work, especially when they are being compared with someone who is; **🔲 expert**: To **the layman** (=laymen in general) all these plants look pretty similar. | If you don't understand what the doctor says, ask to have it explained **in layman's terms** (=in simple language). **2** someone who is not a priest but is a member of a church

'lay-off n [C] an occasion when an employer ends a worker's employment for a temporary period of time because there is not enough work: more lay-offs in the car industry → LAY OFF

lay·out /ˈleɪaʊt/ n [C] **1** the way in which something such as a town, garden, or building is arranged: [+of] the layout of the park | All the flats in the building had the same layout. **2** the way in which writing and pictures are arranged on a page: [+of] the layout of a business letter | page layout software → LAY OUT

lay·o·ver /ˈleɪəʊvə $ -oʊvər/ n [C] AmE a short stay between parts of a journey, especially a long plane journey; **🔲 stopover** BrE

lay·per·son /ˈleɪˌpɜːsən $ -pɜːr-/ n plural **laypersons** or **laypeople** /-ˌpiːpəl/ [C] a LAYMAN or LAYWOMAN

ˌlay 'reader n [C] someone in Christian churches who is not a priest but who has been given authority to lead a religious service

'lay-up n [C] a throw in BASKETBALL made from very close to the basket or from under it

lay·wom·an /ˈleɪˌwʊmən/ n plural **laywomen** /-ˌwɪmɪn/ [C] **1** a woman not trained in a particular

subject or type of work, especially when she is being compared with someone who is; **🔲 expert** **2** a woman who is not a priest but is a member of a church

laze /leɪz/ v [I always + adv/prep] to relax and enjoy yourself in a lazy way: [+in] We spent the afternoon lazing in the sun. | [+about/around] We lazed around, gazing at the views. —**laze** n [singular]

la·zy /ˈleɪzi/ adj comparative **lazier**, superlative **laziest** **1** not liking work and physical activity, or not making any effort to do anything; **🔲 idle**: the laziest boy in the class | He felt too lazy to get out of bed. **2** a lazy period of time is spent doing nothing except relaxing: We spent lazy days relaxing on the beach. —**lazily** adv —**laziness** n [U]

la·zy·bones /ˈleɪzibəʊnz $ -boʊnz/ n plural **lazybones** [C] informal a lazy person – often used in a friendly way to someone you like: Come on, lazybones! Get out of bed.

lb BrE; **lb.** AmE plural **lb** or **lbs** the written abbreviation of **pound** or pounds in weight

lbw /ˌel biː ˈdʌbəljuː/ adv **leg before wicket** a way in which your INNINGS can end in CRICKET, when the ball hits your leg if it is in front of the WICKET

LCD /ˌel siː ˈdiː/ n [C] **liquid crystal display** the part of a watch, CALCULATOR, or small computer where numbers or letters are shown by means of an electric current that is passed through a special liquid

leach /liːtʃ/ also **leach out** v [I,T] technical if a substance leaches or is leached from a larger mass such as the soil, it is removed from it by water passing through the larger mass: The manufacturers say that there is no danger of the aluminium leaching into the water.

lead¹ S1 W1 /liːd/ v past tense and past participle **led** /led/
1 **TAKE SB SOMEWHERE** [I,T] to take someone somewhere by going in front of them while they follow, or by pulling them gently: **lead sb to/into etc sth** A nurse took her arm and led her to a chair. | The horses were **led to safety**. | **lead sb away/down etc** She was led away from the courtroom in tears. | The manager **led the way** through the office. → see box at DIRECT²
2 **GO IN FRONT** [I,T] to go in front of a line of people or vehicles: A firetruck was leading the parade.
3 **BE IN CHARGE** [I,T] to be in charge of an organization, country, or team, or a group of people who are trying to do something: He has led the party for over twenty years. | Some people say she is too old to **lead the country** (=be in charge of its government). | Beckham **led his team to victory**. | **lead an investigation/inquiry/campaign** The investigation will be led by Inspector Scarfe. | They are leading a campaign to warn teenagers about the dangers of drug abuse. | **lead a revolt/rebellion/coup etc** The rebellion was led by the King's brother. | **lead an attack/assault** Nelson preferred to lead the attack himself from the front. | a man who was **born to lead** | a communist-led strike
4 **CAUSE STH TO HAPPEN** [I,T] to cause something to happen or cause someone to do something: [+to] the events that led to the start of the First World War | A degree in English could lead to a career in journalism. | **lead sb into sth** Her trusting nature often led her into trouble. | **lead sb to do sth** What led him to kill his wife? | **lead to sb doing sth** His actions could lead to him losing his job.
5 **CAUSE SB TO BELIEVE STH** [T] to make someone believe something, especially something that is not true: **lead sb to believe/expect/understand sth** He had led everyone to believe that his family was very wealthy. | The hotel was terrible, and not at all what we had been led to expect. | Our research **led** us to the **conclusion** that the present system is unfair.
6 **INFLUENCE** [T] to influence someone to make them do something that is wrong: **lead sb into sth** His brother led him into a life of crime. | He's not a bad boy. He's just easily **led** (=it is easy for other people to persuade him to do things that he should not do).

7 BE MORE SUCCESSFUL [T] to be more successful than other people, companies, or countries in a particular activity: **lead the world/market/pack/field** *US companies lead the world in biotechnology.* | **lead the way** (=be the first to do something, and show other people how to do it) *The Swedes have led the way in data protection.* → LEADING¹ (1)

8 BE WINNING [I,T] to be winning a game, competition etc; ⚡ **lose**: *At half-time, Brazil led 1–0.* | *With 15 laps to go, Schumacher led the race.* | *The polls showed Clinton leading Bush 55 percent to 34 percent.* | **lead by ten points/two goals etc** *Agassi was leading by two sets.*

9 PATH/DOOR ETC [I,T always + adv/prep] used to say where a path, wire etc goes or what place is on the other side of a door: [+to/towards] *The path led down to a small lake.* | [+from/out of] *the major artery leading from the heart* | [+into] *the door leading into the hallway* | **lead sb to/into sth** *The riverside path leads visitors to a small chapel.*

10 LIFE [T] if you lead a particular kind of life, that is what your life is like: **lead a normal/quiet/busy etc life** *If the operation succeeds, Carly will be able to lead a normal life.* | *He has **led a charmed life** (=been very fortunate).* | **lead a life of luxury/poverty etc** | **lead the life of a ...** *She now leads the life of a recluse.* | **lead a double life** (=deceive people by keeping different parts of your life separate and not letting anyone know the whole truth) *Joe had been leading a double life, seeing an ex-model while his wife believed he was on business.* | *They **lead** a nomadic **existence**.*

11 DISCUSSION ETC [T always + adv/prep] to control the way a discussion, conversation etc develops: *I tried to lead the conversation back to the subject of money.*

12 lead sb up the garden path *informal* to deliberately deceive someone

13 lead sb astray a) to encourage someone to do bad or immoral things, which they would not normally do **b)** to make someone believe something that is not true

14 lead nowhere/not lead anywhere to not produce any useful result: *So far police investigations seem to have led nowhere.*

15 lead by example to show the people you are in charge of what you want them to do by doing it yourself: *The best managers lead by example.*

16 lead sb by the nose to influence someone so much that you can completely control everything that they do: *Politicians think they can easily lead people by the nose.*

17 this/that leads (me) to sth used to introduce a new subject that is connected to the previous one: *That leads me to my final point. Where are we going to get the money?*

18 sb has their own life to lead used to say that someone wants to be able to live their life independently, without having to do things that other people want them to do

19 lead sb a merry old dance/a right old dance *BrE* to cause a lot of problems or worries for someone

20 market-led/export-led etc most influenced by the market, by EXPORTS etc: *an export-led economic recovery*

21 lead the eye if a picture, view etc leads the eye in a particular direction, it makes you look in that direction: *marble columns that lead the eye upward*

22 CARD GAME [I,T] to play a particular card as your first card in one part of a card game

lead off *phr v*
1 to start a meeting, discussion, performance etc by saying or doing something: *I'd like to lead off by thanking Rick for coming.* | [+with] *The French team led off with two quick goals in the first five minutes.* | **lead sth ⇔ off** *Hal led the evening off with some folk songs.*
2 lead off (sth) if a road, room etc leads off a place, you can go directly from that place along that road, into that room etc: **lead off from sth** *He pointed down a street leading off from the square.* | *a large room, with doors leading off it in all directions*
3 to be the first player to try to hit the ball in an INNING (=period of play) in a game of baseball

lead sb on *phr v*

to deceive someone, especially to make them think you love them: *He thought she loved him, but in fact she was just leading him on.*

lead on to sth also **lead onto sth** *phr v especially BrE*
to cause something to develop or become possible at a later time: *Alan Turing's work led onto the development of modern computers.*

lead with sth *phr v*
1 if a newspaper or television programme leads with a particular story, that story is the main one: *The Washington Post leads with the latest news from Israel.*
2 to use a particular hand to begin an attack in BOXING, or a particular foot to begin a dance: *Adam led with his left and punched his opponent on the jaw.*

lead up to sth *phr v* [not in passive]
1 if a series of events or a period of time leads up to an event, it comes before it or causes it: *the weeks that led up to her death* | *the events leading up to his dismissal*
2 to gradually introduce an embarrassing, upsetting, or surprising subject into a conversation: *She had already guessed what he was leading up to.*

lead² [S2] [W2] *n*
1 the lead the first position in a race or competition: *She **was in the lead** from start to finish.* | *The Canadians **went into the lead** after only 30 seconds.* | *The goal put Holland **into the lead**.* | *The Bears **took the lead** for the first time this season.*
2 [singular] the amount or distance by which one competitor is ahead of another: *The Chicago Bulls **had a narrow lead** (=were winning by a small number of points).* | [+over] *The Socialists now have a commanding lead over their opponents.*
3 [singular] if someone follows someone else's lead, they do the same as the other person has done: *Other countries are likely to **follow** the U.S.'s **lead**.* | *The Government should **give** industry a **lead** in tackling racism* (=show what other people should do). | *The black population in the 1960s **looked to** Ali **for a lead*** (=looked to him to show them what they should do).
4 take the lead (in doing sth) to be the first to start doing something or be most active in doing something: *The U.S. took the lead in declaring war on terrorism.*
5 [C] a piece of information that may help you to solve a crime or mystery; ⚡ **clue**: *The police have checked out dozens of leads, but have yet to find the killer.*
6 [C] the main acting part in a play, film etc, or the main actor: **play the lead/the lead role** *He will play the lead role in Hamlet.* | *Powers was **cast in the lead role*** (=he was chosen to play it). | **the male/female lead** *They were having trouble casting the female lead.* | *the film's **romantic lead***
7 lead singer/guitarist etc the main singer, GUITARIST etc in a group: [+of/with] *the lead singer of Nirvana*
8 [C] *BrE* a piece of rope, leather, or chain for holding or controlling a dog; ⚡ **leash**: **on a lead** *All dogs must be kept on a lead.*
9 [C] *BrE* a wire used to connect a piece of electrical equipment to the power supply; ⚡ **cord** *AmE* → JUMP LEADS

lead³ /led/ *n* **1** [U] a soft heavy grey metal that melts easily and is poisonous, used to cover roofs, or in the past, for water pipes. It is a chemical ELEMENT: symbol Pb **2** [C,U] the central part of a pencil that makes the marks when you write **3 go down like a lead balloon** *informal* if a suggestion or joke goes down like a lead balloon, people do not like it at all **4** [U] *AmE* old-fashioned bullets: *They filled him full of lead.* **5 leads** [plural] **a)** sheets of lead used for covering a roof **b)** narrow pieces of lead used for holding small pieces of glass together to form a window

lead·ed /ˈledɪd/ *adj* **1** leaded petrol contains lead; ⚡ **unleaded** **2** leaded windows have narrow pieces of lead separating small square or DIAMOND-shaped pieces of glass

L

---

[1] 000, [2] 000, [3] 000, most frequent words in [S] poken and [W] ritten English

leaded lights /ˌledᵻd ˈlaɪts/ n [plural] BrE leaded windows

lead·en /ˈledn/ adj **1** literary a leaden sky or sea is dark grey in colour **2** literary if your body feels leaden, you move slowly, because you are tired, unhappy etc; ◪ **heavy**: She stumbled forward, her legs leaden. **3** dull: a leaden joke **4** a leaden feeling is a feeling of great unhappiness or anxiety **5** made of lead

lead·er S3 W1 /ˈliːdə $ -ər/ n [C]
1 IN CONTROL the person who directs or controls a group, organization, country etc; → **ruler**: [+of] the leader of the local black community | **party/union/ government/opposition etc leader** | **political/military/ religious leader** | the largest ever gathering of **world leaders** (=people who are in charge of countries) | **natural/born leader** (=someone who naturally has all the qualities needed to be a leader) His air of confidence makes him a natural leader.
2 COMPETITION the person or group that is in front of all the others in a race or competition: County Championship leaders of Hampshire
3 PRODUCT/COMPANY the product or company that is the best or most successful: [+in] a world leader in defence and space electronics | These products are firmly established as the **market leaders**.
4 NEWSPAPER BrE a piece of writing in a newspaper giving the paper's opinion on a subject; ◪ **editorial**: The Times leader column
5 MUSICIAN BrE the main VIOLIN player in an ORCHESTRA; ◪ **concertmaster** AmE
6 MUSICAL DIRECTOR AmE someone who directs the playing of a musical group; ◪ **conductor** BrE
7 TAPE technical the part at the beginning of a film or recording tape which has nothing on it
8 BRANCH technical a long thin branch that grows from the stem of a bush or tree beyond other branches

lead·er·ship S3 W2 /ˈliːdəʃɪp $ -ər-/ n
1 [C,U] the position of being the leader of a group, organization, country etc: [+of] the leadership of the Conservative party | **under sb's leadership** Our prospects of winning an election will be better under his leadership. | The United States must now take a firm **leadership role**. | the Conservative **leadership contest** | The next **leadership election** is due in November.
2 [U] the quality of being good at leading a group, organization, country etc: She has great faith in her own **leadership qualities**. | someone with vision and leadership
3 [C also + plural verb BrE] all the people who lead a group, organization, country etc: the country's military leadership | The party leadership are in agreement on this matter.
4 [U] the position of being in front of others in an activity or competition: Leadership in science is important to our nation.

lead-free /ˌled ˈfriː◂ / adj lead-free petrol or paint contains no LEAD; ◪ **unleaded**

lead-in /ˈliːd ɪn/ n [C] remarks made by someone to introduce a radio or television show

lead·ing¹ W2 /ˈliːdɪŋ/ adj [only before noun]
1 best, most important, or most successful: The army **played a leading role** in organizing the attempted coup. | the leading industrial nations | a leading heart specialist | **leading members** of the government
2 leading edge a) technical the part of something that is at the front of it when it moves **b)** the part of an activity where the most modern and advanced equipment and methods are used: [+of] This is the leading edge of medical technology. → LEADING-EDGE
3 leading light a respected person who leads a group or organization, or is important in a particular area of knowledge or activity: The two women were leading lights of the women's union.
4 leading question a question that deliberately tricks

someone into giving the answer you want: Don't ask leading questions.
5 leading lady/man the woman or man who acts the most important female or male part in a film, play etc
→ LEADING ARTICLE

lead·ing² /ˈlediŋ/ n [U] technical LEAD used for covering roofs, for window frames etc

leading ar·ti·cle /ˌliːdɪŋ ˈɑːtɪkəl $ -ˈɑːr-/ n [C] BrE a piece of writing in a newspaper giving the paper's opinion on a subject; ◪ **editorial**

leading-edge /ˌliːdɪŋ ˈedʒ/ adj [only before noun] leading-edge machines, systems etc are the most modern and advanced ones available: leading-edge technologies for military and computer applications

lead-off /ˈliːd ɒf $ -ɒːf/ adj [only before noun] AmE happening or going first or before others

lead story /ˈliːd ˌstɔːri/ n [C] the most important report in a newspaper or news programme, which is put first

lead time /ˈliːd taɪm/ n [U] the time that it takes to make or produce something

lead-up /ˈliːd ʌp/ n [singular] the things that are done in the time before an important event; ◪ **run-up**: the lead-up to the election

leaf¹ S2 W2 /liːf/ n plural **leaves** /liːvz/
1 PLANT [C] one of the flat green parts of a plant that are joined to its stem or branches: a flowering bush with large shiny leaves | [+of] Add a few leaves of fresh basil to the salad. | **be in leaf/come into leaf** (=have or start growing leaves, at a particular time of year) The forest was just coming into leaf.; → see picture at ROSE¹
2 take a leaf out of sb's book to copy the way someone else behaves because you want to be like them or be as successful as they are: They are committing $3m to research. We could take a leaf out of their book.
3 turn over a new leaf to change the way you behave and become a better person: I see fatherhood as a chance to turn over a new leaf.
4 PAGE [C] formal a page of a book: He slipped the letter between the leaves of his notebook. → LOOSE-LEAF, OVERLEAF
5 PART OF TABLE [C] a part of the top of a table that can be taken out to make the table smaller → **shake like a leaf** at SHAKE¹ (2)

leaf² v
leaf through sth phr v to turn the pages of a book quickly, without reading it properly; ◪ **skim through**: She picked up the magazine and leafed through it.

leaf·less /ˈliːfləs/ adj a leafless tree or bush has no leaves on it

leaf·let¹ /ˈliːflᵻt/ n [C] a small book or piece of paper advertising something or giving information on a particular subject: [+on] a leaflet on skin cancer | **hand/ pass/give/send out a leaflet** Students were handing out election leaflets at the station.

leaflet² v [I,T] to give leaflets to people: He's leafleting the neighbourhood.

leaf mould BrE; **leaf mold** AmE n [U] dead decaying leaves that improve soil

leaf·y /ˈliːfi/ adj **1** having a lot of leaves: leafy green vegetables such as spinach **2** having a lot of trees and plants: a leafy suburb

league W2 /liːg/ n [C]
1 a group of sports teams or players who play games against each other to see who is best: He makes his football league debut tomorrow. | the Rugby League **Championship** | **be (at the) top/bottom of the league** (=be the best or the worst team in a group)
2 a group of people or countries who have joined together because they have similar aims, political beliefs etc: the National Socialist League
3 not be in the same league (as sb/sth) also **be in a different league (from sb/sth)** to be not nearly as good or important as someone or something else: They're not in the same league as the French at making wine.
4 be out of your league to not be skilled or experienced

enough to do or deal with something
5 be in league (with sb) to be working with someone secretly, especially for a bad purpose: *Vernon was accused by his enemies of being in league with the devil.*
6 an ancient unit for measuring distance, equal to 3 miles or about 4828 metres on land, and three NAUTICAL MILES or 5556 metres at sea

'league ,table n [C] *especially BrE* a list in which people, teams, or organizations are shown in order of their success or quality: *The government's school league tables are published today.*

leak¹ [S3] /liːk/ v
1 [I,T] if a container, pipe, roof etc leaks, or if it leaks gas, liquid etc, there is a small hole or crack in it that lets gas or liquid flow through: *The roof is leaking in several places.* | *A tanker is leaking oil off the coast of Scotland.*
2 [I always + adv/prep] if a gas or liquid leaks somewhere, it gets through a hole in something; ≡ **seep**: [+into/from/out] *Sea water was leaking into the batteries which powered the electric motors.*
3 [T] to deliberately give secret information to a newspaper, television company etc: *The report's findings had been leaked.* | **leak sth to sb** *civil servants who leak information to the press*
leak out phr v
if secret information leaks out, a lot of people find out about it: *No sooner had the news leaked out than my telephone started ringing.*

leak² n [C] **1** a small hole that lets liquid or gas flow into or out of something: *There is a leak in the ceiling.* | *The boat had sprung a leak* (=a hole had appeared in it). **2 a gas/oil/water etc leak** an escape of gas or liquid through a hole in something: *A gas leak caused the explosion.* **3** a situation in which secret information is deliberately given to a newspaper, television company etc: *It became evident from the leaks that something important was going on.* **4 take/have a leak** *informal* to get rid of waste liquid from your body; ≡ **urinate**

leak·age /'liːkɪdʒ/ n [C,U] **1** when gas, water etc leaks in or out, or the amount of it that has leaked **2** the deliberate spreading of secret information: *leakages of confidential information*

leak·y /'liːki/ adj a container, roof etc that is leaky has a hole or crack in it so that liquid or gas passes through it: *The house had a leaky roof.*

lean¹ [S3] /liːn/ v past tense and past participle **leaned** or **leant** /lent/ *especially BrE*
1 [I always + adv/prep] to move or bend your body in a particular direction: [+forward/back/over etc] *They were leaning forward, facing each other.* | *Lean back and enjoy the ride.* | *She leant towards him and listened.*
2 [I always + adv/prep] to support yourself in a sloping position against a wall or other surface: [+against/on] *He was leaning on the bridge, watching the boats go by.*
3 [I,T always + adv/prep] to put something in a sloping position where it is supported, or to be in that position: **lean (sth) against/on sth** *A huge mirror was leaning against the wall.* | *He leant his bicycle against the fence.*
4 [I] to slope or bend from an upright position: *trees leaning in the wind*
lean on sb phr v
1 to depend on someone for support and encouragement, especially at a difficult time: *The couple lean on each other for support.*
2 *informal* to try to influence someone, especially by

threatening them: *They won't pay unless you lean on them.*
lean towards sth phr v
to tend to support, or begin to support, a particular set of opinions, beliefs etc: *Canada, the UK and Japan leant towards the US view.*

lean² adj **1** thin in a healthy and attractive way: *He was lean, tall, and muscular.* → see box at THIN¹ **2** lean meat does not have much fat on it; ≡ **fatty 3** a lean organization, company etc uses only as much money and as many people as it needs, so that nothing is wasted **4** a lean period is a very difficult time because there is not enough money, business etc: *His wife was a source of constant support during the lean years.* —**leanness** n [U]

lean·ing /'liːnɪŋ/ n [C] a tendency to prefer or agree with a particular set of beliefs, opinions etc; ≡ **inclination**: *his radical political leanings* | [+towards] *a leaning towards the Right*

leant /lent/ v a past tense and past participle of LEAN

'lean-to n [C] a small roughly-made building that is built against the side of a larger building

leap¹ /liːp/ v past tense and past participle **leapt** /lept/ *especially BrE*, **leaped** *especially AmE*
1 [JUMP] **a)** [I always + adv/prep] to jump high into the air or to jump in order to land in a different place: *She leapt over the fence.* | *The smaller animals can easily leap from tree to tree.* → see picture at JUMP¹ **b)** [T] *literary* to jump over something: *Brenda leaped the gate and ran across the field.*
2 [MOVE FAST] [I always + adv/prep] to move very quickly and with a lot of energy: *I leapt up the stairs three at a time.* | *He leapt out of bed.* | *She leapt to her feet* (=stood up quickly) *and started shouting.*
3 [INCREASE] [I] to increase quickly and by a large amount; ≡ **tumble**: [+to] *Profits leapt to £376m.* | *He leapt 27 places to second spot.*
4 leap at the chance/opportunity to accept an opportunity very eagerly: *I leapt at the chance of studying art in Paris.*
5 leap to sb's defence *BrE*; **leap to sb's defense** *AmE* to quickly defend someone: *When her younger brother was being bullied she leapt to his defence.*
6 [HEART] [I] *literary* if your heart leaps, you feel a sudden surprise, happiness, or excitement: *My heart leaped when I saw Paul at the airport.* → **look before you leap** at LOOK¹ (12)
leap out at sb phr v
if a word or phrase in a piece of writing leaps out at you, you notice it particularly, because it is interesting, important etc; ≡ **jump out at**

leap² n [C] **1** a big jump; ≡ **bound**: *He threw a stick into the river and the dog went after it in a flying leap.* **2** a large increase or change: **quantum/great/huge etc leap** *a quantum leap* (=very great increase or change) *in population levels* | [+in] *a 16% leap in pre-tax profits* | [+forward] *the huge leap forward that took place in the 1980s* **3 by/in leaps and bounds** if something increases, develops, grows etc by leaps and bounds, it does it very quickly: *Lifeboat technology has advanced by leaps and bounds.* **4 a leap of (the) imagination** also **an imaginative leap** a mental process that is needed to understand something difficult or see the connection between two very different ideas **5 leap in the dark** something you do without knowing what will happen as a result **6 leap of faith** something you do even though it involves a risk, hoping that it will have a good result

leap·frog¹ /'liːpfrɒg $ -frɔːg, -frɑːg/ n [U] a children's game in which someone bends over and someone else jumps over them

leapfrog² v **leapfrogged**, **leapfrogging** [I,T] to suddenly become better, more advanced etc than people or organizations that were previously better than you: *The company leapfrogged its rivals into a leading position.*

leapt /lept/ v a past tense and past participle of LEAP

leap year n [C] a year, which happens every fourth year, when February has 29 days instead of 28

learn S1 W1 /lɜːn $ lɜːrn/ v past tense and past participle **learned** or **learnt** /lɜːnt $ lɜːrnt/ especially BrE
1 SUBJECT/SKILL [I,T] to gain knowledge of a subject or skill, by experience, by studying it, or by being taught; → **teach**: *What's the best way to learn a language?* | **learn (how) to do sth** *I learnt to drive when I was 17.* | *Hector spent the winter learning how to cope with his blindness.* | *The teacher's task is to help the pupil learn.* | **learn (sth) from sb** *I learned a lot from my father.* | [+about] *Kids can have fun and learn about music at the same time.* | **learn what** *Youngsters must learn what is dangerous and what is not to be feared.* | *The student will **learn from experience** about the importance of planning.* ⚠ Do not say that you 'learn someone something' or 'learn someone how to do something'. Use **teach**: *I taught him how to send an e-mail.*
2 FIND OUT [I,T] formal to find out information or news by hearing it from someone else or reading it; ⊟ **discover**: *I didn't tell her the truth. She would learn it for herself soon enough.* | [+of/about] *He learned about his appointment by telephone yesterday.* | **learn (that)** *Last week I learned that I was pregnant.* | *She was surprised to learn that he was a lot older than she had thought.* | **learn whether/who/why** *I waited to learn whether I'd secured a college place.* | *We have yet to learn who will be the new manager.*
3 REMEMBER [T] to get to know something so well that you can easily remember it; ⊟ **memorize**: *The actors hardly had time to learn their lines before filming started.*
4 CHANGE YOUR BEHAVIOUR [I,T] to gradually understand a situation and start behaving in the way that you should: **learn (that)** *They have to learn that they can't just do whatever they like.* | **learn to do sth** *Young hairdressers must learn to treat the client as a person, not a head of hair.* | *I've told him a hundred times not to bully people, but he **never learns**.* | [+from] *You have to **learn from** your mistakes (=understand why what you did was wrong).* | *the **lessons learned** in the Gulf War*
5 sb has learned their lesson used to say that someone will not do something wrong or stupid again, because they suffered as a result: *I've learned my lesson; I've now got a burglar alarm and a guard dog.*
6 learn (sth) the hard way to understand a situation or develop a skill by learning from your mistakes and bad experiences
7 that'll learn sb! spoken used when something bad has just happened to someone as a result of their actions, especially when they ignored a warning → **live and learn** at LIVE[1] (20)

This graph shows how common the different grammar patterns of the verb **learn** are.

learn sth			
learn to do sth			
learn			
learn (that)			
learn from sb/sth			
learn why/what/how etc			
learn about sth			
other			

10% 20% 30% 40%

learn·ed /ˈlɜːnɪd $ ˈlɜːr-/ adj formal **1** a learned person has a lot of knowledge because they have read

and studied a lot: *a learned professor* **2 learned books/works etc** books etc that are written by people who have a lot of knowledge: *learned works on natural history* —**learnedly** adv

learn·er /ˈlɜːnə $ ˈlɜːrnər/ n [C]
1 someone who is learning to do something

slow learner (=someone who learns things slowly)
quick/fast learner (=someone who learns things quickly)
adult learner
young learner
advanced learner (=someone who has been learning something for a long time)
language learner

[+of] *a new dictionary for learners of business English* | *the needs of **slow learners*** | *attractive grammar books for **adult learners***

2 also **learner driver** BrE someone who is learning to drive a car

learner's ˌpermit n [C] AmE an official document that gives you permission to learn to drive; ⊟ **provisional licence** BrE

learn·ing S3 W2 /ˈlɜːnɪŋ $ ˈlɜːr-/ n [U] knowledge gained through reading and study: *a man of great learning*

learning curve n [C] the rate at which you learn a new skill: *Everyone in the centre has been through a very **steep learning curve** (=they had to learn very quickly).*

learning ˌdifficulties n [plural] a mental problem that affects someone's ability to learn: *a school for children with learning difficulties*

learning disaˌbility n [C,U] a mental problem that affects someone's ability to learn

learnt /lɜːnt $ lɜːrnt/ v a past tense and past participle of LEARN

lease[1] W3 /liːs/ n [C]
1 a legal agreement which allows you to use a building, car etc for a period of time, in return for rent

take out a lease (=start having a lease)
renew a lease (=start having a lease again after it has finished)
a lease expires/runs out (=a lease stops)
the terms of a lease (=the legal details in a lease)
a long lease
a short lease

[+on] *They **took out a lease** on a seven-acre field.* | *The landlord refused to **renew** his **lease**.* | *The 99-year **lease expired** in 1999.* | *Do you understand all **the terms of the lease**?*

2 a new lease of life especially BrE; **a new lease on life** AmE **a)** if something has a new lease of life, it is changed or repaired so that it can continue: *Historic buildings can have a new lease of life through conversion.* **b)** if someone has a new lease of life, they become healthy, active, or happy again after being weak, ill, or tired: *an operation to give her a new lease of life*

lease[2] v [T] **1** to use a building, car etc under a lease: *I'm interested in leasing your cottage.* | **lease sth from sb** *They lease the site from the council.* **2** also **lease out** to let someone use a building, car etc under a lease: **lease sth to sb** *The building was leased to a health club.*; → see box at RENT[1]

lease·back /ˈliːsbæk/ n [C,U] technical an arrangement in which you sell or give something to someone, but continue to use it by paying them rent

lease·hold /ˈliːshəʊld $ -hoʊld/ adj especially BrE leasehold property is property that you will own only for the period of time stated in a lease; → **freehold** —**leasehold** adv

lease·hold·er /ˈliːshəʊldə $ -hoʊldər/ n [C] someone who lives in a leasehold house, apartment etc

leash[1] /liːʃ/ n [C] especially AmE **1** a piece of rope, leather etc fastened to a dog's collar in order to control it; ⊟ **lead** BrE: **on/off a leash** *At her side on a leash* trotted a small grey dog. | *Never leave your dog off the leash outside a store.* **2 keep/have sb on a leash** to control someone – used humorously: *Marcus keeps you on a short leash, does he?*

leash² v [T] *AmE* to put a leash on a dog

least¹ S1 W1 /liːst/ *determiner, pron*
1 at least a) not less than a particular number or amount: *It will take you at least 20 minutes to get there.* | *He had at least £100,000 in savings.* | **at the (very) least** (=not less than and probably much more than) *It would cost $1 million at the very least.* **b)** even if something better is not true or is not done: *At least he didn't lie to me.* | *I don't expect you to pay me, but you could at least cover my expenses.* | *The house still needed a lot of work, but at least the kitchen was finished.* **c)** used when you are correcting or changing something that you have just said: *They all knew I was on their side. At least, that's what they said.* | *I made everything perfectly clear – or at least I thought I did.*
2 at the (very) least used when mentioning the least extreme thing that happens, is needed etc: *Computer viruses are at the very least annoying and often actually destructive.*
3 the least a) the smallest amount: *Women work in those sectors of the job market which pay the least.* | *Which method causes the least damage to the environment?* **b)** used to emphasize how small something is, especially when it hardly exists at all: *I haven't the least idea what you are talking about.* | *He used to wake at the least noise.* **c)** used when you are saying what someone should do in a situation, and suggesting that they should really do more: *The least you could do is give me her phone number.* | *The least they could have given her is some money towards the rent.*
4 not the least/not in the least/not the least bit none at all, or not at all: *I tried to convince them, but they weren't the least interested.* | *I'm not in the least afraid of you any more.* | *His voice was alert, not the least bit sleepy.*
5 to say the least used to show that something is worse or more serious than you are actually saying: *His teaching methods were strange, to say the least.*
6 the least of sb's worries/problems/troubles/concerns something that someone is not worried about because there are other more important problems: *What I looked like was the least of my problems.*
7 it's the least I can do *spoken* used to say that you are very willing to do something or to reply to someone's thanks: *I'll look after them – it's the least I can do.* → **last but not least** at LAST² (3)

least² adv **1** less than anyone or anyone else; OPP **most**: *The journey would impose extra expense on those least able to afford it.* | *It is quite amazing what turns up when you are least expecting it.* | *He's my least favourite member of staff.* **2 least of all** especially not a particular person or thing: *She hardly ever lost her temper – least of all with Anne.* **3 not least** *formal* used to emphasize that something is important: *My mother was upset about his appearance here, not least because she felt it was invading her privacy.*

least-ways /'liːstweɪz/ also **least-wise** /-waɪz/ adv *informal* at least; **F anyway**: *There's no way to cross the mountains, leastways at this time of the year.*

leath-er W3 /'leðə $ -ər/ n
1 [U] animal skin that has been treated to preserve it, and is used for making shoes, bags etc: *The inside of the bag was lined with soft leather.* | *elegant leather boots* → see picture at MATERIAL¹
2 leathers [plural] special leather clothes worn for protection by someone riding a MOTORCYCLE → **run/go hell for leather** at HELL¹ (27)

leath-er-ette /,leðə'ret/ n [U] a cheap material made to look like leather; **F naugahyde** *AmE*

leath-er-y /'leðəri/ adj hard and stiff like leather, rather than soft or smooth: *her leathery brown skin*

leave¹ S1 W1 /liːv/ v past tense and past participle **left** /left/
1 GO AWAY [I,T] to go away from a place or a person:

My baby gets upset when I leave the room. | *Before leaving the train, make sure you have all your belongings with you.* | *Leave the motorway at Junction 7.* | [+at] *The plane leaves at 12.30.* | [+for] *I tried calling him, but he'd already left for work.* | **leave (sth/sb) soon/now/later etc** *If he left immediately, he'd catch the 7.30 train.* | **leave (sth/sb) to do sth** *Frances left work early to meet her mother.* | **leave sb doing sth** *Never leave children playing near water unattended.* | **leave sb to sth** *I'll leave you to it* (=go away and let you continue with what you are doing). | *My youngest boy has not left my side* (=has stayed near me) *since his daddy was killed.* | **leave sb in peace** (=go away from someone so that they can think, work etc alone) *Just a few more questions, then we'll leave you in peace.*
2 STOP [I,T] if you leave your job, home, school etc, you permanently stop doing that job, living at home etc: *Over the past two years, 20 staffers have left.* | **leave home/school/college etc** *How old were you when you left home* (=your parents' home)? | *My daughter got a job after she left school.* | *The lawsuit will be postponed until the president leaves office.* | **leave a job/country/Spain etc** *Many missionaries were forced to leave the country.* | *It seems that Tony has left the band for good* (=permanently). | **leave (sb/sth) to do sth** *Laura left her native England to live in France.*
3 leave sb/sth alone a) to stop annoying or upsetting someone: *Oh, just leave me alone, will you?* | *Leave the boy alone, he can make up his own mind.* **b)** to go away from someone so that they are on their own: *Six-year-old Gemma had been left alone in the house.* **c)** to stop touching something: *Leave that alone. You'll break it.* **d)** also **leave well (enough) alone** to stop being involved in or trying to change a situation: *Why can't they just leave well alone and let us concentrate on teaching?*
4 LET STH/SB STAY [T always + adv/prep] to make or allow something or someone to stay in a place when you go away: **leave sth/sb in/with/behind etc** *Are you leaving the kids with Grandma on Saturday?* | *As soon as I'd shut the door, I realized I'd left the keys inside.* | *Did anybody leave a jacket behind last night?* | *She left her son in the care of a friend.* | **leave sb to do sth** *He left Ruth to find her own way home.* | *Students were left to their own devices* (=left alone and allowed to do whatever they wanted) *for long periods.* | **leave sb for dead** *The girl had been attacked and left for dead.*
5 NOT CHANGE/MOVE STH [T] to let something remain in a particular state, position, or condition: **leave sth on/off/out etc** *You've left your lights on.* | *She must have left the phone off the hook.* | **leave sth open/empty/untidy etc** *I wish you'd stop leaving the door open.* | *The trial left many questions unanswered.* | **leave a space/gap etc** *Leave the next two lines blank for the tutor's comments.* | *Drivers should always leave room for cyclists.* | **leave sth doing sth** *I'll just leave the engine running while I go in.* | *Don't leave tools lying about.* | **leave sth to do sth** *Leave the pots to soak overnight.*
6 RESULT OF ACCIDENT/ILLNESS/EVENT [T] if an event, accident, illness etc leaves you in a particular condition, you are in that condition because of it: *An explosion at a chemical plant has left one worker dead and four injured.* | **leave sb with sth** *Although the infection cleared up, he was left with a persistent cough.* | **leave sb doing sth** *The incident left her feeling confused and hurt.* | *The announcement has left shareholders nursing huge losses.*
7 be left also **have sth left** if something is left, it remains after everything else has gone, been taken away, or used: *I've only got a few dollars left.* | *There were a couple of seats left at the back.* | *We don't have much time left.* | *He pointed to what was left of the house* (=used when very little is left). | *All that was left was a pile of bones.* | [+over] *After we've paid the bills, there's never much left over.* | *They ate some bread rolls*

L

left over from the night before.

8 LETTER/MESSAGE/THING [T] to deliver a message, note, package etc for someone or put it somewhere so that they will get it later: *She left a message on his answerphone.* | **leave sb sth** *Can you leave me some money for the bus?* | **leave sth with sb** *Ian left this note with me.* | **leave sth for sb** *A guy left these flowers for you.*

9 DELAY [T] to not do something or to do it later than you intended: *Leave the dishes. I'll do them later.* | *So much had been **left undone**.* | **leave sth until the last minute/until last** *If you leave your preparation until the last minute, you'll reduce your chances of passing.* | *I left the best bit until last.* | *I want to think about it. Can I **leave it for now**?* | *I'm afraid you've **left it too late** to change your ticket.* | **leave it at that** (=used to say that you will not do any more of something, because you have done enough) *Let's leave it at that for today.*

10 LET SB DECIDE/BE RESPONSIBLE [T] to let someone else decide something or be responsible for something: **leave sth to sb** *Leave it to me. I'll make sure it gets posted.* | *The choice of specialist subject is left entirely to the students.* | **leave it (up) to sb to do sth** *I'll leave it up to you to decide.* | *She leaves it to the reader to draw their own conclusions.* | **leave doing sth to sb** *Is it okay if I leave writing the results to you?* | **leave sth with sb** *I'll fix it for you.* | *He's not the sort to **leave** things **to chance** (=take no action and just wait to see what happens).* | **leave sb with no choice/option** (=force someone to take a particular action) *You leave me with no choice but to fire you.* | **leave sb to do sth** *BrE: Clive moved to London, leaving Edward to run the Manchester office.*

11 HUSBAND/WIFE ETC [I,T] to stop living with or having a relationship with your husband, partner etc: *Martha was always threatening to leave, but I never believed her.* | **leave sb for sb** *Mr Rushworth left his partner of 10 years for a younger woman.*

12 WHEN YOU DIE [T] **a)** to arrange for someone to receive your money, property, etc after you die; ⊟ **bequeath:** *Aunt Alice died, leaving almost $5 million.* | **leave sb sth** *Hugo left me his mother's ring.* | *In his will, he had left all his children a small sum of money.* | **leave sth to sb/sth** *Have you thought of **leaving** a gift **to charity** after you die?* **b)** *leave a wife/children etc* used when someone dies before their wife, children etc: *PC Davis leaves a wife and three small children.*

13 MARK [T] to make a mark that remains afterwards: **leave a mark/stain/scar etc** *The wine had left a permanent mark on the tablecloth.* | *He staggered to the door, **leaving a trail** of blood.* | *Make sure that you don't leave any footprints.*

14 NOT EAT/DRINK [T] if you leave food or drink that you have been given, you do not eat or drink it: *'I'm really hungry now.' 'That's because you left half your lunch.'* | *He rose from the table, **leaving** his brandy **untouched**.*

15 leave sb/sth standing also **leave sb/sth in the dust** *AmE informal* to be much better, quicker, more successful etc than someone or something else: *In terms of fitness, he discovered that Kate left him standing.*

16 leave a lot/something/much to be desired to be very unsatisfactory: *Inspectors say health and safety procedures at the factory leave a lot to be desired.*

17 MATHEMATICS [T] in a sum, to have a particular amount remaining: *Three from seven leaves four.*

18 leave sth aside/to one side to not think about or consider one part of something for a time, so that you can consider another part of it: *Leaving aside for a moment the question of expense, what would your view be of the suggested changes?*

19 leave sb/sth be *old-fashioned* to not upset, speak to, or annoy someone or to not touch something

20 leave go/hold of sth *BrE spoken informal* to stop holding something

21 leave it to sb (to do sth) *AmE spoken informal* used to say that no one should be surprised that someone does

something, because it is typical or expected of them: *Leave it to you to have the whole day planned out!* → **sb can take it or leave it** at TAKE¹ (21); → **be left holding the baby/bag** at HOLD¹ (26)

leave sb/sth ⇔ behind *phr v*

1 to not take someone or something with you when you leave a place: *I think I might have left my wallet behind.* | *He departed for Washington, leaving the children behind with their mother.*

2 if a person, country, or organization is left behind, they do not develop as quickly or make as much progress as other people, countries etc: *In class, a child with poor eyesight can soon get left behind.* | *a fear of being left behind by better-organized rivals*

3 also **leave sb/sth behind you** to permanently stop being involved with a place, person, or situation: *It's time to **leave the past behind**.* | *Although Armstrong overcame the circumstances of his birth, he never really left New Orleans behind.*

4 also **leave sb/sth behind you** to move away from someone or something: *They had left the city behind and were heading into open country.* | *Sarah, with her long legs, soon **left** the rest of us **far behind**.*

5 also **leave sth behind you** to produce a thing or situation that remains after you have gone: *He drove off, leaving behind him a trail of blue smoke.* | *the mess the previous government left behind*

leave off *phr v*

1 to stop doing something: **take up/pick up/continue (sth) etc where sb left off** (=continue something that has stopped for a short time) *Barry took up the story where Justine had left off.* | **leave off doing sth** *BrE informal: 'Will you leave off nagging?' he snarled.*

2 leave sb/sth off (sth) to not include something such as someone's name in a list or other document: *Why was her name left off the list?*

leave sb/sth ⇔ out *phr v*

1 to not include someone or something: *She outlined the case to him, being careful not to leave anything out.* | **leave sb/sth out of sth** *Kidd has been left out of the team.*

2 be/feel left out to feel that you are not accepted or welcome in a situation: *New fathers often feel left out when baby arrives.*

3 leave it out! *BrE spoken* used to tell someone to stop lying, pretending, or being annoying

leave² S3 W2 *n*

1 HOLIDAY [U] time that you are allowed to spend away from your work, especially in the armed forces: *I've applied for three days' leave.* | **on leave** *navy officers home on leave* | *Your basic **annual leave** is 20 days.*

2 *maternity/sick/compassionate leave* time that you are allowed to spend away from work because you have had a baby, because you are ill, or because of a personal problem such as the death of a relative

3 leave of absence a period of time that you are allowed to spend away from work for a particular purpose: *She's been given leave of absence to attend a computer course.*

4 PERMISSION [U] *formal* permission to do something: *All this was done entirely without my leave.* | **leave to do sth** *a petition for leave to appeal to the European court* | **grant/obtain/ask/seek etc leave (to do sth)** *He asked leave to speak to her in private.*

5 without so much as a by your leave *old-fashioned* without asking permission, in a way that seems very rude: *He marched into my office without so much as a by your leave.*

6 take leave of your senses to suddenly start behaving in a strange way: *You want to marry him? Have you taken leave of your senses?*

7 take leave of sb/take your leave *formal* to say goodbye to someone

leav·en¹ /ˈlevən/ also **leav·en·ing** /ˈlevənɪŋ/ *n* **1** [U] *technical* a substance, especially YEAST, that is added to a mixture of flour and water so that it will swell and can be baked into bread; → **unleavened**   **2** [singular, U] *literary* something that makes an event or situation less boring, serious, or sad

leaven² *v* [T] *formal* to make something less boring, serious, or sad

leaves /liːvz/ *n* the plural of LEAF

leave-taking *n* [C] *literary* an act of saying goodbye when you go away

leav·ings /ˈliːvɪŋz/ *n* [plural] *old-fashioned* things that are left because people do not want them

lech, **letch** /letʃ/ *v*

  lech after/over sb *phr v BrE informal* to show sexual desire for someone in a way that is unpleasant or annoying: *a middle-aged man leching after young girls*

lech·er /ˈletʃə $ -ər/ *n* [C] a man who shows his sexual desire for women in a way that is unpleasant or annoying

lech·er·ous /ˈletʃərəs/ *adj* a lecherous man shows his sexual desire for women in a way that is unpleasant or annoying: *a lecherous old man* —**lecherously** *adv*

lech·er·y /ˈletʃəri/ *n* [U] *old-fashioned* sexual desire or pleasure that is considered bad because it is not part of a romantic relationship: *There was a hint of lechery in his eyes.*

lec·tern /ˈlektən $ -ərn/ *n* [C] an object with a sloping surface that you put an open book or notes on while you are speaking to people in public

lec·ture¹ S3 W3 /ˈlektʃə $ -ər/ *n* [C]
1 a long talk on a particular subject that someone gives to a group of people, especially to students in a university; → **speech**: [+on/about] *a lecture on medieval art* | *a series of lectures about the British legal system* | *give/deliver a lecture He regularly gives lectures on modern French literature.* | **go to/attend a lecture** *Very few students ever attended his lectures.* | **lecture hall/theatre/room**
2 an act of criticizing someone or warning them about something in a long, serious talk, in a way that they think is unfair or unnecessary: [+on/about] *My father caught me and gave me a long lecture about the dangers of drink.*

lecture² *v* **1** [T] to talk angrily or seriously to someone in order to criticize or warn them, in a way that they think is unfair or unnecessary: *I wish you'd stop lecturing me!* | **lecture sb about/on sth** *He began to lecture us about making too much noise.* **2** [I] to talk to a group of people on a particular subject, especially to students in a university: [+on] *He lectures on European art at Manchester University.*

lec·tur·er /ˈlektʃərə $ -ər/ *n* [C] **a)** someone who gives lectures, especially in a university: *She's a brilliant lecturer.* **b)** a teacher in a British university or college: [+in] *a lecturer in medieval studies at Edinburgh University*; → see box at TEACHER

lec·ture·ship /ˈlektʃəʃɪp $ -ər-/ *n* [C] a teaching job at a university or college in Britain, in which you give lectures to students: [+in] *He was offered a lectureship in mathematics at Bristol University.*

led /led/ *v* the past tense and past participle of LEAD¹

-led /led/ *suffix* [in adjectives] having a particular thing as the most important cause or influence: *an export-led economic recovery*

ledge /ledʒ/ *n* [C] **1** a narrow flat piece of rock that sticks out on the side of a mountain or cliff: *We crept carefully along the narrow ledge.* | *He leapt onto a ledge of rock.* **2** a narrow shelf: *There's some money on the window ledge (=narrow shelf below the window).*

led·ger /ˈledʒə $ -ər/ *n* [C] a book in which a business, bank etc records how much money it receives and spends

ledger line *n* [C] a line on which you write musical notes that are too high or low to be shown on a STAVE

lee /liː/ *n* **1** **in/under the lee of sth** next to something, and protected from the wind by that thing: *We sat in the lee of a tall hedge.* **2 the lees** *technical* the thick substance that collects at the bottom of a bottle of wine

leech /liːtʃ/ *n* [C] **1** a small soft creature that fixes itself to the skin of animals in order to drink their blood **2** someone who takes advantage of other people by taking their money, food etc: *The family began to see him as a leech.*

leek /liːk/ *n* [C] a vegetable with a long white stem and long flat green leaves, which tastes like an onion → see picture at VEGETABLE¹

leer /lɪə $ lɪr/ *v* [I] to look at someone in an unpleasant way that shows that you think they are sexually attractive: [+at] *She was sick of old men leering at her.* —**leer** *n* [C]

leer·y /ˈlɪəri $ ˈlɪri/ *adj informal* careful in the way that you deal with something or someone because you do not trust them; ◨ **wary**: [+of] *I was very leery of him after I found out he had lied to Jennifer.*

lee·ward /ˈliːwəd, ˈluːəd $ -ərd/ *adj, adv* **1** the leeward side of something is the side that is sheltered from the wind; ◨ **windward**: *We camped on the leeward side of the mountain.* **2** *technical* a leeward direction is the same direction as the wind is blowing; ◨ **windward**: **to leeward** (=in a leeward direction) *The ship cruised slowly to leeward.*

lee·way /ˈliːweɪ/ *n* [U] **1** freedom to do things in the way you want to: [+in] *The government does not have much leeway in foreign policy.* | **leeway to do sth** *Try to give teenagers more leeway to make their own decisions.* **2 make up leeway** *BrE* if you have to make up leeway, you have to do extra work because you have not done as much work as you should have done: *We've got quite a lot of leeway to make up.*

left¹ S1 W1 /left/ *adj* [only before noun]
1 your left side is the side of your body that contains your heart; ◨ **right**: *She held out her left hand.* | *a scar on the left side of his face*
2 on the same side of something as your left side; ◨ **right**: *Take the next left turn.* | *the left bank of the river* | *a pile of papers on the left side of the desk*
3 have two left feet *informal* to move in an awkward way when you are running or doing a sport: *a tall, clumsy-looking boy with two left feet*
4 the left hand doesn't know what the right hand is doing used to say that one part of a group or organization does not know what the other parts are doing

left² *adv* towards the direction or side that is on the left; ◨ **right**: *Turn left just after the school.*

left³ *n* **1 the left/sb's left** the side of your body that contains your heart; ◨ **right**: **on/to the left (of sth)** *Take the next road on the left.* | *Our house is just to the left of the school.* | **on/to sb's left** *On your left you can see the Houses of Parliament.* **2 (from) left to right** from the left side to the right side of something: *The photo shows, from left to right, his daughters Molly, Fiona, and Anne.* **3 the left/the Left** political parties and groups that support the ideas and beliefs of SOCIALISM. They usually want large industries to be owned by the state, and to use taxes to help solve social problems; ◨ **right**: *He has support from the Left.* | *politicians on the left of the party* | *The party is moving further to the left.* **4** [C] a hit made with your left hand; ◨ **right 5 take a left** also **hang a left** *AmE* to turn left: *Take the next left (=turn left at the next road).*

left⁴ *v* the past tense and past participle of LEAVE¹

left field *n* [U] **1** a position in baseball in the left side of the OUTFIELD; → **right field 2 out of/from left field** *informal* something that comes out of left field is unexpected: *People don't know how to react when a question like that comes at them out of left field.*

left-hand *adj* [only before noun] on the left side of something; ◨ **right-hand**: *We live about halfway down the street on the left-hand side.*

left-hand drive *adj* a left-hand drive vehicle is one in which the driver sits on the left; → **right-hand drive**

left-handed *adj* **1** a left-handed person uses their left hand for writing, throwing etc; ◨ **right-handed**

L

2 [only before noun] left-handed tools have been made for left-handed people to use: *left-handed scissors* **3 left-handed compliment** *AmE* a statement that seems to express admiration or praise, but at the same time is insulting; ☒ **backhanded compliment** *BrE*

,**left-'hander** *n* [C] someone who uses their left hand for writing, throwing etc; ☒ **right-hander**

left·ie /'lefti/ *n* another spelling of LEFTY

left·ist /'leftᵻst/ *adj* supporting LEFT-WING ideas or groups; ☒ **rightist**: *a coalition of leftist parties* —**leftist** *n* [C]: *a group of radical leftists*

,**left 'luggage ,office** *n* [C] *BrE* a place in a station, airport etc where you can pay to leave your bags and collect them later

,**left-of-cen·tre** *BrE*; **left-of-center** *AmE adj* supporting ideas and aims that are between the centre and the left in politics; ☒ **right-of-centre**: *a modern left-of-centre party with wide appeal*

left·o·ver¹ /'leftəʊvə $ -oʊvər/ *adj* [only before noun] remaining after all the rest has been used, taken, or eaten: *leftover vegetables* | *a few pieces of leftover carpet*

leftover² *n* **1 leftovers** [plural] food that has not been eaten at the end of a meal: *Give the leftovers to the dog.* **2** [singular] something from an earlier time that still remains, even though it is not really useful or important any more; ☒ **hangover**: [+from] *The headmaster was a leftover from the Victorian era.*

left·wards /'leftwədz $ -wərdz/ *especially BrE*; **leftward** /-wəd $ -wərd/ *AmE adv* on or towards the left; ☒ **rightwards**: *Follow the path leftwards.* —**leftward** *adj*

,**left-'wing** *adj* a left-wing person or group supports the political aims of groups such as SOCIALISTS and COMMUNISTS; ☒ **right-wing**: *a left-wing newspaper* | *a left-wing political organization.* | *She's got very left-wing views.* —**left wing** *n* [singular]: *the left wing of the Labour party* —**left-winger** *n* [C]: *She is supported by left-wingers in the party.*

left·y, leftie /'lefti/ *n plural* **lefties** [C] **1** *informal especially BrE* someone who has left-wing political ideas – used to show disapproval,: *a group of liberals and lefties* **2** *informal especially AmE* someone who uses their left hand for writing, throwing etc —**lefty** *adj*: *I don't get on with his lefty friends.*

leg¹ ⟨S1⟩ ⟨W1⟩ /leg/ *n*
1 BODY PART [C] one of the long parts of your body that your feet are joined to, or a similar part on an animal or insect: *a young boy with skinny legs* | *She fell and broke her leg.* | **four-legged/long-legged etc** *four-legged animals*
2 MEAT [C,U] the leg of an animal when it is cooked and eaten as food: *roast leg of lamb*
3 FURNITURE [C] one of the upright parts that support a piece of furniture: *One of the legs on the table was a bit wobbly.* | *a chair leg* | *a three-legged stool*
4 CLOTHING [C] the part of your trousers that covers your leg: *The legs of my jeans were covered in mud.* | *He rolled up his trouser legs and waded out into the stream.*
5 JOURNEY/RACE [C] one part of a long journey or race: [+of] *the final leg of the Tour de France*
6 SPORT [C] *BrE* one of the series of games in a football competition played between two teams: *Leeds will have to win the second leg if they are to go forward to the finals.*
7 not have a leg to stand on *informal* to be in a situation where you cannot prove or legally support what you say: *If you didn't sign a contract, you won't have a leg to stand on.*
8 get your leg over *BrE informal not polite* to have sex with someone
9 have legs *AmE informal* if a piece of news has legs, people continue to be interested in it and talk about it → **on its last legs** at LAST¹ (9); → **on your last legs** at LAST¹ (8); → **pull sb's leg** at PULL¹ (11); → LEG-PULL, LEG-UP, PEG LEG,

SEA LEGS; → **shake a leg** at SHAKE¹ (9); → **show a leg** at SHOW¹ (23); → **stretch your legs** at STRETCH¹ (7)

leg² *v* **legged, legging** *BrE informal* **leg it** to run in order to escape from someone or something: *We saw him coming, and legged it out of the house.*

leg·a·cy /'legəsi/ *n plural* **legacies** [C] **1** something that happens or exists as a result of something that happened at an earlier time: [+of] *The invasion left a legacy of hatred and fear.* | [+from] *a legacy from the colonial period* **2** money or property that you receive from someone after they die; ☒ **inheritance**: *She received a small legacy from her aunt.*

le·gal ⟨S3⟩ ⟨W1⟩ /'liːgəl/ *adj*
1 if something is legal, you are allowed to do it or have to do it by law; ☒ **illegal**: *What the company has done is perfectly legal.* | *plans to make the carrying of identity cards a legal requirement* | *He had twice the legal limit of alcohol in his bloodstream.* | *a pressure group that is campaigning to make cannabis legal.*
2 [only before noun] concerned with or relating to the law: *free legal advice* | *a costly legal dispute* | *the Scottish legal system* | **the legal profession** (=lawyers)
3 legal action/proceedings the use of the legal system to settle an argument, put right an unfair situation etc: *She threatened to take legal action against the hospital.* → LEGALLY

,**legal 'aid** *n* [U] a system in which a government gives money to people who need a lawyer but cannot afford to pay for one: *They have been granted legal aid and now intend to take their case to court.*

le·gal·ese /,liːgəl'iːz/ *n* [U] *informal* language used by lawyers that is difficult for most people to understand

,**legal 'holiday** *n* [C] *AmE* an official holiday on which most government offices and banks are closed; ☒ **bank holiday** *BrE*

le·gal·ise /'liːgəlaɪz/ *v* a British spelling of LEGALIZE

le·gal·ist·ic /,liːgə'lɪstɪk◂/ *adj* too concerned about small legal details: *a legalistic interpretation of the agreement*

le·gal·i·ty /lɪ'gæləti/ *n* **1** [U] the fact of being allowed by law: [+of] *Several ministers have questioned the legality of the ban.* **2 legalities** [plural] the formal, legal parts of an agreement: *We've sold the house and are just waiting to complete all the legalities.*

le·gal·ize also -ise *BrE* /'liːgəlaɪz/ *v* [T] to make something legal so that people are allowed to do it; ☒ **criminalize**: *Abortion was legalized in the 1960s.* —**legalization** /,liːgəlaɪˈzeɪʃən $ -lə-/ *n* [U]: *a campaign calling for the legalization of certain drugs*

le·gal·ly /'liːgəli/ *adv* **1** according to the law: *They are still legally married.* | *Which of them is legally responsible for the accident?* | *a legally binding agreement* **2** if you can do something legally, you are allowed to do it by law; ☒ **illegally**: *The station can now broadcast legally.*

'**legal pad** *n* [C] a book containing sheets of yellow writing paper with lines on it, of a type sold in the US

'**legal ,system** *n* [C] the laws and the way they work in a particular country: *the British legal system*

,**legal 'tender** *n* [U] coins or bank notes that people can officially use as money in a particular country

leg·ate /'legᵻt/ *n* [C] an important official representative, especially an official representative of the POPE

leg·a·tee /,legə'tiː/ *n* [C] *law* someone who receives money or property from a person who has died

le·ga·tion /lɪ'geɪʃən/ *n* [C] **1** a group of government officials who work in a foreign country and represent their own government in that country: *a member of the British legation in Peking* **2** the building or office where a legation works

le·ga·to /lɪ'gɑːtəʊ $ -toʊ/ *adj, adv technical* music that is played legato is played very smoothly, so that each note connects to the next one without a pause

le·gend /'ledʒənd/ *n* **1** [C,U] an old, well-known story, often about brave people, adventures, or magical events; → **myth**: [+of] *the legend of St George and the* dragon | ancient Greek legends | **according to legend** *According to legend, he escaped by leaping from the cliffs into the sea.* | **Legend has it that** *prisoners were brought here to be executed.* **2** [C] someone who is famous and admired for being extremely good at doing something: **tennis/footballing/music etc legend** *We must put more money into the sport if we want to create the tennis legends of the future.* | *a marvellous player who was **a legend** in his own **lifetime**.* → **living legend** at LIVING[1] (6) **3** [C] *literary* words that have been written somewhere, for example on a sign: *A sign above the door bore the legend 'patience is a virtue'.* **4** [C] *technical* the words that explain a picture or map

le·gen·da·ry /'ledʒəndəri $ -deri/ *adj* **1** very famous and admired: *Lonnie Johnson, the legendary blues guitarist* | *Her singing was legendary.* **2** [only before noun] talked about in a legend; → **mythical**: *The cave is the home of a legendary giant.*

le·ger·de·main /ˌledʒədə'meɪn $ -dʒər-/ *n* [U] *old-fashioned* when you deceive people cleverly: *economic legerdemain*

leg·gings /'legɪŋz/ *n* [plural] **1** tight trousers for women, which stretch to fit the shape of your body **2** a pair of trousers that you wear over other clothes to protect your legs

leg·gy /'legi/ *adj* **1** a woman or child who is leggy has long legs: *a leggy fifteen-year old blonde* **2** a leggy plant has grown too tall very quickly and its stem cannot support its weight very well

le·gi·ble /'ledʒɪbəl/ *adj* written or printed clearly enough for you to read; **2** **illegible**: *Her handwriting was so tiny it was barely legible.* —**legibly** *adv* —**legibility** /ˌledʒɪ'bɪlɪti/ *n* [U]

le·gion[1] /'liːdʒən/ *n* [C] **1** a large group of soldiers, especially in ancient Rome **2** *literary* a large number of people

legion[2] *adj* [not before noun] *literary* very many; **2** **numerous**: *The stories of her adventures were legion.*

le·gion·a·ry /'liːdʒənəri $ -neri/ *n plural* **legionaries** [C] a member of a legion

le·gion·naire /ˌliːdʒə'neə $ -'ner/ *n* [C] a member of a legion, especially the French Foreign Legion

ˌlegion'naire's disˌease *n* [U] a serious disease that affects your lungs

ˈleg irons *n* [plural] metal chains that are put around a prisoner's legs

le·gis·late /'ledʒɪsleɪt/ *v* [I] **1** to make a law about something: **[+on]** *Only Parliament has the power to legislate on constitutional matters.* | **[+for/against]** *The government has promised to legislate against discrimination.* | *We must legislate for equal pay.* | **legislate to do sth** *We must legislate to control these drugs.* **2 legislate for sth** to think about how something may affect what you are doing, and do something to prepare for it: *You can't legislate for bad luck.*

le·gis·la·tion [W2] /ˌledʒɪ'sleɪʃən/ *n* [U] a law or set of laws: *This is a very important **piece of legislation*** (=law). | **[+on]** *the legislation on abortion* | **legislation to do sth** *new legislation to protect children* | **introduce/bring in legislation** *The government has promised to bring in new legislation to combat this problem.* | **under new/existing/current etc legislation** *Both individuals and companies can be prosecuted under the new legislation.*

le·gis·la·tive /'ledʒɪslətɪv $ -leɪtɪv/ *adj* [only before noun] concerned with making laws: *The new assemblies will have no legislative power.* | **legislative assembly/council/body etc** (=one with the power to make laws) *the main legislative body of the EC* | *new legislative measures to stem the flow of drugs into the US* | *legislative elections*

le·gis·la·tor /'ledʒɪsleɪtə $ -ər/ *n* [C] someone who has the power to make laws or belongs to an institution that makes laws

le·gis·la·ture /'ledʒɪsleɪtʃə, -lətʃə $ -ər/ *n* [C] an institution that has the power to make or change laws: **state/national/federal etc legislature** *the state legislature of Virginia*

le·git /lɪ'dʒɪt/ *adj* [not before noun] *spoken informal* **1** legal or allowed by official rules: *Don't worry, the deal's strictly legit.* **2** honest and not trying to deceive people: *Are you sure he's legit?*

le·git·i·mate[1] /lɪ'dʒɪtɪmɪt/ *adj* **1** fair or reasonable: *That's a **perfectly legitimate** question.* | *Most scientists believe **it is legitimate** to use animals in medical research.* **2** acceptable or allowed by law: *Their business operations are perfectly legitimate.* **3** a legitimate child is born to parents who are legally married to each other; **2** **illegitimate** —**legitimately** *adv*: *a legitimately elected government* | *He complained quite legitimately about his treatment.* —**legitimacy** *n* [U]: *Opponents have questioned the legitimacy of the ruling.*

le·git·i·mate[2] /lɪ'dʒɪtɪmeɪt/ *v* [T] the usual American form of LEGITIMIZE

le·git·i·mize also **-ise** *BrE* /lɪ'dʒɪtɪmaɪz/ *v* [T] **1** to make something that is unfair or morally wrong seem acceptable and right: *There is a danger that these films legitimize violence.* **2** to make something official or legal: *Acceptance by the UN would effectively legitimize the regime.* **3** when parents legitimize a child, they get married so that the child becomes LEGITIMATE[1] (3)

leg·less /'legləs/ *adj* **1** [not before noun] *BrE informal* very drunk **2** without legs

Leg·o /'legəʊ $ -oʊ/ *n* [U] *trademark* a toy consisting of small plastic bricks that you fit together to build things

ˈleg-pull *n* [C usually singular] *BrE* a joke in which you make someone believe something that is not true: *My first reaction was that this must be a leg-pull.* → **pull sb's leg** at PULL[1] (11)

ˈleg room *n* [U] space for your legs in front of the seats in a car, theatre etc: *There wasn't enough leg room.*

leg·ume /'legjuːm, lɪ'gjuːm/ *n* [C] *technical* a plant such as a bean plant that has seeds in a POD (=a long thin case) —**leguminous** /lɪ'gjuːmɪnəs/ *adj*

ˈleg-up *n* **give sb a leg-up** *informal* **a)** to help someone to get up to a high place by joining your hands together so they can use them as a step **b)** *BrE* to help someone succeed in their job

leg·work /'legwɜːk $ -wɜːrk/ *n* [U] *informal* the hard boring work that has to be done in order to achieve something: *He has a team of volunteers who do most of the legwork for him.*

lei·sure [W3] /'leʒə $ 'liːʒər/ *n* [U]
1 time when you are not working or studying and can relax and do things you enjoy: *Most people now enjoy shorter working hours and more **leisure time**.* | *Watching television is now the nation's most popular **leisure activity**.* | *The hotel offers various **leisure facilities** such as a swimming pool and sauna.* | *The **leisure industry** (=the business of providing leisure activities) is now an important part of the economy.*
2 at (your) leisure if you do something at your leisure, you do it slowly and without hurrying: *Come round for lunch and then we can discuss it at leisure.* | *Take the leaflets home and read them at your leisure.*
3 gentleman/lady of leisure someone who does not have to work – used humorously

ˈleisure ˌcentre *n* [C] *BrE* a place where people can do many different sports activities, exercise classes etc

lei·sured /'leʒəd $ 'liːʒərd/ *adj* [only before noun] **1** leisured people do not have to work because they are rich: *the leisured aristocracy* **2** doing things slowly because you feel relaxed and are enjoying yourself: *They seemed to live a very leisured life.*

lei·sure·ly /'leʒəli $ 'liːʒərli/ *adj* if you do something in a leisurely way, you do it in a slow, relaxed way,

L

without hurrying: *After lunch we went for a leisurely stroll.* | *working at a leisurely pace* —**leisurely** *adv*: *He sipped leisurely at his drink.*

lei·sure·wear /'leʒəweə $ 'liːʒərwer/ *n* [U] clothes that are made to be worn when you are relaxing or playing sport

leit·mo·tif, **leitmotiv** /'laɪtməʊˌtiːf $ -moʊ-/ *n* [C] **1** *technical* a musical phrase that is repeated several times during a long musical work and represents a particular character or idea **2** something that is seen or heard very many times and so becomes a typical feature of a place, time, or person: *Her designs in clothing became a leitmotif of the 1970s.*

lem·ming /'lemɪŋ/ *n* [C] a small animal that looks like a rat. Lemmings are known for following each other in large numbers and killing themselves by jumping off cliffs into the sea.

lem·on¹ /'lemən/ *n* **1** [C,U] a fruit with a hard yellow skin and sour juice: *a slice of lemon* | *Add a few drops of lemon juice.* → see picture at FRUIT¹ **2** [U] *BrE* a drink that tastes of lemons: *a glass of fizzy lemon* **3** also **lemon yellow** [U] a pale yellow colour **4** [C] *especially AmE informal* something that is useless because it fails to work or to work properly: *I soon realized the van was a lemon.* **5** [C] *BrE informal* a silly person: *He just stood there looking like a real lemon.*

lemon² also **,lemon 'yellow** *adj* pale yellow in colour

lem·on·ade S3 /ˌleməˈneɪd◂/ *n* [C,U] **1** *BrE* a sweet FIZZY drink that tastes of lemons: *a glass of lemonade* | *Would you like a lemonade?* **2** a drink made from lemons, sugar, and water

,lemon 'curd *n* [U] *BrE* a sweet food made from eggs, butter, and lemon juice that is eaten on bread

'lemon ,grass *n* [U] a type of grass that grows in warm countries and is used in cooking

,lemon 'sole *n* [C] a type of flat fish that is cooked and eaten

'lemon ,squeezer *n* [C] a small kitchen tool that you use for getting the juice out of a lemon

lem·on·y /'leməni/ *adj* smelling or tasting of lemons: *a lovely lemony flavour*

le·mur /'liːmə $ -ər/ *n* [C] an animal that looks like a monkey and has a long thick tail

lend S3 W3 /lend/ *v past tense and past participle* **lent** /lent/
1 a) [T] to let someone borrow money or something that belongs to you for a short time; → **borrow**: **lend sth to sb** *I lent my CD player to Dave and I haven't got it back yet.* | **lend sb sth** *The hospital agreed to lend us a wheelchair.* | *Can you lend me £10 until tomorrow?* **b)** [I,T] if a bank or financial institution lends money, it lets someone have it on condition that they pay it back later, often gradually, with an additional amount as INTEREST: *The government is trying to encourage the banks to lend more.* | **lend sth to sb** *A lot of banks are unwilling to lend money to new businesses.* | **lend sb sth** *The building society agreed to lend us £60,000.*
2 lend (sb) a hand to help someone do something, especially something that needs physical effort: *Can you lend me a hand with this?*
3 [T] *formal* to give a situation, event etc a particular quality: **lend sth to sth** *The presence of members of the royal family lent a certain dignity to the ceremony.*
4 lend an ear to listen to someone, especially in a sympathetic way: *He's always prepared to lend a sympathetic ear.*
5 lend itself to sth to be suitable for being used in a particular way: *None of her books really lends itself to being made into a film.*
6 lend (your) support (to sth) to support or help someone: *The government has now lent its support to the campaign.*
7 lend weight/support to sth to make an opinion or belief seem more likely to be correct: *The police have new evidence which lends weight to their theory.*
8 lend your name to sth to announce publicly that you support something that someone is trying to do: *The French prime minister has now lent his name to the protest.*

lender /'lendə $ -ər/ *n* [C] a person or organization that lends money to people on condition that they pay it back: *Several lenders are offering very attractive rates of interest at the moment.*

'lending ,library *n* [C] a library that lends books, records etc for people to use at home; → **reference library**

'lending rate *n* [C] the rate of INTEREST¹ (4) that you have 'to pay to a bank or other financial institution when you borrow money from them; ▣ **interest rate**

length S2 W2 /leŋθ/ *n*
1 SIZE [C,U] the measurement of how long something is from one end to the other; → **breadth**, **width**: *We measured the length and width of the living room.* | **a length of 1 metre/2 feet etc** *Some fish can grow to a length of four feet.* | **2 feet/10 metres etc in length** *The hotel pool is 15 metres in length.* | *You'll need several pieces of string of different lengths.*
2 TIME [C,U] the amount of time that you spend doing something or that something continues; → **duration**: [+of] *Your pension will depend on your length of employment.* | *What's the average length of stay in hospital?* | **(not) for any length of time** (=not for very long) *He wasn't left alone for any length of time.*
3 BOOKS/FILMS ETC [C,U] the amount of writing in a book, or the amount of time that a film, play etc continues: [+of] *We had to cut the length of the book by one third.* | **of this length** *Films of this length* (=as long as this) *are pretty unusual.*
4 run/stretch/walk etc the (full) length of sth to go or move from one end to the other of something: *The wall ran the full length of the garden.* | *They walked the length of the pier.*
5 shoulder-length/knee-length etc reaching down as far as your shoulders etc: *shoulder-length hair* | *an ankle-length dress*
6 go to some/great/any lengths (to do sth) to try very hard or to do whatever is necessary to achieve something that is important to you: *He went to great lengths to keep their name out of the papers.* | *Bella would go to any lengths to fulfil her ambition.*
7 at (some/great etc) length a) if you talk at length about something, you talk about it for a long time: **speak/talk etc at length** *The young people spoke at length about their experiences.* | *We've already discussed the subject at great length.* **b)** *literary* after a long time: *'I don't agree,' she said at length.*
8 the length and breadth of the area/country/land etc in or through every part of a large area: *The police searched the length and breadth of the country.*
9 PIECE [C] a piece of something long and thin: **a length of rope/pipe/wire etc**
10 IN RACES [C] the measurement of a horse, boat etc from one end to the other – used when saying how far the horse, boat etc is ahead of another: **by a/one/two etc lengths** *The horse won by three lengths.*
11 SWIMMING [C] the distance from one end of a swimming pool to the other: **do/swim a length** *She does at least 20 lengths a day.* → **hold sth at arm's length** at ARM¹ (8); → **keep/hold sb at arm's length** at ARM¹ (9); → FULL-LENGTH¹

length·en /'leŋθən/ *v* [I,T] to make something longer or to become longer; ▣ **shorten**: *Can you lengthen this skirt for me?* | *The days lengthened as summer approached.*

length·wise /'leŋθwaɪz/ also **length·ways** /-weɪz/ *BrE adv* in the direction or position of the longest side: *Lay the bricks lengthwise.*

length·y /'leŋθi/ *comparative* **lengthier**, *superlative* **lengthiest** *adj* [usually before noun] **1** continuing for a long time, often too long; ▣ **brief**: *A lengthy period of training is required.* | *An accident is causing some* *lengthy delays.* **2** a speech, piece of writing etc that is lengthy is long and often contains too many details: *a lengthy report*

le·ni·ent /ˈliːniənt/ *adj* not strict in the way you punish someone or in the standard you expect: *the lenient sentences handed down by some judges* | *School examiners say that marking has become more lenient in recent years.* —**leniently** *adv* —**leniency** also **lenience** *n* [U]: *the trend towards greater leniency for most offenders*

lens /lenz/ *n* [C] **1** the part of a camera through which the light travels before it reaches the film: *a standard 50mm lens* → TELEPHOTO LENS, WIDE-ANGLE LENS, ZOOM LENS; → see picture at CAMERA **2** a piece of curved glass or plastic which makes things look bigger, smaller, or clearer when you look through it: *glasses with powerful lenses* | *the lens of the microscope* **3** the clear part inside your eye that FOCUSES so you can see things clearly **4** a CONTACT LENS

lent /lent/ *v* the past tense and past participle of LEND

Lent *n* [U] the 40 days before Easter when some Christians eat less food or stop doing something that they enjoy —**Lenten** *adj*

len·til /ˈlentl, -tl̩/ *n* [C] a small round seed like a bean, dried and used for food

len·to /ˈlentəʊ $ -toʊ/ *adj, adv technical* music that is played lento is played slowly

Le·o /ˈliːəʊ $ ˈliːoʊ/ *n plural* **Leos 1** [U] the fifth sign of the ZODIAC, represented by a lion, which some people believe affects the character and life of people born between July 24 and August 23 **2** [C] someone who was born between July 24 and August 23

le·o·nine /ˈliːənaɪn/ *adj literary* like a lion in character or appearance

leop·ard /ˈlepəd $ -ərd/ *n* [C] **1** a large animal of the cat family, with yellow fur and black spots, which lives in Africa and South Asia → see picture at BIG CAT **2 a leopard can't change its spots** used to say that people cannot change their character

le·o·tard /ˈliːətɑːd $ -ɑːrd/ *n* [C] a tight piece of clothing that looks a little like a woman's SWIMSUIT and is worn for exercise or dancing, especially by women

LEP /ˌel iː ˈpiː/ *adj* [only before noun] *AmE technical* **limited English proficient** relating to someone whose first language is not English and who cannot communicate very well in English: *The number of LEP students has risen since 1993.*

lep·er /ˈlepə $ -ər/ *n* [C] **1** someone who has leprosy **2** someone that people avoid because they have done something that people disapprove of: *They treated me as if I was a leper.*

lep·re·chaun /ˈleprɪkɔːn $ -kɑːn, -kɔːn/ *n* [C] an imaginary creature in the form of a little old man, in old Irish stories

lep·ro·sy /ˈleprəsi/ *n* [U] a very serious infectious disease in which the flesh and nerves are gradually destroyed —**leprous** *adj*

les·bi·an /ˈlezbiən/ *n* [C] a woman who is sexually attracted to other women —**lesbian** *adj* —**lesbianism** *n* [U]

le·sion /ˈliːʒən/ *n* [C] *technical* damage to someone's skin or part of their body such as their stomach or brain, caused by injury or illness: *acute gastric lesions*

less¹ S1 W1 /les/ *adv*

1 not so much or to a smaller degree; ⚡ **more:** *Maybe he would worry less if he understood the situation.* | *In recent years she has appeared in public less frequently.* | **less (...) than** *Tickets were less expensive than I had expected.* | **much/a lot/far less** *Social class matters a lot less than it used to.* | **not ... any the less/no less** (=not less) *Your second point is no less important.* | *It's a common problem but this doesn't make it any the less disturbing.* | *I know he's done a dreadful thing, but I don't love him any the less.* | **be less a... than a...** (=not so much like one thing as another) *'Will you please come with me?' It was less a request than a command.*

2 less than helpful/honest/enthusiastic etc not at all helpful, honest etc: *He was less than enthusiastic about the idea.*

3 less and less used to say that a quality, situation etc gradually decreases; ⚡ **more and more:** *As the years went by, he seemed to care less and less about his reputation.* | *Smoking in the workplace is becoming less and less acceptable.*

4 much/still less used to say that a greater thing is even less true, likely, or possible than the thing you have just mentioned: *These people can scarcely afford to buy food, still less luxury goods like perfume.* | *I didn't think Dave would ever read a book, much less write one himself.*

less² S1 W1 *determiner, pron*

1 a) a smaller amount or not as much; ⚡ **more:** *Doctors recommend eating less salt.* | *People today seem to have less time for each other.* | *Most of us got £4 an hour, but some received even less.* | **[+of]** *The map covered less of the area than I'd thought.* | *Flying is less of a risk than driving.* | **less (...) than** *She knows less than I do about it.* | **less than 10/100 etc** *a distance of less than 100 metres* | **much/a lot less** *It costs much less to go by bus.* **b)** used to mean 'fewer' or 'not as many', although many people think this use is incorrect; ⚡ **more:** *There were less people there than we expected.* → see box at FEW

2 no less a) used to emphasize that an amount or number is large: **no less than** *By 1977, the USA was importing no less than 45% of its oil.* **b)** used to emphasize that the person or thing you are talking about is important or impressive: *Our awards were presented by the mayor, no less.* | *The message came from no less a person than the prime minister.*

3 nothing less than sth used to emphasize how important, serious, or impressive something is: *His appearance in the show was nothing less than a sensation.*

4 less and less a decreasing amount of something; ⚡ **more and more:** *They began spending less and less time together.* | **[+of]** *The band was doing less and less of that kind of music.*

5 in less than no time very quickly or very soon: *In less than no time they found that they owed over $10,000.*

6 less of sth *BrE spoken* used to tell a child to stop doing something: *Less of that noise, please!*

less³ *prep formal* taking away or not including a particular amount: *What is 121 less 36?* | *He gave us our money back, less the $2 service charge.*

-less /ləs/ *suffix* [in adjectives] **1** without something: *I felt powerless.* | *a childless couple* | *tasteless food* **2** not doing or using something: *You're too careless.* | *It's perfectly harmless.* **3** not possible to treat or affect in a particular way: *on countless occasions* | *She's tireless.*

les·see /leˈsiː/ *n* [C] *law* someone who is allowed to use a house, building, land etc for a period of time in return for payment to the owner; → lessor

less·en /ˈlesən/ *v* [I,T] to become smaller in size, importance, or value, or make something do this; ◨ **reduce:** **lessen the risk/chance/possibility etc (of sth)** *Exercise lessens the risk of heart disease.* | **lessen the impact/effect/importance (of sth)** *The new project will lessen the effects of car pollution.* | *Gradually her anxiety lessened.*

less·er /ˈlesə $ -ər/ *adj* [only before noun] **1** *formal* not as large, as important, or as much as something else; ⚡ **greater:** *They originally asked for $5 million, but finally settled for a lesser sum.* | **to a lesser extent/degree** *This was true in Madrid, and to a lesser extent, Valencia and Seville.*; → **lesser mortals** at MORTAL²; → **to a greater or lesser extent** at EXTENT (1) **2 the lesser of two evils** also **the lesser evil** the less unpleasant or harmful of two unpleasant choices **3** *technical* used in the names of some types of animal, bird, or plant that are slightly smaller than the main type —**lesser** *adv*: *the lesser-known artists of the period* | *one of Glasgow's lesser used venues*

L

les·son S2 W3 /'lesən/ *n* [C]
1 LEARNING A SKILL a period of time in which someone is taught a particular skill, for example how to play a musical instrument or drive a car: *piano lessons* | **have/take lessons** *She's started taking driving lessons.* | [+in/on] *lessons in First Aid* | *lessons on road safety*
2 IN SCHOOL *BrE* a period of time in which school students are taught a particular subject; ◳ **class** *AmE*: *Lessons start at 9 o'clock.* | **French/physics/art etc lesson** *I've got a double maths lesson next.* | [+in/on] *Andrew gives private lessons in Spanish.*
3 EXPERIENCE something that provides experience or information that you can learn from and use: **learn a lesson** (=gain useful experience or information) *There were important lessons to be learned from these discoveries.* | *The government has failed to learn the lessons of history.* | [+to] *The men's courage and faith is a lesson to us all.* | *Now* **let that be a lesson to you** all (=be careful to avoid having the same bad experience again).* | *Her fate should be a **salutary lesson** (=one that teaches or warns you about something).*
4 BOOK a part of a book that is used for learning a particular subject, especially in school: *Turn to lesson 25.*
5 CHURCH a short piece that is read from the Bible during a religious ceremony → **sb has learned their lesson** at LEARN (5); → **teach sb a lesson** at TEACH (6)

les·sor /le'sɔː $ -'sɔːr/ *n* [C] *law* someone who allows someone else to use their house, building, land etc for a period of time for payment; → **lessee**

lest /lest/ *conjunction literary* **1** in order to make sure that something will not happen: *She turned away from the window lest anyone see them.* **2** used to show that someone is afraid or worried that a particular thing might happen: **worried/concerned/anxious etc lest ...** *He paused, afraid lest he say too much.* | *She was worried lest he should tell someone what had happened.*

let¹ S1 W1 /let/ *v past tense and past participle* **let**, *present participle* **letting**
1 ALLOW [T not in passive] to allow someone to do something; → **permit**: *I can't come out tonight – my dad won't let me.* | **let sb do sth** *Let Johnny have a go on the computer now.* | *Some people seem to let their kids do whatever they like.* | *Let me have a look at that letter.* | **let sb have sth** (=give something to someone) *I can let you have another £10, but no more.* ⚠ Do not say 'be let to do something', because **let** has no passive form. Use the active form, or use **be allowed to do**: *They let me leave* OR *I was allowed to leave.*
2 NOT STOP STH HAPPENING [T not usually in passive] to not stop something happening, or to make it possible for it to happen: **let sb/sth do sth** *Jenny let the note fall to the ground.* | *Don't let anyone know it was me who told you.* | *Max let the door swing open.* | *Let the cookies cool down before you try them.* | **let yourself be beaten/persuaded/fooled etc** *I stupidly let myself be persuaded to take part in a live debate.*
3 let go a) to stop holding something or someone: *Let go! You're hurting me.* | [+of] *The guard let go of the lead, and the dog lunged forward.* **b)** to accept that you cannot change something and stop thinking or worrying about it: *Sometimes you just have to learn to let go.*
4 let sb go a) to allow someone to leave a place where they have been kept; ◳ **release**: *The police had to let him go through lack of evidence.* | *The hijackers were persuaded to let hostages go.* **b)** to make someone leave their job – used in order to avoid saying this directly: *I'm afraid we had to let several of our staff go.*

SPOKEN PHRASES
5 SUGGEST/OFFER [T not in passive] used to make a suggestion, or to offer help: **let's do sth** *Let's make a start, shall we?* | *Let's all get together over Christmas.* | **Let's not** *jump to conclusions – he might have been*

delayed.* | **let sb do sth** *Let me help you with those bags.* | *Let me give you a piece of advice.* | **let's hope (that)** *Let's hope he got your message in time.* | **don't let's do sth** *BrE informal*: *Don't let's argue like this.*
6 let's see also **let me see** used when you are thinking about or trying to remember something: *Today's date is – let me see, March 20th.* | *Now, let's see, where did I put your application form?*
7 let me think used to say that you need time to think about or remember something: *What was his name, now? Let me think.*
8 let him/her/them etc used to say that you do not care if someone does something they are threatening to do: *'She says she's going to sell her story to the newspapers!' 'Well, let her!'*
9 let's face it/let's be honest used to say that someone must accept an unpleasant fact or situation: *Let's face it, no one's going to lend us any money.*
10 let's just say (that) used to say that you are not going to give someone all the details about something: *'So who did it?' 'Let's just say it wasn't anyone in this family.'*

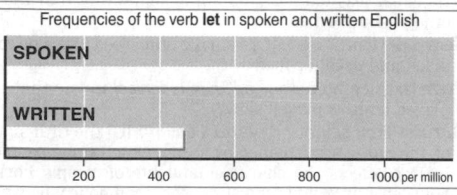

Frequencies of the verb **let** in spoken and written English

SPOKEN

WRITTEN

200   400   600   800   1000 per million

11 let yourself go a) to relax completely and enjoy yourself: *For goodness sake, Peter, why don't you just let yourself go for once?* **b)** to stop looking after yourself properly, for example by not caring about your appearance: *Poor Dad. He's really let himself go since Mum died.*
12 let sth go a) to not punish or criticize someone for something they have done wrong: *OK, I'll let it go this time.* **b)** to stop worrying or thinking too much about something: *It's time to let the past go.* **c)** *informal* to sell something for a particular amount: **let sth go for £20/$200 etc** *I couldn't let it go for less than £300.*
13 WISH [T not in passive] used to say that you wish or hope that something happens, or does not happen: **(not) let sb/sth do sth** *Don't let him be the one who died, she prayed.*
14 let alone used after a negative statement to say that the next thing you mention is even more unlikely: *The baby can't even sit up yet, let alone walk!*
15 let sth drop/rest/lie to stop talking about or trying to deal with something: *It seems the press are not going to let the matter rest.*
16 let slip to accidentally tell someone something that should have been kept secret: [+that] *Liz let slip that she'd seen him quite recently.*
17 RENT [T] *especially BrE* to charge someone an amount of money for the use of a room or building; ◳ **lease**; → **hire, rent**: *Interhome has over 20,000 houses to let across Europe.* | **let sth to sb** *I've let my spare room to a student.* | **let sb sth** *Would you consider letting me the garage for a few months?* | **let sth out to sb** *We let the smaller studios out to local artists.* | **To Let** *written* (=written on a sign outside a building to show that it is available for renting)
18 MATHEMATICS **let sth be/equal/represent sth** *technical* used in mathematics to mean that you give something a particular measurement or value in order to make a calculation: *Let angle A equal the sum of the two opposite sides.*
19 let yourself in for sth *informal* to do something that will cause you a lot of trouble: *I don't think Carol realizes what she's letting herself in for.*
20 never let a day/week/year etc go by without doing sth used to say that someone does a particular thing very regularly: *They never seem to let a year go by without introducing a new version of their software.*

L

21 let the good times roll *informal* used to say that it is time for people to start having fun

22 let sb have it *informal* to attack someone → **let fly (sth)** at FLY¹ (17); → **let it all hang out** at HANG OUT (3); → **live and let live** at LIVE¹ (21); → **let it/her rip** at RIP¹ (5); → **let rip** at RIP¹ (4)

let sb/sth ⇔ **down** *phr v*

1 to not do something that someone trusts or expects you to do: *She had been **let down badly** in the past.* | *The worst feeling is having let our fans down.* | **let the side down** *BrE* (=disappoint a group of people that you belong to)

2 to make someone or something less successful or effective: *McKenzie's judgement rarely lets him down.*

3 to move something or someone to a lower position: *Let down a rope so that I can climb up.* | *Carefully, she let herself down into the water.*

4 let your hair down *informal* to relax and enjoy yourself, especially after working hard: *Visitors young and old let their hair down and enjoyed the show.*

5 let your guard/defences down to relax and stop worrying about what might happen or what someone might find out about you: *Maggie never really lets her guard down, does she?*

6 let sb down lightly/gently to give someone bad news in a way that will not upset them too much: *I get lots of offers, but I try to let them down gently.*

7 *BrE* to allow the air to escape from something so that it loses its shape and becomes flat: *Someone's let my tyres down!*

8 to make a piece of clothing longer by unfolding a folded edge; ◪ **take up**

let sb **in on** sth *phr v*

to tell something that is secret or only known by a few people: *TV chef Raymond Blanc lets us in on the secrets of his kitchen.* | *Would someone mind letting me in on the joke?*

let sb/sth **into** sth *phr v*

1 to tell someone something that is secret or private: *It was time to let the rest of the family into the secret.*

2 [usually passive] *technical* to put something such as a window or a decoration into a wall: *Two large windows were let into the wall each side of the door.*

let sb/sth **off** *phr v*

1 to not punish someone: *I'll let you off this time, but don't do it again.* | [+with] *After checking our identities, the customs men let us off with a warning.* | **let sb off the hook** (=allow someone to escape punishment or criticism) *He'd decided to make Sandra wait before letting her off the hook.* | **let sb off lightly/easily** (=give someone a less serious punishment than they deserve) *I think young criminals are let off far too lightly.*

2 let sb off (sth) if someone in authority lets you off something you should do, they give you permission not to do it: *You've worked hard all week, so I'll let you off today.*

3 let sth ⇔ **off** to make something explode: *One boy had let off a firework in class.* → see picture at EXPLOSION → **let/blow off steam** at STEAM¹ (4)

let on *phr v informal*

to tell something, especially something you have been keeping secret: **let on (that)** *Don't let on that I told you.* | **let on who/why/how etc** *We never did let on how we found out.* | *I'm sure he knows more than he's letting on.*

let out *phr v*

1 let out sth to suddenly make a loud sound such as a shout or cry: **let out a scream/cry/roar etc** *He let out a cry of disbelief.*

2 let sth ⇔ **out** to make a piece of clothing wider or looser, especially because it is too tight

3 let sth ⇔ **out** *BrE* to charge someone an amount of money for the use of a room or building: *We're letting out our son's old room to a student.*

4 *AmE* if a school, college, film etc lets out, it ends and the people attending it can leave: *What time does the movie let out?* → **let the cat out of the bag** at CAT (2)

let up *phr v*

1 to become less severe or harmful: *The wind had*

dropped and the rain gradually let up.

2 to be less severe, unkind, or violent towards someone: *Even when the crowd had scattered, the police didn't let up.*

3 to stop working as hard as you were: *You're doing really well, but you can't afford to let up now.*

let² *n* **1** [C] *BrE* an arrangement in which a house or flat is rented to someone: *An agency is managing the let.* | *a long-term let* **2 without let or hindrance** *law* happening freely without being prevented in any way

-let /lɪt/ *suffix* [in nouns] a small kind of something: *a booklet* | *a piglet*

letch /letʃ/ *a* LECH

let·down /ˈletdaʊn/ *n* [singular] *informal* an event, performance etc that is not as good as you expected it to be; ◪ **disappointment**: *The end of the book was a real letdown.* → **let down** at LET¹

le·thal /ˈliːθəl/ *adj* **1** causing death, or able to cause death; → **fatal**: *a lethal dose of heroin* | *a lethal weapon* | *death by lethal injection* | *a lethal cocktail of drink and pills* | [+to] *These chemicals are lethal to fish.* **2** *informal* likely to be powerful or dangerous – often used humorously: *They were all drinking lethal amounts of tequila!* | *Higher taxes and higher inflation were a lethal combination.*

le·thar·gic /lɪˈθɑːdʒɪk $ -ˈθɑːr-/ *adj* feeling as if you have no energy and no interest in doing anything; ◪ **lazy**: *The hot weather was making us all lethargic.* —**lethargically** /-kli/ *adv*

leth·ar·gy /ˈleθədʒi $ -ər-/ *n* [U] the feeling of being lethargic: *New mothers often complain of lethargy and mild depression.*

let's /lets/ the short form of 'let us', used especially to make suggestions: *Let's go!*

let·ter¹ S1 W1 /ˈletə $ -ər/ *n* [C]

1 a written or printed message that is usually put in an envelope and sent by mail: [+from/to] *I got a long letter from Melanie today.* | *Bart's writing a letter to his parents.* | **post a letter** *BrE*/**mail a letter** *AmE*: *Could you post this letter for me?* | **a letter of thanks/introduction/complaint etc** *Julie received a letter of apology from the hospital.* | *a business letter* → CHAIN LETTER, COVERING LETTER, LETTER OF CREDIT, OPEN LETTER; → **thank-you letter** at THANK-YOU (2)

2 a sign in writing or printing that represents a speech sound: *There are 26 letters in the English alphabet.* | *Fill in the form in **capital letters** (=written in their large form).* → BLOCK LETTERS

3 to the letter paying exact attention to the details of something: *I followed the instructions to the letter, but it still wouldn't work.*

4 the letter of the law the exact words of a law or agreement rather than the intended or general meaning: *employees who stick to the letter of the law in their contracts* → **the spirit of the law** at SPIRIT¹ (11)

5 *AmE* a large cloth letter that you sew onto a jacket, given as a reward for playing in a school or college sports team: *Mark got a letter in soccer.*

L

6 English/American/German etc letters [plural] *formal* the study of the literature of a particular country or language: *a major figure in English letters* → DEAD LETTER, MAN OF LETTERS

letter² *v* **1** [T usually passive] to write, draw, paint etc letters or words on something: *The card was neatly lettered P.A. DUFFY.* | **letter sth in sth** *Several pages are lettered in gold.* **2** [I] *AmE* to earn a LETTER¹ (5) in a sport: [+in] *He lettered in basketball at Brandeis.*

'letter ,bomb *n* [C] a small bomb hidden in a package and sent to someone in order to kill or harm them

let·ter·box /'letəbɒks $ 'letərbaːks/ *n* [C] **1** *BrE* a narrow hole in a door, or a special box outside a house where letters, packages etc are delivered; ▤ **mail box** *AmE*; → see picture at DOOR **2** *BrE* a box in a post office or street, in which letters are posted; ▤ **post box** *BrE*; ▤ **mail box** *AmE*

let·ter·box·ing /'letə,bɒksɪŋ $ -ter,baːks-/ *n* [U] when a film from the cinema is broadcast on television with black bands at the top and bottom of the television screen so that the film will have the same DIMENSIONS as it did on a cinema screen

let·tered /'letəd $ -ərd/ *adj formal* well educated

let·ter·head /'letəhed $ -ər-/ *n* **1** [C] the name and address that is printed at the top of a sheet of writing paper **2** [U] *AmE* paper that has the name and address of a person or business printed at the top of it: *The letter had been written on university letterhead.*

let·ter·ing /'letərɪŋ/ *n* [U] **1** written or drawn letters, especially of a particular type, size, colour etc: *Chinese lettering* **2** the art of writing or drawing letters or words

,**letter of 'credit** *n* [C] an official letter from a bank allowing a particular person to take money from another bank

,**letter-'perfect** *adj AmE* correct in every detail: *a letter-perfect product*

'**letter-size** *adj AmE* letter-size paper is 8½ INCHES wide and 11 inches long

let·ting /'letɪŋ/ *n* [C] *BrE* a house or apartment that can be rented: *short-term holiday lettings* | **a letting agent/agency** (=one that arranges lettings)

let·tuce /'letɪs/ *n* [C,U] a round vegetable with thin green leaves eaten raw in SALADS

'**let-up** also **let·up** *AmE* /'letʌp/ *n* [singular, U] when something unpleasant stops or becomes less difficult, severe etc: **no let-up/not any let-up** *The pressure at work continued without any letup.* | [+in] *Streets were flooded, but still there was no let-up in the rain.* → **let up** at LET¹

leu·ke·mi·a also **leukaemia** *BrE* /luːˈkiːmiə/ *n* [U] a type of CANCER of the blood, that causes weakness and sometimes death

lev·ee /'levi/ *n* [C] a special wall built to stop a river flooding

lev·el¹ S1 W1 /'levəl/ *n* [C]
1 AMOUNT the amount or degree of something, compared to another amount or degree: [+of] *Increased supplies are needed to meet the level of demand.* | **high/ low level** *Dolphins show a high level of intelligence.* | *Inflation dropped to its lowest level in 30 years.* | *At the moment, public interest is at a high level.* | **price/ income etc levels** *the high salary levels of top executives* | *Special attention was paid to minimising* **noise levels**. | *Try to reduce your* **stress levels**. | *the downward trend in annual* **pollution levels**
2 STANDARD a particular standard of skill or ability, for example in education or sport: **at ... level** *Students at this level may have problems with basic grammar.* | *What level do you think you're at?* | **beginner/advanced/ national etc level** *Few athletes can compete at international level.* | *an advanced-level coursebook* → A LEVEL
3 HEIGHT the height of something in relation to the ground or to another object: **at ... level** *Your arms should be at the same level as your desk.* | **eye/knee/**

shoulder etc level (=the same height as your eyes etc) *Skirts this year are just above knee level.* | **water/oil etc level** (=the height of the water etc from the ground or the bottom of a container) *Check the water level in the car radiator.* → GROUND LEVEL, SEA LEVEL
4 FLOOR/GROUND a floor or area of ground that is at a particular height, especially when you can go up or down to other floors or areas: **on ... level** *Didn't we park the car on Level 2?* | *The town is built on different levels.* | *The medical center is on one level* (=so that you do not have to go up or down). → SPLIT-LEVEL
5 RANK OF JOB a particular position in a system that has different ranks of importance: **at ... level** *Training is offered at each level in the department.* | **at board/ management/senior etc level** *Further talks at ministerial level were held.* → HIGH-LEVEL, LOW-LEVEL
6 WAY OF UNDERSTANDING a way of considering or understanding something: **on ... level** *The story can be understood on many different levels.* | **on a personal/ practical/superficial etc level** *I agree with you, but only on a theoretical level.*
7 **at local/state/national etc level** happening within a small area or the whole area of a state, country etc: *These changes are taking place at regional level.*
8 **a level playing field** a situation in which different people, companies, countries, etc can all compete fairly because no one has special advantages: *Small businesses want to compete on a level playing field with larger ones.*
9 **be on the level** *informal* to be honest and legal: *This is all on the level, right?*
10 **descend/sink to sb's level** to behave as badly as someone: *If you hit him back, you'll only be descending to his level.*
11 TOOL a tool used for checking that a surface is flat; ▤ **spirit-level**

level² S1 W2 *adj*
1 flat and not sloping in any direction: *The floors in the old house were not completely level.* | *a level surface suitable for wheelchairs*
2 a) two things that are level are at the same height as each other: [+with] *Your eyes should be level with the top of the screen.* | *The curtains aren't quite level.* **b)** *BrE* two sports teams, competitors etc that are level have the same number of points: [+with] *Before the weekend, Madrid was level with Barcelona.* | *They* **finished level**, *with ten points each.* → LEVEL-PEGGING **c)** having the same value or position as something or someone else: [+with] *Borrowing rates rose to over 8%, roughly level with those in America.* | *He cycled along beside her, keeping level.*
3 do your level best (to do sth) to try as hard as possible to do something: *I'll do my level best to help you.*
4 a level voice/look/gaze a steady voice, look etc, that shows you are calm or determined
5 level teaspoon/cup etc (of sth) an amount of a substance that fills a spoon, cup etc to the top but no more, used as a measure in cooking: *Add one level teaspoon of salt.* → **heaped teaspoon etc** at HEAPED; → **draw level** at DRAW¹ (11)

level³ *v* **levelled, levelling** *BrE*, **leveled, leveling** *AmE* **1** [T] also **level sth** ⇔ **off/out** to make something flat and smooth: *Workers leveled the wet concrete with a piece of wood.* | *Cover with a layer of sand and level it off.* **2** [T] to knock down or destroy a building or area completely: *Bombs levelled a large part of the town.* **3** [I,T] *BrE* to make the score in a game or competition equal: *He dropped the ball into the net to* **level the score** *at 1/1.* | *United went ahead but the visitors levelled in the 73rd minute.* **4 level criticism/ charges/accusations etc at/against sb** to aim criticism etc at a particular person, country etc, especially publicly: *the criticism levelled at the United States* | *Serious allegations were levelled against the minister.*
level sth **at sb/sth** *phr v* to aim something such as a weapon at someone or something: *Slowly he levelled his gun at the tiger.*
level off/out *phr v* **1** to stop going up or down and

continue at the same height: *After climbing steeply, the path levelled off.* | *The plane levelled out at 30,000 feet.*   **2** to stop rising or falling and become steady: *Inflation has begun to level off.*   **3 level sth ⇔ off/out** to make something flat and smooth

level with sb *phr v informal* to speak honestly to someone, after hiding some unpleasant facts from them: *She decided to level with him and tell him how she felt.* → **be on the level** at LEVEL¹ (9)

,**level 'crossing** *n* [C] *BrE* a place where a railway crosses a road, usually protected by gates; ⊟ **railroad crossing** *AmE*

,**level-'headed** *adj* calm and sensible in making judgments or decisions

lev·el·ler *BrE*; **leveler** *AmE* /'levələ $ -ər/ *n* [C] something, especially death or illness, that makes people of all classes and ranks seem equal

,**level-'pegging** *n* be **level-pegging** *BrE* if competitors in a race, election etc are level-pegging, they are equal and it is difficult to know who will win

le·ver¹ /'li:və $ 'levər/ *n* [C]   **1** a stick or handle on a machine or piece of equipment, that you move to operate it: *Pull this lever to open the gate.* → **GEAR LEVER**   **2** a long thin piece of metal that you use to lift something heavy by putting one end under the object and pushing the other end down   **3** something you use to influence a situation to get the result that you want: *Rich countries use foreign aid as a lever to achieve political aims.*

lever² *v* [T]   **1** to move something with a lever: **lever sth off/up/out etc** *He levered the stone into place.*   **2 lever yourself up/onto/out of etc sth** to move your body by pushing on something with your arms to help you: *He slowly levered himself up.*   **3** to make someone leave a particular job, situation etc: **lever sb out** *They're trying to lever him out of his job.*

le·ver·age¹ /'li:vərɪdʒ $ 'le-, 'li:-/ *n* [U]   **1** influence that you can use to make people do what you want: *diplomatic leverage by the US*   **2** the action, power, or use of a lever

leverage² *v* [T] *AmE technical*   **1** to make money available to someone in order to INVEST or to buy something such as a company: *the use of public funds to leverage private investment*   **2** to spread or use RESOURCES (=money, skills, buildings etc that an organization has available), ideas etc again in several different ways or in different parts of a company, system etc: **leverage sth across sth** *Reusable software is leveraged across many applications.*

,**leveraged 'buyout** *n* [C] *technical* when someone borrows money to buy all or most of the STOCK of a company by promising to pay the bank back by selling the company's ASSETS if they cannot pay back the money they borrowed

le·vi·a·than /lɪ'vaɪəθən/ *n* [C] *literary*   **1** something very large and strong: *a leviathan of a ship*   **2** a very large and frightening sea animal

lev·i·tate /'levɪteɪt/ *v* [I,T] to rise and float in the air by magic, or to make someone or something do this —**levitation** /,levɪ'teɪʃən/ *n* [U]

lev·i·ty /'levɪti/ *n* [U] *formal* lack of respect or seriousness when you are dealing with something serious; ⊟ **gravity**

lev·y¹ /'levi/ *v* **levied, levying, levies** [T] to officially say that people must pay a tax or charge: **levy a tax/charge/fine etc (on sth)** *a new tax levied on all electrical goods*

levy² *n plural* **levies** [C] an additional sum of money, usually paid as a tax: [+on] *He wants to impose a levy on landfill waste.*

lewd /lu:d/ *adj* using rude words or movements that make you think of sex: *lewd comments* —**lewdly** *adv* —**lewdness** *n* [U]

lex·i·cal /'leksɪkəl/ *adj technical* dealing with words, or related to words

lex·i·cog·ra·phy /,leksɪ'kɒgrəfi $ -'kɑ:-/ *n* [U] the skill, practice, or profession of writing dictionaries —**lexicographer** *n* [C] —**lexicographical** /,leksɪkə'græfɪkəl‹ / *adj*

lex·i·con /'leksɪkən $ -kɑ:n, -kən/ *n*   **1** the **lexicon** *technical* all the words and phrases used in a language or that a particular person knows   **2** [C] an alphabetical list of words with their meanings, especially on a particular subject or in a particular language: *a lexicon of geographical terms*

lex·is /'leksɪs/ *n* [U] *technical* all the words in a language; ⊟ **vocabulary**

ley /leɪ, liː/ *also* '**ley line** *n* [C] an imaginary line connecting buildings, places etc that is believed to follow an ancient track that has special power

li·a·bil·i·ty W2 /,laɪə'bɪlɪti/ *n*
1 [U] legal responsibility for something, especially for paying money that is owed, or for damage or injury: [+for] *Tenants have legal liability for any damage they cause.* | [+to] *your liability to capital gains tax* | **liability to do sth** *The court ruled there was no liability to pay any refund.*
2 liabilities [plural] *technical* the amount of debt that must be paid; ⊟ **assets**
3 [singular] someone or something that is likely to cause problems for someone: *A kid like Tom would be a liability in any classroom.* | [+to] *The outspoken minister has become a liability to the government.*
4 liability to sth *law* the amount that something is likely to be affected by a particular kind of problem, illness etc → **LIMITED LIABILITY**

li·a·ble /'laɪəbəl/ *adj* [not before noun]   **1 liable to do sth** likely to do or say something or to behave in a particular way, especially because of a fault or natural tendency; ⊟ **likely**: *The car is liable to overheat on long trips.* | *He was liable to just show up without warning.*   **2** legally responsible for the cost of something: [+for] *people who are liable for income tax at a higher rate*   **3** likely to be affected by a particular kind of problem, illness etc; ⊟ **prone**: [+to] *You're more liable to injury when you don't get regular exercise.*   **4** *law* likely to be legally punished or forced to do something by law: [+to/for] *Anyone found trespassing is liable to a maximum fine of $100.*

li·aise /li'eɪz/ *v* [I] to exchange information with someone who works in another organization or department so that you can both be more effective: [+with] *Council officers are liaising closely with local groups.* | [+between] *The education officer liaises between students, schools and colleges.*

li·ai·son /li'eɪzɒn $ 'li:əzɑːn, li'eɪ-/ *n*   **1** [singular, U] the regular exchange of information between groups of people, especially at work, so that each group knows what the other is doing: [+between] *close liaison between the army and police* | [+with] *better liaison with other agencies* | **in liaison with sth** *The project has been set up in liaison with the art department.*   **2** *also* **liaison officer** [C] someone whose job is to talk to different departments or groups and to tell each of them about what the others are doing: [+to] *Renee Ball, liaison to the State Parks Authority*   **3** [C] a secret sexual relationship between a man and a woman, especially a man and a woman who are married but not to each other; → **affair**

li·ar /'laɪə $ -ər/ *n* [C] someone who deliberately says things which are not true: *Are you calling me a liar?*

lib /lɪb/ *n* → **AD-LIB, WOMEN'S LIB**

li·ba·tion /laɪ'beɪʃən/ *n* [C] *formal* a gift of wine to a god

lib·ber /'lɪbə $ -ər/ *n* **women's libber** see WOMEN'S LIB

Lib Dem /,lɪb 'dem‹ / *n* [C] *BrE* the abbreviation of *Liberal Democrat* —**Lib Dem** *adj*

li·bel¹ /'laɪbəl/ *n* [C,U] when someone writes or prints untrue statements about someone so that other people could have a bad opinion of them; → **slander**: **for libel**

L

Holt sued the newspaper for libel. | a libel action/case/trial (=a court case against someone for libel) | *restrictions on press freedom, such as libel laws*

libel² v libelled, libelling *BrE*, libeled, libeling *AmE* [T] to write or print a libel against someone; → **slander**

li·bel·lous *BrE*; **libelous** *AmE* /ˈlaɪbələs/ adj containing untrue written statements about someone which could make other people have a bad opinion of them; → **slanderous**: *libellous gossip*

lib·e·ral¹ W2 /ˈlɪbərəl/ adj
1 willing to understand and respect other people's ideas, opinions, and feelings: *a more liberal attitude towards sexuality* | *I had quite liberal parents.*
2 supporting or allowing gradual political and social changes; ▱ **conservative**: *a more liberal policy on issues of crime and punishment*
3 allowing people or organizations a lot of political or economic freedom: **liberal state/society/democracy etc**
4 generous or given in large amounts: *a liberal supply of drinks* | [+with] *If only they were as liberal with their cash.* → **LIBERALLY**
5 not exact: *a liberal interpretation of the original play*
6 liberal education a kind of education which encourages you to develop a large range of interests and knowledge and respect for other people's opinions

liberal² n [C] someone with liberal opinions or principles; ▱ **conservative**

Liberal n [C] someone who supports or belongs to the former Liberal Party in Britain or the Liberal Party in Canada —**Liberal** adj

liberal ˈarts n [plural] *especially AmE* the areas of learning which develop someone's ability to think and increase their general knowledge, rather than developing technical skills

Liberal ˈDemocrats n [plural] a British political party —**Liberal Democrat** adj

lib·e·ral·is·m /ˈlɪbərəlɪzəm/ n [U] liberal opinions and principles, especially on social and political subjects; ▱ **conservatism**

lib·e·ral·i·ty /ˌlɪbəˈrælɪti/ n [U] *formal* **1** understanding of, and respect for, other people's opinions **2** the quality of being generous

lib·e·ral·ize also **-ise** *BrE* /ˈlɪbərəlaɪz/ v [T] to make a system, laws, or moral attitudes less strict —**liberalization** /ˌlɪbərəlaɪˈzeɪʃən $ -rələ-/ n [U]

lib·e·ral·ly /ˈlɪbərəli/ adv **1** using or including plenty of something, especially in a generous way: *Apply the glue liberally to both surfaces.* | *dark hair liberally sprinkled with grey* **2** with liberal ideas or opinions: *The people around here are more liberally inclined than back home.*

ˈliberal ˌstudies n [plural] *especially BrE* subjects that are taught in order to increase someone's general knowledge and their ability to write, speak, and study more effectively; → **liberal arts**

lib·e·rate /ˈlɪbəreɪt/ v [T] **1** to free someone from feelings or conditions that make their life unhappy or difficult: **liberate sb from sth** *women's freedom to pursue careers liberated from childcare* | *the liberating power of education* **2** to free prisoners, a city, a country etc from someone's control: *A few days later, our armies liberated the city.* —**liberation** /ˌlɪbəˈreɪʃən/ n [U]: *liberation from oppression* | *the liberation of Paris in August 1944* —**liberator** /ˈlɪbəreɪtə $ -ər/ n [C]

lib·e·rat·ed /ˈlɪbəreɪtᵻd/ adj free to behave in the way you want, and not restricted by traditional rules of social and sexual behaviour: *a liberated woman*

lib·er·tar·i·an /ˌlɪbəˈteəriən $ -bərˈter-/ n [C] someone who believes strongly that people should be free to do and think what they want to, without any government control —**libertarian** adj

lib·er·tine /ˈlɪbətiːn $ -ər-/ n [C] *literary* someone who leads an immoral life and always looks for pleasure, especially sexual pleasure —**libertine** adj

lib·er·ty /ˈlɪbəti $ -ər-/ n plural liberties
1 FREEDOM [U] the freedom and the right to do whatever you want without asking permission or being afraid of authority: *the fight for liberty and equality* | **individual/personal liberty** *threats to individual liberty* | **religious/political/economic liberty** *struggles for political liberty*
2 LEGAL RIGHT [C usually plural] a particular legal right: *liberties such as freedom of speech* → **CIVIL LIBERTY**
3 WITHOUT PERMISSION [singular] something you do without asking permission, especially which may offend or upset someone else: **take the liberty of doing sth** *I took the liberty of cancelling your reservation.*
4 be at liberty to do sth *formal* to have the right or permission to do something: *I am not at liberty to discuss these matters.*
5 take liberties with sb/sth **a)** to make unreasonable changes in something such as a piece of writing: *The film-makers took too many liberties with the original novel.* **b)** *old-fashioned* to treat someone without respect by being too friendly too quickly, especially in a sexual way: *He's been taking liberties with our female staff.*
6 at liberty *formal* if a prisoner or an animal is at liberty, they are no longer in prison or enclosed in a small place; ▱ **free**

li·bi·do /lɪˈbiːdəʊ $ -doʊ/ n plural libidos [C,U] *technical* someone's desire to have sex —**libidinous** /lɪˈbɪdɪnəs/ adj

Li·bra /ˈliːbrə/ n **1** [U] the seventh sign of the ZODIAC, represented by a pair of SCALES, which some people believe affects the character and life of people born between September 24 and October 23 **2** also **Libran** [C] someone who was born between September 24 and October 23 —**Libran** adj

li·brar·i·an /laɪˈbreəriən $ -ˈbrer-/ n [C] someone who works in a library —**librarianship** n [U]

li·bra·ry S2 W1 /ˈlaɪbrəri, -bri $ -breri/ n plural libraries [C]
1 a room or building containing books that can be looked at or borrowed; → **bookshop**: *a public library* | **school/college/university library** | *a library book* | **library staff** → see picture at TOWN
2 a group of books, CDs etc, collected by one person
3 a room in a large house where books are kept
4 a set of books, CDs, videos etc that are produced by the same company and have the same general appearance: *a library of modern classics*
5 library pictures/footage *BrE* film or pictures used in a television programme which are not recent

li·bret·tist /lɪˈbretᵻst/ n [C] someone who writes librettos

li·bret·to /lɪˈbretəʊ $ -toʊ/ n plural librettos [C] the words of an OPERA or musical play

lice /laɪs/ n the plural of LOUSE¹

li·cence S3 W2 *BrE*; **license** *AmE* /ˈlaɪsəns/ n
1 DOCUMENT [C] an official document giving you permission to own or do something for a period of time; → **permit**

do sth without a licence
a licence to do sth
apply for a licence
grant/issue a licence
renew a licence
lose your licence (=have your licence taken away)
driving licence *BrE*
driver's license *AmE*
licence fee *BrE* (=the money a licence costs)
licence holder *BrE* (=a person who has a licence)

The dealers applied for an export licence. | *He was arrested for driving without a licence.* | *The Tennessee Valley Authority applied for a license to operate the facility.* | *The owner of land could grant a licence to cut and remove timber.* | *I forgot to renew my*

L

licence. | *Persistent offenders face losing their* **licence**. |
→ DRIVING LICENCE

2 AGREEMENT [C,U] an agreement with a company or organization giving permission to make, sell or use their product: **under licence** *Guinness is brewed under licence in South Africa.* | **single-user/10-user/site licence** (=permission for computer software to be used by a certain number of people or in a certain place only) | *a licence agreement*

3 FREEDOM [U] freedom to do or say what you think is best: *Headteachers should be allowed greater licence in the exercise of their power.*

4 artistic/poetic licence the way in which a painter or writer changes the facts of the real world to make their story, description, or picture of events more interesting or more beautiful

5 EXCUSE [C,U] the freedom or opportunity to behave in a way that is wrong or immoral: **licence to do sth** *Police say it gives youngsters licence to break the law.*

6 licence to print money an opportunity to make a lot of money without much work or effort – especially used to show disapproval

li·cense also **licence** *BrE* /'laɪsəns/ *v* [T usually passive] to give official permission for someone to do or produce something, or for an activity to take place: **be licensed to do sth** *a restaurant which is licensed to sell alcohol* | *The vaccine has been licensed by the US Food and Drug Administration.*

li·censed also **licenced** *BrE* /'laɪsənst/ *adj* **1** *BrE* having a licence to sell alcoholic drinks: *a licensed restaurant* **2** a car, gun etc that is licensed is one that someone has official permission to own or use **3** having been given official permission to do a particular job: *a licensed private investigator*

li·cen·see /ˌlaɪsən'siː/ *n* [C] someone who has official permission to do something

'**license plate** *n* [C] *AmE* one of the signs with numbers on it at the front and back of a car; ☐ **number plate** *BrE*; → see picture at CAR

'**licensing ˌlaws** *n* [plural] the British laws that say when and where you can sell alcohol

li·cen·ti·ate /laɪ'senʃiət/ *n* [C] *formal* someone who has been given official permission to practise a particular art or profession

li·cen·tious /laɪ'senʃəs/ *adj formal* behaving in a sexually immoral or uncontrolled way —**licentiously** *adv* —**licentiousness** *n* [U]

li·chee /'laɪtʃiː/ *n* [C] another spelling of LYCHEE

li·chen /'laɪkən, 'lɪtʃən/ *n* [U] a grey, green, or yellow plant that spreads over the surface of stones and trees; → moss

lick¹ S3 /lɪk/ *v*

1 TONGUE [T] to move your tongue across the surface of something in order to eat it, wet it, clean it etc: *The dog jumped up and licked her face.* | **lick sth ⇔ up** *A cat licked up the drops spilt on the floor.* | **lick sth off sth** *He licked the drops off his upper lip.*

2 SPORT [T] *informal* to defeat an opponent: *I bet we could lick the best teams in Georgia.*

3 FLAMES/WAVES [I,T] *literary* if flames or waves lick something, they touch it again and again with quick movements: [+at/against] *Soon the flames were licking at the curtains.*

4 have (got) sth licked *informal* to have succeeded in dealing with a difficult problem: *Just when you think you've got it licked, it comes back.*

5 lick your lips also lick your chops *AmE* to feel eager and excited because you are expecting to get something good: *Scottish rugby fans are licking their lips in anticipation.*

6 lick your wounds to quietly think about the defeat or disappointment you have just suffered

7 lick sb's boots to obey someone completely because you are afraid of them or want to please them → knock/lick sb/sth into shape at SHAPE¹ (3)

lick² *n* **1** [C usually singular] when you move your tongue across the surface of something: *Can I have a lick of your ice cream?* **2** a lick of paint/colour/etc a small amount of paint etc put onto the surface of something to improve its appearance: *It'll be okay after a lick of paint.* **3** not a lick of sth *AmE old-fashioned* not even a small amount of something: *Ann won't do a lick of work around the house.* **4** [C] *informal* part of a song played on a GUITAR: *a bluesy guitar lick* **5** at a great/fair lick *BrE informal* very fast **6** give sth a lick and a promise **a)** *BrE* to wash or clean something quickly and carelessly **b)** *AmE* to do a job quickly and carelessly **7** [C] *informal* an act of hitting someone

lick·e·ty-split /ˌlɪkəti 'splɪt/ *adv AmE old-fashioned* very quickly

lick·ing /'lɪkɪŋ/ *n* [singular] *informal* **1** a defeat in a sports competition or match; ☐ **hammering**: *We got a real licking in the final.* **2** a severe beating as a punishment

lic·o·rice /'lɪkərɪs, -rɪʃ/ *n* [U] the American spelling of LIQUORICE

lid

toothpaste cap

bottle stopper

saucepan lid

bottle top

drain cover

lid /lɪd/ *n*

1 COVER [C] a cover for the open part of a pot, box, or other container: **dustbin/saucepan etc lid** *the name on the coffin lid* | [+of] *He carefully lifted the lid of the box.* → TOP¹ (4); → see picture at EAT

2 EYE [C] an EYELID

3 keep a/the lid on sth to control a situation very carefully, especially so that it does not cause problems: *keeping the lid on inflation* | *Kline keeps a very tight lid on his private life.*

4 put a/the lid on sth *informal* to do something that finally stops something or ruins or ends someone's plans or hopes: *Let's put a lid on all these rumours.*

5 take the lid off sth also lift the lid on sth to let people know the true facts about a bad or shocking situation: *a documentary that takes the lid off the world of organized crime*

lid·ded /'lɪdɪd/ *adj* **1** heavy-lidded eyes eyes with large EYELIDS **2** a lidded container, pot etc has a lid

li·do /'liːdəʊ, 'laɪ- $ 'liːdoʊ/ *n plural* **lidos** [C] *BrE* an outdoor public area, often at a beach, lake etc, for swimming and lying in the sun

lie¹ S2 W1 /laɪ/ *v past tense* **lay** /leɪ/ *past participle* **lain** /leɪn/ *present participle* **lying**, *third person singular* **lies**

1 FLAT POSITION **a)** [I] to be in a position in which your body is flat on the floor, on a bed etc: [+on/in etc]

[1] 000, [2] 000, [3] 000, most frequent words in [S]poken and [W]ritten English

He was lying on the bed smoking a cigarette. | *Don't lie in the sun for too long.* | **lie there** *For a few minutes he just lay there.* | **lie still/awake etc** *She would lie awake worrying.* | *The dog was lying dead on the floor.* **b)** also **lie down** [I always + adv/prep] to put yourself in a position in which your body is flat on the floor or on a bed: [+on] *Lie flat on the floor.* | [+back] *She lay back against the pillows.* **c)** [I always + adv/prep] to be in a flat position on a surface: [+on/in etc] *The papers were lying neatly on his desk.*; → see box at LAY²

2 EXIST [I always + adv/prep] if a problem, an answer, blame etc lies somewhere, it is caused by, exists, or can be found in that thing, person, or situation: **fault/ blame/responsibility lies with sb** *Part of the blame must lie with social services.* | **the problem/answer etc lies with/in sth** *The difficulty lies in providing sufficient evidence.* | *The strength of the book lies in the fact that the material is from classroom experience.* | **herein/ therein lies the problem/dilemma etc** *And herein lies the key to their achievements.*

3 PLACE [I always + adv/prep] if a town, village, etc lies in a particular place, it is in that place: *The town lies in a small wooded valley.* | *The Tasman Sea lies between Tasmania and Australia.*

4 FUTURE [I always + adv/prep] if something lies ahead of you, lies in the future etc, it is going to happen to you in the future: [+ahead] *How will we cope with the difficulties that lie ahead?* | [+before] *A blank and empty future lay before me.* | *I was wondering what lay in store for us.*

5 CONDITION [linking verb] to be in a particular state or condition: **lie empty/open/hidden etc** *The book lay open on the table.* | *The town now lay in ruins.*

6 lie at the heart/centre/root of sth to be the most important part of something, especially the main cause of it: *the issue that lies at the heart of the present conflict*

7 lie low a) to remain hidden because someone is trying to find you or catch you: *We'll have to lie low until tonight.* **b)** to wait and try not to be noticed by anyone: *He decided to lie low for a while after the report came out.*

8 lie in wait (for sb) a) to remain hidden in a place and wait for someone so that you can attack them: *a giant crocodile lying in wait for its prey* **b)** if something bad lies in wait for you, it is going to happen to you

9 lie (in) second/third/fourth etc (place) *BrE* to be in second, third etc position in a competition: *Liverpool are lying third in the football championship.*

10 lie heavy on sb *formal* if something lies heavy on you, it makes you feel unhappy: *The feelings of guilt lay heavy on him.*

11 DEAD PERSON [I always + adv/prep] if someone lies in a particular place, they are buried there: *Here lies Percival Smythe* (=written on a gravestone).

12 lie in state if an important person who has died lies in state, their body is put in a public place so that people can go and look at the body in order to show their respect for that person → **let sleeping dogs lie** at SLEEP¹ (6)

lie around; lie about *BrE phr v*
1 lie around (sth) if something is lying around, it has been left somewhere in an untidy way, rather than being in its proper place: *If you leave your shoes lying around like that, you'll trip over them.* | *Papers and books lay around the room in complete chaos.*
2 if you lie around, you spend time lying down and not doing anything: *I felt so lazy just lying around on the beach all day.*
lie behind sth *phr v*
if something lies behind an action, it is the real reason for the action, even though it may be hidden: *She soon guessed what lay behind his question.* | *Two basic assumptions lay behind the policy.*
lie down *phr v*
1 to put yourself in a position in which your body is flat on the floor or on a bed: *Just lie down on the bed.*

2 take sth lying down *informal* to accept bad treatment without complaining: *I'm not going to take this lying down!*
lie in *phr v BrE*
to remain in bed in the morning for longer than usual
→ LIE-IN
lie up *phr v BrE*
to hide or rest somewhere for a period of time: *The next day they lay up in a cave.*

lie² *v* **lied, lying, lies** [I] **1** to deliberately tell someone something that is not true: *I could tell from her face that she was lying.* | [+to] *I would never lie to you.* | [+about] *She lied about her age.* | **lie through your teeth** (=say something that is completely untrue) **2** if a picture, account etc lies, it does not show the true facts or the true situation: *Statistics can often lie.* | *The camera never lies.*

lie³ [S3] *n*
1 [C] something that you say or write that you know is untrue

tell (sb) a lie
a complete/outright lie
a big lie
a blatant lie (=a shocking lie)
a bald-faced lie *AmE* **a barefaced lie** *BrE* (=shocking lie)
a white lie (=a lie that is not serious, told to avoid upsetting someone)
a pack of lies (=a completely untrue set of statements)
a tissue of lies *BrE* (=a completely untrue set of statements)
live a lie (=pretend that a situation is satisfactory when it is not)

[+about] *I told her a lie about what I was doing.* | *I always know when he's telling lies.* | *I told them I was Catholic. I used to be Catholic, so it wasn't a complete lie.* | *I don't want to hear a bunch of big lies about what happened.* | *It was obviously a blatant lie.* | *Jones resorted to deception and barefaced lies.* | *those little white lies that we all tell* | *Their whole account of the event was a pack of lies.* | *For years, he had been living a lie.*

2 give the lie to sth *formal* to show that something is untrue: *This report gives the lie to the company's claims.*
3 the lie of the land/ the way the land lies the way that a situation is developing at a particular time: *I want to see how the land lies before I decide whether or not to take the job.*
4 (I) **tell a lie** *BrE spoken* used when you realize that something you have just said is not correct: *It was £25, no, tell a lie, £35.*

'lie de,tector *n* [C] a piece of equipment used especially by the police to check whether someone is lying, by measuring sudden changes in their heart rate: *He was asked to take a lie detector test.*

'lie down *n* [singular] *BrE* a short rest, usually on a bed: *I'm going upstairs to have a lie down.*

liege /liːdʒ/ *n* [C] **1** also **liege lord** a lord who was served and obeyed in the Middle Ages **2** also **liege-man** someone who had to serve and obey a lord in the Middle Ages

'lie-in *n* [singular] *BrE* an occasion when you stay in bed longer than usual in the morning: *I always have a lie-in on a Sunday.*

li·en /'liːən, liːn/ *n* [C + on] *law* the legal right to keep something that belongs to someone who owes you money, until the debt has been paid

lieu /ljuː, luː $ luː/ *n* **in lieu (of sth)** *formal* instead of: *extra time off in lieu of payment*

Lieut *BrE*, **Lieut.** a written abbreviation of *lieutenant*

lieu·ten·ant /lefˈtenənt $ luːˈten-/ *n* [C] **1 a)** a fairly low rank in the armed forces, or an officer of this rank **b)** a fairly high rank in the US police force, or an officer of this rank **2 lieutenant colonel/general/Governor etc** an officer or official with the rank just below COLO-

NEL, GENERAL², GOVERNOR etc   **3** [C] someone who does work for, or in place of, someone in a higher position; ▣ **deputy**

life S1 W1 /laɪf/ *n plural* **lives** /laɪvz/
1 TIME SB IS ALIVE [C,U] the period of time when someone is alive: *Learning goes on throughout life.* | *You have your whole life ahead of you.* | **in sb's life** *For the first time in my life I was happy.* | *I've never been so embarrassed in my life!* | *I've known John all my life* (=since I was born). | *His main aim in life was to have fun.* | *It was one of the best days of my life.* | *The accident scarred him for life* (=for the rest of his life). | *She knew she'd feel guilty for the rest of her life.* | *Raj spent his life caring for others.* | *Bonington spent his entire adult life in France.* | *We don't know much about the poet's early life* (=when he was young). | *Poor diet can lead to a whole range of diseases in later life* (=when you are older). | *She married late in life* (=when she was fairly old). | *He's a life member* (=continuing until he dies) *of the club.*
2 STATE OF BEING ALIVE [C,U] the state of being alive: *The right to life is the most basic of human rights.* | *The riots presented a considerable risk to life and property.* | *Danny was a cheerful little boy who loved life.* | *A seatbelt could save your life.* | *Two firefighters risked their lives to save the children.* | *Thousands lost their lives* (=died) *in the earthquake.* | *an explosion which claimed the lives of* (=killed) *at least 170 miners* | *He has risked life and limb* (=has done very dangerous things) *to photograph some of the world's most dangerous animals.* | *Cuts to the ambulance service could cost lives* (=people could die). | *Misuse of the equipment could endanger the lives of staff and students.* | *He owes his life to* (=he is still alive because of) *the prompt action of a neighbour.* | **take your (own) life** (=deliberately kill yourself) *There's no evidence that she intended to take her own life.* | **take sb's life** (=kill someone) *No-one has the right to take another's life.* | **be fighting for your life** (=be so ill or injured that you might die) *A resident was fighting for his life yesterday, having escaped the blaze.* | **give your life/lay down your life** (=die in order to save other people or because of a strong belief) *He gave his life for the cause of freedom* | **take your life in your (own) hands** (=put yourself in a very dangerous situation) *You take your life in your hands every time you cross this road.*
3 WAY SB LIVES [C usually singular] the way you live your life, and what you do and experience during it: **lead/live/have a ... life** *The operation should enable Bobby to lead a normal life.* | *She just wanted to live a quiet life.* | *Having a baby changes your life completely.* | *The family moved to Australia to start a new life.* | *Ken's whole life revolved around surfing* (=that was the main interest and purpose of his life). | *You shouldn't let your boyfriend rule your life* (=control and affect everything you do). | *My grandmother had a hard life* (=a life full of problems). | *She's led a very sheltered life* (=a life in which you have been protected from unpleasant things). | **a life of crime/poverty/ misery** *He had been drawn into a life of crime.*
4 PARTICULAR SITUATION/JOB [C,U] **a)** the experiences, activities, and ways of living that are typical of being in a particular job, situation, society etc: *Why do so few women enter political life?* | *the British way of life* | **city/country/village etc life** *Noise has become one of the main pollutants of modern city life.* | **army/ student/college etc life** *He missed the routine of army life.* | *Are you enjoying married life?* **b)** the time in your life when you are doing a particular job, are in a particular situation etc: **sb's life as sth** *Now a celebrity chef, he rarely talks about his life as an army cook.* | *Sara admits to having affairs throughout her married life.* | *Most of his working life was spent in the shipyards.*
5 social/personal/sex etc life the activities in your life relating to your friends, your family, sex etc: *I don't need advice about my love life.* | *traditional views of family life* | *Children need a caring and happy home life.*

6 HUMAN EXISTENCE [U] human existence, considered as a variety of experiences and activities: *My Aunt Julia had very little experience of life.* | *Life has a way of changing the best of plans.* | *For some people, religion gives life a meaning.* | **daily/everyday life** *the frustrations and disappointments of everyday life* | *I try to see the funny side of life.*
7 TIME WHEN STH EXISTS/WORKS [C usually singular] **a)** the period of time during which something happens or exists: [+of] *The issues will not be resolved during the life of the present parliament.* | **start/begin/come to life as sth** *The building began life as a monastery.* **b)** the period of time during which something is still good enough to use: [+of] *What's the average life of a passenger aircraft?* | *Careful use can extend the life of your washing machine.* → SHELF LIFE
8 LIVING THINGS [U] **a)** the quality of being alive that people, animals, plants etc have and that objects and dead things do not have: *Ben felt her neck for a pulse or any other sign of life.* | *In the springtime, everything comes to life again.* **b)** living things, such as people, animals, or plants: *Is there life on other planets?* | **human/animal/plant/bird etc life** *The island is rich in bird life.* → WILDLIFE
9 be sb's (whole) life to be the most important thing or person to someone: *Music is Laura's whole life.*
10 life and death also life or death used for emphasizing that a situation, decision etc is extremely urgent and important, especially because someone is at risk of dying: *Don't call me unless it's a matter of life and death.* | *a life or death decision* | *A doctor's job involves life and death situations.*
11 GAME [C] a chance in a game, especially a computer game, in which you can be defeated or do something wrong and can still continue playing: *He's up to level five and still has three lives left.*
12 ACTIVITY [U] activity or movement: *The house was quiet and there was no sign of life.* | *She was always so cheerful and full of life.*
13 INTEREST/EXCITEMENT [U] a quality of being interesting or exciting: *Try to put some life into your writing.* | *The game really came to life after a magnificent goal from Beckham.* | *A gifted teacher can really bring literature to life for his or her students.*
14 come to life/roar into life/splutter into life etc to suddenly start working: *Finally the car spluttered into life.*
15 make life difficult/easier etc to make it difficult, easier etc to do something: *Surely computers are supposed to make life easier, not more complicated!* | [+for] *Why make life difficult for yourself?*
16 the life and soul of the party *BrE*; the life of the party *AmE* someone who enjoys social occasions and is fun and exciting to be with
17 life and limb *formal* your life and physical health – used especially when this is threatened in some way: *She risks life and limb every day in her job as an undercover investigator.*
18 get a life! *spoken* used to tell someone that you think they are boring and should find more exciting things to do: *You guys should just stop moaning and get a life!*
19 that's life also such is life *spoken* used to say that something is disappointing but you have to accept it: *Oh well, that's life!*
20 life's a bitch *spoken not polite* used to say that bad things happen in life
21 this is the life *spoken* used when you are relaxing and doing something you enjoy: *Ah, this is the life! Lying on the beach, sipping cool drinks.*
22 the shock/surprise/game etc of sb's life the biggest shock or surprise, the best game etc that someone has ever had: *I had the surprise of my life when I saw John standing there.* → **have the time of your life** at TIME¹ (41)
23 how's life? *spoken* used to ask someone if they are well, what they have been doing etc: *Hi Bob! How's life?* | *How's life been with you?*

L

24 life goes on *spoken* used to say that you must continue to live a normal life even when something sad or disappointing has happened: *We both miss him, but life goes on.*

25 a life of its own a) if something has a life of its own, it seems to move or work by itself: *The ball seemed to have acquired a life of its own.* **b)** if something has a life of its own, it exists and develops without depending on other things: *Slowly but surely, the project is taking on a life of its own.*

26 cannot for the life of me *spoken* used to say that you cannot remember or understand something even when you try hard: *I couldn't for the life of me remember his name.*

27 life's too short *spoken* used to say that you should not waste time doing something or worrying about something: *Forget about it. Life's too short.* | [+for] *Life's too short for moping about.* | **life's too short to do sth** *Life's too short to bear grudges.*

28 not on your life *spoken* used as a reply to a question or suggestion to say that you definitely will not do something: *'Are you going to go and work for him then?' 'Not on your life!'*

29 the woman/man/girl etc in your life the woman or man you are married to or are having a relationship with – used especially in advertisements: *This is the ideal gift for the man in your life.*

30 PRISON [U] also **life imprisonment** the punishment of being put in prison for the rest of your life: **be sentenced to/get/be given life** | *He was sentenced to life for the murder.* | *I think she should get life.* → LIFE SENTENCE, LIFER

31 ART [U] when you paint, draw etc something you are looking at, especially a person or animal: *She's taking classes in life drawing.* → STILL LIFE

32 frighten/scare the life out of sb *informal* to make someone feel very frightened: *Don't do that! You scared the life out of me!*

33 there's life in the old dog yet *spoken* used to say that although someone or something is old, they are still able to do something – used humorously

34 live/lead/have the life of Riley *informal* to have a very easy and comfortable life and not have to work hard: *He spends all day lounging by the pool and living the life of Riley.*

35 BOOK/FILM [U] the story of someone's life; ▣ **biography**: *Boswell's Life of Johnson*

36 the next life also **the life to come**, **life after death** the time after death, in which some people believe life continues in another form: *She expects to meet her dead husband in the next life.* → **as large as life** at LARGE[1] (7) → **CHANGE OF LIFE**; → **for dear life** at DEAR[3] (6); → **DOUBLE LIFE**; → **high life** at HIGH[1] (22); → **a new lease of life** at LEASE[1] (2); → **quality of life** at QUALITY[1] (5); → **real life** at REAL[1] (3); → **REAL-LIFE**; → **true to life** at TRUE[1] (9); → **WALK OF LIFE**

life as,surance *n* [U] *BrE* LIFE INSURANCE

life belt *n* [C] **1** *BrE* a LIFE BUOY **2** *AmE* a special belt you wear in the water to prevent you from sinking

life·blood /ˈlaɪfblʌd/ *n* [U] **1** the most important thing needed by an organization, relationship etc to continue to exist or develop successfully: [+of] *Communication is the lifeblood of a good marriage.* **2** *literary* your blood

life·boat /ˈlaɪfbəʊt $ -boʊt/ *n* [C] **1** a boat that is sent out to help people who are in danger at sea: **lifeboat crew/station/service** **2** a small boat carried by ships in order to save people if the ship sinks

life ,buoy *n* [C] a large ring made out of material that floats, which you throw to someone who has fallen in the water, to prevent them from drowning

life ,cycle *n* [C] all the different levels of development that an animal or plant goes through during its life

life ex'pectancy *n* [C] **1** the length of time that a person or animal is expected to live **2** the length of time that something is expected to continue to work, be useful etc

life form *n* [C] a living thing such as a plant or animal: *life forms on other planets*

life guard *n* [C] someone whose job at a beach or swimming pool is to help swimmers who are in danger → see picture at SPORTS CENTRE

life ,history *n* [C] all the events and changes that happen during the life of a living thing

life in,surance *n* [U] a type of insurance that someone makes regular payments into so that when they die their family will receive money; ▣ **life assurance**

life ,jacket *BrE n* [C] a piece of clothing that can be filled with air and worn around your upper body to stop you from sinking in the water; ▣ **life vest** *AmE*

life·less /ˈlaɪfləs/ *adj* **1** *literary* dead or appearing to be dead: *Anton's lifeless body was found floating in the lake.* **2** lacking the positive qualities that make something or someone interesting, exciting, or active; ▣ **lively**: *The actors' performances were lifeless.* **3** not living, or not having living things on it: *The surface of the moon is arid and lifeless.* **4** lifeless hair or skin is in bad condition and does not look healthy; ▣ **dull** —**lifelessly** *adv* —**lifelessness** *n* [U]

life·like /ˈlaɪflaɪk/ *adj* a lifelike picture, model etc looks exactly like a real person or thing: *a very lifelike statue*

life·line /ˈlaɪflaɪn/ *n* [C] **1** something which someone depends on completely: [+to] *The telephone is her lifeline to the rest of the world.* | [+for] *The organization has proved to be a lifeline for thousands of needy families.* **2** a rope used for saving people in danger, especially at sea

life·long /ˈlaɪflɒŋ $ -lɒːŋ/ *adj* [only before noun] continuing or existing all through your life: *She became a lifelong friend of ours.* | *David finally realized his lifelong ambition.*

life ,peer *n* [C] someone who has the rank of a British PEER (=lord or lady) but who cannot pass it on to their children

life pre,server *n* [C] *AmE* something such as a LIFE BELT or LIFE JACKET that can be worn in the water to prevent you from sinking

lif·er /ˈlaɪfə $ -ər/ *n* [C] *informal* someone who has been sent to prison for the rest of their life

life raft *n* [C] a small rubber boat that can be filled with air and used by passengers on a sinking ship

life·sav·er /ˈlaɪfseɪvə $ -ər/ *n* [C] **1** someone or something that helps you avoid a difficult or unpleasant situation: *A microwave oven can be a real lifesaver when you're pressed for time.* **2** someone or something that prevents you from dying: *The seatbelt is the biggest single lifesaver in cars.* **3** a LIFE GUARD

life-,saving[1] also **life·sav·ing** /ˈlaɪfˌseɪvɪŋ/ *adj* [only before noun] life-saving medical treatments or equipment are used to help save people's lives: **lifesaving surgery/treatment/drugs etc** *The boy needs a life-saving transplant operation.*

life-saving[2] also **life·sav·ing** /ˈlaɪfˌseɪvɪŋ/ *n* [U] the skills necessary to save a person from drowning: *All of the staff have been trained in lifesaving.*

life ,science *n* [C usually plural] subjects such as BIOLOGY that are concerned with the study of humans, plants, and animals → EARTH SCIENCE, PHYSICAL SCIENCE

life ,sentence *n* [C] the punishment of sending someone to prison for the rest of their life or for a very long time: *Miller is serving a life sentence for murder.*

life-size also **life-sized** *adj* a picture or model of something or someone that is life-size is the same size as they really are: *a life-sized statue of the president*

life·span W3 /ˈlaɪfspæn/ *n* [C] the average length of time that someone will live or that something will continue to work; → **lifetime**: *Men have a shorter lifespan than women.* | **a lifespan of 5 days/10 years etc** *A TV set has an average lifespan of 11 years.*

L

ˈlife ˌstory n [C] the story of someone's whole life: *She insisted on **telling** me her whole **life story.***

ˈlife-ˌstyle /ˈlaɪfstaɪl/ n [C] the way a person or group of people live, including the place they live in, the things they own, the kind of job they do, and the activities they enjoy: *Regular exercise is part of a **healthy lifestyle.*** | *lavish/comfortable/simple etc lifestyle They lead an extremely lavish lifestyle.*

ˈlife support ˌsystem n [C] **1** also **life support machine** a piece of equipment that keeps someone alive when they are extremely ill **2** a piece of equipment that keeps people alive in conditions where they would not normally be able to live, such as in space

ˈlife-ˌthreatening adj a life-threatening situation, illness, or injury could cause a person to die; → **fatal**

ˈlife-ˌtime /ˈlaɪftaɪm/ n [C usually singular] **1** the period of time during which someone is alive or something exists; → **lifespan: during/in sb's lifetime** *During her lifetime she had witnessed two world wars.* | *It's the sort of opportunity you see only **once in a lifetime.*** **2** the chance/experience of a lifetime the best opportunity, experience etc that you will ever have: *It was the holiday of a lifetime.* **3 not in this lifetime** *spoken* not at all; **▣ never**: *'Would you go out with him after he dropped you?' 'Not in this lifetime.'*

ˈlife vest n [C] *AmE* a LIFE JACKET

lift¹ [S2] [W2] /lɪft/ v

1 MOVE STH UPWARDS also **lift up** [T] to move something or someone upwards into the air: *Sophie lifted the phone before the second ring.* | *He lifted the lid on the pot of soup.* | *The lumber was lifted by crane and dropped into the truck.* | *lift sb/sth onto/into/out of etc sth They lifted Andrew onto the bed.* | *lift sb from sth The driver was lifted from the wreck.*

2 PART OF THE BODY also **lift up** [I,T] to move part of your body up to a higher position; **▣ raise: lift your hand/arm/leg etc** *She lifted her hand to knock on the door once again.* | *Pam lifted her shoulders in a little shrug.* | *lift your head/eyes* (=move your head or eyes up so that you can look at something) *She lifted her head to gaze at him.* | *He heard a scream and the hairs on the back of his neck began to lift.*

3 CONTROLS/LAWS [T] to remove a rule or a law that says that something is not allowed: *lift a restriction/an embargo/sanctions etc The government plans to lift its ban on cigar imports.*

4 BY PLANE [T always + adv/prep] to take people or things to or from a place by aircraft: *More troops are being lifted into the area as the fighting spreads.*

5 not lift a finger (to do sth) *informal* to do nothing to help: *He never lifted a finger to help me with the kids.*

6 lift sb's spirits to make someone feel more cheerful and hopeful

7 CLOUDS/MIST [I] if cloud or mist lifts, it disappears

8 SAD FEELINGS [I] if feelings of sadness lift, they disappear: *Jan's depression seemed to be lifting at last.*

9 USE SB'S IDEAS/WORDS [T] to take words, ideas etc from someone else's work and use them in your work, without stating where they came from and as if they were your own words etc: *lift sth from sb/sth The words were lifted from an article in a medical journal.*

10 STEAL [T] *informal* to steal something: *lift sth from sb/sth They had lifted dozens of CDs from the store.*

11 VOICE also **lift up** [T] *literary* if you lift your voice, you speak, shout, or sing more loudly; **▣ raise**

12 INCREASE [T] to make prices, profit etc increase: *The U.S. may use tax cuts to lift the economy.*

13 VEGETABLES [T] to dig up vegetables that grow under the ground: *She was lifting potatoes.*

lift off *phr v*

if an aircraft or spacecraft lifts off, it leaves the ground and rises into the air

lift² [S3] [W3] n

1 IN A BUILDING [C] *BrE* a machine that you can ride in, that moves up and down between the floors in a tall building; **▣ elevator** *AmE: They took the lift down to the bar.* | *It's on the 3rd floor . Let's use the lift.*

2 IN A CAR [C] if you give someone a lift, you take them somewhere in your car; **▣ ride**: *Do you want a lift into town?* | *John gave me a lift home.* | *He very kindly offered me a lift.* → see picture at **STAY**

3 give sb/sth a lift a) to make someone feel more cheerful and more hopeful: *The new park has given everyone in the neighbourhood a lift.* **b)** to make something such as a business, the economy etc operate better: *The Bank of England's announcement gave the stock market a lift today.*

4 LIFTING MOVEMENT [C,U] a movement in which something is lifted or raised up: *She does sit-ups and leg lifts every morning.*

5 WIND/AIRCRAFT [U] the pressure of air that keeps something such as an aircraft up in the air or lifts it higher → **CHAIRLIFT, SKI LIFT**

ˈlift-off n [C,U] the moment when a vehicle that is about to travel in space leaves the ground; → **take-off**

lig·a·ment /ˈlɪɡəmənt/ n [C] a band of strong material in your body, similar to muscle, that joins bones or holds an organ in its place; → **tendon**: *He tore a ligament in his left knee.* | *damaged ankle ligaments*

light¹ [S1] [W1] /laɪt/ n

1 NATURAL/ARTIFICIAL LIGHT a) [U] the energy from the sun, a flame, a lamp etc that allows you to see things: *The morning light came streaming in through the windows.* | *She opened the curtains to let in the light.* | *It was late afternoon and the light was beginning to fade.* | *a pattern of light and shade* | **in/by the light of sth** *Everything looked grey in the dim light of the oil lamp.* | *We sat and talked by the light of the fire.* | **in/into the light** *The man moved forward into the light.* | **good/strong/bright light** *We'll need good light if we want to take the photographs outside.* | **poor/dim/fading light** *In the fading light she could just make out the shape of a tractor.* | **soft/warm light** *The valley was bathed in the soft light of dawn.* | **cold/harsh light** *the cold, harsh light of a winter afternoon* | **blinding/ dazzling light** (=extremely bright light) *We saw a sudden flash of blinding light.* | **a beam/ray/shaft of light** (=a thin line of light) *The clouds parted and a beam of light fell on the field.* **b)** [C] a particular type of light, with its own particular colour, level of brightness etc: *The colours look different in different lights.*

2 LAMP/ELECTRIC LIGHT ETC [C] **a)** an electric light: *Ahead of us we could see the lights of the city.* | *We're having a mixture of wall lights and ceiling lights in different parts of the house.* | **turn/switch/put on a light** *I switched on the light in the bedroom.* | **turn/switch/put off a light** *Don't forget to switch the lights off when you go out.* | **turn/switch/put out a light** *Can you turn the light out downstairs?* | **a light is/comes/goes on** *The lights in the office were still on.* | *The street lights were just beginning to come on.* | *He left a light on in the kitchen.* | **a light is off/out** *Make sure all the lights are off when you leave.* | *Suddenly all the **lights** in the house went out.* | *Can you **turn the light down** (=make it less bright) a bit?* → **the bright lights** at **BRIGHT (13) b)** something such as a lamp that you can carry to give you light: *Shine a light over here, will you?*

3 TRAFFIC CONTROL [C usually plural] one of a set of red, green, and yellow lights used for controlling traffic; **▣ traffic lights**: *We waited for the lights to change.* | *Eventually the lights turned green.* | *The driver had failed to stop at a red light.* → **GREEN LIGHT, RED-LIGHT DISTRICT**

4 ON A VEHICLE [C usually plural] one of the lights on a car, bicycle etc that help you to see at night: *He was dazzled by the lights of oncoming traffic.* | *You've left your lights on.* → **BRAKE LIGHT, HEADLIGHT, PARKING LIGHT;** → see picture at **BICYCLE¹**

5 first light *literary* the first light that appears in the morning sky: *We set out at first light the next day.*

6 be/stand in sb's light to prevent someone from getting all the light they need to see or do something: *Could*

light years ahead of its European competitors. **3 light years ago** *informal* a very long time ago: *It all seems light years ago now.*

lig·nite /ˈlɪgnaɪt/ *n* [U] a soft substance like coal, used as FUEL

lik·a·ble, **likeable** /ˈlaɪkəbəl/ *adj* likable people are nice and easy to like: *a friendly likeable little boy*

like¹ [S1] [W1] /laɪk/ *prep*

1 [SIMILAR] similar to something else, or happening in the same way: *Her hair is dark brown like mine.* | *A club should be like a big family.* | *He eats like a pig!* | **look/sound/feel/taste/seem like** *The garden looked like a jungle.* | *At last he felt like a real soldier.* | *My experience is **very much like** that described in the book.* | *He's **very like** his brother.* | *Sometimes you sound **just like** (=exactly like) my mum!* | *He's growing **more like** his father every day.* | *He looked **nothing like** (=not at all like) the man in the police photograph.* → see box at AS¹

2 what is sb/sth like? *spoken* used when asking someone to describe or give their opinion of a person or thing: *What's their house like inside?* | *What are Dan's parents like?*

3 [EXAMPLE] for example: *Things like glass, paper, and plastic can all be recycled.* | *Try to avoid fatty foods like cakes and biscuits.*

4 [TYPICAL] typical of a particular person: **be like sb to do sth** *It's not like Steven to be late.* | *It's **just like** her to run away from her responsibilities!*

5 like this/that/so *spoken* used when you are showing someone how to do something: *You have to fold the corners back, like so.*

6 just like that *informal* if you do something just like that, you do it without thinking about it or planning it carefully: *You can't give up your job just like that!*

7 something like not much more or less than a particular amount; ▣ **about**: *The machinery alone will cost something like thirty thousand pounds.* | *He's scored something like 60 goals this season.*

8 nothing like *BrE* not at all: *Twenty years ago travel was nothing like as easy as it is now.* | *This will be **nothing like enough** money.*

9 there's nothing like used to say that a particular thing is very enjoyable: *There's nothing like a nice cup of tea!*

10 more like used when giving an amount or number that you think is closer to being right than one that has been mentioned: *The builders say they'll be finished in three months, but I think it'll be more like six.*

11 that's more like it/this is more like it *spoken* used to say that something is better, more correct, or more enjoyable than something else: *That gives us a total of 52 – that's more like it.* | *She sat down by the pool and took a sip of her wine. 'This is more like it,' she said.*

12 more like it *BrE spoken* used when you want to change something that has been said, to make it more true: *'Poor David,' she said. 'Poor Harriet, more like it!'*

13 what are you like! *BrE spoken informal* used in a joking, friendly way, when you are surprised by what someone has just said or done: *'I think she's a lovely lady.' 'What are you like!'*

like² [S1] [W1] *v* [T not usually in progressive]

1 [THINK STH IS NICE] to enjoy something or think that it is nice or good; → **love**; ▣ **dislike**: *I like your jacket.* | *I don't really like classical music.* | *Do you like this colour?* | *I like my coffee quite weak.* | *I don't **like it** when you get angry.* | **How** *do you **like** living in London* (=how much do you like it)? | **like doing sth** *I don't like talking in public.* | **like to do sth** *I like to see people enjoying themselves.* | *In time, I **got to like** her* (=began to like her). | *I **quite like** their new album.* | *We **really liked** the film.* | *The time I **like best** (=like most of all) is the evening when it's cool.* | **like sth about sb/sth** *One of the things I like about John is his sense of humour.* | *I didn't **like the idea** of being a single parent.*

2 [LIKE A PERSON] to think that someone is nice or enjoy being with them: *Jessica's really nice, but I don't*

like her boyfriend. | *You'll like my brother.* | *I **really** like Sam.* | *She's a lovely girl and I **like** her **very much**.*

3 [APPROVE OF STH] to approve of something and think that it is good or right: *I don't like dishonesty.* | *I don't **like the way** he shouts at the children.* | **like doing sth** *He's never liked talking about people behind their backs.* | **like sb doing sth** *I don't like him taking all the credit when he didn't do any of the work.* | **like to do sth** *She doesn't like to swear in front of the children.*

4 [DO STH REGULARLY] to try to do something regularly or make something happen regularly: **like to do sth** *I like to get up early and get a bit of work done before breakfast.* | **like sb to do sth** *We like our students to take part in college sports activities.*

5 [WANT] would like **a)** used to say that you want something or want to do something; → **love**: *I'd like a cheeseburger, please.* | **would like to do sth** *I'd like to see that film.* | *There's something I'd like to tell you.* | *I'd like to apologize for my behaviour yesterday.* | *I'd **just like** to say how grateful we are for your help.* | **would like sb to do sth** *He would like us all to be at the meeting.* **b)** used to ask someone if they want something or want to do something: *Would you like a drink?* | *What would you like to eat?* | *Contact our office if you would like more information.* | **would sb like to do sth** *Would you like to come with us?* | **How would you like** (=would you like) *to spend the summer in Italy?* | **would sb like sb to do sth** *Would you like me to pick you up in the morning?*; → see box at WISH¹

6 whatever/wherever/anything etc you like whatever thing you want, in whatever place you want etc: *You can sit wherever you like.* | *You can choose anything you like from the menu.*

7 as long as you like/as much as you like etc as long, as much etc as you want: *You know you're welcome to stay with us as long as you like.* | *Take as many as you like.*

8 (whether you) like it or not used to emphasize that something unpleasant is true or will happen and cannot be changed: *Like it or not, people are often judged by their appearance.*

9 I'd like to think/believe (that) used to say that you wish or hope something is true, when you are not sure that it is: *I'd like to think that we offer an excellent service.* | *I would like to believe that the company can be successful in the future.*

SPOKEN PHRASES

10 if you like *BrE* **a)** used to suggest or offer something to someone: *I can give you her phone number, if you like.* | *If you like, I could go with you.* **b)** used to agree to something, even if it is not really what you want yourself: *'Shall we get a takeaway on the way home?' 'If you like.'* **c)** used to suggest one possible way of describing something or someone: *We don't have a proper agreement, but we have an informal understanding, if you like.*

11 [ROMANTIC] to think someone is sexually attractive; → **love**: *Do you think Alex likes me?*

12 I'd like to see you/him do sth used to say that you do not believe someone can do something: *I'd like to see you organize a conference!*

13 how would you like sth? used to ask someone to imagine how they would feel if something bad happened to them instead of to you or someone else: *How would you like being left alone for hours in a strange place?* | *How would you like it if someone treated you in that way?*

14 I like that! *BrE* used to say that what someone has said or done is rude and unfair: *I like that! She didn't even say thank you.*

15 like it or lump it used to say that someone must accept a situation or decision they do not like because it cannot be changed

---

like³ *n* **1 sb's likes and dislikes** the things that someone likes and does not like: *We all have our own likes and dislikes when it comes to food.* **2 and the like/and such like** and similar things: *Soldiers, policemen, and the like were all called in to help with the emergency.* |

They believe that the government does not spend enough money on health, education, and such like. **3 the likes of sb/sth** *spoken* **a)** used to talk about someone you do not like or do not approve of: *I don't want you spending time with the likes of him.* **b)** used to talk about people of a particular type: *Information is collected through the likes of the FBI, CIA, and Scotland Yard.* **4 the like of sb/sth** also **sb's/sth's like** *formal* something similar to someone or a particular person or thing, or of equal importance or value: *This will be a show the like of which has never been seen before.* | *The man was a genius. We shall not see his like again.*

like⁴ S1 *adv spoken*
1 used in speech to fill a pause while you are thinking what to say next: *The water was, like, really cold.* | *I was just, like, standing there.*
2 I'm/he's/she's like... a) used to tell the exact words someone used: *I asked Dave if he wanted to go, and he's like, no way!* **b)** used to describe an event, feeling, or person, when it is difficult to describe or when you use a noise instead of words: *She was like, huh?* (=she did not understand)
3 as like as not/like enough *BrE* probably: *The ambulance will be too late, as like as not.*

like⁵ S1 *conjunction*
1 in the same way as. Some people consider this use to be incorrect: *No one else can score goals like he can!* | *Don't talk to me like you talk to a child.*
2 like I say/said *spoken* used when you are repeating something that you have already said: *Like I said, I don't mind helping out on the day.* | *I'm sorry, but, like I say, she's not here at the moment.*
3 *informal* as if. Some people think that this use is not correct English: *He looked at me like I was mad.* | *It looks like it's going to rain.* | *This meat smells like it's gone bad.*

like⁶ S1 W3 *adj* [only before noun] *formal*
1 similar in some way: *The second dispute was sorted out in a like manner.* | *They get on well together because they are **of like mind**.* | *Try to buy two fish **of like size**.*
2 be like to do sth *old use* to be likely to do something

-like /laɪk/ *suffix* [in adjectives] used after a noun to say that something is similar to or typical of the noun: *a jelly-like substance* | *childlike simplicity* | *ladylike behaviour*

like·a·ble /ˈlaɪkəbəl/ *adj* another spelling of LIKABLE

like·li·hood /ˈlaɪklihʊd/ *n* [singular, U] **1** the degree to which something can reasonably be expected to happen; ◲ **probability**: [+of] *Using a seatbelt will reduce the likelihood of serious injury in a car accident.* | **little/lower/high/greater etc likelihood** *There was very little likelihood of her getting the job.* | **likelihood (that)** *They must face the likelihood that the newspaper might go bankrupt.* **2** in all likelihood almost certainly: *If I refused, it would in all likelihood mean I'd lose my job.*

like·ly¹ S1 W1 /ˈlaɪkli/ *adj comparative* **likelier**, *superlative* **likeliest**
1 something that is likely will probably happen or is probably true; ◲ **unlikely**: *Snow showers are likely tomorrow.* | **likely outcome/effects/consequences etc** *What are the likely effects of the law going to be?* | *the most likely cause of the problem* | **likely to do/be sth** *Children who live in the country's rural areas are very likely to be poor.* | **more/less/most/least likely** *Young drivers are more likely to have accidents than older drivers.* | *It is more than likely* (=almost certain) *the votes will have to be counted again.* | *It could have been an accident, but that was hardly likely* (=not very likely). | *He could offer no likely explanation when I asked him.*
2 [only before noun] suitable for a particular purpose: *the three most likely candidates for president* | *One likely source of energy is windpower.*
3 a likely story *spoken* used to tell someone you do not believe what they have just said

likely² *adv* **1** probably: **most/very likely** *I'd very likely have done the same thing in your situation.* | **(as) likely as not** *spoken* (=very probably) *As likely as not, the meeting will take place in the village pub.* **2 not likely!** *spoken especially BrE* used to disagree strongly, or to say that something will not happen: *'He said you'd be giving them a lift.' 'Not likely!'*

like-ˈminded *adj* [usually before noun] having similar interests and opinions: *a chance to meet **like-minded** people* —**like-mindedness** *n* [U]

lik·en /ˈlaɪkən/ *v*
liken sb/sth to sb/sth *phr v formal* to say that someone or something is similar to another person or thing; ◲ **compare**: *Critics have likened the new theater to a supermarket.*

like·ness /ˈlaɪknɪs/ *n* **1** [C,U] the quality of being similar in appearance to someone or something; ◲ **resemblance**: [+to] *Hugh's uncanny likeness to his father* | *I can see the **family likeness**.* **2** [C] a painting or photograph of a person, especially one that looks very like the person: **good/perfect/true etc likeness** | [+of] *That's a remarkable likeness of Julia.*

like·wise /ˈlaɪk-waɪz/ *adv* **1** *formal* in the same way; ◲ **similarly**: *Nanny put on a shawl and told the girls to **do likewise**.* | [sentence adverb]: *The clams were delicious. Likewise, the eggplant was excellent.* **2 likewise** *spoken* used to return someone's greeting or polite statement: *'You're always welcome at our house.' 'Likewise.'*

lik·ing /ˈlaɪkɪŋ/ *n* **1** liking for sb/sth *formal* when you like someone or something: *Jim and Keith **had a liking** and respect for each other.* | *She's developed a liking for theatre.* **2 take a liking to sb/sth** to begin to like someone or something: *He immediately took a liking to Steve.* **3 to your liking** *formal* being just what you wanted: *I hope everything was to your liking, Sir.*

li·lac /ˈlaɪlək/ *n* **1** [C] a small tree with pale purple or white flowers **2** [U] a pale purple colour; ◲ **mauve** —**lilac** *adj: a lilac dress*

lil·li·pu·tian /ˌlɪlɪˈpjuːʃən/ *adj formal* extremely small compared to the normal size of things

Li·lo /ˈlaɪləʊ $ -loʊ/ *n plural* **Lilos** [C] *trademark BrE* a rubber MATTRESS filled with air and used as a bed or for floating on water

lilt /lɪlt/ *n* [singular] a pleasant pattern of rising and falling sound in someone's voice or in music: *the lilt of a Scottish accent* —**lilting** *adj: a lilting melody*

lil·y /ˈlɪli/ *n plural* **lilies** [C] one of several types of plant with large bell-shaped flowers of various colours, especially white → see picture at FLOWER¹ → **gild the lily** at GILD (3); → WATER LILY

lily-liv·ered /ˌlɪli ˈlɪvəd $ -ərd/ *adj old-fashioned* lacking courage

lily of the ˈvalley *n* [C] a plant with several small white bell-shaped flowers

lily-ˈwhite *adj* **1** pure white: *lily-white skin* **2** *informal* morally perfect: *You're not so lily-white yourself!*

li·ma bean /ˈliːmə biːn $ ˈlaɪ-/ *n* [C] a round, flat light green bean that grows in America

limb /lɪm/ *n* [C] **1 out on a limb** alone and without help or support: *All the other countries signed the agreement, leaving Britain out on a limb.* | *He'd **gone out on a limb*** (=taken a risk) *to help us.* **2** an arm or leg **3 strong-limbed/long-limbed etc** having strong, long etc arms and legs **4** a large branch of a tree → **risk life and limb** at RISK² (1); → **tear sb limb from limb** at TEAR² (9)

lim·ber¹ /ˈlɪmbə $ -ər/ *v*
limber up *phr v* to do gentle exercises in order to prepare your muscles for a race, competition etc

limber² *adj* able to move and bend easily

---

1 000, 2 000, 3 000, most frequent words in S poken and W ritten English

lim·bo /'lɪmbəʊ $ -boʊ/ n **1** [singular, U] a situation in which nothing happens or changes for a long period of time, and it is difficult to make decisions or know what to do, often because you are waiting for something else to happen first: **be in limbo** *I'm in limbo now until I know whether I've got the job.* | *[+of] the limbo of his eight years in jail* **2 the limbo** a West Indian dance in which the dancer leans backwards and goes under a stick that is lowered gradually

lime¹ /laɪm/ n **1** [C] a small juicy green fruit with a sour taste, or the tree this grows on → see picture at FRUIT¹ **2** [C] a tree with pleasant-smelling yellow flowers; ◨ **linden** **3** [U] a white substance obtained by burning LIMESTONE, used for making cement, marking sports fields etc; ◨ **quicklime** **4** [U] a light yellowish green colour

lime² v [T] technical to add lime to soil to control acid

lime·ade /ˌlaɪm'eɪd/ n [U] a drink made from the juice of limes

lime 'green n [U] a light yellowish green colour —**lime-green** adj

lime·light /'laɪmlaɪt/ n [singular, U] a situation in which someone receives a lot of attention, especially from newspapers, television etc: **in/out of the limelight** *Tad loves being in the limelight.* | *The president's wife wanted to stay out of the limelight.* | *She's afraid this new actor will steal the limelight from her.* | *his few moments of limelight in front of the cameras*

lim·e·rick /'lɪmərɪk/ n [C] a humorous short poem that has five lines that RHYME

lime·scale /'laɪmskeɪl/ n [U] BrE a hard white or grey substance that forms on the inside of pipes, TAPS and water containers

lime·stone /'laɪmstəʊn $ -stoʊn/ n [U] a type of rock that contains CALCIUM

li·mey /'laɪmi/ n [C] AmE old-fashioned a slightly insulting word for someone from Britain

limits

kerb BrE/
curb AmE

hem

frame

fringe

rim

verge

border

edge

lim·it¹ S2 W2 /'lɪmɪt/ n [C]
1 GREATEST/LEAST ALLOWED the greatest or least amount, number, speed etc that is allowed

set/impose a limit
exceed a limit (=go beyond a limit)
speed limit
time limit
age limit
upper limit (=the highest point something can reach)
lower limit (=the lowest point something can reach)
above/below the limit
strict limit
legal limit

[+to/on] There's a limit on the time you have to take the test. | *My wife and I set a limit on how much we spend on clothes.* | *The cheque must not exceed the limit set by the banker's card.* | *a 55 mph speed limit* | *The time limit for making claims is three months.* | *There's no age limit for applicants.* | *an upper limit for pollution levels* | *His blood alcohol level was 50% above the legal limit.* | *The public would like strict spending limits on political campaigns.*

2 GREATEST AMOUNT POSSIBLE also **limits** the greatest possible amount of something that can exist or be obtained: *[+of] the limits of human knowledge* | *He'd reached the limit of his patience.* | *Our finances are already stretched to the limit* (=we do not have any extra money). | *There's no limit to what you can do if you try.*

3 PLACE also **limits** the furthest point or edge of a place, often one that must not be passed: *He had not been outside the limits of the prison walls for 20 years.* | *The public is not allowed within a 2-mile limit of the missile site.* | *Los Angeles city limits*

4 off limits a) beyond the area where someone is allowed to go: *That area of beach was off limits to us 'city kids'.* **b)** beyond what you are allowed to do or have: *His private life is off limits to the press.*

5 within limits within the time, level, amount etc considered acceptable: *You can come and go when you want – within limits.*

6 be over the limit to have drunk more alcohol than is legal or safe for driving

7 know your limits informal to know what you are good at doing and what you are not good at: *I know my limits. I'm not an administrator.*

8 have your limits spoken to have a set of ideas about what is reasonable to do, and to not accept behaviour that does not follow those ideas: *I have my limits. You will not use that kind of nasty language in class.*

limit² S3 W2 v
1 [T] to stop an amount or number from increasing beyond a particular point: *a decision to limit imports of foreign cars* | **limit sth to sth** *Seating is limited to 500.*
2 [T] to stop someone from doing what they want or from developing and improving beyond a particular point: *A lack of formal education will limit your job opportunities.* | **limit yourself to sth** *I limit myself to two cups of coffee a day.*
3 be limited to sth to exist or happen only in a particular place, group, or area of activity: *The damage was limited to the roof.*

lim·i·ta·tion W3 /ˌlɪmɪ'teɪʃən/ n
1 [U] the act or process of controlling or reducing something: *[+to] Any limitation to the king's power could be permanent.* | *a nuclear limitation treaty* → **damage limitation** at DAMAGE¹ (3)
2 [C usually plural] qualities that stop someone or something from being as good or as effective as you wish they could be; ◨ **weakness**: *[+of] Despite the limitations of the survey, it did suggest some general trends.* | *It's a good little car, but it has its limitations.*
3 [C,U] a rule or condition that stops something from increasing beyond a particular point: *[+on/upon] a limitation on the number of hours children can work* | **put/place/impose limitations** *The new law imposes limitations on campaign contributions.*

lim·it·ed W2 /'lɪmɪtɪd/ adj
1 not very great in amount, number, ability etc: **limited number/amount/time etc** *There are only a limited*

number of tickets available. | My knowledge of the business is limited. | The organization has very **limited resources**. | So far, the education reforms have had only **limited success**. | **(be of) limited use/value** Unfortunately, the drug is of limited value in treating cancer.
2 Limited written abbreviation **Ltd** used after the name of British business companies that have LIMITED LIABILITY

,limited 'company also ,limited lia'bility ,company n [C] a company in Britain whose owners only have to pay a limited amount if the company gets into debt; → **public limited company**

,limited e'dition n [C] a small number of special copies of a book, picture etc which are produced at one time only

,limited lia'bility n [U] technical the legal position of being responsible for paying only a limited amount of debt if something bad happens to yourself or your company

lim·it·ing /ˈlɪmɪ̣tɪŋ/ adj **1** preventing any improvement or increase in something: A **limiting factor** in health care is the way resources are distributed. **2** informal preventing someone from developing and doing what they are interested in: The job's OK, but it's sort of limiting.

lim·it·less /ˈlɪmɪ̣tləs/ adj without a limit or end; ▤ **infinite**: limitless possibilities

lim·o /ˈlɪməʊ $ -moʊ/ n [C] informal a limousine

lim·ou·sine /ˈlɪməzi:n, ˌlɪməˈzi:n/ n [C] **1** a very large, expensive, and comfortable car, driven by someone who is paid to drive **2** a small bus that people take to and from airports in the US

limp[1] /lɪmp/ adj not firm or strong: a limp handshake | His body suddenly **went limp** and he fell down on the floor. —**limply** adv: His arms were **hanging limply**. —**limpness** n [U]

limp[2] v [I] **1** to walk slowly and with difficulty because one leg is hurt or injured: Moreno limped off the field with a foot injury. **2** [always + adv/prep] if a ship or aircraft limps somewhere, it goes there slowly, because it has been damaged: [+into] The damaged liner limped into New York.
    limp along phr v if a company, project etc limps along, it is not successful: The team is limping along in fifth place.

limp[3] n [C] the way someone walks when they are limping: Young walked with **a slight limp**.

lim·pet /ˈlɪmpɪ̣t/ n [C] a small sea animal with a shell, which holds tightly onto the rock where it lives

lim·pid /ˈlɪmpɪ̣d/ adj literary clear or transparent: limpid blue eyes —**limpidly** adv —**limpidity** /lɪm ˈpɪdɪ̣ti/ n [U]

limp-wrist·ed /ˌlɪmp ˈrɪstɪ̣d◂/ adj a limp-wristed man is considered to lack male qualities such as strength; sometimes used to say that a man is HOMOSEXUAL

linch·pin, lynchpin /ˈlɪntʃˌpɪn/ n the linchpin of sth the person or thing in a group, system etc that is most important, because everything depends on them

linc·tus /ˈlɪŋktəs/ n [U] BrE a liquid medicine used for curing coughs

lin·den /ˈlɪndən/ n [C] a LIME tree

line[1] [S1] [W1] /laɪn/ n
1 ON PAPER/ON THE GROUND [C] a long thin mark on a piece of paper, the ground, or another surface: Draw a **straight line** across the top of the page. | Sign your name on the **dotted line** (=line made up of a series of dots). | The edges of the pitch are marked by white lines. | The goalkeeper just managed to stop the ball going over the line. | He raced towards the finishing line.
2 BETWEEN TWO AREAS [C] an imaginary line on the surface of the earth, for example showing where one country or area of land stops and another begins: **county/state line** AmE: He was born in a small town just across the state line. | **line of latitude/longitude** They were still travelling along the same line of longitude. →
INTERNATIONAL DATE LINE

3 OF PEOPLE/THINGS [C] **a)** a row of people or things next to each other: [+of] There was a line of fir trees on either side of the road. | The four men were **standing in a line** on the other side of the table. | A couple of the posts were **out of line** (=not in a straight row). **b)** especially AmE a row of people, cars etc that are waiting one behind the other; ▤ **queue** BrE: I looked in despair at the long line in front of the ticket office. | [+of] I joined the line of vehicles waiting to get into the car park. | The kids were **standing in line** waiting for their teacher. | The woman **next in line** began to mutter to herself. | He tried to **cut in line** (=go in front of other people who are waiting).
4 DIRECTION [C] the direction or imaginary line along which something travels between two places: Light travels **in a straight line**. | A boat came into my **line of vision** (=direction I was looking in). | **line of fire/attack/movement etc** (=the direction in which someone shoots, attacks, moves etc) I was directly in the animal's line of attack. | They knew they needed to block their enemy's **supply lines** (=direction used for carrying supplies of food etc).
5 ON YOUR FACE [C] a line on the skin of someone's face; → **wrinkle**: She frowned, and **deep lines** appeared between her eyebrows. | There were **fine lines** around her eyes. | No one can avoid lines and wrinkles as they get older.
6 PHONE [C] a telephone wire or connection: I'm sorry, **the line is busy** (=someone is already using it). | There seems to be a fault **on the line**. | There was a click, then **the line went dead** (=suddenly stopped working completely). | Henry is **on the line** (=on the phone) from New York. | I **got on the line to** (=phoned) the hospital as soon as I heard about the accident. | I wished he would just **get off the line**. | I'm sorry, it's **a bad line** and I can't hear you. | **Hold the line** (=wait on the phone), please, and I'll put you through to our sales department. | Do you have a separate line for your modem?
7 FOR TRAINS [C] a track that a train travels along: We were delayed because of a problem further along the line. | When you get to central London, take the Victoria Line to Finsbury Park. | **railway line** BrE; **railroad line** AmE: The trail follows a disused railroad line along the edge of the valley.
8 BETWEEN TWO TYPES OF THING [C usually singular] the point at which one type of thing can be considered to be something else or at which it becomes a particular thing: [+between] There is a **fine line** between superstition and religion. | The **dividing line** between luxuries and necessities is constantly changing. | Sometimes he found it hard to **draw the line** between work and pleasure. | Her remarks did not quite **cross the line** into rudeness. | Large numbers of families are living on or near the **poverty line** (=the point at which people are considered to be very poor).
9 SHAPE/EDGE [C usually plural] the outer shape of something long or tall: She was wearing a loose dress which softened the lines of her body. | a modern building with clean, elegant lines.
10 WORDS [C] **a)** a line of written words, for example in a poem or a document: He quoted a few lines from Shakespeare. | Scroll down to line 29. **b)** a remark: He liked to introduce himself with a witty opening line. | This was one of his favourite **chat-up lines** (=remark for impressing someone you want to attract). **c)** [usually plural] words that someone has to learn and say as part of a play or performance: Paul often messed up his lines. | It always took me ages to **learn my lines**.
11 OPINION/ATTITUDE [singular] an opinion or attitude, especially one that someone states publicly and that influences their actions: [+on] I can't agree with the government's line on immigration. | Journalists are often too willing to accept the **official line** (=the opinion that a government states officially). | He found it hard to accept **the party line** (=the official opinion of a political party) on every issue. | **take a tough/firm/hard**

L

line on sth *The school takes a very tough line on drugs.*; → toe the line at TOE²

12 WAY OF DOING STH [C] a particular way of doing something or of thinking about something: **line of argument/reasoning/inquiry etc** *It seemed useless to pursue this line of questioning.* | *Opposition parties soon realized they would have to try a different line of attack.* | *The police are following several different lines of enquiry.* | *We were both thinking along the same lines* (=in the same way). | *In South Africa, the press developed along very different lines* (=in a very different way). | *More groups will now be set up on these lines* (=this way). | *The company's rapid success means it's definitely on the right lines* (=doing something the right way).

13 SERIES OF EVENTS [C usually singular] a series of events that follow each other: [+of] *This is the latest in a long line of political scandals.*

14 IN A WAR [C] the edge of an area that is controlled by an army, where soldiers stay and try to prevent their enemy from moving forward: *They finally broke through the German line.* | *young soldiers who were sent to the front line to fight* | *One regiment was trapped behind enemy lines.* | *Reinforcements were available just behind the lines.*

15 IN A COMPANY/ORGANIZATION [C] a series of levels of authority within an organization: *Decisions are taken by senior officers and fed down through the line of command to the ordinary soldiers.* | *There should be more direct discussion between managers and workers lower down the line.* → LINE MANAGER

16 OF ROPE/WIRE [C] a piece of strong string, rope, or wire used for a particular purpose: *She hung the clothes out on the washing line* (=line for hanging wet clothes on to dry). | *The fishing line* (=line for catching fish) *snapped and the fish got away.*

17 PRODUCT [C] a type of goods for sale in a shop: *The company has just launched a new line of small, low-priced computers.*

18 along these/those lines also **along the lines of sth** similar to something else: *We usually start with general questions along the lines of, 'How do you feel?'* | *They're trying to organize a trip to the beach or something along those lines.*

19 along religious/ethnic/party etc lines if people divide along religious, party etc lines they divide according to the religion, political party, or other group they belong to: *The committee was split along party lines.* | *The community remains divided along religious lines.*

20 on line **a)** using a computer to get information or to communicate with people: *You can book tickets on line.* | *Most of our sales staff now work on line.* → ONLINE **b)** working properly as planned: *a new nuclear reactor which should be on line by 2005* | *If there is a power failure, the emergency generators should come on line within 15 minutes.*

21 drop sb a line *informal* to write a short letter or email to someone: *Drop me a line and let me know how you're getting on.*

22 don't give me that line *spoken* used to say that you do not believe someone's excuse: *I know for a fact you weren't sick yesterday, so don't give me that line.*

23 fall into line/bring sb into line *informal* to start to do what someone else wants you to do, or to make someone do this: *Now that France and Germany have signed up, other countries will soon fall into line.* | *The few party rebels were soon brought into line.*

24 in line with sth if something changes in line with something else, it changes in the same way and at the same rate as it: *Pensions will be increased in line with inflation.*

25 bring sth into line with sth to change a system so that it works according to a particular set of rules, laws etc: *UK immigration procedures will be changed to bring them into line with the latest European ruling.*

26 be out of line *infomal* **a)** to say or do something that

is not acceptable in a particular situation: *You just keep quiet! You're way out of line.* **b)** to not obey someone, or to do something that you should not do: **get/step put of line** *Anybody who steps out of line will be in deep trouble.*

27 be in line for sth/be in line to do sth to be very likely to get or be given something: *I should be in line for promotion soon.* | **first/second/next etc in line for** *He must be first in line for the editor's job.*

28 be first/second/next etc in line to the throne to be the person who has a right to become a future king or queen: *As the oldest son, he was next in line to the throne.*

29 be on the line if something important is on the line, there is a risk that you might lose it or something bad could happen to it: *From now on, all our jobs are on the line.* | *She knew that her whole future was on the line.* | **put yourself/your neck on the line (for sb)** (=risk something bad happening to you) *I've already put myself on the line for you once, and I'm not going to do it again.*

30 be in sb's line *informal* to be the type of thing that someone is interested in or good at: *Acting's not really in my line, I'm afraid.*

31 get a line on sb/sth *informal especially AmE* to get information about someone or something: *We need to get some kind of a line on these guys.*

32 somewhere along the line *informal* at some time during an activity or period of time: *Somewhere along the line, Errol seemed to have lost interest in her.*

33 down the line *informal* later, after an activity or situation has been continuing for a period of time: *There may be more costs further down the line.* | *Now, three years down the line, we're beginning to see the problems with the treatment.*

34 in the line of duty happening or done as part of your job: *firefighters dying in the line of duty*

35 be in the firing line/in the line of fire **a)** to be one of the people who could be criticized or blamed for something: *As one of the President's chief advisers, he's bound to be in the firing line.* **b)** to be in a place where a bullet etc might hit you: *A couple of civilians were caught in the firing line.*

36 PUNISHMENT lines [plural] *BrE* a punishment given to school children that consists of writing the same thing a lot of times: *He got 50 lines for being cheeky to a teacher.*

37 FAMILY [singular] your family, considered as the people you are related to who lived before you and the people who will live after you: *She comes from a long line of actors.* | *It looks as if Joe might be the last of the line* (=the last in his family). | **the male/female line** *This particular gene is passed down through the male line.* | **line of succession** (=the system by which an important position or property is passed from a parent to their children, and then to their children etc) *Henry the Eighth wanted a male heir to ensure the Tudor line of succession.*

38 JOB [C usually singular] the type of work someone does: **line of work/business** *What line of business is he in?* | **in the building/retail etc line** *She's keen to do something in the fashion line.*

39 TRANSPORT [C] a company that provides transport for moving goods by sea, air, road etc: *He runs a transatlantic shipping line.*

40 DRUG [C] *informal* an amount of an illegal drug in powder form, arranged in a line so it can be breathed in through the nose → **draw the line at** at DRAW¹ (16); → **draw a line (between sth)** at DRAW¹ (15); → **where do you draw the line?** at DRAW¹ (17); → **draw a line under sth** at DRAW¹ (18); → **hard line** at HARD¹ (21); → **hook, line and sinker** at HOOK¹ (9); → **lay sth on the line** at LAY² (18) → PICKET LINE; → **the poverty line/level** at POVERTY (2); → **read between the lines** at READ¹ (14)

line² v [T] **1** to sew a piece of material onto the inside or back of another piece to make it stronger or warmer: *Are those curtains lined?* | **line sth with sth** *a leather coat lined with silk* **2** to form a layer over the inner surface of something: *The birds use small leaves for lining their nests.* | **line sth with sth** *The cage should be lined with straw.* **3** to form rows along the sides of something: *Crowds lined the route to the palace.* | **be lined with sth** *The street was lined with small shops.* | *a tree-lined avenue* **4 line your own pockets** to make yourself richer, especially by doing something dishonest – used to show disapproval

line up *phr v* **1** if people line up, or if you line them up, they stand in a row or line, or you make them do this: *Line up, everybody!* | **line sb** ⇔ **up** *He lined us all up in the corridor.* **2 line sth** ⇔ **up** to arrange things in a row: *I lined the bottles up on the sideboard.* **3 line sth** ⇔ **up** to move one thing so that it is in the correct position in relation to something else: [+with] *The windows should be lined up with the door frame.* **4 line sb/sth** ⇔ **up** to arrange for something to happen or for someone to be available for an event: *We've lined up some excellent speakers for tonight.* | *He's already got a new job lined up.* → LINE-UP

lin·e·age /ˈlɪni-ɪdʒ/ *n* [C,U] *formal* the way in which members of a family are DESCENDED from other members; → **line**, ancestry: *a family of ancient lineage*

lin·e·al /ˈlɪniəl/ *adj formal* related directly to someone who lived a long time before you: *lineal descendants*

lin·e·a·ment /ˈlɪniəmənt/ *n* [C usually plural] *formal* **1** a feature of your face **2** a typical quality

lin·e·ar /ˈlɪniə $ -ər/ *adj* **1** consisting of lines, or in the form of a straight line: *a linear diagram* **2** [only before noun] relating to length: *linear measurements* **3** involving a series of connected events, ideas etc, that move or progress from one stage to the next: *linear thinking* —**linearly** *adv* —**linearity** /ˌlɪniˈærˌti/ *n* [U] → LATERAL THINKING

line·back·er /ˈlaɪnˌbækə $ -ər/ *n* [C] a player in American football who tries to TACKLE members of the other team

lined /laɪnd/ *adj* **1** a coat, skirt etc that is lined has a piece of thin material covering the inside; → **lining**: *a fleece-lined jacket* **2** paper that is lined has straight lines printed or drawn across it **3** skin that is lined has WRINKLES on it

line ˌdancing *n* [U] a type of dancing in which people dance in lines, all following the same series of steps

line ˌdrawing *n* [C] a DRAWING consisting only of lines

line·man /ˈlaɪnmən/ *n plural* **linemen** /-mən/ [C] *AmE* **1** a player in American football who plays in the front line of a team: **offensive/defensive lineman 2** someone whose job is to take care of railway lines or telephone wires

line ˌmanagement *n* [U] *BrE* a system of management in which information and instructions are passed from one person to someone immediately higher or lower than them in rank

line ˌmanager *n* [C] *BrE* **1** a manager in a company who is responsible for the main activities of production, sales etc **2 sb's line manager** someone who is one level higher in rank than you in a company and is in charge of your work

lin·en /ˈlɪnˌn/ *n* [U] **1** sheets, TABLECLOTHS etc: *bed linen* | *table linen* **2** cloth made from the FLAX plant, used to make high quality clothes, home decorations etc: *a linen jacket* *old use* underwear → **wash your dirty laundry/linen** at DIRTY[1] (7)

linen ˌcupboard *n* [C] *BrE* a cupboard in which sheets, TOWELS etc are kept; ◾ **linen closet** *AmE*

ˌline of ˈscrimmage *n* [C] a line in American football where the ball is placed at the beginning of a period of play

line-out *n* [C] the way of starting play again in a RUGBY UNION game, when the ball has gone off the field

line ˌprinter *n* [C] a machine that prints information from a computer at a very high speed —**line printing** *n* [U]

lin·er /ˈlaɪnə $ -ər/ *n* **1** [C] a piece of material used inside something, especially in order to keep it clean: *a*

dustbin liner | *nappy liners* → see picture at BAG[1] **2** [C] a large ship for passengers: *an ocean liner* → CRUISE LINER; → see picture at TRIP[1] **3** [C,U] *informal* EYELINER

ˈliner ˌnote *n* [usually plural] printed information about the music or musicians that comes with a CD or record

lines·man /ˈlaɪnzmən/ *n plural* **linesmen** /-mən/ [C] an official in a sport who decides when a ball has gone out of the playing area

ˈline-up *n* [C usually singular] **1** the players in a sports team who play in a particular game: *This was his first match in the starting line-up* (=the players who begin the game). **2** a group of people, especially performers, who have agreed to be involved in an event: *The line-up included top bands Prodigy and Radiohead.* **3** a number of events or programmes arranged to follow each other: *a wonderful line-up of programmes for Christmas and the New Year* **4** *especially AmE* a row of people who stand in front of a WITNESS to a crime, who is then asked if he or she recognizes any of them as the criminal; ◾ **identification parade** *BrE*

-ling /lɪŋ/ *suffix* [in nouns] a small, young, or less important type of something: *a duckling* | *princelings*

lin·ger /ˈlɪŋgə $ -ər/ *v* [I] **1** also **linger on** to continue to exist, be noticeable etc for longer than is usual or desirable: *a taste that lingers in your mouth* | *Unfortunately the tax will linger on until April.* **2** also **linger on** to stay somewhere a little longer, especially because you do not want to leave: [+over] *They lingered over coffee and missed the last bus.* | *I spent a week at Kandersteg and could happily have lingered on.* **3** [always + adv/prep] to continue looking at or dealing with something for longer than is usual or desirable: [+on/over] *Mike let his eyes linger on her face.* | *There's no need to linger over this stage of the interview.* **4** also **linger on** to continue to live although you are slowly dying: *He surprised all the doctors by lingering on for several weeks.*

lin·ge·rie /ˈlænʒəri $ ˌlɑːnʒəˈreɪ, ˈlænʒəri/ *n* [U] women's underwear

lin·ger·ing /ˈlɪŋgərɪŋ/ *adj* [usually before noun] continuing to exist for longer than is usual or desirable: **lingering doubts/suspicions etc** *Any lingering hopes of winning the title soon disappeared.* | *Mr Wilkins suffered a lingering death.* | **lingering smell/aroma/odour** *the lingering aroma of chocolate* —**lingeringly** *adv*

lin·go /ˈlɪŋgəʊ $ -goʊ/ *n* [C usually singular] *informal* **1** a language, especially a foreign one: *I'd like to go to Greece, but I don't speak the lingo.* **2** words or expressions used only by a particular group of people, or at a particular period of time: *academic lingo*

lin·gua fran·ca /ˌlɪŋgwə ˈfræŋkə/ *n* [C] a language used between people whose main languages are different: *English is the lingua franca in many countries.*

lin·gui·ni /lɪŋˈgwiːni/ *n* [plural] long thin flat pieces of PASTA

lin·guist /ˈlɪŋgwˌst/ *n* [C] **1** someone who is good at foreign languages, especially someone who speaks several **2** someone who studies or teaches linguistics

lin·guis·tic ☒ /lɪŋˈgwɪstɪk/ *adj* related to language, words, or linguistics: *a child's linguistic development* —**linguistically** /-kli/ *adv*

lin·guis·tics /lɪŋˈgwɪstɪks/ *n* [U] the study of language in general and of particular languages, their structure, grammar, and history → PHILOLOGY

lin·i·ment /ˈlɪnˌmənt/ *n* [U] a liquid containing oil that you rub on your skin when you feel sore or stiff

lin·ing /ˈlaɪnɪŋ/ *n* [C,U] **1** a piece of material that covers the inside of something, especially a piece of clothing; → **lined**: *a jacket with a silk lining* → see picture at FOOTWEAR; → **every cloud has a silver lining** at CLOUD[1] (6) **2** a substance or material that covers the inside of part of the body: *the lining of the womb*

L

link¹ W2 /lɪŋk/ v
1 be linked if two things are linked, they are related in some way: *Police think the murders are linked.* | **be linked to/with sth** *Some birth defects are linked to smoking during pregnancy.* | **be closely/directly/strongly etc linked** *Our economy is inextricably linked with America's.*
2 MAKE CONNECTION [T] to make a connection between two or more things or people: *A love of nature links the two poets.* | **link sth/sb to/with sth** *Exactly how do we link words to objects?* | **link sb/sth together** *Strong family ties still linked them together.*
3 JOIN [T] to physically join two or more things, people, or places; ◼ **connect**: **link sth/sb to/with sth** *The pipe must be linked to the cold water supply.* | **link sb/sth together** *The climbers were linked together by ropes.* | **link sth and sth** *A long bridge links Venice and the mainland.* | *He walked with her,* **linking arms** (=putting his arm around her arm).
4 SHOW CONNECTION [T] to show or say that there is a connection between two people, situations, or things: **link sb/sth to/with sth** *He denied reports linking him to Colombian drug dealers.*
5 MAKE STH DEPEND ON STH [T] to make one thing or situation depend on another thing or situation: **link sth to sth** *Pay increases will now be linked to performance.* → INDEX-LINKED
6 also **link up** [T] to connect computers, broadcast systems etc, so that electronic messages can be sent between them: **link sth to/with sth** *Local terminals are linked to the central computer.*

link in phr v BrE
1 to connect with another idea, statement, type of work etc, especially in a way that is useful; ◼ **tie in**: [+with] *This point links in with our earlier discussion.*
2 to happen at the same time as something else; ◼ **tie in**: [+with] *Hawk's visit was scheduled to link in with the meeting in Harare.*

link up phr v
1 to connect with something or to make a connection between things, especially so that they can work together: [+with] *The train links up with the ferry at Dover.* | **link sth ⇔ up (with sth)** *The next stage is to link the film up with the soundtrack.*
2 to connect computers, broadcast systems etc so that electronic messages can be sent between them: **link sth ⇔ up (to/with sth)** *All these PCs are linked up to the network.* | *The Internet allows people from all over the world to link up for chat sessions.*
3 to join with someone so that you can do something together: [+with] *We linked up with the Daily Express to help run the campaign.* → LINKUP

link² S3 W2 n [C]
1 a way in which two things or ideas are related to each other: **links between sth (and sth)** *the link between drug use and crime* | *There are a number of links between the two theories.*
2 a relationship or connection between two or more people, countries, organizations etc: [+between] *the close link between teacher and student* | [+with] *The company has strong links with big investors.* | **forge/establish links** *Organizers of the project hope that international links will be forged.*
3 a person or thing that makes possible a relationship or connection with someone or something else: [+with] *For elderly people, TV is a vital link with the outside world.*
4 **rail/road/telephone etc link** something that makes communication or travel between two places possible: *The office has direct computer links to over 100 firms.*
5 one of the rings in a chain
6 **link in the chain** one of the stages involved in a process
7 **the links** a piece of ground near the sea where golf is played; ◼ **golf links**
8 a special word or picture in an Internet document that

you CLICK on to move quickly to another part of the same document or to another document; → **hyperlink**: *Send an email to the above address to report a broken link* (=a link that is not working properly). → CUFF LINK, MISSING LINK; → **weak/weakest link** at WEAK (15)

link·age /'lɪŋkɪdʒ/ n **1** [C,U] formal a LINK² (1): [+between] *the linkage between wages and prices* **2** [C,U] a system of links or connections **3** [singular, U] a condition in a political or business agreement, by which one country or company agrees to do something, only if the other promises to do something in return

'linking ˌverb also **'link verb** n [C] a verb that connects the subject of a sentence with its COMPLEMENT, for example 'seem' in the sentence 'the house seems big'; ◼ **copula**

link·up /'lɪŋk-ʌp/ n [C] a connection between two things, especially organizations or communication systems

lin·net /'lɪnɪt/ n [C] a small brown singing bird

li·no /'laɪnəʊ $ -noʊ/ n [U] BrE informal LINOLEUM

li·no·cut /'laɪnəʊkʌt $ -noʊ-/ n **1** [U] the art of cutting a pattern on a block of linoleum **2** [C] a picture printed from such a block

li·no·le·um /lɪ'nəʊliəm $ -'noʊ-/ n [U] a floor covering made from strong shiny material

Li·no·type /'laɪnəʊtaɪp $ -noʊ-/ n [U] trademark a system for arranging TYPE¹ (3) in the form of solid metal lines

lin·seed /'lɪnsiːd/ n [U] the seed of the FLAX plant

ˌlinseed 'oil n [U] the oil from linseed, used in paints, for protecting wood surfaces etc

lint /lɪnt/ n [U] **1** especially AmE soft light pieces of thread or wool that come off cotton, wool, or other material; ◼ **fluff** BrE **2** BrE soft cotton material used for protecting wounds

lin·tel /'lɪntl/ n [C] a piece of stone or wood across the top of a window or door, forming part of the frame

li·on /'laɪən/ n [C] **1** a large animal of the cat family that lives in Africa and parts of southern Asia. Lions have gold-coloured fur and the male has a MANE (=long hair around its neck); → **lioness**; → see picture at BIG CAT **2** **the lion's share (of sth)** the largest part of something: *The firm has captured the lion's share of the UK market.* **3** **the lion's den** if you go into the lion's den, you go among people who are your enemies

li·on·ess /'laɪənes, -nɪs/ n [C] a female lion

lion-heart·ed /ˌlaɪən 'hɑːtɪd $ 'hɑːr-/ adj written very brave; ◼ **courageous**

li·on·ize also **-ise** BrE /'laɪənaɪz/ v [T] written to treat someone as being very important or famous

lip W2 /lɪp/ n
1 [C] one of the two soft parts around your mouth where your skin is redder or darker: **upper/lower/top/bottom lip** *His bottom lip was swollen.* | *She had big eyes and full lips* (=large and round lips). | *Matt opened the door with a smile on his lips.* | *Marty kissed me right on the lips!* | **thin-lipped/thick-lipped/full-lipped** (=having lips that are thin, or large and round) | *Stephen pursed his lips with distaste* (=brought them together tightly into a small circle). → TIGHT-LIPPED
2 [C] the edge of a hollow or deep place in the land: [+of] *the old road that ran along the lip of the gorge*
3 [C usually singular] the edge of something you use to hold or pour liquid; ◼ **rim**
4 [U] informal talk that is not polite or respectful – used especially by adults to children; ◼ **cheek**: *Don't give me any of your lip!*
5 **my lips are sealed** spoken used to say that you will not tell anyone about a secret
6 **on everyone's lips** being talked about by everyone: *an actress whose name is on everyone's lips* → **bite your lip** at BITE¹ (1); → **lick your lips** at LICK¹ (5); → **not pass sb's lips** at PASS¹ (24); → **read sb's lips** at READ¹ (18); → **smack your lips** at SMACK¹ (3); → **a stiff upper lip** at STIFF¹ (10)

'lip balm n [C,U] a substance used to protect dry lips

'lip gloss n [C,U] a substance used to make lips look very shiny

lip·id /'lɪpᵻd/ n [C] technical one of several types of FATTY substances in living things, such as fat, oil, or WAX

lip·o·suc·tion /'lɪpəʊˌsʌkʃən $ -poʊ-/ n [U] a way of removing fat from someone's body, using SUCTION

lip·py¹ /'lɪpi/ n [C,U] BrE informal LIPSTICK: Wait a minute, I'll just put a bit of lippy on.

lippy² adj BrE informal not showing respect in the way that you speak to someone

lip-read /'lɪp riːd/ v [I,T] to understand what someone is saying by watching the way their lips move, because you cannot hear them —**lip-reading** n [U]

lip·ring /'lɪprɪŋ/ n [C] a small ring that someone puts through their lip, as jewellery

'lip salve n [C,U] BrE a substance used to make sore lips feel better

'lip ˌservice n **pay lip service to sb/sth** to say that you support or agree with something without doing anything to prove it: organizations that pay lip service to career development

lip·stick /'lɪpˌstɪk/ n [C,U] something used for adding colour to your lips, in the shape of a small stick → see picture at MAKE-UP

'lip-synch v [I] to move your lips at the same time as a recording is being played, in order to pretend that you are singing or saying the words —**lip synch** n [U]

liq·ue·fac·tion /ˌlɪkwᵻ'fækʃən/ n [U] technical the act of making something a liquid or of becoming a liquid

liq·ue·fy /'lɪkwᵻfaɪ/ v liquefied, liquifying, liquifies [I,T] formal to become liquid, or make something become liquid

li·queur /lɪ'kjʊə $ lɪ'kɜːr/ n [C,U] a sweet, very strong alcoholic drink, drunk in small quantities after a meal; → liquor

liq·uid¹ /'lɪkwᵻd/ n [C,U] a substance that is not a solid or a gas, for example water or milk: Add a little more liquid to the sauce. → WASHING-UP LIQUID

liquid² adj **1** in the form of a liquid instead of a gas or solid: Children take antibiotics **in liquid form**. | liquid soap **2** technical easily changed into money by being sold or exchanged: Their shares are more liquid than those of many smaller companies. → LIQUID ASSETS **3** liquid refreshment drink, especially alcoholic drink – used humorously **4** literary clear and shiny, like water: liquid green eyes **5** literary liquid sounds are clear and pure

ˌliquid 'assets n [plural] technical the money that a company or person has, and the property they can exchange for money

liq·ui·date /'lɪkwᵻdeɪt/ v **1** [I,T] to close a business or company and sell the things that belong to it, in order to pay its debts **2** [T] technical to pay a debt: The stock was sold to liquidate the loan. **3** [T] informal to kill someone or destroy something that is causing a problem

liq·ui·da·tion /ˌlɪkwᵻ'deɪʃən/ n [C,U] **1** the act of closing a company by selling the things that belong to it, in order to pay its debts: Hundreds of small businesses **went into liquidation** (=were closed). **2** the act of paying a debt

liq·ui·da·tor /'lɪkwᵻdeɪtə $ -ər/ n [C] an official whose job is to close a company and use any money obtained to pay its debts

li·quid·i·ty /lɪ'kwɪdᵻti/ n [U] technical **1** when a business or a person has money or goods that can be sold to pay debts **2** the state of being LIQUID

liq·uid·ize also **-ise** BrE /'lɪkwᵻdaɪz/ v [T] to crush fruit, vegetables etc into a thick liquid

liq·uid·iz·er also **-iser** BrE /'lɪkwᵻdaɪz $ -ər/ n [C] BrE a small electric machine that makes solid foods into liquids; ▤ **blender**

liq·uor /'lɪkə $ -ər/ n [U] **1** especially AmE a strong alcoholic drink such as WHISKY; ▤ **spirit** → LIQUEUR **2** BrE technical any alcoholic drink

liq·uo·rice BrE; **licorice** AmE /'lɪkərɪs, -rɪʃ/ n [U] **1** a black substance produced from the root of a plant, used in medicine and sweets **2** sweets made from this substance

'liquor store n [C] AmE a shop where alcohol is sold; ▤ **off-licence** BrE

lir·a /'lɪərə $ 'lɪrə/ n plural **lire** /-reɪ/ or **liras** [C] the standard unit of money in Malta and Turkey, and used in Italy before the EURO

lisp /lɪsp/ n [singular] a fault in the way someone speaks which makes them pronounce 's' sounds as 'th': She speaks with a slight lisp. —**lisp** v [I,T]

lis·som, **lissome** /'lɪsəm/ adj literary a body that is lissom is thin and graceful; ▤ **lithe**

list¹ S1 W1 /lɪst/ n [C]

1 a set of things, names, numbers etc usually written one below the other, for example so that you can remember or check them

---

make/draw up/write a list
compile a list formal (=make a list)
top a list (=be the most important thing or person on a list)
on a list
a long/short list
price list
shopping list (=a list of things you want to buy)
grocery list AmE (=a list of food you need to buy)
wine list (=a list of wines available in a restaurant)
waiting list (=a list of people who are waiting for something)
mailing list (=a list of people that a company sends information to)
check list (=a list of things you need to check)
guest list (=a list of people invited somewhere)

[+of] a list of activities planned for Saturday | **Make** a **list** of all the things you have to do. | The first person on my list is Mrs Gilling. | a **long list** of words to learn | Do you have an up-to-date **price list**? | Mr Jones has been on the **waiting list** for an operation for 6 months.

---

2 be high/low on a list (of sth) also **be at the top/bottom of a list** to be considered very important or not very important: A good car is high on my list of priorities. → CIVIL LIST; → **be on the danger list** at DANGER (5); → HIT LIST, MAILING LIST, SHORT LIST, WAITING LIST

list² S2 W3 v

1 [T] to write a list, or mention things one after the other: The guidebook lists 1000 hotels and restaurants.
2 [T] to put someone on an official list, especially a hospital or court list: **list sb in fair/stable etc condition** Several passengers were listed in critical condition. | The case was listed for trial in the Crown Court.
3 [I] if a ship lists, it leans to one side

list·ed /'lɪstᵻd/ adj BrE **1** a listed building is one of historical interest in Britain, and is protected by a government order **2** a listed company is one which offers its SHARES for sale on the STOCK EXCHANGE; ▤ **public company**; ▤ **public corporation** AmE

lis·ten¹ S1 W1 /'lɪsən/ v [I]

1 to pay attention to what someone is saying or to a sound that you can hear: Listen! There's a strange noise in the engine. | [+to] We sat around listening to music. | **listen carefully/intently/hard etc** The whole class was listening attentively. | Liz stood still and listened hard (=very carefully). ⚠ **listen** is never followed directly by a noun. It must be followed by **to** and then a noun or a clause: Listen to what I say (NOT listen what I say).
2 spoken used to tell someone to pay attention to what you are going to say: Listen, I want you to come with me.
3 to consider what someone says and accept their advice: I told him not to go, but he just wouldn't listen. |

L

[+**to**] *I wish I'd listened to Dad.* | *She refused to **listen to reason*** (=accept sensible advice).

listen for sth *phr v*
to listen carefully so that you will notice a particular sound: *Listen for the moment when the music changes.*

listen in *phr v*
1 to listen to a broadcast on the radio: [+**to**] *I must remember to listen in to the news.* → **TUNE IN** (1)
2 to listen to someone's conversation when they do not want you to: [+**on**] *It sounded like someone was listening in on us.*

listen out *phr v BrE informal*
to listen carefully so that you will notice a particular sound: [+**for**] *Listen out for the baby in case she wakes up.*

listen up *phr v spoken especially AmE*
used to get people's attention so they can hear what you are going to say: *Hey everybody, listen up!*

listen² *n* **a listen** *BrE informal* an act of listening: *Have a listen to this new album!*

lis·ten·a·ble /'lɪsənəbəl/ *adj informal* pleasant to listen to; → **watchable**

lis·ten·er /'lɪsənə $ -ər/ *n* [C] **1** someone who listens to the radio; → **viewer**: *a new programme for younger listeners* **2** **a good/sympathetic listener** someone who listens carefully and sympathetically to other people

'listening de·vice *n* [C] a piece of equipment that allows you to listen secretly to other people's conversations; ⊟ **bug**

lis·te·ri·a /lɪ'stɪəriə $ -'stɪr-/ *n* [U] a type of BACTERIA that makes you sick

list·ing /'lɪstɪŋ/ *n* **1** [C] an official or public list: [+**of**] *a listing of all households in the district* **2** **listings** [plural] lists of films, plays, and other events, with the times and places at which they will happen **3** [C] if a company has a listing on the STOCK EXCHANGE, it can offer its SHARES for sale

list·less /'lɪstləs/ *adj* feeling tired and not interested in things: *The heat was making me listless.* —**listlessly** *adv* —**listlessness** *n* [U]

'list price *n* [C] a price that is suggested for a product by the people who make it

list·serv /'lɪst‚sɜːv $ -‚sɜːrv/ *n* [C] a computer program that allows a group of people to send and receive e-mail from each other about a particular subject

lit /lɪt/ *v* the past tense and past participle of LIGHT²

lit. also **lit** *BrE* the abbreviation of *literature* or *literary*: *French lit*

lit·a·ny /'lɪtəni/ *n plural* **litanies** [C] **1** a long list of problems, excuses etc – used to show disapproval: [+**of**] *an endless litany of complaints* **2** a long prayer in the Christian church in which the priest says a sentence and the people reply

lite /laɪt/ *adj* [usually before noun] *especially AmE* used in the names of some food or drink products to mean that they have fewer CALORIES or less fat than other similar products: *lite beer*

li·ter /'liːtə $ -ər/ *n* the American spelling of LITRE

lit·e·ra·cy /'lɪtərəsi/ *n* [U] the state of being able to read and write; ⊟ **illiteracy**; → **numeracy**: *a new adult literacy campaign* → COMPUTER LITERACY

lit·e·ral /'lɪtərəl/ *adj* **1** the literal meaning of a word or expression is its basic or original meaning; → **figurative**: **literal meaning/sense/interpretation etc** *A trade war is not a war in the literal sense.* **2** **literal translation** a translation that translates each word exactly instead of giving the general meaning in a more natural way; ⊟ **free** **3** **literal-minded** not showing much imagination —**literalness** *n* [U]

lit·e·ral·ly ⓢ² /'lɪtərəli/ *adv*
1 according to the most basic or original meaning of a word or expression: *The name of the cheese is Dolcelatte, literally meaning 'sweet milk'.* | *I said I felt like*

*quitting, but I didn't **mean** it **literally*** (=I did not mean exactly what I said)*!*
2 **take sb/sth literally** to believe exactly what someone or something says rather than trying to understand their general meaning: *She takes the Bible literally.*
3 used to emphasize that something, especially a large number, is actually true: *The Olympic Games were watched by literally billions of people.*
4 *spoken* used to emphasize a strong expression or word that is not being used in its real or original meaning. Some people consider this use to be incorrect.: *Dad was literally blazing with anger.*

lit·e·ra·ry ⓦ² /'lɪtərəri $ 'lɪtəreri/ *adj* [only before noun]
1 relating to literature: *a literary prize* | **literary criticism** (=the study of the methods used in writing literature)
2 typical of the style of writing used in literature rather than in ordinary writing and talking: *a literary style of writing*
3 liking literature very much, and studying or producing it: *a literary woman*

lit·e·rate /'lɪtər‚ɪt/ *adj* **1** able to read and write; ⊟ **illiterate**; → **numerate** **2** **computer literate/musically literate etc** able to use computers, understand and play music etc **3** well educated

lit·e·ra·ti /‚lɪtə'rɑːti/ *n* **the literati** *formal* a small group of people in a society who know a lot about literature

lit·e·ra·ture ⓦ² /'lɪtərətʃə $ -tʃʊr/ *n* [U]
1 books, plays, poems etc that people think are important and good: *He has read many of the major **works of literature***. | *Italian literature*
2 all the books, articles, etc on a particular subject: [+**on**] *literature on the history of science* | **in the literature** *Several cases of mercury poisoning have been recorded in the literature.*
3 printed information produced by people who want to sell you something or tell you about something: *sales literature*

lithe /laɪð/ *adj* having a body that moves easily and gracefully: *the strong lithe bodies of gymnasts* —**lithely** *adv*

lith·i·um /'lɪθiəm/ *n* [U] a soft silver-white metal that is the lightest known metal, is used in BATTERIES, and is often combined with other metals. It is a chemical ELEMENT: symbol Li

lith·o·graph /'lɪθəɡrɑːf $ -ɡræf/ *n* [C] a printed picture produced by lithography

li·thog·ra·phy /lɪ'θɒɡrəfi $ lɪ'θɑː-/ *n* [U] a method of printing in which a pattern is cut into stone or metal so that ink sticks to some parts of it and not others —**lithographic** /‚lɪθə'ɡræfɪk◂/ *adj*

lit·i·gant /'lɪt‚ɪɡənt/ *n* [C] *law* someone who is making a claim against someone or defending themselves against a claim in a court of law

lit·i·gate /'lɪt‚ɪɡeɪt/ *v* [I,T] *law* to take a claim or complaint against someone to a court of law

lit·i·ga·tion /‚lɪt‚ɪ'ɡeɪʃən/ *n* [U] *law* the process of taking claims to a court of law: *The threat of litigation can be a deciding factor in some business decisions.*

li·ti·gious /lɪ'tɪdʒəs/ *adj formal* very willing to take disagreements to a court of law – often used to show disapproval: *a litigious society* —**litigiousness** *n* [U]

lit·mus /'lɪtməs/ *n* [U] a chemical that turns red when it touches acid, and blue when it touches an ALKALI

'litmus ‚paper *n* [U] paper containing litmus, used to test whether a chemical is an acid or an ALKALI

'litmus ‚test *n* [singular] **1** one detail that is examined in order to help you make a decision about how suitable or acceptable someone or something is: [+**of/for**] *The mayoral election is regarded as the litmus test for the integrity of the electoral process.* **2** a test using litmus paper

li·tre *BrE*; **liter** *AmE* /'liːtə $ -ər/ *n* **1** [C] written abbreviation *l* the basic unit for measuring liquid in the METRIC SYSTEM: [+**of**] *a litre of water* | **litre bottle/drum/**

container etc *a litre bottle of wine* **2 2.6/3.5 etc litre engine** a measurement that shows the size and power of a vehicle's engine; → **cc**: *the Ford's 2.8 litre engine*

lit·ter¹ /ˈlɪtə $ -ər/ n

1 WASTE [U] waste paper, cans etc that people have thrown away and left on the ground in a public place; ⊟ **rubbish, trash, garbage**: *People who drop litter can be fined in some cities.* | *a town with a litter problem*

2 BABY ANIMALS [C] a group of baby animals that a mother gives birth to at the same time: [+of] *a litter of kittens*

3 FOR CAT'S TOILET [U] small grains of a dry substance that is put in the container that a cat uses as a toilet indoors: *cat litter* | *a litter tray*

4 FOREST [U] **leaf litter** dead leaves and other decaying plants on the ground in a forest

5 **a litter of sth** *literary* a group of things that look very untidy: *A litter of notes, papers, and textbooks were strewn on the desk.*

6 FOR ANIMAL'S BED [U] a substance such as STRAW that a farm animal sleeps on

7 BED [C] a chair or bed for carrying important people, used in past times

litter² v **1** also **litter up** [T] if things litter an area, there are a lot of them in that place, scattered in an untidy way: *Clothes littered the floor.* | **litter sth with sth** *The desk was littered with papers.* **2** **be littered with sth** if something is littered with things, there are a lot of those things in it; ⊟ **be full of sth**: *Recent business news has been littered with stories of companies failing.* **3** [I,T] to leave waste paper, cans etc on the ground in a public place **4** [I] *technical* if an animal such as a dog or cat litters, it gives birth to babies

litter bin *BrE* also **litter basket** *BrE* n [C] a container in a public place, for things people throw away, such as papers or cans; ⊟ **rubbish bin, waste bin, trash can** *AmE*, **garbage can** *AmE*; → see picture at BIN¹; → see picture at TOWN

lit·ter·bug /ˈlɪtəbʌg $ -ər-/ also **litter lout** *BrE* n [C] *informal* someone who drops paper, cans etc on the ground in public places

lit·tle¹ S1 W1 /ˈlɪtl/ adj

1 SIZE [usually before noun] small in size: *a little house* | *a cake decorated with little flowers* | *She was cutting the meat up into little bits.* | **little tiny/tiny little** *spoken* (=extremely small) *a little tiny puppy* | **a little something** *informal* (=a small present, or a small amount of food) *I'd like to buy him a little something to thank him.*; → see box at SMALL

2 STH YOU LIKE OR DISLIKE [only before noun] used between an adjective and a noun to emphasize that you like or dislike something or someone, although they are not important, impressive etc: *It could be a nice little business.* | *a useful little gadget* | *It was another of her silly little jokes.* | *a boring little man* | **poor little thing** (=used to show sympathy) *The poor little thing had hurt its wing.*

3 **a little bit a)** a small amount of something: [+of] *With a little bit of luck we should finish by five o'clock.* | *I'm going to give you a little bit of advice.* | *Let me tell you a little bit about myself.* **b)** slightly or to a small degree: *I was a little bit disappointed.*

4 TIME/DISTANCE [only before noun] short in time or distance: *You could have a little sleep in the car.* | *We walked a little way along this path.* | *He arrived a little while ago.*

5 YOUNG **little** children are young: *We didn't have toys like this when I was little.* | **little boy/girl** *two little boys playing in the street* | **sb's little boy/girl** (=someone's son or daughter who is still a child) *Mum, I'm 17 – I'm not your little girl any longer.* | **sb's little brother/sister** (=a younger brother or sister who is still a child) *Her little brother and sister were fighting again.*

6 SLIGHT [only before noun] done in a way that is not very noticeable: *a little smile* | *Nicolo gave a little nod of his head.*

7 UNIMPORTANT [only before noun] **a)** not important: *She gets very angry over little things.* | *There isn't time to discuss every little detail.* **b)** not important – used when you really think that something is important: *There's just that little matter of the £5000 you owe me.*

8 **(just) that little bit better/easier etc** better, easier etc by a small amount that will have an important effect: *Working fewer hours will make life just that little bit easier for me.*

9 **the little woman** *old-fashioned* someone's wife – often used humorously but now considered offensive by many women → **a little bird told me** at BIRD (4)

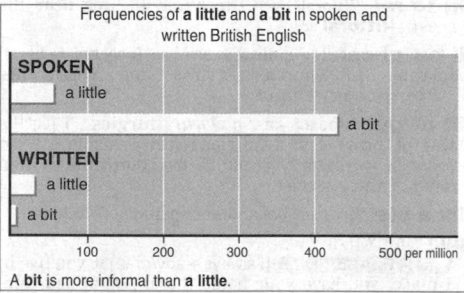

Frequencies of **a little** and **a bit** in spoken and written British English

SPOKEN — a little / a bit
WRITTEN — a little / a bit
100 200 300 400 500 per million

A **bit** is more informal than **a little**.

little² S1 W1 *determiner, pron*

1 only a small amount or hardly any of something: *There's little doubt in my mind that he's guilty.* | *I paid little attention to what the others were saying.* | *Little is known about the causes of the problem.* | *Changes in the law have done little to improve the situation.* | [+of] *Little of their wealth now remains.* | *There's very little money left.* | *Many of the students speak little or no English.* | *He knew little or nothing* (=almost nothing) *about fixing cars.* | *My lawyer advised me to say as little as possible.* | *He did precious little* (=very little) *to help.* | *The laboratory tests are of little real value.* → see box at FEW

2 **a little** a small amount: *Fortunately I had a little time to spare.* | *Susan speaks a little French.* | *A little over half the class can swim.* | *He walked on a little* (=a short distance) *and then turned back.* | **a little more/less** *Would you like a little more milk in your coffee?* | [+of] *The city is regaining a little of its former splendour.*

3 **as little as £5/3 months/10 feet etc** used to emphasize how surprisingly small an amount is: *Prices for his paintings start from as little as £100.* | *The weather can change completely in as little as half an hour.*

4 **what little** also **the little (that)** used to emphasize how small an amount there is, how small an amount is possible etc: *We did what little we could to help.* | *I handed over what little money I had left.*

5 **a little (of sth) goes a long way** *spoken* used to say that only a small amount of something is needed or has a great effect: *A little kindness goes a long way.*

little³ S1 W1 *adv*

1 **a little** slightly or to a small degree; ⊟ **a bit**: *She trembled a little as she spoke.* | *He was a little surprised at her request.* | **a little more/better/further etc** *We'll have to wait a little longer to see what happens.*

2 not much or only slightly: *The town has changed little over the years.* | *The situation has improved very little.* | **little known/understood etc** (=not known about by many people) *a little known corner of the world* | **little more/better etc (than sth)** *His voice was little more than a whisper.*

3 **little did sb know/realize/think etc** used to say that someone did not know or think that something would happen or was true: *Little did I know that the course of my life was about to change.*

4 **little by little** gradually: *Little by little he became accepted by the family.*

5 **more than a little/not a little** *literary* extremely: *Graham was more than a little frightened by what he had seen.*

1 000, 2 000, 3 000, most frequent words in S poken and W ritten English

little 'finger n [C] the smallest finger on your hand; → **pinkie** → see picture at HAND[1]

'Little ,League n a baseball LEAGUE for children in the US

'little ,people n [plural] **1** all the people in a country or organization who have no power: *It's the little people who bear the brunt of taxation.* **2** the little people imaginary people with magic powers, especially Irish LEPRECHAUNS

lit·to·ral /'lɪtərəl/ n [C] *technical* an area near the coast —**littoral** adj

li·tur·gi·cal /lɪ'tɜːdʒɪkəl $ -ɜːr-/ adj [only before noun] relating to church services and ceremonies —**liturgically** /-kli/ adv

lit·ur·gy /'lɪtədʒi $ -ər-/ n plural **liturgies** **1** [C,U] a way of praying in a religious service using a fixed order of words, prayers etc **2** the Liturgy the written form of these services

liv·a·ble /'lɪvəbəl/ adj another spelling of LIVEABLE

live[1] S1 W1 /lɪv/ v

1 IN A PLACE/HOME [I always + adv/prep] if you live in a place, you have your home there: [+in/at/near etc] *They lived in Holland for ten years.* | *He lives just across the street from me.* | *We live only a few miles from the coast.* | *A rather odd family came to live next door to us.* | *As soon as I saw the place, I knew I didn't want to live there.* | *Does Paul still live here?* | *We're still looking for somewhere to live.* | *They've finally found a place to live.* | [+with] *My grandmother came to live with us when I was ten.* | *Most seventeen-year-olds still live at home* (=live with their parents). | *I'm quite happy living alone.* | *The house has 3,600 square feet of living space* (=the areas of a house you live in). | *the number of young people living rough* (=living outside because they have no home) BrE

2 PLANT/ANIMAL [I always + adv/prep] a plant or animal that lives in a particular place grows there or has its home there: [+in/on etc] *These particular birds live on only one island in the Pacific.*

3 AT A PARTICULAR TIME [I always + adv/prep] if you live at a particular time, you are alive then: [+before/in/at] *He lived in the eighteenth century.* | *She lived at a time when women were not expected to work.* | *Gladstone lived during a period of great social change.* | **the best/greatest etc that/who ever lived** (=the best, greatest etc who has been alive at any time) *He's probably the best journalist who ever lived.*

4 BE/STAY ALIVE [I] to be alive or be able to stay alive: *Without light, plants couldn't live.* | *He is extremely ill and not expected to live.* | *The baby only lived a few hours.* | *People on average are living much longer than before.* | *I'll never forget this for as long as I live.* | **live to (be) 80/90 etc/live to the age of 80/90 etc** *My grandmother lived to 85.* | *She lived to the age of 79.* | **have two weeks/six months etc to live** *He knows he's only got a few months to live.* | *He did not live to see* (=live long enough to see) *the realization of his dream.*

5 WAY OF LIFE [I always + adv/prep, T] to have a particular type of life, or live in a particular way: **live in peace/poverty etc** *The people in this country just want to live in peace.* | *People should not live in fear of crime.* | *We live in hope that a cure will be found.* | **live peacefully/quietly/happily etc** *The two communities live peacefully alongside each other.* | *She thought that she would get married and live happily ever after* (=like in a children's story). | *Some people like to live dangerously.* | *Most elderly people prefer to live independently if they can.* | *They earn enough money to live well* (=have plenty of food, clothes etc). | *I just want to live my life in my own way.* | *He's not well enough to live a normal life.* | **live a quiet/active/healthy life** *She lives a very busy life.* | *He had chosen to live the life of a monk.* | *She's now in Hollywood living a life of luxury.* | [+by] *I have always tried to live by my faith* (=according to my

religion). | *We struggle on, living from day to day* (=trying to find enough money each day to buy food etc). | *He was tired of living out of a suitcase* (=spending a lot of time travelling).

6 EARN A LIVING [I] the way that someone lives is the way that they earn money to buy food etc: *Fishing is the way their families have lived for generations.* | **live by doing sth** *They live by hunting and killing deer.*

7 EXCITING LIFE [I] to have an exciting life: *She wanted to get out and live a little.* | *We're beginning to live at last!*

8 IMAGINE STH [I always + adv/prep] to imagine that things are happening to you: [+in] *He lives in a fantasy world.* | [+through] *She lived through her children's lives.* | *You must stop living in the past* (=imagining that things from the past are still happening).

9 BE KEPT SOMEWHERE [I always + adv/prep] BrE informal the place where something lives is the place where it is kept: *Where do these cups live?* | *Those big dishes live in the cupboard next to the fridge.*

10 STILL EXIST/HAVE INFLUENCE [I] if an idea lives, it continues to exist and influence people: *Democracy still lives!* | *His name will live forever.* | *That day will always live in my memory.*

11 living quarters the part of a building where people live, especially a building that is used by many people or is used for several different purposes: *the White House living quarters*

12 living expenses the money you need to spend in order to live, for example on food or a house: *His tuition is paid, but he'll work to cover his living expenses.*

13 living arrangements the way someone organizes how and where they will live: *Her mother disapproved of the living arrangements, saying that two girls living with four boys was bound to cause problems.*

14 live it up *informal* to do things that you enjoy and spend a lot of money: *Sam was living it up in London.*

15 live by your wits to get money by being clever or dishonest, and not by doing an ordinary job

16 live a lie to pretend all the time that you feel or believe something when actually you do not feel that way: *I knew that I could not continue to live a lie.*

17 be living on borrowed time to be still alive after the time that you were expected to die: *She's been living on borrowed time for the last year.*

18 live in sin old-fashioned if people live in sin, they live together and have a sexual relationship without being married; → live together

19 live and breathe sth to enjoy doing something so much that you spend most of your time on it: *Politics is the stuff I live and breathe.*

20 you live and learn *spoken* used to say that you have just learned something that you did not know before

21 live and let live used to say that you should accept other people's behaviour, even if it seems strange

22 you haven't lived (if/until...) *spoken* used to say that someone's life will be boring if they do not do a particular exciting thing: *You haven't lived until you've tasted champagne.*

23 sb will live to regret it used to say that someone will wish that they had not done something: *If you marry him, you'll live to regret it.*

24 live to see/fight another day to continue to live or work after a failure or after you have dealt with a difficult situation: *Hopefully, the company will live to fight another day.*

25 live life to the full to enjoy doing a lot of different things: *She believes in living life to the full.*

26 live high on the hog used to say that someone has a nice life because they have a lot of money and buy expensive things – often used to show disapproval

27 live from hand to mouth to have only just enough money to buy food: *We lived from hand to mouth, never knowing where the next meal was coming from.*

28 long live the King/Queen! etc *spoken* used as an expression of loyal support for a person

29 long live democracy/freedom etc used to say that you hope something continues to exist for a long time: *Long live free education!*

L

live sth ⇔ **down** *phr v*
if someone does not live something down, people never forget about it and never stop laughing at them for it: *She'll never live that down!*

live for sth *phr v*
if you live for something, it is the thing that you enjoy or hope for most in your life: *He lived for his art.* | *She had nothing left to live for.* | *She lives for the day when she can have a house of her own.*

live in *phr v BrE*
if someone lives in, they live in the place where they work; → **live-in**: *Sometimes it can be easier if you have a nanny who lives in.*

live off sb/sth *phr v*
to get your income or food from a supply of money or from another person: *Mom used to live off the interest from her savings.* | *Dad lost his job and we had to live off welfare.* | *Most people in the countryside live off the land* (=live by growing or finding their own food).

live on *phr v*
1 if something lives on, it continues to exist: *Alice's memory will live on.*
2 live on sth to have a particular amount of money to buy food and other necessary things: *I don't know how they manage to live on £55 a week.* | *the number of families who live on benefits*
3 live on sth to eat a lot of a particular type of food: *They live on bread and potatoes.* | *He practically lives on fish and chips!*

live out *phr v*
1 *BrE* if someone lives out, they do not live in the place where they work: *Most home helps prefer to live out.*
2 live out sth to experience or do something that you have planned or hoped for; ■ **fulfil**, **realize**: *The money enabled them to live out their dreams.*
3 live out your life to continue to live in a particular way or place until you die: *He lived out his life in solitude.*

live through sth *phr v*
to experience difficult or dangerous conditions; ■ **endure**: *the generation that lived through the Second World War* | *It was hard to describe the nightmare she had lived through.*

live together *phr v*
if people live together, they live in the same house and have a sexual relationship but are not married; → **live with**: *They lived together for two years before they got married.*

live up to sth *phr v*
if something or someone lives up to a particular standard or promise, they do as well as they were expected to, do what they promised etc: *The bank is insolvent and will be unable to live up to its obligations.* | *The film has certainly lived up to my expectations*.

live with sb/sth *phr v*
1 to accept a difficult situation that is likely to continue for a long time; ■ **put up with**, **tolerate**: *You have to learn to live with stress.* | *He has lived with his illness for most of his life.*
2 to live in the same house as someone and have a sexual relationship with them without being married; → **live together**: *She's living with her boyfriend now.*
3 if something lives with you, it stays in your mind: *That episode has lived with me all my life.*

live² [S3] [W3] /laɪv/ *adj*
1 [LIVING] [only before noun] not dead or artificial; ■ **living**; ■ **dead**: *experiments on live animals* | *Protesters want to stop the export of live sheep and cattle.* | *the number of live births per 1,000 population* | *We were so excited to see real live elephants.*
2 [TV/RADIO] a live television or radio programme is seen or heard on television or radio at the same time as it is actually happening; ■ **prerecorded**: *a live radio phone-in show* | *There will be live TV coverage of tonight's big match.*
3 [MUSIC/THEATRE] a live performance is one in which the entertainer performs for people who are watching, rather than a film, record etc: *A lot of the bars have live music.* | *The band will be giving a live concert perfor-*

mance next week. | *We'll be playing you a track from his new live album* (= ALBUM that was recorded from a live performance). | *It's always different when you perform in front of a live audience* (=an audience watching a live performance).
4 [ELECTRICITY] a wire or piece of equipment that is live has electricity flowing through it: *Be careful – those wires are live.*
5 [BOMBS] a live bomb still has the power to explode because it has not been used: *They came across a field of live, unexploded mines.*
6 [BULLETS] live bullets are real ones that are made of metal and can kill people; ■ **blank**: *Troops fired live ammunition to disperse the crowd.*
7 [ISSUE] a live subject or problem is one that still interests or worries people: *Drink-driving is still very much a live issue.*
8 live coals pieces of coal that are burning: *She threw the paper onto the live coals.*
9 [YOGHURT] live YOGHURT contains BACTERIA that are still alive

live³ /laɪv/ *adv* **1** if something is broadcast live, it is broadcast on television or radio as it is actually happening; → **prerecorded**: *The ceremony will be broadcast live on television.* | *The match will be shown live by the BBC.* **2** if people perform live, they perform in front of people who have come to watch, rather than for a film, record etc: *I love their music, but I've never seen them perform live.* | *The band is playing live in Birmingham tonight.* | *Their latest CD was recorded live* (=recorded at a live performance) *in New York.* **3 go live** when a system or project goes live, people start to use it after it has been planned and discussed for a long time: *Their new information retrieval system went live last month.* | *a new security project which will go live in October*

liv·a·ble especially *BrE*, **livable** especially *AmE* /ˈlɪvəbəl/ *adj* **1** a situation is liveable is satisfactory but not good; ■ **bearable**: *Having the children had made his life more liveable.* **2 a)** also **liveable in** *BrE* good enough to live in; ■ **habitable**: *We need to do more to make the neighborhood more livable.* **b)** nice to live in: *It's one of the most liveable cities in the US.* **3 a livable wage/salary** *AmE* a salary that is enough for you to buy the things you need, such as food, a house etc

lived-in *adj* **1** lived-in places or clothes look as though they have been used or worn a lot – use this to show approval: **a lived-in look/feel** *The most fashionable jeans this winter have a lived-in look.* **2** someone who has a lived-in face looks fairly old and as though they have had a lot of interesting experiences

live-in /ˈlɪv ɪn/ *adj* [only before noun] **1** a live-in job is one in which you live with the family you work for: *a live-in nanny* **2 live-in lover/boyfriend etc** someone who lives with their sexual partner but is not married to them

live·li·hood /ˈlaɪvlihʊd/ *n* [C,U] the way you earn money in order to live: **a means/source of livelihood** *Fishing is the main source of livelihood for many people in the area.* | *It's difficult to earn a livelihood as an artist.* | *Bates says he will lose his livelihood if his driving licence is taken away.*

live·long /ˈlɪvlɒŋ $ -lɔːŋ/ *adj* **all the livelong day** *old-fashioned* a phrase meaning 'all day', used when this seems like a long time to you

live·ly [S3] /ˈlaɪvli/ *adj comparative* **livelier**, *superlative* **liveliest**
1 [PEOPLE] someone who is lively has a lot of energy and is very active: *a lively child*
2 [PLACE/SITUATION] a place or situation that is lively is exciting because a lot of things are happening: *The hotel is situated next to the lively bustling port.* | *the city's lively nightlife*
3 [MUSIC/MOVEMENTS] lively movements or music are very quick and exciting: *a lively Spanish dance*
4 [DISCUSSION/DESCRIPTION ETC] a lively discus-

L

sion, description etc is very interesting and involves a lot of ideas: *The book offers a lively account of her travels.* | *a lively debate on environmental issues*

5 MIND/THOUGHTS someone who has a lively mind is intelligent and interested in a lot of things: *Even Paula has shown a lively interest in politics.* | *Charlie has a very lively imagination* (=he often invents stories, descriptions etc that are not true).

6 COLOUR very bright: *a lively combination of colours*

7 TASTE something that has a lively taste has a strong but pleasant taste: *The wine has a lively fruity flavour.*

8 Look lively! *BrE spoken*; **Step lively!** *AmE spoken* used to tell someone to hurry —**liveliness** *n* [U]

liv·en /'laɪvən/ *v*

liven up *phr v* **1** to become more exciting, or to make an event become more exciting: *The party really livened up when Mattie arrived.* | **liven sth ⇔ up** *Why don't we invite Jane? That'll liven things up!* **2 liven sth ⇔ up** to make something look, taste etc more interesting; ◫ **brighten up**: *Why not liven up the room with some flowers?* **3** to become more interested or excited, or to make someone feel like this: *After a few drinks she livened up a little.*

liv·er /'lɪvə $ -ər/ *n* **1** [C] a large organ in your body that produces BILE and cleans your blood → see picture at HUMAN[1] **2** [C,U] the liver of an animal, used as food

liv·e·ried /'lɪvərid/ *adj* **1** wearing LIVERY: *a liveried servant* **2** *BrE* painted with the colours and designs that represent a company: *liveried aircraft*

liv·er·ish /'lɪvərɪʃ/ *adj BrE old-fashioned* slightly ill, especially after eating or drinking too much

Liv·er·pud·li·an /ˌlɪvəˈpʌdliən $ -vər-/ *n* [C] someone from the city of Liverpool in England —**Liverpudlian** *adj*

liver ˌsausage *BrE*, **liv·er·wurst** *AmE* /'lɪvəwɜːst $ -vərwɜːrst/ *n* [U] a cooked soft SAUSAGE made from LIVER

liv·e·ry /'lɪvəri/ *n plural* **liveries** **1** [C,U] *BrE* the colours and designs used by a company on its property and vehicles **2** [C,U] a special uniform worn by servants in past times **3** [U] the business of keeping and taking care of horses, especially in past times: *a livery stable* → LIVERIED

lives /laɪvz/ *n* the plural of LIFE

live·stock /'laɪvstɒk $ -stɑːk/ *n* [plural, U] animals such as cows and sheep that are kept on a farm

live wire /ˌlaɪv 'waɪə $ -'waɪr/ *n* [C] **1** *informal* someone who is very active and has a lot of energy **2** a wire that has electricity passing through it

liv·id /'lɪvɪd/ *adj* **1** extremely angry; ◫ **furious**: *She was absolutely livid that he had lied.* **2** *formal* a mark on your skin that is livid is dark blue and grey: *livid bruises* **3** *literary* a face that is livid is very pale

liv·ing[1] /'lɪvɪŋ/ *adj* **1** alive now; ▣ **dead**: *He's one of the greatest living composers.* | *The sun affects all living things* (=people, animals, and plants). | *a living language* (=one that people still use) **2 living proof** if someone is living proof of a particular fact, they are a good example of how true it is: **living proof (that)** *I'm living proof that you don't need a college degree to be successful.* | **[+of]** *the living proof of government economic incompetence* **3 in/within living memory** during the time that anyone can remember: *It was the worst storm in living memory.* **4 a living death** a life that is so unpleasant that it seems better to be dead **5 a living hell** a very unpleasant situation that makes you suffer for a long time: *These past few days have been a living hell.* **6 living legend** someone who is famous for being extremely good at something, and who still does that activity: *His music has made him a living legend.* → **scare/frighten the (living) daylights out of sb** at DAYLIGHT (3); → **beat/knock the (living) daylights out of sb/sth** at DAYLIGHT (4)

living[2] S2 *n*

1 [C usually singular] the way that you earn money or the

money that you earn: *It's not a great job, but it's a living.* | *What do you do for a living?* (=what do you do as a job?) | **earn/make a living** *It's hard to make a decent living as a musician.* | **scrape/scratch a living** (=get just enough to eat or live)

2 the living all the people who are alive as opposed to dead people; ▣ **the dead**

3 [U] the way in which someone lives their life: *the stresses of city living*

4 [C] the position or income of a PARISH priest → COST OF LIVING, STANDARD OF LIVING; → **in the land of the living** at LAND[1] (7)

ˌliving 'fossil *n* [C] an ancient animal or plant that still exists and has not changed

'living room *n* [C] the main room in a house where people relax, watch television etc; ◫ **lounge**

'living ˌstandard *n* [C usually plural] the level of comfort and the amount of money that people have; ◫ **standard of living**: *Living standards have improved over the last century.* | *rising living standards* | *There's been a decline in the living standards of old people.*

ˌliving 'wage *n* [singular] a salary that is high enough to allow you to buy the things that you need to live: *jobs that don't even pay a living wage*

ˌliving 'will *n* [C] a document explaining what medical or legal decisions someone should make if you become so ill that you cannot make those decisions yourself

liz·ard /'lɪzəd $ -ərd/ *n* [C] a type of REPTILE that has four legs and a long tail → see picture at REPTILE

ll., ll the abbreviation of *lines*, used in writing to refer to specific lines of a poem etc: *ll. 24–35*

lla·ma /'lɑːmə/ *n* [C] a South American animal with thick hair like wool, and a long neck

LLB *BrE*; **LL.B.** *AmE n* [C] *Bachelor of Laws* a first university DEGREE in law

LLD *BrE*; **LL.D.** *AmE n* [C] *Doctor of Laws* a DOCTORATE in law

LLM *BrE*; **LL.M.** *AmE n* [C] *Master of Laws* a university DEGREE in law that you can get after your first degree

lo /ləʊ $ loʊ/ *interjection* **1** *old use* used to tell someone to look at something that is surprising **2 lo and behold** *spoken* used before mentioning something surprising that happened – used humorously: *We had just been talking about John when, lo and behold, he walked into the room.*

load[1] S2 W3 /ləʊd $ loʊd/ *n* [C]

1 AMOUNT OF STH a large quantity of something that is carried by a vehicle, person etc: **[+of]** *a load of wood* | *The lorry had shed its load* (=the load had fallen off). | *The plane was carrying a full load of fuel.*

2 a load (of sth); **loads (of sth)** *BrE informal* a lot of something: *We got a load of complaints about the loud music.* | *Don't worry, there's loads of time* | **loads to do/see/eat etc** *There's loads to see in Paris.*

3 a bus load/car load/truck load etc the largest amount of something that a vehicle can carry: *a bus load of tourists*

4 a load of crap/bull etc; **a load of rubbish** *BrE spoken not polite* used to say that something is bad, untrue, or stupid: *I thought the game was a load of crap.*

5 WORK the amount of work that a person or machine has to do: *The computer couldn't handle the load and crashed.* | **a light/heavy load** (=not much or a lot of work) *Hans has a heavy teaching load this semester.* | *My work load has doubled since Henry left.* | *They hired more staff in order to* **spread the load**.

6 WORRY a problem or worry that is difficult to deal with: *When someone is depressed, the extra load of having financial problems can make the situation worse.* | *Knowing he was safe was* **a load off** *my mind* (=I felt less worried). | *Coping with ill health was a heavy load to bear.*

7 WASHING a quantity of clothes that are washed together in a washing machine: *I've already done three loads of laundry this morning.*

8 get a load of sb/sth *spoken* used to tell someone to

L

look at or listen to something that is surprising or funny: *Get a load of this! Your stars say you are going to meet someone who's rich.*
9 WEIGHT the amount of weight that something is supporting: *a load-bearing wall* | *It increased the load on the wheels.*
10 ELECTRICITY *technical* an amount of electrical power that is being produced

load² v **1** [I,T] also **load up** to put a large quantity of something into a vehicle or container; ⧉ *unload*: *Have you finished loading up?* | *It took an hour to load the van.* | *Will you help me load the dishwasher?* | **load sth into/onto sth** *Emma loaded all the groceries into the car.* | *He loaded the cups onto a tray.* | **load sth with sth** *She loaded up the car with camping gear.* **2** [T] to put a necessary part into something in order to make it work, for example bullets into a gun or film into a camera: **load sth with sth** *Did you load it with 200 or 400 film?* | **load sth into sth** *Can you load the CD into the player, please?* **3** [I,T] to put a program into a computer, or to be put into a computer: *The program takes a while to load.* | *To load the file, press the 'return' key.* **4** [I] also **load up** if a ship, aircraft etc loads, goods are put onto it: *The first ship to load at the new port was the 'Secil Angola'.* | [+with] *The boat called at Lerwick to load up with fresh vegetables.*

  load sb/sth ⇔ **down** *phr v* **1** [usually passive] to give someone more work or problems than they can deal with; ⧉ **weigh down**: **be/feel loaded down with sth** *Jane felt loaded down with money worries.* **2** to make someone carry too many things; ⧉ **weigh down**: **be loaded down with sth** *I was loaded down with bags so I took a taxi.*

  load up on sth *phr v AmE* to get a lot of something so that you are sure you will have enough; ⧉ **stock up (on)**: *People were loading up on bottled water.*

  load sb **(up) with** sth *phr v* to give someone a lot of things, especially things they have to carry

load·ed /ˈləʊdᵻd $ ˈloʊ-/ *adj*
1 GUN/CAMERA containing bullets, film etc: *a loaded pistol*
2 FULL a loaded vehicle or container is full of things: *a loaded trailer* | *She came back carrying a loaded tray.* | [+with] *a truck loaded with bananas*
3 RICH [not before noun] *informal* very rich: *Giles can afford it – he's loaded.*
4 loaded with sth *informal* full of a particular quality, or containing a lot of something: *snacks loaded with fat* | *paintings loaded with cultural significance*
5 WORD/STATEMENT a loaded word, statement etc has more meanings than you first think and is intended to influence the way you think: *He 'deserved' it? That's a loaded word.* | *There was a loaded silence.*
6 a loaded question a question that is unfair because it is intended to affect your opinions and make you answer in a particular way → **leading question** at LEADING¹ (4)
7 DRUNK [not before noun] *AmE informal* very drunk: *Greg used to come home loaded almost every night.*
8 the dice/odds are loaded against sb/sth used to say that someone or something is unlikely to succeed or win
9 sth is loaded against sb/sth used to say that a system, situation, or organization is unfair and some people have a disadvantage; ⧉ **biased**: *The justice system is loaded against people from ethnic minorities.*
10 loaded dice DICE that have weights in them so that they always fall with the same side on top, used to cheat in games

ˈloading ˌbay *BrE*; **ˈloading dock** *AmE n* [C] an area at the side of a large shop or WAREHOUSE from which goods are taken off or put onto trucks

loaf¹ /ləʊf $ loʊf/ *n plural* **loaves** /ləʊvz $ loʊvz/
1 [C] bread that is shaped and baked in one piece and can be cut into SLICES: *a loaf of bread* | white/wholemeal/granary etc loaf *BrE* | a sliced loaf *BrE*; → see picture at BREAD **2** [C,U] food that has been cut into very small pieces, pressed together, and baked: *a meat*

loaf 3 use your loaf *BrE old-fashioned* used to tell someone to think more carefully about what they are doing

loaf² v [I] *written* to spend time somewhere and not do very much; ⧉ **hang around/round**: [+around/about] *They spend all day loafing around on street corners.*

loaf·er /ˈləʊfə $ ˈloʊfər/ *n* [C] **1** **Loafer** *trademark* a flat leather shoe that does not need to be fastened onto your foot **2** someone who is lazy and does nothing when they should be working

loam /ləʊm $ loʊm/ *n* [U] good quality soil consisting of sand, clay, and decayed plants —**loamy** *adj*

loan¹ S2 W2 /ləʊn $ loʊn/ *n*
1 [C] an amount of money that you borrow from a bank etc

take out a loan (=borrow money)
repay/pay off/pay back a loan (=give back money you have borrowed)
make a loan *AmE* (=give someone a loan)
bank loan (=money lent by a bank)
car/home loan (=a loan to buy a car etc)
personal loan (=money lent to an INDIVIDUAL)
business loan (=money lent to a business)
student loan (=money lent to students to pay for university)
interest-free loan (=a loan on which you only repay the amount you borrowed)
loan repayment

[⊦of] *a loan of £60,000* | *I had to take out a loan to buy my car.* | *It'll be years before we've paid off the loan.* | *The organization was allowed to make loans to private businesses.* | *I'll get a bank loan if necessary.* | *The average home loan is now almost triple what it was at the beginning of the Eighties.* | *An interest-free loan fund is available for students who find themselves in unforeseen financial difficulty.* | *They were unable to keep up with their loan repayments.*

2 [singular] when you lend something to someone: [+of] *Thanks for the loan of your camera.*
3 on loan (from sb/sth) if something or someone is on loan, they have been borrowed. *The book I wanted was out on loan.* | *paintings on loan from the Louvre* | *Cantona initially went on loan to Leeds United.*

loan² v [T] **1** *AmE* to lend someone something, especially money: **loan sb sth** *Can you loan me $5?* | *Jeff's loaned us his car for the weekend.* **2** also **loan out** *BrE* to lend something valuable to someone: *The National Library has loaned several manuscripts.* | **loan sth to sb/sth** *Two of the steam trains have been loaned to other railways.*

ˈloan shark *n* [C] someone who lends money at very high rates of INTEREST and will often use threats or violence to get the money back

loan·word /ˈləʊnwɜːd $ ˈloʊnwɜːrd/ *n* [C] a word taken into one language from another; ⧉ **borrowing**

loath, loth /ləʊθ $ loʊθ/ *adj* be loath to do sth *formal* to be unwilling to do something; ⧉ **reluctant**: *Sarah was loath to tell her mother what had happened.*

loathe /ləʊð $ loʊð/ v [T not in progressive] to hate someone or something very much; ⧉ **detest**: *He loathes their politics.* | **loathe doing sth** *I absolutely loathe shopping.*

loath·ing /ˈləʊðɪŋ $ ˈloʊð-/ *n* [singular, U] a very strong feeling of hatred: [+for] *her loathing for her first husband* | [+of] *a loathing of war* | *The nightmare left her with a sense of fear and loathing.*

loath·some /ˈləʊðsəm $ ˈloʊθ-/ *adj* very unpleasant or cruel; ⧉ **repulsive**: *that loathsome little man*

loaves /ləʊvz $ loʊvz/ *n* the plural of LOAF

lob /lɒb $ lɑːb/ v **lobbed, lobbing** [T always + adv/prep]
1 *informal* to throw something somewhere, especially over a wall, fence etc: *The kids were lobbing pine cones*

L

into the neighbor's yard. **2** to kick or hit a ball in a slow high curve, especially in a game of tennis or football: *Sampras lobbed the ball high over Chang's head.* —**lob** *n* [C]

lob·by¹ /'lɒbi $ 'lɑːbi/ *n plural* **lobbies** [C] **1** a wide passage or large hall just inside the entrance to a public building; **◨ foyer**: *a hotel lobby* | *I'll meet you in the entrance lobby.* → see picture at **STAY** **2 a)** a hall in the British parliament where members of parliament and the public meet **b)** one of the two passages in the British parliament where members go to vote for or against a **BILL 3** [also + plural verb *BrE*] a group of people who try to persuade a government that a particular law or situation should be changed: *the anti-foxhunting lobby* | *a powerful environmental lobby group* **4** an attempt to persuade a government to change a law, make a new law etc: *a mass lobby of Parliament by women's organizations*

lobby² *v* **lobbied, lobbying, lobbies** [I,T] to try to persuade the government or someone with political power that a law or situation should be changed: [+for/against] *The group is lobbying for a reduction in defence spending.* | **lobby sb to do sth** *We've been lobbying our state representative to support the new health plan.* —**lobbyist** *n* [C]

lobe /ləʊb $ loʊb/ *n* [C] **1** the soft piece of flesh at the bottom of your ear; **◨ earlobe 2** *technical* a round part of an organ in your body, especially in your brain or lungs

lo·bot·o·my /lə'bɒtəmi $ lə'bɑː-/ *n plural* **lobotomies** [C] a medical operation to remove part of someone's brain in order to treat their mental problems —**lobotomize** *v* [T]

lob·ster /'lɒbstə $ 'lɑːbstər/ *n* **1** [C] a sea animal with eight legs, a shell, and two large CLAWS → see picture at **SEA FOOD 2** [U] the flesh of a lobster, which is eaten

lob·ster·pot /'lɒbstəpɒt $ 'lɑːbstərpɑːt/ *n* [C] a trap shaped like a basket in which lobsters are caught

lo-cal /ˌləʊ 'kæl◂ $ ˌloʊ-/ *adj* lo-cal food or drink does not contain many CALORIES

lo·cal¹ [S1] [W1] /'ləʊkəl $ 'loʊ-/ *adj* [usually before noun] **1** relating to the particular area you live in, or the area you are talking about: *local hospital* | *local residents* **2** *technical* affecting or limited to one part of your body: *a local infection* | *The tooth was removed under local anaesthetic.*

local² [S3] *n* [C] **1** [usually plural] someone who lives in the place where you are or the place that you are talking about: *We asked one of the locals to recommend a restaurant.* **2** *BrE* a PUB near where you live, especially one where you often drink: *I usually have a pint or two at my local on Friday nights.* **3** *AmE* a bus, train etc that stops at all regular stopping places; → **express 4** *AmE* a branch of a TRADE UNION

local area network *n* [C] *technical* LAN

local authority *n* [C also + plural verb] *BrE* the group of people responsible for the government of a particular area, town, or city in the UK; **◨ local government** *AmE*: *Central government is trying to stop local authorities overspending.*

local call *n* [C] a telephone call to a place near you that does not cost much money; **◪ long-distance**

local colour *BrE*; **local color** *AmE n* [U] additional details in a story or picture that give you a better idea of what a place is really like: *His description of the smells from the market added a touch of local color.*

local council *n* [C also + plural verb BrE] the group of people responsible for providing houses, schools, parks etc in a small area such as a town

lo·cale /ləʊ'kɑːl $ loʊ-/ *n* [C] *formal* the place where something happens or where the action takes place in a book or a film; **◨ setting**: *people who see the countryside as a locale for recreation*

local government *n* [C,U also + plural verb *BrE*] the government of cities, towns etc rather than of a whole country; → **state, national, federal**

local history *n* [U] the history of a particular area

lo·cal·i·ty /ləʊ'kæləti $ loʊ-/ *n plural* **localities** [C] *formal* a small area of a country, city etc; **◨ area**: *weather reports from several different localities* | **in the locality** *Both sea fishing and fresh water angling are available in the locality.*

lo·cal·ize also **-ise** *BrE* /'ləʊkəlaɪz $ 'loʊ-/ *v* [T] *formal* **1** to find out exactly where something is: *A mechanic is trying to localize the fault.* **2** to limit the effect that something has, or the size of area it covers: *They hoped to localize the fighting.* —**localization** /ˌləʊkəlaɪ'zeɪʃən $ ˌloʊkələ-/ *n* [U]

lo·cal·ized also **-ised** *BrE* /'ləʊkəlaɪzd $ 'loʊ-/ *adj* *formal* happening within a small area: *localized flooding* | *a localized infection*

lo·cal·ly [S2] /'ləʊkəli $ 'loʊ-/ *adv* **1** near the area where you are or the area you are talking about: *I live locally, so it's easy to get to the office.* **2** in particular small areas: *Most of the country will be dry, but there will be some rain locally.*

local paper *n* [C] **1** a newspaper that contains mainly local news; → **national 2** *AmE* a newspaper which contains local, national, and international news

local radio *n* [U] a radio service that broadcasts programmes for a particular area of the country; → **national**

local rag *n* [C] *BrE informal* a local newspaper

local time *n* [U] the time of day in a particular part of the world: *We'll arrive in Boston at 4 o'clock local time.*

lo·cate [S3] [W3] /ləʊ'keɪt $ 'loʊkeɪt/ *v* **1** [T] to find the exact position of something: *We couldn't locate the source of the radio signal.* **2** **be located in/near etc sth** to be in a particular position or place; **◨ be situated**: *The business is located right in the center of town.* **3** [T] to put or build something in a particular place: *Large retail chains are usually only prepared to locate stores in areas of high population density.* **4** [I always + adv/prep] *AmE* to come to a place and start a business, company etc there: [+in/at etc] *We are offering incentives for companies to locate in our city.*

Frequencies of the nouns **location**, **place** and **spot** in spoken and written English.

This graph shows that **place** is much more common than **location** or **spot** in both spoken and written English. This is because **place** is the most general of the three words. **Location** is used to mean a particular place or position, especially in relation to other buildings, areas etc. **Spot** is used especially to mean a pleasant place where you spend time.

lo·ca·tion [S3] [W2] /ləʊ'keɪʃən $ loʊ-/ *n* **1** [C] a particular place, especially in relation to other areas, buildings etc: *His apartment is in a really good location.* | *its isolated geographical location* **2** [U] the position of something: [+of] *The map shows the precise location of the crash.*; → see box at **POSITION**¹ **3** [C,U] a place away from a film STUDIO where scenes are filmed: *It was hard to find a suitable location for the*

desert scenes. | **on location** *Most of the movie was shot on location in Africa.*
4 [U] the act of finding the position of something: *The main problem for engineers was the location of underground rivers in the area.*

loch /lɒx, lɒk $ lɑːk, lɑːx/ *n* [C] a lake or a part of the sea partly enclosed by land in Scotland: *Loch Ness*

lo·ci /'ləʊsaɪ $ 'loʊsaɪ, -ki/ *n* the plural of LOCUS

lock¹ S2 W3 /lɒk $ lɑːk/ *v*
1 FASTEN SOMETHING [I,T] to fasten something, usually with a key, so that other people cannot open it. or to be fastened like this: *Did you lock the car? | I can't get this drawer to lock.* → see box at CLOSE¹
2 KEEP IN A SAFE PLACE [T always + adv/prep] to put something in a place and fasten the door, lid etc with a key: **lock sth in sth** *Lock the cat in the kitchen.*
3 FIXED POSITION [I,T] to become fixed in one position and impossible to move, or to make something become fixed: *The wheels suddenly locked.* | **lock sth around/round sth** *He locked his hands around the younger man's throat.* | *A moment later they were* **locked in an embrace** (=holding each other very tightly in a loving or friendly way). | *Their* **eyes locked together** (=they could not look away from each other) *for an instant.*
4 FIXED SITUATION [T usually passive] if you are locked in a situation, you cannot get out of it: **be locked in/into sth** *Security forces and militants are locked in a vicious cycle of killing.* | *The company is locked into a three year contract with PARCO.*
5 be locked in battle/combat/dispute etc to be involved in a long, serious argument or fight with someone: *They are now locked in a bitter custody battle over the three children.*
6 lock arms if people lock arms, they join their arms tightly with the arms of the people on either side: *The police locked arms to form a barrier against the protesters.*
7 lock horns (with sb) to argue or fight with someone: *The band have now locked horns with their record company over the album.* —**lockable** *adj*

lock sb/sth ⇔ **away** *phr v*
1 to put something in a safe place and lock the door, lid etc, ■ **lock up**: *He locked his money away in the safe.*
2 to put someone in prison; ■ **lock up**: *I hope they lock him away for years.*
3 lock yourself away to keep yourself separate from other people by staying in your room, office etc

lock in *phr v*
1 lock sb in (sth) to prevent someone from leaving a room or building by locking the door: *She locked herself in.* | *They locked the director in his office.*
2 lock sth ⇔ in to do something so that a price, offer, agreement etc cannot be changed: *Sell your stocks now to lock in some of the gains of recent months.*
3 lock sth ⇔ in to make the taste, liquid etc remain in something: *This method of cooking locks in the flavour of the meat.*

lock onto sth *phr v*
if a MISSILE or SATELLITE locks onto a TARGET or signal, it finds it and follows it closely

lock sb ⇔ **out** *phr v*
1 to keep someone out of a place by locking the door: [+of] *I locked myself out of the house!*
2 if employers lock workers out, they do not let them enter their place of work until they accept the employers' conditions for settling a disagreement → LOCKOUT

lock up *phr v*
1 to make a building safe by locking the doors, especially at night: *I'll leave you to lock up.* | **lock sth ⇔ up** *Don't forget to lock up the warehouse.*
2 lock sth ⇔ up to put something in a safe place and lock the door, lid etc; ■ **lock away**
3 lock sb ⇔ up to put someone in prison; ■ **lock away**: *Rapists should be locked up.*
4 be locked up (in sth) if your money is locked up, you have put it into a business, INVESTMENT etc and cannot easily use it or use it

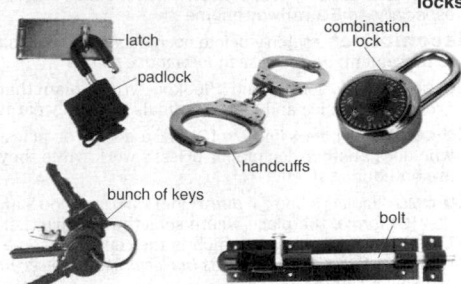

locks

latch
combination lock
padlock
handcuffs
bunch of keys
bolt

lock² S2 *n*
1 FASTENING [C] a thing that keeps a door, drawer etc fastened and is usually opened with a key or by moving a small metal bar: *I'm sorry, there isn't a lock on the bathroom door.* | *The key turned stiffly in the lock.* | *a bike lock* → **pick a lock** at PICK¹ (10); → see picture at LOCK²
2 under lock and key a) kept safely in a box, cupboard etc that is locked: *Dad keeps all his liquor under lock and key.* b) kept in a place such as a prison
3 lock, stock, and barrel including every part of something: *He moved the whole company, lock, stock, and barrel, to Mexico.*
4 HAIR a) [C] a small number of hairs on your head that grow and hang together: [+of] *He gently pushed a lock of hair from her eyes.* b) locks [plural] *literary* someone's hair: *long flowing locks*
5 ON A RIVER ETC [C] a part of a CANAL or river that is closed off by gates so that the water level can be raised or lowered to move boats up or down a slope
6 IN A FIGHT [C] a HOLD which WRESTLERS use to prevent their opponent from moving: *a head lock*
7 VEHICLE [C,U] *BrE* the degree to which a vehicle's STEERING WHEEL can be turned in order to turn the vehicle
8 RUGBY [C] a playing position in the game of RUGBY
9 a lock on sth *AmE* complete control of something: *Pro football still has a lock on male viewers aged 18 to 34.*
→ AIR LOCK, COMBINATION LOCK

lock·er /'lɒkə $ 'lɑːkər/ *n* [C] **1** a small cupboard with a lock in a school, office, sports building etc, where you can leave clothes or possessions while you do something; → see picture at SPORTS CENTRE **2** *AmE* a very cold room used for storing food in a restaurant or factory: *a meat locker*

'locker room *n* [C] a room in a sports building, school etc where people change their clothes and leave them in lockers

lock·et /'lɒkɪt $ 'lɑː-/ *n* [C] a piece of jewellery that you wear around your neck on a chain, with a small metal case in which you can put a picture, a piece of hair etc

lock·jaw /'lɒkdʒɔː $ 'lɑːkdʒɒː/ *n* [U] *informal* TETANUS

'lock ,keeper *n* [C] someone whose job is to open and close the gates of a LOCK on a CANAL

lock·out /'lɒkaʊt $ 'lɑːk-/ *n* [C] a situation when a company does not allow workers to go back to work, especially in a factory, until they accept the employers' conditions → **lock out** at LOCK¹

lock·smith /'lɒk,smɪθ $ 'lɑːk-/ *n* [C] someone who makes and repairs locks

lock·step /'lɒkstep $ 'lɑːk-/ *n* in lockstep *AmE* in exactly the same way or at the same rate

'lock-up *n* [C] **1** a small prison where a criminal can be kept for a short time **2** also **lock-up garage** *BrE* a garage that you can rent to keep cars, goods etc in

lo·co /'ləʊkəʊ $ 'loʊkoʊ/ *adj AmE informal* crazy → IN LOCO PARENTIS

lo·co·mo·tion /,ləʊkə'məʊʃən $,loʊkə'moʊ-/ *n* [U] *formal* or *technical* movement or the ability to move

lo·co·mo·tive¹ /ˌləʊkəˈməʊtɪv $ ˌloʊkəˈmoʊ-/ n [C] *especially AmE* a railway engine

locomotive² *adj* [only before noun] *technical* relating to movement: *an increase in locomotive power*

lo·co·weed /ˈləʊkəʊwiːd $ ˈloʊkoʊ-/ n [C] a plant that grows in America and makes animals ill if they eat it

lo·cum /ˈləʊkəm $ ˈloʊ-/ n [C] *BrE* a doctor or priest who does another doctor's or priest's work while they are on holiday, ill etc

lo·cus /ˈləʊkəs $ ˈloʊ-/ n *plural* loci /ˈləʊsaɪ $ ˈloʊ $ aɪ, -ki/ [C] *formal* the place where something is particularly known to exist, or which is the centre of something: [+of] *The Politburo was the locus of all power in the Soviet Union.*

lo·cust /ˈləʊkəst $ ˈloʊ-/ n [C] an insect that lives mainly in Asia and Africa and flies in a very large group, eating and destroying crops: *a swarm of locusts*

lo·cu·tion /ləʊˈkjuːʃən $ loʊ-/ n *technical* **1** [U] a style of speaking **2** [C] a phrase, especially one used in a particular area or by a particular group of people

lode /ləʊd $ loʊd/ n [C usually singular] an amount of ORE (=metal in its natural form) found in a layer between stones → MOTHER LODE

lode·star /ˈləʊdstɑː $ ˈloʊdstɑːr/ n [singular] *literary* **1** a principle or fact that guides someone's actions **2** the POLE STAR, used to guide ships at sea

lode·stone, loadstone /ˈləʊdstəʊn $ ˈloʊdstoʊn/ n [C,U] *old use* a piece of iron that acts as a MAGNET

lodge¹ /lɒdʒ $ lɑːdʒ/ v
1 lodge a complaint/protest/appeal etc *BrE* to make a formal or official complaint, protest etc: [+with] *He lodged an appeal with the High Court.* | [+against] *They lodged a complaint against the doctor for negligence.*
2 BECOME STUCK [I always + adv/prep, T usually passive] to become firmly stuck somewhere, or to make something become stuck; ◙ **dislodge**: [+in] *The fishbone lodged in her throat.* | be lodged in/between/behind etc sth *The bullet was lodged in his spine.*
3 PUT SB SOMEWHERE [T] to provide someone with a place to stay for a short time: *a building used to lodge prisoners of war* | lodge sb in/at sth *The refugees were lodged in old army barracks.*
4 PUT STH SOMEWHERE [T] *BrE formal* to put something important in an official place so that it is safe: lodge sth with sb *Be sure to lodge a copy of the contract with your solicitor.* | lodge sth in sth *The money was lodged in a Swiss bank account.*
5 STAY SOMEWHERE [I always + adv/prep] *old-fashioned* to pay to live in a room in someone's house: [+at/with etc] *John lodged with a family in Bristol when he first started work.*

lodge² n [C] **1** a small house on the land of a large country house, usually at the main entrance gate **2** a room or small building at the entrance to a college, institution etc for someone whose job is to watch who enters and leaves: *the porter's lodge* **3** a house or hotel in the country or mountains where people can stay when they want to go hunting, shooting etc **4** a local meeting place for some organizations, or the group of people who belong to one of these organizations: *He was a member of a Masonic lodge.* **5** a BEAVER's home **6** *AmE* a traditional home of Native Americans, or the group of people that live in it

lodg·er /ˈlɒdʒə $ ˈlɑːdʒər/ n [C] someone who pays rent for a room in someone's house; ◙ **boarder** *AmE*: *We have decided to take in lodgers to help pay the mortgage.*

lodg·ing /ˈlɒdʒɪŋ $ ˈlɑː-/ n **1** [U] a place to stay: *It's £90 a week for board and lodging (=meals and a room).* **2** [C usually plural] *old-fashioned* a room in someone's house which you live in and pay rent for: *Paul found lodgings in the Marylebone Road.*

'lodging house n [C] *BrE old-fashioned* a building where people can rent rooms to live or stay in; ◙ **boarding house**

loft¹ /lɒft $ lɒːft/ n [C]
1 UNDER A ROOF *BrE* a room or space under the roof of a building, usually used for storing things in; ◙ **attic**: *Our neighbours have just done a loft conversion (=changed the loft into bedrooms).*
2 ON A FARM a raised area in a BARN used for keeping HAY or other crops: *a hayloft*
3 PART OF A ROOM *AmE* a raised area above the main part of a room, usually used for sleeping
4 TYPE OF APARTMENT a space above a business, factory etc that was once used for storing goods, but has been changed into living space: *She's just bought a loft in Manhattan.*
5 FOR BIRDS a set of CAGES used to keep PIGEONS in
6 IN A CHURCH the raised place in a church where the ORGAN or CHOIR is

loft² v [T] to hit a ball very high in GOLF or CRICKET

loft·y /ˈlɒfti $ ˈlɒː-/ adj **1** *literary* lofty mountains, buildings etc are very high and impressive: *He stayed at the ISH, from whose lofty heights he could see across New York.* **2** lofty ideas, beliefs, attitudes etc show high standards or high moral qualities – use this to show approval: *lofty ideals of equality and social justice* | *He had set himself the lofty goal of reaching the world's top five.* **3** seeming to think you are better than other people – used to show disapproval: *She has such a lofty manner.* —**loftily** *adv* —**loftiness** *n* [U]

log¹ S3 /lɒg $ lɒːg, lɑːg/ n [C]
1 a thick piece of wood from a tree: *a roaring log fire* → see picture at FIREPLACE; → see picture at SPLIT¹
2 an official record of events, especially on a journey in a ship or plane: *The captain always keeps a log.*
3 a LOGARITHM → it's as easy as falling off a log at FALL¹ (30); → sleep like a log/top at SLEEP¹ (1)

log² v logged, logging **1** [T] to make an official record of events, facts etc: *All phone calls are logged.* **2** [T] to travel a particular distance or for a particular length of time, especially in a plane or ship: *The pilot has logged 1200 flying hours.* **3** [I,T] to cut down trees
log in/on *phr v* to do the necessary actions on a computer system that will allow you to begin using it: [+to] *You need to log on to your home page.*
log off/out *phr v* to stop using a computer system by giving it particular instructions

lo·gan·ber·ry /ˈləʊgənbəri $ ˈloʊgənbəri/ n *plural* **loganberries** [C] a soft dark red fruit like a large RASPBERRY

log·a·rithm /ˈlɒgərɪðəm $ ˈlɒː-, ˈlɑː-/ n [C] *technical* a number representing another number in a mathematical system so that complicated calculations can be done as simple addition

'log book n [C] **1** *BrE* an official document containing details about a vehicle and the name of its owner **2** an official record of events, especially on a journey in a ship or plane

,log 'cabin n [C] a small house made of LOGS

log·ger /ˈlɒgə $ ˈlɒːgər, ˈlɑː-/ n [C] someone whose job is to cut down trees; ◙ **lumberjack**

log·ger·heads /ˈlɒgəhedz $ ˈlɒːgər-, ˈlɑː-/ n be at **loggerheads (with sb)** if two people are at loggerheads, they disagree very strongly: [+over] *He is at loggerheads with many of his own party over the issue of taxation.*

log·gi·a /ˈlɒdʒiə $ ˈloʊdʒə/ n [C] an open area with a floor and a roof that is built on the side of a house on the ground floor

log·ging /ˈlɒgɪŋ $ ˈlɒː-, ˈlɑː-/ n [U] the work of cutting down trees in a forest

lo·gic /ˈlɒdʒɪk $ ˈlɑː-/ n **1** [singular, U] a way of thinking about something that seems correct and reasonable, or a set of sensible reasons for doing something: [+behind] *The logic behind this statement is faulty.* | [+of] *What's the logic of your argument?* | accept/

follow/see sb's logic *It's easy to understand his logic.* | *There is **a certain logic** in their choice of architect.* | **commercial/industrial/economic logic** *Commercial logic has forced the two parts of the company closer together.* **2** [U] a formal method of reasoning, in which ideas are based on previous ideas **3** [U] technical a set of choices that a computer uses to solve a problem

lo·gic·al S3 /ˈlɒdʒɪkəl $ ˈlɑː-/ *adj*
1 seeming reasonable and sensible; ► **illogical**: *It's a logical site for a new supermarket, with the housing development nearby.* | *a logical conclusion*
2 using a thinking process in which facts and ideas are connected in a correct way: *The detective has to discover the murderer by logical deduction.* —**logically** /-kli/ *adv*: *He tried to think logically.*

lo·gi·cian /ləˈdʒɪʃən $ loʊ-/ *n* [C] someone who studies or is skilled in logic

-logist /lədʒɪst/ *suffix* [in nouns] another form of the suffix -OLOGIST

lo·gis·tic /ləˈdʒɪstɪk $ loʊ-/ also **lo·gis·tic·al** /-tɪkəl/ *adj* relating to the logistics of doing something: *the logistical problems of implementing the proposals* —**logistically** /-kli/ *adv*

lo·gis·tics /ləˈdʒɪstɪks $ loʊ-/ *n* [plural] the practical arrangements that are needed in order to make a plan that involves a lot of people and equipment successful: *the day-to-day logistics involved with mining* | [+of] *the logistics of travelling with small children*

log·jam /ˈlɒgdʒæm $ ˈlɒːg-, ˈlɑːg-/ *n* [C] **1** a situation in which a lot of problems are preventing progress from being made **2** a tightly packed mass of floating LOGS on a river

lo·go /ˈləʊgəʊ $ ˈloʊgoʊ/ *n* [C] a small design that is the official sign of a company or organization

log·roll·ing /ˈlɒgˌrəʊlɪŋ $ ˈlɒːgˌroʊ-, ˈlɑːg-/ *n* [U] *AmE informal* **1** the practice in the US Congress of helping a member to pass a BILL, so that they will do the same for you later **2** The practice of praising or helping someone, so that they will do the same for you later

-logue also **-log** *AmE* /lɒg $ lɒːg, lɑːg/ *suffix* [in nouns] something that is written or spoken: *a monologue* (=a speech by one person)

-logy /lədʒi/ *suffix* [in nouns] another form of the suffix -OLOGY: *mineralogy* (=the study of minerals)

loin /lɔɪn/ *n* **1 loins** [plural] *literary* the part of your body below your waist and above your legs, which includes your sexual organs **2** [C,U] a piece of meat from the lower part of an animal's back: *roast loin of pork* → **gird (up) your loins** at GIRD (1)

loin·cloth /ˈlɔɪnklɒθ $ -klɒːθ/ *n* [C] a piece of cloth that men in some hot countries wear around their waist to cover their sexual organs

loi·ter /ˈlɔɪtə $ -ər/ *v* [I] **1** to stand or wait somewhere, especially in a public place, without any clear reason; ► **hang about, hang around**: *Five or six teenagers were loitering in front of the newsagent's.* **2** to move or do something slowly, or to keep stopping when you should keep moving

loll /lɒl $ lɑːl/ *v* **1** [I always + adv/prep] to sit or lie in a very lazy and relaxed way; ► **lounge**: [+around/about/beside etc] *He lolled back in his chair.* **2** [I,T] if your head or tongue lolls or if you loll your head, you allow it to hang in a relaxed uncontrolled way

lol·li·pop /ˈlɒlipɒp $ ˈlɑːlipɑːp/ *n* [C] a hard sweet made of boiled sugar on a stick; ► **lolly** *BrE*

lollipop lady, lollipop man *n* [C] *BrE* someone whose job is to help children cross a road safely on their way to school

lol·lop /ˈlɒləp $ ˈlɑː-/ *v* [I always +adv/prep] *written* to run with long awkward steps: [+down/up/along etc] *The dog came lolloping up the path.*

lol·ly /ˈlɒli $ ˈlɑːli/ *n plural* **lollies** *BrE informal* **1** [C] frozen juice or ice cream on a stick; ► **ice lolly 2** [C] a hard sweet made of boiled sugar on a stick; ► **lollipop 3** [U] *old-fashioned* money – used humorously

lone /ləʊn $ loʊn/ *adj* [only before noun] **1** used to talk about the only person or thing in a place, or the only person or thing that does something; ► **solitary**: *A lone figure was standing at the bus stop.* | *He was by no means a lone voice criticizing the government.* | *a lone gunman* | *the lone survivor of a shipwreck* **2 lone mother/father/parent etc** *BrE* someone who looks after their children on their own; ► **single**: *a lone-parent family* **3 lone wolf** someone who prefers to be alone

lone·ly S3 /ˈləʊnli $ ˈloʊn-/ *adj comparative* **lonelier**, *superlative* **loneliest**
1 unhappy because you are alone or do not have anyone to talk to; ► **lonesome** *AmE*: *a lonely old man* | *Don't you get lonely being on your own all day?* ⚠ Do not use **lonely** to mean 'without anyone else'. Use **alone**: *She is afraid to travel alone (NOT travel lonely).*
2 a lonely experience or situation makes you unhappy because you are alone or do not have anyone to talk to: *a lonely journey* | **lonely life/existence** *He led a lonely life with few friends.*
3 the lonely [plural] people who are lonely
4 a lonely place is a long way from where people live and very few people go there; ► **lonesome** *AmE*; ► **remote, desolate: lonely place/road/spot** etc —**loneliness** *n* [U]

lonely hearts *n* **lonely hearts club/column/ad** *BrE* a club or an advertisement page of a newspaper that is used by people who want to meet someone that they can have a romantic relationship with

lon·er /ˈləʊnə $ ˈloʊnər/ *n* [C] someone who prefers to be alone or who has no friends: *Ken's always been a bit of a loner.*

lone·some /ˈləʊnsəm $ ˈloʊn-/ *adj AmE* **1** very unhappy because you are alone or have no friends; ► **lonely**: *Beth is lonesome without the children.* **2** a lonesome place is a long way from where people live and very few people go there; ► **lonely, remote**: *a lonesome spot near the canyon* **3 on/by your lonesome** *informal* alone

long¹ S1 W1 /lɒŋ $ lɒːŋ/ *adj comparative* **longer**, *superlative* **longest**
1 GREAT LENGTH measuring a great length from one end to the other; ► **short**: *a long table* | *long hair* | *the longest tunnel in the world* | *He stretched out his long legs.* | *a long line of people*
2 GREAT DISTANCE continuing or travelling a great distance from one place to another; ► **short**: *a long distance* | *Springfield is a long way from Chicago.* | *Liz lives in Cheltenham, which is a long way away.* | **long journey/walk/flight/drive etc** (=a journey etc over a large distance that takes a lot of time) *It's a long walk to the shops from here.*
3 LARGE AMOUNT OF TIME continuing for a large amount of time, or for a larger amount of time than usual; ► **short**: *a long period of time* | *a long history of success* | *He has a long memory.* | **(for) a long time/while** *He's been gone a long time.* | *I haven't been there for a long while.* | *It took a long time to get everything ready.* | *She died a long time ago.* | **long silence/pause/delay etc** *There was a long silence before anybody spoke.* | *She's recovering from a long illness.* | *Doctors often work long hours* (=work for more time than is usual). | **the longest time** *AmE spoken* (=a very long time) *It took me the longest time to figure out how to open the windows.*
4 PARTICULAR LENGTH/DISTANCE/TIME used to talk or ask about a particular length, distance, or time: *How long is your garden?* | *How long is the film?* | *The cable is not quite long enough.* | **two metres/three miles etc long** *The bridge is 140 feet long.* | **two hours/three days etc long** *The speech was twenty minutes long.*
5 WRITING containing a lot of words, letters, names, or pages; ► **short**: *a long novel* | *a long list* | *He has a very long name.* | *He owes money to a list of people as*

long as your arm (=a very long list).

6 CLOTHING covering all of your arms or legs; ▣ short: *a long dress* | *a long-sleeved shirt*

7 TIRING/BORING *spoken* making you feel tired or bored: *It's been a long day*.

8 VOWEL *technical* a long vowel in a word is pronounced for a longer time than a short vowel with the same sound: ▣ short

9 how long is a piece of string? *BrE spoken* used when there is no definite answer to a question: *'How long will it take to finish the project?' 'How long is a piece of string?'*

10 the long and (the) short of it *spoken* used when you are telling someone the most important facts about something rather than all the details: *The long and the short of it is that we missed the train*.

11 the long arm of sb/sth *written* the power of someone or something that has authority, especially to catch and punish someone: *He won't escape the long arm of the law*.

12 long face a sad or disappointed expression on someone's face

13 long in the tooth *informal* too old – used humorously: *I'm getting a bit long in the tooth for this sort of thing*.

14 not long for this world *literary* likely to die or stop existing soon

15 long on sth having a lot of a quality: *He was short on patience, but long on a sense of his own worth*.

16 long odds if there are long odds against something happening, it is very unlikely that it will happen

17 in the long run/term used when talking about what will happen at a later time or when something is finished: *All our hard work will be worth it in the long run*.

18 long shot someone or something with very little chance of success: *Chelsea are a 20–1 long shot to win the championship*.

19 long time no see *spoken* used humorously to say hello when you have not seen someone for a long time

20 take the long view (of sth) to think about the effect that something will have in the future rather than what happens now

21 a long way very much, far, or a great amount or degree: *We're still a long way from achieving our sales targets*. | *Psychiatry has come a long way* (=developed a lot) *since the 1920s*. | *Your contributions will go a long way towards helping children in need* (=will help to reach a goal). | **by a long way/shot** *informal* also **by a long chalk** *BrE* (=used when something is much better, quicker, cheaper etc) *It was his best performance this year, by a long way*. | **not by a long way/shot** *informal* also **not by a long chalk** *BrE* (=not at all or not nearly) *He had not told Rory everything, not by a long shot*.

22 long weekend three or more days, including Saturday and Sunday, when you do not have to go to work or school → at (long) last at LAST³ (2); → it's a long story at STORY (10); → cut/make a long story short at STORY (11); → a little (of sth) goes a long way at LITTLE² (5); → have a long way to go at WAY¹ (19)

long² S1 W1 *adv*

1 for a long time: *Have you been waiting long?* | *Reform of the law is long overdue*. | *long established traditions*

2 used to ask and talk about particular amounts of time: *How long will it take to get there?* | *Try to keep going for as long as possible*. | *It took me longer than I thought it would*.

3 at a time that is a long time before or after a particular time: **long before/after sth** *This all happened long before you were born*. | **long ago/since** *He should have left her long ago*. | *It wasn't long before* (=soon) *Lisa arrived*.

4 for long [usually in questions and negatives] for a long time: *Have you known them for long?* | *I haven't seen her for so long that I've forgotten what she looks like*.

5 as/so long as a) used to say that one thing can happen or be true only if another thing happens or is true: *You can go out to play as long as you stay in the back yard*. b) used to say that one thing will continue to happen or be true if another thing happens or is true at the same time: *As long as we keep playing well, we'll keep winning games*.

6 (for) as long as used to talk about something continuing for the amount of time that you want, need, or is possible: *You can stay for as long as you want*. | *She tried to stay awake for as long as she could*. | *The fruit should be left on the tree as long as possible*.

7 no longer/not any longer used when something used to happen or be true in the past but does not happen or is not true now: *The extra workers won't be needed any longer*. | *It's no longer a secret*.

8 before long soon or in a short time: *Before long a large crowd had gathered outside the building*. | *It's likely that the law will be abolished before long*.

9 sb/sth/it won't be long *spoken* used to say that someone or something will be back, will be ready, will happen etc soon: *Wait here – I won't be long*. | *Dinner won't be long*.

10 all day/year/summer etc long during all of the day etc

11 so long *spoken especially AmE* goodbye

12 long live sb/sth used to show support for a person, idea, principle, or nation: *Long live the King!*

long³ *v* [I] to want something very much, especially when it seems unlikely to happen soon: **long to do sth** *He longed to see her again*. | [+for] *She longed for the chance to speak to him in private*. | **long for sb to do sth** *She longed for him to return*. → LONGED-FOR, LONGING

long. the written abbreviation of *longitude*

long-a·wait·ed, **long awaited** *adj* [only before noun] a long-awaited event, moment etc is one that you have been waiting a long time for: *the long-awaited news of his release from prison*

long·bow /ˈlɒŋbəʊ $ ˈlɔːŋboʊ/ *n* [C] a large BOW made from a long thin curved piece of wood, used in the past for hunting or fighting

long-distance *adj* [only before noun] **1** travelling over a long distance: **long-distance runner** | **long-distance lorry driver** | **long-distance travel/journey/flight/commuting etc 2** long-distance call a telephone call to a place that is far away; ▣ local —**long-distance** *adv*

long di·vi·sion *n* [U] a method of dividing one large number by another

long-drawn-out also **long-drawn** *adj* [only before noun] continuing for a longer time than is wanted or necessary; ▣ protracted: *The official enquiry was a long-drawn-out process*.

longed-for *adj* [only before noun] a longed-for thing or event is one that you want very much: *the birth of her first longed-for child*

lon·gev·i·ty /lɒnˈdʒevɪti $ lɑːn-, lɔːn-/ *n* [U] **1** the amount of time that someone or something lives: [+of] *the greater longevity of women compared with men* | *The worms have a longevity of about two years*. **2** long life or the long time that something lasts: *The ancient Chinese claimed that garlic promoted longevity*. **3** the amount of time that something lasts: [+of] *the longevity of an athlete's career*

long·hand /ˈlɒŋhænd $ ˈlɔːŋ-/ *n* [U] if you write something in longhand, you write it by hand using complete words, rather than TYPING it or using special short forms of words; → shorthand

¹long-haul adj long-haul flight/route/destination etc a long-haul flight etc is over a very long distance; ⓕ **short-haul** → SHORT-HAUL

long·horn /'lɒŋhɔːn $ 'lɔːŋhɔːrn/ n [C] a cow with long horns

long·ing /'lɒŋɪŋ $ 'lɔːŋɪŋ/ n [singular, U] a strong feeling of wanting something or someone: She looked back with longing on the good old days. | [+for] His heart was filled with longing for Cynthia. | [+to] She felt a longing to throw herself into his arms.

long·ing·ly /'lɒŋɪŋli $ 'lɔː-/ adv in a way that shows that you want someone or something very much: She thought longingly of returning to Paris. | look/gaze longingly at sb/sth He looked longingly at the tray of cakes. —**longing** adj

long·ish /'lɒŋɪʃ $ 'lɔːŋɪʃ/ adj informal fairly long; ⓕ **shortish**

lon·gi·tude /'lɒndʒ³₄tjuːd $ 'lɑːndʒ³₄tuːd/ n [C,U] the distance east or west of a particular MERIDIAN (=imaginary line along the Earth's surface from the North Pole to the South Pole), measured in degrees: The town lies at longitude 12° east. → see picture at GLOBE

lon·gi·tu·di·nal /ˌlɒndʒ³₄'tjuːd³ₙəl $ ˌlɑːndʒ³₄'tuː-/ adj technical **1** relating to the development of something over a period of time: longitudinal study/survey/research etc a longitudinal study of unemployed workers **2** going from top to bottom, not across: longitudinal stripes **3** measured according to longitude —**longitudinally** adv

long johns /'lɒŋ dʒɒnz $ 'lɔːŋ dʒɑːnz/ n [plural] warm underwear with long legs

¹long jump n the long jump a sport in which each competitor tries to jump further than anyone else —**long jumper** n [C]

ˌlong-'lasting adj continuing for a long time; ⓕ **short-lived**: The impact of divorce on children can be long-lasting. | long-lasting effect/result

ˌlong-'life adj **1** long-life products continue working longer than ordinary ones: long-life batteries **2** BrE long-life foods stay fresh longer than ordinary ones: long-life milk

ˌlong-'lived /ˌlɒŋ 'lɪvd $ ˌlɔːŋ 'laɪvd/ adj living or existing for a long time; ⓕ **short-lived**: Ostriches are long-lived birds. | the band's long-lived appeal

ˌlong-'lost adj [only before noun] lost or not seen for a long time: long-lost treasures | long-lost brother/cousin/friend etc

ˌlong-playing 'record n [C] an LP; ⓔ **album**; → **single**

ˌlong-'range adj [only before noun] **1** able to hit something that is a long way away; ⓕ **short-range**: long-range nuclear missiles | He scored with a long-range shot. **2** relating to a time that continues far into the future; ⓕ **short-range**: long-range planning/plan/forecast etc a long-range weather forecast | the long-range goal of the project

ˌlong-'running adj [only before noun] used to talk about something that has been continuing for a long time: a long-running saga | long-running dispute/battle/debate/feud etc She was involved in a long-running legal battle. | long-running show/musical/soap opera etc

ˌlong-'serving adj [only before noun] having a particular job or position for a long time: a long-serving member of the committee

long·shore·man /'lɒŋʃɔːmən $ 'lɔːŋʃɔːr-/ n plural longshoremen [C] AmE someone whose job is to load and unload ships at a DOCK; ⓔ **docker** BrE

ˌlong-'sighted adj BrE able to see objects or read things clearly only when they are far from your eyes; ⓕ **short-sighted**; ⓔ **far-sighted** AmE

ˌlong-'standing, long·stand·ing /ˌlɒŋ'stændɪŋ◄ $ ˌlɔːŋ-/ adj having continued or existed for a long time: a long-standing member of the committee | long-standing debate/dispute etc | a long-standing feud between the two families | the long-standing problem of keeping costs down | I have a long-standing arrangement with the bank.

ˌlong-'stay adj [only before noun] BrE **1** relating to care or treatment over a long period of time: long-stay hospital/ward/bed etc | long-stay patient/resident **2** a long-stay car park is a place where people can leave their cars for a long period of time; ⓕ **short-stay**

ˌlong-'suffering adj [usually before noun] patient in spite of problems or other people's annoying behaviour: his long-suffering wife

ˌlong-'term W3 adj [usually before noun] continuing for a long period of time into the future, or relating to what will happen in the distant future; ⓕ **short term**: the long-term future of the fishing industry | the long-term interests of the company | the long-term unemployed (=people who have not had a job for a long time) | the long-term effects of alcohol on the body | long-term plan/strategy/solution | long-term loan/investment → in the long term at TERM¹ (4)

ˌlong-time, long·time /'lɒŋtaɪm $ 'lɔːŋ-/ adj [only before noun] having existed or continued to be a particular thing for a long time: a long-time supporter of civil rights | long-time friend/lover etc

ˌlong ˌwave written abbreviation LW n [U] radio broadcasting or receiving on waves of 1000 metres or more in length; → **medium wave**, **short wave**, **FM**

long-wind·ed /ˌlɒŋ 'wɪnd³d◄ $ ˌlɔːŋ-/ adj **1** continuing to talk for too long or using too many words in a way that is boring: His speeches tend to be rather long-winded. **2** if a way of doing something is long-winded, it is very complicated: The whole process is incredibly long-winded.

loo /luː/ n plural loos [C] BrE informal a toilet: I need to go to the loo (=use the toilet).

loo·fah /'luːfə/ n [C] a rough bath SPONGE, made from the dried inner part of a tropical fruit

look¹ S1 W1 /lʊk/ v

1 SEE [I] to turn your eyes towards something, so that you can see it: We sneaked out while Jessie's mom wasn't looking. | If you look carefully you can see that the painting represents a human figure. | Gina covered her eyes, afraid to look. | [+at] 'It's time we left,' Ian said, looking at his watch. | The men all turned to look at her as she entered the room. | [+away/over/down etc] Dad looked up from his paper and smiled. | 'We can't go out in this weather,' said Bob, looking out of the window.; → see box at SEE¹

2 SEARCH [I] to try to find something: I looked everywhere but Jimmy was nowhere to be found. | [+for] Could you help me look for my contact lens? | If you're looking for a bargain, try the local market. | [+in/under/between etc] Try looking under the bed.

3 SEEM [linking verb] to seem: From the way things look at the moment, the Republicans are unlikely to win this election. | look good/bad etc The future's looking good. | it looks as if/as though/like (=it seems likely that) It looks as if it might rain later. | It looks like they won't be needing us any more. | You made me look really stupid in front of all my friends!

4 APPEARANCE [linking verb] to have a particular appearance: How do I look? | look tired/happy/sad etc You look tired. You should go to bed. | look as if/as though/like He looked as if he hadn't washed for a week. | What did the man look like? | My sister doesn't look anything like me. → look like a million dollars at MILLION (4); → see box at SEEM

5 look daggers at sb informal to look at someone with a very angry expression on your face

6 look sb up and down to look at someone carefully from their head to their feet, as if you were forming an opinion about them

7 look sb in the eye to look directly at someone when you are speaking to them, especially to show that you

L

are not afraid of them or that you are telling the truth: *Owen didn't dare look his father in the eye.*

8 look down your nose at sb/sth to behave as if you think that someone or something is not good enough for you: *He looks down his nose at anyone foreign.*

9 look the other way to ignore something bad that is happening and not try to stop it: *Prison guards looked the other way as the man was attacked by fellow prisoners.*

10 look no further used to say that something you are offering is exactly what someone has been trying to find: *Want a quiet country retreat for your weekend break? Then look no further!*

11 FACE A DIRECTION [I always + adv/prep] if a building looks in a particular direction, it faces that direction: *The cabin looks east, so we get the morning sun.*

12 look before you leap used to say that it is sensible to think about possible dangers or difficulties of something before doing it

13 be looking to do sth *informal* to be planning or expecting to do something: *We're looking to buy a new car early next year.*

SPOKEN PHRASES

14 look a) used to tell someone to look at something that you think is interesting, surprising etc: *Look! There's a fox!* **b)** used to get someone's attention so that you can suggest something or tell them something: *Look. Why don't you think about it and give me your answer tomorrow?* | *Look, I've had enough of this. I'm going home.*

15 look out! used to warn someone that they are in danger; ▤ **watch out**: *Look out! There's a car coming.*

16 look at that! used to tell someone to look at something that you think is interesting, bad etc: *Look at that! What a horrible mess!*

17 look who's here! used when someone arrives unexpectedly: *Well, look who's here! It's Jill and Paul!*

18 don't look now used to say that you have seen someone but do not want them to know you have noticed them: *Oh no! Don't look now but here comes Tony.*

19 look what you're doing/look where you're going etc used to tell someone to be careful: *Look where you're putting your feet! There's mud all over the carpet!*

20 look what you've done! used to angrily tell someone to look at the result of a mistake they have made or something bad they have done: *Look what you've done – my jacket's ruined!*

21 look here *old-fashioned* used to get someone's attention in order to tell them something, especially when you are annoyed with them: *Look here, you can't say things like that to me!*

22 (I'm) just looking used when you are in a shop, to say that you are only looking at things, but do not intend to buy anything now: *'Can I help you?' 'No, thanks. I'm just looking.'*

→ **look kindly on sb/sth** at KINDLY¹ (3)

look after sb/sth *phr v especially BrE*
1 to take care of someone by helping them, giving them what they need, or keeping them safe; ▤ **take care of**: *Don't worry, I'll look after the kids tomorrow.* | *Susan looked after us very well. She's an excellent cook.* | *You could tell that the horse had been **well looked after**.*
2 to be responsible for dealing with something; ▤ **take care of**: *I'm leaving you here to look after the business until I get back.*
3 look after yourself *spoken especially BrE* used when you are saying goodbye to someone in a friendly way
4 can look after yourself to not need anyone else to take care of you: *Don't worry about Maisie – she can look after herself.*

look ahead *phr v*
to think about and plan for what might happen in the future: *Looking ahead, we must expect radical changes to be made in our system of government.*

look around also **look round** *BrE phr v*
1 to try to find something: [+**for**] *Jason's going to start looking around for a new job.*
2 look around/round (sth) to look at what is in a place such as a building, shop, town etc, especially when you are walking: *Do we have to pay to look around the castle?* | *Let's look round the shops.*

look at sb/sth *phr v*
1 to turn your eyes towards something, so that you can see it: *The twins looked at each other and smiled.*
2 to read something quickly in order to form an opinion of it: *I really can't comment on the report – I haven't had time to look at it yet.*
3 to examine something and try to find out what is wrong with it: *You should get the doctor to look at that cut.* | *Can you look at my car? There's a strange noise coming from the front wheel.*
4 to study and think about something, especially in order to decide what to do: *We need to look very carefully at ways of improving our efficiency.*
5 look at sb/sth! *spoken* used to mention someone or something as an example: *You don't have to be smart to be good at music – look at Gary.*
6 to think about something in a particular way; ▤ **see**: *I'd like to be friends again, but Richard doesn't look at it that way.*
7 not much to look at *informal* if someone or something is not much to look at, they are not attractive

look back *phr v*
1 to think about something that happened in the past: [+**on/to**] *When I look back on those days I realize I was desperately unhappy.* | *Looking back on it, I still can't figure out what went wrong.*
2 never look back to become more and more successful, especially after a particular success: *After winning the scholarship he never looked back.*

look down on sb/sth *phr v*
to think that you are better than someone else, for example because you are more successful, or of a higher social class than they are: *Mr Garcia looks down on anyone who hasn't had a college education.*

look for sb/sth *phr v*
1 to try to find something that you have lost, or someone who is not where they should be; ▤ **search for**: *I'm looking for Steve – have you seen him?* | *Detectives are still looking for the escaped prisoner.* → SEARCH² (1)
2 be looking for sb/sth to be trying to find a particular kind of thing or person: *I'm sorry, we're really looking for someone with no family commitments.* | **be (just) what/who you are looking for** *'Salubrious'! That's just the word I was looking for.*
3 be looking for trouble *informal* to be behaving in a way that makes it likely that problems or violence will happen: *They walked into a bar looking for trouble.*

look forward to sth *phr v*
to be excited and pleased about something that is going to happen: *I'm really looking forward to our vacation.* | **look forward to doing sth** *My mother says she's looking forward to meeting you.*; → see box at WAIT¹

look in *phr v informal*
to make a short visit to someone, while you are going somewhere else, especially if they are ill or need help; ▤ **drop in**, **call in**: [+**on**] *I promised to look in on Dad and see if he's feeling any better.*

look into sth *phr v*
to try to find out the truth about a problem, crime etc in order to solve it; ▤ **investigate**: *Police are looking into the disappearance of two children.*

look on *phr v*
1 to watch something happening, without being involved in it or trying to stop it; → **onlooker**: *Only one man tried to help us, the rest just looked on in silence.*
2 look on sb/sth also **look upon sb/sth** to consider someone or something in a particular way, or as a particular thing: [+**as**] *I look on him as a good friend.* | [+**with**] *Strangers to the village are looked upon with a mixture of fear and suspicion.*

look sth ⇔ **out** *phr v*
to search for and find a particular thing among your possessions: *I'll look out some of my old books for you.*

look out for sb/sth *phr v*
1 to pay attention to what is happening around you, so that you will notice a particular person or thing if you see them; → **lookout**: *Look out for your Aunt while you're at the station.* | *He's looking out for a nice apartment downtown.*
2 to try to make sure that someone is treated well: *My older brother always looked out for me when we were kids.* | **look out for yourself/number one** (=think only of the advantages you can get for yourself)

look sth/sb ⇔ **over** *phr v*
to examine something quickly, without paying much attention to detail: *Do you have a few minutes to look these samples over?*

look round *phr v BrE*
to LOOK AROUND

look through sb/sth *phr v*
1 to look for something among a pile of papers, in a drawer, in someone's pockets etc; **□ go through**: *I've looked through all my papers but I still can't find the contract.*
2 to not notice or pretend not to notice someone you know, even though you see them: **look straight/right through sb** *I saw Fiona in the street yesterday and she looked straight through me.*

look to sb/sth *phr v*
1 to depend on someone to provide help, advice etc: [+**for**] *We look to you for support.* | **look to sb to do sth** *They're looking to the new manager to make the company profitable.*
2 to pay attention to something, especially in order to improve it: *We must look to our defences.*

look up *phr v*
1 if a situation is looking up, it is improving; **□ improve, get better**: *Now the summer's here **things are looking up**!*
2 **look** sth ⇔ **up** if you look up information in a book, on a computer etc, you try to find it there: *Look the word up in your dictionary.* | *I'll just look up the train times.*
3 **look** sb ⇔ **up** to visit someone you know, especially when you are in the place where they live for a different reason: *Don't forget to look me up when you come to Atlanta.*

look up to sb *phr v*
to admire or respect someone: *I've always looked up to Bill for his courage and determination.*

look² S1 W1 *n*

1 LOOK AT [C usually singular] an act of looking at something: **have/take a look (at sb/sth)** *Let me have a look at that – I think it's mine.* | *Take a **good look** at the photo and see if you recognize anyone in it.* | *I **took one look** at the coat and decided it wasn't worth £50.* | **have/take a look around** also **have/take a look round** *BrE* (=look at all the things in a particular place) *I have a special interest in old houses. Do you mind if I take a look around?*
2 EXPRESSION [C] an expression that you make with your eyes or face: **give sb a look** *Mike gave him such a severe look he didn't dare argue.* | *Why has Jake been giving me **dirty looks** (=unfriendly looks) all morning?*
3 CONSIDER [singular] an act of examining something and thinking about it: **have/take a look (at sb/sth)** *Have you had a chance to take a look at my proposal yet?* | *I asked the vet to have a **quick look** at the puppies as well.* | *It's time to take a **fresh look** at the old problem of low pay.* | *This month, take a **long hard look** (=examine very carefully) at where your money is going.*
4 SEARCH [singular] an attempt to find something: *I can't find them anywhere.* **Have a look** *yourself.* | *She had a **good look** (=searched carefully) through the files.*
5 APPEARANCE [C usually singular] the appearance that someone or something has: *The area has a very seedy look to it.* | *Mr Flynn had a tired, ill look in his eyes.* | **not like the look of sb/sth** (=think that something

bad has happened or will happen because of something's appearance) *We should turn back now. It's getting dark and I don't like the look of those rain clouds.*
6 WAY STH SEEMS [C] the way something seems to be: *The neighbours are back from holiday **by the looks of it** (=that is how it seems).* | *I don't like **the look of** this new policy (=I do not like the way it seems).*
7 BEAUTY **looks** [plural] physical attractiveness: *Fiona's got everything – looks, money and youth.* | *You get your **good looks** from your mother.* | *When she **lost her looks** (=became less attractive) she found it difficult to get work.*
8 FASHION [singular] a particular style in clothes, hair, furniture etc: *The hippy look is back again.*

look·a·like, **look-alike** /ˈlʊkəlaɪk/ *n* [C] *informal* someone who looks very similar to someone who is famous: *a Madonna lookalike*

look·er /ˈlʊkə $ -ər/ *n* [C] *informal* someone who is attractive, usually a woman

look-in *n BrE informal* **get/have a look-in** [usually in negatives] to have a chance to take part in or succeed in something: *Arsenal barely got a look-in (=were very unsuccessful) during the second half of the match.*

looking glass *n* [C] *old-fashioned* a MIRROR

look·out /ˈlʊk-aʊt/ *n*
1 be on the lookout for sb/sth to continuously watch a place or pay attention in order to find something you want or to be ready for problems or opportunities; → **look out for**: *We're always on the lookout for new business opportunities.* | *Police were on the lookout for anyone behaving suspiciously.*
2 keep a lookout to keep watching carefully for something or someone, especially for danger: [+**for**] *We were instructed to keep a lookout for enemy aircraft.* | *When you're driving, **keep a sharp lookout** (=watch extra carefully) for cyclists.*
3 PERSON [C] someone whose duty is to watch carefully for something, especially for danger
4 PLACE [C] a place for a lookout to watch from

look-'see *n* [singular] *informal* a quick look at something

loom¹ /luːm/ *v* [I] **1** [always + adv/prep] to appear as a large unclear shape, especially in a threatening way: [+**up/out/ahead etc**] *Suddenly a mountain loomed up in front of them.* **2** if a problem or difficulty looms, it is likely to happen very soon: *An economic crisis is **looming on the horizon**.* **3** loom large to seem important, worrying, and difficult to avoid: *Fear of failure loomed large in his mind.*

loom² *n* [C] a frame or machine on which thread is woven into cloth

loon /luːn/ *n* [C] **1** a large North American bird that eats fish and that makes a long high sound **2** *informal* a silly or strange person – used humorously

loon·y¹ /ˈluːni/ *n plural* **loonies** [C] *informal* someone who is crazy or strange: *Her brother's a complete loony.*

loony² *adj informal* silly, crazy, or strange: *a loony idea*

loony bin *n* [C] *informal* an expression meaning a hospital for people who are mentally ill, usually considered offensive; **□ psychiatric hospital**

loop¹ /luːp/ *n* [C]
1 SHAPE OR LINE a shape like a curve or a circle made by a line curving back towards itself, or a piece of wire, string etc that has this shape: **loop of wire/rope/string etc** *A loop of wire held the gate shut.* | **belt loop** (=a loop of material for holding a belt on trousers etc)
2 COMPUTER a set of operations in a computer program that are continuously repeated
3 FILM/MUSIC a film or music loop contains images or sounds that are continuously repeated
4 be in the loop/be out of the loop *informal* to be or not be part of a group of people who make important decisions

L

5 knock/throw sb for a loop *AmE informal* to surprise and upset someone
6 ROAD/RAILWAY *BrE* a road or railway line that leaves the main road or track and then joins it again further on

loop² *v* **1** [I,T] to make a loop or make something into a loop: **loop sth over/around etc sth** *He looped the rope over the post.* **2** [I] to move in a circular direction that forms the shape of a loop: *The ball looped over the goalkeeper into the back of the net.* **3 loop the loop** to fly a plane up and around in a circle so that the plane is UPSIDE DOWN for a time

loop·hole /'lu:phəʊl $ -hoʊl/ *n* [C] a small mistake in a law that makes it possible to avoid doing something that the law is supposed to make you do: **legal/tax loophole** | [+in] *a loophole in the law*

loop·y /'lu:pi/ *adj informal* **1** crazy or strange **2 go loopy** *BrE* **a)** to become extremely angry **b)** to become mentally ill

loose

loose/baggy clothes   tight clothes

loose¹ S3 W3 /lu:s/ *adj*
1 NOT FIRMLY ATTACHED not firmly fastened in place: *a loose floorboard* | *This tooth feels very loose.* | *The screw has **come loose** (=become loose).*
2 NOT ATTACHED not attached to anything else: *loose papers* | *His rear wheel spun on the **loose stones**.* | *The potatoes are sold loose (=not packed in a container).* | *The driver had forgotten to fasten the safety chain and the trailer **came loose** (=become unattached).*
3 NOT TIED TIGHTLY not tied or fastened very tightly: *a loose knot*
4 HAIR if your hair is loose, it hangs freely rather than being tied back: *Her hair fell loose around her shoulders.*
5 CLOTHES loose clothes are big and do not fit your body tightly; ▪ **loosefitting, baggy**; ⊟ **tight**: *a loose sweatshirt*
6 FREE free from being controlled or held in a cage, prison, or institution: **break/get loose** (=escape) *A 34-year old inmate broke loose from the sheriff's office yesterday.* | **turn/let/set sth loose** (=let something go free) *Don't let your dog loose on the beach.*
7 NOT EXACT [usually before noun] not exact or thoroughly done: *a loose translation* | *a **loose interpretation** of the law*
8 NOT VERY CONTROLLED not strictly controlled or organized: **loose federation/alliance/group etc** *a loose federation of political groups* | *loose arrangement* (=an arrangement that can easily be changed)
9 NOT SOLID not pressed tightly together in a solid mass: **loose soil/earth**
10 SPORT not under the control of either team in a game of football, RUGBY etc: *Sheringham was the first player to reach the **loose ball**.*
11 cut loose a) to free yourself from someone or something, or their influence: **cut yourself loose (from sth)** *He cut himself loose from the constraints of family life.* **b)** *AmE informal* to start enjoying yourself in a happy noisy way after a period of controlled behaviour: *I'm ready to cut loose and enjoy the weekend.*
12 let (sth ⇔) loose to speak or behave in an uncon-

trolled way: *She let loose a string of four-letter words.*
13 let sb loose on sth to allow someone to deal with something in the way they want to, when you think they will make mistakes or do something wrong: *Whatever you do, don't let Derek loose on the garden.*
14 be at a loose end also **be at loose ends** *AmE* to have nothing to do: *I was at a loose end so I decided to go see an old movie.*
15 loose ends parts of something that have not been completed or correctly done: *We've nearly finished, but there are still a few **loose ends** to be **tied up** (=dealt with or completed).*
16 loose change coins that you have in your bag or pocket
17 loose cannon someone who cannot be trusted because they say or do things you do not want them to
18 hang/stay loose *AmE spoken* used to tell someone to stay calm, or not to worry about something
19 BODY WASTE having a problem in which the waste from your BOWELS has too much liquid in it: *loose bowels*
20 IMMORAL *old-fashioned* behaving in a way that is considered to be sexually immoral: *a **loose woman** | loose morals*
21 TALK *old-fashioned* not careful about what you say or who is listening: *There's been a bit of **loose talk** about it.* ⚠ Do not confuse the adjective **loose** (=not tight, not firm etc) /luːs/ with the verb **lose** (=no longer have something, be unable to find something etc) which has a different pronunciation /luːz/. —**loosely** *adv: A towel was loosely wrapped around his neck.* | *The film is loosely based on the novel.* —**looseness** *n* [U]

loose² *v* [T] *literary* **1** to make something unpleasant begin: *And now the anger Maggie had feared was loosed.* **2** to make something loose or to untie someone or something, especially an animal **3** to fire an ARROW, a bullet from a gun etc

loose sth on/upon sb/sth *phr v literary* to allow something dangerous or harmful to begin to affect a situation or other people: *the evils loosed upon humanity in World War II*

loose³ *n* **be on the loose** if a criminal or dangerous animal is on the loose, they have escaped from prison or from their cage

loose-'fitting *adj* loose-fitting clothes are big and do not fit your body closely, so that they are comfortable; ▪ **baggy**; ⊟ **tight-fitting, tight**: *a loose-fitting jacket*

loose-'leaf *adj* [only before noun] having pages that can be put in and removed easily: **loose-leaf file/binder/format**

loos·en /'luːsən/ *v* **1** [I,T] to make something less tight or less firmly fastened, or to become less tight or less firmly fastened; ⊟ **tighten**: *You'll need a spanner to loosen that bolt.* | *The screws have loosened.* | *Harry loosened his tie.* → see picture at UNDRESS **2** [T] to make laws, rules etc less strict; ▪ **relax**; ⊟ **tighten**: *Congress has loosened the restrictions on immigration.* **3 loosen your grip/hold a)** to reduce the control or power you have over someone or something: [+on] *The government has loosened its hold on the media considerably.* **b)** to start holding someone or something less tightly than you were before; ⊟ **tighten**: [+on] *He loosened his grip on David's arm.* **4 loosen sb's tongue** to make someone talk more than usual, especially about things they should not talk about

loosen up *phr v* **1** to stop worrying and become more relaxed, or to make someone do this: *She loosened up after she'd had a drink.* | **loosen sb ⇔ up** *His welcoming smile helped loosen her up.* **2** if your muscles loosen up, or if something loosens them up, they stop feeling stiff: **loosen sth ⇔ up** *A massage will loosen up your joints.*

loot¹ /luːt/ *v* [I,T] to steal things, especially from shops or homes that have been damaged in a war or RIOT: *Shops were looted and burned.* —**looter** *n* [C] —**looting** *n* [U]

loot² *n* [U] **1** goods taken by soldiers from a place where they have won a battle; ▪ **plunder** **2** *informal* goods or money that have been stolen; ▪ **spoils** **3** *informal* things that you have bought or been given in large amounts – used humorously: *Jodie came home from the mall with bags of loot.*

lop /lɒp $ lɑːp/ also **lop off** v **lopped**, **lopping** [T] **1** also **lop off** to cut something, especially branches from a tree, usually with a single strong movement; ▤ **chop, chop off**: *Workmen have lopped off more branches in an effort to save the tree.* **2** also **lop off** to reduce an amount, especially of money, by a particular amount: *They lopped £16 off the price.* | **lop sth from sth** *Citicorp plans to lop $1.5 billion a year from its operating costs.*

lope /ləʊp $ loʊp/ also **lope off** v [I always + adv/prep] to run easily with long steps: [+along/across/up etc] *He loped off down the corridor.* —**lope** n [singular]

lop·sid·ed /ˌlɒpˈsaɪdᵻd $ ˌlɑːp-/ adj **1** having one side that is lower or heavier than the other: *a lopsided grin* **2** unequal or uneven, especially in an unfair way: *a lopsided 8–0 victory*

loq·ua·cious /ləˈkweɪʃəs $ loʊ-/ adj formal a loquacious person likes to talk a lot; ▤ **talkative** —**loquacity** /ləˈkwæsᵻti $ loʊ-/ n [U]

lord¹ S3 W2 /lɔːd $ lɔːrd/ n
1 [C] also **Lord** a man who has a rank in the ARISTOCRACY, especially in Britain, or his title; → **lady**: *Lord Salisbury*
2 [C] a man in MEDIEVAL Europe who was very powerful and owned a lot of land: *the feudal lords*
3 my lord BrE spoken used to address a judge or BISHOP, and in the past to address a lord
4 sb's lord and master someone who must be obeyed because they have power over you – used humorously

lord² v **lord it over sb** to behave in a way that shows you think you are better or more powerful than someone else: *He didn't use his position on the council to lord it over people.*

Lord n [singular] **1 a)** a title of God or Jesus Christ, used when praying: *Thank you, Lord, for your blessings.* **b) the Lord** God or Jesus Christ, used when talking about God: *The Lord helps and guides us.* **2 Lord (only) knows** spoken **a)** used when you do not know the answer to something: **Lord knows how/who/where etc** *Lord knows how old she is now.* **b)** used to emphasize that something is true: **Lord only knows** *I tried my best to get this right.* **3 (Good) Lord!/Oh Lord!** spoken said when you are suddenly surprised, annoyed, or worried about something; ▤ **heavens**: *Good Lord! Is that the time?* **4** the title of someone who has a particular type of official job in Britain: *Lord Mayor of London* **5 the Lords** BrE the House of Lords; → **the Commons** **6 Our Lord** a phrase meaning Jesus Christ

lord·ly /ˈlɔːdli $ -ɔːr-/ adj **1** behaving in a way that shows you think you are better or more important than other people: *a lordly disdain for the common man* **2** very big and impressive: *a lordly feast* —**lordliness** n [U]

lord·ship /ˈlɔːdʃɪp $ -ɔːr-/ n [C] **1 your/his lordship** used when talking to or talking about a LORD, or when talking to a British judge or BISHOP (1); → **ladyship** **2 his lordship** BrE spoken a man who thinks he is very important – used humorously: *So when will his lordship be back?*

Lord's Prayer n **the Lord's Prayer** the most important prayer of the Christian religion

lore /lɔː $ lɔːr/ n [U] knowledge or information about a subject, for example nature or magic, that is not written down but is passed from person to person: *According to local lore, a ghost still haunts the castle.*

lor·ry S3 /ˈlɒri $ ˈlɔːri, ˈlɑːri/ n plural **lorries** [C] BrE **1** a large vehicle for carrying heavy goods; ▤ **truck** **2** it fell off the back of a lorry spoken used humorously to say that something was probably stolen

lose S1 W1 /luːz/ v past tense and past participle **lost** /lɒst $ lɔːst/
1 STOP HAVING ATTITUDE/QUALITY ETC [T] to stop having a particular attitude, quality, ability etc, or to gradually have less of it; → **loss**: *I've lost my appetite.* | **lose confidence/interest/hope etc** *The business commu-*

nity has lost confidence in the government. | *Carol lost interest in ballet in her teens.* | *Try not to **lose heart*** (=become sad and hopeless) - *there are plenty of other jobs.* | **lose face** (=stop having as much respect from other people) *A settlement was reached in which neither side lost face.* | **lose weight/height/speed etc** *You're looking slim. Have you lost weight?* | *The plane emptied its fuel tanks as it started losing altitude.* | **lose your sight/hearing/voice/balance etc** *Mr Eyer may lose the sight in one eye.* | *The tour was postponed when the lead singer lost his voice.* | *Julian lost his balance and fell.* | **lose your touch** (=become less skilled at doing something you used to do well) *This latest movie proves Altman is by no means losing his touch.* | *By the time the ambulance arrived, Douglas had lost **consciousness**.* | **lose all sense of time/direction/proportion etc** *When he was writing, he lost all sense of time.* | **lose sight of sth** (=forget an important fact about a situation) *We must never **lose sight of the fact that** man must work in harmony with nature.*
2 NOT WIN [I,T] to not win a game, argument, election, war etc; ▣ **win**; → **defeat**: *They played so badly they deserved to lose.* | *Klinger lost his seat in the election.* | *Arkansas just lost three games in a row.* | *He just can't bear to lose an argument.* | [+to] *The Beavers have dropped only one game since losing to Oregon in January.* | **lose (sth) by 1 goal/10 votes/20 points etc** *The government lost by one vote.* | *The Communist candidate lost by a whisker* (=a very small amount). | *Freddie died in 1982 after **losing** his **battle** against AIDS.* | **lose sb sth** *It was a rash decision, and it lost him the race* (=caused him to lose the race).
3 CANNOT FIND STH [T] to become unable to find someone or something: *I've lost the tickets for tonight's show.* | *I followed her on foot, but lost her in the crowd.* | *It was thought the manuscript had been **lost forever**.* | **be/get lost in the post** BrE **be/get lost in the mail** AmE: *The parcel must have got lost in the post.* | **lose track of sth/sb** (=stop knowing where someone or something is) *He lost track of her after her family moved away.* | **lose sight of sth/sb** (=stop being able to see someone or something) *Don't try to walk in a heavy snowstorm as you may lose sight of your vehicle.* → LOST PROPERTY
4 STOP HAVING STH [T] if you lose something that is important or necessary, you then no longer have it, especially because it has been taken from you or destroyed; → **loss**: *David's very upset about losing his job.* | *Hundreds of people lost their homes in the floods.* | *My family lost everything in the war.* | *He was over the limit and will **lose** his **licence**.* | *90 naval aircraft were lost and 31 damaged.* | **lose a chance/opportunity** *If you hesitate, you may lose the opportunity to compete altogether.* | **lose sth to sb/sth** *We were losing customers to cheaper rivals.* | *She was about to lose her husband to a younger woman.* | *California has lost 90% of its wetlands to development.* | **lose an arm/leg/eye etc** *He lost his leg in a motorcycle accident.* | *He's **lost a lot of blood** but his life is not in danger.* | **lose sb sth** *the mistakes which lost him his kingdom* (=caused him to lose his kingdom)
5 DEATH [T] **a) lose your life** to die: *a memorial to honor those who lost their lives in the war* **b)** if you lose a relative or friend, they die – use this when you want to avoid saying the word 'die'; → **loss**: *One woman in Brooklyn lost a husband and two sons in the gang wars.* | *Sadly, Anna lost the baby* (=her baby died before it was born). | **lose sb to cancer/AIDS etc** *He lost his father to cancer* (=his father died of cancer) *last year.* | *Peter was **lost at sea** when his ship sank.*
6 MONEY [I,T] if you lose money, you then have less money than you had before; → **loss**: [+on] *The company is in debt after losing an estimated $30 million on its dotcom enterprise.* | *Creditors and investors **stand to lose** (=risk losing) vast sums after the company's collapse.* | *A lot of people lost their shirts* (=lost a lot of money) *on Ferraris in the Eighties.* | *It's a great deal – we can't lose!* | **lose sb sth** *The stock market crash lost*

L

the banks £70 million (=caused them to lose £70 million).

7 have nothing to lose *spoken* if you have nothing to lose, it is worth taking a risk because you cannot make your situation any worse: *You might as well apply for the job – you've got nothing to lose.* | **have nothing to lose but your pride/reputation etc** *The working class has nothing to lose but its chains.* (=disadvantages, restrictions etc). | **have a lot/too much to lose** (=used to say that you could make your situation much worse) *These youngsters know they have too much to lose by protesting against the system.*

8 TIME [T] **a)** if you lose time, you do not make progress as quickly as you want to or should: **lose time/2 days/3 hours etc** *Vital minutes were lost because the ambulance took half an hour to arrive.* | *In 1978, 29 million days were lost in industrial action.* | *Come on, there's no time to lose* (=do not waste time). | **lose no time in doing sth** (=do something immediately) *Murdock lost no time in taking out a patent for his invention.* **b)** if a watch, clock etc loses time, it runs too slowly and shows an earlier time than it should; **⊟ gain**

9 lose your way/bearings a) to stop knowing where you are or which direction you should go in: *I lost my way in the network of tiny alleys.* **b)** to become uncertain about your beliefs or what you should do: *The company seems to have lost its way of late.*

10 lose touch (with sb/sth) a) if two people lose touch, they gradually stop communicating, for example by no longer phoning or writing to each other: *I've lost touch with all my old school friends.* | *They lost touch when Di got married and moved away.* **b)** if you lose touch with a situation or group, you are then no longer involved in it and so do not know about it or understand it: *They claim the prime minister has lost touch with the party.* | *It sometimes appears that the planners have lost touch with reality.*

11 lose your temper/cool/rag to become angry: [+with] *Diana was determined not to lose her temper with him.*

12 lose your head to become unable to behave calmly or sensibly: *You've all heard that Nadal lost his head over a girl?*

13 lose your mind to become crazy; **⊟ go crazy, go mad**: *Nicholas looked at her as if she'd lost her mind.*

14 lose it *spoken informal* **a)** to become very angry and upset: *She completely lost it with one of the kids in class.* **b)** also **lose the plot** to become crazy or confused: *I could see people thinking I'd totally lost the plot.*

15 lose yourself in sth to be paying so much attention to something that you do not notice anything else: *She listened intently to the music, losing herself in its beauty.*

16 ESCAPE [T] if you lose someone who is chasing you, you manage to escape from them: *There's a better chance of losing him if we take the back route.*

17 CONFUSE SB [T] *spoken informal* to confuse someone when you are trying to explain something to them: *Explain it again – you've lost me already.*

18 REMOVE STH [T] to remove a part or feature of something that is not necessary or wanted: *You could lose the last paragraph to make it fit on one page.*

19 lose something in the translation/telling to be less good than the original form: *The joke loses something in the translation.* → LOST²; → **lose count** at COUNT² (3); → **lose sleep over sth** at SLEEP² (4)

lose out *phr v*
to not get something good, valuable etc because someone else gets it instead: *The deal will ensure that shareholders do not lose out financially.* | [+to] *He lost out to Roy Scheider for the lead role.* | [+on] *Workers who don't take up training may lose out on promotion.*

los·er /'luːzə $ -ər/ *n* [C] **1** someone who is in a worse situation than they were, because of something that has happened; **⊟ winner**: *If the strike continues, the people of Galway will be the real losers.* **2** someone who is never successful in life, work, or relationships: *What a loser!* | *The guy's a born loser.* **3** someone who has lost a competition, game, election etc; **⊟ winner**: **good/bad loser** (=someone who behaves well or badly after losing)

loss [S2] [W1] /lɒs $ lɒːs/ *n*

1 [C,U] the fact of no longer having something, or of having less of it than you used to have, or the process by which this happens

loss of earnings/income
loss of appetite
loss of interest
loss of confidence
loss of control
loss of faith
loss of memory/memory loss
blood loss/loss of blood
job losses
weight loss
hearing loss

[+of] *The court awarded Ms Dixon £7,000 for damages and **loss of earnings**.* | *a disease which causes fever and a **loss of appetite*** | *This did not explain his apparent **loss of interest** in his wife.* | *her **loss of confidence** in herself* | *a certain feeling of **loss of control*** | *a temporary **loss of memory*** | *The animal was weak through **loss of blood**.* | *The company is closing down two of its factories, leading to 430 **job losses**.* | ***Weight loss** should be gradual.* | *a type of **hearing loss** that affects language development*

2 [C,U] if a business makes a loss, it spends more than it earns: *The company **made a loss** of $250,000 last year.* | *The magazine's losses totaled almost $5 million.* | **profit and loss** | **run/operate etc at a loss** (=to earn less money from something you sell than it costs you to produce it) *Two of the mines are running at a loss.* | *a loss-making rural railway*

3 [C,U] the death of someone: [+of] *She must be feeling very lonely after the loss of her husband.* | *I'm sorry to hear of your family's **sad loss** (=the death of someone you love).* | *US forces withdrew after suffering **heavy losses** (=many deaths).* | *The war has led to a tragic **loss of life**.*

4 be at a loss to be confused and uncertain about what to do or say: *When her son finally left home, Emily felt completely **at a loss**.* | **be at a loss to do sth** *Detectives are so far at a loss to explain the reason for his death.* | *He seemed, for once, **at a loss for words** (=unable to think what to say).*

5 [U] a feeling of being sad or lonely because someone or something is not there any more: *the deep **sense of loss** I felt after my divorce*

6 [singular] a disadvantage caused by someone or something leaving or being removed: [+to] *We see your going as a **great loss** to the company.*

7 that's/it's sb's loss *spoken* said when you think someone is being stupid for not taking a good opportunity: *Well, if he doesn't want to come, it's his loss.* → **cut your losses** at CUT¹ (29); → **a dead loss** at DEAD¹ (10)

'loss ad,juster *n* [C] *BrE* someone who is employed by an insurance company to decide how much should be paid to people who make a CLAIM; **⊟ insurance adjuster** *AmE*

'loss ,leader *n* [C] a product that is sold at a very low price in order to attract customers into a shop

'loss-,making *adj* [only before noun] *especially BrE* a loss-making product or business does not make any money; **⊟ profit-making, profitable**: *The company has sold many of its loss-making businesses to cut debts.*

loss·y /'lɒsi $ 'lɒːsi/ *n* [U] **lossy compression** a way of making a computer file smaller, but which involves losing some of the information in it

lost¹ /lɒst $ lɒːst/ *v* the past tense and past participle of LOSE

lost² [S2] [W3] *adj*

1 CANNOT FIND YOUR WAY if you are lost, you do not know where you are and are unable to find your way somewhere: *'Are you lost?' the driver asked.* | *I got thoroughly **lost** on the way here.* | *a lost child*

2 CANNOT BE FOUND if something is lost, you had it but cannot now find now; ☰ **missing**: *two boys searching for a lost ball* | *The letter never arrived. It must have got lost in the post.*

3 WASTED **a)** lost time or opportunities have not been used in the way that would have given you the greatest advantage: *It'll be impossible to make up the lost time.* | *They didn't change the voting system when they had the chance and now the opportunity has been lost.* **b)** lost sales/business/earnings *etc* sales, business etc that you could have had but did not: *The strike has cost the company £2 million in lost revenue.*

4 feel/be lost to not feel confident about what to do or how to behave: *It's not unusual to feel rather lost when you first start college.* | *She's a great friend and I'd be lost without her.*

5 Get lost! *spoken* used to rudely tell someone to go away or to stop annoying you

6 NOT NOTICING [not before noun] thinking so hard about something, or being so interested in something, that you do not notice what is happening around you: [+in] *Harry just stood there, lost in thought.* | *Amy lay on her bed, totally lost in her book.*

7 get lost (in sth) to be forgotten or not noticed in a complicated process or in a busy time: *It's easy for your main points to get lost in a long speech.*

8 NOT UNDERSTAND be lost to be completely confused by a complicated explanation: *'Do you understand what I mean?' 'Not really. I'm a bit lost.'*

9 be lost on sb if something is lost on someone, they do not understand or want to accept it: *The joke was completely lost on Chris.*

10 be lost for words to be unable to say anything because you are very surprised, upset etc: *For once in her life, she was lost for words.*

11 NOT EXISTING [only before noun] that no longer exists or that you no longer have: *the relics of a lost civilization* | *She wept for her broken dreams and lost youth.*

12 lost cause something that has no chance of succeeding: *Trying to interest my son in classical music is a lost cause.*

13 lost soul someone who does not seem to know where they are or what to do → also used humorously → give sb up for dead/lost etc at GIVE UP (7) → LONG-LOST; → make up for lost time at MAKE UP FOR (4); → there is no love lost between sb and sb at LOVE² (10)

,**lost-and-'found** *n AmE* the lost-and-found a place where things that are lost are kept until someone comes to claim them; ☰ lost property *BrE*

,**lost 'property** *n* [U] *BrE* **1** things that people have lost or accidentally left in a public place, which are kept until someone collects them **2** also Lost Property a place where these things are kept until someone comes to claim them; ☰ lost-and-found *AmE*: *Thankfully, someone had handed my bag into Lost Property.*

lot¹ [S1] [W1] /lɒt $ lɑːt/ *pron, adv*

1 a lot also lots *informal* a large amount or number: *We've spent a lot on the children's education.* | *'How many CDs have you got?' 'Lots.'* | [+of] *They paid a lot of money for that house.* | *I eat a lot of vegetables.* | *There were lots of people at the party.* | an awful lot also a whole lot *informal* (=a very large amount or number) *He spends an awful lot of time on the computer.* | a lot to do/learn/say etc *I still have a lot to learn.* | *It's a great city, with lots to see and do.*

2 a lot also lots *informal* if someone or something is a lot better, faster, easier etc, they are much better, faster etc; ☰ much: *My headache's lots better, thanks.* | *She has a lot more contact with clients these days.* | *You'll get there a lot quicker if you take the motorway.* | *The house is a lot tidier now Chris has left home.*

3 a lot used to say that something happens to a great degree or often: *Things have changed a lot since I was a child.* | *Paul travels a lot on business.* | *I've been worrying a lot about my health.* | *She likes you a lot.*

4 have a lot on your plate *informal* to have a large

number of problems to deal with or a large amount of work to do

5 have a lot on your mind to have a lot of problems that you are worried about: *'You're quiet today.' 'I've got a lot on my mind.'*

6 have a lot on *BrE* to be very busy, with a large number of things to do in a short time: *I can't help you now – I've got rather a lot on.* → thanks a lot at THANKS¹ (1); → a fat lot of good/use at FAT¹ (5); → have a lot to answer for at ANSWER FOR (2)

lot² *n*

1 GROUP OF PEOPLE/THINGS [C] a group of people or things considered together: *Could you help me carry this lot upstairs?* | [+of] *The last lot of people offered £70,000.* | *I did three lots of exams last summer.* | *Come on, you lot, hurry up!* | *His friends are a strange lot.*

2 the lot *especially BrE* the whole of an amount or number of things, people etc: *We'll do everything – cooking, washing, ironing – the lot.* | *I can't believe you ate the whole lot.* | *I think that's the lot* (=everything is included). | the lot of you/them/us (=all of you, them, or us) *Shut up, the lot of you!*

3 SB'S SITUATION [singular] your lot is your work, duties, social position etc, especially when they could be better: *She seems happy enough with her lot.* | *The unions have always tried to improve the lot of their members.*

4 LAND [C] *especially AmE* an area of land used for building on or for another purpose: *the vacant lot* (=empty land) *behind the Commercial Hotel* | *a used-car lot* → PARKING LOT

5 FILM [C] a building and the land surrounding it where films are made; ☰ studio: *the Universal Studios lot*

6 THING TO BE SOLD [C] something, or a group of things, that is sold at an AUCTION: *Lot 54 is a Victorian lamp.*

7 CHOOSING **a)** by lot if someone is chosen by lot, several people each take a piece of paper or an object from a container, and the person who is chosen is the one who gets a particular marked paper or object: *In Athens at that time, judges were chosen by lot.* **b)** draw/cast lots to choose something or someone by lot: *We drew lots to decide who should go first.*

8 throw in/cast your lot with sb/sth to join or support someone or something, and accept that what happens to them will affect what happens to you: *In 1915 Italy threw in her lot with the allies.* → bad lot at BAD¹ (21); → a job lot at JOB (17)

loth /ləʊθ $ loʊθ/ *adj* [not before noun] another spelling of LOATH

lo·tion /'ləʊʃən $ 'loʊ-/ *n* [C,U] a liquid mixture that you put on your skin or hair to clean, SOFTEN, or protect it: *suntan lotion*

lot·sa /'lɒtsə $ 'lɑːt-/ a way of writing 'lots of' to show how it sounds when it is spoken

lot·te·ry [S3] /'lɒtəri $ 'lɑː-/ *n plural* lotteries

1 [C] a game used to make money for a state or a CHARITY in which people buy tickets with a series of numbers on them. If their number is picked by chance, they win money or a prize; → raffle, draw: *a lottery ticket* | *Do you really think winning the lottery would make you happy?* | national/state lottery

2 [C,U] *AmE* a system of choosing who will get something by choosing people's names by chance: by lottery *The State Department issues 55,000 visas each year by lottery.*

3 a lottery a situation in which what happens depends on chance and is not certain to be successful: *That's the trouble with capitalism. It's a lottery.*

lot·to /'lɒtəʊ $ 'lɑːtoʊ/ *n* [C] a game used to make money, in which people buy tickets with a series of numbers on them. If their number is picked by chance, they win money or a prize.

L

lo·tus /'ləʊtəs $ 'loʊ-/ n [C] **1** a white or pink flower that grows on the surface of lakes in Asia and Africa, or the shape of this flower used in decorations **2** a fruit that gives you a pleasant dreamy feeling after you eat it, according to Ancient Greek stories

lotus po.sition n [singular] a way of sitting, used especially in YOGA, in which you sit with your legs crossed and with each foot resting on the top of the opposite leg: *monks sitting in the lotus position*

loud¹ /laʊd/ adj comparative **louder**, superlative **loudest 1** making a lot of noise; ☰ **quiet**: *The book fell to the floor with a loud bang.* | *The music was so loud that I had to shout.* | *'Who's there?' asked David in a loud voice.* **2** someone who is loud talks too loudly and confidently: *The more Tom drank, the louder he became.* **3** loud clothes are too bright or have too many bright patterns; ☰ **garish**, **gaudy**: *a loud checked suit* **4 be loud in your praise/opposition/support etc** to express your approval or disapproval very strongly: *The local business community was loud in its support for the scheme.* —**loudly** adv: *Ben laughed loudly.* | *She spoke more loudly than she intended.* —**loudness** n [U]

> **WORD FOCUS: LOUD**
> *similar words:* **noisy, booming, raucous, rowdy**
> *extremely loud:* **deafening, earsplitting, thunderous**

loud² adv comparative **louder**, superlative **loudest 1** spoken in a way that makes a lot of noise; ☰ **loudly**: *Could you speak a little louder?* | *You've got the telly on too loud.* **2 loud and clear** in a way that is very easy to understand: *The message came through loud and clear.* **3 out loud** in such a way that people can hear you; ☰ **aloud**: *Read it out loud, so we can all hear.* | *Harriet laughed out loud in astonishment.* → **actions speak louder than words** at ACTION¹ (13); → **for crying out loud** at CRY¹ (4)

loud·hail·er /ˌlaʊd'heɪlə $ -ər/ n [C] BrE a piece of equipment with a MICROPHONE, that you can hold in your hand and speak through to make your voice louder; ☰ **megaphone**; ☰ **bullhorn** AmE

loud·mouth /'laʊdmaʊθ/ n [C] not polite someone who talks too much and says offensive or stupid things —**loudmouthed** /'laʊdmaʊθt/ adj: *loudmouthed sports fans*

loud·speak·er /ˌlaʊd'spiːkə, 'laʊdˌspiːkə $ -ər/ n [C] **1** a piece of equipment used to make sounds louder: **from/over/through a loudspeaker** *The voice over the loudspeaker* (=using the loudspeaker) *said the flight was delayed.* **2** a SPEAKER (3)

lough /lɒx, lɒk $ laːk, laːx/ n [C] in Ireland, a lake or a part of the sea almost surrounded by land: *Lough Neagh*

lounge¹ /laʊndʒ/ n [C] **1** a WAITING ROOM at an airport: *the departure lounge* **2** a public room in a hotel or other building, that is used by many people as a place to relax: *the television lounge* **3** BrE the main room in a house where people relax, watch television etc; ☰ **living room** **4** BrE a lounge bar **5** AmE a COCKTAIL BAR → COCKTAIL LOUNGE, SUN LOUNGE

lounge² v [I] **1** [always + adv/prep] to stand, sit, or lie in a lazy or relaxed way: *Nathan was lounging on the grass bank outside the cottage.* **2 lounge around; lounge about** BrE to spend time relaxing and doing nothing, often when you should be doing something; ☰ **laze around**: *James does nothing but lounge around the apartment.*

lounge bar n [C] BrE a comfortable bar in a PUB or hotel; ☰ **saloon bar**; → **public bar**

loung·er /'laʊndʒə $ -ər/ n [C] BrE a SUN LOUNGER

lounge suit n [C] BrE old-fashioned a suit that a man wears during the day, especially to work in an office

louse¹ /laʊs/ n [C] **1** plural **lice** /laɪs/ a small insect that lives on the hair or skin of people or animals **2** plural **louses** informal someone who is nasty and unpleasant

louse² v

louse sth ⇔ up phr v informal to make something worse rather than better, or to spoil something; ☰ **mess up**: *That idiot loused up my chance of promotion.*

lou·sy /'laʊzi/ adj comparative **lousier**, superlative **lousiest 1** especially spoken of very bad quality; ☰ **awful**, **terrible**: *What lousy weather!* | *The food was lousy.* | *a lousy film* **2** spoken **feel lousy** if you feel lousy, you feel ill **3** spoken not very good at doing something; ☰ **hopeless**, **terrible**: [+at/with] *I'm lousy at tennis.* | *Brenda's lousy with kids.* | *a lousy teacher* **4** spoken small, useless, or unimportant: *He left me a lousy fifty cent tip.* **5 be lousy with sth** AmE old-fashioned **a)** a place that is lousy with people of a particular kind is too full of them: *The town was lousy with tourists.* **b)** someone who is lousy with money has a lot more of it than they need

lout /laʊt/ n [C] a rude, violent man; ☰ **yob** —**loutish** adj: *loutish behaviour* —**loutishly** adv —**loutishness** n [U] → LAGER LOUT

lou·vre BrE; **louver** AmE /'luːvə $ -ər/ n [C] **1** a narrow piece of wood, glass etc in a door or window, that slopes towards the outside to let some light in and keep rain or strong sun out **2 louvre window/door** BrE a door or window made of these pieces of wood, glass etc —**louvred** adj: *louvred shutters*

lov·a·ble, loveable /'lʌvəbəl/ adj friendly and attractive: *a sweet lovable child*

love¹ S1 W1 /lʌv/ v

1 ROMANTIC ATTRACTION [T not in progressive] to have a strong feeling of AFFECTION for someone, combined with sexual attraction: *I love you, Tracy.* | *He was the only man she had ever loved.*

2 CARE ABOUT [T not in progressive] to care very much about someone, especially a member of your family or a close friend: *I love my grandad so much.* | *I've always loved children.* | **much-loved/well-loved** *In 1941, her much-loved sister was killed in an accident.* | *Many people feel guilty after the death of a loved one.*

3 LIKE/ENJOY [T] to like something very much or enjoy doing something very much: *I love carrots.* | *Jeff loves his work.* | *I love the way she sings that song.* | *Amy had always loved New York.* | **love doing sth** *I love going out to restaurants.* | **love to do sth** *We all love to talk about ourselves.* | **I'd love to (do sth)** spoken (=used to say that you would really like to do something) *'Would you like to come swimming with us?' 'I'd love to.'* | *I'd have loved to have stayed till the end.* | *I'd love to know just why they did that.*

4 LOYALTY [T not in progressive] to have a strong feeling of loyalty to your country, an institution etc: *Dad's always loved the navy.*

5 I love it! spoken used when you are amused by something, especially by someone else's mistake or bad luck: *'And then her boyfriend walked in and saw her kissing Ray.' 'I love it!'*

6 sb's going to love sth spoken **a)** used to say that someone will enjoy something: *Listen guys, you're going to love this.* **b)** used to say that someone will not be pleased about something: *I'm going to love telling him we've changed our minds again.* → LOVER

love² S1 W1 n

1 FOR FAMILY/FRIENDS [U] a strong feeling of caring about someone, especially a member of your family or a close friend; ☰ **hate**, **hatred**: *What these kids need is love and support.* | [+for] *a mother's love for her child*

2 ROMANTIC [U] a strong feeling of liking someone a lot combined with sexual attraction: [+for] *Their love for each other grew deeper every day.* | **be/fall in love (with sb)** *I think I'm falling in love with Tom.* | **very much in love/madly in love/head over heels in love** *Tara is madly in love with you.* | *When Lynne met Derek, it was love at first sight* (=they loved each other the first time they saw each other). | *a beautiful love song* (=a song about romantic love) | *It's a **love story*** (=a book, film etc about romantic love). | **true love** (=strong romantic love that remains for ever)

3 PERSON YOU LOVE [C] someone that you feel a strong romantic and sexual attraction to: *He was her **first love**.* | **the love of your life** (=the person that you feel or felt the most love for)

4 PLEASURE/ENJOYMENT **a)** [singular, U] a strong feeling of pleasure and enjoyment that something gives you: [+of/for] *my **love** of nature* | *He had a great **love** of music.* | *I **fell in love with** Amsterdam the very first time I visited the city.* **b)** [C] something that gives you a lot of pleasure and enjoyment: *Sailing was her great love.*

5 make love (to/with sb) a) to have sex with someone that you love **b)** *old use* to say LOVING things to someone, to kiss them etc

6 send/give your love (to sb) or **send/give sb your love** to ask someone to give your LOVING greetings to someone else when they see them, write to them etc: *Aunt Mary sends her love.*

7 love (from sb)/lots of love/all my love *written* used at the end of a letter to a friend, a member of your family, or someone you love: *See you soon. Lots of love, Clare.*

8 (my) love *BrE spoken informal* **a)** a word used when you are talking to someone you love; ◧ **darling**: *'Hello, love,' said her father.* **b)** a friendly way of talking to someone who you do not know, especially to a woman or child. Many women consider this to be impolite or offensive: *What's your name, love?*

9 be a love and ... / ... there's a love *BrE spoken* used when you are asking someone, especially children and members of your family, to do something: *Give these to your sisters, there's a love.*

10 there is no love lost between sb and sb if there is no love lost between two people, they dislike each other

11 TENNIS [U] an expression meaning 'no points', used in the game of tennis

12 not for love or/nor money *informal* if you cannot get something or do something for love or money, it is impossible to obtain or to do: *I can't get hold of that book for love nor money.*

13 love triangle a situation in which someone is having a sexual relationship with the partner of a close friend – used especially in newspapers

14 for the love of God *old-fashioned spoken* used to show that you are extremely angry, disappointed etc → **a labour of love** at LABOUR¹ (4)

love af·fair *n* [C] **1** a romantic sexual relationship, usually between two people who are not married to each other → AFFAIR (3) **2** a strong enjoyment of something: [+with] *America's love affair with the automobile*

love·bird /'lʌvbɜːd $ -bɜːrd/ *n* [C] **1 lovebirds** [plural] two people who show by their behaviour that they love each other very much – used humorously **2** a small brightly coloured PARROT

love bite *n* [C] *BrE* a red mark on someone's skin caused by someone else sucking it as a sexual act; ◧ **hickey** *AmE*

love child *n* [C] a child whose parents are not married – used especially in newspapers

loved-'up *adj informal* **1** feeling full of romantic love for someone **2** feeling full of love towards everyone, especially as a result of using the illegal drug ECSTASY: *loved-up clubbers having a ball*

love-'hate re·lationship *n* [C usually singular] if you have a love-hate relationship with someone or something, sometimes you really like or love them, and sometimes you really dislike or hate them: [+with] *her love-hate relationship with professional golf*

love·less /'lʌvləs/ *adj* without love: **loveless marriage/childhood/relationship etc**

love letter *n* [C] a letter that someone writes to tell someone else how much they love them

love life *n* [C,U] the part of your life that involves your romantic and sexual relationships

love·lorn /'lʌvlɔːn $ -lɔːrn/ *adj literary* sad because the person you love does not love you; ◧ **lovesick**

love·ly S2 W3 /'lʌvli/ *adj comparative* **lovelier**, *superlative* **loveliest**

1 *especially BrE* beautiful or attractive: *She had a lovely face.* | *What a lovely house!* | *You **look lovely** in that dress.* | *He was a **lovely little** boy.* | *What a lovely day!*

2 *spoken especially BrE* very pleasant, enjoyable, or good: *Thank you for a lovely evening.* | *That was a lovely cup of tea.*

3 *informal especially BrE* friendly and pleasant: *Richard's a lovely person.*

4 *BrE spoken* used to say that something is not at all enjoyable or good: *'The cat threw up all over the carpet!' 'Lovely!'* | *You've made a lovely mess in here.*

5 lovely and warm/fresh/clean etc *BrE spoken* used to emphasize how good something is: *This bread's lovely and fresh.*

6 *BrE spoken* used to show that you are pleased with something: *Push it right across. That's it, lovely.* —**loveliness** *n* [U]

love·mak·ing /'lʌv,meɪkɪŋ/ *n* [U] sexual activity, especially the act of having sex

love nest *n* [C usually singular] a place where two people who are having a romantic relationship live or meet each other – used humorously

lov·er W3 /'lʌvə $ -ər/ *n* [C]

1 someone's lover is the person they are having a sexual relationship with but who they are not married to; → **mistress**: *He killed his wife's lover.* | *Nicola and I were lovers.* | *a pair of **young lovers***

2 someone who likes something very much: **music lovers** | **animal lovers** | [+of] *lovers of the outdoors*

love seat *n* [C] **1** *AmE* a small SOFA for two people **2** a seat in the shape of an S for two people, designed so that they can face each other

love·sick /'lʌv,sɪk/ *adj* spending all your time thinking about someone you love, especially someone who does not love you: *a lovesick teenager*

lov·ey /'lʌvi/ *n* [C] *BrE spoken informal* a word used to address a woman or child, that many women think is offensive → LUVVIE

lovey-dov·ey /,lʌvi 'dʌvi/ *adj informal* behaviour that is lovey-dovey is too romantic: *a lovey-dovey phone call*

lov·ing /'lʌvɪŋ/ *adj* **1** [only before noun] behaving in a way that shows you love someone: **loving wife/family/parents etc** *the confidence he had gained from having a warm and loving family* | *What that child needs is plenty of **loving care**.* | *He's very loving and affectionate with his sister.* **2** **peace-loving/fun-loving/home-loving etc** thinking that peace, having fun etc is very important: *a peace-loving nation* **3** done with a lot of care and attention: *the loving care with which the house has been restored* —**lovingly** *adv*: *She smiled at him lovingly.* | *the plane he had lovingly built*

low¹ S1 W1 /ləʊ $ loʊ/ *adj comparative* **lower**, *superlative* **lowest**

1 SMALL AMOUNT/LEVEL/VALUE **a)** small, or smaller than usual, in amount, level, or value; ◧ **high**: **low income/pay/wages** *families existing on very low incomes* | *In May, the price of cocoa fell to its lowest level since 1975–76.* | *Morale has been low since the latest round of job-cuts.* | *In this sort of investment, the risks are fairly low.* | *low temperatures* | *the need for low-cost housing* | *a low-security prison* **b) low in sth** having less than the usual amount of a substance or chemical; ◧ **high**: *food that is low in calories* | **low-fat/low-salt etc** *low-alcohol beer* **c) in the low 20s/50s etc** if a number, temperature, or level is in the low 20s, 30s etc, it is between 21 and 23, 31 and 33 etc: *Tonight, temperatures in most areas will be in the low 50s.*

2 HEIGHT **a)** having a top that is not far above the ground; ◧ **high**: *a low wall* | *a long low building* **b)** at a point that is not far above the ground or near the

L

bottom of something; ➡ **high**: *low clouds* | *The sun was low in the sky now.* | *Store raw meat on the lowest shelf.* **c)** below the usual height; ➡ **high**: *a low bridge* | *a low ceiling* | *The river is very low today.*

3 STANDARDS/QUALITY bad, or below an acceptable or usual level or quality; ▣ **poor**; ➡ **high**: *Their safety standards seem to be pretty low.* | *Cost-cutting has led to a lower quality of service.* | *the children's low achievement in school*

4 SUPPLY if you are low on something, or if your supply of something is low, there is not much of it left: **be/get/run low (on sth)** *We're running low on gas.* | *Stocks are getting low.*

5 SOUND a low voice or sound is quiet or deep: *I heard a low moaning noise.* | *The volume is too low – turn it up.* | *a low whisper*

6 LIGHT a light that is low is not bright; ▣ **dim**: *Use low lighting to give the room a romantic atmosphere.*

7 HEAT if you cook something over a low heat or in a low OVEN, you cook it using only a small amount of heat; ➡ **high**

8 BATTERY a BATTERY that is low does not have much power left in it

9 CLOTHES a low dress, BLOUSE etc does not cover your neck and the top of your chest; → **low-cut**

10 UNHAPPY [not before noun] unhappy and without much hope for the future; ▣ **depressed**: *He was feeling a bit low, so I did my best to cheer him up.* | *Terry seems to be in rather **low spirits** today.* → **be at a low ebb** at EBB[1] (2) —**lowness** *n* [U]

low[2] *adv* comparative **lower**, superlative **lowest** **1** in or to a low position or level: *He bent low over the engine.* | *She pulled her hat **low down** over her eyes.* | *I had the radio on low.* **2** near the ground or the bottom of something: *That plane's flying too low!* | *There was a hole **low down** in the hedge.* **3** if you play or sing musical notes low, you play or sing them with deep notes: *Sing those bars an octave lower.* **4 be brought low** *old-fashioned* to become much less rich or important → **search/look high and low** at HIGH[2] (6); → **lay sb low** at LAY[2] (20); → **lie low** at LIE[1] (7)

low[3] *n* [C] **1** a low price, level, or value; ➡ **high**: **fall to/hit/reach etc a new low** (=be worth less than ever before) *The euro has fallen to a new low against the dollar.* | *Public confidence in the legal system is at an **all-time low*** (=much lower or worse than ever before). **2** a very difficult time in someone's personal or working life: **highs and lows (of sth)** (=good times and bad times) *the highs and lows of an actor's life* **3 a)** the lowest point that the temperature reaches during a particular time; ➡ **high**: *The overnight low will be 8° C.* **b)** an area of low pressure in the air; ➡ **high**: *a low moving in over the Pacific* **4 the lowest of the low a)** *informal* someone you think is completely unfair, cruel, immoral etc **b)** someone from a low social class – often used humorously

low[4] *v* [I] *literary* if cattle low, they make a deep sound

low·brow /ˈləʊbraʊ $ ˈloʊ-/ *adj* lowbrow entertainment, newspapers, books etc are easy to understand and are not concerned with serious ideas about art, CULTURE etc – used to show disapproval; ▣ **highbrow**

Low 'Church *n* [U] the part of the Church of England that believes in the importance of faith and studying the BIBLE rather than in religious ceremonies → HIGH CHURCH

low-'class *adj* **1** *old-fashioned* WORKING CLASS; ▣ **high-class**: *a low-class bar* **2** not good quality; ▣ **high-class**

low-'cut *adj* a low-cut dress is shaped so that it shows a woman's neck and the top of her chest

low-down *adj* [only before noun] *informal* dishonest and unkind: *What a low-down, dirty trick.*

low·down /ˈləʊdaʊn $ ˈloʊ-/ *n* **the lowdown (on sth/ sb)** *informal* the most important facts about something: *Ryan gave me **the lowdown** on the meeting.*

'low-end *adj* [usually before noun] *especially AmE* relating to products or services that are less expensive and of lower quality than other products of the same type; ▣ **high-end**: *low-end desktop computers*

low·er[1] /ˈləʊə $ ˈloʊər/ *adj* **1** [only before noun] below something else, especially below something of the same type; ➡ **upper**: *Nina chewed her lower lip anxiously.* | *Ruth went down to the lower deck* (=lower level on a ship). | **your lower limbs** (=your legs) **2** [only before noun] at or near the bottom of something; ➡ **upper**: *the lower slopes of the mountain* | *She suffers with pain in her lower back.* **3** smaller in number or amount; ➡ **higher**: *Temperatures will be lower over the weekend.* **4** [only before noun] less important than something else of the same type; ➡ **higher**: *the lower levels of management*

lower[2] S3 *v*

1 REDUCE [I,T] to reduce something in amount, degree, strength etc, or to become less: *Do you think we should lower the price?* | *After 20 minutes lower the temperature to 325°.* | *drugs to lower blood pressure* | *Helen **lowered** her voice* (=made it quieter) *as they approached.* | *His **voice lowered*** (=became quieter).

2 MOVE DOWN [T] to move something down from higher up; ➡ **raise**: *Very gently, he lowered the dog onto the rug by the fire.* | *The flags were lowered to half-mast.* | *Greg watched as the coffin was lowered.* | **lower yourself** *He lowered himself carefully down from the top of the wall.*

3 lower your eyes/head to look down; ➡ **raise**: *Christina blushed and lowered her eyes.*

4 lower yourself [usually in negatives] to behave in a way that makes people respect you less: *I wouldn't lower myself to speak to her after what she's done.*

5 lower the tone (of sth) to make something not as nice as it was: *They thought an influx of students would lower the tone of the neighborhood.* | *I trust you to lower the tone of the conversation* (=include rude jokes etc in what you say)*!* —**lowered** *adj*: *He leaned forward and spoke in a lowered voice.*

low·er[3] also **lour** *BrE* /ˈlaʊə $ -ər/ *v* [I] *literary* **1** when the sky or the weather lowers, it becomes dark because there is going to be a storm; ▣ **darken**: *lowering clouds* **2** to look threatening or annoyed; ▣ **frown**: *The other driver lowered at us as we passed him.*

lower 'case *n* [U] letters in their small forms, such as a, b, c etc; ▣ **upper case**; → **capital** —**lower case** *adj*: *lower case letters*

lower 'class *n* [C] also **lower classes** [plural] *old-fashioned* the social class that has less money, power, or education than anyone else. This is now considered offensive; → **working class**, **middle class**, **upper class** —**lower-class** *adj*

Lower 'House also **Lower 'Chamber** *n* [singular] a group of elected representatives who make laws in a country, for example the HOUSE OF COMMONS in Britain or the HOUSE OF REPRESENTATIVES in the US; → **upper house**

lower 'orders *n old-fashioned* **the lower orders** an offensive expression for WORKING CLASS people considered as a group

'lower school *n* [C] the classes of a school in Britain that are for younger students, usually aged 11–13

lowest common de'nominator *n* [U] **1** the biggest possible number of people, including people who are very easily influenced or are willing to accept low standards: *Television quiz shows often seem to target the lowest common denominator.* **2** *technical* the smallest number that the bottom numbers of a group of FRACTIONS can be divided into exactly → DENOMINATOR

low-'fat *adj* containing or using only a small amount of fat: *low-fat yoghurt* | *a low-fat diet*

low-'flying *adj* flying close to the ground: *a low-flying aircraft*

low 'gear *n* [C,U] one of a vehicle's GEARS that you use when you are driving at a slow speed

low-'key adj not intended to attract a lot of attention to an event, subject, or thing: *They want the funeral to be as low-key as possible.* | *a low-key military operation*

low-lands /'ləʊləndz $ 'loʊ-/ n [plural] an area of land that is lower than the land around it; → **highlands**: *the Scottish lowlands* —**lowland** adj [only before noun]: *a wild lowland landscape* | *lowland farmers* —**lowlander** n [C]

low-'level adj **1** close to the ground: *low-level bombing attacks on military targets* **2** relating to people who are not in powerful positions or jobs; ☐ **high-level**: *routine, low-level, clerical tasks* **3** at a low degree or strength; ☐ **high-level**: *a low-level tension headache* **4** a low-level computer language is used to give instructions to a computer and is similar to the language that the computer operates in; ☐ **high-level**

'low life n **1** [U] the life and behaviour of people who are involved in criminal or immoral activities: *a novel about low life in Chicago in the 1930s* **2** also **lowlife** [C] AmE informal someone who is involved in crime or who is bad: *Pete turned out to be a real lowlife.* —**lowlife** /'ləʊlaɪf $ 'loʊ-/ adj AmE informal: *Charlie may be lowlife, but he isn't stupid.*

low-lights /'ləʊlaɪts $ 'loʊ-/ n [plural] a dark colour that can be used to change the natural colour of some of your hair; → **highlights**

low-ly /'ləʊli $ 'loʊ-/ adj low in rank, importance, or social class – sometimes used humorously; ☐ **humble**: *He was a lowly assistant gardener.* ⚠ **Lowly** is never an adverb. **Low** is used as an adverb as well as an adjective.

low-'lying adj low-lying land is not far above the level of the sea: *Vast areas of low-lying land have been flooded.*

low-'paid adj providing or earning only a small amount of money: *As part-time, low-paid workers, the women earned very little.*

low-'pitched adj **1** a low pitched musical note or sound is deep; ☐ **high-pitched**: *the low-pitched hum of the generator* **2** low pitched roof a roof that is not steep

'low point n [C] the worst moment of a situation or activity; ☐ **high point**: *The low point in my life was when I was hit by a drunk driver.*

low-'pressure n [U] a condition of the air over a large area that affects the weather; ☐ **high-pressure**

low 'profile n keep a low profile to not go to places or be careful not to do anything that will attract attention to yourself or your actions; ☐ **high profile**: *He's not the sort of politician to keep a low profile for long.*

low-profile adj **1** [usually before noun] not receiving or wanting any attention; ☐ **high-profile**: *The US took a very low-profile role in the talks.* **2** [only before noun] BrE designed to be lower than other things of the same type: *low-profile tyres*

'low-rent adj not expensive or not good quality – used to show disapproval

'low-rise adj [only before noun] a low-rise building does not have many STOREYS; → **high-rise**

low-'risk adj [usually before noun] likely to be safe or without problems; ☐ **high-risk**: *low-risk investments*

'low season n [U] BrE the time of year when fewer people are on holiday and there is less business for hotels etc, and prices are usually lower than normal; ☐ **off-season**; ☐ **high season**

low-'slung adj [only before noun] low and closer to the ground than usual: *a low-slung sports car*

low-'spirited adj unhappy or DEPRESSED

low-tech /ˌləʊ 'tek◂ $ ˌloʊ-/ adj not using the most modern machines or methods in business or industry; ☐ **high-tech**: *He made low-tech, budget space movies.*

low 'tide n [C,U] the time when sea water is at its lowest level; ☐ **high tide**: *You can walk across to the island at low tide.* → see picture at HIGH TIDE

low 'water n [U] the time when the water in a river or the sea is at its lowest level; → **high water**

low 'water ˌmark n [C] a mark showing the lowest level reached by a river or other area of water; → **high water mark**

lox /lɒks $ lɑːks/ n [U] especially AmE SALMON that has been treated with smoke in order to preserve it

loy-al /'lɔɪəl/ adj always supporting your friends, principles, country etc; ☐ **disloyal**: [+to] *The army has remained loyal to the government.* | *a loyal supporter of the team* | *her many years of loyal service to the company* | *loyal customers* —**loyally** adv: *He has always loyally defended the president.*

loy-al-ist /'lɔɪəlɪst/ n [C] **1** someone who continues to support a government or country, especially during a period of change **2 Loyalist** someone from Northern Ireland who believes that Northern Ireland should remain part of the United Kingdom, and not become part of the Republic of Ireland; → **Republican** —**loyalist** adj

loy-al-ty /'lɔɪəlti/ n plural **loyalties** **1** [U] the quality of remaining faithful to your friends, principles, country etc: [+to/towards] *Elizabeth understood her husband's loyalty to his sister.* **2** [C usually plural] a feeling of support for someone or something: **local/regional/tribal/family etc loyalty/loyalties** *In the rural areas, family and tribal loyalties continue to be important.* | *the agony of divided loyalties* (=loyalty to two different or opposing people) *for the children in a divorce*

'loyalty card n [C] a card given by a shop, SUPERMARKET, etc that gives customers who often buy things there advantages such as lower prices, money back on goods etc

loz-enge /'lɒzɪndʒ $ 'lɑː-/ n [C] **1** a small flat sweet, especially one that contains medicine: *a cough lozenge* **2** a shape similar to a square, with two angles of less than 90° opposite each other and two angles of more than 90° opposite each other

LP /ˌel 'piː/ n [C] *long-playing record* a record that turns 33 times per minute, and usually plays for between 20 and 25 minutes on each side; ☐ **album**; → **single, CD**

LPG /ˌel piː 'dʒiː/ also **LP 'gas** n [U] *liquefied petroleum gas* a type of liquid FUEL that is burned to produce heat or power

L-plate /'el pleɪt/ n [C] a flat white square with a red letter L on it, that must be attached to the car of someone who is learning to drive in Britain

LRP /ˌel ɑː 'piː $ -ɑːr-/ n [U] BrE *lead replacement petrol* a special type of PETROL that does not contain LEAD and is meant to be used in older cars

LSD /ˌel es 'diː/ n [U] an illegal drug that makes you see things as more beautiful, strange, frightening etc than usual, or makes you see things that do not exist; ☐ **acid**

Lt. also **Lt** BrE a written abbreviation of *lieutenant*

Ltd the written abbreviation of *limited*, used in the names of companies or businesses; → **Inc., plc**: *M. Dixon & Son Ltd*

lu-bri-cant /'luːbrɪkənt/ n [C,U] a substance such as oil that you put on surfaces that rub together, especially parts of a machine, in order to make them move smoothly and easily

lu-bri-cate /'luːbrɪkeɪt/ v [T] **1** to put a lubricant on something in order to make it move more smoothly: *Lubricate all moving parts with grease.* **2** informal to help things to happen without any problems: *Vic's working day is lubricated by endless cups of coffee.* —**lubrication** /ˌluːbrɪ'keɪʃən/ n [U]

lu-bri-cious /luː'brɪʃəs/ adj formal too interested in sex, in a way that seems unpleasant or unacceptable —**lubriciously** adv

lu-cid /'luːsɪd/ adj **1** expressed in a way that is clear and easy to understand: *You must write in a clear and lucid style.* **2** able to understand and think clearly,

L

used especially about someone who is not always able to do this: *In her more lucid moments the old lady would talk about her past.* —**lucidly** *adv*: *He was lucidly aware of political realities.* —**lucidity** /luːˈsɪdʲti/ *n* [U]

Lu·ci·fer /ˈluːsʲfə $ -ər/ *n* the Devil

luck¹ S2 W3 /lʌk/ *n* [U]

1 SUCCESS also **good luck** good things that happen to you by chance

not have much/any luck
have no luck
have good luck
have more/better luck
have the luck to do sth
can't believe your luck
sheer luck (=used to emphasize something happened only by luck)
a piece of luck
a stroke of luck (=very good luck)
an element of luck (=used to say that luck is involved in something)
dumb luck *AmE* (=good luck that happens by chance, without you planning it at all)

*You're **not having much luck** today, are you?* | *Owen has **had no luck** with job-hunting.* | *He's **had good luck** with his roses this year.* | *We **had the luck to** find good childcare quite quickly.* | *I **couldn't believe my luck** when he showed an interest in me.* | *It was **sheer luck** that we were saved from drowning.* | *It was an incredible **piece of luck.*** | *By **a stroke of luck**, she had spotted the book on a colleague's bookshelf.* | *Often there is **an element of luck** in getting the right answer.* | *It was just **dumb luck** that no one got hurt.* → see box at CHANCE¹

2 bad luck the bad things that happen to someone by chance, not because of something they did: *Bad luck seems to follow me everywhere.* | *I've **had** nothing but **bad luck** since I moved to this town.* | *Lend me some money; I've had a **run of bad luck** (=a series of bad things happened) on the horses recently.*

3 CHANCE when good or bad things happen to people by chance: *You never know who you'll get as a roommate; it's just **a matter of luck**.* | *Roulette is a game of luck.* → see box at CHANCE¹

4 with (any) luck/with a bit of luck *spoken* if things happen in the way that you want; ▤ hopefully: *With a bit of luck, you might get a flight tomorrow.*

5 wish sb (the best of) luck to tell someone that you hope they will be successful in something they are going to do: *She wished me luck in the exam, then left.*

6 good luck/best of luck *spoken* used to tell someone that you hope they will be successful in something they are undertaking: *Good luck in this enormous project you are undertaking.*

7 good luck to sb *spoken* used to say that you do not mind what someone does, because it does not affect you: *I say, good luck to him.*

8 any luck?/no luck? *spoken* used to ask someone if they have succeeded in doing something: *'Oh, there you are. Any luck?' 'No, I didn't catch a single fish.'*

9 be in luck to be able to do or get something, especially when you did not expect to: *You're in luck – it's stopped snowing.*

10 be out of luck to be prevented from getting or doing something by bad luck: *The team were out of luck again at Scarborough on Saturday.*

11 do sth for luck to do something because you think it might bring you good luck: *She crossed her fingers for luck.*

12 just my luck *spoken* used to say that you are not surprised something bad has happened to you, because you are usually unlucky: *I didn't get to the phone in time. Just my luck!*

13 no such luck *spoken* used to say you are disappointed, because something good that you hoped would

happen did not happen: *'Have you Sunday off?' 'No such luck.'*

14 better luck next time used to say that you hope someone will be more successful the next time they try to do something

15 as luck would have it used to say that something happened by chance: *As luck would have it, my best friend is the most wonderful cook in the world.*

16 try/chance your luck to do something because you hope you will be successful, even though you know you may not be: *After the war my father went to Canada to try his luck at farming there.*

17 be down on your luck to have no money because you have had a lot of bad luck over a long period of time: *When someone is down on their luck, friends are very difficult to find.*

18 the luck of the draw the result of chance rather than something you can control

19 some people have all the luck *spoken* used to say that you wish you had what someone else has

20 bad/hard/tough luck *spoken* especially *BrE* used to express sympathy when something unpleasant has happened to someone → **tough luck** at TOUGH¹ (7)

21 with/knowing sb's luck *spoken* used to say that you expect something bad to happen to someone because bad things often do happen to them: *With my luck, I'd lose if I backed the only horse in a one horse race.*

22 worse luck *BrE spoken* unfortunately: *'Would your boyfriend like a drink?' 'He's not my boyfriend, worse luck!'*

23 luck is on sb's side if luck is on someone's side, things go well for them: *Luck was on my side; all the traffic lights were green.*

24 (one) for luck *spoken* used when you take, add, or do something you hope good things happen → HARD-LUCK STORY; → push your luck at PUSH¹ (12)

WORD CHOICE: luck, lucky
⚠ Do not say that someone 'has luck'. Say they **are lucky**: *I was lucky (NOT I had luck) and got to the airport just in time.* | *You're so lucky to live by the sea.*
You can use 'have' with **luck** only when luck has something before it such as 'bad', 'good', 'much', 'any' 'a bit of' etc: *He's had a lot of bad luck recently.* | *Did you have any luck finding your bag?* | *If we have a bit of luck, we'll see her before she leaves.*
⚠ **luck** is an uncountable noun: *Winning was mostly a matter of luck.*
Do not say 'a luck'. To talk about one lucky event you can say **a piece of luck**, **a bit of luck**, or **a stroke of luck**: *Seeing him at that moment was an amazing piece of luck (NOT an amazing luck).*

luck² *v*

luck out *phr v AmE informal* to be lucky: *Yeah, we really lucked out and got a parking space right in front.*

luck·i·ly S3 /ˈlʌkʲli/ *adv* [sentence adverb] used to say that it is good that something happened or was done because if it had not, the situation would be unpleasant or difficult: ▤ fortunately: *Luckily the museum was not damaged by the earthquake.* | **luckily for sb** *Luckily for them, he braked in time.*

luck·less /ˈlʌkləs/ *adj literary* having no luck in something you are trying to do; ▤ unfortunate: *He died in the desert like so many other luckless explorers.*

luck·y S2 W3 /ˈlʌki/ *adj comparative* **luckier**, *superlative* **luckiest**

1 having good luck; ▤ fortunate; ▣ unlucky: **be lucky to do/be sth** *The children were lucky to survive the fire which destroyed their home.* | **lucky enough to do sth** *those of us lucky enough to own our own homes* | **lucky if** *I'll be lucky if I get any of my money back.* | **lucky (that)** *I was tremendously lucky that I didn't die in the accident.* | [+with] *We've been very lucky with the weather.* | **count/consider/think yourself lucky** *Count yourself lucky you've got a husband like Jack.*; → see box at LUCK¹

2 resulting from good luck: *I didn't really know your*

name – it was just a **lucky guess**. | A middle-aged woman had a **lucky escape** when a tree crashed down onto her car. | **it is lucky (that)** It's lucky that no-one was hurt.
3 bringing good luck: a lucky charm
4 lucky you/me etc spoken used to say that someone is fortunate to be able to do something: 'My husband's a rich man, and devoted to me.' 'Lucky you.'
5 be sb's lucky day spoken used to say that something good and often unexpected will happen to someone: We're going to win. I just know it's our lucky day
6 you'll/you'd be lucky spoken used to tell someone that what they want probably will not happen: '£50 should be enough.' 'You'll be lucky!'
7 I/you should be so lucky! spoken used to tell someone that what they want is not likely to happen, especially because it is unreasonable: You want three weeks holiday? You should be so lucky! → **strike it lucky** at STRIKE¹ (19); → **thank your lucky stars** at THANK (3); → **third time lucky** at THIRD¹ (2)

lucky 'dip n BrE **1** [C] a game in which you put your hand into a container filled with small objects, and choose one without looking; ▭ **grab bag** AmE **2** [singular] a situation in which what happens depends on chance; ▭ **lottery**

lu·cra·tive /ˈluːkrətɪv/ adj a job or activity that is lucrative lets you earn a lot of money; ▭ **profitable**: **lucrative business/market/contract etc** He inherited a lucrative business from his father.

lu·cre /ˈluːkə $ -ər/ n **filthy lucre** informal money or wealth   used to show disapproval

Lud·dite /ˈlʌdaɪt/ n [C] someone who is opposed to using modern machines and methods; ▭ **technophobe**

lu·di·crous /ˈluːdɪkrəs/ adj completely unreasonable, stupid, or wrong; ▭ **ridiculous**: It is ludicrous to suggest that I was driving under the influence of alcohol. | The court granted him the ludicrous sum of £100 in damages. | That's a ludicrous idea. —**ludicrously** adv: a ludicrously inadequate army —**ludicrousness** n [U]

lu·do /ˈluːdəʊ $ -doʊ/ n [U] BrE trademark a game played with COUNTERS (=small flat round objects) on a board

lug¹ /lʌɡ/ v **lugged, lugging** [T] informal to pull or carry something heavy with difficulty: **lug sth around/ up/into/onto etc sth** It's a huge book, not something you'd like to lug around. | She began to lug her suitcase up the stairs.

lug² n [C] **1** [usually plural] a part of something that sticks out and can be used as a handle or a support **2** BrE humorous an ear; ▭ **lughole** **3** AmE a rough, stupid, or awkward person: You big lug!

luge /luːʒ/ n [C] a vehicle with blades instead of wheels on which you slide down a track made of ice as a sport

lug·gage /ˈlʌɡɪdʒ/ n [U] the cases, bags etc that you carry when you are travelling; ▭ **baggage** AmE: They searched his luggage for illegal drugs. → **HAND LUGGAGE**; → see picture at STAY

'luggage rack n [C] **1** a shelf in a train, bus etc for putting luggage on **2** AmE a special frame on top of a car that you tie luggage on; ▭ **roof rack** BrE

lug·ger /ˈlʌɡə $ -ər/ n [C] a small boat with one or more sails

lug·hole /ˈlʌɡhəʊl, ˈlʌɡəʊl $ -oʊl/ n [C] BrE humorous an ear

lu·gu·bri·ous /luːˈɡuːbriəs/ adj literary very sad and serious – sometimes used humorously; ▭ **melancholy, morose**: his lugubrious tear-stained face —**lugubriously** adv

lug·worm /ˈlʌɡwɜːm $ -wɜːrm/ n [C] BrE a small WORM that lives in sand by the sea, often used to catch fish

luke·warm /ˌluːkˈwɔːm◂ $ -ˈwɔːrm◂/ adj **1** food, liquid etc that is lukewarm is slightly warm and often not as hot or cold as it should be; ▭ **tepid**: She sipped some lukewarm coffee from her mug. **2** not showing much interest or excitement: His idea got only a **lukewarm response** from the committee.

lull¹ /lʌl/ v [T] **1** to make someone feel calm or as if they want to sleep: The hum of the tyres on the road lulled her to sleep. **2** to make someone feel safe and confident so that they are completely surprised when something bad happens: **lull sb into (doing) sth** The police lulled me into believing that they did not suspect us. | Earthquakes here are rare and this has **lulled** people **into a false sense of security** (=made people think they were safe when they were not).

lull² n [C] **1** a short period of time when there is less activity or less noise than usual: [+in] a brief lull in the conversation | a lull in the fighting **2 the lull before the storm** a short period of time when things are calm that is followed by a lot of activity, noise, or trouble

lul·la·by /ˈlʌləbaɪ/ n plural **lullabies** [C] a slow, quiet song sung to children to make them go to sleep

lum·ba·go /lʌmˈbeɪɡəʊ $ -ɡoʊ/ n [U] pain in the lower part of the back

lum·bar /ˈlʌmbə $ -ər/ adj technical relating to the lower part of the back: pain in the lumbar region

lum·ber¹ /ˈlʌmbə $ -ər/ v **1** [I always + adv/prep] to move in a slow, awkward way: [+up/towards/into/along etc] They lumbered along slowly. | A blue bus lumbered past. **2** [T] informal to give someone a job or responsibility that they do not want: **get/be lumbered with sth** A career was less easy once I was lumbered with a husband and children. **3** [I] AmE to cut down trees in a large area and prepare them to be sold

lumber² n [U] **1** pieces of wood used for building, that have been cut to specific lengths and widths; ▭ **timber** **2** BrE informal large objects that are no longer useful or wanted

lum·ber·jack /ˈlʌmbədʒæk $ -ər-/ n [C] old-fashioned someone whose job is cutting down trees for wood; ▭ **logger**; → see picture at OCCUPATION

lum·ber·man /ˈlʌmbəmən $ -bər-/ n plural **lumbermen** /-mən/ [C] a person or company that cuts down large areas of trees in order to sell them for wood

lum·ber·mill /ˈlʌmbəmɪl $ -bər-/ n [C] AmE a building where trees are cut up to make wood; ▭ **sawmill** BrE

'lumber room n [C] BrE a room where old furniture, broken machines etc are kept

lum·ber·yard /ˈlʌmbəjɑːd $ -bərjɑːrd/ n [C] AmE a place where wood is kept before it is sold

lu·mi·na·ry /ˈluːmɪnəri $ -neri/ n plural **luminaries** [C] someone who is very famous or highly respected for their skill at doing something or their knowledge of a particular subject: luminaries of Parisian society

lu·mi·nes·cence /ˌluːmɪˈnesəns/ n [U] technical or literary a soft shining light: The moonlight gave everything a strange luminescence. —**luminescent** adj

lu·mi·nous /ˈluːmɪnəs/ adj **1** shining in the dark: luminous paint | Her large dark eyes were almost luminous. **2** very brightly coloured, especially in green, pink, or yellow; ▭ **Day Glo**: luminous green socks —**luminously** adv —**luminosity** /ˌluːmɪˈnɒsəti $ -ˈnɑː-/ n [U] technical: the Sun's luminosity

lump¹ S2 /lʌmp/ n [C]
1 a small piece of something solid, without a particular shape: Strain the custard to remove lumps. | [+of] Melt a lump of butter in your frying-pan.
2 a small hard swollen area that sticks out from someone's skin or grows in their body, usually because of an illness: You should never ignore a breast lump.
3 a small square block of sugar: One lump or two?
4 a lump in/to sb's throat a feeling that you want to cry: There was a lump in her throat as she gazed at the child.
5 take your lumps AmE informal to accept the bad things that happen and not let them affect you: According to experts, the company took its lumps but is on the road to profitability.
6 BrE spoken someone who is stupid or CLUMSY: He's a big fat lump.

L

lump² *v* [T] **1 lump it** *informal* to accept a situation or decision you do not like because you cannot change it: *They've been told: take the lower interest rate, or lump it.* | *It's the law so you can* **like it or lump it.** **2** to put two or more different people or things together and consider them as a single group, sometimes wrongly: **lump sth together** *You can't lump the symptoms together and blame them all on stress.* | **lump sb/sth in with sb** *The danger is that people who pay their bills on time will be lumped in with those that don't.*

lump·ec·to·my /ˌlʌmpˈektəmi/ *n plural* **lumpectomies** [C] an operation in which a TUMOUR is removed from someone's body, especially from a woman's breast

lum·pen /ˈlʌmpən, ˈlʊm-/ *adj* **1** relating to the poorest and least educated people from the WORKING CLASS **2** large, heavy, and lumpy: *Her body felt lumpen and awkward.*

lump·ish /ˈlʌmpɪʃ/ *adj* heavy and awkward

lump ˈsum *n* [C] an amount of money given in a single payment: *When you retire you'll get a lump sum of £80,000.*

lump·y /ˈlʌmpi/ *adj* covered with or containing small solid pieces: *a lumpy mattress* → see picture at THICK¹

lu·na·cy /ˈluːnəsi/ *n* [U] **1** a situation or behaviour that is completely crazy; ▣ **madness**: *It would be* **sheer lunacy** *to turn down a job offer like that.* **2** *old-fashioned* mental illness

lu·nar /ˈluːnə $ -ər/ *adj* relating to the moon or to travel to the moon: *studies of the lunar surface* | *a lunar eclipse*

ˌlunar ˈmonth *n* [C] a period of 28 or 29 days between one NEW MOON and the next

lu·na·tic /ˈluːnətɪk/ *n* [C] **1** someone who behaves in a crazy or very stupid way – often used humorously: *This hotel is run by a lunatic!* **2** *old-fashioned* a very offensive word for someone who is mentally ill: *a dangerous lunatic* **3 the lunatic fringe** *BrE* the small group of people in a political group or organization who have the most extreme opinions or ideas —**lunatic** *adj* [only before noun]: *lunatic behaviour*

ˈlunatic aˌsylum *n* [C] *old-fashioned* a hospital where people who are mentally ill are cared for. This word is now considered to be offensive.

lunch¹ S1 W2 /lʌntʃ/ *n* [C,U]
 1 a meal eaten in the middle of the day

eat (your) lunch
have (your) lunch (=eat lunch)
have sth for lunch (=eat a particular food or dish at lunchtime)
go out for lunch
break for lunch (=stop doing something in order to eat lunch)
be at lunch (=not be in your place of work because you are somewhere else having lunch)
take sb (out) to lunch
working lunch (=a lunch during which you also do business)
over lunch (=while eating lunch)
packed lunch *BrE*
bag lunch *AmE* (=food such as sandwiches that you take to work, school etc)
light lunch (=a small meal at lunchtime)
hot lunch (=cooked food, rather than sandwiches)

What's **for lunch**? | *She* **ate** *a small* **lunch** *before the meeting.* | *Perhaps we could* **have lunch** *before you go.* | *I think I'll* **have** *soup for lunch.* | *The two women* **went out for lunch** *together.* | *Let's* **break for lunch** *now.* | *I'm afraid he's* **at lunch** *until two.* | *I'll* **take** *you* **out to lunch** *next time I'm in town.* | *They're having a* **working lunch** *in Mr Savil's office.* | *A dozen senators met* **over lunch** *with the Chinese ambassador.* | *The walk is expected to last all day so bring a* **packed lunch.** | *a café serving* **light lunches** *and snacks* | *The kids get a* **hot lunch** *at school during the winter.* → see box at DINNER

2 there's no (such thing as a) free lunch used to say that you cannot get anything without working for it or paying for it

3 out to lunch *informal* behaving or talking in a strange or crazy way

lunch² *v formal* [I] to eat lunch: [+**with**] *I will be lunching with a client.* | [+**on**] *I lunched on bread and olives.* | [+**at/in**] *We lunched at Maxim's.*

lunch·box /ˈlʌntʃbɒks $ -bɑːks/ *n* [C] a box in which food is carried to school, work etc

ˈlunch break *n* [C] the time in the middle of the day when people at work or at school stop working to eat lunch

ˈlunch ˌcounter *n* [C] *old-fashioned* a place that serves simple meals for lunch, or a small restaurant that is only open at lunchtime

lunch·eon /ˈlʌntʃən/ *n* [C,U] *formal* lunch

ˈluncheon meat *n* [U] meat that has been cooked, then pressed down, and is often sold in a can

ˈluncheon ˌvoucher *n* [C] in Britain, a special ticket that can be used to pay for meals usually given to you by your employer

ˈlunch hour *n* [C] the period of time in the middle of the day when people stop working in order to eat: *I did the shopping during my lunch hour.*

lunch·room /ˈlʌntʃruːm, -rʊm/ *n* [C] *AmE* a large room in a school or office where people can eat

lunch·time S3 /ˈlʌntʃtaɪm/ *n* [C,U] the time in the middle of the day when people usually eat their LUNCH: **at lunchtime** *Some people prefer to eat their main meal at lunchtime.* | *a lunchtime drink*

lung /lʌŋ/ *n* [C] one of the two organs in your body that you breathe with: *Smoking can cause lung cancer.* → see picture at HUMAN¹ → IRON LUNG

lunge /lʌndʒ/ *v* [I] to make a sudden strong movement towards someone or something, especially to attack them: [+**at/forward/towards/out etc**] *The goats lunged at each other with their horns.* | *John lunged forward and grabbed him by the throat.* —**lunge** *n* [C]: *Brad made a lunge towards his opponent, but missed.*

lung·ful /ˈlʌŋfʊl/ *n* [C] the amount of air, smoke etc that you breathe in at one time: [+**of**] *Polly took in a lungful of crisp cool air.*

lu·pus /ˈluːpəs/ *n* [U] one of several diseases that affect the skin and joints

lurch¹ /lɜːtʃ $ lɜːrtʃ/ *v* [I] **1** to walk or move suddenly in an uncontrolled or unsteady way: [+**forward/to/towards/into etc**] *Sam hit the gas and the car lurched forward.* | *He lurched to his feet.* **2 your heart/stomach lurches** used to say that your heart or stomach seems to move suddenly because you feel shocked, frightened etc: *Virginia's heart lurched painfully in her chest.* **3 lurch from one crisis/extreme etc to another** *also* **lurch from crisis to crisis** to seem to have no plan and no control over what you are doing: *The industry lurches from crisis to crisis.*

lurch² *n* [C] **1** a sudden movement: *The train gave a violent lurch.* **2 leave sb in the lurch** to leave someone at a time when you should stay and help them

lure¹ /lʊə, ljʊə $ lʊr/ *v* [T] **1** to persuade someone to do something, especially something wrong or dangerous, by making it seem attractive or exciting: **lure sb into (doing) sth** *People may be lured into buying tickets by clever advertising.* | **lure sb away** *Computer games are luring youngsters away from their lessons.* **2** to attract customers, workers, money etc from another company or place: **lure sb back/away** *The bank launched an advertising campaign to lure back its traditional customers.* | *It's very difficult to lure talent away from Silicon Valley.*

lure² *n* [C] **1** [usually singular] something that attracts people, or the quality of being able to do this: [+**of**] *the lure of easy money* | *Malc wasn't mature enough to resist the lure of drink and drugs.* **2** an object used to attract animals or fish so that they can be caught; ▣ **decoy**

L

lu·rex /'ljʊəreks $ 'lʊr-/ *n* [U] *trademark* a type of thread that looks like metal, usually gold or silver, used in material for making clothes: *gold lurex socks*

lu·rid /'lʊərɪ̯d, 'ljʊərɪ̯d $ 'lʊrɪ̯d/ *adj* **1** a description, story etc that is lurid is deliberately shocking and involves sex or violence; ▣ **explicit**: *lurid headlines* | *He told me in lurid detail what would happen to me.* **2** too brightly coloured; ▣ **gaudy**: *a lurid orange dress* —**luridly** *adv*

lurk /lɜːk $ lɜːrk/ *v* [I] **1** to wait somewhere quietly and secretly, usually because you are going to do something wrong: [+in/behind/beneath/around etc] *She didn't see the figure lurking behind the bushes.* **2** if something such as danger, a feeling etc lurks somewhere, it exists, but you may not see it or know about it: *a dark formless danger, lurking in the shadows* **3** if you lurk in a CHAT ROOM on the Internet, you read what other people are writing to each other, but you do not write any messages yourself: [+in] *I think it's sort of creepy how people lurk in chat rooms.*

lus·cious /'lʌʃəs/ *adj* **1** extremely good to eat or drink: *a luscious and fragrant dessert wine* **2** *informal* very sexually attractive: *her luscious body*

lush¹ /lʌʃ/ *adj* **1** plants that are lush grow many leaves and look healthy and strong: *a lush green mountainous island* | *The fields were lush with grass and flowers.* **2** very beautiful, comfortable, and expensive; ▣ **luxurious**: *lush carpets*

lush² *n* [C] *informal* an ALCOHOLIC

lust¹ /lʌst/ *n* **1** [C,U] very strong sexual desire, especially when it does not include love: *My feelings for Lauren were pure lust.* **2** [singular, U] a very strong desire to have something, usually power or money -used to show disapproval: [+for] *Hitler's lust for power* **3** (a) **lust for life** a strong determination to enjoy life as much as possible – used to show approval: *the happy-go-lucky lust for life so typical of southern Italy*

lust² *v*

lust after/for sb/sth *phr v* **1** to be strongly sexually attracted to someone, and think about having sex with them: *She had secretely lusted after him for years.* **2** to want something very much, especially something that you do not really need: *This is a car to lust after.*

lus·ter /'lʌstə $ -ər/ *n* [singular, U] the American spelling of LUSTRE

lust·ful /'lʌstfəl/ *adj* feeling or showing strong sexual desire: *She ignored his lustful glances.* —**lustfully** *adv*

lus·tre *BrE;* **luster** *AmE* /'lʌstə $ -ər/ *n* [singular, U] **1** an attractive shiny appearance: *Her thick, black hair shone with lustre.* **2** the quality that makes something interesting or exciting: *There'll be a celebrity guest to* **add lustre to** *the occasion.*

lus·trous /'lʌstrəs/ *adj* shining in a soft, gentle way: *Her hair was beautifully dark and lustrous.*

lust·y /'lʌsti/ *adj* strong and healthy; ▣ **powerful**: *the lusty cry of a new-born baby* | *her strong, lusty young husband* —**lustily** *adv*: *Her mother was singing lustily.*

lute /luːt/ *n* [C] a musical instrument like a GUITAR with a round body, played with the fingers or a PLECTRUM (=small piece of plastic, metal etc), especially in the past —**lutenist** /'luːtənɪ̯st/ *n* [C]; → see picture at STRINGED INSTRUMENT

luv /lʌv/ *n BrE informal* an informal way of spelling LOVE: *Come on, luv, don't cry.*

luv·vie /'lʌvi/ *n BrE* **1** another spelling of LOVEY **2** [C] *informal* an actor who behaves to other people in a very friendly way that is not sincere

lux·u·ri·ant /lʌɡ'zjʊəriənt, ləɡ'ʒʊəri- $ ləɡ'ʒʊriənt/ *adj* **1** growing strongly and thickly: *luxuriant black hair* | *luxuriant vegetation* **2** beautiful and pleasant to watch or listen to: *the film's luxuriant visuals* —**luxuriantly** *adv*: *She yawned luxuriantly.* —**luxuriance** *n* [U]

lux·u·ri·ate /lʌɡ'zjʊərieɪt, ləɡ'ʒʊəri- $ ləɡ'ʒʊri-/ *v* [I usually + adv/prep] to relax and enjoy something: [+in] *He ran a hot bath and luxuriated in it for half an hour.*

lux·u·ri·ous /lʌɡ'zjʊəriəs, ləɡ'ʒʊəriəs $ ləɡ'ʒʊriəs/ *adj* very expensive, beautiful, and comfortable: *a luxurious 30-room villa* —**luxuriously** *adv*: *The cabin was luxuriously furnished.*

lux·u·ry /'lʌkʃəri/ *n plural* **luxuries** **1** [U] very great comfort and pleasure, such as you get from expensive food, beautiful houses, cars etc: **in luxury** *She stole to keep her boyfriend in luxury.* | *He was leading* **a life of luxury** *in Australia.* | **luxury hotel/car/home etc** (=expensive and large) *We stayed in a five-star luxury hotel.* | *The dress is lambswool – pure luxury.* **2** [C] something expensive that you do not need, but you buy for pleasure and enjoyment; ▣ **necessity**: *luxuries like chocolate and perfume* **3 afford/have/enjoy the luxury of sth** to have something that is very pleasant or convenient, that you are not always able to have: *For the first time in three years, they actually had the luxury of a whole day together.* → **in the lap of luxury** at LAP¹ (5)

LW the written abbreviation of *long wave*

-ly /li/ *suffix* **1** [in adverbs] in a particular way: *She smiled happily.* | *He was walking slowly.* **2** [in adverbs] considered in a particular way: *Politically speaking it was a rather unwise remark.* | *a financially sound proposal* **3** [in adjectives and adverbs] happening at regular periods of time: *an hourly check* (=done every hour) | *They visit monthly* (=once every month). **4** [in adjectives] like a particular thing in manner, nature, or appearance: *with queenly grace* | *a motherly woman* (=showing the love, kindness etc of a mother)

ly·ce·um /laɪ'siːəm/ *n* [C] *AmE old-fashioned* a building used for public meetings, concerts, speeches etc

ly·chee, litchi /'laɪtʃi/ *n* [C] a small round fruit with a rough pink-brown shell outside and sweet white flesh inside

lych·gate, lichgate /'lɪtʃɡeɪt/ *n* [C] a gate with a roof leading into the area surrounding a church

Ly·cra /'laɪkrə/ *n* [U] *trademark* a material that stretches, used especially for making sports clothes that fit tightly

ly·ing /'laɪ-ɪŋ/ *v* the present participle of LIE

Lyme dis·ease /'laɪm dɪˌziːz/ *n* [U] a serious illness that is caused by a bite from a TICK¹ (2)

lymph /lɪmf/ *n* [U] a clear liquid that is formed in your body and passes into your blood system to fight against infection —**lymphatic** /lɪm'fætɪk/ *adj*

'lymph node *n* [C] also **'lymph gland** a small rounded SWELLING in your body through which lymph passes before entering your blood system

lynch /lɪntʃ/ *v* [T] if a crowd of people lynches someone, they kill them, especially by HANGING them, without using the usual legal process —**lynching** *n* [C]

'lynch mob *n* [singular] a group of people that kills someone by HANGING them, without a legal TRIAL

lynch·pin /'lɪntʃ pɪn/ *n* [C] another spelling of LINCHPIN

lynx /lɪŋks/ *n plural* **lynx** or **lynxes** [C] a large wild cat that has no tail and lives in forests; ▣ **bobcat** *AmE*; → see picture at BIG CAT

lyre /laɪə $ laɪr/ *n* [C] a musical instrument with strings across a U-shaped frame, played with the fingers, especially in ancient Greece

lyr·ic¹ /'lɪrɪk/ *adj* [only before noun] expressing strong personal emotions such as love, in a way that is similar to music in its sounds and RHYTHM: *Wordsworth was one of the greatest lyric poets of his time.*

lyric² *n* **1 lyrics** [plural] the words of a song: *He wrote some great music, but the lyrics weren't that good.* **2** also **lyric 'poem** [C] *technical* a poem, usually a short one, written in a lyric style

L

lyr·i·cal /ˈlɪrɪkəl/ *adj* **1** beautifully expressed in words, poetry, or music: *lyrical love poetry* **2 wax lyrical** to talk about and praise something in a very eager way: *One fisherman waxed lyrical about the variety of fish in the river.* —**lyrically** /-kli/ *adv*

lyr·i·cis·m /ˈlɪrɪ̩sɪzəm/ *n* [U] gentle or romantic emotion, expressed in writing or music: *The lyricism of Tennyson's poetry is magnificent.*

lyr·i·cist /ˈlɪrɪ̩sɪst/ *n* [C] someone who writes the words for songs

The articles are **a** (**an**) and **the**. **A** is the 'indefinite article', and **the** is the 'definite article'. You use **an** instead of **a** if the next word begins with a vowel sound.

When to use 'a' and 'the'

You usually use **a** or **the** in front of countable nouns.

*Can you lend me **a hammer**?* | *We found **the keys** behind **the sofa**.*

You use **a** when you are mentioning something for the first time. You use **the** when you are mentioning something again that you have already talked about.

*She has a car and **a bike**, but she uses **the bike** more often.*

If you use **the** with a noun that you have not mentioned before, you believe that your listener knows which one you mean.

*Have you fed **the cat**?* (=you have only one cat)
*I met him during **the conference**.* (=both you and your listener know which conference)

You use **a** when you are talking about one of several things or people. You use **the** when it is clear that you are talking about a particular thing or person and there is only one.

***A man** I work with told me about it.* (=you work with several men)
***The man** I work with told me about it.* (=you work with only one man)

You also use **a** when you want to talk about a particular type of thing or person.

✔ *I'm training to be **an engineer**.* NOT ✘ *'I'm training to be engineer.'*
✔ *I went out to buy **a newspaper**.* NOT ✘ *'I went out to buy newspaper.'*

With singular nouns such as **world**, **sky**, or **sun**, you use **the** because there is only one of these things in the situation that you are talking about.

*We're going to travel around **the world**.* | *Don't look directly at **the sun**.*

You use **the** when you are talking about buildings, places, and organizations, for example **the bank**, **the theatre**, **the post office** etc.

*I went to **the theatre** last week.* | *She's at **the gym**.*

When NOT to use 'a' and 'the'

Don't use **the** with a countable noun in the plural, when you are talking in general about something.

Tigers are very fierce. | *Prices keep going up.*

There are also many common nouns and phrases which do not use **a** or **the**, for example when talking about meals, illnesses, or ways of travelling.

✔ *Will you have lunch with me?* NOT ✘ *'Will you have the lunch with me?'*
✔ *Her mother has cancer.* NOT ✘ *'Her mother has the cancer.'*
✔ *I go to work by bus.* NOT ✘ *'I go to work by the bus.'*

Most place names do not have **the** in front of them.

✔ *They're visiting Belgium.* NOT ✘ *'They're visiting the Belgium.'*

🛈 **Important exceptions**
Plural names of countries usually have **the** in front of them.

✔ *He's from **the United States**.* NOT ✘ *'He's from United States.'*

Many names of rivers begin with **the**.

✔ *the Mississippi **River*** | ✔ *the **Thames** OR the **River** Thames*

Modal verbs are used to express the following ideas:

Ability

can
could

You use **can** when you are saying that someone is able to do something. In the past tense, you use **could** or **was/were able to**.

> *He **can** speak Russian.* | ***Can** you remember her name?*
> *I **can't** find my shoes.* | ***Could** you hear what she was saying?*
> *Dinosaurs **were able to** run very fast.*

Certainty

must
can't
will

You use **must** when you are saying you are certain that something is true.

> *You **must** be tired after all your hard work.* | *They **must** have left by now.*

If you want to say that you are certain that something is not true, you use **can't**. (Don't use 'must' in this situation.)

> *You **can't** be tired – you've only been working for an hour.*
> *They **can't** have left yet.*

You use **will** when you are saying that something will definitely happen. You can also use **will** when you are talking about something that is always true.

> *I **will** be 18 next year.* | *Oil **will** float on water.*

Intention

will
shall
would

You use **will** when you are saying that you intend to do something. In British English, people sometimes use **shall** (but only with **I** and **we**).

> *The letter says they **will** definitely give us our money back.*
> *I **won't** stay long.* | *I **shall** be going soon.*

You use **would** if there are conditions which control whether something can happen.

> *I **would** leave tomorrow, if I had the money.*

Necessity/ obligation

must
need
have to
have got to

You use **must** when you are saying that it is necessary for something to happen, or it is someone's duty to do something. In spoken English, people often say **have got to** instead of **have to**.

> *I **must** get my hair cut this weekend.* | *All passengers must **wear** seat belts.*
> *The doctor says I've **got to** give up smoking.*

If you want to say that you think that something is not necessary, you use **needn't**, **need not**, or **don't need to**. (Don't use 'must not' in this situation.)

> *You **don't need to** wear a tie if you don't want to.*

If you want to talk about the future, use **will have to** or **will need to**.

> *You **will have to** be home by 10.* | *We'll **need to** leave soon.*

Offers

can
may
shall
will

You use **Can I...?** when you are offering to help someone. **May I...?** is used in formal English. In British English, people sometimes say **shall I...?** You can also offer to help someone by saying **I'll...**

> ***Can** I get you anything from the store?* | ***May** I help you, madam?*
> ***Shall** I carry your bags?* | *I'll open the door for you.*

Permission

can
may
could

You use **can** and **may** when you are giving permission or asking permission to do something. **Could** is more polite than **can**. **May** is used in formal English.

*You **can** go home now.* | ***May** we use your office for a few minutes?*
***Could** I use your phone?*

Possibility

can
may
could
might

You use **can** when you are saying that something is possible.

*You **can** go by bus from London to Liverpool.*

You use **may** or **could** when you are saying that something is possible, but you are not certain about it. In both of the following sentences the stress is placed on the modal verb (**may** or **could**), rather than the main verb.

*You **may** find him in his office.* | *He **could** be in his office.*

You use **might** when you are suggesting that something could happen, but you are very doubtful and uncertain about it.

*He **might** be in his office.*

You also use **could** if there are conditions which control whether something can happen.

*I **could** leave tomorrow, if I had the money.*

Prediction

will
shall

You use **will** when you are saying that something is certain to happen. In British English, people sometimes use **shall** (but only with **I** and **we**).

*The car **will** be there on time, I promise.*
*There's no doubt that we **shall** win.*

Probability

should
ought to

You use **should** and **ought to** when you are saying that something will probably happen, although you are not completely sure.

*We **should** be there by 6 o'clock.* | *We **ought to** be there by 6 o'clock.*
*If you take these tablets, you **should** be all right.*

Requests

can
will
could
would

You use **Can I...?**, **Can you...?**, and **Will you...?** when asking someone to do something.

***Can** I borrow your dictionary?* | ***Can** you hold my bag?*
***Will** you give me a lift to the station?*

Could I...?, **Could you...?**, and **Would you...?** are a little more formal or polite.

***Could** I have another cup of coffee, please?*
*Fiona, **would** you bring another chair, please?*

Suggestions/advice

should
ought to
shall
must

You use **should** and **ought to** when you are suggesting that someone should do something. In British English you use **Shall I/we...?** in questions when suggesting that you do something.

*You **should** get the early flight if you want to be in good time.*
*You **ought to** meet him; he's really nice.* | ***Shall** we leave?*

You use **must** when you are suggesting that someone should do something because you think it is very good.

*You **must** see 'Cinema Paradiso' – it's a really good film.*

What is a phrasal verb?

A phrasal verb is a verb that is made up of two or three words. The first word is a verb, and the second word is a particle (either an adverb or a preposition such as **in**, **up**, or **on**). Examples of common phrasal verbs include **get up**, **turn off**, and **deal with**. There are also some phrasal verbs which have two particles, for example **catch up with** and **look forward to**.

You cannot guess the meaning of a phrasal verb from the meaning of each of the two or three parts. For example, in the sentence *Scientists carried out an experiment*, the meaning of **carry out** (=do) is not related to the normal meaning of 'carry' or the normal meaning of 'out'.

If a verb still keeps its ordinary meaning, even though it is followed by several different prepositions, it is *not* a phrasal verb. For example, in the sentence, *We ran up the hill*, 'run up' is not a phrasal verb. You can use the verb **run** in the sense of 'moving quickly on foot' with several other prepositions or adverbs, including **down**, **in**, and **onto**, and the basic meaning of **run** does not change. However, **run down** and **run in** are also phrasal verbs with their own special meanings.

Phrasal verbs and formality

Phrasal verbs are very commonly used in both spoken and written English. Sometimes a single word can be used instead of the phrasal verb, but often this single word sounds more formal or more technical than the phrasal verb. For example, instead of the phrasal verb **get up** (=leave your bed in the morning), you can use the single verb **rise**, which sounds very formal. Instead of the phrasal verb **stick out** (=point outwards or upwards in a very noticeable way), you can use the single word **protrude**, which sounds formal or technical.

Different types of phrasal verb

Phrasal verbs which do not have an object

Some phrasal verbs do not have an object, for example **stand up** when it means 'move from a sitting position to a standing position'.

James stood up and walked to the window.

Phrasal verbs which must have an object

Some phrasal verbs must have an object, and the object can come either before or after the particle. These are usually called SEPARABLE phrasal verbs. **Turn off** (=make a machine, light etc stop working) is a separable phrasal verb. You can either **turn** *something* **off**, or you can **turn off** *something*.

How do I know where to put the object?

If the object is a pronoun (it/them/him/her etc), the pronoun must come before the particle.

✔ *I turned **it** off.*   NOT   ✗ 'I turned off it.'

If the object is a long phrase, the long phrase usually comes after the particle.

✔ *I turned off **the lights in the**   NOT   ✗ 'I turned the lights in the
front room.   front room off.'

How do I know if the phrasal verb is separable?

The *Longman Dictionary of Contemporary English* uses a special symbol ⇔ between the verb and the particle, which shows you whether the phrasal verb is separable. For example:

> **turn off** *phr v*
> **1 turn sth ⇔ off** to make a machine or piece of electrical equipment such as a television, engine, light etc stop operating by pushing a button, turning a key etc; ▣ **switch off**; ▣ **turn on**: *Don't forget to turn the lights off when you leave.* → see box at CLOSE[1]

Some phrasal verbs must have the object *between* the verb and the particle. For example **get down** (=make someone feel unhappy) always has the object between the verb and the particle. This type of phrasal verb is shown as follows in the dictionary:

> **get down** *phr v*
> **1 MAKE SB SAD get sb down** to make someone feel unhappy and tired: *His lack of social life was beginning to get him down.*

Some other phrasal verbs must have the object *after* the particle. These phrasal verbs are sometimes called NON-SEPARABLE phrasal verbs. **Get at** (=criticize someone in an unkind way) is a non-separable phrasal verb. This type of phrasal verb is shown as follows in the dictionary:

> **get at** sb/sth *phr v*
> **1 CRITICIZE** to keep criticizing someone in an unkind way: *Why is he always getting at me?* | *He felt he was being got at by the other students.*

→ If you want more information on phrasal verbs, the *Longman Phrasal Verbs Dictionary* explains the meaning of and shows how to use 5,000 phrasal verbs.

What is an idiom?

An idiom is a group of words in a particular syntactic relationship that has a special meaning which is different from the meanings of all or some of the individual words. For example, you cannot guess the meaning of **out to lunch** (=talking or behaving in a strange way) from the meanings of the words in the idiom.

Idioms are normally used in a very fixed and limited way. If you want to say that someone is talking or behaving in a strange way, you can say that they are **out to lunch**, but not that they 'have gone out to lunch'.

Idiom and metaphor

If you say, for example, that someone is **cold** towards you, you are not using the word 'cold' in its literal meaning. You are speaking in a metaphorical way. Metaphor is a way of describing something by referring to it as something different. There are several other metaphors that make a link between the feeling of being cold physically and the feeling you have when someone is unfriendly to you, including words such as **cool**, **chilly**, **icy**, and **frosty**.

> *When he arrived home, he received a **cool/chilly** reception.*
> *She looked at him with **icy** contempt.*

Idioms can be seen as metaphors that have become fixed phrases in the language, and are now a usual way of talking about a particular type of situation.

> **Literal meaning**
> *She gave him **a slap in the face**. (=she hit his face)*
>
> **Idiom**
> *The government's decision is seen as **a slap in the face** by environmental groups. (=they think it is very unfair and deliberately intended to offend them)*

Recognizing idioms

Pairs of words

Many idioms consist of pairs of words separated by 'and'. The word order of these pairs cannot be changed.

> *Her previous husband had left her **high and dry**. (=without any money or things that she needed)*
> *The facts were all there **in black and white**. (=in printed form and therefore very clear and definite)*

Similes

Some idioms are similes that have become idiomatic. A simile is an adjective phrase which uses 'as' or 'like':

> *Riding a bike is **as easy as pie**. (=very easy)*
> *The story is **as old as the hills**. (=very old)*
> *The plan worked **like a dream**. (=worked very well)*

Sayings

Many sayings are full sentences, but often only part of the saying is used because the listener already knows what is coming next.

> ***Too many cooks (spoil the broth)**. (=if too many people try to do the same job at the same time, they will do it badly)*
> ***Don't count your chickens (before they're hatched)**. (=you should not make plans that depend on something good happening, because it might not)*

Metaphorical actions that represent a feeling or type of behaviour

Some idioms describe an imaginary action which represents a feeling or type of behaviour.

> *Her family **looked down their noses at** anyone who hadn't been to university.* (=behaved as if they thought that someone or something was not good enough for them)
> *We don't want to **throw the baby out with the bath water**.* (=get rid of good or useful parts of something when you are trying to make it better)
> *There's no need to **get your knickers in a twist**!* (=become upset or annoyed; used in British English)

Phrasal verbs

Phrasal verbs use idiomatic combinations of a verb with a word such as 'up', 'out', 'down' etc.

> *Just tell him to **chill out**!* (=relax and calm down)
> *They **polished off** three plates of sandwiches.* (=ate all of them)
> *She was **leafing through** a magazine.* (=looking at it and quickly turning the pages)

→ Also see **Language Notes** on **Phrasal verbs**.

Variable idioms

Idioms are normally used in a very fixed and limited way. Often, though, English speakers play with idioms by making up their own versions of an existing idiom.

For example there are several different ways of saying that something annoys you, all beginning with the word **drive**.

> *It **drives me crazy**.*
> *It **drives me nuts**.*
> *It **drives me mad**.*
> *It **drives me up the wall**.*
> *It **drives me bananas**.*

Some of these variations are shown in the entry at **drive**, to help you recognize similar expressions if you come across them.

How are idioms shown in the dictionary?

Idioms play an important part in the English language, and it is useful to be able to recognize them and find their meanings. In this dictionary, idioms are usually shown in **bold** at the start of a paragraph. For example, at the entry for **hot**, there are paragraphs which tell you the meaning of the following idioms:

> **7 a hot issue/topic etc** a subject that a lot of people are discussing, especially one that causes a lot of disagreement: *The affair was a hot topic of conversation.* | *one of the hottest issues facing medical science*
> **8 in the hot seat** in an important position and responsible for making difficult decisions
> **9 in hot water** if someone is in hot water, they are in trouble because they have done something wrong: *The finance minister found himself in hot water over his business interests.* | **land/get yourself in hot water** *She got herself in hot water with the authorities.*

→ If you want more information on idioms, the ***Longman Idioms Dictionary*** and the ***Longman American Idioms Dictionary*** show clearly the meaning and use of thousands of spoken and written idioms.

Informal letters

Start with

> *Dear* + first name
> *Hi* + first name (=used in very informal letters)
>
> *It was nice to hear from you.*
> *It was great to see you/It was good to see you.*
> *I'm having a good holiday in.../I'm having a great time in...*
> *Thanks for the...*
> *Sorry I haven't written for so long./Sorry I haven't been in touch.*

End with

> *Look forward to seeing you soon./Look forward to hearing from you soon.*
> *Hope all's well.*
>
> Neutral → *Best wishes (from)*
> *With best wishes*
> *All the (very) best*
>
> Formal → *Yours*
>
> Informal → *Love (from)*
> *Lots of love (from)*
> *All my love*
> *XXXX* (=lots of kisses; used especially when writing to your
> boyfriend or girlfriend)
>
> + your first name

Emails

Emails are often written in a very brief way. Emails to friends and colleagues use informal language as in a conversation. Other emails, for example when writing to companies and organizations, use a style more like that of a formal letter.

Start with

> Informal → *Hi*
> *Hi* + first name
> OR   first name only
> OR   no name and no greeting at all
>
> Neutral → *Dear* + first name

End with

> *Talk to you soon/See you soon/Catch you later* (Informal)
> *Regards/Cheers* (Informal British English)
> *All the best/Best* (Informal)
> *Take care* (Informal)
> *Love* (Informal)
> OR   just the first letter of your first name, for example *M* (Informal)

> ❶ If you are writing a formal email, you can use the same beginnings and
> endings as for formal letters.

Formal letters

Start with

> *Dear Mr/Mrs/Miss/Ms* + family name (you use *Ms* when you don't know if the woman is married or not)
> *Dear Dr/Professor* + family name
> *Dear Sir* (=used when you don't know the man's name)
> *Dear Madam* (=used when you don't know the woman's name)
> *Dear Sir or Madam* (=used when you don't know if you are writing to a man or woman)
> *To Whom it may Concern* (=used when you don't know the person's name)
>
> *I am writing to ask whether/to say that...*
> *I am writing in reply to your advertisement...*
> *Please could you send me/I would appreciate it if you could send me/I would be grateful if you could send me...*
> *I enclose my CV/a cheque for...*

End with

> *Yours truly* (=used in American English)
> *Yours sincerely* (=used in British English when you know the person's name)
> *Yours faithfully* (=used in British English when you don't know the person's name)

Curriculum vitae/resumé

When you are applying for a job or a place on a course, you usually have to send details of your qualifications and your work experience. This information is called your curriculum vitae/CV (in British English), or your résumé (in American English). Models are provided at the back of this dictionary.

Essay writing

dos and don'ts

✔ **dos**

✔ give your essay a clear structure. Make sure that it has an introduction which says what the aim of the essay is, a 'body' (=the main part of the essay, usually consisting of 3 paragraphs), and a conclusion at the end which says what your point was.

✔ link your ideas together so that they are connected in a logical way (→ see **Language Notes** on **Linking ideas**)

✔ give supporting evidence or quotations from other people in order to support the points you want to make, and say where they come from.

✘ **don'ts**

✘ don't mix different ideas together in the same paragraph or sentence.

✘ don't use informal spoken language, and don't use short forms such as can't or won't.

✘ don't overuse phrases such as *I think that...* You can use the form *In my opinion...* or if you want to say what other people think, you can use phrases such as *According to Marx,...* or *It was Marx's view that...* It is also often better to use the passive form: *It has been pointed out that... It has been said that...*

✘ don't copy other people's work. This is known as 'plagiarism' and will cause you to fail your essay. You can give short quotations from other writers to support your arguments, but you must say who and where the quotation is from.

✘ don't feel that you have to use very formal or complicated language. Simple is best.

→ If you would like more guidance on essay writing, you can find information in the **Language Notes** on **Linking ideas**. The *Longman Language Activator* can also help you find the right word and express your ideas clearly.

You know words in English, and you know what they mean, but how do you use them together to form a correct English sentence and link your ideas coherently? Here is a selection of some of the most common problems that students face when linking words together, and some suggestions for different ways of doing this.

Listing ideas in a logical order

One of the most common weaknesses in essays is that the ideas are not linked together in a clear and logical sequence. One simple way of avoiding this problem is to decide exactly which points you want to make, and then number them, using **firstly**, **secondly**, **thirdly** etc, and **lastly**. Instead of **firstly** you can also say **first of all**, **in the first place**, or **to begin with**. Instead of **lastly** you can say **finally**.

Summarizing your ideas

If you want to summarize your ideas at the end of an essay or report, you can begin the summary by saying **in conclusion**, **to conclude**, or **to sum up**.

Adding another idea that supports the previous one

The simple way to do this is to use **also**. Students tend to use **also** too much but there are other expressions which you can use instead, including **furthermore**, **moreover** (both used in formal English), **what is more**, and **besides** (used especially in conversation).

> The country was experiencing severe economic problems. **Furthermore/Moreover**, the unemployment rate was at its highest level for many years.
> Traffic in the city is getting worse. **What is more**, there is a major problem with parking in front of the theatre.
> I didn't want to go to the wedding. **Besides**, I didn't have anything to wear.

If you want to say that something has two different qualities, you can join them together with the word **both**.

> The jacket is **both** stylish and comfortable.

But remember that you can use **both** only with two things. If there are more, then you can say:

> The jacket **combines** stylishness, comfort, and warmth.

If you want to name two qualities that something does not have, you can use **neither ... nor**.

> The jacket is **neither** stylish **nor** warm.

Contrasting different ideas with each other

There are many different ways of pointing out that there is a contrast between two ideas.

> The house is very modern, **but** also very practical.
> He didn't have much experience. **However**, he did have plenty of enthusiasm.
> **Although** in poor health, she continued to carry out her duties.
> We decided to take rooms in Longwood House, **though** we knew we could not really afford the rent.
> What she said was true. It was, **nevertheless**, a little unkind. (=in spite of a fact that you have just mentioned)
> Kelly was a convicted criminal, **and yet** many people admired him. (=even though it is very surprising)
> The old system was very complicated, **whereas** the new one is basically very simple. (=although something is true of one thing, it is not true of another)
> **On the one hand** I suspected a trap, but **on the other** the man seemed perfectly honest.

Saying what the result of something is	There are several expressions you can use, including **so**, **therefore**, **as a result**, and, in formal English, **consequently** and **thus**.

*John's sick, **so** he won't be able to come tonight.*
*The other car was bigger, and **therefore** more comfortable.*
*Many more people have cars now, and **as a result**, village shops have been
    replaced by supermarkets or shopping centres in nearby towns.*
*The flowers never open, and **consequently** no seeds are produced.*
*Most of the evidence was destroyed in the fire. **Thus** it would be almost
    impossible to prove him guilty.*

Saying what the reason for something is	When giving the reason for something you can use **because**, **as**, **due to**, and **owing to**. **Due to** and **owing to** are used especially in official statements when saying that something was caused by a particular event or problem. (However, some speakers of English believe that **due to** is not good English, and that **owing to** is preferred.)

*Many exam candidates lose marks simply **because** they do not read the
    questions properly.*
***Because** he had been in prison, employers were unwilling to offer him a job.*
*We decided to go home **as** it was getting late.*
***As** she was the youngest, she had expected to go first.*
*He is retiring **due to** ill health.*
***Owing to** bad weather, this morning's flight will be delayed.*

Saying what the purpose of something is	You can use **to**, **in order to** (used especially in formal English), and **so (that)** (in informal English the 'that' is often omitted).

*I went to the bank **to** get some money.*
*Some drug users steal **in order to** buy drugs.*
***In order to** be a doctor, you have to study for six years.*
*He used to pretend to be ill **so that** he could get off school.*
*I'm studying English **so** I can go to college.*

Choosing the right thing to say in a particular situation

Pragmatics is the study of how words are used, and what speakers mean, depending on the context and the situation. Simple words with basic meanings such as **please** can be a source of misunderstanding if used inappropriately, and make you sound impolite or unfriendly.

For example if you say *Will you please sit down?* it can sound as if you are talking to a naughty child, particularly if you stress the 'please'. The usual way to ask someone to sit down is to say *Have a seat!* or just say *Please!* and indicate with your hand that you want the other person to sit down.

Feelings and attitudes

When you speak or write to someone, the words or expressions you choose show your feelings about what you are saying.

Approval and disapproval

You can, for example, use **freedom fighter** when you think that someone is fighting against an unfair government and you approve of their actions. If you disapprove, you would call this person a **terrorist**.

Emphasis

There are situations when you may want to use strong words that will emphasize what you are saying. For example, several adjectives can be used to talk about 'anger'. Whichever word you use will show how angry you think someone is: *angry* is not as strong as *furious*, and *fuming* or *livid* are much stronger than *furious*. Similarly, if you say that something is *nice* or *good*, you express a very mild degree of appreciation. But if you say that it is *brilliant* or *fantastic*, you express a strong positive feeling.

Politeness

If you want to be careful and diplomatic, you can use words or expressions that will show that you want to be polite. If for example you don't have a particular opinion on something or a desire to do something, it is better to say *I don't mind* rather than *I don't care*, which can be perceived as rude. Similarly, instead of saying directly that you do not want to do something, it is often better to say that you are *not keen on doing something*.

Vagueness: certainty or uncertainty

When you are making a statement or expressing an idea, you will very often 'modify' what you are saying by using adverbials that express a degree of certainty or uncertainty. For example, if you say *'I'll **probably** go to the party'*, it means that you are not entirely sure that you will, and you want your listener to be aware of your uncertainty. If you say *'I'll **definitely** go to the party'*, you want your listener to know that you are certain to go the party.

You can also use modal verbs to express these feelings and attitudes. For more examples, see the **Language Notes** on **Modal verbs**, and also the language functions below, which explain about politeness and formality in more detail.

Advising someone

The usual way to advise someone is to say **you should...** or **you ought to...**

My tooth hurts.	**You should** *see a dentist.*
Our cat's really fat.	**You shouldn't** *give him so much food then.*
I'm really stressed out.	**You ought to** *try and relax more.*

This can sound quite direct. If you want to make it clear that it is only your opinion or suggestion, you can say **If I were you I'd...** or **I think the best thing is to...**, or you can put your advice in the form of a question and say **Why don't you...?** or **Have you thought of/considered...?**

The car's really hard to start in the mornings.	**If I were you I'd** *take it to a garage.*
I'm really worried about my job.	**Why don't you** *take some time off?*

With people you know very well, you can use much more direct expressions.

> *We're thinking of getting married.*   **Don't do it!**
> *I'm going to give up my course.*   **You mustn't do that!**

If you are advising someone based on your own personal experience, you often begin or end your advice with **take it from me**, or **take my advice**.

> *Dating someone you work with is not always a good idea – **take it from me**!*

Ageeing and disagreeing

Agreeing

> *People should stop using their cars and start using public transport.*   **I agree**. *The roads are too crowded as it is.*
> *I think we've waited long enough.*   **You're right**. *Let's go home.*
> *Why don't we go to the pub?*   **Good idea**.
> *The most important thing is quality.*   **Good point**. (=used in discussions)
> *That meeting was so boring.*   **I know**. *I thought it would never end.*

Agreeing strongly

> *If people do the same work, they should get paid the same money.*   **Absolutely/Exactly/I couldn't agree more!**
> *It's a bit hot today, isn't it?*   **You're telling me!** (=informal)

Agreeing partly

> *You should go and apologize to her.*   **I suppose so**, *but it's not going to be easy.*
> *He has his good points.*   **I guess so**, *but he keeps them well hidden.*

Disagreeing

> *It's really expensive to fly to Paris.*   **No, it isn't**. *It's really cheap.*
> *Women are much tidier than men.*   **That's not right**. *Some men are incredibly tidy.*
> *It's always better to travel alone.*   **That's not** always **true**. *Sometimes it can be really boring.*
> *It's supposed to be a brilliant film.*   **That's not what I've heard**. (=used when saying what other people have told you)
> *Too much money has been wasted on project development.*   **I really don't/can't accept that**.

Disagreeing politely

Just saying 'no' or 'that's not true' can sound very direct, especially when speaking to people you do not know well. If you say **I'm not so sure** or **Are you quite sure (about that)?**, you avoid contradicting what the other person is saying and you sound more polite.

Disagreeing partly

If you disagree with part of what someone is saying, or you think that another thing is far more important, you say **I take/see your point, but...** or **point taken but...**

> *Cheap food means that everyone can afford to eat well.*   **I take/see your point, but** *what about the long-term effects on the environment?*

Disagreeing strongly

If you disagree strongly with someone you know well, you can use direct, informal expressions.

I'm so fat.	**Nonsense!** *You're not fat at all.*
It's all your fault!	**No way!** *It was nothing to do with me.*
The journey shouldn't take more	**You can't be serious!** *It's at least two*
than an hour.	*hours.*

❶ If you use these expressions with people you do not know well, you will often sound very aggressive and rude.

Apologizing

The usual way to apologize is to say **I'm sorry** or just **sorry**. If you are apologizing for something serious, you can say **I'm really sorry**, **I'm awfully/terribly sorry**, or **I'm so sorry**.

Sorry I'm late – the traffic was terrible!
I'm so sorry about the vase. I'll pay for a new one.

In official situations, for example when addressing customers and the public in official announcements, or in formal letters, people say:

We would like to apologize for the delay to your train.
My apologies for not replying earlier.

When apologizing for something not very serious, for example when you have accidentally bumped into someone, you can say **Excuse me** or **I beg your pardon**.

Excuse me! I didn't realize I was standing on your foot!
'That's my seat!' 'Oh, I beg your pardon!'

What to say when someone apologizes

If someone apologizes, you can say **That's OK**, **That's all right**, or **Don't worry about it** to show that you are not bothered by what has happened. In informal English you can also say **No problem**, or **It's no big deal**.

Asking, giving and refusing permission

Asking permission

The usual way to ask permission is to say **Can I...?** **May I...?** is more polite and a little more formal. **Is it all right/OK if I...?** is a little more informal.

Can I go home? | *May I ask you a question?*
Is it all right/OK if I bring a friend?

If you do not know the other person well, or if you think they are likely to refuse, you usually use more indirect expressions, for example **Do you mind if I...?** or **Would you mind if I...?**

Do you mind if I join you? | *Would you mind if I looked at the letter?*
Would it be OK if I left early?

Giving permission

The simplest way of giving permission is to say **yes**. People often use other words instead, for example **of course**, **sure**, and **go ahead**. In more formal English, people say **certainly** and **by all means**.

Can I borrow your paper?	*Of course./Sure.*
Is it all right if I keep this photo?	*Yes, that's fine.*
Do you mind if I smoke?	*Go ahead.*
May I ask you a question?	*Please do!* (British English)
Could we have a copy of the article	*Certainly/By all means.*

Refusing permission

When refusing permission, just saying 'no' can seem very direct. People often say **sorry** or **I'm afraid...** and then give a reason.

Is it all right if I keep this photo?	***Sorry**, but I only have one copy.*
May I look at the files myself?	***I'm afraid** that won't be possible.*
Do you mind if I smoke?	***I'd rather you didn't**. (British English)*

Asking someone to do something

If you are asking for something straightforward and not difficult to do, you can be more direct and use expressions such as **Can you...?**, **Could you...?**, or **Will you...?**

*> **Could you** tell me her name? | **Will you** help me with these bags?*

If you are talking to someone you do not know well, or if you want to ask for something that might be difficult for the other person to do, you usually use more indirect expressions.

*> **Would you mind** waiting outside? | **Do you think you could** come back later?*
***I wonder if you could (possibly)** do some work for me this weekend?*

When asking for things in restaurants and bars, people usually say:

*> **I'll have** a cheese sandwich. | **Can I have** the bill, please?*

Inviting someone

If you know the person well, you can be informal.

*> **How about** a game of tennis? | **What about** dinner tomorrow night?*
***Do you fancy** a pizza? (=used in informal British English)*

If you do not know the person well, or if you think they may refuse, it is often safer to use a more polite expression.

*> **Would you like to** come out for a drink some time?*
***I was wondering if you'd like to** join us for dinner.*
***I hope you don't mind my asking, but** is this your newspaper?*

Accepting an invitation

Do you want to come over for a meal on Friday?	***Sure**.*
How about a drink after work?	***OK/I'd be delighted**. What time?*
Would you like to go skiing with us some time?	*Yes, **I'd like that very much**.*
Would you like to see a film?	***I'd love to**.*
Pizza?	***Cool!** (=I'd like that very much; used especially by young people)*

Refusing an invitation

Do you want to go bowling tonight?	***I'm sorry**, I've got to work.*
How about a drink?	***I'm afraid** I can't. I'm too busy right now.*
Would you like to come to a party this weekend?	***Thanks for asking, but** we're going away on holiday.*

What is collocation?

In English, you can talk about **heavy rain**, **light rain**, and, in British English, **pouring rain**. You do not talk about 'strong rain' or 'mild rain'. **Light** goes well with **rain**, while 'mild' does not. This sort of language behaviour is called collocation. There are lots of cases in English when it is difficult to know which words will go well with the word you want to use, because there are no clear rules. Some words sound right together, while others do not.

Verbs that collocate with nouns

If you want to use a noun in a sentence, you need to know which verb goes with it. For example at **bath**, it is useful to know that you **take a bath**, and that especially in British English people say **have a bath**.

Learners often make mistakes with these verbs. For example they say 'do an effort' instead of **make an effort**, 'do a crime' instead of **commit a crime**, or 'say a joke' instead of **tell a joke**, **make a joke** or **crack a joke**.

Adverbs that collocate with adjectives

There are a number of intensifying adverbs that can be used instead of 'very' or 'extremely' with adjectives, for example **highly controversial** (=very controversial), **deeply offended** (=very offended), and **bitterly disappointed** (=very disappointed).

Often it is difficult to predict which adverb will be used with a particular adjective; some adverbs occur surprisingly often before some adjectives, for example **perfectly normal** (=very normal) and **grossly misleading** (=very misleading).

  ✔ *bitterly ashamed/disappointed/cold* NOT ✗ 'bitterly successful'
  ✔ *highly successful/accomplished* NOT ✗ 'highly divided/grateful'
  ✔ *deeply divided/grateful/unpopular* NOT ✗ 'deeply developed'

Adjectives that collocate with nouns

When you want to describe a noun, there is often a range of different adjectives which you can use. For example when talking about something that might be possible, you can talk about a **strong**, **real**, or **distinct possibility** when something is very possible, or a **remote** or **faint possibility** if something is not very likely.

Helping with collocations

The *Longman Dictionary of Contemporary English* gives you a lot of help with collocations. Common collocations are highlighted in the examples. If the meaning of the collocation is not clear, an explanation is given in brackets. In addition, in over 300 entries, there are special boxes which list the important collocations and provide lots of examples.

---

doubt¹ [S1] [W1] /daʊt/ *n*
  1 [C,U] a feeling of being not sure whether something is true or right

> **have (your) doubts**
> **have no doubts at all**
> **raise doubts** (=make people have doubts)
> **express/voice doubts** (=say that you have doubts)
> **nagging/lingering doubt** (=a doubt that does not go away)
> **serious/grave doubts**
> **an element of doubt** (=a slight doubt)
> **there is little/some/no doubt (that)** (=used to talk about how certain you are about something)
> **not the slightest doubt** (=no doubt at all)
> **without a shadow of a doubt** (=with no doubt at all)
> **cast/throw doubt on sth** (=make someone feel uncertain about something)

Ally was confident that we would be ready on time, but I **had my doubts.** | [+about] *Elizabeth* **had no doubts at all** *about his ability to do the job.*

Extra on the CD-ROM

The CD-ROM of the dictionary contains all the text of the printed book, but in addition contains a further 173,000 collocations with examples.

M, m

M, **m** /em/ *plural* **M's**, **m's** *n* **1** [C,U] the 13th letter of the English alphabet **2** [C] the number 1000 in the system of ROMAN NUMERALS **3** **M6**, **M25** etc the name of a MOTORWAY in Britain

m *also* **m.** **1** the written abbreviation of *metre* or metres **2** the written abbreviation of *mile* or miles **3** the written abbreviation of *million* **4** the written abbreviation of *male* **5** the written abbreviation of *married* **6** the written abbreviation of *medium*, used on clothes to mean an average size

Ma /mɑː/ *ma* *n* [C] *informal* **1** mother: *What's for dinner, Ma?* **2** *old-fashioned* used to mean 'Mrs' in some country areas of the US: *old Ma Harris*

MA *BrE*; **M.A.** *AmE* /ˌem ˈeɪ/ *n* [C] **Master of Arts** a university degree in a subject such as history, languages, or English literature that you can get after your first degree: [+in] *He did an MA in graphic design at Manchester.* | *Vanessa Clark, MA*

ma'am /mæm, mɑːm, məm $ mæm/ *n* **1** *AmE spoken* used to address a woman in a polite and respectful way: *May I help you, ma'am?* **2** *BrE spoken* used to address the Queen or another woman in authority

mac, **mack** /mæk/ *n* [C] *BrE* a coat which you wear to keep out the rain; ⇒ **mackintosh**

Mac /mæk/ *n* **1** [C] *trademark informal* **(Apple) Macintosh** a type of personal computer; → **PC**: *Can you run this software on a Mac?* **2** *AmE spoken old-fashioned* used to address a man whose name you do not know

ma·ca·bre /məˈkɑːbrə, -bə $ -brə, -bər/ *adj* very strange and unpleasant and connected with death or with people being seriously hurt: *a macabre tale* | *a macabre sense of humour*

ma·cad·am /məˈkædəm/ *n* [U] a road surface made of a mixture of broken stones and TAR or ASPHALT; ⇒ **tarmac** *BrE*

mac·a·da·mi·a /ˌmækəˈdeɪmiə/ *n* [C] a sweet white nut that grows on a tropical tree, or the tree that produces this nut

mac·a·ro·ni /ˌmækəˈrəʊni $ -ˈroʊ-/ *n* [U] a type of PASTA in the shape of small tubes: **macaroni cheese** *BrE*/**macaroni and cheese** *AmE* (=macaroni cooked with a cheese sauce); → see picture at PASTA

mac·a·roon /ˌmækəˈruːn/ *n* [C] a small round cake made of sugar, eggs, and crushed ALMONDS or COCONUT

ma·caw /məˈkɔː $ -ˈkɒː/ *n* [C] a large brightly coloured bird like a PARROT, with a long tail

mace /meɪs/ *n* **1** [U] a spice made from the dried shell of a NUTMEG **2** [C] a heavy ball with sharp points on a short metal stick, used in the past as a weapon **3** [C] a decorated stick that is carried by an official in some ceremonies as a sign of power; → **sceptre**

Mace *n* [U] *trademark* a chemical which makes your eyes and skin sting painfully. Police officers sometimes carry Mace in cans to defend themselves.

ma·cer·ate /ˈmæsəreɪt/ *v* [I,T] *technical* to make something soft by leaving it in water, or to become soft in this way

Mach /mæk $ mɑːk/ *n* [U] a unit for measuring speed, especially of an aircraft, in relation to the speed of sound. Mach 1 is the speed of sound, Mach 2 is twice the speed of sound etc: *a plane with a maximum speed of Mach 3*

ma·chet·e /məˈʃeti, məˈtʃeti/ *n* [C] a large knife with a broad heavy blade, used as a weapon or a tool: *a machete attack*

Mach·i·a·vel·li·an /ˌmækiəˈveliən/ *adj* using clever but immoral methods to get what you want; ⇒ **devious**

mach·i·na·tions /ˌmækɪˈneɪʃənz, ˌmæʃɪ-/ *n* [plural] *formal* secret, clever, and often unfair methods used to achieve something – used in order to show disapproval: [+of] *the political machinations of far right groups*

ma·chine¹ S1 W1 /məˈʃiːn/ *n* [C]

1 a piece of equipment with moving parts that uses power such as electricity to do a particular job: **washing/sewing etc machine** *Is the washing machine working now?* | *Could you get me a coffee from the drinks machine?* | *The fax machine is broken.* | **switch/turn a machine on/off** *Turn the machine off before removing the cover.* | **by machine** *The letters are sorted by machine.* | *Did you put my dirty shirts in the machine* (=washing machine)? | *I left a message for you on your machine* (=telephone answering machine). | *The machine* (=cash machine) *wouldn't let me have any money.* → ANSWERING MACHINE, CASH MACHINE, VENDING MACHINE
2 a computer: *My machine's just crashed.*
3 a group of people who control and organize something – often used to show disapproval: *the ruthless bureaucrats of the party machine* | *the government's propaganda machine* | *the powerful American war machine*
4 *informal* a vehicle, especially a MOTORBIKE: *Riders have to learn to handle their machines in all conditions.* | *That's a mean machine* (=very fast and attractive vehicle) *you have there.*
5 a person or animal that does something very well or without having to think about it: *In the tiger, nature has produced the perfect hunting machine.* | *I'm not a golfing machine. I make mistakes just like anyone else.*
6 someone who seems to behave like a machine and to have no feelings or thoughts; ⇒ **automaton**
7 a well-oiled machine something that works very smoothly and effectively: *The office runs like a well-oiled machine.*

WORD CHOICE: machine, device, gadget, appliance
A **machine** is a piece of equipment that uses power to do a particular job. It is usually large and stays in the same place: *a machine that sorts mail* | *a washing machine*
You use the words **device** and **gadget** especially when you think the equipment is very cleverly designed. A **device** is a piece of equipment that does a particular job, for example takes measurements or controls the operation of a machine. It may use electrical power or be used by hand: *a device for detecting blood alcohol levels from breath samples* | *a temperature control device*
A **gadget** is a small piece of equipment that does something useful or impressive: *one of those gadgets that sorts coins* | *kitchen gadgets*
An **appliance** is a piece of electrical equipment used in your home such as a washing machine or fridge. This word is used especially by the companies that produce and sell them: *the world's largest producer of household appliances* | *domestic appliances*

---

machine² *v* [T] **1** to fasten pieces of cloth together using a sewing machine **2** to make or shape something using a machine

ma·chine ˌcode, **ma·chine ˌlanguage** *n* [C,U] *technical* instructions in the form of numbers that are put into a computer

ma·chine gun *n* [C] a gun that fires a lot of bullets very quickly: *There came the sound of men shouting and a burst of machine-gun fire.*

ma·chine-gun *v* **machine-gunned**, **machine-gunning** [T] to shoot at someone or something with a machine gun: *His corporal had been machine-gunned in an ambush.*

ma·chine-head *n* [C] a small button attached to the strings on an instrument such as a GUITAR that you turn in order to make the instrument play in tune

M

ma·chine-made *adj* made using a machine; ⊟ **handmade**

ma,chine-'readable *adj* in a form that can be understood and used by a computer: *information stored in machine-readable form*

ma·chin·e·ry ⓢ₃ /məˈʃiːnəri/ *n* [U]
1 machines, especially large ones: **agricultural/industrial/factory etc machinery** | *The use of heavy machinery has damaged the site.* | *an expensive piece of machinery*
2 a system or set of processes for doing something: [+of] *the machinery of government* | **machinery for (doing) sth** *The company has no effective machinery for resolving disputes.*
3 the parts inside a machine that make it work: *Be careful not to get anything caught in the machinery.*

ma'chine ,tool *n* [C] a tool for cutting and shaping metal, wood etc, usually one that uses electricity

ma'chine ,washable *adj* if clothes are machine washable, it is possible to wash them in a washing machine safely

ma·chin·ist /məˈʃiːnɪst/ *n* [C] someone who operates a machine, especially in a factory: *All the women are highly-skilled machinists.*

ma·chis·mo /məˈtʃɪzməʊ, -ˈkɪz- $ maːˈtʃɪzmoʊ, mə-/ *n* [U] traditional male behaviour that emphasizes how brave, strong, and sexually attractive a man is

mach·o /ˈmætʃəʊ $ ˈmaːtʃoʊ/ *adj informal* behaving in a way that is traditionally typical of men, for example being strong or brave, or not showing your feelings – used humorously or in order to show disapproval: *He's sick of being cast as the hard **macho man** in films.* | *a car with a macho image*

Mac·in·tosh /ˈmækɪntɒʃ $ -taːʃ/ also **Apple Macintosh** also **Mac** *informal n* [C] *trademark* a type of personal computer

mack /mæk/ *n BrE* another spelling of MAC

mack·e·rel /ˈmækərəl/ *n plural* **mackerel** [C,U] a sea fish that has oily flesh and a strong taste: *smoked mackerel*

mack·in·tosh /ˈmækɪntɒʃ $ -taːʃ/ *n* [C] *BrE old-fashioned* a coat which you wear to keep out the rain; ⊟ **mac, raincoat**

ma·cra·mé /məˈkraːmi $ ˌmækrəˈmeɪ/ *n* [U] the art of tying string in patterns to make things

mac·ro /ˈmækrəʊ $ -roʊ/ *n plural* **macros** [C] a set of instructions for a computer, stored and used as a unit: *You can run a macro to change to US spelling.*

macro- /mækrəʊ $ -roʊ/ *prefix technical* large and concerning a whole system rather than particular parts of it; ⊟ **micro**: *macroeconomics* | *macromolecular structures*

mac·ro·bi·ot·ic /ˌmækrəʊbaɪˈɒtɪk◂ $ -kroʊbaɪˈaːtɪk/ *adj* macrobiotic food consists mainly of grains and vegetables, with no added chemicals: *a healthy macrobiotic diet*

mac·ro·cos·m /ˈmækrəʊˌkɒzəm $ -kroʊˌkaː-/ *n* [C] a large, complicated system such as the whole universe or a society, considered as a single unit; ⊟ **microcosm**

mac·ro·ec·o·nom·ics /ˌmækrəʊekəˈnɒmɪks, -iːkə- $ -kroʊekəˈnaː-, -iːkə-/ *n* [U] the study of large economic systems such as those of a whole country or area of the world; → **microeconomics** —**macroeconomic** *adj*

mad ⓢ₂ ⓦ₃ /mæd/ *adj comparative* **madder**, *superlative* **maddest**
1 ANGRY [not before noun] *informal especially AmE* angry; [+at] *Are you still mad at me?* | *We get mad at each other sometimes, like any family.* | [+about] *There's no need to get mad about it!* | *You make make me so mad!* | [+with] *BrE: His wife will be really mad with him.* | **go mad** *BrE* (=become very angry) *Look at this mess! Mum will go mad!* | **hopping mad** (=very angry) | **(as) mad as hell** (=a rude way of saying very angry)

2 CRAZY *especially BrE* crazy or very silly: *He can't possibly get that finished in time. He must be mad!* | *I'd go mad* (=start to feel crazy) *if I was stuck at home all day.* | *He's been driving me mad recently!* | *You've agreed to marry him! Are you mad?* | *Surely no one would be mad enough to fly in this weather?* | *My friends all think I'm stark raving mad* (=completely crazy). | *It's enough to send you barking mad* (=completely crazy). | **as mad as a hatter/March hare** (=completely crazy)

3 UNCONTROLLED *especially BrE* behaving in a wild uncontrolled way, without thinking about what you are doing: **mad dash/rush/panic etc** *We all made a mad dash for the door.* | **mad with grief/fear/jealousy etc** *When she heard of her son's death, she was mad with grief.* | *When Italy scored, the crowd went mad* (=became very excited). | *We went a bit mad* (=spent a lot of money) *and ordered champagne.*
4 be mad about/for/on sb/sth *informal especially BrE* to like someone or something very much; ⊟ **crazy**: *My nine-year-old is mad about Robbie Williams.* | *He's mad about computer games.* | *All the girls at school are mad for him.* | **be mad keen (on sth)** *'Did you enjoy the film?' 'I wasn't mad keen.'* | **be mad for it** (=want to do something very much)
5 MENTALLY ILL *especially BrE old-fashioned informal* mentally ill; ⊟ **insane**: *Mr Rochester's mad wife* | *He turned towards me with a mad look in his eyes.* | *the cartoon figure of the mad scientist*
6 like mad *informal* very much, very quickly, or with a lot of energy: *I caught my thumb in the door and it hurt like mad.* | *She ran like mad to catch the bus.*
7 don't go mad *BrE spoken* used to tell someone not to work too hard, get too excited, or spend too much money: *I know you've got a lot to do but don't go mad.*
8 power-mad/money-mad/sex-mad etc only interested in having power, money etc and doing everything possible to get it: *a power-mad dictator*

mad·am /ˈmædəm/ *n* **1** *formal* used to address a woman in a polite way, especially a customer in a shop; ⊟ **ma'am** *AmE*: *Are you being served, Madam?* **2 Dear Madam** *formal* used at the beginning of a business letter to a woman, when you do not know her name **3 Madam President/Ambassador etc** used to address a woman who has an important official position **4** [C] a woman who is in charge of a BROTHEL **5 a (proper) little madam** *BrE informal* a young girl who is very confident and who expects other people to do everything she wants

Mad·ame /ˈmædəm, məˈdaːm/ *n plural* **Mesdames** /meɪˈdæm $ -ˈdaːm/ used to address or refer to a French-speaking woman, especially one who is married; → **Mademoiselle, Monsieur**: *Madame Lefevre*

mad·cap /ˈmædkæp/ *adj* [only before noun] *old-fashioned* **1** a madcap idea seems crazy and unlikely to succeed: *a madcap scheme* **2** a madcap person behaves in a crazy and often funny way: *He plays a madcap game show host.*

,mad 'cow dis,ease *n* [U] *informal* BSE

mad·den /ˈmædn/ *v* [T usually passive] *literary* to make someone very angry or annoyed: *The unfortunate animal was maddened with pain.*

mad·den·ing /ˈmædənɪŋ/ *adj* very annoying; ⊟ **infuriating**: *maddening delays* —**maddeningly** *adv*: *He moved carefully and maddeningly slowly.*

made /meɪd/ *v* **1** the past tense and past participle of MAKE **2 factory-made/German-made/homemade etc** made in a factory, in Germany, at home etc: *sales of Japanese-made cars* **3 have (got) it made** *informal* to have everything that you need for success or for a happy life: *Nice house, good job, lovely family – you've got it made!* **4 see/find out what sb is (really) made of** *informal* to find out how strong, brave etc someone is or how skilful they are at doing something: *Come on then! Let's see what you're made of.* **5 I'm not made of money** *spoken* used when someone has asked you to pay for something in order to say that you cannot afford it and that you think they are being unreasonable: *I can't buy* you shoes as well – I'm not made of money! **6 be made for each other** informal to be completely suitable for each other, especially as husband and wife: Jacinta and Dermot were made for each other. **7 be made (for life)** informal to be so rich that you will never have to work again: If the deal is successful, I'll be made for life.

Ma·dei·ra /mə'dɪərə $ -'dɪrə/ n [U] a strong sweet wine

Ma'deira cake n [C,U] a kind of plain yellow cake

Mad·e·moi·selle /ˌmædəmwə'zel/ n plural **Mesdemoiselles** /ˌmeɪdəmwə'zel/ used to address or refer to a young French-speaking woman who is not married; → **Madame, Monsieur**: Mademoiselle Dubois

made-to-'measure adj made-to-measure clothes, curtains etc are specially made to fit; ◻ **off-the-peg**

made-to-'order adj made-to-order clothing, furniture etc is made for one particular customer: made-to-order curtains

'made-up adj **1** a story, name, word etc that is made-up is not true or real: She invented a made-up name. **2** wearing MAKE-UP on your face: She was **heavily made-up** (=wearing a lot of make-up).

mad·house /'mædhaʊs/ n [C usually singular] **1** a place with a lot of people, noise, and activity: It's like a madhouse in here. **2** old use a PSYCHIATRIC hospital

mad·ly /'mædli/ adv **1** extremely and in a very strong way: She fell **madly in love** with him. | Suddenly, I felt madly jealous. **2** in a wild, uncontrolled way: The sign swung madly in the wind.

mad·man /'mædmən/ n plural **madmen** /-mən/ [C] **1** someone who behaves in a wild, uncontrolled way: He drives **like a madman**. **2** old-fashioned a man who is mentally ill

'mad ˌmoney n [U] AmE informal money that you have saved so that you can spend it when you see something you want

mad·ness /'mædn‿s/ n [U] **1** especially BrE very stupid behaviour that could be dangerous or have a very bad effect: **it is madness (for sb) to do sth** It would be madness to drive all that way on your own. | Cutting down the forest is **sheer madness** (=completely crazy). **2** serious mental illness; ◻ **insanity**: His family has a history of madness. **3** **moment/fit of madness** when someone does something without thinking clearly: In a moment of madness, I agreed to have the party at my house. → **there's method in/to sb's madness** at METHOD (3)

Ma·don·na /mə'dɒnə $ mə'dɑː-/ n **1 the Madonna** Mary, the mother of Jesus, in the Christian religion **2** [C] a picture or figure of Mary

mad·ri·gal /'mædrɪɡəl/ n [C] a song for several singers without musical instruments, popular in the 16th century

mad·wom·an /'mædwʊmən/ n plural **madwomen** /-ˌwɪmɪn/ [C] old-fashioned a woman who is mentally ill

mael·strom /'meɪlstrəm/ n [C] **1** a confusing situation full of events or strong emotions that is difficult to understand or deal with; ◻ **whirlpool**: [+of] a maelstrom of conflicting emotions **2** dust or water that moves very quickly in circles: A spinning maelstrom of rain swept around the mountain. **3** a violent storm

maes·tro /'maɪstrəʊ $ -roʊ/ n plural **maestros** [C] someone who can do something very well, especially a musician

maf·i·a /'mæfiə $ 'mɑː-, ˌmæ-/ n **1 the Mafia** a large organized group of criminals who control many illegal activities, especially in Italy and the US **2** [singular] a powerful group of people within an organization or profession who support and protect each other: the medical mafia

maf·i·o·so /ˌmæfi'əʊsəʊ $ ˌmɑːfi'oʊsoʊ, ˌmæ-/ n plural **mafiosi** /-si/ [C] a member of the Mafia

mag /mæɡ/ n [C] informal a magazine: music mags

mag·a·zine ⟨S2⟩ ⟨W2⟩ /ˌmæɡə'ziːn $ 'mæɡəziːn/ n [C] **1** a large thin book with a paper cover that contains news stories, articles, photographs etc, and is sold weekly or monthly: **fashion/computer/women's etc magazine** a glossy fashion magazine | She's the editor of a popular women's magazine. | a magazine article | She glanced over the magazine racks. **2** a television or radio programme which is made up of a number of reports: a local news magazine programme **3** the part of a gun that holds the bullets **4** the part that holds the film in a camera or PROJECTOR **5** a room or building for storing weapons, explosives etc

ma·gen·ta /mə'dʒentə/ n [U] a dark reddish purple colour —**magenta** adj

mag·got /'mæɡət/ n [C] a small creature like a WORM that is the young form of a FLY and lives in decaying food, flesh etc

Ma·gi /'meɪdʒaɪ/ n **the Magi** [plural] the three wise men who brought gifts to the baby Jesus, according to the Christian religion

ma·gic¹ /'mædʒɪk/ n [U] **1** the ability of particular people in children's stories to make impossible things happen by saying special words: Do you believe in magic? → **BLACK MAGIC, WHITE MAGIC 2** a special, attractive, or exciting quality: Paris has **lost** some of its **magic** for me over the years. | [+of] the magic of Christmas **3** the skill of doing tricks that look like magic in order to entertain people, or the tricks that are done; ◻ **conjuring 4** **like magic/as if by magic** in a surprising way that seems impossible to explain: As if by magic the waiter suddenly appeared with a tray of drinks. **5** **work/weave your magic** if something or someone works or weaves their magic, they produce a good change or effect in a way that they are often able to do: The warm weather and the beautiful scenery began to work their magic and she started to relax. **6** **work like magic** to be very effective

magic² adj **1** [only before noun] in stories, a magic word or object has special powers that make the person using it able to do impossible things: a book of **magic spells** | a magic sword **2** relating to the skill of doing tricks to entertain people: His best **magic trick** is sawing a lady in half. **3** **magic number/word** a number or word that is particularly important or desired in a particular situation: The magic words 'a million pounds' will get everyone's attention. **4** **the magic word** the word 'please' – used when speaking to children: What's the magic word then, Katie? **5** **magic touch** a special ability to make things work well or to make people happy: She's got a magic touch with babies. **6** **magic moment** a short time which seems beautiful and special: She didn't want to spoil this magic moment. **7** **magic circle** a group of powerful people who are friendly with each other and help each other: His outspokenness denied him access to the magic circle and he was never given high office. **8** BrE spoken very good or very enjoyable; ◻ **great**: 'Did you have a good time?' 'Yeah, it was magic!'

magic³ v **magicked, magicking** BrE

magic sb/sth away phr v to make someone or something disappear or go somewhere by using magic: I wish I could magic us away to a warm beach.

magic sth ⇔ up phr v to make something appear suddenly and unexpectedly

ma·gic·al /'mædʒɪkəl/ adj **1** very enjoyable, exciting or romantic, in a strange or special way: that magical evening we spent together **2** relating to magic or able to do magic: magical powers —**magically** /-kli/ adv

magic 'bullet n [C] **1** a drug or treatment that can cure a disease or illness quickly and easily **2** informal something that solves a difficult problem in an easy way: There's no magic bullet for school reform.

magic 'carpet n [C] in stories, a CARPET that can fly through the air and carry people from one place to another

magic 'eye n [C] a PHOTOELECTRIC CELL

ma·gi·cian /mə'dʒɪʃən/ n [C] **1** a man in stories who can use magic; ▤ **sorcerer, wizard 2** an entertainer who performs magic tricks; ▤ **conjurer**

magic 'lantern n [C] a piece of equipment used in the past to make pictures shine onto a wall or screen

Magic 'Marker n [C,U] trademark a large pen with a thick soft point

magic 'mushroom n [C] a type of MUSHROOM that has an effect like some drugs, and makes you see things that are not really there

magic 'realism, also **magical 'realism** n [U] a style in literature that combines ordinary events with ones like dreams

magic 'wand n [C] **1** a stick used by a MAGICIAN **2** a way to solve problems or difficulties immediately – used humorously: *I wish I could just wave a magic wand and make everything all right.*

ma·gis·te·ri·al /ˌmædʒə'stɪəriəl◂ $ -'stɪr-/ adj **1** a magisterial way of behaving or speaking shows that you think you have authority: *his magisterial voice* **2** a magisterial book is written by someone who has very great knowledge about a subject: *his magisterial study of the First World War* **3** [only before noun] connected with or done by a magistrate —**magisterially** adv

ma·gis·tra·cy /'mædʒɪ̸strəsi/ n [U] **1** the official position of a magistrate, or the time during which someone has this position **2 the magistracy** magistrates considered together as a group

ma·gis·trate /'mædʒɪ̸streɪt, -strɪt/ n [C] someone, not usually a lawyer, who works as a judge in a local court of law, dealing with less serious crimes; ▤ **Justice of the Peace**

Magistrates' Court n [C] one of the courts of law in each area of England and Wales which deal with less serious crimes

mag·ma /'mægmə/ n [U] technical hot melted rock below the surface of the Earth → see picture at VOLCANO

mag·na cum lau·de /ˌmægnə kʊm 'laʊdeɪ, -kʌm 'lɔːdi $ -kʊm 'laʊdi/ adj, adv with high honour – used to show that someone has finished American high school or college at the second of the three highest levels of achievement that students can reach; → **cum laude, summa cum laude**

mag·nan·i·mous /mæg'nænɪ̸məs/ adj kind and generous, especially to someone that you have defeated: *a magnanimous gesture* —**magnanimously** adv —**magnanimity** /ˌmægnə'nɪmɪ̸ti/ n [U]

mag·nate /'mægneɪt, -nɪ̸t/ n [C] a rich and powerful person in industry or business; ▤ **tycoon: steel/oil/shipping etc magnate** *a powerful media magnate*

mag·ne·sia /mæg'niːʃə, -ʒə/ n → MILK OF MAGNESIA

mag·ne·si·um /mæg'niːziəm/ n [U] a common silver-white metal that burns with a bright white flame. It is a chemical ELEMENT: symbol Mg

mag·net /'mægnɪ̸t/ n [C] **1** a piece of iron or steel that can stick to metal or make other metal objects move towards itself **2** something or someone that attracts many people or things: [+for] *The region has become a magnet for small businesses.* | **attract/draw sb/sth like a magnet** *She drew near to her like a magnet.*

mag·net·ic /mæg'netɪk/ adj **1** concerning or produced by MAGNETISM: *magnetic forces* **2** having the power of a magnet or behaving like a magnet: **3 magnetic personality/charm etc** qualities that make other people feel strongly attracted to you —**magnetically** /-kli/ adv

mag,netic 'disk n [C] a DISK containing MAGNETIC TAPE that stores information to be used by a computer

mag,netic 'field n [C] an area around an object that has magnetic power: *the Earth's magnetic field*

mag,netic 'media n [plural, U] magnetic methods of storing information for computers, for example FLOPPY DISKS or MAGNETIC TAPE

mag,netic 'north n [U] the northern direction shown by the needle on a COMPASS → TRUE NORTH

mag,netic 'pole n [C] **1** one of the two points that are not firmly fixed but are near the North and South Poles of the Earth, towards which the needle on a COMPASS points **2** one of two points at the ends of a MAGNET where its power is strongest

mag,netic 'resonance ,imaging n [U] medical **MRI** the process of using strong MAGNETIC FIELDS to make an image of the inside of someone's body for medical reasons

mag,netic 'tape n [U] tape on which sound, pictures, or computer information can be recorded

mag·net·is·m /'mægnɪ̸tɪzəm/ n [U] **1** the physical force that makes two metal objects pull towards each other or push each other apart **2** if someone has magnetism, they have powerful exciting qualities that attract people to them: *his personal magnetism*

mag·net·ize also **-ise** BrE /'mægnɪ̸taɪz/ v [T] **1** to make iron or steel able to pull other pieces of metal towards itself **2** to have a powerful effect on people so that they feel strongly attracted to you: *His dark flashing eyes seemed to magnetize her.* —**magnetization** /ˌmægnɪ̸taɪ'zeɪʃən $ -tə-/ n [U]

mag·ne·to /mæg'niːtəʊ $ -toʊ/ n plural **magnetos** [C] a piece of equipment containing one or more MAGNETS that is used for producing electricity, especially in the engine of a car

'magnet ,school n [C] AmE a school that has more classes in a particular subject than usual, and so attracts students from a wide area

mag·ni·fi·ca·tion /ˌmægnɪ̸fɪ̸'keɪʃən/ n **1** [U] the process of making something look bigger than it is: **at high/low etc magnification** *When viewed at high magnification it is clear that the crystals are quite different.* | **greater levels of magnification** *The colour is evident even under low magnification.* **2** [C] the degree to which something is able to make things look bigger: *binoculars with a magnification of x12* (=which make things look 12 times as big)

mag·nif·i·cent /mæg'nɪfɪ̸sənt/ adj very good or beautiful, and very impressive: *a magnificent performance* | *The twelve-mile coastline has magnificent scenery.* | *She looked magnificent in a long red dress.* —**magnificently** adv —**magnificence** n [U]

mag·ni·fi·er /'mægnɪfaɪə $ -ər/ n [C] an object which makes things look bigger

mag·ni·fy /'mægnɪ̸faɪ/ v **magnified, magnifying, magnifies** [T] **1** to make something seem bigger or louder, especially using special equipment: *At the Sheffield arena, the speakers were magnified ten times on a giant screen.* | *A public address system magnifies all the little noises and coughs.* **2** to make something seem more important than it really is; ▤ **exaggerate:** *The report tends to magnify the risks involved.* **3** formal to make something much worse or more serious: *The results of economic mismanagement were magnified by a series of natural disasters.*

'magnifying ,glass n [C] a round piece of glass with a handle, used to make objects or print look bigger → MAGNIFY; → see picture at OPTICAL

mag·ni·tude /'mægnɪ̸tjuːd $ -tuːd/ n **1** [U] the great size or importance of something: [+of] *They didn't seem to appreciate the magnitude of the problem.* | **of such/this/similar etc magnitude** *We did not think the cuts would be of this magnitude.* | *an increase of this order of magnitude* (=size) **2** [C] technical the degree of brightness of a star **3** [C] technical the force of an EARTHQUAKE

mag·no·li·a /mæɡˈnəʊliə $ -ˈnoʊ-/ n **1** [C] a tree with large white, pink, yellow, or purple flowers **2** [U] a very pale cream colour —**magnolia** adj

mag·num /ˈmæɡnəm/ n [C] **1** a large bottle containing about 1.5 litres of wine, CHAMPAGNE etc **2** a powerful type of gun that you can use with one hand: *a .44 magnum* → see picture at BOTTLE[1]

magnum 'opus n [singular] the most important piece of work by a writer or artist

mag·pie /ˈmæɡpaɪ/ n [C] **1** a bird with black and white feathers and a long tail **2** informal someone who likes collecting things

ma·ha·ra·jah, **maharaja** /ˌmɑːhəˈrɑːdʒə/ n [C] an Indian prince or king

ma·ha·ra·ni, **maharanee** /ˌmɑːhəˈrɑːniː/ n [C] an Indian PRINCESS or queen

ma·ha·rish·i /ˌmɑːhəˈriːʃi/ n [C] a Hindu holy teacher

ma·hat·ma /məˈhætmə $ məˈhɑːt-/ n a title used for a wise and holy man in India

mah·jong, **mahjongg** /ˌmɑː ˈdʒɒŋ $ -ˈʒɑːŋ/ n [U] a Chinese game played with small pieces of wood or bone

ma·hog·a·ny /məˈhɒɡəni $ məˈhɑː-/ n plural **mahoganies 1** [C,U] a type of hard reddish brown wood used for making furniture, or the tree that produces this wood **2** [U] a dark, reddish brown colour —**mahogany** adj

ma·hout /mɑːˈhuːt, məˈhaʊt $ məˈhaʊt/ n [C] someone who rides and trains ELEPHANTS

maid /meɪd/ n [C] **1** a female servant, especially in a large house or hotel: *a kitchen maid* **2** old use a woman or girl who is not married → OLD MAID

maid·en[1] /ˈmeɪdn/ n [C] **1** literary a young girl, or a woman who is not married; ◼ **damsel 2** also **maiden over** in CRICKET, an OVER in which no runs are scored

maiden[2] adj **1 maiden flight/voyage** the first journey that a plane or ship makes **2 maiden speech** BrE the first speech that someone makes in parliament

maiden 'aunt n [C] old-fashioned an AUNT who has never married

maid·en·head /ˈmeɪdnhed/ n old use **1** [U] the state of being a female VIRGIN; ◼ **virginity 2** [C] a HYMEN

maid·en·ly /ˈmeɪdnli/ adj literary old-fashioned used to describe the behaviour of a girl or young woman who is shy about showing her body, talking about sex etc, especially in the past: *maidenly modesty*

'maiden name n [C] a woman's family name before she got married and started using her husband's family name; → **married name**

,maid of 'honour BrE; **maid of honor** AmE n plural **maids of honour** [C] **1** the most important BRIDESMAID at a wedding **2** an unmarried woman who works for a queen or a PRINCESS

maid·ser·vant /ˈmeɪdˌsɜːvənt $ -ɜːr-/ n [C] old-fashioned a female servant

mail[1] S3 W3 /meɪl/ n [U]
1 the letters and packages that are delivered to you: *She's been reading my private mail.* | *When he got to the office he found a mountain of mail waiting for him.* | *He promised to **forward my mail** to my new address.* (=send it from my old home or office) | *He gets sacks of **fan mail**.* (=letters from people who admire him and are his fans) | **hate mail** (=letters from people saying that they hate you)
2 especially AmE the system of collecting and delivering letters and packages; ◼ **post** BrE: *The mail here's really slow and unreliable.* | *The product will be sold mainly through the mail.* | *I'll put the check in the mail tomorrow.* | **by mail** *Did you send the document by mail?* | **registered/express/first-class etc mail** *I sent my application by registered mail.* | *Most reports are sent via **internal mail** (=a system of sending documents to people inside the same organization).*
3 messages that are sent and received on a computer; ◼ **email**: *You should always check your incoming mail*

(=messages that you receive) *every day.* | *Please read the **mail message** for information on the error.*
4 ARMOUR made of small pieces of metal, worn by soldiers in the Middle Ages → VOICE MAIL

mail[2] S3 v [T] especially AmE
1 to send a letter or package to someone; ◼ **post** BrE: **mail sth to sb** *The weekly newsletter is mailed to women all over the country.*
2 to send a document to someone using a computer; ◼ **email**: **mail sth to sb** *Can you mail it to me as an attachment?*
mail sth ⇔ **out** phr v
to send letters, packages etc to a lot of people at the same time; ◼ **send out**: *The department has just mailed out 300,000 notices.*

mail·bag /ˈmeɪlbæɡ/ n [C] **1** a large, strong bag used for carrying mail on trains etc **2** AmE a bag used to deliver letters to people's houses; ◼ **postbag** BrE

mail·bomb /ˈmeɪlbɒm $ -bɑːm/ n [C] a large number of email messages sent to the same computer, with the result that the computer has too much email and cannot work properly any more

mail·box /ˈmeɪlbɒks $ -bɑːks/ n [C] AmE **1** a box, usually outside a house, where someone's letters are delivered or collected → see picture at POSTBOX **2** a container where you post letters; ◼ **postbox** BrE **3** the part of a computer's memory where email messages are stored

'mail ,carrier n [C] AmE old-fashioned someone whose job is to deliver mail; ◼ **mailman**

'mail drop n [C] AmE **1** an address where someone's mail is delivered, which is not where they live **2** a box in a post office where your mail can be left

mail·er /ˈmeɪlə $ -ər/ n [C] especially AmE a container or envelope used for sending something small by post

mail·ing /ˈmeɪlɪŋ/ n **1** [C] something that is sent to people by post, especially to advertise something: *A catalogue and order form are included with this mailing.* | *A mailing had gone out to every school in the country.* **2** [C,U] the process of sending something to people by post: *A very effective mailing of product samples was carried out last year.* | *mailing costs*

'mailing list n [C] **1** a list of names and addresses kept by an organization, so that it can send information or advertising material by post: **on a mailing list** *I have included you on my mailing list for new EFL software.* **2** a list of names and email addresses kept on a computer so that you can send the same message to a group of people at the same time

mail·man /ˈmeɪlmæn/ n plural **mailmen** /-men/ [C] AmE someone who delivers letters and packages to people's houses; ◼ **postman** BrE

,mail 'order n [U] a method of buying and selling in which the buyer chooses goods at home and orders them from a company which sends them by post: **by mail order** *It is available by mail order from Green Life Products.* | *a mail order catalogue*

mail·shot /ˈmeɪlʃɒt $ -ʃɑːt/ n [C] advertisements or information that a company sends to many people at one time by post: *We're sending out a mailshot telling our customers about our new products.*

'mail slot n [C] AmE a LETTERBOX

'mail train n [C] a train that carries letters and packages

maim /meɪm/ v [T] to wound or injure someone very seriously and often permanently: *Landmines still kill or maim about 300 people every month.*

main¹ S1 W1 /meɪn/ adj [only before noun]
1 bigger or more important than all other things, ideas etc of the same kind: *The main reason for living in Spain is the weather.* | *What do you consider to be the main problem?* | *Our main concern is that the children are safe.* | *a summary of the main points of the agreement* | *the main aim of the meeting* | *I'll meet you outside the main entrance.* | *the main bedroom*
2 the main thing *spoken* used to say what is the most important thing in a situation: *As long as you're not hurt, that's the main thing.* | *The main thing is not to panic.* → **an eye for/on/to the main chance** at EYE¹ (22)

main² n **1** [C] a large pipe or wire carrying the public supply of water, electricity, or gas: *The report found that many of Yorkshire's water mains needed replacing.* | *a burst gas main* **2** BrE **a) the mains** the place on a wall where you can connect something to a supply of electricity: *You can run the torch off batteries or plug it into the mains.* | **at the mains** *Make sure that the television is turned off at the mains.* **b) mains gas/water/electricity** gas, water, or electricity supplied to a building through a pipe or wire: *The heater will run off mains gas or bottled gas.* **3 in the main** mostly: *Their job in the main consisted of cleaning and maintaining the building.*

,main 'clause n [C] *technical* a CLAUSE that can stand alone as a complete sentence; → **subordinate clause**

,main 'course n [C] the main part of a meal: *What are you going to have for your main course?* | *starter, main course and dessert*

,main 'drag n **the main drag** AmE *informal* the main street in a town or city where big shops and businesses are: *the restaurants that line the main drag*

main·frame /'meɪnfreɪm/ n [C] a large powerful computer that can work very fast and that a lot of people can use at the same time: *If a problem does occur, a signal is automatically sent to the mainframe.*

main·land /'meɪnlənd, -lænd/ n **the mainland** the main area of land that forms a country, as compared to islands near it that are also part of that country: *flights between a Greek island and the mainland* | **on the mainland** *terrorist attacks both in Northern Ireland and on the mainland* —**mainland** adj [only before noun]: *mainland Britain*

,main 'line n [C] an important railway that connects two cities: *the main line to Moscow* —**mainline** adj [only before noun]: *a mainline station*

main·line¹ /'meɪnlaɪn/ adj [only before noun] accepted by or involving most people in a society; = **mainstream**: *They explicitly denied that they are involved in mainline politics.*

mainline² v [I,T] *informal* to INJECT an illegal drug directly into your blood: *By that time he was mainlining heroin.*

main·ly S2 W2 /'meɪnli/ adv used to mention the main part or cause of something, the main reason for something etc: *Her illness was caused mainly by stress.* | *The workforce is mainly made up of women.* | *I don't go out much, mainly because I have to look after the kids.* | *Increased sales during the summer were mainly due to tourism.* | *We talked about various things – work, mainly.*

main·mast /'meɪnmɑːst, -məst $ -mæst, -məst/ n [C] the largest or most important of the MASTS on a ship

,main 'road n [C] a large and important road: *We live just off the main road.* | *[+to/from/between]* *the main road from Bern to Lausanne*

main·sail /'meɪnsəl $ -seɪl/ n [C] the largest and most important sail on a ship

main·spring /'meɪnsprɪŋ/ n [C] **1 the mainspring of sth** the most important reason or influence that makes something happen: *Christian faith was the mainspring of Peter's life.* | *Small companies are the mainspring of the British economy.* **2** the most important spring in a watch or clock

main·stay /'meɪnsteɪ/ n **the mainstay of sth a)** an important part of something that makes it possible for it to work properly or continue to exist: *Agriculture is still the mainstay of the country's economy.* **b)** someone who does most of the important work for a group or organization: *She was the mainstay of the team.*

main·stream¹ /'meɪnstriːm/ n **the mainstream** the most usual ideas or methods, or the people who have these ideas or methods: *[+of]* *Environmental ideas have been absorbed into the mainstream of European politics.* | *Genet started as a rebel, but soon became part of the literary mainstream.*

mainstream² adj [only before noun] accepted by or involving most people in a society: *Deaf children can often be included in mainstream education.* | *a centre-right candidate supported by all the mainstream political parties*

mainstream³ v [T] AmE to include a child with physical or mental problems in an ordinary class —**mainstreaming** n [U]

'Main Street n **1** the most important street, with many shops and businesses on it, in many small towns in the US; = **high street** BrE **2** [U] AmE ordinary people who believe in traditional American values: *The President's new proposals won't go down too well on Main Street.*

main·tain S3 W2 /meɪn'teɪn, mən-/ v [T]
1 MAKE STH CONTINUE to make something continue in the same way or at the same standard as before: *Careers Officers maintain contact with young people when they have left school.* | *Britain wants to maintain its position as a world power.* | *A lot depends on building and maintaining a good relationship with your customers.* | *The hotel prides itself on maintaining high standards.* | *How can we maintain control of spending?*
2 LEVEL/RATE to make a level or rate of activity, movement etc stay the same: *It is important to maintain a constant temperature inside the greenhouse.* | *This is the most efficient way to build up and maintain a reasonable level of physical fitness.*
3 SAY to strongly express your belief that something is true; = **claim**: **maintain (that)** *Critics maintain that these reforms will lead to a decline in educational standards.* | **maintain your innocence** (=say that you did not commit a crime) *He maintained his innocence and said the allegations were 'ridiculous'.*
4 LOOK AFTER STH to keep a machine, building etc in good condition by checking and repairing it regularly: *The report found that safety equipment had been very poorly maintained.* | *The company is responsible for maintaining public telephone boxes.*
5 PROVIDE MONEY/FOOD to provide someone with the things they need, such as money or food; = **provide for**: *How can you maintain a family on $900 a month?*

main·te·nance S2 W3 /'meɪntənəns/ n [U]
1 the repairs, painting etc that are necessary to keep something in good condition: *the cost of repairs and maintenance* | *[+of]* *The caretaker is responsible for the maintenance of the school buildings.* | *The theatres were closed on Saturday and Sunday for* ***routine maintenance***. | *Engineers are* ***carrying out essential maintenance work*** *on the main line to Cambridge.* | *an evening class in* ***car maintenance*** | **maintenance crew/man/staff** (=someone who looks after buildings and equipment for a school or company)
2 the act of making a state or situation continue: *[+of]* *The purpose of the UN is the maintenance of international peace and security.* | *The maintenance of a firm*

currency plays an important part in the battle against inflation.

3 *BrE* money paid by someone who is DIVORCED to their former wife or husband; ▤ **alimony**: *They have to find the fathers who abandon their children and make them pay maintenance.*

mai·son·ette /ˌmeɪzəˈnet/ *n* [C] *BrE* an apartment, usually on two floors, that is part of a larger house

mai·tre d' /ˌmetrə ˈdiː: $ ˌmeɪ-/ also **mâitre d'hôtel** /ˌmetrə dəʊˈtel $ ˌmeɪtrə doʊ-/ *n* [singular] someone who is in charge of a restaurant, and who welcomes guests, gives orders to the waiters etc

maize /meɪz/ *n* [U] *BrE* a tall plant with large yellow seeds that grow together on a COB (=long hard part), and which are cooked and eaten as a vegetable; ▤ **corn** *AmE*

Maj. also **Maj** *BrE* the written abbreviation of *major*: *Maj. John Wright*

ma·jes·tic /məˈdʒestɪk/ *adj* very big, impressive, or beautiful: *This village is surrounded by majestic mountain scenery.* —**majestically** /-kli/ *adv*

ma·jes·ty /ˈmædʒɪsti/ *n plural* **majesties 1 Your/Her/His Majesty** used when talking to or about a king or queen; → **Your/Her/His Highness**: *The Prime Minister is here to see you, Your Majesty.* | *His Majesty the King* **2** [U] the quality that something big has of being impressive, powerful, or beautiful: [+of] *the pure majesty of the Alps*

ma·jor¹ S3 W2 /ˈmeɪdʒə $ -ər/ *adj*

1 [usually before noun] having very serious or worrying results; ▤ **minor**: *There is a major problem with parking in London.* | *The loss of their goalkeeper through injury was a major setback for the team.* | *He underwent major heart surgery recently.* | *It could have sparked a major confrontation.*

2 [usually before noun] very large or important, when compared to other things or people of a similar kind; ▤ **minor**: **major role/part/factor etc** *Britain played a major role in the negotiations.* | *There are two major political parties in the US.* | *The government's major concern is with preventing accidents on the roads.* | *Smoking is one of the major causes of cancer.* | *the major developments in computer technology* | *a major road*

3 [not before noun] *AmE spoken* very important: *This is major? You got me out of bed for this?*

4 a major KEY is based on a musical SCALE in which there are SEMITONES between the third and fourth and the seventh and eighth notes; → **minor**: *a symphony in D major*

major² *n* [C] **1** an officer of middle rank in the British or US army or MARINES, or in the US airforce → DRUM MAJOR **2** *especially AmE* the main subject that a student studies at college or university: *Her major is history.* **3** *AmE* someone studying a particular subject as their main subject at college or university: *She's a history major.* **4 the majors** [plural] the MAJOR LEAGUES

major³ *v*

major in sth *phr v especially AmE* to study something as your main subject at college or university: *He's majoring in Political Science.*

major on sth *phr v especially BrE* to pay particular attention to one subject or thing: *The company is planning to major on offering the machines we need.*

ma·jor·do·mo /ˌmeɪdʒəˈdəʊməʊ $ -dʒərˈdoʊmoʊ/ *n plural* **majordomos** [C] *old-fashioned* someone in charge of the servants in a large house

ma·jor·ette /ˌmeɪdʒəˈret/ *n* [C] a girl who spins a BATON while marching with a band

major 'general *n* [C] an officer of high rank in the British or US army or the US airforce

ma·jor·i·ty /məˈdʒɒrəti $ məˈdʒɔː-, məˈdʒɑː-/ *n plural* **majorities**

1 MOST PEOPLE OR THINGS [singular also + plural verb *BrE*] most of the people or things in a group; ▤ **minority**: [+of] *The majority of students find it quite hard to live on the amount of money they get.* | **great/vast/overwhelming majority of sth** (=almost all of a group)

In the vast majority of cases the disease is fatal. | **be in the majority** (=form the largest group) *In this city, Muslims are in the majority.* → SILENT MAJORITY

2 MOST VOTES [C] if one person or group wins a majority in an election, they win more votes than other people or groups: **majority of 50/100 etc** *He won by a majority of 500.* | *The Labour Party* **won** *a huge* **majority** *at the last general election.* | **clear/overall/absolute majority** (=a situation in which one party wins more votes in an election than all the other parties) *The party won an absolute majority in Portugal in 1987.* | **small/narrow majority** *The government gained only a narrow majority, with 151 votes against 144.* | **Labour/Conservative etc majority** *The Labour majority was reduced to just 15 seats at the last election.*

3 majority vote/decision/verdict etc a vote or decision in which more people vote for something than vote against it: *The committee usually takes decisions by majority vote.* | *The jury found him guilty by a majority verdict.*

4 majority stake/shareholding etc when one person or group owns a bigger share of a company than other people or groups and so is able to control what happens to the company: *Alex Golding held a majority shareholding in Golding plc.*

5 BECOMING AN ADULT [U] *BrE law* the age when someone legally becomes an adult; ▤ **minority**: **reach majority/the age of majority** *He became a partner in the family firm on reaching his majority.*

ma'jority ˌleader *n* [C] the person who organizes the members of the political party that has the most people elected, in the US House of Representatives or Senate; → **minority leader**

ma,jority 'rule *n* [U] a system of government in which every person in a country has the right to vote and the group which wins the most votes has power: *It took many years of struggle to establish majority rule in South Africa.*

ˌmajor-'league *adj* [only before noun] **1** connected with the Major Leagues: *a major league pitcher* **2** important, large, or having a lot of influence: *a major-league player in California politics*

ˌMajor 'Leagues *n* **the Major Leagues** the group of teams that make up the highest level of American professional baseball; → **Minor Leagues**

ma·jor·ly /ˈmeɪdʒəli $ -ər-/ *adv* [+ adj/adv] *informal* extremely: *I was majorly upset, as you can imagine.*

make¹ S1 W1 /meɪk/ *v past tense and past participle* **made** /meɪd/

1 PRODUCE [T] to produce something, for example by putting the different parts of it together: *I'm going to show you how to make a box for your tools.* | *A family of mice had made their nest in the roof.* | *She made her own wedding dress.* | *The company has been making quality furniture for over 200 years.* | *They met while they were making a film for Australian TV.* | *Make a list of all the things you need.* | **make sb sth** *He made her a toy horse, using just some straw and bamboo twigs.* | **be made from sth** *Paper is made from wood.* | **be made (out) of sth** *a shirt made of silk* | **make sth from/out of sth** *She's very good at making things from old scraps of material.* | **Japanese-made/English-made etc** (=produced in Japan etc) → **make the bed** at BED¹ (1); → see picture at ASSEMBLE

2 DO [T] used with some nouns to say that someone does something: *Anyone can make a mistake.* | *I can't make a decision just yet.* | *I need to make a quick phone call.* | *You could have made more effort to talk to him.* | *He made no attempt to apologize.* | *Could I make a suggestion?* | *There are a few points I'd like to make.* | *The police were called but no arrests were made.* | *I suppose we should make a start on cleaning this room.* | *Stop making such a fuss!*

3 COOK [T] to cook or prepare food or drink: *When*

1 000, 2 000, 3 000, most frequent words in S poken and W ritten English

was the last time you made a cake? | *John was making breakfast in the kitchen.* | *Who's going to make the tea?* | **make sb sth** *I'll make you some sandwiches.*

4 CAUSE [T] to cause something to happen, or cause a particular state or condition: *Its beautiful beaches make this a highly popular area with tourists.* | *It was this movie which made him a star.* | *His attitude made him very unpopular with colleagues.* | *The photo makes her look much older than she really is.* | **make sb/sth do sth** *I like him because he makes me laugh.* | **make sth difficult/easy/possible etc** *The use of computers has made it possible for more people to work from home.* | **make sth the best/worst/most expensive etc** *Over 80,000 people attended, making it the biggest sporting event in the area.* | *The President has **made it clear** that he is not going to change his mind.*

5 FORCE [T] to force someone to do something: **make sb do sth** *My parents always make me do my homework before I go out.* | **be made to do sth** *I was made to wait four hours before I was examined by a doctor.*

6 MARK/HOLE ETC [T] to cause a mark, hole etc to appear: **make a hole/dent/mark etc** *Make a hole in the paper.* | *The cup has made a mark on the table.*

7 make it a) to succeed in getting somewhere in time for something or when this is difficult: *If we run, we should make it.* | [+to] *With blood pouring from his leg, he made it to a nearby house.* **b)** to be successful at something, for example in your job: *He came to the US and not only made it but **made it big** (=was extremely successful).* | *So far, relatively few women have **made it to the top** in the business world.* | [+as] *He was told he had no talent and would never make it as a professional singer.* | [+to] *England look less likely to make it to the finals.* | **make it to manager/director etc** *How did anyone so stupid make it to manager?* **c)** *spoken* to be able to go to an event, meeting etc that has been arranged: *I'm really sorry, but I won't be able to make it on Sunday after all.* | *Nice to see you. I'm glad you could make it.* **d)** *informal* to continue to live after you have been seriously ill or badly injured: *Frank was very ill, and the doctors didn't think he'd make it.* **e)** to manage to deal with a difficult experience: [+through] *I couldn't have made it through those times without the support of my boyfriend.* **f)** used to say or ask what time it is according to your own or someone else's watch: *What time do you make it?* | *I make it ten past three.*

8 make the meeting/the party/Tuesday etc *spoken* to be able to go to something that has been arranged for a particular date or time: *I'm sorry, I can't make Friday after all.* | *Will you be able to make the next meeting?*

9 ACHIEVE STH [T] to succeed in achieving a particular position, rate etc: *He was never good enough to make the team.* | *I don't think we'll make the deadline.*

10 GET MONEY [T] to earn or get money: *The plan could cost you more than you would make.* | *The business **made a profit** of £140 million last year.* | *His one aim in life was to **make money**.* | *She hopes to **make a living** (=earn the money she needs to live) from writing children's books.* | *He's **made a fortune** (=earned a lot of money) selling computers on the Internet.* | **make sth out of sth** *How easy is it to make money out of gardening?*

11 HAVE A QUALITY [linking verb] to have the qualities that are necessary for a particular job, use, or purpose: **+ noun** *I'm sure you will make a very good teacher.* | *The hall would make an ideal venue for a wedding reception.* | *An old cardboard box makes a comfortable bed for a kitten.*

12 make it/that sth *spoken* used to correct what you have just said: *Can we have two cups of coffee, please? No, make that three.*

13 make do to manage with the things that you have, even though this is not really enough: *I hardly had any food in the house so I just had to make do.* | [+with/without] *I usually make do with a cup of coffee for breakfast.* | *For many people, **make do and mend** (=when someone manages with the things they have*

and does not buy anything new) *was a harsh reality.*

14 make yourself heard/understood/known etc to succeed in getting someone to hear you, understand you, or know that you are there: *I had to shout to make myself heard above the music.*

15 BE A TOTAL [linking verb] to be a particular amount when added together: *Two and two make four.* | *There are nine people coming, plus me, which makes ten.*

16 CALCULATE [T] used to say what you have calculated a number to be: *I make that $150 altogether.*

17 SPORTS SCORE [T] to achieve a particular score in a sports game: *Surrey had made 92 by lunchtime.*

18 make sb captain/leader etc to give someone a new job or position in a group, organization etc: *She's now been made a full partner.* | *He was made mayor in 1998.*

19 make believe to pretend or imagine that something is true when it is not: *I tried to make believe she was happy, but knew deep down it wasn't true.* → **MAKE-BELIEVE**

20 make like *informal* to behave as if something is true when it is not: *He makes like he never met me before.*

21 make as if to do sth *literary* to seem as if you are going to do something but then not do it: *She made as if to speak but then stopped.*

22 ARRIVE [T] *old-fashioned* to arrive at or get to a particular place, especially when it is difficult: *I don't think we're going to make the town before nightfall.*

23 make the papers/headlines/front page etc to be interesting or important enough to be printed in a newspaper, reported on television etc: *News of their divorce made the headlines.*

24 make or break to cause something or someone either to be very successful or to fail completely: *Critics can make or break a young performer.* → MAKE-OR-BREAK

25 that makes two of us *spoken* used to say that you agree with someone or that something that is true of them is true of you too: *'I haven't a clue what's going on.' 'That makes two of us.'*

26 MAKE STH PERFECT [T] *informal* to make something complete or successful: *The hat makes the outfit.*

27 make it with sb *old-fashioned informal* to have sex with someone → MADE; → **make sb's day** at DAY (19); → **make friends** at FRIEND (3); → **make good** at GOOD[1] (35); → **make sense** at SENSE[1] (5)

make away with sb/sth *phr v*
1 *informal* to steal something and take it away with you: *Thieves made away with the contents of the safe.*
2 *old-fashioned* to kill someone

make for sth *phr v* [not in passive]
1 to go in the direction of a particular place; ⊟ **head for**: *I think it's time we made for home.*
2 [not in progressive] to cause a particular result or situation: *Both teams are on good form, which should make for a great game.* → **made for each other** at MADE (6)

make sb/sth **into** sth *phr v*
1 to change something so that it has a different form or purpose: *We can make your room into a study.*
2 to change someone's character, job, position in society etc: *The movie made her into a star overnight.*

make sth **of** sb/sth *phr v*
1 to have a particular opinion about or understanding of something or someone: *I didn't know what to make of her.* | *What do you make of the idea?*
2 to use the opportunities that you have in order to become successful: *I want to make something of my life.* | **make sth of yourself** *She has the ambition and talent to make something of herself.*
3 make the most of sth to get as much advantage as you can from a situation while you are able to: *We've only got one day in Paris, so we'd better make the most of it.*
4 make too much of sth to treat something as if it is more important than it really is: *It would be a mistake to make too much of these findings.* → **make much of** sb/sth at MUCH[2] (17)
5 make a day/night/evening of it *informal* to spend a whole day, night etc doing something, because you have chosen to: *We decided to take a picnic and make a day of it.* → **make a go of sth** at GO[2] (3); → **make the best of sth** at BEST[3] (9); → **see what sb is made of** at MADE (4)

make off *phr v*
to leave quickly, especially in order to escape: *The men made off as the police arrived.* | [+**along/across/ through etc**] *The getaway car made off towards Horrocks Avenue.*

make off with sth *phr v* [not in passive] *informal*
to steal something and take it away with you: *Thieves broke into the school and made off with computer equipment worth £40,000.*

make out *phr v*
1 SEE/HEAR make sth ⇔ out to be just able to see or hear something: *He could just make out a dark shape moving towards him.* | **make out who/what etc** *I couldn't make out what he was saying.*
2 UNDERSTAND STH make sth ⇔ out to understand something, especially the reason why something has happened: **make out what/how/why etc** *I couldn't make out what I had done to annoy her.* | *As far as I can make out, he has never been married.*
3 UNDERSTAND SB make sb ⇔ out [usually in questions and negatives] to understand someone's character and the way they behave: *Stuart's a strange guy – I can't make him out at all.*
4 WRITE CHEQUE ETC make sth ⇔ out to write something such as a bill or cheque: *She was making out a list of people to invite.* | *The book gives advice on making out a will.* | [+**to**] *Make the cheque out to 'Spencer Cross Ltd'.*
5 SAY/PRETEND make sb/sth ⇔ out to say that something is true when it is not: *The situation was never as bad as the media made out.* | **make out (that)** *She always tried to make out that I was wrong and she was right.* | **make sb/sth out to be sth** *He makes me out to be some sort of idiot.*
6 make out a case (for sth) to find good reasons that prove something or show why you need something: *I'm sure we can make out a case for hiring another assistant.*
7 SUCCEED *especially AmE* to succeed or progress in a particular way: *How did you make out this morning?*
8 SEX *informal especially AmE* to kiss and touch someone in a sexual way
9 make out like a bandit *AmE informal* to get or win a lot of money: *The lawyers made out like bandits.*

make sth **out of** sb/sth *phr v*
to change a person or thing into something else: *The Olympics can make sporting heroes out of previously little-known athletes.*

make sth/sb ⇔ **over** *phr v*
1 *especially BrE* to officially and legally give money or property to someone else: [+**to**] *He made over the whole estate to his son.*
2 to change someone or something so that they look different or have a different use: *Redgrave has made herself over completely for her movie role.* → MAKEOVER

make towards sth *phr v BrE formal*
to start moving towards something: *She made towards the door.*

make up *phr v*
1 FORM/BE make up sth [not in progressive] to combine together to form something; ▣ **constitute**: *Women make up only a small proportion of the prison population.* | **be made up of sth** *The committee is made up of representatives from every state.*
2 PRETEND STH IS TRUE make sth ⇔ up to pretend that something is true in order to deceive someone: *I think they're making the whole thing up.* → MADE-UP (1)
3 INVENT make sth ⇔ up to produce a new story, song, game etc by thinking: *Nick made up a song about them.* | *When you're the boss you can make up your own rules.* | *I've given talks so many times that now I just make them up as I go along* (=think of things to say as I am speaking).
4 PREPARE make sth ⇔ up to prepare something by mixing things or putting things together: *I could make up a bed for you on the sofa.* | *Can you make up a bottle of milk for the baby?*
5 SB'S FACE make sb ⇔ up to put MAKE-UP (=special coloured substances) on someone's face in order to make them look better or different: *They made him up as an old man for the last act of the play.* | *One lucky winner will have the chance to be made up and photographed.* ⚠ Do not use the verb **make up** when you are talking about putting coloured substances on your own face. Say that you **wear make-up** or **put on make-up**. → MADE-UP (2)
6 NUMBER/AMOUNT make sth ⇔ up *especially BrE* to add to an amount in order to bring it up to the level that is needed: *I saved as much as I could, and my parents made up the rest.* | *The company will be forced to pay $6 million to make up the difference.*
7 TIME/WORK make sth ⇔ up to work at times when you do not usually work, because you have not done as much work as you should: *I'm trying to make up the time I lost while I was sick.* | *Is it OK if I make the work up next week?*
8 FRIENDS also **make it up** *informal* to become friendly with someone again after you have had an argument: [+**with**] *Have you made up with Patty yet?* | *Oh come on! Why don't you just kiss and make up?*
9 FROM CLOTH make sth ⇔ up to produce something from cloth by cutting and sewing: *The dress had been made up to her exact requirements.* | [+**into**] *I plan on making that material up into a dress.* → **make up your mind** at MIND¹ (3)

make up for sth *phr v*
1 to make a bad situation better, or replace something that has been lost: *The team will be anxious to make up for a disappointing start to the season.* | *I don't eat breakfast but I make up for it at lunch.* | *The good days more than make up for the bad ones.* → see box at INCLUDE
2 to have so much of one quality that it is not important that you do not have much of another one: [+**in/ with**] *What Jay lacked in experience, he made up for in enthusiasm.* | *She doesn't have a natural talent but she makes up for it with hard work.*
3 to do something to show that you are sorry for doing something that upset or annoyed someone: *I'm sorry I was late. To make up for it, let me treat you to a meal.*
4 make up for lost time **a)** to work more quickly, or at times when you do not usually work, because something has prevented you from doing the work before: *We rehearsed all day Saturday, to make up for lost time.* **b)** to do a lot of something in an eager way because you have not had a chance to do it before: *Palin didn't travel much as a young man but he's certainly made up for lost time now.*

make up to sb *phr v*
1 make (it) up to sb to do something to show that you are sorry about the problems you have caused someone: *I'll make it up to you somehow.* | *He was looking for a way to make up to her for what he had done.*
2 *BrE informal* to say nice things to someone or be very friendly to them in order to get an advantage for yourself – used in order to show disapproval
3 be made up to captain/manager etc to be given a higher position in an organization: *He was a security guard before he was made up to reception manager.*

WORD CHOICE: made from, made of, made by
When you are talking about the materials that are used to make something, you say that it is **made of** or **made from** those materials.
Use **made from** when the original materials have been completely changed and cannot be recognized: *Paper is made from wood.*
Use **made of** when the original materials have not been completely changed and you can still see them: *a table made of wood*
⚠ Do not use **made by** when you are talking about the materials something is made from: *a small purse made of leather* (NOT *a small purse made by leather*). **Made by** is used to talk about the person or company that made something: *All the furniture in this room was made by my grandfather.*

make² n **1** [C] the name of a particular product or of the company that makes it: *What make is your car?* | [+of] *It's one of the most popular makes of satellite phone on the market.* **2 be on the make** informal to be trying to get money or power – used in order to show disapproval: *He was just a salesman on the make.*

'make-be‚lieve n [U] when you imagine or pretend that something is real or true: *He seems to be living in a world of make-believe.* | *children in the middle of a make-believe adventure*

‚**make-or-'break** adj something that is make-or-break will lead to either success or failure: *This could be a make-or-break speech for the prime minister.*

make·o·ver /'meɪkəʊvə $ -oʊvər/ n [C] **1** if you give someone a makeover, you make them look more attractive by giving them new clothes, a new hair style etc **2** if you give a place a makeover, you make it look more attractive by painting the walls, putting in new furniture etc: *It's time we gave the kitchen a makeover.*

mak·er /'meɪkə $ -ər/ n [C] **1** a person or company that makes a particular type of goods: **car/film/shoe etc maker** *a quality furniture maker* | *a leading Japanese computer maker* | [+of] *The makers of the car claim that it uses up to 50% less fuel than other similar cars.* **2** a machine or piece of equipment that makes something: **coffee/pasta etc maker** *Grind the beans to suit your coffee maker.* **3 decision maker/policy maker/peacemaker etc** someone who does something or makes something happen: *Who's the decision maker in this department?* | *healthcare administrators and policy makers* → TROUBLEMAKER, HOLIDAYMAKER **4 meet your maker** informal to die – used humorously

make·shift /'meɪkʃɪft/ adj made to be used for a short time only when nothing better is available: *The refugees slept in makeshift tents at the side of the road.*

---

make-up

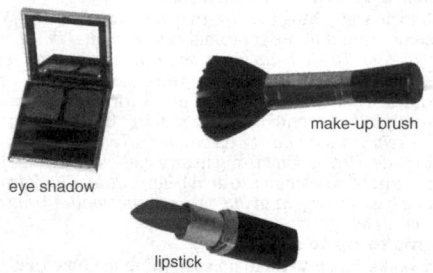

make-up brush

eye shadow

lipstick

'make-up, make·up /'meɪkʌp/ n
1 FOR YOUR FACE [U] coloured substances that are put on your face to improve or change your appearance

wear make-up
have make-up on (=be wearing make-up)
put on/apply make-up
do your make-up (=put on your make-up)
heavy make-up (=a lot of make-up)
eye make-up
stage make-up (=make-up that actors wear in plays)
make-up artist/man/woman (=someone who helps actors put on make-up)

I don't usually wear much make-up. | *Her hair looked untidy, and she had no make-up on.* | *I'm just putting my make-up on, then I'll be ready.* | *girls in heavy make-up* | *Don't you ever wear eye make-up?* → make up at MAKE¹

2 PEOPLE IN A GROUP [singular] the make-up of a group or team is the combination of people that are in it: [+of] *I don't think we should change the make-up of the team.*
3 CHARACTER sb's make-up the qualities that a person has, which form their character: *Pride has always been an important part of his make-up.* | *sb's genetic/*

psychological **make-up** *a possible link between genetic make-up and criminal behaviour*
4 TEST [C] also **make-up test** AmE a test that you take in school when you were not able to take a previous test

'make‚weight /'meɪk‚weɪt/ n [C] a person or thing that is not very important but is included so there is the right number of people or the right amount of something

'make-work n [U] AmE work that is not important but is given to people to keep them busy

mak·ing /'meɪkɪŋ/ n [U] **1** the process of making something: [+of] *companies involved in the making of nuclear weapons* | **cheese making/cider making etc** *a region famous for its cheese making* **2 decision making/policy making** the process of deciding something: *people involved in decision making at the highest level* **3 be the making of sb** to make someone a much better or more successful person: *You'll see – a couple of years abroad will be the making of him.* **4 have the makings of sth** to have the qualities or skills necessary to do a particular job: *He has the makings of a world-class footballer.* **5 be a long time/10 years etc in the making** to take a long time, 10 years etc to make: *a book that was ten years in the making* **6 be of your own making** problems that are of your own making have been caused by you and no one else: *He admits that a lot of his troubles are entirely of his own making.*

mal- /mæl/ prefix bad or badly: *a malformed limb* (=wrongly shaped) | *The children had been maltreated.* (=treated cruelly)

mal·ad·just·ed /,mælə'dʒʌstɪd◂/ adj a maladjusted child behaves badly and is unable to form good relationships with people because they have emotional problems

mal·ad·min·i·stra·tion /,mælədmɪnɪ'streɪʃən/ n [U] formal careless or dishonest management: *He accused the local authority of maladministration.*

mal·a·droit /,mælə'drɔɪt◂/ adj formal not clever or sensitive in the way you deal with people

mal·a·dy /'mælədi/ n plural **maladies** [C] **1** formal a serious problem in society **2** old use an illness

ma·laise /mæ'leɪz, mæ-/ n [singular, U] formal **1** a general problem that is difficult to describe in an exact way: *a general malaise within society* **2** a general feeling that you are slightly ill or not happy in your life

mal·a·prop·is·m /'mæləprɒpɪzəm $ -prɑː-/ n [C] literary an amusing mistake that you make when you use a word that sounds similar to the word you intended to say but means something completely different

ma·lar·i·a /mə'leəriə $ -'ler-/ n [U] a disease that is common in hot countries and that you often get when a type of MOSQUITO bites you —**malarial** adj: *malarial fever*

ma·lar·key /mə'lɑːki $ -'lɑːr-/ n [U] informal things which you think are silly or untrue; ≠ **nonsense**: *I'm not interested in all this scientific malarkey.* | *You don't believe in ghosts and all that malarkey, do you?*

mal·con·tent /'mælkəntent $,mælkən'tent/ n [C] formal someone who is likely to cause trouble because they are not happy with the way things are organized – used in order to show disapproval

male¹ S3 W2 /meɪl/ adj
1 typical of or relating to men or boys; ≠ **female**; → **masculine**: *a deep male voice* | *traditional male values* | *Until now, motor-racing has largely been a male preserve.* (=something that only men have been involved with)
2 a male person or animal cannot have babies or lay eggs; ≠ **female**: *adult male bears* | *Many women earn less than their male colleagues.*
3 a male plant or flower cannot produce fruit; ≠ **female**
4 technical a male PLUG has parts that stick out and that fit into a hole or SOCKET; ≠ **female**

male² W3 n [C]
1 a male animal; ≠ **female**: *The male is usually bigger*

and more brightly coloured than the female.
2 a man; **F** **female**: *Police described her attacker as a white male aged about 25.*

,male 'chauvinist *n* [C] a man who believes that men are better than women and has fixed, traditional ideas about the way men and women should behave – used to show disapproval: *I'm afraid Bill's a bit of a male chauvinist.* | **male chauvinist pig** (=an insulting name for a male chauvinist) —**male chauvinism** *n* [U]

mal·e·dic·tion /ˌmælɪ'dɪkʃən/ *n* [C] *old-fashioned formal* a wish that something bad will happen to someone; **E** **curse**

,male-'dominated *adj* involving mostly men or controlled mostly by men: *a male-dominated profession*

mal·e·fac·tor /'mælɪˌfæktə $ -ər/ *n* [C] *old-fashioned formal* someone who does bad or illegal things

,male 'menopause *n* [singular] a period in the middle of a man's life when he sometimes feels anxious and unhappy because he is getting older – often used humorously

,male-voice 'choir *n* [C] a large group of men who sing together

ma·lev·o·lent /mə'levələnt/ *adj formal* a malevolent person wants to harm other people; **E** **evil**; **F** **benevolent**: **malevolent look/stare/smile etc** *He gave her a dark, malevolent look.* —**malevolence** *n* [U] —**malevolently** *adv*

mal·feas·ance /mæl'fiːzəns/ *n* [U] *law* illegal or dishonest activity

mal·for·ma·tion /ˌmælfɔː'meɪʃən $ -fɔːr-/ *n* [C,U] *technical* when a part of someone's body is badly formed; **E** **deformity**: *children suffering from malformations of the legs and arms*

mal·formed /ˌmæl'fɔːmd◂ $ -'fɔːrmd◂/ *adj technical* if a part of someone's body is malformed, it is badly formed; **E** **deformed**: *malformed limbs*

mal·func·tion /mæl'fʌŋkʃən/ *n* [C] a fault in the way a machine or part of someone's body works: *a malfunction in one of the engines* | **[+of]** *a malfunction of the immune system* | *an equipment malfunction* —**malfunction** *v* [I]: *A warning light seems to have malfunctioned.*

mal·ice /'mælɪs/ *n* [U] **1** the desire to harm someone because you hate them: **with malice** *His eyes gleamed with malice.* | **sheer/pure malice** *She did it out of sheer malice.* | *James bore her no malice* (=did not feel any malice towards her). **2** **with malice aforethought** *law* with the deliberate intention of doing something that is against the law

ma·li·cious /mə'lɪʃəs/ *adj* very unkind and cruel, and deliberately behaving in a way that is likely to upset or hurt someone: *a spiteful and malicious girl* | **malicious gossip/rumour** *I think I know who is responsible for these malicious rumours.* —**maliciously** *adv* —**maliciousness** *n* [U]

ma·lign¹ /mə'laɪn/ *v* [T usually passive] to say unpleasant things about someone that are untrue; **E** **slander**: *She had seen herself repeatedly maligned in the newspapers.* | *a much maligned politician*

malign² *adj formal* harmful; **F** **benign**: *a malign influence*

ma·lig·nan·cy /mə'lɪgnənsi/ *n plural* **malignancies** **1** [C] *medical* a TUMOUR **2** [U] *formal* a feeling of great hatred

ma·lig·nant /mə'lɪgnənt/ *adj* **1** *medical* a malignant disease is one such as CANCER, which can develop in an uncontrolled way and is likely to cause someone's death; **F** **benign**: *She developed a malignant tumour in her breast.* **2** *formal* showing that you hate someone: *a malignant look*

ma·lin·ger /mə'lɪŋgə $ -ər/ *v* [I usually in progressive] to avoid work by pretending to be ill: *He accused Frank of malingering.* —**malingerer** *n* [C]

mall /mɔːl, mæl $ mɔːl/ *n* [C] *especially AmE* a large area where there are a lot of shops, usually a covered

area where cars are not allowed; **E** **shopping centre**: *Let's meet at the mall and go see a movie.* | *a huge new shopping mall* → STRIP MALL

mal·lard /'mælɑːd $ -ərd/ *n* [C] a type of wild duck

mal·le·a·ble /'mæliəbəl/ *adj* **1** *technical* something that is malleable is easy to press or pull into a new shape: *malleable steel* **2** *formal* someone who is malleable can be easily influenced or changed by other people: *a malleable child* —**malleability** /ˌmæliə'bɪlɪti/ *n* [U]

mal·let /'mælɪt/ *n* [C] **1** a wooden hammer with a large end **2** a wooden hammer with a long handle that you use for playing CROQUET or POLO

mal·low /'mæləʊ $ -oʊ/ *n* [C,U] a plant with pink or purple flowers → MARSHMALLOW

mall·rat /'mɔːlræt $ 'mɒːl-/ *n* [C usually plural] *AmE informal* a young person who goes to SHOPPING MALLS a lot in order to be with their friends, not to buy things

mal·nour·ished /ˌmæl'nʌrɪʃt◂ $ -'nɜː-, -'nʌ-/ *adj* someone who is malnourished is ill or weak because they have not had enough good food to eat: *malnourished children*

mal·nu·tri·tion /ˌmælnjʊ'trɪʃən $ -nʊ-/ *n* [U] when someone becomes ill or weak because they have not eaten enough good food: *refugees suffering from malnutrition*

mal·o·dor·ous /mæl'əʊdərəs $ -'oʊ-/ *adj literary* smelling unpleasant; **E** **smelly**

mal·prac·tice /ˌmæl'præktɪs/ *n* [C,U] *law* when a professional person makes a mistake or does not do their job properly and can be punished by a court: *Her doctor was found guilty of malpractice.*

malt /mɔːlt $ mɒːlt/ *n* **1** [U] grain, usually BARLEY, that has been kept in water for a time and then dried. It is used for making beer, WHISKY etc **2** [C] *AmE* a drink made from milk, malt, and ICE CREAM that usually has something else such as chocolate added: *a cheeseburger and a chocolate malt* **3** [C,U] also **malt whisky** a type of high quality WHISKY from Scotland

malt·ed /'mɔːltɪd $ 'mɒːl-/ also **,malted 'milk** *n* [C] *AmE* a MALT (2)

Mal·tese Cross /ˌmɔːltiːz 'krɒs $ ˌmɒːltiːz 'krɒːs/ *n* [C] a cross with four pieces that become wider as they go out from the centre

,malt 'liquor *n* [U] *AmE* a type of beer

mal·treat /mæl'triːt/ *v* [T] to treat a person or animal cruelly; **E** **mistreat**: *The hostages said they were hungry but had not been maltreated.* —**maltreatment** *n* [U]: *evidence of animal maltreatment*

mam /mæm/ *n* [C] mother – used in Scotland and northern England; **E** **mum**

ma·ma¹ /'mɑːmə/ also **mamma** /'mɑːmə/ also **momma** *n* [C] *AmE* a mother – used by or to children; **E** **mummy**: *I want my mama!*

ma·ma² /mə'mɑː/ *n* [C] *BrE old-fashioned* mother

mama's boy /'mɑːməz ˌbɔɪ/ *n* [C] *AmE* a boy or man who lets his mother look after him and protect him too much, so that people think he is weak; **E** **mummy's boy** *BrE*: *You've got to stand up for yourself, stop being such a mama's boy.*

mam·ba /'mæmbə $ 'mɑːmbə, 'mæmbə/ *n* [C] a poisonous African snake that is black or green

mam·bo /'mæmbəʊ $ 'mɑːmboʊ/ *n plural* **mambos** [C] a dance, originally from Cuba, or the music for this dance

mam·ma /'mɑːmə/ *n* another spelling of MAMA¹

mam·mal /'mæməl/ *n* [C] a type of animal that drinks milk from its mother's body when it is young. Humans, dogs, and whales are mammals. —**mammalian** /mæ'meɪliən/ *adj*

M

1 000, **2** 000, **3** 000, most frequent words in **S** poken and **W** ritten English

mam·ma·ry /ˈmæməri/ *adj* [only before noun] *technical* connected with or relating to the breasts: *normal mammary tissue* | *mammary cancer*

ˈmammary ˌgland *n* [C] *technical* the part of a woman's breast that produces milk, or a similar part of a female animal

mam·mo·gram /ˈmæməgræm/ *n* [C] an X-RAY picture of a woman's breasts used to check for signs of CANCER

mam·mo·gra·phy /mæˈmɒɡrəfi $ -ˈmɑː-/ *n* [U] examination of a woman's breasts using X-RAYS to check for signs of CANCER

mam·mon /ˈmæmən/ *n* [U] *formal* money, wealth, and profit, regarded as something bad because people want or think about them too much

mam·moth¹ /ˈmæməθ/ *adj* [only before noun] extremely large; ▣ **enormous**, **gigantic**: *Reforming the prison system would be a mammoth task.* | *a mammoth corporation*

mammoth² *n* [C] an animal like a large hairy ELEPHANT that lived on Earth thousands of years ago

mam·my /ˈmæmi/ *n plural* **mammies** [C] mother – used especially in Ireland

man¹ [S1] [W1] /mæn/ *n plural* **men** /men/
1 MALE PERSON [C] an adult human male; → **woman**: *There were two men and a woman in the car.* | *He's a very kind man.* | *a man's watch* | *Don't keep Hansen waiting – he's a busy man.*
2 STRONG/BRAVE [C usually singular] a man who has the qualities that people think a man should have, such as being brave, strong etc: *Come on, be a man now. No more crying.* | *He wasn't man enough* (=strong or brave enough) *to face up to his responsibilities.* | **make a man (out) of sb** (=make a boy or young man start behaving in a confident way) *Running his own business has really made a man out of Terry.*
3 PERSON [C] a person, either male or female – used especially in formal situations or in the past: *All men are equal in the eyes of the law.* | *a man's right to work*
4 PEOPLE [U] people as a group: *This is one of the worst diseases known to man.* | *the evolution of man* | **prehistoric/stone-age/modern man** (=people who lived at a particular stage of human development)
5 WORKER **a)** [C usually plural] a man who works for an employer: *Why were there no protests from the men at the factory?* **b)** [C] a man who does a job for you, especially repairing something: *Has the man been to fix the TV?* | **gas man/rent man etc** *I waited all day for the gas man.* **c)** **the man from sth** a man who works for a particular company or organization: *Was that the man from the PR agency?*
6 PARTICULAR KIND OF MAN [C] **a)** a man who comes from a particular place, does a particular kind of work, or is connected with a particular organization, especially a university or company: *I think she married a Belfast man.* | *I've been a military man all my life.* | *Even a Harvard man has a lot to learn about politics.* **b)** a man who likes, or likes doing, a particular thing: *I'm more of a jazz man myself.* | *Are you a betting man?*
7 man! *spoken* **a)** used when speaking to an adult male, especially when you are excited, angry etc: *Stop talking nonsense, man!* **b)** used when speaking to someone, especially an adult male: *You look great, man!*
8 SOLDIER [C usually plural] a soldier or SAILOR who is under the authority of an officer: *The Captain ordered his men to fire.*
9 HUSBAND [C] *informal* a woman's husband or boyfriend: **sb's man** *She spent five years waiting for her man to come out of prison.*
10 the man *spoken* **a)** used to talk about a man you dislike, a man who has done something stupid etc: *Don't listen to him – the man's a complete idiot.* **b)** **The Man** *AmE old-fashioned* someone who has authority over you, especially a police officer
11 sb's your man *spoken* used to say that a particular man is the best person for a job, situation etc: *If you need repairs done in the house, Brian's your man.*

12 you da man!, you're the man! *AmE spoken* used to praise someone for having done something well
13 our man *spoken* used by the police to refer to a man that they are watching or trying to find, especially because they think he is responsible for a crime: *Gareth couldn't possibly be our man. He couldn't possibly be a murderer.* | *Perhaps our man parked his car at the station and took the train.*
14 our man in/at sth a man who is the representative of a country or organization in a particular place: *our man in Rome* | *a report on the accident from our man at the scene*
15 men in (grey) suits *informal* the men who control businesses, organizations etc, considered as a group, especially when you think they are boring
16 a man of his word a man you can trust, who will do what he has promised to do: *He had promised to help, and Sally knew that Dr Neil was a man of his word.*
17 a man of few words a man who does not talk very much: *Being a man of few words, his message was short and to the point.*
18 be your own man to behave and think independently without worrying about what other people think: *I'm my own man. I say what I believe.*
19 the man of the moment/hour/year a man who has recently done something important: *Olson was man of the hour when the team beat the Tigers.*
20 it's every man for himself *spoken* used to say that people will not help each other: *In journalism it's every man for himself.*
21 the man in the street; the man on the Clapham omnibus *BrE old-fashioned* the average man or the average person; ▣ **Joe Bloggs/Schmo**: *This kind of music doesn't appeal to the man in the street.*
22 a man of the people a man who understands and expresses the views and opinions of ordinary people: *They want to demonstrate that the prime minister is a man of the people.*
23 a man's man a man who enjoys being with other men and doing sports and activities with them, and is popular with men rather than women: *He enjoyed his reputation as a man's man, but was careful never to neglect his family.*
24 a ladies' man a man who is popular with women and who likes to go out with a lot of different women: *Paul likes to think he's a bit of a ladies' man.*
25 man and boy *BrE* if a man has done something man and boy, he has done it all his life: *I've worked on that farm man and boy.*
26 man and wife if a man and a woman are man and wife, they are married: *I now pronounce you man and wife* (=you are now officially married).
27 live as man and wife if a man and woman live as man and wife, they live together as if they are married, although they are not
28 as one man *written* if a group of people do something as one man, they do it together: *The audience rose as one man to applaud the singers.*
29 to a man/to the last man *written* used to say that all the men in a group do something or have a particular quality: *They were socialists to a man.*
30 man-about-town a rich man who goes out a lot to parties, clubs, theatres etc: *In his designer suit and shiny shoes he looked quite the man about town.*
31 man of God/man of the cloth a priest: *You'd believe a man of the cloth, wouldn't you?*
32 my (good) man *BrE old-fashioned spoken* used when talking to someone of a lower social class – do not use this phrase: *My good man, I really don't think you should be here.*
33 my man *spoken* used by some men to greet a friend: *Jason, my man! How's it going?*
34 your/yer man *spoken* used to talk about a particular man – used mainly in Ireland: *I've got to go and see yer man up this afternoon.*
35 SERVANT [C] *old-fashioned* a male servant: *My man will drive you to the station.*
36 GAME [C] one of the pieces you use in a game such as CHESS

37 every man jack old-fashioned each person in a group: *Spies, every man jack of them, I'd bet.*
38 kick/hit a man when he's down to treat someone badly when you know that they already have problems: *Most of his rivals couldn't resist kicking a man when he was down.*
39 man's best friend a dog
40 the man of the house the most important male member of a family, who is responsible for doing things such as paying bills, making important decisions etc: *Since my father's death, my uncle was the man of the house.* → BEST MAN, MAN-TO-MAN, NEW MAN, OLD MAN; → **be a man/woman of the world** at WORLD[1] (21)

man² v **manned, manning** [T] to work at, use, or operate a system, piece of equipment etc: *A team of volunteers are manning the phones.* | *the first manned spacecraft*

man³ interjection especially AmE used to emphasize what you are saying, especially when you are angry, surprised, disappointed etc: *Man, that was a lucky escape!* | *Oh, man! I can hear the bullets.*

man·a·cle /ˈmænəkəl/ n [C usually plural] an iron ring on a chain that is put around the wrist or ANKLE of a prisoner —**manacle** v [T] —**manacled** adj

man·age S1 W1 /ˈmænɪdʒ/ v
1 BUSINESS [T] to direct or control a business or department and the people, equipment, and money involved in it: *Kerry has been asked to manage a new department.* | *Managing a football team is harder than you think.* | *The company had been very badly managed.* | *a small brewery which has been owned and managed by the same family for over 100 years* → see box at CONTROL²
2 DO STH DIFFICULT [I,T] to succeed in doing something difficult, especially after trying very hard: **manage to do sth** *I finally managed to push the huge animal away.* | *How do you manage to stay so slim?* | *We somehow managed to persuade him.* | *Juventus managed two goals in the last ten minutes.* | *I don't know how I'll manage it, but I'll be there.*
3 DEAL WITH PROBLEMS [I] to succeed in dealing with problems, living in a difficult situation etc: *I don't know how she manages with seven children.* | *We didn't have the proper equipment, but we managed somehow.* | [+without] *How do you manage without a washing machine?* | [+with] *I can't afford to get you a new coat – you'll have to manage with the one you've got.*
4 TIME/MONEY ETC [T] to use your time, money etc sensibly, without wasting it: *Paying a little each month can help you manage your money.* | *You need to learn to manage your time more effectively.* | *Consultants can help academic institutions to manage their resources more efficiently.*
5 LIVE WITHOUT MUCH MONEY [I] to succeed in buying the things that you need in order to live even though you do not have very much money; ⊟ **get by:** *I honestly don't know how we'll manage now Keith's lost his job.* | *It'll be tight, but I guess I'll just about manage.* | [+on] *People like Jim have to manage on as little as $75 a week.*
6 NOT NEED HELP [I,T] spoken to be able to do something or carry something without help: *Can you manage all right, Mum?* | *You'll never manage that suitcase; let me take it.* | *Thank you, but I think I can manage perfectly well on my own.*
7 KEEP TIDY [T] especially BrE to succeed in keeping something neat and tidy: *He'll never manage such a big garden on his own.*
8 CONTROL [T] to control the behaviour of a person or animal, so that they do what you want: *It's hard to manage your children and do the shopping.* | *The horse was huge and vicious. Giles was the only one who could manage her.* → see box at CONTROL²
9 BE STRONG ENOUGH [T] to be able to do something because you are strong enough or healthy enough: *He tried to walk, but managed only a few shaky steps.*
10 EAT/DRINK [T] to be able to eat or drink something: *Could you manage another drink?*

11 CAUSE PROBLEMS [T] to do something that causes problems – used humorously: **manage to do sth** *Andrews has managed to get himself sacked.* | *I don't know how I managed to arrive so late.*
12 **manage a smile/a few words etc** to make yourself say or do something when you do not really want to: *Tom looked tired but still managed a smile.* | **manage to smile/speak/laugh etc** *'Why do you hate me so much?' he managed to say.*
13 HAVE TIME FOR [T] to be able to meet someone or do something, even though you are busy: *Can you manage dinner tonight?* | *'Is there any chance you could work late?' 'I think I could manage an hour.'*

man·age·a·ble /ˈmænɪdʒəbəl/ adj easy to control or deal with; ⊟ **unmanageable:** *Divide the task into manageable sections.* —**manageability** /ˌmænɪdʒəˈbɪlᵻti/ n [U]

man·age·ment S1 W1 /ˈmænɪdʒmənt/ n
1 [U] the activity of controlling and organizing the work that a company or organization does: **good/bad management** *good management and co-operation with staff* | *a lack of management skills* | *a management consultant* | *management training courses*
2 [singular, U also + plural verb BrE] the people who are in charge of a company or organization: *The management has agreed to the policy.* | *The shareholders demanded a change in management.* | *management decisions* | *The factory is under new management.* | **senior/top management** *It is difficult to retain top management.* | *a member of the senior management team* | **middle management** (=the people in charge of small groups within an organization)
3 [U] the way that people control and organize different situations that happen in their lives or their work: [+of] *careful management of the economy* | *traffic management* | *The successful applicant will have experience in project management.* | *courses in time management* | **crisis management** (=when you deal with an unusually difficult or dangerous situation)

management ˈbuyout n [C] when a company's managers buy the company they work for

management conˌsultant n [C] someone who is paid to advise the management of a company how to improve their organization and working methods

man·ag·er S1 W1 /ˈmænɪdʒə $ -ər/ n [C]
1 someone whose job is to manage part or all of a company or other organization: **bank/sales/project etc manager** *She's now assistant marketing manager for the south east area.* | *one of our regional managers* | [+of] *the general manager of Chevrolet* | *a middle manager in a computer company* (=someone who manages a small part of a company) → LINE MANAGER
2 someone who is in charge of training and organizing a sports team: *the new England manager* | [+of] *the manager of Lazio*
3 someone who is in charge of the business affairs of a singer, an actor etc

man·ag·er·ess /ˌmænɪdʒəˈres $ ˈmænɪdʒərᵻs/ n [C] old-fashioned a woman who is in charge of a business, especially a shop or restaurant

man·a·ge·ri·al /ˌmænᵻˈdʒɪəriəl $ -ˈdʒɪr-/ adj relating to the job of a manager: *managerial skills*

managing diˈrector n [C] BrE someone who is in charge of a large company or organization; ⊟ **chief executive officer**

ma·ña·na /mæˈnjɑːnə/ adj, adv a word meaning 'tomorrow', used to talk about someone who seems too relaxed and always delays doing things: *a mañana attitude* —**mañana** n [U]

man-at-ˈarms n plural **men-at-arms** [C] old use a soldier

man·a·tee /ˈmænətiː/ n [C] a large sea animal with FLIPPERS and a large flat tail which eats plants

Man·cu·ni·an /mænˈkjuːniən/ n [C] someone from the city of Manchester in England —**Mancunian** adj

man·da·la /'mændələ, mæn'dɑːlə/ n [C] a picture of a circle around a square, that represents the universe in the Hindu and Buddhist religions

mandarin /'mændərɪn/ n [C] **1** also **mandarin orange** a kind of small orange with skin that is easy to remove **2** BrE an important government official who people think has too much power: *Civil Service mandarins* **3** an important government official in the former Chinese EMPIRE

Man·da·rin n [U] the official language of China, spoken by most educated Chinese people

mandarin 'orange n [C] a MANDARIN

man·date¹ /'mændeɪt/ n **1** [C] if a government or official has a mandate to make important decisions, they have the authority to make the decisions because they have been elected by the people to do so: **mandate to do sth** *The President was elected with a **clear mandate** to tackle violent crime.* | [+for] *a **popular mandate** for election reform* | [+from] *I **sought a mandate** from my constituents to oppose this tax.* | **have/be given a mandate** *Sometimes a President thinks he has more of a mandate than he really does.* **2** [C] an official instruction given to a person or organization, allowing them to do something: *Matters debated in meetings do not become a mandate automatically.* **3** [C,U] the power given to one country to govern another country

man·date² /mæn'deɪt/ v [T] **1** *formal* to tell someone that they must do a particular thing: *These measures were mandated by the IMF.* | **mandate that** *Justice mandates that we should treat all candidates equally.* **2** [usually passive] to give someone the right or power to do something: *The committee was mandated to co-ordinate measures to help Poland.*

man·dat·ed /mæn'deɪtᵻd/ adj [only before noun] a mandated country has been placed under the control of another country: *mandated territories*

man·da·to·ry /'mændətəri $ -tɔːri/ adj if something is mandatory, the law says it must be done; ⊟ **compulsory, obligatory;** → *discretionary:* [+for] *Crash helmets are mandatory for motorcyclists.* | *Murder carries a **mandatory** life **sentence**.* | *The Council has **made it mandatory** for all nurses to attend a refresher course every three years.*

man·di·ble /'mændᵻbəl/ n [C] *technical* **1** the jaw bone of an animal or fish, especially the lower jaw **2** the outside part of a bird's beak **3** the part of an insect's mouth that it uses for eating

man·do·lin, mandoline /ˌmændə'lɪn/ n [C] a musical instrument with eight metal strings and a round back, played with a PLECTRUM (=small piece of plastic, metal etc)

man·drake /'mændreɪk/ n [C] a poisonous plant that was once thought to have magic powers

man·drill /'mændrᵻl/ n [C] a large monkey that lives in West Africa and that has a red and blue face

mane /meɪn/ n [C] **1** the long hair on the back of a horse's neck, or around the face and neck of a lion **2** *literary* a person's long thick hair: *her mane of hair*

'man-eater n [C] **1** a wild animal that kills and eats people **2** a woman who people think is frightening because she has many sexual partners – used humorously —**man-eating** adj: *a man-eating shark*

ma·neu·ver /mə'nuːvə $ -ər/ n, v the American spelling of MANOEUVRE

ma·neu·ve·ra·ble /mə'nuːvərəbəl/ adj the American spelling of MANOEUVRABLE

ma·neu·ve·ring /mə'nuːvərɪŋ/ n [C,U] the American spelling of MANOEUVRING

man·ful·ly /'mænfəli/ adv *old-fashioned* in a brave, determined way: *Joe struggled manfully with his case and rucksack.*

man·ga·nese /'mæŋgəniːz/ n [U] a grey-white metal that breaks easily and is used to make steel and glass. It is a chemical ELEMENT: symbol Mn

mange /meɪndʒ/ n [U] a skin disease of animals that makes them lose their fur

man·ger /'meɪndʒə $ -ər/ n [C] a long open container that horses, cattle etc eat from

mange·tout /ˌmɒnʒ'tuː $ ˌmɑːnʒ-/ n [C] BrE a long flat green vegetable whose outer part is eaten as well as the seeds; ⊟ **snowpea** AmE

man·gle¹ /'mæŋgəl/ v [T] **1** to damage or injure something badly by crushing or twisting it: *The trap closed round her leg, badly mangling her ankle.* **2** to spoil something such as a speech or piece of music, by saying or playing it badly: *The orchestra had mangled Bach's music.* —**mangled** adj [only before noun]: *the mangled remains of the aircraft*

mangle² n [C] a machine used in former times to remove water from washed clothes by pressing them between two ROLLERS

man·go /'mæŋgəʊ $ -goʊ/ n plural **mangoes** [C] a tropical fruit with a thin skin and sweet yellow flesh → see picture at FRUIT¹

man·grove /'mæŋgrəʊv $ -groʊv/ n [C] a tropical tree that grows in or near water and grows new roots from its branches: *a mangrove swamp*

mang·y /'meɪndʒi/ adj **1** suffering from MANGE: *thin mangy dogs* **2** *informal* dirty and in bad condition: *a mangy-looking rug*

man·han·dle /'mænhændl/ v [T] **1** to push or handle someone roughly: **manhandle sb into/through etc sth** *It had ended with Tony physically manhandling her out of the house.* **2** to move a heavy object using force: **manhandle sth into/on to/across etc sth** *We lifted it off the truck and manhandled it into the workshop.*

man·hole /'mænhəʊl $ -hoʊl/ n [C] a hole in the surface of a road covered by a lid. It is used to examine underground pipes, wires etc

man·hood /'mænhʊd/ n **1** [U] qualities such as strength, courage, and sexual power, that people think a man should have: *Why did he feel he had to prove his manhood in the company of women?* **2** [U] the state of being a man and no longer a boy; → **womanhood**: **reach/attain manhood** *He had barely reached manhood when he married.* **3** [U] *literary* all the men of a particular nation: *America's manhood* **4** [singular] *especially literary* a PENIS

'man-hour n [C] the amount of work done by one person in one hour: *The main structure takes only about 40 man-hours to erect.*

man·hunt /'mænhʌnt/ n [C] an organized search for someone who might have committed a crime, or a prisoner who has escaped: *Police have launched a nationwide manhunt.*

ma·ni·a /'meɪniə/ n [C,U] **1** a strong desire for something or interest in something, especially one that affects a lot of people at the same time; ⊟ **craze**: [+for] *the Victorian mania for butterfly collecting* | **religious/football/disco etc mania** *Keep-fit mania has hit some of the girls in the office.* **2** *medical* a serious mental illness

ma·ni·ac /'meɪniæk/ n [C] **1** *informal* someone who behaves in a stupid or dangerous way; ⊟ **lunatic**: *He leapt into the car and drove like a maniac to the hospital.* | *Suddenly this maniac ran out into the middle of the road.* **2** **religious/sex maniac** *informal* someone who you think is too involved or interested in religion or sex; ⊟ **freak**: *The woman's a sex maniac if you ask me.* **3** someone who is mentally ill: **homicidal maniac** (=one who kills people)

ma·ni·a·cal /mə'naɪəkəl/ adj behaving as if you are crazy —**maniacally** /-kli/ adv

man·ic /'mænɪk/ adj **1** *informal* behaving in a very anxious or excited way: *She seemed slightly manic.* | *Mortimer continued to shoot, a manic grin on his* face. **2** *medical* relating to a feeling of great happiness or excitement that is part of a mental illness

manic de'pression *n* [U] a mental illness that causes someone to feel very strong emotions of happiness and sadness in a short period of time

manic de'pressive *n* [C] someone with manic depression

man·i·cure /'mænɨkjʊə $ -kjʊr/ *n* [C,U] a treatment for the hands that includes cutting and polishing the nails; → **pedicure** —**manicure** *v* [T]; → see picture at **NAIL**[1]

man·i·cured /'mænɨkjʊəd $ -kjʊrd/ *adj* **1** manicured hands or fingers have nails that are neatly cut and polished: *slim,* **perfectly manicured** *fingers* **2** manicured gardens or LAWNS are very neat and tidy: *The ball rolled across the immaculately manicured lawn.*

man·i·cur·ist /'mænɨkjʊərɨst $ -kjʊr-/ *n* [C] someone whose job is to cut and polish people's nails

man·i·fest[1] /'mænɨfest/ *v* [T] *formal* **1** to show a feeling, attitude etc: *The shareholders have manifested their intention to sell the shares.* | **manifest sth in/as/through sth** *A dog's protective instincts are manifested in increased alertness.* **2 manifest itself** to appear or to become easy to see: *His illness began to manifest itself at around this time.*

manifest[2] *adj formal* plain and easy to see; **⊟ obvious, patent**: *a manifest error of judgment* | **be made/ become manifest** (=be clearly shown) *Their devotion to God is made manifest in ritual prayer.* —**manifestly** *adv*: *a manifestly unfair system*

manifest[3] *n* [C] a list of passengers or goods carried on a ship, plane or train: *the ship's cargo manifest*

man·i·fes·ta·tion /ˌmænɨfe'steɪʃən $ -fə-/ *n formal* **1** [C] a very clear sign that a particular situation or feeling exists: [+of] *These latest riots are a clear manifestation of growing discontent.* **2** [C,U] the act of appearing or becoming clear: [+of] *Manifestation of the disease often doesn't occur until middle age.*

man·i·fes·to /ˌmænɨ'festəʊ $ -toʊ/ *n plural* **manifestos** [C] a written statement by a political party, saying what they believe in and what they intend to do: *the Labour Party's election manifesto* | *The Tories are due to publish their manifesto tomorrow.*

man·i·fold[1] /'mænɨfəʊld $ -foʊld/ *adj formal* many and of different kinds: *The reasons for this situation are manifold.*

manifold[2] *n* [C] *technical* an arrangement of pipes through which gases enter or leave a car engine

man·i·kin, mannikin /'mænɨkɨn/ *n* [C] **1** a model of the human body, used for teaching art or medicine **2** *literary* a very small man

ma·nil·a, manilla /mə'nɪlə/ *n* [U] strong brown paper used for making envelopes: *a large manila envelope*

ma·nip·u·late /mə'nɪpjʊleɪt/ *v* [T] **1** to make someone think and behave exactly as you want them to, by skilfully deceiving or influencing them: *He was one of those men who manipulated people.* | *You have the constant feeling you are being manipulated.* | **manipulate sb into (doing) sth** *The thought that any parent would manipulate their child into seeking fame just appalled me.* **2** to work skilfully with information, systems etc to achieve the result that you want: *software designed to store and manipulate data* | *You can integrate text with graphics and manipulate graphic images.* **3** *medical* to move and press bones or muscles to remove pain in them **4** to use skill in moving or handling something: *The workmen manipulated some knobs and levers.* —**manipulation** /mə,nɪpjʊ'leɪʃən/ *n* [U]: *There were allegations of political manipulation.* | *manipulation of photographic images*

ma·nip·u·la·tive /mə'nɪpjʊlətɪv $ -leɪ-/ *adj* **1** clever at controlling or deceiving people to get what you want – used in order to show disapproval: *She was sly, selfish, and manipulative.* **2** *technical* relating

---

to the ability to handle objects in a skilful way: *Before a child can learn a musical instrument he or she first needs to acquire the necessary manipulative skills.* **3** [only before noun] *technical* relating to the skill of moving bones and joints into the correct position

ma·nip·u·la·tor /mə'nɪpjʊleɪtə $ -ər/ *n* [C] someone who is skilful at getting what they want by cleverly controlling or deceiving other people

man·kind /ˌmæn'kaɪnd/ *n* [U] all humans considered as a group; **⊟ humankind, man**; → **womankind**: *Since earliest times, mankind has been fascinated by fire.* | *one of the most important events in* **the history of mankind**

man·ky /'mæŋki/ *adj BrE informal* looking dirty and unattractive; **⊟ mangy**: *a manky old sweater*

man·ly /'mænli/ *adj* having qualities that people expect and admire in a man, such as being brave and strong; **⊟ masculine**: *a deep manly voice* —**manliness** *n* [U]

man-'made *adj* **1** man-made materials and substances are not natural; **⊟ artificial**; **⊟ natural**: *fabrics made using a combination of natural and man-made fibres* **2** made by people, rather than by natural processes: *Europe's largest man-made lake*

man·na /'mænə/ *n* [U] **1 manna from heaven** something very good that you get when you did not expect to, just when you really need it **2** the food which, according to the Bible, was provided by God for the Israelites in the desert after their escape from Egypt

man·ne·quin /'mænɨkɨn/ *n* [C] **1** a model of the human body, used for showing clothes in shop windows **2** *old-fashioned* a woman whose job is to wear fashionable clothes and show them to people; **⊟ model**

man·ner S3 W2 /'mænə $ -ər/ *n*
1 [singular] *formal* the way in which something is done or happens: **manner of (doing) sth** *It seemed rather an odd manner of deciding things.* | *He felt some guilt over the manner of her death.* | **in a ... manner** *I had hoped you would behave in a more responsible manner.* | *The issue will be resolved in a manner that is fair to both sides.* | **criticism of the manner in which** *the bishop was appointed* | **in the usual/normal etc manner** *The matter should be submitted to the accounts committee in the usual manner.*
2 [singular] the way in which someone behaves towards or talks to other people: *She has a calm relaxed manner.* | [+towards] *Something in Beth's manner towards him had changed.* | *Sophie resented his high-handed manner.*
3 manners [plural] polite ways of behaving in social situations

---

have good/bad manners
it's good/bad manners to do sth
perfect/impeccable manners
table manners (=the polite way of eating at a table)
mind your manners (=used to tell someone to behave politely)
sb has no manners (=someone often behaves in a way that is not polite)
remember your manners (=behave politely)
forget your manners (=behave in an impolite way)
where are your manners? *BrE* (=used to tell a child that he or she is behaving impolitely)

Her children all had such **good manners.** | **It's bad manners** *to talk with your mouth full* (=talk and eat at the same time). | *His* **manners were impeccable.** | *Dad gave us a lecture about our* **table manners.** | *You* **mind your manners,** *young man!* | *'Lesley just got up and left.' 'Some people* **have no manners.'** | *Good heavens, child,* **where are your manners?**

---

4 manners [plural] *formal* the customs of a particular

M

group of people: *a book about the life and manners of Victorian London*

5 in a manner of speaking in some ways, though not exactly: *'Are you his girlfriend?' Nicola asked. 'In a manner of speaking.'*

6 all manner of sth *formal* many different kinds of things or people: *We would discuss all manner of subjects.* | *The British Isles have been conquered by all manner of people.*

7 in the manner of sb/sth *formal* in the style that is typical of a particular person or thing: *a painting in the manner of the early Impressionists*

8 what manner of...? *literary* what kind of: *What manner of son would treat his mother in such a way?*

9 not by any manner of means *BrE spoken formal* not at all: *I haven't lost my interest in politics by any manner of means.*

10 (as) to the manner born if you do something new as to the manner born, you do it in a natural confident way, as if you have done it many times before → BEDSIDE MANNER, COMEDY OF MANNERS

man·nered /ˈmænəd $ -ərd/ *adj* **1 well-mannered/ bad-mannered etc** polite, impolite etc in the way you behave in social situations: *He is the most well-mannered, well-behaved boy I know.* **2** behaviour, speech, or writing that is mannered is not natural and is intended to make people admire you – used in order to show disapproval: *Hickstone gave a very mannered performance in the lead role.*

man·ner·is·m /ˈmænərɪzəm/ *n* [C] a way of speaking or moving that is typical of a particular person: *He has the same mannerisms as his father.*

man·ni·kin /ˈmænɪkɪn/ *n* another spelling of MANIKIN

man·nish /ˈmænɪʃ/ *adj* a woman who is mannish, or who wears mannish clothes, looks or behaves like a man – used especially when this is considered unattractive: *She had strong, almost mannish features.* | *a mannish jacket* —**mannishly** *adv*

man·o a man·o /ˌmænəʊ ɑː ˈmænəʊ $ ˌmɑːnoʊ ɑː ˈmɑːnoʊ/ *adv* with only two people involved; **one-to-one**: *He finally faced up to his father, mano a mano, telling him he was going to leave college.*

ma·noeu·vra·ble *BrE*; **maneuverable** *AmE* /məˈnuːvərəbəl/ *adj* if something, especially a vehicle, is manoeuvrable, it can be moved or turned easily: *a ship which was surprisingly fast and manoeuvrable* —**manoeuvrability** /məˌnuːvərəˈbɪləti/ *n* [U]

ma·noeu·vre¹ *BrE*; **maneuver** *AmE* /məˈnuːvə $ -ər/ *n* **1** [C] a skilful or careful movement that you make, for example in order to avoid something or go through a narrow space: *A careful driver will often stop talking before carrying out a complex manoeuvre.* **2** [C,U] a skilful or carefully planned action intended to gain an advantage for yourself: *They tried by diplomatic maneuvers to obtain an agreement.* **3** manoeuvres [plural] military activities, such as pretending to fight a battle, which are done as practice or training; **exercises**: *Large-scale military manoeuvres are being carried out near the border.* | **on manoeuvres** *troops on night manoeuvres* **4 room for manoeuvre/freedom of manoeuvre** the possibility of changing your plans or decisions in order to achieve what you want: *As I see it, Lisa, you don't really have a great deal of room for manoeuvre.*

manoeuvre² *BrE*; **maneuver** *AmE v* **1** [I,T always + adv/prep] to move or turn skilfully or to move or turn something skilfully, especially something large and heavy: *She managed to manoeuvre expertly into the parking space.* | **manoeuvre yourself into/out of sth** *Josh manoeuvred himself out of bed and hobbled to the door.* | *We manoeuvred the TV in front of the sofa.* **2** [I,T] to use cleverly planned and often dishonest methods to get the result that you want: **manoeuvre**

sb into/out of sth *It was a well-organized plan to maneuver company president John Woolford out of office.* | *Businesses manoeuvred to have their industry organized to their own advantage.*

ma·noeu·vring *BrE*; **maneuvering** *AmE* /məˈnuːvərɪŋ/ *n* [C,U] the use of clever and sometimes dishonest methods to get what you want: *diplomatic manoeuvrings* | *months of political manoeuvring*

man of ˈletters *n plural* **men of letters** [C] a male writer, especially one who writes NOVELS or writes about literature

man-of-ˈwar also **man-o'-war** /ˌmæn ə ˈwɔː $ -ˈwɔːr/ *n plural* **men-of-war** [C] a ship with guns that was used in the past in sea battles

man·or /ˈmænə $ -ər/ *n* [C] **1** also **manor house** a big old house with a large area of land around it **2** the land that belonged to an important man, under the FEUDAL system **3** *BrE informal* the area that a group of police officers are responsible for; **patch**, **turf**

ma·no·ri·al /məˈnɔːriəl/ *adj* [only before noun] relating to a manor: *a study based on manorial records*

man·pow·er /ˈmænˌpaʊə $ -paʊr/ *n* [U] all the workers available for a particular kind of work: *a lack of trained manpower* | *a scheme to increase police manpower*

man·qué /ˈmɒŋkeɪ $ mɑːŋˈkeɪ/ *adj* **artist/actor/ teacher etc manqué** someone who could have been successful as an artist etc, but never became one

man·sard /ˈmænsɑːd $ -ɑːrd/ also **ˈmansard roof** *n* [C] *technical* a roof whose lower part slopes more steeply than its upper part

manse /mæns/ *n* [C] the house of a Christian minister, especially in Scotland

man·ser·vant /ˈmænˌsɜːvənt $ -ɜːr-/ *n* [C] *old-fashioned* a male servant, especially a man's personal servant; **valet**

-manship /mənʃɪp/ *suffix* [in U nouns] a particular art or skill: *seamanship* (=sailing skill) | *statesmanship* (=skill at being a political or government leader)

man·sion /ˈmænʃən/ *n* [C] **1** a very large house: *a beautiful country mansion* **2** Mansions used in Britain in the names of some apartment buildings: *19 Carlyle Mansions*

ˈman-sized also **ˈman-size** *adj* [only before noun] **1** large and considered suitable for a man: *a man-sized breakfast* | *man-size tissues* **2** about the same size as a man: *man-sized plants*

man·slaugh·ter /ˈmænˌslɔːtə $ -ˌslɔːtər/ *n* [U] *law* the crime of killing someone illegally but not deliberately; → **homicide**, **murder**: *She was cleared of murder but found guilty of manslaughter.*

man·tel·piece /ˈmæntlpiːs/ also **man·tel** /ˈmæntl/ *especially AmE*, **man·tel·shelf** /ˈmæntlʃelf/ *BrE n* [C] a wooden or stone shelf which is the top part of a frame surrounding a FIREPLACE: *The clock on the mantelpiece struck 10.* → see picture at FIREPLACE

man·tis /ˈmæntɪs/ *n plural* **mantises** or **mantids** /-tɪdz/ [C] a PRAYING MANTIS

man·tle¹ /ˈmæntl/ *n* **1 take on/assume/wear the mantle of sth** *formal* to accept or have an important duty or job: *It is up to Europe to take on the mantle of leadership in environmental issues.* **2 a mantle of snow/darkness etc** *literary* something such as snow or darkness that covers a surface or area: *A mantle of snow lay on the trees.* **3** [C] a loose piece of outer clothing without sleeves, worn especially in former times **4** [C] a cover that is put over the flame of a gas or oil lamp to make it shine more brightly **5** [singular] *technical* the part of the Earth around the central CORE → see picture at GLOBE

mantle² *v* [T] *literary* to cover the surface of something

man-to-ˈman *adj* [only before noun] *informal* **1** if two men have a man-to-man talk, they discuss something in an honest, direct way **2** playing a sport in such a way that one person on your team tries to stay close to one person on the other team —**man-to-man** adv: *You two need to discuss this man-to-man.*

man·tra /'mæntrə/ n [C] **1** a word or sound that is repeated as a prayer or to help people MEDITATE: **recite/repeat a mantra** *He closed his eyes and began to recite a Buddhist mantra.* **2** a word or phrase representing a rule or principle which someone often uses, but which other people often find annoying or boring: *The Treasury Secretary has stuck to his mantra that 'a strong dollar is in America's interest'.* **3** a piece of holy writing in the Hindu religion

man·u·al¹ /'mænjuəl/ adj **1** manual work involves using your hands or your physical strength rather than your mind; ▤ **blue-collar**: **manual job/labour/worker etc** *low-paid manual jobs* | *People in manual occupations have a lower life expectancy.* **2** operated or done by hand or without the help of electricity, computers etc; ▤ **automatic**: *a manual typewriter* | *a five-speed manual gearbox* | *It would take too long to do a manual search of all the data.* **3** relating to how well you use your hands to make or do things: *No great manual dexterity* (=skill in using your hands) *is required to perform the technique.* —**manually** adv

manual² n [C] **1** a book that gives instructions about how to do something, especially how to use a machine: **instruction/training/reference etc manual** | *Consult the computer manual if you have a problem.* | *a user manual* **2** **on manual** if a machine is on manual, it can only be operated by hand and not AUTOMATICALLY

man·u·fac·ture¹ /ˌmænjᵿˈfæktʃə $ -ər/ v [T] **1** to use machines to make goods or materials, usually in large numbers or amounts: *the company that manufactured the drug* | *manufactured goods* **2** to invent an untrue story, excuse etc; ▤ **fabricate**: *If the media can manufacture stories like this, who are we supposed to believe?* **3** technical if your body manufactures a particular useful substance, it produces it

manufacture² n **1** [U] the process of making goods or materials using machines, usually in large numbers or amounts: *Cost will determine the methods of manufacture.* **2** **manufactures** [plural] technical goods that are produced in large quantities using machinery

man·u·fac·tur·er S3 W2 /ˌmænjᵿˈfæktʃərə $ -ər/ n [C] also **manufacturers** [plural] a company that makes large quantities of goods: *Read the manufacturer's instructions before using your new dishwasher.* | *The fridge was sent back to the manufacturers.*

man·u·fac·tur·ing W3 /ˌmænjᵿˈfæktʃərɪŋ/ n [U] the process or business of producing goods in factories: *Thousands of jobs had been lost in manufacturing.* | *the manufacturing industry*

ma·nure /mə'njʊə $ mə'nʊr/ n [U] waste matter from animals that is mixed with soil to improve the soil and help plants grow —**manure** v [T]

man·u·script /'mænjᵿskrɪpt/ n [C] **1** a book or piece of writing before it is printed: **in manuscript** *I read his novel in manuscript.* | *Unfortunately, parts of the original manuscript have been lost.* **2** a book or document written by hand before printing was invented: *a fine collection of medieval manuscripts*

Manx /mæŋks/ adj from or relating to the Isle of Man or its people: *the Manx government*

Manx 'cat n [C] a breed of cat that has no tail or only a very short tail

man·y S1 W1 /'meni/ determiner, pron, adj
1 a large number of people or things; ▤ **few**; → **more**, **most**, **much**: *Many people have to use a car to travel to work.* | *I don't have many friends.* | *My mother has lived in Spain for many years.* | *Do you get many visitors?* | *Some of the houses have bathrooms but many do not.* | *His third novel is regarded by many* (=a lot of people) *as his best.* | [+of] *Many of our staff work part-time.* | *There are plenty of cafes and bars, many of them*

serving excellent food. | *There are so many things we disagree about.* | **Not many** (=only a few) *people can afford my services.* | *You've been reading too many romantic novels* (=more than you should). | *One job loss is one too many* (=one more than is acceptable, needed etc). | **the many people/things etc** *We should like to thank the many people who have written to us offering their support.* | **many hundreds/thousands/millions** *military equipment worth many millions of dollars* | **a great many/a good many/very many** (=a very large number) *Most of the young men went off to the war, and a great many never came back.* | *It all happened a good many years ago.*
2 **how many** used to ask or talk about how large a number or quantity is: *How many sisters do you have?* | *I didn't know how many tickets to buy.*
3 **as many** a number that is equal to another number: *They say the people of Los Angeles speak 12 languages and teach just as many in the schools.* | **as many (...) as** *Grandfather claimed to have as many medals as the general.* | *There weren't as many people at the meeting as we had hoped.* | **in as many days/weeks/games etc** *A great trip! We visited five countries in as many days* (=in five days). | **twice/three times etc as many** *The company now employs four times as many women as men.*
4 **as many as 50/1000 etc** used to emphasize how surprisingly large a number is: *As many as 10,000 civilians are thought to have fled the area.*
5 **many a sth** formal or old-fashioned a large number of people or things: *Many a parent has had to go through this same painful process.* | *I've sat here many a time* (=often) *and wondered what happened to her.*
6 **many's the time/day etc (that/when)** old-fashioned used to say that a particular thing has happened often: *Many's the time we've had to borrow money in order to get through the month.*
7 **have had one too many** informal to be drunk: *Don't pay any attention to him – he's had one too many.*
8 **many thanks** written used especially in formal letters to thank someone for something: [+for] *Many thanks for your letter of 17 March.*
9 **the many** formal a very large group of people, especially the public in general: *This war is another example of the few sacrificing their lives for the many.* → **in as many words** at WORD¹

GRAMMAR
Many is used mainly in questions and negative sentences: *Were there many people at the party?* | *There weren't many people at the party.*
In other sentences, phrases like **a lot of** and **plenty of** are used instead: *Slovakia has a lot of small towns* (NOT *Slovakia has many small towns*).
However, **many** can be used in formal English: *Many politicians expressed concern about the high level of defence spending.*
Many can also be used after **too**, **so**, and **as**: *There are too many mistakes in this work.* | *I didn't realize I had so many friends.* | *Bring as many people as you want.*
⚠ Do not use 'and' after **many** and before an adjective: *There are not many interesting Sunday newspapers* (NOT *There are not many and interesting Sunday newspapers*).

man-year n [C] technical the amount of work done by one person in a year, used as a measurement: *The project will take five man-years to complete.*

many-'sided adj consisting of many different qualities or features: *a complex many-sided personality*

Mao·ri /'maʊri/ n **1** [C] someone who belongs to the race of people that first lived in New Zealand and now forms only a small part of the population **2** [U] the language used by the Maori people —**Maori** adj: *Maori children*

M

map 1004

M

map¹ [S2] [W2] /mæp/ *n* [C]
1 a drawing of a particular area for example a city or country, which shows its main features, such as its roads, rivers, mountains etc: *According to the map we should turn left.* | *I'll draw a map of where we live.* | *on a map I'm just trying to find Vancouver Island on the map.* | *[+of] a large-scale map of Mexico City* | **street/road/route map** *a full colour street map of Amsterdam* | *Do you know how to read a map* (=understand the information it gives)*?*

reading a map

2 a drawing of an area showing some kind of special feature, for example the type of rocks, weather, population etc; ⊟ **chart**: *an archaeological map of the area* | *the colour weather map in the newspaper* | **political map** (=one showing where political parties have power, or where countries are)
3 put sth on the map to make a place famous: *It was the Olympic Games that really put Seoul on the map.*
4 off the map *informal* a long way from any large town: *It's a small place in Nebraska. Right off the map.* → **wipe sth off the map** at WIPE¹ (8)

map² *v* **mapped, mapping** [T] **1** to make a map of a particular area: *He spent the next fifteen years mapping the Isle of Anglesey.* **2** to discover or show information about something, especially about its shape or arrangement, or how it moves or works: *The points at which stress and anxiety emerge can be mapped.*
 map onto sth *phr v* to match something or have a direct relationship with something
 map sth ⇔ **out** *phr v* to plan carefully how something will happen: *Her own future had been mapped out for her by wealthy and adoring parents.*

ma·ple /'meɪpəl/ *n* **1** also **maple tree** [C] a tree which grows mainly in northern countries such as Canada. Its leaves have five points and turn red or gold in autumn. **2** [U] the wood from a maple

maple 'syrup *n* [U] a sweet sticky liquid obtained from some kinds of maple tree which is eaten especially on PANCAKES

map-,reading *n* [U] the practice of using a map to find which way you should go —**map-reader** *n* [C]

mar /mɑː $ mɑːr/ *v* **marred, marring** [T] to make something less attractive or enjoyable; ⊟ **spoil**: *Their wedding was marred by the death of Jenny's mother a week earlier.* | *A frown marred his handsome features.*

Mar. also **Mar** *BrE* the written abbreviation of *March*

mar·a·bou, marabout /'mærəbuː/ *n* [C] a large African STORK (=a long-legged bird)

ma·ra·cas /məˈrækəz $ -'rɑː-, -'ræ-/ *n* [plural] a pair of hollow balls with handles, filled with small objects, that you shake and use as a musical instrument

mar·a·schi·no /,mærə'skiːnəʊ‹, -'ʃiː- $ -noʊ‹/ *n* [U] a sweet alcoholic drink made from a type of black CHERRY

maraschino 'cherry *n* [C] a CHERRY that has been kept in maraschino. Maraschino cherries are used to decorate alcoholic drinks or cakes.

mar·a·thon¹ /'mærəθən $ -θɑːn/ *n* [C] **1** a long race of about 26 miles or 42 kilometres: *the Boston Marathon* | *Garcia ran the marathon in just under three hours.* **2** an activity that continues for a long time and needs a lot of energy, patience, or determination: *We finished the job but it was quite a marathon.*

marathon² *adj* [only before noun] a marathon event continues for a long time and needs a lot of energy, patience, or determination: *a marathon round of negotiations*

mar·a·thon·er /'mærəθɒnə $ -θɑːnər/ also **'marathon ,runner** *n* [C] someone who runs in a marathon: *an Olympic marathoner*

ma·raud·ing /məˈrɔːdɪŋ $ -'rɒː-/ *adj* [only before noun] *written* a marauding person or animal moves around looking for something to destroy or kill: *marauding street gangs* —**marauder** *n* [C]

mar·ble /'mɑːbəl $ 'mɑːr-/ *n* **1** [U] a type of hard rock that becomes smooth when it is polished, and is used for making buildings, STATUES etc: *The columns were of white marble.* | *a marble statue* **2** [C] a small coloured glass ball that children roll along the ground as part of a game **3 marbles** [U] a game played by children using marbles **4 lose your marbles** *informal* to start behaving in a crazy way; ⊟ **go mad** **5** [C] a STATUE or SCULPTURE made of marble

mar·bled /'mɑːbəld $ 'mɑːr-/ *adj* **1** having an irregular pattern of lines and colours: *a marbled book cover* | *marbled meat* (=with lines of fat in it) **2** made of marble: *Footsteps rang out along the marbled hallway.*

march¹ /mɑːtʃ $ mɑːrtʃ/ *v* **1** [I] if soldiers or other people march somewhere, they walk there quickly with firm regular steps: *[+across/along/past etc] On 29 August the royal army marched into Inverness.* | *[+on] He gathered his troops and prepared to march on the capital* (=march to the capital in order to attack it). | **Quick march!** (=an order to tell people to start marching) *We marched 50 km across the foothills.* **2** [I always + adv/prep] if a large group of people march somewhere, they walk there together to express their ideas or protest about something: *An estimated 5,000 people marched through the city to demonstrate against the factory closures.* | *[+on] Outraged citizens marched on City Hall* (=marched to City Hall), *demanding the police chief's resignation.* **3** [I always + adv/prep] to walk somewhere quickly and with determination, often because you are angry: *[+off/out etc] Brett marched out of the office, slamming the door behind him.* **4** [T always + adv/prep] to force someone to walk somewhere with you, often pushing or pulling them roughly: **march sb to/into etc sth** *Mr Carter marched us to the principal's office.* **5 be given/get your marching orders** *BrE informal* to be ordered to leave, especially because someone no longer wants you to work for them or no longer wants a relationship with you **6 time marches on** used to say that as time goes by, situations change and things do not remain the same

march² *n* [C] **1** an organized event in which many people walk together to express their ideas or protest about something: *In the end the police decided not to ban the march.* | **protest/civil rights/peace etc march** *I went on a lot of peace marches when I was a student.* **2** when soldiers walk with firm regular steps from one place to another: *From Calais the general led his forces on a long march southwards.* **3 on the march a)** an army that is on the march is marching somewhere **b)** a belief, idea etc that is on the march is becoming stronger and more popular: *Fascism is on the march again in some parts of Europe.* **4 a day's march/two weeks' march etc** the distance a group of soldiers can march in a particular period of time: *Lake Van was still three days' march away.* **5 the march of time/history/progress etc** *formal* the way that things happen or change over time and cannot be stopped: *You can't control the march of science.* | *She was desperate to halt the march of time upon her face and figure.* **6** a piece of music for people to march to: *military marches* | *a funeral march* **7 marches** [plural] the area around the border between England and Wales or between England and Scotland → **steal a march on** at STEAL¹ (8)

March *n* [C,U] written abbreviation **Mar.** the third month of the year, between February and April: *next/last March She started work here last March.* | *in March The theatre opened in March 2001.* | *on March 6th There's a meeting on March 6th.* | *on 6th March BrE: I wrote to my bank on 6th March.* | *March 6 AmE: The hospital is scheduled to open March 6.*

march·er /'mɑːtʃə $ 'mɑːrtʃər/ *n* [C] a member of a group of people that are walking somewhere in order to express their ideas or protest about something; → **demonstrator**, **protester**: *civil rights marchers*

'marching ,band *n* [C] a group of musicians who march as they play musical instruments

mar·chio·ness /ˌmɑːʃəˈnes $ ˈmɑːrʃənəs/ *n* [C] **1** the wife of a MARQUIS **2** a woman who has the rank of MARQUIS

'march-past *n* [singular] when soldiers march past an important person during a ceremony: *300 war veterans took part in the parade and march-past.*

Mar·di Gras /ˌmɑːdi ˈɡrɑː $ ˈmɑːrdi ɡrɑː/ *n* [U] the day before LENT begins, or the music, dancing etc that happen on this day in some countries

mare /meə $ mer/ *n* [C] **1** a female horse or DONKEY; → **stallion, filly 2 mare's nest a)** a discovery that seems important but is actually of no value **b)** a confused situation or a very untidy place

mar·ga·rine /ˌmɑːdʒəˈriːn, ˌmɑːɡə- $ ˈmɑːrdʒərɪn/ *n* [U] a yellow substance similar to butter but made from vegetable or animal fats, which you eat with bread or use for cooking

mar·ga·ri·ta /ˌmɑːɡəˈriːtə $ ˌmɑːr-/ *n* [C] an alcoholic drink made with TEQUILA and LEMON or LIME juice

marge /mɑːdʒ $ mɑːrdʒ/ *n* [U] *BrE spoken informal* margarine

mar·gin S3 W3 /ˈmɑːdʒɪn $ ˈmɑːr-/ *n* [C]
1 the empty space at the side of a page: *Someone had scribbled a note **in the margin**.* | *Use double spacing and wide margins to leave room for comments.*
2 the difference in the number of votes, points etc that exists between the winners and the losers of a competition or election: **by a wide/narrow/significant etc margin** *They're a world-class team and it was no surprise that they won by such a wide margin.* | **by a margin of 10 points/100 votes etc** *The bill was approved by a margin of 55 votes.*
3 the difference between what it costs a business to buy or produce something and what they sell it for: *Margins are low and many companies are struggling.* | *Within 10 years they had a gross **profit margin** of 50%.*
4 [usually singular] an additional amount of something such as time, money, or space that you include in order to make sure that you are successful in achieving something: *It'll take about 30 minutes to dry but I'd allow a **safety margin** of, say, another 10 minutes.*
5 margin of error the degree to which a calculation might or can be wrong: *The survey has a margin of error of 2.1%.*
6 margin for error how many mistakes you can make and still be able to achieve something: *At this late stage in the competition there is absolutely no margin for error.*
7 *technical* or *literary* the edge of something, especially an area of land or water: *the western margin of southern Africa*
8 on the margin(s) a person on the margins of a situation or group has very little power, importance or influence; **on the fringes**: *unemployed youths living on the margins of society*

mar·gin·al /ˈmɑːdʒɪnəl $ ˈmɑːr-/ *adj* **1** a marginal change or difference is too small to be important: *a marginal increase in the unemployment figures* | *a marginal improvement in profits* **2** *technical* relating to a change in cost, value etc when one more thing is produced, one more dollar is earned etc: *marginal revenue* **3 marginal seat/constituency** *BrE* a SEAT in a parliament or similar institution, which can be won or lost by a small number of votes **4** marginal people or groups are not considered powerful or important; **mainstream**: *The album contains too many songs by marginal bands.* **5** [only before noun] written in a margin: *marginal notes*

mar·gin·al·ize also **-ise** *BrE* /ˈmɑːdʒɪnəlaɪz $ ˈmɑːr-/ *v* [T] to make a person or a group of people unimportant and powerless in an unfair way: *Female employees complained of being marginalized by*

management. **—marginalized** *adj* **—marginalization** /ˌmɑːdʒɪnəlaɪˈzeɪʃən $ ˌmɑːrdʒɪnələ-/ *n* [U]

mar·gin·al·ly /ˈmɑːdʒɪnəl-i $ ˈmɑːr-/ *adv* not enough to make an important difference; **slightly**: *Gina's grades have improved marginally since last term.* | *The new system is only marginally more efficient than the old one.*

ma·ri·a·chi /ˌmæriˈɑːtʃi $ ˌmɑː-/ *n* [U] a kind of Mexican dance music

mar·i·gold /ˈmærɪɡəʊld $ -ɡoʊld/ *n* [C] a plant with yellow or orange flowers

mar·i·jua·na /ˌmærɪˈwɑːnə, -ˈhwɑːnə/ *n* [U] an illegal drug smoked like a cigarette, made from the dried leaves of the HEMP plant; **cannabis**

ma·rim·ba /məˈrɪmbə/ *n* [C] a musical instrument like a XYLOPHONE

ma·ri·na /məˈriːnə/ *n* [C] a small port or area of water where people keep boats that are used for pleasure

mar·i·nade /ˌmærɪˈneɪd/ *n* [C,U] a mixture of oil and spices in which meat or fish is put for a time before cooking

mar·i·nate /ˈmærɪneɪt/ also **mar·i·nade** /ˈmærɪneɪd/ *v* [I,T] to put meat or fish in a marinade, or to be left in a marinade for some time: **marinate (sth) in sth** *fish marinated in olive oil, garlic and vinegar*

ma·rine /məˈriːn/ *adj* [only before noun] **1** relating to the sea and the creatures that live there: *the enormous variety of **marine life*** | *the effects of oil pollution on **marine mammals*** | *marine biology* **2** relating to ships or the navy; **maritime**

Marine *n* [C] a soldier who serves on a ship, especially a member of the Royal Marines or the US Marine Corps

Ma'rine Corps *n* **the Marine Corps** one of the main parts of the US armed forces, consisting of soldiers who serve on ships

mar·i·ner /ˈmærɪnə $ -ər/ *n* [C] *literary* a SAILOR

mar·i·o·nette /ˌmæriəˈnet/ *n* [C] a PUPPET whose arms and legs are moved by pulling strings

mar·i·tal /ˈmærɪtl/ *adj* [only before noun] relating to marriage: *marital problems* | *the increase in marital breakdown* | *marital bliss* (=the state of being very happily married – used humorously)

,marital 'status *n* [U] whether someone is married – used especially on official forms: *Marital status: married/single/divorced* | *questions about age, sex and marital status*

mar·i·time /ˈmærɪtaɪm/ *adj* [only before noun] **1** relating to the sea or ships; **marine**: *San Francisco has lost nearly all of its maritime industry.* **2** near the sea: *the Canadian maritime provinces*

mar·jo·ram /ˈmɑːdʒərəm $ ˈmɑːr-/ *n* [U] a herb that smells sweet and is used in cooking

mark¹ S3 W2 /mɑːk $ mɑːrk/ *n* [C]
1 DIRT a spot or dirty area on something that spoils its appearance: *I can't get these marks out of my T-shirt.* | *His feet left dirty **marks** all over the floor.* | *Police said the **skid marks** (=marks left by a car's tyres) were over 30 feet long.*
2 DAMAGED AREA a cut, hole, or other small sign of damage: **burn/scratch/bite etc mark** *a burn mark on the kitchen table* | *There were scratch marks all over the victim's body.*
3 COLOURED AREA a small area of darker or lighter colour on a plain surface such as a person's skin or an animal's fur: *The kitten is mainly white with black marks on her back.* → **BIRTHMARK**
4 WRITING a shape or sign that is written or printed: *What do those strange marks at the top mean?* | *Make a mark at the bottom of the page.*
5 LEVEL/NUMBER a particular level, number, amount

etc: **pass/reach/approach etc the ... mark** *The tempera-ture is not expected to reach the 20 degree mark in the next few days.* | *In 1976 unemployment in Britain passed the one million mark.*

6 STUDENT'S WORK *especially BrE* a letter or number given by a teacher to show how good a student's work is; ⊟ **grade** *AmE*: **good/high mark** *The highest mark was a B+.* | *Her marks have been a lot lower this term.* | *She always gets good marks.* | **pass mark** (=the mark you need in order to pass an exam) *The pass mark was 75%.* | **full/top marks** (=the highest possible mark)

7 full/top marks for effort/trying/persistence etc *BrE spoken* used to praise someone for trying hard to do something, even though they did not succeed: *I have to give you top marks for determination.*

8 high/low mark approval or disapproval of something or of the way someone has done something: *Parents gave the kit high marks.* | *his low marks as transpor-tation chief*

9 make/leave your mark to become successful or famous: *It took Hughes only two games to make his mark.* | [+as] *Dorsey made his mark as a pianist in the 1920s.* | [+on/in] *Cobb has left his mark on baseball history.*

10 leave/make its mark on sb/sth to affect someone or something so that they change in a permanent or very noticeable way: *Singers like Franklin and Redding helped gospel music make its mark on popular culture.* | *Growing up during the war had left its mark on her.*

11 off the mark/wide of the mark not correct; ⊟ **inac-curate**: *Our cost estimate was way off the mark.*

12 be a mark of sth to show that someone or something is a particular thing, has a particular quality etc; ⊟ **be a sign of sth**: *The ability to perform well under pressure is the mark of a true champion.*

13 a mark of respect/honour/affection etc something that happens or is done to show respect, honour etc: [+for] *The plaque awarded to Grant is a mark of recog-nition for his years of service.* | *There was a two-minute silence as a mark of respect for the dead.*

14 Mark 2/6 etc also **mark 2/6 etc a)** *especially BrE* a particular type or model of a car, machine etc: *an old Mark 2 Ford Cortina* **b)** a measurement used in Britain for the temperature of a gas OVEN: *Cook for 40 minutes at gas mark 6.*

15 hit/miss the mark a) to hit or miss the thing that you were shooting at **b)** to succeed or fail to have the effect you wanted: *Although it contains a certain amount of truth, this theory ultimately misses the mark.*

16 be quick/slow/first etc off the mark *informal* to be quick, slow, first etc to understand things or react to situations: *You'll have to be quick off the mark if you want to find a job around here.*

17 not up to the mark *BrE* **a)** not good enough: *Her work just isn't up to the mark.* **b)** old-fashioned not well and healthy: *I'm not feeling quite up to the mark today.*

18 the halfway mark the point in a race, journey, or event that is half way between the start and the finish

19 bear the mark of sth a) to show the physical signs of something which happened in the past: *His face bore the marks of many missions.* **b)** if something bears the mark of something or someone, it has signs that show who or what made it or influenced it: *His speech bore all the marks of his military background.*

20 on your mark(s), get set, go! *spoken* said in order to start a race

21 MONEY the standard unit of money used in Ger-many before the EURO

22 SIGNATURE *old use* a sign in the form of a cross, used by someone who is not able to write their name
⚠ Do not use **mark** when you mean a particular type of product. Use **make** or **brand**: *an expensive make of camera* | *a well-known brand of toothpaste* → EXCLAMATION MARK; → **overstep the mark** at OVERSTEP (2); → PUNCTUATION MARK, QUESTION MARK, SPEECH MARKS

mark² S3 W2 *v*

1 WRITE ON STH [T] to write or draw on something, so that someone will notice what you have written: *I've marked the pages you need to look at.* | **mark sth with sth** *When you're done, put your sheet in the envelope marked with your name.* | **mark sth on sth** *Peter marked his name on the first page.* | **mark sth personal/fragile/urgent etc** *a document marked 'confidential'* | **mark sb present/absent** (=write on an official list that someone is there or not there, especially in school) *Any student who is more than 20 minutes late for class will be marked absent.* | *All school uniform should be clearly marked with the child's name.*

2 DAMAGE [I,T] to make a mark on something in a way that spoils its appearance or damages it, or to become spoiled in this way: *Take off your shoes so you don't mark the floor.* | *The disease had marked her face for life.* | *The table marks easily, so please be careful.*

3 CELEBRATE [T] to celebrate an important event: *celebrations to mark Australia Day* | **mark sth with sth** *Carter's 90th birthday will be marked with a large party at the Savoy Hotel.* | *Mrs Lawson was presented with a gold watch to mark the occasion.*

4 SHOW POSITION [T] to show where something is: *A simple wooden cross marked the spot.* | *He had marked the route on the map in red.* | **mark sth with sth** *Troop positions were marked with colored pins.* | *She placed a bookmark between the pages to mark her place.*

5 YEAR/MONTH/WEEK [T] if a particular year, month, or week marks an important event, the event happened on that date during a previous year: *This week marks the 250th anniversary of the birth of Joseph Priestley.*

6 SHOW A CHANGE [T] to be a sign of an important change or an important stage in the development of something: *Her latest novel marks a turning point in her development as a writer.* | *The move seemed to mark a major change in government policy.* | *These elections mark the end of an era.*

7 QUALITY/FEATURE [T usually passive] if something is marked by a particular quality or feature, it is a typical or important part of that thing; ⊟ **character-ize**: *The villages of East Anglia are marked by beautiful churches with fine towers.*

8 STUDENT'S WORK [T] *especially BrE* to read a piece of written work and put a number or letter on it to show how good it is; ⊟ **grade** *AmE*: *I've got a pile of exam papers to mark.*

9 SPORT [T] *especially BrE* to stay close to a player of the opposite team during a game; ⊟ **guard** *AmE*

10 be marking time to spend time not doing very much except waiting for something else to happen: *I was just marking time until a better job came up.*

11 mark time if soldiers mark time, they move their legs as if they were marching, but remain in the same place

12 (you) mark my words! *spoken* used to tell someone that they should pay attention to what you are saying: *They're going to regret firing me, you mark my words.*

13 mark you *BrE old-fashioned* used to emphasize something you say; ⊟ **mind you**: *Her uncle's just given her a car – given, mark you, not lent.* → MARKED

mark sb/sth ⇔ **down** *phr v*

1 to write something down, especially in order to keep a record: *Mark down everything you eat on your daily chart.* | **mark sb/sth down as sth** *The teacher marked him down as absent.*

2 to reduce the price of something; ⊟ **mark up**; → **markdown**: *Winter coats have been marked down from $80 to $50.*

3 *especially BrE* to give a student a lower result in a test, paper etc because they have made mistakes: *Students will be marked down for failing to follow directions.*

mark sb/sth **down as** sth *phr v*
BrE to consider someone or something to be a particu-lar type of person or thing: *When I first saw Gilbert play I marked him down as a future England player.*

mark sb/sth ⇔ **off** *phr v*

1 to make an area separate by drawing a line around it, putting a rope around it etc: *The competitors' arena had* been marked off with cones.

2 to make a mark on a list to show that something has been done or completed; ▤ **tick off, check off**: *Mark off each of the names on the list as I call them out.*

3 *BrE* to make something or someone different from other things or people of a similar type; ▤ **distinguish**: [+**from**] *Sara's natural flair for languages marked her off from the other students.*

mark sb/sth ⇔ **out** *phr v*
1 to show the shape or position of something by drawing lines around it: *A volleyball court had been marked out on the grass.*
2 *BrE* to make someone or something seem very different from or better than other similar people or things: **mark sb/sth out as sth** *His stunning victory marked him out as the very best horse of his era.* | **mark sb out for sth** *She seemed marked out for success.*

mark sth ⇔ **up** *phr v*
1 to increase the price of something, so that you sell it for more than you paid for it; ▥ **mark down**: *Compact discs may be marked up as much as 80%.* → MARK-UP
2 to write notes or instructions for changes on a piece of writing, music etc: *I have to mark up the pages and send them back to the printer.*

mark·down /'mɑːkdaʊn $ 'mɑːrk-/ *n* [C] a reduction in the price of something: [+**of**] *a markdown of 15%*

marked W3 /mɑːkt $ mɑːrkt/ *adj*
1 [only before noun] very easy to notice; ▤ **noticeable**: *a marked lack of enthusiasm* | *The patient showed a marked improvement in her condition after changing medication.* | *Miller's organized desk stood **in marked contrast to** the rest of the office.*
2 marked man/woman a person who is in danger because someone wants to harm them —**markedly** /'mɑːk<u>ɪ</u>dli $ 'mɑːr-/ *adv*: *Johnson and Rivera have markedly different leadership styles.*

mark·er /'mɑːkə $ 'mɑːrkər/ *n* [C] **1** an object, sign etc that shows the position of something: *He buried the bodies in a single grave with a wooden cross as a marker.* **2** something which shows that a quality or feature exists or is present; ▤ **mark**: [+**of/for**] *antibodies which are a marker of hepatitis* | *the use of slang as a marker of social identity* **3** also **marker pen** *BrE* a large pen with a thick point made of FELT, used for marking or drawing things → MAGIC MARKER **4 put/lay/set down a marker** *BrE* to say or do something that clearly shows what you will do in the future

marker pen *n* [C] *BrE* a MARKER (3)

mar·ket¹ S1 W1 /'mɑːk<u>ɪ</u>t $ 'mɑːr-/ *n*
1 PLACE TO BUY THINGS [C] **a)** a time when people buy and sell goods, food etc, or the place, usually outside or in a large building, where this happens: *I usually buy all my vegetables at the market.* | **fish/fruit and vegetable/flower etc market** *There's a good antiques market here on Sundays.* | **street market** (=with a lot of different people selling things from tables, STALLS etc in the street) **b)** *AmE* a shop that sells food and things for the home; ▤ **grocery store**
2 the market a) the STOCK MARKET: *Most analysts are forecasting a further downturn in the market.* | *As soon as she graduated from college, she started to **play the market** (=risk money on the stock market).* | *The markets (=all the stock markets in the world) are better prepared for a weakening economy than they were ten years ago.* **b)** the total amount of trade in a particular kind of goods: *Honda is trying to increase its **market share***. | *the state of the art market* | **the housing/property etc market** *Investors in the property market are worried about rising inflation.* | [+**in**] *the world market in aluminum* → BEAR MARKET, BULL MARKET **c)** the system in which all prices and wages depend on what goods people want to buy, how many they buy etc: *The president believes prices should be determined by the market, not the government.* → FREE MARKET
3 on the market available for people to buy: *The manufacturers say the device will be on the market by May.* | *Handguns are freely available **on the open***

market (=for anyone to buy). | *They knew it wasn't a good time to sell their house, but they still **put it on the market** (=offered it for sale).* | *a revolutionary new drug that has just **come onto the market** ⚠ Do not say 'in the market'. Say **on the market**.
4 COUNTRY/AREA [C] a particular country or area where a company sells its goods or where a particular type of goods is sold: *Our main overseas market is Japan.* | **international/home/UK etc market** *The domestic market makes up about 75% of their sales.* | [+**for**] *The world's largest market for illegal drugs is the United States.*
5 PEOPLE WHO BUY [singular] the number of people who want to buy something, or the type of people who want to buy it: [+**for**] *The market for specialist academic books is pretty small.* | *He's been trying to determine if **there is a market** for his invention.* | **niche/specialist market**
6 be in the market for sth to be interested in buying something: *This is a bad time to be in the market for a new car.*
7 the job/labour market the people looking for work, and the number of jobs that are available: *The job market has been badly hit by the recession.*
8 a buyer's/seller's market a time that is better for buyers because prices are low, or better for sellers because prices are high: *I'll look for a house next year when it's more of a buyer's market.* → **corner the market** at CORNER² (3); → **price yourself out of the market** at PRICE² (4)

market² *v* [T] **1** to try to persuade people to buy a product by advertising it in a particular way, using attractive packages etc: *If you could ever figure out how to market this you'd make a fortune.* | **market sth for sb** *They plan to market the toy for children aged 2 to 6.* | **market sth as sth** *Electric cars are being marketed as safe for the environment.* **2** to make a product available in shops: *The turkeys are marketed ready-to-cook.*

mar·ket·a·ble /'mɑːk<u>ɪ</u>təbəl $ 'mɑːr-/ *adj* marketable goods, skills etc can be sold easily because people want them: *The program is designed to provide students with real, marketable skills.* —**marketability** /ˌmɑːk<u>ɪ</u>tə'bɪl<u>ɪ</u>ti $ ˌmɑːr-/ *n* [U]

market ˌday *n* [C,U] *BrE* the day in the week when there is a market in a particular town

market-ˌdriven *adj* market-driven activities, products, developments etc are a result of public demand for a particular product, service, or skill: *a market-driven economy*

ˌmarket eˈconomy *n* [C] an economic system in which companies are not controlled by the government but decide what they want to produce or sell, based on what they believe they can make a profit from

mar·ket·eer /ˌmɑːk<u>ɪ</u>'tɪə $ ˌmɑːrk<u>ɪ</u>'tɪr/ also **mar·ket·er** /'mɑːk<u>ɪ</u>tə $ 'mɑːrk<u>ɪ</u>tər/ *n* [C] someone who sells goods or services —**marketeering** *n* [U]

ˌmarket ˈforces *n* [plural] the way that the behaviour of buyers and sellers affects the levels of prices and wages, without any influence from the government

ˌmarket ˈgarden *n* [C] *BrE* an area of land where vegetables and fruit are grown so that they can be sold; ▤ **truck farm** *AmE* —**market gardener** *n* [C]

mar·ket·ing S3 W3 /'mɑːk<u>ɪ</u>tɪŋ $ 'mɑːr-/ *n* [U] the activity of deciding how to advertise a product, what price to charge for it etc, or the type of job in which you do this: *a clever marketing ploy* | *Company sales improved dramatically following a $2 million marketing campaign.* | *a career in **sales and marketing*** | *Cushman is director of marketing for a chain of Italian restaurants.* | *You should contact the company's UK marketing manager.*

ˌmarket ˈleader *n* [C] the company that sells the most of a particular type of product, or the product that is the most successful one of its type: *the UK market leader in sports shoes*

'market-led adj BrE MARKET-DRIVEN

mar·ket·mak·er /'mɑːkɪ̯t,meɪkə $ 'mɑːrkɪ̯t,meɪkər/ n [C] BrE technical an organization such as a bank or a BROKER who keeps a supply of STOCKS and SHARES available for people who want to buy them

mar·ket·place /'mɑːkɪ̯tpleɪs $ 'mɑːr-/ n [C] **1** the marketplace the part of business activity that is concerned with buying and selling goods in competition with other companies: *Some retailers worry that new regulations will hurt their ability to compete in the marketplace.* **2** an open area in a town where a market is held

market 'price n [C] the price of something on a MARKET at a particular time

market re'search n [U] a business activity which involves collecting information about what goods people buy and why they buy them: *They had to conduct market research, then advertise the product.*

'market share n [C,U] the PERCENTAGE of sales in a MARKET that a company or product has

'market town n [C] BrE a town where there is an outdoor market, usually once or twice a week

market 'value n [C,U] **1** the value of a product, building etc based on the price that people are willing to pay for it, rather than the cost of producing it or building it **2** the total value of all the SHARES on a STOCK MARKET, or the value of a particular company's shares

mark·ing /'mɑːkɪŋ $ 'mɑːr-/ n **1** [C usually plural, U] things painted or written on something, especially something such as an aircraft, road, vehicle etc: *The marking on the road is unclear.* | *There were strange markings on the walls of the cave.* **2** [C usually plural, U] the coloured patterns and shapes on an animal's fur, on leaves etc: *This particular dolphin is noted for its distinctive black and white markings.* | *the vivid markings of the angelfish* **3** [U] especially BrE the activity of checking students' written work; ▤ **grading** AmE: *I have to do a lot of marking tonight.* | *the setting and marking of exams*

mark·ka /'mɑːkə $ 'mɑːr-/ n plural **markkaa** /-kɑː/ [C] the standard unit of money used in Finland before the Euro

marks·man /'mɑːksmən $ 'mɑːrks-/ n plural **marksmen** /-mən/ [C] someone who can shoot a gun very well

marks·man·ship /'mɑːksmənʃɪp $ 'mɑːrks-/ n [U] the ability to shoot a gun very well

'mark-up BrE; **mark·up** AmE /'mɑːkʌp $ 'mɑːrk-/ n [C] an increase in the price of something, especially from the price a shop pays for something to the price it sells it for; → **mark up**: *The retailer's mark-up is 50%.*

marl /mɑːl $ mɑːrl/ n [U] **1** soil consisting of LIME and CLAY **2** cloth which has pale threads running through another colour: *a jacket available in black or grey marl*

mar·lin /'mɑːlɪ̯n $ 'mɑːr-/ n plural **marlin** [C] a large sea fish with a long sharp nose, which people hunt for sport

mar·ma·lade /'mɑːməleɪd $ 'mɑːr-/ n [U] a JAM made from fruit such as oranges, LEMONS or GRAPEFRUIT, usually eaten at breakfast

mar·mo·set /'mɑːməzet $ 'mɑːrməset, -zet/ n [C] a type of small monkey with long hair and large eyes that lives in Central and South America

mar·mot /'mɑːmət $ 'mɑːr-/ n [C] a small European or American animal with fur and short front legs which lives under the ground

ma·roon¹ /mə'ruːn/ n [U] a dark brownish red colour —**maroon** adj

maroon² v [T usually passive] to be left in a place where there are no other people and where you cannot escape: *The car broke down and left us marooned in the middle of nowhere.*

marque /mɑːk $ mɑːrk/ n [C] BrE the well-known name of a type of car or other product, especially an expensive one: *the prestigious Ferrari marque*

mar·quee /mɑːˈkiː $ mɑːr-/ n [C] **1** BrE a large tent at an outdoor event or large party, used especially for eating or drinking in **2** AmE a large sign above the door of a theatre or cinema which covers the entrance and gives the name of the play or film **3** AmE **marquee player, actor etc** someone who people want to see because they are good or famous

mar·quess /'mɑːkwɪ̯s $ 'mɑːr-/ n [C] BrE a MARQUIS

mar·quet·ry /'mɑːkɪ̯tri $ 'mɑːr-/ n [U] a pattern made of coloured pieces of wood laid together, or the art of making these patterns

mar·quis /'mɑːkwɪ̯s $ 'mɑːr-/ n [C] a man who, in the British system of NOBLE titles, has a rank between DUKE and EARL: *the Marquis of Bath*

mar·riage S2 W2 /'mærɪdʒ/ n

1 [C,U] the relationship between two people who are married, or the state of being married

happy/unhappy marriage
mixed marriage (=between people of different races or religions)
arranged marriage (=your parents choose the person who you marry)
loveless marriage
a marriage breaks down (=it ends because of disagreements)
the breakdown/break-up of your marriage (=the end of your marriage)
sex before marriage/outside marriage
be born outside marriage (=be born when your parents are not married)
propose marriage formal (=ask someone to marry you)
consummate a marriage (=make your marriage complete by having sex)
annul a marriage formal (=a court or church leader officially ends a marriage)

She has three daughters from a previous marriage. | *One in three marriages ends in divorce.* | [+to] *his marriage to Marilyn Monroe* | [+between] *In Denmark they have legalized marriage between gay couples.* | *They have a very **happy marriage**.* | *children of **mixed marriages*** | *Women were often forced into **arranged marriages**.* | *She felt trapped in a **loveless marriage**.* | *She moved to London after **the break-up of her marriage**.* | *My parents disapprove of **sex before marriage**.* | *More than half of all births in the region are **outside marriage**.*

2 [C] the ceremony in which two people get married; ▤ **wedding**: *The marriage took place at St Bartholomew's church.*

3 by marriage if you are related to someone by marriage, they are married to someone in your family, or you are married to someone in theirs: *her cousin by marriage*

mar·riage·a·ble /'mærɪdʒəbəl/ adj old-fashioned suitable for marriage: *a girl of marriageable age*

'marriage ,bureau n [C] BrE old-fashioned an organization that helps people find partners to marry

'marriage cer,tificate n [C] an official document that proves that two people are married

,marriage 'guidance n [U] BrE, **marriage 'counseling** AmE advice given to people who are having difficulties in their marriage

'marriage ,licence BrE, **marriage license** AmE n [C] an official written document saying that two people are allowed to get married

'marriage lines n [plural] BrE old-fashioned a MARRIAGE CERTIFICATE

,marriage of con'venience n [C] **1** an agreement between two or more countries, businesses, or people that is only made for political or economic reasons **2** a marriage for political or economic reasons, not for love

'marriage ,vow n [C usually plural] a promise that you make during the marriage ceremony

mar·ried S2 W2 /'mærid/ adj
1 having a husband or a wife: *Are you married or*

single? | They've been married for eight years. | Married men earn 70 percent more than single men. | [+**to**] Nicole is married to my brother. | We're **getting married** (=marrying) next month. | **married couple/man/ woman** a happily married man | When she first came to London, she was **newly married** and out of work. | So, how do you like **married life**? ⚠ Do not say 'be married with' someone or 'get married with' someone. Say **be married to** someone or **get married to** someone.
2 be married to sth to give most of your time and attention to a job or activity: I was married to my job.

WORD FOCUS: MARRIED
single not married | **divorced** if you are divorced, you have officially ended your marriage to someone | **engaged** if you are engaged to be married, you have formally agreed to marry someone in the future | **widowed** if you are widowed, your husband or wife has died | **be living together** to be living as a couple in the same house without being married | **spouse** formal the person you are married to | **partner** your husband, wife, boyfriend, or girlfriend | **marital status** whether you are single or married – used on official forms

mar·row /'mærəʊ $ -roʊ/ n **1** [U] the soft fatty substance in the hollow centre of bones; ▤ **bone marrow:** a bone marrow transplant **2** [C,U] BrE a large long dark green vegetable that grows on the ground **3 chilled/frozen/shocked etc to the marrow** BrE literary very cold, shocked etc

'**marrow bone** n [C,U] BrE a large bone that contains a lot of marrow

mar·ry S1 W2 /'mæri/ v **married, marrying, marries 1** [I,T] if you marry someone, you become their husband or wife; → **married:** He married Bea in 1925. | I'm going to ask her to marry me on St Valentine's Day. | She **married young** (=at a young age), and was divorced when her children were tiny. | People in higher social classes are more likely to **marry late** (=when they are older than is usual). | Sophia had, in a sense, **married beneath her** (=married someone of a lower social class than her). ⚠ In spoken English, **get married** is more common than **marry.**
2 [T] to perform the ceremony at which two people get married: The priest who married us was really nice.
3 [T] to find a husband or wife for one of your children: **marry sb to sb** She was determined to marry all of her daughters to rich men.
4 also **marry up** [T] formal to combine two different ideas, designs, tastes etc together: **marry sth with/to sth** The building's design marries a traditional style with modern materials. | **marry sth and sth** He writes fiction that marries up realism and the supernatural.
5 not the marrying kind not the type of person who wants to get married: I'm just not the marrying kind.

WORD FOCUS: MARRY
wedding the ceremony at which people get married | **bride** the woman who is getting married | **bridegroom/ groom** the man who is getting married | **the best man** a friend of the groom, who helps him and gives a speech | **bridesmaid** a woman or girl who helps the bride | **matron of honour** BrE/**honor** AmE a married woman who helps the bride on her wedding day | **reception** the meal after the wedding | **honeymoon** the holiday that people go on after they get married | **hen night** BrE/ **bridal shower** AmE a party before the wedding for the bride | **stag night** BrE/**bachelor party** AmE a party before the wedding for the groom | **propose** to ask someone to marry you | **get engaged** to formally agree to marry each other → ENGAGEMENT, DIVORCE

marry into sth phr v
to join a family or social group by marrying someone who belongs to it: She married into a very wealthy family.

marry sb ⇔ **off** phr v
to find a husband or wife for someone – used in order to show disapproval: [+**to**] They married her off to the first young man who came along.

Mars /mɑːz $ mɑːrz/ n the small red PLANET that is fourth in order from the sun and is nearest the Earth; → **Martian:** the enormous volcanoes known to exist on Mars → see picture at SOLAR SYSTEM

Mar·seil·laise /ˌmɑːseɪˈez $ ˌmɑːr-/ n **the Marseillaise** the national song of France

marsh /mɑːʃ $ mɑːrʃ/ n [C,U] an area of low flat ground that is always wet and soft; → **bog, swamp** —**marshy** adj: The crane lives in marshy habitats.

mar·shal¹ /'mɑːʃəl $ 'mɑːr-/ n [C] **1** an officer of the highest rank in the army or air force of some countries: Marshal Zhukov | the Marshal of the Royal Airforce **2** an official in charge of an important public event or ceremony: Heston has been named **grand marshal** of the parade. **3** a person who controls crowds, traffic etc at a sports event or other public event: I could see a marshal on the finish line waving a yellow flag. **4 federal/US marshal** AmE a police officer employed by the national government to make sure people do what a COURT ORDER says they must do **5** AmE the officer in charge of a fire department

marshal² v **marshalled, marshalling** BrE, **marshaled, marshaling** AmE [T] **1** to organize your thoughts, ideas etc so that they are clear, effective, or easy to understand: **marshal your thoughts/arguments etc** Briggs paused for a moment as if to marshal his thoughts. **2** to organize all the people or things that you need in order to be ready for a battle, election etc: The general **marshalled** his **forces** for a major offensive. | Senator Bryant attempted to **marshal support** for the measure. **3** to control or organize a large group: Gently, Ginny marshalled her guests into a better position.

'**marshalling ˌyard** n [C] BrE a place where railway WAGONS are brought together to form trains

'**marsh gas** n [U] gas formed from decaying plants under water in a MARSH; ▤ **methane**

marsh·land /'mɑːʃlænd $ 'mɑːrʃ-/ n [U] an area of low wet ground that is always soft

marsh·mal·low /ˌmɑːʃˈmæləʊ $ 'mɑːrʃmeloʊ/ n [C,U] a very soft light white or pink sweet, made of sugar and egg WHITE

mar·su·pi·al /mɑːˈsuːpiəl $ mɑːr-/ n [C] an animal such as a KANGAROO which carries its babies in a pocket of skin on its body —**marsupial** adj

mart /mɑːt $ mɑːrt/ n [C] **1** AmE a place where goods are sold – used especially in the names of shops: the largest furniture mart in the region | K-Mart **2** BrE a market, especially one where animals are sold

mar·ten /'mɑːt̬n, -tn $ 'mɑːrtn/ n [C] a small animal with a long body and a tail that lives mainly in trees and that eats smaller animals: a pine marten

mar·tial /'mɑːʃəl $ 'mɑːr-/ adj [only before noun] connected with war and fighting: martial music → COURT MARTIAL

ˌ**martial ˈart** n [C usually plural] a sport such as JUDO or KARATE, in which you fight with your hands and feet. Martial arts were developed in Eastern Asia: a martial arts expert

ˌ**martial ˈlaw** n [U] a situation in which the army controls an area instead of the police, especially because of fighting against the government: **impose/ declare martial law** The government may declare martial law in response to the latest violence in the region. | In May, **martial law** was **lifted** (=ended) in most areas. | **under martial law** According to press reports, the country is now under martial law.

Mar·tian /'mɑːʃən $ 'mɑːr-/ n [C] an imaginary creature from the PLANET Mars —**Martian** adj

mar·tin /'mɑːt̬n $ 'mɑːrtn/ n [C] a small bird like a SWALLOW

M

mar·ti·net /ˌmɑːtɪˈnet $ ˌmɑːr-/ n [C] *formal* someone who is very strict and makes people obey rules exactly; ☐ **disciplinarian**: *The woman in charge was a martinet who treated us like children.*

Mar·ti·ni /mɑːˈtiːni $ mɑːr-/ n [C,U] *trademark* an alcoholic drink made by mixing GIN or VODKA with VERMOUTH: *a dry* (=not sweet) *Martini*

mar·tyr¹ /ˈmɑːtə $ ˈmɑːrtər/ n [C] **1** someone who dies for their religious or political beliefs and is admired by people for this: *St. Stephen, the first Christian martyr* | [+to] *He was a martyr to the cause of racial harmony.* | *The army has been held back because the government is reluctant to make martyrs of the protesters.* **2** someone who tries hard to get other people's sympathy by complaining about how hard their life is – used to show disapproval: *I think she rather relishes the role of martyr.* **3 be a martyr to sth** *BrE spoken* to suffer a lot because of an illness, problem, or bad situation: *She's a martyr to her arthritis.*

martyr² v [T usually passive] if someone is martyred, they are killed because of their religious beliefs: *Becket was martyred in 1170.* | **be martyred for sth** *Catherine was martyred for her faith.*

mar·tyr·dom /ˈmɑːtədəm $ ˈmɑːrtər-/ n [U] death as a martyr: *In that year, thousands of Christians suffered martyrdom for their faith.*

mar·tyred /ˈmɑːtəd $ ˈmɑːrtərd/ adj **a martyred look/expression/air etc** *especially BrE* an unhappy look or expression that is intended to make other people feel sorry for you: *He did not reply, but got into the car glumly, with a martyred expression.*

mar·vel¹ /ˈmɑːvəl $ ˈmɑːr-/ v **marvelled, marvelling** *BrE*, **marveled, marveling** *AmE* [I,T] to feel or express great surprise or admiration at something, especially someone's behaviour: *'The man is a genius,' marvelled Claire.* | [+at/over] *I marvelled at my mother's ability to remain calm in a crisis.* | *Visitors to Rome marvel over the beauty of the city.* | **marvel that** *I marvelled that anyone could be so stupid.*

marvel² n [C] something or someone that is extremely useful or skilful; ☐ **miracle, wonder**: *an engineering marvel* | *I don't know how he did it – he's an absolute marvel!* | [+of] *the marvels of modern science*

mar·vel·lous S2 *BrE*; **marvelous** *AmE* /ˈmɑːvələs $ ˈmɑːr-/ adj extremely good, enjoyable, impressive etc; ☐ **wonderful**: *'How was your holiday?' 'Marvellous!'* | *We had a marvellous time.* | *I can't stand him, but my wife thinks he's marvellous.* | *It's marvellous what they can do these days.* —**marvellously** adv

Marx·is·m /ˈmɑːksɪzəm $ ˈmɑːr-/ n [U] the system of political thinking invented by Karl Marx, which explains changes in history as the result of a struggle between social classes

Marx·ist¹ /ˈmɑːksɪst $ ˈmɑːr-/ adj relating to or based on Marxism: *a Marxist perspective*

Marxist² n [C] someone who agrees with Marxism

mar·zi·pan /ˈmɑːzɪˌpæn $ ˈmɑːrtsə-, ˌmɑːrzə-/ n [U] a sweet food made from ALMONDS, sugar, and eggs, used to make sweets and for covering cakes

masc. also **masc** *BrE* the written abbreviation of *masculine*

mas·ca·ra /mæˈskɑːrə $ mæˈskærə/ n [U] a dark substance used to colour your EYELASHES and make them look thicker

mas·cot /ˈmæskət, -kɒt $ -kɑːt/ n [C] an animal or toy, or a person dressed as an animal, that represents a team or organization, and is thought to bring them good luck: *the official mascot of the 2002 World Cup* | *Rocky the Raccoon, the team mascot*

mas·cu·line /ˈmæskjəlɪn/ adj **1** having qualities considered to be typical of men or of what men do; ☐ **feminine**: *They're nice curtains, but I'd prefer something a little more masculine.* | *She has a very masculine voice.* | *Hunting was a typically masculine occupa-*

tion. **2** in some languages, a masculine noun, PRONOUN etc belongs to a class of words that have different INFLECTIONS from FEMININE or NEUTER words: *The word for 'book' is masculine in French.*

mas·cu·lin·i·ty /ˌmæskjʊˈlɪnəti/ n [U] the features and qualities considered to be typical of men; ☐ **femininity**: *Children's ideas of masculinity tend to come from their fathers.* | *boys trying to prove their masculinity*

ma·ser /ˈmeɪzə $ -ər/ n [C] *technical* a piece of equipment that produces a very powerful electric force; → **laser**

mash¹ /mæʃ/ also **mash up** v [T] to crush something, especially a food that has been cooked, until it is soft and smooth: *Mash the bananas.* —**mashed** adj: *mashed potatoes* —**masher** n [C]: *a potato masher;* → see picture at POTATO

mash² n [U] **1** *BrE informal* potatoes that have been boiled and then crushed and mixed with milk until they are smooth: *bangers* (=sausages) *and mash* **2** a mixture of MALT or crushed grain and hot water, used to make beer or WHISKY **3** a mixture of grain cooked with water to make a food for animals

mashed /mæʃt/ adj [not before noun] *BrE informal* very drunk or strongly affected by drugs: *We got completely mashed last night.*

mask¹ /mɑːsk $ mæsk/ n [C] **1** something that covers all or part of your face, to protect it or to hide it: *a surgical face mask* | *He was attacked and robbed by two people wearing masks.* **2** something that covers your face, and has another face painted on it, which is used for ceremonies or special occasions: *a Halloween mask* **3** [usually singular] an expression or way of behaving that hides your real emotions or character; ☐ **front**: *Her sarcasm is a mask for her insecurity.* **4** a substance that you put on your face and leave there for a short time to clean the skin or make it softer; ☐ **face pack**: *a facial mask* → DEATH MASK, GAS MASK

mask² v [T] **1** if a smell, taste, sound etc is masked by a stronger one, it cannot be noticed because of the stronger one: *Liz turned on a radio to mask the noise.* | *Air-fresheners mask bad smells instead of removing them.* **2** to hide your feelings or the truth about a situation: *Men often mask their true feelings with humour.* **3** to cover or hide something so that it cannot be clearly seen: *The new accommodation block has all but masked the original building.*

masked /mɑːskt $ mæskt/ adj wearing a mask: *Masked gunmen opened fire on the bus.*

masked 'ball n [C] a formal dance at which everyone wears masks

masking tape n [U] long narrow paper that is sticky on one side, used especially to protect the edge of an area which you are painting

mas·o·chis·m /ˈmæsəkɪzəm/ n [U] **1** sexual behaviour in which someone gains pleasure from being hurt or punished; → **sadism, sado-masochism** **2** behaviour that makes it seem that someone wants to suffer or have problems: *Unconscious masochism seemed to drive her from one disaster to the next.* —**masochist** n [C] —**masochistic** /ˌmæsəˈkɪstɪk◄/ adj: *masochistic behavior* —**masochistically** /-kli/ adv

ma·son /ˈmeɪsən/ n [C] a STONEMASON

Mason n [C] a FREEMASON

Mason-Dix·on line /ˌmeɪsən ˈdɪksən laɪn/ n [singular] the border between the American states of Pennsylvania and Maryland, considered as the dividing line between the northern and southern US

Ma·son·ic /məˈsɒnɪk $ -ˈsɑː-/ adj involved or connected with FREEMASONRY: *a Masonic lodge*

Mason jar n [C] *trademark AmE* a glass pot with a tight lid, used for preserving fruit and vegetables; ☐ **Kilner jar** *BrE*

ma·son·ry /ˈmeɪsənri/ n [U] **1** the bricks or stone from which a building, wall etc has been made: *Several people were buried under falling masonry.* **2** the skill of building with stone

Masonry n [U] FREEMASONRY

masque /mɑːsk $ mæsk/ n [C] a type of play popular in England in the 16th and 17th centuries that included music, dancing, and songs: *a Court masque*

mas·que·rade[1] /ˌmæskəˈreɪd/ n **1** [C] a formal dance or party where people wear MASKS and unusual clothes **2** [C,U] a way of behaving or speaking that hides your true thoughts or feelings; ◼ **pretence**: *She didn't really love him, but she kept up the masquerade for the children's sake.*

masquerade[2] v [I] to pretend to be something or someone different: [+as] *A number of police officers masqueraded as demonstrators.* | *Some of these breakfast foods are just candy masquerading as cereals.* | [+under] *He was masquerading under a false name.*

mass[1] W2 /mæs/ n
 1 LARGE AMOUNT a) [C] a large amount of a substance which does not have a definite or regular shape: *The food had congealed into a sticky mass.* | [+of] *a high mass of rock* **b)** [C usually singular] a large amount or quantity of something: [+of] *a huge mass of data* **c)** **masses of sth** BrE informal a large amount of something, or a lot of people or things: *Masses of books covered every surface in the room.*
 2 CROWD [singular] a large crowd: [+of] *There was a mass of people around the club entrance.* | *The road was blocked by a solid mass of protesters.*
 3 the masses all the ordinary people in society who do not have power or influence: *The trains provided cheap travel for the masses.*
 4 the mass of people/the population/workers etc most of the people in a group or society; ◼ **the majority**: *The war is strongly supported by the mass of the population.*
 5 CHURCH CEREMONY also **Mass a)** [C,U] the main ceremony in some Christian churches, especially the Roman Catholic Church, which celebrates the last meal that Jesus Christ ate: *What time do you go to mass?* | *morning/evening/midnight etc Mass Will I see you at morning Mass?* | **say/celebrate Mass** (=perform this ceremony as a priest) → HIGH MASS **b)** [C] a piece of music written to be performed at the ceremony of mass: *Mozart's Mass in C minor*
 6 SCIENCE [U] *technical* the amount of material in something: *The sun makes up 99.9% of the mass of our solar system.* → CRITICAL MASS

mass[2] W3 adj [only before noun] involving or intended for a very large number of people: *a mass protest* | *weapons of mass destruction* | *the problem of mass unemployment* | **mass marketing/entertainment etc** *a mass marketing campaign* | *Email has made mass mailings possible at the touch of a button.*

mass[3] v [I,T] to come together, or to make people or things come together, in a large group; ◼ **gather**: **mass (sth) behind/along/in etc sth** *Western reports say that troops have been massing in the region since December.* | *grey clouds massing behind the mountains* | *Both countries have massed troops along the border.*

mas·sa·cre[1] /ˈmæsəkə $ -ər/ n **1** [C,U] when a lot of people are killed violently, especially people who cannot defend themselves: *the only survivor of the massacre* | [+of] *the massacre of several hundred prodemocracy demonstrators* | **the Boston/Peterloo/Harperville etc massacre** *the infamous Peterloo massacre of 1819* **2** [C] informal a very bad defeat in a game or competition: *United lost in a 9–0 massacre.*

massacre[2] v [T] **1** to kill a lot of people or animals in a violent way, especially when they cannot defend themselves: *The army massacred more than 150 unarmed civilians.* | *Tens of thousands of dolphins and small whales are brutally massacred every year.* → see box at KILL[1] **2** informal to defeat someone very badly in a game, competition etc: *The Cougars massacred the*

Bucs last night, 38 – 7. **3** informal to spoil part of a play, a song etc by performing it very badly: *Unfortunately, Jones absolutely massacres the role of Ophelia.*

mas·sage[1] /ˈmæsɑːʒ $ məˈsɑːʒ/ n [C,U] the action of pressing and rubbing someone's body with your hands, to help them relax or to reduce pain in their muscles or joints: *Massage helps ease the pain.* | *Why don't you **have a massage**?* | *Joan **gave** me a **gentle neck massage**.* | **body/shoulder/foot etc massage** *A full-body massage lasts around one hour.*

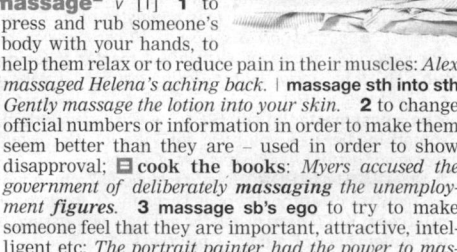
massage

massage[2] v [T] **1** to press and rub someone's body with your hands, to help them relax or to reduce pain in their muscles: *Alex massaged Helena's aching back.* | **massage sth into sth** *Gently massage the lotion into your skin.* **2** to change official numbers or information in order to make them seem better than they are – used in order to show disapproval; ◼ **cook the books**: *Myers accused the government of deliberately massaging the unemployment figures.* **3 massage sb's ego** to try to make someone feel that they are important, attractive, intelligent etc: *The portrait painter had the power to massage the king's ego or to expose his flaws.*

ˈ**massage parlour** BrE; **massage parlor** AmE /$ ˌ.ˈ.ˌ.ˈ/ n [C] **1** a BROTHEL (=place where people pay to have sex) - used to pretend that it is not a brothel **2** a place where you pay to have a massage

masse → EN MASSE

massed /mæst/ adj [only before noun] in a large group: **massed ranks/forces** *I look around me at the massed ranks of reporters.* | **massed choir/band** BrE (=several choirs or bands singing or playing together as one large group)

mas·seur /mæˈsɜː, mə- $ -ˈsɜːr/ n [C] someone who gives MASSAGES

mas·seuse /mæˈsɜːz $ mæˈsuːz, mə-/ n [C] **1** a woman who gives MASSAGES → see picture at OCCUPATION **2** a PROSTITUTE

mas·sif /ˈmæsiːf $ mæˈsiːf/ n [C] a group of mountains forming one large solid shape

mas·sive S2 W3 /ˈmæsɪv/ adj
 1 very large, solid, and heavy: *The bell is massive, weighing over 40 tons.* | *the castle's massive walls*
 2 unusually large, powerful, or damaging: *My phone bill is going to be massive this month.* | *massive increases in the number of homeless* | *Club members can get a massive discount of £50.* | **massive stroke/heart attack etc** *Simpkins suffered a massive stroke.* | **massive argument/row etc** BrE: *I had a massive argument with her.*
 3 BrE informal extremely good: *Listen to this. It's a massive song.* —**massively** adv: *The president was massively popular.*

ˈ**mass-market** adj [only before noun] designed for sale to as wide a range of people as possible: **mass-market paperback/novel/film etc** *a mass-market paperback priced at $8.99* —**mass market** n [C]

ˌ**mass ˈmedia** n **the mass media** all the people and organizations that provide information and news for the public, including television, radio, and newspapers: *The crime received heavy coverage in the mass media.*

ˌ**mass ˈmurderer** n [C] someone who has murdered a lot of people

ˌ**mass-proˈduced** adj produced in large numbers using machinery, so that each object is the same and can be sold cheaply; → **mass production**: *mass-produced furniture* —**mass-produce** *v* [T]

,**mass pro'duction** *n* [U] when products are made in large numbers by machines so that they can be sold cheaply; → **mass-produced**

,**mass 'transit** *n* [U] *technical* methods of transport by which large numbers of people can travel around a city: *The city has virtually no mass transit.*

mast /mɑːst $ mæst/ *n* [C] **1** a tall pole on which the sails or flags on a ship are hung → see picture at WRECK[1] **2** *BrE* a tall metal tower that sends out radio and television signals: *a radio mast* **3** a tall pole on which a flag is hung → HALF-MAST

mas·tec·to·my /mæˈstektəmi/ *n plural* **mastectomies** [C] *medical* a medical operation to remove a breast

mas·ter[1] /ˈmɑːstə $ ˈmæstər/ *n* [C]
1 SKILLED PERSON someone who is very skilled at something: [+of] *Runyon was a master of the short story.* | *a master of disguise* | *Hitchcock was an acknowledged master of suspense.* | **master at (doing) sth** *She's a master at manipulating people.* | *a work of art by a true master*
2 be a past master (at sth) *BrE* to be very good at doing something because you have done it a lot: *He's a past master at getting free drinks out of people.*
3 MAN WITH AUTHORITY *old-fashioned* **a)** a man who has control or authority over servants or workers; → **mistress**: *You'll have to ask the master's permission.* **b)** the male owner of a dog; → **mistress**
4 be your own master to be in control of your own life or work: *Determined to be his own master, Simmons quit in 1998 and started working freelance.*
5 be master of your own fate/destiny *literary* to be in complete control of what happens to you: *Our country must be master of its own economic destiny.*
6 ORIGINAL a document, record, etc from which copies are made: *I gave him the master to copy.*
7 Master of Arts/Science/Education etc a university DEGREE in an ARTS subject, a science subject etc that you can get after your first degree → **MA, M.SC., MED, MPHIL;** → **Bachelor of Arts/Science/Education** etc at BACHELOR (2)
8 TEACHER **a)** *BrE old-fashioned* a male teacher; → **headmaster, mistress b)** also **Master** a wise person whose ideas and words other people accept and follow: *a Zen master*
9 YOUNG BOY also **Master** *old-fashioned* used when speaking or referring to a young boy: *How's young Master Toby today?*
10 UNIVERSITY OFFICIAL also **Master** the person who is in charge of some university colleges in the UK: *the Master of Trinity College, Cambridge*
11 CAPTAIN *old-fashioned* someone who is in charge of a ship → GRAND MASTER, OLD MASTER, QUIZMASTER

master[2] *v* [T] **1** to learn a skill or a language so well that you have no difficulty with it: *the skills needed to master a new language* | *I never quite mastered the art of walking in high heels.* **2** to manage to control a strong emotion; ▣ **overcome**: *He had learned to master his fear of heights.*

master[3] *adj* [only before noun] **1** a master copy of a document, recording etc is the one from which copies are made: **master list/copy/recording etc** *We've lost the master disk.* **2** most important or main: *the master control center at NASA* **3** **master craftsman/chef/plumber etc** someone who is very skilled at a particular job, especially a job that involves working with your hands: *a society of master chefs*

,**master-at-'arms** *n* [C] an officer with police duties on a ship

'**master ,bedroom** *n* [C] the largest bedroom in a house or apartment, often with its own bathroom

mas·ter·class, **master class** /ˈmɑːstəˌklɑːs $ ˈmæstərˌklæs/ *n* [C] a lesson, especially in music, given to very skilful students by someone famous

mas·ter·ful /ˈmɑːstəfəl $ ˈmæstər-/ *adj* **1** controlling people or situations in a skilful and confident way: *Klein handled the situation in a masterful way.* **2** done with great skill and understanding; ▣ **masterly**: *a masterful analysis of the text* —**masterfully** *adv*: *Jack strode masterfully into the room.*

'**master key** *n* [C] a key that will open all the door locks in a building

mas·ter·ly /ˈmɑːstəli $ ˈmæstərli/ *adj* done or made very skilfully; ▣ **masterful**: *He gave a masterly display in round one of the World Chess Championship.*

mas·ter·mind[1] /ˈmɑːstəmaɪnd $ ˈmæstər-/ *n* [singular] someone who plans and organizes a complicated operation, especially a criminal operation: *a criminal mastermind* | [+of/behind] *He is suspected of being the mastermind behind the bombings.*

mastermind[2] *v* [T] to think of, plan, and organize a large, important, and difficult operation: *The project was masterminded by Morris, then aged 29.* | *Ridley, as commerce secretary, masterminded the privatisation.*

,**Master of 'Arts** *n* [C] an MA

,**master of 'ceremonies** *n* [C] someone who introduces guests or performers at a social or public occasion; ▣ **emcee**: *the master of ceremonies for the Miss World Pageant*

,**Master of 'Science** *n* [C] an MS or an M.SC.

mas·ter·piece /ˈmɑːstəpiːs $ ˈmæstər-/ *n* [C] **1** a work of art, a piece of writing or music etc that is of very high quality or that is the best that a particular artist, writer etc has produced; ▣ **masterwork**: *Mary Shelley was just 18 when she wrote the horror masterpiece 'Frankenstein'.* **2** a very good example of something: [+of] *The shark is a masterpiece of evolution.*

'**master plan** *n* [C usually singular] a detailed plan for controlling everything that happens in a complicated situation: *The job losses were part of a master plan aimed at transforming the structure of the company.* | *a master plan to modernize the health care system*

'**master ,race** *n* [C] a race of people who consider themselves better than other races, and who believe that they should rule over them

mas·ter's /ˈmɑːstəz $ ˈmæstərz/ *n* [C] *informal* a MASTER'S DEGREE

'**master's de,gree** also **master's** *informal n* [C] a university DEGREE such as an MA, M.SC., or M.S., that you can get by studying for one or two years after your first degree

mas·ter·stroke /ˈmɑːstəstrəʊk $ ˈmæstərstroʊk/ *n* [C] a very clever, skilful, and often unexpected action that is completely successful: *That ad campaign was an absolute masterstroke.* | [+of] *a masterstroke of diplomacy*

'**master ,switch** *n* [C] the switch that controls the supply of electricity to the whole of a building or area

mas·ter·work /ˈmɑːstəwɜːk $ ˈmæstərwɜːrk/ *n* [C] a painting, SCULPTURE, piece of music etc that is the best that someone has done; ▣ **masterpiece**: *'Otello' is Verdi's riveting masterwork.*

mas·ter·y /ˈmɑːstəri $ ˈmæs-/ *n* [U] **1** thorough understanding or great skill: [+of] *She possesses complete technical mastery of her instrument.* **2** complete control or power over someone or something: [+of/over] *humankind's mastery over the environment*

mast·head /ˈmɑːsthed $ ˈmæst-/ *n* [C] **1** the name of a newspaper, magazine etc printed in a special design at the top of the first page **2** the top of a MAST on a ship

mas·tic /ˈmæstɪk/ *n* [U] a type of glue that does not crack or break when it is bent

mas·ti·cate /ˈmæstɪˌkeɪt/ *v* [I,T] *formal* to chew food —**mastication** /ˌmæstɪˈkeɪʃən/ *n* [U]

mas·tiff /ˈmæstɪf/ also **bull mastiff** *n* [C] a large, strong dog, often used to guard houses

mas·ti·tis /mæˈstaɪtɪs/ n [U] a painful swelling of the breast or UDDER (=the part of some animals that gives milk)

mas·tur·bate /ˈmæstəbeɪt $ -tər-/ v [I,T] to give yourself or another person sexual pleasure by touching or rubbing the sexual organs —**masturbation** /ˌmæstəˈbeɪʃən $ -tər-/ n [U]

mat¹ /mæt/ n [C]   **1** a small piece of thick rough material which covers part of a floor: *Wipe your feet on the mat.*   **2** a small flat piece of wood, cloth etc which protects a surface, especially on a table: *She wrote her number on a **beer mat** (=a mat for putting a glass of beer on). | a mouse mat (=for a computer mouse) → PLACE MAT   **3** a piece of thick soft material used in some activities for people to sit on, fall onto etc: *a yoga mat | a prayer mat → see picture at SPORTS CENTRE*   **4 go to the mat (for sb/sth)** to do everything you can to solve a difficult problem, win an argument, support someone etc: *The mayor is willing to go to the mat on this issue.*   **5** a thick mass of something such as hairs or leaves; → **matted**: [+of] *a floating mat of vegetation → MATTING*

mat² adj another spelling of MATT

mat·a·dor /ˈmætədɔː $ -ɔːr/ n [C] a man who fights and kills BULLS during a BULLFIGHT; ☰ **bullfighter**

match¹ [S3] [W3] /mætʃ/ n
1 [GAME] [C] *especially BrE* an organized sports event between two teams or people: *It's our last match of the season. | cricket/football/tennis etc match | They're preparing for a **big** (=important) **match** tomorrow. | [+against/between/with] the match between Nigeria and Ireland | home/away match (=a match played at a team's own sports ground, or at a different ground) Good teams win their home matches. | McClaire's goal earned him the title of **man of the match** (=the person in a team who plays best).*
2 [FIRE] [C] a small wooden or paper stick with a special substance at the top, that you use to light a fire, cigarette etc: *a box of matches | Don't let your children play with matches. | strike/light a match (=rub a match against a surface to produce a flame) Peg struck a match and lit the candle. | I tore up the letter and put a match to it (=made it burn, using a match).*
3 [COLOURS/PATTERNS] [singular] something that is the same colour or pattern as something else, or looks attractive with it: [+for] *That shirt's a perfect match for your blue skirt.*
4 [GOOD OPPONENT] [singular] someone who is much stronger, cleverer etc than their opponents: *Carlos was **no match for** the champion. | This time you've **met your match**, Adam Burns! I'm not giving up without a fight! | Guerrilla tactics proved **more than a match for** the Soviet military machine.*
5 shouting match *also* slanging match *BrE* a loud angry argument in which two people insult each other: *The meeting degenerated into a shouting match.*
6 [MARRIAGE] [singular] a marriage or two people who are married: *They're **a perfect match**. | a match made in heaven (=a marriage of two people who are exactly right for each other) | Claire **made a good match** (=married someone suitable).*
7 [SUITABILITY] [singular] a situation in which something is suitable for something else, so that the two things work together successfully: [+between] *We need to establish a match between students' needs and teaching methods. → mix and match at MIX¹ (6)*

match² [S2] [W2] v
1 [LOOK GOOD TOGETHER] [I,T] if one thing matches another, or if two things match, they look attractive together because they are a similar colour, pattern etc; → **matching**: *We painted the cabinets green to match the rug. | Do you think this outfit matches? | a beech dining table with four chairs to match (=chairs that match it)*
⚠ Do not say that one thing 'matches to' or 'matches with' another. Say that one thing **matches** another or that two things **match**.
2 [LOOK THE SAME] [I,T] two things that match look the same because they are a pair: *Your socks don't match.*

M

3 [SEEM THE SAME] [I,T] if two things match, or if one matches the other, there is no important difference between them: *The suspect matched the descriptions provided by witnesses. | Their actions do not match their words. | match exactly/closely/perfectly The copy closely matches the original.*
4 [SUITABLE] [T] to be suitable for a particular person, thing, or situation; ☰ **suit**: *Teaching materials should match individual students' needs. | We'll help you find a home that will match your requirements. | **well-matched/ill-matched** a well-matched pair*
5 [CONNECT] [T] to put two people or things together that are similar to or somehow connected with each other: *match sth to/with sth Can you name the animals and match them to the correct countries? | All checked-in baggage must be matched with a passenger travelling on the aircraft.*
6 [BE EQUAL] [T] to be equal to something in value, size, or quality: *His strength is matched by his intelligence. | Few cities in Europe can match the cultural richness of Berlin. | Fancy designer labels tend to come with fancy price tags to match. | evenly/equally matched The two candidates are fairly evenly matched.*
7 [MAKE EQUAL] [T] to make something equal to something else: *match sth to sth Lindsey matched her steps to those of the other girl as they walked. | an attempt to match financial resources to need*
8 [GIVE MONEY] [T] to give a sum of money that is equal to a sum given by someone else: *The government has promised to match any private donations to the earthquake fund.*
9 [COMPETITION] [T usually passive] if you are matched against someone else in a game or competition, you are competing against them: *be matched against/with sb Agassi will be matched with Sampras in the men's final.*

match up phr v
1 match sb/sth ⇔ up to put two people or things together that are related to or suitable for each other: *The employment agency exists to match up graduates and IT companies. | [+with] My mother spent her life trying to match me up with various women.*
2 if two things match up, they seem the same or are connected in some way: *Their accounts just don't match up. | [+with] The DNA samples found on her body did not match up with a sample taken from the accused.*
3 match up to sb's hopes/expectations/ideals etc to be as good as you hoped, expected etc; ☰ **measure up to**: *Unfortunately, the product's performance did not match up to the manufacturer's promise.*

match·book /ˈmætʃbʊk/ n [C] a small folded piece of thick paper containing paper matches

match·box /ˈmætʃbɒks $ -bɑːks/ n [C] a small box containing matches

match-fit adj [not before noun] *BrE* a sports player who is match-fit is well and fit enough to play —**match-fitness** n [U]: *A question mark still hangs over Beckham's match-fitness.*

match·ing /ˈmætʃɪŋ/ adj [only before noun] having the same colour, style, or pattern as something else: *a necklace with matching earrings*

match·less /ˈmætʃləs/ adj *literary* more intelligent, beautiful etc than anyone or anything else; ☰ **unparalleled**: *the matchless beauty of the Parthenon*

match·mak·er /ˈmætʃˌmeɪkə $ -ər/ n [C] someone who tries to find a suitable partner for someone else to marry —**matchmaking** n [U]: *Perhaps we should do a little bit of matchmaking and introduce them.*

match-play n [singular] a method of scoring in golf based on the number of holes that are won, rather than the number of STROKES needed to reach each hole

match point n   **1** [U] a situation in tennis when the person who wins the next point will win the

---

match **2** [C] the point that a player must win in order to win a tennis match; → **game point**

match·stick /'mætʃ,stɪk/ n [C] **1** a wooden MATCH **2 matchstick men/figures** BrE people in pictures who have been drawn with thin lines to represent their arms, legs, and bodies, as if by a child; ⬛ **stick person** AmE

match·wood /'mætʃwʊd/ n [U] very small pieces of wood: *Their boat was shattered into matchwood against the rocks and sank instantly.*

mate¹ S3 /meɪt/ n
1 SB YOU DO STH WITH [C] someone you work with, do an activity with, or share something with: **class/ team/work etc mate** *Dad's office mates are throwing a party for him.* | **house/flat/room mate** (=someone you share a house, room etc with)
2 FRIEND [C] BrE informal **a)** a friend: *I'm going out with my mates tonight.* | **good/best mate** *He's good mates with John.* | *Most of my **school mates** are black.* **b)** used as a friendly way to address a man: *What's the time, mate?*
3 ANIMAL [C] the sexual partner of an animal
4 HUSBAND/WIFE [C] AmE a husband or wife – used especially in magazines; ⬛ **partner**: *How do women choose their mates?*
5 SAILOR [C] a ship's officer who is one rank below the captain
6 NAVY OFFICER [C] a US Navy PETTY OFFICER
7 builder's/plumber's/electrician's etc mate BrE someone who works with and helps a skilled worker
8 GAME [C,U] CHECKMATE in the game of CHESS

mate² v **1** [I] if animals mate, they have sex to produce babies: [+**with**] *It's quite common for male birds to mate with several females.* **2** [T] to put animals together so that they will have sex and produce babies:

Rabbits can be mated as early as six months old. **3** [T] to achieve the CHECKMATE of your opponent in CHESS

ma·ter /'meɪtə, 'mɑː- $ 'meɪtər/ n [C] BrE old-fashioned mother – now used humorously; → **pater** → ALMA MATER

ma·te·ri·al¹ S1 W1 /mə'tɪəriəl $ -'tɪr-/ n
1 [C,U] cloth used for making clothes, curtains etc; ⬛ **fabric**: *curtain material* | *scraps of material* | *a cape made of a soft material*
2 [C,U] a solid substance such as wood, plastic, or metal: *materials like wood or stone* | **organic/plant material** *Animals depend on plant material for food.* | *harmful **radioactive material*** | *a paper company which imports **raw materials** (=substances which have not been treated) from North America.* | *recycled material*
3 [U] also **materials** [plural] the things that are used for making or doing something: **reading/writing etc material(s)** *Videos often make good teaching material.* | *a supply of **building materials*** | *artists' materials*
4 [U] information or ideas used in books, films etc: *His act contains a lot of new material.* | [+**for**] *Anita is collecting material for a novel.* | *the **raw material** (=information that has not been carefully examined) for an article*
5 officer/executive etc material someone who is good enough for a particular job or position: *He's a good soldier, but not really officer material.*

material² W3 adj [usually before noun]
1 relating to your money, possessions, living conditions etc, rather than the needs of your mind or soul; ⬛ **spiritual**: **material goods/possessions/wealth etc** *The spiritual life is more important than material possessions.* | *a society that places high importance on **material rewards***
2 relating to the real world and physical objects, rather than religious or SPIRITUAL things: *According to some, **the material world** is all that exists.*

materials

chrome toaster

gold watch

silver bracelet

tin box

iron horseshoe

steel tap BrE/ faucet AmE

wooden barrel

concrete block

plastic mixing bowl

rubber gloves

paper fan

silk hat

fur hat

woolly hat

nylon tights

glass jar

cotton blouse

cardboard box

leather belt

3 *law* important and needing to be considered when making a decision: *material evidence* | [+to] *facts material to the investigation* **4** *formal* important and having a noticeable effect: *material changes to the schedule* → MATERIALLY

ma·te·ri·al·is·m /məˈtɪəriəlɪzəm $ -ˈtɪr-/ n [U] **1** the belief that money and possessions are more important than art, religion, moral beliefs – used in order to show disapproval: *a reaction to a world full of shallow materialism* **2** the belief that only physical things really exist —**materialist** adj: *materialist philosophy* —**materialist** n [C]: *We confess to being hopeless materialists, surrounded by our own neat stuff.*

ma·te·ri·al·is·tic /mə,tɪəriəˈlɪstɪk◂ $ -,tɪr-/ adj concerned only with money and possessions rather than things of the mind such as art, religion, or moral beliefs – used in order to show disapproval: *He's so materialistic.* | *the materialistic values of American society* —**materialistically** /-kli/ adv

ma·te·ri·al·ize also **-ise** BrE /məˈtɪəriəlaɪz $ -ˈtɪr-/ v [I] **1** to happen or appear in the way that you expected: *Problems were expected, but they never materialized.* | *The money we had been promised failed to materialize.* **2** to appear in an unexpected and strange way: *The figure of a man suddenly materialized in the shadows.* —**materialization** /mə,tɪəriəlaɪˈzeɪʃən $ -lə-/ n [U]

ma·te·ri·al·ly /məˈtɪəriəli $ -ˈtɪr-/ adv **1** formal in a big enough or strong enough way to change a situation: *This would materially affect US security.* **2** [sentence adverb] in relation to possessions and money, rather than the needs of a person's mind or soul; **■** spiritually: *Materially, we are better off than ever before.*

ma·té·ri·el /mə,tɪəriˈel $ -,tɪr-/ n [U] formal supplies of weapons used by an army

ma·ter·nal /məˈtɜːnl $ -ɜːr-/ adj **1** typical of the way a good mother behaves or feels; → **paternal**: *Annie was wonderfully warm and maternal.* | *She seems to have a strong maternal instinct* (=desire to have babies and take care of them). **2** [only before noun] relating to a mother or to being a mother; → **paternal**: *the relationship between maternal age and infant mortality* **3** maternal grandfather/aunt etc your mother's father, sister etc —**maternally** adv

ma·ter·ni·ty¹ /məˈtɜːnəti $ -ɜːr-/ adj [only before noun] relating to a woman who is PREGNANT or who has just had a baby; → **paternity**: *a blue maternity dress* | **maternity benefits/pay etc** (=money that the government or employers give to a woman after she has had a baby)

maternity² n [U] the state of being a mother

ma'ternity ,leave n [U] time that a mother is allowed to spend away from work when she has a baby; → **paternity leave**: **on maternity leave** *Karen will be on maternity leave next month.*

mat·ey¹ /ˈmeɪti/ adj BrE informal behaving as if you were someone's friend: [+with] *She's been very matey with the boss lately.*

matey² n BrE informal used by men as a very informal or disrespectful way of speaking to another man

math S2 /mæθ/ n [U] AmE mathematics; **■** **maths** BrE: *Tim's good at math and science.* | *a set of simple math problems* (=questions that are related to math) | *She's learning calculus in math class.* | *a math test*

math·e·mat·i·cal /,mæθ₃ˈmætɪkəl◂/ adj **1** relating to or using mathematics: **mathematical equation/ calculation/formula etc** | *mathematical analysis* | *the development of mathematical skills* | *a mathematical genius* **2** [only before noun] calculating things in a careful, exact way: *The whole trip was planned with mathematical precision.* **3** **mathematical certainty** something that is completely certain to happen **4** **a mathematical chance (of sth)** a very small chance that something will happen —**mathematically** /-kli/ adv

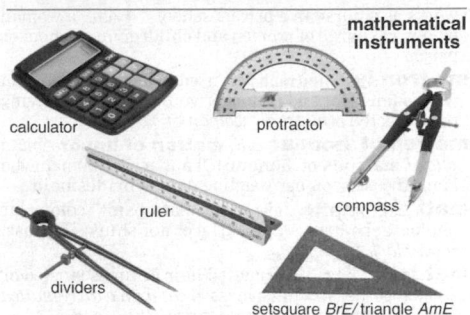

mathematical instruments

calculator
protractor
ruler
compass
dividers
setsquare BrE/ triangle AmE

math·e·ma·ti·cian /,mæθ₃mə'tɪʃən/ n [C] someone who studies or teaches mathematics, or is a specialist in mathematics

math·e·mat·ics /,mæθ₃ˈmætɪks/ n [U] the science of numbers and of shapes, including ALGEBRA, GEOMETRY, and ARITHMETIC

maths S2 /mæθs/ n [U] BrE informal mathematics; **■** **math** AmE: *the new maths teacher* | *maths lessons* | *She got top marks in maths and chemistry.*

mat·i·née /ˈmætₐneɪ $,mætn'eɪ/ n [C] **1** a performance of a play or film in the afternoon **2** AusE informal sexual INTERCOURSE in the daytime

'matinée ,idol / $ ..'. ,../ n [C] old-fashioned an actor who is very popular with women

'matinée ,jacket / $ ..'. ,../ n [C] BrE old-fashioned a short coat for a baby

mat·ing /ˈmeɪtɪŋ/ n [U] sex between animals: *the mating season*

mat·ins mattins /ˈmætₐnz $ ˈmætnz/ n [U] the first prayers of the day in the Christian religion; **■** **morning prayer**

ma·tri·arch /ˈmeɪtriɑːk $ -ɑːrk/ n [C] a woman, especially an older woman, who controls a family or a social group; → **patriarch**

ma·tri·ar·chal /,meɪtriˈɑːkl $ -ˈɑːr-/ adj **1** ruled or controlled by women: *a matriarchal society* **2** relating to or typical of a matriarch; → **patriarchal**

ma·tri·ar·chy /ˈmeɪtriɑːki $ -ɑːr-/ n plural matriarchies [C,U] **1** a social system in which the oldest woman controls a family and its possessions; → **patriarchy** **2** a society in which women hold all the power; → **patriarchy**

mat·ri·cide /ˈmætrₐsaɪd/ n [U] formal the crime of murdering your mother; → **parricide**, **patricide**

ma·tric·u·late /məˈtrɪkjₐleɪt/ v [I] formal to officially begin studying at a university or, in the US, at a school or college: [+at] *Aged only 15, he matriculated at the University of Leipzig.* | *matriculated students* —**matriculation** /mə,trɪkjₐˈleɪʃən/ n [U]

mat·ri·mo·ny /ˈmætrₐməni $ -mooni-/ n [U] formal the state of being married; **■** **marriage**: *They were joined together in holy matrimony.* —**matrimonial** /,mætrₐˈmooniəl $ -ˈmoo-/ adj

ma·trix /ˈmeɪtrɪks/ n plural matrices /-trₐsiːz/ or matrixes [C] technical **1** an arrangement of numbers, letters, or signs in rows and COLUMNS that you consider to be one amount, and that you use in solving mathematical problems: *a matrix table* **2** a situation from which a person or society can grow and develop: *the cultural matrix* **3** a living part in which something is formed or develops, such as the substance from which your FINGERNAILS grow **4** a MOULD (=hollow container) into which melted metal, plastic, etc is poured to form a shape **5** the rock in which hard stones or jewels have formed → **DOT-MATRIX PRINTER**

ma·tron /ˈmeɪtrən/ n [C] **1** literary an older married woman **2** BrE old-fashioned a nurse who is in charge of the other nurses in a hospital **3** BrE a woman who

M

works as a nurse in a private school   **4** *AmE* a woman who is in charge of women and children in a school or prison

ma·tron·ly /ˈmeɪtrənli/ *adj* used to describe a woman who is fairly fat and no longer young – to avoid saying this directly: *a matronly woman of 50*

matron of ˈhonour *BrE*; **matron of honor** *AmE n plural* **matrons of honour** [C] a married woman who helps the BRIDE on her wedding day; → **bridesmaid**

matt *BrE*, **matte** /mæt/ *adj* matt paint, colour, or photographs have a dull surface, not shiny; ⊟ **gloss**: *matt black*

mat·ted /ˈmætɪd/ *adj* matted hair or fur is twisted or stuck together in a thick mass: *a cat with a dirty matted coat* | [+with] *Her hair was matted with blood.*

mat·ter¹ S1 W1 /ˈmætə $ -ər/ *n*
1 SUBJECT/SITUATION [C] a subject or situation that you have to think about or deal with

> a serious/important matter
> a personal/private matter
> a simple/easy matter (=something that is easy to do)
> financial/legal/political/religious matters
> a matter of importance
> a matter of/for concern
> a matter for discussion/negotiation/consideration etc
> be a matter for sb (to decide) (=be something that a particular person should deal with)
> be no laughing matter (=something very serious)
> the heart/crux of the matter (=the most important part of something)
> raise a matter with sb (=discuss something with someone)
> let the matter rest/drop (=decide to stop worrying about something)
> matters arising from/ out of sth (=things that come from or are connected with a particular event)
> the matter at hand/in hand (=the thing you are dealing with now)

*There are more **important matters** we need to discuss.* | *It was **a personal matter**, and she had no intention of talking to any journalist about it.* | *It will be **a simple matter** to find her.* | *She held strong views on **religious matters**.* | *He consulted Landers on all **matters of importance**.* | *Safety standards in the industry have been **a matter of concern** for many years.* | *The legal arrangements for the sale are **matters for negotiation**.* | *This **is a matter for** the German people to decide.* | *The whole situation may seem funny now, but it **was no laughing matter** at the time.* | *Charles no longer loved her. That was **the crux of the matter**.* | *I decided to **raise the matter** with my boss.* | *He was too curious to **let the matter drop**.* | *There are a number of **matters arising** out of this.* | *We need to concentrate on **the matter in hand**.*

2 matters [plural] a situation that you are in or have been describing: *Maybe some of these suggestions will help to improve matters.* | *Matters can be more easily sorted out once you get to the resort.* | *His long absences didn't help matters* (=made the situation worse). | **to make matters worse** (=used to say that something makes a bad situation worse) *The team has lost the last two games and, to make matters worse, two of its best players are injured.* | **to complicate matters further** (=used to say that something makes a complicated situation more complicated) *To complicate matters further, the law on this issue has been changed.*
3 MATERIAL [U] **a)** the material that everything in the universe is made of, including solids, liquids, and gases: *particles of matter* **b)** waste/solid/organic/vegetable etc matter a substance that consists of waste material, solid material etc **c)** a yellow or white substance in wounds or next to your eye
4 as a matter of fact *spoken* used when adding more details about what you have just said: *'Have you had many visitors yet?' 'No, as a matter of fact you're the*

first.' | *I knew him when we were in college – as a matter of fact we were on the same course.* → MATTER-OF-FACT
5 what's the matter?/something's the matter/nothing's the matter etc *spoken* used to ask or talk about why someone seems worried, unhappy, or ill, why something about a situation seems wrong, or why a machine seems not to be working properly: *What's the matter? You look as though you've been crying.* | *'Is something the matter?' 'Just a headache – I'll be fine in a minute.'* | *You look worried. Is there anything the matter?* | *What's the matter with Bill?* | *What's the matter with your eye? It looks red.* | *I know something's the matter. You're frightened of something.* | *Nothing's the matter, honestly, I'm fine.* | *There was nothing the matter with it* (=it was all right) *when I lent it to him.* | *She had something the matter with her back.*
6 the truth/fact of the matter is (that) *spoken* used when saying what you think is really true concerning a situation: *The truth of the matter is that we don't know exactly how the disease is spread.*
7 for that matter used to say that what you are saying about one thing is also true about something else: *Ben never touched beer, or any kind of alcohol for that matter.* | *He's an artist who has never been as well-known here, or for that matter as well-respected, as he has been in the USA.*
8 be (quite) a different matter also **be (quite) another matter** *especially BrE* used to say that a situation or action is very different from the one you have just mentioned, and may not be as easy, pleasant etc: *She didn't mind seeing him in a group but an intimate dinner in a restaurant was another matter altogether.*
9 take matters into your own hands to deal with a problem yourself because other people have failed to deal with it: *Local people took matters into their own hands and hired their own security guards.*
10 it's only/just a matter of time used to say that something will definitely happen in the future: *It can only be a matter of time before someone is seriously injured.*
11 a matter of life and/or death a situation that is extremely serious or important, especially one in which someone could die: *The quality of the ambulance service is a matter of life and death.* | *Can't it wait? It's hardly a matter of life or death, is it?*
12 be a matter of opinion used to say that people have different opinions about something, especially when you yourself have a negative opinion: *Whether or not he is any good as a manager is a matter of opinion.*
13 be a matter of (personal) taste/choice/preference used to say that different people like different things: *I can't say which wine is best – it's a matter of personal taste.*
14 be a matter of principle to be something that you feel you must or must not do, because of your moral principles: *She couldn't take the money. It was a matter of principle.*
15 be a matter of doing sth used to say that an action involves doing something: **be simply/largely/merely etc a matter of doing sth** *Reducing the number of road deaths is not simply a matter of improving roads.*
16 a matter of seconds/weeks/hours etc only a few seconds, weeks etc: *The ambulance arrived in a matter of minutes.* | *The bullet missed his head **by a matter of** inches.*
17 as a matter of sth because of a particular belief or quality: *He invited her as a matter of courtesy.* | *As a matter of fairness, he should be allowed to give his version of events.*
18 as a matter of interest *BrE spoken* used when you ask or tell someone something that interests you but is not important: *Just as a matter of interest, which school did you go to?*
19 as a matter of urgency if something is done or should be done as a matter of urgency, it is done or should be done very soon: *That procedure should be streamlined as a matter of urgency.*
20 as a matter of course/routine if something is done as a matter of course or routine, it is the correct and

usual thing to do in a particular situation: *We will contact your former employer as a matter of course.*

21 no matter how/whether/what etc also **no matter the ...** used to say that something is true or that something happens whatever the situation is: *Feeding a baby is a messy job no matter how careful you are.* | *I'm determined to visit Japan no matter what it costs.* | *He visited her every day no matter the weather.*

22 no matter what *spoken* used to say that you will definitely do something: *I'll call you tonight, no matter what.*

23 no matter *spoken formal or old-fashioned* used to say that something is not important and will not affect a situation: *'I'm afraid I forgot to bring a towel.' 'No matter, I've got one you can borrow.'*

24 it's a matter of fact (that) used to say that something is a fact: *It's a matter of fact that the team have not performed as well this season.*

25 the little/small matter of sth *spoken* something that is not important or not difficult – used when you really think something is important or difficult: *He seemed unworried by the small matter of the war that was in progress.* | *There's the small matter of tonight's game if we are to reach the finals.*

26 no matter that used to say that something is not important and will not affect a situation: *I would always be an outsider here – no matter that I spoke fluent Spanish.*

27 reading/printed etc matter things that are written for people to read: *As well as textbooks and other printed matter, courses may include video and audio cassettes.* → GREY MATTER, SUBJECT MATTER; → **not mince matters** at MINCE¹ (3); → **mind over matter** at MIND¹ (43)

matter² S1 W3 *v*

1 [I not in progressive] to be important, especially to be important to you, or to have an effect on what happens: **it doesn't etc matter** *Will it matter if I'm a little late?* | *If I have to stay late at work tonight, it won't matter because we can go out another night.* | **it doesn't etc matter who/why/what etc** *It doesn't matter what you wear, as long as you look neat and tidy.* | *Does it matter what I think?* | **it doesn't etc matter that** *It does not matter that the gun was in fact unloaded.* | *Do you think it matters that the cups and saucers don't match?* | **it doesn't matter about sth** *Just give me $5 – it doesn't matter about the rest.* | [+to] *He had lost many of the people who mattered to him.* | **matter a lot/a great deal** *It mattered a great deal to her what other people thought of her.* | **not matter much/matter little** *I don't think it matters much what you study.* | *campaigning on issues that* **really matter** | **all that matters/the only thing that matters** *All that matters is that you're safe.* | *Money was the only thing that mattered to him.* | *I don't care what it looks like –* **what matters is** *that it works.* | *At last she was with the man she loved and* **nothing else mattered.** | *She said very little during the meal.* **Not that it mattered** (=it was not important).

2 it doesn't matter *spoken* **a)** used to tell someone that you are not angry or upset about something, especially something that they have done: *'I've spilled some coffee on the carpet.' 'It doesn't matter.'* **b)** used to say that you do not mind which one of two things you have: *'Red or white wine?' 'Oh, either. It doesn't matter.'*

3 what does it matter? *spoken* used to say that something is not important: *It all happened so long ago now, what does it matter?* | *What does it matter how old I am?*

matter-of-'fact *adj* showing no emotion when you are talking about something exciting, frightening, upsetting etc: [+about] *Jan was surprisingly matter-of-fact about her divorce.* | **matter-of-fact voice/tone** *Use a matter-of-fact tone when disciplining your children.* —**matter-of-factly** *adv*

mat·ting /'mætɪŋ/ *n* [U] strong rough material, used for making MATS: *straw matting*

mat·tins /'mætˌnz $ 'mætnz/ *n* another spelling of MATINS

mat·tock /'mætək/ *n* [C] a tool used for digging, with a long handle and a metal blade

mat·tress /'mætrˌs/ *n* [C] the soft part of a bed that you lie on: **firm/soft/hard etc mattress** *an old, lumpy mattress*

ma·tu·ra·tion /ˌmætʃʊ'reɪʃən/ *n* [U] *formal* the period during which something grows and develops: *cell maturation*

ma·ture¹ /mə'tʃʊə $ -'tʃʊr/ *adj*

1 SENSIBLE someone, especially a child or young person, who is mature behaves in a sensible and reasonable way, as you would expect an adult to behave; ☒ **immature**: *Laura is very mature for her age.* | *We're* **mature enough** *to disagree on this issue but still respect each other.*

2 FULLY GROWN fully grown and developed: *Mature apple trees are typically 20 feet tall.* | *The new leader wants his country to be seen as a mature democracy.* | *The human brain isn't* **fully mature** *until about age 25.* | **physically/emotionally/sexually mature** *Most girls are sexually mature by about 14 years of age.*

3 WINE/CHEESE ETC *BrE* mature cheese, wine etc has a good strong taste which has developed during a long period of time: *mature cheddar*

4 OLDER a polite or humorous way of describing someone who is no longer young; ☒ **middle-aged**: *wedding fashions for mature brides* | *a respectable gentleman* **of mature years.**

5 NOVEL/PAINTING ETC a mature piece of work by a writer or an artist is done late in their life and shows a high level of understanding or skill: *His mature work reveals a deep sense of enjoyment of nature.*

6 on mature reflection/consideration *formal* after thinking carefully and sensibly about something for a long time: *On mature reflection we have decided to decline their offer.*

7 FINANCIAL a mature BOND or POLICY is ready to be paid

8 mature market/industry *technical* a mature industry or market is one where growth is quite low and there are fewer competitors than before —**maturely** *adv*: *If you want us to treat you as an adult, you have to act maturely.*

mature² *v* **1** [I] to become fully grown or developed: *As the fish matures, its colours and patternings change.* | [+into] *She has matured into a fine writer.* **2** [I] to become sensible and start to behave sensibly and reasonably, like an adult: *He has matured a lot since he left home.* | *He wants to prove just how much he has matured both as a player and as a man.* **3** [I] if a financial arrangement such as a BOND or an insurance POLICY matures, it becomes ready to be paid **4** [I,T] if cheese, wine etc matures, or if it is matured, it develops a good strong taste over a period of time: *Few beers brewed in Britain are matured in the bottle.* | *The olives are pulped, then left to mature for three years.*

ma,ture 'student *n* [C] *BrE* a student at a university or college who is over 25 years old

ma·tu·ri·ty /mə'tʃʊərˌti $ -'tʃʊr-/ *n* [U] **1** the quality of behaving in a sensible way like an adult; ☒ **immaturity**: *Beth shows a maturity way beyond her 16 years.* | *One day you'll have the maturity to understand.* **2** the time or state when someone or something is fully grown or developed: **at maturity** *The tree will reach only 5 feet at maturity.* | **reach/come to/grow to maturity** *These insects reach* **full maturity** *after a few weeks.* | *the era when the Republic came to* **political maturity** | **sexual/emotional/physical maturity** *He lacks the emotional maturity to appreciate poetry.* **3** the time when a financial arrangement such as a BOND or an insurance POLICY becomes ready to be paid

mat·zo, matzoh /'mɒtsə $ 'mɑː-/ *n plural* **matzos** [C,U] **1** a large thin piece of flat bread, eaten by Jewish people during PASSOVER **2** a type of flour used to make

---

1 000, 2 000, 3 000, most frequent words in S poken and W ritten English

bread, cakes etc especially by Jewish people during PASSOVER: *herrings dipped in matzo and fried*

maud·lin /ˈmɔːdlɪn $ ˈmɒː-/ *adj* **1** talking or behaving in a sad, silly, and emotional way, especially when drunk: **get/grow/become maudlin** *Sir Ralph was becoming maudlin after his third glass of claret.* **2** a maudlin song, story, film etc tries too hard to make people feel emotions such as love or sadness and seems silly: *a song that is tender without being maudlin*

maul /mɔːl $ mɒːl/ *v* [T] **1** if an animal mauls someone, it injures them badly by tearing their flesh: *A mentally ill man was mauled after climbing into the lions' enclosure at London Zoo.* **2** to strongly criticize something, especially a new book, play etc: *Her latest book was absolutely mauled by the critics.* **3** to touch someone in a rough sexual way which they think is unpleasant: *What makes you think you've got the right to maul me like that?* **4** *informal* to defeat someone very easily – used especially in sports reports: *Stanford have looked quite good lately. They absolutely mauled Notre Dame last weekend.* —**mauling** *n* [singular]: *Juppe got a mauling over the government's failure to fulfil its promises.*

maun·der /ˈmɔːndə $ ˈmɒːndər/ *v* [I] *especially BrE* to talk or complain about something for a long time in a boring way: [+**on/about**] *What are you maundering on about, George?*

Maun·dy Thurs·day /ˌmɔːndi ˈθɜːzdi, -deɪ $ ˌmɒːndi ˈθɜːrz-/ *n* [U] the Thursday before Easter

mau·so·le·um /ˌmɔːsəˈliːəm $ ˌmɒː-/ *n* [C] a large stone building made specially to contain the body of a dead person, or the dead bodies of an important family: *the Lenin Mausoleum*

mauve /məʊv $ moʊv/ *n* [U] a pale purple colour —**mauve** *adj*: *mauve flowers*

ma·ven /ˈmeɪvən/ *n* [C] *AmE* someone who knows a lot about a particular subject: **food/fashion/sports etc maven** *A food maven could also be called a gourmet.*

mav·e·rick /ˈmævərɪk/ *n* [C] an unusual person who has different ideas and ways of behaving from other people, and is often very successful: *He's always been a bit of a maverick.* —**maverick** *adj* [only before noun]: *a maverick detective*

maw /mɔː $ mɒː/ *n* [C] **1** *formal* something which seems to swallow or use up things completely: [+**of**] *Millions of dollars were poured into the maw of defense spending.* **2** *literary* an animal's mouth or throat

mawk·ish /ˈmɔːkɪʃ $ ˈmɒː-/ *adj* showing too much emotion in a way that is embarrassing; ⊟ **sentimental**: *a mawkish love story* —**mawkishly** *adv* —**mawkishness** *n* [U]

max¹ /mæks/ *n* [C] *informal* **1** the abbreviation of *maximum*: *Five people will fit, but that's the max.* **2 to the max** to the greatest degree possible: *We had the air conditioner turned up to the max.* —**max** *adj, adv*: *Let's say two hours to get there, max.*

max² *v*

max out *phr v AmE informal* **1 max sth ⇔ out** to use something such as money or supplies so that there is none left: *I maxed out my Visa.* **2** to do too much, eat too much etc: [+**on**] *'Want a beer?' 'Nah, I maxed out on booze this weekend.'*

max·im /ˈmæksɪm/ *n* [C] a well-known phrase or saying, especially one that gives a rule for sensible behaviour

max·i·mal /ˈmæksɪməl/ *adj technical* as much or as large as possible: *the right conditions for a maximal increase in employment* —**maximally** *adv*

max·i·mize also **-ise** *BrE* /ˈmæksɪmaɪz/ *v* [T] **1** to increase something such as profit or income as much as possible; ⊟ **minimize**: **maximize profit/revenue etc** *The company's main function is to maximize profit.* **2** to CLICK on a special part on a window on a computer screen so that it becomes as big as the

screen; ⊟ **minimize 3** to use something in a way that gives you the greatest practical value or the best results: *We need to maximize the space.* | **maximize opportunities/chances etc** *The career center will help you maximize your opportunities.* —**maximization** /ˌmæksɪmaɪˈzeɪʃən $ -sɪmə-/ *n* [U]

max·i·mum¹ S2 W3 /ˈmæksɪməm/ *adj* [only before noun] the maximum amount, quantity, speed etc is the largest that is possible or allowed; ⊟ **minimum**: *The car has a maximum speed of 120 mph.* | *They made maximum use of the resources available.* | *To get the maximum benefit, do the exercises slowly.* | *Display the hologram under a strong light for maximum effect.* | *The plant is operating* **at maximum capacity**. | **maximum amount/number etc** *Work out the maximum amount you can afford to spend.* | *The award will consist of a lump sum to a* **maximum value** *of $5000.* | **maximum sentence/penalty/fine etc** *She faces a maximum penalty of life in prison.*

maximum² *n* [C] the largest number or amount that is possible or is allowed: [+**of**] *He faces a maximum of seven years in prison.* | *The company will reimburse you* **up to a maximum** *of $1000.* | *We might have a third child, but that's* **the absolute maximum**.

may¹ S1 W1 /meɪ/ *modal verb*

1 POSSIBILITY if something may happen or may be true, there is a possibility that it will happen or be true but this is not certain; ⊟ **might**: *I may be late, so don't wait for me.* | *Some chemicals may cause environmental damage.* | *There may not be enough money to pay for the repairs.* | *Well, I may have been wrong.* | *They may have called while you were out.* | *It* **may be that** *Minoan ships were made and repaired here.* | *Your job* **may well** *involve some travelling* (=it is fairly likely).

2 POSSIBLE TO DO STH if something may be done, completed etc in a particular way, that is how it is possible to do it; ⊟ **can**: *The problem may be solved in a number of different ways.*

3 ALLOWED a) used to say that someone is allowed to do something; ⊟ **can**: *Thank you. You may go now.* | *There is a set of rules to show what members may and may not do.* | *You may sit down or stand, just as you wish.* | *No one may own more than 10% of the shares.* **b)** **may I/we ...?** *spoken formal* used to ask politely for permission to do something: *May I come in and wait?* | *May we use your office for a few minutes?*

4 IN POLITE EXPRESSIONS *spoken formal* used to say, ask, or suggest something in a polite way: *All these things, if I may say so, are entirely irrelevant.* | *Who, may I ask, is Wotherspoon?* | *May I suggest that you consider the matter further before taking any action.*

5 ALTHOUGH used to say that even though one thing is true, something else which seems very different is also true: *I may be slow, but at least I don't make stupid mistakes.* | *Although this may sound like a simple process, great care is needed.* | *Strange as it may seem, I always felt I belonged here.*

6 may as well *spoken* used to suggest that someone should do something, because there is no good reason to do anything else; ⊟ **might as well**: *If there's nothing more to do, we may as well go to bed.* | *You may as well tell us now – we'll find out sooner or later.*

7 may sb/sth do sth *formal* used to express a wish or hope: *We pray for those who died – may they rest in peace.* | *It is a fine tradition and long may it continue!*

8 PURPOSE *formal* used after 'so that' or 'in order that' to say that someone does something in order to make something else possible: *The hero sacrifices his life so that his friend may live.*

9 be that as it may *formal* in spite of what you have just mentioned: *Perhaps there isn't one single system that will work for everyone. Be that as it may, we all need order in our lives.*

10 may well used to say that there is a good reason for a reaction, question, or feeling: *'What's all the noise?' 'You* **may well ask**.'

may² *n* [U] *BrE* the white or pink flowers of the HAWTHORN

May n [C,U] the fifth month of the year, between April and June: *next/last May She started work here last May.* | *in May The theatre opened in May .* | *on May 6th We don't have any meetings on May 6th, do we?* | *on 6th May BrE: An agreement was signed on 6th May 1977.* | *May 6 AmE: Michael's getting married May 6.*

may·be [S1] [W2] /'meɪbi/ adv [sentence adverb]
1 used to say that something may happen or may be true but you are not certain; ▣ **perhaps**: *Maybe it's all just a big misunderstanding.* | *'Do you think he'll come back?' 'Maybe.'* | *Maybe they're right, but maybe not.* | *You have talent, maybe even genius.* | *He said he'd finish the work soon – maybe tomorrow.*
2 *spoken* used to reply to a suggestion or idea when either you are not sure if you agree with it, or you do not want to say 'yes' or 'no': *'I think Sheila would be an excellent manager.' 'Maybe.'*
3 used to show that you are not sure of an amount or number: *The problems really started maybe two or three years ago.* | *He looked like he was thirty, maybe thirty-five years old.*
4 *spoken* used to make a suggestion you are not quite sure about: *If the bill doesn't seem right, maybe you should give them a call.* | *Maybe I can ride the bicycle and follow you.*

may·day /'meɪdeɪ/ n [singular] a radio signal used to ask for help when a ship or plane is in serious danger; → SOS

May Day n [C,U] the first day of May, when LEFT-WING political parties in some countries celebrate, and when people traditionally celebrate the arrival of spring

may·est /'meɪəst/ v thou mayest old use you may

may·fly /'meɪflaɪ/ n plural **mayflies** [C] a small insect that lives near water, and only lives for a short time

may·hem /'meɪhem/ n [U] an extremely confused situation in which people are very frightened or excited; ▣ **chaos**: *There was complete mayhem after the explosion.* | **cause/create/wreak mayhem** *For some children, the first fall of snow is an opportunity to create mayhem.*

may·n't /'meɪənt/ BrE old-fashioned the short form of 'may not'

may·o /'meɪəʊ $ -oʊ/ n [U] informal mayonnaise

may·on·naise /ˌmeɪə'neɪz $ 'meɪəneɪz/ n [U] a thick white sauce, made of raw egg YOLKS and oil, often eaten on sandwiches or SALAD

mayor /meə $ 'meɪər/ n [C] **1** the person who has been elected to lead the government of a town or city: *the election of the London mayor* **2** someone who is chosen or elected each year in Britain to represent a town or city at official public ceremonies —**mayoral** adj: *mayoral duties*

mayor·al·ty /'meərəlti $ 'meɪərəlti/ n [U] formal the position of mayor, or the period when someone is mayor

mayor·ess /'meər¦s $ 'meɪər¦s/ n [C] BrE the wife of a mayor, or a woman who shares the work of a mayor

may·pole /'meɪpəʊl $ -poʊl/ n [C] a tall pole around which people danced on May Day in the past

mayst /meɪst/ v thou mayst old use you may

may've /'meɪəv/ spoken the short form of 'may have': *You may've heard this story before.*

maze /meɪz/ n [C] **1** a complicated and confusing arrangement of streets, roads etc: **maze of streets/ paths/tunnels etc** *the maze of narrow streets* | *I was led through a maze of corridors.* **2** a large number of rules, instructions etc which are complicated and difficult to understand: **maze of rules/regulations etc** *a maze of new laws* **3** a specially designed system of paths, often in a park or public garden, which is difficult to find your way through: *We got completely lost in the maze.* | *the famous Hampton Court maze* **4** a children's game on paper in which you try to draw a line through a complicated group of lines without crossing any of them

ma·zur·ka /mə'zɜːkə $ -ɜːr-/ n [C] a fast traditional Polish dance, or the music for this dance

MB /ˌem 'biː/ also **Mb** the written abbreviation of *megabyte* or megabytes

MBA also **M.B.A.** AmE /ˌem biː 'eɪ/ n [C] *Master of Business Administration* a university degree in the skills needed to be in charge of a business that you can get after your first degree. A person who has this degree is also called an MBA: **do/have an MBA** | *Rick is a 32-year-old MBA from Harvard.*

MBE /ˌem biː 'iː/ n [C] *Member of the Order of the British Empire* a special honour given to some British people for things they have done for their country

MC /ˌem 'siː/ n [C] **1** *Master of Ceremonies* someone who introduces guests or performers at a social or public occasion; ▣ **emcee** **2** the person in a RAP group who holds the MICROPHONE and says the words to the songs **3** *Military Cross* a MEDAL given to British army officers for being brave

McCoy /mə'kɔɪ/ n **the real McCoy** informal something that is real and is not a copy, especially something valuable: *In the movie, the two thieves try to discover whether the banknotes are fakes or the real McCoy, with hilarious results.*

m-com·merce /'em ˌkɒmɜːs $ -ˌkɑːmɜːrs/ n [U] *mobile commerce* the buying or selling of goods and services using a radio connection to the Internet, for example using a LAPTOP or MOBILE PHONE; → e-commerce

MD BrE; **M.D.** AmE /ˌem 'diː/ n **1** [C] *Doctor of Medicine* a university DEGREE in medicine that you can get after your first degree **2** [C] BrE the abbreviation of *managing director*; → CEO **3** [U] the abbreviation of *muscular dystrophy*

me [S1] [W1] /mi; strong miː/ pron [object form of 'I']
1 used by the person speaking or writing to refer to himself or herself: *Stop, you're hurting me.* | *He bought me a drink.* | *Give that book to me.* | *She's two years older than me.* | *That's me, standing on the left.*
2 me too spoken used to tell someone that you feel the same way as they do, that you are in a similar situation etc: *'I'm hungry!' 'Me too.'*
3 me neither also **nor me** spoken used to say that you agree with a negative statement that someone has just made: *'I can't believe he's fifty.' 'Me neither.'*

ME /ˌem 'iː/ n **1** [U] BrE *myalgic encephalomyelitis* an illness that makes you feel very tired and weak and can last for a long time: *ME sufferers* **2** [C] AmE the abbreviation of medical examiner

me·a cul·pa /ˌmeɪə 'kʊlpə/ interjection used humorously to admit that something is your fault

mead /miːd/ n **1** [U] an alcoholic drink made from HONEY: *a glass of mead* **2** [C] literary a meadow: *the flowery mead*

mead·ow /'medəʊ $ -doʊ/ n [C] a field with wild grass and flowers → see picture at COUNTRY

mead·ow·lark /'medəʊlɑːk $ -doʊlɑːrk/ n [C] a brown North American bird with a yellow breast

mea·gre BrE; **meager** AmE /'miːgə $ -ər/ adj a meagre amount of food, money etc is too small and is much less than you need: *a meagre diet of bread and beans* | **meagre income/earnings/wages etc** *He supplements his meager income by working on Saturdays.* | *a school with meagre resources* —**meagrely** adv —**meagreness** n [U]

meal [S2] [W2] /miːl/ n
1 [C] an occasion when you eat food, for example breakfast or dinner, or the food that you eat on that occasion

> go (out) for a meal
> ask sb out for a meal
> take sb (out) for a meal
> have/eat a meal
> cook/prepare/make a meal
> enjoy your meal! (=I hope you like your food)

M

evening/midday meal
the main meal of the day
a three/five-course meal
a decent/proper meal
a hot meal
a full meal (=a complete meal)
a square meal (=a meal with enough good food to keep you healthy)

After the movie we went for a meal in a Chinese restaurant. | *Why don't you ask him out for a meal?* | *He was always taking her out for meals in fancy restaurants.* | *We must have a meal together some time.* | *Mavis ate her meal in silence.* | *My mom was helping me prepare the meal.* | *The price includes accommodation, breakfast, and evening meals.* | *Dinner is the main meal of the day for most people.* | *a five-course meal in an expensive French restaurant* | *All I need is a bath, a decent meal, and a good long sleep.* | *The soldiers were looking forward to a hot meal.* | *The cinnamon roll has as many calories as a full meal.* | *You need to have three square meals a day.*

⚠ Do not say 'take a meal'. Say **have a meal.**
2 [U] grain that has been crushed into a powder, for making flour or animal food → BONEMEAL
3 make a meal (out) of sth *BrE informal* to spend too much time or effort doing something: *He made a real meal out of parking the car.*

WORD FOCUS: MEAL
meals at different times of day: **breakfast, brunch, lunch, tea** *BrE*, **dinner, supper**
a meal outside: **picnic, barbecue** also **barbie** *informal*, **cookout** *AmE*
when you quickly eat a little food: **snack, a bite to eat**
a very big meal for a lot of people: **banquet, feast**
parts of a meal: **starter** *BrE*, **appetizer** *AmE* (the first course) | **main course/entree** *especially AmE*, **side dish** (eaten with the main course) | **dessert** *also* **pudding, sweet** *BrE* (sweet food eaten at the end of the meal)

mea·lie /'miːli/ *n* [C,U] *informal* MAIZE, or a piece of maize

meals-on-'wheels *n* a service run by the government in Britain in which hot meals are taken to old or sick people in their homes

'meal ,ticket *n* [C] **1** *informal* something or someone that you depend on to give you money or food: *There were times when he suspected he was just a meal ticket to her.* **2** a card that you buy and then use to get meals at school or work, or at a special event: *The meal ticket is $15 and includes three meals with beverages.*

meal·time /'miːltaɪm/ *n* [C,U] a time during the day when you have a meal: **at mealtimes** *The only time I see the boys is at mealtimes.*

meal·y /'miːli/ *adj* **1** fruit or vegetables that are mealy are dry and do not taste good: *These apples are kind of mealy.* **2** containing MEAL

mealy-'mouthed *adj* not brave enough or honest enough to say clearly and directly what you really think – used in order to show disapproval: *Most people felt Mr Major fought a pretty mealy-mouthed campaign in which radical ideas were either dropped or blunted.*

mean¹ S1 W1 /miːn/ *v* [T] *past tense and past participle* **meant** /ment/
1 HAVE A PARTICULAR MEANING [not in progressive] to have or represent a particular meaning: *What does 'patronizing' mean?* | *The red light means 'Stop'.* | *The report fails to define what is meant by the term 'key issues'.* | **mean (that)** *This light means you're running low on fuel.*
2 INTEND TO SAY STH [not in progressive] to intend a particular meaning when you say something: **mean (that)** *I meant we'd have to leave early – that's all.* | *It's pretty obvious what she means.* | **(do) you mean** *spoken*

(=used to check you have understood what someone intended to say) *Do you mean you've changed or Chris has changed?* | **do/if you know/see what I mean?** *spoken* (=used to check that someone understands you) *I want to buy her something really special, if you know what I mean.* | *We're still married but living apart in the same house, if you see what I mean.* | *Oh yeah! I see what you mean.* (=I understand what you are trying to say) | **What I mean is**, *I don't feel alone anymore'* (=used to explain more about what you have said). | *'I didn't really like him.'* **'I know what you mean**, *I didn't get on with him either* (=used to say you understand and have had the same experience). | *'In three hours' time, I'll be a free man.'* **'How do you mean?'** (=used to ask someone to explain what they have just said)
3 INTEND TO DO STH to intend to do something or intend that someone else should do something: **mean to do sth** *I've been meaning to ask you if you want to come for a meal next week.* | *I didn't mean to upset you.* | **mean sb/sth to do sth** *I didn't mean this to happen at all.* | *I never meant you to find out.* | **mean for sb to do sth** *especially AmE*: *I didn't mean for her to get hurt.* | *I'm sure she didn't mean it* (=you did not intend to upset or hurt someone). | **mean no harm/offence/disrespect** (=not intend to harm, offend etc someone) *I'm sure he didn't mean any harm.* | *He may sound a bit rude at times, but he means well* (=intends to be helpful or kind, even if it does not seem like that). | *I wasn't criticizing you, I really meant it for the best* (=wanted to be helpful, although my actions had the wrong effect).
4 RESULT IN STH [not in progressive] to have a particular result or involve something: *The merger will mean the eventual closure of the company's Sydney office.* | *Don't let him see you. It will only mean trouble.* | **mean (that)** *The high cost of housing means that many young people can't afford to buy a house.* | **mean doing sth** *My new job will mean travelling all over the world.* | *Dieting also means being careful about which foods you buy.*
5 BE FAMILIAR [not in progressive] if a name, word etc means something to you, you are familiar with it or you understand it: *He said his name was 'Randall' but it meant nothing to me* (=I was not familiar with it). | *Does the name Bryce mean anything to you?* | *You need to use analogies which will mean something to the reader.*
6 SAY STH SERIOUSLY [not in progressive] to be serious about what you are saying or writing: *With children, if you say 'no', you have to mean it.* | *I meant what I said earlier.* | *You don't really mean that, do you?*
7 HOW IMPORTANT SB/STH IS [not in progressive] used for saying how important someone or something is to you: **mean sth to sb** *I know how much your work means to you.* | *The medal meant a lot to him.* | **mean the world to sb/mean everything to sb** (=be very important to someone) *He meant the world to her.* | *Time meant nothing* (=it was not important) *to me while I was travelling.* | *Of course the relationship meant something to me.*
8 SHOW STH IS TRUE/WILL HAPPEN [not in progressive] to be a sign that something is true or will happen: **mean (that)** *Finding a lump does not necessarily mean you have cancer.* | *Clear skies mean that it will be a cold night.* | *Just because he's been in prison, it doesn't mean that he's violent.*

SPOKEN PHRASES

Frequencies of the verb **mean** in spoken and written English.

SPOKEN			
WRITTEN			
	1000	2000	3000 per million

9 what do you mean ...? **a)** used when you do not understand what someone is trying to say: *'You'll be careful won't you?' 'What do you mean?'* **b)** used when

you are very surprised or annoyed by what someone has just said: *What do you mean, you've cancelled the trip?* | *What do you mean by that?* **c)** used when you are very annoyed by what someone has just done: *What do you mean by calling me at this time of night?* **10** SAY WHICH PERSON/THING used to say that a particular person or thing is the one that you are talking about, pointing to etc: *'Hey you!' 'Do you mean me?'* | *I meant the pink dress, not the red one.*
11 I mean a) used when explaining or giving an example of something, or when pausing to think about what you are going to say next: *You're more of an expert than me. I mean, you've got all that experience.* | *It's just not right. I mean, it's unfair isn't it?* **b)** used to quickly correct something you have just said: *She plays the violin, I mean the viola, really well.*
12 see what I mean? used when something that happens proves what you said before: *See what I mean? Every time she calls me up she wants me to do something for her.*
13 that's what I mean used when someone is saying the same thing that you were trying to say earlier: *'We might not have enough money.' 'That's what I mean, so we'd better find out the price first.'*
14 I mean to say used when adding a reason or explanation for something you have just said, especially something you feel strongly about: *Of course she wants to see the children, I mean to say, it's only natural isn't it?*

15 mean business to be determined to do something: *This decision shows the public that we mean business.*
16 be meant to do sth **a)** if you are meant to do something, you should do it, especially because someone has told you to or because you are responsible for it: *Come on, Ellen, you're meant to be helping me.* | *I thought the police were meant to protect people.* **b)** to be intended to do something: *The diagram is meant to show the different stages of the process.*
17 be meant to be good/excellent/bad etc used to say that you have heard or read that something is good, bad etc: *The play is meant to be really good.*
18 be meant for sb/sth to be intended for a particular person or purpose: *a book meant for children*
19 be meant for sb if two people are meant for each other, they are very suitable as partners for each other: *They were meant for each other.* | *She's meant for him.*
20 sb was never meant for sth/to be sth used to say that someone is not at all suitable for a particular job or activity: *I was never meant for the army.*
21 sth was meant to be/happen used to say that you think a situation was certain to happen and that no one could have prevented it: *Dan left me after a month so I guess it just wasn't meant to be.*
22 know/understand what it means to be sth to have experienced a particular situation, so that you know what it is like: *I know what it means to be alone in a foreign country.*

mean² *adj comparative* **meaner**, *superlative* **meanest**
1 CRUEL cruel or not kind: *That was a mean thing to do.* | *I felt a bit mean asking him to help.* | *It's a mean trick to play on someone.* | *It was mean of him not to invite her.* | [+to] *Don't be so mean to her!*
2 NOT GENEROUS *BrE* not wanting to spend money, or not wanting to use much of something; ▣ **stingy**; ▣ **cheap** *AmE*: *He's too mean to buy a present for his wife.* | [+with] *He's always been mean with his money.* | *It was supposed to be garlic bread, but they'd been a bit mean with the garlic.*
3 no mean feat/achievement/task etc something that is very difficult to do, so that someone who does it deserves to be admired: *They sold 1 million cards in the first year of business – no mean feat, given the problems many businesses are facing.*
4 be no mean performer/player etc to be very good at doing something: *Kinnock is no mean performer on the rugby field.*
5 a mean sth *informal* used to say that something is very good or that someone is very good at doing something:

He plays a mean game of poker. | *They serve a mean Sunday brunch at the restaurant on Fourth Street.*
6 AVERAGE [only before noun] *technical* average: *The study involved 60 patients with a mean age of 58.2 years.* | *The mean annual rainfall was 852 mm.*
7 POOR [only before noun] *literary* poor or looking poor: *She walked briskly through the mean and dirty streets.*
—**meanly** *adv* —**meanness** *n* [U]

mean³ *n* **1** the mean *technical* the average amount, figure, or value: *The mean of 7, 9 and 14 is 10.* **2** the/a mean between sth and sth a method of doing something which is between two very different methods, and better than either of them: *It's a case of finding the mean between firmness and compassion.* → MEANS

me·an·der /miˈændə $ -ər/ *v* [I] **1** if a river, stream, road etc meanders, it has a lot of bends rather than going in a straight line: [+along/across/down etc] *The river meandered gently along the valley floor.* **2** [always + adv/prep] to walk to somewhere in a slow relaxed way rather than take the most direct way possible: [+along/through etc] *Cows still meander through these villages.* **3** also meander on if a conversation or piece of writing meanders on, it is too long and has no purpose or structure —**meanderings** *n* [plural]: *his aimless meanderings through Europe* —**meander** *n* [C]

mean·ie, **meany** /ˈmiːni/ *n* [C] *spoken* an unkind person used especially by children: *Don't be such a meanie!*

mean·ing S2 W1 /ˈmiːnɪŋ/ *n*
1 OF A WORD/SIGN ETC [C,U] the thing or idea that a word, expression, or sign represents: [+of] *I don't know the precise meaning of the word 'gleaned'.* | *The expression has two very different meanings in English.*
2 IDEAS IN SPEECH/BOOK ETC [C,U] the thoughts or ideas that someone wants you to understand from what they say, do, write etc: [+of] *The meaning of her words was clear. We'd lost our jobs.* | [+behind] *She hardly dared to understand the meaning behind his statement.* | get/understand sb's meaning (=understand what they are trying to tell you) *He's become a bit more than a friend, if you get my meaning.*
3 what's the meaning of this? *spoken* used to demand an explanation: *What's the meaning of this? I asked you to be here an hour ago!*
4 PURPOSE/SPECIAL QUALITY [U] the quality that makes life, work etc seem to have a purpose or value: *Life seemed to have lost its meaning since Janet's death.* | *Her studies no longer seemed to have any meaning.* | *For many people it is religion that gives meaning to their existence.*
5 TRUE NATURE [U] the true nature and importance of something: [+of] *We seem to have forgotten the true meaning of Christmas.*
6 (not) know the meaning of sth to have, or not have, experience and understanding of a particular situation or feeling: *Living in a warzone, the children knew the meaning of fear.* | *Guilty! She doesn't know the meaning of the word!*

mean·ing·ful /ˈmiːnɪŋfəl/ *adj* **1** having a meaning that is easy to understand and makes sense: *Without more data we cannot make a meaningful comparison of the two systems.* | *Teaching history to five-year-olds in a meaningful way can be very difficult.* | [+to] *Rules must be put in a context that is meaningful to the children.* **2** meaningful look/glance/smile etc a look that clearly expresses the way someone feels, even though nothing is said: *Sam and Barbara exchanged meaningful glances.* **3** serious, important, or useful: *They want a chance to do meaningful work.* | *I want a mature and meaningful relationship.* | *a meaningful conversation* —**meaningfully** *adv*

mean·ing·less /ˈmiːnɪŋləs/ *adj* **1** having no purpose or importance and therefore not worth doing or having: *He said a few meaningless words to his*

M

hostess and looked around the room. | a repetitive and meaningless task | **absolutely/utterly/completely meaningless** a statistic that is absolutely meaningless | **virtually/fairly/largely meaningless** **2** not having a meaning that you can understand or explain: *Chinese characters are just meaningless symbols to me.*
—**meaninglessness** n [U]

means S2 W2 /miːnz/ n plural **means**
1 METHOD [C] a way of doing or achieving something
means of transport (=a way of travelling, for example using a car, bus, bicycle etc)
means of communication
means of escape
means of identification (=an official document that shows who you are)
means of expression (=a way of expressing your feelings, opinions etc)
a means of doing sth
have no means of doing sth
use any means (=use any method, even if it is illegal or causes harm to other people)
by unlawful/illegal/unfair means
(whether) by fair means or foul (=using unfair methods if necessary)

[+of] *For most people, the car is still their main **means of transport**.* | *The only **means of communication** was sign language.* | *The window was our only **means of escape**.* | *Do you have any **means of identification**?* | *art as a **means of expression*** | *Homework should not be used as **a means of** controlling children.* | *I **had no means of** telling him I would be late.* | *Brian was prepared to **use any means** to get what he wanted.* | *They had entered the country **by unlawful means**.* | *the means by which performance is assessed*

2 MONEY [plural] the money or income that you have: **have the means to do sth** *I don't have the means to support a family.* | *Paying for your children to go to a private school is **beyond the means of** most people* (=too expensive for most people). | *Try to live **within** your **means*** (=only spending what you can afford). | *His father was a **man of means*** (=a rich man).
3 by all means! *spoken* used to mean 'of course' when politely allowing someone to do something or agreeing with a suggestion: *'Can I bring Alan?' 'By all means!'*
4 by no means/not by any means not at all: *It is by no means certain that the game will take place.* | *She's not a bad kid, by any means.*
5 by means of sth *formal* using a particular method or system: *The blocks are raised by means of pulleys.*
6 a means to an end something that you do only to achieve a result, not because you want to do it or because it is important: *For Geoff, the job was simply a means to an end.*
7 the means of production the material, tools, and equipment that are used in the production of goods → ways and means at WAY¹ (1)

mean-'spirited adj not generous or sympathetic

'means test n [C] an official check in order to find out whether someone is poor enough to need money from the government —**means-tested** adj: *means-tested benefits*

meant /ment/ v the past tense and past participle of MEAN

mean-time /'miːntaɪm/ adv **1** also **in the meantime** in the period of time between now and a future event, or between two events in the past; ⊟ **meanwhile**: *The doctor will be here soon. In the meantime, try and relax.* | *I didn't see her for another five years, and in the meantime she had got married and had a couple of kids.* **2 for the meantime** for the present time, until something happens: *The power supply should be back soon – for the meantime we'll have to use candles.*

mean-while W2 /'miːnwaɪl/ adv [sentence adverb]
1 while something else is happening: *Cook the sauce*

over a medium heat until it thickens. Meanwhile start boiling the water for the pasta.
2 also **in the meanwhile** in the period of time between two events: *The flight will be announced soon. Meanwhile, please remain seated.* | *I knew I wouldn't get my exam results for several weeks, and I wasn't sure what to do in the meanwhile.*
3 used to compare two things, especially if they are completely different and are happening at the same time: *The incomes of male professionals went up by almost 80%. Meanwhile, part-time women workers saw their earnings fall.*

mean·y /'miːni/ n plural **meanies** another spelling of MEANIE

mea·sles /'miːzəlz/ n [U] also **the measles** an infectious illness in which you have a fever and small red spots on your face and body. People often have measles when they are children. → GERMAN MEASLES

meas·ly /'miːzli/ adj informal very small and disappointing in size, quantity, or value – used to show disapproval: *All I got was a measly £5.*

mea·su·ra·ble /'meʒərəbəl/ adj **1** large or important enough to have an effect that can be seen or felt; ⊟ **noticeable**: *The law has had little measurable effect since it was introduced two years ago.* **2** able to be measured: *measurable results* —**measurably** adv: *The company is working to make its environmental performance measurably better.*

mea·sure¹ S2 W2 /'meʒə $ -ər/ v
1 [T] to find the size, length, or amount of something, using standard units such as INCHES, metres etc: *The rainfall was measured over a three-month period.* | **measure sb for sth** (=measure someone in order to make clothes for them) *She was being measured for her wedding dress.* | **measure sth in sth** *We can measure the energy that food provides in calories.* | **measuring jug/cup/tape** (=one used for measuring)
2 [T] to judge the importance, value, or true nature of something; ⊟ **assess**: *Doctors say it is too early to measure the effectiveness of the drug.* | **measure sth by sth** *Education shouldn't be measured purely by examination results.*
3 [linking verb] to be a particular size, length, or amount: *The room measures 6x6 metres.* | *The earthquake measured 6.5 on the Richter scale.*
4 [T] if a piece of equipment measures something, it shows or records a particular kind of measurement: *An odometer measures the number of miles your car travels.*

measure sb/sth **against** sb/sth phr v
to judge someone or something by comparing them with another person or thing: *Bridget did not think she had to measure herself against some ideal standard.* | *Measured against our budget last year, $2.7 million seems small.*

measure sth ⇔ **off** phr v
to measure a particular length or distance, and make a mark so that you can see the beginning and end: *He measured off three yards of rope.*

measure sth ⇔ **out** phr v
to take a specific amount of liquid, powder etc from a larger amount: *Measure out 100 grams of flour.*

measure up phr v
1 to be good enough to do a particular job or to reach a particular standard: *We'll give you a week's trial in the job to see how you measure up.* | [+to] *How will the Secretary General measure up to his new responsibilities?*
2 to measure something before you do something, for example before you put in new furniture, cupboards etc: *I'd better measure up before I start laying the carpet.* | **measure sth ⇔ up** *Measure up any items that you want to keep in the kitchen.*

measure² W3 n [C]
1 ACTION an action, especially an official one, that is intended to deal with a particular problem; ⊟ **step**: *Measures are being taken to reduce crime in the city.* | **drastic/tough/extreme etc measures** *drastic measures*

to reduce traffic problems | New **safety measures** were being demanded after last night's horrific train crash. | The new bridge was erected as a **temporary measure** to replace the one which was destroyed by floods. | **precautionary/preventative measure** (=something done to stop something bad from happening) He was kept in hospital overnight as a precautionary measure.

2 half measures things done to deal with a difficult situation that are not effective or firm enough: This was no time for half measures and compromises.

3 SIGN/PROOF be a measure of sth formal be a sign of the importance, strength etc of something, or a way of testing or judging something: The flowers and tears at the funeral were a measure of the people's love for her. | Exam results are not necessarily a **true measure** of a student's abilities.

4 AMOUNT a measure of sth an amount of something good or something that you want, for example success or freedom: The new law gives local governments a significant measure of control over their own finances. | I met a number of sportsmen who had achieved a measure of success (=some success).

5 UNIT OF MEASUREMENT **a)** an amount or unit in a measuring system: a table of **weights and measures** **b)** a standard amount of an alcoholic drink

6 in large measure/in some measure a lot or quite a lot – used when talking about the reason or cause of something: The improvements **are due in large measure** to his leadership.

7 in equal measure used when the amount of one thing is the same as the amount of another thing: I was angry and embarrassed in equal measure.

8 for good measure in addition to what you have already done, given, or included: Why don't you try phoning them one more time, for good measure?

9 beyond measure very much or very great – used when you want to emphasize what you are saying: Her work has **improved beyond measure**.

10 the full measure of sth formal the whole of something: Ralph received the full measure of his mother's devotion.

11 in full measure formal if someone gives something back in full measure, they give back as much as they received: They returned our hospitality in full measure.

12 have/get the measure of sth to become familiar with something, so that you can control or deal with it

13 have/get the measure of sb BrE to know what someone's strengths and weaknesses are, so that you are able to deal with them or defeat them: She soon got the measure of her opponent.

14 THING USED FOR MEASURING something used for measuring, for example a piece of wood or a container → TAPE MEASURE

15 MUSIC a group of notes and RESTS, separated from other groups by vertical lines, into which a piece of music is divided; ▣ bar BrE → MADE-TO-MEASURE; → give sb short measure at SHORT¹ (23)

mea·sured /ˈmeʒəd $ -ərd/ adj if you do something in a measured way, you do it in a careful and controlled way, not in an excited or sudden way: a measured response to the problem | She spoke **in measured tones**.

mea·sure·less /ˈmeʒələs $ -ʒər-/ adj literary too great to be measured: Otto had measureless charm.

mea·sure·ment W3 /ˈmeʒəmənt $ -ʒər-/ n
1 [C] the length, height etc of something: **waist/chest/leg etc measurement** What's your waist measurement? | **take/make measurements** (=measure something) Take measurements of the room before you buy any new furniture. | **take sb's measurements** (=measure someone in order to make or get clothes for them) The assistant took my measurements and showed me what was available in my size.
2 [U] the act of measuring something: [+of] the measurement of performance | **accurate measurement** of body temperature

measuring jug BrE; **measuring cup** AmE n [C] a container used for measuring liquids in cooking → see picture at EAT

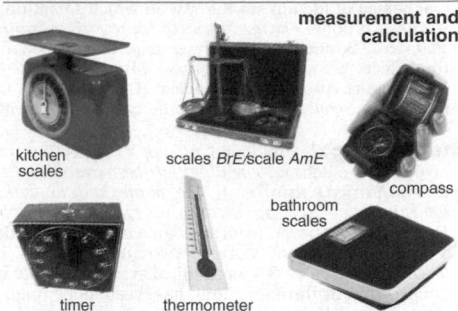

measurement and calculation

kitchen scales

scales BrE/scale AmE

compass

bathroom scales

timer

thermometer

M

measuring tape n [C] a TAPE MEASURE

meat S2 W3 /miːt/ n
1 [C,U] the flesh of animals and birds eaten as food: I gave up eating meat a few months ago. | raw meat | a meat pie | a selection of cold meats | **red meat** (=a dark-coloured meat such as BEEF) | **white meat** (=meat that is pale in colour, for example CHICKEN)
2 [U] something interesting or important in a talk, book, film etc: There's **no meat to** their arguments. | We then got down to **the real meat of** the debate (=the main and most interesting part of it).
3 sb doesn't have much meat on him/her BrE need some (more) meat on your bones AmE informal used to say that someone looks very thin
4 one man's meat is another man's poison used to say that something that one person likes may not be liked by someone else
5 be easy meat BrE informal if someone is easy meat, they are easy to defeat, deceive, or hurt: [+ for] San Marino should be easy meat for England in next week's match.
6 the meat and potatoes AmE informal the most important or basic parts of a discussion, decision, piece of work etc: Let's get down to the meat and potatoes. How much are you going to pay me for this?
7 be meat and drink to sb BrE to be something that someone enjoys doing or finds very easy to do because they have done it many times before: The first five questions in the quiz were about football, which was meat and drink to Brian.

meat·ball /ˈmiːtbɔːl $ -bɒːl/ n [C] a small round ball made from small pieces of meat, herbs, and egg or BREADCRUMBS pressed together. Meatballs are often served with a sauce.

meat grinder n [C] AmE a machine that cuts meat into very small pieces by forcing it through small holes; ▣ mincer BrE

meat·loaf /ˈmiːtləʊf $ -loʊf/ n plural meatloaves /-ləʊvz $ -loʊvz/ [C,U] meat, herbs, and other foods mixed and baked together in the shape of a LOAF

meat-packing n [U] AmE the preparation of animals that have been killed so that they can be sold as meat: the meat-packing industry —**meat-packer** n [C]

meat·y /ˈmiːti/ adj **1** containing a lot of meat, or tasting strongly of meat: a delicious meaty gravy **2** informal big and fat, with a lot of flesh: meaty forearms **3** informal containing a lot of interesting ideas or information: a meaty article | The lecture wasn't very meaty. **4** meaty role an interesting or important character that an actor is playing in a play or film: her first meaty role as an actress

mec·ca /ˈmekə/ n [singular] **1** a place that many people want to visit for a particular reason; ▣ **magnet**: [+for] Florence is a mecca for students of Art History. **2** Mecca a city in Saudi Arabia which is the holiest city of Islam

me·chan·ic /mɪˈkænɪk/ n **1** [C] someone who is skilled at repairing motor vehicles and machinery: a garage mechanic → see picture at OCCUPATION **2** the

M

mechanics of (doing) sth the way in which something works or is done: *The mechanics of the process are quite complex.* **3 mechanics** [U] the science that deals with the effects of forces on objects: *fluid mechanics* → QUANTUM MECHANICS **4 mechanics** [U] the study of machines: *Steven is planning to go to college to study mechanics.*

me·chan·i·cal /mɪˈkænɪkəl/ *adj* **1** affecting or involving a machine: *The flight has been cancelled due to mechanical failure.* | *The plane had to make an emergency landing because of mechanical problems.* **2** using power from an engine or machine to do a particular kind of work: *a mechanical digger* | *a mechanical device* **3** a mechanical action, reply etc is done without thinking, and has been done many times before: *He was asked the same question so many times that the answer became mechanical.* **4** someone who is mechanical understands how machines work **5** *technical* relating to or produced by physical forces: *the mechanical properties of solids* —**mechanically** /-kli/ *adv: The actors spoke their lines mechanically, hardly caring about the meaning.* | *I'm not very mechanically minded* (=good at understanding how machines work and repairing them).

me,chanical engin'eering *n* [U] the study of the design and production of machines and tools —**mechanical engineer** *n* [C]

me,chanical 'pencil *n* [C] *AmE* a pencil made of metal or plastic, with a thin piece of LEAD (=the part that you write with) inside; **目 propelling pencil** *BrE*

mech·a·nis·m /ˈmekənɪzəm/ *n* [C] **1** part of a machine or a set of parts that does a particular job: *the brake mechanism* | *a clock mechanism* **2** a system that is intended to achieve something or deal with a problem: **mechanism for (doing) sth** *existing mechanisms for decision making* | **mechanism to do sth** *The Army has set up mechanisms to help jobless ex-soldiers get work.* → EXCHANGE RATE MECHANISM **3** a system or a way of behaving that helps a living thing to avoid or protect itself from something difficult or dangerous: **defence/control/survival mechanism** *When a person is ill, the body's natural defence mechanisms come into operation.* **4** the way that something works: [+of] *the mechanism of the brain*

mech·a·nis·tic /ˌmekəˈnɪstɪk◂/ *adj* tending to explain the behaviour of things in the natural world as if they were machines: *a mechanistic view of the universe* —**mechanistically** /-kli/ *adv*

mech·a·nized also **-ised** *BrE* /ˈmekənaɪzd/ *adj* **1** a mechanized system or process now uses machines instead of people or animals; **目 automated**: *Car production is now highly mechanized.* **2** a mechanized army unit uses TANKS and other ARMOURED military vehicles —**mechanize** *v* [T] —**mechanization** /ˌmekənaɪˈzeɪʃən $ -nə-/ *n* [U]: *increasing mechanization of agriculture*

med /med/ *adj* [only before noun] *informal* an abbreviation of MEDICAL: *med school* | *a med student*

Med *n* **the Med** *BrE informal* the Mediterranean Sea or the area surrounding it

MEd *BrE*; **M.Ed.** *AmE* /ˌem ˈed/ *n* [C] *Master of Education* a university DEGREE in teaching that you can get after your first degree; → BEd

med·al¹ /ˈmedl/ *n* [C] a flat piece of metal, usually shaped like a coin, that is given to someone who has won a competition or who has done something brave: **gold/silver/bronze medal** *She won a gold medal at the last Olympics.* | *the bronze medal winner* | *The two boys were awarded medals for their bravery.* → **deserve a medal** at DESERVE (3); → see picture at PRIZE¹

medal² *v* **medalled, medalling** *BrE*, **medaled, medaling** *AmE* [I] to win a medal at a competition, especially at the Olympic Games: [++ in] *Germany has the potential to medal at least four times in gymnastics this year.*

me·dal·li·on /mɔˈdæliən/ *n* [C] a piece of metal shaped like a large coin, worn as jewellery on a chain around the neck: *a silver medallion*

med·al·list *BrE*; **medalist** *AmE* /ˈmedl-ɪst/ *n* [C] someone who has won a medal in a competition: *the Olympic gold medallist*

Medal of 'Honor *n* [C] the most important medal given by the US to a soldier, sailor etc who has done something extremely brave

med·dle /ˈmedl/ *v* [I] **1** to deliberately try to influence or change a situation that does not concern you, or that you do not understand; **目 interfere**: [+in] *I don't like other people meddling in the way I run this prison.* | *He accused the US of meddling in China's internal affairs.* | [+with] *I'm not the sort of newspaper owner who meddles with editorial policy.* **2** *BrE* to touch something which you should not touch, especially in a careless way that might break it: [+with] *You have no right to come in here meddling with my things.* —**meddler** *n* [C] —**meddling** *n* [U] —**meddling** *adj* [only before noun]: *meddling politicians*

med·dle·some /ˈmedlsəm/ *adj* a meddlesome person becomes involved in situations that do not concern them, in a way that annoys people; **目 interfering**: *a meddlesome old woman*

me·di·a [S2] [W2] /ˈmiːdiə/ *n*

1 the media all the organizations, such as television, radio, and newspapers, that provide news and information for the public, or the people who do this work

---

the national/local media
the news media
media attention/coverage/interest/speculation
media hype (=when the media give something too much attention, and try to make it seem much more important or better than it really is)
media event (=an event that the media gives a lot of attention to)
media circus (=a disapproving word for all the people from the media who report events, and all the attention they give to these events)

The scandal was widely reported in the national media. | *The role of the news media in forming public opinion is very important.* | *The 11-day trial generated intense media interest.* | *A great deal of media hype surrounded the release of the group's latest CD.* | *There will be another war somewhere else and the whole international media circus will move on.*

2 the plural of MEDIUM → MASS MEDIA, MULTIMEDIA

med·i·ae·val /ˌmediˈiːvəl◂ $ ˌmiː-/ *adj* another spelling of MEDIEVAL

me·di·an¹ /ˈmiːdiən/ *n* [C] **1** *AmE* also **'median strip** a narrow area of land that separates the two sides of a big road in order to keep traffic travelling in different directions apart; **目 central reservation** *BrE* **2** *technical* the middle number or measurement in a set of numbers or measurements that have been arranged in order **3** *technical* a line passing from one of the points of a TRIANGLE to the centre of the opposite side

median² *adj* **1** being the middle number or measurement in a set of numbers or measurements that have been arranged in order; → **average**: *The median age of the group is 42.* **2** in or passing through the middle of something

'media ,studies *n* [U] the study of how newspapers, radio, television etc work and how they affect society

me·di·ate /ˈmiːdieɪt/ *v* **1** [I,T] to try to end a quarrel between two people, groups, countries etc: [+between] *UN officials mediated between the rebel fighters and the government.* | *The former president has agreed to mediate the peace talks.* | [+in] *The court was set up to mediate in civil disputes.* **2** [T usually passive] *formal or technical* to change the effect or influence of something, especially to make the effect less bad: *Exercise may mediate the effects of a bad diet.* —**mediation** /ˌmiːdiˈeɪʃən/ *n* [U]

me·di·a·tor /'miːdieɪtə $ -ər/ *n* [C] a person or organization that tries to end a quarrel between two people, groups, countries etc by discussion

med·ic /'medɪk/ *n* [C] **1** *BrE informal* a medical doctor **2** *BrE informal* a medical student **3** *AmE* someone in the army who is trained to give medical treatment; → **paramedic**

Med·i·caid /'medɪkeɪd/ *n* [U] a system in the US by which the government helps to pay the cost of medical treatment for poor people; → **Medicare**

med·i·cal¹ [S2] [W2] /'medɪkəl/ *adj* relating to medicine and the treatment of disease or injury: *medical research* | *medical staff* | *a medical student* | *a patient's* **medical history** (=the illnesses they have had) | **medical records** (=which show what illnesses and treatment someone has had) | **medical attention/treatment/care** *The injury required urgent medical attention.* | the **medical profession** (=doctors, nurses, and other people who treat people who are ill) —**medically** /-kli/ *adv*: *medically qualified personnel* | *medically fit*

medical² also **medical exami'nation** *n* [C] *BrE* an examination of your body by a doctor to see if you are healthy; ▣ **physical** *AmE*

medical cer,tificate *n* [C] an official piece of paper signed by a doctor saying that you are too ill to work or that you are completely healthy; → **sick note**

medical ex'aminer *n* [C] *AmE* a doctor who examines dead people's bodies in order to find out how they died, especially if they died in a sudden or unusual way

medical ,officer *n* [C] a doctor working in the armed forces

medical prac'titioner *n* [C] *BrE formal* a doctor

medical school *n* [C,U] a college or university where people study to become doctors

me·dic·a·ment /mɪ'dɪkəmənt, 'medɪ-/ *n* [C] *formal* a substance used to treat a disease

Med·i·care /'medɪkeə $ -ker/ *n* [U] a system by which the US government helps to pay for the medical treatment of old people; → **Medicaid**

med·i·cat·ed /'medɪkeɪtɪd/ *adj* medicated soap or SHAMPOO contains a substance to help small medical problems of your skin or hair

med·i·ca·tion /,medɪ'keɪʃən/ *n* [C,U] medicine or drugs given to people who are ill: **be on medication (for sth)** *He's on medication for high blood pressure.*

me·di·ci·nal /mə'dɪsənəl/ *adj* **1** used for treating medical problems; → **medical**: *Garlic is believed to have* **medicinal properties** (=contain things that can cure medical problems). **2 for medicinal purposes a)** used in a humorous way to say that you drink alcohol because it is good for your health: *I keep a bottle of brandy handy – purely for medicinal purposes.* **b)** for use as a medicine: *herbs used in medieval times for medicinal purposes* —**medicinally** *adv*

medi·cine [S2] [W3] /'medsən $ 'medɪsən/ *n* **1** [C,U] a substance used for treating illness, especially a liquid you drink: *Medicines should be kept out of the reach of children.* | *Have you been* **taking** *your* **medicine?** | *a medicine bottle* | **medicine chest/cabinet** (=for keeping medicine in) ⚠ Do not say that you 'drink medicine'. Say that you **take** your **medicine**. **2** [U] the treatment and study of illnesses and injuries: *She studied medicine at John Hopkins University.* | *the remarkable achievements of* **modern** *medicine* | **complementary/alternative/folk** etc **medicine** | *traditional Chinese medicine* **3 the best medicine** the best way of making you feel better when you are sad: *Laughter is the best medicine.* **4 give someone a dose/taste of their own medicine** to treat someone as badly as they have treated you **5 take your medicine (like a man)** to accept an unpleasant situation or a punishment that you deserve, without complaining

medicine man or **medicine ,woman** *n* [C] a person in a Native American tribe who is considered to have the ability to cure illness and disease; → **shaman**, **witch-doctor**

med·i·co /'medɪkəʊ $ -koʊ/ *n plural* **medicos** [C] *informal* a MEDIC

med·i·e·val [W3] **mediaeval** /,medi'iːvəl $,miː-/ *adj* **1** connected with the Middle Ages (=the period between about AD 1100 and 1500): *These spices were first brought to Italy from the East in medieval times.* | *a medieval castle* **2** very old or old-fashioned – used in a humorous or disapproving way: *The plumbing in this house is positively medieval!*

me·di·o·cre /,miːdi'əʊkə◂ $ -'oʊkər◂ / *adj* not very good; ▣ **second rate**: *I thought the book was pretty mediocre.* | *a mediocre student* —**mediocrity** /,miːdi'ɒkrəti $ -'ɑːk-/ *n* [U]

med·i·tate /'medɪteɪt/ *v* **1** [I] to think seriously and deeply about something: [+on/upon] *She sat quietly, meditating on the day's events.* **2** [I] to spend time sitting in a silent, calm state, in order to relax completely or for religious purposes: *I try to meditate for half an hour every evening.* **3** [T] *formal* to plan to do something, usually something unpleasant: *Silently she meditated revenge.*

med·i·ta·tion /,medɪ'teɪʃən/ *n* **1** [U] the practice of emptying your mind of thoughts and feelings, in order to relax completely or for religious reasons: *Yoga involves breathing exercises, stretching, and meditation.* → TRANSCENDENTAL MEDITATION **2** [C usually plural, U] the act of thinking deeply and seriously about something: *She found him sitting alone, deep in meditation.* | *Rob interrupted his father's meditations.* **3** [C usually plural] serious thoughts about a particular subject: [+on] *meditations on death and loss*

med·i·ta·tive /'medɪtətɪv $ -teɪtɪv/ *adj* **1** thinking deeply and seriously about something: *She was in a meditative mood.* **2** relating to the practice of emptying your mind of thoughts and feelings, in order to relax completely or for religious reasons: *meditative techniques* —**meditatively** *adv*

Med·i·ter·ra·ne·an¹ /,medɪtə'reɪniən◂ / *n* **a)** the **Mediterranean** the sea that is surrounded by the countries of southern Europe, North Africa, and the Middle East **b)** the area of southern Europe that surrounds the Mediterranean Sea

Mediterranean² *adj* relating to the Mediterranean Sea, or typical of the area of southern Europe around it: *a Mediterranean country* | *a plant normally only found in a* **Mediterranean climate**

me·di·um¹ [S3] /'miːdiəm/ *adj* **1** of middle size, level, or amount: *What size shirt does he wear – small, medium or large?* | **(of) medium height/length/build** *She's of medium height.* | *hair of medium length* | *Fry the onions over a* **medium heat** *until they are golden.* | **medium to large** *companies* ⚠ Use **average**, not 'medium', when you want to say that someone's level of skill or activity is neither high nor low: *Her standard is average (NOT Her standard is medium).* **2** also **medium rare** meat that is medium or medium rare is partly cooked but still slightly pink inside; → **rare**, **well-done** **3 medium dry** medium dry wine is slightly sweeter than dry wine **4 medium brown/blue** etc a colour which is neither light nor dark: *His jacket's a medium brown colour.*

medium² *n plural* **media** /-diə/ *or* **mediums** [C] **1** a way of communicating information and news to people, such as newspapers, television etc; → **media**: *Advertising is a powerful medium.* **2** a way of expressing your ideas, especially as a writer or an artist: [+for] *the novel as a medium for satire* | *the visual*

[1] 000, [2] 000, [3] 000, most frequent words in [S]poken and [W]ritten English

M

media (=painting and films)　**3 medium of instruction** a language that is used for teaching: *English is still the main medium of instruction in Nigeria.*　**4 medium of exchange** money or other ways of paying for things　**5** *technical* a substance or material in which things grow or exist: *a good growing medium for tomatoes*　**6** *technical* a substance through which a force travels* → MAGNETIC MEDIA; → a happy medium* at HAPPY (8)

medium³ *n plural* **mediums** [C] someone who claims to have the power to receive messages from dead people

'**medium-sized** also '**medium-size** *adj* not small but not large either: *a medium-sized business*

'**medium ,term** *n* [singular] the period of time a few weeks or months ahead of the present; → **short-term**, **long-term**: **in the medium term** *The company's prospects look good in the medium term.* | *medium term investments*

'**medium ,wave** written abbreviation **MW** *n* [U] a system of radio broadcasting using radio waves between 100 and 1000 metres in length; → **long wave**, **FM**

med·ley /'medli/ *n* [C]　**1** a group of songs or tunes sung or played one after the other as a single piece of music: [+of] *He played a medley of Beatles songs.*　**2** [usually singular] a mixture of different types of the same thing which produces an interesting or unusual effect: [+of] *an exotic medley of smells* | *a medley of architectural styles*　**3** a swimming race in which the competitors swim using four different STROKES: *the 400 metres individual medley*

meek /miːk/ *adj* very quiet and gentle and unwilling to argue with people: *He was always so meek and mild.* —**meekly** *adv*: *'All right,' said Neil meekly.* —**meekness** *n* [U]

meet¹ [S1] [W1] /miːt/ *v past tense and past participle* **met** /met/

1 SEE SB AT AN ARRANGED PLACE [I,T not in passive] to go to a place where someone will be at a particular time, according to an arrangement, so that you can talk or do something together: *Meet me at 8.00.* | *I'll meet you by the main reception desk.* | **meet (sb) for sth** *Why don't we meet for lunch on Friday?* | *We arranged to meet outside the theatre.*

2 SEE SB BY CHANCE [I,T not in passive] to see someone by chance and talk to them; ▣ **bump into**: *You'll never guess who I met in town.* | *I was worried I might meet Henry on the bus.*

3 SEE SB FOR THE FIRST TIME [I,T not in passive] to see and talk to someone for the first time, or be introduced to them: *We first met in Florence.* | *I met my husband at university.* | *Jane, come and meet my brother.* | **nice/pleased to meet you** (=used to greet someone politely when you have just met them for the first time) *'This is my niece, Sarah.' 'Pleased to meet you.'* | **(it was) nice meeting you** (=used to say goodbye politely to someone you have just met for the first time)

4 SEE SB AT AN AIRPORT/STATION ETC [T] to be waiting for someone at an airport, station etc when they arrive in a plane or train: *My dad met us at the station.* | *I'll come and meet you off the plane.*

5 COME TOGETHER TO DISCUSS STH [I] to come together in the same place in order to discuss something: *The committee meets once a month.* | *The two groups will meet next week to discuss the project.*

6 COMPETE AGAINST SB [I,T not in passive] to play against another person or team in a competition, or to fight another army in a war: *Manchester United will meet Blackburn Rovers in the sixth round of the Cup.* | *The two armies finally met on the battlefield at Stamford Bridge.*

7 JOIN OR TOUCH [I,T not in passive] if two things meet, they touch or join at a particular place: *The two roads meet just north of Flagstaff.* | *Their hands met under the table.*

8 EXPERIENCE A PROBLEM OR SITUATION [T] to experience a problem, attitude, or situation; ▣

encounter, **come across**: *Wherever she went she met hostility and prejudice.*

9 **meet a problem/challenge** to deal with a problem or something difficult that you have to do: *The new building will mean that we can meet the challenge of increasing student numbers.*

10 **meet a need/demand/requirement/condition etc** to do something that someone wants, needs, or expects you to do or be as good as they need, expect etc: *The company says it is unable to meet the workers' demands for higher wages.* | *The service is tailored to meet your needs.* | *beaches which meet European standards of cleanliness*

11 **meet a deadline** to finish something at the time it is meant to be finished: *We are still hoping to meet the November deadline.*

12 **meet a goal/target etc** to achieve something that you are trying to achieve: *It's virtually impossible to meet the weekly sales targets.* | *The scheme does not meet its objectives.*

13 **meet a debt/cost/expense etc** to make a payment that needs to be made: *The government has promised to meet the cost of clearing up after the floods.*

14 **there's more to sb/sth than meets the eye** used to say that someone or something is more interesting, intelligent etc than they seem to be

15 **our/their eyes meet** if two people's eyes meet, they look at each other: *Our eyes met momentarily, then he looked away.* | *His eyes met Nina's and she smiled.*

16 **meet sb's eye(s)/gaze/glance etc** to look directly at someone who is looking at you: *Ruth looked down, unable to meet his eye.* | *She turned to meet his gaze.*

17 **meet your eye(s)** if something meets your eyes, you see it: *An extraordinary scene met our eyes as we entered the room.*

18 **meet your match** to compete against an opponent who is stronger or more skilful than you are: *I think he might have met his match in Simon.*

19 **meet sb halfway** to do some of the things that someone wants, in order to reach an agreement with them

20 **meet (sth) head-on a)** if two moving vehicles meet head-on, they are facing each other and hit each other suddenly and violently **b)** if you meet a problem head-on, you deal with it directly without trying to avoid it

21 **meet your death/end** to die in a particular way: *He met his death at the hands of enemy soldiers.*

22 **meet your maker** to die – used humorously

23 **meet your Waterloo** to finally be defeated after you have been successful for a long time → **make ends meet** at END¹ (18)

meet up *phr v*

1 to meet someone in order to do something together: *We often meet up after work and go for a drink.* | [+with] *I've got to go now, but I'll meet up with you later.*

2 if roads, paths etc meet up, they join together at a particular place: [+with] *The path eventually meets up with the main road.*

meet with sb/sth *phr v*

1 to have a meeting with someone: *Representatives of EU countries will meet with senior American politicians to discuss the trade crisis.*

2 also **be met with sth** to get a particular reaction or result: **meet with opposition/disapproval etc** *His comments have met with widespread opposition.* | **meet with support/approval etc** *Her ideas have met with support from doctors and health professionals.* | **meet with success/failure** (=succeed or fail) *Our attempts at negotiation finally met with some success.*

3 **meet with an accident** *formal* to be injured or killed in an accident

meet² *n* [C]　**1 track meet** *especially AmE* a sports competition between people running races, jumping over bars etc　**2** *BrE* an occasion when a group of people riding horses go out to hunt FOXES

meet³ *adj old use* right or suitable

,**meet-and-'greet** n [C] **1** an event that is organized for famous musicians, writers, artists etc to meet and talk to their FANS: *There will be a meet-and-greet after the show.* **2** a service that sends people to greet and help a person or group when they arrive at an airport **3** an event in which parents go to their child's school and meet the teachers and other people who work there

meet·ing S1 W1 /'miːtɪŋ/ n [C]

1 an event at which people meet to discuss and decide things

have/hold a meeting
go to/attend a meeting
be in/at a meeting
call a meeting (=decide there will be a meeting)
public meeting
emergency meeting
general meeting *especially BrE* (=a meeting that anyone can come to)
committee/staff/board meeting (=a meeting of a particular group of people)
summit meeting (=a meeting between leaders of governments)

We're **having** *a* **meeting** *next week to discuss the matter.* | *Over a hundred and fifty people* **attended** *the* **meeting.** | *Mrs Lavelle* **is in a meeting** *at the moment.* | *The minister has* **called** *an emergency* **meeting.** | [+about/on] *There was a* **public meeting** *about the future of the gallery.* | [+with] *I've got a meeting with Mr Edwards this afternoon.* | [+of] *a meeting of senior politicians* | [+between] *a meeting between unions and management* | *Are you coming to the* **committee meeting** *this evening?*

2 the meeting *formal* all the people who are at a meeting: *I'd like to put a few ideas before the meeting.*
3 [usually singular] when people meet each other by chance or because they have arranged to do this: *I had felt drawn to Alice ever since our first meeting.*
4 a sports competition or a set of races for horses
5 meeting of minds a situation in which two people have very similar ideas and understand each other very well: *There was a real meeting of minds between the two leaders.*
6 an event at which a group of Quakers (=a Christian religious group) pray together

'**meeting-house** n [C] a building where Quakers (=a Christian religious group) pray together

'**meeting place** n [C] a building or place where people meet: *The pub is a popular meeting place for local teenagers.*

meg /meg/ n [C] *informal* a MEGABYTE

meg·a /'megə/ *adj informal* very big and impressive or enjoyable: *Their first record was a mega hit.* —**mega** *adv*

mega- /megə/ *prefix* **1** [in nouns] a million – used with units of measurement: *1000 megawatts of electricity* **2** *informal* extremely: *Her family is mega-rich!* **3** very big: *a megastore*

meg·a·bit /'megəbɪt/ n [C] *technical* a million BITS

meg·a·bucks /'megəbʌks/ n [plural] *informal* a very large amount of money: *She's earning megabucks now.*

meg·a·byte /'megəbaɪt/ n [C] written abbreviation **MB** or **Mb** a unit for measuring computer information, equal to 1,024 KILOBYTES, and used less exactly to mean one million BYTES

meg·a·hertz /'megəhɜːts $ -ɜːr-/ n *plural* **megahertz** [C] written abbreviation **MHz** a unit for measuring FREQUENCY, especially of radio signals, equal to one million HERTZ

meg·a·lith /'megəlɪθ/ n [C] a large tall stone put in an open place by people in ancient times, possibly as a religious sign —**megalithic** /ˌmegə'lɪθɪk◂/ *adj*

meg·a·lo·ma·ni·a /ˌmegələʊ'meɪniə $ -loʊ-/ n [U] when someone wants to have a lot of power for themselves and enjoys having control over other people's lives, sometimes as part of a mental illness

meg·a·lo·ma·ni·ac /ˌmegələʊ'meɪniæk $ -loʊ-/ n [C] someone who wants to have a lot of power for themselves and enjoys having control over other people's lives —**megalomaniac** *adj*

meg·a·phone /'megəfəʊn $ -foʊn/ n [C] a piece of equipment like a large horn which you talk through to make your voice sound louder, when you are speaking to a crowd

meg·a·star /'megəstaː $ -staːr/ n [C] *informal* a very famous singer or actor

meg·a·ton /'megətʌn/ n [C] a unit for measuring the power of an explosive, equal to the power of one million TONS of TNT (=a powerful explosive): *a five megaton atomic bomb*

meg·a·watt /'megəwɒt $ -waːt/ n [C] written abbreviation **MW** a million WATTS

mei·shi /'meɪʃiː/ n *plural* **meishi** [C] a card that shows a business person's company, position, name, address etc, used in Japan; ▤ **business card**

mel·a·mine /'meləmiːn/ n [U] a material like plastic that is used to make a hard smooth surface on tables and shelves

mel·an·cho·li·a /ˌmelən'kəʊliə $ -'koʊ-/ n [U] *old-fashioned* a feeling of great sadness and lack of energy

mel·an·chol·ic /ˌmelən'kɒlɪk◂ $ -'kaː-/ *adj literary* feeling very sad

mel·an·chol·y¹ /'melənkəli $ -kaːli/ *adj* very sad: *The music suited her melancholy mood.*

melancholy² n [U] *formal* a feeling of sadness for no particular reason: *He sank into deep melancholy.*

me·lange /meɪ'lɑːnʒ/ n [singular] *formal* a mixture of different things: [+of] *The population is a melange of different cultures.*

mel·a·nin /'melənɪn/ n [U] a natural dark brown colour in human skin, hair, and eyes

mel·a·no·ma /ˌmelə'nəʊmə $ -'noʊ-/ n [C] *technical* a TUMOUR on a person's skin which causes CANCER

mel·a·to·nin /ˌmelə'təʊnɪn $ -'toʊ-/ n [U] a HORMONE that is sometimes used as a drug to help you sleep

Mel·ba toast /ˌmelbə 'təʊst $ -'toʊst/ n [U] a type of thin dry TOAST that breaks easily

meld /meld/ v [I,T] if two things meld, or if you meld them, they combine into one thing: **meld (sth) with sth** *He melded country music with blues to create rock and roll.* | [+into] *The raindrops melded into a sheet of water.*

mel·ée /'meleɪ $ 'meɪleɪ, meɪ'leɪ/ n [C usually singular] a situation in which a lot of people rush around in a confused way: *It's amazing that no one was hurt in the melée.*

mel·li·flu·ous /mɪ'lɪfluəs/ *adj formal* a mellifluous voice or piece of music sounds pleasantly smooth

mel·low¹ /'meləʊ $ -loʊ/ *adj*
1 NOT BRIGHT a mellow colour or light looks soft, warm, and not too bright: *the mellow golden light of early evening*
2 NOT LOUD OR HARSH a mellow sound is pleasant and smooth: *a warm, mellow voice*
3 NOT STRONG IN FLAVOUR mellow wine or fruit has a smooth, pleasant taste: *its smooth, mellow flavour*
4 NOT STRICT someone who is mellow is gentle and calm and does not criticize other people, because they have a lot of experience of life
5 RELAXED if you feel mellow, you feel calm and relaxed, especially after drinking alcohol —**mellowness** n [U]

mellow² v [I,T] **1** if someone mellows or is mellowed, they become gentler and more sympathetic: *Paul's certainly mellowed over the years.* | *Two pints of beer had mellowed my father.* **2** if colours mellow or are mellowed, they begin to look warm and soft: *The bricks had mellowed to a soft red.* **3** if wine mellows or is mellowed, its taste becomes smoother

M

mellow (sb) **out** phr v AmE informal to become relaxed and calm, or to make someone like this

me·lod·ic /mɔ'lɒdɪk $ -'lɑː-/ adj **1** formal something that sounds melodic sounds like music or has a pleasant tune: Their music is loud and not very melodic. | a deep melodic voice **2** technical concerned with the main tune in a piece of music: There is very little melodic variation in the piece.

me·lo·di·ous /mɔ'ləʊdiəs $ -'loʊ-/ adj formal something that sounds melodious sounds like music or has a pleasant tune: He spoke in a quiet melodious voice. —**melodiously** adv

mel·o·dra·ma /'melədrɑːmə $ -drɑːmə, -dræmə/ n [C,U] **1** a story or play in which very exciting or terrible things happen, and in which the characters and the emotions they show seem too strong to be real: He was behaving like a character in a Victorian melodrama. **2** a situation in which people become more angry or upset than is really necessary: Come on, there's no need for all this melodrama.

mel·o·dra·mat·ic /ˌmelədrə'mætɪk◂/ adj if you behave in a melodramatic way, you become more angry or upset than is really necessary: Stop being so melodramatic! —**melodramatically** /-kli/ adv

mel·o·dy /'melədi/ n plural **melodies** [C,U] a tune: They played some lovely melodies. | a haunting melody

mel·on /'melən/ n [C,U] a large round fruit with sweet juicy flesh → see picture at FRUIT[1]

melt /melt/ v
1 BECOME LIQUID [I,T] if something solid melts or if heat melts it, it becomes liquid; → freeze, thaw: It was warmer now, and the snow was beginning to melt. | Melt the butter in a saucepan.
2 DISAPPEAR [I] also **melt away** to gradually disappear: Opposition to the government melted away. | His anger slowly melted.
3 BECOME LESS ANGRY [I] to become less angry and begin to feel more gentle and sympathetic: She melted under his gaze. | My heart just melted when I saw her crying.
4 melt in your mouth if food melts in your mouth, it is soft and tastes very nice
5 melt into sb's arms/embrace literary to allow someone to hold you in their arms and feel that you love them: Closing her eyes, she melted into his embrace. → butter wouldn't melt in sb's mouth at BUTTER[1] (2)

melt away phr v
1 if a crowd of people melts away, the people gradually leave: The demonstrators melted away at the first sign of trouble.
2 to gradually disappear: Her determination to take revenge slowly melted away.

melt sth ⇔ **down** phr v
to heat a metal object until it becomes a liquid, especially so that you can use the metal again: A lot of the gold was melted down and used for making jewellery.

melt into sth phr v
1 to gradually change into something else: Her irritation melted into pity.
2 to gradually become hidden by something: He is trying to melt into the background.

melt·down /'meltdaʊn/ n [C,U] **1** a very dangerous situation in which the material inside a NUCLEAR REACTOR melts and burns through its container, allowing RADIOACTIVITY to escape **2** a situation in which prices fall by a very large amount or an industry or economic situation becomes much weaker: The stock market crash might lead to financial meltdown.

melt·ing /'meltɪŋ/ adj [usually before noun] written if someone gives you a melting look or speaks to you in a melting voice, it makes you feel pity or love for them —**meltingly** adv

'melting point n [C,U] the temperature at which a solid substance becomes a liquid

'melting pot n [singular] **1** a place where people from different races, countries, or social classes come to live together: New York has always been a great melting pot. **2** a situation or place in which many different ideas are discussed **3 in the melting pot** BrE an idea or situation that is still in the melting pot is likely to change

mem·ber S1 W1 /'membə $ -ər/ n [C]
1 a person or country that belongs to a group or organization

committee/party/union/board etc member (=a member of a particular group)
member of staff/staff member
member of sb's family
member of the public
member of society (=a citizen)
senior/junior member
leading member (=one of the most important members)
active member
founder member (=a member of an organization who also started that organization)
member state/country/nation (=a country that belongs to a particular international organization)
card-carrying member (=a member who is very active in a group)
full member (=a member in the most complete way)
associate member (=a member who does not have all the rights of a full member)

The majority of **union members** voted in favour of a strike. | [+of] He is a **member of** the local tennis club. | We offer training to all **members of staff**. | The other **members of** his **family** were against the marriage. | Copies of the report are available to schools and **members of the public**. | a problem which should concern every **member of society** | a **senior member of** the ruling party | **leading members of** the government | In her youth she was an **active member of** the Campaign for Nuclear Disarmament (CND). | He is a **founder member of** the Prison Reform Trust. | a meeting of all UN **member states** | a **card-carrying member** of the Communist Party | Turkey is not yet a **full member of** the EU.

2 one of a particular group of animals or plants: [+of] The plant is a **member of** the lily **family**. | Wolves and domestic dogs are **members of** the same **species**.
3 BrE a Member of Parliament: [+for] the member for Truro
4 formal a man's sex organ; ⊟ penis

Member of 'Parliament n plural **Members of Parliament** [C] MP someone who has been elected to represent people in a parliament

mem·ber·ship S2 W2 /'membəʃɪp $ -ər-/ n
1 [U] when someone is a member of a club, group, or organization

apply for membership
renew your membership (=apply to become a member again after your membership has ended)
union/church/party etc membership (=membership of a particular group)
full membership (=membership with all the rights that can be allowed to members)
membership card
membership fees

[+of] Greece first **applied for membership** of the EU in 1975. | [+in] AmE: I forgot to **renew** my **membership** in the sailing club. | You should carry your **membership card** with you at all times. | **Membership fees** are being increased this year.

2 [singular also + plural verb BrE] all the members of a club, group, or organization: The membership voted to change the rules about women members.
3 [singular] the number of people who belong to a club, group, or organization: We're trying to increase our membership. | The club now has a membership of over 2,000.

mem·brane /ˈmembreɪn/ n [C,U] **1** a very thin piece of skin that covers or connects parts of your body: *Loud noise can damage the delicate membrane in the ear.* **2** a very thin layer of material that covers something —**membranous** /ˈmembrənəs/ adj

me·men·to /mɪˈmentəʊ $ -toʊ/ n plural **mementos** [C] a small thing that you keep to remind you of someone or something: [+of] *I kept the bottle as a memento of my time in Spain.*

mem·o S3 /ˈmeməʊ $ -moʊ/ n plural **memos** [C] a short official note to another person in the same company or organization: *I sent him a memo reminding him about the meeting.* | [+to/from] *a memo from the managing director to all heads of department*

mem·oir /ˈmemwɑː $ -wɑːr/ n [C] **1 memoirs** [plural] a book by someone important and famous in which they write about their life and experiences: *Lady Thatcher had just published her memoirs.* **2** formal a short piece of writing about a person or place that you knew well, or an event that you experienced

mem·o·ra·bil·i·a /ˌmemərəˈbɪliə/ n [plural] things that you keep or collect because they are connected with a famous person, event, or time: *a collection of war memorabilia*

mem·o·ra·ble /ˈmemərəbəl/ adj very good, enjoyable, or unusual, and worth remembering: *We want to make this a truly memorable day for the children.* —**memorably** adv

mem·o·ran·dum /ˌmeməˈrændəm/ n plural **memoranda** /-də/ or **memorandums** [C] **1** formal a MEMO **2** law a short legal document that contains the important details of an agreement

me·mo·ri·al¹ /mɪˈmɔːriəl/ adj [only before noun] done or made in order to remind people of someone who has died: **memorial service/ceremony** *A memorial service will be held at 7 pm on Saturday.*

memorial² n **1** [C] something, especially a stone with writing on it, that reminds people of someone who has died: [+to] *The hospital was built as a memorial to King Edward VII.* | **permanent/lasting memorial** *An appeal has been launched to build a lasting memorial to the composer.* **2** [singular] an achievement that reminds people of someone who has died: [+to] *The garden is a memorial to one of the finest Victorian gardeners.* → WAR MEMORIAL

Me'morial ˌDay n [U] a national holiday in the US on the last Monday in May to remember soldiers who have died in wars

me·mo·ri·a·lize also **-ise** BrE /mɪˈmɔːriəlaɪz/ v [T] to do something so that a person or event will be remembered by people

memoriam → IN MEMORIAM

mem·o·rize also **-ise** BrE /ˈmeməraɪz/ v [T] to learn words, music etc so that you know them perfectly

mem·o·ry S1 W1 /ˈmeməri/ n plural **memories**
1 ABILITY TO REMEMBER [C,U] someone's ability to remember places, experiences etc

have a good/excellent memory
have a bad/poor/terrible etc memory
have a memory like a sieve (=have a very bad memory)
have a long memory (=be able to remember things for a long time)
have a short memory (=only remember something for a short time, and soon forget it)
from memory (=using your memory, and not using notes or written instructions)
lose your memory (=lose your ability to remember things)
short-term memory (=your ability to remember things you have just seen, heard, or experienced)
long-term memory (=your ability to remember events that happened a long time ago)
remain/stay/be etched in your memory (=be remembered for a long time)
if my memory serves me correctly/right (=used to say that you are almost certain you have remembered correctly)

My memory's not as good as it once was. | [+for] *She has a terrible memory for names.* | *Those of you with long memories will remember this song.* | *The pianist played the whole piece from memory.* | *I'm speaking from memory, but I believe it was last May.* | *The first symptom of the disease is often short-term memory loss.* | *The image has remained in my memory ever since.* | *If my memory serves me correctly, he lived in Paris for a while.*

2 STH YOU REMEMBER [C usually plural] something that you remember from the past about a person, place, or experience: [+of] *She talked about her memories of the war.* | **happy/fond/bad etc memories** *He has lots of happy memories of his stay in Japan.* | *My most vivid memory is not the accident itself but being in the ambulance.* | *One of my earliest childhood memories is of my mother reading stories to me by the fire.* | *Those old songs bring back memories.*

3 COMPUTER **a)** [C] the part of a computer where information can be stored: *The data is stored in the computer's memory.* **b)** [U] the amount of space that can be used for storing information on a computer: *128 Mb of memory* | *Personal computers now have much increased memory capacity.*

4 in/within memory during the time that people can remember: *the worst floods in living memory* (=since the earliest time that people now alive can remember) | *It's certainly the best England team in recent memory.* | *The disaster was within the memory of many men still working at the station.*

5 in memory of sb if something is done or made in memory of someone, it is done to remember them and remind other people of them after they have died: *a statue in memory of those who died in the war* | *She set up a charitable fund in her father's memory.*

6 sb's memory the way you remember someone who has died: *She died over 40 years ago but her memory lives on* (=people still remember her). | **to sb's memory** *There's a bench to his memory in the local park.*

7 a walk/trip down memory lane when you spend some time remembering the past: *She returned to her old school yesterday for a trip down memory lane.*

8 sb's memory is playing tricks on them spoken used to say that someone is remembering things wrongly: *My memory must be playing tricks on me; I'm sure I put that book on the desk.* → **commit sth to memory** at COMMIT (9); → **jog sb's memory** at JOG¹ (3) → PHOTOGRAPHIC MEMORY; → **refresh sb's memory** at REFRESH (2)

'**memory bank** n [C] the part of a big computer system that stores information

'**memory hog** n [C] informal **1** a computer program that uses a lot of memory **2** someone who uses computer programs that use a lot of the power available, so that other people on the network have trouble using their programs —**memory-hogging** adj [only before noun]

mem·sahib /ˈmemˌsɑːb $ -ˌsɑːhɪb, -ˌsɑːb/ n [C] old-fashioned a European woman – used in India

men /men/ n the plural of MAN

men·ace¹ /ˈmenəs/ n **1** [C] something or someone that is dangerous; ▤ **threat**: [+of] *It's the only way to deal with the menace of drug dealing.* | [+to] *That man's a menace to society. He should be locked away.* | *the growing menace of oil pollution at sea* **2** [U] a threatening quality, feeling, or way of behaving: *There was menace in his voice.* | **air/sense of menace** *There was a sense of menace as the sky grew darker.* **3** [C] a person, especially a child that is annoying or causes trouble; ▤ **nuisance**: *My little brother's a real menace.* **4 with menaces** BrE law if someone asks another person for something with menaces, they use threats of violence to get what they want: *He was charged with demanding money with menaces.*

M

menace² v [T] formal to threaten: *The elephants are still menaced by poachers.*

men·ac·ing /'menɪsɪŋ/ adj making you expect something unpleasant; ▤ **threatening**: *dark menacing clouds | a low menacing laugh | His tone grew more menacing.* —**menacingly** adv: *He moved towards her menacingly.*

mé·nage /'meɪnɑːʒ $ məˈnɑːʒ/ n [C] formal all the people who live in a particular house; ▤ **household**

ménage à trois /ˌmeɪnɑːʒ ɑː ˈtrwɑː $ məˌnɑːʒ-/ n [singular] a sexual relationship involving three people who live together

me·na·ge·rie /mɪˈnædʒəri/ n [C] a group of wild animals kept privately or for the public to see

mend¹ /mend/ v
1 [REPAIR] [T] **a)** to repair a tear or hole in a piece of clothing: *My father used to mend our shoes.* **b)** BrE to repair something that is broken or not working; ▤ **fix**: *When are you going to mend that light in the hall? | Tim can mend any broken toy.* → see box at REPAIR¹
2 [BECOME HEALTHY] [I] informal if a broken bone mends, it becomes whole again: *His leg isn't mending as quickly as he'd expected.*
3 mend your ways to improve the way you behave after behaving badly for a long time: *If he doesn't mend his ways, he'll be asked to leave.*
4 mend (your) fences to try to become friendly with someone again after you have offended them or argued with them: *Is it too late to mend fences with your ex-wife?*
5 [END A QUARREL] [T] to end a quarrel or difficult situation by dealing with the problem that is causing it: *I've tried to mend matters between us, but she's still very angry.*

mend² n [C] **1 be on the mend** to be getting better after an illness or after a difficult period: *He's had flu, but he's on the mend. | signs that the economy is on the mend* **2** a place in something where it has been repaired

men·da·cious /menˈdeɪʃəs/ adj formal not truthful: *mendacious propaganda* —**mendaciously** adv

men·da·ci·ty /menˈdæsɪti/ n [U] formal the quality of not being truthful

mend·er /'mendə $ -ər/ n [C] someone who repairs something

men·di·cant /'mendɪkənt/ n [C] formal someone who asks people for money in order to live, usually for religious reasons —**mendicant** adj

mend·ing /'mendɪŋ/ n [U] clothes that need to be repaired

men·folk /'menfəʊk $ -foʊk/ n [plural] old-fashioned the men in a particular society, family etc; → **womenfolk**: *Many women took in washing to supplement the income of their menfolk.*

me·ni·al¹ /'miːniəl/ adj menial work is boring, needs no skill, and is not important: *a menial job | She did menial tasks about the house.*

menial² n [C] someone who does menial work, especially a servant in a house

men·in·gi·tis /ˌmenɪnˈdʒaɪtɪs/ n [U] a serious illness in which the outer part of the brain becomes swollen

men·o·pause /'menəpɔːz $ -pɔːz/ n [singular, U] the time when a woman stops MENSTRUATING, which usually happens around the age of 50; → **male menopause**: *After the menopause a woman cannot bear a child.* —**menopausal** /ˌmenəˈpɔːzəl◂ $ -ˈpɔː-/ adj

me·no·rah /məˈnɔːrə/ n [C] a Jewish CANDLESTICK that holds seven CANDLES

mensch /menʃ/ n [C] AmE spoken someone that you like and admire, especially because they have done something good for you

men·ses /'mensiːz/ n [plural] medical the blood that flows out of a woman's body each month

men's room n [C] especially AmE the men's toilet; ▤ **gents** BrE; → **ladies' room**

men·stru·al /'menstruəl/ adj relating to the time each month when a woman loses blood, or the blood that she loses: *the menstrual cycle*

menstrual 'period n [C] formal the time each month when a woman menstruates; ▤ **period**

men·stru·ate /'menstrueɪt/ v [I] when a woman menstruates, usually every month, blood flows from her body —**menstruation** /ˌmenstruˈeɪʃən/ n [C,U]

mens·wear /'menzweə $ -wer/ n [U] clothing for men – used especially in shops: *the menswear department*

-ment /mənt/ suffix [in nouns] used to form a noun from a verb to show actions, the people who do them, or their results: *the government* (=the people who govern a country) | *the replacement of something* (=the action of replacing something) | *some interesting new developments* —**-mental** /mentl/ suffix [in adjectives]: *governmental*

men·tal [S2] [W2] /'mentl/ adj
1 [only before noun] relating to the health or state of someone's mind; → **psychiatric**: *The centre provides help for people suffering from mental illness. | Stress has an effect on both your physical and mental health.*
2 [only before noun] relating to the mind and thinking, or happening only in the mind: *a child's mental development | You need to develop a positive mental attitude.* | **mental picture/image** (=a picture that you form in your mind) *I tried to get a mental picture of him from her description.*
3 make a mental note to make a special effort to remember something: *Sarah made a mental note to ask Janine about it later.*
4 mental block a difficulty in remembering something or in understanding something: *I got a complete mental block as soon as the interviewer asked me a question.*
5 go mental BrE spoken informal **a)** to get very angry **b)** to start behaving in an uncontrolled or excited way
6 [not before noun] BrE informal thinking or behaving in a way that seems crazy or strange: *He must be mental!* —**mentally** adv: *She's obviously mentally ill.*

mental 'age [S3] n [C] a measure of someone's ability to think, understand etc, expressed as the average age of a child with that level of ability: *a 25-year-old man with a mental age of seven*

mental a'rithmetic n [U] the act of adding numbers together, multiplying them etc in your mind, without writing them down: *I did a quick bit of mental arithmetic.*

'mental ˌhospital n [C] old-fashioned a hospital where people with mental illnesses are treated; ▤ **psychiatric hospital**

men·tal·i·ty /menˈtælɪti/ n plural **mentalities** [C] a particular attitude or way of thinking, especially one that you think is wrong or stupid: *a get-rich-quick mentality | I can't understand the mentality of the people who are behind this kind of violence.*

mentally 'handicapped adj old-fashioned a mentally handicapped person has a problem with their brain, often from the time they are born, that affects their ability to think or control their body movements

men·thol /'menθɒl $ -θɔːl, -θɑːl/ n [U] a substance that smells and tastes of MINT, used to give cigarettes and sweets a special taste

men·tho·la·ted /'menθəleɪtɪd/ adj containing menthol

men·tion¹ [S1] [W1] /'menʃən/ v [T]
1 to talk or write about something or someone, usually quickly and without saying very much or giving details: *Was my name mentioned at all? | Some of the problems were mentioned in his report.* | **mention sth to sb** *I mentioned the idea to Joan, and she seemed to like it.* | **mention (that)** *He mentioned that he was having problems, but he didn't explain.* | **It's worth mentioning** (=it is important enough to mention) *that they only studied a very small number of cases.* | **As I mentioned earlier**, *there have been a lot of changes recently.* | *She mentioned in passing* (=mentioned in a quick unimportant way) *that you had just been to Rome.* | *now you*

mention it (=used to say that you had not thought about something until the speaker mentioned it) *Now you mention it, I haven't seen her around lately.* | **fail/omit/ neglect to mention sth** (=not mention something you should mention) *The report failed to mention that most of the landowners do not live on their properties.* ⚠ Do not say 'mention about' something. **Mention** is followed by a direct object: *She didn't mention her mother.*
2 don't mention it *spoken* used to say politely that there is no need for someone to thank you for helping them: *'Thanks for the ride home!' 'Don't mention it.'*
3 not to mention sth used to introduce an additional thing that makes a situation even more difficult, surprising, interesting etc: *Pollution has a negative effect on the health of everyone living in the city, not to mention the damage to the environment.* | *It's too far to walk, **not to mention the fact that** it'll probably be closed by now anyway.*
4 be mentioned in dispatches *BrE* to have your name on an official list of people who have been brave in battle, as an honour

mention² *n* [C usually singular, U] when someone mentions something or someone in a conversation, piece of writing etc: [+of] *He **made no mention** of his wife's illness.* | **at the mention of sth** *At the mention of a trip to the seaside, the children got very excited.* | *They all **get a mention** (=they are all mentioned) in the book.* | **deserve/merit (a) mention** *There is one other person who deserves **special mention** (=is especially worth mentioning for something they have done).* → HONOURABLE MENTION

men·tor /ˈmentɔː $ -tɔːr/ *n* [C] an experienced person who advises and helps a less experienced person

men·tor·ing /ˈmentɔːrɪŋ/ *n* [U] a system where people with a lot of experience, knowledge etc advise and help other people at work or young people preparing for work

men·u S3 /ˈmenjuː/ *n* [C]
1 a list of all the kinds of food that are available for a meal, especially in a restaurant: *Could we have the menu, please?* | **on the menu** *Is there any fish on the menu?* | *a three course **set menu** (=dishes which you do not choose for yourself)*
2 a list of things on a computer screen which you can ask the computer to do: *Select PRINT from the main menu.* | **pull-down/drop-down menu** (=a list of choices which appears when you CLICK ON a place on the screen) | **menu-driven** (=operated by using a menu)

me·ow /miˈaʊ/ *n, v* the usual American spelling of MIAOW

MEP /ˌem iː ˈpiː/ *n* [C] **Member of the European Parliament** someone who has been elected as a member of the Parliament of the European Union

mer·can·tile /ˈmɜːkəntaɪl $ ˈmɜːrkəntiːl, -taɪl/ *adj* [only before noun] *formal* concerned with trade; ☐ **commercial**: *mercantile law*

Mer·ca·tor pro·jec·tion /məˌkeɪtə prəˈdʒekʃən $ mərˌkeɪtər-/ also **Mercator's projection** *n* [singular] the usual way a map of the world is drawn

mer·ce·na·ry¹ /ˈmɜːsənəri $ ˈmɜːrsəneri/ *n plural* **mercenaries** [C] a soldier who fights for any country or group that will pay him: *an army of foreign mercenaries* | *a mercenary soldier*

mercenary² *adj* only interested in the money you may be able to get from a person, job etc: *She did it for purely mercenary reasons.* | *a mercenary attitude*

mer·cer·ized cot·ton also **-ised** *BrE* /ˌmɜːsəraɪzd ˈkɒtn $ ˌmɜːrsəraɪzd ˈkɑːtn/ *n* [U] cotton that has been treated with chemicals to make it shiny and strong

mer·chan·dise¹ W3 /ˈmɜːtʃəndaɪz, -daɪs $ ˈmɜːr-/ *n* [U] *formal* goods that are being sold: *A range of official Disney merchandise was on sale.* | *They inspected the merchandise carefully.*

merchandise² *v* [T] to try to sell goods or services using methods such as advertising; ☐ **market**: *If the product is properly merchandised, it should sell very well.*

mer·chan·dis·ing /ˈmɜːtʃəndaɪzɪŋ $ ˈmɜːr-/ *n* [U] **1** toys, clothes, and other products relating to a popular film, sports team, singer etc: *The concerts generated £3 million in ticket and merchandising sales.* **2** the way in which shops and businesses try to sell their products: *the director of merchandising*

mer·chant /ˈmɜːtʃənt $ ˈmɜːr-/ *n* [C] **1 wine/coal/ timber etc merchant** someone whose job is to buy and sell wine, coal etc or a small company that does this: *He had a job with an Edinburgh wine merchant.* **2** *old-fashioned* someone who buys and sells goods in large quantities: *the son of a wealthy merchant* **3 con merchant/speed merchant etc** *BrE informal* someone who is involved in a particular activity, such as tricking people or driving very fast

mer·chant·a·ble /ˈmɜːtʃəntəbəl $ ˈmɜːr-/ *adj* of **merchantable quality** *law* in a suitable condition to be sold

merchant bank *n* [C] a bank that provides services for businesses —**merchant banker** *n* [C]

mer·chant·man /ˈmɜːtʃəntmən $ ˈmɜːr-/ *n plural* **merchantmen** /-mən/ [C] *old-fashioned* a ship used for carrying goods

merchant navy *BrE*; **merchant marine** *AmE n* [singular] all of a country's ships that are used for trade, not war, and the people who work on these ships: *John worked as a chef in the merchant navy.*

merchant seaman *n* [C] a sailor in the merchant navy

mer·ci·ful /ˈmɜːsɪfəl $ ˈmɜːr-/ *adj* **1 merciful death/ end/release** a death or end to something that seems fortunate because it ends someone's suffering: *I think my uncle's death was a merciful release for my poor aunt.* **2** being kind to people and forgiving them rather than punishing them or being cruel: *Merciful God, save us.*

mer·ci·ful·ly /ˈmɜːsɪfəli $ ˈmɜːr-/ *adv* fortunately or luckily, because a situation could have been much worse: *Mercifully, I managed to stop the car just in time.* | *The journey was mercifully brief.*

mer·ci·less /ˈmɜːsɪləs $ ˈmɜːr-/ *adj* **1** cruel and showing no kindness or forgiveness: *a merciless attack* | *a merciless killer* **2 merciless heat/cold/wind etc** heat, cold etc that is very great or strong and unpleasant, and does not stop: *It brings some relief from the merciless summer heat.* —**mercilessly** *adv*: *He teased his sister mercilessly.*

mer·cu·ri·al /mɜːˈkjʊəriəl $ mɜːrˈkjʊr-/ *adj* **1** *literary* having feelings that change suddenly and without warning: *an actor noted for his mercurial temperament* **2** *literary* quick and clever: *her mercurial wit* **3** *technical* containing mercury

mercury *n* [U] /ˈmɜːkjəri $ ˈmɜːr-/ a heavy silver-white poisonous metal that is liquid at ordinary temperatures, and is used in THERMOMETERS. It is a chemical ELEMENT: symbol Hg

Mer·cu·ry *n* the PLANET that is nearest the sun: *Temperatures on Mercury reach as high as 700 K.* → see picture at SOLAR SYSTEM

mer·cy /ˈmɜːsi $ ˈmɜːrsi/ *n* **1** [U] if someone shows mercy, they choose to forgive or to be kind to someone who they have the power to hurt or punish: *He showed **no mercy** to his enemies.* | *God **have mercy** on his soul.* | **beg/cry/plead for mercy** *The boy was screaming and begging for mercy.* **2 at the mercy of sb/sth** unable to do anything to protect yourself from someone or something: *After the boat's motor failed, they were at the mercy of the weather.* | *She was completely at his mercy.* **3 mercy flight/mission etc** a journey taken to bring help to people: *a mercy mission to help homeless refugees* **4 leave sb to sb's (tender) mercies** to let someone be dealt with by another person, who may treat them very badly or strictly – used humorously **5 throw yourself on sb's mercy** to ask someone to help you or forgive you when you are in a very bad

M

situation   **6 it's a mercy (that)** *spoken* used to say that it is lucky that a worse situation was avoided: *It's a mercy the accident happened so near the hospital.* → **be thankful/grateful for small mercies** at SMALL¹ (13)

mercy ˌkilling *n* [C,U] the act of killing someone who is very ill or old so that they do not have to suffer any more; ◨ **euthanasia**

mere¹ W3 /mɪə $ mɪr/ *adj superlative* **merest** [only before noun, no comparative]
1 used to emphasize how small or unimportant something or someone is: *She lost the election by a mere 20 votes.* | *He's a mere child.* | *It can't be a mere coincidence that they left at the same time.*
2 used to emphasize that something which is small or not extreme has a big effect or is important: *The merest little noise makes him nervous.* | *The mere thought of food made her feel sick.* | *The mere fact that the talks are continuing is a positive sign.*

mere² *n* [C] *literary* a lake

mere·ly S2 W2 /'mɪəli $ 'mɪrli/ *adv*
1 used to emphasize how small or unimportant something or someone is; ◨ **only**: *He's merely a boy – you can't expect him to understand.*
2 used to emphasize that nothing more than what you say is involved; ◨ **just**: *We're merely good friends.* | *He merely shrugged and walked away.*
3 not merely/rather than merely used before the less important of two ideas in a sentence to emphasize the more important idea: *It's not merely a matter of cost, but whether she's old enough to go on holiday alone.* | *It's important to write these goals down, rather than merely think about them.*

mer·e·tri·cious /ˌmerɪ'trɪʃəs◂/ *adj formal* something that is meretricious seems attractive but has no real value or is not based on the truth: *meretricious research* —**meretriciousness** *n* [U]

merge /mɜːdʒ $ mɜːrdʒ/ *v*   **1** [I,T] to combine, or to join things together to form one thing: [+with] *The bank announced that it was to merge with another of the high street banks.* | *The company plans to merge its subsidiaries in the US.* | **merge sth into sth** *proposals to merge the three existing health authorities into one* | [+together] *The villages have grown and merged together over the years.*   **2** [I] if two things merge, or if one thing merges into another, you cannot clearly see them, hear them etc as separate things: [+into] *She avoided reporters at the airport by merging into the crowds.* | [+with] *Memories seemed to merge with reality.*

merg·er /'mɜːdʒə $ 'mɜːrdʒər/ *n* [C] the joining together of two or more companies or organizations to form one larger one: [+of/between] *a proposed merger between two of the largest software companies* | [+with] *There has been a lot of talk about a merger with another leading bank.* | *merger negotiations*

me·rid·i·an /mə'rɪdiən/ *n*   **1** [C] one of the imaginary lines from the North Pole to the South Pole, drawn on a map of the Earth   **2 the meridian** *technical* the highest point reached by the sun or another star, when seen from a point on the Earth's surface

me·ringue /mə'ræŋ/ *n* [C,U] a light sweet food made by mixing sugar and the white part of eggs together very quickly and then baking it

me·ri·no /mə'riːnəʊ $ -noʊ/ *n plural* **merinos** [C,U] a type of sheep with long wool, or cloth made from this wool

mer·it¹ /'merɪt/ *n*   **1** [C] an advantage or good feature of something: [+of] *The film has the merit of being short.* | *The merit of the report is its realistic assessment of the changes required.* | *The great merit of the project is its flexibility and low cost.* | *Each of these approaches to teaching has its merits.* | *Tonight's meeting will weigh up the relative merits of the two candidates.*   **2** [U] *formal* a good quality that makes someone or something deserve praise: *There is never any merit in being second best.* | **have (some) merit/be of merit**

(=be good) *The suggestion has some merit.* | **on merit** *All students are selected solely on merit* (=because they are good). | **artistic/literary merit** *a film lacking any kind of artistic merit*   **3 judge/consider etc sth on its (own) merits** to judge something only on what you see when you look at it rather than on what you know from other people or things: *It's important to judge each case on its merits.*

mer·it² *v* [T not in progressive] *formal* to be good, important, or serious enough for praise or attention; ◨ **deserve**: *The results have been encouraging enough to merit further investigation.* | *It's a fascinating book which merits attention.*

mer·i·toc·ra·cy /ˌmerɪ'tɒkrəsi $ -'tɑː-/ *n plural* **meritocracies** [C]   **1** a social system that gives the greatest power and highest social positions to people with the most ability   **2 the meritocracy** the people who have power in a meritocracy —**meritocratic** /ˌmerɪtə'krætɪk◂/ *adj*

mer·i·to·ri·ous /ˌmerɪ'tɔːriəs◂/ *adj formal* very good and deserving praise

mer·maid /'mɜːmeɪd $ 'mɜːr-/ *n* [C] in stories, a woman who has a fish's tail instead of legs and who lives in the sea

mer·ri·ly /'merɪli/ *adv*   **1** *written* in a happy way, or in a way that makes you feel happy: *Sylvia laughed merrily.*   **2** *literary* quickly and in a pleasant way: *The fire soon began to burn merrily.* | *The clock ticked merrily in the corner.*   **3** not thinking about possible problems that might happen as a result of what you are doing – used to show disapproval; ◨ **blithely**: *Meanwhile, the company is merrily pushing ahead with its plans.*

mer·ri·ment /'merɪmənt/ *n* [U] *literary* laughter, fun, and enjoyment: *Her eyes sparkled with merriment.* | *the sounds of merriment*

mer·ry /'meri/ *adj*   **1 Merry Christmas!** used to say that you hope someone will have a happy time at Christmas; ◨ **Happy Christmas**   **2** *literary* happy; ◨ **cheerful, jolly**: *He marched off, whistling a merry tune.* | *He's a lovely man with merry eyes and a wide smile.*   **3 the more the merrier** *spoken* used to say that you are happy for other people to join you in what you are doing: *'Do you mind if I bring Tony?' 'No, of course not. The more the merrier.'*   **4** [not before noun] *BrE informal* slightly drunk; ◨ **tipsy**   **5 make merry** old-fashioned to enjoy yourself by drinking, singing, laughing, etc: *Christmas is a time to eat, drink and make merry.*   **6** *old use* pleasant: *the merry month of June* —**merriness** *n* [U] → **play (merry) hell with sth** at HELL¹ (25); → **lead sb a merry old dance** at LEAD¹ (19)

ˈmerry-go-ˌround *n*   **1** [C] a machine that turns around and around, and has model animals or cars for children to sit on; ◨ **carousel** *AmE*; ◨ **roundabout** *BrE*   **2** [singular] a series of similar events that happen very quickly one after another: [+of] *the endless Washington merry-go-round of parties and socializing*

mer·ry·mak·ing /'meri,meɪkɪŋ/ *n* [U] *literary* fun and enjoyment, especially drinking, dancing, and singing

me·sa /'meɪsə/ *n* [C] a hill with a flat top and steep sides, in the southwestern US

mes·ca·line, **mescalin** /'meskəliːn/ *n* [U] a drug made from a CACTUS plant that makes people imagine that they can see things that do not really exist

mesh¹ /meʃ/ *n*   **1** [C,U] material made from threads or wires that have been woven together like a net, or a piece of this material: *The windows were covered in wire mesh to keep out flies.* | *a mesh fence*   **2** [C usually singular] *literary* a complicated or difficult situation or system: [+of] *She had felt trapped by the old mesh of loyalty and shame.*

mesh² *v* [I]   **1** if two ideas or things mesh, they fit together very well: [+with] *His own ideas did not mesh with the views of the party.*   **2** if two parts of an engine or machine mesh, they fit closely together and connect with each other

mes·mer·ic /mezˈmerɪk/ *adj* very attractive or having a very powerful effect, so that people cannot think of anything else: *a mesmeric performance* | *the mesmeric hum of the bees*

mes·mer·ize also **-ise** *BrE* /ˈmezmə raɪz/ *v* [T usually in passive] if you are mesmerized by someone or something, you cannot stop watching them or listening to them because they are so attractive or have such a powerful effect; ⊟ **captivate**: *The first time I saw Diana I was mesmerized by her beauty.* —**mesmerizing** *adj*

mes·quite /meˈskiːt/ *n* [C,U] an American tree or bush, or the wood from it that is used to give food a special taste when cooking on a BARBECUE

mess¹ [S2] /mes/ *n*

1 DIRTY/UNTIDY [singular, U] if there is a mess somewhere or a place is a mess, things there are dirty or not neatly arranged: *What a mess!* | *Sorry – the place is a bit of a mess.* | *When I got home, the house was a complete mess.* | *in a mess BrE: The burglars left the house in an awful mess.* | *You can make cookies if you promise not to make a mess in the kitchen.* | **clear/clean up the mess** *Whoever is responsible for this mess can clear it up immediately!* | *She hates mess.*

2 PROBLEMS/DIFFICULTIES [singular, U] a situation in which there are a lot of problems and difficulties, especially as a result of mistakes or carelessness: *My life's such a mess.* | *in a mess The economy is still in a terrible mess.* | *You got us into this mess, Terry. You can get us out of it.* | *All she could do was pray that, somehow, she might be able to sort out the mess she had got herself into.*

3 make a mess of (doing) sth to do something badly: *I feel I've made a real mess of my marriage.* | *Many people make a mess of handling money.*

4 PERSON **be a mess** *informal* if someone is a mess, they look dirty and untidy, or are in a bad emotional state

5 a mess of sth *AmE informal* a lot of something: *a mess of fresh fish* .

6 ARMY/NAVY [C] a room in which members of the army, navy etc eat and drink together: *We had lunch in the officers' mess.*

7 WASTE SUBSTANCE [C,U] *BrE informal* solid waste from an animal: *The dog's made a mess on the carpet.*

mess² [S3] *v*

1 [I] to make something look untidy or dirty: *He scratched his head and messed his hair even more.*

2 [I,T] *BrE* if an animal or person messes something, they use the wrong place as a toilet: *He was so drunk that he messed the bed.*

3 no messing *spoken informal* used to say that something was done very easily: *Williams won very comfortably, no messing.*

4 [I] to have meals in a room where members of the army, navy etc eat together

mess around also **mess about** *BrE phr v informal*

1 to spend time lazily, doing things slowly and in a way that is not planned: *He spent his vacation messing around on the farm.*

2 to behave in a silly way when you should be paying attention or doing something sensible; ⊟ **fool around**: *Stop messing around and get ready for school.*

3 mess sb around to cause a lot of problems for someone, especially by changing your mind often and not being completely honest: *Don't mess me about – I want the money you promised me.*

mess around with sb/sth also **mess about with sb/sth** *BrE phr v informal*

1 to have a sexual relationship with someone that you should not have a sexual relationship with: *She'd been messing around with another man.*

2 to spend time playing with something, repairing it etc: *Dave likes messing around with old cars.*

3 to use something and make annoying changes to it: *Who's been messing around with my camera?*

mess up *phr v informal*

1 mess sth ⇔ **up** to spoil or ruin something, especially something important or something that has been care-

fully planned: *It took me ages to get this right – I don't want some idiot to mess it up.* | *She felt she'd messed up her whole life.*

2 mess sth ⇔ **up** to make something dirty or untidy: *Who messed up the kitchen?*

3 to make a mistake and do something badly: *I think I messed up on the last question.* | **mess sth** ⇔ **up** *It doesn't matter if you mess it up, you can always try again.*

4 mess sb ⇔ **up** to make someone have emotional or mental problems: *I messed up my kids.*

5 mess sb ⇔ **up** *AmE informal* to hurt someone especially by hitting them

mess with sb/sth *phr v informal*

1 to get involved with someone or something that may cause problems or be dangerous: *Don't mess with drugs.*

2 to deceive someone or cause trouble for them: *You mess with me, and I'll rip your head off.*

3 to try changing something, especially in a way that damages or spoils it

mes·sage [S1] [W2] /ˈmesɪdʒ/ *n* [C]

1 a spoken or written piece of information that you send to another person or leave for them

---

get/receive a message

leave a message

send a message

take a message (=give a telephone message from someone to someone else)

pass on/relay a message (–give someone a message from someone else)

urgent/important message

telephone/fax message

mail/email message (=a message sent by computer)

text message (=on a mobile phone)

message of thanks/congratulations/support/sympathy etc

*Did you **get my message**? | [+from] There's a message from Karen on the answerphone.* | *[+for] I have an **urgent message** for you.* | *He **left a message** saying he would probably be a little late.* | *I use the internet mainly for **sending** email **messages**.* | *I'm sorry, she's out right now, **can I take a message**?* | *He wanted me to **pass on a message** to the police.* | *The family would like to express their thanks to all those who sent **messages of sympathy** after Jack's tragic accident.*

---

2 [usually singular] the main or most important idea that someone is trying to tell people about in a film, book, speech etc: *The message of the film is that good always triumphs over evil.* | *The result of this legal battle **sends an important message to** people in similar situations.* | *It's perfectly possible to **get your message across** (=communicate what you want to say) without being so angry.* | *They use illustrations to **convey** their **message**.*

3 get the message *informal* to understand what someone means or what they want you to do: *OK, I get the message – I'm going!*

4 a piece of written information which appears on a computer screen to tell the user about something, especially a problem: **error/warning message** *I keep getting an error message when I try to log on.*

5 on/off message stating or not stating the official opinion of the political party you belong to

6 keep to the message to always emphasize your political party's most important ideas when you are trying to gain people's support: *Don't confuse the voters. Keep to the message.*

'message board *n* [C] a place on a website where you can read or leave messages; ⊟ **electronic bulletin board**

mes·sag·ing /ˈmesɪdʒɪŋ/ *n* [U] the system or process of sending messages using electronic equipment: *an electronic messaging system*

---

[1] 000, [2] 000, [3] 000, most frequent words in [S]poken and [W]ritten English

messed 'up adj informal someone who is messed up has emotional or mental problems because of something that has happened to them

mes·sen·ger¹ /'mesɪndʒə, -sən- $ -ər/ n [C] **1** someone whose job is to deliver messages or documents, or someone who takes a message to someone else **2 blame/shoot the messenger** to be angry with the person who tells you about something bad, instead of the person who caused it to happen

messenger² v [T] to send a letter, package etc somewhere using a messenger

'messenger ,boy n [C] someone who delivered messages to other people as a job in the past

'mess hall n [C] a large room where soldiers eat

mes·si·ah /mɪ'saɪə/ n [singular] **1 the Messiah a)** Jesus Christ, who Christians believe has been sent by God to save the world from evil **b)** a great religious leader who, according to Jewish belief, will be sent by God to save the world **2** someone who people believe will solve all their problems: *The club was in desperate need of a new footballing messiah.*

mes·si·an·ic /ˌmesi'ænɪk◂/ adj formal **1** someone who has messianic beliefs wants to make very big social or political changes: *Many young people have an admirable messianic zeal about them.* **2** relating to or involving the Messiah

Mes·srs BrE; **Messrs.** AmE /'mesəz $ -ərz/ the plural of MR, used especially in the names of companies: *Messrs Ford and Dobson*

mess·y S3 /'mesi/ adj comparative **messier**, superlative **messiest**
1 dirty or untidy: *a messy room* | *Sorry the place is so messy, I haven't had time to clear up.* → see picture at TIDY¹
2 informal a messy situation is complicated and unpleasant to deal with: *He's just been through a particularly messy divorce.*
3 making someone or something dirty or untidy: *messy jobs like plumbing, plastering, and tiling* —**messily** adv —**messiness** n [U]

mes·ti·zo /me'stiːzəʊ $ -zoʊ/ n plural **mestizos** [C] someone who has one Hispanic parent and one Native American parent

met /met/ v the past tense and past participle of MEET

meta- /metə/ prefix **1** beyond or at a higher level: *metaphysical* (=beyond ordinary physical things) **2** relating to a change of state or position: *metabolism* (=the process of changing food into energy)

met·a·bol·ic /ˌmetə'bɒlɪk◂ $ -'bɑː-/ adj [only before noun] relating to your body's metabolism: **(high/low) metabolic rate** *Fish normally have a high metabolic rate.* | *Exercise can increase your metabolic rate.* | *the metabolic activity of the brain*

me·tab·o·lis·m /mɪ'tæbəlɪzəm/ n [C,U] the chemical processes by which food is changed into energy in your body: *This drug speeds up your metabolism.* | **protein/carbohydrate/alcohol etc metabolism** *The vast majority of alcohol metabolism occurs in the liver.* | **[+of]** *the metabolism of fat by the liver*

me·tab·o·lize also **-ise** BrE /mɪ'tæbəlaɪz/ v [T] to change food in your body into energy and new cells, using chemical processes

met·a·da·ta /'metədeɪtə/ n [plural, U] information that describes what is contained in large computer DATABASES, for example who wrote the information, what it is for, and in what form it is stored

met·al S2 W2 /'metl/ n [C,U] a hard, usually shiny substance such as iron, gold, or steel; → **metallic**: *The gate is made of metal.* | *a small black metal box* | *They traded in gold and other **precious metals*** (=valuable metals used especially for making jewellery). | *The old trucks were sold as **scrap metal*** (=old metal that is melted and used again). → **HEAVY METAL**

met·a·lan·guage /'metəˌlæŋgwɪdʒ/ n [C,U] words that are used for talking about or describing language

'metal de,tector n [C] **1** a machine used to find pieces of metal that are buried under the ground **2** a special frame that you walk through at an airport, used to check for weapons made of metal

'metal fa,tigue n [U] weakness in metal that makes it likely to break, caused for example by frequent shaking over a long period

me·tal·lic /mɪ'tælɪk/ adj **1** a metallic noise sounds like pieces of metal hitting each other: *The key turned in the lock with a loud metallic click.* | *The pans made a metallic clatter as they crashed to the floor.* **2** a metallic voice is rough, hard, and unpleasant: *He spoke in a thin, metallic voice.* **3** a metallic colour shines like metal: *He drives a metallic red van.* **4** a metallic taste is bitter and unpleasant, like metal: *The gum left a horrible metallic taste in my mouth.* **5** made of metal or containing metal: *metallic particles*

met·al·lur·gy /mɪ'tælədʒi $ 'metələːrdʒi/ n [U] the scientific study of metals and their uses —**metallurgist** n [C] —**metallurgical** /ˌmetə'lɜːdʒɪkəl◂ $ -'lɜːr-/ adj

met·al·work /'metlwɜːk $ -wɜːrk/ n [U] **1** objects made by shaping metal: *a huge collection of antique metalwork* **2** the activity or skill of making metal objects: *Students can study woodwork or metalwork.* —**metalworker** n [C]; → see picture at HANDICRAFT

met·a·mor·phose /ˌmetə'mɔːfəʊz $ -'mɔːrfoʊz/ v [I,T] formal to change completely and become something different, or to make something change in this way: **[+into]** *From an easygoing young girl, she had metamorphosed into a neurotic middle-aged woman.*

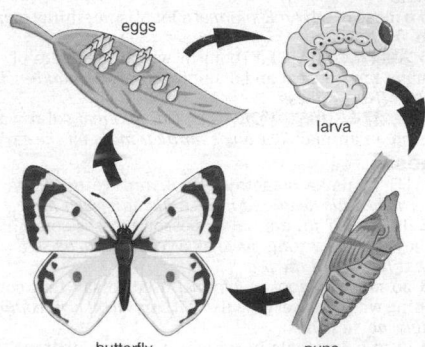

metamorphosis

eggs

larva

butterfly pupa

met·a·mor·pho·sis /ˌmetə'mɔːfəsɪs $ -'mɔːr-/ n plural **metamorphoses** /-siːz/ [C,U] **1** formal a process in which something changes completely into something very different; ⊟ **transformation**: *It took me some time to undergo the metamorphosis from teacher to lecturer.* | *the metamorphosis of China under Deng's economic reforms* **2** a process in which a young insect, FROG etc changes into another stage in its development: *Beetles undergo a complete metamorphosis in their life cycle.*

met·a·phor /'metəfə, -fɔː $ -fɔːr/ n [C,U] **1** a way of describing something by referring to it as something different and suggesting that it has similar qualities to that thing; → **simile**: *She uses some wonderful images and metaphors in her writing.* | *a very creative use of metaphor* **2 mixed metaphor** the use of two different metaphors at the same time to describe something, especially in a way that seems silly or funny **3** something that represents a general idea or quality: **[+for]** *Their relationship is a metaphor for the failure of communication in the modern world.*

met·a·phor·i·cal /ˌmetə'fɒrɪkəl◂ $ -'fɔː-, -'fɑː-/ adj **1** a metaphorical use of a word is not concerned with real objects or physical events, but with ideas or events of a non-physical kind: *The word has a metaphorical as well as a literal meaning.* **2** used to show that you are using a metaphor: *his need to escape from the metaphorical chains that held him* —**metaphorically** /-kli/ *adv*: *She was, literally and metaphorically, in perfect shape.*

met·a·phys·i·cal /ˌmetəˈfɪzɪkəl◂/ *adj* concerned with the study of metaphysics: *A lot of scientists don't like discussing metaphysical matters.*

met·a·phys·ics /ˌmetəˈfɪzɪks/ *n* [U] the part of PHIL-OSOPHY that is concerned with trying to understand and describe the nature of truth, life, and REALITY

mete /miːt/ *v*
  mete sth ⇔ **out** *phr v formal* if you mete out a punishment, you give it to someone: [+to] *He felt he had a right to mete out physical punishment to the children.* | *Judges are meting out increasingly harsh sentences for car theft.*

me·te·or /ˈmiːtiə $ -ər/ *n* [C] a piece of rock or metal that travels through space, and makes a bright line in the night sky when it falls down towards the Earth: *Astronomers track large meteors using radar.* | *a meteor shower* (=a lot of meteors that fall down towards the Earth at the same time)

me·te·or·ic /ˌmiːtiˈɒrɪk◂ $ -ˈɔːrɪk, -ˈɑːrɪk/ *adj* **1** happening very suddenly and quickly: *her meteoric rise from dancer to professional actress* | *The company has experienced meteoric growth.* | *The scandal ended his **meteoric** political career.* **2** technical from a METEOR: *meteoric iron* —**meteorically** /-kli/ *adv*: *His career faded as meteorically as it grew.*

me·te·o·rite /ˈmiːtiəraɪt/ *n* [C] a piece of rock or metal from space that has landed on Earth

me·te·o·rol·o·gy /ˌmiːtiəˈrɒlədʒi $ -ˈrɑː-/ *n* [U] the scientific study of weather conditions —**meteorologist** *n* [C]: *The storms have baffled meteorologists in the United States.* —**meteorological** /ˌmiːtiərəˈlɒdʒɪkəl◂ $ -ˈlɑː-/ *adj*: *satellites that provide meteorological data to the National Weather Service*

me·ter¹ /ˈmiːtə $ -ər/ *n* [C] **1** a machine that measures and shows the amount of something you have used or the amount of money that you must pay: **water/gas/electricity meter** | *A man came to **read** the electricity **meter**.* | *The taxi driver left the meter running while I ran in to pick up my bags.* **2** a machine that measures the level of something: **sound-level/light etc meter** **3** also **parking meter** a machine which you put money into when you park your car next to it **4** the American spelling of METRE

meter² *v* [T] to measure how much of something is used, and how much you must pay for it, by using a meter: *All our water is metered now.*

-meter /miːtə, mɪtə $ -tər/ *suffix* [in nouns] an instrument for measuring something: *a speedometer*

ˈmeter maid *n* [C] *AmE old-fashioned* a woman whose job is to make sure that cars are not parked illegally; ⧉ **traffic warden** *BrE*

meth·a·done /ˈmeθədəʊn $ -doʊn/ *n* [U] a drug that is often given to people who are trying to stop taking HEROIN

me·thane /ˈmiːθeɪn $ ˈme-/ *n* [U] a gas that you cannot see or smell, which can be burned to give heat: *Methane is one of the principal gases contributing to the greenhouse effect.*

meth·a·nol /ˈmeθənɒl $ -nɔːl, -nɑːl/ *n* [U] a type of poisonous alcohol that can be made from wood

me·thinks /mɪˈθɪŋks/ *v past tense* **methought** /-ˈθɔːt $ -ˈθɒːt/ [T] *old use* I think: *Methinks he is mistaken.*

meth·od S1 W1 /ˈmeθəd/ *n*
1 [C] a planned way of doing something, especially one that a lot of people know about and use: *traditional teaching methods* | *I think we should try again using a different method.* | **method of/for (doing) sth** *Today's methods of birth control make it possible for a couple to choose whether or not to have a child.* | *effective methods*

for the storage and retrieval of information
2 [U] *formal* a well-organized and well-planned way of doing something: *There's no method in the way they do their accounts.*
3 there's method in/to sb's madness used to say that even though someone seems to be behaving strangely, there is a sensible reason for what they are doing

me·thod·i·cal /mɪˈθɒdɪkəl $ -ˈθɑː-/ *adj* **1** a methodical way of doing something is careful and uses an ordered system: *He always checked every detail in a methodical way.* | *a methodical approach to answering questions* **2** a methodical person always does things carefully, using an ordered system: *She's a very methodical person.* | *He had a neat, methodical mind.* —**methodically** /-kli/ *adv*: *He went through the papers methodically, one by one.*

Meth·o·dist /ˈmeθədɪst/ *n* [C] someone who belongs to a Christian religious group that follows the ideas of John Wesley —**Methodist** *adj*: *a Methodist chapel* —**Methodism** *n* [U]

meth·o·dol·o·gy /ˌmeθəˈdɒlədʒi $ -ˈdɑː-/ *n plural* **methodologies** [C,U] the set of methods and principles that you use when studying a particular subject or doing a particular kind of work: **methodology for (doing) sth** *We've been developing a new methodology for assessing new products.* | *There are some differences in methodology between the two studies.* —**methodological** /ˌmeθədəˈlɒdʒɪkəl◂ $ -ˈlɑː-/ *adj*: *There are a few methodological issues we need to discuss.* —**methodologically** /-kli/ *adv*: *The study was methodologically flawed.*

me·thought /mɪˈθɔːt $ -ˈθɒːt/ *v* the past tense of METHINKS

meths /meθs/ *n* [U] *BrE informal* METHYLATED SPIRITS

Me·thu·se·lah /məˈθjuːzələ $ -ˈθuː-/ *n* **as old as Methuselah** very old

meth·yl al·co·hol /ˌmeθɪl ˈælkəhɒl, ˌmiːθaɪl- $ -hɔːl/ *n* [U] *technical* a poisonous alcohol that can be made from wood; ⧉ **methanol**

meth·yl·at·ed spir·its /ˌmeθɪleɪtɪd ˈspɪrɪts/ *n* [U] a type of alcohol that is burned in lamps, heaters etc

me·tic·u·lous /mɪˈtɪkjɪləs/ *adj* very careful about small details, and always making sure that everything is done correctly: *He kept meticulous accounts.* | *Their planning and preparation were meticulous.* | *He cleaned the tools with meticulous care.* | *The book describes his journey in meticulous detail.* | [+in] *He was meticulous in his use of words.* | [+about] *He has always been so meticulous about his appearance.* —**meticulously** *adv*: *The attack was meticulously planned and executed.*

met·i·er /ˈmetieɪ, ˈmeɪ- $ meˈtjeɪ, ˈmetjeɪ/ *n* [C usually singular] *formal* someone's metier is the type of work or activity that they enjoy doing because they have a natural ability to do it well: *Acting is not my metier.*

me-ˈtoo *adj* [only before noun] *informal* a me-too product is one that a company begins to sell after it has seen that other companies are successful with the same type of product – used to show disapproval

me·tre S2 W3 *BrE*; **meter** *AmE* /ˈmiːtə $ -ər/ *n*
1 [C] written abbreviation *m* the basic unit for measuring length in the METRIC SYSTEM
2 [C,U] the arrangement of sounds in poetry into patterns of strong and weak beats; → **rhythm**

-metre *BrE*; **-meter** *AmE* /miːtə, mɪtə $ -tər/ *suffix* [in nouns] part of a metre, or a number of metres: *a millimetre* | *a kilometer*

met·ric /ˈmetrɪk/ *adj* **1** using or connected with the METRIC SYSTEM of weights and measures; → **imperial**: *a metric tonne* | *The parts all come in metric sizes now.* **2** metrical

met·ri·cal /ˈmetrɪkəl/ *adj technical* written in the form of poetry, with a pattern of strong and weak beats

M

met·ri·ca·tion /ˌmetrɪˈkeɪʃən/ n [U] the change to using the METRIC SYSTEM of weights and measures: *Most businesses are in favour of metrication.*

metric system n the metric system the system of weights and measures that is based on the kilogram and the metre

metric ton n [C] a unit for measuring weight, equal to 1000 kilograms

met·ro /ˈmetrəʊ $ -troʊ/ n plural **metros** [C] a railway system that runs under the ground below a city: *the Paris Metro* | *It'll be quicker to go on the metro.* | *a metro station*

met·ro·nome /ˈmetrənəʊm $ -noʊm/ n [C] a piece of equipment that makes a regular repeated sound like a clock, showing the speed at which music should be played

me·trop·o·lis /mɪˈtrɒpəlɪs $ -ˈtrɑː-/ n [C] a very large city that is the most important city in a country or area: *The city has become a huge, bustling metropolis.*

met·ro·pol·i·tan /ˌmetrəˈpɒlɪtən◂ $ -ˈpɑː-/ adj [only before noun] **1** relating or belonging to a very large city: *a metropolitan area of South Australia* **2** technical relating to France, rather than its COLONIES: *metropolitan France*

Metropolitan Police n the Metropolitan Police the police force that is responsible for the London area

met·tle /ˈmetl/ n [U] **1** courage and determination to do something even when it is very difficult: **test/show/prove your mettle** *a crisis which will test the prime minister's mettle* **2 on your mettle** BrE if you are on your mettle, you are ready to try as hard as possible because your abilities are being tested: *We'll have to be on our mettle from the start.* | **keep/put sb on their mettle** *This was just his way of keeping me on my mettle.*

met·tle·some /ˈmetlsəm/ adj literary full of energy and determination

mew /mjuː/ v [I] if a cat mews, it makes a soft high crying sound: *The cat mewed at me.* —**mew** n [C]

mews /mjuːz/ n [plural] BrE a small street or area surrounded by buildings in a city, where horses used to be kept, but where people now live

Mex·i·can¹ /ˈmeksɪkən/ adj relating to Mexico or its people: *the Mexican government* | *the Mexican border* | *Mexican food*

Mexican² n [C] someone from Mexico

Mexican wave n [singular] BrE the effect that is made when all the people watching a sport stand up, move their arms up and down, and sit down again one after the other in a continuous movement that looks like a wave moving on the sea

mez·za·nine /ˈmezəniːn, ˈmetsə- $ ˈmezə-/ n [C] **1** a small floor that is built between two other floors in a building: *A young woman was sitting at a desk on the mezzanine floor.* **2** AmE the lowest BALCONY in a theatre, or the first few rows of seats in that balcony

mez·zo /ˈmetsəʊ $ -oʊ/ adv **mezzo forte/piano etc** technical not too loud, softly etc – used in instructions for performing music

mezzo-so·pra·no also **mezzo** n [C] a female singing voice that is lower than a SOPRANO but higher than an ALTO, or a woman with a voice like this

mez·zo·tint /ˈmetsəʊˌtɪnt, ˈmedzəʊ- $ -oʊ-/ n [C,U] a picture printed from a metal plate that is polished in places to produce areas of light and shade

MFA /ˌem ef ˈeɪ/ n [C] AmE **Master of Fine Arts** a university DEGREE in a subject such as painting or drawing

mg plural **mg** or **mgs** the written abbreviation of *milligram* or milligrams

MHz the written abbreviation of *megahertz*

mi /miː/ n [U] the third note in a musical SCALE according to the SOL-FA system

MI5 /ˌem aɪ ˈfaɪv/ n a secret British government organization whose job it is to keep Britain safe from attack by enemies inside the country, such as foreign SPIES or TERRORISTS: *a government agent working for MI5*

MI6 /ˌem aɪ ˈsɪks/ n a secret British government organization that sends people to foreign countries to try and find out secret political and military information: *He used to work for MI6.* | *the head of MI6*

MIA /ˌem aɪ ˈeɪ/ n [C] AmE **missing in action** a soldier who has disappeared in a battle and who may still be alive: *There are still more than 500 MIAs.*

mi·aow, meow /miˈaʊ/ v [I] if a cat miaows, it makes a crying sound —**miaow** n [C]: *The cat jumped away with a loud miaow.*

mi·as·ma /miˈæzmə, maɪ-/ n [singular] literary **1** dirty air or a thick unpleasant mist that smells bad: *He looked up at me through a miasma of cigarette smoke.* | *A foul miasma lay over the town.* **2** an evil influence or feeling that seems to surround a person or place: [+of] *The miasma of defeat hung over them.*

mi·ca /ˈmaɪkə/ n [U] a mineral that separates easily into small flat transparent pieces of rock, often used to make electrical instruments

mice /maɪs/ n the plural of MOUSE

Mich·ael·mas /ˈmɪkəlməs/ n [C,U] 29th September, a Christian holy day in honour of Saint Michael

mick /mɪk/ n [C] taboo an offensive word for someone from Ireland. Do not use this word.

mick·ey /ˈmɪki/ n **take the mickey (out of sb)** BrE informal to make someone look silly, often in a friendly way, for example by copying them or by pretending something is true when it is not: *He's always taking the mickey out of me.*

Mickey Mouse adj informal small and not at all important: *The charity has been described as a Mickey Mouse operation.* | *a Mickey Mouse job*

mi·cro /ˈmaɪkrəʊ $ -kroʊ/ n plural **micros** [C] a small computer

micro- /maɪkrəʊ, -krə $ -kroʊ, -krə/ prefix [in nouns, adjectives and adverbs] extremely small; → **macro-, mini-**: *microelectronics* | *a micro-organism*

mi·crobe /ˈmaɪkrəʊb $ -kroʊb/ n [C] an extremely small living thing which you can only see if you use a MICROSCOPE. Some microbes can cause diseases

mi·cro·bi·ol·o·gy /ˌmaɪkrəʊbaɪˈɒlədʒi $ -kroʊbaɪˈɑːl-/ n [U] the scientific study of very small living things such as BACTERIA —**microbiologist** n [C] —**microbiological** /ˌmaɪkrəʊbaɪəˈlɒdʒɪkəl $ -kroʊbaɪəˈlɑː-/ adj: *a microbiological examination of the fibres found near the body*

mi·cro·brew /ˈmaɪkrəʊˌbruː $ -kroʊ-/ n [C] a type of beer that is only produced in small quantities

mi·cro·brew·e·ry /ˈmaɪkrəʊˌbruːəri $ -kroʊ-/ n plural **microbreweries** [C] a small company that makes only a small amount of beer to sell, and often has a restaurant where the beer is served

mi·cro·chip /ˈmaɪkrəʊˌtʃɪp $ -kroʊ-/ also **chip** n [C] a very small piece of SILICON containing a set of electronic parts which is used in computers and other machines: *Japan's largest producer of microchips* | *the microchip industry*

mi·cro·cli·mate /ˈmaɪkrəʊˌklaɪmɪt $ -kroʊ-/ n [C] the weather patterns in one small area, which are different from the weather patterns in the surrounding area: *The valley has its own unique microclimate.*

mi·cro·com·put·er /ˈmaɪkrəʊkəmˌpjuːtə $ -kroʊkəmˌpjuːtər/ n [C] a small computer

mi·cro·cos·m /ˈmaɪkrəʊkɒzm $ -kroʊkɑː-/ n [C] a small group, society, or place that has the same qualities as a much larger one; → **macrocosm**: [+of] *New York's mix of people is a microcosm of America.* | *in microcosm All the problems of society can be seen here* *in microcosm.* —**microcosmic** /ˌmaɪkrəʊˈkɒzmɪk $ -krəʊˈkɑːz-/ *adj: the forces which we see at work on a microcosmic scale*

mi·cro·dot /ˈmaɪkrəʊdɒt $ -krəʊdɑːt/ *n* [C] a secret photograph of something such as a document which is reduced to a very small size so that it can easily be hidden

mi·cro·ec·o·nom·ics /ˌmaɪkrəʊekəˈnɒmɪks, -iːkə- $ -krəʊekəˈnɑː-, -iːkə-/ *n* [U] the study of small economic systems that are part of national or international systems; ➔ **macroeconomics** —**microeconomic** *adj*

mi·cro·e·lec·tron·ics /ˌmaɪkrəʊɪlekˈtrɒnɪks $ -krəʊɪlekˈtrɑː-/ *n* [U] the practice or study of designing very small electrical CIRCUITS that are used in computers: *the latest developments in microelectronics* —**microelectronic** *adj: a new system that has been developed using microelectronic technology*

mi·cro·en·gi·neer·ing /ˌmaɪkrəʊendʒɪˈnɪərɪŋ $ -krəʊendʒɪˈnɪr-/ *n* [U] the activity of designing structures and machines that are extremely small —**microengineer** *n* [C]

mi·cro·fiche /ˈmaɪkrəʊfiːʃ $ -krəʊ-/ *n* [C,U] a sheet of microfilm which can only be read using a special machine, especially in a library: **on microfiche** *Details of all members are now available on microfiche.*

mi·cro·film /ˈmaɪkrəʊfɪlm $ -krəʊ-/ *n* [C,U] a type of film on which pictures and writing can be made very small, so that large amounts can be stored easily: **on microfilm** *Most of the daily newspapers are available on microfilm.*

mi·cro·fi·nance /ˈmaɪkrəʊˌfaɪnæns $ -krəʊfˌɑːnæns/ *n* [U] a system that allows people in poor countries to borrow small amounts of money to help them start a small business

mi·cro·light /ˈmaɪkrəʊlaɪt $ -krəʊ-/ *n* [C] a very light small plane for one or two people ➔ see picture at AERIAL[1]

mi·cro·man·age /ˈmaɪkrəʊˌmænɪdʒ $ -krəʊ-/ *v* [T] to organize and control all the details of another person's work in a way that they think is annoying —**micromanagement** *n* [U]

mi·crom·e·ter /maɪˈkrɒmɪtə $ -ˈkrɑːmɪtər/ *n* [C] an instrument for measuring very small distances

mi·crom·e·tre *BrE;* **micrometer** *AmE* /ˈmaɪkrəʊˌmiːtə $ -krəʊˌmiːtər/ *also* **mi·cron** /ˈmaɪkrɒn $ -krɑːn/ *n* [C] a unit for measuring length. There are one million micrometres in one metre.

mi·cro·or·gan·is·m /ˌmaɪkrəʊˈɔːɡənɪzəm $ -krəʊˈɔːr-/ *n* [C] a living thing that is so small that it cannot be seen without a MICROSCOPE

mi·cro·phone /ˈmaɪkrəfəʊn $ -foʊn/ *n* [C] a piece of equipment that you speak into to record your voice or make it louder when you are speaking or performing in public: *She spoke confidently into the microphone.* | *They searched the room for hidden microphones.*

mi·cro·pro·ces·sor /ˈmaɪkrəʊˌprəʊsesə $ -krəʊˌprɑːsesər/ *n* [C] the central CHIP in a computer, which controls most of its operations

micro·scooter *n* [C] a vehicle like a child's SCOOTER, but smaller and lighter. It is used as a toy, and also by adults, especially as a way of travelling short distances.

mi·cro·scope /ˈmaɪkrəskəʊp $ -skoʊp/ *n* [C] **1** a scientific instrument that makes extremely small things look larger: **under/through a microscope** *Abnormalities in the cells can be seen quite clearly under a microscope.* | *Each sample was examined through a microscope.*; ➔ see picture at OPTICAL **2 put sth under the microscope** to examine a situation very closely and carefully: *Our prison system is being put under the microscope after an alarming number of deaths and suicides this year.*

mi·cro·scop·ic /ˌmaɪkrəˈskɒpɪk $ -ˈskɑː-/ *adj* **1** extremely small and therefore very difficult to see: *a microscopic speck of dust* | *Inspectors discovered microscopic cracks in the hull of the submarine.* **2** [only

before noun] using a microscope: *The cells were identified through microscopic analysis.* —**microscopically** /-kli/ *adv: The seeds are microscopically small.*

mi·cro·sec·ond /ˈmaɪkrəʊˌsekənd $ -krəʊ-/ *n* [C] one millionth of a second

mi·cro·sur·ge·ry /ˈmaɪkrəʊˌsɜːdʒəri $ -krəʊˌsɜːr-/ *n* [U] medical treatment in which a part of someone's body is repaired or removed using very small instruments or LASERS

mi·cro·wave[1] /ˈmaɪkrəweɪv/ *n* [C] **1** also **,micro-wave 'oven** a type of OVEN that cooks food very quickly using very short electric waves instead of heat: *I'll heat it up in the microwave.* ➔ see picture at EAT **2** a very short electric wave that is used in cooking food and sending messages by radio, and in RADAR

microwave[2] *v* [T] to cook something in a microwave oven: *You can heat it up under the grill or microwave it.* —**microwaveable, microwavable** *adj: a new range of microwavable snacks*

mid /mɪd/ *prep literary* among or in the middle of

mid- /mɪd/ *prefix* middle: *a young woman in her mid-twenties* | *The mid-sixties were a turning point in sports car design.* | *in mid-July* | *He stopped mid-sentence.* | **mid-morning/afternoon/week etc**

mid·air /ˌmɪdˈeə◂ $ -ˈer◂/ *n* **in midair** in the air or the sky, away from the ground: *The planes collided in midair.* —**midair** *adj* [only before noun]: *a midair collision*

Mi·das touch /ˈmaɪdəs ˌtʌtʃ/ *n* **the Midas touch** if someone has the Midas touch, everything they do is successful and makes money for them: *a talented young businessman with the Midas touch*

,mid At'lantic *adj* **1 mid Atlantic accent** a way of speaking that uses a mixture of American and British English sounds and words: *She spoke in a soft mid Atlantic accent.* **2 mid-Atlantic states/region** the US states that are on the Atlantic coast, approximately between New Jersey and Maryland

mid·day /ˌmɪdˈdeɪ◂ $ ˈmɪd-deɪ/ *n* [U] the middle of the day, at or around 12 o'clock; ➔ **midnight: at/around/by etc midday** *I'm meeting him at midday.* | *I got there around midday.* | *By midday it had begun to warm up.* | *We stopped off in Colchester for our **midday meal.*** | *the full heat of the **midday sun***

mid·den /ˈmɪdn/ *n* [C] *old use* a pile of animal waste or things such as food that have been thrown away

mid·dle[1] S1 W2 /ˈmɪdl/ *n*
1 CENTRE PART **the middle** the part that is nearest the centre of something, and furthest from the sides, edges, top, bottom etc: [+of] *We rowed out towards the **middle of the lake.*** | **in the middle (of sth)** *Jo was standing in the middle of the room.* | *Those are my two brothers, and that's me in the middle.* | *The meat was burnt on the outside and raw in the middle.* | *a huge hole **right in the middle** of the lawn* | **through the middle (of sth)** *The new road will go **right through the middle** of the wood.* | **down the middle (of sth)** *Draw a line down the middle of the page.*
2 TIME/EVENT **the middle** the part of an event or period of time that is between the beginning and the end: [+of] *events which took place around the middle of the last century* | **in the middle (of sth)** *I'm going to stay with some friends in the middle of May.* | *He gets killed in the middle of the film.* | **the middle of the night/day** *I got a phone call from her in the middle of the night!* | **the middle of the week/month/year etc** *Everything should be sorted out by the middle of next year.*
3 SCALE/RANGE **the middle** the level or position that is between two extreme positions, for example between the best and the worst: *There are plenty of small houses for sale, and quite a lot of very large ones, but very little in the middle.* | [+of] *In tests, I always seem to finish around the middle of the class.*

1 000, 2 000, 3 000, most frequent words in S poken and W ritten English

4 BODY [C usually singular] the part of your body around your waist and stomach: *sb's middle He was holding a towel around his middle.*

5 be in the middle of (doing) sth to be busy doing something: *Can I call you back – I'm in the middle of a meeting.* | *I was in the middle of sorting some papers when the phone rang.*

6 in the middle of sth if you are in the middle of something, it is happening to you or around you: *At that time Britain was in the middle of a recession.* | *The company is in the middle of a takeover battle.*

7 in the middle of nowhere a long way from the nearest big town: *They live miles away, in the middle of nowhere.*

8 divide/split sth down the middle to divide something into equal halves or groups: *We put all the money together and then split it down the middle.* | *The voters are split down the middle on this issue.* → piggy in the middle at PIGGY¹ (2)

middle² S1 W2 *adj* [only before noun]
1 CENTRE nearest the centre and furthest from the edge, top, end etc: *driving in the middle lane of the motorway* | *the middle drawer of the filing cabinet*
2 TIME/EVENT half of the way through an event or period of time: *They spent the middle part of their vacation in Florida.* | *the middle part of the day*
3 SCALE/RANGE between two extreme levels or positions, for example between the best and worst, the biggest and smallest etc: *a car in the middle price range* | *the middle ranks of the army* | *a middle-income family*
4 in your middle twenties/thirties etc about 25, 35 etc years old
5 middle brother/child/daughter etc the brother etc who is between the oldest and the youngest
6 middle course/way etc a way of dealing with something that is between two opposite and often extreme ways: [+**between**] *The party is seeking to find a middle way between extreme right-wing and left-wing policies.* | *I try to steer a middle course between keeping control of the project and giving responsibility to others.*
7 Middle English/French etc an old form of English, French etc, used in the Middle Ages (=between 1100 and 1500 AD)

,middle 'age *n* [U] the period of your life between the ages of about 40 and 60, when you are no longer young but are not yet old: *Men who smoke are more likely to have heart attacks in middle age.*

,middle-'aged *adj* **1** between the ages of about 40 and 60: *a middle-aged businessman* **2** someone who seems middle-aged seems rather dull and does not do exciting or dangerous things: *Living with Henry had made her feel middle-aged.* **3** middle-aged spread fat that many people develop around their waist as they grow older

,Middle 'Ages *n* the Middle Ages the period in European history between about 1100 and 1500 AD

,Middle A'merica *n* **1** the middle part of the United States, which is not on the east or west coasts **2** Americans who are neither very rich nor very poor and who have traditional ideas and beliefs

mid·dle·brow /'mɪdlbraʊ/ *adj* middlebrow books, television programmes etc are of fairly good quality but are not very difficult to understand; → highbrow, lowbrow

,middle 'C *n* [U] the musical note C, which is the middle note on a piano

,middle 'class *n* [C] the social class that includes people who are educated and work in professional jobs, for example teachers or managers; → lower class, upper class, working class: *This led to the creation of a new, affluent middle class.* | *Home ownership was once a privilege of the middle classes.*

,middle-'class *adj* **1** typical of people who are educated and work in professional jobs: *a middle-class*

family | *They lived a comfortable middle-class life.* **2** middle-class attitudes and ideas are typical of middle-class people and are often concerned with the idea that people should work hard, have a good education, and try to earn enough money to live a comfortable life

,middle 'distance *n* the middle distance the part of a picture or view that is between the nearest part and the part that is furthest away: *She just stood there gazing into the middle distance.*

'middle-,distance *adj* [only before noun] a middle-distance race is neither very short nor very long, for example 800 or 1500 metres

,middle 'ear *n* [singular] the part just inside your ear

,Middle 'East *n* the Middle East the area that includes Iran and Egypt and the countries which are between them; → Far East —**Middle Eastern** *adj*

,middle 'finger *n* [C] the longest finger on your hand

,middle 'ground *n* [U] ideas that are not extreme, and that people who oppose each other can agree about: *The negotiators could find no middle ground.*

mid·dle·man /'mɪdlmæn/ *n plural* middlemen /-men/ [C] someone who buys things in order to sell them to someone else, or who helps to arrange business deals for other people: *He acts as a middleman for British companies seeking contracts in the Gulf.* | *Buy direct from the manufacturer and cut out the middleman* (=avoid using a middleman).

,middle 'management *n* [U] managers who are in charge of small groups of people, but do not take important decisions that affect the whole organization —**middle manager** *n* [C]

,middle 'name *n* [C] **1** the name that is between your first name and your family name **2** sth is sb's middle name *informal* used to say that someone has a personal quality very strongly: *Don't worry – discretion is my middle name.*

,middle-of-the-'road *adj* **1** middle-of-the-road ideas or opinions are not extreme, and so most people are likely to agree with them: *a party offering safe, middle-of-the-road policies* **2** middle-of-the-road voters or politicians have ideas that are not extreme **3** *informal* ordinary and not new, different, or exciting: *Their first album was quite good, but the second was very middle-of-the-road stuff.*

,middle-'ranking *adj* having a responsible job or position, but not among the most important people in a company: *middle-ranking officers and bureaucrats*

'middle school *n* [C,U] **1** a school in Britain for children between the ages of 8 and 12 **2** a school in the US for children between the ages of 11 and 14

,middle-'sized *adj* neither very large nor very small: *a middle-sized company*

mid·dle·weight /'mɪdlweɪt/ *n* [C] a BOXER who weighs less than 72.58 kilograms, and who is heavier than a WELTERWEIGHT but lighter than a LIGHT HEAVYWEIGHT

,Middle 'West *n* the Middle West another form of the MIDWEST

mid·dling /'mɪdlɪŋ/ *adj informal* of average size, quality, ability etc: *a tennis player of middling talent*

mid·field /'mɪdfiːld/ *n* [U] **1** the middle part of the area where a game such as football is played: *He plays in midfield.* | *an excellent midfield player* **2** the members of a football team who play in the midfield: *The midfield did very well in the first half.*

mid·field·er /'mɪdfiːldə $ -ər/ *n* [C] a player in a game of football who usually plays in the midfield

midge /mɪdʒ/ *n* [C] a small flying insect that can bite people

midg·et¹ /'mɪdʒɪt/ *n* [C] **1** *taboo* a very offensive word for someone who is very short because their body has not grown normally. Do not use this word.; → dwarf **2** *BrE informal* someone who is not very tall

M

midget² adj [only before noun] very small: *a midget submarine*

mid·i /'mɪdi/ adj **midi skirt/dress/coat** a skirt, dress etc that comes to the middle of the lower leg; → **mini**

MIDI /'mɪdi/ n [U] technical **musical instrument digital interface** a system that allows computers to communicate with electronic musical instruments

Mid·lands /'mɪdləndz/ n **the Midlands** the central part of England —**Midland** adj —**Midlander** n [C]

mid·life cri·sis also **mid-life crisis** /ˌmɪdlaɪf ˈkraɪsəs/ n [C] a period of worry and lack of confidence that some people experience when they are about 40 or 50 years old and begin to feel that they are getting old

mid·night /'mɪdnaɪt/ n [U] 12 o'clock at night; → **midday**: **at midnight** *The train is due in at midnight.* | **after/before midnight** *We stayed there until way after midnight.* | *You can't phone her now – it's* **gone midnight** (=after midnight)! | *By the time he arrived, it was well* **past midnight** (=after midnight). | **at/on the stroke of midnight** (=at exactly midnight) *The treaty will come into force on the stroke of midnight tonight.* | *He's gone for a midnight swim.* ⚠ Do not say 'in the midnight'. If you mean 'at 12 o'clock at night' say **at midnight** and if you mean 'very late at night' say **in the middle of the night**. → **burn the midnight oil** at BURN¹ (20)

ˌmidnight ˈblue n [U] a very dark blue colour —**midnight blue** adj

ˌmidnight ˈsun n **the midnight sun** the sun that you can see in the middle of the night in summer in the far north or south of the world

mid·point /'mɪdpɔɪnt/ n [C usually singular] a point that is half of the way through or along something: [+of] *At the midpoint of the study, all those taking part were interviewed again.*

ˈmid-range adj [only before noun] mid-range products and services are not the most expensive or the cheapest; → **top-of-the-range**

mid·riff /'mɪdrɪf/ n [C] the part of the body between your chest and your waist

mid·sec·tion /'mɪdˌsekʃən/ n [C usually singular] the middle part of something or of someone's body: *There are 24 missiles in the submarine's midsection.*

mid·ship·man /'mɪdʃɪpmən/ n plural **midshipmen** /-mən/ [C] someone who is training to become an officer in the British navy

midst¹ /mɪdst/ n **1 in the midst of sth a)** if you are in the midst of an event or situation, it is happening around you: *The government is in the midst of a major crisis.* **b)** in the middle of a place or a group of things or people: *We were sitting in the midst of an elegant and well-dressed audience.* **2 in our/their midst** formal in a particular group: *I fear we have an enemy in our midst.*

midst² prep old use surrounded by people or things

mid·stream /ˌmɪdˈstriːm/ n [U] **1 in midstream** when something has started and is still happening: *They had to drop the experiment in midstream.* | *He interrupted the official in midstream* (=while the official was still speaking). **2** the middle part of a river: **in midstream** *The boat had anchored in midstream.* —**midstream** adv

mid·sum·mer /ˌmɪdˈsʌmə $ -ər/ n [U] the middle of summer: *a perfect midsummer afternoon*

ˌMidsummer ˈDay also **ˌMidsummer's ˈDay** n [C,U] BrE the 24th of June

mid·term¹ /ˌmɪdˈtɜːm $ -ˈtɜːrm/ n **1** [U] the middle period of an elected government's time in power **2** [C] AmE a test that students take in the middle of a SEMESTER or QUARTER

mid·term² /'mɪdtɜːm $ -tɜːrm/ adj [only before noun] **1** in the middle of an elected government's time in power: *midterm elections* **2** AmE in the middle of a SEMESTER or QUARTER; → **half-term**: *midterm tests*

mid·town /ˌmɪdˈtaʊn $ / adj, adv AmE in the area of a city that is quite near the centre but is not the main business area; → **downtown, uptown** —**midtown** n [U]

mid·way /ˌmɪdˈweɪ $ ˈmɪdweɪ/ adj, adv **1** between two places, and the same distance from each of them; ⊟ **halfway**: [+between] *The city is midway between Edinburgh and London.* **2** when half a period of time has passed; ⊟ **halfway**: [+through] *Leeds scored midway through the first half.*

mid·week /ˌmɪdˈwiːk $ ˈmɪdwiːk/ adj, adv on one of the middle days of the week: *There are often discounts available for midweek travel.* —**midweek** n [U]: *The match will be played in midweek.*

Mid·west /ˌmɪdˈwest/ n **the Midwest** the central area of the United States —**Midwestern** adj

mid·wife /'mɪdwaɪf/ n plural **midwives** /-waɪvz/ [C] a specially trained nurse whose job is to help women when they are having a baby

mid·wif·e·ry /'mɪdˌwɪfəri $ -ˌwaɪfəri/ n [U] the skill or work of a midwife

mid·win·ter /ˌmɪdˈwɪntə $ -ər/ n [U] the middle of winter: *The mountains look beautiful in midwinter.*

mid·year /'mɪdjɪə $ -jɪr/ n [U] the middle of the year: *Sales had improved by midyear.* —**midyear** adj [only before noun]: *a midyear review*

mien /miːn/ n [singular] literary a person's typical expression or appearance: *her sorrowful mien*

miffed /mɪft/ adj spoken slightly annoyed or upset: *I felt a bit miffed that no one had told me about the trip.*

might¹ S1 W1 /maɪt/ modal verb negative short form **mightn't**

1 POSSIBILITY **a)** if something might happen or might be true, there is a possibility that it may happen or may be true, but you are not at all certain: *I might be a few minutes late.* | *She might not want to come with us.* | *I suppose he might have missed the train.* | *This* **might well** *be her last public performance* (=it is fairly likely). | *One of the guards* **might easily** *panic and shoot someone* (=it is likely). **b)** used as the past tense of 'may' when reporting that someone talked or thought about the possibility of something: *George said he might be able to help you.* | *I thought they might have gone home.* | *She was worried that we might get hurt.* **c)** used to say that something was a possibility in the past but did not actually happen: *It was terrifying. We might have been killed.*

2 SUGGESTING used to suggest politely what someone should do: *If you need more information, you might try the Internet.* | *I thought we might go to the new Chinese restaurant on the High Street.* | *It might be a good idea to put those plants in the shade.* | *We're going to a concert. You might like to come with us.*

3 ASKING PERMISSION **a)** spoken especially BrE used to politely ask for permission to do something: *Might I borrow your pen?* | *I wonder if I might speak to your son.* **b)** used when reporting that someone asked for permission to do something: *He asked if he might come in and look around.*

4 SB SHOULD HAVE DONE STH used when you are annoyed because someone has not not done something that you think they should do: *You might at least say thank you.* | *They might have cleaned up before they left.*

5 PAST PURPOSE used after 'so that' or 'in order that' to say that someone did something in order to make something else happen or be possible: *I asked for names and addresses so that I might pass on details to the police.*

6 might I say/ask/add etc spoken especially BrE used to politely give more information, ask a question, interrupt etc: *Might I ask how old you are?* | *Might I just say how lovely it is to see everyone here today.*

7 I might say/add spoken used to emphasize what you are saying: *I was, I might say, not surprised.*

8 I might have known/guessed etc spoken used to say that you are not surprised at a situation: *I might have known it was you!* | *I might have guessed I'd get no sympathy from my family.*

9 might (just) as well **a)** used to suggest that someone

M

should do something, because there is no good reason to do anything else: *I suppose we might as well go home.* **b)** used to say that the effect of an action or situation is the same as if it was another one: *They might as well have a badge on them saying 'Steal me'.* | *He might as well have been a million miles away.*

10 ALTHOUGH used to say that even though something is perhaps true, something different or opposite is also true: *He might be nearly seventeen but he's still very immature.* | *Surprising as it might seem, some tourists actually enjoy the British weather.* | *Although she might understand his beliefs, she could not accept them.* | *Try as I might* (=although I tried hard), *I couldn't work out the answer.*

11 FORMAL QUESTION used to ask a question in a formal and rather unfriendly way: *And who might you be, young man?*

12 might well used to say that there is a good reason for a reaction, question, or feeling: *'What do they hope to achieve?' 'You might well ask.'* | *a system of which we in Britain might well be envious* | *This caused a few gasps, as well it might.*

might² *n* [U] **1** great strength and power: *two individuals who took on the might of the English legal system* | *He swung the axe again with all his might.* **2 might is right** *BrE*; **might makes right** *AmE* used to say that powerful people and countries are able to do whatever they want, especially when you disapprove of this

'might-have-,beens *n* [plural] things that you wish had happened in the past but which never did

might·i·ly /'maɪtᵊli/ *adv* **1** very: *a mightily impressive piece of work* | *I was mightily relieved when we landed at Manchester airport.* **2** *literary* using great strength: *We laboured mightily to rebuild the walls.*

might·n't /'maɪtənt/ *informal especially BrE* the short form of 'might not'

might·y¹ /'maɪti/ *adj comparative* **mightier**, *superlative* **mightiest** *literary* very strong and powerful, or very big and impressive: *the mighty Mississippi river* | *a mighty army* → **high and mighty** at HIGH¹ (26)

mighty² *adv AmE informal* very: *You seem mighty sure of your facts.* | *They got out of there mighty fast, I can tell you.*

mi·graine /'miːgreɪn, 'maɪ- $ 'maɪ-/ *n* [C,U] an extremely bad headache, during which you feel sick and have pain behind your eyes: *I won't be coming this evening – I've got a migraine* | **bad/severe migraine** *He suffers from severe migraine.*

mi·grant /'maɪgrənt/ *n* [C] **1** someone who goes to live in another area or country, especially in order to find work; → **emigrant, immigrant: migrant worker/labourer** *A lot of factory work is done by migrant workers.* | **economic migrant** (=someone who goes to live in another country because they are likely to find a better job there) **2** a bird or animal that travels regularly from one part of the world to another

mi·grate /maɪˈgreɪt $ ˈmaɪgreɪt/ *v* [I + from/to] **1** if birds or animals migrate, they travel regularly from one part of the world to another **2** if people migrate, they go to live in another area or country, especially in order to find work; → **emigrate**

mi·gra·tion S2 /maɪˈgreɪʃən/ *n* [C,U] **1** when large numbers of people go to live in another area or country, especially in order to find work **2** when birds or animals travel regularly from one part of the world to another

mi·gra·to·ry /'maɪgreɪtəri, 'maɪgrətəri $ 'maɪgrətɔːri/ *adj* involved in or relating to migration: *migratory birds*

mike¹ /maɪk/ *n* [C] *informal* a MICROPHONE → **OPEN MIKE**

mike² *v*

mike sb ⇔ **up** *phr v informal* to fix a MICROPHONE to someone so that their voice can be recorded or made louder

mi·la·dy /mɪˈleɪdi/ *n* another spelling of M'LADY

mild¹ /maɪld/ *adj comparative* **milder**, *superlative* **mildest**

1 WEATHER fairly warm; ☒ **cold**: *We had an exceptionally mild winter last year.* | *a mild climate*

2 ILLNESS a mild illness or health problem is not serious: *He suffered a mild heart attack.* | *Sometimes the symptoms can be quite mild.* | *a mild case of food poisoning* | *a mild form of diabetes*

3 FEELINGS a mild feeling is not very strong: *Both men looked at her in mild surprise.* | *a feeling of mild irritation*

4 FOOD/TASTE not very strong or hot-tasting: *a mild curry* | *a cheese with a pleasant mild flavour*

5 CRITICISM a mild criticism does not criticize strongly

6 PROBLEMS/SITUATIONS not serious enough to cause much suffering: *The recession in Germany has been comparatively mild.* | *a mild setback*

7 PEOPLE a mild person has a gentle character and does not easily get angry: *a mild, well-mannered man* | *His voice was soft and mild.*

8 DRUGS/CHEMICALS a mild drug or chemical does not have a very strong effect: *a mild painkiller* | *a mild herbicide*

9 SOAP ETC soft and gentle to your skin: *a mild shampoo*

10 LANGUAGE mild words or language are not very rude or offensive: *I heard him mutter a mild swear word.* —**mildness** *n* [U] → MILDLY

mild² *n* [U] *BrE* dark beer with a slightly sweet taste; → **bitter**

mil·dew /'mɪldjuː $ -duː/ *n* [U] a white or grey substance that grows on walls or other surfaces in wet, slightly warm conditions —**mildewed** *adj*

mild·ly /'maɪldli/ *adv* **1** slightly: *The drug is only mildly addictive.* | *I felt mildly depressed.* **2 to put it mildly** *spoken* used to say that you could use much stronger words to describe something: *Losing two members of staff was unfortunate, to put it mildly.* **3** in a gentle way without being angry: *'Of course I don't mind,' she answered mildly.*

,mild-'mannered *adj* gentle and polite

mile S1 W1 /maɪl/ *n* [C]

1 written abbreviation **m** a unit for measuring distance, equal to 1760 YARDS or about 1609 metres: *It's forty miles from here to the Polish border.* | *an area 50 miles wide and 150 miles long* | *We walked about half a mile.* | *He was driving at 70 miles per hour.*

2 the mile a race that is a mile in length: *the first man to run the mile in under four minutes*

3 miles *informal* a very long distance: [+from] *We were miles from home, and very tired.* | [+away] *You can't go to Portsmouth, it's miles away.* | **for miles** *You can see for miles from here.* | *They lived in a little cottage* **miles from anywhere** (=a long way from the nearest town).

4 go the extra mile to try a little harder in order to achieve something, after you have already used a lot of effort: *The president expressed his determination to go the extra mile for peace.*

5 stick out/stand out a mile *informal* to be very easy to see or notice: *It sticks out a mile that you're new here.*

6 can see/spot/tell sth a mile off *informal* if you can see something a mile off, it is very easy to notice: *You can tell a mile off that he likes you.*

7 be miles away *spoken* to not be paying attention to anything that is happening around you: *'Kate!' 'Sorry, I was miles away!'*

8 miles older/better/too difficult etc *BrE informal* very much older, better, too difficult etc; ☒ **loads**: *The second film's miles better.*

9 by a mile *informal* by a very large amount: *He was the best player on the pitch by a mile.*

10 miles out *BrE informal* a measurement, guess, or calculation that is miles out is completely wrong

11 join the mile high club *informal* to have sex in a plane → NAUTICAL MILE; → **run a mile** at RUN¹ (38)

mile·age /ˈmaɪlɪdʒ/ n **1** [C usually singular, U] the number of miles a vehicle has travelled since it was made: *Always check the mileage before you buy a second-hand car.* **2** [C usually singular, U] the number of miles someone travels in a vehicle in a particular period of time: *Look for a car hire agreement that offers unlimited mileage.* **3** [C usually singular, U] the number of miles a vehicle can travel using a particular amount of FUEL: *The car's average mileage is 22.73 miles per gallon.* **4** [U] the amount of use or advantage you get from something: *The newspapers wanted to get as much mileage from the story as they could.* **5** [C usually singular, U] also **mileage allowance** an amount of money that is paid to someone for each mile that they travel when they use their own car for work: *Community nurses are paid a mileage allowance.* **6** [U] the number of miles that is covered by a country's roads or railways: *plans to treble the country's railway mileage*

mile·om·e·ter, **milometer** /maɪˈlɒmɪtə $ -ˈlɑːmɪtər/ n [C] BrE an instrument in a car that shows how many miles it has travelled; ▤ **odometer** AmE; → see picture at CAR

mile·post /ˈmaɪlpəʊst $ -poʊst/ n [C] AmE **1** a post next to a road or railway that shows the distance in miles to the next town **2** a MILESTONE (1)

mil·er /ˈmaɪlə $ -ər/ n [C] a person or horse that competes in races one mile long

mile·stone /ˈmaɪlstəʊn $ -stoʊn/ n [C] **1** a very important event in the development of something; ▤ **milepost** AmE: [+in] *an important milestone in South African history* | *The treatment of diabetes reached a significant milestone in the 1970s.* **2** a stone next to a road that shows the distance in miles to the next town

mi·lieu /ˈmiːljɜː $ miːˈljɜː, -ˈljuː/ n plural **milieux** /-ljɜːz, -ljɜː $ -ˈljɜːz, -ˈljuːz, -ˈjɜː, -ˈljuː/ or **milieus** [C] formal the things and people that surround you and influence the way you live and think: *Proust's work reflected his own social and cultural milieu.* | *She never felt happy in a student milieu.*

mil·i·tant /ˈmɪlɪtənt/ adj a militant organization or person is willing to use strong or violent action in order to achieve political or social change: *militant political activists* | *a militant animal rights group* | *After the assassination of Martin Luther King, black leaders became more militant.* —**militant** n [C]: *right-wing militants* —**militancy** n [U]: *an increase in trade union militancy* —**militantly** adv: *a militantly anti-communist group*

mil·i·ta·ris·m /ˈmɪlɪtərɪzəm/ n [U] the belief that a country should build up its military forces and use them to protect itself and get what it wants: *a country emerging from 20 years of militarism and political repression* —**militarist** n [C] —**militaristic** /ˌmɪlɪtəˈrɪstɪk◂/ adj: *a militaristic regime*

mil·i·ta·rized also **-ised** BrE /ˈmɪlɪtəraɪzd/ adj **1** a militarized area is one that has a lot of soldiers and weapons in it: *Kaliningrad is a highly militarized zone.* **2** organized like an army: *the militarized police force*

mil·i·ta·ry¹ [S2] [W1] /ˈmɪlɪtəri $ -teri/ adj **1** used by, involving, or relating to the army, navy, or airforce: *a military helicopter* | *military equipment* | *The government has threatened to take military action if the rebels do not withdraw from the area.* | *The United States is prepared to use military force to achieve its aims.* | *a raid by European military forces* (=the army, navy, or air force) **2** **with military precision** if you do something with military precision, you do it in a very organized and exact way: *The trips are planned with military precision.* —**militarily** adv: *Europe may have to intervene militarily if the crisis worsens.*

military² n **the military** [also + plural verb BrE] the military forces of a country; ▤ **the forces**: *He was never tempted to join the military.* | **in the military** *My brother is in the military.* | *The military were sent in to break up the demonstration.*

Military A'cademy n [C] **1** a national college where people are trained to be officers in the military forces **2** a private school in the US that gives students military training

Military 'Cross n [C] a MEDAL given to British army officers for being brave in battle

military po'lice n **the military police** a special police force whose job is to deal with members of the army etc who break the rules

military 'service n [U] the system in which every adult, or every male adult, in a country has to spend a period of time in the army, navy, or air force; → **draft**: *More and more men are refusing to do military service.*

mil·i·tate /ˈmɪlɪteɪt/ v

militate against sth phr v formal to prevent something or make it less likely to happen: *Environmental factors militate against building the power station in this area.*

mi·li·tia /məˈlɪʃə/ n [C] a group of people trained as soldiers, who are not part of the permanent army: *He joined the local militia as soon as he was 16.* | *a militia leader* | *a left-wing militia group*

mi·li·tia·man /məˈlɪʃəmən/ n plural **militiamen** /-mən/ [C] a member of a militia

milk¹ [S2] [W3] /mɪlk/ n
1 [U] a white liquid produced by cows or goats that is drunk by people: *a bottle of milk* | *Would you like some milk in your tea?* | *a pint of semi-skimmed milk*
2 [U] a white liquid produced by female animals and women for feeding their babies: *mothers who believe that breast milk is best for their babies* | *The tiny fox cubs drink nothing but their mother's milk.*
3 [U] a liquid or juice produced by particular plants, especially the COCONUT
4 [C,U] a thin white liquid used to clean or protect skin; ▤ **lotion**: *a mild facial cleansing milk*
5 **the milk of human kindness** literary the kind and sympathetic behaviour of most ordinary people → EVAPORATED MILK; → **cry over spilt milk** at CRY¹ (3); → **land of milk and honey** at LAND¹ (8)

milk² v [T] **1** informal to get as much money or as many advantages as you can from a situation, in a very determined and sometimes dishonest way: **milk sb/sth for sth** *Their landlord regularly milks them for extra money by claiming for damage to his property.* | *He seems to be milking the incident for all it's worth* (=getting as much from it as possible). **2** to take milk from a cow or goat: *I helped to milk the cows.* —**milking** n [U]: *They had risen at 5.30 to do the milking.*

milk 'chocolate n [U] chocolate that has milk added to it; → **plain chocolate**

'milk churn n [C] BrE a tall round metal container with a lid, used to carry milk from farms

'milk float n [C] BrE an electric vehicle that is used for delivering milk to people's houses

'milking ma,chine n [C] a machine used for taking milk from cows

'milking ,parlour BrE; **milking parlor** AmE n [C] a building on a farm where milk is taken from cows

milk·maid /ˈmɪlkmeɪd/ n [C] a woman in the past whose job was to get milk from cows on a farm

milk·man /ˈmɪlkmən/ n plural **milkmen** /-mən/ [C] someone in Britain whose job is to deliver milk to people's houses each morning

milk of mag'nesia n [U] a thick white liquid medicine used for stomach problems

'milk ,product n [C usually plural] a food such as cheese or cream that is made from milk: *I've tried to cut down on milk products.*

milk 'pudding n [C] BrE a sweet food made of rice or other grains baked with milk and sugar

[1] 000, [2] 000, [3] 000, most frequent words in [S]poken and [W]ritten English

M

milk round *n BrE* **1** [C] the regular journey a milkman makes every day to deliver milk **2 the milk round** a series of visits to universities in Britain that large companies make each year in order to find students they may want to employ

milk run *n* [C] *informal* **1** *BrE* a familiar, easy journey that you do regularly **2** *AmE* a train journey or regular plane flight with stops in many places

milk shake *n* [C] **1** *BrE* a sweet drink made of milk with fruit or chocolate added **2** *AmE* a sweet drink made of milk, ICE CREAM, and fruit or chocolate

milk sop /'mɪlksɒp $ -saːp/ *n* [C] *old-fashioned* a boy or man who is too gentle and weak, and who is afraid to do anything difficult or dangerous

milk tooth *n plural* **milk teeth** [C] *BrE* one of the first set of teeth that babies and young children have; ▣ **baby tooth**

milk weed /'mɪlkwiːd/ *n* [U] a common North American plant that produces a bitter white substance when its stem is broken

milk y /'mɪlki/ *adj* **1** containing a lot of milk: *a cup of milky coffee* **2** looking, smelling, or tasting like milk: *a sweet, milky flavour* **3** milky skin is white and smooth: *her beautiful milky complexion* **4** *literary* white or pale: *His eyes were a pale milky blue.*

Milky Way *n* **the Milky Way** the pale white band of stars that can be seen across the sky at night

mill

pepper mill   coffee mill

mill¹ W3 /mɪl/ *n* [C]
1 GRAIN a building containing a large machine for crushing grain into flour
2 COTTON/CLOTH/STEEL a factory that produces materials such as cotton, cloth, or steel: **cotton/steel/paper etc mill** *an old Victorian cotton mill*
3 coffee/pepper mill a small machine for crushing coffee or pepper
4 go through the mill to go through a time when you experience a lot of difficulties and problems: *He's really been through the mill recently.*
5 put sb through the mill to make someone answer a lot of difficult questions or do a lot of difficult things in order to test them: *It was a three day course and they really put us through the mill.*
6 MONEY *AmE* a unit of money equal to 1/10 of a cent, used in setting taxes and for other financial purposes
7 MILLION *spoken* a million: *Are you saying they paid a quarter of a mill for that house?* → RUN-OF-THE-MILL; → **(all) grist to the mill** at GRIST

mill² *v* [T] **1** to crush grain, pepper etc in a mill: *All our flours are milled using traditional methods.* | *Add some freshly milled black pepper.* **2** to press, roll, or shape metal in a machine
mill around/about (sth) *phr v informal* if a lot of people mill around, they move around a place in different directions without any particular purpose: *Crowds of students were milling around in the street.* | *There were a lot of people milling around the entrance.*

mil·len·ni·um /mɪ'leniəm/ *n plural* **millennia** /-niə/ [C] **1** a period of 1000 years: *people who have inhabited this land for millennia* **2** [usually singular] the time when a new 1000-year period begins: *the beginning of a new millennium* | *events which took place at the turn of the last millennium* —**millennial** *adj*

mill·er /'mɪlə $ -ər/ *n* [C] someone who owns or works in a mill which makes flour

mil·let /'mɪlət/ *n* [U] the small seeds of a plant similar to grass, used as food

milli- /mɪlɪ̩, mɪlɪ/ *prefix* [in nouns] a 1000th part of a unit: *a millilitre* (=0.001 litres)

mil·li·bar /'mɪlɪ̩baː $ -baːr/ *n* [C] a unit for measuring the pressure of the ATMOSPHERE (=the mixture of gases surrounding the Earth)

mil·li·gram also **milligramme** *BrE* /'mɪlɪ̩græm/ *n* [C] written abbreviation **mg** a unit for measuring weight. There are 1000 milligrams in one gram.

mil·li·li·tre *BrE*; **milliliter** *AmE* /'mɪlɪ̩liːtə $ -ər/ *n* [C] written abbreviation **ml** a unit for measuring an amount of liquid. There are 1000 millilitres in one litre.

mil·li·me·tre S3 *BrE*; **millimeter** *AmE* /'mɪlɪ̩miːtə $ -ər/ *n* [C] written abbreviation **mm** a unit for measuring length. There are 1000 millimetres in one metre.

mil·li·ner /'mɪlɪ̩nə $ -ər/ *n* [C] someone who makes and sells women's hats

mil·li·ne·ry /'mɪlɪ̩nəri $ -neri/ *n* [U] *formal* **1** the making and selling of women's hats **2** hats

mil·lion /'mɪljən/ *number, n plural* **million** *or* **millions** **1** the number 1,000,000: *Each of the books sold more than a million copies.* | **two/three/four etc million** *seven million dollars* | *£37 million of new investment* | **millions of pounds/dollars etc** *Millions of pounds were lost in Western aid.* **2** an extremely large number of people or things: **a million** *I've got a million ideas.* | **millions of sth** *She seems to have millions of friends.* **3 not/never in a million years** *spoken* used to emphasize that something is impossible or very unlikely to happen: *She'll never believe me. Not in a million years.* **4 look/feel like a million dollars/bucks** *informal especially AmE* to look very attractive or feel very happy and healthy **5 in a million** *informal* **a)** the best of all possible people or things: *She's a wife in a million.* | *He's so generous. He's* **one in a million.** **b)** used to show how unlikely something is: *It was a* **chance in a million** *that we'd find a fossil.* —**millionth** *adj: The park has just received its millionth visitor.* —**millionth** *n* [C]

mil·lion·aire /ˌmɪljə'neə $ -'ner/ *n* [C] someone who is very rich and has at least a million pounds or dollars: *an American millionaire* | *a millionaire businessman*

mil·lion·air·ess /ˌmɪljə'neərɪ̩s $ -'ner-/ *n* [C] *old-fashioned* a woman who is very rich and has at least a million pounds or dollars

mil·li·pede /'mɪlɪ̩piːd/ *n* [C] a long thin creature with a very large number of legs; → **centipede**

mil·li·sec·ond /'mɪlɪˌsekənd/ *n* [C] a unit for measuring time. There are 1000 milliseconds in one second.

mill·pond /'mɪlpɒnd $ -paːnd/ *n* [C] a very small lake that supplies water to turn the wheel of a WATERMILL

mill·stone /'mɪlstəʊn $ -stoʊn/ *n* [C] **1** one of the two large circular stones that crush grain into flour in a MILL **2 a millstone round/around sb's neck** something that causes a lot of problems for someone, and that they cannot get rid of: *Inflation is still a millstone round the neck of British businesses.*

mill·wheel /'mɪlwiːl/ *n* [C] *especially BrE* a large wheel that is turned by water flowing past it to provide power to the machinery in a WATERMILL

mil·om·e·ter /maɪ'lɒmɪtə $ -'laːmɪtər/ *n* another spelling of MILEOMETER

mime¹ /maɪm/ n [C,U] the use of movements to express what you want to say without using words, or a play where the actors use only movements: *The children learn through role-play, dance and mime.* | *They will **perform** a short **mime** later.* | *a professional **mime** artist*

mime² v [I,T] **1** to describe or express something, using movements not words: *Stan put a finger to his mouth, miming 'shush'.* | **mime doing sth** *Soundlessly, she mimed picking up a phone and speaking into it.* **2** to pretend to play or sing a piece of music, without making any sound: [+to] *Singers on television often mime to pre-recorded tapes.*

mi·met·ic /mɪ'metɪk/ adj technical copying the movements or appearance of someone or something else

mim·ic¹ /'mɪmɪk/ v mimicked, mimicking [T] **1** to copy the way someone speaks or behaves, especially in order to make people laugh; ◨ imitate, take off: *He could mimic all the teachers' accents.* | *'I'm so sorry,' she mimicked.* **2** to behave or operate in exactly the same way as something or someone else: *Europe should not try to mimic Japan: we have to find our own path to successful modernisation.* | *The drug mimics the action of the body's own chemicals.* **3** if an animal mimics something, it looks or sounds very like it: *a fly whose size and shape exactly mimics that of the wasp* —**mimicry** n [U]: *He has a gift for mimicry.*

mimic² n [C] a person or animal that is good at copying the movements, sound, or appearance of someone or something else; → impressionist, impersonator

mi·mo·sa /mɪ'məʊzə $ -'moʊsə/ n [C,U] **1** a tree with small yellow flowers that grows in hot countries **2** AmE a mixture of CHAMPAGNE and orange juice, or a glass of this; ◨ Buck's Fizz BrE

min. **1** the written abbreviation of *minimum* **2** the written abbreviation of *minute* or minutes

min·a·ret /ˌmɪnə'ret, 'mɪnəret/ n [C] a tall thin tower on a MOSQUE, from which Muslims are called to prayer

min·a·to·ry /'mɪnətəri $ -tɔːri/ adj formal threatening to hurt someone or something

mince¹ /mɪns/ v **1** [T] also **mince sth** ⇔ **up** to cut food, especially meat, into very small pieces, usually using a machine: *minced lamb* | *Mince the meat up with some onion and garlic.* **2** [I always + adv/prep] to walk with very quick, short steps in a way that looks unnatural or silly: *She was mincing about in her high-heeled shoes.* **3 not mince (your) words** to say exactly what you think, even if this might offend people: *Tom didn't mince words and told me straight away that I had failed.*

mince² n [U] BrE meat, especially BEEF, that has been cut into very small pieces using a special machine; ◨ ground beef AmE

mince·meat /'mɪns-miːt/ n [U] **1** a mixture of dried fruits that you use to make sweet dishes **2 make mincemeat of sb/sth** informal to completely defeat someone in an argument, fight, or game: *I knew that a good lawyer would make mincemeat of him if I allowed him to give evidence.*

ˌmince 'pie n [C] a PIE filled with mincemeat, especially one that people eat at Christmas

minc·er /'mɪnsə $ -ər/ n [C] BrE a machine that cuts meat into very small pieces by forcing it through small holes; ◨ meat grinder AmE

mind¹ S1 W1 /maɪnd/ n

1 ABILITY TO THINK AND IMAGINE [C,U] your thoughts or your ability to think, feel, and imagine things: *It is impossible to understand the complex nature of the **human mind**.* | *Mind and body are closely related.* | *Meditation involves focusing the mind on a single object or word.* | **in sb's mind** *There was no doubt in my mind that it was the right decision to make.* | *Do you have a clear picture in your mind of what you want?* | *A plan began to form in his mind.* | *The event is still fresh in most people's minds.* | **independence/**

strength/flexibility of mind *men who were chosen for their independence of mind*

2 change your mind to change your decision, plan, or opinion about something: *I was afraid that Liz would change her mind and take me back home.* | [+about] *If you change your mind about the colour scheme, it's easy to just paint over it.*

3 make up your mind/make your mind up a) to decide which of two or more choices you want, especially after thinking for a long time: *I wish he'd hurry up and make his mind up.* | [+about] *He couldn't make up his mind about what to do with the money.* | **make up your mind whether** *Karen couldn't make up her mind whether to apply for membership or not.* **b)** to become very determined to do something, so that you will not change your decision: *No more argument My **mind is made up**.* | **make up your mind to do sth** *He had clearly made up his mind to end the affair.* | **make up your mind that** *I made up my mind there and then that I would never get married.* **c)** to decide what your opinion is about someone or something: [+about] *I could never really make my mind up about him.* | *You're old enough to **make your own mind up** about smoking.*

4 have sb/sth in mind (for sth) to have an idea about who or what you want for a particular purpose: *It was a nice house, but it wasn't quite **what we had in mind**.* | *Did you have anyone in mind for the job?* | *Have you any particular colour in mind for the bedroom?*

5 bear/keep sb/sth in mind to remember or think about someone or something when you are doing something: *It's a good idea – I'll keep it in mind.* | *You must always keep the reader in mind when writing a report.* | *Floor tiles can be difficult to clean – **worth keeping in mind** when you choose a new floor.* | **bear/keep in mind that** *Bear in mind that the price does not include flights.* | *More money should be given to housing, **bearing in mind** (=because of) the problem of homelessness.*

6 with sb/sth in mind considering someone or something when doing something, and taking suitable action: *Most gardens designed with children in mind are safe but dull.* | *With these aims in mind, the school operates a broad-based curriculum.*

7 on your/sb's mind a) if something is on your mind, you keep thinking or worrying about it: *She looked as though he **had something on his mind**.* | *Sorry I forgot. I've **got a lot on my mind** (=a lot of problems to worry about) at the moment.* **b)** if something is on your mind, that is what you are thinking about: *She's the type of person who just says what's on her mind.*

8 get/put sb/sth out of your mind also **put sb/sth to the back of your mind** to stop yourself thinking about someone or something: *I just can't seem to get her out of my mind.* | *You've got to try and put him out of your mind.* | *She put her disappointment to the back of her mind and concentrated on Dana.*

9 cross/enter sb's mind also **come into sb's mind** [not in progressive] if something crosses your mind, you have a thought or idea: *It never **crossed** my **mind that** Lisa might be lying.* | *Suddenly a horrible thought came into my mind.*

10 go/run/flash etc through sb's mind if something goes through your mind, you have a thought, especially for a short time: *She knew what was going through his mind.* | *All kinds of questions ran through my mind.* | *After the accident, one of the things that went through my mind was whether I would be able to drive again.*

11 come/spring to mind [not in progressive] if something comes or springs to mind, you suddenly or immediately think of it: *I just used the first excuse which sprang to mind.* | *A memory of last night came to mind, and he smiled.* | *Fatherhood doesn't immediately spring to mind when you think of James.* ⚠ Do not say that something 'comes to your mind' or 'springs to your mind'. Say that it **comes to mind** or **springs to mind**.

12 CHARACTER [C] used to talk about the way that someone thinks and the type of thoughts they have: *He*

M

has a very devious mind. | *My naturally suspicious mind thought he might be lying.*

13 INTELLIGENCE [C usually singular] your intelligence and ability to think, rather than your emotions: *a mind trained to react with split-second accuracy* | **a brilliant/enquiring/logical etc mind** *a bright child with an enquiring mind*

14 INTELLIGENT PERSON [C] someone who is very intelligent, especially in a particular subject or activity; ▤ **brain**: *This is one of the issues that has most interested military minds.* | *Some of the finest minds in the country are working on the project.*

15 state/frame of mind the way someone is thinking and feeling at a particular time: *What happened had a lot to do with my state of mind at the time.* | **in a good/positive/relaxed etc frame of mind** *She returned from lunch in a happier frame of mind.* | **in the right/wrong frame of mind** *You have to be in the right frame of mind to play well.*

16 to/in my mind used to show you are giving your opinion about something: *The Internet, to my mind, represents information exchange at its best.*

17 go/turn over sth in your mind to keep thinking about something because you are trying to understand it or solve a problem: *Corbett rode along, turning over in his mind what Bruce had said.*

18 be the last thing on sb's mind also **be the furthest thing from sb's mind** to be the thing that someone is least likely to be thinking about: *Insurance was the last thing on my mind when we set off that day.*

19 take/keep/get sb's mind off sth to make someone stop thinking and worrying about something: *Going back to work helped take my mind off my Ian's death.* | *Want a game? It might* **take** *your* **mind off things.**

20 set/put sb's mind at rest also **set/put sb's mind at ease** to make someone feel less worried or anxious: *If you're worried, see a doctor to set your mind at rest.*

21 it/that is a load/weight off sb's mind *informal* used to say that someone does not have to worry about something any more

22 prey on sb's mind also **play on sb's mind** if a problem preys on your mind, you cannot stop thinking about it: *Finally, she broached the subject that had been playing on her mind for days.*

23 no one in their right mind ... also **who in their right mind ...?** *informal* used to say that someone must be stupid or crazy to do something: *Who in their right mind would want to do that job?* | *No woman in her right mind would go out with a man like him.*

24 be out of your mind *informal* to be stupid or crazy: *He must have been out of his mind to employ her.*

25 be out of your mind with worry/grief etc also **be worried/bored etc out of your mind** to be extremely worried, bored etc: *It was getting late and I was out of my mind with worry.*

26 go out of your mind also **lose your mind** *informal* to become mentally ill or very worried, bored etc: *Nicole looked at him as if he'd gone out of his mind.*

27 sb's mind goes blank also **sb's mind is a blank** *informal* if your mind goes blank, you suddenly cannot remember something: *For some inexplicable reason, her mind went completely blank.* | *His heart was thumping and his mind was a complete blank.*

28 go (right/clean) out of sb's mind also **slip sb's mind** if something goes out of your mind, you forget it, especially because you are very busy: *I'm sorry. So much has been happening, it went clean out of my mind.* | *It had completely* **slipped** *her* **mind that** *Dave still had a key to the house.*

29 bring/call sth to mind a) to make you think of someone or something: *The wine's sweet nutty taste calls to mind roasted chestnuts.* **b)** *formal* to remember something: *The only thing I could call to mind was something my mother once said.*

30 put sb in mind of sb/sth [not in progressive] *formal* to remind someone of someone or something: *The girl put me in mind of my own daughter.*

31 stick/stay in sb's mind if a name, fact etc sticks in your mind, you remember it for a long time: *For some reason, the name really stuck in Joe's mind.* | *One line from the poem had stayed in her mind.*

32 be of one mind/of the same mind/of like mind *formal* to have the same opinions as someone else: *It can be difficult to meet others of like mind.* | **[+on/about]** *The council and the government are of one mind on the long-term objective.*

33 have a mind of your own a) to have strong opinions about things, and make your own decisions without being influenced by other people: *She's a woman without fear, with a mind of her own, who says what she thinks.* **b)** if an object has a mind of its own, it seems to control itself and does not work or move in the way you want it to: *The bicycle seemed to have a mind of its own and I couldn't steer it straight.*

34 put/set/turn your mind to sth to decide that you want to achieve something and try very hard to do it: *I think anyone can lose weight if they set their mind to it.*

35 sb's mind is not on sth if your mind is not on what you are doing, you are not thinking much about it because you are thinking or worrying about something else: *His mind didn't seem to be on the game at all.*

36 keep your mind on sth to keep paying attention to something, even though it is difficult: *He could hardly keep his mind on what she was saying.* | **keep your mind on the job/task in hand** *Making notes is the best way of keeping your mind on the task at hand.*

37 sb's mind wanders if your mind wanders, you no longer pay attention to something, especially because you are bored: *Her mind was beginning to wander.*

38 sb's mind is racing if your mind is racing, you are thinking very quickly and hard about something because you are excited, frightened etc: *He tried to reassure her, but Carrie's mind was racing.*

39 it's all in the mind used to tell someone that they have imagined something and it does not really exist: *He's one of those doctors who say you're not really sick and it's all in the mind.*

40 in your mind's eye if you see something in your mind's eye, you imagine or remember clearly what it looks like: *She paused, imagining the scene in her mind's eye.*

41 have it in mind *formal* to intend to do something: **have it in mind to do sth** *For a long time I had it in mind to write a book about my experiences.* | **have it in mind that** *I had it in mind that one day I might move to Spain.*

42 have half a mind to do sth *spoken* **a)** also **have a good mind to do sth** used to say that you might do something to show that you disapprove of something someone has done: *I've a good mind to tell him exactly what I think.* | *I've half a mind to stop him seeing her altogether.* **b)** used to say that you may decide to do something: *I've half a mind to come with you tomorrow.*

43 mind over matter used to say that you can use your thoughts to control physical feelings or an unpleasant situation: *I'm scared, yes, but it's a case of mind over matter.* → **in/at the back of your mind** at BACK² (6); → **blow sb's mind** at BLOW¹ (15); → **cast your mind back** at CAST¹ (9); → **a closed mind** at CLOSED (4); → **be in/at/to the forefront of sb's mind/attention** at FOREFRONT (2); → **give sb a piece of your mind** at PIECE¹ (13); → **great minds think alike** at GREAT¹ (15); → **know your own mind** at KNOW¹ (50); → **the mind boggles** at BOGGLE; → **meeting of minds** at MEETING (5) → **ONE-TRACK MIND**; → **an open mind** at OPEN¹ (16); → **out of sight, out of mind** at SIGHT¹ (8); → **presence of mind** at PEACE (3); → **PRESENCE OF MIND**; → **read sb's mind** at READ¹ (15); → **set your heart/mind/sights on (doing) sth** at SET¹ (13); → **be of sound mind** at SOUND³ (5); → **speak your mind** at SPEAK (7); → **be in two minds** at TWO (9)

mind² S1 W2 *v*

1 FEEL ANNOYED [I,T not in progressive or passive, usually in questions and negatives] to feel annoyed or upset about something: *I don't mind the heat, in fact I quite like it.* | *The expression on Dan's face showed that he did mind, very much.* | *I wouldn't have minded if she'd asked me first.* | **mind doing sth** *Did you mind* *being away from home for so long?* | **mind sb doing sth** *Don't your parents mind you staying out so late?* | **mind that** *He didn't mind that other people in the village thought him odd.*

2 not mind doing sth to be willing to do something: *I don't mind driving if you're tired.*

3 NOT CARE WHICH ONE not mind [I,T not in progressive or passive] *especially BrE* if you do not mind what someone does or what happens, you do not have a strong opinion about it: *'Do you want to go out now or later?' 'I don't really mind.'* | **not mind what/who/where** etc *I don't mind where we go.*

4 mind your own business *informal* to not ask questions about a situation that does not involve you: *Why don't you just mind your own business and leave me in peace?* | *I wish he'd mind his own business.*

5 be minding your own business to be doing something ordinary on your own when something unexpected happens to you: *My father was just driving along, minding his own business, when suddenly a brick came through the window.*

SPOKEN PHRASES

6 never mind **a)** used to tell someone not to worry or be upset about something: *'We haven't done very well, have we?' 'Never mind. At least we tried.'* | [+about] *Never mind about the car. You're safe, and that's the main thing.* **b)** used to say that something is not possible or likely, because even a less extreme thing is not possible or likely: *Well, you would have hardly got a bed in that room, never mind anything else.* | *I don't think I could walk that far, never mind run that far.* **c)** used to tell someone that it is not important to do or consider something now, often because something else is more important: *Never mind me – what about you? What have you been doing?* | *Never mind the dishes – I'll do them later.* | **never mind doing sth** *Never mind looking at the boys, we're supposed to be playing tennis.* | **never mind why/how etc** *Never mind how I got here. Tell me what happened.*

7 I wouldn't mind (doing) sth used to say that you would like something: *'Can I get you anything to drink?' 'I wouldn't mind a coffee.'* | *She's gorgeous! I wouldn't mind looking like that!*

8 would/do you mind...? **a)** used to politely ask someone's permission: **would you mind if** *Would you mind if I opened the window?* | *Would you mind if I came with you?* | *I'll have to leave early, do you mind?* **b)** used to politely ask someone to do something: **would you mind doing sth?** *Would you mind waiting outside?* | *'Do you want me to carry this bag for you?' 'Would you mind?'* **c)** used to angrily ask or tell someone to do something: **would you mind doing sth?** *Would you mind telling me what you're doing in here?* | *Would you mind shutting up for a minute?*

9 mind you also **mind** *BrE* used when saying something that is almost the opposite of what you have just said, or that explains or emphasizes it: *He looks very young in this photo. Mind you, it was taken years ago.* | *I love hot weather, but not too hot, mind.*

10 WARNING mind! *BrE* used to warn someone to be careful because they might hurt themselves or someone else, or damage something: *Mind that bike, James!* | *Mind you don't fall.* | **mind your head/fingers etc** *Mind your head – the ceiling's a bit low.* | **mind how/where/who etc** *It's slippery, so mind where you're walking.*

11 mind how you go *BrE* used when saying goodbye to someone, to tell them to take care

12 mind you do sth *BrE* used to tell someone to do something: *Mind you behave yourself.*

13 never you mind *especially BrE* used to tell someone that you are not going to tell them something because it is private or secret: *'What's that you were saying to Dad?' 'Never you mind.'*

14 do you mind! used to say to someone that you are annoyed with them because of something they have just done or said: *Do you mind! I just washed that floor!*

15 if you don't mind also **if you wouldn't mind a)** used to check that someone is willing to do something or let you do something: *If you don't mind, I think I'll go to bed now.* | *I'd like to stay a while longer if you don't mind.* | *We'll go there together – **that's if you don't mind.*** **b)** used when you are annoyed to tell someone what to do or what you are going to do: *Now, if you don't mind, I'd like to get back to bed.* **c)** used humorously or rudely to correct something someone has said: *The name's John, not Jonathan, if you don't mind.* **d)** used to refuse someone's offer politely: *'Do you want to come for a drink?' 'I won't if you don't mind. I've got a lot of work to do.'*

16 if you don't mind my saying so/if you don't mind me asking used when you are saying or asking something that you think might offend someone: *You're looking tired, if you don't mind my saying so.* | *How old are you, if you don't mind me asking?*

17 I don't mind admitting/telling you/saying etc used to emphasize what you are saying, especially when it could make you seem silly: *I don't mind admitting that I was really scared.*

18 don't mind me **a)** used to tell someone not to pay any attention to you: *If you want to get on and do something, please don't mind me.* **b)** used when you are annoyed because someone is not paying any attention to you: *Don't mind me! I only live here!*

19 don't mind her/him etc used to say sorry for someone else's behaviour: *Don't mind her. She doesn't mean to be hurtful.*

20 (I) don't mind if I do *old-fashioned* used humorously to accept something such as food or drink that has been offered to you

21 TAKE CARE OF STH/SB [T] *BrE* **a)** to be responsible for something for a short time; ▣ **watch**: *Will you mind my bag while I buy my ticket?* **b)** to take care of a child while their parents are not there; ▣ **look after**: *My sister minds the baby while I'm at yoga.*

22 mind the shop *BrE*, **mind the store** *AmE informal* to be in charge of something, while the person who is usually in charge is not there

23 mind your manners/language/p's and q's to be careful about what you say or how you behave so that you do not offend anyone: *She gave him a frown and told him to mind his manners.*

24 OBEY [T not in progressive] *AmE* to obey someone's instructions or advice: *Some dogs will mind instructions better than others.*

mind out *phr v* [always in imperative or infinitive] *BrE* used to warn someone to be careful: *Mind out. The plates are hot.*

'mind-,bending *adj* [usually before noun] *informal* **1** mind-bending drugs have a strong effect on your mind and make you have very strange feelings and experiences **2** difficult to understand: *Infinity in space is a mind-bending concept.*

'mind-,blowing *adj informal* very exciting, shocking, or strange: *a mind-blowing experience*

'mind-,boggling *adj informal* difficult to imagine and very big, strange, or complicated: *a problem of mind-boggling complexity*

mind·ed /'maɪndᵻd/ *adj* **1** serious-minded/evil-minded etc having a particular attitude or way of thinking: *a very serious-minded girl who studies hard* | *a tough-minded businessman* **2** be minded to do sth *formal* to want or intend to do something

mind·er /'maɪndə $ -ər/ *n* [C] *BrE* someone who is employed to protect another person; ▣ **bodyguard** → CHILDMINDER

mind·ful /'maɪndfəl/ *adj* **mindful of sth** *formal* remembering a particular rule or fact and thinking about it when you are making decisions about what to do; ▣ **conscious of**: *The school is mindful of its responsibilities towards all the children.*

M

mind·less /'maɪndləs/ adj **1** completely stupid and without any purpose; ▣ **senseless**: *His drinking bouts often ended in acts of mindless violence.* **2** if something is mindless, you can do it or watch it without thinking or using your mind: *Doug was watching something mindless on television.* | *the mindless routine of military discipline* **3 mindless of sth** not paying attention to something, especially something dangerous or unpleasant: *After lunch we explored the city, mindless of the rain.* —**mindlessly** adv

'**mind ,reader** n [C] someone who knows what someone else is thinking without being told

mind·set /'maɪndset/ n [C] someone's general attitude, and the way in which they think about things and make decisions: *The company seems to have a very old-fashioned mindset.*

mine¹ ⑤1 /maɪn/ pron [possessive form of 'I'] used by the person speaking or writing to refer to something that belongs to or is connected with himself or herself: *It was Glen's idea, not mine.* | *'Is that your car?' 'No, mine is parked over the road.'* | *You've got good legs – mine are too thin.* | *His English is better than mine.* | **of mine** *I want you to meet an old friend of mine.*

mine² ⑤2 W3 n [C]
1 a deep hole or holes in the ground that people dig so that they can remove coal, gold, TIN etc: **coal/gold/copper etc mine** *one of the largest coal mines in the country* | **in/down a mine** *the time when children used to work down the mines*
2 a type of bomb that is hidden just below the ground or under water and that explodes when it is touched: *They learnt how to set ambushes and* **lay mines** (=put them in place). | *The ship* **struck** *a mine and sank.* →
LANDMINE
3 a mine of information (about/on sth) someone or something that can give you a lot of information about a particular subject and that is therefore very useful or helpful: *The website is a mine of information about all forms of cancer.*

mine³ v **mined**, **mining 1** [I,T usually passive] to dig large holes in the ground in order to remove coal, gold etc: *Copper has been mined here since the sixteenth century.* | *This area has been mined for over 300 years.* | [+for] *The company first started mining for salt in 1851.* **2** [T usually passive] to hide bombs in the sea or under the ground: *All the roads leading to the village had been mined.*

mine·field /'maɪnfiːld/ n **1** [C] an area where a lot of bombs have been hidden just below the ground or under water: *They realized they had wandered into a minefield.* **2** [singular] a situation in which there are a lot of dangers and difficulties, and it is difficult to make the right decision: *Choosing the right school can be a bit of a minefield.* | [+of] *The new Administration has to pick its way through the minefield of legislation.* | **legal/financial/political etc minefield** *The legalisation of cannabis is a political minefield.*

min·er /'maɪnə $ -ər/ n [C] someone who works under the ground in a mine to remove coal, gold etc: **coal/gold etc miner** *a strike by coal miners*

min·e·ral /'mɪnərəl/ n [C] **1** a substance that is formed naturally in the earth, such as coal, salt, stone, or gold. Minerals can be dug out of the ground and used: *The area is very* **rich in minerals.** | *a country with few* **mineral resources 2** a natural substance such as iron that is present in some foods and is important for good health: *Fish is a rich source of vitamins and minerals.*

min·e·ral·o·gy /ˌmɪnəˈrælədʒi $ -ˈrɑː-, -ˈræ-/ n [U] the scientific study of minerals —**mineralogist** n [C]

'**mineral ,water** n [C,U] water that comes from under the ground and contains a lot of minerals: *a glass of mineral water*

mine·shaft /'maɪnʃɑːft $ -ʃæft/ n [C] a deep narrow hole that goes into the ground to a mine

min·e·stro·ne /ˌmɪnɪ'strəʊni $ -'stroʊ-/ also **,min-estrone 'soup** n [U] a type of soup containing vegetables and small pieces of PASTA

mine·sweep·er /'maɪnˌswiːpə $ -ər/ n [C] a ship with special equipment for removing bombs from under water —**minesweeping** n [U]

mine·work·er /'maɪnˌwɜːkə $ -ˌwɜːrkər/ n [C] someone who works in a mine

min·gle /'mɪŋɡəl/ v **mingled**, **mingling 1** [I,T] if two feelings, sounds, smells etc mingle, they mix together with each other: *Add the mint and allow the flavours to mingle.* | [+with] *Her perfume mingled with the smell of woodsmoke from the fire.* | **be mingled with sth** *Her excitement was mingled with a slight feeling of fear.* **2** [I] if you mingle at a party, you move around the room and talk to lots of different people: [+with] *She was eager to mingle with the other guests.*

min·gy /'mɪndʒi/ adj BrE informal not at all generous

min·i /'mɪni/ n [C] a MINISKIRT

mini- /mɪni, mɪni/ prefix very small or short, compared with others of the same kind: *All the hotel's bedrooms have a mini-bar, telephone and radio.* | *a mini-screen TV*

min·ia·ture¹ /'mɪnɪtʃə $ 'mɪniətʃər/ adj [only before noun] much smaller than normal: *miniature roses* | *a miniature railway* | *He looked like a* **miniature version** *of his father.*

miniature² n **1 in miniature** exactly like something or someone but much smaller: *She's her mother in miniature.* **2** [C] a very small painting, usually of a person **3** [C] a very small bottle containing an alcoholic drink: *a miniature of whiskey*

,**miniature 'golf** n [U] AmE a type of GOLF game, played for fun, in which you hit a small ball through passages, over bridges and small hills etc; ▣ **crazy golf** BrE

min·ia·tur·ist /'mɪnɪtʃərɪst $ 'mɪniətʃur-/ n [C] someone who paints very small pictures for money

min·ia·tur·ize also **-ise** BrE /'mɪnɪtʃəraɪz $ 'mɪniə-/ v [T] to make something in a very small size —**miniaturized** adj: *a miniaturized listening device*

'**mini-bar** also **min·i·bar** /'mɪnibɑː $ -bɑːr/ n [C] a small FRIDGE in a hotel bedroom, in which drinks are kept → see picture at STAY

min·i·bus /'mɪnibʌs/ n [C] especially BrE a small bus with seats for six to twelve people

min·i·cab /'mɪnikæb/ n [C] BrE a taxi that you have to order by telephone, not one that you can stop in the street

min·i·com·put·er /'mɪnikəmˌpjuːtə $ -ər/ n [C] a computer that is larger than a PERSONAL COMPUTER and smaller than a MAINFRAME, used by businesses and other large organizations

'**Mini ,Disc** n [C] trademark a very small, round DISK that is used for recording music

min·im /'mɪnɪm/ n [C] BrE a musical note that continues for the length of two CROTCHETS; ▣ **half note** AmE

min·i·mal /'mɪnɪməl/ adj very small in degree or amount, especially the smallest degree or amount possible: *The storm caused only minimal damage* | *The cost to taxpayers would be minimal.* | *This is a practical course, with only a minimal amount of theory.* —**minimally** adv: *Rates of truancy from school have only increased minimally.*

min·i·mal·is·m /'mɪnɪməlɪzəm/ n [U] a style of art, design, music etc that uses only a very few simple ideas or patterns —**minimalist** adj: *minimalist Christmas decorations* —**minimalist** n [C]

min·i·mart /'mɪnimɑːt $ -mɑːrt/ n [C] AmE a small shop that stays open very late, selling food, cigarettes etc

min·i·mize also **-ise** BrE /'mɪnimaɪz/ v [T] **1** to reduce something that is difficult, dangerous, or unpleasant to the smallest possible amount or degree; ▣ **maximize**: *Every effort is being made to minimize civilian casualties.* | *The rail company is bringing in more trains in an effort to minimize disruption to* travellers. **2** to make something seem less serious or important than it really is; ◨ **play down**: *We must not minimize the problem of racial discrimination.* **3** to make a document or program on your computer very small when you are not using it but still want to keep it open; ◪ **maximize**: *Click on the top of the window to minimize it.*

min·i·mum[1] [S2] [W3] /'mɪnᵻməm/ *adj* [only before noun] the minimum number, degree, or amount of something is the smallest or least that is possible, allowed, or needed; ◪ **maximum**: *The minimum number of students we need to run the course is fifteen.* | *The minimum age for retirement is 55.* —**minimum** *adv*: *You'll need two tons of cement, minimum.*

minimum[2] *n* [singular] **1** the smallest amount of something or number of things that is possible or necessary; ◪ **maximum**: **a minimum of two hours/ £1000 etc** *The judge recommended that he should serve a minimum of 12 years.* | **[+of]** *He achieved enviable results with the minimum of effort.* | **absolute/bare minimum** (=the very least amount or number) *Prison inmates are kept in tiny cells, with the bare minimum of furniture.* | **keep/reduce sth to a minimum** *She had reduced her consumption of fat and sugar to an absolute minimum.* **2 at a/the minimum** used to say that if nothing else is done, this one thing should be done: *At a minimum, we must recruit two new teachers.*

minimum se'curity prison *n* [C] *AmE* a prison that does not restrict prisoners' freedom as much as ordinary prisons; ◨ **open prison** *BrE*

minimum 'wage *n* [singular] the lowest amount of money that an employer can legally pay to a worker: *Most of the junior office staff are on the minimum wage* (=being paid the lowest legal amount).

min·ing /'maɪnɪŋ/ *n* [U] the work or industry of getting gold, coal etc out of the earth: **coal/gold etc mining** *the coal mining industry*

min·ion /'mɪnjən/ *n* [C usually plural] someone's minions are the people who just obey their orders and do unskilled work – used humorously: *I was shown into the office by one of her minions.*

mini-'roundabout *n* [C] *BrE* a white circle painted on the ground where several roads meet. Vehicles must drive round the circle in one direction only.

min·i·se·ries /'mɪnɪˌsɪəriz $ -ˌsɪr-/ *n* [C] a television film that is divided into several parts. Each part is shown on a different evening

min·i·skirt /'mɪnɪskɜːt $ -skɜːrt/ *n* [C] a very short skirt; ◨ **mini**

min·is·ter[1] [S1] [W1] /'mɪnᵻstə $ -ər/ *n* [C]
1 a politician who is in charge of a government department, in Britain and some other countries: **[+of]** *the Minister of Agriculture* | **[+for]** *the Minister for Foreign Affairs* | **foreign/defence/finance etc minister** *a meeting of EU foreign ministers* | *a senior* **Cabinet minister** → PRIME MINISTER
2 a priest in some Christian churches; → **pastor**, **vicar**: *a Baptist minister*
3 someone whose job is to represent their country in another country, but who is lower in rank than an AMBASSADOR

minister[2] *v* [I] to work as a priest: *Rev Wilson spent 20 years ministering in some of New York's poorest areas.*
minister to sb/sth *phr v formal* to give help to someone who needs it, especially someone who is sick or old: *She spent much time ministering to the sick.* | *ministering to the needs of other people*

min·is·ter·i·al /ˌmɪnᵻ'stɪəriəl $ -'stɪr-/ *adj* [only before noun] connected with or relating to government ministers: *a ministerial meeting* | *The project was approved at ministerial level.*

minister of 'state *n* [C] a member of the government in Britain who has an important job in a government department but is not in charge of it

min·i·stra·tions /ˌmɪnᵻ'streɪʃənz/ *n* [plural] *formal* the giving of help to people who are ill or who need the help of a priest: *Despite the ministrations of the surgeon poor Lucy died on the 22 July.*

min·is·try [W2] /'mɪnᵻstri/ *n plural* **ministries**
1 [C] a government department that is responsible for one of the areas of government work, such as education or health: **[+of]** *the Ministry of Agriculture* | **foreign/justice/finance etc ministry** *a Defence Ministry spokesman*
2 the ministry the profession of being a church leader, especially in the Protestant church: *Converted in his early teens, he* **entered the ministry** (=started working as a church leader) *in 1855.*
3 [C usually singular] the work done by a priest or other religious person as a result of their religious beliefs: *the ministry of Jesus*

min·i·van /'mɪnivæn/ *n* [C] *AmE* a large car with seats for six to eight people; ◨ **people carrier** *BrE*

mink /mɪŋk/ *n plural* **mink** *or* **minks** **1** [C,U] a small animal with soft brown fur, or the very valuable fur of this animal which is used to make coats, hats etc: *a mink coat* **2** [C] a coat or jacket made of mink

min·now /'mɪnəʊ $ -noʊ/ *n* [C] **1** a very small fish that lives in rivers and lakes **2** an organization or company that is small and unimportant: *one of the minnows of the computer industry*

mi·nor[1] [S2] [W2] /'maɪnə $ -ər/ *adj*
1 small and not very important or serious, especially when compared with other things; ◪ **major**: *We have made some minor changes to the program.* | *a relatively minor error* | *a minor road* | *They played only a minor role in local government.* | **minor injury/illness/operation etc** (=one that is not very serious or dangerous) *He escaped with only minor injuries.*
2 based on a particular type of musical SCALE: *Mahler's Symphony No. 3 in D minor* | *a minor key*

minor[2] *n* [C] **1** *law* someone who is below the age at which they become legally responsible for their actions: *This film contains material unsuitable for minors.* **2** *AmE* the second main subject that you study at university for your degree; ◪ **major**: *I'm taking history as my minor.* **3 the minors** the MINOR LEAGUES

minor[3] *v*
minor in sth *phr v AmE* to study a second main subject as part of your university degree; ◪ **major**: *Sid minored in political science.*

mi·nor·i·ty [S3] [W2] /maɪ'nɒrᵻti $ mə'nɔː-, mə'nɑː-/ *n plural* **minorities**
1 [singular also + plural verb] a small group of people or things within a much larger group; ◪ **majority**: *Gaelic is still spoken in Ireland by a tiny minority.* | **[+of]** *A small minority of young people does drink excessively.* | *Only a minority of people support these new laws.* | **small/tiny/substantial/significant minority** *Gay men are a small but significant minority.* | **minority report** (=a report by a minority of a group who do not agree with the others)
2 [C usually plural] **a)** a group of people of a different race, religion etc from most other people in that country: *People from* **ethnic minorities** *often face prejudice and discrimination.* | *the very large Russian minorities in Ukraine and Moldova* | *children from* **minority groups** | *the teaching of* **minority languages** *in schools* | **minority leader/businessman/student etc** *AmE: a school with a high proportion of minority students* **b)** *AmE* someone who belongs to a group like this: *Businesses are under pressure to hire minorities and women.*
3 be in the/a minority to form less than half of a group: *Boys are very much in the minority at the dance class.*
4 be in a minority of one to be the only person in a group who has a particular opinion
5 [U] *law* the period of time when someone is below the age at which they become legally responsible for their actions

mi.nority 'government n [C] a government that does not have enough politicians in a parliament to control parliament and take decisions without the support of other parties

mi'nority .leader n [C] AmE the leader of the political party that has fewer politicians in CONGRESS than the leading party; → **majority leader**

M .minor-'league** adj [only before noun] **1** connected with the Minor Leagues: a minor-league team **2** not as important, powerful, or successful as others of the same kind: Collins and Reynolds were just minor-league crooks.

.Minor 'Leagues n the Minor Leagues the groups of teams that form the lower levels of American professional BASEBALL; → **Major Leagues**

min.ster /'mɪnstə $ -ər/ n [C] BrE a large or important church: a carol service at the minster | York Minster

min.strel /'mɪnstrəl/ n [C] **1** a singer or musician in the Middle Ages **2** one of a group of white singers and dancers who pretended to be black while performing in popular shows in the 1920s

mint¹ /mɪnt/ n **1** [U] a small plant with green leaves that have a fresh smell and taste and are used in cooking: new potatoes sprinkled with chopped mint | roast lamb with **mint sauce** | Decorate with a **sprig of mint**. **2** [C] a sweet that tastes of PEPPERMINT (=a type of mint with a strong fresh taste): We sat in the back row, sucking mints. | Would you like a mint? **3 in mint condition** looking new and in perfect condition: A copy in mint condition would fetch about £2000. **4 a mint** informal a large amount of money: She **made a mint** on the stock exchange last year. **5** [C] a place where coins are officially made: coins issued by the Royal Mint

mint² v [T] to make a coin: Only 2,000 of the special commemorative coins are being minted.

mint.ed /'mɪntɪd/ adj **1** newly/freshly minted a newly minted word, phrase, idea etc has been invented or produced very recently: some newly minted theatrical stories **2** minted food and drinks have mint added to them: Serve with minted peas.

.mint 'julep n [C] AmE a drink in which alcohol and sugar are mixed with ice and mint leaves are added

mint.y /'mɪnti/ adj tasting or smelling of mint: a fresh, minty flavour

min.u.et /.mɪnju'et/ n [C] a slow dance of the 17th and 18th centuries, or a piece of music for this dance

mi.nus¹ /'maɪnəs/ prep **1** used to show that one number or quantity is being SUBTRACTED from another; **⊟ plus**: 17 minus 5 is 12 (17 − 5 = 12). | The payment will be refunded to you minus a small service charge. **2** informal without something that would normally be there, or that used to be there: He came back minus a couple of front teeth.

minus² n [C] **1** something that is a disadvantage because it makes a situation unpleasant; **⊟ drawback**; **⊟ plus**: There are both pluses and minuses to living in a big city. **2** a MINUS SIGN

minus³ adj **1** [only before noun] BrE used to talk about a disadvantage of a thing or situation; **⊟ plus**: 'Any minus points?' 'Well, the engine is rather noisy.' | **On the minus side**, there is no free back-up service if things go wrong. **2** less than zero – used especially when talking about temperatures: At night temperatures sometimes fall to minus 30°. | a minus quantity **3** A minus/B minus etc a mark used in a system of judging students' work. An 'A minus' is slightly lower than an 'A', but higher than a 'B'.; **⊟ plus**

min.us.cule /'mɪnəskjuːl/ adj extremely small; **⊟ minute**: a minuscule amount of food | Her office is minuscule.

'minus .sign also **minus** n [C] a sign (-) showing that a number is less than zero, or that the second of two numbers is to be SUBTRACTED from the first → **PLUS SIGN**

min.ute¹ S1 W1 /'mɪnɪt/ n [C]
1 TIME a unit for measuring time. There are 60 minutes in one hour: It takes me ten minutes to walk to work. | The train arrived at four minutes past eight. | He returned a few minutes later. | I'll meet you at the car in five minutes. | **a one/two/three etc minute sth** a ten minute bus ride
2 the last minute the last possible time, just before it is too late: **at the last minute** He cancelled his trip to England at the last minute. | **until the last minute** If you leave your essay until the last minute, you'll almost certainly panic. → LAST-MINUTE
3 by the minute also **every minute, minute by minute** used to say that something continues quickly becoming greater, stronger etc: She was getting angrier by the minute. | His voice was getting stronger every minute.
4 love/enjoy/hate etc every minute (of sth) informal if you love, enjoy etc every minute of an activity or experience, you love, enjoy etc all of it: I went camping for a week and enjoyed every minute of it.
5 within minutes very soon after something has happened: The ambulance was there within minutes. | **within minutes of doing sth** He had his car stolen within minutes of arriving at the office.
6 a minute a very short period of time; **⊟ moment**: Sam thought for a minute, then smiled at his brother. | Can I have a quick word? It won't take a minute (=it won't take very long).

SPOKEN PHRASES

7 in a minute very soon: Wait here. I'll be back in a minute. | Mr Gregson will be with you in a minute.
8 wait a minute/just a minute/hold on a minute/hang on a minute a) used to tell someone you want them to wait for a short time while you do or say something else: Just a minute, Margaret, I want to introduce you to Betty. | Wait a minute, let me see if I understand this correctly. **b)** used to tell someone to stop speaking or doing something for a short time because they have said or done something wrong: Hold on a minute! That can't be right.
9 (at) any minute (now) used to say that something will or may happen extremely soon: We're expecting them any minute now.
10 have you got a minute? BrE; **do you have a minute?** AmE used to ask someone if you may talk to them for a short time: Have you got a minute? I need to ask you some questions.
11 the minute (that) sb does sth as soon as someone does something: Tell him I need to see him the minute he arrives.
12 not think/believe/etc for one minute used to say that you certainly do not think something, believe something etc: I don't think for one minute that he'll do it but I have to ask.
13 this minute immediately: Johnny! Get inside, this minute! | You don't have to tell me **right this minute**.

---

14 the next minute immediately afterwards: I put down the phone and the next minute it rang again.
15 one minute ... the next (minute) ... used to say that a situation suddenly changes: One minute they're madly in love and the next they've split up again.
16 MEETING minutes [plural] an official written record of what is said and decided at a meeting: Will you **take the minutes** (=write them down)? | **[+of]** Has everyone seen the minutes of last month's meeting?
17 MATHEMATICS technical one of the sixty parts into which a degree of an angle is divided. It can be shown as a symbol after a number. For example, 78° 52′ means 78 degrees 52 minutes. → UP-TO-THE-MINUTE

mi.nute² /maɪ'njuːt $ -'nuːt/ adj **1** extremely small: You only need a minute amount. | Her handwriting is minute. **2** paying careful attention to the smallest details: a minute examination of the rock | He explained the plan **in minute detail**. —**minutely** adv: She studied the letter minutely.

min·ute³ /'mɪnɪt/ v [T] *especially BrE* to make an official note of something in the record of a meeting: *This discussion is off the record and should not be minuted.*

minute hand /'mɪnɪt hænd/ n [C] the long thin piece of metal that points to the minutes on a clock or watch; → **hour hand**

min·ute·man /'mɪnɪtmæn/ n plural **minutemen** /-men/ [C] *AmE* one of a group of men in the past who were not official soldiers but who were ready to fight at any time

mi·nu·ti·ae /maɪ'njuːʃiaɪ, mᵻ- $ mᵻ'nuː-/ n [plural] very small and exact details: [+of] *Most people are not interested in the minutiae of the research, just its conclusions.*

minx /mɪŋks/ n [C] *old-fashioned* an attractive young woman who does not show respect and who is good at getting what she wants in a clever way

mips /mɪps/ *technical* **millions of instructions per second** used to say how fast a computer works

mir·a·cle /'mɪrəkəl/ n [C] **1** something very lucky or very good that happens which you did not expect to happen or did not think was possible: *It's a miracle you weren't killed! | By some miracle, we managed to catch the plane. | the **economic miracle** of the 1950s. | She's our miracle baby. |* **small/minor miracle** (=something lucky but not very important) *The fence's survival in these winds seems like a minor miracle.* **2** an action or event believed to be caused by God, which is impossible according to the ordinary laws of nature: *Do you believe in miracles?* **3** **miracle cure/drug** a very effective medical treatment that cures even serious diseases: *There is no miracle cure for diabetes.* **4** **work/ perform miracles** to have a very good effect or achieve a very good result: *Maybe you should try yoga – it worked miracles for me.* **5** **a miracle of sth** a very good example of something: *The concert tour was an absolute miracle of organization. | a miracle of modern engineering*

mi·rac·u·lous /mɪ'rækj˟ləs/ adj **1** very good, completely unexpected, and often very lucky: *She made a miraculous recovery from her injuries. | They had a miraculous escape when their car plunged into a river.* **2** a miraculous action or event is believed to be caused by God, and is impossible according to the ordinary laws of nature: *miraculous powers of healing* —**miraculously** adv: *Miraculously, no one was killed.*

mi·rage /'mɪrɑːʒ $ mᵻ'rɑːʒ/ n [C] **1** an effect caused by hot air in a desert, which makes you think that you can see objects when they are not actually there **2** a dream, hope, or wish that cannot come true; ⊟ **illusion**: *Perhaps we are just chasing a mirage.*

mire /maɪə $ maɪr/ n [U] *literary* **1** deep mud: *The wheels got stuck in the mire.* **2** **the mire** a bad or difficult situation that you cannot seem to escape from; ⊟ **quagmire**: *The Party sank deeper into the mire of conflict.* **3** **drag sb's name through the mire** to say bad things about someone in public, so that other people have a bad opinion of them

mired /maɪəd $ maɪrd/ adj [not before noun] *literary* **1** stuck in a bad situation and unable to get out or make progress: [+in] *a government mired in scandal and controversy* **2** stuck in mud or covered in mud

mir·ror¹ [S3] [W3] /'mɪrə $ -ər/ n [C]
1 a piece of special glass that you can look at and see yourself in: **in a mirror** *She was studying her reflection in the mirror. | He spends hours **in front of the mirror**! | When I **looked in the mirror** I couldn't believe it. I looked fantastic!* → see picture at BEDROOM
2 a mirror on the inside or side of a vehicle, which the driver uses to see what is behind: *Check your **rear-view mirror** before you drive away. | a **wing mirror** →* see picture at MOTORBIKE

3 **a mirror of sth** something that gives a clear idea of what something else is like: *We believe the polls are an accurate mirror of public opinion.*

mirror² v [T] if one thing mirrors another, it is very similar to it and may seem to copy or represent it: *Henry's sad smile mirrored that of his son. | The economic recovery in Britain was mirrored in the US.*

mirror image n [C] **1** an image of something in which the right side appears on the left, and the left side appears on the right **2** something that is either very similar to something else or is the complete opposite of it: [+of] *The situation is a mirror image of the one Republicans faced 25 years ago.*

mirror site n [C] a website that is an exact copy of another one, but which is in a different place on the Internet

mirth /mɜːθ $ mɜːrθ/ n [U] *literary* happiness and laughter: *Her body began to shake with mirth.* —**mirthful** adj

mirth·less /'mɜːθləs $ 'mɜːrθ-/ adj *literary* mirthless laughter or a mirthless smile does not seem to be caused by real amusement or happiness: *'Now it's your turn,' he said with a mirthless grin.* —**mirthlessly** adv: *He smiled mirthlessly.*

mis- /mɪs/ prefix **1** bad or badly: *misfortune* (=bad luck) | *He's been misbehaving.* **2** wrong or wrongly: *a miscalculation | I misunderstood you.* **3** used to refer to an opposite or the lack of something: *What caused this anger and mistrust* (=lack of trust)?

mis·ad·ven·ture /ˌmɪsəd'ventʃə $ -ər/ n **1** **death by misadventure** *BrE law* the official name for a death caused by an accident: *A verdict of death by misadventure was recorded.* **2** [C,U] *literary* bad luck or an accident

mis·al·li·ance /ˌmɪsə'laɪəns/ n [C] *formal* a situation in which two people or organizations have agreed to work together, marry each other etc, but are not suitable for each other: *It was a hopeless misalliance.*

mis·an·thro·pist /mɪs'ænθrəpᵻst/ also **mis·an·thrope** /'mɪsənθrəup $ -θroup/ n [C] *formal* someone who does not like other people and prefers to be alone —**misanthropic** /ˌmɪsən'θrɒpɪk◂ $ -'θrɑː-/ adj —**misanthropy** /mɪs'ænθrəpi/ n [U]

mis·ap·ply /ˌmɪsə'plaɪ/ v **misapplied, misapplying, misapplies** [T usually passive] to use something incorrectly or for a wrong purpose: *In your case the rules have been misapplied.* —**misapplication** /ˌmɪsæplᵻ'keɪʃən/ n [U]: *a misapplication of the law*

mis·ap·pre·hen·sion /ˌmɪsæprɪ'henʃən/ n [C] *formal* a mistaken belief or a wrong understanding of something; ⊟ **misunderstanding**: **under a misapprehension** *You seem to be under a misapprehension. | I think we should clear up this misapprehension.*

mis·ap·pro·pri·ate /ˌmɪsə'prəuprieɪt $ -'prou-/ v [T] *formal* to dishonestly take something that someone has trusted you with, especially money or goods that belong to your employer; ⊟ **embezzle**: *He claimed the finance manager had misappropriated company funds.* —**misappropriation** /ˌmɪsəprəupri'eɪʃən $ -prou-/ n [U]: *the misappropriation of public funds*

mis·be·got·ten /ˌmɪsbɪ'ɡɒtn◂ $ -'ɡɑː-/ adj [only before noun] *old-fashioned* **1** a misbegotten plan, idea, etc is not likely to succeed because it is badly planned or not sensible **2** a misbegotten person is completely stupid or useless: *You misbegotten fool!*

mis·be·have /ˌmɪsbɪ'heɪv/ v [I] also **misbehave yourself** to behave badly, and cause trouble or annoy people; ⊟ **behave**: *George has been misbehaving at school. | Students have a tendency to misbehave themselves at exam time.*

mis·be·ha·viour *BrE*; **misbehavior** *AmE* /ˌmɪsbɪ'heɪvjə $ -ər/ n [U] bad behaviour that is not

[1] 000, [2] 000, [3] 000, most frequent words in [S] poken and [W] ritten English

M

acceptable to other people; ◻ **misconduct**: *Even the most minor forms of misbehaviour were punished.*

mis·cal·cu·late /mɪsˈkælkjʊ̩leɪt/ v [I,T] **1** to make a mistake when deciding how long something will take to do, how much money you will need etc: *We miscalculated how long it would take to get there.* **2** to make a wrong judgment about a situation: *Tim had miscalculated: Laura would never disobey her father.*

mis·cal·cu·la·tion /ˌmɪsˌkælkjʊ̩ˈleɪʃən/ n [C] **1** a mistake made in deciding how long something will take to do, how much money you will need etc **2** a wrong judgment about a situation

mis·car·riage /ˌmɪsˈkærɪdʒ, ˈmɪskærɪdʒ/ n [C,U] if a woman who is going to have a baby has a miscarriage, she gives birth before the baby is properly formed and it dies; → **abortion**, **stillbirth**: *She had two miscarriages before she had her first child.* | *One in five pregnancies ends in miscarriage.*

mis,carriage of 'justice n plural **miscarriages of justice** [C,U] a situation in which someone is wrongly punished by a court of law for something they did not do: *the victim of a serious miscarriage of justice*

mis·car·ry /ˌmɪsˈkæri/ v **miscarried**, **miscarrying**, **miscarries** **1** [I,T] to give birth to a baby before it is properly formed and able to live; → **abort**: *She miscarried when she was 10 weeks pregnant.* | *Many babies with serious disabilities are miscarried.* **2** [I] formal if a plan miscarries, it is not successful

mis·cast /ˌmɪsˈkɑːst $ -ˈkæst/ v past tense and past participle **miscast** [T usually in passive] to choose an unsuitable actor to play a particular character in a play or film; → **cast**: *She was hopelessly miscast in her last film.*

mis·ce·ge·na·tion /ˌmɪsɪ̩dʒɪˈneɪʃən $ -sedʒ-/ n [U] formal when people of different races have a sexual relationship or have children together

mis·cel·la·ne·ous /ˌmɪsəˈleɪniəs◂/ adj [only before noun] a miscellaneous set of things or people includes many different things or people who do not seem to be connected with each other: *a miscellaneous assortment of books* | *They receive a grant of £1094 to cover the cost of miscellaneous expenses.*

mis·cel·la·ny /mɪˈseləni $ ˈmɪsɪ̩leɪni/ n plural **miscellanies** [C] a group of different things: [+of] *He earned his living from a miscellany of jobs.*

mis·chance /ˌmɪsˈtʃɑːns $ -ˈtʃæns/ n [C,U] formal bad luck, or a situation that results from bad luck: *If by some mischance the government get elected again, I think taxes will rise.*

mis·chief /ˈmɪstʃɪ̩f/ n **1** [U] bad behaviour, especially by children, that causes trouble or damage, but no serious harm: *Now run along, and don't get into mischief.* | *They've got enough toys to keep them out of mischief for a while.* | *If you can't see Nick, you can be sure he's up to some mischief* (=behaving badly and causing trouble or damage). **2** [U] the pleasure or enjoyment of playing tricks on people or embarrassing them: *Kiki's eyes were bright with mischief.* **3** **make mischief** informal to deliberately cause quarrels or unfriendly feelings between people: [+**between**] *I didn't want to make mischief between them.* **4** **do yourself a mischief** BrE informal to injure yourself slightly: *If you try to lift that box, you'll do yourself a mischief.* **5** [U] formal damage or harm that is done to someone or to their property: *The jury cleared him of the charge of criminal mischief.*

'mischief-,maker n [C] someone who deliberately causes trouble or quarrels; ◻ **stirrer**

mis·chie·vous /ˈmɪstʃɪ̩vəs/ adj **1** someone who is mischievous likes to have fun, especially by playing tricks on people or doing things to annoy or embarrass them: *Their sons are noisy and mischievous.* | **mischievous smile/look etc** *Gabby looked at him with a mis-*chievous grin.* | *There was a mischievous gleam in her eyes.* **2** causing trouble or quarrels deliberately: *a mischievous remark* —**mischievously** adv: *He grinned mischievously.* —**mischievousness** n [U]

mis·con·ceived /ˌmɪskənˈsiːvd◂/ adj a misconceived idea, plan, method etc is not a good one because it is based on a wrong understanding of something: *His arguments are totally misconceived.* | *His criticisms are misconceived and misplaced.*

mis·con·cep·tion /ˌmɪskənˈsepʃən/ n [C,U] an idea which is wrong or untrue, but which people believe because they do not understand the subject properly; ◻ **fallacy**; → **preconception**: **popular/common misconception** *There is a popular misconception that too much exercise is bad for you.* | **misconception that** *Refugees have the misconception that life is great over here.* | [+**about**] *many people's misconceptions about the blind and deaf*

mis·con·duct /ˌmɪsˈkɒndʌkt $ -ˈkɑːn-/ n [U] formal bad or dishonest behaviour by someone in a position of authority or trust: *a doctor who has been accused of* **professional misconduct** | *He was fired for* **serious misconduct**. | *She was found guilty of* **gross misconduct** (=very serious misconduct).

mis·con·struc·tion /ˌmɪskənˈstrʌkʃən/ n [C,U] formal an incorrect or mistaken understanding of something: *Your ideas are open to misconstruction.*

mis·con·strue /ˌmɪskənˈstruː/ v [T] formal to MISUNDERSTAND something that someone has said or done: *His behaviour could easily be misconstrued.*

mis·count /ˌmɪsˈkaʊnt/ v [I,T] to count wrongly: *Sorry, I miscounted – we need ten copies, not nine.* | *The votes were deliberately miscounted.*

mis·cre·ant /ˈmɪskriənt/ n [C] formal a bad person who causes trouble, hurts people etc

mis·deed /ˌmɪsˈdiːd/ n [C] formal a wrong or illegal action: *He now repents of his past misdeeds.*

mis·de·mea·nour BrE; **misdemeanor** AmE /ˌmɪsdɪˈmiːnə $ -ər/ n [C] **1** formal a bad or unacceptable action that is not very serious: *Alfred beat his children for even the smallest misdemeanour.* **2** law a crime that is not very serious; → **felony**

mis·di·ag·nose /ˌmɪsdaɪəɡˈnəʊz $ -ˈnoʊs-/ v [T] to give an incorrect explanation of an illness, a problem in a machine etc: **misdiagnose sth as sth** *Her condition was misdiagnosed as arthritis.*

mis·di·rect /ˌmɪsdɪ̩ˈrekt, -daɪ-/ v [T usually in passive] **1** formal to use your effort, energy, abilities etc on doing the wrong thing: *Without well-defined goals, it is likely that efforts will be misdirected.* | *Their criticism is misdirected.* **2** if a judge misdirects a JURY (=the group of people who decide a legal case), he or she gives them incorrect information about the law **3** formal to send someone or something to the wrong place: **misdirect sb/sth to sth** *Our mail was misdirected to the wrong street.* —**misdirection** /-ˈrekʃən/ n [U]

mi·ser /ˈmaɪzə $ -ər/ n [C] someone who is not generous and does not like spending money

mis·e·ra·ble /ˈmɪzərəbəl/ adj **1** extremely unhappy, for example because you feel lonely, cold, or badly treated: *I've been so miserable since Patrick left me.* | *I spent the weekend feeling miserable.* | *Janice looks really miserable.* | *Why do you make yourself miserable by taking on too much work?* | **as miserable as sin** BrE (=very miserable) **2** especially BrE always bad-tempered, DISSATISFIED, or complaining: *He's a miserable old devil.* **3** [usually before noun] making you feel very unhappy, uncomfortable etc: *They endured hours of backbreaking work in miserable conditions.* | *Mosquito bites can make life miserable.* **4** miserable weather is cold and dull, with no sun shining: *It was a miserable grey day.* | *two weeks of miserable weather* **5** [only before noun] very small in amount, or very bad in quality: *I can hardly afford the rent on my miserable income.* | *The team gave a miserable perfor-*

mance. **6 miserable failure** *BrE* a complete failure: *Her attempts to learn to drive had been a miserable failure.* —**miserably** *adv*: *I failed miserably in my duty to protect her.*

mi·ser·ly /ˈmaɪzəli $ -zər-/ *adj* **1** a miserly amount or quantity is one that is much too small; ⊟ **measly**, **paltry**: *We were offered a miserly 4% pay rise.* **2** a miserly person is not generous and does not like spending money; ⊟ **mean** —**miserliness** *n* [U]

mis·e·ry S3 /ˈmɪzəri/ *n plural* **miseries**
1 [C,U] great suffering that is caused for example by being very poor or very sick: *What we are witnessing here is human misery on a vast scale.* | *the misery of unemployment* | *the miseries of war*
2 [C,U] great unhappiness: *She looked away so that Tom wouldn't see her misery.* | *His face was a picture of sheer misery.* | *The news plunged him into* **abject misery**.
3 make sb's life a misery *BrE* to cause so much trouble for someone that they cannot enjoy their life: *Competitive mothers can make their daughters' lives a misery.*
4 put sth/sb out of their misery a) *informal* to make someone stop feeling worried, especially by telling them something they are waiting to hear: *Go on, put them out of their misery and announce the winner.* **b)** to kill a sick or injured animal in order to end its suffering; ⊟ **put down**: *I think you should put the poor creature out of its misery.*
5 [C] *BrE spoken* someone who is always complaining and never enjoys anything: *Don't be such a misery.* | *What's the matter with you,* **misery guts** (=a name for someone like this)?

mis·field /ˌmɪsˈfiːld/ *v* [I,T] to make a mistake in catching or throwing the ball in some ball games, such as CRICKET —**misfield** /ˈmɪsfiːld/ *n* [C]

mis·fire /ˌmɪsˈfaɪə $ -ˈfaɪr/ *v* [I] **1** if a plan or joke misfires, it goes wrong and does not have the result that you intended; → **backfire**: *His attempt at a joke misfired.* | *I was worried that the plan might misfire.* **2** if an engine misfires, the petrol mixture does not burn at the right time **3** if a gun misfires, the bullet does not come out

mis·fit /ˈmɪsˌfɪt/ *n* [C] someone who does not seem to belong in a particular group of people, and who is not accepted by that group, because they are very different from the other group members: *I was very conscious of being a misfit at school.* | *a social misfit*

mis·for·tune /mɪsˈfɔːtʃən $ -ɔːr-/ *n* [C,U] very bad luck, or something that happens to you as a result of bad luck: *It seems the banks always profit from farmers' misfortunes.* | **have the misfortune to do/of doing sth** *The French soldiers had the misfortune to be caught in the crossfire.*

mis·giv·ing /mɪsˈɡɪvɪŋ/ *n* [C,U] a feeling of doubt or fear about what might happen or about whether something is right: [+**about**] *Despite her misgivings about leaving the baby, she decided to accompany her husband.* | **grave/serious/deep misgivings** *Some politicians have expressed grave misgivings about the scheme.* | *Opponents of nuclear energy* **have deep misgivings** *about its safety.* | *She eyed the distant shoreline with misgiving.*

mis·guid·ed /mɪsˈɡaɪdɪd/ *adj* **1** intended to be helpful but in fact making a situation worse: *He described the government's economic policy as misguided.* | *a misguided attempt to bring her parents back together* **2** a misguided idea or opinion is wrong because it is based on a wrong understanding of a situation: *His parents still clung to the misguided belief that his common sense would keep him out of serious trouble.* —**misguidedly** *adv*: *The company misguidedly thought that expansion was the best way to survive.*

mis·han·dle /ˌmɪsˈhændl/ *v* [T] **1** to deal with a situation badly, because of a lack of skill or care: *The prime minister admitted that the crisis had been mis-*handled. **2** to treat something roughly, often causing damage: *Some of the goods had been mishandled and damaged.*

mis·hap /ˈmɪshæp/ *n* [C,U] a small accident or mistake that does not have very serious results: *I had a* **slight mishap** *with one of the glasses.* | *a series of mishaps* | **without mishap** *Only one horse finished the course without mishap.*

mis·hear /ˌmɪsˈhɪə $ -ˈhɪr/ *v past tense and past participle* **misheard** /-ˈhɜːd $ -ˈhɜːrd/ [I,T] to not hear properly what someone says, so that you think they said something different: *It seemed a strange question.; I wondered if I had misheard.* | *You must have misheard him.*

mis·hit /ˌmɪsˈhɪt/ *v past tense and past participle* **mishit**, *present participle* **mishitting** [T] to hit a ball badly in a game or sport: *He completely mishit his shot.* —**mishit** /ˈmɪshɪt/ *n* [C]

mish·mash /ˈmɪʃmæʃ/ *n* [singular] *informal* a mixture of a lot of very different things that are put together in a way that is not organized; ⊟ **hodge-podge**: [+**of**] *The magazine is a jumbled mishmash of jokes, stories, and serious news.*

mis·in·form /ˌmɪsɪnˈfɔːm $ -ɔːrm/ *v* [T usually passive] to give someone information that is incorrect: *I am afraid you've been misinformed.*

mis·in·for·ma·tion /ˌmɪsɪnfəˈmeɪʃən $ -fər-/ *n* [U] incorrect information, especially when deliberately intended to deceive people; → **disinformation**

mis·in·ter·pret /ˌmɪsɪnˈtɜːprɪt $ -ɜːr-/ *v* [T] to not understand the correct meaning of something that someone says or does, or of facts that you are considering; ⊟ **misread**, **misconstrue**: *Some parts of the report could be misinterpreted.* | **misinterpret sth as sth** *She had misinterpreted his silence as anger.* —**misinterpretation** /ˌmɪsɪntɜːprɪˈteɪʃən $ -tɜːr-/ *n* [C,U]: *a misinterpretation of the test results*

mis·judge /ˌmɪsˈdʒʌdʒ/ *v* [T] **1** to form a wrong or unfair opinion about a person or a situation: *The government misjudged the mood of the electorate.* | *I think you've misjudged her.* **2** to guess an amount or distance wrongly: *I misjudged the speed of the car coming towards me.* —**misjudgment** also **misjudgement** *BrE n* [C,U]: *He accused the government of a serious foreign policy misjudgment.*

mis·lay /ˌmɪsˈleɪ/ *v past tense and past participle* **mislaid** /-ˈleɪd/ [T] to put something somewhere, then forget where you put it; ⊟ **lose**, **misplace**: *I've mislaid my glasses again.* | *Sometimes students' work does get lost or mislaid.*

mis·lead /ˌmɪsˈliːd/ *v past tense and past participle* **misled** /-ˈled/ [T] to make someone believe something that is not true by giving them information that is false or not complete: **mislead sb about/over sth** *Politicians have misled the public over the dangers of these chemicals.* | *Don't be misled by appearances, he's a good worker.* | **mislead sb into believing/thinking etc sth** *Don't be misled into thinking that scientific research is easy.*

mis·lead·ing /mɪsˈliːdɪŋ/ *adj* likely to make someone believe something that is not true: *The article was misleading, and the newspaper has apologized.* | **seriously/highly/grossly etc misleading** *These figures are highly misleading.* —**misleadingly** *adv*: *The diagrams are misleadingly simple.*

mis·man·age /ˌmɪsˈmænɪdʒ/ *v* [T] if someone mismanages something they are in charge of, they deal with or manage it badly: *The nation's finances had been badly mismanaged.* —**mismanagement** *n* [U]: *the government's mismanagement of the crisis*

mis·match /ˈmɪsmætʃ/ *n* [C] a combination of things or people that do not work well together or are not suitable for each other: [+**between**] *the mismatch*

M

between the demand for health care and the supply —**mismatched** /ˌmɪsˈmætʃtɪ/ adj: a mismatched couple

mis·name /ˌmɪsˈneɪm/ v [T] to give something a name that is wrong or not suitable: a dreary little place that was misnamed the Grand Hotel

mis·no·mer /mɪsˈnəʊmə $ -ˈnoʊmər/ n [C] a wrong or unsuitable name: 'Silent movie' is a misnomer since the movies usually had a musical accompaniment.

mi·so·gy·nist /mɒˈsɒdʒɪnɪst $ mɪˈsɑː-/ n [C] formal a man who hates women —**misogynist, misogynistic** adj: deeply misogynist attitudes —**misogyny** n [U]

mis·place /ˌmɪsˈpleɪs/ v [T] to lose something for a short time by putting it in the wrong place; ⊟ **mislay**: Oh dear, I seem to have misplaced the letter.

mis·placed /ˌmɪsˈpleɪstɪ/ adj misplaced feelings of trust, love etc are wrong and unsuitable, because the person that you have these feelings for does not deserve them: I realized that my trust in him was misplaced. | She stuck with him through a misplaced sense of loyalty.

mis·print /ˈmɪs-prɪnt/ n [C] a small mistake, especially a spelling mistake, in a book, magazine etc

mis·pro·nounce /ˌmɪsprəˈnaʊns/ v [T] to pronounce a word or name wrongly —**mispronunciation** /ˌmɪsprənʌnsiˈeɪʃən/ n [C,U]

mis·quote /ˌmɪsˈkwəʊt/ v [T] to make a mistake in reporting what someone else has said: Dr Hall said he had been misquoted in the press. —**misquotation** /ˌmɪskwəʊˈteɪʃən $ -kwoʊ-/ n [C,U]

mis·read /ˌmɪsˈriːd/ v past tense and past participle **misread** /-ˈred/ [T] **1** to make a wrong judgment about a person or situation; ⊟ **misinterpret**: I think she misread the situation. | He may be misreading her intentions. **2** to read something incorrectly: The doctor must have misread the notes. —**misreading** n [C,U]: a misreading of the situation

mis·re·port /ˌmɪsrɪˈpɔːt $ -ˈpɔːrt/ v [T usually passive] to give an incorrect or untrue account of an event or situation: The facts of the story have been misreported.

mis·rep·re·sent /ˌmɪsreprɪˈzent/ v [T] to deliberately give a wrong description of someone's opinions or of a situation: These statistics grossly misrepresent the reality. —**misrepresentation** /ˌmɪsreprɪzenˈteɪʃən/ n [C,U]: a misrepresentation of the truth

mis·rule /ˌmɪsˈruːl/ n [U] formal bad government: The country has suffered years of misrule by a weak and corrupt government.

miss¹ S1 W2 /mɪs/ v

1 NOT DO STH/FAIL TO DO STH [T] to not go somewhere or do something, especially when you want to but cannot: I'm absolutely starving — I missed lunch. | He missed 20 games after breaking a bone in his wrist. | She was upset at missing all the excitement. | **miss doing sth** He had missed being elected by a single vote.
2 NOT HIT/CATCH [I,T] to fail to hit or catch an object that is close to you, or to fail to hit a distant object that you are aiming at: Every time she missed the ball she became more angry. | He fired, missed and loaded again. | The bullet **narrowly missed** her heart.
3 FEEL SAD ABOUT SB [T] to feel sad because someone you love is not with you: She missed her family badly. | Will you miss me? | John will be **sorely missed** by his family and friends.
4 FEEL SAD ABOUT STH [T] to feel sad because you do not have something or cannot do something you had or did before: I miss the car, but the bus system is good. | **miss doing sth** Ben knew he would miss working with Sabrina.
5 TOO LATE [T] to be too late for something: We got there late and missed the beginning of the movie. | **miss the train/bus etc** I overslept and missed the train.
6 **miss a chance/opportunity** to fail to use an opportunity to do something: He certainly wasn't going to miss the chance of making some extra money. | Don't miss the

chance to see the breathtaking Dolomite Mountains. | The **opportunity** was **too good to miss** so we left immediately.
7 NOT SEE/HEAR [T] to not see, hear, or notice something, especially when it is difficult to notice: Maeve's sharp eyes missed nothing. | Perhaps there's something the police have missed. | It's a huge hotel on the corner. **You can't miss it** (=it is very easy to notice or recognize). | **You don't miss much**, do you (=you are good at noticing things)? | John **didn't miss a trick** (=noticed every opportunity to get an advantage) when it came to cutting costs.
8 **miss the point** to not understand the main point of what someone is saying
9 sth **is not to be missed** used to say that someone should do something while they have the opportunity: A journey on one of the steam trains is certainly not to be missed!
10 AVOID STH [T] to avoid something bad or unpleasant: If we leave now we should miss the traffic. | **miss doing sth** As he crossed the street, a bus just missed hitting him. | They **narrowly missed** being killed in the fire.
11 I **wouldn't miss it for the world** spoken used to say that you really want to go to an event, see something etc: 'Come to the party.' 'I will. I wouldn't miss it for the world.'
12 NOTICE STH ISN'T THERE [T] to notice that something or someone is not in the place you expect them to be: I didn't miss my wallet till it came to paying the bill.
13 **miss the mark** to not achieve something you were trying to do: Their efforts to improve quality have somewhat missed the mark.
14 **miss the boat** informal to fail to take an opportunity that will give you an advantage: You'll miss the boat if you don't buy shares now.
15 **without missing a beat** if you do something without missing a beat, you do it without showing that you are surprised or shocked: She handled all of their questions without missing a beat.
16 sb's **heart misses a beat** used to say that someone is very excited, surprised, or frightened: Glancing up at Rick's face, she felt her heart miss a beat .
17 ENGINE [I] if an engine misses, it stops working for a very short time and then starts again

miss out phr v
1 to not have the chance to do something that you enjoy and that would be good for you: Some children miss out because their parents can't afford to pay for school trips. | [+on] Prepare food in advance to ensure you don't miss out on the fun!
2 **miss sb/sth ⇔ out** BrE to not include someone or something: Make sure you don't miss any details out.

miss² S2 n
1 **Miss** used in front of the family name of a woman who is not married to address her politely, to write to her, or to talk about her; → **Mrs, Ms, Mr**: I'd like to make an appointment with Miss Taylor. △ Some unmarried women prefer to be addressed as **Ms** because it does not draw attention to whether or not they are married. → see also note at MR
2 **Miss Italy/Ohio/World** etc used to refer to a woman who represents a country, city etc in a beauty competition
3 YOUNG WOMAN spoken used as a polite way of speaking to a young woman whom you do not know her name; → **madam, sir**: Excuse me, miss, you've dropped your umbrella.
4 TEACHER BrE spoken used by children when speaking to a female teacher, whether she is married or not; → **sir**: I know the answer, Miss.
5 **give sth a miss** BrE informal to decide not to do something: I'd better give the coffee a miss. I'm due at a meeting in half an hour. '
6 NOT HIT/CATCH [C] an occasion when you fail to hit, catch, or hold something: Will he score a goal this time? No, no it's a miss.

7 YOUNG GIRL [C] *BrE spoken* a young girl, especially one who has been bad or rude: *She's a cheeky little miss.* → HIT-AND-MISS; → **near miss** at NEAR² (6)

mis·sal /'mɪsəl/ *n* [C] a book containing all the prayers said during each Mass for a whole year in the Roman Catholic church

mis·shap·en /ˌmɪsˈʃeɪpən, mɪˈʃeɪ-/ *adj* not the normal or natural shape: *an old woman struggling to walk on misshapen feet* | *misshapen carrots*

mis·sile /'mɪsaɪl $ 'mɪsəl/ *n* [C]   **1** a weapon that can fly over long distances and that explodes when it hits the thing it has been aimed at: *a **nuclear missile*** | *a missile attack*   **2** an object that is thrown at someone in order to hurt them: *Demonstrators threw missiles at the police.* → BALLISTIC MISSILE, CRUISE MISSILE, GUIDED MISSILE

miss·ing /'mɪsɪŋ/ *adj*   **1** something that is missing is not in its usual place, so that you cannot find it: *We found the missing piece of the jigsaw under the chair.* | *The keys have been missing for ages.* | [+from] *Two bottles were missing from the drugs cupboard.* | **go missing** *BrE: The scissors have gone missing again.*   **2** if part of something is missing, it is no longer attached or has been destroyed: *Two of her front teeth were missing.* | *The last page of the diary was missing.* | [+from] *There's a button missing from your shirt.*   **3** someone who is missing has disappeared, and no one knows if they are alive or dead: *Two crew members survived, but two are still missing.* | **go missing** *BrE: Nearly 100,000 young people go missing in Britain each year.* | *When Lily did not come home, her parents called the police to **report** her **missing**.*   **4** not present or not included in something: [+from] *Why is my name missing from the list?* | *Something was missing from her life.*   **5** **missing in action** a soldier who is missing in action has not returned after a battle and their body has not been found

missing ˈlink *n* [C]   **1** a piece of information that you need in order to solve a problem: *Could this be the missing link in the search for a cure for cancer?*   **2** **the missing link** an animal which was a stage in the development of humans from APES, whose bones have not yet been found

missing ˈperson *n plural* **missing persons** [C] someone who has disappeared and whose family has asked the police to try to find them

mis·sion /'mɪʃən/ *n* [C]
1 AIR FORCE/ARMY ETC an important job that involves travelling somewhere, done by a member of the airforce, army etc, or by a spacecraft: *He was sent on over 200 missions before being killed in action.* | [+to] *the first manned space mission to Mars* | *US troops taking part in the **peacekeeping mission***
2 JOB an important job that someone has been given to do, especially when they are sent to another place: *Her mission was to improve staff morale and output.* | **on a mission** *scientists on a mission to the rainforest, to study possible medicinal uses of plants* | **rescue/ diplomatic/fact-finding etc mission** *a group of US congressmen on a fact-finding mission to Northern Ireland*
3 DUTY something that you feel you must do because it is your duty; ☰ **calling, vocation**: *Momich's mission was to help young people in his local community.* | *His main **mission in life** is to earn as much money as possible.*
4 PURPOSE the purpose or the most important aim of an organization: *The mission of International House is to enable students of different cultures to live together and build life-long friendships.* → MISSION STATEMENT
5 GOVERNMENT a group of important people who are sent by their government to another country to discuss something or collect information; ☰ **delegation**: *a British trade mission to Moscow*
6 RELIGION a) religious work that involves going to a foreign country in order to teach people about Christianity or help poor people **b)** a building where this kind of work is done, or the people who work there
7 mission accomplished used when you have success-

fully achieved something that you were trying to do
8 woman/man with a mission someone who is very determined to achieve what they are trying to do – often used humorously

mis·sion·a·ry¹ /'mɪʃənəri $ -neri/ *n plural* **missionaries** [C] someone who has been sent to a foreign country to teach people about Christianity and persuade them to become Christians

missionary² *adj* [only before noun]   **1** relating to the work of missionaries: *missionary work* | *a missionary hospital*   **2 missionary zeal** if you do something with missionary zeal, you do it with great eagerness, because you believe strongly that it is a good thing to do: *a young English teacher, who taught poetry with missionary zeal*

ˈmissionary poˌsition *n* the missionary position the sexual position in which the woman lies on her back with the man on top of her and facing her

ˈmission ˌcontrol *n* [U] the people on earth who communicate with and guide a spacecraft

ˈmission ˌcreep *n* [U] *AmE* a series of gradual changes in the aim of a group of people, with the result that they do something different from what they planned to do at the beginning

ˈmission ˌstatement *n* [C]   **1** an official statement about the aims of a company or organization   **2 personal mission statement** a clear statement about what you want to achieve with your life: *Use a personal mission statement to chart your career course.*

mis·sis /'mɪsɪz/ *n* another spelling of MISSUS

mis·sive /'mɪsɪv/ *n* [C] *literary* a letter – often used humorously: *An anonymous missive had been pushed under her door.*

mis·spell /ˌmɪsˈspel/ *v past tense and past participle* **misspelt** /-ˈspelt/ *or* **misspelled** [T] to spell a word wrongly —**misspelling** *n* [C,U]

mis·spend /ˌmɪsˈspend/ *v past tense and past participle* **misspent** /-ˈspent/ [T]   **1 misspent youth** someone who had a misspent youth wasted their time or behaved badly when they were young – often used humorously   **2** to use time or money badly or wrongly: *Carey admitted misspending company funds.*

mis·step /'mɪs-step/ *n* [C] *AmE* a mistake, especially one that is caused by not understanding a situation correctly: *A misstep here could cost millions of dollars.*

mis·sus, missis /'mɪsɪz/ *n* [singular] *spoken informal*   **1** a man's wife, or girlfriend who lives with him: *How's the missus?*   **2** *BrE* used when speaking to a woman whose name you do not know: *Hey, missus, are these your kids?*

mist¹ /mɪst/ *n*   **1** [C,U] a light cloud low over the ground that makes it difficult for you to see very far; → **fog**: *We could just see the outline of the house through the mist.* | *Next morning, the whole town was **shrouded in mist** (=covered in mist).*   **2 lost in the mists of time** if something such as a fact or secret is lost in the mists of time, no one remembers it because it happened so long ago: *The real reasons for the war are now lost in the mists of time.*   **3 see sth through a mist of tears** *literary* to see something while you are crying

mist² *v* [T] to cover something with very small drops of liquid in order to keep it wet: *The plant has to be misted every day.*
mist over *phr v*   **1** if someone's eyes mist over, they become filled with tears: *His eyes misted over at the memory of his wife.*   **2** to mist up
mist up *phr v* if a piece of glass mists up, or if something mists it up, it becomes covered with very small drops of water so that you cannot see through it: **mist sth ⇔ up** *I can't see where I'm going, with the windows all misted up like this.*

mis·take¹ S2 W2 /mɪˈsteɪk/ n
1 [C] something that has been done in the wrong way, or an opinion or statement that is incorrect; → **error**

make a mistake
be full of mistakes/be littered with mistakes (=have a lot of mistakes in it)
spelling mistake
silly mistake
common mistake
honest mistake (=something not done deliberately)
admit your mistake (=admit that you have made a mistake)
correct a mistake
it is a mistake to think/assume/imagine etc that
there must be some mistake (=used when you think someone has made a mistake)

[+in] *We may have made a mistake in our calculations.* | *a mistake in the law* | *Ivan's work is always full of mistakes.* | *The article was littered with spelling mistakes.* | *One silly mistake cost them the match.* | *The most common mistake is to plant them too deep.* | *Please believe me. It was an honest mistake.* | *Did he admit his mistake?* | *He warned that correcting the mistakes of the present administration would not be easy.* | *It is a mistake to think that violence can bring a solution to our problems.* | *There must be some mistake with the bill.*

⚠ Do not say 'do a mistake'. Say **make a mistake.**; → see box at FAULT¹

2 [C] something you do that is not sensible or has a bad result: *Buying the house seemed a great idea at the time, but now I can see it was a mistake.* | *It's your decision, but I warn you – you're making a mistake.* | **make the mistake of doing sth** *I stupidly made the mistake of giving them my phone number.* | **big/terrible/ghastly etc mistake** *Marrying him was the biggest mistake she ever made.* | *It proved to be a costly mistake.* | *She only realized her mistake when it was too late.* | *Some of our decisions were wrong, but you have to learn from your mistakes.* | **make the same mistake (again/twice)** *I don't intend to make the same mistake again.*
3 by mistake if you do something by mistake, you do it without intending to; ◙ **accidentally**; ◙ **deliberately, on purpose**: *Someone must have left the door open by mistake.* | *I'm sorry, this letter is addressed to you – I opened it by mistake.*
4 we all make mistakes *spoken* used to tell someone not to be worried because they have made a mistake
5 make no mistake (about it) *spoken* used to emphasize that what you are saying is true, especially when you are warning about something serious or dangerous: *Make no mistake, this is the most serious threat our industry has ever seen.*
6 and no mistake *BrE spoken informal* used to emphasize the description you have just given: *Miles was a heartbreaker, and no mistake!*

mistake² v *past tense* **mistook** /-ˈstʊk/ *past participle* **mistaken** /-ˈsteɪkən/ [T] **1** to understand something wrongly: *She mistook my meaning entirely.* | *Ken mistook her concern, thinking she was interested in him for another reason.* **2 you can't mistake sb/sth** used to say that someone or something is very easy to recognize: *You can't mistake her. She's the one with the long red hair.* **3 there is no mistaking sb/sth** used to say that you are certain about something: *There's no mistaking whose children they are – they all look just like Joe.*
mistake sb/sth for sb/sth *phr v* to wrongly think that one person or thing is someone or something else: *A woman mistook him for a well-known actor, and asked him for his autograph.* | *The doctor mistook the symptoms for blood poisoning.*

mis·tak·en /mɪˈsteɪkən/ *adj* **1 be mistaken** if you are mistaken, you are wrong about something that you thought you knew or saw: *It can't have been my car. You must be mistaken.* | *I thought he said 12 o'clock, but I*

might have been mistaken. | *We bought the rug in Turkey, if I'm not mistaken.* **2 mistaken belief/idea/impression/view etc** a mistaken belief etc is not correct: *Marijuana has few withdrawal effects, and this has given rise to the mistaken belief that it is not addictive.* —**mistakenly** *adv*

mis,taken i'dentity n [U] a situation in which someone believes that they have seen a particular person when in fact it was someone else – used especially in relation to crimes: *The police arrested someone, but it turned out to be a case of mistaken identity.*

mis·ter /ˈmɪstə $ -ər/ n **1 Mister** the full form of MR
⚠ In people's names, Mister is always written **Mr. 2** *spoken especially AmE* used to address a man whose name you do not know: *Thanks, mister.*

mis·time /ˌmɪsˈtaɪm/ v [T] to do something at not quite the right time.: *He mistimed his kick and missed the ball.*

mis·tle·toe /ˈmɪsəltəʊ $ -toʊ/ n [U] a plant with small white berries, which grows on trees. It is traditional to kiss people under a piece of mistletoe at Christmas.

mis·took /mɪˈstʊk/ v the past tense of MISTAKE

mis·treat /ˌmɪsˈtriːt/ v [T] to treat a person or animal badly, especially in a cruel way; ◙ **ill-treat, maltreat**: *Security forces are accused of mistreating prisoners.* —**mistreatment** n [U]

mis·tress /ˈmɪstrɪs/ n [C] **1** a woman that a man has a sexual relationship with, even though he is married to someone else: *The Prince had shocked society by living openly with his mistress.* **2** *BrE old-fashioned* a female teacher; → **master**: *the new English mistress* **3** the female owner of a dog, horse etc; → **master 4** *old-fashioned* the female employer of a servant; → **master**: *The maid looked nervously at her mistress.* **5 be (a/the) mistress of sth** if a woman is a mistress of something, she is in control of it, highly skilled at it etc; → **master**: *She appeared to be very much the mistress of the situation.* **6 Mistress** *old use* used with a woman's family name as a polite way of speaking to her; → **master**

mis·tri·al /ˌmɪsˈtraɪəl/ n [C] a TRIAL in a court of law which is unfair, so that a new trial has to be held: *The defense attorney argued that the judge should declare a mistrial.*

mis·trust¹ /mɪsˈtrʌst/ n [U] the feeling that you cannot trust someone, especially because you think they may treat you unfairly or dishonestly; ◙ **suspicion, distrust**: [+of] *He had a deep mistrust of the legal profession.*

mistrust² v [T] to not trust someone, especially because you think they may treat you unfairly or dishonestly; ◙ **distrust**: *As a very small child she had learned to mistrust adults.* —**mistrustful** *adj*: *Some people are very mistrustful of computerised banking.*

mist·y /ˈmɪsti/ *adj* **1** misty weather is weather with a lot of mist: *a cold, misty morning* **2** *literary* if your eyes are misty, they are full of tears, especially because you are remembering a time in the past: *He paused, his eyes growing misty.* | *Whenever Maria sees a picture of her mother, she gets misty-eyed.* **3** not clear or bright: *Without my glasses everything is just a misty blur.*

mis·un·der·stand /ˌmɪsʌndəˈstænd $ -ər-/ v *past tense and past participle* **misunderstood** [I,T] to fail to understand someone or something correctly: *Rachel, you must have misunderstood her! Ellie would never say something like that.* | *Don't misunderstand me. She's a very nice person when you get to know her.*

mis·un·der·stand·ing /ˌmɪsʌndəˈstændɪŋ $ -ər-/ n **1** [C,U] a problem caused by someone not understanding a question, situation, or instruction correctly: *There must have been some misunderstanding. I didn't order all those books.* **2** [C] an argument or disagreement that is not very serious – often used humorously: *Terry had a little misunderstanding with the police last night.*

mis·un·der·stood/ˌmɪsʌndəˈstʊd $ -ɚ-/ adj used to describe someone who is not liked by other people in a way that is unfair, because they do not understand him or her: *Rodman claims that he is misunderstood, and that the media has always portrayed him unfairly.*

mis·use¹/ˌmɪsˈjuːz/ v [T]   **1** to use something for the wrong purpose, or in the wrong way, often with harmful results: *Even harmless drugs can be misused.* | *The term 'schizophrenia' is often misused.* | *There is concern that the judges might misuse their power.*   **2** to treat someone badly or unfairly

mis·use²/mɪsˈjuːs/ n [C,U] the use of something in the wrong way or for the wrong purpose; ▤ **abuse**: *a system designed to prevent credit card misuse* | **drug/ alcohol misuse** *Children who begin smoking when young are at greater risk from drugs misuse.* | [+of] *a scandalous misuse of public funds*

mite/maɪt/ n [C]   **1** a very small creature that lives in plants, CARPETS etc   **2** *spoken* a small child, especially one that you feel sorry for: *Poor mite! You must be starving!*   **3 a mite** slightly; ▤ **a bit**: *She's a mite shy.* | *It's a mite too big for the box.*   **4 a mite of sth** old-fashioned a small amount of something

mi·ter/ˈmaɪtə $ -ɚ/ n the American spelling of MITRE

mit·i·gate/ˈmɪtɪɡeɪt/ v [T] *formal* to make a situation or the effects of something less unpleasant, harmful, or serious; ▤ **alleviate**: *Measures need to be taken to mitigate the environmental effects of burning more coal.*

mit·i·gat·ing /ˈmɪtɪɡeɪtɪŋ/ adj **mitigating circumstances/factors** facts about a situation that make a crime or bad mistake seem less serious: *Judges often give reduced sentences where there are mitigating circumstances.*

mit·i·ga·tion /ˌmɪtɪˈɡeɪʃən/ n [U]   **1 in mitigation** *law* if you say something in mitigation, you try to make someone's crime or mistake seem less serious or show that they were not completely responsible: *The captain added, in mitigation, that the engines may have been faulty.*   **2** *formal* a reduction in how unpleasant, harmful, or serious a situation is: *His marriage had brought a slight mitigation of the monotony of his existence.*

mi·tre *BrE*; **miter** *AmE* /ˈmaɪtə $ -ɚ/ n [C]   **1** a tall pointed hat worn by BISHOPS and ARCHBISHOPS   **2** also **mitre joint** a joint between two pieces of wood, in which each piece is cut at an angle

mitt/mɪt/ n [C]   **1** a type of GLOVE that does not have separate parts for each finger; ▤ **mitten**: *ski mitts* | *an oven mitt* (=a thick glove used to protect your hand when you hold hot pans)   **2** a type of leather GLOVE used to catch a ball in BASEBALL   **3** *informal especially BrE* someone's hand: *Robert's put his sticky mitts all over it.*

mit·ten/ˈmɪtn/ n [C] a type of GLOVE that does not have separate parts for each finger → see picture at GLOVE

mix¹ S2 W3 /mɪks/ v

1 [I,T] if you mix two or more substances or if they mix, they combine to become a single substance, and they cannot be easily separated: *Oil and water don't mix.* | **mix (sth) with sth** *Shake the bottle well so that the oil mixes with the vinegar.* | *The powder is mixed with cold water to form a paste.* | *Mix the soured cream with ketchup and tomatoes.* | **mix sth together** *First mix the butter and sugar together, then add the milk.* | **mix sth in** *Mix in 75g of butter.* | **mix sth into sth** *Mix the herbs into the sauce.*

2 [T] to combine two or more different activities, ideas, groups of things etc: *Their musical style mixes elements of Eastern culture and Western pop.* | **mix sth with sth** *His books mix historical fact with fantasy.* | *I don't like to* **mix business with pleasure** (=combine business and social activities at the same time).

3 [I] to meet, talk, and spend time with other people, especially people you do not know very well; ▤ **socialize**: [+with] *Charlie doesn't mix well with the other children.*

4 not mix if two different ideas, activities etc do not mix, there are problems when they are combined:

Smoking and babies don't mix.

5 [T] also **mix up** to prepare something, especially food or drink, by mixing things together: *Will you mix us some martinis, Bill?*

6 mix and match to choose to put different things together from a range of possibilities: *They can mix and match their uniform, wearing either a sweatshirt or blouse with trousers or a skirt.*

7 [T] *technical* to control the balance of sounds in a record or film

8 mix it (up) *informal* to get involved in a fight with someone: *You don't want to mix it with him. He's been drinking since noon.*

mix sb/sth ⇔ up phr v

1 to make the mistake of thinking that someone or something is another person or thing; ▤ **confuse**, **muddle up**: [+with] *I always mix him up with his brother. They look so much alike.* | *I think you might be mixing up Wetherall and Newton.* | *I must have got the times mixed up.*

2 to change the way things have been arranged, often by mistake, so that they are no longer in the same order: *My papers got all mixed up.* | *Books on Scottish history were mixed up with books on volcanoes.*

3 to make someone feel confused: *They kept trying to mix me up.*

4 to prepare something by mixing things together: *It was hard work mixing up four tonnes of cement.* → MIXED UP, MIX-UP

mix² n   **1** [singular] the particular combination of things or people in a group or thing: [+of] *a good mix of people* | *We felt that between us we had the right mix of skills.* | *a complicated mix of colours and textures* | *the region's rich ethnic mix* (=people of different races)   **2** [C,U] a combination of substances that you mix together to make something such as a cake; ▤ **mixture**: **cake/soup etc mix** *Add water to the cake mix and bake at 375°F.*   **3** [C] a particular arrangement of sounds, voices, or different pieces of music used on a POP record: *the dance mix*

mixed S2 /mɪkst/ adj

1 [only before noun] consisting of several different types of things or people: *a very mixed group of women* | *a mixed salad*

2 mixed feelings/emotions if you have mixed feelings or emotions about something, you are not sure whether you like, agree with or feel happy about it: [+about] *I had mixed feelings about meeting Laura again.* | *He watched with mixed emotions.*

3 mixed reaction/response/reviews etc if something gets a mixed reaction etc, some people say they like it or agree with it, but others dislike it or disagree with it: *The film has had mixed reviews from the critics.* | *Media coverage of the event was mixed.*

4 *especially BrE* for both males and females: *a mixed school*

5 a mixed blessing something that is good in some ways but bad in others: *Having your parents living nearby is a mixed blessing.*

6 a mixed bag a) a group of things or people that are all very different from each other: [+of] *The concert was a mixed bag of classical and modern music.* | *Club-goers are a mixed bag these days, and so are the places they go clubbing.* **b)** something that includes both good and bad parts: *The meat was very good, but the vegetables were rather a mixed bag.*

7 (of) mixed race having parents of different races: *children of mixed race*

8 in mixed company when you are with people of both sexes: *It's not the sort of joke you tell in mixed company.* → **mixed metaphor** at METAPHOR (2)

mixed a·bil·i·ty adj [only before noun] a mixed ability school or class teaches all children of the same age together, even if they have different levels of ability: *a mixed ability group* | *mixed ability teaching*

M

,mixed 'doubles *n* [U] a game in a sport such as tennis in which a man and a woman play against another man and woman

,mixed e'conomy *n* [C] an economic system in which some industries are owned by the government and some are owned by private companies

,mixed 'farming *n* [U] a system of farming in which you grow crops and keep animals

,mixed 'grill *n* [C] *BrE* a dish consisting of meats such as SAUSAGE, BACON, LIVER etc which have all been GRILLED

,mixed 'marriage *n* [C,U] a marriage between two people from different races or religions

,mixed 'media *n* [U] a combination of substances or materials that are used in a painting, SCULPTURE etc

,mixed 'up *adj* **1 be/get mixed up in sth** to be involved in an illegal or dishonest activity: *He's the last person I'd expect to be mixed up in something like this.* | *I'd have to be crazy to get mixed up in that kind of thing.* **2 be/get mixed up with sb** to be involved with someone who has a bad influence on you: *When he left college he got mixed up with the wrong people.* **3** [not before noun] confused, for example because you have too many different details to remember or think about: *I get all mixed up over the money whenever I travel abroad.* **4** also **mixed-up** *informal* confused and suffering from emotional problems; ▤ **screwed up**: *She's just a crazy mixed-up kid.* → **mix up** at MIX[1]; → MIX-UP

mix·er /'mɪksə $ -ər/ *n* [C] **1** a piece of equipment used to mix things together: *an electric food mixer* | *a cement mixer* | *a shower mixer* → see picture at EAT **2** a piece of equipment or computer software which is used to control the sound levels or picture quality of a recording or film, or a person whose job is to use this equipment: *an audio mixer* **3** a drink that can be mixed with alcohol, especially to make a COCKTAIL: *We can use tonic water or orange juice as mixers.* **4 good mixer** someone who finds it easy to talk to people they do not know: *Media people need to be good mixers and good talkers.* **5** *AmE old-fashioned* a party held so that people who have just met can get to know each other better: *Are you going to the freshman mixer?*

'mixer tap *n* [C] *BrE* a TAP which both hot and cold water come through together

'mixing bowl *n* [C] a large bowl used for mixing things such as flour and sugar for making cakes → see picture at MATERIAL[1]

mix·tape /'mɪksteɪp/ *n* [C] a piece of music that is produced by mixing different voices or musical instruments that have already been recorded: *All types of electronic dance music mixtapes for sale.* | *mixtape CDs*

mix·ture S3 W3 /'mɪkstʃə $ -ər/ *n*
1 [C] a combination of two or more different things, feelings, or types of people: [+of] *The town is a mixture of the old and the new.* | *The mixture of different people living in the city* | *She felt a strange mixture of excitement and fear.* | *a mixture of emotions*
2 [C,U] a liquid or other substance made by mixing several substances together, especially in cooking; → **compound**: [+of] *Fill the bread with a mixture of lettuce, tomatoes, and cucumbers.* | *Pour the mixture into four small dishes.*
3 [C] *technical* a combination of substances that are put together but do not mix with each other

'mix-up *n* [C] *informal* a mistake that causes confusion about details or arrangements: [+in] *Geoffrey rushed in late pleading a mix-up in his diary.* | [+between] *A council official blamed a mix-up between departments.* | [+over] *There was a mix-up over the hotel booking.*

miz·zen /'mɪzən/ *n* [C] **1** also **mizzen mast** the MAST behind the main mast on a sailing ship **2** also **mizzen sail** the main sail on a mizzen on a sailing ship

Mk the written abbreviation of *mark*

ml *plural* ml *or* mls the written abbreviation of *millilitre* or millilitres

m'lady, milady /mɪˈleɪdi/ *n old use* used by a servant to address a woman who belongs to a NOBLE family: *Will that be all, m'lady?*

MLitt, M.Litt. /,em 'lɪt/ *n* [C] *BrE Master of Letters* a university degree that you can get at some British universities by studying for two years after your first degree

M'lord /mᵊˈlɔːd $ -ˈlɔːrd/ *n* **1** used to address a judge **2** *old use* used by a servant to address a man who belongs to a NOBLE family

M'lud /mᵊˈlʌd/ *n* used to address a judge in a British court of law (=short for 'my lord')

mm[1] the written abbreviation of *millimetre* or millimetres

mm[2] /m/ used when someone else is speaking and you want to show that you are listening, that you agree with them, or that you are thinking about what they have said: *'That's okay, isn't it?' 'Mm yeah.'* | *Mm, I see what you mean.*

mne·mon·ic /nɪˈmɒnɪk $ nɪˈmɑː-/ *n* [C] something such as a poem or a sentence that you use to help you remember a rule, a name etc —**mnemonic** *adj*

mo /məʊ $ moʊ/ *n* [singular] *BrE spoken* a very short period of time; ▤ **moment**: *Wait a mo!* | *I'll be back in a mo.*

mo. *AmE* the written abbreviation of *month*

M.O. also MO *BrE* /,em 'əʊ $ -'oʊ/ *n* **1** [singular] *modus operandi* a way of doing something that is typical of a particular person or group **2** [C] *especially BrE medical officer* an army doctor

moan[1] /məʊn $ moʊn/ *v* **1** [I,T] *informal* to complain in an annoying way, especially in an unhappy voice and without good reason: *'I feel seasick already,' she moaned.* | [+about] *A lot of people moaned about the parking problems.* | [+at] *BrE: My mum never stops moaning at me.* | **moan that** *He's always moaning that we use too much electricity.* | *He moaned and groaned all the way there.* **2** [I] to make a long low sound expressing pain, unhappiness, or sexual pleasure; ▤ **groan**: *She moaned and cried out in pain.* **3** [I] *literary* if the wind moans, it makes a long low sound: *They could hear the wind moaning in the trees.* —**moaner** *n* [C] *BrE: Dad's a gloomy old moaner.*

moan[2] *n* [C] **1** a long low sound expressing pain, unhappiness, or sexual pleasure: [+of] *There was a moan of pain from the injured man.* | *She gave a little moan of pleasure.* | *a low moan* **2 have a moan (about sth)** *BrE informal* to complain about something: *We were just having a moan about work.* **3** *literary* a low sound made by the wind

moat /məʊt $ moʊt/ *n* [C] **1** a deep wide hole, usually filled with water, dug around a castle as a defence **2** a deep wide hole dug around an area used for animals in a ZOO to stop them from escaping —**moated** *adj*

mob[1] /mɒb $ mɑːb/ *n* [C] **1** a large noisy crowd, especially one that is angry and violent: [+of] *a mob of a few hundred demonstrators* | *They were immediately surrounded by the mob.* | *The leadership had been criticized for giving in to* **mob rule** (=when a mob controls the situation rather than the government or the law). **2** *informal* a group of people of the same type; ▤ **gang**: [+of] *The usual mob of teenagers were standing on the corner.* | **the heavy mob** *BrE* (=group of strong violent men) *What happens if they send the heavy mob round to find him?* **3 the Mob** the MAFIA (=a powerful organization of criminals) **4 the mob** *old use* an insulting expression meaning all the poorest and least educated people in society **5 mob of sheep/cattle** *AusE* a large group of sheep or cattle

mob[2] *v* **mobbed, mobbing** [T] **1** if people mob a famous person, they rush to get close to them and form a crowd around them: *Fans ran onto the pitch and mobbed the batsman.* **2** if a group of birds or animals mob another bird or animal, they all attack it

'mob cap *n* [C] a light cotton hat with a decorative edge, worn by women in the 18th and 19th centuries

mo·bile¹ /'məʊbaɪl $ 'moʊbəl, -biːl/ *adj* **1** not fixed in one position, and easy to move and use in different places: *mobile air-conditioners* **2** moving or able to move from one job, area, or social class to another: *a more mobile workforce | People these days are much more socially mobile. | an upwardly mobile* (=moving to a higher social scale) *professional* **3** able to move or travel easily; ⯈ **immobile**: *She's more mobile now that she has her own car.* **4** mobile library/shop/clinic etc *BrE* a shop etc that is kept in a vehicle and driven from place to place: *Two mobile units provide healthcare in rural villages.* **5** mobile mouth/face/features *written* features that can change their expression quickly: *His mobile features registered amusement.*

mo·bile² /'məʊbaɪl $ 'moʊbiːl/ *n* [C] **1** *BrE* a MOBILE PHONE; ⯈ **cellphone** *AmE*: *Give me a call on my mobile. | Have you got my mobile number?* **2** a decoration made of small objects tied to wires or string which is hung up so that the objects move when air blows around them

,**mobile 'home** *n* [C] **1** *AmE* a type of house made of metal, that can be pulled by a vehicle and moved to another place **2** *BrE* a large CARAVAN which always stays in the same place and is used as a house; ⯈ **trailer** *AmE*

,**mobile 'phone** *n* [C] a telephone that you can carry with you and use in any place; ⯈ **cellular phone** *AmE*: *mobile phone users* → see picture at OFFICE

> mobile phone *BrE*/
> cellular phone *AmE*

mo·bil·i·ty /məʊ'bɪləti $ moʊ-/ *n* [U] **1** the ability to move easily from one job, area, or social class to another: *social mobility | [+of] There is greater mobility of labour* (=movement of workers) *between jobs and areas. | upward/downward mobility jobs and opportunities for upward mobility* **2** the ability to move easily: *It improves the strength and mobility of joints. | The key to the army's effectiveness is its increased mobility. | mobility allowance BrE* (=money paid to sick or disabled people to help pay for transport)

mo·bil·ize also **-ise** *BrE* /'məʊbɪlaɪz $ 'moʊ-/ *v* **1** [T] to encourage people to support something in an active way: *an attempt to mobilize popular opinion | a campaign to mobilize support for the strike* **2** [T] to start to use the things or people you have available in order to achieve something: *They failed to mobilize their resources effectively.* **3** [I,T] if a country mobilizes or mobilizes its army, it prepares to fight a war; → **demobilize** **4** [T] to help something to move more easily: *The physiotherapist mobilizes the patient's shoulder.* —**mobilization** /ˌməʊbɪlaɪ'zeɪʃən $ ˌmoʊbələ-/ *n* [C,U]: *the mobilization of public opinion*

mob·ster /'mɒbstə $ 'mɑːbstər/ *n* [C] *especially AmE* a member of an organized criminal group; ⯈ **gangster**

moc·ca·sin /'mɒkəsɪn $ 'mɑː-/ *n* [C] a flat comfortable shoe made of soft leather

moch·a /'mɒkə $ 'moʊkə/ *n* [U] **1** a type of coffee **2** a combination of coffee and chocolate

moch·ac·ci·no /ˌmɒkə'tʃiːnəʊ $ ˌmoʊkə'tʃiːnoʊ/ *n plural* **mochaccinos** [C,U] a drink made of strong coffee, chocolate or COCOA, and hot milk

mock¹ /mɒk $ mɑːk/ *v* **1** [I,T] *formal* to laugh at someone or something and try to make them look stupid by saying unkind things about them or by copying them; ⯈ **make fun of**: *Opposition MPs mocked the government's decision. | 'Running away?' he mocked. | It's easy for you to mock, but we put a lot of work into this play.* **2** [T] *formal* to make something seem completely useless: *Violent attacks like this mock the peace process.* —**mocking** *adj*: *Her tone was mock-*

ing. —**mockingly** *adv*: *His lips twisted mockingly.* —**mocker** *n* [C]

mock sth ⇔ **up** *phr v* to make a FULL-SIZE model of something so that it looks real → MOCK-UP

mock² *adj* [only before noun] **1** not real, but intended to be very similar to a real situation, substance etc: *war games with mock battles | a mock interview | mock marble floors* **2** mock surprise/horror/indignation etc surprise etc that you pretend to feel, especially as a joke: *She threw her hands up in mock horror.*

mock³ *n* **1** mocks [plural] *BrE* school examinations taken as practice before official examinations: *I'm revising for my mocks.* **2** make mock of sb *literary* to mock someone

mock- /mɒk $ mɑːk/ *prefix* **1** used to show that an attitude or feeling is pretended, not real: *a mock-serious expression | His frown was mock-severe.* **2** copying a particular style, especially of building: *a mock-Tudor fireplace*

mock·ers /'mɒkəz $ 'mɑːkərz/ *n* put the mockers on sth *BrE informal* to spoil an event or someone's plans, or to bring someone bad luck: *Without wishing to put the mockers on things, I'd like to know where the money is going to come from.*

mock·e·ry /'mɒkəri $ 'mɑː-/ *n* **1** make a mockery of sth to make something such as a plan or system seem completely useless or ineffective: *This building plan makes a mockery of the government's environmental policy.* **2** [U] when someone laughs at someone or something or shows that they think they are stupid: *There was a hint of mockery in his voice.* **3** [singular] something that is completely useless or ineffective: *She said that the trial had been a mockery.*

mock·ing·bird /'mɒkɪŋbɜːd $ 'mɑːkɪŋbɜːrd/ *n* [C] an American bird that copies the songs of other birds

,**mock 'turtleneck** *n* [C] *AmE* a type of TURTLENECK SWEATER

'**mock-up** *n* [C] a full size model of something, made before the real thing is built, or made for a film, show etc: *[+of] a mock-up of the system | a mock-up of a submarine* → mock up at MOCK¹

mod /mɒd $ mɑːd/ *n* [C] *BrE* a member of a group of young people in Britain in the 1960s who wore a particular type of neat clothes, listened to SOUL MUSIC, and drove MOTOR SCOOTERS; → **rocker**

mo·dal¹ /'məʊdl $ 'moʊdl/ *n* [C] a modal verb

modal² *adj technical* **1** [only before noun] modal meanings are concerned with the attitude of the speaker to the hearer or to what is being said **2** related to or written in a musical MODE (5) —**modality** /məʊ'dæləti $ moʊ-/ *n* [U]

,**modal aux'iliary** *n* [C] a modal verb

,**modal 'verb** also **modal** *n* [C] *technical* one of these verb forms: can, could, may, might, shall, should, will, would, must, ought to, used to, need, had better, and DARE. They are all used with other verbs to express ideas such as possibility, permission, or intention; → **auxiliary verb**

mod cons /ˌmɒd 'kɒnz $ ˌmɑːd 'kɑːnz/ *n* all mod cons *BrE informal* all the things that are fitted in modern houses to make life easy and comfortable: *a property with many interesting features and all mod cons*

mode W3 /məʊd $ moʊd/ *n* [C] **1** *formal* a particular way or style of behaving, living or doing something: *[+of] the most efficient mode of transport | They have a relaxed mode of life that suits them well. | Western modes of thought* **2** *technical* a particular way in which a machine or piece of equipment can operate: *Set the monitor to 256 colour mode. | To get out of the 'auto' mode on the camera, turn the knob to 'M'.* **3** be in work mode/holiday mode etc *informal* to have a particular feeling or way of thinking or behaving, because of the situation you are in: *With only minutes to go, we were now in panic mode.* **4 be the mode** *formal* to be fashionable at a particular time: *Long skirts were then the mode.* **5** *technical* one of various systems of arranging notes in music, such as MAJOR and MINOR in Western music → À LA MODE, MODISH

M

mod·el[1] [S2] [W1] /ˈmɒdl $ ˈmɑːdl/ *n* [C] **1** SMALL COPY a small copy of a building, vehicle, machine etc, especially one that can be put together from separate parts: [+of] *They showed us a model of the building.* | *a **working model** (=one with parts which move) of a steam engine* **2** FASHION someone whose job is to show clothes, hair styles etc by wearing them at fashion shows or for photographs: *a top fashion model* | *a male model* **3** TYPE OF CAR ETC a particular type or design of a vehicle or machine: *Renault are introducing three new models at the show.* | *Our dishwasher is the **latest model** (=newest design).* | *the 2.8 litre V6 model* **4** DESCRIPTION a computer representation or scientific description of something: [+of] *Scientists are building computer models of the ocean currents.* **5** SB/STH TO COPY someone or something which people want to copy because they are successful or have good qualities: [+for] *It served as a model for other cities.* | *He used English medieval architecture as his model.* | ***role model** (=someone that you try to copy because they have qualities you would like to have) Good teachers can act as **positive role models**.* **6** model of efficiency/virtue etc someone or something that has a lot of a good quality: *She was a model of honesty and decency.* **7** ART someone who is employed by an artist or photographer to be painted or photographed

model[2] *adj* **1 model aircraft/train/car etc** a small copy of an aircraft, train etc, especially one that a child can play with or put together from separate parts: *He spent hours playing with his model railway.* | *She builds model aeroplanes in her spare time.* **2 model wife/ employee/student etc** a wife, EMPLOYEE (=worker) etc who is considered to be good because they do everything they should; ◼ **exemplary**: *His lawyers tried to show him as a model husband and father.* **3 model prison/farm/school etc** a prison etc that has been specially designed or organized to be as good as possible

model[3] *v* **modelled, modelling** *BrE*, **modeled, modeling** *AmE* **1** [I,T] to wear clothes at a fashion show or in magazine photographs in order to show them to people: *She's modeling Donna Karan's fall collection.* | *Claire modelled for a few years when she was in her twenties.* **2 model yourself on sb** *BrE*; **model yourself after sb** *AmE* to try to be like someone else because you admire them: *Jim had always modelled himself on his great hero, Martin Luther King.* **3 be modelled on sth** to be designed in a way that copies another system or way of doing something: *Their education system is modelled on the French one.* **4** [T] to do a computer representation or scientific description of a situation or event: *They used a computer to model the possible effects of global warming.* **5** [T] to make something by shaping clay, wood etc —**modeller** *n* [C]

mod·el·ling *BrE*; **modeling** *AmE* /ˈmɒdl-ɪŋ $ ˈmɑː-/ *n* [U] **1** the work of a fashion model: *a career in modelling* **2** the process of making a scientific or computer model of something to show how it works or to understand it better: [+of] *computer modelling of the system* | *economic modelling* **3** the activity of making models of objects

mo·dem /ˈməʊdəm, -dem $ ˈmoʊ-/ *n* [C] a piece of electronic equipment that allows information from one computer to be sent along telephone wires to another computer

mod·e·rate[1] /ˈmɒdərɪt $ ˈmɑː-/ *adj* **1** not very large or very small, very hot or very cold, very fast or very slow etc: *Even moderate amounts of alcohol can be dangerous.* | *a moderate degree of success* | *a student of only moderate ability* | *Moderate exercise, such as walking or swimming, is recommended.* | *Bake the pie for 30 minutes in a moderate oven.* | *moderate to strong winds* **2** having opinions or beliefs, especially about politics, that are not extreme and that most people consider reasonable; ◼ **extreme**: *the more moderate members of the party* | *a moderate politician* **3** staying within reasonable or sensible limits; ◼ **immoderate**: *a moderate smoker* | *moderate wage demands* → MODERATELY

mod·e·rate[2] /ˈmɒdəreɪt $ ˈmɑː-/ *v* [I,T] **1** *formal* to make something less extreme or violent, or to become less extreme or violent: *The students moderated their demands.* | *He learnt to moderate his anger.* **2** *BrE* to do the work of a MODERATOR

mod·e·rate[3] /ˈmɒdərɪt $ ˈmɑː-/ *n* [C] someone whose opinions or beliefs, especially about politics, are not extreme and are considered reasonable by most people; ◼ **extremist**, **hardliner**: *He's coming under pressure from moderates in the party.*

mod·e·rate·ly /ˈmɒdərɪtli $ ˈmɑː-/ *adv* **1** fairly, but not very; ◼ **reasonably**: *a moderately successful film* | *He did moderately well in the exams.* **2** in a way which is not extreme or stays within reasonable limits: *He drinks moderately.* **3 moderately priced** neither cheap nor expensive: *Both hotels are moderately priced.*

mod·e·ra·tion /ˌmɒdəˈreɪʃən $ ˌmɑː-/ *n* [U] **1 in moderation** if you do something in moderation, such as drinking alcohol or eating certain foods, you do not do it too much; ◼ **to excess**: *Some people think drinking in moderation can prevent heart disease.* **2** *formal* control of your behaviour, so that you keep your actions, feelings, habits etc within reasonable limits: [+in] *Moderation in diet is the way to good health.* | *He encouraged moderation and toleration on religious issues.* **3** *formal* reduction in force, degree, speed etc

mod·e·ra·to /ˌmɒdəˈrɑːtəʊ $ ˌmɑːdəˈrɑːtoʊ/ *adj, adv* at an average speed – used as an instruction on how fast to play a piece of music

mod·e·ra·tor /ˈmɒdəreɪtə $ ˈmɑːdəreɪtər/ *n* [C] **1** someone whose job is to control a discussion or an argument between people **2** *BrE* someone who makes sure that an examination is fair, and that the marks given are fair and correct **3** a religious leader who is in charge of the council of the Presbyterian and United Reformed Churches

mod·ern [S1] [W1] /ˈmɒdn $ ˈmɑːdərn/ *adj* **1** [only before noun] belonging to the present time or most recent time; ◼ **contemporary**: *Such companies must change if they are to compete **in the modern world**.* | *They are the youngest children **in modern times** to face murder charges.* | *Smaller families are a feature of **modern society**.* | *Computers are an essential part of **modern life**.* | *a book about **modern history*** | *The original supermarkets were small by modern standards.* | **Modern Greek/Hebrew etc** *(=the form of the language used today)* **2** made or done using the most recent designs or methods; ◼ **up-to-date**: *A lot of progress has been made with the use of **modern technology**.* | *advances in **modern medicine*** | *modern surgical techniques* **3** [only before noun] modern art, music, literature etc uses styles that have been recently developed and are very different from traditional styles; ◼ **contemporary**: *an exhibition of **modern art*** | *modern dance* **4** having very recent attitudes or ways of behaving; ◼ **progressive**; ◼ **traditional**: *The school is very modern in its approach to sex education.* → SECONDARY MODERN

modern-day *adj* [only before noun] existing in the present time – used when comparing someone or something to a person or thing in the past; ◼ **present-day**, **contemporary**: *She's a modern-day Joan of Arc.* | *The modern-day diet has too little fiber in it.*

mod·ern·is·m /'mɒdənɪzəm $ 'mɑːdər-/ n [U] a style of art, building etc that was popular especially from the 1940s to the 1960s, in which artists used simple shapes and modern artificial materials; → **post-modernism**: _the rise of modernism in Paris_ — **modernist** adj, n [C]: _the modernist school_

mod·ern·ist·ic /ˌmɒdə'nɪstɪk◄ $ -ˌmɑːdər-/ adj designed in a way that looks very modern and very different from previous styles; **adj traditional**: _a mod-ernistic office building_

mo·der·ni·ty /mɒ'dɜːnˌti $ mə'dɜːr-/ n [U] formal the quality of being modern: _a conflict between tradition and modernity_

mod·ern·ize also **-ise** BrE /'mɒdənaɪz $ 'mɑːdər-/ v **1** [T] to make something such as a system or build-ing more modern: _They need more funds to modernize the country's telephone system._ | _a tastefully modernized old farmhouse_ **2** [I] to start using more modern meth-ods and equipment: _The business will lose money if it doesn't modernize._ —**modernizer** n [C]: _the conflict between the modernizers and the conservatives_ —**modernization** /ˌmɒdənaɪ'zeɪʃən $ ˌmɑːdərnə-/ n [C,U]: _the modernization of the railway system_

ˌmodern 'language n [C] BrE a language which is used now, especially a European language such as French or Italian, studied as a subject at school or university: _a degree in modern languages_

ˌmodern pen'tathlon n [singular] a sports competi-tion that involves running, swimming, riding horses, FENCING, and shooting guns

mod·est /'mɒdˌst $ 'mɑː-/ adj
1 NOT PROUD someone who is modest does not want to talk about their abilities or achievements; **adj immodest, boastful**: [+about] _He was always mod-est about his role in the Everest expedition._ | _You're too modest! You've been a huge help to us._
2 NOT BIG not very great, big, or expensive: _a modest increase in costs_ | _She had saved a modest amount of money._ | _The new service proved a modest success._ | _a modest house with a small garden_ | _his modest ambitions_
3 SHY shy about showing your body or attracting sexual interest, because you are easily embarrassed; **adj immodest**: _She was a modest girl, always keeping covered, even in summer._
4 CLOTHES old-fashioned modest clothing covers the body in a way that does not attract sexual interest: _a modest knee-length dress_ —**modestly** adv: _'I was just lucky,' he said modestly._ | _modestly priced meals_

mod·es·ty /'mɒdˌsti $ 'mɑː-/ n [U] **1** a modest way of behaving or talking: _'Anyone else would have done the same thing,' he said with typical modesty._ **2** unwill-ingness to show your body or do anything that may attract sexual interest **3** in all modesty spoken used when you want to talk about something good you have done, but you do not want to seem too proud: _I think in all modesty that I can take some small credit for the team's success._ **4** modesty forbids spoken used when saying jokingly that you do not want to talk about your achievements → **false modesty** at FALSE (4)

mod·i·cum /'mɒdɪkəm $ 'mɑː-/ n a modicum of sth formal a small amount of something, especially a good quality: _a modicum of common sense_

mod·i·fi·ca·tion /ˌmɒdˌfˌ'keɪʃən $ ˌmɑː-/ n **1** [C] a small change made in something such as a design, plan, or system: [+to] _We've made one or two modifi-cations to the original design._ | _They have used the same process for almost 50 years with only minor modifica-tions._ **2** [C,U] the act of modifying something, or the process of being modified: [+of] _The review resulted in the modification of our security procedures._ | [+in] _Knowledge of the ill effects of tobacco has led to a modification in smoking behaviour._

mod·i·fi·er /'mɒdˌfaɪə $ 'mɑːdˌfaɪər/ n [C] technical a word or group of words that gives additional informa-tion about another word. Modifiers can be adjectives (such as 'fierce' in 'the fierce dog'), adverbs (such as

'loudly' in 'the dog barked loudly'), or phrases (such as 'with a short tail' in 'the dog with a short tail').

mod·i·fy /'mɒdˌfaɪ $ 'mɑː-/ v **modified, modifying, modifies** [T] **1** to make small changes to something in order to improve it and make it more suitable or effective; **adj adapt**: _The feedback will be used to modify the course for next year._ | _The regulations can only be modified by a special committee._ | **modify sth to do sth** _The seats can be modified to fit other types of vehicle._ **2** technical if an adjective, adverb etc modi-fies another word, it describes something or limits the word's meaning. In the phrase 'walk slowly', the adverb 'slowly' modifies the verb 'walk'.

mod·ish /'məʊdɪʃ $ 'moʊ-/ adj old-fashioned modish ideas, designs etc are modern and fashionable —**modishly** adv

mod·u·lar /'mɒdjˌlə $ 'mɑːdʒələr/ adj consisting of separate parts or units which can be put together to form something, often in different combinations: _a modular course in business studies_ | _Most colleges now use the modular system of teaching._ | _modular furniture_

mod·u·late /'mɒdjˌleɪt $ 'mɑːdʒə-/ v **1** [T] formal to change the sound of your voice **2** [T] to change a process or activity to make it more controlled, slower, less strong etc: _These drugs modulate the disease pro-cess._ **3** [I + from/to] technical to move from one KEY to another in a piece of music using a series of related CHORDS **4** [T] technical to change the form of a radio signal so that it can be broadcast more effectively —**modulation** /ˌmɒdjˌ'leɪʃən $ ˌmɑːdʒə-/ n [C,U]

mod·ule W2 /'mɒdjuːl $ 'mɑːdʒuːl/ n [C]
1 especially BrE one of the separate units that a course of study has been divided into. Usually students choose a number of modules to study: _a module in mathematics_ | _You choose five modules in the first year._
2 technical one of several parts of a piece of computer software that does a particular job
3 a part of a spacecraft that can be separated from the main part and used for a particular purpose
4 one of several separate parts that can be combined to form a larger object, such as a machine or building

mo·dus op·e·ran·di /ˌməʊdəs ˌɒpə'rændi $ ˌmoʊdəs ˌɑːpə-/ n [singular] formal M.O. a way of doing something that is typical of a particular person or group

modus vi·ven·di /ˌməʊdəs vɪ'vendi $ ˌmoʊ-/ n [sin-gular] formal an arrangement between people with very different opinions or habits that allows them to live or work together without quarrelling

mog·gy, moggie /'mɒgi $ 'mɑːgi, 'mɒːgi/ n plural **moggies** [C] BrE informal a cat

mo·gul /'məʊgəl $ 'moʊ-/ n [C] movie/media/gambling etc mogul a BUSINESSMAN or BUSINESSWOMAN who has great power and influence in a particular industry

mo·hair /'məʊheə $ 'moʊher/ n [U] expensive wool made from the hair of the ANGORA goat: _a mohair sweater_

Mo·ham·me·d /məʊ'hæmˌd, mə- $ moʊ-/ n the Arab PROPHET who founded the religion of Islam

Mo·hi·can /məʊ'hiːkən $ moʊ-/ BrE; **Mo·hawk** /'məʊhɔːk $ 'moʊhɑːk/ AmE n [C] a hairstyle in which the hair is cut off the sides of the head, and the hair on top of the head is made to stick up and is sometimes brightly coloured —**Mohican** adj: _a Mohican haircut_; → see picture at HAIRSTYLE

moi /mwɑː/ pron spoken me – used humorously to disagree with a negative description of yourself: _Diffi-cult, moi?_

moi·e·ty /'mɔɪˌti/ n plural **moieties** [C] law or literary a half share

moire /mwɑː $ mwɑːr, mwɑː'reɪ/ n [U] a type of silk with a pattern that looks like waves

moist /mɔɪst/ adj slightly wet, especially in a way that is pleasant or suitable: _Make sure the soil is moist before planting the seeds._ | _a rich, moist chocolate cake_ | _warm_ *moist air* | *Her eyes were moist* (=she was almost crying). —**moistness** *n* [U]

moist·en /'mɔɪsən/ *v* [T] to make something slightly wet: *Moisten the clay if it seems too dry.* | *She moistened her lips* (=made her lips wet with her tongue).

mois·ture /'mɔɪstʃə $ -ər/ *n* [U] small amounts of water that are present in the air, in a substance, or on a surface: *Plants use their roots to absorb moisture from the soil.* | *Your skin's moisture content varies according to weather conditions.*

mois·tur·ize also **-ise** *BrE* /'mɔɪstʃəraɪz/ *v* [I,T] **1** to make your skin less dry by using special cream: *You should cleanse, tone and moisturize every day for healthy looking skin.* **2 moisturizing cream/lotion/oil etc** cream, oil etc which you put on your skin or hair to make it less dry

mois·tur·iz·er also **-iser** *BrE* /'mɔɪstʃəraɪzə $ -ər/ *n* [C,U] cream that you put on your skin to make it less dry

mo·lar /'məʊlə $ 'moʊlər/ *n* [C] one of the large teeth at the back of the mouth that are used for breaking up food; → **incisor** —**molar** *adj*

mo·las·ses /mə'læsɪz/ *n* [U] *AmE* a thick dark sweet liquid that is obtained from raw sugar plants when they are being made into sugar; ▣ **treacle** *BrE*

mold /məʊld $ moʊld/ *n, v* the American spelling of MOULD —**molding** *n*

mol·der /'məʊldə $ 'moʊldər/ *v* the American spelling of MOULDER

mold·y /'məʊldi $ 'moʊl-/ *adj* the American spelling of MOULDY

mole /məʊl $ moʊl/ *n* [C] **1** a small dark furry animal which is almost blind. Moles usually live under the ground. **2** a small dark brown mark on the skin that is slightly higher than the skin around it **3** someone who works for an organization while secretly giving information to its enemies

mol·e·cule /'mɒlɪkjuːl $ 'mɑː-/ *n* [C] the smallest unit into which any substance can be divided without losing its own chemical nature, usually consisting of two or more atoms: *The molecules of oxygen gas contain just two atoms.* —**molecular** /mə'lekjʊlə $ -ər/ *adj*: *molecular structure*

mole·hill /'məʊl,hɪl $ 'moʊl-/ *n* [C] a small pile of earth made by a MOLE → **make a mountain out of a molehill** at MOUNTAIN (4)

mole·skin /'məʊl,skɪn $ 'moʊl-/ *n* [U] **1** thick cotton cloth with a soft surface: *moleskin trousers* **2** the skin of a MOLE

mo·lest /mə'lest/ *v* [T] **1** to attack or harm someone, especially a child, by touching them in a sexual way or by trying to have sex with them; ▣ **abuse**: *men who molest young boys* **2** *old-fashioned* to attack and physically harm someone: *a dog that was molesting sheep* —**molester** *n* [C] —**molestation** /,məʊle'steɪʃən $,moʊ-/ *n* [U]: *sexual molestation* → CHILD MOLESTER

moll /mɒl $ mɑːl/ *n* [C] *especially AmE old-fashioned informal* a criminal's girlfriend: *a gangster's moll*

mol·li·fy /'mɒlɪfaɪ $ 'mɑː-/ *v* **mollified, mollifying, mollifies** [T] *formal* to make someone feel less angry and upset about something; ▣ **placate**: *A policewoman attempted to mollify her.* | *Nature reserves were set up around new power stations to mollify local conservationists.*

mol·lusc *BrE*; **mollusk** *AmE* /'mɒləsk $ 'mɑː-/ *n* [C] a type of sea or land animal that has a soft body covered by a hard shell: *snails and other molluscs* —**molluscan** /mə'lʌskən/ *adj*: *molluscan prey*

mol·ly·cod·dle /'mɒli,kɒdl $ 'mɑːli,kɑːdl/ *v* [T] to treat someone too kindly and to protect them too much from anything unpleasant: *He had been mollycoddled as a young boy.*

Mol·o·tov cock·tail /,mɒlətɒf 'kɒkteɪl $,mɑːlətɔːf 'kɑːk-, ,mɒːl-/ *n* [C] a simple bomb consisting of a bottle filled with petrol with a piece of cloth in the end

molt /məʊlt $ moʊlt/ *v* the American spelling of MOULT

mol·ten /'məʊltən $ 'moʊl-/ *adj* [usually before noun] molten metal or rock has been made into a liquid by being heated to a very high temperature: *molten iron* | **molten lava** (=liquid rock from a VOLCANO)

mol·to /'mɒltəʊ $ 'moʊltoʊ, 'mɒːl-/ *adv* very – used in musical instructions: **molto allegro** (=very fast)

mo·lyb·de·num /mə'lɪbdənəm/ *n* [U] a hard silver-white metal that is used to make steel stronger. It is a chemical ELEMENT: symbol Mo

mom ⟨S1⟩ ⟨W2⟩ /mɒm $ mɑːm/ *n* [C] *AmE informal* mother; ▣ **mum** *BrE*: *Mom, can I go over to Lisa's house?* | *My mom says I have to stay home tonight.*

,mom-and-'pop *adj* [only before noun] *AmE* a mom-and-pop business is owned and managed by a family or a husband and wife: *a real mom-and-pop restaurant*

mo·ment ⟨S1⟩ ⟨W1⟩ /'məʊmənt $ 'moʊ-/ *n* [C]

1 POINT IN TIME a particular point in time: *It was one of the most exciting moments in his life.* | **at this/that moment** (=used for emphasis) *Just at that moment there was a knock on the door.* | *She may be in trouble at this very moment and trying to call you.* | *I remember the moment when I first saw him after the operation.* | *Quinn always seems to be in the right place at the crucial moment.* | **I just this moment** (=only a very short time ago) *arrived and already Dan wants to know when I'm leaving.* | **At this moment in time** *it would be inappropriate to comment on the situation.* | **From that moment on** (=after that time) *we were the best of friends.* ⚠ Do not say **in that moment** when you mean 'at that particular time'. Say **at that moment**: *At that moment, everything stopped.*

2 SHORT TIME a very short period of time: *He was here a moment ago.* | *Can you spare a few moments to answer some questions?* | **in a moment** (=very soon) *I'll come back to that point in a moment.* | **for a moment** *It was quiet for a moment, then Rae spoke.* | **after a moment** *'I don't understand,' said Louise after a moment.* | *A moment later we heard a splash.* | **wait/just a moment** (=used when you want someone to wait a short time while you do or say something) *Just a moment; let me put these away first.* | *We have to be ready to leave at a moment's notice* (=very quickly).

3 at the moment *BrE especially spoken, AmE formal* now: *Julia's on holiday in Spain at the moment.* | *At the moment, the situation in Haiti is very tense.*

4 for the moment used to say that something is happening or is true now but will probably change in the future: *Well, for the moment we're just friends.* | *For the moment the rain had stopped.*

5 the moment (that) sb does sth as soon as someone does something: *He said he'd phone you the moment he got home.*

6 the last moment if you do something at the last moment or if something happens at the last moment, it happens at the last possible time: **at the last moment** *The operation was cancelled at the last moment.* | *She always leaves everything to the last moment.*

7 (at) any moment extremely soon: *The plumber should be here any moment now.* | *The roof could collapse at any moment.*

8 OPPORTUNITY [usually singular] a particular time when you have a chance to do something: *His wife Denise was there to share his big moment* (=opportunity to do something great). | **choose/pick your moment** (=try to choose the best time to do something) *He picked his moment carefully to tell them the news.* | *This was her moment and she knew she had to take it.*

9 moment of madness/weakness/panic etc a short period of time when you do not feel or behave as normal and often do or say something which you later wish you had not done or said: **in a moment of sth** *In a moment of madness I agreed to go with him.* | *He experienced a brief moment of panic.*

10 one moment ... the next/from one moment to the

next used to say that a situation changes very suddenly, often in a way which you do not expect or cannot explain: *One moment she's kissing me, the next she doesn't want to see me again.* | *You never know what's going to happen from one moment to the next.*
11 not believe/think/do sth for a/one moment *especially spoken* used to say that you did not believe, expect etc something at all: *He didn't fool me for a moment.* | *She had never for one moment imagined that it could happen to her.*
12 of the moment the person, idea, word etc of the moment is the one that is most important or popular at the present time: *They interview personalities on a topic of the moment.* | *the mood of the moment*
13 have its/your moments to have periods of being good or interesting: *a movie that had its moments*
14 not a moment too soon almost too late: *The ambulance finally arrived, and not a moment too soon.*
15 the moment of truth the time when you will find out if something will work properly, be successful etc
16 of great moment *old-fashioned* important

mo·men·tar·i·ly /ˈmoumɒntərəli $ ˌmoumənˈterəli/ *adv* **1** for a very short time; ⊟ **briefly:** *She was momentarily lost for words.* | *Jimmy paused momentarily.* **2** *AmE* very soon: *Mr Johnson will be with you momentarily.*

mo·men·ta·ry /ˈmoumɒntəri $ ˈmoumənteri/ *adj* continuing for a very short time; ⊟ **brief:** *There was a momentary pause.*

mo·men·tous /məʊˈmentəs, mə- $ moʊ-, mə-/ *adj* a momentous event, change, or decision is very important because it will have a great influence on the future: *a momentous decision* | *Momentous events are taking place in the US.* | *His colleagues all recognized that this was a momentous occasion.* | *one of the most momentous days in British sport*

mo·men·tum /məʊˈmentəm, mə- $ moʊ-, mə-/ *n* [U] **1** the ability to keep increasing, developing, or being more successful: **gain/gather momentum** *The campaign for reform should start to gather momentum in the new year.* | *incentives to* **maintain** *the* **momentum** *of European integration* | *Governments often* **lose momentum** *in their second term of office.* | [+of] *the momentum of increasing immigration* | [+towards] *the momentum towards economic union* **2** the force that makes a moving object keep moving: **gain/gather momentum** (=move faster) *The wheel was allowed to roll down the slope, gathering momentum as it went.* | *Pratt, without* **losing** *any* **momentum** *at all, passed them both and won the race.* **3** *technical* the force or power that is contained in a moving object and is calculated by multiplying its weight by its speed: [+of] *the momentum of a particle*

mom·ma /ˈmɒmə $ ˈmɑːmə/ *n AmE* another spelling of MAMA[1]

mom·my [S3] /ˈmɒmi $ ˈmɑːmi/ *n plural* **mommies** [C] *AmE* mother – used by or to young children; ⊟ **mummy** *BrE*

ˈmommy ˌtrack *n* [C] *AmE informal* a situation in which women with children have less opportunity to make large amounts of money or become very successful at their jobs, for example because they are not able to work as many hours as other people

Mon. also **Mon** *BrE* the written abbreviation of *Monday*

mon·arch /ˈmɒnək $ ˈmɑːnərk, -ɑːrk/ *n* [C] a king or queen —**monarchic** /məˈnɑːkɪk $ -ɑːr-/ also **monarchical** *adj*: *the old monarchical system*

mon·arch·ist /ˈmɒnəkəst $ ˈmɑːnər-/ *n* [C] someone who supports the idea that their country should be ruled by a king or queen

mon·ar·chy /ˈmɒnəki $ ˈmɑːnərki/ *n plural* **monarchies** **1** [U] the system in which a country is ruled by a king or queen: *the abolition of the monarchy* **2** [C] a country that is ruled by a king or queen; → **republic** **3 the monarchy** the king or queen of a country,

and his or her family: *People are going to be questioning the role of the monarchy more and more.*

mon·as·tery /ˈmɒnəstri $ ˈmɑːnəsteri/ *n plural* **monasteries** [C] a place where MONKS live; → **convent, nunnery**

mo·nas·tic /məˈnæstɪk/ *adj* **1** relating to MONKS or life in a monastery: *the monastic life* | *a monastic community* | *Roman Catholic* **monastic orders** (=groups of monks) **2** similar to a MONK'S way of living, for example being quiet, simple, or not having sex: *He led a rather monastic lifestyle.* —**monasticism** /-tɪˌsɪzəm/ *n* [U]: *early medieval monasticism*

Mon·day /ˈmʌndi, -deɪ/ *n* [C,U] written abbreviation **Mon.** the day between Sunday and Tuesday: **on Monday** *It was raining on Monday.* | *The president announced Monday that he would cancel the debt. AmE* | **Monday morning/afternoon etc** *Let's go out for a meal on Monday night.* | **last Monday** *Kelly arrived last Monday.* | **this Monday** *The UK office will open for business this Monday.* | **next Monday** (=Monday of next week) *Shall we meet next Monday?* | **a Monday** (=one of the Mondays in the year) *My birthday's on a Monday this year.*

mon·e·ta·ris·m /ˈmʌnɪtərɪzəm $ ˈmɑː-/ *n* [U] the belief that the best way to manage a country's ECONOMY is for the government to control and limit the amount of money that is available and being used: *the monetarism of the 1980s* —**monetarist** *adj, n* [C]: *a monetarist view of the economy*

mon·e·ta·ry [W3] /ˈmʌnɪtəri $ ˈmɑːnəteri/ *adj* [only before noun] relating to money, especially all the money in a particular country: *the government's tight monetary policy* | *objects of little monetary value*

mon·e·tize also **-ise** *BrE* /ˈmʌnətaɪz $ ˈmɑː-/ *v* [T] *technical* to change government BONDS and debts into money

mon·ey [S1] [W1] /ˈmʌni/ *n* [U]
1 what you earn by working and can use to buy things. Money can be in the form of notes and coins or cheques, and can be kept in a bank

spend money
make/earn money
make money (=make a profit)
lose money (=not make a profit, so that a business owes more than it earns)
cost money/cost a lot of money
save money
lend/borrow/owe money
waste money (on sth)
be a waste of money
charge (sb) money
raise money
pay money (for sth)
give sb their money back/refund sb's money
a sum/an amount of money
get/earn good money (=be paid good wages)

Don't **spend** *all your* **money** *on the first day of your holiday!* | *She doesn't* **earn** *very much* **money.** | *He's working for a finance company now, and* **making** *loads of* **money.** | *At last the business is starting to* **make money.** | *The company is* **losing money** *and may have to close down.* | *The repairs will* **cost** *quite a lot of* **money.** | *We're not going on holiday this year because we're trying to* **save money.** | *Could you* **lend** *me some* **money?** | *I don't want to* **borrow money** *from the bank unless I really have to.* | *They* **charge** *huge amounts of* **money** *for their services.* | *We're trying to* **raise money** *to help children with cancer.* | *If you are not completely satisfied with our products, we will* **give you your money back.** | *He was left a large* **sum of money.** | *You can* **earn good money** *as a computer programmer.*

2 money in the form of coins or notes that you can carry around with you; ⊟ **cash:** *You'll find some money*

M

in my purse. | I didn't **have** any **money on me** (=I was not carrying any money). | **Swiss/Japanese/Turkish etc money** Don't forget to get some Swiss money before you leave. | We can **change** some **money** at the airport (=change it into the money of another country).
3 someone's wealth, including all the property and other things they own: The family **made** their **money** in the woollen trade. | He had **lost** all his **money** gambling.
4 the **money** informal the amount of money that you earn for doing a job: It sounds quite an interesting job, but I don't know what the money's like yet. | You have to work long hours and the money's terrible!
5 pay good money for sth spoken to spend a lot of money on something: Don't let the children jump around on the sofa. I paid good money for that.
6 put/pump/pour money into sth to give money to a company or business so that it will become successful and you will earn money from it in the future: No one's going to put money into the company while the market is so unstable.
7 there's money (to be made) in sth spoken used to say that you can earn a lot of money from doing a particular job or type of business: There's a lot of money in sport these days. | Teaching can be very rewarding, but there's no money in it.
8 I'm not made of money spoken used to say that you cannot afford something when someone asks you to pay for it.
9 have money to burn to have more money than you need, so that you spend it on unnecessary things: Unless you've got money to burn, these expensive guitars are probably not for you.
10 get your money's worth to get something worth the price that you paid: At that price, you want to make sure you get your money's worth.
11 be in the money informal to have a lot of money suddenly, or when you did not expect to
12 money is no object informal used to say that someone can spend as much money as they want to on something
13 for my money spoken used when giving your opinion about something to emphasize that you believe it strongly: For my money, he's one of the best TV comedians ever.
14 put (your) money on sth to risk money on the result of a race or competition
15 I'd put (my) money on sth spoken used to say that you feel sure that something will happen
16 my money's on sb/sth also the smart money's on sb/sth spoken used to say that you feel sure someone will win a race or competition, or that something will happen
17 money for old rope BrE spoken money that you earn very easily by doing a job that is not difficult
18 put your money where your mouth is informal to show by your actions that you really believe what you say
19 money talks spoken used to say that people with money have power and can get what they want
20 be (right) on the money AmE spoken to be completely correct or right: You were right on the money when you said that he would have to resign.
21 marry (into) money to marry someone whose family is rich → MONIES, BLOOD MONEY, HUSH MONEY, POCKET MONEY; → give sb a (good) run for their money at RUN² (11); → have a (good) run for your money at RUN² (12); → throw money at sth at THROW¹ (19)

WORD CHOICE: money, cash, change, currency
Money is the most general word for the notes and coins that you use for buying things: Can I borrow some money? | Put the money straight in your purse.
Use **cash** when you want to emphasize that you mean notes and coins, and not cheques, credit cards etc: You have to pay in cash – they don't accept cheques.
⚠ Do not say 'pay by cash'. Say **pay in cash**.

Use **change** when you mean money in the form of coins, or the money you get back when you pay for something with more money than it cost: I need some change for the phone. | He left the shop without waiting for his change.
Use **currency** to refer to the money of a particular country: You'll need about £500 worth of Japanese currency.

mon·ey·bags /'mʌnibægz/ n [singular] informal someone who has a lot of money – used humorously
money ,belt n [C] a special belt that you can carry money in while you are travelling
mon·ey·box /'mʌnibɒks $ -baːks/ n [C] especially BrE a box in which children put their money to save it
mon·eyed, monied /'mʌnid/ adj [only before noun] old-fashioned formal rich: the monied classes
mon·ey·grab·bing /'mʌnigræbɪŋ/ also **mon·ey·grub·bing** /'mʌnigrʌbɪŋ/ adj [only before noun] informal determined to get a lot of money, even by unfair or dishonest methods: people who are exploited by moneygrabbing employers —**moneygrabber, moneygrubber** n [C]
money ,laundering n [U] when money that has been obtained illegally is put into legal businesses or bank accounts in different countries, so that it is difficult for people to discover where it came from: The country is a major centre for money laundering. | He will now face trial on money laundering charges.
mon·ey·lend·er /'mʌni,lendə $ -ər/ n [C] someone whose business is to lend money to people, especially someone who makes people pay back a lot more money than they have borrowed —**moneylending** n [U]: Most of his fortune came from moneylending.
mon·ey·mak·er /'mʌni,meɪkə $ -ər/ n [C] a product or business that earns a lot of money; ⊟ **money-spinner** BrE —**money-making** adj [only before noun]: money-making schemes
money ,market n [C] all the banks and other institutions that buy, sell, lend, or borrow money, especially foreign money, for profit
money ,order n [C] an official document that you buy in a post office or a bank and send to someone so that they can exchange it for money in a bank; → postal order
money-,spinner n [C] BrE a MONEYMAKER: We're hoping the show will be a real money-spinner.
money sup·ply n [singular] technical all the money that exists in a country's economic system at a particular time: his policy of controlling the money supply and cutting public spending
-monger /mʌŋgə $ maːŋgər, mʌŋ-/ suffix [in nouns] **1** someone who sells a particular thing: a fishmonger **2** rumour-monger/gloom-monger/doom-monger etc someone who says unpleasant things: The rumour-mongers have been busy again. | the economic gloom-mongers → WARMONGER
mon·gol /'mɒŋgəl $ 'maːŋ-/ n [C] taboo old-fashioned a very offensive word for someone with DOWN'S SYNDROME. Do not use this word. —**mongolism** n [U]
mon·goose /'mɒŋguːs $ 'maːŋ-/ n plural mongooses [C] a small furry tropical animal that kills snakes and rats
mon·grel /'mʌŋgrəl $ 'maːŋ-, 'mʌŋ-/ n [C] a dog that is a mix of several different breeds
mon·ied /'mʌnid/ adj another spelling of MONEYED
mon·ies, moneys /'mʌniz/ n [plural] law money: If we are no longer able to provide the holiday you booked, we will return to you all monies paid.
mon·i·ker /'mɒnɪkə $ 'maːnɪkər/ n [C] informal a name, especially one that you choose for yourself or give something – used humorously
mon·i·tor¹ [S3] [W3] /'mɒnɪtə $ 'maːnɪtər/ v [T]
1 to carefully watch and check a situation in order to see how it changes over a period of time: Patients who are given the new drug will be asked to monitor their progress. | The government is **monitoring** the situation

very **closely.** | *The temperature is* **carefully**
monitored. | monitor what/how etc *We need a better
system for monitoring what is going on.*; → see box at
CONTROL²
2 to secretly listen to other people's telephone calls,
foreign radio broadcasts etc: *He suspected that his
phone calls were being monitored.*

monitor² *n* [C]
1 SCREEN a television or part of a computer with a
screen, on which you can see pictures or information:
television/TV/computer monitor *She was staring at her
computer monitor.* | **on a monitor** *We could watch what
was happening on the TV monitor.*
2 PIECE OF EQUIPMENT FOR MEASURING a piece of
equipment that measures and shows the level, speed,
temperature etc of something: *a heart monitor* | *The
noise monitor recorded 98 decibels.*
3 SB WHO WATCHES AN ACTIVITY someone whose
job is to watch an activity or a situation to see how it
changes or develops, or to make sure that it is fair and
legal: *UN monitors will remain in the country to super-
vise the elections.* | **peace/human rights etc monitors**
The UN is sending peace monitors to the area.
4 CHILD a child who has been chosen to help a teacher
in some way in class
5 SB WHO LISTENS TO RADIO someone whose job is
to listen to news or messages on a radio and report on
them

monk /mʌŋk/ *n* [C] a member of an all-male religious
group that lives apart from other people in a MONASTERY;
→ nun —**monkish** *adj*

mon·key¹ /ˈmʌŋki/ *n* [C] **1** a small brown animal
with a long tail, which uses its hands to climb trees and
lives in hot countries **2** *informal* a small child who is
very active and likes to play tricks: *Stop that, you little
monkey!* **3** monkey business *informal* bad or dishonest behaviour **4** not give a monkey's *BrE spoken
informal* to not care at all about something: *To be honest
I don't give a monkey's what they do.* **5** make a
monkey (out) of sb to make someone seem stupid **6** a
monkey on your back *AmE informal* a serious problem
that makes your life very difficult, especially being
dependent on drugs

monkey² *v*
monkey around also **monkey about** *BrE phr v
informal* to behave in a stupid or careless way: *Stop
monkeying around and listen to me!*

monkey bars *n* [plural] *AmE* a structure of bars for
children to climb and play on; ◻ **climbing frame** *BrE*

monkey nut *n* [C] *BrE informal* a PEANUT in its shell

mon·key·shines /ˈmʌŋkiʃaɪnz/ *n* [plural] *AmE old-
fashioned informal* silly tricks or jokes

monkey wrench *n* [C] *especially AmE* **1** a tool that
is used to hold or turn things of different widths;
◻ **adjustable spanner** *BrE* **2** throw a monkey
wrench in the works *AmE informal* to do something that
will cause problems or spoil someone's plans;
◻ **throw/put a spanner in the works** *BrE*

mon·o¹ /ˈmɒnəʊ $ ˈmɑːnoʊ/ *n* [U] *informal* **1** *AmE* an
infectious illness that makes your LYMPH NODES swell and
makes you feel weak and tired for a long time afterwards; ◻ **glandular fever** *BrE* **2** a system of recording or broadcasting sound, in which the sound comes
from only one direction; → stereo

mono² *adj* using a system of recording or broadcasting sound in which all the sound comes from only one
direction; → stereo: *an old mono recording*

mono- /mɒnəʊ, -nə $ -noʊ, -nə/ *prefix* one: *a mono-
plane* (=a plane with only one wing on each side) | *a
monolingual dictionary* (=dealing with only one language)

mon·o·chrome /ˈmɒnəkrəʊm $ ˈmɑːnəkroʊm/
adj **1** in shades of only one colour, especially shades
of grey: *We looked out over the grey, monochrome
landscape.* **2** a monochrome picture or screen uses
only the colours black, white, and grey; ◻ **colour:** *a*

monochrome computer monitor —**monochromatic**
/ˌmɒnəkrəˈmætɪk◂ $ ˌmɑː-/ *adj*

mon·o·cle /ˈmɒnəkəl $ ˈmɑː-/ *n* [C] a round piece of
glass that you put in front of one eye to help you see
better

mo·nog·a·my /məˈnɒɡəmi $ məˈnɑː-/ *n* [U] **1** the
custom of being married to only one husband or wife;
→ **bigamy**, **polygamy** **2** when a person or animal has
a sexual relationship with only one partner:
*Monogamy is rare in most animal groups, but is com-
mon among birds.* —**monogamous** *adj*: *We live in a
monogamous society.* —**monogamously** *adv*

mon·o·gram /ˈmɒnəɡræm $ ˈmɑː-/ *n* [C] a design that
is made using the first letters of someone's names and
is put on pieces of clothing or other possessions
—**monogrammed** *adj*

mon·o·graph /ˈmɒnəɡrɑːf $ ˈmɑːnəɡræf/ *n* [C] an
article or short book that discusses a subject in detail

mon·o·ling·ual /ˌmɒnəˈlɪŋɡwəl◂ $ ˌmɑːnə-/ *adj*
speaking or using only one language; → **bilingual**,
multilingual: *a monolingual dictionary*

mon·o·lith /ˈmɒnəlɪθ $ ˈmɑː-/ *n* [C] **1** a large, pow-
erful organization that cannot change quickly and does
not consider the ideas or feelings of the people it
affects: *It is misleading to see the legal system as a
monolith.* **2** a large tall block of stone, especially one
that was put in place in ancient times, possibly for
religious reasons

mon·o·lith·ic /ˌmɒnəˈlɪθɪk◂ $ ˌmɑː-/ *adj* **1** a mono-
lithic building is very large, solid, and impressive **2** a
monolithic organization, political system etc is very
large and powerful and difficult to change: *a monolithic
movie company*

mon·o·logue also **monolog** *AmE* /ˈmɒnəlɒɡ
$ ˈmɑːnl-ɒːɡ, -ɑːɡ/ *n* [C] a long speech by one person; →
soliloquy, **dialogue**: *Henry looked up, then continued
his monologue.*

mon·o·ma·ni·a /ˌmɒnəʊˈmeɪniə $ ˌmɑːnoʊ-/ *n* [U]
formal a very strong interest in one particular idea or
subject which prevents you from thinking about anything else: *an obsession with food that verged on mono-
mania* **monomaniac** /-niæk/ *n* [C]

mon·o·nu·cle·o·sis /ˌmɒnəʊnjuːkliˈəʊs̩s
$ ˌmɑːnoʊnukliˈoʊ-/ *n* [U] *medical* MONO¹ (1)

mon·o·plane /ˈmɒnəʊpleɪn $ ˈmɑːnoʊ-/ *n* [C] a plane
with only one wing on each side; → **biplane**

mo·nop·ol·is·tic /məˌnɒpəˈlɪstɪk◂ $ -ˌnɑː-/ *adj* con-
trolling or trying to control an industry or business
activity completely: *The company wants to maintain its
monopolistic position.*

mo·nop·o·lize also **-ise** *BrE* /məˈnɒpəlaɪz $ -ˈnɑː-/ *v*
[T] **1** to have complete control over something so that
other people cannot share it or take part in it: *The
company has monopolized the soft drinks market.* | *He
monopolized the conversation all evening.* **2** to use a
lot of someone's time or attention: *Virtually all her
time and energy is now monopolized by the children.*
—**monopolist** *n* [C]

mo·nop·o·ly /məˈnɒpəli $ məˈnɑː-/ *n plural* **monopo-
lies** **1** [C] if a company or government has a
monopoly of a business or political activity, it has
complete control of it so that other organizations
cannot compete with it: [+of] *They are demanding an
end to the Communist Party's monopoly of power.* | *the
state monopoly of television* | [+on/in] *For years Bell
Telephone had a monopoly on telephone services in the
US.* | *a monopoly in copper trading* **2** [C] a large
company that controls all or most of a business
activity: *The company will become a state-owned
monopoly.* **3** [singular] if someone has a monopoly on
something, that thing belongs to them, and no one else
can share it: *Teachers do not have a monopoly on
educational debate.*

M

mon·o·rail /ˈmɒnəʊreɪl $ ˈmɑːnə-/ n **1** [C,U] a railway system that uses a single RAIL, usually high above the ground **2** [C] a train on a monorail system

mon·o·sod·i·um glu·tam·ate /ˌmɒnəʊˌsəʊdiəm ˈgluːtəmeɪt $ ˌmɑːnəsoʊ-/ n [U] MSG

mon·o·syl·lab·ic /ˌmɒnəsɪˈlæbɪk◂ $ ˌmɑː-/ adj **1** someone who speaks in a monosyllabic way does not say very much and does not try to be friendly: *He made monosyllabic replies to my questions.* **2** technical a monosyllabic word has only one SYLLABLE

mon·o·syl·la·ble /ˈmɒnəˌsɪləbəl $ ˈmɑː-/ n [C] technical a word with one SYLLABLE

mon·o·the·is·m /ˈmɒnəʊθiˌɪzəm $ ˈmɑːnə-/ n [U] the belief that there is only one God; → **polytheism** —**monotheist** n [C] —**monotheistic** /ˌmɒnəʊθiˈɪstɪk◂ $ ˌmɑːnə-/ adj: *monotheistic religions*

mon·o·tone /ˈmɒnətəʊn $ ˈmɑːnətoʊn/ n [singular] a sound or way of speaking or singing that continues on the same note without getting any louder or softer, and therefore sounds very boring: *He answered all the lawyer's questions in a dull monotone.*

mo·not·o·nous /məˈnɒtənəs $ məˈnɑː-/ adj boring because of always being the same: *a monotonous diet* | *a little boy who wet his bed with monotonous regularity* —**monotonously** adv: *The rain poured monotonously out of the grey sky.*

mo·not·o·ny /məˈnɒtəni $ məˈnɑː-/ n [U] the quality of being always the same, which makes something boring, especially someone's life or work: [+of] *She wanted to escape the monotony of her everyday life.* | **relieve/break the monotony** *He suggested a card game to relieve the monotony of the journey.*

mo·nox·ide /məˈnɒksaɪd $ məˈnɑːk-/ n → CARBON MONOXIDE

Mon·sieur /məˈsjɜː $ -ˈsjɜːr/ n plural **Messieurs** /meɪˈsjɜːz $ -ˈsjɜːrz/ used when speaking to or about a French-speaking man; → **Madame**, **Mademoiselle**: *Monsieur Lacombe*

Mon·si·gnor /mɒnˈsiːnjə $ mɑːnˈsiːnjər/ n used when speaking to or about a priest of high rank in the Roman Catholic Church: *Monsignor Delgard*

mon·soon /mɒnˈsuːn $ mɑːn-/ n [C] **1** [usually singular] the season, from about April to October, when it rains a lot in India and other southern Asian countries **2** the heavy rain that falls during the monsoon, or the wind that brings the rain

mon·ster¹ /ˈmɒnstə $ ˈmɑːnstər/ n [C]
1 IN STORIES an imaginary or ancient creature that is large, ugly, and frightening: *the remains of a prehistoric monster* | *the search for the Loch Ness Monster*
2 CRUEL PERSON someone who is very cruel and evil: *Only a monster could kill all those women.*
3 CHILD a small child, especially one who is behaving badly – used humorously: *I've got to get home and feed this little monster.*
4 STH LARGE informal an object, animal etc that is unusually large: *Did you see the fish Dad caught? It was a monster!* | *There's a monster of a spider in the bath!*
5 DANGEROUS PROBLEM a dangerous or threatening problem, especially one that develops gradually and is difficult to manage

monster² adj [only before noun] informal unusually large; ☐ **giant**: *a monster cat* | *The song was a monster hit.*

mon·stros·i·ty /mɒnˈstrɒsəti $ mɑːnˈstrɑː-/ n plural **monstrosities** [C] something large and ugly, especially a building: *a concrete monstrosity*

mon·strous /ˈmɒnstrəs $ ˈmɑːn-/ adj **1** very wrong, immoral, or unfair: *It's monstrous to charge that much for a hotel room.* | *Such monstrous injustice is hard to understand.* **2** unusually large: *a monstrous nose* **3** unnatural or ugly and frightening; ☐ **hideous**: *a*

monstrous shadow on the stairs —**monstrously** adv: *He was ugly and monstrously fat.* | *It was monstrously unfair.*

mon·tage /ˈmɒntɑːʒ $ mɑːnˈtɑːʒ/ n **1** [U] the process of making a whole picture, film, or piece of music or writing by combining parts of different pictures, films etc in an interesting and unusual way **2** [C] something made by combining parts of different pictures, films etc in an interesting and unusual way: [+of] *a montage of flowers* | *a photo montage*

month S1 W1 /mʌnθ/ n [C]
1 one of the 12 named periods of time that a year is divided into: **this/last/next month** *Phil is coming home for a visit next month.* | *She'll be thirteen this month.* | *I hope I'll have finished the work by the end of the month.* | *She earns about £350 a month* (=each month). | *We update the schedule at least once a month.* | **the month of May/June etc** *It snowed heavily during the month of January.*
2 a period of about four weeks: *She has an eight-month-old daughter.* | *He'll be away for two months.* | *The symptoms she suffered varied from month to month* (=every few weeks she had different medical problems). | *a month-long transport strike*
3 months a long time, especially several months: *Redecorating the kitchen took months.* | **for/in months** *I haven't seen him for months.*
4 month after month used to emphasize that something happens regularly or continuously for a period of time: *I felt I was doing the same old thing week after week, month after month.*
5 month by month used when you are talking about a situation that develops slowly and steadily over a period of time: *Unemployment figures are rising month by month.*
6 never/not in a month of Sundays especially BrE spoken used to emphasize that something will definitely never happen: *You won't find someone to do that job in a month of Sundays.*

month·ly¹ S3 /ˈmʌnθli/ adj [only before noun]
1 happening once a month: *The mortgage is payable in monthly instalments.* | *a monthly publication*
2 used to talk about the total amount of something that is received, paid, measured, or calculated in a month: *a monthly salary of $850* | *a monthly rainfall of four inches*
3 a monthly ticket, PASS etc can be used for a period of one month —**monthly** adv: *They meet monthly to discuss progress.*

monthly² n plural **monthlies** [C] a magazine that appears once a month: *a leading women's monthly*

mon·ty /ˈmɒnti $ ˈmɑːn-/ n **the full monty** informal something that includes everything possible

mon·u·ment /ˈmɒnjᵿmənt $ ˈmɑː-/ n [C] **1** a building, STATUE, or other large structure that is built to remind people of an important event or famous person; → **memorial**: *He erected a monument on the spot where his daughter was killed.* | [+to] *a fitting monument to the men who died in the battle* **2** a very old building or place that is important historically: *Ancient monuments are protected by law.* **3** be a monument to sb/sth to show clearly the result of someone's qualities, beliefs, or actions: *The company is a monument to Sir Peter's energy and vision.* → NATIONAL MONUMENT

mon·u·ment·al /ˌmɒnjᵿˈmentl◂ $ ˌmɑː-/ adj **1** [usually before noun] a monumental achievement, piece of work, etc is very important and is usually based on many years of work: *a monumental contribution to the field of medicine* | *Charles Darwin's monumental study, 'The Origin of Species'* **2** [only before noun] extremely large, bad, good, impressive etc: *Banks and building societies were yesterday accused of monumental incompetence.* | *a monumental task* | *There was a monumental traffic jam on the freeway.* **3** [only before noun] relating to a monument or built as a monument: *a monumental arch*

mon·u·ment·al·ly /ˌmɒnjᵿˈmentəli $ ˌmɑː-/ *adv* extremely – usually used of negative qualities: *It was a monumentally stupid thing to do.*

moo /muː/ *v* [I] if a cow moos, it makes a long low sound —**moo** *n* [C]

mooch /muːtʃ/ *v* [T] *AmE informal* to get something by asking someone to give you it, instead of paying for it; ▣ **scrounge** *BrE*: **mooch sth off sb** *He tried to mooch a drink off me.*

   mooch around/about *phr v BrE informal* to move around slowly without any purpose and doing very little: *Beth was happy to mooch around for hours in her nightdress.*

mood S3 W3 /muːd/ *n*

1 WAY YOU FEEL [C] the way you feel at a particular time

in a good mood (=happy)
in a bad mood (=angry)
in a foul mood (=in a very bad mood)
in a confident/optimistic mood
in a holiday/party/festive mood
put sb in a good/bad etc mood (=make someone feel happy, angry etc)
get into the mood (=start to feel that you are ready and want to do something)
mood of confidence/optimism/despair/gloom etc
the general mood (=among a group of people)
the mood of the time/moment
sb's mood changes
mood swings (=sudden big changes in someone's mood)
lighten sb's mood (=make someone happier)
reflect/capture sb's mood (=show what someone is feeling)

*You're **in a good mood** this morning!* | *The manager was **in a foul mood** and was shouting at everyone.* | *The players are all **in a confident mood**.* | *What kind of mood is she in today?* | *The good weather **put him in an excellent** mood for breakfast.* | *It usually takes me a couple of days to **get into** the holiday **mood**.* | *The mood of the crowd was unpredictable.* | *the growing **mood of confidence** in East-West relations* | *the **general mood** of depression in the office* | *Why had her **mood changed** so dramatically?* | *a mental disorder characterized by severe **mood swings*** | *The weather did little to **lighten** their mood.* | *The movie accurately **reflects the mood of the time**.*

2 be in a mood to feel unhappy, impatient, or angry and to refuse to speak normally to other people: *He's been in a real mood all day.* | *Don't talk to her. She's **in one of her moods** (=used about someone who is often unhappy, angry etc).*

3 be/feel in the mood for sth to feel that you would like to do something: *We really felt in the mood for a party.* | *I don't want to talk about it now. I'm not in the mood.*

4 be in no mood for sth/to do sth to not want to do something, or be determined not to do something: *I was in no mood for a joke.* | *George was in no mood to be sociable.*

5 WAY A PLACE OR EVENT FEELS [singular] the way that a place, event, book, film etc seems or makes you feel: *The opening shot of dark, rainy streets sets the mood for the whole film.*

6 GRAMMAR [C] *technical* one of the sets of verb forms in grammar: the INDICATIVE (=expressing a fact or action), the IMPERATIVE (=expressing a command), the INTERROGATIVE (=expressing a question) or the SUBJUNCTIVE (=expressing a doubt or wish)

ˈmood-ˌaltering *adj* [only before noun] mood-altering drugs or substances affect your mind and change the way you think or feel

ˈmood ˌmusic *n* [U] music that is supposed to make you have particular feelings, especially romantic ones

mood·y /ˈmuːdi/ *adj* **1** annoyed or unhappy: *Keith had seemed moody all morning.* **2** often changing quickly from being in a good temper to being in a bad temper; ▣ **temperamental**: *a moody teenager* | *Lewis*

was aggressive, eccentric, moody, and brilliantly clever. **3** moody places, films, pictures, and music make you feel slightly sad, lonely, or perhaps frightened: *the moody grey sea in the dawn light* —**moodily** *adv*: *She was staring moodily into the fire.* —**moodiness** *n* [U]

moo·la, moolah /ˈmuːlə/ *n* [U] *AmE informal* money

moon¹ W3 /muːn/ *n*

1 the moon/the Moon the round object that you can see shining in the sky at night, and that moves around the Earth every 28 days: *The Americans landed on the moon in 1969.* | *the craters on the surface of the moon* → see picture at SOLAR SYSTEM

2 [C usually singular] the appearance or shape of the moon at a particular time: *a clear night with a bright moon* | *a thin crescent moon* | *It was raining and there was no moon* (=the moon could not be seen). → FULL MOON, HALF MOON, NEW MOON

3 [C] a round object that moves around a PLANET other than Earth: *the moons of Saturn*

4 ask for the moon also **cry for the moon** *BrE informal* to ask for something that is difficult or impossible to obtain: *There's no point in crying for the moon.*

5 over the moon *BrE informal* very happy: *She's over the moon about her new job.*

6 many moons ago *literary* a long time ago: *It all happened many moons ago.* → **once in a blue moon** at ONCE¹ (15); → **promise sb the moon** at PROMISE¹ (3)

moon² *v* [I,T] *informal* to bend over and show your BUTTOCKS as a joke or a way of insulting someone

   moon about/around *phr v BrE informal* to spend your time lazily, moving around with no real purpose: *I wish you'd stop mooning about and do something useful!*

   moon over sb/sth *phr v old-fashioned* to spend your time thinking about someone that you are in love with: *She sits mooning over his photograph for hours.*

moon·beam /ˈmuːnbiːm/ *n* [C] a shining line of light from the moon

ˈmoon boot *n* [C] a thick warm boot made of cloth or plastic, worn in snow and cold weather

moon·less /ˈmuːnləs/ *adj* a moonless sky or night is dark because the moon cannot be seen: *a cloudy, moonless night*

moon·light¹ /ˈmuːnlaɪt/ *n* [U] **1** the light of the moon: **in the moonlight** *The water looked silver in the moonlight.* | **pale/silver moonlight** *The hills were bathed in pale moonlight.* | **by moonlight** *We dined by moonlight.* **2 do a moonlight (flit)** *BrE* to leave a place secretly in the middle of the night in order to avoid paying money that you owe: *They did moonlight flits from one awful apartment to another.*

moonlight² *v* [I] *informal* **1** to have a second job in addition to your main job, especially without the knowledge of the government tax department: *She's been moonlighting as a waitress in the evenings.* **2** *BrE* to do paid work although you are getting money from the government because you do not officially have a job —**moonlighter** *n* [C] —**moonlighting** *n* [U]: *He's been doing some moonlighting for another company.*

moon·lit /ˈmuːnˌlɪt/ *adj* [only before noun] lit by the moon: *a moonlit garden*

moon·scape /ˈmuːnskeɪp/ *n* [singular] an area of land with no plants that looks like the surface of the moon

moon·shine /ˈmuːnʃaɪn/ *n* [U] *informal* **1** especially *AmE* strong alcoholic drink that is produced illegally **2** *BrE* an idea or statement that is silly or wrong and does not deserve serious attention; ▣ **nonsense**: *He regarded her plans as romantic moonshine.*

moon·stone /ˈmuːnstəʊn $ -stoʊn/ *n* [C,U] a milky-white stone used in making jewellery: *a moonstone necklace*

M

1 000, 2 000, 3 000, most frequent words in S poken and W ritten English

M

moon·struck /'muːnstrʌk/ *adj informal* slightly crazy, especially because you are in love

moor¹ /mʊə $ mʊr/ *n* [C usually plural] *especially BrE* a wild open area of high land, covered with rough grass or low bushes and HEATHER, that is not farmed because the soil is not good enough: *They went grouse shooting up on the moors.* | *the Yorkshire moors*

moor² *v* [I,T] to fasten a ship or boat to the land or to the bottom of the sea using ropes or an ANCHOR: *Two or three fishing boats were moored alongside the pier.*

Moor *n* [C] one of the Muslim people from North Africa who entered Spain in the 8th century and ruled the southern part of the country until 1492

moor·hen /'mʊəhen $ 'mʊr-/ *n* [C] *BrE* a black bird that lives beside streams and lakes

moor·ing /'mʊərɪŋ $ 'mʊr-/ *n* [C] **1 moorings** [plural] the ropes, chains, ANCHORS etc used to fasten a ship or boat to the land or the bottom of the sea: **break free of/slip its moorings** *The great ship slipped her moorings and slid out into the Atlantic.* **2** the place where a ship or boat is moored: *a temporary mooring*

Moor·ish /'mʊərɪʃ $ 'mʊr-/ *adj* relating to the Moors: *Moorish architecture*

moor·land /'mʊələnd $ 'mʊr-/ *n* [U] also **moorlands** [plural] *especially BrE* wild open countryside covered with rough grass and low bushes: *large areas of open moorland* —**moorland** *adj*: *a bleak moorland road*

moose /muːs/ *n plural* **moose** [C] a large brown animal like a DEER that has very large flat ANTLERS (=horns that grow like branches) and lives in North America, northern Europe, and parts of Asia

moot¹ /muːt/ *adj* **1 a moot point/question** something that has not yet been decided or agreed, and about which people have different opinions: *Whether these controls will really reduce violent crime is a moot point.* **2** *AmE* a situation or possible action that is moot is no longer likely to happen or exist: *The fear that airstrikes could endanger troops is moot now that the army is withdrawing.*

moot² *v* **be mooted** to be suggested for people to consider: *The question of changing the membership rules was mooted at the last meeting.*

moot court *n* [C] *AmE* a court in which law students practise holding TRIALS

mop¹ /mɒp $ mɑːp/ *n* [C] **1** a thing used for washing floors, consisting of a long stick with threads of thick string or a piece of SPONGE fastened to one end: *a mop and bucket* **2** a thing used for cleaning dishes, consisting of a short stick with a piece of SPONGE fastened to one end **3** [usually singular] *informal* a large amount of thick, often untidy hair: [+of] *He ran a hand through his mop of fair hair.*

mop² *v* **mopped**, **mopping** **1** [I,T] to wash a floor with a wet mop: *She carried on mopping the floor.* → see picture at CLEAN **2** [T] to dry your face by rubbing it with a cloth or something soft; ▣ **wipe**: *It was so hot he had to keep stopping to mop his face.* | *The doctor mopped his brow* (=removed sweat from his forehead) *with a handkerchief.* **3** [I,T] to remove liquid from a surface by rubbing it with a cloth or something soft: **mop sth from sth** *She gently mopped the blood from the wound.* | *He mopped the sweat from his face.* | **mop sth away** *She mopped the tears away with a lacy handkerchief.* **4 mop the floor with sb** *AmE* to completely defeat someone, for example in a game or argument; ▣ **wipe the floor with sb** *BrE*: *We mopped the floor with the team from Pomona High.*

mop sth/sb ⇔ **up** *phr v* **1** to remove liquid with a mop, a cloth, or something soft, especially in order to clean a surface; ▣ **wipe up**: *Mop the sauce up with your bread.* | *He mopped up the spilt milk.* **2** to remove or deal with something which you think is undesirable or dangerous, so that it is no longer a problem: *The usual solution is to send in infantry to mop up any remaining*

opposition. | *The rebellion has been crushed, but mopping-up operations may take several weeks.*

mope /məʊp $ moʊp/ *v* [I] to feel sorry for yourself, without making any effort to do anything or be more happy: *Don't lie there moping on a lovely morning like this!* | *The week he died, we all sat around and moped.*

mope around/about (sth) *phr v BrE* to move around a place in a sad, slow way, especially because you feel unhappy about the situation you are in: *She spends her days moping around the house.* | *Stephen didn't expect her to mope about while he was away on business.*

mo·ped /'məʊped $ 'moʊ-/ *n* [C] a small two-wheeled vehicle with an engine; → **motorcycle**

mop·pet /'mɒpɪt $ 'mɑː-/ *n* [C] *informal* a small child

mo·quette /mɒ'ket $ moʊ-/ *n* [U] a thick soft material used for covering furniture: *a moquette armchair*

mo·raine /mə'reɪn/ *n* [C] *technical* a mass of earth or pieces of rock moved along by a GLACIER and left in a line at the bottom of it

mor·al¹ S3 W2 /'mɒrəl $ 'mɔː-/ *adj*
1 [only before noun] relating to the principles of what is right and wrong behaviour, and with the difference between good and evil; → **morally, ethical**: *It is easy to have an opinion on a moral issue like the death penalty for murder.* | **moral philosophy** | **moral standards/ values/principles** *I think you can run a business to the highest moral standards.* | *If we accept that certain babies should be allowed to die, we place doctors in a **moral dilemma**.* | *Man is gifted with a **moral sense** by which he distinguishes good from evil.*
2 [only before noun] based on your ideas about what is right, rather than on what is legal or practical: *The book places a high **moral value** on marriage and the family unit.* | *The UN feels that it has the **moral authority** (=influence because people accept that its beliefs are right) to send troops to the area.* | **moral duty/obligation/responsibility** *A man has a moral duty to obey the law.* | *It isn't just **lack of moral fibre** (=lack of the emotional strength to do what you believe is right) which leads to a rising divorce rate.*
3 moral support encouragement that you give by expressing approval or interest, rather than by giving practical help: *Dad came along to give me some moral support.*
4 moral victory a situation in which you show that your beliefs are right and fair, even if you do not win: *Through Joan of Arc, France won a great moral victory.*
5 always behaving in a way that is based on strong principles about what is right and wrong; ▣ **immoral, amoral**: *a moral man of high integrity*
6 take/claim/seize the moral high ground to claim that you are the only person who does what is morally right in a situation, with the intention of being noticed and considered to be good by the public

moral² *n* [C] **1 morals** [plural] principles or standards of good behaviour, especially in matters of sex; → **ethics**: *the morals and customs of the Victorian period* | *Values and morals are independent of religious faith.* | *the corruption of **public morals** (=the standards of behaviour, especially sexual behaviour, expected by society) | *a young woman of **loose morals** (=low standards of sexual behaviour – often used humorously) **2** a practical lesson about what to do or how to behave, which you learn from a story or from something that happens to you; → **message**: [+of] *The moral of the film was that crime does not pay.*

mo·rale /mə'rɑːl $ mə'ræl/ *n* [U] the level of confidence and positive feelings that people have, especially people who work together, who belong to the same team etc: *A win is always good for morale.* | **low/high morale** *low staff morale* | *The failed coup caused a dramatic loss of morale within the army.* | **boost/raise/improve/ build morale** *There is a need to raise morale in the teaching profession.* | *the Prince's **morale-boosting** (=intended to raise morale) mission to the war-torn* *country* | maintain/keep up/restore morale *The media feels pressure to keep the morale of the country up in war time.*

mor·al·ist /ˈmɒrəlᵻst $ ˈmɔː-/ n [C]   **1** someone who has very strong beliefs about what is right and wrong and how people should behave – used to show disapproval: *a narrow-minded moralist*   **2** a teacher of moral principles

mor·al·ist·ic /ˌmɒrəˈlɪstɪk◂ $ ˌmɔː-/ adj with very strong beliefs about what is right and wrong, especially when this makes you judge other people's behaviour: *It's difficult to talk to teenagers about drugs without sounding too moralistic.*

mo·ral·i·ty /məˈrælᵻti/ n [U]   **1** beliefs or ideas about what is right and wrong and about how people should behave: *sexual morality* | **public/private/personal morality** *the decline in standards of personal morality* | *The authorities are protectors of public morality.* | **conventional/traditional morality** *a lack of concern for conventional morality*   **2** the degree to which something is right or acceptable: [+of] *a discussion on the morality of abortion*

mor·al·ize also **-ise** *BrE* /ˈmɒrəlaɪz $ ˈmɔː-/ v [I] to tell other people your ideas about right and wrong behaviour, especially when they have not asked for your opinion; ▣ **preach**: *politicians moralizing about people's sexual behaviour*

mor·al·ly /ˈmɒrəli $ ˈmɔː-/ adv   **1** according to moral principles about what is right and wrong: *What you did wasn't illegal, but it was **morally wrong**.* | *There is a belief that village life is somehow morally superior to city life.* | *Such hypocrisy is morally indefensible.* | *The Constitution is not morally neutral but is based on certain central values.*   **2 morally certain** *old-fashioned* certain about something that cannot be proved: *I am morally certain that he is incapable of deliberately harming anyone.*

moral ma·jority n **the moral majority** the group of people in a society who have strong moral beliefs and think they are always right. In the US there is an organized group called the Moral Majority, who have strong Christian principles: *Smokers today are often made to feel like social outcasts by the moral majority.*

mo·rass /məˈræs/ n   **1** [singular] a complicated and confusing situation that is very difficult to get out of: *We're trying to drag the country out of its economic morass.* | [+of] *They were **stuck** in a **morass** of paperwork.*   **2** [C] *literary* a dangerous area of soft wet ground; ▣ **marsh**

mor·a·to·ri·um /ˌmɒrəˈtɔːriəm $ ˌmɔː-/ n plural **moratoriums** or **moratoria** [C usually singular]   **1** an official stopping of an activity for a period of time: [+on] *a moratorium on nuclear testing*   **2** a law or an agreement that gives people more time to pay their debts: *a two-year moratorium on interest payments*

mor·bid /ˈmɔːbᵻd $ ˈmɔːr-/ adj   **1** with a strong and unhealthy interest in unpleasant subjects, especially death: *morbid fascination/curiosity a morbid fascination with instruments of torture* | *The trip was made all the worse by Frankie's **morbid fear** of flying.* | *His head was full of morbid thoughts.*   **2** *medical* relating to or caused by a disease: *a morbid gene* —**morbidly** adv —**morbidity** /mɔːˈbɪdᵻti $ mɔːr-/ n [U]

mor·dant /ˈmɔːdənt $ ˈmɔːr-/ adj **mordant wit/satire/humour** *formal* unkind and insulting humour etc that is also funny; ▣ **biting**: *The play's mordant comedy makes for compelling viewing.*

more¹ S1 W1 /mɔː $ mɔːr/ adv   **1** [used before an adjective or adverb to form the comparative] having a particular quality to a greater degree; ▣ **less**: *You'll have to be more careful next time.* | *Can't it be done more quickly?* | **much/a lot/far more** *Children generally feel much more confident working in groups.* | **more ... than** *It was a lot more expensive than I had expected.* | *Your health is more important than anything else.* | *Children can often do these puzzles more easily than adults.* | *Selling goods abroad is **no**

---

more **difficult** (=not more difficult) *than selling to the home market.* △ Do not use **more** with the -er form of an adjective or adverb: *I'll be smarter than before* (NOT *I'll be more smarter than before*).
  2 used to say that something happens a greater number of times or for longer; ▣ **less**: *I promised Mum that I'd help more with the housework.* | *You need to get out of the house more.* | **more than** *Children are using the library more than they used to.* | *He travels around **a lot more** now that he has a car.*
  3 used to say that something happens to a greater degree; ▣ **less**: *She cares **a lot more** for her dogs than she does for me.* | **more than** *It's his manner I dislike, more than anything else.*
  4 more and more used to say that a quality, situation etc gradually increases; ▣ **increasingly**: *More and more, we are finding that people want to continue working beyond 60.* | *As the disease worsened, he found walking more and more difficult.*
  5 more or less almost: *a place where the ground was more or less flat* | *They've settled here more or less permanently.* | *He more or less accused me of lying.*
  6 once more a) again, and often for the last time: *May I thank you all once more for making this occasion such a big success.* | *Once more the soldiers attacked and once more they were defeated.* **b)** used to say that someone or something returns to the situation they were in before: *Within a year, England was once more at war with France.*
  7 not any more also **no more** *literary* if something does not happen any more, it used to happen but does not happen now: *Sarah doesn't live here any more.*
  8 more than happy/welcome/likely etc very happy, welcome, likely etc – used to emphasize what you are saying: *The store is more than happy to deliver goods to your home.* | *The police are more than likely to ban the match.*
  9 the more ..., the more/less ... used to say that if a particular activity increases, another change happens as a result: *The more I thought about it, the less I liked the idea.*
  10 be more sth than sth to be one thing rather than another: *It was more a worry than a pleasure.*
  11 more than a little *formal* fairly: *The lectures were more than a little disappointing.*
  12 no more does/has/will etc sb *spoken old-fashioned* used to say that a negative statement is also true about someone else; ▣ **nor**, **neither**: *'He didn't know the reason for his leaving.' 'No more do I* (=neither do I)*'.*
  13 no more ... than used to emphasize that someone or something does not have a particular quality or would not do something: *He's no more fit to be a priest than I am.* → **more often than not** at OFTEN (5); → **more fool you/him etc** at FOOL¹ (7); → **that's more like it/this is more like it** at LIKE¹ (11)

more² S1 W1 determiner, pron [comparative of 'many' and 'much']
  1 a greater amount or number; ▣ **less, fewer**: *We should spend more on health and education.* | **more (...) than** *More people are buying new cars than ever before.* | **much/a lot/far more** *Diane earns a lot more than I do.* | **more than 10/100 etc** *Our plane took off more than two hours late.* | *More than a quarter of the students never finished their courses.* | [+of] *Viewers want better television, and more of it.* | *Perhaps next year more of us will be able to afford holidays abroad.*
  2 an additional number or amount; ▣ **less**: *I really am interested. Tell me more.* | *We need five more chairs.* | **a little/many/some/any more** *Can I have a little more time to finish?* | *Are there any more sandwiches?* | *I have **no more** questions.* | [+of] *You'd better take some more of your medicine.* | *Don't waste any more of my time.*
  3 more and more an increasing number or amount; ▣ **less and less**: *More and more people are moving to the cities.*
  4 not/no more than sth used to emphasize that a

particular number, amount, distance etc is not large: *It's a beautiful cottage not more than five minutes from the nearest beach.* | *Opinion polls show that no more than 30% of people trust the government.*

5 the more ..., the more/less ... used to say that if an amount of something increases, another change happens as a result: *It always seems like the more I earn, the more I spend.*

6 be more of sth than sth to be one thing rather than another: *It was more of a holiday than a training exercise.*

7 no more than a) used to say that something is not too much, but exactly right or suitable: *It's no more than you deserve.* | *Eline felt it was no more than her duty to look after her husband.* **b)** also **little more than** used to say that someone or something is not very great or important: *He's no more than a glorified accountant.* | *He left school with little more than a basic education.*

8 (and) what's more used to add more information that emphasizes what you are saying: *I've been fortunate to find a career that I love and, what is more, I get well paid for it.*

9 no more sth used to say that something will or should no longer happen: *No more dreary winters – we're moving to Florida.* → **more's the pity** at PITY¹ (4)

more·ish /ˈmɔːrɪʃ/ *adj BrE spoken* food or drink that is moreish tastes very good, and makes you want to have more of it

more·o·ver W2 /mɔːrˈəʊvə $ -ˈoʊvər/ *adv* [sentence adverb] *formal* in addition – used to introduce information that adds to or supports what has previously been said: *The rent is reasonable and, moreover, the location is perfect.* | *The source of the information is irrelevant. Moreover, the information need not be confidential.* ⚠ **Moreover** is very formal and not common in spoken English. Use **besides** or **also** instead.

mo·res /ˈmɔːreɪz/ *n* [plural] *formal* the customs, social behaviour, and moral values of a particular group: *contemporary social and sexual mores*

morgue /mɔːg $ mɔːrg/ *n* [C] **1** a building or room, usually in a hospital, where dead bodies are kept until they are buried or CREMATED; ☐ **mortuary** **2** a place that has become very quiet and dull – used humorously: *This place is like a morgue.*

mor·i·bund /ˈmɒrɪbʌnd $ ˈmɔː-, ˈmɑː-/ *adj* **1** a moribund organization, industry, etc is no longer active or effective and may be coming to an end: *The region's heavy industry is still inefficient and moribund.* | *A cut in interest rates will help the country's moribund housing market.* **2** *literary* slowly dying: *The patient was moribund by the time the doctor arrived.*

Mor·mon /ˈmɔːmən $ ˈmɔːr-/ *n* [C] a member of a religious organization formed in 1830 in the US, officially called The Church of Jesus Christ of Latterday Saints —**Mormon** *adj* —**Mormonism** *n* [U]

morn /mɔːn $ mɔːrn/ *n* [C usually singular] *literary* morning

morn·ing¹ S1 W1 /ˈmɔːnɪŋ $ ˈmɔːr-/ *n* [C,U]
1 the early part of the day, from when the sun rises until 12 o'clock in the middle of the day

in the morning(s)
on Monday/Friday/Saturday etc morning
tomorrow morning
yesterday morning
this morning (=today in the morning)
(the) next morning
late morning
early morning
morning sun/light/mist

It was a nice sunny morning. | *I hated those cold winter mornings.* | *Classes start in the morning and go through the whole day.* | *He stayed in bed late on Sunday morning.* | *I'll see you tomorrow morning.* | *I only met her yesterday morning.* | *I'm not feeling too good this morning.* | *Next morning I went to the*

bank. | *It was still only late morning.* | *He took the early morning train.* | *a copy of the morning paper*

2 the part of the day from 12 o'clock at night until 12 o'clock in the middle of the day: **two/four o'clock in the morning** *The phone rang at three in the morning.* | *It's four o'clock in the morning.* | *I woke up in the small hours of the morning* (=very early, before dawn).
3 in the morning if something will happen in the morning, it will happen during the morning of the following day: *I'll deal with that in the morning.*
4 mornings during the morning of each day: *She works mornings at the local school.*
5 morning, noon, and night used to emphasize that something happens a lot or continuously: *I was on duty morning, noon, and night.* → COFFEE MORNING

morning² *interjection* used to greet someone in the morning: *Morning, Dave. How are you?*

morning-ˈafter pill *n* [C] a drug that a woman can take a few hours after having sex to prevent her from becoming PREGNANT

ˈmorning coat *n* [C] a formal black coat with a long back that is worn as part of morning dress

ˈmorning dress *n* [U] *especially BrE* men's formal clothes that include a morning coat, trousers, and a TOP HAT, worn at daytime ceremonies such as weddings

ˌmorning ˈglory /$ ˈ.. ˌ../ *n* [C,U] a plant that has white, blue, or pink flowers that open in the morning and close in late afternoon

ˌMorning ˈPrayer *n* [U] a morning church service in the Church of England and the Episcopal Church in the US; ☐ **matins**

ˈmorning room *n* [C] *old-fashioned* a comfortable room that is used in the morning, usually in a large house

ˈmorning ˌsickness *n* [U] a feeling of sickness that some women have during the morning when they are PREGNANT, usually in the early months

ˌmorning ˈstar *n* [singular] a bright PLANET, usually Venus, that you can see in the eastern sky when the sun rises

ˈmorning suit *n* [C] a man's suit that is worn at formal ceremonies during the day, especially weddings

mo·roc·co /məˈrɒkəʊ $ məˈrɑːkoʊ/ *n* [U] fine soft leather used especially for covering books

mo·ron /ˈmɔːrɒn $ -rɑːn/ *n* [C] **1** *informal not polite* a very offensive word for someone who you think is very stupid; ☐ **idiot**: *Don't leave it there, you moron!* **2** *technical old-fashioned* someone whose intelligence has not developed to the normal level —**moronic** /məˈrɒnɪk $ -ˈrɑː-/ *adj*: *a moronic grin*

mo·rose /məˈrəʊs $ -ˈroʊs/ *adj* bad-tempered, unhappy, and silent: *Daniel seems very morose and gloomy.* —**morosely** *adv*: *He stared morosely at the floor.* —**moroseness** *n* [U]

morph /mɔːf $ mɔːrf/ *v* [I,T] to develop a new appearance or change into something else, or to make something do this: [+into] *The river flooded its banks and morphed into a giant sea that swamped the town.*

mor·pheme /ˈmɔːfiːm $ ˈmɔːr-/ *n* [C] *technical* the smallest unit of meaning in a language. The words 'so', 'the' and 'boy' consist of one morpheme. 'Boys' consists of two morphemes, 'boy' and 's'.: *the past tense morpheme* | *the plural morpheme*

Mor·phe·us /ˈmɔːfiəs, -fjuːs $ ˈmɔːr-/ *n* **in the arms of Morpheus** *literary* asleep

mor·phi·a /ˈmɔːfiə $ ˈmɔːr-/ *n* [U] *old-fashioned* morphine

mor·phine /ˈmɔːfiːn $ ˈmɔːr-/ *n* [U] a powerful and ADDICTIVE drug used for stopping pain and making people calmer

morph·ing /ˈmɔːfɪŋ $ ˈmɔːr-/ *n* [U] a computer method that is used to make one image gradually change into a different one

mor·phol·o·gy /mɔːˈfɒlədʒi $ mɔːrˈfɑː-/ *n plural* **morphologies** *technical* **1** [U] the study of the MOR-

PHEMES of a language and of the way in which they are joined together to make words; → **syntax** **2** [U] the scientific study of the form and structure of animals and plants **3** [C,U] the structure of an object or system or the way it was formed —**morphological** /ˌmɔːfəˈlɒdʒɪkəl◂ $ ˌmɔːrfəˈlɑː-/ *adj: the morphological features of cells* —**morphologically** /-kli/ *adv*

mor·ris danc·ing /ˈmɒrɟs ˌdɑːnsɪŋ $ ˈmɔːrɟs ˌdænsɪŋ, ˈmɑː-/ *n* [U] traditional English country dancing performed by men wearing white clothes decorated with small bells —**morris dancer** *n* [C]

mor·row /ˈmɒrəʊ $ ˈmɔːroʊ, ˈmɑː-/ *n* **1 the morrow** *old use* **a)** the next day; 🔲 **tomorrow**: *on the morrow* *They were to arrive on the morrow.* **b)** the future: *Take no thought for the morrow* (=do not worry about the future). **2 on the morrow of sth** *literary* immediately after a particular event: *on the morrow of victory* **3 good morrow** *old use* GOOD MORNING

Morse code /ˌmɔːs ˈkəʊd $ ˌmɔːrs ˈkoʊd/ *n* [U] a system of sending messages in which the alphabet is represented by signals made of DOTS (=short signals) and DASHES (=long signals) in sound or light: **in Morse code** *a message in Morse code*

mor·sel /ˈmɔːsəl $ ˈmɔːr-/ *n* [C] a very small amount of something, especially a small piece of food; 🔲 **scrap**: [+**of**] *a morsel of bread* | *a morsel of scandal* | *birds searching for **tasty morsels***

mor·tal[1] /ˈmɔːtl $ ˈmɔːrtl/ *adj* **1** not able to live for ever; 🔲 **immortal**: *Her father's death reminded her that she was mortal.* **2 mortal blow/danger/wound etc a)** something very serious, that may cause the end of something: *The computer has dealt a mortal blow to traditional printing methods.* | *Our health service is in mortal danger.* **b)** something that causes death or may cause death; → **lethal**: *Near the end of the battle, he received a mortal wound.* | *the screams of men in **mortal combat*** (=fighting until one person kills the other) **3 mortal enemy/foe** an enemy that you hate very much and will always hate: *He glared at Claudia as if she were his mortal enemy.* **4 mortal fear/dread/terror** extreme fear: *She lives in mortal fear of her husband's anger.* **5 sb's mortal remains** *formal* someone's body, after they have died: *the churchyard where his mortal remains lie* (=where his body is buried) **6** *literary* human – used especially when comparing humans with gods, SPIRITS etc: *Both gods and mortal men found her captivating.* **7 mortal coil** *literary* life or the state of being alive: *when Hubbard **shuffled off this mortal coil*** (=died)

mortal[2] *n* [C] **1 lesser/ordinary/mere mortals** ordinary people, as compared with people who are more important, more powerful, or more skilled – used humorously: *She dines in the executive suite, while we lesser mortals use the staff cafeteria.* **2** *literary* a human – used especially when comparing humans with gods, SPIRITS etc

mor·tal·i·ty /mɔːˈtæləti $ mɔːr-/ *n plural* **mortalities** **1** [U] also **mor'tality ˌrate** /ˈ.../ the number of deaths during a particular period of time among a particular type or group of people: *Mortality from heart disease varies widely across the world.* | **infant/child/maternal/adult mortality** *an appallingly high **infant mortality rate*** (=number of babies who die) **2** [U] the condition of being human and having to die; 🔲 **immortality**: *My mother's death forced me to face the fact of my **own mortality**.* **3** [C] *technical* a death: *mortalities from cancer*

mor·tal·ly /ˈmɔːtəl-i $ ˈmɔːr-/ *adv* **1** in a way that will cause death; 🔲 **fatally**: *He regarded the **mortally** wounded man with no pity in his heart.* **2** extremely or greatly: *He was mortally afraid of upsetting her.* | *I tried to be tactful, but he seemed to be mortally offended.*

ˌ**mortal 'sin** *n* [C,U] something that you do that is so bad, according to the Roman Catholic Church, that your soul will be punished for ever after death unless you ask to be forgiven

mor·tar /ˈmɔːtə $ ˈmɔːrtər/ *n* **1** [U] a mixture of CEMENT or LIME, and sand and water, used in building for holding bricks or stones together **2** [C] a heavy gun that fires bombs or SHELLS in a high curve: *A cameraman was killed when his vehicle came under **mortar fire**.* | *a **mortar attack*** **3** [C] a stone bowl in which substances are crushed with a PESTLE (=tool with a heavy round end): *You'll need a pestle and mortar to grind the spices.* → **bricks and mortar** at BRICK[1] (2)

mor·tar·board /ˈmɔːtəbɔːd $ ˈmɔːrtərbɔːrd/ *n* [C] a black cap with a flat square top worn by members of some universities on formal occasions

mort·gage[1] W3 /ˈmɔːgɪdʒ $ ˈmɔːr-/ *n* [C] **1** a legal arrangement by which you borrow money from a bank or similar organization in order to buy a house, and pay back the money over a period of years: *Your building society or bank will help arrange a mortgage.* | *They've **taken out** a 30 year **mortgage*** (=they will pay for their house over a period of 30 years). | *We decided to use Fred's redundancy money to **pay off** the **mortgage*** (=pay back all the money we borrowed for a mortgage). | ***Mortgage rates** are set to rise again in the spring.* | *She was having trouble meeting her **mortgage payments**.* **2** the amount of money you borrow in the form of a mortgage: *If you earn £20,000 per year, then you may be able to get a mortgage of £60,000.*

mortgage[2] *v* [T] **1** if you mortgage your home, land, or property, you borrow money, usually from a bank, and if you cannot pay back the money within a particular period of time, the bank has the right to sell your property in order to get the money you owe it: *We mortgaged our house to start Paul's business.* **2 mortgage the/sb's future** to borrow money or do something that is likely to cause problems in the future, that other people will have to deal with: *The report explains how governments are mortgaging their nations' futures.*

mort·ga·gee /ˌmɔːgəˈdʒiː $ ˌmɔːr-/ *n* [C] a person or organization that lends money to people to buy property

mort·ga·gor /ˈmɔːgɪdʒə $ ˈmɔːrgɪdʒər/ *n* [C] a person who borrows money from a bank or other organization in order to buy property

mor·ti·cian /mɔːˈtɪʃən $ mɔːr-/ *n* [C] *AmE* someone whose job is to arrange funerals and prepare bodies to be buried; 🔲 **undertaker** *BrE*

mor·ti·fied /ˈmɔːtɟfaɪd $ ˈmɔːr-/ *adj* extremely offended, ashamed, or embarrassed: **mortified to hear/find etc** *Nora was mortified to discover that her daughter had been out drinking.* —**mortification** /ˌmɔːtɟfɟˈkeɪʃən $ ˌmɔːr-/ *n* [U]

mor·ti·fy /ˈmɔːtɟfaɪ $ ˈmɔːr-/ *v* **mortified, mortifying, mortifies** [T] **1** to cause someone to feel extremely embarrassed or ashamed **2 mortify the flesh/yourself** *formal* to try to control your natural physical desires and needs by making your body suffer pain —**mortifying** *adj*

mor·tise, mortice /ˈmɔːtɟs $ ˈmɔːr-/ *n* [C] *technical* a hole cut in a piece of wood or stone so that the shaped end of another piece will fit there firmly; → **tenon**

ˈ**mortise lock** *n* [C] *BrE* a strong lock that fits into a hole cut in the edge of a door; 🔲 **dead bolt** *AmE*

mor·tu·a·ry[1] /ˈmɔːtʃuəri $ ˈmɔːrtʃueri/ *n plural* **mortuaries** [C] **1** *BrE* a building or room, for example in a hospital, where dead bodies are kept before they are buried or CREMATED; 🔲 **morgue** **2** *AmE* the place where a body is kept before a funeral and where the funeral is sometimes held

mortuary[2] *adj* [only before noun] *formal* connected with death or funerals: *a mortuary urn*

M

mosaic /məʊˈzeɪ-ɪk $ moʊ-/ n **1** [C,U] a pattern or picture made by fitting together small pieces of coloured stone, glass etc: *rooms decorated with wall paintings and mosaics* | *a 3rd century Roman mosaic floor* **2** [C usually singular] a group of different things that exist next to each other or together: [+of] *The forest floor was a mosaic of autumn colours.* | *the complex mosaic of world cultures*

Mo·sa·ic adj relating to Moses, the great leader of the Jewish people in ancient times: *the Mosaic law*

Mo·ses bas·ket /ˈməʊzɪz ˌbɑːskɪ̯t $ ˈmoʊzɪz ˌbæ-/ n [C] BrE a large basket with handles, in which a baby can sleep and be carried

mo·sey /ˈməʊzi $ ˈmoʊ-/ v [I always + adv/prep] AmE informal **1** to walk somewhere in a slow relaxed way – used humorously: *I guess I'll mosey on down to the store now.* **2** **I'd better mosey along/be moseying along** I should leave now: *I'd better mosey along – it's getting late.* —**mosey** n [singular]

mosh /mɒʃ $ mɑːʃ/ v [I] informal to dance very violently at a concert with loud ROCK or PUNK music

'mosh pit n [C] informal an area in front of the stage at a ROCK or PUNK concert where people dance with a lot of energy, often hitting their bodies against other people

Mos·lem /ˈmɒzlɪ̯m $ ˈmɑːz-/ n [C] another spelling of MUSLIM —**Moslem** adj

mosque /mɒsk $ mɑːsk/ n [C] a building in which Muslims worship

mos·qui·to /məˈskiːtəʊ $ -toʊ/ n plural **mosquitoes** or **mosquitos** [C] a small flying insect that sucks the blood of people and animals, sometimes spreading the disease MALARIA → see picture at INSECT

mos'quito net n [C] a net placed over a bed as a protection against mosquitoes

moss /mɒs $ mɒːs/ n [C,U] a very small green plant that grows in a thick soft furry mass on wet soil, trees, or rocks —**mossy** adj: *a high, mossy wall*

most¹ S1 W1 /məʊst $ moʊst/ adv
1 [used before an adjective or adverb to form the superlative] having the greatest amount of a particular quality; ◨ **least**: *She's one of the most experienced teachers in the district.* | *The most important thing is to stay calm.* | *A recent study showed that gardening is easily the most popular activity among the over 50s.* | *We shall find out which system works most effectively.* | *It is the kind of tea most often served in Chinese restaurants.*
2 to a greater degree or more times than anything else: *What annoyed him most was the way she wouldn't even listen.* | *I guess the food I eat most is pasta.* | *Most of all, I just felt sad that it was over.*
3 [+adj/adv] formal very: *Thank you for a most interesting evening.* | *I was most surprised to hear of your engagement.*
4 AmE informal almost: *He plays poker most every evening.*

> **GRAMMAR**
> When you mean 'nearly all' use **most**, not **the most**: *Most pupils wanted to go to university (NOT The most pupils wanted to go to university).*
> Use **the most** when you are comparing one person or thing with all others: *It was the most terrifying experience of my life.*
> In spoken English, you can also use **the most** when you are talking about just two people or things: *Who's the most talented – Will or Gareth?* but some users of English think that this use is incorrect and use **the more** instead: *Who is the more talented – Will or Gareth?*
> ⚠ Do not use **most** with the -est form of an adjective or adverb: *one of the hardest things to do (NOT one of the most hardest things to do)*

most² S1 W1 determiner, pron [the superlative of 'many' and 'much']
1 nearly all of the people or things in a group, or nearly

all of something; ◨ **the majority**: *Like most people, I try to take a vacation every year.* | *Most research in this field has been carried out by the Russians.* | [+of] *It was Sunday and most of the shops were shut.* | *Most of what Hannah told me wasn't true.* | *Some were barefoot, most were in rags.* | **most of the time/most days etc** (=usually) *Most of the time it's very quiet here.* | *Most evenings we just stay in and watch TV.*
2 a larger amount or number than anyone or anything else: **the most** *The team that scores the most points wins.* | *Which class has the most children in it?* | *It's unfair that you should have to pay the most when you earn so little.* | *The animal that caused most trouble was a little black puppy.*
3 the largest number or amount possible: *The aim is to help patients to obtain most benefit from their treatment.* | **the most** *The most you can hope to achieve is just to get him to listen to your ideas.*
4 **at (the) most** used to say that you think an amount cannot be larger than the amount you are mentioning: *It'll take 20 minutes at the most.* | *There were at most 50 people in the audience.* | *The boy looked nine at the very most* (=he was probably younger).
5 **for the most part** used to say that something is generally true but not completely true: *For the most part, people seemed pretty friendly.*
6 **make the most of sth/get the most out of sth** to gain the greatest possible advantage from something: *Charming and friendly, she will help you make the most of your visit.* | *advice on how to get the most out of your computer*

-most /məʊst $ moʊst/ suffix [in adjectives] nearest to something: *the northernmost town in Sweden* (=the town that is furthest to the north) | *the topmost branches of the tree*

most·ly S2 W3 /ˈməʊstli $ ˈmoʊst-/ adv used to talk about most members of a group, most occasions, most parts of something etc; ◨ **mainly**: *Green teas are mostly from China or Japan.* | *There were about fifteen people in the lounge, mostly women.* | *He blamed his parents. Mostly he blamed his dad.*

MOT /ˌem əʊ ˈtiː $ -oʊ-/ also ˌ**MO'T test** n [C] a test in Britain that all cars more than three years old must pass every year in order to show that they are still safe to be driven: *My car's just failed its MOT.* | *an MOT certificate*

mote /məʊt $ moʊt/ n [C] old-fashioned a very small piece of dust

mo·tel /məʊˈtel $ moʊ-/ n [C] a hotel for people who are travelling by car, where you can park your car outside your room → see picture at STAY

mo·tet /məʊˈtet $ moʊ-/ n [C] a piece of music on a religious subject

moth /mɒθ $ mɒːθ/ n [C] an insect related to the BUTTERFLY that flies mainly at night and is attracted to lights. Some moths eat holes in cloth → see picture at INSECT

moth·ball¹ /ˈmɒθbɔːl $ ˈmɒːθbɒːl/ n [C usually plural] **1** a small ball made of a strong-smelling chemical, used for keeping moths away from clothes **2** **in/into mothballs** kept but not used for a long time: *With the end of the Cold War, several warships were put into mothballs.*

mothball² v [T] to stop using a factory, equipment etc or to not continue with a plan, temporarily but possibly for a long time: *The hospital manager said the project would be mothballed until funding became available.*

'moth-ˌeaten adj **1** cloth that is moth-eaten has had holes eaten in it by moths: *a moth-eaten sweater* **2** old and in bad condition: *a moth-eaten old sofa*

moth·er¹ S1 W1 /ˈmʌðə $ -ər/ n [C]
1 a female parent of a child or animal: *His mother and father are both doctors.* | **mother of two/three etc** (=mother of two/three etc children) *Janet is a full-time teacher and a mother of two.* | *the relationship between mother and child* | *Goodnight, Mother.* | *Mother said they'd met at university.* | *If food is scarce, the mother*

will feed the smaller, weaker chicks. | **mother cat/bird/ hen etc** (=an animal that is a mother)

2 be (like) a mother to sb to care for someone as if you were their mother: *She's like a mother to them. If they need anything she always helps out.*

3 like a mother hen if someone behaves like a mother hen, they try to protect their children too much and worry about them all the time

4 learn/be taught sth at your mother's knee to learn something when you are a very young child: *the prayers which he had been taught at his mother's knee*

5 the mother of sth a) the origin or cause of something: *Westminster is known as 'the mother of parliaments'.* | *Necessity is the mother of invention* (=people have good ideas when the situation makes it necessary). **b)** *informal* a very severe or extreme type of something, usually something bad: *I woke up with the mother of all hangovers.*

6 *spoken especially AmE* something very large and usually very good: *a real mother of a car*

7 *AmE taboo spoken* MOTHERFUCKER

8 Mother used to address the woman who is in charge of a CONVENT

mother² v [T] to look after and protect someone as if you were their mother, especially by being too kind and doing everything for them: *I don't like being mothered!*

moth·er·board /ˈmʌðəbɔːd $ -ɔːrbɪrd/ n [C] *technical* a board where all the CIRCUITS of a computer are placed

mother country n [C usually singular] **1** someone's mother country is the country where they or their family were born and to which they feel a very strong emotional connection, even if they are no longer living there; ◼ **motherland** **2** a powerful country that controls or used to control a less powerful country: *The bond between the mother country and her former colonies grew stronger.*

Mother Earth n the world, considered as the place or thing from which all life comes

moth·er·fuck·er /ˈmʌðəˌfʌkə $ -ðərˌfʌkər/ n [C] *AmE taboo spoken* a very offensive word for someone that you dislike very much or that you are very angry with. Do not use this word. **—motherfucking** *adj*

moth·er·hood /ˈmʌðəhʊd $ -ðər-/ n [U] the state of being a mother: *the challenge of combining a career with motherhood* | *teenagers who are unprepared for motherhood*

moth·er·ing /ˈmʌðərɪŋ/ n [U] the process of caring for children in the way that a mother does: *mothering skills* | *Babies and young children need mothering.*

Mothering Sunday n [C,U] *BrE old-fashioned* MOTHER'S DAY

mother-in-law n plural **mothers-in-law** [C] the mother of your wife or husband

moth·er·land /ˈmʌðəlænd $ -ðər-/ n [C usually singular] someone's motherland is the country where they were born and to which they feel a strong emotional connection; ◼ **mother country, fatherland**: *They are willing to die for the motherland.*

moth·er·less /ˈmʌðələs $ -ðər-/ adj a motherless child is one whose mother has died: *homes for children who had been left motherless*

mother lode, **moth·er·lode** /ˈmʌðələʊd $ -ðərloʊd/ n [C usually singular] *AmE* **1** a mine that is full of gold, silver etc **2** a place where you can find a lot of a particular type of object: [+of] *The catalog is a mother lode of men's gadgets and toys.*

moth·er·ly /ˈmʌðəli $ -ðər-/ adj a motherly woman is loving and kind, like a good mother; → **maternal**: *her motherly instincts* | *She was a plump, motherly woman in her fifties.* **—motherliness** n [U]

Mother Nature n used to talk about nature, especially when it is thought of as a force that affects people and the world: *How could Mother Nature have dealt such a savage blow?*

Mother of God n a title for Mary, the mother of Jesus Christ, used in the Roman Catholic Church

mother-of-pearl n [U] a pale-coloured hard smooth shiny substance that forms the inside of some SHELLFISH, and is used for making buttons, jewellery etc

mother's boy *BrE* a man or boy who allows his mother to protect him too much and is considered weak; ◼ **mama's boy** *AmE*

Mother's Day n [C,U] a day on which people give cards and presents to their mothers

mother ship n [C] a large ship or spacecraft from which smaller boats or spacecraft are sent out

Mother Superior n [C usually singular] the woman who is in charge of a CONVENT

mother-to-be n plural **mothers-to-be** [C] a woman who is going to have a baby

mother tongue n [C] *especially BrE* your mother tongue is the first and main language that you learnt when you were a child; ◼ **native language/tongue**: *children for whom English is not their mother tongue*

mo·tif /məʊˈtiːf $ moʊ-/ n [C] **1** an idea, subject, or image that is regularly repeated and developed in a book, film, work of art etc: *The theme of creation is a recurrent motif in Celtic mythology.* **2** a small picture or pattern used to decorate something plain: *a white T-shirt with a blue fish motif* **3** an arrangement of notes that is often repeated in a musical work

mo·tion¹ W3 /ˈməʊʃən $ ˈmoʊ-/ n

1 MOVEMENT [U] the process of moving or the way that someone or something moves: [+of] *the motion of the planets* | *The rocking motion of the boat made Sylvia feel sick.* | *Newton's first law of motion*

2 MOVING YOUR HEAD OR HAND [C] a single movement of your hand or head, especially one made in order to communicate something; ◼ **gesture**: [+of] *He summoned the waiter with a motion of his hand.* | *Doyle glanced back at Bodie, and made a slight motion with his head.*

3 SUGGESTION AT A MEETING [C] a proposal that is made formally at a meeting, and then is usually decided on by voting: *The motion was defeated by 201 votes to 159.* | **motion to do sth/motion that** *We will now vote on the motion that membership charges should rise by 15%.* | **pass/carry/approve a motion** (=accept it by voting) *The motion was carried unanimously.* | *I urge you to support this motion.* | **propose/put forward/ table a motion** (=make a proposal) *I'd like to propose a motion to move the weekly meetings to Thursdays.* | *The motion was seconded* (=formally supported) *by Mr. Levin.* | *The attorneys filed a motion* (=made a proposal in a court) *for a temporary restraining order.*

4 in motion *formal* moving from one place or position to another: *The end doors are not to be used when the train is in motion.*

5 set/put sth in motion to start a process or series of events that will continue for some time: *The Church voted to set in motion the process allowing women to be priests.* | *Once the house had been sold, Jane set the wheels in motion* (=started the process) *to find somewhere smaller to live.*

6 go through the motions (of doing sth) to do something because you have to do it, without being very interested in it: *I feel so bored at work, like I'm just going through the motions.*

7 BODY WASTE [C] solid waste material that comes out when you empty your BOWELS - used especially by doctors and nurses → SLOW MOTION, TIME AND MOTION STUDY

motion² v [I,T] to give someone directions or instructions by moving your hand or head; ◼ **signal**: **motion (for) sb to do sth** *The police officer motioned for me to pull over.* | **motion to sb to do sth** *He motioned to the barman to refill their glasses.* | **motion sb forward/away etc** *His father motioned him forward.* | **motion sb into/to sth** *I saw her motioning me into the room.*

M

moun·tain·side /ˈmaʊntˌn̩saɪd $ ˈmaʊntən-/ n [C] the side of a mountain: *Great rocks rolled down the mountainside.*

moun·tain·top /ˈmaʊntˌn̩tɒp $ ˈmaʊntəntɑːp/ n [C] the top part of a mountain

moun·te·bank /ˈmaʊntɪbæŋk/ n [C] *literary* a dishonest person who tricks and deceives people

moun·ted /ˈmaʊntˌd/ adj **1** riding on a horse: *the mounted police* | *Jean was mounted on a grey mare.* **2** fixed firmly to a larger thing: *The statue was mounted on a marble base.* | *music blasting from wall-mounted speakers*

Mount·ie /ˈmaʊnti/ n [C] *informal* a member of the Royal Canadian Mounted Police

mount·ing[1] adj /ˈmaʊntɪŋ/ [only before noun] gradually increasing – often used about things that cause problems or trouble: *There was mounting pressure on him to resign.* | *The government has come under mounting criticism in the press.* | *They faced mounting debts.* | *There's mounting evidence of a link between obesity and some forms of cancer.*

mounting[2] n [C] an object to which other things, especially parts of a machine, are fastened to keep them in place: *The engine is supported by four rubberized mountings.*

mourn /mɔːn $ mɔːrn/ v [I,T] **1** to feel very sad and to miss someone after they have died; ▤ **grieve for:** *Hundreds of people gathered to mourn the slain president.* | [+for] *They mourned for their children, killed in the war.* | **mourn sb's death/loss/passing** *She still mourns the death of her husband.* **2** to feel very sad because something no longer exists or is no longer as good as it used to be: *The old steam trains were much-loved, and we all mourn their passing.*

mourn·er /ˈmɔːnə $ ˈmɔːrnər/ n [C] someone who attends a funeral

mourn·ful /ˈmɔːnfəl $ ˈmɔːrn-/ adj very sad: *Durant was thin, mournful and silent.* | *the slow, mournful music of the bagpipes* —**mournfully** adv

mourn·ing /ˈmɔːnɪŋ $ ˈmɔːr-/ n [U] **1** great sadness because someone has died: *The Armenian authorities declared May 29 a national day of mourning.* | **in mourning** (=feeling great sadness) *It was the custom to visit those in mourning and sit quietly with them.* **2** black clothes worn to show that you are very sad that someone has died: *She was recently widowed and wearing mourning.*

mouse S2 W3 /maʊs/ n [C]
1 plural **mice** /maɪs/ a small furry animal with a pointed nose and a long tail that lives in people's houses or in fields: *The cat laid a dead mouse at my feet.* | *a field mouse*
2 plural **mouses** a small object connected to a computer by a wire, which you move with your hand to give instructions to the computer: *Select the printer icon and then click the left mouse button.* ➔ see picture at OFFICE
3 plural **mice** *informal* a quiet, nervous person ➔ **play cat and mouse** at CAT (4); ➔ **quiet as a mouse** at QUIET[1] (1)

mouse mat also **mouse pad** AmE n [C] a small piece of flat material with a special surface which you move a computer mouse on ➔ see picture at OFFICE

mouse·trap /ˈmaʊs-træp/ n [C] a trap for catching mice ➔ see picture at TRAP[1]

mous·sa·ka /muːˈsɑːkə/ n [C,U] a Greek dish made from meat, cheese, and AUBERGINES

mousse /muːs/ n [C,U] **1 a)** a sweet food made from a mixture of cream, eggs, and fruit or chocolate which is eaten when it is cold: *chocolate mousse* | *raspberry mousse* **b)** a food that is mixed and cooked with cream or eggs so that it is very light: *salmon mousse* **2** a

substance full of small bubbles that you put in your hair to make it look thicker or to hold its style in place

mous·tache also **mustache** AmE /məˈstɑːʃ $ ˈmʌstæʃ/ n [C] hair that grows on a man's upper lip; ➔ **beard:** *He's shaved off his moustache.*

mous·tached also **mustached** AmE /məˈstɑːʃt $ ˈmʌstæʃt/ adj [usually before noun] having a moustache: *a young, moustached British officer*

mous·tach·i·oed /məˈstɑːʃiəʊd, -ˈstæ- $ -oʊd/ adj another spelling of MUSTACHIOED

mous·y, mousey /ˈmaʊsi/ adj **1** mousy hair is a dull brown colour **2** a mousy woman is quiet and unattractive

mouth[1] S2 W1 /maʊθ/ n plural **mouths** /maʊðz/ [C]
1 FACE the part of your face which you put food into, or which you use for speaking: *He lifted his glass to his mouth.* | *The old man had a cigarette dangling from the corner of his mouth.* | *Liam was fast asleep with his mouth wide open.* | *She put her hand to her lips, trying not to laugh with her mouth full* (=with food in her mouth). | *She kissed him full on the mouth* (=directly on the mouth). | *I burnt the roof of my mouth* (=the top inside part) *on some hot soup.* | *She stared at him open-mouthed* (=looking very surprised or shocked). | *Karen felt dry-mouthed and sick.*
2 keep your mouth shut *informal* **a)** to not tell other people about a secret: *He demanded £2000 to keep his mouth shut.* **b)** to not say something even if you think it: *I wished that I'd kept my mouth shut.*
3 open your mouth to prepare to speak: *'I'll go,' Travis said quickly before she could open her mouth.* | **open your mouth to say/speak/protest etc** *Julia opened her mouth to reply, but they were interrupted.*
4 (you) watch your mouth *spoken informal* used to tell someone not to speak in such a rude way
5 ENTRANCE the entrance to a large hole or CAVE: *As the train entered the mouth of the tunnel, the lights came on.*
6 RIVER the part of a river where it joins the sea: *the mouth of the River Tees*
7 BOTTLE/CONTAINER the open part at the top of a bottle or container
8 big mouth *informal* if someone has a big mouth, they say too much or tell another person's secrets
9 me and my big mouth/you and your big mouth etc *spoken* used to criticize yourself or another person for saying something that should not have been said: *Oops, I shouldn't have said that. Me and my big mouth.*
10 mouth to feed/hungry mouth someone who you must provide food for, especially one of your children: *To these parents, a new baby is just another hungry mouth.*
11 make your mouth water if food makes your mouth water, it smells or looks so good you want to eat it immediately: *The smell of the cooked fish made her mouth water.* ➔ MOUTH-WATERING
12 down in the mouth *informal* unhappy: *Tim's looking very down in the mouth.*
13 out of the mouths of babes (and sucklings) used humorously when a small child has just said something clever or interesting
14 be all mouth BrE *spoken* if someone is all mouth, they talk a lot about what they will do but are not brave enough to actually do it ➔ **be born with a silver spoon in your mouth** at BORN[2] (8); ➔ **by word of mouth** at WORD[1] (13); ➔ **be foaming at the mouth** at FOAM[2] (2); ➔ **put your foot in your mouth** at FOOT[1] (15); ➔ **put your money where your mouth is** at MONEY (18); ➔ **put words into sb's mouth** at WORD[1] (21); ➔ **shut your mouth** at SHUT[1] (2); ➔ **shoot your mouth off** at SHOOT[1] (12) ➔ FOUL-MOUTHED, MEALY-MOUTHED

mouth[2] /maʊð/ v [T] **1** to move your lips in the same way you do when you are saying words, but without making any sound: *She silently mouthed the words 'Good luck'.* | *Philip mouthed something through the glass which she did not hear.* **2** to say things that you do not really believe or that you do not understand: *The* *players mouthed clichés about what they hoped to do at the World Cup.* | *They mouthed the usual platitudes.*

mouth off *phr v informal* to complain angrily and noisily about something, or talk as if you know more than anyone else: [+**at/to**] *You should have heard Pete mouthing off at Joe.* | [+**about**] *Morris was mouthing off about his former team.*

mouth·ful /'maʊθfʊl/ *n* [C]   **1** an amount of food or drink that you put into your mouth at one time: *Michael told his story between mouthfuls.* | [+**of**] *Betty drank a mouthful of beer.* | *He took a mouthful of his pudding.*   **2 (a bit of) a mouthful** *informal* a long word or phrase that is difficult to say: *Her real name is a bit of a mouthful, so we just call her Dee.*   **3 give sb a mouthful** *informal especially BrE* to speak angrily to someone, often swearing at them   **4 say a mouthful** *AmE informal* to say a lot of true and important things about something in a few words

mouth ,organ *n* [C] a small musical instrument that you play by blowing or sucking and moving it from side to side near your mouth; ➡ **harmonica**

mouth·piece /'maʊθpiːs/ *n* [C]   **1** the part of a musical instrument, telephone etc that you put in your mouth or next to your mouth: *Ben put his hand over the mouthpiece and shouted to me.*   **2** [usually singular] a person, newspaper etc that expresses the opinions of a government or a political organization: [+**of**] *The newspaper was the mouthpiece of the National Democratic Party.*

mouth-to-mouth resusci'tation also **mouth-to-'mouth** *n* [U] a method used to make someone start breathing again by blowing air into their mouth; ➡ **CPR**

mouth ,ulcer *BrE*, **canker sore** *AmE n* [C] a sore area in the mouth of people or animals, caused by illness or a disease

mouth·wash /'maʊθwɒʃ $ -wɒːʃ, -wɑːʃ/ *n* [C,U] a liquid used to make your mouth smell fresh or to get rid of infection in your mouth

mouth-,watering *adj* food that is mouth-watering looks or smells extremely good: *a mouth-watering aroma coming from the kitchen*

mouth·y /'maʊθi/ *adj informal* someone who is mouthy talks a lot and says what they think even if it is rude

mov·a·ble¹, **moveable** /'muːvəbəl/ *adj* able to be moved and not fixed in one place or position: *a teddy bear with movable arms and legs*

movable², **moveable** *n* [C usually plural] *law* a personal possession such as a piece of furniture

movable 'feast *n* [C] *BrE*   **1** *informal* something that happens at different times, so that you are not sure exactly when it will happen   **2** a special religious day, such as Easter, the date of which changes

move¹ S1 W1 /muːv/ *v*

1 CHANGE PLACE [I,T] to change from one place or position to another, or to make something do this: *Please keep the doors closed while the train is moving.* | *'Come on,' Sue said. No one moved.* | *Could you move your car, please? It's blocking the road.* | **move quickly/ slowly/steadily etc** *The plane moved slowly along the runway, then stopped.* | [+**away/out/to/towards etc**] *He moved closer to her.* | *Becca moved down the steps and into the yard.* | [+**about/around**] *I could hear someone moving around upstairs.* | *The bar was so crowded you could hardly move.* | *At Christmas, you couldn't move for toys in this house* (=there were a lot of toys). | *Paul couldn't move a muscle* (=could not move at all) *he was so scared.*

2 NEW HOUSE/OFFICE [I,T] if a person or company moves, or if you move them, they go to live or work in a different place: *We've moved seven or eight times in the last five years.* | [+**to/into/from**] *When are you moving to Memphis?* | *They've moved into bigger offices in London.* | **move sb to/into/from sth** *He had to move his mother into a nursing home.* | *The company is moving its sales center downtown.* | **move house/home** *BrE* (=go to live in a different house) *My parents kept*

moving house because of my dad's job.

3 CHANGE OPINION ETC a) [I] to change from one opinion or way of thinking to another; **◱ shift**: *Neither side is willing to move on the issue of territory.* | [+**towards/away from**] *The two political parties have moved closer towards each other in recent months.* | *At this stage, children move further away from the influence of their parents, and depend more on their friends.* **b)** [T] to persuade someone to change their opinion: *She won't be moved – it doesn't matter what you say to her.*

4 PROGRESS [I] to make progress in a particular way or at a particular rate: *Things moved quickly once the contract was signed.* | *The negotiations seem to be moving in the right direction.* | **get/keep things moving** *The plan should boost employment and get things moving in the economy.*

5 TAKE ACTION [I] to start taking action, especially in order to achieve something or deal with a problem: [+**on/against**] *The governor has yet to move on any of the recommendations in the report.* | **move fast/quickly/ swiftly** *You'll have to move fast if you want to get a place on the course.*

6 CHANGE JOB/CLASS ETC [I,T] to change to a different job, class etc, or to make someone change to a different job, class etc; **◱ transfer**: **move sb to/into/ from sth** *Several students were moved from the beginners' class into the intermediate one.* | *He spent five years at KLP, before moving to IMed as a manager.*

7 EMOTION [T] to make someone feel strong emotions, especially of sadness or sympathy: **be deeply/genuinely/profoundly moved** *Russell was deeply moved by what he heard.* | *His speech moved the audience to tears.* ➡ **MOVING** (1)

8 CAUSE SB TO DO STH [T] to cause someone to do something: **move sb to do sth** *Seeing her there had moved him to think about the time they had together.* | **be/feel moved to do sth** *I have never before felt moved to write, but I feel I must protest.*

9 TIME/ORDER [T] to change the time or order of something: **move sth to/from sth** *Could we move the meeting to Thursday?*

10 CHANGE SUBJECT [I] to start talking or writing about a different subject: [+**away from/off/to etc**] *We seem to be moving away from the main point of the discussion.* ➡ **MOVE ON⁴**

11 get moving also **move it** *spoken* used to tell someone to hurry: *Come on, get moving or you'll be late for school.*

12 it's time I was moving/we ought to get moving etc *spoken* used to say that you need to leave or go somewhere: *I think it's time we were moving.* | *I ought to get moving – I have to be up early tomorrow.*

13 GAMES [I,T] to change the position of one of the objects used to play a game such as CHESS

14 AT A MEETING [I,T] *formal* to officially make a proposal at a meeting: **move that** *The chairman moves that the meeting be adjourned.* | **move to do sth** *I move to approve the minutes as read.* | **move an amendment** *BrE* (=suggest a change) *They want to move an amendment to the bill.*

15 GO FAST [I] *informal* to travel very fast: *This car can really move!*

16 BE BOUGHT [I] if things of a particular kind are moving, they are being bought, especially at a particular rate: *The highest-priced homes are still moving slowly.*

17 move with the times to change the way you think and behave, as society changes: *If the resorts want to keep attracting tourists, they need to move with the times.*

18 move in ... circles/society/world to spend a lot of time with a particular type of people and know them well: *She spent time in England, where she moved in high society.* ➡ **move the goalposts** at GOALPOST (2); ➡ **move in for the kill** at KILL² (2); ➡ **move heaven and earth** at HEAVEN (9); ➡ **when the spirit moves you** at SPIRIT¹ (15)

M

move along *phr v*
1 if a process or situation is moving along, or if you move it along, it continues and makes progress: *Construction of the bridge is moving along.* | **move sth along** *I hope we can move things along and get the negotiations going again.*
2 move sb ⇔ along to officially order someone to leave a public place: *A queue formed by the gates, and a policeman tried to move people along.*

move around *phr v*
to change where you live very frequently, especially so that you live in many different parts of a country: *My dad was in the army, so we moved around a lot.*

move away *phr v*
to go to live in a different area: *My best friend moved away when I was ten.*

move down (sth) *phr v*
to change to a lower group, rank, or level: *Interest rates have moved down.* | *A drop in wages has meant that these families have moved down the social and economic scale.*

move in *phr v*
1 also **move into sth** to start living in a new home; **🔲 move out**: *When are you moving in?* | *Mom and Dad had always planned to move into a smaller house when we grew up.*
2 to start living with someone in the same home: [+with] *Steve's going to move in with her.*
3 to start being involved in and controlling a situation that someone else controlled previously: *The big multinationals moved in and started pushing up prices.* | [+on] *Investors moved in on a group of car enthusiasts and took over the market.*
4 to go towards a place or group of people, in order to attack them or take control of them: [+on] *Police moved in on the demonstrators in the square.*

move off *phr v especially BrE*
if a vehicle or group of people moves off, it starts to leave: *Do not forget to check behind the car before you move off.*

move on *phr v*
1 CHANGE JOB/CLASS to leave your present job, class, or activity and start doing another one: *I enjoyed my job, but it was time to move on.* | [+to] *When you finish, move on to the next exercise.* | **move on to higher/better things** (=get a better job or social position – used humorously) *Jeremy's leaving the company to move on to higher things.*
2 CHANGE/DEVELOP **a)** to develop in your life, and change your relationships, interests, activities etc: *I've moved on since high school, and now I don't have much in common with some of my old friends.* | [+from] *She has long since moved on from the roles of her youth.* **b)** to change, progress, improve, or become more modern as time passes: *By the time the software was ready, the market had moved on.*
3 move sb on *BrE* to order someone to leave a particular place – used especially about police: *The police arrived on the scene and began moving the protesters on.*
4 CHANGE SUBJECT to start talking about a new subject in a discussion, book etc: *Before we move on, does anyone have any questions?*
5 CONTINUE JOURNEY to leave the place where you have been staying and continue to another place: *After three days we decided it was time to move on.* | [+to] *The exhibition has now moved on to Edinburgh.*
6 TIME if time, the year etc moves on, the time passes: *As time moves on, I'd like the children to play more challenging music.*
7 *time is moving on BrE spoken* used to say that you must leave soon or do something soon, because it is getting late: *Time's moving on – we'd better get back to the car.*

move out *phr v*
1 to leave the house where you are living now in order to go and live somewhere else; **🔲 move in**: *He moved out, and a year later they were divorced.* | [+of] *They moved out of London when he was little.*
2 if a group of soldiers moves out, they leave a place
3 *AmE spoken* to leave: *Are you ready to move out?*

move over *phr v*
1 to change position so that there is more space for someone else: *Move over a little, so I can get in.*
2 to start using a different system, doing a different type of work etc: [+to] *Most companies have moved over to computer-aided design systems.*
3 to change jobs, especially within the same organization or industry: [+from] *The company's new publisher just moved over from Villard Books.*
4 move over Madonna/Walt Disney/CD-ROMs etc used when saying that something new is becoming more popular than something older – used humorously: *Move over, Armani, there's a new designer taking the fashion scene by storm.*

move up *phr v*
1 to get a better job in a company, or change to a more advanced group, higher rank, or higher level: *To move up, you'll need the right training.* | *Share prices moved up this month.* | [+to] *The kids learn fast, and can't wait to move up to the junior team.* | *He was **moving up the ladder** (=getting higher and higher positions), getting experience of command.* | *He's **moved up in the world** (=got a better job or social position) in the last few years, and his new flat shows it.*
2 *especially BrE* to change position in order to make more space for other people or things or be near someone else: *There's room for one more if everyone moves up a bit.*

move² S2 W1 *n* [C]
1 DECISION/ACTION something that you decide to do in order to achieve something: *She's still thinking about her next move.* | **move to do sth** *the Board's recent moves to cut interest rates* | *Most of the council members are reluctant to **make** such a drastic **move**.* | *The authorities have **made no move** to resolve the conflict.* | *a **good/wise/smart etc move** She decided to learn as much about it as she could, which seemed like a wise move.* | *Taking the position was a good **career move** (=a decision that will improve the type of jobs you can do).* | *there are **moves afoot (to do sth)** BrE* (=there are plans, especially secret ones) *It seems there could be moves afoot to close the centre.*
2 MOVEMENT [usually singular] when someone moves for a short time in a particular direction: *Good gymnasts rehearse their moves mentally before a competition.* | *He **made no move** to come any nearer.* | *Martin **made a move** towards the door.* | **watch/follow sb's every move** *His green eyes followed Cissy's every move.* | *One **false move** (=move in the wrong direction) and I'll shoot.*
3 PROGRESS/CHANGE a change, especially one which improves a situation: [+towards/from/against/to] *the country's move towards democracy* | *a move away from traditional industries such as coal mining* | *Much more research is being done, which is **a move in the right direction**.*
4 be on the move a) to be travelling from one place to another: *The rebel army is on the move.* **b)** to be busy and active: *Roy is constantly on the move.* **c)** to be changing and developing a lot, especially in a way that improves things: *Museums are on the move, adding exhibits that entertain and educate.*
5 get a move on *spoken* used to tell someone to hurry
6 make the first move to do something first, especially in order to end a quarrel or start a relationship: *Men say they like it when women make the first move.*
7 GAMES when you change the position of one of the objects in a game such as CHESS: *Several moves later, Ron took his king.* | *It's your move, Janet* (=it is your turn to move an object).

8 **make a move** *BrE informal* to leave a place: *It's getting late – we ought to make a move.*
9 **GOING TO A NEW PLACE** [usually singular] when you leave one house, office etc, and go to live or work in a different one: *The move to a larger office building is long overdue.*

move·a·ble /'mu:vəbəl/ *adj* another spelling of MOVABLE

---

movement (animals)

pounce

slither

gallop

hover   stalk

move·ment S1 W1 /'mu:vmənt/ *n*
1 **PEOPLE WORKING TOGETHER** [C] a group of people who share the same ideas or beliefs and who work together to achieve a particular aim: **civil rights/feminist/peace etc movement** *the civil rights movement of the 1960s* | **movement to do sth** *Mendes led a movement to stop destruction of the rain forest.* | [+for] *the movement for independence*
2 **POSITION/PLACE** [C,U] **a)** when someone or something changes position or moves from one place to another: *the dancer's graceful movements* | [+of] *A slight movement of the curtains showed where she was hiding.* | *the movement of goods across the border* | *He motioned to the door with a movement of his head.* **b)** a planned change in the position of a group of soldiers: *reports of* **troop movements** *in the area*
3 **CHANGE/DEVELOPMENT** [U] a gradual change or development in a situation or in people's attitudes or opinions: *There's been no movement in the peace talks since Thursday.* | [+towards/away from] *a movement towards equality with men in the workplace*
4 **sb's movements** the places where someone goes and the things they do during a certain period: *Police are trying to trace Carter's movements since Tuesday.*
5 **MUSIC** [C] one of the main parts into which a piece of music is divided, especially a SYMPHONY
6 **CLOCK/WATCH** [C usually singular] the moving parts of a piece of machinery, especially a clock or watch
7 **BODY WASTE** [C] *formal* when you get rid of waste matter from your BOWELS

mov·er /'mu:və $ -ər/ *n* [C] **1 mover and shaker** *informal* an important person who has power and influence over what happens in a situation: *He's one of the movers and shakers in Florida politics.* **2** someone or something that moves in a particular way: *Hummingbirds are quick movers.* **3** *especially AmE* someone whose job is to move furniture, boxes etc from one house to another when someone changes where they live **4** something that moves things from one place to another: *an earth mover* **5** a STOCK or SHARE that people are buying and selling a lot of **6** someone who makes a formal proposal at a meeting: *the mover of the motion*

→ PRIME MOVER

mov·ie S2 W2 /'mu:vi/ *n* [C] *especially AmE*
1 a film made to be shown at the cinema or on television

watch/see a movie
go to a movie also take in a movie *informal*
appear in/be in/star in a movie
make/shoot a movie
show/screen a movie
horror/action/sci-fi etc movie
silent movie
big-budget/low-budget movie
hit movie (=very successful movie)
movie star (=a famous movie actor)
movie director/producer

Do you want to **see a movie** *tonight?* | *Maybe we'll* **go to a movie.** | *It was like one of those old John Wayne movies.* | *She* **starred** *with Humphrey Bogart* **in the movie** *'Casablanca'.* | *They don't* **make movies** *like that any more.* | *The* **movie** *was* **shot** *entirely on location in India.* | *Many people were shocked when the* **movie** *was first* **shown.** | *She once played the innocent victim in a* **horror movie.** | *Spielberg's latest* **hit movie** | [+about] *a movie about two gay teenagers who fall in love* | *a big Hollywood* **movie star**

2 **the movies a)** the cinema: *We* **took** *the kids* **to the movies.** | *In those days, we* **went to the movies** *every week.* | **at the movies** *Why were you at the movies all by yourself?* **b)** films in general, and the events in them: **in (the) movies** *He couldn't believe his luck. It was the sort of thing that only happened in the movies.* **c)** the business of producing films: *a career in the movies*

mov·ie·go·er /'mu:vi,gəʊə $ -,goʊər/ *n* [C] *especially AmE* someone who goes to see films at the cinema, especially regularly; ⊟ **cinemagoer** *BrE*

mov·ie·mak·er /'mu:vi,meɪkər $ -ər/ *n* [C] *especially AmE* a FILM-MAKER

movie star *n* [C] *especially AmE* a famous film actor or actress; ⊟ **film star** *BrE*

movie theater *n* [C] *AmE* a building where you go in order to watch films; ⊟ **cinema** *BrE*

mov·ing /'mu:vɪŋ/ *adj* **1** making you feel strong emotions, especially sadness or sympathy: **deeply/very/profoundly moving** *Bayman's book about his illness is deeply moving.* | *a moving account/story etc a moving account of his childhood in Ireland* | *Attending the memorial service was a* **moving experience.** **2** [only before noun] changing from one position to another: *a moving stage* | **fast/slow moving etc** *Be careful when changing lanes in fast-moving traffic.* | *an archer learning to hit a* **moving target 3 a moving target** something that is changing continuously, so that it is very difficult to criticize it or compete against it: *The company is constantly improving the system, making it a moving target.* **4 the moving spirit** *formal* someone who makes something start to happen: *Mr Arkwright was the moving spirit behind the founding of the union.* —**movingly** *adv*: *She spoke movingly about her father's last days.*

moving picture *n* [C] *old-fashioned especially AmE* a film made to be shown at the cinema

moving staircase *n* [C] *old-fashioned* an ESCALATOR

moving van *n* [C] *AmE* a large vehicle used for moving furniture from one house to another; ⊟ **removal van** *BrE*

mow /məʊ $ moʊ/ *v past tense* **mowed**, *past participle* **mown** /məʊn $ moʊn/ [I,T] **1** to cut grass using a machine: *It's time to* **mow** *the lawn again.* **2 new-mown hay/grass etc** recently cut grass etc

mow *sb* ⇔ **down** *phr v informal* **1** to kill large numbers of people at the same time, especially by shooting them: *The soldiers were mown down by machine gun fire.* **2** to kill someone by driving into

1 000, 2 000, 3 000, most frequent words in S poken and W ritten English

M

them fast: *He was sentenced to two years in prison for mowing down a nine-year old girl.*

mow·er /'məʊə $ 'moʊər/ *n* [C] **1** a machine used for cutting grass; ▤ **lawnmower** **2** *old use* someone who mows

mox·ie /'mɒksi $ 'mɑː-/ *n* [U] *AmE informal* courage and determination: *He's a small kid, but he has plenty of moxie.*

moz·za·rel·la /ˌmɒtsə'relə $ ˌmɑː-/ *n* [U] a white Italian cheese that is often used on PIZZA

MP /ˌem 'piː/ *n* [C] **1** *Member of Parliament* someone who has been elected to a parliament to represent people from a particular area of the country: *Ken Newton, MP* | *a Labour MP* | [+for] *She's the MP for Liverpool North.* **2** *informal* a member of the MILITARY POLICE

MP3 /ˌem pi: 'θriː/ *n* [C] *trademark* a recording of music that can be DOWNLOADED from the Internet

MP3 player *n* [C] a machine or computer program that plays music which has been DOWNLOADED from the Internet

MPEG /'em peg/ *n* [C] *technical* **Moving Picture Experts Group** a type of computer FILE used on the Internet that contains sound and video material; ➔ **JPEG**

mpg /ˌem pi: 'dʒiː/ *miles per gallon* used to describe the amount of petrol used by a car: *do 30/40 etc mpg* *BrE* *get 30/40 etc mpg* *AmE*: *a car that does 35 mpg*

mph /ˌem pi: 'eɪtʃ/ *miles per hour* used to describe the speed of something, especially a vehicle or the wind: *high winds of up to 140 mph*

MPhil, M.Phil. /ˌem 'fɪl/ *n* [C] *BrE* **Master of Philosophy** a university degree in a subject such as history, languages, or English literature, that you can get after your first degree; ➔ **PhD**

MPV /ˌem pi: 'viː/ *n* [C] *BrE* **multi-purpose vehicle** a large car for up to eight people; ▤ **minivan** *AmE*

Mr *BrE*; **Mr.** *AmE* /'mɪstə $ -ər/ **1** used before a man's family name to be polite when you are speaking to him, writing to him, or talking about him: *Mr Smith is the headteacher.* | *Mr. John Smith* | *Mr and Mrs Smith* **2** used when speaking to a man in an official position: *Mr Chairman* | *Mr. President* ➔ **MADAM** (3) **3 Mr Right** a man who would be the perfect husband for a particular woman: *She's finally found Mr. Right.* **4 Mr Big** *informal* the leader or most important person in a group, especially a criminal group **5 Mr Clean** *informal* someone who is honest and always obeys the law **6 Mr Sarcasm/Mr Messy/Mr Forgetful etc** *spoken* used humorously to say that someone has a particular quality or behaves in a particular way: *I don't think we need any more comments from Mr Sarcasm here.* ➔ **no more Mr Nice Guy!** at GUY¹ (5)

MRI /ˌem ɑːr 'aɪ/ *n medical* **1** [U] **magnetic resonance imaging** the process of using strong MAGNETIC FIELDS to make a picture of the inside of someone's body for medical reasons; ➔ **CTscan, X-ray** **2** [C] a picture of the inside of someone's body produced with MRI equipment: *Brian had an MRI taken Sunday.*

Mrs *BrE*; **Mrs.** *AmE* /'mɪsɪz/ **1** used before a married woman's family name to be polite when you are speaking to her, writing to her, or talking about her; ➔ **miss, Mrs**: *Mrs. Smith* | *Mrs Meddeman heads the fundraising committee.* | *Mr and Mrs David Smith* ⚠ Some married women prefer to be addressed as **Ms** because it does not draw attention to whether or not they are married. ➔ see also note at MR **2 Mrs Tidy/Mrs Efficient/Mrs Nosy etc** *spoken* used humorously to say that a woman has a particular quality or behaves in a particular way: *Mrs Superefficient has already taken care of it.*

ms *n plural* **mss** [C] the written abbreviation of **manuscript**

Ms *BrE*; **Ms.** *AmE* /mɪz, məz/ used before a woman's family name when she does not want to be called 'Mrs' or 'Miss', or when you do not know whether she is married or not; ➔ **miss, Mrs**: *Dear Ms Johnson, ...*

MS /ˌem 'es/ *n* [U] **multiple sclerosis** a serious illness that gradually destroys the nerves, causing weakness and inability to move

M.S. /ˌem 'es/ *n* [C] *AmE* **Master of Science** a university degree in a science subject that you can get after your first degree

M.Sc. also **MSc** *BrE* /ˌem es 'siː/ *n* [C] **Master of Science** a university degree in a science subject that you can get after your first degree

MSG /ˌem es 'dʒiː/ *n* **1** [U] **monosodium glutamate** a chemical that is added to food to make it taste better **2** also **msg** [C] **message** used especially in TEXT MESSAGES sent or received on a MOBILE PHONE

Mt. also **Mt** *BrE* the written abbreviation of **mount**: *Mt. Everest*

MTV /ˌem ti: 'viː/ *n trademark* **music television** a television company that broadcasts popular music and videos of the songs

much¹ S1 W1 /mʌtʃ/ *adv*
1 by a great amount: **much better/greater/easier etc** *Henry's room is much bigger than mine.* | *These shoes are much more comfortable.* | *I'm feeling very much better, thank you.* | **much too big/old etc** *He was driving much too fast.* | **much the best/most interesting etc** *BrE*: *It's much the best way to do it.*
2 a) used to ask or talk about the degree of a difference: **how much older/smaller etc** *She kept weighing herself to see how much heavier she was getting.* **b)** used to ask or talk about how big an additional amount of something is: **how much more/longer/further** *How much longer do we have to wait?* | *How much further is it?* **c)** used to emphasize the difference you are mentioning: **how much better/nicer/easier etc** *I was surprised to see how much better she was looking.* | *How much better life would be if we returned to the values of the past!*
3 used to talk about a strong feeling or something that is done often: **how/however much** *You know how much I care about you.* | *I think you have to accept the pain, however much it hurts.* | *He talks too much.* | *We're looking forward to your visit so much.* | *Thank you very much!* | **much loved/admired/discussed etc** *The money will buy much needed books for the school.*
4 not ... much a) only a little or hardly at all: *'Did you enjoy it?' 'No, not much.'* | *She isn't much younger than me.* | *Tony hasn't changed much in the last ten years.* **b)** used to say that something does not often happen: *We don't go to the theatre much any more.* | *Kids don't play outside as much as they used to.* ➔ **LITTLE³** (2)
5 much like sth/much as also **much the same (as sth)** used to say that something is very similar to something else: *The house was very much as I'd remembered it.* | *The taste is much like butter.* | *Plants are classified in much the same way as animals.*
6 much to sb's surprise/embarrassment etc *formal* used to say that someone feels very surprised, embarrassed etc when something happens: *Much to my relief, the conversation turned to another topic.*
7 much less used to say that a greater thing is even less true, likely, or possible than the thing you have just mentioned: *The shelves were lined with books which neither Hugo nor Sally would ever open, much less read.*
8 much as although: *Much as I like Bob, I wouldn't want to live with him.*
9 not so much...as... used to say that one description of someone or something is less suitable or correct than another: *She was not so much nervous as impatient for the journey to be over.* ➔ **so much the better** at BETTER³ (2)

much² S1 W1 *determiner, pron*
1 [in informal English 'much' is used mainly in questions and negatives] a large amount of something: *I don't have much money with me.* | *Was there much traffic?* | *He didn't say much about his trip.* | *Do you get much chance to travel in your job?* | *After much consideration*

we have finally arrived at a decision. | [+of] Much of the city was destroyed in the attack. | **(far/much/rather/a little) too much** There was too much work for one person. | It would cost far too much to have the thing repaired. | It was such a small thing to have caused so much trouble.
2 how much used to ask or talk about the amount or cost of something: How much is that dress? | How much flour should I use in the sauce? | I know how much hard work goes into looking after a baby.
3 as much an amount that is equal and not less: **as much (...) as** I hope you have as much fun as I did. | Just do as much as you can.
4 as much as 10/100 etc used to emphasize how surprisingly large an amount is: Some machines cost as much as £20,000.
5 used in negative expressions to say that something is not important, interesting, good etc: **not/nothing much** 'What are you doing?' 'Oh, not much, really.' | There's nothing much we can do to help. | **I don't think much** of that idea (=I do not think it is good). | The car may **not be much to look at** (=does not look good) but it's very reliable. | It's the best book he's written, but **that's not saying much** (=none of his books are very good).
6 not be much of a sth to not be a good example of something or not be very good at something: I'm not much of a dancer, I'm afraid. | It wasn't really much of a storm.
7 be too much for sb to be too difficult for someone to do or bear: The effort of climbing the stairs had been too much for the old man. | The shock had been too much for her – she never recovered.
8 not be up to much BrE spoken to be fairly bad: The restaurant's very grand but the food isn't up to much.
9 there is not much in it informal used to say that there is little difference between two things or amounts: 'Isn't the woollen carpet more expensive?' 'A little, perhaps, but there's not much in it.'
10 think/say etc as much to think or say the thing that has just been mentioned: Carson strongly disapproved of the plan and said as much at the meeting. | 'Max was lying all the time.' ' I thought as much.'
11 it was as much as sb could do to do sth used to say that someone only succeeded in doing something with great difficulty: He looked so stupid, it was as much as I could do to stop myself from laughing.
12 not/without so much as sth used when you are surprised or annoyed that someone did not do something: They left without so much as saying goodbye. | He'd received not so much as a thank you from Tiffany.
13 so much for sth used to say that a particular action, idea, statement etc was not useful or did not produce the result that was hoped for: He's late again. So much for good intentions.
14 I'll say this/that much for sb/sth used when saying one good thing about someone or something when they are being criticized a lot: Well, he does admit it when he's wrong, I'll say that much for him.
15 as much again an additional amount that is equal: The car only cost me £1500 but it cost as much again to get it insured.
16 be a bit much/be too much BrE spoken used to say that someone's behaviour is unacceptable or impolite: It's a bit much expecting you to pay for it all.
17 make much of sb/sth formal to treat a person or thing as though you think they are very important or special: The press made much of the discovery. | They've always made much of their nephews and nieces.

GRAMMAR
When **much** is a quantifier, it is used mainly in questions and negative sentences: Was there much mess? | I don't have much time. In sentences which are not questions or negative sentences, phrases like 'a lot of' and 'plenty of' are used instead: Kurama has a lot of snow (NOT Kurama has much snow).
Much can also be used after **too, so**, and **as**: We've wasted too much time. | She cried so much her head ached. | Drink as much wine as you want.

⚠ Do not use **much** before countable nouns. Use **many** or **a lot of**: There are too many advertisements on television (NOT There are too much advertisements on television).
When **much** is an adverb, it is mainly used before comparative adjectives: He looks much older than 35. | Some people are much more fortunate than others.
Much can also be used before some adjectives in questions and negative questions: She doesn't look much different with her new hairstyle.
⚠ Do not use **much** before adjectives in sentences that are not questions or negative sentences. Use **very**: Tea and coffee taste very different (NOT Tea and coffee taste much different).
Much can also be used before some past participles acting as adjectives: Education is a much discussed government service. | a much admired writer This use is mainly found in formal and literary English.

much-'heralded adj [only before noun] a much-heralded event, product etc has been talked about a lot before it happens or becomes available: Ford's much-heralded new sports car
much·ness /'mʌtʃnɪs/ n **be much of a muchness** BrE informal to be very similar in standard, quality etc: It was hard to choose between the candidates – they were all much of a muchness.
much-'vaunted adj [only before noun] a much-vaunted plan, achievement etc is one that people say is very good or important, especially when this may not be true: the president's much-vaunted health care plan
muck¹ /mʌk/ n [U] informal **1** dirt, mud, or another sticky substance that makes something dirty: Come on, let's wipe that muck off your face. **2** BrE waste matter from animals, sometimes put on land to make plants grow better; ▣ manure: special machinery for spreading muck onto the fields | dog muck **3** BrE something that is unpleasant or of very bad quality: How can you eat that muck? It looks disgusting. | I'm not surprised she left. He treated her like muck (=very badly). **4 make a muck of sth** BrE informal to do something very badly and make a lot of mistakes; ▣ muck up: I really made a muck of the exam. **5 as common as muck** BrE informal very common or of a low social class
muck² v
muck about/around phr v BrE informal **1** to behave in a silly way, especially when you should be working or paying attention to something; ▣ mess around: Stop mucking about and listen! | Some of the boys were mucking around on bikes in the middle of the road. **2 muck sb about/around** to cause trouble for someone, especially by changing your mind a lot or not doing what you promised to do; ▣ mess sb around: The company kept mucking us around and changing the price.
muck in phr v BrE informal **1** to do your share of the work that is necessary in order to get a job done: If we all muck in, we could get the whole house painted by the end of the week. **2** to share space with other people: [+with] There are only three bedrooms. Do you mind mucking in with the other boys?
muck sth ⇔ **out** phr v BrE to clean the place where a farm animal lives: You have to muck out the stables every day in the winter.
muck sth ⇔ **up** phr v informal **1** BrE to do something badly, so that you fail to achieve something; ▣ mess up: I really mucked up my driving test first time. **2** to spoil something, especially an arrangement or plan; ▣ mess up: The bad weather mucked up our plans for a picnic. **3** BrE to make something dirty; ▣ mess up: Who's mucked up the carpet in here?
muck·heap /'mʌkhiːp/ n [C] BrE a pile of MANURE (=animal waste matter) on farm land
muck·rak·ing /'mʌk-reɪkɪŋ/ n [U] the practice of telling or writing unpleasant and perhaps untrue

M

M

multimedia 'messaging n [U] a form of sending and receiving written messages to and from MOBILE PHONES that makes it possible to combine the written message with pictures, video, and sound

mul·ti·mil·lion /ˌmʌltiˈmɪljən◂/ adj **multimillion-pound/multimillion-dollar etc** worth or costing many millions of pounds, dollars etc: a multimillion-dollar lawsuit

mul·ti·mil·lio·naire /ˌmʌltiˌmɪljəˈneə $ -ˈner/ n [C] someone who has many millions of pounds or dollars

mul·ti·na·tion·al¹ /ˌmʌltiˈnæʃənəl◂/ adj **1** a multinational company has factories, offices, and business activities in many different countries: a multinational media corporation **2** involving people from several countries: the UN's multinational peace-keeping force

multinational² n [C] a large company that has offices, factories etc in many different countries: Multinationals have made large investments in Thailand.

mul·ti·par·ty /ˌmʌltiˈpɑːti◂ $ -ˈpɑːr-/ adj [only before noun] involving or including more than one political party: a multiparty democracy

multi-player 'gaming n [U] the playing of computer games on the Internet by more than one person at the same time, using different computers

mul·ti·ple¹ /ˈmʌltɪpəl/ adj [only before noun] many, or involving many things, people, events etc: Baxter was rushed to the hospital with multiple stab wounds. | Having multiple partners increases your risk of sexual diseases. | His new album includes multiple versions of the same songs.

multiple² n [C] **1** a number that contains a smaller number an exact number of times: [+of] 20 is a multiple of 5. **2** BrE technical a MULTIPLE STORE

multiple 'birth n [C] when more than one baby is born to the same mother at the same time: The number of multiple births has risen sharply.

multiple 'choice adj a multiple choice examination or question shows several possible answers, and you have to choose the correct one

multiple person'ality n [C] if someone has a multiple personality, they are mentally ill because they have two or more completely separate PERSONALITIES that each behave differently: multiple personality disorder

multiple scle'rosis n [U] medical MS a serious illness that gradually destroys your nerves, making you weak and unable to walk

multiple 'store n [C] BrE technical a CHAIN STORE

mul·ti·plex¹ /ˈmʌltɪpleks/ also **multiplex 'cinema** BrE n [C] a cinema that has several different rooms in which it can show films

multiplex² adj technical having many different parts

mul·ti·plex·er /ˈmʌltɪpleksə $ -ər/ n [C] technical a piece of computer equipment that is used to send several electrical signals using only one connection, especially with a MODEM —**multiplexing** n [U]

mul·ti·pli·ca·tion /ˌmʌltɪplɪˈkeɪʃən/ n **1** a method of calculating in which you add a number to itself a particular number of times; → **division** **2** formal a large increase in the size, amount, or number of something: a multiplication of the number of forms to fill out

multipli'cation sign n [C] a sign (×) showing that one number is multiplied by another

multipli'cation ,table n [C] a list, used especially by children in school, that shows the results when each number between one and twelve is multiplied by each number between one and twelve

mul·ti·pli·ci·ty /ˌmʌltɪˈplɪsɪti/ n [singular, U] formal a large number or great variety of things: [+of] the multiplicity of courses available to language students

mul·ti·ply /ˈmʌltɪplaɪ/ v **multiplied, multiplying, multiplies** **1** [I,T] to do a calculation in which you add a number to itself a particular number of times; →

divide: Children will learn to multiply in the second grade. | **multiply sth by sth** Multiply the total by 12. **2** [I,T] to increase by a large amount or number, or to make something do this: The amount of information available has multiplied. | Smoking multiplies the risk of heart attacks and other health problems. **3** [I] to breed: Bacteria multiply quickly in warm food.

mul·ti·pur·pose /ˌmʌltiˈpɜːpəs◂ $ -ˈpɜːr-/ adj [usually before noun] able to be used for many different purposes: a multipurpose building | a multipurpose tool

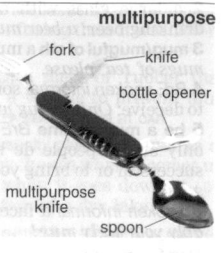

multipurpose

fork — knife
— bottle opener
multipurpose knife
spoon

mul·ti·ra·cial /ˌmʌltiˈreɪʃəl◂/ adj including or involving several different races of people; → **multicultural**: a multiracial society

mul·ti·skill·ing /ˈmʌltiˌskɪlɪŋ/ n [U] when someone is trained to do several different jobs within the same company

multi-'storey¹ adj [only before noun] BrE a multi-storey building has many levels or floors

multi-storey² n [C] BrE spoken a multi-storey CAR PARK

mul·ti·task /ˈmʌltitɑːsk $ -tæsk/ v [I] to do several things at the same time: The successful applicant for this job must be able to multitask. —**multitasker** n [C]

mul·ti·task·ing /ˈmʌltitɑːskɪŋ $ -tæs-/ n [U] **1** a computer's ability to do more than one job at a time **2** when a person does more than one thing at a time: Women are traditionally supposed to be good at multitasking.

mul·ti·tude /ˈmʌltɪtjuːd $ -tuːd/ n [C] **1** a multitude of sb/sth formal or literary a very large number of people or things: I had never seen such a multitude of stars before. | a multitude of possible interpretations **2** the multitude(s) ordinary people, especially when they are thought of as not being very well educated: Political power has been placed in the hands of the multitude. **3** literary or biblical a large crowd of people: Clamoring multitudes demanded a view of the Pope. **4** cover/hide a multitude of sins to make faults or problems seem less clear or noticeable – used humorously: Patterned carpet can hide a multitude of sins (=the carpet is dirty, but the pattern hides it).

mul·ti·tu·di·nous /ˌmʌltɪˈtjuːdɪnəs◂ $ -ˈtuː-/ adj formal very many: language in all its multitudinous forms

mul·ti·vit·a·min /ˈmʌltiˌvɪtəmɪn, -ˌvaɪ- $ -ˌvaɪ-/ n [C] a PILL or liquid containing many different VITAMINS

mum¹ [S1] [W2] /mʌm/ n [C]
1 BrE mother; ▣ mom AmE
2 mum's the word spoken used to tell someone that they must not tell other people about a secret

mum² adj **keep mum** informal to not tell anyone about a secret

mum·ble /ˈmʌmbəl/ v [I,T] to say something too quietly or not clearly enough, so that other people cannot understand you; → **mutter**: He bumped into someone and mumbled an apology. | Stop mumbling! | **mumble to yourself** A woman on the corner was mumbling to herself. —**mumble** n [C]

mum·bo-jum·bo /ˌmʌmbəʊ ˈdʒʌmbəʊ $ -boʊ ˈdʒʌmboʊ/ n [U] informal technical language that is difficult to understand and seems to have no sense: a bunch of legal mumbo-jumbo

mum·mer /ˈmʌmə $ -ər/ n [C] an actor in a simple traditional play that does not have words —**mumming** n [U]

mum·mi·fy /ˈmʌmɪfaɪ/ v **mummified, mummifying, mummifies** [T] to preserve a dead body by putting special oils on it and wrapping it with cloth —**mummification** /ˌmʌmɪfɪˈkeɪʃən/ n [U]

mum·my S2 /ˈmʌmi/ *n plural* **mummies** [C]
1 *BrE* mother – used especially by young children or when you are talking to young children; ■ **mommy** *AmE*: *Mummy, can I play outside?*
2 a dead body that has been preserved by wrapping it in cloth, especially in ancient Egypt

'mummy's boy *n* [singular] *BrE informal* a MOTHER'S BOY

mumps /mʌmps/ *n* [U] also **the mumps** an infectious illness which makes your neck swell and become painful

mum-to-'be *n plural* **mums-to-be** [C] *BrE informal* a MOTHER-TO-BE

munch /mʌntʃ/ *v* [I,T] to eat something noisily: [+on/at] *Barry sat munching on an apple.* | *They'd **munched** their **way through** (=eaten all of) three packets of biscuits.*

munch·ies /ˈmʌntʃiz/ *n* [plural] *informal* **1** the munchies a feeling of wanting to eat something, especially food that is not healthy for you: **have/get the munchies** *Get me a packet of crisps – I have the munchies.* **2** *AmE* foods that are easy to pick up and eat, especially foods served at a party

mun·dane /mʌnˈdeɪn/ *adj* **1** ordinary and not interesting or exciting; ■ **boring**: *Initially, the work was pretty mundane.* | *The mundane task of setting the table can be fun on holidays.* **2** *literary* concerned with ordinary daily life rather than religious matters; ■ **worldly**

mung bean /ˌmʌŋ ˈbiːn/ *n* [C,usually plural] a small green bean, usually eaten as a BEANSPROUT

mu·ni·ci·pal /mjuːˈnɪsɪpəl $ mjʊ-/ *adj* relating to or belonging to the government of a town or city: *the municipal waste dump* | *municipal elections* —**municipally** *adv*

mu·ni·ci·pal·i·ty /mjuː,nɪsˈpælti $ mjʊ-/ *n plural* **municipalities** [C] a town, city, or other small area, which has its own government to make decisions about local affairs, or the officials in that government: *the municipality of Berkeley* | *an elected municipality*

mu·nif·i·cent /mjuːˈnɪfsənt $ mjʊ-/ *adj formal* very generous: *a munificent gift* —**munificence** *n* [U]: *the munificence of the museum's benefactors*

mu·ni·tions /mjuːˈnɪʃənz $ mjʊ-/ *n* [plural] military supplies such as bombs and guns: *a munitions factory* —**munition** *adj* [only before noun]

mu·ral /ˈmjʊərəl $ ˈmjʊrəl/ *n* [C] a painting that is painted on a wall, either inside or outside a building; → **fresco** —**mural** *adj* [only before noun]

mur·der[1] S3 W2 /ˈmɜːdə $ ˈmɜːrdər/ *n*
1 [C,U] the crime of deliberately killing someone; → **manslaughter**

> commit (a) murder
> investigate a murder
> accuse sb of murder/charge sb with murder
> a brutal murder
> attempted murder (=the crime of trying to kill someone)
> first-degree murder *AmE* (=the most serious type of murder under US law)
> mass murder (=of a large number of people)
> murder victim
> murder weapon
> murder investigation/inquiry
> murder case/trial
> murder charge

> *On the night the **murder** was **committed**, he was out of the country.* | *The man **accused of** her **murder** will appear in court today.* | [+of] *the **brutal murder** of a young child* | *He was found guilty of **attempted murder**.* | *She was charged with two counts of **first degree murder**.* | *The mother of the **murder victim** wept in court.* | *Police are still searching for the **murder weapon**.* | *Detectives have launched a **murder investigation**.*

2 get away with murder *informal* to do anything you want, even things that are wrong, without being pun-

---

ished: *She lets those kids get away with murder.*
3 be murder *spoken* to be very difficult or unpleasant: *It's murder doing the shopping on Saturdays.* | *The traffic was murder this morning.*
4 be murder on sth *spoken* to harm or damage something else: *These new shoes are murder on my feet.* → **scream blue murder** at SCREAM[1] (1)

murder[2] *v* [T] **1** to kill someone deliberately and illegally: *He was convicted of murdering a policeman.* | *Thousands of civilians were brutally murdered during the civil war.* | *the murdered man* → see box at KILL[1] **2** *informal* to spoil a song, play etc by performing it very badly: *It's a good song, but they murdered it.* **3 sb will murder you** *spoken* used to tell someone that another person will be very angry with them: *Your dad'll murder you when he hears about it.* **4 I could murder a beer/pizza etc** *BrE spoken* used to say that you are very hungry or thirsty and want a particular food or drink **5** *informal* to defeat someone completely: *They murdered us in the final.*

mur·der·er /ˈmɜːdərə $ ˈmɜːrdərər/ *n* [C] someone who murders another person: *a convicted murderer* | *his brother's murderer*

mur·der·ess /ˈmɜːdərs $ ˈmɜːr-/ *n* [C] *old-fashioned* a woman who murders another person

mur·der·ous /ˈmɜːdərəs $ ˈmɜːr-/ *adj* **1** very dangerous and likely to kill people: *a murderous attack* | *murderous drug dealers* **2 murderous look/expression/glare etc** an expression or look which shows that someone is very angry —**murderously** *adv*

murk /mɜːk $ mɜːrk/ *n* [U] *literary* darkness caused by smoke, dirt, or clouds; ■ **gloom**

murk·y /ˈmɜːki $ ˈmɜːr-/ *adj* **1** dark and difficult to see through: *murky water* **2** complicated and difficult to understand; ■ **obscure**: *The laws on intellectual property are murky.* | *the **murky waters** (=complicated subject) of sexuality and jealousy* **3** involving dishonest or illegal activities that are kept secret; ■ **shady**: *a murky world of fraud and secret deals* | *a politician with a murky past* —**murkiness** *n* [U]

mur·mur[1] /ˈmɜːmə $ ˈmɜːrmər/ *v* **1** [I,T] to say something in a soft quiet voice that is difficult to hear clearly: *'Well done,' murmured George.* | *The girl murmured something polite, and smiled.* | *Julie turned over and murmured in her sleep.* **2** [I] to make a soft, low sound: *The wind murmured through the trees.* **3** [I + against] *literary especially BrE* to complain to friends and people you work with, but not officially —**murmuring** *n* [C,U]: *murmurings of discontent*

murmur[2] *n* [C] **1** a soft low sound made by people speaking quietly or a long way away: [+of] *the murmur of voices in the other room* | *She replied in a low murmur.* | **murmur of agreement/surprise/regret etc** (=one that expresses a particular feeling) *There was a murmur of agreement from the crowd.* **2** a complaint, but not a strong or official complaint: [+of] *There have been murmurs of discontent over the new rules.* **3 do sth without a murmur** to do something without complaining, especially when this is surprising: *They signed the form without a murmur.* **4** the soft low sound made by water, the wind etc: *the murmur of the little brook* **5 heart murmur** an unusual sound made by the heart, which shows that there may be something wrong with it

Mur·phy's law /ˌmɜːfiz ˈlɔː $ ˌmɜːrfiz ˈlɒː/ *n* [U] *informal especially AmE* a tendency for bad things to happen whenever it is possible for them to do so – used humorously; ■ **sod's law** *BrE*

mus·cle[1] S2 W3 /ˈmʌsəl/ *n*
1 [C,U] one of the pieces of flesh inside your body that you use in order to move, and that connect your bones together

> arm/leg/neck/stomach etc muscles
> the muscles in your leg/arm/stomach etc
> strengthen/build up your muscles

pull/strain a muscle (=injure a muscle)
flex your muscles (=bend your arm muscles so that people can see how strong you are)
muscle tissue/fibres (=the material that muscles are made of)
muscle tone (=the firmness of your muscles)

*Relax your **stomach muscles**, then stretch again.* | *Regular exercise will help to **strengthen your muscles**.* | *Beckham has **pulled a muscle** in his thigh and won't play tomorrow.* → see picture at HUMAN[1]

2 not move a muscle to stay completely still: *The soldier stood without moving a muscle.*
3 [U] power or influence: **military/economic/political etc muscle** *The unions have a lot of political muscle.* | *The agreement will give the UN some muscle to enforce human rights.*
4 [U] physical strength and power: *It **took muscle** to work in an old-fashioned kitchen.* | **put some muscle into it** (=used to tell someone to work harder) → **flex your muscles** at FLEX[1] (2)

muscle[2] *v* **muscle your way into/through etc sth** to use your strength to go somewhere: *Joe and Tony muscled their way through the crowd.*

muscle in *phr v* to use your power to get involved in or take control of something that someone else was doing, especially in business – used to show disapproval: [+**on**] *Banks are muscling in on the insurance business.*

mus·cle·bound /ˈmʌsəlbaʊnd/ *adj* having large stiff muscles because of too much physical exercise: *musclebound weight-lifters*

mus·cled /ˈmʌsəld/ *adj* having large muscles; ⊟ **muscular**: *He had a good body, tanned and well-muscled.*

mus·cle·man /ˈmʌsəlmæn/ *n plural* **musclemen** /-men/ [C] **1** a man who has developed big strong muscles by doing exercises **2** a strong man who is employed to protect someone, usually a criminal

Mus·co·vite /ˈmʌskəvaɪt/ *n* [C] someone from the city of Moscow in Russia —**Muscovite** *adj*

mus·cu·lar /ˈmʌskjᵊlə $ -ər/ *adj* **1** having large, strong muscles: *She was fast and strong, with a slender, muscular body.* | *He's very muscular.* **2** concerning or affecting the muscles: *muscular injuries* —**muscularity** /ˌmʌskjᵊˈlærᵊti/ *n* [U]

muscular dys·tro·phy /ˌmʌskjᵊlə ˈdɪstrəfi $ -lər-/ *n* [U] a serious illness in which the muscles become weaker over a period of time

mus·cu·la·ture /ˈmʌskjᵊlətʃə $ -tʃʊr/ *n* [singular, U] *medical* all the muscles in the body, considered as a group

muse[1] /mjuːz/ *v* **1** [T] to say something in a way that shows you are thinking about it carefully: *'Somewhere,' he mused, 'I've heard your name before.'* **2** [I] to think about something for a long time: [+**on/over/about/upon**] *He mused on how different his life would have been, had he not met Louisa.* —**musing** *n* [C,U]: *her gloomy musings* —**musingly** *adv*

muse[2] *n* [C] **1** someone's muse is the force or person that makes them want to write, paint, or make music, and helps them to have good ideas; ⊟ **inspiration**: *Rossetti's wife and creative muse* **2** also **Muse** one of the nine ancient Greek goddesses who each represented a particular art or science: *the Muse of History*

mu·se·um S3 W2 /mjuːˈziəm $ mjʊ-/ *n* [C] a building where important CULTURAL, historical, or scientific objects are kept and shown to the public: *the Museum of Modern Art* | *The museum has an extensive collection of early photographs.* → see picture at TOWN

muˈseum ˌpiece *n* [C] **1** something or someone that is very old-fashioned – often used humorously: *Some of the weapons used by the rebels are museum pieces.* **2** an object that is so valuable or interesting that it should be in a museum

mush[1] /mʌʃ/ *n* **1** [singular, U] an unpleasant soft substance, especially food, which is partly liquid and partly solid: *The boiled vegetables had **turned to mush**.* | *She trudged through the mush of fallen leaves.* **2 turn/go to mush** if your brains, heart etc turn to mush, you cannot think clearly or sensibly: *If you watch too much TV, your brains will turn to mush.* **3** [U] *AmE* a thick PORRIDGE made from CORNMEAL **4** [U] a book, film etc that is about love and is SENTIMENTAL: *poetry and mush like that*

mush[2] /mʊʃ/ *n BrE spoken* used to speak to someone in an angry way: *Oi, mush! Get your hands off my car!*

mush[3] /mʌʃ/ *interjection* used to tell a team of dogs that pull a SLEDGE over snow to start moving

mush·room[1] /ˈmʌʃruːm, -rʊm/ *n* [C] one of several kinds of FUNGUS with stems and round tops, some of which can be eaten; → **toadstool**: *mushroom soup* → MAGIC MUSHROOM; → see picture at VEGETABLE[1]

mushroom[2] *v* [I] to grow and develop very quickly: *New housing developments mushroomed on the edge of town.*

ˈmushroom ˌcloud *n* [C usually singular] a large cloud shaped like a mushroom, which is caused by a NUCLEAR explosion

mush·y /ˈmʌʃi/ *adj* **1** soft, wet, and unpleasant: *Cook for two minutes until soft but not mushy.* **2** expressing or describing love in a silly way: *mushy romance novels*

ˌmushy ˈpeas *n* [plural] *BrE* soft cooked PEAS, eaten especially in the north of England

mu·sic S1 W1 /ˈmjuːzɪk/ *n* [U]
1 a series of sounds made by instruments or voices in a way that is pleasant or exciting

listen to music
play music
write/compose music
pop/rock/jazz/classical/country music
live music (=music that is played by musicians on stage)
recorded music
background music
piece of music
music lover

*I often **listen to music** when I'm in the car.* | *What's your favourite kind of music?* | *a record featuring the music of George Harrison* | *The band was **playing music** from the show 'South Pacific'.* | *Nyman **writes** the **music** for most of Peter Greenaway's films.* | *a **country music** radio station* | *A lot of the bars round here have **live music** at weekends.* | *A new **piece of music** was specially written for the occasion.* | *He was a keen **music lover**.*

2 the art of writing or playing music: *Peter's studying music at college.* | *music lessons* | **music business/industry etc** *a career in the music business*
3 a set of written marks representing music, or paper with the written marks on it: *I left my music at home.* | *McCartney never learned to **read music**.* → SHEET MUSIC
4 be music to your ears if someone's words are music to your ears, they make you very happy or pleased
5 set/put sth to music to write music so that the words of a poem, play etc can be sung → **face the music** at FACE[2] (7)

GRAMMAR
⚠ Do not say 'musics' or 'a music'. **Music** is an uncountable noun: *I love listening to music.*
⚠ Do not say 'music band' or 'music group'. Say **band** or **group**: *Why don't we form a band?* | *My favourite group is S Club 7.* You can also use a word that describes a type of music before **band** or **group**: *a jazz band* | *a rock group*
⚠ Do not say 'music concert'. Say **concert**: *It was the first time I'd been to a concert.* You can also use a word that describes a type of music before **concert**: *pop concerts* | *a classical music concert*

mu·sic·al¹ S3 W3 /ˈmjuːzɪkəl/ adj
1 [only before noun] relating to music or consisting of music: *a musical version of the fairy tale 'Cinderella'* | *When he began his musical career, King played only for black audiences.*
2 good at or interested in playing or singing music: *She's very musical and loves to sing.*
3 having a pleasant sound like music: *a sweet musical voice* → MUSICALLY

musical² n [C] a play or film that includes singing and dancing: *Webber had three musicals playing in London at one time.* | **Broadway/West End musical** (=one that is performed in New York's or London's important theatres) *Carroll appeared in a number of Broadway musicals.*

ˌmusical ˈchairs n [U] **1** a children's game in which all the players must sit down on a chair when the music stops, but there is always one chair less than the number of people playing **2** a situation in which people change jobs for no good reason or with no useful result: *Scott is now the finance director, after a long game of musical chairs among top management.*

ˌmusical ˈcomedy n [C] old-fashioned a musical, especially one from the early 20th century

ˌmusical ˈinstrument n [C] something that you use for playing music, such as a piano or GUITAR; ◨ **instrument**

mu·sic·ally /ˈmjuːzɪkli/ adv **1** in a way that is related to music: *It's not as good a show, musically, as 'The Most Happy Fella'.* **2** in a way that sounds like music: *A small fountain splashed musically in the courtyard.*

ˈmusic ˌbox n [C] a box that plays a musical tune when you open it

ˈmusic hall n BrE **1** [U] a type of entertainment in the theatre in the 19th and early 20th century consisting of performances by singers, dancers, and people telling jokes; ◨ **vaudeville 2** [C] a theatre used for music hall shows

mu·si·cian /mjuːˈzɪʃən $ mjʊ-/ n [C] someone who plays a musical instrument, especially very well or as a job: *a talented young musician*

mu·si·cian·ship /mjuːˈzɪʃənʃɪp $ mjʊ-/ n [U] skill in playing music

mu·si·col·o·gy /ˌmjuːzɪˈkɒlədʒi $ -ˈkɑː-/ n [U] the study of music, especially the history of different types of music —**musicologist** n [C]

ˈmusic stand n [C] a metal frame for holding written music, so that you can read it while playing an instrument or singing

musk /mʌsk/ n [U] **1** a substance with a strong smell that is used to make PERFUME **2** written a strong smell, especially the way a person smells: *the musk of sweat and muscle* —**musky** adj

mus·ket /ˈmʌskɪt/ n [C] a type of gun used in the past

mus·ket·eer /ˌmʌskɪˈtɪə $ -ˈtɪr/ n [C] a soldier in the past who used a musket

musk·mel·on /ˈmʌskˌmelən/ n [C] a type of sweet MELON; ◨ **cantaloupe**

ˈmusk ox n plural **musk oxen** [C] a large animal with long brown or black hair and curved horns, which lives in northern Canada and Greenland

musk·rat /ˈmʌskræt/ n [C] an animal which lives in water in North America

Mus·lim /ˈmʊzlɪm, ˈmʌz-, ˈmʊs-/ n [C] someone whose religion is Islam —**Muslim** adj

mus·lin /ˈmʌzlɪn/ n [U] a very thin cotton cloth used for making dresses and curtains, especially in the past

mu·so /ˈmjuːzəʊ $ -zoʊ/ n plural **musos** [C] BrE informal someone who plays popular music or knows a lot about it

muss¹ /mʌs/ also **muss up** v [T] informal especially AmE to make something untidy, especially someone's hair: *Briscoe reached down and mussed the boy's hair.*

muss² n **no muss, no fuss** used to say that something can be done easily and without problems – used humorously: *It works every time, no muss, no fuss.*

mus·sel /ˈmʌsəl/ n [C] a small sea animal, with a soft body that can be eaten and a black shell that is divided into two parts → see picture at SEAFOOD

must¹ S1 W1 /məst; strong mʌst/ modal verb negative short form **mustn't**
1 past tense **had to** to have to do something because it is necessary or important, or because of a law or order; → **have, oblige**: *All passengers must wear seat belts.* | *It's getting late. I really must go.* | *You must work hard.* | *We must all be patient.* | *Must I pay now?* | *For the engine to work, the green lever must be in the 'up' position.* | *Accidents must be reported to the safety officer.*
2 used in negative sentences to say that something should not happen, because of a rule or law or because of the situation: *You mustn't talk to your mother like that.* | *This book must not be removed from the library.* | *We must never forget how much we owe to these brave men.* | *No one must disturb him while he's sleeping.*
3 used to say you think something is very likely to be true or very likely to have happened: *Sam must be nearly 90 years old now.* | *His new car must have cost around £20,000.* | *You must have been really upset.* | *There must be something wrong with the engine.* | *Karl must've seen 'Star Wars' six or seven times.*
4 especially BrE spoken used to suggest that someone should do something, especially because you think they will enjoy it or you think it is a good idea: *You must come and stay with us in London sometime.* | *'We must do this again,' he said. 'I've enjoyed it thoroughly.'*
5 especially BrE spoken used to say that you intend or want to do something: *I must call her tonight.*
6 I must admit/say/confess spoken used to emphasize what you are saying: *I must say, it gave me quite a shock.*
7 (why) must you...? spoken used to tell someone that their behaviour upsets or annoys you: *Must you spoil everything?* | *Why must you always be so suspicious?*
8 a must-have/must-see/must-read etc informal something that is so good, exciting, or interesting that you think people should have it, see it etc: *The exhibit is a must-see for anyone interested in Japanese art.* | *a must-read novel*
9 if you must (do sth) spoken used to tell someone that they are allowed to do something, but that you do not approve of it or agree with it: *All right, come along, if you must.* | *If you must smoke, please go outside.*
10 if you must know spoken used when you answer a question that you think someone should not have asked, because it is slightly impolite: *Well, if you must know, I'm thirty-six.* → **you must be joking** at JOKE² (2)

must² /mʌst/ n [C usually singular] something that you must do or must have: *Warm clothes are a must in the mountains.*

mus·tache /məˈstɑːʃ $ ˈmʌstæʃ/ n the usual American spelling of MOUSTACHE

mus·ta·chi·oed, moustachioed /məˈstæʃiəʊd, -ˈstɑː- $ -ʃioʊd/ adj having a MOUSTACHE, especially a large one

mus·tang /ˈmʌstæŋ/ n [C] a small wild horse in North America

mus·tard /ˈmʌstəd $ -ərd/ n [U] **1** a yellow sauce with a strong taste, eaten especially with meat **2** a plant with yellow flowers and seeds that are used to make mustard sauce **3** a yellow-brown colour **4 cut the mustard** informal to be good enough to do something: *Other magazines have tried to copy ZAPP, but have never quite cut the mustard.* → **keen as mustard** at KEEN¹ (4)

ˈmustard gas n [U] a poisonous gas that burns the skin, first used during the First World War

mus·ter¹ /ˈmʌstə $ -ər/ v **1** [T] also **muster up sth** to get enough courage, confidence, support etc to do something, especially with difficulty; ➡ **summon (up)**: **muster (up) the courage/confidence/energy etc to do sth** *Finally I mustered up the courage to ask her out.* | *Senator Newbolt has been trying to muster support for his proposals.* | *'It's going to be fine,' replied David, with as much confidence as he could muster.* **2** [I,T] if soldiers muster, or if someone musters them, they come together in a group; ➡ **gather**: *In April 1185, he began to muster an army.*

muster² n **1 pass muster (as sth)** to be accepted as good enough for something: *I wasn't sure that our clothing would pass muster at the club door.* **2** [C] *literary* a gathering together of soldiers so that they can be counted, checked etc

must·n't /ˈmʌsənt/ the short form of 'must not': *You mustn't tell Jerry what I've bought.*

must·y /ˈmʌsti/ adj a musty room, house, or object has an unpleasant smell, because it is old and has not had any fresh air for a long time: *the musty smell of old books*

mu·ta·ble /ˈmjuːtəbəl/ adj formal able or likely to change; ⬦ **immutable** —**mutability** /ˌmjuːtəˈbɪləti/ n [U]

mu·tant /ˈmjuːtənt/ n [C] **1** an animal or plant that is different in some way from others of the same kind, because of a change in its GENETIC structure **2** something that is very different from others of the same type, in a way that is strange or bad – often used humorously —**mutant** adj [only before noun]

mu·tate /mjuːˈteɪt $ ˈmjuːteɪt/ v [I] **1** if an animal or plant mutates, it becomes different from others of the same kind, because of a change in its GENETIC structure: *Simple organisms like bacteria mutate rapidly.* **2** to change and develop a new form: *Technology continues to mutate at an alarming rate.*

mu·ta·tion /mjuːˈteɪʃən/ n [C,U] **1** a change in the GENETIC structure of an animal or plant that makes it different from others of the same kind **2** *technical* a change in a speech sound, especially a vowel, because of the sound of the one next to it

mute¹ /mjuːt/ adj **1** *written* someone who is mute does not speak, or refuses to speak; ⬦ **silent**: *Billy continued to stand there, mute and defiant.* **2** *old-fashioned* someone who is mute is unable to speak —**mutely** adv

mute² v [T] **1** *formal* to make the sound of something quieter, or make it disappear completely: *Excess noise can be reduced by muting alarms and telephones.* **2** to make a musical instrument sound softer **3** *formal* to reduce the level of criticism, protest, discussion etc that is happening: *The incident so shocked all the students that it muted further protest.*

mute³ n [C] **1** a small piece of metal, rubber etc that you place over or into a musical instrument to make it sound softer **2** *old-fashioned* someone who cannot speak ➡ **DEAF MUTE**

mut·ed /ˈmjuːtɪd/ adj [usually before noun] **1** muted sounds, voices etc are quieter than usual; ⬦ **subdued**: *Everyone was sitting round discussing the accident in muted voices.* **2** a muted reaction to something is not expressed strongly: *There was muted agreement from most of the people in the room.* | *The speech received only a muted response from the unions.* **3** a muted colour or light is soft and gentle, not bright: *muted pinks and blues* **4** a muted musical instrument has been made to sound softer

mu·ti·late /ˈmjuːtɪleɪt/ v [T] **1** to severely and violently damage someone's body, especially by cutting or removing part of it: *The prisoners had been tortured and mutilated.* | *extra protection for mental patients who might mutilate themselves* **2** to damage or change something so much that it is completely spoiled: *The*

sculpture was badly mutilated in the late eighteenth century. —**mutilation** /ˌmjuːtɪˈleɪʃən/ n [C,U]

mu·ti·neer /ˌmjuːtɪˈnɪə $ ˌmjuːtnˈɪr/ n [C] someone who is involved in a mutiny

mu·ti·nous /ˈmjuːtɪnəs $ -tn-əs/ adj **1** *written* showing by your behaviour or appearance that you do not want to obey someone; ⬦ **rebellious**: *There was a mutinous look in Rosie's eyes.* **2** involved in a mutiny —**mutinously** adv

mu·ti·ny /ˈmjuːtɪni $ -tn-i/ n plural **mutinies** [C,U] when soldiers, SAILORS, etc refuse to obey the person who is in charge of them, and try to take control for themselves: [+against] *He led a mutiny against the captain.* —**mutiny** v [I]: *The soldiers had mutinied over the non-payment of wages.*

mutt /mʌt/ n [C] *informal* a dog that does not belong to any particular breed; ⬦ **mongrel**

mut·ter /ˈmʌtə $ -ər/ v **1** [I,T] to speak in a low voice, especially because you are annoyed about something, or you do not want people to hear you: **mutter to yourself** *'I never want to come here again,' he muttered to himself.* | *Elsie muttered something I couldn't catch and walked off.* | *'He's such an unpleasant man,' Alyssa muttered under her breath.* | [+about] *What are you two muttering about?* **2** [I] to complain about something or express doubts about it, but without saying clearly and openly what you think: [+about] *Some senators muttered darkly about the threat to national security.* —**mutter** n [singular]: *His voice subsided to a mutter.* —**muttering** n [C,U]: *The mutterings about his leadership continued to grow.*

mut·ton /ˈmʌtn/ n [U] **1** the meat from a sheep; ➡ **lamb 2 mutton dressed as lamb** *BrE* used to describe, in a disapproving way, someone who is wearing clothes that are usually worn by younger people

mutton chop whiskers n [plural] hair that a man allows to grow on the sides of his cheeks

mu·tu·al /ˈmjuːtʃuəl/ adj **1** mutual feelings such as respect, trust, or hatred are feelings that two or more people have for each other; ➡ **reciprocal**: **mutual respect/trust/understanding etc** *Mutual respect is necessary for any partnership to work.* | *European nations can live together in a spirit of mutual trust.* | *I didn't like Dev, and the feeling seemed to be mutual.* | *The two men were a mutual admiration society, gushing about how much they were learning from each other.* **2** [only before noun] mutual support, help etc is support that two or more people give each other: *MAMA puts new mothers in touch with each other, for mutual support and friendship.* **3** **mutual agreement/consent** when two or more people both agree to something: *In the end the relationship was ended by mutual agreement.* **4 mutual friend/interest** a friend or interest that two people both have: *We discovered a mutual interest in drama.*

mutual fund n [C] *AmE* an arrangement managed by a company, in which you can buy SHARES in many different businesses; ⬦ **unit trust** *BrE*

mu·tu·al·ly /ˈmjuːtʃuəli/ adv **1 mutually acceptable/beneficial/convenient etc** something that is mutually acceptable etc is acceptable etc to both or all the people involved: *We eventually arrived at a figure that was mutually acceptable.* **2 mutually exclusive** two ideas or beliefs that are mutually exclusive cannot both exist or be true at the same time

muu-muu /ˈmuː muː/ n [C] *AmE* a long loose dress

Mu·zak /ˈmjuːzæk/ n [U] *trademark* recorded music that is played continuously in airports, shops etc

muz·zle¹ /ˈmʌzəl/ n [C] **1** the nose and mouth of an animal, especially a dog or horse **2** a cover that you put over a dog's mouth to stop it from biting people **3** the open end of a gun, where the bullets come out

muzzle² v [T] **1** to prevent someone from saying what they think in public; ⬦ **gag**: *an attempt by the* government to muzzle the country's media   **2** to put a muzzle over a dog's mouth so that it cannot bite people

muz·zy /'mʌzi/ *adj BrE* unable to think clearly, especially because you are ill, sleepy, or drunk: *Juliet's head felt muzzy, and she hoped she hadn't a cold coming on.*

MW   **1** the written abbreviation of *medium wave*   **2** the written abbreviation of *megawatt* or megawatts

my¹ [S1] [W1] /maɪ/ *determiner* [possessive form of 'I']
1 used by the person who is speaking to show that something belongs to or is connected with himself or herself: *Have you seen my car keys?* | *My mother phoned last night.* | *I'm sure you don't want to listen to all my problems.* | *Even my own family wouldn't believe me.* | *an apartment of my own*
2 my goodness/my God etc used when you are surprised or shocked about something: *Oh my God! I've missed the train.*
3 my dear/darling/love etc used when talking or writing to someone that you love or like a lot: *Happy Birthday, my love.*

my² *interjection* used when you are surprised, IMPRESSED, or upset: *My! Look at the size of that tree!* | *'It's 3:30.' 'Oh my, I'm going to be late!'*

my·col·o·gy /maɪ'kɒlədʒi $ -'kɑː-/ *n* [U] the study of different types of FUNGUS

my·nah bird /'maɪnə bɜːd $ -bɜːrd/ also **mynah** *n* [C] a large dark Asian bird that can copy human speech

my·o·pi·a /maɪ'əʊpiə $ -'oʊ-/ *n* [U]   **1** when someone does not think about the future, especially about the possible results of a particular action – used in order to show disapproval; ▪ **short-sightedness**   **2** *medical* the inability to see clearly things that are far away; ▪ **short-sightedness** *BrE*; ▪ **nearsightedness** *AmE*

my·o·pic /maɪ'ɒpɪk $ -'ɑːpɪk/ *adj*   **1** unwilling or unable to think about the future, especially about the possible results of a particular action – used in order to show disapproval; ▪ **short-sighted**: *the government's myopic attitude to environmental issues*   **2** *medical* unable to see things clearly that are far away; ▪ **short-sighted** *BrE*; ▪ **near-sighted** *AmE* —**myopically** /-kli/ *adv*

myr·i·ad¹ /'mɪriəd/ *adj* [usually before noun] *written* very many: *the myriad causes of homelessness* | *a myriad We were plagued by a myriad tiny flies.*

myriad² *n* **a myriad of sth/myriads of sth** a very large number of things: *We're still studying a myriad of options.*

myrrh /mɜː $ mɜːr/ *n* [U] a substance that comes from trees and is used for making PERFUME and INCENSE

myr·tle /'mɜːtl $ 'mɜːr-/ *n* [C] A small tree with shiny green leaves and white flowers that smell nice

my·self [S1] [W1] /maɪ'self/ *pron* [reflexive form of 'I']
1 used by the person speaking or writing to show that they are affected by their own action: *I blame myself for what has happened.* | *I can look after myself.* | *I'm making myself a sandwich.*
2 a) used to emphasize 'I' or 'me': *Why do I always have to do everything myself?* | *They say it's a beautiful place, but I myself have never been there.* **b)** used after 'like', 'as', or 'except' instead of 'me': *No one is to blame except myself.*
3 (all) by myself a) alone: *I'd like to be by myself for a while.* **b)** without help from anyone else: *I painted the house all by myself.*
4 not feel/be myself *informal* used when the person speaking does not feel well, or is not able to behave normally, for example because he or she is upset or ill: *I haven't been feeling myself lately.* | *Sorry, I'm not myself today. I've had some bad news.*
5 have sth (all) to myself to not have to share something with anyone else: *Everyone else had gone out and I had the apartment all to myself.*

mys·te·ri·ous /mɪ'stɪəriəs $ -'stɪr-/ *adj*   **1** mysterious events or situations are difficult to explain or understand: *The police are investigating the mysterious*

M

deaths of children at the hospital. | *Benson later disappeared in mysterious circumstances.* | *There's something mysterious going on.*   **2** a mysterious person is someone who you know very little about and who seems strange or interesting; ▪ **enigmatic**: *I decided to find out more about my mysterious new neighbour.* | *a mysterious stranger*   **3** someone who behaves in a mysterious way says very little about what they are doing, in a way that makes you want to know more; ▪ **secretive**: [+about] *Helen's being very mysterious about her plans.* | *She hid her thoughts behind a mysterious smile.* —**mysteriously** *adv*: *Jackson had mysteriously disappeared.*

mys·te·ry¹ [W3] /'mɪstəri/ *n plural* **mysteries**
1 [C usually singular] an event, situation etc that people do not understand or cannot explain because they do not know enough about it

remain a mystery
be a mystery (to sb)
it's a mystery
solve/unravel a mystery (=find an explanation for it)
the mystery deepens (=it becomes more difficult to understand)
a complete mystery
an unsolved mystery
be one of life's (little) mysteries (=be something that you will never understand – used humorously)

Twenty years after the event, his death **remains a mystery**. | *The way her mind worked* **was** *always a* **mystery** *to him.* | *'Why did he do it?' 'I don't know.* **It's a complete mystery**.' | *The police never* **solved** *the* **mystery** *of Gray's disappearance.* | *But why would anyone want to kill Jack?* **The mystery deepened**. | *What happened to the paintings after that is an* **unsolved mystery**. | *I don't know how he got the job – it's* **one of life's little mysteries**. | *How life began on Earth is one of the great mysteries of science.*

2 [U] the quality that something or someone has when they seem strange, secret, or difficult to understand or explain: *Her dark glasses gave her an* **air of mystery**. | *Annie knew that there was some* **mystery surrounding** *her birth.* | **be shrouded/veiled in mystery** *The circumstances of his death were veiled in mystery.*
3 [C usually plural] a subject, activity etc that is very complicated, secret, or difficult to understand, and that people want to learn about: **the mysteries of sth** *his introduction to the mysteries of the perfume business*
4 [C] also **murder mystery** a story, film, or play about a murder, in which you are not told who the murderer is until the end: *an Agatha Christie mystery*

mystery² *adj* [only before noun] used to describe someone or something that people do not recognize or know anything about, especially when this causes great interest: **mystery man/woman** *Who was the mystery woman spotted on board the yacht with the prince?* | *a* **mystery virus**

mystery play *n* [C] a religious play from the Middle Ages, based on a story from the Bible

mystery tour *n* [C] *BrE* a trip, usually by bus, in which people do not know exactly where they will be taken

mys·tic¹ /'mɪstɪk/ *n* [C] someone who practises MYSTICISM

mystic² *adj* another word for MYSTICAL

mys·tic·al /'mɪstɪkəl/ also **mystic** *adj* [usually before noun]   **1** involving religious, SPIRITUAL, or magical powers that people cannot understand: *music's spiritual and mystical powers*   **2** relating to mysticism: *a mystic ritual* —**mystically** /-kli/ *adv*

mys·ti·cism /'mɪstɪˌsɪzəm/ *n* [U] a religious practice in which people try to get knowledge of truth and to become united with God through prayer and MEDITATION

mys·ti·fy /'mɪstɪˌfaɪ/ *v* **mystified, mystifying, mystifies** [T] if something mystifies you, it is so strange or

na·ked S3 /ˈneɪkɪd/ adj

1 not wearing any clothes or not covered by clothes; ◨ **nude**; → **bare**: *The children ran naked through the yard.* | *a picture of a naked man* | *They found the body lying* **half** *naked in the grass.* | *The governor ordered the prisoner to be* **stripped** *naked and whipped.* | **stark naked** also **buck naked/naked as a jaybird** *AmE* (=completely naked)

2 the naked eye if you can see something with the naked eye, you can see it without using anything to help you, such as a TELESCOPE: **visible to/with the naked eye** *The mite is just visible to the naked eye.* | *Through his telescope he could see millions of stars that were* **invisible to the naked eye.**

3 weak and unable to protect yourself: *Standing in front on his first day of teaching, Brad* **felt** *completely naked.*

4 naked truth/self-interest/aggression etc truth, SELF-INTEREST, AGGRESSION etc that is not hidden and is shocking: *The President condemned the invasion as an act of naked aggression.*

5 naked light/flame/sword etc a light, flame etc that is not enclosed by a cover: *A naked light bulb dangled from the ceiling.* —**nakedly** *adv* —**nakedness** *n* [U]

nam·by-pam·by /ˌnæmbi ˈpæmbi◂/ adj *informal* too weak and gentle and not strict or TOUGH enough: *For some people soccer has a reputation as a rather namby-pamby sport.* —**namby-pamby** *n* [C]

name¹ S1 W1 /neɪm/ n

1 OF A PERSON [C] what someone is called: *Her name is Mandy Wilson.* | *What's your name?* | *Can I have your* **last name?** | *She* **called** *him by his* **first name** (=she used his first name when talking to him). | *Please leave your* **full name** (=complete name) *and address with reception.* | *She didn't* **give** (=say) *her* **name.** | *I heard someone* **call** (=say or shout) *my* **name.** | **Sign** *your* **name** (=write it) *on the dotted line.* | *Can you* **put** *my* **name** *on the list?* | *It's a big school but the principal* **knows everyone by name** (=can recognize everyone and address them by their name). | *I* **knew him by name only** (=I knew his name, but didn't know what he looked like). | **under the name (of) sth** (=using a different name from your real name) *HH Munro wrote under the name Saki.* | **(go) by the name of sth** (=used to say that someone has or uses a particular name) *a young politician who went by the name of Tony Blair*

2 OF A THING OR PLACE [C] what a thing, organization, or place is called: [+of] *What's the name of the street?* | *The name of the company has changed.* | [+for] *Edo was the ancient name for Tokyo.* | *The flower's* **common name** (=name that is used by ordinary people, not its scientific name) *is forget-me-not.*

3 REPUTATION [singular] the opinion that people have about a person or organization; ◨ **reputation**: *He didn't want to do anything to damage the* **good name** *of the company.* | *The restaurant got a* **bad name** *for slow service.* | *They* **give** *the rest of the fans* **a bad name.** | *The company* **has a name** *for reliability.* | **make your name/make a name for yourself** (=become famous for something) *He quickly made a name for himself in the Parisian art world.* | **clear your name** (=prove that you did not do something bad or illegal)

4 FAMOUS PERSON/COMPANY/PRODUCT [C] *informal* a person, company, or product that is very famous or is known by many people: **big/famous/household name** *some of the biggest names in show business* | *It made the company into a household name* (=a very well known person or thing).

5 call sb names to use unpleasant words to describe someone in order to insult or upset them: *The other kids used to call me names.* | **call sb all the names under the sun** (=use many unpleasant words to describe someone)

6 in sb's **name/in the name of sb a)** if something is in someone's name, it officially belongs to them or is for them to use: *The house is in my husband's name.* | *I've*

booked a table in the name of Steinmann. **b)** *formal* as someone else's official representative: *I claim this land in the name of the King!*

7 sth has sb's name on it something that seems to be appropriate for or deserved by a particular person: *The match had England's name on it* (=they will win it).

8 in the name of religion/freedom/science etc using religion, freedom etc as the reason why something is done – used especially when you disapprove of what someone is doing: *cruel experiments on animals carried out in the name of science* | *the things people do in the name of love*

9 have sth to your name *informal* to have or own something – used to emphasize that someone has very little or a lot of something: *He died* **without a penny to his name** (=very poor). | *He didn't have a qualification to his name.*

10 the name of the game *informal* the most important thing in a particular activity or situation: *Quality, that's the name of the game.*

11 cannot put a name to sth *spoken* used to say that someone is not able to say what something is called: *I know the tune but I can't put a name to it.*

12 take sb's name in vain to talk about someone without showing respect for them: *How dare you* **take the Lord's name in vain** (=swear using a word such as 'God' or 'Jesus')?

13 in name only/alone if a situation exists in name only, it does not really exist even though officially people say it does: *a democracy in name only* | *He was president in name only.*

14 in all/everything but name if something is true in all but name, it is really true, even though people do not officially say that it is true: *She was his wife in all but name.*

15 sb's name is mud *informal* used to say that people are angry with someone because of something he or she has done – used especially humorously: *If anything goes wrong, your name will be mud.* → **drag sb's name through the mud** at DRAG¹ (10); → PEN NAME

---

name² S2 W2 v [T]

1 GIVE SB A NAME to give someone or something a particular name; → **call**: **name sb John/Ann etc** *We named our daughter Sarah.* | **name sb/sth after sb/sth** (=give someone or something the same name as another person or thing) *He was named after his father.* | *The street is named after the famous South African leader, Nelson Mandela.* | **name sth for sb/sth** *AmE* (=give something the same name as a person or thing) *The college is named for George Washington.* | **man/woman etc named sth** (=someone with a particular name) *some guy named Bob Dylan* ⚠ To talk about the name of a person or thing, it is more usual to say **called** rather than **named**: *He had a friend called Mick.*

2 SAY SB'S OR STH'S NAME to say what the name of someone or something is, especially officially: *The two* *murder victims have yet to be named.* | **name sb as sth** *The woman who was shot has been named as Mary Radcliff.* | *She has secret information and is threatening to* **name names** (=name the people who were involved in something, especially something bad or illegal). | *They're a lot better than some airlines I* **could name**. | **name and shame** *BrE* (=say publicly who is responsible for something illegal that has happened, or who has not achieved a particular standard)

3 CHOOSE SB to officially choose someone or something, especially for an important job or prize: **name sb/sth (as) sth** *The film was named best foreign film.* | *Quinn has been named as the new team manager.* | **name sb to sth** *AmE: Fitzgerald was named to the committee by the chairman.*

4 **to name but a few/a handful/three** etc used after a short list of things or people to say that there are many more you could mention

5 **you name it (they've got it)!** *spoken* used after a list of things to mean that there are many more you could mention: *Clothes, books – you name it, they sell it!*

6 **name the day/date** to decide on a date for your wedding

7 **name your price** *spoken* to say how much you are willing to pay for something or sell something for

'**name brand** *n* [C] *AmE* a popular and well-known product name —**name-brand** *adj* [only before noun]: *name-brand climbing gear* → BRAND NAME

'**name-,calling** *n* [U] when people use unpleasant words to describe someone in order to insult or upset them: *playground teasing including name-calling*

'**name-check** *v* [T] to mention a particular product, person, business etc in something such as an advertisement or speech, or to mention them in order to thank them —**namechecking** *n* [U]

'**name day** *n* [C] the day each year when people of some Christian religions celebrate the particular SAINT (=holy person) whose name they have been given

'**name-,dropping** *n* [U] when someone mentions the name of a famous person they have met or have some connection with, in order to seem impressive to other people – used humorously or to show disapproval: *I didn't want to be accused of name-dropping.* —**name-drop** *v* [I] —**name-dropper** *n* [C]

name·less /'neɪmləs/ *adj* **1** **who shall remain nameless** *spoken* used when you want to say that someone has done something wrong but without mentioning their name, especially to criticize them in a friendly way: *A certain person, who shall remain nameless, forgot to lock the front door.* **2** [only before noun] a nameless person is someone whose name is not known: *the work of some nameless 13th century writer* **3** [only before noun] a nameless thing does not have a name: *He lay still in his nameless grave.* **4** [only before noun] *literary* nameless emotions are very strong and difficult to describe in words: *He managed to calm her nameless fears.* **5** [only before noun] *literary* too terrible to name or describe: *nameless horrors*

name·ly /'neɪmli/ *adv formal* or *written* used when saying the names of the people or things you are referring to: *Three students were mentioned, namely John, Sarah and Sylvia.*

name·plate /'neɪmpleɪt/ *n* [C] a piece of metal or plastic fastened to something, showing the name of the owner or maker, or the person who lives or works in a place

name·sake /'neɪmseɪk/ *n* **sb's namesake** another person, especially a more famous person, who has the same name as someone: *Like his famous namesake, young Washington had a brave, adventurous spirit.*

'**name tag** *n* [C] a small sign with your name on it that you wear

'**name-tape** *n* [C] *BrE* a small piece of cloth with your name on it that is sewn onto clothes, especially school children's clothes; ▤ **label** *AmE*

nan[1] /næn/ also **nan·na** /'nænə/ *n* [C] *BrE informal* grandmother – used by children; ▤ **nanny**

nan[2], **naan** /nɑːn/ also '**nan bread** *n* [U] a type of bread made without YEAST and eaten with Indian food

nan·ny /'næni/ *n plural* **nannies** [C] **1** a woman whose job is to take care of the children in a family, usually in the family's own home: *She found a job as a nanny with a wealthy Italian family.* **2** *BrE informal* grandmother – used by children; ▤ **nan** **3** **the nanny state** *especially BrE* a government which tries to control the lives of its citizens too much

'**nanny goat** *n* [C] a female goat; → **billy goat**

nano- /'nænəʊ $ -oʊ/ *prefix* [in nouns] one BILLIONTH part of a unit: *nanometre* (=a billionth of a metre)

nan·o·sec·ond /'nænəʊ,sekənd $ -noʊ-/ *n* [C] a unit for measuring time. There are a BILLION nanoseconds in a second.

nan·o·tech·nol·o·gy /,nænəʊtek'nɒlədʒi $ -noʊtek- 'nɑː-/ *n* [U] *technical* a science which involves developing and making extremely small but very powerful machines

nap[1] /næp/ *n* **1** [C] a short sleep, especially during the day: **have/take a nap** *I usually take a nap after lunch.* | *an* **afternoon nap** **2** [singular] the soft surface on some cloth and leather, made by brushing the short fine threads or hairs in one direction → PILE[1] (7)

nap[2] *v* **napped**, **napping** [I] **1** **be caught napping** *informal* to not be ready to deal with something when it happens, although you should be ready for it: *The German team were caught napping and Beckham scored the winning goal.* **2** to sleep for a short time during the day

na·palm /'neɪpɑːm $ -pɑːm, -pɑːlm/ *n* [U] a substance made from petrol that was used in bombs by US forces to burn fields and villages during the Vietnam war

nape /neɪp/ *n* [singular] *literary* the bottom part of the back of your neck, where the hair ends: *the soft warm nape of her neck*

naph·tha·lene /'næfθəliːn/ also **naph·tha** /'næfθə/ *n* [U] a type of oil used for FUEL or for making chemicals

nap·kin /'næpkᵻn/ *n* [C] **1** a square piece of cloth or paper used for protecting your clothes and for cleaning your hands and lips during a meal; ▤ **serviette** **2** a SANITARY PAD

'**napkin ,ring** *n* [C] a small ring which a napkin can be kept in

nap·py S3 /'næpi/ *n plural* **nappies** [C] *BrE* a piece of soft cloth or paper worn by a baby between its legs and fastened around its waist to hold its liquid and solid waste; ▤ **diaper** *AmE*: *Excuse me while I* **change the baby's nappy.** | *a* **dirty nappy** | **disposable nappies** (=nappies which are made to be used once and thrown away) | **nappy rash** (=sore skin caused by wet nappies)

narc[1] /nɑːk $ nɑːrk/ *n* [C] *AmE informal* a police officer who deals with the problem of illegal drugs

narc[2] *v* [I + on] *AmE informal* to secretly tell the police about someone else's criminal activities, especially activities involving illegal drugs

nar·cis·sis·m /'nɑːsᵻsɪzəm $ 'nɑːr-/ *n* [U] when someone is too concerned about their appearance or abilities or spends too much time admiring them – used to show disapproval: *He went to the gym every day, driven purely by narcissism.* —**narcissist** *n* [C] —**narcissistic** /,nɑːsᵻ'sɪstɪk $,nɑːr-/ *adj*

nar·cis·sus /nɑː'sɪsəs $ nɑːr-/ *n plural* **narcissi** /-saɪ/ [C] a yellow or white spring flower, such as the DAFFODIL → see picture at FLOWER[1]

nar·cot·ic[1] /nɑː'kɒtᵻk $ nɑːr'kɑː-/ *n* [C] **1** **narcotics** [plural] *especially AmE* strong illegal drugs such as HEROIN or COCAINE: *the narcotics trade* | **narcotics agent** (=a police officer who deals with the problems of narcotics) **2** a type of drug which makes you sleep and reduces pain

narcotic[2] *adj* **1** [only before noun] *especially AmE* relating to illegal drugs: *narcotic addiction* **2** a narcotic drug takes away pain or makes you sleep

nark /nɑːk $ nɑːrk/ n [C] informal especially BrE someone who is friendly with criminals and who secretly tells the police about their activities; ⊟ **informer**

narked /nɑːkt $ nɑːrkt/ also **nark·y** /ˈnɑːki $ ˈnɑːr-/ adj [not before noun] BrE informal angry about something someone has done: There's no need to **get narked** about it!

nar·rate /nəˈreɪt $ ˈnæreɪt, næˈreɪt, nə-/ v [T] formal **1** to explain what is happening in a film or television programme as part of the film or programme: a wildlife film narrated by David Attenborough **2** to tell a story by describing all the events in order, for example in a book: The main character narrates the story.

nar·ra·tion /nəˈreɪʃən $ næ-, nə-/ n [C,U] **1** a spoken description or explanation which is given during a film, play etc **2** formal the act of telling a story

nar·ra·tive /ˈnærətɪv/ n formal **1** [C] a description of events in a story, especially in a NOVEL: At several points in the narrative the two stories cross. **2** [U] the process or skill of telling a story —**narrative** adj: a narrative poem | narrative structure

nar·ra·tor /nəˈreɪtə $ ˈnæreɪtər, næˈreɪtər, nə-/ n [C] **1** the person who tells the story in a book or a play **2** the person who describes or explains what is happening in a film or television programme but who is not seen

nar·row¹ S3 W2 /ˈnærəʊ $ -roʊ/ adj
1 NOT WIDE measuring only a small distance from one side to the other, especially in relation to the length; ⊟ **wide**; → **broad: narrow street/road/path etc** a long narrow road | the narrow passage between the cottage and the house | his narrow bed | The stairs were very narrow. | a long, narrow band of cloud → see picture at THIN¹
2 narrow escape a situation in which you only just avoid danger, difficulties, or trouble: A woman **had a narrow escape** yesterday when her car left the road. | He was shaken by his narrow escape from death.
3 narrow victory/defeat/majority/margin etc a win etc that is only just achieved or happens by only a small amount; → **slim**: The president won a narrow victory in the election. | He persuaded a narrow majority of the party to support the government. | Scotland eventually won the match by the narrow margin of 5–4.
4 IDEAS/ATTITUDES a narrow attitude or way of looking at a situation is too limited and does not consider enough possibilities: You've got a very **narrow view** of life. | Some teachers have a narrow vision of what art is. → NARROW-MINDED
5 narrow sense/definition a meaning of a word that is exact or limited: I use the word 'neighbour' in its more precise or narrower sense.
6 LIMITED limited in range or number of things: The company offered only a narrow range of financial services. —**narrowness** n [U] → NARROWLY, NARROWS; → the straight and narrow at STRAIGHT³ (2)

narrow² v [I,T] **1** to make something narrower or to become narrower: He **narrowed** his eyes and gazed at the horizon. | The track divided into two and narrowed. **2** if a range, difference etc narrows, or if something narrows it, it becomes less: The choice of goods available is narrowing. | The economic gap between the two halves of the country was beginning to narrow.
narrow sth ⇔ **down** phr v to reduce the number of things included in a range: The police have narrowed down their list of suspects. | [+to] I've narrowed it down to one of two people (=there are now only two people to choose between).

ˈnarrow ˌboat n [C] BrE a long, narrow boat for use on CANALS

ˈnarrow ˌgauge n [C,U] a size of railway track of less than standard width: a narrow gauge railway

1 by only a small amount: He was narrowly defeated in the election. | One bullet struck his car, narrowly missing him. | A man narrowly escaped death when a fire broke out in his home on Sunday morning. **2** in a limited way: The law is being interpreted too narrowly. | These big general issues should be broken down into more narrowly focused questions.

narrow-ˈminded / $ ˈ.. ˌ../ adj unwilling to accept or understand new or different ideas, opinions, or customs; ⊟ **prejudiced**; ⊟ **broadminded**: His attitude is narrow-minded and insensitive. | narrow-minded nationalism —**narrow-mindedness** n [U]

nar·rows /ˈnærəʊz $ -roʊz/ n [plural] **1** a narrow area of water between two pieces of land which connects two larger areas of water: There are really three lakes, joined by narrows. **2** AmE a narrow part of a river, lake etc

na·ry /ˈneəri $ ˈneri/ adv old-fashioned **nary a sth** not one: They said nary a word.

NASA /ˈnæsə/ n National Aeronautics and Space Administration a US government organization that controls space travel and the scientific study of space

na·sal¹ /ˈneɪzəl/ adj **1** [only before noun] related to the nose: the nasal passage **2** a sound or voice that is nasal comes mainly through your nose: He spoke in a high nasal voice. **3** [only before noun] technical a nasal CONSONANT or vowel such as /n/ or /m/ is one that is produced completely or partly through your nose —**nasally** adv

nasal² n [C] technical a particular speech sound such as /m/, /n/, or /ŋ/ that is made through your nose

nas·cent /ˈnæsənt/ adj [usually before noun] formal coming into existence or starting to develop: the country's nascent democracy | their nascent manufacturing industries

nas·tur·tium /nəˈstɜːʃəm $ -ɜːr-/ n [C] a garden plant with orange, yellow, or red flowers and circular leaves

nas·ty S2 /ˈnɑːsti $ ˈnæsti/ adj comparative **nastier**, superlative **nastiest**
1 BEHAVIOUR nasty behaviour or remarks are extremely unkind and unpleasant: a nasty temper | the nasty things that were being written about her | There's a nasty streak in her character. | Drivers often have a **nasty habit** of driving too close to cyclists. | [+to] Don't be so nasty to your mum (=do not treat her unkindly). | **get/turn nasty** especially BrE (=suddenly start behaving in a threatening way) When Harry refused, Don turned nasty and went for him with both fists.
2 PERSON someone who is nasty behaves in an unkind and unpleasant way: I went to school with him – he was nasty then and he's nasty now. | You're a **nasty little brute!**
3 EXPERIENCE/SITUATION a nasty experience, feeling, or situation is unpleasant: **nasty shock/surprise** It gave me a nasty shock. | **nasty feeling/suspicion** I had a nasty feeling that a tragedy was going to happen. | Life has a **nasty habit** of repeating itself. | He had a nasty **accident** while riding in the forest. | When you feel you've been cheated, it always **leaves a nasty taste in the mouth** (=makes you feel upset or angry afterwards). | The weather **turned nasty** towards the evening.
4 SIGHT/SMELL ETC having a bad appearance, smell, taste etc: What's that nasty smell? | They were **cheap and nasty** watches, the kind you see on special offer in petrol stations.
5 INJURY/ILLNESS severe or very painful: a nasty cut | He was carried off the field with a nasty injury.
6 SUBSTANCE a nasty substance is dangerous: nasty chemicals
7 a nasty piece of work BrE someone who is dishonest, violent, or likely to cause trouble —**nastily** adv —**nastiness** n [U] → VIDEO NASTY

na·tal /ˈneɪtl/ adj technical relating to birth: Green turtles return to their natal island to breed.

natch /nætʃ/ adv [sentence adverb] spoken informal used to say that something is exactly as you would expect; ▤ **naturally**: 'What does he drive?' 'A BMW, natch.'

na·tion S3 W2 /'neɪʃən/ n [C]
1 a country, considered especially in relation to its people and its social or economic structure: the President's radio broadcast to the nation | an independent nation | the world's leading industrial nations △ In most situations, it is more usual to say **country**: I've been to countries all over the world. | Do you like this country?
2 a large group of people of the same race and language: the Cherokee nation

na·tion·al¹ S1 W1 /'næʃənəl/ adj
1 related to a whole nation as opposed to any of its parts; → **local**: Religion matters very much at a national level. | Between 1929 and 1933 America's national income fell by more than half. | There are strong indications that the Prime Minister will call national elections in May.
2 relating to one particular nation as opposed to other nations; → **international**: We refuse to sign any treaty that is against our national interests.
3 [only before noun] owned or controlled by the central government of a country: the National Institute for Space Research | the country's national airline → NATION-ALLY

national² n [C] someone who is a citizen of a particular country but is living in another country; → **alien, citizen, subject**: Foreign nationals were advised to leave the country. | French/EU/Japanese etc national Turkish nationals who are living in the UK

national 'anthem n [C] the official song of a nation that is sung or played on public occasions

national 'costume n [C,U] special clothing traditionally worn by the people of a particular country: folk dancers in national costume

National Cur'riculum n the National Curriculum the course of study that most students follow in England and Wales between the ages of five and 16

national 'debt n [C usually singular] the total amount of money owed by the government of a country: The government taxed fuel highly in order to finance the national debt.

national 'dress n [U] NATIONAL COSTUME

National 'Grid n the National Grid the system of electricity lines across Britain

National 'Guard n the National Guard a military force in each state of the US which can be used when it is needed by the state or the US government

National 'Health ,Service n the National Health Service the NHS the state system for providing health care in Britain, paid for by taxes

National In'surance n [U] a system of insurance organized by the British government into which workers and employers make regular payments, and which provides money for people who are unemployed, old, or ill

na·tion·al·ise /'næʃənəlaɪz/ v BrE another spelling of NATIONALIZE

na·tion·al·is·m /'næʃənəlɪzəm/ n [U] **1** the desire by a group of people of the same race, origin, language etc to form an independent country: Scottish nationalism **2** love for your own country and the belief that it is better than any other country; → **patriotism**: Under his leadership, a strong sense of nationalism emerged.

na·tion·al·ist¹ /'næʃənəlɪst/ adj [only before noun] **1** a nationalist organization, party etc wants to gain or keep political independence for their country and people: the Scottish Nationalist Party | the rise of the nationalist movement **2** a nationalist organization or party believes that their country is the most important or the best

nationalist² n [C] **1** someone who is involved in trying to gain or keep political independence for their country and people: Welsh nationalists **2** someone who believes their country is best

na·tion·al·is·tic /,næʃənə'lɪstɪk◂/ adj someone who is nationalistic believes that their country is better than other countries; → **patriotic**: They were encouraging nationalistic sentiment among the students.

na·tion·al·i·ty /,næʃə'nælɪti/ n plural nationalities **1** [C,U] the state of being legally a citizen of a particular country; → **citizenship**: people of the same nationality | French/Brazilian etc nationality He has British nationality. | dual nationality (=the state of being a citizen of two countries) **2** [C] a large group of people with the same race, origin, language etc: the different nationalities within the former USSR

na·tion·al·ize also **-ise** BrE /'næʃənəlaɪz/ v [T] if a government nationalizes a very large industry such as water, gas, or the railways, it buys it or takes control of it; → **privatize**: The British government nationalized the railways in 1948. | a **nationalised industry** —**nationalization** /,næʃənəlaɪ'zeɪʃən $ -nələ-/ n [C,U]

National 'League n [singular] one of the two groups that professional baseball teams in the US and Canada are divided into

na·tion·al·ly /'næʃənəli/ adv by or to everyone in the nation: a nationally recognised qualification | The programme will be broadcast nationally.

national 'monument n [C] a building, special feature of the land etc that is kept and protected by a government for people to visit

national 'park n [C] land which is protected by a government because of its natural beauty or historical or scientific interest, and which people can visit: Yosemite National Park

national se'curity n [U] the idea that a country must keep its secrets safe and its army strong in order to protect its citizens: The number of people who join the army is so low that it is beginning to threaten national security.

national 'service n [U] the system of making all adults spend a period of time in the army, navy, or air force

National 'Trust n the National Trust a British organization which owns and takes care of many beautiful old buildings and areas of countryside in England and Wales

na·tion·hood /'neɪʃənhʊd/ n [U] the state of being a nation

nation 'state n [C] a nation that is a politically independent country: European union is seen as a threat to the sovereignty of the nation state.

na·tion·wide /,neɪʃən'waɪd◂, 'neɪʃənwaɪd/ adj [usually before noun] happening or existing in every part of the country: a nationwide search for a missing British tourist | nationwide television —**nationwide** adv: We have 350 sales outlets nationwide.

na·tive¹ W3 /'neɪtɪv/ adj
1 COUNTRY [only before noun] your native country, town etc is the place where you were born; → **home**: They never saw their native land again. | He spent most of his professional life outside his native Poland.
2 native New Yorker/population/inhabitants etc a person or people who come from or have always lived in a particular place
3 native language/tongue the language you spoke when you first learned to speak; ▤ **first language**: English is not the native language for almost half of our overseas visitors.
4 PLANT/ANIMAL growing, living, produced etc in one particular place; ▤ **indigenous**: Singapore has many **native species** of palm. | [+to] These fish are native to North America.
5 ART/CUSTOM [only before noun] native customs, traditions etc are related to people who lived in a

N

particular country before European people arrived there: *the native traditions of Peru* | *stalls selling native jewelry* | *native folklore*
6 NATURAL [only before noun] a native ability is one that you have naturally from birth: *her native wit*
7 go native to behave, dress, or speak like the people who live in the country where you have come to stay or work – used humorously: *Austen has been living in New Guinea so long he's gone native.*

native² *n* [C] **1** a person who was born in a particular place: [+of] *a native of Switzerland* **2** someone who lives in a place all the time or has lived there a long time: [+of] *He has become a native of Glasgow.* **3** [usually plural] *not polite* a word used by white people in the past to refer to the people who lived in America, Africa, southern Asia etc before European people arrived, now considered offensive: *He was not certain whether the natives were friendly.* **4** a plant or animal that grows or lives naturally in a place: [+of] *The bear was once a native of Britain.*

Native A'merican *n* [C] someone who belongs to one of the races that lived in North America before Europeans arrived

native 'speaker *n* [C] someone who has learned a particular language as their first language, rather than as a foreign language; → **non-native speaker**: *For the spoken language, students are taught by native speakers.* | [+of] *a native speaker of English*

Na·tiv·i·ty /nə'tɪvəti/ *n plural* **Nativities 1** the **Nativity** the birth of Jesus Christ **2** [C] a picture or model of the baby Jesus Christ and his parents in the place where he was born: *a Nativity scene with all the animals*

Na'tivity ,play *n* [C] a play telling the story of the birth of Jesus Christ, performed by children at Christmas: *the school's Nativity play*

NATO /'neɪtəʊ $ -toʊ/ *n* **North Atlantic Treaty Organization** a group of countries including the US and several European countries, which give military help to each other: *our allies in NATO* | *a NATO country*

nat·ter¹ /'nætə $ -ər/ *v* [I] *BrE informal* to talk for a long time about unimportant things; ☐ **chat**: [+to/with] *Sometimes she would pick up the telephone and natter to Charles.* | [+about] *Lynne's been nattering on about the wedding for weeks.*

natter² *n* [singular] *BrE informal* the act of talking about unimportant things; ☐ **chat**: *We sat down and had a natter and a cup of tea.*

nat·ty /'næti/ *adj informal* neat and fashionable in appearance: *a natty suit* | *He was a natty dresser.* —**nattily** *adv*

nat·u·ral¹ S2 W1 /'nætʃərəl/ *adj*
1 NATURE existing in nature and not caused, made, or controlled by people; → **artificial**, **man-made**: *the study of the natural world* (=trees, rivers, animals, plants etc) | *an area of spectacular natural beauty* | *natural disasters* (=things such as floods or EARTHQUAKES) | *death from natural causes* | *the need for natural light in offices*

natural lake

artificial pond

2 NORMAL normal and as you would expect; ☑ **unnatural, abnormal**: *At the time, accepting his offer had seemed the most natural thing in the world.* | *it is natural (for sb) to do sth It's not natural for a child of his age to be so quiet.* | *It's only natural that he should be interested in what happens.* | *It was a perfectly natural* (=not surprising) *mistake to make.*
3 BEHAVIOUR a natural tendency or type of behaviour is part of your character when you are born, rather than one that you learn later: *Babies have a natural fear of falling.*
4 ABILITY having a particular quality or skill without needing to be taught and without needing to try hard: *a natural musician* | *Cheryl has a natural elegance about her.* | *his natural ability with figures*
5 RELAXED behaving in a way that is normal and shows you are relaxed and not trying to pretend: *Be cool, be natural.*
6 PARENT/CHILD [only before noun] **a)** someone's natural parent or child is their real parent or child, who is BIOLOGICALLY related to them: *An adopted young person has the right to trace his natural parents.* **b)** *old-fashioned* if someone is the natural child of someone, their parents were not married to each other: *He was rumoured to be the natural son of a duke.*
7 REAL not connected with gods, magic, or SPIRITS; ☑ **supernatural**: *I'm sure there's a perfectly natural explanation.*
8 natural justice/law justice that is based on human reason alone
9 FOOD with nothing added to change the taste: *natural yoghurt*
10 MUSIC *technical* a musical note that is natural has been raised from a FLAT by one SEMITONE or lowered from a SHARP by one semitone; → **sharp, flat** —**naturalness** *n* [U]: *Manufacturers now choose to emphasize the naturalness of the ingredients used in their products.*

natural² *n* [C] **1 be a natural** to be good at doing something without having to try hard or practise: *People think I am a natural, but I've had to work at it.* **2** *technical* **a)** a musical note that has been changed from a FLAT to be a SEMITONE higher, or from a SHARP to be a semitone lower **b)** the sign in written music that shows this kind of musical note

'natural-born *adj* **natural-born singer/story-teller etc** someone who has always had a particular quality or skill without having to learn it

,natural 'childbirth *n* [U] a method of giving birth to a baby in which a woman chooses not to be given drugs to reduce the pain

,natural 'gas *n* [U] gas used for heating and lighting, taken from under the earth or under the sea

,natural 'history *n* [U] the study of plants, animals, and minerals: *the Natural History Museum*

nat·u·ral·is·m /'nætʃərəlɪzəm/ *n* [U] a style of art or literature which tries to show the world and people exactly as they are

nat·u·ral·ist /'nætʃərəlɪst/ *n* [C] someone who studies plants or animals

nat·u·ral·is·tic /,nætʃərə'lɪstɪk◂/ *also* **naturalist** *adj* painted, written etc according to the ideas of naturalism —**naturalistically** /-kli/ *adv*

nat·u·ral·ize *also* **-ise** *BrE* /'nætʃərəlaɪz/ *v* **be naturalized** if someone who was born outside a particular country is naturalized, they become a citizen of that country —**naturalization** /,nætʃərəlaɪ'zeɪʃən $ -lə-/ *n* [U]

nat·u·ral·ly S2 W3 /'nætʃərəli $ -tʃərəli, -tʃɑrli/ *adv*
1 [sentence adverb] use this to say that something is normal and not surprising: *Naturally, you'll want to discuss this with your wife.* | *Naturally enough, she wanted her child to grow up fit and strong.*
2 *spoken* use this to say 'yes' when you agree with someone or when you think the person who asked the question should know that your reply will be 'yes': *'Am I allowed in?' 'Naturally.'*
3 in a way that is the result of nature, not of someone's actions: *My hair is naturally curly.* | **come naturally (to sb)** (=be easy for you to do because you have a natural ability) *Speaking in public seems to come quite naturally to her.*
4 in a relaxed manner without trying to look or sound

,**natural phi'losophy** n [U] *old use* science

,**natural re'source** / $,... '../ n [C usually plural] things that exist in nature and can be used by people, for example oil, trees etc: *a country with abundant natural resources*

,**natural 'science** n [C,U] chemistry, biology, and physics, considered together as subjects for study, or one of these subjects

,**natural se'lection** n [U] *technical* the process by which only plants and animals that are naturally suitable for life in their environment will continue to live and breed, while all others will die out; → **evolution** → **survival of the fittest** at SURVIVAL (2)

,**natural 'wastage** n [U] a reduction in the number of people employed by an organization, which happens when people leave their jobs and the jobs are not given to anyone else

na·ture S1 W1 /'neɪtʃə $ -tʃər/ n
1 PLANTS/ANIMALS ETC also **Nature** [U] everything in the physical world that is not controlled by humans, such as wild plants and animals, earth and rocks, and the weather: *We grew up in the countryside, surrounded by the beauties of nature.* | *nature conservation* | **the laws/forces of nature** *The inhabitants of the island fight a constant battle against the forces of nature.* | **in nature** *All these materials are found in nature.* | *Disease is* **nature's way** *of keeping the population down.*
2 SB'S CHARACTER [C,U] someone's character: *a child with a happy, easy-going nature* | **sb's nature** *It's just not in Jane's nature to lie.* | **by nature** *She was by nature a very affectionate person.* | *I tried appealing to his* **better nature** (=his feelings of kindness) *but he wouldn't agree to help us.* | *Of course she's jealous – it's only* **human nature** (=the feelings and ways of behaving that all people have).
3 QUALITIES OF STH [singular, U] the qualities or features that something has: [+of] *They asked a lot of questions about the nature of our democracy.* | *He examined the nature of the relationship between the two communities.* | **exact/precise/true nature** *The exact nature of the problem is not well understood.* | **different/ political/temporary etc in nature** *Any government funding would be temporary in nature.* | *Capitalist society is* **by its very nature** *unstable.*
4 TYPE [singular] a particular kind of thing: **of a personal/political/difficult etc nature** *The support being given is of a practical nature.* | **of this/that nature** *I never trouble myself with questions of that nature.*
5 **in the nature of things** according to the natural way things happen: *In the nature of things, there is bound to be the occasional accident.*
6 **be in the nature of sth** *formal* to be similar to a type of thing: *The enquiry will be more in the nature of a public meeting than a formal hearing.*
7 **let nature take its course** to allow events to happen without doing anything to change the results: *Sometimes the best cure for an illness is just to let nature take its course.*
8 **back to nature** a style of living in which people try to live simply and not use modern machines: *city workers who want to* **get back to nature** *in their holidays* → **be/become second nature (to sb)** at SECOND¹ (10); → **the call of nature** at CALL² (12)

'**nature re,serve** n [C] an area of land in which animals and plants are protected

'**nature ,trail** n [C] a path through the countryside that is designed so that you can see interesting plants, animals etc along the way

na·tur·ist /'neɪtʃərˌɪst/ n [C] someone who enjoys not wearing any clothes because they believe it is natural and healthy to do this; ▤ **nudist** —**naturism** n [U]

na·tur·o·path /'neɪtʃərəpæθ/ n [C] someone who tries to cure illness using natural things such as plants, rather than drugs —**naturopathy** /,neɪtʃə'rɒpəθi $ -'rɑː-/ n [U] —**naturopathic** /,neɪtʃərə'pæθɪkⵟ / adj

naught /nɔːt $ nɒːt/ pron *old use* nothing: *All their plans* **came to naught** (=failed).

naugh·ty /'nɔːti $ 'nɒːti, 'nɑːti/ adj
1 DISOBEDIENT a naughty child does not obey adults and behaves badly; ▤ **good:** *You're a very naughty boy! Look what you've done!*
2 SLIGHTLY BAD *BrE* if an adult does something naughty, they do something that is not right or good, but is not very serious: *I felt a bit naughty going off on my own, leaving the children behind.*
3 INVOLVING SEX naughty jokes/magazines/films etc *BrE old-fashioned* naughty jokes, magazines, films etc deal with sex, especially in a humorous way; → **rude, blue** —**naughtily** adv —**naughtiness** n [U]

nau·se·a /'nɔːziə, -siə $ 'nɒːziə, -ʃə/ n [U] *formal* the feeling that you have when you think you are going to VOMIT (=bring food up from your stomach through your mouth); ▤ **sick: feeling/wave of nausea** *A feeling of nausea suddenly came over me.* → AD NAUSEAM

nau·se·ate /'nɔːzieɪt, -si- $ 'nɒːzi-, -ʃi-/ v [T] to make someone feel that they are going to VOMIT: *The thought of food nauseated me.* | *She felt dizzy and nauseated.*

nau·se·at·ing /'nɔːzieɪtɪŋ, -si- $ 'nɒːzi-, -ʃi-/ adj **1** making you feel that you are going to VOMIT; ▤ **sickening:** *the nauseating smell of rotting fish* **2** making you feel annoyed or offended; ▤ **disgusting:** *his nauseating remarks* —**nauseatingly** adv

nau·se·ous /'nɔːziəs, -siəs $ -'nɒːziəs, -ʃəs/ adj **1** *especially AmE* feeling that you are going to VOMIT; ▤ **sick:** *I felt slightly nauseous.* | *The taste made me nauseous.* **2** *formal* making you feel that you are going to VOMIT: *a nauseous smell*

nau·ti·cal /'nɔːtɪkəl $ 'nɒː-/ adj relating to ships, boats, or sailing: *All the waiters were dressed in nautical attire.*

,**nautical 'mile** n [C] a unit for measuring distance at sea, equal to about 1.15 miles or 1852 metres

na·val /'neɪvəl/ adj [only before noun] relating to the navy or used by the navy: *a naval officer* | *naval battles*

nave /neɪv/ n [C] the long central part of a church

na·vel /'neɪvəl/ n [C] **1** the small hollow or raised place in the middle of your stomach; ▤ **belly button, tummy button 2 gaze at/contemplate your navel** to spend too much time thinking about your own problems – used humorously

nav·i·ga·ble /'nævɪgəbəl/ adj a river, lake etc that is navigable is deep and wide enough for ships to travel on —**navigability** /,nævɪgə'bɪlɪti/ n [U]

nav·i·gate /'nævɪgeɪt/ v **1** [I,T] to find which way you need to go when you are travelling from one place to another: *I'll drive, you take the map and navigate.* | *Early explorers used to* **navigate by the stars.** | **navigate your way through/to/around sth** *We managed to navigate our way through the forest.* **2** [I,T] to understand or deal with something complicated: *A solicitor will help you navigate the complex legal system.* | [+through] *I am currently trying to navigate through a whole stack of information on the subject.* **3** [T] to sail along a river or other area of water: *The river is too dangerous to navigate.* **4** [I,T] to find your way around on a particular website, or to move from one website to another: *The magazine's website is easy to navigate.*

nav·i·ga·tion /,nævɪ'geɪʃən/ n [U] **1** the science or job of planning which way you need to go when you are travelling from one place to another: *compasses and other instruments of navigation* **2** when someone sails a ship along a river or other area of water: *Navigation becomes more difficult further up the river.* **3** when you CLICK on words, pictures etc in order to move between documents that are connected on the Internet —**navigational** adj [only before noun]

nav·i·ga·tor /'nævɪgeɪtə $ -tər/ n [C] an officer on a ship or aircraft who plans which way it should go when it is travelling from one place to another

criticized: *If we don't make some changes we'll all get it in the neck.*
8 by a neck *informal* if a race, especially a horse race, is won by a neck, the winner is only a very short distance in front: *Our horse won by a neck.*
9 LAND a narrow piece of land that comes out of a wider part: *a neck of land between a lake and the sea*
10 (hang) around your neck if something hangs around your neck, it keeps causing you problems → **be breathing down sb's neck** at BREATHE (5); → **I'll wring sb's neck** at WRING (6); → **pain in the neck** at PAIN[1] (3); → **risk your neck** at RISK[2] (1); → **save sb's neck** at SAVE[1] (11); → **stick your neck out** at STICK OUT (3)

neck[2] *v* [I usually in progressive] *informal* if two people are necking, they kiss for a long time in a sexual way —**necking** *n* [U]

neck·band /'nekbænd/ *n* [C] a narrow piece of material around the neck of a piece of clothing

neck·er·chief /'nekətʃiːf $ -ər-/ *n* [C] a square piece of cloth that is folded and worn tied around the neck

neck·lace /'nek-ləs/ *n* [C] a string of jewels, BEADS etc or a thin gold or silver chain to wear around the neck: **pearl/gold/diamond etc necklace** *She was wearing a coral necklace.*; → see picture at JEWELLERY

neck·let /'nek-lət/ *n* [C] a short necklace

neck·line /'nek-laɪn/ *n* [C usually singular] the shape made by the upper edge of a piece of woman's clothing around or below the neck: *a square neckline* | **low/plunging neckline** (=leaving part of the chest uncovered) *Her evening gown had a plunging neckline.*

neck·tie /'nektaɪ/ *n* [C] *AmE formal* a man's tie

nec·ro·man·cy /'nekrəmænsi/ *n* [U] **1** magic, especially evil magic **2** *literary* the practice of claiming to talk with the dead —**necromancer** *n* [C]

nec·ro·phil·i·a /ˌnekrəʊˈfɪliə, -krə $ -kroʊ-, -krə-/ *n* [U] sexual interest in dead bodies

ne·crop·o·lis /nəˈkrɒpələs $ -ˈkrɑː- / *n* [C] an area of land where dead people are buried, especially a large ancient one; ◼ **cemetery**: *the extensive necropolis which served the Etruscan city of Caere*

nec·tar /'nektə $ -ər/ *n* [U] **1** the sweet liquid that BEES collect from flowers **2** thick juice made from particular fruit: *mango nectar* **3** the drink of the gods, in the stories of ancient Greece

nec·ta·rine /'nektəriːn $ ˌnektəˈriːn/ *n* [C] a type of fruit like a PEACH that has a smooth skin, or the tree that produces this fruit

née /neɪ/ used to say what a married woman's family name was when she was born. 'Née' is put after her married name and before her old name; → **maiden name**: *Mrs Elizabeth Davis, née Williams*

need[1] S1 W1 /niːd/ *v*
1 [T not in progressive] to have to have something or someone, because you cannot do something without them, or because you cannot continue or cannot exist without them; ◼ **require**: *You don't really need a car.* | *Plants need light in order to survive.* | *The camcorder needs a new battery.* | *Are you sure that you have everything you need?* | **need sth for sth** *I need glasses for reading.* | **need sb to do sth** *I need you to help me with the cooking.* | **need sth desperately/badly/urgently** *More blood donors are urgently needed.* | **much needed/badly needed** *a much needed boost to the local economy*
2 [T not in progressive] to feel that you want something very much: *I need a drink.* | *If you need anything, just say.* | **need to do sth** *She said she needed to go out for a walk.*
3 need to do sth used when saying that someone should do something or has to do something: *He needs to see a doctor straightaway.* | *I need to catch up on my office work.* | *You need to let me know by Monday if you want to take part.*
4 [modal] *BrE* used in negative sentences when saying that something is not necessary or not always true; →

have to: **need not/needn't** *You needn't stay long.* | *Going to the dentist need not necessarily be a painful experience.* | **need not have done sth/need not do sth** *You needn't have spent all that money.* | *I needn't have worried.* | **need I/we etc do sth** *BrE old-fashioned: Need we leave so soon?* | **sb need never do sth** *Jim need never find out what I said.*
5 [T] used when saying that something should have something done to it, or has to have something done to it: **sth needs doing** *The house needed painting.* | *Does this shirt need ironing?* | **sth needs to be checked/cleaned/done etc** *The engine will need to be completely checked.* | *The pie doesn't need to be refrigerated.* | **need a (good) wash/clean/cut etc** (=ought to be washed, cleaned etc) *His hair needs a wash.*
6 [T] if a job needs a quality or skill, you must have that quality or skill in order to do it well: *The job needs a lot of patience.* | *Being a teacher needs a high level of motivation.*
7 I need hardly say/tell/remind etc *BrE* used when you think people should already know what you are going to say: *I need hardly remind you that this information is confidential.*
8 you need only do sth/all you need do is ... *BrE* used when saying that you only have to do something in order to do something else: *We need only look at the building to see how much money it will take to repair.* | *All we need do is threaten them.*
9 need I ask/need I say more/ need I go on etc? *BrE* used to say that it is not necessary to say more or ask about something, because the rest is clear: *She's lazy, slow, and stubborn. Need I say more?*
10 that's all I need/that's just what I didn't need *spoken* used when saying that you did not want something to happen, especially when it seems annoying: *'There's a customer for you on the phone.' 'That's all I need!'*
11 need sth like a hole in the head *informal* used when saying that you definitely do not need something
12 who needs it/them? *spoken* **a)** used to say you are not interested in something: *Make-up, who needs it?* **b)** used to say that someone or something is actually very important to you: *Kids? Who needs them!*

need² S1 W1 *n*

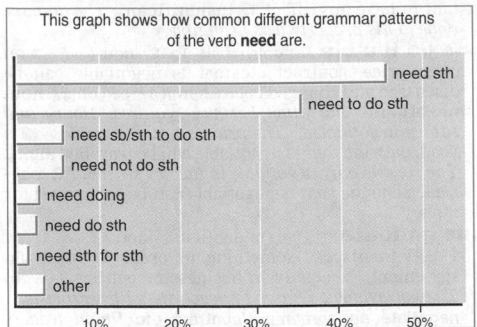

This graph shows how common different grammar patterns of the verb **need** are.

1 [singular] a situation in which something is necessary, especially something that is not happening yet or is not yet available: [+**for**] *Managers should explain the need for change.* | *There's an* **urgent need** *for more nurses.* | *There's a* **growing need** *for new housing in many rural areas.* | **a need to do sth** *We fully recognize the need to improve communications.* | **stress/emphasize/underline etc the need (for sth)** *She stressed the need for regular meetings.* | *Training courses are held in London and in other centres* **as the need arises** (=whenever it is necessary). | *I'll work all night* **if need be** (=if it is necessary).
2 [singular,U] a strong feeling that you want something, want to do something, or that you must have something: [+**for**] *the need for job satisfaction* | **feel the need (to do sth)** *Jack did not feel the need to boast about his success.* | *You're welcome to come back and talk any time, if ever you feel the need.*
3 [C usually plural] what someone needs to have in order to live a normal healthy comfortable life: *She works to provide for her family's* **basic needs**. | **sb's needs** *Environmentalists argue that the organization fails to address the needs of third world farmers.* | **meet/satisfy a need** (=provide something that people want or need) *The charity exists to meet the needs of elderly people.* | *Schools must satisfy the needs of their pupils.* | *We have loans to meet your* **every need**.
4 **there's no need (for sb) to do sth a)** used to say that someone does not have to do something: *There's no need for you to come if you don't want to.* | *There's no need to feel sorry for him.* **b)** spoken used to tell someone to stop doing something: *There's no need to shout!*
5 **be in need of sth a)** to need help, advice, money etc, because you are in a difficult situation: *This project is* **in urgent need** *of funding.* | *He is homeless and* **in desperate need** *of help.* **b)** to need to be cleaned, repaired, or given attention in some way: *The church was* **in dire** (=very great) *need of repair.*
6 **have no need of sth** to not need something: *She believes him and has no need of further proof.*
7 [U] when you do not have enough food or money: *cases of severe need in the inner cities* | **in need** *We must care for those in need.*
8 **in your hour of need** when you are in trouble and need someone to help you: *How could she abandon her father now, in his hour of need?* → SPECIAL NEEDS

need·ful /'niːdfəl/ *adj old use* necessary: *needful expenditure*

nee·dle¹ /'niːdl/ *n* [C]
1 SEWING **a)** a small thin piece of steel, with a point at one end and a hole in the other, used for sewing; → **pin**: *a needle and thread* | *a tapestry needle* **b)** a KNITTING NEEDLE; → see picture at SEWING
2 DRUGS a very thin, pointed steel tube at the end of a SYRINGE, which is pushed into your skin to put a drug or medicine into your body or to take out blood: *She carried hypodermic needles and syringes in her bag.* | *Drug users are at risk when they share needles.*
3 POINTER a long thin piece of metal on a scientific instrument that moves backwards and forwards and

points to numbers or directions: *a compass needle*
4 MEDICAL TREATMENT a long, very thin piece of metal used in ACUPUNCTURE (=a kind of medical treatment originally used in China)
5 LEAF a small needle-shaped leaf, especially from a PINE tree: *pine needles*
6 RECORDS the very small, pointed part in a RECORD PLAYER that touches the record in order to play it
7 **like looking for a needle in a haystack** *informal* used to say that something is almost impossible to find: *Finding out which file you want can be like looking for a needle in a haystack.* → PINS AND NEEDLES

needle² *v* [T] *informal* to deliberately annoy someone by making unkind remarks or jokes about them; ⏹ **rib**, **tease**: *I just said that to Charlie to needle him.*

nee·dle·point /'niːdlpɔɪnt/ *n* [U] pictures made by covering a piece of material with small stitches; → **embroidery**

need·less /'niːdləs/ *adj* **1** **needless to say** used when you are telling someone something that they probably know or expect: *Needless to say, any contributions of money will be gratefully received.* **2** needless troubles, suffering, loss etc are unnecessary because they could easily have been avoided; ⏹ **unnecessary**: *The report caused needless anxiety to women who have attended the clinic.* | *We need to bring to an end these needless deaths.* | *Charles hates needless waste.*
—**needlessly** *adv*: *Over 2,600 Australians are dying needlessly every year of heart attacks.*

nee·dle·wom·an /'niːdl,wʊmən/ *n plural* **needle-women** /-,wɪmɪn/ [C] a woman who is good at sewing

nee·dle·work /'niːdlwɜːk $ -wɜːrk/ *n* [U] the activity or art of sewing, or things made by sewing

need·n't /'niːdnt/ *especially BrE* the short form of 'need not': *I needn't have put on this thick coat.*

need-to-ˈknow *adj* **on a need-to-know basis** if information is given to people on a need-to-know basis, they are given only the details that they need at the time when they need them: *Access to the manufacturing process is on a strictly need-to-know basis.*

need·y /'niːdi/ *adj* **1** **a)** having very little food or money: *a needy family* **b)** **the needy** needy people: *money to help the needy* **2** needing and wanting a lot of love and attention

ne'er /neə $ ner/ *adv literary* never

'ne'er-do-ˌwell *n* [C] *old use* a lazy useless person

ne·far·i·ous /nɪ'feəriəs $ -'fer-/ *adj formal* evil or criminal: *nefarious activities such as drug trafficking and fraud*

neg. *also* **neg** *BrE* the written abbreviation of **negative**

ne·gate /nɪ'geɪt/ *v* [T] *formal* **1** to prevent something from having any effect: *Efforts to expand the tourist industry could be negated by reports that the sea is highly polluted.* **2** to state that something does not exist or is untrue; ⏹ **deny**

ne·ga·tion /nɪ'geɪʃən/ *n* **1** [singular, U] when something is made to have no effect or be the opposite of what it should be: *Much of what passes for Christianity is a negation of Christ's teachings.* **2** [U] when someone says no or disagrees: *He shook his head in silent negation.*

neg·a·tive¹ S2 W2 /'negətɪv/ *adj*
1 BAD harmful, unpleasant, or not wanted; ⏹ **positive**: *My drinking was starting to have a negative effect on my work.* | *the negative aspects of ageing* | *On the negative side, it will cost a lot.*
2 NOT LIKING SB/STH considering only the bad qualities of a situation, person etc and not the good ones; ⏹ **positive**: *students with a negative attitude to school* | *They have a uniformly negative image of the police.* | *Jean rarely sounded so negative about her mother.*
3 NO/NOT **a)** saying or meaning 'no': **negative answer/reply/response** *He gave a negative answer without any explanation.* **b)** containing one of the words 'no', 'not',

N

'nothing', 'never' etc; ⊟ **affirmative**
4 SCIENTIFIC TEST not showing any sign of the chemical or medical condition that was being looked for; ⊟ **positive**: *The pregnancy test was negative.* | *A person can be recently infected by HIV and have a negative result.*
5 ELECTRICITY *technical* a negative CHARGE is carried by ELECTRONS; ⊟ **positive**
6 NUMBER/QUANTITY less than zero; ⊟ **minus**; ⊟ **positive**: *negative numbers* | *a negative return on our investment* (=a loss)
7 BLOOD *technical* used in the names of blood types, meaning not having RHESUS FACTOR; ⊟ **positive**
—**negatively** *adv*

N

negative² *n* [C] **1** an image on a photographic film that shows dark areas as light and light areas as dark, from which the final picture is printed: *black and white photographic negatives* **2** a statement or expression that means 'no'; ⊟ **affirmative**: **answer/reply in the negative** *formal* (=say 'no') *The majority of people, when asked whether or not they are creative, will **reply in the negative.*** **3** something bad or harmful: *The negatives outweigh the positives on this issue.* **4** a negative result from a chemical or scientific test: *The test will give a proportion of false negatives.*

negative³ *v* [T] *formal* **1** to refuse to accept a proposal or request **2** to prove something to be untrue

,**negative 'equity** *n* [U] *BrE* a situation in which someone owes more money on a MORTGAGE (=arrangement to borrow money to pay for a house) than they would receive if they sold their house

neg·a·tiv·i·ty /,negə'tɪvɨti/ *n* [U] an attitude in which someone considers only the bad qualities of a situation, person etc, not the good ones

ne·glect¹ /nɪ'glekt/ *v* [T] **1** to fail to look after someone or something properly: *She smoked and drank, neglected the children, and left the clothes unmended.* | *a neglected garden* | *The building has been badly neglected.* **2** to pay too little attention to something: *Many of these ideas have been neglected by modern historians.* | *The police officer was accused of neglecting his duty* (=not doing everything he should). **3** **neglect to do sth** *formal* to not do something: *You neglected to mention that they had a second album released during 1991.*

neglect² *n* [U] **1** failure to look after something or someone, or the condition of not being looked after: [+of] *Tenants are complaining about the landlord's neglect of the property.* | **years/decades/centuries etc of neglect** *After years of neglect, the roads were full of potholes.* | *The whole district had an air of abandonment and neglect.* **2** failure to pay proper attention to something: [+of] *Five officers were court-martialled for cowardice or neglect of duty.*

ne·glect·ful /nɪ'glektfəl/ *adj formal* not looking after something properly, or not giving it enough attention: [+of] *She became more and more neglectful of her responsibilities.* —**neglectfully** *adv*

neg·li·gee /'neglɨʒeɪ $,neglɨ'ʒeɪ/ *n* [C] a very thin, pretty coat, worn over a NIGHTDRESS

neg·li·gence /'neglɪdʒəns/ *n* [U] failure to take enough care over something that you are responsible for: *negligence in carrying out safety procedures* | *The bridge's architect was sued for criminal negligence.*

neg·li·gent /'neglɪdʒənt/ *adj* **1** not taking enough care over something that you are responsible for, with the result that serious mistakes are made; ⊟ **irresponsible**; ⊟ **responsible**: **negligent in (doing) sth** *The report stated that Dr Brady had been negligent in not giving the patient a full examination.* | *Mr Brown was found guilty of negligent driving.* **2** *literary* a negligent manner or way of dressing is careless, but in a pleasantly relaxed way: *He gave a negligent shrug.* —**negligently** *adv*

neg·li·gi·ble /'neglɪdʒɨbəl/ *adj* too slight or unimportant to have any effect; ⊟ **insignificant**: *The damage done to his property was negligible.*

ne·go·ti·a·ble /nɪ'gəʊʃiəbəl, -ʃə- $ -'goʊ-/ *adj* **1** an offer, price, contract etc that is negotiable can be discussed and changed before being agreed on; ⊟ **non-negotiable**: *Part-time barman required. Hours and salary negotiable.* | *The price is not negotiable.* **2** a road, path etc that is negotiable can be travelled along: *The road is only negotiable in the dry season.* **3** *technical* a cheque that is negotiable can be exchanged for money

ne·go·ti·ate S3 W3 /nɪ'gəʊʃieɪt $ -'goʊ-/ *v*
1 [I,T] to discuss something in order to reach an agreement, especially in business or politics: [+with] *The government refuses to negotiate with terrorists.* | **negotiate an agreement/contract etc** *Union leaders have negotiated an agreement for a shorter working week.* | *His first aim is to get the warring parties back to **the negotiating table** (=used to refer to official discussions).*
2 [T] to succeed in getting past or over a difficult place on a path, road etc: *Guido swung the steering-wheel round to negotiate a corner.*

ne·go·ti·a·tion S2 W2 /nɪ,gəʊʃi'eɪʃən $ -,goʊ-/ *n* [C usually plural, U] official discussions between the representatives of opposing groups who are trying to reach an agreement, especially in business or politics: [+with] *The negotiations with the company had reached a crucial stage.* | [+between] *This follows private negotiations between the landowner and the leisure centre.* | [+on/over] *He is trying to involve community leaders in negotiations on reform.* | **open/enter into negotiations (with sb)** (=start official discussions) *The government opened negotiations with the IMF for another loan.* | *the next **round of** arms **negotiations*** | *The price is generally **open to negotiation** (=is not fixed and can be discussed).*

ne·go·ti·a·tor /nɪ'gəʊʃieɪtə $ -'goʊʃieɪtər/ *n* [C] someone who takes part in official discussions, especially in business or politics, in order to try and reach an agreement: *the chief union negotiator*

Ne·gress /'niːgrɨs/ *n* [C] *old-fashioned* a word for a black woman, which is now usually considered offensive

Ne·gro /'niːgrəʊ $ -groʊ/ *n plural* **Negroes** [C] *old-fashioned* a word for a black person, which is now usually considered offensive —**negro** *adj*

,**Negro 'spiritual** *n* [C] a SPIRITUAL²

neigh /neɪ/ *v* [I] if a horse neighs, it makes a long loud noise —**neigh** *n* [C]

neigh·bour S2 W2 *BrE*; **neighbor** *AmE* /'neɪbə $ -bər/ *n* [C]
1 someone who lives next to you or near you: *One of the neighbors complained about the noise from the party.* | *FBI agents were interviewing all their friends and neighbors.* | *Our **next-door neighbours** (=the people who live in the house next to us) say they'll look after our cat for us while we're away.*
2 a country that is next to another one; → **bordering**: *Israel and its Arab neighbours*
3 someone or something that is next to another person or thing of the same type: *The teacher saw Phil passing a note to his neighbour.* | *The garden was divided from its neighbour by a high wall.*

neigh·bour·hood *BrE*; **neighborhood** *AmE* /'neɪbəhʊd $ -ər-/ *n* [C] **1** an area of a town or city: *She grew up in a quiet neighborhood of Boston.* | *The hotel is situated in a peaceful residential neighbourhood* (=area where there are houses rather than factories or shops). | *a neighbourhood school* **2** **the neighbourhood** the area around you or around a particular place, or the people who live there: *Be quiet! You'll wake up the whole neighbourhood!* | **in the neighbourhood** *Is there a good Chinese restaurant in the neighborhood?* **3** **(something) in the neighbourhood of £500/30% etc** a little more or a little less than a particular number or amount; ▤ **approximately**: *The painting is worth something in the neighborhood of $3000.*

,neighbourhood 'watch *BrE*; **neighborhood watch** *AmE n* [U] a system, organized by a group of neighbours, in which members of the group regularly watch each other's houses in order to prevent crime

neigh·bour·ing *BrE*; **neighboring** *AmE* /'neɪbərɪŋ/ *adj* [only before noun] near the place where you are or the place you are talking about; ▤ **nearby**; → **bordering**: *The fair attracted hundreds of people from the neighbouring towns and villages.*

neigh·bour·ly *BrE*; **neighborly** *AmE* /'neɪbəli $ -ər-/ *adj* behaving in a friendly and helpful way towards the people who live next to you or towards the countries that are next to you: *the importance of good neighbourly relations between the two countries* —**neighbourliness** *n* [U]

nei·ther[1] W3 /'naɪðə $ 'niːðər/ *determiner, pron* not one or the other of two people or things; → **either**: *'Would you like tea or coffee?' 'Neither, thanks.'* | *It was a game in which neither team deserved to win.* | [+of] *Neither of them can cook.* | *Thompson had two strategies, **neither of which** seems to have worked very well.* | *We asked both John and Jerry, but **neither one** could offer a satisfactory explanation.* → see box at NONE[1]

neither[2] S2 W3 *adv* used to show that a negative statement is also true about another person or thing; → **either**: **neither does/can/will etc sb** *'I don't have any money.' 'Neither do I.'* | *Tom didn't believe a word she said, and neither did the police.* | *'I don't like horror movies.' 'Me neither.'*

neither[3] *conjunction* **1** neither ... nor ... used when mentioning two things that are not true or possible: *Neither Oleg's mother nor his father spoke English.* | *The equipment is neither accurate nor safe.* ⚠ Do not say 'neither ...or ...'. Say **not ...or ...** or **neither ...nor ...**: *We don't know or care where he is. Neither he nor his wife eats meat.* **2 be neither here nor there** *spoken* used to say that something is not important because it does not affect a fact or situation; ▤ **irrelevant**: *The fact that she needed the money for her children is neither here nor there – it's still stealing.* **3 be neither one thing nor the other** *spoken* used to say that something or someone cannot be described as either one of two types of thing or person, but is somewhere in the middle of the two: *The New York Times is neither one thing nor the other. It's not really a city newspaper and it's not really a national newspaper either.* **4** *formal* used to add another negative statement about someone or something; ▤ **nor**: *The authorities were not sympathetic to the students' demands, neither would they tolerate any disruption.*

nel·ly, nellie /'neli/ *n* **not on your nelly** *BrE spoken old-fashioned* used to tell someone humorously or rudely that you are definitely not going to do something

nem·e·sis /'neməsɪs/ *n* [singular] **1** an opponent or enemy that is likely to be impossible for you to defeat, or a situation that is likely to be impossible for you to deal with: **meet/face your nemesis** *In the final he will meet his old nemesis, Pete Sampras.* **2** *literary* a punishment that is deserved and cannot be avoided

neo- /niːəʊ, niːə $ niːoʊ, niːə/ *prefix* [in nouns and adjectives] based on a style, set of ideas, or political system that existed in the past; ▤ **new**: *neo-Georgian architecture* | *neo-fascists*

ne·o·clas·sic·al /,niːəʊ'klæsɪkəl◂ $,niːoʊ-/ *adj* neoclassical art or ARCHITECTURE copies the style of ancient Greece or Rome: *a palace built in a neoclassical style*

ne·o·co·lo·ni·al·is·m /,niːəʊkə'ləʊniəlɪzəm $,niːoʊkə'loʊ-/ *n* [U] when a powerful country uses its economic and political influence to control another country —**neocolonialist** *adj*

Ne·o·lith·ic, neolithic /,niːəʊ'lɪθɪk◂/ *adj* relating to the last period of the STONE AGE, about 10,000 years ago,

when people began to live together in small groups and make stone tools and weapons: *a Neolithic burial ground*

ne·ol·o·gis·m /niː'ɒlədʒɪzəm $ -'ɑːl-/ *n* [C] *formal* a new word or expression, or a word used with a new meaning; ▤ **coinage**

ne·on /'niːɒn $ -ɑːn/ *n* [U] a colourless gas that is found in small quantities in the air and is used in glass tubes to produce a bright light in electric advertising signs. It is a chemical ELEMENT: symbol Ne: **neon lights/signs** (=ones that use neon) *the neon lights of Las Vegas* | *A neon sign flashed on and off above the door.*

ne·o·na·tal /,niːəʊ'neɪtl◂ $ -oʊ-/ *adj* [only before noun] *technical* relating to babies that have just been born; → **antenatal, postnatal**: *neonatal care* | *nurses working in neonatal units*

,neo-'Nazi *n* [C] someone who believes that white people are better than people of other races, and who often behaves violently

ne·o·phyte /'niːəfaɪt/ *n* [C] *formal* **1** someone who has just started to learn a particular skill, art, job etc **2** a new member of a religious group

neph·ew /'nefjuː, 'nev- $ 'nef-/ *n* [C] the son of your brother or sister, or the son of your husband's or wife's brother or sister; → **niece, uncle, aunt**

nep·o·tis·m /'nepətɪzəm/ *n* [U] the practice of unfairly giving the best jobs to members of your family when you are in a position of power: *allegations of nepotism and corruption* —**nepotistic** /,nepə'tɪstɪk◂/ *adj* → CRONYISM, JOBS FOR THE BOYS at JOB (15)

Nep·tune /'neptjuːn $ -tuːn/ *n* the PLANET that is eighth in order from the sun: *the discovery of Neptune in 1846* → see picture at SOLAR SYSTEM

nerd /nɜːd $ nɜːrd/ *n* [C] *informal* **1** someone who seems only interested in computers and other technical things – used to show disapproval; ▤ **geek**: *a computer nerd* **2** someone who seems very boring and unfashionable, and is not good at communicating with other people in social situations —**nerdy** *adj*: *nerdy glasses*

nerve[1] S3 W3 /nɜːv $ nɜːrv/ *n*

1 WORRIED FEELINGS **nerves** [plural] **a)** used to talk about someone being worried or frightened: **sb's nerves are on edge/in tatters/frayed** (=someone feels very worried or frightened) | **calm/steady your nerves** (=stop yourself feeling worried or frightened) *Sean drank a large glass of brandy to calm his nerves.* | **be a bundle/bag of nerves** (=be extremely worried or frightened) *I remember you were a bundle of nerves on your wedding day.* **b)** the feeling of being worried or a little frightened: *A lot of people **suffer from nerves** before they go on stage.* | *'What's wrong with Rachel?' 'It's just nerves. She's got her driving test tomorrow.'* | **exam/first-night etc nerves**

2 BODY PART [C] nerves are parts inside your body which look like threads and carry messages between the brain and other parts of the body: *a condition which affects the nerves in the back* | **trapped nerve** *BrE*/**pinched nerve** *AmE* (=a nerve that has been crushed between two muscles etc, causing a lot of pain)

3 COURAGE [U] courage and confidence in a dangerous, difficult, or frightening situation: **the nerve to do sth** *Not many people **have the nerve** to stand up and speak in front of a large audience.* | *She finally **found the nerve** to tell him she wanted a divorce.* | *It **takes a lot of nerve** to report a colleague for sexual harassment.* | **lose your nerve** (=suddenly become very nervous so that you cannot do what you intended to do) *Jensen would've won if he hadn't lost his nerve.* | **hold/keep your nerve** (=remain calm in a difficult situation) *It's hard to keep your nerve when people keep interrupting you.*

4 **get on sb's nerves** *informal* if someone gets on your nerves, they annoy you, especially by doing something all the time: *She's always moaning. It really gets on my nerves.*

5 LACK OF RESPECT [singular] *spoken* if you say someone has a nerve, you mean that they have done something unsuitable or impolite, without seeming to be embarrassed about behaving in this way; ➡ **cheek**: *He's got a nerve asking for more money.* | *'She didn't say sorry or anything.' 'What a nerve!'* | **have the nerve to do sth** *She lets me do all the work, and then she has the nerve to criticize my cooking.*

6 touch/hit a (raw) nerve to mention something that makes someone upset, angry, or embarrassed, especially accidentally: *Without realizing, he had touched a raw nerve.*

7 nerves of steel the ability to be brave and calm in a dangerous or difficult situation: *The job requires nerves of steel.* ➡ **strain every nerve** at STRAIN² (6)

nerve² *v* **nerve yourself to do sth/for sth** to force yourself to be brave enough to do something difficult or dangerous: *The parachutist nerved himself for the jump.*

nerve cell *n* [C] a NEURON

nerve centre *BrE*; **nerve center** *AmE n* [C] the place from which a system, activity, organization etc is controlled: *the ship's nerve center*

nerve gas *n* [U] a poisonous gas that is used in war to kill or PARALYSE people

nerve·less /'nɜːvləs $ 'nɜːrv-/ *adj written* used to describe someone's fingers when they cannot hold something firmly, especially because they have had a shock: *The key fell from her suddenly nerveless fingers.*

nerve-racking, nerve-wracking *adj* a nerve-racking situation makes you feel very nervous or worried: *Speaking in public can be a nerve-wracking experience.* | *Fran faced a nerve-racking wait for her test results.*

ner·vous S3 W3 /'nɜːvəs $ 'nɜːr-/ *adj*
1 worried or frightened about something, and unable to relax; ➡ **anxious**: [+about] *She was so nervous about her exams that she couldn't sleep.* | *I wish you'd stop looking at me like that. You're making me nervous.* | **feel/get nervous** *Paul always gets nervous whenever he has to give a presentation.* | **nervous smile/laugh/look/glance** *'Don't be silly,' she said with a nervous laugh.* *'There's no such thing as ghosts.'* | By the time I got into the interview *I was a nervous wreck* (=was extremely nervous). | [+of] *We were all a bit nervous of him at first* (=frightened of him).
2 often becoming worried or frightened, and easily upset: *She's a nervous, sensitive child.* | *The film is unsuitable for people of a nervous disposition* (=who are easily frightened).
3 [only before noun] related to the nerves in your body: **nervous condition/illness/disorder** *She was suffering from a nervous condition.* | *He had a nervous twitch* (=his body made small, uncontrolled movements).
4 nervous exhaustion/strain a mental condition in which you feel very tired, usually caused by working too hard or by a difficult emotional problem — **nervously** *adv*: *She smiled nervously.* —**nervousness** *n* [U]: *Mike's nervousness showed in his voice.*

WORD CHOICE: nervous, anxious, annoyed, irritated
If you are **nervous**, you cannot relax because you are worried about something that you have to do: *I was nervous about my job interview.* | *He sounded really nervous when he first started speaking.*
If you are **anxious**, you are very worried about something that may happen or may have happened, over which you feel you have no control: *When she didn't come home from school her parents began to get anxious.*
Do not use **nervous** to talk about angry feelings. Use **annoyed** or **irritated**.
If you are **annoyed**, you feel slightly angry with someone because of what they have done: *I was annoyed that he kept me waiting.*

If you are **irritated**, you are made slightly angry by something that keeps happening: *Irritated by their giggling, he told them to be quiet.*
⚠ If someone is irritating you, you can say that they **get on your nerves** (NOT 'on your nervous'): *His fidgeting is getting on my nerves.*

nervous breakdown *n* [C] a mental illness in which someone becomes extremely anxious and tired and cannot deal with the things they usually do: *Colin came close to having a nervous breakdown last year.*

nervous system *n* [C] your nerves, brain, and SPINAL CORD, with which your body feels pain, heat etc and your movements are controlled

nerv·y /'nɜːvi $ 'nɜːr-/ *adj informal* **1** nervous and easily frightened: *She was all tired and nervy.* **2** *AmE* brave and confident

-ness /nəs/ *suffix* [in nouns] used to form nouns from adjectives: *loudness* | *sadness*

nest¹ /nest/ *n* [C]
1 BIRDS a place made or chosen by a bird to lay its eggs in and to live in: *a bird's nest* | *In May the females build a nest and lay their eggs.* | *Young eagles are ready to leave the nest after only two months.*
2 INSECTS/ANIMALS a place where insects or small animals live: *a field mouse's nest*
3 leave/fly the nest to leave your parents' home and start living somewhere else when you are an adult: *Both daughters were of an age where they wanted to fly the nest.*
4 nest of spies/thieves/intrigue etc a place where people are secretly doing a lot of illegal or dishonest things
5 nest of tables/boxes etc a set of tables etc that fit inside each other ➡ **feather your nest** at FEATHER² (1); ➡ **mare's nest** at MARE (2); ➡ **LOVE NEST**

nest² *v* **1** [I] to build or use a nest: *They say eagles used to nest in those rocks.* **2** [T] to organize information, especially in a computer program, so that some of the information is recognized as separate but is included or contained in a larger part of the information: *Phrases are nested in the dictionary entry for the first major word.*

nest egg *n* [C] an amount of money that you have saved so that you can use it for something special in the future: *They had to use part of their retirement nest egg to pay for their son's college fees.*

nes·tle /'nesəl/ *v* **1** [I,T always + adv/prep] to move into a comfortable position, pressing your head or body against someone or against something soft: *Sarah lay there peacefully, the child nestling by her side.* | *He nestled his head against her shoulder.* **2** [I always + adv/prep] *literary* to be surrounded by something, especially hills or countryside: *a tiny village nestling among the foothills of the French Alps*

nest·ling /'nestlɪŋ, 'neslɪŋ/ *n* [C] a very young bird that cannot leave its nest because it is not yet able to fly

net¹ W3 /net/ *n*
1 INTERNET the Net also **the net** the system that allows millions of computer users around the world to exchange information; ➡ **the web**: *Bruce spends most evenings surfing the Net* (=looking at information in different places on the Internet). | **on the Net** *You might find something on the Net.*
2 FOR FISHING/CATCHING THINGS [C] something used for catching fish, insects, or animals which is made of threads or wires woven across each other with regular spaces between them: *a fishing net* | *a butterfly net* ➡ see picture at FISHING
3 FOR SPORTS [C] **a)** the thing that players must hit the ball over in games such as tennis **b)** the thing behind the posts that players try to kick or hit the ball into in games such as football or HOCKEY; ➡ **goal**: *Henry kicked the ball into the back of the net.*
4 FOR KEEPING THINGS OUT [C] something used for keeping things out, for example insects or birds, which is made of threads woven across each other with

regular spaces between them: *a mosquito net*
5 MATERIAL [U] very thin material made from fine threads woven together, with small spaces between: *net curtains*
6 slip through the net if criminals slip through the net, they avoid attempts by the police etc to catch them
7 fall/slip through the net if someone or something falls or slips through the net, a system which was designed to help or check them has not succeeded in doing this: *In a class of 30 children it is easy for some to slip through the net and learn nothing.*
8 cast/spread your net wide to consider or try as many things as possible in order to find what you want: *Record companies are casting their nets wide in search of new talent.* → FISHNET STOCKINGS, HAIRNET, SAFETY NET, NETTING

net² also **nett** *BrE adj* [only before noun] **1** the net amount is the final amount that remains after all the other amounts have been taken away; → gross: *The net profit* (=after taxes, costs etc) *was up 16.3% last month.* | *The company reported a net loss of $56 million last year.* | *Vernon estimates the company's net worth at over $8 billion.* | *The United States is a net importer of beef* (=it imports more than it exports). **2** net result/effect the final result or effect of something: *The net result will be higher costs to the consumer.* **3** net weight the weight of something without its container
—**net** *adv: He earns $40,000 net.* | *jars of coffee weighing 450 grams net*

net³ W2 *v* netted, netting
1 [T] *informal* to earn a particular amount of money as a profit after tax has been paid: *I was netting around $64,000 a year.*
2 [T] to succeed in getting something, especially by using your skill: *The company has recently netted several large contracts.* | *An undercover sweep netted 22 suspects in one evening.*
3 [I,T] *informal* to hit or kick the ball into the net in sport; → score: *Sheringham has netted nine goals for United so far this season.*
4 [T] to catch a fish in a net: *We netted three fish in under an hour.*

net·ball /ˈnetbɔːl $ -bɔːl/ *n* [U] a game similar to BASKETBALL played in Britain, especially by girls

neth·er /ˈneðə $ -ər/ *adj* [only before noun] *literary* lower down – often used humorously: *exploring the nether regions of East Sussex*

net·i·quette /ˈnetiket/ *n* [U] *informal* the commonly accepted rules for polite behaviour when communicating with other people on the Internet

net·i·zen /ˈnetˌzən/ *n* [C] *informal* someone who uses the Internet, especially someone who uses it in a responsible way: *China and India will soon have far larger numbers of netizens than any Western nation.*

net·pre·neur /ˈnetprənɜː $ -nɜːr/ also
net·re·pre·neur /ˈnetrəprənɜː $ -nɜːr/ *n* [C] *informal* someone who has started an Internet business

net·speak /ˈnetspiːk/ *n* [U] the expressions, technical words, SLANG etc commonly used on the Internet: *a glossary of netspeak terms*

nett /net/ *adj* a British spelling of NET²

net·ting /ˈnetɪŋ/ *n* [U] material consisting of string, wire etc that has been woven into a net; → mesh: *a fence of wire netting*

net·tle¹ /ˈnetl/ also **stinging nettle** *n* [C] a wild plant with rough leaves that sting you → grasp the nettle at GRASP¹ (4); → STINGING NETTLE

nettle² *v* be nettled (by sth) *informal* to be annoyed by what someone says or does: *She was nettled by Holman's remark.*

'nettle rash *n* [C,U] *BrE* a medical condition that causes areas of red spots on your skin

net·work¹ W3 /ˈnetwɜːk $ -wɜːrk/ *n* [C]
1 a system of lines, tubes, wires, roads etc that cross each other and are connected to each other: *Hungary's telephone network* | *a high-speed European rail network* | [+of] *an elaborate network of canals* | *the*

network of blood vessels in the body
2 a group of radio or television stations, which broadcast many of the same programmes, but in different parts of the same country: *the four biggest TV networks* | *You're listening to the American Armed Forces Network.*
3 a set of computers that are connected to each other so that they can share information
4 a group of people, organizations etc that are connected or that work together: [+of] *It's important to build up a network of professional contacts.* → the old-boy network at OLD BOY (2)

network² *v* **1** [I,T] to connect several computers together so that they can share information **2** [I] to meet and talk with people who have similar jobs to yours, especially because they may be useful for your work **3** [I,T] to broadcast a radio or television programme on several different CHANNELS at the same time

net·work·ing /ˈnetwɜːkɪŋ $ -wɜːr-/ *n* [U] the practice of meeting other people involved in the same kind of work, to share information, support each other etc: *I'm hoping to do some networking at the conference.*

neu·ral /ˈnjʊərəl $ ˈnʊr-/ *adj technical* relating to a nerve or the NERVOUS SYSTEM: *signs of neural activity*

neural com'puter *n* [C] a computer that is designed to operate in a way similar to the human brain
—**neural computing** *n* [U]

neu·ral·gia /njʊˈrældʒə $ nʊ-/ *n* [U] *medical* a sharp pain along the length of a nerve —**neuralgic** *adj*

neural 'network also **neural 'net** *n* [C] a set of computers that are connected to each other, which share information and operate in a way that is supposed to be similar to the human brain: *By 1989, they were using neural networks to assess credit risks.*

neuro- /ˈnjʊərəʊ, -rə $ ˈnʊroʊ, -rə/ *prefix* also **neur-** /njʊər $ nʊr/ *technical* relating to the nerves: *a neurosurgeon*

neu·ro·in·for·mat·ics /ˌnjʊərəʊɪnfəˈmætɪks $ ˌnʊroʊɪnfər-/ *n* [U] a scientific study which combines NEUROSCIENCE (=the study of the brain) and INFORMATION SCIENCE (=the collecting, storing, and arranging of information, especially using powerful computers)

neu·rol·o·gy /njʊˈrɒlədʒi $ nʊˈrɑː-/ *n* [U] *medical* the scientific study of the NERVOUS SYSTEM and its diseases —**neurologist** *n* [C] —**neurological** /ˌnjʊərəˈlɒdʒɪkəl $ ˌnʊrəˈlɑː-/ *adj: a neurological disease*

neu·ron /ˈnjʊərɒn $ ˈnʊrɑːn/ also **neu·rone** /-rəʊn $ -roʊn/ *n* [C] a type of cell that makes up the NERVOUS SYSTEM and sends messages to other parts of the body or the brain; ◻ **nerve cell**

'neu·ro·science /ˈnjʊərəʊ, saɪəns $ ˈnʊroʊ-/ *n* [U] the scientific study of the brain

neu·ro·sis /njʊˈrəʊsˌs $ nʊˈroʊ-/ *n* plural **neuroses** /-siːz/ [C,U] *medical* a mental illness that makes someone unreasonably worried or frightened

neu·rot·ic /njʊˈrɒtɪk $ nʊˈrɑː-/ *adj* **1** unreasonably anxious or afraid: *He seemed a neurotic, self-obsessed man.* **2** *technical* relating to or affected by neurosis: *neurotic disorders* —**neurotic** *n* [C]: *She accused him of being a neurotic.* —**neurotically** /-kli/ *adv*

neu·ter¹ /ˈnjuːtə $ ˈnuːtər/ *adj technical* a neuter noun, PRONOUN etc belongs to a class of words that have different INFLECTIONS from MASCULINE or FEMININE words; → gender

neuter² *v* [T] **1** to remove part of the sex organs of an animal so that it cannot produce babies; → spay: *a neutered tomcat* **2** to remove power from something or to stop something from being effective – used to show disapproval: *Plans to reform local government are designed to neuter local democracy.*

neu·tral¹ /ˈnjuːtrəl $ ˈnuː-/ *adj*
1 IN AN ARGUMENT ETC not supporting any of the people or groups involved in an argument or disagree-

N

ment: *I always tried to remain neutral when they started arguing.* | *Clive decided to adopt a neutral position.* | *The British government acted as a neutral observer during the talks.*
2 IN A WAR a country that is neutral does not support any of the countries involved in a war: *During World War II, Sweden was neutral.* | **neutral territory/waters** (=land or sea that is not controlled by any of the countries involved in a war)
3 on neutral ground/territory in a place that is not connected with either of the people, groups, or countries that are involved in a discussion, argument, war, or competition: *The talks will be held on neutral ground.*
4 LANGUAGE language, words etc that are neutral are deliberately chosen to avoid expressing any strong opinion or feeling: *the neutral language of an official news report*
5 VOICE/EXPRESSION if someone says something in a neutral voice, or if they have a neutral expression on their face, they do not show how they are feeling: *Bragg said in a neutral voice, 'The investigation has been closed down.'*
6 COLOUR a neutral colour is a colour such as grey, light brown, or cream: *Neutral tones give the room a feeling of space.*
7 WIRE a neutral wire, for example in a PLUG, has no electrical CHARGE[1] (7)
8 CHEMICAL a neutral substance is neither acid nor ALKALINE: *The plant prefers a neutral or slightly acidic soil.* | *a neutral pH of 7.0* —**neutrally** *adv*

neutral[2] *n* **1** [U] the position of the GEARS of a car or machine when no power is being sent from the engine to the wheels or other moving parts: **in/into neutral** *When you start the engine, make sure the car's in neutral.* | *Put the car into neutral.* **2** [C] a country, person, or group that is not involved in an argument or disagreement **3** [C usually plural] a neutral colour

neu·tral·i·ty /njuːˈtrælɪti $ nuː-/ *n* [U] the state of not supporting either side in an argument or war —**neutralist** /ˈnjuːtrəlɪst $ ˈnuː-/ *adj, n* [C]

neu·tral·ize also **-ise** *BrE* /ˈnjuːtrəlaɪz $ ˈnuː-/ *v* [T] **1** to prevent something from having any effect: *Rising prices neutralize increased wages.* **2** *technical* to make a substance chemically NEUTRAL: *a medicine that neutralizes the acid in the stomach* **3** to make an area NEUTRAL in a war **4** to destroy something that is dangerous to you during a war —**neutralization** /ˌnjuːtrəlaɪˈzeɪʃən $ ˌnuːtrələ-/ *n* [U]

neu·tri·no /njuːˈtriːnəʊ $ nuːˈtriːnoʊ/ *n plural* **neutrinos** [C] *technical* something that is smaller than an atom and has no electrical charge

neu·tron /ˈnjuːtrɒn $ ˈnuːtrɑːn/ *n* [C] *technical* a part of an atom that has no electrical charge

ˈneutron ˌbomb *n* [C] a type of NUCLEAR bomb that kills people but is not intended to cause much damage to buildings, roads etc

nev·er S1 W1 /ˈnevə $ -ər/ *adv*
1 not at any time, or not once: *He's never been to Australia.* | *I'm never going back there again, not as long as I live.* | *It is never too late to give up smoking.* | **Never had/did/was** etc *Never had she been so confused.* | **never ever** (=used to emphasize what you are saying) *I'll never ever forgive him for leaving me.* | **Never again** (=never after a particular time) *would he return to Naples.* | **never in all my life** (=used to emphasize how bad something was) *Never in all my life have I felt so humiliated.* | **never for one moment** (=used to emphasize that you never thought something) *She had never for one moment imagined that it could happen to her.* | **sb/sth has never been known to do sth** (=used to say that something is strange because it has never happened before) *Max had never been known to leave home without telling anyone.* ⚠ Do not use another negative word (e.g. 'not') with **never**. Use **ever** with **not**: *I've never seen her.* | *I haven't ever seen her.*

2 you never know *spoken* used to say that something which seems unlikely may happen: *Try it! You never know, you might be lucky.*
3 I never knew (that) *spoken* used to mean that you did not know something until now: *I never knew you played the guitar!*
4 never so much as used to emphasize that someone did not do something, especially when this seems surprising: *I do everything for him, and he's never so much as made me a cup of coffee.*
5 that would/will never do *spoken* used to say that you would not want something to happen: *Someone might discover our secret and that would never do.*
6 never! *BrE spoken* used when you are very surprised by something: *'They're getting married next month.' 'Never!'* | *He's never going to cycle all the way to Manchester!* | *Well I never! I wouldn't have thought she was that old!*
7 (no) I never! *BrE spoken* used to say that you did not do something bad that someone has said you did. Many teachers think this is not correct English: *'You cheated, didn't you?' 'No, I never.'*
8 never say never *informal* used to say that you should not say that you will never do something, because there is always a small possibility that you might do it
9 never say die used to encourage someone not to give up
10 never fear *spoken old-fashioned* used to tell someone not to worry: *She'll be back, never fear.* → **never the twain shall meet** at TWAIN (2)

ˌnever-ˈending *adj* seeming to continue for a very long time; ⊟ **endless**: *Keeping the house neat and clean is a never-ending battle.*

nev·er·more /ˌnevəˈmɔː $ -vərˈmɔːr/ *adv literary* never again

ˌnever-ˈnever *n* on the never-never *BrE old-fashioned informal* if you buy something on the never-never, you buy it by making small regular payments over a long period; ⊟ **on hire purchase**

ˌnever-ˈnever land *n* [U] an imaginary place where everything is perfect

nev·er·the·less S3 /ˌnevəðəˈles $ -vər-/ *adv formal* in spite of a fact that you have just mentioned; ⊟ **nonetheless**: *What you said was true. It was, nevertheless, a little unkind.*

new S1 W2 /njuː $ nuː/ *adj*
1 RECENTLY MADE recently made, built, invented, written, designed etc; ⚡ **old**: *the city's new hospital* | *the new issue of 'Time' magazine* | *new products on the market* | *The hardest part of this job is understanding the new technology.* | *a new range of drugs*
2 RECENTLY BOUGHT recently bought: *Do you like my new dress?* | *They've just moved into their new home.*
3 NOT THERE BEFORE having just developed: *new leaves on the trees* | *a young man with new ideas* | *a new generation of women writers* | **new hope/confidence/optimism etc** (=hope etc that you have only just started to feel) *a medical breakthrough that offers new hope to cancer patients*
4 NOT USED BEFORE not used or owned by anyone before; ⚡ **used, second hand**: *New and second hand books for sale.* | *I got a used video camera for £300 – it would have cost £1000 if I'd bought it new.* | *Someone had driven into the back of his brand new* (=completely new) *car.* | *a spanking new* (=completely new) *conference centre*
5 like new/as good as new in excellent condition: *Your watch just needs cleaning and it'll be as good as new.*
6 UNFAMILIAR not experienced before: *Learning a new language is always a challenge.* | *Living in the city was a new experience for Philip.* | [+to] *This idea was new to him.* | **that's a new one on me** *spoken* (=used to say that you have never heard something before) *'The office is going to be closed for six weeks this summer.' 'Really? That's a new one on me.'*
7 RECENTLY ARRIVED having recently arrived in a place, joined an organization, or started a new job: *You're new here, aren't you?* | [+to/at] *Don't worry if*

you make mistakes. You're still new to the job. | **new member/employee/student** etc *training for new employees* | **new kid on the block** *informal* (=the newest person in a job, school etc) *It's not always easy being the new kid on the block.* | **the new boy/girl** *BrE* (=the newest person in a job, organization etc – used humorously)

8 RECENTLY CHANGED recently replaced or different from the previous one; ⊞ **old**: *Have you met Keith's new girlfriend?* | *I'll let you have my new phone number.* | *the new regime in Beijing*

9 RECENTLY DISCOVERED recently discovered: *the discovery of a new planet* | *new oilfields in Alaska* | *important new evidence that may prove her innocence*

10 MODERN modern: *the new breed of politicians*

11 VEGETABLES [only before noun] new potatoes, CARROTS etc are grown early in the season and eaten when young

12 new life/day/era a period that is just beginning, especially one that seems to offer better opportunities: *They went to Australia to start a new life there.*

13 be/feel like a new man/woman to feel much healthier and have a lot more energy than before, or to have a different attitude: *I lost 19 pounds and felt like a new man.*

14 new arrival **a)** someone who has recently arrived or started work somewhere **b)** a new baby: *The children are thrilled with the new arrival.*

15 new blood new members of a group or organization who will bring new ideas and be full of energy: *What we need in this company is some new blood.*

16 new broom someone who has just started work in a high position in an organization and who is expected to make a lot of changes: *The company seems set to make a fresh start under a new broom.*

17 what's new? *spoken especially AmE* used as a friendly greeting to mean 'how are you?'

18 the new new ideas, styles etc: *This charming hotel is a delightful blend of the old and the new.*

19 sth ... is the new ... *BrE* used to say that something is thought to be the new fashion that will replace an existing thing: *Don't you know that vodka is the new water, my dear?*

20 new-made/new-formed/new-laid etc recently made, formed etc → **a new lease of life** at LEASE[1] (2); → **turn over a new leaf** at LEAF[1] (3) —**newness** *n* [U]

New 'Age[1] *adj* relating to SPIRITUAL beliefs, types of medicine, and ways of living that are not traditional Western ones: *the New Age movement*

New Age[2] *n* (the) New Age New Age beliefs and ways of living

New Age 'traveller *n* [C usually plural] a member of a group of people in Britain who refuse to live the way other people live in ordinary society, and go from place to place living in vehicles

new·bie /'nju:bi $ 'nu:-/ *n* [C] *informal* someone who has just started doing something, especially using the Internet or computers

new·born /'nju:bɔːn $ 'nuːbɔːrn/ *adj* **newborn child/baby/son** etc a child that has just been born —**newborn** *n* [C]

new·com·er /'njuːkʌmə $ 'nuːkʌmər/ *n* [C] **1** someone who has only recently arrived somewhere or only recently started a particular activity; → **novice**: [+to] *I'm a relative newcomer to the retail business.* | *a special award for the most promising newcomer* **2** something that did not exist before: [+to] *The most glamorous newcomer to the Volkswagen Golf range is the revamped GTi 16 valve.*

new e'conomy *n* [singular] an economic system that is based on computers and modern technology, and is therefore dependent on educated workers: *As we move into a new economy, trade unions will have to reinvent themselves to stay relevant.* —**new economy** *adj*: *new economy methods*

new·fan·gled /ˌnjuːˈfæŋɡəld◂ $ ˌnuː-/ *adj* [only before noun] recently designed or produced – usually used to show disapproval or distrust: *newfangled ideas about children's education*

'new-found *adj* [only before noun] recently obtained, found, or achieved: *He enjoyed his new-found freedom.* | *the children's new-found friends*

'new-look *adj* [only before noun] different from before, especially more modern or more attractive: *the new-look Labour party* | *the new-look Brazilian football team*

new·ly W3 /'njuːli $ 'nuːli/ *adv* newly elected/formed/arrived etc elected etc very recently: *the newly appointed director* | *newly fallen snow*

new·ly·weds /'njuːliwedz $ 'nuː-/ *n* [plural] a man and a woman who have recently married —**newlywed** *adj*

New 'Man *n plural* **New Men** [C] a man who is considered to be very modern because he shares the work of looking after his children, cooking, cleaning the home etc

new 'media *n* [U] things such as the internet, DVDs etc that use very modern technology

new 'money *n* [U] **1** people who have become rich by working, rather than by getting money from their families **2** money that makes someone rich and that is recently earned, rather than from their families

new 'moon *n* **1** [C usually singular] the moon when it first appears in the sky as a thin CRESCENT **2** [U] the time of the month at which the moon is first seen → **full moon, half moon**

new po'tato *n plural* **new potatoes** [C] a small potato that is taken from the ground early, and that has a very good taste

new 'rich *n* the new rich [plural] *AmE* people who have recently or suddenly become very rich, as opposed to people whose families have always been rich —**new rich** *adj*

news S1 W1 /njuːz $ nuːz/ *n* [U]

1 information about something that has happened recently

good/bad news
great/wonderful/terrible etc news
news that
welcome news (=good news)
the latest news
a piece/bit of news
have some news (for sb)
tell sb some news
hear some news
break the news (to sb) (=tell someone about something for the first time)
welcome the news (=be happy about something)
greet the news with sth
news spreads

I'm not sure how he's going to react to the news. | *The good news is that tomorrow will be fine and sunny.* | *You seem upset – not bad news, I hope?* | *We are delighted at the news that our daughter is expecting a baby.* | *The fall in house prices will be welcome news for first-time buyers.* | [+on] *What's the latest news on your university application?* | *David's just told me an interesting piece of news.* | *Do you have any news for me?* | [+of/about] *Everyone is shocked by the news of the arrests.* | *Sit down and tell me all your news.* | *Have you heard the news? We're going to get married.* | *How would he break the news to Mary that he'd been lying to her?* | *People living near a disused factory have welcomed the news that it is to be demolished.* | *Friday's news was greeted with enthusiasm in Denmark.* | *News of the tragedy spread quickly around the town.*

2 reports of recent events in the newspapers or on the

N

radio or television: *a late evening news broadcast* | *We've got the* **news headlines** *coming up at half past twelve.* | *a news and current affairs programme* | *Here's the sports news from Jane Murray.* | *the* **latest news** *from the Olympic stadium* | [+**about/on/of**] *news on the latest developments in the talks* | **news that** *Several evening papers carried the news that a cabinet minister was about to resign.* | **local/regional/national/international news** | *Twenty years ago environmental issues rarely* **made the news** (=were considered important enough to be in the news). | **be in the news** *Hong Kong is in the news this morning.* | *His resignation was* **front page news** (=was important news). | **news story/report/item** *Never before has a news story triggered such sensational sales of the newspaper.*

3 the news a regular television or radio programme that gives you reports of recent events: *the ten o'clock news* | *Let's* **watch the news**. | *Be quiet. I want to* **listen to the news**. | **on the news** *It must be true – I heard it on the news last night.* | **switch/turn/put on the news** (=turn the television or radio on so that you can watch or hear the news)

4 be good/bad news for sb if the facts about something are good or bad news for someone, they are likely to make life better or worse for them: *There is no legal market for African ivory, which is good news for the elephants.*

5 he's/she's bad news *informal* used to say that someone is likely to cause trouble: *Stay away from that guy, he's bad news.*

6 be news if someone or something is news, people are interested in them at the moment and want to know about them: *European fashions* **are big news** *right now in the States.*

7 that's news to me! *spoken* used when you are surprised or annoyed because you have not been told something earlier: *'The meeting's been cancelled.' 'That's news to me!'*

8 I've got news for you *spoken* used to say that you are going to tell someone the facts about something, which they will probably not like to hear: *You may think I'm finished, but I've got news for you – I'll be back.*

9 no news is good news *spoken* used when you have not received any news about someone and you hope this means that nothing bad has happened △ **News** is an uncountable noun. Use singular forms with it, not plural: *The news was good (NOT were good).* | *I was surprised by this news (NOT these news).*

ˈnews ˌagency *n* [C] an organization that collects news stories and supplies them to newspapers, radio, and television

news·a·gent /ˈnjuːzˌeɪdʒənt $ ˈnuːz-/ *n* [C] *BrE* **1** someone who owns or works in a shop that sells newspapers, magazines, sweets and cigarettes **2 newsagent's** a shop which sells magazines, sweets and cigarettes

ˈnews ˌblackout *n* [C] a period of time when news about a particular event is not allowed to be reported: *The Indian government has* **imposed** *a* **news blackout** *in Srinagar.*

ˈnews ˌbulletin *n* [C] **1** *BrE* a short news programme on radio or television, reporting only the most important information **2** *AmE* a very short news programme on radio or television, broadcast suddenly in the middle of another programme when something very important has happened; ☐ **newsflash** *BrE*

news·cast /ˈnjuːzkɑːst $ ˈnuːzkæst/ *n* [C] *AmE* a news programme on radio or television

news·cast·er /ˈnjuːzˌkɑːstə $ ˈnuːzˌkæstər/ *n* [C] *especially AmE* someone who reads the news on radio or television; ☐ **newsreader** *BrE*

ˈnew school, new-school *adj* [only before noun] *informal* using new ideas in a type of music or art: *new school hip hop artists*

ˈnews ˌconference *n* [C] a meeting at which someone, especially someone famous or important, speaks to people who work for newspapers or news programmes; ☐ **press conference**: *The chairman told a news conference that some members of staff would lose their jobs.* | **at/in a news conference** *At a news conference yesterday, the two men described their ordeal.*

news·flash /ˈnjuːzflæʃ $ ˈnuːz-/ *n* [C] *especially BrE* a very short news programme on radio or television, broadcast suddenly in the middle of another programme when something very important has happened; ☐ **news bulletin** *AmE*: *We interrupt this programme to bring you a newsflash.*

news·group /ˈnjuːzgruːp $ ˈnuːz-/ *n* [C] a discussion group on the Internet, with a place where people with a shared interest can exchange messages

news·hound /ˈnjuːzhaʊnd $ ˈnuːz-/ *n* [C] *informal* someone who collects information for a newspaper or news programme; → **journalist**

news·let·ter /ˈnjuːzˌletə $ ˈnuːzˌletər/ *n* [C] a short written report of news about a club, organization, place etc that is sent regularly to people who are interested: *The society publishes a newsletter three times a year.*

news·man /ˈnjuːzmæn $ ˈnuːz-/ *n plural* **newsmen** /-men/ [C] someone who writes or reports news for a newspaper, radio, or television

news·pa·per [S2] [W2] /ˈnjuːsˌpeɪpə $ ˈnuːzˌpeɪpər/ *n* **1** [C] a set of large folded sheets of printed paper containing news, articles, pictures, advertisements etc which is sold daily or weekly; ☐ **paper**

> **in the newspaper**
> **local/national newspaper**
> **daily/weekly/Sunday newspaper**
> **newspaper article/report**
> **newspaper reporter/editor/columnist**
> **newspaper cutting/clipping** (=an article that has been cut out of a newspaper)

She had read about it **in the newspapers**. | *I saw an interesting article in the* **local newspaper**. | *I always buy a* **daily newspaper**. | *a series of* **newspaper articles** *about life in Cuba* | *The case attracted* **newspaper reporters** *from all over the world.* | *He was looking through a pile of old* **newspaper clippings**.

2 [U] sheets of paper from old newspapers: *Wrap the plates in newspaper to stop them from breaking.* | *Bella laid the flowers out carefully on a* **sheet of newspaper**. **3** [C] a company that produces a newspaper: *He works for a local newspaper.*

> **WORD FOCUS: NEWSPAPER**
> **the press** newspapers in general | **the media** newspaper, TV, and radio | **tabloid** a newspaper that does not contain much serious news, and mainly has short articles and photographs | **broadsheet** *BrE/***quality paper** *AmE* a newspaper that mostly contains reports about serious news | **journalist/reporter** someone whose job is writing articles for newspapers | **headline** the title of a newspaper report, written in big letters | **article** a piece of writing about something in a newspaper | **column** an article that appears regularly in a newspaper, in which someone writes about their opinions | **editorial** a piece of writing in which the newspaper gives its comments on recent events | **the front page** (which has the main news stories) | **the back page** (which has the less important news, and news about sport) | **the sports/television/fashion/arts etc page**

news·pa·per·man /ˈnjuːspeɪpəˌmæn $ ˈnuːzpeɪpər-/ *n plural* **newspapermen** /-men/ [C] someone who writes or reports news for a newspaper

ˈnewspaper ˌstand *n* [C] a NEWSSTAND

news·print /ˈnjuːzˌprɪnt $ ˈnuːz-/ *n* [U] cheap paper used mostly for printing newspapers on

news·read·er /'nju:z,ri:də $ 'nu:z,ri:dər/ n [C] BrE someone who reads the news on television or radio

news·reel /'nju:zri:l $ 'nu:z-/ n [C] a short film of news that was shown in cinemas in the past

'news re,lease n [C] an official statement giving information to the newspapers, radio, and television; ◨ **press release**: *The University has issued a news release announcing the results of their experiments.*

news·room /'nju:zrʊm, -ru:m $ 'nu:z-/ n [C] the office in a newspaper or broadcasting company where news is received and news reports are written

'news-sheet n [C] a small newspaper with only a few pages

news·stand /'nju:zstænd $ 'nu:z-/ n [C] a place on a street where newspapers and magazines are sold

news·wom·an /'nju:z,wʊmən $ 'nu:z-/ n plural **newswomen** /-,wɪmɪn/ [C] a woman who writes or reports for a newspaper, radio, or television

news·wor·thy /'nju:z,wɜːði $ 'nu:z,wɜːrði/ adj important or interesting enough to be reported in newspapers, on the radio, or on television: *newsworthy events*

news·y /'nju:zi $ 'nu:zi/ adj informal a newsy letter is from a friend or relative and contains a lot of interesting news

newt /nju:t $ nu:t/ n [C] a small animal with a long body, four short legs, and a tail, which lives partly in water and partly on land

New 'Testament n the New Testament the part of the Bible which describes the life of Jesus Christ and what he taught, and the life of the first Christians; → **Gospel, Old Testament**

New·toni·an /nju:'təʊniən $ nu:'toʊ-/ adj relating to the laws of physics that were discovered by the scientist Isaac Newton: *Newtonian mechanics*

'new town n [C] one of several complete towns built in Britain since 1946

,new variant CJ'D n [U] a brain disease that kills people, which may be caused by eating BEEF that is affected by BSE; → **mad cow disease**

,new 'wave n **1** [C] a group of people who try to introduce new ideas in music, films, art, politics etc: [+of] *a new wave of feminism in the sixties and early seventies* **2** [U] also **New Wave** a type of music that was popular in the 1970s and early 1980s, which uses SYNTHESIZERS and a strong beat, and in which the words are sung without much emotion

New 'World n the New World a) North, Central, and South America; → **Old World**: *Christopher Columbus's voyage of discovery to the New World* b) wines from the New World are from non-European countries such as South Africa, New Zealand, and the United States —**New World** adj

,New 'Year, new year n [U] **1** also **the New Year** the time when people celebrate the beginning of a new year: *We're going to spend Christmas and the New Year with my parents.* | *The business will be closed over New Year.* | **Happy New Year** (=used as a greeting) | *Our neighbours invited us round to* **see in the new year** (=celebrate the beginning of the year). **2 the new year** the first few weeks of the year: *Prices are expected to go up in the new year.*

,New Year reso'lution, ,New Year's reso'lution n [C] a decision to do something better or to stop doing something bad in the new year: *I haven't made any New Year resolutions - I never stick to them anyway.*

,New Year's 'Day n [singular, U] 1st January, the first day of the year

,New Year's 'Eve n [singular, U] 31st December, the last day of the year

New Zea·land /nju: 'zi:lənd $ nu:-/ adj relating to New Zealand or its people

New Zea·land·er /nju: 'zi:ləndə $ nu: 'zi:ləndər/ n [C] someone from New Zealand

next¹ S1 W1 /nekst/ determiner, adj **1** the next event, day, time etc is the one that happens after the present one, or the previous one: *I just missed my flight to Chicago. When's the next one?* | *We'll look at the proposals at the next meeting.* | *Over the next couple of months, try to relax more and get more exercise.* | **next week/year/Monday etc** *We're hoping to open the factory some time next year.* | **the next day/week etc** (=on or during the following day, week etc) *She called me and we arranged to meet the next day.* | **(the) next time** *Next time I go skiing, I'll wear warmer clothes.* **2** the next house, room, place etc is the one that is nearest to where you are now: *Turn left at the next corner.* | *We could hear them arguing in the next room.* → **NEXT TO** **3** the next person or thing in a list, series etc comes after the one that you are dealing with now: *Read the next two chapters before Friday.* | *Do they have the next size up* (=a slightly bigger size)? **4 next biggest/most common etc** almost as big, more common etc than the one you are talking about: *Cancer-related diseases are the next biggest killers.* **5 the next best thing** the thing or situation that is almost as good as the one you really want: *If I can't be home for Christmas, phoning you on the day is the next best thing.* **6 the next thing I/she etc knew** informal used when something surprising happens very suddenly: *The next thing I knew, I was lying face down on the pavement.* **7 as the next man/person** as any other man or person: *I am as keen to do well as the next man.*

next² S1 W1 adv **1** immediately afterwards: *With John here, you never know what will happen next.* | *Next, put it in the oven for 20 minutes.* **2** the next time: *When I next saw her she completely ignored me.*

next³ pron **1** the person or thing in a list, series etc that comes after the person or thing you are dealing with now: *What's next on the shopping list?* | **the next to do sth** *Who will be the next to go?* **2 the day/week etc after next** the day, week etc that follows the next one: *Have you remembered it's Susie's birthday the week after next?* **3 the next to last** the one before the last one: *the next to last day of their visit* **4 next (please)** used to tell someone that it is now their turn to speak or their turn to do something **5 be next in line** to be the next person, especially to have a job or position

,next 'door¹ adv **1** in the house, room etc next to yours or someone else's: *the boy next door* | *Her office is just next door.* **2 next door to sth** next to another building, room etc: *They live next door to the fish and chip shop.*

next door² n [U] BrE informal the people living in the house or apartment next to yours; ◨ **neighbour**: *Have you seen next door's new car?*

'next-door adj [only before noun] **1 next-door neighbour** the person who lives in the house or apartment next to yours **2 next-door apartment/office etc** the apartment etc that is next to yours

,next of 'kin n [plural, U] your closest living relative or relatives: *May I have your name, address and next of kin, please?*

'next to prep **1** very close to someone or something, with nothing in between; ◨ **beside**: *There was a little girl sitting next to him.* **2 next to nothing** very little: *He knows next to nothing about antiques.* **3** used to give a list of things you like, hate etc in order to say what is first on the list: *Next to soccer, I like playing*

N

N

tennis best. **4** in comparison with someone or something: *Next to her, I'm a very poor cook.* **5 the next to last** the one before the last one: *We'll need to buy some more wine. This is the next to last bottle.* **6 next to impossible/useless etc** almost impossible, useless etc: *This crossword puzzle is next to impossible.*

nex·us /ˈneksəs/ *n* [singular] *formal* a connection or network of connections between a number of people, things, or ideas: [+of] *a nexus of social relationships*

NGO /ˌen dʒiː ˈəʊ $ -ˈoʊ/ *n* [C] **non-governmental organization** an organization which helps people, protects the environment etc and which is not run by a government

NHS /ˌen eɪtʃ ˈes/ *n* **the NHS the National Health Service** the British system that provides free medical treatment for everyone, and is paid for by taxes: *NHS hospitals* | **on the NHS** (=free from the NHS) *Can I get my glasses on the NHS?*

ni·a·cin /ˈnaɪəsɪn/ *n* [U] a type of VITAMIN that is good for your skin and your NERVOUS SYSTEM

nib /nɪb/ *n* [C] **1** the pointed metal part at the end of a pen → see picture at TIP¹ **2 his/her nibs** *old-fashioned informal* someone in authority or someone who thinks they are important: *And how's his nibs this morning?*

nib·ble¹ /ˈnɪbəl/ *v* **1** [I,T] to eat small amounts of food by taking very small bites: *He nibbled the biscuit cautiously.* | [+at] *There's a fish nibbling at my bait.* | [+on] *He nibbled on a piece of raw carrot.*; → see picture at BITE¹ **2** [T] to gently bite someone in a loving way: *He began to nibble her ear affectionately.*

nibble away at sth *phr v* to take away small amounts of something so that the total amount is gradually reduced: *All these expenses are nibbling away at our savings.* | *The Scottish National Party is at last beginning to nibble away at Labour's huge majority.*

nibble² *n* [C] **1** a small bite of something: [+of] *She took a nibble of her cookie.* **2 nibbles** [plural] *informal* small things to eat, like CRISPS and PEANUTS, especially at a party **3** a small amount of interest in something: *We've had the house on the market for a month and not even had a nibble yet.*

NiCad /ˈnaɪkæd/ *n* [C] *trademark* **nickel-cadmium** a type of BATTERY that can be RECHARGED, and that is used in cameras and small electronic equipment

nice S1 W2 /naɪs/ *adj*

1 GOOD pleasant, attractive, or enjoyable: *They've got a very nice house.* | *Did you have a nice time?* | *It's such a nice day* (=good weather), *why not go for a swim?* | *What a nice surprise!* | **look/taste/smell nice** *You look nice in that suit.* | *Mm, something smells nice!* | **nice big/new/long etc** *a nice long holiday* | *a nice new car* | **nice and warm/clean/easy/quiet etc** *The house seemed nice and tidy.* | *One of the nice things about Christmas is having all the family together.* ⚠ You can use **nice and** followed by another adjective after *be The weather was nice and warm.* But before a noun you must leave out 'and' *a nice hot* (NOT *nice and hot*) *drink*

2 FRIENDLY friendly, kind, or polite: *Dave's a really nice guy.* | *That's not a very nice thing to say about your sister!* | [+about] *Tim spilt wine all over the sofa, but Martha was very nice about it.* | [+to] *They were very nice to me while I was ill.* | **it is nice of sb (to do sth)** *It was nice of you to help.* | *He told me, in the nicest possible way, that I was interfering too much.*

3 STH YOU WANT used to say what you like or what you think would be good or useful: *It's quite nice to live so close to work.* | **it is nice to do sth** *It would be nice to have a break.* | **that'd be nice** (=used to accept an offer or agree with a suggestion) *'Would you like a cup of coffee?' 'Yes, that'd be nice.'* | *I thought it would be a nice idea to send them some flowers.* | *It would be nice if you could let us know in advance.*

SPOKEN PHRASES
4 it's nice to know (that) used to mean that you feel happier when you know something: *I still haven't heard any news – it would be nice to know what's happening.* | *It's nice to know that there's someone nearby if she needs help.*
5 have a nice day! *AmE* used to say goodbye to someone, especially to customers in shops and restaurants when they are leaving
6 nice to meet you used as a friendly greeting when you meet someone for the first time: *Hello. It's nice to meet you at last.*
7 (it's been) nice meeting/talking to you used when you say goodbye to someone you have met for the first time
8 NOT NICE *BrE* used in a humorous or angry way when you really think that something or someone is not at all good or pleasant: *That's a nice way to treat a friend, I must say!* | *Well, we're in a nice mess now.*
9 nice try used when someone has made a guess or suggestion, or has attempted to do something, to say that it is good, but not quite correct or successful: *'We could phone Mark to come and pick us up.' 'Nice try, Clive, but we haven't got his number.'*
10 nice one! *BrE* used when someone has just said or done something clever, amusing, or helpful: *'Dad said he'd help pay for it.' 'Nice one!'*

11 be (as) nice as pie *BrE* if someone is as nice as pie, they are not angry with you when you were expecting them to be
12 nice work if you can get it *BrE* used humorously to say that someone has a very easy or enjoyable job, especially one which you would like to do
13 DETAIL *formal* involving a very small difference or detail: *a nice point of law*
14 RESPECTABLE *old-fashioned* having high standards of moral and social behaviour: *What's a nice girl like you doing in a place like this?*
15 nice ... shame about the ... *BrE* used when saying that part of something is good or well done, but a more important part is bad or badly done: *Nice video, shame about the song.* —**niceness** *n* [U]: *The first thing you noticed about him was his niceness.* → no more Mr Nice Guy! at GUY (5)

WORD FOCUS: NICE
person: **lovely, pleasant, charming, sweet, adorable**
thing/place/activity/time: **lovely, pleasant, delightful**

nice-looking *adj* attractive; → **good-looking**: *a nice-looking young man* | *a nice-looking car*

nice·ly S3 /ˈnaɪsli/ *adv*
1 WELL in a satisfactory, pleasant, or attractive way: *He was handsome and nicely dressed.* | *The table fits in nicely with the rest of the furniture.* | *The wound healed up nicely.* | *The garden's coming along very nicely now* (=it is growing well).
2 IN A FRIENDLY/PLEASANT WAY in a pleasant, polite, or friendly way: *I'm sure he'll help if you ask him nicely.*
3 be doing nicely *BrE* to be successful and be earning a lot of money: *The business is doing quite nicely.* | *I've heard Malcolm's doing very nicely for himself out in Japan.*
4 that will do nicely *BrE spoken* used when saying that something is very suitable and is just what you want: *'Will cheese sandwiches be okay?' 'Yes, that'll do nicely.'*
5 EXACTLY *formal* exactly or carefully: *a nicely calculated distance*

ni·ce·ty /ˈnaɪsəti/ *n plural* **niceties 1** [C usually plural] a small detail or point of difference, especially one that is usually considered to be part of the correct way of doing something: *social niceties* | *legal niceties* | [+of] *the niceties of political diplomacy* **2 to a nicety** *formal* exactly

niche¹ /niːʃ, nɪtʃ $ nɪtʃ, niːʃ/ *n* **1** [C] if you find your niche, you find a job or activity that is very suitable for you: *Amanda soon found her niche at the club.* | *He's managed to create a niche for himself in local politics.*

2 [singular] an opportunity to sell a product or service to a particular group of people who have similar needs, interests etc: [+in] *He spotted a niche in the market.* **3** [C] a hollow place in a wall, often made to hold a STATUE

niche² *adj* [only before noun] relating to selling goods to a particular small group of people who have similar needs, interests etc: *niche marketing* | *a niche market* | *a niche product*

nick¹ /nɪk/ *n* **1 in the nick of time** just before it is too late, or just before something bad happens: *Luckily, help arrived in the nick of time.* **2 in good nick/in bad nick etc** *BrE informal* in good condition or in bad condition: *It's an old car but it's still in good nick.* **3** [C] a very small cut made on the edge or surface of something **4 the nick** *BrE informal* a POLICE STATION

nick² *v* [T] **1** *BrE informal* to steal something; ⚑ **pinch, steal**: *Someone's nicked my wallet.* | **nick sth from sb/sth** *You nicked those pens from my desk.* **2** to make a small cut in the surface or edge of something, usually by accident: *He nicked his hand on some broken glass.* **3** *BrE informal* if the police nick you, they catch you and charge you with a crime; ⚑ **arrest**: *You're nicked!*

nick·el /ˈnɪkəl/ *n* **1** [U] a hard silver-white metal that is often combined with other metals, for example to make steel. It is a chemical ELEMENT: symbol Ni **2** [C] a coin in the US or Canada that is worth five cents

nickel-and-ˈdime¹ *v* [T] *AmE informal* to not give enough attention or money to something, with the result that it is not dealt with effectively

nickel-and-dime² *adj* [only before noun] *AmE* unimportant or involving little money

nick·name /ˈnɪkneɪm/ *n* [C] a name given to someone, especially by their friends or family, that is not their real name and is often connected with what they look like or something they have done: [+for] *We had nicknames for all the teachers.* | *Stephen earned himself the nickname Hawkeye.* —**nickname** *v* [T]: *She was nicknamed Sunny because of her happy nature.*

nic·o·tine /ˈnɪkətiːn/ *n* [U] a substance in tobacco which makes it difficult for people to stop smoking

ˈnicotine ˌpatch *n* [C] a small piece of material containing nicotine which you stick on your skin to help you stop smoking

niece /niːs/ *n* [C] the daughter of your brother or sister, or the daughter of your wife's or husband's brother or sister; → **nephew, aunt, uncle**

nif·ty /ˈnɪfti/ *adj informal* something that is nifty is good because it is clever, skilful, or effective: *a nifty little gadget for squeezing oranges*

nig·gard·ly /ˈnɪɡədli $ -ər-/ *adj old-fashioned* **1** a niggardly gift, amount, salary etc is much too small and is given unwillingly: *niggardly wages* | *a niggardly 2% increase* **2** unwilling to spend money or be generous; ⚑ **stingy**: *a niggardly person*

nig·ger /ˈnɪɡə $ -ər/ *n* [C] *taboo* a very offensive word for a black person. Do not use this word.

nig·gle¹ /ˈnɪɡəl/ *v* **1** [T] if something niggles you, you keep worrying about it or feeling annoyed about it and you cannot forget it; → **bug**: *Something's been niggling her all day.* | *It niggles me that we can't go home yet and get warm.* **2** [I] to argue or make criticisms about small unimportant details: *She niggled over every detail of the bill.*

niggle² *n* [C] **1** a slight feeling: *a niggle of doubt* **2** a slight criticism or complaint **3** a slight physical pain: *a niggle in his knee*

nig·gling /ˈnɪɡəlɪŋ/ *adj* **1 niggling doubt/worry/suspicion etc** a slight doubt etc that you cannot stop thinking about; ⚑ **nagging**: *a niggling injury or problem is a slight one that does not go away*

nigh /naɪ/ *adv* **1 nigh on** *old-fashioned* almost: *There were nigh on 40 people there.* **2** *literary* near or soon: *Winter draws nigh* (=will start soon). → **WELL-NIGH**

night S1 W1 /naɪt/ *n* [C,U]
1 WHEN IT IS DARK the dark part of each 24-hour period when the sun cannot be seen and when most people sleep; ⚑ **day**

> **last night**
> **at night** (=when it is night)
> **in/during the night** (=at a particular point in the night)
> **in the middle of the night**
> **all night (long)**
> **by night** (=at night, rather than in the day)
> **at this time of night** (=used when you are surprised)
> **in/at the dead of night** *literary* (=in the middle of the night when it is quiet)
> **spend/stay a night somewhere**
> **stay the night** (=sleep at the house of someone you are visiting)
> **night train/bus/flight**
> **night falls** *written* (=it starts to become dark)
> **the night air**
> **the night sky**

> *It was a cold moonlit night.* | *I didn't sleep too well last night.* | *At night the temperature drops below zero.* | *He woke up twice during the night.* | *The party went on all night.* | *Many animals hunt by night.* | *Who could be calling at this time of night?* | *an attack in the dead of night* | *We spent the first two nights of our vacation in a cheap motel.* | *If you miss the last bus home, you can always stay the night.* | *We took the night train to Glasgow.* | *Night was beginning to fall.* | *the cold night air*

2 EVENING the time during the evening until you go to bed: *We had a really good meal last night.* | *They stay in and watch television every night.* | *She recognised him from the night before* (=the previous evening). | *My parents are coming for dinner tomorrow night.* | **Friday/Saturday etc night** *There's a party at Ben's place on Saturday night.* | *We were on our way back from a night out* (=an evening when you go to a party, restaurant, theatre etc) *at the theatre.* | *Anna doesn't like him walking home late at night.* | **quiz night/student night etc** (=an evening when a particular event happens, especially at a bar, club etc)

3 nights if you do something nights, you do it regularly or often at night: *I work nights, so I'm usually asleep during the day.*

4 night! *spoken* used to say goodbye to someone when it is late in the evening or when they are going to bed; ⚑ **good night**: *Night! See you tomorrow!*

5 night night! *spoken* used to say goodbye to someone, especially a child, when they are going to bed

6 night and day/day and night all the time: *The store is guarded day and night.* | *We had to work night and day to get it finished.*

7 night or day/day or night at any time: *You can call me any time, night or day.*

8 night after night every night for a long period: *He's out drinking night after night.*

9 first night/opening night the first performance of a play or show; → **premiere**: *We saw 'Riverdance' on its opening night.*

10 spend the night with sb/spend the night together to sleep with someone and have sex with them: *And you thought we spent the night together?*

11 a good night's sleep a night when you sleep well: *You'll feel better after a good night's sleep.*

12 (have a) late/early night to go to bed later or earlier than usual: *I think I'll have an early night.* → **LATE-NIGHT**

13 last thing at night at the end of the day, just before you go to bed: *You should water plants either first thing in the morning or last thing at night.* → **NIGHTLY**

night·cap /ˈnaɪtkæp/ *n* [C] **1** an alcoholic drink that you have at the end of the evening, just before you go to bed **2** a soft hat that people used to wear in bed

night class n [C] a class which takes place during the evening for people who work during the day

night·clothes /ˈnaɪtkləʊðz, -kləʊz $ -kloʊ-/ n [plural] clothes that you wear in bed

night·club /ˈnaɪtklʌb/ n [C] a place where people go to dance and drink which is open late at night

night de·pository n [C] AmE a special hole in the outside wall of a bank into which a customer can put money or documents safely when the bank is closed; ⊟ **night safe** BrE

night·dress /ˈnaɪtdres/ n [C] a piece of clothing, like a thin dress, that a woman wears in bed

night ,duty n [U] work that is done during the night: **on night duty** She is on night duty at the hospital.

night·fall /ˈnaɪtfɔːl $ -fɒːl/ n [U] old-fashioned the time when it begins to get dark in the evening; ⊟ **dusk**: Don't worry, we'll be back by nightfall.

night·gown /ˈnaɪtgaʊn/ n [C] old-fashioned a night-dress

night·hawk /ˈnaɪthɔːk $ -hɒːk/ n [C] AmE informal someone who enjoys staying awake all night; ⊟ **night owl**

night·ie /ˈnaɪti/ n [C] informal a NIGHTDRESS

nigh·tin·gale /ˈnaɪtɪŋgeɪl/ n [C] a small bird that sings very beautifully, especially at night

night·life /ˈnaɪtlaɪf/ n [U] entertainment in the evening: The hotel is only a five minute walk from both the beach and the nightlife.

night·light /ˈnaɪtlaɪt/ n [C] a small electric light that you put in a child's room at night

night·ly /ˈnaɪtli/ adj happening every night: the nightly talk show —**nightly** adv: The band plays twice nightly in the bar.

nightmare

nightmare

daydream

night·mare /ˈnaɪtmeə $ -mer/ n [C] **1** a very frightening dream: [+about] Years after the accident I still **have nightmares** about it. | a **recurring nightmare** (=one which you have again and again) **2** [usually singular] a very difficult, unpleasant, or frightening experience or situation: Traffic was a nightmare. | [+for] This has been an absolute nightmare for me and my family. | **nightmare of (doing) sth** the nightmare of going through divorce | It was every teacher's **worst nightmare** (=the worst thing which could have happened). | a nightmare journey **3** something terrible that you fear may happen in the future: [+of] the nightmare of a nuclear war | **nightmare scenario** (=the worst or most frightening situation that you can imagine) —**nightmarish** adj

night owl n [C] informal someone who enjoys staying awake all night

night ,porter n [C] BrE someone who works at the main entrance of a hotel during the night

night safe n [C] BrE a special hole in the outside wall of a bank into which a customer can put money or documents safely when the bank is closed; ⊟ **night depository** AmE

night school n [U] classes that take place in the evening for people who work during the day

night shift n [C] **1** a period of time at night when people regularly work, especially in a factory: **on the night shift** She's on the night shift this week. **2** the group of people who work on the night shift: The night shift was just arriving.

night·shirt /ˈnaɪt-ʃɜːt $ -ʃɜːrt/ n [C] a long loose shirt that someone, especially a man, wears in bed

night spot n [C] a place people go to at night for entertainment: my favourite New York night spot

night·stand /ˈnaɪtstænd/ n [C] AmE a small table beside a bed; ⊟ **bedside table** BrE

night·stick /ˈnaɪt,stɪk/ n [C] AmE a short thick stick carried as a weapon by police officers; ⊟ **truncheon** BrE

night·time /ˈnaɪt-taɪm/ n [U] the time during the night; 🞂 **daytime**: **at nighttime** animals that hunt at nighttime

night ,watchman n [C] someone whose job is to guard a building at night —**night watch** n [U]

night·wear /ˈnaɪtweə $ -wer/ n [U] clothes that you wear in bed at night

nig·nog /ˈnɪg nɒg $ -nɑːg/ n [C] BrE taboo old-fashioned a very offensive word for a black person. Do not use this word.

ni·hil·is·m /ˈnaɪᵻlɪzəm/ n [U] **1** the belief that nothing has any meaning or value **2** the idea that all social and political institutions should be destroyed —**nihilist** n [C] —**nihilistic** /ˌnaɪᵻˈlɪstɪk◂/ adj

-nik /nɪk/ suffix [in nouns] someone who is connected with a particular activity or set of beliefs: a peacenik (=someone who supports peace)

nil [S3] /nɪl/ n [U]
1 nothing; ⊟ **zero**: The new machine reduced labour costs to almost nil.
2 BrE the number zero, used in sports results: Our team won by two goals to nil.

nim·ble /ˈnɪmbəl/ adj **1** able to move quickly and easily with light neat movements; ⊟ **agile**: nimble fingers | a nimble climber **2** **a nimble mind/brain/wit** an ability to think quickly or understand things easily —**nimbly** adv —**nimbleness** n [U]

nim·bus /ˈnɪmbəs/ n plural **nimbuses** or **nimbi** /-baɪ/ **1** [C,U] technical a dark cloud that may bring rain or snow **2** [C] a HALO

nim·by /ˈnɪmbi/ n plural **nimbies** [C] **not in my backyard** someone who does not want a particular activity or building near their home – used to show disapproval —**nimby** adj

NiMH /nɪm/ n [C] **nickel-metal hydride** a type of BATTERY that can be RECHARGED and that is used in cameras and small electronic equipment

nin·com·poop /ˈnɪŋkəmpuːp/ n [C] old-fashioned a stupid person

nine /naɪn/ number **1** the number 9: He's only been in this job for nine months. | We open at nine (=nine o'clock). | Kay was taught by her mother till she was nine (=nine years old). **2** **nine times out of ten** almost always: Nine times out of ten we can solve the problem over the phone. **3** **a nine days' wonder** a thing or event that makes people very excited for a short time **4** **have nine lives** to make lucky escapes from dangerous situations 🞂 **dressed up to the nines** at DRESSED (4); 🞂 **be on cloud nine** at CLOUD[1] (5)

9/11 /ˌnaɪn ɪˈlevən/ *n* [U] *especially AmE* September 11, 2001, when TERRORISTS used planes to attack New York and Washington: *the terrifying events of 9/11* | *a 9/11 disaster relief fund*

nine·pins /ˈnaɪnˌpɪnz/ *n* [U] **1** a game in which you roll a ball at nine bottle-shaped objects to try to hit them so that they fall **2 drop/go down like ninepins** if people or things drop like ninepins, many of them fall down or become ill or injured suddenly all at the same time: *It's just three weeks into the season and players are dropping like ninepins.*

nine·teen /ˌnaɪnˈtiːn◂/ *number* **1** the number 19: *It was nineteen minutes past seven.* | *I was only nineteen* (=19 years old). **2 nineteen to the dozen** if you talk nineteen to the dozen, you talk very quickly and without stopping —**nineteenth** *adj, pron*: *in the nineteenth century* | *her nineteenth birthday* | *I'm planning to leave on the nineteenth* (=the 19th day of the month).

nineteenth hole *n* **the nineteenth hole** an expression used humorously by GOLF players meaning the bar where they drink after playing

nine to five *adv* between nine o'clock and five o'clock, the normal working hours of an office worker: *She didn't like working nine to five.* —**nine-to-five** *adj*: *a nine-to-five job*

nine·ty /ˈnaɪnti/ *number* **1** the number 90 **2 the nineties** [plural] also **the '90s, the 1990s** the years from 1990 to 1999: *America was far richer in the nineties.* | **the early/mid/late nineties** *The industry received a lot of bad publicity in the early nineties.* **3 be in your nineties** to be aged between 90 and 99: **early/mid/late nineties** *My grandfather was in his early nineties when he died.* **4 in the nineties** if the temperature is in the nineties, it is between 90 degrees and 99 degrees: **in the low/mid/high nineties** *Temperatures were still in the high nineties.* —**ninetieth** *adj*: *her ninetieth birthday*

nin·ja /ˈnɪndʒə/ *n* [C] in the past, a Japanese fighter with special skills

nin·ny /ˈnɪni/ *n plural* **ninnies** [C] *old-fashioned* a silly person

ninth[1] /naɪnθ/ *adj* coming after eight other things in a series: *in the ninth century* | *her ninth birthday* —**ninth** *pron*: *I'm planning to leave on the ninth* (=ninth day of the month).

ninth[2] *n* [C] one of nine equal parts of something

nip[1] /nɪp/ *v* **nipped, nipping** **1** [I always + adv/prep] *BrE informal* to go somewhere quickly or for a short time; ⊟ **pop**: *Have we time to nip down the pub for a quick drink?* | *Another car nipped in* (=moved quickly into a space) *in front of me.* | *I've got to nip home and change my clothes.* **2** [I,T] to bite someone or something lightly: *She gently nipped the lobe of his ear.* | [+at] *The fish swam all around her and nipped at her legs.* **3 nip sth in the bud** to prevent something from becoming a problem by stopping it as soon as it starts: *Try to nip this kind of bad behaviour in the bud.* **4** [T] *BrE* to suddenly and quickly press something tightly between two fingers, edges, or surfaces; → **pinch**: *Sally nipped her cheeks to make them look less pale.* | *He nipped his finger in the door.* **5** [I,T] *written* if cold weather or the wind nips at part of your body or at a plant, it hurts or damages it: [+at] *The frost nipped at our fingers.*

nip sth ⇔ **off** *phr v* to remove a small part of something, especially a plant, by pressing it tightly between your finger and thumb: *She nipped off a dead flower.*

nip[2] *n* [C] **1** the act or result of biting something lightly or pressing something between two fingers, edges, or surfaces: *His dog gave me a painful nip on the leg.* **2** a small amount of strong alcoholic drink: [+of] *a nip of brandy* **3 a nip in the air** coldness in the air **4 nip and tuck** *AmE informal* **a)** equally likely to happen or not happen: *We made it to the airport, but it was nip and tuck.* **b)** if two competitors are nip and tuck in a race or competition, they are doing equally

well; ⊟ **neck and neck**: *The fourth quarter was nip and tuck, but the Bulls won 92–90.*

nipp·er /ˈnɪpə $ -ər/ *n* [C] *BrE informal* a child

nip·ple /ˈnɪpəl/ *n* [C] **1** the small dark circular part of a woman's breast. Babies suck milk through their mother's nipples. **2** one of the two small dark circular parts on a man's chest **3** *AmE* the rubber part on a baby's bottle that a baby sucks milk through; ⊟ **teat** *BrE* **4** a part in an engine or machine made of rubber or plastic and shaped like a nipple. It has a hole in it which liquid can flow or be poured through.

nip·py /ˈnɪpi/ *adj informal* **1** weather that is nippy is slightly cold; ⊟ **chilly**: *It's a bit nippy out there.* **2** *BrE* moving quickly or able to move quickly: *a nippy little car*

nir·va·na /nɪəˈvɑːnə, nɜː- $ nɪr-, nɜːr-/ *n* [U] **1** the final state of complete knowledge and understanding that is the aim of believers in Buddhism **2** a condition of great happiness and a feeling of peace

ni·si /ˈnaɪsaɪ/ *n* → DECREE NISI

nit /nɪt/ *n* [C] **1** an egg of a LOUSE (=a small insect that sucks blood), that is sometimes found in people's hair **2** *BrE informal* a silly person

nit-picking *n* [U] *informal* when someone argues about small unimportant details or tries to find small mistakes in something: *Soames was getting impatient with his daughter's constant nitpicking.* —**nitpicking** *adj* —**nitpicker** *n* [C]

ni·trate /ˈnaɪtreɪt, -trət/ *n* [C,U] used in the name of substances containing NITROGEN and OXYGEN. Nitrates are often used to improve soil: *potassium nitrate* | *high levels of nitrates in drinking water*

ni·tric ac·id /ˌnaɪtrɪk ˈæsɪd/ *n* [U] a powerful acid that is used in explosives and other chemical products

ni·tro·gen /ˈnaɪtrədʒən/ *n* [U] a gas that has no colour or smell, and that forms most of the Earth's air. It is a chemical ELEMENT: symbol N

ni·tro·gly·ce·rine, nitroglycerin /ˌnaɪtrəʊˈɡlɪsərɪn, -riːn $ -troʊˈɡlɪsərɪn/ *n* [U] a chemical used to make a powerful liquid explosive and also in some medicines

ni·trous ox·ide /ˌnaɪtrəs ˈɒksaɪd $ -ˈɑːk-/ *n* [U] a type of gas used by DENTISTS to reduce pain; ⊟ **laughing gas**

nit·ty-grit·ty /ˌnɪti ˈɡrɪti/ *n informal* **the nitty-gritty** the basic and practical facts of a subject or activity: *Let's get down to the nitty-gritty and work out the costs.*

nit·wit /ˈnɪt-wɪt/ *n* [C] *informal* a silly person

nix[1] /nɪks/ *v* [T] *AmE informal* to answer no to something or say that you will not allow something: *They nixed the idea of filming in Ireland.*

nix[2] *adv AmE old-fashioned* no

no[1] [S1] [W1] /nəʊ $ noʊ/ *adv*

1 used to give a negative reply to a question, offer, or request; ⊟ **yes**: *'Are you Italian?' 'No, I'm Spanish.'* | *'Do you want any more?' 'No thanks.'* | *'Could you help me write this?' 'No, sorry, I haven't got time at the moment.'* | *He wanted to take me to a disco but I said no.* | *Sixty percent of people voted no.* | *If you're asking whether I feel the same way about her, the answer is no.*

SPOKEN PHRASES
2 used to say that you disagree with a statement: *'You're always complaining about work.' 'No, I'm not!'*
3 used to say that you agree with a negative statement: *'They shouldn't drive so fast.' 'No, it's really dangerous.'*
4 used to tell someone not to do something: *No, Jimmy, don't touch that switch.*
5 used to show that you are shocked, surprised, annoyed, or disappointed by what someone has just told you, or by what has just happened: *'She's nearly fifty.' 'No, you're kidding!'* | *Oh no, I've lost my wallet!*
6 used to correct what you have just said: *He's the director, no, the assistant director, of the company.*

N

7 won't take no for an answer if someone won't take no for an answer, they are determined that you should agree to do something: *He insists on taking us all out to dinner and he won't take no for an answer.*
8 used before COMPARATIVES to mean 'not even a small amount': *I'll pay you $75 and no more.* | *You're no better than the rest of them.* → **no longer** at LONG² (7)

no² S1 W1 *determiner*
1 not one or not any: *There's no food left in the fridge.* | *No trains will be affected by this incident.* | *a house with no central heating* | *There's no excuse for that kind of behaviour.*
2 used on signs to say that something is not allowed: *No parking* | *No smoking*
3 in no time *informal* very soon or very quickly: *We'll be home in no time.*
4 there's no doing sth *spoken* used to emphasize that it is not possible to do something: *There's no knowing what this lunatic will do next.* | *There is no denying the suffering of these families* (=they are definitely suffering).
5 used to emphasize that the opposite of a particular description is true: *That girl's no fool* (=she is intelligent). | *Larry's no friend of mine.* | *If he has to do it all himself, it will be no bad thing* (=a good thing). | *a question of no great importance*

no³ *n plural* **noes 1** [singular] a negative answer or decision: *The answer was a definite no.* **2** [C] a vote against a proposal in parliament

No. also **no.** *plural* **Nos** the written abbreviation of *number*: *Mozart's piano concerto no. 27*

No. 10 /ˌnʌmbə ˈten $ -bər-/ *n* **No. 10 Downing Street** the address of the official home of the British PRIME MINISTER

'no-ac,count also **'no-count** *adj* [only before noun] *AmE old-fashioned informal* a no-account person does not achieve very much because they are so lazy: *a no-account drifter who died of drink*

No·ah's ark /ˌnəʊəz ˈɑːk $ ˌnoʊəz ˈɑːrk/ *n* in the Bible, the large boat built by Noah to save his family and the animals from a flood that covered the earth

nob /nɒb $ nɑːb/ *n* [C] *BrE old-fashioned* a rich person with a high social position

'no ball *n* [C] an act of BOWLING the ball in the game of CRICKET in a way that is not allowed by the rules

nob·ble /ˈnɒbəl $ ˈnɑː-/ *v* [T] *BrE informal* **1** to make someone do what you want by illegally offering them money or threatening them; → **bribe**: *The jury had been nobbled and the case had to be reheard.* **2** to prevent a horse from winning a race, especially by giving it drugs **3** to get someone's attention, especially in order to persuade them to do something: *I was nobbled by my deaf old aunt and couldn't get away.*

No·bel Prize /nəʊˌbel ˈpraɪz, ˌnəʊbel- $ noʊ-/ *n* [C] one of six prizes given each year for important work in science, literature, ECONOMICS, or work towards world peace

no·bil·i·ty /nəʊˈbɪləti, nə- $ noʊ-, nə-/ *n* **1 the nobility** the group of people in some countries who belong to the highest social class and have titles such as 'Duke' or 'Countess'; ☰ **the aristocracy 2** [U] the quality of being noble: *the nobility of his intentions*

no·ble¹ /ˈnəʊbəl $ ˈnoʊ-/ *adj* **1** morally good or generous in a way that is admired: *It's very noble of you to spend all your weekends helping the old folk.* | *noble ideals* **2** [only before noun] belonging to the nobility: **noble family/blood/birth etc** *a member of an ancient noble family* | *The Marquis would have to marry a woman of noble blood.* **3** something that is noble is very impressive and beautiful: *the old church with its noble tower* **4 noble gas/metal** *technical* a noble gas or metal is not affected chemically by other substances → BASE METAL **5 noble savage** *literary* someone who comes from a society that is less developed or interested in

money than western countries, making them morally better than people who live in western countries

noble² *n* [C] a member of the highest social class with a title such as 'Duke' or 'Countess' → COMMONER

no·ble·man /ˈnəʊbəlmən $ ˈnoʊ-/ *n plural* **noblemen** /-mən/ [C] a man who is a member of the highest social class and has a title such as 'Duke'

no·blesse o·blige /nəʊˌbles əˈbliːʒ $ noʊ-/ *n* [U] the idea that people who belong to a high social class should behave in a kind and generous way towards people of a lower social class

no·ble·wom·an /ˈnəʊbəlˌwʊmən $ ˈnoʊ-/ *n plural* **noblewomen** /-ˌwɪmɪn/ [C] a woman who is a member of the highest social class and has a title such as 'Duchess'

no·bly /ˈnəʊbli $ ˈnoʊ-/ *adv* **1** in a morally good or generous way that should be admired: *They chose to die nobly rather than to betray their king.* **2 nobly born** *literary* having parents who are members of the NOBILITY

no·bod·y¹ S1 W2 /ˈnəʊbədi $ ˈnoʊbəːdi, -bədi/ *pron*
1 no one: *I knocked on the door but nobody answered.* ⚠ Do not spell this as two words, or the meaning changes: *There was nobody there* (=no person). *There was no body there* (=not a dead body).
2 like nobody's business very much, very well, or very fast: *We get along like nobody's business.* → **be nobody's fool** at FOOL¹ (5)

nobody² *n plural* **nobodies** [C] someone who is not important and has no influence: *I was a nothing and a nobody with everything to prove.*

,no-'brainer *n* [singular] a decision that is easy, and that you do not need to think about, used when you want to emphasize that it is really very easy: *Joining the savings plan is a no-brainer. Just do it.*

,no-'claims ,bonus *n* [C] in Britain, a reduction in the amount that you have to pay for car insurance, because you have not claimed any money during a particular period

,no-'confidence *n* [U] **vote of no-confidence/no-confidence vote/motion of no-confidence etc** an official vote where people can say if they no longer think someone or something is good enough: *fears that he may lose a vote of no-confidence in parliament* | *The chairman has survived four no-confidence motions.*

'no-count *adj* another form of NO-ACCOUNT

noc·tur·nal /nɒkˈtɜːnl $ nɑːkˈtɜːr-/ *adj* **1** an animal that is nocturnal is active at night: *Hamsters are nocturnal creatures.* **2** *formal* happening at night: *Rebecca paid a nocturnal visit to the flat.*

noc·turne /ˈnɒktɜːn $ ˈnɑːktɜːrn/ *n* [C] a piece of music, especially a soft beautiful piece of piano music

nod¹ W2 /nɒd $ nɑːd/ *v* **nodded, nodding** [I,T]
1 to move your head up and down, especially in order to show agreement or understanding; → **shake**: *I asked her if she was ready to go, and she nodded.* | *Mom nodded her head sympathetically.* | **nod your approval/ agreement etc** (=show your approval etc by nodding) *Corbett nodded his acceptance.*
2 to move your head down and up again once in order to greet someone or give someone a sign to do something: [+at] *The judge nodded at the foreman to proceed.* | [+to] *She nodded to us as she walked by.*
3 have a nodding acquaintance (with sth) to know a little about a subject but not a lot: *Students will need to have a nodding acquaintance with at least three languages.*
4 have a nodding acquaintance (with sb) also **be on nodding terms (with sb)** *BrE* to know someone but not very well

nod off *phr v*
to begin to sleep, usually when you do not intend to and are sitting somewhere: *I missed the movie because I kept nodding off.*

nod² *n* **1** [C] an act of nodding: *The woman greeted us with a nod of the head.* | *I showed the doorman my card* *and he gave a friendly nod.*   **2 give sb the nod/get the nod from sb** *informal* to give or be given permission to do something: *We're waiting for the boss to give us the nod on this one.*   **3 on the nod** *BrE informal* by general agreement and without people discussing it: *The chairman's proposals are usually passed on the nod.*   **4 a nod's as good as a wink** *BrE* used to tell someone that you have understood something, although it was said in an indirect way → **the land of nod** at LAND[1] (9)

no·dal /'nəʊdl $ 'noʊ-/ *adj* [only before noun] *technical* being or connected with a node: *the nodal point of the transport system*

nod·dle /'nɒdl $ 'nɑːdl/ *n* [C] *BrE old-fashioned informal* your head or brain: *It's easy enough to do if you just use your noddle* (=think).

node /nəʊd $ noʊd/ *n* [C] *technical*   **1** the place on the stem of a plant from which a leaf or branch grows   **2** a place where lines in a network cross or join   **3** a part of a computer network where messages can be received or sent   **4** a LYMPH NODE

nod·ule /'nɒdjuːl $ 'nɑːdʒuːl/ *n* [C] a small round raised part, especially a small swelling on a plant or someone's body —**nodular** *adj*

No·el /nəʊˈel $ noʊ-/ *n* [U] CHRISTMAS - used especially in songs and on cards

noes /nəʊz $ noʊz/ *n* the plural of NO[3]

no-ˈfault *adj* [only before noun] *law*   **1** a no-fault DIVORCE is one in which both people agree not to be married any longer and do not have to say whose fault this is   **2** no-fault car insurance will pay for the damage done in an accident, even if you caused the accident

no-ˈfly ˌzone *n* [C] an area that only particular aircraft are allowed to enter, and in which other aircraft could be attacked

no-ˈfrills *adj* [only before noun] a no-frills product or service includes only basic features and is not of the highest possible quality: *no-frills accommodation*

nog·gin /'nɒgɪn $ 'nɑː-/ *n* [C] *old-fashioned*   **1** a small amount of an alcoholic drink   **2** *informal* your head or brain: *Use your noggin* (=think).

ˌno-ˈgo ˌarea *n* [C]   **1** an area that people should not go to because it is very dangerous: *This part of the city was a no-go area for the police.*   **2** a subject that cannot be discussed because it is private or because it may offend people: *She made it clear that her private life was a no-go area.*

ˌno-holds-ˈbarred *adj* [only before noun] a no-holds-barred discussion, situation etc is one in which there are no rules or limits: *Viewers had been promised a no-holds-barred interview with the former mayor.*

ˌno-ˈhoper *n* [C] *BrE* a person or animal who you think has no chance of winning something or of being successful: *a bunch of complete no-hopers*

no·how /'nəʊhaʊ $ 'noʊ-/ *adv AmE informal* not in any way or in any situation – usually used humorously: *I never liked her nohow.*

noir → FILM NOIR

noise¹ [S2] [W2] /nɔɪz/ *n*
1 [C,U] a sound, especially one that is loud, unpleasant, or frightening; ⊟ **sound**: *What's that noise?* | [+of] *the noise of the traffic* | *Try not to **make** a **noise** when you go upstairs.* | *gurgling/banging/crackling etc* **noise** *There was a strange whistling noise in his ears.* | *There was* **a lot of noise** *outside.* | *Noise levels have been reduced by 20%.* | *traffic/engine/background etc* **noise** *the problem of aircraft noise near airports*
2 (make) encouraging/optimistic etc noises (about sth) *BrE* to say things which suggest what your opinion or attitude is, without saying it directly: *Both sides were making hopeful noises about the hostages.*
3 make (all) the right noises (about sth) to say the things that other people want or expect to hear: *The health minister seems to be making all the right noises.*
4 make noises about doing sth to say that you are considering doing something: *He is now making noises about starting his own business.*

5 make a (lot of) noise about sth *BrE* to talk about something a lot, so that people will notice it – used in order to show disapproval: *modern men who make a noise about the fact that they know how to look good*
6 [U] *technical* unwanted signals produced by an electrical CIRCUIT
7 [U] *technical* pieces of unwanted information that can prevent a computer from working effectively
8 noises off the sounds, voices etc that come from actors who are not on the stage at the time → BIG NOISE

noise² *v* **be noised abroad/about/around** *old-fashioned especially BrE* if news or information is noised abroad, people are talking about it: *Rumours of an election are being noised abroad.*

noise·less·ly /'nɔɪzləsli/ *adv written* without making any sound; ⊟ **silently**: *We crept noiselessly down the hall.* —**noiseless** *adj: his noiseless footsteps*

ˈnoise polˌlution *n* [U] very loud or continuous noise which is considered unpleasant and harmful to people

noi·some /'nɔɪsəm/ *adj literary* very unpleasant: *noisome smells*

nois·y [S3] /'nɔɪzi/ *adj comparative* **noisier**, *superlative* **noisiest**
1 someone or something that is noisy makes a lot of noise; ⊟ **quiet**: *The kids have been really noisy today.* | *a noisy engine*
2 a place that is noisy is full of noise: *The bar was very noisy.* —**noisily** *adv: He blew his nose noisily.*

no·mad /'nəʊmæd $ 'noʊ-/ *n* [C] a member of a tribe that travels from place to place instead of living in one place all the time, usually in order to find grass for their animals

no·mad·ic /nəʊˈmædɪk $ noʊ-/ *adj*   **1** nomadic people are nomads: *nomadic herdsmen*   **2** if someone leads a nomadic life, they travel from place to place and do not live in any one place for very long: *The son of an airforce pilot, he had a somewhat nomadic childhood.*

ˈno-man's-ˌland *n* [singular, U]   **1** an area of land that no one owns or controls, especially an area between two borders or opposing armies   **2** a situation or type of activity that is not either of two things or is a combination of two things: [+between] *the no-man's land between art and science*

nom de guerre /ˌnɒm də ˈgeə $ ˌnɑːm də ˈger/ *n plural* **noms de guerre** [C] *formal* a name that someone uses instead of their real name, especially someone who is fighting in a war

nom de plume /ˌnɒm də ˈpluːm $ ˌnɑːm-/ *n plural* **noms de plume** [C] *formal* a name used by a writer instead of their real name; ⊟ **pen name**

no·men·cla·ture /nəʊˈmeŋklətʃə $ 'noʊmən-kleɪtʃər/ *n* [U] *formal* a system of naming things, especially in science: [+of] *the nomenclature of science* | *zoological nomenclature*

nom·i·nal /'nɒmɪnəl $ 'nɑː-/ *adj*   **1 nominal sum/charge/fee etc** a very small sum of money, especially when compared with what something would usually cost or what it is worth: *A nominal charge is made for use of the tennis courts.*   **2** officially described as being something, when this is not really true: *the nominal head of the rebellion* | *Their conversion to Christianity was only nominal.*   **3 nominal value/rate/income etc** *technical* a nominal value etc does not show what something is really worth or really costs, because it does not take into account changes in the price of other goods and services; ⊟ **real**: *If prices rise and the nominal wage remains constant, the real wage falls.*   **4** *technical* relating to nouns or used as a noun: *the nominal use of the present participle*

nom·i·nal·ly /'nɒmɪnəli $ 'nɑː-/ *adv* officially described as being something, when this is not really true: *a nominally Christian country* | *He was nominally in charge of his father's printing company.*

N

N

,**non-scien'tific** *adj* not using scientific methods to collect information and form opinions: *The report is based on non-scientific data.*

non·sense |S3| /'nɒns.əns $ 'nɑːnsens/ *n* [U]
1 STUPID/UNTRUE ideas, opinions, statements etc that are not true or that seem very stupid; ⊟ **rubbish** BrE: *'I'm a prisoner in my own home.' 'Nonsense!'* | absolute/utter/complete nonsense *'Nobody cares about me.' 'That's absolute nonsense, Mary!'* | [+about] *all this nonsense about health foods* | *If you ask me, these modern teaching methods are **a load of nonsense** (=a lot of nonsense).* | *He was **talking** utter **nonsense** as usual.* | **be a nonsense** BrE: *The government's housing policy is a nonsense.* | *By 1832 the idea had become an economic nonsense.* | **it is (a) nonsense to do sth** *It is nonsense to say that mistakes are never made.*
2 ANNOYING BEHAVIOUR behaviour that is stupid and annoying: *You're to **stop** that **nonsense**, do you hear me?* | **not stand/put up with/take any nonsense** (=not accept such behaviour) *She won't stand any nonsense from the kids in her class.*
3 WITHOUT MEANING speech or writing that has no meaning or cannot be understood: *Computer programs look like complete nonsense to me.*
4 **make (a) nonsense of sth** BrE to make an action, system, or plan useless or ineffective: *Having the army still in power makes a nonsense of last year's elections.*
5 nonsense poems/verse/rhymes poetry that is humorous because it does not have a normal sensible meaning

non·sen·si·cal /nɒn'sens.ɪkəl $ nɑːn-/ *adj* ideas, actions, or statements that are nonsensical are not reasonable or sensible: *This is a nonsensical argument.*

non seq·ui·tur /ˌnɒn 'sekwɪtə $ ˌnɑːn 'sekwɪtər/ *n* [C] a statement which does not seem to be connected in a reasonable or sensible way with what was said before

,**non-'slip** *adj* a non-slip surface prevents you from slipping and falling: *a non-slip bath mat*

,**non-'smoker** *n* [C] someone who does not smoke: *an area reserved for non-smokers*

,**non-'smoking** *adj* **1** a non-smoking area is one where you are not allowed to smoke: *a non-smoking restaurant* **2** [only before noun] used to describe someone who does not smoke: *a non-drinking, non-smoking fitness fanatic*

,**non-spe'cific** *adj* **1** [only before noun] a non-specific medical condition could have one of several causes: *children with non-specific abdominal pain* **2** not exact or detailed, or not relating to one particular thing; → **vague**: *The description was deliberately non-specific.*

,**non-'standard** *adj* **1** non-standard ways of speaking are not usually considered to be correct by educated speakers of a language: *Non-standard dialects of English are regional dialects.* **2** not the usual size or type: *a non-standard disk size*

non·start·er /ˌnɒn'stɑːtə $ ˌnɑːn'stɑːrtər/ *n* [C usually singular] *informal* an idea, a plan, or a person that has no chance of success: *In its present form the scheme is a non-starter.*

,**non-'stick** *adj* a non-stick cooking pan has a special inside surface which prevents food from sticking to it

non·stop /ˌnɒn'stɒp◂ $ ˌnɑːn'stɑːp◂/ *adj* [usually before noun] without any stops or pauses; → **continuous**: *a **nonstop** flight to Los Angeles* —**nonstop** *adv*: *She talked nonstop for over an hour.*

,**non-'threatening** *adj* not making someone feel afraid or worried: *It is important to create a safe, non-threatening environment for children.*

,**non-'toxic** *adj* not poisonous or harmful to your health: *non-toxic paint*

,**non-tra'ditional** *adj* [only before noun] different from the way something happened or from what was considered typical in the past: *older, non-traditional university students* | *non-traditional workdays*

,**non-'union** also ,**non-'unionized** *adj* **1** [usually before noun] non-union workers do not belong to a TRADE UNION (=official organization for workers) **2** businesses or organizations that are non-union do not officially accept TRADE UNIONS, or do not employ their members

non·ver·bal /ˌnɒn'vɜːbəl◂ $ ˌnɑːn'vɜːr-/ *adj* not using words: *nonverbal forms of communication* —**nonverbally** *adv*

,**non-'violence** *n* [U] the practice of opposing a government without using violence, for example by not obeying laws; → **passivity**: *She was committed to non-violence.* | *a policy of non-violence*

,**non-'violent** *adj* not using or not involving violence; → **peaceful**: *a non-violent protest against the government* | *an increase in the amount of violent and non-violent crime*

,**non-'white** *n* [C] someone who does not belong to a white race —**non-white** *adj*

noo·dle /'nuːdl/ *n* [usually plural] a long thin piece of food made from a mixture of flour, water, and eggs, usually cooked in soup or boiling water: *Serve the meat with rice or noodles.*

nook /nʊk/ *n* [C] **1** *literary* a small quiet place which is sheltered by a rock, a big tree etc: *a shady nook* **2** a small space in a corner of a room: *the table in the breakfast nook* **3** **every nook and cranny** every part of a place: *We searched every nook and cranny.*

nook·ie, nooky /'nʊki/ *n* [U] *informal* the activity of having sex – used humorously

noon /nuːn/ *n* [U] 12 o'clock in the daytime; ⊟ **midday**: **at/before/by noon** *We left home at noon.* | *He rarely gets up before noon.* | *We met at **12 noon**.* → **morning, noon, and night** at MORNING¹ (5)

noon·day /'nuːndeɪ/ *adj* [only before noun] *literary* happening or appearing at noon; ⊟ **midday**: *It was impossible to work in the heat of the **noonday** sun.*

'**no one** |S1| |W2|, **no-one** *pron* not anyone; ⊟ **nobody**: *No one likes being criticized.* | *There's no one else I really want to invite apart from you.* | *Has no one phoned about the car?* | *No one can say I didn't warn you.* ⚠ Do not use another negative word (e.g. 'not') with **no one**. Use **anyone** with **not**: *No one came.* | *Didn't anyone come?*

noose /nuːs/ *n* [C] a ring formed by the end of a piece of rope, which closes more tightly as it is pulled, used especially for killing someone by hanging them

nope |S3| /nəʊp $ noʊp/ *adv spoken informal* used to say 'no' when you answer someone: *'Hungry?' 'Nope, I just ate.'*

'**no place** *adv informal especially AmE* nowhere: *There's no place left to hide.*

nor |S2| |W1| /nɔː $ nɔːr/ *conjunction, adv*
1 **neither ... nor ...** used when mentioning two things that are not true or do not happen: *He can neither read nor write.* (=he cannot read or write) | *Hilary was neither shocked nor surprised by the news.* | *Neither Matt nor Julie said anything* (=Matt did not say anything and Julie did not say anything).
2 *formal* used after a negative statement in order to introduce another negative statement containing a similar kind of information: *I don't expect children to be rude, nor do I expect to be disobeyed.* | *It was not my fault, nor his.*
3 BrE used after a negative statement to say that the negative statement is also true for someone or something else: *'I don't want to go.' 'Nor do I.'* | *They couldn't understand it at the time, and nor could we.* → NEITHER³

nor'- /nɔː $ nɔːr/ *prefix* a PREFIX meaning 'north', used especially by sailors: *nor'east* | *nor'west*

Nor·dic /'nɔːdɪk $ 'nɔːr-/ *adj* relating to the Northern European countries of Denmark, Norway, Sweden, Iceland, and Finland, or to their people; → **Scandinavian**: *the Nordic countries*

norm /nɔːm $ nɔːrm/ *n* [C] **1** the usual or normal situation, way of doing something etc: **be/become the**

norm *Short term contracts are now the norm with some big companies.* | *Joyce's style of writing was a striking departure from the literary norm.* **2 norms** [plural] generally accepted standards of social behaviour: *terrorists who violate the norms of civilized society* | **social/cultural etc norms 3 the norm** the normal or average standard: **above/below the norm** *28% of children tested below the norm.*

nor·mal[1] [S1] [W1] /'nɔːməl $ 'nɔːr-/ *adj*
1 usual, typical, or expected: *A normal working week is 40 hours.* | **it is normal (for sb) to do sth** *It's normal to feel nervous before an exam.* | **quite/perfectly etc normal** *Her room was untidy, but that was quite normal.* | *She was assessed in the normal way, and placed on the waiting list.* | *All I want is to lead a normal life.*
2 someone as normal is mentally and physically healthy and does not behave strangely ⊟ **abnormal**: *He seems a perfectly normal little boy.* | *They can't be normal to do something like that.*

normal[2] *n* [U] the usual state, level, or amount: *Thankfully, train services are now back to normal.* | *Slowly her heartbeat returned to normal.* | **above/below normal** *Car sales are still below normal for the time of year.* | **higher/larger/less etc than normal** *The journey took longer than normal.*

nor·mal·i·ty /nɔːˈmælɪti $ nɔːr-/ also **nor·mal·cy** /'nɔːməlsi $ 'nɔːr-/ *AmE n* [U] a situation in which things happen in the usual or expected way: *We're hoping for a return to normality as soon as possible.* | *We'll soon get back to some semblance of normality.*

nor·mal·ize also **-ise** *BrE* /'nɔːməlaɪz $ 'nɔːr-/ *v* [I,T] **1** if you normalize a situation, or if it normalizes, it becomes normal again: *Journalists are reporting that the situation has now normalized.* **2** if two countries normalize relations, or if relations normalize, the two countries behave in a normal way towards each other again: *Relations between the countries were formally normalized in 1997.* —**normalization** /ˌnɔːməlaɪˈzeɪʃən $ ˌnɔːrmələ-/ *n* [U]

nor·mal·ly [S1] [W2] /'nɔːməli $ 'nɔːr-/ *adv*
1 usually: *The journey normally takes about two hours.* | [sentence adverb]: *Normally, I park behind the theatre.*
2 in a normal way; ⊟ **abnormally**: *The system seems to be working normally now.*

Nor·man /'nɔːmən $ 'nɔːr-/ *adj* **1** built in the style that was popular during the 11th and 12th centuries in Europe: *a Norman church* **2** relating to the Normans, the northern French people who took control of England in the 11th century

nor·ma·tive /'nɔːmətɪv $ 'nɔːr-/ *adj formal* describing or establishing a set of rules or standards of behaviour: *normative guidelines for senators*

Norse[1] /nɔːs $ nɔːrs/ *adj* [only before noun] relating to the people of ancient Scandinavia or their language: *Norse legends*

Norse[2] *n* [U] the language that was spoken by the people of ancient Scandinavia

Norse·man /'nɔːsmən $ 'nɔːrs-/ *n plural* **Norsemen** /-mən/ [C] *literary* a VIKING

north[1] [S1] [W2] , **North** /nɔːθ $ nɔːrθ/ written abbreviation *N n* [singular, U]
1 the direction that is at the top of a map of the world, above the Equator. It is on the left if you are facing the rising sun: *Which way is north?* | **from/towards the north** *winds blowing from the north* | **to the north (of sth)** *Cheshunt is a few miles to the north of London.*
2 the north a) the northern part of a country or area: *The North will be dry and bright.* | [+of] *the north of England* **b)** the richer countries of the world, especially Europe and North America

north[2], **North** written abbreviation *N adj* [only before noun] **1** in the north or facing the north: *The north side of the building doesn't get much sun.* | *He lives in North Wales.* **2** a north wind comes from the north

north[3] written abbreviation *N adv* **1** towards the north: *The birds fly north in summer.* | [+of] *Chicago is four hours north of Indianapolis.* | *a north-facing window* **2 up north** *informal* to or in the north of the country: *They've moved up north.*

north·bound /'nɔːθbaʊnd $ 'nɔːrθ-/ *adj* travelling or leading towards the north: *a northbound bus* | *the northbound lane of the A1*

north-ˈcountry *adj* in or from the north of England: *a low north-country voice*

north·east[1], **Northeast** /ˌnɔːθˈiːst◂ $ ˌnɔːrθ-/ written abbreviation *NE n* [U] **1** the direction that is exactly between north and east **2 the northeast** the northeastern part of a country —**northeast** *adv*: *He headed northeast across the open sea.*

northeast[2], **Northeast** written abbreviation *NE adj* **1** a northeast wind comes from the northeast **2** in the northeast of a place: *the northeast outskirts of Las Vegas*

north·east·er /ˌnɔːθˈiːstə $ ˌnɔːrθˈiːstər/ *n* [C] a strong wind or storm coming from the northeast

north·east·er·ly /ˌnɔːθˈiːstəli $ ˌnɔːrθˈiːstərli/ *adj* **1** towards or in the northeast: *They set off in a northeasterly direction.* **2** a northeasterly wind comes from the northeast

north·east·ern /ˌnɔːθˈiːstən $ ˌnɔːrθˈiːstərn/ written abbreviation *NE adj* in or from the northeast part of a country or area: *the northeastern states of the US*

north·east·wards /ˌnɔːθˈiːstwədz $ ˌnɔːrθˈiːstwərdz/ also **northeastward** *adv* towards the northeast —**northeastward** *adj*

nor·ther·ly /'nɔːðəli $ 'nɔːrðərli/ *adj* **1** towards or in the north: *We set off in a northerly direction.* **2** a northerly wind comes from the north

nor·thern [S2] [W2] , **Northern** /'nɔːðən $ 'nɔːrðərn/ written abbreviation *N adj* in or from the north of a country or area: *a man with a northern accent* | *Northern Europe*

nor·thern·er also **Northerner** /'nɔːðənə $ 'nɔːrðərnər/ *n* [C] someone from the northern part of a country

northern ˈhemisphere, **Northern Hemisphere** *n* the northern hemisphere the half of the world that is north of the Equator

Northern ˈLights *n* the Northern Lights bands of coloured light that are seen in the night sky in the most northern parts of the world; ⊟ **aurora borealis**

nor·thern·most /'nɔːðənməʊst $ 'nɔːrðərnmoʊst/ *adj* furthest north: *the northernmost tip of the island*

North ˈPole *n* the North Pole the most northern point on the surface of the Earth → MAGNETIC POLE, SOUTH POLE

north·wards /'nɔːθwədz $ 'nɔːrθwərdz/ also **northward** *adv* towards the north: *We sailed northwards.* —**northward** *adj*: *the northward journey*

north·west[1], **Northwest** /ˌnɔːθˈwest◂ $ ˌnɔːrθ-/ written abbreviation *NW n* [U] **1** the direction that is exactly between north and west **2 the northwest** the northwestern part of a country —**northwest** *adv*: *She rode northwest toward Boulder.*

northwest[2], **Northwest** written abbreviation *NW adj* **1** a northwest wind comes from the northwest **2** in the northwest of a place: *the northwest suburbs of the city*

north·west·er /ˌnɔːθˈwestə $ ˌnɔːrθˈwestər/ *n* [C] a strong wind or storm coming from the northwest

north·west·er·ly /ˌnɔːθˈwestəli $ ˌnɔːrθˈwestərli/ *adj* **1** towards or in the northwest: *We headed off in a northwesterly direction.* **2** a northwesterly wind comes from the northwest

north·west·ern /ˌnɔːθˈwestən $ ˌnɔːrθˈwestərn/ written abbreviation *NW adj* in or from the northwest part of a country or area: *a town in northwestern Canada*

---

[1] 000, [2] 000, [3] 000, most frequent words in [S]poken and [W]ritten English

N

north·west·wards /ˌnɔːθˈwestwədz $ ˌnɔːrθ-ˈwestwərdz/ also **northwestward** adv towards the northwest —**northwestward** adj

nos. also **Nos.** the written abbreviation of *numbers*: nos. 17–33

nose[1] S2 W2 /nəʊz $ noʊz/ n
1 ON YOUR FACE [C] the part of a person's or animal's face used for smelling or breathing; → **nasal**, **nostril**

> big/long nose
> hooked nose/Roman nose (=a nose that curves out near the top)
> snub nose (=a small nose that curves up at the end)
> blow your nose (=clear your nose by blowing strongly into a piece of cloth)
> wipe your nose
> pick your nose (=remove dirt from your nose with your finger)
> punch sb on the nose
> break your nose
> your nose is running (=liquid is coming out of your nose)
> runny nose (=when liquid is coming out of your nose)
> blocked nose (=you cannot breathe easily through your nose)
> wrinkle your nose
> the bridge of your nose (=the upper part, between your eyes)

> *He's got a really **big nose**.* | *He took out a tissue and* **blew** *his* **nose**. | *Stop **picking** your* **nose**! | *Someone* **punched** *him* **on the nose**. | *He* **broke his nose** *playing football.* | *Rachel had a sore throat and* **runny nose** *all day yesterday.* | *Tina* **wrinkled** *her* **nose** *as if she was smelling bad meat.*

2 (right) under sb's nose **a)** if something bad or illegal happens under someone's nose, they do not notice it even though it is happening very close to them and they should have noticed it: *The drugs were smuggled in right under the noses of the security guards.* **b)** if something is right under someone's nose, they cannot see it even though it is very close to them: *The key was right under my nose all the time.*
3 stick/poke your nose into sth to become involved in something that does not concern you, in a way that annoys people; → **nosy**: *She always has to stick her nose into matters that do not concern her.*
4 keep your nose out (of sth) *spoken* to avoid becoming involved in something that does not concern you: *I wish he'd keep his nose out of my business!*
5 turn your nose up (at sth) *informal* to refuse to accept something because you do not think it is good enough for you: *My children turn their noses up at home cooking.*
6 with your nose in the air behaving as if you are more important than other people and not talking to them: *She just walked past with her nose in the air.*
7 have a (good) nose for sth to be naturally good at finding and recognizing something: *a reporter with a good nose for a story*
8 get (right) up sb's nose *BrE spoken* to annoy someone very much: *I wish he wouldn't keep interrupting. It really gets up my nose.*
9 keep your nose clean *spoken* to make sure you do not get into trouble, or do anything wrong or illegal: *Sid's got to keep his nose clean or he'll end up back in prison.*
10 on the nose *AmE spoken* exactly: *He gets up at 6 a.m. on the nose every morning.*
11 keep your nose to the grindstone *informal* to work very hard, without stopping to rest: *Jim had decided he was going to keep his nose to the grindstone.*
12 have your nose in a book/magazine/newspaper to be reading a book etc, especially with a lot of interest: *She always had her nose in a book.*
13 by a nose if a horse wins a race by a nose, it only just wins

14 have a nose around *BrE spoken* to look around a place in order to try to find something, when there is no one else there
15 put sb's nose out of joint *informal* to annoy someone, especially by attracting everyone's attention away from them: *His nose has been a bit out of joint ever since Marion got here.*
16 nose to tail *especially BrE* cars, buses etc that are nose to tail are in a line without much space between them: *Traffic was nose to tail for three miles.*
17 PLANE [C] the pointed front end of a plane, ROCKET etc
18 SMELL [singular] the smell of a wine or tobacco; ⊟ **bouquet** → HARD-NOSED, BROWN-NOSE; → cut off your nose to spite your face at CUT OFF (10); → NOSE JOB; → lead sb by the nose at LEAD[1] (16); → look down your nose at sb/sth at LOOK[1] (8); → pay through the nose at PAY[1] (16); → as plain as the nose on your face at PLAIN[1] (1); → poke your nose into sth at POKE[1] (7); → powder your nose at POWDER[2] (2); → rub sb's nose in it/in the dirt at RUB[1] (9); → thumb your nose at sb/sth at THUMB[2] (2)

nose[2] v [always + adv/prep I,T] if a vehicle, boat etc noses forward, or if you nose into it forward, it moves forward slowly; ⊟ **edge**: nose its way along/through etc sth *The bus nosed its way along the street.* | *She carefully nosed the car forward through the traffic.*
  nose around (sth) also **nose about (sth)** *BrE phr v informal* to look around a place in order to try to find something, when there is no one else there: *What were you doing nosing around in my office?*
  nose into sth *phr v informal* to try to find out private information about someone or something, especially in a way that is annoying
  nose sth ⇔ **out** *phr v informal* **1** to discover some information that someone else does not want you to discover: *The media always manage to nose out some interesting facts about a politician's past life.* **2** to defeat someone by a very small amount in a race, competition etc

nose·bag /ˈnəʊzbæg $ ˈnoʊz-/ n [C] *BrE* a bag that holds food and is hung around a horse's head

nose·bleed /ˈnəʊzbliːd $ ˈnoʊz-/ n [C] if you have a nosebleed, blood suddenly starts flowing from your nose

nose·cone /ˈnəʊzkəʊn $ ˈnoʊzkoʊn/ n [C] the pointed front part of an aircraft, MISSILE, or ROCKET

nose·dive[1] /ˈnəʊzdaɪv $ ˈnoʊz-/ n [C] **1** a sudden very large fall in the price, value, or condition of something: *The pound took a nosedive on the foreign exchange market today.* | *The economy went into a nosedive.* **2** a sudden steep drop made by a plane with its front end pointing towards the ground: *Everyone screamed as the plane suddenly went into a nosedive.*

nosedive[2] v [I] **1** if a price, value, or condition of something nosedives, it suddenly goes down or gets much worse; ⊟ **plummet**: *Sales have nosedived since January.* **2** if a plane nosedives, it drops suddenly and steeply with its front end pointing towards the ground

nose·gay /ˈnəʊzgeɪ $ ˈnoʊz-/ n [C] *old-fashioned* a small arrangement of flowers

'nose job n [C] *informal* a medical operation on someone's nose to improve its appearance; → **plastic surgery**, **cosmetic surgery**

nos·ey /ˈnəʊzi $ ˈnoʊ-/ adj another spelling of NOSY

nosh[1] /nɒʃ $ nɑːʃ/ n [U] *informal* **1** *BrE* food **2** *AmE* a small amount of food eaten between meals; ⊟ **snack**

nosh[2] v [I] *informal* to eat

no-'show n [C] someone who does not arrive or appear somewhere they were expected to be, for example at a restaurant or a meeting: *The bad weather meant there were a lot of no-shows at the game.*

'nosh-up n [singular] *BrE informal* a big meal

no-'smoking adj NON-SMOKING

nos·tal·gia /nɒˈstældʒə $ nɑː-/ *n* [U] a feeling that a time in the past was good, or the activity of remembering a good time in the past and wishing that things had not changed: [+**for**] *nostalgia for the good old days* | *He looked back on his university days with a certain amount of nostalgia.* | *a **wave of nostalgia** for how great life was in the 1960s*

nos·tal·gic /nɒˈstældʒɪk $ nɑː-/ *adj* if you feel nostalgic about a time in the past, you feel happy when you remember it, and in some ways you wish that things had not changed: *Seeing those old school photographs has made me **feel** quite **nostalgic**.* | *a **nostalgic look** back at the 1950s* | [+**about**] *He remained nostalgic about his days as a young actor.* —**nostalgically** /-kli/ *adv*: *Tim spoke nostalgically of his first visit to Peru.*

nos·tril /ˈnɒstrɪl $ ˈnɑː-/ *n* [C] one of the two holes at the end of your nose, through which you breathe and smell things: *The smell of gunpowder filled his nostrils.* | *the horse's **flaring nostrils** (=widened nostrils)*

nos·trum /ˈnɒstrəm $ ˈnɑː-/ *n* [C] *formal* an idea that someone thinks will solve a problem easily, but will probably not help at all: *an economic nostrum*

nos·y¹, nosey /ˈnəʊzi $ ˈnoʊ-/ *adj comparative* **nosier,** *superlative* **nosiest** always wanting to find out things that do not concern you, especially other people's private affairs: *Don't be so nosy! It's none of your business.* | *a nosy neighbor* —**nosiness** *n* [U] —**nosily** *adv*

nosy² *n BrE informal* **a nosy** a thorough look around a place, especially somewhere that belongs to someone else and is private: *I'd love to have a good old nosy in Josey's room!*

‚nosy 'parker *n* [C] *BrE informal* someone who is too interested in finding out about other people's affairs – used to show disapproval

not S1 W1 /nɒt $ nɑːt/ *adv*
1 used to make a word, statement, or question negative: *Most of the stores do not open until 10am.* | *She's not a very nice person.* | *You were wrong not to inform the police.* | *'Can we go to the park?' 'No, not today, dear.'* | **not at all/not ... at all** (=used to emphasize what you are saying) *The changes were not at all surprising.* | *I do not like his attitude at all.* → NO¹ → N'T
2 used in order to make a word or expression have the opposite meaning: *Edinburgh isn't far now.* | *The food is **not very** good there.* | **not a lot/much/many etc** (=only a few, only a little etc) *Not much is known about the disease.* | *Not many people have read the report.* | *Most of the hotels are **not that** cheap (=they are fairly expensive).*
3 used instead of a whole phrase, to mean the opposite of what has been mentioned before it: *No one knows if the story is true **or not**.* | *I hope to see you tomorrow, but if not, leave me a message.* | *'Is Mark still sick?' 'I hope not.'* → SO¹ (4)
4 not only in addition to being or doing something: **not only ... (but) also ...** *Shakespeare was not only a writer but also an actor.* | **not only do/will/can etc** *Not only do the nurses want a pay increase, they want reduced hours as well.*
5 not a/not one not any person or thing: *Not one of the students knew the answer.* | *There wasn't a cloud in the sky.* | *Not a single person said thank you.*
6 not that ... used before a sentence or phrase to mean the opposite of what follows it, and to make the previous sentence seem less important: *Sarah has a new boyfriend – **not that I care** (=I do not care).* | *Janice had lost some weight, **not that it mattered** (=it did not matter).*
7 not at all *spoken especially BrE* used to be polite when someone has thanked you or asked you to do something: *'Would you mind helping me with my suitcase?' 'Not at all.'*
8 - not! *spoken* used, especially by young people, to say that you really mean the opposite of what you have just

said: *I really enjoy spending my day working here – not!*
⚠ Do not use another negative word (no, nothing, nobody, never etc) with **not**. Use **any, anything, anybody, ever** etc: *I haven't got any (NOT haven't got no) money.* | *I didn't know anybody (NOT didn't know nobody).* → **not half** at HALF³ (5); → **not to say** at SAY¹ (44)

no·ta·ble /ˈnəʊtəbəl $ ˈnoʊ-/ *adj* [usually before noun] important, interesting, excellent, or unusual enough to be noticed or mentioned: **notable feature/example** *A notable feature of the church is its unusual bell tower.* | **notable achievement/success/victory** | *Every country in the world signed the treaty, with one **notable exception** - the United States.* | [+**for**] *The town is notable for its busy open-air market.*

no·ta·bles /ˈnəʊtəbəlz $ ˈnoʊ-/ *n* [plural] important or famous people: *local notables*

no·ta·bly W3 /ˈnəʊtəbli/ *adv*
1 used to say that a person or thing is a typical example or the most important example of something; 🔲 **especially, in particular**: *Some early doctors, notably Hippocrates, thought that diet was important.*
2 *formal* in a way that is clearly different, important, or unusual: *Emigration has notably increased over the past five years.* | *Notably absent from his statement was any hint of an apology.*

no·ta·rized also **-ised** *BrE* /ˈnəʊtəraɪzd $ ˈnoʊ-/ *adj law* signed by a NOTARY

no·ta·ry /ˈnəʊtəri $ ˈnoʊ-/ also **‚notary 'public** *n plural* **notaries** [C] someone, especially a lawyer, who has the legal power to make a signed statement or document official

no·ta·tion /nəʊˈteɪʃən $ noʊ-/ *n* [C,U] a system of written marks or signs used to represent something such as music, mathematics, or scientific ideas

notch¹ /nɒtʃ $ nɑːtʃ/ *n* [C] **1** a level on a scale that measures something, for example quality or achievement: *Her new book is several notches above anything else she has written.* | *Jackson raised his voice by a notch.* | *The Spartans turned it up a notch in the second half.* **2** a V-shaped cut or hole in a surface or edge: *Cut a notch near one end of the stick.* **3** *AmE* a passage between two mountains or hills → TOP-NOTCH

notch² *v* [T] **1** to cut a V-shaped mark into something, especially as a way of showing the number of times something has been done **2** *AmE* to notch something up

notch sth ⇔ **up** *phr v* to achieve something, especially a victory or a particular total or score: *The Houston Astros have **notched up** another **win**.*

note¹ S1 W1 /nəʊt $ noʊt/ *n*
1 TO REMIND YOU a) [C] something that you write down to remind you of something: *Dave **made a note of** her address and phone number.* | *Keep a careful note of any problems you have with the software.* b) **make a (mental) note to do sth** to decide that you must remember to do something later: *He made a mental note to arrange a time to meet her.*
2 FOR STUDYING notes [plural] information that a student writes down during a lesson, from a book etc: *Can I borrow your lecture notes?* | **take/make notes** (=write notes) *I read the first chapter and took notes.*
3 SHORT LETTER [C] a short informal letter: *I was going to **write** Kathy a **note**, but I decided to call her instead.* | *This is just a **quick note** to let you know that I won't be in the office tomorrow.* | *a **suicide note** (=a note telling someone that you are going to kill yourself)* | *a **thank you note** (=a note to say thank you for something)*
4 OFFICIAL LETTER [C] an official letter or document: **sick note** *BrE* (=a note saying that you are too ill to go to work or school) | **delivery note** (=a document showing that goods have been delivered) | **diplomatic note** (=a formal letter from one government to another) → CREDIT NOTE, PROMISSORY NOTE

N

5 ADDITIONAL INFORMATION [C] a short piece of writing at the bottom of a page or at the end of a book or document which gives more information about something written in the main part: *The notes are at the back of the book.* | **explanatory/guidance notes** *A set of guidance notes is provided to assist applicants in completing the form.* → FOOTNOTE (1)

6 MUSIC [C] a particular musical sound, or a symbol representing this sound: **high/low note** *She has a good voice but has trouble hitting the high notes.*

7 MONEY [C] *BrE* also **bank note** a piece of paper money worth a particular amount of money; ▤ **bill** *AmE*; → **coin**: *a ten-pound note*

8 FEELING OR QUALITY [singular] a type of feeling or quality when someone speaks or does something: [+of] *There was a note of doubt in her voice.* | *He brought a note of realism into the debate.* | **on a ... note** (=speaking in a particular way) *She ended her speech on a personal note.* | *On a more serious note, I'd like to thank everyone for all their support.*

9 hit/strike the right/wrong note to succeed or not succeed in being right and suitable for a particular occasion: *Bush is hoping to hit the right note again with voters.*

10 take note (of sth) to pay attention to something; ▤ **notice**: *People were beginning to take note of her talents as a writer.* | *His first album made the music world* **stand up and take note**.

11 sb/sth of note *formal* important, interesting, or famous: *The college has produced several architects of note.* | *The village has a number of buildings of note.*

12 worthy/deserving of note important or interesting and deserving particular attention; → **noteworthy**: *three recent novels that are especially worthy of note* → **compare notes** at COMPARE¹ (5)

note² v [T] *formal* **1** to notice or pay careful attention to something: *He carefully noted the time when they left the building.* | **note (that)** *Please note that the bill must be paid within ten days.* | *It should be noted that parking without a permit attracts a charge of £5.* | **note how** *Note how she is holding her racket.* **2** to mention something because it is important or interesting: **note that** *The judge noted that Miller had no previous criminal record.*

note sth ⇔ **down** *phr v* to write something down so that you will remember it: *Note down the main points you want to include in your essay.*

note·book /'nəʊtbʊk $ 'noʊt-/ *n* [C] **1** a book made of plain paper on which you can write notes → see picture at STATIONERY **2** also **notebook computer** a small computer that you can carry with you; → **laptop**

'note card *n* [C] *AmE* a small folded piece of paper with a picture on it, for writing a short letter; ▤ **note-let** *BrE*

not·ed /'nəʊtɪd $ 'noʊ-/ *adj* well known or famous, especially because of some special quality or ability; → **renowned**: *a noted author* | [+for] *The city is noted for its 18th-century architecture.*

note·let /'nəʊtlɪt $ 'noʊt-/ *n* [C] *BrE* a small folded piece of paper with a picture on it, for writing a short letter; ▤ **note card** *AmE*

note·pad /'nəʊtpæd $ 'noʊt-/ *n* [C] a group of sheets of paper fastened together at the top, used for writing notes

note·pa·per /'nəʊt,peɪpə $ 'noʊt,peɪpər/ *n* [U] paper used for writing letters or notes; → **writing paper**: **headed notepaper** (=with the sender's address printed on it)

note·wor·thy /'nəʊt,wɜːði $ 'noʊt,wɜːr-/ *adj* important or interesting enough to deserve your attention: *a noteworthy achievement*

not-for-'profit *adj* [only before noun] *especially AmE* NON-PROFIT

noth·ing¹ [S1] [W1] /'nʌθɪŋ/ *pron*
1 not anything or no thing

nothing else/nothing more
know nothing (about sb/sth)
do/say/hear nothing
absolutely nothing
nothing at all/nothing whatsoever
virtually/practically nothing
nothing wrong
nothing new
nothing untoward (=nothing unusual or bad)

Nothing ever happens in this town. | *There's nothing in this box.* | *There was* **nothing else** *the doctors could do.* | *He had* **nothing more** *to say.* | *We* **know nothing about** *her family.* | *I couldn't just stand by and* **do nothing**. | *I promised to* **say nothing** *about it to anyone.* | *We've* **heard nothing** *from her for weeks.* | *There's* **absolutely nothing** *to be ashamed of.* | *'Do you know much about business?' '* **Nothing at all**.' | *She had eaten* **virtually nothing** *at supper.* | *There's* **nothing wrong** *with the data.* | *There's* **nothing new** *about this.* | *A brief search was made but they found* **nothing untoward**.

2 nothing but only: *She'd had nothing but bad luck.*

3 have nothing against sb/sth if you have nothing against someone or something, they do not annoy or offend you: *I have nothing against him personally.*

4 something which is considered unimportant, not interesting, or not worth worrying about: *'What have you been doing?' 'Nothing. Just sitting here.'* | *There's nothing on television tonight.* | *'What did you do last weekend?' 'Oh,* **nothing much**.' | *Politics* **meant nothing** (=was not important) *to me for years.* | *The meal was* **nothing special** (=it was not unusual or interesting) *- just fish with a cheese sauce.*

5 *especially AmE* zero; ▤ **nil** *BrE*: *We beat them ten to nothing.*

6 have/be nothing to do with sb/sth if you have nothing to do with someone or something, or if someone or something has nothing to do with you, you are not involved or connected with it: *He said that he had nothing to do with the decision.* | *As I said, it's nothing to do with me.* | *That's got nothing to do with you.* | *I* **want nothing to do with** (=do not want to be involved) *the whole thing.* | *My staff had* **nothing whatsoever** *to do with this.*

7 for nothing a) without paying for something or being paid for something: *Why pay a plumber when my brother will do it for nothing?* **b)** if you do something for nothing, you make an effort but do not get the result you expected and wanted: *We went all that way for nothing.*

8 no money or payment at all: *This service will cost you nothing.* | *When a car has done that many miles, it's worth nothing.*

9 there's nothing like sth used to say that something is very good: *There's nothing like a long hot bath after a day's climbing.*

10 there's nothing in/to sth used to say that what people are saying about someone or something is not true: *It seems there's nothing in the rumours that she's pregnant.*

11 if nothing else used to emphasize one good quality or feature that someone or something has, while suggesting that it might be the only good one: *If nothing else, the report points out the need for better math education.*

12 come to nothing if a plan or action comes to nothing, it does not continue or does not achieve anything

13 be nothing if not sth used to emphasize a particular quality that someone or something has: *You've got to admit – he's nothing if not persistent.*

14 nothing doing *spoken* used to refuse to do something

15 (there's) nothing to it *spoken* used to say that something is easy to do: *Anyone can use a computer. There's nothing to it!*

16 it was nothing/think nothing of it *spoken* used when someone has thanked you a lot for something you have done for them: *'Thank you so much.' 'Oh, it was nothing.'*

17 nothing of the sort/kind *spoken* used to say strongly or angrily that something is not true or will not happen: *'I'll pay.' 'You'll do nothing of the sort!'*

18 have nothing on sb *informal* if someone has nothing on you, they are not better than you at something: *She's got nothing on you when it comes to writing.*

19 there's nothing for it but to do sth *BrE* used when there is only one thing you can do in a particular situation: *There was nothing for it but to go back the way we came.* ⚠ Do not use another negative word (e.g. 'not') with **nothing**. Use **anything** with **not**: *Nothing happened.* | *Didn't anything happen?* → **sweet nothings** at SWEET¹ (13); → **to say nothing of** at SAY¹ (46); → **nothing on earth** at EARTH¹ (9)

nothing² *adv* **1 be/seem/look nothing like sb/sth** to have no qualities or features that are similar to someone or something else: *She's nothing like her brother.* | *She looked nothing like her photograph.* **2 be nothing less than sth** also **be nothing short of sth** used to emphasize that something or someone has a particular quality or seems to be something: *His behaviour was nothing short of rudeness.*

noth·ing·ness /ˈnʌθɪŋnəs/ *n* [U] **1** empty space or the complete absence of everything: *Natalie found him looking into nothingness.* **2** the state of not existing: *Is there only nothingness after death?*

no·tice¹ ⑤¹ Ⓦ² /ˈnəʊtɪs $ ˈnoʊ-/ *v* [I,T not in progressive]
1 if you notice something or someone, you realize that they exist, especially because you can see, hear, or feel them: *He noticed a woman in a black dress sitting across from him.* | *I didn't notice any smoke.* | *Have you noticed any change in him?* | **notice (that)** *I noticed that her hands were shaking.* | *He never seems to notice when people take advantage of him.* | **notice who/what/how etc** *She hadn't noticed before quite how grey his hair was.* | **notice sb/sth doing sth** *Did you notice him leaving the party early?*
2 be noticed/get (sb) noticed to get attention, or to make someone get attention: *These clothes will get you noticed and enhance your image.*
3 sb can't help noticing sth also **sb can't help but notice sth** if someone can't help noticing something, they realize that it exists or is happening even though they are not deliberately trying to pay attention to it: *I couldn't help noticing the bruises on her arm.*

This graph shows how common the different grammar patterns of the verb **notice** are.

notice sth/sb				
notice (that)				
notice				
notice who/what/how etc				
notice sb/sth doing sth				
other				

10%	20%	30%	40%

notice² ⑤² Ⓦ² *n*
1 ATTENTION [U] when you notice or pay attention to someone or something: *I waved but they took no notice.* | **not take any/much notice (of sth)** *I did not take much notice of her suggestions.* | *I hope you'll take notice of what I'm going to tell you.* | *This problem may have escaped your notice so far* (=you may not have noticed it). | *This never came to my notice* (=I never knew about this). | *There are several important matters that I'd like to bring to your notice* (=that I would like you to know about).
2 ON PAPER [C] a written or printed statement that gives information or a warning to people; → **sign**: *The notice on the wall said 'No smoking'.* | *I'll put up a notice about the meeting.* | **obituary notices** (=about people who have just died) *in the newspaper*

3 TIME TO PREPARE [U] information or a warning about something that is going to happen; → **warning**: **without notice** *These rules are subject to change without notice.* | **sufficient/reasonable notice** *They didn't give me sufficient notice.* | **advance/prior notice** *When you're on the mailing list, you'll receive advance notice of upcoming events.* | **ten days'/three months' etc notice** (=a warning ten days etc before) *They closed the factory, giving the workers only a week's notice.* | *Firefighters were prepared to rush out at a moment's notice.* | [+of] *his failure to give notice of his intention to alter the property* | **notice to do sth** *I've been given notice to quit my flat* (=I have been told that I must leave by a certain date). | *Union members served strike notice* (=warned that they would go on strike) *late last night.*
4 until further notice from now until another change is announced: *The office is closed until further notice.*
5 hand in your notice/give (your) notice to tell your employer that you will be leaving your job soon; ⊟ **resign**: *Jim gave notice on Thursday.*
6 at short notice *BrE*, **on short notice** *AmE* if you do something at short notice, you do not have very much time to prepare for it: *The trip was planned on short notice.* | *Thanks for agreeing to see me at such short notice.* | *a cancellation* **at very short notice**
7 BOOK/PLAY ETC [C usually plural] a statement of opinion, especially one written for a newspaper or magazine, about a new play, book, film etc; ⊟ **review**: *The new play got* **mixed notices** (=some good, some bad) *in the newspapers.* → **sit up (and take notice)** at SIT UP (5)

no·tice·a·ble /ˈnəʊtɪsəbəl $ ˈnoʊ-/ *adj* easy to notice: *Alcohol has a noticeable effect on the body.* | *It was* **noticeable** *that many of them avoided answering the question.* | **noticeable difference/change/increase etc** *a noticeable improvement in air quality* —**noticeably** *adv: She has become noticeably more confident.* | *The children were noticeably affected by the divorce.*

no·tice·board /ˈnəʊtɪsˌbɔːd $ ˈnoʊtɪsˌbɔːrd/ *n* [C] *BrE* a special board on a wall which notices can be fastened to; ⊟ **bulletin board**

no·ti·fi·a·ble /ˈnəʊtɪfaɪəbəl $ ˈnoʊ-/ *adj BrE technical* a notifiable disease or crime is one that by law must be reported to the government or to the police

no·ti·fi·ca·tion /ˌnəʊtɪfɪˈkeɪʃən $ ˌnoʊ-/ *n* [C,U] formal official information about something: **prior/advance notification** *I was given no prior notification.* | [+of] *You should receive notification of the results within a week.* | **official/written/formal notification** *We received official notification that Harry was missing.*

no·ti·fy /ˈnəʊtɪfaɪ $ ˈnoʊ-/ *v* **notified, notifying, notifies** [T] to formally or officially tell someone about something; ⊟ **inform**: **notify sb of sth** *You will be notified of any changes in the system.* | **notify sb that** *In August we were notified that our article had been rejected.*

no·tion Ⓦ³ /ˈnəʊʃən $ ˈnoʊ-/ *n* [C]
1 an idea, belief, or opinion: [+of] *misguided notions of male superiority* | *The traditional notion of marriage goes back thousands of years.* | *She had only a* **vague notion** *of what she wanted to do.* | **notion that** *the notion that human beings are basically good* | *She had* **no notion** *what he meant.* | **accept/challenge/reject etc a notion** *They reject the notion of group guilt.*
2 notions [plural] *AmE* small things such as thread and buttons that are used for sewing

no·tion·al /ˈnəʊʃənəl $ ˈnoʊ-/ *adj* [usually before noun] existing only as an idea or plan, and not existing in reality: *Their calculations were based on a notional minimum wage.*

no·to·ri·e·ty /ˌnəʊtəˈraɪəti $ ˌnoʊ-/ *n* [U] the state of being famous or well-known for something that is bad or that people do not approve of: **of notoriety** *John is*

⊡ 000, ⊡ 000, ⊡ 000, most frequent words in ⑤poken and Ⓦritten English

nuclear 'bomb n [C] a very powerful bomb that uses NUCLEAR energy to kill a lot of people and destroy large areas

nuclear de'terrence n [U] the threat of using NUCLEAR weapons as a way to stop an enemy from attacking

nuclear dis'armament n [U] the process or activity of getting rid of NUCLEAR weapons

nuclear 'family n [C] a family unit that consists only of a husband, wife and children; → **extended family**

nuclear 'fission n [U] the splitting of the NUCLEUS (=central part) of an atom which results in a lot of power being produced

nuclear-'free adj [usually before noun] places that are nuclear-free do not allow NUCLEAR materials to be carried, stored, or used in that area: a **nuclear-free zone**

nuclear 'fusion n [U] a NUCLEAR reaction in which the NUCLEI (=central parts) of atoms join together, which produces power without producing any waste

nuclear 'physics n [U] the area of physics which is concerned with the structure and features of the NUCLEUS (=central part) of atoms

nuclear re'actor n [C] a large machine that produces NUCLEAR energy, especially as a means of producing electricity

nuclear 'waste n [U] waste material from NUCLEAR REACTORS, which is RADIOACTIVE: the problems of nuclear waste disposal

nu·cle·ic ac·id /njuːˌkliːɪk ˈæsɪd, -ˌkleɪ- $ nuː-/ n [C,U] one of the two acids, DNA and RNA, that exist in the cells of all living things

nu·cle·us /ˈnjuːkliəs $ ˈnuː-/ n plural nuclei /-kliaɪ/ [C] **1** the central part of an atom, made up of NEUTRONS, PROTONS, and other ELEMENTARY PARTICLES **2** the central part of almost all the cells of living things **3** a small, important group at the centre of a larger group or organization: [+of] the nucleus of an effective team | Marantz and Grohl form the nucleus of the Atlanta operation.

nude¹ /njuːd $ nuːd/ adj **1** not wearing any clothes; ▣ **naked**: I did some work as a **nude model** when I was in college. | Have you ever **posed nude** (=been photographed or painted while nude)? **2** done by or involving people who are not wearing any clothes: There are several **nude scenes** in the film. | I have no desire to go to a **nude beach** (=a beach where people wear no clothes).

nude² n **1** [C] a painting, STATUE etc of someone not wearing clothes **2** in the nude not wearing any clothes: He was standing there in the nude.

nudge /nʌdʒ/ v **1** [T] to push someone gently, usually with your elbow, in order to get their attention: Jill nudged him in the ribs. **2** [T always + adv/prep] to move something or someone a short distance by gently pushing: She nudged the glass towards me. | David nudged me out of the way. **3** [I always + adv/prep] to move forward slowly by pushing gently: nudge your way to/through etc (sth) I started to nudge my way to the front of the crowd. **4** [T always + adv/prep] to gently persuade or encourage someone to take a particular decision or action: nudge sb into/towards sth We're trying to nudge them towards a practical solution. **5** [T] to almost reach a particular level or amount: Outside the temperature was nudging 30 degrees Celsius. —**nudge** n [C]: Hannah gave me a gentle **nudge**.

nud·ist /ˈnjuːdɪst $ ˈnuː-/ n [C] someone who enjoys not wearing any clothes because they believe it is natural and healthy; ▣ **naturist** —**nudism** n [U]

nu·di·ty /ˈnjuːdɪti $ ˈnuː-/ n [U] the state of not wearing any clothes: The play contains scenes of nudity.

nu·ga·to·ry /ˈnjuːgətəri $ ˈnuːgətɔːri/ adj formal having no value

nug·get /ˈnʌgɪt/ n [C] **1** a small rough piece of a valuable metal found in the earth: a **gold nugget** **2** a

small, round piece of food: chicken nuggets **3** **nugget of information/wisdom etc** a piece of valuable information, advice etc: It took months to extract that nugget of information from them.

nui·sance S3 /ˈnjuːsəns $ ˈnuː-/ n **1** [C usually singular] a person, thing, or situation that annoys you or causes problems: a real/awful/terrible etc nuisance The dogs next door are a real nuisance. | What a nuisance! BrE: What a nuisance! I've forgotten my ticket. | I hate to be a nuisance.../Sorry to be a nuisance... I hate to be a nuisance, but could you move your car to the other side of the street? | Stop making a nuisance of yourself (=annoying other people with your behaviour)! | It's a nuisance having to get up that early on a Sunday morning. **2** [C,U] law the use of a place or property in a way that causes public annoyance: The nightclub has been declared a **public nuisance**.

nuke¹ /njuːk $ nuːk/ v [T] informal **1** to attack a place using NUCLEAR weapons **2** to cook food in a MICROWAVE OVEN: Nuke it for two minutes.

nuke² n [C] informal a NUCLEAR weapon

null /nʌl/ adj **null and void** law an agreement, contract etc that is null and void has no legal force; ▣ **invalid**: The contract was **declared null and void.**

nul·li·fy /ˈnʌlɪfaɪ/ v **nullified, nullifying, nullifies** [T] **1** law to officially state that something has no legal force: The election results were nullified because of voter fraud. **2** formal to make something lose its effect or value: Recent inflation could nullify the economic growth of the last several years. —**nullification** /ˌnʌlɪfɪˈkeɪʃən/ n [U]

nul·li·ty /ˈnʌlɪti/ n [U] law the fact that a marriage or contract no longer has any legal force: a decree of nullity

numb¹ /nʌm/ adj **1** a part of your body that is numb is unable to feel anything, for example because you are very cold: My fingers were so numb I could hardly write. | The anaesthetic made his whole face **go numb. 2** unable to think, feel, or react in a normal way: numb with shock/fear/terror etc I just sat there, numb with fear. —**numbly** adv: She watched numbly as Matt walked away. —**numbness** n [U]: It caused some numbness in my hand.

numb² v [T] **1** to make someone unable to feel pain or feel things they are touching: The cold had numbed her fingers. | the numbing effect of the drug **2** to make someone unable to think, feel, or react in a normal way: He was numbed by the shock of his wife's death.

number¹ S1 W1 /ˈnʌmbə $ -bər/ n **1 NUMBER** [C] a word or sign that represents an amount or a quantity; → **numeral, figure**: They wrote various numbers on a large sheet of paper. | They wrote her lucky number. | an **even number** (=2, 4, 6, 8, 10 etc) | an **odd number** (=1, 3, 5, 7, 9 etc) | **round number** (=a number ending in 0) A million pounds seemed a suitably round number. | be good/bad/no good with numbers informal (=to be good, bad etc at calculating things using numbers) → CARDINAL NUMBER, ORDINAL NUMBER, PRIME NUMBER, WHOLE NUMBER
2 PHONE [C] a phone number: My new number is 502–6155. | sb's home/office/work number I gave him my home number. | mobile/fax number What's your mobile number? | Sorry, you have the wrong number.
3 IN A SET/LIST [C] a number used to show the position of something in an ordered set or list: Answer question number 4. | a number 17 bus → E NUMBER, NO. 10, NUMBER ONE
4 FOR RECOGNIZING SB/STH [C] a set of numbers used to name or recognize someone or something: model/account etc number What is your account number, please? | Press 1 to change the printer number. | Did you get the number (= REGISTRATION number) of the car? BrE → BOX NUMBER, PIN, SERIAL NUMBER
5 AMOUNT [C,U] an amount of something that can be counted; ▣ **quantity**: the number of sth The number of cars on our roads rose dramatically last year. | a number

of sth *We have been friends for a number of years.* | a **large/small/significant/growing etc number of sth** *Doctors believe only a tiny number of people are at risk.* | *The lake produces **a good number of** (=a lot of) salmon each season.* | *There was an unusually **high number of** entries in the competition.* | *They were printed **in** limited numbers.* | *Young people have been leaving the countryside **in large numbers** for urban areas.* | *Today's case **brings the number of** successful prosecutions in the region **to** (=makes the number rise to) thirty-four.* | *There could be **any number of** (=many) reasons why she's late.* | *The condors have dwindled to an estimated sixty **in number**.*
6 numbers [plural] how many people there are, especially people attending an event or doing an activity together: *Can you give me some idea of numbers?* | **student/client etc numbers** *Visitor numbers increase in the summer.* | *The **sheer weight of numbers** (=large number of people) on stage made the performance more impressive.*
7 **MUSIC** [C] a piece of popular music that forms part of a longer performance: *Madonna sang several numbers from her latest album.* → PRODUCTION NUMBER
8 **MAGAZINE** [C] *BrE* a copy of a magazine or newspaper printed on a particular date; 🔲 **issue**: [+of] *I was reading the latest number of 'Surfing'.* | **back numbers** (=old copies) *of The Times*
9 have sb's number *informal* to understand something about someone that helps you deal with them: *Judy had always had his number.*
10 black/elegant etc (little) number *informal* a black, ELEGANT etc dress or suit, especially a woman's: *She was wearing a chic little number.*
11 sb's number comes up someone has the winning number in a competition
12 sb's number is up also **sb's number has come up** *informal* a) used to say that someone will stop being lucky or successful b) used to say that someone will die – used humorously: *She told her husband she didn't mind going when her number was up.*
13 the numbers a) information about something that is shown using numbers: *Chris, have you got the numbers yet?* b) an illegal game in the US in which people risk money on the appearance of a combination of numbers in a newspaper: ***playing the numbers***
14 by numbers if you do something by numbers, you do it in a basic way by following a set of simple instructions – used to show disapproval: *The last thing we want is teaching by numbers.*
15 do a number on sb/sth *informal* to hurt or damage someone or something badly: *Tod really did a number on the old house. I don't envy the new tenants.*
16 beyond/without number *literary* if things are beyond number, there are so many of them that no one could count them all
17 **GROUP OF PEOPLE** [U] *formal* a group of people: **one/two/several etc of our/their number** *Only three of our number could speak Italian.* | *They wanted to choose a leader from **among their** own **number**.*
18 **GRAMMAR** [U] *technical* the form of a word, depending on whether one thing or more than one thing is being talked about: *'Horses' is plural in number, while 'horse' is singular.*

number² *v* **1** [T] to give a number to something that is part of an ordered set or list: *They haven't numbered the pages of the report.* | *All the seats in the theatre are numbered.* | *Each check is **numbered consecutively**.* | *a **numbering system*** | **number sth (from) 1 to 10/100 etc** *Number the questions 1 to 25.* **2** [linking verb] if people or things number a particular amount, that is how many there are: *The population of the town numbered about 5,000.* | *The men on strike now number 5% of the workforce.* **3 sb's/sth's days are numbered** used to say that someone or something cannot live or continue for much longer: *I knew my days were numbered at that firm.* **4 number among sth/be numbered among sth** *formal* to be included as one of a particular group: *He was a successful corporate lawyer who numbered*

among his clients J.P. Morgan and Standard Oil. **5** [T] *literary* to count something: *Who can number the stars?* **number off** *phr v BrE* if soldiers number off, each one calls out their number when their turn comes; 🔲 **count off** *AmE*

'number ,cruncher *n* [C] *informal* someone whose job involves working with numbers, such as an ACCOUNTANT

'number ,crunching *n* [U] *informal* the process of working with a lot of numbers and calculating results —**number-crunching** *adj*

num·ber·less /ˈnʌmbələs $ -bər-/ *adj literary* too many to be counted; 🔲 **countless**: *numberless fish*

,number 'one¹ *n* **1** [U] the best, most important, or most successful person or thing in a group: *Until his marriage, his job was number one in his life.* | *Shearson is number one in the market this year.* **2** [C,U] the musical record that is the most popular at a particular time: *number one in the charts* | *They've had three number ones.* **3 look out for number one** also **look after number one** *spoken* to look after yourself and not worry about other people, in a way that may seem SELFISH **4** [singular, U] *spoken informal* a word meaning URINE, used especially with children to avoid saying this directly

,number 'one² *adj* **1** most important or successful in a particular situation: *The University of Maine has the number one hockey team in the country.* | *Sweden's number one model* **2** first on a list of several things to be considered, done etc: *item number one on the agenda* | *This has got to be our number one task.*

'number ,plate *n* [C] *BrE* one of the signs with numbers and letters on it at the front and back of a car; → **registration number**; 🔲 **license plate** *AmE*; → see picture at CAR

,Number 'Ten *n* **Number Ten Downing Street** the address of the official home of the British Prime Minister

,number 'two *n* [singular, U] *spoken informal* a word meaning solid waste from your BOWELS, used especially with children to avoid saying this directly; → **number one**

numb·skull, numskull /ˈnʌmskʌl/ *n* [C] *informal* a very stupid person; 🔲 **idiot**: *Look what you've done now, you numbskull!*

nu·me·ra·cy /ˈnjuːmərəsi $ ˈnuː-/ *n* [U] the ability to do calculations and understand simple mathematics; → **literacy**: *The report suggests that students need to improve their numeracy skills.*

nu·me·ral /ˈnjuːmərəl $ ˈnuː-/ *n* [C] a written sign such as 1, 2, or 3 that represents a number; → **figure** —**numeral** *adj*

nu·me·rate /ˈnjuːmərət $ ˈnuː-/ *adj* able to do calculations and understand simple mathematics; → **literate**

nu·me·ra·tion /ˌnjuːməˈreɪʃən $ ˌnuː-/ *n* [C,U] *technical* a system of counting or the process of counting

nu·me·ra·tor /ˈnjuːməreɪtə $ ˈnuːməreɪtər/ *n* [C] *technical* the number above the line in a FRACTION, for example 5 is the numerator in ⅝; → **denominator**

nu·mer·i·cal /njuːˈmerɪkəl $ nuː-/ *adj* expressed or considered in numbers: *a numerical code* | *The home team tried to utilize their numerical advantage* (=the fact that they had more players than the other team). | *Make sure the files are organized **in numerical order**.* —**numerically** /-kli/ *adv*

nu·me·rous 🔲W3🔲 /ˈnjuːmərəs $ ˈnuː-/ *adj* many: *Numerous attempts have been made to hide the truth.* | *The two leaders have worked together on **numerous occasions**.* | **too numerous to mention/list** *The individuals who have contributed to this book are far too numerous to mention.*

1 000, 2 000, 3 000, most frequent words in S poken and W ritten English

N

nu·mi·nous /ˈnjuːmᵻnəs $ ˈnuː-/ adj literary having a mysterious and holy quality, which makes you feel that God is present

nu·mis·mat·ics /ˌnjuːmᵻzˈmætɪks $ ˌnuː-/ n [U] the activity of collecting and studying coins and MEDALS

nu·mis·ma·tist /njuːˈmɪzmətᵻst $ nuː-/ n [C] someone who collects and studies coins and MEDALS

nun /nʌn/ n [C] someone who is a member of a group of religious women that live together in a CONVENT; → **monk**

nun·ci·o /ˈnʌnsiəʊ $ -sioʊ/ n plural **nuncios** [C] a representative of the Pope in a foreign country

nun·ne·ry /ˈnʌnəri/ n plural **nunneries** [C] old use a CONVENT

nup·tial /ˈnʌpʃəl/ adj [only before noun] formal relating to marriage or the marriage ceremony; → **wedding**: a nuptial mass | nuptial bliss

nup·tials /ˈnʌpʃəlz/ n [plural] formal a wedding

nurse¹ S3 W3 /nɜːs $ nɜːrs/ n [C]
1 someone whose job is to look after people who are ill or injured, usually in a hospital: The nurse is coming to give you an injection. | The school nurse sent Sara home. | a male nurse | a senior nurse | a student nurse (=someone who is learning to be a nurse) | a psychiatric nurse (=a nurse for people who are mentally ill) | a community nurse → DISTRICT NURSE, STAFF NURSE, VETERINARY NURSE; → see picture at OCCUPATION
2 old-fashioned a woman employed to look after a young child; ⊟ **nanny** → NURSERY NURSE, WET NURSE

nurse² v
1 SICK PEOPLE **a)** [T] to look after someone who is ill or injured: He's been nursing an elderly relative. | After Ray's operation, Mrs Stallard **nursed** him **back to health**. **b)** [I usually in progressive] to work as a nurse: She spent several years nursing in a military hospital.
2 REST [T not in passive] to rest when you have an illness or injury so that it will get better: Shaw has been nursing a sore ankle, and is not expected to play on Sunday.
3 FEED A BABY **a)** [I,T] old-fashioned if a woman nurses a baby, she feeds it with milk from her breasts; ⊟ **breastfeed**: information on nutrition for nursing mothers **b)** [I] if a baby nurses, it sucks milk from its mother's breast
4 YOUR FEELINGS [T not in passive] to keep a feeling or idea in your mind for a long time, especially an angry feeling: **nurse a grudge/grievance/ambition etc** For years he had nursed a grievance against his former employer.
5 TAKE CARE OF STH [T] to take special care of something, especially during a difficult situation: **nurse sth through/along etc** He bought the hotel in 1927 and managed to nurse it through the Depression.
6 DRINK [T] informal if you nurse a drink, especially an alcoholic one, you drink it very slowly: Oliver sat at the bar, nursing a bottle of beer.
7 HOLD [T] literary to hold something carefully in your hands or arms close to your body: a child nursing a kitten

nurse·maid /ˈnɜːsmeɪd $ ˈnɜːrs-/ n [C] old-fashioned a woman employed to look after young children

nurse prac·ti·tion·er n [C] a nurse who is trained to do some of the work that is usually done by a doctor

nur·se·ry /ˈnɜːsəri $ ˈnɜːr-/ n plural **nurseries** [C] **1** a place where young children are taken care of during the day while their parents are at work **2** a place where plants and trees are grown and sold **3 nursery education/unit/teacher etc** BrE education etc for young children from three to five years old → NURSERY SCHOOL **4** a room in a hospital where babies that have just been born are looked after **5** old-fashioned a baby's BEDROOM or a room in a house where young children play

nur·se·ry·man /ˈnɜːsərimən $ ˈnɜːr-/ n plural **nurserymen** /-mən/ [C] BrE someone who grows plants and trees in a nursery

nursery nurse n [C] BrE someone who has been trained to look after young children

nursery rhyme n [C] a short traditional poem or song for children

nursery school n [C] a school for children who are between three and five years old; ⊟ **kindergarten**

nursery slope n [C] BrE a slope that is not very steep, where people are taught to SKI

nurs·ing /ˈnɜːsɪŋ $ ˈnɜːr-/ n [U] the job or skill of looking after people who are ill, injured, or old: I'd love to go into nursing. | the nursing profession | psychiatric nursing

nursing home n [C] a place where people who are old and ill can live and be looked after; ⊟ **old people's home**

nur·tur·ance /ˈnɜːtʃərəns $ ˈnɜːr-/ n [U] formal loving care and attention that you give to someone

nur·ture¹ /ˈnɜːtʃə $ ˈnɜːrtʃər/ v [T usually passive] formal **1** to help a plan, idea, feeling etc to develop: European union is an ideal that has been nurtured since the post-war years. | a hatred of foreigners nurtured by the media **2** to feed and take care of a child or a plant while it is growing: plants nurtured in the greenhouse

nurture² n [U] formal the education and care that you are given as a child, and the way it affects your later development and attitudes

nuts

hazelnuts

coconuts almonds

pine nuts pistachios peanuts

nut¹ S3 /nʌt/ n [C]
1 FOOD a dry brown fruit inside a hard shell, that grows on a tree: a pine nut | roasted nuts | We were sitting round the fire **cracking nuts** (=opening them).
2 TOOL a small piece of metal with a hole through the middle which is screwed onto a BOLT to fasten things together: Use a wrench to loosen the nut.
3 CRAZY PERSON informal someone who is crazy or behaves strangely: My dad is such a nut. | What are you, some kind of nut?
4 golf/opera etc nut informal someone who is very interested in golf etc; → **fanatic**: You don't have to be a sports nut to enjoy skiing.
5 SEX ORGAN nuts [plural] informal a man's TESTICLES
6 the nuts and bolts of sth informal the practical details of a subject or job: the nuts and bolts of government
7 tough/hard nut informal someone who is difficult to deal with: He may have softened a bit in his old age but he's still a tough nut.
8 a hard/tough nut to crack a difficult problem or situation: Celtic have lost only once this season and will be a tough nut to crack.
9 be off your nut BrE spoken informal to be crazy: You must be off your nut!
10 do your nut BrE spoken to become very angry or worried: I didn't get home till three – my mum did her nut!
11 HEAD BrE spoken old-fashioned your head or brain: **sb's nut** Oh come on, use your nut!

nut² v **nutted, nutting** [T] BrE spoken to hit someone with your head; ⊟ **headbutt**: He just turned round and nutted me!

,nut-'brown adj dark brown in colour

nut·case /'nʌtkeɪs/ n [C] informal someone who behaves in a crazy way; ☐ **idiot**: He's a complete nutcase.

nut·crack·er /'nʌt,krækə $ -ər/ n [C] also **nut-crackers** BrE a tool for cracking the shells of nuts

nut·house /'nʌthaʊs/ n [C] **1** informal a place that is loud, unpleasant, and not organized: I don't want to spend another night in this nuthouse. **2** old-fashioned informal a PSYCHIATRIC hospital

nut·meg /'nʌtmeg/ n [U] a brown powder made from the seed of a tropical tree, which is used as a spice

nu·tra·ceu·ti·cals /,njuːtrə'sjuːtɪkəlz $,nuːtrə-'suː-/ n [plural] foods that are designed to improve health and lower the risk of disease, for example by increasing the amount of VITAMINS in them, or removing some of the FAT; ☐ **functional foods**

nu·tri·ent /'njuːtriənt $ 'nuː-/ n [C] a chemical or food that provides what is needed for plants or animals to live and grow: The plant absorbs nutrients from the soil. —**nutrient** adj

nu·tri·ment /'njuːtrɪmənt $ 'nuː-/ n [U] formal a substance that gives plants and animals what they need in order to live and grow; ☐ **nourishment**

nu·tri·tion /njuː'trɪʃən $ nuː-/ n [U] **1** the process of giving or getting the right type of food for good health and growth; → **malnutrition**: Nutrition and exercise are essential to fitness and health. | a nutrition expert | **poor/good nutrition** Poor nutrition can cause heart disease in later life. **2** the science that deals with the effects of food, VITAMINS etc on people's health

nu·tri·tion·al /njuː'trɪʃənəl $ nuː-/ adj relating to the substances in food that help you to stay healthy: Cooking vegetables for too long lessens their **nutritional value**. | the nutritional requirements of pregnant women | nutritional deficiencies —**nutritionally** adv

nu·tri·tion·ist /njuː'trɪʃənɪst $ nuː-/ n [C] someone who has a special knowledge of nutrition

nu·tri·tious /njuː'trɪʃəs $ nuː-/ adj food that is nutritious is full of the natural substances that your body needs to stay healthy or to grow properly: Wholemeal bread is more nutritious than white bread. | Nuts and fruit make nutritious snacks. | The cookbook contains many simple yet **highly nutritious** meals.

nu·tri·tive /'njuːtrɪtɪv $ 'nuː-/ adj **1** relating to nutrition **2** formal nutritious

nuts¹ /nʌts/ adj [not before noun] informal **1** crazy: Are you nuts? | I'm going to **go nuts** (=become crazy) if I don't find a new job soon. | Turn that radio off. It's **driving** me **nuts** (=annoying me very much). **2 go nuts** spoken **a)** to become very excited because something good has just happened: The crowd went nuts after the third touchdown. **b)** to become very angry

about something: Mom's going to go nuts if you don't clean this mess up. **3 be nuts about/over sb/sth** to like someone or something very much: My wife is nuts about kids.

nuts² interjection AmE old-fashioned **1** used to emphasize that something bad or annoying has happened: Nuts! Now we're going to be late for the movie. **2 nuts to sb/sth** used when you are angrily refusing to listen to someone or do something: 'Nuts to that,' he sneered, and left.

nut·shell /'nʌtʃel/ n [C] **1 in a nutshell** used when you are stating the main facts about something in a short, clear way: Okay, that's our proposal in a nutshell. Any questions? **2** the hard outer part of a nut

nut·ter /'nʌtə $ -ər/ n [C] BrE informal a crazy person; ☐ **idiot**: an absolute nutter

nut·ty /'nʌti/ adj **1** informal crazy: It's another of his nutty ideas. | She's **nutty as a fruitcake** (=completely crazy). **2** tasting like, or containing, nuts: This coffee has a rich nutty flavour. | a nutty cake

nuz·zle /'nʌzəl/ also **nuzzle up** v [I always + adv/prep, T] to gently rub or press your nose or head against someone to show you like them: Evan leaned forward and began nuzzling her shoulder. | [+against] The horses were nuzzling up against each other.

NVQ /,en viː 'kjuː/ n [C] **National Vocational Qualification** an examination relating to the skills and knowledge involved in a particular type of work. NVQs are taken in Britain, usually by people who are already working.

NW the written abbreviation of **northwest** or **northwestern**

N-word also **N word** /'en wɜːd $ -wɜːrd/ n **the N-word** used when you are talking about the word 'nigger' but do not want to say it because it is offensive; → **f-word**

ny·lon /'naɪlɒn $ -lɑːn/ n **1** [U] a strong artificial material that is used to make plastics, clothes, rope etc: nylon fabric | The tent was made of nylon. → see picture at MATERIAL¹ **2 nylons** [plural] old-fashioned women's STOCKINGS that are made of nylon

nymph /nɪmf/ n [C] **1** one of the SPIRITS of nature who, according to ancient Greek and Roman stories, appeared as young girls living in trees, mountains, streams etc **2** literary a beautiful girl or young woman

nym·phet /nɪm'fet, 'nɪmfɪt $ nɪm'fet/ n [C] a young girl who is very sexually attractive

nym·pho·ma·ni·ac /,nɪmfə'meɪniæk/ also **nym·pho** /'nɪmfəʊ $ -foʊ/ informal n [C] a woman who wants to have sex often, usually with a lot of different men; ☐ **sex maniac** —**nymphomania** /-niə/ n [U]

NZ the written abbreviation of **New Zealand**

O, o

O, o /əʊ $ oʊ/ *plural* **O's, o's** *n* **1** [C,U] the 15th letter of the English alphabet **2** [U] *spoken* zero: *My phone number is six o four double two* (=60422). **3** [U] a common type of blood

O /əʊ $ oʊ/ *interjection* **1** used when praying to a god or, in the past, when speaking to someone in great authority: *O Lord, in you I put my trust.* **2** another form of OH

o' /ə/ *prep* 'of' written as people sometimes say it informally: *a drop o' whisky* → O'CLOCK

oaf /əʊf $ oʊf/ *n* [C] someone who is stupid or awkward, especially a man —**oafish** *adj*

oak S3 /əʊk $ oʊk/ *n* [C,U] a large tree that is common in northern countries, or the hard wood of this tree: *an oak door*

oak·en /ˈəʊkən $ ˈoʊ-/ *adj* [only before noun] *literary* made of oak: *an oaken chest*

oa·kum /ˈəʊkəm $ ˈoʊ-/ *n* [U] small pieces of old rope used for filling up small holes in the sides of wooden ships

OAP /ˌəʊ eɪ ˈpiː $ ˌoʊ-/ *n* [C] *BrE* **old age pensioner** a person who is old enough to receive a PENSION from the state: *special rates for OAPs*

oar /ɔː $ ɔːr/ *n* [C] **1** a long pole with a wide flat blade at one end, used for rowing a boat; → **paddle** **2** **put/stick/get your oar in** *BrE informal* to get involved in a conversation or situation when the other people do not want you to: *We were getting along fine until you stuck your oar in.*

oar·lock /ˈɔːlɒk $ ˈɔːrlɑːk/ *n* [C] *AmE* one of the small pieces of metal on a rowing boat that holds the oars

oars·man /ˈɔːzmən $ ˈɔːrz-/ *n plural* **oarsmen** /-mən/ [C] someone who rows a boat, especially in races; → **rower**

oars·wom·an /ˈɔːzˌwʊmən $ ˈɔːrz-/ *n plural* **oarswomen** /-ˌwɪmɪn/ [C] a woman who rows a boat, especially in races

o·a·sis /əʊˈeɪsɪs $ oʊ-/ *n plural* **oases** /-siːz/ [C] **1** a place with water and trees in a desert **2** a peaceful or pleasant place that is very different from everything around it: **an oasis of calm/serenity/tranquillity etc** *The park was an oasis of peace.*

oast house /ˈəʊst haʊs $ ˈoʊst-/ *n* [C] *BrE* a round building with a pointed top, built for drying HOPS

oat /əʊt $ oʊt/ *adj* [only before noun] made of OATS: *oat biscuits*

'oat cake *n* [C] *BrE* a BISCUIT made of oatmeal

oath /əʊθ $ oʊθ/ *n plural* **oaths** /əʊðz $ oʊðz/ [C] **1** a formal and very serious promise: **oath of loyalty/allegiance/obedience etc (to sb)** *an oath of allegiance to the Queen* | **swear/take an oath** *Servicemen have to swear an oath of loyalty to their country.* | *The president took the oath of office* (=promised to do a government job well before beginning it). **2** *law* a formal promise to tell the truth in a court of law: **on/under oath** *The evidence was given under oath.* | *Witnesses are required to take the oath* (=make this promise). **3** *written* an offensive word or phrase that expresses anger, surprise, shock etc: *He was shouting out oaths as they led him away.*

oat·meal /ˈəʊtmiːl $ ˈoʊt-/ *n* [U] **1** *BrE* crushed OATS used in cooking, especially for making BISCUITS or PORRIDGE **2** *AmE* a soft breakfast food made by boiling crushed OATS; ⊟ **porridge** *BrE* **3** a light brown colour

oats /əʊts $ oʊts/ *n* [plural] the grain from which flour or oatmeal is made and that is used in cooking, or in food for animals → **sow your wild oats** at SOW[1] (3)

ob·du·rate /ˈɒbdjʊrət $ ˈɑːbdʊ-/ *adj formal* very determined not to change your beliefs, actions, or feelings, in a way that seems unreasonable; ⊟ **stubborn**: *They argued, but he remained obdurate.* —**obduracy** *n* [U] —**obdurately** *adv*

o·be·di·ence /əˈbiːdiəns/ *n* [U] when someone does what they are told to do, or what a law, rule etc says they must do; ⊟ **disobedience**: [+to] *obedience to God* | **in obedience to sth** | *He lived in obedience to the church's teachings.* | **blind/unquestioning/complete obedience** (=complete obedience without any thought) *With blind obedience, I allowed my father to organize my life.* | *obedience classes for dogs and their owners*

o·be·di·ent /əˈbiːdiənt/ *adj* **1** always doing what you are told to do, or what the law, a rule etc says you must do; ⊟ **disobedient**: *an obedient child* | [+to] *citizens who are obedient to the law* **2** **your obedient servant** *old use* a phrase used to end a very formal letter —**obediently** *adv*

o·bei·sance /əʊˈbeɪsəns $ oʊ-/ *n* [C,U] *literary* respect and obedience to someone or something, often shown by bending your head or the upper part of your body: **make/pay obeisance (to sb/sth)** *They made obeisance to the sultan.*

ob·e·lisk /ˈɒbəlɪsk $ ˈɑː-, ˈoʊ-/ *n* [C] a tall pointed stone PILLAR, built to remind people of an event or of someone who has died

o·bese /əʊˈbiːs $ oʊ-/ *adj* very fat in a way that is unhealthy; → see box at FAT[1]

o·be·si·ty /əʊˈbiːsˌti $ oʊ-/ *n* [U] when someone is very fat in a way that is unhealthy

o·bey /əʊˈbeɪ, ə- $ oʊ-, ə-/ *v* [I,T] to do what someone in authority tells you, or what a law or rule says you must do; ⊟ **disobey**: *The little boy made no effort to obey.* | *'Sit!' he said, and the dog obeyed him instantly.* | **obey an order/command** *Soldiers are expected to obey orders without questioning them.* | **obey the law/rules** *Failure to obey the law can lead to a large fine.* ⚠ Do not say 'obey to' someone or something. **Obey** may be followed directly by a noun: *He refused to obey their orders* (NOT *He refused to obey to their orders*).

ob·fus·cate /ˈɒbfəskeɪt $ ˈɑːb-/ *v* [T] *formal* to deliberately make something unclear or difficult to understand —**obfuscation** /ˌɒbfəˈskeɪʃən $ ˌɑːb-/ *n* [U]

ob/gyn /ˌəʊbiː ˈɡaɪn $ ˌoʊ-/ *n informal especially AmE* **1** [U] the part of medical science that deals with OBSTETRICS and GYNAECOLOGY **2** [C] a doctor who works in this part of medical science

o·bit /ˈəʊbɪt $ ˈoʊ-/ *n* [C] *informal* an obituary

o·bit·u·a·ry /əˈbɪtʃuəri $ -tʃueri/ *n plural* **obituaries** [C] an article in a newspaper about the life of someone who has just died

ob·ject[1] S3 W2 /ˈɒbdʒɪkt $ ˈɑːb-/ *n*
1 THING [C] a solid thing that you can hold, touch, or see but that is not alive: *an everyday object such as a spoon* | *a small metal object* | *scientists studying plants, animals, or inanimate objects* (=things that are not alive) → UFO
2 AIM [singular] the purpose of a plan, action, or activity; → **goal**, **aim**: [+of] *The object of the game is to improve children's math skills.* | *My object was to explain the decision simply.* | *The customer will benefit most, and that is the object of the exercise* (=the purpose of what you are doing). ⚠ Do not use **object** to mean 'the thing you are working towards and hope to achieve'. Use **objective**: *We have not yet achieved our objective* (NOT *our object*).
3 **an object of pity/desire/ridicule etc** someone or something that is pitied, wanted etc: *She feared becoming an object of ridicule.* | *sports cars and other objects of desire* | **an object of study** → SEX OBJECT
4 **money/expense is no object** used to say that you are willing to spend a lot of money to get something: *Money's no object; I want the best.*
5 **object lesson** an event or story that shows you the right or wrong way of doing something: [+in] *The way ants work is an object lesson in order and organization.*

6 GRAMMAR [C] **a)** a noun or pronoun representing the person or thing that something is done to, for example 'the house' in 'We built the house.'; **☐ direct object b)** a noun or pronoun representing the person or thing that is joined by a PREPOSITION to another word or phrase, for example 'the table' in 'He sat on the table.' **c)** the person who is involved in the result of an action, for example 'her' in 'I gave her the book.'; **☐ indirect object**; → **subject**
7 COMPUTER [C] a combination of written information on a computer and instructions that act on the information, for example in the form of a document or a picture: *multimedia data objects*

ob·ject² S2 /əb'dʒekt/ *v*
1 [I] to feel or say that you oppose or disapprove of something: *If no one objects, I would like Mrs Harrison to be present.* | **object to (doing) sth** *Robson* **strongly objected** *to the terms of the contract.* | *I objected to having to rewrite the article.* | **I object** (=used in formal arguments, for example in a court of law) *Mr. Chairman, I object. That is an unfair allegation.*
2 [T] to state a fact or opinion as a reason for opposing or disapproving of something: **object that** *The group objected that the policy would prevent patients from receiving the best treatment.* | *'My name's not Sonny,' the child objected.* → OBJECTOR

'object ˌcode *n* [U] MACHINE CODE

ob·jec·ti·fy /əb'dʒektⁱ¹faɪ/ *v* **objectified, objectifying, objectifies** [T] *formal* to treat a person or idea as a physical object: *a culture that objectifies women* —**objectification** /əb,dʒektⁱf¹ə'keɪʃən/ *n* [U]

ob·jec·tion S3 /əb'dʒekʃən/ *n*
1 [C,U] a reason that you have for opposing or disapproving of something, or something you say that expresses this

raise/voice/make an objection (to sth)
have no objection (to sth)
strong objection
moral objection
religious objection
do sth over the objections of sb (=do something despite someone's objections)

Her objection was that he was too young. | [+to] *Lawyers* **raised** no **objections** *to the plan.* | *Normally he would* **have no objection** *to the whole world knowing his business.* | *Local residents raised* **strong objections** *to the building application.* | *He had* **moral objections** *to killing animals for food.* | *the* **religious objections** *of some parents* | *The bill was passed* **over the objections** *of many Democrats.*

2 objection! *spoken formal* said by lawyers to a judge in a court when they think that what another lawyer has just said should not be allowed

ob·jec·tion·a·ble /əb'dʒekʃənəbəl/ *adj formal* unpleasant and likely to offend people; **☐ offensive**: *objectionable odours* | *This programme contains scenes some viewers may* **find objectionable**. —**objectionably** *adv*

ob·jec·tive¹ W3 /əb'dʒektɪv/ *n* [C]
1 something that you are trying hard to achieve, especially in business or politics; **☐ goal**

achieve/meet an objective
accomplish an objective (=achieve an objective)
have an objective
set an objective (=decide what your objective is)
main/primary/principal objective
clear/specific objective
career objectives
business objectives

He vowed to **achieve** *certain* **objectives** *before the end of his presidency.* | *the best way to* **accomplish** *your* **objectives** | *The degree program* **has** *two main* **objectives.** | *Managers should* **set** *specific performance* **objectives** *for their teams.* | *The* **main objective** *was to improve children's knowledge of geography.* | *A* **clear**

objective was set and adhered to. | *One of your first* **business objectives** *should be to get your own office.*
2 a place that you are trying to reach, especially in a military attack: *The 4th Division's objective was a town twenty miles to the east.*

objective² S3 *adj*
1 based on facts, or making a decision that is based on facts rather than on your feelings or beliefs; **☐ subjective**: **objective assessment/measurement/description etc** *It's hard to give an objective opinion about your own children.* | *Scientists need to be objective when doing research.* | **purely/totally/completely objective** *the importance of a completely objective, independent press*
2 *formal* existing outside the mind as something real, not only as an idea: *The world has an objective reality.* —**objectivity** /,ɒbdʒek'tɪvⁱ¹ti $,ɑːb-/ *n* [U]

ob·jec·tive·ly /əb'dʒektɪvli/ *adv* if you consider something objectively, you try to think about the facts, and not be influenced by your own feelings or opinions: *Look at your skills objectively when deciding on a career change.*

ob·jec·tor /əb'dʒektə $ -tər/ *n* [C] someone who states or shows that they oppose something: [+to] *objectors to the new motorway* → CONSCIENTIOUS OBJECTOR

'object-ˌoriented *adj* object-oriented computer programming languages are based on objects that are arranged in a HIERARCHY: *object-oriented programming* | *object-oriented languages*

ob·jet d'art /,ɒbʒeɪ 'dɑː $,ɑːbʒeɪ 'dɑːr/ *n plural* **objets d'art** *(same pronunciation)* [C] a small object used for decoration, such as a work of art

ob·la·tion /ə'bleɪʃən/ *n* [C,U] *formal* a gift that is offered to God or a god, or the act of offering the gift

ob·li·gate /'ɒblⁱ¹geɪt $ 'ɑːb-/ *v* [T usually passive] *especially AmE* **1** to make someone have to do something, because it is the law, their duty, or the right thing to do; **☐ oblige**: **obligate sb to do sth** *Tenants are obligated to pay their rent on time.* **2 be/feel obligated** to feel that you must do something because it is right or because someone has done something for you, **☐ be/feel obliged**: **be/feel obligated to do sth** *Ava felt obligated to help her mother, even if it meant leaving college.* | **be/feel obligated to sb** *Watson felt obligated to him for the loan.* → OBLIGE

ob·li·ga·tion W3 /,ɒblⁱ¹'geɪʃən $,ɑːb-/ *n* [C,U] a moral or legal duty to do something

have an obligation (to do sth)
be under an obligation (to do sth) (=have an obligation)
be under no obligation (to do sth)
meet/fulfil an obligation (=do something that is your duty)
honour an obligation *formal* (=meet an obligation)
impose an obligation *formal* (=make someone have an obligation)
owe sb an obligation *formal* (=feel that you must do something for someone)
moral/legal/social obligation
contractual obligation (=something that a contract says you must do)
a sense of obligation

[+to] *America's obligation to its allies* | *Employers* **have an obligation** *to treat all employees equally.* | *Parents* **are under a** *legal* **obligation** *to educate their children.* | *You* **are under no obligation to** *buy any more books.* | *Greater resources are needed to* **meet** *these* **obligations.** | *the rights and* **obligations imposed on** *them by treaties* | *The government must pay for health care for war veterans – it is an* **obligation** *we* **owe** *to them.* | *a* **moral obligation** *to help the poor* | *He stayed with the team out of a* **sense of obligation**.

ob·lig·a·to·ry /ə'blɪgətəri $ -tɔːri/ *adj* **1** *formal* something that is obligatory must be done because of a law, rule etc; ◼ **compulsory**, **mandatory**: **it is obligatory for sb (to do sth)** *It is obligatory for companies to provide details of their industrial processes.* **2** [only before noun] used humorously to describe something that is always done or included in a particular situation: *She offered him the obligatory cup of tea.*

o·blige S3 /ə'blaɪdʒ/ *v formal*
1 [T usually passive] if you are obliged to do something, you have to do it because the situation, the law, a duty etc makes it necessary: **oblige sb to do sth** *The minister was obliged to report at least once every six months.* | *Circumstances had obliged him to sell the business.* | **feel obliged to do sth** (=feel that you have a duty to do something) *Many parents feel obliged to pay for at least part of the wedding.* ⚠ Do not use **oblige** when you are talking about making someone do something they do not want to do. Use **force** or **make**: *No one can force (NOT oblige) you to stay in a job that you hate.*
2 [I,T] to do something that someone has asked you to do: *It's always a good idea to oblige important clients.* | **happy/glad/ready etc to oblige** *If you need a ride home, I'd be happy to oblige.*
3 I'd be obliged if *spoken formal* used to make a polite request: *I'd be obliged if you'd treat this matter as strictly confidential.*
4 (I'm) much obliged (to you) *spoken old-fashioned* used to thank someone very politely

Frequencies of **be obliged to**, **must**, and **have to/have got to** in spoken and written English.

This graph shows that the expressions **have to** and **have got to** are much more common in spoken English than **must** or **be obliged to**. **Have got to** is only used in British English. **Must** is more common in written English. **Be obliged to** is much less common than the others and is only used to say that someone must do something because of a rule or law, or because the situation forces them to do it.

o·blig·ing /ə'blaɪdʒɪŋ/ *adj* willing and eager to help: *The shop assistant was very obliging.* —**obligingly** *adv*

o·blique¹ /ə'bliːk/ *adj* **1** not expressed in a direct way; ◼ **indirect**: *an oblique reference to his drinking problem* **2** not looking, pointing etc directly at something: *an oblique glance* **3 oblique line/stroke etc** a sloping line etc **4 oblique angle** *technical* an angle that is not 90 degrees —**obliquely** *adv*

oblique² *n* [C] *BrE* a mark (/) used for writing FRACTIONS or for separating numbers, letters, words etc; ◼ **slash**

o·blit·er·ate /ə'blɪtəreɪt/ *v* [T] **1** to destroy something completely so that nothing remains: *Hiroshima was nearly obliterated by the atomic bomb.* **2** to remove a thought, feeling, or memory from someone's mind: *Nothing could obliterate the memory of those tragic events.* **3** to cover something completely so that it cannot be seen: *Then the fog came down, obliterating everything.* —**obliteration** /ə,blɪtə'reɪʃən/ *n* [U]

o·bliv·i·on /ə'blɪviən/ *n* [U] **1** when something is completely forgotten or no longer important: **sink/slip/pass etc into oblivion** *Wind power presents too many advantages to be allowed to sink into oblivion.* | *The loser's name has been* **consigned to oblivion** (=completely forgotten). **2** the state of being unconscious

or of not noticing what is happening: *the oblivion of sleep* | *He had drunk himself into oblivion.*

o·bliv·i·ous /ə'blɪviəs/ *adj* [not before noun] not knowing about or not noticing something that is happening around you; ◼ **unaware**: **[+of/to]** *He seemed oblivious to the fact that he had hurt her.* | **seemingly/apparently oblivious** *Congress was seemingly oblivious to these events.* —**obliviousness** *n* [U]

ob·long /'ɒblɒŋ $ 'ɑːblɒːŋ/ *adj* **1** *BrE* an oblong shape has four straight sides at 90 degrees to each other, two of which are longer than the other two; ◼ **rectangular**: *an oblong table* **2** *AmE* an oblong shape is much longer than it is wide: *an oblong leaf* —**oblong** *n* [C]

ob·lo·quy /'ɒbləkwi $ 'ɑːb-/ *n* [U] *formal* **1** very strong, offensive criticism **2** loss of respect and honour

ob·nox·ious /əb'nɒkʃəs $ -'nɑːk-/ *adj* very offensive, unpleasant, or rude: *She's really obnoxious.* | *an obnoxious idea* | *obnoxious odours* —**obnoxiously** *adv* —**obnoxiousness** *n* [U]

o·boe /'əʊbəʊ $ 'oʊboʊ/ *n* [C] a wooden musical instrument like a narrow tube, which you play by blowing air through a REED —**oboist** *n* [C]

ob·scene /əb'siːn/ *adj* **1** relating to sex in a way that is shocking and offensive; → **rude**: *Bradford made an* **obscene gesture**. | *obscene phone calls* (=calls from an unknown person saying obscene things) | *obscene photographs* **2** extremely unfair, immoral, or unpleasant, especially in a way that makes you angry: *Some players earn obscene amounts of money.* | *an obscene act of cruelty* —**obscenely** *adv*

ob·scen·i·ty /əb'senəti/ *n plural* **obscenities** **1** [U] sexually offensive language or behaviour, especially in a book, play, film etc: *laws against obscenity* **2** [C usually plural] a sexually offensive word or action; → **swear**: *drunken youths screaming obscenities*

ob·scu·ran·tis·m /,ɒbskjʊ'ræntɪzəm $,ɑːb-/ *n* [U] *formal* the practice of deliberately stopping ideas and facts from being known —**obscurantist** *adj*

ob·scure¹ /əb'skjʊə $ -'skjʊr/ *adj* **1** not well known and usually not very important: *an obscure poet* | *The details of his life remain obscure.* **2** difficult to understand: *obscure legal phrases* | *For some obscure reason, the group is very popular.* —**obscurely** *adv*

obscure² *v* [T] **1** to make something difficult to know or understand: *Recent successes have* **obscured the fact** *that the company is still in trouble.* **2** to prevent something from being seen or heard clearly: *The view was obscured by mist.*

ob·scu·ri·ty /əb'skjʊərəti $ -'skjʊr-/ *n plural* **obscurities** **1** [U] the state of not being known or remembered: **fade/slide/sink etc into obscurity** *The group produced two albums before disappearing into obscurity.* | **live/work/remain etc in obscurity** *O'Brien died in obscurity.* | **from obscurity to sth** *She rose from obscurity to stardom.* **2** [C,U] something that is difficult to understand, or the quality of being difficult to understand: *obscurities in the text*

ob·se·quies /'ɒbsɪkwiz $ 'ɑːb-/ *n* [plural] *formal* a funeral ceremony

ob·se·qui·ous /əb'siːkwiəs/ *adj* very eager to please or agree with people who are powerful – used in order to show disapproval; ◼ **servile**: *an obsequious smile* —**obsequiously** *adv* —**obsequiousness** *n* [U]

ob·ser·va·ble /əb'zɜːvəbəl $ -ɜːr-/ *adj* something that is observable can be seen or noticed; → **noticeable**: *an observable change in behaviour* —**observably** *adv*

ob·ser·vance /əb'zɜːvəns $ -ɜːr-/ *n* **1** [U] when someone obeys a law or does something because it is part of a religion, custom, or ceremony: **[+of]** *the observance of a peace agreement* | *the strict observance of Islam* | *the Memorial Day observance* **2** [C] something you do as part of a ceremony, especially a religious ceremony: *religious observances*

ob·ser·vant /əb'zɜːvənt $ -ɜːr-/ *adj* **1** good or quick at noticing things: *a quiet and observant person* | *Supervisors are trained to be observant.* | *the writer's* **observant eye** *for detail* **2** obeying laws, religious rules etc: *observant Jews*

ob·ser·va·tion W3 /ˌɒbzə'veɪʃən $ ˌɑːbzər-/ *n*
1 [C,U] the process of watching something or someone carefully for a period of time

> **be under observation** (=being watched carefully)
> **keep sb under observation**
> **sb's powers of observation** (=someone's ability to notice things)
> **close/careful/detailed observation**
> **direct observation**
> **personal observation**

[+of] *Bloomfield's approach to linguistics was based on observation of the language.* | *He spent two nights under* **under close observation** *in hospital.* | *His orders were to* **keep** *the men* **under observation**. | *Art classes help develop children's* **powers of observation**. | *Careful observation suggests that this is not the case.* | *Detailed observations were carried out on the behaviour of the students.* | *From their* **direct observations**, *children absorb a model of marriage.*

2 [C] something that you notice when watching something or someone: *Some interesting observations emerged from this research.*

3 [C] a spoken or written remark about something you have noticed: [+on] *Darwin's observations on the habits of certain birds* [+about] | *Paz* **makes** *some* **observations** *about the role of the critic.*

4 [U] the act of obeying a law etc; ◨ observance
—**observational** *adj*

obser'vation ,post *n* [C] a position from which an enemy can be watched

obser'vation ,tower *n* [C] a tall structure built so that you can see a long way, used to watch prisoners, look for forest fires etc

ob·ser·va·to·ry /əb'zɜːvətəri $ əb'zɜːrvətɔːri/ *n plural* **observatories** [C] a special building from which scientists watch the moon, stars, weather etc

ob·serve W2 /əb'zɜːv $ -ɜːrv/ *v*
1 [T not in progressive] *formal* to see and notice something: *Scientists have observed a drop in ozone levels over the Antarctic.* | **observe that** *It was observed that 40 percent of patients had high blood pressure.* | **observe sb doing sth** *Officers observed him driving at 90 miles per hour.* | *Predators have been observed to avoid attacking brightly coloured species.*

2 [I,T] to watch something or someone carefully: *The police have been observing his movements.* | *One student performs the experiment, while his partner observes.* | **observe what/how/where** *Observe how the people in the group interact.*

3 [T] *formal* to say or write what you have noticed about a situation: *'Sid looks ill,' Doherty observed.* | **observe that** *Keynes observed that humans fall into two classes.*

4 [T] to do what you are supposed to do according to a law or agreement; ◨ obey: *So far the ceasefire has been observed by both sides.*

5 [T] to do things and obey laws that are part of a religion or custom

ob·serv·er /əb'zɜːvə $ -ɜːrvər/ *n* [C] **1** someone who regularly watches or pays attention to particular things, events, situations etc: [+of] *an observer of nature* | *political observers* | *Observers are predicting a fall in interest rates.* **2** someone who attends meetings, classes, events etc to check what is happening: *The UN sent observers to the peace talks.* | *Independent observers monitored the elections.* **3** someone who sees or looks at something: *reports from observers at sea and on dry land* | **casual observer** (=someone looking at something but not very carefully) *A casual observer would have guessed his age at 70.*

ob·sess /əb'ses/ *v* **1** [T usually passive] if something or someone obsesses you, you think or worry about them all the time and you cannot think about anything else – used to show disapproval: **be obsessed by/with sth/sb** *A lot of young girls are obsessed by their weight.* | *Jody's been obsessed with some lifeguard for months.* **2 be obsessing about/over sth/sb** *informal* to think about something or someone much more than is necessary or sensible: *Stop obsessing about your hair. It's fine.*

ob·ses·sion /əb'seʃən/ *n* [C,U] an extreme unhealthy interest in something or worry about something, which stops you from thinking about anything else

> **become an obsession**
> **unhealthy/dangerous obsession**
> **sexual obsession**
> **national/American/British etc obsession**
> **to the point of obsession**
> **border on/upon obsession** (=be almost as bad as an obsession)

Gambling **became an obsession**, *and he eventually lost everything.* | [+with] *an* **unhealthy obsession** *with being thin* | *The current obsession with exam results is actually harming children's education.* | *The game pachinko became a* **national obsession.** | *He has an enthusiasm for art,* **to the point of obsession** *in my opinion.* | *She looked after him with a devotion* **bordering on obsession.**

— **obsessional** *adj*

ob·ses·sive[1] /əb'sesɪv/ *adj* thinking or worrying about something all the time, so that you do not think about other things enough – used to show disapproval: *an obsessive concern with cleanliness and order* | **obsessive about (doing) sth** *I try to stay fit, but I'm not obsessive about it.* —**obsessively** *adv*

obsessive[2] *n* [C] *BrE technical* someone whose behaviour is obsessive

ob,sessive-com'pulsive *adj technical* someone who is obsessive-compulsive tends to repeat particular actions in a way that is not necessary, because they have strong anxious feelings: *obsessive-compulsive behaviour*

ob·sid·i·an /əb'sɪdiən/ *n* [U] a type of rock that looks like black glass

ob·so·les·cence /ˌɒbsə'lesəns $ ˌɑːb-/ *n* [U] **1** when something becomes old-fashioned and no longer useful, because something newer and better has been invented **2 planned/built-in obsolescence** when a product is designed so that it will soon become unfashionable or impossible to use and will need replacing: *the planned obsolescence of some software*

ob·so·les·cent /ˌɒbsə'lesənt◂ $ ˌɑːb-/ *adj formal* becoming obsolete

ob·so·lete /'ɒbsəliːt $ ˌɑːbsə'liːt/ *adj* no longer useful, because something newer and better has been invented; → **out-of-date**: *obsolete weapons* | *computer hardware that quickly* **became obsolete** | *Will computers* **render** (=make) *books* **obsolete**?

ob·sta·cle /'ɒbstəkəl $ 'ɑːb-/ *n* [C]
1 something that makes it difficult to achieve something

> **put/place obstacles in the way (of sth)**
> **overcome an obstacle**
> **remove an obstacle**
> **main/biggest/greatest obstacle**
> **major/serious obstacle**
> **insuperable obstacle** (=one that makes it impossible to achieve something)
> **formidable obstacle** (=a very difficult obstacle)
> **legal obstacle**
> **political obstacle**

[+to] *Fear of change is an obstacle to progress.* | *The tax* **puts obstacles in the way of** *companies trying to*

develop trade overseas. | Women still have to **overcome** many **obstacles** to gain equality. | We want to **remove** all **obstacles** to travel between the two countries. | the single **biggest obstacle** to a Conservative victory in the next election | There are **formidable obstacles** on the road to peace.
2 an object which blocks your way, so that you must try to go around it

'obstacle course n [C] **1** a line of objects which people have to jump over, climb through etc in a race **2** a series of difficulties which must be dealt with to achieve a particular aim **3** an area of land with special equipment that soldiers must run through, climb over etc, as part of their training; ◩ **assault course** BrE

'obstacle race n [C] BrE a type of race in which runners have to jump over or climb through various objects

ob·ste·tri·cian /ˌɒbstɪ̥ˈtrɪʃən $ ˌɑːb-/ n [C] a doctor who has special training in obstetrics

ob·stet·rics /əbˈstetrɪks/ n [U] the part of medical science that deals with the birth of children —**obstetric** adj

ob·sti·nate /ˈɒbstᵻ̥nᵻ̥t $ ˈɑːb-/ adj **1** determined not to change your ideas, behaviour, opinions etc, even when other people think you are being unreasonable; ◩ **stubborn**: He was the most obstinate man I've ever met. | Don't be so obstinate! | an **obstinate refusal** to obey **2** [only before noun] BrE difficult to deal with or get rid of: obstinate stains | a complex and obstinate issue —**obstinately** adv —**obstinacy** n [U]

ob·strep·e·rous /əbˈstrepərəs/ adj formal noisy and refusing to do what someone asks; → **awkward** —**obstreperously** adv

ob·struct /əbˈstrʌkt/ v [T] **1** to block a road, passage etc; ◩ **block**: A small aircraft was obstructing the runway. | The column obstructed our view of the stage. **2** to prevent someone from doing something or something from happening, by making it difficult; ◩ **block**: The group is trying to obstruct the peace process. | He was fined for obstructing the work of the police.

ob·struc·tion /əbˈstrʌkʃən/ n **1** [C,U] when something blocks a road, passage, tube etc, or the thing that blocks it; ◩ **blockage**: an operation to remove an obstruction from her throat | Police can remove a vehicle that is **causing an obstruction**. | [+of] an unlawful obstruction of the highway; → see picture at BARRIER **2** [U] when someone or something prevents or delays a legal or political process: [+of] the obstruction of vital legislation | He was found guilty of **obstruction of justice**. **3** [U] an offence in football, HOCKEY etc in which a player gets between an opponent and the ball

ob·struc·tion·is·m /əbˈstrʌkʃənɪzəm/ n [U] formal when someone tries to prevent or delay a legal or political process —**obstructionist** n [C]

ob·struc·tive /əbˈstrʌktɪv/ adj **1** trying to prevent someone from doing something, by deliberately making it difficult for them: an obstructive official | obstructive tactics **2** medical relating to a blocked tube, passage etc in the body: obstructive symptoms

ob·tain S2 W2 /əbˈteɪn/ v formal
1 [T] to get something that you want, especially through your own effort, skill, or work; ◩ **get**: **obtain sth from sb/sth** Further information can be obtained from head office. | You will need to obtain permission from the principal. | **obtain sth through sth** the results obtained through these surveys
2 [I not in progressive] if a situation, system, or rule obtains, it continues to exist: These conditions no longer obtain.

ob·tain·a·ble /əbˈteɪnəbəl/ adj formal able to be obtained: The form is obtainable at your local post office.

ob·trude /əbˈtruːd/ v [I,T] formal if something obtrudes, or you obtrude something, it becomes noticeable where it is not wanted → **INTRUDE**

ob·tru·sive /əbˈtruːsɪv/ adj noticeable in an unpleasant or annoying way; ◩ **unobtrusive**: obtrusive TV antennas | The waiters were friendly and not obtrusive.

ob·tuse /əbˈtjuːs $ -ˈtuːs/ adj formal slow to understand things, in a way that is annoying: 'But why?' said Charles, being deliberately obtuse. —**obtuseness** n [U]

ob,tuse 'angle n [C] technical an angle between 90 and 180 degrees; → **acute angle**

ob·verse /ˈɒbvɜːs $ ˈɑːbvɜːrs/ n [singular] **1** formal the opposite of a particular situation or feeling; ◩ **opposite**: [+of] The obverse of victory is defeat. **2** the **obverse** technical the front side of a coin or MEDAL; ◩ **reverse**

ob·vi·ate /ˈɒbvieɪt $ ˈɑːb-/ v [T] formal to prevent or avoid a problem or the need to do something; ◩ **eliminate**: The new treatment **obviates the need** for surgery.

ob·vi·ous S2 W2 /ˈɒbviəs $ ˈɑːb-/ adj
1 easy to notice or understand: The obvious way of reducing pollution is to use cars less. | For **obvious reasons** the police cannot give any more details about the case. | The most **obvious example** of an information source is a dictionary. | The obvious question is – does his invention work? | The quality of his cooking is **immediately obvious**. | **it is obvious (that)** It was obvious that Gina was lying. | [+to] It might be obvious to you, but it isn't to me.
2 behaving in a way that shows you want something very badly, when other people think this behaviour is not suitable: I know you really like him, but you don't have to be so obvious about it.
3 **the/an obvious choice** the person or thing that you would expect everyone to choose: Teaching is an obvious choice of career if you like working with children.
4 **the obvious thing (to do)** what clearly seems the best thing to do: The obvious thing is to speak to her before you make a decision.
5 **state the obvious** to say something that is already obvious so it is not necessary to say it: It is stating the obvious, but regular measurement of blood pressure is essential in older people. —**obviousness** n [U]

ob·vi·ous·ly S1 W2 /ˈɒbviəsli $ ˈɑːb-/ adv used to mean that a fact can easily be noticed or understood: We're obviously going to need more help. | Your research has obviously been very thorough. | Obviously, this is going to take some time. | Cost is obviously important. | She frowned and was obviously puzzled.

oc·ca·sion[1] S1 W2 /əˈkeɪʒən/ n
1 TIME **a)** [C] a time when something happens: **on ... occasion** I've seen Jana with them on several occasions. | On this occasion we were sitting in a park in Madrid. | She had met Zahid on two separate occasions. **b)** [singular] a suitable or favourable time: [+for] This was the occasion for expressions of friendship by the two presidents. ⚠ Do not use **occasion** when you mean 'a time when it is possible for you to do what you want to do'. Use **opportunity** or **chance**: Do not waste this opportunity (NOT this occasion).
2 SPECIAL EVENT [C] an important social event or ceremony: I'm saving this bottle of champagne for a **special occasion**. | They presented him with a gift to **mark the occasion** (=celebrate it). | [+of] His funeral was a great occasion of public mourning.
3 CAUSE/REASON [U] formal a cause or reason: His remark **was the occasion of** a bitter quarrel. | I **had occasion to** call on him last year.
4 **if (the) occasion arises** formal if a particular action ever becomes necessary: If ever the occasion arises when I want advice, you're the first person I'll come to.
5 **on occasion** sometimes but not often: On occasion prisoners were allowed visits from their families.
6 **on the occasion of sth** formal at the time of an important event: on the occasion of his second wedding → **rise to the occasion** at RISE[1] (9); → **a sense of occasion** at SENSE[1] (1)

occasion² *v* [T] *formal* to cause something: *She had a long career break occasioned by her husband's job being moved to Paris.* | **occasion sb sth** *Your behaviour has occasioned us a great deal of anxiety.*

oc·ca·sion·al S3 W3 /əˈkeɪʒənəl/ *adj* [only before noun] happening sometimes but not often or regularly: *He made occasional visits to London.* | *They had an occasional coffee together after shopping.* | *He only has occasional use of a car.* | *We should have enough money left for the occasional trip.*

oc·ca·sion·al·ly S2 W3 /əˈkeɪʒənəli/ *adv* sometimes, but not regularly and not often: *Occasionally Alice would look up from her books.* | *We only see each other very occasionally* (=rarely). → **FREQUENCY**

oc'casional ˌtable *n* [C] a small light table that can be easily moved

Oc·ci·dent /ˈɒksɪdənt $ ˈɑːksɪdənt, -dent/ **the Occident** *literary* the western part of the world, especially Europe and the Americas; → **Orient**

oc·ci·den·tal /ˌɒksɪˈdentəl◂ $ ˌɑːk-/ *n* [C] *old-fashioned* someone from the western part of the world —**occidental** *adj*

oc·cult¹ /ˈɒkʌlt, əˈkʌlt $ əˈkʌlt, ˈɑːkʌlt/ *n* **the occult** mysterious practices and powers involving magic and SPIRITS: *He was a strange man who dabbled in the occult.* —**occultist** *n* [C]

occult² *adj* [only before noun] magical and mysterious: *occult practices* | *the occult powers*

oc·cu·pan·cy /ˈɒkjʊpənsi $ ˈɑːk-/ *n* [U] *formal* **1** the number of people who stay, work, or live in a room or building at the same time: **single/multiple occupancy** *single occupancy room rates* | *Hotels in Tokyo enjoy over 90% occupancy.* **2** someone's use of a building, hotel, or other space, for living or working in, or the period during which they live or work there: *The day for changing from one occupancy to the next was on a Saturday.*

oc·cu·pant /ˈɒkjʊpənt $ ˈɑːk-/ *n* [C] **1** someone who lives in a house, room etc; → **resident**: *The furniture had been left by the previous occupants.* | [+of] *Police are still trying to trace the occupants of the house which was destroyed by fire.* **2** someone who is in a room, vehicle etc at a particular time: *Neither of the car's two occupants was injured.*

oc·cu·pa·tion S3 W3 /ˌɒkjʊˈpeɪʃən $ ˌɑːk-/ *n*
1 [C] a job or profession: *Please state your name, address and occupation.* | *professional and managerial occupations* | *manual occupations* → see box at **JOB**
2 [U] when a large group of people enter a place and take control of it, especially by military force: [+of] *the German occupation of France* | **under occupation** *The area is under occupation* (=controlled by a foreign army).
3 [C] a way of spending your time; ☐ **pastime**: *One of my childhood occupations was collecting stamps.*
4 [U] when someone lives or stays in a building or place: *When the first scientists came to the region they found little evidence of human occupation.*

oc·cu·pa·tion·al /ˌɒkjʊˈpeɪʃənəl◂ $ ˌɑːk-/ *adj* [only before noun] relating to, or caused by your job: *occupational pension schemes* | *an occupational health centre* | *occupational disease* | *Getting injured is an occupational hazard* (=a risk that always exists in a particular job or activity) *of the sport.* —**occupationally** *adv*

ˌoccupational 'therapist *n* [C] someone whose job is to help people get better after an illness by giving them activities to do

ˌoccupational 'therapy *n* [U] the job of an occupational therapist

oc·cu·pied /ˈɒkjʊpaɪd $ ˈɑːk-/ *adj* **1** [not before noun] busy doing something: [+with] *His time was*

1 000, 2 000, 3 000, most frequent words in S poken and W ritten English

O

occupations

gardener

optician *BrE*/ optometrist *AmE*

nurse

dentist

teacher

photographer

doctor

welder

decorator

lumberjack

courier

policeman/policewoman

waiter

masseuse

florist

mechanic

chef

occupied with the children. | *She's **fully occupied** with work.* | *The museum has enough exhibits to **keep** anyone **occupied** for an hour or two.* | *I kept myself occupied by watching television.* **2** [not before noun] a bed, chair, room etc that is occupied is being used: *Sorry, this seat is occupied.* **3** an occupied place is controlled by an army from another country: *occupied territories*

oc·cu·pi·er /'ɒkjʊpaɪə $ 'ɑːkjʊpaɪər/ n [C] especially BrE **1** someone who lives in or uses a particular house, piece of land etc; → **resident**: *A large proportion of occupiers now own their homes.* **2** a member of an army that has occupied a city or country by force → **owner-occupier** at OWNER-OCCUPIED

oc·cu·py S3 W2 /'ɒkjʊpaɪ $ 'ɑːk-/ v occupied, occupying, occupies [T]
1 STAIN A PLACE to live or stay in a place: *He occupies the house without paying any rent.* | *The building was purchased and occupied by its new owners last year.*
2 FILL TIME if something occupies you or your time, you are busy doing it: *Football occupies most of my leisure time.* | **occupy sb with (doing) sth** *Only six percent of police time is occupied with criminal incidents.*
3 CONTROL BY FORCE to enter a place in a large group and keep control of it, especially by military force; → **invade**: *an occupying army* | *Students occupied Sofia university on Monday.*
4 FILL SPACE to fill a particular amount of space: *Family photos occupied almost the entire wall.*
5 occupy sb's mind/thoughts/attention if something occupies your mind etc, you think about that thing more than anything else; → **preoccupy**: *Work will occupy your mind and help you forget about him.*
6 USE to use something such as a room, seat, or bed: *Many patients who are occupying hospital beds could be transferred to other places.*
7 OFFICIAL POSITION to have an official position or job: *Before becoming prime minister, he had already occupied several cabinet posts.* → **occupied**

oc·cur S1 W1 /ə'kɜː $ ə'kɜːr/ v occurred, occurring [i] formal
1 to happen: *A third of accidental deaths occur in the home.* | *The explosion occurred at 5.30 a.m.*
2 [always + adv/prep] to happen or exist in a particular place or situation: [+in/among etc] *Whooping cough occurs mainly in young children.* | *The highest rates of unemployment occur in the inner urban areas.*
  occur to sb phr v
  if an idea or thought occurs to you, it suddenly comes into your mind: **it occurs to sb to do sth** *I suppose it didn't occur to you to phone the police?* | *It never seems to occur to my children to contact me.* | **it occurs to sb (that)** *It had never occurred to him that he might be falling in love with her.*

oc·cur·rence /ə'kʌrəns $ ə'kɜː-/ n **1** [C] something that happens; → **occurrence: frequent/rare/common occurrence** *Laughter was a rare occurrence in his classroom.* | *Flooding in the area is a common occurrence.* **2** [singular] the fact of something happening: [+of] *The frequent occurrence of earthquakes in the area means that the buildings must be specially designed to withstand the force.*

OCD /ˌəʊ siː 'diː $ ˌoʊ-/ n [U] medical **obsessive-compulsive disorder** a form of mental illness in which a person does the same thing again and again and cannot stop doing it, for example washing their hands many times a day

o·cean S3 W2 /'əʊʃən $ 'oʊ-/ n
1 the ocean especially AmE the great mass of salt water that covers most of the Earth's surface; ⊟ **the sea**: *She stood on the beach, gazing at the ocean.* | *I like to swim in the ocean when it's warm enough.*
2 [C] one of the very large areas of sea on the Earth's surface: *the Pacific Ocean*

3 oceans of sth informal a lot of something, especially a liquid: *oceans of champagne* → **a drop in the ocean** at DROP² (8)

o·cean·front /'əʊʃən,frʌnt $ 'oʊ-/ adj [only before noun] AmE on the land along the edge of an ocean; ⊟ **seafront** BrE: *oceanfront houses*

o·cean·go·ing /'əʊʃən,gəʊɪŋ $ 'oʊʃən,goʊ-/ adj [only before noun] an oceangoing ship is designed to sail across the sea rather than a river or lake: *an oceangoing tanker*

o·ce·an·ic /ˌəʊʃi'ænɪk◂ $ ˌoʊ-/ adj [usually before noun] relating to the ocean: *an oceanic island* | *oceanic waters*

o·cean·og·ra·phy /ˌəʊʃən'ɒgrəfi $ ˌoʊʃən'ɑːg-/ n [U] the scientific study of the ocean —**oceanographer** n [C]

o·ce·lot /'ɒsɪlɒt $ 'ɑːsɪlɑːt, 'oʊ-/ n [C] a large American wild cat that has a pattern of spots on its back

och /ɒx $ ɒːx/ interjection used in Scotland and parts of Ireland to express surprise or to emphasize a remark

o·chre BrE; **ocher** AmE /'əʊkə $ 'oʊkər/ n [U] **1** a type of reddish-yellow earth used in paints **2** the reddish-yellow colour of ochre —**ochre** adj

ock·er /'ɒkə $ 'ɑːkər/ n [C] an Australian man – used in Australia and New Zealand: *G'day Ocker!*

o'clock S1 W3 /ə'klɒk $ ə'klɑːk/ adv **one o'clock/two o'clock etc** one of the times when the clock shows the exact hour as a number from 1 to 12: *It's already 9 o'clock.* | *The meeting is at 10 o'clock.*

O'CLOCK
Do not use **o'clock** for times that include minutes or parts of an hour: *ten past nine* (NOT *ten past nine o'clock*) | *I get up at 6.30* (NOT *6.30 o'clock*)
Do not use **o'clock** when the time is written in the form 1.00, 2.00, 3.00 etc. Write *1 o'clock, 2 am,* or simply *3.00.*

OCR /ˌəʊ siː 'ɑː $ ˌoʊ siː 'ɑːr/ n [U] technical **optical character recognition** computer software that recognizes numbers and letters of the alphabet which are written on paper, so that information from paper documents can be SCANNED into a computer

-ocracy /ɒkrəsi $ ɑːk-/ also **-cracy** suffix [in nouns] government by a particular sort of people or according to a particular principle: *democracy* (=government by the people) | *meritocracy* (=government by people with the most ability)

-ocrat /əkræt/ also **-crat** suffix [in nouns] **1** someone who believes in a particular principle of government: *a democrat* (=someone who believes in government by the people) **2** a member of a powerful or governing social class or group: *a technocrat* (=a scientist who controls an organization or country) —**-ocratic** /əkrætɪk/ suffix —**-ocratically** /əkrætɪkli/ suffix

Oct. also **Oct** BrE the written abbreviation of *October*

oc·ta·gon /'ɒktəgən $ 'ɑːktəgɑːn/ n [C] a flat shape with eight sides and eight angles —**octagonal** /ɒk'tægənəl $ ɑːk-/ adj: *an octagonal tower*

oc·tane /'ɒkteɪn $ 'ɑːk-/ n [U] a type of HYDROCARBON that is in FUEL and is used as a measure of its quality: *low octane petrol* | *high octane fuel*

oc·tave /'ɒktɪv, -teɪv $ 'ɑːk-/ n [C] **a)** the range of musical notes between the first note of a SCALE and the last one **b)** the first and last notes of a musical SCALE played together

oc·tet /ɒk'tet $ ɑːk-/ n [C] **1** eight singers or musicians performing together **2** a piece of music for an octet

octo- /ɒktəʊ $ ɑːktoʊ/ prefix eight, or having eight: *octagon* (=a shape with eight sides) | *octopus* (=a sea creature with eight arms)

Oc·to·ber /ɒk'təʊbə $ ɑːk'toʊbər/ n [C,U] written abbreviation **Oct.** the tenth month of the year, between September and November: **next/last October** *We moved in last October.* | **in October** *You're going to be busy in*

October. | **on October 6th** *We begin on October 6th.* | **on 6th October** *BrE: They were arrested on 6th October.* | **October 6** *AmE: The baby was baptized Monday, October 6.*

oc·to·ge·nar·i·an /ˌɒktəʊdʒɔ̩'neəriən, -tə- $ ˌɑːk-toʊ-/ *n* [C] someone who is between 80 and 89 years old

oc·to·pus /'ɒktəpəs $ 'ɑːk-/ *n plural* **octopuses** *or* **octopi** /-paɪ/ [C] a sea creature with eight TENTACLES (=arms)

oc·u·lar /'ɒkjɵlə $ 'ɑːkjɵlər/ *adj medical* relating to your eyes or your ability to see: *ocular muscles*

oc·u·list /'ɒkjɵlɨst $ 'ɑːk-/ *n* [C] *old-fashioned* a doctor who examines and treats people's eyes

OD /ˌəʊ 'diː $ ˌoʊ-/ *v* **OD'd, OD'ing, OD's** [I] *informal* **1** *overdose* to take too much of a drug so that it is dangerous: [+on] *He OD'd on sleeping tablets.* **2** to see, hear, eat etc too much of something: [+on] *children who OD on video games* —**OD** *n* [C]

o·da·lisque /'əʊdəlɪsk $ 'oʊ-/ *n* [C] *literary* a beautiful female slave in former times

odd S1 W3 /ɒd $ ɑːd/ *adj comparative* **odder**, *superlative* **oddest**

1 STRANGE different from what is normal or expected, especially in a way that you disapprove of or cannot understand: *It was an odd thing to say.* | *an odd way to behave* | *They're an odd couple.* | *There was something odd about him.* | *What she did was unforgivable, but the odd thing was he didn't seem to mind.* | *She was holding an extremely odd-looking weapon.* | **it is/seems odd (that)** *It seemed odd that he wanted a picture of me.*; → see box at UNUSUAL

2 the odd occasion/day/moment/drink etc *especially BrE* a few occasions, days etc that happen at various times but not often and not regularly; ▣ **occasional**: *Lack of sleep doesn't matter on the odd occasion.* | *I take the odd day off work.* | *I like the odd glass of wine with my dinner.* | *Jo smokes the odd cigarette.*

3 VARIOUS [only before noun] not specially chosen or collected: *Any odd scrap of paper will do.*

4 NOT IN A PAIR/SET [only before noun] separated from a pair or set: *an odd shoe* | **odd socks/gloves etc** (=not a matching pair of socks etc) *He was wearing odd socks.*

5 odd number a number that cannot be divided exactly by two, for example 1, 3, 5, 7 etc; ▣ **even number**

6 20-odd/30-odd etc *spoken* a little more than 20 etc: *I have another 20-odd years to work before I retire.*

7 the odd man/one out *BrE* someone or something that is different from the rest of the group or not included in it: *Which shape is the odd one out?* | *I was always the odd one out at school.* —**oddness** *n* [U] → ODDLY

odd·ball /'ɒdbɔːl $ 'ɑːdbɒːl/ *n* [C] *informal* someone who behaves in a strange or unusual way —**oddball** *adj: a rather oddball sense of humour*

odd·i·ty /'ɒdɨti $ 'ɑː-/ *n plural* **oddities** **1** [C] a strange or unusual person or thing: *In a class of 120 students there were four women including myself, and I still felt rather an oddity.* **2** [C,U] a strange quality in someone or something: *60s fashions that are remembered for their oddity*

odd-'job man *n* [C] *BrE* a man who does various jobs in people's houses or gardens

odd 'jobs *n* [plural] small jobs of different types: *I've got a few odd jobs to do this weekend.*

odd·ly /'ɒdli $ 'ɑːdli/ *adv* **1** in a strange or unusual way: *She's been behaving oddly this week.* **2** also **oddly enough** [sentence adverb] used to say that something seems strange or surprising: *Oddly enough, someone asked me the same question only yesterday.*

odd·ments /'ɒdmənts $ 'ɑːd-/ *n* [plural] small things of no value, or pieces of a material that were not used when something was made: *You can make a patchwork quilt from oddments of silk and cotton.*

odds S3 /ɒdz $ ɑːdz/ *n* [plural]

1 PROBABILITY the odds how likely it is that something will or will not happen: *The odds are* (=it is

likely) *that he will commit the same crime again.* | [+of] *You can narrow the odds of a nasty accident happening in your home by being more safety-conscious.* | [+against] *The odds against a plane crash are around a million to one.* | *I'm afraid that the odds are heavily against her winning* (=it is not likely). | *The odds are in favour of a Russian victory* (=it is likely). | *What are the odds* (=how likely is it) *that they will mess up?* | *a new company that has beaten the odds and succeeded* (=it was not likely to succeed, but it did)

2 DIFFICULTIES difficulties which make a good result seem very unlikely

against (all) the odds (=although there are great difficulties)
overcome the odds (=succeed although there are great difficulties)
battle against the odds
the odds are stacked against sb (=there are great difficulties)
impossible odds
enormous/heavy/overwhelming odds

Against all the odds, he recovered from his terrible injuries. | *The South Africans overcame the odds to beat Australia.* | *The hospital's director has been battling against the odds to improve patient care.* | *The odds are stacked against the young birds, especially in winter.* | *Their job was to hold on despite impossible odds, in order to give the rest of the army time to strike.* | *a little company that battled its way, despite enormous odds, to success*

3 be at odds **a)** to disagree: [+with] *Briggs found himself at odds with his colleagues.* | [+over/on] *The two politicians were at odds over what was the truth.* **b)** if two statements, descriptions, actions etc are at odds with each other, they are different although they should be the same: [+with] *Mark's account of what happened is at odds with Dan's.* | *She gave him a sweet smile, totally at odds with the look of dislike in her eyes.*

4 HORSE RACING ETC the numbers that show how much money you will win if you BET on the winner of a horse race or other competition: *The odds are 6–1.* | [+of] *At odds of 10–1 he bet a hundred pounds* | **(at) long/short odds** (=high or low numbers, that show a high or low risk of losing) *Everyone was surprised when Desert Zone won the race, at very long odds.* | **lay/offer (sb) odds** *BrE: They are laying odds of 8–1 that the Conservatives will win the next election.*

5 it makes no odds *BrE spoken* used to say that what someone does or what happens is not important: *Pay me now or later – it makes no odds.*

6 pay over the odds *BrE informal* to pay a higher price than is usual or reasonable: *Most residents live in tiny apartments and pay over the odds for them too.*

odds and 'ends also **odds and 'sods** *BrE informal n* [plural] small things of various kinds without much value: *He didn't keep much in his desk – just a few odds and ends.*

odds-'on *adj* **1** odds-on favourite the person, horse etc that is most likely to win a race or other competition **2** *BrE informal* very likely: **it's odds on (that)** *It's odds on that she won't come.* | **be odds-on to do sth** *They must have felt they were odds-on to win.*

ode /əʊd $ oʊd/ *n* [C] a poem or song written in order to praise a person or thing: [+to] *Keats' 'Ode to a Nightingale'*

o·di·ous /'əʊdiəs $ 'oʊ-/ *adj formal* extremely unpleasant: *an odious little man* —**odiously** *adv*

o·di·um /'əʊdiəm $ 'oʊ-/ *n* [U] *formal* a strong feeling of hatred that a lot of people have for someone because of something they have done: *Internationally Reagan attracted odium for his militarism.*

o·dom·e·ter /əʊ'dɒmɨtə $ oʊ'dɑːmɨtər/ *n* [C] an instrument in a vehicle that shows how many miles or kilometres the vehicle has travelled; ▣ **milometer** *BrE*;
→ see picture at CAR

o·dor /'əʊdər $ 'oʊdər/ *n* the American spelling of ODOUR

o·do·rif·er·ous /ˌəʊdər'ɪfərəs◂ $ ˌoʊ-/ *adj* old-fashioned ODOROUS

o·dor·less /'əʊdələs $ 'oʊdər-/ *adj* the American spelling of ODOURLESS

o·do·rous /'əʊdərəs $ 'oʊ-/ *adj literary* or *technical* having a smell: *odorous gases*

o·dour *BrE*; **odor** *AmE* /'əʊdə $ 'oʊdər/ *n* [C,U] a smell, especially an unpleasant one: [+of] | *the faint odour of damp* | **strong/unpleasant/pungent/offensive etc odour** *obnoxious odours from a factory* → BODY ODOUR

o·dour·less *BrE*; **odorless** *AmE* /'əʊdələs $ 'oʊdər-/ *adj* having no smell: *a colorless, odorless liquid*

od·ys·sey /'ɒdɪsi $ 'ɑː-/ *n* [C] *literary* **1** a series of experiences that teach you something about yourself or about life: *a spiritual odyssey* **2** a long journey with a lot of adventures or difficulties: **on an odyssey** *They departed Texas on a three-year odyssey that took them as far as Japan.*

OECD /ˌəʊ iː siː $ 'diː $ ˌoʊ-/ *n* **the OECD** *the Organization for Economic Cooperation and Development* a group of rich countries who work together to develop trade and economic growth

oe·di·pal /'iːdɪpəl $ 'e-/ *adj* [usually before noun] related to an Oedipus complex

Oe·di·pus com·plex /'iːdɪpəs ˌkɒmpleks $ 'edɪpəs ˌkɑːm-/ *n* according to Freudian PSYCHOLOGY, when a son unconsciously feels sexual desire for his mother, combined with a hatred for his father

o'er /əʊə $ ɔːr/ *adv, prep literary* over – used especially in poetry

oe·soph·a·gus *BrE*, **esophagus** *AmE* /ɪ'sɒfəgəs $ ɪ'sɑː-/ *n plural* **oesophaguses** *or* **oesophagi** /-gaɪ/ [C] the tube which food passes down from your mouth to your stomach → **digestive system** at DIGESTIVE

oes·tro·gen *n* [U] *BrE*, **estrogen** *AmE* /'iːstrədʒən $ 'es-/ a substance that is produced in a woman's OVARIES that causes changes in her body and prepares it for having babies

oeu·vre /'ɜːvrə $ 'ʊvrə/ *n* [C usually singular] *formal* all the works of an artist or writer: *the oeuvre of Van Gogh*

of S1 W1 /əv, ə; *strong* ɒv $ əv, ə; *strong* ɑːv/ *prep*
1 used to show what a part belongs to or comes from: *the back of the house* | *the last scene of the movie* | *the end of the day*
2 used to show who something or someone belongs to or has a connection with: *a friend of Mark's* | *Avocado salad is a favourite of mine.* | *Product inspection is the responsibility of the employees themselves.*
3 used when talking about a feature or quality that something has: *the cost of the meal* | *the beauty of the scenery* | *the length of the swimming-pool*
4 used to show what group one or more things or people belong to: *some of the students* | *'Sunflowers' is one of his best-known paintings.* | *Two of the guests are vegetarian.* | *a member of the baseball team*
5 used to show what type of substance or thing you are referring to, when talking about an amount: *two kilos of sugar* | *millions of dollars* | *a bar of chocolate*
6 used to say what something contains: *a cup of coffee* | *several packets of cigarettes* | *truckloads of refugees*
7 used to say what type of things or people are in a group: *a herd of elephants* | *his circle of friends* | *a bunch of bananas*
8 a) used to state specifically which thing of the general type mentioned you are referring to: *the city of New York* | *the art of painting* | *the problem of unemployment* **b)** used to state specifically what a particular number, amount, age etc is: *at the age of 52* | *an increase of 3%*
9 used to talk about things produced by a famous or skilled writer, artist etc: *the plays of Shakespeare* | *the paintings of Picasso* | *the work of a great architect*
10 used to say what a story, some news etc is about, or

what a picture, map etc shows: *a story of love and loss* | *news of his arrest* | *a photo of Elizabeth* | *a map of Indonesia*
11 a) used after nouns that refer to actions, or to people who do something, in order to show who or what the action is done to: *the cancellation of the meeting* | *the killing of innocent children* | *supporters of the project* **b)** used after nouns that refer to actions in order to show who or what does the action: *the ringing of the phone* | *the arrival of a visitor*
12 used after some adjectives that describe feelings, to show who or what the feeling is directed towards: *He's always been frightened of spiders.* | *Most children want their parents to feel proud of them.*
13 used when referring to the day, moment etc when something happened: *the day of the accident* | *the week of the festival* | *I was at home* **at the time** *of the murder.*
14 used to say where something is in relation to a place or thing: **north/south etc of sth** *a historic seaside town 99 km south of London* | **to the left/right of sth** *To the left of the sofa is a table.* | *I live within a mile of here.*
15 used to describe a person or thing by saying what their main qualities or features are: *Albright was seen as a woman of great determination.* | *It's an area of considerable historical interest.*
16 used to say what someone's age is: *He has two children, a boy of twelve and a girl of fifteen.*
17 it is kind/stupid/careless etc of sb (to do sth) used to say that someone's action shows a particular quality: *It was kind of you to remember my birthday.*
18 used to say where someone comes from: *the people of China* | *Jesus of Nazareth*
19 used to show the country, organization, or group in which someone has a particular position: *King Philip II of Spain* | *the secretary of the tennis club*
20 used in dates before the name of the month: *the 27th of July*
21 used to say when something happened: *the presidential election of 1825* | *one of the biggest upsets of recent years*
22 *AmE spoken* used in giving the time, to mean 'before'; ⊟ **to** *BrE*: *It's* **a quarter of seven** (=6.45).
23 used to show the cause of someone's death: *He died of cancer.*
24 *literary* used to say what material has been used to make something: *a dress of pure silk*
25 **of an evening/of a weekend etc** *BrE* in the evenings, at WEEKENDS etc: *We often used to walk by the river of an evening.*

GRAMMAR
To refer to someone or something that belongs to or is connected with someone, it is usual to use **–'s** or **–s'** (NOT of) with short noun phrases: *Dad's car* (NOT *the car of Dad*) | *a child's bike* (NOT *the bike of a child*) | *my sister's boyfriend* (NOT *the boyfriend of my sister*) | *the miners' strike* (NOT *the strike of the miners*)
When referring to one of several people or things belonging to or connected with someone, or when using 'this' or 'that', use **of + mine/yours/his/hers/ours/theirs**: *a friend of mine* (NOT *a friend of me*) | *a relation of ours* (NOT *a relation of us*) | *that car of yours* (NOT *that car of you*)
To talk about the person who sang, wrote, painted, or composed a particular work, use **by** not **of**: *a song by Mariah Carey* (NOT *of Mariah Carey*)

---

of 'course S1 W1 *adv*
1 used to show that other people probably already know what you are saying is true, or expect to hear it: *Well, she won, of course.* | *You should of course keep copies of all your correspondence.* | *Of course there will be some difficult times ahead.*
2 *spoken* also **course** *informal* used to emphasize that you are saying 'yes' when someone asks your permission to do something: *'Can I ring you back in a minute?' 'Yes, of course.'* | *'Is it OK if I have another cup of coffee?' 'Course, help yourself.'*
3 *spoken* also **course** *informal* used to emphasize that

what you are saying to someone is true or correct: *'Do you really believe her?' 'Of course I do!'* | *'I hope this idea of yours works.' 'Course it'll work.'*

4 *spoken* used to show that you accept or agree with what someone has just said: *'Don't get angry. She's only thirteen.' 'Of course.'* | *'The correct answer is 83.' 'Oh, yes, of course.'*

5 of course not/course not *spoken* used to emphasize that you are saying 'no' to something: *'Have you been reading my e-mail?' 'Of course not!'* | *'Do you mind if I bring a friend?' 'No, of course not.'*

POLITENESS

Use **of course** as a polite and friendly way of agreeing to something: *'Can I borrow your pen?'- 'Of course'.* | *Of course I'll help you.* | *'Do you mind if I smoke?' – 'Of course not'.*

Do not use **of course** as a reply when someone asks you for information, because this can sound rude and unfriendly. If, for example, you asked someone: *'Is this the Swallow Hotel?'* and they said: *'Of course it is'* it would sound as though they thought the answer was obvious and that you were stupid to ask them.

off¹ [S1] [W1] /ɒf $ ɔːf/ *adv, prep, adj*

1 away from a place: *He got into his car and drove off.* | *Suddenly they turned off and parked in a side road.* | *Once we were off the main freeway, the trip felt more like a vacation.* | *Her husband was off on a business trip somewhere.* | *Are you ready? Off we go.* | *I must be off now* (=I must leave). | *They were off to Italy* (=leaving to go to Italy) *and wanted to make an early start.*

2 not on something, or removed from something: *Keep off the grass.* | *As he leaned forward, his hat fell off.* | *Someone had taken the mirror off the wall.* | *Take your coat off.* | *I was trying to scrape the mud off my boots.*
⚠ Do not say 'off of' something. Say **off** something: *Get off the bus at the airport* (NOT *Get off of the bus at the airport*).

3 out of a bus, train, plane etc; 🔒 **on**: *I'll get off at the next stop.* | *Everyone got off the train at Winnipeg.*

4 a machine, piece of equipment etc that is off is not working or operating; 🔒 **on**: *Will someone switch the radio off?* | *Make sure all the lights are off.*

5 not at work, school etc because you are ill or on holiday; → **absent**: *My secretary's been off with flu for the past week.* | *Clare had to stay off school because her mother was ill.* | *You look tired. Why don't you take tomorrow off?* | *He needs more time off duty for relaxation and rest.* | *'Going to work today, mum?' 'No. It's my day off today.'*

6 *informal* from someone: *My brother once borrowed some money off him.* | *I got this necklace off a woman outside the market.*

7 a) used to say how far away something is: *We could see the cliffs of Shetland about two miles off.* | *Kara's home was a long way off across the sea.* **b)** used to say how much time there is between now and a future event: *With the exams now only a week off, I had to study hard.* | *Christmas seemed a long way off.* **c)** used to say how likely or unlikely something is: *Any kind of peace agreement still seems a long way off.*

8 a) only a short distance away from a place: *Our hotel was just off the main street.* | *an island off the coast of France* **b)** connected to a particular room, area, road etc: *There's a small bathroom off the main bedroom.* | *a narrow street leading off the corner of the square*

9 used to say that a price is reduced by a particular amount: *If you buy more than ten, they knock 10% off.*

10 if an event which has been arranged is off, it will not now take place; → **cancelled**, **postponed**: *The wedding's off.* | *The race may have to be called off if the bad weather continues.*

11 *BrE informal* behaviour that is off is rude or is not acceptable: *She walked out before the end of your lecture, which I thought was a bit off.* | *Look, I know when someone's being off with me.*

12 used to say how much of something someone has: **be well/badly off for sth** *The school's fairly well off for*

books these days. | **How are you off for** sports equipment? (=do you have enough?) → WELL-OFF, BADLY OFF, BETTER OFF

13 off and on also **on and off** for short periods but not regularly, over a long period of time: *We've been going out together for five years, off and on.*

14 no longer wanting or liking something: *Toby's been off his food for a few days.* | **go off sth/sb** *BrE*: *I used to enjoy tennis, but I've gone off it a bit now.* | *She seems to have gone off Mark since he's grown a beard.*

15 no longer taking something such as a drug or medicine; 🔒 **on**: *The operation was a success, and she's off the morphine.*

16 a) food that is off is no longer fresh enough to eat; → **rotten, sour**: *Ugh! The milk's off.* | *Do you think the meat's gone off?* **b)** used to say that a particular kind of food is not available in a restaurant although it's on the MENU: *I'm sorry, the fish pie is off today, sir.*

17 *AmE* not as good as usual: *Sales figures for last year were a little off compared with those of the previous year.*

18 *AmE* not correct or not right: *Our calculations were off. I guess again.* → **right off**, at RIGHT³ (2); → **straight off**, at STRAIGHT¹ (7); → **off the top of your head**, at TOP¹ (18); → **noises off** at NOISE¹ (8)

off² *adj* [only before noun] **1 off day/week etc** a day, week etc when you are not doing something as well as you usually do: *Brian never usually loses his temper – he must be* **having an off day**. **2 off period/season etc** a period or season which is not as busy as other times of the year: *In the off season, there's hardly anyone staying at the hotel.* **3** *BrE* used to talk about a pair of things such as wheels on a car, to mean the one on the right; 🔒 **near**

off³ *n BrE* **1 the off** the start of a race or a journey: *The horses were in line, ready for the off.* **2 from the off** from the beginning of something: *She was doubtful about the interview from the off.*

off⁴ *v* [T] *AmE informal* to kill someone: *The guy who did this ought to be offed.*

,**off-'air** *adj* [only before noun] not being broadcast on the radio or television at the present moment; 🔒 **on air**: *off-air television recordings*

of·fal /'ɒfəl $ 'ɔː-, 'ɑː-/ *n* [U] *BrE* the inside parts of an animal, for example the heart, LIVER, and KIDNEYS used as food

,**off-'balance**, **off balance** *adj* [not before noun] **1** in an unsteady position and likely to fall: **throw/knock/push etc sb off-balance** *The sudden movement of the ship knocked them both off balance.* **2 catch/throw sb off-balance** to surprise or shock someone because they are not prepared for something that happens: *I was thrown off-balance by some of the more difficult questions I was asked.*

off·beat /,ɒf'biːt◄ $,ɔːf-/ *adj informal* unusual and not what people normally expect, especially in an interesting way: *offbeat humour* | *She's a little offbeat, but she's a wonderful actress.*

,**off-'Broadway** *adj, adv* an off-Broadway play is one that is performed outside the Broadway entertainment area in New York City and does not involve as much money as the famous plays on Broadway

,**off-'centre** *BrE*; **off-center** *AmE adj* [not before noun] not exactly in the centre of something: *Place the photo slightly off-centre, so that there is more space on the page.*

'**off-chance, off chance** *n* **on the off-chance** if you do something on the off-chance that something will happen, you do it hoping that it will happen although it is unlikely: *I just came to see you on the off-chance that Pippa might be here.*

O

off-ˈcolour _BrE_; **off-color** _AmE adj_ **1** sexually offensive: _off-color jokes_ **2** [not before noun] _BrE_ slightly ill: _She's been feeling a bit off-colour lately._

off-cut _n_ [C] _especially BrE_ a piece of wood, paper etc that is left after the main piece has been cut and removed

off-ˈduty _adj_ if someone such as a policeman, nurse, or soldier is off-duty, they are not working: _an off-duty guard_ | _I shall be off-duty on Thursday._

of·fence W3 _BrE_; **offense** _AmE_ /əˈfens/ _n_
1 [C] an illegal action or a crime

> criminal offence
> serious/minor offence
> **first offence** (=the first illegal thing that someone has done)
> commit an offence
> **capital offence** (=a crime for which death is the punishment)
> **federal offense** _AmE_ (=a very serious offence against the law of the US, rather than against state law)
> driving/parking etc offence
> it is an offence to do sth
> **make sth an offence/make it an offence to do sth**
> a punishable offence
> an offence punishable by/with sth

> _The possession of stolen property is a **criminal offence.** | Punishment for a **first offence** is a fine. | His solicitor said he **committed** the **offence** because he was heavily in debt. | The bill **makes it an offence to** carry a knife._ | [+**against**] _sexual offences against children_

2 [U] when you offend or upset someone by something you do or say: **cause/give offence** _The problem was how to say 'no' to her without causing offence._ | _Don't be upset by what he said; he **meant no offence** (=did not intend to offend anyone)._
3 no offence _spoken_ used to tell someone that you hope that what you are going to say or do will not offend them: _No offense, but this cheese tastes like rubber._
4 take offence (at sth) to feel offended because of something someone says or does: _I think he took offence at my lack of enthusiasm._
5 [U] _formal_ the act of attacking: _the weapon of offence used during the attack_

of·fend /əˈfend/ _v_ **1** [I,T] to make someone angry or upset by doing or saying something that they think is rude, unkind etc: _His remarks deeply offended many Scottish people._ | **be offended by/at sth** _Liddy was offended by such a personal question._ | _The careful language is designed not to offend._ **2** [T] to seem bad or unacceptable to someone: _A solution must be found that doesn't offend too many people._ | _Some of these new buildings really offend the eye (=look very ugly)._ **3** [I] _formal_ to commit a crime or crimes: _Many of the young men here are likely to offend again._ **4** [I,T] _formal_ to be against people's feelings of what is morally acceptable: [+**against**] _Broadcasters have a responsibility not to offend against good taste and decency._

of·fend·ed /əˈfendɪd/ _adj_ someone who is offended is angry and upset by someone's behaviour or remarks: **feel/look/sound offended** _Stella was beginning to feel a little offended._ | _I knew that Piers would be **deeply offended.** | I get very offended when he talks to me like that._ | _radio listeners who are **easily offended**_

of·fend·er /əˈfendə $ -ər/ _n_ [C] **1** someone who is guilty of a crime: _Community punishment is used for less serious offenders._ | _At 16, Scott was already a **persistent offender** (=someone who has been caught several times for committing crimes)._ → FIRST OFFENDER, SEX OFFENDER, YOUNG OFFENDER **2** someone or something that is the cause of something bad: _Among causes of air pollution, car exhaust fumes may be the **worst offender.**_

of·fend·ing /əˈfendɪŋ/ _adj_ [only before noun] **1** the **offending ...** the thing that is causing a problem – often used humorously: _I decided to have the offending tooth removed._ **2** relating to or guilty of an illegal offence: _offending behaviour_ | _the offending vehicle_ **3** making people feel angry or insulted: _his offending remarks_

of·fense¹ /əˈfens/ _n_ the usual American spelling of OFFENCE

of·fense² /əˈfens $ ˈɒːfens, ˈɑː-/ _n_ [U] _AmE_ the part of a game such as American football, which is concerned with getting points and winning, or the group of players who do this; **F** **defense:** _The Bears are going to have to work on their offense this season._

of·fen·sive¹ /əˈfensɪv/ _adj_ **1** very rude or insulting and likely to upset people; **F** **inoffensive:** _I found her remarks **deeply offensive.** | [+**to**] crude jokes that are offensive to women_ | _offensive behaviour_ **2** _formal_ very unpleasant: _an offensive smell_ **3** [only before noun] for attacking → DEFENSIVE¹ (1): _Jan was convicted of possessing an **offensive weapon.** | The troops took up offensive positions._ **4** _AmE_ relating to getting points and winning a game, rather than stopping the other team from getting points; **F** **defensive:** _the Jets' offensive strategy_ **—offensively** _adv_: _Rick's remarks were offensively racist._ **—offensiveness** _n_ [U]

offensive² _n_ [C] **1** a planned military attack involving large forces over a long period: _a **military offensive** | A major **offensive** was **launched** on August 22._ **2 go on the offensive** also **take the offensive** to start attacking or criticizing someone before they start attacking or criticizing you: _Republicans went on the offensive over soaring gasoline prices._ | _The international coalition was ready to take the offensive._ **3 charm/diplomatic offensive** a planned set of actions intended to influence a lot of people

offer

offering   refusing

of·fer¹ S1 W1 /ˈɒfə $ ˈɒːfər, ˈɑː-/ _v_
1 [T] to ask someone if they would like to have something, or to hold something out to them so that they can take it: **offer sb sth** _Can I offer you something to drink?_ | _They offered him a very good job, but he turned it down._ | **offer sth to sb** _Maureen lit a cigarette and offered one to Lucy._ | _The drama school offers places to students who can show talent._
2 [I,T] to say that you are willing to do something: _I don't need any help, but it was nice of you to offer._ | **offer to do sth** _My dad has offered to pick us up._ | _The newspaper offered to apologise for the article._
3 [T] to provide something that people need or want: **offer advice/help/support etc** _Your doctor should be able to offer advice on diet._ | **offer an opportunity/chance/possibility** _The course offers the opportunity to specialize in the final year._ | _A number of groups **offer** their **services** free of charge._ | _The Centre offers a wide range of sports facilities._ | **offer sth to sb** _I did what I could to offer comfort to the family._
4 have sth to offer (sb) to have qualities, opportunities etc that people are likely to want or enjoy: _Canada **has much to offer** in terms of location and climate._ | _He felt he **had nothing to offer** her that she wanted._
5 [T] to say that you are willing to pay a particular amount of money for something: **offer (sb) sth for sth** _They've offered us £75,000 for the house._ | _The police are offering a reward for any information._
6 offer (up) a prayer/sacrifice etc to pray to God or give something to God

7 offer itself *formal* if an opportunity to do something offers itself, it becomes available to you: *I'll raise the subject when a suitable occasion offers itself.*
8 offer your hand (to sb) to hold out your hand in order to shake hands with someone

offer² [S2] [W1] *n* [C]
1 a statement saying that you are willing to do something for someone or give them something: **offer of help/support/friendship etc** *Thank you for your offer of help.* | *The company* **withdrew** *their* **offer** *of employment.* | *Have you had any* **job offers**? | **accept/take up an offer** (=say yes to an offer) *She accepted their offer of rent-free accommodation.* | **turn down/refuse/decline an offer** (=say no to an offer) *I can't turn down the offer of a free trip to Milan!* | **offer to do sth** *His offer to resign will be accepted.*
2 an amount of money that you are willing to pay for something: *Will you* **accept** *their* **offer**? | **make (sb) an offer (for/on sth)** (=offer a particular amount of money for something) *Within 20 minutes they were prepared to make us an offer.* | *The company* **made an offer of** *$5 million for the site.* | **a generous/good offer** *'I'll be interested if Newcastle make me a good offer,' said the 25-year-old striker.* | **be open to offers** (=be ready to consider people's offers and lower your original price) *We're asking £2500, but we're open to offers.* → O.N.O.
3 a reduction of the price of something in a shop for a short time; → **discount**: *All* **special offers** *advertised in this brochure are subject to availability .* | [+on] *There's a* **free offer** *on orders over £45.* | *To* **take advantage of** *this* **offer** (=buy something at the reduced price), *complete the attached forms.*
4 on offer a) available to be bought, chosen, or used: *Activities* **on** *offer* **include** *sailing, rowing, and canoeing.* | *I was impressed with the designs on offer.* **b)** *BrE* for sale for a short time at a cheaper price than usual: *Lean minced beef is on offer this week.*
5 under offer *BrE* if a house that is for sale is under offer, someone has offered to buy it for a particular price

of·fer·ing /ˈɒfərɪŋ $ ˈɒː-, ˈɑː-/ *n* [C] **1** a book, play, piece of music etc that someone has written recently: *the latest offering from Nancy Griffith* **2** something that is given to God **3** something that is given as a present to please someone → **burnt offering** at BURNT² (2); → PEACE OFFERING

of·fer·to·ry /ˈɒfətəri $ ˈɒːfətɔːri, ˈɑː-/ *n plural* **offertories** [C] *formal* **1** the money people give during a religious ceremony in church; ▤ **collection 2** the offering of the bread and wine to God at a Christian church service

off-'guard *adj* [not before noun] **catch/take sb off-guard** to surprise someone by happening when they are not expecting something or prepared for it: *The sudden snow storm caught us all off-guard.*

off·hand¹ /ˌɒfˈhænd◂ $ ˌɒːf-/ *adj* **1** *BrE* not very friendly towards someone when you are talking to them: *She said you were a bit offhand with her this afternoon.* | *an offhand tone of voice* **2** said or done without thinking or planning: *an offhand remark* —**offhandedly** *adv* —**offhandedness** *n* [U]

offhand² *adv* immediately, without time to think about it or find out about something: *I can't remember offhand where the file is.*

of·fice [S1] [W1] /ˈɒfɪs $ ˈɒː-, ˈɑː-/ *n*
→ see picture on next page
1 BUILDING [C] a building that belongs to a company or organization, with rooms where people can work at desks: *The department occupies an office just a mile from the White House.* | **main/head office** (=the most important office) *The head office is in Edinburgh.* | *Did you go to* **the office** (=the office where you work) *today?* | **at the office** *Have a nice day at the office.* | **local/regional office** *The agency has a network of regional offices.* | **office staff/workers/equipment etc** *Office staff need well-designed desks and chairs.* | *the increased demand for office space*

2 ROOM [C] a room where someone has a desk and works, on their own or with other people: *the manager's office* | *Sorry, Ann's not in her office right now.* | *Dan shares an office with Lisa.*
3 office hours a) the time between about 9:00 in the morning and 5:00 in the afternoon, when people in offices are working: *Can you phone again during office hours?* **b)** *AmE* the time during the day or week when students can meet with their teacher in the teacher's office: *Professor Lee's office hours are from 2 to 4 on Mondays and Thursdays.*
4 JOB [C,U] an important job or position with power, especially in government: *the office of President* | **in office** *She was celebrating ten years in office.* | *A provisional military government* **took office** (=started in an important job or position). | **hold office** (=have a particular important job or position) *Trujillo held office as finance minister.* | *a five year* **term of office** (=period of time working in an important job)
5 Office used in the names of some government departments: *the Foreign Office* | *the Office of the District Attorney*
6 PLACE FOR INFORMATION [C] a room or building where people go to ask for information, buy tickets etc: **information/ticket etc office** *the tourist office* | *Is there a lost property office?* → BOX OFFICE, POST OFFICE, REGISTRY OFFICE
7 DOCTOR [C] *AmE* the place where a doctor or DENTIST examines or treats people; ▤ **surgery** *BrE*
8 sb's good offices/the good offices of sb *formal* help given by someone who has authority or can influence people: **through the good offices of sb** *I managed to obtain a visa through the good offices of a friend in the Service.*

'office ,boy *n* [C] *old-fashioned* a boy or young man who does simple jobs in an office

'office ,building also **'office ,block** *BrE n* [C] a large building with many offices in it, especially ones that belong to different companies → see picture at TOWN

'office ,holder *n* [C] someone who has an official position, especially in the government

,office 'party *n* [C] a party, especially one held before Christmas, in the office of a company, government department etc for the people who work there

of·fi·cer [S1] [W1] /ˈɒfɪsə $ ˈɒːfɪsər, ˈɑː-/ *n* [C]
1 someone who is in a position of authority in the army, navy etc: **an army/naval/military etc officer** | *a* **commanding officer** *of the SAS*
2 someone who is in a position in an organization or the government: *a prison officer* | *the chief medical officer* | *a former Cabinet officer* | *the public information officer* → CHIEF EXECUTIVE OFFICER; → **press officer** at PRESS OFFICE; → PROBATION OFFICER, RETURNING OFFICER
3 a member of the police; ▤ **police officer, policeman, policewoman**: *a request for 400 more officers*
4 Officer *AmE* a title for a policeman or policewoman: *Officer Murdoch*

of·fi·cial¹ [S3] /əˈfɪʃəl/ *n* [C] someone who is in a position of authority in an organization: *a government official* | *senior administration officials*

official² [S3] [W2] *adj*
1 approved of or done by someone in authority, especially the government: *an official investigation into the causes of the explosion* | *the official policy on education* | *official statistics about illegal drug use* | *You will have to get official permission first.* | *Finally the letter of appointment came, making it all official.*
2 relating to or done as part of an important job or position: **an official visit/engagement etc** *The President was leaving for a four-day official tour of Mexico.* | *the Queen's performance of* **official duties** | *They dined in an official capacity with other European leaders.* | *the Lord Mayor's official residence*
3 an official explanation, account etc is one that is given formally and publicly, but may not be true: *Many doubted the official version of events.* | *The* **official line** (=what is said publicly by people in authority) *was that*

O

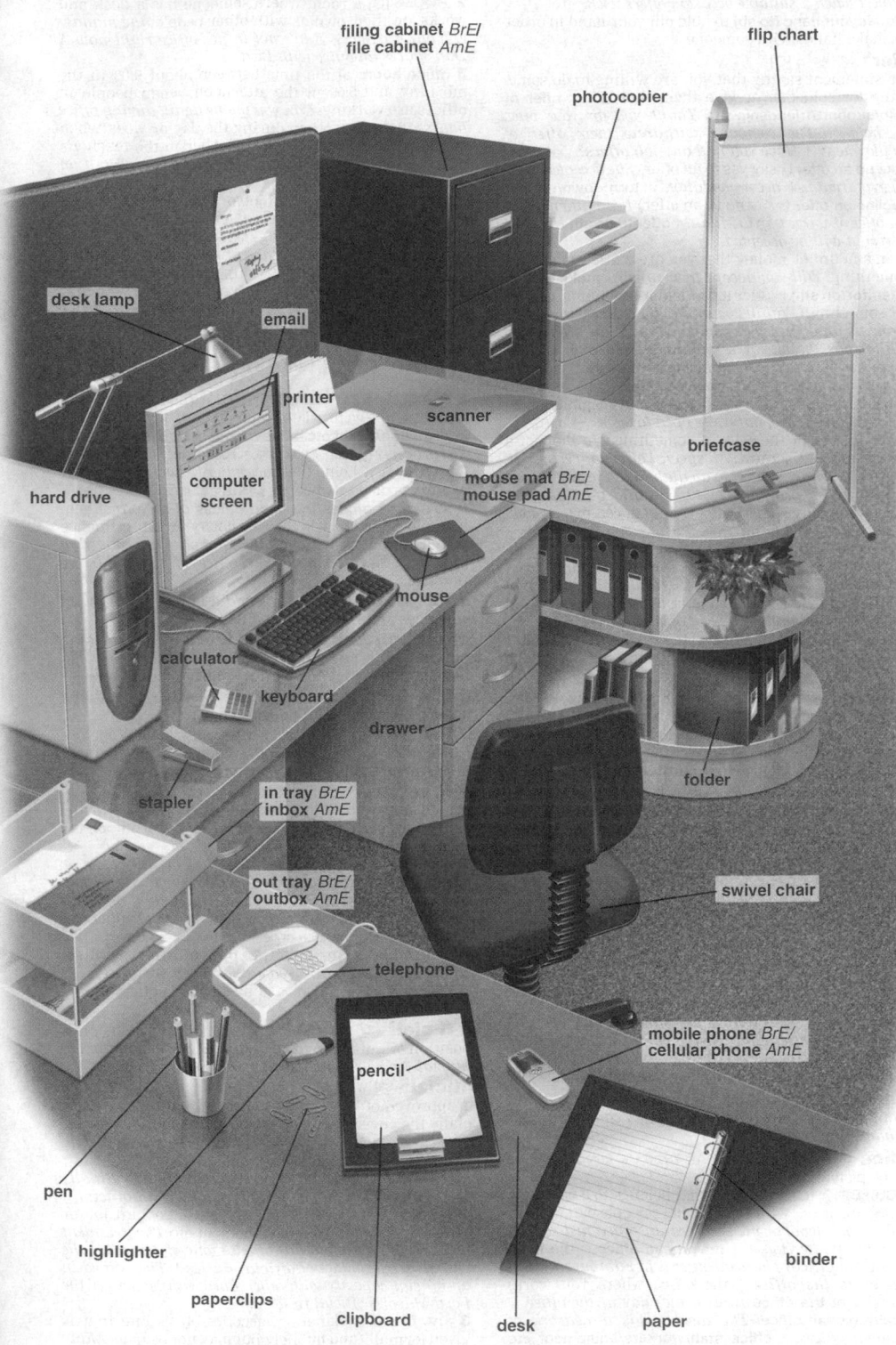

filing cabinet *BrE/*
file cabinet *AmE*

flip chart

photocopier

desk lamp

email

printer

scanner

briefcase

computer screen

mouse mat *BrE/*
mouse pad *AmE*

hard drive

mouse

calculator

keyboard

drawer

folder

stapler

in tray *BrE/*
inbox *AmE*

out tray *BrE/*
outbox *AmE*

swivel chair

telephone

mobile phone *BrE/*
cellular phone *AmE*

pen

pencil

highlighter

paperclips

clipboard

desk

paper

binder

the troops were there to protect the King.
4 chosen to represent someone or an organization, or do something for them: *the company's official logo* | *the official representative from the American administration*
5 an official event is a formal, public event: *The official opening of the institute was in May.*

of·fi·cial·dom /ə'fɪʃəldəm/ *n* [U] government departments or the people who work in them – used when you think they are not helpful; → **bureaucracy**

of·fi·cial·ese /ə,fɪʃə'iːz/ *n* [U] *informal* a way of talking or writing used by government officials, that is unnecessarily difficult to understand

of·fi·cial·ly /ə'fɪʃəli/ *adv* **1** publicly or formally: *The new church was officially opened on July 5th.* | *Nothing has yet been officially announced.* | *The scheme was officially launched in May.* | *Has the company officially confirmed the appointment?* | *the number of officially recognized political parties* **2** [sentence adverb] according to what someone says publicly, even though this may not be true: *Officially, the talks never took place* .

of·ficial re·ceiver *n* [C] *BrE* someone whose job is to take care of the financial affairs of a company or a person that is BANKRUPT

of·fi·ci·ate /ə'fɪʃieɪt/ *v* [I] to perform official duties, especially at a religious ceremony

of·fi·cious /ə'fɪʃəs/ *adj* too eager to tell people what to do – used to show disapproval: *an officious traffic warden* —**officiously** *adv* —**officiousness** *n* [U]

off·ing /'ɒfɪŋ $ 'ɒː-, 'ɑː-/ *n* **be in the offing** to be likely to happen soon: *Big changes were in the offing.*

off-'key *adj* music that is off-key sounds unpleasant because it is played slightly above or below the correct PITCH; → **in tune**: *The band sounded slightly off-key.* —**off-key** *adv*: *Someone upstairs was singing off-key.*

off-'kilter *adj* **1** not completely straight or correctly balanced: *The paintings were slightly off-kilter.* **2** unusual in a strange or interesting way: *her off-kilter sense of humour*

off-,licence *n* [C] *BrE* a shop that sells wine, beer, and other alcoholic drinks, in bottles or cans; **≣ liquor store** *AmE*

off 'limits *adj* **be off limits a)** if a place is off limits, you are not allowed to go there; **≣ out of bounds**: [+to/for] *Footpaths are, of course, off limits to bikers.* **b)** if a subject is off limits, you are not allowed to talk about it: *Unlike most group discussions, nothing was off limits.*

off·line /,ɒf'laɪn $,ɒːf-/ *adv* **1** with your computer not connected to the Internet; **≣ online**: *I work offline most of the day.* **2** if computer equipment is offline, it is not directly connected to the computer; **≣ online**: *The printer was offline all morning.* —**offline** *adj*: *offline storage*

off·load /,ɒf'ləʊd $,ɒːf'loʊd/ *v* **1** [T] to get rid of something that you do not want by giving it or selling it to someone else: **offload sth onto sb** *The dealer had offloaded some of the shares onto a willing client.* **2 offload your worries/emotions/problems etc** *BrE* to tell someone about your worries etc in order to make yourself feel better **3** [T] to take something off a truck or ship: *The men offloaded their cargo.*

off-'message *adj, adv* a politician who is off-message says things that are different from the ideas of the political party they belong to; **≣ on-message**

off-'peak *adj especially BrE* **1** off-peak hours or periods are times that are less busy because fewer people want to do or use something: *Telephone charges are lower during off-peak periods.* **2** off-peak travel, electricity etc is cheaper because it is done or used at less busy times —**off-peak** *adv*

off-'piste *adj* not on the usual SKI slopes: *off-piste skiing* —**off-piste** *adv*

off·print /'ɒfprɪnt $ 'ɒːf-/ *n* [C] *technical* an article from a magazine that is printed and sold separately

off-,putting *adj BrE* if someone's behaviour or the appearance of something is off-putting, you do not like it or you think it is unattractive: *Some women found the competitive style of the discussions off-putting.* —**off-puttingly** *adv* → **put sb/sth off** at PUT

off-ramp *n* [C] *AmE* a road for driving off a FREEWAY; **≣ slip road** *BrE*

off-'road *adj* [usually before noun] **1** designed to be used on rough ground as well as on roads: *an off-road vehicle* **2** going over rough ground: *off-road cycling* | *off-road tracks* —**off-road** *adv*

off-'screen *adv* when a film actor is not acting; **≣ on-screen**: *What's he like off-screen?* —**off-screen** *adj*: *off-screen romances*

off-'sea,son *n* **the off-season a)** the time of year when not many people are taking holidays ; **≣ low season**; → **high season** : in the off-season *Most hotels are closed in the off-season.* **b)** *AmE* the time of year when a sport is not usually played; **≣ close season** *BrE* —,**off-'season** *adj, adv*: *Take advantage of our special off-season fares.*

off·set¹ /'ɒfset, ,ɒf'set $ 'ɒːfset, ,ɒːf'set/ *v past tense and past participle* **offset**, *present participle* **offsetting** [T] **1** if the cost or amount of something offsets another cost or amount, the two things have an opposite effect so that the situation remains the same: *Cuts in prices for milk, butter, and cheese will be offset by direct payments to farmers.* | **offset sth against sth** *He was able to offset his travel expenses against tax.* **2** to make something look better by being close to it and different: *His blonde hair offset a deep tan.*

off·set² /'ɒfset $ 'ɒːf-/ *adj* relating to a method of printing in which ink is put onto ROLLERS and the paper then passes between the rollers —**offset** *n* [U]

off·shoot /'ɒfʃuːt $ 'ɒːf-/ *n* [C] **1** something such as an organization which has developed from a larger or earlier one: [+of] *The company was originally an off-shoot of Bell Telephones.* | *the Mafia and its off-shoots* **2** a new stem or branch on a plant

off·shore /,ɒf'ʃɔː $,ɒːf'ʃɔːr‹ / *adj* **1** in or under the sea and not far from the coast; → **inshore, onshore**: *offshore oil fields* | *an offshore island* **2 offshore banks/companies/investments etc** banks etc that are based abroad in a country where you pay less tax than in your home country: *offshore financial centres* **3 offshore wind/current etc** a wind etc that is blowing or moving away from the land; **≣ onshore** —**offshore** *adv*: *a boat anchored offshore*

off·side¹ /,ɒf'saɪd‹ $,ɒːf-/ *adj, adv* in a position, usually ahead of the ball, where you are not allowed to play the ball in sports such as SOCCER and HOCKEY; **≣ onside**

off·side² /'ɒfsaɪd $ 'ɒːf-/ *n* **the offside** *BrE* the side of a car that is nearest to the middle of the road when you are driving it; → **nearside** —**offside** *adj*: *the offside headlight*

off-'site *adj, adv* happening away from a particular place, especially a place of work; **≣ on-site**: *the off-site disposal of harmful waste* | *A small team worked off-site on the project.*

off·spring /'ɒf,sprɪŋ $ 'ɒːf-/ *n plural* **offspring** [C] **1** someone's child or children – often used humorously: *a young mother trying to control her off-spring* **2** an animal's baby or babies: *a lion and its offspring*

off·stage /,ɒf'steɪdʒ‹ $,ɒːf-/ *adv* **1** just behind or to the side of a stage in a theatre, where the people watching a play cannot see; **≣ onstage**: *There was a loud crash offstage.* **2** when an actor is not acting: *Offstage, Peter seemed a shy sort of person.* —**offstage** *adj*: *offstage noises*

off-street *adj* **off-street parking** places for parking that are not on public streets

≣ 1 000, **2** 000, **3** 000, most frequent words in **S** poken and **W** ritten English

someone you like: *Good old Keith!* | *You poor old thing!*

13 a good old sth also **a right old sth** *BrE spoken* used to talk about something you enjoy: *We had a good old talk.*

14 old devil/rascal etc *spoken* used to talk about someone you like and admire: *You old devil! You were planning this all along!*

15 old fool/bastard/bat etc *spoken not polite* used to talk very rudely about someone you do not like: *the stupid old cow*

16 the old guard a group of people within an organization or club who do not like changes or new ideas: *He'll never manage to persuade the old guard.*

17 be an old hand (at sth) to have a lot of experience of something: *I'm an old hand at this game.*

18 be old before your time to look or behave like someone much older than you, especially because of difficulties in your life

19 for old times' sake if you do something for old times' sake, you do it to remind yourself of a happy time in the past

20 the old country *especially AmE* the country that you were born in, but that you no longer live in, used especially to mean Europe

21 an old head on young shoulders *BrE* a young person who seems to think and behave like an older person

22 pay/settle an old score to punish someone for something wrong that they did to you in the past

23 of/from the old school old-fashioned and believing in old ideas and customs: *a doctor of the old school*

24 old wives' tale a belief based on old ideas that are now considered to be untrue

25 of old *literary* from a long time ago in the past: *the knights of old*

26 Old English/Old Icelandic etc an early form of English, Icelandic etc

---

WORD FOCUS: OLD

PEOPLE: **elderly** a polite word used to describe someone who is old | **middle-aged** aged between about 50 and 60 years old | **senior citizen/senior** *AmE*/**pensioner** *BrE*/**retiree** *AmE* someone over 60 who has stopped working | **senile** old and mentally ill | **ancient/geriatric, be getting on, be past it, be over the hill, be no spring chicken** informal words and expressions used to describe someone who is old, often used humorously | **geriatric** geriatric medicine, care, hospitals etc are for old people

THINGS/PLACES: **ancient** ancient civilizations, cities, buildings, traditions etc existed many hundreds of years ago | **prehistoric** existing many thousands of years ago | **antique** antique furniture, jewellery etc is old and often valuable

---

old 'age n [U] the part of your life when you are old: *You need to start putting money away for your old age.* | **in (sb's) old age** *My mother had a very lively mind, even in her old age.*

old age 'pension n [C,U] *BrE* money that is paid regularly by the state to old people who do not work any more; ▤ **social security** *AmE*

old age 'pensioner n [C] *BrE* **OAP** someone who does not work any more and who receives an old age pension

Old 'Bill n the Old Bill *BrE informal* the police

old 'boy n [C] **1** *BrE* a man who used to be a student at a school: *an old boys' reunion* **2** the old-boy network the system by which men who went to the same school, belong to the same club etc use their influence to help each other **3** *BrE spoken* an old man: *He's a nice old boy.* **4** *BrE old-fashioned* used when speaking to a male friend: *How are you, old boy?* → OLD GIRL

old·e /'əʊldi $ 'oʊldi/ *adj* an old-fashioned spelling of 'old', used in the names of shops, products etc to make them seem traditional and attractive: *ye olde tea shop*

old e'conomy n [singular] also **the Old Economy** an economic system that is based on older types of

---

industry such as steel, energy, and machinery: *Is the Old Economy really dead?* —**old economy** *adj* [only before noun]: *old economy practices*

old·en /'əʊldən $ 'oʊld-/ *adj* **in (the) olden days** also **in olden times** a long time ago: *People didn't travel so much in the olden days.*

Old English 'Sheepdog n [C] a large dog with long thick grey and white hair

old-es'tablished *adj* [only before noun] having existed, been in business etc for a long time: *old-established merchant banks*

olde-world·e /ˌəʊldi 'wɜːldi‹ $ ˌoʊldi 'wɜːr-/ *adj BrE informal* a place that is olde-worlde has been decorated so that it looks old-fashioned: *an olde-worlde pub*

old-'fashioned *adj* **1** not considered to be modern or fashionable any more: *She wears really old-fashioned clothes!* | *old-fashioned farming methods* | *The idea seems rather old-fashioned now.* **2** someone who is old-fashioned has ideas, attitudes etc that were more usual in the past than now: *He's very old-fashioned when it comes to music.*

old fo·gey /ˌəʊld 'fəʊgi $ ˌoʊld 'foʊ-/ n [C] *informal* someone who is boring and has old-fashioned ideas about things, especially someone old

old 'folk *BrE* also **old 'folks** *especially AmE* n [plural] old people – an expression used when talking about old people in a kind way

old 'folks' home n [C] *informal* a place where old people live and are looked after when they are unable to look after themselves; ▤ **old people's home**, **nursing home**

old girl n [C] *BrE* **1** a woman who is a former student of a school: *an old girls' reunion* **2** *spoken* an old woman: *She's a nice old girl!* → OLD BOY

Old 'Glory n [U] *AmE informal* the flag of the US

old-growth *adj* [only before noun] old-growth forests/rainforest/timber etc forests etc that have been growing in a place for a long time, rather than ones planted more recently

old 'hat *adj* [not before noun] if something is old hat, a lot of people have said or done the same thing before and it is therefore not new or interesting: *Most of this is probably old hat to you, isn't it?*

old·ie /'əʊldi $ 'oʊldi/ n [C] *informal* someone or something that is old, especially an old film or song → GOLDEN OLDIE

old·ish /'əʊldɪʃ $ 'oʊld-/ *adj* fairly old: *an oldish woman*

old 'lady n sb's old lady old-fashioned informal someone's wife, mother, or girlfriend: *Where's your old lady?*

old 'lag n [C] *BrE old-fashioned* someone who has been in prison many times

old 'maid n [C] *old-fashioned not polite* an offensive word for a woman who has never married and is not young any more; ▤ **spinster**

old 'man n [C] **1** old-fashioned informal someone's husband, father, or boyfriend: *I heard her old man beats her.* **2** *BrE old-fashioned* used when speaking to a male friend: *Could I have a word with you, old man?*

old 'master, Old Master n [C] a famous painter, especially from the 15th to 18th century, or a painting by one of these painters: *a priceless collection of old masters*

old 'money n [U] people who come from families that have had a lot of money for a long time, which gives them a high social position: *He invited both the smart set and Perth's old money.*

Old 'Nick n *BrE old-fashioned* the Devil

old 'people's home n [C] *BrE* a place where old people live and are cared for when they are too old to live by themselves; ▤ **nursing home**

old 'salt n [C] *old-fashioned* a SAILOR who has had a lot of experience of sailing

'old-school adj [only before noun] old-fashioned, or relating to ideas from the past: *He was one of the last old-school comics.*

.old school 'tie n **the old school tie** BrE the situation that exists when people who went to the same private school use their influence to help each other get work or other advantages: *a system based on social class and the old school tie*

old·ster /'əʊldstə $ 'oʊldstər/ n [C] *informal* an old person

'old-style adj [only before noun] similar to the type of something that existed in the past: *old-style communism*

.Old 'Testament n **the Old Testament** the first part of the Christian Bible containing ancient Hebrew writings about the time before the birth of Christ; → **New Testament**

'old-time adj [only before noun] typical of what used to exist, be done etc in the past: *old-time remedies*

.old 'timer n [C] **1** someone who has been doing a job or living in a place for a long time and knows a lot about it **2** *especially AmE* an old man

.old 'woman n [C] BrE *old-fashioned informal* **1** sb's old woman someone's wife or mother **2** a man who pays too much attention to small, unimportant details — **old womanish** adj

'old-world adj [only before noun] an old-world place or quality is attractive because it is old or reminds you of the past: *The town has retained much of its old-world charm.*

.Old 'World n **the Old World** the Eastern HEMISPHERE, especially Europe, Asia, and Africa; → **New World** *the civilizations of the Old World*

ole /əʊl $ oʊl/ adj [only before noun] *written* used to represent the way some people say 'old': *my ole man*

o·le·ag·i·nous /ˌəʊliˈædʒɪnəs $ ˌoʊ-/ adj *technical* containing, producing, or like oil

o·le·an·der /ˌəʊliˈændə $ ˌoʊliˈændər/ n [C,U] a green bush with white, pink, or purple flowers

O lev·el /'əʊ ˌlevəl $ 'oʊ-/ n [C,U] *Ordinary level* an examination in a range of subjects, done by students in schools in England and Wales, usually at the age of 15 or 16. In 1988, O levels were replaced by GCSEs. → **GCSE, A Level**

ol·fac·to·ry /ɒlˈfæktəri $ ɑːl-, oʊl-/ adj [only before noun] *technical* connected with the sense of smell: *the olfactory cells in the nose*

ol·i·garch /'ɒlɪɡɑːk $ 'ɑːlɪɡɑːrk/ n [C] a member of a small group of people who run a country or organization — **oligarchic** /ˌɒlɪˈɡɑːkɪk◂ $ ˌɑːlɪˈɡɑːr-/ adj

ol·i·gar·chy /'ɒlɪɡɑːki $ 'ɑːlɪɡɑːrki/ n plural **oligarchies** **1** [C usually singular] a small group of people who run a country or organization, or a country that is run by a small group of people **2** [U] when a country or organization is run by a small group of people: *Eventually oligarchy took over from democracy.*

ol·i·gop·o·ly /ˌɒlɪˈɡɒpəli $ ˌɑːlɪˈɡɑː-/ n plural **oligopolies** [C] *technical* the control of all or most of a business activity by very few companies, so that other organizations cannot easily compete with them

ol·ive /'ɒlɪv $ 'ɑː-/ n **1** [C] a small, bitter, egg-shaped black or green fruit, used as food and for making oil **2** [C] also **olive tree** a tree that produces olives, grown especially in Mediterranean countries: *an olive grove* **3** [U] also **olive green** a deep yellowish green colour **4** **olive skin/complexion** skin colour that is typical of people from countries such as Greece, Italy, or Turkey **5** **extend/offer/hold out etc an olive branch (to sb)** to do or say something in order to show that you want to end an argument with someone — **olive** adj: *an olive sweatshirt*

.olive 'oil n [C,U] a pale yellow or green oil obtained from olives and used in cooking

-ologist /ɒlədʒɪst $ aːl-/ also **-logist** suffix [in nouns] a person who studies or has knowledge of a particular kind of science: *a biologist*

-ology /ɒlədʒi $ aːl-/ also **-logy** suffix [in nouns] **1** the study of something, especially something scientific: *geology* (=the study of rocks and the Earth) | *climatology* (=the study of climate) | *Egyptology* (=the study of ancient Egypt) **2** the things studied by a particular science: *The geology* (=structure of the rocks etc) *of north Devon is particularly interesting.* —**-ological** /ɒlədʒɪkəl $ -laː-/ suffix [in adjectives] —**-ologically** /ɒlədʒɪkli $ əlaː-/ suffix [in adverbs]: *geologically interesting*

O·lym·pi·ad /əˈlɪmpi-æd/ n [C] *formal* a particular occasion of the modern Olympic Games: *the 25th Olympiad*

O·lym·pi·an¹ /əˈlɪmpiən/ adj [only before noun] **1** like a god, especially by being calm and not concerned about ordinary things: *He viewed the world with Olympian detachment.* **2** relating to the ancient Greek gods: *Olympian mythology*

Olympian² n [C] someone who is taking part in, or who has taken part in, the Olympic Games – used especially in news reports: *the American Olympians*

O·lym·pic /əˈlɪmpɪk/ adj [only before noun] relating to the Olympic Games: *an Olympic gold medal*

O.lympic 'Games also **Olympics** n [plural] **the Olympic Games/the Olympics** an international sports event held every four years in different countries: *the 1976 Olympic Games*

OM /ˌəʊ ˈem $ ˌoʊ-/ n [C] *Order of Merit* a special HONOUR given to someone by the Queen of England

om·buds·man /'ɒmbʊdzmən $ 'aːm-/ n plural **ombudsmen** /-mən/ [C] someone who deals with complaints made by ordinary people against the government, banks, insurance companies etc

o·me·ga /'əʊmɪɡə $ oʊˈmeɡə, -'miː-, -'meɪ-/ n the last letter of the Greek alphabet

ome·lette also **omelet** AmE /'ɒmlɪt $ 'aːm-/ n [C] **1** eggs mixed together and cooked in hot fat, sometimes with other foods added: *a cheese omelette* **2** **you can't make an omelette without breaking eggs** used to say that it is impossible to achieve anything important without causing a few problems

o·men /'əʊmən $ 'oʊ-/ n [C] a sign of what will happen in the future: *The car won't start. Do you think it's an omen?* | **a good/bad/ill omen** *The mist seemed like a bad omen and Sara's heart sank a little.* | [+of] *He will regard your presence as an omen of good fortune.* | [+for] *It's a good omen for the future.*

om·i·nous /'ɒmɪnəs $ 'aː-/ adj making you feel that something bad is going to happen: *'How long will she be ill?' he asked. There was an ominous silence.* | *The car is making an ominous rattling sound.* —**ominously** adv: *The sky looked ominously dark.*

o·mis·sion /əʊˈmɪʃən, ə- $ oʊ-, ə-/ n **1** [U] when you do not include or do not do something: [+of] *The omission of her name was not a deliberate act.* | [+from] *his omission from the team* **2** [C] something that has been omitted: *Copies of the lists were posted so that omissions could be corrected.* | **serious/notable/major omission** *Your failing to note her mistakes is a serious omission.* | **a glaring omission** (=one that is very bad and easily noticed)

o·mit /əʊˈmɪt, ə- $ oʊ-, ə-/ v omitted, omitting [T] **1** to not include someone or something, either deliberately or because you forget to do it; ▤ **leave out**: *Please don't omit any details, no matter how trivial they may seem.* | **omit sth from sth** *Lisa's name had been omitted from the list of honor students.* **2** **omit to do sth** *formal* to not do something, either because you forgot or deliberately: **omit to mention/say/tell etc** *Oliver omitted to mention that he was married.*

omni- /ɒmni $ aːm-/ prefix [in nouns and adjectives] everything or everywhere; → **all**: *an omnivore* (=an animal that eats all kinds of food)

om·ni·bus¹ /'ɒmnɪbəs, -bʌs $ 'ɑːm-/ *n* [C] **1** *BrE* a radio or television programme consisting of several programmes that have previously been broadcast separately: *the Saturday **omnibus edition** of 'Brookside'* **2** a book containing several stories, especially by one writer, that have already been printed separately: ***Omnibus editions** of novels tend to be too heavy to be read with comfort.* **3** *BrE old-fashioned* a bus

omnibus² *adj* [only before noun] *AmE* an omnibus law contains several different laws collected together: *an omnibus civil rights bill*

om·nip·o·tent /ɒm'nɪpətənt $ ɑːm-/ *adj formal* able to do everything; 🔲 **all-powerful** —**omnipotence** *n* [U]

om·ni·pres·ent /ˌɒmnɪ'prezənt◂ $ ˌɑːm-/ *adj formal* present everywhere at all times —**omnipresence** *n* [U]: *the omnipresence of God*

om·nis·cient /ɒm'nɪsiənt, -'nɪʃənt $ ɑːm'nɪʃənt/ *adj formal* knowing everything: *the book's omniscient narrator* —**omniscience** *n* [U]

om·ni·vore /'ɒmnɪvɔː $ 'ɑːmnɪvɔːr/ *n* [C] an animal that eats both meat and plants; → **carnivore, herbivore**

om·niv·o·rous /ɒm'nɪvərəs $ ɑːm-/ *adj* **1** an animal that is omnivorous eats both meat and plants; → **carnivorous, herbivorous 2** *formal* interested in everything, especially in all books: *an **omnivorous** reader*

on¹ S1 W1 /ɒn $ ɑːn, ɔːn/ *prep*
1 ON A SURFACE **a)** touching a surface or being supported by a surface: *Leave your things on the table over there.* | *People were sunbathing on the grass.* | *The little girl was sitting on her father's shoulders.* → see box at AT **b)** used to say that someone or something moves so that they are then touching or supported by a surface: *snow falling on the mountainsides* | *He threw himself on the bed.*
2 SUPPORTING YOUR BODY used to say what part of someone's body is touching the ground or another surface and supporting their weight: *She was on her feet in no time.* | *He was on his hands and knees searching for something.* | *Can you stand on your head?*
3 PART HIT/TOUCHED used to say what part of someone or something is hit or touched: *I wanted to punch him on the nose.* | *Matt kissed her on the cheek.*
4 WRITTEN/SHOWN used to say where something is written or shown: *There's a diagram on page 25.* | *He wrote his phone number on a piece of paper.*
5 ATTACHED attached to or hanging from something: *She hung her coat on a hook.* | *Dogs must be kept on a lead at all times.*
6 PLACE in a particular place: *The town is right on the border.* | *Is there a water supply on the island?* | *He grew up on a ranch in California.* | *a store on Fifth Avenue*
7 POSITION in a particular position in relation to something else: *You'll see the school on your left.* | *They live on the opposite side of the town.*
8 LOOKING/POINTING looking or pointing towards something or someone: *His eyes were on the stranger standing in the doorway.* | *She trained her binoculars on the house.*
9 DAY/DATE during a particular day: *They'll be here on Tuesday.* | *I was born on July 1st.* | *We'll see you on Christmas Eve.*
10 AFFECTING/RELATING TO affecting or relating to someone or something: *a tax on cigarettes* | *his influence on young people* | *There will be new restrictions on the sale of weapons.* | *What effect will these changes have on the tourist industry?*
11 ABOUT about a particular subject: *Do you have any books on India?* | *You can get information on local services by calling this number.* | *an international conference on global warming*
12 ORDERS/ADVICE as a result of someone's order, request, or advice: *He was killed on the king's orders.* |

I accepted the offer on the advice of my lawyer.
13 EAT/DRINK used to talk about what someone usually eats or drinks: *They live mainly on beans, lentils and rice.* | *Is your baby on solid food yet?*
14 TRANSPORT **a)** in or into a bus, train, plane etc; 🔲 **off**: *Did you manage to sleep on the plane?* | *Tommy should be on the six o'clock train.* | *She got on the first bus that came along.* **b)** riding something: *a statue of the king on horseback* | *I'll probably come on my bike.*
15 MONEY receiving money for a job or as a regular payment: *He's on quite a good salary now.* | *She must be on at least £50,000 a year.* | *the difficulties faced by families on low incomes*
16 FUEL using a particular type of FUEL or power: *Most buses run on diesel.* | *Does it work on mains electricity?*
17 MEDICINE/DRUGS taking a particular drug or medicine regularly; 🔲 **off**: *Are you still on antibiotics?* | *The doctor put her on Prozac.* | *A lot of these kids are on heroin by the age of twelve.*
18 what's sb on? *spoken* used to say that someone is behaving in a very strange way, as if they are taking an illegal drug
19 USING EQUIPMENT using a machine or piece of equipment: *He's been on the computer all afternoon.* | *Is Rachel still on the phone?*
20 MUSICAL INSTRUMENTS playing a musical instrument: *He played a short piece on the piano.* | *The album features Rick Wakeman on keyboards.*
21 RADIO/TELEVISION being broadcast by radio or television: *What's on TV tonight?* | *Did you hear that programme on the radio last night?*
22 RECORDED used to say in what form information is stored or music, films etc are recorded: *The movie is now available on video and DVD.* | *I always keep a backup copy on disk.*
23 ACTIVITY/JOURNEY taking part in an activity or travelling somewhere: *She's on a course all this week.* | *I met him on vacation in Canada.* | *My girlfriend is often away on business trips.*
24 INCLUDED included in a group or team of people or in a list: *Are you still on the management committee?* | *Mr Edwards is no longer on the staff here.* | *Whose team are you on?* | *There was no steak on the menu.* | *What's the next item on the agenda?*
25 WHEN STH HAPPENS *formal* as soon as someone has done something or as soon as something has happened: *Couples are presented with a bottle of wine on their arrival at the hotel.* | *All patients are examined on admission to the hospital.* | **on doing sth** *What was your reaction on seeing him?*
26 COMPARED WITH STH compared with another person or thing: *This essay is a definite improvement on your last one.* | *Sales are 10% up on last year.*
27 CARRYING STH *informal* if you have something on you, you have it in your pocket, your bag etc: *I don't have any money on me.*
28 PAY be on sb *spoken* used to say who is going to pay for something: *The drinks are on me!* | *Each table will get a bottle of champagne on the house* (=paid for by the restaurant, hotel etc).
29 TELEPHONE NUMBER used to say what number you should use in order to telephone someone; 🔲 **at** *AmE*: *You can contact me on this number.*
30 CAUSING SB PROBLEMS used when something bad happens to you, for example when something you are using suddenly stops working, or someone you have a relationship with suddenly leaves you: *Suddenly the telephone went dead on me.* | *Dorothy's first husband walked out on her.*

on² S1 W1 *adj, adv* [not before noun]
1 CONTINUING used to say that someone continues to do something or something continues to happen, without stopping: *We decided to play on even though it was snowing.* | *He went **on and on** (=talked for a very long time) about his job all evening.*
2 FURTHER if you move, walk etc on, you move forward or further towards something: *If you walk on*

a little, you can see the coast. | *We drove on towards Manchester.*

3 LATER later than or after a particular time: *Now, forty years on, this is one of the most successful theatres in the country.* | *From that moment on I never believed a word she said.*

4 WEARING STH if you have something on, you are wearing it: *All he **had on** was a pair of tattered shorts.* | ***Put** your coat **on**. It's freezing outside.*

5 ATTACHED used to say that something is attached to something else, especially when it is in the correct position; ⊡ **off**: *Is the cover on properly?* | *Remember to put the lid back on.*

6 WRITTEN used to say that something is written somewhere: *He was wearing a badge with his name on.*

7 TRANSPORT in or into a bus, train etc; ⊡ **off**: *The train stopped and two people got on.*

8 LIGHT/MACHINE if a machine, light etc is on, it is operating; ⊡ **off**: *Who left all the lights on?* | *The TV's on, but nobody seems to be watching it.* | *He sat down at the desk and switched on the computer.*

9 BEING BROADCAST if a radio or television programme etc is on, it is being broadcast: *What time is 'Star Trek' on?*

10 EVENTS if an event is on, it has been arranged and is happening or will happen; ⊡ **off**: *The transport union has confirmed that the strike is definitely on.* | *I'd avoid the city centre – there's some kind of procession on.* | *Is the party still on tonight or have they cancelled it?*

11 PERFORMING/SPEAKING performing or speaking in public: *You're on in two minutes.*

12 WORKING if you are on at a particular time, you are doing your job at that time: *I'm not on again until 2 o'clock tomorrow.*

13 have sth on *informal* if you have something on, there is something that you must do: *I haven't got anything on tomorrow, so I could see you then.* | *We've got a lot on at the moment.*

14 on and off also **off and on** for short periods but not regularly over a long period of time: *He's been smoking for 10 years now, on and off.*

15 be/go/keep on at sb *informal* to keep complaining to someone or asking someone to do something, especially when this annoys them: *I've been on at him to fix that cupboard for weeks now.* | *I wish you wouldn't go on at me the whole time!*

16 be/go/keep on about sth *BrE informal* to keep talking about something, in a way that is boring or annoying: *He's always going on about money.* | *I don't know what you're on about!*

17 be not on *BrE spoken* if something is not on, it is not acceptable or reasonable: *I'm sorry, what you're suggesting is just not on!*

18 be on for sth *spoken* to be ready or willing to do something that someone has suggested: *Right, how many of you are on for a drink after work?*

19 you're on *spoken* used tell someone that you accept a BET or an invitation to compete against them: *'I bet you £20 he won't turn up.' 'You're on!' →* ONTO

o.n.o. *BrE or near/nearest offer* used in advertisements to show that you are willing to sell something for slightly less money than you have said in the advertisement: *Bicycle for sale: £60 o.n.o.*

'**on-air** *adj* [only before noun] broadcast while actually happening; ⊡ **off-air**: *an on-air interview*

'**on-board** *adj* [only before noun] carried on a ship, plane, car etc: *an on-board computer*

once[1] S1 W1 /wʌns/ *adv*

1 on one occasion only: *I've only met her once.* | *Paul's been to Wexford once before.* | **(just) the once** *BrE spoken*: *Mrs Peterson came in to see Ruth just the once.*

2 once a week/once every three months etc one time every week etc, as a regular activity or event: *Staff meetings take place once a week.* | *They took separate holidays at least once every two years.*

3 at some time in the past, but not now: *Sonya and Ida had once been close friends.* | *She and her husband had*

once owned a house like this. | **once-great/proud etc** *It was sad to see the once-great man looking so frail.* | *the once-mighty steel industry*

4 in the past, at a time that is not stated: *I once ran 21 miles.* | *Marx once described religion as the 'opium of the people'.*

5 at once a) immediately or without delay: *Now, go upstairs at once and clean your room!* | *When I saw him I recognized him at once.* **b)** together, at the same time: *I can't do two things at once!* | *Don't all talk at once.*

6 once more/once again a) again, after happening several times before: *I looked at myself in the mirror once more.* | *Once again she's refusing to help.* **b)** used to say that a situation changes back to its previous state: *The crowds had all gone home and the street was quiet once more.* **c)** *formal* used before you repeat something that you said before: *Once again, it must be stressed that the pilot was not to blame.*

7 all at once a) if something happens all at once, it happens suddenly when you are not expecting it: *All at once there was a loud banging on the door.* **b)** together, at the same time: *A lot of practical details needed to be attended to all at once.*

8 (every) once in a while sometimes, although not often: *I do get a little anxious once in a while.* | *I saw her in the shop every once in a while.*

9 never once/not once used to emphasize that something has never happened: *I never once saw him get angry or upset.* | *Not once did they finish a job properly.*

10 (just) for once used to say that something unusual happens, especially when you wish it would happen more often: *Be honest for once.* | *Just for once, let me make my own decision.* | *For once Colin was speechless.*

11 once and for all a) if you deal with something once and for all, you deal with it completely and finally: *Let's settle this matter once and for all.* **b)** *BrE spoken* used to emphasize your impatience when you ask or say something that you have asked or said many times before: *Once and for all, will you switch off that television!*

12 once or twice a few times: *I wrote to him once or twice, but he didn't answer.*

13 (just) this once *spoken* used to emphasize that this is the only time you are allowing something, asking for something etc, and it will not happen again: *Go on, lend me the car, just this once.* | *I'll make an exception this once.*

14 once upon a time a) *spoken* at a time in the past that you think was much better than now: *Once upon a time you used to be able to leave your front door unlocked.* **b)** a long time ago – used at the beginning of children's stories

15 once in a blue moon *informal* very rarely: *It only happens like this once in a blue moon.*

16 do sth once too often to repeat a bad, stupid, or dangerous action with the result that you get punished or cause trouble for yourself: *He tried that trick once too often and in the end they caught him.*

17 once a ..., always a ... *spoken* used to say that people stay the same and cannot change the way they behave and think: *Once a thief, always a thief.*

18 once is/was enough *spoken* used to say that after you have done something one time you do not need or want to do it again

19 once bitten, twice shy used to say that people will not do something again if it has been a bad experience

once[2] S1 W1 *conjunction* from the time when something happens: *Once I get him a job, he'll be fine.* | *Once in bed, the children usually stay there.*

'**once-over** *n* **give sth the/a once-over a)** to look at someone or something quickly to check what they are like **b)** to clean or tidy something quickly

on·col·o·gy /ɒŋˈkɒlədʒi $ ɑːŋˈkɑː-/ *n* [U] the part of medical science that deals with CANCER and TUMOURS
—**oncologist** *n* [C]

on·com·ing /ˈɒn,kʌmɪŋ $ ˈɑːn-, ˈɒːn-/ adj **oncoming car/traffic etc** a car etc that is coming towards you: *He crashed into an oncoming car.*

one¹ [S1] [W1] /wʌn/ number

1 the number 1: *They had one daughter.* | *one hundred and twenty-one pounds* | *Come back at one* (=one o'clock). | *Katie's almost one* (=one year old).

2 one or two a small number of people or things; ▣ a few: *There are one or two things to sort out before I leave.* | [+of] *One or two of us knew him quite well.*

3 in ones and twos BrE alone or in pairs, rather than in large numbers or groups: *Guests arrived in ones and twos.*

one² [S1] [W1] pron plural **ones**

1 used to mean someone or something of a type that has already been mentioned or is known about: *'Have you got a camera?' 'No.' 'You should buy one'* (=buy a camera). | *The train was crowded so we decided to catch a later one* (=catch a later train). | **the one(s) (that/who/which)** *The only jokes I tell are the ones that I hear from you.* | **this one/that one/these ones/those ones** *I like all the pictures except this one.*

2 used to mean someone or something from a group that has been mentioned or is about to be mentioned: *The children seemed upset. One was crying.* | [+of] *This is one of my favourite books.*

3 used to talk about a particular person or thing in comparison with other similar people or things: [+of] *One of the men sounded furious,* **the other** *frightened.* | *She has two daughters.* **One** *is a primary school teacher,* **the other** *a musician.*

4 the one(s) who/that the person or people who: *I was the one who had been attacked, not Richard.* | **The only ones** *who will benefit are the shareholders.*

5 one by one used when one person or thing in a group does something, then the next, then the next, especially in a regular way: *One by one each soldier approached the coffin and gave a final salute.*

6 one after another/one after the other if events happen one after the other, they happen without much time between them: *One after another, tropical storms battered the Pacific coastline.*

7 (all) in one if someone or something is many different things all in one, they are all those things: *It's a TV, radio and VCR all in one.*

8 formal used to mean people in general, including yourself: *One can never be too careful.* | *Great pictures make one think.* ⚠ This is a very formal use. People usually say or write **you** instead of 'one': *You can never be too careful.*

9 I, for one, ... used to emphasize that you believe something, will do something etc and hope others will do the same: *I, for one, am proud of the team's effort.*

10 ... for one used to give an example of someone or something: *There were several other people absent that afternoon, weren't there? Mr Ashton for one.*

11 be one up (on sb)/get one up on sb to have or get an advantage over someone → ONE-UPMANSHIP

12 put one over on sb informal to trick someone: *No one's going to put one over on me!*

13 be at one with sb/sth a) to feel very calm or relaxed in the situation or environment you are in: *She felt as she always did in these mountains: peaceful, without care,* **at one with** *nature.* **b)** formal to agree with someone about something: *He was at one with Wheatley on the need to abandon free trade.*

14 informal used in particular phrases to mean 'an alcoholic drink': *How about a quick one at the pub?* | **have had one too many** (=have drunk too much alcohol) | **(have) one for the road** (=have one last alcoholic drink before you leave a place)

15 the one about ... spoken a joke or humorous story: *Have you heard the one about the chicken who tried to cross the road?*

16 as one written if many people do something as one,

they all do it at the same time: *The whole team stood up as one.*

17 a difficult/hard/good etc one a particular kind of problem, question, story etc: *'What do you attribute your long life to?' 'Oh that's a difficult one'.*

18 one and the same the same person or thing: *Muhammad Ali and Cassius Clay are one and the same.*

19 not/never be one to do sth informal to never do a particular thing, because it is not part of your character to do it: *Tom is not one to show his emotions.*

20 not/never be (a great) one for (doing) sth informal to not enjoy a particular activity, subject etc: *I've never been a great one for watersports.*

21 one of us spoken used to say that someone belongs to the same group as you, or has the same ideas, beliefs etc: *You can talk in front of Terry – he's one of us.*

22 one and all old-fashioned or formal everyone: *Apologies to one and all.*

23 got it in one! BrE spoken used to say that someone has correctly guessed or understood something immediately: *'You're not painting the house again are you?' 'Got it in one!'*

24 little/young ones spoken used by some people to mean 'children', especially young children: *She's got four little ones.*

25 you are/he is a one BrE old-fashioned used to say that someone's behaviour is amusing, strange or surprising: *You are a one!* → ONE-TO-ONE

one³ [S1] [W1] determiner

1 used to emphasize a particular person or thing: *One person I find very difficult is Bob.* | *If there's one thing I can't stand, it's people who bite their nails.*

2 one day/morning/year etc a) on a particular day, morning etc in the past: *One morning I was sitting at my desk when a policeman knocked at my door.* **b)** used to talk about a day, morning etc in the future which is not yet exactly known or decided: *We should go out for a drink one evening.* | *One day she hopes to move to the South Coast.*

3 used to talk about a particular person or thing in comparison with other similar people or things: *Why does my card work in* **one** *cash machine and not in* **another**?

4 It's one thing to ... it's (quite) another to used to say that the second thing mentioned is very different from the first, and is often much more difficult to do: *It's one thing to say we have a goal; it's another to actually act on it.*

5 for one thing used to introduce a reason for what you have just said: *He couldn't bring himself to say what he thought.* **For one thing,** *she seldom stopped to listen.* **For another,** *he doubted that he could make himself clear.*

6 be one crazy woman/be one interesting job etc spoken especially AmE to be a very crazy woman, be a very interesting job etc: *You're one lucky guy.*

7 formal used before the name of someone you do not know or have not heard of before; ▣ **a certain**: *He was accused of stealing a horse from one Peter Wright.*

one⁴ adj [only before noun] **1** only: *Her one concern was to get to the door without being seen.* | *Claire is the one person I can trust.* **2 one and only a)** used to emphasize that someone is very famous: *the one and only Frank Sinatra* **b)** used to emphasize that something is the only one of its kind: *I even tried my one and only French joke on them.*

one⁵ n [C usually plural] AmE a piece of paper money worth one dollar: *I don't have any ones.*

one an·oth·er [S3] [W3] pron each other: *Liz and I have known one another for years.* | *They often stay at one another's houses.*

one-armed ˈbandit n [C] a machine with a long handle, into which you put money in order to try to win more money; ▣ **slot machine;** ▣ **fruit machine** BrE

one-di·men·sion·al adj simple and not considering or showing all the parts of something – used to show disapproval: *the novel's one-dimensional characters*

'one-horse adj **1 one-horse town** informal a small and boring town **2 one-horse race** a race, competition etc which a particular person or thing looks likely to win easily

,one-'liner n [C] a very short joke or humorous remark

'one-man adj [only before noun] performed, operated, controlled etc by one person: He does a **one-man show** in Las Vegas. | a one-man business

,one-man 'band n [C] **1** informal an organization or activity in which one person does everything: The company is really a one-man band. **2** a street musician who plays several instruments at the same time

one·ness /'wʌnn‿s/ n [U] a peaceful feeling of being part of a whole: [+with] a sense of oneness with nature

,one-night 'stand n [C] **1** informal **a)** an occasion when two people have sex, but do not meet each other again: I'm not into one-night stands. **b)** a person that you have sex with once and do not see again **2** a performance of music or a play that is given only once in a particular place

'one-off¹ adj [only before noun] BrE happening or done only once, not as part of a regular series; ◳ **one-shot** AmE: It's yours for a **one-off payment** of only £200.

,one-'off² n [C] BrE **1** something that is done or made only once: The deal was a one-off. **2** informal someone who is completely different from anyone else

,one-on-'one adj between only two people: Virtually all instruction is in small groups or one-on-one. **—one-on-one** adv: Often, the employer just called in the drivers and bargained with them directly, one-on-one.

,one-parent 'family n [C] a family in which there is only one parent who lives with the children; ◳ **single parent family**

'one-piece adj [only before noun] consisting of only one piece, not separate parts: a one-piece bathing suit

on·er·ous /'ɒnərəs, 'əʊ- $ 'ɑː-, 'oʊ-/ adj formal work or a responsibility that is onerous is difficult and worrying or makes you tired: an onerous task

one·self /wʌn'self/ pron formal the REFLEXIVE form of ONE³ (2): It is only through study that one really begins to know oneself.

'one-shot adj [only before noun] AmE happening or done only once; ◳ **one-off** BrE: This is a one-shot deal. If it doesn't work, it's over.

,one-'sided adj **1** considering or showing only one side of a question, subject etc in a way that is unfair; → **biased, balanced**: The newspapers give a very one-sided account of the war. **2** an activity or competition that is one-sided is one in which one person or side is much stronger or does much more than the other: a very boring, one-sided game | The conversation was very one-sided. **—one-sidedly** adv **—one-sidedness** n [U]

,one-size-fits-'all adj [only before noun] **1** a one-size-fits-all attitude, method, plan etc is designed to please everyone or be suitable for every situation, often with the result that it is not successful: a one-size-fits-all public education program **2** one-size-fits-all clothes are designed so that people of any size can wear them

'one-star adj [only before noun] a one-star hotel, restaurant etc has been judged to be not of a very high standard

'one-stop adj **one-stop shop/store etc** a shop where you can buy many different things

'one-time adj [only before noun] former: Neil McMurtry, a one-time bus driver, is the lead singer.

,one-to-'one adj **1** between only two people: tuition on a one-to-one basis **2** matching each other exactly: a one-to-one correspondence between letters and sounds **—one-to-one** adv: I need to discuss it with him one-to-one.

,one-track 'mind n **have a one-track mind** to be continuously thinking about one particular thing, especially sex

,one-'two n [C] a movement in which a BOXER hits his opponent with one hand and then quickly with the other: Ali gives his opponent **the old one-two**, and it's all over.

one-up·man·ship /wʌn'ʌpmənʃɪp/ n [U] attempts to make yourself seem better than other people, no matter what they do

,one-'way adj [usually before noun] **1** a one-way street is one in which vehicles are only allowed to travel in one direction: the town's **one-way system 2** especially AmE a one-way ticket is for travelling from one place to another but not back again; ◳ **round-trip**; ◳ **single** BrE **3** a one-way process, relationship etc is one in which only one person makes any effort or provides anything

,one-way 'mirror n [C] a mirror which can be used as a window by people secretly watching from the other side of it

'one-woman adj [only before noun] performed, operated, controlled etc by only one woman: a **one-woman show**

on·go·ing /'ɒnˌɡəʊɪŋ $ 'ɑːnˌɡoʊɪŋ, 'ɔːn-/ adj continuing, or continuing to develop: their ongoing search for a new director | ongoing negotiations | The discussions are still ongoing. → **go on** at GO¹

on·ion S3 /'ʌnjən/ n [C,U] a round white vegetable with a brown, red, or white skin and many layers. Onions have a strong taste and smell: Chop the onions finely. | red onions | home-made onion soup → see picture at VEGETABLE¹

on·ion·skin /'ʌnjənskɪn/ n [U] AmE very thin light paper, used in the past especially for writing letters

on·line /'ɒnlaɪn $ 'ɑːn-, 'ɔːn-/ adj **1** connected to other computers through the Internet, or available through the Internet; ◳ **offline**: All the city's schools will be online by the end of the year. **2** directly connected to or controlled by a computer; ◳ **off-line**: an online printer **—online** adv: The reports are not available online yet.

,online 'auction n [C] a type of website in which you can sell things to the person who offers you the highest price

,online 'banking also **Internet banking** n [U] a service provided by banks so that people can find out information about their bank account, pay bills etc using the Internet

on·look·er /'ɒnˌlʊkə $ 'ɑːn-, 'ɔːn-/ n [C] someone who watches something happening without being involved in it: A crowd of onlookers had gathered at the scene of the accident. → **look on** at LOOK¹

on·ly¹ S1 W1 /'əʊnli $ 'oʊn-/ adv
1 not more than a particular number, age etc: Naomi was only 17 when she got married. | There are only a few cars on the island. | It's only eight o'clock.
2 used to say that something or someone is not very important, serious etc: It was only a joke. | It's an interesting job, but it's only temporary. | They're only small cuts, nothing life-threatening.
3 nothing or no one except a particular person or thing: Only the president can authorize a nuclear attack. | We use only the best ingredients. | **women/ men/residents etc only** The car park is for staff only.
4 used to say that something happens or is possible in one particular situation or place and no others, or for one particular reason: I'll tell you, but **only if** you don't tell anyone else. | I ate the food, but **only because** I was starving. | The transfer takes place **only when** the data is complete.
5 no earlier than a particular time: **only yesterday/ last week/recently** 'When did you e-mail her?' 'Only yesterday.' | **only then did/would/could etc sb do sth** (=at that moment and not before) Only then did she tell him about the attack.

O

6 only just *BrE* **a)** a very short time ago ago: *She's only just got up.* **b)** almost not; ☐ **barely**: *I only just finished my essay in time.*

7 can only hope/wait etc used to say that it is not possible to do more than hope etc: *We can only hope it won't rain on the day.*

8 I can only think/suppose/assume (that) *spoken* used when you are giving a reason for something, to say that you do not know something for certain but think that this is the only possible reason: *I can only assume that it was a mistake.*

9 I only wish/hope *spoken* used to express a strong wish or hope: *'What's happening?' 'I only wish I knew.'*

10 if only *spoken* used to express a strong wish: *If only he'd call!*

11 you'll only *spoken* used to tell someone that what they want to do will have a bad effect: *Don't interfere – you'll only make things worse.*

12 you only have to read/look at/listen to etc sth *spoken* used to say that it is easy to know that something is true because you can see or hear things that prove it: *You only have to look at the statistics to see that things are getting worse.*

13 only to used to say that someone did something, with a disappointing or surprising result: *I arrived only to find that the others had already left.*

14 only too very: *Prices have risen sharply, as we know only too well.* | *Mark was only too happy to agree with her.* → **not only ... but (also)** at NOT (4); → **only have eyes for sb** at EYE¹ (32); → **for sb's eyes only** at EYE¹ (25)

only² S1 W1 *adj* [only before noun]

1 used to say that there is one person, thing, or group in a particular situation and no others: *I was the only woman there.* | *He is our only child.* | *I was the only one who disagreed.* | *Cutting costs is the only solution.* | *She's the only person for this job.*

2 the only thing/problem is ... *spoken* used when you are going to mention a problem or disadvantage: *I could take you. The only thing is Dan might need the car.*

3 an only child a child who has no brothers or sisters → **the one and only** at ONE⁴ (2); → **(only) time will tell** at TIME¹ (36)

only³ *conjunction spoken* used like 'but' to give the reason why something is not possible: *I'd offer to help, only I'm really busy just now.*

on-'message *adj* [not before noun] *adv* a politician who is on-message says things that are in agreement with the ideas of his or her political party, especially when it appears that he or she is not thinking enough about these ideas; ☐ **off-message**

on-'off *adj* [only before noun] **1** happening sometimes and not at other times: *an on-off relationship* | *She had an on-off obsession with Mikey.* **2** an on-off switch is the thing you press to make a piece of electrical equipment start and stop working

on·o·mat·o·poe·ia /ˌɒnəmætəˈpiːə $ ˌɑːn-/ *n* [U] *technical* the use of words that sound like the thing that they are describing, for example 'hiss' or 'boom' —**onomatopoeic** *adj*

'on-ramp *n* [C] *AmE* a road for driving onto a FREEWAY; ☐ **slip road** *BrE*

on·rush /ˈɒnrʌʃ $ ˈɑːn-, ˈɒːn-/ *n* [singular] a strong fast movement forward, or the sudden development of something: [+of] *the first onrush of the epidemic* —**onrushing** *adj*: *the onrushing tide*

on-'screen, onscreen *adj, adv* appearing on a computer screen, or on a television or cinema screen: *An on-screen tutorial is included in the price of the software.* | *onscreen violence*

on·set /ˈɒnset $ ˈɑːn-, ˈɒːn-/ *n* **the onset of sth** the beginning of something, especially something bad: *the onset of winter*

on·shore /ˌɒnˈʃɔː $ ˌɑːnˈʃɔːr, ˌɒːn-/ *adj* [only before noun] *adv* **1** on the land, not in the sea; → **offshore**,

inshore: *onshore oil production* **2** onshore winds are moving from the sea towards the land; → **offshore**

on·side /ˌɒnˈsaɪd $ ˌɑːn-, ˌɒːn-/ *adj, adv* in a position where you are allowed to play the ball in sports such as football; ☐ **offside**

,on-'site *adj* [only before noun] *adv* at the place or on the area of land that you are talking about; ☐ **off-site**: *on-site car parking* | *Accommodation is provided on-site.*

on·slaught /ˈɒnslɔːt $ ˈɑːnslɔːt, ˈɒːn-/ *n* [C] **1** a large violent attack by an army: [+on/against] *In December they launched a full-scale onslaught on the capital.* **2** strong criticism of someone: [+on/against] *his public onslaught on the Conservatives* | **under the onslaught of sth** *He praised his wife for her dignity under the onslaught of the tabloid press.* **3** **the onslaught of sth** the effect of something that is unpleasant and could cause damage: *plants that will survive the onslaught of winter*

on·stage /ˌɒnˈsteɪdʒ $ ˌɑːn-, ˌɒːn-/ *adj, adv* on the stage in a theatre; ☐ **offstage**: *Even today I get nervous before I go onstage.*

,on 'stream, on-stream *adj, adv* **come/be on stream** if something new comes on stream, it starts to be used or done: *Costs should fall as new technology comes on-stream.*

'on-the-job *adj, adv* [only before noun] while working, or at work; → **in-service, in-house**: *on-the-job training*

'on-the-spot *adj* [only before noun] done immediately while you are at a particular place: *Doctors can often give on-the-spot treatment.* → **on the spot** at SPOT¹ (5)

onto S1 W2 *also* **on to** /ˈɒntə; *before vowels* ˈɒntʊ $ ˈɑːn-, ˈɒːn-/ *prep*
1 used to say that someone or something moves to a position on a surface, area, or object: *She watched him walk onto the platform.* | *Don't jump onto* (=into) *the bus while it's moving.* | *Pour the syrup on to the egg mixture.* | *The car rolled over onto its side.* | **down/out/up etc onto sth** *Let's get back onto the highway.*
2 used to say that a room, door, or window faces towards something or allows movement into another place: *The dining room looks out onto a pretty garden.* | *a gate leading on to a broad track*
3 be onto sb *informal* **a)** *also* **get onto sb** *especially BrE* to speak to someone in order to tell them or ask them something: *A number of people have been onto me complaining about the noise.* | *Get onto the Press Office and find out what's happening.* **b)** to know that a particular person did something wrong or committed a crime: *The police are onto him.*
4 be onto sth *informal* **a)** to have discovered or produced something new and interesting: *With the new show, we were onto something big.* | **be onto a good thing/a winner** *I think she's onto a real winner with this song.* **b)** *also* **get onto sth** to be dealing with something or start dealing with something: *I'll get onto it right away.*

on·tol·o·gy /ɒnˈtɒlədʒi $ ɑːnˈtɑː-/ *n* [U] a subject of study in PHILOSOPHY that is concerned with the nature of existence —**ontological** /ˌɒntəˈlɒdʒɪkəl $ ˌɑːntəˈlɑː-/ *adj*

o·nus /ˈəʊnəs $ ˈoʊ-/ *n* [singular] *formal* the responsibility for something: **the onus is on sb to do sth** *The onus is on the prosecution to provide proof of guilt.*

on·ward /ˈɒnwəd $ ˈɑːnwərd, ˈɒːn-/ *adj* [only before noun] moving forward or continuing: *The company offers flights to Amsterdam with onward travel to The Hague.* | *the onward march of science*

on·wards /ˈɒnwədz $ ˈɑːnwərdz, ˈɒːn-/ *usually* **onward** *AmE adv* **1 from ... onwards** beginning at a particular time or age and continuing after that: *from the 1980s onwards* **2** *literary* forwards: *He walked onwards to the head of the lake.* **3 onwards and upwards** used to say that the development, increase, or progress of something continues: *With exports strong, the business is moving **onwards and upwards**.*

on·yx /ˈɒnɪks $ ˈɑː-/ *n* [U] a stone with lines of different colours in it, often used in jewellery

oo·dles /'u:dlz/ *n* **oodles of sth** *informal* a large amount of something: *They've got oodles of money.*

oof /u:f/ *interjection* a sound that you make when you have been hit, especially in the stomach

ooh /u:/ *interjection* said when you think something is very beautiful, unpleasant, surprising etc: *Ooh, that's nice!*

ooh la la /,u: lɑ: 'lɑ:/ *interjection* said when you think that something or someone is surprising, unusual, or sexually attractive – used humorously

oomph /ʊmf/ *n* [U] *informal* a quality that makes something attractive and exciting and that shows energy: *It's not a bad song, but it needs more oomph.*

oops /ʊps/ *interjection* said when someone falls or makes a small mistake: *Oops, I've spelt that wrong.*

'oops-a-,daisy *interjection* said when a child falls

ooze¹ /u:z/ *v* [I always + adv/prep, T] **1** if a thick liquid oozes from something or if something oozes a thick liquid, that liquid flows from it very slowly: [+**from/out of/through**] *The ice cream was melting and oozing out of its wrapper.* | *A cut on his cheek was still oozing blood.* **2** to show a lot of a particular quality or feeling: *Andrew laughed gently,* **oozing charm.**

ooze² *n* **1** [U] very soft mud, especially at the bottom of a lake or sea **2** [singular] a very slow flow of liquid

ooz·y /'u:zi/ *adj informal* soft and wet like mud: *a black, oozy mess*

op /ɒp $ ɑ:p/ *n* [C] *BrE informal* a medical operation; 🔲 **operation**: *He's had a minor heart op.*

o·pac·i·ty /əʊ'pæsⱥti $ oʊ-/ *n* [U] **1** the quality that something has when it is difficult to see through; → **opaque 2** the quality that something has when it is difficult to understand

o·pal /'əʊpəl $ 'oʊ-/ *n* [C,U] a type of white stone with changing colours in it, often used in jewellery

o·pa·les·cent /,əʊpə'lesənt◂ $,oʊ-/ *adj literary* having colours that shine and seem to change: *an opalescent sky*

o·paque /əʊ'peɪk $ oʊ-/ *adj* [usually before noun] **1** opaque glass or liquid is difficult to see through and often thick; 🔲 **transparent**: *a shower with an opaque glass door* **2** *formal* difficult to understand: *an opaque style of writing* —**opaqueness** *n* [U]

'op art *n* [U] art that uses patterns which seem to move or to produce other shapes as you look at them

op. cit. /,ɒp 'sɪt $,ɑ:p-/ an abbreviation used in formal writing to refer to a book that has been mentioned before

OPEC /'əʊpek $ 'oʊ-/ *n* **Organization of Petroleum Exporting Countries** an organization of countries that produce and sell oil

,op-'ed *adj AmE* **op-ed page/article** a page in a newspaper that has articles containing opinions on various subjects, or one of these articles

o·pen¹ S1 W1 /'əʊpən $ 'oʊ-/ *adj*
1 DOOR/CONTAINER ETC not closed, so that things, people, air etc can go in and out or be put in and out; 🔲 **closed**, **shut**: *He threw the door open and ran down the stairs.* | *an open window* | *The gates swung silently* **open.** | *The bar door flew open and a noisy group burst in.* | *All the windows were wide open* (=completely open). | *She looked at the open suitcase with surprise.* | *There was an open bottle of wine on the table.*
2 EYES/MOUTH not closed, so that your EYELIDS or your lips are apart: *I was so sleepy, I couldn't keep my eyes* **open.** | *He was fast asleep with his mouth wide open.*
3 NOT ENCLOSED [only before noun] not enclosed, or with no buildings, walls, trees etc: *There was open ground at the end of the lane.* | *open spaces such as parks and gardens* | *open countryside/country At weekends people want to leave the town for open countryside.* | *A shoal of fish swam past heading for the* **open sea** (=part of the sea away from land). | *The car's performance is good, especially going fast on the* **open road** (=a road without traffic where you can drive fast).

4 NOT COVERED without a roof or cover: *The president was riding with his wife in an open car.* | *Martin was struggling with the sails on the open deck.* | *an open drain* | **open to the sky/air/elements** *Many of the tombs had been robbed and left open to the sky.*
5 the open air outdoors: **in the open air** *The dancing was outside, in the open air.* | *Jane wanted to rush to the door and get out into the open air.* → OPEN-AIR
6 BUSINESS/BUILDING ETC [not before noun] ready for business and allowing customers, visitors etc to enter; 🔲 **closed**, **shut**: *The museum is open daily in the summer months.* | *The offices are also open at weekends.* | *After the security alert, most of the firms affected were* **open for business** *on Monday morning.* | *The villagers are anxious that their local school is kept open.* | *I declare this exhibition open* (=officially say that it is now open).
7 NOT RESTRICTED allowing everyone, or everyone in a group, to take part in something, know about something, or have a chance to win something: [+**to**] *The competition is open to all readers in the UK.* | *In many schools, governors' meetings are not* **open to the public.** | *The discussion was then* **thrown open** *for the audience's questions.* | *an open meeting* | *The men's race appears* **wide open** (=anyone could win it). | *The painting would fetch several hundred dollars on the* **open market** (=a market in which anyone can buy or sell).
8 OPPORTUNITY [not before noun] if an opportunity, possible action, job etc is open to you, you have the chance to do it: *The job is being kept open for her.* | [+**to**] *The 1960s was a period when greater opportunities were open to women.* | *So what other* **options** *are open to us?* | *There is only one course of action open to the local authority.*
9 NOT SECRET [only before noun] actions, feelings, intentions etc that are open are not hidden or secret: *Her father watched her with open admiration.* | *open hostility between the two nations* | *The party was calling for more* **open government** (=when the government makes information freely available). | *The case will be tried* **in open court** (=in a court where everything is public). | *It is* **an open secret** (=it is supposed to be secret, but most people know about it) *that she is having an affair with another man.*
10 HONEST honest and not wanting to hide any facts from other people: [+**with**] *The couple are quite open with each other about their feelings.* | [+**about**] *She was quite open about her ambitions.* | *his friendly, open manner*
11 CLOTHES not fastened: *the open neck of his shirt* | *She was wearing an open jacket.*
12 NOT YET DECIDED needing more discussion or thought before a decision can be made: *The matter remains* **an open question.** | [+**to**] *The new rates of pay are open to negotiation.* | *The test results are open to interpretation.* | **keep/leave your options open** *Officers investigating her death are keeping their options open.*
13 open to sth **a)** likely to suffer from something or be affected by something: *The magazine's editor is* **open to criticism** *in allowing the article to be printed.* | *The regulations are open to abuse by companies.* | *He has left himself* **open to** *accusations of dishonesty.* **b)** willing to consider something new or to accept something new: *Teachers need to be open to children's ideas.* | *The committee is open to suggestions.* | *The owners of the building want to sell and are open to offers.*
14 NOT BLOCKED if a road or line of communication is open, it is not blocked and can be used: *We try to* **keep** *the mountain roads* **open** *all through the winter.*
15 SPREAD APART spread apart instead of closed, curled over, etc: *At night the flowers were open.* | *Johnson raised an open hand.* | *He was sitting in bed with a book lying open* (=with its pages apart so it can be read) *on his knees.*
16 an open mind if you have an open mind, you deliberately do not make a decision or form a definite

opinion about something: *It's important to **keep an open mind** as you study the topic.*

17 be open to question/doubt if something is open to question, there are doubts about it: *Whether the new situation is an improvement is open to question.*

18 welcome/greet sb/sth with open arms to be very pleased to see someone or something: *Mike will be welcomed back into the team with open arms.*

19 an open invitation a) an invitation to visit someone whenever you like b) something that makes it easier for criminals to steal, cheat etc: [+to] *The lack of security measures provides an open invitation to crime.*

20 be an open book to be something that you know and understand very well: *The natural world was an open book to him.*

21 the door is open there is an opportunity for someone to do something: [+to] *Schoolgirls are being told that the door is open to them to pursue careers in science.*

22 keep your eyes/ears open to keep looking or listening so that you will notice anything that is important, dangerous etc

23 open weave/texture cloth with an open weave or texture has wide spaces between the threads → **keep an eye open (for sth)** at EYE¹ (14); → **with your eyes open** at EYE¹ (19); → OPEN-EYED

open² [S1] [W1] *v*

1 DOOR/WINDOW ETC [I,T] to move a door, window etc so that people, things, air etc can pass through, or to be moved in this way: *Jack opened the window.* | *He opened the drawer of the desk.* | *She heard a door open and then close.*

2 CONTAINER/PACKAGE [T] to unfasten or remove the lid, top, or cover of a container, package etc: *Louise opened a bottle of wine.* | *He opened the letter and began to read it.* | *The children were opening their presents.* | *Mark was about to open a beer when the doorbell rang.*

3 EYES [I,T] to raise your EYELIDS so that you can see, or to be raised in this way: *Barry was awake long before he opened his eyes.* | *Carrie smelled coffee and her eyes opened reluctantly.*

4 MOUTH [I,T] to move your lips apart, or to be moved in this way: *He opened his mouth but couldn't think what to say.*

5 START OPERATING [I,T] also **open up** if a place such as an office, shop, restaurant etc opens or is opened, it starts operating or providing a service: *Sarah had recently opened an office in Genoa.* | *French and Scandinavian offices are due to open in the autumn.* | *The Forestry Commission has opened a plant centre selling rare plants.* | *The centre has been a great success since it opened its doors a year ago.*

6 SHOP/RESTAURANT ETC [I] also **open up** to start business, letting in customers or visitors, at a particular time: *What time do the banks open?* | *The bakery opens early.*

7 START AN ACTIVITY [T] to start an activity, event, or set of actions: *The US attorney's office has opened an investigation into the matter.* | *An inquest into the deaths will be opened next week.*

8 COMPUTER [T] to make a document or computer program ready to use: *Click on this icon to open the File Manager.*

9 MEETING/EVENT [I,T] if a meeting etc opens or is opened in a particular way, it starts in that way: *Hughes, opening the Conference, made a dramatic plea for peace.* | [+with] *The concert opens with Beethoven's Egmont Overture.*

10 OFFICIAL CEREMONY [T] to perform a ceremony in which you officially state that a building is ready to be used: *The new County Hall building was officially opened by the King.*

11 SPREAD/UNFOLD [I,T] to spread something out or unfold something, or to become spread out or unfolded: *She opened her umbrella.* | *John opened his hand to show her he wasn't holding anything.* | *The flowers only open during bright weather.* | *I sat down and opened my*

book. | *She opened the curtains* (=pulled the two curtains apart). | *Dave opened his arms* (=stretched his arms wide apart) *to give her a hug.*

12 MAKE A WAY THROUGH [T] to make it possible for cars, goods etc to pass through a place: *They were clearing away snow to open the tunnel.* | *The peace treaty promises an end to war and **opens** the **borders** between the two countries.*

13 FILM/PLAY ETC [I] to start being shown to the public: *Paula and Rachael star as mother and daughter in the play, which opens tonight.* | *The film opened yesterday to excellent reviews.*

14 open an account to start an account at a bank or other financial organization by putting money into it: *Mary was in the bank to ask about opening a current account.*

15 open fire (on sth) to start shooting at someone or something: *Troops opened fire on the rioters.*

16 open the door/way to sth also **open doors** to make an opportunity for something to happen: *Research on genes should open the door to exciting new medical treatments.* | *If the record is successful, it could open doors for my career.*

17 open sb's eyes (to sth) to make someone realize something that they had not realized before: *The purpose of the training is to open managers' eyes to the consequences of their own behaviour.*

18 open your mind (to sth) to be ready to consider or accept new ideas

19 open your heart (to sb) to tell someone your real thoughts and feelings because you trust them

20 the heavens opened *literary* it started to rain heavily → **open the floodgates** at FLOODGATE

open onto/into sth *phr v*
if a room, door etc opens onto or into another place, you can enter that other place directly through it: *The door opens onto a long balcony.*

open out *phr v*
1 if a road, path, or passage opens out, it becomes wider: [+into] *Beyond the forest the path opened out into a track.*
2 *BrE* if someone opens out, they become less shy

open up *phr v*
1 OPPORTUNITY if opportunities open up, or a new situation opens them up, they become available or possible: *With a microscope, a whole new world of investigation opens up.* | **open sth ⇔ up** *The new international agreement opens up the possibility of much greater co-operation against terrorism.*
2 LAND open sth ⇔ up if someone opens up an area of land, they make it easier to reach and ready for development: *The new road will open up 300 acres of prime development land.*
3 DOOR/CONTAINER ETC to open something that is closed, locked, or covered: *Open up, this is the police!* | **open sth ⇔ up** *He opened up his case and took out a clean sweater.*
4 SHOP/OFFICE ETC a) if a shop, office etc opens up or is opened up, someone starts it b) if a shop, office etc opens up at a particular time, it starts business at that time
5 DISAGREEMENT/DISCUSSION open sth ⇔ up to start a discussion or argument: *The article was written with the intention of opening up a public debate.*
6 COMPETITION/RACE if someone opens up a lead in a competition or race, they increase the distance or number of points by which they are winning
7 TALK to stop being shy and say what you really think: *Last night was the first time that Ken had opened up about his feelings.*
8 WITH A GUN to start shooting
9 HOLE/CRACK ETC if a hole, crack etc opens up or is opened up, it appears and becomes wider

open³ *n* **1** in the open outdoors: *In the summer, we camped in the open.* **2** (out) in the open information that is out in the open is not hidden or secret: *By now the whole affair was in the open.* | *She never let her* *dislike for him come out into the open.* | *All these concerns need to be brought out into the open.*

,**open-'air** *adj* [usually before noun] happening or existing outdoors; ⊟ **outdoor**: *open-air concerts* | *an open-air swimming pool*

,**open-and-shut 'case** *n* [C usually singular] a legal case or other matter that is easy to prove or decide because the facts are very clear

,**open 'bar** *n* [C] *AmE* a bar at an occasion such as a wedding, where drinks are served free

o·**pen·cast** /'əʊpənkɑːst $ 'oʊpənkæst/ *adj* [usually before noun] *BrE* an opencast mine is one where coal is taken out of holes in the ground near the surface, not from deep under the ground: *opencast mining*

'**open day** *n* [C] *BrE* a day when a school or an organization invites the public to come in and see the work that is done there

,**open-'door ,policy** *n* [C]   **1** the principle of allowing people and goods to move into a country freely: *They're pushing forward economic reform and an open-door policy.*   **2** the principle of allowing anyone to come to a place at any time, for example in order to discuss something

,**open-'ended** *adj*   **1** something that is open-ended does not have a definite answer or definite rules about how it must be done: *an open-ended question* | *These interviews are fairly open-ended.*   **2** without a particular ending time: *an open-ended agreement*

o·**pen·er** /'əʊpənə $ 'oʊpənər/ *n* [C]   **1** a tool that is used to open cans, bottles etc: *a can opener* | *a bottle opener*   **2** the first of a series of games in a sports competition: *They are hoping to win tomorrow's opener against New Zealand.*   **3 for openers a)** *BrE* as a beginning or first stage: *For openers, the band played a couple of old Beatles songs.* **b)** *AmE* used to give one reason, explanation etc for something, although there are others you might mention later too: *It's tough being a reporter. For openers, there are the long hours.*

,**open-'eyed** *adj, adv* awake, or with your eyes open: *She lay there open-eyed.*

,**open-faced 'sandwich** also ,**open-face 'sandwich** *n* [C] *AmE* a single piece of bread with meat, cheese etc on top; ⊟ **open sandwich** *BrE*

,**open-'handed** *adj*   **1** generous and friendly: *an open-handed offer of help*   **2** done with your hand open: *an open-handed slap*

open-heart·ed /ˌəʊpən 'hɑːt⅃d $ ˌoʊpən 'hɑːr-/ *adj* kind, sympathetic, and friendly: *They gave us an open-hearted welcome.*

,**open-heart 'surgery** *n* [U] a medical operation in which doctors operate on someone's heart, while a machine keeps the PATIENT'S blood flowing

,**open 'house** *n*   **1** [C] *AmE* a day when a school or organization invites the public to come in and see the work that is done there: *Parents are invited to attend the open house next Thursday.*   **2** [U] *BrE* if it is open house at someone's home, people are always welcome to visit at any time: *He kept open house for a wide range of artists and writers.*   **3** [C] a party at someone's house that you can come to at any time during a particular period: *We're having an open house Sunday, noon to 5pm.*   **4** [C] *AmE* an occasion when someone who is selling their house lets everyone who is interested in buying it come to see it

o·**pen·ing**¹ /'əʊpənɪŋ $ 'oʊ-/ *n*   **1** [C] the time when a new building, road etc is used for the first time, or when a public event begins, especially when it involves a special ceremony: [+of] *the official opening of the new theatre* | *the opening of the Cannes film festival*   **2** [C] a hole or space in something: [+in] *a narrow opening in the fence*   **3** [C usually singular] the beginning or first part of something: [+of] *at the opening of the trial*   **4** [C] a job that is available: *There are very few openings in scientific research.*   **5** [C] a chance for someone to do or say something: [+for] *His question left an opening for me to say exactly what I thought.*

  6 [U] when something opens, or is opened: [+of] *I was startled by the sudden opening of the door.*

opening² *adj* [only before noun] first or beginning: *the opening match of the season* | *the opening chapter of the book* | *the chairman's opening remarks*

'**opening ,hours** *n* [plural] *BrE* the hours when a shop, bank, bar etc is open to the public

,**opening 'night** *n* [C,U] the first night that a new play, film etc is shown to the public; ⊟ **first night**

'**opening time** *n* [C,U] the time that a business opens to the public; ⊠ **closing time**: *We arrived at the pub just before opening time.*

,**opening 'up** *n* **the opening up of sth** when something is made less restricted and more available to people: *the opening up of opportunities for women* | *the opening up of new areas to cultivation*

,**open-jaw 'fare** *n* [C] the price you pay to travel on a plane, train etc when this includes travel to a place and travel back from a different place

,**open 'letter** *n* [C] a letter to an important person, which is printed in a newspaper or magazine, usually in order to protest about something

o·**pen·ly** /'əʊpənli $ 'oʊ-/ *adv* in a way that does not hide your feelings, opinions, or the facts: *Sarah **talked openly** about her problems.* | *He was **openly critical** of his colleagues.*

,**open 'market** *n*   **1 on the open market** goods that are bought and sold on the open market are sold publicly rather than privately: *The painting would fetch millions of dollars if it was **sold on the open market**.*   **2** [C usually singular] a system which makes it easy to buy and sell goods with other countries, because there are few restrictions: *There is now an open market within the European Community.*

,**open 'marriage** *n* [C] a marriage in which both partners accept that they will have sex with other people

,**open 'mike** *n* [U] *AmE* a time when anyone is allowed to tell jokes, sing etc in a bar or club

,**open-'minded** *adj* willing to consider and accept other people's ideas and opinions; ⊠ **narrow-minded**: [+about/towards] | *She's quite open-minded about sex.*   —**openmindedness** *n* [U]

,**open-'mouthed** *adj, adv* with your mouth wide open, because you are very surprised or shocked: *We stared open-mouthed as the plane came down.*

,**open-'necked** *adj* an open-necked shirt is worn with the top button undone

o·**pen·ness** /'əʊpənn⅃s $ 'oʊ-/ *n* [U]   **1** the quality of being honest and willing to talk about things: [+of] *the openness of American society* | [+about] *her openness about her problems*   **2** the quality of being willing to accept new ideas or people: [+to/towards] *the importance of openness to change*   **3** the quality of not being enclosed: [+of] *the vast openness of the African plains*

,**open-'plan** *adj* *BrE* an open-plan office, school etc does not have walls dividing it into separate rooms

,**open 'primary** *n* [C] a PRIMARY ELECTION in the US in which any voter may vote for someone from any party

,**open 'prison** *n* [C] *BrE* a prison that does not restrict the freedom of prisoners as much as ordinary prisons

,**open 'sandwich** *n* [C] *BrE* a single piece of bread with meat, cheese etc on top; ⊟ **open-faced sandwich** *AmE*

'**open ,season** *n* [singular,U]   **1** *BrE* the time each year when it is legal to kill particular animals, birds, or fish as a sport; ⊠ **close season**: [+for] *the open season for deer*   **2 open season (on sb)** a time when a lot of people criticize someone, or a group of people: *It seems to be open season on politicians just now.*

ˌopen ˈsesame *n* [singular] *BrE* an easy way to achieve something that is usually very difficult: [+**to**] *A university degree isn't always an open sesame to a good job.*

ˈopen ˌsystem *n* [C] *technical* a computer system that can be connected with similar computer systems made by other companies

ˌopen-ˈtoed *adj* **open-toed sandals/shoes** shoes that do not cover the end of your toes

ˌopen ˈverdict *n* [C] an official decision in a British court saying that the exact cause of someone's death is not known: *The jury* ***returned an open verdict.*** | *He said there was some doubt over the way Grant had died, and* ***recorded an open verdict.***

ˌopen ˈvowel *n* [C] *technical* a vowel such as /a/ that is pronounced with your tongue flat on the bottom of your mouth

o·pen·work /ˈəʊpənˌwɜːk $ ˈoʊpənˌwɜːrk/ *adj* [only before noun] an openwork object has a pattern of open spaces between the material that it is made from: *an openwork stone screen*

op·e·ra /ˈɒpərə $ ˈɑː-/ *n* **1** [C] a musical play in which all of the words are sung; → **operetta**: *We* ***go to the opera*** (=go to a performance of opera) *regularly.* | *an* ***opera singer*** **2** [U] these plays considered as a form of art —**operatic** /ˌɒpəˈrætɪk◂ $ ˌɑː-/ *adj*: *operatic performances* —**operatically** /-kli/ *adv* → GRAND OPERA, SOAP OPERA

op·e·ra·ble /ˈɒpərəbəl $ ˈɑː-/ *adj* **1** a system which is operable is working; ≠ **inoperable**: *Less than half the rail network was operable.* **2** a medical condition that is operable can be treated by an operation; ≠ **inoperable**

ˈopera house *n* [C] a theatre where operas are performed: *the Sydney Opera House*

op·e·rate S3 W2 /ˈɒpəreɪt $ ˈɑːp-/ *v*
1 MACHINE a) [T] to use and control a machine or equipment: *The Lewis family operated a number of boats on the canal.* | *Clive was experienced in operating the computers.* **b)** [I always + adv/prep] if a machine operates in a particular way, it works in that way: [+**in/at**] *Check that the equipment is operating in a safe manner.* | *The bus is designed to operate in all weather conditions.* | *Most freezers operate at below -18°C.*
2 BUSINESS/ORGANIZATION a) [I] if a business or organization operates in a particular place or way, it works in that place or way: [+**in/within/from**] *a design company operating from offices in Seattle.* | *A playgroup operates on the campus.* | *They were trying to reduce* ***operating costs.*** **b)** [T] to control a business or organization: *Nuns are operating an emergency hospital.*
3 SYSTEM/PROCESS/SERVICE [I,T] if a system, process, or service operates, or if you operate it, it works: *The whole tax system is now operating more efficiently.* | *The new law doesn't operate in our favour.* | *The car parks operate a pay-as-you-leave system.* | *The bus company operates a Monday to Saturday service.*
4 MEDICAL [I] to cut into someone's body in order to repair or remove a part that is damaged: *Doctors had to operate to remove the bullet.* | [+**on**] *the surgeon who operated on Taylor's knee* ⚠ A surgeon does not 'operate' a part of a person's body. He or she **operates on** it: *They need to operate on her stomach (NOT operate her stomach).*
5 WORK [I] to do your job or try to achieve things in a particular way: *Most people just can't operate in noisy, crowded conditions.* | *Older children often like to operate independently.*
6 SOLDIERS/POLICE [I] if soldiers or police officers are operating in an area, they are working in that area: [+**in**] *Security patrols now operate in some of the most dangerous parts of the city.* | *enemy submarines operating in the Mediterranean*
7 operate as sth to have a particular purpose: *The foam operates as a very effective filter.* | *The car's service manual is designed to operate as a guide for owners.*
8 LAWS/PRINCIPLES [I] to have an effect on something: *the laws of evolution operating on each species*

ˈoperating room *n* [C] *AmE* an OPERATING THEATRE

ˈoperating ˌsystem *n* [C] a system in a computer that helps all the programs in it to work together

ˈoperating ˌtable *n* [C] a special table in an operating theatre which a person lies on when they are having an operation

ˈoperating ˌtheatre *n* [C] *BrE* a room in a hospital where operations are done; = **operating room** *AmE*

op·e·ra·tion S1 W1 /ˌɒpəˈreɪʃən $ ˌɑːp-/ *n*
1 MEDICAL [C] the process of cutting into someone's body to repair or remove a part that is damaged

> **have an operation**
> **undergo an operation** *formal* (=have an operation)
> **perform an operation**
> **major/minor operation**
> **emergency operation**
> **routine operation** (=an operation that is often performed)
> **life-saving operation**

a heart bypass operation | [+**on/for**] *She's going to need an operation on her ankle.* | *He* ***had an operation*** *to reduce the swelling in his brain.* | *She* ***underwent*** *a minor* ***operation*** *on her elbow in the summer.* | *the surgeon who* ***performed the operation*** | *The poor man had two* ***major operations*** *in two weeks.* | *an* ***emergency operation*** *to save his sight* | *a* ***routine*** *knee* ***operation*** | *The first indications were that the* ***life-saving operation*** *had gone well.*

⚠ Do not say that someone 'takes an operation'. Say that they **have an operation.**
2 BUSINESS/ORGANIZATION [C] a business, company, or organization: *The firm set up its own property development operation.* | *a microchip manufacturing operation* | *Nolan and Barnes were both involved in the operation.*
3 WORK/ACTIVITIES [C,U] the work or activities done by a business or organization, or the process of doing this work: *Many small businesses fail in the first year of operation.* | *The Education Business Partnership has* ***been in operation*** *since 1989.*
4 ACTIONS [C] a set of planned actions or activities for a particular purpose: *The UN rescue operation started shortly after dawn.*
5 MACHINE/SYSTEM [U] the way the parts of a machine or system work together, or the process of making a machine or system work: *The aircraft's engine operation was normal.* | **in operation** *Protective clothing must be worn when the machine is in operation.* | *The device has a single button, allowing for easy operation.* | *Careful checks must be made before the factory commences operation.* | *The new investment system* ***came into operation*** *in 1999.*
6 PRINCIPLE/LAW/PLAN ETC [U] the way something such as a principle or law works or has an effect: **in operation** *a clear example of the law of gravity in operation* | **come/go into operation** (=begin to have an effect) *The new rule comes into operation on February 1.* | **put/bring sth into operation** (=make something start to work) *A scheme is being brought into operation to see how these changes would work.*
7 MILITARY/POLICE ACTION [C] a planned military or police action, especially one that involves a lot of people: *Britain will carry out a joint* ***military operation*** *with the US.*
8 COMPUTERS [C] an action done by a computer

op·e·ra·tion·al /ˌɒpəˈreɪʃənəl◂ $ ˌɑːp-/ *adj* **1** [not before noun] working and ready to be used: *The boat should be operational by this afternoon.* | *The new system* ***became operational*** *in March.* | *Our main offices are now* ***fully operational.*** → OPERATIVE[1] (1) **2** [only before noun] relating to the operation of a business, government etc: *Patco accepted full responsibility for operational management.* —**operationally** *adv*

,operational re'search, **,operations re'search** *n* [U] the study of the best ways to build and use machines or plan organizations

op·e·ra·tive¹ /'ɒpərətɪv $ 'ɑːpərə-, 'ɑːpəreɪ-/ *adj* **1** working and able to be used; ✗ **inoperative**: *Only one runway is operative.* | *the steps to be taken before the scheme can become operative* → OPERATIONAL (1) **2 the operative word** used when you repeat a word from a previous sentence to draw attention to its importance: *The new system offers fast solutions. Fast being the operative word.* **3** relating to a medical operation: *patients undergoing operative procedures*

operative² *n* [C] **1** a worker, especially a factory worker – used in business: *the company's overseas operatives* **2** someone who does work that is secret in some way, especially for a government organization: **CIA/FBI/intelligence etc operatives**

op·e·ra·tor /'ɒpəreɪtə $ 'ɑːpəreɪtər/ *n* [C] **1** someone who works on a telephone SWITCHBOARD, who you can call for help: *Hello, operator? Could you put me through to Room 31?* **2** someone who operates a machine or piece of equipment: **machine/computer/radio etc operator** | *computers which can be used by untrained operators* **3** a person or company that operates a particular business: *new regulations affecting taxi operators* | *Julian travelled with Caribbean Connection, the UK's leading Caribbean tour operator* (=company that arranges holidays). | *a private operator running regular passenger services* **4** someone who is good at achieving things by persuading people to help or agree with them: *Monsieur Valentin was a formidable political operator.* | *He may not look it, but Newman is a smooth operator* (=someone who is good at persuading people but who you feel you cannot trust).

op·e·ret·ta /,ɒpə'retə $,ɑːp-/ *n* [C] a funny or romantic musical play in which some of the words are spoken and some are sung; → **opera**

oph·thal·mic /ɒf'θælmɪk $ ɑːf-/ *adj* [only before noun] *medical* relating to the eyes and the illnesses that affect them: *an ophthalmic surgeon*

oph·thal·mol·o·gy /,ɒfθæl'mɒlədʒi $,ɑːfθæl'mɑː-/ *n* [U] *medical* the study of the eyes and diseases that affect them —**ophthalmologist** *n* [C]

o·pi·ate /'əʊpiət, -eɪt $ 'oʊ-/ *n* [C] **1** a drug that contains OPIUM. Opiates can be used to reduce severe pain and help people to sleep. **2** something that makes people stop thinking about the problems in their lives so that they stop trying to make their lives better – used to show disapproval: *Hollywood movies were seen as an opiate for the people.*

o·pine /əʊ'paɪn $ oʊ-/ *v* [T] *formal* to say what your opinion is about something: *opine that The headmistress opined that the trip would make a nice change.*

o·pin·ion S1 W2 /ə'pɪnjən/ *n*
1 [C,U] your ideas or beliefs about a particular subject

in sb's opinion
general/popular opinion (=what most people think about something)
public opinion (=what ordinary people think about something)
sb's personal opinion
difference of opinion
a matter of opinion
ask (for) sb's opinion
express/give/state an opinion
strong opinion
keep your opinions to yourself (=not say what you really think)
contrary to popular opinion (=despite what most people think)

[+**about**] *The two women had very different opinions about drugs.* | [+**of**] *What's your opinion of Cathy?* |

[+**on**] *He asked his wife's opinion on every important decision.* | *It's a terrible shame,* **in my opinion,** *that the building was knocked down.* | *The* **general opinion** *is that the new law is a good thing.* | *Politicians should listen to* **popular opinion.** | *These are just my own* **personal opinions.** | *Whether or not this is useful is a* **matter of opinion.** | *Everyone has the right to* **express an opinion.** | *Contrary to popular opinion, chocolate is quite good for you.* | *Jody is a person with very* **strong opinions.**

⚠ Do not say 'according to someone's opinion'. Say either **according to** someone or **in** someone's **opinion**. → VIEW¹ (1); → **in my humble opinion** at HUMBLE¹ (3)

2 [C] judgement or advice from a professional person about something: *When choosing an insurance policy it's best to* **get** *an* **opinion.** | *My doctor says I need an operation, but I've asked for a* **second opinion** (=advice from a second doctor to make sure that the first advice is right). | *They took the painting to get an* **expert opinion** (=an opinion from someone who knows a lot).
3 have a high/low/good/bad etc opinion of sb/sth to think that someone or something is very good or very bad: *They have a very high opinion of Paula's work.*
4 be of the opinion (that) to think that something is true: *I was firmly of the opinion that we should not give Jackson any more money.* → **a difference of opinion** at DIFFERENCE (6); → **be a matter of opinion** at MATTER¹ (12); → **PUBLIC OPINION**

o·pin·ion·at·ed /ə'pɪnjəneɪtɪd/ *adj* expressing very strong opinions about things: *I found him very arrogant and opinionated.*

o'pinion-,makers *n* [plural] people such as politicians or JOURNALISTS who have a lot of influence on the way other people think

o'pinion poll *n* [C] the process of asking a large group of people the same questions in order to find out what most people think about something: *An opinion poll showed that 70% of adults were against legalizing drugs.*

o·pi·um /'əʊpiəm $ 'oʊ-/ *n* [U] a powerful illegal drug made from POPPY seeds. Drugs made from opium are used to reduce severe pain; → **heroin**

o·pos·sum /ə'pɒsəm $ -'pɑː-, 'pɑːsəm/ *n* [C] also **possum** one of various small animals from America and Australia that have fur and climb trees

opp. the written abbreviation of *opposite*

op·po·nent W3 /ə'pəʊnənt $ ə'poʊ-/ *n* [C]
1 someone who you try to defeat in a competition, game, fight, or argument: *Graf's opponent in today's final will be Sukova.* | **leading/main/chief opponent** *During the primary elections, McCain was Bush's leading opponent.* | **formidable/worthy opponent** *In debate he was a formidable opponent.* | *He is admired even by his* **political opponents.**
2 someone who disagrees with a plan, idea, or system and wants to try to stop or change it: [+**of**] *Rodgers was not an opponent of the new airport.* | **bitter/vocal/outspoken opponent** *an outspoken opponent of gun control*

op·por·tune /'ɒpətjuːn $,ɑːpər'tuːn/ *adj formal* **1 an opportune moment/time** a time that is suitable for doing something: *I waited, hoping for an opportune moment to discuss the possibility of a raise.* **2** done at a very suitable time; ✗ **inopportune**: *an opportune remark* | *The law reforms were opportune and important.* —**opportunely** *adv*

op·por·tun·is·m /,ɒpə'tjuːnɪzəm $,ɑːpər'tuː-/ *n* [U] using every opportunity to gain power, money, or unfair advantages – used to show disapproval: *He accused the diary's publishers of blatant opportunism.*

op·por·tun·ist /,ɒpə'tjuːnɪst $,ɑːpər'tuː-/ *n* [C] **1** someone who uses every opportunity to gain power, money, or unfair advantages – used to show disapproval: *Voters dislike opportunists – politicians who*

change their policies according to opinion polls.
2 someone who commits a crime because they have a chance to, and not because they planned to: *Most burglars are opportunists.* | *an opportunist crime* —**opportunist** *adj*: *the opportunist policies of wartime leaders* —**opportunistic** /ˌɒpətjuːˈnɪstɪk◂ $ ˌɑːpərtuː-/ *adj*: *opportunistic thefts from cars*

op·por·tu·ni·ty S1 W1 /ˌɒpəˈtjuːnəti $ ˌɑːpərˈtuː-/ *n*
plural **opportunities**
1 [C,U] a chance to do something or an occasion when it is easy for you to do something

> **opportunity to do sth**
> **ideal/perfect opportunity**
> **rare/unique opportunity**
> **once-in-a-lifetime opportunity**
> **ample opportunity**
> **golden opportunity** (=a very good opportunity)
> **wasted/lost/missed opportunity** (=one you do not use)
> **take/seize/use an opportunity**
> **provide/present/open up an opportunity**
> **an opportunity comes (along/up)**
> **an opportunity arises**
> **take the/this opportunity to do sth** (=use a chance to say something you want to say)
> **at the first/earliest opportunity** (=as soon as possible)
> **at every (possible) opportunity** (=whenever possible)
> **land of opportunity** (=a country where you have a lot of good opportunities)
> **window of opportunity** (=a time when you can do something)

*This is an **ideal opportunity** to save money on a holiday to Crete.* | *[+for] Games and songs provide the **perfect opportunity** for classroom interaction and language development.* | *It was a **rare opportunity** to see how ordinary people lived.* | *For many athletes, the Olympics is a **once-in-a-lifetime opportunity**.* | *I saw it as a **golden opportunity** – the chance I'd been waiting for all along.* | *a classic example of **missed opportunity*** | *an event that would **provide an opportunity** for meaningful debate* | *When the **opportunity** for promotion came, I wanted to be ready.* | *I'd like to **take this opportunity** to thank you for all your hard work.* | *53% of students leave school **at the earliest opportunity**.* | *He likes to make his opinions known **at every opportunity**.* | *the view of America as a **land of opportunity*** | *Our **window of opportunity** for winning the championship is the next couple of seasons.*

2 [C] a chance to get a job or improve your situation at work: *There are fewer opportunities for new graduates this year.* → **equal opportunities** at EQUAL¹ (2)

op·pose W3 /əˈpəʊz $ əˈpoʊz/ *v* [T]
1 to disagree with something such as a plan or idea and try to prevent it from happening or succeeding: *Congress is continuing to oppose the President's healthcare budget.*
2 to fight or compete against another person or group in a battle, competition, or election: *He is opposed by two other candidates.*

op·posed /əˈpəʊzd $ əˈpoʊzd/ *adj* [not before noun] **1 be opposed to sth** to disagree with something such as a plan or system: *Most of us are opposed to the death penalty.* **2** two ideas that are opposed to each other are completely different from each other: *The principles of capitalism and socialism are **diametrically opposed** (=completely opposite).* **3 as opposed to sth** used to compare two things and show that they are different from each other: *Students discuss ideas, as opposed to just copying from books.*

op·pos·ing /əˈpəʊzɪŋ $ əˈpoʊ-/ *adj* [only before noun] **1** opposing teams, groups, or forces are competing, arguing, or fighting against each other: *The opposing armies were preparing for war.* | *The Socialist Party has split into two opposing camps.* **2** opposing ideas,

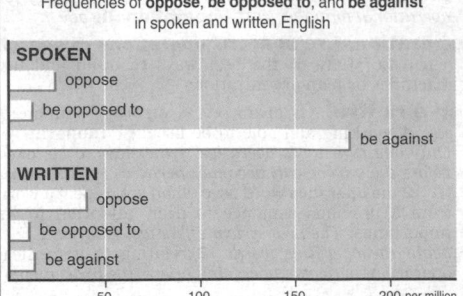

Frequencies of **oppose**, **be opposed to**, and **be against** in spoken and written English

This graph shows that it is much more usual in spoken English to say that you **are against** something, rather than to say that you **oppose** it or **are opposed to** it. This is because **be against** is more informal and more general than **oppose** and **be opposed to**, which often suggest not only disagreeing with and disapproving of something, but also taking action to prevent it.

opinions etc are completely different from each other: *Throughout the negotiations Hurst and Jevons took opposing views.*

op·po·site¹ S2 W2 /ˈɒpəzət $ ˈɑːp-/ *prep*
1 especially BrE if one thing or person is opposite another, they are facing each other: *The people sitting opposite us looked very familiar.* | *on the wall opposite the door* ⚠ Do not say that one thing is 'opposite to' or 'opposite of' another. Say that one thing is **opposite** another: *There's a car park opposite the hotel.*; → see box at FRONT¹
2 play/star/appear etc opposite sb to act with someone in a film, especially as the two main characters: *a comedy in which he stars opposite Julia Roberts*

opposite² *adj* [only before noun] **1** as different as possible from something else: *I thought the medicine would make him sleep, but it **had the opposite effect**.* | **at the opposite end of the scale/spectrum** *two parties at opposite ends of the political spectrum* | **At the opposite extreme**, *Ashworth's style is very simple and modern.* | *Bob was quicker than Ed? It's usually **the opposite way round**.* | *[+to] a political philosophy that was opposite to everything she believed in* **2** the opposite direction, way etc is directly away from someone or something: *She turned and walked off **in the opposite direction**.* | *But the sign was pointing **the opposite way**.* **3** the opposite side, corner, edge etc of something is on the other side of the same area, often facing it: *The store was **on the opposite side** of the street.* | *the drawing on the opposite page* | *They work **at opposite ends of the country*** (=a long distance apart), *so only see each other at weekends.* **4 the opposite sex** the other sex. If you are a man, women are the opposite sex: *members of the opposite sex* **5 sb's opposite number** someone who has the same job in another similar organization: *a meeting with her opposite number at the Department of Health*

opposite³ *n* [C] **1** a person or thing that is as different as possible from someone or something else: *[+of] What's the opposite of 'optimistic'?* | *She's quite shy, **the exact opposite** of Becky.* | *The two men were **complete opposites** - Simon tall and fair, Clive short and dark.* | *If anything, **the opposite** was true.* | *Is it sensible to think of masculine/feminine as **polar opposites** (=exactly or completely opposite)?* **2 not ... just/quite the opposite** used to say that something is completely different from what has just been said: *I didn't feel sleepy at all – just the opposite, in fact.* **3 opposites attract** used to say that often people who have completely different characters become friends or are attracted to each other

opposite⁴ *adv especially BrE* in a position on the other side of the same area: *Hannah lives just opposite.*

op·po·si·tion S2 W1 /ˌɒpəˈzɪʃən $ ˌɑːp-/ *n*
1 [U] strong disagreement with, or protest against, something such as a plan, law, or system

face/meet with opposition
overcome opposition
arouse opposition/arouse the opposition of sb (=make
  someone feel disagreement)
strong/fierce/intense/stiff opposition
public opposition
in opposition to sth

[+**to**] *There was a great deal of opposition to the war.* |
[+**from**] *They* **face opposition** *from local residents as
well as from environmentalists.* | *He is confident in his
ability to* **overcome** *all* **opposition** *with his personal
charm.* | *The proposals have* **aroused the opposition**
of teachers. | *Strong opposition resulted in rejection of
the bill.* | *Plans to turn the site into a £600 million leisure
complex have met with* **stiff opposition**. | *Much* **public
opposition** *to the new law remained.* | *Workers found
themselves* **in opposition to** *local interests.*

2 the opposition in some countries such as Britain, the
main political party in the parliament that is not part
of the government: *the leader of the Opposition* | *the
three main* **opposition parties**
3 in opposition in some countries such as Britain, a
political party that is in opposition is in parliament,
but is not part of the government: *The Socialists were
elected to power after 10 years in opposition.*
4 [C,U also + plural verb *BrE*] the people who you are
competing against: *They played well against good
opposition.*
5 [C,U] *formal* when two things are completely opposite: [+**between**] *the opposition between capitalism and
socialism*

op·press /ə'pres/ *v* [T often passive] **1** to treat a
group of people unfairly or cruelly, and prevent them
from having the same rights that other people in
society have: *native tribes oppressed by the authorities* **2** to make someone feel unhappy, worried, or
uncomfortable: *The gloom in the chapel oppressed her.*

op·pressed /ə'prest/ *adj* **1** a group of people who
are oppressed are treated unfairly or cruelly and are
prevented from having the same rights as other people
have: *oppressed minorities* | **the oppressed** (=people
who are oppressed) **2** someone who is oppressed feels
unhappy, worried, or uncomfortable

op·pres·sion /ə'preʃən/ *n* [U] when someone treats a
group of people unfairly or cruelly and prevents them
from having the same rights as other people have:
political/racial/sexual etc oppression *They suffered
years of political oppression.* | *the struggle against
oppression*

op·pres·sive /ə'presɪv/ *adj* **1** powerful, cruel, and
unfair: *an oppressive military regime* **2** weather that
is oppressive is unpleasantly hot with no movement of
air: *the* **oppressive heat** *of the afternoon* **3** a situation
that is oppressive makes you unhappy, worried, or
uncomfortable: *an oppressive silence* | *an oppressive
atmosphere* —**oppressively** *adv*

op·pres·sor /ə'presə $ -ər/ *n* [C] a person or group
that treats people unfairly or cruelly, and prevents
them from having the same rights that other people in
society have

op·pro·bri·um /ə'prəubriəm $ ə'prou-/ *n* [U] *formal*
strong criticism or disapproval, especially expressed
publicly

opt /ɒpt $ ɑːpt/ *v* [I] to choose one thing or do one thing
instead of another: [+**for**] *We finally opted for the wood
finish.* | **opt to do sth** *Many young people are opting to
go on to college.*
  opt in *phr v* to decide to join a group or system: [+**to**]
  Employees have the choice to opt in to the scheme.
  opt out *phr v* **1** to avoid doing a duty: [+**of**] *You can't
  just opt out of all responsibility for the child!* **2** to
  decide not to be part of a group or system: [+**of**] *Britain
  wants to opt out of the new European regulations.* **3** if
  a school or hospital in Britain opts out, it decides to
  control the money that it is given by the government,
  instead of being controlled by local government

op·tic /'ɒptɪk $ 'ɑːp-/ *adj* [only before noun] relating to
the eyes: *the optic nerve*

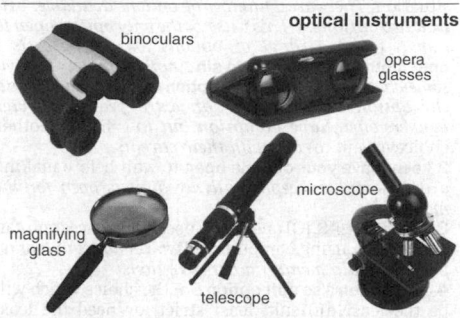

optical instruments

binoculars
opera
glasses
microscope
magnifying
glass
telescope

op·ti·cal /'ɒptɪkəl $ 'ɑːp-/ *adj* relating to machines or
processes which are concerned with light, images, or
the way we see things: *microscopes and other* **optical
instruments** —**optically** /-kli/ *adv*

optical 'character recog,nition *n* [U] *technical*
computer software that recognizes numbers and letters
of the alphabet which are written on paper, so that
information from paper documents can be SCANNED into
a computer

optical 'fibre *BrE*; **optical fiber** *AmE n* [C,U] a long
thin thread of glass or plastic along which information
can be sent through a phone or computer system, using
light

optical il'lusion *n* [C] a picture or image that tricks
your eyes and makes you see something that is not
actually there

op·ti·cian /ɒp'tɪʃən $ ɑːp-/ *n* [C] **1** *BrE* someone who
tests people's eyes and sells GLASSES in a shop; ▤ **optometrist** *AmE*; → see picture at OCCUPATION **2** *AmE* someone who makes LENSES for GLASSES

op·tics /'ɒptɪks $ 'ɑːp-/ *n* [U] the scientific study of
light and the way we see

op·ti·mal /'ɒptɪməl $ 'ɑːp-/ *adj formal* the best or most
suitable; ▤ **optimum**

op·ti·mis·m /'ɒptɪmɪzəm $ 'ɑːp-/ *n* [U] a tendency to
believe that good things will always happen; ▤ **pessimism**: **grounds/cause/reason for optimism** *Recent
results must give some cause for optimism.* | *There are
grounds for* **cautious optimism**. | **mood/sense of opti-
mism** *a new sense of optimism in the country* | **optimism
(that)** *There was optimism that an agreement could be
reached.* | [+**about**] *I don't share his optimism about our
chances of success.*

op·ti·mist /'ɒptɪmɪst $ 'ɑːp-/ *n* [C] someone who
believes that good things will happen; ▤ **pessimist**:
He's an **eternal optimist** (=he always believes that
good things will happen).

op·ti·mis·tic /,ɒptɪ'mɪstɪk◄ $,ɑːp-/ *adj* **1** believing
that good things will happen in the future; ▤ **pessi-
mistic**: [+**about**] *Bankers are* **cautiously optimistic**
about the country's economic future. | **optimistic (that)**
*We are still relatively optimistic that the factory can be
saved.* | *Andrew took a more optimistic view.* **2** think-
ing that things will be better, easier, or more successful
than is actually possible: *an optimistic estimate* | **over-
optimistic** *BrE*: *somewhat over-optimistic expectations*

op·ti·mize also **-ise** *BrE* /'ɒptɪmaɪz $ 'ɑːp-/ *v* [T] to
improve the way that something is done or used so that
it is as effective as possible: *They need to optimize the
use of available resources.*

op·ti·mum /'ɒptɪməm $ 'ɑːp-/ *adj* [only before noun]
the best or most suitable for a particular purpose or in
a particular situation: *optimum conditions for growth* |
*This design makes the optimum use of the available
space.* —**optimum** *n* [singular]

op·tion S1 W2 /'ɒpʃən $ 'ɑ:p-/ n
1 CHOICE [C] a choice you can make in a particular situation: *There are a number of options available.* | *He had two options.* | *This was not the only option open to him.* | [+for] *a range of options for cutting costs* | **one/another option is to do sth** *Another option is to rent somewhere for six months.* | **option of doing sth** *She had the option of staying for an extra year.* | *Teenage mothers often* **have no option but to** (=have no other choice except to) *live with their parents.*
2 keep/leave your options open to wait before making a decision: *I'm keeping all my options open for the moment.*
3 COMPUTERS [C] one of the possible choices you can make when using computer software: *Select an option from the main menu.* | *a list of options*
4 easy option also **soft option** *BrE* the choice which will be the least difficult, least strict, or need the least effort, which someone might choose because they are lazy: *Is community service just a soft option for criminals?*
5 RIGHT TO BUY/SELL [C] *formal* the right to buy or sell something in the future: [+on] *The government has agreed to buy 20 planes, with an option on a further 10.* | *Connor now owns 302,000 shares and options.*
6 AT SCHOOL/UNIVERSITY [C] *BrE* one of the subjects that you can choose to study at school for an examination, or as part of a course at a college or university: *advice on choosing your options*
7 STH ADDITIONAL [C] something that is offered in addition to the standard equipment when you buy something new, especially a car
8 first option the chance to buy or get something before anyone else: [+on] *They've agreed to give us the first option on their apartment.*

op·tion·al /'ɒpʃənəl $ 'ɑ:p-/ adj if something is optional, you do not have to do it or use it, but you can choose to if you want to; 🔁 compulsory: *three optional courses* | *The other excursions are optional.* | **optional extra** *BrE*: *Leather seats are an optional extra.*

op·tom·e·trist /ɒp'tɒmɪtrɪst $ ɑ:p'tɑ:-/ n [C] *AmE* someone who tests people's eyes and orders GLASSES for them; 🔁 **optician** *BrE* → see picture at OCCUPATION

'opt-out n [C] *BrE* **1** when a person or group chooses not to join a system or accept an agreement: *an opt-out clause* | [+on/from] *the government's opt-out on the euro* **2** when a school or hospital in Britain chooses to control its own money, instead of being controlled by local government: *an opt-out school*

op·u·lent /'ɒpjʊlənt $ 'ɑ:p-/ adj *formal* **1** very beautiful, with a lot of decoration, and made from expensive materials; 🔁 luxurious: *evening dresses in opulent fabrics* **2** very rich and spending a lot of money: *Europe's opulent elite* —**opulence** n [U]: *the size and opulence of the rooms*

o·pus /'əʊpəs $ 'oʊ-/ n plural **opuses** or **opera** /'ɒpərə $ 'ɑ:-/ [usually singular] **1** a piece of music by a great musician, numbered according to when it was written: *Beethoven's Opus 95* **2** *formal* an important work of art by a famous writer, painter etc → MAGNUM OPUS

or S1 W1 /ə; strong ɔ: $ ər; strong ɔ:r/ conjunction
1 POSSIBILITIES/CHOICES used between two words or phrases to show that either of two things is possible, or used before the last in a list of possibilities or choices: *Shall we go out to the cinema or stay at home?* | *You can have ham, cheese or tuna.* | *... or anything/ something spoken* (=or something of the same kind) *Would you like a coffee or something?* | *She wasn't involved in drugs or anything like that.* | *Grapes are usually either green or red.* | *He's going to do it whether we like it or not.* | *You must do the job yourself or else employ someone else to do it.* → EITHER[1]
2 AND NOT used after a negative verb when you mean not one thing and also not another thing: *He doesn't have a television or a video.* | *Sonia never cleans or even offers to wash the dishes.*

3 AVOIDING BAD RESULT used to say that something bad could happen if someone does not do a particular thing: *Wear your coat or you'll catch cold.* | *Hurry up or we'll be late.* | *I had to defend myself or else he'd have killed me.* | *You'd better hand over the money,* **or else** (=used to threaten someone).
4 CORRECTION used to correct something that you have said or to give more specific information: *It's going to snow tomorrow, or that's what the forecast says.* | *John picked us up in his car,* **or rather** *his dad's car which he'd borrowed.* | *We've cleaned it all up, or at least most of it.*
5 PROOF used to prove that something must be true, by saying that the situation would be different if it was not true: *He must be at home, or his car wouldn't be here.* | *It's obviously not urgent or else they would have called us straight away.*
6 UNCERTAIN AMOUNTS used to show that you are guessing at an amount or number because you cannot be exact: *The boy was three or four years of age.* | *I saw Donald leaving a minute or two ago.* | *There's a motel* **a mile or so** *down the road* (=about a mile or possibly a little more).

-or /ə $ ər/ suffix [in nouns] **1** someone who does something or is doing something: *an actor* (=someone who acts) | *an inventor* | *a translator* **2** something that does something: *a calculator* (=a machine which calculates) | *a word processor* → -ER[2], -AR

or·a·cle /'ɒrəkəl $ 'ɔ:-, 'ɑ:-/ n [C] **1** someone who the ancient Greeks believed could communicate with the gods, who gave advice to people or told them what would happen **2** a message given by an oracle **3** a person or book that gives advice and information – used humorously

o·rac·u·lar /ɒ'rækjʊlə, ə- $ ɔ:'rækjʊlər, ə-/ adj *formal* from or like an oracle

o·ral¹ /'ɔːrəl/ adj **1** spoken, not written: *oral history* | *an oral agreement* **2** relating to or involving the mouth: *oral hygiene* —**orally** adv: *The drug should be taken orally.* | *The statement may be given orally or in writing.*

oral² also **'oral ex,am** n [C] **1** *especially BrE* a spoken test, especially in a foreign language: *I've got my French oral tomorrow.* **2** *AmE* a spoken test for a university degree

,oral contra'ceptive n [C] a drug that a woman takes by mouth, so that she can have sex without having a baby; 🔁 pill

,oral 'sex n [U] the activity of touching someone's sex organs with the lips and tongue, to give sexual pleasure

'oral ,surgeon n [C] a DENTIST who performs operations in the mouth

or·ange S3 /'ɒrɪndʒ $ 'ɔ:-, 'ɑ:-/ n
1 [C] a round fruit that has a thick orange skin and is divided into parts inside: *orange juice* | *orange peel* | *Peel the oranges and divide them into segments.* | *orange groves* (=where orange trees grow) → see picture at FRUIT[1]
2 [U] a colour that is between red and yellow: *a bright shade of orange* —**orange** adj: *an orange shirt*

or·ange·ade /,ɒrɪndʒ'eɪd $,ɔ:-, ,ɑ:-/ n [C,U] a drink that tastes like oranges

or·an·ge·ry /'ɒrɪndʒəri $ 'ɔ:-, 'ɑ:-/ n plural **orangeries** [C] *old-fashioned* a place, usually next to a large expensive house, where orange trees are grown

o·rang·u·tang /ɔ:,ræŋuː'tæŋ $ ə'ræŋətæŋ/ also **orang-utan** /-tæn/ n [C] a large APE with long arms and long orange-brown hair

o·ra·tion /ə'reɪʃən, ɔ:-/ n [C] a formal public speech

or·a·tor /'ɒrətə $ 'ɔ:rətər, 'ɑ:-/ n [C] *formal* someone who is good at making speeches and persuading people

or·a·to·ri·o /,ɒrə'tɔ:riəʊ $,ɔ:rə'tɔ:rioʊ, ,ɑ:-/ n plural **oratorios** [C] a long piece of music in which a large group of people sing

or·a·tory /'ɒrətri $ 'ɔ:rətɔ:ri, 'ɑ:-/ n plural **oratories** **1** [U] the skill of making powerful speeches

2 [C] a small building or part of a church where people can go to pray —**oratorical** /ˌɒrəˈtɒrɪkəl◂ $ ˌɔːrəˈtɔːr-, ˌɑːrəˈtɑː-/ adj

orb /ɔːb $ ɔːrb/ n [C] **1** literary a bright ball-shaped object, especially the sun or the moon: *the red orb of the sun* **2** a ball decorated with gold, carried by a king or queen on formal occasions as a sign of power

or·bit¹ /ˈɔːbɪt $ ˈɔːr-/ v [I,T] to travel in a curved path around a much larger object such as the Earth, the sun etc: *The satellite orbits the Earth every 48 hours.*

orbit² n [C] **1** the curved path travelled by an object which is moving around another much larger object such as the Earth, the sun etc: [+**around**] *the Moon's orbit around the Earth* | **in/into orbit** *The Space Shuttle is now in orbit.* | *The telecommunications satellite went into orbit at the end of last year.* **2** formal the area of power and influence of a person, organization etc: **within the orbit of sth** *countries within the orbit of the British commonwealth*

or·bit·al¹ /ˈɔːbɪtl $ ˈɔːr-/ adj **1** relating to the orbit of one object around another: *the Earth's orbital path* **2** BrE an orbital road goes around a large city: *the M25, London's orbital motorway*

orbital² n [C] BrE a road that goes around a large city to keep the traffic away from the centre; ◨ **ring road**

or·chard /ˈɔːtʃəd $ ˈɔːrtʃərd/ n [C] a place where fruit trees are grown: *a cherry orchard*

or·ches·tra /ˈɔːkɪ̬strə $ ˈɔːr-/ n **1** [C also + plural verb BrE] a large group of musicians playing many different kinds of instruments and led by a CONDUCTOR: *the Berlin Symphony Orchestra* | *the school orchestra* **2 orchestra section/seats** AmE the area of seats in a theatre close to and on the same level as the stage

or·ches·tral /ɔːˈkestrəl $ ɔːr-/ adj relating to or written for an orchestra: *orchestral music*

orchestra pit n [C] the space below the stage in a theatre where the musicians sit

or·ches·trate /ˈɔːkɪ̬streɪt $ ˈɔːr-/ v [T] **1** written to organize an important event or a complicated plan, especially secretly: *The riots were orchestrated by anti-government forces.* | *a carefully orchestrated promotional campaign* **2** to arrange a piece of music so that it can be played by an orchestra —**orchestration** /ˌɔːkɪ̬ˈstreɪʃən $ ˌɔːr-/ n [C,U]

or·chid /ˈɔːkɪ̬d $ ˈɔːr-/ n [C] a plant that has flowers which are brightly coloured and unusually shaped → see picture at FLOWER¹

or·dain /ɔːˈdeɪn $ ɔːr-/ v [T] **1** to officially make someone a priest or religious leader; → **ordination**: *Desmond Tutu was ordained in 1960.* | **ordain sb (as) sth** *The church voted to allow women to be ordained as priests.* **2** formal to order that something should happen: **ordain that** *The King ordained that deer should not be hunted without a royal licence.*

or·deal /ɔːˈdiːl, ˈɔːdiːl $ ɔːrˈdiːl, ˈɔːrdiːl/ n [C] a terrible or painful experience that continues for a period of time

> go through an ordeal
> face an ordeal
> survive an ordeal
> recover from an ordeal
> spare sb the ordeal of doing sth (=not make someone have to do something)
> terrible/dreadful ordeal
> terrifying ordeal

> [+of] *She then had to go through the ordeal of giving evidence.* | *She was forced to face the ordeal of withdrawal symptoms.* | *He was beginning to wonder if he would survive the ordeal.* | *Teresa had a transplant in 1989 and was just recovering from that ordeal when she suffered a brain hemorrhage.* | *Soon the whole terrifying ordeal would be over.*

or·der¹ [S1] [W1] /ˈɔːdə $ ˈɔːrdər/ n

1 [FOR A PURPOSE] **a) in order to do sth** for the purpose of doing something: *Samuel trained every day in order to improve his performance.* | *In order to understand*

---

how the human body works, you need to have some knowledge of chemistry. **b) in order for/that** formal so that something can happen or so that someone can do something: *Sunlight is needed in order for the process of photosynthesis to take place in plants.*

2 [ARRANGEMENT] [C,U] the way that things or events are arranged in relation to each other, for example showing whether something is first, second, third etc; ◨ **sequence: in (...) order** *The photographs can be viewed in any order.* | *Make a list of what you have to do, and put them in order with the most important at the top.* | **in order of importance/priority/preference etc** *Students learn the verbs in order of difficulty.* | **do sth in order** (=do things one after another, according to a plan) *Then they call out our names in order and we answer yes or no.* | *Your paragraphs are not arranged in a logical order.* | *My files are in alphabetical order.* | **in the right/correct order** *Replace all the pieces in the correct order.* | **out of order/in the wrong order** *Be careful not to get the cards in the wrong order.* | *He always shaves his face in the same order, right side, then left.* | **in reverse order** (=in the opposite order to what is usual) | **in descending/ascending order** (=starting with the highest or lowest number) *The leaflet gives details of all the hotels in the area in descending order of price.*

3 [INSTRUCTION] [C usually plural] an instruction to do something that is given by someone in authority

> an/the order to do sth
> give/issue an order
> follow/obey orders
> take orders from sb
> receive an order
> have (strict) orders to do sth/be under (strict) orders to do sth (=have been told to do something)
> court order
> doctor's orders (=when the doctor says you must do something)
> by order of sb/on the orders of sb

> *The captain had to give the order to abandon ship.* | *I followed your orders to the letter* (=I did exactly what you ordered). | *I'm not taking orders from him!* | *He received a direct order from the President.* | *She is under strict orders to have a complete rest.* | *The government obtained a court order requiring the editor to reveal his source.* | *I've got to take it easy – doctor's orders.* | *The company cannot be identified by order of the court.*

4 [CONTROLLED SITUATION] [U] a situation in which rules are obeyed and authority is respected: *the breakdown of law and order* | *The riots are a threat to public order.* | **keep order/keep sb in order** (=stop people from behaving badly) *The physics teacher couldn't keep order in any class.* | *She had trouble keeping her teenage sons in order.* | *The army was called in to restore order.*

5 [WELL-ORGANIZED STATE] [U] a situation in which everything is controlled, well organized, and correctly arranged: *Let's have some order in here.* | *You need to put your financial affairs in order.* | *She keeps her room in good order.*

6 [FOR FOOD OR DRINK] [C] **a)** a request for food or drink in a restaurant or bar: *The waiter took our orders.* | **last orders** BrE (=the last time you can order a drink before a bar closes) *Last orders now please!* **b)** the food or drink you have asked for in a restaurant or bar: *When our order finally arrived we were very hungry indeed.* → SIDE ORDER

7 [FOR GOODS] [C] **a)** a request by a customer for a company to supply goods: *Goods will be sent within 24 hours of receiving your order.* | *You can always cancel your order if you change your mind.* | *The government has placed an order for* (=asked a company to supply) *new weapons.* | *Please complete the enclosed order form.* | **on order** (=asked for, but not yet received) *My bicycle is on order.* | **make/supply sth to order** (=produce something especially for a particular customer)

They make hand-made shoes to order. **b)** goods that you have ordered from a company: *Your order has arrived – you can collect it from the store any time.* → MAIL ORDER
8 be out of order a) if a machine or piece of equipment is out of order, it is not working: *The phone is out of order again.* **b)** *BrE informal* if someone's behaviour is out of order, it is unacceptable; **☰ out of line** *AmE* **c)** to be breaking the rules in a committee, court, parliament etc: *The MP's remarks were ruled out of order.*
9 be in order a) if something is in order, it is correct or right: *Everything is in order.* **b)** to be a suitable thing to do or say on a particular occasion: *I hear congratulations are in order.* **c)** if an official document is in order, it is legal and correct: *Is your passport in order?* **d)** if something that you do is in order, it is allowed by the rules in a committee, court, parliament etc
10 be in (good) working/running order in good condition or working well: *She keeps her bicycle in good working order.*
11 SOCIAL/ECONOMIC SITUATION [singular] the political, social, or economic situation at a particular time: **social/political order** *He called the rioters a threat to the social order.* | *The people of South Africa wanted a* **new order**. | *He dared to challenge the* **established** (=traditional) *order.*
12 be the order of the day a) to be suitable for a particular occasion or situation: *Casual clothes are the order of the day.* **b)** to be very common at a particular time – used especially when you disapprove of something: *Sexual explicitness is the order of the day.*
13 the order of things the way that life and the world are organized and intended to be: *People accepted the class system as part of the* **natural order of things**.
14 of a high order/of the highest order also of the first order of a very good kind or of the best kind: *an achievement of the highest order*
15 withdraw/retreat in good order to move away from the enemy in war in an organized way
16 in the order of sth/of the order of sth also **on the order of sth** *AmE* a little more or a little less than a particular amount, especially a high amount; **☰ approximately**: *a figure in the order of $7 million*
17 RELIGIOUS GROUP [C] a society of MONKS or NUNS (=people who live a holy life according to religious rules): *the Benedictine Order* | [+of] *the order of Jesuits*
18 take (holy) orders to become a priest
19 SECRET SOCIETY [C] an organization or society whose members meet for secret ceremonies
20 OFFICIAL HONOUR [C] a group of people who have received a special official reward from a king, president etc for their services or achievements: *the Order of the Garter*
21 MONEY [C] an official piece of paper that can be exchanged for money → MONEY ORDER, POSTAL ORDER
22 the lower orders *BrE old-fashioned* people who belong to the lowest social class
23 ANIMALS/PLANTS [C] *technical* a group of animals or plants that are considered together because they EVOLVED from the same plant or animal → CLASS¹ (5), SPECIES
24 COMPUTER [C] *AmE* a list of jobs that a computer has to do in a particular order; **☰ queue** *BrE*
25 Order! Order! *spoken* used to ask people to stop talking in a meeting or parliament → PECKING ORDER, POINT OF ORDER, STANDING ORDER; → **call sb/sth to order** at CALL¹ (16); → **set/put your own house in order** at HOUSE¹ (7); → **be given/get your marching orders** at MARCH¹ (5); → **in short order** at SHORT¹ (22); → **under starter's orders** at STARTER; → **tall order** at TALL

order² [S2] [W2] v
1 ASK FOR FOOD/DRINK [I,T] to ask for food or a drink in a restaurant, bar etc: *Anne ordered another glass of wine.* | *Are you ready to order?* | *He sat down and* **ordered a meal**.
2 ASK FOR GOODS [I,T] to ask for goods or services to be supplied: *I've ordered a new computer from the*

supplier. | **order sb sth** *I'll order you a taxi.*
3 TELL SB TO DO STH [T] to tell someone that they must do something, especially using your official power or authority: *The court ordered his release from prison.* | *'Stay right there,' she ordered.* | **order sb to do sth** *Tom was ordered to pay £300 as compensation.* | *Her doctor had ordered her to rest for a week.* | **be ordered back to sth** *The soldiers were ordered back to their units.* | **order that** *He ordered that the house be sold.*
4 ARRANGE [T] to arrange something in an order: *The list is ordered alphabetically.*
  order sb around also **order sb about** *BrE phr v* to give someone orders in an annoying or threatening way: *How dare he order her about like that?*
  order sb ⇔ out *phr v* to order soldiers or police to go somewhere to stop violent behaviour by a crowd: *The governor decided to order out the National Guard.*

'order ˌbook *n* [C usually plural] *especially BrE* a record of how many goods or services a company has been asked to provide, which shows how successful it is financially: *Our order books are full at the moment.*

or·dered /ˈɔːdəd $ ˈɔːrdərd/ also **well-ordered** *adj* well arranged or controlled: *an ordered existence* | *a well-ordered household* → DISORDERED

or·der·ing /ˈɔːdərɪŋ $ ˈɔːr-/ *n* [C,U] the way in which something is arranged, or the act of arranging something: *a different ordering*

or·der·ly¹ /ˈɔːdəli $ ˈɔːrdərli/ *adj* **1** arranged or organized in a sensible or neat way; **☰ disorderly**: **(an) orderly sth** *The tools were arranged in orderly rows.* | *She needs to organize her ideas in a more orderly way.* **2** peaceful or well-behaved; **☰ disorderly**: **(an) orderly sth** *The elections were conducted* **in an orderly fashion**. | *They waited in a dignified and orderly manner outside the church.* —**orderliness** *n* [U]

orderly² *n plural* **orderlies** [C] **1** someone who does unskilled jobs in a hospital **2** a soldier who does unskilled jobs

ˌorder of ˈmagnitude *n plural* **orders of magnitude** [C] **1** if something is an order of magnitude greater or smaller than something else, it is ten times greater or smaller in size or amount **2** the scale of the size of something: *That was a problem but this crisis is of a different order of magnitude.*

'order ˌpaper *n* [C] a list of subjects to be discussed in the British Parliament

'or·di·nal ˌnumber also **or·di·nal** /ˈɔːdɪnəl $ ˈɔːrdənəl/ *n* [C] one of the numbers such as first, second, third etc which show the order of things → CARDINAL NUMBER

or·di·nance /ˈɔːdɪnəns $ ˈɔːrdənəns/ *n* [C] **1** *AmE* a law, usually of a city or town, that forbids or restricts an activity: *a city ordinance that says parks must be closed at 11 p.m.* **2** an order given by a ruler or governing organization: *a Royal ordinance*

or·di·nand /ˈɔːdɪnænd $ ˈɔːrdn-/ *n* [C] a person who is preparing to become a priest

or·di·na·ri·ly /ˈɔːdənərɪli, ˌɔːdənˈeərɪli $ ˌɔːrdənˈerɪli/ *adv* **1** [sentence adverb] usually: *Ordinarily, he didn't like to go to the movies.* | *This is not the price at which the CD is ordinarily sold.* **2** in an ordinary or normal way

or·di·na·ry [S1] [W2] /ˈɔːdənəri $ ˈɔːrdəneri/ *adj*
1 average, common, or usual, not different or special: *It's just an ordinary camera.* | *The book is about* **ordinary people**. | *Art should be part of* **ordinary life**. | *It is good because it is written in friendly, ordinary language.* | **out of the ordinary** (=unusual or unexpected) *Anything out of the ordinary made her nervous.* | **in the ordinary way** *BrE* (=as normal) *The money is taxed as income in the ordinary way.* | **sb/sth is no ordinary ...** (=used to say someone or something is very special) *This is no ordinary car.* | *Ruiz is no ordinary prisoner.*
2 not particularly good or impressive: *I thought the paintings were pretty ordinary.* —**ordinariness** *n* [U]

'Ordinary ˌlevel *n* [C,U] O LEVEL

,ordinary 'seaman n [C] a low rank in the British Navy

,ordinary 'shares n [plural] *technical* the largest part of a company's CAPITAL, which is owned by people who have the right to vote at meetings and to receive part of the company's profits

or·di·na·tion /ˌɔːdɪˈneɪʃən $ ˌɔːr-/ n [C,U] the act or ceremony in which someone is made a priest; → **ordain**: *the ordination of women*

ord·nance /ˈɔːdnəns $ ˈɔːr-/ n [U] **1** large guns with wheels; ▣ **artillery 2** weapons, explosives, and vehicles used in fighting

,Ordnance 'Survey ,map n [C] BrE a map which shows all the roads, paths, hills etc of an area in detail

or·dure /ˈɔːdjʊə $ ˈɔːrdʒər/ n [U] *formal* dirt, especially waste matter from the body

ore /ɔː $ ɔːr/ n [C,U] rock or earth from which metal can be obtained: *iron ore* | *veins of rich ore*

or·e·ga·no /ˌɒrɪˈɡɑːnəʊ $ əˈreɡənoʊ/ n [U] a plant used in cooking, especially in Italian cooking

or·gan W3 /ˈɔːɡən $ ˈɔːr-/ n [C]
1 BODY PART **a)** a part of the body, such as the heart or lungs, that has a particular purpose

> **internal organs**
> **vital organs** (=most important organs for life, for example the heart and brain)
> **sexual/reproductive/sex organs**
> **organ transplant** (=an operation to put an organ from one person's body into another's)
> **organ donor** (=someone who gives an organ for an organ transplant)
>
> *the liver, heart, and other **internal organs*** | *loss of blood flow to his **vital organs*** | *Extra doses of the hormone caused the animals' **reproductive organs** to develop sooner than usual.* | *In Arizona, 480 people are waiting for **organ transplants**.* | *dying people who have agreed to be **organ donors*** **b)** a PENIS - used because you want to avoid saying this directly

2 MUSICAL INSTRUMENT **a)** also **pipe organ** a large musical instrument used especially in churches, with KEYS like a piano and large pipes that air passes through to produce the sound **b)** an electronic musical instrument that produces music similar to a pipe organ, but that does not have pipes: *an electronic organ*
3 ORGANIZATION *formal* an organization that is part of, or works for, a larger organization or group: [+of] *The courts are organs of government.* | *the decision-making organs*
4 NEWSPAPER/MAGAZINE *formal* a newspaper or magazine which gives information, news etc for an organization or group: [+of] *the **official organ** of the Communist Party*

or·gan·die also **organdy** AmE /ˈɔːɡəndi $ ˈɔːr-/ n [U] very thin stiff cotton cloth, used as dress material

'organ ,grinder n [C] a musician who plays a BARREL ORGAN in the street

or·gan·ic /ɔːˈɡænɪk $ ɔːr-/ adj
1 FARMING relating to farming or gardening methods of growing food without using artificial chemicals, or produced or grown by these methods: ***Organic farming** is better for the environment.* | *organic gardening* | **organic food/vegetables/milk etc** | *The shop sells organic food.* | *organic wine* → see picture at ENVIRONMENT
2 DEVELOPMENT change or development which is organic happens in a natural way, without anyone planning it or forcing it to happen: *The company's path to success was by means of organic growth.*
3 LIVING THINGS living, or produced by or from living things; ▣ **inorganic**: *Adding **organic matter** such as manure can improve the soil.* | *Bacteria act on **organic waste**.*
4 PART OF STH an organic system or relationship is one in which the parts or people fit well and in a comfortable way with each other: *an **organic relationship** between the individual and his community* | *They believe in the **organic unity** of the universe.*

5 BODY ORGANS relating to the organs of the body: *organic diseases* —**organically** /-kli/ adv: *organically produced cheese* | *A writer's style must develop organically.*

or,ganic 'chemistry n [U] the study of substances containing CARBON; → **inorganic chemistry**

or·gan·is·m S3 /ˈɔːɡənɪzəm $ ˈɔːr-/ n [C]
1 an animal, plant, human, or any other living thing: *All **living organisms** have to adapt to changes in environmental conditions.* | *Genes operate together in determining the characteristics of an **individual organism**.*
2 a system made up of parts that are dependent on each other: *A society is essentially an organism.*

or·gan·ist /ˈɔːɡənɪst $ ˈɔːr-/ n [C] someone who plays the ORGAN: *a church organist*

or·gan·i·za·tion S2 W1 also **-isation** BrE /ˌɔːɡənaɪˈzeɪʃən $ ˌɔːrɡənə-/ n
1 [C] a group such as a club or business that has formed for a particular purpose: *The public expect high standards from any large organization.* | *the World Trade Organization* | *a voluntary organization which helps disabled people with their transport needs* | *an illegal terrorist organization* | ***international organizations** such as the UN*
2 [U] planning and arranging something so that it is successful or effective: *Putting on a show of this kind involves considerable organisation.* | [+of] *The college has helped Anne with the organization of the event.*
3 [U] the way in which the different parts of a system are arranged and work together: [+of] *There needs to be a change in the organization of the health service.*
—**organizational** adj: *organizational skills*

or·gan·ize S1 W2 also **-ise** BrE /ˈɔːɡənaɪz $ ˈɔːr-/ v
1 [T] to make the necessary arrangements so that an activity can happen effectively: *The course was organized by a training company.* | *Students need to learn how to organize their work.*
2 [T] to manage a group of people who are doing something: *The lawyer helped to organize a group of parents who took action for their children.* | **organize yourself** *The scientists need to organize themselves and work as a team.*
3 [T] to arrange something so that it is more ordered or happens in a more sensible way: *He doesn't need you to organize his life for him.* | *Organize yourself to arrive at places on time.*
4 [T] to arrange things in a particular order or pattern: *We are learning about how genes are organized.*
5 [I,T] to form a TRADE UNION or persuade people to join one: *The law gives workers the right to organize and bargain collectively.*

or·gan·ized S3 also **-ised** BrE /ˈɔːɡənaɪzd $ ˈɔːr-/ adj
1 involving people working together in an effective and well planned way; ▣ **disorganized**: *Organized groups of citizens are more successful at changing the government's mind.* | *Organized networks of thieves are stealing cattle.* | **organized religion** (=a religion that has lasted for a long time with leaders and many followers)
2 **well/badly/carefully etc organized** arranged or ordered well, badly, carefully etc: *a carefully organized campaign* | *I want to work with a well organized team.* | *a **highly organized** (=well organized) social system*
3 achieving your aims in an effective, ordered, and sensible way: *It will take me a few days to **get organized**.*

,organized 'crime n [U] a large and powerful organization of criminals: *Organized crime is involved in drug trafficking.*

or·gan·iz·er also **-iser** BrE /ˈɔːɡənaɪzə $ ˈɔːrɡənaɪzər/ n [C] someone who makes the arrangements for something that is planned to happen: *The organizers had expected about 50,000 people to attend the concert.*

or·gan·o·gram /ɔːˈɡænəɡræm $ ˈɔːr-/ *n* [C] a drawing that shows the different ranks of the people working in an organization

or·gas·m /ˈɔːɡæzəm $ ˈɔːr-/ *n* [C,U] the greatest point of sexual pleasure: *women who have never had an orgasm*

or·gas·mic /ɔːˈɡæzmɪk $ ɔːr-/ *adj* **1** *informal* extremely exciting or enjoyable: *an orgasmic experience* **2** relating to orgasm

or·gy /ˈɔːdʒi $ ˈɔːr-/ *n plural* **orgies** [C] **1** a wild party with a lot of eating, drinking, and sexual activity: *the drunken orgies of their youth* **2** sexual activity in a group **3** **an orgy of sth** used to emphasize that people suddenly do a lot of a particular activity, especially far too much of it: *an orgy of spending* | *an orgy of violence* —**orgiastic** /ˌɔːdʒiˈæstɪk◂ $ ˌɔːr-/ *adj*

o·ri·ent¹ /ˈɔːrient, ˈɒri- $ ˈɔː-/ also **orientate** *BrE v* **1** **be oriented to/towards/around sth/sb** to give a lot of attention to one type of activity or one type of person: *a course that is oriented towards the needs of businessmen* | *A lot of the training is orientated around communications skills.* | *The organization is strongly oriented towards research* **2** **orient yourself a)** to find exactly where you are by looking around you or using a map; → **disorient, disorientated**: *She looked at the street names, trying to orient herself.* **b)** to become familiar with a new situation: [+to] *It takes new students a while to orientate themselves to college life.*

o·ri·ent² /ˈɔːrient, ˈɒri- $ ˈɔː-/ *n* **the Orient** *old-fashioned* the eastern part of the world, especially China and Japan → **the East** at EAST (1a); → OCCIDENT

o·ri·en·tal¹ /ˌɔːriˈentl◂ , ˌɒri- $ ˌɔː-/ *adj* relating to or from the eastern part of the world, especially China and Japan: *a beautiful oriental rug* | *oriental art*

oriental² also **Oriental** *n* [C] *old-fashioned not polite* a word for someone from the eastern part of the world, especially China or Japan, now considered offensive → OCCIDENTAL

o·ri·en·tal·ist /ˌɔːriˈentəlɪst, ˌɒri- $ ˌɔː-/ *n* [C] someone who studies the languages and culture of oriental countries

o·ri·en·tate /ˈɔːrienteit, ˈɒri- $ ˈɔː-/ *v* a British word for ORIENT¹; 🖪 **disorientate**

o·ri·en·tat·ed /ˈɔːrienteitɪd, ˈɒ- $ ˈɔː-/ *adj* a British word for ORIENTED

o·ri·en·ta·tion /ˌɔːrienˈteiʃən, ˌɒri- $ ˌɔː-/ *n formal* **1** [C,U] the type of activity or subject that a person or organization seems most interested in and gives most attention to: [+towards/to] *The company needs to develop a stronger orientation towards marketing its products.* | *How can we get students to adopt a serious orientation to learning?* | [+of] *He was unhappy with the commercial orientation of the organization.* **2** [C,U] the political opinions or religious beliefs that someone has: **political/religious orientation** *The meeting is open to everyone, whatever their political or religious orientation.* | *The party has a broadly socialist orientation.* **3** **sexual orientation** the fact that someone is HETEROSEXUAL or HOMOSEXUAL: *Discrimination on the grounds of sexual orientation is still far too widespread.* **4** [U] a period of time during which people are trained and prepared for a new job or course of study: *This is orientation week for all the new students.* **5** [C] the angle or position of an object, or the direction in which it is facing

o·ri·ent·ed /ˈɔːrientɪd, ˈɒri- $ ˈɔː-/ also **orientated** *BrE adj* giving a lot of time, effort, or attention to one particular thing: *A lot of the younger students don't seem to be politically oriented at all.* | *She's very career orientated.* | *The country's economy is export oriented.*

o·ri·en·teer·ing /ˌɔːrienˈtiəriŋ, ˌɒri- $ ˌɔːrienˈtɪr-/ *n* [U] a sport in which people have to find their way quickly across an area in the countryside that they do not know, using a map and a COMPASS → see picture at OUTDOOR

or·i·fice /ˈɒrɪfɪs $ ˈɔː-, ˈɑː-/ *n* [C] *formal* **1** one of the holes in your body, such as your mouth, nose etc: *various bodily orifices* **2** a hole or entrance

o·ri·ga·mi /ˌɒriˈɡɑːmi $ ˌɔː-/ *n* [U] the Japanese art of folding paper to make attractive objects

or·i·gin W2 /ˈɒrɪdʒɪn $ ˈɔː-, ˈɑː-/ *n* [C,U] **1** also **origins** [plural] the place or situation in which something begins to exist: [+of] *a new theory to explain the origins of the universe* | **in origin** *Most coughs are viral in origin.* | *The word is French in origin.* | *The tradition has its origins in the Middle Ages.* | *old folk tales of unknown origin* | **country/place of origin** (=where something came from) *All meat should be clearly labelled with its country of origin.* **2** also **origins** [plural] the country, race, or type of family which someone comes from; → **extraction**: **of French/German/Asian etc origin** *Two thirds of the pupils are of Asian origin.* | *The form asks for information about the person's ethnic origin.* | *Immigrants rarely return to their country of origin.* | *She never forgot her humble origins* (=low class or social position).

o·rig·i·nal¹ S1 W1 /əˈrɪdʒɪnəl, -dʒənəl/ *adj* **1** **FIRST** [only before noun] existing or happening first, before other people or things: *The land was returned to its original owner.* | *The kitchen still has many original features* (=parts that were there when the house was first built). | *the original meaning of the word* | *The original plan was to fly out to New York.* **2** **NEW** completely new and different from anything that anyone has thought of before: *I don't think George is capable of having original ideas!* | *That's not a very original suggestion.* | *a highly original design* | *His work is truly original.* **3** **A WORK OF ART** [only before noun] an original work of art is the one that was made by the artist and is not a copy: *The original painting is now in the National Gallery in London.* | *an original Holbein drawing*

original² *n* [C] **1** a work of art or a document that is not a copy, but is the one produced by the writer or artist: *The colours are much more striking in the original.* | *I'll keep a copy of the contract, and give you the original.* **2** **in the original** in the language that a book, play etc was first written in, before it was translated: *I'd prefer to read it in the original.* **3** *informal* someone whose behaviour, clothing etc is unusual and amusing

o·rig·i·nal·i·ty /əˌrɪdʒɪˈnælɪti/ *n* [U] when something is completely new and different from anything that anyone has thought of before: [+of] *I was impressed by the originality of the plan.* | *Her earlier work shows a lot of originality.* | *A lot of his designs lack originality.* | *a young writer of great originality*

o·rig·i·nal·ly S2 W2 /əˈrɪdʒɪnəli, -dʒənəli/ *adv* in the beginning, before other things happened or before things changed: *The family originally came from France.* | *The building was originally used as a prison.* | *We originally intended to stay for just a few days.* | [sentence adverb]: *Originally, we had planned a tour of Scotland but we didn't go in the end.*

o,riginal 'sin *n* [U] the tendency to behave in bad or evil ways, which is in all people according to the Christian religion

o·rig·i·nate /əˈrɪdʒɪneit/ *v* **1** [I always + adv/prep, not in progressive] *formal* to come from a particular place or start in a particular situation: *How did the plan originate?* | [+from] *A lot of our medicines originate from tropical plants.* | [+in] *Many Christmas traditions originated in Germany.* | [+with] *The idea originated with the ancient Greek philosophers.* | [+as] *The town originated as a small fishing port.* **2** [T] to have the idea for something and start it: *The technique was originated by an Italian artist.*

o·rig·i·na·tor /əˈrɪdʒɪneitə $ -ər/ *n* [C] the person who first has the idea for something and starts it: [+of] *Professor Adams was the originator of the project.*

or·i·ole /ˈɔːriəʊl $ -oʊl/ n [C] **1** a North American bird that is black with a red and yellow STRIPE on its wing **2** a European bird with black wings and a yellow body

or·mo·lu /ˈɔːməluː $ ˈɔːr-/ n [U] a gold-coloured mixture of metals that does not contain real gold: *an ormolu clock*

or·na·ment¹ /ˈɔːnəmənt $ ˈɔːr-/ n **1** [C] a small object that you keep in your house because it is beautiful rather than useful: *a shelf covered with books and ornaments* | *china ornaments* **2** [U] decoration that is added to something: *The building style is plain, with very little ornament.* | **for ornament** *The coins were only ever used for ornament, not as currency.*

or·na·ment² /ˈɔːnəmənt $ ˈɔːr-/ v **be ornamented with sth** to be decorated with something: *a silver goblet ornamented with pearls* | **richly/exquisitely/lavishly etc ornamented** *a table richly ornamented with carvings*

or·na·men·tal /ˌɔːnəˈmentl◂ $ ˌɔːr-/ adj designed to make something look attractive rather than to be used for a particular purpose: *ornamental gardens* | *The pillars in the centre are purely ornamental.*

or·na·men·ta·tion /ˌɔːnəmenˈteɪʃən $ ˌɔːr-/ n [U] decoration on an object that makes it look attractive: *a bronze plate with gold ornamentation*

or·nate /ɔːˈneɪt $ ɔːr-/ adj covered with a lot of decoration: *an ornate gold mirror* —**ornately** adv: *an ornately carved chair*

or·ne·ry /ˈɔːnəri $ ˈɔːr-/ adj AmE behaving in an unreasonable and often angry way, especially by doing the opposite of what people want you to do: *an ornery kid*

or·ni·thol·o·gist /ˌɔːnɪˈθɒlədʒɪst $ ˌɔːrnɪˈθɑː-/ n [C] someone who studies birds

or·ni·thol·o·gy /ˌɔːnɪˈθɒlədʒi $ ˌɔːrnɪˈθɑː-/ n [U] the scientific study of birds —**ornithological** /ˌɔːnɪθəˈlɒdʒɪkəl◂ $ ˌɔːrnɪθəˈlɑː-/ adj

or·phan¹ /ˈɔːfən $ ˈɔːr-/ n [C] a child whose parents are both dead: *The war has left thousands of children as orphans.* | **orphan girl/boy/child** *a poor little orphan girl*

orphan² v **be orphaned** to become an orphan: *She was orphaned when her parents died in a plane crash.*

or·phan·age /ˈɔːfənɪdʒ $ ˈɔːr-/ n [C] a large house where children who are orphans live and are taken care of: *He was raised in an orphanage.*

or·tho·don·tics /ˌɔːθəˈdɒntɪks $ ˌɔːrθəˈdɑːn-/ n [U] the skill or job of helping teeth to grow straight when they have not been growing correctly —**orthodontic** adj: *orthodontic treatment*

or·tho·don·tist /ˌɔːθəˈdɒntɪst $ ˌɔːrθəˈdɑːn-/ n [C] a DENTIST whose job is to help teeth to grow straight when they have not been growing correctly

or·tho·dox /ˈɔːθədɒks $ ˈɔːrθədɑːks/ adj **1** orthodox ideas, methods, or behaviour are accepted by most people to be correct and right; ☐ **conventional**: *orthodox medical treatments* | *He challenged the orthodox views on education.* **2** someone who is orthodox has the opinions and beliefs that are generally accepted as being right, and does not have new or different ideas: *Orthodox economists believe that a recession is now inevitable.* | *an orthodox Marxist* **3** believing in all the traditional beliefs, laws, and practices of a religion: *an orthodox Jew*

Orthodox 'Church n [C,U] one of the Christian churches in Greece, eastern Europe, and parts of Asia

or·tho·dox·y /ˈɔːθədɒksi $ ˈɔːrθədɑː-/ n plural **orthodoxies** [C,U] an idea or set of ideas that is accepted by most people to be correct and right: *He challenged the political orthodoxy of his time.* | *These ideas have now become part of educational orthodoxy.*

or·thog·ra·phy /ɔːˈθɒgrəfi $ ɔːrˈθɑː-/ n [U] technical the way in which words are spelled —**orthographic** /ˌɔːθəˈgræfɪk◂ $ ˌɔːr-/ adj —**orthographically** /-kli/ adv

or·tho·pe·dic also **orthopaedic** BrE /ˌɔːθəˈpiːdɪk◂ $ ˌɔːr-/ adj **1** relating to the medical treatment of problems that affect a people's bones or muscles: *an orthopaedic surgeon* | *the orthopedic ward in the hospital* **2** **orthopedic bed/chair/shoe etc** one that is designed to help treat medical problems that affect people's bones or muscles —**orthopedically** /-kli/ adv

or·tho·pe·dics also **orthopaedics** BrE /ˌɔːθəˈpiːdɪks $ ˌɔːr-/ n [U] the part of medicine that treats illnesses or injuries that affect people's bones or muscles

or·tho·pe·dist also **orthopaedist** BrE /ˌɔːθəˈpiːdɪst $ ˌɔːr-/ n [C] a doctor with special training in orthopedics

-ory¹ /əri $ ɔːri, əri/ suffix [in nouns] a place or thing that is used for doing something: *an observatory* (=a place from where people watch something, especially the stars)

-ory² suffix [in adjectives] describes something that does a particular thing: *an explanatory note* (=that gives an explanation) | *a congratulatory telegram* (=that congratulates someone)

Os·car /ˈɒskə $ ˈɑːskər/ n [C] a prize that is given each year in the US for the best film, actor etc in the film industry: **[+for]** *Who got the Oscar* (=won it) *for best actress?* | *The film won five Oscars.*

os·cil·late /ˈɒsɪleɪt $ ˈɑːsə-/ v [I] **1** formal to keep changing between two extreme amounts or limits: *The stock market is oscillating wildly at the moment.* | **[+between]** *His income oscillated between £1500 and £2000 a month.* **2** formal to keep changing between one feeling or attitude and another: **[+between]** *Her attitude towards me oscillated between friendship and hostility.* **3** to move backwards and forwards in a regular way: *The needle on the dial began to oscillate.* **4** technical if an electric current oscillates, it changes direction very regularly and very frequently

os·cil·la·tion /ˌɒsɪˈleɪʃən $ ˌɑːsə-/ n [C,U] **1** formal oscillations are frequent changes between two extreme amounts or limits: **[+in/of]** *oscillations in the value of the dollar* | **[+between]** *oscillating between growth and decline* **2** formal oscillations are frequent changes between one feeling or attitude and another: *The drug causes oscillations of mood in some people.* **3** technical a regular movement of something from side to side: *the oscillations of a pendulum* **4** technical a regular change in direction of an electrical current

os·cil·la·tor /ˈɒsɪleɪtə $ ˈɑːsəleɪtər/ n [C] technical a machine that produces electrical oscillations

-oses /əʊsiːz $ oʊ-/ suffix the plural form of the suffix -OSIS

o·si·er /ˈəʊziə, ˈəʊʒə $ ˈoʊziər, ˈoʊʒər/ n [C] a WILLOW tree whose branches are used for making baskets

-osis /ˈəʊsɪs $ oʊ-/ suffix plural -oses /əʊsiːz $ oʊ-/ [in nouns] **1** a diseased condition: *silicosis* (=a lung disease) | *neuroses* (=medical conditions that affect the mind) **2** a condition or process: *a metamorphosis* (=change from one state to another) —**-otic** /ɒtɪk $ aːtɪk/ suffix [in adjectives]: *neurotic* | *hypnotic* —**-otically** /ɒtɪkli $ aːt-/ suffix [in adverbs]

os·mo·sis /ɒzˈməʊsɪs $ aːzˈmoʊ-/ n [U] **1** if you learn facts or understand ideas by osmosis, you gradually learn them by hearing them often: **by osmosis** *Children learn new languages by osmosis.* | *He seems to absorb information through a* **process of osmosis**. **2** technical the gradual process of liquid passing through a MEMBRANE —**osmotic** /ɒzˈmɒtɪk $ aːzˈmaː-/ adj

os·prey /ˈɒspreɪ $ ˈaːspri, -preɪ/ n [C] a type of large bird that kills and eats fish

os·si·fy /ˈɒsɪfaɪ $ ˈaː-/ v **ossified, ossifying, ossifies 1** [I] formal to become unwilling to consider new ideas or change your behaviour **2** [I,T] technical to change into bone or to make something change into bone —**ossification** /ˌɒsɪfɪˈkeɪʃən $ ˌaːs-/ n [U]

os·ten·si·ble /ɒ'stensᵻbəl $ ɑː-/ adj seeming to be the reason for or the purpose of something, but usually hiding the real reason or purpose: **ostensible reason/ purpose/aim** The ostensible reason for his resignation was ill health.

os·ten·si·bly /ɒ'stensᵻbli $ ɑː-/ adv if something is ostensibly true, people say that it is true but it is not really true: She stayed behind at the office, ostensibly to work.

os·ten·ta·tion /ˌɒstən'teɪʃən, -ten- $ ˌɑː-/ n [U] formal when you deliberately try to show people how rich or clever you are, in order to make them admire you: Her lifestyle was remarkably free from ostentation.

os·ten·ta·tious /ˌɒstən'teɪʃəs◂, -ten- $ ˌɑː-/ adj **1** something that is ostentatious looks very expensive and is designed to make people think that its owner must be very rich: She carried her car keys on an ostentatious gold key ring. | an ostentatious display of wealth **2** someone who is ostentatious likes to show everyone how rich they are: He was vain and ostentatious. —**ostentatiously** adv

osteo- /ɒstiəʊ, -tiə $ ɑːstioʊ, -tiə/ prefix technical relating to bones

os·te·o·ar·thri·tis /ˌɒstiəʊɑː'θraɪtᵻs $ ˌɑːstioʊɑːr-/ n [U] a medical condition which makes your knees and other joints stiff and painful

os·te·o·path /'ɒstiəpæθ $ 'ɑː-/ n [C] someone who is trained to treat people using osteopathy → CHIROPRACTOR

os·te·op·a·thy /ˌɒsti'ɒpəθi $ ˌɑːsti'ɑː-/ n [U] a way of treating medical problems such as back pain by moving and pressing the muscles and bones

os·te·o·po·ro·sis /ˌɒstiəʊpə'rəʊsᵻs $ ˌɑːstioʊpə-'roʊ-/ n [U] a medical condition in which your bones become weak and break easily: the risk of developing osteoporosis

os·tler /'ɒslə $ 'ɑːslər/ also **hostler** AmE n [C] a man who took care of guests' horses at a hotel in the past

os·tra·cize also **-ise** BrE /'ɒstrəsaɪz $ 'ɑː-/ v [T] if a group of people ostracize someone, they refuse to accept them as a member of the group: She was afraid that if she spoke up her colleagues would ostracize her. | He was ostracized by the other students. —**ostracism** /-sɪzəm/ n [U]: He suffered years of ostracism.

os·trich /'ɒstrɪtʃ $ 'ɒː-, 'ɑː-/ n [C] **1** a large African bird with long legs, that runs very quickly but cannot fly **2** informal someone who does not deal with difficult problems but tries to pretend that they do not exist

OTC /ˌəʊ tiː 'siː◂ $ ˌəʊ-/ the abbreviation of **over-the-counter**

OTE /ˌəʊ tiː 'iː $ ˌoʊ-/ BrE **on target earnings** used in advertisements for jobs to say that the EMPLOYEE will receive the complete pay only if they succeed in doing as much work or selling as many things as the employer wants them to, and will get less pay if they do not succeed

oth·er S1 W1 /'ʌðə $ 'ʌðər/ determiner, adj, pron **1** THE SECOND OF TWO used to refer to the second of two people or things, which is not the one you already have or the one you have already mentioned: **the/your other** I can't find my other shoe. | One man was arrested, but **the other one** got away. | He kept shifting awkwardly from one foot to the other. | She took it for granted that each knew who the other was.
2 THE REST used to refer to all the people or things in a group apart from the one you have already mentioned or the one that is already known about: **the/your other** The other hotels are all full. | She's much brighter than all the other children in her class. | I chose this coat in the end because **the other ones** were all too expensive. | **the/your others** I can see Julie, but where have all the others gone?
3 ADDITIONAL used to refer to additional people or things of the same kind: There are one or two other problems I'd like to discuss. | I've got some other friends

I'd like to invite. | Have you **any other** questions? | **among others** (=used when mentioning one or more examples) The guests included, among others, Elizabeth Taylor and Michael Jackson.
4 DIFFERENT used to refer to a different person or thing from the one you have already mentioned or the one that is already known about: David and Jessica were playing with two other children. | You'd better change into some other clothes. | Do you envy other women who seem to manage their lives better? | Can we discuss this **some other** time? | There is **no other** job I would rather do. | Saudi Arabia produces more oil than **any other** country. | I hope you will learn to show more respect for others (=other people). | **some ... others** Some people are at greater risk than others.
5 OPPOSITE used to refer to the thing that is opposite you, furthest from you, or moving away from you: **the other side/end/direction etc** You can park on the other side of the street. | He lives at the other end of the road. | She drove off in the other direction.
6 other than apart from a particular person or thing; ☐ **except**: The truth was known to no one other than herself. | He doesn't eat pork, but other than that he'll eat just about anything.
7 none other than sb used to emphasize that the person involved in something is famous, impressive, or surprising: Johnson's defence lawyer was none other than Joe Beltrami.
8 the other way around/round the opposite of what you have just mentioned: I always thought that rugby was a rougher game than football, but in fact it's the other way round. | Students practise translating from French to English and the other way around.
9 the other day/morning/week etc used to say that something happened recently, without saying exactly when: I saw Rufus the other day.
10 something/someone/somewhere etc or other used when you are not being specific about which thing, person, place etc you mean: It'll be here somewhere or other. | We'll get the money somehow or other.
11 in other words used when you are expressing an idea or opinion again in a different and usually simpler way: The tax only affects people on incomes of over $200,000 – in other words, the very rich. | So he is a fraud, a common thief in other words.
12 the other woman used to refer to a woman with whom a man is having a sexual relationship, even though he already has a wife or partner: He left his wife and child and moved in with the other woman. ⚠ When **other** is used before a noun, it never has an 's': We visited other places (NOT others places). → ANOTHER → EACH OTHER; → every other at EVERY (5); → on the one hand ... on the other hand at HAND¹ (5)

oth·er·ness /'ʌðənᵻs $ 'ʌðər-/ n [U] when something is strange and different

oth·er·wise S1 W2 /'ʌðəwaɪz $ 'ʌðər-/ adv **1** [sentence adverb] used when saying what bad thing will happen if something is not done: You'll have to go now, otherwise you'll miss your bus. | Put your coat on, otherwise you'll get cold.
2 [sentence adverb] used when saying what would have happened or might have happened if something else had not happened: We were delayed at the airport. Otherwise we would have been here by lunch time. | They got two free tickets to Canada, otherwise they'd never have been able to afford to go.
3 say/think/decide etc otherwise to say, think, or decide something different: The government claims that the economy is improving, but this survey suggests otherwise. | A lot of people think otherwise.
4 except for what has just been mentioned: He was tired but otherwise in good health. | [sentence adverb]: I could hear the distant noise of traffic. Otherwise all was still. | [+ adj/adv]: This spoiled an otherwise excellent piece of work. | Their arrival livened up an otherwise dull afternoon.
5 or otherwise especially BrE used to refer to the opposite of what has just been mentioned: We welcome

any comments from viewers, favourable or otherwise. | *The truth or otherwise of this diagnosis would be revealed in the future.*

6 otherwise engaged *formal* busy doing something else: *I'm afraid I will be otherwise engaged that day.*

7 otherwise known as also called: *Albert DeSalvo, otherwise known as the Boston Strangler*

8 *formal* in a different way: *people who smoke or otherwise abuse their bodies*

9 it cannot be otherwise/how can it be otherwise? *formal* used to say that it is impossible for something to be different from the way it is: *Life in the military is hard – how can it be otherwise?*

oth·er·world·ly /ˌʌðə'wɜːldli◂ $ ˌʌðər'wɜːr-/ *adj* relating to religious thoughts and ideas rather than with normal daily life

o·ti·ose /'əʊtiəʊs, 'əʊʃəs $ 'əʊʃiəʊs, 'əʊti-/ *adj formal* unnecessary

OTT /ˌəʊ tiː 'tiː $ ˌoʊ-/ *adj BrE informal* **over-the-top** remarks, behaviour etc that are OTT are so extreme or unreasonable that they seem stupid or offensive

ot·ter /'ɒtə $ 'ɑːtər/ *n* [C] an animal with smooth brown fur that swims in rivers and eats fish

ot·to·man /'ɒtəmən $ 'ɑː-/ *n* [C] a piece of furniture like a large box with a soft top, used as a seat, for resting your feet on when you are sitting, or for storing things

ou·bli·ette /ˌuːbli'et/ *n* [C] a small room in an old castle where prisoners were kept for a long time

ouch /aʊtʃ/ *interjection* a sound that you make when you feel sudden pain: *Ouch! That hurt!*

oughta /'ɔːtə $ 'ɒːtə/ *modal verb informal* a way of saying 'ought to' – used especially in writing to show how it is pronounced by some people: *You oughta tell your mom.*

oughtn't /'ɔːtnt $ 'ɒː-/ the short form of 'ought not': *You oughtn't to drive if you're tired.*

ought to S1 W2 /'ɔːt tuː $ 'ɒːt-/ *modal verb*

1 used to say that someone should do something because it is the best or most sensible thing to do; ⊟ **should**: *You really ought to quit smoking.* | *The company ought to be making changes in its marketing strategy.* | *What sort of crimes ought the police to concentrate on?* | *You were not enjoying yourself when you ought to have been studying.*

2 used to make a suggestion about something you think is a good idea, especially in a social situation; ⊟ **should**: *We ought to get together some time soon.* | *You ought to meet him; he's really nice.* | *We ought to get her some flowers for her birthday.* | *I ought to call Brian.*

3 used to say that someone should do something or something should happen, because it is morally right or fair; ⊟ **should**: *You ought to be ashamed of yourself.* | *The courts ought to treat black and white defendants in exactly the same way.* | *Many people felt that America ought not to take part in the war.*

4 used to say that you think something will probably happen, is probably true etc; ⊟ **should**: *He left two hours ago, so he ought to be there by now.* | *They ought to win – they've trained hard enough.* | *That ought to be enough potatoes for eight people.* | *New technology ought to make this easier.*

Oui·ja board /'wiːdʒə bɔːd $ 'wiːdʒi bɔːrd/ *n* [C] *trademark* a board with letters and signs on it, which some people believe can be used to receive messages from dead people

ounce S3 /aʊns/ *n* [C] written abbreviation *oz*

1 a unit for measuring weight, equal to 28.35 grams. There are 16 ounces in a pound. → FLUID OUNCE

2 an ounce of sense/truth/decency etc any sense, truth etc at all: *If you had an ounce of sense you wouldn't believe him!*

3 every (last) ounce of courage/energy/strength etc all the courage, energy etc that you have: *Every ounce of attention was focused on our common goal.*

4 an ounce of prevention (is worth a pound of cure) used to say that it is better to prevent a problem before

it happens than to try to solve it after it has happened

5 not an ounce of fat (on sb) if there is not an ounce of fat on someone, they are thin and usually look healthy

our S1 W1 /aʊə $ aʊr/ *determiner* [possessive form of 'we']

1 belonging to or connected with us: *a picture of our grandchildren* | *You can stay at our house.* | *We must preserve our natural environment.* | *We must each take responsibility for our own actions.*

2 *spoken* used to show that the person mentioned is your child, brother, or sister – used in northern England: *Our Sharon did really well in her exams.*

ours S1 /aʊəz $ aʊrz/ *pron* [possessive form of 'we'] used to refer to something that belongs to or is connected with us: *I'll show you to your room. Ours is next door.* | *The main difference between our brains and those of monkeys is that ours are bigger.* | *No, that's not ours.* | **of ours** *The Thackers are friends of ours.*

our·selves S1 W3 /aʊə'selvz $ aʊr-/ *pron*

1 used by the person speaking to show that they and one or more other people are affected by their own action: *We prepared ourselves for the long journey ahead.* | *It was strange seeing ourselves on television.*

2 a) used to emphasize 'we' or 'us': *We built the house ourselves.* | *As parents ourselves, we understand the problem* **b)** used after 'as', 'like', or 'except' instead of 'us': *More help is needed for people like ourselves.*

3 (all) by ourselves a) alone: *We weren't supposed to play by ourselves near the pond.* **b)** without help from anyone else: *I knew that Tim and I wouldn't be able to do the whole job by ourselves.*

4 (all) to ourselves without having to share something with any other people: *We had the house to ourselves.*

-ous /əs/ *suffix* [in adjectives] describes something that has a particular quality: *dangerous* (=full of danger) | *spacious* (=with a lot of space)

oust /aʊst/ *v* [T] to force someone out of a position of power, especially so that you can take their place: **oust sb from sth** *The Communists were finally ousted from power.*

ous·ter /'aʊstə $ -ər/ *n* [U] *AmE* when someone is removed from a position of power or from a competition – used in news reports: **sb's ouster/the ouster of sb** *the ouster of the brutal dictatorship*

out¹ S1 W1 /aʊt/ *adv*

1 FROM INSIDE from inside an object, container, building, or place; ⊞ **in**: *She opened her suitcase and took out a pair of shoes.* | *Lock the door on your way out.* | *Charlotte went to the window and looked out.* | *Out you go!* (=used to order someone to leave a room) | [+of] *The keys must have fallen out of my pocket.* | *Get out of here!* | *Someone had torn several pages out of her diary.* | *I don't think I'd have the courage to jump out of a plane.* | *All the roads out of the city were snowbound.* | **out came/jumped etc** *The egg cracked open and out came a baby chick.*

2 OUTSIDE not inside a building; ⊟ **outside**: *Many of the homeless have been sleeping out for years.* | *Children were out playing in the snow.* | *Brrr, it's cold out there.*

3 NOT AT HOME **a)** away from your home, office etc, especially for a short time; ⊞ **in**: *Did anyone call while I was out?* | *My parents are both out at the moment.* | *He went out at 11 o'clock.* **b)** to or in a place that is not your home, in order to enjoy yourself: *You should get out and meet people.* | *Let's eat out tonight* (=eat in a restaurant). | *At first he was too shy to ask her out.* | **be/get out and about** (=go to places where you can meet people) *Most teenagers would rather be out and about with their friends.*

4 DISTANT PLACE **a)** in or to a place that is far away or difficult to get to: *He went out to New Zealand.* | *They've rented a farmhouse right out in the country.* **b)** used to say how far away something is: *The Astra Satellite is travelling some 23,000 miles out in space.* | [+of] *a little* *village about five miles out of Birmingham*

5 GIVEN TO MANY PEOPLE used to say that something is given to many people: *The examination will start when all the question papers have been handed out.* | *Have you sent out the invitations yet?*

6 GET RID OF STH used to say that someone gets rid of something or makes it disappear: *Have you thrown out yesterday's paper?* | *Mother used washing soda to get the stains out.*

7 NOT BURNING/SHINING a fire or light that is out is no longer burning or shining: *Turn the lights out when you go to bed.* | *The firefighters arrived, and within minutes the fire was out.*

8 SUN/MOON ETC if the sun, moon, or stars are out, they have appeared in the sky: *When the sun came out, a rainbow formed in the sky.*

9 FLOWERS if the flowers on a plant are out, they have opened: *It's still February and already the primroses are out.*

10 COMPLETELY/CAREFULLY used to say that something is done carefully or completely: *I spent all morning cleaning out the kitchen cupboards.* | *In the summer months the soil dries out quickly.*

11 NOT INCLUDED not included in a team, group, competition etc: *The Welsh team was surprisingly knocked out in the semi finals.* | [+of] *Daniels will be out of the team until he recovers from his injury.*

12 COME FROM STH used to say where something comes from or is taken from: [+of] *A lot of good music came out of the hippy culture in the 1960s.* | *The money is automatically taken out of your bank account every month.*

13 AWAY FROM THE EDGE OF STH away from the main part or edge of something: *I swam out into the middle of the lake.* | *A long peninsula juts out into the sea.* | [+of] *She stuck her head out of the window to see what was happening.*

14 NOT WORKING especially AmE if a machine, piece of equipment etc is out, it is not working: *I don't believe it – the elevator's out again!* → **be out of order** at ORDER[1] (8)

15 PRODUCT used to say that a product is available to be bought: *Is the new Harry Potter book out yet?* | *Sony have brought out a new portable music system.*

16 NOT IN A SITUATION no longer in a particular state or situation: [+of] *She's not completely cured, but at least she's out of danger.* | *This whole situation is getting out of control.* | *How long have you been out of work now?* | *Karen waved until the car was **out of sight** (=too far away to be seen).*

17 HAVING LEFT AN INSTITUTION **a)** having left the institution where you were: [+of] *a kid just out of college* | *His wife isn't out of hospital yet.* **b)** no longer in prison: *Once he was out, he returned to a life of crime.*

18 NOT FASHIONABLE no longer fashionable; 🔁 **in**: *You can't wear that – maxi skirts have been out for years.*

19 NOT SECRET no longer a secret: *Her secret was out.* | *The word's out that Mel Gibson is in town.* | *Eventually the truth came out.*

20 read/shout etc sth out (loud) to say something in a voice that is loud enough for others to hear: *Someone called out my name.* | *We all listened as he read the statement out loud.*

21 UNCONSCIOUS not conscious: *She fainted – she was out for about ten minutes.* | *How hard did you hit him? He's **out cold**.*

22 NONE LEFT used to say that there is none of something left because you have used it all, sold it all etc: *The album was sold out within minutes.* | [+of] *We're out of milk.* | *They've run out of ideas.*

23 before the day/year etc is out before the day, year etc has ended: *Don't cry, I'll be back before the week's out.*

24 NOT CORRECT if a measurement, result etc is out, it is wrong because the numbers have not been calculated correctly: *He was out in his calculations, so there was a lot of carpet left over.* | *The bill was out by over*

£10. | *Their forecast was **way out**.* → **not far off/out/wrong** at FAR[1] (2)

25 be out for sth/be out to do sth informal to have a particular intention: *Andrew's just out for a good time.* | *I was convinced he was out to cheat me.*

26 NOT IN POWER used to say that someone, especially a political party, no longer has power or authority; 🔁 **in**: *It's time we voted the Republicans out.* | [+of] *The party has been out of office for a long time.*

27 ON STRIKE BrE used to say that someone has stopped working as a way of protesting about something: *The railway workers have come out in sympathy with the miners.*

28 HOMOSEXUAL if a HOMOSEXUAL is out, they have told people that they are homosexual

29 NOT POSSIBLE spoken if a particular suggestion or activity is out, it is not possible: *We don't have enough money to rent a car, so that's out.*

30 SEA when the TIDE is out, the sea by the shore is at its lowest level; 🔁 **in**: *You can walk across the sands when the tide is out.*

31 SPORT **a)** a player or team that is out in a game such as CRICKET or baseball is no longer allowed to BAT: *Sussex were all out for 365.* **b)** a ball that is out in a game such as tennis or BASKETBALL is not in the area of play; 🔁 **in**

32 out with it! spoken used to tell someone to say something which they have been unwilling to say or have difficulty saying: *OK, out with it! What really happened?*

33 REASON because of a particular feeling that you have: [+of] *They obeyed him out of fear rather than respect.* | *Just out of curiosity, why did you take that job?*

34 MADE OF STH used to say what substance or materials a particular thing is made of: [+of] *a tombstone carved out of black marble* | *toy boats made out of old tin cans*

35 HOW MANY OF A GROUP used to say how common something is, or how large a part of a group you are talking about: **9 out of 10/three out of four etc** *Nine out of ten students pass the test first time.* | *Apparently they've lost three games out of seven already.*

36 out of it informal **a)** slightly unhappy because you feel different from the rest of a group of people and cannot share their fun, conversation etc: *I felt a bit out of it because I was the only one who couldn't speak French.* **b)** unable to think clearly because you are tired or drunk, or have taken drugs: *You were really out of it last night. What were you drinking?*

37 out there **a)** in a place that could be anywhere except here: *My real father is out there and one day I plan to find him.* **b)** where someone or something can be noticed by many people: *Jerry Lewis is out there all the time raising money for disabled kids.*

38 out front especially AmE **a)** in front of something, especially a building, where everyone can see you: *There's a blue car out front.* **b)** taking a leading position: *As a civil rights leader, he was always out front.* **c)** informal very honest and direct: *Molly is very out front in talking about her mistakes.* → **out of your mind** at MIND[1] (24) ; → **out of the blue** at BLUE[2] (4) ; → **out of luck** at LUCK[1] (10) ; → **out of this world** at WORLD[1] (15) ; → **be out of the question** at QUESTION[1] (9) ; → **out front** at FRONT[1] (8) ; → **out back** at BACK[2] (2) ; → **out of sorts** at SORT[1] (10)

⚠ Do not confuse **outdoors** (with an –s) and **outdoor** (without an –s). **Outdoors** is an adverb: *I like playing outdoors.* **Outdoor** is an adjective that can only be used before a noun: *outdoor activities such as fishing*

out² [S1] [W1] *prep informal especially AmE* from the inside to the outside of something – many teachers of British English consider it incorrect to use 'out' as a PREPOSITION: *Karen looked out the window at the back yard.* | *Get out the car and push with the rest of us!*

out³ *v* **1** [T usually passive] to publicly say that someone is HOMOSEXUAL when that person would prefer to keep it secret: *Several gay politicians have been outed in recent months.* **2 murder/the truth etc will out!** used to say that it is difficult to hide a murder, the truth etc

out⁴ *n* **1** [singular] an excuse to avoid doing an activity or to avoid being blamed for something: *I'm busy on Sunday, so that gives me an out.* **2** [C] an act of making a player in baseball lose the chance to score a point **3 on the outs (with sb)** *AmE informal* arguing or not agreeing with someone: *Wilson is on the outs with his family because of his relationship with that woman.*
→ INS AND OUTS

out- /aʊt/ *prefix* **1** used to form nouns and adjectives from verbs that are followed by 'out': *an outbreak of flu* (=from 'break out') | *outspoken comments* (=from 'speak out') **2** [in nouns and adjectives] outside or beyond something: *an outbuilding* (=small building away from the main building) | *outlying areas* (=far from the centre) **3** [in verbs] being or becoming bigger, further, greater etc than someone or something else: *He's outgrown his clothes* (=become too big for them). | *She outlived her brother* (=he died before her). **4** [in verbs] doing better than someone, so that you defeat them: *I can out-argue you any day.* | *She outran him.*

out·age /ˈaʊtɪdʒ/ *n* [C] *AmE* a period of time during which a service such as the electricity supply cannot be provided; ⊞ **power cut** *BrE*: *a power outage*

out-and-'out *adj* [only before noun] used to emphasize that someone is definitely a particular kind of person or thing; ⊞ **complete**: *He's an out-and-out liar.*

out·back /ˈaʊtbæk/ *n* **the outback** the Australian countryside far away from cities, where few people live

out·bid /aʊtˈbɪd/ *v* **outbid, outbidding** [T] to offer a higher price than someone else, especially at an AUCTION

out·board mo·tor /ˌaʊtbɔːd ˈməʊtə $ -bɔːrd ˈmoʊtər/ *n* [C] a motor attached to the back end of a small boat

out·bound /ˈaʊtbaʊnd/ *adj* moving away from you or away from a town, country etc; ⊞ **inbound**: *outbound traffic* | *the outbound flight*

out·box , **out box** /ˈaʊtbɒks $ -bɑːks/ *n* [C] **1** the place in a computer email program where messages that you have not sent yet are stored → INBOX **2** *AmE* a container on an office desk that is used to hold letters, documents etc that have been dealt with and are ready to be taken away by someone such as a secretary; ⊞ **out tray** *BrE*

out·break /ˈaʊtbreɪk/ *n* [C] if there is an outbreak of fighting or disease in an area, it suddenly starts to happen: *a cholera outbreak* | [+of] *outbreaks of fighting* | *the outbreak of World War II* → **break out** at BREAK

out·build·ing /ˈaʊtˌbɪldɪŋ/ *n* [C] a building near a main building, for example a BARN or SHED: *a farmhouse with a few outbuildings*

out·burst /ˈaʊtbɜːst $ -bɜːrst/ *n* [C] **1** something you say suddenly that expresses a strong emotion, especially anger: *He later apologized for his outburst.* | **emotional/violent/angry outburst** *his father's violent outbursts of temper* | [+of] *an outburst of anger* **2** a sudden short increase in an activity: [+of] *an outburst of creative energy* | *outbursts of violence*

out·cast /ˈaʊtkɑːst $ -kæst/ *n* [C] someone who is not accepted by the people they live among, or who has been forced out of their home: *Smokers often feel as though they are being treated as social outcasts.* —**outcast** *adj*

out·class /aʊtˈklɑːs $ -ˈklæs/ *v* [T] to be or do something much better than someone or something else: *He won his next race, completely outclassing his rivals.*

out·come [W3] /ˈaʊtkʌm/ *n* [C] the final result of a meeting, discussion, war etc – used especially when no one knows what it will be until it actually happens; ⊟ **result**: [+of] *It was impossible to predict the outcome of the election.* | *People who had heard the evidence at the trial were surprised at the outcome.*

out·crop /ˈaʊtkrɒp $ -krɑːp/ also **out·crop·ping** /-krɒpɪŋ $ -krɑː-/ *AmE n* [C] a rock or group of rocks above the surface of the ground: *Below us was a pool surrounded by rocky outcrops.*

out·cry /ˈaʊtkraɪ/ *n* [C usually singular,U] an angry protest by a lot of ordinary people: *The closure of the local hospital has caused a huge **public outcry**.* | [+against/about/over] *a national outcry about the lack of gun control laws* | [+from] *The proposed changes caused an **angry outcry** from residents.*

out·dat·ed /ˌaʊtˈdeɪtɪd◂/ *adj* **1** if something is outdated, it is no longer considered useful or effective, because something more modern exists; → **old-fashioned**: *outdated teaching methods* | *a factory with outdated equipment* | *His writing style is now boring and outdated.* **2** outdated information is not recent and may no longer be correct: *This estimate was made on the basis of outdated figures.*

out·did /aʊtˈdɪd/ *v* the past tense of OUTDO

out·dis·tance /aʊtˈdɪstəns/ *v* [T] to run, ride etc faster than other people, especially in a race, so that you are far ahead: *Lewis quickly outdistanced the other runners.*

out·do /aʊtˈduː/ *v past tense* **outdid** /-ˈdɪd/ *past participle* **outdone** /-ˈdʌn/, *third person singular* **outdoes** /-ˈdʌz/ [T] **1** to be better or more successful than someone else at doing something: *When it comes to speed of response, a small firm can outdo a big company.* | **outdo sb in sth** *skaters trying to outdo each other in grace and speed* **2 not to be outdone** in order not to let someone else do better or seem better than you: *Not to be outdone, other computer manufacturers are also donating machines to schools.*

out·door /ˌaʊtˈdɔː◂ $ -ˈdɔːr◂/ *adj* **1** [only before noun] existing, happening, or used outside, not inside a building; ⊟ **indoor**: *a huge outdoor market* | *outdoor recreational activities* | *outdoor clothing* | *a healthy outdoor life* **2 outdoor type** someone who enjoys camping, walking in the countryside etc

out·doors¹ /ˌaʊtˈdɔːz $ -ˈdɔːrz/ *adv* outside, not in a building; ⊟ **out of doors**; ⊟ **indoors**: *It's warm enough to eat outdoors tonight.* | *He wants a job that will let him work outdoors.*; → see box at OUT¹

outdoors² *n* → see picture on next page **the (great) outdoors** the countryside far away from buildings and cities: *a woman with a taste for adventure in the great outdoors*

out·door·sy /aʊtˈdɔːzi $ -ˈdɔːr-/ *adj informal* an outdoorsy person enjoys outdoor activities

out·er /ˈaʊtə $ -ər/ *adj* [only before noun] **1** on the outside of something; ⊟ **inner**: *Remove the tough outer leaves before cooking.* **2** further from the centre of something; ⊟ **inner**: *the outer suburbs* **3** relating to objects, activities etc that are part of the world, as opposed to your own thoughts and feelings; ⊟ **inner**: *His inner conflict is related to struggles in the outer world.*

out·er·most /ˈaʊtəməʊst $ -tərmoʊst/ *adj* [only before noun] furthest from the middle; ⊟ **innermost**: *the outermost stars*

O

snowboarding

caving *BrE*/
spelunking *AmE*

skydiving

whitewater rafting

archery

rock climbing

canoeing

hillwalking *BrE*

mountain biking

abseiling *BrE*/
rappelling *AmE*

cross-country skiing

orienteering

,outer 'space n [U] the space outside the Earth's air, where the PLANETS and stars are: *creatures from outer space* (=from another planet)

out·er·wear /'aʊtəweə $ -tərwer/ n [U] clothes such as coats that are worn over other clothes

out·face /aʊt'feɪs/ v [T] *formal* to deal bravely with a difficult situation or opponent

out·fall /'aʊtfɔːl/ n [C] a place where water flows out, especially from a DRAIN or river: *a sewage outfall*

out·field /'aʊtfiːld/ n **the outfield a)** the part of a CRICKET or baseball field furthest from the player who is BATTING; → **infield b)** the players in this part of the field; → **infield** —**outfielder** n [C]

out·fit[1] [S3] /'aʊtfɪt/ n [C]
1 a set of clothes worn together, especially for a special occasion: *She bought a new outfit for the party.* | *a cowboy outfit*
2 *informal* a group of people who work together as a team or organization: *My outfit was sent to Italy during the war.* | *a small advertising outfit in San Diego*
3 BrE a set of equipment that you need for a particular purpose or job; ☐ **kit**: *a tyre repair outfit*

outfit[2] v **outfitted, outfitting** [T] to provide someone or something with a set of clothes or equipment, especially ones that are needed for a particular purpose: **outfit sb/sth with sth** *a car outfitted with dual controls for driver training* | **outfit sb in sth** *Members outfit themselves in Civil War clothing.*

out·fit·ter /'aʊtfɪtə $ -ər/ n [C] **1** BrE old-fashioned a shop that sells men's clothes **2** AmE a shop that sells equipment for outdoor activities such as camping

out·flank /aʊt'flæŋk/ v [T] **1** to gain an advantage over an opponent, especially in politics: *The Tories found themselves outflanked by Labour on the issue of law and order.* **2** to go around the side of a group of enemies during a battle and attack them from behind

out·flow /'aʊtfləʊ $ -floʊ/ n [C] **1** when money, goods etc leave a bank, country etc: [+of] *the outflow of capital from the developed countries* **2** the flow of water or air from something: [+of] *an outflow of gas escaping from the main duct* | *the outflow valve*

out·fox /aʊt'fɒks $ -'fɑːks/ v [T] to gain an advantage over someone by using your intelligence; ☐ **outsmart**

out·go·ing /,aʊt'gəʊɪŋ◂ $ -'goʊ-/ adj **1** someone who is outgoing likes to meet and talk to new people: *We're looking for someone with an outgoing personality.* **2** outgoing president/chancellor etc someone who will soon finish their time as president etc **3** [only before noun] going out or leaving a place; ☐ **incoming**: *the tray for outgoing mail* | *outgoing phone calls*

out·go·ings /'aʊt,gəʊɪŋz $ -,goʊ-/ n [plural] BrE the money that you have to spend regularly, for example on rent or food: *List all your outgoings for a month.*

out·grow /aʊt'grəʊ $ -'groʊ/ v past tense **outgrew** /-'gruː/ past participle **outgrown** /-'grəʊn $ -'groʊn/ [T] **1** to grow too big for something; ☐ **grow out of**: *They outgrew their clothes so quickly.* | *Harry outgrew his cot when he was about two.* **2** to no longer do or enjoy something that you used to do, because you have grown older and changed: *Most children eventually outgrow a tendency toward travel sickness.* **3** if a business outgrows a building, it begins to have too many people or too much work to fit into the building: *His furniture-making business soon outgrew his garage.* **4** to grow or increase faster than someone or something else: *a population outgrowing its resources*

out·growth /'aʊtgrəʊθ $ -groʊθ/ n [C] **1** something that develops from something else, as a natural result of it: [+of] *Crime is often an outgrowth of poverty.* **2** technical something that grows out of something else

out·house /'aʊthaʊs/ n [C] **1** BrE a small building which is near to and belongs to a larger main building; ☐ **outbuilding 2** AmE a small building over a hole in the ground that is used as a toilet, in a camping area or, in the past, behind a house; ☐ **privy** BrE

out·ing /'aʊtɪŋ/ n **1** [C] a short trip that a group of people take for pleasure: **a family/school etc outing** *a class outing to the ballet* | [+to] *an outing to the beach* | **on an outing** *They had gone on an outing to the pool for Robert's birthday.* **2** [C,U] when someone publicly says that someone else is HOMOSEXUAL, when that person does not want anyone to know

out·land·ish /aʊt'lændɪʃ/ adj strange and unusual: *outlandish clothes* | *Her story seemed so outlandish.*

out·last /aʊt'lɑːst $ -'læst/ v [T] to continue to exist or be effective for a longer time than something else: *Smith outlasted his rivals in the council to become leader in 1996.* | *A leather sofa will usually outlast a cloth one.* → **OUTLIVE**

out·law[1] /'aʊtlɔː $ -lɒː/ v [T] to completely stop something by making it illegal: *The bill would have outlawed several types of guns.*

outlaw[2] n [C] someone who has done something illegal, and who is hiding in order to avoid punishment – used especially about criminals in the past

out·lay /'aʊtleɪ/ n [C,U] the amount of money that you have to spend in order to start a new business, activity etc; → **expense, cost: small/modest/considerable/large etc outlay** *For a relatively small outlay, you can start a home hairdressing business.* | [+on] *House buyers usually have a large initial outlay on carpets and furniture.*

out·let /'aʊtlet, -lɪt/ n [C] **1** a way of expressing or getting rid of strong feelings: [+for] *Is football a good outlet for men's aggression?* | *an outlet for creativity* **2 a)** formal a shop, company, or organization through which products are sold: *Benetton has* **retail outlets** *in every major European city.* | *a fast-food outlet* **b)** a shop that sells things for less than the usual price, especially things from a particular company or things of a particular type **3** AmE a place on a wall where you can connect electrical equipment to the supply of electricity; ☐ **power point** BrE **4** a pipe or hole through which something such as a liquid or gas can flow out: *a waste water outlet*

'outlet ,mall n [C] AmE a SHOPPING MALL where clothes are sold for less than the usual price, often because they are no longer fashionable or are slightly damaged

out·line[1] /'aʊtlaɪn/ n **1** [C,U] the main ideas or facts about something, without the details: *a research proposal outline* | [+of] *an outline of world history* | **broad/rough/general outline** *a broad outline of the committee's plans* | **in outline** *A debt reduction scheme was agreed in outline* (=people agreed on its main points). **2** [C,U] a line around the edge of something which shows its shape: [+of] *The outlines of animals were cut into the rock.* | *an* **outline map** *of Europe* | **in outline** *figures drawn in outline* **3** [C] a plan for a piece of writing in which each new idea or fact is separately written down: *Always write an outline for your essays.*

outline[2] v [T] **1** to describe something in a general way, giving the main points but not the details: *The new president outlined plans to deal with crime, drugs, and education.* **2** [usually passive] to show the edge of something, or draw around its edge, so that its shape is clear: *a map with our property outlined in red* | *trees outlined against the sky*

out·live /aʊt'lɪv/ v [T] **1** to remain alive after someone else has died: *She outlived her husband by twenty years.* **2** to continue to exist after something else has ended or disappeared; → **outlast**: *Good books have a way of outliving those who want to ban them.* **3 outlive its/your usefulness** to become no longer useful: *The docks have outlived their usefulness.*

out·look /'aʊtlʊk/ n [C] **1** your general attitude to life and the world: [+on] *He's got a good* **outlook on** *life.* | *Exercise will improve your looks and your outlook.* | **positive/optimistic outlook** *She still has an*

2 not yet done, solved, or paid: *We've got quite a few debts still outstanding.* | *an outstanding issue*
3 very great or clear: *The question of who is in charge is of outstanding importance.*

out·stand·ing·ly /aʊt'stændɪŋli/ *adv* extremely well: *He played outstandingly.* | *She performed outstandingly well in her examinations.* | *an outstandingly talented musician*

out·stay /aʊt'steɪ/ *v* [T] to stay somewhere longer than someone else → **outstay your welcome** at WELCOME³ (3)

out·stretched /ˌaʊt'stretʃt◂/ *adj* stretched out to full length: **outstretched arms/hands/fingers** *She ran to meet them with outstretched arms.*

out·strip /aʊt'strɪp/ *v* **outstripped**, **outstripping** [T] **1** to do something better than someone else or be more successful: *We outstripped all our competitors in sales last year.* **2** to be greater in quantity than something else: *Demand for new aircraft production is outstripping supply.* **3** to run or move faster than someone or something else: *Speeding at 90 mph, Denny outstripped police cars for an hour.*

out·ta /'aʊtə/ *prep AmE informal* used in writing to represent the spoken form 'out of': *I've got to get outta here.*

out-take also **out·take** *AmE* /'aʊt-teɪk/ *n* [C] a piece of a film or television show that is removed before it is broadcast, especially because it contains a mistake

out tray *n* [C] a box on an office desk where you put work and letters which are ready to be posted or taken away; → **in tray**

out·vote /aʊt'vəʊt $ -'voʊt/ *v* [T usually passive] to defeat a person by winning more votes than them: *France was outvoted on that issue.*

out·ward /'aʊtwəd $ -wərd/ *adj* **1** [only before noun] relating to how a person or situation seems to be, rather than how it really is; **f** **inward**: *The economy and outward appearance of the area have changed considerably.* | *His clenched fist was the only outward sign of his anger.* **2** **outward journey/voyage etc** a journey in which you are travelling away from home **3** [only before noun] directed towards the outside or away from a place: *the outward flow of oil*

out·ward·ly /'aʊtwədli $ -wərd-/ *adv* according to the way people or things seem; **f** **inwardly**: *Calvin remained outwardly calm, but inside he was very angry.* | *Outwardly, at least, he was an optimist.*

out·wards /'aʊtwədz $ -wərdz/ also **outward** *AmE adv* towards the outside or away from the centre of something; **f** **inwards**: *The door opens outwards.* | **facing/looking/spreading etc outwards** *Stand with your elbows pointing outwards.*

out·weigh /aʊt'weɪ/ *v* [T] to be more important or valuable than something else: *The benefits of the scheme outweigh the disadvantages.*

out·wit /aʊt'wɪt/ *v* **outwitted**, **outwitting** [T] to gain an advantage over someone using tricks or clever plans: *a wolf that had outwitted hunters for years*

out·work /'aʊtwɜːk $ -wɜːrk/ *n* [U] work for a business that is done by people at home —**outworker** *n* [C]

out·worn /ˌaʊt'wɔːn◂ $ -'wɔːrn◂/ *adj* [only before noun] old-fashioned, and no longer useful or important; → **worn out**: *outworn traditions*

ou·zo /'uːzəʊ $ -zoʊ/ *n* [U] a Greek alcoholic drink that is drunk with water

o·va /'əʊvə $ 'oʊ-/ *n* the plural form of OVUM

o·val /'əʊvəl $ 'oʊ-/ *n* [C] a shape like a circle, but wider in one direction than the other —**oval** *adj*: *an oval mirror*

Oval 'Office *n* **the Oval Office** the office of the US president, in the White House in Washington DC

o·var·i·an /əʊ'veəriən $ oʊ'ver-/ *adj* relating to the ovary: *ovarian cancer*

o·va·ry /'əʊvəri $ 'oʊ-/ *n plural* **ovaries** [C] **1** the part of a female that produces eggs **2** the part of a female plant that produces seeds

o·va·tion /əʊ'veɪʃən $ oʊ-/ *n* [C] *formal* if a group of people give someone an ovation, they CLAP to show approval: *The Chancellor's entrance was greeted with a* **standing ovation** (=everyone stood up). | *Fans gave the rock group a thunderous ovation.*

ov·en S3 /'ʌvən/ *n* [C]
1 a piece of equipment that food is cooked inside, shaped like a metal box with a door on the front; → **cooker, stove**: *Preheat the oven to 200 degrees C.* | *Press the mixture onto the bread and bake in a hot oven for 10 minutes.*
2 **like an oven** *informal* uncomfortably hot → **have a bun in the oven** at BUN (5)

ov·en·proof /'ʌvənpruːf/ *adj* ovenproof dishes, plates etc will not be harmed by the high temperatures in an oven

oven-'ready *adj BrE* oven-ready food is already prepared when you buy it, so you only have to cook it: *a five-pound oven-ready turkey*

ov·en·ware /'ʌvənweə $ -wer/ *n* [U] cooking pots that can be put in a hot oven without cracking

o·ver¹ S1 W1 /'əʊvə $ 'oʊvər/ *prep*
1 ABOVE above or higher than something, without touching it; **f** **under**: *A lamp hung over the table.* | *She leaned over the desk to answer the phone.* | *The sign over the door said 'Mind your head'.* | *We watched a helicopter flying low over the harbour.*
2 COVERING on something or covering it; **f** **under**: *Over the body lay a thin white sheet.* | *She wore a large jacket over her sweater.* | *Mind you don't spill coffee over my best tablecloth.*
3 ACROSS from one side of something to the other side of it: *Somehow the sheep had jumped over the fence.* | *The road over the mountains is steep and dangerous.* | *a bridge over the River Thames* | *Their house has a magnificent view over the bay.*
4 ON THE OTHER SIDE on the opposite side of something from where you already are: *There's a bus stop just over the road.* | *They live over the river in Richmond.*
5 DOWN FROM STH down from the edge of something: *The car plunged over a cliff.*
6 IN MANY PARTS OF STH in or to many parts of a particular place, organization, or thing: *He used to wander over the moors, losing all track of time.* | **all over (sth)** (=in every part) *They said they had cleaned up but there were bottles all over the place.* | *Scientists from all over the world gather here.*
7 NO LONGER AFFECTED if you are over an illness or a bad experience or situation, you are no longer affected by it; → **recover**: *I think we're over the worst of the crisis now.* | *He had a fever last night, but he seems to be over it now.* | *Sybil has never got over the shock of her mother's death.* | *I'm over him now* (=I am no longer in love with him).
8 MORE THAN more than a particular number, amount, or level; **f** **under**: *The Japanese were producing over 100 million tons of steel.* | *toys suitable for children over the age of three* | *drivers who go over the speed limit* | **the over-30s/50s etc** (=people who are more than a particular age) *a social club for the over-60s*
9 DURING during: *Will you be home over the summer vacation?* | *Over a period of ten years he stole a million pounds from the company.* | *Can we talk about this over dinner?* → see box at SINCE
10 CONCERNING about a particular subject, person or thing: *He's having problems over his income tax.* | *a row over public expenditure* | *There is concern over the bad image of the legal profession.*
11 CONTROLLING in control of or influencing someone or something: *Genghiz ruled over an empire that stretched from Persia across to China.* | *She had great personal influence and power over her followers.*
12 BETTER used to say that someone or something is more successful or better than someone or something

else: *Ipswich's 3–1 win over Manchester City* | *Can Labour maintain its lead over the Conservatives?* | *It has one great advantage over its rivals.*

13 **BY TELEPHONE/RADIO** using something such as a telephone or radio: *I don't want to talk about this over the telephone.* | *I heard the news over the radio.*

14 **over and above** in addition to something: *He gets a travel allowance over and above his existing salary.*

15 **LOUDER THAN STH** making a sound louder than another sound: *'What?' he yelled over the noise of the engine and the wind.*

16 **PREFERRING** if you choose one thing over another, you choose that thing rather than the other: *What is your main reason for choosing one restaurant over another?*

over² S1 W1 *adv, adj*

1 **FALLING DOWN** from an upright position into a position of lying on a surface: *He was so drunk he fell over in the road.* | *Mind you don't knock the candle over.* | *Engineers are working to prevent the tower from toppling over.*

2 **BENDING/FOLDING** so that someone or something is no longer straight or flat, but is bent or folded in the middle: *As Sheila bent over, a sudden pain shot up her back.* | *He folded the paper over and put it in his pocket.*

3 **ACROSS a)** from one side of an object, space, or area to the other side: *There are only three canoes so some people will have to swim over.* | *The wall was crumbling where children had climbed over.* | *I went over (=crossed the room, street etc) to say hello, but Vincent didn't recognize me.* | *[+to] We flew over to the US to visit my Aunt Polly.* | *[+from] One of my cousins is coming over from France with his wife and daughter.* | *Come over here and see what I've found.* **b)** in a place that is on the other side of a space or area: *Bill lives over on the other side of town.* | *She was standing over by the window.* | *Do you see that building over there?*

4 **IN OR TO A PLACE** in or to a particular house, city etc: *You really should come over and see our new house.* | *I spent the whole day over at Gabby's place.* | *We could drive over to Oxford this afternoon.*

5 **FINISHED** if an event or period of time is over, it has finished: *Is the meeting over yet?* | **over (and done) with** (=used about something unpleasant) *I'm so glad the mid-term exams are over and done with.* | *You'd better give them the bad news. Do it now – get it over with.*

6 **TO THE SIDE** towards one side: *The bus pulled over to the side of the road.* | *Would you move over, so I can sit next to you.*

7 **GIVING** from one person or group to another: *The attacker was ordered to hand over his weapon.* | *Most of the money has been signed over to his children.*

8 **CHANGING** from one position or system to another: *The guards change over at midnight.* | *We switched over from electricity to gas because it was cheaper.*

9 **TURNING** so that the bottom or the other side of something can now be seen: *Turn the box over and open it at that end.* | *Josh rolled over and went back to sleep.*

10 **MORE THAN** more than or higher than a particular number, amount, or level; E **under**: *Almost 40% of women are size 14 or over.* | *People earning £33,000 and over will pay the higher rate of tax.*

11 **VERY/TOO** used before an adjective or adverb to mean 'very' or 'too': *She didn't seem over pleased when I asked her to wait.* | *Perhaps we were all over enthusiastic about the project.*

12 **REMAINING** an amount of something that is over is what remains after some of it has been used: *There should be some money over when I've paid all the bills.* | *There was a little food left over from the party.*

13 **COVERED** used to show that something is completely covered with a substance or material: *Most of the windows have been boarded over.* | *Parts of the river were iced over.* | *[+with] The door had been painted over with a bright red varnish.*

14 **ABOVE** above someone or something: *We stood on the roof watching the planes fly over.*

15 **TALKING/THINKING/READING** in a detailed and careful way: *After talking it over with my wife, I've decided to retire.* | *I'll need time to read the contract over before I sign.* | *Think it over carefully before you make a decision.*

16 **AGAIN** *AmE* if you start or do something over, you do it again: *I got mixed up and had to start over.*

17 **over and over (again)** many times: *The way to learn the script is to say it to yourself over and over again.*

18 **twice over/three times over etc a)** used to say how many times the same thing happens: *He sings each song twice over.* | *The pattern is repeated many times over.* **b)** used to say by how much an amount is multiplied: *Trade between the two countries has increased five times over.*

19 **all over again** used to emphasize that you do the whole of something again from the beginning, or that the same thing happens again: *Their first plan had gone wrong, so they had to start all over again.* | *We had quarrelled about the money before, and now it was happening all over again.*

20 **over to sb** used to say that it is now someone else's turn to do something, to speak etc: *I've done my best. Now it's over to the professionals.*

21 **RADIO MESSAGE** *spoken* used when communicating by radio to show that you have finished speaking: *Are you hearing me loud and clear? Over.*

22 **over against sth** *formal* used to say what something is compared to or preferred to: *The Celtic Church maintained the Greek calendar over against that of Rome.*

over³ *n* [C] the period of time in the game of CRICKET during which six or eight balls are thrown by the same BOWLER in one direction

over- /ˈəʊvə $ ˈoʊvər/ *prefix* **1** too much: *overpopulation* | *overcooked vegetables* | *overweight* **2** above; beyond; across: *overhanging branches* | *overhead telephone wires* | *the overland route* (=not by sea or air) **3** outer: *an overcoat* **4** additional: *We were working overtime.* (=working beyond the usual time)

over-a'chiever *n* [C] someone who works very hard to be successful, and is very unhappy if they do not achieve everything they want to; E **underachiever**

o·ver·act /ˌəʊvərˈækt $ ˌoʊ-/ *v* [I] to act in a play with too much emotion or movement – used to show disapproval —**overacting** *n* [U]

o·ver·ac·tive /ˌəʊvərˈæktɪv $ ˌoʊ-/ *adj* too active, in a way that produces a bad result; E **underactive**: *an overactive thyroid gland* | *Such fears are nothing more than the product of an overactive imagination.*

over-'age *adj* too old for a particular purpose or activity; E **under-age**: *Leyton was over-age for recruitment into the army.*

o·ver·all¹ S3 W2 /ˌəʊvərˈɔːl $ ˌoʊvərˈɒːl/ *adj* [only before noun] considering or including everything: *The overall cost of the exhibition was £400,000.* | *The overall result is an increase in population.* | *An overall winner and a runner-up were chosen.* | *We don't want all the details now, just the overall picture.* ⚠ Do not say 'in the overall' or 'on the overall'. Say **on the whole**: *In spite of the film's many faults, on the whole it's worth seeing.*

overall² *adv* **1** considering or including everything: *Williams came fifth overall.* | *What will it cost, overall?* **2** [sentence adverb] generally: *Overall, prices are still rising.*

o·ver·all³ /ˈəʊvərɔːl $ ˈoʊvərɒːl/ *n* **1** [C] *BrE* a loose-fitting piece of clothing like a coat, that is worn over clothes to protect them **2** **overalls** [plural] *AmE* heavy cotton trousers with a piece covering your chest, held up by pieces of cloth that go over your shoulders; E **dungarees** *BrE* **3** **overalls** [plural] *BrE* a piece of clothing like a shirt and trousers in one piece that is worn over other clothes to protect them; ⊟ **coveralls** *AmE*

ˌoverall maˈjority *n* [C] *BrE* **1** more votes than all the other political parties together: *The Conservatives had a huge overall majority in the House of Commons.* **2** the difference between the number of votes gained by the winning party and the total votes gained by all the other parties: *an overall majority of 28*

o·ver·arch·ing /ˌəʊvərˈɑːtʃɪŋ◂ $ ˌoʊvərˈɑːr-/ *adj* [only before noun] including or influencing every part of something: *The crisis gave an overarching justification to the government's policy.*

o·ver·arm /ˈəʊvərɑːm $ ˈoʊvərɑːrm/ *adj, adv* especially *BrE* an overarm throw in a sport is when you throw the ball with your arm high above your shoulder; → **underarm**

o·ver·awe /ˌəʊvərˈɔː $ ˌoʊvərˈɒː/ *v* [T usually passive] to make someone feel respect or fear, so that they are nervous or unable to say or do anything: *He was totally overawed by his father.* —**overawed** *adj*

o·ver·bal·ance /ˌəʊvəˈbæləns $ ˌoʊvər-/ *v* [I,T] **1** *BrE* to fall over or nearly fall over because you lose balance **2** *AmE* **OUTWEIGH**

o·ver·bear /ˌəʊvəˈbeə $ ˌoʊvərˈber/ *v past tense* **overbore** /-ˈbɔː $ -ˈbɔːr/ *past participle* **overborne** /-ˈbɔːn $ -ˈbɔːrn/ [T usually passive] to defeat someone or something: *She is independent-minded enough not to be easily overborne by her husband.*

o·ver·bear·ing /ˌəʊvəˈbeərɪŋ $ ˌoʊvərˈber-/ *adj* always trying to control other people without considering their wishes or feelings; ⊟ **domineering**: *a bossy, overbearing wife*

o·ver·bid /ˌəʊvəˈbɪd $ ˌoʊvər-/ *v* **overbid, overbidding** **1** [I + for] to offer too high a price for something, especially at an AUCTION **2** [I,T] to offer more than the value of your cards in a card game such as BRIDGE

o·ver·bite /ˈəʊvəbaɪt $ ˌoʊvərˈbaɪt-/ *n* [C] a condition in which someone's upper teeth are too far in front of their lower teeth

o·ver·blown /ˌəʊvəˈbləʊn◂ $ ˌoʊvərˈbloʊn/ *adj* made to seem greater or more impressive than something really is; ⊟ **exaggerated**: *He's not really a scientist; he's just an overblown fraud.*

o·ver·board /ˈəʊvəbɔːd $ ˈoʊvərbɔːrd/ *adv* **1** over the side of a ship or boat into the water: *One of the crew fell overboard and drowned.* | *Man overboard!* (=said when someone falls off a boat) **2** **go overboard** to do or say something that is too extreme for a particular situation: *I hope politicians will not go overboard in trying to control the press.* **3** **throw sth overboard** to get rid of an idea, system etc that is considered to be useless or unnecessary

o·ver·book /ˌəʊvəˈbʊk $ ˌoʊvər-/ *v* [I,T] to sell more tickets for a theatre, plane etc than there are seats available: *overbooked hotels*

o·ver·bur·den /ˌəʊvəˈbɜːdn $ ˌoʊvərˈbɜːrdn/ *v* [T usually passive] to give an organization, person, or system more work or problems than they can deal with: *Health services have been overburdened and are unable to care for many older people.* | *a manager overburdened with work*

o·ver·came /ˌəʊvəˈkeɪm $ ˌoʊvər-/ *v* the past tense of OVERCOME

o·ver·ca·pa·ci·ty /ˌəʊvəkəˈpæsɪ̧ti $ ˌoʊvər-/ *n* [singular,U] the situation in which an industry or factory cannot sell as much as it produces

o·ver·cast /ˌəʊvəˈkɑːst◂ $ ˌoʊvərˈkæst◂/ *adj* dark with clouds: *a chilly overcast day* | *The sky was overcast and a light rain began to fall.*

o·ver·charge /ˌəʊvəˈtʃɑːdʒ $ ˌoʊvərˈtʃɑːrdʒ/ *v* **1** [I,T] to charge someone too much money for something; ⊟ **undercharge**: *They were being over-*

charged for cheap beer. **2** [T] to put too much power into a BATTERY or electrical system

o·ver·charged /ˌəʊvəˈtʃɑːdʒd $ ˌoʊvərˈtʃɑːrdʒd/ *adj* [I] full of emotion or excitement: *the stadium's overcharged atmosphere*

o·ver·coat /ˈəʊvəkəʊt $ ˈoʊvərkoʊt/ *n* [C] a long thick warm coat

o·ver·come [S3] [W3] /ˌəʊvəˈkʌm $ ˌoʊvər-/ *v past tense* **overcame** /-ˈkeɪm/ *past participle* **overcome** [T] **1** to successfully control a feeling or problem that prevents you from achieving something: *He struggled to overcome his shyness.* | *Her financial problems could no longer be overcome.* **2** [usually passive] if smoke or gas overcomes someone, they become extremely sick or unconscious because they breathe it: *The engineer was working on the freezer when he was overcome by gas.* **3** if an emotion overcomes someone, they cannot behave normally because they feel the emotion so strongly: [+with] *Charles was overcome with grief.* **4** to fight and win against someone or something: *Australia overcame the Netherlands 2–1.*

o·ver·com·pen·sate /ˌəʊvəˈkɒmpənseɪt, -pen- $ ˌoʊvərˈkɑːm-/ *v* [I] to try to correct a weakness or mistake by doing too much of the opposite thing: [+for] *Zoe overcompensates for her shyness by talking a lot.* —**overcompensation** /ˌəʊvəkɒmpənˈseɪʃən, -pen- $ ˌoʊvərkɑːm-/ *n* [U]

o·ver·cook /ˌəʊvəˈkʊk $ ˌoʊvər-/ *v* [T] to cook food for too long; ⊟ **undercook**: *overcooked chicken*

o·ver·crowd·ed /ˌəʊvəˈkraʊdɪ̧d◂ $ ˌoʊvər-/ *adj* filled with too many people or things: *Staff had to work in overcrowded conditions.* | *overcrowded housing*

o·ver·crowd·ing /ˌəʊvəˈkraʊdɪŋ $ ˌoʊvər-/ *n* [U] when there are too many people or things in one place: *relieve/ease/reduce overcrowding There are plans to relieve overcrowding in the village.* | *the prison's chronic overcrowding problem*

o·ver·de·vel·oped /ˌəʊvədɪˈveləpt◂ $ ˌoʊvər-/ *adj* **1** if a city or area is overdeveloped, too many houses, buildings, roads etc have been built there: *an overdeveloped country* **2** too great or large: *You have an overdeveloped sense of duty.*

o·ver·do /ˌəʊvəˈduː $ ˌoʊvər-/ *v past tense* **overdid** /-ˈdɪd/, *past participle* **overdone** /-ˈdʌn/, *third person singular* **overdoes** /-ˈdʌz/ [T] **1** to do something more than is suitable or natural: *Analysts believe that worries about the economy are overdone.* | *Use a few drawings and photographs, but don't overdo it.* **2 overdo it** to work too hard or be too active so that you become tired: *You mustn't overdo it – if you're tired, just sit down and start again.* **3** to use too much of something: *I think I overdid the salt.*

o·ver·done /ˌəʊvəˈdʌn◂ $ ˌoʊvər-/ *adj* cooked too much; ⊟ **underdone**: *The beef was overdone.*

o·ver·dose¹ /ˈəʊvədəʊs $ ˈoʊvərdoʊs/ *n* [C] **1** too much of a drug taken at one time: [+of] *a massive overdose of heroin* | *She took an overdose and died two days later.* **2** too much of something, especially something harmful: [+of] *an overdose of sun*

o·ver·dose² /ˌəʊvəˈdəʊs $ ˌoʊvərˈdoʊs/ *v* [I] *OD* to take too much of a drug at one time, so that it harms you or kills you: [+on] *She overdosed on sleeping pills.*

o·ver·draft /ˈəʊvədrɑːft $ ˈoʊvərdræft/ *n* [C] *BrE* the amount of money you owe to a bank when you have spent more money than you had in your account: *a £250 overdraft* | *Many students have a free overdraft facility* (=agreement with their bank to have an overdraft up to a particular limit).

o·ver·drawn /ˌəʊvəˈdrɔːn $ ˌoʊvərˈdrɒːn/ *adj* [not before noun] if you or your bank account is overdrawn, you have spent more than you had in your account and so you owe the bank money: *I try not to go overdrawn if possible.* | [+by] *My account is overdrawn by £300.*

o·ver·dressed /ˌəʊvəˈdrest◂ $ ˌoʊvər-/ *adj* dressed in clothes that are too formal for the occasion; 🔲 **underdressed**: *She felt overdressed in her smart suit.* —**overdress** *v* [I]

o·ver·drive /ˈəʊvədraɪv $ ˈoʊvər-/ *n* [U] **1** an additional GEAR which allows a car to go fast while its engine produces the least power necessary **2 go into overdrive/be in overdrive** to start being very active or working very hard: *Her career has gone into overdrive.*

o·ver·due /ˌəʊvəˈdjuː◂ $ ˌoʊvərˈduː◂/ *adj* **1** not done, paid, returned etc by the time expected: *an overdue gas bill* | *The library books are overdue.* | *The baby was a week overdue* (=it was expected to be born a week ago). **2** something that is overdue should have happened or been done a long time ago: [+for] *He was overdue for a shave.* | *We welcome this announcement and think it's* **long overdue**.

o·ver·eat /ˌəʊvərˈiːt $ ˌoʊ-/ *v past tense* **overate** /-ˈet, -ˈeɪt $ -ˈeɪt/ *past participle* **overeaten** /-ˈiːtn/ [I] to eat too much, or eat more than is healthy

o·ver·egg /ˌəʊvərˈeg $ ˌoʊ-/ *v* **overegg the pudding** *BrE informal* to do more than is necessary, or add something that is not needed

o·ver·em·pha·size also **-ise** *BrE* /ˌəʊvərˈemfəsaɪz $ ˌoʊ-/ *v* [T] to give something more importance than it deserves or than is suitable: *In the past the exam had been overemphasized.* | *The importance of adequate preparation* **cannot be overemphasized** (=used to say that something is very important). —**overemphasis** /-fəsɪs/ *n* [singular]: *There has been an overemphasis on content rather than methodology.*

o·ver·es·ti·mate[1] /ˌəʊvərˈestɪmeɪt $ ˌoʊ-/ *v* [T] **1** to think something is better, more important etc than it really is; 🔲 **underestimate**: *He tends to overestimate his own abilities.* | *The importance of training in health and safety* **cannot be overestimated** (=is extremely important). **2** to guess an amount or value that is too high; 🔲 **underestimate**: *Most patients overestimated how long they had had to wait to see a doctor.*

o·ver·es·ti·mate[2] /ˌəʊvərˈestɪmɪt $ ˌoʊ-/ *n* [C] a calculation, judgement, or guess that is too large: *The figure of 30% is clearly an overestimate.*

o·ver·ex·cit·ed /ˌəʊvərɪkˈsaɪtɪd $ ˌoʊ-/ *adj* someone who is overexcited is very excited and not behaving sensibly: *Some of the boys became overexcited.*

o·ver·ex·pose /ˌəʊvərɪkˈspəʊz $ ˌoʊvərɪkˈspoʊz/ *v* [T] **1** to allow too much light to reach the film when taking or developing a photograph; → **underexpose 2 be overexposed** to appear too many times on television, in the newspapers etc, so that people lose interest in you and you become less popular

over-ex'posure *n* [U] **1** when too much light, RADIATION etc reaches someone's skin, a photographic film etc and is harmful **2** when someone receives too much attention from television, the newspapers etc

o·ver·ex·tend /ˌəʊvərɪkˈstend $ ˌoʊ-/ *v* [T] **1** to try to do or use too much of something, causing problems, illness, or damage: **overextend yourself** *Be careful not to overextend yourself. You've been very ill.* **2** to spend more money than you actually have: *Jackson's company became overextended financially.* —**overextended** *adj*

o·ver·feed /ˌəʊvəˈfiːd $ ˌoʊvər-/ *v past tense and past participle* **overfed** /-ˈfed/ [T] to give someone too much food

o·ver·fill /ˌəʊvəˈfɪl $ ˌoʊvər-/ *v* [T] to put too much of something into a container: *He had overfilled the jug.*

o·ver·fish·ing /ˌəʊvəˈfɪʃɪŋ $ ˌoʊvər-/ *n* [U] the process of taking too many fish from the sea, a river etc, so that the number of fish in it becomes too low

o·ver·flow[1] /ˌəʊvəˈfləʊ $ ˌoʊvərˈfloʊ/ *v* [I,T] **1** if a river, lake, or container overflows, it is so full that the liquid or material inside flows over its edges: *The drains flooded and water overflowed down the main street.* | *The river had overflowed its banks.* | [+with]

wastebins overflowing with plastic cups **2** to have a lot of something: [+with] *The garden overflows with colour.* | *He was overflowing with good ideas.* **3** if a place overflows with people or people overflow into a place, there are too many of them to fit into it: [+with] *Hospitals were reported to be overflowing with dead and wounded.* | [+into] *The house was full and people were overflowing into the street.* **4** to have a very strong feeling: [+with] *My heart was overflowing with gratitude.* **5 be filled to overflowing (with sth)** to be completely full: *One wall was filled to overflowing with books.*

o·ver·flow[2] /ˈəʊvəfləʊ $ ˈoʊvərfloʊ/ *n* **1** [singular] the amount of something or the number of people that cannot be contained in a place because it is already full: *The overflow will be accommodated in another hotel.* | [+of] *the overflow of water from the lake* **2** [C] a pipe through which water flows out of a container when it becomes too full

o·ver·fly /ˌəʊvəˈflaɪ $ ˌoʊvər-/ *v past tense* **overflew** /-ˈfluː/ *past participle* **overflown** /-ˈfləʊn $ -ˈfloʊn/ *present participle* **overflying**, *third person singular* **overflies** [T] to fly over an area or country in an aircraft

o·ver·ground /ˈəʊvəɡraʊnd $ ˈoʊvər-/ *adj* [only before noun] used to describe a train system that runs on the surface of the ground rather than below it; 🔲 **underground**: *an overground railway*

overgrown

an overgrown garden   a well-kept garden

o·ver·grown /ˌəʊvəˈɡrəʊn◂ $ ˌoʊvərˈɡroʊn◂/ *adj* **1** covered with plants that have grown in an uncontrolled way: [+with] *The garden will be overgrown with weeds by the time we get back.* **2** when grass or plants are overgrown, they have grown in an uncontrolled way: *a lawn with overgrown grass* **3 overgrown schoolboy/child** an adult who behaves like a child – used to show disapproval: *Stop acting like an overgrown schoolboy.*

o·ver·growth /ˈəʊvəɡrəʊθ $ ˈoʊvərɡroʊθ/ *n* [U] plants and branches of trees growing above your head, usually in a forest

o·ver·hand /ˈəʊvəhænd $ ˈoʊvər-/ *adj, adv AmE* an overhand throw in a sport is when you throw the ball with your arm above the level of your shoulder; → **underhand**

o·ver·hang[1] /ˌəʊvəˈhæŋ $ ˌoʊvər-/ *v past tense and past participle* **overhung** /-ˈhʌŋ/ [I,T] to hang over something or stick out above it

o·ver·hang[2] /ˈəʊvəhæŋ $ ˈoʊvər-/ *n* [C,usually singular] **1** a rock, roof etc that hangs over something else: *We stood under the overhang while it rained.* **2** the amount by which something hangs over something else: *a five-foot overhang*

o·ver·haul[1] /ˌəʊvəˈhɔːl $ ˌoʊvərˈhɒːl/ *v* [T] **1** to repair or change the necessary parts in a machine, system etc that is not working correctly: *A mechanic is coming to overhaul the engine.* **2** to change a system or method in order to improve it: *All the community's decision-making institutions need to be overhauled.*

o·ver·haul² /ˈəʊvəhɔːl $ ˈoʊvərhɒːl/ n [C] **1** necessary changes or repairs made to a machine or system: *The car needs a complete overhaul.* **2** when a system or method is changed in order to improve it: [+of] *an overhaul of the tax system*

o·ver·head¹ /ˌəʊvəˈhed◂ $ ˌoʊvər-/ adv above your head or in the sky: *Bullets whizzed overhead.* | *A plane flew overhead.* —**overhead** adj: *overhead wires*

o·ver·head² /ˈəʊvəhed $ ˈoʊvər-/ n **1** [U] AmE, **overheads** [plural] BrE money spent regularly on rent, insurance, electricity, and other things that are needed to keep a business operating: *Their offices are in London so the overheads are very high.* **2** [C] a piece of transparent material used with an overhead projector to show words, pictures etc

overhead pro·jec·tor n [C] OHP a piece of electrical equipment used when giving a talk, which shows words or pictures on a wall or large screen so that many people can see them

o·ver·hear /ˌəʊvəˈhɪə $ ˌoʊvərˈhɪr/ v past tense and past participle **overheard** /-ˈhɜːd $ -ˈhɜːrd/ [T] to accidentally hear what other people are saying, when they do not know that you have heard: *I overheard part of their conversation.* | **overhear sb saying sth** *She overheard the management discussing pay rises.* | **overhear sb say (that)** *We overheard the teacher say there would be a pop quiz today.* | *I couldn't help overhearing your argument.* → EAVESDROP

o·ver·heat /ˌəʊvəˈhiːt $ ˌoʊvər-/ v [I,T] **1** to become too hot, or to make something too hot: *I think the engine's overheating again.* | *Try not to overheat the sauce.* **2** if a country's ECONOMY overheats, or if something overheats it, it grows too fast and this leads to increases in prices, salaries, interest rates etc

o·ver·heat·ed /ˌəʊvəˈhiːtɪd◂ $ ˌoʊvər-/ adj **1** too hot: *an overheated waiting room* **2** an overheated ECONOMY grows too fast, leading to increases in prices, salaries, interest rates etc **3** too full of anger or excitement: *her overheated imagination*

o·ver·hung /ˌəʊvəˈhʌŋ $ ˌoʊvər-/ v the past tense and past participle of OVERHANG¹

o·ver·in·dulge /ˌəʊvərɪnˈdʌldʒ $ ˌoʊ-/ v **1** [I] to eat or drink too much: *It's hard not to overindulge at Christmas.* **2** [T] to let someone have everything they want, or always let them do what they want: *Penny was overindulged by her parents.* —**overindulgence** n [U]

o·ver·joyed /ˌəʊvəˈdʒɔɪd $ ˌoʊvər-/ adj [not before noun] extremely pleased or happy: **overjoyed to hear/find/see etc sth** *He was overjoyed to see his mother again.* | [+at] *She wasn't exactly overjoyed at the prospect of looking after two small boys.* | **overjoyed (that)** *Her parents were overjoyed that she'd been found alive.*

o·ver·kill /ˈəʊvəkɪl $ ˈoʊvər-/ n [U] more of something than is necessary or desirable: *More television coverage of the election would be overkill.*

o·ver·la·den /ˌəʊvəˈleɪdn◂ $ ˌoʊvər-/ adj filled with too many people or things: *overladen buses*

o·ver·laid /ˌəʊvəˈleɪd $ ˌoʊvər-/ v the past tense and past participle of OVERLAY

o·ver·land /ˌəʊvəˈlænd◂ $ ˌoʊvər-/ adv across land, not by sea or air: *They plan to travel overland to China.* —**overland** adj: *an overland route*

o·ver·lap¹ /ˌəʊvəˈlæp $ ˌoʊvər-/ v **overlapped, overlapping** [I,T] **1** if two or more things overlap, part of one thing covers part of another thing: *One of Jilly's front teeth overlaps the other.* | *The tiles on the roof overlap.* **2** if two subjects, ideas etc overlap, they include some but not all of the same things: *Maxwell's responsibilities overlap yours, so you will be sharing some of the work.* | [+with] *The study of sociology overlaps with the study of economics.* | *two great men with overlapping interests* **3** if two activities or periods of time overlap, the second one starts before the first one has finished: *The second phase of development overlaps the first.* | [+with] *My vacation overlaps with yours.*

o·ver·lap² /ˈəʊvəlæp $ ˈoʊvər-/ n [C,U] the amount by which two activities, ideas, things etc overlap: [+between] *There is considerable overlap between the girls' and boys' test results.* | [+of] *an overlap of about two centimetres* | *a large degree of overlap*

o·ver·lay¹ /ˌəʊvəˈleɪ $ ˌoʊvər-/ v past tense and past participle **overlaid** [T] **1** to cover or be on top of something: **be overlaid with sth** *The wood is overlaid with silver.* **2** if one quality, sound etc overlays another, it is added to it and is often stronger or more noticeable: *The roar of the engines was overlaid by a loud banging.*

o·ver·lay² /ˈəʊvəleɪ $ ˈoʊvər-/ n [C] **1** something which covers something else: *the brass fire surround with its decorative overlay* **2** a transparent sheet with a picture or drawing on it which is put on top of another picture to change it **3** an additional quality or feeling: *sad stories with an overlay of humour*

o·ver·leaf /ˌəʊvəˈliːf $ ˈoʊvərliːf/ adv on the other side of the page: *See the diagram overleaf.*

o·ver·lie /ˌəʊvəˈlaɪ $ ˌoʊvər-/ v past tense **overlay** /-ˈleɪ/ past participle **overlain** /-ˈleɪn/ present participle **overlying** [T] technical to lie over something: *Clay overlies chalk in the southern mountains.*

o·ver·load /ˌəʊvəˈləʊd $ ˌoʊvərˈloʊd/ v past participle **overloaded** or **overladen** /-ˈleɪdn/ [T] **1** to put too many things or people on or into something: *Be careful not to overload the washing machine.* | **be/become overloaded with sth** *The bus was overloaded with tourists and their luggage.* **2** to put too much electricity through an electrical system or piece of equipment: *Don't overload the lighting circuit.* **3** to give someone too much work or information to deal with: **be/become overloaded with sth** *All the staff are overloaded with work.* —**overload** /ˈəʊvələʊd $ ˈoʊvərloʊd/ n [C,U]: *the modern day information overload* | *an overload of urgent daily business*

o·ver·long /ˌəʊvəˈlɒŋ◂ $ ˌoʊvərˈlɒːŋ◂/ adj continuing for too long: *an overlong performance*

o·ver·look /ˌəʊvəˈlʊk $ ˌoʊvər-/ v [T] **1** to not notice something, or not see how important it is; ▤ **miss**: *It is easy to overlook a small detail like that.* | *Nobody could overlook the fact that box office sales were down.* **2** to forgive someone's mistake, bad behaviour etc and take no action: *She found him entertaining enough to overlook his faults.* **3** if a house, room etc overlooks something, it has a view of it, usually from above: *Our room overlooks the ocean.*

o·ver·lord /ˈəʊvələːd $ ˈoʊvərlɔːrd/ n [C] someone with great power over a large number of people, especially in the past

o·ver·ly /ˈəʊvəli $ ˈoʊvər-/ adv too or very: *Your views on economics are overly simplistic.* | *I'm not overly fond of cats.*

o·ver·man·ning /ˌəʊvəˈmænɪŋ $ ˌoʊvər-/ n [U] a situation in which a company, industry etc has more workers than are needed; ▤ **overstaffing** —**overmanned** adj

o·ver·much /ˌəʊvəˈmʌtʃ $ ˌoʊvər-/ adv literary too much or very much: *At his age, he didn't care overmuch about impressing people.*

o·ver·night¹ /ˌəʊvəˈnaɪt $ ˌoʊvər-/ adv **1** for or during the night: *Pam's staying overnight at my house.* **2** suddenly or surprisingly quickly: *He became a millionaire overnight.* | **happen/appear/change overnight** *Reputations are not changed overnight.* ⚠ Do not talk about 'an overnight' because overnight is never a noun. It is either an adverb or an adjective.

o·ver·night² /ˈəʊvənaɪt $ ˈoʊvər-/ adj **1** happening during the night or for the night: *an overnight flight to Chicago* | *overnight accommodation in London* **2** happening surprisingly quickly: *The show was an overnight success.* | *his overnight decision to become a vegetarian*

'overnight ,bag n [C] a bag containing everything you need for a night away from home: *He packed an overnight bag and left.*

,over-opti'mistic adj expecting that things will be better than is possible or likely: *over-optimistic forecasts of economic growth*

o·ver·paid /,əʊvə'peɪd $,oʊvər-/ adj given more money for a job than you deserve; ☲ **underpaid**: *grossly overpaid football players*

o·ver·pass /'əʊvəpɑːs $ 'oʊvərpæs/ n [C] AmE a structure like a bridge that allows one road to go over another road

o·ver·pay /,əʊvə'peɪ $,oʊvər-/ v past tense and past participle **overpaid** **1** [T] to pay someone more money than they deserve; ☲ **underpay**: *Most big companies continue to overpay their top executives.* **2** [I,T] to pay too much money for something; ☲ **underpay**: *Try to recover any tax you have overpaid.* —**overpayment** n [C,U]

o·ver·play /,əʊvə'pleɪ $,oʊvər-/ v [T] **1** to make something seem more important than it is; ☲ **underplay**: *His role in the group's success has been overplayed.* **2** **overplay your hand** to behave too confidently because you think you are in a stronger position than you actually are: *The unions overplayed their hand in the end and failed to get the pay rise they wanted.*

o·ver·pop·u·la·tion /,əʊvəpɒpjₐ'leɪʃən $,oʊvərpɑːp-/ n [U] when there are too many people living in a particular place: *efforts to reduce overpopulation* —**overpopulated** /,əʊvə'pɒpjₐleɪtₐd $,oʊvər'pɑːp-/ adj: *our overpopulated cities*

o·ver·pow·er /,əʊvə'paʊə $,oʊvər'paʊr/ v [T] **1** to take control of someone physically because you are stronger: *The security guards soon overpowered the man.* **2** if a smell, taste, or emotion overpowers you, it affects you very strongly: *Her scent overpowered his senses.* | *She was overpowered by grief.*

o·ver·pow·er·ing /,əʊvə'paʊərɪŋ $,oʊvər'paʊr-/ adj **1** very strong; → **intense**: *an overpowering smell of rotten flesh* | *He felt an overpowering desire to slap her.* **2** someone who is overpowering has such a strong character that they make other people feel uncomfortable or afraid; ☲ **overbearing** —**overpoweringly** adv

o·ver·priced /,əʊvə'praɪst $,oʊvər-/ adj something that is overpriced is more expensive than it should be

o·ver·print /,əʊvə'prɪnt $,oʊvər-/ v [T] to print additional words over a document, stamp etc that already has printing on it

o·ver·pro·duc·tion /,əʊvəprə'dʌkʃən $,oʊvər-/ n [U] the act of producing more of something than people want or need: *the systematic overproduction of food*

o·ver·pro·tec·tive /,əʊvəprə'tektɪv $,oʊvər-/ adj so anxious to protect someone from harm that they restrict their freedom: *overprotective parents*

o·ver·qual·i·fied /,əʊvə'kwɒlₐfaɪd $,oʊvər'kwɑː-/ adj if you are overqualified for a particular job, you have more experience or training than is needed; ☲ **underqualified**: *I'm having trouble finding another job – everyone says I'm overqualified.*

o·ver·ran /,əʊvə'ræn $,oʊ-/ v the past tense of OVERRUN

o·ver·rated /,əʊvə'reɪtₐd $,oʊ-/ adj not as good or important as some people think or say; ☲ **underrated**: *a vastly overrated film* —**overrate** v [T]

o·ver·reach /,əʊvə'riːtʃ $,oʊ-/ v **overreach yourself** to try to do more than you have the power, ability, or money to do: *The company overreached itself financially.*

o·ver·re·act /,əʊvəri'ækt $,oʊ-/ v [I] to react to something with too much emotion, or by doing something that is unnecessary: [+to] *You always overreact to criticism.* | *Many investors overreacted to the stock market crash.* —**overreaction** /-ri'ækʃən/ n [singular,U]: *Their response was an overreaction.*

o·ver·ride /,əʊvə'raɪd $,oʊ-/ v past tense **overrode** /-'rəʊd $ -'roʊd/ past participle **overridden** /-'rɪdn/ [T] **1** to use your power or authority to change someone else's decision: *The EU commission exercised its power to override British policy.* **2** to be regarded as more important than something else: *The needs of the mother should not override the needs of the child.* **3** to stop a machine doing something that it does by itself: *Can you override the automatic locking system?* —**override** /'əʊvəraɪd $ 'oʊ-/ n [C]: *a manual override*

o·ver·rid·ing /,əʊvə'raɪdɪŋ $,oʊ-/ adj [only before noun] more important than anything else: *a question of overriding importance* | *Their overriding concern is with efficient crime control.*

o·ver·ripe /,əʊvə'raɪp $,oʊ-/ adj overripe fruit and vegetables are past the point of being ready to eat and are too soft: *overripe bananas*

o·ver·rule /,əʊvə'ruːl $,oʊ-/ v [T] to change an order or decision that you think is wrong, using your official power: *The House of Lords overruled the decision of the Court of Appeal.* | *They have the power to overrule the local council.*

o·ver·run¹ /,əʊvə'rʌn $,oʊ-/ v past tense **overran** /-'ræn/, past participle **overrun**, present participle **overrunning** **1** [T usually passive] if unwanted things or people overrun a place, they spread over it in great numbers: **be overrun by/with sth** *a tiny island overrun by tourists* | *The house was overrun with mice.* **2** [I,T] to take more time or money than intended: *The final speaker overran by at least half an hour.* **3** [T usually passive] if soldiers overrun a place, they take control of it: *Poland was overrun by the Russian army.*

o·ver·run² /'əʊvərʌn $ 'oʊ-/ n [C] an amount of time or money that is larger than was planned or intended: *cost overruns of £2 billion*

o·ver·seas¹ W3 /,əʊvə'siːz‹ $,oʊvər-/ adv to or in a foreign country that is across the sea; → **abroad**: *Chris is going to work overseas.* | *Most applications came from overseas.*

o·ver·seas² /'əʊvəsiːz $ 'oʊvər-/ adj [only before noun] coming from, existing in, or happening in a foreign country that is across the sea; → **home**: *overseas students* | *overseas investment*

o·ver·see /,əʊvə'siː $,oʊvər-/ v past tense **oversaw** /-'sɔː $ -'sɒː/ past participle **overseen** /-'siːn/ [T] to be in charge of a group of workers and check that a piece of work is done satisfactorily; ☲ **supervise**: *A team leader was appointed to oversee the project.*

o·ver·seer /'əʊvəsɪə $ 'oʊvərsiːər/ n [C] someone who is in charge of a project, group of workers etc, and who makes sure that the job is done properly; ☲ **supervisor**

o·ver·sell /,əʊvə'sel $,oʊvər-/ v past tense and past participle **oversold** /-'səʊld $ -'soʊld/ [T] **1** to praise someone or something too much: *Tourism on the island is oversold.* **2** to sell more of something than is actually available

o·ver·sen·si·tive /,əʊvə'sensₐtɪv‹ $,oʊvər-/ adj easily upset or offended: *Don't you think you're being a bit oversensitive?*

o·ver·sexed /,əʊvə'sekst‹ $,oʊvər-/ adj having more interest in or desire for sex than is usual

o·ver·shad·ow /,əʊvə'ʃædəʊ $,oʊvər'ʃædoʊ/ v [T] **1** to make someone or something else seem less important: *Her interest in politics began to overshadow her desire to be a poet.* | *The achievement of the men's team was overshadowed by the continuing success of the women's team.* **2** to make an occasion or period of time less enjoyable by making people feel sad or worried: *The threat of war overshadowed the summer of 1939.* **3** if a tall building, mountain etc overshadows a place, it is very close to it and much taller than it: *a dark valley overshadowed by towering peaks*

⬚1 000, ⬚2 000, ⬚3 000, most frequent words in ⬚S poken and ⬚W ritten English

o·ver·shoe /'əʊvəʃuː $ 'oʊvər-/ n [C] a rubber shoe that you wear over an ordinary shoe to keep your feet dry

o·ver·shoot /,əʊvə'ʃuːt $,oʊvər-/ v past tense and past participle **overshot** /-'ʃɒt $ -'ʃɑːt/ [I,T] **1** to accidentally go a little further than you intended: *The plane overshot the runway and plunged into a ditch.* **2** to spend more money than you had intended: *The school has overshot its cash limit.* —**overshoot** /'əʊvəʃuːt $ 'oʊvər-/ n [C]

o·ver·sight /'əʊvəsaɪt $ 'oʊvər-/ n [C,U] **1** a mistake in which you forget something or do not notice something: *I assure you that this was purely an oversight on my part.* **2** have oversight of sth to be in charge of something: *He has general oversight of all training courses.*

o·ver·sim·pli·fy /,əʊvə'sɪmplɪfaɪ $,oʊvər-/ v **oversimplified, oversimplifying, oversimplifies** [I,T] to describe something in a way that is too simple and ignores many facts: *To describe all these people as refugees is to oversimplify the situation.* —**oversimplification** /,əʊvəsɪmplɪfɪ'keɪʃən $,oʊvər-/ n [C,U]

o·ver·sized /,əʊvə'saɪzd◂ $,oʊvər-/ also **o·ver·size** /-'saɪz◂/ adj bigger than usual or too big: *an oversized jacket*

o·ver·sleep /,əʊvə'sliːp $,oʊvər-/ v past tense and past participle **overslept** /-'slept/ [I] to sleep for longer than you intended: *Sorry I'm late. I overslept.* → **sleep in** at SLEEP¹

o·ver·spend /,əʊvə'spend $,oʊvər-/ v past tense and past participle **overspent** /-'spent/ [I,T] to spend more money than you can afford: *The hospital has overspent its budget by £70,000.* —**overspend** /'əʊvəspend $ 'oʊvər-/ n [C]: *an overspend of £200,000*

o·ver·spill /'əʊvə,spɪl $ 'oʊvər-/ n [singular,U] *BrE* people who move out of a big city because there are too many people living there, and go to live in new houses outside the city: *an overspill of workers from London*

o·ver·staffed /,əʊvə'stɑːft◂ $,oʊvər'stæft◂/ adj an overstaffed company, organization etc has more workers than it needs; ⊟ **understaffed**

o·ver·state /,əʊvə'steɪt $,oʊvər-/ v [T] to talk about something in a way that makes it seem more important, serious etc than it really is; ⊟ **exaggerate**; ⊟ **understate**: *To say that all motorists speed in residential areas is overstating the case.* | *The importance of a child's early years cannot be overstated* (=is very important). —**overstatement** n [C,U]: *It's an overstatement to say that the man's a fool.*

o·ver·stay /,əʊvə'steɪ $,oʊvər-/ v [T] to stay somewhere longer than you are allowed to; ⊟ **outstay**: *They overstayed their visas and were arrested.* → **overstay your welcome** at WELCOME³ (3)

o·ver·step /,əʊvə'step $,oʊvər-/ v **overstepped, overstepping** [T] **1** overstep the limits/bounds/boundaries to do something that is not acceptable or allowed: *He has overstepped the bounds of acceptable behaviour.* **2** overstep the mark to offend someone by doing or saying things that you should not do or say: *She overstepped the mark and lost her job.*

o·ver·stock /,əʊvə'stɒk $,oʊvər'stɑːk/ v [I,T] to obtain more of something than is needed —**overstock** /'əʊvəstɒk $ 'oʊvərstɑːk/ n [C]

o·ver·stretch /,əʊvə'stretʃ $,oʊvər-/ v [T] to try to do more than you are able to, or to use more money, supplies etc than you have: *an overstretched social services department* | **overstretch yourself** *Problems only arise when people overstretch themselves.*

o·ver·sub·scribed /,əʊvəsəb'skraɪbd◂ $,oʊvər-/ adj if something is oversubscribed, too many people have said that they want to use it or have it: *All good schools are oversubscribed.*

o·ver·sup·ply /'əʊvəsəplaɪ $ 'oʊvər-/ n plural **oversupplies** [C,U] the state of having more of something than you need or can sell: *an oversupply of computers*

o·vert /'əʊvɜːt, əʊ'vɜːt $ 'oʊvɜːrt, oʊ'vɜːrt/ adj overt actions are done publicly, without trying to hide anything; ⊟ **covert**: *an overt attempt to silence their political opponents* | *Overt race discrimination is illegal.* —**overtly** adv: *an overtly political message*

o·ver·take /,əʊvə'teɪk $,oʊvər-/ v past tense **overtook** /-'tʊk/ past participle **overtaken** /-'teɪkən/ **1** [I,T] to go past a moving vehicle or person because you are going faster than them and want to get in front of them: *He pulled out to overtake the van.* | *Never try to overtake on a bend.* **2** [T] to develop or increase more quickly than someone or something else and become more successful, more important, or more advanced than them: *Television soon overtook the cinema as the most popular form of entertainment.* | *Hingis has now overtaken her in the world tennis rankings.* **3** [T] if something bad, especially a feeling, overtakes you, it happens to you suddenly and has a strong effect on you; → **overcome**: **be overtaken by sth** *She was overtaken by emotion and started to cry.* | *A terrible sense of panic overtook him.* **4** be overtaken by events if you are overtaken by events, the situation changes, so that your plans or ideas are not useful any more: *The diplomatic negotiations were soon overtaken by events.*

o·ver·tax /,əʊvə'tæks $,oʊvər-/ v [T] **1** to make someone do more than they are really able to, so that they become very tired: **overtax yourself** *Be careful you don't overtax yourself.* **2** to make people pay too much tax

over-the-'counter adj [only before noun] **1** over-the-counter drugs can be obtained without a PRESCRIPTION (=a written order) from a doctor **2** *AmE* **OTC** over-the-counter business shares are ones that do not appear on an official STOCK EXCHANGE list

over-the-'top adj *BrE informal* **OTT** remarks, behaviour etc that are over-the-top are so extreme or unreasonable that they seem stupid or offensive: *It's a bit over-the-top to call him a fascist.*

o·ver·throw¹ /,əʊvə'θrəʊ $,oʊvər'θroʊ/ v past tense **overthrew** /-'θruː/, past participle **overthrown** /-'θrəʊn $ -'θroʊn/ [T] **1** to remove a leader or government from power, especially by force; ⊟ **oust**: *Rebels were already making plans to overthrow the government.* **2** to get rid of the rules, ideas, or systems of a society

o·ver·throw² /'əʊvəθrəʊ $ 'oʊvərθroʊ/ n [U] the defeat and removal from power of a leader or government, especially by force: [+of] *The organization was dedicated to the overthrow of capitalism.* | *the overthrow of Mussolini*

o·ver·time /'əʊvətaɪm $ 'oʊvər-/ n [U]

1 time that you spend working in your job in addition to your normal working hours

work/do overtime
paid/unpaid overtime
overtime payment/pay
on overtime

six hours' overtime | *They're **working overtime** to get the job finished.* | *He's been **doing** a lot of **overtime** recently.* | *Many employees work countless hours of **unpaid overtime**.* | *Many of our offices will be working **on overtime** until the end of the year.*

2 the money that you are paid for working more hours than usual: *He earns £450 a week, including overtime.*
3 be working overtime *informal* to be very active: *As she put down the phone, her brain was working overtime.* | *His senses were working overtime.*
4 *AmE* a period of time added to the end of a sports game to give one of the two teams a chance to win; ⊟ **extra time** *BrE*: **in overtime** *Steve Smith scored all nine of the Hawks' points in overtime.*

o·ver·tired /,əʊvə'taɪəd $,oʊvər'taɪrd/ adj very tired, so that you cannot think or do things normally and become annoyed easily

o·ver·tone /ˈəʊvətəʊn $ ˈoʊvərtoʊn/ n **1** overtones [plural] signs of an emotion or attitude that is not expressed directly; → **undertone**: [+of] *There were overtones of anger in his voice.* | **racial/sexual etc overtones** *football songs with violent overtones* | **political/religious overtones** (=having a connection to politics or religion that is not directly expressed) *The decision may have political overtones.* **2** [C] *technical* a higher musical note that sounds together with the main note

o·ver·took /ˌəʊvəˈtʊk $ ˌoʊvər-/ v the past tense of OVERTAKE

o·ver·top /ˌəʊvəˈtɒp $ ˌoʊvərˈtɑːp/ v **overtopped**, **overtopping** [T] *formal* to be higher or more important than something

o·ver·ture /ˈəʊvətʃʊə, -tʃʊə, -tʃə $ ˈoʊvərtʃʊr, -tʃər/ n **1** [C] a short piece of music written as an introduction to a long piece of music, especially an OPERA **2** overtures [plural] an attempt to begin a friendly relationship with a person, country etc: *They began making overtures to the Irish government.* | *She had rejected his overtures.* **3 be an overture** if an event is an overture to a more important event, it happens just before it and makes you expect it

o·ver·turn /ˌəʊvəˈtɜːn $ ˌoʊvərˈtɜːrn/ v **1** [I,T] if you overturn something, or if it overturns, it turns upside down or falls over on its side: *Leslie jumped to her feet, overturning her chair.* | *His car overturned, trapping him inside.* **2 overturn a decision/verdict etc** to change a decision or result so that it becomes the opposite of what it was before: *His conviction was overturned by the Court of Appeal.* **3** [T] to suddenly remove a government from power, especially by using violence; ▤ **overthrow**

o·ver·use /ˌəʊvəˈjuːz $ ˌoʊvər-/ v [T] to use something too much, especially so that it is not effective any more or it is damaged: *Students tend to overuse certain words.* —**overuse** /-ˈjuːs/ n [U]: *the overuse of natural resources*

o·ver·val·ue /ˌəʊvəˈvælju $ ˌoʊvər-/ v [T] to believe or say that something is more valuable or more important than it really is —**overvaluation** /ˌəʊvəvæljuˈeɪʃən $ ˌoʊvər-/ n [U]

o·ver·view /ˈəʊvəvjuː $ ˈoʊvər-/ n [C] a short description of a subject or situation that gives the main ideas without explaining all the details: [+of] *an overview of the issues involved* | **provide/give an overview** *The document provides a general overview of the bank's policies.* | **broad/general overview** *This chapter gives a broad overview of the main concerns facing employers.*

o·ver·ween·ing /ˌəʊvəˈwiːnɪŋ $ ˌoʊvər-/ adj *formal* too proud and confident – used to show disapproval; ▤ **arrogant**: *overweening ambition* —**overweeningly** adv

o·ver·weight /ˌəʊvəˈweɪt◂ $ ˌoʊvər-/ adj **1** someone who is overweight is too heavy and fat; → **underweight: 10 kilos/20 lbs etc overweight** *Sally was fifty pounds overweight.* | *He is slightly overweight.* → see box at FAT¹ **2** something such as a package that is overweight weighs more than it is supposed to weigh; → **underweight**: *My luggage was overweight by five kilos.*

o·ver·whelm /ˌəʊvəˈwelm $ ˌoʊvər-/ v [T usually passive]
1 EMOTION if someone is overwhelmed by an emotion, they feel it so strongly that they cannot think clearly: **be overwhelmed by sth** *Harriet was overwhelmed by a feeling of homesickness.* | **be overwhelmed with sth** *The children were overwhelmed with excitement.* | *Grief overwhelmed me.*
2 TOO MUCH if work or a problem overwhelms someone, it is too much or too difficult to deal with: **be overwhelmed by sth** *We were overwhelmed by the number of applications.* | **overwhelm sb with sth** *They would be overwhelmed with paperwork.*
3 SURPRISE SB to surprise someone very much, so that they do not know how to react: **be overwhelmed by**

sth *I was completely overwhelmed by his generosity.* | *We were overwhelmed by the sheer size of the place.*
4 DEFEAT SB to defeat an army completely: *In 1532 the Spaniards finally overwhelmed the armies of Peru.*
5 WATER *literary* if water overwhelms an area of land, it covers it completely and suddenly

o·ver·whelm·ing /ˌəʊvəˈwelmɪŋ $ ˌoʊvər-/ adj **1** having such a great effect on you that you feel confused and do not know how to react: *an overwhelming sense of guilt* | *She felt an overwhelming desire to hit him.* | *She found the city quite overwhelming when she first arrived.* **2** very large or greater, more important etc than any other: *There is overwhelming evidence that smoking damages your health.* | *An overwhelming majority of the members were against the idea.* | *The proposal has been given overwhelming support.* | *The British Air Force succeeded despite overwhelming odds against them.* —**overwhelmingly** adv: *Congress voted overwhelmingly in favor of the bill.*

o·ver·win·ter /ˌəʊvəˈwɪntə $ ˌoʊvərˈwɪntər/ v [I,T] to live through the winter, or to make it possible for something to live through the winter: *These birds generally overwinter in tropical regions.*

o·ver·work¹ /ˌəʊvəˈwɜːk $ ˌoʊvərˈwɜːrk/ v [I,T] to work too much or to make someone work too much: *You've been overworking – why don't you take a week off?* | *Have they been overworking you again?*

overwork² n [U] too much hard work: *a heart attack brought on by overwork*

o·ver·worked /ˌəʊvəˈwɜːkt◂ $ ˌoʊvərˈwɜːrkt◂/ adj **1** made to work too hard: *an overworked doctor* | *They're overworked and understaffed.* **2** a word or phrase that is overworked is used too much and has become less effective: *overworked metaphors*

o·ver·wrought /ˌəʊvəˈrɔːt◂ $ ˌoʊvərˈrɒːt◂/ adj very upset, nervous, and worried: *Clara was tired and overwrought after all the problems of the last few days.*

o·ver·zeal·ous /ˌəʊvəˈzeləs◂ $ ˌoʊvər-/ adj too eager about something you believe in strongly: *overzealous fans*

o·vi·duct /ˈəʊvɪdʌkt $ ˈoʊvə-/ n [C] *technical* one of the two tubes in a woman or female animal through which eggs pass to the WOMB

o·vip·a·rous /əʊˈvɪpərəs $ oʊ-/ adj *technical* an animal, fish, bird etc that is oviparous produces eggs that develop outside its body

o·void /ˈəʊvɔɪd $ ˈoʊ-/ adj *formal* shaped like an egg —**ovoid** n [C]

ov·u·late /ˈɒvjᵿleɪt $ ˈɑːv-/ v [I] when a woman or female animal ovulates, she produces eggs inside her body —**ovulation** /ˌɒvjᵿˈleɪʃən $ ˌɑːv-/ n [U]

o·vum /ˈəʊvəm $ ˈoʊ-/ n plural **ova** /-və/ [C] *technical* an egg, especially one that develops inside the mother's body

ow /aʊ/ interjection used to express sudden pain: *'Ow, that hurts!'*

owe [S2] [W3] /əʊ $ oʊ/ v [T]
1 MONEY to need to pay someone for something that they have done for you or sold to you, or to need to give someone back money that they have lent you; → **borrow, lend: owe sb money/£10 etc** *I owe my brother $50.* | **owe sth for sth** *I still owe you for the taxi.* | *How much do I owe you* (=often used to show that you want to pay for something)? | **owe sth to sb** *the money owed to credit card companies*
2 STH DONE/GIVEN to feel that you should do something for someone or give someone something, because they have done something for you or given something to you: *He asked for help from a colleague who owed him a favour.* | **owe sb a drink/letter etc** *I owe Shaun a letter; I must write soon.* | *Thanks a lot for being so understanding about all this –* **I owe you one** (=used to thank someone who has helped you, and to say that you are willing to help them in the future)! | **owe sb** (=be in a position in which someone has helped you, so that

you should help them) *Let's go and see Joe – he owes me!*
3 owe sb an explanation/apology to feel that you should give someone an explanation of why you did something, or say you are sorry: *You owe him an apology.*
4 HELP TO ACHIEVE STH **a)** to have something or achieve something because of what someone else has done: owe sth to sb *He probably owes his life to her prompt action.* **b)** to know that someone's help has been important to you in achieving something: owe sb a lot/owe sb a great deal *'I owe my parents a lot,' he admitted.* | *He owes a great deal to his publishers.* | owe it all to sb/owe everything to sb *I owe it all to you.* | owe sb a debt (of gratitude) *the debt that we owe to our teachers*
5 GOOD EFFECT to be successful because of the good effect or influence of something or someone: [+to] *Their success owes more to good luck than to careful management.* | *Pearson's work owed much to the research of his friend, Hugh Kingsmill.*
6 owe it to sb to do sth to feel you should do something for someone, because they have helped you or given you support: *You owe it to your supporters not to give up now.*
7 owe it to yourself to do sth to feel you should try to achieve something because it is what you deserve: *You owe it to yourself to take some time off.*
8 owe loyalty/allegiance etc to sb to have a duty to obey someone: *provinces owing allegiance to the Emperor*
9 think that the world owes you a living to be unwilling to work in order to get things, and expect them to be provided for you – used to show disapproval

ow·ing /'əʊɪŋ $ 'oʊ-/ *adj* [not before noun] *especially BrE* if money is owing, it has not yet been paid to the person who should receive it; → outstanding: *You need to pay the amount owing, plus the interest.*

'owing to *prep formal* because of something: *Owing to a lack of funds, the project will not continue next year.* | *Flight BA213 has been delayed owing to fog.*

> **WORD CHOICE: owing to, due to, because of, thanks to**
> Owing to and due to are slightly formal. They are often used in official notices and public statements: *Owing to bad weather, this morning's flight will be delayed.* | *He is retiring due to ill health.*
> ⚠ Owing to and due to are prepositions (they come immediately before a noun). They are not conjunctions (they cannot connect two parts of a sentence): *I had to wait hours because the plane was delayed* (NOT *I had to wait hours owing to the plane was delayed*).
> In spoken English, it is more usual to use **because of** than owing to or due to: *All my clothes got wet because of the storm* (NOT *owing to the storm*).
> **Thanks to** is used to explain why something good has happened: *Thanks to the success of his first album, he is now a wealthy man.*

owl /aʊl/ *n* [C] a bird with large eyes that hunts at night → see picture at BIRD OF PREY

owl·et /'aʊlɪt/ *n* [C] a young owl

owl·ish /'aʊlɪʃ/ *adj* looking like an owl and seeming serious and clever: *He was an owlish man, with little round glasses.* —**owlishly** *adv*

own¹ S1 W1 /əʊn $ oʊn/ *adj, pron* [always after a possessive]
1 used to emphasize that something belongs to or is connected with a particular person or thing and not any other: *Bring your own equipment.* | *Every dance has its own rhythm.* | *The yacht was intended for the king's own personal use.* | *His face was only a few inches from her own.* | of your own *We have problems of our own.* | *I'd like to have a place of my own* (=my own home). | your very own (=used to add more emphasis) *One day I want to have a horse of my very own.* | sth to call your own/which you can call your own (=something that belongs to you) *She just wanted a place to call her*

own.
2 used to emphasize that someone did or made something without the help or involvement of anyone else: *She makes a lot of her own clothes.* | *We encourage students to develop their own ideas.* | *It's your own fault for leaving the window open.*
3 (all) on your own **a)** alone: *I've been living on my own for four years now.* | *He didn't want to be left on his own.* **b)** without anyone's help: *You can't expect him to do it all on his own.* | *I can manage on my own, thanks.*
4 for your own good/safety/benefit etc if you do something for someone's own good etc, you do it to help them even though they might not like it or want it: *I'm only telling you this for your own good.* | *He was kept away from the other prisoners for his own safety.*
5 too nice/clever etc for your own good used to say that someone has too much of a good quality so that it may be a disadvantage: *Stephen can be too generous for his own good.*
6 get your own back (on sb) *informal* to do something bad to someone who has harmed you, as a way of punishing them; → revenge: *She wanted to get her own back on Liz for ruining her party.*
7 be your own man/woman to have strong opinions and intentions that are not influenced by other people: *Hilary's very much her own woman.*
8 make sth your own to change or deal with something in a way that makes it seem to belong to you: *Great singers can take an old song and make it their own.*
⚠ Use **own** only after possessive words like my, John's, the company's etc → come into your own at COME¹ (6); → hold your own at HOLD¹ (24)

own² S2 W2 *v* [T not in progressive]
1 to have something which belongs to you, especially because you have bought it, been given it etc and it is legally yours; → possess: *The building is owned by the local council.* | *You need to get permission from the farmer who owns the land.* | *Many more people now own their own homes.* | *the cost of owning a car* | publicly/privately owned *BrE* (=belonging to the government or a private organization) *a privately owned company*
2 as if/as though/like you own the place *informal* to behave in a way that is too confident and upsets other people: *She acts like she owns the place!* | *They walked in as if they owned the place.*
3 *old-fashioned* to admit that something is true: own (that) *I own that I judged her harshly at first.* | [+to] *I must own to a feeling of anxiety.*

own up *phr v*
to admit that you have done something wrong, especially something that is not serious: *Come on, own up. Who broke it?* | own up to (doing) sth *No one owned up to breaking the window.* | *He was too frightened to own up to his mistake.* | *He still wouldn't own up to the fact that he'd lied.*

own 'brand *adj BrE* own brand goods are specially produced and sold by particular shops and have the name of the shop on them; ◼ store brand *AmE: Tesco's own brand tomato sauce*

own·er S2 W2 /'əʊnə $ 'oʊnər/ *n* [C] someone who owns something: [+of] *I met the owner of the local hotel.* | original/previous/new owner *the club's new owners* | *He was now the proud owner of a bright red sports car.* | car-owner/dog-owner etc *Dog-owners have been warned to keep their animals under control.* | home-owner (=someone who owns their house)

owner-'occupied *adj* houses, apartments etc that are owner-occupied are lived in by the people who own them: *Most of these properties are owner-occupied.* —**owner-occupier** *n* [C]

own·er·ship S3 W3 /'əʊnəʃɪp $ 'oʊnər-/ *n* [U] the fact of owning something: [+of] *a dispute over the ownership of the land* | public/private/state ownership *The company was returned to private ownership in mid-1987.* | *The price of home ownership is increasing.*

own 'goal *n* [C] *BrE* **1** a GOAL that you accidentally score against your own team without intending to in a game of football, HOCKEY etc **2** *informal* an action or remark that has the opposite effect from what you intended: *The minister's admission turned out to be a spectacular own goal.*

own 'label *adj* [U] *BrE* OWN BRAND

ox /ɒks $ ɑːks/ *n plural* **oxen** /'ɒksən $ 'ɑːks-/ [C] **1** a BULL whose sex organs have been removed, often used for working on farms **2** a large cow or BULL

Ox·bridge /'ɒks,brɪdʒ $ 'ɑːks-/ *n* [U] the universities of Oxford and Cambridge; → **redbrick**

ox·cart /'ɒkskɑːt $ 'ɑːkskɑːrt/ *n* [C] a vehicle pulled by oxen that was used in the past

'ox-eye *n* [C] a yellow flower like a DAISY

ox·ford /'ɒksfəd $ 'ɑːksfərd/ *n AmE* **1 oxfords** [plural] a type of leather shoes that fasten with SHOELACES **2** [C] a type of shirt made of thick cotton

ox·ide /'ɒksaɪd $ 'ɑːk-/ *n* [C,U] a substance which is produced when a substance is combined with oxygen: *iron oxide*

ox·i·dize also **-ise** *BrE* /'ɒksɪ̣daɪz $ 'ɑːk-/ *v* [I,T] *technical* to combine with oxygen, or make something combine with oxygen, especially in a way that causes RUST —**oxidation** /,ɒksɪ̣'deɪʃən $,ɑːk-/ also **oxidization** /,ɒksɪ̣daɪ'zeɪʃən $,ɑːksɪ̣də-/ *n* [U]

Oxon used after the title of a degree from Oxford University: *David Jones BA (Oxon)*

ox·tail /'ɒksteɪl $ 'ɑːks-/ *n* [U] the meat from the tails of cattle, used especially in soup

ox·y·a·cet·y·lene /,ɒksiə'setəliːn◂ $,ɑːksiə'setl-iːn◂ , -ən◂/ *n* [U] *technical* a mixture of oxygen and ACETYLENE that produces a hot white flame that can cut steel

ox·y·gen /'ɒksɪdʒən $ 'ɑːk-/ *n* [U] a gas that has no colour or smell, is present in air, and is necessary for most animals and plants to live. It is a chemical ELEMENT: symbol O

ox·y·gen·ate /'ɒksɪdʒəneɪt $ 'ɑːk-/ *v* [T] *technical* to add oxygen to something —**oxygenation** /,ɒksɪdʒə'neɪʃən $,ɑːk-/ *n* [U]

'oxygen bar *n* [C] a bar where you pay to breathe pure oxygen, or oxygen that has a pleasant smell, so that you can relax and have more energy

'oxygen mask *n* [C] a piece of equipment that fits over someone's mouth and nose to provide them with oxygen

'oxygen tent *n* [C] a piece of equipment shaped like a tent that is put around people who are very ill in hospital, to provide them with oxygen

ox·y·mo·ron /,ɒksi'mɔːrɒn $,ɑːksi'mɔːrɑːn/ *n* [C] *technical* a deliberate combination of two words that seem to mean the opposite of each other, such as 'cruel kindness'

o·yez /əʊ'jez $ oʊ-/ *interjection* a word used by law officials or by TOWN CRIERS in the past to get people's attention

oy·ster /'ɔɪstə $ -ər/ *n* [C] **1** a type of SHELLFISH that can be eaten cooked or uncooked, and that produces a jewel called a PEARL → see picture at SEAFOOD **2 the world is your oyster** used to tell someone that they can achieve whatever they want

'oyster bed *n* [C] an area at the bottom of the sea where oysters live

oz *BrE*; **oz.** *AmE* the written abbreviation of *ounce* or ounces

Oz /ɒz $ ɒːz/ *n BrE, AusE informal* a short way of saying Australia

o·zone /'əʊzəʊn $ 'oʊzoʊn/ *n* [U] **1** *technical* a poisonous blue gas that is a type of oxygen **2** *informal* air near the sea, thought to be fresher and healthier

ozone-'friendly *adj* not containing chemicals that damage the ozone layer: *an ozone-friendly aerosol* → see picture at ENVIRONMENT

'ozone ,layer *n* [singular] a layer of gases in the sky that prevents harmful RADIATION from the sun from reaching the Earth: *the hole in the ozone layer*

P, p

P, p /piː/ *plural* **P's, p's** *n* [C,U] the 16th letter of the English alphabet → **mind your p's and q's** at MIND² (23)

P *BrE* the written abbreviation of *provisional*, used on cars to show that the driver is a learner and has a PROVISIONAL LICENCE → **P-PLATE**

p. also **p** *BrE* **1** the written abbreviation of *page* → P.P. **2** *BrE* the abbreviation of *penny* or *pence*: *The bus fare was only 50p.* **3** used in written music to show that a part should be played or sung quietly

p & p *BrE* the written abbreviation of *postage and packing*: *Please send 80p to cover p & p.*

pa /pɑː/ *n* [C] *old-fashioned informal* father – used by children or when speaking to children

p.a. the written abbreviation of *per annum*

PA /ˌpiː ˈeɪ/ *n* [C] **1** [usually singular] **public address system** electronic equipment that makes someone's voice loud enough to be heard by large groups of people **2** *BrE* **personal assistant** someone who works as a secretary for one person

PAC /ˌpiː eɪ ˈsiː, pæk/ *n* [C] *AmE* the abbreviation of *political action committee*

pace¹ W3 /peɪs/ *n*

1 SPEED OF EVENTS/CHANGES [singular] the speed at which something happens or is done

> **pace of change/reform/growth**
> **pace of life**
> **at your own pace** (=at the pace that suits you)
> **at a rapid/slow/steady etc pace**
> **at breakneck pace** (=extremely fast)
> **gather pace** (=happen more quickly)
> **keep up the pace** (=continue to do something or happen as quickly as before)
> **at a snail's pace** (=very slowly)

*The **pace of change** in our lives is becoming faster and faster.* | *Here in Bermuda, the **pace of life** is very slow.* | *Public spending continues to rise **at a steady pace**.* | *Children learn best by studying **at their own pace**.* | *The company had been growing **at breakneck pace** until last year.* | *Support for European unity began to **gather pace**.* | *If they can **keep up the pace**, they should have finished by early next week.* | *Things are changing, but **at a snail's pace**.*

⚠ Do not say 'in your own pace' or 'on your own pace'. Say **at your own pace**.

2 WALK/RUN [singular] the speed at which someone walks, runs, or moves: [+of] *You need to step up the pace of your exercises.* | **at a slow/leisurely/brisk etc pace** *Lucy set off at a leisurely pace back to the hotel.* | *He quickened his pace, longing to be home.* | *Traffic slowed to a walking pace.*

3 STEP [C] a single step when you are running or walking, or the distance you move in one step: [+backwards/towards/forwards etc] *He took a pace towards the door.* | *Rebecca walked a few paces behind her mum.*

4 **keep pace (with sth/sb)** to change or increase as fast as something else, or to move as fast as someone else: *Salaries have not always kept pace with inflation.* | *The supply of materials cannot keep pace with demand.* | *Slow down! I can't keep pace with you.*

5 **go through your paces** also **show your paces** to show how well you can do something

6 **put sb/sth through their paces** to make a person, vehicle, animal etc show how well they can do something: *The test driver puts all the cars through their paces.*

7 **set the pace a)** if a company sets the pace, it does something before its competitors or to a better standard: [+in] *Japanese firms have been setting the pace in electronic engineering.* **b)** also **set a brisk/cracking etc pace** *BrE* to go faster than the other competitors in a race, who then try to achieve the same speed: *The Italians set the pace for the first eight laps.*

8 **force the pace** to make something happen or develop more quickly than it would do normally: [+on] *measures designed to force the pace on alternative energy policies*

9 **be able to stand the pace** to be able to deal with situations where you are very busy and have to think and act very quickly: *If you can stand the pace, working in advertising pays well.*

pace² *v* **1** [I always + adv/prep, T] to walk first in one direction and then in another many times, especially because you are nervous: *I found Mark at the hospital, pacing restlessly up and down.* | **pace the floor/room** *Sam stood up and paced the floor, deep in thought.* **2** **pace yourself a)** to control the speed that you move at in a race, so that you still have energy left near the end: *Nicky paced herself and came through the ranks to win.* **b)** to organize your life and activities so that you do not have too much to do: *You need to pace yourself and decide which tasks are the most important.* **3** [T] also **pace sth ⇔ off**, **pace sth ⇔ out** to measure a distance by walking across it with steps of equal length: *The director paced out the length of the stage.*

pace·mak·er /ˈpeɪsˌmeɪkə $ -ər/ *n* [C] **1** a small machine that is placed inside someone's chest in order to help their heart beat regularly **2** also **pacesetter** a person or horse who goes to the front in a race and sets the speed that the others must try to achieve

pace·set·ter /ˈpeɪsˌsetə $ -ər/ also **pacemaker** *n* [C] **1** a person or team that is winning in a competition, and that others have to try to defeat: *That left him three strokes behind the pacesetter, Parry.* **2** a person or company that is considered to be a leader in a particular area of activity: *a new company, now seen as the industry's pacesetter* **3** → PACEMAKER (2)

pa·chin·ko /pəˈtʃɪŋkəʊ $ -koʊ/ *n* [U] a game that is popular in Japan, in which you can win money or prizes by making balls fall into particular places in a special machine

pach·y·derm /ˈpækɪdɜːm $ -dɜːrm/ *n* [C] *technical* an animal with thick skin, such as an ELEPHANT

pa·cif·ic /pəˈsɪfɪk/ *adj literary* peaceful and loving or wanting peace: *a normally pacific community*

Pa·cific 'Rim *n* **the Pacific Rim (countries)** the countries around the Pacific Ocean, such as Japan, Australia, and the west coast of the US, considered as an economic group

pac·i·fi·er /ˈpæsɪˌfaɪə $ -faɪər/ *n* [C] **1** *AmE* a rubber object that you give a baby to suck so that it does not cry; ▭ **dummy** *BrE* **2** something that makes people calm

pac·i·fis·m /ˈpæsɪˌfɪzəm/ *n* [U] the belief that war and violence are always wrong

pac·i·fist /ˈpæsɪfɪst/ *n* [C] someone who believes that wars are wrong and who refuses to use violence —**pacifist** *adj* [only before noun]: *the pacifist movement*

pac·i·fy /ˈpæsɪˌfaɪ/ *v* **pacified, pacifying, pacifies** [T] **1** to make someone calm, quiet, and satisfied after they have been angry or upset: *'You're right,' Rita said, in order to pacify him.* **2** to stop groups of people from fighting or protesting, often by using force: *Economic reforms are needed to pacify and modernize the country.*

pack¹ S2 W3 /pæk/ *v*

1 CLOTHES [I,T] also **pack up** to put things into cases, bags etc ready for a trip somewhere: *I forgot to pack my razor.* | *Have you finished packing yet?* | **pack your things/belongings** *Kelly packed her things before breakfast.* | **pack a bag/case** *You'd better pack your* bags. *We're leaving in an hour.* | **pack sb sth** *Shall I pack us a picnic?*

2 GOODS [T] also **pack up** to put something into a box or other container, so that it can be moved, sold, or stored: **pack sth in/into sth** *Now wild mushrooms are available all year, packed in handy 25g boxes.*

3 CROWD [I always + adv/prep,T] to go in large numbers into a space, or to make people or animals do this, until the space is too full: [+into/in/onto] *50,000 fans packed into the stadium.* | *The sheep had been packed into a truck and transported without food or water.*

4 PROTECT STH [T] to cover or fill an object with soft material so that it does not get damaged: [+in/with] *Glass must be packed in several layers of paper.*

5 SNOW/SOIL ETC to press snow, soil, sand etc down so that it becomes hard and firm: **pack sth down** *Pack the soil down firmly.*

6 pack your bags *informal* to leave a place and not return, especially because of a disagreement

7 pack a gun *AmE informal* to carry a gun

8 pack a (hard/hefty/strong etc) punch also **pack a wallop** *informal* to have a very strong or impressive effect: *The Spanish wine, with the flavour of honey, packed quite a punch.* → **send sb packing** at SEND (11)

pack sth ⇔ **away** *phr v*
to put something back in a box, case etc where it is usually kept: *Christmas was over and the decorations packed away.*

pack in *phr v*
1 pack sth ⇔ **in** also **pack sth into sth** to do a lot in a limited period of time, or fit a lot of information, ideas etc into a limited space: *We packed a lot of sightseeing into two weeks.* | *In an essay of 2000 words, you can pack a lot in.*

2 pack sb ⇔ **in** *informal* if a film, play etc packs people in, it attracts large numbers to come and see it: *Any film starring Tom Cruise always packs them in.*

3 pack sth ⇔ **in** *BrE informal* to stop doing a job or activity that you are not enjoying: *After one year, I packed in university.* | *Sometimes I feel like packing it all in and going off travelling.*

4 pack it in *BrE spoken* used to tell someone to stop doing something that is annoying you

5 *BrE informal* if a machine packs in, it stops working because there is something wrong with it; ■ **pack up**: *Halfway to the airport, the engine packed in.*

pack sb/sth **off** *phr v informal*
to send someone to stay somewhere for a period of time: [+to] *My parents used to pack us off to camp every summer.*

pack up *phr v*
1 to put things into cases, bags etc ready for a trip somewhere: *Most of the holidaymakers had packed up and gone.* | **pack sth** ⇔ **up** *I gave her a hand packing up her clothes and stuff.*

2 pack sth ⇔ **up** to put something into a box or other container, so that it can be moved, sold, or stored: *Don't worry. The removal men will pack everything up.*

3 *informal* to finish work at the end of the day: *'What time do you pack up?' 'Oh, about six.'*

4 *BrE informal* if a machine packs up, it stops working because there is something wrong with it; ■ **pack in**: *The photocopier's packed up again.*

5 pack sth ⇔ **up** *BrE informal* to stop doing something, especially a job: *He packed up his teaching job after only three months.*

pack² S2 W3 *n* [C]
1 THINGS WRAPPED TOGETHER something wrapped in paper or packed in a box and then sent by post or taken somewhere: [+of] *a pack of three T-shirts* | *Send away for your free information pack today.* → SIX-PACK (1)

2 SMALL CONTAINER especially *AmE* a small container, usually made of paper, that something is sold in; ■ **packet** *BrE*: [+of] *a pack of cigarettes* | *a 10 oz. pack of frozen peas;* → see box at PACKAGE¹

3 BAG especially *BrE* a bag that you carry on your back, especially when climbing or walking, used to

---

carry equipment, clothes etc; ■ **rucksack** *BrE*; ■ **backpack**

4 CARDS also **pack of cards** a complete set of PLAYING CARDS; ■ **deck**; → see picture at SPLIT

5 ANIMALS a group of wild animals that hunt together, or a group of dogs trained to hunt together: *a wolf pack* | [+of] *a pack of hounds*

6 GROUP OF PEOPLE a group of the same type of people, especially a group who you do not approve of: [+of] *A pack of reporters were waiting outside.*

7 pack of lies *informal* something you are told that is completely untrue: *Don't believe what it says in the paper – it's a pack of lies.*

8 Cub/Brownie pack a group of children who belong to a particular children's organization → CUB SCOUT, BROWNIE, GIRL SCOUT

9 ON A WOUND a thick soft piece of cloth that you press on a wound to stop the flow of blood; ■ **compress** → ICE PACK

pack·age¹ S2 W2
/'pækɪdʒ/ *n* [C]   **package**
1 something wrapped in paper, packed in a box and then sent by mail or delivered; ■ **parcel** *BrE*: *There's a package here for a Miami Lakes address.*

2 *AmE* the paper or plastic container that food or other goods are sold in; ■ **packet** *BrE*: [+of] *a package of meat*

package/parcel

3 a set of ideas or services that are suggested or offered all together as a group: **package of measures/proposals/incentives etc** *The government has announced a package of measures to assist affected areas.* | **aid/financial/benefits etc package** | *Many banks are offering financial packages for students.*

4 a set of related programs sold together for use on a computer: **software/word-processing/graphics etc package**

WORD CHOICE: package, packet, packaging, packing, pack

⚠ Do not confuse these similar words.

A **package** is a parcel, usually sent by post: *A package containing a bomb was delivered to her home.*
In American English, a **package** is also a paper or plastic container that food etc is sold in: *a package of cookies*
In British English, a **packet** is a box, bag, or some other container that things are sold in: *a packet of biscuits* | *a packet of crisps.* A **packet** can also sometimes be called a **pack**: *a pack of cigarettes.* This meaning of **pack** is also used in American English.
In American English, a **packet** is a small flat paper or plastic container for something such as tomato ketchup or sugar. The British word for this is **sachet**.
Packaging is material that is put round things that are sold, to protect them or to encourage people to buy them: *It's the same old stuff in better packaging.*
Packing is material that is put around things to protect them, especially from getting damaged in the post: *Carefully remove the computer from its foam packing.*

---

package² *v* [T usually passive] **1** also **package up** to put food or other goods into a bag, box etc ready to be sold or sent: *The code informs us where and when a product was packaged.* | *The videos were packaged up, ready for distribution.* **2** to prepare something for sale, especially by making it attractive or interesting to a particular group of people: *books that are packaged for mass readership*

package deal *n* [C] **1** also **package holiday** *BrE* a holiday organized by a company at a fixed price that includes the cost of travel, hotel etc: *a cheap package deal to Tenerife* **2** an offer or agreement which includes several things that you must buy or accept together: *The Commission attempted to bring all three proposals into one package deal.*

package tour n [C] a PACKAGE DEAL (1)

pack·ag·ing /ˈpækɪdʒɪŋ/ n [U]   **1** the container or material that a product is sold in: *plastic packaging* → see box at PACKAGE¹   **2** the process of wrapping something for sale: *the date of packaging*   **3** a way of making something seem attractive and interesting to people: *the packaging of the company image*

pack animal n [C] an animal used for carrying heavy loads, for example a horse

packed /pækt/ adj   **1** extremely full of people: *a packed courtroom* | [+with] *The island was packed with tourists.*   **2 packed with/full of sth** containing a lot of a particular type of thing: *a new magazine packed with exciting recipes*   **3** [not before noun] if you are packed, you have put everything you need into cases ready to go somewhere   **4 tightly/loosely/densely packed** pressed, arranged etc closely or not closely together: *houses tightly packed in rows*

packed lunch n [C] *BrE* food such as sandwiches and fruit that you take with you to work, school etc for LUNCH

packed out adj [not before noun] *BrE informal* a cinema, restaurant etc that is packed out is completely full of people

pack·er /ˈpækə $ -ər/ n [C] someone who works in a factory, putting things into containers

pack·et S2 /ˈpækɪt/ n [C]
1 a) *BrE* a container made of paper, plastic, or CARDBOARD that something is sold in: [+of] *a packet of envelopes* | *a packet of cigarettes* | *a cereal packet* → see box at PACKAGE¹ **b)** *AmE* a small flat paper or plastic container that a liquid or powder is sold in; ⊟ **sachet** *BrE*: *packets of ketchup and mustard* → see picture at CONTAINER
2 *especially BrE* a small flat package that is sent by post or delivered to someone: *Paul tore open the packet as soon as it arrived.* → PAY PACKET
3 cost a packet *BrE informal* to cost a lot of money: *I bet that car cost him a packet.*
4 *technical* a quantity of information that is sent as a single unit from one computer to another on a network or on the Internet

packet boat n [C] *old-fashioned* a boat that carries letters, packages etc and usually passengers at regular times

packet-switching n [C] a method of sending information stored on a computer, usually across the Internet. Long messages are broken into pieces and put together again when they are received.

pack horse n [C] a horse used for carrying heavy loads

pack ice n [U] a mass of ice floating in the sea

pack·ing /ˈpækɪŋ/ n [U]   **1** when you put things into cases or boxes so that you can send or take them somewhere: *I can do my packing the night before we leave.*   **2** the material used for packing things so that they can be sent somewhere: *Use plenty of packing.* → see box at PACKAGE¹

packing case n [C] a large strong wooden box in which things are packed to be sent somewhere

pack rat n [C] *AmE informal* someone who collects and stores things that they do not really need

pack trip n [C] a trip through the countryside on horses, for fun or as a sport; ⊟ **pony-trekking** *BrE*

pact /pækt/ n [C] a formal agreement between two groups, countries, or people, especially to help each other or to stop fighting: *the Warsaw pact* | **make/sign a pact** *The two countries signed a non-aggression pact.* | [+with] *a defence pact with the USA* | [+between] *a peace pact between the rebels and the government* → SUICIDE PACT

pad¹ S3 /pæd/ n [C]
1 SOFT MATERIAL a thick flat object made of cloth or rubber, used to protect or clean something, or to make something more comfortable: [+of] *Press on the wound with a large pad of cotton wool.* | *Use an abrasive pad for stubborn stains.* | **knee/elbow/shin/shoulder pad** (=a pad that you wear to protect a part of your body when you are playing a sport); → see picture at ACCIDENT, SANITARY PAD
2 PAPER several sheets of paper fastened together, used for writing or drawing: **writing/sketch/memo/legal etc pad** *a box of paints and a sketch pad* | *Keep a telephone pad and a pen to hand.* | *a pad of paper*
3 FLAT GROUND a piece of flat ground where small aircraft can land: **launch/landing/helicopter pad** *The hospital has built a helicopter pad.*
4 ANIMAL'S FOOT the flesh on the bottom of the foot of a cat, dog, etc
5 APARTMENT *old-fashioned informal* someone's apartment or the room where they live
6 WATER PLANT the leaf of a WATER LILY → LAUNCH PAD, HELICOPTER PAD

pad² v **padded, padding**   **1** [I always + adv/prep] to walk softly and quietly: [+across/through/along etc] *The cat came padding silently back to its home.* | *She padded barefoot down the stairs.*   **2** [T] also **pad (sth) out** *BrE* to fill or cover something with a soft material in order to protect it or make it more comfortable: **pad sth with sth** *jackets padded out with a soft cotton filling*   **3** [T] *AmE* to dishonestly make bills more expensive than they should be: *padding the bills of Medicare patients*   **4** [T] also **pad (sth) out** to make a speech or piece of writing longer by adding unnecessary words or details: *Don't pad out your answer to make it seem impressive.* | [+with] *His autobiography is padded with boring anecdotes.*

pad·ded /ˈpædɪd/ adj filled or covered with a soft material to make it thicker or more comfortable: *The shoes are padded to protect the foot.* | *a padded headrest*

padded cell n [C] a special room in a hospital for people who are mentally ill. The room has thick soft material on the walls so that the person in it cannot get hurt.

pad·ding /ˈpædɪŋ/ n [U]   **1** soft material used to fill or cover something: *a helmet with protective padding*   **2** unnecessary and uninteresting details or words that are added to make a sentence, speech etc longer – used to show disapproval

pad·dle¹ /ˈpædl/ n   **1** [C] a short pole that is wide and flat at the end, used for moving a small boat in water; → oar   **2** [singular] *BrE* when you walk for pleasure without shoes or socks in water that is not very deep: *If it's not too cold, we can go for a paddle.*   **3** [C] *AmE* a small round flat BAT with a short handle, used for hitting the ball in TABLE TENNIS: *a ping-pong paddle*   **4** [C] a tool like a flat spoon, used for mixing food → DOG PADDLE

paddle² v **paddled, paddling**   **1** [I,T] to move a small light boat through water, using one or more paddles: [+along/upstream/towards etc] *I desperately tried to paddle for the shore.* | *She and her husband paddled a canoe down the Mississippi.* → ROW³   **2** [I] *BrE* to walk for pleasure without shoes or socks in water that is not very deep; ⊟ **wade** *AmE*: *children paddling in the sea*   **3** [I] to swim with short, quick movements: *The dog was paddling furiously after the ducks.*   **4** [T] *AmE informal* to hit a child with a piece of wood as a punishment   **5 paddle your own canoe** *BrE informal* to do things yourself, without help from anyone else

paddle steamer also **paddle boat** *BrE* n [C] a large old-fashioned boat that moves by using steam to drive a large wheel attached to the side

paddling pool n [C] *BrE* a small pool or plastic container of water which is not very deep, for children to play in; ⊟ **wading pool** *AmE*

pad·dock /'pædək/ n [C] **1** especially BrE a small field in which horses are kept **2** a piece of ground where horses are brought together before a race so that people can look at them

pad·dy /'pædi/ also **'paddy field** n plural **paddies** [C] a field in which rice is grown in water; **目 rice paddy**

Paddy n plural **Paddies** [C] taboo an offensive word for someone from Ireland. Do not use this word.

'paddy ˌwagon n [C] AmE informal a police vehicle used to carry prisoners

pad·lock /'pædlɒk $ -lɑːk/ n [C] a lock that you can put on a gate, door, bicycle etc: He undid the padlock and eased back the lid. —**padlock** v [T]; → see picture at LOCK²

pa·dre /'pɑːdreɪ, -ri/ n [C] informal a priest, especially one in the army

pae·an /'piːən/ n [C] literary a happy song of praise, thanks, or victory

paed·e·rast BrE; **pederast** AmE /'pedəræst/ n [C] formal a man who has sex with a young boy —**paederasty** n [U]

pae·di·a·tri·cian BrE; **pediatrician** AmE /ˌpiːdiə'trɪʃən/ n [C] a doctor who deals with children and their illnesses

pae·di·at·rics BrE; **pediatrics** AmE /ˌpiːdi'ætrɪks/ n [U] the area of medicine that deals with children and their illnesses —**paediatric** adj: a pediatric hospital

pae·do·phile BrE; **pedophile** AmE /'piːdəfaɪl/ n [C] someone who is sexually attracted to children

pa·el·la /paɪ'elə $ pɑː-/ n [U] a Spanish dish made with rice, pieces of meat, fish, and vegetables

pa·gan¹ /'peɪɡən/ adj pagan religious beliefs and customs do not belong to any of the main religions of the world, and may come from a time before these religions: ancient pagan temples

pagan² n [C] **1** also **Pagan** someone who believes in a pagan religion **2** someone with few or no religious beliefs – used humorously —**paganism** n [U]

page¹ [S1] [W1] /peɪdʒ/ n [C]
1 [PAPER] one side of a piece of paper in a book, newspaper, document etc, or the sheet of paper itself

(on) page 5/20/360 etc
the top/bottom of the page
the front/back page (=of a newspaper)
the opposite/facing page
over the page BrE (=on the next left-hand page)
the sports/fashion/financial etc pages (=pages about sports, fashion, money etc in a newspaper)
full/half page
turn a page
flick through the pages (of sth) (=turn the pages without reading carefully)
see/turn to/go to page 22, 49 etc
jump/leap off the page (=be very easy to notice)
a blank/new/clean/fresh page (=a page that you have not written on yet)

The address is given **on page 15**. | You'll find the answers at **the bottom of the page**. | Her picture appeared on **the front page** of a local newspaper. | Complete the booking form on the **opposite page**. | The answers are **over the page**. | I never read the **business pages**. | a **full page** article | a **half-page** ad | a **400 page** novel | She waited, idly **turning the pages** of a magazine. | He took out a notebook, and **flicked through** the pages. | For full details **see page** 99. | One name seemed to **leap off the page** from the list of candidates. | Start each section of your essay on a **new page**.

2 [COMPUTER] all the writing etc that you can see at one time on a computer screen: a **web page** (=a single screen of writing, pictures etc on a website)
3 [YOUNG PERSON] AmE a student, usually a student, who works as a helper to a member of the US Congress
4 on the same page if a group of people are on the same page, they are working well together and have

the same aims: We need to get environmentalists and businesses on the same page to improve things.
5 [BOY] **a)** a boy who served a KNIGHT during the Middle Ages as part of his training **b)** a PAGEBOY (2)
6 [SERVANT] a boy who in the past served a person of high rank
7 a page in history an important event or period of time

page² v [T] **1** to call someone's name out in a public place, especially using a LOUDSPEAKER, in order to find them: She hurried to the reception desk and asked the girl to page her husband. **2** to send a message to someone's PAGER asking them to go somewhere or telephone someone: He was constantly being paged during meetings. | the paging network
  page down phr v to press a special key on a computer that makes the screen show the page after the one you are reading: It's not there, so page down and see if you can find it.
  page through sth phr v AmE to look at a book, magazine etc by turning the pages quickly
  page up phr v to press a special key on a computer that makes the screen show the page before the one you are reading

pag·eant /'pædʒənt/ n [C] **1** an organized public show, often performed outdoors, where people dress in decorated or unusual clothes: a colourful pageant of Scotland's past **2** AmE a public competition for young women in which their appearance, and sometimes other qualities, are compared and judged; **目 beauty contest** **3** the pageant of sth literary a series of historical events that are interesting and important: the pageant of African history

pag·eant·ry /'pædʒəntri/ n [U] impressive ceremonies or events, involving many people wearing special clothes: [+of] the pageantry of a military ceremony

page·boy /'peɪdʒbɔɪ/ n [C] **1** BrE a boy who helps the BRIDE as part of a wedding ceremony; → **bridesmaid** **2** old-fashioned a young man who works in a hotel, club etc, delivering messages, carrying bags etc **3** a woman's HAIRSTYLE in which very straight hair is cut shorter at the front than at the back, and turned under at the ends

pag·er /'peɪdʒə $ -ər/ n [C] a small machine you can carry in your pocket that can receive signals from a telephone. It tells you when someone has sent you a message, or wants you to telephone them, for example by making a noise; **目 beeper**

'page ˌtraffic n [U] technical the number of people who read a page in a magazine, newspaper etc

pa·gi·na·tion /ˌpædʒ̩'neɪʃən/ n [U] technical the process of giving a number to each page of a book, magazine etc —**paginate** /'pædʒ̩neɪt/ v [T]

pa·go·da /pə'ɡəʊdə $ -'ɡoʊ-/ n [C] a Buddhist TEMPLE (=religious building) that has several levels with a decorated roof at each level

pah /pɑː/ interjection BrE used to show that you disapprove strongly of something

paid [S2] /peɪd/ v the past tense and past participle of PAY → put paid to sth at PUT (15)

ˌpaid-'up adj BrE informal **1** a fully paid-up member of sth if someone is a fully paid-up member of a particular group, they strongly support what that group likes or believes in: a fully paid-up member of the celebrity circuit **2** paid-up member someone who has paid the money needed to be a member of a club, political party etc: The competition is open to all paid-up members of the Women's Institute.

pail /peɪl/ n [C] especially AmE **1** a metal or wooden container with a handle, used for carrying liquids; **目 bucket**: a milk pail | [+of] a pail of water **2** also **pailful** /-fʊl/ the amount of liquid a pail will hold

pain[1] S2 W2 /peɪn/ n

1 [C,U] the feeling you have when part of your body hurts

have a pain in your stomach/leg/side etc
be in pain
chest pain/back pain/neck pain etc
severe/terrible/chronic pain
sharp pain (=a short but severe pain)
excruciating pain (=very severe pain)
dull pain (=one that is not severe but continues for a long time)
nagging pain (=one that continues for a long time and keeps BOTHERING you)
shooting pain (=a severe pain that starts in one place then quickly moves to another)
ease/relieve/kill pain
pain relief/control
inflict pain (on sb)
labour pains (=pain felt by a woman who is starting to have a baby)
aches and pains (=slight feelings of pain that are not very serious)

[+in] *The pain in her jaw had come back.* | *I had a nasty pain in my leg.* | *Greg was in a lot of pain.* | *If you suffer from back pain, consult your doctor before attempting this exercise.* | *The patient complained of severe chest pains.* | *She felt a sharp pain in her stomach* | *Morphine is used to relieve pain.* | *drugs for pain relief* | *She hated the thought of anyone inflicting pain on an animal.* | *a few minor aches and pains*
→ GROWING PAINS (2)

2 [C,U] the feeling of unhappiness you have when you are sad, upset, etc: *the pain and grief of bereavement* | **cause (sb) pain/inflict pain on sb** *She hated to say the words, for fear of causing pain.*

3 be a pain (in the neck) *spoken* also **be a pain in the ass/arse/backside/butt** *not polite* to be very annoying: *There were times when Joe could be a real pain in the neck.* | *It's a pain, having to go upstairs to make the coffee every time.*

4 take/go to (great) pains to do sth also **take pains with/over sth** to make a special effort to do something: *He's taken great pains to improve his image.*

5 be at pains to do sth to be especially careful to make sure people understand what you are saying or what you plan to do: *Roy was at pains to point out that English was the only exam he'd ever failed.*

6 for your pains as a reward for something you worked to achieve – used especially when this is disappointing: *I fetched the file, and all I got for my pains was a dirty look from Simon.*

7 on/under pain of death at the risk of being killed as punishment, if you do not obey: *Communist activity was prohibited on pain of death.*

WORD FOCUS: PAIN
pain in different parts of your body: **headache, backache, toothache, earache, stomach ache, my leg/arm/neck etc hurts**
to feel a lot of pain: **be in agony**
what you say when something hurts: **ouch**
→ **painful, sore, twinge**

pain[2] *v* [T] **it pains sb to do sth** *formal* used to say that it is very difficult and upsetting for someone to have to do something

'pain ,barrier *n* **the pain barrier** in sport, the point that you reach when you continue trying to do something, even though you are in pain, very tired, or injured: *Iona reached the final, but she had to go through the pain barrier to get there.*

pained /peɪnd/ *adj* **pained expression/look/voice etc** someone's expression, voice etc that shows they are worried, upset, or slightly annoyed: *He sat stiffly, with a pained expression on his face.*

pain·ful /'peɪnfəl/ *adj* **1** making you feel very upset, or very difficult and unpleasant for you; ⊟ **painless**:

painful memories/experience etc *He sobbed as he recalled the painful memory.* | *Venice was a painful reminder of her marriage.* | *He and his wife took the painful decision to switch off their son's life support machine.* | *the long and painful process of growing up* | **painful to do sth** *It can be painful to leave the house in which you were born.* | [+for/to] *The divorce was painful for both of us.* | *Even hearing his name was painful to her.* **2** if a part of your body is painful, it hurts: *stiff, painful joints* | *Is your arm very painful?* | *The neck becomes swollen and painful to the touch* (=hurts when you touch it). **3** causing physical pain: *a painful blow on the head* | **excruciatingly/extremely painful** *an excruciatingly painful death* | **painful to do sth** *He was finding it painful to breathe.* **4** if someone's behaviour or a performance is painful, it is so bad that it embarrasses people: **painful to watch/listen/hear to etc** *It's painful to watch her making the best of a terrible script.* ⚠ Do not use **painful** to mean 'feeling pain': *He didn't feel much pain (NOT feel very painful) at first!*

pain·ful·ly /'peɪnfəli/ *adv* **1** very – used to emphasize a bad or harmful quality that someone or something has: *painfully thin arms* | *As a teenager, I was painfully shy.* | *The road to peace is a painfully slow process.* | *We are only too painfully aware of the damage his actions have caused.* | **painfully obvious/clear/evident/apparent** *It was painfully obvious he'd rather not see her again.* **2** with pain or causing pain: *Robyn swallowed painfully.* **3** needing a lot of effort: *all the knowledge that he had so painfully acquired*

pain·kill·er /'peɪn,kɪlə $ -ər/ *n* [C] a medicine which reduces or removes pain: *an overdose of painkillers*

pain·kill·ing /'peɪn,kɪlɪŋ/ *adj* [only before noun] able to reduce or remove pain: *painkilling drugs*

pain·less /'peɪnləs/ *adj* **1** causing no pain: *a painless death* **2** not difficult or unpleasant to do: *The train is a quick and painless way to travel.* | *The interview was relatively painless.* —**painlessly** *adv*

pains·tak·ing /'peɪnz,teɪkɪŋ/ *adj* [usually before noun] very careful and thorough: *The work had been done with painstaking attention to detail.* | *Chris described in painstaking detail what had happened.* —**painstakingly** *adv*: *The old painting was painstakingly restored.*

paint[1] S2 W3 /peɪnt/ *n* [U]

1 a liquid that you put on a surface, using a brush to make the surface a particular colour: *a can of blue paint* | *Wet paint* (=used as a warning on signs when something has just been painted) | *The whole house could do with a fresh coat of paint.* | **peeling/flaking paint** (=old paint that is starting to come off the surface) | *All this room needs is a lick of paint* (=paint used to make a place more attractive).

2 paints tubes or dry blocks of a coloured substance, used for painting pictures: *acrylic and oil paints*

paint[2] S2 W3 *v*

1 [I,T] to put paint on a surface: *The ceiling needs painting.* | **brightly painted** *houses* | **paint sth (in) blue/red/green etc** *We painted the door blue.* | *Paint the walls in a contrasting colour.* | *The living room was painted in pastel shades of pink and blue.*

2 [I,T] to make a picture, design etc using paint: *A white cross was painted on the door.* | *Turner is famous for painting landscapes.* | **paint in oils/watercolours etc** (=paint using a particular type of paint) *He paints mainly in acrylics.*

3 [T] to put a coloured substance on part of your face or body to make it different or more attractive: *The children's faces were painted to look like animals.* | *She'd painted her toenails with red nail polish.*

4 [T] to describe someone or something in a particular way: **paint sb/sth as sth** *She's often been painted as a tough businesswoman.* | **paint a grim/rosy/gloomy picture of sb/sth** *Dickens painted a grim picture of Victorian life.* | *The article painted him in a bad light* (=described him in a way that made him seem bad).

5 paint the town (red) *informal* to go out to bars, clubs etc **to enjoy yourself** → **not be as black as you are painted** at BLACK¹ (10)

    paint sth ⇔ **out** phr v
to cover part of a picture or sign with paint so that it can no longer be seen: *The name of the firm had been partially painted out.*

    paint over sth phr v
to cover a picture or surface with new paint: *Much of the original decoration was painted over.*

paint·ball /'peɪntbɔːl $ -bɒːl/ n [U] a game in which you shoot small containers of paint at people

paint·box /'peɪntbɒks $ -bɑːks/ n [C] a small box containing dry paint that you mix with water

paint·brush /'peɪntbrʌʃ/ n [C] a brush for spreading paint on a surface → see picture at BRUSH¹

paint·er /'peɪntə $ -ər/ n [C] **1** someone who paints pictures; ▣ **artist**: *Gerry's ambition was to become a portrait painter.* **2** someone whose job is painting houses or other buildings: **painter and decorator** BrE

paint·er·ly /'peɪntəli $ -tər-/ adj written typical of painters or painting: *painterly images*

paintings

still life

landscape

abstract

portrait

paint·ing S3 W2 /'peɪntɪŋ/ n
1 [C] a painted picture that you put on a wall for people to see: *a collection of valuable paintings* | [+of] *There was a large painting of his father on the wall.* | *Can you help me* **hang** *this* **painting** (=put it on a wall)? → OIL PAINTING
2 [U] the act or skill of making a picture, using paints: *Degas's style of painting* | *the Cubist school of painting* (=a particular style used by a group of people)
3 [U] the work of covering a wall, house etc with paint: **painting and decorating** BrE

'paint job n [singular] informal if a car has a paint job, it is painted again: *old cars that are given a quick paint job before being sold*

'paint ˌstripper n [U] a powerful chemical substance used to remove paint from walls, doors etc

paint·work /'peɪntwɜːk $ -wɜːrk/ n [U] paint on a car, house etc: *She noticed the peeling paintwork.*

pair¹ S2 W2 /peə $ per/ n plural **pairs** or **pair** [C]
1 JOINED TOGETHER an object that is made from two similar parts that are joined together: **pair of trousers/scissors/glasses etc** *two pairs of jeans* | *a pair of black tights*
2 BELONGING TOGETHER two things of the same type that are used together: [+of] *a new pair of sandals* | **pair of hands/eyes/legs etc** *She felt as if every pair of eyes in the room was on her.* | *earrings, £5 a pair* | *a pair of skis* | *We have five pairs of free tickets to give away.*
3 in pairs in groups of two: *We* **worked in pairs** *for the role-play exercise.* | *The leaves of the tree are arranged in pairs.*
4 TWO PEOPLE two people who are standing or doing something together, or who have some type of connection with each other; → **couple**: *The pair are looking for sponsorship from local businesses.* | [+of] *a pair of dancers* ⚠ Do not use **pair** to talk about a husband and wife (or two people in a similar relationship). Use **couple**: *They're such a nice couple* (NOT *pair*).
5 the pair of you/them BrE spoken used when you are angry or annoyed with two people: *Oh, get out, the pair of you.*
6 TWO ANIMALS **a)** a male and a female animal that come together in order to BREED: [+of] *a pair of doves* | *a breeding pair* **b)** old use two horses that work together
7 I've only got one pair of hands spoken used to say that you are busy and cannot do any more than you are already doing
8 an extra pair of hands someone who helps you do something when you are busy: *Having an extra pair of hands during busy periods can take the pressure off.*
9 a safe pair of hands someone you can trust and depend on because they are sensible – used especially in news reports: *Colleagues regard him as a safe pair of hands.*

pair² v **1** [I,T usually passive] to put people or things into groups of two, or to form groups of two: **be paired with sb** *We were each paired with a newcomer to help with training.* **2** also **pair up** [I] if animals pair, they come together in order to BREED
    pair off phr v to come together or bring two people together to have a romantic relationship: *All the others were pairing off and I was left on my own.* | **pair sb off with sb** *My aunt was forever pairing me off with unsuitable men.*
    pair up phr v **1** BrE to become friends and start to have a relationship: *We learned later that he and Tanya had paired up.* **2** to work together to do something or to put two people together to do something: *They first paired up in the screen adaptation of 'Grease'.* | **pair sb** ⇔ **up** *They have paired up writers and artists, and commissioned linked works.* **3** if animals pair up, they come together in order to BREED

pais·ley /'peɪzli/ n [U] a pattern consisting of curved shapes used on cloth: *a paisley shawl*

pa·ja·mas /pə'dʒɑːməz $ -'dʒɑː-, -'dʒæ-/ n [plural] the American spelling of PYJAMAS

pak choi /ˌpæk 'tʃɔɪ $ ˌpɑːk-/ BrE; **bok choy** AmE n [U] a green vegetable similar to CABBAGE that is used in Chinese cooking

Pa·ki /'pæki/ n [C] BrE taboo a very offensive word for someone from Pakistan or India. Do not use this word.

Pak·i·sta·ni¹ /ˌpækɪ'stɑːni‹ $ -'stæni/ adj relating to Pakistan or its people

Pakistani² n [C] someone from Pakistan: *a 20-year-old Pakistani*

pal¹ /pæl/ n [C] **1** informal a close friend; → **mate**: *We've been pals since we were at school.* | *an* **old pal** (=a friend you have had for a long time) **2** spoken used to speak to a man in an unfriendly way: *Look, pal, I don't want you hanging around.*

pal² v **palled, palling**
    pal around phr v AmE if you pal around with someone, you do things together as friends: [+with] *It was nice having someone to pal around with.*
    pal up phr v BrE to become someone's friend: [+with] *She palled up with Neil while travelling round Europe.*

pal·ace W3 /'pælɪs/ n [C]
1 the official home of a person of very high rank, especially a king or queen – often used in names: *Buckingham Palace*
2 **the Palace** especially BrE the people who live in a palace – used in news reports: *The Palace has*

announced that the Duke and Duchess are to separate. **3** a large, beautifully decorated house: *the splendid palaces of Florence*

palace revo·lution also **palace 'coup** *n* [C] a situation in which the people who work for a leader take control and remove that leader's power: *He deposed his father in a palace coup.*

pal·a·din /ˈpælədɪn/ *n* [C] a KNIGHT (=a soldier of high rank) in the Middle Ages who was very brave and loyal

palaeo- /ˈpæliəʊ, peɪ- $ peɪlioʊ/ *prefix* another spelling of PALEO-

pal·ae·o·lith·ic /ˌpæliəʊˈlɪθɪk◂, ˌpeɪ- $ ˌpeɪliə-/ *adj* a British spelling of PALEOLITHIC

pal·ae·on·tol·o·gy /ˌpæliɒnˈtɒlədʒi, ˌpeɪ- $ ˌpeɪliɑːnˈtɑː-/ *n* [U] a British spelling of PALEONTOLOGY

pal·at·a·ble /ˈpælətəbəl/ *adj* **1** palatable food or drink has a pleasant or acceptable taste; **₣** **unpalatable**: *a very palatable wine* **2** an idea, suggestion etc that is palatable is acceptable; **₣** **unpalatable**: [+to] *They changed the wording of the advertisement to make it more **palatable** to women.* | *The truth, as always, is slightly less palatable.*

pal·ate /ˈpælət/ *n* **1** [C] the ROOF (=top inside part) of your mouth → CLEFT PALATE, SOFT PALATE **2** [C,U] the sense of taste, and especially your ability to enjoy or judge food: *It tasted very strange, at least to my untrained palate.* | *a collection of dishes to tempt your palate*

pa·la·tial /pəˈleɪʃəl/ *adj* a palatial building etc is large and beautifully decorated: *a palatial country residence*

pa·lat·i·nate /pəˈlætɪnət/ *n* [C] in the past, an area which was controlled by someone who represented the ruler

pa·la·ver /pəˈlɑːvə $ -ˈlævər/ *n* [singular, U] *especially BrE informal* unnecessary trouble and anxiety that makes something seem more important than it really is: *We could have done without all this palaver.* | *What a palaver over nothing!*

pale¹ W3 /peɪl/ *adj*
1 having a skin colour that is very white, or whiter than it usually is: *He looked very pale and drawn.* | **turn/go pale** | *He suddenly went pale.* | *Sharon went **deathly pale** and looked as if she might faint.* | *an elderly, **pale-faced** woman*
2 a pale colour has more white in it than usual; → **deep**; **₣** **light**: *pale blue curtains*
3 pale light is not bright: *the pale gray dawn*
4 pale imitation (of sth) something that is similar to, but not as good as, something else: *The cheese is a pale imitation of real Parmesan.*

pale² *v* [I] **1** *literary* if your face pales, it becomes whiter than usual because you have had a shock: *Kent's face paled when he saw that Rob had a knife.* **2 pale into insignificance** to seem much less important when compared to something bigger, worse, more serious etc: *The amounts of money involved pale into insignificance when compared with the sums spent each year on research.* **3 pale in/by comparison** to seem small or unimportant compared to something else: [+to/with] *Today's economic problems pale in comparison with those of the 1930s.*

pale³ *n* **beyond the pale** offensive or unacceptable: *His opinions are entirely beyond the pale.*

pale 'ale *n* [C,U] *BrE old-fashioned* a type of light-coloured beer that is sold in bottles

paleo-, palaeo- /ˈpæliəʊ, peɪ- $ peɪlioʊ/ *prefix technical* relating to very ancient times

pal·e·o·lith·ic also **palaeolithic** *BrE* /ˌpæliəʊˈlɪθɪk◂, ˌpeɪ- $ ˌpeɪlioʊ-/ often **Paleolithic** *adj* relating to the STONE AGE (=the period of time thousands of years ago when people used stone tools and weapons): *a paleolithic axe* → NEOLITHIC

pal·e·on·tol·o·gy, palaeontology /ˌpæliɒnˈtɒlədʒi, ˌpeɪ- $ ˌpeɪliɑːnˈtɑː-/ *n* [U] the study of FOSSILS

(=ancient bones, plants etc that have been preserved in rock) —**paleontologist** *n* [C]

pal·ette /ˈpælət/ *n* [C] **1** a thin, curved board that an artist uses to mix paints, holding it by putting his or her thumb through a hole at the edge **2** [usually singular] the colours that a particular artist uses or the colours in a particular painting **3** the choice of colours or shapes that are available in a computer program

palette knife *n* [C] a knife that bends easily and is not sharp, used for spreading a substance, for example in cooking or painting

pa·li·mo·ny /ˈpæliməni $ -moʊni/ *n* [U] *especially AmE* an amount of money that a law court orders someone to pay regularly to a former partner that they were living with but were not married to

pal·imp·sest /ˈpælɪmpsest/ *n* [C] *technical* an ancient document on which the original writing has been covered over with new writing

pal·in·drome /ˈpælɪndrəʊm $ -droʊm/ *n* [C] a word or phrase such as 'deed' or 'level', which is the same when you spell it backwards

pal·ing /ˈpeɪlɪŋ/ *n* [C,U] a wooden or metal post that is pointed at the top, or a fence made of these posts: *A new paling had been erected around the yard.* | *iron palings*

pal·i·sade /ˌpælɪˈseɪd/ *n* [C] **1** a strong fence made of pointed posts **2** also **palisades** *AmE* a line of high straight cliffs, especially beside water

pall¹ /pɔːl $ pɒːl/ *v* [I not in progressive] *literary* if something palls, it becomes less interesting or enjoyable because you have experienced it before: *Gradually, the novelty of city life began to pall.*

pall² *n* [C] **1** [usually singular] a thick, dark cloud of smoke, dust etc: **pall of smoke/dust/ash etc** *A pall of thick grey smoke hung over the buildings.* **2 a pall of sth** *literary* an unpleasant quality that seems to be in a place or situation: *The area is enveloped in a pall of neglect.* **3** a cloth used to cover a COFFIN (=a box containing a dead body)

pal·la·di·um /pəˈleɪdiəm/ *n* [U] a soft silver-white metal that is often combined with gold and silver, and used to cover an object with a very thin layer of metal. It is a chemical ELEMENT: symbol Pd

pall·bear·er /ˈpɔːlˌbeərə $ ˈpɒːlˌberər/ *n* [C] someone who helps to carry a COFFIN at a funeral

pal·let /ˈpælət/ *n* [C] **1** a large frame, used for storing or carrying heavy things: *wooden pallets* **2** a rough cloth bag filled with STRAW, used in the past for sleeping on

pal·li·ate /ˈpælieɪt/ *v* [T] *formal* to reduce the effects of illness, pain etc without curing them: *Chosen carefully, the oils may not only palliate but also cure the condition.*

pal·li·a·tive /ˈpæliətɪv $ -ətɪv, -eɪtɪv/ *n* [C] **1** *formal* something done to make a bad situation seem better, but which does not solve the problem: *short-term economic palliatives* **2** *medical* a medical treatment that will not cure an illness but will reduce the pain —**palliative** *adj* [usually before noun]: *palliative care*

pal·lid /ˈpælɪd/ *adj* **1** very pale, especially in a way that looks weak or unhealthy: *pallid cheeks* **2** not very interesting: *a pallid performance*

pal·lor /ˈpælə $ -ər/ *n* [singular, U] when someone's skin is very pale in a way that makes them look weak or unhealthy: *A sleepless night had added to her pallor.*

pal·ly /ˈpæli/ *adj* [not before noun] *BrE informal* very friendly with someone: *She's pally with Steven.*

palm¹ /pɑːm $ pɑːm, pɑːlm/ *n* [C]
1 PART OF HAND the inside surface of your hand, in which you hold things: **in sb's palm** *She looked at the coins in her palm.* | *He held the pebble **in the palm of his hand**.* → see picture at HAND¹
2 TREE also **palm tree** a tropical tree which grows near beaches or in deserts, with a long straight trunk and large pointed leaves at the top: *coconut palms*
3 hold/have sb in the palm of your hand to have a strong

influence on someone, so that they do what you want them to do

4 read sb's palm to tell someone what is going to happen to them in the future by looking at the lines on their hand → **cross sb's palm (with silver)** at CROSS[1] (18); → **grease sb's palm** at GREASE[2] (2)

palm² v [T] to hide something in the palm of your hand, especially when you are performing a magic trick or stealing something

palm sth ⇔ **off** phr v to persuade someone to accept or buy something that is not of good quality or is not the thing that they really want: [+on/onto] He tried to palm off his old books onto me. | [+as] Dealers sometimes palm off fakes as genuine works of art.

palm sb **off with** sth phr v to give someone an explanation that is not true but that you hope they will accept

palm·ist /'pɑːmɪ̣st $ 'pɑːm-, 'pɑːlm-/ n [C] BrE someone who claims they can tell what will happen to a person by looking at the lines on the palm of their hand

palm·ist·ry /'pɑːmɪ̣stri $ 'pɑːm-, 'pɑːlm-/ n [U] the art of looking at the palm of a person's hand to tell what will happen to them in the future

palm oil n [U] the oil obtained from the nut of an African PALM TREE

palm reader n [C] a PALMIST

palm-sized adj **palm-sized computer/PC/PDA** a palm-sized computer, PC etc is small enough to fit in your hand

Palm Sunday n the Sunday before Easter in the Christian Church

palm·top /'pɑːmtɒp $ 'pɑːmtɑːp, 'pɑːlm-/ n [C] a very small computer that you can hold in your hand; → **laptop, notebook**

palm tree also **palm** n [C] a tropical tree which grows near beaches or in deserts, with a long straight trunk and large pointed leaves at the top

pal·o·mi·no /ˌpælə'miːnəʊ ◂ -noʊ◂/ n plural **palominos** [C] a horse that is a golden or cream colour, with a white MANE and tail

pal·pa·ble /'pælpəbəl/ adj formal **1** a feeling that is palpable is so strong that other people notice it and can feel it around them; ⊟ **impalpable**: There was a palpable sense of relief among the crowd. **2** [only before noun] complete: What he said is palpable nonsense. —**palpably** adv: This was palpably untrue.

pal·pate /pæl'peɪt $ 'pælpeɪt/ v [T] medical to touch part of someone's body in order to examine it

pal·pi·tate /'pælpɪ̣teɪt/ v [I] if your heart palpitates, it beats quickly in an irregular way

pal·pi·ta·tions /ˌpælpɪ̣'teɪʃənz/ n [plural] if you have palpitations, your heart beats quickly in an irregular way

pal·sy /'pɔːlzi $ 'pɒːl-/ n [U] **1** an illness that makes your arms and legs shake because you cannot control your muscles **2** old use PARALYSIS → CEREBRAL PALSY

pal·sy-wal·sy /ˌpælzi 'wælzi/ adj BrE spoken very friendly with someone – used especially when you disapprove of this

pal·try /'pɔːltri $ 'pɒːl-/ adj **1** a paltry amount of something is too small to be useful or important: **paltry sum** of money | He received only a paltry £25 a day. **2** formal unimportant or worthless: paltry issues

pam·pas /'pæmpəs, -pəz/ n **the pampas** the large flat areas of land covered with grass in some parts of South America

pampas grass n [U] a type of tall grass with silver-white feathery flowers

pam·per /'pæmpə $ -ər/ v [T] to look after someone very kindly, for example by giving them the things that they want and making them feel warm and comfortable: She spent her childhood as the pampered daughter of a wealthy family. | **pamper yourself** Pamper yourself with a stay in one of our luxury hotels.

pam·phlet /'pæmflɪ̣t/ n [C] a very thin book with paper covers, that gives information about something; → **leaflet**: a political pamphlet

pam·phle·teer /ˌpæmflɪ̣'tɪə $ -'tɪr/ n [C] someone who writes pamphlets giving political opinions

pans

cooking pot   frying pan

saucepan   roasting pan

pan¹ /pæn/ n [C]

1 FOR COOKING a round metal container that you use for cooking, usually with one long handle and a lid; ⊟ **saucepan**: a frying pan | pots and pans | Cook the pasta in a large pan of boiling water.

2 FOR BAKING CAKES ETC AmE a metal container for baking things in; ⊟ **tin** BrE: a cake pan

3 OPEN CONTAINER AmE a wide, usually round, open container with low sides, used for holding liquids

4 TOILET BrE the bowl of a toilet

5 go down the pan BrE informal to be wasted or become useless or ruined: The business is rapidly going down the pan. → WARMING PAN; → **a flash in the pan** at FLASH² (5)

pan² v **panned, panning**

1 CRITICIZE [T] informal to strongly criticize a film, play etc in a newspaper or on television or radio: The movie was panned by the critics.

2 CAMERA a) [I always + adv/prep] if a film or television camera pans in a particular direction, it moves in that direction and follows the thing that is being filmed: The camera panned slowly across the crowd. b) [I,T] to move a camera in this way

3 GOLD [I,T] to wash soil in a metal container in order to separate gold from other substances: [+for] panning for gold in Alaska

pan out phr v to happen or develop in a particular way: We'll have to see how things pan out.

pan- Pan- /pæn/ prefix including all people: pan-African unity

pan·a·cea /ˌpænə'sɪə/ n [C] something that people think will make everything better and solve all their problems; ⊟ **cure-all**: [+for] There is no panacea for the country's economic problems.

pa·nache /pə'næʃ, pæ-/ n [U] a way of doing things that makes them seem easy and exciting, and makes other people admire you; → **style**: with panache They played and sang with great panache.

pan·a·ma hat /ˌpænəmɑː 'hæt/ also **panama** /ˌpænə'mɑː◂, 'pænəmɑː/ n [C] a light hat for men, made from STRAW

pan·cake /'pænkeɪk/ n **1** [C] a thin flat round cake made from flour, milk, and eggs, that has been cooked in a flat pan and is eaten hot; → **crêpe 2** [U] very thick MAKE-UP for your face, that is worn especially by actors

Pancake Day, Pancake Tuesday n [C,U] BrE SHROVE TUESDAY, when people in Britain traditionally eat pancakes

pan·cre·as /'pæŋkriəs/ n [C] a GLAND inside your body, near your stomach, that produces INSULIN and a liquid that helps your body to use the food that you eat —**pancreatic** /ˌpæŋkri'ætɪk◂/ adj

pan·da /'pændə/ n [C] **1** a large black and white animal that looks like a bear and lives in the mountains of China → see picture at BEAR² **2** a small animal with red-brown fur and a long tail that lives in the south-eastern Himalayas

'**Panda car** n [C] BrE informal a small black and white police car

pan·dem·ic /pæn'demɪk/ n [C] technical a disease that affects people over a very large area or the whole world; → **endemic**, **epidemic**: the AIDS pandemic —**pandemic** adj

pan·de·mo·ni·um /ˌpændɪ'məʊniəm $ -'moʊ-/ n [U] a situation in which there is a lot of noise because people are angry, confused or frightened; 🔲 **chaos**: There was complete **pandemonium** in the kitchen. | When the verdict was read **pandemonium broke out** in the courtroom.

pan·der /'pændə $ -ər/ v
pander to sb/sth phr v to give someone anything they want in order to please them, even if it seems unreasonable or unnecessary – used to show disapproval: Some newspapers feel they have to pander to the prejudices of their readers. | Highly trained staff will **pander to** your **every whim**.

Pan·do·ra's box /pæn,dɔːrəz 'bɒks $ -'bɑːks/ n **open a Pandora's box** to do or start something that will cause a lot of other problems: The report could open up a Pandora's box of claims from similar cases.

pane /peɪn/ n [C] a piece of glass used in a window or door: a window pane | a pane of glass → WINDOWPANE

pan·e·gyr·ic /ˌpænɪ'dʒɪrɪk/ n [C] old-fashioned formal a speech or piece of writing that praises someone or something a lot

pan·el [S1] [W2] /'pænl/ n [C]
1 GROUP OF PEOPLE [also + plural verb BrE] **a)** a group of people with skills or SPECIALIST knowledge who have been chosen to give advice or opinions on a particular subject: [+of] A panel of experts has looked at the proposal. | **on a panel** There will be at least three senior doctors on the panel. **b)** a group of well-known people who answer questions on a radio or television programme; → **panellist**: **on a panel** We have two senior politicians on our panel tonight. **c)** AmE a group of people who are chosen to listen to a case in a court of law and to decide the result; 🔲 **jury**: The panel spent 14 hours going over the evidence.
2 PIECE OF SOMETHING **a)** a flat piece of wood, glass etc with straight sides, which forms part of a door, wall, fence etc: a stained glass panel | There were a few panels missing from the fence. **b)** a piece of metal that forms part of the outer structure of a vehicle: One of the door panels was badly damaged and had to be replaced. **c)** a piece of material that forms part of a piece of clothing: a skirt made in six panels
3 instrument/control panel a board in a car, plane, boat etc that has the controls on it
4 PICTURE a thin board with a picture painted on it → SOLAR PANEL

pan·elled BrE; **paneled** AmE /'pænld/ adj covered or decorated with flat pieces of wood: [+with/in] The walls were panelled with oak.

pan·el·ling BrE; **paneling** AmE /'pænəl-ɪŋ/ n [U] long or square pieces of wood that are used to cover and decorate walls

pan·el·list BrE; **panelist** AmE /'pænəl-ɪst/ n [C] one of a group of well-known people who answer questions on a radio or television programme

'**panel pin** n [C] BrE a short, thin nail that is used for fastening thin pieces of wood together

'**panel truck** n [C] AmE a small motor vehicle used for delivering goods

pang /pæŋ/ n [C] a sudden feeling of pain, sadness etc: **pang of jealousy/guilt/remorse/regret** She felt a sudden pang of guilt. | **hunger pangs**

pan·han·dle¹ /'pæn,hændl/ n [C] AmE a long, thin area of land that sticks out from a larger area: the Texas panhandle

panhandle² v [I] especially AmE informal to ask for money in the streets; 🔲 **beg**: homeless people panhandling in the subway —**panhandler** n [C]

pan·ic¹ [S3] /'pænɪk/ n
1 [C usually singular, U] a sudden strong feeling of fear or nervousness that makes you unable to think clearly or behave sensibly: **in (a) panic** The children fled in panic. | a feeling of **sheer panic** (=complete panic) | She **got into a panic** when she couldn't find the tickets. | The whole nation is **in a state of panic** following the attacks. | She suffers from terrible **panic attacks**.
2 [C usually singular, U] a situation in which people are suddenly made very anxious, and make quick decisions without thinking carefully: [+over/about] the recent panic over the safety of baby milk | **panic buying/selling** a wave of panic selling in Hong Kong
3 [singular] especially BrE a situation in which you have a lot to do and not much time to do it in; → **rush**: the usual last minute panic just before the deadline
4 panic stations BrE a situation in which everyone is busy and anxious because something needs to be done urgently: It was panic stations here on Friday.

panic² v panicked, panicking [I,T] to suddenly feel so frightened that you cannot think clearly or behave sensibly, or to make someone do this: He started to panic when he saw the gun. | **Don't panic!** We'll soon get you out of there. | **panic sb into doing sth** The protests became more violent and many people were panicked into leaving the country.

'**panic ˌbutton** n [C] **1** a button that you can press to call for help if you are being attacked **2** **press/push the panic button** BrE to do something quickly without thinking enough about it, because something unexpected or dangerous has suddenly happened

pan·ic·ky /'pænɪki/ adj informal very nervous and anxious: By 10 o'clock she was starting to get a bit panicky.

'**panic-ˌstricken** adj so frightened that you cannot think clearly or behave sensibly: Lucy suddenly looked panic-stricken.

pan·ni·er /'pæniə $ -ər/ n [C] **1** one of a pair of baskets or bags that you carry one on each side of an animal or a bicycle; → **saddlebag** **2** a basket in which someone carries a load on their back

pan·o·ply /'pænəpli/ n [singular] formal **1** an impressive show of special clothes, decorations etc, especially at an important ceremony: [+of] a glorious panoply of colours **2** a large number of people or things: [+of] a panoply of men in grey suits | **full/entire/whole panoply of sth** (=the whole range of something)

pan·o·ra·ma /ˌpænə'rɑːmə $ -'ræmə/ n [C usually singular] **1** an impressive view of a wide area of land: [+of] The tower offers a panorama of the city. | a breathtaking panorama of mountains **2** a description or series of pictures that shows all the features of a subject, historical period etc: [+of] a panorama of life in England 400 years ago —**panoramic** /ˌpænə'ræmɪk◂/ adj: a panoramic view of the valley

pan·pipes /'pænpaɪps/ n [plural] a simple musical instrument made of short wooden pipes of different lengths, that you play by blowing across their open ends

pan·sy /'pænzi/ n plural pansies [C] **1** a small garden plant with brightly coloured flowers **2** informal not polite an offensive word for a man who seems weak and too much like a woman

pant /pænt/ v **1** [I] to breathe quickly with short noisy breaths, for example because you have been running or because it is very hot: He came in panting after running up the steps. | He was **panting for breath**. | The dog lay panting on the doorstep. **2** [T] to say something while you are panting: 'I can't run any farther,' she panted. —**pant** n [C]

pant for sth *phr v* to want something very much: *He came in panting for a cup of tea.*

pan·ta·loons /ˌpæntəˈluːnz/ *n* [plural] *old-fashioned* long trousers with wide legs, that become tight at the bottom of your legs

pan·tech·ni·con /pænˈteknɪkən $ -kɑːn/ *n* [C] *BrE old-fashioned* a REMOVAL VAN

pan·the·is·m /ˈpænθi-ɪzəm/ *n* [U] the religious idea that God and the universe are one thing and that God is present in all natural things —**pantheist** *n* [C] —**pantheistic** /ˌpænθiˈɪstɪk◂/ *adj*

pan·the·on /ˈpænθiən $ -θiɑːn/ *n* [C] **1** all the gods of a particular people or nation: *the Roman pantheon* **2** *literary* a group of famous and important people: [+of] *a leading figure in the pantheon of 20th century artists* **3** a religious building that is built in honour of all gods

pan·ther /ˈpænθə $ -ər/ *n* [C] **1** a large wild animal that is black and a member of the cat family → see picture at BIG CAT **2** *AmE* a COUGAR

pan·ties /ˈpæntiz/ *n* [plural] *especially AmE* a piece of women's underwear that covers the area between their waist and the top of their legs; ◨ **knickers** *BrE*: *a pair of lacy panties*

pan·ti·hose /ˈpæntihəʊz $ -hoʊz/ *n* [plural] *AmE* another spelling of PANTYHOSE

pan·tile /ˈpæntaɪl/ *n* [C usually plural] *BrE* a curved TILE used for covering a roof

pan·to /ˈpæntəʊ $ -toʊ/ *n plural* **pantos** [C,U] *BrE informal* pantomime

pan·to·graph /ˈpæntəɡrɑːf $ -ɡræf/ *n* [C] *technical* **1** an instrument used to make a smaller or larger exact copy of a drawing, plan etc **2** a thing on top of an electric train which takes electric power from an electric power line above it

pan·to·mime /ˈpæntəmaɪm/ *n* **1** [C,U] a type of play for children that is performed in Britain around Christmas, in which traditional stories are performed with jokes, music, and songs **2** [C,U] a method of performing using only actions and not words, or a play performed using this method; ◨ **mime** **3** [C] *BrE* a situation or behaviour that is silly

pan·try /ˈpæntri/ *n plural* **pantries** [C] a very small room in a house where food is kept; ◨ **larder**

pants¹ S3 /pænts/ *n* [plural]
1 *especially AmE* a piece of clothing that covers you from your waist to your feet and has a separate part for each leg; ◨ **trousers** *BrE*: *She was wearing dark blue pants and a white sweater.*
2 *BrE* a piece of underwear that covers the area between your waist and the top of your legs; ◨ **underpants** *AmE*; → **knickers**, **briefs**, **boxer shorts**
3 bore/scare etc the pants off sb *informal spoken* to make someone feel very bored, very frightened etc: *She always bores the pants off me.*
4 beat the pants off sb *AmE spoken* to defeat someone very easily in a game or competition; ◨ **thrash**
5 sb puts his pants on one leg at a time *AmE spoken* used to say that someone is just like everyone else: *Go on, ask him for his autograph – he puts his pants on one leg at a time just like you do.*
6 (since sb was) in short pants *BrE informal* since someone was a very young boy: *I've known Eric since he was in short pants.* → **do sth by the seat of your pants** at SEAT¹ (10); → **catch sb with their pants down** at CATCH¹ (6); → **wear the pants/trousers** at WEAR¹ (7)

pants² *adj* [not before noun] *BrE spoken informal* very bad: *The concert was pants.*

pant·suit /ˈpæntsuːt, -sjuːt $ -suːt/ *n* [C] *AmE* a woman's suit consisting of a jacket and matching trousers

pan·ty·hose, **pantihose** /ˈpæntihəʊz $ -hoʊz/ *n* [plural] *AmE* a very thin piece of women's clothing that covers their legs from the toes to the waist and is usually worn with dresses or skirts; ◨ **tights** *BrE*

pan·ty·lin·er /ˈpæntilaɪnə $ -ər/ *n* [C] a very thin SANITARY PAD

---

pap /pæp/ *n* [U] **1** films, programmes, books etc that are badly made or badly written, are intended for entertainment only, and have no serious value: *Hollywood produces a lot of pap.* **2** *especially BrE* very soft food that does not have a strong taste, like the food that babies eat → PAP SMEAR

pa·pa /pəˈpɑː $ ˈpɑːpə/ *n* [C] *old-fashioned* a way of talking to or about your father: *Good morning, Papa!*

pa·pa·cy /ˈpeɪpəsi/ *n* **1 the papacy** the position and authority of the Pope **2** [U] the time during which a Pope is in power

pap·a·dum /ˈpæpədəm $ ˈpɑː-/ *n* another spelling of POPPADOM

pa·pal /ˈpeɪpəl/ *adj* [only before noun] relating to the Pope: *a challenge to papal authority*

pap·a·raz·zi /ˌpæpəˈrætsi $ ˌpɑːpəˈrɑː-/ *n* [plural] photographers who follow famous people in order to take photographs they can sell to newspapers

pa·pa·ya /pəˈpaɪə/ *n* [C] the large yellow-green fruit of a tropical tree

pa·per¹ S1 W1 /ˈpeɪpə $ -ər/ *n*
1 FOR WRITING/WRAPPING [U] material in the form of thin sheets that is used for writing on, wrapping things etc: **piece/sheet of paper** *Write it down on a piece of paper.* | **scrap/slip of paper** (=a small piece of paper) | *recycled paper* | *a box wrapped in plain brown paper* | *flowers made from* **tissue paper** (=very light thin paper) | **writing/wrapping paper** *sheets of writing paper*; → see picture at MATERIAL¹; → see picture at OFFICE
⚠ When **paper** refers to the material that you write on, it is an uncountable noun. Do not say that something is written on 'a paper'. Say that it is written on **a piece of paper.**
2 NEWSPAPER [C] a newspaper: *Have you seen today's paper?* | *You'll read about it in tomorrow's papers.* | **Sunday/evening/daily paper** *The story was all over the Sunday papers.* | **local/national/trade paper** *Why don't you put an ad in the local paper?*
3 DOCUMENTS/LETTERS papers [plural] **a)** pieces of paper with writing on them that you use in your work, at meetings etc: *I left some important papers in my briefcase.* **b)** documents and letters concerning someone's private or public life: *While I was organizing Simon's papers I came across his diaries.* **c)** *divorce papers* documents concerning a DIVORCE **d)** official documents such as your PASSPORT, IDENTITY CARD etc: *My papers are all in order* (=they are legal and correct). → WHITE PAPER, GREEN PAPER, ORDER PAPER
4 on paper a) if you put ideas or information on paper, you write them down: **put/get sth down on paper** *You need to get some of these thoughts down on paper.* **b)** if something seems true on paper, it seems to be true as an idea, but may not be true in a real situation; ◨ **in theory**: *It's a nice idea on paper, but you'll never get it to work.*
5 EXAMINATION [C] *BrE* a set of printed questions used as an examination in a particular subject, and the answers people write: *an exam paper* | *I have a stack of papers to mark.* | **history/French etc paper** *The geography paper was really easy.*
6 SPEECH/PIECE OF WRITING [C] a piece of writing or a talk on a particular subject by someone who has made a study of it: *a scientific paper* | [+on] *a paper on psychology* | *Professor Usborne gave a* **paper** *on recent developments in his field.*
7 PIECE OF SCHOOLWORK [C] *especially AmE* a piece of writing that is done as part of a course at school or university; ◨ **essay**: [+on] *a paper on the Civil War*
8 OFFICIAL PUBLICATION [C] a report prepared by a government or committee on a question they have been considering or a proposal for changes in the law: *We will publish a* **discussion paper** *on the future of the BBC.* | [+on] *the 1998 White Paper on political reform* | *a* **working paper** (=a report that is not final) *on funding the Health Service*
9 FOR WALLS [C,U] paper for covering and decorating

the walls of a room; ☐ **wallpaper**: *a floral paper*
10 FINANCIAL [C,U] STOCKS and SHARES that can be bought and sold on a financial market
11 TOILET [U] soft thin paper used for cleaning yourself after you have used the toilet; ☐ **toilet paper, toilet roll**
12 not worth the paper it is written on/printed on if something such as a contract is not worth the paper it is written on, it has no value because whatever is promised in it will not happen → **put/set pen to paper** at PEN¹ (3); → WASTE PAPER

paper² *adj* [only before noun] **1** made of paper: *a paper bag* **2** written or printed on paper: *The brochure is available in electronic and paper versions.* **3 paper qualifications** an expression meaning documents showing that you have passed particular examinations, used specially when you think that experience and knowledge are more important: *Paper qualifications are no guide to ability.* **4** existing only as an idea but not having any real value: *paper profits* (=a record of the value of something, that is not real until the thing is sold) | *paper promises*

paper³ *v* [T] **1** to decorate the walls of a room by covering them with special paper; ☐ **wallpaper**
2 paper over the cracks to try to hide disagreements or difficulties: *We need to discuss disagreements honestly without papering over the cracks.*

pa·per·back /'peɪpəbæk $ -ər-/ *n* [C] a book with a stiff paper cover; → **hardback**: *a shelf full of paperbacks* | **in paperback** *Her first novel sold over 20,000 copies in paperback.*

pa·per·boy /'peɪpəbɔɪ $ -ər-/ *n* [C] a boy who delivers newspapers to people's houses

'paper chase *n* [C] *informal* an official process that prevents you from doing something quickly because it involves writing or reading a lot of documents; → **bureaucracy, red tape**

pa·per·clip /'peɪpəklɪp $ -ər-/ *n* [C] a small piece of curved wire used for holding sheets of paper together → see picture at OFFICE

'paper ,fastener *n* [C] *BrE* a small metal object like a button used to hold several pieces of paper together

'paper girl *n* [C] a girl who delivers newspapers to people's houses

'paper knife *n* [C] *BrE* a knife for opening envelopes

'paper 'money *n* [U] money made of paper, not coins; → **note**

'paper-,pusher *n* [C] someone whose job is doing unimportant office work; ☐ **pen pusher** *BrE*; ☐ **pencil pusher** *AmE*

'paper round *BrE*, **'paper route** *AmE n* [C] the job of delivering newspapers to a group of houses

'paper shop *n* [C] *BrE* a shop that sells newspapers and magazines, and also things such as tobacco, sweets, and cards; ☐ **newsagent** *BrE*

,paper-'thin *adj* very thin: *paper-thin walls*

,paper 'tiger *n* [C] an enemy or opponent who seems powerful but actually is not

,paper 'towel *n* [C] a sheet of soft thick paper that you use to dry your hands or to clean up small amounts of liquid, food etc

pa·per·weight /'peɪpəweɪt $ -ər-/ *n* [C] a small heavy object used to hold pieces of paper in place

pa·per·work /'peɪpəwɜːk $ -pərwɜːrk/ *n* [U] **1** work such as writing letters or reports, which must be done but is not very interesting: *Police work involves so much paperwork these days.* **2** the documents that you need for a business deal, a journey etc: *I'm leaving the solicitors to sort out the paperwork.*

pa·per·y /'peɪpəri/ *adj* something such as skin or leaves that is papery is very dry and thin and a little stiff

pap·ier-mâ·ché /ˌpæpieɪ 'mæʃeɪ, ˌpeɪpər- $ ˌpeɪpər məˈʃeɪ, ˌpæpjeɪ-/ also **paper-mâché** /ˌpeɪpə-

$ ˌpeɪpər/ *AmE n* [U] a soft substance made from a mixture of paper, water, and glue, which becomes hard when it dries and is used for making pots and other objects

pa·pist /'peɪpɪst/ *n* [C] an insulting word for a member of the Roman Catholic Church, used especially by Protestants

pa·poose /pəˈpuːs $ pæ-/ *n* [C] **1** *BrE* a type of bag attached to a frame, which you use to carry a baby on your back **2** *old use* a Native American baby or young child

pap·ri·ka /'pæprɪkə, pəˈpriːkə $ pəˈpriːkə/ *n* [U] a red powder made from a type of sweet PEPPER, used for giving a slightly hot taste to meat and other food

'Pap smear *n* [C] *AmE* a medical test that takes cells from a woman's CERVIX and examines them for signs of CANCER; ☐ **smear test** *BrE*

pa·py·rus /pəˈpaɪrəs/ *n plural* **papyruses** *or* **papyri** /-raɪ/ **1** [U] a plant like grass that grows in water **2** [C,U] a type of paper made from papyrus and used in ancient Egypt, or a piece of this paper

par /pɑː $ pɑːr/ *n* [U] **1 be on a par (with sth)** to be at the same level or standard: *The wages of clerks were on a par with those of manual workers.* | *We will have Christmas decorations on a par with anything on show at the MetroCentre.* **2 be below/under par a)** to feel a little ill or lacking in energy: *I've been feeling a little under par the last couple of weeks.* **b)** also **not be up to par** to be less good than usual or below the proper standard: *None of the people who'd auditioned were really up to par.* | *The champion was playing well below par.* **3 be par for the course** to be what you would normally expect to happen – used to show disapproval: *Long hours and tough working conditions are often par for the course in catering.* **4** the number of STROKES a good player should take to hit the ball into a hole in the game of GOLF: *The last hole is a par five.* **5** also **par value** *technical* the value of a STOCK or BOND that is printed on it when it is first sold: *bonds sold at 97% of their par value* | **at/above/below/under par** *The notes are currently trading at 10% above par.* → PAR EXCELLENCE

par·a¹ /'pærə/ *n* [C] *BrE informal* a PARATROOPER

para² also **par** the written abbreviation of *paragraph*

para- /pærə/ *prefix* **1** beyond: *the paranormal* (=strange unnatural events, beyond normal experience) **2** very similar to something: *terrorists wearing paramilitary uniforms* **3** relating to a profession and helping more highly trained people: *a paramedic* (=someone who helps a doctor) | *a paralegal* (=someone who helps a lawyer) **4** relating to PARACHUTES: *a paratrooper* | *paragliding*

par·a·ble /'pærəbəl/ *n* [C] a short simple story that teaches a moral or religious lesson, especially one of the stories told by Jesus in the Bible

pa·rab·o·la /pəˈræbələ/ *n* [C] *technical* a curve in the shape of the imaginary line an object makes when it is thrown high in the air and comes down a little distance away —**parabolic** /ˌpærəˈbɒlɪk◂ $ -ˈbɑː-/ *adj*

par·a·ce·ta·mol /ˌpærəˈsiːtəmɒl, -ˈset- $ -mɑːl, -mɒːl/ *n plural* **paracetamol** *or* **paracetamols** [C,U] *BrE* a common drug used to reduce pain, which does not contain ASPIRIN

par·a·chute¹ /'pærəʃuːt/ *n* [C] a piece of equipment fastened to the back of people who jump out of planes, which makes them fall slowly and safely to the ground: *a parachute jump* → see picture at AERIAL¹

parachute² *v* **1** [I always + adv/prep] to jump from a plane using a parachute: [+into] *They parachuted into Vietnam in 1968.* **2** [T always + adv/prep] to drop something from a plane with a parachute: **parachute sth to/into sth** *Supplies have been parachuted into the area.*

par·a·chut·ist /'pærəʃuːtɪst/ *n* [C] someone who jumps from a plane with a parachute

pa·rade¹ /pəˈreɪd/ *n* [C] **1** a public celebration when musical bands, brightly decorated vehicles etc move down the street: *a victory parade* | *the St Patrick's Day parade* **2** a military ceremony in which soldiers stand or march together so that important people can examine them: *a military parade* | **on parade** (=be standing or marching in a parade) *troops on parade* **3** a line of people moving along so that other people can watch them: *a fashion parade* **4** a series of people, events etc that seems to never end: [+of] *She had a constant parade of young men coming to visit her.* **5** *BrE* a street with a row of small shops → IDENTIFICATION PARADE, HIT PARADE

parade² v

1 PROTEST/CELEBRATE [I always + adv/prep] to walk or march together to celebrate or protest about something: [+around/past etc] *The marchers paraded peacefully through the capital.*

2 SHOW STH [T] if you parade your skills, knowledge, possessions etc, you show them publicly in order to make people admire you; ◼ **show off**: *Young athletes will get a chance to parade their skills.*

3 WALK AROUND [I always + adv/prep] to walk around, especially in a way that shows that you want people to notice and admire you: [+around/past etc] *A trio of girls in extremely tight shorts paraded up and down.*

4 SHOW SB [T always + adv/prep] if prisoners are paraded on television or through the streets, they are shown to the public, in order to prove that the people holding them are important or powerful: *The prisoners were paraded in front of the TV cameras.*

5 PROUDLY SHOW [T] to proudly show something or someone to other people, because you want to look impressive to them; ◼ **show off**: *She paraded her new team.* | *war medals paraded for public admiration*

6 SOLDIERS [I,T] if soldiers parade, or if an officer parades them, they march together so that an important person can watch them

7 parade as sth/be paraded as sth if something parades as something else that is better, someone is pretending that it is the other better thing – used to show disapproval: *It's just self-interest parading as concern for your welfare.*

pa'rade ˌground *n* [C] a place where soldiers practise marching or standing together in rows

par·a·digm /ˈpærədaɪm/ *n* [C] **1** *technical* a model or example that shows how something works or is produced: [+of] *the basic paradigm of the family tree* **2** *formal* a very clear or typical example of something: [+of] *Pius XII remained the paradigm of what a pope should be.* —**paradigmatic** /ˌpærədɪgˈmætɪk◂/ *adj* —**paradigmatically** /-kli/ *adv*

'paradigm ˌshift *n* [C] an important change in which the usual way of thinking or doing something is replaced by another way of thinking or doing something

par·a·dise /ˈpærədaɪs/ *n* **1** [U] a place or situation that is extremely pleasant, beautiful, or enjoyable: *a beautiful tropical paradise* | *The hotel felt like paradise after two weeks of camping.* | *A home near the sea is my idea of paradise.* **2** [singular] a place that has everything you need for doing a particular activity: *The market is a shopper's paradise.* | [+for] *Hawaii is a paradise for surfers.* **3** Paradise [singular] **a)** in some religions, a perfect place where people are believed to go after they die, if they have led good lives; → **heaven b)** according to the Bible, the garden where the first humans, Adam and Eve, lived → BIRD OF PARADISE; → be living in a fool's paradise at FOOL¹ (9)

par·a·dox /ˈpærədɒks $ -dɑːks/ *n* **1** [C] a situation that seems strange because it involves two ideas or qualities that are very different: *It's a paradox that in such a rich country there can be so much poverty.* **2** [C] a statement that seems impossible because it contains two opposing ideas that are both true: *The paradox is that fishermen would catch more fish if they fished less.* **3** [U] the use of statements that are a paradox in writing or speech —**paradoxical** /ˌpærəˈdɒksɪkəl◂ $ -ˈdɑːk-/ *adj*

par·a·dox·i·cal·ly /ˌpærəˈdɒksɪkli $ -ˈdɑːk-/ *adv* in a way that is surprising because it is the opposite of what you would expect: *Paradoxically, the prohibition of liquor caused an increase in alcoholism.*

par·af·fin /ˈpærəf₁ɪn/ *n* [U] **1** *BrE* a kind of oil used for heating and in lamps, made from PETROLEUM or coal; ◼ **kerosene** *AmE* **2** also **paraffin wax** *BrE* a soft white substance used for making CANDLES, made from PETROLEUM or coal

par·a·glid·ing /ˈpærəˌglaɪdɪŋ/ *n* [U] a sport in which you jump off a hill or out of a plane and use a PARACHUTE to fly for long distances before floating back down to the ground → see picture at AERIAL¹

par·a·gon /ˈpærəgən $ -gɑːn/ *n* [C] someone who is perfect or is extremely brave, good etc – often used humorously: [+of] *a paragon of virtue*

par·a·graph S3 W3 /ˈpærəgrɑːf $ -græf/ *n* [C] part of a piece of writing which starts on a new line and contains at least one sentence: *the opening paragraphs of the novel* —**paragraph** *v* [T]

par·a·keet /ˈpærəkiːt/ *n* [C] a small brightly coloured bird with a long tail

par·a·le·gal /ˌpærəˈliːgəl/ *n* [C] *AmE* someone whose job is to help lawyers do their work

par·al·lel¹ /ˈpærəlel/ *n* [C] **1** a relationship or similarity between two things, especially things that exist or happen in different places or at different times: [+with] *Entering the world of fine art, she found many parallels with the world of fashion.* | [+between] *There are many parallels between Yeats and the Romantic poets.* | *books that attempt to draw parallels between brains and computers* **2** in parallel with sb/sth together with and at the same time as something else: *She wanted to pursue her own career in parallel with her husband's.* **3** have no parallel/be without parallel be greater, better, worse etc than anything else: *The poverty of hill farmers had no parallel.* **4** an imaginary line drawn on a map of the Earth, that is parallel to the EQUATOR: *the 38th parallel*

parallel² *adj* **1** two lines, paths etc that are parallel to each other are the same distance apart along their whole length: *Lines AB and CD are parallel.* | *two parallel roads* | [+to] *She was travelling parallel to her previous route.* | [+with] *The railway is parallel with the canal.* | *Take the road running parallel to the main road just after the village.* **2** *formal* similar and happening at the same time: *Social changes in Britain are matched by parallel trends in some other countries.*

parallel³ *v* past tense and past participle **paralleled**, present participle **paralleling** also past tense and past participle **parallelled**, present participle **parallelling** *BrE* [T] *written* if one thing parallels another, they happen at the same time or are similar, and seem to be related: *The rise in greenhouse gases parallels the reduction in the ozone layer.* | *His career parallels that of his father.*

ˌparallel 'bars *n* [plural] two wooden bars that are held parallel to each other on four posts, used in GYMNASTICS

par·al·lel·is·m /ˈpærəlelɪzəm/ *n* [singular, U] *written* the state of being PARALLEL with something: *There is a parallelism between fatigue and the ability to sleep.*

par·al·lel·o·gram /ˌpærəˈleləgræm/ *n* [C] a flat shape with four sides in which each side is the same length as the side opposite it and parallel to it; → **rectangle**

ˌparallel 'processing *n* [U] *technical* when several computers work on a single problem at one time, or the process by which a single computer can perform several operations at the same time

par·a·lyse *BrE*; **paralyze** *AmE* /ˈpærəlaɪz/ *v* [T] **1** if something paralyses you, it makes you lose the ability to move part or all of your body, or to feel it: *Her*

P

1 000, 2 000, 3 000, most frequent words in S poken and W ritten English

legs were partly paralysed in the crash. **2** to make something unable to operate normally: *Fear of unemployment is paralysing the economy.* | *Motor traffic was paralysed in much of the city.*

par·a·lysed *BrE*; **paralyzed** *AmE* /'pærəlaɪzd/ *adj* **1** unable to move part or all of your body or feel it: *The accident left him permanently paralysed.* | **paralysed from the neck/chest/waist down** **2** unable to think clearly or deal with a situation: [+**by/with**] *paralysed by fear* | *paralyzed with shock* | *He stood paralysed for a moment, and then ran away.*

pa·ral·y·sis /pə'ræləsɪs/ *n* [U] **1** the loss of the ability to move all or part of your body or feel things in it: *paralysis of the lower body* | *The snake's poison causes paralysis.* **2** a state of being unable to take action, make decisions, or operate normally: *a period of political paralysis* → INFANTILE PARALYSIS

par·a·lyt·ic¹ /ˌpærə'lɪtɪk◀/ *adj* **1** [not before noun] *BrE informal* very drunk **2** [only before noun] suffering from paralysis —**paralytically** /-kli/ *adv*

paralytic² *n* [C] *old-fashioned* someone who is PARALYSED

par·a·lyze /'pærəlaɪz/ the American spelling of PARALYSE

par·a·med·ic /ˌpærə'medɪk/ *n* [C] someone who has been trained to help people who are hurt or to do medical work, but who is not a doctor or nurse —**paramedical** *adj* [usually before noun]

pa·ram·e·ter /pə'ræmɪtə $ -ər/ *n* [C usually plural] a set of fixed limits that control the way that something should be done: *The inquiry has to stay within the parameters laid down by Congress.*

par·a·mil·i·ta·ry /ˌpærə'mɪlɪtəri $ -teri◀/ *adj* [usually before noun] **1** a paramilitary organization is an illegal group that is organized like an army: *extremist paramilitary groups* **2** relating to, or helping a military organization: *the paramilitary police* —**paramilitary** *n* [C]

par·a·mount /'pærəmaʊnt/ *adj formal* more important than anything else: *During a war the interests of the state are paramount, and those of the individual come last.* | *Women's role as mothers is **of paramount importance** to society.* —**paramountcy** *n* [U]

par·a·mour /'pærəmʊə $ -mʊr/ *n* [C] *literary* someone who you have a romantic or sexual relationship with, but who you are not married to

par·a·noi·a /ˌpærə'nɔɪə/ *n* [U] **1** an unreasonable belief that you cannot trust other people, or that they are trying to harm you or have a bad opinion of you **2** *medical* a mental illness that makes someone believe that they are very important and that people hate them and are trying to harm them

par·a·noi·ac /ˌpærə'nɔɪæk◀/ *adj* paranoid —**paranoiac** *n* [C]

par·a·noid /'pærənɔɪd/ *adj* **1** believing unreasonably that you cannot trust other people, or that they are trying to harm you or have a bad opinion of you: **be/become/get paranoid** *Malcolm got really paranoid, deciding that there was a conspiracy out to get him.* | [+**about**] *He has always been paranoid about his personal security.* **2** *medical* suffering from a mental illness that makes you believe that other people are trying to harm you: *a patient suffering from paranoid schizophrenia*

par·a·nor·mal /ˌpærə'nɔːməl◀ $ -'nɔːr-/ *adj* **1** paranormal events cannot be explained by science and seem strange and mysterious; → **supernatural**: *ghosts and other paranormal phenomena* **2** **the paranormal** strange and mysterious events in general: *researchers investigating the paranormal*

par·a·pet /'pærəpɪt, -pet/ *n* [C] **1** a low wall at the edge of a high roof, bridge etc **2** a protective wall of earth or stone built in front of a TRENCH in a war **3** **put/stick your head above the parapet** *BrE* to take a risk

par·a·pher·na·li·a /ˌpærəfə'neɪliə $ -fər-/ *n* [U] **1** a lot of small things that belong to someone, or are needed for a particular activity: *an electric kettle and all the paraphernalia for making tea and coffee* | *travelling paraphernalia* **2** the things and events that are connected with a particular activity, especially those which you think are unnecessary: *all the usual paraphernalia of bureaucracy*

par·a·phrase¹ /'pærəfreɪz/ *v* [T] to express in a shorter, clearer, or different way what someone has said or written: *To paraphrase Finkelstein, mathematics is a language, like English.*

paraphrase² *n* [C] a statement that expresses in a shorter, clearer, or different way what someone has said or written

par·a·ple·gia /ˌpærə'pliːdʒə, -dʒiə/ *n* [U] inability to move your legs and the lower part of your body; → **paralysis**

par·a·ple·gic /ˌpærə'pliːdʒɪk◀/ *n* [C] someone who is unable to move the lower part of their body, including their legs; → **paralysed** —**paraplegic** *adj*

par·a·psy·chol·o·gy /ˌpærəsaɪ'kɒlədʒi $ -'kɑː-/ *n* [U] the scientific study of mysterious abilities that some people claim to have, such as knowing what will happen in the future

par·a·quat /'pærəkwɒt $ -kwɑːt/ *n* [U] *trademark* a strong poison used to kill WEEDS; → **weed killer**

par·a·sail·ing /'pærəˌseɪlɪŋ/ *n* [U] a sport in which you wear a PARACHUTE and are pulled behind a motor boat so that you fly through the air

par·as·cend·ing /'pærəˌsendɪŋ/ *n* [U] a sport in which you wear a PARACHUTE, and are pulled along by a car so that you go up into the sky and float back down to the ground

par·a·site /'pærəsaɪt/ *n* [C] **1** a plant or animal that lives on or in another plant or animal and gets food from it **2** *informal* a lazy person who does not work but depends on other people – used to show disapproval

par·a·sit·ic /ˌpærə'sɪtɪk◀/ also **par·a·sit·i·cal** /-'sɪtɪkəl/ *adj* **1** living in or on another plant or animal and getting food from them: *parasitic fungi* **2** a parasitic person is lazy, does no work, and depends on other people **3** a parasitic disease is caused by parasites —**parasitically** /-kli/ *adv*

par·a·sol /'pærəsɒl $ -sɒːl, -sɑːl/ *n* [U] a type of UMBRELLA used to provide shade from the sun

par·a·troop·er /'pærəˌtruːpə $ -ər/ *n* [C] a soldier who is trained to jump out of a plane using a PARACHUTE

par·a·troops /'pærətruːps/ *n* [plural] a group of paratroopers that fights together as a military unit

par·boil /'pɑːbɔɪl $ 'pɑːr-/ *v* [T] to boil something until it is partly cooked

par·cel¹ S3 /'pɑːsəl $ 'pɑːr-/ *n* [C]
1 *especially BrE* an object that has been wrapped in paper or put in a special envelope, especially so that it can be sent by post; ▤ **package**: *The parcel was delivered last week.* | *He sends regular food parcels to his family in Libya.* | [+**of**] *a parcel of clothes and blankets*; → see picture at PACKAGE¹
2 an area of land that is part of a larger area which has been divided up: [+**of**] *a parcel of farmland*
3 *BrE* a small quantity of food that has been wrapped up, usually in PASTRY → **be part and parcel of sth** at PART¹ (28)

parcel² *v* **parcelled, parcelling** *BrE*, **parceled, parceling** *AmE*
parcel sth ⇔ **off** *phr v AmE* to divide something into small parts so that it can be sold: *The new owner has parceled off many of the company's assets.*
parcel sth ⇔ **out** *phr v* to divide or share something among several people: *They didn't want the federal government parceling out food supplies.*
parcel sth ⇔ **up** *phr v BrE* **1** to make something into a parcel by wrapping it up: *She parcelled up the photos.* **2** to divide something into small parts, espe-

cially so that it is easier to deal with: *University education is often parcelled up into specialist teaching units.*

'parcel ,bomb *n* [C] *BrE* a bomb which is wrapped like a parcel and sent by post, and is intended to explode when it is opened

'parcel post *n* [U] the slowest and cheapest system of sending parcels by post in the US

parch /pɑːtʃ $ pɑːrtʃ/ *v* [T] if the sun or wind parches something, it makes it very dry

parched /pɑːtʃt $ pɑːrtʃt/ *adj* **1** very dry, especially because of hot weather: *the parched African landscape* | *He raised the water bottle to his parched lips.* **2 be parched** *informal* to be very thirsty

Par·chee·si /pɑːˈtʃiːzi $ pɑːr-/ *n* [U] *AmE trademark* a children's game in which you move a small piece of plastic around a board after throwing DICE

parch·ment /ˈpɑːtʃmənt $ ˈpɑːr-/ *n* **1** [U] a material used in the past for writing on, made from the skin of a sheep or a goat **2** [U] thick yellow-white writing paper, sometimes used for official documents **3** [C] a document written on parchment

pard·ner /ˈpɑːdnə $ ˈpɑːrdnər/ *n AmE spoken* used humorously when speaking to someone you know well: *Howdy, pardner!*

par·don¹ [S2] /ˈpɑːdn $ ˈpɑːrdn/ also **,pardon 'me** *interjection*
1 used when you want someone to repeat something because you did not hear it: *'Hurry up Jonathan!' 'Pardon?' 'I said hurry up!'* → see box at EXCUSE¹
2 *BrE* used to say 'sorry' after you have made an impolite sound such as a BURP; ◨ **excuse me**

pardon² *v* [T] **1** to officially allow someone who has been found guilty of a crime to go free without being punished: *The two spies were pardoned yesterday by the President.* **2** [not in progressive] *formal* to forgive someone for behaving badly; ◨ **forgive: pardon sb for sth** *He could never pardon her for the things she had said.* **3 sb may be pardoned for doing sth** used to say that it is easy to understand why someone has done something or why they think something: *Anyone reading the advertisement might be pardoned for thinking that the offer was genuine.* **4 pardon me** *spoken* **a)** used to say 'sorry' politely when you have accidentally pushed someone or interrupted them: *Oh, pardon me, I didn't mean to disturb you.* **b)** used to say 'sorry' politely after you have made an impolite sound such as a BURP **c)** used before you politely correct someone or disagree with them: *James, if you'll pardon me, you've got it all wrong.* **d)** used to politely get someone's attention in order to ask them a question; ◨ **excuse me:** *Pardon me, can you direct me to City Hall?* **5 pardon me for interrupting/asking/saying** *spoken* used to politely ask if you can interrupt someone, ask them a question, or tell them something: *Pardon me for saying so, but you don't look well.* **6 pardon my ignorance/rudeness etc** *spoken* used when you want to say something which you think may make you seem not to know enough or not to be polite enough: *Pardon my ignorance, but what does OPEC stand for?* **7 if you'll pardon the expression** *spoken* used when you are saying that you are sorry for using an impolite phrase: *It was a bit of a cock-up, if you'll pardon the expression.* **8 pardon my French** *spoken* used humorously to say that you are sorry for using a swear word **9 pardon me for breathing/living** *spoken* used when you are annoyed because you think someone has answered you angrily for no good reason: *'Shut up, Callum!' 'Well, pardon me for breathing.'*

pardon³ *n* [C] **1** an official order allowing someone who has been found guilty of a crime to go free without being punished: **grant/give sb a pardon** *Tyler was convicted but was granted a **royal pardon** (=one given by a king or queen).* **2 ask/beg sb's pardon (for sth)** *old-fashioned* to ask someone to forgive you: *Walter begged her pardon for all the pain he had caused her.* → **I beg your pardon** at BEG (4)

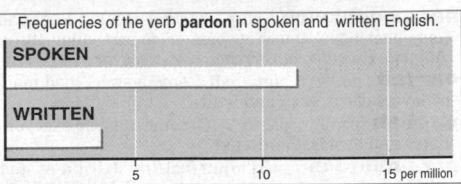
Frequencies of the verb **pardon** in spoken and written English.

| SPOKEN | | | |
| WRITTEN | | | |

5   10   15 per million

par·don·a·ble /ˈpɑːdənəbəl $ ˈpɑːr-/ *adj formal* pardonable mistakes are not very bad and can be forgiven; ◨ **forgivable:** *He had made the pardonable mistake of trusting the wrong person.* —**pardonably** *adv*

pare /peə $ per/ *v* [T] **1** to cut off the outer layer of something, using a sharp knife: *Pare the rind from the fruit.* **2** to reduce the amount, number, or size of something as much as you can: *The firm has not been able to pare costs fast enough to match competitors.* | *The country's defences have been **pared to the bone** (=reduced as far as possible).*
pare sth ⇔ **down** *phr v* to reduce something, especially by making a lot of small reductions: *The list was pared down for the final interviews.* —**pared-down** *adj: Even in its pared-down form, the contract was unacceptable.*

par·ent [S1] [W1] /ˈpeərənt $ ˈper-/ *n* [C]
1 the father or mother of a person or animal: *Children under fourteen should be accompanied by a parent.* | *The eggs are guarded by both parents.* | *Melissa's spending the weekend at her parents' house.* → BIRTH PARENT; → **foster parents** at FOSTER² (3); → **lone parent** at LONE (2); → ONE-PARENT FAMILY, SINGLE PARENT
2 something that produces other things of the same type: *New shoots appear near the parent plant.*
3 a company which owns a smaller company or organization: *Land Rover's new parent*

par·ent·age /ˈpeərəntɪdʒ $ ˈper-/ *n* [U] someone's parents and the country and social class they are from: *an English-born man with Irish parentage* | *He was born in France in 1670 **of unknown parentage** (=nobody knows who his parents were).*

pa·rent·al /pəˈrentl/ *adj* relating to being a parent and especially to being responsible for a child's safety and development: *parental responsibility* | *Opening a new school will increase parental choice.* | *Parental consent is required before the operation can take place.*

pa,rental 'leave *n* [U] time that a parent is allowed to spend away from work with his or her baby

'parent ,company *n* [C] a company that controls a smaller company or organization

pa·ren·the·sis /pəˈrenθɪsɪs/ *n plural* **parentheses** /-siːz/ [C usually plural] **1** a round BRACKET: **in parentheses** *The figures in parentheses refer to page numbers.* **2 in parenthesis** *BrE*; **in parentheses** *AmE* if you say something in parenthesis, you say it while you are talking about something else in order to add information or explain something: *In parenthesis, I should add that the results have not yet been proven.* → PUNCTUATION MARK

par·en·thet·i·cal /,pærənˈθetɪkəl◂/ also **par·en·thet·ic** /-ˈθetɪk◂/ *adj formal* said or written while you are talking or writing about something else in order to explain something or add information: *parenthetical references to his childhood* —**parenthetically** /-kli/ *adv*

par·ent·hood /ˈpeərənthʊd $ ˈper-/ *n* [U] the state of being a parent: *Story-reading should be one of the great joys of parenthood.*

par·ent·ing /ˈpeərəntɪŋ $ ˈper-/ *n* [U] the skill or activity of looking after your own children: *The program aims to teach young men parenting skills.*

'parents-in-,law *n* [plural] the parents of your husband or wife

,parent-'teacher associ,ation *n* [C] a PTA

par ex·cel·lence /ˌpɑːr ˈeksəlɑːns $ -eksəˈlɑːns/ adj [only after noun] the very best of a particular thing: *Auguste Escoffier, masterchef par excellence*

par·fait /pɑːˈfeɪ $ pɑːr-/ n [U] AmE a sweet food made of layers of ICE CREAM and fruit

pa·ri·ah /pəˈraɪə, ˈpæriə/ n [C] someone who everyone hates and avoids; **⊟ outcast**

par·i·mu·tu·el /ˌpæriˈmjuːtʃuəl/ n **1** [U] a system in which the money that people have risked on a horse race is shared between the people who have won: *parimutuel betting* **2** [C] AmE a machine used to calculate the amount of money that people can win when they risk it on horse races

par·ings /ˈpeərɪŋz $ ˈper-/ n [plural] especially BrE thin narrow pieces of something that have been cut off; → **pare**: *nail parings | cheese parings*

par·ish /ˈpærɪʃ/ n [C] **1** the area that a priest in some Christian churches is responsible for: *Father Doyle moved to a new parish.* **2** BrE a small area, especially a village, that has its own local government: *elections to the parish council*

parish 'church n [C] BrE the main Christian church in a particular area

parish 'clerk n [C] BrE an official who works for a Christian church in a particular town or area

pa·rish·ion·er /pəˈrɪʃənə $ -ər/ n [C] someone who lives in a parish, especially someone who regularly goes to a Christian church there

parish 'pump adj [only before noun] BrE old-fashioned concerned only with what happens in a small local area: *parish pump politics*

parish 'register n [C] BrE an official record of the births, deaths, and marriages in a parish

Pa·ris·i·an /pəˈrɪziən $ pəˈrɪʒən, -ˈriː-/ n [C] someone from the city of Paris in France —**Parisian** adj

par·i·ty /ˈpærəti/ n [U] **1** the state of being equal, especially having equal pay, rights, or power; **⊟ equality**: [+with] *Women workers are demanding parity with their male colleagues.* **2** technical equality between the units of money from two different countries

park¹ S1 W2 /pɑːk $ pɑːrk/ n [C]
1 a large open area with grass and trees, especially in a town, where people can walk, play games etc: *Let's go for a walk in the park. | a park bench | a flat overlooking Hyde Park* → see picture at TOWN
2 a large area of land in the country which has been kept in its natural state to protect the plants and animals there: **national/state/county park** *the Lake District National Park*
3 BrE a large enclosed area of land, with grass and trees, around a big house in the countryside
4 the park BrE informal the field where a game of football or RUGBY is played; **⊟ the pitch**: *He was easily the best player on the park.*
5 AmE informal the field where a game of baseball is played → AMUSEMENT PARK, BALL PARK (1), CAR PARK, NATIONAL PARK, SAFARI PARK, SCIENCE PARK, THEME PARK, TRAILER PARK

park² S2 v
1 [I,T] to put a car or other vehicle in a particular place for a period of time: *You can't park here – it's private property. | I couldn't find anywhere to park. | She parked the car on the drive. | a line of parked cars*
2 [T] spoken to put something in a particular place for a period of time, especially in a way that annoys someone: **park sth on/in etc sth** *He parked a load of papers on my desk.*
3 park yourself informal to sit down in a particular place, especially with the intention of staying a long time: [+on/in etc] *Connie parked herself on the sofa.*

par·ka /ˈpɑːkə $ ˈpɑːrkə/ n [C] a thick warm jacket with a HOOD

park and 'ride n [U] a system in which you leave your car outside a busy town and then take a special bus to the centre of the town

park·ing S3 /ˈpɑːkɪŋ $ ˈpɑːr-/ n [U]
1 the act of parking a car or other vehicle: *No Parking | a £45 parking fine* | **parking space/place/spot** *I couldn't find a parking space near the shops.*
2 spaces in which you can leave a car or other vehicle: *Free parking is available at the hotel.*

parking ,brake n [C] AmE a piece of equipment in a car which prevents it from moving when it is parked; **⊟ handbrake** BrE

parking ,garage / $ ˈ.. .,./ n [C] AmE a building with open sides in a public place where cars can be parked

parking ,light n [C] AmE one of two small lights next to each of the main lights at the front of a car → see picture at CAR

parking ,lot n [C] AmE an open area for cars to park in; **⊟ car park** BrE

parking ,meter n [C] a machine at the side of a road which you have to put money into if you park your car next to it → see picture at TOWN

parking ,ticket n [C] an official notice fixed to a vehicle, saying that you have to pay money because you have parked your car in the wrong place or for too long

Par·kin·son's dis·ease /ˈpɑːkɪnsənz dɪˌziːz $ ˈpɑːr-/ also **Parkinson's** n [U] a serious illness in which your muscles become very weak and your arms and legs shake

Parkinson's ,law n [U] the idea that the amount of work you have to do increases to fill the amount of time you have to do it in – used humorously

park ,keeper n [C] someone whose job is to look after a public park in British towns

park·land /ˈpɑːk-lænd $ ˈpɑːrk-/ n [U] **1** BrE an area of land with grass and trees, surrounding a big house in the countryside: *The hotel is set in ten acres of parkland.* **2** land with grass and trees which is used as a park: *a narrow strip of parkland*

park ,ranger n [C] AmE a RANGER (1)

park·way /ˈpɑːkweɪ $ ˈpɑːrk-/ n [C] **1** AmE a wide road with an area of grass and trees in the middle or along the sides **2** BrE used to talk about railway stations that have large areas for cars to park

par·ky /ˈpɑːki $ ˈpɑːrki/ adj BrE informal cold; **⊟ chilly**: *It's a bit parky outside today.*

par·lance /ˈpɑːləns $ ˈpɑːr-/ n **1 in medical/advertising etc parlance** expressed in the words that a particular group of people would use: *In military parlance this is known as a fast retreat.* **2 in common parlance** expressed in the words that most people use: *These schemes are known in common parlance as 'private pensions'.*

par·lay /ˈpɑːli $ ˈpɑːrleɪ/ v [T] AmE to use advantages that you already have, such as your skills, experience, or money, and increase their value by using all your opportunities well: **parlay sth into sth** *He owned five movie theaters, which he eventually parlayed into hotels.*

par·ley /ˈpɑːli $ ˈpɑːrli/ n [C] old-fashioned a discussion in which enemies try to achieve peace —**parley** v [I]

par·lia·ment W2 /ˈpɑːləmənt $ ˈpɑːr-/ n
1 [C] [also + plural verb BrE] the group of people who are elected to make a country's laws and discuss important

national affairs; → **government**, **MP**: *They demanded a free parliament and press.*
2 Parliament [singular also + plural verb *BrE*] the main law-making institution in the UK, which consists of the HOUSE OF COMMONS and the HOUSE OF LORDS: *The bill was passed by Parliament in April.* | **enter/get into Parliament** (=be elected as a member of Parliament) | **in Parliament** *He failed to win a seat in Parliament.* | **before Parliament** *The new laws will be placed before Parliament.* → HUNG PARLIAMENT
3 [C] the period during which the British Parliament meets: *We expect to get these laws passed during the present parliament.*

par·lia·men·tar·i·an /ˌpɑːləmənˈteəriən $ ˌpɑːrlə-mənˈter-/ n [C] a member of a parliament, especially one who is very experienced; → **MP**

par·lia·men·ta·ry W3 /ˌpɑːləˈmentəriˌ $ ˌpɑːrl-/ adj relating to, or governed by a parliament: *the world's oldest parliamentary democracy*

par·lor /ˈpɑːlə $ ˈpɑːrlər/ n [C] the American spelling of PARLOUR

par·lour *BrE*; **parlor** *AmE* /ˈpɑːlə $ ˈpɑːrlər/ n [C] **1** **ice cream/funeral/tattoo parlour** a shop or type of business that provides a particular service **2** *old-fashioned* a room in a house which has comfortable chairs and is used for meeting guests → MILKING PARLOUR

parlour game n [C] *BrE old-fashioned* a game that can be played indoors, such as a guessing game or a word game

parlour maid n [C] *BrE* a female servant who was employed in large houses in the past to clean the rooms and serve guests

par·lous /ˈpɑːləs $ ˈpɑːr-/ adj formal in a very bad or dangerous condition: *The country's police force was in a parlous state in 1990.*

Par·me·san /ˌpɑːmɪˈzænˌ $ ˈpɑːrmɪˌzɑːn, -zæn/ also **Parmesan 'cheese** n [U] a hard Italian cheese

pa·ro·chi·al /pəˈrəʊkiəl $ -ˈroʊ-/ adj **1** only interested in things that affect your local area – used to show disapproval: *Local newspapers tend to be very parochial.* **2** [only before noun] relating to a particular church and the area around it: *the parochial church council* —**parochialism** n [U]

pa'rochial ˌschool n [C] *AmE* a private school which is run by or connected with a church

par·o·dy¹ /ˈpærədi/ n plural **parodies** **1** [C,U] a piece of writing, music etc or an action that copies someone or something in an amusing way: [+of] *a brilliant parody of classical dance* | **in a parody of sth** *He swung the door wide open in a parody of welcome.* | *Her performance contains a strong element of self-parody* (=when someone makes fun of their own style). **2** [C] something that is not a correct or acceptable example of something: [+of] *Although his comment was a parody of the truth, Diana was upset by it.* | *The trial was a parody of justice* (=very unfair).

parody² v **parodied, parodying, parodies** [T] to copy someone or something in a way that makes people laugh: *His style has often been parodied.* —**parodist** n [C]

pa·role¹ /pəˈrəʊl $ -ˈroʊl/ n [U] permission for someone to leave prison, on the condition that they promise to behave well: **on parole** *He was released on parole after serving two years.* | *She will become eligible for parole in 19 months.*

parole² v [T] to allow someone to leave prison on the condition that they promise to behave well

pa'role ˌboard n [C] the people who decide if a prisoner should get permission to leave prison

par·ox·ys·m /ˈpærəksɪzəm/ n [C] **1** a sudden expression of strong feeling that you cannot control: [+of] *Had she cut her wrists in a paroxysm of guilt?* **2** a sudden, short attack of pain, coughing, shaking etc

par·quet /ˈpɑːkeɪ, ˈpɑːki $ pɑːrˈkeɪ/ n [U] small flat blocks of wood fitted together in a pattern that cover the floor of a room: *a parquet floor*

par·ri·cide /ˈpærɪˌsaɪd/ n [U] formal the crime of killing your father, mother, or any other close relative; → **matricide, patricide**

par·rot¹ /ˈpærət/ n [C] **1** a tropical bird with a curved beak and brightly coloured feathers that can be taught to copy human speech → see picture at FEED¹ **2 parrot fashion** *BrE* if you learn something parrot fashion, you repeat what someone has just said without understanding it; → **by heart**: *We recited poems parrot fashion.* → **sick as a parrot** at SICK¹ (10)

parrot² v [T] to repeat someone else's words or ideas without really understanding what you are saying – used to show disapproval: *He just parroted his father's opinions.*

par·ry /ˈpæri/ v **parried, parrying, parries** **1** [I,T] to defend yourself against someone who is attacking you by pushing their weapon or hand to one side; ◫ **deflect**: *It is far easier to parry a direct blow than to stop it forcibly.* **2** [T] to avoid answering a question that is difficult to answer or that someone does not want to answer: *He parried all her questions about his work.* —**parry** n [C]

parse /pɑːz $ pɑːrs/ v [T] technical to describe the grammar of a word when it is in a particular sentence, or the grammar of the whole sentence —**parser** n [C]

Par·see, Parsi /ˈpɑːˈsiː $ ˈpɑːrsiː/ n [C] a member of an ancient Persian religious group in India —**Parsee** adj

par·si·mo·ni·ous /ˌpɑːsɪˈməʊniəsˌ $ ˌpɑːrsɪˈmoʊ-/ adj formal extremely unwilling to spend money —**parsimoniously** adv —**parsimony** /ˈpɑːsɪˌməni $ ˈpɑːrsɪˌmoʊni/ n [U]

pars·ley /ˈpɑːsli $ ˈpɑːr-/ n [U] a herb with curly leaves, used in cooking or as decoration on food

pars·nip /ˈpɑːsnɪp $ ˈpɑːr-/ n [C,U] a vegetable with a thick white or yellowish root

par·son /ˈpɑːsən $ ˈpɑːr-/ n [C] old-fashioned a Christian priest or minister

par·son·age /ˈpɑːsənɪdʒ $ ˈpɑːr-/ n [C] the house where a parson lives

ˌparson's 'nose n [C] *BrE informal* the piece of flesh at the tail end of a bird, usually a chicken, that has been cooked; ◫ **pope's nose** *AmE*

part¹ S1 W1 /pɑːt $ pɑːrt/ n
1 PIECE [C] a piece or feature of something such as an object, area, or period of time: [+of] *The front part of the car was damaged.* | *In parts of Canada, French is the first language.* | *For part of the day, you will be outside doing practical work.* | *The cost of living is becoming unbearable for retired people in our part of the world* (=where we live). | *More heat is lost through the head than any other part of the body.* | **the early/later/latter/last part** *in the early part of the nineteenth century* | **the best/worst part** *The best part of the holiday was the food.* | **the first/final/last part etc** *You can see the final part of that series on Tuesday.* | **part two/three etc** *I shall be explaining this further in Part Two.* | **the hard/easy part** *Getting Dad to agree will be the hard part.* | **different parts/all parts of sth** *The jobs attracted people from all parts of the world.* | **integral/vital/important part** *the traditions that are an integral part of Jewish life* | **in parts** *The film is very violent in parts.* △ Do not say 'most part of'. Say **most of**: *We spent most of (NOT most part of) the morning shopping.*
2 MACHINE/OBJECT [C] one of the separate pieces that something such as a machine or piece of equipment is made of: *Lay all the parts out before you start assembling the model.* | *engine parts* | **spare parts** (=kept for when a part breaks, needs replacing etc)
3 NOT ALL part of sth some, but not all, of a particular

P

thing: *Part of the money will be spent on a new playground.* | *Part of the castle was destroyed by fire.* | **part of me/him etc** *Part of me hates him* (=I partly hate him).* | **(only) part of the story/problem/explanation etc** *Poor working conditions are only part of the problem.*

4 INVOLVEMENT play a part if something or someone plays a part in something else, they are involved in it: [+in] *Health education will play a part in preparing us for old age.* | *Britain should **play its full part** in the negotiations.* | **play a big/important part in sth** *Pictures play an important part in publishing.*

5 have a part to play (in sth) to have a particular job or be responsible for something: *The church used to have a more important part to play in the community.*

6 take part to be involved in an activity, sport, event etc with other people: [+in] *About 400 students took part in the protest.* | *She wanted to take part but she was too ill.* | **take an active/leading part** *At college I took an active part in student politics.* ⚠ Do not say 'take a part in' something. Say **take part in** something.

7 take/have/play no part in sth to not be involved in something: *She took no part in the fighting.*

8 want no part of sth to not want to be involved in something: *There was a plan to change the production style, and he wanted no part of it.*

9 the best/better part of sth nearly all of something: *We waited for the best part of an hour.*

10 a good/large part of sth a lot or more than half of something: *A large part of the budget will be spent on advertising.*

11 the greater/major part of sth most of something: *They controlled the greater part of North Africa.*

12 in part to some degree, but not completely; ☐ **partly**: *His reluctance to help could, in part, be explained by his poor eyesight.*

13 in large part/for the most part mostly, or in most places: *Success was due in large part to good teamwork.* | *For the most part he worked patiently.*

14 be (a) part of sth to be included or involved in something: *Falling over is part of learning how to ski.* | *If you decide to work for our organisation, you will be part of a great team.*

15 form (a) part of sth to be one of the things that make up something larger or more important: *Practical work **forms an integral part of** the course.*

16 HAIR [C usually singular] *AmE* a PARTING

17 ACTING [C] the words and actions of a particular character in a play or film; ☐ **role**: *Could someone **take the part of** Romeo, please?* | *Katharine's **playing the part of** Mary in the school play.*

18 MUSIC [C] the music that one type of instrument or voice within a group plays or sings: *The violin part is difficult.* | *The choir sings in four-part harmony.*

19 QUANTITY [C] used to say how much of each substance there is or should be in a mixture: *Prepare the glue with one **part** powder to three **parts** water.* | *The sulphur dioxide level in the air was 32 parts per billion.*

20 look the part a) to look like a typical person of a particular type: *In his smart suit, he certainly looked the part.* b) to perform well and seem likely to be successful – used in sports reports: *He's beginning to look the part on the soccer field.*

21 dress the part to wear suitable clothes for something: *She's got a new high-powered job, and she's certainly dressing the part.*

22 sb's part in sth what a particular person did in an activity that was shared by several people, especially something bad: *He was imprisoned for six years for his part in the murder.*

23 in/round these parts in the particular area that you are in: *We don't get many tourists in these parts.*

24 take sb's part *BrE formal* to support someone in a quarrel or argument; ☐ **take sb's side**: *Dad always takes my brother's part when we argue.*

25 for my/his part etc *formal* used when saying what a particular person thinks or does, as opposed to other people: *For my part, I prefer living in the country.*

26 on sb's part/on the part of sb used when describing a particular person's feelings or actions: *It was probably just a mistake on her part.* | *There has never been any jealousy on my part.*

27 take sth in good part *old-fashioned* to accept jokes or criticism about you without being upset

28 be part and parcel of sth to be a necessary feature of something: *Working irregular hours is all part and parcel of being a journalist.*

29 man/woman of many parts someone who is able to do many different things: *He was a man of many parts: writer, literary critic and historian.*

part² *v* **1** [I,T] *written* to move the two sides of something apart, or to move apart, making a space in the middle: *When he parted the curtains, the sunlight flooded into the room.* | *The crowd parted to let him through.* | *Ralph's lips parted in a delighted smile.* **2** [I] *written* to separate from someone, or end a relationship with them: *They parted on amicable terms.* | [+from] *He has parted from his wife.* **3** be parted (from sb) to be prevented from being with someone: *They were hardly ever parted in thirty years of marriage.* | *He hates being parted from the children.* **4** part company (with sb) a) to go in different directions after having gone in the same direction: *The two women parted company outside their rooms.* b) to end a relationship with someone: *George parted company with the band in 1996.* c) to disagree with someone about something: *He parted company with Lloyd George over post-war diplomacy.* **5** [T] if you part your hair, you comb some of your hair in one direction and the rest in the other direction

part with sth *phr v* to give something to someone else, although you do not want to: *I'm reluctant to part with any of the kittens, but we need the money.*

part³ *adv* **1** part sth, part sth if something is part one thing, part another, it consists of both of those things: *The exams are part written, part practical.* | *The room is part sitting room, part bedroom.* **2** not completely; ☐ **partly**: *The project is part funded by the council.* | *The object was part hidden by the grass.*

part⁴ *adj* **1** part payment payment of only a part of something, not all of it: *I gave them £10 in part payment.* **2** part owner someone who is one of the people who own something

par·take /pɑːˈteɪk $ pɑːr-/ *v* past tense **partook** /-ˈtʊk/, past participle **partaken** /-ˈteɪkən/ [I] *formal* **1** to eat or drink something: [+of] *Grandmother likes to partake of a small glass of sherry before lunch.* **2** to take part in an activity or event; ☐ **participate**: [+in] *a woman's fundamental right to partake in club affairs*

partake of sth *phr v formal* to have a certain amount of a particular quality

par·terre /pɑːˈteə $ pɑːrˈter/ *n* [C] *formal* a part of a garden with areas of flowers surrounded by low HEDGES in a formal pattern

part ex'change *n* [C,U] *BrE* a way of buying a new car, television etc in which you give your old car, television etc as part of the payment; ☐ **trade in** *AmE*: *The company **takes** the buyer's property **in part exchange**.*

par·the·no·gen·e·sis /ˌpɑːθɪnəʊˈdʒenɪsɪs $ ˌpɑːrθɪnoʊ-/ *n* [U] *technical* the production of a new plant or animal from a female without the sexual involvement of the male

par·tial /ˈpɑːʃəl $ ˈpɑːr-/ *adj* **1** not complete: *The exhibition was only a partial success.* | *a partial solution to traffic congestion in Oxford* **2** be partial to sth *formal* to like something very much: *I'm very partial to cream cakes.* **3** unfairly supporting one person or one group against another; ☐ **impartial**

par·ti·al·i·ty /ˌpɑːʃiˈælɪti $ ˌpɑːr-/ *n* [U] **1** unfair support of one person or one group against another; ☐ **bias**: *the problem of partiality in news reporting* **2** partiality for sth *formal* a special liking for something: *a partiality for Moorish architecture*

par·tial·ly /ˈpɑːʃəli $ ˈpɑːr-/ *adv formal* not completely; ◼ **partly**: *The operation was only partially successful.* | *Remember that you are partially responsible for their unhappiness.*

partially sighted *adj* unable to see well; → **blind**: *Reading aids have been provided for partially sighted pupils.*

par·tic·i·pant W3 /pɑːˈtɪsɪ̥pənt $ pɑːr-/ *n* [C] someone who is taking part in an activity or event: [+in] *an active participant in the negotiations*

par·tic·i·pate W3 /pɑːˈtɪsɪ̥peɪt $ pɑːr-/ *v* [I] *formal* to take part in an activity or event: *Some members refused to participate.* | [+in] *Everyone in the class is expected to participate actively in these discussions.* | *They welcomed the opportunity to participate fully in the life of the village.* ⚠ **Participate** is never followed directly by a noun. Say that you **participate in** something: *Everyone can participate in an election (NOT Everyone can participate an election).*

par·ti·ci·pa·tion W3 /pɑːˌtɪsɪ̥ˈpeɪʃən $ pɑːr-/ *n* [U] the act of taking part in an activity or event: *Thank you for your participation.* | [+in] *We want more participation in the decision-making.* | *entertainment with plenty of audience participation*

par·ti·ci·pa·tory /pɑːˌtɪsɪ̥ˈpeɪtəri◂ $ pɑːrˈtɪsɪ̥pətɔːri/ *adj* [usually before noun] *formal* a participatory way of organizing something, making decisions etc is one that involves everyone who will be affected: *a participatory democracy*

par·ti·cip·i·al /ˌpɑːtɪ̥ˈsɪpiəl $ ˌpɑːr-/ *adj technical* using a participle, or having the form of a participle

par·ti·ci·ple /ˈpɑːtɪ̥sɪpəl, pɑːˈtɪsɪpəl $ ˈpɑːr-/ *n* [C] *technical* one of the forms of a verb that are used to make tenses. In English, PRESENT PARTICIPLES end in -ing and PAST PARTICIPLES usually end in -ed or -en.

par·ti·cle /ˈpɑːtɪkəl $ ˈpɑːr-/ *n* [C] **1** a very small piece of something: *dust particles* | [+of] *tiny particles of soil* **2 not a particle of truth/evidence etc** no truth etc at all: *There's not a particle of truth in what he says.* **3** one of the very small pieces of matter that an atom consists of **4** *technical* an adverb or PREPOSITION that can combine with a verb to form a PHRASAL VERB

particle ac·cel·er·a·tor *n* [C] a machine used in scientific studies which makes the very small pieces of matter that atoms are made of move at high speeds

particle physics *n* [U] the study of the way that parts of atoms develop and behave

par·tic·u·lar¹ S1 W1 /pəˈtɪkjʊ̥lə $ pərˈtɪkjʊ̥lər/ *adj* **1** [only before noun] a particular thing or person is the one that you are talking about, and not any other; → **certain, specific**: *In this particular case, no one else was involved.* | *Most students choose one particular area for research.* | *a particular type of food* **2** special or great: *You should pay particular attention to spelling.* | *For no particular reason, he quit the job.* | **of particular interest/concern/importance etc** *Of particular concern is the rising cost of transportation.* | **anything/nothing/something particular** *I had nothing particular planned.* **3** very careful about choosing exactly what you like and not easily satisfied; ◼ **fussy**: [+about] *Marty's very particular about his food.*

particular² *n* **1 in particular** especially: *It was a good concert – I enjoyed the last song in particular.* | **anything/anyone/anywhere in particular** *Was there anything in particular that you wanted to talk about?* | **nothing/no one/nowhere in particular** *'What did you want?' 'Oh, nothing in particular.'* **2 particulars** [plural] the facts and details about a job, property, legal case etc: [+of] *You may be required to give particulars of the change in your financial position.* | *For further particulars, contact the College secretary.* | *Send your particulars* (=details such as your name, address, profession etc) *to the address above.* **3 in every particular/in all particulars** *formal* in every detail: *The documents were identical in almost every particular.*

par·tic·u·lar·i·ty /pəˌtɪkjʊ̥ˈlærɪ̥ti $ pər-/ *n plural* **particularities** *formal* **1** [U] a quality that makes something different from all others: *the particularity of her style of writing* **2** [U] the quality of being exact and paying attention to details **3** [C] a detail

par·tic·u·lar·ize also **-ise** *BrE* /pəˈtɪkjʊ̥ləraɪz $ pər-/ *v* [I,T] *formal* to give the details of something; ◼ **itemize**

par·tic·u·lar·ly S1 W1 /pəˈtɪkjʊ̥ləli $ pərˈtɪkjʊ̥lərli/ *adv*
1 more than usual or more than others; ◼ **especially**: *Steve was in a particularly bad mood when he got back.* | *The restaurant is particularly popular with young people.* | *We are hoping to expand our business, particularly in Europe.* | *British farmers, particularly those producing lamb, are very worried.*
2 not particularly a) not very: *I'm not particularly impressed with their performance.* **b)** *spoken* not very much: *'Do you want to come to the party?' 'Not particularly.'*

par·tic·u·lates /pəˈtɪkjʊ̥ləts, -leɪts $ pər-/ *n* [plural] harmful dust in the air, especially produced by car engines

part·ing¹ /ˈpɑːtɪŋ $ ˈpɑːr-/ *n* **1** [C,U] an occasion when two people leave each other: *an emotional parting at the airport* | *the moment of parting* | **on parting** *He gave her a light kiss on parting.* **2** [C] *BrE* the line on your head made by dividing your hair with a comb; ◼ **part** *AmE: a centre parting* **3 parting of the ways** the point at which two people or organizations decide to separate

parting² *adj* **1 a parting kiss/gift/glance etc** a kiss etc that you give someone as you leave **2 parting shot** an unpleasant remark that you make just as you are leaving, especially at the end of an argument: *As her parting shot, she told me never to phone her again.*

par·ti·san¹ /ˌpɑːtɪ̥ˈzæn $ ˈpɑːrtɪ̥zən, -sən/ *adj* **1** strongly supporting a particular political party, plan or leader, usually without considering the other choices carefully: *British newspapers are highly partisan.* **2** relating to the fighting of an armed group against an enemy that has taken control of its country: *the nature of partisan warfare*

partisan² *n* [C] **1** someone who strongly supports a political party, plan, or leader: *a media campaign to represent Democrats as angry partisans* **2** a member of an armed group that fights against an enemy that has taken control of its country —**partisanship** *n* [U]

par·ti·tion¹ /pɑːˈtɪʃən $ pər-, pɑːr-/ *n* **1** [C] a thin wall that separates one part of a room from another **2** [U] the action of separating a country into two or more independent countries: [+of] *the partition of India*

partition² *v* [T + into] to divide a country, building, or room into two or more parts
partition sth ⇔ **off** *phr v* to divide part of a room from the rest by using a partition: *They partitioned off part of the living room to make a study.*

par·ti·tive /ˈpɑːtɪ̥tɪv $ ˈpɑːr-/ *n* [C] *technical* a word which comes before a noun and shows that only part of something is being described, for example the word 'some' in the phrase 'some of the cake' —**partitive** *adj*

part·ly S2 W2 /ˈpɑːtli $ ˈpɑːr-/ *adv* to some degree, but not completely: *The poor weather was partly responsible for the crash.* | *The company's problems are partly due to bad management.* | *It is partly because of her sick mother that she hasn't taken the job abroad.* | *The group is funded partly by the government.*

part·ner¹ S3 W2 /ˈpɑːtnə $ ˈpɑːrtnər/ *n* [C]
1 MARRIAGE ETC one of two people who are married, or who live together and have a sexual relationship; → **husband, wife**: *Discuss your worries with your partner.* | *Only 29% of lone parents receive financial support from their former partners.* | *a sexual partner*
2 BUSINESS one of the owners of a business: *She's a*

3 pass sth ⇔ out to give something, such as books or papers, to everyone in a group; ⊟ **hand out, distribute**

pass over phr v
1 pass sb ⇔ over [usually in passive] if you pass someone over for a job, you choose someone else who is younger or lower in the organization than them: *This is the second time I've been **passed over for promotion*** (=someone else has been given a higher job instead of me).
2 pass over sth if you pass over a remark or subject, you do not spend any time discussing it: *I want to pass over this quite quickly.* | *I think we'd better pass over that last remark.*

pass sth ⇔ **up** phr v
to not make use of a chance to do something: **pass up a chance/opportunity/offer** *I don't think you should pass up the opportunity to go to university.*

pass² S2 W3 n [C]
1 DOCUMENT an official piece of paper which shows that you are allowed to enter a building or travel on something without paying: *The guard checked our passes.* | *They issued us with free passes to the theatre.* | *You can buy a cheap one-day **bus pass**.*
2 EXAM/TEST a successful result in an examination; ⌗ **fail**: *You will need at least three passes to get onto the course.* | [+in] *Did you get a pass in English?* | *The **pass mark*** (=the mark you need to be successful) *is 55%.*
3 SPORT when you kick, throw, or hit a ball to another member of your team during a game: *That was a brilliant pass by Holden.*
4 make a pass at sb *informal* to try to kiss or touch another person with the intention of starting a sexual relationship with them
5 ROAD/PATH a high road or path that goes between mountains to the other side: *a narrow, winding mountain pass*
6 STAGE one part of a process that involves dealing with the whole of a group or thing several times: *On the first pass we eliminated all the candidates who didn't have the right experience.*
7 AIRCRAFT a movement in which an aircraft flies once over a place which it is attacking
8 come to a pretty/sorry pass *old-fashioned informal* if things have come to a pretty or sorry pass, a situation has become very bad

pass·a·ble /ˈpɑːsəbəl $ ˈpæ-/ adj **1** formal fairly good, but not excellent: *The food was excellent and the wine was passable.* | *He can do a passable imitation of the maths teacher.* **2** a road or river that is passable is not blocked, so you can travel along it or across it; ⌗ **impassable**

pass·a·bly /ˈpɑːsəbli $ ˈpæs-/ adv in a way that is fairly good, but not excellent: *There were one or two passably funny jokes but it was mostly dull.*

pas·sage S3 W2 /ˈpæsɪdʒ/ n
1 IN A BUILDING [C] a long narrow area with walls on either side which connects one room or place to another; → **corridor**: *My office is just along the passage.* | *We walked down a narrow passage to the back of the building.* | *an underground passage*
2 FROM A BOOK ETC [C] a short part of a book, poem, speech, piece of music etc: [+from/of] *He read out a short passage from the Bible.*
3 MOVEMENT [U] formal the movement of people or vehicles along a road or across an area of land: [+of] *The bridge isn't strong enough to allow the passage of heavy vehicles.* | *Both sides agreed to allow the **free passage** of medical supplies into the area.* | *He was guaranteed **safe passage** out of the country.*
4 OF A LAW [U] when a new law is discussed and accepted by a parliament or Congress: [+through] *The bill was amended several times during its passage through Congress.* | *They are expecting the new legislation to have quite a **rough passage*** (=be discussed and criticized a lot) *through parliament.*

5 JOURNEY [C] old-fashioned a journey on a ship: [+to] *My parents couldn't afford the passage to America.*
6 INSIDE SB'S BODY [C] a tube in your body that air or liquid can pass through: *the nasal passages*
7 WAY THROUGH [singular] a way through something: [+through] *The police forced a passage through the crowd.*
8 the passage of time the passing of time: *With the passage of time, things began to look more hopeful.* → **rite of passage** at RITE (2)

pas·sage·way /ˈpæsɪdʒweɪ/ n [C] a PASSAGE (1): *He led me down a narrow passageway.*

pass·book /ˈpɑːsbʊk $ ˈpæs-/ n [C] a book in which a record is kept of the money you put into and take out of a bank account

pas·sé /ˈpæseɪ, ˈpɑː- $ pæˈseɪ/ adj formal no longer modern or fashionable

pas·sel /ˈpæsəl/ n [C] AmE old-fashioned a group of people or things: [+of] *a whole passel of kids*

pas·sen·ger S3 W2 /ˈpæsɪndʒə, -sən- $ -ər/ n [C]
1 someone who is travelling in a vehicle, plane, boat etc, but is not driving it or working on it: *Neither the driver nor the passengers were hurt.* | **passenger train/ plane/ship** *a crash involving a passenger train* | **bus/ rail/airline passengers** *Rail passengers now face even longer delays.*
2 BrE someone in a group who does not do their share of the group's work: *The company can't afford to carry any passengers.*

passenger seat n [C] the seat in the front of a vehicle next to the driver → see picture at CAR

pass·er·by /ˌpɑːsəˈbaɪ $ ˌpæsər-/ n plural **passersby** [C] someone who is walking past a place by chance: *They sell drinks to passersby.*

pas·sim /ˈpæsɪm/ adv formal used to show that a person or subject is referred to many times in a book or article

pass·ing¹ /ˈpɑːsɪŋ $ ˈpæ-/ n [U] **1 the passing of time/the years** the process of time going by: *Most of the old traditions have died out with the passing of time.* | *The passing of the years had done nothing to improve his temper.* **2 mention/note sth in passing** if you say something in passing, you mention it while you are mainly talking about something else: *He did mention his brother's wife, but only in passing.* **3** the passing of something is the fact that it has ended: *The old regime was defeated, and few people mourned its passing.* **4** the passing of a person is their death – use this when you want to avoid using the word 'death': *Nothing could fill the gap in her life left by his passing.*

passing² adj [only before noun] **1** going past a place or person: *Michael watched the passing cars.* | *A passing motorist stopped to help.* **2 passing days/weeks/ years etc** literary the days, weeks, years etc that pass: *Her grief became less intense with the passing years.* | *With each passing day she grew stronger.* **3** a passing thought or feeling is short and not very serious: *He had only ever shown a **passing interest** in sport.* **4** a passing remark is one that you make while you are talking about something else: *He made only a passing reference to her achievements.*

pas·sion W3 /ˈpæʃən/ n
1 [C,U] a very strong feeling of sexual love; → **desire**: *His eyes were burning with passion.* | [+for] *her passion for a married man*
2 [C,U] a very strong belief or feeling about something: **with passion** *He spoke with considerable passion about the importance of art and literature.* | *The issue arouses **strong passions**.*
3 [C] a very strong liking for something: [+for] *his passion for football* | *Gardening was her great passion.*
4 fly into a passion literary to suddenly become very angry → **crime of passion** at CRIME (5)

Passion n **the Passion** the suffering and death of Jesus Christ

pas·sion·ate /ˈpæʃənɨt/ adj **1** showing or involving very strong feelings of sexual love: *He had a brief but passionate love affair with an older woman.* | *a very passionate young man* | *a passionate lover* | *a passionate kiss* **2** someone who has a passionate belief believes something very strongly: *a passionate supporter of women's rights* | *He had a passionate belief in justice.* **3** if you are passionate about something, you like it a lot: *She developed a passionate interest in wild flowers.* | [+about] *I've always been passionate about football.* —**passionately** adv: *He kissed her passionately.* | *Peter is passionately involved in environmental issues.*

pas·sion·flow·er /ˈpæʃənˌflaʊə $ -ˌflaʊr/ n [C] a climbing plant with large attractive flowers

passion fruit n [C,U] a small fruit which has a brown skin and many seeds

pass·ion·less /ˈpæʃənləs/ adj with no strong feelings of love: *a dull, passionless marriage*

passion play n [C] a play that tells the story of the suffering and death of Jesus Christ

pas·sive¹ /ˈpæsɪv/ adj **1** someone who is passive tends to accept things that happen to them or things that people say to them, without taking any action; → **impassive**: *Kathy seems to take a very passive role in the relationship.* | *their passive acceptance of their fate* **2** technical a passive verb or sentence has as its subject the person or thing to which an action is done, as in 'His father was killed in a car accident.' → **ACTIVE¹** (6) —**passively** adv: *He listened passively as his sentence was read out.* —**passivity** /pæˈsɪvɨti/ n [U]

passive² n the passive technical the passive form of a verb, for example 'was destroyed' in the sentence 'The building was destroyed during the war.' → **ACTIVE²**

passive re·sistance n [U] a way of protesting against something or opposing a government without using violence: *They tried to achieve their aims by passive resistance.*

passive smoking n [U] especially BrE the act of breathing in smoke that is in the air around you when someone else is smoking cigarettes

passive voice n [singular] the **PASSIVE²**

pas·siv·ize also **-ise** BrE /ˈpæsɪvaɪz/ v [I,T] technical to make a verb **PASSIVE**, or to become passive

pass·key /ˈpɑːs-kiː $ ˈpæs-/ n [C] a key that will open several different locks in a building

Pass·o·ver /ˈpɑːsəʊvə $ ˈpæsoʊvər/ n [U] also **the Passover** a Jewish religious holiday when people remember the escape of the Jews from Egypt

pass·port S3 /ˈpɑːspɔːt $ ˈpæspɔːrt/ n [C]
1 a small official document that you get from your government, that proves who you are, and which you need in order to leave your country, and enter other countries: **British/French/American etc passport** *She was born in New York and has an American passport.* | **have/hold a passport** *Do you hold a British passport?* | *All people entering the country will need a valid passport.* | *He got into Europe with a false passport.* | *I need to check that your passport is in order.*
2 passport to success/health/romance etc something that makes it easy for you to achieve success, good health etc: *She saw a good diet as a passport to good health.* | *Don't assume that winning a talent contest is a passport to success.*

passport con·trol n [U] the place where your passport is checked when you leave or enter a country; → **immigration**: *It took us ages to get through passport control.*

pass·word /ˈpɑːswɜːd $ ˈpæswɜːrd/ n [C] **1** a secret group of letters or numbers that you must type into a computer before you can use a system or program: *Enter your password, then click on the 'proceed' icon.* | *Give your user name and password.* **2** a secret word or phrase that someone has to say before they are allowed to enter a place such as a military camp

past¹ S1 W1 /pɑːst $ pæst/ adj
1 **PREVIOUS** [only before noun] done, used, or experienced before now: *Judging by her past performance, Jane should do very well.* | *From past experience she knew that it was no use arguing with him.* | *Study some past exam papers to get an idea of the questions.*
2 **RECENT** [only before noun] used to refer to a period up until now: *the events of the past year* | *During the past two weeks twelve people have died of the disease.* | *She has been feeling tired for the past few days.*
3 **FINISHED** finished or having come to an end: *Winter is past and spring has come at last.* | *writers from past centuries* | *a tradition rooted in times* **long past**
4 **FORMER** [only before noun] having held a particular position in the past or achieved a particular honour in the past: **past president/member/winner etc** *a past president of the golf club* | *a celebration for past and present employees of the newspaper* | *Bruce Jenner, a past Olympic champion*
5 **GRAMMAR** [only before noun] relating to the PAST TENSE

past² S1 W2 prep, adv
1 later than a particular time: *It's ten past nine.* | *I should be finished by half past* (=30 minutes after the hour). | *It was past midnight when the party ended.* | *Come on Annie, it's* **long past** *your bedtime.*
2 further than a particular place: *The hospital's just up this road, about a mile past the school.* | *There are parking spaces over there,* **just past** (=a little further than) *the garage.*
3 up to and beyond a person or place, without stopping: *She waved as she drove past.* | *Will you be going past my house on your way home?* | **straight/right past** (=used to emphasize that someone passes close to you and does not stop) *Monica hurried straight past me and down the steps.*
4 if a period of time goes past, it passes: *Weeks went past without any news.* | *The hours seemed to fly past.*
5 beyond or no longer at a particular point or stage: *The roses were already past their best.* | *Reid never really got past the stage of copying other artists.* | *A pot of yoghurt* **well past** *its sell-by date* | *an Italian singer who was then past her prime* (=no longer strong and active) | *I'm past caring about my appearance* (=I do not care about it any more).
6 **I wouldn't put it past sb (to do sth)** spoken used to say that you would not be surprised if someone did something bad or unusual because it is typical of them to do that type of thing: *I wouldn't put it past Colin to cheat.*
7 **past it** BrE spoken too old to be able to do what you used to do, or too old to be useful: *People seem to think that just because I'm retired, I'm past it.*
8 **be past due** AmE something that is past due has not been paid or done by the time it should have been

past³ S1 W2 n
1 the past a) the time that existed before the present: **in the past** *The lake was smaller in the past.* | *Good manners have become* **a thing of the past** (=something that does not exist any more). | *It's time she stopped* **living in the past** (=thinking only about the past) *and began to think about her future.* | **the recent/immediate/distant past** *She allowed her mind to drift towards the recent past.* | *I did a law degree some time* **in the dim and distant past** (=a long time ago). b) the PAST TENSE
2 **all in the past** spoken used to say that an unpleasant experience has ended and can be forgotten: *You mustn't think about it. It's all in the past now.*
3 [singular] the past life or existence of someone or something: *At some time in its past the church was rebuilt.* | *The woman who ran the bar had a very* **shady past** (=events in her past which might be considered bad).

P

pasta

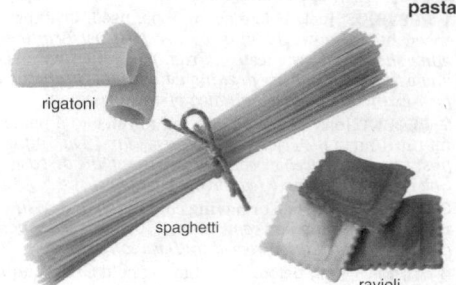

rigatoni

spaghetti

ravioli

pas·ta /ˈpæstə $ ˈpɑː-/ n [U] an Italian food made from flour, eggs, and water and cut into various shapes, usually eaten with a sauce: *I eat a lot of pasta.*

paste¹ /peɪst/ n **1** meat/fish/tomato etc paste a soft smooth food, made by crushing meat, fish etc **2** [C,U] a soft thick mixture that can easily be shaped or spread: *Mix the powder with enough water to make a smooth paste.* **3** [C,U] a type of glue that is used for sticking paper onto things: *wallpaper paste* **4** [U] pieces of glass that are used in jewellery to look like valuable stones

paste² v **1** [T always + adv/prep] to stick something to something else using glue: *A notice had been pasted to the door.* **2** [I,T] to make words that you have removed or copied appear in a new place on a computer screen; → **copy, cut**: *Data can be pasted into word processing documents.* → PASTE-UP, PASTING

paste·board /ˈpeɪstbɔːd $ -bɔːrd/ n [U] flat stiff CARD-BOARD made by sticking sheets of paper together

pas·tel¹ /ˈpæstl $ pæˈstel/ n **1 a)** [C,U] a small coloured stick for drawing pictures with, made of a substance like CHALK **b)** [C] a picture drawn with pastels **2** [C usually plural] a light colour such as pale blue or pink: *a room beautifully furnished in soft pastels*

pastel² adj [only before noun] **1** pastel colours are light and pale: *pastel blue* | *The walls were painted in pastel shades.* **2** drawn using pastels: *a set of four small pastel drawings*

paste-up n [C] a piece of paper with writing and pictures stuck on it that shows what a page will look like when a book or magazine is produced

pas·teur·ized also **-ised** BrE /ˈpɑːstʃəraɪz, -stə-$ ˈpæs-/ adj a liquid, usually milk, that is pasteurized has been heated using a special process in order to kill any harmful BACTERIA in it —**pasteurize** v [T] —**pasteurization** /ˌpɑːstʃəraɪˈzeɪʃən -stə-$ ˌpæstʃərə-/ n [U]

pas·tiche /pæˈstiːʃ/ n **1** [C] a piece of writing, music, film etc that is deliberately made in the style of someone or something else; → **parody**: [+of] *The film is a pastiche of the Hollywood Wild West.* **2** [C] a work of art that consists of a variety of different styles put together **3** [U] the practice of making a piece of writing, music, film etc using the style of something else or using a variety of different styles

pas·tille /pæˈstiːl/ n [C] especially BrE a small round sweet, sometimes containing medicine for a sore throat; ⊟ **lozenge**: *fruit pastilles*

pas·time /ˈpɑːstaɪm $ ˈpæs-/ n [C] something that you do because you think it is enjoyable or interesting; → **hobby**: *Reading was her favourite pastime.*

past·ing /ˈpeɪstɪŋ/ n **1** [U] the activity of moving words from one place to another on a computer screen: *cutting and pasting* **2** [singular] informal an easy defeat of someone in a game or competition **3** [singular] BrE informal a severe beating

past 'master n [C] someone who is very skilled at doing something and has done it many times before; ⊟ **expert: past master at (doing) sth** *She's a past master at exploiting other people.*

pas·tor /ˈpɑːstə $ ˈpæstər/ n [C] a Christian priest in some Protestant churches: *the pastor of Carr's Lane Congregational church* | *Pastor Martin Niemoller*

pas·tor·al /ˈpɑːstərəl $ ˈpæ-/ adj **1** relating to the duties of a priest, minister etc towards the members of their religious group: *his pastoral work among the congregation* **2** literary typical of the simple peaceful life in the country: *a charming pastoral scene* **3** relating to the duties of a teacher in advising students about their personal needs rather than their school-work: *pastoral care at the school*

past 'participle n [C] technical the form of a verb used with the verb 'to have' in PERFECT tenses (for example 'eaten' in 'I have eaten'), or with the verb 'to be' in the PASSIVE (for example 'changed' in 'it was changed'), or sometimes as an adjective (for example 'broken' in 'a broken leg')

past 'perfect n [singular] technical the form of a verb that shows that the action described by the verb was completed before a particular time in the past, formed in English with 'had' and a past participle —**past perfect** adj

pas·tra·mi /pəˈstrɑːmi/ n [U] smoked BEEF that contains a lot of spices

pas·try S3 /ˈpeɪstri/ n plural **pastries** **1** [U] a mixture of flour, butter, and milk or water, used to make the outer part of baked foods such as PIES **2** [C] a small sweet cake, made using pastry: *a Danish pastry*

past 'tense n [C] a form of a verb that shows that something happened or existed before the present time, typically a form such as 'walked', as in 'I walked away'

pas·tur·age /ˈpɑːstʃərɪdʒ $ ˈpæs-/ n [U] pasture

pas·ture¹ /ˈpɑːstʃə $ ˈpæstʃər/ n [C,U] **1** land or a field that is covered with grass and is used for cattle, sheep etc to feed on: *large areas of rough upland pasture* | *the lush pastures of the southern counties* **2 put sth/sb out to pasture a)** to move cattle, horses etc into a field to feed on the grass **b)** informal to make someone leave their job because you think they are too old to do it well **3 pastures new/greener pastures** a new and exciting or better job, place, or activity – used humorously: *I'd like to say goodbye to Paul who leaves us for pastures new.*

pasture² v **1** [T] to put animals outside in a field to feed on the grass **2** [I + on] if animals pasture on a particular area of land, they eat the grass that is growing there

pas·ture·land /ˈpɑːstʃəlænd $ ˈpæstʃər-/ n [U] pasture

past·y¹ /ˈpeɪsti/ adj a pasty face looks very pale and unhealthy

past·y² /ˈpæsti/ n plural **pasties** [C] BrE a small PASTRY case filled with meat, vegetables etc and baked: *a Cornish pasty*

pasty-faced /ˈpeɪsti feɪst/ adj having a very pale face that looks unhealthy

pat¹ /pæt/ v **patted, patting** [T] **1** to lightly touch someone or something several times with your hand flat, especially to give comfort; → **stroke**: *He patted the dog affectionately.* **2 pat sb/yourself on the back** to praise someone or yourself for doing something well: *You can pat yourselves on the back for a job well done.*

pat² n [C] **1** a friendly act of touching someone with your hand flat: *Mrs Dodd gave the child a pat on the head.* **2 pat of butter** a small flat amount of butter **3 a pat on the back** informal praise for something that you have done well: *Alex deserves a pat on the back for all his hard work.* → COWPAT

pat³ adj [usually before noun] a pat answer or explanation seems too quick and too simple and sounds as if it has been used before: *There are no pat answers to these questions.*

pat⁴ adv **1 have sth off pat** BrE; **have sth down pat** AmE to know something thoroughly so that you can say it, perform it etc immediately without thinking about it; → **off by heart 2 stand pat** AmE to refuse to change your opinion or decision

patch¹ /pætʃ/ n [C]
1 PART OF AN AREA a small area of something that is different from the area around it: [+of] *We finally found a patch of grass to sit down on.* | *Belinda watched a patch of sunlight move slowly across the wall.* | *Look out for icy patches on the road.* | *a cat with a white patch on its chest* | *He combs his hair over his bald patch.*
2 OVER A HOLE a small piece of material that is sewn on something to cover a hole in it: *a jacket with leather patches at the elbows*
3 FOR GROWING STH a small area of ground for growing fruit or vegetables: *a strawberry patch*
4 COMPUTER a small computer program that is added to software to solve problems
5 EYE a piece of material that you wear over your eye to protect it when it has been hurt: *He had a black patch over one eye.*
6 DECORATION AmE a small piece of cloth with words or pictures on it that you can sew onto clothes; ▢ **badge** BrE
7 a bad/difficult/sticky/rough patch informal a period of time when you are having a lot of difficulty: *Gemma's going through a bad patch right now.*
8 sb's patch BrE informal an area that someone knows very well because they work or live there; ▢ **turf**: *Policemen know what's going on in their home patch.*
9 not be a patch on sb/sth BrE informal to be much less attractive, good etc than something or someone else: *The second film isn't a patch on the first.*

patch² v also **patch up** [T + with] to repair a hole in something by putting a piece of something else over it
  patch sth ⇔ **together** phr v to make something quickly or carelessly from a number of different pieces or ideas: *A new plan was quickly patched together.*
  patch sth/sb ⇔ **up** phr v **1** to end an argument because you want to stay friendly with someone: *Try to patch up your differences before he leaves.* | **patch it/things up (with sb)** *He went back to patch things up with his wife.* **2** to repair a hole in something by putting a piece of something else over it: *We'll have to patch up the hole in the roof.* **3** to give quick and basic medical treatment to someone who is hurt: *We patched up the wounded as best we could.*

pa·tchou·li /pəˈtʃuːli/ n [U] a type of PERFUME made from the leaves of a SE Asian bush

patch·work /ˈpætʃwɜːk $ -wɜːrk/ n **1** [U] a type of sewing in which many coloured squares of cloth are stitched together to make one large piece: *a patchwork quilt* → see picture at HANDICRAFT **2** [singular] something that is made up of a lot of different things: [+of] *a patchwork of woods and fields, typical of the English countryside* | *The area was a patchwork of local industries.*

patch·y /ˈpætʃi/ adj **1** happening or existing in some areas but not in others: *patchy fog* **2** not complete enough to be useful: *His knowledge of French remained pretty patchy.* | *There is only patchy evidence of the animal's existence.* **3** especially BrE good in some parts but bad in others: *I thought the performance was patchy.* —**patchiness** n [U]

pate /peɪt/ n [C] old use the top of your head: *his bald pate*

pâ·té /ˈpæteɪ $ pɑːˈteɪ, pæ-/ n [C,U] a soft food made from meat or fish, that you can spread on bread

pa·tel·la /pəˈtelə/ n [C] technical your KNEE CAP

pa·tent¹ /ˈpeɪtnt, ˈpæ- $ ˈpæ-/ n [C,U] a special document that gives you the right to make or sell a new INVENTION or product that no one else is allowed to copy:

[+on/for] *He applied for a patent for a new method of removing paint.* | *He wants to take out a patent on his new type of dustbin.* | *The drugs are protected by patent.*

patent² adj [only before noun] **1** protected by a patent: *a patent lock* **2** patent lie/nonsense/impossibility etc formal used to emphasize that something is clearly a lie etc; ▢ **obvious** → PATENTLY

patent³ v [T] to obtain a special document giving you the right to make or sell a new INVENTION or product

patent leath·er /ˌpeɪtnt ˈleðə◂ $ ˌpætnt ˈleθər/ n [U] thin shiny leather, usually black: *patent leather shoes*

pa·tent·ly /ˈpeɪtntli $ ˈpæ-/ adv formal very clearly: *The treatment is patently not working.* | **patently false/untrue** *To say that the proposal has no disadvantages at all is patently untrue.* | *It's patently obvious that you're in love with her.*

patent medi·cine /ˌpeɪtnt ˈmedsən $ ˌpætnt ˈmedʒsən/ n [C] a medicine which can be bought without a PRESCRIPTION (=a written order from your doctor); ▢ **over-the-counter**

pa·ter /ˈpeɪtə $ -ər/ n [C] BrE old-fashioned father

pa·ter·fa·mil·ias /ˌpeɪtəfəˈmiːliæs $ ˌpɑːtərfəˈmiːliəs/ n [C] formal a father or a man who is the head of a family

pa·ter·nal /pəˈtɜːnl $ -ɜːr-/ adj **1** paternal feelings or behaviour are like those of a kind father towards his children: *Dan took a paternal interest in my work.* **2** paternal grandmother/uncle etc your father's mother, brother etc —**paternally** adv → MATERNAL

pa·ter·nal·is·m /pəˈtɜːnəl-ɪzəm $ -ɜːr-/ n [U] when people in charge of an organization or society protect the members and give them what they need but do not allow them any freedom or responsibility —**paternalistic** /pəˌtɜːnəlˈɪstɪk◂ $ -ɜːr-/ also **paternalist** adj

pa·ter·ni·ty /pəˈtɜːnɪti $ -ɜːr-/ n [U] law the fact of being the father of a particular child, or the question of who the child's father is: *The paternity of the child is in dispute.*

pa'ternity ˌleave n [U] a period of time that the father of a new baby is allowed away from work; → **maternity leave, parental leave**

pa'ternity ˌsuit n [C] a legal action in which a mother asks a court of law to find proof that a particular man is the father of her child, usually in order to claim financial support from him

path S2 W2 /pɑːθ $ pæθ/ n plural **paths** /pɑːðz $ pæðz/ [C]
1 TRACK a track that has been made deliberately or made by many people walking over the same ground: *I walked nervously up the garden path towards the front door.* | *a well-worn path across the grass* | **Follow the path** *along the river to the bridge.* | *a path leading to the summer house* → see picture at COUNTRY
2 WAY THROUGH STH the space ahead of you as you move along: [+through] *Police cleared a path through the protesters.* | *Damian blocked their path.*
3 DIRECTION the direction or line along which something or someone is moving: **in sth's/sb's path** *The tornado destroyed everything in its path.* | **into the path of sth** *She walked into the path of an oncoming vehicle.*
4 PLAN a plan or series of actions that will help you achieve something, especially over a long period of time: *a career path* | **path to freedom/success/independence etc** *She saw a college degree as her path to success.* | **the same/a different path** *I hope you will choose a different path.*
5 sb's paths cross if two people's paths cross, they meet by chance: *Our paths did not cross again.* → **beat a path (to sb's door)** at BEAT¹ (16); → **off the beaten path** at BEATEN (1) → FLIGHT PATH; → **lead sb up the garden path** at LEAD¹ (12); → **stand in sb's path** at STAND¹ (30)

P

pa·thet·ic S3 /pə'θetɪk/ *adj*
1 something or someone that is pathetic is so useless, unsuccessful, or weak that they annoy you: *You're pathetic! Here, let me do it.* | *I know it sounds pathetic now, but at the time I was frightened.* | *Vic made a pathetic attempt to apologise.*
2 making you feel pity or sympathy: *The child looked a pathetic sight.* —**pathetically** /-kli/ *adv*: *She whimpered pathetically.*

pa,thetic 'fallacy *n* [U] *technical* the idea of describing the sea, rocks, weather etc in literature as if they were human

path·find·er /'pɑ:θ,faɪndə $ 'pæθ,faɪndər/ *n* [C] *especially AmE* **1** someone who goes ahead of a group and finds the best way through unknown land **2** a person who discovers new ways of doing things; ◻ **trailblazer**

path·o·gen /'pæθədʒən, -dʒen/ *n* [C] *technical* something that causes disease in your body —**pathogenic** /,pæθə'dʒenɪk◂/ *adj*

path·o·log·i·cal /,pæθə'lɒdʒɪkəl◂ $ -'lɑː-/ *adj* **1** pathological behaviour or feelings happen regularly, and are strong, unreasonable, and impossible to control: *a pathological hatred of women* | *a pathological liar* **2** a mental or physical condition that is pathological is caused by disease: ***pathological conditions*** *such as cancer* **3** relating to pathology —**pathologically** /-kli/ *adv*: *Stephen was almost pathologically jealous of his brother.*

pa·thol·o·gy /pə'θɒlədʒi $ -'θɑː-/ *n* [U] the study of the causes and effects of illnesses —**pathologist** *n* [C]

pa·thos /'peɪθɒs $ -θɑːs/ *n* [U] the quality that a person, situation, film, or play has that makes you feel pity and sadness: *the pathos of the woman trying to keep her lover*

path·way /'pɑ:θweɪ $ 'pæθ-/ *n* [C] **1** a path **2** a series of nerves that pass information to each other

pa·tience S3 /'peɪʃəns/ *n* [U]
1 the ability to continue waiting or doing something for a long time without becoming angry or anxious; ◼ **impatience**: *I wouldn't have the patience to sit sewing all day.* | **infinite/unlimited/endless** patience *a good listener who has infinite patience*
2 the ability to accept trouble and other people's annoying behaviour without complaining or becoming angry: *You'll need patience and understanding if you're going to be a teacher.* | **have little/no patience with sb** *She has no patience with time-wasters.* | **lose/run out of patience (with sb)** (=stop being patient and get angry) *I'm beginning to lose patience with you people.* | *It will take time and patience to get these changed accepted.* | *Celia's patience suddenly snapped and she told them to shut up.* | **the patience of Job/the patience of a saint** (=very great patience when someone is annoying you) | *Henry's negative attitude is beginning to try my patience* (=make me lose my patience).
3 (have) patience used to tell someone to wait calmly: *Patience, my dear. Some things take time.*
4 *BrE* a card game for one player; ◻ **solitaire** *AmE*

pa·tient¹ S2 W1 /'peɪʃənt/ *n* [C] someone who is receiving medical treatment from a doctor or in a hospital → see picture at EXAMINE

patient² W3 *adj* able to wait calmly for a long time or to accept difficulties, people's annoying behaviour etc without becoming angry; ◼ **impatient**: *You'll just have to be patient and wait till I'm off the phone.* | [+with] *Louise was very patient with me.* —**patiently** *adv*: *He waited patiently for Katherine to speak.*

pat·i·na /'pætɪnə $ pə'tiːnə/ *n* [singular] **1** a greenish layer that forms naturally on the surface of COPPER or BRONZE **2** a smooth, shiny surface that gradually develops on wood, leather etc **3** **a patina of wealth/success etc** the appearance of being wealthy, successful etc

pat·i·o /'pætiəʊ $ -oʊ/ *n plural* **patios** [C] a flat hard area near a house, where people sit outside → see picture at PATIO

'patio ,doors *n* [plural] *especially BrE* glass doors that open from a living room onto a patio

pa·tis·se·rie /pə'tiːsəri, -'tɪs-/ *n* [C] a shop that sells cakes and PIES, especially French cakes, or the cakes it sells

pa·tois /'pætwɑː/ *n plural* **patois** /-twɑːz/ [C,U] a spoken form of a language used by the people of a small area and different from the national or standard language

pa·tri·arch /'peɪtriɑːk $ -ɑːrk/ *n* [C] **1** an old man who is respected as the head of a family or tribe → MATRIARCH **2** a BISHOP in the early Christian church **3** a BISHOP of the Orthodox Christian churches who is very high in rank

pa·tri·arch·al /,peɪtri'ɑːkəl◂ $ -'ɑːr-/ *adj* **1** ruled or controlled only by men: *a patriarchal society* **2** relating to being a patriarch, or typical of a patriarch; → **matriarchal**

pa·tri·arch·y /'peɪtriɑːki $ -ɑːr-/ *n plural* **patriarchies** [C,U] **1** a social system in which men have all the power **2** a social system in which the oldest man rules his family and passes power and possessions on to his sons → MATRIARCHY

pa·tri·cian /pə'trɪʃən/ *adj* **1** typical of a member of the highest class in society: *a patrician manner* **2** belonging to the high class of people that governed in ancient Rome —**patrician** *n* [C] → PLEBEIAN

pat·ri·cide /'pætrɪsaɪd/ *n* [U] the crime of murdering your father; → **matricide**, **parricide**

pat·ri·mo·ny /'pætrɪməni $ -moʊni/ *n* [singular, U] *formal* property given to you after the death of your father, which was given to him by your grandfather etc; ◻ **inheritance**

pat·ri·ot /'pætriət, -triɒt, 'peɪ- $ 'peɪtriət, -triɑːt/ *n* [C] someone who loves their country and is willing to defend it – used to show approval

pat·ri·ot·ic /,pætri'ɒtɪk◂, ,peɪ- $,peɪtri'ɑːtɪk◂/ *adj* having or expressing a great love of your country; → **nationalistic**: *patriotic songs* | *I'm not very patriotic.* —**patriotism** /'pætriətɪzəm, 'peɪ- $ 'peɪ-/ *n* [U]

pa·trol¹ /pə'trəʊl $ -'troʊl/ *v* **patrolled**, **patrolling** [T] **1** to go around the different parts of an area or building at regular times to check that there is no trouble or danger: *Armed guards patrolled the grounds.* | *an area patrolled by special police units* **2** to drive or walk around an area in a threatening way: *Gangs of youths patrolled the streets at night.*

patrol² *n* **1** [C,U] when someone goes around different parts of an area at regular times to check that there is no trouble or danger: **on patrol** *police on patrol in the city centre* | *The security forces increased their patrols in the area.* **2** [C] a group of police, soldiers, vehicles, planes etc sent out to search a particular area: *a US border patrol* | **patrol boat/car** (=used by the army or police) **3** [C] a small group of BOY SCOUTS or GUIDES → HIGHWAY PATROL

pa'trol car *n* [C] a police car that drives around the streets of a city

pa·trol·man /pə'trəʊlmən $ -'troʊl-/ *n plural* **patrolmen** /-mən/ [C] **1** *AmE* a police officer who regularly walks or drives around a particular area to try to prevent crime **2** someone employed by a car owners' association in Britain who goes to give help to drivers by the road

pa·tron /'peɪtrən/ *n* [C] **1** someone who supports the activities of an organization, for example by giving money: *a wealthy patron* | [+of] *a patron of the arts* **2** a famous person who is officially involved with an organization, such as a CHARITY, and whose name is used to help advertise it **3** *formal* someone who uses a particular shop, restaurant, or hotel: *facilities for disabled patrons*; → see box at CUSTOMER

pat·ron·age /ˈpætrənɪdʒ $ ˈpeɪ-, ˈpæ-/ n [U] **1** the support, especially financial support, that is given to an organization or activity by a patron **2** AmE formal the support that you give a particular shop, restaurant etc by buying their goods or using their services; ▤ **custom** BrE: Thank you for your patronage. **3** a system by which someone in a powerful position gives people help or important jobs in return for their support

pa·tron·ess /ˈpeɪtrənˌes/ n [C] a woman who supports the activities of a person or organization, by giving money or using their name in advertising; → **patron**

pat·ron·ize /ˈpætrənaɪz $ ˈpeɪ-, ˈpæ-/ v [T] **1** to talk to someone in a way which seems friendly but shows that you think they are not as intelligent or do not know as much as you: Don't patronize me! | The program focuses on kids' interests without patronizing them. **2** formal to use or visit a shop, restaurant etc **3** to support or give money to an organization or activity

pat·ro·niz·ing /ˈpætrənaɪzɪŋ $ ˈpeɪ-, ˈpæ-/ adj someone who is patronizing talks to you in a way that shows they think you are less intelligent or important than them: a patronizing attitude | a patronizing tone | I don't mean to sound patronizing. —**patronizingly** adv

patron 'saint n [C] a Christian SAINT who people believe gives special protection to a particular place, activity, or person: [+of] St. Christopher, the patron saint of travellers

pat·sy /ˈpætsi/ n plural patsies [C] especially AmE informal someone who is easily tricked or deceived, especially so that they take the blame for someone else's crime

pat·ter¹ /ˈpætə $ -ər/ v [I] if something, especially water, patters, it makes quiet sounds as it keeps hitting a surface lightly and quickly: [+on] rain pattering on the window panes

patter² n **1** [singular] the sound made by something as it keeps hitting a surface lightly and quickly: [+of] the patter of footsteps | the **pitter patter** of rain-drops **2** [singular, U] fast, continuous, and usually amusing talk, used by someone telling jokes or trying to sell something: It's difficult to look at the cars without getting the **sales patter**. **3** the **patter of tiny feet** used humorously to mean that someone is going to have a baby: Are we going to hear the patter of tiny feet?

pat·tern¹ S3 W1 /ˈpætən $ ˈpætərn/ n [C]
1 the regular way in which something happens, develops, or is done: Weather patterns have changed in recent years. | [+of] changing **patterns of behaviour** among students | The child showed a normal **pattern of development**. | [+in] They noticed patterns in the data. | A general **pattern** began to **emerge**. | Their descriptions seemed to **follow a set pattern** (=always develop in the same way). | His behavior **fits a pattern** of violent acts.
2 a) a regularly repeated arrangement of shapes, colours, or lines on a surface, usually as decoration: a black and white striped pattern | [+of] a pattern of dots **b)** a regularly repeated arrangement of sounds or words: A sonnet has a fixed rhyming pattern.
3 [usually singular] a thing, idea, or person that is an example to copy: The book **set the pattern for** over 40 similar historical romances.
4 a shape used as a guide for making something, especially a thin piece of paper used when cutting material to make clothes: a dress pattern
5 a small piece of cloth, paper etc that shows what a larger piece will look like; ▤ **sample**

pattern² v [T] **1** be **patterned on/after sth** to be designed or made in a way that is copied from something else: The exam system is patterned after the one used in Japan. **2** literary to form a pattern on something: Tiny white flowers patterned the ground like confetti.

pat·terned /ˈpætənd $ -ərnd/ adj decorated with a pattern: a patterned carpet | a brightly patterned dress | [+with] wallpaper patterned with roses

pat·tern·ing /ˈpætənɪŋ $ -tər-/ n [U] **1** technical the development of particular ways of behaving, thinking, doing things etc that are the result of copying and repeating actions, language etc: cultural patterning | [+of] the patterning of parent-child relation-ships **2** patterns of a particular kind, especially on an animal's skin

pat·ty /ˈpæti/ n plural patties [C] small, flat pieces of cooked meat or other food: a beef patty

pau·ci·ty /ˈpɔːsˌti $ ˈpɒː-/ n [singular] formal less than is needed of something; ▤ **lack**: [+of] a paucity of information

paunch /pɔːntʃ $ pɒːntʃ/ n [C] a man's fat stomach —**paunchy** adj

pau·per /ˈpɔːpə $ ˈpɒːpər/ n [C] old-fashioned some-one who is very poor

pause¹ W3 /pɔːz $ pɒːz/ v
1 [I] to stop speaking or doing something for a short time before starting again: [+for] She paused for a moment. | He **paused for breath**, then continued up the hill. | 'No,' he replied, without **pausing for thought**. | **pause to do sth** Joe paused to consider his answer.
2 [I,T] to push a button on a tape player, CD player, computer etc in order to make a tape, CD etc stop playing for a short time

pause² n [C] **1** a short time during which someone stops speaking or doing something before starting again: There was a pause while Alice changed the tape. | After a **long pause**, she went on. | [+in] an awkward pause in the conversation **2** also **pause button** a control which allows you to stop a CD PLAYER, VIDEO RECORDER etc for a short time and start it again **3** a mark (⌢) over a musical note, showing that the note is to be played or sung longer than usual **4** give sb **pause (for thought)** to make someone stop and consider carefully what they are doing: an avoidable accident that should give us all pause for thought

pave /peɪv/ v [T usually passive] **1** to cover a path, road, area etc with a hard level surface such as blocks of stone or CONCRETE: [+with] The city centre streets are paved with dark local stone. | a paved court-yard **2** pave the **way for sth** to make a later event or development possible by producing the right condi-tions: The Supreme Court decision paved the way for further legislation on civil rights. **3** the streets are **paved with gold** used to say that it is easy to become rich quickly in a particular place

pave·ment /ˈpeɪvmənt/ n **1** [C] BrE a hard level surface or path at the side of a road for people to walk on; ▤ **sidewalk** AmE: A small group of journalists waited on the pavement outside her house. | a pavement café → see picture at TOWN **2** [U] AmE the hard surface of a road: As she fell off the bike, her head hit the pavement. **3** [C,U] any paved surface or area; ▤ **pav-ing** **4** pound/hit the **pavement** to work very hard to get something, especially a job, by going to a lot of different places: He spent the next six months pounding the pavement in search of a job.

pa·vil·ion /pəˈvɪljən/ n [C] **1** a temporary building or tent which is used for public entertainment or EXHIBI-TIONS and is often large with a lot of space and light: the German pavilion at the World Trade Fair **2** BrE a building beside a sports field, especially a CRICKET field, used by the players and people watching the game **3** AmE a very large building with big open areas used for sports and other public events: victory before a home crowd at Maples Pavilion

pav·ing /ˈpeɪvɪŋ/ n **1** [U] material used to form a hard level surface on a path, road, area etc: brick paving **2** [U] an area covered in a hard level surface such as blocks of stone or CONCRETE **3** [C] a paving stone

'paving stone also **'paving slab** BrE n [C] one of the flat pieces of stone that are used to make a hard surface to walk on

P

severe penalties for late payment of taxes. | [+in] *Most hotels here accept payment in dollars.* | **Payment** can be **made** by cheque or credit card. | *We do accept* **payment in instalments** (=paying in small amounts over a period of time). | *She demanded* **payment in advance.** | **in payment for sth** (=in order to pay for something) *cheques received in payment for goods supplied* | **on payment of sth** (=when an amount has been paid) *Any item can be reserved on payment of a deposit.*

3 payment in kind a way of paying for something with goods or services instead of money

pay·off /ˈpeɪɒf $ -ɒːf/ n [C] **1** an advantage or profit that you get as a result of doing something: *With electric cars there is a big environmental payoff.* **2** a payment that is made to someone, often illegally, in order to stop them from causing you trouble; → **bribe**: *Union leaders allegedly received huge payoffs from the company's bosses.* **3** a payment made to someone when they are forced to leave their job; → **redundancy**: *The average payoff to staff was about £2000.*

pay·o·la /peɪˈəʊlə $ -ˈoʊlə/ n [U] *informal especially AmE* **1** the illegal practice of paying someone to use their influence to make people buy what your company is selling **2** the money that is paid to someone to use their influence

pay·out /ˈpeɪ-aʊt/ n [C] a large payment of money to someone, for example from an insurance claim or from winning a competition: *There should be a big payout on this month's lottery.* | *Some of the victims have been offered massive* **cash payouts.**

pay ˌpacket n [C] *BrE* **1** the amount of money someone earns **2** an envelope containing someone's wages

pay-per-ˈview adj [only before noun] a pay-per-view television CHANNEL makes people pay for each programme they watch; → **pay TV** —**pay-per-view** n [U]

pay phone n [C] a public telephone that you can use when you put in a coin or a CREDIT CARD

pay rise *BrE*; **pay raise** *AmE* n [C] an increase in the amount of money you are paid for doing your job: *Some company directors have awarded themselves huge pay rises.* | *a 4% pay raise*

pay·roll /ˈpeɪrəʊl $ -roʊl/ n **1 on the payroll** if someone is on the payroll of a company, they are employed by that company: *The company now has 350 people on the payroll.* **2** [U] the activity of managing salary payments for workers in a company: *the payroll department* | *a computerized payroll system* **3** [C,U] the total amount of wages paid to all the people working in a particular company or industry: *the annual payroll was $88 million*

payroll ˌtax n [C,U] a tax that is taken from someone's wages and given directly to the government; → **income tax**

pay·slip /ˈpeɪslɪp/ *BrE*, **pay stub** *AmE* n [C] a piece of paper that an employed person gets every time they are paid, showing the amount they have been paid and the amount that has been taken away for tax

pay ˈTV also **pay teleˈvision** n [U] television CHANNELS that you must pay to watch; → **pay-per-view**

PC¹ /ˌpiː ˈsiː◂/ n [C] **1** *personal computer* a computer that is used by one person at a time, either at home or at work: *People can use their PC's to do their banking from home.* **2** *BrE* **police constable** a police officer of the lowest rank

PC² adj *politically correct* used to describe language, behaviour, and attitudes that are carefully chosen so that they do not offend or insult anyone: *It's not PC to describe people as disabled.*

PˈC ˌCard n [C] *trademark* **personal computer card** a small flat object which stores information that can be added to some computers

pcm *per calendar month* used in writing when stating the amount of rent to be paid each month

PCP /ˌpiː siː ˈpiː/ n [C] *AmE* **primary care physician** a doctor you go to when you are ill, who may treat you or advise you to see a SPECIALIST (=a doctor who deals with a particular part of the body)

PDA /ˌpiː diː ˈeɪ/ n [C] **personal digital assistant** a very small light computer that you can carry with you, and that you use to store information such as telephone numbers, addresses, and APPOINTMENTS. Some PDAs can send and receive email, and connect to the Internet

PDF /ˌpiː diː ˈef/ n [U] *technical* **portable document format** a way of storing computer FILES so that they can be easily read when they are moved from one computer to another

PDQ /ˌpiː diː ˈkjuː/ adv *informal* **pretty damn quick** used to say that something should be done immediately

PDT /ˌpiː diː ˈtiː/ the abbreviation of *pacific daylight time*

PE *BrE*; **P.E.** *AmE* /ˌpiː ˈiː/ n [U] **physical education** sport and physical activity taught as a school subject: *a PE teacher*

pea /piː/ n [C] **1** a round green seed that is cooked and eaten as a vegetable, or the plant on which these seeds grow: *roast chicken with peas and carrots* → see picture at VEGETABLE¹ **2 like two peas in a pod** *informal* exactly the same in appearance, behaviour etc

pea-brained adj *informal* stupid: *a pea-brained idiot*

peace S2 W2 /piːs/ n

1 NO WAR [singular, U] a situation in which there is no war or fighting

be at peace (with sb) (=not be involved in a war)
make peace (=agree to stop fighting)
live in peace (=live without fighting)
bring peace to somewhere
world peace
lasting peace
uneasy peace
peace talks/negotiations/conference
peace treaty/agreement/accord
peace movement/march/campaigner/protester
the peace process

The country is **at peace with** *its neighbours for the first time in years.* | *By the end of the century, France had* **made peace with** *Britain.* | *a city where people of different religions have* **lived** *together* **in peace** *for centuries* | *efforts to* **bring peace** *to the region* | *a dangerous situation which threatens* **world peace** | [+between] *a* **lasting peace** *between the two sides* | *An* **uneasy peace** *continued until 1939.* | *the Northern Ireland* **peace talks** | *an international* **peace conference** | *the* **peace treaty** *that ended the First World War* | *the Middle East* **peace process**

2 NO NOISE/INTERRUPTIONS [U] a very quiet and pleasant situation in which you are not interrupted: **in peace** *I'll leave you now and let you get dressed in peace.* | *I wish she would just* **leave** *me* **in peace.** | *All I want is some* **peace and quiet.**

3 CALM/NOT WORRIED [U] a feeling of being calm, happy, and not worried: *the search for* **inner peace** | *Having household insurance is supposed to give you* **peace of mind.** | *Lynn seems to be more* **at peace with** *herself these days* (=calm, satisfied, no longer worried about anything).

4 make (your) peace with sb to end a quarrel with a person or group, especially by telling them you are sorry: *Ann wanted to make her peace with her father before he died.*

5 keep the peace to stop people from fighting, arguing, or causing trouble: *The US is sending troops overseas in order to keep the peace.*

6 hold/keep your peace *formal old-fashioned* to keep quiet even though you would like to say something

7 disturb the peace *law* to behave in a noisy or violent way: *Macklin was charged with disturbing the peace.* → **breach of the peace** at BREACH¹ (5)

8 rest in peace words that are said during a funeral service for someone who has died, or written on a GRAVESTONE; → RIP

peace·a·ble /ˈpiːsəbəl/ adj literary **1** someone who is peaceable does not like fighting or arguing; → **pacifist**; ⊟ **violent, aggressive**: He's always been a very peaceable man. **2** a peaceable situation or way of doing something is calm, without any violence or fighting: We are now hoping for a peaceable end to this dispute. —**peaceably** adv: The two communities live together quite peaceably.

'peace ˌdividend n [singular] the money that is saved on weapons and is available for other purposes, when a government reduces its military strength because the risk of war has been reduced

peace·ful ⑤₃ /ˈpiːsfəl/ adj
1 **QUIET/CALM** a peaceful time, place, or situation is quiet and calm without any worry or excitement: We had a peaceful afternoon without the children. | It's very peaceful out here in the woods.
2 **NO WAR** not involving war, fighting, or violence: peaceful protest/demonstration There was a large but peaceful demonstration outside the US Embassy. | peaceful solution/conclusion/settlement We must try to find a peaceful solution to the conflict. | peaceful means/way/manner/method a political change achieved by peaceful and democratic means | the use of nuclear power for peaceful purposes | The countries in Europe have established a **peaceful co-existence** (=they exist together without fighting).
3 **NOT LIKING VIOLENCE** peaceful people do not like violence and do not behave in a violent way; → **non-violent**: a noisy but peaceful group of demonstrators —**peacefully** adv: She was sleeping peacefully. —**peacefulness** n [U]

peace·keep·ing /ˈpiːsˌkiːpɪŋ/ adj [only before noun] **peacekeeping force/troops etc** a group of soldiers who are sent to a place in order to stop two opposing groups from fighting each other: The United Nations has decided to send a peacekeeping force into the area. —**peacekeeper** n [C]: a group of UN peacekeepers

'peace-ˌloving adj believing strongly in peace rather than war: a peace-loving nation

peace·mak·er /ˈpiːsmeɪkə $ -ər/ n [C] someone who tries to persuade other people or countries to stop fighting: The US sees itself as a peacemaker in the region.

'peace ˌoffering n [C] something you give to someone to show them that you are sorry and want to be friendly, after you have annoyed or upset them

'peace pipe n [C] a pipe which Native Americans use to smoke tobacco, which is shared in a ceremony as a sign of peace; ⊟ **pipe of peace**

peace·time /ˈpiːstaɪm/ n [U] a period of time when a country is not fighting a war; ⊟ **wartime**: **in peacetime** the highest military award given in peacetime

peach¹ /piːtʃ/ n **1** [C] a round juicy fruit that has a soft yellow or red skin and a large, hard seed in the centre, or the tree that this fruit grows on → see picture at FRUIT¹ **2** [U] a pale pinkish-orange colour **3** [singular] old-fashioned something or someone that you think is very good: Anderton scored **a peach of a** goal. | Jan's **a real peach**. **4 peaches and cream** used to describe skin that is an attractive pink colour: a peaches and cream complexion

peach² adj pinkish-orange in colour: peach curtains

Peach Mel·ba /ˌpiːtʃ ˈmelbə/ n [C,U] half a peach served with ice cream and RASPBERRY juice

peach·y /ˈpiːtʃi/ adj **1** tasting or looking like a peach: a delicious peachy flavour **2** AmE informal very good or pleasant

pea·cock /ˈpiːkɒk $ -kɑːk/ n [C] a large bird, the male of which has long blue and green tail feathers that it can lift up and spread out

pea·fowl /ˈpiːfaʊl/ n [C] a peacock or peahen

pea ˈgreen n [U] a light green colour —**pea green** adj

pea·hen /ˈpiːhen/ n [C] a female PEACOCK

peak¹ ⓦ₃ /piːk/ n [C]
1 **TIME** [usually singular] the time when something or someone is best, greatest, highest, most successful etc: **at sth's peak** The British Empire was at its peak in the mid 19th century. | Sales this month have **reached** a new peak. | Most athletes **reach** their peak in their mid 20s. | He's **past** his peak as a tennis player. | Oil production is down from its peak of two years ago. | **at the peak of sth** Hotel rooms are difficult to find at the peak of the holiday season. | the **peaks and troughs** of the US economy (=high and low points)
2 **MOUNTAIN a)** the sharply pointed top of a mountain: snow-capped **mountain peaks** | jagged peaks **b)** a mountain; → **summit**: Mount McKinley is Alaska's highest peak.
3 **POINT** a part that forms a point above a surface or at the top of something: Whisk the egg whites until they form stiff peaks.
4 **HAT** especially BrE the flat curved part of a cap that sticks out in front above your eyes; ⊟ **visor** AmE

peak² v [I] to reach the highest point or level: Sales peaked in August, then fell sharply. | **[+at]** Wind speeds peaked at 105 mph yesterday.

peak³ adj [only before noun] **1** used to talk about the best, highest, or greatest level or amount of something: Gasoline prices are 14% below the peak level they hit in November. | a shampoo designed to keep your hair **in peak condition** | If you phone during the day you pay the **peak rate** for calls. | periods of **peak demand** for electricity **2** BrE the peak time or period is when the greatest number of people are doing the same thing, using the same service etc: Extra buses run at **peak times**. | Hotel prices rise during the **peak season**.

peak·ed¹ /ˈpiːkd/ adj AmE looking pale and ill; ⊟ **peaky** BrE: You're **looking** a little peaked this morning.

peaked² /piːkt/ adj BrE a peaked cap or hat has a flat curved part at the front above the eyes → see picture at HAT

pea·ky /ˈpiːki/ adj informal BrE looking pale and ill; ⊟ **peaked¹** AmE: He's **looking** a bit peaky today.

peal¹ /piːl/ n [C] **1** a sudden loud sound of laughter: **[+of]** We could hear **peals of laughter** coming from the hall. **2** a loud sound of thunder; ⊟ **clap**: **[+of]** A loud **peal of thunder** crashed directly overhead. **3** the loud ringing sound made by a bell: A sudden **peal of bells** broke the silence. **4** technical a musical pattern made by ringing a number of bells one after the other

peal² v [I] **1** also **peal out** if bells peal, they ring loudly: The bells pealed out on Christmas Day. **2** literary to make a loud sound: Lightning flashed and thunder pealed.

pea·nut /ˈpiːnʌt/ n **1** [C] a pale brown nut in a thin shell which grows under the ground; ⊟ **groundnut**: a packet of roasted peanuts → see picture at NUT¹ **2 peanuts** informal a very small amount of money: The hotel workers get **paid peanuts**. | I'm tired of **working for peanuts**.

ˌpeanut ˈbutter / $ '.. ˌ../ n [U] a soft food made from crushed peanuts, which is eaten on bread or used in cooking

pear ⑤₃ /peə $ per/ n [C] a sweet juicy fruit that has a round base and is thinner near the top, or the tree that produces this fruit → see picture at FRUIT¹

pearl /pɜːl $ pɜːrl/ n
1 **JEWEL** [C] a small round white object that forms inside an OYSTER, and is a valuable jewel: a **pearl necklace** | a **string of pearls** (=a NECKLACE made of pearls)
2 **HARD SUBSTANCE** [U] a hard shiny substance of various colours formed inside some SHELLFISH, which is used for making buttons or to make objects look attractive; ⊟ **mother-of-pearl**
3 pearls of wisdom wise remarks – used especially

P

peep² n [C] **1** a quick or secret look at something: [+at/into] *Jon took a peep at his watch.* **2** a peep *informal* a sound that someone makes, or something that they say, especially a complaint: *There has not been a peep out of them since bedtime. | a peep of protest* **3** a short high sound, like the sound a mouse or a young bird makes: *the peep of a chick | loud peeps from the smoke alarm* **4** also **peeps** *informal* a word meaning 'people', used in magazines

peep·bo /'piːpbəʊ $ -boʊ/ *interjection, n* [U] PEEKABOO

peep·hole /'piːphəʊl $ -hoʊl/ n [C] a small hole in a door or wall that you can see through; → **spy hole**

peeping Tom /ˌpiːpɪŋ 'tɒm $ -'tɑːm/ n [C] someone who secretly watches people, especially people who are taking off their clothes, having sex etc

peep·show /'piːpʃəʊ $ -ʃoʊ/ n [C] **1** a type of show in which a man pays for a woman to take her clothes off while he watches through a window **2** a box containing moving pictures that you look at through a small hole

peer¹ /pɪə $ pɪr/ n [C] **1** [usually plural] *formal* your peers are the people who are the same age as you, or who have the same type of job, social class etc: *American children did less well in math than their peers in Japan. | Staff members are trained by their peers.* → PEER GROUP, PEER PRESSURE **2** a member of the British NOBILITY; → **House of Lords, peerage** → LIFE PEER

peer² v [I always + adv/prep] to look very carefully at something, especially because you are having difficulty seeing it: *He was peering through the wet windscreen at the cars ahead. | Philippa peered into the darkness.*

peer·age /'pɪərɪdʒ $ 'pɪr-/ n **1** the peerage all the British peers considered as a group **2** [C] the rank of a British peer

peer·ess /'pɪərɪ̥s $ 'pɪr-/ n [C] a woman who is a member of the British NOBILITY

peer group n [C] a group of people, especially people who are the same age, social class etc as yourself: *the TV shows that are popular with his peer group*

peer·less /'pɪələs $ 'pɪr-/ adj *written* better than any other: *the peerless blues musician B.B. King*

peer ,pressure n [U] a strong feeling that you must do the same things as other people of your age if you want them to like you: *Teenagers often start smoking because of peer pressure.*

peer-to-'peer also **P2P** adj **peer-to-peer architecture/network/technology etc** a computer system etc in which all of the computers are connected to each other and they do not need a SERVER (=a main computer that controls all the others): *How will peer-to-peer technology be important to the average Internet user?*

peeve /piːv/ → **pet hate/pet peeve** at PET³ (2)

peeved /piːvd/ adj *informal* annoyed: [+at] *Peeved at his silence, she left.*

peev·ish /'piːvɪʃ/ adj easily annoyed by small and unimportant things; → **bad-tempered**: *The kids were peevish after so long in the car.* —**peevishly** adv —**peevishness** n [U]

pee·wit /'piːwɪt/ n [C] a LAPWING

peg¹ /peg/ n [C]
1 SHORT STICK a short piece of wood, metal, or plastic that is attached to a wall or fits into a hole, used especially to hang things on or to fasten things together: *Sarah hung her coat on the peg. | a table fitted together with pegs | a pattern made with coloured pegs on a board*
2 HANGING WET CLOTHES *BrE* a small plastic or wooden object used to fasten wet clothes to a thin rope to dry; ◻ **clothespeg**; ◻ **clothespin** *AmE*
3 TENT a pointed piece of wood or metal that you push into the ground in order to keep a tent in the correct position
4 take/bring sb down a peg (or two) to make someone

realize that they are not as important or skilled as they think they are: *Evans is an arrogant bully who needs taking down a peg or two.*
5 MUSICAL INSTRUMENT a wooden screw used to make the strings of a VIOLIN, GUITAR etc tighter or looser; ◻ **tuning peg**
6 a peg to hang sth on *BrE* something that is used as a reason for doing, discussing, or believing something: *As a peg to hang it on, the tournament had the 100th anniversary of Nehru's birth.*
7 DRINK *BrE old-fashioned* a small amount of strong alcoholic drink, especially WHISKY or BRANDY → **square peg in a round hole** at SQUARE¹ (12)

peg² v **pegged, pegging** [T] **1** to set prices, wages etc at a particular level, or set them in relation to something else: **peg sth at sth** *The dividend was pegged at 6.1p.* | **peg sth to sth** *a currency pegged to the American dollar* **2** to fasten something somewhere with a peg: *The tent flap was pegged open. | Outside, a woman was pegging sheets to a washing line.*

peg sb/sth as sth phr v to believe or say that someone has a particular type of character, or that a situation has particular qualities: *I'd had him pegged as a troublemaker.*

peg away phr v *BrE informal* to work hard and with determination: [+at] *She pegged away at her essay.*

peg sb/sth ⇔ back phr v *BrE* to stop someone from winning in a sport or from increasing the amount by which they are winning – used in news reports: *They were pegged back by an equaliser from Jameson.*

peg out phr v **1** *BrE informal* to die, or to fall down because you are tired **2 peg sth ⇔ out** *BrE* to fasten wet clothes to a washing line to dry **3 peg sth ⇔ out** to mark a piece of ground with wooden sticks

peg·board, peg board /'pegbɔːd $ -bɔːrd/ n [C,U] thin board with holes in it, into which you can put pegs or hooks to hang things on

peg leg n [C] *informal* an artificial leg, especially a wooden one

pe·jo·ra·tive /pɪ'dʒɒrətɪv $ -'dʒɔː-, -'dʒɑː-/ adj *formal* a word or expression that is pejorative is used to show disapproval or to insult someone: *For hard-line Republicans, the word 'liberal' had become a pejorative term.* —**pejoratively** adv

peke /piːk/ n [C] *informal* a Pekinese dog

Pe·kin·ese, Pekingese /ˌpiːkɪ'niːz◂/ n plural **Pekinese, Pekingese** [C] a very small dog with a short flat nose and long silky hair

pe·lag·ic /pɪ'lædʒɪk/ adj *technical* relating to or living in the deep sea, far from shore: *pelagic fish*

pel·i·can /'pelɪkən/ n [C] a large water bird that catches fish for food and stores them in a deep bag of skin under its beak

pelican 'crossing n [C] a place on some roads in Britain where someone who wants to cross the road can stop the traffic by pushing a button that changes the TRAFFIC LIGHTS → ZEBRA CROSSING

pel·la·gra /pə'lægrə/ n [U] a disease that makes you feel tired and that causes problems with your skin and CENTRAL NERVOUS SYSTEM, caused by a lack of a type of B VITAMIN

pel·let /'pelɪ̥t/ n [C] **1** a small ball of a substance: *food pellets for rabbits* **2** a small ball of metal made to be fired from a gun: *shotgun pellets*

pell-mell /ˌpel 'mel◂/ adv *old-fashioned* quickly and in an uncontrolled way: *The children ran pell-mell out of school.*

pel·lu·cid /pə'luːsɪ̥d/ adj *literary* very clear; ◻ **transparent**: *a pellucid stream*

pel·met /'pelmɪ̥t/ n [C] *BrE* a narrow piece of wood or cloth above a window that hides the rod that the curtains hang on; ◻ **valance** *AmE*

pelt¹ /pelt/ v **1** [T] to attack someone by throwing a lot of things at them: **pelt sb with sth** *The marchers were pelted with rocks and bottles.* **2** [I,T] to be raining very heavily; → **pour**: *Rain pelted the windows. | It's pelt-*

ing down out there. | *the cold wind and **pelting rain***
3 [I always + adv/prep] *informal* to run somewhere very fast: *Three huge dogs came pelting into the street.*

pelt² n [C] **1** the skin of a dead animal, especially with the fur or hair still on it; → **hide** **2** the fur or hair of a living animal **3** (at) full pelt *BrE* moving as fast as possible: *Nancy ran at full pelt to the school.*

pel·vic /'pelvɪk/ *adj* in or relating to the pelvis

pel·vis /'pelvɪs/ n [C] the set of large wide curved bones at the base of your SPINE, to which your legs are joined → see picture at SKELETON

pem·mi·can /'pemɪkən/ n [U] dried meat, beaten into small pieces and pressed into flat round shapes

pen¹ [S2] /pen/ n
1 [C,U] an instrument for writing or drawing with ink; → **pencil**, **biro**: *a ballpoint pen* | *a felt-tip pen* | **in pen** *Please fill out the form in pen.* | *a **pen and ink** drawing* → see picture at OFFICE
2 [C] a small piece of land enclosed by a fence to keep farm animals in: *a sheep pen* → PLAYPEN
3 put/set pen to paper to begin to write
4 [C] *AmE informal* a short form of PENITENTIARY

pen² v **penned**, **penning** [T] *literary* to write something such as a letter, a book etc, especially using a pen: *a song penned by George Clinton*
pen sb/sth ⇔ **up/in** phr v **1** to shut an animal in a small enclosed area **2 be penned up/in** to be restricted or forced to remain in a small place: *Norma felt restless and penned in.*

pe·nal /'piːnl/ *adj* **1** [only before noun] relating to the legal punishment of criminals, especially in prisons: *the penal system* | **penal colony/settlement** (=a special area of land where prisoners are kept) **2 penal servitude** *law* when someone is punished by being kept in prison and made to do hard physical work **3** *BrE* very severe: *penal rates of interest*

penal ,code n [C] a set of laws and the punishments for not obeying those laws

pe·nal·ize also **-ise** *BrE* /'piːnəl-aɪz $ 'piː-, 'pe-/ v [T] **1** to punish someone or treat them unfairly: **penalize sb for (doing) sth** *Two students were penalized very differently for the same offence.* | *Women feel professionally penalized for taking time off to raise children.* **2** to punish a team or player in sports by giving an advantage to the other team: *The team was penalized for wasting time.*

pen·al·ty [S3] [W3] /'penlti/ n plural **penalties** [C]
1 a punishment for breaking a law, rule, or legal agreement: *No littering. Penalty $500.* | [+for] *The penalty for a first offense is a fine.* | **severe/stiff/heavy penalty** *Drug dealers face severe penalties.* | *If he is convicted, he could receive **the death penalty** (=be killed as a punishment).*
2 something bad that happens to you because of something you have done or because of the situation you are in: **penalty of (doing) sth** *One of the penalties of being famous is the loss of privacy.* | *If you don't do the job right, you will **pay the penalty**.*
3 a disadvantage in sports given to a player or team for breaking a rule: *Woodson received a penalty.*
4 a chance to kick the ball or hit the PUCK into the GOAL in a game of football, RUGBY, or ICE HOCKEY, given because the other team has broken a rule: *Townsend **kicked a penalty** (=in a rugby game) in the last minute.* | *Leeds were awarded a penalty.*

penalty ,area n [C] the area in front of the GOAL in football. The team opposing you is given a PENALTY if you break a rule there.

penalty ,box n [C] **1** an area off the ice where a player in ICE HOCKEY must wait after not obeying a rule **2** a penalty area

penalty ,clause n [C] the part of a contract which says what someone will have to pay or do if they do not obey the agreement, for example if they do not complete work on time

penalty ,kick n [C] a PENALTY (4)

penalty ,point n [C] *BrE* a note made on a driver's LICENCE to show that they have done something wrong while they were driving. If someone gets 12 penalty points they are no longer allowed to drive a car.

penalty 'shoot-out n [C] an occasion when each team in a football match takes penalty kicks until one team misses the GOAL - used as a way of deciding which team will win when the ordinary part of the match has ended in a DRAW

pen·ance /'penəns/ n **1** [C usually singular, U] something that you must do to show that you are sorry for something you have done wrong, especially in some religions: **do/perform penance** *We prayed and did penance together.* | [+for] *as a penance for his sins* **2** [singular] something that you have to do but do not enjoy doing: *Working in the garden was a kind of penance.*

pence /pens/ n *BrE* **p** a plural of PENNY: *a few pence* | *a 20 pence stamp*

pen·chant /'pɒnʃɒn, 'pentʃənt $ 'pentʃənt/ n **a/sb's penchant for sth** if you have a penchant for something, you like that thing very much and try to do it or have it often: *a penchant for fast cars*

pen·cil¹ [S2] /'pensəl/ n [C,U] an instrument that you use for writing or drawing, consisting of a wooden stick with a thin piece of a black or coloured substance in the middle: *a sharp pencil* | *a blue pencil* | **in pencil** *a note written in pencil* | *a pencil sketch* → EYEBROW PENCIL; → see picture at OFFICE; → see picture at STATIONERY

pencil² v **pencilled**, **pencilling** *BrE*, **penciled**, **penciling** *AmE* [T] to write something or make a mark with a pencil: *a name pencilled on the envelope*
pencil sb/sth ⇔ **in** phr v to make an arrangement for a meeting or other event, knowing that it might have to be changed later: *Pickford has been pencilled in as Robson's replacement.*

'pencil case, **'pencil box** n [C] a bag or box to carry pens and pencils in → see picture at CASE¹

'pencil ,pusher n [C] *AmE* someone who has a boring, unimportant job in an office

'pencil ,sharpener n [C] a small instrument with a blade inside, used to make pencils sharp → see picture at STATIONERY

'pencil ,skirt n [C] a long narrow straight skirt

pen·dant /'pendənt/ n [C] a jewel, stone etc that hangs from a thin chain that you wear around your neck; → **necklace**: *a ruby pendant*

pen·dent /'pendənt/ *adj* *literary* or *technical* hanging from something: *a pendent lamp*

pend·ing¹ /'pendɪŋ/ *prep* *formal* while waiting for something, or until something happens: *Sales of the drug have been stopped, pending further research.*

pending² *adj* **1** *formal* not yet decided or settled: *Many trade disputes are pending, awaiting the outcome of the talks.* **2** *formal* something that is pending is going to happen soon: *the pending election* **3 pending file/tray** *BrE* a container for keeping papers, letters etc that have not yet been dealt with; → **in-tray, out-tray**

pen·du·lous /'pendjʊləs $ -dʒə-/ *adj* *literary* hanging down loosely and swinging freely: *pendulous breasts*

pen·du·lum /'pendjʊləm $ -dʒə-/ n [C] **1** a long metal stick with a weight at the bottom that swings regularly from side to side to control the working of a clock **2 the pendulum** used to talk about the tendency of ideas, beliefs etc to change regularly to the opposite: *After several years of Republican government, **the pendulum** undoubtedly **swing** back and voters will elect a Democrat.* | [+of] *the pendulum of fashion*

pen·e·trate /'penɪtreɪt/ v
1 GO THROUGH [I,T] to enter something and pass or spread through it, especially when this is difficult; → **pierce**: *bullets that penetrate thick armour plating* | *Sunlight barely penetrated the dirty windows.* | [+into] *Explorers penetrated deep into unknown regions.*

who understands or is like ordinary people). | **the people's party/army etc** (=belonging to or popular with the ordinary people) *the People's Liberation Army* | *Diana – the people's princess* **b)** *AmE* used in court cases to represent the government of the US or of a particular state: *The People vs. Romero*
5 sb's **people** [plural] **a)** the people that a king or leader rules or leads: *The king ordered his people to prepare for war.* **b)** the people who work for a person or organization: *A manager's job is to make his or her people feel part of the system.* **c)** *old-fashioned* your relatives, especially your parents, grandparents etc: *Do your people live round here?*
6 of all people *spoken* used to say that someone is the person you would least or most expect to do something: *Why should he, of all people, get a promotion?* | *You of all people should have known better.*
7 TO GET ATTENTION [plural] *AmE spoken informal* used to get the attention of a group of people: *Listen up, people!* → LITTLE PEOPLE

people² *v* [T usually passive] *formal* **1** if a country or area is peopled by people of a particular type, they live there; ☰ **inhabit: be peopled by/with sb** *an island peopled by hardy seafolk* **2** if a story or someone's imagination is peopled by people of a particular type, it is full of them: **be peopled by/with sb** *Her world was peopled with imaginary friends.*

people ,carrier also **'people ,mover** *n* [C] a large car with about eight seats, used especially by people with families; ☰ **mini-van** *AmE*

pep¹ /pep/ *v* **pepped, pepping**
pep sb/sth ⇔ **up** *phr v informal* to make something or someone more active or interesting: *The team needs a few new players to pep it up.*

pep² *n* [U] *informal* physical energy: *an enthusiastic player, full of pep* → PEP TALK

pep·per¹ S3 /'pepə $ -ər/ *n*
1 [U] a powder that is used to add a hot taste to food: *salt and pepper* → BLACK PEPPER, WHITE PEPPER
2 [C] a hollow, red, green, or yellow vegetable, eaten either raw or cooked with other food; ☰ **bell pepper** *AmE*; → see picture at VEGETABLE¹ → SWEET PEPPER, CAYENNE PEPPER, RED PEPPER

pepper² *v* [T] **1** [usually passive] if something is peppered with things, it has a lot of those things in it or on it: **be peppered with sth** *a speech peppered with amusing stories* | *The surface of the moon is peppered with craters.* **2** if bullets pepper something, they hit it several times: *Machine gun fire peppered the front of the building.* **3** pepper sb with questions *AmE* to ask someone a lot of questions, one after the other: *Reporters peppered him with questions.* **4** to add pepper to food: *Pepper the steak well.* | *peppered salami*

,pepper-and-'salt also **salt-and-pepper** *adj* pepper-and-salt hair is starting to become grey

pep·per·corn /'pepəkɔːn $ 'pepərkɔːrn/ *n* [C] the small dried fruit that is crushed to make pepper

,peppercorn 'rent *n* [C] *BrE* a very low rent

'pepper mill *n* [C] a piece of kitchen equipment used to crush peppercorns to make pepper

pep·per·mint /'pepə,mɪnt $ -ər-/ *n* **1** [U] a plant with a strong taste and smell, often used in sweets **2** [C] a sweet with the taste of peppermint

pep·pe·ro·ni /,pepə'rəuni $ -'rou-/ *n* [C,U] an Italian SAUSAGE with a strong taste

'pepper pot *BrE;* **'pepper ,shaker** *AmE n* [C] a small container with little holes in the top, used for shaking pepper onto food

'pepper ,spray *n* [C,U] a substance used especially by the police for controlling people. It contains red pepper and is SPRAYED into people's eyes to make them blind for a short time

pep·per·y /'pepəri/ *adj* **1** tasting or smelling of pepper **2** *informal* becoming annoyed easily; ☰ **irritable**

'pep pill *n* [C] *informal* a PILL containing a drug that gives you more energy or makes you feel happier for a short time

'pep ,rally *n* [C] *AmE* a meeting at a school before a sports event, when CHEERLEADERS lead the students in encouraging their team to win

pep·sin /'pepsᵻn/ *n* [U] *technical* a liquid in your stomach that changes food into a form that your body can use

'pep squad *n* [C] *AmE* a group of CHEERLEADERS who perform at school sports events or pep rallies

'pep talk *n* [C] *informal* a short speech intended to encourage someone to work harder, win a game etc: *Alam gave the Pakistani team a pep talk.*

pep·tic ul·cer /,peptɪk 'ʌlsə $ -ər/ *n* [C] a painful ULCER inside someone's stomach

per S3 W1 /pə; *strong* pɜ $ pər; *strong* pɜːr/ *prep*
1 per hour/day/week etc during each hour etc: *The park attracts 4 million visitors per year.* | *miles/kilometres per hour* (=used for measuring speed) *a speed limit of 40 miles per hour*
2 for each: *How much does it cost per kilo?* | *rooms costing £40 per night* | *Admission is £9.95 per adult.* | *My car does 12 miles per litre* (=for each litre of petrol). | *The meal cost $25 per head* (=for or by each person).
3 as per sth *formal* according to something: *The work was carried out as per your instructions.*
4 as per usual/normal *spoken* used when something annoying happens which has often happened before: *Jenny was late, as per usual.* → PER ANNUM, PER CAPITA

per·am·bu·la·tion /pə,ræmbjᵿ'leɪʃən/ *n* [C] *old-fashioned* a walk around a place, especially a slow walk for pleasure —**perambulate** /pə'ræmbjᵿleɪt/ *v* [I,T]

per·am·bu·la·tor /pə'ræmbjᵿleɪtə $ -ər/ *n* [C] *BrE old-fashioned* a PRAM

per an·num /pər 'ænəm/ *written abbreviation* **p.a.** *adv formal* for each year: *a salary of $40,000 per annum*

per·cale /pə'keɪl $ pər-/ *n* [C,U] a type of cotton cloth, used especially for making sheets

per cap·i·ta /pə 'kæpᵻtə $ pər-/ *adj, adv formal* used to describe the average amount of something in a particular place, calculated according to the number of people who live there: *the country's per capita income* | *the number of crimes that occur per capita*

per·ceive W3 /pə'siːv $ pər-/ *v* [T not in progressive]
1 *written* to understand or think of something or someone in a particular way; → **perception: perceive sth/sb as sth** *Even as a young woman she had been perceived as a future chief executive.* | **perceive sth/sb to be sth** *Often what is perceived to be aggression is simply fear.* | *Children who do badly in school tests often perceive themselves to be failures.*
2 *formal* to notice, see, or recognize something; → **perceptive:** *That morning, he perceived a change in Franca's mood.* | *Cats are not able to perceive colour.* | **perceive that** *He perceived that there was no other way out of the crisis.*

per·cent¹ S3 also **per cent** *BrE* /pə'sent $ pər-/ *adj, adv*
1 5 percent (5%)/10 percent (10%) etc equal to five, ten etc parts out of a total of 100 parts: *a 10% increase in house prices* | *a company with a forty percent stake in the project* ⚠ Use **percent** only with a number (30 percent, 9 percent etc). If you mean 'an amount expressed as part of a total' use **percentage:** *A high percentage (NOT percent) of the population was illiterate.*
2 a/one hundred percent completely: *I agree with you a hundred percent.*

percent² S3 W3 also **per cent** *BrE n* **5 percent (5%)/10 percent (10%) etc** an amount equal to five, ten etc parts out of a total of 100 parts: *The bank charges interest at 14%.* | **[+of]** *80 percent of the population voted.*

per·cen·tage W3 /pəˈsentɪdʒ $ pər-/ n
1 [C,U] an amount expressed as if it is part of a total which is 100: [+of] *The percentage of school leavers that go to university is about five per cent.* | *Tax is paid as a percentage of total income.* | **high/low/small percentage** *A high percentage of married women have part-time jobs.* | *Interest rates fell by six* **percentage points** (=6%). | *The numbers are small* **in percentage terms** (=when calculated as a percentage). | **percentage change/increase etc** *Crime figures showed significant percentage increases.* ⚠ If the noun that follows **a percentage of** is plural, use a plural verb: *Only a small percentage of people are interested in politics.*
2 [C usually singular] a share of the profits: *She gets a percentage for every record sold.*
3 there is no percentage in doing sth *BrE informal* used to say that doing something is not going to help or be useful: *There's no percentage in worrying.*

per·cen·tile /pəˈsentaɪl $ pər-/ n [C] *technical* one of 100 equal-sized parts that a group of people can be divided into – used especially when comparing people's scores in a test or levels of health

per·cep·ti·ble /pəˈseptɪbəl $ pər-/ adj *formal* something that is perceptible can be noticed, although it is very small; ⏸ **imperceptible**: *a small but perceptible change* | *The sound was* **barely perceptible**.
—perceptibly adv: *the light dimmed perceptibly*

per·cep·tion W3 /pəˈsepʃən $ pər-/ n
1 [C,U] the way you think about something and your idea of what it is like: [+of] *children's perceptions of the world* | *the* **public perception** *of the government's performance*
2 [U] the way that you notice things with your senses of sight, hearing etc: *drugs that alter perception* | *visual perception*
3 [U] the natural ability to understand or notice things quickly: *Ross shows unusual perception for a boy of his age.*

per·cep·tive /pəˈseptɪv $ pər-/ adj someone who is perceptive notices things quickly and understands situations, people's feelings etc well – used to show approval: *a perceptive young man* | *highly perceptive comments* | *You're right.* **That's** very **perceptive of you.**
—perceptively adv **—perceptiveness** n [U]

perch¹ /pɜːtʃ $ pɜːrtʃ/ n [C] **1** a branch or stick where a bird sits **2** *informal* a high place or position, especially one where you can sit and watch something: *She watched the parade from her perch on her father's shoulders.* **3** a type of fish that lives in lakes and rivers → see picture at FRESHWATER

perch² v **1 be perched on/above etc sth** to be in a position on top of something or on the edge of something: *a house perched on a cliff above the town* **2 perch (yourself) on sth** to sit on top of something or on the edge of something: *Bobby had perched himself on a tall wooden stool.* **3** [I + on] if a bird perches on something, it flies down and sits on it

per·chance /pəˈtʃɑːns $ pərˈtʃæns/ adv *old use* or *literary* **1** perhaps: *One day perchance I shall tell you.* **2** by chance: *Leave now, lest perchance he find you.*

per·cip·i·ent /pəˈsɪpiənt $ pər-/ adj *formal* quick to notice and understand things; ⏸ **perceptive**
—percipience n [U]

per·co·late /ˈpɜːkəleɪt $ ˈpɜːr-/ v **1** [I] if an idea, feeling, or piece of information percolates through a group, it gradually spreads: [+through/down] *The message has begun to percolate through the organization.* | *These ideas were slow to percolate.* **2** [I always + adv/prep] if liquid, light, or air percolates somewhere, it passes slowly through a material that has very small holes in it: [+through/down/into] *Rainwater percolates down through the rock.* **3** [I,T] also **perk** if coffee percolates, or if you percolate it, you make it in a special pot in which hot water goes up through a tube and then passes down through crushed coffee beans
—percolation /ˌpɜːkəˈleɪʃən $ ˌpɜːr-/ n [C,U]

per·co·la·tor /ˈpɜːkəleɪtə $ ˈpɜːrkəleɪtər/ n [C] a special pot in which coffee is percolated

per·cus·sion /pəˈkʌʃən $ pər-/ n [U] **1** musical instruments such as drums, bells etc which you play by hitting them: *Tonight we have Paul Duke* **on percussion** (=playing a percussion instrument). | *a range of* **percussion instruments** → BRASS (2), STRINGED INSTRUMENT, WIND INSTRUMENT, WOODWIND **2 the percussion (section)** the people in an ORCHESTRA or band that play musical instruments such as drums, bells etc **3** *formal* the sound or effect of two things hitting each other with great force **—percussionist** n [C]

per·cus·sive /pəˈkʌsɪv $ pər-/ adj [usually before noun] relating to or sounding like percussion instruments: *On the piano such chords have a fine percussive effect.*

per di·em¹ /pə ˈdiːəm $ pər-/ n [C] *AmE* **1** an amount of money that an employer pays a worker for each day that is worked **2** an amount of money that a worker is allowed to spend when doing his or her job, for example on a business trip: *a per diem allowance*

per diem² adv *AmE formal* for each day or on each day: *workers who are paid per diem*

per·di·tion /pəˈdɪʃən $ pər-/ n [U] *old use* **1** punishment after death **2** complete destruction or failure: *an alcoholic on the road to perdition*

per·e·gri·na·tion /ˌperɪɡrɪˈneɪʃən/ n [C] *literary* a long journey: *His peregrinations took him to India.*

per·e·grine fal·con /ˌperɪɡrɪn ˈfɔːlkən $ -ˈfɔːl-, -ˈfɑːl-/ also **peregrine** n [C] a hunting bird with a black and white spotted front

pe·remp·to·ry /pəˈremptəri/ adj *formal* peremptory behaviour, speech etc is not polite or friendly and shows that the person speaking expects to be obeyed immediately: *a peremptory demand for silence* **—peremptorily** adv

pe·ren·ni·al¹ /pəˈreniəl/ adj **1** continuing or existing for a long time, or happening again and again: *Lack of resources has been a* **perennial problem** *since the beginning.* | *Teddy bears are a* **perennial favorite** *with children.* **2** a plant that is perennial lives for more than two years; → **annual** **—perennially** adv

perennial² n [C] a plant that lives for more than two years → HARDY PERENNIAL (1)

per·e·stroi·ka /ˌperɪˈstrɔɪkə/ n [U] a Russian word meaning 'rebuilding', used to describe the social, political, and economic changes that happened in the former USSR in the 1980s, just before the end of the Communist government; → **glasnost**

per·fect¹ S2 W2 /ˈpɜːfɪkt $ ˈpɜːr-/ adj
1 not having any mistakes, faults, or damage; ⏸ **imperfect**: *His English was perfect.* | *The car was in perfect condition.* | *You're very lucky to have perfect teeth.* | *perfect performance* | **In a perfect world**, *we wouldn't need an army.*
2 as good as possible, or the best of its kind: *The weather was perfect the whole week.* | *a perfect example of Gothic architecture* | *The clothes were a perfect fit.* | *a perfect solution to the problem* | *Ronnie was in perfect health.* | **perfect timing** (=used when something happens at exactly the right time) *Good, you're home. Perfect timing – dinner's on the table.*
3 exactly what is needed for a particular purpose, situation, or person; ⏸ **ideal**: *That's perfect! Just the way I wanted it to look.* | *Crusty bread is the perfect accompaniment to this soup.* | [+for] *The land is perfect for sheep farming.* | **perfect way/place/time etc to do sth** *She thought she'd found the perfect place to live.* | **perfect day/place/person etc for sth** *a perfect day for a picnic* | *the perfect actor for the part*
4 nobody's perfect *spoken* said when you are answering someone who has criticized you or someone else: *So I made a mistake! Nobody's perfect.*
5 have a perfect right to do sth used to emphasize that it is reasonable for someone to do something: *He has a*

describe someone or something that is annoying you: *Tell those perishing kids to shut up!* —**perishingly** *adv*

per·i·style /ˈperɪstaɪl/ *n* [C] *technical* a row of PILLARS around an open space in a building, or the open space itself

per·i·to·ni·tis /ˌperɪtəˈnaɪtɪs $ -tnˈaɪ-/ *n* [U] *technical* a serious condition in which the inside wall of someone's ABDOMEN (=part around and below your stomach) becomes infected and painful

per·i·win·kle /ˈperɪwɪŋkəl/ *n* **1** [C] a small plant with light blue or white flowers that grows close to the ground **2** [C] a small sea animal that lives in a shell and can be eaten; ➔ **winkle**

per·jure /ˈpɜːdʒə $ ˈpɜːrdʒer/ *v* **perjure yourself** *law* to tell a lie after promising to tell the truth in a court of law —**perjured** *adj: perjured evidence* —**perjurer** *n* [C]

per·ju·ry /ˈpɜːdʒəri $ ˈpɜːr-/ *n* [U] *law* the crime of telling a lie after promising to tell the truth in a court of law, or a lie told in this way: *Hall was found guilty of perjury.*

perk[1] /pɜːk $ pɜːrk/ *n* [C usually plural] something that you get legally from your work in addition to your wages, such as goods, meals, or a car: *theatre tickets and other perks* | [+of] *the perks of working at a large law firm* | *I only eat here because it's free* – **one of the perks of the job.**

perk[2] *v* [I,T] *informal* to PERCOLATE (3)

perk up *phr v informal* **1** to become more cheerful, active, and interested in what is happening around you, or to make someone feel this way: *She seemed kind of tired, but she perked up when Helen came over.* | **perk sb ⇔ up** *There's no doubt coffee perks you up.* **2** to become more active, more interesting, more attractive etc, or to make something do this: **perk sth ⇔ up** *A little chili will perk up the sauce.*

perk·y /ˈpɜːki $ ˈpɜːrki/ *adj informal* confident, happy, and active: *a perky salesgirl* —**perkily** *adv* —**perkiness** *n* [U]

perm[1] /pɜːm $ pɜːrm/ *n* [C] a process in which you make straight hair curly by using chemicals, or hair that has been treated in this way; ➔ **permanent** *AmE: a very curly perm*

perm[2] *v* [T] **1** to make straight hair curly by using chemicals: *I'm going to have my hair permed.* | *her blonde permed hair* **2** *BrE* to choose and combine a number of football games from the list given in the FOOTBALL POOLS in order to try to win money —**perming** *n* [U]: *a home perming kit*

per·ma·frost /ˈpɜːməfrɒst $ ˈpɜːrməfrɒːst/ *n* [U] a layer of soil that is always frozen in countries where it is very cold

per·ma·nent[1] S2 W2 /ˈpɜːmənənt $ ˈpɜːr-/ *adj* continuing to exist for a long time or for all the time in the future; ➔ **temporary**: *He gave up a permanent job in order to freelance.* | *a permanent change in your eating habits* | *The blindness that the disease causes will be permanent.* | *Miller soon became a permanent fixture* (=someone or something that is always there) *on the team.* —**permanence** also **permanency** *n* [U]: *the permanence of parental love* | *our desire for some sense of permanence*

permanent[2] *n* [C] *AmE* a PERM[1]

per·ma·nent·ly /ˈpɜːmənəntli $ ˈpɜːr-/ *adv* always, or for a very long time: *The accident left him permanently disabled.*

permanent 'press *n* [U] a process used to treat cloth so that it does not WRINKLE easily, or cloth that has been treated in this way

permanent 'wave *n* [C] *old-fashioned* a PERM[1]

per·me·a·ble /ˈpɜːmiəbəl $ ˈpɜːr-/ *adj technical* material that is permeable allows water, gas etc to pass through it; ➔ **impermeable**: *the permeable cell membrane* —**permeability** /ˌpɜːmiəˈbɪlɪti $ ˌpɜːr-/ *n* [U]

per·me·ate /ˈpɜːmieɪt $ ˈpɜːr-/ *v* **1** [I always + adv/prep, T] if liquid, gas etc permeates something, it enters it and spreads through every part of it: *The smell of diesel oil permeated the air.* | [+through/into] *Rain permeates through the ground to add to ground water levels.* **2** [T] if ideas, beliefs, emotions etc permeate something, they are present in every part of it: *Racism continues to permeate our society.* | *Emotion permeates every one of O'Connor's songs.*

per·mis·si·ble /pəˈmɪsɪbəl $ pər-/ *adj formal* allowed by law or by the rules; ➔ **allowable**; ➔ **impermissible**: *the maximum permissible level of radiation*

per·mis·sion S2 W3 /pəˈmɪʃən $ pər-/ *n* [U] when someone is officially allowed to do something

ask/request/apply for permission
give/grant permission
get/obtain/receive permission
have permission (to do sth)
refuse/deny (sb) permission
with/without (sb's) permission
special/written permission
by kind permission of sb *formal* (=used for saying who allowed something)

You must **ask permission** *before taking any photographs inside the church.* | *They didn't* **have permission** *to cross the frontier.* | *Who* **gave** *him* **permission** *to leave class early?* | [+from] *He* **obtained permission** *from his boss before talking to the press.* | [+for] *the Council's decision to* **refuse permission** *for the development* | *Pages may not be copied* **without the permission** *of the publisher.* | **With your permission,** *I should like to visit Mrs Thorne.* | *The paintings are reproduced* **by kind permission** *of the National Gallery.*

⚠ **Permission** is an uncountable noun. Do not say 'a permission' or 'the permission'. ➔ PLANNING PERMISSION

per·mis·sive /pəˈmɪsɪv $ pər-/ *adj* not strict, and allowing behaviour that many other people would disapprove of: *parents who are too permissive* | *a permissive society* —**permissiveness** *n* [U]: *permissiveness in education*

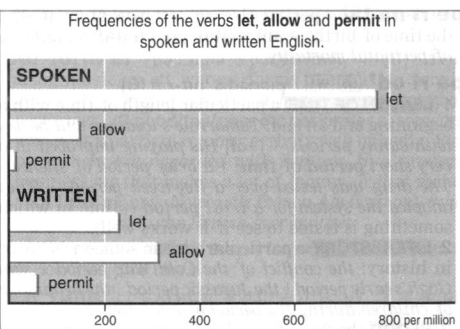

Frequencies of the verbs **let**, **allow** and **permit** in spoken and written English.

This graph shows that **let** is much more common in spoken English than **allow** and **permit**. **Allow** is more common in written English. **Permit** is more formal than **let** and **allow**, and is used especially when talking about rules or laws.

per·mit[1] W3 /pəˈmɪt $ pər-/ *v* permitted, permitting *formal*

1 [T] to allow something to happen, especially by an official decision, rule, or law: *Smoking is only permitted in the public lounge.* | **permit sb to do sth** *As a punishment, she was not permitted to attend any school activities.* | **permit sth in/near etc sth** *Dogs are not permitted inside the shop.* | **permit sth** *The bill would permit workers twelve weeks of unpaid leave for family emergencies.* | *He had more than the permitted level of alcohol in his blood.*

2 [I,T] to make it possible for something to happen: *The large windows permit a clear view of the lake.* | **permit sb to do sth** *The moon permitted me to see a little way* into the distance. | I'll see you after the meeting, **if time permits** (=if it finishes early enough). | We'll have a picnic at the beach, **weather permitting** (=if the weather is good enough).

per·mit² /'pɜːrmɪt $ 'pɜːr-, pər'mɪt/ n [C] an official written statement giving you the right to do something: [+for] A permit is required for fishing in the canal. | **travel/parking/export etc permit** Hikers need a camping permit for overnight stays in the park. → WORK PERMIT

per·mu·ta·tion /,pɜːmjʊ'teɪʃən $,pɜːr-/ n [C] one of the different ways in which a number of things can be arranged: a sandwich shop that sells every possible permutation of meat and bread → COMBINATION

per·ni·cious /pə'nɪʃəs $ pər-/ adj formal very harmful or evil, often in a way that you do not notice easily: the pernicious effects of poverty | the media's pernicious influence —**perniciously** adv

per,nicious a'naemia n [U] medical a severe form of ANAEMIA (=too few red blood cells in the blood)

per·nick·e·ty /pə'nɪkʲti $ pər-/ adj BrE informal worrying too much about small and unimportant things; ⊟ **fussy**

per·o·ra·tion /,perə'reɪʃən/ n [C] **1** technical the last part of a speech, in which the main points are repeated **2** formal a long speech that sounds impressive but does not have much meaning

per·ox·ide /pə'rɒksaɪd $ -'rɑːk-/ n [U] a liquid chemical used to make hair light in colour or to kill BACTERIA: her waist-length **peroxide blonde** hair (=hair made light yellow using peroxide)

per·pen·dic·u·lar¹ /,pɜːpən'dɪkjʊlə◄ $,pɜːrpən-'dɪkjʊlər◄/ adj **1** not leaning to one side or the other but exactly vertical; → **vertical, horizontal**: a perpendicular line | a perpendicular wall of rock **2 be perpendicular to sth** if one line is perpendicular to another line, they form an angle of 90 degrees; ⊟ **at right angles to**: a road perpendicular to the highway **3 Perpendicular** in the style of 14th and 15th century English churches, which are decorated with straight, upright lines —**perpendicularly** adv

perpendicular² n [singular] an exactly vertical position or line

per·pe·trate /'pɜːpʲtreɪt $ 'pɜːr-/ v [T] formal to do something that is morally wrong or illegal; → **commit**: Who could have perpetrated such a dreadful crime? —**perpetration** /,pɜːpʲ'treɪʃən $,pɜːr-/ n [U]

per·pe·tra·tor /'pɜːpʲtreɪtə $ 'pɜːrpʲtreɪtər/ n [C] formal someone who does something morally wrong or illegal; → **culprit**: The perpetrators were never caught. | [+of] The perpetrators of racially motivated violence must be punished.

per·pet·u·al /pə'petʃuəl $ pər-/ adj [usually before noun] **1** continuing all the time without changing or stopping; ⊟ **continuous**: the perpetual noise of the machines | a little girl with a perpetual smile **2** repeated many times in a way that annoys you; ⊟ **continual**: my mother's perpetual nagging **3** literary permanent: the perpetual snows of the mountaintops —**perpetually** adv

per,petual 'motion n [U] the ability of a machine to always continue moving without getting energy from anywhere else, which is not considered possible

per·pet·u·ate /pə'petʃueɪt $ pər-/ v [T] to make a situation, attitude etc, especially a bad one, continue to exist for a long time: an education system that perpetuates the divisions in our society —**perpetuation** /pə,petʃu'eɪʃən $ pər-/ n [U]

per·pe·tu·i·ty /,pɜːpʲ'tjuːʲti $,pɜːrpʲ'tuː-/ n in **perpetuity** law for all future time; ⊟ **forever**: The land had been promised to the Indian tribes in perpetuity.

per·plex /pə'pleks $ pər-/ v [T] if something perplexes you, it makes you feel confused and worried because it is difficult to understand; ⊟ **puzzle**: Shea's symptoms perplexed the doctors. —**perplexing** adj: a perplexing problem

per·plexed /pə'plekst $ pər-/ adj confused and worried by something that you do not understand; ⊟ **puzzled**: The student looked at him, perplexed. | Perplexed investors tried to work out what the deal meant. —**perplexedly** /pə'pleksʲdli, -'plekstli $ pər-/ adv

per·plex·i·ty /pə'pleksʲti $ pər-/ n plural **perplexities 1** [U] the feeling of being confused or worried by something you cannot understand **2** [C usually plural] something that is complicated or difficult to understand: moral perplexities

per·qui·site /'pɜːkwʲzɪt $ 'pɜːr-/ n [C] formal a PERK¹

per·ry /'peri/ n [U] especially BrE an alcoholic drink made from PEARS

per se /,pɜː 'seɪ $,pɜːr 'siː, -'seɪ, ,per 'seɪ/ adv formal used to say that something is being considered alone, not with other connected things: The color of the shell per se does not affect the quality of the egg.

per·se·cute /'pɜːsɪkjuːt $ 'pɜːr-/ v [T] **1** to treat someone cruelly or unfairly over a period of time, especially because of their religious or political beliefs: The Puritans left England to escape being persecuted . **2** to deliberately cause difficulties for someone by annoying them often; ⊟ **harass**: Like many celebrities, she complained of being persecuted by the press. —**persecutor** n [C] —**persecution** /,pɜːsɪ'kjuːʃən $,pɜːr-/ n [C,U]: the persecution of writers who criticize the government

perse'cution ,complex n [C] a mental illness in which someone believes that other people are trying to harm them

per·se·ver·ance /,pɜːsʲ'vɪərəns $,pɜːrsʲ'vɪr-/ n [U] determination to keep trying to achieve something in spite of difficulties – use this to show approval: It took perseverance to overcome his reading problems.

per·se·vere /,pɜːsʲ'vɪə $,pɜːrsʲ'vɪr/ v [I] to continue trying to do something in a very determined way in spite of difficulties – use this to show approval: It can be tricky at first, but persevere. | [+with] He persevered with his task until he had succeeded in collecting an armful of firewood. | **persevere in (doing) sth** She had persevered in her claim for compensation. **persevering** adj

Per·sian¹ /'pɜːʃən, -ʒən $ 'pɜːrʒən/ adj relating to Iran, its people, or its language, especially in the time when it was called Persia: the Persian Empire | a Persian carpet

Persian² n **1** [C] someone from Iran, especially in the time when it was called Persia **2** [U] the language used in Iran; ⊟ **Farsi**

,Persian 'cat n [C] a cat with long silky hair

per·sim·mon /pə'sɪmən $ pər-/ n [C] a soft orange-coloured fruit that grows in hot countries

per·sist /pə'sɪst $ pər-/ v **1** [I,T] to continue to do something, although this is difficult, or other people oppose it: **persist in (doing) sth** He persisted in his refusal to admit responsibility. | [+with] She persisted with her studies in spite of financial problems. | 'I don't think it's right,' John persisted. **2** [I] if something bad persists, it continues to exist or happen: If the pain persists, you must see a doctor.

per·sis·tence /pə'sɪstəns $ pər-/ n [U] **1** determination to do something even though it is difficult or other people oppose it: Her persistence paid off when she was offered the job of manager. | 'Why can't I come?' repeated Will with **dogged persistence**. **2** when something continues to exist or happen, especially for longer than is usual or desirable: [+of] the persistence of high unemployment in the post-war years

per·sis·tent /pə'sɪstənt $ pər-/ adj **1** [usually before noun] continuing to exist or happen, especially for longer than is usual or desirable: persistent rumours | persistent headaches | a persistent problem | persistent

Uganda and Romania adds a wider perspective.
2 [U] a sensible way of judging and comparing situations so that you do not imagine that something is more serious than it really is: *I think Viv's **lost all sense of perspective**.* | *The figures have to be **put into perspective**.* | **get/keep sth in perspective** (=judge the importance of something correctly)
3 [U] a method of drawing a picture that makes objects look solid and shows distance and depth, or the effect this method produces in a picture: *the artist's use of perspective*
4 [C] *formal* a view, especially one in which you can see a long way into the distance

Per·spex /'pɜːspeks $ 'pɜːr-/ n [U] *trademark BrE* a strong type of plastic that can be used instead of glass

per·spi·ca·cious /ˌpɜːspɪ'keɪʃəs◂ $ ˌpɜːr-/ adj *formal* good at judging and understanding people and situations; ▤ **perceptive** —**perspicaciously** adv —**perspicacity** /-'kæsɨti/ n [U]

per·spi·ra·tion /ˌpɜːspə'reɪʃən $ ˌpɜːr-/ n [U] *formal* liquid that appears on your skin when you are hot or nervous; ▤ **sweat**; → **antiperspirant**: *He wiped the beads of perspiration (=drops) from his brow.*

per·spire /pə'spaɪə $ pər'spaɪr-/ v [I] *formal* if you perspire, parts of your body become wet, especially because you are hot or have been doing hard work; ▤ **sweat**: *Willie was perspiring heavily.*

per·suade S2 W2 /pə'sweɪd $ pər-/ v [T]
1 to make someone decide to do something, especially by giving them reasons why they should do it, or asking them many times to do it: **persuade sb to do sth** *I finally managed to persuade her to go out for a drink with me.* | **persuade sb into doing sth** *Don't let yourself be persuaded into buying things you don't want.* | **try/manage/fail to persuade sb** *I'm trying to persuade your dad to buy some shares.* | **attempt/effort to persuade sb** *Leo wouldn't agree, despite our efforts to persuade him.* | **little/a lot of/no persuading** *He took a lot of persuading to come out of retirement* (=it was hard to persuade him). | *He was fairly **easily persuaded**.*
2 to make someone believe something or feel sure about something; ▤ **convince**: *I am not persuaded by these arguments.* | **persuade sb (that)** *She'll only take me back if I can persuade her that I've changed.* | **persuade sb of sth** *McFadden must persuade the jury of her innocence.*

per·sua·sion /pə'sweɪʒən $ pər-/ n **1** [U] the act of persuading someone to do something: *After a little gentle persuasion, Debbie agreed to let us in.* | *It had taken a great deal of persuasion to get him to accept.* | *She used all her **powers of persuasion** (=skill at persuading people) to convince Tilly that it was the right thing to do.* **2** [C] *formal* a particular type of belief, especially a political or religious one: **political/religious persuasion** *We need people with talent, whatever their political persuasions.* | *politicians **of all persuasions*** **3** *of the ... persuasion* *formal* of a particular type – often used humorously: *an ancient bed of the iron persuasion*

per·sua·sive /pə'sweɪsɪv $ pər-/ adj able to make other people believe something or do what you ask: *Trevor can be very persuasive.* | **persuasive argument/evidence** *a persuasive argument against capital punishment* —**persuasively** adv —**persuasiveness** n [U]

pert /pɜːt $ pɜːrt/ adj **1** a girl or woman who is pert is amusing, but slightly disrespectful: *Angie gave him one of her pert little glances.* **2** a pert part of the body is small, firm, and attractive: *a pert bottom* —**pertly** adv —**pertness** n [U]

per·tain /pə'teɪn $ pər-/ v
pertain to sth phr v *formal* to relate directly to something: *legislation pertaining to employment rights*

per·ti·na·cious /ˌpɜːtɨ'neɪʃəs◂ $ ˌpɜːr-/ adj *formal* continuing to believe something or to do something

in a very determined way; ▤ **tenacious** —**pertinaciously** adv —**pertinacity** /-'næsɨti/ n [U]

per·ti·nent /'pɜːtɨnənt $ 'pɜːr-/ adj *formal* directly relating to something that is being considered; ▤ **relevant**: *He asked me a lot of very pertinent questions.* | [+to] *The last point is particularly pertinent to today's discussion.* —**pertinently** adv —**pertinence** n [U]

per·tur·ba·tion /ˌpɜːtə'beɪʃən $ ˌpɜːrtər-/ n **1** [C,U] *technical* a small change in the movement, quality, or behaviour of something: *climatic perturbations* **2** [U] *formal* worry about something that has happened or will happen

per·turbed /pə'tɜːbd $ pər'tɜːrbd/ adj *formal* worried about something that has happened or will happen: *William looked a little perturbed.* | [+by/at/about] *He didn't seem perturbed by the noises outside.* | **perturbed that** *He was perturbed that she didn't look happy.* —**perturb** v [T]: *My unexpected arrival didn't perturb him in the least.*

pe·ruse /pə'ruːz/ v [T] *formal* to read something, especially in a careful way: *She leant forward to peruse the document more closely.* —**perusal** n [C,U]

perv /pɜːv $ pɜːrv/ n [C] *BrE spoken informal* a PERVERT —**pervy** adj

per·vade /pə'veɪd $ pər-/ v [T] *formal* if a feeling, idea, or smell pervades a place, it is present in every part of it: *A spirit of hopelessness pervaded the country.*

per·va·sive /pə'veɪsɪv $ pər-/ adj existing everywhere: *the pervasive influence of television* | *the all-pervasive mood of apathy* —**pervasiveness** n [U]

per·verse /pə'vɜːs $ pər'vɜːrs/ adj behaving in an unreasonable way, especially by deliberately doing the opposite of what people want you to do: *He gets perverse satisfaction from embarrassing people.* —**perversely** adv: *Perversely, she was irritated by his kindness.*

per·ver·sion /pə'vɜːʃən, -ʒən $ pər'vɜːrʒən/ n [C,U] **1** a type of sexual behaviour that is considered unnatural and unacceptable **2** the process of changing something that is natural and good into something that is unnatural and wrong, or the result of such a change: [+of] *a perversion of the true meaning of democracy*

per·ver·si·ty /pə'vɜːsɨti $ pər'vɜːr-/ n [U] the quality of being perverse: *Max refused the money out of sheer perversity.*

per·vert¹ /pə'vɜːt $ pər'vɜːrt/ v [T] **1** to change something in an unnatural and often harmful way: *Genetic scientists are often accused of perverting nature.* **2** to influence someone so that they begin to think or behave in an immoral way; ▤ **corrupt**: *TV violence perverts the minds of young children.* **3** **pervert the course of justice** *law* to deliberately prevent a fair examination of the facts about a crime

per·vert² /'pɜːvɜːt $ 'pɜːrvɜːrt/ n [C] someone whose sexual behaviour is considered unnatural and unacceptable

per·vert·ed /pə'vɜːtɨd $ pər'vɜːr-/ adj **1** morally wrong: *He derives a perverted pleasure from hurting other people.* | *the perverted logic of terrorism* **2** sexually unacceptable or unnatural

pe·se·ta /pə'seɪtə/ n [C] the standard unit of money used in Spain before the EURO

pes·ky /'peski/ adj [only before noun] *informal especially AmE* annoying: *Those pesky kids!*

pe·so /'peɪsəʊ $ -soʊ/ n plural **pesos** [C] the standard unit of money in the Philippines and in various Latin American countries including Mexico, Cuba, and Colombia

pes·sa·ry /'pesəri/ n plural **pessaries** [C] **1** a small block of medicine which a woman puts into her VAGINA in order to cure an infection or to stop herself becoming PREGNANT **2** an instrument put into a woman's VAGINA to support her WOMB

pes·si·mi·sm /'pesɨmɪzəm/ n [U] a tendency to believe that bad things will happen; ▤ **optimism**: [+about/over] *There is deep pessimism about the future.*

pes·si·mist /'pesɪmɪst/ n [C] someone who always expects that bad things will happen; → **optimist**: *Don't be such a pessimist!*

pes·si·mis·tic /ˌpesɪ'mɪstɪk◂/ adj expecting that bad things will happen in the future or that something will have a bad result; → **optimistic**: *a pessimistic view of life* | [+about] *He remains deeply pessimistic about the peace process.* —**pessimistically** /-kli/ adv

pest /pest/ n [C] **1** a small animal or insect that destroys crops or food supplies; → **vermin**: *a chemical used in pest control* **2** informal an annoying person, especially a child

pes·ter /'pestə $ -ər/ v [I,T] to annoy someone, especially by asking them many times to do something: *She'd been pestered by reporters for days.* | **pester sb for sth** *I can't even walk down the street without being continually pestered for money.* | **pester sb to do sth** *The kids have been pestering me to buy them new trainers.*

'pester ˌpower n [U] the ability that children have to make their parents buy things or do things for them by asking them again and again

pes·ti·cide /'pestɪsaɪd/ n [C,U] a chemical substance used to kill insects and small animals that destroy crops; → **herbicide**

pes·ti·lence /'pestɪləns/ n [C,U] literary a disease that spreads quickly and kills a lot of people

pes·ti·len·tial /ˌpestɪ'lenʃəl/ also **pes·ti·lent** /'pestɪlənt/ adj **1** literary extremely unpleasant and annoying **2** old use causing disease

pes·tle /'pesəl, 'pestl/ n [C] a short stick with a heavy round end, used for crushing things in a MORTAR (=a special bowl)

pes·to /'pestəʊ $ -oʊ/ n [U] a sauce made from BASIL, GARLIC, PINE NUTS, OLIVE OIL, and cheese

pet¹ /pet/ n **1** [C] an animal such as a cat or a dog which you keep and care for at home: *Rabbits can make very good pets.* | **pet dog/cat/bird etc** *He was bitten by his pet dog.* | *pet food* | *a pet shop* → TEACHER'S PET **2** BrE spoken used when speaking to someone you like or love: *Don't cry, pet.*

pet² v **petted, petting** [T] to touch and move your hand gently over someone, especially an animal or a child; → **stroke**: *Our cat loves being petted.* → PETTING

pet³ adj **1** pet project/theory/subject a plan, idea, or subject that you particularly like or are interested in **2** pet hate BrE; pet peeve AmE something that you strongly dislike because it always annoys you: *TV game shows are one of my pet hates.* → PET NAME

pet·a·flop /'petəflɒp $ -flɑːp/ n [C usually plural] a unit that measures how fast a computer works. One petaflop is one million BILLION operations every second

pet·al /'petl/ n [C] one of the coloured parts of a flower that are shaped like leaves: *rose petals* | *The flower has seven petals.* → see picture at ROSE¹

pe·tard /pɪ'tɑːd $ -ɑːrd/ n → be hoist with/by your own petard at HOIST¹ (2)

pe·ter /'piːtə $ -ər/ v
peter out phr v to gradually become smaller, less, weaker etc and then come to an end: *The road became narrower and eventually petered out.* | *Public interest in the environment is in danger of petering out.*

Peter → rob Peter to pay Paul at ROB (2)

peth·i·dine /'peθɪdiːn/ n [U] a drug used to reduce severe pain, given especially to women who are giving birth

pet·it bour·geois /ˌpeti 'bʊəʒwɑː, -bʊə'ʒwɑː $ ˌpeti bʊr'ʒwɑː, pə,tiː-/ adj another spelling of PETTY BOURGEOIS

pe·tite /pə'tiːt/ adj a woman who is petite is short and attractively thin

petit four /ˌpeti 'fʊə, -'fɔː $ -'fʊr, -'fɔːr/ n plural **petits fours** [C] a small sweet cake or BISCUIT served with coffee

pe·ti·tion¹ /pɪ'tɪʃən/ n [C] **1** a written request signed by a lot of people, asking someone in authority to do something or change something: [+for/against] *a petition against the new road* | *They wanted me to sign a petition against experiments on animals.* | *Local residents have drawn up a petition to protest the hospital closure.* | *petition drive AmE* (=an attempt to get a lot of people to sign a petition) **2** law an official letter to a law court, asking for a legal case to be considered: [+for] *She is threatening to file a petition for divorce.* **3** formal a formal prayer or request to someone in authority or to God

petition² v [I,T] **1** to ask the government or an organization to do something by sending them a petition: **petition sb to do sth** *Villagers petitioned the local authority to provide better bus services.* | [+against/for] *Residents are petitioning against the new road.* **2** law or formal to make a formal request to someone in authority, to a court of law, or to God: [+for] *More and more couples are petitioning for divorce.*

pe·ti·tion·er /pɪ'tɪʃənə $ -ər/ n [C] **1** someone who writes or signs a petition **2** law someone who asks for a legal case to be considered in a court of law

petit mal /ˌpeti 'mæl/ n [U] medical a form of EPILEPSY which is not very serious → GRAND MAL

'pet ˌname n [C] a special name you call someone who you like very much

pet·rel /'petrəl/ n [C] a black and white sea bird

Pe·tri dish /'piːtri dɪʃ/ n [C] a small clear dish with a cover which is used by scientists, especially for growing BACTERIA

pet·ri·fied /'petrɪfaɪd/ adj **1** extremely frightened, especially so frightened that you cannot move or think: [+of] *I'm petrified of spiders.* | **petrified with fright/fear** *He was petrified with fear when he saw the gun.* **2** petrified wood/trees etc wood, trees etc that have changed into stone over a long period of time —**petrify** v [T]

pet·ro·chem·i·cal /ˌpetrəʊ'kemɪkəl $ -troʊ-/ n [C] any chemical substance obtained from PETROLEUM or natural gas: *the petrochemical industry*

pet·ro·dol·lars /'petrəʊˌdɒləz $ -troʊˌdɑːlərz/ n [plural] money earned by the sale of oil: *the flow of petrodollars into the American economy*

pet·rol [S3] /'petrəl/ n [U] BrE a liquid obtained from PETROLEUM that is used to supply power to the engine of cars and other vehicles; → **gasoline** AmE: *unleaded petrol* | *petrol prices* | *The petrol tank is leaking.*

'petrol bomb n [C] BrE a simple bomb consisting of a bottle filled with petrol and a lighted cloth; → **molotov cocktail**

pe·tro·le·um /pɪ'trəʊliəm $ -'troʊ-/ n [U] oil that is obtained from below the surface of the Earth and is used to make petrol, PARAFFIN, and various chemical substances: *petroleum-based products*

pe,troleum 'jelly n [U] VASELINE

'petrol ˌstation n [C] BrE a place where you can take your car and fill it with petrol; → **gas station** AmE

PET scan /'pet skæn/ n [C] medical *positron emission tomography scan* a type of medical test that can produce a picture of areas in your body where cells are very active, for example the brain or where a TUMOUR is growing

pet·ti·coat /'petikəʊt $ -koʊt/ n [C] BrE a piece of women's underwear like a thin skirt or dress that is worn under a skirt or dress; → **slip**

pet·ti·fog·ging /'petiˌfɒgɪŋ $ -ˌfɑː-, -ˌfɔː-/ adj BrE old-fashioned too concerned with small details

pet·ting /'petɪŋ/ n [U] **1** the activity of kissing and touching someone as part of a sexual activity → HEAVY PETTING **2** the action of touching and moving your hand gently over an animal → PET²

'petting zoo n [C] AmE part of a ZOO which has animals in it for children to touch

pet·tish /'petɪʃ/ adj PETULANT —**pettishly** adv

pet·ty /'peti/ adj **1** a petty problem, detail etc is small and unimportant; → **trivial**: *petty squabbles* | *petty* *restrictions* **2** unkind and caring too much about small unimportant things: *How can she be so petty?* | *petty jealousy and spitefulness* **3** petty crime a crime that is not serious, for example stealing things that are not very valuable **4 petty criminal/thief etc** a criminal whose crimes are not very serious **5** a petty official is not important – used especially when they use their power as if they were important: *Some petty bureaucrat wanted all the documents in triplicate.* —**pettiness** *n* [U]: *the pettiness of Hollywood*

,petty **'bourgeois** also **petit bourgeois** / $,.. .'./ *adj* **1** paying too much attention to things such as social position, money, and possessions – used to show disapproval **2** belonging to the group of lower MIDDLE CLASS people —**petty bourgeois** *n* [C]

,petty **'cash** *n* [U] a small amount of money that is kept in an office for making small payments

,petty **'larceny** *n* [U] *law* the crime of stealing things that are worth only a small amount of money

,petty **'officer** *n* [C] an officer of low rank in the Navy

pet·u·lant /'petʃələnt/ *adj* behaving in an unreasonably impatient and angry way, like a child —**petulantly** *adv*: *'Which one?' he demanded petulantly.* —**petulance** *n* [U]

pe·tu·ni·a /pɪ'tjuːniə $ pɪ'tuː-/ *n* [C] a garden plant which has pink, purple, or white TRUMPET -shaped flowers

pew[1] /pjuː/ *n* [C] **1** a long wooden seat in a church **2 take a pew** *BrE spoken* used humorously to invite someone to sit down

pew[2] *interjection AmE spoken* used when something smells very bad

pew·ter /'pjuːtə $ -ər/ *n* [U] a grey metal made by mixing LEAD and TIN: *a pewter plate*

PG /,piː 'dʒiː/ *n* [singular, U] *BrE* **parental guidance** used to show that a film includes parts that parents may feel are not suitable for young children

PGCE /,piː dʒiː siː 'iː/ *n* [C] *Postgraduate Certificate of Education BrE* a course and examination in teaching done by someone who already has a university degree: *I came to Birmingham to do a PGCE.*

pH /piː 'eitʃ/ also **p'H ,value** *n* [singular] a number on a scale of 0 to 14 which shows how acid or ALKALINE a substance is: [+of] *soil with a pH of 3.1*

pha·lanx /'fælæŋks $ 'fei-/ *n plural* **phalanxes** [C] *formal* a large group of people or things standing close together so that it is difficult to go through them: [+of] *A solid phalanx of policemen blocked the road.*

phal·lic /'fælɪk/ *adj* like or relating to a phallus: *phallic symbols*

phal·lus /'fæləs/ *n* [C] **1** a model of the male sex organ, used to represent sexual power **2** the male sex organ; **◻ penis**

phan·tas·m /'fæntæzəm/ *n* [C,U] *literary* something that exists only in your imagination; **◻ illusion**

phan·tas·ma·go·ri·a /,fæntæzmə'gɒriə $ fæn-,tæzmə'gɔːriə/ *n* [C] *literary* a confused, changing, strange scene, like something from a dream —**phantasmagorical** /-'gɒrɪkəl $ -'gɔː-/ *adj*

phan·ta·sy /'fæntəsi/ *n* an old spelling of FANTASY

phan·tom[1] /'fæntəm/ *n* [C] *literary* **1** the image of a dead person or strange thing that someone thinks they see; **◻ ghost 2** something that exists only in your imagination

phantom[2] *adj* [only before noun] **1** *literary* seeming to appear to someone: *a phantom ship* **2** not real, but seeming real to the person affected: *a phantom pregnancy* **3** made to seem real in order to deceive people: *Phantom contracts were used to make the company seem more successful than it was.* **4** used humorously to describe an unknown person that you blame for something annoying: *The phantom pen stealer strikes again!*

Pha·raoh , **pharaoh** /'feərəʊ $ 'feroʊ/ *n* [C] a ruler of ancient Egypt

Phar·i·see /'færɪsiː/ *n* **1 the Pharisees** [plural] a group of Jews who lived at the time of Christ and who believed in strictly obeying religious laws **2** [C] someone who pretends to be religious or morally good, but who is not sincere —**Pharisaic** /,færɪ'seɪ-ɪk‹ / *adj*

phar·ma·ceu·ti·cal /,fɑːmə'sjuːtɪkəl‹ $,fɑːrmə-'suː-/ *adj* [only before noun] relating to the production of drugs and medicines: *the pharmaceutical industry* | *pharmaceutical products*

phar·ma·ceu·ti·cals /,fɑːmə'sjuːtɪkəlz $,fɑːrmə-'suː-/ *n* [plural] *technical* drugs and medicines

phar·ma·cist /'fɑːməsɪst $ 'fɑːr-/ *n* [C] someone whose job is to prepare medicines in a shop or hospital

---

WORD CHOICE: pharmacist, pharmacy, chemist, chemist's, drugstore
A **pharmacist** is someone who prepares and sells medicines. This is the usual word in American English, but in British English **pharmacist** is slightly technical and it is more usual to use the word **chemist**.
The place where a pharmacist works is a **pharmacy**. This can be a shop, part of a shop, or part of a hospital. **Pharmacy** is the usual word in American English. In British English, you usually refer to the part of a hospital that prepares and gives out medicines as a **pharmacy**, but the usual word for a shop where medicines are prepared and sold is a **chemist** or a **chemist's**.
In Britain chemists usually also sell other things, such as beauty and baby products. A shop like this in the United States is called a **drugstore**.

---

phar·ma·col·o·gy /,fɑːmə'kɒlədʒi $,fɑːrmə'kɑː-/ *n* [U] the scientific study of drugs and medicines —**pharmacologist** *n* [C] —**pharmacological** /,fɑːməkə'lɒdʒɪkəl‹ $,fɑːrməkə'lɑː-/ *adj*

phar·ma·co·poe·ia /,fɑːməkə'piːə $,fɑːr-/ *n* [C] *technical* an official book giving information about medicines

phar·ma·cy /'fɑːməsi $ 'fɑːr-/ *n plural* **pharmacies 1** [C] a shop or a part of a shop where medicines are prepared and sold; **◻ chemist**: *an all-night pharmacy* **2** [C] the place where medicines are prepared in a hospital **3** [U] the study or practice of preparing drugs and medicines

phar·yn·gi·tis /,færɪn'dʒaɪtɪs/ *n* [U] a medical condition in which you have a sore swollen pharynx

phar·ynx /'færɪŋks/ *n plural* **pharynges** /fə'rɪndʒiːz/ [C] the tube that goes from the back of your mouth to the place where the tube divides for food and air

phase[1] **W2** /feɪz/ *n* [C]
1 one of the stages of a process of development or change: *a new drug that is in the experimental phase* | [+of] *The first phase of renovations should be finished by January.* | **in phases** *The work will be carried out in phases.* | *It's just **a phase** he's **going through**.*
2 out of phase (with sth) *BrE* not happening together in the right way: *Nizan's views were out of phase with the political climate of the time.*
3 in phase (with sth) *BrE* happening together in the right way: *The electrical work will be carried out in phase with the other renovations.*
4 *technical* one of a fixed number of changes in the appearance of the moon or a PLANET when it is seen from the Earth

phase[2] *v* [T usually passive] to make something happen gradually in a planned way: *The closure of the regional offices was phased over an 18-month period.* | *a phased withdrawal of military forces*
   phase sth ⇔ **in** *phr v* to gradually start using a new system, law, process etc: *The new tests will be phased in over the next two years.*
   phase sth ⇔ **out** *phr v* to gradually stop using or providing something: *The subsidy for company cars is to be phased out next year.*

phat /fæt/ also **'phat-ass** AmE adj informal fashionable, attractive, or desirable – used by young people: *a phat song* | *These shoes are just so phat.*

PhD BrE, **Ph.D.** AmE /ˌpiː eɪtʃ ˈdiː/ n [C] **Doctor of Philosophy** a university degree of a very high level, which involves doing advanced RESEARCH: [+in] *He's got a PhD in Biochemistry.* | *Jacqueline Hope, PhD* | **do/start/finish a PhD**

pheas·ant /ˈfezənt/ n [C,U] a large bird with a long tail, often shot for food, or the meat of this bird

phe·nom /fɪˈnɒm $ -ˈnɑːm/ n [C] AmE informal a PHENOMENON (2): *a 16-year old guitar phenom*

phe·nom·e·nal /fɪˈnɒmɪnəl $ -ˈnɑː-/ adj very great or impressive: *the phenomenal success of computer games in recent years* | **phenomenal growth/rise/increase** *California had experienced a phenomenal growth in population.* | *He has learned a phenomenal amount in the last two years.* | *The results have been phenomenal.* —**phenomenally** adv: *The group have been phenomenally successful in Europe.*

phe·nom·e·nol·o·gy /fɪˌnɒmɪˈnɒlədʒi $ fɪˌnɑːmɪˈnɑː-/ n [U] the part of PHILOSOPHY that deals with people's feelings, thoughts, and experiences

phe·nom·e·non W3 /fɪˈnɒmɪnən $ fɪˈnɑːmɪnɑːn, -nən/ n plural **phenomena** /-nə/ [C]
1 something that happens or exists in society, science, or nature, especially something that is studied because it is difficult to understand: [+of] *the growing phenomenon of telecommuting* | *Homelessness is not a new phenomenon.* | **natural/historical/social etc phenomenon** *Language is a social and cultural phenomenon.*
2 something or someone that is very unusual because of a rare quality or ability that they have

pher·o·mone /ˈferəməʊn $ -moʊn/ n [C usually plural] a chemical that is produced by people's and animals' bodies and is thought to influence the behaviour of other people or animals

phew /fjuː/ interjection used when you feel tired, hot, or RELIEVED: *Phew! We finally did it.*

phi·al /ˈfaɪəl/ n [C] a small bottle, especially for liquid medicines; ▣ **vial**: [+of] *a phial of morphine*

Phi Be·ta Kap·pa /ˌfaɪ ˌbiːtə ˈkæpə $ -ˌbeɪtə-/ n an American society for university and college students who have done well in their studies

-phil /fɪl/ suffix another form of the suffix -PHILE

phi·lan·der·er /fɪˈlændərə $ -ər/ n [C] old-fashioned a man who has sex with many women, without intending to have any serious relationships —**philandering** adj —**philandering** n [U]

phil·an·throp·ic /ˌfɪlənˈθrɒpɪk $ -ˈθrɑː-/ adj a philanthropic person or institution gives money and help to people who are poor or in trouble —**philanthropically** /-kli/ adv

phi·lan·thro·pist /fɪˈlænθrəpɪst/ n [C] a rich person who gives a lot of money to help poor people

phi·lan·thro·py /fɪˈlænθrəpi/ n [U] the practice of giving money and help to people who are poor or in trouble

phi·lat·e·ly /fɪˈlætəli/ n [U] the activity of collecting stamps for pleasure —**philatelic** /ˌfɪləˈtelɪk/ adj —**philatelist** /fɪˈlætəlɪst/ n [C]

-phile /faɪl/ also **-phil** suffix [in nouns] someone who likes something: *a bibliophile* (=someone who likes books) | *an Anglophile* (=someone who likes English or British things)

Phil·har·mon·ic /ˌfɪləˈmɒnɪk, ˌfɪlhɑː- $ ˌfɪlərˈmɑː-, ˌfɪlhɑːr-/ adj, n [C] used in the names of ORCHESTRAS: *the Berlin Philharmonic*

-philia /fɪliə/ suffix [in nouns] **1** technical a tendency to feel sexually attracted in a way that is not approved of or not normal: *necrophilia* (=a sexual attraction to dead bodies) **2** a love of something: *Francophilia* (=a love of French things)

-philiac /fɪliæk/ suffix [in nouns] technical someone who feels sexually attracted in a way that is not approved of: *a necrophiliac*

phi·lip·pic /fɪˈlɪpɪk/ n [C] literary a strong angry speech publicly attacking someone

phil·is·tine /ˈfɪlɪstaɪn $ -stiːn/ n [C] someone who does not like or understand art, literature, music etc: *When it comes to art, the man's a philistine.* —**philistine** adj —**philistinism** n [U]

phi·lol·o·gy /fɪˈlɒlədʒi $ -ˈlɑː-/ n [U] old-fashioned the study of words and of the way words and languages develop —**philologist** n [C] —**philological** /ˌfɪləˈlɒdʒɪkəl $ -ˈlɑː-/ adj → LINGUISTICS

phi·los·o·pher /fɪˈlɒsəfə $ -ˈlɑːsəfər/ n [C] **1** someone who studies and develops ideas about the nature and meaning of existence, truth, good and evil etc: *Plato, Aristotle, and other Greek philosophers* **2** someone who thinks deeply about the world, life etc

phi,losopher's 'stone n [singular] an imaginary substance that was thought in the past to have the power to change any other metal into gold

phil·o·soph·i·cal /ˌfɪləˈsɒfɪkəl $ -ˈsɑː-/ also **phil·o·soph·ic** /-ˈsɒfɪk $ ˈsɑː-/ adj **1** relating to philosophy: *the philosophical problem of whether there is free will* | *a philosophical argument* **2** calmly accepting a difficult or unpleasant situation which cannot be changed: [+about] *Some old people are philosophical about death.* | *He was by nature a philosophical person.* —**philosophically** /-kli/ adv

phi·los·o·phize also **-ise** BrE /fɪˈlɒsəfaɪz $ -ˈlɑː-/ v [I] to talk about serious subjects in detail or for a long time

phi·los·o·phy W3 /fɪˈlɒsəfi $ -ˈlɑː-/ n plural **philosophies**
1 [U] the study of the nature and meaning of existence, truth, good and evil, etc: *Emma studies philosophy at university.* | [+of] *the philosophy of science*
2 [C] the views of a particular philosopher or group of philosophers: [+of] *the philosophy of Aristotle*
3 [C] the attitude or set of ideas that guides the behaviour of a person or organization: *The company explained their management philosophy.* | *The idea that you should treat others as you would like them to treat you is a fine philosophy of life.* → NATURAL PHILOSOPHY

phil·tre also **philter** AmE /ˈfɪltə $ -ər/ n [C] literary a magic drink that makes someone fall in love

phle·bi·tis /flɪˈbaɪtɪs/ n [U] medical a condition in which there is swelling and roughness on the inside surface of a VEIN (=tube that carries blood through your body)

phlegm /flem/ n [U] **1** the thick yellowish substance produced in your nose and throat, especially when you have a cold; ▣ **mucus** **2** unusual calmness in worrying, frightening, or exciting situations

phleg·mat·ic /flegˈmætɪk/ adj calm and not easily excited or worried: *The taxi driver, a phlegmatic man in middle age, showed no surprise at this request.* —**phlegmatically** /-kli/ adv

phlox /flɒks $ flɑːks/ n [C,U] **1** a tall garden plant with pink, purple, or white flowers **2** AmE a low, spreading plant with pink or white flowers

-phobe /fəʊb $ foʊb/ suffix [in nouns] someone who dislikes or hates something: *a xenophobe* (=someone who hates foreigners) | *a technophobe* (=someone who dislikes and fears modern technology such as computers)

pho·bi·a /ˈfəʊbiə $ ˈfoʊ-/ n [C,U] a strong unreasonable fear of something: [+about] *Owen has a phobia about snakes.* | *Some children suffer from school phobia.* —**phobic** adj

-phobia /fəʊbiə $ foʊ-/ suffix [in nouns] **1** technical a strong unreasonable dislike or fear of something, which may be part of a mental illness: *claustrophobia* (=fear of being in a small enclosed space) | *aquaphobia* (=fear of water) **2** a dislike or hatred of something: *Anglophobia* (=a dislike of English or British things)

P

-phobic /fəʊbɪk $ foʊ-/ *suffix technical* **1** [in nouns] someone who has a strong unreasonable fear of something: *He's a claustrophobic* (=he fears small enclosed places). **2** [in adjectives] suffering from or connected with a strong unreasonable fear of something: *I'm a bit agoraphobic* (=I am afraid of crowds and open places).

phoe·nix /'fi:nɪks/ *n* [C] **1** a magic bird that is born from a fire, according to ancient stories **2 rise like a phoenix from the ashes** to become successful again after seeming to have failed completely

phon- /fən, fəʊn, fɒn $ fən, foʊn, fɑːn/ *prefix* another form of the prefix PHONO-

phone¹ S1 W2 /fəʊn $ foʊn/ *n* [C]
1 a telephone

answer the phone
come to the phone
phone number
the phone rings
the phone goes dead (=you can no longer hear the person you were speaking to on the telephone)
phone conversation
by phone/over the phone (=using the telephone)
on the phone (=speaking on the telephone)
off the phone (=no longer using the telephone)
phone company
mobile phone/mobile *BrE*
cellphone/cellular phone *especially AmE*

Louise got up to **answer** *the* **phone**. | *She's too busy to* **come to the phone** *right now. Can you call back later?* | *What's your* **phone number***?* | *The* **phone** *rang. It was Pam.* | *Before he could answer,* **the phone went dead.** | *a secret tape of Diana's* **phone conversations** | *Much of his work is done* **by phone.** | *Who was that on the* **phone***?* | *I wish Amy would get* **off the phone.** →
CELLPHONE → MOBILE PHONE → PAY PHONE

2 the part of a telephone into which you speak; ▤ **receiver**: *She* **picked up the phone** *and dialled.* | *Jean* **put the phone down** (=after she had finished her conversation) *and burst out laughing.* | *He* **put the phone down on** *me* (=before I had finished speaking).

phone² S1 also **phone up** *v* [I,T]
to speak to someone by telephone; ▤ **telephone**: *I'll phone you this evening.* | *Why didn't they phone the police?* | *For information phone 01279-623772.* | *Stevie phoned to say that he was going to be late.* | *I kept phoning her up, asking to meet her.* | *Tell him to phone back* (=telephone again at a later time) *tomorrow.*
⚠ You do not 'phone to' someone or 'phone to' a number. **Phone** is followed immediately by a noun: *She phoned her friend Judy.* | *Just phone 01279-623772 and I'll come and get you.* → see box at CALL¹

phone in *phr v*
1 to telephone the place where you work, especially in order to report something: *I'll phone in and let them know.* | **phone sth** ⇔ **in** *I'll phone the report in tomorrow morning.* | *She* **phoned in sick** (=telephoned to say that she was ill and could not come to work).
2 to telephone a radio or television show to give your opinion or ask a question: *There's still time to phone in before the end of the programme.* → PHONE-IN

-phone /fəʊn $ foʊn/ *suffix* **1** [in nouns] an instrument or machine relating to sound or hearing, especially a musical instrument: *earphones* (=for listening to a radio etc) | *a saxophone* **2** [in nouns] *technical* someone who speaks a particular language: *a Francophone* (=someone who speaks French) **3** [in adjectives] speaking a particular language: *Francophone nations* (=nations where French is spoken)

phone book *n* [C] a book that contains an alphabetical list of the names, addresses, and telephone numbers of all the people who have a telephone in a particular area; ▤ **telephone directory**

phone booth *n* [C] a small structure that is partly or completely enclosed, containing a public telephone

phone box *n* [C] *BrE* a small structure that is partly or completely enclosed, containing a public telephone

phone call *n* [C] when you speak to someone on the telephone; ▤ **call, telephone call**: *I need to* **make a quick phone call.** | *I got a* **phone call** *from someone called Mike.* | *obscene phone calls*

phone·card /'fəʊnkɑːd $ 'foʊnkɑːrd/ *n* [C] a plastic card that can be used in some public telephones instead of money

phone-in *n* [C] a radio or television programme in which you hear ordinary people expressing opinions or asking questions over the telephone

pho·neme /'fəʊniːm $ 'foʊ-/ *n* [C] *technical* the smallest unit of speech that can be used to make one word different from another word, such as the 'b' and the 'p' in 'big' and 'pig' —**phonemic** /fə'niːmɪk/ *adj* —**phonemically** /-kli/ *adv*

pho·ne·mics /fə'niːmɪks/ *n* [U] *technical* the study and description of the phonemes of languages

phone sex *n* [U] the activity of talking with someone on the telephone about sex in order to become sexually excited: *She claimed the relationship consisted mainly of him calling her up to* **have phone sex.**

phone-tapping *n* [U] the activity of listening secretly to other people's telephone conversations using special electronic equipment

pho·net·ic /fə'netɪk/ *adj technical* **1** relating to the sounds of human speech **2** using special signs, often different from ordinary letters, to represent the sounds of speech: *a phonetic alphabet* | *phonetic symbols*

pho·net·ics /fə'netɪks/ *n* [U] the science and study of speech sounds —**phonetician** /ˌfəʊnɪ'tɪʃən, ˌfɒn- $ ˌfoʊ-/ *n* [C]

phone tree *n* [C] *informal* a list of all the telephone numbers of the people in an organization, showing who should call who if there is important information that everyone should know

pho·ney also **phony** *AmE* /'fəʊni $ 'foʊ-/ *adj informal* **1** false or not real, and intended to deceive someone; ▤ **fake**: *a phoney American accent* **2** someone who is phoney is insincere and pretends to be something they are not —**phoney** *n* [C]: *He's a complete phoney!* —**phoniness** *n* [U]

phoney war *n* [singular] a period during which a state of war officially exists but there is no actual fighting

phon·ic /'fɒnɪk, 'fəʊ- $ 'fɑː, 'foʊ-/ *adj technical* **1** relating to sound **2** relating to speech sounds

phon·ics /'fɒnɪks, 'fəʊ- $ 'fɑː-, 'foʊ-/ *n* [U] a method of teaching people to read in which they are taught to recognize the sounds that letters represent

phono- *prefix* /fəʊnəʊ, -nə, fɒnə $ foʊnoʊ, -nə, fɑːnə/ also **phon-** *technical* **1** relating to the voice or speech: *phonetics* (=the science of speech sounds) **2** relating to sound: *a phonoreceptor* (=a hearing organ)

pho·no·graph /'fəʊnəgrɑːf $ 'foʊnəgræf/ *n* [C] *AmE old-fashioned* a RECORD PLAYER

pho·nol·o·gy /fə'nɒlədʒi $ -'nɑː-/ *n* [U] *technical* the study of the system of speech sounds in a language, or the system of sounds itself —**phonologist** *n* [C] —**phonological** /ˌfəʊnə'lɒdʒɪkəl◂, ˌfɒn- $ ˌfoʊnə'lɑː-/ *adj* —**phonologically** /-kli/ *adv*

pho·ny /'fəʊni $ 'foʊ-/ *adj* the usual American spelling of PHONEY

phoo·ey /'fuːi/ *interjection* used to express strong disbelief or disappointment

phos·gene /'fɒzdʒiːn $ 'fɑːz-/ *n* [U] a poisonous gas used in war and in industry

phos·phate /'fɒsfeɪt $ 'fɑːs-/ *n* [C,U] **1** one of the various forms of a SALT of PHOSPHORUS, often used in industry **2** [usually plural] a substance containing a phosphate used for making plants grow better

phos·pho·res·cence /ˌfɒsfə'resəns $ ˌfɑːs-/ *n* [U] a slight steady light that can only be noticed in the dark

phos·pho·res·cent /ˌfɒsfə'resənt◂ $ ˌfɑːs-/ *adj* shining slightly in the dark but producing little or no heat: *a strange phosphorescent light*

phos·pho·rus /'fɒsfərəs $ 'fɑːs-/ *n* [U] a poisonous yellowish chemical substance that starts to burn when it is in the air, and shines in the dark. It is a chemical ELEMENT: symbol P —**phosphoric** /fɒs'fɒrɪk $ fɑːs'fɔː-, fɑːs'fɑː-, 'fɑːsfərɪk/ *adj*: *phosphoric acid*

pho·to S2 W2 /'fəʊtəʊ $ 'foʊtoʊ/ *n plural* **photos** [C] *informal* a photograph: [+of] *I'll send Mom a photo of Sammy.* | *Can you take a photo of me and Rachel?*

photo- /fəʊtəʊ, -tə $ foʊtoʊ, -tə/ *prefix technical* **1** relating to light: *photosensitive paper* (=paper that changes when light touches it) **2** relating to photography: *photo-journalism* (=the use of photographs in reporting news)

'**photo booth** *n* [C] a small structure in which you can sit to have photographs taken by a machine

pho·to·call /'fəʊtəʊˌkɔːl $ 'foʊtoʊˌkɒːl/ *n* [C] an occasion during which a professional photographer takes pictures of a famous person or group of people

pho·to·cop·i·er /'fəʊtəʊˌkɒpiə $ 'foʊtəˌkɑːpiər/ *n* [C] a machine that makes photographic copies of documents → see picture at OFFICE

pho·to·cop·y¹ /'fəʊtəʊˌkɒpi $ 'foʊtəˌkɑːpi/ *n plural* **photocopies** [C] a photographic copy, especially of something printed, written, or drawn: *I sent him the original document, not a photocopy.*

photocopy² *v* **photocopied, photocopying, photocopies** [T] to make a photographic copy of something: *Leave the papers with me and I'll get them photocopied.* —**photocopying** *n* [U]: *Could you do some photocopying for me tomorrow?*

pho·to·e·lec·tric /ˌfəʊtəʊ-ɪ'lektrɪk◂ $ ˌfoʊtoʊ-/ *adj* using an electrical current that is controlled by light

ˌ**photoelectric 'cell** *n* [C] **1** an electronic instrument that changes light into electricity **2** an electronic instrument that uses light to start an electrical effect, often used in BURGLAR ALARMS

ˌ**photo 'finish** *n* [C] the end of a race in which the leading runners finish so close together that a photograph of it has to be examined to decide which is the winner

Pho·to·fit /'fəʊtəʊfɪt $ 'foʊtoʊ-/ *n* [U] *trademark BrE* a way of making a picture of a face using photographs of parts of different faces, used to help the police catch a criminal

pho·to·gen·ic /ˌfəʊtə'dʒenɪk◂, ˌfəʊtəʊ- ˌfoʊtə-/ *adj* always looking attractive in photographs: *Helen is very photogenic.*

pho·to·graph¹ S2 W2 /'fəʊtəgrɑːf $ 'foʊtəgræf/ also **photo** *informal n* [C] a picture obtained by using a camera and film that is sensitive to light: *a colour photograph* | *a black and white photograph* | [+of] *I wish I had a photograph of Thomas.* | *He took a photograph of the hotel.* | *Tim was looking through an old photograph album* (=book in which you put photographs). | *Did you see Leo's photograph* (=a photograph of Leo) *in the newspaper?*

photograph² *v* **1** [T] to take a photograph of someone or something: *Kate agreed to let me photograph her.* | *He stood by the tree to be photographed.* **2** **photograph well** to look attractive in photographs: *Cilla does not photograph well.*

pho·tog·ra·pher /fə'tɒgrəfə $ -'tɑːgrəfər/ *n* [C] someone who takes photographs, especially as a professional or as an artist: *a fashion photographer* → see picture at OCCUPATION

pho·to·graph·ic /ˌfəʊtə'græfɪk◂ $ ˌfoʊ-/ *adj* relating to photographs, using photographs, or used in producing photographs: *photographic film* | *photographic equipment* | *The software allows you to scan photographic images on your personal computer.* —**photographically** /-kli/ *adv*

ˌ**photographic 'memory** *n* [C] if you have a photographic memory, you can remember exactly every detail of something you have seen

pho·tog·ra·phy /fə'tɒgrəfi $ -'tɑː-/ *n* [U] the art, profession, or method of producing photographs or the scenes in films: *He did fashion photography for Vogue magazine.* | *the National Museum of Photography*

pho·to·jour·nal·is·m /ˌfəʊtəʊ'dʒɜːnəl-ɪzəm $ ˌfoʊtoʊ'dʒɜːr-/ *n* [U] the job or activity of reporting news stories in newspapers and magazines using mainly photographs instead of words

pho·ton /'fəʊtɒn $ 'foʊtɑːn/ *n* [C] *technical* a unit of ENERGY that carries light and has zero MASS

ˌ**photo oppor'tunity** *n* [C] a chance for someone such as a politician to be photographed for a newspaper in a way that will make them look good

pho·to·sen·si·tive /ˌfəʊtəʊ'sensɪtɪv◂ $ ˌfoʊtə'sen-/ *adj* reacting to light, for example by changing colour or producing an electrical current: *photosensitive paper*

pho·to·sen·si·tize also **-ise** *BrE* /ˌfəʊtəʊ'sensɪtaɪz $ ˌfoʊtə'sen-/ *v* [T] to make something photosensitive

ˌ**photo shoot** *n* [C] an occasion during which a professional photographer takes pictures of a fashion model or an actor for advertisements

Pho·to·stat /'fəʊtəstæt $ 'foʊ-/ *n* [C] *trademark* a photographic copy of a document, or a type of machine used for making one —**Photostat** *v* [T]

pho·to·syn·the·sis /ˌfəʊtəʊ'sɪnθɪsɪs $ ˌfoʊtə'sɪn-/ *n* [U] *technical* the production by a green plant of special substances like sugar that it uses as food, caused by the action of sunlight on CHLOROPHYLL (=the green substance in leaves) —**photosynthesize** *v* [I,T]

phras·al /'freɪzəl/ *adj* consisting of or relating to a phrase or phrases

ˌ**phrasal 'verb** *n* [C] a group of words that is used like a verb and consists of a verb with an adverb or PREPOSITION after it, for example 'set off' or 'look after'. In this dictionary, phrasal verbs are marked 'phr v'.

phrase¹ W3 /freɪz/ *n* [C]
1 a group of words that together have a particular meaning, especially when they express the meaning well in a few words: *She used the phrase 'survival of the fittest'.* | *Edward Heath's famous phrase, 'the unacceptable face of capitalism'*
2 *technical* a group of words without a FINITE verb, especially when they are used to form part of a sentence, such as 'walking along the road' and 'a bar of soap' → CLAUSE (2), SENTENCE¹ (1)
3 a short group of musical notes that is part of a longer piece → **to coin a phrase** at COIN² (2); → **a turn of phrase** at TURN² (11); → **turn a phrase** at TURN¹ (20)

WORD FOCUS: PHRASE
similar words: **expression, idiom, cliche, metaphor, saying, turn of phrase**

phrase² *v* [T] **1** to express something in a particular way: *Polly tried to think how to phrase the question.* | *Sorry, I phrased that badly.* **2** to perform music in order to produce the full effect of separate musical phrases

phrase·book /'freɪzbʊk/ *n* [C] a book that explains phrases of a foreign language, for people to use when they travel to other countries

phra·se·ol·o·gy /ˌfreɪzi'ɒlədʒi $ -'ɑː-/ *n* [U] the way that words and phrases are chosen and used in a particular language or subject

phras·ing /'freɪzɪŋ/ *n* [U] **1** the way that something is said: *I don't remember her exact phrasing.* **2** a way of playing music, reading poetry etc that separates the notes, words, or lines into phrases

phre·nol·ogy /frə'nɒlədʒi $ -'nɑː-/ *n* [U] the study of the shape of people's heads as a way of finding out what their characters and abilities are, which was popular in the 19th century —**phrenologist** *n* [C]

phut /fʌt/ n go phut BrE informal if a machine goes phut, it stops working completely: *The microwave's gone phut.*

phwoar /fwɔː/ interjection BrE informal used to show that you think someone is sexually attractive: *Phwoar! Look at her!*

phyl·lo /ˈfiːləʊ $ -loʊ/ n [U] another spelling of FILO

phy·lum /ˈfaɪləm/ n plural **phyla** /-lə/ [C] technical one of the large groups into which scientists divide plants, animals, and languages

physi- /fɪzɪ/ prefix another form of PHYSIO-

phys·i·cal[1] ⓢ2 ⓦ1 /ˈfɪzɪkəl/ adj
1 BODY NOT MIND related to someone's body rather than their mind or emotions; → **mental, emotional**: *She was in constant physical pain.* | *the physical and emotional needs of young adults* | *people with severe physical disabilities* | *Don't be put off by his physical appearance.* | *He was obsessed with physical fitness.*
2 SEX a physical relationship involves sex rather than just friendship: *My attraction to him was totally physical.* | *Their physical relationship had never been very good.*
3 PERSON informal someone who is physical likes touching people a lot: *She's a very physical person.*
4 VIOLENT involving touching someone in a rough or violent way: *Football can be a very physical game.* | *I was a bit worried that the argument might become physical.*
5 REAL/SOLID relating to real objects that you can touch, see, or feel: *the physical world around us* | *the physical environment* | *They were kept in appalling physical conditions.*
6 NATURAL relating to or following natural laws: *a physical explanation for this phenomenon*
7 SCIENCE [only before noun] a physical science is an area of scientific study that is related to PHYSICS: *physical chemistry* —**physicality** /ˌfɪzɪˈkælɪti/ n [U]: *the physicality of sport* → **PHYSICALLY**

physical[2] also **physical examin'ation** n [C] a thorough examination of someone's body by a doctor, in order to discover whether they are healthy or have any illnesses or medical problems

physical edu'cation n [U] PE sport and physical exercise that are taught as a school subject

physical ge'ography n [U] the study of the Earth's surface and of its rivers, mountains etc

phys·i·cally ⓢ3 /ˈfɪzɪkli/ adv
1 in relation to your body rather than your mind or emotions; → **mentally, emotionally**: *She is young and physically fit.* | *Do you find him physically attractive?* | *I felt physically sick at the thought.* | *children who have been physically abused*
2 physically possible/impossible possible or not possible according to the laws of nature: *It would be physically impossible to carry everything at once.*

physically 'challenged adj AmE someone who is physically challenged has a problem with their body that makes it difficult for them to do things that other people can do easily

physical 'science n [U] also **the physical sciences** [plural] the sciences, for example CHEMISTRY and PHYSICS, that are concerned with studying things that are not living

physical 'therapist n [C] AmE someone whose job is to give physical therapy; ⊟ **physiotherapist** BrE

physical 'therapy n [U] AmE a treatment that uses special exercises, rubbing, heat etc to treat medical conditions and problems with muscles; ⊟ **physiotherapy** BrE

phy·si·cian /fɪˈzɪʃən/ n [C] formal especially AmE a doctor

phys·i·cist /ˈfɪzɪsɪst/ n [C] a scientist who has special knowledge and training in PHYSICS

phys·ics /ˈfɪzɪks/ n [U] the science concerned with the study of physical objects and substances, and of natural forces such as light, heat, and movement

phys·i·o /ˈfɪziəʊ $ -zioʊ/ n plural **physios** **1** [C] informal a PHYSIOTHERAPIST **2** [U] PHYSIOTHERAPY

physio- /fɪziəʊ, -ziə $ -zioʊ, -ziə/ also **physi-** prefix **1** relating to nature and living things: *physiology* (=study of how the body works) **2** physical: *physiotherapy* (=treatment using exercises etc)

phys·i·og·no·my /ˌfɪziˈɒnəmi $ -ˈɑː-, -ˈɑːg-/ n plural **physiognomies** [C] technical the general appearance of a person's face

phys·i·ol·o·gy /ˌfɪziˈɒlədʒi $ -ˈɑː-/ n [U] **1** the science that studies the way in which the bodies of living things work: *a book on biochemistry and physiology* **2** the way the body of a person or an animal works; → **anatomy**: *the physiology of the brain*

phys·i·o·ther·a·pist /ˌfɪziəʊˈθerəpɪst $ -zioʊ-/ n [C] someone whose job is to give physiotherapy; ⊟ **physical therapist** AmE

phys·i·o·ther·a·py /ˌfɪziəʊˈθerəpi $ -zioʊ-/ n [U] a treatment that uses special exercises, rubbing, heat etc to treat medical conditions and problems with muscles; ⊟ **physical therapy** AmE

phy·sique /fɪˈziːk/ n [C] the size and appearance of someone's body: *She didn't have the physique to be a dancer.* | *He had good health and a strong physique.*

pi /paɪ/ n [U] technical a number that is represented by the Greek letter (π) and is equal to the distance around a circle, divided by its width

pi·a·nis·si·mo /ˌpiːəˈnɪsɪˌməʊ $ -moʊ/ adj, adv technical played or sung very quietly

pi·a·nist /ˈpiːənɪst $ piˈænɪst, ˈpiːə-/ n [C] someone who plays the piano

pi·an·o[1] ⓢ3 /piˈænəʊ $ -noʊ/ n plural **pianos** [C] a large musical instrument that has a long row of black and white KEYS. You play the piano by sitting in front of it and pressing the keys: *Jean accompanied her on the piano.* | **a piano lesson/teacher etc** *a wonderful piano player*

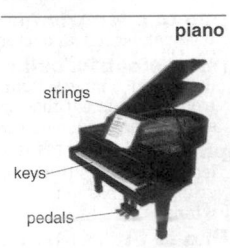
piano
strings
keys
pedals

piano[2] adj, adv technical played or sung quietly

pi·ano ac'cordion n [C] BrE an ACCORDION

pi·ano 'bar n [C] a bar where someone plays the piano for entertainment

pi·an·o·for·te /piˌænəʊˈfɔːti $ -noʊˈfɔːrteɪ/ n [C] old-fashioned a piano

pi·a·no·la /ˌpiːəˈnəʊlə $ -ˈnoʊ-/ n [C] trademark a piano that is played by machinery inside it. A long roll of paper with holes cut in it gradually turns and works the machinery, pressing down the KEYS on the piano to produce music; ⊟ **player piano**

pi'ano stool n [C] a small seat that you sit on while you play the piano

pi·az·za /piˈætsə $ -ˈɑːt-/ n [C] a large square open area between the houses in a town or city, where people often meet or sit together

pic /pɪk/ n [C] informal a picture or film

pic·a·dor /ˈpɪkədɔː $ -dɔːr/ n [C] a man in a BULLFIGHT who rides a horse, and annoys and weakens the BULL by sticking a long spear into it

pic·a·resque /ˌpɪkəˈresk◂/ adj a picaresque story tells the amusing and unlikely adventures of a character who travels to a lot of different places

pic·a·yune /ˌpɪkəˈjuːn/ adj AmE written small and unimportant: *A few cuts and bruises are picayune compared to what might have happened.*

pic·ca·lil·li /ˌpɪkəˈlɪli/ n [U] BrE a hot-tasting sauce that is made with small pieces of vegetables and eaten with cold meat

pic·co·lo /ˈpɪkələʊ $ -loʊ/ *n plural* **piccolos** [C] a musical instrument that looks like a small FLUTE

pick¹ S1 W1 /pɪk/ *v* [T]

1 CHOOSE STH to choose a person or thing, for example because they are the best or most suitable: *Students have to pick three courses from a list of 15.* | *I don't know which colour to pick.* | *Who's going to pick the team for the match on Saturday?* | **pick sb/sth for sth** *I wasn't picked for the hockey team.* | **pick sb/sth as sth** *The hotel was picked as the best small hotel in the area.* | **pick sb to do sth** *He was picked to run in the 100 metres.* | *Russell spoke slowly, picking his words (=choosing what to say) very carefully.* → PICKED

2 FLOWERS/FRUIT ETC to remove a flower, fruit, nut etc from a plant or tree: *We picked some blackberries to eat on the way.* | *Amy picked a small bunch of wild flowers.* | *a dish of freshly picked peas*

3 REMOVE STH [always + adv/prep] to remove something carefully from a place, especially something small: **pick sth from sth** *Ahmed picked the melon pips from his teeth.* | **pick sth off (sth)** *She was nervously picking bits of fluff off her sweater.* | **pick sth out of sth** *The goalkeeper spent a lot of his time picking the ball out of the back of the net.*

4 pick your way through/across/among etc sth to walk in a slow careful way, choosing exactly where to put your feet down: *She picked her way between the puddles.* | *He picked his way down the narrow staircase.*

5 pick your nose to remove MUCUS from your nose with your finger: *Don't pick your nose!*

6 pick your teeth to remove bits of food from between your teeth with your finger or a small pointed object

7 pick sb's brains to ask someone who knows a lot about something for information and advice about it: *Have you got a minute? I need to pick your brains.*

8 pick a quarrel/fight (with sb) to deliberately start a quarrel or fight with someone: *I could see he was trying to pick a fight with me.*

9 pick and choose to choose only the best people or things, or only the ones that you really like: *Come on, you haven't got time to pick and choose.*

10 pick a lock to use something that is not a key to unlock a door, drawer etc: *It's quite easy to pick the lock on a car door.*

11 pick a hole in sth to make a hole in something by pulling it with your fingers: *He had picked a hole in his jumper.*

12 pick holes in sth *informal* to criticize an idea or a plan by saying what its weak points are: *It's easy to pick holes in her argument.*

13 pick sth clean to remove all the meat from a bone when you are eating

14 pick sb's pocket to quietly steal something from someone's pocket; → **pickpocket**

15 pick a winner *informal* to choose someone or something very good

16 pick sth to pieces *informal* to criticize something very severely and in a very detailed way: *I'm fed up with having my work picked to pieces.*

17 MUSICAL INSTRUMENT *AmE* to play a musical instrument by pulling at its strings with your fingers; ⊟ pluck → **have a bone to pick with sb** at BONE¹ (10)

pick at sth *phr v*

1 to eat only small amounts of food because you do not feel hungry or do not like the food: *Paige could only pick at her meal, forcing down a mouthful or two.*

2 to touch something many times with your fingers, pulling it slightly: *She was picking at her skirt.*

pick sb/sth ⇔ off *phr v*

to point a weapon carefully at one person or animal in a group, and then shoot them: *There were gunmen in some of the buildings who picked off our men as they went past.*

pick on sb/sth *phr v spoken*

1 to behave in an unfair way to someone, for example by blaming them or criticizing them unfairly: *Why don't you pick on someone else for a change?*

2 *BrE* to choose a particular person or thing: *Just pick*

on one job and try to get that finished.

pick sb/sth ⇔ out *phr v*

1 CHOOSE to choose someone or something from a group: *She picked out a navy blue dress.* | *His story was picked out as the best by the judges.*

2 RECOGNIZE to recognize someone or something in a group of people or things: *She was able to pick out her father at the other side of the room.* | *I picked out Valerie's voice from among the general conversation.*

3 SEE if you can pick something out, you can see it but not very clearly: *I could just pick out some letters carved into the stone.*

4 SHOWN CLEARLY [usually passive] if something is picked out, it is in a different colour or material from the background, so that it can be clearly seen: *His name was picked out in gold lettering.*

5 PLAY A TUNE to play a tune on a musical instrument slowly or with difficulty: *He sat at the piano and picked out a simple tune.*

pick over sth *phr v*

to examine a group of things very carefully in order to choose the ones you want: *She was sitting at the kitchen table picking over a pile of mushrooms.*

pick through sth *phr v*

to search through a pile of things to find things that you want: *Police are still picking through the rubble looking for clues to the cause of the explosion.*

pick up *phr v*

1 LIFT STH/SB UP **pick sth/sb ⇔ up** to lift something or someone up: *He picked up the letter and read it.* | *The phone rang and I picked it up.* | *Mummy, can you pick me up?* → see box at HOLD¹

2 pick yourself up to get up from the ground after you have fallen: *Carol picked herself up and brushed the dirt off her coat.*

3 TIDY STH **pick sth ⇔ up** *AmE* to make a room or building tidy: *Pick up your room before you go to bed.*

4 GET STH **pick sth ⇔ up** *informal* **a)** to get or win something: *He's already picked up three major prizes this year.* **b)** to buy something or get it from a shop etc: *I picked up an evening paper on the way home.* | *For more details, pick up a leaflet in your local post office.* **c)** to get an illness: *I picked up a virus while I was in America.*

5 COLLECT **pick sth ⇔ up** to collect something from a place: *I'll pick my things up later.* | *She just dropped by to pick up her mail.*

6 LET SB INTO A VEHICLE **pick sb ⇔ up** to let someone get into your car, boat etc and take them somewhere: *I'll pick you up at the station.* | *The survivors were picked up by fishing boats from nearby villages.*

7 LEARN **pick sth ⇔ up** to learn something by watching or listening to other people: *I picked up a few words of Greek when I was there last year.* | *Mary watched the other dancers to see if she could pick up any tips.*

8 NOTICE **pick sth ⇔ up** to notice something that is not easy to notice, such as a slight smell or a sign of something: *I picked up a faint smell of coffee.* | *The dogs picked up the scent and raced off.* | *We picked up their tracks again on the other side of the river.*

9 RADIO/SIGNALS **pick sth ⇔ up** if a machine picks up a sound, movement, or signal, it is able to notice it or receive it: *The sensors pick up faint vibrations in the Earth.* | *I managed to pick up an American news broadcast.*

10 SEX **pick sb ⇔ up** to become friendly with someone you have just met because you want to have sex with them: *young women sitting around in bars waiting to be picked up*

11 START AGAIN **a)** if you pick up where you stopped or were interrupted, you start again from that point: *We'll meet again in the morning and we can pick up where we left off.* **b)** **pick sth ⇔ up** if you pick up an idea that has been mentioned, you return to it and develop it further: *I'd like to pick up what you said* *earlier.* | *This same theme is picked up in his later works.*

12 IMPROVE a) if a situation picks up, it improves: *Her social life was picking up at last.* | *The economy is finally beginning to pick up again.* | *We've been through a bit of a bad patch, but things are picking up again now.* b) pick sb up if a medicine or drink picks you up, it makes you feel better; → **pick-me-up**

13 ROAD pick sth ⇔ up if you pick up a road, you go onto it and start driving along it: *We take the A14 to Birmingham and then pick up the M5.*

14 TRAIN/BUS pick sth ⇔ up if you pick up a train, bus etc you get onto it and travel on it

15 pick up speed/steam to go faster: *The train was gradually picking up speed.*

16 pick up the bill/tab (for sth) *informal* to pay for something: *Why should the taxpayer pick up the tab for mistakes made by a private company?*

17 WIND if the wind picks up, it increases or grows stronger

18 COLOUR pick sth ⇔ up if one thing picks up a colour in something else, it has an amount of the same colour in it so that the two things look nice together: *I like the way the curtains pick up the red in the rug.*

19 CRIMINAL pick sb ⇔ up if the police pick someone up, they take them somewhere to answer questions or to be locked up: *He was picked up by police as he was trying to leave the country.*

20 pick up the pieces (of sth) to try to make your life normal again after something very bad has happened to you: *Thousands of victims of the earthquake are now faced with the task of picking up the pieces of their lives.*

21 pick up the threads (of sth) if you pick up the threads of something that you were doing, you try to return to it and start doing it again after it stopped or was changed: *Now that the war was over they could pick up the threads of their lives again.*

22 pick your feet up *spoken* used to tell someone to walk properly or more quickly

pick up after sb *phr v informal*
to tidy things that someone else has left untidy: *I'm tired of picking up after you!*

pick up on sth *phr v*
1 to notice something about the way someone is behaving or feeling, even though they are trying not to show it: *Children pick up on our worries and anxieties.*
2 to return to a point or an idea that has been mentioned and discuss it more: *I'd like to pick up on a point that Steven made earlier.*
3 pick sb up on sth to criticize someone slightly for something they have said: *I knew he was lying and I should have picked him up on it.*

pick² n **1** [U] if you can have your pick or take your pick of different things, you can choose which one you want: *Have a look at the menu and take your pick.* | *He knew he could take his pick of any of the girls in the office.* | *Sarah could have her pick of any university in the country.* | have/get first pick (of sth) *She always gets first pick of the videos.* **2** the pick of sth *informal* the best things in a group: *In tonight's programme we'll be discussing the pick of this month's new movies.* | *There were fifteen candidates for the job, and he was the pick of the bunch* (=the best one). **3** [C] *informal* your pick is the person or thing that you have chosen from a group; ⊟ **choice**: *There are a lot of good horses in the race, but Archimedes would be my pick.* **4** [C] a PICKAXE **5** [C] *informal* a small, flat object that you use for pulling at the strings of a musical instrument such as a GUITAR; ⊟ **plectrum** → **ICE PICK**

pick-and-'mix *adj BrE* if something is pick-and-mix, you are free to choose the things or parts that you want and not choose the rest: *Students can select parts of the course on a pick-and-mix basis.*

pick·axe *BrE*; **pickax** *AmE* /'pɪk-æks/ *n* [C] a large tool that you use for breaking up the ground. It consists of a curved iron bar with a sharp point on each end and a long handle

picked /pɪkt/ *adj* [only before noun] picked people have been specially chosen because they are very suitable for a particular job; → **handpicked**

pick·er /'pɪkə $ -ər/ *n* [C] cotton picker/fruit picker etc a person or machine that picks fruit or vegetables

pick·et¹ /'pɪkɪt/ *n* [C] **1** a) when a group of people stand or march in front of a shop, factory, government building etc to protest about something or to stop people from going in during a STRIKE: *There was a mass picket* (=one involving a lot of people) *by students outside the main office of the university.* | [+of] *They organized a picket of the power station.* b) a person or the group of people involved in a picket: *The pickets persuaded some drivers not to enter the factory.* → **FLYING PICKET 2** a soldier or a group of soldiers with the special duty of guarding a military camp: *He's on picket duty tonight.*

picket² *v* **1** [I,T] to stand or march in front of a shop, factory, government building etc to protest about something or to stop people from going in during a STRIKE: *Protesters are still picketing outside the White House gates.* | *a group of picketing miners* **2** [T] to place soldiers around or near a place as guards —**picketing** *n* [U]: *The new law will still allow peaceful picketing.*

'picket ,fence *n* [C] *AmE* a fence made up of a line of strong pointed sticks that are fixed in the ground

'picket ,line *n* [C] a group of people who stand outside a factory and try to prevent people from going in or coming out during a STRIKE: on a picket line *So far, there has been very little violence on the picket line.* | *Very few workers were willing to cross the picket line.*

pick·ings /'pɪkɪŋz/ *n* [plural] *informal* money or profits that you can get easily from a situation: *There were rich pickings* (=a lot of money) *to be had from the stock market.* | *There are easy pickings for thieves at these big outdoor concerts.* | slim/lean/meagre pickings *Companies are put off investing in poor areas because of the meagre pickings to be had.*

pick·le¹ /'pɪkəl/ *n* **1** [C,U] *BrE* a thick cold sauce that is made from pieces of vegetables preserved in VINEGAR. It is usually eaten with cold meat or cheese: *cheese and pickle sandwiches* | *a selection of cold meats and pickles* **2** [C] *AmE* a CUCUMBER preserved in VINEGAR or salt water, or a piece of this; ⊟ **gherkin** *BrE* **3** be in a (pretty) pickle *old-fashioned* to be in a very difficult situation and not know what to do

pickle² *v* [T] to preserve food in VINEGAR or salt water

pick·led /'pɪkəld/ *adj* **1** pickled vegetables or fruits have been preserved in VINEGAR or salt water: *pickled onions* **2** *old-fashioned informal* drunk

'pick-me-up *n* [C] *informal* a drink or medicine that makes you feel happier and gives you more energy

pick·pock·et /'pɪk,pɒkɪt $ -,pɑːk-/ *n* [C] someone who steals things from people's pockets, especially in a crowd

'pick-up *n*
1 VEHICLE [C] *especially AmE* a small truck with low sides that is used for carrying goods
2 IMPROVEMENT [C] an improvement in something which will be good for economic success: [+in] *There are signs of a pick-up in high street spending.*
3 COLLECTION [C,U] an occasion when someone or something is collected from a place: *The price includes travel from your local pick-up point in the UK to your hotel in Paris.* | *trash pick-up*
4 PERSON [C] *informal* a stranger that you meet in a bar, at a party etc and have sex with
5 MUSIC [C] an electronic part on a musical instrument, especially an electric GUITAR, that makes the sound louder
6 SPEED [U] *AmE* the rate at which a vehicle can increase its speed; ⊟ **acceleration**: *It was a small car, but it had good pick-up.*

'pick-up ,truck *n* [C] *AmE* a PICK-UP (1)

pick·y /'pɪki/ *adj informal* someone who is picky only likes particular things and not others, and so is not easy to please: *He's a very picky eater.*

pic·nic¹ /'pɪknɪk/ n [C] **1** if you have a picnic, you take food and eat it outdoors, especially in the country: *We decided to have a picnic down by the lake.* | **go on/for a picnic** *We could go on a picnic today.* | *a picnic table* | *There is free parking for visitors, as well as a restaurant and picnic area* (=a special area with tables where people can have a picnic). | **picnic site/spot/place** (=a place that is suitable or pleasant for a picnic) *We found a lovely picnic spot by the river.* | **picnic basket/hamper** (=a container in which you can carry food for a picnic); → see picture at TABLE¹ ⚠ Do not say 'do a picnic' or 'make a picnic'. Say **have a picnic. 2** *BrE* the food that you take to eat outdoors on a picnic: *We'll take a picnic with us.* | **picnic lunch/tea/supper** *We ate our picnic lunch by the river.* **3 be no picnic** *informal* if something is no picnic, it is very difficult and needs a lot of effort or hard work: *Bringing up six children is no picnic!*

picnic² v **picnicked, picnicking** [I] to have a picnic: *We picnicked on the beach.* —**picnicker** n [C]: *The area is very popular with picnickers.*

pic·to·gram /'pɪktəgræm/ n [C] **1** a picture that represents a word or phrase **2** a mathematical drawing that shows numbers or amounts in the form of pictures

pic·to·ri·al /pɪk'tɔːriəl/ adj using or relating to paintings, drawings, or photographs: *a pictorial record of their journey*

pic·ture¹ S1 W1 /'pɪktʃə $ -ər/ n
1 PAINTING/DRAWING [C] shapes, lines etc painted or drawn on a surface, showing what someone or something looks like: *The room had several pictures on the walls.* | *a book with pictures in it* | [+of] *I like that picture of the two horses.* | **draw/paint a/sb's picture** *Draw a picture of your house.* | *He asked her permission to paint her picture* (=paint a picture of her).
2 PHOTOGRAPH [C] a photograph: [+of] *That's a great picture of you, Dad!* | **take sb's picture/take a picture of sb** *I asked the waiter if he'd mind taking our picture.* | **wedding/holiday etc pictures** *Would you like to see the wedding pictures?*
3 TELEVISION [C] an image that appears on a television or cinema screen: [+of] *upsetting pictures of the famine in Africa* | *satellite pictures from space*
4 DESCRIPTION/IDEA [C usually singular] a description or idea of what something is like: [+of] *Once the research is complete, we'll have a clearer picture of the outcome.* | *an overall picture of the country's health needs* | *What sort of picture is starting to emerge?* | **paint a bleak/happy/rosy etc picture** (=describe something in a particular way) *The film paints a bleak picture of life in the inner city.* | *The article gives a vivid picture of the way artists at the studio collaborated.* | *Detectives are trying to build up a picture of the kidnapper.*
5 SITUATION [singular] the general situation in a place, organization etc: *The worldwide picture for tribal people remains grim.* | *the wider political picture* | *Checks throughout the region revealed a similar picture everywhere.* | **big/bigger/wider picture** *We were so caught up with the details, we lost sight of the big picture* (=the situation considered as a whole).
6 MENTAL IMAGE [C usually singular] an image or memory that you have in your mind: *Sarah had a mental picture of Lisbon.* | *He had a vivid picture in his mind.*
7 put/keep sb in the picture to give someone all the information they need to understand a situation, especially one that is changing quickly: *I'm just going now, but Keith will put you in the picture.*
8 get the picture *informal* to understand a situation: *You've said enough. I get the picture.*
9 out of the picture if someone is out of the picture, they are no longer involved in a situation: *Injury has effectively put Woods out of the picture as far as international matches are concerned.*
10 FILM a) [C] a film: *It was voted the year's best picture.* **b) the pictures** [plural] *BrE* the cinema: *Would*

you like to go to the pictures?
11 be the picture of health/innocence/despair etc to look very healthy etc: *Head bowed and sobbing, she was the picture of misery.* → **pretty as a picture** at PRETTY² (7)

picture² v [T] **1** to imagine something by making an image in your mind: *Tom, picturing the scene, smiled.* | **picture sb/sth as sth** *Rob had pictured her as serious, but she wasn't like that.* | **picture sb doing sth** *I can't picture him skiing. He's so clumsy!* | **picture what/how** *Picture what it would be like after a nuclear attack.* **2** [usually passive] to show someone or something in a photograph, painting, or drawing: *She is pictured with her mum Christine and sister Kelly.* **3** [usually passive] to describe something in a particular way: **be pictured as sth** *She's been pictured as a difficult, demanding woman.*

picture book n [C] a book for children with many pictures in it

picture card n [C] *BrE* a COURT CARD

picture-perfect adj *AmE* exactly right in appearance or quality: *The bride looked picture-perfect.*

picture postcard n [C] a POSTCARD with a photograph or picture on it

picture-postcard adj [only before noun] a picture-postcard place is very pretty: *picture-postcard villages*

picture rail n [C] *BrE* a long narrow piece of wood fixed high on a wall, used for hanging pictures from

pic·tur·esque /ˌpɪktʃəˈresk◂/ adj **1** a picturesque place is pretty and interesting in an old-fashioned way: *a quiet fishing village with a picturesque harbour* **2** picturesque language uses unusual, interesting, or sometimes rude words to describe something: *a picturesque account of his trip to New York*

picture window n [C] a large window made of a single piece of glass

pid·dle /'pɪdl/ v [I] *informal* to URINATE
piddle around phr v to waste time doing things that are not important

pid·dling /'pɪdlɪŋ/ adj *informal* small and unimportant

pid·gin /'pɪdʒən/ n [C,U] **1** a language that is a mixture of two other languages, which people who do not speak each other's languages well use to talk to each other **2 pidgin English/French etc** English, French etc that is mixed with the words or grammar of another language

pie S2 /paɪ/ n [C,U]
1 fruit baked inside a PASTRY covering: **slice/piece of pie** *Would you like another piece of apple pie?*; → see picture at DESSERT
2 *BrE* meat or vegetables baked inside a PASTRY or potato covering: *I had a steak and kidney pie with chips.*
3 slice/share/piece of the pie a share of something such as money, profits etc: *The smaller companies want a bigger share of the pie.*
4 pie in the sky something good that someone says will happen, but which you think is impossible or unlikely: *Hope of a cure is just pie in the sky.* → MUD PIE, PIE CHART; → **easy as pie** at EASY¹ (1); → **eat humble pie** at HUMBLE¹ (6); → **have a finger in every pie** at FINGER¹ (7); → **be as nice as pie** at NICE (11)

pie·bald /'paɪbɔːld $ -bɒːld/ adj a piebald animal has black and white areas on its body: *a piebald horse*

piece¹ S1 W1 /piːs/ n [C]
1 AMOUNT an amount of something that has been separated from the main part: [+of] *He broke off a piece of bread and gave it her.* | *Cut off a piece of wood 5 cm in length.* | *His trousers were held up with a piece of string.* | *Would you like a small or a large piece?* | **cut/divide etc sth into pieces** *She cut the cake into four equal pieces.* | *Chop the potato into bite-sized pieces.*
2 PART one of the parts that something divides or breaks into: [+of] *a piece of broken glass* | *Individual pieces of text can be cut and pasted to their correct position.* | **in pieces** *The china dish lay in pieces on the*

floor. | *jigsaw pieces* | *His father had taught him how to* **take** *a gun* **to pieces.** | *The shelving* **comes to pieces** (=divides into separate parts) *for easy transport.* | *The shower head just* **came to pieces** (=broke into separate parts) *in my hand.* | *The fireplace was carefully dismantled* **piece by piece** (=one part at a time).

3 SINGLE ITEM a single thing of a particular type, or something that is one of several similar things: [+of] *Pass me another piece of paper.* | *You should eat three pieces of fruit a day.* | *She was wearing a single piece of jewellery.* | *You need to examine every piece of evidence first.* | *an excellent piece of work* | *a major piece of legislation* | *a piece of equipment* | **four-piece/60-piece etc** (=consisting of four, 60 etc separate parts) *a five-piece band* | *a three-piece suite* (=two chairs and a SOFA)

4 SMALL AMOUNT [usually singular] a small amount of something that is interesting, useful, or unusual in some way: **piece of advice/information/gossip etc** *Let me give you a piece of advice.* | *We're witnessing a piece of history in the making.* | **piece of luck/good fortune** *It really was an extraordinary piece of luck.*

5 LAND an area of land: [+of] *a piece of waste ground* | *a dispute about a piece of land*

6 fall to pieces a) to become old and in bad condition: *All my clothes are falling to pieces.* | *They've let that lovely old house fall to pieces around them.* **b)** to no longer be successful or working well: *The economy is falling to pieces.*

7 go to pieces if a person or what they do goes to pieces, they are so upset or nervous that they cannot live, work, or perform as they should: *He just went to pieces after his wife died.* | *Her performance goes to pieces when her father is watching.*

8 smash/rip/tear sth to pieces to damage something badly by breaking it into many parts: *His arm was ripped to pieces by a shark.* | *Wear thick gloves, otherwise you'll tear your fingers to pieces.*

9 pull/rip/tear sb/sth to pieces to criticize someone or their ideas very severely: *Donna could tear your work to pieces, and frequently did.*

10 ART/MUSIC ETC something that has been produced by an artist, musician, or writer: **piece of music/ writing/sculpture etc** *some unusual pieces of sculpture* | *The LSO will perform a much-loved concert piece.*

11 NEWS ITEM a short ARTICLE in a newspaper or magazine or part of a television or radio programme that is about a particular subject: [+about/on] *Did you read that piece in the Observer about censorship?* | *Robert* **wrote** *a short* **piece** *on the earthquake.*

12 in one piece *informal* if you arrive somewhere in one piece, you are not injured: *Cheer up. At least you're* **still in one piece.** | *Ring mum and let her know we* **got here in one piece.**

13 give sb a piece of your mind *informal* to tell someone that you are very angry with them: *After the game he gave the players a piece of his mind.*

14 be a piece of cake *informal* to be very easy to do: *Landing this type of aircraft is a piece of cake for an experienced pilot.*

15 be a piece of piss *BrE spoken not polite* to be very easy to do

16 a piece of the action *informal* a share of the money from a business activity: *And will foreign firms* **get a piece of the action?**

17 be (all) of a piece a) if the things someone says or does are all of a piece, they are part of the typical behaviour of that person: [+with] *Sexist language is all of a piece with the way some men treat women.* **b)** to be the same or similar in all parts: *The architecture here is all of a piece.*

18 MONEY **a)** a coin of a particular value: **ten pence/ fifty-cent etc piece** *Have you change for a 50-cent piece?* **b)** *old use* a coin: *Robert slipped two gold pieces into the man's hand.*

19 GAMES a small object used in a game such as CHESS

20 GUN *AmE informal* a small gun

21 be a piece of shit/crap *spoken not polite* used to

show that you do not respect someone or something they say

22 piece of ass *AmE informal not polite* an offensive expression for a woman. Do not use this expression. → **how long is a piece of string?** at LONG¹ (9)

piece² v

piece *sth* ⇔ **together** *phr v* **1** to use all the information you have about a situation in order to discover the truth about it: *Police are trying to piece together his movements before the murder.* | *Her early life has been pieced together from several different sources.* **2** to put all the separate parts of an object into the correct order or position: *He slowly pieced together the torn fragments of a letter.*

pi·èce de ré·sis·tance /piˌes də reziːˈstɑːns/ *n* [C] the best or most important thing in a series, which comes after everything else: *The pièce de résistance was a stunning goal in the last minute of the match.*

piece·meal /ˈpiːsmiːl/ *adj* a process that is piecemeal happens slowly and in stages that are not regular or planned properly: *The buildings have been adapted* **in a piecemeal fashion.** | *a piecemeal approach to the problem* —**piecemeal** *adv*: *The new fire regulations have been introduced piecemeal.*

piece·work /ˈpiːswɜːk $ -wɜːrk/ *n* [U] work for which you are paid according to the number of things that you produce rather than the number of hours that you spend working: *bargaining over piecework rates*

ˈpie ˌchart *n* [C] a circle divided into parts by lines coming from the centre to show how big the different parts of a total amount are → see picture at CHART¹

pied /paɪd/ *adj* [only before noun] used in the names of birds that are black and white: *a pied wagtail*

pied-à-terre /ˌpjeɪd æ ˈteə $ pi̩ˌed ɑː ˈter/ *n* [C] a small apartment or house, often in the centre of a city or town, that is not your main home but which you own and stay in sometimes: *They kept a pied-à-terre in London for theatre evenings.*

ˌpie-ˈeyed *adj old-fashioned informal* very drunk

pier /pɪə $ pɪr/ *n* [C] **1** a structure that is built over and into the water so that boats can stop next to it or people can walk along it: *a yacht moored at a pier* | *strolling along Brighton Pier* **2** a thick stone, wooden, or metal post that is used to support something

pierce /pɪəs $ pɪrs/ *v* **1** [T] to make a small hole in or through something, using an object with a sharp point: *Steam the corn until it can easily be pierced with a fork.* | *Rose underwent emergency surgery after a bullet pierced her lung.* | **pierce a hole in/through sth** *Pierce small holes in the base of the pot with a hot needle.* **2 have your ears/nose etc pierced** to have a small hole made in your ears, nose etc so that you can wear jewellery through the hole: *I had my belly-button pierced.* | *pierced ears* **3** [I,T always + adv/prep] *literary* if sound or light pierces something, you suddenly hear or see it: *The darkness was pierced by the beam from the lighthouse.* | *A sudden scream pierced the silence.* | [+through] *The men's lanterns pierced through the dense mist.* **4 pierce sb's heart** to make someone feel a strong emotion such as pain, sadness, or love: *Her memories sometimes pierced her heart.* **5** [T] to force a way through something: *Leicester rarely threatened to pierce the Manchester United defence.*

pierc·ing¹ /ˈpɪəsɪŋ $ ˈpɪr-/ *adj*

1 EYES/LOOK *literary* someone with piercing eyes is looking at you and seems to know what you are thinking: *There was mockery now in those piercing blue eyes.* | *She felt foolish and unsure under his* **piercing gaze.** | *He gave her a* **piercing look.**

2 SOUND a sound that is piercing is high, sharp, and unpleasant: *He grinned and let out a piercing whistle.* | *a piercing scream*

3 WIND a piercing wind is very cold

4 PAIN causing a lot of pain: *She felt a piercing sensation in her arm.*

5 EMOTION [only before noun] affecting your feelings

very deeply in a sad way: *a piercing moment of regret*
—**piercingly** *adv*: *It was piercingly cold.* | *She looked at him piercingly.*

piercing² *n* [C,U] a hole made through part of your body so that you can put jewellery there, or the process of making these holes

pi·e·ty /'paɪəti/ *n* [U] when you behave in a way that shows respect for your religion; → **pious**: *an act of Christian piety*

pif·fle /'pɪfəl/ *n* [U] *old-fashioned informal* nonsense

pif·fling /'pɪflɪŋ/ *adj BrE old-fashioned informal* piffling amounts are very small and therefore useless

pig¹ S2 /pɪg/ *n* [C]

1 ANIMAL a farm animal with short legs, a fat body, and a curved tail. Pigs are kept for their meat, which includes PORK, BACON and HAM; **hog** *AmE*: *He kept pigs and poultry.*

2 PERSON *spoken* **a)** someone who eats too much or eats more than their share: *You greedy pig, you ate all the candy!* | *I made a bit of a pig of myself* (=ate too much) *at dinner.* **b)** someone who is unpleasant in some way, for example unkind or very untidy: *They live like pigs in that house over the road.* | *You can tell him from me he's an ignorant pig.* | **(male) chauvinist pig** (=a man who thinks women are not equal to men)

3 POLICE *taboo informal* an offensive word for a police officer. Do not use this word.

4 a pig (of a sth) *BrE spoken* something that is very difficult or unpleasant to do: *They're improving, and they're a pig of a team to beat.*

5 make a pig's ear of sth *BrE spoken* to do something very badly: *Someone's made a right pig's ear of these repairs.*

6 in a pig's eye *AmE spoken informal* used to show that you do not believe what someone is saying

7 pig in a poke *spoken* something that you bought without seeing it first and that is not as good or valuable as you expected: *What if the car you buy turns out to be a pig in a poke?*

8 pigs might fly *spoken* used to say that you do not think something will happen: *'Someone might have handed in your pass.' 'Yes, and pigs might fly.'*

pig² *v* **pigged**, **pigging**
pig out *phr v informal* to eat a lot of food all at once: [+on] *I found Sam in front of the TV, pigging out on pizza and fries.*

pi·geon S3 /'pɪdʒən/ *n* [C] a grey bird with short legs that is common in cities → CARRIER PIGEON, CLAY PIGEON SHOOTING, HOMING PIGEON; → see picture at BITE¹

pigeon-'chested *adj* someone who is pigeon-chested has a very narrow chest that sticks out

pi·geon·hole¹ /'pɪdʒənhəʊl $ -hoʊl/ *n* [C] one of a set of small open boxes fixed to a wall. You leave letters, messages etc for particular people in the boxes.

pigeonhole² *v* [T] to unfairly consider a person, activity etc as belonging to a particular type or group: **pigeonhole sb/sth as sth** *Patsy was pigeonholed as a Country and Western singer, but that's too simple.*

pigeon-'toed *adj* someone who is pigeon-toed has feet that turn towards each other as they walk

pig·ge·ry /'pɪgəri/ *n plural* **piggeries** [C] *BrE* a pig farm, or the place on a farm where pigs are kept

pig·gy¹ /'pɪgi/ *n plural* **piggies** [C] **1** a pig – used by children or when you are talking to children **2 piggy in the middle** *BrE* **a)** *informal* someone who is involved in an argument between two opposing sides, but does not know who they should support: *What have I got myself into? I'm piggy in the middle between Guido and Silvia!* **b)** a game in which two people throw a ball backwards and forwards between them, while a third person in the middle tries to catch it; **keep-away** *AmE*

piggy² *adj* **piggy eyes** small unattractive eyes: *His little piggy eyes were red with hatred.*

pig·gy·back¹ /'pɪgibæk/ also **'piggyback ,ride** *n* [C] if you give someone, especially a child, a piggyback,

you carry them high on your shoulders, supporting them with your hands under their legs —**piggyback** *adv*

piggyback² *v* [I] *informal* to use something that is bigger, better, or more successful in order to help another product or project succeed: [+on/onto] *videos that piggyback onto the success of proven TV programs*

'piggy-bank *n* [C] a small container, usually in the shape of a pig, in which children can save coins

pig·head·ed /,pɪg'hedɪd◂/ *adj* determined to do things the way you want and refusing to change your mind, even when there are good reasons to do so; **stubborn**: *Never have I met a woman so obstinate, so pigheaded!* —**pigheadedness** *n* [U]: *It was just sheer pigheadedness on his part.*

'pig ,iron *n* [U] a form of iron that is not pure

pig·let /'pɪglɪt/ *n* [C] a young pig

pig·ment /'pɪgmənt/ *n* [C,U] a natural substance that makes skin, hair, plants etc a particular colour: *Melanin is the dark brown pigment of the hair, skin and eyes.* | *The artist Sandy Lee uses natural pigments in her work.*

pig·men·ta·tion /,pɪgmən'teɪʃən/ *n* [U] *technical* the natural colour of living things: *The dark pigmentation gives protection from the sun's rays.*

pig·my /'pɪgmi/ *n plural* **pigmies** another spelling of PYGMY

pig·pen /'pɪgpen/ *n* [C] *AmE* **1** a building where pigs are kept; **pigsty** **2** *informal* a very dirty or untidy place; **pigsty**

pig·skin /'pɪg,skɪn/ *n* **1** [U] leather made from the skin of a pig: *a pigskin suitcase* **2** [singular] *AmE informal* the ball used in American football: *We started tossing the pigskin around.*

pig·sty /'pɪgstaɪ/ *n plural* **pigsties** [C] **1** a building where pigs are kept; **pigpen** *AmE* **2** *informal* a very dirty or untidy place; **pigpen** *AmE*: *The house was a pigsty, as usual.* → see picture at HOME¹

pig·swill /'pɪg,swɪl/ *n* [U] *BrE* waste food that is fed to pigs

pig·tail /'pɪgteɪl/ *n* [C] lengths of hair that have been twisted together into a PLAIT *She wore her hair in pigtails.* → BUNCH¹ (5), PLAIT², BRAID¹ (2), PONYTAIL; → see picture at HAIRSTYLE

pike /paɪk/ *n* [C] **1** *plural* **pike** a large fish that eats other fish and lives in rivers and lakes → see picture at FRESHWATER **2** a long-handled weapon with a sharp blade, used in the past **3 come down the pike** *AmE* to happen or become known: *The world is being turned upside down by the string of multimedia technologies coming down the pike.* **4** *AmE spoken* a TURNPIKE

pik·er /'paɪkə $ -ər/ *n* [C] *AusE* someone who avoids difficult situations, especially ones involving money

pike·staff /'paɪkstɑːf $ -stæf/ *n* **as plain as a pikestaff** *BrE old-fashioned* very clear and easy to understand: *None of us worked it out, though it was as plain as a pikestaff when you thought about it.*

pi·laff, pilaf /'piːlæf $ pɪ'lɑːf/ *n* [C,U] a pilau

pi·las·ter /pɪ'læstə $ -ər/ *n* [C] a flat square COLUMN attached to the wall of a building for decoration

Pi·la·tes /pɪ'lɑːtiz/ *n* [U] a type of exercise based on YOGA and dance that you do with special equipment which makes you push, pull, and stretch, so that your body moves more easily and becomes stronger

pi·lau /'piːlaʊ $ pɪ'loʊ/ *n* [C,U] *BrE* a dish made of rice, vegetables, and sometimes meat: *mushroom pilau*

pil·chard /'pɪltʃəd $ -ərd/ *n* [C] *BrE* a small fish that lives in the sea and that can be eaten

pile¹ S2 /paɪl/ *n*

1 ARRANGEMENT OF THINGS [C] a group of several things of the same type that are put on top of each other; **stack**: [+of] *His mother came in carrying a pile* *of ironing in her arms.* | *Flora shuffled through a pile of magazines.* | **put sth in/into a pile** *She tidied up the books and put them in* **neat piles** | *He balanced the plate on* **the top of a pile** *of books.* → see picture at **BUNDLE**[1]

2 LARGE AMOUNT [C] a large amount of something arranged in a shape that looks like a small hill: [+of] *piles of melting snow* | *All that remained of the old house was a pile of rubble.* | *Sophie stooped to throw another branch on the pile.* | *He began to* **sweep** *the pieces of glass* **into** *a pile.*

3 a pile of sth also **piles of sth** *informal* a lot of something: *We've had piles of letters from viewers.* | *another pile of directives from the EU*

4 the bottom of the pile *BrE* the weakest or least important position in a society or organization: *I soon discovered I was at the bottom of the pile in the office hierarchy.* | *She always puts her own needs to the bottom of the pile.*

5 the top of the pile *BrE* the best or highest position in a society or organization: *It's been 20 years since a British tennis player was at the top of the pile.*

6 HOUSE [C] a very large old house: *They've just bought an 18th-century pile in Surrey.*

7 MATERIAL [C,U] the soft surface of short threads on a CARPET or some types of cloth: **thick/deep pile** *Her feet sank into the thick pile of the rug.* | *a deep pile carpet* → NAP[1] (2)

8 POST [C] *technical* a heavy wooden, stone, or metal post, used to support something heavy

9 make a/your pile *informal* to make a lot of money: *He had made his pile in the wholesale business.*

10 piles [plural] painfully swollen BLOOD VESSELS near a person's ANUS

pile² *v* [T] **1** [always + adv/prep] to fill a place or container or cover a surface with a large amount of things: **pile sth into/onto sth** *He piled bread and milk into his basket.* | *Melissa piled spaghetti onto her plate.* | **be piled with sth** *a chair piled with velvet cushions* | *The room was* **piled high** *with boxes* (=filled with a lot of boxes).* **2** also **pile up** to arrange things in a pile: *Ma stacked the cups and piled the plates.* | **pile sth on/onto sth** *She brushed her hair and piled it carefully on top of her head.*

pile in also **pile into sth** *phr v* if people pile in, they get into a vehicle very quickly: *Pierre came to pick them up, and they all piled in.*

pile sth ⇔ **on** *phr v informal* **1 pile it on/pile on the drama** to talk about something in a way that makes it seem much worse than it really is; **≡ exaggerate**: *I know I'm piling it on a bit, but there is a serious point to be made.* **2 pile on the pressure/agony** to show that you are much better than your opponent in a game: *England piled on the pressure from the start.* **3 pile on the pounds** to gain a lot of body weight: *She slimmed down a couple of years ago but has piled on the pounds again.*

pile out *phr v* if people pile out, they leave a place or get out of a vehicle quickly and in a disorganized way: *Edward parked by the river and we all piled out.*

pile up *phr v* **1** to increase in quantity or amount, in a way that is difficult to manage: *It wasn't long before the debts were piling up.* | *The traffic starts piling up around this time.* | *The work has a tendency to pile up if I'm not careful.* **2 pile sth** ⇔ **up** to arrange things in a pile: *tiny doughnuts piled up in a dish* → PILE-UP

pile driver *n* [C] **1** a machine for pushing heavy posts into the ground **2** *BrE informal* a very hard hit

pile-up *n* [C] a traffic accident involving many vehicles: *a motorway pile-up*

pil·fer /'pɪlfə $ -ər/ *v* [I,T] to steal things that are not worth much, especially from the place where you work: [+from] *She was sacked after being caught pilfering from the till.* —**pilferer** *n* [C]: *an office pilferer* —**pilfering** *n* [U]

pil·grim /'pɪlgrⁱm/ *n* [C] a religious person who travels a long way to a holy place: *pilgrims visiting a holy shrine*

pil·grim·age /'pɪlgrⁱmɪdʒ/ *n* [C,U] **1** a journey to a holy place for religious reasons: **make a pilgrimage/go on (a) pilgrimage** *the chance to go on pilgrimage to Mecca* **2** a journey to a place connected with someone or something famous: *Presley's home has become a* **place of pilgrimage**.

pill¹ S3 /pɪl/ *n*

1 [C] a small solid piece of medicine that you swallow whole: *He has to* **take pills** *to control his blood pressure.* | **sleeping pills** | *a bottle of* **vitamin pills**

2 the Pill/the pill a pill taken regularly by some women in order to prevent them having babies: **on the Pill** *My doctor advised me to go on the pill* (=start taking it regularly).

3 sugar/sweeten the pill to do something to make an unpleasant job or situation less unpleasant for the person who has to accept it

4 be a pill *AmE informal* if someone, especially a child, is a pill, they are annoying: *Luke can be a real pill sometimes.* → **a bitter pill (to swallow)** at BITTER¹ (7); → MORNING-AFTER PILL

pill² *v* [I] *AmE* if a piece of clothing pills, especially a SWEATER, it forms little balls on the surface of the cloth after it has been worn or washed

pil·lage /'pɪlɪdʒ/ *v* [I,T] if soldiers pillage a place in a war, they steal a lot of things and do a lot of damage; **≡ plunder** —**pillage** *n* [U] —**pillager** *n* [C]

pil·lar /'pɪlə $ -ər/ *n* [C] **1 a)** a tall upright round post used as a support for a roof or bridge: *Eight massive stone pillars supported the roof.* **b)** a tall upright round post, usually made of stone, put up to remind people of an important person or event **2 pillar of society/the community/the church etc** somebody who is an important and respected member of a group, and is involved in many public activities: *Mr Fitzwilliam had been seen as a pillar of the community.* **3** a very important part of a system of beliefs or ideas: [+of] *One of the pillars of a civilized society must be that everyone has equal access to the legal system.* **4 be driven/pushed from pillar to post** to have to go from one person or situation to another without achieving much or being able to settle: *The poor kid has been pushed from pillar to post.* **5 be a pillar of strength** if someone is a pillar of strength, they are there to give you help and support at a difficult time: *Christine's been a pillar of strength to me.* **6 pillar of dust/smoke/flame etc** a tall upright mass of dust, smoke, flame etc

pillar box *n* [C] *BrE old-fashioned* a large red tube-shaped box for posting letters that stands on streets in Britain; **≡ postbox**; → **letterbox**

pillar-box 'red *n* [U] *BrE* a very bright red colour —**pillar-box red** *adj*

pill·box /'pɪlbɒks $ -baːks/ *n* [C] **1** a small round box for holding PILLS **2** a small, strong, usually circular shelter with a gun inside it, built as a defence **3** also **pillbox 'hat** a small round hat for a woman

pil·lion /'pɪljən/ *n* [singular] *BrE* the seat behind the driver of a MOTORCYCLE: *a pillion passenger* —**pillion** *adv*: *Tom had never* **ridden pillion** *before.*

pil·lock /'pɪlək/ *n* [C] *BrE informal* a very stupid person

pil·lo·ry¹ /'pɪləri/ *v* **pilloried, pillorying, pillories** [T usually passive] if someone is pilloried, they are publicly criticized by a lot of people, especially in newspapers etc: *The education secretary was pilloried by the press for his latest proposals.*

pillory² *n* plural **pillories** [C] a wooden frame with holes for someone's head and hands to be locked into, used in the past as a way of publicly punishing someone → **the stocks** at STOCK¹ (9)

pil·low¹ S3 /'pɪləʊ $ -loʊ/ *n* [C]

1 a cloth bag filled with soft material that you put your head on when you are sleeping: *I'll be asleep as soon as my head hits the pillow.* → CUSHION¹ (1); → see picture at BED¹

2 pillow fight a game in which children hit each other with pillows

3 pillow talk *informal* conversation between lovers in bed

pillow² *v* [T always + adv/prep] *literary* to rest your head somewhere: *His head was pillowed on his arm.*

pil·low·case, **'pillow case** /'pɪləʊkeɪs $ -loʊ-/ *n* [C] a cloth cover for a pillow

pi·lot¹ W3 /'paɪlət/ *n* [C]

1 someone who operates the controls of an aircraft or spacecraft: *an airline pilot | a fighter pilot | The official report into the accident says that it was caused by **pilot error** (=a mistake by the pilot).*

2 someone with a special knowledge of a particular area of water, who is employed to guide ships across it: *a harbour pilot*

3 pilot study/project/scheme etc a small study, project etc which is carried out as a test to see if an idea, product etc will be successful: *a pilot scheme which could be extended to other areas*

4 a television programme that is made in order to test whether people like it and would watch it: *a pilot for a new sitcom* → AUTOMATIC PILOT

pilot² *v* [T] **1** to guide an aircraft, spacecraft, or ship as its pilot **2** to test a new idea, product etc on people to find out whether it will be successful: *The new exams are currently being piloted in a number of areas.* **3** *literary* to help someone to go to a place **4** *BrE* to be responsible for making sure that a new law or plan is officially approved: **pilot sth through sth** *The Bill was piloted through Parliament by the health minister.*

'pilot light *n* [C] a small gas flame that burns all the time and is used for lighting larger gas burners

'pilot ,officer *n* [C] a middle rank in the Royal Air Force, or someone who has this rank

'pilot ,whale *n* [C] a small WHALE with black skin

pi·men·to /pɪˈmentəʊ $ -toʊ/ also **pim·i·en·to** /-'mjentəʊ $ -toʊ/ *n plural* **pimentos** [C,U] a small red PEPPER which does not have a very strong taste

pimp /pɪmp/ *n* [C] a man who makes money by controlling PROSTITUTES —**pimp** *v* [I]

pim·per·nel /'pɪmpənel $ -ər-/ *n* [C] a small wild plant with flowers in various colours, especially red

pim·ple /'pɪmpəl/ *n* [C] a small raised red spot on your skin, especially on your face —**pimply** *adj*: *a pimply eighteen-year-old* → GOOSE PIMPLES

pin¹ S3 /pɪn/ *n* [C]

1 FOR JOINING/FASTENING **a)** a short thin piece of metal with a sharp point at one end, used especially for fastening together pieces of cloth while making clothes **b)** a thin piece of metal used to fasten things together, especially broken bones; → see picture at SEWING

2 JEWELLERY *AmE* a piece of metal, sometimes containing jewels, that you fasten to your clothes to wear as a decoration; ⊟ brooch *BrE*

3 ELECTRICAL *BrE* one of the pieces of metal that sticks out of an electric PLUG: *a three-pin plug*

4 BOWLING one of the bottle-shaped objects that you try to knock down in a game of BOWLING

5 you could hear a pin drop *spoken* used to say that it is very quiet and no one is speaking

6 PART OF BOMB a short piece of metal which you pull out of a HAND GRENADE to make it explode a short time later

7 GOLF a metal stick with a flag at the top which marks the holes on a GOLF COURSE

8 for two pins I'd … *BrE old-fashioned* used to say that you would like to do something to someone because they have annoyed you: *For two pins, I'd just send them all home.*

9 pins [plural] *BrE informal* legs → DRAWING PIN, PIN MONEY, PINS AND NEEDLES (1), ROLLING PIN, SAFETY PIN

pin² *v* **pinned**, **pinning** [T always + adv/prep] **1** to fasten something somewhere, or to join two things together, using a pin: **pin sth to/on sth** *Can you pin this to the notice board? | He pinned the name tag on his*

---

jacket. | **pin sth up** *She had photos of her kids pinned up next to her desk.* **2** to make someone unable to move by putting a lot of pressure or weight on them: **pin sb/sth to sth** *He pinned her arms to her sides.* | **pin sb against sth** *Albert got him pinned against the wall.* | **pin sb down** *They managed to pin him down until the police arrived.* | **be pinned under/beneath sth** *Her body was pinned under the weight of the car.*

pin sb/sth ⇔ down *phr v* **1** to make someone give clear details or make a definite decision about something: [+to] *Did you manage to pin him down to a definite date? | He's impossible to pin down.* **2** to understand something clearly or be able to describe it exactly: **hard/difficult to pin down** *The flavour was hard to pin down.* **3** if soldiers etc involved in fighting are pinned down, they cannot move from their position because someone is shooting at them: *The rebels have been pinned down in a camp to the south of the river.*

pin sth **on** sb/sth *phr v* **1** to blame someone for something, often unfairly: *Don't try to **pin the blame on** me! | They're trying to pin the murder on the boyfriend.* **2 pin your hopes/faith on sth/sb** to hope that something will happen or someone will help you, because all your plans depend on this: *Chris is pinning his hopes on getting into Yale.*

PIN /pɪn/ also **'PIN ,number** *n* [C] *personal identification number* a number that you use when you get money from a machine using a plastic card

pi·ña co·la·da /ˌpiːnə kəˈlɑːdə/ *n* [C,U] an alcoholic drink made from COCONUT juice, PINEAPPLE juice, and RUM

pin·a·fore /'pɪnəfɔː $ -fɔːr/ *n* [C] **1** also **'pinafore ,dress** *BrE* a dress that does not cover your arms and under which you wear a shirt or BLOUSE; ⊟ **jumper** *AmE* **2** also **pinny** *BrE informal* a loose piece of clothing that does not cover your arms, worn over your clothes to keep them clean

pin·ball /'pɪnbɔːl $ -bɒːl/ *n* [U] a game played on a machine with a sloping board which a ball rolls down while the player tries to prevent it reaching the bottom

pince-nez /ˌpæns 'neɪ, ˌpɪns-/ *n* [plural] glasses worn in the past that were held in position on the nose by a spring, instead of by pieces fitting round the ears

pin·cer /'pɪnsə $ -ər/ *n* **1** [C usually plural] one of the pair of CLAWS that some SHELLFISH and insects have, used for holding and cutting food, and for fighting **2 pincers** [plural] a tool made of two crossed pieces of metal used for holding things tightly

'pincer ,movement *n* [C] a military attack in which two groups of soldiers come from opposite directions in order to trap the enemy between them

pinch¹ /pɪntʃ/ *v* **1** [T] to press a part of someone's skin very tightly between your finger and thumb, especially so that it hurts: *We have to stop her pinching her baby brother. | He pinched her cheek.* **2** [T] *BrE informal* to steal something, especially something small or not very valuable: *Someone's pinched my coat!* **3** [T] to press something between your finger and thumb: *Pinch the edges of the pastry together to seal it.* **4** [I,T] if something you are wearing pinches you, it presses painfully on part of your body, because it is too tight: *Her new shoes were pinching.* **5 sb has to pinch themselves** used when a situation is so surprising that the person involved needs to make sure that they are not imagining it: *Sometimes she had to pinch herself to make sure it was not all a dream.* **6** [T usually passive] *BrE old-fashioned* to ARREST someone

pinch sth ⇔ **out** *phr v* to remove a small part of a plant with your fingers: *Pinch out any side shoots to make the plant grow upwards.*

pinch² *n* [C] **1 pinch of salt/pepper etc** a small amount of salt, pepper etc that you can hold between your finger and thumb: *Add a pinch of salt to taste.* **2** when you press someone's skin between your finger and thumb: *She gave him a playful pinch.* **3 at**

pipe·work /ˈpaɪpwɜːk $ -wɜːrk/ *n* [U] the pipes that are part of a building, machine, or structure: *The houses all have lead pipework.*

pip·ing¹ /ˈpaɪpɪŋ/ *n* [U] **1** a thin tube of cloth, usually with string inside, sewn onto clothing, furniture etc as decoration **2** several pipes, or a system of pipes, used to send liquid or gas in or out of a building

piping² *adv* **piping hot** piping hot liquid or food is very hot: *piping hot coffee*

pip·it /ˈpɪpɪt/ *n* [C] a small brown or grey singing bird

pip·pin /ˈpɪpɪn/ *n* [C] a small sweet apple

pip·squeak /ˈpɪpskwiːk/ *n* [C] *old-fashioned* someone that you think is not worth respecting or paying attention to, especially because they are small or young

pi·quant /ˈpiːkənt/ *adj* **1** having a pleasantly spicy taste: *a piquant wild mushroom sauce* **2** interesting and exciting —**piquantly** *adv* —**piquancy** *n* [U]: *The production retains its original piquancy.*

pique¹ /piːk/ *n* [U] **1** a feeling of being annoyed or upset, especially because someone has ignored you or insulted you: *He stormed out in a fit of pique.* **2** also **piqué** a type of material made of cotton, silk, or RAYON

pique² *v* **1** [T usually passive] to make someone feel annoyed or upset, especially by ignoring them or making them look stupid: *Privately, Zarich was piqued that his offer was rejected.* **2 pique your interest/curiosity** *especially AmE* to make you feel interested in something or someone: *She was hostile to him, which piqued his curiosity.*

pi·ra·cy /ˈpaɪərəsi $ ˈpaɪrə-/ *n* [U] **1** the crime of illegally copying and selling books, tapes, videos, computer programs etc; → **pirate**: *software piracy* **2** the crime of attacking and stealing from ships at sea **3** the crime of making illegal television or radio broadcasts

pi·ra·nha /pɑ̱ˈrɑːnə $ -ˈrɑːnjə, -ˈrænə/ *n* [C] a South American fish with sharp teeth that lives in rivers and eats flesh

pi·rate¹ /ˈpaɪərət $ ˈpaɪrət/ *n* [C] **1** someone who sails on the seas, attacking other boats and stealing things from them; → **piracy** **2** someone who dishonestly copies and sells another person's work; → **piracy**: *Computer game pirates cost the industry twenty million pounds a year.* | **pirate videos/CDs/software etc** **3** pirate radio/TV (station) illegal radio or television broadcasts, or the station sending them out —**piratical** /paɪˈrætɪkəl, pɑ̱-/ *adj literary*

pirate² *v* [T] to illegally copy and sell another person's work such as a book, video, or computer program: *pirated video tapes*

pir·ou·ette /ˌpɪruˈet/ *n* [C] a dance movement in which the dancer turns very quickly, standing on one toe or the front part of one foot —**pirouette** *v* [I]

pis·ca·to·ri·al /ˌpɪskəˈtɔːriəl◂/ *adj formal* relating to fishing or people who go fishing

Pis·ces /ˈpaɪsiːz/ *n* **1** [U] the 12th sign of the ZODIAC, represented by two fish, which some people believe affects the character and life of people born between February 20 and March 20 **2** [C] also **Piscean** someone who was born between February 20 and March 20 —**Piscean** /ˈpaɪsiən, paɪˈsiːən/ *adj*

piss¹ /pɪs/ *v* [I] *spoken not polite* **1** to URINATE **2 piss in the wind** to waste time or effort trying to do something that is impossible **3 it is pissing down (with rain)** *BrE* used to say that it is raining very heavily **4 piss yourself (laughing)** *BrE* to laugh a lot, especially when you cannot stop laughing: *They were all copying my accent and pissing themselves laughing.* **5 piss all over sb** *BrE* to thoroughly defeat a person or a team **6 not have a pot to piss in** to be extremely poor **7 go piss up a rope!** *AmE* used to tell someone to go away

piss about/around *phr v BrE spoken not polite* **1** to waste time doing stupid things with no purpose or plan; ☐ **mess about/around**: *Stop pissing*

about and get some work done! **2 piss sb about/around** to treat someone badly by not doing what you have promised to do, or by not being honest with them; ☐ **mess sb about/around**: *I wish he'd say yes or no – he's been pissing me around for weeks.*

piss sth ⇔ **away** *phr v spoken not polite* to waste something in a very stupid way: *I was earning quite a lot but I pissed it all away.*

piss off *phr v spoken not polite* **1 piss sb** ⇔ **off** to annoy someone very much: *The way she treats me really pisses me off.* **2** *BrE* to go away – used especially to tell someone to go away: *Now piss off and leave me alone!* | *He pissed off before we got there.* **3** *BrE* used to say no or to refuse to do something

piss² *n spoken not polite* **1** [singular] an act of URINATING: **go for/have/take a piss** *I need to have a piss.* **2** [U] URINE **3 take the piss (out of sb/sth)** *BrE* to annoy someone by laughing at them or making them seem stupid; → **piss-take**: *The kids always take the piss out of some teachers.* **4 be on the piss** *BrE* to be at a PUB or club, drinking a lot of alcohol: *'Where's Jo?' 'Out on the piss somewhere.'* **5 be full of piss and vinegar** *AmE* to be full of energy → **be a piece of piss** at PIECE¹ (15)

piss-ant, piss·ant /ˈpɪsænt/ *n* [C] *AmE informal not polite* an offensive word for an annoying person with a weak character

piss ˌartist *n* [C] *BrE informal not polite* a very offensive word for someone who drinks a lot of alcohol

pissed /pɪst/ *adj* [not before noun] *informal* **1** *BrE* drunk: *They rolled in pissed at three in the morning.* | **pissed as a newt/pissed out of your head** (=extremely drunk) **2** *AmE* PISSED OFF

pissed ˈoff also **pissed** *AmE adj* [not before noun] *informal* annoyed, disappointed, or unhappy: *You get really pissed off applying for jobs all the time.* | [+with/at] *I was pissed off with the way some people were behaving.* | *Judy's pissed at Carol.*

pis·ser /ˈpɪsə $ -ər/ *n* [C] *informal not polite* an offensive word for a difficult job or activity, or a bad or annoying situation: *The real pisser was investing so much time and effort for zero return.*

piss·head /ˈpɪshed/ *n* [C] *BrE informal not polite* a very offensive word for someone who drinks a lot of alcohol

piss-ˈpoor *adj informal not polite* very bad in quality: *All the local beers were piss-poor imitations.*

piss-take *n* [C usually singular] *BrE informal not polite* something you do to make people laugh at someone, especially by copying them in a funny way: *The record is a piss-take of people who have a high opinion of themselves.* → **take the piss out of sb/sth** at PISS² (3)

piss-up *n* [C] *BrE informal not polite* an occasion when people drink a lot of alcohol together: *We had a good piss-up on my birthday.*

pis·sy /ˈpɪsi/ *adj* [not before noun] *spoken not polite* **1** angry or annoyed and treating people badly: *Stacey gets pissy if we tease her.* **2** small or unimportant and annoying

pis·ta·chi·o /pɑ̱ˈstɑːʃiəʊ $ pɑ̱ˈstæʃioʊ/ *n plural* **pistachios** [C] a small green nut: *pistachio ice cream* → see picture at NUT¹

piste /piːst/ *n* [C] *BrE* a snow-covered slope which has been prepared for people to SKI down → OFF-PISTE

pis·til /ˈpɪstl/ *n* [C] *technical* the female part of a flower that produces seeds

pis·tol /ˈpɪstl/ *n* [C] a small gun you can use with one hand; → **handgun, revolver**

pistol-whip *v* pistol-whipped, pistol-whipping [T] to hit someone many times with a pistol

pis·ton /ˈpɪstən/ *n* [C] a part of an engine consisting of a short solid piece of metal inside a tube, which moves up and down to make the other parts of the engine move

piston ring *n* [C] a circular metal spring used to stop gas or liquid escaping from between a piston and the tube that it moves in

pit¹ /pɪt/ *n* [C]

1 HOLE a) a hole in the ground, especially one made by digging: *The female digs a pit in which to lay the eggs.* | *a five-foot deep pit* → SANDPIT **b)** a large hole in the ground from which stones or minerals are obtained by digging: **gravel/sand/chalk pit**

2 MINE *especially BrE* a coal mine: *Dad first went down the pit* (=worked in a coal mine) *when he was 15 years old.* | *a national strike against* **pit closures** (=when a coal mine is closed permanently)

3 MARK a small hollow mark in the surface of something, especially on your skin as the result of a disease: *the deep pits left by smallpox*

4 UNTIDY PLACE [usually singular] *spoken* a house or room that is dirty, untidy, or in bad condition

5 be the pits *spoken informal* to be extremely bad: *The company refused to pay – I think it's the pits.*

6 in/at the pit of your stomach if you have a feeling in the pit of your stomach, you have a sick or tight feeling in your stomach, usually because you are nervous or afraid: *I had a feeling in the pit of my stomach that something terrible was going to happen.*

7 CAR RACING the pits the place beside the track in a car race where cars can come in for petrol, new tyres etc → PIT STOP

8 IN A THEATRE an ORCHESTRA PIT

9 IN A GARAGE a hole in the floor of a garage that lets you get under a car to repair it: *an inspection pit*

10 a/the pit of sth *literary* a situation which makes you feel very bad: *Just thinking about the future plunged her into* **a pit of despair**.

11 IN FRUIT *especially AmE* the single large hard seed in some fruits; ▣ **stone** *BrE*: *a peach pit*

12 BODY PART *informal* an ARMPIT

13 BUSINESS *AmE* the area of a STOCK EXCHANGE where people buy and sell shares; ▣ **floor** *BrE*

pit² *v* **pitted, pitting** **1** [T usually passive] to put small marks or holes in the surface of something: **be pitted with sth** *The whole street was pitted with potholes.* **2** [T] *especially AmE* to take out the single hard seed inside some fruits; ▣ **stone**: *Peel and pit two avocados.* **3** [I] *AmE* to stop in a car race to get petrol or have your car repaired → PITTED

pit sb/sth **against** sb/sth *phr v* to test someone's strength, ability, power etc in a competition or fight against someone or something else: *We'll be pitting our team against the champions.* | **pit your wits against sb** (=compete against someone using your intelligence or knowledge) *Pit your wits against family or friends!* | **pit yourself against sth/sb** *The men had to pit themselves against the forces of nature.*

pit out *phr v AmE informal* to SWEAT so much that your clothes become wet under your arms

pit·a bread /'pɪtə bred $ 'piː-/ *n* the American spelling of PITTA BREAD

'pit-a-,pat *adv informal* PITTER-PATTER

,pit bull 'terrier also **'pit bull** *n* [C] a small but extremely strong and sometimes violent fighting dog

pitch¹ W3 /pɪtʃ/ *n*

1 SPORTS FIELD [C] *BrE* a marked out area of ground on which a sport is played; ▣ **field**: **football/cricket/ rugby etc pitch** *the world-famous Wembley football pitch* | *He ran the length of the pitch and scored.* | **on the pitch** (=playing a sport) *Jack was on the pitch for his school in the Senior Cup Final.*

2 STRONG FEELINGS/ACTIVITY [singular, U] a strong level of feeling about something or a high level of an activity or a quality: *The controversy* **reached** *such a* **pitch** (=become so strong) *that the paper devoted a whole page to it.* | **a pitch of excitement/excellence/ perfection etc** (=a high level of excitement etc) *He screamed at her in a pitch of fury.* | *The goal roused the crowd to* **fever pitch** (=a very excited level).

3 MUSIC a) [singular, U] how high or low a note or other sound is: *Ultrasonic waves are at a higher pitch than the human ear can hear.* **b)** [U] the ability of a musician to play or sing a note at exactly the correct level: *She's got* **perfect pitch**.

4 PERSUADING [C] *informal* the things someone says to persuade people to buy something, do something, or accept an idea: *an aggressive salesman with a fast-talking* **sales pitch** | **make a/sb's pitch (for sth)** (=try to persuade people to do something) *He made his strongest pitch yet for standardized testing in schools.*

5 BASEBALL [C] a throw of the ball, or a way in which it can be thrown: *His first pitch was high and wide.*

6 BLACK SUBSTANCE [U] a black, sticky substance that is used on roofs, the bottoms of ships etc to stop water coming through: *The night was* **as black as pitch** (=very dark). → PITCH-BLACK, PITCH-DARK

7 SHIP/AIRCRAFT [U] an up and down movement of a ship or an aircraft; → roll: *the* **pitch and roll** *of the ship*

8 SLOPE [singular, U] the degree to which a roof slopes or the sloping part of a roof: *the steep pitch of the roof*

9 STREET/MARKET [C] *BrE* a place in a public area where someone who sells things to people goes to sell things or where an entertainer goes to sell things or perform: *We found the boy at his usual pitch at the bottom of the Acropolis.* → **queer sb's pitch/queer the pitch for sb** at QUEER³

pitch² *v*

1 THROW [T always + adv/prep] to throw something with a lot of force, often aiming carefully: *She crumpled up the page and pitched it into the fire.*

2 BALL GAMES a) [I,T] to aim and throw a ball in baseball: [+to] *Stanton pitched to two batters in the ninth inning.* **b)** [I] if a ball pitches in CRICKET or golf, it hits the ground **c)** [T] to hit the ball in a high curve in golf **d)** [T] to make the ball hit the ground when you are BOWLING in CRICKET → see picture at THROW¹

3 FALL [I,T always + adv/prep] to fall or be moved suddenly in a particular direction, or to make someone or something do this: **pitch (sb/sth) forward/backward/ over etc** *She slipped and pitched forward onto the ground.* | **pitch sb/sth into/onto/through etc sth** *Without a seatbelt, you can easily be pitched right through the windscreen.*

4 SHIP/PLANE [I] if a ship or an aircraft pitches, it moves up and down in an uncontrolled way with the movement of the water or air → ROLL² (4), YAW

5 SET A LEVEL [T usually passive] **a)** to set a speech, examination, explanation etc at a particular level of difficulty: **pitch sth at a high level/the right level etc** *The projects were pitched at a number of different levels.* | *Some questions were pitched too high for intermediate students.* **b)** *BrE* to set prices at a particular level: **pitch sth at sth** *Room rates are pitched at £69 for a single.*

6 AIM PRODUCT [T usually passive] to aim a product at a particular type of organization, group of people etc, or to describe it in a particular way, in order to sell it: **pitch sth at sb/sth** *The new machine will be pitched at users in the hotel and air reservation business.* | **pitch sth as sth** *It is pitched as a cheaper alternative to other workstations.*

7 BUSINESS DEALS [I,T] *informal* to try to persuade someone to do business with you, buy something etc: **pitch for business/contracts/custom etc** *Booksellers are keen to pitch for school business.* | [+to] *For many companies, pitching to investors has become almost a full-time job.* | *sales reps pitching new gadgets*

8 VOICE/MUSIC [T always + adv/prep] if you pitch your voice or another sound at a particular level, the sound is produced at that level: **pitch sth high/low etc** *Her voice is pitched a little too high.* → HIGH-PITCHED, LOW-PITCHED

9 pitch a tent/pitch camp to set up a tent or a camp for a short time: *Try and pitch your tent on level ground.*

10 SLOPE [I always + adv/prep] to slope down: **pitch gently/steeply etc** *The roof pitches sharply to the rear of the house.* → PITCHED

11 pitch sb a line *AmE informal* to tell someone a story or give them an excuse that is difficult to believe: *She pitched me some line about a bomb scare on the metro.*

P

pitch in phr v informal
1 to join others and help with an activity: *If we all pitch in, we'll have it finished in no time.* | [+with] *Everyone pitched in with efforts to entertain the children.*
2 to join others and pay part of the money towards something: *They all pitched in and the money was collected within a few days.*
3 BrE to start to eat hungrily: *Pitch in – there's plenty.*
pitch into sb/sth phr v BrE informal
1 to suddenly start criticizing someone or hitting them: *She pitched into me as soon as I started to speak.*
2 to start doing something, especially quickly and eagerly: *Rick pitched into decorating the house at once.*
pitch up phr v BrE spoken
to arrive somewhere; ■ **turn up**: *Wait a bit longer – Bill hasn't pitched up yet.*

‚pitch-and-'putt n [U] BrE a game of golf played on a very small course

‚pitch-'black adj completely black or dark: *The lights were off and it was pitch-black.* —**pitch-black** n [U]

pitch·blende /'pɪtʃblend/ n [U] a dark shiny substance dug from the earth, from which URANIUM and RADIUM are obtained

‚pitch-'dark adj completely dark: *Outside it was pitch-dark and pouring with rain.*

pitched /pɪtʃt/ adj a pitched roof is sloping rather than flat

‚pitched 'battle n [C] **1** a big battle between armies or large groups of people: *a pitched battle between the rival groups* **2** an angry and usually long argument: *She wanted to avoid another pitched battle with her son.*
→ SKIRMISH

pitch·er /'pɪtʃə $ -ər/ n [C] **1** the player in baseball who throws the ball **2** AmE a container for holding and pouring a liquid, with a handle and a shaped part to help the liquid flow out; ■ **jug** BrE: *a pitcher of water* → see picture at JUG **3** BrE a large clay container with two handles, used in the past for holding and pouring a liquid

pitch·fork¹ /'pɪtʃfɔːk $ -fɔːrk/ n [C] a farm tool with a long handle and two long curved metal points, used especially for lifting HAY (=dried grass)

pitchfork² v [T] BrE to put someone suddenly into a situation for which they are not properly prepared: *pitchfork sb into sth She was pitchforked into power by the early death of her husband James V.*

pitch·out /'pɪtʃaʊt/ n [C] a ball in baseball that the PITCHER deliberately throws too far to the side for it to be hit

'pitch pine n [C,U] a type of PINE tree that grows in North America, or the wood from this tree

pit·e·ous /'pɪtiəs/ adj literary expressing suffering and sadness in a way that makes you feel pity: *She gave a long piteous cry.* —**piteously** adv

pit·fall /'pɪtfɔːl $ -fɔːl/ n [C usually plural] a problem or difficulty that is likely to happen in a particular job, course of action, or activity: [+of] *He gave me advice on how to avoid the pitfalls of the legal process.* | *the pitfalls associated with the purchase of a used car*

pith /pɪθ/ n [U] **1** a white substance just under the outside skin of oranges and similar fruit: *Peel the oranges with a sharp knife to remove all pith.* → see picture at FRUIT¹ **2** a soft white substance that fills the stems of some plants

pit·head /'pɪt-hed/ n [C] BrE the entrance to a coal mine and the buildings around it

‚pith 'helmet n [C] a large light hat worn especially in the past in hot countries, to protect your head from the sun

pith·y /'pɪθi/ adj if something that is said or written is pithy, it is intelligent and strongly stated, without wasting any words: *Press releases must be short and pithy.* | *a series of pithy quotations* —**pithily** adv

pit·i·a·ble /'pɪtiəbəl/ adj formal making you feel pity: *the pitiable victims of war* —**pitiably** adv

pit·i·ful /'pɪtɪfəl/ adj **1** someone who is pitiful looks or sounds so sad and unfortunate that you feel very sorry for them; → **pity**: *The refugees were a pitiful sight.* **2** a pitiful amount is very small: *The fee was pitiful – only about £60.* **3** very bad in quality: *His performance was pitiful – five goals flew past him.* —**pitifully** adv: *The dog was pitifully thin.*

pit·i·less /'pɪtɪləs/ adj **1** showing no pity and not caring if people suffer; ■ **cruel**: *a pitiless tyrant* | *the pitiless bombing of Guernica* **2** literary pitiless wind, rain, or sun is very severe and shows no sign of changing: *a night of pitiless rain* —**pitilessly** adv

pi·ton /'piːtɒn $ -taːn/ n [C] a piece of metal used in ROCK CLIMBING that you attach onto a rock to hold the rope

'pit ‚pony n [C] a small horse that was used in the past for moving coal in a mine in Britain

'pit stop n [C] **1** a time when a driver in a car race stops in the PITS to get more petrol or have repairs done **2** **make a pit stop** AmE informal to stop when driving on a long journey, for food, petrol, or to go to the toilet

pit·ta bread BrE; **pita bread** AmE /'pɪtə bred $ 'piːtə-/ n [C,U] a type of bread which is flat and hollow. It can be cut open and filled with food → see picture at BREAD

pit·tance /'pɪtəns/ n [singular] a very small amount of money, especially wages, that is less than someone needs or deserves: **earn/be paid a pittance** *The musicians earn a pittance.* | **work/be sold for a pittance** *The crop was sold for a pittance.* | *She raised three children on a pittance.*

pit·ted /'pɪtɪd/ adj **1** covered with small marks or holes on the surface: *a red-faced man with pitted cheeks* | [+with] *The desert roads are pitted with potholes.* **2** a pitted fruit has had the single hard seed removed from it: *pitted olives*

pit·ter-pat·ter /'pɪtə ‚pætə $ 'pɪtər ‚pætər/ adv literary with quick light beats or steps: *Anna's heart went pitter-patter as she opened the letter.* —**pitter-patter** n [singular]: *the pitter-patter of small feet running up the stairs*

pi·tu·i·ta·ry /pə'tjuːɪtəri $ -'tuːəteri/ also **pi'tuitary ‚gland** n plural **pituitaries** [C] the small organ at the base of your brain which produces HORMONES that control the growth and development of your body —**pituitary** adj

pit·y¹ [S3] /'pɪti/ n
1 a pity spoken used to show that you are disappointed about something and you wish things could happen differently; ■ **shame**: **(it's a) pity (that)** *It's a pity that he didn't accept the job.* | *It's a great pity Joyce wasn't invited.* | *I like Charlie. Pity he had to marry that awful woman.* | *A pity we can't find the guy who did it.* | **what/that's a pity** *'Are you married?' 'No.' 'What a pity.'* | **it's a pity to do sth** *It would be a pity to give up now – you've nearly finished.*
2 [U] sympathy for a person or animal who is suffering or unhappy; → **piteous, pitiable, pitiful, pitiless**: [+for] *He looked exhausted, but Marie felt no pity for him.* | *I listened to Jason's story with pity.* | *I hated the thought of being an object of pity* (=someone who other people feel sorry for). | **take/have pity on sb** (=feel sorry for someone and treat them with sympathy) *He sounded so upset that Leah started to take pity on him.*
3 for pity's sake BrE spoken used to show that you are very annoyed and impatient: *For pity's sake just shut up and let me drive!*
4 more's the pity spoken especially BrE used after describing a situation, to show that you wish it was not true: *Sue's not coming, more's the pity.*

pity² v **pitied, pitying, pities** [T not usually in progressive] to feel sorry for someone because they are in a very bad situation: *I pity anyone who has to feed a* *family on such a low income.* | *Sam pitied his grand-mother there alone, never going out.* | *Pity the poor teachers who have to deal with these kids.*

pit·y·ing /ˈpɪtiɪŋ/ *adj* pitying look/smile/glance a look or smile that shows you feel pity for someone: *Ellen gave me a pitying look.*

piv·ot¹ /ˈpɪvət/ *n* [C] **1** a central point or pin on which something balances or turns **2** [usually singular] also **pivot point** the most important thing in a situation, system etc, which other things depend or are based on: **the pivot on/around which sth turns/revolves** *Iago's lie is the pivot on which the play turns.* | [+of] *West Africa was the pivot of the chocolate trade.*

pivot² *v* **1** [I,T] to turn or balance on a central point, or to make something do this: [+on] *The table-top pivots on two metal pins.* **2** [I] to turn quickly on your feet so that you face in the opposite direction: *Magee pivoted and threw the ball to first base.*

  pivot on/around sth *phr v* to depend on or be based on one important thing, event, or idea: *His argument will pivot on the growing cost of legal fees.*

piv·ot·al /ˈpɪvətəl/ *adj* more important than anything else in a situation, system etc: *The Bank of England has a pivotal role in the London money market.* | [+to] *The talks are pivotal to the success of the country.*

pix /pɪks/ *n* [plural] *informal* pictures or photographs

pix·el /ˈpɪksəl/ *n* [C] *technical* the smallest unit of an image on a computer screen

pix·e·lat·ed, **pixellated** /ˈpɪksəˌleɪtɪd/ *adj technical* consisting of pixels, especially large pixels that produce an unclear image: *pixelated photographs*

pix·ie, **pixy** /ˈpɪksi/ *n* [C] an imaginary creature that looks like a very small human being, has magical powers, and likes to play tricks on people

piz·za S2 /ˈpiːtsə/ *n* [C,U] a food made of thin flat round bread, baked with tomato, cheese, and sometimes vegetables or meat on top: *a slice of pizza* → see picture at FAST FOOD

'pizza ˌparlor *n* [C] *AmE* a restaurant that serves pizza; ⊟ **pizzeria**

piz·zazz /pəˈzæz/ *n* [U] *informal* something that has pizzazz is exciting and has a strong interesting style: *Their new album has plenty of pizzazz.*

piz·ze·ri·a /ˌpiːtsəˈriːə/ *n* [C] a restaurant that serves pizza → see picture at EAT

piz·zi·ca·to /ˌpɪtsɪˈkɑːtəʊ $ -toʊ/ *n* [U] musical notes played by pulling on the strings of an instrument —**pizzicato** *adv, adj*

pj's, **PJ's** /ˌpiː ˈdʒeɪz/ *n* [plural] *informal* the abbreviation of *pyjamas*

Pk *BrE*; **Pk.** *AmE* the written abbreviation of *park*

pkg. *AmE* the written abbreviation of *package*

pkt the written abbreviation of *packet*

pl. also **pl** *BrE* the written abbreviation of *plural*

Pl. also **Pl** *BrE* the written abbreviation of *Place*, used in addresses: *3 Palmerston Pl., Edinburgh*

plac·ard /ˈplækɑːd $ -ərd/ *n* [C] a large notice or advertisement on a piece of card, which is put up or carried in a public place: *a huge placard saying 'Welcome to Derbyville'*

pla·cate /pləˈkeɪt $ ˈpleɪkeɪt/ *v* [T] *formal* to make someone stop feeling angry; ⊟ **appease**: *These changes did little to placate the unions.* —**placatory** /pləˈkeɪtəri, ˈplækətəri $ ˈpleɪkətɔːri/ *adj*: *a placatory smile*

place¹ S1 W1 /pleɪs/ *n* [C]

1 AREA/SPACE/BUILDING ETC a space or area, for example a particular point on a surface or a room, building, town, city etc: *Make sure you keep the key in a safe place.* | *I've spent the day dashing about from place to place.* | *The place was full of screaming children.* | *He was threatening to burn the place down.* | *She had never been back to the place where the accident happened.* | *The theatre bar was our usual meeting place.* | *We were living then in a place called Alberiga.* | *The wall was*

quite damp in places (=in some places). | [+for] *This is a great place for a holiday.* | **a place to do sth** *I couldn't find a place to park.* | *Did the accident happen at your* **place of work** (=the place where you work)? | *The Great Mosque has been a* **place of worship** *for Muslims for centuries.* → see box at POSITION¹

2 HOME *informal* a house or apartment where someone lives: *They've got quite a big place on the outskirts of Leeds.* | **sb's place** *Do you want to come back to my place for coffee?* | *It took us ages to find a place to live.* | *He's staying with us until he can find a place of his own.*

3 **take place** to happen, especially after being planned or arranged: *The next meeting will take place on Thursday.* | *Talks between the two sides are still taking place.* | *Major changes are taking place in society.*

4 SPACE TO SIT OR PUT STH a space where someone can sit, or a space where you can put something: *I might arrive a bit late, so could you save me a place?* | *There are still a few places left on the coach.* | *Make sure you put everything back in its proper place.* | [+for] *Can you find a good place for this vase?*

5 POINT IN BOOK/SPEECH a point that you have reached in a book or a speech: *This would be a good place to stop and answer any questions that people have.* | *I used a bookmark so that I wouldn't* **lose** *my* **place** (=forget the point that I had reached).

6 OPPORTUNITY TO DO STH if someone has a place somewhere, they have the opportunity to go there or join in an activity: [+in] *If you don't come to training you might lose your place in the team.* | *We've been trying to find her a place in a residential home.* | [+on] *He was offered a place on the management committee.* | *There are still a couple of places left on the course.* | [+at] *I've been offered a place at York University.*

7 ROLE/POSITION the ROLE or important position that someone or something has in a situation or in society: **sb's place** *the old idea that a woman's place is in the home* | [+in] *He finally reached the summit of Everest and secured his place in history.* | *Working has a very important place in all our lives.*

8 **in place a)** in the correct position: *The chairs for the concert were nearly all in place.* | *The glass was* **held in place** *by a few pieces of sellotape.* **b)** existing and ready to be used: *Funding arrangements are already in place.*

9 **in place of sb/sth** also **in sb's/sth's place** instead of someone or something else: *In place of our advertised programme, we will have live coverage of the special memorial service.* | *The company flag had been taken down and in its place hung the Union Jack.* | *If I refused to go, they would send someone else in my place.*

10 **take the place of sb/sth** also **take sb's/sth's place** to exist or be used instead of someone or something else; ⊟ **replace**: *Natural methods of pest control are now taking the place of chemicals.* | *I had to find someone to take Jenny's place.*

11 **in sb's place** used to talk about what you would do if you were in someone else's situation: *What would you do in my place?* | *Try to* **put yourself in my place** *and think how you would feel.*

12 **be no place for sb** to be a completely unsuitable place for someone: *This is no place for a child.*

13 **first/second/third etc place** first, second etc position in a race or competition: *He took second place in the long jump.* | **in first/second etc place** *I finished in third place.*

14 **in the first place a)** used to introduce a series of points in an argument, discussion etc: *In the first place, I'm too busy, and in the second I don't really want to go.* **b)** used to talk about what someone did or should have done at the start of a situation: *I wish I'd never got involved in the first place!*

15 **take second place (to sb/sth)** to be less important than someone or something else: *She wasn't prepared to take second place in his life.*

16 **take your places** used to tell people to go to the

correct place or position that they need to be in for an activity: *If you would like to take your places, the food will be served shortly.*
17 all over the place *informal* **a)** everywhere: *There was blood all over the place.* **b)** in a very untidy state: *She came in with her hair all over the place.*
18 put sb in their place to show someone that they are not as clever or important as they think they are: *I soon put him in his place.*
19 out of place a) not suitable for a particular situation or occasion: *He never seemed to feel out of place at social functions.* | *The paintings looked strangely out of place.* **b)** not in the correct or usual position: *The kitchen was spotlessly clean, with nothing out of place.*
20 it is not sb's place (to do sth) if it is not your place to do something, you do not have the duty or right to do it: *It's not your place to criticize me!*
21 have no place *formal* to be completely unacceptable: [+in] *Capital punishment has no place in a modern society.*
22 fall into place a) if things fall into place in your mind, you suddenly realize and understand what is really happening: *Things were beginning to fall into place in my mind.* | *Everything suddenly fell into place.* **b)** if plans or events fall into place, they start to happen in the way that you hoped they would: *Eventually I got a job, and my life began to fall into place.*
23 be going places *informal* to start becoming successful in your life: *William is a young man who is definitely going places*; → **have/take pride of place** at PRIDE¹ (6)

place² S3 W1 *v*
1 POSITION [T always + adv/prep] to put something somewhere, especially with care; ⊟ **put**: *She poured the doctor a cup of tea and placed it on the table.* | *He carefully placed the folder back in his desk drawer.*
2 SITUATION [T always + adv/prep] to put someone or something in a particular situation; ⊟ **put**: *The government is being placed under pressure to give financial help to farmers.* | *Children must not be placed at risk.* | *Some areas of the city have been placed under curfew.* | *This places me in a very difficult position.*
3 IN A JOB/HOME [T] *formal* to find a suitable job or home for someone: *Some unemployed people can be very difficult to place.* | *He was later placed with a foster family.*
4 ARRANGE STH [T] to arrange for something to be done: *He placed an advertisement in the local paper.* | *You can place orders by telephone.* | *I had no idea which horse I should place a bet on.*
5 HOW GOOD/IMPORTANT [T always + adv/prep] to say how good or important you think someone or something is: *I would place health quite high on my list of priorities.* | **places sb/sth above/before sb/sth** *Some museums seem to place profit above education.*
6 place value/importance/emphasis etc on sth to decide that something is important: *Most people place too much value on money.* | *The company places a lot of emphasis on training.*
7 can't place sb to recognize someone, but be unable to remember where you have met them before: *I've seen her somewhere before, but I can't quite place her.*
8 be well/ideally etc placed a) to be in a good situation where you have the ability or opportunity to do something: **be well/ideally placed to do sth** *The company is now well placed to compete in Europe.* **b)** *BrE* to be in a good place or position: [+for] *The hotel is well placed for most of London's theatres.*
9 RACES be placed first/second etc to be first, second etc in a race or competition

pla·ce·bo /plə'si:bəʊ $ -boʊ/ *n plural* **placebos** [C] **1** a harmless substance given to a sick person instead of medicine, without telling them it is not real. Placebos are often used in tests in which some people take real medicine and others take a placebo, so that doctors can compare the results to see if the real medicine works properly. **2 placebo effect** when

someone feels better after taking a placebo, even though it has not had any effect on their body
'place card *n* [C] a small card with someone's name on it, which is put on a table to show where they are going to sit
'place kick *n* [C] in RUGBY or AMERICAN FOOTBALL, an occasion when the ball is kicked after it has been placed or held on the ground
'place mat *n* [C] a board or piece of cloth that you put on a table for each person who is eating there, so that the table is protected from the plates, knives etc
place·ment /'pleɪsmənt/ *n* [C,U] **1** the act of finding a place for someone to live or work: *The centre provides a job placement service.* | [+of] *the placement of children in foster homes* | *They lived on campus, but this was just a temporary placement.* **2** *BrE* a job, usually as part of a course of study, which gives you experience of a particular type of work: **on placement** *Students are sent out on placement for training.* | *a forty-five day placement in a factory* **3** when something is placed somewhere or when you decide where something should go: [+of] *the placement of fire hydrants along the city's streets*
'place name *n* [C] the name of a particular place, such as a town, mountain etc: *Many of the place names are Scottish in origin.*
pla·cen·ta /plə'sentə/ *n* [C] an organ that forms inside a woman's UTERUS to feed an unborn baby —**placental** *adj* [only before noun]: *placental blood*
'place ,setting *n* [C] an arrangement on a table of knives, forks, glasses etc to be used by one person
plac·id /'plæsɪd/ *adj* **1** a placid person does not often get angry or upset and does not usually mind doing what other people want them to: *a large, placid baby* | *She sat still, placid and waiting.* **2** calm and peaceful: *The lake was placid and still under the moonlight.* —**placidly** *adv*: *Dobbs stood at the entrance, placidly smoking his pipe.* —**placidity** /plə'sɪdɪti/ *n* [U]
plac·ing /'pleɪsɪŋ/ *n* [C] *BrE* the position of someone or something in a competition or ordered list: *Hancock and Smith took the top two placings.*
pla·gia·ris·m /'pleɪdʒərɪzəm/ *n* **1** [U] when someone uses another person's words, ideas, or work and pretends they are their own: *The journal accused the professor of plagiarism.* **2** [C] an idea, phrase, or story that has been copied from another person's work, without stating where it came from: *claims that there are plagiarisms in the new software* —**plagiarist** *n* [C]
pla·gia·rize also **-ise** *BrE* /'pleɪdʒəraɪz/ *v* [I,T] to take words or ideas from another person's work and use them in your work, without stating that they are not your own: *He accused other scientists of plagiarizing his research.*
plague¹ /pleɪg/ *n* **1** [C] a disease that causes death and spreads quickly to a large number of people: *drops in population levels due to plagues and famines* **2** [U] also **the plague** a very infectious disease that produces high fever and swollen places on the body, and often leads to death, especially BUBONIC PLAGUE; → **Black Death**: *The plague caused 100,000 deaths in London alone in the 1600s.* **3** a plague of rats/locusts etc an uncontrolled and harmful increase in the numbers of a particular animal or insect: *A plague of squirrels is threatening our forests.* → **avoid sb/sth like the plague** at AVOID (2)
plague² *v* [T] **1** [usually passive] to cause pain, suffering, or trouble to someone, especially for a long period of time: **be plagued by/with sth** *He was plagued by eye troubles.* | *Financial problems continued to plague the company.* **2** to annoy someone, especially by asking for something many times or asking them many questions: **plague sb with sth** *The kids have been plaguing me with questions.*
plaice /pleɪs/ *n plural* **plaice** [C,U] a flat sea fish that is eaten

plaid /plæd/ *n* **1** [U] a pattern of crossed lines and squares, used especially on cloth; ▤ **tartan** *BrE*: *a plaid shirt* **2** [C] a piece of plaid cloth worn over the shoulder and across the chest by people from Scotland as part of their NATIONAL COSTUME

plain¹ S2 W3 /pleɪn/ *adj*
1 CLEAR very clear, and easy to understand or recognize; ▤ **obvious**: **it is plain (that)** *It was plain that Giles was not going to agree.* | *The advantages were plain to see.* | *You have made your feelings plain enough.* | **Let me make it plain** (=state it clearly). *We do not want you here.* | **make yourself plain** (=make what you are saying clear) *If you do that again you will be severely punished. Do I make myself plain?* | **as plain as day/the nose on your face** (=very clear)
2 in plain English/language in clear and simple words, without using technical language: *The document, written in plain English, tells you about your new policy.*
3 SIMPLE without anything added or without decoration; ▤ **simple**: *a plain white blouse* | *a plain wooden table* | *plain yoghurt* | *a plain gold wedding ring* | *Your essay should be written on **plain paper*** (=paper with no lines on it).
4 HONEST showing clearly and honestly what is true or what you think about something; ▤ **frank**, **candid**: *Let's have some plain, truthful answers.* | *I don't know, and that's **the plain truth.** | **The plain fact** is people still buy books.*
5 EMPHASIS [only before noun] *spoken* used to emphasize that a particular type of behaviour, attitude etc is involved, usually a bad one: *His motive was plain greed.* | *When you told him his house was too cold that was just plain bad manners.*
6 NOT BEAUTIFUL not beautiful or attractive – often used because you want to avoid saying this directly: *Mrs Cookson was a rather plain woman.* | **plain Jane** (=used to talk about a woman who is not beautiful)
7 in plain clothes police officers in plain clothes are not wearing uniform → PLAIN-CLOTHES
8 (just) plain Mr/Mrs etc *spoken* used to show that someone does not have or use a special title: *I don't call him Uncle – just plain Bill.*
9 be plain sailing to be very easy to do or achieve: *If you can answer the first question, the rest of the test should be plain sailing.*
10 in plain sight *AmE* if something is in plain sight, it is easy to see or notice, especially when it should be hidden: *Don't leave your valuables in plain sight.*
—**plainness** *n* [U]

plain² *n* **1** also **plains** [C] a large area of flat dry land; → **prairie**: *The grassy plain gave way to an extensive swamp.* | *the vast plains of central China* **2** [U] the ordinary stitch in KNITTING

plain³ *adv informal* used to emphasize an adjective, usually one referring to a bad quality: *It's just plain crazy to spend all your pay as soon as you get it.*

plain·chant /'pleɪntʃɑːnt $ -tʃænt/ *n* [U] PLAINSONG

plain 'chocolate *n* [U] *BrE* chocolate made without milk and with very little sugar; ▤ **dark chocolate**

plain-'clothes *adj* [only before noun] plain-clothes police are police who wear ordinary clothes so that they can work without being recognized

plain 'flour *n* [U] *BrE* flour that contains no BAKING POWDER; → **self-raising flour**

plain·ly /'pleɪnli/ *adv* **1** in a way that is easy to understand or recognize: *Mrs Gorman was plainly delighted.* | *The first part of that argument is plainly true.* | *We could hear Tom's voice plainly over the noise of the crowd.* | [sentence adverb]: *Plainly the laws are not effective.* **2** speaking honestly, and without trying to hide the truth: *She told him plainly that she had no intention of marrying him.* **3** simply or without decoration: *a plainly dressed young girl* | *The room was very plainly furnished.*

plain·song /'pleɪnsɒŋ $ -sɔːŋ/ also **plainchant** *n* [U] a type of old Christian church music in which people sing a simple tune without musical instruments

plain·spo·ken /ˌpleɪn'spəʊkən◄ $ -'spoʊ-/ *adj* saying exactly what you think, especially in a way that people think is honest rather than rude: *a straightforward, plainspoken man*

plain·tiff W3 /'pleɪntɪf/ *n* [C] someone who brings a legal action against another person in a court of law; ▤ **complainant** *BrE*; → **defendant**

plain·tive /'pleɪntɪv/ *adj* a plaintive sound is high, like someone crying, and sounds sad: **plaintive cry/voice/sound etc** *the plaintive cry of the seagull* —**plaintively** *adv*

plait¹ /plæt $ pleɪt, plæt/ *v* [T] *BrE* to twist three long pieces of hair or rope over and under each other to make one long piece; ▤ **braid** *AmE*: *She plaited her hair hurriedly.* | *a plaited leather belt*

plait² *n* [C] *BrE* a length of something, usually hair, that has been plaited; ▤ **braid** *AmE*: **in plaits** *Jenni wore her hair in plaits.*

plan¹ S1 W1 /plæn/ *n* [C]
1 INTENTION something you have decided to do: *His plan is to get a degree in economics and then work abroad for a year.* | *There's been a **change of plan** - we're not going to Ibiza after all.* | *We don't have any **plans for** the weekend – why don't you come over?* | *Julia's been busy **making plans for** (=preparing for) her wedding.* | **sb's best plan** *BrE* (=the best course of action) *Your best plan would be to catch a taxi.*
2 METHOD/ARRANGEMENT a set of actions for achieving something in the future, especially a set of actions that has been considered carefully and in detail: *an ambitious economic recovery plan* | [+for] *Managers denied there are any plans for a merger.* | **plan to do sth** *plans to turn the site of the factory into a park* | **keep/stick to a plan** *If we keep to the plan the work should be completed in two weeks.* | **work out/draw up/devise a plan** *They devised a plan to reduce costs.* | *If everything **goes according to plan** (=happens in the way that was arranged) the first stage will be completed by December.* | *Jane explained her **plan of action**.*
3 MAP a drawing similar to a map, showing roads, towns, and buildings: [+of] *a street plan of London*
4 DRAWING **a)** *technical* a drawing of a building, room, or machine as it would be seen from above, showing the shape, size, and position of the walls, windows, and doors → ELEVATION (4), SECTION¹ (7), GROUND PLAN (1) **b)** a drawing that shows exactly how something will be arranged: *I have to organise a **seating plan** for the dinner.*
5 plan A, Plan A your first plan, which you will use if things happen the way you expect: *We're going to find a restaurant and buy a meal. That's Plan A.*
6 plan B, Plan B your second plan, which you can use if things do not happen the way you expect: *It's time to put Plan B into action.*

plan² S1 W1 *v* **planned, planning**
1 [I,T] to think carefully about something you want to do, and decide how and when you will do it: *He immediately began planning his escape.* | *Talks are planned for next week.* | *The wedding was fine and everything **went as planned** (=happened the way it had been planned).* | **plan to do sth** *Maria didn't plan to kill Fiona. It was an accident.* | **plan ahead/plan for the future** *Now that you're pregnant you'll have to plan ahead.*
2 [T] to intend to do something: **plan to do sth** *He said he planned to write his essay tonight.* | **plan on doing sth** *When do you plan on going to Geneva?* | *The former president is planning a return to politics.*
3 [T] to think about something you are going to make, and decide what it will be like; ▤ **design**: *Planning a small garden is often difficult.* | *The system needs to be planned carefully.*

plan sth ⇔ **out** *phr v*
to plan something carefully, considering all the possible problems: *I'll get the maps so we can plan out our route.* → PLANNING

plate 1250

chemicals on it that are sensitive to light
9 BASEBALL [C usually singular] the place where the person hitting the ball stands
10 COMPETITION **the ... Plate** used in the names of sports competitions or races in which the winner gets a silver plate: *This horse won the Galway Plate.*
11 TEETH [C] **a)** a thin piece of plastic shaped to fit inside a person's mouth, into which FALSE TEETH are fixed **b)** *BrE* a thin piece of plastic with wires fixed to it, that some people wear in their mouth to make their teeth straight; ◧ **brace** *BrE* → HOTPLATE

plate² *v* [T] **be plated with sth a)** to be covered with a thin covering of gold or silver: *a beautiful necklace, plated with 22 carat gold* | **gold-plated/silver-plated** *a gold-plated watch* **b)** to be covered in sheets of a hard material such as metal: *The ship had been heavily plated with protective sheets.*

plat·eau¹ /'plætəʊ $ plæ'toʊ/ *n plural* **plateaus** or **plateaux** /-təʊz $ -'toʊz/ [C] **1** a large area of flat land that is higher than the land around it **2** a period during which the level of something does not change, especially after a period when it was increasing: *Inflation rates have reached a plateau.*

plateau² *v* [I] if something plateaus, it reaches and then stays at a particular level: *The athletic footwear market has not yet plateaued.*

plate·ful /'pleɪtfʊl/ *n* [C] all the food that is on a plate: [+of] *a plateful of toast*

plate 'glass *n* [U] big pieces of glass made in large thick sheets, used especially in shop windows

plate·let /'pleɪtlᵻt/ *n* [C] one of the very small flat round cells in your blood that help it become solid when you bleed, so that you stop bleeding

plate tec'tonics *n* [U] *technical* the study of the forming and movement of the large sheets of rock that form the surface of the Earth

plat·form W3 /'plætfɔːm $ -fɔːrm/ *n* [C]
1 TRAIN *especially BrE* the raised place beside a railway track where you get on and off a train in a station: *The Edinburgh train will depart from platform six.*
2 FOR SPEECHES a stage for people to stand on when they are making a speech, performing etc: *a small raised platform at one end of the room*
3 POLITICS **a)** [usually singular] the main ideas and aims of a political party, especially the ones that they state just before an election; → **plank**: *a strong women's rights platform* | *the Labour party platform* **b)** a chance for someone to express their opinions, especially their political opinions: [+for] *The conference provides a platform for people on the left wing of the party.*
4 STRUCTURE a tall structure built so that people can stand or work above the surrounding area: *an oil exploration platform*
5 COMPUTERS the type of computer system or software that someone uses: *the UNIX platform* | *a multimedia platform*
6 EXPRESS IDEAS an opportunity to express your ideas to a large number of people: [+for] *We mustn't give these groups a platform for their propaganda.*
7 BUS *BrE* the open part at the back of some DOUBLE-DECKER buses, where passengers get on and off
8 SHOES **platforms** also **platform shoes** [plural] shoes that have a thick layer of wood, leather etc under the front part and the heel

'platform ,game *n* [C] *technical* a computer game in which the action happens against a background that does not move

plat·ing /'pleɪtɪŋ/ *n* [U] a thin layer of metal that covers another metal surface: *gold plating*

plat·i·num /'plætᵻnəm/ *n* [U] **1** a silver-grey metal that does not change colour or lose its brightness, and is used in making expensive jewellery and in industry. It is a chemical ELEMENT: symbol Pt: *a platinum ring* **2** if a music recording goes platinum, at least a million

copies of it have been sold: *Eight of Denver's albums went platinum.* | *a platinum disc*

,platinum 'blonde *n* [C] *informal* a woman whose hair is a silver-white colour, especially because it has been coloured with chemicals —**platinum blonde** *adj*

plat·i·tude /'plætᵻtjuːd $ -tuːd/ *n* [C] *formal* a statement that has been made many times before and is not interesting or clever – used to show disapproval: *His excuse was the platitude 'boys will be boys.'* —**platitudinous** /,plætᵻ'tjuːdᵻnəs◂ $ -'tuː-/ *adj*

pla·ton·ic /plə'tɒnɪk $ -'tɑː-/ *adj* a relationship that is platonic is just friendly and is not a sexual relationship: *a platonic friendship*

pla·toon /plə'tuːn/ *n* [C] a small group of soldiers which is part of a COMPANY and is led by a LIEUTENANT

plat·ter /'plætə $ -ər/ *n* [C] **1** *especially AmE* a large plate from which food is served: *a serving platter* | [+of] *a platter of turkey and vegetables* **2** chicken/seafood etc platter chicken, fish etc with vegetables or other foods on a large plate, served in a restaurant

plat·y·pus /'plætᵻpəs/ *n* [C] a small furry Australian animal that has a beak and feet like a duck, lays eggs, and produces milk for its young

plau·dits /'plɔːdᵻts $ 'plɒː-/ *n* [plural] *formal* praise and admiration: **win/draw/receive etc plaudits** *Her performance won plaudits from the critics.*

plau·si·ble /'plɔːzᵻbəl $ 'plɒː-/ *adj* **1** reasonable and likely to be true or successful; ◧ **implausible**: *His story certainly sounds plausible.* | *a plausible explanation* **2** someone who is plausible is good at talking in a way that sounds reasonable and truthful, although they may in fact be lying: *a plausible liar* —**plausibly** *adv* —**plausibility** /,plɔːzᵻ'bɪlᵻti $,plɒː-/ *n* [U]

play¹ S1 W1 /pleɪ/ *v*
1 CHILDREN [I,T] when children play, they do things that they enjoy, often with other people or with toys: *Kids were playing and chasing each other.* | **play catch/house/tag/school etc** *Outside, the children were playing cowboys and Indians.* | [+with] *Did you like to play with dolls when you were little?* | *Parents need to spend time just playing with their children.*
2 SPORTS/GAMES **a)** [I,T] to take part or compete in a game or sport: *Karen began playing basketball when she was six.* | *If you feel any pain, you shouldn't play.* | *Men were sitting in the park, playing cards.* | [+against] *Bristol will play against Coventry next week.* | *She's playing Helen Evans in the semi-final.* (=playing against her) | [+for] *Moxon played for England in ten test matches.* **b)** [T] to use a particular piece, card, person etc in a game or sport: *Harrison played a ten of spades.* | *The Regents played Eddie at center* (=used him as a player in that position) *in the game against Arizona.* **c)** [I,T] to take a particular position on a team: *Garvey played first base for the Dodgers.* **d)** [T] to hit a ball in a particular way or to a particular place in a game or sport: *She played the ball low, just over the net.*
3 MUSIC [I,T] to perform a piece of music on a musical instrument: *He's learning to play the piano.* | *She played a Bach prelude.* | *Haden has played with many jazz greats.* | *A small orchestra was playing.*
4 RADIO/CD ETC [I,T] if a radio, CD etc plays, or if you play it, it produces sound, especially music: *The bedside radio played softly.* | **play a record/CD/tape etc** *DJs playing the latest house and techno tracks*
5 THEATRE/FILM **a)** [T] to perform the actions and say the words of a particular character in a theatre performance, film etc: *Streep plays a shy, nervous woman.* | **play a role/part/character etc** *Playing a character so different from herself was a challenge.* **b)** [I] if a play or film is playing at a particular theatre, it is being performed or shown there: *'Macbeth' is playing at the Theatre Royal in York.* **c)** [T] if actors play a theatre, they perform there in a play
6 play a part/role to have an effect or influence on something: [+in] *A good diet and fitness play a large part in helping people live longer.*
7 play ball **a)** to throw, kick, hit, or catch a ball as a

game or activity: *Jim and Karl were playing ball in the backyard.* **b)** to do what someone wants you to do: *So far, the company has refused to play ball, preferring to remain independent.*

8 **PRETEND** [linking verb] to behave as if you are a particular kind of person or have a particular feeling or quality, even though it is not true: *the accusation that scientists are playing God* | *Some snakes fool predators by playing dead.* | *'What do you mean?' 'Don't play dumb.'* (=pretend you do not know something) | **play the idiot/the teacher etc** *Susan felt she had to play the good wife.* | *He played the fool* (=behaved in a silly way) *at school instead of working.*

9 **BEHAVE** [T always + adv/prep] to behave in a particular way in a situation, in order to achieve the result or effect that you want: *How do you want to play this meeting?* | **Play it safe** (=avoid risks) *and make sure the eggs are thoroughly cooked.* | **play it carefully/cool etc** *If you like him, play it cool, or you might scare him off.*

10 **play games** to hide your real feelings or wishes in order to achieve something in a clever or secret way – used to show disapproval: *Stop playing games, Luke, and tell me what you want.*

11 **play sth by ear a)** to decide what to do according to the way a situation develops, without making plans before that time: *We'll see what the weather's like and play it by ear.* **b)** if someone can play a musical instrument by ear, they can play a tune without looking at written music

12 **play a joke/trick/prank on sb** to do something to someone as a joke or trick

13 **play the game a)** to do things in the way you are expected to do them or in a way that is usual in a particular situation: *If you want a promotion, you've got to play the game.* **b)** *BrE* to behave in a fair and honest way

14 **play the race/nationalist/environmentalist etc card** to use a particular subject in politics in order to gain an advantage: *a leader who is skillfully playing the nationalist card to keep power*

15 **play your cards right** to say or do things in a situation in such a way that you gain as much as possible from it: *Who knows? If you play your cards right, maybe he'll marry you.*

16 **play your cards close to your chest** to keep secret what you are doing in a situation

17 **play into sb's hands** to do what someone you are competing with wants you to do, without realizing it: *If we respond with violence, we'll be playing into their hands, giving them an excuse for a fight.*

18 **play for time** to try to delay something so that you have more time to prepare for it or prevent it from happening: *The rebels may be playing for time while they try to get more weapons.*

19 **play tricks (on you)** if your mind, memory, sight etc plays tricks on you, you feel confused and not sure about what is happening: *It happened a long time ago, and my memory might be playing tricks on me.*

20 **play the market** to risk money on the STOCK MARKET as a way of trying to earn more money

21 **play the system** to use the rules of a system in a clever way, to gain advantage for yourself: *Accountants know how to play the tax system.*

22 **play second fiddle (to sb)** to be in a lower position or rank than someone else

23 **play hard to get** to pretend that you are not sexually interested in someone so that they will become more interested in you

24 **SMILE** [I always + adv/prep] *written* if a smile plays about someone's lips, they smile slightly

25 **play hooky** *AmE*; **play truant** *BrE* to stay away from school without permission

26 **play with fire** to do something that could have a very dangerous or harmful result: *Dating the boss's daughter is playing with fire.*

27 **LIGHT** [I always + adv/prep] *written* if light plays on something, it shines on it and moves on it: *the sunlight playing on the water*

28 **WATER** [I] *written* if a FOUNTAIN plays, water comes from it

29 **play the field** to have sexual relationships with a lot of different people

30 **play fast and loose with sth** to not be careful about what you do, especially by not obeying the law or a rule: *They played fast and loose with investors' money.*

31 **play a hose/light on sth** to point a HOSE or light towards something so that water or light goes onto it

play around also **play about** *BrE phr v*
1 to have a sexual relationship with someone who is not your usual partner: [+with] *Wasn't she playing around with another man?* | *It was years before I realized he'd been playing around.*
2 to try doing something in different ways, to see what would be best, especially when this is fun: [+with] *Play around with the ingredients if you like.*
3 to behave in a silly way or waste time, when you should be doing something more serious; ⊟ **fool around**: *When the teacher wasn't looking, we used to play about a lot.*

play around with sth also **play about with sth** *BrE phr v*
to keep moving or making changes to something in your hands; ⊟ **fiddle with**: *Will you stop playing around with the remote control!*

play along *phr v*
1 to pretend to agree to do what someone wants, in order to avoid annoying them or to get an advantage: *She felt she had to play along or risk losing her job.*
2 **play sb along** *BrE* to tell someone something that is not true because you need their help in some way

play at sth *phr v*
1 **What is sb playing at?** *BrE spoken* used when you do not understand what someone is doing or why they are doing it, and you are surprised or annoyed: *What do you think you're playing at?*
2 if you play at doing something, you do not do it properly or seriously: **play at doing sth** *He's still playing at being an artist.*
3 *BrE* if children play at doctors, soldiers etc, they pretend to be doctors, soldiers etc: **play at being sth** *a fourteen-year-old playing at being a grown woman*

play sth ⇔ **back** *phr v*
to play something that has been recorded on a machine so that you can listen to it or watch it: *He played back his answering machine messages.*

play sth ⇔ **down** *phr v*
to try to make something seem less important or less likely than it really is: *Management has been playing down the possibility of job losses.* | **play down the importance/seriousness/significance of sth** *The White House spokeswoman sought to play down the significance of the event.*

play off *phr v*
1 *BrE* if people or teams play off, they play the last game in a sports competition, in order to decide who is the winner: *The top two teams will play off at Twickenham for the county title.*
2 **play off sb/sth** *AmE* to deliberately use a fact, action, idea etc in order to make what you are doing better or to get an advantage: *The two musicians played off each other in a piece of inspired improvisation.*

play sb **off against** sb *phr v*
to encourage one person or group to compete or argue with another, in order to get some advantage for yourself: *The house seller may try to play one buyer off against another, to raise the price.*

play on/upon sth *phr v*
to use a feeling, fact, or idea in order to get what you want, often in an unfair way: *The ad plays on our emotions, showing a doctor holding a newborn baby.*

play sth ⇔ **out** *phr v*
1 if an event or situation is played out or plays itself out, it happens: *It will be interesting to see how the election plays itself out.*
2 if people play out their dreams, feelings etc, they

often in a way that annoys other people: *Miranda, pleased with herself for getting it right, sat down.*

pleas·er /'pliːzə $ -ər/ *n* **crowd-pleaser/audience-pleaser etc** someone or something that people like a lot: *A chocolate dessert is a sure crowd-pleaser.*

pleas·ing /'pliːzɪŋ/ *adj formal* giving pleasure, enjoyment, or satisfaction: *a pleasing sound* | [+to] *a design that is pleasing to the eye* —**pleasingly** *adv*: *a pleasingly relaxed atmosphere*

plea·sur·a·ble /'pleʒərəbəl/ *adj formal* enjoyable: *a pleasurable experience* —**pleasurably** *adv*

plea·sure S2 W2 /'pleʒə $ -ər/ *n*
1 [U] the feeling of happiness, enjoyment, or satisfaction that you get from an experience; → **pleasant**: **with pleasure** *She sipped her drink with obvious pleasure.* | **for pleasure** *a book to read for pleasure* | *The garden has given pleasure to many people.* | **take pleasure in (doing) sth** *I shall take great pleasure in telling everyone the truth.*
2 [C] an activity or experience that you enjoy very much; → **pleasant**: *the simple pleasures of life* | **be a pleasure to read/work with/watch etc** *Carol was a pleasure to work with.*
3 (it's) my pleasure *spoken* used when someone has thanked you for doing something and you want to say that you were glad to do it
4 [singular] *spoken formal* used to be polite when you are meeting someone, asking for something, agreeing to do something etc: **have the pleasure of (doing) sth** *May I have the pleasure of seeing you again?* | *It's been a pleasure to meet you.* | **It'll be a pleasure/With pleasure** (=used to respond to a request) *'Give the kids a hug for me.' 'With pleasure.'*
5 at your pleasure *formal* if you can do something at your pleasure, you can do it when you want to and in the way you want to
6 at his/her Majesty's pleasure *BrE law* if someone is put in prison at his or her Majesty's pleasure, there is no fixed limit to the time they have to spend there

'pleasure ,boat also **'pleasure ,craft** *n* [C] a boat that someone uses for fun rather than for business

'pleasure ,seeker *n* [C] *written* someone who does things just for enjoyment without considering other people

pleat /pliːt/ *n* [C usually plural] a flat narrow fold in a skirt, a pair of trousers, a dress etc

pleat·ed /'pliːt̬d/ *adj* a pleated skirt, dress etc has a lot of flat narrow folds

pleath·er /'pleðə $ -ər/ *n* [U] an artificial material that looks like leather and is used to make clothes: *a pleather jean jacket*

pleb /pleb/ *n* [C usually plural] *BrE informal* an insulting word meaning someone who is from a low social class – often used humorously: *Plebs like me could never have such perfect manners.* —**plebby** *adj*

plebe /pliːb/ *n* [C] *AmE informal* a student in their first year at a military college

ple·be·ian¹ /plɪ'biːən/ *adj* relating to ordinary people and what they like, rather than to people from a high social class – used to show disapproval: *a man with plebeian tastes*

plebeian² *n* [C] **1** an insulting word for someone who is from a low social class **2** an ordinary person who had no special rank in ancient Rome; ⧉ **patrician**

pleb·is·cite /'plebɪ̬sɪt $ -saɪt/ *n* [C,U] *formal* a system by which everyone in a country or area votes on an important decision that affects the whole country or area: [+on] *a plebiscite on independence*; → **referendum**

plec·trum /'plektrəm/ *n* [C] *especially BrE* a small thin piece of plastic, metal, or wood that you use for playing some musical instruments with strings, such as a GUITAR; ⧉ **pick**

pled /pled/ *v AmE* a past tense and past participle of PLEAD

pledge¹ /pledʒ/ *n* [C]
1 PROMISE *formal* a serious promise or agreement, especially one made publicly or officially: [+for] *a pledge of support for the plan* | **pledge to do sth** *the government's pledge to make no deals with terrorists* | **make/take/give a pledge** *Parents make a pledge to take their children to rehearsals.* | **keep/fulfil/honour a pledge** *Eisenhower fulfilled his election pledge to end the war in Korea.*
2 MONEY a promise to give money to an organization: *Donors have made pledges totaling nearly $4 million.* | [+of] *a pledge of $200 to the public TV station*
3 SOMETHING VALUABLE something valuable that you leave with someone else as proof that you will do what you have agreed to do
4 US COLLEGES someone who has promised to become a member of a FRATERNITY or SORORITY at an American university

pledge² *v* [T]
1 PROMISE to make a formal, usually public, promise that you will do something: **pledge sth to sth/sb** *Moore pledged $100,000 to the orchestra at the fund-raising dinner.* | **pledge to do sth** *The new governor pledged to reduce crime.* | **pledge that** *Herrera pledged that his company will give aid to schools.* | **pledge (your) support/loyalty/solidarity etc** *He pledged his cooperation.* | **pledge yourself to (do) sth** *Trade unions pledged themselves to resist the government plans.*
2 MAKE SB PROMISE to make someone formally promise something: *Employees were pledged to secrecy.*
3 LEAVE STH to leave something with someone as a PLEDGE¹ (3)
4 US COLLEGES to promise to become a member of a FRATERNITY or SORORITY at an American university

Pleis·to·cene /'plaɪstəsiːn/ *adj* belonging to the period in the Earth's history that started about two million years ago and ended about 10,000 years ago, when much of the Earth was covered with ice

ple·na·ry /'pliːnəri/ *adj* [only before noun] *formal* **1** involving all the members of a committee, organization etc: *The conference ended with a plenary debate.* **2** plenary powers are complete powers with no limit: *He was given plenary powers to negotiate with the rebels.* —**plenary** *n* [C]

plen·i·po·ten·tia·ry /ˌplenɪpə'tenʃəri $ -ʃieri/ *n plural* **plenipotentiaries** [C] *formal or technical* someone who has full power to take action or make decisions, especially as a representative of their government in a foreign country —**plenipotentiary** *adj*

plen·i·tude /'plenɪ̬tjuːd $ -tuːd/ *n* [U] *literary* **1 a plenitude of sth** a large amount of something: *a plenitude of wealth* **2** completeness or fullness

plen·te·ous /'plentiəs/ *adj literary* plentiful

plen·ti·ful /'plentɪfəl/ *adj* more than enough in quantity: *a plentiful supply of food* —**plentifully** *adv*

plen·ty¹ S1 W1 /'plenti/ *pron* a large quantity that is enough or more than enough: [+of] *Make sure she gets plenty of fresh air.* | *No need to hurry – you've got plenty of time.* | *There's plenty to do and see in New York.* | *There are plenty more chairs in the next room.*

plenty² *adv informal* **1 plenty big/fast/warm etc enough** used to emphasize that something is more than big enough, fast enough etc: *This apartment's plenty big enough for two.* **2** *AmE* a lot or very: *I'd practiced plenty.* | *I was plenty nervous.*

plenty³ *n* [U] *formal* **1** a situation in which there is a lot of food and goods available for people: *a land of plenty* **2 in plenty** in large supply or more than enough: *There was food and wine in plenty.*

pleth·o·ra /'pleθərə/ *n* **a plethora of sth** *formal* a very large number of something, usually more than you need: *a plethora of suggestions*

pleu·ri·sy /ˈpluərɪ̯si $ ˈplur-/ n [U] a serious illness which affects your lungs, causing severe pain in your chest

Plex·i·glas, **plexiglass** /ˈpleksɪglɑːs $ -glæs/ n [U] AmE trademark a strong clear type of plastic that can be used instead of glass; ▤ **Perspex** BrE

plex·us /ˈpleksəs/ n → SOLAR PLEXUS

pli·a·ble /ˈplaɪəbəl/ adj **1** able to bend without breaking or cracking: a shoe made of soft, pliable leather **2** easily influenced and controlled by other people: Senior officials would have preferred a more pliable government. —**pliability** /ˌplaɪəˈbɪlɪ̯ti/ n [U]

pli·ant /ˈplaɪənt/ adj **1** soft and moving easily in the way that you want: Isabel was pliant in his arms. | her pliant lips **2** easily influenced and controlled by other people: Pliant judges have been a problem in the past. —**pliantly** adv —**pliancy** n [U]

pli·ers /ˈplaɪəz $ -ərz/ n [plural] a small tool made of two crossed pieces of metal, used to hold small things or to bend and cut wire: a pair of pliers

plight¹ /plaɪt/ n [usually singular] a very bad situation that someone is in: [+of] the **desperate plight** of the flood victims | the country's **economic plight**

plight² v **plight your troth** old use to promise someone that you will marry them

plim·soll /ˈplɪmsəl, -səʊl $ -səl, -soʊl/ n [C] BrE a cotton shoe with a flat rubber SOLE; ▤ **sneaker** AmE

Plimsoll line also **Plimsoll mark** n [C] BrE a line painted on the outside of a ship, showing how low in the water it can safely be when it is loaded

plinth /plɪnθ/ n [C] especially BrE a square block, usually made of stone, that is used as the base for a PILLAR or STATUE → see picture at STAND²

Pli·o·cene /ˈplaɪəsiːn/ adj belonging to the period in the Earth's history that started about 13 million years ago and continued about 12 million years

plod /plɒd $ plɑːd/ v **plodded**, **plodding** [I always + adv/prep] to walk along slowly, especially when this is difficult: [+through/up/across etc] The horse plodded up the hill. | [+on/along/back] Jake kept plodding on.
  plod on/along phr v to work slowly or make slow progress, especially in a way that is boring: For years he had plodded along in a series of boring office jobs.

plod·der /ˈplɒdə $ ˈplɑːdər/ n [C] informal **1** BrE someone who works slowly and is not very clever **2** someone who walks or does something slowly

plod·ding /ˈplɒdɪŋ $ ˈplɑː-/ adj slow or thorough and not exciting: plodding research

plonk¹ /plɒŋk $ plɑːŋk, plɔːŋk/ v [T always + adv/prep] especially BrE informal **1** also **plonk sth down** to put something down somewhere, especially in a noisy and careless way; ▤ **plunk** AmE: You can plonk those bags down anywhere in my room. | **plonk sth on/onto/beside etc sth/sb** He plonked a couple of glasses on the table. | **plonk yourself (down)** to sit down heavily and then relax: We plonked ourselves down in front of the telly and opened a couple of beers.

plonk² n [U] BrE informal cheap wine

plonk·er /ˈplɒŋkə $ ˈplɑːŋkər, ˈplɔːŋ-/ n [C] BrE informal not polite an offensive word for a stupid person

plop¹ /plɒp $ plɑːp/ n [C] the sound made by something when it falls or is dropped into liquid: **with a plop** The soap fell into the bath with a loud plop.

plop² v **plopped**, **plopping** **1** [I always + adv/prep] to fall somewhere, making a sound like something dropping into water: [+into/out of/onto etc] The frog plopped back into the pond. **2** [T] to drop something, especially into a liquid, so that it makes a sound: **plop sth into sth** I plopped a couple of ice cubes into the drink. **3** **plop (yourself) down** to sit down or lie down heavily: She plopped down on the sofa beside me.

plo·sive /ˈpləʊsɪv $ ˈploʊ-/ n [C] technical a CONSONANT sound that is made by completely stopping the flow of air out of your mouth and then suddenly letting it out, as when saying /b/ or /t/ —**plosive** adj

plot¹ /plɒt $ plɑːt/ n [C]
1 **PLAN** a secret plan by a group of people, to do something harmful or illegal: **plot to do sth** a plot to bomb the UN headquarters | [+against] a plot against the king | The court heard how she and her lover **hatched a plot** (=planned a plot) to kill her husband. | The **plot** to overthrow the military government was **foiled** (=prevented from being successful). | an **assassination plot**
2 **STORY/FILM** the events that form the main story of a book, film, or play: The plot was a little confusing. | We discover that Jack isn't as innocent as he seems, as the **plot unfolds** (=gradually becomes clearer).
3 **the plot thickens** used to say that events seem to be becoming more complicated – often used humorously
4 **PIECE OF LAND a)** a small piece of land for building or growing things on: a two acre **plot of land** | a **vegetable plot b)** a piece of land that a particular family owns in a CEMETERY, in which members of the family are buried when they die: a **burial plot**
5 **DRAWING** AmE a drawing that shows the plan of a building at ground level; ▤ **ground plan** → **lose the plot** at LOSE (14)

plot² v **plotted**, **plotting 1** [I,T] to make a secret plan to harm a person or organization, especially a political leader or government: **plot to do sth** They had plotted to blow up the White House. | [+against] He suspected that the military were **secretly plotting** against him. | The minister was found guilty of plotting the downfall of the government. | the story of a woman who plots revenge **2** [T] also **plot out** to draw marks or a line to represent facts, numbers etc: We **plotted a graph** to show the increase in sales figures this year. | **plot sth on sth** You can plot all these numbers on one diagram for comparison. **3** [T] also **plot out** to mark, calculate, or follow the path of an aircraft or ship, for example on a map: We **plotted a course** across the Pacific.

plot·ter /ˈplɒtə $ ˈplɑːtər/ n [C] **1** someone who makes a secret plan to harm a person or organization, especially a political leader or government: The plotters were caught and executed. **2** a computer program that turns facts, numbers etc into a GRAPH or CHART

plough¹ also **plow** AmE /plaʊ/ n [C] **1** a piece of farm equipment used to turn over the earth so that seeds can be planted **2** **under the plough** BrE formal land that is under the plough is used for growing crops → SNOW PLOUGH (1)

plough² also **plow** AmE v **1** [I,T] to turn over the earth using a plough so that seeds can be planted: In those days the land was plowed by oxen. | a **ploughed field 2** [I always + adv/prep] to move with a lot of effort or force: [+through/up/across etc] We ploughed through the thick mud. **3** **plough a lonely/lone furrow** BrE literary to do a job or activity that is different from those done by other people, or to do it alone
  plough ahead phr v to continue to do something in spite of opposition or difficulties: [+with] The government will plough ahead with tests this year, despite a boycott from teachers.
  plough sth ⇔ **back** phr v to use money that you have earned from a business to make the business bigger and more successful: [+into] Companies can **plough back** their **profits** into new equipment.
  plough into sb/sth phr v to crash into something or someone, especially while driving, because you are unable to stop quickly enough: I plowed into the car in front.
  plough on phr v to continue doing something that is difficult or boring: [+with] Julia ploughed on with the endless exam papers. | He looked displeased but she **ploughed on regardless**.
  plough through sth phr v to read all of something, even though it is boring and takes a long time: Most staff will never want to plough through the manuals that come with the software.

P

plough sth ⇔ **up** phr v to break up the surface of the ground by travelling over it many times: *Horses plough up the paths and make them muddy for walkers.*

Plough /plaʊ/ n BrE **the Plough** the group of seven bright stars that can be seen only from the northern part of the world; ⊟ **the Big Dipper** AmE

plough·boy /ˈplaʊbɔɪ/ n [C] BrE old use a boy who led a horse that pulled a plough

plough·man /ˈplaʊmən/ n plural **ploughmen** /-mən/ [C] BrE old use a man whose job was to guide a plough that was being pulled by a horse

ploughman's 'lunch n [C] BrE a simple meal that people eat especially in PUBS, consisting of bread, cheese, SALAD and PICKLE

plough·share BrE; **plowshare** AmE /ˈplaʊʃeə $ -ʃer/ n [C] **1** the broad curved metal blade of a PLOUGH, which turns over the soil **2 turn/beat swords into ploughshares** to stop fighting and start living in peace

plov·er /ˈplʌvə $ -ər/ n [C] a small bird that lives near the sea

plow /plaʊ/ n, v the usual American spelling of PLOUGH

ploy /plɔɪ/ n [C] a clever and dishonest way of tricking someone so that you can get an advantage: *His usual ploy is to pretend he's ill.* | *ploy to do sth a smart ploy to win votes*

PLS, **pls** the written abbreviation of *please*, used in email or TEXT MESSAGES

pluck¹ /plʌk/ v

1 PULL STH [T] written to pull something quickly in order to remove it: **pluck sth from/off etc sth** *He plucked a couple of plastic bags from the roll.* | *Reaching up, she plucked an apple off the tree.*

2 pluck your eyebrows to make your EYEBROWS the shape you want, by pulling out some of the hairs

3 TAKE SB/STH AWAY [T always + adv/prep] to take someone away from a place or situation that is dangerous or unpleasant in a quick and unexpected way: **pluck sb/sth from/out of sth** *Some refugee children were plucked out of the country in a number of mercy missions.* | *She was **plucked from obscurity** (=made suddenly famous) by a Hollywood film producer.* | *Three survivors were **plucked to safety** after being in the sea for 7 hours.*

4 CHICKEN [T] to pull the feathers off a dead chicken or other bird before cooking it

5 pluck up (the) courage (to do sth) to force yourself to be brave and do something that you are afraid of doing: *He finally plucked up enough courage to ask her out.*

6 MUSIC [I,T] to pull the strings of a musical instrument: [+at] *Someone was plucking at the strings of an old guitar.*

7 pluck sth out of the air also pluck something out of thin air to say or suggest a number, name etc that you have just thought of, without thinking about it carefully: *I'm plucking a figure out of the air here, but let's say it'll cost about $15,000.*

pluck at sth phr v
to pull something quickly several times with your fingers, especially because you are nervous or to attract attention: *Kitty's hands plucked at her black cotton skirt.* | *The little boy plucked at her sleeve.*

pluck² n [U] old-fashioned courage and determination: *It takes a lot of pluck to stand up to a bully.*

pluck·y /ˈplʌki/ adj informal brave and determined – often used in newspapers: *Plucky Denise saved her younger sister's life.*

plug¹ S3 /plʌg/ n [C]
1 ELECTRICITY **a)** a small object at the end of a wire that is used for connecting a piece of electrical equipment to the main supply of electricity: *The plug on my iron needs changing.* | *an electric plug* **b)** informal especially BrE a place on a wall where electrical equipment can be connected to the main electricity supply; ⊟ **socket**; ⊟ **outlet** AmE

2 BATH a round flat piece of rubber used for stopping the water flowing out of a bath or SINK: *the bath plug*

3 ADVERTISEMENT informal a way of advertising a book, film etc by mentioning it publicly, especially on television or radio: **put/get in a plug (for sth)** *During the show she managed to put in a plug for her new book.*

4 IN AN ENGINE informal the part of a petrol engine that makes a SPARK, which makes the petrol start burning; ⊟ **spark plug**: *Change the plugs every 10,000 miles.*

5 pull the plug (on sth) informal to prevent a plan, business etc from being able to continue, especially by deciding not to give it any more money: *The Swiss entrepreneur has pulled the plug on any further investment in the firm.*

6 TO FILL A HOLE an object or substance that is used to fill or block a hole, tube etc: [+of] *You can fill any holes with plugs of matching wood.* → EARPLUG

7 FOR HOLDING SCREWS BrE a small plastic tube put in a hole to hold a screw tightly

8 A PIECE OF STH a piece of something pressed tightly together: *a plug of tobacco*

plug² v plugged, plugging [T] **1** also plug up to fill or block a small hole: *We used mud to plug up the holes in the roof.* **2** to advertise a book, film etc by mentioning it on television or radio: *Arnie was on the show to plug his new movie.* **3** plug the gap to provide something that is needed, because there is not enough: *With so few trained doctors, paramedics were brought in to plug the gap.* **4** AmE old-fashioned to shoot someone

plug away phr v to keep working hard at something: [+at] *If you keep plugging away at it, your English will improve.*

plug sth ⇔ **in** phr v to connect a piece of electrical equipment to the main supply of electricity, or to another piece of electrical equipment: *'Is your printer working?' 'Wait a minute – it's not plugged in.'*

plug into sth phr v **1** plug (sth) into sth to connect one piece of electrical equipment to another, or to be connected: *Your phone can be plugged into the cigarette lighter socket in your car.* | *Games consoles plug into the back of the TV.* **2** informal to realize that something is available to be used and use it: *A lot of students don't plug into all the research facilities we have.*

plug and 'play n [U] technical the ability of a computer and a new piece of equipment to be used together as soon as they are connected

plug·hole /ˈplʌghəʊl $ -hoʊl/ n [C] BrE **1** the hole in a bath or SINK that the water flows out of, and which you can put a plug into; ⊟ **drain** AmE **2 go down the plughole** informal **a)** if work or effort goes down the plughole, it is completely wasted: *Two years of hard work went right down the plughole.* **b)** if a business goes down the plughole, it fails and has to close

'plug-in¹ adj [only before noun] able to be connected to the electricity supply, or to another piece of electrical equipment: *a plug-in microphone*

plug·in², **plug·in** /ˈplʌgɪn/ n [C] technical a piece of computer software that can be used in addition to existing software in order to make particular programs work properly

plum¹ /plʌm/ n **1** [C] a small round juicy fruit which is dark red, purple, or yellow and has a single hard seed, or the tree that produces this fruit: *juicy ripe plums* → see picture at FRUIT¹ **2** [U] a dark purple-red colour **3** [C] informal something very good that other people wish they had, such as a good job or a part in a play: *The first job I had was a real plum.* → PLUM PUDDING

plum² adj **1** plum job/role/assignment etc informal a good job etc that other people wish they had: *He landed a plum role in a TV mini-series.* **2** having a dark purple-red colour

plum·age /ˈpluːmɪdʒ/ n [U] the feathers covering a bird's body: *the parrot's brilliant blue plumage*

plumb¹ /plʌm/ v [T] **1** plumb the depths (of despair/misery/bad taste etc) to feel an unpleasant emotion in a very extreme way, or to behave in a way that is extremely unpleasant or morally bad: *When his wife left* *him, Matt plumbed the very depths of despair.* | *That night they plumbed the depths of treachery and horror, and murdered the king as he slept.* **2** to succeed in understanding something completely; ▤ **fathom**: *Psychologists try to plumb the deepest mysteries of the human psyche.*

  plumb sth ⇔ **in** *phr v* to connect a piece of equipment such as a washing machine to the water supply

plumb² *adv* **1** [always + adv/prep] *informal* exactly: *The bullet hit him plumb between the eyes.* **2** *AmE informal* completely – often used humorously: *The whole idea sounds plumb crazy to me.*

plumb³ *adj technical* **1** exactly upright or level **2 out of plumb** not exactly upright or level

plumb·er /ˈplʌmə $ -ər/ *n* [C] someone whose job is to repair water pipes, baths, toilets etc

plumb·ing /ˈplʌmɪŋ/ *n* [U] **1** the pipes that water flows through in a building: *We keep having problems with the plumbing.* **2** the work of fitting and repairing water pipes, baths, toilets etc

ˈplumb line *n* [C] a piece of string with a small heavy object tied to one end, used for measuring the depth of water, or for checking whether something such as a wall is built exactly upright

plume¹ /pluːm/ *n* [C] **1** a cloud of smoke, dust etc which rises up into the air: **plume of smoke/dust/gas/ spray etc** *A black plume of smoke rose above the city.* **2** a large feather or bunch of feathers, especially one that is used as a decoration on a hat → **NOM DE PLUME**

plume² *v* [I] *literary* to rise or come out in a cloud: *No smoke plumed out of the factory's great chimneys.*

plumed /pluːmd/ *adj* [only before noun] decorated with feathers: *a knight with a plumed helmet*

plum·met /ˈplʌmɪt/ also **plummet down** *v* [I] **1** to suddenly and quickly decrease in value or amount; ▤ **plunge**: *plummet from sth to sth Profits plummeted from £49 million to £11 million.* | *House prices have plummeted down.* **2** to fall suddenly and quickly from a very high place; ▤ **plunge**: *The plane plummeted towards the earth.*

plum·my /ˈplʌmi/ *adj* **1** *BrE informal* a plummy voice sounds very UPPER-CLASS **2** like a PLUM in taste, colour etc: *a plummy wine*

plump¹ /plʌmp/ *adj* **1** slightly fat in a fairly pleasant way – used especially about women or children, often to avoid saying the word fat: *The nurse was a cheerful plump woman.* | *The baby's nice and plump.* → see box at **FAT¹** **2** round and full in a way that looks attractive: *plump, soft pillows* | *plump juicy tomatoes* —**plumpness** *n* [U]

plump² *v* **1** also **plump up** [T] to make CUSHIONS, PILLOWS etc rounder and softer by shaking or hitting them **2 plump (yourself) down** to sit down suddenly and heavily; ▤ **plonk 3** [T always + adv/prep] to put something down suddenly and carelessly; ▤ **plonk**: *Plump the bags down anywhere you like.* **4** also **plump up** [I,T] if dried fruit plumps up, or if you plump it up, it becomes fatter and softer when in liquid: *Soak the apricots and raisins until the fruit plumps up.*

  plump for sth/sb *phr v BrE informal* to choose something or someone after thinking carefully about it: *Finally we plumped for a bottle of champagne.*

ˌplum ˈpudding *n* [C,U] *BrE* CHRISTMAS PUDDING

ˈplum toˌmato *n* [C] a type of tomato shaped like a PLUM, often used in cooking

plun·der¹ /ˈplʌndə $ -ər/ *v written* **1** [I,T] to steal large amounts of money or property from somewhere, especially while fighting in a war: *The rich provinces of Asia Minor were plundered by the invaders.* **2** [T] to use up all or most of the supplies of something in a careless way: *Unlicensed fishermen have plundered tuna stocks.* | *the egotism of man as he plunders our planet* —**plunderer** *n* [C]

plunder² *n* [U] *written* **1** things that have been stolen during a violent attack, especially during a war:

Henry's army returned loaded down with plunder. **2** the act of plundering: *fear of invasion and plunder*

plunge¹ /plʌndʒ/ *v* **1** [I,T always + adv/prep] to move, fall, or be thrown suddenly forwards or downwards: [+off/into etc] *Her car swerved and plunged off the cliff.* | *Both the climbers had plunged to their deaths.* **2** [I] if a price, rate etc plunges, it suddenly decreases by a large amount: *The unemployment rate plunged sharply.* | [+to] *Oil prices have plunged to a new low.* | *In the recession, the company's profits plunged 60%.* **3** [I] *literary* if a ship plunges, it moves violently up and down because of big waves

  plunge in also **plunge into sth** *phr v* **1** to start talking or doing something quickly and confidently, especially without thinking about it first: *It's a difficult situation. You can't just plunge in and put everything right.* | *'I don't agree,' she said, plunging into the conversation.* **2** to jump or DIVE into water: *He stripped off and plunged into the sea.* **3 plunge sth ⇔ in** also **plunge sth into sth** to push something firmly and deeply into something else: *He open the bag and plunged his hand in.* | *Plunge the pasta into boiling water.* | *Repeatedly she plunged the knife into his chest.*

  plunge (sb/sth) **into** sth *phr v* to suddenly experience a difficult or unpleasant situation, or to make someone or something do this: *A strike would plunge the country into chaos.* | *The house was suddenly plunged into darkness.* | *After the war, the family plunged into debt.*

plunge² *n* **1 take the plunge** to decide to do something important or risky, especially after thinking about it for a long time: *We took the plunge and set up our own business.* **2** [C] a sudden large decrease in the price, value etc of something: [+in] *a dramatic plunge in house prices* **3** [C usually singular] a sudden movement down or forwards: *The plane began a **headlong plunge** towards the Earth.* **4** [C usually singular] when someone suddenly becomes involved in something new: [+into] *his sudden plunge into marriage* **5** [C usually singular] a jump or DIVE into water, or a quick swim: [+in/into] *a quick plunge in the lake*

plung·er /ˈplʌndʒə $ -ər/ *n* [C] **1** a tool for clearing waste that is blocking a kitchen or bathroom pipe. It consists of a straight handle with a rubber cup on the end. **2** *technical* a part of a machine that moves up and down

ˌplunging ˈneckline *n* [C] if a woman's dress or shirt has a plunging neckline, the top part at the front is very low

plunk /plʌŋk/ *v* [T always + adv/prep] *AmE informal* **1** also **plunk sth down** to put or place something somewhere, especially in a noisy, sudden, or careless way; ▤ **plonk** *BrE*: *plunk sth in/on etc sth plans to plunk a theme park on the site* **2 plunk (yourself) down** to sit down suddenly or heavily and then relax; ▤ **plonk** *BrE*: *Why don't you plunk yourself down with a good book?*

  plunk sth ⇔ **down** *phr v* to spend an amount of money on something: *She plunked down $250 for a silver necklace.*

plu·per·fect /pluːˈpɜːfɪkt $ -ɜːr-/ *n* **the pluperfect** *technical* the PAST PERFECT tense of a verb

plu·ral¹ /ˈplʊərəl $ ˈplʊr-/ *n* [C] a form of a word that shows you are talking about more than one thing, person etc. For example, 'dogs' is the plural of 'dog': **in the plural** *'Sheep' remains the same in the plural.* | [+of] *What's the plural of 'mouse'?*

plural² *adj* **1** a plural word or form shows you are talking about more than one thing, person etc. For example 'we' is a plural PRONOUN **2** *formal* a plural society, system, or culture is one with people from many different religions, races etc: *Britain has developed into a plural society.*

plu·ral·is·m /'pluǝrǝlizǝm $ 'plur-/ n [U] formal when people of many different races, religions, and political beliefs live together in the same society, or the belief that this can happen successfully: a nation characterized by cultural pluralism —**pluralist** n [C] —**pluralistic** /,pluǝrǝ'lɪstɪk◂ $,plur-/ —**pluralist** adj: a pluralist society

plu·ral·i·ty /plu'rælǝti/ n plural pluralities **1** [C usually singular] formal a large number of different things: [+of] the plurality of factors affecting the election **2** [C,U] especially AmE technical if one person or party receives a plurality in an election, they receive more votes than any of the other people or parties, but fewer votes than the total number of votes that all the others receive together: The Democrats won only a plurality of the votes cast. **3** [U] technical when a noun is plural

plus¹ S1 W2 /plʌs/ prep
1 used to show that one number or amount is added to another; ▪ minus: Three plus six equals nine. (3 + 6 = 9) | The total cost was $10, 000, plus 14% interest.
2 and also: There are numerous clubs, plus a casino.
3 plus or minus used to say that a number may be more or less by a certain amount: There may be a variation of plus or minus 5% in the prices that are quoted.

plus² n [C] **1** informal something that is an advantage: major/definite/big etc plus Some knowledge of Spanish is a definite plus in this job. **2** a PLUS SIGN; ▪ minus

plus³ adj **1** [only before noun] used to talk about an advantage or good feature of a thing or situation; ▪ minus: Another of the Beach Club's plus points is that it's right in the middle of town. | This is not an exciting car to drive, but on the plus side it is extremely reliable. **2** used after a number to mean an amount which is more than that number: an income of $50,000 plus | Most children start school when they're five plus. **3** more than zero – used especially when talking about temperatures; ▪ minus: Daytime temperatures barely reached plus 5°. **4** A plus/B plus etc a mark used in a system of judging students' work. An 'A plus' is slightly higher than an 'A'.

plus⁴ conjunction informal used to add more information: He's been studying hard for exams. Plus he's been working in a bar at night.

,plus 'fours n [plural] short loose trousers that are fastened just below the knee. Men wore them in the past, especially when playing golf.

plush¹ /plʌʃ/ adj informal very comfortable, expensive, and of good quality: a plush hotel | Their casino is the plushest in town.

plush² n [U] a silk or cotton material with a thick soft surface: plush curtains

'plus sign also **plus** especially BrE n [C] the sign (+), showing that you should add two or more numbers together, or that a number is more than zero

Plu·to /'plu:tǝʊ $ -toʊ/ n the PLANET that is furthest from the sun and is the smallest in the SOLAR SYSTEM: the discovery of Pluto in 1930 → see picture at SOLAR SYSTEM

plu·toc·ra·cy /plu:'tɒkrǝsi $ -'tɑːk-/ n plural plutocracies [C] a ruling class or government that consists of rich people, or a country that is governed by rich people

plu·to·crat /'plu:tǝkræt/ n [C] someone who has power because they are rich – used to show disapproval: champagne-drinking plutocrats —**plutocratic** /,plu:tǝ'krætɪk◂/ adj

plu·to·ni·um /plu:'tǝʊniǝm $ -'toʊ-/ n [U] a RADIOACTIVE metal that is used in the production of NUCLEAR power, and in nuclear weapons. It is a chemical ELEMENT: symbol Pu

ply¹ /plaɪ/ v **plied, plying, plies 1** ply your trade literary to work at your business, especially buying and selling things on the street: In some areas, drug dealers openly ply their trade on street corners. **2** [I,T always +

adv/prep] written if a ship, bus etc plies between two places or across a place, it does that journey regularly: [+between/across etc] Two ferries ply between Tripoli and Malta every day. **3** ply for hire/trade BrE to try and get customers or passengers, in order to do business: Continental airlines ply for trade in the UK. **4** [T] old use or literary to use a tool skilfully

ply sb with sth phr v **1** to keep giving someone large quantities of food or drink: The local people plied me with beer, until I could barely move. **2** ply sb with questions to keep asking someone questions

ply² n plural ply [C] a unit for measuring the thickness of thread, rope, plywood etc, based on the number of threads or layers that it has: a sweater in 4-ply yarn

ply·wood /'plaɪwʊd/ n [U] a material made of several thin layers of wood that are stuck together to form a strong board

p.m. also **pm** BrE /pi: 'em/ used after numbers expressing the time, to show that it is between NOON and MIDNIGHT; → a.m.: The meeting starts at 2.30 pm.

PM /,pi: 'em/ n [C] BrE informal the PRIME MINISTER: a meeting with the PM

PMS /,pi: em 'es/ n [U] premenstrual syndrome the unpleasant physical and emotional feelings that many women have before their PERIOD starts

PMT /,pi: em 'ti:/ n [U] BrE premenstrual tension the unpleasant physical and emotional feelings that many women have before their PERIOD starts

pneu·mat·ic /nju:'mætɪk $ nʊ-/ adj [usually before noun] **1** technical filled with air: pneumatic tyres **2** worked by air pressure: a pneumatic pump

pneu,matic 'drill n [C] especially BrE a large powerful tool worked by air pressure and used for breaking up hard materials, especially road surfaces; ▣ **jackhammer** AmE

pneu·mo·ni·a /nju:'mǝʊniǝ $ nʊ'moʊ-/ n [U] a serious illness that affects your lungs and makes it difficult for you to breathe: She was taken to hospital, suffering from pneumonia.

PO BrE, **P.O.** AmE **1** the written abbreviation of post office → PO BOX **2** BrE the written abbreviation of postal order

poach /pǝʊtʃ $ poʊtʃ/ v
1 COOK [T] **a)** to cook an egg in or over gently boiling water, without its shell: poached eggs on toast → see picture at EGG¹ **b)** to gently cook food, especially fish, in a small amount of boiling water, milk etc: Poach the salmon in white wine and water.
2 ANIMALS [I,T] to illegally catch or shoot animals, birds, or fish, especially on private land without permission: Deer have been poached here for years.
3 PEOPLE [T] to persuade someone who belongs to another organization, team etc to leave it and join yours, especially in a secret or dishonest way: That company's always poaching our staff. | [+from] Several of their reporters were poached from other papers.
4 STEAL IDEAS [T] to take and use someone else's ideas unfairly or illegally: [+from] characters poached from Shakespeare
5 poach on sb's territory/preserve BrE to do something that is someone else's responsibility, especially when they do not want you to do it —**poaching** n [U]: the poaching of elephants for their ivory tusks

poach·er /'pǝʊtʃǝ $ 'poʊtʃǝr/ n [C] **1** someone who illegally catches or shoots animals, birds, or fish, especially on private land without permission **2** poacher turned gamekeeper BrE someone who used to do illegal things or have a bad attitude to authority, and who has now changed completely – used especially of someone who is now in a position of authority **3** BrE a pan with small containers shaped like cups used for poaching eggs

PO Box BrE, **P.O. Box** AmE /'pi: ǝʊ bɒks $ -oʊ bɑːks/ n [C] post office box used before a number as an address at a post office where letters to you can be sent: Write to P.O. Box 714, Key Largo, Florida.

pocked /pɒkt $ pɑːkt/ *adj* covered with small holes or marks; ◼ **pockmarked**: [+with] *His face was pocked with scars.*

pock·et¹ S2 W2 /'pɒkᵻt $ 'pɑː-/ *n* [C]
1 IN CLOTHES a type of small bag in or on a coat, trousers etc that you can put money, keys etc in: *Luke came in with his hands in his pockets.* | **jacket/trouser etc pocket** *The keys are in my trouser pocket.* | [+of] *the inside pocket of his jacket* | *The policeman told me to turn out my pockets* (=take everything out of them).
2 MONEY the amount of money that you have to spend: *There are eight hotels, with a price range to* **suit every pocket.** | **from/out of/into your own pocket** *Dan had to pay for the repairs out of his own pocket.* | *He was accused of diverting some of the firm's money into his own pocket.* | *The deepening recession has* **hit** *people's* **pockets.** | *For investors with* **deep pockets** (=a lot of money), *the Berlin property market is attractive.*
3 SMALL CONTAINER a small bag or piece of material fastened to something so that you can put things into it: *Please read the air safety card in the pocket of the seat in front.*
4 SMALL AREA/AMOUNT a small area or amount of something that is different from what surrounds it: [+of] *In some parts, there are still pockets of violence and unrest.* | *pockets of air inside the hull of the ship*
5 be in sb's pocket to be controlled or strongly influenced by someone in authority, and willing to do whatever they want: *The judge was in the defense lawyer's pocket.*
6 have sth in your pocket to be certain to win something such as a competition or election: *The Democrats had the election in their pocket.*
7 out of pocket *especially BrE informal* if you are out of pocket, you have less money than you should have, especially as a result of making a mistake or being unlucky: *If he loses the deal, he'll be badly out of pocket.*
8 be/live in each other's pockets *BrE informal* if two people are in each other's pockets, they are together too much
9 GAME a small net on a POOL, SNOOKER, or BILLIARD table, which you try to hit balls into → see picture at POOL¹ → AIR POCKET; → **burn a hole in your pocket** at BURN¹ (17); → **line your own pockets** at LINE² (4); → **pick sb's pocket** at PICK¹ (14)

pocket² *v* [T] **1** to put something into your pocket: *Maggie locked the door and pocketed the keys.* **2** to steal money, especially money that you are responsible for: *One inspector had pocketed up to $500,000 in bribes.* **3** to get a large amount of money, win a prize etc, especially in a way that seems very easy or slightly dishonest: *Johnston pocketed $2,500 in prize money.* **4** to hit a ball into a pocket in the game of POOL, SNOOKER and BILLIARDS; ◼ **pot**

pocket³ *adj* [only before noun] small enough to be carried in your pocket: *a pocket dictionary*

pocket battleship *n* [C] a fairly small fighting ship

pock·et·book /'pɒkᵻtbʊk $ 'pɑː-/ *n* [C] **1** *AmE* the amount of money that you have, or your ability to pay for things; ◼ **pocket** *BrE: The aim was to provide a car for every age and pocketbook.* | *Older voters are most concerned about* **pocketbook issues** (=that concern money). **2** *AmE old-fashioned* a HANDBAG **3** *AmE old-fashioned* a WALLET **4** *BrE old-fashioned* a NOTEBOOK

pocket calculator *n* [C] a small piece of electronic equipment that you use to do calculations

pocket change *n* [U] *AmE* **1** a small or unimportant amount of money: *The money is nothing – pocket change to them.* **2** coins that you carry in your pocket

pock·et·ful /'pɒkᵻtfʊl $ 'pɑː-/ *n* [C] the amount that can fit in a pocket: [+of] *a pocketful of coins*

pocket handkerchief *n* [C] *old-fashioned* a HANDKERCHIEF

pocket-handkerchief *adj* [only before noun] *BrE informal* a pocket-handkerchief garden or area of land is very small and usually square

pocket knife *n plural* **pocket knives** [C] a small knife with one or more blades that fold into the handle; ◼ **penknife**

pocket money *n* [U] **1** *BrE* a small amount of money that parents give regularly to their children, usually every week or month; ◼ **allowance** *AmE: How much pocket money do you get?* **2** *informal* a small amount of extra money that you earn in order to spend it on things you want: *I give a few private lessons too, for pocket money.*

pocket-sized also **pocket-size** *adj* [usually before noun] *BrE* small enough to fit into your pocket or be carried easily: *pocket-sized dictionaries*

pocket veto *n* [C] a method used by the US President to stop a BILL (=proposal for a new law). The President keeps the proposal without signing it until Congress is not working any more.

pock·mark /'pɒkmɑːk $ 'pɑːkmɑːrk/ *n* [C] a hollow mark on someone's skin or on the surface of something

pock·marked /'pɒkmɑːkt $ 'pɑːkmɑːrkt/ *adj* covered with hollow marks or holes: *a pockmarked skin*

pod /pɒd $ pɑːd/ *n* [C] **1** a long narrow seed container that grows on various plants, especially PEAS and beans: *a pea pod* → **like two peas in a pod** at PEA (2) **2** a part of a space vehicle that can be separated from the main part: *a space pod* **3** a long narrow container for petrol or other substances, especially one carried under an aircraft wing **4** a group of sea animals, such as WHALES or DOLPHINS, that swim together **5** a container which holds the eggs of some types of insects

p.o.'d /ˌpiː 'əʊd $ -'oʊd/ *adj AmE spoken* very annoyed: *She was really p.o.'d when she didn't get the job.*

podg·y /'pɒdʒi $ 'pɑː-/ *adj BrE* another form of PUDGY

po·di·a·trist /pəˈdaɪətrᵻst/ *n* [C] *especially AmE* a doctor who takes care of people's feet and treats foot diseases; ◼ **chiropodist** *BrE* —**podiatry** *n* [U]

po·di·um /'pəʊdiəm $ 'poʊ-/ *n* [C] **1** a small raised area for a performer, speaker, or musical CONDUCTOR to stand on **2** *AmE* a high sloping surface for putting an open book or notes on while you are giving a speech to a lot of people – some people think that this use is incorrect; ◼ **lectern**: *Several speakers took the* **podium** (=spoke from it) *that night.*

po·dunk /'pəʊdʌŋk $ 'poʊ-/ *adj AmE informal* a podunk place is small and unimportant: *Bob's from some podunk town in Iowa.*

po·em S3 /'pəʊᵻm $ 'poʊ-/ *n* [C] a piece of writing that expresses emotions, experiences, and ideas, especially in short lines using words that RHYME (=end with the same sound); → **poet**, **poetry**: [+about] *I decided to write a poem about how I felt.*

po·et W3 /'pəʊᵻt $ 'poʊ-/ *n* [C] someone who writes poems; → **poem**

po·et·ess /ˌpəʊᵻˈtes◂ $ 'poʊᵻtᵻs/ *n* [C] *old-fashioned* a female poet

po·et·ic /pəʊˈetɪk $ poʊ-/ also **po·et·ic·al** /-ˈetɪkəl/ *adj* **1** relating to poetry, or typical of poetry: *poetic expression* **2** having qualities of deep feeling or graceful expression: *poetic language* —**poetically** /-kli/ *adv*

po·etic justice *n* [U] a situation in which someone suffers, and you think they deserve it because they did something bad: *After the way she treated Sam, it's only poetic justice that Dave left her.*

po·etic licence *BrE*; **poetic license** *AmE n* [U] the freedom that poets and other artists have to change facts, ignore grammar rules etc, because what they are making is poetry or art

poet laureate *n plural* **poets laureate** [C] a poet who is chosen by a king, queen, president etc to write poems on important national occasions

po·et·ry W3 /'pəʊᵻtri $ 'poʊ-/ *n* [U]
1 poems in general, or the art of writing them; → **poem**, **poet**: *He reads a lot of poetry.* | *a poetry*

point of 'sale also **,point of 'purchase** n [singular] the place or shop where a product is sold: *Under the new law, cigarette advertising will only be allowed at the point of sale.*

,point of 'view n plural **points of view** [C] **1** a particular way of thinking about or judging a situation: **scientific/technical/business etc point of view** *From an economic point of view, the new development will benefit the town greatly.* **2** someone's own personal opinion or attitude about something: *I respect your point of view, but I'm not sure I agree with you.* | **from sb's point of view** *From my point of view, there is no way they can win.*

point·y /'pɔɪnti/ adj informal POINTED (1)

poise¹ /pɔɪz/ n [U] **1** a calm, confident way of behaving, combined with an ability to control your feelings or reactions in difficult situations: *Louisa seems to have much more poise and confidence.* **2** a graceful way of moving or standing, so that your body seems balanced and not awkward: *the poise of a dancer* | *She's pretty, but lacks poise.*

poise² v [T always + adv/prep] to put or hold something in a carefully balanced position, especially above something else: **poise sth over/above sth** *He poised the bottle over her glass. 'More wine?'*

poised /pɔɪzd/ adj **1** [not before noun] not moving, but ready to move or do something at any moment: [+for] *She waited by the door like a small animal poised for flight.* | [+on] *His finger was poised on the camera's shutter release.* | **poised to do sth** *He stood on the edge of the roof, poised to jump.* **2** [not before noun] completely ready to do something or for something to happen, when it is likely to happen soon: **poised to do sth** *Spain was poised to become the dominant power in Europe.* | **poised on the brink/edge of sth** *The economy is poised on the edge of collapse.* **3 poised between sth and sth** to be in a position or situation in which two things have an equally strong influence: *The world stood poised between peace and war.* **4** behaving in a calm, confident way, and able to control your feelings and reactions: *Abigail walked to the microphone, poised and confident.*

poi·son¹ /'pɔɪzən/ n **1** [C,U] a substance that can cause death or serious illness if you eat it, drink it etc: *Belladonna and red arsenic are deadly poisons.* | *a box of rat poison* (=poison to kill rats) | *He swallowed some type of poison.* **2** [C] something such as an emotion or idea that makes you behave badly or become very unhappy: *Hatred is a poison that will destroy your life.* **3 what's your poison?** old fashioned spoken a humorous way of asking which alcoholic drink someone would like → **one man's meat is another man's poison** at MEAT (4)

poison² v [T] **1** to give someone poison, especially by adding it to their food or drink, in order to harm or kill them: *She was accused in 1974 of poisoning her second husband, Charles.* | *He killed several people by poisoning their tea.* | **poison sb with sth** *Helms attempted to poison his whole family with strychnine.* **2** if a substance poisons someone, it makes them sick or kills them: *Thousands of children were poisoned by radiation.* **3** to make land, rivers, air etc dirty and dangerous, especially by the use of harmful chemicals: *Pesticides are poisoning our rivers.* **4** to have very harmful and unpleasant effects on someone's mind, emotions, or a situation: *Her childhood had been poisoned by an abusive stepfather.* | *The law will only serve to poison relations between the US and Mexico.* | *Television violence is poisoning the minds of young people.* —**poisoner** n [C]

,poison 'gas n [U] gas that causes death or serious injury, used especially against an enemy in a war: *There are reports that poison gas is being used against the rebels.*

poi·son·ing /'pɔɪzənɪŋ/ n [C,U] **1** illness caused by swallowing, touching, or breathing in a poisonous substance: **alcohol/lead/radiation etc poisoning** (=caused by a particular substance) *a case of alcohol poisoning* **2** the act of giving poison to someone: *An autopsy revealed no evidence of poisoning.* → FOOD POISONING

,poison 'ivy n [U] a North American plant that has an oily substance on its leaves that makes your skin hurt and ITCH if you touch it

,poison 'oak n [U] a North American plant with leaves similar to an OAK tree's, that makes your skin hurt and ITCH if you touch it

poi·son·ous /'pɔɪzənəs/ adj **1** containing poison or producing poison: *Some mushrooms are extremely poisonous.* | *poisonous gases such as hydrogen sulfide* | *poisonous substances* | *She was bitten on the ankle by a poisonous snake.* | [+to] *The berries are poisonous to birds.* **2** full of bad and unfriendly feelings: *the poisonous atmosphere of the office* **3** BrE someone who is poisonous seems to get pleasure from causing arguments, unhappiness etc: *That poisonous bastard Lucett told Morris I was seeing his wife.* —**poisonously** adv

,poison-'pen letter n [C] a letter that is not signed and that says bad things about the person it has been sent to

,poison 'pill n [C] technical informal something in a company's financial or legal structure that is intended to make it difficult for another company to take control of it

poke¹ /pəʊk $ poʊk/ v

1 WITH A FINGER/STICK ETC [I,T] to quickly push your finger or some other pointed object into something or someone: **poke sb/sth with sth** *Andy poked the fish with his finger to see if it was still alive.* | **poke sb in the eye/arm/ribs etc** *Be careful with that umbrella or you'll poke someone in the eye.* | [+at] *He was poking at the dust with a stick, making little patterns.*

2 THROUGH A SPACE/HOLE [T always + adv/prep] to move or push something through a space or opening: **poke sth in/into/through sth** *He poked a hand into one of his pockets.* | *One of the nurses poked her head around the door.*

3 BE SEEN [I always + adv/prep] if something is poking through or out of something else, you can see part of it but not all of it: [+out] *Ella looked at the tiny face poking out of the blanket.* | [+through] *Weeds had started poking through the cracks in the patio.*

4 poke a hole to make a hole or hollow area in something by pushing something pointed into or through it: [+into/in/through] *Poke a hole in the dough, and then form it into a rounded shape.*

5 poke holes in sth to find mistakes or problems in a plan or in what someone has said: *Defense attorneys tried to poke holes in Rodger's story.*

6 poke fun at sb to make fun of someone in an unkind way: *Some of the kids were poking fun at Judy because of the way she was dressed.*

7 poke your nose into sth informal to take an interest in or get involved in someone else's private affairs, in a way that annoys them: *I'm sick of your mother poking her nose into our marriage.*

8 poke the fire to move coal or wood in a fire with a stick to make it burn better

9 SEX [T] spoken not polite to have sex with a woman

poke along phr v AmE informal
to move very slowly: *He kept the car in the slow lane, poking along at about 40 miles an hour.*

poke around also **poke about** BrE phr v informal
1 to look for something, especially by moving a lot of things around: [+in] *James began poking about in the cupboard, looking for the sugar.*
2 to try to find out information about other people's private lives, business etc, in a way that annoys them: [+in] *Stop poking around in my business!*
3 poke around (sth) to spend time in shops, markets etc looking at nothing in particular; **▪ browse**: *I spent Sunday afternoon poking around an old bookshop.*

P

poke into sth *phr v informal*
to try to find out information about other people's private lives, business etc, in a way that annoys them

poke² *n [C]* **1 give sb/sth a poke** to quickly push your fingers, a stick etc into something or someone: *Vanessa gave me a playful poke in the ribs.* **2** *AmE informal* a criticism of someone or something: *Bennett took a poke at the President's refusal to sign the bill.*

pok·er /'pəʊkə $ 'poʊkər/ *n* **1** [U] a card game that people usually play for money: *Can you play poker?* **2** [C] a metal stick used to move coal or wood in a fire to make it burn better → see picture at FIREPLACE

poker-'faced *adj* showing no expression on your face: *a poker-faced officer* —**poker face** *n* [singular]

po·ker·work /'pəʊkəwɜːk $ 'poʊkərwɜːrk/ *n* [U] pictures or patterns burned onto the surface of wood or leather with hot tools, or the art of making these pictures

pok·ey /'pəʊki $ 'poʊ-/ *n* [C] *AmE old-fashioned informal* a prison

pok·y, pokey /'pəʊki $ 'poʊ-/ *adj informal* **1** *BrE* too small and not very pleasant or comfortable: *The whole family was crammed into two poky little rooms.* **2** *AmE* doing things very slowly, especially in a way that is annoying: *I got behind some poky driver on the freeway.*

pol /pɒl $ pɑːl/ *n* [C] *AmE informal* a politician – used in newspapers: *He's just another Washington pol.*

Po·lack, Polak /'pəʊlæk $ 'poʊ-/ *n* [C] *AmE taboo* a very offensive word for someone from Poland. Do not use this word.

po·lar /'pəʊlə $ 'poʊlər/ *adj* **1** close to or relating to the North Pole or the South Pole: *As our climate warms up, the polar ice caps will begin to melt.* **2 polar opposite/extreme** something that is the complete or exact opposite of something else: *Ortega's cheerful landscapes are the polar opposites of Miller's dark, troubled portraits.* **3** *technical* relating to one of the POLES of a MAGNET

polar 'bear /$ '.. ./ *n* [C] a large white bear that lives near the North Pole

po·lar·ise /'pəʊləraɪz $ 'poʊ-/ *v* a British spelling of POLARIZE

po·lar·i·ty /pə'lærəti/ *n plural* **polarities** [C,U] **1** *formal* a state in which people, opinions, or ideas are completely different or opposite to each other: [+between] *the polarity between the intellect and the emotions* **2** *technical* the state of having either a positive or negative electric charge

po·lar·ize also **-ise** *BrE* /'pəʊləraɪz $ 'poʊ-/ *v* [I,T] *formal* to divide into clearly separate groups with opposite beliefs, ideas, or opinions, or to make people do this: *The issue has polarized the country.* —**polarization** /ˌpəʊləraɪˈzeɪʃən $ ˌpoʊlərə-/ *n* [U]

Po·lar·oid /'pəʊlərɔɪd $ 'poʊ-/ *n* [C] *trademark* **1** a camera that uses a special film to produce a photograph very quickly **2** a photograph taken with a Polaroid camera: *Why don't you send us a few Polaroids of the new house?*

pole¹ W3 /pəʊl $ poʊl/ *n* [C]
1 STICK/POST a long stick or post usually made of wood or metal, often set upright in the ground to support something: *a telephone pole*
2 the most northern or most southern point on a PLANET, especially the Earth: *the distance from pole to equator* | **the North/South Pole** *Amundsen's expedition was the first to reach the South Pole.*; → see picture at GLOBE
3 be poles apart two people or things that are poles apart are as different from each other as it is possible to be: *Both are brilliant pianists, though they're poles apart in style.*
4 OPPOSITE IDEAS/BELIEFS one of two situations, ideas, or opinions that are the complete opposite of each other: **at a/one/opposite poles** *We have enormous wealth at one pole, and poverty and misery at the other.* | *Washington and Beijing are at opposite poles* (=think in two completely different ways) *on this issue.*

5 ELECTRICAL a) one of two points at the ends of a MAGNET where its power is the strongest b) one of the two points at which wires can be attached to a BATTERY in order to use its electricity

pole² *v* [I,T] *BrE* to push a boat along in the water using a pole

Pole *n* [C] someone from Poland

pole·axed /'pəʊlækst $ 'poʊl-/ *adj* [not before noun] *especially BrE* **1** *informal* very surprised and shocked: *I was poleaxed when I heard I'd passed the exam.* **2** unable to stand because something has hit you very hard: *He staggered and collapsed as if poleaxed.*

pole·cat /'pəʊlkæt $ 'poʊl-/ *n* [C] **1** a small dark brown wild animal that lives in northern Europe and can defend itself by producing a bad smell **2** *AmE informal* a SKUNK

po·lem·ic /pə'lemɪk/ *n formal* **1** [C] a written or spoken statement that strongly criticizes or defends a particular idea, opinion, or person: *Before long, the dispute degenerated into fierce polemics.* **2** [U] also **polemics** the practice or skill of making written or spoken statements that strongly criticize or defend a particular idea, opinion, or person

po·lem·i·cal /pə'lemɪkəl/ also **polemic** *adj formal* using strong arguments to criticize or defend a particular idea, opinion, or person: *The reforms were attacked in a highly polemical piece in the 'New Yorker'.* —**polemically** /-kli/ *adv*

pole po,sition *n* [C,U] the front position at the beginning of a car or bicycle race

Pole Star *n* **the Pole Star** a star that is almost directly over the North Pole and that can be seen from the northern part of the world

pole vault *n* **the pole vault** the sport of jumping over a high bar using a long pole —**pole vaulter** *n* [C] —**pole vaulting** *n* [U]

po·lice¹ S1 W1 /pə'liːs/ *n* [plural]
1 the people who work for an official organization whose job is to catch criminals and make sure that people obey the law: *Police surrounded the courthouse.* | *Several police were injured during the rioting.* | *Armed police stormed the building.*
2 the police the official organization whose job is to catch criminals and make sure that people obey the law: *Quick! Call the police!* | *Did you report the robbery to the police?* | *He was arrested by the police for dangerous driving.* | *a police car* ⚠ **Police** is a plural noun. Do not say 'a police'. Say a **police officer**, a **policeman**, or a **policewoman**: *The police were called.* | *A police officer came.* → MILITARY POLICE, SECRET POLICE

po·lice² *v* [T] **1** to keep control over a particular area in order to make sure that laws are obeyed and that people and property are protected, using a police or military force: *The army was brought in to police the city centre.* **2** to control a particular activity or industry by making sure that people follow the correct rules for what they do: *The agency was set up to police the nuclear power industry.* → POLICING

po,lice 'constable *n* [C] *BrE formal* **PC** a police officer of the lowest rank

po'lice de,partment *n* [C] *AmE* the official police organization in a particular area or city

po'lice dog *n* [C] a dog trained by the police to find hidden drugs or catch criminals

po'lice force *n* [C] the official police organization in a country or area: *Jones joined the police force in 1983.*

po·lice·man [S2] [W3] /pə'liːsmən/ *n plural* **policemen** /-mən/ [C] a male police officer → see picture at OCCU-PATION

po'lice ,officer *n* [C] a member of the police

po'lice state *n* [C] a country where the government strictly controls people's freedom to meet, write, or speak about politics, travel etc

po'lice ,station *n* [C] the local office of the police in a town, part of a city etc

po·lice·wom·an /pə'liːs,wʊmən/ *n plural* **police-women** /-,wɪmɪn/ [C] a female police officer

po·lic·ing /pə'liːsɪŋ/ *n* [U] **1** the way that the police are used to keep control over a particular area and to protect people and property: *The community is demanding a less aggressive style of policing.* | [+of] *the policing of the city* **2** the way that an industry or activity etc is controlled in order to make sure that people obey the rules: *In the last twenty years the industry has had no oversight or policing.* → POLICE

pol·i·cy [S3] [W1] /'pɒlɪsi $ 'pɑː-/ *n plural* **policies** **1** [C,U] a way of doing something that has been officially agreed and chosen by a political party, business, or other organization: **foreign/economic/public etc policy** *a foreign policy adviser* | *The company has adopted a strict no-smoking policy.* | [+on/towards] *government policy on higher education* | *US policy towards China* | **it is (sb's) policy to do sth** *It is hospital policy to screen all mothers with certain risk factors.* **2** [C] a contract with an insurance company, or an official written statement giving all the details of such a contract: *an **insurance policy*** | *There's a clause in the policy that I'd like to discuss.* | *I've just **renewed** the **policy** (=arranged for it to continue).* | *Does the **policy cover** theft and fire?* | *You can **take out** a **policy** (=buy one) for as little as $11.00 a month.* **3** [C] a particular principle that you believe in and that influences the way you behave: **it is sb's policy to do sth** *It's always been my policy not to gossip.*

pol·i·cy·hold·er /'pɒlɪsi,həʊldə $ 'pɑːlɪsi,hoʊldər/ *n* [C] someone who has bought insurance for something

pol·i·cy·mak·er /'pɒlɪsi,meɪkə $ 'pɑːlɪsi,meɪkər/ *n* [C] someone who decides what an organization's or government's policies will be

po·li·o /'pəʊliəʊ $ 'poʊlioʊ/ *also* **po·li·o·my·e·li·tis** /,pəʊliəʊmaɪə'laɪtɪs $,poʊlioʊ-/ *technical n* [U] a serious infectious disease of the nerves in the SPINE, that often results in someone being permanently unable to move particular muscles

pol·i sci /,pɒli 'saɪ $,pɑː-/ *n* [U] *AmE informal* the abbreviation of *political science*

Pol·ish¹ /'pəʊlɪʃ $ 'poʊ-/ *adj* relating to Poland, its people, or its language

Polish² *n* **1** **the Polish** [plural] people from Poland **2** [U] the language used in Poland

pol·ish¹ /'pɒlɪʃ $ 'pɑː-/ *v* [T] **1** to make something smooth, bright, and shiny by rubbing it: *I spent all afternoon polishing the silver.* | **polish sth with sth** *Polish the lenses with a piece of tissue.*; → see picture at CLEAN **2** to improve a piece of writing, a speech etc by making slight changes to it before it is completely finished: *Your essay is good, you just need to polish it a bit.* —**polishing** *n* [U]

polish

polish sb/sth ⇔ **off** *phr v informal* **a)** to finish food, work etc quickly or easily: *Sam polished off the rest of the pizza.* **b)** *AmE* to kill or defeat a person or animal when they are weak or wounded: *He was polished off with a shotgun blast to the face.*

polish sth ⇔ **up** *phr v* **1** *also* **polish up on sth** to improve a skill or an ability by practising it: *You should polish up your Spanish before you go to Chile.* **2** to make something seem better or more attractive to other people: *The company needs to polish up its image.* **3** to polish something

polish² *n* **1** [C,U] a liquid, powder, or other substance that you rub into a surface to make it smooth and shiny: **furniture/shoe/floor etc polish** → FRENCH POL-ISH **2** [singular] *especially BrE* an act of polishing a surface to make it smooth and shiny: *An occasional polish will keep wall tiles looking good.* **3** [U] a high level of skill or style in the way someone performs, writes, or behaves: *Carla's writing has potential, but it lacks polish.* **4** [singular] the smooth shiny appearance of something produced by polishing → **spit and polish** at SPIT² (5)

pol·ished /'pɒlɪʃt $ 'pɑː-/ *adj* **1** shiny because of being rubbed, usually with polish: *highly polished boots* **2** done with great skill and style: *a polished performance* | *a polished piece of writing* **3** polite, confident, and graceful: *a polished and confident man*

pol·ish·er /'pɒlɪʃə $ 'pɑːlɪʃər/ *n* [C] a machine used to polish something: *an electric floor polisher*

pol·it·bu·ro /'pɒlɪtbjʊərəʊ, $ 'pɑːlətbjʊroʊ/ *n plural* **politburos** [C] the most important decision-making committee of a Communist party or Communist government

po·lite [S3] /pə'laɪt/ *adj* **1** behaving or speaking in a way that is correct for the social situation you are in, and showing that you are careful to consider other people's needs and feelings; **🔁 rude, impolite**: *She's always very polite.* | *polite, well-behaved children* | *a clear but polite request* | **it is polite (of sb) to do sth** *We left the party as soon as it was polite to do so.* | *It's not polite to talk with your mouth full.* **2** you make polite conversation, remarks etc because it is considered socially correct to do this, but not necessarily because you believe what you are saying: **polite remarks/conversation/interest etc** *While they ate, they made polite conversation about the weather.* | *Jan expressed polite interest in Edward's stamp collection.* | *I know Ian said he liked her singing, but he was **only** being polite.* **3** in polite society/circles/company among people who are considered to have a good education and correct social behaviour – often used humorously: *You can't use words like that in polite company.* —**politely** *adv*: *'Can I help you?' she asked politely.* —**politeness** *n* [U]

pol·i·tic /'pɒlɪtɪk $ 'pɑː-/ *adj formal* sensible and likely to gain you an advantage; **🔁 prudent**: **it is politic to do sth** *It would not be politic to ignore the reporters.* → POLITICS, BODY POLITIC

po·lit·i·cal [S3] [W1] /pə'lɪtɪkəl/ *adj* **1** relating to the government, politics, and public affairs of a country; → **politically**: *Education is now a major political issue.* | *a time of political and social change* | **political party/system/institutions** *The U.S. has two main political parties.* | *The UN is seeking a political solution rather than a military one.* | *political jokes* | *the workers' struggle for political power* **2** relating to the ways that different people have power within a group, organization etc: *a purely political decision* | *The appointment was given to Wellington, mainly for political reasons.* **3** [not before noun] interested in or active in politics: *Most students aren't very political.* **4** **political football** a difficult problem which opposing politicians argue about or which each side deals with in a way that will bring them advantage: *Funding of the health service has become a political football.*

po,litical 'action com,mittee n [C] AmE **PAC** an organization formed by a business, UNION, or INTEREST GROUP to help raise money for politicians who support their ideas

po,litical a'sylum n [U] the right to stay in another country if you cannot live safely in your own country because of the political situation there: *Refugees were seeking political asylum in Britain.* | *No country would grant* (=give) *him political asylum.*

po,litical cor'rectness n [U] language, behaviour, and attitudes that are carefully chosen so that they do not offend or insult anyone – used especially when you think someone is too careful in what they say or how they behave; → **PC**, **politically correct**: *Political correctness has had an impact on the language people use to describe women.*

po,litical e'conomy n [U] the study of the way nations organize the production and use of wealth

po,litical ge'ography n [U] the study of the way the Earth's surface is divided up into different countries, rather than the way it is marked by rivers, mountains etc; → **physical geography**

po·lit·ic·ally /pə'lɪtɪkli/ adv in a political way: *Women were becoming more politically active.* | *a politically sensitive issue* | [sentence adverb]: *Politically, raising the minimum wage is good for the Democrats.*

po,litically cor'rect adj **PC** language, behaviour, and attitudes that are politically correct are carefully chosen so that they do not offend or insult anyone; 🔒 **politically incorrect**: *politically correct textbooks*

po,litically incor'rect adj language, behaviour, or attitudes that are politically incorrect might offend or insult someone: *politically incorrect jokes*

po,litical ma'chine n [singular] AmE the system used by people with the same political interests to make sure that political decisions give advantages to themselves or to their group: *the Chicago mayor's political machine*

po,lit,ical 'prisoner n [C] someone who is in prison because they have opposed or criticized the government of their own country

po,litical 'science n [U] the study of politics and government —**political scientist** n [C]

pol·i·ti·cian W2 /,pɒlɪ'tɪʃən $,pɑː-/ n [C]
1 someone who works in politics, especially an elected member of the government: *politicians who are trying to get the minority vote* | *a British Labour politician*
2 someone who is skilled at dealing with people or using the situation within an organization to gain an advantage: *the office politician*

po·li·ti·cize also **-ise** BrE /pə'lɪtɪˌsaɪz/ v [T] **1** to make a subject or a situation more political: *The Olympic Games should not be politicized.* **2** to make someone become more involved in political activities: *He became politicised during his years in prison.* —**politicized** adj: *Abortion is a highly politicized issue.* —**politicization** /pə,lɪtɪsaɪ'zeɪʃən $ -sə-/ n [U]

pol·i·tick·ing /'pɒlɪtɪkɪŋ $ 'pɑː-/ n [U] political activity, usually done to gain support for yourself or your political group: *the politicking at the party conference*

po·lit·i·co /pə'lɪtɪkəʊ $ -koʊ/ n [C] a politician or someone who is active in politics – usually used to show disapproval: *a slick politico*

politico- /pəlɪtɪkəʊ $ -koʊ/ prefix [used in adjectives] relating to both politics and something else: *politico-economic factors*

pol·i·tics S2 W2 /'pɒlɪtɪks $ 'pɑː-/ n
1 [U also + plural verb BrE] ideas and activities relating to gaining and using power in a country, city etc; → **political**, **politician**: *a good understanding of politics in China* | *modern American politics* | *Politics have always interested Anita.* | **national/local etc politics** *Brooke's been involved in city politics since college.* | *The president should stand above* **party politics** (=working only for your political PARTY).
2 [U] the profession of being a politician: *Flynn retired*

from politics in 1986. | *Her father's trying to enter politics.* | *Smith went into politics in his early twenties.*
3 [plural] the activities of people who are concerned with gaining personal advantage within a group, organization etc: *I'm tired of dealing with all of the office politics.* | *Her art examines sexual politics* (=how power is shared between men and women).* | [+of] *the politics of race and class at American universities*
4 [plural] someone's political beliefs and opinions: *I assume her politics must be fairly conservative.*
5 [U] especially BrE the study of political power and systems of government; ▣ **political science**: *Tom is studying for a degree in politics.*

pol·i·ty /'pɒlɪti $ 'pɑː-/ n plural **polities** [C,U] formal a particular form of political or government organization, or a condition of society in which political organization exists

pol·ka /'pɒlkə, 'pəʊlkə $ 'poʊlkə/ n [C] a very quick, simple dance for people dancing in pairs, or a piece of music for this dance —**polka** v [I]

'polka dot n [C] one of a number of round spots that form a pattern, especially on cloth used for clothing: *a white scarf with red polka dots* —**polka-dot** adj: *a polka-dot dress*

poll¹ W3 /pəʊl $ poʊl/ n
1 [C] the process of finding out what people think about something by asking many people the same question, or the record of the result; ▣ **opinion poll**, **survey**: *A recent poll found that 80% of Californians support the governor.* | *Polls indicate that education is the top issue with voters.* | *Labour is ahead in the polls.* | *The latest public opinion poll showed that 25% of us consider ourselves superstitious.* | **conduct/carry out/do a poll** *a poll conducted by USA Today* | [+on] *a poll on eating habits* | [+of] *a poll of 1000 people*
2 go to the polls to vote in an election: *10 million voters went to the polls.*
3 [singular] BrE the process of voting in an election, or the number of votes recorded: *Labour won the election with 40% of the poll.* | *The result of the poll won't be known until around midnight.*
4 the polls the place where you can go to vote in an election: *The polls will close in an hour.*

poll² v [T] **1** to ask a lot of people the same questions in order to find out what they think about a subject: *18% of the women we polled said their husbands had a drinking problem.* **2** to get a particular number of votes in an election: *Labour polled just 4% of the vote.*

pol·lard /'pɒləd, -lɑːd $ 'pɑːlərd/ v [T usually passive] BrE to cut the top off a tree in order to make the lower branches grow more thickly

pol·len /'pɒlən $ 'pɑː-/ n [U] a fine powder produced by flowers, which is carried by the wind or by insects to other flowers of the same type, making them produce seeds

'pollen count n [C] a measure of the amount of pollen in the air, usually given as a guide for people who are made ill by it: *The pollen count was high yesterday.*

pol·li·nate /'pɒlɪneɪt $ 'pɑː-/ v [T] to give a flower or plant pollen so that it can produce seeds: *flowers pollinated by bees* —**pollination** /,pɒlɪ'neɪʃən $,pɑː-/ n [U]

poll·ing /'pəʊlɪŋ $ 'poʊ-/ n [U] **1** when people vote in a political election: *Polling started at 8.00 this morning.* | **heavy/light polling** (=with many or few people voting) **2** when a person or an organization asks a lot of people the same questions in order to find out what they think about a subject

'polling booth n [C] BrE a small partly enclosed place in a polling station where you can vote secretly in an election

polling day *n* [C] *BrE* the day on which people vote in an election

polling ˌstation *BrE*; **polling ˌplace** *AmE n* [C] the place where people go to vote in an election

poll·ster /ˈpəʊlstə $ ˈpoʊlstər/ *n* [C] someone who works for a company that prepares and asks questions to find out what people think about a particular subject

poll tax *n* [C] a tax of a particular amount that is collected from every citizen of a country

pol·lut·ant /pəˈluːtənt/ *n* [C] a substance that makes air, water, soil etc dangerously dirty, and is caused by cars, factories etc: **air/environmental/water etc pollutants** *New regulations will reduce hazardous air pollutants.* | *a dumping ground for* **toxic pollutants** | **chemical/industrial etc pollutants** *industrial pollutants in the lake*

pol·lute /pəˈluːt/ *v* [T] **1** to make air, water, soil etc dangerously dirty and not suitable for people to use: *beaches polluted by raw sewage* | *The factory pollutes the air and water.* | **heavily/severely/badly etc polluted** *The island has been seriously polluted by a copper mine.* | **pollute sth with sth** *The rivers had been polluted with aluminium.* **2** to spoil or ruin something that used to be good: *an artist spiritually polluted by money and fame* **3 pollute sb's mind** to give someone immoral thoughts and spoil their character: *Violence on television is polluting the minds of our children.*

pol·lut·ed /pəˈluːtɪd/ *adj* dangerously dirty and not suitable for people to use: *one of the most polluted areas in the world* | **polluted air/water/rivers etc** *The project's aim is to clean up polluted land.* | **heavily/seriously/severely polluted** *The lake is seriously polluted.*

pol·lut·er /pəˈluːtə $ -ər/ *n* [C] a person or organization that causes pollution: *The polluter should pay for the cost of the clean-up.* | **big/major/main etc polluter** *a list of Canada's worst polluters*

pol·lu·tion W2 /pəˈluːʃən/ *n* [U]
1 the process of making air, water, soil etc dangerously dirty and not suitable for people to use, or the state of being dangerously dirty: *California's tough anti-pollution laws* | **air/water/soil pollution** *air pollution from traffic fumes* | **pollution prevention/standards/control** *The costs of pollution control must be considered.*
2 substances that make air, water, soil etc dangerously dirty: *a plan to* **reduce pollution** | **industrial/chemical etc pollution** *the effects of industrial pollution on the population* | *The chemicals have been identified as a* **source of pollution.** → NOISE POLLUTION; → see picture at ENVIRONMENT

Pol·ly·an·na /ˌpɒliˈænə $ ˌpɑː-/ *n* [C usually singular] someone who is always happy and always thinks something good is going to happen

po·lo /ˈpəʊləʊ $ ˈpoʊloʊ/ *n* [U] a game played between two teams of players who ride on horses and hit a small ball with long-handled wooden hammers → WATER POLO

polo neck *n* [C] *BrE* a shirt or SWEATER that has a high collar that folds down and fits closely around the neck; 🔲 **turtleneck** *AmE*: *a polo-neck sweater*

polo shirt *n* [C] a shirt that has a collar, a few buttons near the neck, and is pulled on over the head

pol·ter·geist /ˈpɒltəɡaɪst $ ˈpoʊltər-/ *n* [C] a GHOST that makes objects move around and causes strange noises

pol·y /ˈpɒli $ ˈpɑːli/ *n plural* **polys** [C] *BrE informal* a POLYTECHNIC

poly- /pɒli $ pɑː-/ *prefix* many: *polysyllabic* (=with three or more SYLLABLES)

pol·y·es·ter /ˈpɒliestə, ˌpɒliˈestə◂ $ ˈpɑːliestər/ *n* [U] an artificial material used to make cloth: *a blue polyester shirt*

pol·y·eth·y·lene /ˌpɒliˈeθəliːn $ ˌpɑː-/ *n* [U] *AmE* a strong light plastic used to make bags, sheets for covering food, small containers etc; 🔲 **polythene** *BrE*

po·lyg·a·my /pəˈlɪɡəmi/ *n* [U] the practice of having more than one husband or wife at the same time; → **bigamy, monogamy** —**polygamous** *adj*: *polygamous societies*

pol·y·glot /ˈpɒliɡlɒt $ ˈpɑːliɡlɑːt/ *adj formal* speaking or using many languages; 🔲 **multilingual**: *a polyglot population* —**polyglot** *n* [C]

pol·y·gon /ˈpɒliɡən $ ˈpɑːliɡɑːn/ *n* [C] *technical* a flat shape with three or more sides —**polygonal** /pəˈlɪɡənəl/ *adj*

pol·y·graph /ˈpɒliɡrɑːf $ ˈpɑːliɡræf/ *n* [C] a piece of equipment that is used by the police to find out whether someone is telling the truth; 🔲 **lie detector**: *The suspect was given a polygraph test.*

pol·y·he·dron /ˌpɒliˈhiːdrən $ ˌpɑː-/ *n* [C] *technical* a solid shape with many sides

pol·y·math /ˈpɒlimæθ $ ˈpɑː-/ *n* [C] *formal* someone who has a lot of knowledge about many different subjects

pol·y·mer /ˈpɒlimə $ ˈpɑːlimər/ *n* [C] a chemical COMPOUND that has a simple structure of large MOLECULES

pol·y·mor·phous /ˌpɒliˈmɔːfəs◂ $ ˌpɑːliˈmɔːr-/ also **pol·y·mor·phic** /-fɪk◂/ *adj technical* having many forms, styles etc during the stages of development

pol·y·no·mi·al /ˌpɒliˈnəʊmiəl $ ˌpɑːliˈnoʊ-/ *n* [C] *technical* a statement in ALGEBRA that contains several different numbers and signs which are equal to a specific amount: *polynomial equations*

pol·yp /ˈpɒlɪp $ ˈpɑː-/ *n* [C] **1** a small lump that grows inside your body because of an illness, but is not likely to harm you **2** a very simple sea animal that has a body like a tube: *a coral polyp*

po·lyph·o·ny /pəˈlɪfəni/ *n* [U] a type of music in which several different tunes or notes are sung or played together at the same time —**polyphonic** /ˌpɒliˈfɒnɪk◂ $ ˌpɑːliˈfɑː-/ *adj*

pol·y·pro·py·lene /ˌpɒliˈprəʊpɪliːn $ ˌpɑːliˈproʊ-/ *n* [U] a hard light plastic material

po·lys·e·mous /pəˈlɪsɪməs, ˌpɒliˈsiːməs $ ˌpɑːliˈsiːməs◂/ *adj technical* a polysemous word has two or more different meanings —**polysemy** /pəˈlɪsɪmi, ˈpɒlɪˌsiːmi $ ˈpɑːlɪˌsiːmi, pəˈlɪsɪmi/ *n* [U]

pol·y·sty·rene /ˌpɒliˈstaɪriːn◂ $ ˌpɑː-/ *n* [U] *BrE* a soft light plastic material that prevents heat or cold from passing through it, used especially for making containers; 🔲 **Styrofoam**

pol·y·syl·lab·ic /ˌpɒliˈlæbɪk◂ $ ˌpɑː-/ *adj technical* a polysyllabic word has three or more SYLLABLES —**polysyllable** /ˈpɒliˌsɪləbəl $ ˈpɑː-/ *n* [C]

pol·y·tech·nic /ˌpɒliˈteknɪk $ ˌpɑː-/ *n* [C] **1** a type of British college similar to a university, which provided training and degrees in many subjects, and existed until 1993 **2** a word used in the names of high schools or colleges in the US, where you can study technical or scientific subjects: *Baltimore Polytechnic Institute*

pol·y·the·is·m /ˈpɒliθiːɪzəm $ ˈpɑː-/ *n* [U] the belief that there is more than one god; → **monotheism** —**polytheistic** /ˌpɒliθiˈɪstɪk◂ $ ˌpɑː-/ *adj*

pol·y·thene /ˈpɒlɪθiːn $ ˈpɑː-/ *n* [U] *BrE* a strong light plastic used to make bags, sheets for covering food, small containers etc; 🔲 **polyethylene** *AmE*

pol·y·un·sat·u·ra·ted /ˌpɒliʌnˈsætʃəreɪtɪd◂ $ ˌpɑː-/ *adj* polyunsaturated fats or oils come from vegetables and plants, and are considered to be better for your health than animal fats; → **saturated fat** —**polyunsaturate** /-rɪt/ *n* [C]

pol·y·u·re·thane /ˌpɒliˈjʊərəθeɪn $ ˌpɑːliˈjʊr-/ *n* [U] a plastic used to make paints and VARNISH

pom /pɒm $ pɑːm/ also **pommy** or **pommie** *n* [C] *not polite* an offensive word for someone from Britain, used in Australia and New Zealand

po·made /pəˈmeɪd, pəˈmɑːd $ poʊˈmeɪd/ *n* [U] a sweet-smelling oily substance men used to rub on their hair to make it smooth, especially in the past

po·man·der /pəˈmændə, pəʊ- $ ˈpoʊmændər/ *n* [C] a box or ball that contains dried flowers and HERBS and is used to make clothes or a room smell pleasant

pom·e·gran·ate /ˈpɒmɪˌgrænɪt $ ˈpɑːmə-/ *n* [C] a round fruit that has a lot of small juicy red seeds that you can eat and a thick reddish skin

pom·mel /ˈpʌməl/ *n* [C] **1** the high, rounded part at the front of a horse's SADDLE **2** the round end of a sword handle

'pommel horse *n* [C] a piece of equipment used in GYMNASTICS that has two handles on top, which you hold on to when you jump or swing over it

pom·my, **pommie** /ˈpɒmi $ ˈpɑː-/ *n plural* **pommies** [C] a POM

pomp /pɒmp $ pɑːmp/ *n* [U] *formal* all the impressive clothes, decorations, music etc that are traditional for an important official or public ceremony: *The queen's birthday was celebrated with great* **pomp and ceremony**. | *all the* **pomp and circumstance** (=an impressive ceremony) *of a treaty signing*

pom·pom /ˈpɒmpɒm $ ˈpɑːmpɑːm/ *also* **pom·pon** /-pɒn $ -pɑːn/ *n* [C] **1** a small soft ball used as a decoration on clothing, especially hats **2** a large round ball of loose plastic strings connected to a handle, used by CHEERLEADERS

pom·pous /ˈpɒmpəs $ ˈpɑːm-/ *adj* someone who is pompous thinks that they are important, and shows this by being very formal and using long words – used to show disapproval: *He seems rather pompous.* | *the book's pompous style* —**pompously** *adv* —**pomposity** /pɒmˈpɒsɪti $ pɑːmˈpɑː-, / *also* **pompousness** /ˈpɒmpəsnəs ˈpɑːm-/ *n* [U]

ponce¹ /pɒns $ pɑːns/ *n* [C] *BrE informal* **1** *taboo* an offensive word for a man who dresses or behaves in a way that is typical of women or who people think is a HOMOSEXUAL. Do not use this word. **2** a PIMP

ponce² *v*
  ponce about/around *phr v BrE informal* to waste time doing silly things: *He's been poncing about all day.*

pon·cho /ˈpɒntʃəʊ $ ˈpɑːntʃoʊ/ *n plural* **ponchos** [C] a type of coat consisting of one large piece of cloth, with a hole in the middle for your head

ponc·y, **poncey** /ˈpɒnsi $ ˈpɑː-/ *adj BrE informal not polite* an offensive word used about people or things that seem typical of HOMOSEXUAL men: *a poncy suit*

pond S3 /pɒnd $ pɑːnd/ *n* [C]
1 a small area of fresh water that is smaller than a lake, that is either natural or artificially made
2 across the pond *also* **on the other side of the pond** *informal* on the other side of the Atlantic Ocean in the US or in Britain: *my cousins from across the pond*

pon·der /ˈpɒndə $ ˈpɑːndər/ *v* [I,T] *formal* to spend time thinking carefully and seriously about a problem, a difficult question, or something that has happened; ▣ **consider**: *He continued to ponder the problem as he walked home.* | [+on/over/about] *The university board is still pondering over the matter.* | **ponder how/what/whether** *Jay stood still for a moment, pondering whether to go or not.*

pon·der·ous /ˈpɒndərəs $ ˈpɑːn-/ *adj* **1** slow or awkward because of being very big and heavy: *an elephant's ponderous walk* **2** boring, very serious, and seeming to progress very slowly: *a ponderous and difficult book* | *The system, though ponderous, works.* —**ponderously** *adv* —**ponderousness** *n* [U]

'pond scum *n* [U] **1** *AmE informal* someone that you do not like, respect, or trust: *He's lower than pond scum.* **2** ALGAE

pong /pɒŋ $ pɑːŋ/ *n* [C usually singular] *BrE informal* an unpleasant smell: *an awful pong in the fridge* —**pong** *v* [I]

pon·tiff /ˈpɒntɪf $ ˈpɑːn-/ *n* [C] *formal* the Pope

pon·tif·i·cal /pɒnˈtɪfɪkəl $ pɑːn-/ *adj formal* **1** relating to the Pope **2** speaking as if you think your judgment or opinion is always right

pon·tif·i·cate¹ /pɒnˈtɪfɪˌkeɪt $ pɑːn-/ *v* [I] to give your opinion about something in a way that shows you think you are always right: [+about/on] *Politicians are always pontificating about education.*

pon·tif·i·cate² /pɒnˈtɪfɪkɪt $ pɑːn-/ *n* [C] the position or period of being Pope

pon·toon /pɒnˈtuːn $ pɑːn-/ *n* **1** [C] one of several metal containers or boats that are fastened together to support a floating bridge **2** [C] one of two hollow metal containers fastened to the bottom of a plane so that it can come down onto water and float **3** [U] *BrE* a card game, usually played for money; ▣ **blackjack** *AmE*

pon'toon bridge *n* [C] a floating bridge which is supported by several pontoons

po·ny¹ /ˈpəʊni $ ˈpoʊ-/ *n plural* **ponies** [C] a small horse → **PIT PONY, SHETLAND PONY**

pony² *v* **ponied, ponying, ponies**
  pony up (sth) *phr v AmE informal* to find or produce a particular amount of money: *All investors had to pony up a minimum of $5000.*

po·ny·tail /ˈpəʊniteɪl $ ˈpoʊ-/ *n* [C] hair tied together at the back of your head and falling like a horse's tail → see picture at **HAIRSTYLE**

'pony-trekking *n* [U] *BrE* the activity of riding through the countryside on ponies

poo /puː/ *n informal* **1** [C,U] solid waste from the BOWELS; ▣ **poop** *AmE* **2** [C usually singular] the act of passing waste from the BOWELS; ▣ **poop** *AmE* —**poo** *v* [I,T] *informal*

pooch /puːtʃ/ *n* [C] *informal* a dog – often used humorously

poo·dle /ˈpuːdl/ *n* [C] **1** a dog with thick curly hair **2 be sb's poodle** *BrE informal* if someone is another person's poodle, they always do what the other person tells them to do

poof¹ /pʊf, puːf/ *also* **poof·ter** /ˈpʊftə, ˈpuːf- $ -ər/ *n* [C] *BrE taboo informal* a very offensive word for a HOMOSEXUAL man. Do not use this word.

poof² *interjection* used when talking about something that happened suddenly: *Then poof! She was gone.*

poof·y /ˈpʊfi, ˈpuːfi/ *adj* **1** *AmE* poofy hair or clothes look big and soft or filled with air: *a blouse with big poofy sleeves* **2** *BrE informal not polite* an offensive word meaning typical of a HOMOSEXUAL man

pooh /puː/ *interjection* **1** *BrE* used when there is a very unpleasant smell; ▣ **pew** *AmE* **2** *old-fashioned* used when you think an idea, suggestion, effort etc is stupid or not very good: *Pooh! You can't finish that paper by tomorrow.*

pooh-bah /ˈpuː bɑː/ *n* [C] *informal* someone who is important or powerful – used to show that you do not respect them very much: *the pooh-bahs of the technology industry*

pooh-'pooh *v* [T] *informal* to say that you think that an idea, suggestion, effort etc is silly or not very good: *He pooh-poohed herbal remedies at first.*

pool

cue ball
pool balls — cue
pocket — cushion
baize
pool table

pool¹ S2 W2 /puːl/ *n*
1 FOR SWIMMING [C] a hole or container that has been specially made and filled with water so that people can swim or play in it; ▣ **swimming pool**: *They have a nice pool in their backyard.* | *a shallow pool*

suitable for children

2 AREA OF WATER [C] a small area of still water in a hollow place: *pools of water with tiny fish in them* | *Mosquitoes breed in stagnant pools of water.*

3 pool of water/blood/light etc a small area of liquid or light on a surface: *A guard found him lying in a pool of blood.* | *a pool of light formed by the street lamp above*

4 GAME [U] a game in which you use a stick to hit numbered balls into holes around a table, which is often played in bars: **shoot/play pool** *We went to the pub and played pool.*

5 GROUP OF PEOPLE [C] a group of people who are available to work or to do an activity when they are needed: [+of] *a pool of talented applicants to choose from* | *The region has a large and talented labour pool.*

6 SHARED MONEY/THINGS [C usually singular] a number of things or an amount of money that is shared by a group of people: *Both partners put money into a common pool.*

7 the pools a system in Britain in which people try to win money each week by guessing the results of football games: *I do the pools sometimes.* | *Dad won £40 on the pools.*

8 SPORTS [C] *AmE* a game in which people try to win money by guessing the result of a sports game, or the money that is collected from these people for this: *the office basketball pool*

pool² v [T] to combine your money, ideas, skills etc with those of other people so that you can all use them: *Investors agreed to pool their resources to develop the property.* | *The students worked together, pooling their knowledge.*

pool hall n [C] *AmE* a building where people go to play pool

pool room n [C] a room used for playing pool, especially in a bar

pool·room /'pu:lrum, -ru:m/ n *old-fashioned* [C] a pool hall

pool·side /'pu:lsaɪd/ adj [only before noun] near or on the side of a swimming pool: *a poolside bar* —**poolside** n [singular]: *We met down at the poolside.*

poop¹ /pu:p/ n **1** [U] *AmE informal* solid waste from the BOWELS; ➡ **poo** *BrE* **2** [singular] *AmE informal* the act of passing waste from the BOWELS; ➡ **poo** *BrE*

poop² v [I] *AmE informal* to pass solid waste from the BOWELS; ➡ **poo** → **PARTY POOPER**

poop out phr v *AmE informal* **1** to stop trying to do something because you are tired, bored etc: *Dan pooped out about halfway through the race.* **2** to decide not to do something you have already said you would do, because you are tired or not interested: [+on] *'Is Bill coming along?' 'Nah, he's pooping out on us.'* **3** if a machine or piece of equipment poops out, it stops working: *The laptop's battery pooped out after only two hours.*

poop deck n [C] the floor on the raised part at the back of an old sailing ship

pooped /pu:pt/ also **pooped 'out** adj [not before noun] *AmE informal* very tired; ➡ **exhausted**: *I was really pooped by the end of the day.*

poop·er scoop·er /'pu:pə ˌsku:pə $ -pər ˌsku:pər/ n [C] *informal* a small SPADE and a container, used by dog owners for removing their dogs' solid waste from the streets

poo-poo n [C,U] *informal* POO

poop sheet n [C] *AmE informal* written official instructions or information

poor S1 W1 /pɔ: $ pur/ adj *comparative* **poorer**, *superlative* **poorest**

1 NO MONEY a) having very little money and not many possessions; ➡ **rich**: *Her family were so poor they couldn't afford to buy her new clothes.* | *An area where poor people lived* | *one of the poorest countries in the world* | *a poor part of Chicago* (=where a lot of poor people live) | *My grandparents grew up dirt poor*

(=very poor). | **desperately/extremely poor** *Many of the families are desperately poor.* **b)** the poor [plural] people who are poor: *It's the government's responsibility to help the poor.* | the rural/urban/working poor *tax relief for the working poor*

2 NOT GOOD not as good as it could be or should be: *The soil in this area is very poor.* | *poor rates of pay* | *He blames himself for the team's poor performance.* | of poor quality (=not made well or not made of good materials) *The jacket was of very poor quality.* | poor hearing/eyesight/memory *Her hearing is poor, so speak fairly loudly.* | make/do a poor job of doing sth *The builders did a really poor job of fixing our roof.*

3 SYMPATHY [only before noun] *spoken* used to show sympathy for someone because they are so unlucky, unhappy etc: *Poor kid, he's had a rough day.* | *You poor thing, you've had a hard time of it, haven't you?* | *Poor old Ted was sick for weeks.*

4 NOT GOOD AT STH not good at doing something: *a poor public speaker* | [+at] *He's poor at sports.*

5 HEALTH someone whose health is poor is ill or weak for a long period of time: *My parents are both in rather poor health.*

6 poor in sth lacking something that is needed: *The country is poor in natural resources.*

7 a poor second/third etc the act of finishing a race, competition etc a long way behind the person ahead of you: *McLean won easily, and Benson was a poor second.* | come (in) a poor second/third etc *BrE: The Socialists came a poor second with 26.5% of the vote.*

8 the poor man's sb used to say that someone is like a very famous performer, writer etc but is not as good as they are: *He was the poor man's Elvis Presley.*

9 the poor man's sth used to say that something can be used for the same purpose as something else, and is much cheaper: *Herring is the poor man's salmon.*

10 poor relation *BrE* someone or something that is not treated as well as other members of a group or is much less successful than they are: [+of] *Theatre musicians tend to be the poor relations of the musical profession.* → be in bad/poor taste at TASTE¹ (6); → POORLY

WORD FOCUS: words meaning POOR
be hard up/be broke also be skint *BrE informal* to have very little money at the present time and be unable to buy the things that you want | destitute having no money and nowhere to live, especially because something terrible has happened | poverty-stricken very poor

poor boy also **po' boy** /'pɔ: bɔɪ/ n [C] *AmE* a sandwich made with a long bread roll – used especially in the southern US; ➡ **submarine sandwich**

poor·house /'pɔ:haus $ 'pur-/ n [C] **1** the state of not having any money: *If Jimmy keeps spending like this, he's going to end up in the poorhouse.* **2** a building where very poor people in the past could live and be fed, which was paid for with public money; ➡ **workhouse**

poor·ly¹ /'pɔ:li $ 'purli/ adv badly: *Jana's doing poorly in school.* | *poorly educated workers* | *The article was poorly written.*

poorly² adj *BrE informal* ill: *Matt's wife's been very poorly.*

poorly 'off adj [not before noun] *BrE* someone who is poorly off does not have very much money; ➡ **well off**

poo·tle /'pu:tl/ v [I + about/around] *BrE spoken* to spend time pleasantly, doing things that are not very important

pop¹ S3 /pop $ pɑ:p/ v popped, popping

1 COME OUT/OFF [I always + adv/prep] to come suddenly or unexpectedly out of or away from something: [+out/off/up etc] *The top button popped off my shirt.* | *The ball popped out of Smith's hands and onto the ground.* | out/up popped sth *The egg cracked open and out popped a tiny head.* | *The lid popped open and juice spilled all over the floor.*

2 GO QUICKLY [I always + adv/prep] *especially BrE spoken* to go somewhere quickly, suddenly, or in a way that you did not expect: [+**in/out/by** etc] *Why don't you pop by the next time you're in town?* | *I need to pop into the drugstore for a second.* | [+**round**] *BrE: Could you pop round to the shop for some bread?*

3 QUICKLY PUT STH [T always + adv/prep] *especially BrE informal* to quickly put something somewhere, usually for a short time: **pop sth in/around/over** etc *I'll just pop these cakes into the oven.* | **pop sth round sth** *BrE: Barry popped his head round the door to say hello.*

4 SHORT SOUND [I,T] to make a short sound like a small explosion, or to make something do this: *The wood sizzled and popped in the fire.*

5 BURST [I,T] to burst, or to make something burst, with a short explosive sound: *A balloon popped.*

6 EARS [I] if your ears pop, you feel the pressure in them suddenly change, for example when you go up or down quickly in a plane

7 sb's eyes popped (out of their head) *especially BrE spoken* used to say that someone looked extremely surprised or excited

8 pop into your head/mind to suddenly think of something: *All at once an idea popped into her head.*

9 pop the question *informal* to ask someone to marry you: *Hasn't Bill popped the question yet?*

10 pop pills *informal* to take PILLS too often, or to take too many at one time

11 HIT [T] *AmE spoken* to hit someone: *If you say that again, I'll pop you one.*

12 POPCORN [I,T] to cook POPCORN until it swells and bursts open, or to be cooked in this way

13 pop your clogs *BrE humorous* to die

pop off *phr v informal*
to die suddenly

pop sth ⇔ **on** *phr v BrE spoken*
1 to quickly put on a piece of clothing: *Here, pop on your pyjamas and then we'll read a story.*
2 to quickly turn on a piece of electrical equipment: *Pop the kettle on, would you?*

pop out *phr v informal*
if words pop out, you suddenly say them without thinking first: *I didn't mean to say it like that – it just popped out.*

pop up *phr v*
to appear, sometimes unexpectedly: *Click here, and a list of files will pop up.* | *Her name keeps popping up in the newspapers.* → POP-UP

pop² [S3] [W3] *n*
1 MUSIC [U] modern music that is popular, especially with young people, and usually consists of simple tunes with a strong beat; → **pop music**: *a new pop record* | *a pop star* | *a pop festival*
2 SOUND [C] a sudden short sound like a small explosion: *the pop of a champagne cork* | *The balloon went* **pop** (=made a sudden short sound).
3 DRINK [C,U] *informal* a sweet drink with bubbles but no alcohol, or a glass or can of this drink; ▤ **soda**: *a bottle of pop* | *Can you get me a pop while you're up?*
4 take a pop at sb *BrE informal* to criticize someone in public: *When you're a professional footballer, you expect people to take a pop at you now and again.*
5 $7/$50/25¢ etc a pop *AmE spoken* used when each of something costs a particular amount of money: *Tickets for the show are a hundred bucks a pop.*
6 FATHER [C] also **Pops** *AmE old-fashioned* father – used especially when you are talking to your father
7 pops *AmE* CLASSICAL music that most people know, especially people who do not usually like this type of music: *a pops concert* | *the Boston Pops Orchestra*

pop. the written abbreviation of *population*

pop art *n* [U] a type of art that was popular in the 1960s, which shows ordinary objects, such as advertisements, or things you see in people's homes

pop·corn /'pɒpkɔːn $ 'pɑːpkɔːrn/ *n* [U] a kind of corn that swells and bursts open when heated, and is usually eaten warm with salt or sugar as a SNACK

pop culture *n* [U] music, films, products etc in a particular society that are familiar to and popular with most ordinary people in that society

Pope /pəʊp $ poʊp/ *n* [C] **1** the leader of the Roman Catholic church; → **papal**: *The Pope will visit El Salvador this year.* | *Pope John XXIII* **2** Is the Pope (a) Catholic? *informal* used to say that something is clearly true or certain – used humorously: *'Do you think they'll win?' 'Is the Pope Catholic?'*

pop·e·ry /'pəʊpəri $ 'poʊ-/ *n* [U] *taboo especially BrE* an offensive word for the Roman Catholic religion. Do not use this word.

pop-'eyed *adj informal* **1** having your eyes wide open, because you are surprised, excited, or angry **2** having eyes that stick out slightly

pop fly *n* [C] a type of hit in baseball in which the ball is hit straight up into the air

pop group *n* [C] *especially BrE* a group of people who sing and perform POP MUSIC

pop-gun *n* [C] a toy gun that fires small objects, such as CORKS, with a loud noise

pop·ish /'pəʊpɪʃ $ 'poʊ-/ *adj taboo especially BrE* offensive word for something that is related to the Roman Catholic religion. Do not use this word.

pop·lar /'pɒplə $ 'pɑːplər/ *n* [C] a very tall straight thin tree that grows very fast

pop·lin /'pɒplɨn $ 'pɑːp-/ *n* [U] a strong shiny cotton cloth

pop music *n* [U] modern music that is popular, especially with young people, and usually consists of simple tunes with a strong beat

pop·o·ver /'pɒpəʊvə $ 'pɑːpoʊvər/ *n* [C] *AmE* a light, hollow MUFFIN (=small cake) made with eggs, milk, and flour

pop·pa /'pɒpə $ 'pɑːpə/ *n AmE* another spelling of PAPA

pop·pa·dom, **poppadum** /'pɒpədəm $ 'pɑː-/ *n* [C] a large circular piece of very thin flat Indian bread cooked in oil

pop·per /'pɒpə $ 'pɑːpər/ *n* **1** [C] *BrE informal* a small metal thing that is used to fasten clothes, which works when you press its two parts together; ▤ **snap** *AmE* **2 poppers** [plural] *informal* an illegal drug in the form of a liquid, which people take for pleasure by breathing it in

pop·pet /'pɒpɨt $ 'pɑː-/ *n* [C] *BrE spoken* used to talk to or about a child or animal you like very much: *Come here, poppet.*

pop psy'chology *n* [U] ways of dealing with personal problems that are made popular on television or in books, but are not considered scientific

pop·py /'pɒpi $ -'pɑː-/ *n plural* **poppies** [C] a plant that has brightly coloured, usually red, flowers and small black seeds

pop·py·cock /'pɒpikɒk $ 'pɑːpikɑːk/ *n* [U] *old-fashioned* nonsense

pop·py·seed /'pɒpisiːd $ 'pɑː-/ *n* [U] the small black seeds of the poppy plant, used in cakes, bread etc

pop quiz *n* [C] *AmE* a short test that a teacher gives without any warning, in order to check whether students have been studying

Pop·si·cle /'pɒpsɨkəl $ 'pɑːp-/ *n* [C] *AmE trademark* a food made of juice that is frozen onto sticks; ▤ **ice lolly** *BrE*

pop star *n* [C] a famous and successful entertainer who plays or sings POP MUSIC

pop·u·lace /'pɒpjɨləs $ 'pɑː-/ *n* [singular also + plural verb *BrE*] *formal* the people who live in a country: *the effects of the war on the local populace*

pop·u·lar [S2] [W1] /'pɒpjɨlə $ 'pɑːpjələr/ *adj*
1 liked by a lot of people; ▤ **unpopular**: *Hilary was popular at school.* | *a popular holiday resort* | *Coffee is probably the most popular drink in the world.* | **hugely/ enormously/immensely** etc **popular** *Guerrero's music is hugely popular in Latin America.* | [+**with/among**] *The President is very popular with Jewish voters.*

2 [only before noun] done by a lot of people in a society, group etc: *the closest popular vote in U.S. presidential history* | *The government has little* **popular support** *among women voters.* | *Kaplan's latest recording has received considerable* **popular acclaim** (=it is liked by a lot of people). | **popular belief/opinion/view** (=a belief, opinion etc that a lot of people have) *a survey of Hispanic-American popular opinion* | *Contrary to* **popular belief** (=in spite of what many people believe), *gorillas are basically shy, gentle creatures.* | *a* **popular movement** *for democracy*
3 [only before noun] relating to ordinary people, or intended for ordinary people: *Wintour's writing is full of references to American* **popular culture.** | *Steele was ridiculed by the popular press.* → POP MUSIC

pop·u·lar·i·ty /ˌpɒpjʊˈlærɪti $ ˌpɑː-/ n [U] when something or someone is liked or supported by a lot of people: [+of] *The popularity of the Internet has soared.* | *The president's* **popularity** *has* **declined** *considerably.* | **gain/grow/increase in popularity** (=start to be liked by many people) *Country music is growing in popularity.*

pop·u·lar·ize also **-ise** BrE /ˈpɒpjʊləraɪz $ ˈpɑː-/ v [T] **1** to make something well known and liked: *Bob Marley popularized reggae music in the 1970s.* **2** to make a difficult subject or idea able to be easily understood by ordinary people who have no special knowledge about it: *Skinner was the psychologist who popularized behavior modification.* —**popularization** /ˌpɒpjʊləraɪˈzeɪʃən $ ˌpɑːpjʊlərə-/ n [U]

pop·u·lar·ly /ˈpɒpjʊləli $ ˈpɑːpjʊlər-/ adv by most or many people: *The President of Korea is popularly elected every five years.* | **popularly believed/thought/ called etc** *Vitamin C is popularly believed to prevent colds.* | *The Church of Jesus Christ of Latter-Day Saints is* **popularly known as** *the Mormon Church.*

pop·u·late /ˈpɒpjʊleɪt $ ˈpɑː-/ v [T usually passive] if an area is populated by a particular group of people, they live there: *The highlands are populated mainly by peasant farmers.* | **densely/heavily/highly/thickly populated** (=with a lot of people) *one of the most densely populated areas in the world* | **sparsely/thinly/lightly populated** (=with very few people)

pop·u·la·tion S2 W1 /ˌpɒpjʊˈleɪʃən $ ˌpɑː-/ n
1 [C] the number of people living in a particular area, country etc: [+of] *India has a population of more than 1 billion.* | **population explosion/boom** (=a quick increase in the population of an area)
2 [C usually singular] all of the people who live in a particular area: *Most of the world's population doesn't get enough to eat.* | **white/French/urban etc population** (=part of the group of people who live in a particular area who are white, French etc) *South Florida has a large Jewish population.*
3 centre of population/population centre a city, town etc: *Cromer is the main centre of population in this area.*

pop·u·list /ˈpɒpjʊlɪst $ ˈpɑː-/ adj relating to or representing ordinary people, rather than rich or very highly educated people: *a populist campaign* —**populist** n [C] —**populism** n [U]

pop·u·lous /ˈpɒpjʊləs $ ˈpɑː-/ adj formal a populous area has a large population in relation to its size: *Hong Kong is one of the most populous areas in the world.*

pop-up¹ adj **1 pop-up book/card etc** a book, card etc with a picture that stands up when you open the pages **2 pop-up menu/window** a MENU or WINDOW that can appear suddenly on a computer screen while you are using it

pop-up² n [C] a WINDOW, often containing an advertisement, that suddenly appears on a computer screen, especially when you are looking at a website

porce·lain /ˈpɔːslɪn $ ˈpɔːrsələn/ n [U] **1** a hard shiny white substance that is used for making expensive plates, cups etc; → **china:** *a porcelain vase* **2** plates, cups etc made of this

porch /pɔːtʃ $ pɔːrtʃ/ n [C] **1** BrE an entrance covered by a roof outside the front door of a house or church **2** AmE a structure built onto the front or back entrance of a house, with a floor and a roof but no walls

por·cine /ˈpɔːsaɪn $ ˈpɔːr-/ adj formal looking like or relating to pigs

por·cu·pine /ˈpɔːkjʊpaɪn $ ˈpɔːr-/ n [C] an animal with long, sharp parts growing all over its back and sides

pore¹ /pɔː $ pɔːr/ n [C] one of the small holes in your skin that liquid, especially SWEAT, can pass through, or a similar hole in the surface of a plant

pore² v
pore over sth phr v to read or look at something very carefully for a long time: *She was poring over a book.*
⚠ Do not confuse **pore** with the verb **pour,** which has the same pronunciation but means 'to make liquid flow'.

pork /pɔːk $ pɔːrk/ n [U] **1** the meat from pigs: *pork chops* **2** AmE informal government money spent in a particular area in order to get political advantages – used to show disapproval: *a bill filled with pork projects*

pork barrel n [singular, U] AmE informal a government plan to increase the amount of money spent in a particular area, done in order to gain a political advantage – used to show disapproval: *pork-barrel spending*

pork·er /ˈpɔːkə $ ˈpɔːrkər/ n [C] **1** a young pig that is made fat before being killed for food **2** informal a fat person – often used humorously

pork pie n [C] BrE a small round PIE which contains pieces of cooked pork

pork rinds n [plural] AmE small pieces of pig fat that have been cooked in hot oil and are eaten as a SNACK

pork·y¹ /ˈpɔːki $ ˈpɔːrki/ adj informal fat – often used humorously

porky² also **porky pie** n plural **porkies** [C] BrE informal a lie: *Was he* **telling porkies** *again?*

porn /pɔːn $ pɔːrn/ also **porn·o** /ˈpɔːnəʊ $ ˈpɔːrnoʊ/ n [U] informal pornography: *the porn industry* | *a porno movie* → HARD PORN, SOFT PORN

por·nog·ra·phy /pɔːˈnɒgrəfi $ pɔːrˈnɑːg-/ n [U] magazines, films etc that show sexual acts and images in a way that is intended to make people feel sexually excited —**pornographer** n [C] —**pornographic** /ˌpɔːnəˈgræfɪk◂ $ ˌpɔːr-/ adj: *pornographic websites*

po·rous /ˈpɔːrəs/ adj **1** allowing liquid, air etc to pass slowly through many very small holes: *porous material* **2** easy to pass through or get into something: *the porous border between Haiti and the Dominican Republic*

por·poise /ˈpɔːpəs $ ˈpɔːr-/ n [C] a sea animal that looks similar to a DOLPHIN and breathes air

por·ridge /ˈpɒrɪdʒ $ ˈpɑː-, ˈpɔː-/ n [U] **1** OATS that are cooked with milk or water and served hot for breakfast; ▣ **oatmeal** AmE **2** BrE informal a period of time spent in prison: **do porridge** (=spend time in prison)

port¹ W2 /pɔːt $ pɔːrt/ n
1 WHERE SHIPS STOP [C,U] a place where ships can be loaded and unloaded: **be in port** *We'll have two days ashore while the ship is in port.* | **come into port/leave port** *The ferry was about to leave port.*
2 TOWN [C] a town or city with a HARBOUR or DOCKS where ships can be loaded or unloaded: *Britain's largest port*
3 COMPUTER [C] a part of a computer where you can connect another piece of equipment, such as a PRINTER
4 WINE [U] strong sweet Portuguese wine that is usually drunk after a meal: *a glass of port*
5 SIDE OF SHIP [U] the left side of a ship or aircraft when you are looking towards the front; ▣ **starboard:** *on the port side* | **to port** *The plane tilted to port.*
6 any port in a storm spoken used to say that you should take whatever help you can when you are in trouble, even if it has some disadvantages → PORT OF CALL

port² v [T] to move software from one computer system to another: **port sth from/to sth** *Can Windows applications be ported to Unix?* —**porting** n [U]

por·ta·ble¹ /ˈpɔːtəbəl $ ˈpɔːr-/ adj **1** able to be carried or moved easily: *a portable radio* **2** a portable computer program can be used on different computer systems **3 portable benefits** AmE health insurance, PENSION PLANS etc that workers can keep when they move from one job to another —**portability** /ˌpɔːtəˈbɪləti $ ˌpɔːr-/ n [U]

portable² n [C] a piece of electronic equipment that can be easily carried or moved: *Get a portable, not a big TV.*

port·age /ˈpɔːtɪdʒ $ ˈpɔːr-/ n [U] when people carry small boats over land from one river to another

Por·ta·kab·in /ˈpɔːtəkæbɪn $ ˈpɔːr-/ n [C] BrE trademark a very small building that can be used as a temporary office, CLASSROOM etc, and can be moved by truck

por·tal /ˈpɔːtl $ ˈpɔːrtl/ n [C] **1** a website that helps you find other websites **2** [usually plural] literary a tall and impressive gate or entrance to a building

Porta Potti, porta-potty /ˈpɔːtə ˌpɒti $ ˈpɔːrtə ˌpɑːti/ n [C] AmE trademark a toilet that is in a small plastic building that can be moved

port·cul·lis /pɔːtˈkʌlɪs $ pɔːrt-/ n [C] a strong iron gate that can be lowered over the entrance of a castle

por·tend /pɔːˈtend $ pɔːr-/ v [T] literary to be a sign that something is going to happen, especially something bad: *strange events that portend disaster*

por·tent /ˈpɔːtent $ ˈpɔːr-/ n [C] literary a sign or warning that something is going to happen; ◨ **omen**: [+of] *Some people believe the raven is a portent of death.*

por·ten·tous /pɔːˈtentəs $ pɔːr-/ adj **1** literary showing that something important is going to happen, especially something bad: *Recent developments are as portentous as the collapse of the Berlin Wall.* **2** trying to appear important and serious: *a portentous film*

por·ter /ˈpɔːtə $ ˈpɔːrtər/ n **1** [C] someone whose job is to carry people's bags at railway stations, airports etc **2** [C] BrE someone in charge of the entrance to a hotel, hospital etc **3** [C] BrE someone whose job is to carry heavy goods at markets **4** [C] AmE someone whose job is to look after the part of a train where people sleep **5** [C] AmE someone whose job is to look after a building by cleaning it, repairing things etc **6** [U] old-fashioned a dark brown bitter beer

por·ter·house steak /ˌpɔːtəhaus ˈsteɪk $ ˌpɔːrtər-/ n [C,U] a thick, flat piece of high quality BEEF

port·fo·li·o /pɔːtˈfəuliəu $ pɔːrtˈfouliou/ n plural **portfolios** [C] **1** a large flat case used especially for carrying pictures, documents etc **2** a set of pictures or other pieces of work that an artist, photographer etc has done: *You'll need to prepare a portfolio of your work.* **3** a group of STOCKS owned by a particular person or company: *an investment portfolio* **4** BrE the work that a particular government official is responsible for: *the foreign affairs portfolio*

port·hole /ˈpɔːthəul $ ˈpɔːrthoul/ n [C] a small round window on the side of a ship or plane

por·ti·co /ˈpɔːtɪkəu $ ˈpɔːrtɪkou/ n plural **porticoes** or **porticos** [C] a covered entrance to a building, consisting of a roof supported by PILLARS

por·tion¹ /ˈpɔːʃən $ ˈpɔːr-/ n **1** [C] a part of something larger, especially a part that is different from the other parts: [+of] *The front portion of the rocket breaks off.* | *The rent on his portion of the apartment was $500 a month.* | **significant/substantial/major/good portion** *The main character's childhood takes up a good portion of the film.* **2** [C] an amount of food for one person, especially when served in a restaurant; ◨ **serving, helping**: *Do you have any children's portions?* | [+of] *a huge portion of roast beef* | *He served generous portions* (=large portions) *of soup from a black pot.* **3** [usually singular] a share of something, such as responsibility, blame, or a duty, that is divided between a small number of people: [+of] *The other driver must bear a portion of the blame for the accident.*

portion² v

portion sth ⇔ **out** phr v BrE to divide something into parts and give it to several people: [+among] *The money was portioned out among them.*

port·ly /ˈpɔːtli $ ˈpɔːr-/ adj written someone who is portly, especially an old man, is fat and round: *a portly old gentleman*

port·man·teau /pɔːtˈmæntəu $ pɔːrtˈmæntou/ n plural **portmanteaus** or **portmanteaux** /-təuz $ -touz/ [C] old-fashioned a very large SUITCASE that opens into two parts

port'manteau ˌword n [C] technical a portmanteau word is made by combining the sound and meaning of two other words, for example 'edutainment' combines 'education' and 'entertainment'

ˌport of 'call n plural **ports of call** [C usually singular] **1** informal one of a series of places that you visit: *My first port of call will be the post office.* **2** a port where a ship stops on a journey from one place to another

ˌport of 'entry n plural **ports of entry** [C] a place, such as a port or airport, where people or goods can enter a country

por·trait¹ /ˈpɔːtrɪt $ ˈpɔːr-/ n [C] **1** a painting, drawing, or photograph of a person: *a family portrait* | [+of] *the artist's portrait of his mother* | *She's been commissioned to paint Jackson's portrait.*; → see picture at PAINTING **2** a description or representation of something: [+of] *a portrait of working life in America* → SELF-PORTRAIT

portrait² adj if a piece of paper, a page, a photograph etc is in a portrait position, it is placed on a surface or hung on a wall with its longer edges at the sides; ◨ **landscape**

por·trai·ture /ˈpɔːtrɪtʃə $ ˈpɔːrtrɪtʃər/ n [U] formal the art of painting or drawing pictures of people

por·tray /pɔːˈtreɪ $ pɔːr-/ v [T] **1 portray sb/sth as sth** to describe or show someone or something in a particular way, according to your opinion of them; ◨ **depict**: *Romantic artists portrayed nature as wild and powerful.* | *The President likes to portray himself as a friend of working people.* **2** to describe or represent something or someone; ◨ **depict**: *His most famous painting portrayed the death of Nelson.* | *Religion was portrayed in a negative way.* **3** to act the part of a character in a play, film, or television programme; ◨ **play**: *She portrays a dancer in the hit film.*

por·tray·al /pɔːˈtreɪəl $ pɔːr-/ n [C,U] the way someone or something is described or shown in a book, film, play etc: [+of] *the newspapers' portrayal of Islamic culture* | **accurate/realistic etc portrayal** *The film is not an accurate portrayal* (=correct portrayal) *of his life.*

Por·tu·guese¹ /ˌpɔːtʃʊˈgiːz $ ˌpɔːr-/ adj relating to Portugal, its people, or its language

Portuguese² n **1 the Portuguese** [plural] people from Portugal **2** [U] the language used in Portugal, Brazil, and some other countries

ˌPortuguese man-of-'war n [C] a very large, poisonous JELLYFISH

pose¹ [W3] /pəuz $ pouz/ v
1 CAUSE PROBLEM [T] to exist in a way that may cause a problem, danger, difficulty etc: **pose a threat/danger/risk** *Officials claim the chemical poses no real threat.* | **pose sth to/for sb/sth** *The events pose a challenge to the church's leadership.* | *Rising unemployment is posing serious problems for the administration.*
2 PICTURE [I] to sit or stand in a particular position in order to be photographed or painted, or to make someone do this: [+for] *We posed for photographs.*
3 **pose a question** to ask a question, especially one that needs to be carefully thought about: *In her book she poses the question, 'How much do we need to be happy?'*
4 **pose as sb** to pretend to be someone else, in order to deceive people: *Bryce was caught posing as a lawyer.*
5 TO IMPRESS PEOPLE [I] to dress or behave like a

rich and fashionable person in order to make other people notice you or admire you

pose² n [C] **1** the position in which someone stands or sits, especially in a painting, photograph etc: **in a pose** *a painting of the Duchess in a dramatic pose* | *Ann* **struck a pose** (=stood or sat in a particular position) *and smiled for the camera.* **2** behaviour in which someone pretends to have a quality or social position they do not really have, usually in order to make other people notice them or admire them: *Her confidence was merely a pose to hide her uncertainty.*

pos·er /'pəʊzə $ 'poʊzər/ n [C] *informal* **1** *BrE* also **po·seur** /pəʊ'zɜː $ poʊ'zɜːr/ someone who pretends to have a quality or social position they do not really have, usually in order to make people notice or admire them: *You meet a lot of posers in this job.* **2** a difficult question: *That's a real poser.*

posh¹ /pɒʃ $ pɑːʃ/ adj *informal* **1** a posh restaurant, hotel, car etc is expensive and looks as if it is used or owned by rich people: *a posh private school* **2** *BrE* upper class: *Her parents are terribly posh.*

posh² adv *BrE informal* **talk posh** to talk in an upper class way

pos·it /'pɒzɪt $ 'pɑː-/ v [T] *formal* to suggest that a particular idea should be accepted as a fact: **posit that** *He posited that each planet moved in a perfect circle.*

po·si·tion¹ S3 W1 /pə'zɪʃən/ n
1 WAY OF STANDING/SITTING ETC [C] the way someone is standing, sitting, or lying: *Lie in a* **comfortable position***.* | *Frankie* **shifted** *his* **position** *so that his knees would not become cramped.* | **sitting/kneeling/ standing position** *I struggled up into a sitting position.*
2 SITUATION [C] usually singular] the situation that someone is in, especially when this affects what they can and cannot do

> **in sb's position**
> **in the same/a similar position**
> **in a good/strong position (to do sth)**
> **in an enviable position** (=in a situation that other people would like to be in)
> **in a difficult/awkward/impossible position**
> **a position of strength** (=a situation in which you can get what you want)
> **financial/legal position**
> **strengthen/weaken sb's position** (=put someone in a better or worse situation)

I'm not sure what I would do if I were **in your position***.* | *We're* **in a strong position***, but we mustn't take victory for granted.* | *Next week we will be* **in a** *much* **better** *position to comment.* | *She is* **in the enviable position** *of having three job offers.* | *You're putting me in rather* **a difficult position***.* | *We must negotiate from a* **position of strength***.* | *the company's precarious* **financial position**

3 PLACE WHERE SB/STH IS [C] the place where someone or something is, especially in relation to other objects and places: [+of] *the position of the sun in the sky* | *Our hotel was in a superb* **central position** *near St Mark's Square.* | *the* **strategic position** (=useful or important position) *of Egypt in relation to the Arabian peninsula*
4 CORRECT PLACE [C,U] the place where someone or something is needed or supposed to be: **into position** *He pulled the ladder into position.* | **in/out of position** *All parking signs have now been placed in position.*
5 DIRECTION [C] the direction in which an object is pointing: **vertical/upright/horizontal position** *Make sure the container remains in an upright position.* | *She turned the switch to the 'on' position.*
6 OPINION [C] an opinion or judgment on a particular subject, especially the official opinion of a government, a political party, or someone in authority; ⊟ **attitude**: [+on] *What's the party's position on tax reform?* | *The principal* **took the position that** *the*

students didn't need music classes.* | *I hope you'll* **reconsider** *your* **position***.*
7 JOB [C] *formal* a job: **sb's position as sth** *Bill took up his new* **position** *as Works Director in October.* | [+of] *She has* **held** *the* **position** *of Chief Financial Officer since 1992.* | *Bruce is thinking of* **applying for** *the* **position***.* | *I'm sorry, the* **position has been filled** (=someone has been found to do the job).; → see box at **JOB**
8 LEVEL/RANK [C,U] someone's or something's level, authority, or importance in a society or organization: **the position of sb** *the position of women in society* | **position of power/authority/influence etc** *Many of his supporters used their positions of power for personal advantage.* | *As a priest, he was in a* **position of trust***.* | **abuse your position as sth** (=use your authority wrongly)
9 **be in a position to do sth** to be able to do something because you have the ability, money, or power to do it: *When I know all the facts, I'll be in a position to advise you.*
10 **be in no position to do sth** to be unable to do something because you do not have the ability, money, or power to do it: *You're unemployed and in no position to support a family.* | *Ned says I'm always late? He's in* **no position to talk** (=should not criticize he does the same thing).
11 RACE/COMPETITION [C,U] the place of someone or something in a race or competition in relation to the other people or things: **(in) 2nd/3rd/4th etc position** *Alesi* **finished** *in third* **position***.*
12 SPORTS [C] the area where someone plays in a sport, or the type of actions they are responsible for doing: *What* **position** *do you* **play***?*
13 **jockey/manoeuvre/jostle for position** to try to get an advantage over other people who are all trying to succeed in doing the same thing: *Firms adopt different strategies as they jockey for position.*
14 ARMY [C usually plural] a place where an army has put soldiers, guns etc: *an attack on the enemy positions*

> **WORD CHOICE: position, place, location, where, there**
> **Place** is a very general word for talking about where something or someone is: *the place where they live* | *Put this in a safe place.*
> **Position** can be used to talk about the place where something is in relation to other things or places: *the position of the table in the room*
> **Location** is used mainly in formal or business English to talk about where a building is: *a house in a central location* | *the location of the new headquarters*
> In ordinary spoken English, it is more usual to use words like **where, there, somewhere, anywhere** to talk about the place where something or someone is: *This is where (NOT the place where) I live.* | *My shoes were in the hall but they're not there (NOT in that place) now.* | *Let's have lunch somewhere different (NOT in a different place) today.*

position² v [T always + adv/prep] to carefully put something in a particular position: *Position the cursor before the letter you want to delete.* | **position yourself** *I positioned myself where I could see the door.*

pos·i·tion·al /pə'zɪʃənəl/ adj [only before noun] relating to the position or job of someone or something: *positional power or authority*

po'sition ,paper n [C] a written statement that shows how a department, organization etc intends to deal with something

pos·i·tive¹ S2 W2 /'pɒzɪtɪv $ 'pɑː-/ adj
1 ATTITUDE if you are positive about things, you are hopeful and confident, and think about what is good in a situation rather than what is bad; ⊟ **negative**: [+about] *You've got to be more positive about your work.* | **positive attitude/approach/outlook etc** *She's got a really positive attitude to life.* | *the power of* **positive thinking** | *'* **Think positive***!' she advised herself.*
2 GOOD THING good or useful; ⊟ **negative**

something positive
positive thing/aspect
positive effect/result/outcome
positive experience
be/have a positive influence (on sb)
positive role model (=someone good or successful that
   people want to be like)
make a positive contribution (=do something good in a
   situation)
on the positive side/on a positive note (=used when
   saying what is good about a situation)
in a positive light (=showing the good things about
   something)

---

*At least **something positive** has come out of the
situation.* | *Write down all the **positive things** about
your life.* | *The rural environment was having a **posi-
tive effect** on the children's health.* | *It's been a very
positive experience for her.* | *TV can **be a positive
influence**.* | *the **positive contribution** to the commu-
nity **made** by many older people* | *It's been a difficult
time but, **on the positive side**, I feel physically fine.* |
*Women should be portrayed **in a** more **positive light**.*

---

3 ACTION if you take positive action, you do something definite in order to try and achieve something:
*We need to **take positive steps** to improve the situation
of families in poverty.* | ***Positive action** was required.* |
*It's a relief to know that **something positive** is being
done.*
4 SUPPORT expressing support, agreement, or
approval; ☒ **negative: positive response/reaction** *The
response we've had from the public has been very
positive.* | *a lot of **positive feedback** from the
people of this city.* | [+**about**] *Most people have been very
positive about the show.*
5 SURE [not before noun] very sure, with no doubt at
all that something is right or true; ☒ **certain: positive
(that)** *Are you **absolutely positive** you locked the door?* |
'Are you sure about that?' 'Positive.'
6 SIGN showing that something is likely to succeed or
improve: *The fact that he's breathing on his own again is
a **positive sign**.*
7 PROOF positive **proof/evidence/identification** etc
proof etc that shows that there is no doubt that something is true: *The witness made a positive identification.*
8 SCIENTIFIC TEST showing signs of the medical condition or chemical that is being looked for; ☒ **nega-
tive**: *The test results came back positive.* | *athletes who
had **tested positive** for banned substances* | *children
who are HIV positive*
9 EMPHASIS [only before noun] spoken used to emphasize how good or bad something is; ☒ **total**: *The journey was a positive nightmare.*
10 NUMBER technical a positive number is more than
zero; ☒ **negative**
11 ELECTRICITY technical having the type of electrical charge that is carried by PROTONS; ☒ **negative**: *a
positive charge*

positive² *n* [C] a quality or feature that is good or
useful; ☒ **negative**: *You can find positives in any
situation.* | *Always emphasise **the positive**.* → FALSE
POSITIVE

,positive discrimi'nation *n* [U] *BrE* the practice of
giving a particular number of jobs, places at university
etc to people who are often treated unfairly because of
their race, sex etc; ☒ **affirmative action** *AmE*

pos·i·tive·ly /'pɒzɪtɪvli $ 'pɑː-/ *adv* **1** used to
emphasize that something is true, especially when this
seems surprising: *Some holiday destinations are **positively dangerous**.* **2** in a way that shows you agree
with something or want it to succeed; ☒ **negatively**: *It
is hoped that the industry will respond positively to this
new initiative.* **3** in a way that shows you are thinking
about what is good in a situation rather than what is
bad: *They're encouraged to **think positively** about
themselves and their future.* | *Change should be
accepted and be viewed positively.* **4** in a way that
leaves no doubt: *'You certainly won't!' Katherine said*

---

positively. | *The blood was never **positively identified**
as the victim's.* **5** spoken used to emphasize that you
really mean what you are saying; ☒ **definitely**: *This is
positively the last time you'll hear me say this.* **6** positively **charged** technical having the type of electrical
charge that is carried by PROTONS

pos·i·tiv·is·m /'pɒzɪtɪvɪzm $ 'pɑː-/ *n* [U] a type of
PHILOSOPHY based only on facts which can be scientifi-
cally proved, rather than on ideas —**positivist** *adj, n*
[C]

pos·i·tron /'pɒzɪtrɒn $ 'pɑːzɪtrɑːn/ *n* [C] technical a
very small piece of matter that has the same mass as an
ELECTRON but has a positive electrical CHARGE

poss /pɒs $ pɑːs/ *adj BrE informal* **1 if poss** if pos-
sible: *Please send a photo if poss.* **2 as soon as poss** as
soon as possible: *I need them back as soon as poss.*

pos·se /'pɒsi $ 'pɑːsi/ *n* [C] **1** informal a group of the
same kind of people: [+**of**] *I was surrounded by a posse
of photographers.* **2** a group of men gathered together
by a SHERIFF (=local law officer) in the US in past times
to help catch a criminal **3** *AmE informal* **a)** someone's
group of friends – used especially by young people **b)** a
group of friends from a particular place who share an
interest in RAP, HIP-HOP, or HOUSE music; ☒ **massive** *BrE*

pos·sess W3 /pə'zes/ *v* [T not in progressive]
1 formal to have a particular quality or ability: *Different
workers possess different skills.* | *He no longer possessed
the power to frighten her.* ⚠ In spoken English it is much
more usual to use **have** or **have got**: *He has a lot of talent.*
2 formal or law to have or own something: *Neither of
them possessed a credit card.* | *Campbell was found
guilty of possessing heroin.*
3 what possessed sb (to do sth)? spoken used to say
that you cannot understand why someone did something stupid: *What on earth possessed her to do it?*
4 literary if a feeling possesses you, you suddenly feel it
very strongly and it affects your behaviour: *A mad rage
possessed her.*

pos·sessed /pə'zest/ *adj* **1** if someone is possessed, their mind is controlled by something evil: *She
was convinced he was **possessed by the devil**.* | **like a
man/woman possessed** literary (=with a lot of energy
or violence) **2 be possessed of sth** literary to have a
particular quality, ability etc: *She was possessed of a
fine and original mind.* → SELF-POSSESSED

pos·ses·sion W3 /pə'zeʃən/ *n*
1 HAVING STH [U] formal if something is in your
possession, you own it, or you have obtained it from
somewhere: **in sb's possession** *The house has been in
the family's possession since the 1500s.* | *That informa-
tion is not in our possession.* | **in possession of sth** *She
was found in possession of stolen goods.* | *How did the
painting come into your possession* (=how did you get
it)? | *The finance company now **has possession of** the
house.* | *We didn't **take possession of** (=get and start
using) the car until a few days after the auction.*
2 STH YOU OWN [C usually plural] something that you
own or have with you at a particular time; ☒ **belongings**: *He had sold all his possessions and left the
country.* | *I packed my remaining possessions into the
trunk.* | **treasured/prized/precious possession** (=one
that is very important to you) *This old violin had been
her father's most treasured possession.* | *Prisoners were
allowed no **personal possessions**.*
3 CRIME [U] law the crime of having illegal drugs or
weapons with you or in your home: [+**of**] *He was
arrested and **charged with possession** of cocaine.*
4 SPORT [U] when a person or team has control of the
ball in some sports: **win/lose/gain etc possession** *Pitts-
burgh got possession and scored.*
5 COUNTRY [C usually plural] a country controlled or
governed by another country: *France's former **colonial
possessions***
6 EVIL SPIRITS [U] a situation in which someone's

---

① 000, ② 000, ③ 000, most frequent words in Ⓢpoken and Ⓦritten English mind is being controlled by something evil: *Was it a case of demonic possession?*

7 in (full) possession of your faculties/senses able to think in a clear and intelligent way, and not crazy or affected by old age

8 possession is nine-tenths of the law used to say that if you have something, you are likely to be able to keep it, even if it is not yours

pos·ses·sive¹ /pəˈzesɪv/ *adj* **1** wanting someone to have feelings of love or friendship for you and no one else: [+of/about] *She was terribly possessive of our eldest son.* **2** unwilling to let other people use something you own: [+of/about] *He's so possessive about his new car.* **3** technical used in grammar to show that something belongs to someone or something: *possessive pronoun/form/case etc the possessive pronouns 'ours' and 'mine'* —**possessively** *adv* —**possessiveness** *n* [U]

pos·ses·sive² *n* [C] technical an adjective, PRONOUN, or form of a word that shows that something belongs to someone or something

pos·ses·sor /pəˈzesə $ -ər/ *n* [C] formal someone who owns or has something – often used humorously: [+of] *He's now the proud possessor of two satellite dishes.*

pos·si·bil·i·ty S2 W2 /ˌpɒsɨˈbɪlɨti $ ˌpɑː-/ *n plural* **possibilities**

1 [C,U] if there is a possibility that something is true or that something will happen, it might be true or it might happen

possibility (that)
possibility of (doing) sth
a strong/real/distinct possibility (=something that is quite likely to happen)
a remote/faint possibility (=something that is very unlikely to happen)
not beyond the bounds/realms of possibility (=not impossible, but unlikely)
within the bounds/realms of possibility (=possible)
raise the possibility (=say or show that something may be possible)

There's always a possibility that he might go back to Seattle. | *the possibility of an enemy attack* | *There was no possibility of changing the voting procedure.* | *A peace settlement now looks like a real possibility.* | *Tomorrow, there's a remote possibility of snow on high ground.* | *They might get married – it's not beyond the bounds of possibility.* | *The study raises the possibility that dieting is bad for your health.*

2 [C usually plural] an opportunity to do something, or something that can be done or tried: **possibilities for/of (doing) sth** *exciting possibilities for reducing costs* | *Archer began to explore the possibilities of opening a club in the city.* | *The US has not yet exhausted all diplomatic possibilities* (=tried everything possible). | *the range of possibilities offered to students*

3 have possibilities if something has possibilities, it could be made into something much better; ⊟ **have potential**: *The house has great possibilities.* ⚠ Possibility or opportunity? → see note at OPPORTUNITY

pos·si·ble¹ S1 W1 /ˈpɒsɨbəl $ ˈpɑː-/ *adj*

1 if something is possible, it can be done or achieved; ⚡ **impossible**

it is possible (for sb) to do sth
make it possible (for sb) to do sth
if (at all) possible (=if it is possible to do it)
where/whenever/wherever possible (=every time you have an opportunity)
do everything possible
(in) every way possible
technically possible (=possible using the scientific knowledge available)
theoretically possible (=possible but difficult and unlikely to be done)
humanly possible (=possible for anyone)

Is it possible to get tickets for the game? | *It might be possible for the documents to be sent over.* | *Computer technology makes it possible for many people to work from home.* | *I want to avoid the rush hour traffic if possible.* | *I walk or use public transport whenever possible.* | *We are doing everything possible to track down the killer.* | *Our staff will help you in every way possible.* | *Even if it were technically possible, we do not have the money to do it.* | *She decided to stay as far away from him as was humanly possible.*

2 as soon/quickly/much etc as possible as soon, quickly etc as you can: *I need the money as soon as possible.* | *Sharon always does as little work as possible.* | *The original features of the house have been preserved as far as possible* (=as much as possible).

3 a possible answer, cause etc might be true: *There seem to be only two possible explanations.* | *the possible causes of a child's learning difficulties* | *it is possible (that)* | *It's possible that the letter got lost in the post.*

4 a possible event or thing might happen or exist: *Heavy rain is possible later in the day.* | *the possible effect on the health of local people* | *You need to look at the possible consequences of your actions.* | *In Hollywood, anything is possible* (=anything can happen, even though it may seem very unlikely).

5 the best/biggest/fastest etc possible the best etc that can exist or be achieved: *Try to get the best possible price.* | *What is the worst possible thing that could happen?*

6 would it be possible (for sb) to do sth? *spoken* used when asking politely if you can do or have something: *Would it be possible to speak to Oliver?*

possible² *n* [C] someone or something that might be suitable or acceptable for a particular purpose: *Frank's a possible for the job.*

pos·si·bly S1 W2 /ˈpɒsɨbli $ ˈpɑː-/ *adv*

1 used when saying that something may be true or likely, although you are not completely certain; ⊟ **perhaps, maybe**: *This last task is possibly the most difficult.* | *It will take three weeks, possibly longer.* | *'Will you be here tomorrow?' 'Possibly.'* | *'Was it murder?' 'Quite possibly* (=it is very likely).'

2 *spoken* used to emphasize that you are very surprised or shocked by something, or you cannot understand it: *How could anyone possibly do such a thing?*

3 could/can you possibly *spoken* used when making a polite request: *Could you possibly close that window?*

4 used to emphasize that someone will do or has done everything they can to help or to achieve something: *We shall be contributing as much as we possibly can to the campaign.* | *Doctors did everything they possibly could to save his life.*

5 used to emphasize that you cannot do something, or that something cannot or could not happen or be done: **can't/couldn't possibly** *I can't possibly allow you to go home in this weather.* | *She couldn't possibly have heard what was said.*

pos·sum /ˈpɒsəm $ ˈpɑː-/ *also* **opossum** *n* [C] **1** one of various types of small furry animals that climb trees and live in America or Australia **2 play possum** *informal* to pretend to be asleep or dead so that someone will not annoy or hurt you

post¹ S3 W3 /pəʊst $ poʊst/ *n*

1 JOB [C] formal a job, especially an important one in a large organization; ⊟ **position**

apply for a post
offer sb a post
appoint sb to a post
take up a post (=start a new job)
hold a post (=have a job)
fill a post
resign (from) a post/leave a post
senior/junior post
teaching/administrative/government post

I applied for the post and was asked to attend an interview. | *She was offered the post of ambassador to India.* | *He will take up his post as Head of Modern Languages in September.* | *Goddard has held the post since 1998.* | *Unfortunately they were unable to find a suitable person to* **fill** *the* **post**. | *Mr Thomson* **resigned** *his £50,000 a year* **post** *in April.* | *She now holds a* **senior post** *in the Department of Education.* | *the creation of 4000 new* **teaching posts** → see box at JOB

2 POSTAL SYSTEM the post *BrE* the official system for carrying letters, packages etc from one place to another; ◼ **mail**: **by post** *The winners will be notified by post.* | **in the post** *Your letter must have got lost in the post.* | *I'll* **put** *a copy of the book* **in the post** (=send it). | **through the post** *A parcel arrived through the post.*

3 LETTERS [U] *BrE* letters, packages etc that are sent and delivered; ◼ **mail**: *Was there any* **post** *for me today?* | *Emma was* **opening** *her* **post**.

4 COLLECTION/DELIVERY [singular,U] *BrE* when letters are collected or delivered; ◼ **mail**: *What time does* **the post go** (=get collected)? | **(the) first/second/last post** (=the first, second etc collection or delivery of letters each day) *Applications must arrive* **by first post** *on September 23.* | **catch/miss the post** (=post your letter in time for it to be collected, or not in time); → **by return (of post)** at RETURN[2] (11)

5 PIECE OF WOOD/METAL [C] a strong upright piece of wood, metal etc that is fixed into the ground, especially to support something: *a* **fence post** → BEDPOST, GATEPOST (1), LAMP-POST, SIGNPOST[1] (1)

6 FOOTBALL/HOCKEY ETC [C] one of the two upright pieces of wood between which players try to kick or hit the ball in football, HOCKEY etc; ◼ **goalpost**: *The ball hit the post and bounced off.*

7 NEWSPAPER [singular] used in the names of some newspapers: *the Washington Post*

8 SOLDIER/GUARD ETC sb's post the place where a soldier, guard etc is expected to be in order to do their job: **at sb's post** *By 5 am the soldiers were already at their posts.* | *No one was allowed to* **leave** *their* **post**.

9 border/military/customs/police post a place, especially one on a border, where soldiers or police are guarding, checking etc something

10 RACE the post also the finishing post the place where a race finishes, especially a horse race: *Mr Magic was first* **past the post**.

11 INTERNET MESSAGE [C] also **posting** a message sent to an Internet discussion group so that all members of the group can read it: *There was* **post** *after post criticizing the Minister.* → **as deaf as a post** at DEAF (1); → **be driven/passed from pillar to post** at PILLAR (4); → **pip sb at the post** at PIP[2] (1) → FIRST-PAST-THE-POST

post² S3 *v* [T]

1 LETTER *BrE* to send a letter, package etc by post; ◼ **mail**: *She's just gone to* **post** *a letter.* | **post sth (off) to sb** *Did you remember to post the card to my parents?* | **post sb sth** *I posted Barry the cheque last Friday.*

2 post sth through sb's door/letter box *BrE* to push something through someone's LETTERBOX: *I'll post the key through your letterbox when I leave.*

3 JOB [usually passive] if you are posted somewhere, your employer sends you to work there, usually for several years: **post sb to France/London etc** *He joined the British Army and was posted to Germany.* | **post sb abroad/overseas**

4 PUBLIC NOTICE also **post up** to put up a public notice about something on a wall or notice board: *The exam results were posted on the bulletin board yesterday.*

5 GUARD to make someone be in a particular place in order to guard a building, check who enters or leaves a place, watch something etc; ◼ **station**: *Guards were to be posted around nuclear power stations.*

6 keep sb posted *spoken* to regularly tell someone the most recent news about something: [+on] *I'll keep you posted on his progress.*

7 PROFIT/LOSS ETC *especially AmE* to officially record and announce information about a company's financial situation or a country's economic situation: *Cisco Systems* **posted** *record* **profits** *and* **sales** *for the third fiscal quarter.*

8 INTERNET MESSAGE to put a message or computer document on the Internet so that other people can see

it: *Could you* **post** *those new flyers on David's website?*

9 be posted missing *BrE* if a soldier is posted missing, it is announced officially that they have disappeared

10 post bail *law especially AmE* to pay a specific amount of money in order to be allowed to leave prison before your TRIAL

post- /pəʊst $ poʊst/ *prefix* later than or after something: *the postwar years* (=the years after a particular war) | *the post-1979 Conservative government*

post·age /ˈpəʊstɪdʒ $ ˈpoʊs-/ *n* [U] the money charged for sending a letter, package etc by post: *How much is the postage for a postcard?* | **postage and packing** *BrE*/**postage and handling** *AmE* (=the charge for packing and sending something you have bought) *It's yours for £13.99, including postage and packing.*

ˈ**postage ˌmeter** *n* [C] *AmE* a machine used by businesses which puts a mark on letters and packages to show that postage has been paid; ◼ **franking machine** *BrE*

ˈ**postage stamp** *n* [C] *formal* a stamp

post·al /ˈpəʊstl $ ˈpoʊs-/ *adj* [only before noun] **1** relating to the official system which takes letters from one place to another: *the U.S.* **postal service** | **postal workers** | *an increase in postal charges* **2** relating to sending things by post: *Candidates are chosen by a* **postal ballot** *of all party members.* | **postal vote** *BrE*: *Housebound voters should register early for a postal vote.* **3** go postal *AmE informal* to become very angry and behave in a violent way

ˈ**postal ˌorder** *n* [C] *BrE* an official document that you buy in a post office and send to someone so that they can then exchange it for money; ◼ **money order** *AmE*

post·bag /ˈpəʊstbæg $ ˈpoʊst-/ *n* *BrE* **1** [singular] all the letters received by an important person, television programme etc on a particular occasion: *We've had an enormous postbag on the recent programme changes.* **2** [C] a bag for carrying letters, used by the person who delivers them; ◼ **mailbag** *AmE*

post·box /ˈpəʊstbɒks $ ˈpoʊstbɑːks/ *n* [C] *BrE* a box in a public place, into which you put letters that you want to send; ◼ **letter box** *BrE*; ◼ **mailbox** *AmE*

UK postbox   US mailbox

postbox

post·card /ˈpəʊstkɑːd $ ˈpoʊstkɑːrd/ *n* [C] a card that can be sent in the post without an envelope, especially one with a picture on it: *Don't forget to send us a postcard!*

post·code /ˈpəʊstkəʊd $ ˈpoʊstkoʊd/ *n* [C] *BrE* a group of numbers and letters that you write at the end of an address on an envelope, package etc. The postcode shows the exact area where someone lives and helps the post office deliver the post more quickly; ◼ **zip code** *AmE*

post·date /ˌpəʊstˈdeɪt $ ˌpoʊst-/ *v* [T] **1** if you postdate a cheque, you write it with a date that is later than the actual date, so that it will not become effective until that time; → **backdate 2** to happen, live, or be made later in history than something else; → **predate**: *Some of the mosaics postdate this period.*

ˌ**post ˈdoctoral** *adj* [only before noun] relating to study done after a PhD: *post doctoral research*

post·er S3 /ˈpəʊstə $ ˈpoʊstər/ *n* [C] a large printed notice, picture, or photograph, used to advertise something or as a decoration: *A team of volunteers were* **putting up posters**. | *a poster campaign for the election* | [+for] *the poster for the exhibition* | [+of] *posters of old movie stars*; → see picture at BEDROOM

poster child *n* [C usually singular] *AmE*
1 a child with a particular illness or physical problem

whose picture appears on a poster advertising the work of an organization that helps children with that problem **2** someone or something that represents a particular quality, idea etc – often used humorously: *Dillon is the poster child for wasted talent.*

poste res·tante /ˌpəʊst ˈrestɒnt $ ˌpəʊst reˈstɑːnt/ *n* [U] *BrE* a post office department which keeps letters for people who are travelling, until they arrive to collect them

pos·te·ri·or¹ /pɒˈstɪəriə $ pɑːˈstɪriər/ *adj* [only before noun] *technical* near or at the back of something; ⚒ **anterior**: *the posterior part of the brain*

posterior² *n* [C] the part of the body you sit on – used humorously; ⚒ **buttocks, bottom**

pos·ter·i·ty /pɒˈsterəti $ pɑː-/ *n* [U] *formal* all the people in the future who will be alive after you are dead: **preserve/record/keep etc sth for posterity** *a priceless work of art that must be kept for posterity*

'poster paint *n* [C,U] brightly coloured paint that contains no oil, used especially by children to paint pictures

post·game /ˌpəʊstˈgeɪm $ ˌpəʊst-/ *adj* [only before noun] *AmE* happening after a sports game: *postgame celebrations*

ˌpost-'grad *n* [C] *BrE informal* a postgraduate —**post-grad** *adj*

post·grad·u·ate¹ /ˌpəʊstˈgrædjuɪt $ ˌpəʊst-ˈgrædʒuːt/ *n* [C] *especially BrE* someone who is studying at a university to get a MASTER'S DEGREE or a PHD; ⚒ **graduate student** *AmE*

postgraduate² *adj* [only before noun] **1** *especially BrE* relating to studies done at a university after completing a first degree; ⚒ **graduate** *AmE*: *postgraduate degrees* **2** *AmE* relating to studies done after completing a PHD; ⚒ **post doctoral**

ˌpost-'haste *adv literary* very quickly: *He departed post-haste for Verdun.*

post·hu·mous /ˈpɒstjʊ̬məs $ ˈpɑːstʃə-/ *adj* happening, printed etc after someone's death: *a posthumous collection of his articles* —**posthumously** *adv*: *He was posthumously awarded the Military Cross.*

post·ie also **'post-ie** /ˈpəʊsti $ ˈpoʊ-/ *n* [C] *BrE informal* a POSTMAN

ˌpost-in'dustrial *adj* relating to the period in the late 20th century when the older types of industry became less important, and computers became more important: *the post-industrial information-based society*

post·ing /ˈpəʊstɪŋ $ ˈpoʊs-/ *n* [C] **1** if a soldier, a representative of a country etc gets a posting somewhere, they are sent there to do their job: [+to] *shortly before his posting to South Africa* | *a diplomatic posting* **2** also **post** a message sent to an Internet discussion group so that all members of the group can read it **3** *AmE* a public notice, especially one advertising a job: *job postings*

'Post-it also **'Post-it ˌnote** *n* [C] *trademark* a small piece of coloured paper that sticks to things, used for leaving notes for people

post·man /ˈpəʊstmən $ ˈpoʊst-/ *n plural* **postmen** /-mən/ [C] *BrE* someone whose job is to collect and deliver letters; ⚒ **mailman** *AmE*

post·mark /ˈpəʊstmɑːk $ ˈpoʊstmɑːrk/ *n* [C] an official mark made on a letter, package etc to show when and where it was posted —**postmark** *v* [T]: *The letter was postmarked Iowa.*

post·mas·ter /ˈpəʊstˌmɑːstə $ ˈpoʊstˌmæstər/ *n* [C] someone who is in charge of a post office

post·men·o·paus·al /ˌpəʊstmenəˈpɔːzəl $ ˌpoʊstmenə-ˈpɒː-/ *adj* a postmenopausal woman has gone through the MENOPAUSE (=when she stops having her monthly flow of blood)

post·mis·tress /ˈpəʊstˌmɪstrɪs $ ˈpoʊst-/ *n* [C] old-fashioned a woman who is in charge of a post office

post·mod·ern /ˌpəʊstˈmɒdn $ ˌpoʊstˈmɑːdərn/ *adj* **1** relating to or influenced by postmodernism: *postmodern architecture* **2** used to describe styles, attitudes etc that are typical of the social life that is found in many western countries now, in which television, video, the buying of goods and services etc are very important: *postmodern culture*

post·mod·ern·is·m /ˌpəʊstˈmɒdən-ɪzəm $ ˌpoʊst-ˈmɑːdərn-/ *n* [U] a style of building, painting, writing etc, developed in the late 20th century, that uses a mixture of old and new styles as a reaction against MODERNISM —**postmodernist** *adj*: *postmodernist fiction* —**postmodernist** *n* [C]

post-mor·tem, **post-mor·tem** /ˌpəʊstˈmɔːtəm $ ˌpoʊstˈmɔːr-/ *n* [C] **1** also **post mortem examin'ation** an examination of a dead body to discover why the person died; ⚒ **autopsy**: [+on] *A post-mortem on the body revealed that the victim had been strangled.* | **do/carry out/conduct a post-mortem 2** *especially BrE* an examination of a plan or event that failed, done to discover why it failed: [+on] *a post-mortem on the company's poor results*

post·na·tal /ˌpəʊstˈneɪtl $ ˌpoʊst-/ *adj* [only before noun] relating to the time after a baby is born: *postnatal care* | **postnatal depression** (=an illness in which a woman feels very unhappy and tired after her baby is born)

'post ˌoffice *n* **1** [C] a place where you can buy stamps, send letters and packages etc **2 the Post Office** the national organization which is responsible for collecting and delivering letters

'post office ˌbox *n* [C] *formal* a PO BOX

ˌpost-'operative *adj* [only before noun] relating to the time after someone has had a medical operation: *post-operative care*

post·paid /ˌpəʊstˈpeɪd $ ˌpoʊst-/ *adj* costing nothing to send because the amount has already been paid: *The kit costs $33.95 postpaid.*

post·par·tum /ˌpəʊstˈpɑːtəm $ ˌpoʊstˈpɑːr-/ *adj* technical relating to the time immediately after a woman has a baby; ⚒ **postnatal**

post·pone /pəʊsˈpəʊn $ poʊsˈpoʊn/ *v* [T] to change the date or time of a planned event or action to a later one; ⚒ **put back**; ⚒ **bring forward**: *The match had to be postponed until next week.* | **postpone doing sth** *They've decided to postpone having a family for a while.* | *His trial has been postponed indefinitely* (=no one knows when it will happen). —**postponement** *n* [C,U]

post·pran·di·al /ˌpəʊstˈprændiəl $ ˌpoʊst-/ *adj* [only before noun] *formal especially BrE* happening immediately after a meal – often used humorously: *a postprandial nap*

post·script /ˈpəʊsˌskrɪpt $ ˈpoʊs-/ *n* [C] *PS* **1** a message written at the end of a letter after you have signed your name **2** extra details or information that you add after a story or account: [+to] *There's an interesting postscript to this tale.*

post·sea·son /ˈpəʊstˌsiːzən $ ˈpoʊst-/ *adj* [only before noun] *AmE* relating to the time after the usual sports season is over; ⚒ **preseason**: *a postseason game* —**postseason** *n* [singular]

post·sec·ond·a·ry /ˌpəʊstˈsekəndəri $ ˌpoʊst-ˈsekənderi/ *adj* relating to schools or education after you have finished HIGH SCHOOL

ˌpost-traumatic 'stress dis,order *n* [U] *medical* **PTSD** a mental illness which can develop after a very bad experience such as a plane crash

pos·tu·late¹ /ˈpɒstjʊ̬leɪt $ ˈpɑːstʃə-/ *v* [T] *formal* to suggest that something might have happened or be true: **postulate that** *It has been postulated that the condition is inherited.* —**postulation** /ˌpɒstjʊ̬ˈleɪʃən $ ˌpɑːstʃə-/ *n* [C,U]

pos·tu·late² /'pɒstjʊleɪt $ 'pɑːstʃə-/ *n* [C] *formal* something believed to be true, on which an argument or scientific discussion is based: [+of] *the basic postulates of Marxism*

pos·tur·al /'pɒstʃərəl $ 'pɑːs-/ *adj* [only before noun] *formal* relating to the way you sit or stand: *postural problems*

pos·ture /'pɒstʃə $ 'pɑːstʃər/ *n* **1** [C,U] the way you position your body when sitting or standing: **good/bad etc posture** *Poor posture can lead to muscular problems.* | *her upright posture* **2** [singular] the way you behave or think in a particular situation: [+towards] *He tends to adopt a defensive posture towards new ideas.*

pos·tur·ing /'pɒstʃərɪŋ $ 'pɑːs-/ *n* [C,U] *formal* **1** when someone pretends to have a particular opinion or attitude: *He dismissed the Senator's comments as 'political posturing'.* **2** when someone stands or moves in a way that they hope will make other people notice and admire them —**posture** *v* [I]

post-'war *adj* [only before noun] happening or existing after a war, especially the Second World War; ➡ PRE-WAR: *post-war Britain* | **post-war period/years/era** *food rationing in the immediate post-war years* —**post-war** *adv* ➡ PRE-WAR

po·sy /'pəʊzi $ 'poʊ-/ *n plural* **posies** [C] a small BUNCH of flowers

pots

teapot

flowerpot

paint pots

cooking pot

coffee pot

fondue pot

pot¹ S2 W3 /pɒt $ pɑːt/ *n*
1 COOKING [C] a container used for cooking which is round, deep, and usually made of metal: **pots and pans** | [+of] *There was a big pot of soup on the stove.*; ➡ see picture at PAN¹
2 FOR A PLANT [C] a container for a plant, usually made of plastic or baked clay: *herbs growing in pots*
3 TEA/COFFEE [C] a container with a handle and a small tube for pouring, used to make tea or coffee: *Is there any tea left in the pot?* | [+of] *I'll make a pot of coffee.* ➡ COFFEE POT, TEAPOT
4 FOR FOOD, PAINT ETC [C] *BrE* a round container for storing foods such as JAM that are slightly liquid, or for substances such as glue or paint: [+of] *a pot of blue paint* | **jam/paint/yoghurt etc pot**; ➡ see picture at CONTAINER
5 BOWL/DISH ETC [C] a dish, bowl, plate, or other container that is made by shaping clay and then baking it; ➡ pottery: *an earthenware pot*
6 **go to pot** *informal* if something such as a place or an organization goes to pot, it becomes much worse or fails because no one is taking care of it: *The government has let the whole country go to pot.*
7 **pots of money** *BrE informal* a lot of money: *They've got pots of money in the bank.* | *He's hoping to make pots of money from the deal.*
8 MONEY **the pot a)** money that is available to do something, especially money that people have collected: **in the pot** *So far we've got £150 in the pot.* **b)** all the money that people have risked in a card game, and which can be won: **in the pot** *There was $1000 in the pot.*
9 DRUG [U] *old-fashioned informal* MARIJUANA: *Michael was smoking pot with some friends.*
10 **(a case of) the pot calling the kettle black** *informal*

used humorously to say that you should not criticize someone for something, because you have done the same thing or have the same fault
11 STOMACH [C] a POTBELLY
12 HIT A BALL [C] *BrE* the act of hitting a ball into one of the POCKETS (=holes at the edge of the table) in games such as BILLIARDS, POOL, and SNOOKER
13 TOILET [C] *informal* a toilet ➡ CHAMBER POT, CHIMNEY POT, FLOWERPOT, LOBSTERPOT, MELTING POT

pot² *v* **potted, potting** [T]
1 PLANTS also **pot up** *BrE* to put a plant into a pot filled with soil: *Pot the seedlings after 2–3 weeks.*
2 BALL *BrE* to hit a ball into one of the POCKETS (=holes at the edge of the table) in games such as BILLIARDS, POOL, and SNOOKER; ⊟ **pocket**
3 SHOOT *BrE* to shoot at animals in order to kill them

po·ta·ble /'pəʊtəbəl $ 'poʊ-/ *adj formal* potable water is safe to drink

pot·ash /'pɒtæʃ $ 'pɑː-/ *n* [U] a type of potassium used especially in farming to make the soil better

po·tas·si·um /pə'tæsiəm/ *n* [U] a common soft silver-white metal that usually exists in combination with other substances, used for example in farming. It is a chemical ELEMENT: symbol K

potato

chips *BrE*/ French fries *AmE*

roast potatoes

mashed potatoes

boiled potatoes

po·ta·to S2 /pə'teɪtəʊ $ -toʊ/ *n plural* **potatoes**
1 [C,U] a round white vegetable with a brown, red, or pale yellow skin, that grows under the ground: **roast/fried/boiled/mashed potato** | **jacket potato** (=cooked in its skin) | *Marie stood at the sink, peeling potatoes* (=cutting off the skin). ➡ see picture at VEGETABLE¹
2 [C] a plant that produces potatoes

po'tato ,crisp *BrE*; **po'tato ,chip** *AmE n* [C] a very thin round piece of potato cooked in oil and eaten cold, sold in packages

po'tato ,peeler *n* [C] a small tool like a knife, used for removing the skin of a potato

potbellied 'stove *n* [C] *AmE* a small round metal STOVE that you burn wood or coal in for heating or cooking, used especially in the past

pot·bel·ly /'pɒt,beli $ 'pɑːt-/ *n plural* **potbellies** [C] a large round unattractive stomach that sticks out —**potbellied** [adj]

pot·boil·er /'pɒt,bɔɪlə $ 'pɑːt,bɔɪlər/ *n* [C] a book or film that is produced quickly to make money and which is not of very high quality, especially one that is exciting or romantic

pot·bound /'pɒtbaʊnd $ 'pɑːt-/ *adj BrE* a plant that is potbound cannot grow any more because its roots have grown to fill the pot it is in

po·teen /pə'tʃiːn, -'tiːn/ *n* [U] Irish WHISKY made secretly and illegally to avoid paying tax

P

po·ten·cy /'pəʊtənsi $ 'poʊ-/ n [singular,U] **1** the power that something has to influence people: [+of] *the potency of his arguments* | *The myth of male superiority was losing its potency.* **2** the strength of something, especially a drug, on your mind or body: [+of] *the potency of the drug* **3** also **sexual potency** the ability of a man to have sex: *loss of potency after age 40*

po·tent /'pəʊtənt $ 'poʊ-/ adj **1** having a very powerful effect or influence on your body or mind; ▣ **powerful**: *potent drugs* | *a potent symbol of oppression* | *Advertising is a potent force in showing smoking as a socially acceptable habit.* | *A good company pension scheme remains a potent weapon for attracting staff.* **2** powerful and effective: *The treaty requires them to get rid of their most potent weapons.* **3** a man who is potent is able to have sex or able to make a woman PREGNANT; ▣ **impotent** —**potently** adv

po·ten·tate /'pəʊtənteɪt $ 'poʊ-/ n [C] literary a ruler in the past, who had great power over his people

po·ten·tial¹ [S3] [W2] /pə'tenʃəl/ adj [only before noun] likely to develop into a particular type of person or thing in the future; ▣ **possible**: **potential customer/buyer/client** *new ways of attracting potential customers* | **potential benefit/problem** *the potential benefits of the new system* | **potential danger/threat/risk** *the potential risks to health associated with the drug*

potential² [W3] n [U] **1** the possibility that something will develop in a particular way, or have a particular effect: [+for] *The company certainly has the potential for growth.* | [+of] *the potential of the Internet to create jobs* **2** if people or things have potential, they have a natural ability or quality that could develop to make them very good: **have/show potential** *She has the potential to become a champion.* | **with potential** *a young player with great potential* | **achieve/fulfil/realize your (full) potential** (=succeed as well as you possibly can) **3** technical the difference in VOLTAGE between two points on an electrical CIRCUIT

po·ten·ti·al·i·ty /pə,tenʃi'æləti/ n plural **potentialities** [C] formal an ability or quality that could develop in the future

po·ten·tial·ly /pə'tenʃəli/ adv [+ adj/adv] something that is potentially dangerous, useful etc is not dangerous etc now, but may become so in the future: *a potentially dangerous situation*

pot·ful /'pɒtfʊl $ 'pɑːt-/ n [C] the amount a pot can contain

pot·hold·er /'pɒt,həʊldə $ 'pɑːt,hoʊldər/ n [C] a piece of thick material that you use to protect your hands when you pick up a hot cooking pan

pot·hole /'pɒthəʊl $ 'pɑːthoʊl/ n [C] **1** a large hole in the surface of a road, caused by traffic and bad weather, which makes driving difficult or dangerous **2** BrE a long hole that goes deep under the ground, formed by natural processes —**potholed** adj

pot·hol·ing /'pɒt,həʊlɪŋ $ 'pɑːt,hoʊl-/ n [U] BrE the sport of climbing down POTHOLES and underground CAVES; ▣ **caving** —**potholer** n [C]

po·tion /'pəʊʃən $ 'poʊ-/ n [C] **1** literary a drink intended to have a special or magical effect on the person who drinks it, or which is intended to poison them: *a magic potion* | *a love potion* **2** a medicine, especially one that seems strange or old-fashioned

pot luck BrE, **pot·luck** AmE /,pɒt'lʌk◂ $,pɑːt-/ n **1** take pot luck a) to choose something without knowing very much about it, and hope that it will be what you want: *We hadn't booked a hotel so we had to take pot luck.* b) to have a meal at someone's home in which you eat whatever they have available, rather than food which has been specially bought for the occasion: *I'm not sure what there is in the fridge – you'll have to take pot luck.* **2** [C] AmE a meal in which everyone who is invited brings something to eat: *Can*

you bring a salad? It's a potluck. | **potluck meal/dinner etc** *a potluck supper at the church*

pot 'pie n [C] AmE meat and vegetables covered with PASTRY and baked in a deep dish

'pot plant n [C] BrE a plant that is grown indoors in a pot

pot·pour·ri /,pəʊpʊ'riː $,poʊ-/ n **1** [U] a mixture of pieces of dried flowers and leaves kept in a bowl to make a room smell pleasant **2** [singular] a mixture of things that are not usually put together, for example different pieces of music or writing: [+of] *a potpourri of literary styles*

'pot roast n [C] a dish that consists of a piece of meat cooked slowly in a pan with potatoes and other vegetables

'pot shot n **take a pot shot at sb/sth a)** to shoot at someone or something without aiming very carefully: *The boy took a pot shot at a pigeon with his air gun.* **b)** to criticize someone or something unfairly without thinking carefully about it: *He enjoys taking pot shots at the government whenever the opportunity arises.*

pot·ted /'pɒtɪd $ 'pɑː-/ adj [only before noun] **1** growing indoors in a pot: *a potted plant* **2** potted history/biography/version BrE a short and simple explanation or description that gives only the most important facts about someone or something **3** BrE potted meat or fish has been cooked and stored in a container, usually in the form of a PASTE for spreading on bread

pot·ter¹ /'pɒtə $ 'pɑːtər/ n [C] someone who makes pots, dishes etc out of clay

potter² also **potter about/around** v [I] BrE to spend time doing pleasant things that are not important without hurrying; ▣ **putter** AmE: *I spent the morning pottering about in the garden.* —**potterer** n [C]

,potter's 'wheel n [C] a piece of equipment that turns around, onto which wet clay is placed so that it can be shaped by hand into a pot

pot·ter·y /'pɒtəri $ 'pɑː-/ n plural **potteries 1** [U] objects made out of baked clay: *Native American pottery* **2** [U] clay that has been shaped and baked in order to make pots, dishes etc: *a pottery bowl* **3** [U] the activity of making pots, dishes etc out of clay: *a pottery class* → see picture at HANDICRAFT **4** [C] a factory where pottery objects are made

'potting shed n [C] BrE a small building, usually made of wood, where garden tools, seeds etc are kept

pot·ty¹ /'pɒti $ 'pɑːti/ adj BrE informal **1** crazy or silly: *What a potty idea!* | *You must be potty!* **2 drive sb potty** if something or someone is driving you potty, they are annoying you, especially if they are making it difficult for you to continue what you are doing **3 be potty about sb/sth** to like someone very much, or be very interested in something: *She's potty about riding.* —**pottiness** n [U]

potty² n plural **potties** [C] **1** a container used by very young children as a toilet **2 go potty** AmE to use the toilet – used by young children or when speaking to them: *Do you need to go potty?* **3 potty mouth** AmE spoken someone who has or is a potty mouth uses offensive words **4 potty break** AmE informal a time when you stop what you are doing, especially when driving a car, so that you can use the toilet – used humorously

'potty-,training n [U] the process of teaching a very young child to use a potty or toilet —**potty-train** v [T] —**potty-trained** adj

pouch /paʊtʃ/ n [C] **1** a small leather, cloth, or plastic bag that you can keep things in, and which is sometimes attached to a belt: [+of] *a leather pouch of tobacco* | *a money pouch* → see picture at BAG¹ **2** especially AmE a large bag for carrying letters or papers: *a mail pouch* **3** a pocket in the side of a bag such as a RUCKSACK **4** a pocket of skin on the stomach which MARSUPIALS such as KANGAROOS use for carrying their babies **5** a fold of skin like a bag which animals such as HAMSTERS or SQUIRRELS have inside each cheek to carry and store food

pouffe, **pouf** /puːf/ n [C] BrE a soft piece of furniture like a large CUSHION, which you can sit on or rest your feet on

poul·tice /ˈpəʊltɪs $ ˈpoʊl-/ n [C] something that is put on someone's skin to make it less swollen or painful, often made of a wet cloth with milk, herbs, or clay on it

poul·try /ˈpəʊltri $ ˈpoʊl-/ n **1** [plural] birds such as chickens and ducks that are kept on farms in order to produce eggs and meat **2** [U] meat from birds such as chickens and ducks

pounce /paʊns/ v [I] to suddenly move forward and attack someone or something, after waiting to attack them: *The cat was hiding in the bushes, ready to pounce.* | [+**on**] *Kevin pounced on Liam and started hitting him.*; → see picture at MOVEMENT —**pounce** n [C]
   pounce on sb/sth phr v **1** to criticize someone's mistakes or ideas very quickly and eagerly: *Teachers are quick to pounce on students' grammatical errors.* **2** to eagerly take an opportunity as soon as it becomes available: *When they offered O'Leary the chance to become manager, he pounced on it.*

pound¹ S1 W2 /paʊnd/ n
1 WEIGHT [C] written abbreviation *lb* a unit for measuring weight, equal to 16 OUNCES or 0.454 kilograms: [+**of**] *a pound of apples* | *Moira* **weighs** *about 130* **pounds**. | *The grapes* **cost** *$2* **a pound**.
2 MONEY also **pound sterling** [C] **a)** £ the standard unit of money in Britain, which is divided into 100 pence: *They spent over a thousand pounds.* | *a multi-million pound business* | *a five pound note* **b)** the (British) pound the value of British money compared with the value of the money of other countries: *The pound was up against the dollar.* **c)** the standard unit of money in various other countries, such as Egypt and the Sudan
3 FOR DOGS AND CATS [C usually singular] a place where dogs and cats that have been found on the street are kept until their owners come to get them
4 FOR CARS [C] a place where cars that have been illegally parked are kept until their owners pay money to get them back
5 get/take/demand etc your pound of flesh to get the full amount of work, money etc that someone owes you, even though it makes them suffer and you do not really need it
6 TELEPHONE [U] AmE the POUND KEY

pound² v
1 HIT [I,T] to hit something very hard several times and make a lot of noise, damage it, break it into smaller pieces etc: *He began pounding the keyboard of his computer.* | [+**against/on**] *Thomas pounded on the door with his fist.* | *Waves pounded against the pier.* | **pound sth against/on sth** *Green pounded his fist on the counter.*
2 HEART [I] if your heart or blood is pounding, your heart is beating very hard and quickly: [+**with**] *Patrick rushed to the door, his heart pounding with excitement.* | *She ran, her* **heart pounding in her chest**.
3 HEAD [I] if your head is pounding, it feels painful, especially because you have a headache or you have been using a lot of effort
4 MOVE [I always + adv/prep, T] to walk or run quickly with heavy loud steps: [+**along/through/down etc**] *I could hear him pounding up the stairs.* | *a policeman pounding his beat* | *Runners will be pounding the pavement this weekend during the London Marathon.*
5 ATTACK WITH BOMBS [T] to attack a place continuously for a long time with bombs: *Enemy forces have been pounding the city for over two months.*
   pound sth ⇔ **out** phr v
to play music loudly: *The Rolling Stones were pounding out one of their old numbers.*

pound·age /ˈpaʊndɪdʒ/ n [U] **1** technical an amount charged for every pound in weight, or for every British £1 in value **2** informal weight

pound cake n [C] a heavy cake made from flour, sugar, and butter

pound·er /ˈpaʊndə $ -ər/ n a 3-pounder/24-pounder/185-pounder etc **a)** an animal, fish, or person that weighs 3 pounds, 24 pounds etc **b)** a gun that fires a SHELL that weighs 3 pounds, 24 pounds etc

pound·ing /ˈpaʊndɪŋ/ n **1** [singular,U] the action or the sound of something hitting a surface very hard many times: [+**of**] *the pounding of the waves on the rocks below* **2** [singular,U] the action or sound of your heart beating **3 take a pounding a)** to be completely defeated: *Manchester United took a real pounding.* **b)** to be hit or attacked many times and often badly damaged: *The ship had taken a pounding on the rocks.*

pound key n [C] AmE the button on a telephone that has the SYMBOL (#) on it

pound sign n [C] **1** BrE the SYMBOL (£), used for a pound in British money **2** AmE the SYMBOL (#), used especially on a telephone; ⊟ **hash** BrE

pound 'sterling n [singular] the standard unit of money in Britain, which is divided into 100 pence

pour S2 W3 /pɔː $ pɔːr/ v
1 LIQUID [T] to make a liquid or other substance flow out of or into a container by holding it at an angle: *She poured coffee for everyone.* | **pour sth into/out/down etc (sth)** *Pour the oil into a frying pan and heat.* | **pour sth away** (=get rid of something) *The wine was so bad I just poured it away.* | **pour sb sth** *Why don't you pour yourself another drink?*
2 LIQUID/SMOKE [I always + adv/prep] if a lot of liquid or smoke pours out, it comes out from somewhere in very large amounts: [+**from/down/out**] *Smoke was pouring out of the upstairs windows.* | *Blood was pouring from his nose.*
3 RAIN also **pour down** [I] to rain heavily without stopping: *It's pouring now.* | *It poured all night.* | **it's pouring with rain/it poured with rain** BrE: *It was pouring down with rain at three o'clock.*
4 PEOPLE OR THINGS [I always + adv/prep] if a lot of people or things pour into or out of a place, a lot of them arrive or leave at the same time: [+**into/out of/from etc**] *The crowds began pouring out of the stadium.* | *Offers of help poured in from all over the country.*
5 LIGHT [I always + adv/prep] if light is pouring into or out of a place, a lot of light is coming in or out: [+**into/out of**] *Light was pouring into the courtyard.*
6 pour cold water on/over sth to criticize someone's plan, idea, or desire to do something so much that they no longer feel excited about it
7 pour scorn on sb/sth to say that something or someone is stupid and not worth considering
8 pour oil on troubled waters to try to stop a quarrel, for example by talking to people and making them calmer
9 pour it on **a)** to behave or talk in a particular way in order to make people like you or feel sorry for you **b)** AmE informal to try very hard in order to do something, especially in order to win a game: *The Raiders really poured it on in the second quarter.*
10 pour on the charm to behave in a very nice and polite way, in order to make someone like you
   pour sth **into** sth phr v
if people pour money into something, they provide a lot of money for it over a period of time, in order to make it successful: *They've poured thousands of pounds into developing the business.*
   pour sth ⇔ **out** phr v
if you pour out your thoughts, feelings etc, you tell someone all about them, especially because you feel very unhappy: *She poured out all her troubles to him.* | **pour out your heart/soul** (=tell someone all your feelings, including your most secret ones)

P

pour·ing /'pɔːrɪŋ/ *adj* pouring rain is very heavy rain

pout /paʊt/ *v* [I,T] to push out your lower lip because you are annoyed or unhappy, or in order to look sexually attractive: *He sounded like a pouting child.* | *Her full lips pouted slightly.* —**pout** *n* [C] —**pouty** *adj*

pov·er·ty W3 /'pɒvəti $ 'pɑːvərti/ *n*
1 [U] the situation or experience of being poor; → **poor**, **impoverished**

> **live/grow up/die in poverty**
> **fight/combat poverty** (=try to end poverty)
> **alleviate/relieve poverty** (=improve poverty)
> **extreme/severe poverty**
> **abject/grinding/dire poverty** (=extreme poverty)
> **urban/rural poverty** (=poverty of people in cities or the countryside)

> *Millions of elderly people **live in poverty**.* | *We need an effective strategy to **fight poverty**.* | *continued efforts to **alleviate poverty** and raise living standards* | *scenes of **abject poverty*** | *the causes of **urban poverty***

2 the poverty line also **the poverty level** *AmE* the income below which a person or a family is officially considered to be very poor and in need of help: *20% of the population now live **below the poverty line**.*
3 the poverty trap a situation in which a poor person without a job cannot afford to take a low paying job because they would lose the money they receive from the government
4 [singular,U] *formal* a lack of a particular quality: [+of] *The novel shows a surprising poverty of imagination.*

poverty-,stricken *adj* extremely poor: *poverty-stricken families*

pow /paʊ/ *interjection* used to represent the sound of a gun firing, an explosion, or someone hitting another person hard, especially in children's COMICS

POW /,piː əʊ 'dʌbəlju: $ -oʊ-/ *n* [C] A PRISONER OF WAR

pow·der¹ /'paʊdə $ -ər/ *n* **1** [C,U] a dry substance in the form of very small grains: *curry powder* | *talcum powder* | **Grind** *the sugar **into a powder**.* | *The paint is supplied **in powder form**.* | **milk/custard etc powder** (=a powder that you add water to in order to change it into a liquid) **2** [U] also **face powder** a type of powder that you put on your face in order to make it look smoother and to give it more colour **3 a powder keg** a dangerous situation or place where violence or trouble could suddenly start: *Since the riot, the city has been a powder keg waiting to explode.* **4** [U] also **powder snow** dry light snow: *There's a foot of powder on the slopes.* **5** [U] GUNPOWDER **6 keep your powder dry** to wait calmly until you see how a situation develops before deciding what to do

powder² *v* **1** [T] to put powder on something, especially your skin: *She was powdering her face.* **2 powder your nose** an expression meaning to go to the TOILET, used by women to avoid saying this directly: *She's just gone to powder her nose.*

,powder 'blue *n* [U] a pale blue colour —**powder blue** [adj]

pow·dered /'paʊdəd $ -ərd/ *adj* **1** produced or sold in the form of a powder: *powdered milk* **2** covered with powder

,powdered 'sugar *n* [U] *AmE* sugar in a powder form; ⊟ **icing sugar** *BrE*

'powder puff *n* [C] a small round piece of soft material used by women to spread POWDER on their face or body

'powder room *n* [C] a room with a toilet for women, especially in a public place – used to avoid saying this directly

pow·der·y /'paʊdəri/ *adj* **1** like powder or easily broken into powder: *powdery snow* **2** covered with powder

pow·er¹ S1 W1 /'paʊə $ paʊr/ *n*
1 CONTROL [U] the ability or right to control people or events; → **powerful**, **powerless**: *We all felt that the chairman had too much power.* | [+over] *People should have more power over the decisions that affect their lives.* | *the enormous **economic power** of the US* | *Workers had little **political power**.* | *the **balance of power** between management and unions* | *He was engaged in a bitter **power struggle** with the director* (=a situation in which groups or leaders try to get control).* | *Nothing will change until there are more women in **positions of power**.* | **power-mad/power-crazy/power-hungry** *power-hungry politicians* | *The bishops had almost **absolute power**.* | *the power **wielded** by unelected civil servants* (=which they have and use)
2 GOVERNMENT [U] the position of having political control of a country or government: **in power** *The dictator had been in power for seven years.* | *the party **in power*** | **come/rise to power** (=start having political control) *De Gaulle came to power in 1958.* | *They **seized power** in a military coup.*
3 INFLUENCE [U] the ability to influence people or give them strong feelings; → **powerful**, **powerless**: [+of] *the power of his writing* | *the immense power of television* | *the **pulling power*** (=ability to attract people or attention) *of major celebrities* | **student/black/consumer etc power** (=the political or social influence a particular group has)
4 RIGHT/AUTHORITY [C,U] the right or authority to do something: *The police have been given special powers to help them in the fight against terrorism.* | **power to do sth** *The committee has the power to order an enquiry.* | **power of arrest/veto etc** *The chairman has the power of veto on all decisions.*
5 ABILITY [C,U] a natural or special ability to do something: *After the accident she lost the **power of speech*** (=ability to speak).* | **powers of observation/concentration/persuasion** *a writer's powers of observation* | *your mental powers* | *a stone with magical powers*
6 ENERGY [U] energy that can be used to make a machine work or to make electricity: **nuclear/wind/solar etc power** *Many people are opposed to the use of nuclear power.* | *the search for renewable **sources of power*** | **under power** *The ship was able to leave port **under its own power*** (=without help from another machine, ship etc).*
7 earning/purchasing/bargaining etc power the ability to earn money, buy things etc: *Property in the city is beyond the purchasing power of most people.* | *your bargaining power in pay negotiations*
8 STRENGTH [U] the physical strength or effect of something; → **powerful**: *the power of a cheetah's long legs* | *The power of the explosion smashed windows across the street.*
9 ELECTRICITY [U] electricity that is used in houses, factories etc: *Make sure the power is switched off first.* | **power cut/failure/outage** (=a short time when the electricity supply is not working) *Parts of the country have had power cuts because of the storms.* | *The power came back on.*
10 air/sea power the number of planes or ships that a country has available to use in a war
11 STRONG COUNTRY [C] a country that is strong and important and can influence events, or that has a lot of military strength; → **powerful**, **powerless**: *Egypt is still a major power in the Middle East.* | **world power** (=a country that can influence events in different parts of the world)
12 be in/within sb's power (to do sth) if it is in someone's power to do something, they have the authority or ability to do it: *I wish it was within my power to change the decision.* | **do everything/all in your power** *The ambassador promised to do everything in his power to get the hostages released.*
13 be beyond sb's power (to do sth) if it is beyond someone's power to do something, they do not have the authority or ability to do it: *It's beyond the power of the court to make such a decision.*
14 be in sb's power *literary* to be in a situation in which someone has complete control over you

15 do sb a power of good *BrE informal* to make someone feel more healthy, happy, and hopeful about the future: *It looks as if your holiday has done you a power of good.*
16 MATHEMATICS [C] if a number is increased to the power of three, four, five etc, it is multiplied by itself three, four, five etc times
17 the powers that be the unknown people who have important positions of authority and power, and whose decisions affect your life: *The powers that be don't want the media to get hold of the story.*
18 LENS [U] *technical* the ability of a LENS, for example in a pair of GLASSES or a MICROSCOPE, to make things look bigger
19 the powers of good/evil/darkness unknown or magical forces that people believe can influence events in a good or evil way
20 a power in the land *old-fashioned* someone who has a lot of power and influence in a country
21 the power behind the throne someone who secretly controls and influences decisions made by the leader or government of a country, but who does not have an official government position
22 power trip *informal* if you are on a power trip, you are enjoying your power or authority in a way that other people think is unpleasant → STAYING POWER, BALANCE OF POWER, HIGH-POWERED

power² *v* **1** [T usually passive] to supply power to a vehicle or machine: *It's powered by a Ferrari V12 engine.* **2** [I always + adv/prep] to move with a lot of force and speed: *His strong body powered through the water.* → HIGH-POWERED

power sth ⇔ up *phr v* to make a machine start working: *Never move a computer while it is powered up.*

power³ *adj* [only before noun] **1** driven by an electric motor: *power tools* | *power shower* **2 power breakfast/ lunch etc** *informal* a meal at which people meet to discuss business **3 power suit** *informal* clothes which you wear at work to make you look important or confident

power-assisted 'steering *n* [U] POWER STEERING
'power base *n* [C] an area or group of people whose support makes a politician or leader powerful: *the party's traditional power base*
pow·er·boat /'pauəbəut $ 'pauərbout/ *n* [C] a powerful MOTORBOAT that is used for racing
'power ,broker, power-broker *n* [C] someone who controls or influences which people get political power in an area —**power-broking** *n* [U]
'power cut *n* [C] *BrE* a period of time when there is no electricity supply; ⧉ **power failure**; ⧉ **power outage** *AmE*
'power ,dressing *n* [U] when you wear a particular style of clothes in order to emphasize how important or powerful you are, especially at work
'power drill *n* [C] a tool for making holes that works by electricity
pow·ered /'pauəd $ paurd/ *adj* working or moving using a means of power such as electricity, a motor etc: *a powered wheelchair* | **battery-powered/nuclear-powered/mains powered** *a nuclear-powered submarine* | **high-powered/low-powered** *a high-powered engine* → HIGH-POWERED
'power ,failure *n* [C] a period of time when there is no electricity supply
pow·er·ful W2 /'pauəfəl $ 'paur-/ *adj*
1 IMPORTANT a powerful person, organization, group etc is able to control and influence events and other people's actions; → **powerless**: *He was one of the most powerful men in Bohemia.* | *a very influential and powerful family* | *rich and powerful nations*
2 SPEECH/FILM ETC having a strong effect on someone's feelings or opinions: *a powerful speech* | **powerful reasons/arguments** (=reasons that make you think that something must be true) | *Good teamwork is a powerful tool* (=very effective method) *for effective management.*

3 FEELING/EFFECT a powerful feeling or effect is very strong or great: *Immigrants have had a powerful influence on the local culture.* | *a powerful sense of tradition*
4 MACHINE/WEAPON ETC a powerful machine, engine, weapon etc is very effective and can do a lot: *a new generation of more powerful PCs* | *a machine that is immensely powerful* | *a powerful 24 valve engine* | *a powerful telescope*
5 PHYSICALLY STRONG physically strong: *Jed was a powerful, well-built man.* | *The females are smaller and less powerful than the males.*
6 A LOT OF FORCE a powerful blow, explosion etc has a lot of force: *an explosion ten times more powerful than the Hiroshima bomb* | *a powerful right-foot shot on goal* | *winds powerful enough to uproot trees*
7 MEDICINE a powerful medicine or drug has a very strong effect on your body
8 TEAM/ARMY ETC a powerful team, army etc is very strong and can easily defeat other teams or armies: *a powerful fighting force*
9 QUALITY very strong, bright, loud etc: *a powerful singing voice* | *the powerful headlights* —**powerfully** *adv*: *Christie is very powerfully built.* → ALL-POWERFUL

pow·er·house /'pauəhaus $ 'paur-/ *n* [C] *informal*
1 an organization or place where there is a lot of activity or where a lot of things are produced: *Europe's industrial powerhouse* **2** someone who is very strong or has a lot of energy: *a powerhouse of a man*
pow·er·less /'pauələs $ 'paur-/ *adj* unable to stop or control something because you do not have the power, strength, or legal right to do so; → **powerful**: *He felt so powerless.* | **powerless to do sth** *Local police were powerless to stop them doing it again.* | [+against] *The villagers were powerless against the rising flood water.* —**powerlessly** *adv* —**powerlessness** *n* [U]: *a sense of frustration and powerlessness*
'power line *n* [C] a large wire carrying electricity above or under the ground: *overhead power lines*
'power-nap *n* [C] a short sleep in the middle of the day that helps you to have more energy, do your job better, and make better decisions
,power of at'torney *n plural* **powers of attorney** [C,U] *law* the legal right to make financial decisions, sign documents etc for another person
'power ,outage *n* [C] *AmE* a period of time when there is no electricity supply; ⧉ **power failure**; ⧉ **power cut** *BrE*
'power ,pack *n* [C] something that is easily carried from which a piece of electrical equipment can get power, for example a BATTERY
'power plant *n* [C] **1** a building where electricity is produced to supply a large area; ⧉ **power station** **2** the machine or engine that supplies power to a factory, plane, car etc
'power point *n* [C] *BrE* a place on a wall where electrical equipment can be connected to the electricity supply; ⧉ **socket**
'power ,politics *n* [U] when a country or person attempts to get power and influence by using or threatening to use force or other actions, especially against another country
'power-,sharing *n* [U] an arrangement in which different groups, such as political parties, share the power to make decisions: *proposals for power-sharing between Catholics and Protestants in Northern Ireland*
'power ,station *n* [C] *especially BrE* a building where electricity is produced to supply a large area: *Chernobyl nuclear power station* | **coal-fired/gas-fired power station**; → see picture at ENERGY
'power ,steering also **power assisted steering** *n* [U] a system for STEERING a vehicle which uses power from the vehicle's engine and so needs less effort from the driver: *Most new cars now have power steering.*

P

prayer was that she would pass her exams.
4 prayers [plural] a regular religious meeting in a church, school etc, at which people pray together: *Prayers are at 8 o'clock.*
5 not have a prayer (of doing sth) *informal* to have no chance of succeeding: *He tried hard, but he didn't have a prayer.* | *They don't have a prayer of winning.*
6 an/the answer to sb's prayers *informal* something that someone wants or needs very much: *The job was an answer to my prayers.* → **on a wing and a prayer** at WING¹ (10)

prayer book *n* [C] a book containing prayers that is used in some Christian church services

prayer mat also **prayer rug** *n* [C] a small cloth on which Muslims kneel when praying

prayer wheel *n* [C] a drum-shaped object with prayers on it or inside it, which Tibetan Buddhists turn on a pole as a way of praying

praying 'mantis also **mantis** *n* [C] a large insect that eats other insects

pre- /priː/ *prefix* **1** before someone or something; → **ante-**: *prewar* (=before a war) **2** in preparation: *a prearranged signal* | *Preset the video.*

preach /priːtʃ/ *v* **1** [I,T] to talk about a religious subject in a public place, especially in a church during a service: [+to] *Christ began preaching to large crowds.* | [+on/about] *The vicar preached a sermon about the prodigal son.* | *He traveled the southern states, preaching the gospel.* **2** [T] to talk about how good or important something is and try to persuade other people about this: *Alexander has been preaching patience.* | **preach the virtues/merits/benefits of sth** *a politician preaching the virtues of a free market* **3** [I] to give someone advice, especially about their behaviour, in a way that they think is boring or annoying: [+about] *grown-ups preaching about the evils of drugs* **4 preach to the converted/choir** to talk about what you think is right or important to people who already have the same opinions as you → **practise what you preach** at PRACTISE (5)

preach·er /'priːtʃə $ -ər/ *n* [C] someone who talks about a religious subject in a public place, especially at a church

preach·y /'priːtʃi/ *adj informal* trying too much to persuade people to accept a particular opinion – used to show disapproval: *a preachy TV show*

pre·am·ble /priˈæmbəl $ 'priːæmbəl/ *n* [C,U] *formal* a statement at the beginning of a book, document, or talk, explaining what it is about: [+to] *the preamble to the American Constitution* | *Harding gave him the news without preamble* (=without saying anything else before it).

pre·ar·ranged /ˌpriːəˈreɪndʒd◂/ *adj* planned or decided before: *At a prearranged signal, everyone stood up.* —**prearrangement** *n* [U]

pre·but·tal /priˈbʌtl/ *n* [C] a statement that a politician makes saying that a criticism of them is false or unfair, before the criticism has been made; → **rebuttal**: *Wiggins issued a prebuttal against his opponent's speech, even before the text was delivered to reporters.*

pre·car·i·ous /prɪˈkeəriəs $ -ˈker-/ *adj* **1** a precarious situation or state is one which may very easily or quickly become worse: *Her health remained precarious, despite the treatment.* | *the company's precarious financial position* **2** likely to fall, or likely to cause someone to fall: *a precarious mountain trail* —**precariously** *adv*: *a cup of tea balanced precariously on her knee* —**precariousness** *n* [U]

pre·cast /ˌpriːˈkɑːst◂ $ -ˈkæst◂/ *adj* precast CONCRETE is already formed into the shapes needed to build something

pre·cau·tion /prɪˈkɔːʃən $ -ˈkɒː-/ *n* [C usually plural] something you do in order to prevent something dangerous or unpleasant from happening: *Fire precautions*

were neglected. | **as a precaution** *The traffic barriers were put there as a safety precaution.* | [+against] *Save your work often as a precaution against computer failure.* | **wise/sensible precaution** *The trails are well marked, but carrying a map is a wise precaution.* | *Vets took precautions to prevent the spread of the disease.* | **take the precaution of doing sth** *I took the precaution of insuring my camera.*

pre·cau·tion·a·ry /prɪˈkɔːʃənəri $ -ˈkɒːʃəneri/ *adj* done in order to prevent something dangerous or unpleasant from happening: *More troops were sent to the area as a precautionary measure.*

pre·cede [W3] /prɪˈsiːd/ *v* [T] *formal* **1** to happen or exist before something or someone, or to come before something else in a series; → **preceding**: *a type of cloud that precedes rain* | *Lunch will be preceded by a short speech from the chairman.* **2** to go somewhere before someone else: *The guard preceded them down the corridor.*

pre·ce·dence /'presɪdəns/ *n* [U] when someone or something is considered to be more important than someone or something else, and therefore comes first or must be dealt with first; ▣ **priority**: [+over] *Do we want a society where appearance takes precedence over skill or virtue?* | *Guests were seated in order of precedence.* | *Safety must be given precedence.*

pre·ce·dent /'presɪdənt/ *n* **1** [C] an action or official decision that can be used to give support to later actions or decisions: *a legal precedent* | **set/create a precedent** *UN involvement in the country's affairs would set a dangerous precedent.* | [+for] *precedents for what courts will accept as 'fair'* **2** [C,U] something of the same type that has happened or existed before: [+for] *There's not much precedent for men taking leave when their baby is born.* | **without precedent** *An epidemic on this scale is without precedent.* **3** [U] the way that things have always been done: **break with precedent** (=do something in a new way)

pre·ced·ing /prɪˈsiːdɪŋ/ *adj* [only before noun] *formal* happening or coming before the time, place, or part mentioned; ▣ **previous**; ◪ **following**: **preceding days/weeks/months/years** *income tax paid in preceding years* | **preceding chapter/paragraph/page etc** *the diagram in the preceding chapter*

pre·cept /'priːsept/ *n* [C] *formal* a rule on which a way of thinking or behaving is based: *basic moral precepts*

pre·cinct /'priːsɪŋkt/ *n* **1** [C] **shopping/pedestrian precinct** *BrE* an area of a town where people can walk and shop, and where cars are not allowed **2** [C] *AmE* one of the areas that a town or city is divided into, so that elections or police work can be organized more easily **3** [C] *AmE* the main police station in a particular area of a town or city **4 precincts** [plural] the area that surrounds an important building: *the precincts of the cathedral*

pre·cious¹ /'preʃəs/ *adj* **1** something that is precious is valuable and important and should not be wasted or used without care: **precious seconds/minutes/hours/time** *We cannot afford to waste precious time.* | *planes disrupting precious supplies of medicine and food* | *our planet's precious resources* **2** rare and worth a lot of money: **precious gem/stone/jewel** *a statue covered with precious jewels* **3** precious memories or possessions are important to you because they remind you of people you like or events in your life: [+to] *The doll is cracked and worn, but it's precious to me because it was my mother's.* **4** [only before noun] *spoken* used to show that you are annoyed that someone seems to care too much about something: *I never touched your precious car!* **5** *spoken* used to speak to someone you love, especially a baby or small child: *Come sit by me, precious.* **6** *AmE spoken* used in order to describe someone or something that is small and pretty; ▣ **cute**: *The kids gave me that ornament. Isn't it precious?* **7** *formal* too concerned about style or detail in your writing or speech, so that it does not seem

natural: *His early work is rather precious and juvenile.*
—**preciously** *adv* —**preciousness** *n* [U]

precious[2] *adv informal* **precious little/few** very little or very few: *I had precious little time for reading.*

precious 'metal *n* [C,U] a rare and valuable metal such as gold or silver

precious 'stone *n* [C] a rare and valuable jewel such as a DIAMOND or an EMERALD; → **semi-precious**

pre·ci·pice /ˈpresɪpɪs/ *n* [C]   **1** a very steep side of a high rock, mountain or cliff: *A loose rock tumbled over the precipice.*   **2** a dangerous situation in which something very bad could happen: *The stock market is on the edge of a precipice.*

pre·cip·i·tate[1] /prɪˈsɪpɪteɪt/ *v*   **1** [T] *formal* to make something serious happen suddenly or more quickly than was expected; ◨ **hasten**: *The riot was precipitated when four black men were arrested.*   **2** [I,T + out] *technical* to separate a solid substance from a liquid by chemical action, or to be separated in this way
precipitate sb into sth *phr v formal* to force someone or something into a particular state or condition: *The drug treatment precipitated him into a depression.*

pre·cip·i·tate[2] /prɪˈsɪpɪtət/ *n* [C] *technical* a solid substance that has been chemically separated from a liquid

precipitate[3] *adj formal* happening or done too quickly, and not thought about carefully; ◨ **hasty**: *a precipitate decision* —**precipitately** *adv*

pre·cip·i·ta·tion /prɪˌsɪpɪˈteɪʃən/ *n*   **1** [U] *technical* rain, snow etc that falls on the ground, or the amount of rain, snow etc that falls   **2** [C,U] *technical* a chemical process in which a solid substance is separated from a liquid   **3** [U] *formal* the act of doing something too quickly in a way that is not sensible

pre·cip·i·tous /prɪˈsɪpɪtəs/ *adj*   **1** very sudden: *a precipitous decline in stock prices*   **2** dangerously high or steep: *a precipitous path*   **3** *formal* happening or done too quickly, and not thought about carefully: *a precipitous marriage* —**precipitously** *adv*

pré·cis /ˈpreɪsiː $ preɪˈsiː/ *n plural* **précis** /-siːz $ -ˈsiːz/ [C] *especially BrE* a statement which gives the main idea of a piece of writing, speech etc; ◨ **summary, abstract** *AmE*: *a précis of the report* —**précis** *v* [T]

pre·cise W3 /prɪˈsaɪs/ *adj*   **1** precise information, details etc are exact, clear, and correct; ◨ **exact**: *precise sales figures* | *It was difficult to get precise information.* | *'She's a lot older than you, isn't she?' 'Fifteen years, to be precise.'*   **2** [only before noun] used to emphasize that you are referring to an exact thing; ◨ **exact**: *At that precise moment, her husband walked in.* | *The precise cause of the disease is unknown.* | *the precise location of the ship* | *the precise nature of their agreement*   **3** someone who is precise is very careful about small details or about the way they behave: *a precise, careful woman* | *with precise movements of his hands*

pre·cise·ly S2 W3 /prɪˈsaɪsli/ *adv*   **1** exactly and correctly; ◨ **exactly**: *Temperature can be measured precisely.* | *He arrived at precisely 4 o'clock.* | **precisely what/how/where etc** *It is difficult to know precisely how much impact the changes will have.* | *What, precisely, does that mean?* | *Lathes make wheels, or, more precisely, they make cylindrical objects.*   **2** used to emphasize that a particular thing is completely true or correct: *Women in these jobs are paid less precisely because most of the jobs are held by women rather than men.* | *She's precisely the kind of person we're looking for.*   **3** *spoken formal* used to say that you completely agree with someone: *'It needs to be dealt with now.' 'Precisely, before it gets any worse.'*

pre·ci·sion[1] /prɪˈsɪʒən/ *n* [U] the quality of being very exact or correct: **with precision** *The work was carried out with military precision* (=the work was done in a carefully planned and exact way).

precision[2] *adj* [only before noun]   **1** made or done in a very exact way: *precision engineering* | *precision bombing*   **2** **precision tool/instrument** a precision tool or instrument is used for making or measuring something in a very exact way

pre·clude /prɪˈkluːd/ *v* [T] *formal* to prevent something or make something impossible: *rules that preclude experimentation in teaching methods* | **preclude sb from doing something** *Age alone will not preclude him from standing as a candidate.*

pre·co·cious /prɪˈkəʊʃəs $ -ˈkoʊ-/ *adj* a precocious child shows intelligence or skill at a very young age, or behaves in an adult way – sometimes used to show disapproval in British English: *a precocious child who walked and talked early* —**precociously** *adv* —**precociousness** also **precocity** /prɪˈkɒsɪti $ -ˈkɑː-/ *n* [U]

pre·cog·ni·tion /ˌpriːkɒgˈnɪʃən $ -kɑːg-/ *n* [U] *formal* the knowledge that something will happen before it actually does

pre·con·ceived /ˌpriːkənˈsiːvd/ *adj* [only before noun] preconceived ideas, opinions etc are formed before you really have enough knowledge or experience: *preconceived notions about art* | *We started from scratch with no preconceived ideas.*

pre·con·cep·tion /ˌpriːkənˈsepʃən/ *n* [C] a belief or opinion that you have already formed before you know the actual facts, and that may be wrong: [+about/of] *I had the same preconceptions about life in South Africa that many people have.*

pre·con·di·tion /ˌpriːkənˈdɪʃən/ *n* [C] something that must happen or exist before something else can happen: [+of/for] *A ceasefire is a precondition for talks.*

pre·cooked /ˌpriːˈkʊkt◂/ *adj* precooked food has been partly or completely cooked before it is sold so that it can be quickly heated up later —**precook** *v* [T]

pre·cur·sor /prɪˈkɜːsə $ -ˈkɜːrsər/ *n* [C] *formal* something that happened or existed before something else and influenced its development: [+of/to] *a precursor of modern jazz*

pre·date /priːˈdeɪt/ *v* [T] to happen or exist earlier in history than something else: *The kingdom predates other African cultures by over 3,000 years.*

pre·da·tion /prɪˈdeɪʃən/ *n* [U] *technical* when an animal kills and eats another animal

pred·a·tor /ˈpredətə $ -ər/ *n* [C]   **1** an animal that kills and eats other animals; → **prey**   **2** someone who tries to use another person's weakness to get advantages: *a sexual predator*

predator

pred·a·to·ry /ˈpredətəri $ -tɔːri/ *adj*   **1** a predatory animal kills and eats other animals for food   **2** trying to use someone's weakness to get advantages for yourself – used to show disapproval: *predatory pricing*

predator and prey

pre·de·ces·sor /ˈpriːdɪsesə $ ˈpredɪsesər/ *n* [C]   **1** someone who had your job before you started doing it; ◨ **successor**: *Kennedy's predecessor as president was the war hero Dwight Eisenhower.*   **2** a machine, system etc that existed before another one in a process of development; ◨ **successor**: *The new BMW has a more powerful engine than its predecessor.*

pre·des·ti·na·tion /prɪˌdestɪˈneɪʃən, ˌpriːdes-/ *n* [U] the belief that God has decided everything that will happen and that people cannot change this

[1] 000, [2] 000, [3] 000, most frequent words in [S]poken and [W]ritten English

pre·fec·ture /ˈpriːfektʃʊə $ -tʃər/ *n* [C] a large area which has its own local government in some countries: *Saitama prefecture*

pre·fer S2 W2 /prɪˈfɜː $ -ˈfɜːr/ *v* **preferred, preferring** [T not in progressive]
1 to like someone or something more than someone or something else, so that you would choose it if you could; → **preference**: *This type of owl prefers a desert habitat.* | *She prefers her coffee black.* | *the government's preferred option* | **prefer sb/sth to sb/sth** *a child that prefers his imaginary world to reality* | *Employees said they would prefer more flexible working hours.* | **prefer to do sth** *I prefer to wear clothes made of natural fibers.* | *Or, if you prefer, you can email us.* | **prefer doing sth** *Chantal prefers travelling by train.* | **prefer that** *We prefer that our teachers have a degree in early childhood education.*
2 I would prefer it if *spoken* **a)** used to say that you wish a situation was different: *Sales have gone down, and obviously we'd prefer it if that didn't happen.* **b)** used when telling someone politely not to do something: *I'd prefer it if you didn't smoke in front of the children.*
3 prefer charges *BrE law* to make an official statement that someone has done something illegal

pref·e·ra·ble /ˈprefərəbəl/ *adj* better or more suitable: *For this dish, fresh herbs and garlic are preferable.* | *In warm weather, clothes made of natural fabrics are infinitely preferable* (=much better). | **preferable to (doing) sth** *Being taught in a small group is far preferable to being in a large, noisy classroom.*

pref·e·ra·bly /ˈprefərəbli/ *adv* used in order to show which person, thing, place, or idea you think would be the best choice: *Students must take two years of a foreign language, preferably Spanish.*

pref·e·rence W3 /ˈprefərəns/ *n*
1 [C,U] if you have a preference for something, you like it more than another thing and will choose it if you can; → **prefer**: *Do you have a colour preference?* | [+for] *a cultural preference for boy babies* | *Parents may be able to express a preference as to the school their child will attend.* | *The amount of sugar you add will depend on personal preference.* | *Many elderly people expressed a strong preference to live in their own homes.* | **in preference to sth** (=rather than something) *Use clear English in preference to technical language.*
2 [C,U] when someone is treated more favourably than other people, often when he or she has been treated unfairly in the past: *Racial preferences are a way to make up for years of discrimination against minorities.* | **give/show preference (to sb)** *In allocating housing, preference is given to families with young children.*
3 sexual preference someone's sexual preference is whether they want to have sex with men or women

pref·e·ren·tial /ˌprefəˈrenʃəl◂/ *adj* [only before noun] preferential treatment, rates etc are deliberately different in order to give an advantage to particular people: *preferential credit terms for reliable borrowers* —**preferentially** *adv*

pre·fer·ment /prɪˈfɜːmənt $ -ɜːr-/ *n* [U] *formal* when someone is given a more important job

pre·fig·ure /ˌpriːˈfɪgə $ -gjər/ *v* [T] *formal* to be a sign that something will happen later

pre·fix¹ /ˈpriːfɪks/ *n* [C] **1** *technical* a group of letters that is added to the beginning of a word to change its meaning and make a new word, such as 'un' in 'untie' or 'mis' in 'misunderstand'; → **affix, suffix 2** a number or letter that comes before other numbers or letters, especially a group of numbers that comes before a telephone number when you are calling someone in a different area **3** *old-fashioned* a title such as 'Ms' or 'Dr' used before someone's name; ⊟ **title**

prefix² *v* [T] **1** to add a prefix to a word, name, or set of numbers **2** *formal* to say something before the main part of what you have to say

preg·nan·cy /ˈpregnənsi/ *n plural* **pregnancies** [C,U] when a woman is pregnant (=has a baby growing inside her body): *This drug should not be taken during pregnancy.* | *her third pregnancy* | *teenage pregnancies* | *a pregnancy test*

preg·nant S3 /ˈpregnənt/ *adj*
1 if a woman or female animal is pregnant, she has an unborn baby growing inside her body; → **pregnancy**: *medical care for pregnant women* | *I knew right away that I was pregnant.* | *I thought I was too old to get pregnant.* | **twenty weeks/three months etc pregnant** *She's about five months pregnant.* | [+with] *Maria was pregnant with her second child.* | *I didn't mean to get her pregnant* (=make her pregnant). | *His wife was heavily pregnant* (=almost ready to give birth).
2 pregnant pause/silence a pause or silence which is full of meaning or emotion: *He stopped, and there was a pregnant pause.*
3 pregnant with sth *formal* containing a lot of a quality: *Every phrase in this poem is pregnant with meaning.*

pre·heat /ˌpriːˈhiːt/ *v* [T] to heat an oven to a particular temperature before it is used to cook something: *Preheat the oven to 375 degrees.*

pre·hen·sile /prɪˈhensaɪl $ -səl/ *adj technical* a prehensile tail, foot etc can curl around things and hold on to them

pre·his·tor·ic /ˌpriːhɪˈstɒrɪk◂ $ -ˈstɔː-, -ˈstɑː-/ *adj* **1** relating to the time in history before anything was written down: *prehistoric burial grounds* | *prehistoric animals* **2** very old-fashioned – used humorously: *a prehistoric attitude towards women*

pre·his·to·ry /priːˈhɪstəri/ *n* [U] the time in history before anything was written down

pre·judge /ˌpriːˈdʒʌdʒ/ *v* [T] to form an opinion about someone or something before you know or have considered all the facts – used to show disapproval: *Shepherd's case was prejudged by the media before her trial.* —**prejudgment** *n* [C,U]

prej·u·dice¹ /ˈpredʒʊdɪs/ *n* **1** [C,U] an unreasonable dislike and distrust of people who are different from you in some way, especially because of their race, sex, religion etc – used to show disapproval: *Women still face prejudice in the workplace.* | *It takes a long time to overcome these kinds of prejudices.* | [+against] *a cultural prejudice against fat people* | **racial/sexual prejudice** *Asian pupils complained of racial prejudice at the school.* **2 without prejudice (to sth)** *law* without harming or affecting something: *He was able to turn down the promotion without prejudice, and applied again several years later.* **3 to the prejudice of sth** *formal* in a way that has a harmful effect or influence on something

prejudice² *v* [T] **1** to influence someone so that they have an unfair or unreasonable opinion about someone or something: *There was concern that reports in the media would prejudice the jury.* | **prejudice sb against sth** *My own schooldays prejudiced me against all formal education.* **2** to have a bad effect on the future success or situation of someone or something: *A criminal record will prejudice your chances of getting a job.* | *He refused to comment, saying he did not wish to prejudice the outcome of the talks.*

prej·u·diced /ˈpredʒʊdɪst/ *adj* **1** having an unreasonable dislike of someone or something, especially a dislike of a group of people who belong to a different race, sex, or religion – used to show disapproval: *Some officers were racially prejudiced.* | *an intolerant and prejudiced man* | [+against] *The early Christian church was prejudiced against the Jews.* | *Environmentalists are prejudiced against the dam.* **2** seriously affected by a bad situation: *The council must provide housing for young people whose welfare is seriously prejudiced.*

prej·u·di·cial /ˌpredʒʊˈdɪʃəl/ *adj formal* having a bad effect on something: *prejudicial testimony*

P

prel·ate /'prelɪt/ n [C] a BISHOP, CARDINAL, or other important priest in the Christian church

pre·lim·i·na·ry¹ /prɪ'lɪmɪ̯nəri $ -neri/ adj [only before noun] happening before something that is more important, often in order to prepare for it: *the preliminary stages of the competition | a preliminary draft | [+to] The discussions were preliminary to preparing a policy paper.*

preliminary² n plural **preliminaries** [C usually plural] **1** something that is said or done first, to introduce or prepare for something else: [+to] *Pilot studies are a useful preliminary to large research projects. | After the usual preliminaries, the chairman made his announcement.* **2** one of the games in the first part of a competition, when it is decided who will go on to the main competition: *Four teams will be eliminated in the preliminaries.*

pre·lit·e·rate /priː'lɪtərɪ̯t/ adj a society that is preliterate has not developed a written language; → **illiterate**

pre-loved /ˌpriː 'lʌvd◂/ adj a pre-loved house, pet etc has already been owned by someone else – used especially in advertisements to suggest the previous owner cared strongly about the object, animal etc

prel·ude /'prelju:d/ n [C] **1 a prelude to sth** if an event is a prelude to a more important event, it happens just before it and makes people expect it: *Living together as a prelude to marriage is now considered acceptable in many countries.* **2** a short piece of music, especially one played at the beginning of a longer musical piece or before a church ceremony: *Chopin's preludes | an organ prelude*

pre·mar·i·tal /priː'mærɪ̯təl/ adj happening or existing before marriage: *premarital sex*

pre·ma·ture /'premətʃə, -tʃʊə, ˌpremə'tʃʊə $ ˌpriːmə'tʃʊr/ adj **1** happening before the natural or proper time: *his premature death due to cancer | premature ageing of the skin* **2** a premature baby is born before the usual time of birth: *a premature birth | The baby was six weeks premature.* **3** done too early or too soon: *a premature order to attack | Any talk of a deal is premature.* | **it is premature (for sb) to do sth** *It would be premature to accuse anyone until the investigation is complete.* —**prematurely** adv: *The baby was born prematurely.*

pre·med, pre-med /ˌpriː'med/ adj AmE relating to classes that prepare a student for medical school, or to the students who are taking these classes: *a premed student* —**premed,, pre-med** /'priːmed/ n [U]

pre·med·i·tat·ed /priː'medɪ̯teɪtɪd $ prɪ-/ adj a premeditated crime or attack is planned in advance and done deliberately: *premeditated murder*

pre·med·i·ta·tion /priːˌmedɪ̯'teɪʃən $ prɪ-/ n [U] the act of thinking about something and planning it before you actually do it

pre·men·stru·al /priː'menstruəl/ adj happening or relating to the time just before a woman's PERIOD (=the time each month when blood flows from her body)

pre,menstrual 'syndrome n [U] *PMS* the tiredness, headache, bad temper etc experienced by some women in the days before their PERIOD; ◲ **premenstrual tension** BrE

pre,menstrual 'tension n BrE [U] *PMT* the tiredness, headache, bad temper etc experienced by some women in the days before their PERIOD

prem·i·er¹ /'premiə $ prɪ'mɪr/ n [C] a PRIME MINISTER - used in news reports: *the Irish Premier*

premier² adj [only before noun] formal best or most important: *one of Dublin's premier hotels*

prem·i·ere, première /'premiə $ prɪ'mɪr/ n [C] the first public performance of a film, play, or piece of music: *Rossini's work had its premiere at the Paris Opera. | a movie premiere | the play's world premiere* (=the first performance in the world) —**premiere** v [I,T]: *The movie premiered on December 21, 1937.*

prem·i·er·ship /'premiəʃɪp $ prɪ'mɪrʃɪp/ n [C,U] the period when someone is PRIME MINISTER

prem·ise W3 /'premɪs/ n
1 premises [plural] the buildings and land that a shop, restaurant, company etc uses: *Schools may earn extra money by renting out their premises. | business premises |* **off the premises** *The manager escorted him off the premises.* | **on the premises** *The wonderful desserts are made on the premises.*
2 [C] also **premiss** BrE a statement or idea that you accept as true and use as a base for developing other ideas: *The idea that there is life on other planets is the central premise of the novel.* | **premise that** *the premise that an accused person is innocent until they are proved guilty*

prem·ised /'premɪst/ adj **be premised on/upon sth** to be based on a particular idea or belief: *The program is premised on the idea that drug addiction can be cured.*

pre·mi·um¹ /'priːmiəm/ n **1** [C] the cost of insurance, especially the amount that you pay each year: *insurance premiums* **2** [C] an additional amount of money, above a standard rate or amount: *Consumers are prepared to* **pay a premium** *for organically grown vegetables. | Top quality cigars are being* **sold at a premium**. **3 be at a premium** if something is at a premium, people need it or want it, but there is little of it available or it is difficult to get: *During the Olympic Games, accommodation will be at a premium.* | **space/time is at a premium** *Foldaway furniture is the answer where space is at a premium.* **4 put/place a premium on sth** to consider one quality or type of thing as being much more important than others: *Modern economies place a premium on educated workers.* **5** [U] especially AmE good quality petrol

premium² adj **1** of very high quality: *premium ice cream | the current consumer trend for premium products |* **premium quality** *British potatoes* **2 premium price/rate** premium prices and rates are higher than usual ones: *People are prepared to pay premium prices for quality products. | Calls are charged at the premium rate of 60p per minute.*

'premium ,bond n [C] a document that you buy from the government in Britain, which gives you the chance to win a large amount of money each month

'premium rate adj BrE **premium rate number/line/ service** a telephone connection to a particular service or company that costs a lot more than the usual rate when you call it because the company you are calling takes some of the money that you pay

pre·mo·ni·tion /ˌpreməˈnɪʃən, ˌpriː-/ n [C] a strange feeling that something, especially something bad, is going to happen: [+of] *a premonition of death |* **premonition that** *When Anne didn't arrive, Paul* **had a premonition that** *she was in danger.*

pre·mon·i·to·ry /prɪˈmɒnɪ̯təri $ -ˈmɑːnɪ̯tɔːri/ adj formal giving a warning that something unpleasant is going to happen: *premonitory symptoms of the disease*

pre·na·tal /ˌpriːˈneɪtl◂/ adj [only before noun] relating to unborn babies and the care of PREGNANT women; ◲ **antenatal** BrE: *prenatal care | prenatal screening* —**prenatally** adv

pre·nup·tial a·gree·ment /ˌpriːˌnʌpʃəl əˈgriːmənt/ also **pre-nup** /'priːnʌp/ informal n [C] a legal document that is written before a man and a woman get married, in which they agree things such as how much money each will get if they DIVORCE

pre·oc·cu·pa·tion /priːˌɒkjʊ̯ˈpeɪʃən $ -ˌɑːk-/ n **1** [singular,U] when someone thinks or worries about something a lot, with the result that they do not pay attention to other things: [+with] *the current preoccupation with sex and scandal | The management's*

P

preoccupation with costs and profits resulted in a drop in quality and customer service. **2** [C] something that you give all your attention to: **main/chief/central etc preoccupation** *Their main preoccupation was how to feed their families.*

pre·oc·cu·pied /priːˈɒkjᵿpaɪd $ -ˈɑːk-/ *adj* thinking about something a lot, with the result that you do not pay attention to other things: *What's wrong with Cindy? She seems a little preoccupied.* | [+with] *He's completely preoccupied with all the wedding preparations at the moment.*

pre·oc·cu·py /priːˈɒkjᵿpaɪ $ -ˈɑːk-/ *v* **preoccupied**, **preoccupying**, **preoccupies** [T] *formal* if something preoccupies someone, they think or worry about it a lot

pre·op·e·ra·tive /priːˈɒpərətɪv $ -ˈɑːp-/ *adj medical* relating to the time before a medical operation; **⚡ postoperative**: *the patient's preoperative assessment*

pre·or·dained /ˌpriːɔːˈdeɪnd◂ $ -ɔːr-/ *adj formal* if something is preordained, it is certain to happen in the future because God or FATE has decided it: *Is everything we do preordained?*

pre-owned /ˌpriː ˈəʊnd◂ $ -ˈoʊnd◂/ *adj* if something that is for sale is pre-owned, it has been owned and used by someone else before – used especially in advertisements to make something not sound old; **⚡ secondhand** *BrE*; **⚡ used** *AmE*: *pre-owned cars*

prep¹ /prep/ *n* [U] *BrE informal* work that is done by students on their own, after classes have finished – used in private schools; **⚡ homework**

prep² *v* past participle **prepped**, present participle **prepping** *AmE informal* **1** [T] to prepare someone for an operation or an examination **2** [T] to prepare food for cooking in a restaurant **3** [I] to prepare for something that you are going to do: *I have to prep for my afternoon class.*

prep. also **prep** *BrE* the written abbreviation of **preposition**

pre·pack·aged /ˌpriːˈpækɪdʒd◂/ *adj* prepackaged foods have already been prepared when you buy them, so that they are ready to eat, or only have to be heated: *prepackaged microwave meals*

pre·packed /ˌpriːˈpækt◂/ *adj* prepacked food or other goods are wrapped before they are sent to the shop where they are sold: *prepacked vegetables*

pre·paid /ˌpriːˈpeɪd◂/ *adj* if something is prepaid, it is paid for before it is needed or used: *The shipping charges are prepaid.* | *a prepaid envelope*

prep·a·ra·tion S2 W3 /ˌprepəˈreɪʃən/ *n*
1 [U] the process of preparing something: *This dish is good for dinner parties because much of the preparation can be done ahead of time.* | [+for] *Business training is a good preparation for any career.* | [+of] *the preparation of the budget* | **do sth in preparation for sth** (=in order to prepare for something) *He is practising every day, in preparation for the ice-skating championship.* | *Plans for the new school* **are** now **in preparation.** | *a course in food service and* **food preparation**
2 preparations [plural] arrangements for something that is going to happen: [+for] *Preparations for the upcoming Olympic Games are nearing completion.* | *Preparations are being made for the President's visit.* | *The festival was a great success, and* **preparations are underway** (=have started) *for another one next summer.*
3 [C] *formal* a mixture that has been prepared and that is used for a particular purpose, especially as a medicine or to make your skin more attractive: *a new preparation for cleansing the skin*

pre·par·a·to·ry /prɪˈpærətəri $ -tɔːri/ *adj* **1** [only before noun] done in order to get ready for something: *preparatory talks to clear the way for a peace settlement* | *preparatory drawings* | *A lot of preparatory work still needs to be done.* **2 preparatory to sth** *formal* before something else and in order to prepare for it: *The partners held several meetings preparatory to signing the agreement.*

pre·paratory school *n* [C] **1** a private school in Britain for children between the ages of 8 and 13 **2** a private school in the US that prepares students for college

pre·pare S1 W1 /prɪˈpeə $ -ˈper/ *v*
1 MAKE STH [T] **a)** to make a meal or a substance: *Prepare the sauce while the pasta is cooking.* | *When we got home, Stephano was busy preparing dinner.* ⚠ It is fairly formal to say that someone prepares a meal. It is more usual to say that they **make** a meal or **cook** a meal: *Bella was making dinner.* **b)** to write a document, make a programme etc: *Health and safety officers will investigate the site and prepare a report.* | *Green set himself the task of preparing a map of this remote area.*
2 MAKE PLANS/ARRANGEMENTS [I,T] to make plans or arrangements for something that will happen in the future; **⚡ get ready**: *The 45 year-old explorer has been preparing for his latest expedition to the Arctic.* | **prepare to do sth** *Her parents were busy preparing to go on holiday.* | *The prosecution wanted more time to prepare their case.*
3 MAKE STH READY [T] to make something ready to be used: *Prepare the soil, then plant the seedlings 8 inches apart.* | **prepare sth for sb/sth** *Coulthard's team were up all night preparing the car for the race.*
4 MAKE YOURSELF READY [T] to make yourself mentally or physically ready for something that you expect to happen soon: **prepare yourself (for sth)** *The letter arrived, and we prepared ourselves for bad news.* | *Can you just give me a couple more moments to prepare myself?* | **prepare yourself for a race/fight etc** *The Chicago Bears are busy preparing themselves for the big game.* | **prepare to do sth** *Buy the album, and prepare to be amazed.*
5 MAKE SB READY [T] to provide someone with the training, skills, experience etc that they will need to do a job or to deal with a situation: **prepare sb for sth** *a course that prepares students for English examinations* | *Schools should do more to prepare children for the world of work.* | *What does a coach do to prepare his team for the Superbowl?*
6 prepare the way/ground for sb/sth to make it possible for something to be achieved, or for someone to succeed in doing something: *Curie's research prepared the way for the work of modern nuclear scientists.*

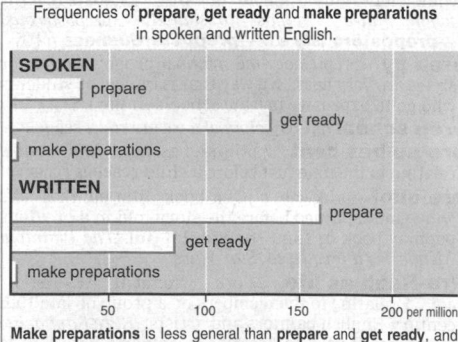

Frequencies of **prepare**, **get ready** and **make preparations** in spoken and written English.

SPOKEN — prepare / get ready / make preparations
WRITTEN — prepare / get ready / make preparations
50   100   150   200 per million

Make preparations is less general than **prepare** and **get ready**, and is usually used to talk about making a large number of arrangements for something important that is going to happen.

pre·pared S2 /prɪˈpeəd $ -ˈperd/ *adj*
1 be prepared to do sth to be willing to do something, especially something difficult or something that you do not usually do: *You have to be prepared to take risks in this kind of work.* | *How much is she prepared to pay?*
2 READY TO DEAL WITH STH [not before noun] ready to do something or deal with a situation: [+for] *I wasn't prepared for all their questions.* | **well/fully/inadequately etc prepared** *Luckily, we were well prepared for the storm.* | **ill-prepared** (=not ready to deal with a

P

⟦1⟧ 000, ⟦2⟧ 000, ⟦3⟧ 000, most frequent words in ⟦S⟧poken and ⟦W⟧ritten English

difficult situation) *The country was ill-prepared to fight another war.* | *There was no news and we were* **prepared for the worst** (=expected something very bad).
3 I'm not prepared to do sth *spoken* used when saying strongly that you refuse to do something: *I'm not prepared to sit here and listen to this rubbish!*
4 MADE EARLIER planned, made, or written at an earlier time, so that it is ready when it is needed: *The president read out a* **prepared statement.**

pre·pared·ness /prɪ'peədnɪs, -'peər̯d- $ -'perəd-, -'perd-/ *n* [U] *formal* **1** when someone is ready for something: *the country's lack of military preparedness* **2** when someone is willing to do something: *their preparedness to break the law*

pre-pay /'priː peɪ/ *adj* [only before noun] pre-pay MOBILE PHONE systems make you pay before you use the service, rather than sending you a demand for money after you have been using it

pre·pay /priː'peɪ/ *v past tense and past participle* **prepaid** [I,T] to pay for something before you need it or use it —**prepayment** *n* [C,U]

pre·pon·de·rance /prɪ'pɒndərəns $ -'pɑːn-/ *n formal* **1** a preponderance of sth if there is a preponderance of people or things of a particular type in a group, there are more of that type than of any other: *There is a preponderance of female students in the music department.* **2** a preponderance of the evidence *law* most of the EVIDENCE in a law case

pre·pon·de·rant /prɪ'pɒndərənt $ -'pɑːn-/ *adj formal* main, most important, or most frequent —**preponderantly** *adv*: *the preponderantly female staff at the factory*

pre·pon·de·rate /prɪ'pɒndəreɪt $ -'pɑːn-/ *v* [I] *formal* to be more important or frequent than something else

prep·o·si·tion /ˌprepə'zɪʃən/ *n* [C] a word that is used before a noun, PRONOUN, or GERUND to show place, time, direction etc. In the phrase 'the trees in the park', 'in' is a preposition —**prepositional** *adj*

prepositional 'phrase *n* [C] *technical* a phrase beginning with a preposition, such as 'in bed' or 'at war'

pre·pos·sess·ing /ˌpriːpə'zesɪŋ◂/ *adj formal* looking attractive or pleasant: *a prepossessing smile*

pre·pos·ter·ous /prɪ'pɒstərəs $ -'pɑːs-/ *adj formal* completely unreasonable or silly; ■ **absurd**: *The whole idea sounds absolutely preposterous!* —**preposterously** *adv* —**preposterousness** *n* [U]

prep·py /'prepi/ *adj AmE informal* preppy clothes or styles are very neat, in a way that is typical of students who go to expensive private schools in the US

'prep school *n* [C,U] *informal* a PREPARATORY SCHOOL

pre·pu·bes·cent /ˌpriːpjuː'besənt◂/ *adj formal* relating to the time just before a child reaches PUBERTY

pre·quel /'priːkwəl/ *n* [C] a book, film etc that tells you what happened before the story told in a previous popular book or film; → **sequel**: [+to] *'The Phantom Menace' is a prequel to 'Star Wars'.*

Pre-Raph·ae·lite /ˌpriː 'ræfəlaɪt $ -'ræfiə-/ *adj* **1** relating to the members of a group of late 19th century English painters and artists: *a Pre-Raphaelite painting* **2** used to describe a woman's hair that is long and curly —**Pre-Raphaelite** *n* [C]

pre·re·cord /ˌpriːrɪ'kɔːd $ -'kɔːrd/ *v* [T] to record music, a radio programme etc on a machine so that it can be used later: *a prerecorded interview* —**prerecording** *n* [C,U]

pre·req·ui·site /priː'rekwɪzɪt/ *n* [C] *formal* something that is necessary before something else can happen or be done: [+for/of/to] *A reasonable proficiency in English is a prerequisite for the course.*

pre·rog·a·tive /prɪ'rɒgətɪv $ -'rɑː-/ *n* [C usually singular] a right that someone has, especially because of their importance or social position: [+of] *Education was once the prerogative of the elite.* | *Arriving late is a*

woman's prerogative. | *the royal prerogative* (=the rights of kings and queens)

pres. also **pres** *BrE* **1** the written abbreviation of *present* **2** the written abbreviation of *president*

pres·age /'presɪdʒ, prɪ'seɪdʒ/ *v* [T] *formal* to be a sign that something is going to happen, especially something bad: *The large number of moderate earthquakes that have occurred recently could presage a larger quake soon.* —**presage** *n* [C]: *a presage of doom*

Pres·by·te·ri·an /ˌprezbɪ'tɪəriən◂ $ -'tɪr-/ *n* [C] a member of a Protestant church, which is one of the largest churches in the US, and is the national church of Scotland —**Presbyterian** *adj* —**Presbyterianism** *n* [U]

pres·by·ter·y /'prezbɪtəri $ -teri/ *n plural* **presbyteries** [C] **1** a local court or council of the Presbyterian church or the area controlled by that church **2** a house in which a Roman Catholic priest lives **3** the eastern part of a church, behind the area where the CHOIR (=singers) sits

pre·school[1], **pre-school** /'priːskuːl/ *adj* relating to the time in a child's life before they are old enough to go to school: *preschool children*

preschool[2] *n* [C,U] *AmE* a school for children between two and five years of age; ■ **kindergarten** *BrE*

preschool·er /ˌpriː 'skuːlə $ -ər/ *n* [C] *AmE* a child who does not yet go to school, or who goes to preschool

pre·sci·ent /'presiənt $ 'preʃənt, 'priː-/ *adj formal* able to imagine or know what will happen in the future —**prescience** *n* [U]

pre·scribe /prɪ'skraɪb/ *v* [T] **1** to say what medicine or treatment a sick person should have; → **prescription**: prescribe sb sth *If these don't work I may have to prescribe you something stronger.* | prescribe sth for sth *the drugs prescribed for his stomach pains* **2** *formal* to state officially what should be done in a particular situation: *What punishment does the law prescribe for this crime?*

pre·scribed /prɪ'skraɪbd/ *adj* decided by a rule: *All schools must follow the prescribed curriculum.*

pre·script /'priːˌskrɪpt/ *n* [C] *formal* an official order or rule

pre·scrip·tion /prɪ'skrɪpʃən/ *n* [C] **1** a piece of paper on which a doctor writes what medicine a sick person should have, so that they can get it from a PHARMACIST; → **prescribe**: [+for] *a prescription for sleeping pills* | *We are trying to cut the price of* **prescription drugs**. | *a* **repeat prescription** (=one that you have regularly) | **fill a prescription** *AmE* (=get the drugs a doctor has written that you need) *I got the prescription filled on the way home.* **2** a particular medicine or treatment ordered by a doctor for a sick person: *If you're pregnant, you can get free prescriptions.* **3** **on prescription** *BrE*, **by prescription** *AmE* a drug that you get on prescription can only be obtained with a written order from the doctor; → **over the counter** **4** an idea or suggestion about how you should behave, or how to make a situation, activity etc successful: [+for] *The party's main prescription for educational problems was to give schools more money.*

pre·scrip·tive /prɪ'skrɪptɪv/ *adj* **1** saying how something should or must be done, or what should be done: *prescriptive teaching methods* **2** stating how a language should be used, rather than describing how it is used; ■ **descriptive**: *prescriptive grammar* **3** prescriptive right *BrE law* a right that has existed for so long that it is as effective as a law —**prescriptively** *adv*

pre·seas·on /ˌpriː'siːzən◂/ *adj* [only before noun] preseason matches, training etc happen in the time immediately before a sport's normal SEASON: *preseason training*

pres·ence S2 W2 /'prezəns/ *n*
1 [U] when someone or something is present in a particular place; ■ **absence**: *Your presence is requested at the club meeting on Friday.* | [+of] *Tests revealed the*

...e of poison in the blood.
presenc... presence of sb also **in sb's presence** formal
2 in th... presence of someone or in the same place as them: *He was*
with so... ...ned not to complain in the presence of the
determin... ...asked you not to smoke in my presence. | *I... nurse. |*
3 APPEARANCE/MANNER [U] the ability to appear
impressive... to people because of your appearance or
the way you... behave: *a man of great presence*
4 OFFICIAL GROUP [singular] a group of people, especially soldie...s, who are in a place to control what is
happening: *We will increase police presence in local*
communities. | *Soldiers still maintain a military pres-
ence in the area.*
5 BUSINESS [C usually singular] the ability to gain
sales because your business is strong or noticeable: *a
company with a strong presence in all major world
markets*
6 SPIRIT [C usually singular] a spirit or influence that
cannot be seen but is felt to be near: *They felt a strange
presence in the deserted house.*
7 make your presence felt to have a strong and noticeable effect on the people around you or the situation
you are in: *She was a very pretty girl and made her
presence felt almost at once.*

presence of 'mind *n* [U] the ability to deal with a
dangerous situation calmly and quickly: **have the presence of mind to do sth** *I'm glad she had the presence of
mind to take down the car's registration number.*

pres·ent¹ S2 W2 /'prezənt/ *adj*
1 PLACE [not before noun] in a particular place;
↔ **absent** [+at/in] *Foreign observers were present at the
elections.* | *the gases present in the earth's atmosphere*
2 MEMORY [not before noun] to be felt strongly or
remembered for a long time: [+in] *The memory of her
brother's death is still present in her mind.*
3 TIME [only before noun] happening or existing now:
*the present situation of the millions of people who are
suffering poverty and disease* | **At the present time** *we
have no explanation for this.*
4 the present day also **the present** in the time now, or
modern times: *The practice has continued from medieval times to the present day.*
5 the present also **the present tense** *technical* the form
of the verb that shows an existing state or action: *the
present tense of the verb 'to be'*
6 all present and correct *BrE*, **all present and
accounted for** *AmE* used to say that everyone who is
supposed to be in a place, at a meeting etc is now here
7 present company excepted *spoken* used when you
are criticizing a group of people and you want to tell
the people you are with that they are not included in
the criticism: *Women are never satisfied with anything!
Present company excepted, of course.* → PRESENTLY

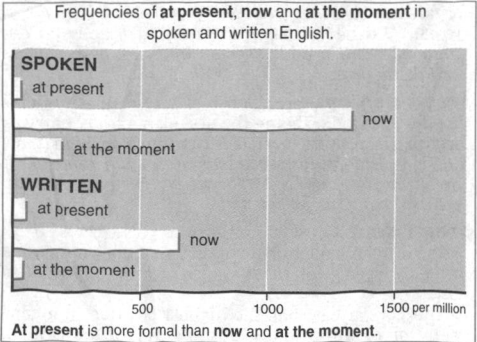

Frequencies of **at present**, **now** and **at the moment** in
spoken and written English.

SPOKEN
at present
now
at the moment

WRITTEN
at present
now
at the moment

500   1000   1500 per million

At present is more formal than **now** and **at the moment**.

pre·sent² S2 W1 /prɪ'zent/ *v*
1 GIVE [T] to give something to someone, for example
at a formal or official occasion: **present sb with sth** *He
was presented with a bottle of champagne.* | *She was
presented with an award.* | **present sth to sb/sth** *The
computer centre presented a cheque for £500 to cancer
research.*

2 CAUSE STH TO HAPPEN [T] to cause something to
happen or exist: **present sb with sth** *I knew I had
presented her with an impossible task.* | **present a
problem/difficulty** *Large classes present great problems
to many teachers.*
3 present yourself to talk and behave in a particular
way when you meet people: *He presents himself well.*
4 DESCRIPTION [T] to show or describe someone or
something: *The artist was determined to present an
accurate picture.* | *We'll present the information using a
chart.* | **present sb as sth** *Shakespeare presents the hero
as a noble man doomed to make mistakes.* | **present
yourself as sth** *The government presents itself as being
sensitive to environmental issues.*
5 SPEECH [T] to give a speech in which you offer an
idea, plan etc to be considered or accepted: *Our manager is due to present the report at the end of the
month.* | **present sth to sb** *On January 3 the company
will present its plans to the bank.*
6 DOCUMENT/TICKET [T] to show something such as
an official document or ticket to someone in an official
position: *You must present your passport to the customs
officer.*
7 THEATRE/CINEMA [T] to give a performance in a
theatre, cinema etc, or broadcast a programme on
television or radio: *Edinburgh Theatre Company presents 'The Wind in the Willows'*
8 TELEVISION/RADIO [T] *BrE* if you present a television or radio programme, you introduce its different
parts; ▤ **host** *AmE*: *Thursday's The Late Show was
presented by Cynthia Rose.*
9 APPEARANCE [T] to give something or someone a
particular appearance or style: *The restaurant likes to
present food with style.*
10 sth presents itself if a situation, opportunity etc
presents itself, it suddenly happens or exists: *I'll tell
her as soon as the opportunity presents itself.*
11 FORMALLY INTRODUCE SB [T] to formally introduce someone to another person, especially to someone of a very high rank: *I was presented to the Queen in
1964.*
12 present your apologies/compliments etc *formal*
used to greet someone, say sorry to them etc very
politely: *Mrs. Gottlieb presents her apologies and
regrets she will not be able to attend.*
13 ILLNESS [I,T] *medical* to show an illness by having a
particular SYMPTOM (=sign of an illness): *The doctor
asked whether any of the children had been presenting
any unusual symptoms.* | *Three of the five patients
presented with fever and severe headaches.*

pres·ent³ /'prezənt/ *n* **1** [C] something you give
someone on a special occasion or to thank them for
something; ▤ **gift**: *I was searching for a present for
Mark.* | **birthday/Christmas present** | *I gave her a very
special present for her birthday.* **2 the present a)** the
time that is happening now: *Stop worrying about the
past and live in the present.* | *The film is set sometime
between 1995 and the present.* | *'When do you want to
start?' 'Well, there's **no time like the present** (=used to
say that if you are going to do something at all, you
should do it now).'* **b)** *technical* the form of the verb that
shows what exists or is happening now; ▤ **the present
tense 3 at present** at this time; ▤ **now**: *The item you
want is not available at present.* | *At present, the airport
handles 110 flights a day.* **4 for the present** something
that exists or will be done for the present exists now
and will continue for a while, though it may change in
the future: *The company is still in business, at least for
the present.*

pre·sent·a·ble /prɪ'zentəbəl/ *adj* tidy and attractive
enough to be seen or shown to someone: *She's a pre-
sentable young woman.* | *Let's tidy up and **make the
house a bit more presentable.*** | *I must go and **make
myself presentable.*** —**presentably** *adv*

pre·sen·ta·tion [S2] [W3]
/ˌprezənˈteɪʃən
$ ˌpriːzen-, -zən / n

1 GIVE PRIZE [C] the act of giving someone a prize or present at a formal ceremony: *the presentation ceremony* | *Dr Evans thanked him for coming to* **make** the **presentations.** | [+of] *the presentation of prizes*

presentation

giving a presentation

2 TALK [C] an event at which you describe or explain a new product or idea: *We will begin a series of presentations to help the public fully understand our system.* | **make/give a presentation** *I'm going to ask each of you to make a short presentation.*

3 WAY OF SAYING/SHOWING [U] the way in which something is said, offered, shown, or explained to others: [+of] *desktop devices for the presentation of information* | *the presentation of evidence*

4 PROOF [U] when you show something to someone so that it can be checked or considered: [+of] *the presentation of the identity documents* | **on presentation of sth** *Club members will be admitted on presentation of their membership cards.*

5 PERFORMANCE [C] the act of performing a play: [+of] *I went to see the National Theatre's presentation of Arthur Miller's 'The Last Yankee'.*

6 BABY [C,U] *medical* the position in which a baby is lying in its mother's body just before it is born: *a breech presentation*

7 presentation copy a book that is given to someone, especially by the writer or PUBLISHER —**presentational** *adj*

'present-day *adj* [only before noun] modern or existing now: *present-day Sicily*

pres·en·tee·is·m /ˌprezənˈtiːɪzəm/ n [U] a situation when people spend a lot of time at work, even if they are ill or could take a holiday, because they want their employers to see that they are working very hard; → **absenteeism**

pre·sent·er /prɪˈzentə $ -ər/ n [C] *BrE* someone who introduces the different parts of a television or radio show; ⊟ **host** *AmE*: *the presenter of BBC 2's Newsnight*

pre·sen·ti·ment /prɪˈzentɪmənt/ n [C] *formal* a strange feeling that something is going to happen, especially something bad; ⊟ **premonition**: [+of] *a presentiment of disaster*

pres·ent·ly /ˈprezəntli/ *adv formal* **1** in a short time; ⊟ **soon**: *The doctor will be here presently.* | *Presently, I fell asleep.* **2** especially *AmE* at the present time; ⊟ **now**: *The range of courses presently available has grown.* | *Your case is presently being investigated.*

ˌpresent 'participle n [C] *technical* a PARTICIPLE that is formed in English by adding 'ing' to the verb, as in 'sleeping'. It can be used in COMPOUND forms of the verb to show CONTINUOUS tenses, as in 'she's sleeping', or as an adjective, as in 'the sleeping child'.

ˌpresent 'perfect n **the present perfect** the form of a verb that shows what happened during a period of time up to and including the present, formed in English with the present tense of the verb 'have' and a PAST PARTICIPLE, as in 'he has gone'

ˌpresent 'tense n **the present tense** *technical* the form of the verb that shows what exists or is happening now; ⊟ **the present**

pres·er·va·tion /ˌprezəˈveɪʃən $ -zər-/ n [U] **1** when something is kept in its original state or in good condition; → **preserve**: [+of] *Eliot campaigned for the preservation of London's churches.* | *We are working for the preservation of the environment.* | *the preservation of our cultural heritage* | *methods of food preser-*

vation **2** the act of making sure that a situation continues without changing: [+of] *the preservation of peace in the region* **3** the degree to which something has remained unchanged or unharmed by weather, age etc: *The arena is in an exceptionally fine state of preservation.* → SELF-PRESERVATION

pres·er·va·tion·ist /ˌprezəˈveɪʃənɪst $ -zər-/ n [C] someone who works to prevent historical places, buildings etc from being destroyed

preser'vation ˌorder n [C] in Britain, an official order that something, especially an area of countryside or an old building, must be preserved and not damaged: *a tree preservation order*

pre·ser·va·tive /prɪˈzɜːvətɪv $ -ɜːr-/ n [C,U] a chemical substance that is used to prevent things from decaying, for example food or wood: *food that contains no artificial preservatives*

pre·serve¹ [W3] /prɪˈzɜːv $ -ɜːrv/ v [T]
1 to save something or someone from being harmed or destroyed; → **preservation**: *We must encourage the planting of new trees and preserve our existing woodlands.*
2 to make something continue without changing: *the responsibility of the police to preserve the peace* | *Norma tried to preserve a normal family life in difficult circumstances.*
3 to store food for a long time after treating it so that it will not decay: *black olives preserved in brine* —**preservable** *adj* —**preserver** n [C] → WELL-PRESERVED

preserve² n **1** [C usually plural] a substance made from boiling fruit or vegetables with sugar, salt, or VINEGAR: *homemade fruit preserves* **2** [singular] an activity that is only suitable or allowed for a particular group of people: *Banking used to be a male preserve.* | [+of] *The civil service became the preserve of the educated middle class.* **3** [C] an area of land or water that is kept for private hunting or fishing

pre-set /ˌpriː ˈset/ *adj* [usually before noun] decided or set at an earlier time: *The heating automatically switches on and off at pre-set temperatures.*

pre-shrunk /ˌpriː ˈʃrʌŋk◂/ *adj* pre-shrunk clothes are sold after they have been made smaller by being washed; → **shrink**: *pre-shrunk jeans*

pre·side /prɪˈzaɪd/ v [I] to be in charge of a formal event, organization, ceremony etc: *I shall be pleased to preside at your meetings.* | *Mr Justice Waller, presiding judge for the north east*

preside over sth *phr v* **1** to be in a position of authority at a time when important things are happening: *The government seemed to be presiding over large-scale unemployment.* **2** to be the head of a company or organization: *Finch presided over the company for 30 years.* **3** to be in charge of a meeting or activity: *The chairman will preside over an audience of architects and developers.*

pres·i·den·cy /ˈprezɪdənsi/ n plural **presidencies** [C] the position of being the president of a country or organization, or the period of time during which someone is president: *Roosevelt was elected four times to the presidency of the US.* | *There were few real improvements during his presidency.*

pres·i·dent [S2] [W2] /ˈprezɪdənt/ n [C]
1 the official leader of a country that does not have a king or queen: [+of] *the President of France* | *President Bush*
2 the person who has the highest position in a company or organization: [+of] *the president of General Motors*

ˌpresident-e'lect n [singular] someone who has been elected as a new president, but who has not yet started the job

pres·i·den·tial /ˌprezɪˈdenʃəl◂/ *adj* [usually before noun] relating to a president: *a presidential election* | *the party's presidential candidate*

pre·sid·i·um, praesidium /prɪ'sɪdiəm, -'zɪ-/ n *plural* **presidia** /-diə/ [C] a committee chosen to represent a large political organization, especially in a COMMUNIST country

press¹ [S2] [W2] /pres/ n

1 NEWS **a)** the press [also + plural verb *BrE*] people who write reports for newspapers, radio, or television: *the freedom of the press* | *The press have been very nasty about him.* **b)** reports in newspapers and on radio and television: *To judge from the press, the concert was a great success.* | *press reports* | *The band has received good press coverage* (=the reports written about something in newspapers). | **local/national etc press** *The story was widely covered in the national press.* | **tabloid/popular etc press**

2 **get/be given a bad press** to be criticized in the newspapers or on radio or television: *The government's policy on mental health care is getting an increasingly bad press.*

3 **get/have a good press** to be praised in the newspapers or on radio or television: *Our recycling policy is getting a good press.*

4 PRINTING [C] **a)** a business that prints and sometimes also sells books: *the Clarendon Press* **b)** also **printing press** a machine that prints books, newspapers, or magazines

5 MACHINE [C] a piece of equipment used to put weight on something in order to make it flat or to force liquid out of it: *a trouser press* | *a flower press*

6 PUSH [C usually singular] *especially BrE* a light steady push against something small: *Give the button another press.*

7 **go to press** if a newspaper, magazine, or book goes to press, it begins to be printed: *All information was correct at the time we went to press.*

8 CROWD [singular + of] *especially BrE* a crowd of people pushing against each other

press² [S1] [W2] v

1 AGAINST STH [T always + adv/prep] to push something firmly against a surface; ◨ **push**: *Manville kept his back pressed flat against the wall.* | *She pressed the gas pedal and the car leapt forwards.* | *He pressed a card into her hand before leaving.*

2 BUTTON [T] to push a button, switch etc to make a machine start, a bell ring etc; ◨ **push**: *Lily pressed the switch and plunged the room into darkness.* | *Press control, alt, delete to log on to the computer.*

3 CLOTHES [T] to make clothes smooth using a hot iron; ◨ **iron**: *I'll need to press my suit.*

4 CROWD [I always + adv/prep] to move in a particular direction by pushing: *The car rocked as the crowd pressed hard against it.*

5 PERSUADE [I,T] to try hard to persuade someone to do something, especially by asking them many times: *I felt that if I had pressed him he would have lent me the money.* | **press sb to do sth** *The police pressed her to remember all the details.* | **press sb for sth** *The manufacturers are pressing the government for action.* | [+for] *We must continue to press for full equality.* | *I was pressing my claim for custody of the child.*

6 HEAVY WEIGHT [T] to put pressure or a weight on something to make it flat, crush it etc: *pressed flowers* | *At this stage the grapes have to be pressed.*

7 HOLD SB/STH CLOSE [T] to hold someone or something close to you: **press sb/sth to you** *He reached out and pressed her to him.*

8 **press sb's hand/arm** to hold someone's hand or arm tightly for a short time, to show friendship, sympathy etc: *Sometimes he was too ill to speak, and just pressed my hand.*

9 **press charges** to say officially that someone has done something illegal and must go to court

10 **be pressed for time/cash etc** to not have enough time, money etc: *a government department that is pressed for both time and money*

11 GIVE [T] to offer something to someone and try to make them take it: **press sth on sb** *I pressed money on him, but he refused to take it.*

12 EXERCISE [T] to push a weight up from your chest using only your arms, without moving your legs or feet

13 **press sb/sth into service** to persuade someone to help you, or to use something to help you do something because of an unexpected problem or need: *The army was pressed into service to fight the fires.*

14 **press the flesh** to shake hands with a lot of people – used humorously: *The President reached into the crowd to press the flesh.*

15 **press sth home a)** to push something into its place: *Jane slammed the door and pressed the bolt home.* **b)** to repeat or emphasize something, so that people remember it: *He decided it was the time to press his point home.*

16 **press home your advantage** to try to succeed completely, using an advantage that you have gained

17 RECORD [T] to make a copy of a record, CD etc → **be hard pressed to do sth** at HARD² (5)

press on *phr v*

also **press ahead** to continue to continue doing something, especially working, in a determined way: *We'll talk about your suggestion later – now let's just press on.* | [+with] *Shall we press ahead with the minutes of the last meeting?*

'press ,agency n [C] an organization that gets news from a country and supplies it to newspapers, television news etc all over the world

'press ,agent n [C] someone whose job is to supply photographs or information about a particular actor, musician etc to newspapers, radio, or television

'press ,baron n [C] *BrE* someone who owns and controls one or more important national newspapers

'press box n [C] an area at a sports STADIUM where people from newspapers, radio, or television sit

'press ,conference n [C] a meeting held by a person or group at which they answer questions from people who write or present news reports: *The Green Party held a press conference the next day.*

'press corps n [C] a group of news REPORTERS working at the place where something important is happening: *the White House press corps*

'press ,cutting also **'press ,clipping** n [C] a short piece of writing or a picture, cut out from a newspaper or magazine

pressed /prest/ adj **be pressed for time/money etc** to not have enough time, money etc

'press ,gallery n [C] an area above or at the back of a hall, used by news REPORTERS

'press-gang¹ v [T] **1** **press-gang sb into doing sth** *informal* to force someone to do something: *I don't want to press-gang you into doing something you're not happy with.* **2** to force men to work on a ship, by taking them from the streets – done in the past

'press-gang² n [C] a group of people in the past who took young men away using force in order to make them come to work on a ship

pres·sie, prezzie /'prezi/ n [C] *BrE spoken* a present

'press·ing¹ /'presɪŋ/ adj needing to be discussed or dealt with very soon; ◨ **urgent**: **pressing problem/matter/need etc** *Poverty is a more pressing problem than pollution.*

pressing² n **1** [C] a thing or group of things, especially records or CDs, that have been made by pressing plastic or metal into shape: *The CD, released in October, sold out a first pressing of 1,500 in just four months.* **2** [C,U] the act of pressing something: *The olives are heat treated during the second pressing.*

press·man /'presmæn/ n *plural* **pressmen** /-men/ [C] *BrE informal* someone who writes news reports

'press ,office n [C] the office of an organization or government department which gives information to the newspapers, radio, or television —**press officer** n [C]

P

'press re,lease *n* [C] an official statement giving information to the newspapers, radio, or television

'press ,secretary *n* [C] a secretary to an important organization or person, who gives information about them to the newspapers, radio, or television

'press-up *n* [C] *BrE* a type of exercise in which you lie facing the ground, and push your body up with your arms; ☐ **push-up** *AmE*

press-up

pres·sure¹ S1 W1
/'preʃə $ -ər/ *n*
1 PERSUADE [U] an attempt to persuade someone by using influence, arguments, or threats: *They are* **putting pressure on** *people to vote yes.* | **be/come under pressure to do sth** *The minister was under pressure to resign.* | **be/come**

press-up *BrE*/
push-up *AmE*

sit-up

under pressure from sb (to do sth) *I was under pressure from my parents to become a teacher.* | *The Labour government came under pressure from the trade unions.* | [+for] *Pressure for change has become urgent.* | [+on] *the pressure on all of us to keep slim* | *He* **exerts pressure** *on his kids to get them to do as he wants.* | *You must never* **give in to pressure.**
2 ANXIETY/OVERWORK [C,U] a way of working or living that causes you a lot of anxiety, especially because you feel you have too many things to do: [+of] *I feel I'm not able to cope well with the pressures of life.* | [+on] *The pressure on doctors is increasing steadily.* | **under pressure** *I'm under constant pressure at work.* | *The* **pressures of work** *can make you ill.* | *a* **high pressure** *job* | *athletes who show* **grace under pressure** (=who behave well when they are anxious)
3 CAUSING CHANGE [C,U] events or conditions that cause changes and affect the way a situation develops, especially in ECONOMICS or politics: *inflationary pressures* | *Analysts expect the pound to* **come under pressure.** | **relieve/reduce pressure (on sb/sth)** *Slowing the arms race relieved pressure on the Soviet economic system.* | *The 1990s* **brought** *increased economic* **pressure to bear on** *all business activities.*
4 WEIGHT [U] the force or weight that is being put on to something: [+of] *The pressure of the water turns the wheel.* | *the pressure of his hand on my arm*
5 GAS/LIQUID [C,U] the force produced by the quantity of gas or liquid in a place or container: *The gas containers burst* **at high pressure.**
6 WEATHER [C,U] a condition of the air in the Earth's ATMOSPHERE, which affects the weather: **high/low pressure** *A ridge of high pressure is building up strongly over the Atlantic.* → PEER PRESSURE

pressure² *v* [T] *especially AmE* to try to make someone do something by making them feel it is their duty to do it; ☐ **pressurize** *BrE*: **pressure sb into doing sth** *You want to enjoy food, not to be pressured into eating the right things.* | **pressure sb to do sth** *Don't feel we are pressuring you to give what you can't afford.*

'pressure ,cooker *n* [C] **1** a tightly-covered cooking pot in which food is cooked very quickly by the pressure of hot steam **2** a situation or place that causes anxiety or difficulties: *the pressure cooker of soccer management*

pres·sured /'preʃəd $ -ərd/ *adj* feeling worried, or making you feel worried, because of the number of things you have to do; ☐ **pressurized** *BrE*: *a highly pressured job*

'pressure group *n* [C] a group or organization that tries to influence the opinions of ordinary people and

persuade the government to do something; → **interest group**: *environmental pressure groups*

'pressure point *n* [C] **1** a place or situation where there may be trouble: *a pressure point for racial tension* **2** a place on the body that can be pressed, either to stop bleeding or to help make you feel better

pres·sur·ize also **-ise** *BrE* /'preʃəraɪz/ *v* [T] to persuade someone to do something by making them feel it is their duty to do it; ☐ **pressure**: **pressurize sb into doing sth** *It is not a good idea to pressurize children into playing a musical instrument.* | **pressurize sb to do sth** *Everyone is being pressurized to vote.*

pres·sur·ized also **-ised** *BrE* /'preʃəraɪzd/ *adj* **1** if a container or space is pressurized, the air, gas, or liquid inside it is kept at a controlled pressure: *a pressurized aircraft cabin* | *a pressurized water reactor* **2** *BrE* feeling worried, or making you feel worried, because of the number of things you have to do; ☐ **pressured**: *I feel very pressurized at the moment.*

pres·tige¹ /pre'stiːʒ/ *n* [U] the respect and admiration that someone or something gets because of their success or important position in society: [+of] *the prestige of having your work shown at a top London gallery* | *The king wanted to* **enhance** *his* **prestige** *through war.* | *This little-known British firm has now* **gained** *considerable* **prestige.** | *the personal prestige attached to owning a large property*

prestige² *adj* [only before noun] a prestige project, product etc is one of high quality that people respect you for having or being involved in: *tiny roles in prestige films* | *a prestige car*

pres·ti·gious /pre'stɪdʒəs $ -'stiː-, -'stɪ-/ *adj* admired as one of the best and most important: *a prestigious literary award* | *a* **highly prestigious** *university*

pres·to¹ /'prestəʊ $ -toʊ/ *adj, adv* technical played or sung very quickly

presto² *n plural* **prestos** [C] *technical* a piece of music, or part of one, that is played or sung very quickly

presto³ *interjection AmE* said when something happens suddenly in a way that seems unbelievable or magical; ☐ **hey presto** *BrE*: *You just press a button and presto! A drink appears.*

pre-stressed /ˌpriː 'strest◂/ *adj* pre-stressed CONCRETE has been made stronger by having wires put inside it

pre·su·ma·bly S1 W3 /prɪ'zjuːməbli $ -'zuː-/ *adv* used to say that you think something is probably true: *It's raining, which presumably means that your football match will be cancelled.* | [sentence adverb]: *He's dead now, presumably?*

pre·sume S3 /prɪ'zjuːm $ -'zuːm/ *v*
1 [T] to think that something is true, although you are not certain; ☐ **assume**: *Each of you will make a speech, I presume?* | *'Are his parents still alive?' '**I presume so.'** |* **presume that** *I presume we'll be there by six o'clock.* | **presume sb/sth to be sb/sth** *From the way he talked, I presumed him to be your boss.* | **be presumed to do sth** *The temple is presumed to date from the first century BC.*
2 [T] to accept something as true until it is shown to not be true, especially in law; ☐ **assume**: *We must presume innocence until we have evidence of guilt.* | **be presumed dead/innocent etc** *Their nephew was missing, presumed dead.*
3 [I] *formal* to behave without respect or politeness by doing something that you have no right to do: **presume to do something** *I would never presume to tell you what to do.*
4 [T usually in present tense] *formal* to accept something as being true and base something else on it; ☐ **presuppose**: *The Ancient History course presumes some knowledge of Greek.* | **presume that** *I presume that someone will be there to meet us when we arrive.*
5 presume on/upon sb's friendship/generosity etc to unfairly ask someone for more than you should,

because they are your friend, are generous etc: *It would be presuming on his generosity to ask him for money.*

pre·sump·tion /prɪˈzʌmpʃən/ n **1** [C] something that you think is true because it is very likely: **presumption that** *the presumption that their wealth is the result of crime* | **on the presumption that** | *On the presumption that the doctor knows best, I took the medicine.* **2** [C,U] *law* the act of thinking something is true, bad, or good until it is shown to not be true, bad, or good: [+of] *the presumption of innocence* | [+against/ in favour of] *a strong presumption against development in national parks* **3** [U] *formal* behaviour that seems rude and too confident: *She was enraged by his presumption.*

pre·sump·tive /prɪˈzʌmptɪv/ adj *formal* or *technical* based on a reasonable belief about what is likely to be true: *a presumptive diagnosis* —**presumptively** adv

pre·sump·tu·ous /prɪˈzʌmptʃuəs/ adj *formal* doing something that you have no right to do and that seems rude: **is it presumptuous (of sb) to do sth** *Would it be presumptuous of me to ask why you are so miserable?* —**presumptuously** adv —**presumptuousness** n [U]

pre·sup·pose /ˌpriːsəˈpəʊz $ -ˈpoʊz/ v [T] *formal* **1** to depend on something that is believed to exist or to be true; **◨ assume**: *The idea of heaven presupposes the existence of God.* | **presuppose that** *Your argument presupposes that Dickens was a social reformer.* **2** to have to happen if something is true: *Without struggle there can be no progress, and struggle presupposes winners and losers.*

pre·sup·po·si·tion /ˌpriːsʌpəˈzɪʃən/ n *formal* **1** [C] something that you think is true, although you have no proof; **◨ assumption**: **presupposition that** *Hick's presupposition is that all religions believe in the same God.* **2** [U] when you think something is true even though you have no proof

pre-tax /ˌpriː ˈtæks◂/ adj pre-tax profits or losses are the profits or losses of a company before tax has been taken away: ***Pre-tax profits fell 26.6% to £3.1 million.*** —**pre-tax** adv

pre·teen /ˌpriːˈtiːn◂/ adj relating to or made for children who are 11 or 12 years old: *preteen clothing* —**preteen** /ˈpriːtiːn/ n [C]

pre·tence *BrE*; **pretense** *AmE* /prɪˈtens $ ˈpriːtens/ n [singular,U] **1** a way of behaving which is intended to make people believe something that is not true: **pretence that** *the pretence that the old system could be made to work* | **pretence of/at (being/doing) sth** *a pretence at seriousness* | *Tollitt **made no pretense** of being surprised.* | *How long are you going to **keep up the pretence** of being ill?* | **abandon/give up/drop a pretence** *Abandoning any pretence at politeness, they ran for the door.* | **under the pretence of (doing) sth** *John waited for her under the pretence of tying his shoelaces.* | *It was all an **elaborate pretence**.* **2** **under/on false pretences** without telling the truth about yourself or your intentions: *You brought me here under false pretences!*

pre·tend¹ S2 W3 /prɪˈtend/ v
1 [I,T] to behave as if something is true when in fact you know it is not, in order to deceive people or for fun: **pretend (that)** *We can't go on pretending that everything is OK.* | *Let's pretend we're on the moon.* | **pretend to do sth** *She pretended not to notice.* | *He's not asleep – he's just pretending.* | *To **pretend ignorance** of the situation would be irresponsible.* | *I can't marry her and to **pretend otherwise** would be wrong.*
2 [T usually in negatives] to claim that something is true, when it is not: **pretend (that)** *I can't pretend I understand these technical terms.* (=I admit I do not understand them) | **pretend to do/be sth** *The book doesn't pretend to be for beginners.*

pretend² adj imaginary or not real – used especially by children: *We sang songs around a pretend campfire.*

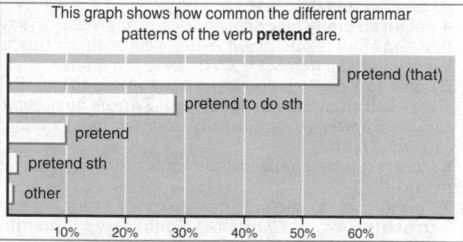
This graph shows how common the different grammar patterns of the verb **pretend** are.

- pretend (that)
- pretend to do sth
- pretend
- pretend sth
- other

10%　20%　30%　40%　50%　60%

pre·tend·ed /prɪˈtendɪd/ adj something that is pretended appears to be real but is not: *Her eyes widened in pretended astonishment.*

pre·tend·er /prɪˈtendə $ -ər/ n [C] someone who claims to have a right to be king, leader etc, when this is not accepted by many people: [+to] *the pretender to the English throne*

pre·tense /prɪˈtens $ ˈpriːtens/ n the American spelling of PRETENCE

pre·ten·sion /prɪˈtenʃən/ n [C usually plural,U] **1** an attempt to seem more important, more intelligent, or of a higher class than you really are: [+to] *Lilith resented Adam's pretensions to superiority.* | *the humbleness and **lack of pretension** of Jordan's cafe* **2** a claim to be or do something: **pretension(s) to be sth** *The group don't **have any pretensions** to be pop stars.* | [+to] *a large village with pretensions to the status of a small town*

pre·ten·tious /prɪˈtenʃəs/ adj if someone or something is pretentious, they try to seem more important, intelligent, or high class than they really are in order to be impressive; **◨ unpretentious**: *a pretentious film* —**pretentiously** adv —**pretentiousness** n [U]

pret·er·ite also **preterit** *AmE* /ˈpretərət/ n **the preterite** *technical* the tense or verb form that expresses a past action or condition —**preterite** adj

pre·ter·nat·u·ral /ˌpriːtəˈnætʃərəl◂ $ -tər-/ adj *formal* **1** beyond what is usual or normal: *He felt possessed of a preternatural strength and fearlessness.* **2** strange, mysterious, and unnatural: *the preternatural green light* —**preternaturally** adv: *The town was preternaturally quiet.*

pre·text /ˈpriːtekst/ n [C] a false reason given for an action, in order to hide the real reason: [+for] *The incident **provided the pretext** for war.* | **on/under the pretext of doing sth** *Tom called at her apartment on the pretext of asking for a book.* | **on/under the pretext that** *He left immediately on the pretext that he had a train to catch.* | *He'll phone **on some pretext** or other.*

pret·ti·fy /ˈprɪtɪfaɪ/ v **prettified, prettifying, prettifies** [T] to change something with the intention of making it more attractive, but often with the effect of spoiling it: *attempts to prettify the harbour*

pret·ty¹ S2 W3 /ˈprɪti/ adv [+ adj/adv] *spoken*
1 fairly or more than a little: *I'm pretty sure he'll say yes.* | *She still looks pretty miserable.* → see box at RATHER
2 very: *Dinner at Luigi's sounds pretty good to me.*
3 **pretty well/much** almost completely: *He hit the ball pretty well exactly where he wanted it.* | *The guard left us pretty much alone.* | *They're all pretty much the same.*
4 **pretty nearly** also **pretty near** *AmE* almost: *The shock of Pat's death pretty near killed Roy.* → **be sitting pretty** at SIT (9)

pretty² S3 W3 adj comparative **prettier**, superlative **prettiest**
1 a woman or child who is pretty has a nice, attractive face: *a pretty little girl* | *Maria looks much prettier with her hair cut short.* → see box at BEAUTIFUL
2 something that is pretty is pleasant to look at or listen to but is not impressive: *a pretty dress* | *The tune is pretty.* | *What a pretty little garden!*
3 **not a pretty sight** very unpleasant to look at – sometimes used humorously: *After a night's drinking,*

P

Al was not a pretty sight.

4 not just a pretty face *spoken* used humorously to say that someone is intelligent, when people think this is surprising: *I'm not just a pretty face, you know!*

5 come to a pretty pass *old-fashioned* used to say that a very bad situation has developed: ***Things have come to a pretty pass**, if you can't say what you think without causing a fight.*

6 cost a pretty penny *old-fashioned* to cost a lot of money

7 pretty as a picture *old-fashioned* very pretty
—**prettily** *adv*: *Charlotte sang very prettily.*
—**prettiness** *n* [U]

pret·zel /ˈpretsəl/ *n* [C] a hard salty type of bread baked in the shape of a stick or a loose knot

pre·vail /prɪˈveɪl/ *v* [I not in progressive] *formal* **1** if a belief, custom, situation etc prevails, it exists among a group of people at a certain time: [+in/among etc] *the economic conditions which prevail in England and Wales* | *I admired the creativity which prevailed among the young writers.* **2** if a person, idea, or principle prevails in a fight, argument etc, they are successful in the end: *Justice will prevail.* | **common sense prevails/reason prevails** (=a sensible decision is made) *He considered lying, but then common sense prevailed.* | [+over/against] *Your inner strength will enable you to prevail over life's obstacles.*

prevail on/upon sb *phr v formal* to persuade someone: **prevail on/upon sb to do sth** *She prevailed upon her father to say nothing.*

pre·vail·ing /prɪˈveɪlɪŋ/ *adj* [only before noun] **1** existing or accepted in a particular place or at a particular time; ◨ **current**: *The **prevailing mood** of public opinion remained hostile.* | *the **prevailing** economic **conditions** in Northern Ireland* **2 prevailing wind** a wind that blows over a particular area most of the time

prev·a·lent /ˈprevələnt/ *adj* common at a particular time, in a particular place, or among a particular group of people: [+in/among etc] *Solvent abuse is especially prevalent among younger teenagers.* | *the prevalent belief in astrology* —**prevalence** *n* [singular,U]: *the prevalence of deafness in older age groups*

pre·var·i·cate /prɪˈværɪkeɪt/ *v* [I,T] *formal* to try to hide the truth by not answering questions directly: *'I'm not sure,' he prevaricated.* —**prevarication** /prɪˌværɪˈkeɪʃən/ *n* [C,U]

pre·vent S2 W1 /prɪˈvent/ *v* [T] to stop something from happening, or stop someone from doing something: *The rules are intended to prevent accidents.* | **prevent sb (from) doing sth** *His back injury may prevent him from playing in tomorrow's game.* | *We were prevented from entering the site.* | *Wrap small ornaments in paper to prevent them being damaged.* —**preventable** *adj*: *preventable diseases* | *Every one of these deaths is preventable.*

pre·vent·a·tive /prɪˈventətɪv/ *adj* PREVENTIVE: *preventative measures* —**preventatively** *adv*

pre·ven·tion /prɪˈvenʃən/ *n* [U] when something bad is stopped from happening: [+of] *Educating new drivers is important for the **prevention of accidents**.* | **crime/accident/fire etc prevention** *Effective crime prevention must be our main goal.* | *a fire prevention officer* | *You know what they say, **prevention is better than cure** (=it is better to stop something bad from happening than to remove the problem once it has happened).*

pre·vent·ive /prɪˈventɪv/ also **preventative** *adj* [only before noun] intended to stop something you do not want to happen, such as illness, from happening: *preventive health programs* | **preventive action/measure** *While travelling abroad, take preventive measures to avoid illness.* —**preventively** *adv*

pre,ventive de'tention *n* [U] *BrE law* a system in which people who are guilty of many crimes are kept in prison for a long time

pre,ventive 'medicine *n* [U] medical treatment, advice, and health education that is designed to prevent disease happening rather than cure it

pre-verb·al /ˌpriː ˈvɜːbəl◂ $ -ɜːr-/ *adj* [only before noun] *technical* happening before a child has learned to speak: *the pre-verbal stages*

pre·view¹ /ˈpriːvjuː/ *n* [C] **1** an occasion when you can see a film, play, painting etc before it is shown to the public: [+of] *a **sneak preview** of the new fashions for autumn* | *the press preview of the show* (=when people who write for newspapers, television etc could see it) **2** a description of a film, television programme, show etc that people will be able to see soon

preview² *v* [T] **1** to see or describe something before it is shown to the public: *Journalists will be able to preview the exhibition tomorrow.* **2** to show or perform something before it is shown to the public: *The band will preview their new album on 2nd March.*

pre·vi·ous S1 W1 /ˈpriːviəs/ *adj*
1 [only before noun] having happened or existed before the event, time, or thing that you are talking about now: *I've met him before on two previous occasions.* | *She has two children from a previous marriage.* | *Do you have any previous experience of this type of work?* | *The lawyer told the judge that Kennedy had no previous convictions.*
2 the previous day/chapter/owner etc the one that came immediately before the one you are talking about now: *I had met them the previous day.* | *as we said in the previous chapter* | *The trees had been planted by the previous owner.*
3 previous to sth *formal* before a particular time or event: *There were almost no women MPs previous to 1945.*

pre·vi·ous·ly S3 W2 /ˈpriːviəsli/ *adv* before now or before a particular time: *Almost half the group had previously been heavy smokers.* | **two days/three years etc previously** (=two days, three years etc before) *Six months previously he had smashed up his car.*; → see box at AGO

pre-war /ˌpriː ˈwɔː◂ $ -ˈwɔːr◂/ *adj* [usually before noun] happening or existing before a war, especially the Second World War; ◨ **post-war**: *pre-war Britain*

prey¹ /preɪ/ *n* **1** [singular,U] an animal, bird etc that is hunted and eaten by another animal; ◨ **predator**: *a tiger stalking its prey* → see picture at PREDATOR **2 bird/beast of prey** a bird or animal which lives by killing and eating other animals **3 be/fall prey to sb/sth** if someone falls prey to someone or something bad, they are harmed or affected by them: *Street children in this part of the world often fall prey to drug dealers.* | *They are prey to nameless fears.* **4 easy prey a)** someone who can easily be deceived or harmed: *He was easy prey for the two conmen who called at his house.* **b)** an animal which is easily caught by another: *Fish at the surface of the water are easy prey for eagles.*

prey² *v*
prey on sb/sth *phr v* **1** if an animal or bird preys on another animal or bird, it hunts and eats it; → **predator**: *Cats prey on birds and mice.* **2** to try to deceive or harm weaker people: *religious cults that specialize in preying on young people* **3 prey on sb's mind** to make someone worry continuously: *The accident has been preying on my mind all week.*

prez·zie /ˈprezi/ *n* [C] *BrE spoken* a present

price¹ S1 W1 /praɪs/ *n*
1 [C,U] the amount of money you have to pay for something

high/low price
prices go up/rise/increase/soar
prices go down/fall/drop
prices fluctuate (=prices go up and down)
a price rise/increase
a reduction/fall/drop in prices
put up/increase/raise prices
cut/lower/slash prices (=make them lower)
agree (on) a price/fix a price

price freeze (=when prices are kept at the same level)
price war (=when shops try to have the lowest prices)

People are prepared to pay high prices for designer clothes. | [+of] *The price of fuel keeps going up.* | *House prices in this area are falling.* | *Oil prices fluctuated significantly during October.* | *fears of massive electricity price increases* | *a sharp rise in food prices* | *a drop in the price of coal* | *They have cut the price of their products by almost 30 per cent.* | [+for] *We agreed on a price for the bike.* | *Tesco is selling two bottles of champagne for the price of one!* → see box at COST¹ → ASKING PRICE, COST PRICE, LIST PRICE, MARKET PRICE

2 [singular] the unpleasant things that you must suffer in order to be successful, free etc: [+of] *He's never at home, but that's the price of success.* | *The awful boat journey was a small price to pay for freedom.* | *They may pay a high price for their few years of glory.* | *She was finally made senior executive, but at what price!*
3 half/full price used to talk about half the usual price of something, or the actual usual price: *I bought these jeans at half price in the sale.*
4 at a price for a lot of money: *You can get goat's cheese at the local delicatessen – at a price!*
5 at any price whatever the cost and difficulties may be: *She was determined to have a child at any price.*
6 not at any price used to say that you would not do something, even for a lot of money: *Sorry, that painting's not for sale at any price.*
7 put a price on sth to give something a financial value: *You can't put a price on what a mother does for her children.*
8 What price fame/glory etc? *usually spoken* used to suggest that something was not worth achieving because too many bad things have happened as a result: *What price progress?*
9 be beyond price to be extremely valuable or important
10 price on sb's head a reward for catching or killing someone
11 everyone has their price used to say that you can persuade people to do anything if you give them what they want → **cheap at the price** at CHEAP¹ (8); → **name your price** at NAME² (7); → **pay the price** at PAY¹ (9)

price² v [T] **1** [usually in passive] to decide the price of something that is for sale: *a reasonably priced apartment* | **be priced at sth** *Tickets are priced at £75 each.* **2** to put the price on goods to show how much they cost **3** to compare the prices of things: *We spent Saturday morning pricing microwaves.* **4 price yourself out of the market** to demand too much money for the services or goods that you are selling

price con·trol n [C,U] a system in which the government decides the prices of things

price ·fixing n [U] **1** a system in which the government decides the prices of things; ◳ **price control 2** an agreement between producers and sellers of a product to set its price at a high level

price ·index n [C] a list of particular goods and services and how much their prices change each month → RETAIL PRICE INDEX

price·less /'praisləs/ adj **1** extremely valuable: *priceless antiques* **2** a quality or skill that is priceless is extremely important or useful: *The ability to motivate people is a priceless asset.* **3** *informal* extremely funny or silly: *The look on his face was priceless.*

price list n [C] a list of prices for things being sold

price sup·port n [U] a system in which the government keeps the price of a product at a particular level by giving the producer money or buying the product itself

price tag n [C] **1** a piece of paper with a price on it that is attached to something in a shop **2** the amount that something costs: *It's difficult to put a price tag on such a project* (=say how much it costs).

price war n [C] a situation in which several companies reduce the prices of what they sell, because they are all trying to get the most customers

pric·ey, **pricy** /'praisi/ adj informal expensive: *The clothes are beautiful but very pricey.*

pric·ing /'praisiŋ/ n [U] the act of deciding the price of something that you sell: *a competitive pricing policy*

prick¹ /prik/ v **1** [T] to make a small hole in something using something sharp: *Prick the sausages before you grill them.* | **prick yourself/prick your finger** (=accidentally make a hole in your skin) *She had pricked her finger on a rose thorn.* **2** [I,T] if something pricks a part of your body, or if it pricks, you feel small sharp pains; → **prickle:** *Angry tears pricked her eyes.* | *a curious pricking sensation* **3 prick sb's conscience** if something pricks someone's conscience or their conscience pricks them, they feel guilty or ashamed: *Her conscience pricked her as she told the lie.* **4 prick (up) its ears** if an animal pricks up its ears, it raises them to listen to a sound: *The rabbit stopped suddenly, pricking up its ears.* **5 prick (up) your ears** if you prick up your ears or your ears prick up, you listen carefully because you have heard something interesting: *Jay pricked up his ears when I mentioned a vacation.*

prick sth ⇔ **out** phr v BrE to place young plants in soil after you have grown them from seed

prick² n [C]
1 PERSON *spoken not polite* a very offensive word for a stupid unpleasant man
2 SEX ORGAN *informal not polite* a PENIS
3 POINT ENTERING **a)** a slight pain you get when something sharp goes into your skin: *I didn't feel the prick of the needle.* **b)** BrE an act of pricking something: *Give the sausages a prick.* → PINPRICK
4 EMOTION a sudden slight feeling you get when you are unhappy about something: [+of] | *She felt a prick of resentment when she saw them together.*
5 prick of conscience an uncomfortable feeling that you have done something wrong

prick·le¹ /'prikəl/ n [C] **1** a long thin sharp point on the skin of some animals or the surface of some plants **2** if you feel a prickle of fear, anger, or excitement, you feel slightly afraid, angry, or excited in a way that makes your skin feel slightly cold and uncomfortable: [+of] *She felt a prickle of fear as she realized that she was alone.*

prickle² v **1** [I,T] if something prickles your skin, it makes it sting slightly: *A cold breeze prickled his face.* | *His hair prickled my neck.* | [+on] *He felt sweat prickle on his forehead.* **2** [I] if your skin prickles, it begins to sting slightly: *Her skin was prickling uncomfortably.* **3** [I] BrE if your eyes prickle, they sting slightly because you are going to cry: *She felt her eyes prickle. 'It was awful,' she whispered.* | *My eyes prickled with tears.* **4** [I] if you prickle, you feel slightly angry, excited, or afraid: [+with] *The thought of meeting him made her prickle with excitement.* | [+at] *She felt herself prickle* (=become angry) *at his tone of voice.*

prick·ly /'prikli/ adj **1** covered with thin sharp points: *a plant with prickly leaves* → see picture at SURFACE **2** if your skin feels prickly, it stings slightly: *His skin felt painful and prickly.* | *The base of my neck was prickly with sweat.* **3** something that is prickly makes your skin sting slightly: *a prickly woollen sweater* **4** *informal* someone who is prickly gets annoyed or offended easily: *She was prickly and sharp with me.* | *As she got older, she became more prickly and forgetful.* **5** a prickly subject causes a lot of disagreements and difficulties: *We finally turned to the prickly question of who was going to pay.* —**prickliness** n [U]

prickly ·heat n [U] a skin condition in which you get uncomfortable red spots on your skin. Prickly heat is caused by too much strong sun on your skin.

P

1 000, 2 000, 3 000, most frequent words in S poken and W ritten English

prickly 'pear n [C,U] a type of CACTUS that has yellow flowers and red fruit. The fruit is also called a prickly pear.

pric·y /'praɪsi/ adj another spelling of PRICEY

pride[1] S3 W3 /praɪd/ n

1 FEELING OF PLEASURE [U] a feeling that you are proud of something that you or someone connected with you has achieved; → **proud**

with pride
great/immense pride
take pride in sth (=feel proud of something)
a sense of pride
glow with pride/feel a glow of pride/your heart swells with pride (=feel very proud)
national pride (=a feeling that you are proud of your country)
civic pride (=a feeling that you are proud of your town or city)

He wore his medals with pride. | [+in] *He takes great pride in his children's achievements.* | *The people have a sense of pride in their community.* | *His heart swelled with pride when his daughter came in.* | *She felt a glow of pride when her name was announced for the prize.* | *Success in sport is a source of national pride.*

2 RESPECT [U] a feeling that you like and respect yourself and that you deserve to be respected by other people; → **proud**: **sb's pride** *It hurt his pride when his wife left him.* | *I think that getting a job would give him his pride back.* | *She didn't try to hide her anger and injured pride.* | *It's a matter of pride for some men that their wives don't have to work.*

3 TOO MUCH PRIDE [U] a belief that you are better than other people and do not need their help or support; → **proud**: **sb's pride** *His pride wouldn't allow him to ask for help.* | *She ought to swallow her pride* (=ignore or forget her feelings of pride) *and call him.*

4 take pride in your work/appearance etc to do something very carefully and well, in a way that gives you a lot of satisfaction: *Your should take more pride in your work.* | *She took great pride in her appearance.*

5 sb's pride and joy a person or thing that someone is very proud of: *His garden is his pride and joy.*

6 the pride of sth a) the thing or person that the people in a particular place are most proud of: *Wigan's rugby team was the pride of the town.* **b)** the best thing in a group: *a beautiful Japanese sword that is the pride of our collection*

7 have/take pride of place if something has or takes pride of place, it is put in the best place for people to see because it is the thing you are most proud of: *A large photograph of the children had pride of place on the sitting room wall.*

8 LIONS [C] a group of lions: *A young lion had strayed some distance from the pride.*

pride[2] v **pride yourself on (doing) sth** to be especially proud of something that you do well, or of a good quality that you have: *a restaurant that prides itself on speed of service* | *She prides herself on being a good listener.*

priest W3 /priːst/ n [C]
1 someone who is specially trained to perform religious duties and ceremonies in the Christian church
2 a man with religious duties and responsibilities in some non-Christian religions

priest·ess /'priːstes/ n [C] a woman with religious duties and responsibilities in some non-Christian religions

priest·hood /'priːsthʊd/ n **1 the priesthood** if someone is in the priesthood, they are a Christian priest: *He is celebrating 30 years in the priesthood.* | *There has been a decline in the number of people joining the priesthood.* **2** [C usually singular,U] all the priests of a particular religion or country: *an attempt to reduce the influence of the priesthood in the country*

priest·ly /'priːstli/ adj [usually before noun] like a priest, or relating to a priest: *priestly robes*

prig /prɪg/ n [C] someone who behaves in a morally good way and shows that they disapprove of the way other people behave – used to show disapproval: *Don't be such a prig! It's only a bit of harmless fun!* —**priggish** adj: *a rather priggish, old-fashioned man* —**priggishness** n [U]

prim /prɪm/ adj **1** very formal and careful in the way you speak and behave, and easily shocked by anything rude: *She looked prim and nervous in her best hat and coat.* | *a very prim and proper young lady* **2** prim clothes are neat and formal: *a prim suit* —**primly** adv

pri·ma bal·le·ri·na /ˌpriːmə ˌbæləˈriːnə/ n [C] the main woman dancer in a group of BALLET dancers

pri·ma·cy /'praɪməsi/ n [singular,U] formal if someone or something has primacy, they are the best or most important person or thing: [+of] *the primacy of the family* | *We must give primacy to education.*

prima don·na /ˌpriːmə ˈdɒnə $ -ˈdɑːnə/ n [C] **1** the most important woman singer in an OPERA company **2** someone who thinks that they are very good at what they do, and demands a lot of attention and praise from other people: *In my view, football players are a bunch of over-paid prima donnas.*

pri·mae·val /praɪˈmiːvəl/ adj a British spelling of PRIMEVAL

pri·ma fa·cie /ˌpraɪmə ˈfeɪʃi $ -ʃə/ adj [only before noun] law based on what seems to be true when you first consider a situation, even though it may later be proved to be untrue: *prima facie evidence* | *a prima facie case of professional misconduct*

pri·mal /'praɪməl/ adj [only before noun] formal primal feelings or actions seem to belong to a part of people's character that is ancient and animal-like: *a primal fear of the unknown*

pri·ma·ri·ly W3 /'praɪmərəli $ praɪˈmerəli/ adv mainly: *The advertisement is aimed primarily at children.*

pri·ma·ry[1] S3 W2 /'praɪməri $ -meri/ adj
1 [usually before noun] most important; ⊟ **main**: *Our primary concern is to provide the refugees with food and healthcare.* | *Many of the villagers rely on fishing as their primary source of income.* | **primary purpose/aim/objective** *Their primary objective is to make money.* | *Personal safety is of primary importance.*
2 [only before noun] especially BrE relating to the education of children between five and eleven years old; ⊟ **elementary** AmE; → **secondary**: *a primary teacher* | *primary education* | *teaching at primary level*
3 happening or developing before other things: *a primary tumour* | *Counselling was given as a primary therapy for depression.*

primary[2] n plural **primaries** [C] **1** a primary election **2** BrE a primary school

primary 'care n [U] basic medical treatment that you receive from a doctor who is not a SPECIALIST: *a primary care physician* (=a doctor who provides primary care)

primary 'colour n [C] one of the three colours red, yellow, and blue, which you can mix together to make any of the other colours

primary e'lection n [C] an election in the US at which people vote to decide who will be a party's CANDIDATE for a political position in the main election

primary 'health care also **primary care** n [U] the medical care that someone receives first when they become ill or have an accident

primary 'school n [C] BrE a school for children between five and 11 years old in England and Wales; ⊟ **elementary school** AmE

primary 'source n [C] a document, book etc that contains information that has been obtained by people's experiences and not taken from other documents, books etc; → **secondary source**

,primary 'stress n [C,U] technical the strongest force that is put on a part of a long word when you say it, like the force given to 'pri' in 'primary'. It is shown in this dictionary by the mark (').

pri·mate /'praɪmeɪt/ n [C] a member of the group of animals that includes monkeys and humans

Pri·mate /'praɪmət/ n [C] the most important priest in a country, especially in the Church of England; ➡ **archbishop**

prime[1] /praɪm/ adj [only before noun]   **1** most important; ➡ **main**: Smoking is the prime cause of lung disease. | Our prime concern is providing jobs for all young school leavers. | He was named as the **prime suspect** in the murder investigation. | Good management is of **prime importance** in business.   **2** of the very best quality or kind: prime rib of beef | prime agricultural land | The hotel is in a prime location overlooking the valley.   **3 be a prime candidate/target (for sth)** to be the person or thing that is most suitable or most likely to be chosen for a particular purpose: The school is a prime candidate for closure. | Old people are a prime target for thieves.   **4 prime example** a very typical example of something: Blakey Hall is a prime example of a 19th century building.

prime[2] n [singular] the time in your life when you are strongest and most active: **in your prime** She's now forty and still in her prime. | He is now **past his prime**. | a man **in the prime of life** | a young singer who was tragically **cut off in** her **prime** (=died while she was in her prime)

prime[3] v [T]   **1** |PREPARE SB| to prepare someone for a situation so that they know what to do: **prime sb with sth** Did you prime her with what to say? | **prime sb for sth** He had a shower and primed himself for action. | **prime sb to do sth** He had been primed to say nothing about it.   **2** |A GUN| to prepare a gun or bomb so that it can fire or explode   **3** |PAINT| to put a special layer of paint on a surface, in order to prepare it for the next layer: All metal surfaces will have to be primed.   **4 prime the pump** informal to encourage a business, industry, or activity to develop by putting money or effort into it   **5** |WATER| to pour water into a water pump in order to make it ready to work

,Prime 'Minister, **prime minister** abbreviation PM n [C] the most important minister and leader of the government in some countries which have a parliament: the British Prime Minister | He first became prime minister in 1982. | [+of] the Prime Minister of Turkey

,prime 'mover n [C]   **1** someone who helps to make something happen and has great influence in the way it develops: [+in/of/behind] He was a prime mover in the bid to get better pay for West Indian cricketers. | She was a prime mover of social change in the nineteenth century.   **2 Prime Mover** a way of referring to God

,prime 'number n [C] a number that can be divided only by itself and the number one. For example, three and seven are prime numbers.

prim·er /'praɪmə $ -ər/ n   **1** [C,U] paint that you put on the surface of wood, metal etc before you put on the main layer of paint   **2** [C] a tube that contains explosive and is used to fire a gun or explode a bomb   **3** /'praɪmə $ 'prɪmər/ [C] AmE a book that contains basic information about something: [+on/of] a primer on Italian wines | a primer of good management techniques   **4** [C] old-fashioned a school book that contains very basic facts about a subject

'prime ,rate n [C] the lowest rate of interest at which companies can borrow money from a bank; ➡ **base rate**

'prime ,time n [U] the time in the evening when the largest number of people are watching television: a prime time entertainment programme | prime time television | prime time audiences | a speech that was broadcast live during prime time

pri·me·val also **primaeval** BrE /praɪˈmiːvəl/ adj   **1** belonging to the earliest time in the existence of the universe or the Earth: Primeval clouds of gas formed themselves into stars.   **2** very ancient: primeval forests   **3** primeval feelings are very strong and seem to come from a part of people's character that is ancient and animal-like: the primeval urge to reproduce

prim·i·tive[1] /'prɪmɪtɪv/ adj   **1** |WAY OF LIFE| belonging to a simple way of life that existed in the past and does not have modern industries and machines; ➡ **advanced**, **modern**: a primitive society | a primitive nomadic tribe | the tools used by primitive man | primitive art   **2** |NOT MODERN| something that is primitive is very simple and does not have the extra modern parts that would make it faster, better, more comfortable etc; ➡ **advanced**, **modern**: The first station buildings were quite primitive. | The local hospital care is primitive and unreliable. | Conditions at the camp are very primitive. | a primitive steam engine   **3** |ANIMALS/PLANTS| a primitive animal or plant has a simple structure or body: primitive life-forms that live deep in the ocean | a primitive single-celled creature   **4** |FEELINGS| primitive feelings are not based on reason, and seem to come from a part of people's character that is ancient and animal-like: the primitive instinct of survival | primitive desires —**primitively** adv —**primitiveness** n [U]

primitive[2] n [C] an artist who paints simple pictures like those of a child

pri·mo·gen·i·ture /ˌpraɪməʊˈdʒenɪtʃə $ -moʊˈdʒenɪtʃər/ n [U] law the system by which property that is owned by a man goes to his oldest son after his death

pri·mor·di·al /praɪˈmɔːdiəl $ -ˈmɔːr-/ adj formal   **1** existing at the beginning of time or the beginning of the Earth: the primordial seas   **2** primordial feelings are very strong and seem to come from the part of people's character that is ancient and animal-like: He was driven on by a primordial terror.   **3 the primordial soup** the mixture of gases and other substances that people believe existed before the beginning of life on Earth

primp /prɪmp/ v [I,T] old-fashioned to make yourself look attractive by arranging your hair, putting on MAKE-UP etc: She spends hours primping in front of the mirror.

prim·rose /'prɪmrəʊz $ -roʊz/ n   **1** [C] a small wild plant with pale yellow flowers, or the flower from this plant: a bunch of primroses   **2** also **primrose yellow** [U] a pale yellow colour   **3 the primrose path** literary a way of life that is full of pleasure but causes you harm after a period of time

prim·u·la /'prɪmjʊlə/ n [C] a small wild or garden plant with brightly coloured flowers

Pri·mus /'praɪməs/ also **'Primus stove** n [C] trademark BrE a piece of equipment for STOVE (=a piece of equipment for cooking) that burns oil and can be easily carried around, used especially when camping

prince [W3] /prɪns/ n [C]   **1** the son of a king, queen, or prince; ➡ **princess**: Prince William   **2** a male ruler of a small country or state: Prince Rainier of Monaco   **3 the prince of sth/a prince among sth** literary the man who is best at something: the prince of sculptors

,Prince 'Charming n [C] informal a perfect man who a young woman might dream about meeting – often used humorously: She is still waiting to find her Prince Charming.

,prince 'consort n [C] a title that is sometimes given to the husband of a ruling queen

prince·ly /'prɪnsli/ adj [only before noun]   **1** a princely amount of money is very large – often used humorously to mean a very small amount of money: My savings had now reached **the princely sum of** £30. |

a far from princely salary **2** *formal* impressive or generous: *princely buildings* | *A princely welcome awaited them.* **3** belonging or relating to a prince: *a princely state*

Prince of Wales /ˌprɪns əv 'weɪlz/ *n* **the Prince of Wales** a title given to the first son of a British king or queen

prin·cess /ˌprɪn'ses◂ $ 'prɪnsəs/ *n* [C] **1** a close female relation of a king and queen, especially a daughter; → **prince**: *Princess Anne* **2** the wife of a prince

Princess 'Royal *n* **the Princess Royal** a title given to the first daughter of a British king or queen

prin·ci·pal¹ W2 /'prɪnsˌpəl/ *adj* [only before noun] most important; ▤ **main**: *His principal reason for making the journey was to visit his family.* | *Teaching is her principal source of income.* | *the principal character in the book* → **PRINCIPALLY**

principal² *n*
1 SCHOOL [C] *AmE* someone who is in charge of a school; ▤ **headteacher** *BrE*: *a small school with just three teachers and the principal*
2 UNIVERSITY/COLLEGE [C] *BrE* someone who is in charge of a university or college
3 BUSINESS [C] *AmE* the main person in a business or organization, who can make important business decisions and is legally responsible for them: *The principal of the business has an office in New York.*
4 PERFORMER [C] the main performer in a play or in a group of musicians, dancers etc: *She later became a principal with the Royal Ballet.*
5 MONEY [singular] *technical* the original amount of money that is lent to someone, not including any of the INTEREST

principal 'boy *n* [C] *BrE* the main male character in a PANTOMIME, usually played by a young woman

prin·ci·pal·i·ty /ˌprɪnsˌ'pælˌti/ *n plural* **principalities** [C] **1** a country that is ruled by a prince **2** **the Principality** *BrE* Wales

prin·ci·pally /'prɪnsˌpli/ *adv* mainly: *The money is principally invested in stocks and shares.* | *He was principally a landscape painter.* | *We met principally to discuss the future of the school.*

prin·ci·ple S3 W1 /'prɪnsˌpəl/ *n*
1 MORAL RULE [C,U] a moral rule or belief about what is right and wrong, that influences how you behave: *Schools try to teach children a set of principles.* | *He prided himself on his high moral principles* (=strong ideas about how it is right or wrong to behave) | *He's got no principles at all!* | *He refused to give me any more money as a matter of principle.* | *against sb's principles It's against my principles to accept gifts from clients.* | *man/woman of principle* (=a man or woman with strong moral ideas) *He considered himself to be a man of principle.*
2 IDEA BEHIND STH [C] the basic idea that a plan or system is based on: *The general principle is that education should be available to all children up to the age of 16.* | *basic/fundamental/guiding principle the basic principles of business management* | *[+of] the principles of French law* | *principle that Reflexology is based on the principle that specific areas on the feet correspond to different parts of the body.* | *on a principle The project worked on the principle that each person's experience was equally valuable.* | *[+behind] the principles behind government policies* | *He called for a return to first principles* (=the most important ideas) *of road safety for children.* | *Similar principles apply in the case of older children* (=the principles are the same as others that have been mentioned).
3 *in principle* **a)** if something is possible in principle, there is no good reason why it should not happen, but it has not actually happened yet: *In principle, the new software should make the accounting system a lot simpler.* **b)** if you agree to something in principle, you

agree about a general plan or idea but have not yet considered the details: *They have accepted the idea in principle.* | *The government has agreed in principle to a referendum.*
4 RULES OF A PROCESS [C] a rule which explains the way something such as a machine works, or which explains a natural force in the universe: *Archimedes' principle* | *[+of] the basic principles of physics* ⚠ Do not confuse the noun **principle** (=a basic rule) with the noun and adjective **principal**, which have the same pronunciation but different meanings.

prin·ci·pled /'prɪnsˌpəld/ *adj formal* **1** someone who is principled has strong opinions about what is morally right and wrong: *principled stand/opposition/objection etc He took a principled stand against the legislation.* **2** based on clear and definite ideas: *an attempt to reduce prison sentences in a principled way*

print¹ S2 W3 /prɪnt/ *v*
1 WORDS **a)** [I,T] to produce words, numbers, or pictures on paper, using a machine which puts ink onto the surface: *I need to make a few changes before I print the document.* | *The company's name was printed in bold letters across the top of the page.* | *a printed letter* | *The printer's switched on but it won't print.* | *As a newspaper publisher he understood the power of the printed word* (=words that are printed on paper). **b)** [I] when a computer document prints, a printed copy of it is produced: *Press return, then the document should print.*
2 BOOKS/NEWSPAPERS [T] to produce many printed copies of a book, newspaper etc: *Over five million copies of the paper are printed every day.* | *When the book was first written no publisher would print it.*
3 IN A NEWSPAPER [T] to print a report of something or a letter, speech etc in a newspaper or magazine; ▤ **publish**: *The Express was the first paper to print the story.* | *The Telegraph has printed numerous articles on this subject over the last three years.* | *I wrote to the newspaper but my letter wasn't printed.*
4 PHOTOGRAPH [T] to produce a photograph from a photographic film: *It usually takes a couple of hours for the pictures to be developed and printed.*
5 CLOTH [T] to decorate cloth with a pattern that is put all over its surface by a machine: *a skirt printed with brightly coloured flowers* | *a printed silk shirt*
6 WRITE [I,T] to write words by hand without joining the letters: *Please print your name clearly in the top right hand corner of the page.*
7 MAKE A MARK [T] to make a mark on a surface or in a soft substance by pressing something on to it: *print sth on/in sth The mark of the man's shoe was printed in the mud.* → **a licence to print money** at LICENCE (6)
 print sth ⇔ **off/out** *phr v*
to produce a printed copy of a computer document: *Could you print a copy off for me?* | *I'll print the file out and then we can look at it.*

print² W3 *n*
1 BOOKS/NEWSPAPERS [U] writing that has been printed, for example in books or newspapers: *There was no print at all on the backs of the tickets.* | *in print* (=printed in a book, newspaper etc) *It must be really exciting to see your work in print.* | *the pleasure of seeing my name in print* | *Very little of his poetry actually got into print* (=was printed).
2 *be in print* if a book is in print, new copies of it are still being printed: *After fifty years, the book is still in print.*
3 *be out of print* if a book is out of print, it is no longer being printed and you cannot buy new copies
4 LETTERS [U] the letters in which something is printed: *The book is also available in large print.* | *The print quality of the new printer is excellent.*
5 *the small/fine print* the details of a legal document, which are often printed in very small writing: *Always read the small print before signing anything.*
6 MARK [C] a mark that is made on a surface by something that has been pressed onto it: *His feet left deep prints in the soft soil.*

7 prints [plural] the marks that are made by the pattern of lines on the ends of your fingers; ▣ **fingerprints**: *The police found a set of prints on the car door.*
8 CLOTH [C,U] cloth, especially cotton, on which a coloured pattern has been printed: *a lovely selection of floral prints | She was wearing a cotton print dress.*
9 PHOTOGRAPH [C] a photograph that has been produced from a film: *Why don't you order an extra set of prints? | a colour print*
10 PICTURE [C] **a)** a picture that is made by cutting lines onto a piece of metal or wood and then printing it onto paper **b)** a copy of a painting that is produced by taking a photograph of it and printing it onto paper

print·a·ble /ˈprɪntəbəl/ *adj* suitable to be printed and read by everyone; ▣ **unprintable**: *Her remarks were scarcely printable* (=were very rude).

printed 'circuit *n* [C] a set of connections in a piece of electrical equipment consisting of thin lines of metal on a board

printed ˌmatter *n* [U] printed articles – used especially about advertisements that can be sent by post at a cheap rate

print·er W3 /ˈprɪntə $ -ər/ *n* [C]
1 a machine which is connected to a computer and can make a printed record of computer information: *a laser printer | a colour printer* → see picture at OFFICE
2 someone who is employed in the trade of printing

print·ing /ˈprɪntɪŋ/ *n* **1** [U] the act or process of making a book, magazine, etc using a machine that puts ink onto paper: *the invention of printing | the printing industry | a printing error* **2** [C] an act of printing a number of copies of a book: *The first printing of her book was 10,000 copies.* **3** [U] a method of writing when you write each letter separately rather than joining the letters of a word

printing ink *n* [U] a type of ink that dries very quickly and is used in printing books and newspapers etc

printing press also **printing ma,chine** *n* [C] a machine that prints newspapers, books etc; ▣ **press**

print·out /ˈprɪntˌaʊt/ *n* [C,U] a sheet or length of paper with printed information on it, produced by a computer

print run *n* [C] the number of books or magazines that are printed at the same time

pri·on /ˈpraɪɒn, ˈpriː- $ -ɑːn/ *n* [C] a very small piece of PROTEIN that is thought to cause some brain diseases such as BSE

pri·or¹ W3 /ˈpraɪə $ praɪr/ *adj*
1 existing or arranged before something else or before the present situation; ▣ **previous**: *You do not need any prior knowledge of the subject. | Changes may not be made without the prior approval of the council. | Vegetarian meals are provided by prior agreement. | Some prior experience with the software is needed.*
2 prior warning/notice a warning or announcement made before something happens: *The society must give customers prior notice before changing the cost. | The bomb exploded without any prior warning.*
3 prior to sth *formal* before: *All the arrangements should be completed prior to your departure.*
4 prior claim a person's right to something which is considered more important than another person's right to the same thing: *His own children have a prior claim to the business.*

pri·or² *n* [C] **1** the man in charge of a PRIORY **2** the priest next in rank to the person in charge of an ABBEY **3** *informal* a previous occasion when someone was found guilty of a crime: *two priors for homicide*

pri·or·ess /ˈpraɪərəs/ *n* [C] the woman in charge of a PRIORY

pri·o·ri·tize also **-ise** *BrE* /praɪˈɒrətaɪz $ -ˈɔːr-/ *v* [T] **1** to put several things, problems etc in order of importance, so that you can deal with the most important ones first: *You need to prioritize your tasks.* **2** to deal with one thing first, because it is the most impor-

tant: *The public wants to see the fight against crime prioritized.* —**prioritization** /praɪˌɒrətaɪˈzeɪʃən $ -ˌɔːrət̬ə-/ *n* [U]

pri·or·i·ty¹ S2 W2 /praɪˈɒrəti $ -ˈɔːr-/ *n plural* **priorities**
1 [C,U] the thing that you think is most important and that needs attention before anything else: *The club's priority is to win the League.* | **first/top/main priority** *The children are our first priority. | After several burglaries in the area, security is now a high priority* (=very important and needing attention soon). | *With so little money available, repairs must remain a low priority* (=not important and not needing attention soon). | *The customer is high on our list of priorities. | List your tasks in order of priority* (=most important first).
2 [U] the right to be given attention first and before other people or things: [+over] *Buses should have priority over other road users. | A young person who has finished the course will be given priority over one who has not. | I want to start work on the garden but the house must take priority.*
3 get your priorities right also **get your priorities straight** *AmE* to know what is most important and needs attention first: *We need to get our priorities right.*

priority² *adj* before other people or things: *Members receive priority bookings and reduced ticket prices to all concerts.*

pri·o·ry /ˈpraɪəri/ *n plural* **priories** [C] a building where a group of MONKS or NUNS, (=men or women living a religious life) live which is smaller and less important than an ABBEY

prise *BrE*; **prize** *AmE* /praɪz/ *v* [T always + adv/prep] to move or lift something by pushing it away from something else: *I tried to prise the lid off.*
prise sth out of sb also **prise sth from sb** *phr v* to get something such as information or money from someone when they do not want to give it to you: *I more or less had to prise it out of him.*

pris·m /ˈprɪzəm/ *n* [C] **1** a transparent block of glass that breaks up white light into different colours **2** *technical* a solid object with matching ends and several sides which are the same width all the way up

pris·mat·ic /prɪzˈmætɪk/ *adj* **1** using or containing a PRISM: *a prismatic compass* **2** a prismatic colour is very clear and bright

pris·on S2 W2 /ˈprɪzən/ *n*
1 [C,U] a building where people are kept as a punishment for a crime, or while they are waiting to go to court for their TRIAL; ▣ **jail**; → **prisoner, imprison**

in prison
out of prison
put sb in prison/send sb to prison
release sb from prison/let sb out of prison
get out of prison
escape from prison
go to prison
prison sentence (=a punishment which consists of a period of time in prison)
prison officer/warder (=someone who works in a prison and guards the prisoners)
prison cell (=a prisoner's room in a jail)
*He visits his Dad in prison every week.	Ricky has been out of prison for 3 years now.	They'll probably put him in prison for a long time.	Helen was sent to prison for attacking a man with a knife.	The two men were arrested only a week after they were released from prison.	Three terrorists escaped from Brixton Prison.	an increase in the number of women going to prison	Mr Gunn received a ten year prison sentence.*

⚠ Do not say 'the prison' unless you are referring to a

particular building: *She was sent to prison.* | *He spent five years in prison.* | *They live opposite the prison.*
2 [U] the system that deals with keeping people in a prison: *the **prison service*** | *Does prison deter criminals from offending again?*
3 [C] an unpleasant place or situation which it is difficult to escape from: *The farm felt like a prison for her.*

prison camp *n* [C] a special prison in which prisoners of war are kept

pris·on·er S3 W2 /ˈprɪzənə $ -ər/ *n* [C]
1 someone who is kept in a prison as a legal punishment for a crime or while they are waiting for their TRIAL; → **guard, imprison**: *Relationships between the staff and the prisoners are good.* | *Prisoners here only serve short sentences.* | **remand prisoner** *BrE* (=someone who is in prison waiting for their trial) | *The organization is arguing for the release of political prisoners* (=people in prison because of their political opinions).
2 someone who is taken by force and kept somewhere; ◧ **captive**: **hold/keep sb prisoner** *The guerillas kept her prisoner for three months.* | *He was being held prisoner.* | *Our pilot was **taken prisoner.*** | *The army advanced, **taking** 200,000 **prisoners.***
3 someone who is in a place or situation from which they cannot escape: *He is a prisoner of his own past.*

prisoner of 'conscience *n* [C] someone who is put in prison because of their political ideas

prisoner of 'war *n* [C] a soldier, member of the navy etc who is caught by the enemy during a war and kept as a prisoner

prison 'visitor *n* [C] someone who visits prisoners in Britain to help them

pris·sy /ˈprɪsi/ *adj informal* behaving very correctly and easily shocked by anything rude – used to show disapproval —**prissily** *adv* —**prissiness** *n* [U]

pris·tine /ˈprɪstiːn/ *adj* **1** extremely fresh or clean: *a pristine white shirt* **2** something that is pristine is in the same condition as when it was first made: *The car has been restored to **pristine condition.*** **3** not spoiled or damaged in any way: *pristine African rainforest*

prith·ee /ˈprɪði/ *interjection old use* please

priv·a·cy /ˈprɪvəsi, ˈpraɪ- $ ˈpraɪ-/ *n* [U] **1** the state of being able to be alone, and not seen or heard by other people: *With seven people squashed in one house, you don't get much privacy.* **2** the state of being free from public attention: *each individual's right to privacy*

pri·vate¹ S1 W1 /ˈpraɪvət/ *adj*
1 NOT FOR THE PUBLIC for use by one person or group, not for everyone; ◧ **public**: *Morris has a private jet.* | *He made some notes for his private use.* | *Many communists objected to any form of **private property.***
2 NOT GOVERNMENT [only before noun] not related to, owned by, or paid for by the government; ◧ **public**: *a private hospital* | *There is private ownership of property in a market economy.* | *private education* | **go private** *BrE* (=pay for medical treatment instead of getting it free at a public hospital)
3 FOR ONLY A FEW a private meeting, conversation etc involves only two people or a small number of people, and is not for other people to know about: *I need to have a private discussion with you.* | *Are you alone? I just wanted a private word.*
4 SECRET private feelings, information, or opinions are personal or secret and not for other people to know about: *Jack's private opinion was that she was selfish.* | *Don't read that – it's private.*
5 NOT PUBLICLY KNOWN used about someone who is not known to the public or not working for the government or another organization: *a private citizen* | *The painting was sold to a private collector.* | *Seven police and three **private individuals** needed medical attention.*
6 NOT WORK separate from and not related to your work or your official position: *The president is paying a*

private visit to Europe. | *He enjoys everything he does in both his professional and his **private life.***
7 QUIET PLACE quiet and without a lot of people: *Why don't we go upstairs where it's more private?*
8 PERSON [only before noun] a private person is one who likes being alone, and does not talk much about their thoughts or feelings: *He's a very private man.*
9 **private joke** a joke made between friends, family members etc that other people do not understand; → **privately**

pri·vate² *n* **1 in private** without other people being present: *I need to speak to you in private.* **2** [C] a soldier of the lowest rank **3 privates** [plural] *informal* PRIVATE PARTS

private de'tective *n* [C] someone who can be employed to look for information or missing people, or to follow people and report on what they do

private edu'cation *n* [U] education which parents pay for, rather than free education provided by the government

private 'enterprise *n* [U] the economic system in which private businesses are allowed to compete freely with each other, and the government does not control industry; → **private sector**

pri·va·teer /ˌpraɪvəˈtɪə $ -ˈtɪr/ *n* [C] **1** an armed ship in the past that was not in the navy but attacked and robbed enemy ships carrying goods **2** someone who sailed on a privateer

private 'eye *n* [C] *informal* a PRIVATE DETECTIVE

private 'income *n* [C,U] money that someone gets regularly, not from working but because they own part of a business or have money which earns INTEREST

private in'vestigator *n* [C] a PRIVATE DETECTIVE

private ,law *n* [U] *law* the part of the law relating to ordinary people, private property, and relationships

private ,limited 'company *n* [C] a company whose shares are not bought and sold on the STOCK MARKET and can only pass to another person with the agreement of other SHAREHOLDERS

pri·vate·ly /ˈpraɪvətli/ *adv* **1** with no one else present; ◧ **in private**: *I must talk to you privately.* **2** if you feel or think something privately, you do not tell anyone about it: *Laura praised the pictures, though she privately thought they were rather ordinary.* | [sentence adverb]: *Privately, Harriet had to agree.* **3** not publicly or as part of your work: [sentence adverb]: *Privately, senior officials agreed that not many people had voted.* **4** *especially BrE* using or involving private rather than government institutions: *Both children are privately educated.* | *a privately-owned company*

private 'medicine *n* [U] *BrE* the system in which medical treatment and advice is not provided by the government but is paid for by the patient or their insurance company; → **NHS**

private 'member *n* [C] *BrE* a member of parliament who is not a minister in the government

private 'member's ,bill *n* [C] a law introduced to the British parliament by a member of parliament who is not a minister in the government

private 'parts *n* [plural] the sex organs – used when you want to avoid naming them directly

private 'patient *n* [C] *BrE* someone who pays for medical treatment or advice, rather than receiving it free through the government's system

private 'practice *n* [C,U] **1** the business of a professional person that is independent of a bigger or government-controlled organization: *Richard set up in private practice.* **2** *AmE* the business of a professional person, especially a doctor, who works alone rather than with others

private school *n* [C] a school that is not supported by government money, where education must be paid for by the children's parents; → **public school, state school**

private 'secretary *n* [C] **1** a secretary who is employed to help one person, especially with personal business **2** *BrE* a CIVIL SERVANT whose job is to help a government minister: *a parliamentary private secretary*

,private 'sector *n* **the private sector** the industries and services in a country that are owned and run by private companies, and not by the government; → **public sector**: *pay increases in the private sector*

,private 'soldier *n* [C] *BrE formal* a soldier of the lowest rank; **◫ private**

,private 'view also **,private 'viewing** *n* [C] an occasion when a few people are invited to see a show of paintings before the rest of the public

pri·va·tion /praɪˈveɪʃən/ *n* [C,U] *formal* a lack or loss of the things that everyone needs, such as food, warmth, and shelter: *the privations of wartime*

pri·vat·i·za·tion also **-isation** *BrE* /ˌpraɪvətaɪˈzeɪʃən $ -tə-/ *n* [C,U] the act of privatizing something

pri·vat·ize also **-ise** *BrE* /ˈpraɪvətaɪz/ *v* [T] if a government privatizes an organization, industry, or service that it owns or controls, it sells it; → **nationalize**

priv·et /ˈprɪvɪt/ *n* [U] a bush with leaves that stay green all year, often grown to form a HEDGE

priv·i·lege¹ W3 /ˈprɪvəlɪdʒ/ *n*
1 [C] a special advantage that is given only to one person or group of people: *He had no special privileges and was treated just like every other prisoner.* | [+of] *the privilege of a good education*
2 [singular] something that you are lucky to have the chance to do, and that you enjoy very much: **the privilege of doing sth** *Today, we have the privilege of listening to two very unusual men.* | **the privilege to do sth** *I had the great privilege to play for Yorkshire.* | *It is a privilege to hear her play.*
3 [U] a situation in which people who are rich or of a high social class have many more advantages than other people: *wealth and privilege*
4 [U] a situation in which doctors, lawyers etc are allowed to keep information about their discussions with their patients or CLIENTS secret from other people
5 [C,U] the right to do or say something unacceptable without being punished, especially in parliament: **breach of privilege** (=a breaking of the rules about what a member of parliament can do or say)

privilege² *v* [T] *formal* to treat some people or things better than others

priv·i·leged /ˈprɪvəlɪdʒd/ *adj* **1 a)** having advantages because of your wealth, social position etc; **◲ underprivileged**: *Students from a privileged background have an advantage at university.* | *Only the privileged few can afford private education.* **b)** the **privileged** [plural] people who are privileged **2** having a special advantage or a chance to do something that most people cannot do: *Kylie feels fortunate to be in such a privileged position because of her successful TV career.* | **be privileged to do sth** *I was privileged to lead the team.* **3** *law* privileged information is private and is not allowed to be made public by law

priv·y¹ /ˈprɪvi/ *adj* **1 be privy to sth** sharing in the knowledge of facts that are secret: *Colby was privy to the committee's decisions.* **2** *old use* secret and private —**privily** *adv*

privy² *n* *plural* **privies** [C] a toilet, especially one outside a house in a small separate building

,Privy 'Council *n* **the Privy Council** a group of important people in Britain who advise the king or queen on political affairs —**Privy Councillor** *n* [C]

,privy 'purse, Privy Purse *n* **the privy purse** money given by the British government to the king or queen for their personal use

prix fixe /ˌpriː ˈfiːks, -ˈfɪks/ *adj AmE* a prix fixe meal is a complete meal served for a fixed price

prize¹ S2 W2 /praɪz/ *n* [C]
1 something that is given to someone who is successful in a competition, race, game of chance etc: *In this month's competition you could win a prize worth £3000.* | *The first prize has gone to Dr John Gentle.* | [+for] *The prize for best photography has been won by a young Dutch photographer.* | *Scientists from Oxford shared the Nobel Prize for Medicine in 1945.* | *The prizes are awarded* (=given) *every year to students who have shown original thinking in their work.*
2 something that is very valuable to you or that it is very important to have: *Fame was the prize.*
3 no prizes for guessing sth *spoken* used to say that it is very easy to guess something: *No prizes for guessing what she was wearing.*

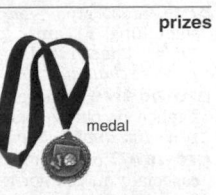
prizes
medal

trophy

prize² *adj* [only before noun] **1** good enough to win a prize or having won a prize: *He has spent months cultivating what he hopes are prize flowers.* → **PRIZE-WINNING 2** very good or important: *The Picasso painting is a prize exhibit in the museum.* **3 prize money** money that is given to the person who wins a competition, race etc **4 a prize idiot/fool** *informal* a complete idiot, fool etc

prize³ *v* [T] **1** to think that someone or something is very important or valuable: *He is someone who prizes truth and decency above all things.* | *The company's shoes are highly prized by fashion conscious youngsters.* **2** the American spelling of PRISE

prized /praɪzd/ *adj* extremely important or valuable to someone: *The child held the bag as tightly as if it were her most prized possession.*

'prize day *n* [C] *BrE* an occasion at a school, usually once a year, when prizes are given to children who have done well in particular subjects

'prize·fight /ˈpraɪzfaɪt/ *n* [C] **1** *BrE* a public BOXING match in which two men fight each other without boxing gloves, in order to win money **2** *AmE* a professional BOXING match —**prizefighter** *n* [C] —**prizefighting** *n* [U]

'prize-,giving *n* [C] *BrE* a ceremony at which people are given prizes, especially at a school: *the annual school prize-giving* | *a glittering prize-giving ceremony*

'prize-,winning *adj* [only before noun] a prize-winning thing or person has won a prize: *a prize-winning novel* | *a prize-winning pianist* —**prize winner** *n* [C]

pro¹ /prəʊ $ proʊ/ *n* *plural* **pros** [C] **1** someone who is paid to do something, especially play a sport, that other people do for pleasure; **◲ professional**; **◲ amateur**: *a tennis pro* | *the small gap between top amateurs and pros in golf* **2** *informal* also **old pro** someone who has had a lot of experience with a particular type of situation: *Cathy's an old pro at organizing raffles.* **3 pros and cons** the advantages and disadvantages of something: **the pros and cons of (doing) sth** *We discussed the pros and cons of going to university.* **4** *BrE old-fashioned informal* a PROSTITUTE → **PRO FORMA, PRO RATA**

pro² *adj informal* **1** paid to do something, especially play a sport that other people do for pleasure; **◲ professional**: **turn/go pro** *Most young talented players are determined to turn pro.* **2** *AmE* played or done by people who are paid for what they do: *pro basketball*

pro³ *prep* if you are pro an idea, suggestion etc, you support it: *As a party, they had always been pro family.*

P

pro- /prəʊ $ proʊ/ *prefix* **1** supporting or approving of something; ◨ **anti-**: *pro-American* | *the pro-choice lobby* **2** *technical* doing a job instead of someone: *the pro-vice-chancellor*

pro·ac·tive /prəʊˈæktɪv $ proʊ- / *adj* making things happen or change rather than reacting to events: *a proactive approach to staffing requirements*

pro-am /ˌprəʊ ˈæm◂ $ ˌproʊ-/ *n* [C] a competition, especially in golf, for PROFESSIONALS (=people who play for money) and AMATEURS (=people who play just for pleasure) —**pro-am** *adj*

prob·a·bil·i·ty /ˌprɒbəˈbɪləti $ ˌprɑː-/ *n* **1** [C,U] how likely something is, sometimes calculated in a mathematical way: **the probability of (doing) sth** *The probability of winning the lottery is really very low.* | *There's a* **high probability** *that the children will follow a different career.* | **probability that** *There is a 95% probability that she will not have the disease.* | *You must decide whether,* **on the balance of probabilities**, *he committed the crime.* **2** [singular] what is likely or something that is likely: *The probability is that smaller businesses will not have to pay the tax.* | *A peace agreement now seems a probability rather than a possibility.* | **high/strong probability** *projects that have a high probability of making profits* **3** *in all probability* very probably: *Mistakes could and, in all probability, would occur.*

prob·a·ble¹ /ˈprɒbəbəl $ ˈprɑː-/ *adj* likely to exist, happen, or be true: *The probable cause of the fire was faulty wiring.* | *Success is* **highly probable.** | **it is probable (that)** *It seems probable that the accident has damaged her brain.* | **probable outcome/consequence/result** *The probable result of global warming will be a rise in sea levels.*

probable² *n* [C] someone who is likely to be chosen for a team, to win a race etc

prob·a·bly ⑤1 Ⓦ1 /ˈprɒbəbli $ ˈprɑː-/ *adv* used to say that something is likely to happen, likely to be true etc: *It will probably take about a week.* | *This would probably be a good time to take a break.* | *It's probably the best movie I have ever seen.* | [sentence adverb]: *'Are you going to be able to do this?' 'Yes, probably.'* | *'Is she going to send it back?' ' Probably not, no.'* | **very/most probably** *The building will be replaced, most probably by a modern sports centre.*

pro·bate¹ /ˈprəʊbeɪt, -bət $ ˈproʊbeɪt/ *n* [U] *law* the legal process of deciding that someone's WILL has been properly made

probate² *v* [T] *AmE law* to prove that a WILL is legal

pro·ba·tion /prəˈbeɪʃən $ proʊ-/ *n* [U] **1** a system that allows some criminals not to go to prison or to leave prison, if they behave well and see a probation officer regularly, for a particular period of time: *The judge sentenced Jennings to three years' probation.* | **(put/place sb) on probation** *He pleaded guilty and was placed on probation.* **2** a period of time, during which an employer can see if a new worker is suitable: *a three month probation period* | **on probation** *Some people are appointed on probation.* **3** *AmE* a period of time in which you must improve your work or behave well so that you will not have to leave your job: *I'm afraid I have no choice but to* **put** *you* **on probation.** —**probationary** *adj*: *a probationary period*

pro·ba·tion·er /prəˈbeɪʃənə $ proʊˈbeɪʃənər/ *n* [C] **1** someone who has recently started a job, especially nursing or teaching, and who is being tested to see whether they are suitable for it **2** someone who has broken the law, and has been put on probation

pro'bation officer *n* [C] someone whose job is to watch, advise, and help people who have broken the law and are on probation

probe¹ /prəʊb $ proʊb/ *v* [I,T] **1** to ask questions in order to find things out, especially things that other people do not want you to know: [+into] *I don't want to probe too deeply into your personal affairs.* | *Police*

probed claims that he had sold drugs. **2** to look for something or examine something, using a long thin object: *Jules probed the mud gingerly with a stick.*

probe² *n* [C] **1** a long thin metal instrument that doctors and scientists use to examine parts of the body **2** a SPACE PROBE **3** an INVESTIGATION in which many questions are asked to discover the truth about something: *a police corruption probe*

prob·ing /ˈprəʊbɪŋ $ ˈproʊ-/ *adj* **1** designed to find things out, especially things that other people do not want you to know: *probing questions* **2** watching carefully and intelligently: *his probing eyes* —**probingly** *adv*

pro·bi·ot·ic /ˌprəʊbaɪˈɒtɪk◂ $ ˌproʊbaɪˈɑː-/ *n* [C,U] a food or other substance that contains BACTERIA and is used in a positive way to improve health, or the use of this type of food to improve health: *Probiotics have been reported to enhance digestion.* | *probiotic yoghurt*

pro·bi·ty /ˈprəʊbəti $ ˈproʊ-/ *n* [U] *formal* complete honesty: *I have always found Bentner to be a model of probity in our dealings.*

prob·lem ⑤1 Ⓦ1 /ˈprɒbləm $ ˈprɑː-/ *n* [C]
1 DIFFICULTY a situation that causes difficulties

have a problem
big/serious/major problem
cause a problem
deal with/sort out a problem
solve/fix/overcome a problem
address/tackle a problem
pose/present a problem
a problem arises/occurs/comes up (=it happens)
economic/financial problems
personal problem (=a problem in someone's private life)
money/family problems
drink/drug problem (=when someone drinks too much alcohol or takes too many drugs)
thorny/knotty problem (=a difficult problem)

[+of] *the problem of race relations* | [+with] *I've been* **having** *a few* **problems** *with my car.* | *She was older than me, but that wasn't a problem.* | *new ways of* **dealing with** *the* **problem** *of street crime* | *Does this mean that all our* **problems** *are* **solved?** | *They still have some* **serious problems** *to* **overcome.** | *new measures aimed at* **tackling** *the* **drug problem** | *The shortage of teachers* **poses** *a* **major problem.** | *The country has huge* **economic problems.** | *He had to take some time off work due to* **personal problems.** | *The marriage ended because of her husband's* **drink problem.** | *We still haven't sorted out the* **thorny problem** *of where exactly the money is going to come from.*
→ see box at TROUBLE¹

2 something wrong with your health or with part of your body: **health problem/problem with your health** *Does she have any long-term health problems?* | **back/heart/kidney etc problem** *If you have back problems you should avoid lifting heavy objects.* | **hearing problem** *Many people with hearing problems try to hide their condition.* | **weight problem** *She refuses to admit to herself that she has a weight problem.* | **emotional/psychological problem** *Is this a sign of some kind of deeper psychological problem?*
3 QUESTION a question for which you have to find the right answer, using mathematics or careful thought: *She gave us 20* **mathematical problems** *to solve.*
4 no problem *spoken* **a)** used to say that you are happy to do something or for someone else to do something: *'Can I bring a friend?' 'Sure, no problem.'* **b)** used after someone has said thank you or said that they are sorry: *'Thanks for all your help.' 'No problem!'*
5 the (only) problem is (that) ... *spoken* used before saying what the main difficulty in a situation is: *The problem is, there isn't enough time.*
6 that's your/his etc problem *spoken* used to say rudely that someone else is responsible for dealing with a situation, not you: *If you miss the train, that's your problem.*

7 it's/that's not my problem *spoken* used to say rudely that you are not responsible for dealing with a particular problem and are not willing to help: *'We've got a serious staffing shortage.' 'That's not my problem.'*
8 What's your/his etc problem? *spoken informal* used when you think that someone is behaving in a way that is unreasonable
9 Do you have a problem with that? *spoken informal* used to ask someone why they seem to disagree with you, in a way that shows that you are annoyed
10 problem child/family/drinker etc a child etc whose behaviour causes problems for other people

prob·lem·at·ic /ˌprɒbləˈmætɪk◂ $ ˌprɑː-/ *adj* involving problems and difficult to deal with: *The reforms could turn out be **highly problematic**.*

problem page *n* [C] *BrE* a page in a magazine where letters are printed about people's personal problems, and answers are suggested

problem-solving *n* [U] when you find ways of doing things, or answers to problems: *tasks that involve problem-solving* | *employees with good problem-solving skills*

pro bo·no /ˌprəʊ ˈbəʊnəʊ $ ˌprəʊ ˈbəʊnəʊ/ *adj, adv* used to describe work that someone, especially a lawyer, does without getting paid

pro·bos·cis /prəˈbɒsɪs $ -ˈbɑː-/ *n plural* **probosces** /-siːz/ *or* **proboscises** [C] **1** a long thin tube that forms part of the mouth of some insects and WORMS **2** the long thin nose of some animals such as an ELEPHANT

probs /prɒbz $ prɑːbz/ *n* **no probs** *BrE spoken informal* used to say that you will be able to do something easily and with no problems: *It'll be ready by six – no probs.*

pro·ce·du·ral /prəˈsiːdʒərəl/ *adj* [only before noun] *formal* connected with a procedure, especially in a law court: *procedural rules*

pro·ce·dure S3 W2 /prəˈsiːdʒə $ -ər/ *n* [C,U]
1 a way of doing something, especially the correct or usual way; → **process**: [+for] *What's the procedure for applying for a visa?* | **correct/proper/normal etc procedure** *This is standard procedure for getting rid of toxic waste.* | **legal/court/parliamentary etc procedures** *All schools have disciplinary **procedures** they must follow.* | *On board, we were given the usual talk on **safety procedures** (=what to do if an accident happens, or to prevent an accident).*
2 a medical treatment or operation: *Liposuction is a minor **surgical procedure**.*

pro·ceed S3 W3 /prəˈsiːd/ *v* [I]
1 *formal* to continue to do something that has already been planned or started; → **proceeds**: [+with] *The government was determined to proceed with the election.* | *Before proceeding further, we must define our terms.*
2 *formal* to continue: *Work is **proceeding according to plan**.*
3 proceed to do sth to do something after doing something else first – used sometimes to express surprise or annoyance: *Sammy took off his coat and proceeded to undo his boots.*
4 [always +adv/prep] *formal* to move in a particular direction: [+to/towards/into etc] *Passengers for Miami*

should proceed to gate 25. ⚠ Do not confuse **proceed** and **precede**, which have different meanings and slightly different pronunciations.
  proceed against sb *phr v law*
to begin a legal case against someone
  proceed from sth *phr v formal*
to happen or exist as a result of something: *ideas that proceed from a disturbed state of mind*
  proceed to sth *phr v formal*
if you proceed to the next part of an activity, job etc, you do or take part in the next part of it; ▤ **go on to**: *players who proceed to the finals of the competition*

pro·ceed·ing W2 /prəˈsiːdɪŋ/ *n*
1 the proceedings also **the proceeding** an event or a series of things that happen: *We watched the proceedings in the street below.* | *At this point in the proceedings, my doctor offered me a choice.*
2 [C usually plural] when someone uses a court of law to deal with a legal case: **begin/open/take proceedings (against sb)** *She has begun **divorce proceedings**.* | *John is taking **legal proceedings** against his ex-partner.*
3 the proceedings *formal* the official written records of a meeting, society etc: [+of] *the proceedings of the conference*

pro·ceeds /ˈprəʊsiːdz $ ˈprəʊ-/ *n* [plural] *formal* the money that is obtained from doing something or selling something: *We sold the business and bought a villa in Spain with the proceeds.* | [+of/from] *The proceeds of the concert will go to charity.*

pro·cess¹ S2 W1 /ˈprəʊses $ ˈprɑː-/ *n* [C]
1 a series of actions that are done in order to achieve a particular result: *the Israeli-Egyptian **peace process*** | *Repetition can help the learning process.* | [+of] *the process of economic change* | **slow/lengthy/laborious etc process** *Getting fit again has been a long slow process.* | *the **mental processes** involved in decision-making*
2 a series of things that happen naturally and result in gradual change: [+of] *the **natural process** of evolution* | *Coal forms by a **slow process** of chemical change.* | *the digestive process*
3 be in the process of (doing) sth to have started doing something and not yet be finished: *The company is in the process of moving to new offices.*
4 be in process if something is in process, it is happening now: *There was an armed revolt in process.*
5 in the process while you are doing something or something is happening: *I spilt the coffee, burning myself in the process.*
6 process of elimination a way of finding the right answer, the truth etc by gradually deciding that none of the other answers are possible: **by (a) process of elimination** *I solved the problem by a process of elimination.*
7 a method of making or producing goods: *the car **production process*** | *Recycling is an industrial process.* → DUE PROCESS

process² *v* [T] **1** to make food, materials, or goods ready to be used or sold, for example by preserving or improving them in some way: *Goats' cheese may be processed in many ways.* | *Two million workers are employed processing goods for electronic firms.* **2** to deal with an official document, request etc in the usual way: **process an application/claim/transaction etc** *All university applications are processed through this system.* **3** to deal with information using a computer: *The new network will enable data to be processed more speedily.* **4** to print a picture from a photographic film
→ DATA PROCESSING, WORD PROCESSOR

pro·cess³ /prəˈses/ *v* [I always + adv/prep] *formal* to walk or move along in a very slow and serious way, especially as part of a group

pro·cessed /ˈprəʊsest $ ˈprɑː-/ *adj* [only before noun] processed food has substances added to it before it is sold, in order to preserve it, improve its colour etc:

processed cheese/meat/fish etc | *the artificial colourings and flavourings in processed foods*

pro·ces·sion /prəˈseʃən/ *n* **1** [C,U] a line of people or vehicles moving slowly as part of a ceremony; → **parade:** *funeral/wedding/carnival etc* **procession** | *They* **marched in procession** *to the Capitol building.* → see picture at DEMONSTRATION **2** [C] several people or things of the same type, appearing or happening one after the other: [+of] *an endless procession of visitors*

pro·ces·sion·al /prəˈseʃənəl/ *adj* [only before noun] relating to or used in a procession

pro·ces·sor /ˈprəʊsesə $ ˈprɑːsesər/ *n* [C] **1** the central part of a computer that deals with the commands and information it is given; ▤ **central processing unit** **2** a machine or person that processes food or other materials before they are sold or used: *US tuna processors* → FOOD PROCESSOR

pro-'choice *adj* someone who is pro-choice believes that women have a right to have an ABORTION; → **pro-life:** *the pro-choice lobby*

pro·claim /prəˈkleɪm $ proʊ-/ *v* [T] *formal* **1** to say publicly or officially that something important is true or exists; → **proclamation:** *The President proclaimed the republic's independence.* | **proclaim that** *Protesters proclaimed that the girl was innocent.* | **proclaim sb sth** *His son was immediately proclaimed king.* **2** to show something clearly or be a sign of something: *The stripes on her uniform proclaimed her seniority.*

proc·la·ma·tion /ˌprɒkləˈmeɪʃən $ ˌprɑː-/ *n* [C,U] an official public statement about something that is important, or when someone makes such a statement; → **proclaim:** *The authorities* **issued a proclamation** *forbidding public meetings.* | [+of] *the proclamation of Lithuania's independence*

pro·cliv·i·ty /prəˈklɪvₖti $ proʊ-/ *n plural* **proclivities** [C] *formal* a tendency to behave in a particular way, or to like a particular thing – used especially about something bad: [+to/towards/for] *The child* **showed no proclivity** *towards aggression.* | *his sexual proclivities*

pro·con·sul /ˌprəʊˈkɒnsəl $ proʊˈkɑːn-/ *n* [C] someone who governed a part of the ancient Roman Empire

pro·con·su·late /ˌprəʊˈkɒnsjₐlₐt $ proʊˈkɑːnsəl-/ also **pro·con·sul·ship** /-səlʃɪp/ *n* [C] the rank of a proconsul, or the time when someone was a proconsul

pro·cras·ti·nate /prəˈkræstₐneɪt/ *v* [I] *formal* to delay doing something that you ought to do, usually because you do not want to do it; ▤ **put off:** *People often procrastinate when it comes to paperwork.* —**procrastination** /prəˌkræstₐˈneɪʃən/ *n* [U]

pro·cre·ate /ˈprəʊkrieɪt $ ˈproʊ-/ *v* [I,T] *formal* to produce children or baby animals; ▤ **reproduce** —**procreation** /ˌprəʊkriˈeɪʃən $ ˌproʊ-/ *n* [U]

proc·tor /ˈprɒktə $ ˈprɑːktər/ *n* [C] *AmE* someone who watches students in an examination to make sure that they do not cheat; ▤ **invigilator** *BrE* —**proctor** *v* [T]

pro·cu·ra·tor /ˈprɒkjₐreɪtə $ ˈprɑːkjₐreɪtər/ *n* [C] **1** an official with legal powers, especially in the former Soviet Union, the Roman Catholic Church or the ancient Roman Empire: *the Procurator General of the Ukraine* **2** **procurator fiscal** an official in Scotland who decides whether someone should be sent to court for a TRIAL

pro·cure /prəˈkjʊə $ proʊˈkjʊr/ *v* [T] *formal* **1** to obtain something, especially something that is difficult to get: **procure sth for sb** *He was accused of procuring weapons for terrorists.* **2** to provide a PROSTITUTE for someone —**procurable** *adj* —**procurement** *n* [U]: *the procurement of raw materials from abroad* —**procurer** *n* [C]

prod¹ /prɒd $ prɑːd/ *v* **prodded, prodding** [I,T] **1** to quickly push something or someone with your finger or a pointed object; ▤ **poke:** *'Don't go to sleep,' she said, prodding me in the ribs.* | [+at] *Theo prodded at the dead snake.* **2** to make someone do something by

persuading or reminding them that it is necessary, especially when they are lazy or unwilling: **prod sb into (doing) sth** *It had prodded Ben into doing something about it.* | *The strike may* **prod** *the government* **into action.** —**prodding** *n* [U]: *He's a bright kid, but he needs prodding.*

prod² *n* [C usually singular] **1** *especially BrE* a quick pushing movement, using your finger or a pointed object; ▤ **poke:** *'Go on,' he whispered,* **giving** *me a* **prod** *in the back.* **2** *BrE* when you persuade or remind someone to do something: *Why don't you ring the shop and* **give** *them a* **prod?** **3** a pointed instrument used for pushing animals, to make them move: *a* **cattle prod**

prod·i·gal¹ /ˈprɒdₐgəl $ ˈprɑː-/ *adj* [usually before noun] *formal* **1** **prodigal son/daughter** someone who leaves their family and home without the approval of their family, but who is sorry later and returns **2** spending money, wasting time etc in a careless way; ▤ **extravagant:** *a prodigal lifestyle*

prodigal² *n* [C] *literary* someone who spends money carelessly and wastes their time – used humorously

pro·di·gious /prəˈdɪdʒəs/ *adj* [usually before noun] very large or great in a surprising or impressive way: **prodigious amounts/quantities of sth** *Some galaxies seem to release prodigious amounts of energy.* | *the artist's prodigious output* —**prodigiously** *adv*

prod·i·gy /ˈprɒdₐdʒi $ ˈprɑː-/ *n plural* **prodigies** [C] a young person who has a great natural ability in a subject or skill: **child/infant prodigy** | *Mozart was a musical prodigy.*

pro·duce¹ ⓢ¹ ⓦ¹ /prəˈdjuːs $ -ˈduːs/ *v* [T] **1** **CAUSE** to cause a particular result or effect; → **product:** *New drugs are producing remarkable results.* | *a rise in sea-level produced by climatic change* | *As a policy, it did not* **produce the desired effect.** → see box at PRODUCE² **2** **CREATE/MAKE** to make, write etc something to be bought, used, or enjoyed by people; → **product, production:** *The factory produces an incredible 100 cars per hour.* | *How did you manage to produce a meal so quickly?* → MASS-PRODUCED **3** **MAKE NATURALLY** to grow something or make it naturally; → **product, production:** *This region produces the grapes used in champagne.* | *Plants produce oxygen.* **4** **SHOW** if you produce an object, you bring it out or present it, so that people can see or consider it: *When challenged, he produced a gun.* | *They were unable to produce any statistics to verify their claims.* **5** **PLAY/FILM** if someone produces a film or play, they find the money for it and control the way it is made; → **producer:** *Costner produced and directed the film.* **6** **BABY** to give birth to a baby or young animals: *An adult cat may produce kittens three times a year.*

prod·uce² /ˈprɒdjuːs $ ˈproʊduːs/ *n* [U] food or other things that have been grown or produced on a farm to be sold: **agricultural/organic etc produce** *fresh local produce* | **dairy produce** *BrE* (=milk, butter, cheese etc)

> **WORD CHOICE: produce (v), produce (n), product**
> The verb **produce** is pronounced /prəˈdjuːs $ -ˈduːs/.
> The noun **produce** is pronounced /ˈprɒdjuːs $ ˈproʊduːs/ and is used to mean 'food that has been grown to be sold': *We sell tinned goods and fresh produce* (=fruit and vegetables).
> The usual noun used to mean 'something that is produced to be sold' is **product:** *Their latest product is a games console.* | *the packaging of food products*

pro·duc·er ⓦ³ /prəˈdjuːsə $ -ˈduːsər/ *n* [C] **1** someone whose job is to control the preparation of a play, film, or broadcast, but who does not direct the actors: **television/film/theatre producer** | *Hollywood producers and movie stars* **2** also **record producer** someone whose job is to organize and direct the recording and production of a record **3** a person, company, or country that makes or grows goods, foods, or materials; → **consumer**: [+of] *South Carolina is the fourth largest producer of tobacco.* | **coffee/wine/car etc producer** *leading oil producers*

prod·uct S1 W1 /ˈprɒdʌkt $ ˈprɑː-/ n
1 [C,U] something that is grown or made in a factory in large quantities, usually in order to be sold; → **produce**, **production**: **agricultural/dairy/software etc products** *consumer products such as VCRs* | *The London factory assembles the finished product.* | *He works in marketing and product development.* → see box at PRODUCE²
2 the product of sth a) if someone is the product of a particular background or experience, their character is typical of that background or the result of that experience: *Paula was the product of a sheltered middle-class home.* **b)** if something is the product of a particular situation, process etc, it is the result of that situation or process: *The report was the product of four years' hard work.*
3 [C] *technical* the number you get by multiplying two or more numbers in MATHEMATICS
4 [C] something that is produced through a natural or chemical process: *Hemoglobin is a product of red blood cells.*

pro·duc·tion S1 W1 /prəˈdʌkʃən/ n
1 [U] the process of making or growing things to be sold, especially in large quantities; → **produce**, **product**: [+of] *the production of consumer goods* | **food/oil/milk etc production** *agricultural production and distribution* | **production costs/facilities/processes etc** *high-tech production methods* | **be in production** (=being produced) *By September, the new motors were in production.* | **go into/out of production** (=begin to be produced in large numbers, or stop being produced) *The new model will go into production next year.*
2 [U] the amount of goods that are made or grown: **increase/rise/fall etc in production** *a drop in oil and gas production* | **production levels/targets etc**
3 [U] when something is produced through a natural process: [+of] *the skin's natural production of oil*
4 [C,U] a play, film, broadcast etc that is produced for the public, or the process of producing it: *the new Shakespeare production at the Arts Theatre* | *In 1992, Green moved into video production.*
5 on/upon (the) production of sth *formal* when you show something: *Entrance is only permitted on production of a ticket.*

▶ **production line**

pro·duc·tion ·line n [C] a line of machines and workers in a factory, each doing one job in the process of making of a product before passing it to the next machine or worker; ◨ **assembly line**

pro·duc·tion ·number n [C] a scene in a MUSICAL with a lot of people singing and dancing

pro·duc·tive /prəˈdʌktɪv/ adj **1** producing or achieving a lot; ◨ **unproductive**: *Most of us are more productive in the morning.* | *a highly productive meeting* **2** [only before noun] relating to the production of goods, crops, or wealth: *the economy's productive capacity* **3 productive of sth** *formal* causing or resulting in something: *The meeting was productive of several good ideas.* —**productively** adv

prod·uc·tiv·i·ty /ˌprɒdʌkˈtɪvəti, -dək- $ ˌprɑː-/ n [U] the rate at which goods are produced, and the amount produced, especially in relation to the work, time, and money needed to produce them: **increase/improve/**

raise **productivity** *ways of increasing productivity* | **high productivity** *levels in manufacturing* | *It cost the country $4 million in* **lost productivity**.

ˈproduct ˌplacement n [U] a form of advertising in which a company arranges for one or more of its products to appear in a television programme or film

prof /prɒf $ prɑːf/ n [C] **1** *informal* a PROFESSOR **2 Prof.** the written abbreviation of *professor*, used in front of names

pro·fane¹ /prəˈfeɪn/ adj *formal* **1** showing a lack of respect for God or holy things: *profane language* **2** related to ordinary life, not religion or holy things; ◨ **secular**; ◨ **sacred**: *sacred and profane art*

profane² v [T] *formal* to treat something holy with a lack of respect

pro·fan·i·ty /prəˈfænəti/ n plural **profanities** **1** [C usually plural] offensive words or religious words used in a way that shows you do not respect God or holy things **2** [U] behaviour that shows you do not respect God or holy things

pro·fess /prəˈfes/ v [T] *formal* **1** to say that you do, are etc something, especially when it is not really true: **profess to do/be sth** *The government professes to care about the poor.* | *He professed to be an expert on Islamic art.* **2 profess your innocence** to say that you did not do something bad, especially a crime: *In court, the man was still professing his innocence.* **3** to state a personal feeling or belief openly: *He finally made up his mind to* **profess** *his* **love** *for her.* | **profess yourself (to be) sth** *He professed himself satisfied with the results.* **4** to have a religion or belief: *Matt professed no religion.*

pro·fessed /prəˈfest/ adj [only before noun] *formal* **1** used to describe a belief that someone has stated openly: *a professed atheist* **2** used to describe a feeling or attitude that someone says they have, but which may not be true: *Their professed aim is to encourage democracy.*

pro·fes·sion S3 W3 /prəˈfeʃən/ n
1 [C] a job that needs a high level of education and training: **the legal/medical/teaching etc profession** *members of the teaching profession* | **enter/go into/join a profession** *Some students enter other professions such as arts administration.* | *people who work in* **the professions** (=doctors, lawyers etc) | **by profession** *Johnson was a barrister by profession.* | *nurses, social workers, and other people in* **the caring professions** (=ones that involve looking after people) → see box at JOB
2 [singular, also + plural verb *BrE*] all the people who work in a particular profession: *the* **medical profession**
3 [C] *formal* a statement of your belief, opinion, or feeling: [+of] *a profession of faith*
4 the oldest profession the job of being a PROSTITUTE - used humorously

pro·fes·sion·al¹ S2 W1 /prəˈfeʃənəl/ adj
1 JOB [only before noun] **a)** relating to a job that needs special education and training: *What professional qualifications does he have?* | *It is essential to get good* **professional advice**. | *You may need to seek* **professional help**. **b)** relating to your job or work and not to your private life: *professional contacts*
2 WELL TRAINED showing that someone has been well trained and is good at their work: *This business plan looks very professional.* | *a more professional approach to work*
3 PAID doing a job, sport, or activity for money, rather than just for fun; → **amateur**: *a professional tennis player* | *a professional army* | **turn/go professional** (=start to do something as a job)
4 TEAM/EVENT done by or relating to people who are paid to do a sport or activity; → **amateur**: *a professional hockey team* | *The golf tournament is a professional event.*
5 professional person/man/woman etc someone who

works in a profession, or who has an important position in a company or business: *We'd prefer to rent the house to a professional couple.*
6 professional liar/complainer etc someone who lies or complains too much – used humorously —**professionalization** /prəˌfeʃənəlaɪˈzeɪʃən $ -lə-/ n [U]: *the increasing professionalization of childcare services* —**professionalize** /prəˈfeʃənəlaɪz/ v [T]

professional² W3 n [C]
1 someone who earns money by doing a job, sport, or activity that many other people do just for fun; → **amateur**: *Hurd signed as a professional in 1998.* | *top snooker professionals*
2 someone who works in a job that needs special education and training, such as a doctor, lawyer, or ARCHITECT: *health professionals* (=doctors, nurses etc)
3 someone who has a lot of experience and does something very skillfully: *You sing like a real professional.*
4 tennis/golf/swimming etc professional someone who is very good at a sport and is employed by a private club to teach its members

pro,fessional 'foul n [C] in football, if someone commits a professional foul, they deliberately do something that is against the rules in order to prevent another player from scoring

pro·fes·sion·al·is·m /prəˈfeʃənəlɪzəm/ n [U] **1** the skill and high standards of behaviour expected of a professional person: *the dedication and professionalism of our staff* **2** BrE the practice of using professional players in sports: *Professionalism has raised the standard of rugby immensely.*

pro·fes·sion·al·ly /prəˈfeʃənəli/ adv **1** as part of your work: *Do you need to use English professionally?* **2** in a way that shows high standards and good training: *The magazine wasn't very professionally designed.* **3** as a paid job rather than just for fun: *a chance to play football professionally* **4** by someone who has the necessary skills and training: *The carpet should be professionally fitted.*

pro,fessional 'wrestling n [U] a form of entertainment in which people, usually men, fight each other in a way that has been planned before the event —**professional wrestler** n [C]

pro·fes·sor /prəˈfesə $ -ər/ n [C] **1** BrE a teacher of the highest rank in a university department: *Professor Barclay* | **professor of Chinese/economics/religion etc** *She's been named the professor of English.* **2** AmE a teacher at a university or college: *Ted's a college professor.* | **biology/history/French etc professor** *Who's your chemistry professor?* → ASSISTANT PROFESSOR, ASSOCIATE PROFESSOR; → see box at TEACHER

pro·fes·so·ri·al /ˌprɒfəˈsɔːriəl $ ˌprɑː-/ adj relating to the job of a professor, or considered typical of a professor: *a new professorial chair* | *His beard gives him a very professorial look.* —**professorially** adv

pro·fes·sor·ship /prəˈfesəʃɪp $ -sər-/ n [C] the job or position of a university or college professor: *a professorship in Japanese*

prof·fer /ˈprɒfə $ ˈprɑːfər/ v [T] formal **1** to offer something to someone, especially by holding it out in your hands: *Sarah took the glass proffered by the attendant.* | **proffer sb sth** *Poirot proffered him a cigarette.* **2** to give someone advice, an explanation etc: *the proffered invitation*

pro·fi·cien·cy /prəˈfɪʃənsi/ n [U] a good standard of ability and skill: [+in/with/at] *a high level of proficiency in English* | *Nick's proficiency with computers is well-known.*

pro·fi·cient /prəˈfɪʃənt/ adj able to do something well or skillfully: [+in/at] *Martha's proficient in Swedish.* | *There's only one way to become proficient at anything – practice!* | *a proficient typist* —**proficiently** adv

pro·file¹ W3 /ˈprəʊfaɪl $ ˈproʊ-/ n [C]
1 HEAD a side view of someone's head: *Dani has a*

lovely profile. | **in profile** *I only saw her face in profile.*
2 DESCRIPTION a short description that gives important details about a person, a group of people, or a place: *a job profile* | [+of] *a short profile of the actor*
3 high profile something that is high profile is noticed by many people or gets a lot of attention: *Jack runs a department with a high public profile.* | *The star has a high profile in Britain.*
4 keep a low profile to behave quietly and avoid doing things that will make people notice you
5 raise sb's profile if a person or an organization raises its profile, it gets more attention from the public: *an advertising campaign designed to raise the bank's profile*
6 SHAPE an edge or shape of something seen against a background: *the sharp profile of the western foothills against the sky*

profile² v [T] to write or give a short description of someone or something: *The new Chief Executive was profiled in yesterday's newspaper.*

pro·fil·ing /ˈprəʊfaɪlɪŋ $ ˈproʊ-/ n [U] **1** offender profiling BrE the process of studying a crime, especially a murder, and making judgments about the character of the person who committed it **2** AmE when people who belong to a particular race or group are stopped and searched, for example by the police or at airports, because the police think that they are more likely to commit crimes: *racial profiling* **3** when companies collect information about people that they wish to sell something to

prof·it¹ S1 W1 /ˈprɒfɪt $ ˈprɑː-/ n
1 [C,U] money that you gain by selling things or doing business, after your costs have been paid; ⚡ loss; → revenue

at a profit
make/earn/turn a profit
big/huge/healthy/substantial/handsome/hefty profit (=a large profit)
profits are up/down
profits rise/increase/grow
profits soar/leap (=profits increase by a lot)
profits fall/drop
profits slump/plunge (=profits fall by a lot)
boost profits (=make them increase)
maximize profits (=get as much profit as possible)
net profit (=after tax and costs are paid)
gross profit (=before tax and costs are paid)
pre-tax profit (=before tax is paid)
trading/operating profit

Our daily profit is usually around $500. | *She sold the business and bought a farm with the profits.* | *They sold their house at a healthy profit.* | *Few independent movies turn a profit.* | *The property company made a huge profit on the deal.* | *Profits are up by a third.* | *Marston's profits rose last year to $17 million.* | *The group's pre-tax profits slumped to £25.5m.* | *They were able to report a small trading profit.*

2 [U] formal an advantage that you gain from doing something: *There's no profit in letting meetings drag on.* → NON-PROFIT

profit² v [I,T] **1** formal to be useful or helpful to someone: **profit sb to do sth** *It might profit you to learn about the company before your interview.* | [+by/from] *There are lessons in these stories that all children can profit by.* **2** to get money from doing something: [+by/from] *Some industries, such as shipbuilding, clearly profited from the war.*

prof·it·a·bil·i·ty /ˌprɒfɪtəˈbɪləti $ ˌprɑː-/ n [U] when a business or an activity makes a profit, or the amount of profit it makes: *a decline in company profitability*

prof·it·a·ble /ˈprɒfɪtəbəl $ ˈprɑː-/ adj producing a profit or a useful result; ⚡ unprofitable: *The advertising campaign proved very profitable.* | *a highly profitable business* | *a profitable afternoon* —**profitably** adv

profit and loss ac·count n [C] BrE a financial statement showing a company's income, spending, and profit over a particular period

prof·it·eer·ing /ˌprɒfɪˈtɪərɪŋ $ ˌprɑːfɪˈtɪr-/ n [U] the process of making unfairly large profits, especially by selling things that are very difficult to get at very high prices —**profiteer** n [C]: black market profiteers —**profiteer** v [I]

pro·fit·e·role /prəˈfɪtərəʊl $ -roʊl/ n [C] BrE a small round PASTRY with a sweet filling and chocolate on the top

prof·it·less /ˈprɒfɪtləs $ ˈprɑː-/ adj formal not making a profit, or not useful to do —**profitlessly** adv

profit-making adj [usually before noun] a profit-making organization or business makes a profit

profit margin n [C] the difference between the cost of producing something and the price at which you sell it

profit sharing n [U] a system by which all the people who work for a company receive part of its profits

profits warning n [C] BrE technical an occasion when a company announces that its profit for a particular period of time will be less than expected

prof·li·gate /ˈprɒflɪɡət $ ˈprɑː-/ adj formal **1** wasting money or other things in a careless way; ◨ **wasteful**: profligate spending | the profligate use of energy resources **2** behaving in an immoral way and not caring that your behaviour is bad —**profligacy** n [U] —**profligate** n [C]

pro for·ma /ˌprəʊ ˈfɔːmə $ ˌproʊ ˈfɔːr-/ adj, adv formal if something is approved, accepted etc pro forma, this is part of the usual way of doing things and does not involve any actual choice or decision: pro forma approval

pro forma invoice n [C] BrE a document like a bill that is sent to the customer to show what a price would be if he or she made an order; ◨ **quotation**

pro·found /prəˈfaʊnd/ adj **1** having a strong influence or effect: profound effect/influence/impact/consequence etc Tolstoy's experiences of war had a profound effect on his work. | The mother's behaviour has a profound impact on the developing child. | profound changes in society **2** showing strong, serious feelings; ◨ **deep**: a profound sense of guilt **3** showing great knowledge and understanding; ◨ **deep**: a profound question | Jenner is a profound thinker. **4** literary deep or far below the surface of something; ◨ **deep**: Her work touches something profound in the human psyche. **5** complete: profound deafness —**profoundly** adv: profoundly disturbing news

pro·fun·di·ty /prəˈfʌndɪti/ n plural **profundities** formal **1** [U] when someone or something shows great knowledge and understanding, or strong, serious feelings; ◨ **depth**: The cartoon version lacks the profundity of the original text. **2** [C usually plural] something that someone says that shows great knowledge and understanding: the profundities of her speech

pro·fuse /prəˈfjuːs/ adj produced or existing in large quantities: He made **profuse apologies**. | Profuse sweating is one of the symptoms of heat exhaustion. —**profusely** adv: The wound was bleeding profusely. —**profuseness** n [U]

pro·fu·sion /prəˈfjuːʒən/ n [singular,U] formal a very large amount of something: [+of] The house was overflowing with a profusion of strange ornaments. | **in profusion** Cornflowers grow in profusion in the fields.

pro·gen·i·tor /prəʊˈdʒenɪtə $ proʊˈdʒenɪtər/ n [C] **1** formal someone who first thought of an idea: [+of] a progenitor of cubism **2** technical a person or animal that lived in the past, to whom someone or something living now is related; ◨ **ancestor**

prog·e·ny /ˈprɒdʒəni $ ˈprɑː-/ n [U] **1** formal the babies of animals or plants; ◨ **offspring 2** someone's children – used humorously; ◨ **offspring**: Sarah with her numerous progeny **3** something that devel-

ops from something else: [+of] Connolly's book is the progeny of an earlier TV series.

pro·ges·ter·one /prəʊˈdʒestərəʊn $ proʊˈdʒestəroʊn/ n [U] a female sex HORMONE which prepares the body for having a baby, and which is also used in CONTRACEPTIVE drugs

prog·na·thous /prɒɡˈneɪθəs $ prɑːɡ-/ adj technical having a jaw that sticks out more than the rest of the face

prog·no·sis /prɒɡˈnəʊsɪs $ prɑːɡˈnoʊ-/ n plural **prognoses** /-siːz/ [C] **1** a doctor's opinion of how an illness or disease will develop; → **diagnosis**: good/poor prognosis Doctors said Blake's long-term prognosis is good. **2** formal a judgment about the future, based on information or experience: [+of] a hopeful prognosis of the country's future development

prog·nos·ti·ca·tion /prɒɡˌnɒstɪˈkeɪʃən $ prɑːɡˌnɑːs-/ n [C,U] formal a statement about what you think will happen in the future; ◨ **forecast**: gloomy prognostications —**prognosticate** /prɒɡˈnɒstɪkeɪt $ prɑːɡˈnɑːs-/ v [T]

pro·gram¹ W1 /ˈprəʊɡræm $ ˈproʊ-/ n [C] **1** a set of instructions given to a computer to make it perform an operation: a word processing program **2** the American spelling of PROGRAMME

program² v **programmed, programming** [T] **1** to give a computer a set of instructions that it can use to perform a particular operation: program sth to do sth attempts to program computers to produce and understand speech | Any large high-speed computer can be programmed to learn. **2** the American spelling of programme → PROGRAMMER

pro·gram·ma·ble /ˈprəʊɡræməbəl $ ˈproʊ-/ adj able to be controlled by a computer or electronic program: a programmable heating system

pro·gramme¹ S1 W1 BrE; **program** AmE /ˈprəʊɡræm $ ˈproʊ-/ n [C]

1 PLAN a series of actions which are designed to achieve something important: the US space program | programme to do sth a United Nations programme to control the spread of AIDS | [+of] a programme of economic reforms

2 TELEVISION/RADIO something that you watch on television or listen to on the radio: What's your favourite **television programme**? | news and current affairs programmes | [+about/on] There's a programme about killer whales next. | **see/watch a programme**

3 EDUCATION AmE a course of study: Stanford University's MBA program | a research program

4 IMPROVEMENTS actions that have been planned to keep something in good condition or improve something: a new fitness programme

5 PLAY/CONCERT a small book or piece of paper that gives information about a play, concert etc and who the performers are: a theatre programme

6 LIST OF EVENTS a series of planned activities or events, or a list showing what order they will come in: [+for] What's the programme for tomorrow? | [+of] a programme of exhibitions throughout the year

7 MACHINE a series of actions done in a particular order by a machine such as a washing machine: The light goes off when it finishes the programme. → PROGRAM¹

pro·gramme² BrE; **program** AmE v [T] **1** to set a machine to operate in a particular way: programme sth to do sth I've programmed the video to come on at ten. → PROGRAM² **2 be programmed** if a person or animal is programmed socially or biologically to do something, they do it without thinking: be programmed to do sth All birds of this species are programmed to build their nests in the same way. **3** to arrange for something to happen as part of a series of planned events or activities: What's programmed for this afternoon?

able to: *I'll try my best to get tickets, but I can't promise anything.*
5 I promise you *spoken* used to emphasize a promise, warning, or statement: *I promise you, it does work!*

promise² [S3] [W2] *n*

1 [C] a statement that you will definitely do or provide something or that something will definitely happen: [+of] *a promise of help* | [+to] *his promise to his father* | **promise to do sth** *She made a promise to visit them once a month.* | **promise that** *his promise that the job would be mine* | **keep/break a promise** (=to do or fail to do something you promised) *Don't make promises you can't keep.* | *I might have to break my promise.* | *I'll never lie to you again. You have my promise.* | *You have my* **solemn promise.**
2 [U] signs that something or someone will be good or successful: *a young man full of promise* | *Bill* **shows** *great* **promise** *as a goalkeeper.* | *She didn't* **fulfil** *her* **early promise.**
3 [singular,U] a sign that something, usually something good, may happen: [+of] *the promise of spring* | *The letter gave a promise of greater happiness.*

Promised Land *n* **the Promised Land a)** the land of Canaan, which was promised by God to Abraham and his people in the Bible **b)** a situation or place which people have been wanting to be in because they will be safe and happy

prom·is·ing /ˈprɒmɪsɪŋ $ ˈprɑː-/ *adj* showing signs of being successful or good in the future: *a promising career in law* | *a promising young actor* | *a promising start* —**promisingly** *adv*

prom·is·so·ry note /ˈprɒmɪsəri ˌnəʊt $ ˈprɑːmɪsɔːri ˌnoʊt/ *n* [C] *technical* a document promising to pay money before a particular date

pro·mo /ˈprəʊməʊ $ ˈproʊmoʊ/ *n plural* **promos** [C] *informal* a short film that advertises an event or product: *a promo video*

prom·on·to·ry /ˈprɒməntəri $ ˈprɑːməntɔːri/ *n plural* **promontories** [C] a long narrow piece of land which sticks out into the sea: *a rocky promontory*

pro·mote [S3] [W2] /prəˈməʊt $ -ˈmoʊt/ *v* [T]
1 ENCOURAGE to help something to develop or increase: *a meeting to promote trade between Taiwan and the U.K.* | *Fertilizer promotes leaf growth.*
2 BETTER JOB [usually passive] to give someone a better, more responsible job in a company; ⧆ **demote**: **promote sb to sth** *Helen was promoted to senior manager.*
3 SELL to help sell a new product, film etc by offering it at a reduced price or by advertising it: *She's in London to promote her new book.*
4 SPORT [usually passive] *BrE* if a sports team is promoted, they play in a better group of teams the next year; ⧆ **relegate**: **promote sb to sth** *They have been promoted to the First Division.*
5 PERSUADE to try to persuade people to support or use something: *John Major promoted the idea of a classless society.*
6 ARRANGE to be responsible for arranging a large public event such as a concert or a sports game

pro·mot·er /prəˈməʊtə $ -ˈmoʊtər/ *n* [C] **1** someone who arranges and advertises concerts or sports events: *a boxing promoter* **2** someone who tries to persuade people to support or use something: *promoters of solar energy*

pro·mo·tion [S3] [W3] /prəˈməʊʃən $ -ˈmoʊ-/ *n*
1 [C,U] a move to a more important job or position in a company or organization: *I want a job with good prospects for promotion.* | [+to] *Your promotion to Senior Editor is now official.*
2 [C,U] an activity intended to help sell a product, or the product that is being promoted: *a winter sales promotion*
3 [U] the activity of persuading people to support something: [+of] *the promotion of energy conservation*
4 [U] the activity of helping something to develop or

increase: [+of] *the promotion of international environmental cooperation*
5 [U] *BrE* when a sports team moves into a better group of teams; ⧆ **relegation**

pro·mo·tion·al /prəˈməʊʃənəl $ -ˈmoʊ-/ *adj* promotional films, events etc advertise something: *a promotional video*

prompt¹ /prɒmpt $ prɑːmpt/ *v* **1** [T] to make someone decide to do something: **prompt sb to do sth** *What prompted you to buy that suit?* **2** [T] to make people say or do something as a reaction: *The decision prompted an outcry among prominent US campaigners.* **3** [T] to help a speaker who pauses, by suggesting how to continue: *'I can't decide.' said Beatrice. 'Decide what?' prompted Marlon.* **4** [T] to ask someone to do something on a computer: *A message will appear which will prompt you for certain information.* **5** [I,T] to remind an actor of the next words in a speech

prompt² *adj* **1** done quickly, immediately, or at the right time: *Prompt action must be taken.* | *a prompt payment is requested.* | *a prompt response* **2** [not before noun] someone who is prompt arrives or does something at the right time and is not late: *Lunch is at two. Try to be prompt.* —**promptness** *n* [U]

prompt³ *adv BrE informal* at the time mentioned and no later; ⧆ **sharp** *AmE*: *The bus will leave at 8 o'clock prompt.*

prompt⁴ *n* [C] **1** a word or words said to an actor in a play, to help them remember what to say **2** a sign on a computer screen which shows that the computer has finished one operation and is ready to begin the next

prompt·er /ˈprɒmptə $ ˈprɑːmptər/ *n* [C] someone who tells actors in a play what words to say when they forget

prompt·ly /ˈprɒmptli $ ˈprɑː-/ *adv* **1** at the right time without being late; ⧆ **on time**: *She arrived promptly.* **2** immediately: *She turned off the alarm and promptly went back to sleep.* **3** without delay: *A reply came very promptly.*

Proms /prɒmz $ prɑːmz/ *n* **the Proms** plural *BrE informal* a series of PROMENADE CONCERTS held every year in Britain

prom·ul·gate /ˈprɒməlɡeɪt $ ˈprɑː-/ *v* [T] *formal* **1** to spread an idea or belief to as many people as possible **2** to make a new law come into effect by announcing it officially —**promulgator** *n* [C] —**promulgation** /ˌprɒməlˈɡeɪʃən $ ˌprɑː-/ *n* [U]

pron. also **pron** *BrE* the written abbreviation of *pronoun*

prone /prəʊn $ proʊn/ *adj* **1** likely to do something or suffer from something, especially something bad or harmful: [+to] *Some plants are very prone to disease.* | **prone to do sth** *Kids are all prone to eat junk food.* | **accident-prone/injury-prone** etc *He's always been accident-prone.* **2** *formal* lying down with the front of your body facing down; ⧆ **prostrate**: *His eyes shifted to the prone body on the floor.* —**proneness** *n* [U] —**prone** *adv*: *Jack lay prone on his bed.*

prong /prɒŋ $ prɑːŋ/ *n* [C] **1** a thin sharp point of something such as a fork that has several points: *sticking out like the prongs of a garden fork* **2** one of two or three ways of achieving something which are used at the same time: [+of] *the second prong of the attack* —**pronged** *adj*: *a two-pronged fork*

pro·nom·i·nal /prəʊˈnɒmɪnəl $ proʊˈnɑː-/ *adj technical* related to or used like a PRONOUN —**pronominally** *adv*

pro·noun /ˈprəʊnaʊn $ ˈproʊ-/ *n* [C] a word that is used instead of a noun or noun phrase, such as 'he' instead of 'Peter' or 'the man' → DEMONSTRATIVE PRONOUN, PERSONAL PRONOUN

pro·nounce /prəˈnaʊns/ *v* **1** [T] to make the sound of a letter, word etc, especially in the correct way; → **pronunciation**: *How do you pronounce your name?* **2** [T] to officially state that something is true: **pronounce sb/sth sth** *The victim was pronounced dead* on arrival. | I now pronounce you man and wife. **3** [I,T] to give a judgment or opinion: The scheme was pronounced a failure. | [+on/upon] He used to pronounce on matters he knew nothing about. **4** [I,T] law to give a legal judgment: **pronounce sentence** (=tell a court of law what punishment a criminal will have)

pro·nounce·a·ble /prəˈnaʊnsəbəl/ adj a word, name etc that is pronounceable is easy to say

pro·nounced /prəˈnaʊnst/ adj very great or noticeable: a pronounced Polish accent | This disability is more pronounced in men. —**pronouncedly** /prəˈnaʊnsɪdli/ adv

pro·nounce·ment /prəˈnaʊnsmənt/ n [C] formal an official public statement: [+on] the Pope's last pronouncement on birth control

pron·to /ˈprɒntəʊ $ ˈprɑːntoʊ/ adv spoken informal quickly or immediately: You'd better get back here pronto.

pro·nun·ci·a·tion /prəˌnʌnsiˈeɪʃən/ n **1** [C,U] the way in which a language or a particular word is pronounced: [+of] Do you know the **correct pronunciation** of these Gaelic names? **2** [singular] a particular person's way of pronouncing a word or words

proof¹ [S2] [W3] /pruːf/ n
1 EVIDENCE [C,U] facts, information, documents etc that prove something is true: [+of] proof of the existence of life on other planets | This latest interview was further proof of how good at her job Cara was. | **proof of purchase/ownership/identity** Do you have any proof of purchase? (=something to prove that you bought and paid for something) | You'll need your passport **as proof** of identity. | **proof (that)** Do you have any proof that this man stole your bag? | There is no proof that the document is authentic. | Laboratory tests gave **conclusive proof** that the meat presents no risk to human health. | He's **living proof** (=his experience or life shows it is true) that footballers can still play at the highest level into their late thirties. | **proof positive** (=definite proof that cannot be doubted) We received 800 applications last year, proof positive that the college is highly regarded by parents and students. | **burden/onus of proof** law (=used to say who has to show that something is true or not in a legal case) The burden of proof lies on the defendant.
2 COPY [C usually plural] technical a copy of a piece of writing or a photograph that is checked carefully before the final printing is done: Can you check these proofs?
3 MATHEMATICS [C] **a)** a test in mathematics of whether a calculation is correct **b)** a list of reasons that shows a THEOREM (=statement) in GEOMETRY to be true
4 the proof of the pudding (is in the eating) used to say that you can only know whether something is good or bad after you have tried it
5 ALCOHOL [U] a measurement of the strength of some types of alcoholic drink, especially SPIRITS : 70% proof vodka (=that contains 70% pure alcohol) BrE | 70 proof vodka (=that contains 35% pure alcohol) AmE

proof² adj be proof against sth literary to be too strong or good to be affected by something bad: Their defences are proof against most weapons.

proof³ v [T] BrE **1** [usually passive] to treat a material with a substance in order to protect it against water, oil etc: **proof sth against sth** climbing gear proofed against water **2** to proofread something

-proof /pruːf/ suffix **1** [in adjectives] used to describe something which a particular thing cannot harm or pass through, or which protects people against that thing: a bulletproof car | a waterproof jacket | an ovenproof dish (=that cannot be harmed by heat) **2** [in adjectives] used to describe something which cannot easily be affected or damaged by someone or something: a childproof container | vandal-proof **3** [in verbs] to treat or make something so that a particular thing cannot harm it or pass through it, or so that it gives protection against it: soundproof a room (=so that sound cannot get into or out of it)

proof·read /ˈpruːfriːd/ also **proof** past tense and past participle **proofread** /-red/ v [I,T] to read through something that is written or printed in order to correct any mistakes in it —**proofreader** n [C] —**proofreading** n [U]: a proofreading job

prop¹ /prɒp $ prɑːp/ v propped, propping [T always + adv/prep] to support something by leaning it against something, or by putting something else under, next to, or behind it: **prop sth against/on sth** He propped his bike against a tree. | Can we **prop** the window **open** with something?

prop sth ⇔ **up** phr v **1** to prevent something from falling by putting something against it or under it: The builders are trying to prop up the crumbling walls of the church. | [+against] paintings propped up against the wall **2** to help an ECONOMY, industry, or government so that it can continue to exist, especially by giving money: The government introduced measures to prop up the stock market. **3** prop yourself up to hold your body up by leaning against something: [+on/against/with] She propped herself up on one elbow.

prop² n [C] **1** an object placed under or against something to hold it in a particular position **2** [usually plural] a small object such as a book, weapon etc, used by actors in a play or film: Anna looks after costumes and props. | stage props **3** something or someone that helps you to feel strong: She was becoming an emotional prop for him. **4** informal a PROPELLER **5** also **prop forward** one of the players in a RUGBY team, who is large and strong and holds up the SCRUM

prop·a·gan·da /ˌprɒpəˈɡændə $ ˌprɑː-/ n [U] information which is false or which emphasizes just one part of a situation, used by a government or political group to make people agree with them: the spreading of political propaganda | Nazi/Communist etc propaganda | propaganda exercise/campaign (=something done to show one political opinion) | They have mounted a propaganda campaign against Western governments. | the government propaganda machine (=people who produce propaganda) —**propagandize** also -**ise** BrE v [I,T] —**propagandist** n [C]

prop·a·gate /ˈprɒpəɡeɪt $ ˈprɑː-/ v formal **1** [T] formal to spread an idea, belief etc to many people: The group launched a website to propagate its ideas. **2** [I,T] if you propagate plants, or if they propagate, they start to grow from a parent plant to produce new plants: Propagate your plants in fresh soil. **3** [T] if an animal, insect, etc propagates itself or is propagated, it increases in number; ⊟ reproduce —**propagation** /ˌprɒpəˈɡeɪʃən $ ˌprɑː-/ n [U]

prop·a·gat·or /ˈprɒpəɡeɪtə $ ˈprɑːpəɡeɪtər/ n [C] **1** someone who spreads ideas, beliefs etc **2** a covered box of soil in which young plants or seeds are placed so that they can grow

pro·pane /ˈprəʊpeɪn $ ˈproʊ-/ n [U] a colourless gas used for cooking and heating

pro·pel /prəˈpel/ v propelled, propelling [T] **1** to move, drive, or push something forward; → **propulsion**: a boat propelled by a small motor | One of our students was unable to propel her wheelchair up the ramp. | **propel yourself along/through etc** She used the sticks to propel herself along. **2** written to make someone move in a particular direction, especially by pushing them: He took her arm and propelled her towards the door. **3** to move someone into a new situation or make them do something: **propel sb to/into sth** The film propelled her to stardom. | Company directors were propelled into action.

pro·pel·lant /prəˈpelənt/ n [C,U] **1** an explosive for firing a bullet or ROCKET **2** gas which is used in an AEROSOL to SPRAY out a liquid —**propellant** adj

pro·pel·ler /prəˈpelə $ -ər/ n [C] a piece of equipment consisting of two or more blades that spin around, which makes an aircraft or ship move

proposition² v [T] formal to suggest to someone that they have sex with you: *Here, prostitutes constantly proposition tourists.*

pro·pound /prə'paʊnd/ v [T] formal to suggest an idea, explanation etc for other people to consider: *The theory of natural selection was first propounded by Charles Darwin.*

prop·py /'prɒpi $ 'prɑːpi/ adj AusE unable to walk or run well; ▤ **lame**

pro·pri·e·ta·ry /prə'praɪətəri $ -teri/ adj formal **1** especially BrE a proprietary product is one that is sold under a TRADE NAME; ▣ **generic**: *a proprietary brand of insecticide* | *proprietary software products* **2** relating to who owns something: *They have proprietary rights to the data.* | *He has no proprietary interest in the farm* (=he does not own any part of it). **3** proprietary behaviour makes it seem that you think you own something or someone

pro·pri·e·tor /prə'praɪətə $ -ər/ n [C] formal an owner of a business: [+of] *the proprietor of a small hotel and restaurant* | **newspaper/garage/cafe etc proprietor**

pro·pri·e·to·ri·al /prə,praɪə'tɔːriəl/ adj behaving or feeling as if you own something or someone: [+about] | *She felt proprietorial about the valley.* —**proprietorially** adv

pro·pri·e·tress /prə'praɪətr‿əs/ n [C] old-fashioned a woman who owns a business

pro·pri·e·ty /prə'praɪəti/ n formal **1** [singular,U] correctness of social or moral behaviour; ▣ **impropriety**: [+of] *They discussed the propriety of treating ill children against the wishes of the parents.* | **with propriety** *They conducted themselves with propriety.* **2** **the proprieties** especially BrE the accepted rules of correct social behaviour: *strict in observing the proprieties*

props /prɒps $ prɑːps/ interjection informal used when you want to say publicly that someone has done something good: **props to sb for (doing) sth** *Props to Chris for all of his volunteer work.*

pro·pul·sion /prə'pʌlʃən/ n [U] technical the force that drives a vehicle forward; → **propel**: **rocket/wind/nuclear/jet propulsion** | *research into liquid hydrogen as a means of propulsion* —**propulsive** /-sɪv/ adj

pro ra·ta /prəʊ 'rɑːtə $ proʊ 'reɪtə/ adj [only before noun] especially BrE a payment or share that is pro rata is calculated according to how much of something is used, how much work is done, etc: *Fees are calculated on a pro rata basis.* —**pro rata** adv

pro·rate /prəʊ'reɪt $ proʊ-/ v [T usually passive] AmE to calculate a charge, price, etc according to the actual amount of service received rather than by a standard sum

pro·sa·ic /prəʊ'zeɪ-ɪk, prə- $ proʊ-, prə-/ adj boring or ordinary: *a prosaic writing style* | *The reality, however, is probably more prosaic.* —**prosaically** /-kli/ adv

pro·sce·ni·um /prə'siːniəm, prəʊ- $ prə-, proʊ-/ n [C] technical the part of a theatre stage that is in front of the curtain: **the proscenium arch** (=the arch over the stage where the curtain can be attached)

pro·scribe /prəʊ'skraɪb $ proʊ-/ v [T] formal to officially say that something is not allowed to exist or be done; ▣ **forbid**, **prohibit**: *The Act proscribes discrimination on the grounds of race.* —**proscription** /-'skrɪpʃən/ n [C,U]

prose /prəʊz $ proʊz/ n [U] written language in its usual form, as opposed to poetry

pros·e·cute /'prɒsɪkjuːt $ 'prɑː-/ v **1** [I,T] to charge someone with a crime and try to show that they are guilty of it in a court of law: *Shoplifters will be prosecuted.* | **prosecute sb for (doing) sth** *Buxton is being prosecuted for assault.* | **prosecute sb under a law/Act etc** *The company is to be prosecuted under the Health and Safety Act.* **2** [I,T] if a lawyer prosecutes a case, he or she tries to prove that the person charged with a crime is guilty; → **defend**: *Mrs Lynn Smith,*

prosecuting, said the offence took place on January 27. **3** [T] formal to continue doing something: *We cannot prosecute the investigation further.*

pros·e·cu·tion W3 /,prɒsɪ'kjuːʃən $,prɑː-/ n **1** [C,U] when a charge is made against someone for a crime, or when someone is judged for a crime in a court of law: *a criminal prosecution* | [+for] *Walters could face prosecution for his role in the robbery.* | [+of] *the prosecution of war criminals* | *The evidence is not sufficient to bring a prosecution against him.*
2 **the prosecution** the lawyers who try to prove in a court of law that someone is guilty of a crime; → **defence**: *the chief witness for the prosecution*
3 [U] formal when you do something that is your job: *the prosecution of her duties*

pros·e·cu·tor /'prɒsɪkjuːtə $ 'prɑːsɪkjuːtər/ n [C] a lawyer who is trying to prove in a court of law that someone is guilty of a crime

pros·e·lyt·ize also **-ise** BrE /'prɒsələtaɪz $ 'prɑː-/ v [I,T] formal to try to persuade someone to join a religious group, political party etc – used especially when you disapprove of this —**proselytizer** n [C] —**proselytizing** n [U]

pros·o·dy /'prɒsədi $ 'prɑː-/ n [U] technical the patterns of sound and RHYTHM in poetry and spoken language, or the rules for arranging these patterns —**prosodic** /prə'sɒdɪk $ -'sɑː-/ adj

pros·pect¹ S2 W2 /'prɒspekt $ 'prɑː-/ n **1** [C,U] the possibility that something will happen: **prospect of doing sth** *I see no prospect of things improving here.* | *There is every prospect* (=a strong possibility) *of the weather remaining dry this week.* | [+for] *There are good prospects for growth in the retail sector.* | **prospect that** *There's a real prospect that England will not qualify for the World Cup.*
2 [singular] a particular event which will probably or definitely happen in the future – used especially when you want to talk about how you feel about it: [+of] *The prospect of marriage terrified Alice.* | *Greeks face the prospect of new general elections next month.* | *He relishes the prospect of a fight.* | **daunting/exciting etc prospect** | **be excited/alarmed/concerned etc at the prospect (of sth)** *She wasn't exactly overjoyed at the prospect of looking after her niece.*
3 **prospects** [plural] chances of future success: *I had no job, no education, and no prospects.* | **job/career prospects** *Job prospects for graduates don't look good.*
4 [C] a person, job, plan etc that has a good chance of success in the future
5 **in prospect** formal likely to happen in the near future: *A new round of trade talks is in prospect.*
6 [C usually singular] formal a view of a wide area of land, especially from a high place

pro·spect² /prə'spekt $ 'prɑːspekt/ v [I] **1** to examine an area of land or water, in order to find gold, silver, oil etc: [+for] *The company is prospecting for gold in Alaska.* **2** to look for something, especially business opportunities: [+for] *salesmen prospecting for new customers*

pro·spec·tive /prə'spektɪv/ adj [only before noun] **1** **prospective employee/candidate/buyer etc** someone who is likely to do a particular thing or achieve a particular position **2** likely to happen: *the prospective costs of providing pensions*

pro·spec·tor /prə'spektə $ 'prɑːspektər/ n [C] someone who looks for gold, minerals, oil etc

pro·spec·tus /prə'spektəs/ n [C] **1** especially BrE a small book that advertises a school, college, new business etc **2** a document produced by a company that wants the public to buy its shares

pros·per /'prɒspə $ 'prɑːspər/ v [I] if people or businesses prosper, they grow and develop in a successful way, especially by becoming rich or making a large profit: *Businesses across the state are prospering.*

pro·sper·i·ty /prɒ'sperⁱti $ prɑː-/ n [U] when people have money and everything that is needed for a good life: *a time of economic prosperity* | [+of] *the future prosperity of the country*

pros·per·ous /'prɒspərəs $ 'prɑː-/ adj formal rich and successful: *a prosperous landowner*; → see box at **RICH**

pros·tate /'prɒsteɪt $ 'prɑː-/ also **'prostate ˌgland** n [C] an organ in the body of male MAMMALS that is near the BLADDER and that produces a liquid in which SPERM are carried

pros·the·sis /prɒs'θiːsⁱs $ prɑːs-/ n plural **prostheses** /-siːz/ [C] medical an artificial leg, tooth, or other part of the body which takes the place of a missing part —**prosthetic** /-'θetɪk/ adj

pros·ti·tute¹ /'prɒstⁱtjuːt $ 'prɑːstⁱtuːt/ n [C] someone, especially a woman, who earns money by having sex with people

prostitute² v **1** [T] if someone prostitutes a skill, ability, important principle etc, they use it in a way that does not show its true value, usually to earn money: *Friends from the theater criticized him for prostituting his talent in the movies.* **2 prostitute yourself** to work as a prostitute

pros·ti·tu·tion /ˌprɒstⁱ'tjuːʃən $ ˌprɑːstⁱ'tuːʃən/ n [U] the work of prostitutes

pros·trate¹ /'prɒstreɪt $ 'prɑː-/ adj **1** lying on your front with your face towards the ground: *They found him lying prostrate on the floor.* | *prostrate body/figure/form* **2** too shocked, upset, weak etc to be able to do anything: [+with] *Julie was prostrate with grief after her father's death.* —**prostration** /prɒ'streɪʃən $ prɑː-/ n [C,U]

pro·strate² /prə'streɪt $ 'prɑːstreɪt/ v **1 prostrate yourself** to lie on your front with your face towards the ground, especially as an act of religious WORSHIP or as a sign of your willingness to obey someone **2** [T usually passive] to make someone too shocked, upset, or weak to be able to do anything

pro·tag·o·nist /prəʊ'tægənⁱst $ proʊ-/ n [C] formal **1** the most important character in a play, film, or story; ▣ **main character** **2** one of the most important people taking part in a competition, battle, or struggle: *the main protagonists in the conflict* **3** one of the most important supporters of a social or political idea: [+of] *a protagonist of educational reform*

pro·te·an /'prəʊtiən, prəʊ'tiːən $ 'proʊtiən, proʊ-/ adj literary able to keep changing or to do many things

pro·tect ▣S2 ▣W2 /prə'tekt/ v
1 [I,T] to keep someone or something safe from harm, damage, or illness; → **protection, protective**: *Are we doing enough to protect the environment?* | **protect sb/sth from sth** *The cover protects the machine from dust.* | **protect sb/sth against sth** *Physical exercise can protect you against heart disease.* | [+against] *Waxing your car will help protect against rust.*
2 [T usually passive] if an insurance company protects your home, car, life, etc, it agrees to pay you money if things are stolen or damaged or you are hurt or killed; ▣ **cover**: *Unemployment insurance means that you are partially protected if you lose your job.*
3 [T] to help the industry and trade of your own country by taxing or restricting foreign goods

pro·tect·ed /prə'tektⁱd/ adj a protected animal, plant, area, or building is one that it is illegal to harm or damage: *Spotted owls are a protected species.*

pro·tec·tion ▣S2 ▣W2 /prə'tekʃən/ n
1 [U] when someone or something is protected: [+of] *the protection of the environment* | [+against/from] *evidence that vitamin C gives protection against cancer* | [+for] *This law provides protection for threatened animals and plants.* | **for protection** *The police were issued with body armour for extra protection.*
2 [C,U] something that protects: **as (a) protection (against sth)** *Magee pulled up his collar as protection against the breeze.*
3 [U] the promise of payment from an insurance

company if something bad happens; ▣ **coverage**
4 [U] CONTRACEPTION: *Do you have any protection?*
5 [U] when criminals threaten to damage your property or hurt you unless you pay them money: *protection money* | *a protection racket* (=the illegal activity of demanding money for protection)

pro·tec·tion·is·m /prə'tekʃənɪzəm/ n [U] when a government tries to help industries in its own country by taxing or restricting foreign goods —**protectionist** adj —**protectionist** n [C]

pro·tec·tive /prə'tektɪv/ adj **1** [only before noun] used or intended for protection: *protective clothing* | *Sunscreen provides a protective layer against the sun's harmful rays.* **2** wanting to protect someone from harm or danger: [+towards] *I can't help feeling protective towards my kids.* | [+of] *He's very protective of his younger brother.* **3** intended to give an advantage to your own country's industry: *protective tariffs* —**protectively** adv —**protectiveness** n [U]

pro·tective 'custody n [U] a situation in which the police make you stay somewhere to protect you from people who could harm you: **in/into protective custody** *The children were taken into protective custody.*

pro·tec·tor /prə'tektə $ -ər/ n [C] someone or something that protects someone or something else

pro·tec·tor·ate /prə'tektərⁱt/ n [C] a country that is protected and controlled by a more powerful country

prot·é·gé /'prɒtəʒeɪ $ 'proʊ-/ n [C] someone, especially a young person, who is taught and helped by someone who has influence, power, or more experience: *She attempted to encourage her young protégé.*

pro·tein ▣W2 /'prəʊtiːn $ 'proʊ-/ n [C,U] one of several natural substances that exist in food such as meat, eggs, and beans, and which your body needs in order to grow and remain strong and healthy

pro tem /ˌprəʊ 'tem $ ˌproʊ-/ also **pro tem·po·re** /-'tempəreɪ/ adj [only after noun] formal happening or existing now, but only for a short time: *the president pro tem of the Senate*

pro·test¹ ▣W3 /'prəʊtest $ 'proʊ-/ n
1 [C,U] something that you do to show publicly that you think that something is wrong and unfair, for example taking part in big public meetings, refusing to work, or refusing to buy a company's products

protest march/rally
hold/stage/mount a protest
in protest (at sth)
peaceful protest
violent/angry protest
public protest
street protest
protest group/movement

[+against] *protests against the Vietnam war* | *protest marches against the government's policy on immigration* | *A small group of demonstrators staged a peaceful protest outside the UN Headquarters.* | *5000 employees came out on strike in protest at the poor working conditions.* | *Three people died yesterday in violent street protests.* | *the protest movements of the 1960s*

2 [C] words or actions that show that you do not want someone to do something or that you dislike something very much: [+from] *I turned off the TV, despite loud protests from the kids.* | **without protest** *He accepted his punishment without protest.* | *She ignored his protests and walked away.* | *The programme caused a storm of protest* (=a lot of angry protest). | *The announcement was met with howls of protest.*
3 do sth under protest to do something while making it clear that you do not want to do it: *The bill was eventually paid under protest.* ⚠ The noun **protest** is pronounced with the emphasis on the first syllable

▣1▣ 000, ▣2▣ 000, ▣3▣ 000, most frequent words in ▣S▣ poken and ▣W▣ ritten English

/ˈprəʊtest $ ˈproʊtest/. The verb is pronounced with the emphasis on the second syllable /prəˈtest /.

pro·test² /prəˈtest/ v **1** [I,T] to come together to publicly express disapproval or opposition to something: [+against/at/about] *Thousands of people blocked the street, protesting against the new legislation.* | **protest sth** *AmE: Students protested the decision.* **2** [I,T] to say that you strongly disagree with or are angry about something because you think it is wrong or unfair: *'I don't see why I should take the blame for this!' she protested.* | **protest that** *Clive protested that he hadn't been given enough time to do everything.* **3** [T] to state very firmly that something is true, when other people do not believe you: **protest (that)** *Sarah protested that she wasn't Mick's girlfriend.* | *Years later, he is still protesting his innocence.*

Prot·es·tant /ˈprɒtɪˌstənt $ ˈprɑː-/ n [C] a member of a part of the Christian church that separated from the Roman Catholic church in the 16th century —**Protestant** adj —**Protestantism** n [U]

prot·es·ta·tion /ˌprɒtɪˈsteɪʃən ˌprəʊ- $ ˌprɑː-, ˌproʊ-/ n [C] formal a strong statement saying that something is true or not true, when other people believe the opposite: [+of] *protestations of innocence*

pro·test·er /prəˈtestə $ -ər/ n [C] someone who takes part in a public activity such as a DEMONSTRATION in order to show their opposition to something

proto- /prəʊtəʊ, -tə $ proʊtoʊ, -tə/ prefix technical existing or coming before other things of the same type: *a proto-fascist group* | *a prototype*

pro·to·col /ˈprəʊtəkɒl $ ˈproʊtəkɒːl, -kɑːl/ n **1** [U] a system of rules about the correct way to behave on an official occasion: *a breach of diplomatic protocol* **2** formal **a)** an international agreement between two or more countries: *the Montreal protocol on the protection of the ozone layer* **b)** a written record of a formal or international agreement, or an early form of an agreement **3** [C] technical an established method for connecting computers so that they can exchange information **4** [C] technical a set of rules that are followed when doing a scientific EXPERIMENT or giving someone medical treatment

pro·ton /ˈprəʊtɒn $ ˈproʊtɑːn/ n [C] a very small piece of matter with a positive electrical CHARGE that is in the central part of an atom; → **electron, neutron**

pro·to·plas·m /ˈprəʊtəplæzəm $ ˈproʊ-/ n [U] technical the colourless substance that forms the cells of plants and animals

pro·to·type /ˈprəʊtətaɪp $ ˈproʊ-/ n [C] **1** the first form that a new design of a car, machine etc has, or a model of it used to test the design before it is produced: [+of/for] *a working prototype of the new car* **2** someone or something that is one of the first and most typical examples of a group or situation

pro·to·typ·i·cal /ˌprəʊtəˈtɪpɪkəl $ ˌproʊ-/ adj very typical of a group or type: *prototypical behaviour*

pro·to·zo·an /ˌprəʊtəˈzəʊən $ ˌproʊtəˈzoʊən/ also **pro·to·zo·on** /-ˈzəʊɒn $ -ˈzoʊɑːn/ n plural **protozoa** /-ˈzəʊə $ -ˈzoʊə/ or **protozoans** [C] a very small living thing that has only one cell —**protozoan** adj

pro·trac·ted /prəˈtræktɪd/ adj used to describe something that continues for a long time, especially if it takes longer than usual, necessary, or expected; ◫ lengthy: **protracted negotiations/discussions/debate etc** *the expense of a protracted legal battle*

pro·trac·tor /prəˈtræktə $ proʊˈtræktər/ n [C] a piece of plastic in the shape of a half-circle, which is used for measuring and drawing angles → see picture at MATHEMATICS

pro·trude /prəˈtruːd $ proʊ-/ v [I] written to stick out from somewhere: [+from] *The envelope was protruding from her bag.*

pro·tru·sion /prəˈtruːʒən $ proʊ-/ n [C] formal something that sticks out

pro·tu·be·rance /prəˈtjuːbərənt $ -ˈtuː-/ n [C] formal something that sticks out: *This dinosaur is recognizable by the protuberance on the top of its head.* —**protuberant** adj

proud S2 W3 /praʊd/ adj comparative **prouder**, superlative **proudest**
1 PLEASED feeling pleased about something that you have done or something that you own, or about someone or something you are involved with or related to; → **pride**; ◫ **ashamed**: [+of] *Her parents are very proud of her.* | *You should be proud of yourself.* | *His past record is certainly something to be proud of.* | **be justly/rightly proud of sth** (=have good reasons for being proud) *The company is justly proud of its achievements.* | **proud to do/be sth** *Seven-year-old Ian is proud to have earned his red belt in karate.* | **proud (that)** *She was proud that the magazine had agreed to publish one of her stories.* | *Seth was the proud owner of a new sports car.*
2 **proudest moment/achievement/possession** the moment etc that makes you feel most proud: *His proudest moment was winning the European Cup final.*
3 TOO HIGH OPINION thinking that you are more important, skilful etc than you really are – used to show disapproval; → **pride**: *a proud man who would not admit his mistakes*
4 GREAT SELF-RESPECT having respect for yourself, so that you are embarrassed to ask for help when you are in a difficult situation; → **pride**: *Some farmers were too proud to ask for government help.*
5 do sb proud a) informal to make people feel proud of you by doing something well: *I tried to do my country proud.* **b)** old-fashioned to treat someone well by providing them with good food or entertainment
6 IMPRESSIVE literary tall and impressive —**proudly** adv

prove S2 W1 /pruːv/ v past tense **proved**, past participle **proved** or **proven** /ˈpruːvən/ especially AmE
1 SHOW STH IS TRUE [T] to show that something is true by providing facts, information etc; → **proof**: *You're wrong, and I can prove it.* | **prove (that)** *Tests have proved that the system works.* | **prove sth to sb** *I knew he had done it, but there was no way I could prove it to Eddie.* | **prove sb's guilt/innocence** *He claims the police destroyed records that could prove the officer's guilt.* | **prove sb wrong/innocent etc** *They say I'm too old, but I'm going to prove them all wrong.* | **To prove his point** (=show that he was right), *he mentioned several other experiments which had produced similar results.* ⚠ You **prove** something **to** someone: *I will prove to you (NOT prove you) that I'm right.*
2 BE [linking verb] if someone or something proves difficult, helpful, a problem etc, they are difficult,

helpful, a problem etc: *The recent revelations may prove embarrassing to the President.* | **prove to be sth** *The design proved to be a success.*

3 **prove yourself/prove something (to sb)** to show how good you are at doing something: *When I first started this job, I felt I had to prove myself.*

4 **prove yourself (to be)** sth to show other people that you are a particular type of person: *She's proved herself to be a very reliable worker.*

5 **what is sb trying to prove?** *spoken* said when you are annoyed by someone's actions and do not understand them

6 **prove a point** if someone does something to prove a point, they do it to show that they are right or that they can do something: *I'm not going to run the marathon just to prove a point.*

7 BREAD [I] if DOUGH (=unbaked bread mixture) proves, it rises and becomes light because of the YEAST in it

8 LAW [T] *law* to show that a WILL has been made in the correct way ⚠ Do not use 'prove' to mean 'make something better.' Use **improve**: *a chance to improve your English* —**provable** *adj*

prov·en[1] /'pruːvən, 'prəʊvən $ 'pruːvən, 'pruːvən/ *adj* [usually before noun] tested and shown to be true or good, or shown to exist: *a player of proven ability* | *a telephone system with a proven track record* (=past performance showing how good it is) *of reliability*

prov·en[2] /'pruːvən/ *v especially AmE* a past participle of PROVE

prov·e·nance /'prɒvənəns $ 'prɑː-/ *n* [U] *formal* the place where something originally came from: *The provenance of the paintings is unknown.* | **(of) dubious/doubtful provenance** (=used to suggest that something may have been stolen) *artworks of doubtful provenance*

prov·erb /'prɒvɜːb $ 'prɑːvɜːrb/ *n* [C] a short well-known statement that gives advice or expresses something that is generally true. 'A penny saved is a penny earned' is an example of a proverb; → **saying**

pro·ver·bi·al /prəˈvɜːbiəl $ -ɜːr-/ *adj* **1** the proverbial sth used when you describe something using part of a well-known expression: *The store had everything including the proverbial kitchen sink.* **2** relating to a proverb: *a proverbial expression* **3** well-known by a lot of people: *His modesty is proverbial.* —**proverbially** *adv*

pro·vide[S1][W1] /prəˈvaɪd/ *v* [T]
1 to give something to someone or make it available to them, because they need it or want it; → **provision**: *Tea and biscuits will be provided.* | **provide sth for sb** *The hotel provides a shoe-cleaning service for guests.* | **provide sb with sth** *The project is designed to provide young people with work.*
2 to produce something useful as a result: *We are hoping the enquiry will provide an explanation for the accident.* | **provide sb with sth** *The search provided the police with several vital clues.*
3 **provide that** *formal* if a law or rule provides that something must happen, it states that it must happen

provide against sth *phr v formal*
to make plans in order to deal with a bad situation that might happen: *Health insurance will provide against loss of income if you become ill.*

provide for sb/sth *phr v*
1 to give someone the things they need to live, such as money, food etc: *Without work, how can I provide for my children?*
2 *formal* if a law, rule, or plan provides for something, it states that something will be done and makes it possible for it to be done: *The new constitution provides for a 650-seat legislature.*
3 *formal* to make plans in order to deal with something that might happen in the future: *Commanders failed to provide for an attack by sea.*

or **provide** something **for** someone: *He provided me with everything (NOT provided me everything) I needed.* | *They did not provide enough paper for everyone (NOT to everyone).*
To **provide for** someone means to support them by giving them the things they need to live: *She has to provide for her four children (NOT provide her four children).*

pro·vid·ed[S3][W2] /prəˈvaɪdɪd/ also **pro'vided that** *conjunction* used to say that something will only be possible if something else happens or is done; 🔳 **providing**: *He can come with us, provided he pays for his own meals.*

Prov·i·dence, providence /'prɒvɪdəns $ 'prɑː-/ *n* [U] *literary* a force which is believed by some people to control what happens in our lives and to protect us: *divine providence*

prov·i·dent /'prɒvɪdənt $ 'prɑː-/ *adj formal* careful and sensible in the way you plan things, especially by saving money for the future

prov·i·den·tial /ˌprɒvɪˈdenʃəl◂ $ ˌprɑː-/ *adj formal* a providential event is a lucky one —**providentially** *adv*

pro·vid·er /prəˈvaɪdə $ -ər/ *n* [C] **1** a company or person that provides a service: *an Internet service provider* **2** someone who supports a family: *A widow, she is the sole provider* (=the only one) *for her family.*

pro·vid·ing[S2] /prəˈvaɪdɪŋ/ also **pro'viding that** *conjunction* used to say that something will only be possible if something else happens or is done; 🔳 **provided**: *You can borrow the car, providing I can have it back by six o'clock.*

prov·ince[W3] /'prɒvɪns $ 'prɑː-/ *n*
1 also **Province** [C] one of the large areas into which some countries are divided, and which usually has its own local government: *a Chinese province*
2 **the provinces** the parts of a country that are not near the capital
3 [singular] *formal* a subject that someone knows a lot about or something that only they are responsible for: [+of] *Computers were once the exclusive province of scientists and mathematicians.*

pro·vin·cial[1] /prəˈvɪnʃəl/ *adj* **1** [only before noun] relating to or coming from a province: *a provincial election* | *the provincial government of Quebec* **2** relating to or coming from the parts of a country that are not near the capital: *a provincial town* **3** old-fashioned and not interested in anything new or different – used to show disapproval: *provincial attitudes*

provincial[2] *n* [C] someone who comes from a part of a country that is not near the capital, especially someone who is not interested in anything new or different – often used to show disapproval

pro·vin·cial·is·m /prəˈvɪnʃəlɪzəm/ *n* [U] provincial attitudes

'proving ground *n* [C] **1** a place or situation in which something new is tried or tested: [+for] *High-crime areas are proving grounds for new police officers.* **2** *technical* an area for scientific testing, especially of vehicles

pro·vi·sion[1][S3][W1] /prəˈvɪʒən/ *n*
1 [C usually singular,U] when you provide something that someone needs now or in the future: [+of] *the provision of childcare facilities* | [+for] *provision for people with disabilities* | *He made provisions for his wife and his children in his will.*
2 **provisions** [plural] food, drink, and other supplies, especially for a journey: *We had enough provisions for two weeks.*
3 [C] a condition in an agreement or law: *The agreement includes a provision for each side to check the other side's weapons.* | **under the provisions of sth** *Under the provisions of the Act, employers must supply safety equipment.*

provision² v [T] formal to provide someone or something with a lot of food and supplies, especially for a journey

pro·vi·sion·al /prə'vɪʒənəl/ adj formal likely or able to be changed in the future: a **provisional government** | We accept provisional bookings by phone. —**provisionally** adv: The meeting has been provisionally arranged for the end of May.

pro,visional 'licence n [C] BrE an official document that you must have when you are learning to drive; ⊟ **learner's permit** AmE

pro·vi·so /prə'vaɪzəʊ $ -zoʊ/ n plural **provisos** [C] formal a condition that you ask for before you will agree to something: **with the proviso that** The money was given to the museum with the proviso that it is spent on operating costs.

prov·o·ca·tion /,prɒvə'keɪʃən $,prɑː-/ n [C,U] an action or event that makes someone angry or upset, or is intended to do this; → **provoke: without provocation** She claims that Graham attacked her without any provocation. | He was accused of **deliberate provocation**. | Julie has a tendency to burst into tears **at the slightest provocation**.

pro·voc·a·tive /prə'vɒkətɪv $ -'vɑː-/ adj **1** provocative behaviour, remarks etc are intended to make people angry or upset, or to cause a lot of discussion: **provocative comment/remark/statement** The minister's provocative remarks were widely reported in the press. | a **provocative act** by a terrorist group | She was accused of being **deliberately provocative**. **2** provocative clothes, movements, pictures etc are intended to make someone sexually excited: **provocative images** of young girls —**provocatively** adv

pro·voke /prə'vəʊk $ -'voʊk/ v [T] **1** to cause a reaction or feeling, especially a sudden one; → **provocation: provoke a protest/an outcry/criticism etc** The proposal provoked widespread criticism. | The decision to invade provoked storms of protest. | **provoke debate/discussion** | The novel has provoked fierce debate in the US. | **provoke sb into (doing) sth** She hopes her editorial will provoke readers into thinking seriously about the issue. | **provoke sb to do sth** Emma, though still at school, was provoked to help too. **2** to make someone angry, especially deliberately: The dog would not have attacked if it hadn't been provoked. | **provoke sb into (doing) sth** Paul tried to provoke Fletch into a fight.

Prov·ost, provost /'prɒvəst $ 'proʊvoʊst/ n [C] **1** the person in charge of a college in some British universities, especially at Oxford or Cambridge **2** an important official at a university in the US **3** old use the leader of the council in some Scottish towns and cities

prow /praʊ/ n [C] especially literary the front part of a ship or boat

prow·ess /'praʊɪs/ n [U] formal great skill at doing something: his physical prowess | military prowess

prowl¹ /praʊl/ v [I,T] **1** if an animal prowls, it moves around an area quietly, especially because it is hunting another animal **2** if someone prowls, they move around an area slowly and quietly, especially because they are involved in a criminal activity or because they are looking for something: gangs of teenagers **prowling the streets** | [+around/about] BrE: Irene prowled restlessly around the room.

prowl² n **be/go on the prowl (for sth/sb) a)** if an animal is on the prowl, it is hunting **b)** if someone is on the prowl, they are moving around different places, looking for an opportunity to do something: local men **out on the prowl** (=looking for people to have a sexual relationship with) in the city's bars and nightclubs | She's always on the prowl for bargains.

prowl·er /'praʊlə $ -ər/ n [C] a person who follows someone or hides near their house, especially at night,

in order to frighten or harm them or to steal something: The police were called after a prowler was spotted near their home.

prox·i·mate /'prɒksɪmət $ 'prɑːk-/ adj formal **1** a proximate cause is a direct one **2** nearest in time, order, or family relationship; ⊟ **close**

prox·im·i·ty /prɒk'sɪmɪti $ prɑːk-/ n [U] formal nearness in distance or time: [+to] We chose the house for its proximity to the school. | [+of] the proximity of the Bahamas to the States | Here the rich and the poor live **in close proximity** (=very near to each other).

prox·y /'prɒksi $ 'prɑːksi/ n plural **proxies 1 by proxy** if you do something by proxy, you arrange for someone else to do it for you: You can vote by proxy. **2** [C,U] someone who you choose to represent you, especially to vote for you: [+for] a husband acting as proxy for his wife **3** [C + for] formal something used to represent something else that you want to measure

proxy² adj [only before noun] involving the use of a proxy: a proxy vote

prude /pruːd/ n [C] someone who is very easily shocked by anything relating to sex – used to show disapproval

pru·dence /'pruːdəns/ n [U] a sensible and careful attitude that makes you avoid unnecessary risks: financial prudence

pru·dent /'pruːdənt/ adj sensible and careful, especially by trying to avoid unnecessary risks: prudent house buyers | **it is prudent (for sb) to do sth** It might be prudent to get a virus detector for the network.

pru·den·tial /pruː'denʃəl/ adj old-fashioned PRUDENT

prud·er·y /'pruːdəri/ n [U] the behaviour or attitude of people who are too easily shocked by things relating to sex – used to show disapproval

prud·ish /'pruːdɪʃ/ adj very easily shocked by things relating to sex – used to show disapproval: American culture is in many ways still fairly prudish. —**prudery** n [U] —**prudishly** adv —**prudishness** n [U]

prune¹ /pruːn/ v [T] **1** also **prune sth ⇔ back** to cut off some of the branches of a tree or bush to make it grow better: The roses need pruning. **2** especially BrE to make something smaller by removing parts that you do not need or want: The company is pruning staff in order to reduce costs. | The original version of the text has been pruned quite a bit.

prune² n [C] a dried PLUM, often cooked before it is eaten: stewed prunes

pru·ri·ent /'prʊəriənt $ 'prʊr-/ adj formal having or showing too much interest in sex – used to show disapproval: prurient interests —**pruriently** adv —**prurience** n [U]

prus·sic ac·id /,prʌsɪk 'æsɪd/ n [U] a very poisonous acid

pry /praɪ/ v **pried, prying, pries 1** [I] to try to find out details about someone else's private life in an impolite way: I **don't want to pry**, but I need to ask you one or two questions. | [+into] reporters prying into the affairs of celebrities **2** [T always + adv/prep] especially AmE to force something open, or force it away from something else; ⊟ **prize** BrE: We finally managed to pry the door open with a screwdriver. **3 away from prying eyes** in private, where people cannot see what you are doing

pry sth out of sb/sth phr v AmE to get money or information from someone with a lot of difficulty: If you want to know his name, you have to pry it out of her.

PS also **P.S.** AmE /,piː 'es/ n [C] **postscript** a note written at the end of a letter, adding more information: She added a PS to say 'hi' to my brother. | Best wishes, Julie. PS Maggie sends her love.

psalm /sɑːm $ sɑːm, sɑːlm/ n [C] a song or poem praising God, especially in the Bible

psalm·ist /'sɑːmɪst $ 'sɑːm-, 'sɑːlm-/ n [C] someone who has written a psalm

psal·ter /'sɔːltə $ 'sɒːltər/ n [C] a book containing the psalms from the Bible

psal·ter·y /ˈsɔːltəri $ ˈsɒːl-/ n plural **psalteries** [C] an ancient musical instrument with strings stretched over a board

pse·phol·o·gy /seˈfɒlədʒi $ siːˈfɑː-/ n [U] BrE technical the study of how people vote in elections —**psephologist** n [C]

pseud /sjuːd $ suːd/ n [C] BrE a person who pretends to know a lot about a subject and talks about it in a complicated way in order to make other people admire them – used to show disapproval

pseudo- /sjuːdəʊ $ suːdoʊ/ prefix false or not real: pseudo-intellectuals (=people who pretend to be clever) | She dismisses astrology as pseudo-science.

pseu·do·nym /ˈsjuːdənɪm $ ˈsuː-/ n [C] an invented name that a writer, artist etc uses instead of their real name: **under a pseudonym** He wrote under the pseudonym 'Silchester'. —**pseudonymous** /sjuːˈdɒnₐməs $ suːˈdɑː-/ adj: He was the pseudonymous author. —**pseudonymously** adv

pso·ri·a·sis /səˈraɪəsₐs/ n [U] a skin disease that causes rough red areas where the skin comes off in small pieces

psst /pst/ interjection a sound people make when they want to attract someone's attention without other people noticing: Psst! Guess what?

PST /ˌpiː es ˈtiː/ the abbreviation of Pacific Standard Time

psych¹ /saɪk/ v
  psych sb ↔ out phr v informal to do or say things that will make your opponent in a game or competition feel nervous or confused, so that it is easier for you to win
  psych sb up phr v informal if you psych yourself up or if someone psychs you up, you get mentally prepared before doing something so that you feel confident: **psych yourself up (for sth)** We both knew we had to psych ourselves up for the race.

psych² /saɪk/ n spoken informal **1** [U] a short form of PSYCHOLOGY: I'm a psych major now. **2** [C] a short form of PSYCHIATRIST

psy·che n [C usually singular] technical or formal someone's mind, or their deepest feelings, which control their attitudes and behaviour: Freud's account of **the human psyche** | A characteristic of the feminine psyche is to seek approval from others.

psy·che·del·ic /ˌsaɪkₐˈdelɪk/ adj [usually before noun] **1** psychedelic drugs such as LSD make you HALLUCINATE (=see things that do not exist) **2** having or using bright colours or strange sounds, and representing the experiences people have when they use drugs such as LSD: a psychedelic light show | Fashion designers look back to the 1960s with dazzling psychedelic prints. —**psychedelically** /-kli/ adv —**psychedelia** /-ˈdiːliə/ n [U]: Sixties psychedelia

psy·chi·at·ric /ˌsaɪkiˈætrɪk/ adj relating to the study and treatment of mental illness: a psychiatric hospital | a psychiatric nurse | Charles was suffering from a psychiatric disorder (=mental illness). —**psychiatrically** /-kli/ adv

psy·chi·a·trist /saɪˈkaɪətrₐst $ sə-/ n [C] a doctor trained in the treatment of mental illness; → psychologist

psy·chi·a·try /saɪˈkaɪətri $ sə-/ n [U] the study and treatment of mental illnesses; → psychology

psy·chic¹ /ˈsaɪkɪk/ adj [no comparative] **1** also **psy·chi·cal** /ˈsaɪkɪkəl/ relating to the power of the human mind to do strange or surprising things that cannot be explained by reason: a spiritual healer with **psychic powers** | a documentary on psychic phenomena **2** someone who is psychic has the ability to know what other people are thinking or what will happen in the future; → clairvoyant: You don't have to be psychic to know what Maggie is thinking. **3** also **psychical** affecting the mind rather than the body: psychic disorders (=illnesses) —**psychically** /-kli/ adv

psychic² n [C] someone who has mysterious powers, especially the ability to receive messages from dead people or to know what will happen in the future

psy·cho /ˈsaɪkəʊ $ -koʊ/ n plural **psychos** [C] informal someone who is mentally ill and who may behave in a violent or strange way —**psycho** adj

psycho- /saɪkəʊ, -kə $ -koʊ, -kə/ prefix also **psych-** technical relating to the mind and the mental processes, rather than the body: a psychoanalyst

psy·cho·ac·tive /ˌsaɪkəʊˈæktɪv $ -koʊ-/ adj psychoactive drugs have an effect on your mind

psy·cho·a·nal·y·sis /ˌsaɪkəʊ-əˈnælₐsₐs $ -koʊ-/ n [U] medical treatment that involves talking to someone about their life, feelings etc in order to find out the hidden causes of their problems —**psychoanalytic** /ˌsaɪkəʊ-ænəˈlɪtɪk $ -koʊænl-ˈɪtɪk/ adj: psychoanalytic theory —**psychoanalytical** adj —**psychoanalytically** /-kli/ adv

psy·cho·an·a·lyst /ˌsaɪkəʊˈænəl-ₐst $ -koʊ-/ n [C] someone who treats patients using psychoanalysis

psy·cho·an·a·lyze also **-yse** BrE /ˌsaɪkəʊˈænəlaɪz $ -koʊ-/ v [T] to treat someone using psychoanalysis

psy·cho·bab·ble /ˈsaɪkəʊˌbæbəl $ -koʊ-/ n [U] informal language that sounds scientific but is not really, that some people use when talking about their emotional problems – used to show disapproval

psy·cho·bi·ol·o·gy /ˌsaɪkəʊbaɪˈɒlədʒi $ -koʊbaɪˈɑː-/ n [U] the study of the body in relation to the mind

psy·cho·dra·ma /ˈsaɪkəʊˌdrɑːmə $ -koʊˌdrɑːmə, -ˌdræmə/ n **1** [C,U] a way of treating mental illness in which people are asked to act in a situation together to help them understand their emotions **2** [C] a serious film, play etc that examines the minds and feelings of the characters, rather than what happens

psy·cho·ki·ne·sis /ˌsaɪkəʊkaɪˈniːsₐs $ -koʊkₐ-/ n [U] the moving of solid objects using only the power of the mind, which some people believe is possible —**psychokinetic** /-kaɪˈnetɪk $ -kₐˈne-/ adj —**psychokinetically** /-kli/ adv

psy·cho·log·i·cal W3 /ˌsaɪkəˈlɒdʒɪkəl $ -ˈlɑː-/ adj **1** relating to the way that your mind works and the way that this affects your behaviour: Sleep disorders are a serious **psychological problem**. | Freud's psychological theories | What was the patient's **psychological state?**
2 relating to what is in someone's mind rather than what is real: Max says he's ill, but I'm sure it's psychological.
3 **psychological warfare** behaviour intended to make your opponents lose confidence or feel afraid
4 **the psychological moment** BrE informal the exact time in a situation when you have the best chance to achieve what you want —**psychologically** /-kli/ adv: psychologically disturbed patients

psy·chol·o·gist /saɪˈkɒlədʒₐst $ -ˈkɑː-/ n [C] someone who is trained in psychology; → psychiatrist: a clinical psychologist

psy·chol·o·gy W3 /saɪˈkɒlədʒi $ -ˈkɑː-/ n plural **psychologies**
1 [U] the study of the mind and how it influences people's behaviour: educational/social etc psychology experts in the field of developmental psychology
2 [U] the mental processes involved in believing in something or doing a certain activity: [+of] research into the psychology of racism
3 [C,U] what someone thinks or believes, and how this affects what they do: the psychology of three-year-olds | mob psychology | You have to use psychology to get people to stop smoking.

psy·cho·met·ric /ˌsaɪkəʊˈmetrɪk $ -koʊ-/ adj relating to the measurement of mental abilities and qualities: psychometric tests

P

2 [T] if a newspaper or magazine publishes a letter, article etc, it prints it for people to read; → **publication**: *We love reading your letters and we try to publish as many as possible.*
3 [T usually passive] to make official information such as a report available for everyone to read; → **publication**: *The latest unemployment figures will be published tomorrow.*
4 [I,T] if a writer, musician etc publishes their work, they arrange for it to be printed and sold: *University teachers must publish regularly to gain promotion.*
5 publish and be damned *BrE* used to say that you should take a risk in saying what you think is true, although the result may be harmful to you

pub·lish·er W3 /ˈpʌblɪʃə $ -ər/ *n* [C] a person or company whose business is to arrange the writing, production, and sale of books, newspapers etc

pub·lish·ing /ˈpʌblɪʃɪŋ/ *n* [U] the business of producing books and magazines: *Tony wants to get a job in publishing.* | *a new publishing house* (=publishing company) → DESKTOP PUBLISHING

puce /pjuːs/ *adj* dark brownish purple in colour —**puce** *n* [U]

puck /pʌk/ *n* [C] a hard flat circular piece of rubber that you hit with the stick in the game of ICE HOCKEY

puck·er /ˈpʌkə $ -ər/ also **pucker up** *v* **1** [I,T] if part of your face puckers, or if you pucker it, it becomes tight or stretched, for example because you are going to cry or kiss someone: *Her mouth puckered, and she started to cry.* **2** [I] if cloth puckers, it gets lines or folds in it and is no longer flat —**pucker** *n* [C] —**puckered** *adj*

puck·ish /ˈpʌkɪʃ/ *adj* [usually before noun] *literary* showing that you are amused by other people, and like to make jokes about them: *a puckish grin* —**puckishly** *adv*

pud /pʊd/ *n* [C,U] *BrE informal* a PUDDING: *What's for pud?*

pud·ding S3 /ˈpʊdɪŋ/ *n* [C,U]
1 *especially BrE* a hot sweet dish, made from cake, rice, bread etc with fruit, milk or other sweet things added
2 *especially AmE* a thick sweet creamy dish, usually made with milk, eggs, sugar, and flour, and served cold: *chocolate pudding*
3 *BrE* a sweet dish served at the end of a meal: **for pudding** *There's ice-cream for pudding.* → DESSERT
4 *BrE* a hot dish made of a mixture of flour, fat etc, with meat or vegetables inside: *steak and kidney pudding* → BLACK PUDDING, CHRISTMAS PUDDING, MILK PUDDING, PLUM PUDDING, YORKSHIRE PUDDING; → **the proof of the pudding is in the eating** at PROOF[1] (4)

pudding basin *n* [C] *BrE* a deep round dish in which puddings are cooked

pud·dle /ˈpʌdl/ *n* [C] a small pool of liquid, especially rain water: *Children splashed through the puddles.* | [+of] *He had fallen asleep, his head resting in a puddle of beer.* —**puddle** *v* [I] *literary*: *Rain trickled down the glass, puddling on the window sills.*

pu·den·dum /pjuːˈdendəm/ *n plural* **pudenda** /-də/ [C] *technical* the sexual organs on the outside of the body, especially a woman's

pudg·y /ˈpʌdʒi/ *adj* fairly fat: *the baby's pudgy little legs* —**pudginess** *n* [U]

pueb·lo /ˈpwebləʊ $ -loʊ/ *n plural* **pueblos** [C] a small town, especially in the south west U.S.

puer·ile /ˈpjʊəraɪl $ ˈpjʊrəl/ *adj formal* silly and stupid; ⊟ **childish**: *a puerile joke* —**puerility** /pjʊˈrɪləti/ *n* [U]

puff[1] /pʌf/ *v* **1** [I] to breathe quickly and with difficulty after the effort of running, carrying something heavy etc: *George puffed and panted and he tried to keep up.* | [+along/up etc] *An old man puffed up to them.* | *He caught up with Gary, puffing for breath.* → **huff and puff** at HUFF[1] (1) **2** [I,T] also **puff away** to breathe in and out while smoking a cigarette or PIPE:

[+at/on] *Kinane sat in silence, puffing thoughtfully at his pipe.* **3** [I always + adv/prep, T] if smoke, steam etc puffs from somewhere, or if something puffs it, it comes out in little clouds: *Steam puffed out of the chimney.* | *The boiler was puffing thick black smoke.* | *Don't puff smoke into my face.* **4** [I always + adv/prep] to move in a particular direction, sending out little clouds of steam or smoke: *The train puffed steadily across the bridge.*

puff sth ⇔ out *phr v* **puff out your cheeks/chest** to make your cheeks or chest bigger by filling them with air: *Henry puffed out his chest proudly.*

puff up *phr v* **1** to become bigger by increasing the amount of air inside, or to make something bigger in this way: *The pastry will puff up while it bakes.* | **puff sth ⇔ up** *Birds puff up their feathers to keep warm.* **2** if a part of your body puffs up, it swells painfully because of injury or infection: *My eye had puffed up because of a mosquito bite.*

puff[2] *n* **1** [C] the action of taking the smoke from a cigarette, PIPE etc into your LUNGS: [+on/at] *He laughed and took a puff on his cigar.* **2** [C] a sudden small movement of wind, air, or smoke: *puff of smoke/wind/air/steam etc The dragon disappeared in a puff of smoke.* **3 cheese/jam/cream etc puff** a piece of light PASTRY with a soft mixture inside **4** [U] *BrE informal* your breath: *I was out of puff* (=had difficulty breathing). **5** [C] also **puff piece** a piece of writing or a speech that praises someone too much – used to show disapproval

puff·ball /ˈpʌfbɔːl $ -bɒːl/ *n* [C] a type of round white FUNGUS that bursts to send out its seeds

puffed /pʌft/ *adj* [not before noun] *BrE informal* breathing quickly because you have been using a lot of energy: *I'm too puffed to dance any more.*

puffed up *adj* [not before noun] behaving in a way that shows you are too pleased with yourself and your achievements – used to show disapproval: *I was so puffed up with my own importance in those days.*

puff·er /ˈpʌfə $ -ər/ *n* [C] **1** *BrE informal* a small piece of equipment containing medicine which you breathe in through your mouth, to help you breathe more easily; ⊟ **inhaler**: *Asthma can be made worse by using puffers too often.* **2** a type of tropical fish that can fill itself with air so that it looks almost round

puf·fin /ˈpʌfɪn/ *n* [C] a North Atlantic sea bird with a black and white body and a large brightly coloured beak

puff pastry *n* [U] a type of very light PASTRY made of many thin layers

puff·y /ˈpʌfi/ *adj* **1** if a part of your body is puffy, it is swollen: *Her eyes were puffy from crying.* **2** soft and full of air: *puffy white clouds* —**puffiness** *n* [U]

pug /pʌɡ/ *n* [C] a small short-haired dog with a wide flat face, a very short nose, and a curly tail

pu·gi·list /ˈpjuːdʒəlɪst/ *n* [C] *old-fashioned formal* a BOXER —**pugilism** *n* [U] —**pugilistic** /ˌpjuːdʒəˈlɪstɪk/ *adj*

pug·na·cious /pʌɡˈneɪʃəs/ *adj formal* very eager to argue or fight with people: *The professor had been pugnacious and irritable.* —**pugnaciously** *adv* —**pugnacity** /pʌɡˈnæsəti/ *n* [U]

puke[1] /pjuːk/ also **puke up** *v* [I,T] *informal* **1** to bring food back up from your stomach through your mouth; ⊟ **vomit**: *He puked all over the carpet.* **2 make you (want to) puke** *informal* to make you feel very angry: *That kind of greed makes me puke!*

puke[2] *n* [U] *informal* food brought back up from your stomach through your mouth; ⊟ **vomit**

puk·ey, puky /ˈpjuːki/ *adj informal* very unpleasant or unattractive

puk·ka, pukha /ˈpʌkə/ *adj BrE informal* real or properly made and of good quality: *pukka food*

pul·chri·tude /ˈpʌlkrɪtjuːd $ -tuːd/ *n* [U] *formal* physical beauty

pull¹ S1 W1 /pʊl/ v

1 MOVE STH TOWARDS YOU [I,T] to use your hands to make something or someone move towards you or in the direction that your hands are moving; ➡ **push**: *Mom! Davey's pulling my hair!* | **pull sb/sth into/away from/over etc sth** *He pulled her down into her seat.* | **pull sth open/shut** *She pulled open the door and hurried inside.*

2 REMOVE [T] to use force to take something from the place where it is fixed or held: *She has to have two teeth pulled.* | **pull sth out/off/away etc** *Vicky had pulled the arm off her doll.*

3 MAKE STH FOLLOW YOU [T] to be attached to something or hold something and make it move behind you in the direction you are going: *a tractor pulling a trailer*

4 TAKE STH OUT [T always + adv/prep] to take something out of a bag, pocket etc with your hand: *He pulled out his wallet and said 'let me pay'.* | *Ben pulled a pen from his pocket.* | **pull a gun/knife (on sb)** (=take one out, ready to use it)

5 CLOTHING [T always + adv/prep] to put on or take off a piece of clothing, usually quickly: [+**on/off/up/down etc**]

6 MOVE YOUR BODY a) [I,T always + adv/prep] to move your body or part of your body away from someone or something: **pull sth away/free** *She tried to pull her hand free, but it was held fast.* | **pull sth out of/from sth** *She struggled fiercely, trying to pull her arm out of his grasp.* | [+**away/back**] *She pulled away from him.* **b)** **pull yourself up/to your feet etc** to hold onto something and use your strength to move your body towards it: *Benny pulled himself up from the floor with difficulty.*

7 MUSCLE [T] to injure one of your muscles by stretching it too much during physical activity; ➡ **strain**: *Paul pulled a muscle trying to lift the freezer.*

8 pull strings to secretly use your influence with important people in order to get what you want or to help someone else: *Francis pulled strings to get him out of trouble.*

9 pull the/sb's strings to control something or someone, especially when you are not the person who is supposed to be controlling them: *It was widely believed that Montagu was secretly pulling the strings behind the prime minister.*

10 TRICK/CRIME [T] *informal* to succeed in doing something illegal or dishonest or in playing a trick on someone: *The gang have pulled another bank robbery.* | *He was trying to **pull a fast one** (=deceive you) when he told you he'd paid.* | **pull a stunt/trick/joke** *Don't you ever pull a stunt like that again!*

11 pull sb's leg to tell someone something that is not true, as a joke: *I haven't won, have I? You're pulling my leg.*

12 pull the other one (it's got bells on) *BrE spoken* used to tell someone that you think they are joking or not telling the truth: *Your dad's a racing driver? Pull the other one!*

13 SWITCH [T] to move a control such as a switch, LEVER, or TRIGGER towards you to make a piece of equipment work: *She raised the gun, and pulled the trigger.*

14 pull the curtains/blinds to open or close curtains or BLINDS: *It was already getting dark so he pulled the curtains.*

15 CROWD/VOTES ETC [T] if an event, performer etc pulls crowds or a politician pulls a lot of votes, a lot of people come to see them or vote for them: *Muhammad Ali can still pull the crowds.*

16 ATTRACT/INFLUENCE [T] to attract or influence someone or their thoughts or feelings: *The city's reputation for a clean environment has pulled new residents from other states.*

17 SEXUALLY ATTRACT [I,T] *BrE spoken* to attract someone in order to have sex with them or spend the evening with them: *He knew he could pull any girl he wanted.*

18 STOP EVENT [T] to stop a planned event from taking place: *They pulled the concert.*

19 pull sb's licence *informal* to take away someone's LICENCE to do something, especially to drive a car, because they have done something wrong

20 STOP A VEHICLE [I,T] to drive a vehicle somewhere and stop; to stop somewhere: **pull sth into/towards/down etc sth** *She pulled the car into a side street.* | *The bus pulled to a halt.*

21 CAR [I] if a car pulls to the left or right as you are driving, it moves in that direction because of a problem with its machinery

22 sth is like pulling teeth used to say that it is very difficult or unpleasant to persuade someone to do something: *Getting him to do his homework is like pulling teeth.*

23 BEER [T] *BrE* to get beer out of a BARREL by pulling a handle: *The barman laughed and began to pull a couple of pints.*

24 pull a punch to deliberately hit someone with less force than you could do, so that it hurts less ➡ **not pull any punches** at PUNCH² (6)

25 CRICKET/GOLF/BASEBALL [I,T] to hit the ball in CRICKET, golf, or baseball so that it does not go straight but moves to one side

26 ROW A BOAT [I,T] to make a boat move by using OARS ➡ **pull/make a face** at FACE¹ (2); ➡ **pull your finger out** at FINGER¹ (12); ➡ **pull rank (on sb)** at RANK¹ (5); ➡ **pull the rug (out) from under sb's feet** at RUG (3); ➡ **pull the plug (on sth)** at PLUG¹ (5); ➡ **pull your socks up** at SOCK¹ (3); ➡ **pull your weight** at WEIGHT¹ (12); ➡ **pull the wool over sb's eyes** at WOOL (4)

pull ahead *phr v*
if one vehicle pulls ahead of another, it gets in front of it by moving faster: *Schumacher pulled ahead of Montoya as the two drivers approached the first corner of the race.*

pull apart *phr v*
1 pull sth ⇔ apart to separate something into pieces: *Pull the meat apart with two forks.*
2 pull sb ⇔ apart to make the relationships between people in a group bad or difficult: *His drinking pulled the family apart.*
3 pull sth ⇔ apart to carefully examine or criticize something: *The selection committee pulled each proposal apart.*
4 pull sb/sth ⇔ apart to separate people or animals when they are fighting: *The fight ended only when the referee pulled the two players apart.*
5 if something pulls apart, it breaks into pieces when you pull on it

pull at/on sth *phr v*
1 to take hold of something and pull it several times: *Mary was pulling nervously at her hair.*
2 to take smoke from a pipe or cigarette into your lungs: *He pulled hard on the cigarette.*
3 to take a long drink from a bottle or glass

pull away *phr v*
1 to start to drive away from a place where you had stopped: *He waved as he pulled away.*
2 to move ahead of a competitor by going faster or being more successful: [+**from**] *Nkoku is pulling away from the other runners.*

pull back *phr v*
1 to decide not to do or become involved in something: [+**from**] *In the end, he pulled back from financing the film.*
2 to get out of a bad situation or dangerous place, or to make someone else do this: [+**from**] *Many banks are pulling back from international markets.* | **pull sb ⇔ back** *They are preparing to pull back their forces.*
3 pull sth ⇔ back *BrE* if a team that is losing pulls back a GOAL or some points, it succeeds in scoring a goal or some points: *Our play improved and we pulled back two goals.*

P

pull down *phr v*
1 pull sth ⇔ down to destroy something or make it stop existing: *My old school was pulled down.*
2 pull down sth to earn a particular amount of money: *Real estate stocks pulled down total returns of 35.7 percent.*
3 pull sb down to make someone less successful, happy, or healthy: *Her problems have really pulled her down.*
4 pull down a menu to make a computer program show you a list of the things it can do

pull for sb/sth *phr v*
informal to encourage a person or team to succeed: *The crowd were pulling for me to do well.*

pull in *phr v*
1 if a driver pulls in, they move to the side of the road and stop: *She pulled in to let the ambulance pass.*
2 if a train pulls in, it arrives at a station; **⊟ pull out**
3 pull sb/sth ⇔ in to attract business, money, people etc: *a publicity stunt to pull in the crowds*
4 pull in sth *informal* if you pull in a lot of money, you earn it
5 pull sb ⇔ in if a police officer pulls someone in, they take them to a police station because they think that person may have done something wrong

pull off *phr v*
1 pull sth ⇔ off *informal* to succeed in doing something difficult: *The goalkeeper pulled off six terrific saves.*
2 pull off (sth) to drive a car off a road in order to stop, or to turn into a smaller road: *We pulled off the road to get some food.*

pull on sth *phr v*
to PULL AT something

pull out *phr v*
1 a) to drive onto a road from another road or from where you have stopped: *Don't pull out! There's something coming.* **b)** to drive over to a different part of the road in order to get past a vehicle in front of you: *I pulled out to overtake a bus.*
2 if a train pulls out, it leaves a station; **⊟ pull in**
3 to stop doing or being involved in something, or to make someone do this: *McDermott pulled out with an injury at the last minute.* | [+of] *They are trying to pull out of the agreement.* | pull sb out of sth *He threatened to pull his son out of the team.*
4 to get out of a bad situation or dangerous place, or to make someone or something do this: *Jim saw that the firm was going to be ruined, so he pulled out.* | pull sb/sth ⇔ out *Most of the troops have been pulled out.* | [+of] *when the country was still pulling out of a recession* → **pull out all the stops** at STOP² (7)

pull over *phr v*
to drive to the side of the road and stop your car, or to make someone else do this: *The policeman signalled to him to pull over.* | pull sb/sth ⇔ over *He pulled the car over.* | *A cop pulled him over and gave him a speeding ticket.*

pull (sb) through *phr v*
1 to stay alive after you have been very ill or badly injured, or to help someone do this: *His injuries are severe but he's expected to pull through.* → **bring (sb) through** at BRING
2 to succeed in doing something very difficult, or to help someone to do this: *He relied on his experience to pull him through.*

pull together *phr v*
1 if a group of people pull together, they all work hard to achieve something: *If we all pull together, we'll finish on time.*
2 pull yourself together to force yourself to stop behaving in a nervous, frightened, or uncontrolled way: *With an effort Mary pulled herself together.*
3 pull sth together to improve something by organizing it more effectively: *We need an experienced manager to pull the department together.*

pull up *phr v*
1 to stop the vehicle that you are driving: *He pulled up in front of the gates.*

2 pull up a chair/stool etc to get a chair, etc and sit down next to someone who is already sitting
3 pull sb up *especially BrE* to stop someone who is doing something wrong and tell them you do not approve: [+on] *I felt I had to pull her up on her lateness.* → **pull sb up short** at SHORT² (7)

pull² *n*
1 ACT OF MOVING STH [C] an act of using force to move something towards you or in the same direction that you are moving; **⊟ push**: *He gave her a sharp **pull** forward.*
2 FORCE [C usually singular] a strong physical force that makes things move in a particular direction: *the gravitational pull of the moon*
3 ATTRACTION [C usually singular] the ability to attract someone or have a powerful effect on them: [+of] *After about a year I gave in to the pull of fatherhood.*
4 INFLUENCE [singular,U] *informal* special influence or power over other people: *His family's name gives him a lot of pull in this town.*
5 CLIMB [singular] *BrE* a difficult climb up a steep road: *It was a long pull up the hill.*
6 MUSCLE [C usually singular] an injury to one of your muscles, caused by stretching it too much during exercise: *a groin pull*
7 SMOKE/DRINK [C] an act of taking the smoke from a cigarette, pipe etc into your LUNGS or of taking a long drink of something: [+on/at] *She took a long pull on her cigarette.*
8 HANDLE [C] a rope or handle that you use to pull something: *He popped the ring pull on another can of lager.*
9 CRICKET/GOLF/BASEBALL [C] a way of hitting the ball in CRICKET, golf, or baseball so that it does not go straight, but moves to one side

pull·back /'pʊlbæk/ *n* [C] **1** the act of moving soldiers away from the area where they were fighting: [+from] *The government is planning to implement a second pullback from the area.* **2** a reduction in the value, amount, or level of something: *a significant pullback in the stock market*

pull-down 'menu *n* [C] a list of things a computer program can do. You make a pull-down menu appear on the computer screen by CLICKING on a special word with a MOUSE

pul·let /'pʊlɪt/ *n* [C] a young chicken that is in its first year of laying eggs

pul·ley /'pʊli/ *n* [C] a piece of equipment consisting of a wheel over which a rope or chain is pulled to lift heavy things

'pulling ,power *n* [U] *BrE* the ability of someone or something to attract people: *Madonna's pulling power filled the Arena for 10 nights.*

Pull·man /'pʊlmən/ *n* [C] a very comfortable train carriage, or a train made up of these carriages

'pull-on *adj* [only before noun] pull-on clothes or shoes do not have any buttons, ZIPS etc, so you just pull them on to wear them

'pull-out, pull·out /'pʊlaʊt/ *n* [C] **1** the act of an army, business etc leaving a particular place: *The pull-out of troops will begin soon.* **2** part of a book or magazine that is designed to be removed and read separately: *a pull-out on home PCs*

pull·o·ver /'pʊl,əʊvə $ -,oʊvər/ *n* [C] a piece of WOOLLEN clothing without buttons that you wear on the top half of your body; **⊟ sweater**

'pull tab *n* [C] *AmE* a small piece of metal attached to a can of food, drink etc that you pull in order to open it; **⊟ ring-pull** *BrE*

'pull-up *n* [C] *BrE* an exercise in which you use your arms to pull yourself up towards a bar above your head; **⊟ chin-up** *AmE*

pul·mo·na·ry /'pʊlmənəri, 'pʌl- $ -neri, 'pʌl-/ *adj* [only before noun] *medical* relating to the lungs, or having an effect on the lungs

pulp¹ /pʌlp/ n

1 SOFT SUBSTANCE [singular,U] a very soft substance that is almost liquid, made by crushing plants, wood, vegetables etc: *Mash the bananas* **to a pulp**. | *timber grown for* **wood pulp** (=used for making paper) | *a soft pulp of leaves and mud*

2 FRUIT/VEGETABLE [U] the soft inside part of a fruit or vegetable: *Halve the melon and scoop out the pulp.*

3 BOOKS/FILM ETC [U] *AmE* books, magazines, films etc that are badly written and that contain lots of sex, violence etc: *an ad in a pulp magazine* | **pulp fiction**

4 beat sb to a pulp *informal* to seriously injure someone by hitting them many times

5 TOOTH [U] part of the inside of a tooth —**pulpy** *adj*: *Cook slowly until soft and pulpy.*

pulp² v [T] **1** to beat or crush something until it becomes very soft and almost liquid: *pulped apples* **2** [usually passive] to beat or hit someone's face or body very badly: *His body was pulped by the impact of the train.* **3** to make wood or old books and newspapers into paper: *wood pulping techniques* | *Unsold novels are sent to be pulped.*

pul·pit /ˈpʊlpɪt/ n [C usually singular] a raised structure inside a church at the front that a priest or minister stands on when they speak to the people: **in/from the pulpit** *Rev. Dawson addressed the congregation from the pulpit.*

pul·sar /ˈpʌlsɑː $ -sɑːr/ n [C] an object like a star that is far away in space and produces RADIATION and RADIO WAVES; → **quasar**

pul·sate /pʌlˈseɪt $ ˈpʌlseɪt/ v [I] **1** to make sounds or movements that are strong and regular like a heart beating: *I could see the veins in his neck pulsating.* | *pulsating music* **2** *literary* to be strongly affected by a powerful emotion or feeling: [+**with**] *The whole city seemed to pulsate with excitement.*

pul·sa·tion /pʌlˈseɪʃən/ n [C,U] *technical* a beat of the heart or any regular movement that can be measured: *the pulsations of the baby's heart* | *muscular pulsation*

pulse¹ /pʌls/ n

1 HEART [C usually singular] **a)** the regular beat that can be felt, for example at your wrist, as your heart pumps blood around your body; → **heartbeat**: *The doctor listened to his breathing and* **checked** *his pulse.* | *His breathing was shallow and his* **pulse** *was* **weak**. | **find/detect a pulse** (=check that someone is alive by trying to feel the beat of their pulse) *In an emergency it can be difficult to find a pulse.* | *She felt his neck. There was no pulse.* **b)** also **pulse rate** the number of heart beats per minute: **take/feel sb's pulse** (=count how many times someone's heart beats in a minute, usually by feeling their wrist) | *Her* **pulse raced** (=beat very quickly) *with excitement.*

2 MUSIC [C,U] a strong regular beat in music: *the distant pulse of a steel band*

3 SOUND/LIGHT/ELECTRICITY [C] an amount of sound, light, or electricity that continues for a very short time

4 FEELINGS/OPINIONS [U] the ideas, feelings, or opinions that are most important to a particular group of people or have the greatest influence on them at a particular time: *Clinton had an uncanny ability to sense the pulse of the nation.*

5 FOOD pulses [plural] seeds such as beans, PEAS, and LENTILS that you can eat → **have/keep your finger on the pulse** at FINGER¹ (6)

pulse² v **1** [I] to move or flow with a steady quick beat or sound: *She felt the blood* **pulsing through** *her veins.* | *Colored lights pulsed in time to the music.* **2** [I] if a feeling or emotion pulses through someone, they feel it very strongly: [+**through**] *Excitement pulsed through the crowd.* **3** [I,T] to push a button on a FOOD PROCESSOR to make the machine go on and off regularly, rather than work continuously: *Pulse several times until the mixture looks like oatmeal.*

pul·ver·ize also **-ise** *BrE* /ˈpʌlvəraɪz/ v [T usually passive] **1** to crush something into a powder: *The*

seeds can be used whole or pulverized into flour. **2** *informal* to completely defeat someone: *Stewart completely pulverized the opposition.* —**pulverized** *adj*: *pulverized coal* —**pulverization** /ˌpʌlvəraɪˈzeɪʃən $ -rə-/ n [U]

pu·ma /ˈpjuːmə/ n [C] a COUGAR → see picture at BIG CAT

pum·ice /ˈpʌmɪs/ also **'pumice stone** n **1** [U] very light grey rock from a VOLCANO that is crushed to a powder and used for cleaning **2** [C] a piece of pumice stone that you rub on your skin to clean it or make it soft

pum·mel /ˈpʌməl/ v **pummelled, pummelling** *BrE*, **pummeled, pummeling** *AmE* [T] **1** to hit someone or something many times quickly, especially using your FISTS (=closed hands); ◼ **beat**: *Diane leaned over and pummeled the pillows.* | **pummel sth with sth** *She flew at him, pummelling his chest with her fists.* | [+**at**] *The cook pummelled at the dough.* | *The platoon was pummeled by heavy machine-gun fire.* **2** *informal* to completely defeat someone at a sport

pump¹ S3 /pʌmp/ n

1 [C] a machine for forcing liquid or gas into or out of something: **water/air/beer etc pump** (=for moving water, air etc) | **hand/foot pump** (=operated by your hand or foot) | **petrol pump/gas pump** (=for putting petrol into cars) | **stomach pump** (=for removing the contents of someone's stomach); → see picture at BICYCLE¹

2 [C usually plural] **a)** *BrE* a flat light shoe for dancing, exercise, sport etc **b)** *AmE* a woman's plain shoe with no LACES, BUCKLES etc: *a pair of leather pumps*

3 [C] an act of pumping → HEAT PUMP; → **all hands to the pumps** at HAND¹ (38); → **prime the pump** at PRIME³ (4); → PARISH PUMP

pump² v

1 MOVE IN A DIRECTION [T always + adv/prep] to make liquid or gas move in a particular direction, using a pump: **pump sth into/out of/through sth** *The fire department is still pumping floodwater out of the cellars.*

2 MOVE FROM UNDER GROUND [T] to bring a supply of water, oil etc to the surface from under the ground: *We were able to pump clean water from several of the wells.* | **pump gas** *AmE* (=put gasoline into a car) *He got a job pumping gas for the hotel guests.*

3 MOVE IN AND OUT [I] also **pump away** to move very quickly in and out or up and down: *My heart was pumping fast.*

4 USE A PUMP [I] also **pump away** to operate a pump: [+**at**] *The furnace man's job was to pump away furiously at the bellows.*

5 COME OUT [I always + adv/prep] if a liquid pumps from somewhere, it comes out suddenly in small amounts: [+**from/out of**] *Blood pumped from the wound.*

6 ASK QUESTIONS [T] *informal* to ask someone a lot of questions in order to get information from them: **pump sb for sth** *I tried to pump him for information about their other contacts.*

7 DRUGS **pump sb full of sth** *informal* to put a lot of drugs into someone's body: *athletes pumped full of steroids*

8 EXERCISE **pump iron** *informal* to do exercises by lifting heavy weights

9 MEDICAL TREATMENT **have your stomach pumped** to have a medical treatment to remove things you have swallowed, using a pump

pump sth **into** sb/sth *phr v*

1 pump bullets into sb/sth *informal* to shoot someone several times

2 pump money into sth to put a lot of money in a project, INVESTMENT etc

pump out *phr v*

1 if something such as music, information, or a supply of products pumps out, or if someone pumps it out, a lot of it is produced: *Music pumped out from the loudspeakers.* | **pump sth ⇔ out** *propaganda pumped out by the food industry*

P

2 pump sth ⇔ out to remove liquid from something, using a pump: *You'll have to pump the boat out.*

pump sth/sb ⇔ up *phr v*
1 to fill a tyre, AIRBED etc with air until it is full; ⊟ **inflate**
2 *informal* to increase the value, amount, or level of something: *The US was able to pump up exports.* | *Come on, pump up the volume!* (=play music louder)
3 to increase someone's excitement, interest etc

ˈpump-ˌaction *adj* [only before noun] a pump-action piece of equipment is operated by pulling or pressing a part in or out so that the contents come out in short bursts: **pump-action shotgun/rifle**

pum·per·nick·el /ˈpʌmpənɪkəl $ ˈpʌmpər-/ *n* [U] a heavy dark brown bread

pump·kin /ˈpʌmpkɪ̣n/ *n* **1** [C,U] a very large orange fruit that grows on the ground, or the inside of this fruit: *pumpkin pie* → see picture at VEGETABLE[1] **2** *AmE* used when speaking to someone you love

ˈpump-ˌpriming *n* [U] the process of trying to help a business, industry, or country to develop by giving it money

pun[1] /pʌn/ *n* [C] an amusing use of a word or phrase that has two meanings, or of words that have the same sound but different meanings; ⊟ **play on words**: | **forgive/excuse/pardon the pun** (=used to show you know you are making a pun) | **no pun intended** (=used to show you do not mean to make a joke about something) *The clergy prey (no pun intended) on bereaved families.*

pun[2] *v* **punned, punning** [I] to make a pun: [+on] *In this line, Hamlet puns on the meaning of 'saw'.*

punch[1] S3 /pʌnʃ/ *v* [T]
1 HIT to hit someone or something hard with your FIST (=closed hand): *He punched me and knocked my teeth out.* | **punch sb on/in sth** *He punched Jack in the face.*
2 MAKE HOLES to make a hole in something, using a metal tool or other sharp object: *The guard punched my ticket and I got on.* | *These bullets can punch a hole through 20 mm steel plate.*
3 PUSH BUTTONS to push a button or key on a machine: *Just punch the button to select a track.*
4 punch holes in sb's argument/idea/plans etc to criticize someone's views, idea, plans etc by showing why they are wrong
5 punch the air to make a movement like a punch towards the sky, to show that you are very pleased: *He punched the air in triumph.*
6 punch sb's lights out *informal* to hit someone hard in the face
7 punch the clock *AmE informal* to record the time that you start or finish work by putting a card into a special machine
8 CATTLE *AmE old-fashioned* to move cattle from one place to another

punch in *phr v*
1 *AmE* to record the time that you arrive at work, by putting a card into a special machine; ⊟ **clock in** *BrE*
2 punch sth ⇔ in to put information into a computer by pressing buttons or keys

punch out *phr v AmE*
1 to record the time that you leave work, by putting a card into a special machine; ⊟ **clock out** *BrE*
2 punch sb out to hit someone so hard that they become unconscious

punch[2] *n* **1** [C] a quick strong hit made with your FIST (=closed hand): [+in/on] *a punch in the kidneys* | *I managed to land a punch on his chin.* | *The two men started throwing punches* (=trying to hit each other). **2** [singular,U] a strong effective way of expressing things that makes people interested: *30 years after it was written, Orton's 'Entertaining Mr Sloane' still packs a punch.* **3** [C,U] a drink made from fruit juice, sugar, water, and usually some alcohol: *a glass of hot punch* **4** [C] a metal tool for cutting

holes or for pushing something into a small hole **5 a one-two punch** two bad events that happen close together: *A meteorite collided with Earth at the same time, delivering a one-two punch to the magnetic field.* **6 not pull any/your punches** to express disapproval or criticism clearly, without trying to hide anything: *The inquiry report doesn't pull any punches in apportioning blame.* **7 beat sb/sth to the punch** *informal* to do or get something before anyone else does: *Hitachi has beaten its competitors to the punch with its new palmtop.* **8 as pleased as punch** *old-fashioned* very happy: *He's as pleased as punch about the baby.* → **pack a (hard) punch** at PACK[1] (8)

Punch and Ju·dy show /ˌpʌntʃ ən ˈdʒuːdi ʃəʊ $ -ʃoʊ/ *n* [C] a traditional type of entertainment for children, especially at British SEASIDE towns, that uses PUPPETS

punch·bag /ˈpʌntʃbæg/ *BrE*; **ˈpunching bag** *AmE n* [C] **1** a heavy leather bag hung from a rope, that is punched for exercise or training **2** a person who is hit, criticized strongly, or blamed, even though they have done nothing wrong: *a young wife whose husband used her as a punching bag*

ˈpunch bowl *n* [C] a large bowl in which punch (=a mixed drink) is served

ˈpunch-drunk *adj* **1** *informal* very confused, especially because you have had a lot of bad luck or have been treated badly **2** a BOXER who is punch-drunk is suffering brain damage from being hit on the head

ˈpunched card also **ˈpunch card** *n* [C] a card with a pattern of holes in it that was used in the past for putting information into a computer

ˈpunch·line, ˈpunch line /ˈpʌntʃlaɪn/ *n* [C usually singular] the last few words of a joke or story, that make it funny or surprising

ˈpunch-up *n* [C] *BrE informal* a fight

punch·y /ˈpʌntʃi/ *adj* a punchy piece of writing or speech is short but very clear and effective —**punchiness** *n* [U]

punc·til·i·ous /pʌŋkˈtɪliəs/ *adj formal* very careful to behave correctly and follow rules: [+about] *Joe was always punctilious about repaying loans.* —**punctiliously** *adv* —**punctiliousness** *n* [U]

punc·tu·al /ˈpʌŋktʃuəl/ *adj formal* arriving, happening, or being done at exactly the time that has been arranged; ⊟ **on time**: *She's always very punctual for appointments.* | *the punctual payment of invoices* —**punctually** *adv* —**punctuality** /ˌpʌŋktʃuˈæləti/ *n* [U]

punc·tu·ate /ˈpʌŋktʃueɪt/ *v* **1** [T] to divide written work into sentences, phrases, etc using COMMAS, FULL STOPS etc **2** [T usually passive] *literary* to be interrupted by something, especially when this is repeated: *The silence was occasionally punctuated by laughter.*

punc·tu·a·tion /ˌpʌŋktʃuˈeɪʃən/ *n* [U] the marks used to divide a piece of writing into sentences, phrases etc

punctuˈation mark *n* [C] a sign, such as a COMMA or QUESTION MARK, used to divide a piece of writing into sentences, phrases, etc

punc·ture[1] /ˈpʌŋktʃə $ -ər/ *n* [C] **1** *BrE* a small hole made accidentally in a tyre; ⊟ **flat** *AmE*: *She was cycling home when she had a puncture.* | **slow puncture** (=one that lets air out very slowly) **2** a small hole made by a sharp point, especially in someone's body: *puncture wounds*

puncture[2] *v* **1** [I,T] if a tyre punctures, or if you puncture it, a small hole appears in it: *A piece of glass punctured the back tyre.* **2** [T] to make a small hole in something: *One bullet punctured his lung.* | *Pressurized container – do not puncture.* **3** [T] to interrupt a period of silence by making a noise: *There was a stunned silence, punctured by shrill laughter.* **4** [T] to suddenly destroy someone's hopes or beliefs, making them feel unhappy, embarrassed, or confused: *He wasn't hurt, but his dignity was punctured.*

pun·dit /'pʌndɪt/ n [C] someone who is often asked to give their opinion publicly of a situation or subject: **political/media/TV etc pundits** *If you believe the fashion pundits, we'll all be wearing pink this year.*

pun·gent /'pʌndʒənt/ adj **1** having a strong taste or smell: **pungent smell/aroma/odour etc** *the pungent odour of garlic* **2** *formal* pungent speech or writing is clever and direct, and usually criticizes someone or something strongly: *He expressed some fairly pungent criticisms.* —**pungently** adv —**pungency** n [U]

pun·ish /'pʌnɪʃ/ v [T] **1** to make someone suffer because they have done something wrong or broken the law; → **punishment**, **punitive**: *Smacking is not an acceptable way of punishing a child.* | *He promised to punish severely any officials found guilty of electoral fraud.* | **punish sb for (doing) sth** *It's unfair to punish a whole class for the actions of one or two students.* | *They deserve to be punished for putting passengers at risk.* | *I felt I was being punished for what my mother had done.* | **punish sb by doing sth** *My parents decided to punish me by withdrawing financial support.* | **punish sb with sth** *The House voted to punish the senator with a formal reprimand.* **2** [usually passive] if a crime is punished in a particular way, anyone who is guilty of it is made to suffer in that way; → **punishment**, **punitive**: **[+by/with]** *In some societies, theft is punished by death.* **3 punish yourself** to make yourself feel guilty or bad for something you have done: *If you fail, don't punish yourself.*

pun·ish·a·ble /'pʌnɪʃəbəl/ adj in law, a punishable act can be punished: *a punishable offence* | **[+by/with]** *a crime punishable by death*

pun·ish·ing /'pʌnɪʃɪŋ/ adj [usually before noun] difficult, tiring, or extreme: *He set himself a **punishing schedule** of conferences.* | *a series of punishing defeats* | *a punishing exercise regime*

pun·ish·ment W3 /'pʌnɪʃmənt/ n **1** [C,U] something that is done in order to punish someone, or the act of punishing them; → **punitive**: *The Court decides what **punishment** to **impose**.* | **[+for]** *the punishment for treason* | **[+by]** *punishment by whipping* | **as (a) punishment** *I was sent to bed as a punishment.* | *The gunmen will not **escape punishment**.* | **harsh/severe punishment** *He got a six-year jail sentence, a harsh punishment for a first offense.* **2** [U] *informal* rough physical treatment: *tough plants that can **take** any amount of **punishment*** → **CAPITAL PUNISHMENT**

pu·ni·tive /'pjuːnətɪv/ adj [usually before noun] **1** intended to punish someone: **punitive action/measures etc** *The agency sent a letter, but took no punitive action.* | *The jury awarded **punitive damages** (=money paid to someone who is the victim of a crime).* | *The government is expected to **take punitive steps** against offenders.* **2 punitive taxes/price increases etc** taxes etc that are so high that it is difficult for people to pay them: *The US could impose **punitive tariffs** on exports.*

Pun·ja·bi /pʌn'dʒɑːbiː/ n **1** [U] the language used in the Punjab **2** [C] someone from the Punjab —**Punjabi** adj

punk /pʌŋk/ n **1** [U] also **,punk 'rock** a type of loud music popular in the late 1970s and 1980s **2** [C] also **punk rocker** someone who likes punk music and wears things that are typical of it, such as torn clothes, metal chains, and coloured hair: *punk hairstyles* **3** [C] *AmE informal* a young man who fights and breaks the law **4** [U] *AmE* a substance that burns without a flame that is used to light FIREWORKS etc

pun·kah /'pʌŋkə/ n [C] in the past, a large FAN that was hung across a room and was swung backwards and forwards by hand

pun·net /'pʌnɪt/ n [C] *BrE* a small square box used to hold soft fruits such as STRAWBERRIES

punt¹ /pʌnt/ n **1** BOAT [C] a long thin boat with a flat bottom that you move by pushing a long pole against the bottom of the river

2 a punt the activity of travelling in a punt: *a punt down the river* **3** KICK [C usually singular] in RUGBY or American football, the action of kicking the ball after dropping it from your hands: *a 45-yard punt* **4** MONEY [C] the standard unit of money used in the Republic of Ireland before the EURO

punt² v **1** [I,T] to go on a river in a punt: **[+along/down/past etc]** *Pete punted us back to the boatyard.* **2** [T] **a)** in RUGBY or American football, to drop the ball from your hands and kick it: *He punted the ball 40 yards.* **b)** to kick a ball hard so that it goes a long way

punt·er /'pʌntə $ -ər/ n [C] **1** *BrE informal* someone who buys a product or service; customer: **average/typical/ordinary punter** *The technical details mean nothing to the average punter.* | *You need something to **pull in the punters** (=attract them).* **2** *BrE informal* someone who BETS on the result of a horse race etc **3** the player who punts the ball in American football

pu·ny /'pjuːni/ adj **1** a puny person is small, thin, and weak: *a puny little guy* | **puny arms** **2** not effective or impressive: **puny effort/attempt** | *a puny attempt at humour* | *Our efforts look puny beside Fred's.* **3** a puny amount of money is too small: *She was awarded a puny £1,000 in compensation.*

pup /pʌp/ n [C] **1** a young dog; puppy: *a spaniel pup* | *a **litter of pups** (=several pups born to the same mother at the same time)* **2** a young SEAL or OTTER **3** *old-fashioned* a young man who is rude or too confident **4 be sold a pup/buy a pup** *BrE old-fashioned* to be tricked into buying something that is not worth what you paid for it

pu·pa /'pjuːpə/ n plural **pupae** /-piː/ also **pupas** AmE [C] an insect at the stage before it becomes adult, when it is protected by a special cover: *moth pupae* —**pupal** adj [only before noun]: *the pupal stage*; → see picture at METAMORPHOSIS

pu·pate /pjuː'peɪt $ 'pjuːpeɪt/ v [I] *technical* to become a pupa

pu·pil S2 W1 /'pjuːpəl/ n [C] **1** *especially BrE* someone who is being taught, especially a child: *About 20 pupils study music here.* | *staff and pupils* | *a **star pupil** (=a very good one)* | *a third-grade pupil* → see box at STUDENT **2** the small black round area in the middle of your eye; → **iris**

pup·pet /'pʌpɪt/ n [C] **1** a model of a person or animal that you move by pulling wires or strings, or by putting your hand inside it: **puppet show/theatre/play** *a 20-minute puppet show* | **glove/hand/finger puppet** **2** a person or organization that allows other people to control them and make their decisions: **[+of]** *The government is in danger of becoming a mere puppet of the military.* | **puppet government/regime/state** *(=a government etc controlled by a more powerful country or organization)*

pup·pe·teer /ˌpʌpɪ'tɪə $ -'tɪr/ n [C] someone who performs with puppets

pup·pet·ry /'pʌpɪtri/ n [U] the art of performing with puppets

pup·py S3 /'pʌpi/ n plural **puppies** [C] **1** a young dog: *a six-month-old puppy* **2 this/that puppy** *AmE spoken informal* used instead of the name of a thing, especially when you do not know the name: *How do you turn this puppy off?*

puppy fat n [U] *BrE informal* fat on a child's body, that disappears as they get older; baby fat *AmE*: *Carol had shed her puppy fat and was now very elegant.*

puppy love n [U] a young person's romantic love for someone, which other people do not think is serious: *a bad case of puppy love*

pup tent n [C] *AmE* a small TENT for two people

etc: *The boy was provided with an interpreter, pursuant to the Individuals with Disabilities Act.*

pur·sue S3 W2 /pə'sjuː $ pər'suː/ v [T]

1 to continue doing an activity or trying to achieve something over a long period of time; → **pursuit**: *She plans to **pursue** a **career** in politics.* | *Students should **pursue** their own **interests**, as well as do their school work.* | **pursue a goal/aim/objective etc** *companies that pursue the traditional goal of profits* | *a campaign promise to **pursue policies** that will help the poor*

2 pursue the matter/argument/question etc to continue trying to find out about or persuade someone about a particular subject: *Janet did not dare **pursue the matter further**.* | *The defence pursued the question of Dr Carrington's state of mind.*

3 to chase or follow someone or something, in order to catch them, attack them etc; → **pursuit**: *Briggs ran across the field with one officer pursuing him.*

4 to keep trying to persuade someone to have a relationship with you: *I was pleased, but somewhat embarrassed, when she pursued me.*

pur·su·er /pə'sjuːə $ pər'suːər/ n [C] someone who is chasing you: *They managed to escape their pursuers.*

pur·suit /pə'sjuːt $ pər'suːt/ n **1** [U] when someone tries to get, achieve, or find something in a determined way; → **pursue**: [+of] *the pursuit of liberty and happiness* | *the pursuit of war criminals* | **in (the) pursuit of sth** *People are having to move to other areas in pursuit of work.* **2** [U] when someone chases or follows someone else; → **pursue**: **in pursuit** *There were four police cars in pursuit.* | *The quarterback sprinted toward the end zone with Jansen **in hot pursuit** (=following closely behind).* **3** [C usually plural] *formal* an activity such as a sport or HOBBY, which you spend a lot of time doing: *pursuits such as swimming and tennis*

pu·ru·lent /'pjʊərələnt $ 'pjʊr-/ adj *technical* containing or producing PUS —**purulence** n [U]

pur·vey /pɜː'veɪ $ pɜːr-/ v [T] *formal* to supply goods, services, information etc to people: *DJ Dominic purveys a unique brand of music.*

pur·vey·or /pɜː'veɪə $ pɜːr'veɪər/ n [C usually plural] *formal* a business that supplies goods, services, or information: *purveyors of farmyard fresh poultry*

pur·view /'pɜːvjuː $ 'pɜːr-/ n **within/outside the purview of sb/sth** *formal* within or outside the limits of someone's job, activity, or knowledge: *This matter comes within the purview of the Department of Health.*

pus /pʌs/ n [U] a thick yellowish liquid produced in an infected part of your body: *a wound oozing pus*

push¹ S1 W2 /pʊʃ/ v

1 MOVE [I,T] to make someone or something move by pressing them with your hands, arms etc; ◻ **pull**: *It didn't move, so she pushed harder.* | *I promised to push him on the swings for as long as he wanted.* | *shoppers pushing their grocery carts* | **push sb/sth away/back/aside etc** *She pushed him away.* | *Maria pushed her hair back from her forehead.* | **push sb/sth towards/into etc sth** *Philip pushed him towards the door.* | **push sth open/shut** *I slowly pushed the door open.*

2 BUTTON/SWITCH [I,T] to press a button, switch etc in order to make a piece of equipment start or stop working; ◻ **press**: *I got in and pushed the button for the fourth floor.* | *Push the green button to start the engine.*

3 TRY TO GET PAST [I] to use your hands, arms etc to make people or things move, so that you can get past them: *Don't push. Everyone will get a turn.* | **push (your) way past/through/into etc** *A fat man pushed past me in his rush to leave.* | *She pushed her way to the front.*

4 ENCOURAGE [T] to encourage or force someone to do something or to work hard: *Encourage your kids to try new things, but try not to **push** them too hard.* | *athletes who **push** their bodies to the **limit*** | **push yourself** *He's been pushing himself too hard, working 12-hour days.* | **push sb into (doing) sth** *My husband pushed me into leaving the job.* | **push sb to do sth** *The*

teachers pushed the students to achieve.

5 PERSUADE [I,T] to try to persuade people to accept your ideas, opinions etc in order to achieve something: *The president is trying to push his agenda in Congress.* | [+for] *He was **pushing hard** for welfare reform.* | **push to do sth** *Company representatives are pushing to open foreign markets to their products.* | **push sth on sb** *We don't try to push our religion on anyone.*

6 CHANGE [T always + adv/prep] to change someone's situation, or to make a situation change, especially when some people do not want it to change: *The law would push even more children into poverty.* | *attempts to push the peace process forward*

7 INCREASE/DECREASE [T always + adv/prep] to increase or decrease an amount, value, or number: **push sth up/down** *Slow sales have pushed down orders.* | **push sth higher/lower** *New technology has pushed the cost of health care even higher.*

8 ARMY [I always + adv/prep] if an army pushes somewhere, it moves in that direction: *The army was pushing north.* | *We pushed deep into enemy territory.*

9 ADVERTISE [T] *informal* to try to sell more of a product by advertising it a lot: *Sports stars earn big bucks for pushing everything from shoes to soft drinks.*

10 DRUGS [T] *informal* to sell illegal drugs → **PUSHER**

11 be pushing 40/50 etc *informal* to be nearly 40, 50 etc years old

12 push your luck/push it *informal* to do something or ask for something, especially something you have done or asked for before, when this is likely to annoy someone or involves a risk: *If she doesn't want to go, don't push it.* | *It's 26 miles, so you're pushing your luck if you try to hike it in a day.*

13 push sth out of your mind also **push sth to the back of your mind** to try not to think about something, especially something bad or worrying: *He pushed the thought out of his mind and tried to concentrate.*

14 push (sb's) buttons *informal* to make someone feel strong emotions: *Movies shouldn't be afraid to push a few buttons.*

15 push the boat out *BrE informal* to spend more money than you usually do, on something special: *Push the boat out and get tickets to the theatre or ballet.*

16 push the point to keep trying to make someone accept your opinion in a way that they think is annoying

17 push the envelope *AmE* to do something that is new and that goes beyond the limits of what has already been done in a particular area of activity: [+of/on] *ideas that push the envelope of design and construction*

18 be pushing up (the) daisies *informal* to be dead – used humorously → **PUSHED, PUSHING**

push ahead phr v
to continue with a plan or activity, especially in a determined way: [+with] *Quinlan decided to push ahead with the deal.*

push along phr v
must/should etc be pushing along BrE spoken used to say that you think it is time for you to leave a place: *It's getting late – I think we should be pushing along.*

push sb **around** also **push sb about** *BrE* phr v
to tell someone what to do in an impolite or threatening way: *Europeans sometimes feel the Americans are trying to push them around.*

push sb/sth **aside** phr v
1 push sth ⇔ aside to try to forget about something, especially something unpleasant, so that you can give your attention to what you are doing: *She pushed aside her anger, forcing herself to focus on her work.*
2 to force someone out of their job or position, taking the job in their place: *Primakov was pushed aside but later became head of Intelligence.*

push yourself **forward** phr v
BrE to try to make other people notice you: *Rupert was a quiet type, not one to push himself forward.*

push in phr v
BrE informal to go in front of other people who are already waiting in a line for something, instead of going to the back of the line: *A couple of boys pushed in*

REVOLUTION etc by using force: *The uprising was put down by the police and the army.*

5 PAY **put sth ⇔ down** to pay part of the total cost of something, so that you can pay the rest later: [+**on**] *They put down a deposit on the goods until Christmas.*

6 BABY **put sb down** to put a baby in its bed: *We try to put Amy down at six every evening.*

7 put the phone down to put the RECEIVER back onto the telephone when you have finished speaking to someone; ◨ **hang up**: [+**on**] *She put the phone down on me* (=suddenly ended the conversation).

8 KILL **put sth ⇔ down** to kill an animal without causing it pain, usually because it is old or sick; ◨ **put sth to sleep**: *We had to have the dog put down.*

9 I couldn't put it down spoken used to say that you found a book, game etc extremely interesting: *Once I'd started reading it I just couldn't put it down.*

10 AIRCRAFT **put (sth) down** if an aircraft puts down or if a pilot puts it down, it lands, especially because of an EMERGENCY: *The engine failed and the plane put down in the sea.*

11 put down a motion/an amendment to suggest a subject, plan, change in the law etc for a parliament or committee to consider

12 LEAVE PASSENGER **put sb down** BrE to stop a vehicle so that passengers can get off at a particular place: *He asked the taxi to put him down at the end of the road.*

  put sb down as sth *phr v*
to guess what someone is like or what they do, without having much information about them: *I didn't think he was unfriendly. I put him down as shy.*

  put sb down for sth *phr v*

1 to put someone's name on a list so that they can take part in an activity, join an organization etc: *They put themselves down for a training course.*

2 put sb down for £5/£20 etc especially BrE to write someone's name on a list with an amount of money that they have promised to give

  put down to sth *phr v*

1 to think that something is caused by something else: *I was having difficulty reading, which I put down to the poor light.*

2 put it down to experience to try not to feel too upset about failure, especially when you learn something useful from it: *Everyone gets rejected from time to time; put it down to experience.*

  put forth sth *phr v*

1 to suggest an idea, explanation etc, especially one that other people later consider and discuss; ◨ **submit**: *Arguments were put forth for changing some of the rules of the game.*

2 put forth leaves/shoots/roots etc formal if a tree or bush puts forth leaves etc, it begins to grow them

  put sth ⇔ forward *phr v*

1 to suggest a plan, proposal etc, for other people to consider or discuss; ◨ **propose**: *They put forward a number of suggestions.*

2 to suggest formally that you or someone else should be considered for a particular job, membership of an organization etc: *Her name was put forward for the lead role in the play.*

3 to arrange for an event to start at an earlier time or date: [+**to**] *The men's final has been put forward to 1:30.*

4 put a clock/watch forward BrE to make a clock or watch show a later time; ◨ **set forward** AmE

  put in *phr v*

1 put sth ⇔ in to fix a piece of equipment somewhere and connect it so that it is ready to be used; ◨ **instal**: *We decided to have a new bathroom put in.*

2 put sth ⇔ in to spend time or use energy working or practising something: *Dorothy had put in a lot of hard work during her six years as chairperson.*

3 put in sth written to interrupt someone in order to say something: *'How old are you?' 'Sixteen.' 'I'm sixteen too,' put in Dixie.*

4 put sth ⇔ in to ask for something in an official way: *She put in an insurance claim.* | *We must put in an order by tonight.* | **put in for sth** *I put in for a pay increase.*

5 put your faith/trust/confidence in sb/sth to trust someone or something or believe that they can do something: *I'm putting my faith in the appeal judges.*

6 put in sth to do something in a particular way, especially a performance in a play, film, race etc: *He put in a brilliant performance in the British Grand Prix.*

7 put in an appearance to go to a social event, meeting etc for a short time: *There was an hour yet before she needed to put in an appearance at the restaurant.*

8 if a ship puts in, it enters a port

  put sth **into** sth *phr v*

1 to make money available to be used for a particular purpose: *The government appears to be putting more money into education.*

2 to use a lot of energy etc when you are doing an activity: *Candidates put a lot of time and effort into gaining qualifications.*

3 to add a quality to something: *These simple recipes put more fun into eating.*

  put sb/sth **off** *phr v*

1 put sth ⇔ off to delay doing something or to arrange to do something at a later time or date, especially because there is a problem or you do not want to do it now; ◨ **delay**, **procrastinate**: *The match has been put off until tomorrow because of bad weather.* | **put off doing sth** *I put off going to the doctor but I wish I hadn't.*

2 put sb ⇔ off BrE to make you dislike something or not want to do something: *Don't let the restaurant's decor put you off – the food is really good.* | **put sb off (doing) sth** *Don't let your failures put you off trying harder.*

3 put sb off to make someone wait because you do not want to meet them, pay them etc until later; ◨ **stall**: *When he calls, put him off as long as you can.*

4 put sb off (sth) BrE to make it difficult for someone to pay attention to what they are doing by talking, making a noise, moving etc: *It puts me off when you watch me all the time.*

5 put sb off (sth) BrE to let someone leave a vehicle at a particular place: *I'll put you off at the supermarket.*

  put sb/sth **on** *phr v*

1 CLOTHES **put sth ⇔ on** to put a piece of clothing on your body; ◨ **take off**: *He took off his uniform and put on a sweater and trousers.* | *I'll have to put my glasses on; I can't read the sign from here.*

2 ON SKIN **put sth ⇔ on** to put MAKE-UP, cream etc on your skin: *I've got to put this cream on twice a day.*

3 AFFECT/INFLUENCE STH **put sth on sth** to do something that affects or influences someone or something else: *The government put a limit on imports of textiles.* | *Pat was putting pressure on him to leave his wife.*

4 START EQUIPMENT **put sth ⇔ on** to make a light or a piece of equipment start working by pressing or turning a button or switch; ◨ **switch on**, **turn on**: *He got up and put on the light.* | *Shall I put the kettle on?*

5 MUSIC **put sth ⇔ on** to put a record, tape, or CD into a machine and start playing it: *She put on some music while they ate.*

6 PRETEND **put sth ⇔ on** to pretend to have a particular feeling, opinion, way of speaking etc especially in order to get attention: *Sheila's not really that upset; she's just putting it on.* | *Leaving the court, the families all tried to **put on a brave face** (=not show that they were sad or worried).*

7 put on weight/12 lbs/4 kg etc to become fatter and heavier; ◨ **gain**: *Rosie's put on five kilos since she quit smoking.*

8 EVENT/CONCERT/PLAY ETC **put sth ⇔ on** to arrange for a concert, play etc to take place, or to perform in it: *One summer the children put on a play.*

9 SHOW WHAT YOU CAN DO **put sth ⇔ on** to show what you are able to do or what power you have: *The team need to put on another world-class performance.*

10 COOK **put sth ⇔ on** to start cooking something: *Shall I put the pasta on now?*

11 PROVIDE STH **put sth ⇔ on** BrE to provide a service for people, especially a special one: *BA is putting on extra flights to cover the Christmas rush.*

P

P

12 you're putting me on! *spoken especially AmE* used to tell someone that you think they are joking: *He wouldn't do that – you're putting me on.*
13 `RISK MONEY` put sth on sth to risk an amount of money on the result of a game, race etc; ▣ **bet**: *We put £50 on Brazil to win the Cup.*
14 `ADD` put sth on sth to add an amount of money or tax onto the cost of something: *Can smokers really complain if more tax is put on cigarettes?*
15 `TELEPHONE` put sb ⇔ on to give someone the telephone so that they can talk to someone who is telephoning: *Can you put Janet on?*

put sb onto sb/sth *phr v*
BrE informal to give someone information about something interesting or useful that they did not know about: *Jo put us onto this fantastic French restaurant.*

put out *phr v*
1 `FIRE/CIGARETTE ETC` put sth ⇔ out to make a fire etc stop burning; ▣ **extinguish**: *The rescue services are still trying to put out the fires.*
2 `LIGHT` put sth ⇔ out to make a light stop working by pressing or turning a button or switch; ▣ **switch off**
3 `MAKE AVAILABLE` put sth ⇔ out to put things where people can find and use them: *The girls helped her to put out the cups and plates.*
4 feel/be put out to feel upset or offended: *We were a little put out at not being invited to the wedding.*
5 `MAKE EXTRA WORK` put sb out to make extra work or cause problems for someone: *Mary can't come to dinner tonight. She hopes it won't put you out.*
6 put yourself out to make an effort to do something that will help someone: *They had put themselves out to entertain her during her visit.*
7 `TAKE OUTSIDE` put sth ⇔ out to take something outside your house and leave it there: *Remember to put the cat out before you go to bed.* | **put the rubbish/garbage etc out** (=put unwanted things outside your house to be taken away) | **put the washing out** (=put clothes outside to dry)
8 put your tongue out to push your tongue out of your mouth, especially as a rude sign to someone
9 put your hand/foot/arm out to move your hand etc forward and away from your body: *He put out his hand toward her.*
10 `MAKE UNCONSCIOUS` put sb out to make someone unconscious before a medical operation
11 put your back out to injure your back
12 `PRODUCE STH` put sth ⇔ out to broadcast or produce something for people to read or listen to: *They put out a half-hour programme on young refugees.*
13 put out feelers to try to discover information or opinions by listening to people or watching what is happening: *He had already put out feelers with local employers but they hadn't been interested.*
14 `SHIP` if a ship puts out, it starts to sail
15 `HAVE SEX` *AmE informal* if a woman puts out, she has sex with a man
16 `BASEBALL` put sb out to prevent a baseball player from running around the BASES, for example, by catching the ball that they have hit

put sth ⇔ **over** *phr v*
1 *BrE* to succeed in telling other people your ideas, opinions, feelings, etc: *The advert puts over the message clearly and simply: nuclear power is clean.*
2 put one/sth over on sb *informal* to deceive someone into believing something that is not true or that is useless: *Nobody could put one over on him.*

put through *phr v*
1 put sb/sth ⇔ through to connect someone to someone else on the telephone: [+to] *Could you put me through to Eddie?*
2 put sb through school/college/university to pay for someone to study at school, college etc: *She worked as a waitress and put herself through school.*
3 put sb through sth to make someone do or experience something difficult or unpleasant: *The soldiers were put through eight weeks of basic training.* | *They really*

put me through it at the interview.
4 put sth ⇔ through to do what is necessary in order to get a plan or suggestion accepted or approved: *Production will start up again when these changes have been put through.*

put sth ⇔ **together** *phr v*
1 to prepare or produce something by collecting pieces of information, ideas etc: *It took all morning to put the proposal together.*
2 to form people or things into a group: *We are currently putting together a sales and marketing team.*
3 to make a machine, model etc by joining all the different parts; ▣ **assemble**: *I can't work out how to put this table together.*
4 more ... than the rest/the others/everything else put together used to say that one amount is greater than the total of a set of amounts: *Paul seemed to have more money than the rest of us put together.*

put sth **towards** sth *phr v*
to use some money in order to pay part of the cost of something: *Alec put the money towards a trip to Australia.*

put sb **under** *phr v*
if a doctor puts you under, they give you drugs to make you unconscious before SURGERY

put up *phr v*
1 `BUILD` put sth ⇔ up to build something such as a wall, fence, building etc; ▣ **erect**: *They're putting up several new office blocks in the centre of town.*
2 `FOR PEOPLE TO SEE` put sth ⇔ up to put a picture, notice etc on a wall so that people can see it: *Can I put up some posters?* | *The shops have started to put up Christmas decorations.*
3 `ATTACH STH` put sth ⇔ up to attach a shelf, cupboard etc to a wall: *My Dad put up five shelves.*
4 `INCREASE` put sth ⇔ up *BrE* to increase the cost or value of something; ▣ **raise**: *Most big stores admit they daren't put prices up for fear of losing their customers.*
5 `RAISE` put sth ⇔ up to raise something to a higher position: *I put up my hand and asked to leave the room.* | *Philip put his hood up because it was raining.*
6 `LET SB STAY` put sb up to let someone stay in your house and give them meals: *I was hoping Kenny could put me up for a few days.*
7 `STAY SOMEWHERE` *BrE* to stay in a place for a short time: [+at/in/with] *We can put up at a hotel for the night.*
8 put up a fight/struggle/resistance to show great determination to oppose something or get out of a difficult situation: *Gina put up a real fight to overcome the disease.* | *The rebels have put up fierce resistance.*
9 put up sth to give an amount of money for a particular purpose: *The paper put up a reward for information on the murder.*
10 `MAKE AVAILABLE` put sth up to make something or someone available for a particular purpose: [+for] *They put their house up for sale.* | *The baby was put up for adoption.*
11 put up a proposal/argument/case etc to explain a suggestion or idea so that other people can think about it or discuss it: *If you can put up a good enough case, the board will provide the finance.*
12 `ELECTIONS` put sb ⇔ up to suggest someone as a suitable person to be elected to a position: *I was put up for the committee.*
13 put up or shut up *spoken informal* used to tell someone that they should either do what needs to be done or stop talking about it

put sb **up to** sth *phr v*
to encourage someone to do something stupid or dangerous: *'Did Shirley put you up to this?' 'No, it was my own idea.'*

put up with sb/sth *phr v*
to accept an unpleasant situation or person without complaining: *She put up with his violent temper.*

pu·ta·tive /ˈpjuːtətɪv/ *adj* [only before noun] *formal* believed or accepted by most people: *the putative father of her child*

put-down n [C usually singular] something you say that is intended to make someone feel stupid or unimportant; ⊟ **snub**: *She was tired of his put-downs.*

put-on n [C usually singular] *AmE informal* something you say or do to try to make someone believe something that is not true

put 'out adj [not before noun] *BrE* upset or offended: *She felt put out that she hadn't been consulted.*

pu·tre·fy /ˈpjuːtrɪfaɪ/ v **putrefied**, **putrefying**, **putrefies** [I] *formal* if a dead animal or plant putrefies, it decays and smells very bad —**putrefaction** /ˌpjuːtrɪˈfækʃən/ n [U]

pu·trid /ˈpjuːtrɪd/ adj **1** dead animals, plants etc that are putrid are decaying and smell very bad: *the putrid smells from the slaughterhouses* **2** *informal* very unpleasant: *a putrid green colour*

putsch /pʊtʃ/ n [C] a secretly planned attempt to remove a government by force: *the communist putsch*

putt /pʌt/ v [I,T] to hit a golf ball lightly a short distance along the ground towards the hole —**putt** n [C] —**putting** n [U]: *I was practising my putting.*

put·tee /ˈpʌti $ pʌˈtiː/ n [C usually plural] a long piece of cloth that soldiers wrapped around each leg from the knee down, as part of their uniform in the past

put·ter¹ /ˈpʌtə $ -ər/ n [C] a type of GOLF CLUB (=stick), used to hit the ball a short distance towards or into the hole → see picture at GOLF

putter² v [I always + adv/prep] **1** *AmE* also **putter around** to spend time doing things that are not very important in a relaxed way; ⊟ **potter** *BrE*: *I puttered around for a while, cleaning up the kitchen.* **2** *AmE* to walk or move slowly and without hurrying: *A little boy puttered along the sidewalk.* **3** *BrE informal* to make the low sound that a vehicle makes when it is moving slowly: *A motor boat puttered by.*

putting green n [C] **1** also **green** one of the smooth areas of grass on a GOLF COURSE where you hit the ball along the ground into the hole **2** *BrE* a smooth area of grass with special holes in it for playing a simple type of golf

put·ty /ˈpʌti/ n [U] **1** a soft whitish substance that becomes hard when it dries and that is used to fix glass into window frames **2 be putty in sb's hands** to be easily controlled or influenced by someone

put-up job n [C usually singular] *informal* an event that seems real but has actually been arranged in order to deceive someone: *It's been suggested the kidnapping was a put-up job.*

put-upon adj *informal* someone who feels put-upon thinks that other people are treating them unfairly by expecting them to do too much

putz¹ /pʌts/ n [C] *AmE informal not polite* **1** an offensive word for someone, especially a man, who is stupid, annoying, and unpleasant **2** a PENIS

putz² /pʌts, pʊts/ v

putz around phr v *AmE informal* to spend time doing very little, or not doing anything important: *I've just been putzing around this morning.*

puz·zle¹ /ˈpʌzəl/ n [C] **1** a game or toy that has a lot of pieces that you have to fit together; → **jig-saw**: *a child's wooden puzzle* **2** a game in which you have to think hard to solve a difficult question or problem: *a crossword puzzle* **3** [usually singular] something that is difficult to understand or explain: [+of] *the puzzle of how the sun works* | *The meaning of the poem has always been a puzzle.* | *He thought he had solved the puzzle.* **4 piece of the puzzle** a piece of information that helps you to understand part of a difficult question, mystery etc

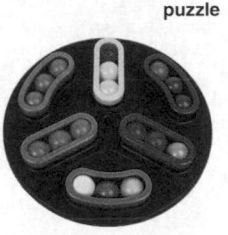
puzzle

puzzle² v [T] to confuse someone or make them feel slightly anxious because they do not understand something: *a question that continues to puzzle scientists* | *He was puzzled by the reactions to his remark.* | *What puzzles me is why his books are so popular.*

puzzle sth ⇔ **out** phr v to solve a confusing or difficult problem by thinking about it carefully: *He lay looking at the ceiling, trying to puzzle things out.*

puzzle over sth phr v to think for a long time about something because you cannot understand or solve it: *The class puzzled over a poem by Shakespeare.*

puz·zled /ˈpʌzəld/ adj confused and unable to understand something: *'Dinner?' Sam asked, looking puzzled.* | [+about/as to/at] *John seemed puzzled about what the question meant.* | **puzzled that** *Harry was puzzled that Nicholas didn't seem to recognize him.* | **puzzled look/expression/frown etc** *Alice read the letter with a puzzled expression on her face.*

puz·zle·ment /ˈpʌzəlmənt/ n [U] *formal* a feeling of being confused and unable to understand something

puz·zler /ˈpʌzlə $ -ər/ n [C] *informal* something that is difficult to understand or explain

puz·zling /ˈpʌzlɪŋ/ adj confusing and difficult to understand or explain: *a puzzling fact* | *Gary found her reaction puzzling.*

PVC /ˌpiː viː ˈsiː◂/ n [U] a type of plastic, used to make pipes, window frames, clothes etc

pvt. *AmE* a written abbreviation of *private*, the lowest military rank in the army

p.w. *BrE per week* used in writing to show that something happens, is paid etc each week: *Rent is £55 p.w.*

PX /ˌpiː ˈeks/ n [C] a shop selling food and other supplies on a US military base

pyg·my¹, **pigmy** /ˈpɪgmi/ n *plural* **pygmies** [C] **1** also **Pygmy** someone who belongs to a race of very small people, especially one of the tribes of central Africa **2** someone who is not as good, intelligent, strong etc as other people in the same group – used in order to show disapproval: *a literary pygmy*

pygmy² adj [only before noun] used to describe a type of animal or plant that is much smaller than other similar types: *a pygmy elephant*

py·ja·mas *BrE*; **pajamas** *AmE* /pəˈdʒɑːməz $ -ˈdʒæ-, -ˈdʒɑː-/ n [plural] **1** a soft pair of trousers and a top that you wear in bed: *striped pyjamas* **2** loose trousers that are tied around the waist, worn by Muslim men or women —**pyjama** adj [only before noun]: *pyjama bottoms* → **the cat's pyjamas** at CAT (5)

py·lon /ˈpaɪlən $ -lɑːn, -lən/ n [C] **1** a tall metal structure that supports wires carrying electricity **2** *AmE* one of a set of plastic CONES placed on a road to control traffic and protect people working there

PYO *BrE written* the abbreviation of *pick your own*, used by farms that let you pick fruit and vegetables to buy

pyr·a·mid /ˈpɪrəmɪd/ n [C] **1** a large stone building with four TRIANGULAR (=three-sided) walls that slope in to a point at the top, especially in Egypt and Central America **2** [usually singular] a system, society, company etc that is organized in different levels, so that there is a small number of people at the top and a much larger number of people at the bottom: *different levels of the management pyramid* | *At the bottom of the pyramid are the poor.* **3** a pile of objects that have been put into the shape of a pyramid: [+of] *a pyramid of oranges* **4** an object shaped like a pyramid —**pyramidal** /pɪˈræmɪdl/ adj

pyramid ˌscheme also **Pon·zi scheme** /ˈpɒnzi skiːm $ ˈpɑːn-/ n [C] a dishonest and often illegal way of selling INVESTMENTS, in which money from people who INVEST later is used to pay people in the system who have already invested

'pyramid ,selling n [U] a business activity in which the main income comes from people who buy the right to sell products, rather than from the sale of the products themselves. Pyramid selling is illegal in many places.

pyre /paɪə $ paɪr/ n [C] a high pile of wood on which a dead body is placed to be burned in a funeral ceremony: *a funeral pyre*

Py·rex /'paɪreks/ n [U] *trademark* a special type of strong glass that does not break when it gets very hot and that is used to make cooking dishes, plates etc

py·ri·tes /paɪ'raɪtiːz $ pə-/ n [U] a mix of SULPHUR with a type of metal, usually iron, or iron and COPPER; → **fool's gold**: *iron pyrites*

py·ro·ma·ni·ac /ˌpaɪrəʊ'meɪniæk $ -rə-/ n [C] *medical* someone who suffers from a mental illness that gives them a strong desire to start fires —**pyromania** n [U]

py·ro·tech·nics /ˌpaɪrəʊ'tekniks $ -rə-/ n **1** [plural] *formal* or *technical* a public show of FIREWORKS **2** [U] *technical* the skill or business of making FIRE-WORKS **3** [plural] an impressive show of someone's skill as a public performer, musician etc: *the guitar pyrotechnics of Eric Clapton* —**pyrotechnic** adj: *a pyrotechnic display*

Pyr·rhic vic·to·ry /ˌpɪrɪk 'vɪktəri/ n [C] a victory in which the person who wins suffers so much that the victory was hardly worth winning

py·thon /'paɪθən $ -θɑːn, -θən/ n [C] a large tropical snake that kills animals for food by winding itself around them and crushing them

P

Q, q

Q, q /kjuː/ *plural* **Q's, q's** *n* [C,U] the 17th letter of the English alphabet → **mind your p's and q's** at MIND[2] (23) → Q-TIP

Q., **q.** also **Q, q** *BrE* the written abbreviation of *question*: *a Q and A session* (=a time when people can ask questions and get answers) → FAQ

QB *AmE* the written abbreviation of *quarterback*

QC /ˌkjuː ˈsiː/ *n* [C] **Queen's Counsel** a BARRISTER of high rank in the British legal system; → **KC**

QED /ˌkjuː iː ˈdiː/ the abbreviation of the Latin phrase *quod erat demonstrandum*, used to say that a fact or event proves that what you say is true

qt *BrE*; **qt.** *AmE* the written abbreviation of *quart* or quarts

q.t. /ˌkjuː ˈtiː/ *n* **on the q.t.** *old-fashioned* secretly

Q-tip /ˈkjuː tɪp/ *n* [C] *trademark AmE* a short stick with cotton at each end, used especially for cleaning your ears

qtr. the written abbreviation of *quarter*

qua /kwɑː, kweɪ $ kwɑː/ *prep formal* used to show you are talking about the basic nature or job of someone or something: *Money, qua money, cannot provide happiness.* → SINE QUA NON

quack[1] /kwæk/ *v* [I] to make the sound that ducks make

quack[2] *n* [C] **1** the sound a duck makes **2** someone who pretends to be a doctor – used in order to show disapproval: *quacks selling weight-loss drugs* **3** *BrE informal* a doctor: *You'd better go and see the quack with that burn.*

quack[3] *adj* [only before noun] relating to the activities or medicines of someone who pretends to be a doctor: *a quack remedy*

quack·er·y /ˈkwækəri/ *n* [U] the activities of someone who pretends be a doctor

quad /kwɒd $ kwɑːd/ *n* [C] **1** *informal* a square open area with buildings all around it, especially in a school or college **2** *informal* a QUADRUPLET **3 quads** [plural] *informal* QUADRICEPS

quad bike *n* [C] *BrE* a small vehicle, similar to a MOTORCYCLE but with four wide wheels, usually ridden on rough paths or fields; ▤ **four wheeler** *AmE*

quadr- /kwɒdr $ kwɑːdr/ *prefix* another form of QUADRI-

quad·ran·gle /ˈkwɒdræŋɡəl $ ˈkwɑː-/ *n* [C] **1** *formal* a square open area with buildings all around it, especially at a school or college; ▤ **quad** **2** *technical* a flat shape that has four straight sides

quad·rant /ˈkwɒdrənt $ ˈkwɑː-/ *n* [C] **1** a quarter of a circle **2** an instrument for measuring angles, used when sailing or looking at the stars

quad·ra·phon·ic, **quadrophonic** /ˌkwɒdrəˈfɒnɪk◂ $ ˌkwɑːdrəˈfɑː-/ *adj* using a system of sound recording, broadcasting etc in which sound comes from four different SPEAKERS at the same time; → **mono**, **stereo**

quad·rat·ic e·qua·tion /kwɒˌdrætɪk ɪˈkweɪʒən $ kwɑː-/ *n* [C] *technical* an EQUATION such as $ax^2+by+c=z$, which includes numbers or quantities multiplied by themselves

quadri- /kwɒdrɪ $ kwɑː-/ also **quadru-, quadr-** *prefix* four or four times: *a quadrilateral* (=shape with four straight sides) | *a quadruped* (=animal with four legs)

quad·ri·ceps /ˈkwɒdrɪseps $ ˈkwɑː-/ *n plural* **quadriceps** [C] the large muscle at the front of your THIGH

quad·ri·lat·er·al /ˌkwɒdrɪˈlætərəl◂ $ ˌkwɑː-/ *n* [C] *technical* a flat shape with four straight sides —**quadrilateral** *adj*

qua·drille /kwəˈdrɪl $ kwɑː-/ *n* [C] a dance, popular especially in the 19th century, in which the dancers form a square

qua·dril·lion /kwɒˈdrɪljən $ kwɑː-/ *number* **1** the number one followed by 15 zeros **2** *BrE old use* the number one followed by 24 zeros

quad·ri·ple·gic /ˌkwɒdrɪˈpliːdʒɪk◂ $ ˌkwɑː-/ *n* [C] someone who is permanently unable to move any part of their body below their neck; → **paraplegic**: *A car accident left him a quadriplegic.* —**quadriplegia** *n* [U] —**quadriplegic** *adj*

quad·ro·phon·ic /ˌkwɒdrəˈfɒnɪk◂ $ ˌkwɑːdrəˈfɑː-/ *adj* another spelling of QUADRAPHONIC

quadru- /kwɒdru $ kwɑː-/ *prefix* another form of QUADRI-

quad·ru·ped /ˈkwɒdruped $ ˈkwɑːdrə-/ *n* [C] *technical* an animal that has four legs; → **biped**

quad·ru·ple[1] /ˈkwɒdrʊpəl, kwɒˈdruː- $ kwɑːˈdruː-/ *v* [I,T] to increase and become four times as big or as high, or to make something increase in this way; → **double**, **triple**: *Food prices quadrupled during the war.* | *The company has quadrupled its profits in just three years.*

quadruple[2] *adj, predeterminer* **1** four times as big or as many; → **double**, **triple**: *The subjects were given quadruple the normal dosage of the drug.* **2** involving four things of the same kind: *a quadruple murder*

quad·ru·plet /ˈkwɒdrʊplɪt $ kwɑːˈdruːp-/ *n* [C] one of four babies born at the same time to the same mother; ▤ **quad**

quaff /kwɒf, kwɑːf $ kwɑːf, kwæf/ *v* [T] *literary* to drink a lot of something quickly; ▤ **knock back**: *Wedding guests quaffed champagne.*

quag·mire /ˈkwæɡmaɪə, ˈkwɒɡ- $ ˈkwæɡmaɪr/ *n* [C usually singular] **1** an area of soft wet muddy ground: *In the rainy season the roads become a quagmire.* **2** a difficult or complicated situation: *The Balkan situation became a political and military quagmire.*

quail[1] /kweɪl/ *n* [C,U] a small fat bird with a short tail that is hunted for food or sport, or the meat from this bird

quail[2] *v* [I] *literary* to be afraid and show it by shaking a little bit or moving back slightly; ▤ **shrink**: [+at] *She quailed visibly at the sight of the prison walls.*

quaint /kweɪnt/ *adj* unusual and attractive, especially in an old-fashioned way: *a quaint little village in Yorkshire*

quake[1] /kweɪk/ *v* [I] **1** to shake or tremble, usually because you are very frightened: **quake with fear/fright/anger etc** *Richmond was quaking with fury.* **2 quake in your boots** *informal* to feel very afraid – used humorously **3** if the earth, a building etc quakes, it shakes violently: *The explosion made the whole house quake.*

quake[2] *n* [C] an EARTHQUAKE

Quak·er /ˈkweɪkə $ -ər/ *n* [C] a member of the Society of Friends, a Christian religious group that meets without any formal ceremony or priests and that is opposed to violence —**Quaker** *adj*

qual·i·fi·ca·tion S2 W3 /ˌkwɒlɪfɪˈkeɪʃən $ ˌkwɑː-/ *n* **1** [C usually plural] if you have a qualification, you have passed an examination or course to show you have a particular level of skill or knowledge in a subject: **academic/vocational/professional/educational etc qualifications** *the academic qualifications needed for university entrance* | **technical/secretarial/medical etc qualifications** *jobs that require technical qualifications* | *Applicants should have an EFL qualification and a year's teaching experience.* | [+in] *She gained a qualification in marketing.* | *40 percent of the prisoners lack any qualifications.* | **paper qualifications** *BrE* (=official qualifications rather than experience or personal qualities)

2 [C usually plural] a skill, personal quality, or type of experience that makes you suitable for a particular job or position: [+for] *health and fitness qualifications for membership in the Territorial Army* | **qualification to do sth** *There have been questions about his qualifica-*

tions to lead the company. | *Does he have the right qualifications to become a Supreme Court Justice?*
3 [U] when a person or team reaches a necessary standard, for example by passing an examination or defeating another team: *Upon qualification, you can expect to find work abroad fairly easily.* | [+**for**] *the US qualification for the World Cup*
4 [C,U] something that you add to a statement to limit its effect or meaning; ◢ **reservation**: *I welcome without qualification the Minister's proposal.*

GRAMMAR

Qualification is usually plural. **Qualifications** are all the examination passes and skills you need to do a particular job: *Academic qualifications (NOT qualification) are not necessary to do this job.*
When **qualification** is used in the singular form in British English, it means 'a degree, a certificate, a diploma etc': *a qualification in business studies.* Speakers of American English usually mention the specific name of the degree, diploma etc they are talking about, e.g. **high school diploma, college degree, teaching certificate** etc.
⚠ Do not say 'study a qualification'. Say **study for a qualification.**

---

qual·i·fied S3 /'kwɒlɪfaɪd $ 'kwɑː-/ *adj*
1 having suitable knowledge, experience, or skills, especially for a particular job: **well/suitably/highly qualified** *Dawn is well qualified for her new role.* | **qualified to do sth** *The guides are qualified to lead groups into the mountains.* | *If you don't speak German, you're not qualified to comment.*
2 having passed a professional examination: **qualified doctor/teacher/accountant etc** *There are qualified instructors on hand to advise you.* | **highly/fully qualified** *a fully qualified nurse* | *a **professionally qualified** social worker* | *Are you **medically qualified**?* | **qualified to do sth** *He's qualified to teach biology at high school level.*
3 [usually before noun] limited in some way; → **partial**: **qualified approval/support** *The proposal received qualified approval.* | *The program was considered a **qualified success.** | Is it worth the money? The answer is a **qualified yes.**

qual·i·fi·er /'kwɒlɪfaɪə $ 'kwɑːlɪfaɪər/ *n* [C] **1** someone who has reached the necessary standard for entering a competition, especially by defeating other competitors: *He's among the qualifiers for the Lancome Trophy at Paris.* **2** a game that you have to win in order to be able to take part in a competition: *the World Cup qualifier against the Netherlands* **3** *technical* a word or phrase that limits or adds to the meaning of another word or phrase

qual·i·fy S2 W3 /'kwɒlɪfaɪ $ 'kwɑː-/ *v* **qualified, qualifying, qualifies**
1 HAVE A RIGHT [I,T] to have the right to have or do something, or to give someone this right: *Free school lunches are given to children who qualify.* | [+**for**] *You may qualify for unemployment benefit.* | **qualify sb/sth for sth** *Membership qualifies you for a discount on purchases.*
2 PASS EXAM [I] to pass an examination or finish a course of study that you need in order to do something: [+**as**] *I finally qualified as a pilot.* | *After qualifying, doctors spend at least two years working in hospitals.*
3 BE CONSIDERED STH [I] to have all the necessary qualities to be considered to be a particular thing: [+**as**] *It doesn't qualify as a date if you bring your children with you.*
4 GIVE SB SKILLS/KNOWLEDGE [T] if something qualifies you to do something, you have the necessary skills, knowledge, ability etc to do it: **qualify sb for sth** *Fluency in three languages qualifies her for work in the European Parliament.* | **qualify sb to do sth** *The certificate qualifies you to work as a dental assistant.*
5 SPORT [I] to reach the necessary standard to enter or continue in a competition or sports event: [+**for**] *She*

qualified for a spot on the U.S. Olympic speed skating team.
6 ADD SOMETHING [T] to add to something that has already been said, in order to limit its effect or meaning: *Could I just qualify that last statement?*
7 GRAMMAR [T] if a word or phrase qualifies another word or phrase, it limits or adds to the meaning of it

qual·i·ta·tive /'kwɒlɪtətɪv $ 'kwɑːlɪteɪ-/ *adj formal* relating to the quality or standard of something rather than the quantity: **a qualitative analysis/study/research** *a qualitative study of educational services* —**qualitatively** *adv*: *Women's experiences are qualitatively different from men's.* → **quantitative**

qual·i·ty¹ S1 W1 /'kwɒlɪti $ 'kwɑː-/ *n plural* **qualities**
1 [C,U] how good or bad something is: **air/water etc quality** *The recent hot, humid weather is affecting air quality.* | [+**of**] *the quality of research into the disease* | **be of poor/good/high etc quality** *Much of the land was of poor quality.* | *Use only high quality ingredients.*
2 [C usually plural] something that people may have as part of their character, for example courage or intelligence; → **characteristic**: *He shows strong **leadership qualities.** | the **personal qualities** necessary to be a successful salesman* | [+**of**] *the qualities of honesty and independence*
3 [C] something that is typical of one thing and makes it different from other things, for example size, colour etc: *the drug's addictive quality* | [+**of**] *the physical and chemical qualities of the rock*
4 [U] a high standard: *his pride in the quality of his craftsmanship* | *wines of quality*
5 **quality of life** how good or bad your life is, shown for example by whether or not you are happy, healthy, able to do what you want etc: *drugs that improve the quality of life for very ill patients*

quality² *adj* [only before noun] **1** [no comparative] very good – used especially by people who are trying to sell something: *quality child-care at prices people can afford* | *quality double glazing* **2** **quality newspapers/ press etc** *BrE* newspapers etc intended for educated readers

'quality as,surance *n* [U] the practice of checking the quality of goods or services that a company sells, so that the standard continues to be good

'quality con,trol *n* [U] the practice of checking goods as they are produced to be sure that their quality is good enough —**quality controller** *n* [C]

'quality ,time *n* [U] the time that you spend giving someone your full attention, especially time that you spend with your children when you are not busy: *Do you spend enough quality time with your children?*

qualm /kwɑːm $ kwɑːm, kwɑːlm/ *n* [C usually plural] a feeling of slight worry or doubt because you are not sure that what you are doing is right: *Despite my qualms, I took the job.* | *The manager **has no qualms about** dropping players who do not perform well.*

quan·da·ry /'kwɒndəri $ 'kwɑːn-/ *n plural* **quandaries** [C] a difficult situation or problem, especially one in which you cannot decide what to do: **in a quandary** *Kate was in a quandary over whether to go or not.*

quan·go /'kwæŋɡəʊ $ -ɡoʊ/ *n plural* **quangos** [C] an independent organization in Britain, started by the government but with its own legal powers

quan·ta /'kwɒntə $ 'kwɑːn-/ *n* the plural of QUANTUM

quan·ti·fi·er /'kwɒntɪfaɪə $ 'kwɑːntɪfaɪər/ *n* [C] *technical* a word or phrase such as 'much', 'few', or 'a lot of' that is used with a noun to show quantity

quan·ti·fy /'kwɒntɪfaɪ $ 'kwɑːn-/ *v* **quantified, quantifying, quantifies** [T] to calculate the value of something and express it as a number or an amount: *an attempt to quantify the region's social and economic decline* | **difficult/impossible to quantify** *The damage caused to the tourist industry is difficult to quantify.* —**quantifiable** *adj*: *The cost of unemployment to the government is quite easily quantifiable.*

quan·ti·ta·tive /ˈkwɒnt‖tətɪv $ ˈkwɑːnt‖teɪ-/ *adj formal* relating to amounts rather than to the quality or standard of something: **quantitative analysis/methods/ data etc** *We need to do a proper quantitative analysis of this problem.*; → **qualitative** —**quantitatively** *adv*

quan·ti·ty S3 W2 /ˈkwɒnt‖ti $ ˈkwɑːn-/ *n plural* **quantities**
1 [C,U] an amount of something that can be counted or measured: [+of] *The police also found a quantity of ammunition in the flat.* | *Add 50 grams of butter, and the same quantity of sugar.* | **a large/small/vast etc quantity of sth** *He had consumed a large quantity of alcohol.* | *Huge quantities of oil were spilling into the sea.* | **in large/small/sufficient etc quantities** *Buy vegetables in small quantities, for your immediate use.* | *Your work has improved in quantity and quality this term.* △ Do not say 'a big quantity'. Say **a large quantity**.
2 [U] the large amount of something: *The sheer quantity of text meant that people did not read the whole of their newspaper.*
3 in quantity in large amounts: *It's a lot cheaper if you buy it in quantity.* → **be an unknown quantity** at UNKNOWN[1] (4)

quantity sur·vey·or *n* [C] *BrE* someone whose job is to calculate the amount of materials needed to build something, how long it will take to build, and how much it will cost

quan·tum /ˈkwɒntəm $ ˈkwɑːn-/ *n plural* **quanta** /-tə/ [C] *technical* a unit of energy in NUCLEAR PHYSICS

quantum leap also **quantum jump** *n* [C] a very large and important development or improvement: [+in] *There has been a quantum leap in the range of the wines sold in the UK.* | *The treatment of breast cancer has taken a quantum leap forward.*

quantum me·chan·ics *n* [U] the scientific study of the way that atoms and smaller parts of things behave

quantum theory *n* [U] the idea that energy, especially light, travels in separate pieces and not in a continuous form

quar·an·tine[1] /ˈkwɒrəntiːn $ ˈkwɔː-/ *n* [U] a period of time when a person or animal is kept apart from others in case they are carrying a disease: **in quarantine** *The monkeys were kept in quarantine for 31 days.*

quarantine[2] *v* [T] to keep a person or animal apart from others for a period of time in case they are carrying a disease

quark /kwɑːk, kwɔːk $ kwɔːrk, kwɑːrk/ *n* [C] *technical* a very small part of something, which is smaller than an atom

quar·rel[1] /ˈkwɒrəl $ ˈkwɔː-, ˈkwɑː-/ *n* [C] *especially BrE* **1** an angry argument or disagreement: *I think they've had a quarrel.* | [+with] *Jacob left after a quarrel with his wife.* | [+about/over] *They had a quarrel about some girl.* | [+between] *Had there been any quarrel between you?* | *Are you trying to pick a quarrel* (=deliberately start one)? **2** a reason to disagree with something or argue with someone: [+with] *My only quarrel with this plan is that it's going to take far too long.* | *I have no quarrel with the court's verdict.*

quarrel[2] *v* **quarrelled, quarrelling** *BrE*, **quarreled, quarreling** *AmE* [I] to have an argument: *I wish you two would stop quarreling.* | [+with] *I always seem to be quarrelling with my parents.* | [+about] *We're not going to quarrel about a few dollars.*
  quarrel with sth *phr v* to disagree with something or complain about something: *Nobody could quarrel with the report's conclusions.*

quar·rel·some /ˈkwɒrəlsəm $ ˈkwɔː-, ˈkwɑː-/ *adj especially BrE* someone who is quarrelsome quarrels a lot with people; ☐ **argumentative**: *He became quarrelsome after drinking too much.*

quar·ry[1] /ˈkwɒri $ ˈkwɔː-, ˈkwɑː-/ *n plural* **quarries 1** [C] a place where large amounts of stone or sand are dug out of the ground: *a slate quarry* **2** [sin-

gular] the person or animal that you are hunting or chasing: *Briefly, the hunter and his quarry glared at each other.*

quarry[2] *v* **quarried, quarrying, quarries** [T] to dig stone or sand from a quarry: **quarry sth for sth** *The rock here is quarried for building stones.* | **quarry sth from sth** *Chalk is quarried from the surrounding area.* —**quarrying** *n* [U]

quarry tile *n* [C usually plural] a clay TILE that has not been GLAZED. Quarry tiles are used to cover floors.

quart /kwɔːt $ kwɔːrt/ *n* [C] written abbreviation **qt** a unit for measuring liquid, equal to two PINTS. In Britain this is 1.14 litres, and in the US it is 0.95 litres.

quar·ter[1] S1 W2 /ˈkwɔːtə $ ˈkwɔːrtər/ *n* [C]
1 AMOUNT one of four equal parts into which something can be divided; → **half**, **third**: **a/one quarter (of sth)** *a quarter of a mile* | *roughly one quarter of the city's population* | *It's about a page and a quarter.* | **three quarters (of sth)** (=75%) *three quarters of a million pounds* | **the first/second etc quarter** *in the last quarter of the 19th century* | *Cut the cake into quarters.* → see picture at QUICHE △ Say **a quarter of** something, not 'quarter of' something.
2 PART OF AN HOUR a period of 15 minutes: *I'll meet you in a quarter of an hour.* | *She arrived three quarters of an hour* (=45 minutes) *late.* | **(a) quarter to (sth)** also **(a) quarter of (sth)** *AmE* (=15 minutes before the hour) *It's a quarter of two.* | **(a) quarter past (sth)** *BrE* also **(a) quarter after (sth)** *AmE* (=15 minutes after the hour) *I'll meet you at a quarter past ten.*
3 MONEY a coin used in the US and Canada worth 25 cents
4 THREE MONTHS a period of three months, used especially when discussing business and financial matters: **the first/second/third/fourth quarter** *The company's profits rose by 11% in the first quarter of the year.* | *Our database is updated every quarter.* → QUARTERLY (1)
5 SPORT one of the four equal periods of time into which games of some sports are divided: **the first/ second/third/fourth quarter** *The home side took the lead in the second quarter.*
6 PART OF A CITY [usually singular] an area of a town: *I found a small flat in the student quarter.* | *Granada's ancient Arab quarter* | *a historic quarter of the city*
7 HOME **quarters** [plural] the rooms that are given to someone to live in as part of their job, especially servants or soldiers: *The top floor provided **living quarters** for the kitchen staff.* | *Most of the officers live in **married quarters*** (=houses where soldiers live with their wives).
8 COLLEGE *AmE* one of the four periods into which a year at school or college is divided, continuing for 10 to 12 weeks; → **semester**: *What classes are you taking this quarter?*
9 MOON the period of time twice a month when you can see a quarter of the moon's surface
10 in/from ... quarters among or from different groups of people: *Offers of financial help came from several quarters.* | *Doubts were expressed in many quarters.*
11 all quarters of the Earth/globe *literary* everywhere in the world
12 give/receive no quarter *literary* if someone gives no quarter, they do not show any pity or gentleness when dealing with someone, especially an enemy: *It was a fight to the death, with no quarter given.* → **at close quarters** at CLOSE[2] (20)

quarter[2] *v* [T] **1** to cut or divide something into four parts; → **halve**: *Quarter the tomatoes and place them round the dish.* **2** [usually passive] *formal* to provide someone with a place to sleep and eat, especially soldiers: *Our troops were quartered in Boston until June.*

Q

cessful or will not continue to exist: *A big question mark hangs over the company's future.*

question ,master *n* [C] *BrE* the person who asks the questions in a QUIZ game on television or radio; ▤ **quizmaster**

ques·tion·naire /ˌkwestʃə'neə, ˌkes- $ -'ner/ *n* [C] a written set of questions which you give to a large number of people in order to collect information: **fill in/fill out/complete a questionnaire** (=answer all the questions in it) *All staff were asked to fill in a questionnaire about their jobs.* △ Do not use **questionnaire** to mean 'a study in which many people are asked questions to find out their opinions or behaviour'. Use **survey**: *We conducted a survey (NOT a questionnaire) to find out what students think about sport.*

question tag *n* [C] *technical* a phrase such as 'isn't it?', 'won't it?', or 'does she?' that you add to the end of a statement to make it a question or to check that someone agrees with you, as in the sentence: 'You're from Hamburg, aren't you?'

queue

a queue of people

queue¹ S3 /kjuː/ *n* [C]
1 *BrE* a line of people waiting to enter a building, buy something etc, or a line of vehicles waiting to move; ▤ **line** *AmE*: **be/stand/wait in a queue** *We stood in a queue for half an hour.* | *You'll have to* **join the queue.** | [+of] *a queue of people waiting for the bus* | [+for] *the queue for the toilets* | **queue to do sth** *There was a long queue to get into the cinema.* | **the front/head/back/end of a queue** *At last we got to the front of the queue.*
2 *BrE* all the people who are waiting to have or get something: *You'll have to join the housing queue.* | [+for] *the queue for kidney transplant operations* | *It is possible to* **jump the queue** (=get something before people who have been waiting longer) *if you are prepared to pay for your treatment.*
3 *technical* a list of jobs that a computer has to do in a particular order: *the print queue*
4 a number of telephone calls to a particular number that are waiting to be answered → **the dole queue** at DOLE¹ (2)

queue² *v* also **queue up** [I] *BrE* **1** to form or join a line of people or vehicles waiting to do something or go somewhere; ▤ **line up** *AmE*: [+for] *Some of the people queuing for tickets had been there since dawn.* | **queue (up) to do sth** *We had to queue up for ages to get served.* **2** if people are queueing up to do something, they all want to do it very much: **queue up to do sth** *The school is one of the best, and parents are queueing up to send their children there.* | **queue up for sth** *Actresses are queuing up for the part.*

queue-jumping *n* [U] *BrE* when someone unfairly gets something before other people who have been waiting longer —**queue-jump** *v* [I]

quib·ble¹ /'kwɪbəl/ *v* [I] to argue about small unimportant details: [+about/over] *Let's not quibble over minor details.*

quibble² *n* [C] a small complaint or criticism about something unimportant: *I've just got a few minor quibbles.*

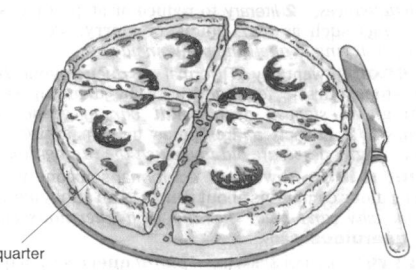

quarter

quiche /kiːʃ/ *n* [C,U] a PIE without a top, filled with a mixture of eggs, cheese, vegetables etc

quick¹ S1 W2 /kwɪk/ *adj comparative* **quicker,** *superlative* **quickest**
1 SHORT TIME lasting for or taking only a short time: *That was quick! I thought you'd be another hour.* | *It's probably quicker by train.* | *Have we got time for a quick drink?* | *What's the quickest way to the station?* | *We stopped to have a quick look at the church.* | *Three bombs went off* **in quick succession** (=quickly, one after the other).
2 FAST moving or doing something fast: *She walked with short, quick steps.* | *They were great people to work with – very quick, very efficient.*
3 NO DELAY happening very soon, without any delay; ▤ **speedy**: *I had to make a* **quick decision.** | *We've put the house on the market and we're hoping for a* **quick sale.** | *We need a* **quick response** *from the government.* | *Robertson's* **quick thinking** *had saved the little girl's life.*
4 CLEVER able to learn and understand things fast: *Jane's very witty and very quick.* | *She's a* **quick learner.** | *He's a good interviewer, tough and* **quick on the uptake** (=able to understand quickly what someone is saying).
5 be quick used to tell someone to hurry: *If you want to come with me you'll have to be quick – I'm leaving in ten minutes.* | *'Can I just finish this first?' 'OK, but* **be quick about it.'**
6 be quick to do sth to react quickly to what someone says or does: *The government was quick to deny any involvement in the attacks.*
7 quick fix *informal* a solution to a problem that can be done quickly, but is not a good or permanent solution: *There's no quick fix for stopping pollution.* | *Congress is trying to avoid quick-fix solutions.*
8 have a quick temper to get angry very easily
9 be quick on the draw a) to be able to pull a gun out quickly in order to shoot **b)** *AmE informal* to be good at reacting quickly and intelligently to difficult questions or in difficult situations —**quickness** *n* [U] → QUICKLY

quick² *interjection* used to tell someone to hurry or come quickly: *Quick! We'll miss the bus!*

quick³ S3 *adv* quickly – many teachers think this is not correct English; ▤ **fast**: *Come quick! Larry's on TV!* | *It all happened pretty quick.* | *Quick as a flash* (=very quickly) *she replied, 'That's not what I've heard!'*

quick⁴ *n* **1 the quick** the sensitive flesh under your fingernails and toenails: *Her nails were bitten to the quick.* **2 cut/sting/pierce sb to the quick** if a remark or criticism cuts you to the quick, it makes you feel extremely upset: *She was cut to the quick by the accusation.* **3 the quick and the dead** *biblical* all people, including those who are alive and those who are dead

quick·en /'kwɪkən/ *v* [I,T] **1** *written* to become quicker or make something quicker: *Ray glanced at his watch and quickened his pace* (=began to walk faster). | *Companies are finding it hard to cope with the quickening pace of technological change.* | **your heart/pulse/breathing quickens** (=your heart beats faster because you are afraid, excited etc) *She caught sight of*

Rob and felt her heart quicken. **2** *formal* if a feeling quickens, or if something quickens it, it becomes stronger or more active; ▤ **increase**: *This policy served only to quicken anti-government feeling*.

quick·en·ing /'kwɪkənɪŋ/ *n* [U] the first movements of a baby that has not been born yet

quick·fire /'kwɪkfaɪə $ -faɪr/ *adj* [only before noun] done very quickly, one after the other: *Contestants have to answer a series of quickfire questions*.

quick·ie /'kwɪki/ *n* [C] *informal* **1** something that you can do quickly and easily: *I've got a question for you – it's just a quickie*. **2** a sexual act that you do quickly – used humorously —**quickie** *adj* [only before noun]: *a quickie divorce*

quick·lime /'kwɪk-laɪm/ *n* [U] a white powder that is made by heating LIMESTONE

quick·ly ⑤1 ⑩1 /'kwɪkli/ *adv*
1 fast: *We need to get this finished as quickly as possible*. | *Kids grow up so quickly these days*.
2 after only a very short time; ▤ **soon**: *I realized fairly quickly that this wasn't going to be easy*.
3 for a short time: *I'll just quickly nip into that shop*. | *'Have you talked to Vera about it yet?' 'Just quickly.'*

quick·sand /'kwɪksænd/ *n* [C,U] **1** wet sand that is dangerous because you sink down into it if you try to walk on it **2** a bad situation that keeps getting worse, and that you cannot escape from

quick·sil·ver /'kwɪkˌsɪlvə $ -ər/ *n* [U] **1** *old use* the metal MERCURY **2** *literary* something that is like quicksilver changes or moves quickly in a way that you do not expect: *His mood changed like quicksilver.* —**quicksilver** *adj*: *his quicksilver temperament*

quick·step /'kwɪkstep/ *n* [C] a dance with fast movements of the feet, or music for this dance

quick-'tempered *adj* someone who is quick-tempered becomes angry very easily; ▤ **bad-tempered**

quick-'witted *adj* able to think and understand things quickly; ▤ **slow-witted**: *Toby was quick-witted and entertaining*. | *a quick-witted reply*

quid ⑤2 /kwɪd/ *n plural* **quid** [C] *BrE informal*
1 one pound in money: *She earns at least 600 quid a week*.
2 be quids in to make a good profit: *If this deal comes off, we'll be quids in*.

quid pro quo /ˌkwɪd prəʊ 'kwəʊ $ -proʊ 'kwoʊ/ *n plural* **quid pro quos** [C] something that you give or do in exchange for something else, especially when this arrangement is not official: [+**for**] *There's a quid pro quo for everything in politics – you'll soon learn that*.

qui·es·cent /kwi'esənt, kwaɪ-/ *adj formal* not developing or doing anything, especially when this is only a temporary state

qui·et¹ ⑤2 ⑩2 /'kwaɪət/ *adj comparative* **quieter**, *superlative* **quietest**
1 NO NOISE not making much noise, or making no noise at all: *We'll have to be quiet so as not to wake the baby*. | *It's a nice car. The engine's really quiet*. | *I'll be as quiet as a mouse* (=very quiet).
2 NOT SPEAKING **a)** not saying much or not saying anything: *You're very quiet, Mom – is anything the matter?* | *I didn't know anything about it so I just kept quiet*. | **quiet confidence/satisfaction/desperation** (=having a particular feeling but not talking about it) *a woman whose life of quiet desperation threatens to overwhelm her* | **quiet authority/dignity** (=not saying much but making other people have a particular feeling about you) *Jack's air of quiet authority* **b)** someone who is quiet does not usually talk very much: *a strange, quiet girl*
3 (be) quiet! *spoken* used to tell someone to stop talking or making a noise: *Tanya, be quiet! I'm on the phone*. | *Quiet, you lot!*
4 keep quiet/keep quiet about sth to keep information secret: *You're getting married? You kept that quiet!*
5 NO ACTIVITY/PEOPLE without much activity or without many people: *It was a Sunday, about three o'clock, and the streets were quiet* . | *I'd love to go on holiday somewhere where it's nice and quiet*. | *I'm going to have a quiet night in* (=an evening when you stay at home and relax). | *Anthony met her in the bar, and they found a quiet corner where they could talk*.
6 BUSINESS if business is quiet, there are not many customers; ▤ **slack**: *August is a quiet time of year for the retail trade*.
7 keep sb quiet to stop someone from talking, complaining, or causing trouble: *Give the kids some crayons – that will keep them quiet for a while*.
8 have a quiet word (with sb) *especially BrE* to talk to someone privately when you want to criticize them or tell them about something serious: *Brian's just not keeping up with the workload. Can you have a quiet word?* ⚠ Do not confuse **quiet** (=with little noise) and **quite** (=fairly) even though they have similar spellings. —**quietness** *n* [U] → QUIETLY

> **WORD FOCUS: QUIET**
> **voice, sound**: low, soft, muffled, hushed, subdued
> **place**: peaceful, calm, sleepy, tranquil
> **completely quiet**: silent, you could hear a pin drop
> **what you say when you want someone to be quiet**: sh, shut up *not polite*, be quiet, keep it down *BrE informal*

quiet² *n* [U] **1** the state of being quiet, calm, and peaceful: *We were enjoying the quiet of the forest*. | *I've had an awful day – now I just want some peace and quiet*. **2** silence: *Can I have some quiet, please?* **3 on the quiet** *BrE informal* secretly: *We found out he'd been doing some freelance work on the quiet*.

qui·et·en /'kwaɪətn/ *BrE*, **quiet** *AmE v* **1** [I,T] also **quieten down** *BrE* to become calmer and less noisy or active, or to make someone or something do this: *Javed Miandad appealed for calm, but he failed to quieten the protesters*. | *Quiet down and get ready for bed!* | *Things tend to quieten down after Christmas*. **2** [T] to reduce a feeling such as fear or worry: *I managed to quieten her fears*.

qui·et·is·m /'kwaɪətɪzəm/ *n* [U] *formal* when you accept situations and do not try to change them

qui·et·ly ⑤3 ⑩3 /'kwaɪətli/ *adv*
1 without making much noise: *Rosa shut the door quietly*. | *'I'm sorry,' she said quietly*. | *a quietly-spoken man* (=one who always speaks quietly)
2 in a way that does not attract attention: *The mayor had been aiming to quietly turn over control of the city's water to private business interests*. | *The government hoped that their early mishandling of the crisis could be quietly forgotten*.
3 without protesting, complaining, or fighting: *Now are you gonna come quietly, or do I have to use force?* | *Speculation is growing that Grogan will be replaced at the end of the season, and he is unlikely to go quietly*.
4 quietly confident *especially BrE* fairly confident of success, but without talking proudly about it: *Adam came out of the interview feeling quietly confident*.

qui·e·tude /'kwaɪətjuːd $ -tuːd/ *n* [U] *formal* calmness, peace, and quiet; ▤ **calm**

qui·e·tus /kwaɪ'iːtəs, kwi'eɪtəs $ kwaɪ'iːtəs/ *n* [singular] *formal* **1** the death of a person **2** the end of something

quiff /kwɪf/ *n* [C] *BrE* a part of a man's hair style where the hair stands up at the front above his forehead → see picture at HAIRSTYLE

quill /kwɪl/ *n* [C] **1** also **quill pen** a pen made from a large bird's feather, used in the past **2** a stiff bird's feather **3** one of the long pointed things that grow on the back of a PORCUPINE

quilt /kwɪlt/ *n* [C] a warm thick cover for a bed, made by sewing two layers of cloth together, with feathers or a thick material in between them; → **duvet**; → see picture at BED¹

quilt·ed /ˈkwɪltɪd/ *adj* quilted cloth consists of layers held together by lines of stitches that cross each other: *a quilted bath robe*

quilt·ing /ˈkwɪltɪŋ/ *n* [U] the work of making a quilt, or the material and stitches that you use

quin /kwɪn/ *n* [C] *BrE informal* a QUINTUPLET

quince /kwɪns/ *n* [C,U] a hard yellow fruit like a large apple, used in cooking

quin·ine /ˈkwɪniːn $ ˈkwaɪnaɪn/ *n* [U] a drug used for treating fevers, especially MALARIA

quint /kwɪnt/ *n* [C] *AmE informal* a QUINTUPLET

quin·tes·sence /kwɪnˈtesəns/ *n* **the quintessence of sth** *formal* a perfect example of something: *John is the quintessence of good manners.*

quin·tes·sen·tial /ˌkwɪntɪˈsenʃəl◂/ *adj* being a perfect example of a particular type of person or thing; ▣ **typical**: *'Guys and Dolls' is the quintessential American musical.* —**quintessentially** *adv*: *a place that is quintessentially English*

quin·tet /kwɪnˈtet/ *n* [C] **1** five singers or musicians who perform together **2** a piece of music written for five performers; → **quartet, sextet, trio**

quin·tu·plet /ˈkwɪntjʊplɪt, kwɪnˈtjuːp- $ kwɪnˈtʌp-/ *n* [C] one of five babies born to the same mother at the same time; → **quadruplet, sextuplet**

quip /kwɪp/ *v* **quipped, quipping** [T] to say something clever and amusing: *'Giving up smoking is easy,' he quipped. 'I've done it hundreds of times.'* —**quip** *n* [C]: *an amusing quip*

quire /kwaɪə $ kwaɪr/ *n* [C] *technical* 24 sheets of paper

quirk /kwɜːk $ kwɜːrk/ *n* [C] **1** something strange that happens by chance: [+of] *Years later, by a strange quirk of fate, she found herself sitting next to him on a plane.* **2** a strange habit or feature of someone's character, or a strange feature of something: *Like every computer, this one has its little quirks.*

quirk·y /ˈkwɜːki $ -ɜːr-/ *adj* unusual, especially in an interesting way: *I like his quirky sense of humour.* —**quirkily** *adv* —**quirkiness** *n* [U]

quis·ling /ˈkwɪzlɪŋ/ *n* [C] *old-fashioned* someone who helps an enemy country that has taken control of their own country

quit /kwɪt/ *v past tense and past participle* **quit** *also* **quitted** *BrE present participle* **quitting** **1** [I,T] *informal* to leave a job, school etc, especially without finishing it completely: *He quit his job after an argument with a colleague.* | *I quit school at 16.* | *She has decided to quit show business.* | *People are now calling on the chairman to quit.* **2** [I,T] *especially AmE* to stop doing something, especially something that is bad or annoying; → **give up**: *The majority of smokers say that they would like to quit the habit.* | *Quit it, Robby, or I'll tell mom!* | *We've done what we can. Let's quit.* | **quit doing sth** *Doctors have given him six months to live if he doesn't quit drinking.* | *I wish you'd all quit complaining.* **3** [I,T] *BrE law* to leave a house or apartment that you have been renting: *The landlord gave them **notice to quit** the premises within seven days.* **4** **be quit of sth** *BrE formal* to no longer have to suffer or be involved with something bad: *The people now long to be quit of war.* **5** [T] *formal* to leave a place: *It was fourteen years since he had quit Russia.*

quite S1 W1 /kwaɪt/ *predeterminer, adv*
1 fairly or very, but not extremely; → **pretty**: *The food in the canteen is usually quite good.* | *He seems quite upset about it all.* | *I'm quite willing to help.* | *Amy's at university now and doing quite well.* | *I got a letter from Sylvia quite recently.* | **quite a sth** *He's quite a good soccer player.* | **quite like/enjoy** *BrE: I quite like Chinese food.* ⚠ Quite goes before, not after, **a** or **an**: *quite a short time (NOT a quite short time);* → see box at RATHER
2 **quite a lot/bit/few** a fairly large number or amount: *He's got quite a lot of friends.* | *Quite a few towns are now banning cars from their shopping centres.*

3 [+ adj/adv] *BrE* completely: *I'm sorry. That's quite impossible.* | *What she's suggesting is quite ridiculous!* | *I think you've had quite enough to drink already!* | *That's quite a different matter.*
4 **not quite** not completely: *They weren't quite ready so we waited in the car.* | *I'm not quite sure where she lives.* | *Dinner's almost ready, but not quite.*
5 **not quite why/what/where etc** not exactly why, what, where etc: *I must admit, the play wasn't quite what we expected.*
6 **quite a sth/quite some sth** *BrE* used before a noun to emphasize that something is very good, large, interesting etc: *That was quite a party you had last night.* | *The engines make quite a noise.* | *It's quite some distance away.*
7 **quite a/some time** *especially BrE* a fairly long time: *We've been waiting for quite some time now.*
8 **quite right** *BrE* used to show that you agree strongly with someone: *'I refused to do any more work until I'd been paid.' 'Quite right. They can't expect you to work for nothing.'*
9 **that's quite all right** *BrE* used to reply to someone that you are not angry about something they have done: *'I'm sorry we're so late.' 'That's quite all right.'*
10 **quite/quite so** *BrE formal* used to show that you agree with what someone is saying; ▣ **exactly**: *'They really should have thought of this before.' 'Yes, quite.'*
11 **quite something** *especially BrE* used to say that someone or something is very impressive: *It's quite something to walk out on stage in front of 20,000 people.*

quits /kwɪts/ *adj informal* **1** **be quits** *BrE* if two people are quits, neither one owes anything to the other; ▣ **straight**: *I'll give you £10, and then we're quits.* **2** **call it quits a)** to agree that a debt or argument is settled: *Just give me $20 and we'll call it quits.* **b)** to stop doing something: *After twenty-five years as a teacher, he's decided to call it quits.*

quit·ter /ˈkwɪtə $ -ər/ *n* [C] *informal* someone who does not have the determination or courage to finish something that is difficult

quiv·er¹ /ˈkwɪvə $ -ər/ *v* [I] to shake slightly because you are cold, or because you feel very afraid, angry, excited etc; ▣ **tremble**: *The child was quivering in her arms.* | *Her mouth quivered slightly as she turned away.* | **quiver with indignation/anger etc** *I lay there quivering with fear.* | *His voice was quivering with rage.*

quiv·er² *n* [C] **1** a slight trembling: **quiver of fear/anxiety/anticipation etc** *I felt a quiver of excitement run through me.* **2** a long case for carrying ARROWS

quix·ot·ic /kwɪkˈsɒtɪk $ -ˈsɑː-/ *adj* quixotic ideas or plans are not practical and are based on unreasonable hopes of improving the world: *This is a vast, exciting, and perhaps quixotic project.*

quiz¹ /kwɪz/ *n plural* **quizzes** [C] **1** a competition or game in which people have to answer questions: *a love quiz in a magazine* | *a **general knowledge quiz*** | **quiz show** *especially BrE: I get fed up with television quiz shows.* | **quiz night** *BrE: a quiz night held in the local pub* **2** *AmE* a short test that a teacher gives to a class: *a biology quiz* → POP QUIZ

quiz² *v* **quizzed, quizzing** [T] to ask someone a lot of questions; ▣ **question**: **quiz sb about sth** *Four men have been quizzed about the murder, but no one has yet been charged.* | **quiz sb on/over sth** *They quizzed me on my involvement in the scheme.*

quiz·mas·ter /ˈkwɪzˌmɑːstə $ -ˌmæstər/ *n* [C] *BrE* someone who asks people questions during a quiz; ▣ **question master**

quiz·zi·cal /ˈkwɪzɪkəl/ *adj* a quizzical expression is one that shows that you do not understand something and perhaps think it is slightly amusing: **a quizzical look/expression/smile** *He sat and watched her, a quizzical look on his face.* —**quizzically** /-kli/ *adv*

quo /kwəʊ $ kwoʊ/ → QUID PRO QUO, STATUS QUO

quoit /kwɔɪt, kɔɪt/ *n* **1** **quoits** [U] a game in which you throw rings over a small upright post **2** [C] the

Q

ring that you throw in this game   **3** [C] a small circle made of large vertical stones in ancient times

Quon·set hut /ˈkwɒnset ˌhʌt $ ˈkwɑːn-/ n [C] *AmE trademark* a long metal building with a curved roof where soldiers live or things are stored

Quorn /kwɔːn $ kwɔːrn/ n [U] *BrE trademark* a vegetable substance that you can use in cooking instead of meat

quo·rum /ˈkwɔːrəm/ n [singular] the smallest number of people who must be present at a meeting so that official decisions can be made: *We need a quorum of seven.*

quo·ta /ˈkwəʊtə $ ˈkwoʊ-/ n [C]
1 an official limit on the number or amount of something that is allowed in a particular period

> **impose/introduce a quota** (=officially start a quota)
> **set a quota** (=say what the quota for something will be)
> **lift/end/scrap a quota**
> **import/export quota**
> **strict quota**

[+on] *The government has **imposed quotas** on the export of timber.* | *The government has decided to **scrap quotas** on car imports.* | [+for] *Several countries have now **set quotas** for cod fishing.* | *There are plans to introduce **strict immigration quotas.***

2 an amount of something that someone is expected to do or achieve: [+of] *Each person was given a quota of tickets to sell.* | [+for] *In the 1990s the Navy couldn't **fill** its quota for new recruits.* | **meet/make/achieve a quota** *Workers only get paid if they make their quota.* | **sales/production quota** *They're worried that they won't achieve this year's sales quota.*

3 an amount of something that you think is fair, right, or normal; ⬛ **fair share**: [+of] *The committee has had **more than** its quota of problems.* | *I think I've had my quota of coffee for the day.*

4 *BrE* a particular number of votes that someone needs to get to be elected in an election

quot·a·ble /ˈkwəʊtəbəl $ ˈkwoʊ-/ adj a quotable remark or statement is interesting, clever, or amusing: *a speech full of witty, quotable phrases*

quo·ta·tion /kwəʊˈteɪʃən $ kwoʊ-/ n   **1** [C] a sentence or phrase from a book, speech etc which you repeat in a speech or piece of writing because it is interesting or amusing; ⬛ **quote**: [+from] *a quotation from the Bible* | *The following quotation is taken from a nineteenth century travel diary.* | *a dictionary of quotations*   **2** [C] a written statement of exactly how much money something will cost; → **estimate**: [+for] *Ask the builder to **give** you a written **quotation** for the job.* | *a quotation for car insurance* | *Get a couple of **quotations** from different companies before you decide which one to use.*   **3** [U] the act of quoting something that someone else has written or said

quo'tation ˌmark n [C usually plural] one of a pair of marks (' ') or (" ") that are used in writing to show that you are recording what someone has said; ⬛ **inverted comma** *BrE*

quote¹ [S2] [W3] /kwəʊt $ kwoʊt/ v
1 [I,T] to repeat exactly what someone else has said or written: [+from] *She quoted from a newspaper article.* | *He **quoted** a short **passage** from the Bible.* | *A military spokesman was **quoted as saying** that the border area is now safe.* | **quote sb on sth** *Can I quote you on that?*
2 [T] to give a piece of information that is written down somewhere: *You can order by phoning our hotline and quoting your credit card number.* | *He quoted a figure of 220 deaths each year from accidents in the home.*
3 [T] to give something as an example to support what you are saying; ⬛ **cite**: *Mr Jackson quoted the case of an elderly man who had been evicted from his home.* | **quote sth as sth** *He quoted the example of France as a country with an excellent rail service.* | *The nurses' union was **quoted as an example** of a responsible trade union.*
4 [T] to tell a customer the price you will charge them for a service or product: *They quoted a price of £15,000.* | **quote sth for sth** *The firm originally quoted £6,000 for the whole job.*
5 [T] to give the price of a share or CURRENCY: *The pound was quoted this morning at just under $1.46.* | *The company is now **quoted on the stock exchange** (=people can buy and sell shares in it).*
6 (I) **quote** *spoken* used when you are going to repeat what someone else has said, to emphasize that it is exactly the way they said it: *The minister said, quote: 'There will be no more tax increases this year.'*
7 **Quote ... unquote** *spoken* used at the beginning and end of a word or phrase that someone else has said or written, to emphasize that you are repeating it exactly

quote² [S2] n [C]
1 a sentence or phrase from a book, speech etc which you repeat in a speech or piece of writing because it is interesting or amusing; ⬛ **quotation**: [+from] *a quote from the minister's speech*
2 **in quotes** words that are in quotes are written with QUOTATION MARKS around them to show that someone said those words
3 a statement of how much it will probably cost to build or repair something; ⬛ **estimate**: *Always get a quote before proceeding with repair work.*

quoth /kwəʊθ $ kwoʊθ/ v [T] *old use* **quoth I/he/she etc** a way of saying 'I said', 'he said' etc

quo·tid·i·an /kwəʊˈtɪdiən $ kwoʊ-/ adj *literary* ordinary, and happening every day

quo·tient /ˈkwəʊʃənt $ ˈkwoʊ-/ n [C]   **1** the amount or degree of a quality, feeling etc in a person, thing, or situation: *Is all this healthy food supposed to increase my happiness quotient?*   **2** *technical* the number which is obtained when one number is divided by another

Qu·r'an /kɔːˈrɑːn, kə- $ kəˈræn, -ˈrɑːn/ n **the Qur'an** another spelling of KORAN (=the holy book of Islam)

q.v. *quod vide* used to tell readers to look in another place in the same book for a piece of information

qwert·y /ˈkwɜːti $ ˈkwɜːrti/ adj *especially BrE* a qwerty KEYBOARD on a computer or TYPEWRITER has the keys arranged in the usual way for English-speaking countries, with Q,W,E,R,T, and Y on the top row

Q

R, r

R, r /ɑː $ ɑːr/ *n plural* **R's, r's** **1** [C,U] the 18th letter of the English alphabet **2** [singular, U] *AmE* used to describe a film that has been officially approved as only suitable for people over 17 → **THREE R'S**

R **1** *AmE* the written abbreviation of *Republican*, used after a politician's name to show that he or she belongs to the Republican Party in the US; → **D**: *Steve Gunderson (R)* **2** *BrE* the written abbreviation of *regina* (=queen), used after the name of the queen of the United Kingdom: *Elizabeth R* **3** also **R.** the written abbreviation of *river*, used especially on maps → **R & B, R & D, R & R**

R & B /ˌɑːr ən ˈbiː/ *n* [U] *rhythm and blues* a style of popular music that is a mixture of BLUES and JAZZ

R & D /ˌɑːr ən ˈdiː/ *n* [U] *research and development* the part of a business concerned with studying new ideas and planning new products

R & R /ˌɑːr ənd ˈɑː $ -ˈɑːr/ *n* [U] *especially AmE rest and relaxation* a holiday, especially one given to people in the army, navy etc after a long period of hard work or during a war: *He was enjoying a few hard-earned days of R and R.*

rab·bi /ˈræbaɪ/ *n* [C] a Jewish priest

rab·bi·nate /ˈræbɪ̯nᵻt, -neɪt/ *n* **the rabbinate** rabbis considered together as a group

rab·bin·i·cal /rəˈbɪnɪkəl/ *adj* relating to the writings or teaching of rabbis

rab·bit¹ [S3] /ˈræbɪ̯t/ *n* **1** [C] a small animal with long ears and soft fur, that lives in a hole in the ground **2** [U] the fur or meat of a rabbit

rabbit² *v*

rabbit on *phr v BrE informal* to talk for a long time in an uninteresting or annoying way; ▣ **go on:** [+about] *He kept rabbiting on about the environment.*

rabbit punch *n* [C] *BrE* a quick hit on the back of the neck, done with the side of your hand

rabbit ,warren *n* [C] **1** an area under the ground where a lot of wild rabbits live; ▣ **warren;** → **bur-row** **2** a building with a lot of narrow passages, or a place with a lot of narrow streets, where you can easily get lost; ▣ **warren**

rab·ble /ˈræbəl/ *n* [singular] a noisy crowd of people: [+of] *a rabble of angry youths*

rabble-,rousing *n* [U] when someone deliberately makes a crowd of people angry and violent, especially in order to achieve political aims: *He accused union leaders of rabble-rousing.* —**rabble-rousing** *adj*: *a rabble-rousing speech* —**rabble-rouser** *n* [C]

rab·id /ˈræbɪ̯d, ˈreɪ-/ *adj* **1** having very extreme and unreasonable opinions: *a group of rabid right-wing fanatics* **2** a rabid animal is suffering from rabies

ra·bies /ˈreɪbiːz/ *n* [U] a very dangerous disease that affects dogs and other animals, and that you can catch if you are bitten by an infected animal

rac·coon, racoon /rəˈkuːn, ræ- $ ræ-/ *n* **1** [C] a small North American animal with black fur around its eyes and black and grey rings on its tail **2** [U] the skin and thick fur of a raccoon: *a raccoon coat*

race¹ [S2] [W2] /reɪs/ *n*

1 **SPORT** [C] a competition in which people or animals compete to run, drive etc fastest and finish first: **in a race** *He will be the youngest runner in the race.* | *She finished second in the race.* | [+between] *the annual boat race between Oxford and Cambridge Universities* | *Over 80 cars will* **take part in** *the race.* | *She has* **won** *her last four races.* | *There are only three days to go until*

the **big race** (=important race).

2 **PEOPLE** **a)** [C,U] one of the main groups that humans can be divided into according to the colour of their skin and other physical features; → **ethnic group**: *The school welcomes children* **of all races.** | *a person of* **mixed race** | *The law forbids discrimination on the grounds of race or religion.* → **HUMAN RACE b)** [singular] *informal* a group of people who are similar in some way: [+of] *The 1960s produced a new race of young novelists.* | *Are schools breeding* (=producing) *a race of children incapable of making decisions for themselves?*

3 **GET/DO STH FIRST** [singular] a situation in which one group of people tries to obtain or achieve something before another group does: **the race to do sth** *More and more drug companies are joining the race to beat cancer.* | *The race is on* to develop more environmentally friendly forms of energy. → **ARMS RACE, RAT RACE**

4 **DO STH QUICKLY** [singular] a situation in which you have to do something very quickly because you have very little time available: **a race to do sth** *It is now a race to find the killer.* | **race against time/against the clock** *The pilot then began a desperate race against time to land the plane before it ran out of fuel.*

5 **PRIZE/POWER** [singular] a situation in which people are competing with each other to win a prize or obtain a position of power: [+for] *Mr Bird has now officially joined the race for the White House.* | *He* **is no longer in the race for** *academic awards.* | **race to do sth** *the race to host the next Olympic Games*

6 **HORSE RACE** **the races** an occasion when horse races are held: **at the races** *We spent a day at the races.* → **play the race card** at PLAY¹ (14)

race² *v*

1 **SPORT** **a)** [I,T] to compete against someone or something in a race: [+against] *She'll be racing against some of the world's top athletes.* | [+in] *Stevens will not be racing in the final due to a knee injury.* | **race sb up/down sth etc** *I'll race you to the end of the road.* **b)** [T] to use an animal or a vehicle to compete in a race: *He will be racing a Ferrari in this year's Formula One championships.*

2 **MOVE QUICKLY** [I,T always + adv/prep] to move very quickly or take someone or something to a place very quickly: *He raced into the village on his bike.* | *I had to race home for my bag.* | **race sb to sth etc** *She was raced to hospital.* | **race to do sth** *He raced to meet her.*

3 **DO STH QUICKLY** [I] to try to do something very quickly because you want to be the first to do it, or because there is very little time available: **race to do sth** *Investors are racing to buy shares in the new hi-tech companies.* | **race against time/the clock** *The astronauts are racing against time to repair the spaceship.*

4 **HEART/MIND** [I] if your heart or mind races, it works harder and faster than usual, for example because you are afraid or excited: *My heart was racing and my knees shook uncontrollably.* | *My mind was racing, trying to think where I had seen him before.*

5 **ENGINE** [I] if an engine races, it runs too fast

race car *n* [C] *AmE* a RACING CAR

race·card /ˈreɪskɑːd $ -kɑːrd/ *n* [C] *BrE* a list of the races that will happen at a horse racing event, and the horses that will take part in each race

race·course /ˈreɪskɔːs $ -kɔːrs/ *n* [C] *BrE* a grass track on which horses race; ▣ **racetrack** *AmE*

race·go·er /ˈreɪsɡəʊə $ -ɡoʊər/ *n* [C] *BrE* someone who goes regularly to watch horse races

race·horse /ˈreɪshɔːs $ -hɔːrs/ *n* [C] a horse specially bred and trained for racing

race ,meeting *n* [C] *BrE* an occasion when horse races are held at a particular place

rac·er /ˈreɪsə $ -ər/ *n* [C] someone who competes in a race

race re,lations *n* [plural] the relationship that exists between people from different countries, religions etc who are now living in the same place: *We need to do more to promote good race relations.* | *Community leaders are working to improve race relations in the city.*

race riot n [C] violent fighting between people of different countries, religions etc who now live in the same country

race-track /'reɪs-træk/ n [C] **1** a track on which runners or cars race **2** AmE a grass track on which horses race; ◨ **racecourse** BrE

ra·cial /'reɪʃəl/ adj
1 [only before noun] relating to the relationships between different races of people who now live in the same country or area

racial discrimination/prejudice/harassment/hatred
racial attack/violence/abuse
racial segregation (=when people of different races are kept apart)
racial equality/harmony
racial tension

*a victim of **racial discrimination** | This part of the community needs to be protected from **racial prejudice**. | evidence of **racial harassment** | the campaign for **racial equality** | the need for tolerance and **racial harmony***

2 relating to the various races that humans can be divided into; → **ethnic**: *a broad range of racial and ethnic groups | people of different racial origin* —**racially** adv: *They live in a racially mixed area. | Police officers believe the attack was racially motivated.*

ra·cial·is·m /'reɪʃəlɪzəm/ n [U] BrE old-fashioned RACISM —**racialist** n, adj

rac·ing¹ [S3] /'reɪsɪŋ/ n [U]
1 the sport of racing horses; ◨ **horse racing**: *watching the racing on television | today's racing results* → FLAT RACING
2 car/bike/greyhound etc racing the sport of racing cars etc

racing² adj [only before noun] designed or bred to go very fast and be used for racing: *racing pigeons | a racing yacht*

racing car n [C] a very fast car that is specially designed for races

ra·cis·m /'reɪsɪzəm/ n [U] **1** unfair treatment of people, or violence against them, because they belong to a different race from your own: *The government has promised to continue the fight against racism. | the problem of racism in schools* **2** the belief that different races of people have different characters and abilities, and that your own race is the best

rac·ist /'reɪsɪst/ n [C] someone who believes that people of their own race are better than others, and who treats people from other races unfairly and sometimes violently – used to show disapproval: *He denied being a racist.* —**racist** adj: *the victim of a racist attack | racist violence | racist remarks*

rack¹ /ræk/ n [C] **1** a frame or shelf that has bars or hooks on which you can put things: *a wine rack | a magazine rack* → LUGGAGE RACK, ROOF-RACK **2 the rack** a piece of equipment that was used in the past to make people suffer severe pain by stretching their bodies: *Thousands of people were tortured on the rack.* **3 on the rack** BrE informal in a very difficult situation: *The company is now well and truly on the rack.* **4 go to rack and ruin** if a building goes to rack and ruin, it gradually gets into a very bad condition because no one has looked after it: *The house had been left to go to rack and ruin.* **5** AmE a three-sided frame used for arranging the balls at the start of a game of SNOOKER or POOL **6 a rack of lamb/pork** a fairly large piece of meat from the side of an animal, that contains several RIB bones **7 off the rack** AmE if you can buy something off the rack, you can buy it in a shop rather than having it specially made; ◨ **off the peg** BrE: *A lot of designer clothes are now available off the rack.*

rack² v **1** [T usually passive] to make someone suffer great mental or physical pain: *Great sobs racked her body.* | **be racked by/with sth** *Her face was racked with pain. | Liza was racked by guilt.* **2 rack your brains** to try very hard to remember or think of something: *I*

racked my brains, trying to remember his name.

rack sth ⇔ up phr v informal to get a number or amount of something, especially a number of points in a competition: *He racked up 41 points.*

rack·et /'rækɪt/ n **1** [singular] informal a loud noise: *The old machine used to make an awful racket.* **2** [C] informal a dishonest way of obtaining money, such as by threatening people or selling them illegal goods: **drugs/gambling/smuggling etc racket** *Police believe he is involved in an international smuggling racket.*; → **protection racket** at PROTECTION (5) **3** [C] also **racquet** a specially shaped piece of wood or metal that you use for hitting the ball in games such as tennis, that has a circle filled with tight strings at one end; → **bat**: *a tennis racket* → see picture at BAT¹

rack·e·teer /,rækɪ'tɪə $ -'tɪr/ n [C] someone who earns money through crime and illegal activities

rack·e·teer·ing /,rækɪ'tɪərɪŋ $ -'tɪr-/ n [U] when someone earns money through crime and illegal activities: *people involved in smuggling and racketeering | He has been arrested on racketeering charges.*

rac·on·teur /,rækɒn'tɜː $ -kɑːn'tɜːr/ n [C] formal someone who is good at telling stories in an interesting and amusing way

ra·coon /rə'kuːn, ræ- $ ræ-/ n another spelling of RACCOON

rac·quet /'rækɪt/ n [C] another spelling of RACKET (3)

rac·quet·ball /'rækɪtbɔːl $ -bɒːl/ n [U] an indoor game in which two or four players hit a small ball against the four walls of the court; → **squash**

rac·y /'reɪsi/ adj racy writing is exciting and entertaining and often about sex: *a racy novel*

rad /ræd/ adj informal exciting or interesting: *Have you guys seen Wendy's new place? It's so rad.*

ra·dar /'reɪdɑː $ -ɑːr/ n [C,U] a piece of equipment that uses radio waves to find the position of things and watch their movement; → **sonar**: *The coastline can now be monitored by radar. | We could see the plane quite clearly on the radar screen.*

radar trap n [C] a set of equipment that uses radar to catch drivers who are going faster than the legal speed limit; → **speed trap**

rad·dled /'rædld/ adj BrE someone who looks raddled looks old or tired: *her raddled face*

ra·di·al /'reɪdiəl/ adj arranged in a circular shape with bars or lines coming from the centre: *radial roads leading out of the city centre*

radial tyre BrE; **radial tire** AmE n [C] a car tyre with wires inside the rubber that go completely around the wheel to make it stronger and safer

ra·di·ance /'reɪdiəns/ n [U] literary **1** great happiness that shows in someone's face and makes them look attractive: *a young face full of radiance* **2** a soft gentle light: *the moon's radiance*

ra·di·ant /'reɪdiənt/ adj **1** full of happiness and love, in a way that shows in your face and makes you look attractive: *She looked radiant in a white silk dress.* | **radiant smile** | [+with] *They were both radiant with happiness.* **2** [only before noun] literary very bright: *a lovely day with clear blue skies and radiant sun* **3** [only before noun] technical radiant heat or energy is sent out in the form of waves —**radiantly** adv: *She looked radiantly beautiful.*

ra·di·ate /'reɪdieɪt/ v **1** [I,T] if someone radiates a feeling, or if it radiates from them, it is very easy to see that this is how they feel: *He radiated calm confidence.* | [+from] *Kindness radiated from her.* **2** [I always + adv/prep, T] if something radiates light or heat, or if light or heat radiates from something, the light or heat is sent out in all directions: *The log fire radiated a warm cosy glow.* | [+from] *Heat radiated from the glowing coals.* **3** [I always + adv/prep] if things radiate

R

from a central point, they spread out in different directions from that point: [+out/from] *There were tiny lines radiating from the corners of her eyes.*

ra·di·a·tion /ˌreɪdiˈeɪʃən/ *n* [U] **1** a form of energy that comes especially from NUCLEAR reactions, which in large amounts is very harmful to living things: *An accident at the power station could result in large amounts of radiation being released.* | *a lethal dose of radiation* **2** energy in the form of heat or light that is sent out as waves that you cannot see: *Sun creams work by blocking harmful ultraviolet radiation.*

radi'ation ˌsickness *n* [U] an illness that is caused when your body receives too much radiation

ra·di·a·tor /ˈreɪdieɪtə $ -ər/ *n* [C] **1** a thin metal container that is fastened to a wall and through which hot water passes to provide heat for a room **2** the part of a car or aircraft which stops the engine from getting too hot

rad·i·cal¹ W3 /ˈrædɪkəl/ *adj*
1 CHANGE/DIFFERENCE a radical change or difference is very big and important: *They are proposing radical changes to the way the company is run.* | *a radical reform of the tax system* | *There are radical differences between the two organizations.*
2 OPINIONS radical ideas are very new and different, and are against what most people think or believe; → conservative: *He has put forward some very radical ideas.* | *I was shocked by her radical views.* | *a radical approach to education*
3 PEOPLE someone who is radical has ideas that are very new and different, and against what most people think or believe: *a radical left-wing politician* | *a radical feminist*
4 GOOD *AmE informal* very good or enjoyable: *That was one radical party last night!* —**radically** /-kli/ *adv*: *a radically different method of production* | *a radically new approach to the problem*

radical² *n* [C] someone who has new and different ideas, especially someone who wants complete social and political change; → conservative: *radicals on the extreme left wing of the party* —**radicalism** *n* [U]

rad·i·cal·ize also **-ise** *BrE* /ˈrædɪkəlaɪz/ *v* [T] to make people accept new and different ideas, especially ideas about complete social and political change

ra·dic·chi·o /ræˈdiːtʃiəʊ, -kiəʊ $ -kiəʊ/ *n* [U] a type of plant used in SALADS that is red and has a bitter taste

rad·i·i /ˈreɪdiaɪ/ *n* the plural of RADIUS

ra·di·o¹ S1 W2 /ˈreɪdiəʊ $ -diəʊ/ *n*
1 a) [C] a piece of electronic equipment which you use to listen to programmes that are broadcast, such as music and news: **turn/switch the radio on/off** *I sat down and turned on the radio.* **b)** [U] programmes that are broadcast on the radio: *I don't really listen to the radio very much.* | **on the radio** *Did you hear the interview with the Prime Minister on the radio this morning?* | **radio programme/show** *He's got his own radio show now.* | **local/national radio** *She works for a local radio station.*
2 a) [C] a piece of electronic equipment, for example on a plane or ship, which can send and receive spoken messages: **over the radio** *We received a call for help over the ship's radio.* **b)** [U] when messages are sent or received in this way: **by radio** *We should be able to reach them by radio.* | *We've lost radio contact with the plane.*

radio² *v* [I,T] to send a message using a radio: [+for] *The ship radioed for help.* | **radio sb for sth** *We radioed London for permission to land.*

radio

radio- /ˈreɪdiəʊ $ -diəʊ/ *prefix technical* using radio waves: *radiopaging* (=calling people by radio)

ra·di·o·ac·tive /ˌreɪdiəʊˈæktɪv◂ $ -diəʊ-/ *adj* a radioactive substance is dangerous because it contains RADIATION (=a form of energy that can harm living things): *the problem of how to dispose of radioactive waste* | *a consignment of highly radioactive plutonium*

ˌradioactive ˈdating *n* [U] *AmE* a scientific method of calculating the age of a very old object by measuring the amount of a certain substance in it; ■ **carbon dating** *BrE*

ˌradioactive ˈwaste *n* [U] harmful radioactive substances that remain after energy has been produced in a NUCLEAR REACTOR

ra·di·o·ac·tiv·i·ty /ˌreɪdiəʊækˈtɪvÖti $ -diəʊ-/ *n* [U] the sending out of RADIATION (=a form of energy) when the NUCLEUS (=central part) of an atom has broken apart: *the discovery of radioactivity* | *high levels of radioactivity*

ˈradio ˌbeacon *n* [C] a tower that sends out radio signals to help aircraft stay on the correct course

ra·di·o·car·bon dat·ing /ˌreɪdiəʊkɑːbən ˈdeɪtɪŋ $ -diəʊkɑːr-/ *n* [U] *formal* CARBON DATING

ˌradio-casˈsette ˌplayer *n* [C] a piece of equipment that contains both a radio and a CASSETTE PLAYER

ˌradio-conˈtrolled *adj* controlled from far away using radio signals: *a radio-controlled toy car*

ra·di·o·gram /ˈreɪdiəʊɡræm $ -diəʊ-/ *n* [C] *BrE* a piece of furniture, popular in the 1950s, which contained a radio and a record player

ra·di·og·ra·pher /ˌreɪdiˈɒɡrəfə $ -ˈɑːɡrəfər/ *n* [C] someone whose job is to take X-RAY photographs of the inside of people's bodies, or who treats people for illnesses using an X-ray machine

ra·di·og·ra·phy /ˌreɪdiˈɒɡrəfi $ -ˈɑːɡ-/ *n* [U] the taking of X-RAY photographs of the inside of people's bodies for medical purposes

ra·di·ol·o·gist /ˌreɪdiˈɒlədʒ\u0323st $ -ˈɑː-/ *n* [C] a hospital doctor who is trained in the use of RADIATION to treat people

ra·di·ol·o·gy /ˌreɪdiˈɒlədʒi $ -ˈɑː-/ *n* [U] the study and medical use of RADIATION

ˌradio-ˈtelephone *n* [C] a telephone that works by sending and receiving radio signals and can be used in a car, boat etc

ˌradio ˈtelescope *n* [C] a piece of equipment that collects RADIO WAVES from space and is used to find stars and other objects in space

ra·di·o·ther·a·py /ˌreɪdiəʊˈθerəpi $ -diəʊ-/ *n* [U] treatment of illnesses using RADIATION; → **radiation therapy** —**radiotherapist** *n* [C]

ˈradio ˌwave *n* [C usually plural] a form of electric energy that can move through air or space

rad·ish /ˈrædɪʃ/ *n* [C] a small vegetable whose red or white root is eaten raw and has a strong spicy taste

ra·di·um /ˈreɪdiəm/ *n* [U] a white metal that is RADIOACTIVE and is used in the treatment of diseases such as CANCER. It is a chemical ELEMENT: symbol Ra

ra·di·us /ˈreɪdiəs/ *n plural* **radii** /-diaɪ/ [C] **1** the distance from the centre to the edge of a circle, or a line drawn from the centre to the edge; → **diameter 2** an area that covers a particular distance in all directions from a central point: *The shock of the explosion was felt over a radius of forty miles.* | **within a 10-mile/200-metre etc radius** *There are more than a dozen golf courses within a 15-mile radius of St Andrews.* **3** *technical* the outer bone of the lower part of your arm

ra·don /ˈreɪdɒn $ -dɑːn/ *n* [U] a RADIOACTIVE gas that is used in the treatment of diseases such as CANCER. It is a chemical ELEMENT: symbol Rn

rad·waste /ˈrædweɪst/ *n* [U] *AmE* RADIOACTIVE WASTE

RAF /ˌɑːr eɪ ˈef, ræf/ *n* **the RAF** *the Royal Air Force* the British AIR FORCE

raf·fi·a /ˈræfiə/ n [U] a soft substance like string that comes from the leaves of a PALM tree and is used for making baskets, hats, MATS etc

raf·fish /ˈræfɪʃ/ adj literary behaving or dressing in a way which is not respected by many people but which is still confident and attractive: an interesting character with a raffish air —**raffishly** adv —**raffishness** n [U]

raf·fle¹ [S3] /ˈræfəl/ n [C] a competition or game in which people buy numbered tickets and can win prizes: a woman selling **raffle tickets**

raffle² also **raffle off** v [T] to offer something as a prize in a raffle

raft /rɑːft $ ræft/ n [C]   **1** a flat floating structure, usually made of pieces of wood tied together, used as a boat   **2 a raft of sth** a large number of things: The company has launched a whole raft of new software products.   **3** a flat floating structure that you can sit on, jump from etc when you are swimming   **4** a small flat rubber boat filled with air, used for example if a boat sinks

raf·ter /ˈrɑːftə $ ˈræftər/ n [C usually plural] one of the large sloping pieces of wood that form the structure of a roof: The club was **packed to the rafters** (=very full).

raft·ing /ˈrɑːftɪŋ $ ˈræf-/ n [U] the activity of travelling on a raft, especially as a sport: white-water rafting → see picture at OUTDOOR

rag¹ /ræg/ n
1 CLOTH [C,U] a small piece of old cloth, for example one used for cleaning things: He wiped his boots dry with an old rag. | an oily rag
2 NEWSPAPER [C] informal a newspaper, especially one that you think is not particularly important or of good quality: He writes for the **local rag**.
3 in **rags** wearing very old torn clothes: Children in rags begged money from the tourists.
4 from **rags to riches** becoming very rich after starting your life very poor: He likes to tell people of his rise from rags to riches. → RAGS-TO-RICHES
5 MUSIC [C] a piece of RAGTIME music
6 STUDENTS' EVENT [C] BrE an event organized by students every year in order to make money for people who are poor, sick etc: rag week → **glad rags** at GLAD (7); → **like a red rag to a bull** at RED¹ (5); → **lose your rag** at LOSE (11)

rag² v **ragged**, **ragging** [T] BrE old-fashioned to laugh at someone or play tricks on them; ⊟ **tease**

ra·ga /ˈrɑːɡə/ n [C]   **1** a piece of Indian music based on an ancient pattern of notes   **2** one of the ancient patterns of notes that are used in Indian music

rag·a·muf·fin /ˈræɡəˌmʌfˌn/ n [C] literary a dirty young child wearing torn clothes

ˌrag-and-ˈbone-man n plural **rag-and-bone-men** [C] BrE a man who goes around the streets buying and collecting old clothes and other things that people no longer want

rag·bag /ˈræɡbæɡ/ n [singular] BrE a mixture of very different things that do not seem to fit together well: [+of] a ragbag of leftover bits of food

ˌrag ˈdoll / $ˈ. ./ n [C] a soft DOLL made of cloth

rage¹ /reɪdʒ/ n [C,U]   **1** a strong feeling of uncontrollable anger: Sobbing with rage, Carol was taken to the hospital. | **in a rage** Sam became quite frightening when he was in a rage. | **cry/scream/roar etc of rage** Just then, she heard Mr Evan's bellow of rage. | **red/dark/ purple with rage** His face was red with rage. | **trembling/ shaking with rage** Forester stared at his car, trembling with rage. | **seething/incandescent with rage** (=as angry as a person can possibly be) Animal rights supporters were incandescent with rage. | Richens was 17 when he **flew into a rage** and stabbed another teenager.   **2 be all the rage** informal to be very popular or fashionable: DiCaprio became all the rage after starring in the film 'Titanic'.   **3 rage for sth** a situation in which something is very popular or fashionable: the rage for mobile phones

rage² v   **1** [I,T] written to feel very angry about something and show this in the way you behave or speak: [+at/against] He was sorry he had raged at her earlier. | 'How was I to know!' Jenny raged.   **2** [I] if something such as a battle, a disagreement, or a storm rages, it continues with great violence or strong emotions: Civil war has been raging in the country for years. | A debate is raging about what form pensions should take. | Outside, a storm was raging. | [+on] The battle raged on (=continued).   **3** [I] if a fire or illness rages, it spreads fast and is hard to control: The fire raged for twelve hours and fifteen people died. | A great cholera epidemic raged across Europe in 1831.   **4** [I] informal to have fun with a group of people in a wild and uncontrolled way: We couldn't wait to go out and rage.

-rage /reɪdʒ/ suffix [in nouns] **road-rage/air-rage etc** when someone becomes extremely angry and violent while they are driving, on a plane etc: He was attacked in a road-rage incident.

rag·ga /ˈræɡə/ n [U] a form of popular music from the West Indies

rag·ged /ˈræɡˌd/ adj
1 CLOTHES ETC also **rag·ged·y** /ˈræɡˌdi/ especially AmE torn and in bad condition: the ragged blankets on the bed | a raggedy hat
2 PEOPLE wearing clothes that are old and torn: Crowds of ragged children played among the rocks.
3 UNEVEN also **raggedy** having a rough uneven edge or surface: The old photograph looked a little ragged at the edges. | a ragged hole | raggedy hair
4 NOT REGULAR not regular or together: The crowd gave a ragged cheer. | ragged breathing
5 TIRED informal tired after using a lot of effort: He looked ragged, so I told him to go to bed. | He **ran** United's defence **ragged** (=made them do a lot of work).
6 be on the ragged edge AmE informal to be feeling very tired or upset —**raggedly** adv: raggedly dressed | She was breathing raggedly. —**raggedness** n [U]

rag·ing /ˈreɪdʒɪŋ/ adj [only before noun]   **1** very great and hard to control: a raging appetite | I was in a raging temper.   **2** continuing strongly and showing no signs of ending: a raging debate | raging inflation | The show was a raging success.   **3** a raging headache etc is very painful: Richard developed a raging headache and had to lie down. | a raging fever (=a very high body temperature)   **4** continuing or moving with great natural force: a raging storm | a raging sea | The fire had become a raging blaze.

rag·lan /ˈræɡlən/ adj if a coat, SWEATER etc has raglan sleeves, the sleeves are joined with a sloping line from the arm to the neck

ra·gout /ræˈɡuː, ˈræɡuː $ ræˈɡuː/ n [C,U] a mixture of vegetables and meat boiled together; ⊟ **stew**

ˌrags-to-ˈriches adj [only before noun] a rags-to-riches story is about someone who becomes very rich after starting life very poor

rag·tag /ˈræɡtæɡ/ adj [only before noun] informal a ragtag group is not tidy or properly organized: a ragtag fighting force

rag·time /ˈræɡtaɪm/ n [U] a type of music and dancing that has a strong beat and was popular in the US in the early part of the 20th century

ˈrag trade n **the rag trade** BrE informal the business of making and selling clothes, especially women's clothes; ⊟ **the fashion industry**

rag·weed /ˈræɡwiːd/ n [U] a North American plant that produces a substance which causes HAY FEVER

rag·wort /ˈræɡwɜːt $ -wɜːrt/ n [U] a common plant with yellow flowers, and leaves with uneven edges

raid¹ /reɪd/ n [C]   **1** a short attack on a place by soldiers, planes, or ships, intended to cause damage but not take control: a bombing raid | an **air raid** warning siren | [+on/against] The colonel led a successful raid against a rebel base. | **launch/carry out/stage a raid** The army launched several cross-border raids last night. →

R

AIR RAID **2** a surprise visit made to a place by the police to search for something illegal: *a police raid* | *an FBI raid* | [+on] *Four people were arrested during a raid on a house in London.* | *a dawn raid* (=one made very early in the morning) **3** an attack by criminals on a building where they believe they can steal money or drugs: *a bank raid* | [+on] *an armed raid on a shop in Glasgow* → RAM-RAIDING **4** *technical* an attempt by a company to buy enough SHARES in another company to take control of it

raid² v [T] **1** if police raid a place, they make a surprise visit to search for something illegal: *Police found illegal weapons when they raided five homes yesterday.* **2** to make a sudden military attack on a place: *air bases on the mainland from which the island could be raided* | *raiding party* (=a group taking part in an attack) **3** to go into a place and steal things: *A gang of thieves raided three homes in the area.* **4** to go to a place that has supplies of food or drink and take some because you are hungry: *Peter went into the kitchen to raid the fridge.*

raid·er /'reɪdə $ -ər/ n [C] someone who goes into a place and steals things: *an armed raider* | *Masked raiders carried out a bank robbery today.*

rail¹ S2 W2 /reɪl/ n
1 [U] the railway system; → **train**: *the American rail system* | *a high-speed rail network* | *Passengers want a better rail service.* | *the Channel Tunnel and its rail links with London* | *by rail We continued our journey by rail.* | *I need to buy a rail ticket.* | *cheap rail fares*
2 [C] one of the two long metal tracks fastened to the ground that trains move along
3 [C] a bar that is fastened along or around something, especially to stop you from going somewhere or from falling: *Several passengers were leaning against the ship's rail.* → GUARDRAIL, HANDRAIL
4 [C] a bar that you use to hang things on: *a towel rail* | *a curtain rail*
5 go off the rails *informal* to start behaving in a strange or socially unacceptable way: *At 17 he suddenly went off the rails and started stealing.*
6 back on the rails happening or functioning normally again: *The coach was credited with putting the team back on the rails.*

rail² v **1** [T] to enclose or separate an area with rails; → **cordon off**: *rail sth off/in The police railed off the area where the accident happened.* **2** [I,T] *formal* to complain angrily about something, especially something that you think is very unfair: [+against/at] *Consumers rail against the way companies fix prices.*

rail·card /'reɪlkɑːd $ -kɑːrd/ n [C] *BrE* a small card that allows you to travel by train at a lower price than the usual price: *a student railcard*

rail·head /'reɪlhed/ n [C] the end of a railway line

rail·ing /'reɪlɪŋ/ n [C] **1** also **railings** [plural] a metal fence that is made of a series of upright bars: *a small park surrounded by railings* → see picture at FENCE¹; → see picture at TOWN **2** one of the bars in some railings

rail·le·ry /'reɪləri/ n [U] *formal* friendly joking about someone: *affectionate raillery*

rail·road¹ /'reɪlrəʊd $ -roʊd/ n [C] *AmE* a railway or the railway: *The supplies were sent on the railroad.* | *a railroad station*

railroad² v [T] to force or persuade someone do something without giving them enough time to think about it: *railroad sb into doing sth The workers were railroaded into signing the agreement.*

railroad ‚crossing n [C] *AmE* a LEVEL CROSSING

rail trail n [C] *AmE* a path that used to be a railway track but that has been covered with a hard surface for people to walk, run, or ride bicycles on

rail·way S2 W2 /'reɪlweɪ/ n [C] *BrE* a system of tracks along which trains run, or a system of trains; ▤ **railroad** *AmE*: *a railway company*

'railway line n [C] *BrE* **1** one of the two metal tracks fixed to the ground that trains move along; ▤ **railroad track, train track** *AmE* **2** a part of the railway system that connects two places; ▤ **railroad line** *AmE*: *an old disused railway line*

rail·way·man /'reɪlweɪmən/ n plural **railwaymen** /-mən/ [C] *BrE* someone who works on a train or railway

'railway ‚station n [C] *BrE* a place where trains stop for passengers to get on and off; ▤ **train station**; ▤ **railroad station** *AmE*: *I'll meet you outside the main railway station.*

rai·ment /'reɪmənt/ n [U] *literary* clothes

rain¹ S2 W2 /reɪn/ n
1 [U] water that falls in small drops from clouds in the sky: *a night of wind and rain* | *in the rain I left my bicycle out in the rain.* | *heavy/torrential/pouring rain* (=a lot of rain) *There will be heavy rain in most parts of the country.* | *The light rain had stopped.* | *a heavy shower of rain* | *An inch of rain fell in an hour.* | *As the first drops of rain fell, they ran for cover.* | *It was pouring with rain* (=it was raining very hard) *and Laura only had a thin dress on.* | *It looks like rain* (=there are dark rain clouds), *so let's go inside.* → ACID RAIN, RAIN DROP, RAINY
2 the rains heavy rain that falls during a particular period in the year in tropical countries; ▤ **monsoon**: *Last year, the rains came on time in April.*
3 rain of sth a large number of things falling or moving through the air together: *The archers sent a rain of arrows towards the enemy.*
4 (come) rain or shine *spoken* whatever happens or whatever the weather is like: *Don't worry. We'll be there – rain or shine.* —**rainless** adj → **right as rain** at RIGHT¹ (9)

rain² v **1 it rains** if it rains, drops of water fall from clouds in the sky: *Outside it was still raining.* | *It's starting to rain.* | *rain heavily/hard It must have rained quite hard last night.* | *it's raining cats and dogs spoken* (=it is raining very hard) **2 rain (down) blows/blows rain down** if you rain blows onto someone, you hit them many times: *She attacked the man, raining blows on his head and shoulders.* **3 it never rains but it pours** *spoken* used to say that as soon as one thing goes wrong, a lot of other things go wrong as well

rain down phr v to fall in large quantities: [+on] *Bombs rained down on the city.*

be rained off *BrE*; **be rained out** *AmE* phr v if an event or activity is rained off or rained out, it has to stop because there is too much rain: *The match was rained off.*

rain·bow /'reɪnbəʊ $ -boʊ/ n [C] a large curve of different colours that can appear in the sky when there is both sun and rain

'rain check n [C] **1 take a rain check (on sth)** *informal especially AmE* used to say that you will do something in the future but not now: *'Care for a drink?' 'I'll take a rain check, thanks.'* **2** *AmE* a ticket for an outdoor event, such as a sports game, that you can use again if it rains and the action stops

rain·coat /'reɪnkəʊt $ -koʊt/ n [C] a coat that you wear to protect yourself from rain

'rain drop, rain·drop /'reɪndrɒp $ -drɑːp/ n [C] a single drop of rain

rain·fall /'reɪnfɔːl $ -fɒːl/ n [C,U] the amount of rain that falls on an area in a particular period of time: *We've had a long period of low rainfall.* | *The city has received only half its average rainfall of four inches.*

'rain ‚forest, rain·for·est /'reɪnfɒrɪst $ -fɔː-, -fɑː-/ n [C,U] a tropical forest with tall trees that are very close together, growing in an area where it rains a lot: *the destruction of the rain forest*

'rain gauge n [C] an instrument that is used for measuring the amount of rain that falls somewhere

rain·proof /'reɪnpruːf/ adj able to keep rain out; → **waterproof**: *a rainproof jacket*

rain·storm /'reɪnstɔːm $ -ɔːrm/ n [C] a sudden heavy fall of rain; ▤ **downpour**

rain·y /ˈreɪni/ adj **1** a rainy period of time is one when it rains a lot: *a cold **rainy day** in October* | *I hate **rainy weather**.* | *the **rainy season*** **2 save sth for a rainy day** to save something, especially money, for a time when you will need it

raise¹ S2 W1 /reɪz/ v [T]
1 MOVE HIGHER to move or lift something to a higher position, place, or level: *Can you raise the torch so I can see?* | *William raised his hat and smiled at her.* | ***Raise your hand** if you know the right answer.*
2 INCREASE to increase an amount, number, or level; ◄ lower: *Many shops have raised their prices.* | *The university is working to raise the number of students from state schools.* | *a campaign to **raise awareness** of meningitis* | *Dr Hayward intends to **raise** the museum's **profile*** (=make it more well-known).
3 COLLECT MONEY to collect money that you can use to do a particular job or help people: *The Trust hopes to raise $1 million to buy land.* | *They are **raising funds** to help needy youngsters.* | *a concert to **raise money** for charity* → FUNDRAISING
4 IMPROVE to improve the quality or standard of something: *Changing the law cannot raise standards.* | *The team need to raise their game.*
5 START A SUBJECT to begin to talk or write about a subject that you want to be considered or a question that you think should be answered; ◄ bring up: *He did not raise the subject again.* | *I'd like to raise the issue of publicity.* | *Betty **raised** the important **question** of who will be in charge.*
6 CAUSE A REACTION to cause a particular emotion or reaction: *This attack **raises fears** of increased violence against foreigners.* | *The way the research was carried out **raises doubts** about the results.*
7 MOVE EYES OR FACE to move your eyes, head, or face so that you are looking up; ◄ lower: *Albert raised his eyes and stared at Ruth.* | *'No,' he said without raising his head.*
8 MOVE UPRIGHT also **raise up** to move or lift yourself into an upright position; ◄ lower: **raise yourself** *Adele raised herself from the pillows.* | *He raised himself up on one elbow to watch.*
9 CHILDREN especially AmE to look after your children and help them grow; ◄ bring up BrE: *Stan's dad died, leaving his mother to raise three sons alone.* | *It was time for Dean to settle down and **raise a family**.* | *Anne married a Jew, despite being raised a Catholic.* | *The new generation was the first to be raised on processed food.* | *Camus was **born and raised** in Algeria.*
10 raise a smile to smile when you are not feeling happy, or to make someone smile when they are not feeling happy: *I couldn't raise a smile.*
11 ANIMALS OR PLANTS to look after animals or grow plants so that they can be sold or used as food: *He raised cattle in Nebraska when he was young.* | *Jim retired to raise raspberries.*
12 COLLECT PEOPLE to collect together a large group of people, especially soldiers: *The rebels quickly raised an army.*
13 raise your eyebrows to show surprise, doubt, disapproval etc by moving your EYEBROWS upwards: *Blanche raised her eyebrows in surprise.*
14 raise eyebrows if something raises eyebrows, it surprises people: *The band's new sound will raise some eyebrows.*
15 raise your voice to speak loudly or shout because you are angry: *He's never raised his voice to me.* | *I could hear raised voices in the next room.*
16 raise your glass spoken to celebrate someone's happiness or success by holding up your glass and drinking from it: *Ladies and gentlemen, will you raise your glasses to the bride and groom.*
17 raise the alarm BrE to warn people about a danger so that they can take action: *Sam stayed with his injured friend while a passing motorist raised the alarm.*
18 raise the spectre of sth literary to make people feel afraid that something frightening might soon happen: *The violence has raised the spectre of civil war.*
19 raise its (ugly) head if a question or problem raises its head, it appears and has to be dealt with: *Another problem then raised its ugly head.*
20 CARD GAME to make a higher BID than an opponent in a card game: *I'll raise you $100.*
21 raise hell informal to complain in a very angry way about something you think is not acceptable: *I'll raise hell with whoever is responsible for this mess.*
22 raise hell/Cain especially AmE to behave in a wild, noisy way that upsets other people: *The kids next door were raising hell last night.*
23 raise the roof to make a very loud noise when singing, celebrating etc
24 SPEAK TO SB to speak to someone on a piece of radio equipment; ◄ contact, get: *They finally managed to raise him at Miller's sheep farm.*
25 WAKE SB literary to wake someone who is difficult to wake: *Try as he might he could not raise her.*
26 DEAD PERSON old use to make someone who has died live again: *Jesus raised Lazarus from the grave.*
27 raise a siege/embargo formal to allow goods to go in and out of a place again after they have been stopped by force or by a law
28 BUILD formal to build something such as a MONUMENT; ◄ erect
29 raise 2/4/10 etc to the power of 2/3/4 etc technical to multiply a number by itself a particular number of times: *2 raised to the power of 3 is 8.*

raise² n [C] AmE an increase in the money you earn; ◄ rise BrE
raised /reɪzd/ adj higher than the surrounding area or surface: *a raised platform*
rai·sin /ˈreɪzən/ n [C] a dried GRAPE
rai·son d'être /ˌreɪzɒn ˈdetrə $ -zoʊn-/ n [singular] the reason why something exists, why someone does something etc: *Commerce was the town's raison d'être.*
Raj /rɑːdʒ/ n **the (British) Raj** the rule of the British government in India before India became independent in 1947
ra·jah, **raja** /ˈrɑːdʒə/ n [C] the king or ruler of an Indian state
rake¹ /reɪk/ n **1** [C] a gardening tool with a row of metal teeth at the end of a long handle, used for making soil level, gathering up dead leaves etc: *a garden rake* → see picture at GARDENING **2** [C] old-fashioned a man who has many sexual relationships, drinks too much alcohol etc **3** [singular] the angle of a slope: *the rake of the stage*
rake² v **1** [I,T] to move a rake across a surface in order to make the soil level, gather dead leaves etc: **rake sth over/up** *She raked the soil over to loosen the weeds.* **2** [I always + adv/prep] to search a place very carefully for something: [+through/around] *I've been raking*

through my drawers looking for those tickets. **3** [T] to point something such as a gun, camera, or strong light, and keep moving across an area; ◨ **sweep**: *The searchlight raked the open ground around the prison.* | **rake sth with sth** *They raked the room with gunfire.* **4** [T] to push a stick backwards and forwards in a fire in order to remove ASHES **5 rake over the past/old coals** to keep talking about something that happened in the past that people would prefer you not to mention **6 rake your fingers (through sth)** to pull your fingers through something or across a surface: *Ken raked his fingers through his hair.*

rake sth ⇔ **in** *phr v informal* to earn a lot of money without trying very hard: *Lou's been raking in the dollars since he opened his business.* | *If someone opened a burger bar, they'd really rake it in.*

rake sth ⇔ **up** *phr v informal* **1** to talk about something from the past that people would prefer you not to mention; ◨ **dredge up**: *It upsets Dad when that story is raked up again.* **2** also **rake sth** ⇔ **together** to collect things or people together for a purpose, but with difficulty: *They could only rake up $300.*

'rake-off *n* [C] *informal* a dishonest share of profits; → **cut**: *The taxi driver gets a rake-off from the hotel.*

rak·ish /'reɪkɪʃ/ *adj* **1** if a man looks rakish, or wears rakish clothes, he dresses nicely and looks confident and relaxed; ◨ **stylish**: *a rakish uniform* **2 at a rakish angle** if you wear a hat at a rakish angle, you do not wear it straight, and this makes you look relaxed and confident **3** *old-fashioned* a rakish man has a lot of sexual relationships, wastes money, and drinks too much alcohol —**rakishly** *adv*

ral·ly¹ /'ræli/ *n plural* **rallies** [C] **1** a large public meeting, especially one that is held outdoors to support a political idea, protest etc: *About 1,000 people attended the **rally** in Hyde Park.* | *We decided to **hold a rally** to put pressure on the government.* | *a **mass rally** (=large rally) in support of the pay claim* | **political/election/peace etc rally** *He was shot dead while addressing an election rally.* → PEP RALLY **2** a car race on public roads: *a **rally driver*** **3** an occasion when something, especially the value of shares, becomes stronger again after a period of weakness or defeat: *a late rally in the Tokyo stock market* **4** a continuous series of hits of the ball between players in a game such as tennis

rally² *v* **rallied, rallying, rallies** **1** [I,T] to come together, or to bring people together, to support an idea, a political party etc: [+to] *Fellow Republicans rallied to the President's defense.* | **rally to do sth** *Surely the local business community could have rallied to raise the cash.* | *an attempt to **rally support** for the party* **2** [I] to become stronger again after a period of weakness or defeat; → **recover**: *After a shaky start, he rallied and won the title in style.* | *The Tokyo stock market rallied later in the day.*

rally around (sb) also **rally round (sb)** *BrE phr v informal* if a group of people rally round, they all try to help you when you are in a difficult situation: *Her friends all rallied round when she was ill.*

'rallying ˌcry *n* [singular] a word or phrase used to unite people in support of an idea: *'Land and Liberty' was the rallying cry of revolutionary Mexico.*

'rallying ˌpoint *n* [singular] an idea, event, person etc that makes people come together to support something they believe in: [+for] *a rallying point for the struggle against apartheid*

ram¹ /ræm/ *v* **rammed, ramming** **1** [I,T] to run or drive into something very hard: *In the latest raid, thieves used his van to ram a police car.* | [+into] *He lost control of his truck and rammed into a van, killing two people.* **2** [T always + adv/prep] to push something into a position, using great force: *First, you'll have to ram the posts into the ground.* | *I rammed my foot down on the brake.* **3 ram sth down sb's throat** to try to make someone accept an idea or opinion by repeating it

many times, especially when they are not interested **4 ram sth home** to make sure someone fully understands something by emphasizing it and by providing a lot of examples, proof etc: *a police video ramming home the dangers of driving fast in fog*

ram² *n* [C] **1** an adult male sheep; → **ewe** **2** a BATTERING RAM **3** a machine that hits something again and again to force it into a position

RAM /ræm/ *n* [U] *technical **random access memory*** the part of a computer that acts as a temporary store for information so that it can be used immediately; → **ROM**: *a model with 128 MB of RAM*

Ram·a·dan /'ræmədæn, -dɑːn, ˌræmə'dɑːn, -'dæn/ *n* [U] the ninth month of the Muslim year, during which Muslims do not eat or drink anything during the day while it is light

ram·ble¹ /'ræmbəl/ *v* [I] **1** to talk for a long time in a way that does not seem clearly organized, so that other people find it difficult to understand you: *She's getting old and she tends to ramble a bit.* **2** [always + adv/prep] *BrE* to go on a walk in the countryside for pleasure; → **hike**: *There's plenty to discover as you ramble around this little island.* **3** a plant that rambles grows in all directions

ramble on *phr v BrE* to talk or write for a long time in a way that other people find boring; ◨ **go on**: [+about] *My father kept rambling on about the war.*

ramble² *n* [C] *BrE* **1** a walk in the countryside for pleasure; → **hike**: *I quite like the idea of **going for a ramble** one weekend.* **2** a speech or piece of writing that is very long and does not seem to be clearly organized: *In a ten-page ramble, Barre explains why he wrote the book.*

ram·bler /'ræmblə $ -ər/ *n* [C] **1** *BrE* someone who goes for walks in the countryside for pleasure **2** a plant, especially a rose, that grows in all directions

ram·bling¹ /'ræmblɪŋ/ *adj* [usually before noun] **1** a rambling building has an irregular shape and covers a large area: *a rambling old farmhouse* **2** rambling speech or writing is very long and does not seem to have any clear organization or purpose: *a long rambling letter*

rambling² *n* [U] *BrE* the activity of going for walks in the countryside for pleasure

ram·blings /'ræmblɪŋz/ *n* [plural] speech or writing that goes on for a long time and does not seem to have any clear organization or purpose: *He refused to listen to their mad ramblings.*

ram·bunc·tious /ræm'bʌŋkʃəs/ *adj AmE* noisy, full of energy, and behaving in a way that cannot be controlled: *three rambunctious kids*

ram·e·kin /'ræmɪkən, 'ræmkən/ *n* [C] a small dish in which food for one person can be baked and served

ram·i·fi·ca·tion /ˌræmɪfɪ'keɪʃən/ *n* [C usually plural] *formal* an additional result of something you do, which may not have been clear when you first decided to do it; → **implications**: *an agreement which was to **have significant ramifications** for British politics* | [+of] *the practical ramifications of taking on a new job* | **legal/political/economic etc ramifications** *the environmental ramifications of the road-building program*

ramp¹ /ræmp/ *n* [C] **1** a slope that has been built to connect two places that are at different levels: *Ramps are needed at exits and entrances for wheelchair users.* → see picture at BARRIER **2** *AmE* a road for driving onto or off a large main road; ◨ **slip road** *BrE: Take the Lake Drive ramp at Charles Street.* | **off-/on-ramp** *They missed the off-ramp to Manhattan.*

ramp² *v*

ramp sth ⇔ **up** *phr v* **1** to try to persuade people that a company's SHARES are worth more than they really are: *To ramp up a share price during a takeover bid is unacceptable.* **2** if a company ramps up an activity, it increases it: *Producers can quickly ramp up production.* —**ramp-up** *n* [C usually singular]

ram·page¹ /ræm'peɪdʒ, 'ræmpeɪdʒ/ v [I] to rush about in groups, acting in a wild or violent way: [+through] *Drunken football fans rampaged through the streets.*

rampage² n **on the rampage** rushing about in a wild and violent way, often causing damage: *gangs of youths on the rampage* | *Rioters went on the rampage through the town.*

ram·pant /'ræmpənt/ adj **1** if something bad, such as crime or disease, is rampant, there is a lot of it and it is very difficult to control; → **rife**, **widespread**: *Pickpocketing is rampant in the downtown area.* | *The country has high unemployment and **rampant inflation**.* **2** a plant that is rampant grows and spreads quickly, in a way that is difficult to control —**rampantly** adv

ram·part /'ræmpɑːt $ -ɑːrt/ n [C usually plural] a wide pile of earth or a stone wall built to protect a castle or city in the past

'ram-,raiding n [U] *BrE informal* the crime of driving a car into a shop window in order to steal goods from the shop —**ram-raid** n [C]: *a ram-raid on a jeweller's shop* —**ram-raider** n [C]

ram·rod /'ræmrɒd $ -rɑːd/ n [C] **1 straight/stiff as a ramrod** sitting or standing with your back straight and your body stiff **2** a stick for cleaning a gun or pushing GUNPOWDER into an old-fashioned gun

ram·shack·le /'ræmʃækəl/ adj a ramshackle building or vehicle is in bad condition and in need of repair; ⊟ **tumbledown**: *a ramshackle old cottage*

ran /ræn/ v the past tense of RUN

ranch /rɑːntʃ $ ræntʃ/ n [C] **1** a very large farm in the western US and Canada where sheep, cattle, or horses are bred **2** a RANCH HOUSE

ranch·er /'rɑːntʃə $ 'ræntʃər/ n [C] someone who owns or works on a ranch

'ranch house n [C] **1** *AmE* a house built on one level, usually with a roof that does not slope very much; → **bungalow**; → see picture at HOUSE **2** a house on a ranch in which the rancher lives

ranch·ing /'rɑːntʃɪŋ $ 'ræn-/ n [U] the activity or business of operating a ranch: *cattle ranching*

ran·cid /'rænsɪd/ adj oily or fatty food that is rancid smells or tastes unpleasant because it is no longer fresh: *rancid butter*

ran·cour *BrE*; **rancor** *AmE* /'ræŋkə $ -ər/ n [U] *formal* a feeling of hatred and anger towards someone you cannot forgive because they harmed you in the past; → **resentment**: **without rancour** *He spoke openly about the war without a trace of rancour.*

rand /rænd/ n plural **rand** [C] the standard unit of money in South Africa

ran·dom /'rændəm/ adj **1** happening or chosen without any definite plan, aim, or pattern: *The company has introduced random drug testing of its employees.* | *A few random shots were fired.* | *We looked at a **random sample** of 120 families.* | *a **random selection** of women who were in the shop* **2 at random** without any definite plan, aim, or pattern: **choose/select/pick sth at random** *The gang picked their victims at random.* —**randomly** adv: *seven **randomly chosen** numbers* —**randomness** n [U]

,random 'access ,memory n [U] *technical* RAM

ran·dom·ize also **-ise** *BrE* /'rændəmaɪz/ v [T] *technical* to choose things in a way that is not carefully controlled or planned in order to do a scientific test: *The numbers have been randomized.* | *a randomized trial of a new drug*

rand·y /'rændi/ adj *BrE informal* full of sexual desire; ⊟ **horny**: *She was feeling very randy.*

rang /ræŋ/ v the past tense of RING

range¹ [S1] [W1] /reɪndʒ/ n
1 VARIETY OF THINGS/PEOPLE [C usually singular] a number of people or things that are all different, but are all of the same general type: [+of] *a range of services* | *The drug is effective against a range of bacteria.* | **wide/broad/whole/full range of sth** *students from a wide range of backgrounds* | *They give advice on a whole range of subjects.* | **narrow/limited range of sth** *A fairly narrow range of people are responsible for key decisions.*

2 LIMITS [C] the limits within which amounts, quantities, ages etc vary: **age/price/temperature etc range** *toys suitable for children in the pre-school age range* | *a temperature range of 72–85°* | **in/within a ... range** *Your blood pressure's well within the normal range.* | **in the range (of) sth to sth** *a salary in the range of $25,000 to $30,000* | *Even the cheapest property was **out of** our **price range*** (=too expensive for us).

3 PRODUCTS [C] a set of similar products made by a particular company or available in a particular shop: [+of] *a new range of kitchenware* | *A company from Darlington has just launched its latest range of fashion jewellery.* | *The watches in this range are priced at £24.50.* | *We have a very large **product range**.* → MID-RANGE, TOP-OF-THE-RANGE

4 DISTANCE a) [C,U] the distance over which a particular weapon can hit things: [+of] *missiles with a range of 3000 km* | **within range (of sth)** *We waited until the enemy was within range.* | **out of/beyond range (of sth)** *I ducked down to get out of range of the gunshots.* | **at close/short/point-blank range** (=from very close) *Both men had been shot at point-blank range.* → LONG-RANGE, SHORT-RANGE **b)** [C,U] the distance within which something can be seen or heard: **within range (of sth)** *a handsome man who drew admiring glances from any female within range* | *any spot within range of your radio signal* | **out of/beyond range (of sth)** *Joan hoped that the others were out of range of her mother's voice.* | *One way to see birds **at close range** is to attract them into your own garden.* **c)** [C] the distance which a vehicle such as an aircraft can travel before it needs more FUEL etc: [+of] *The plane has a range of 3,600 miles.*

5 MUSIC [C usually singular] all the musical notes that a particular singer or musical instrument can make: *His **vocal range** is amazing.*

6 MOUNTAINS/HILLS [C] a group of mountains or hills, usually in a line: *a land of high **mountain ranges** and deep valleys* | **range of mountains/hills** *the longest range of hills in the Lake District*

7 PLACE FOR SHOOTING [C] an area of land where you can practise shooting or where weapons can be tested: *a **rifle range*** | *the police **shooting range***

8 ABILITY [C,U] the number of different things that someone, especially an actor or actress, does well: *an actor of extraordinary range and intensity*

9 LAND [C,U] *AmE* a large area of land covered with grass, on which cattle are kept

10 COOKING [C] **a)** *AmE* a COOKER **b)** *BrE* a large piece of kitchen equipment in which you make a fire and use this heat to cook food; → **stove**: *a coal-fired **kitchen range*** → FREE-RANGE

range² [W3] v
1 INCLUDE [I always + adv/prep] **a)** to include a variety of different things or people in addition to those mentioned: **range from sth to sth** *The show had a massive audience, ranging from children to grandparents.* **b)** if prices, levels, temperatures etc range from one amount to another, they include both those amounts and anything in between: **range from sth to sth** *There were 120 students whose ages ranged from 10 to 18.* | **range between sth and sth** *The population of these cities ranges between 3 and 5 million.* | **range in age/size/price etc** *The shoes range in price from $25 to $100.*

2 DEAL WITH MANY SUBJECTS [I] to deal with a wide range of subjects or ideas in a book, speech, conversation etc: [+over] *The conversation had ranged over a variety of topics, from sport to current affairs.* | *The discussion **ranged widely**.*

3 MOVE AROUND [I always + adv/prep] to move around in an area without aiming for a particular place; ⊟ **wander**: [+over/through] *Cattle ranged over the pastures in search of food.*

R

4 range yourself with/against sb/sth *formal* to publicly state your agreement with, or opposition to, a particular group's beliefs and ideas: *individuals who had ranged themselves against the authorities*
5 ARRANGE *BrE* [T always + adv/prep] *formal* to put things in a particular order or position: *In the dining room, team photographs were ranged along the wall.*

rang·er /'reɪndʒə $ -ər/ *n* [C] **1** someone whose job is to look after a forest or area of countryside: *a park ranger* **2** also **ranger guide** a girl who belongs to a part of the Guide Association in Britain, for girls between the ages of 14 and 19

rang·y /'reɪndʒi/ *adj* with long thin strong legs: *a tall, rangy boy*

rank¹ W3 /ræŋk/ *n*
1 POSITION IN ARMY/ORGANIZATION [C,U] the position or level that someone holds in an organization, especially in the police or the army, navy etc: [+of] *officers below the rank of Colonel* | *He held* (=had) *the rank of Chief Inspector.* | **rise to/be promoted to/attain the rank of sth** *During the war Harold had risen to the rank of major.* | **high/senior/low/junior rank** *an officer of junior rank* | *He was sentenced to prison and stripped of his rank* (=had his rank taken from him).
2 the ranks a) the people who belong to a particular organization or group: **in/within ... ranks** *There were splits in the party ranks on this issue.* | *The Democrats now face opposition from within their own ranks.* | [+of] *Most are recruited from the ranks of people who studied Latin and Greek at university.* | *That summer I left school and* **joined the ranks of** (=became one of) *the unemployed.* **b)** all the members of the army, navy etc who are not officers: *He rose from the ranks to become a Field Marshal* (=he became an officer after starting as an ordinary soldier).
3 break ranks to behave in a way which is different from other members of a group, especially when they expect your support: [+with] *He was the first to break ranks with Ceausescu and publicly criticise his policies.*
4 LINE [C] a rank of people or things is a line or row of them: [+of] *Silently, ranks of police edged closer to the crowds.* | *Everyone lines up in ranks, all facing the instructor.* | **rank after rank/rank upon rank** (=a lot of things or people in a row) *On the shelves were rank after rank of liquor bottles.*
5 pull rank (on sb) *informal* to use your authority over someone to make them do what you want, especially unfairly: *You may just have to pull rank and tell them.*
6 QUALITY [singular] the degree to which something or someone is of high quality: *While none of these pictures is* **of the first rank** (=of the highest quality), *some are of interest.*
7 SOCIAL CLASS [C,U] someone's position in society: *people of all ranks in society* | *He came from a* **family of rank** (=one from a high social class).
8 TAXI [C] also **taxi rank** a place where taxis wait in a line to be hired: *I called a taxi from the rank outside.* → **close ranks** at CLOSE¹ (17)

rank² *v* **1 a)** [I always + adv/prep, not in progressive] to have a particular position in a list of people or things that have been put in order of quality or importance: [+as/among] *Today's match ranks as one of the most exciting games that these two have ever played.* | *We rank among the safest countries in the world.* | [+with/alongside] (=be of the same importance or quality) *Cuvier wanted to turn natural history into a science that would rank with physics and chemistry.* | **rank high/low** *He ranked high among the pioneers of 20th century chemical technology.* **b)** [T] to decide the position of someone or something on a list based on quality or importance: **be ranked fourth/number one etc** *Agassi was at that time ranked sixth in the world.* | *It is not always easy to* **rank** *the students* **in order of** *ability.* **2** [T] *AmE* to have a higher rank than someone else; ▪ **outrank**: *A general ranks a captain.* **3** [T] to

arrange objects in a line or row: *There were several pairs of riding boots ranked neatly in the hall.*

rank³ *adj* **1** if something is rank, it has a very strong unpleasant smell: **rank smell/odour** *the rank odour of sweat and urine* **2** [only before noun] used to emphasize a bad or undesirable quality; ▪ **total**: *an example of this government's rank stupidity* | *They make us look like* **rank amateurs** (=not at all good or professional). **3** rank plants are too thick and have spread everywhere: *rank grass and weeds*

rank and ˈfile *n* **the rank and file** the ordinary members of an organization rather than the leaders: *The rank and file of the party had lost confidence in the leadership.* —**rank-and-file** *adj* [only before noun]: *the rank-and-file members of the trade union*

rank·ing¹ /'ræŋkɪŋ/ *n* [C] a position on a scale that shows how good someone or something is when compared with others: *She is now fifth in the world rankings.*

ranking² *adj* [only before noun] *especially AmE* a ranking person has a high, or the highest, position in an organization or is one of the best at an activity: *the panel's ranking Democrat, William Clay* | *He's the ship's ranking officer* (=the one with the highest rank).

-ranking /ræŋkɪŋ/ *suffix* used to say where someone or something is on a scale that shows how good they are, or what position they have, compared with other people or things: **high/top/low/middle-ranking** *a top-ranking tennis player*

ran·kle /'ræŋkəl/ *v* [I,T] if something rankles, you still remember it angrily because it upset you or annoyed you a lot: *His comments still rankled.*

ran·sack /'rænsæk/ *v* [T] **1** to go through a place, stealing things and causing damage: *The whole flat had been ransacked.* **2** to search a place very thoroughly, often making it untidy: **ransack sth for sth** *She ransacked the wardrobe for something to wear.*

ran·som¹ /'rænsəm/ *n* [C] **1** an amount of money that is paid to free someone who is held as a prisoner: *The kidnappers were* **demanding a ransom** *of $250,000.* | *The government refused to* **pay the ransom.** | **ransom demand/note** *There has still been no ransom demand.* | *He's got the* **ransom money.** **2 hold sb for ransom** also **hold sb to ransom** *BrE* to keep someone prisoner until money is paid: *His daughter was kidnapped and held for ransom.* **3 hold sb to ransom** *BrE* to put someone in a situation where they have no choice and are forced to agree to your demands: *He has accused the nurses of holding the government to ransom by threatening to strike.*

ransom² *v* [T] to pay an amount of money so that someone who is being held as a prisoner is set free: *They were all ransomed and returned unharmed.*

rant /rænt/ *v* [I,T] to talk or complain in a loud excited and rather confused way because you feel strongly about something: [+about] *She was still ranting about the unfairness of it all.* | *Why don't you stop* **ranting and raving** *for a minute and listen?* —**rant** *n* [C]: *a 15-minute rant about the evils of modern society*

rant·ings /'ræntɪŋz/ *n* [plural] a long speech in which someone complains about something in a loud excited and rather confused way

rap¹ /ræp/ *n*
1 MUSIC [C,U] also **rap music** a type of popular music in which the words of a song are not sung, but spoken in time to music with a steady beat: *a popular rap song*
2 KNOCK [C] a series of quick sharp hits or knocks; → **tap**: *She was woken by a sharp rap on the door.*
3 CRIME [C] *AmE informal* a statement by the police saying that someone is responsible for a serious crime; ▪ **charge**: *murder/robbery etc rap The kid's been cited twice on drunk-driving raps.* → RAP SHEET
4 take the rap (for sth) to be blamed or punished for a mistake or crime, especially unfairly: *Bo was left to take the rap for Victor's murder.*
5 beat the rap *AmE informal* to avoid being punished for a crime

6 a rap on/over the knuckles a) *informal* a punishment or criticism that is not very severe: *The New York Post received an official rap over the knuckles for the way it reported the story.* **b)** if someone gives a child a rap on the knuckles, they hit them on the back of their hand as a punishment
7 a bum/bad rap *especially AmE informal* unfair treatment or punishment: *Cleveland always **gets a bum rap** in the press.*

rap² *v* **rapped, rapping**
1 HIT [I,T] to hit or knock something quickly several times; → **tap**: *She rapped the table with her pen.* | [+on/at] *Angrily she rapped on his window.*
2 MUSIC [I] to say the words of a rap song
3 CRITICIZE [T] to criticize someone angrily – used especially in news reports; ☐ **slam**: *a film rapped by critics for its excessive violence*
4 SAY also **rap out** [T] to say something loudly, suddenly, and in a way that sounds angry: *'Come on,' he rapped impatiently.*
5 rap sb on/over the knuckles also **rap sb's knuckles a)** to punish or criticize someone for something, but not very severely: *He had his knuckles rapped sharply for meddling in foreign policy.* **b)** to punish a child by hitting them on the back of their hand

ra·pa·cious /rəˈpeɪʃəs/ *adj formal* always wanting more money, goods etc than you need or have a right to; ☐ **greedy**: *rapacious landlords* —**rapaciously** *adv* —**rapacity** /rəˈpæsɨti/ *n* [U]

rape¹ /reɪp/ *v* [T] to force someone to have sex, especially by using violence: *She had been raped and stabbed.*

rape² *n* **1** [C,U] the crime of forcing someone to have sex, especially by using violence: *Police are investigating a series of violent rapes in the town.* | *He was arrested and charged with rape.* | *He always denied that he was guilty of rape.* | *a **rape victim*** | *the **gang rape** of a 17-year-old girl* | *He was convicted of **attempted rape**.* **2** [U] also **oilseed rape** *BrE* a European plant with yellow flowers, grown as animal food and for its oil; ☐ **canola** *AmE* **3** the rape of sth the unnecessary destruction of something, especially the environment: *companies which profit from the rape of the Earth*

rap·id W3 /ˈræpɨd/ *adj* happening or done very quickly and in a very short time; → **fast, quick**: *The patient made a rapid recovery.* | **rapid growth/expansion/development/increase** *rapid population growth* | *a period of **rapid decline*** | *He fired three times **in rapid succession** (=one after another).* —**rapidity** /rəˈpɪdɨti/ *n* [U]: *Their debts mounted with alarming rapidity.*

rapid-fire *adj* [only before noun] **1** rapid-fire questions, jokes etc are said quickly, one after another **2** a rapid-fire gun fires shots quickly, one after another

rap·id·ly /ˈræpɨdli/ *adv* very quickly and in a very short time: *The disease was spreading more rapidly than expected.* | **rapidly growing/changing/expanding** etc *the rapidly changing world of technology*

rapid-re'sponse *adj* [only before noun] **1** relating to a person or group of people whose job is to react quickly to a dangerous or important situation, such as a military attack, and find a solution to the problem: **rapid-response forces/team/unit** etc **2** relating to something which allows someone to react quickly to information they have received: *a rapid-response system* —**rapid response** *n* [U]

rap·ids /ˈræpɨdz/ *n* [plural] part of a river where the water looks white because it is moving very fast over rocks

rapid 'transit ,system also **,rapid 'transit** *n* [C] *AmE* a system for moving people quickly around a city using trains

ra·pi·er /ˈreɪpiə $ -ər/ *n* [C] a long thin sword with two sharp edges

rap·ist /ˈreɪpɨst/ *n* [C] a person who has RAPED someone (=forced them to have sex, especially using violence): *She later found out that he was a convicted rapist.*

rap·pel /ræˈpel/ *v* **rappelled, rappelling** [I] *AmE* to go

---

down a cliff or rock by sliding down a rope and touching the rock or cliff with your feet; ☐ **abseil** *BrE* —**rappel** *n* [C]

rap·per /ˈræpə $ -ər/ *n* [C] someone who speaks the words of a RAP song

rap·port /ræˈpɔː $ -ɔːr/ *n* [singular, U] friendly agreement and understanding between people; → **relationship**: [+with/between] *He had an excellent rapport with his patients.* | **establish/build up/develop (a) rapport** *He always found he could build up a good rapport with children.*

rap·proche·ment /ræˈprɒʃmɒŋ, ræˈprəʊʃ- $,ræprouʃˈmɑːŋ/ *n* [singular, U] *formal* the establishment of a good relationship between two countries or groups of people, after a period of unfriendly relations: [+between/with] *I hope for a rapprochement between our two countries.*

'rap sheet *n* [C] *AmE informal* a list kept by the police of someone's criminal activities

rapt /ræpt/ *adj written* so interested in something that you do not notice anything else: *They listened with **rapt attention**.* | *the **rapt expression** on his face*

rap·ture /ˈræptʃə $ -ər/ *n* [U] **1** *literary* great excitement and happiness: *The boys gazed up at him in rapture.* **2 be in raptures/go into raptures** *BrE formal* to express or feel great pleasure and happiness about something: [+over/about/at] *She went into raptures about the climate, the food, the spring flowers.*

rap·tu·rous /ˈræptʃərəs/ *adj* [usually before noun] expressing great happiness or admiration – used especially in news reports: *She was greeted with **rapturous applause**.* | **rapturous reception/welcome** *He was given a rapturous welcome.* —**rapturously** *adv*

rare S3 W2 /reə $ rer/ *adj comparative* **rarer,** *superlative* **rarest**
1 not seen or found very often, or not happening very often; ☐ **common**; → **unusual**: *This species of plant is becoming increasingly rare.* | *I only saw Helen on the **rare occasions** when I went into her shop.* | **it is rare (for sb/sth) to do sth** *It is rare to find such an interesting group of people.* | *It is very rare for her to miss a day at school.*
2 meat that is rare has only been cooked for a short time and is still red; → **underdone, well-done**: *I like my steak rare.*
3 [only before noun] *BrE old-fashioned* very good or surprising: *We had a **rare old** time at the party.*

rar·e·fied /ˈreərɨfaɪd $ ˈrer-/ *adj* [usually before noun] **1** a rarefied place, organization, or type of activity is only available to or understood by a small group of people – used to show disapproval: *the rarefied atmosphere of academia* **2** rarefied air is the air in high places, which has less oxygen than usual

rare·ly W2 /ˈreəli $ ˈrerli/ *adv* not often; ☐ **frequently**: *She very rarely complains.* | *This method is rarely used in modern laboratories.*

rar·ing /ˈreərɪŋ $ ˈrer-/ *adj informal* **1 raring to go**

very eager to start an activity: *They woke up early and were raring to go.* **2 raring to do sth** *BrE* very eager to do something: *The children were raring to get outdoors.*

rar·i·ty /ˈreərˌti $ ˈrer-/ *n plural* **rarities 1 be a rarity** to not happen or exist very often: *Visitors were a rarity in the village.* **2** [C] something that is valuable or interesting because it is rare: *Some of these plants are national rarities.* **3** [U] the quality of being rare: *Such stamps are expensive because of their rarity.*

ras·cal /ˈrɑːskəl $ ˈræs-/ *n* [C] **1** a child who behaves badly but whom you still like **2** *old-fashioned* a dishonest man; ⊟ **scoundrel**

rash¹ /ræʃ/ *adj* if you are rash, you do things too quickly, without thinking carefully about whether they are sensible or not; → **foolish**: *Please Jessie, don't do anything rash.* | *Don't go making any rash decisions about your future!* | *It was rather rash of you to lend them your car.* —**rashly** *adv*: *I rashly agreed to look after the children.* —**rashness** *n* [U]

rash² *n* [C] **1** a lot of red spots on someone's skin, caused by an illness: *She had a nasty rash on her arm.* | **come/break out in a rash** (=get a rash) *My mother comes out in a rash if she eats seafood.* | **nappy** *BrE*/**diaper** *AmE* **rash** | *Most babies get nappy rash at some stage.* | *a heat rash* (=a rash caused by heat) **2 rash of sth** *informal* a large number of unpleasant events, changes etc within a short time; ⊟ **spate of sth**: *There's been a rash of car thefts in the city centre.*

rash·er /ˈræʃə $ -er/ *n* [C] *BrE* a thin piece of BACON or HAM: [+of] *a rasher of bacon*

rasp¹ /rɑːsp $ ræsp/ *v* **1** [I,T] to make a rough unpleasant sound: *my father's rasping voice* | *'Stop!' he rasped.* **2** [T] to rub a surface with something rough

rasp² *n* **1** [singular] a rough unpleasant sound: [+of] *the harsh rasp of her breathing* **2** [C] a metal tool with a rough surface that is used for shaping wood or metal

rasp·ber·ry /ˈrɑːzbəri $ ˈræzberi/ *n plural* **raspberries** [C] **1** a soft sweet red berry, or the bush that this berry grows on: *a bowl of fresh raspberries* | *raspberry jam* → see picture at FRUIT¹ **2** *informal* a rude sound that you make by putting your tongue out and blowing: **blow a raspberry** also **give a raspberry** *AmE*: *She blew a raspberry at him as he drove off.*

Ras·ta /ˈræstə/ *n* [C] *informal* a Rastafarian

Ras·ta·fa·ri·an /ˌræstəˈfeəriən◂ $ -ˈfer-/ *n* [C] someone who believes in a religion that is popular in Jamaica, which has Haile Selassie as its religious leader, and has the belief that one day black people will return to Africa —**Rastafarian** *adj* —**Rastafarianism** *n* [U]

Ras·ta·man /ˈræstəmæn/ *n plural* **Rastamen** /-men/ [C] *informal* a male Rastafarian

rat¹ /ræt/ *n* [C] **1** an animal that looks like a large mouse with a long tail **2** *spoken* someone who has been disloyal to you or deceived you: *But you promised to help us, you rat!* **3 look like a drowned rat** to look very wet and uncomfortable **4 (like) rats leaving the sinking ship** used to describe people who leave a company, organization etc when it is in trouble → RAT RACE, RATS; → **smell a rat** at SMELL² (7)

rat² *v* **ratted, ratting** [I] *informal* **1** if someone rats on you, they tell someone in authority about something wrong that you have done; ⊟ **grass on**: [+on] *They'll kill you if they find out you've ratted on them!* **2** *BrE* to not do what you had promised to do; ⊟ **go back on**, **renege on**: [+on] *He accused the government of ratting on its promises to the disabled.*

rat sb ⇔ **out** *AmE informal* if someone rats you out, they are disloyal to you, especially by telling someone in authority about something wrong that you have done: *You can't rat out your teammates.*

rat-arsed *adj BrE informal* extremely drunk

rat-a-ˈtat also **rat-a-tat-ˈtat** *n* [singular] the sound of knocking, especially on a door

rat·bag /ˈrætbæg/ *n* [C] *BrE informal* an unpleasant person

ratch·et¹ /ˈrætʃət/ *n* [C] a machine part consisting of a wheel or bar with teeth on it, which allows movement in only one direction

ratchet² *v*

ratchet up *phr v* to increase something by a small amount, especially after a series of increases, or to increase in this way: **ratchet sth** ⇔ **up** *Raising the minimum wage would ratchet up real incomes in general.* | *The debate will ratchet up a notch on Wednesday when the Commission publishes its report.*

rate¹ S1 W1 /reɪt/ *n* [C]

1 NUMBER the number of times something happens, or the number of examples of something within a certain period: **birth/unemployment/crime etc rate** *Australia's unemployment rate rose to 6.5% in February.* | *a rapid increase in the divorce rate* | **high/low rate of sth** *areas with high rates of crime* | **success/failure rate** (=the number of times that something succeeds or fails) *It's a new technique and the failure rate is quite high.* | *Immediately his heart rate* (=the number of beats per minute) *increased.* | *at a rate of sth Asylum seekers were entering Britain at a rate of 1,600 per day.* → BIRTHRATE, DEATH RATE

2 MONEY a charge or payment that is set according to a standard scale: **at (a) ... rate** *people who pay tax at the highest rate* | **at a rate of sth** *They only pay tax at a rate of 5%.* | **interest/exchange/mortgage etc rate** *another reduction in the mortgage rate* | **rate of pay/tax/interest etc** *Nurses are demanding higher rates of pay.* | **special/reduced/lower rate** *Some hotels offer special rates for children.* | **hourly/weekly rate** (=the amount someone is paid per hour or week) *What's the hourly rate for cleaning?* | *$20 an hour is the going rate* (=the usual amount paid) *for private tuition.* → BASE RATE; → **cut-rate** at CUT-PRICE; → EXCHANGE RATE, INTEREST RATE, PRIME RATE

3 SPEED the speed at which something happens over a period of time: [+of] *an attempt to slow down the rate of economic growth* | **at (a) ... rate** *Children learn at different rates.* | *Our money was running out at an alarming rate.* | **at a rate of sth** *Iceland is getting wider at a rate of about 0.5 cm per year.*

4 at any rate *spoken* **a)** used when you are stating one definite fact in a situation that is uncertain or unsatisfactory; ⊟ **anyway**: *They've had technical problems – at any rate that's what they told me.* **b)** used to introduce a statement that is more important than what was said before; ⊟ **anyway**: *Well, at any rate, the next meeting will be on Wednesday.*

5 at this rate *spoken* used to say what will happen if things continue to happen in the same way as now: *At this rate we won't ever be able to afford a holiday.*

6 first-rate/second-rate/third-rate of good, bad, or very bad quality: *a cheap third-rate motel*

7 at a rate of knots *BrE informal* very quickly: *Jack's getting through the ironing at a rate of knots!*

8 rates [plural] a local tax, paid before 1990 by owners of buildings in Britain

rate² *v* **1 a)** [T] to think that someone or something has a particular quality, value, or standard: *The company seems to rate him very highly* (=think he is very good). | **be rated (as) sth** *Rhodes is currently rated the top junior player in the country.* **b)** [I] to be considered as having a particular quality, value, or standard: [+as] *That rates as one of the best meals I've ever had.* **2** [T] *BrE informal* if you rate someone or something, you think they are very good: *I never rated him.* **3 rate sb's chances (of doing sth)** *BrE spoken* if you do not rate someone's chances of achieving something, you do not think that it is likely that they will achieve it: *I don't rate your chances of getting a ticket for the Leeds game.* | *How do you rate your chances tomorrow* (=do you think you will be successful?)*?* **4** [T] *informal especially AmE* to deserve something: *They rate a big thank-you for all their hard work.* | *a local incident that didn't rate a mention in the national press* **5 be rated G/U/PG/X etc** if a film is rated G, U etc, it is officially

,rate of ex'change *n* [C] the EXCHANGE RATE

,rate of re'turn *n* [singular] a company's profit for a year, expressed as a PERCENTAGE of the money that the company has spent during the year

rate·pay·er /'reɪtpeɪə $ -ər/ *n* [C] *BrE* someone who pays taxes that are used to provide local services

ra·ther S1 W1 /'rɑːðə $ 'ræðər/ *predeterminer, adv*
1 fairly or to some degree: *I was rather surprised to see him with his ex-wife.* | *He was limping rather badly.* | *My own position is rather different.* | *Abigail's always been rather a difficult child. BrE* | *Isn't it rather late* (=a little too late) *to start changing all the arrangements?* | *Actually I rather like the new style of architecture. BrE* | *It was a nice house, but rather too small for a family of four. BrE* | *The task proved to be rather more difficult than I had expected. BrE*
2 would rather used to say that you would prefer to do or have something: *I'd rather have a quiet night in front of the TV.* | *We could eat later if you would rather do that.* | *'I think you'd better ask her.' 'I'd rather not* (=I do not want to).' | **would rather ... than ...** *I'd rather die than apologize to Helen.* | *I'd rather you didn't go out alone* (=I do not want you to go).
3 rather than instead of: *I think you'd call it a lecture rather than a talk.* | *Rather than go straight on to university why not get some work experience first?* | *Bryson decided to quit rather than accept the new rules.*
4 or rather used before correcting something that you have said, or giving more specific information: *We all went in Vic's car, or rather his father's.*
5 not ... but rather ... used to say that one thing is not true but a different thing is true: *The problem is not their lack of funding, but rather their lack of planning.*
6 rather you/him/her/them than me *spoken* used to say that you are glad that you are not going to be doing something that someone else will be doing
7 Rather! *BrE spoken old-fashioned* used to agree with someone

---

WORD CHOICE: rather, fairly, quite, pretty
Rather, fairly, quite, and **pretty** are all used to say that something is true to some degree, but not completely or extremely: *She's rather shy.* | *You should find the test fairly easy.* | *It took quite a long time (NOT a quite long time).* | *His English is pretty good.*
Rather is fairly formal but can be used in spoken English, especially British English. In American English it is more usual to use **pretty**. In both American and British English, **pretty** is more usual in speech than in writing.
Quite can also be used in front of an adjective or adverb, and in British English a verb, to mean 'completely'. This is a fairly formal use: *You are quite wrong.* | *I quite understand your feelings.*

---

rat·i·fy /'rætɪfaɪ/ *v* **ratified, ratifying, ratifies** [T] to make a written agreement official by signing it: **ratify a treaty/an agreement/a decision etc** *We hope that the republics will be willing to ratify the treaty.* —**ratification** /ˌrætɪfɪ'keɪʃən/ *n* [U]: *an attempt to delay ratification of the treaty*

rat·ing /'reɪtɪŋ/ *n* **1** [C] a level on a scale that shows how good, important, popular etc someone or something is: *By the end of the year the Prime Minister's approval rating* (=how many people agreed with his policies) *had fallen as low as 12 percent.* → CREDIT RATING **2 the ratings** a list that shows which films, television programmes etc are the most popular: *CBS will end the series if it continues to drop in the ratings.* **3** [singular] a letter that shows whether or not a film is suitable for children: *'The Godfather' had an X-rating when it was first shown.* **4** [C] *BrE* a SAILOR in the navy who is not an officer

ra·ti·o S3 W3 /'reɪʃiəʊ $ 'reɪʃoʊ/ *n plural* **ratios** [C] a relationship between two amounts, represented by a pair of numbers showing how much bigger one amount is than the other; → **proportion**: the ratio of

sth to sth *The ratio of nursing staff to doctors is 2:1.* | [+**between**] *the ratio between profits and incomes*

ra·tion¹ /'ræʃən $ 'ræ-, 'reɪ-/ *n* **1** [C,U] a fixed amount of something that people are allowed to have when there is not enough, for example during a war: **food/clothes/meat etc ration** *the weekly meat ration* | *a coal ration of 4 kg a month* | **on ration** *Even wool was on ration in the war.* **2 rations** [plural] a fixed amount of food given to a soldier or member of a group: *emergency food rations* | *The prisoners were queuing for their meagre rations* (=small rations). | *We were on short rations* (=given a smaller amount than usual). **3** [singular] an amount of something that you think is reasonable or normal: [+**of**] *holidaymakers who like a generous ration of open-air activity*

ration² *v* [T] **1** [usually passive] to control the supply of something because there is not enough: *Fuel was rationed during the war.* **2** to allow someone only a small amount of something: *the need to ration health care resources* | *diets which ration fat* | **ration sb/sth to sth** *He rationed himself to 4 cigarettes a day.* | *I try to ration the children's television viewing to an hour a day.*

ra·tion·al /'ræʃənəl/ *adj* **1** rational thoughts, decisions etc are based on reasons rather than emotions; **≠ irrational**: *Parents need to be fully informed so they can make a rational decision.* | *I'm sure there's a rational explanation for all this.* | *It's impossible to have a rational conversation with him.* **2** a rational person is able to think calmly and sensibly; **≠ irrational**: *Culley was quite rational at the time of her baby's death.* **3** *formal* able to make sensible judgments: *Man is a rational animal.* —**rationally** *adv*: *We were too shocked to think rationally.* —**rationality** /ˌræʃə'nælɪti/ *n* [U]

ra·tio·nale /ˌræʃə'nɑːl $ -'næl/ *n* [C usually singular] *formal* the reasons for a decision, belief etc: [+**behind/for/of**] *The rationale behind the changes is not at all evident.* | *The rationale for using this teaching method is to encourage student confidence.*

ra·tion·al·is·m /'ræʃənəlɪzəm/ *n* [U] *technical* the belief that your actions should be based on scientific thinking rather than emotions or religious beliefs: *philosophers who accept scientific rationalism*

ra·tion·al·ist /'ræʃənəlɪst/ *n* [C] someone who bases their actions on rationalism —**rationalist, rationalistic** /ˌræʃənə'lɪstɪk◂/ *adj*

ra·tion·al·ize also **-ise** *BrE* /'ræʃənəlaɪz/ *v* [I,T] **1** if you rationalize behaviour that is wrong, you invent an explanation for it so that it does not seem as bad: *When he fouls up, Glen always finds a way to rationalize what he's done.* **2** *BrE* to make a business more effective by removing unnecessary workers, equipment etc: *Our systems will be rationalized over the coming months.* —**rationalization** /ˌræʃənəlaɪ'zeɪʃən $ -lə-/ *n* [C,U]: *a major rationalization of the aircraft industry*

ra·tion·ing /'ræʃənɪŋ/ *n* [U] when the amount of food, petrol etc that people are allowed to have is limited by the government: **fuel/clothes/food etc rationing** *News of bread rationing created panic buying.*

'rat race *n* **the rat race** the unpleasant situation experienced by people working in big cities, when they continuously compete for success and have a lot of STRESS in their lives: **get out of/quit the rat race** *the story of a couple who quit the rat race*

'rat run *n* [C] *BrE* a quiet street that drivers use as a quick way of getting to a place, rather than using a main road: *The road has become a rat run for traffic avoiding the town centre.*

rats /ræts/ *interjection informal* used to show annoyance: *Rats! I forgot to buy any bread.*

'rats' tails *n BrE* **in rats' tails** if your hair is in rats' tails, it hangs down in separate pieces because it is wet or dirty

judged to be suitable or unsuitable for people of a particular age to see → X-RATED

R

rat·tan /rə'tæn/ n [U] the plant used to make WICKER furniture: *rattan chairs*

rat·tle¹ /'rætl/ v **1** [I,T] if you rattle something, or if it rattles, it shakes and makes a quick series of short sounds: *Dan banged on her door and rattled the handle.* | *The window rattled in the wind.* | *Bottles rattled as he stacked the beer crates.* → see box at SHAKE¹ **2** [I] if a vehicle rattles somewhere, it travels there while making a rattling sound: [+along/past/over etc] *The cart rattled along the stony road.* | *An old blue van rattled into view.* **3** [T] *informal* to make someone lose confidence or become nervous: *His mocking smile rattled her more than his anger.* | *It was hard not to get rattled when the work piled up.* | *His confidence was rattled by the accident.* **4 rattle sb's cage** spoken *informal* to annoy someone – used humorously: *Who rattled your cage?*

rattle around phr v BrE to live in a building that is much too big for you: [+in] *Dad and I rattled around miserably in the house after Mum died.*

rattle sth ⇔ **off** phr v to say several pieces of information or a list quickly and easily from memory: *An officer rattled off some statistics about the aid program.*

rattle on phr v BrE informal to talk quickly for a long time about boring things; ⊟ **go on**: [+about] *Nancy would rattle on for hours about her grandchildren.*

rattle through sth phr v BrE informal to do something quickly because you want to finish it

rattle up sth phr v BrE if a sports player rattles up a number of points, they get that number of points very quickly: *The West Indies had rattled up 411 for 5 when rain stopped play.*

rattle² n **1** [C,U] a short repeated sound, made when something shakes: *They listened anxiously to every rattle and creak in the house.* | [+of] *the rattle of chains* | *the faint rattle of distant gunfire* → DEATH RATTLE **2** [C] a baby's toy that makes a noise when it is shaken **3** [C] BrE an object that people shake to make a loud noise and show excitement or encouragement, for example at ceremonies or sports games

rat·tler /'rætlə $ -ər/ n [C] informal a rattlesnake

rat·tle·snake /'rætlsneɪk/ n [C] a poisonous American snake that shakes its tail to make a noise when it is angry

rat·tle·trap /'rætl,træp/ adj [only before noun] AmE a rattletrap vehicle is old and in bad condition

rat·tling /'rætlɪŋ/ adv **a rattling good yarn/story/read** BrE old-fashioned a good exciting story

rat·ty /'ræti/ adj **1** BrE informal becoming annoyed quickly or easily; ⊟ **irritable**: *I feel guilty about getting ratty with the children.* **2** AmE informal dirty and in bad condition; → **shabby**: *a ratty old sofa* | *ratty hair*

rau·cous /'rɔːkəs $ 'rɒ-/ adj **1** sounding unpleasantly loud: *He burst into raucous laughter.* | *raucous cheers* **2** impolite, noisy, and violent: *A group of raucous students spilled out of the bar.* | *The atmosphere became increasingly raucous.* —**raucously** adv

raunch·y /'rɔːntʃi $ 'rɒ-/ adj informal intended to be sexually exciting, in a way that seems immoral or shocking; → **sexy**: *a raunchy magazine* | *The show was quite raunchy.*

rav·age /'rævɪdʒ/ v [T usually passive] to damage something very badly: *a country ravaged by civil war* | *His health was gradually ravaged by drink and drugs.*

rav·ag·es /'rævɪdʒɪz/ n literary **the ravages of sth** the damage caused by something: *a building that has survived the ravages of time* | *the ravages of war*

rave¹ /reɪv/ v [I] **1 rave about/over sth** to talk about something you enjoy or admire in an excited way; ⊟ **enthuse**: *Now I understand why travelers rave about Lapland.* | *The customers were raving over our homemade chili.* **2** to talk in an angry, uncontrolled, or crazy way: [+at] *He started raving at me* | [+on] *BrE:*

Lisa raved on about how awful it all was. | *He was still* **ranting and raving** *the next morning.*

rave² n [C] **1** a big event where people dance to loud music with a strong beat and often take drugs: *an all-night rave* | *rave music* | *rave parties* → RAVER **2** strong praise for a new play, book etc: *The play got raves from the critics.*

rave³ adj **rave reviews/notices/reports** strong praise for a new play, book etc, especially in a newspaper or magazine: **win/receive/earn rave reviews** *The performance earned them rave reviews from critics.*

ra·ven¹ /'reɪvən/ n [C] a large shiny black bird

raven² adj [only before noun] literary raven hair is black and shiny

rav·e·ning /'rævənɪŋ/ adj literary ravening animals are hungry and dangerous: *a pack of ravening wolves*

rav·e·nous /'rævənəs/ adj very hungry; → **starving**: *I'm absolutely ravenous.* | *a ravenous appetite* —**ravenously** adv: *I was ravenously hungry.*

rav·er /'reɪvə $ -ər/ n [C] BrE informal **1** someone who goes to a RAVE: *Police believe many of the ravers were on drugs.* **2** someone who has an exciting social life and goes to a lot of parties

ra·vine /rə'viːn/ n [C] a deep narrow valley with steep sides; ⊟ **gorge**

rav·ing¹ /'reɪvɪŋ/ adj [only before noun] informal **1** talking or behaving in a crazy way: *a raving lunatic* **2** especially BrE used to emphasize that someone or something has a lot of a particular quality: *She was no raving beauty, but at least she looked smart.*

raving² adv **(stark) raving mad/bonkers** informal completely crazy

rav·ings /'reɪvɪŋz/ n [plural] crazy things that someone says: [+of] *the ravings of a demented man*

rav·i·o·li /,rævi'əʊli $ -'oʊli/ n [U] small PASTA squares filled with meat or cheese → see picture at PASTA

rav·ish /'rævɪʃ/ v [T] literary **1** to force a woman to have sex; ⊟ **rape** **2** to badly harm something: *a landscape ravished by drought*

rav·ish·ing /'rævɪʃɪŋ/ adj literary very beautiful; ⊟ **stunning**: *She looked ravishing.* | *a ravishing smile* —**ravishingly** adv

raw¹ /rɔː $ rɒː/ adj

1 FOOD not cooked: *raw meat* | *grated raw carrots* | *Cabbage can be eaten raw.*

2 SUBSTANCES raw substances are in a natural state and not treated or prepared for use; → **refined**: *raw silk* | *In its raw state, cocoa is very bitter.* | *Raw sewage had been dumped in the river.* | *The cost of our raw materials has risen significantly.*

3 INFORMATION raw information is collected but not organized, examined, or developed: *software to convert raw data into usable information* | *His time here provided the raw material for his novel.* | *Warhol used everyday items as the raw ingredients of his art.*

4 EMOTIONS raw feelings are strong and natural, but not fully controlled: *raw passion* | *Linda didn't want to see Roy while her emotions were still raw.* | *It took raw courage to admit she was wrong.*

5 BODY if a part of your body is raw, the skin there is red and painful: *The skin on my feet was rubbed raw.*

6 INEXPERIENCED not experienced or not fully trained: *Most of our soldiers are raw recruits.*

7 touch/hit a raw nerve to upset someone by something you say: *Seeing his face, Joanne realized she'd touched a raw nerve.*

8 raw deal unfair treatment: *Customers are getting a raw deal and are rightly angry.*

9 WEATHER very cold: *She shivered in the raw morning air.*

10 ART music, art, language etc that is raw is simple, direct, and powerful, but not fully developed: *Her voice has a raw poetic beauty.* | *His early sketches are raw and unpretentious.*

11 raw talent someone with raw talent is naturally good at something, but has not developed their ability

yet: *He has the raw talent to become a star.*
12 raw edge the edge of a piece of material before it
has been sewn: *Turn over the raw edges and stitch.*
—**rawness** *n* [U]

raw² *n* **1 in the raw a)** seen in a way that does not hide
cruelty and violence: *He went on the streets to experience
life in the raw.* | *It was my first exposure to India in the
raw.* **b)** *informal* not wearing any clothes; **⊟ in the
nude**: *sunbathing in the raw* **2 catch/touch sb on the
raw** *BrE* to say or do something that upsets someone:
She flinched, caught on the raw by his question.

raw·hide /'rɔːhaɪd $ 'rɒː-/ *n* [U] leather that is in its
natural state

ray /reɪ/ *n* [C] **1** a straight narrow beam of light from
the sun or moon: *The room darkened as a cloud hid the
sun's rays.* | [+of] *Rays of light filtered through the
trees.* **2** a beam of heat, electricity, or other form of
energy → COSMIC RAY, GAMMA RAY, X-RAY¹ **3 a ray of hope/
light etc** something that provides a small amount of
hope or happiness in a difficult situation: *a treatment
that offers a ray of hope for cancer sufferers* **4 a ray of
sunshine** someone who is happy and makes a difficult
situation seem better **5 catch some/a few rays** *informal* to sit or lie in the sun: *Let's go out and catch a few
rays.* **6** a large flat sea fish with a long pointed tail

ray·on /'reɪɒn $ -ɑːn/ *n* [U] a smooth artificial cloth
used for making clothes: *a rayon shirt*

raze /reɪz/ *v* [T usually passive] to completely destroy a
town or building: *In 1162 Milan was razed to the
ground by imperial troops.*

ra·zor /'reɪzə $ -ər/ *n* [C] **1** a tool with a sharp blade,
used to remove hair from your skin; → **shaver**: *an
electric razor* | *a disposable razor* → see picture at
SHAVE¹ **2 be on a razor/razor's edge** *BrE* to be in a
difficult position where a mistake could be dangerous:
Politically we are on a razor edge.

'razor blade *n* [C] a small flat blade with a very sharp
edge, used in a razor

razor-'sharp *adj* **1** very sharp: *razor-sharp
teeth* **2** intelligent and able to think quickly: *He has a
razor-sharp mind.*

razor-'thin *adj AmE* razor-thin victory/margin in an
election, a razor-thin victory is won by only a small
number of votes

'razor ,wire *n* [U] strong wire with sharp edges, used
to keep people out of a building, area of land etc

razz /ræz/ *v* [T] *AmE informal* to make jokes that insult
or embarrass someone; **⊟ tease**: *Eddie was razzed by
his teammates after the game.*

raz·zle /'ræzəl/ *n* be/go (out) on the razzle *BrE spoken
informal* to go somewhere such as a party, bar etc to
enjoy yourself

razz·ma·tazz /,ræzmə'tæz/ also **raz·za·ma·tazz**
/,ræzə-/ also **'razzle-,dazzle** *n* [U] noisy exciting
activity that is intended to attract people's attention:
the razzmatazz of showbusiness

RC the written abbreviation of *Roman Catholic*

-rd /d $ rd/ *suffix* used with ORDINAL numbers ending in 3,
except 13: *the 3rd (=third) of June* | *his 53rd birthday*

Rd. also **Rd** *BrE* the written abbreviation of *Road*, used
in addresses

R.D. /,ɑː 'diː $,ɑːr-/ *n* [U] *AmE* **rural delivery** the
postal system for country areas

RDA /,ɑː diː 'eɪ $,ɑːr-/ *n* [singular] **recommended daily
allowance** the amount of substances such as VITAMINS
that you should have every day

re¹ /riː/ *prep written formal* used in business letters to
introduce the subject: *re your enquiry of the 19th
October*

re² /reɪ/ *n* [singular] the second note in a musical SCALE →
SOL-FA

re- /riː/ *prefix* **1** again: *They're rebroadcasting the
play.* **2** again in a better way: *She asked me to redo the
essay.* **3** back to a former state: *After years of separation they were finally reunited.*

're /ə $ ər/ the short form of 'are'

RE /,ɑːr 'iː/ *n* [U] *BrE* **Religious Education** a subject
taught in schools

reach¹ S1 W1 /riːtʃ/ *v*
1 DEVELOPMENT [T] if someone or something
reaches a particular point in their development, they
get to that point: **reach the point/level/stage etc** *I had
reached the point where I was earning a good salary.* |
*The kids have reached the age when they can care for
themselves.*
2 RATE/AMOUNT [T] if something reaches a particular rate, amount etc, it increases until it is at that rate
or amount: *By 2008, that figure is expected to reach 7
million.* | *wind speeds reaching up to 180 mph* | *Prices
rose steadily to* **reach record levels**.
3 SUCCEED [T] to successfully agree on something
with other people: **reach a decision/agreement etc** *The
theatre has reached an agreement with striking actors.* |
It took the jury three days to **reach** a **verdict**. | *The talks
will continue until a* **conclusion** is **reached**.
4 TOUCH a) [I,T always + adv/prep] to move your arm
in order to touch or lift something with your hand: *She
reached into her bag and produced a business card.* | *He
reached down to help her to her feet.* | [+for] *Kelly
reached for his gun.* | *Luisa* **reached out** *her* **hand** *to
stroke the cat.* **b)** [I,T not in progressive] to touch something by stretching out your arm: *It's no good – I can't
reach.* | *She's too small to reach the table.* **c)** [T] to get
something from a high place by stretching up your
arm: **reach sth down** *She fell while reaching down a
vase from the top shelf.*
5 LENGTH/HEIGHT [I always + adv/prep, T not in pro-
gressive] to be big enough, long enough etc to get to a
particular point: *The phone lead isn't long enough to
reach the bedroom.* | *a skirt that reaches halfway down
her legs* | **reach as far as sth/reach down to sth** *Her hair
reaches down to her waist.*
6 ARRIVE [T] to arrive at a place: *We reached London
late at night.* | *The pyramids can be reached by public
transport.*
7 SPEAK TO SB [T] if you reach someone, you succeed
in speaking to them on the telephone; **⊟ contact**: *I can
probably reach him on his mobile.*
8 BE SEEN/HEARD [T] if a message, television programme etc reaches a lot of people, they hear it or see
it: *Cable TV* **reaches** a *huge* **audience**.
9 INFORMATION [T] if information reaches you, you
hear about it: *The news reached us in Lahore.*
10 COMMUNICATE [T] to succeed in making someone
understand or accept what you tell them; **⊟ get
through to**: *I just can't seem to reach Ed anymore.*
11 reach for the stars to aim for something that is very
difficult to achieve
   reach out to sb *phr v*
to show people that you are interested in them and
want to listen to them: *So far, his administration has
failed to reach out to hardline Republicans.*

reach² *n* **1** [singular,U] the distance that you can
stretch out your arm to touch something: **out of/be-
yond (sb's) reach** *Keep chemicals out of the reach of
children.* | **within reach (of sb)** *Keep a glass of water
within reach.* **2** [singular,U] within (easy) reach of sth
close to a place: *The tourist attractions are within easy
reach of the hotel.* **3** the limit of someone's power or
ability to do something: **beyond the reach of sb** *He lives
in Paraguay, well beyond the reach of the British
authorities.* **4 reaches** [plural] **a)** the parts of a place
that are furthest from the centre: **the further/outer
reaches of sth** *the further reaches of the jungle* **b)** the
straight part of a river between two bends: *the* **upper
reaches** *of the Nile* **5 the higher/lower reaches of sth**
the high or low levels of an organization or system:
*They lingered in the lower reaches of the Football
League.*

re·act S3 W3 /ri'ækt/ *v* [I]
1 BEHAVIOUR/FEELINGS to behave in a particular

1 000, 2 000, 3 000, most frequent words in S poken and W ritten English

way or show a particular emotion because of something that has happened or been said; → **respond**: [+**to**] *How did Wilson react to your idea?* | *He **reacted angrily** to the suggestion that he had lied.* | *She **reacted** very **badly** (=was very upset) when her parents split up.* | *You have to **react quickly** to circumstances.* | **react by doing sth** *The government reacted by declaring all strikes illegal.* → OVERREACT

2 CHEMICALS *technical* if a chemical substance reacts, it changes when it is mixed with another chemical substance: [+**with**] *The calcium reacts with sulphur in the atmosphere.*

3 PRICES if prices or financial markets react to something that happens, they increase or decrease in value because of it: [+**to**] *Oil prices **reacted sharply** (=reacted a lot) to news of the crisis in the Middle East.* | *The market reacted favourably to the announcement.*

4 BECOME ILL to become ill when a chemical or drug goes into your body, or when you eat a particular kind of food; → **respond**: [+**to**] *Quite a lot of children **react badly** to antibiotics.*

react against sth *phr v*
to show that you dislike someone else's ideas or ways of doing something, by deliberately doing the opposite: *He **reacted strongly** against his religious upbringing.*

re·ac·tion S2 W2 /riˈækʃən/ *n*

1 TO A SITUATION/EVENT [C,U] something that you feel or do because of something that has happened or been said; → **response**: *What was Jeff's reaction when you told him about the job?* | [+**to**] *the government's reaction to the fuel crisis* | **bring/provoke/produce a reaction** *The news brought an angry reaction from unions.* | **sb's first/immediate reaction** *His first reaction was to deny everything.* | **instinctive/gut reaction** (=what you immediately feel before you have time to think) *My gut reaction was not to trust him.* | *There were **mixed reactions** (=different people reacting in different ways) to the strike.* | **in reaction to sth** *An emergency fund was set up in reaction to the famine.*

2 MOVING QUICKLY **reactions** [plural] your ability to move quickly when something dangerous happens suddenly: *a skilled driver with very **quick reactions***

3 TO FOOD/DRUGS [C] if you have a reaction to a drug or to something you have eaten, it makes you ill: [+**to**] *a reaction to the immunization* | **have/suffer a reaction** *She had a **severe allergic reaction** to the drug.* | **cause/bring on/trigger a reaction** *Certain foods are more likely than others to cause **allergic reactions**.*

4 SCIENCE [C,U] **a)** a chemical change that happens when two or more substances are mixed together: *a **chemical reaction** in the soil* **b)** a physical force that is the result of an equally strong physical force in the opposite direction

5 CHANGE [singular] a change in people's attitudes, behaviour, fashions etc that happens because they disapprove of the way in which things were done in the past: [+**against**] *a reaction against the traditional values of the nineteenth century*

6 AGAINST CHANGE [U] *formal* strong and unreasonable opposition to all social and political changes: *The revolutionary movement was crushed by **the forces of reaction**.* → CHAIN REACTION

re·ac·tion·a·ry[1] /riˈækʃənəri $ -ʃəneri/ *adj* very strongly opposed to any social or political change – used to show disapproval: *reactionary attitudes*

reactionary[2] *n plural* **reactionaries** [C] someone who strongly opposes any social or political change – used to show disapproval

re·ac·tiv·ate /riˈæktɪ̥veɪt/ *v* [T] to make something start working again

re·ac·tive /riˈæktɪv/ *adj* **1** reacting to events or situations rather than starting or doing new things yourself: *a reactive foreign policy* **2** *technical* a reactive substance changes when it is mixed with another substance: *a highly reactive chemical*

re·ac·tor /riˈæktə $ -ər/ *n* [C] a NUCLEAR REACTOR

read[1] S1 W1 /riːd/ *v past tense and past participle* **read** /red/

1 WORDS/BOOKS [I,T] to look at written words and understand what they mean: *I can't read your writing.* | *She picked up the letter and read it.* | *Read the instructions carefully before you start.* | *children who are just learning to read and write* | *Her books are quite **widely read** (=read by a lot of people).* | *When I was young, I **read** every one of his books **from cover to cover**.* (=read all of something because you are very interested)

2 FIND INFORMATION [I,T not in progressive] to find out information from books, newspapers etc: *You can't believe everything you read in the papers.* | [+**about**] *Did you read about what happened to that guy in Florida?* | [+**of**] *I was shocked when I read of his death.* | **read (that)** *I read last week that the disease is on the increase.*

3 READ AND SPEAK [I,T] to say the words in a book, newspaper etc so that people can hear them: **read sb sth** *Daddy, will you read me a story?* | **read (sth) to sb** *Our mother reads to us every evening.* | *Teachers should read more poetry to children.* | *He glanced at the letter and began to **read** it **aloud**.*

4 MUSIC/MAPS ETC [T] to look at signs or pictures and understand what they mean: *He plays the violin very well but can't actually read music.* | *Are you any good at map reading?*

5 COMPUTER [T] *technical* if a computer can read a DISK, it can take the information that is on the disk and put it into its memory

6 UNDERSTAND STH IN A PARTICULAR WAY [T always + adv/prep] to understand a situation, remark etc in one of several possible ways; ◳ **interpret**: *I wasn't sure how to read his silence.* | **read sth as sth** *She shook her head, and I read this as a refusal.* | *The poem can be read as a protest against war.* | **read sth well/accurately** (=understand something correctly) *He had accurately read the mood of the nation.*

7 HAVE WORDS ON [T not in progressive] used to say what words are on a sign, in a letter etc; ◳ **say**: *A sign on the outer door read: 'No Entry'.*

8 STYLE OF WRITING [I] if something reads well, badly etc, it has been written well, badly etc: *I think in general the report **reads well**.*

9 **read sth as/for sth** to replace one word or number with another one, usually with the correct one: *Please read £50 as £15.* | *For 'November'* (=instead of November) *on line 6, read 'September'.*

10 MEASURING [T] **a)** to look at the number or amount shown on a measuring instrument: *Someone should be coming to read the gas meter.* **b)** if a measuring instrument reads a particular number, it shows that number: *The thermometer read 46 degrees.*

11 AT UNIVERSITY [I,T] *BrE* to study a subject at a university: *I read history at Cambridge.* | [+**for**] *He wants to read for a law degree.*

12 **take it as read (that)** *especially BrE* to feel certain that something is true although no one has told you it is true; ◳ **assume**: *You can take it as read that we will support the project.*

13 **take sth as read** to accept that a report or statement is correct without reading it or discussing it: *We'll take the secretary's report as read.*

14 **read between the lines** to guess someone's real feelings from something they say or write, when they do not tell you directly: *Reading between the lines, I'd say Robert's not very happy.*

15 **read sb's mind/thoughts** to guess what someone else is thinking: *'Want some coffee?' 'You read my mind.'*

16 **can read sb like a book** if you can read someone like a book, you know them so well that you immediately know what they are thinking or feeling

17 **read sb's palm** to look carefully at someone's hand, in order to find out about their future

18 **read sb's lips** to understand what someone is saying by watching the way their lips move. People who cannot hear do this. → LIP-READ

19 **read my lips** *spoken* used to tell someone that you really mean what you are saying: *Read my lips: I will not let you down.*

R

20 do you read me? *spoken* used to ask someone whether they can hear you when you are speaking to them by radio
21 well-read/widely-read someone who is well-read has read a lot of books and knows a lot about many subjects: *She is intelligent and extremely well-read.* → READING; → **read (sb) the riot act** at RIOT¹ (4)

read sth ⇔ **back** *phr v*
to read out loud something that you have just written down: [+**to**] *Can you read that last bit back to me?*
read for sth *phr v*
to say some of the words that are said by a particular character in a play, as a test of your ability to act
read sth **into** sth *phr v*
to think that a situation, action etc has a meaning or importance that it does not really have: *It was only a casual remark. I think you're reading too much into it.*
read sth ⇔ **out** *phr v*
to read and say words that are written down, so that people can hear: *Why don't you read out the name of the winner?* | [+**to**] *He read the last few sentences out to me.*
read sth ⇔ **through/over** *phr v*
to read something carefully from beginning to end in order to check details or find mistakes; ◨ **check over/ through**: *Read the contract over carefully before you sign it.* | *Spend a couple of minutes just reading through your essay.*
read up on sth also **read** sth ⇔ **up** *BrE phr v*
to read a lot about something because you will need to know about it: *You'll enjoy traveling more if you read up on the history of the countries you'll be visiting.*

read² *n* [singular] *informal* **1** *BrE* if you have a read, you spend time reading: *I sat down to **have a nice quiet read**.* | [+**of**] *I had a quick read of the report before I left.* **2 a good read** something that you enjoy reading: *I thought his last book was a really good read.*

read·a·ble /ˈriːdəbəl/ *adj* **1** interesting and enjoyable to read, and easy to understand; ◨ **unreadable**: **very/highly/eminently readable** *The book is informative and highly readable.* **2** writing or print that is readable is clear and easy to read; ◨ **legible** —**readability** /ˌriːdəˈbɪləti/ *n* [U] → MACHINE-READABLE

read·er [S3] [W2] /ˈriːdə $ -ər/ *n* [C]
1 [SB WHO READS] someone who reads books, or who reads in a particular way: *The book will appeal to young readers.* | *I've always been an **avid reader** (=someone who reads a lot).* | [+**of**] *He's a great reader of crime fiction.* | **a fast/slow reader**
2 [OF A NEWSPAPER/MAGAZINE] someone who reads a particular newspaper or magazine regularly: *The newspaper gradually lost readers during the 1980s.*
3 [BOOK] an easy book for children who are learning to read or for people who are learning a foreign language
4 [TEACHER] *Reader* an important teacher in a British university: [+**in**] *a Reader in Sociology at Bristol University* → MIND READER, NEWSREADER

read·er·ship /ˈriːdəʃɪp $ -ər-/ *n* [C,U] **1** all the people who read a particular newspaper or magazine regularly: [+**of**] *a magazine with a readership of 60,000* | *They are hoping that the paper will have quite a **wide readership**.* **2** the job that a Reader has in a British university: *a readership in linguistics*

read·i·ly [W3] /ˈredɪli/ *adv*
1 quickly and easily: *Boats are **readily available** to visitors.* | *The information is **readily accessible** on the Internet.*

2 quickly, willingly, and without complaining: *Jack readily agreed to help.*

read·i·ness /ˈredinəs/ *n* **1** [U] when you are prepared for something, or when something is ready to be used: **in readiness (for sth)** *They stacked the firewood in readiness for the evening campfire.* **2** [singular, U] willingness to do something: **readiness to do sth** *He stressed the government's readiness to take tough action against terrorists.*

read·ing [W2] /ˈriːdɪŋ/ *n*
1 [ACTIVITY/SKILL] [U] the activity or skill of understanding written words: *She loves reading.* | *Reading is taught using a combination of several methods.*
2 [BOOKS] [U] books and other things that you can read: *Her main reading seems to be mystery novels.* | *a bit of **light reading** (=things that are easy and enjoyable to read) for my holiday* | *There's a list of **further reading** (=other things you can read) at the end of each chapter.* | *a supply of interesting **reading material***
3 [ACT OF READING] [singular] when you read something: *The book is quite difficult **on first reading**.* | *a **close reading** of the text (=when you read it very carefully)*
4 [UNDERSTANDING] [C] your way of understanding what a particular statement, situation, event etc means; ◨ **interpretation**: [+**of**] *What's your reading of the government's response to this crisis?*
5 [TO A GROUP] [C] **a)** an occasion when a piece of literature is read to a group of people: *a poetry reading at the bookstore* **b)** a piece of writing, especially from the Bible, that is read to a group of people: *The first reading is from Corinthians I, Chapter 3.*
6 **make (for) interesting/fascinating/compelling etc reading** to be interesting etc to read: *Your report made fascinating reading.*
7 [MEASUREMENT] [C] a number or amount shown on a measuring instrument: *We **take** temperature **readings** every two hours.*
8 [IN PARLIAMENT] [C] one of the occasions in the British Parliament or the US Congress when a suggested new law is discussed: *the second reading of the Industrial Relations Bill*

re·ad·just /ˌriːəˈdʒʌst/ *v* **1** [I] to get used to a new situation, job, or way of life: *It takes time to readjust after a divorce.* | [+**to**] *Former soldiers often struggle to readjust to life outside the army.* **2** [T] to make a small change to something or to its position: *He readjusted his glasses.* | *We may need to readjust these figures slightly.* —**readjustment** *n* [C,U]

read-only 'memory *n* [U] *technical* ROM

'read-out *n* [C] information that is produced by a computer and shown on a screen; → **printout**: *a readout of all the sales figures*

read·y¹ /ˈredi/ *adj*
1 [PREPARED] [not before noun] if you are ready, you are prepared for what you are going to do: *Come on. Aren't you ready yet?* | *When the doorbell rang he was **ready and waiting**.* | **ready to do sth** *Everything's packed, and we're ready to leave.* | [+**for**] *I don't feel that I'm ready for my driving test yet.* | *I felt strong, fit, and **ready for anything**.* | [+**with**] *At the end of the lecture, I was ready with questions.* | *Why does it take you so long to **get ready** to go out?* | **make ready** (=prepare to start doing something) *We made ready for our journey home.* | **when you're ready** (=said to tell someone that you are ready for them to start doing something) | **ready when you are** (=said to tell someone that you are ready to do what you have arranged to do together) → PREPARE
2 [FOR IMMEDIATE USE] [not before noun] if something is ready, someone has prepared it and you can use it immediately: *When will supper be ready?* | **ready to use/eat etc** *The computer is now set up and ready to use.* | [+**for**] *Is everything ready for the exhibition?* | *I've got to **get a room ready** for our guests.*
3 **have sth ready** to have something near you so that you can use it if you need to: *I had my calculator ready.*

4 be/feel ready for sth *spoken* to need or want something as soon as possible: *I'm really ready for a vacation.*

5 be ready to do sth *informal* to be likely to do something soon: *She looked ready to burst into tears.*

6 WILLING [not before noun] very willing to do something: **ready to do sth** *He was always ready to help us.* | *She was ready and willing to work hard.*

7 QUICK [only before noun] available or coming without delay: *They need to have ready access to police files.* | *a ready supply* of drink | *I had no ready answer to his question.* | *an intelligent man with a ready wit*

8 ready money/cash money that you can spend immediately: *The company is short of ready cash.*

9 ready, steady, go! *BrE*; **get ready, get set, go!** *AmE spoken* used to tell people to start a race → READILY, READINESS; → rough and ready at ROUGH¹ (15)

ready² *v* **readied**, **readying**, **readies** [T] *formal* to make something or someone ready for something; ◗ **prepare**: **ready sb/sth for sth** *I tried to ready him for the bad news.*

ready³ *n* **1 at the ready** available to be used immediately: *Soldiers stood around with weapons at the ready.* **2 the readies** *BrE informal* money that you can use immediately: *I'm getting a new car as soon as I can scrape together the readies.*

ready⁴ *adv* **ready cooked/prepared etc** already cooked, prepared etc by someone else: *They seem to live on ready cooked meals.*

ready-'made *adj* [only before noun] **1** ready-made food or goods are already prepared or made, and ready for you to use immediately: *a ready-made spaghetti sauce* **2** ready-made ideas or reasons are provided for you, so that you do not have to think of them yourself: *The rain gave us a ready-made excuse to stay at home.*

ready 'meal *n* [C] *BrE* a meal that has already been cooked and is sold ready to eat

ready-to-'wear *adj* *old-fashioned* ready-to-wear clothes are made in standard sizes, not made specially to fit one person

re·af·firm /ˌriːəˈfɜːm $ -ɜːrm/ *v* [T] to formally state an opinion, belief, or intention again, especially after someone has questioned you or expressed a doubt; ◗ **reiterate**: *The party reaffirmed its commitment to nuclear disarmament.* | **reaffirm that** *The government has reaffirmed that education is a top priority.* —**reaffirmation** /ˌriːæfəˈmeɪʃən $ -fər-/ *n* [C,U]

re·af·for·es·ta·tion /ˌriːəfɒrɪˈsteɪʃən $ -fɔː-, -fɑː-/ *n* [U] *BrE technical* REFORESTATION

re·a·gent /riˈeɪdʒənt/ *n* [C] *technical* a substance that shows that another substance in a COMPOUND exists, by causing a chemical REACTION

real¹ S1 W1 /rɪəl/ *adj*

1 IMPORTANT something that is real exists and is important: *There is a real danger that the disease might spread.* | *We need to tackle the real problems of unemployment and poverty.* | *There is no real reason to worry.*

2 NOT ARTIFICIAL something that is real is actually what it seems to be and not false or artificial; ◗ **fake**: *a coat made of real fur* | *She had never seen a real live elephant before.* | *Artificial flowers can sometimes look better than the real thing.*

3 NOT IMAGINARY something that is real actually exists and is not just imagined: *The children know that Santa Claus isn't a real person.* | *Dreams can sometimes seem very real.* | *Things don't happen quite that easily in real life.*

4 the real world used to talk about the difficult experience of living and working with other people, rather than being protected at home, at school, or at college: *the shock of leaving university and going out into the real world*

5 TRUE [only before noun] actual and true, not invented: *That's not her real name.* | *What was the real reason you quit your job?*

6 FEELINGS a real feeling or emotion is one that you actually experience and is strong; ◗ **genuine**: *There was a look of real hatred in her eyes.* | *I got a real sense of achievement when my work was first published.*

7 RIGHT QUALITIES [only before noun] a real thing has all the qualities you expect something of that type to have: *I remember my first real job.* | *Simon was her first real boyfriend.*

SPOKEN PHRASES

8 FOR EMPHASIS [only before noun] used to emphasize how stupid, beautiful, terrible etc someone or something is: *Thanks – you've been a real help.* | *The house was a real mess.*

9 for real seriously, not just pretending: *After two trial runs we did it for real.*

10 are you for real? *AmE* used when you are very surprised or shocked by what someone has done or said

11 get real! used to tell someone that they are being very silly or unreasonable

12 keep it real to behave in an honest way and not pretend to be different from how you really are

---

13 MONEY [only before noun] a real increase or decrease in an amount of money is one you calculate by including the general decrease in the value of money over a period of time: *a real increase of 6% in average wages* | *The average value of salaries has fallen in real terms* (=calculated in this way).

real² *adv AmE spoken* very: *He's real cute.* | *It was real nice to see you again.*

real 'ale *n* [C,U] *BrE* beer that has been made in the traditional way, not in a large factory

real es·tate *n* [U] *especially AmE* **1** property in the form of land or houses: *a fall in the value of real estate* **2** the business of selling houses or land

real estate ˌagent *n* [C] *AmE* someone whose job is to sell houses or land for other people; ◗ **estate agent** *BrE*

re·a·lign /ˌriːəˈlaɪn/ *v* [T] **1** to change the way in which something is organized; ◗ **reorganize**: *The company is planning to realign its sales operations.* **2 realign yourself with sb** to begin to support and work together with someone again: *They have tried to realign themselves with the communists.* **3** to change the position of something slightly so that it is in the correct position in relation to something else: *You'll have to realign your text columns.*

re·a·lign·ment /ˌriːəˈlaɪnmənt/ *n* [C,U] **1** when something is changed and organized in a different way; ◗ **reorganization**: [+of] *a realignment of the company's management structure* **2** when people stop supporting one group and start to support and work together with a different group: [+of] *There is now a need for a realignment of political parties.* **3** when the parts of something are arranged so that they return to their correct positions in relation to each other: *the realignment of several major roads*

real·is·m /ˈrɪəlɪzəm/ *n* [U] **1** the ability to accept and deal with difficult situations in a practical way, based on what is possible rather than what you would like to happen: *He has hope, but also a scientist's sense of realism.* **2** the quality of being or seeming real: *the realism of the horses on the carousel* **3** also **Realism** the style of art and literature in which things, especially unpleasant things, are shown or described as they really are in life; → **idealism, romanticism**: *the tough realism of his early works*

real·ist /ˈrɪəlɪst/ *n* [C] **1** someone who accepts that things are not always perfect, and deals with problems or difficult situations in a practical way: *She had always been a realist, not a dreamer.* **2** a writer, painter etc who shows or describes things, especially unpleasant things, as they really are in life

rea·lis·tic S3 /rɪəˈlɪstɪk/ *adj*
1 judging and dealing with situations in a practical way according to what is actually possible rather than

what you would like to happen; **⊟ unrealistic: it is not realistic to do sth** *It's just not realistic to expect a promotion so soon.* | [+**about**] *You need to be realistic about the amount you can do in a day.*
2 a realistic aim or hope is one that it is possible to achieve; **⊟ unrealistic:** *Is this a realistic target?* | *I don't think they have a **realistic chance** of winning.*
3 realistic pictures or stories show things as they are in real life: *a realistic portrayal of life in Victorian Britain*

rea·lis·tic·ally /rɪəˈlɪstɪkli/ *adv* **1** if you think about something realistically, you think about it in a practical way and according to what is actually possible: *You can't realistically expect to win the whole competition.* | [sentence adverb]: *Realistically, we're not going to get this finished this week.* **2** if you describe or show something realistically, you describe or show it as it is in real life: *realistically painted toy soldiers* | *The novel realistically depicts immigrant life at the beginning of the last century.*

re·al·i·ty [S2] [W2] /riˈæləti/ *n plural* **realities**
1 [C,U] what actually happens or is true, not what is imagined or thought: *the distinction between fantasy and reality* | *TV is used as an **escape from reality**.* | *I think the government has **lost touch with reality** (=no longer understands what is real or true).* | *political realities* | **harsh/grim/stark reality** *Millions of people live with the harsh realities of unemployment.* | *the **reality is that** The reality is that young people will not go into teaching until salaries are higher.* | *The paperless office may one day **become a reality**.*
2 in reality used to say that something is different from what people think: *In reality, violent crimes are still extremely rare.*
3 [U] the fact that something exists or is happening: *She had never accepted the reality of her pregnancy.* → **VIRTUAL REALITY**

re'ality ˌcheck *n* [C usually singular] *informal* an occasion when you consider the facts of a situation, as opposed to what you would like or what you have imagined: *It's time for a reality check. The Bears aren't as good a team as you think.*

rea·liz·a·ble also **-isable** *BrE* /ˈrɪəlaɪzəbəl/ *adj* **1** possible to achieve; **⊟ achievable:** *Is this a realizable goal?* **2** in a form that can be changed into money easily: *the company's realizable assets*

re·a·li·za·tion also **-isation** *BrE* /ˌrɪəlaɪˈzeɪʃən $ -lə-/ *n* [singular, U] **1** when you understand something that you had not understood before: [+**of**] *I was shocked by the realization of what I had done.* | **realization that** *the realization that she might never recover from her illness* | *There is a **growing realization** that we must manage the earth's resources more carefully.* **2** *formal* when you achieve something that you had planned or hoped for; **⊟ achievement:** [+**of**] *the realization of his dreams* **3** *technical* when you change something into money by selling it: *the realization of assets*

rea·lize [S1] [W1] also **-ise** *BrE* /ˈrɪəlaɪz/ *v* [T not usually in progressive]
1 UNDERSTAND to know and understand something, or suddenly begin to understand it: **realize (that)** *I suddenly realized that the boy was crying.* | *Do you realize you're an hour late?* | **realize who/what/how etc** *I'm sorry, I didn't realize who you were.* | *It took us a while to realize the extent of the tragedy.* | *It was only later that I realized my mistake.*
2 ACHIEVE *formal* to achieve something that you were hoping to achieve: *She never realized her ambition of winning an Olympic gold medal.* | *a young singer who has not yet realized her full potential* (=achieved as much as she can achieve)
3 sb's worst fears were realized used to say that the thing that you were most afraid of has actually happened: *His worst fears were realized when he heard that Chris had been arrested.*
4 MONEY a) *formal* to obtain or earn an amount of money: *The campaign realized $5000.* | *We realized a*

small profit on the sale of the house. **b)** realize an asset *technical* to change something that you own into money by selling it

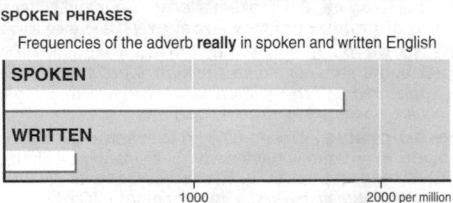

WORD CHOICE: realize, recognize
If you **realize** a fact, you know and understand it, or begin to understand it: *Do you realize how dangerous this is?* | *I realized that the job was going to take longer than I thought.*
If you **recognize** a fact or problem, you accept that it exists: *We recognize that many students need extra help.* | *The government does not recognize the need for more funding.*
⚠ **Realize** is not followed by 'about' or 'of': *She already had a boyfriend, but I didn't realize this* (NOT *didn't realize about this*).

'real-life *adj* [only before noun] actually happening in life, not invented in a book: *a real-life drama* | *real-life problems*

real·ly [S1] [W1] /ˈrɪəli/ *adv*
1 VERY very; **⊟ extremely:** *a really good film* | *It was really cold last night.* | *He walks really slowly.* | *I'm really, really sorry.*
2 THE REAL SITUATION used when you are talking about what actually happened or is true, rather than what people might wrongly think: *Why don't you tell us what really happened?* | *Oliver's not really her brother.* | *I never know what he's really thinking.* | *She seems unfriendly at first, but she's really very nice.*

SPOKEN PHRASES

Frequencies of the adverb **really** in spoken and written English

SPOKEN	
WRITTEN	

| 1000 | 2000 per million |

3 DEFINITELY used to emphasize something you are saying: *We really need that extra money.* | *I really don't mind.* | *I'm absolutely fine, Dad – really.*
4 NOT TRUE used in questions when you are asking someone if something is true and suggesting that you think it is not true; **⊟ honestly:** *Do you really think she's doing this for your benefit?* | *Do you really expect me to believe that?*
5 a) really? used to show that you are surprised by what someone has said: *'He's Canadian.' 'Really?'* **b) really?** used in conversation to show that you are listening to or interested in what the other person is saying: *'We had a great time in Florida.' 'Really? How lovely.'* **c)** *AmE* used to show that you agree with someone: *'Glen can be such a jerk.' 'Yeah, really!'* **d)** especially *BrE* used to show that you are angry or disapprove of something: *Really, Larry, you might have told me!*
6 not really used to say 'no' or 'not' in a less strong way: *'Do you want to come along?' 'Not really.'* | *I don't really know what he's doing now.*
7 should/ought really used to say what someone should do, especially when they are probably not going to do it: *You should really go and see a doctor.*
8 really and truly also **really, truly** *AmE* to emphasize a statement or opinion: *He was really and truly a brilliant comedian.*

realm /relm/ *n* [C] **1** *written* a general area of knowledge, activity, or thought: *the spiritual realm* | [+**of**] *an idea that belongs in the realm of science fiction* **2 within the realms of possibility** also **not beyond the realm(s) of possibility** used, often humorously, to

[1] 000, [2] 000, [3] 000, most frequent words in [S]poken and [W]ritten English

say that something is possible even though you think it is not very likely: *I suppose it's not beyond the realms of possibility.* **3** *literary* a country ruled by a king or queen

re·al·pol·i·tik /reɪˈɑːlpɒlɪtiːk $ -pɑː-/ *n* [U] politics based on practical situations and needs rather than on moral principles or ideas

ˌreal ˈproperty *n* [U] *law* REAL ESTATE (1)

ˈreal-time *adj* [only before noun] *technical* a real-time computer system deals with information as fast as it receives it: *a real-time operating system* —**real time** *n* [U]: *The images are created in real time.*

Real·tor, realtor /ˈrɪəltə, -tɔː $ -ər, -ɔːr/ *n* [C] *trademark AmE* a REAL ESTATE AGENT

real·ty /ˈrɪəlti/ *n* [U] *AmE* REAL ESTATE

ream¹ /riːm/ *n* [C] **1 reams** [plural] *informal* a large amount of writing on paper: [+of] *reams of notes* **2** *technical* a standard amount of paper, 500 pieces in the US or 480 pieces in Britain

ream² *v* [T] *AmE informal* to treat someone badly, especially by cheating

re·an·i·mate /riːˈænɪ̯meɪt/ *v* [T] *formal* to give new strength to someone or something or the energy to start again

reap /riːp/ *v* **1** [T] to get something, especially something good, as a result of what you have done: **reap the benefit/reward/profit (of sth)** *Those who do take risks often reap the rewards.* **2 you reap what you sow** used to say that if you do bad things, bad things will happen to you, and if you do good things, good things will happen to you **3** [I,T] *old-fashioned* to cut and collect a crop of grain; → **harvest** —**reaper** *n* [C] → GRIM REAPER

re·ap·pear /ˌriːəˈpɪə $ -ˈpɪr/ *v* [I] to appear again after not being seen for some time: *In March, his cancer reappeared.* | *Many of these ideas reappear in his later books.* —**reappearance** *n* [C,U]

re·ap·praise /ˌriːəˈpreɪz/ *v* [T] to examine something again in order to consider whether you should change it or your opinion of it; ⧉ **reassess:** *People began to reappraise their values.* —**reappraisal** *n* [C,U]

rear¹ /rɪə $ rɪr/ *n* **1** *formal* **the rear** the back part of an object, vehicle, or building, or a position at the back of an object or area; ⧉ **front: at/to the rear (of sth)** *a garden at the rear of the house* | *The hotel overlooks the river to the rear.* | **in the rear (of sth)** *a passenger travelling in the rear of a car* **2** [C] also **rear end** *informal* the part of your body which you sit on; ⧉ **bottom** **3 bring up the rear** to be at the back of a line of people or in a race: *Carole was left to bring up the rear.*

rear² *v* **1** [T] to look after a person or animal until they are fully grown; ⧉ **raise:** *It's a good place to rear young children.* | *The birds have been successfully reared in captivity.* **2** also **rear up** [I] if an animal rears, it rises up to stand on its back legs; → **buck:** *The horse reared and threw me off.* **3** also **rear up** [I] if something rears up, it appears in front of you and often seems to be leaning over you in a threatening way: *A large rock, almost 200 feet high, reared up in front of them.* **4 be reared on sth** to be given a particular kind of food, books, entertainment etc regularly while you are a child: *children reared on TV and video games* **5 rear its ugly head** if a problem or difficult situation rears its ugly head, it appears and is impossible to ignore: *The problem of drug-taking in sport has reared its ugly head again.*

rear³ *adj* [only before noun] at or near the back of something, especially a vehicle; ⧉ **front:** *the rear door of the car* | *Knock at the rear entrance.*

ˌrear ˈadmiral *n* [C] a high rank in the navy

rear·guard /ˈrɪəgɑːd $ ˈrɪrgɑːrd/ *n* **1 fight a rear-guard action a)** to make a determined effort to prevent a change that you think is bad, although it seems too late to stop it: *They have been fighting a rearguard action to stop a supermarket being built on the land.* **b)**

if an army fights a rearguard action, it defends itself at the back against an enemy that is chasing it **2** [singular] the group of soldiers who defend the back of an army against an enemy that is chasing it

re·arm /riːˈɑːm $ -ˈɑːrm/ *v* [I,T] to obtain weapons again or provide someone else with new weapons: *They returned to base to rearm.* —**rearmament** *n* [U]

rear·most /ˈrɪəməʊst $ ˈrɪrmoʊst/ *adj* [only before noun] furthest back; ⧉ **last:** *the rearmost seats*

re·ar·range /ˌriːəˈreɪndʒ/ *v* [T] **1** to change the position or order of things: *She set about rearranging the furniture in the living room.* **2** to change the time of a meeting etc: *My secretary will phone to rearrange the appointment.* —**rearrangement** *n* [C,U]

rear·view mir·ror /ˌrɪəvjuː ˈmɪrə $ ˌrɪrvjuː ˈmɪrər/ *n* [C] a mirror inside a car etc that lets the driver see the area behind the car → see picture at CAR

rear·ward /ˈrɪəwəd $ ˈrɪrwərd/ *adj* in or towards the back of something —**rearwards** also **rearward** *adv*

rea·son¹ S1 W1 /ˈriːzən/ *n*

1 CAUSE [C] why someone decides to do something, or the cause or explanation for something that happens

> reason (that)
> reason why
> reason for (doing) sth
> reason to do sth
> a good reason
> a compelling reason (=a reason that persuades you)
> give a reason (for sth)
> for some reason (or other/or another) (=for a reason that you do not know)
> for personal reasons
> for sentimental reasons (=because of your feelings, not for practical reasons)
> for the simple reason (that)
> for obvious reasons
> for reasons of sth
> for reasons best known to himself/themselves etc (=used when someone does something surprising)
> no/any reason whatsoever
> have your reasons (=have a secret reason for doing something)
> see no reason why/to do sth
> by reason of sth *formal* (=because of something)

The reason I called was to ask about the plans for Saturday. | *We'd like to know the **reason why** she didn't accept the job.* | *People give many different **reasons for** wanting to change jobs.* | *They must have had a **good reason to** do it.* | [+behind] *He explained the reasons behind the decision.* | *He wouldn't **give** the **reasons for** his decision.* | *For some reason or other, he couldn't come that day.* | *She wants to change her job **for** purely **personal reasons.*** | *I kept the photos **for sentimental reasons.*** | *She didn't answer **for the simple reason** that she couldn't think of anything to say.* | *For obvious reasons, we've changed all the names.* | *The tower is closed **for reasons of** safety.* | *For reasons best known to herself, she's sold the house and left the country.* | *There is **no reason whatsoever** to doubt her story.* | 'Why did you tell him?' 'Oh, I **had my reasons.'** | *I **see no reason** why it shouldn't work.* → see box at CAUSE¹

2 GOOD OR FAIR [U] a fact that makes it right or fair for someone to do something: **(no) reason to do sth** *There is no reason to panic.* | *She **has reason to** feel guilty.* | *We **have reason to believe that** the goods were stolen.* | *I know I'm late, but **that's no reason** to shout at me.* | *Under the circumstances, we **had every reason** (=had very good reasons) to be suspicious.* | **with (good) reason** (=based on something sensible) *Natalie was alarmed by the news, and with reason.*

3 all the more reason why/to do sth *spoken* used to say that what has just been mentioned is an additional reason for doing what you have suggested: *But surely that's all the more reason to act quickly.*

4 GOOD JUDGMENT [U] sensible judgment and understanding; ⧉ **sense:** *There's reason in what he* *says.* | *They're not prepared to **listen to reason*** (=be persuaded by someone's sensible advice). | *There's no way of making my father **see reason*** (=accept advice and make a sensible decision).

5 within reason within sensible limits: *You can go anywhere you want, within reason.*

6 go/be beyond (all) reason to be more than is acceptable or reasonable: *Their demands go beyond all reason.*

7 ABILITY TO THINK [U] the ability to think, understand, and form judgments that are based on facts: *the human **power of reason*** | **lose your reason** old-fashioned (=become mentally ill)

8 no reason *spoken* used when someone asks you why you are doing something and you do not want to tell them: *'Why d'you want to go that way?' 'Oh, no reason.'*

→ **no rhyme or reason** at RHYME¹ (4); → **it stands to reason** at STAND¹ (32)

reason² v **1** [T] to form a particular judgment about a situation after carefully considering the facts: **reason (that)** *They reasoned that other businesses would soon copy the idea.* **2** [I] to think and make judgments: *the ability to reason*

reason sth ⇔ **out** *phr v* to find an explanation or solution to a problem, by thinking of all the possibilities; ◼ **work out**

reason with sb *phr v* to talk to someone in an attempt to persuade them to be more sensible: *I tried to reason with her.*

rea·son·a·ble [S1] [W2] /'riːzənəbəl/ *adj*
1 fair and sensible; ◼ **unreasonable:** *a reasonable request* | *Be reasonable - you can't expect her to do all the work on her own!* | *I thought it was a **perfectly reasonable** (=completely reasonable) question.* | **it is reasonable to do sth** *It seems reasonable to assume they've been tested.* | *He had **reasonable grounds** (=good reasons but no proof) for believing the law had been broken.* | **a reasonable explanation/excuse** *It sounded like a **reasonable enough** excuse to me.*
2 fairly good, but not especially good; ◼ **average:** *She has a reasonable chance of doing well in the exam.*
3 a reasonable amount is fairly large: *I've got a reasonable amount of money saved.*
4 reasonable prices are not too high; ◼ **fair:** *good food at a reasonable price*
5 beyond (a) reasonable doubt *law* if something is proved beyond reasonable doubt, it is shown to be almost certainly true —**reasonableness** *n* [U]

rea·son·a·bly [S2] [W3] /'riːzənəbli/ *adv*
1 [+ adj/adv] quite or to a satisfactory degree, but not completely: *The car is in reasonably good condition.* | *He's doing reasonably well at school.*
2 in a way that is right or fair: *He can't reasonably be expected to have known that.*
3 in a sensible way: *Despite her anger, she had behaved very reasonably.*

rea·soned /'riːzənd/ *adj* [only before noun] based on careful thought, and therefore sensible; ◼ **logical:** *reasoned argument*

rea·son·ing /'riːzənɪŋ/ *n* [U] a process of thinking carefully about something in order to make a judgment: **scientific/logical/legal reasoning** | [+behind] *What is the reasoning behind this decision?*

re·as·sem·ble /ˌriːə'sembəl/ *v* **1** [T] to bring together the different parts of something to make a whole again, after they have been separated: *The equipment had to be dismantled and reassembled at each new location.* **2** [I] if a group of people reassemble, they meet together again after a period apart: *Parliament reassembled after a seven-week break.*

re·as·sert /ˌriːə'sɜːt $ -'sɜːrt/ *v* [T] **1 reassert your authority/power/control** to do or say something to make your position stronger after a period when it seemed weak: *The Prime Minister aimed to reassert his authority.* **2** to state a fact or opinion again, often more strongly or more clearly: *He used the opportunity to reassert his position on energy policy.* **3 reassert itself** if something reasserts itself, it returns or becomes stronger after a period when it was missing or weak: *At last, common sense had reasserted itself.*

re·as·sess /ˌriːə'ses/ *v* [T] to think about something again carefully in order to decide whether to change your opinion or judgment about it; ◼ **reappraise:** *This has caused us to reassess the way we approach our planning.* —**reassessment** *n* [C,U]

re·as·sur·ance /ˌriːə'ʃʊərəns $ -'ʃʊr-/ *n* [C,U] something that is said or done which makes someone feel calmer and less worried or frightened about a problem: *Parents are looking for reassurance about their children's safety.* | **give/offer/provide reassurance** *They are offering practical help and reassurance.* | **reassurance that** *We have been given reassurances that the water is safe to drink.*

re·as·sure /ˌriːə'ʃʊə $ -'ʃʊr/ *v* [T] to make someone feel calmer and less worried or frightened about a problem or situation: *Teachers reassured anxious parents.* | **reassure sb (that)** *He tried to reassure me that my mother would be okay.*

re·as·sur·ing /ˌriːə'ʃʊərɪŋ◂ $ -'ʃʊr-/ *adj* making you feel less worried or frightened: *a reassuring smile* | **it is reassuring (for sb) to do sth** *It's reassuring to know that problems are rare.* —**reassuringly** *adv*

re·bate /'riːbeɪt/ *n* [C] an amount of money that is paid back to you when you have paid too much tax, rent etc: *You may be entitled to a tax rebate.*

reb·el¹ /'rebəl/ *n* [C] **1** someone who opposes or fights against people in authority: *Anti-government rebels attacked the town.* | **rebel forces/soldiers** | *the rebel leader* **2** someone who refuses to do things in the normal way, or in the way that other people want them to: *Alex has always been a bit of a rebel.*

re·bel² /rɪ'bel/ *v* **rebelled, rebelling** [I] **1** to oppose or fight against someone in authority or against an idea or situation which you do not agree with: [+against] *teenage boys rebelling against their parents* **2** *written* if your stomach, legs, mind etc rebel, you cannot do or believe something you think you should: *He knew he ought to eat, but his stomach rebelled.*

re·bel·lion /rɪ'beljən/ *n* [C,U] **1** an organized attempt to change the government or leader of a country, using violence; → **coup, revolution:** *an armed rebellion* | [+against] *a rebellion against the military regime* | **in rebellion** *The Bretons rose in rebellion against the King.* | **suppress/crush a rebellion** (=use violence to stop it) **2** when someone opposes or fights against people in authority or ideas which they do not agree with: *a rebellion by right-wing members of the party* | [+against] *rebellion against traditional values*

re·bel·lious /rɪ'beljəs/ *adj* **1** deliberately not obeying people in authority or rules of behaviour: *rebellious teenagers* | *He's always had a **rebellious streak** (=a tendency to rebel).* **2** fighting against the government of your own country: *rebellious minorities* —**rebelliously** *adv* —**rebelliousness** *n* [U]

re·birth /ˌriː'bɜːθ $ -'bɜːrθ/ *n* **1** [singular] *formal* when an important idea, feeling, or organization becomes strong or popular again: [+of] *a rebirth of nationalism*

R

school are music and recess. **3** [C] a space in the wall of a room, especially for shelves, cupboards etc; ▤ **alcove** **4 the recesses of sth** the inner hidden parts of something: *the deep recesses of the cave* | *fears hidden away in the darker recesses of her mind*

re·cess² /rɪ'ses $ 'riːses, rɪ'ses/ *v* [I] especially AmE if a government, law court etc recesses, it officially stops work for a period of time

re·cessed /rɪ'sest $ 'riːsest, rɪ'sest/ *adj* fitted into a part of a wall that is further back than the rest of the wall: *a recessed bookshelf*

re·ces·sion S2 W3 /rɪ'seʃən/ *n* [C,U] a difficult time when there is less trade, business activity etc in a country than usual: *the economic recession of the early 1980s* | *There is deep recession in the UK.* | **into/out of recession** *attempts to pull the country out of recession*

re·ces·sion·a·ry /rɪ'seʃənəri $ -ʃəneri/ *adj* relating to a recession or likely to cause one: *recessionary pressures*

re·ces·sive /rɪ'sesɪv/ *adj* technical a recessive GENE is passed to children from their parents only if both parents have the gene; ▤ **dominant**

re·charge /ˌriːˈtʃɑːdʒ $ -ɑːr-/ *v* [T] **1** to put a new supply of electricity into a BATTERY **2 recharge your batteries** informal to get back your strength and energy again: *I'm going to spend a week in the mountains to recharge my batteries.* —**rechargeable** *adj*: *rechargeable batteries*

re·charg·er /ˌriːˈtʃɑːdʒə $ -ˈtʃɑːrdʒər/ *n* [C] a machine that recharges a BATTERY

re·cher·ché /rəˈʃeəʃeɪ $ rəʃerˈʃeɪ/ *adj* formal a recherché subject, idea, word etc is uncommon and has been chosen to make people admire your knowledge

re-chip /riːˈtʃɪp/ *v* **re-chipped, re-chipping** [T] to put a new computer CHIP into a piece of electronic equipment such as a MOBILE PHONE or a computer games machine so that you can use software that you are not supposed to use, or use a service that you have not paid for

re·cid·i·vist /rɪˈsɪdɪˌvɪst/ *n* [C] technical a criminal who starts doing illegal things again, even after he or she has been punished —**recidivism** *n* [U]

re·ci·pe S3 /ˈresɪpi/ *n* [C] **1** a set of instructions for cooking a particular type of food: [+for] *a recipe for tomato soup* | *a recipe book* **2 be a recipe for sth** to be likely to cause a particular result, often a bad one: *She said that five small boys on skis was a recipe for disaster, not a holiday.*

re·cip·i·ent /rɪˈsɪpiənt/ *n* [C] formal someone who receives something: [+of] *the recipient of the Nobel Peace Prize*

re·cip·ro·cal /rɪˈsɪprəkəl/ *adj* formal a reciprocal arrangement or relationship is one in which two people or groups do or give the same things to each other; → **mutual**: *He spoke of the necessity for a reciprocal relationship that would be useful for all sides.* | *Such treaties provide reciprocal rights and obligations.* —**reciprocally** /-kli/ *adv*

re·cip·ro·cate /rɪˈsɪprəkeɪt/ *v* **1** [I,T] formal to do or give something, because something similar has been done or given to you: *When he spoke I was expected to reciprocate with some remark of my own.* **2** [T] to feel the same about someone as they feel about you: *It was a hopeless love that could not possibly be reciprocated.* —**reciprocation** /rɪˌsɪprəˈkeɪʃən/ *n* [U]

re·ci·pro·ci·ty /ˌresɪˈprɒsɪti $ -ˈprɑː-/ *n* [U] formal a situation in which two people, groups, or countries give each other similar kinds of help or special rights

re·cit·al /rɪˈsaɪtl/ *n* [C] **1** a performance of music or poetry, usually given by one performer: *a piano recital* | [+of] *a recital of classical favourites* **2** formal a spoken description of a series of events: [+of] *a long recital of her adventures*

re·ci·ta·tion /ˌresɪˈteɪʃən/ *n* [C,U] **1** an act of saying a poem, piece of literature etc that you have learned, for people to listen to: *recitations from the great poets* **2** a spoken description of an event or a series of events: [+of] *He went into a recitation of his life from the earliest years.*

re·ci·ta·tive /ˌresɪtəˈtiːv/ *n* [C,U] technical a speech set to music that is sung by one person and continues the story of an OPERA (=musical play) between the songs

re·cite /rɪˈsaɪt/ *v* **1** [I,T] to say a poem, piece of literature etc that you have learned, for people to listen to: *She recited a poem that she had learnt at school.* **2** [T] to tell someone a series or list of things: *Len recited the breakfast menu – cereal, bacon and eggs, and toast.* —**reciter** *n* [C]

reck·less /ˈrekləs/ *adj* not caring or worrying about the possible bad or dangerous results of your actions: *He was accused of causing death by reckless driving.* | *a reckless disregard for safety* | *He dashed into the burning house with reckless abandon* (=without caring about the danger). —**recklessly** *adv* —**recklessness** *n* [U]

reck·on S2 W3 /ˈrekən/ *v* [T not in progressive] **1** spoken especially BrE to think or suppose something: **reckon (that)** *Do you reckon he'll agree to see us?* | *The police reckon that whoever killed Dad was with him earlier that day.* | *'There's nothing we can do about it.' 'You reckon* (=used to express doubt or disagreement)?' **2** to guess a number or amount, without calculating it exactly: **reckon (that)** *We reckon that sitting in traffic jams costs us around $9 billion a year in lost output.* | **reckon sth to be sth** *The average selling price for flats in the area was reckoned to be around £11,000.* **3** [usually passive] to think that someone or something is a particular kind of person or thing: **be reckoned to be sth** *The Lowsons were reckoned to be very good farmers.* | *Moving house is reckoned to be nearly as stressful as divorce.* | **be reckoned as sth** *An earthquake of magnitude 7 is reckoned as a major quake.* **4** formal to calculate an amount: *The expression 'full moon' means the fourteenth day of the moon reckoned from its first appearance.*

reckon on sth *phr v* BrE
to expect something to happen, when you are making plans: *We were reckoning on a profit of about half a million a year.* | **reckon on doing sth** *I was reckoning on getting at least 60% of the votes.*

reckon sth ⇔ **up** *phr v* BrE old-fashioned
to add up amounts, costs etc in order to get a total; ▤ **calculate**: *Pat was reckoning up the cost of everything in her mind.*

reckon with sb/sth *phr v*
1 sb/sth to be reckoned with someone or something that is powerful and must be regarded seriously as a possible opponent, competitor, danger etc: *Barcelona will be a force to be reckoned with this season.* | *The principal was certainly a woman to be reckoned with.* **2 not reckon with sb/sth** to not consider a possible problem when you are making plans: *I had not reckoned with the excitement in the popular press.* **3 have sb/sth to reckon with** to have to deal with someone or something powerful: *Any invader would have the military might of NATO to reckon with.*

reckon without sb/sth *phr v* BrE
if you are reckoning without something, you do not expect it and are not prepared for it: *They doubted that Fiona could finish the course, but they reckoned without her determination.*

reck·on·ing /ˈrekənɪŋ/ *n* **1** [U] calculation that is based on a careful guess rather than on exact knowledge: **by sb's reckoning** *By my reckoning, we have 12,000 clients.* **2** [C usually singular, U] a time when you are judged or punished for your actions, or when they have results that affect you: *We know that you will not forget their crimes when their day of reckoning comes.* | *In the final reckoning, the president failed to achieve his major goals.* **3 in/into/out of the reckoning** BrE among or not among those who are likely to win or be successful, especially in sport: *He had a knee injury, which put him out of the reckoning.* → DEAD RECKONING

re·claim /rɪˈkleɪm/ v [T] **1** to get back an amount of money that you have paid; ▣ **claim back**: *You may be entitled to reclaim some tax.* **2** to make an area of desert, wet land etc suitable for farming or building: *Large areas of land will be reclaimed for a new airport.* **3** to get back something that you have lost or that has been taken away from you: *I want to reclaim the championship that I lost in 1999.* **4** to obtain useful products from waste material; → **recycle**: *You can reclaim old boards and use them as shelves.* —**reclamation** /ˌrekləˈmeɪʃən/ n [U]: *land reclamation*

re·cline /rɪˈklaɪn/ v **1** [I] *formal* to lie or lean back in a relaxed way: [+in/on] *I spent Sunday reclining in a deck chair.* | *A solitary figure was reclining on the grass.* **2** [I,T] if you recline a seat, or if it reclines, you lower the back of the seat so that you can lean back in it: **reclining seat/chair**

re·clin·er /rɪˈklaɪnə $ -ər/ n [C] *especially AmE* a chair in which you can lean back at different angles

re·cluse /rɪˈkluːs $ ˈrekluːs/ n [C] someone who chooses to live alone, and does not like seeing or talking to other people: *She became a recluse after her two sons were murdered.* —**reclusive** /rɪˈkluːsɪv/ adj

rec·og·ni·tion ⟨S3⟩ ⟨W2⟩ /ˌrekəgˈnɪʃən/ n
1 [singular, U] the act of realizing and accepting that something is true or important: [+of] *Don's recognition of the importance of Suzy in his life* | **recognition that** *There is general recognition that the study techniques of many students are weak.* | **formal/official recognition** *official recognition of the need for jail reform*
2 [singular, U] public respect and thanks for someone's work or achievements: *He has achieved recognition and respect as a scientist.* | *The importance of voluntary organizations in the economy still needs to be given recognition.* | **in recognition of sth** *He was presented with a gold watch in recognition of his service to the company.*
3 [U] the act of knowing someone or something because you have known or learned about them in the past: *He stared at her, but there was no sign of recognition.* | **change beyond/out of all recognition** (=change completely) *The bakery business has changed beyond all recognition in the last 10 years.*
4 [U] the act of officially accepting that an organization, government, person etc has legal or official authority: [+of] *the recognition of Latvia as an independent state* | **international/diplomatic recognition** *the government's failure to achieve international recognition*
5 **speech recognition** the ability of a computer to recognize speech: *speech recognition systems*

rec·og·nize ⟨S1⟩ ⟨W1⟩ also **-ise** BrE /ˈrekəgnaɪz, ˈrekən-/ v [T]
1 [not in progressive] to know who someone is or what something is, because you have seen, heard, experienced, or learned about them in the past: *I didn't recognize you in your uniform.* | *It was malaria, but Dr Lee hadn't recognized the symptoms.* → see box at REALIZE
2 to officially accept that an organization, government, document etc has legal or official authority: *British medical qualifications are recognized in Canada.* | **recognize sth as sth** *The World Health Organization has recognized alcoholism as a disease since 1951.*
3 to accept or admit that something is true: **recognize (that)** *One must recognise that homesickness is natural.* | **recognize what/how/who etc** *It is important to recognize how little we know about this disease.*; → see box at REALIZE
4 [usually in passive] if something is recognized by people, they realize that it is important or very good: *Alexander tried to get his work recognized by the medical profession.* | **be recognized as sth** *Lawrence's novel was eventually recognized as a work of genius.* | *a*

recognized authority on Roman pottery
5 to officially and publicly thank someone for something they have done, by giving them a special honour: *He was recognized for having saved many lives.* —**recognizable** /ˈrekəgnaɪzəbəl, -kən-, ˌrekəgˈnaɪ-/ adj: *His face was instantly recognizable.* —**recognizably** adv

re·coil /rɪˈkɔɪl/ v [I] **1** to move back suddenly and quickly from something you do not like or are afraid of: [+from/at] *She recoiled from his touch as if she had been slapped.* **2** to feel such a strong dislike of a particular situation that you want to avoid it: [+from/at] *He recoils from everything in life that demands hard work.* | *We recoil in horror from the thought of subjecting someone to extreme pain.* **3** if a gun recoils, it moves backwards very quickly after it has been fired —**recoil** /ˈriːkɔɪl/ n [singular, U]: *The recoil of the gun sent him flying backwards.*

rec·ol·lect /ˌrekəˈlekt/ v [T] to be able to remember something: *All I recollect is a grey sky.* | **recollect that** *She recollected sadly that she and Ben used to laugh a lot.* | **recollect how/when/what etc** *Can you recollect how your brother reacted?* | **recollect doing sth** *I recollect seeing Ryder some years ago in Bonn.*

rec·ol·lec·tion /ˌrekəˈlekʃən/ n *formal* **1** [C] something from the past that you remember: *My earliest recollections are of my mother bending over my cot.* **2** [U] an act of remembering something: **have no recollection (of sth)** (=not remember) *I have no recollection of how I found my way there in the dark.* | **to (the best of) my recollection** (=used when you are unsure if you remember correctly) *To the best of my recollection, she drives a Mercedes.* | *Noone, to my recollection, gave a second thought to the risks involved.*

re·com·mence /ˌriːkəˈmens/ v [I,T] to begin something again after it has stopped

rec·om·mend ⟨S3⟩ ⟨W2⟩ /ˌrekəˈmend/ v [T]
1 to advise someone to do something, especially because you have special knowledge of a situation or subject: **recommend (that)** *I recommend that you get some professional advice.* | *Doctors strongly recommend that fathers should be present at their baby's birth.* | **recommend doing sth** *I would never recommend using a sunbed on a regular basis.* | *Sleeping tablets are not recommended in this case.* | *It is dangerous to exceed the recommended dose.*
2 to say that something or someone is good, or suggest them for a particular purpose or job: *I recommend the butter chicken – it's delicious.* | *Can you recommend a good lawyer?* | **recommend sth to sb** *I recommend this book to anyone with an interest in chemistry.* | **recommend sth for sth/sb** *Which type of oil do you recommend for my car?* | **recommend sb for sth** *I have decided to recommend you for the directorship.* | **highly/thoroughly recommend** *The hotel is highly recommended.*
3 **sth has much/little/nothing to recommend it** used to say that something has many, few, or no good qualities: *The town itself has little to recommend it.*

rec·om·men·da·tion ⟨W3⟩ /ˌrekəmenˈdeɪʃən/ n
1 [C] official advice given to someone, especially about what to do: *We will review the case and make a recommendation to the client.* | [+for] *recommendations for school reform* | [+of] *the main recommendations of the report* | **recommendation that** *We are making no recommendation that children should use Standard English.* |

games **2** *AmE* a room in a private house, where you can relax, play games etc; ☐ **games room** *BrE*

re·crim·i·na·tion /rɪˌkrɪmᵻ'neɪʃən/ *n* [C usually plural, U] when you blame or criticize someone for something that has happened: *Bitter accusations and recriminations followed the disaster.*

rec room /'rek ruːm, -rʊm/ *n* [C] *AmE informal* a RECREATION ROOM

re·cruit¹ /rɪ'kruːt/ *v* **1** [I,T] to find new people to work in a company, join an organization, do a job etc: *We're having difficulty recruiting enough qualified staff.* | *Many government officials were recruited from private industry.* **2** [I,T] to get people to join the army, navy etc; → **conscript**: *Most of the men in the village were recruited that day.* **3** [T] to persuade someone to do something for you: **recruit sb to do sth** *I recruited three of my friends to help me move.* —**recruiter** *n* [C] —**recruitment** *n* [U]

recruit² *n* [C] **1** someone who has just joined the army, navy, or AIR FORCE; → **conscript**: **new/raw/fresh recruit** (=one who is completely untrained) *Drill sergeants have eight weeks to turn fresh recruits into soldiers.* **2** someone who has recently joined an organization, team, group of people etc: *New recruits are sent to the Atlanta office for training.*

rec·tal /'rektəl/ *adj medical* relating to the RECTUM

rec·tan·gle /'rektæŋgəl/ *n* [C] a shape that has four straight sides, two of which are usually longer than the other two, and four 90° angles at the corners; → **square**

rec·tan·gu·lar /rek'tæŋgjᵿlə $ -ər/ *adj* having the shape of a rectangle

rec·ti·fy /'rektᵻfaɪ/ *v* **rectified, rectifying, rectifies** [T] *formal* to correct something that is wrong; ☐ **put right**: *I did my best to rectify the situation, but the damage was already done.* —**rectification** /ˌrektᵻfᵻ'keɪʃən/ *n* [C,U]

rec·ti·lin·e·ar /ˌrektᵻ'lɪniə◂ $ -ər◂/ *adj technical* consisting of straight lines

rec·ti·tude /'rektᵻtjuːd $ -tuːd/ *n* [U] *formal* behaviour that is honest and morally correct

rec·tor /'rektə $ -ər/ *n* [C] **1** a priest in some Christian churches who is responsible for a particular area, group etc; → **vicar 2** the person in charge of certain colleges and schools

rec·to·ry /'rektəri/ *n plural* **rectories** [C] a house where the priest of the local church lives; → **vicarage**

rec·tum /'rektəm/ *n plural* **rectums** or **recta** /-tə/ [C] *medical* the lowest part of your BOWELS

re·cum·bent /rɪ'kʌmbənt/ *adj formal* lying down on your back or side

re·cu·pe·rate /rɪ'kjuːpəreɪt, -'kuː-/ *v* **1** [I] to get better again after an illness or injury; ☐ **recover**: [+from] *Coles is recuperating from a sprained ankle.* **2** [T] *especially BrE* to get back money that you have spent or lost in business; ☐ **recoup, recover**: *We've recuperated our losses.* **3** [I] to return to a more normal condition after a difficult time; ☐ **recover**: *Winston proposed several ways for the industry to recuperate.* —**recuperation** /rɪˌkjuːpə'reɪʃən, -ˌkuː-/ *n* [U]

re·cu·pe·ra·tive /rɪ'kjuːpərətɪv, -'kuː- $ -pəreɪtɪv/ *adj* [only before noun] recuperative powers, abilities etc help someone or something get better again, especially after an illness: *a recuperative vacation*

re·cur /rɪ'kɜː $ -ɜːr/ *v* **recurred, recurring** [I] **1** if something, especially something bad or unpleasant, recurs, it happens again: *There is a danger that the disease may recur.* | *Love is a recurring theme in the book.* | **recurring dream/nightmare 2** *technical* if a number or numbers after a DECIMAL POINT recur, they are repeated for ever in the same order

re·cur·rence /rɪ'kʌrəns $ -'kɜːr-/ *n* [C usually singular, U] *formal* an occasion when something that has happened before happens again: [+of] *after the recurrence*

of a back problem | *Measures must be taken to stop a recurrence of last night's violence.*

re·cur·rent /rɪ'kʌrənt $ -'kɜːr-/ *adj* happening or appearing several times: *recurrent minor illnesses* | *Political revolution is a recurrent theme in Riley's books.* —**recurrently** *adv*

re·cy·cla·ble /ˌriː'saɪkləbəl/ *adj* used materials or substances that are recyclable can be recycled: *recyclable cardboard packaging* —**recyclable** *n* [C usually plural] *AmE*

re·cy·cle /ˌriː'saɪkəl/ *v* **1** [I,T] to put used objects or materials through a special process so that they can be used again: *We take all our bottles to be recycled.* | *packaging made of* **recycled paper 2** [T] to use something such as an idea, writing etc again instead of developing something new: *The fashion world just keeps recycling old ideas.*

re·cy·cling /ˌriː'saɪklɪŋ/ *n* **1** [U] the process of treating used objects or materials so that they can be used again: *Recycling is important to help protect our environment.* → see picture at ENVIRONMENT **2** [singular] *AmE informal* things that are to be recycled: *Don't forget to take out the recycling.* → see picture at BIN¹

red¹ S1 W1 /red/ *adj comparative* **redder**, *superlative* **reddest**
1 COLOUR having the colour of blood: *We painted the door* **bright red.** | *a red balloon* → BLOOD-RED; → **cherry red** at CHERRY (3); → SCARLET
2 HAIR hair that is red has an orange-brown colour
3 FACE if you go red, your face becomes a bright pink colour, especially because you are embarrassed or angry: **go/turn red** *Every time you mention his name, she goes bright red.*
4 WINE red wine is a red or purple colour; → **white**
5 like a red rag to a bull *BrE* also **like waving a red flag in front of a bull** *AmE* very likely to make someone angry or upset: *Just mentioning his ex-wife's name was like a red rag to a bull.*
6 roll out the red carpet/give sb the red carpet treatment to give special treatment to an important visitor
7 not one red cent *AmE informal* used to emphasize that you mean no money at all: *I wouldn't give him one red cent for that car.*
8 POLITICS *informal* COMMUNIST or extremely LEFT-WING political views – used to show disapproval —**redness** *n* [U] → **paint the town red** at PAINT² (5)

red² *n* **1** [C,U] the colour of blood: *I like the way the artist uses red in this painting.* | *the reds and yellows of the trees* | *The corrections were marked in red* (=in red ink). **2** [C,U] red wine; → **white**: *a nice bottle of red* **3** be in the red *informal* to owe more money than you have; ☐ **be in the black;** → **overdrawn**: *This is the airline's fourth straight year in the red.* **4** [C] *informal* someone who has COMMUNIST or very LEFT-WING political opinions – used especially in the past to show disapproval → **see red** at SEE¹ (35)

red a·lert *n* [C usually singular, U] a warning that there is very great danger: **be (put/placed) on red alert** *All the hospitals are on red alert.*

red 'blood cell also **red 'corpuscle** *n* [C] one of the cells in your blood that carry oxygen to every part of your body; → **white blood cell**

red-'blooded *adj* **red-blooded male/Englishman/American etc** used to emphasize that someone has all of the qualities that a typical man, Englishman etc is supposed to have – used humorously

red·brick /'redbrɪk/ *adj* a redbrick university is one of the British universities built in the late 19th or early 20th century, rather than an older university; → **Oxbridge**

red 'card *n* [C] a red card held up by the REFEREE in a football match, to show that a player has done something against the rules and will not be allowed to play for the rest of the game; → **yellow card**

red·coat /'redkəʊt $ -koʊt/ *n* [C] a British soldier during the 18th and 19th centuries

Red 'Crescent n the Red Crescent an organization in Muslim countries that helps people who are suffering as a result of war, floods, disease etc

Red 'Cross n the Red Cross an international organization that helps people who are suffering as a result of war, floods, disease etc

red·cur·rant /ˌred'kʌrənt‹ $ -'kɜːr-/ n [C] a very small red fruit that grows on bushes in northern Europe

red·den /'redn/ v [I,T] written to become red, or to make something red: *Sue's face reddened.*

red·dish /'redɪʃ/ adj slightly red: *reddish-brown lipstick*

re·dec·o·rate /riː'dekəreɪt/ v [I,T] to change the way a room looks by painting it, changing the curtains etc —**redecoration** /riːˌdekə'reɪʃən/ n [U]

re·deem /rɪ'diːm/ v [T] formal
1 IMPROVE STH to make something less bad; ⊟ **make up for**: *Olivier's performance redeemed an otherwise second-rate play.* | redeeming quality/feature etc (=the one good thing about an unpleasant person or thing) *The hotel had a single redeeming feature – it was cheap.*
2 redeem yourself to do something that will improve what other people think of you, after you have behaved badly or failed: *He spent the rest of the game trying to redeem himself after a first-minute mistake.*
3 GET MONEY FOR STH to exchange a piece of paper representing an amount of money for that amount of money or for goods equal in cost to that amount of money: *You can redeem the coupon at any store.*
4 RELIGION to free someone from the power of evil, especially in the Christian religion → **REDEEMER**
5 redeem a promise/pledge formal to do what you promised to do: *The government found itself unable to redeem its election pledges.*
6 GET STH BACK to buy back something which you left with someone you borrowed money from: **redeem sth from sth** *He finally redeemed his watch from the pawnbroker.*

re·deem·a·ble /rɪ'diːməbəl/ adj able to be exchanged for money or goods: *Stamps are redeemable for merchandise or cash.*

Re·deem·er /rɪ'diːmə $ -ər/ n literary the Redeemer Jesus Christ

re·demp·tion /rɪ'dempʃən/ n [U] **1** the state of being freed from the power of evil, believed by Christians to be made possible by Jesus Christ **2** the act of exchanging a piece of paper worth a particular amount of money for money, goods, or services **3** past/beyond redemption too bad to be saved, repaired, or improved **4** technical the exchange of SHARES, BONDS etc for money —**redemptive** /-tɪv/ adj

re·de·ploy /ˌriːdɪ'plɔɪ/ v [T] to move someone or something to a different place or job: *There are plans to redeploy 200 employees in the next six months.* —**redeployment** n [U]

re·de·vel·op /ˌriːdɪ'veləp/ v [T] to make an area more modern by putting in new buildings or changing or repairing the old ones: *The old docks are being redeveloped as a business park.*

re·de·vel·op·ment /ˌriːdɪ'veləpmənt/ n [C,U] the act of redeveloping an area, especially in a city: *redevelopment of the city's downtown area*

red eye n take the red eye AmE informal to take a journey in a plane that continues all night: *I took the red eye to LA.*

red-'faced adj embarrassed or ashamed: *Red-faced officials ordered an investigation into the cause of the accident.*

red 'flag n [C] AmE something that shows or warns you that something might be wrong, illegal etc

red 'giant n [C] a large star that is near the middle of its life and shines with a reddish light

red-'handed adj catch sb red-handed to catch someone at the moment when they are doing something wrong: *Earl was caught red-handed taking the money.*

red·head /'redhed/ n [C] someone who has red hair

red 'herring n [C] a fact or idea that is not important but is introduced to take your attention away from the points that are important

red-'hot adj **1 a)** metal or rock that is red-hot is so hot that it shines red: *The poker glowed red-hot in the fire.* **b)** informal very hot: *Be careful with those plates – they're red-hot.* **2** informal extremely active, exciting, or interesting: *a red-hot news story* | *The Braves have been red-hot in the last few games.* **3** a red-hot feeling is very strong: *red-hot anger* **4 red-hot favourite** BrE the team or person who most people believe will win a competition

re·dial /ˌriː'daɪəl/ v redialled, redialling BrE, redialed, redialing AmE [I,T] to DIAL a telephone number again

re·di·rect /ˌriːdaɪ'rekt, -dɪ-/ v [T] **1** to use something for a different purpose: *She was good at redirecting the children's energy into something useful.* **2** to send something in a different direction: *The flight was redirected to Cleveland.* **3** BrE to send someone's letters to their new address from an address they have left; ⊟ **forward** —**redirection** /-'rekʃən/ n [U]

re·dis·trib·ute /ˌriːdɪ'strɪbjuːt/ v [T] to give something to each member of a group so that it is divided up in a different way from before: **redistribute income/wealth/resources etc** *a programme to redistribute wealth from the rich to the poor*

re·dis·tri·bu·tion /ˌriːdɪstrɪ'bjuːʃən/ n [U] the act of redistributing something, especially money or land: [+of] *a major redistribution of land*

red-'letter day n [C] informal a day that you will always remember because something special happened that made you very happy

red-'light district n [C] the area of a town or city where there are many PROSTITUTES

red 'meat n [U] dark coloured meat such as BEEF or LAMB; → **white meat**

red·neck /'rednek/ n [C] AmE informal a person who lives in a country area of the US, is uneducated, and has strong unreasonable opinions – used in order to show disapproval: *a redneck bar*

re·do /riː'duː/ v past tense **redid** /-'dɪd/ past participle **redone** /-'dʌn/ third person singular **redoes** /-'dʌz/ [T] **1** to do something again: *You'll have to redo this piece of work.* **2** to change the way a room is decorated: *We're having the kitchen redone.*

red·o·lent /'redl-ənt/ adj **1** formal making you think of something; ⊟ **reminiscent**: [+of] *a style redolent of the sixties* **2** literary smelling strongly of something: [+of/with] *The bar was redolent with the smell of stale cigarette smoke.*

re·dou·ble /riː'dʌbəl/ v redouble your efforts to greatly increase your effort as you try to do something: *Both sides redoubled their efforts to end the war.*

re·doubt /rɪ'daʊt/ n [C] formal a small hidden place, for example where soldiers hide themselves when they are fighting

re·doubt·a·ble /rɪ'daʊtəbəl/ adj literary someone who is redoubtable is a person you respect or fear: *He had never met a more redoubtable fighter.*

re·dound /rɪ'daʊnd/ v redound to sb's credit/honour etc formal to improve people's opinion of someone

red 'pepper n **1** [C] a red vegetable which you can eat raw or use in cooking: *stuffed red peppers* **2** [U] a spicy red powder used in cooking; ⊟ **cayenne pepper**

re·dress¹ /rɪ'dres/ v [T] formal to correct something that is wrong or unfair: *Little could be done to redress the situation.* | *Affirmative action was meant to redress the balance* (=make the situation fair) *for minorities.*

re·dress² /rɪ'dres $ 'riːdres/ n [U] formal money that someone pays you because they have caused you harm or damaged your property; ⊟ **compensation**: *The only hope of redress is in a lawsuit.*

R

needed. **4** [U] the process of making a substance more pure: *sugar refinement* | [+**of**] *the refinement of cocaine* **5** [U] the quality of being polite and well-educated, in a way that is typical of someone from a high social class: *a woman of great refinement*

re·fin·e·ry /rɪˈfaɪnəri/ *n plural* **refineries** [C] a factory where something such as oil or sugar is made purer: *oil/petroleum/sugar refinery*

re·fit /ˌriːˈfɪt/ *v* **refitted**, **refitting** [I,T] to make a ship, aircraft, building etc ready to be used again, by doing repairs and putting in new machinery: *The ship was completely refitted five years ago.* —**refit** /ˈriːfɪt/ *n* [C,U]

re·fla·tion /riːˈfleɪʃən/ *n* [U] *technical* the process of increasing the amount of money being used in a country in order to increase trade; → **inflation, deflation** —**reflate** /riːˈfleɪt/ *v* [I,T] —**reflationary** *adj*

re·flect [S2] [W1] /rɪˈflekt/ *v*
1 IMAGE [T usually passive] if a person or a thing is reflected in a mirror, glass, or water, you can see an image of the person or thing on the surface of the mirror, glass, or water: **be reflected in sth** *She could see her face reflected in the car's windshield.*
2 BE A SIGN OF STH [T not usually in progressive] to show or be a sign of a particular situation or feeling: *The drop in consumer spending reflects concern about the economy.* | **be reflected in sth** *The increasing racial diversity of the US is reflected in the latest census statistics.* | **reflect who/what/how etc** *How much you're paid reflects how important you are to the company.*
3 LIGHT/HEAT/SOUND a) [T] if a surface reflects light, heat, or sound, it sends back the light etc that reaches it: *Wear something white – it reflects the heat.* **b)** [I always + adv/prep] if light, heat, or sound reflects off something it reaches, it comes back from it
4 THINK ABOUT STH [I,T] to think carefully about something, or to say something that you have been thinking about: [+**on**] *He had time to reflect on his successes and failures.* | **reflect that** *Moe reflected that he had never seen Sherry so happy.*
reflect on/upon sb/sth *phr v*
to influence people's opinion of someone or something, especially in a bad way: *If my children are rude, that reflects on me as a parent.*

re‚flected 'glory *n* [U] respect or admiration that is given to someone, not because of what they are or what they have done, but because of what someone they know has done: *I certainly don't want to* **bask in** *any reflected glory.*

re·flec·tion [S3] [W3] /rɪˈflekʃən/ *n*
1 [C] an image that you can see in a mirror, glass, or water: *Can you see your reflection in the glass?*
2 [C,U] careful thought, or an idea or opinion based on this: *A moment's reflection will show the stupidity of this argument.* | **on/upon reflection** *At first I disagreed, but on reflection* (=after thinking carefully about it), *I realized she was right.*
3 [C] something that shows what something else is like, or that is a sign of a particular situation: [+**of**] *His speech was an accurate reflection of the public mood.* | **be a reflection on sb/sth** (=show how good or bad someone or something is) *On some level, a student's grades are a reflection on the teacher.*
4 [U] the action or process of light, heat, or sound being thrown back from a surface

re·flec·tive /rɪˈflektɪv/ *adj* **1** a reflective surface reflects light: *reflective tape* **2** thinking quietly about something: *She was in a reflective mood.* **3** showing that something is true about a situation: [+**of**] *TV is reflective of society's more liberal views on sex.*

re·flec·tor /rɪˈflektə $ -ər/ *n* [C] **1** a small piece of plastic that is fastened to a bicycle or to a piece of clothing, so that it can be seen more easily at night → see picture at BICYCLE[1] **2** a surface that reflects light

re·flex /ˈriːfleks/ *n* [C] **1 reflexes** [plural] **a)** the natural ability to react quickly and well to sudden situa-

tions: **have good/quick/slow reflexes** *A tennis player needs to have very quick reflexes.* **b)** a sudden uncontrolled movement that your muscles make as a natural reaction to a physical effect: *The doctor* **tested** *Jenny's* **reflexes** (=especially by hitting her knee with a special rubber hammer). **2 reflex action** something that you do without thinking, as a reaction to a situation

re·flex·ive /rɪˈfleksɪv/ *adj technical* a reflexive verb or PRONOUN shows that the action in a sentence affects the person or thing that does the action. In the sentence 'I enjoyed myself', 'myself' is reflexive —**reflexive** *n* [C] —**reflexively** *adv*

re·flex·ol·o·gy /ˌriːflekˈsɒlədʒi $ -ˈsɑː-/ *n* [U] a type of ALTERNATIVE medicine in which areas of the feet are touched or rubbed in order to cure medical problems in other parts of the body

re·for·est·a·tion /riːˌfɒrɪˈsteɪʃən $ -ˌfɔː-, -ˌfɑː-/ *n* [U] the practice of planting trees in an area where they were previously cut down, in order to grow them for industrial use or to improve the environment; ⊡ **deforestation**

re-form /ˌriːˈfɔːm $ -ɔːrm/ *v* [I,T] to start to exist again or to make something start to exist again: *At the end of the year, the company re-formed.*

re·form[1] /rɪˈfɔːm $ -ɔːrm/ *v* **1** [T] to improve a system, law, organization etc by making a lot of changes to it, so that it operates in a fairer or more effective way: *plans to radically reform the tax system* **2** [I,T] to change your behaviour and become a better person, or to make someone do this: *Greeley says he's a genuinely reformed character.* | *a reformed criminal*

reform[2] [W2] *n* [C,U] a change or changes made to a system or organization in order to improve it: [+**of**] *a reform of the legal system* | **economic/political/educational reform** *a much-needed programme of economic reform* | **Reforms were made** *to revive the economy.* | **far-reaching/sweeping/radical reforms** *The Prime Minister is calling for sweeping reforms of the NHS.*

re·for·mat /ˌriːˈfɔːmæt $ -ɔːr-/ *v* **reformatted**, **reformatting** [T] if you reformat a document, you change the way it is organized or arranged, for example the amount of space between lines: *The books will be condensed and reformatted for electronic reading.*

ref·or·ma·tion /ˌrefəˈmeɪʃən $ -fər-/ *n* **1** [C,U] *formal* when something is completely changed in order to improve it **2 the Reformation** the religious changes in Europe in the 16th century, that resulted in the Protestant churches being established

re·for·ma·to·ry /rɪˈfɔːmətəri $ rɪˈfɔːrmətɔːri/ *n plural* **reformatories** [C] *AmE old use* a REFORM SCHOOL

re·form·er /rɪˈfɔːmə $ -ɔːrmər/ *n* [C] someone who works to improve a social or political system: *a great social reformer*

re·form·ist /rɪˈfɔːmɪst $ -ɔːr-/ *adj* wanting to change systems or situations, especially in politics: *the reformist wing of the party* —**reformist** *n* [C]

re'form school *n* [C] *AmE* a special school where young people who have broken the law are sent

re·fract /rɪˈfrækt/ *v* [T] *technical* if glass or water refracts light, the light changes direction when it passes through the glass or water —**refraction** /rɪˈfrækʃən/ *n* [U]

re·frac·to·ry /rɪˈfræktəri/ *adj* **1** *formal* deliberately not obeying someone in authority and being difficult to deal with or control; ⊡ **unruly** **2** *medical* a refractory disease or illness is hard to treat or cure

re·frain[1] /rɪˈfreɪn/ *v* [I] *formal* to not do something that you want to do; → **abstain**: **refrain from (doing) sth** *Please refrain from smoking in this area.*

refrain[2] *n* [C] **1** part of a song or poem that is repeated, especially at the end of each VERSE; → **chorus** **2** *formal* a remark or idea that is often repeated: *Our proposal met with the constant refrain that the company could not afford it.*

re·fresh /rɪˈfreʃ/ *v* **1** [T] to make someone feel less tired or less hot: *A shower will refresh you.* | **refresh**

yourself (with sth) *He refreshed himself with a glass of iced tea.* **2 refresh sb's memory** to make someone remember something: *I looked at the map to refresh my memory of the route.* **3 refresh sb's drink** *AmE* to add more of an alcoholic drink to someone's glass; ⬛ **top sb up** *BrE: Can I refresh your drink?* **4** [I,T] *technical* if you refresh your computer screen while you are connected to the Internet, you make the screen show any new information that has arrived since you first began looking at it; ⬛ **update** —**refreshed** *adj: Jen returned from vacation feeling relaxed and refreshed.*

re·fresh·er ,course also **re·fresh·er** /rɪˈfreʃə $ -ər/ *n* [C] a training course, usually a short one, that teaches you about new developments in a particular subject or skill, especially one that you need for your job

re·fresh·ing /rɪˈfreʃɪŋ/ *adj* **1** making you feel less tired or less hot: *a refreshing drink* | *The breeze felt refreshing.* **2** pleasantly different from what is familiar and boring: *It made a refreshing change to talk to someone new.* —**refreshingly** *adv*

re·fresh·ment /rɪˈfreʃmənt/ *n formal* **1 refreshments** [plural] small amounts of food and drink that are provided at a meeting, sports event etc: *Refreshments will be served after the meeting.* **2** [U] food and drink in general: *We worked all day without refreshment.* | **liquid refreshment** (=alcoholic drink – used humorously) *I was in need of some liquid refreshment.* **3** [U] the experience of being made to feel less tired or hot

re·fried beans /ˌriːfraɪd ˈbiːnz/ *n* [plural] a Mexican dish in which beans that have already been cooked are crushed and then FRIED with spices

re·fri·ge·rate /rɪˈfrɪdʒəreɪt/ *v* [T] to make something such as food or liquid cold in a refrigerator in order to preserve it: *Refrigerate the mixture overnight.* —**refrigeration** /rɪˌfrɪdʒəˈreɪʃən/ *n* [U]

re·fri·ge·ra·tor /rɪˈfrɪdʒəreɪtə $ -ər/ *n* [C] *BrE formal* or *AmE* a large piece of electrical kitchen equipment, shaped like a cupboard, used for keeping food and drink cool; ⬛ **fridge**; → **freezer**

re·fuel /ˌriːˈfjʊəl/ *v* refuelled, refuelling *BrE*, refueled, refueling *AmE* **1** [I,T] to fill a plane or vehicle with FUEL before continuing a journey: *The plane was refuelled in Dubai.* **2** [T] to make feelings, emotions, or ideas stronger: *The attack refuelled fears of war.*

ref·uge /ˈrefjuːdʒ/ *n* **1** [U] shelter or protection from someone or something: **take/seek refuge (in sth)** *During the frequent air-raids, people took refuge in their cellars.* **2** [C] a place that provides shelter, or protection from danger: *a **wildlife refuge*** | [+from] *A huge oak tree provided a refuge from the storm.* | [+for] *a refuge for battered wives*; → see picture at STAY

ref·u·gee W3 /ˌrefjʊˈdʒiː/ *n* [C] someone who has been forced to leave their country, especially during a war, or for political or religious reasons: *Refugees were streaming across the border.* | **refugee camps**

re·fund¹ /ˈriːfʌnd/ *n* [C] **1** an amount of money that is given back to you if you are not satisfied with the goods or services that you have paid for: *They refused to give me a refund.* | *Return your purchase within 14 days for a **full refund**.* | *You should go down there and demand a refund.* **2 tax refund** money that you get back from the government when it has taken too much money in taxes from your salary

re·fund² /rɪˈfʌnd/ *v* [T] to give someone their money back, especially because they are not satisfied with the goods or services they have paid for; → **reimburse**: *I took the radio back, and they refunded my money.*

re·fur·bish /ˌriːˈfɜːbɪʃ $ -ɜːr-/ *v* [T] *especially BrE* **1** to decorate and repair something such as a building or office in order to improve its appearance; → **renovate**: *The Grand Hotel has been completely refurbished.* **2** to change and improve a plan, idea, or skill —**refurbishment** *n* [C,U]

re·fus·al /rɪˈfjuːzəl/ *n* [C,U] when you say firmly that you will not do, give, or accept something: **refusal to do sth** *His refusal to pay the fine got him into even more trouble.* | **flat/blunt/point-blank refusal** (=an immediate

direct refusal) *His request was met with a blunt refusal.* | [+of] *They couldn't understand her refusal of a scholarship to Yale.*

re·fuse¹ S2 W1 /rɪˈfjuːz/ *v*
1 [I] to say firmly that you will not do something that someone has asked you to do: *She asked him to leave, but he refused.* | **refuse to do sth** *I absolutely refuse to take part in anything that's illegal.* | **flatly refuse/refuse point-blank (to do sth)** (=refuse immediately and directly without giving a reason) *Mom flatly refused to go back into the hospital.* | *When he offered all that money, I **could hardly refuse** (=could not refuse), could I?*
2 [I,T] to say no to something that you have been offered; ⬛ **turn down**: *She refused a second piece of cake.* | *The offer seemed too good to refuse.* → see picture at OFFER¹
3 [T] to not give or allow someone something that they want, especially when they have asked for it officially: **refuse sb sth** *She was refused a work permit.*

ref·use² /ˈrefjuːs/ *n* [U] *formal* waste material that has been thrown away; ⬛ **rubbish** *BrE*; ⬛ **trash, garbage** *AmE*: *a refuse dump* | **household/domestic refuse** | **refuse collection**

re·fute /rɪˈfjuːt/ *v* [T] *formal* **1** to prove that a statement or idea is not correct; ⬛ **rebut**: **refute a hypothesis/a claim/an idea etc** *an attempt to refute Darwin's theories* **2** to say that a statement is wrong or unfair; ⬛ **deny**: **refute an allegation/a suggestion etc** *She refuted any allegations of malpractice.* —**refutable** *adj* —**refutation** /ˌrefjʊˈteɪʃən/ *n* [C,U]

reg. also **reg** *BrE* /redʒ/ **1** the written abbreviation of **registration** **2 L reg./M reg. etc** *BrE* used to show what year a car was first REGISTERED, based on the first letter of its NUMBER PLATE: *a Y reg. BMW*

re·gain /rɪˈɡeɪn/ *v* [T] **1** to get something back, especially an ability or quality, that you have lost; ⬛ **recover**: *The family never quite regained its former influence.* | *He somehow managed to **regain** his **balance**.* | *Government forces have **regained control** of the city.* | *When she **regained consciousness** (=woke up after being unconscious), she was lying on the floor.* | *He looked stunned, but he soon **regained** his **composure** (=became calm again).* | *The doctors don't know if he will ever regain the use of his legs.* **2** *literary* to reach a place again

re·gal /ˈriːɡəl/ *adj formal* typical of a king or queen, suitable for a king or queen, or similar to a king or queen in behaviour, looks etc: *a ceremony of regal splendour* | *James watched with regal detachment.* —**regally** *adv*

re·gale /rɪˈɡeɪl/ *v*
regale sb with sth *phr v written* to entertain someone by telling them about something: *Bailey regaled the customers with tales of our exploits.*

re·ga·li·a /rɪˈɡeɪliə/ *n* [U] traditional clothes and decorations, used at official ceremonies: *the royal regalia* (=worn by a king or queen) | *a pipe band **in full regalia*** (=wearing all their traditional clothes, decorations etc)

re·gard¹ S3 /rɪˈɡɑːd $ -ɑːrd/ *n*
1 ADMIRATION/RESPECT [U] respect and admiration for someone or something: [+for] *Jan's regard for his great talent* | *Burt **had high regard** for his old law professor, Dr. Finch* (=he respected him a lot). | *The voters **hold her in high regard** (=respect or admire her).* | *Teachers are held in low regard in this society* (=are not respected or admired).
2 ATTENTION/CONSIDERATION [U] *formal* attention or consideration that is shown towards someone or something: [+for] *She has no regard for other people's feelings.* | **pay/show regard** *One must show proper regard for the law.* | **little/no/scant regard (for sb/sth)** *The present administration has demonstrated little regard for environmental issues.* | *All students must*

have access to quality education **without regard to** *wealth or class.*

3 with/in regard to sth *formal* relating to a particular subject: *US foreign policy with regard to Cuba*

4 in this/that regard *formal* relating to something you have just mentioned: *The company's problems, in this regard, are certainly not unique.*

5 regards [plural] good wishes – used when sending your good wishes to someone or when ending a short letter or message: *My husband **sends his regards**.* | *Hope to see you soon. Regards, Chris* | **(with) kind/best regards** (=used to end a letter in a friendly but rather formal way)

6 [singular] *literary* a long look without moving your eyes

regard² [S2] [W1] *v* [T]

1 [not in progressive] to think about someone or something in a particular way: **regard sb/sth as sth** *Paul seemed to regard sex as sinful and immoral.* | *Edith was **widely regarded** as* (=considered by many people to be) *eccentric.* | *His work is **highly regarded*** (=regarded as very good) *by art experts.*

2 *formal* to look at someone or something, in a particular way: *She stood back and regarded him coldly.*

3 as regards sth *formal* relating to a particular subject – use this when you want to talk or write about a particular subject: *As regards a cure for the disease, very few advances have been made.*

re·gard·ing [S3] /rɪˈɡɑːdɪŋ $ -ɑːr-/ *prep formal* a word used especially in letters or speeches to introduce the subject you are writing or talking about; **◨ concerning, with regard to**: *Regarding your recent inquiry, I have enclosed a copy of our new brochure.*

re·gard·less /rɪˈɡɑːdləs $ -ɑːr-/ *adv* **1** without being affected or influenced by something: [+of] *The law requires equal treatment for all, regardless of race, religion, or sex.* **2** if you continue doing something regardless, you do it in spite of difficulties or other people telling you not to: **carry on/go on regardless** *BrE* (=continue what you are doing) *You get a lot of criticism, but you just have to carry on regardless.*

re·gat·ta /rɪˈɡætə/ *n* [C] a sports event at which there are races for rowing boats or sailing boats

re·gen·cy /ˈriːdʒənsi/ *n plural* **regencies** [C,U] a period of government by a REGENT (=person who governs instead of a king or queen)

Regency *adj* Regency buildings, furniture etc are from or in the style of the period 1811–1820 in Britain

re·gen·e·rate /rɪˈdʒenəreɪt/ *v* **1** [T] *formal* to make something develop and grow strong again: *efforts to regenerate the US economy* | *The Marshall Plan sought to regenerate the shattered Europe of 1947.* **2** [I,T] *technical* to grow again, or make something grow again: *Small nodules form as the liver cells regenerate.* —**regenerative** /-nərətɪv/ *adj*: *a regenerative process* —**regeneration** /rɪ,dʒenəˈreɪʃən/ *n* [U]: *a new strategy for urban regeneration*

re·gent /ˈriːdʒənt/ *n* [C] someone who governs instead of a king or queen, because the king or queen is ill, absent, or still a child —**regent** *adj* [only after noun]: *the Prince Regent*

reg·gae /ˈreɡeɪ/ *n* [U] a kind of popular music originally from Jamaica, with a strong regular beat

re·gi·cide /ˈredʒɪsaɪd/ *n formal* **1** [U] the crime of killing a king or queen **2** [C] someone who kills a king or queen

re·gime [W2] /reɪˈʒiːm/ *n* [C]

1 a government, especially one that was not elected fairly or that you disapprove of for some other reason: *The regime got rid of most of its opponents.* | **military/ totalitarian/fascist regime** | **brutal/oppressive/corrupt regime**

2 a particular system – used especially when talking about a previous system, or one that has just been introduced: **under a regime** *Under the new regime, all*

sheep and cattle will be regularly tested for disease.

3 a special plan of food, exercise etc that is intended to improve your health; **◨ regimen**: *a dietary regime*

re·gi·men /ˈredʒɪmən/ *n* [C] *formal* a special plan of food, exercise etc that is intended to improve your health; **◨ regime**: [+of] *a regimen of morning stretching exercises* | *Patients maintain a strict dietary regimen.*

re·gi·ment¹ /ˈredʒɪmənt/ *n* [C] **1** a large group of soldiers, usually consisting of several BATTALIONS **2** a large number of people, animals, or things: [+of] *a regiment of ants* —**regimental** /,redʒɪˈmentl◂/ *adj*: *the regimental commander*

re·gi·ment² /ˈredʒɪment/ *v* [T usually passive] to organize and control people firmly and usually too strictly: *the regimented routine of boarding school* —**regimentation** /,redʒɪmenˈteɪʃən/ *n* [U]

re·gion [S1] [W1] /ˈriːdʒən/ *n* [C]

1 a large area of a country or of the world, usually without exact limits; **◨ area**: *efforts to bring peace to the region* | [+of] *the Choco region of Columbia* | **coastal/border/central etc region** *Flooding is likely in some coastal regions of the Northeast during the early part of the week.*

2 a particular part of someone's body; **◨ area**: *the lower back region* | [+of] *a region of the brain*

3 (somewhere) in the region of sth used to describe an amount of time, money etc without being exact: *a grant somewhere in the region of £2,500*

4 the regions *BrE* the parts of a country that are away from the capital city: *a government policy to relocate jobs from the capital to the regions*

re·gion·al [S1] [W2] /ˈriːdʒənəl/ *adj* [usually before noun] relating to a particular region or area; **→ local**: *local and regional government* | *regional variations in farming practice* | *a slight regional accent* —**regionally** *adv*: *goods sold locally and regionally*

re·gion·al·is·m /ˈriːdʒənəlɪzəm/ *n* [U] loyalty to a particular region of a country and the desire for it to be more independent politically

re·gis·ter¹ [S3] [W3] /ˈredʒɪstə $ -ər/ *n*

1 OFFICIAL LIST [C] an official list of names of people, companies etc, or a book that has this list: [+of] *the official register of births, deaths, and marriages* | *Have you signed the **hotel register**?* | *Police want a **national register** of DNA samples.* | **the electoral register** (=official list of voters) | **call/take the register** *BrE old-fashioned* (=say the names of the students in a class, to check who is there)

2 LANGUAGE STYLE [C,U] *technical* the words, style, and grammar used by speakers and writers in a particular situation or in a particular type of writing: **formal/informal register** *letters written in a formal register*

3 MUSIC [C] *technical* the range of musical notes that someone's voice or a musical instrument can reach: **the upper/middle/lower register** *the upper register of the cello*

4 MACHINE [C] a CASH REGISTER

5 HEATING CONTROL [C] *AmE* a movable metal plate that controls the flow of air in a HEATING or COOLING SYSTEM; **◨ vent**

register² [W3] *v*

1 ON A LIST [I,T] to put someone's or something's name on an official list: *The tanker is registered in Rotterdam.* | [+for] *How many students have registered for English classes?* | [+with] *You must bring your insurance card with you when you register with a dentist or doctor.* | **register a birth/death/marriage** *The baby's birth was registered this morning.* | **be registered (as) unemployed/disabled etc** *BrE* (=be on an official list of a particular group)

2 STATE YOUR OPINION [T] *formal* to officially state your opinion about something so that everyone knows what you think or feel: *The delegation **registered** a formal **protest** with US embassy officials Wednesday.*

3 REALIZE [I usually in negatives, T] if something

registers, or if you register it, you realize or notice it, and then remember it: *She had told me her name before, but I guess it didn't register.* | *I'd been standing there for several minutes before he registered my presence.*
4 MEASUREMENT [I,T] if an instrument registers an amount or if something registers on it, the instrument shows that amount: *The thermometer registered 98.6°.* | *The earthquake registered 7.2 on the Richter scale.*
5 SHOW A FEELING [T] *formal* to show or express a feeling: *Her face registered shock and anger.*
6 MAIL [T] *BrE* to send a package, letter etc by REGISTERED POST: *Did you register the parcel?*

,registered 'nurse also **RN** *n* [C] someone who has been trained and is officially allowed to work as a nurse

,registered 'office *n* [C] the office of a company in Britain, to which all letters and official documents must be sent

,registered 'post *n* [U] *BrE* a way of insuring something that you send by post in case it gets lost or damaged; ▣ **certified mail** *AmE*

'register ,office *n* [C] *BrE* a REGISTRY OFFICE

re·gis·trar /ˌredʒɹ̩ˈstrɑː◂ $ ˈredʒɹ̩strɑːr/ *n* [C] **1** someone who is in charge of official records of births, marriages, and deaths **2** an official of a college or university who deals with the running of the college **3** *BrE* a hospital doctor who has finished his or her training but is of a lower rank than a CONSULTANT

re·gis·tra·tion S3 /ˌredʒɹ̩ˈstreɪʃən/ *n*
1 [U] the act of recording names and details on an official list: [+of] *the registration of motor vehicles* | *Student registration* (=for a course of study) *starts the first week in September.* | *The registration fee is $75.*
2 [C] *AmE* an official piece of paper containing details about a motor vehicle and the name of its owner: *May I see your license and registration, ma'am?*

regi'stration ,number *n* [C] *BrE* the official set of numbers and letters shown on the front and back of a vehicle on the NUMBER PLATE

re·gis·try /ˈredʒɹ̩stri/ *n plural* **registries** [C] **1** a place where information used by an organization is kept, especially official records or lists **2** *BrE technical* used when saying where something, especially a ship, is officially REGISTERED: *the registry of the vessel*

'registry ,office *n* [C] a local government building in Britain where you can get married, and where births, marriages, and deaths are officially recorded

re·gress /rɪˈgres/ *v* [I] *technical* to go back to an earlier and worse condition, or to a less developed way of behaving; ▣ **progress**: *The patient had regressed to a state of childish dependency.*

re·gres·sion /rɪˈgreʃən/ *n* [C,U] **1** the act of returning to an earlier condition that is worse or less developed; ▣ **progression 2** *technical* the act of thinking or behaving as you did at an earlier time of your life, such as when you were a child

re·gres·sive /rɪˈgresɪv/ *adj* returning to an earlier, less advanced state, or causing something to do this – used to show disapproval; ▣ **progressive**: *Many considered the changes to the welfare laws a regressive step.*

re'gressive ,tax *n* [C] a tax that has less effect on the rich than on the poor

re·gret¹ /rɪˈgret/ *v* regretted, regretting [T] **1** to feel sorry about something you have done and wish you had not done it: *I've never regretted the decision.* | *Don't do anything you might regret.* | **regret doing sth** *I now regret leaving school so young.* | **regret (that)** *He was beginning to regret that he'd come along.* | **bitterly/ deeply/greatly regret** *It was a stupid thing to do and I bitterly regret it.* | *If we don't act now, we'll* **live to regret it** (=we'll regret it in the future). **2** [not in progressive] *formal* used in official letters or statements when saying that you are sorry or sad about something: *We regret any inconvenience caused to our customers.* | **regret (that)** *I regret that I will be unable to attend.* | **regret to say/inform/tell** *I regret to inform you that your contract will not be renewed.*

regret² *n* **1** [C usually plural, U] sadness that you feel about something, especially because you wish it had not happened: [+about] *I have no regrets about leaving.* | **great/deep regret** *She has already expressed deep regret for what happened.* | **with regret** *I decided with some regret that it was time to move on.* | *It is* **with great regret** *that I must decline your offer.* | *to sb's* **regret** *I lost touch with her, much to my regret.* **2** **give/ send your regrets** *formal* to say that you are unable to go to a meeting, accept an invitation etc: *My father was ill and had to send his regrets.*

re·gret·ful /rɪˈgretfəl/ *adj* someone who is regretful feels sorry or disappointed: *She apologized and sounded genuinely regretful.*

re·gret·ful·ly /rɪˈgretfəli/ *adv* **1** feeling sad because you do not want to do what you are doing: *'I must go,' he said regretfully.* **2** [sentence adverb] *formal* used to talk about a situation that you wish was different or that you are sorry about; ▣ **regrettably**: *Regretfully, we do not have time to continue this discussion now.*

re·gret·ta·ble /rɪˈgretəbəl/ *adj* something that is regrettable is unpleasant, and you wish things could be different; ▣ **unfortunate**: *This was a very regrettable error.* | **it is regrettable that** *It's regrettable that classical music receives so little attention.*

re·gret·ta·bly /rɪˈgretəbli/ *adv* used to talk about a situation that you wish was different or that you are sorry about; ▣ **regretfully**: [sentence adverb]: *Regrettably, he will not be able to come.*

re·group /ˌriːˈɡruːp/ *v* **1** [I,T] to form a group again in order to be more effective, or to make people do this: *The Allies regrouped and launched a new attack.* | *The Russians retreated, needing to regroup their forces.* **2** [I] *AmE* to stop and think about something, so that you can start to do something again in a better way: *I paused for a minute to regroup.*

reg·u·lar¹ S2 W2 /ˈreɡjʊlə $ -ər/ *adj*
1 EVERY HOUR/DAY/WEEK ETC happening every hour, every week, every month etc, usually with the same amount of time in between; ▣ **irregular**: *The company holds regular meetings with employees.* | *His breathing was slow and regular.* | *Trains will run at* **regular intervals** *from 11am to 4pm.* | *We hear from him* **on a regular basis.** | *He phones us every Sunday at six,* **regular as clockwork** (=always at the same time). | *a* **regular job** (=a job that you do during normal working hours)
2 OFTEN [only before noun] happening or doing something very often; ▣ **irregular**: *a regular occurrence* | *Regular exercise helps keep your weight down.* | **regular customer/visitor** *He's one of the bar's regular customers.* | *Penn Station was* **in regular use** (=people used it often) *until the 1960s.*
3 USUAL [only before noun] *especially AmE* normal or usual: *He has returned to his regular duties.* | *Our regular opening hours are 10 am to 7pm.*
4 EQUAL DISTANCE with the same amount of space between each thing and the next; ▣ **irregular**: *The pipes were placed* **at regular intervals.** | *a carpet with*

a regular pattern of flowers
5 ORDINARY *especially AmE* ordinary, without any special feature or qualities: *a regular type of guy*
6 NORMAL SIZE [only before noun] *especially AmE* of a normal or standard size: *a regular Coke*
7 SHAPE evenly shaped with parts or sides of equal size: *a regular hexagon* | *He's very handsome, with strong regular features* (=an evenly shaped face).
8 GRAMMAR *technical* a regular verb changes its forms in the same way as most verbs, for example its past tense and past participle end in 'ed'. The verb 'dance' is regular, but the verb 'be' is not; **⊟ irregular**
9 EMPHASIZING [only before noun] *BrE informal* used to emphasize what you think someone is like; **⊟ real**: *He's a regular little dictator!*
10 regular army/troops/soldier a regular army etc is permanent, and exists whether there is a war or not
11 be/keep regular *informal* **a)** to get rid of waste from your BOWELS often enough to be healthy **b)** a woman who is regular has her MENSTRUAL PERIOD at the same time each month

regular² n **1** [C] *informal* someone who often goes to the same bar, restaurant etc or who takes part in an activity very often: *The barman knows all the regulars by name.* **2** [C] a soldier whose permanent job is in the army **3** [U] *AmE* petrol that contains LEAD

reg·u·lar·i·ty /ˌregjʊ'lærᵻti/ n plural **regularities** **1** [U] when the same thing keeps happening often, especially with the same amount of time between each occasion when it happens: *Climate change is disrupting the regularity of the seasons.* | **with alarming/increasing etc regularity** *Our team kept losing with monotonous regularity* (=in a way that seems boring or annoying). **2** [C,U] when something is arranged in an even way: *the regularity of his features*

reg·u·lar·ize also **-ise** *BrE* /'regjʊləraɪz/ v [T] to make a situation that has existed for some time legal or official —**regularization** /ˌregjʊləraɪ'zeɪʃən $ -rə-/ n [U]

reg·u·lar·ly S3 W3 /'regjʊləli $ -ərli/ adv
1 at the same time each day, week, month etc: *We meet regularly, once a month.*
2 often: *I see them pretty regularly.* | *It's important to exercise regularly.*
3 evenly arranged or shaped: *The plants are regularly spaced.* | *regularly shaped crystals*

reg·u·late /'regjʊleɪt/ v [T] **1** to control an activity or process, especially by rules: *strict rules regulating the use of chemicals in food* **2** to make a machine or your body work at a particular speed, temperature etc: *People sweat to regulate their body heat.*

reg·u·la·tion¹ S2 W2 /ˌregjʊ'leɪʃən/ n
1 [C] an official rule or order: *There seem to be so many rules and regulations these days.* | [+on] *new regulations on imports* | *regulations governing the safety of toys* | **building/planning/fire/health regulations** *The local authority is introducing new planning regulations.* | *All companies must comply with the regulations.* | **under ... regulations** *Under the new regulations, all staff must have safety training.*
2 [U] control over something, especially by rules: [+of] *the regulation of public spending*

regulation² adj [only before noun] used or worn because of official rules: *The girls were all wearing regulation shoes.*

reg·u·la·tor /'regjʊleɪtə $ -ər/ n [C] **1** an instrument for controlling the temperature, speed etc of something: *a heat regulator* **2** someone who makes sure that a system operates properly or fairly: *traffic safety regulators*

reg·u·la·to·ry /ˌregjʊ'leɪtəri $ 'regjʊlətɔːri/ adj formal a regulatory authority has the official power to control an activity and to make sure that it is done in a

satisfactory way: **regulatory body/authority/agency** *New drugs have been approved by the regulatory authority.*

re·gur·gi·tate /rɪ'gɜːdʒᵻteɪt $ -ɜːr-/ v [T] formal **1** to bring food that you have already swallowed, back into your mouth; → **vomit**: *Some birds and animals regurgitate food to feed their young.* **2** to repeat facts, ideas etc that you have read or heard without thinking about them yourself – used to show disapproval: *She tries to get students to think critically, not just regurgitate facts.* —**regurgitation** /rɪˌgɜːdʒᵻ'teɪʃən $ -ɜːr-/ n [U]

re·hab /'riːhæb/ n [U] the process of curing someone who has an alcohol or drugs problem: *a rehab program* | **in rehab** *I spent three months in rehab.*

re·ha·bil·i·tate /ˌriːhə'bɪlᵻteɪt/ v [T] **1** to help someone to live a healthy, useful, or active life again after they have been seriously ill or in prison: *a special unit for rehabilitating stroke patients* **2** to make people think that someone or something is good again after a period when people had a bad opinion of them: *The Prime Minister seems to be trying to rehabilitate the former defence secretary.* **3** to improve a building or area so that it returns to the good condition it was in before; → **renovate**: *A lot of the older houses have now been rehabilitated.* —**rehabilitation** /ˌriːhəbɪlᵻ'teɪʃən/ n [U]: *the rehabilitation of mentally ill patients*

re·hash /riː'hæʃ/ v [T] **1** to use the same ideas again in a new form that is not really different or better – used to show disapproval: *He simply rehashed the same story.* **2** to repeat something that was discussed earlier, especially in an annoying way: *This issue has been rehashed so many times already.* —**rehash** /'riːhæʃ/ n [C]: *It was just a rehash of last year's show.*

re·hears·al /rɪ'hɜːsəl $ -ɜːr-/ n **1** [C,U] a time when all the people in a play, concert etc practise before a public performance: [+for/of] *a rehearsal for 'Romeo and Juliet'* | **in rehearsal** *The dialogue was worked out by actors in rehearsal.* → **DRESS REHEARSAL** **2** [C] a time when all the people involved in a big event practise together before it happens: *a wedding rehearsal*

re·hearse /rɪ'hɜːs $ -ɜːrs/ v **1** [I,T] to practise or make people practise something such as a play or concert in order to prepare for a public performance: *I think we need to rehearse the first scene again.* | [+for] *The band was rehearsing for their world tour.* **2** [T] to practise something that you plan to say to someone: *She had carefully rehearsed her resignation speech.* **3** [T] formal to repeat an opinion that has often been expressed before

re·heat /ˌriː'hiːt/ v [T] to make a meal or drink hot again: *I reheated some soup for lunch.*

rehome /ˌriː'həʊm $ -'hoʊm/ v [T] to arrange for a pet to have a new owner and home, especially a pet that has been looked after in a SHELTER: *The kittens have been rehomed.*

re·house /ˌriː'haʊz/ v [T] to put someone in a new or better home: *All flood victims will be rehoused as soon as possible.*

reign¹ /reɪn/ n [C] **1** the period when someone is king, queen, or EMPEROR: [+of] *changes that took place during Charlemagne's reign* | *the reign of James I* **2** the period when someone is in charge of an organization, team etc: *during his reign at the Education Department* **3** a period during which something is the most powerful or most important feature of a place: [+of] *the reign of Stalinism in Russia* **4** reign of terror a period when a ruler or a government kills many of their political opponents

reign² v [I] **1** to rule a nation or group of nations as their king, queen, or EMPEROR: *George VI reigned from 1936 to 1952.* | [+over] *Pharaohs reigned over Egypt for centuries.* **2** literary if a feeling or quality reigns, it exists strongly for a period of time: *For several minutes confusion reigned.* | *Silence reigned while we waited for news.* **3** reigning champion the most recent winner of a competition: *Can he defeat the reigning Wimbledon champion?* **4** reign supreme if someone or something reigns supreme, they are the most important part of a situation or time: *It was a time when romance reigned supreme.*

re·im·burse /ˌriːɪmˈbɜːs $ -ˈɜːrs/ *v* [T] *formal* to pay money back to someone when their money has been spent or lost: **reimburse sb for sth** *The company will reimburse you for travel expenses.* **—reimbursement** *n* [C,U]

rein¹ /reɪn/ *n* **1** [C usually plural] a long narrow band of leather that is fastened around a horse's head in order to control it; → **bridle** **2 give (full/free) rein to sth** to allow an emotion or feeling to be expressed freely: *He gave free rein to his imagination.* **3 give sb (a) free rein** to give someone complete freedom to do a job in whatever way they choose **4 keep a tight rein on sb/sth** to control something strictly: *The finance director keeps a tight rein on spending.* **5 take/hand over the reins** to take or give someone control over an organization or country: *Owens will officially take over the reins in a few weeks.*

rein² *v*
rein sth ⇔ in also **rein sth ⇔ back** *BrE phr v* **1** to start to control a situation more strictly: *The government is reigning in public expenditure.* **2** to make a horse go more slowly by pulling on the reins

re·in·car·nate /ˌriːɪnˈkɑːneɪt $ -ɑːr-/ *v* be reincarnated to be born again in another body after you have died

re·in·car·na·tion /ˌriːɪnkɑːˈneɪʃən $ -ɑːr-/ *n* **1** [U] the belief that after someone dies their soul lives again in another body **2** [C] the person or animal that contains the soul of a dead person or animal: [+of] *She thinks she is a reincarnation of Cleopatra.*

rein·deer /ˈreɪndɪə $ -dɪr/ *n plural* **reindeer** [C] a large DEER with long wide ANTLERS (=horns), that lives in cold northern areas

re·in·force W3 /ˌriːɪnˈfɔːs $ -ˈfɔːrs/ *v* [T]
1 to give support to an opinion, idea, or feeling, and make it stronger: *The film reinforces the idea that women should be pretty and dumb.*
2 to make part of a building, structure, piece of clothing etc stronger
3 to make a group of people, especially an army, stronger by adding people, equipment etc

reinforced 'concrete *n* [U] CONCRETE with metal bars in it to make it stronger

re·in·force·ment /ˌriːɪnˈfɔːsmənt $ -ˈfɔːrs-/ *n* **1 reinforcements** [plural] more soldiers, police etc who are sent to a battle, fight etc to make their group stronger: *The police called for reinforcements.* **2 positive/negative reinforcement** positive reinforcement is when you give someone praise or rewards for their behaviour or work, so they want to continue doing well. Negative reinforcement is when you give someone punishments or criticism when their behaviour or work is bad, so that they want to improve to avoid punishments again: *We need to give students plenty of positive reinforcement.* **3** [U] the act of making something stronger: *The bridge needs some structural reinforcement.*

re·in·state /ˌriːɪnˈsteɪt/ *v* [T] **1** if someone is reinstated, they are officially given back their job after it was taken away **2** to make something such as a law, system, or rule exist again: *California reinstated the death penalty in 1977.* **—reinstatement** *n* [C,U]

re·in·sure /ˌriːɪnˈʃʊə $ -ˈʃʊr/ *v* [T] *technical* to share the insurance of something between two or more companies, so that there is less risk for each **—reinsurance** *n* [U] **—reinsurer** *n* [C]

re·in·tro·duce /ˌriːɪntrəˈdjuːs $ -ˈduːs/ *v* [T] to start using something again or bring something back to an area after it had not been used or had not existed there for some time; **■ bring back**: *plans to reintroduce a capital-gains tax on securities* **—reintroduction** /-ˈdʌkʃən/ *n* [U]

re·in·vent /ˌriːɪnˈvent/ *v* [T] **1** to make changes to an idea, method, system etc in order to improve it or make

it more modern; **■ reform**: *plans to reinvent the American educational system* **2 reinvent yourself** to do something differently from before, especially in order to improve or change the way people think of you: *Bowie has constantly reinvented himself during his long career.* **3 reinvent the wheel** *informal* to waste time trying to find a way to do something when someone else has already discovered the best way to do it

re·in·vest /ˌriːɪnˈvest/ *v* [I,T] to use money you have earned from INVESTMENTS to buy additional investments: **reinvest sth in sth** *She reinvested the dividends in mutual funds.* **—reinvestment** *n* [U]

re·is·sue /ˌriːˈɪʃuː, -ˈɪsjuː $ -ˈɪʃuː/ *v* [T] to produce a record, book etc again, after it has not been available for some time: *an early jazz record reissued on CD* **—reissue** *n* [C]

re·it·e·rate /riːˈɪtəreɪt/ *v* [T] *formal* to repeat a statement or opinion in order to make your meaning as clear as possible; **■ restate**: *Let me reiterate the most important points.* | **reiterate that** *Lawyers reiterated that there was no direct evidence against Mr Evans.* **—reiteration** /riːˌɪtəˈreɪʃən/ *n* [C,U]: *a reiteration of his previous statement*

re·ject¹ S2 W2 /rɪˈdʒekt/ *v* [T]
1 OFFER/SUGGESTION/IDEA to refuse to accept, believe in, or agree with something; **■ accept**: *Sarah rejected her brother's offer of help.* | **reject sth as sth** *Gibson rejected the idea as 'absurd'.* | *Dexter flatly rejected* (=completely rejected) *calls for his resignation.* | *His proposal was rejected outright* (=completely rejected).
2 NOT CHOOSE SB to not choose someone for a job, course of study etc; **■ accept**: *It's obvious why his application was rejected.*
3 PRODUCT to throw away something that has just been made, because its quality is not good enough: *If inspectors find a defective can, the batch is rejected.*
4 NOT LOVE SB to refuse to give someone any love or attention: *Children feel abandoned or rejected if they don't see their parents regularly.*
5 ORGAN if your body rejects an organ, after a TRANSPLANT operation, it does not accept that organ

re·ject² /ˈriːdʒekt/ *n* [C] **1** a product that has been rejected because there is something wrong with it: *a shop selling cheap rejects* **2** someone who is not accepted or liked by another person, or by other people: *They felt that they were society's rejects.*

re·jec·tion /rɪˈdʒekʃən/ *n* **1** [C,U] the act of not accepting, believing in, or agreeing with something; **■ acceptance**: [+of] *What are the reasons for his rejection of the theory?* **2** [C,U] the act of not accepting someone for a job, school etc; **■ acceptance**: *They sent me a rejection letter.* **3** [U] a situation in which someone stops giving you love or attention: *He was left with a feeling of rejection and loss.*

re·jig /riːˈdʒɪg/ *BrE*; **re·jig·ger** /riːˈdʒɪgə $ -ər/ *AmE v* **rejigged, rejigging** [T] *informal* to arrange or organize something in a different way; **■ reorganize**: *plans to rejig the schedule*

re·joice /rɪˈdʒɔɪs/ *v* [I] **1** *literary* to feel or show that you are very happy: [+at/over/in] *His family rejoiced at the news.* | *We rejoiced in our good fortune.* **2 rejoice in the name/title (of) sth** *BrE* to have a name or title that is silly or amusing: *He rejoices in the name of Pigg.*

re·joic·ing /rɪˈdʒɔɪsɪŋ/ *n* [U] also **rejoicings** [plural] *literary* a situation in which a lot of people are very happy because they have had good news: [+at/over] *There was great rejoicing at the victory.*

re·join¹ /ˌriːˈdʒɔɪn/ *v* [T] to go back to a group of people, organization etc that you were with before: *She rejoined her friends in the lounge.* | *In 1938 he rejoined the Socialists.*

re·join² /rɪˈdʒɔɪn/ *v* [T] *literary* to say something in reply, especially rudely or angrily; **■ retort**: *'I don't care!' she rejoined.*

re·li·ance /rɪ'laɪəns/ n [singular, U] when someone or something is dependent on someone or something else; ◨ **dependence**: [+on/upon] *the country's reliance on imported oil* | *the country's **heavy reliance** on trade*

re·li·ant /rɪ'laɪənt/ adj dependent on someone or something: [+on/upon] *Most companies are now reliant on computer technology.* → SELF-RELIANT

rel·ic /'relɪk/ n [C] **1** an old object or custom that reminds people of the past or that has lived on from a past time: *Roman relics found in a field* | [+of] *the books and photos, relics of Rob's university days* | *Everything in the house seemed old and untouched, like relics of an ancient time.* **2** a part of the body or clothing of a holy person which is kept after their death because it is thought to be holy

re·lief S2 W2 /rɪ'liːf/ n
1 COMFORT [singular, U] a feeling of comfort when something frightening, worrying, or painful has ended or has not happened; → **relieve**: *I felt a huge surge of relief and happiness.* | *He watched with relief as the girl nodded.* | **in relief** *He laughed in relief.* | *No one was hurt, and we all **breathed a sigh of relief**.* | **it is a relief to see/have/know etc sth** *I hate to say it, but it was a relief to have him out of the house.* | **to sb's relief** *To my relief, they spoke English.* | **what a relief/ that's a relief** *The doctor said it was just the flu. What a relief!*
2 REDUCTION OF PAIN [U] when something reduces someone's pain or unhappy feelings: *Marijuana can provide **pain relief** for some cancer patients.* | [+of] *the relief of suffering* | [+from] *The cool room provided relief from the terrible heat outdoors.*
3 HELP [U] money, food, clothes etc given to people who are poor or hungry: *money raised for the **relief effort*** | *disaster/famine/flood etc relief famine relief for victims of the drought*
4 REPLACEMENT [U] a person or group of people that replaces another one and does their work after they have finished: *the relief for the military guard* | *a relief driver*
5 DECORATION [C,U] a way of decorating wood, stone etc with a shape or figure that is raised above the surface, or the decoration itself; → **bas relief**: **in relief** *figures carved in relief*
6 bring/throw sth into relief also stand out in relief to make something very noticeable, or to be very noticeable: **sharp/stark relief** *The tree stood out in stark relief against the snow.* | *The article throws into sharp relief the differences between the two theories.*
7 light/comic relief a funny moment during a serious film, book, or situation: *a moment of comic relief*
8 MONEY [U] *old-fashioned especially AmE* money given by the government to help people who are poor, old, unemployed etc; ◨ **welfare**: **on relief** *families on relief during the Depression*
9 WAR [U] *formal* the act of freeing a town when it has been surrounded by an enemy: [+of] *the relief of Mafeking*
10 MAP **in relief** if you show a part of the Earth's surface in relief, you show the differences in height between different parts of it → TAX RELIEF

re'lief map n [C] a map that shows the different heights of mountains, valleys etc by printing them in a different colour or by raising some parts

re'lief road n [C] *BrE* a road that vehicles use to avoid heavy traffic, usually built for this purpose: *an eastern relief road for city traffic*

re·lieve S3 /rɪ'liːv/ v [T]
1 PAIN to reduce someone's pain or unpleasant feelings; → **relief**: *Drugs helped to relieve the pain.* | **relieve tension/pressure/stress etc** *Some people eat for comfort, to relieve their anxieties.*
2 PROBLEM to make a problem less difficult or serious: *programs aimed at relieving unemployment*
3 REPLACE SB to replace someone when they have completed their duty or when they need a rest: *The*

guard will be relieved at midnight.
4 relieve yourself a polite expression meaning to URINATE - often used humorously
5 BORING to make something less dull and boring: *a plain wall relieved by flecks of blue and yellow* | **relieve the boredom/monotony** *The books helped relieve the boredom of waiting.*
6 WAR *formal* to free a town which an enemy has surrounded

relieve sb of sth phr v
1 *formal* to help someone by taking something from them, especially a job they do not want to do or something heavy that they are carrying: *A secretary was hired to relieve her of some of the administrative work.* | *He rose and relieved her of her bags.*
2 relieve sb of their post/duties/command etc *formal* to take away someone's job because they have done something wrong: *After the defeat General Meyer was relieved of his command.*
3 to steal something from someone – used humorously: *A couple of guys relieved him of his wallet.*

re·lieved /rɪ'liːvd/ adj feeling happy because you are no longer worried about something; → **relief**: **greatly/ immensely/extremely etc relieved** *She looked immensely relieved when she heard the news.* | **relieved to see/hear/know sth** *His mother was relieved to see him happy again.* | **relieved (that)** *I felt relieved that Ben would be there.* | *A relieved smile spread over his face.*

re·li·gion S2 W2 /rɪ'lɪdʒən/ n
1 [U] a belief in one or more gods: *The U.S. Constitution promises freedom of religion.* | *a course on philosophy and religion*
2 [C] a particular system of this belief and all the ceremonies and duties that are related to it: *people of different religions* | *the Islamic religion* | *The tribe practised a religion that mixed native beliefs and Christianity.*
3 find/get religion to suddenly become interested in religion in a way that seems strange to other people: *Miller found religion in prison.*
4 sth is (like) a religion used when saying that something is very important to someone and they are extremely interested in it and spend a lot of time doing it, watching it etc: *Football was a religion in my family.*

WORD FOCUS: RELIGION
faith one of the world's main religions, for example Islam, Hinduism, Buddhism, Judaism, or Christianity | **church** a Christian religious group, for example the Catholic Church | **sect** a religious group that is part of a larger religious group but has slightly different beliefs, for example a Buddhist sect | **cult** an extreme religious group that is not part of an established religion | **faith community** a group of people living in the same area, who have a particular religion | **secular** not relating to religion or any religious group
→ religious, devout, orthodox, holy, sacred, atheist, agnostic

re·li·gious S2 W2 /rɪ'lɪdʒəs/ adj
1 relating to religion in general or to a particular religion: *I don't share her **religious beliefs**.* | *a religious school* | *the dates of major religious observances such as Easter or Christmas*
2 believing strongly in your religion and obeying its rules carefully: *a **deeply religious** person* —**religiosity** /rɪ,lɪdʒi'ɒsɪti $ -'aːrs-/ n [U]

re·li·gious·ly /rɪ'lɪdʒəsli/ adv **1** if you do something religiously, you are always very careful to do it: *He exercises religiously every morning.* **2** in a way that is related to religion: *a religiously diverse country*

re·lin·quish /rɪ'lɪŋkwɪʃ/ v [T] *formal* to let someone else have your position, power, or rights, especially unwillingly; ◨ **give up**: *No one wants to relinquish power once they have it.* | **relinquish sth to sb** *Stultz relinquished control to his subordinate.*

rel·i·qua·ry /'relɪkwəri $ -kweri/ n plural **reliquaries** [C] *technical* a container for religious objects that are related to holy people

rel·ish¹ /ˈrelɪʃ/ v [T] to enjoy an experience or the thought of something that is going to happen: **relish the prospect/thought/idea** I don't relish the thought of you walking home alone. | **relish the chance/opportunity** He relishes the chance to play Hamlet.

relish² n **1** [U] great enjoyment of something: **with relish** I ate **with great relish**, enjoying every bite. **2** [C,U] a thick spicy sauce made from fruits or vegetables, and usually eaten with meat: a hot dog with mustard and relish

re·live /ˌriːˈlɪv/ v [T] to remember or imagine something that happened in the past so clearly that you experience the same emotions again: The girls watch the tape, eager to relive their victory against UCLA.

re·load /ˌriːˈləʊd $ -ˈloʊd/ v [I,T] **1** to put something into a container again, especially bullets into a gun **2** if you reload a page on the Internet, you ask for the information shown on that page to be sent to your computer again, usually because there has been a problem or because you want the information to be as new as possible

re·lo·cate /ˌriːləʊˈkeɪt $ riːˈloʊkeɪt/ v [I,T] if a person or business relocates, or if they are relocated, they move to a different place: [+to] A lot of firms are relocating to the North of England. | [+in] businesses that relocate in depressed areas | **relocate sb/sth to sth** The residents were relocated to temporary accommodation while the work was being done. —**relocation** /ˌriːləʊˈkeɪʃən $ -loʊ-/ n [U]

re·luc·tance /rɪˈlʌktəns/ n [singular, U] when someone is unwilling to do something, or when they do something slowly to show that they are not very willing: Wells finally agreed, but with reluctance. | **reluctance to do sth** a reluctance to share information

re·luc·tant /rɪˈlʌktənt/ adj slow and unwilling: She gave a reluctant smile. | **reluctant to do sth** Maddox was reluctant to talk about it. —**reluctantly** adv: Reluctantly, he agreed.

re·ly S2 W2 /rɪˈlaɪ/ v relied, relying, relies **rely on/upon** sb/sth phr v
1 to trust or depend on someone or something to do what you need or expect them to do; → **reliable**, **reliance**: I knew I could rely on David. | **rely on sb/sth to do sth** Many working women rely on relatives to help take care of their children. | [+for] Many people now rely on the Internet for news.
2 to depend on something in order to continue to live or exist: For its income, the company **relies heavily** on only a few contracts. | [+for] They have to rely on the river for their water.

re·main S1 W1 /rɪˈmeɪn/ v
1 [I always + adv/prep, linking verb] to continue to be in the same state or condition: Please remain seated until all the lights are on. | We remained friends. | The boy remained silent. | [+as] Despite the job losses, Parker remained as manager. | **remain unclear/unchanged/ unanswered etc** Many scientists remain unconvinced by the current evidence.
2 [I] formal to stay in the same place without moving away; ⊟ **stay**: [+at/in/with etc] She was too ill to remain at home. | The refugees were allowed to remain in the UK. ⚠ In spoken English it is more usual to use **stay**.
3 [I] to continue to exist or be left after others have gone, been used, or been destroyed: Little of the original building remains. | The score is tied, with fifteen minutes remaining. | **What remains of** his original art collection is now in the city museum.
4 [I] to be left after other things have been dealt with: **remain to be done** Several points remain to be settled. | **There remained** a few jobs still to be finished. | **The fact remains that** racism is still a considerable problem.
5 it remains to be seen used to say that it is still uncertain whether something will happen or is true: It remains to be seen whether the operation was successful.

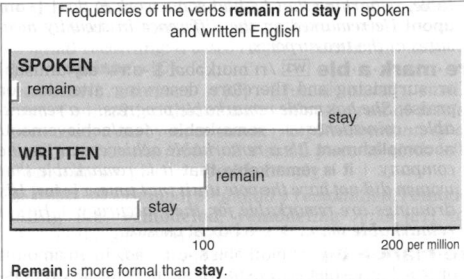

Frequencies of the verbs **remain** and **stay** in spoken and written English

SPOKEN — remain / stay
WRITTEN — remain / stay
100 ... 200 per million
Remain is more formal than **stay**.

re·main·der /rɪˈmeɪndə $ -ər/ n **1 the remainder** the part of something that is left after everything else has gone or been dealt with; ⊟ **the rest**: The remainder must be paid by the end of June. | [+of] He spent the remainder of his police career behind a desk. **2** [C] **a)** the number you get when you subtract one number from another number **b)** the number that is left when you divide one number by another number: Fifteen divided by four gives you a remainder of 3.

re·main·ing W2 /rɪˈmeɪnɪŋ/ adj [only before noun] the remaining people or things are those that are left when the others have gone, been used, or been dealt with: The few remaining guests were in the kitchen. | Add the remaining ingredients and simmer for 30 minutes. | The only remaining question is whether we can raise the money.

re·mains W3 /rɪˈmeɪnz/ n [plural]
1 the parts of something that are left after the rest has been destroyed or has disappeared: [+of] On the table were the remains of the evening meal. | extensive Roman remains (=of ancient buildings) at Arles
2 the body of someone who has died: Her remains are buried in Westminster.

re·make¹ /ˈriːmeɪk/ n [C] a record or film that has the same music or story as one that was made before: [+of] a remake of 'Cape Fear'

re·make² /ˌriːˈmeɪk/ v past tense and past participle remade /-ˈmeɪd/ [T] **1** to film a story or record a piece of music again: It was remade as a musical. **2** to build or make something again: She remade her wedding dress to fit her daughter.

re·mand¹ /rɪˈmɑːnd $ rɪˈmænd/ v [T usually passive] law **1** BrE to send someone back from a court of law, to wait for their TRIAL: Smith was **remanded in custody** (=kept in prison) until Tuesday. | He's been **remanded on bail** for a month (=allowed to leave the law court and go home to wait for trial). **2** AmE to send a case to be dealt with in another court: The court remanded the case for trial.

remand² n [U] BrE the period of time that someone spends in prison before their TRIAL: **on remand** Evans committed suicide while on remand in Parkhurst prison. | remand prisoners

re'mand ˌcentre n [C] BrE a place like a prison where people are kept while waiting for a TRIAL

re'mand ˌhome n [C] BrE a place like a prison where young people are kept while waiting for a TRIAL

re·mark¹ S3 W3 /rɪˈmɑːk $ -ɑːrk/ n
1 [C] something that you say when you express an opinion or say what you have noticed; ⊟ **comment**: The Senator denied **making the remark**. | **a sexist/ critical/personal etc remark** He was fired for making racist remarks during an interview.
2 remarks [plural] the things you say in a formal speech: **introductory/opening/concluding remarks** the chairman's introductory remarks | **in sb's remarks** Caldwell, in his remarks, emphasized the need for cooperation.

remark² v [T] to say something, especially about something you have just noticed: 'This house must be very old,' he remarked. | **remark that** Anderson left the

from a distance, using radio or electronic signals: *a missile guided by remote control* **3** [U] a type of computer software that lets you use a particular computer by connecting it to another one that is far away —**remote-controlled** *adj*

re,mote interro'gation *n* [U] the process of calling your own telephone when you are away from your home or office so that you can listen to messages that people have left on your ANSWERING MACHINE

re·mote·ly /rɪ'məʊtli $ -'moʊt-/ *adv* **1** by only a small amount; **⊟ slightly**: *The brew tasted only remotely of beer.* **2** not remotely interested/funny/possible etc used to emphasize that someone or something is not at all interested, funny etc: *There was nothing remotely new in this idea.* **3** from far away: *remotely operated vehicles*

re,mote 'sensing *n* [U] the use of SATELLITES to obtain pictures and information about the Earth

re,mote 'working *n* [U] when people do their work at home, using a computer that is connected to the computer system in an office; **⊟ homeworking**

re·mould[1] *BrE*; **remold** *AmE* /ˌriː'məʊld $ -'moʊld/ *v* [T] *formal* to change an idea, system, way of thinking etc: *Mergers have forced organizations to remould themselves.*

re·mould[2] /'riːməʊld $ -moʊld/ *n* [C] *BrE* an old tyre with a new surface, that you can use again

re·mount /ˌriː'maʊnt/ *v* [I,T] to get onto a horse, bicycle etc again

re·mov·a·ble /rɪ'muːvəbəl/ *adj* easy to remove: *a sofa with removable cloth covers*

re·mov·al [S3] /rɪ'muːvəl/ *n* [C,U]
1 when something is taken away from, out of, or off the place where it is; → **remove**: [+of] *the removal of rubbish*
2 when you get rid of something so that it does not exist any longer: *stain removal*
3 when someone is forced out of an important position or dismissed from a job: [+from] *the mayor's removal from office*
4 *BrE* the process of taking furniture from your old house to your new one: **removal company/man etc** *The removal men have been in and out all day.*

re'moval van *n* [C] *BrE* a large vehicle used for moving furniture and other things from one house to another

re·move[1] [S2] [W1] /rɪ'muːv/ *v* [T]
1 TAKE AWAY to take something away from, out of, or off the place where it is: *Remove the old wallpaper and fill any holes in the walls.* | **remove sth from sth** *Reference books may not be removed from the library.*
2 GET RID OF to get rid of something so that it does not exist any longer: *a cleaner that will remove wine stains* | *The college removed rules that prevented women from enrolling.*
3 FROM A JOB to force someone out of an important position or dismiss them from a job: **remove sb from sth** *Congress could remove the President from office.*
4 CLOTHES *formal* to take off a piece of clothing: *He removed his hat and gloves.*
5 be far removed from sth to be very different from something: *The events in the newspaper article were far removed from reality.*
6 cousin once/twice etc removed the child, GRANDCHILD etc of your COUSIN, or your cousin's father, grandfather etc

remove[2] *n* [C,U] *especially BrE formal* a distance or amount by which two things are separated: **at a remove** *The X-ray operator works at a safe remove in a separate room.*

re·mov·er /rɪ'muːvə $ -ər/ *n* [C,U] **paint/nail varnish/stain etc remover** a substance that removes paint marks etc

REM sleep /'rem sliːp/ *n* [U] *technical* **rapid eye movement sleep** a period during sleep when your eyes move quickly, when you are dreaming

re·mu·ne·ra·tion /rɪˌmjuːnə'reɪʃən/ *n* [C,U] *formal* the pay you give someone for something they have done for you: *high rates of remuneration* —**remunerate** /rɪ'mjuːnəreɪt/ *v* [T]

re·mu·ne·ra·tive /rɪ'mjuːnərətɪv $ -nəreɪtɪv/ *adj* *formal* making a lot of money

re·nais·sance /rɪ'neɪsəns $ 'renə,sɑːns/ *n* [singular] a new interest in something, especially a particular form of art, music etc, that has not been popular for a long period: [+in] *a renaissance in wood carving over the last few years*

Renaissance *n* **1 the Renaissance** the period of time in Europe between 14th and 17th centuries, when art, literature, PHILOSOPHY, and scientific ideas became very important and a lot of new art etc was produced **2** Renaissance art/furniture/architecture etc art, furniture etc belonging to the Renaissance period

Re,naissance 'man / $,... './ **Re,naissance 'woman** / $,... '../ *n* [C] a man or woman who can do many things well, such as writing and painting, and who knows a lot about many different subjects

re·nal /'riːnl/ *adj* [only before noun] *technical* relating to the KIDNEYS: *acute renal failure*

re·name /ˌriː'neɪm/ *v* [T usually passive] to give something a new name: **rename sth sth** *Myddleton Way was renamed Allende Avenue.*

re·nas·cent /rɪ'næsənt/ *adj* [only before noun] *formal* becoming popular, strong, or important again: *Voters have come back to a renascent Labour Party.*

rend /rend/ *v past tense and past participle* **rent** /rent/ [T] *literary* to tear or break something violently into pieces

ren·der /'rendə $ -ər/ *v* [T] **1** to cause someone or something to be in a particular condition: **render sb/sth impossible/harmless/unconscious etc** *He was rendered almost speechless by the news.* | *The blow to his head was strong enough to render him unconscious.* **2** *formal* to give something to someone or do something, because it is your duty or because someone expects you to: *an obligation to render assistance to those in need* | **render a decision/opinion/judgment** etc *It is unlikely that the court will render an opinion before November 5.* | *a bill of $3200 for services rendered* (=for something you have done) **3** to express or present something in a particular way: **render sth as sth** *She made a sound that in print is rendered as 'harrumph.'* | **render sth sth** *Infrared film renders blue skies a deep black.* | **render sth in sth** *a sculpture rendered in bronze* **4** **render sth into English/Russian/Chinese etc** *formal* to translate something into English, Russian etc **5** *technical* to spread PLASTER or CEMENT on the surface of a wall: *a brick wall that has been rendered and whitewashed* **6** to melt the fat of an animal as you cook it: *Steam the goose to render some of the fat.*

ren·der·ing /'rendərɪŋ/ *n* **1** [C] someone's performance of a play, piece of music etc; **⊟ rendition**: [+of] *a spirited rendering of the national anthem* **2** [C] the way an expression, piece of writing etc is translated or explained, or the way an event, situation etc is described: **accurate/literal etc rendering of sth** *a faithful rendering of historical events* **3** [C,U] *BrE* a material made of CEMENT and sand, used on the outside walls of buildings

ren·dez·vous[1] /'rɒndɪvuː, -deɪ- $ 'rɑːndeɪ-/ *n plural* **rendezvous** /-vuːz/ **1** [C] an arrangement to meet someone at a particular time and place, often secretly: [+with] *He made a rendezvous with her in Times Square.* | *plans for a secret rendezvous* **2** [C usually singular] a place where two or more people have arranged to meet: *Boats picked us up at pre-arranged rendezvous.* **3** [C] a bar, restaurant etc where people like to meet: *a popular rendezvous for media people*

rendezvous[2] *v* [I] **1** to meet someone at a time or place that was arranged earlier; **⊟ meet up**: [+with]

We'll rendezvous with James in Nicosia. **2** if two spacecraft, aircraft, or military vehicles rendezvous, they meet, for example to move supplies from one to the other

ren·di·tion /ren'dɪʃən/ n **1** [C usually singular, U] someone's performance of a play, piece of music etc: *He gave a moving rendition of Lennon's 'Imagine'.* **2** [C] a translation of a piece of writing: [+of] *an English rendition of a Greek poem*

ren·e·gade /'renɪɡeɪd/ n [C] literary someone who leaves one side in a war, politics etc in order to join the opposing side – used to show disapproval: *a renegade army unit*

re·nege /rɪ'niːɡ, rɪ'neɪɡ $ rɪ'nɪɡ, rɪ'niːɡ/ v [I] formal **renege on an agreement/deal/promise etc** to not do something you have promised or agreed to do; ◪ **go back on**: *The fighters had reneged on a pledge to release foreign prisoners.*

re·new /rɪ'njuː $ rɪ'nuː/ v [T] **1** to arrange for an agreement or official document to continue for a further period of time: **renew sb's contract/licence/membership etc** *I need to renew my passport this year.* **2** formal to begin doing something again after a period of not doing it; ◪ **resume**: *Local people have renewed their efforts to save the school.* | *Police renewed their appeal for witnesses.* | **renew a friendship/acquaintance etc** (=become friendly with someone again) **3** to remove something that is old or broken and put a new one in its place; ◪ **replace**: *The window frames need to be renewed.* **4 renew a book** to arrange to borrow a library book for a further period of time

re·new·a·ble /rɪ'njuːəbəl $ rɪ'nuː-/ adj **1** if an agreement or official document is renewable, you can make it continue for a further period of time after it ends; ◪ **non-renewable**: *It's a six-month lease but it's renewable.* | *a renewable visa* **2** [usually before noun] renewable energy replaces itself naturally, or is easily replaced because there is a large supply of it: *renewable energy* such as solar power | *an industry based on renewable resources* → see picture at ENVIRONMENT

re·new·al /rɪ'njuːəl $ -'nuː-/ n [singular, U] **1** when an activity, situation, or process begins again after a period when it had stopped: [+of] *a renewal of the recent conflict* | *Spring is a time of renewal.* **2** when you make an agreement or official document continue for a further period of time after it ends: [+of] *the renewal of our annual licence* | *Mark's contract comes up for renewal at the end of this year.* **3 inner city/urban renewal** when the poor areas of towns are improved by making new jobs, industries, homes etc

re·newed /rɪ'njuːd $ -'nuːd/ adj **1** [only before noun] starting again, especially with increased interest or strength: **renewed interest/confidence/enthusiasm etc** *renewed concern about farming methods* | *The festival went ahead, despite renewed protests.* **2** [not before noun] feeling healthy and relaxed again, after feeling ill or tired

ren·net /'renɪt/ n [U] a substance used for making milk thicker in order to make cheese

re·nounce /rɪ'naʊns/ v [T] **1** if you renounce an official position, title, right etc, you publicly say that you will not keep it any more; ◪ **give up**: *Edward renounced his claim to the French throne.* | *She renounced her citizenship.* **2** to publicly say or show that you no longer believe in something, or will no longer behave in a particular way; ◪ **reject**: *These groups must renounce violence if there is to be progress towards peace.* | *Young people renounced capitalism in favour of peace and love.*

ren·o·vate /'renəveɪt/ v [T] to repair a building or old furniture so that it is in good condition again: *The hotel has been renovated and redecorated.* —**renovation** /ˌrenə'veɪʃən/ n [C,U]

re·nown /rɪ'naʊn/ n [U] formal when you are famous and a lot of people admire you for a special skill, achievement, or quality; ◪ **acclaim**: **international/public etc renown** *He has won world renown for his films.* | *He achieved some renown as a football player.*

re·nowned /rɪ'naʊnd/ adj known and admired by a lot of people, especially for a special skill, achievement, or quality; ◪ **famous**: [+for] *an island renowned for its beauty* | [+as] *He's renowned as a brilliant speaker.* | **renowned author/actor/photographer etc** *a world renowned expert in the field*

rent¹ S2 W3 /rent/ v
1 [I,T] to regularly pay money to live in a house or room that belongs to someone else, or to use something that belongs to someone else: *Most students rent rooms in their second year.* | *I'd rather have my own house than rent.* | **rent sth from sb** *Some farmers rent their land from the council.*
2 also **rent out** [T] to let someone live in a house, room etc that you own, or use your land, in return for money; ◪ **let** BrE: **rent sth (out) to sb** *She rents out two rooms to students.*
3 [T] especially AmE to pay money for the use of something for a short period of time; ◪ **hire** BrE: *Will you rent a car while you're in Spain?*
rent at/for sth phr v
if a house rents at or for an amount of money, that is how much you must pay to use it: *Houses here rent for at least $2,500 a week.*

WORD CHOICE: rent, hire, lease
Rent is used to talk about paying to live in or use a building that is owned by someone else: *We rented an apartment together.*
In American English, you also **rent** a car or electrical equipment: *The TV is rented.*
In British English, you can use **rent** or **hire**, but it is more usual to say that you **hire** a car: *You can hire a car at the airport.*
Lease is used to talk about renting buildings, cars, or equipment over a long period of time, especially for business use: *If you upgrade computers regularly, it may work out cheaper to lease them.*

---

rent² n **1** [C,U] the money that someone pays regularly to use a room, house etc that belongs to someone else: *I pay the rent at the beginning of every month.* | **high/low/reasonable etc rent** *Shop rents are extremely high.* | [+of] *an annual rent of £8,000* **2** [C,U] especially AmE an amount of money that you pay to use a car, boat etc that belongs to someone else: *The rent was only $20 an hour.* **3 for rent** available to be rented: *Luxury villas for rent.* **4** [C] formal a large tear in something made of cloth: *huge rents in the curtains*

rent³ v the past tense and past participle of REND

rent·al /'rentl/ n **1** [C usually singular, U] the money that you pay to use a car, television, or other machine over a period of time: **car/television/telephone etc rental** *The price includes accommodation and car rental.* | *Video rental is usually £3.* | **line rental** BrE (=the money that you pay to use a telephone line) **2** [C,U] an arrangement to rent something for a period of time, or the act of doing this: **rental contract/scheme/service etc** *Could you sign the rental agreement?* **3** [C] especially AmE something that you rent, especially a house or car: *companies that provide rentals*

'rent boy n [C] BrE informal a young man who has sex with other men in return for money

'rent con·trol n [U] when a city or a state uses laws to control the cost of renting houses and apartments

rent·ed /'rentɪd/ adj **rented accommodation/housing/apartment etc** houses etc that people pay rent for

ˌrent-'free adj, adv without payment of rent: *rent-free accommodation* | *He lives there rent-free.*

'rent ˌrebate n [C] BrE money that some people get from the local government to help them pay their rent

'rent strike n [C] an occasion when all the people living in a group of houses or apartments refuse to pay their rent, as a protest against something

re·nun·ci·a·tion /rɪ,nʌnsi'eɪʃən/ n [C,U] *formal* when someone makes a formal decision to no longer believe in something, live in a particular way etc; → **renounce**: [+of] *Eastern Europe's renunciation of Communism*

re·o·pen /ri'əʊpən $ -'oʊ-/ v [I,T] **1** if a theatre, restaurant etc reopens, or if it is reopened, it opens again after a period when it was closed: *The swimming pool will reopen in May.* **2** if you reopen a discussion, law case etc, or if it reopens, you begin it again after it had stopped: **reopen a case/question/debate etc** *attempts to reopen the issue of the power station's future* **3** if a government reopens the border of their country, or if the border reopens, people are allowed to pass through it again after it had been closed

re·or·der /ri'ɔːdə $ -'ɔːrdər/ v [I,T] **1** to order a product to be supplied again: *Could you reorder more of this fabric?* **2** to change the way that things are ordered or arranged: *The whole system needs reordering.*

re·or·gan·ize also **-ise** BrE /riː'ɔːgənaɪz $ -'ɔːr-/ v [I,T] to arrange or organize something in a new way: *Our office is being completely reorganized.* —**reorganization** /ri,ɔːgənaɪ'zeɪʃən $ -,ɔːrgənə-/ n [C,U]: *a major reorganization of child care services*

rep /rep/ n **1** [C] *informal* a SALES REPRESENTATIVE **2** [C] someone who speaks officially for a company, organization, or group of people; ▪ **representative**: **staff/ union/company etc rep** *You need to speak to the students' rep.* | *Safety reps have the right to stop the job when workers are in danger.* **3** [C] AmE a REPRESENTA-TIVE **4** [C,U] REPERTORY, or a repertory theatre or company: *Most actors start off in rep.* **5** [C] AmE spoken a REPUTATION **6** [C] one exercise that you do in a series of exercises; ▪ **repetition**: *Do 15 reps of each exercise.*

Rep. **1** the written abbreviation of *Representative*, used before names: *Rep. Bud Shuster* **2** the written abbreviation of *Republican*

re·paid /rɪ'peɪd/ v the past tense and past participle of REPAY

re·pair¹ S3 /rɪ'peə $ -'per/ v [T] **1** to fix something that is damaged, broken, split, or not working properly; ▪ **mend** BrE: *Dad was up the ladder, repairing the roof.* | *Where can I get my shoes repaired?* **2** *formal* to do something to remove harm that you have caused; ▪ **mend** BrE: *Neil tried to repair the damage that his statements had caused.* → IRREPARABLE
    repair to sth *phr v*
    old-fashioned to go to a place: *Shall we repair to the drawing room?* —**repairer** n [C]

WORD CHOICE: repair, fix, mend
Repair is slightly more formal than **fix** or **mend**. You can **repair** anything that is broken or damaged, or has a hole in it: *He repairs old furniture.* | *It cost too much to get the car repaired.* | *The roof needs repairing in a few places.*
In British English, **fix** and **mend** have the same meaning, but people more often use **fix** to talk about repairing a machine, vehicle etc and **mend** to talk about repairing holes in clothes, roads, roofs, and fences.
In American English, **mend** is usually only used to talk about repairing things with holes in them, especially clothes and shoes.

repair² S3 W3 n **1** [C,U] something that you do to fix a thing that is damaged, broken, or not working: [+to] *repairs to the roads* | **make/carry out/do repairs** *His job is to make minor repairs on all the machines.* | *The church tower is in need of repair.* | **structural/housing/motorway etc repairs** *an extensive programme of building repairs* | **beyond repair** *Many of the paintings were beyond repair* (=so damaged that they cannot be mended). | **under repair** (=being repaired) *Is the bridge still under repair?* | *They did a good repair job on the roof.*

2 in good/poor etc repair in good or bad condition: *Garden tools should be kept in good repair.*

re·pair·a·ble /rɪ'peərəbəl $ -'per-/ adj [not before noun] able to be fixed

re·pair·man /rɪ'peəmæn $ -'per-/ n plural **repairmen** /-men/ [C] someone whose job is to repair things: *the TV repairman*

rep·a·ra·tion /,repə'reɪʃən/ n formal **1 reparations** [plural] money paid by a defeated country after a war, for all the deaths, damage etc it has caused: *The government agreed to pay reparations to victims.* **2** [C,U] when you give something to someone or do something for them because you have done something wrong to them in the past: **make reparation (to sb) for sth** *Offenders must make reparation for their crimes through community service.*

rep·ar·tee /,repɑː'tiː $,repər'tiː/ n [U] conversation which is fast and full of intelligent and amusing remarks and replies: *witty repartee*

re·past /rɪ'pɑːst $ rɪ'pæst/ n [C] formal a meal

re·pat·ri·ate /riː'pætrieɪt $ riː'peɪ-/ v [T] **1** to send someone back to their own country; → **deport**: *After the war, prisoners were repatriated.* **2** to send profits or money you have earned back to your own country

re·pay /rɪ'peɪ/ v past tense and past participle **repaid** [T] **1** to pay back money that you have borrowed: **repay a loan/debt etc** *Your mortgage will be repaid over 25 years.* | **repay sb sth** *I'll repay you the money you lent me next week.* **2** to do something for someone, or give them something, in return for helping you: **repay sb for sth** *How can we repay him for everything he's done?* | *I'd like to buy them something to repay all their kindness.* **3** if something repays your time, effort etc, it is worth the time or effort you have spent

re·pay·a·ble /rɪ'peɪəbəl/ adj [not before noun] money that is repayable at a particular time has to be paid back by that time: [+over] *The loan is repayable over 10 years.*

re·pay·ment /rɪ'peɪmənt/ n **1** [U] when you pay back money that you have borrowed: [+of] *the repayment of debt* **2** [C usually plural] an amount of money that you pay regularly until you do not owe any more: *monthly mortgage repayments of £330* | *Do you worry about meeting* (=paying) *your loan repayments?*

re·peal /rɪ'piːl/ v [T] if a government repeals a law, officially ends that law —**repeal** n [U]

re·peat¹ S2 W2 /rɪ'piːt/ v [T]
1 SAY AGAIN to say or write something again: *Can you repeat your question?* | *Sorry – could you repeat that?* | **repeat that** *Nick patiently repeated that he had to work that day.* | *It is not, I repeat not, my fault.* | *'I promise,' she repeated.* | **repeat yourself** (=say something that you have said before, usually by mistake) *Elderly people tend to repeat themselves.*
2 DO AGAIN to do something again: *Repeat the exercises twice a day.* | *We must not repeat the mistakes of the past.* | **repeat a class/grade/year** (=do the same class at school again the following year) *The team are hoping to repeat their success* (=achieve the same good result) *of last season.*
3 LEARN to say something that someone else has just said, especially in order to learn it: **repeat (sth) after sb** *Repeat after me: amo, amas, amat ...*
4 TELL to tell someone something that you have heard, especially something secret: *Here's what happened, but don't repeat it.*
5 BROADCAST to broadcast a television or radio programme again: *The series will be repeated in the autumn.*
6 sth doesn't bear repeating used to say that you do not want to repeat what someone has said, especially because it is rude: *Her comments don't bear repeating!* → **history repeats itself** at HISTORY (8)
    repeat on sb *phr v* BrE
    if food repeats on you, its taste keeps coming back into your mouth after you have eaten it

repeat² n [C] **1** [usually singular] an event that is very like something that happened before: [+of] *The match was basically a repeat of last year's game at Wembley.* | *It was a terrible journey – I hope we don't have a **repeat performance*** (=have the same thing happen again) *on the way home.* **2** a television or radio programme that has been broadcast before: *'Is it a repeat?' 'No, it's a new series.'* **3** repeat order/prescription *BrE* an order of goods or a PRESCRIPTION of medicine that is the same as one you had before **4** *technical* the sign that tells a performer to play a piece of music again, or the music that is played again

re·peat·a·ble /rɪ'piːtəbəl/ *adj* [not usually before noun] **1 not repeatable** too rude to repeat – used about something someone says; ◨ **unrepeatable 2** able to be repeated: *I hope these results are repeatable.*

re·peat·ed /rɪ'piːtᵻd/ *adj* [only before noun] done or happening again and again: *repeated calls for change* | *repeated attempts to kill him*

re·peat·ed·ly /rɪ'piːtᵻdli/ *adv* many times: *Graham was repeatedly warned not to work so hard.*

re·peat·er /rɪ'piːtə $ -ər/ n [C] *technical* a gun that you can fire several times before you have to load it again

re·pel /rɪ'pel/ v **repelled**, **repelling 1** [T] if something repels you, it is so unpleasant that you do not want to be near it, or it makes you feel ill; → **repulsive**: *The smell repelled him.* **2** [T] to make someone who is attacking you go away, by fighting them: *The army was ready to repel an attack.* **3** [T] to keep something or someone away from you: *a lotion that repels mosquitoes* **4** [I,T] *technical* if two things repel each other, they push each other away with an electrical force; ◨ **attract**: *Two positive charges repel each other.*

re·pel·lent¹ /rɪ'pelənt/ *adj* very unpleasant; → **repulsive**: *She found him physically repellent.* | [+to] *The sight of blood is repellent to some people.*

repellent², **repellant** n [C,U] a substance that keeps insects away: **insect/mosquito/bug etc repellent**

re·pent /rɪ'pent/ v [I,T] *formal* to be sorry for something and wish you had not done it – used especially when considering your actions in a religious way: [+of] *He repented of his sins before he died.*

re·pen·tance /rɪ'pentəns/ n [U] when you are sorry for something you have done

re·pen·tant /rɪ'pentənt/ *adj formal* sorry for something wrong that you have done; ◨ **unrepentant**

re·per·cus·sion /ˌriːpə'kʌʃən $ -pər-/ n [C usually plural] the effects of an action or event, especially bad effects that continue for some time; → **consequence**: [+for] *The collapse of the company had repercussions for the whole industry.* | [+on] *There were **serious repercussions** on his career.* | [+of] *the repercussions of the crisis* | **political/social/economic etc repercussions**

rep·er·toire /'repətwɑː $ -pərtwɑːr/ n [C usually singular] **1** all the plays, pieces of music etc that a performer or group knows and can perform: **in sb's repertoire** *The group include some techno in their repertoire.* | [+of] *a **wide repertoire** of songs* **2** the total number of things that someone or something is able to do: *the behavioral repertoire of infants*

rep·er·to·ry /'repətəri $ 'repərtɔːri/ n plural **repertories 1** [U] a type of theatre work in which actors perform different plays on different days, instead of doing the same play for a long time: *a repertory company* **2** [C] *formal* a repertoire

rep·e·ti·tion /ˌrepᵻ'tɪʃən/ n **1** [U] doing or saying the same thing many times: [+of] *The job involved the **constant repetition** of the same movements.* | *Children used to learn by repetition.* **2** [C,U] something that happens again, especially something bad: [+of] *a repetition of the same problem*

rep·e·ti·tious /ˌrepᵻ'tɪʃəs◂/ *adj* involving the same actions or using the same words many times, in a way that is boring: *repetitious work*

re·pet·i·tive /rɪ'petᵻtɪv/ *adj* done many times in the same way, and boring: **repetitive work/tasks/jobs** *repetitive tasks like washing and ironing* | *The song was dreary and repetitive.* —**repetitively** *adv*

re·petitive 'strain ˌinjury n [U] *medical* **RSI** pains in your hands, arms etc caused by doing the same hand movements many times, especially by using a computer KEYBOARD or MOUSE

re·phrase /ˌriː'freɪz/ v [T] to say or write something again using different words to express what you mean in a way that is clearer or more acceptable: *OK. Let me rephrase the question.*

re·place S2 W1 /rɪ'pleɪs/ v [T] **1** to start using something instead of another person, or start being used instead of another thing: *I'm replacing Sue on the team.* | *Lectures have replaced the old tutorial system.* **2** to remove someone from their job or something from its place, and put a new person or thing there: *Two of the tyres had to be replaced.* | **replace sth with sth** *They replaced the permanent staff with part-timers.* **3** if you replace something that has been broken, stolen etc, you get a new one; → **irreplaceable**: *I'll replace the vase I broke as soon as possible.* **4** to put something back where it was before: *He replaced the book on the shelf.* —**replaceable** *adj*

re·place·ment W3 /rɪ'pleɪsmənt/ n **1** [U] when you get something that is newer or better than the one you had before: *Our old car is badly in need of replacement.* | *replacement windows* **2 knee/hip/joint replacement** an artificial knee etc that replaces a damaged one, given to people in a medical operation **3** [C] someone or something that replaces another person or thing: [+for] *It was difficult to find a replacement for Ted.*

re·plat·form /ˌriː'plætfɔːm $ -fɔːrm/ v *BrE* be replatformed if a train is replatformed, passengers have to get on it in a different part of the station from the one they were originally told to go to: *The replatformed 19:47 to Leeds will now leave from platform six.*

re·play¹ /ˌriː'pleɪ/ v [T] **1** [usually passive] to play a game again because neither team won the first time: *The match will be replayed on Wednesday.* **2** to show again on television something that has been recorded: *Highlights of the race were replayed on the news.*

re·play² /'riːpleɪ/ n [C] **1** a game that is played again because neither team won the first time: *Milan won the semi-final replay 3–0.* **2** a part of a game of sport that has been recorded on video tape or film, and that is shown again, especially in order to examine it more clearly: *You can see on the replay that the goalkeeper was fouled.* → ACTION REPLAY **3** *informal* something that is done exactly as it was before: [+of] *a replay of the same old mistakes*

re·plen·ish /rɪ'plenɪʃ/ v [T] *formal* to put new supplies into something, or to fill something again: *More vaccines are needed to replenish our stocks.* —**replenishment** n [U]

re·plete /rɪ'pliːt/ *adj* [not before noun] **1** *formal* full of something: [+with] *Literature is replete with tales of power.* **2** *old-fashioned* very full of food or drink

rep·li·ca /'replᵻkə/ n [C] an exact copy of something, especially a building, a gun, or a work of art: [+of] *an **exact replica** of the Taj Mahal* | *replica guns*

rep·li·cate /'replᵻkeɪt/ v **1** [T] *formal* if you replicate someone's work, a scientific study etc, you do it again, or try to get the same result again: *There is a need for further research to replicate these findings.* **2** [I,T] *technical* if a VIRUS or a MOLECULE replicates, or if it replicates itself, it divides and produces exact copies of itself: *the ability of DNA to replicate itself* —**replication** /ˌreplᵻ'keɪʃən/ n [C,U]

R

re·ply¹ [S3] [W2] /rɪˈplaɪ/ v replied, replying, replies
1 [I,T] to answer someone by saying or writing something: *I asked Clive where he was going, but he didn't reply.* | *Sorry it took me so long to reply.* | *'Did you see Simon today?' 'Of course,' Nathalie replied with a smile.* | [+to] *Has Ian replied to your letter yet?* | **reply that** *Mills replied that he was staying at his parents' flat.*
2 [I] to react to an action by doing something else: **reply (to sth) with sth** *The rebel troops replied to government threats with increased violence.*

reply² [S2] [W3] n plural replies [C]
1 something that is said, written, or done as a way of replying; ▤ **answer**: *I tried calling, but there was no reply.* | [+to] *We still haven't received a reply to our letter.* | *Stephen made no reply.*
2 **in reply (to sth)** formal as a way of replying to something: *I am writing in reply to your letter of 1st June.*
3 **without reply** BrE if a sports team gets a number of points or GOALS without reply, their opponents do not score

re·ply-'paid adj BrE a reply-paid envelope is one which you can send back to an organization without a stamp because they have already paid for this

re·po man /ˈriːpəʊ mæn $ -poʊ/ n [C] AmE informal someone whose job is to REPOSSESS (=take away) cars that have not been paid for

re·port¹ [S2] [W1] /rɪˈpɔːt $ -ɔːrt/ n [C]
1 a written or spoken description of a situation or event, giving people the information they need; → **account**: [+of/on/about] *Martens gave a report on his sales trip to Korea.*
2 a piece of writing in a newspaper about something that is happening, or part of a news programme; → **reporter**: *According to recent news reports, two of the victims are Americans.* | [+on/of] *media reports of the food shortages*
3 an official document that carefully considers a particular subject: [+on] *a recent report on child abuse*
4 information that something has happened, which may or may not be true: [+of] *Police received reports of a bomb threat at the airport at 11:28 p.m.* | **report that** *a report that he had been killed*
5 BrE a written statement by teachers about a child's work at school, which is sent to his or her parents; ▤ **report card** AmE
6 BrE someone who works for a particular manager: *Only Gordon's direct reports are attending the course.*
7 formal the noise of an explosion or shot: *a loud report*

report² [S3] [W1] v
1 [NEWS] [I,T] to give people information about recent events, especially in newspapers and on television and radio; → **reporter**: *This is Gavin Williams, reporting from the United Nations in New York.* | *We aim to report the news as fairly as possible.* | *The incident was widely reported in the national press.* | [+on] *The Times sent her to Bangladesh to report on the floods.* | **report that** *Journalists in Cairo reported that seven people had been shot.* | **report doing sth** *Witnesses reported seeing three people flee the scene.*
2 **be reported to be/do sth** used to say that a statement has been made about someone or something, but you do not know if it is true; → **allege**: *The stolen necklace is reported to be worth $57,000.*
3 [JOB/WORK] [I,T] to tell someone about what has been happening, or what you are doing as part of your job: **report (to sb) on sth** *I've asked him to come back next week and report on his progress.*
4 [PUBLIC STATEMENT] [T] to officially give information to the public: *Doctors have reported a 13% increase in the number of people with heart disease.*
5 [CRIME/ACCIDENT] [T] to tell the police or someone in authority that an accident or crime has happened: *I'd like to report a theft.* | **report sth to sb** *All accidents must be reported to the safety officer.* | **report sb/sth missing/injured/killed** *The plane was reported missing.*

6 [COMPLAIN] [T] to complain about someone to people in authority: **report sb for sth** *Polish referee Ryszard Wojoik reported two Leeds United players for violent conduct.* | **report sb to sb** *Hadley's drinking problem led co-workers to report him to the supervisor.*
7 [ARRIVAL] [I] to go somewhere and officially state that you have arrived: [+to] *All visitors must report to the site office.* | *All soldiers were required to report for duty* (=arrive and be ready for work) *on Friday.*
8 **report sick** to officially tell your employers that you cannot to work because you are ill
report back phr v
to give someone information about something that they asked you to find out about: [+to] *The committee has 60 days to report back to Congress.* | [+on] *Students were asked to report back on their results.*
report to sb phr v
to be responsible to someone at work and be managed by them: *He will report to Greg Carr, Boston Technology's chief executive.*

re·port·age /rɪˈpɔːtɪdʒ, ˌrepɔːˈtɑːʒ $ -ɔːr-/ n [U] formal the reporting or describing of events in newspapers, on television, or on the radio; → **reporting**

re'port card n [C] AmE a written statement by teachers about a child's work at school, which is sent to his or her parents; ▤ **report** BrE

re·port·ed·ly /rɪˈpɔːtɪdli $ -ɔːr-/ adv [sentence adverb] according to what some people say: *Her husband's assets are reportedly worth over $15 million.*

re,ported 'speech n [U] technical in grammar, words that are used to tell what someone says without repeating their actual words. 'She said she didn't feel well' is an example of reported speech; ▤ **indirect speech**; ▣ **direct speech**

re·port·er [S3] /rɪˈpɔːtə $ -ˈpɔːrtər/ n [C] someone whose job is to write about news events for a newspaper, or to tell people about them on television or on the radio; → **correspondent, journalist**: *a news reporter*

re·port·ing /rɪˈpɔːtɪŋ $ -ɔːr-/ n [U] the activity of writing about news events for a newspaper or telling people about them on television or on the radio; → **reportage**: *news reporting*

re·pose¹ /rɪˈpəʊz $ -ˈpoʊz/ n [U] formal or literary a state of calm or comfortable rest: **in repose** *His face looked less hard in repose.*

repose² v [I always + adv/prep] formal or literary **1** if something reposes somewhere, it has been put there **2** if someone reposes somewhere, they rest there **3** **repose your trust/hope etc in sb** to trust someone to help you

re·pos·i·to·ry /rɪˈpɒzɪtəri $ rɪˈpɑːzətɔːri/ n plural **repositories** [C] formal **1** a place or container in which large quantities of something are stored; ▤ **store**: [+of/for] *a fire-proof repository for government papers* **2** a person or book that has a lot of information: [+of/for] *Bob is a repository of football statistics.*

re·pos·sess /ˌriːpəˈzes/ v [T] to take back cars, furniture, or property from people who had arranged to pay for them over a long time, but cannot now continue to pay for them; → **bailiff, repo man**: *Eventually the bailiffs came to repossess the flat.* —**repossession** /-ˈzeʃən/ n [C,U]

rep·re·hen·si·ble /ˌreprɪˈhensəbəl/ adj formal reprehensible behaviour is very bad and deserves criticism: *I find their behaviour morally reprehensible.*

re·pre·sent /ˌriːprɪˈzent/ v [T] to give, offer, or send something again, especially an official document: *The phone company re-presented the bill for payment.*

rep·re·sent [S2] [W1] /ˌreprɪˈzent/ v
1 [SPEAK FOR SB] [T] to officially speak or take action for another person or group of people: *Mr Kobayashi was chosen to represent the company at the conference.*
2 [IN COURT] [T] to speak officially for someone in a court of law: **represent yourself** *She decided to represent*

herself (=speak for herself without a lawyer) *during the trial.*
3 BE STH [linking verb] to form or be something; → **amount to**: *European orders represented 30 percent of our sales last year.* | **represent a change/an advance/an increase etc** *This treatment represents a significant advance in the field of cancer research.*
4 GOVERNMENT [T] to have been elected to a parliament, council etc by the people in a particular area: *He represents the Congressional District of Illinois.*
5 SIGN [T] to be a sign or mark that means something; ▤ **stand for**: *Brown areas represent deserts on the map.*
6 SYMBOL [T] to be a symbol of something; ▤ **symbolize**: *He hated the school and everything it represented.*
7 SPORTS [T] if you represent your country, school, town etc in a sport, you take part in a sports event for that country etc: *Her greatest ambition was to represent her country at the Olympics.*
8 be represented if a group, organization, area etc is represented at an event, people from it are at the event: *All the local clubs were represented in the parade.*
9 DESCRIBE [T] to describe someone or something in a particular way, especially in a way that is not true; ▤ **portray**; → **depict**: **represent sb/sth as sth** *The article represents the millionaire as a simple family man.* | *He had represented himself as an employee in order to gain access to the files.*
10 ART [T] if a painting, STATUE, piece of music etc represents something or someone, it shows them: *Paintings representing religious themes were common in medieval times.*

rep·re·sen·ta·tion [S3] [W2] /ˌreprɪzenˈteɪʃən/ n
1 [U] when you have someone to speak, vote, or make decisions for you: *Minority groups need more effective parliamentary representation.* | *There has been a decline in union representation in the auto industry.* → PROPORTIONAL REPRESENTATION
2 [C] a painting, sign, description etc that shows something: [+of] *The clock in the painting is a symbolic representation of the passage of time.*
3 [U] the act of representing someone or something: [+of] *She received praise for her effective representation of Garcia during the trial.*
4 [C usually plural] *formal especially BrE* a formal complaint or statement: [+about] *A group of students made representations to the college about the poor standard of the accommodation.*
5 make false representations *law* to describe or explain something in a way that you know is not true

rep·re·sen·ta·tion·al /ˌreprɪzenˈteɪʃənəl/ adj a representational painting or style of art shows things as they actually appear in real life; ▤ **figurative**

rep·re·sen·ta·tive[1] /ˌreprɪˈzentətɪv◂/ adj **1** typical of a particular group or thing: [+of] *The latest incident is representative of a wider trend.* **2** including examples of all the different types of something in a group: *The pollsters asked a **representative sample** of New York residents for their opinions.* **3** a representative system of government allows people to vote for other people to represent them in the government: *a representative democracy*

representative[2] [S3] [W2] n [C]
1 someone who has been chosen to speak, vote, or make decisions for someone else; ▤ **delegate**: *a union representative* | [+of] *an elected representative of the people*
2 Representative a member of the House of Representatives, the Lower House of Congress in the United States

re·press /rɪˈpres/ v [T] **1** to stop yourself from doing something you want to do: *Brenda repressed the urge to shout at him.* | *I repressed a smile.* **2** if someone represses upsetting feelings, memories etc, they do not allow themselves to express or think about them: *He had long ago repressed the painful memories of his childhood.* **3** to control a group of

people by force; → **suppress**, **oppress**: *The police were widely criticized for their role in repressing the protest movement.*

re·pressed /rɪˈprest/ adj **1** having feelings or desires that you do not allow yourself to express or think about, especially sexual feelings; ▤ **frustrated**: *a repressed middle-aged woman* **2** repressed feelings or desires are ones which you do not allow yourself to express or think about: *repressed anger*

re·pres·sion /rɪˈpreʃən/ n [C,U] **1** when someone does not allow themselves to express feelings or desires which they are ashamed of, especially sexual ones – used when you think someone should express these feelings: *sexual repression* | [+of] *the repression of desire* **2** cruel and severe control of a large group of people; → **suppression**, **oppression**: [+of] *brutal repression of members of the Communist party*

re·pres·sive /rɪˈpresɪv/ adj **1** a repressive government or law controls people in a cruel and severe way; ▤ **oppressive**: *a repressive regime* | *repressive measures* **2** not allowing the expression of feelings or desires, especially sexual ones —**repressively** adv —**repressiveness** n [U]

re·prieve[1] /rɪˈpriːv/ n [C] **1** a delay before something bad happens or continues to happen; → **respite**: [+from] *Shoppers will get a temporary reprieve from the new sales tax.* **2** an official order stopping the killing of a prisoner as a punishment: **give/grant sb a reprieve** *The US Supreme Court voted against granting Smith a reprieve* (=against giving him one).

reprieve[2] v [T usually passive] **1** to officially stop a prisoner from being killed as a punishment **2** to change a decision to close a factory, school etc or get rid of something

rep·ri·mand /ˈreprɪmɑːnd $ -mænd/ v [T] to tell someone officially that something they have done is very wrong; → **scold**, **tell off**: **reprimand sb for (doing) sth** *The military court reprimanded him for failing to do his duty.* —**reprimand** n [C]: *a severe reprimand*

re·print[1] /ˌriːˈprɪnt/ v [T] to print a book, story, newspaper article etc again

re·print[2] /ˈriːprɪnt/ n [C] **1** an occasion when more copies of a book are printed because all the copies of it have been sold **2** a book that is printed again

re·pri·sal /rɪˈpraɪzəl/ n [C,U] something violent or harmful which you do to punish someone for something bad they have done to you; → **revenge**, **retaliation**: *They didn't tell the police for fear of reprisal.* | [+against] *There were reprisals against unarmed civilians.* | **in reprisal (for sth)** *Alfred was shot in reprisal for the killing of a rival gang member.*

re·prise[1] /rɪˈpriːz/ n [C] when all or part of something, especially a piece of music, is repeated

reprise[2] v [T] to act the same part again, play the same tune again etc

re·proach[1] /rɪˈprəʊtʃ $ -ˈprəʊtʃ/ n *formal* **1** [U] criticism, blame, or disapproval: *'You don't need me,' she said quietly, without reproach.* **2** [C] a remark that expresses criticism, blame, or disapproval: *He argued that the reproaches were unfair.* **3 above/beyond reproach** impossible to criticize; ▤ **perfect**: *His behaviour throughout this affair has been beyond reproach.* **4 a reproach to sb/sth** something that should make a person, society etc feel bad or ashamed: *These derelict houses are a reproach to the city.*

reproach[2] v [T] **1** *formal* to blame or criticize someone in a way that shows you are disappointed at what they have done: **reproach sb for/with sth** *He publicly reproached his son for his behavior.* **2 reproach yourself** to feel guilty about something that you think you are responsible for: [+for/with] *You've got nothing to reproach yourself for – it was his own decision.*

re·proach·ful /rɪˈprəʊtʃfəl $ -ˈprəʊtʃ-/ adj a reproachful look, remark etc shows that you are criti-

R

cizing someone or blaming them: *She gave her daughter a reproachful glance.* —**reproachfully** *adv*

rep·ro·bate /'reprəbeɪt/ *n* [C] *formal* someone who behaves in an immoral way – often used humorously —**reprobate** *adj*

re·pro·cess /riːˈprəʊses $ -ˈprɑː-/ *v* [T] to treat a waste substance so that it can be used again

re·pro·duce /ˌriːprəˈdjuːs $ -ˈduːs/ *v* 1 [I,T] if an animal or plant reproduces, or reproduces itself, it produces young plants or animals: *The turtles return to the coast to reproduce.* 2 [T] to make a photograph or printed copy of something: *Klimt's artwork is reproduced in this exquisite collector's book.* 3 [T] to make something happen in the same way as it happened before; ⬛ **repeat**; → **copy**: *British scientists have so far been unable to reproduce these results.* 4 [T] to make something that is just like something else; → **copy**: *With a good set of speakers, you can reproduce the orchestra's sound in your own home.* —**reproducible** *adj*

re·pro·duc·tion /ˌriːprəˈdʌkʃən◂/ *n* 1 [U] the act or process of producing babies, young animals, or plants: *Scientists studied the reproduction, diet, and health of the dolphins.* | *sexual reproduction* 2 [U] the act of producing a copy of a book, picture, piece of music etc: [+of] *Unauthorized reproduction of this publication is strictly forbidden.* 3 [C] a copy of a work of art, piece of furniture etc: [+of] *a reproduction of Vincent Van Gogh's 'Sunflowers'* | **reproduction furniture/chairs etc** *a reproduction Louis XIV table*

re·pro·duc·tive /ˌriːprəˈdʌktɪv◂/ *adj* [only before noun] 1 relating to the process of producing babies, young animals, or plants: *the human reproductive system* | *reproductive organs* 2 relating to the copying of books, pictures, music etc

re·proof /rɪˈpruːf/ *n* *formal* 1 [U] blame or disapproval: *She greeted me with a look of cold reproof.* 2 [C] a remark that blames or criticizes someone: *a mild reproof*

re·prove /rɪˈpruːv/ *v* [T] *formal* to criticize someone for something that they have done; ⬛ **tell off: reprove sb for (doing) sth** *Employees were reproved for smoking in the building's restrooms.*

re·prov·ing /rɪˈpruːvɪŋ/ *adj* *formal* expressing criticism of something that someone has done —**reprovingly** *adv*

reptiles

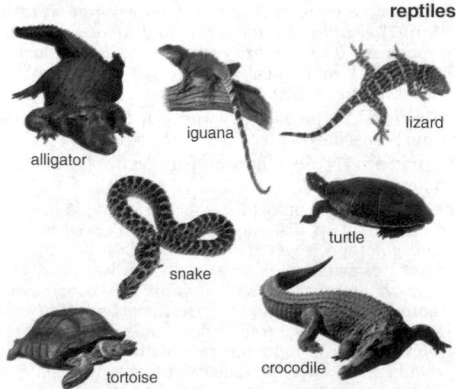

iguana
lizard
alligator
turtle
snake
tortoise
crocodile

rep·tile /ˈreptaɪl $ ˈreptl/ *n* [C] 1 a type of animal, such as a snake or LIZARD, whose body temperature changes according to the temperature around it, and that usually lays eggs to have babies 2 *informal* someone who is unpleasant or cannot be trusted —**reptilian** /repˈtɪliən/ *adj*

re·pub·lic W2, **Republic** /rɪˈpʌblɪk/ *n* [C] a country governed by elected representatives of the people, and led by a president, not a king or queen; → **democracy**,

monarchy: *the former Federal Republic of Germany* | *Nine republics took part in the referendum.*

re·pub·li·can¹ /rɪˈpʌblɪkən/ *n* [C] 1 someone who believes in government by elected representatives only, with no king or queen 2 **Republican** a member or supporter of the Republican Party in the US; → **Democrat** 3 **Republican** someone from Northern Ireland who believes that Northern Ireland should become part of the Republic of Ireland, not the United Kingdom; → **loyalist** —**republicanism** *n* [U]

republican² *adj* relating to or supporting a system of government that is not led by a king or queen; → **democratic**

Re'publican ˌParty *n* **the Republican Party** one of the two main political parties in the US; → **Democratic Party**

re·pu·di·ate /rɪˈpjuːdieɪt/ *v* [T] *formal* 1 to refuse to accept or continue with something; ⬛ **reject**: *He repudiated all offers of friendship.* 2 to state or show that something is not true or correct: *The book repudiates the racist stereotypes about black women.* —**repudiation** /rɪˌpjuːdiˈeɪʃən/ *n* [U]

re·pug·nance /rɪˈpʌgnəns/ *n* [U] *formal* a strong feeling of dislike for something; ⬛ **disgust**

re·pug·nant /rɪˈpʌgnənt/ *adj* *formal* very unpleasant and offensive; ⬛ **repellent**: **deeply/utterly/wholly etc repugnant** | *I find his political ideas totally repugnant.* | [+to] *Animal experiments are morally repugnant to many people.*

re·pulse /rɪˈpʌls/ *v* [T] *formal* 1 if something or someone repulses you, you think that they are extremely unpleasant; ⬛ **disgust**: *The very thought of his cold clammy hands repulsed me.* 2 to fight someone and successfully stop their attack on you: *Government troops repulsed an attack by rebel forces.* 3 to refuse an offer of friendship or help in a way that is rude —**repulse** *n* [singular]

re·pul·sion /rɪˈpʌlʃən/ *n* 1 [singular,U] a feeling that you want to avoid something or move away from it, because it is extremely unpleasant; ⬛ **revulsion**: *I felt a mixture of amazement and repulsion.* 2 [U] *technical* the electric or MAGNETIC force by which one object pushes another one away from it

re·pul·sive /rɪˈpʌlsɪv/ *adj* 1 extremely unpleasant, in a way that almost makes you feel sick; ⬛ **revolting, disgusting**: *Many people find slugs repulsive.* 2 *technical* repulsive forces push objects away from each other —**repulsively** *adv* —**repulsiveness** *n* [U]

re·pur·pose /ˌriːˈpɜːpəs $ -ˈpɜːr-/ *v* [T] if something such as equipment, a building, or a document is repurposed, it is used in a new way that is different from its original use, without having to be changed very much; → **adapt**: *We put a lot of material up on our website simply by repurposing our existing catalog.*

rep·u·ta·ble /ˈrepjᵿtəbəl/ *adj* respected for being honest or for doing good work; ⬛ **reliable**, ⬛ **disreputable: reputable firm/company** *If you have a burglar alarm fitted, make sure it is done by a reputable company.*

rep·u·ta·tion W3 /ˌrepjᵿˈteɪʃən/ *n* [C] the opinion that people have about someone or something because of what has happened in the past: [+for] *Judge Kelso has a reputation for being strict but fair.* | [+as] *In her last job she acquired a reputation as a troublemaker.* | **earn/gain/establish a reputation as sth** *His approach had won him a reputation as a tough manager.* | **a good/bad reputation** *a hotel with a good reputation for its food* | *The service at Heron Lodge failed to **live up to** its reputation* (=be as good or bad as people say it is).

re·pute /rɪˈpjuːt/ *n* [U] *formal* reputation: **of good/high/international etc repute** *a man of high repute* | **of (some) repute** (=having a good reputation) *a hotel of some repute*

re·put·ed /rɪˈpjuːtᵻd/ *adj* according to what some people say, but not definitely: **be reputed to be/do sth** *She is reputed to be extremely wealthy.* | *the reputed leader of the Crips gang* | *The painting was sold for a reputed $3 million.*

re·put·ed·ly /rɪˈpjuːtɪdli/ adv [sentence adverb] according to what some people say; ▯ **reportedly**; → **allegedly**: *The committee had reputedly spent over $3000 on 'business entertainment'.*

re·quest¹ S2 W2 /rɪˈkwest/ n [C]
1 a polite or formal demand for something: [+for] *They have made an urgent request for international aid.* | **request that** *Anderson repeated his request that we postpone the meeting.* | **at sb's request** (=because someone asked for it to be done) *The study was done at the request of the Chairman.* | **on request** (=if you ask for it) *Further details will be sent on request.* | **by request** *There were no flowers at the funeral, by request.*
2 a piece of music that is played on the radio because someone has asked for it

request² S3 v [T] formal to ask for something in a polite or formal way: *To request more information, please call our toll free number.* | *You have to request permission if you want to take any photographs.* | **request that** *The prosecution has requested that all charges against Hodgkins are dropped.* | **request sb to do sth** *All club members are requested to attend the annual meeting.* | **request sth from sb** *The Police Committee requested a grant from the Government to cover the extra expense.*

req·ui·em /ˈrekwiəm, -em/ also ˌrequiem ˈmass n [C] **1** a Christian ceremony in which prayers are said for someone who has died **2** a piece of music written for a requiem

re·quire S1 W1 /rɪˈkwaɪə $ -ˈkwaɪr/ v [T not in progressive]
1 to need something: *Campbell's broken leg will probably require surgery.* | *What's required is a complete reorganization of the system.* | *Most house plants require regular watering.*
2 if you are required to do or have something, a law or rule says you must do it or have it: **be required to do sth** *You are required by law to wear a seat belt.* | **require that** *Regulations require that students attend at least 90% of the lectures.* | *The bill failed to get the required number of votes.*

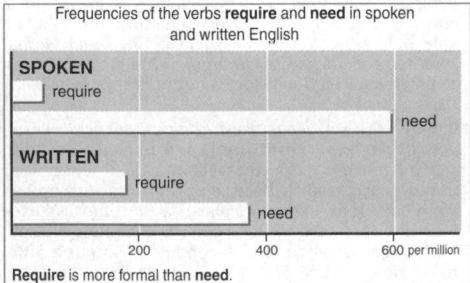

Frequencies of the verbs **require** and **need** in spoken and written English

SPOKEN
require
need

WRITTEN
require
need

200   400   600 per million

Require is more formal than **need**.

re·quire·ment S2 W2 /rɪˈkwaɪəmənt $ -ˈkwaɪr-/ n [C usually plural]
1 something that someone needs or asks for: *The refugees' main requirements are food and shelter.* | [+of] *Potatoes can provide one-third of our daily requirement of vitamin C.* | **meet/fulfil/satisfy a requirement** (=have or do what is necessary) *The new computer system will meet all our requirements.* | **surplus to requirements** BrE (=more than is needed) *The increase in gas-fired power stations means traditional coal ones are becoming surplus to requirements.*
2 something that must be done because of a law or rule: *If you are installing a new bathroom, it has to **meet** the **requirements** of the Building Regulations.* | *Two measures have been introduced as **legal requirements**.*
3 something, especially good examination results, that a college, employer etc says you must have in order to do something: [+for] *English 4 is a requirement for English majors.* | *To find out about **entry requirements** for students, write to the college admissions board.* | *The **minimum requirement** for the post was a degree in engineering.*

req·ui·site¹ /ˈrekwɪzɪt/ adj [only before noun] formal needed for a particular purpose; ▯ **necessary**, **required**: *He lacks the requisite qualifications.*

requisite² n [C usually plural] formal something that is needed for a particular purpose: [+of/for] *He lacked the moral requisites for marriage.* → PREREQUISITE

req·ui·si·tion /ˌrekwəˈzɪʃən/ v [T] if someone in authority, especially the army, requisitions a building, vehicle, or food, they officially demand to have it during an EMERGENCY such as a war; ▯ **commandeer**: *The building was requisitioned as a military hospital for the duration of the war.* —**requisition** n [C,U]

re·quite /rɪˈkwaɪt/ v [T] formal to give or do something in return for something done or given to you

re-re·lease /ˌriː rɪˈliːs/ v [T] if a CD, record, or film is re-released, it is produced and sold or shown for a second time, usually with small changes —**re-release** /ˈriː rɪliːs/ n [C]

re-route /ˌriːˈruːt $ -ˈruːt, -ˈraʊt/ v [T] to send vehicles, planes, telephone calls etc to a different place from the one where they were originally going; ▯ **redirect**

re·run¹ /ˈriːrʌn/ n [C] **1** a film or television programme that is being shown again on television; ▯ **repeat**: *We watched a rerun of 'I Love Lucy.'* **2** something that happens in the same way as something that happened before; ▯ **repeat**: *The government wants to avoid a rerun of last year's crisis.*

re·run² /riːˈrʌn/ v past tense **reran** /-ˈræn/ , past participle **rerun** present participle **rerunning** [T] **1** to show a film or television programme again on television; ▯ **repeat** **2** to do something in the same way as before; ▯ **repeat** **3** to arrange for a race or competition to be held again; ▯ **repeat**

re·sale /ˈriːseɪl/ n [U] the activity of selling goods that you have bought from someone else; → **resell**

re·sched·ule /ˌriːˈʃedjuːl $ -ˈskedʒʊl, -dʒəl/ v [T] **1** to arrange for something to happen at a different time from the one that was previously planned: **reschedule sth for sth** *The press conference has been rescheduled for March 19.* **2** technical to arrange for a debt to be paid back later than was previously agreed —**rescheduling** n [singular,U]

re·scind /rɪˈsɪnd/ v [T] to officially end a law, or change a decision or agreement

res·cue¹ /ˈreskjuː/ v [T] to save someone or something from a situation of danger or harm: *Survivors of the crash were rescued by helicopter.* | **rescue sb/sth from sb/sth** *She died trying to rescue her children from the blaze.* —**rescuer** n [C]

rescue² n [C,U] **1** when someone or something is rescued from danger: *a daring rescue at sea* | [+of] *Storms delayed the rescue of the crash victims.* | *Rescue workers arrived at the scene two hours later.* | **rescue mission/operation** *The rescue operation proved successful.* **2** **come to the/sb's rescue a)** to save someone who is in a dangerous situation: *A lifeboat came to the yachtsman's rescue.* **b)** to help someone who is having problems or difficulties: *Carol's brother came to the rescue and sent her $1000.*

re·search¹ S2 W1 /rɪˈsɜːtʃ, ˈriːsɜːtʃ $ -ɜːr-/ n [U] also **researches** formal
1 serious study of a subject, in order to discover new facts or test new ideas: [+into/on] *research into the causes of cancer* | **scientific/medical/historical etc research** | *a research team* | **do/conduct/undertake research** *I'm still doing research for my thesis.* | *Gould was helped in his researches by local naturalists.*
2 the activity of finding information about something that you are interested in or need to know about: *It's a good idea to **do some research** before you buy a house.*; → **investigation** → MARKET RESEARCH

re·search² /rɪˈsɜːtʃ $ -ɜːr-/ v [I,T] **1** to study a subject in detail, especially in order to discover new facts or test new ideas; → **investigate**: *He's been researching* *material for a documentary.* | [+**into**] *Ten years ago I began researching into the role of women in trade unions.* **2** to get all the necessary facts and information for something: *This book has been very well researched.* —**researcher** *n* [C]

re·search and de·velopment *n* [U] R & D

re·sell /ˌriːˈsel/ *v past tense and past participle* **resold** /ˈsəʊld $ -ˈsoʊld/ [T] to sell something that you have bought; → **resale**: *The retailer resells the goods at a higher price.*

re·sem·blance /rɪˈzembləns/ *n* [C,U] if there is a resemblance between two people or things, they are similar, especially in the way they look; → **similarity**: [+**between**] *The resemblance between Susan and her sister was remarkable.* | **bear a (close/striking/uncanny etc) resemblance to sb/sth** (=look like) *Tina bears a striking resemblance to her mother.* | **bear little/no resemblance to sb/sth** *What happens in the film bears little resemblance to what actually happened.*

re·sem·ble /rɪˈzembəl/ *v* [T not in progressive or passive] to look like or be similar to someone or something: *It's amazing how closely Brian and Steve resemble each other.* | *He grew up to resemble his father.*

re·sent /rɪˈzent/ *v* [T] to feel angry or upset about a situation or about something that someone has done, especially because you think that it is not fair: **resent (sb) doing sth** *I resented having to work such long hours.* | **bitterly/deeply/strongly resent** *She bitterly resented his mother's influence over him.* | *Paul resented the fact that Carol didn't trust him.*

re·sent·ful /rɪˈzentfəl/ *adj* feeling angry and upset about something that you think is unfair; ◨ **bitter**: [+**of/about/at etc**] *She felt resentful at not being promoted.* —**resentfully** *adv* —**resentfulness** *n* [U]

re·sent·ment /rɪˈzentmənt/ *n* [U] a feeling of anger because something has happened that you think is unfair; ◨ **bitterness**: [+**at/against/of etc**] *She was filled with deep resentment at being passed over for promotion.* | **feel/harbour/bear resentment** *He felt considerable resentment towards Sheila for making him work late.*

res·er·va·tion [S3] /ˌrezəˈveɪʃən $ -zər-/ *n*

1 [C] an arrangement which you make so that a place in a hotel, restaurant, plane etc is kept for you at a particular time in the future; → **booking**: *a dinner reservation* | *Customers are advised to make seat reservations well in advance.*

2 [C,U] a feeling of doubt because you do not agree completely with a plan, idea, or suggestion: **have/ express reservations (about sth)** *I had serious reservations about his appointment as captain.* | *We condemn their actions without reservation* (=completely).

3 [C] an area of land in the US kept separate for Native Americans to live on: *a Navajo reservation*

4 [C] *AmE* an area of land where wild animals can live without being hunted; ◨ **reserve**; ◨ **preserve** *AmE*: *a wildlife reservation*

re·serve¹ [W3] /rɪˈzɜːv $ -ɜːrv/ *v* [T]

1 to arrange for a place in a hotel, restaurant, plane etc to be kept for you to use at a particular time in the future; → **book**: **reserve sth for sb/sth** *I'd like to reserve a table for two.* | *Do you have to reserve tickets in advance?*

2 to keep something so that it can be used by a particular person or for a particular purpose; ◨ **set aside**: **reserve sth for sb/sth** *A separate room is reserved for smokers.* | *reserved parking spaces*

3 *especially written* to keep part of something for use at a later time during a process – used especially when describing how to cook something; ◨ **keep, save**: *Reserve a little of the mixture to sprinkle over the top of the pie.*

4 to use or show something only in one particular situation: **reserve sth for sb/sth** *She spoke in a tone of voice she usually reserved for dealing with officials.*

5 reserve the right to do sth *formal* if you reserve the right to do something, you will do it if you think it is necessary – used especially in notices or official documents: *The management reserves the right to refuse admission.*

6 reserve (your) judgment (on sth) *spoken* to not give your opinion about something until a later time when you have more information

reserve² *n*

1 **SUPPLY** [C usually plural] a supply of something kept to be used if it is needed: *$10 million in cash reserves* | *oil reserves* | [+**of**] *Somehow Debbie maintained an inner reserve of strength.*

2 **in reserve** ready to be used if needed: *We always keep some money in reserve, just in case.*

3 **PERSONAL QUALITY** [U] a quality in someone's character that makes them not like expressing their emotions or talking about their problems; → **shyness**: *She overcame her own natural reserve.*

4 **PLAYER** [C] an extra player who plays in a team if one of the other players is injured or ill; → **substitute**

5 **TEAM** **the reserves** *BrE* a team that plays when the usual team cannot do so

6 **MILITARY** **the reserve** also **the reserves** an extra military force that a country has in addition to its usual army, navy etc which can be used if needed; → **reservist**

7 **FOR ANIMALS/PLANTS** [C] *BrE* an area of land where wild animals and plants are protected; ◨ **reservation** *AmE*, **preserve** *AmE*: *a wildlife reserve* → **NATURE RESERVE**

8 **FOR NATIVE AMERICANS** [C] a RESERVATION

9 **PRICE** [C] also **reserve price** a price below which something will not be sold, especially in an AUCTION

re·served /rɪˈzɜːvd $ -ɜːr-/ *adj* unwilling to express your emotions or talk about your problems; → **shy**: *Ellen was a shy, reserved girl.*

re·serv·ist /rɪˈzɜːvɪ̈st $ -ɜːr-/ *n* [C] someone in the RESERVE

res·er·voir /ˈrezəvwɑː $ -ərvwɑːr, -vɔːr/ *n* [C] **1** a lake, especially an artificial one, where water is stored before it is supplied to people's houses → see picture at COUNTRY **2** a large amount of something that is available and has not yet been used: [+**of**] *She found she had reservoirs of unexpected strength.* **3** *technical* a part of a machine or engine where a liquid is kept before it is used

re·set¹ /ˌriːˈset/ *v past tense and past participle* **reset**, *present participle* **resetting** [T] **1** to change a clock, control, machine etc so that it shows a different time or number, or is ready to be used again **2** to put a broken bone back into its correct place so that it grows back together correctly **3** to restart a computer without switching the power off; → **reboot** **4** to put a jewel into a new piece of jewellery —**reset** /ˈriːset/ *n* [C,U]

re·set² /ˈriːset/ *adj* **reset button/switch** a control that is used to make a machine or instrument ready to work again

re·set·tle /ˌriːˈsetl/ *v* **1** [I,T] to go to live in a new country or area, or to help people do this: *The tribesmen were forcibly resettled by the government.* **2** [T] to start using an area again as a place to live: *The area was resettled in the latter half of the century.* —**resettlement** *n* [U]

re·shuffle /ˌriːˈʃʌfəl, ˈriːʃʌfəl/ *n* [C] *especially BrE* when the jobs of people who work in an organization are changed around, especially in a government; ◨ **reorganize**: *a Cabinet reshuffle* —**reshuffle** /ˌriːˈʃʌfəl/ *v* [T]

re·side /rɪˈzaɪd/ *v* [I always + adv/prep] *formal* to live in a particular place: *He spent most of his time in Rutherglen, where his family resided.*

reside in sth/sb *phr v formal* **1** to be present in or consist of something: *Joe's talent resides in his storytelling abilities.* **2** also **reside within sth/sb** if a power, right etc resides in something or someone, it belongs to them: *Executive power resides in the President.*

res·i·dence /'rezɪ̩dəns/ n **1** [C] *formal* a house, especially a large or official one: *the ambassador's official residence* **2** [U] legal permission to live in a country for a certain period of time; ⊟ **residency**: *a residence permit* | **permanent/temporary residence** *Jeff has permanent residence in Canada, but is still a US citizen.* **3** [U] *formal* the state of living in a place; ⊟ **residency**: *Rome was his main* **place of residence**. **4 artist/writer etc in residence** an artist etc who has been officially chosen by a college or other institution to work there **5 take up residence** *formal* to start living in a place: *He took up residence in Chicago.* **6 in residence** *formal* living in a place at a particular time: *The emperor was in residence at his summer palace.*

'residence ˌhall n [C] *AmE* a large building where many students live at a university; ⊟ **dormitory** *AmE*; ⊟ **hall of residence** *BrE*

res·i·den·cy /'rezɪ̩dənsi/ n *plural* **residencies** **1** [U] legal permission to live in a country for a certain period of time; ⊟ **residence 2** [C,U] when an artist, writer, musician etc does work at a college or other institution for a period of time; ⊟ **residence 3** [U] the state of living in a place; ⊟ **residence 4** [U] *especially AmE* a period of time when a doctor receives special training in a particular type of medicine, especially at a hospital

res·i·dent¹ [S2] [W3] /'rezɪ̩dənt/ n [C]
1 someone who lives or stays in a particular place: *the residents of Westville*
2 *AmE* a doctor working at a hospital where he or she is being trained; ⊟ **registrar** *BrE*

resident² adj **1** *formal* living in a place: [+in] *Many retired British people are now resident in Spain.* **2** [only before noun] living or working in a particular place or institution: *a resident tutor* | *The resident population of mental hospitals has fallen by 20%.* **3** [only before noun] belonging to a particular group of people – used humorously: *He's our* **resident expert** *on computer games.*

res·i·den·tial [W3] /ˌrezɪ̩'denʃəl̩/ adj
1 a residential part of a town consists of private houses, with no offices or factories; → **suburban**: *a quiet residential neighbourhood*
2 relating to homes rather than offices or businesses; → **domestic**: *telephone services for residential customers*
3 residential course/school etc *especially BrE* if you are on a residential course, you are living in the institution where you are studying

ˌresidential 'care n [U] a system in which people who are old or ill live together in a special house and are looked after by professionals

ˌresidential 'home n [C] a special house in which old or ill people live and are looked after by professionals; ⊟ **nursing home**

ˌresidential 'treatment faˌcility also **ˌresidential 'treatment ˌcenter** n [C] *formal especially AmE* a place that gives treatment to people with mental problems or problems with drugs or alcohol

ˌresident phy'sician n [C] *AmE* a RESIDENT¹ (2)

'residents' associˌation n [C] *BrE* a group of people who meet to discuss the problems and needs of the area where they live

re·sid·u·al /rɪ'zɪdʒuəl/ adj [only before noun] *formal* remaining after a process, event etc is finished: *the residual effects of drug treatment* | **residual income** (=the money left from what you earn after you have paid your taxes)

re·sid·u·als /rɪ'zɪdʒuəlz/ n [plural] money that is paid to an actor, writer etc when their work is broadcast again

re·sid·u·a·ry /rɪ'zɪdʒuəri $ -eri/ adj [only before noun] *BrE law* relating to all the money and property that remains after a person has died, and after any bills have been paid

res·i·due /'rezɪ̩dju: $ -du:/ n **1** [C,U] a substance that remains on a surface, in a container etc and cannot be removed easily, or that remains after a chemical process: [+from] *residue from sewage treatment plants* | *The flies* **leave a sticky residue** *on crops.* | *Rinse off any soap residue.* **2** [C] *formal* the part of something that is left after the rest has gone or been taken away: [+of] *The residue of the stock was sold.*

re·sign [W3] /rɪ'zaɪn/ v [I,T]
1 to officially announce that you have decided to leave your job or an organization; → **quit**: [+from] *She resigned from the government last week.* | [+as] *He resigned as Governor of Punjab in August.* | **resign your post/seat/position etc** *Tom has since resigned his membership of the golf club.*
2 resign yourself to (doing) sth to make yourself accept something that is bad but cannot be changed; → **resigned**: *Josh resigned himself to the long walk home.* | *At sixteen, I resigned myself to the fact that I'd never be a dancer.*

res·ig·na·tion [W3] /ˌrezɪg'neɪʃən/ n
1 [C,U] when you officially announce that you have decided to leave your job or an organization, or a written statement that says you will be leaving; → **notice**: *The governor refused to* **accept** *Cox's* **resignation**. | *a* **letter of resignation** | **hand in/tender your resignation** (=officially say that you want to resign)
2 [U] when someone calmly accepts a situation that cannot be changed, even though it is bad: *She gave a sigh of resignation.* | **with resignation** *He accepted her decision with resignation.*

re·signed /rɪ'zaɪnd/ adj **1 be resigned to (doing) sth** to calmly accept a situation that is bad, but cannot be changed: *She's resigned to spending Christmas on her own.* | *Sam was* **resigned to the fact that** *he would never be promoted.* **2 a resigned** look, voice etc shows that you are making yourself accept something that you do not like: *'We'll have to leave,' she said with a resigned sigh.* —**resignedly** /rɪ'zaɪnɪ̩dli/ adv

re·sil·i·ence /rɪ'zɪliəns/ also **re·sil·i·en·cy** /-ənsi/ n [U] **1** the ability to become strong, happy, or successful again after a difficult situation or event; → **toughness**: [+of] *the resilience of youth* | *People showed remarkable resilience during the war.* **2** the ability of a substance such as rubber to return to its original shape after it has been pressed or bent

re·sil·i·ent /rɪ'zɪliənt/ adj **1** able to become strong, happy, or successful again after a difficult situation or event; → **tough**: *Children are often very resilient.* | *The company proved* **remarkably resilient** *during the recession.* **2** strong and not easily damaged by being pulled, pressed etc: *boots with tough resilient soles* | *Any chemical treatment will leave hair less resilient than before.* —**resiliently** adv

res·in /'rezɪ̩n/ n **1** [U] a thick sticky liquid that comes out of some trees; → **sap 2** [C,U] a type of plastic —**resinous** adj

re·sist [W3] /rɪ'zɪst/ v
1 [I,T usually in negatives] to stop yourself from having something that you like very much or doing something that you want to do: **cannot resist (doing) sth** *I just can't resist chocolate.* | *She can never resist buying new shoes.* | **it is hard/difficult/impossible to resist sth** *It's hard to resist an invitation like that.* | **resist the temptation/urge to do sth** *She resisted the temptation to laugh.* | *They only wanted 3 dollars for it, so how could I resist?*
2 [T] to try to prevent a change from happening, or prevent yourself from being forced to do something: *He resisted pressure to resign.* | **resist doing sth** *For months the company has resisted changing its accounts system.* | **strongly/fiercely/vigorously etc resist** *The proposal was strongly resisted by the police.*
3 [I,T] to use force to stop something from happening: **strongly/fiercely/firmly etc resist** *Demonstrators*

violently resisted attempts to remove them from the building. | *He was charged with trying to resist arrest.* **4** [T] to not be changed or harmed by something: *your ability to resist infection*

re·sist·ance S2 W3 /rɪˈzɪstəns/ n
1 AGAINST CHANGE [singular,U] a refusal to accept new ideas or changes: [+to] *people's resistance to change* | [+from] *The no-smoking policy was introduced with little resistance from staff.*
2 FIGHTING [singular,U] fighting against someone who is attacking you: **put up/offer resistance** *Rebel gunmen have put up strong resistance.*
3 AGAINST INFECTION/ILLNESS [singular,U] the natural ability of a person, animal, or plant to stop diseases or difficult conditions from harming them: [+to] *the body's resistance to infection* | *disease resistance*
4 wind/air/water resistance the way in which wind, air, or water can cause a moving object such as a car, plane, or boat to slow down
5 ELECTRICITY [U] the ability of a substance to stop the flow of an electric current through it
6 the resistance also the Resistance an organization that secretly fights against an enemy that controls their country
7 the line/path of least resistance if you follow the path of least resistance, you avoid making difficult decisions and choose the easiest solution to a problem – often used to show disapproval: *Many people don't make changes because they're following the path of least resistance.* | *Kirk always just takes the line of least resistance.* → PASSIVE RESISTANCE

re·sis·tant /rɪˈzɪstənt/ adj **1** not damaged or affected by something; → proof: [+to] *an infection that's resistant to antibiotics* | *heat-resistant/stain-resistant/fire-resistant etc shock-resistant rubber* **2** opposed to something and wanting to prevent it from happening: [+to] *Many managers are resistant to change.*

re·sis·tor /rɪˈzɪstə $ -ər/ n [C] a piece of wire or other material used for increasing electrical resistance

re·sit /ˌriːˈsɪt/ v past tense and past participle **resat** /-ˈsæt/ present participle **resitting** [T] BrE to take an examination again, because you failed it or did not do well enough; ⊟ **retake** —**re·sit** /ˈriːsɪt/ n [C]

re·skill·ing /ˌriːˈskɪlɪŋ/ n [U] BrE the practice of teaching people new skills, to help them find a new job

res·o·lute /ˈrezəluːt/ adj doing something in a very determined way because you have very strong beliefs, aims etc; ⊠ **irresolute**: *resolute opposition* | *resolute leadership* | *She remained resolute in her belief that the situation would improve.* —**resolutely** adv: *Mia resolutely refused to talk about her illness.*

res·o·lu·tion W3 /ˌrezəˈluːʃən/ n
1 DECISION [C] a formal decision or statement agreed on by a group of people, especially after a vote: **pass/adopt/approve a resolution** *The resolution was passed by a two-thirds majority.* | *a resolution calling for a ban on dumping nuclear waste* | *They have failed to comply with the resolution.*
2 SOLUTION [singular,U] when someone solves a problem, argument, or difficult situation: [+of] *a forum for the resolution of commercial disputes*
3 PROMISE [C] a promise to yourself to do something; → resolve: **resolution to do sth** *Carol made a resolution to work harder at school.* | *New Year's resolution* (=a resolution made on January 1st)
4 DETERMINATION [U] strong belief and determination: *Then, with sudden resolution, she stood up.*
5 CLEAR PICTURE [C,U] the power of a television, camera, MICROSCOPE etc to give a clear picture: **high/low resolution** (=how clear or unclear the picture is)

re·solve¹ W3 /rɪˈzɒlv $ rɪˈzɑːlv, rɪˈzɔːlv/ v [T]
1 to find a satisfactory way of dealing with a problem or difficulty; ⊟ **solve**; → settle: **resolve a dispute/conflict/problem etc** *The crisis was resolved by negotiations.* | *Barnet was desperate for money to resolve his financial problems.*
2 formal to make a definite decision to do something: **resolve to do sth** *After the divorce she resolved never to marry again.* | **resolve that** *Mary resolved that she would stop smoking.*
3 to make a formal decision, especially by voting: **resolve to do sth** *The Senate resolved to accept the President's proposals.*
4 technical to separate something into its different parts: *DNA samples were extracted and resolved.*
resolve (sth) into sth phr v
1 technical to separate into parts, or to separate something: *This mixture will resolve into two separate compounds.*
2 resolve (itself) into sth formal to gradually change into something; ⊟ **become**: *The argument resolved itself into an uneasy truce.*

re·solve² n [U] formal strong determination to succeed in doing something: *Recent events strengthened her resolve to find out the truth.*

res·o·nance /ˈrezənəns/ n **1** [U] the resonance of a sound is its quality of being deep and loud and continuing for a long time **2** [C,U] formal the special meaning or importance that something has for you because it relates to your own experiences: *a tradition that has little resonance in the 21st century* | *His words will have resonance for many musicians.* **3** [C,U] technical sound that is produced or increased in one object by sound waves from another object

res·o·nant /ˈrezənənt/ adj **1** a resonant sound is deep, loud, and clear, and continues for a long time: *the violin's smooth, resonant tone* **2** resonant with sth literary filled with a particular meaning, quality, or sound: *prints resonant with traditions of Russian folk art* **3** technical resonant materials increase any sound produced inside them —**resonantly** adv

res·o·nate /ˈrezəneɪt/ v [I] **1** if something such as an event or a message resonates, it seems important or good to people, or continues to do this: [+with] *an idea that resonates with many voters* **2** to make a deep loud clear sound that continues for a long time; → resound: *The music resonated through the streets.* **3** to make a sound that is produced as a reaction to another sound
resonate with sth phr v **1** formal to be full of a particular meaning or quality: *literature that resonates with biblical imagery* **2** to be full of a particular sound: *a hall resonating with laughter*

res·o·na·tor /ˈrezəneɪtə $ -ər/ n [C] a piece of equipment that makes the sound of a musical instrument louder

re·sort¹ W3 /rɪˈzɔːt $ -ɔːrt/ n [C]
1 a place where a lot of people go for holidays: **seaside/beach/ski etc resort** *Aspen, a ski resort in Colorado* | *Lagoon Reef is one of the best resort hotels.*
2 last/final resort what you will do if everything else fails: **as a last resort** *Drug treatment should only be used as a last resort.* | **of last resort** *a weapon of last resort* | **in the last resort** BrE: *Economic sanctions will be used only in the last resort.*
3 first resort what you will do first before you try other things: *In the past, your family was the first resort when looking for a job.*
4 resort to sth formal when you must use or depend on something because nothing better is available: **without resort to sth** *We hope they will be able to resolve the situation without resort to force.*

resort² v
resort to sth phr v to do something bad, extreme, or difficult because you cannot think of any other way to deal with a problem: *Officials fear that extremists may resort to violence.* | **resort to doing sth** *Vets have had to resort to killing the animals.*

re·sound /rɪˈzaʊnd/ v [I] **1** if a place resounds with a sound, it is full of that sound: [+with] *The stadium resounded with cheers.* | [+to] *By now, the whole room was resounding to the sound of the team's chants.* **2** if a sound such as a musical note resounds, it continues loudly and clearly for quite a long time; → **resonate**: [+through/around etc] *a horn resounding through the forest* **3** *formal* to be mentioned or talked about a lot: *The war still resounds in the country's folklore.*

re·sound·ing /rɪ'zaʊndɪŋ/ *adj* **1** **resounding success/victory/defeat etc** a very great or complete success, victory etc: *The show was a resounding success.* **2** [only before noun] a resounding noise is so loud that it seems to continue for a few seconds: *a resounding thud* —**resoundingly** *adv*

re·source¹ [S2] [W1] /rɪ'zɔːs, -'sɔːs $ 'riːsɔːrs/ *n*
1 LAND/OIL/COAL ETC [C usually plural] something such as useful land, or minerals such as oil or coal, that exists in a country and can be used to increase its wealth: *Canada's vast mineral resources* | *a country rich in* **natural resources**
2 MONEY/PROPERTY ETC **resources** [plural] all the money, property, skills etc that you have available to use when you need them: *She had no* **financial resources.** | *Only* **limited resources** *are available to the police.* | **pool your resources** (=put together all the resources that each of you can provide) → HUMAN RESOURCES
3 PERSONAL QUALITIES **resources** [plural] personal qualities, such as courage and determination, that you need to deal with a difficult situation: *He proved that he has considerable* **inner resources.**
4 EDUCATIONAL [C] something such as a book, film, or picture used by teachers or students to provide information: *resources for learning* | *a valuable new computer resource* | **resource room/centre**
5 PRACTICAL ABILITY [U] *formal* the ability to deal with practical problems; ⊟ **resourcefulness**: *a man of great resource*

re·source² /rɪ'zɔːs, -'sɔːs $ -'sɔːrs/ *v* [T usually passive] to provide money or other resources for something: *The program wasn't adequately resourced.*

re·source·ful /rɪ'zɔːsfəl, -'sɔːs- $ -ɔːr-/ *adj* good at finding ways of dealing with practical problems: *a woman who is energetic and resourceful* —**resourcefully** *adv* —**resourcefulness** *n* [U]

re·spawn /ˌriː'spɔːn $ -ɒːn/ *v* [I,T] if a character in a computer game respawns or is respawned, they are born again after being killed

re·spect¹ [S1] [W1] /rɪ'spekt/ *n*
1 ADMIRATION [U] when you admire someone, especially because of their personal qualities, knowledge, or skills; → **admiration**: [+for] *I have the greatest respect for Jane's work.* | **win/earn/gain the respect of sb** *She has earned the respect of her fellow athletes.* | *He* **commands** (=has and deserves) *the respect of everyone in the profession.*
2 CONSIDERATION [U] when you regard something or someone as important and are careful not to harm them, treat them rudely etc; ⊟ **disrespect**: [+for] *Out of respect for the wishes of her family, the affair was not reported in the media.* | *The boys showed a complete* **lack of respect** *for authority.* | **with respect** *Old people deserve to be* **treated with respect.**
3 **with (the greatest) respect/with (all) due respect** *spoken formal* say this before disagreeing with someone when you want to be polite: *With respect, I think you're wrong.*
4 FOR DANGER [singular,U] a careful attitude towards something or someone that could be dangerous: [+for] *My fear turned into a respect for the sea.* | *People should have a* **healthy respect** *for alcohol* (=a sensible careful attitude towards it).
5 **in one respect/in some respects etc** used to say that something is true in one way, in some ways etc: *In many respects the new version is not as good as the old one.* | *Mum is very stubborn, and Kim takes after her in that respect.* → see box at CASE¹
6 GREETINGS **respects** [plural] *formal* polite greetings: **give/send your respects (to sb)** *Give my respects to your wife.* | **pay your respects (to sb)** *BrE* (=make a polite visit) *I've come to pay my respects to Mrs O'Hara.*

7 **pay your last respects (to sb)** to go to someone's funeral
8 **in respect of sth** *formal* concerning or in relation to something: *This is especially true in respect of the UK.*
9 **with respect to sth** *formal* **a)** concerning or in relation to something: *the freedom of a property owner to make a contract with respect to his property* **b)** used to introduce a new subject, or to return to one that has already been mentioned: *With respect to your request, I am not yet able to agree.* → SELF-RESPECT

respect² *v* [T] **1** [not in progressive] to admire someone because they have high standards and good qualities such as fairness and honesty; → **admire**: **respect sb for (doing) sth** *She respected him for his honesty.* | *I respect his views, although I do not agree with them.* **2** to be careful not to do anything against someone's wishes, rights etc: *She said she wanted to leave, and her father* **respected** *her* **wishes.** | *I would like you to respect my privacy.* | *the need to respect human rights* **3** to not break a rule or law: *The President is expected to respect the constitution.*

re·spect·a·ble /rɪ'spektəbəl/ *adj* **1** someone who is respectable behaves in a way that is considered socially acceptable: *hard-working, respectable people* | *a respectable family* | *Put a tie on – it'll make you look more respectable.* **2** good or satisfactory; ⊟ **decent**: *a respectable income* | *Her exam results were respectable enough.* —**respectably** *adv* —**respectability** /rɪˌspektə'bɪləti/ *n* [U]

re·spect·ed /rɪ'spektɪd/ *adj* admired by many people because of your good work or achievements: *He's one of the most respected managers in the game.* | **highly/well/widely/greatly respected** *a highly respected journalist*

re·spect·er /rɪ'spektə $ -ər/ *n* **1** **be no respecter of persons** *formal* to affect all people in the same way, whether or not they are rich or powerful: *Disease is no respecter of persons.* **2** **be a respecter of sth** to have respect for something such as a law or organization: *She is a respecter of the rights of all religious groups.*

re·spect·ful /rɪ'spektfəl/ *adj* feeling or showing respect; ⊟ **disrespectful**: *They listened in respectful silence.* | [+of] *He was always respectful of my independence.* —**respectfully** *adv* —**respectfulness** *n* [U]

re·spect·ing /rɪ'spektɪŋ/ *prep formal* about or relating to something: *A discussion took place respecting the provision of science teaching.*

re·spec·tive /rɪ'spektɪv/ *adj* [only before noun] used before a plural noun to refer to the different things that belong to each separate person or thing mentioned: *We all went back to our respective homes to wait for news.* | *the respective roles of teachers and students*

re·spec·tive·ly [W3] /rɪ'spektɪvli/ *adv* in the same order as the things you have just mentioned: *The cups and saucers cost £5 and £3 respectively.*

res·pi·ra·tion /ˌrespə'reɪʃən/ *n* [U] *technical* the process of breathing → ARTIFICIAL RESPIRATION

res·pi·ra·tor /'respəreɪtə $ -ər/ *n* [C] **1** a piece of equipment that pumps air in and out of someone's lungs if they are too ill or weak to breathe; ⊟ **ventilator**: *The baby was immediately put on a respirator.* **2** a piece of equipment that you wear over your nose and mouth to help you breathe in a place where there is harmful gas, smoke etc; → **gas mask**

re·spi·ra·to·ry /rɪ'spɪrətəri, 'respəreɪtəri, rɪ'spaɪərə- $ 'respərətɔːri, rɪ'spaɪrə-/ *adj formal* or *technical* relating to breathing or your lungs: *respiratory disease*

re·spire /rɪ'spaɪə $ -'spaɪr/ *v* [I] *technical* to breathe

res·pite /'respɪt, -paɪt $ -pɪt/ *n* [singular, U] **1** a short time when something bad stops happening, so that the situation is temporarily better: [+from] *The trip was a welcome respite from the pressures of work.* | *a* **brief respite** *from persecution* | **without respite** *The pain went on without respite.* **2** a short period of time

R

before you have to do something that you do not like: *We have a few days' respite before we have to pay them.*

respite care *n* [U] temporary care for people who are too old or ill to look after themselves, which allows the people who usually look after them to rest

re·splen·dent /rɪˈsplendənt/ *adj formal* very beautiful, bright, and impressive in appearance: [+in] *She looked resplendent in a silk dress.* —**resplendently** *adv*

re·spond S2 W2 /rɪˈspɒnd $ rɪˈspɑːnd/ *v*
1 [I] to do something as a reaction to something that has been said or done; ⊟ **react**: [+to] *Responding to the news, Mr Watt appealed for calm.* | **respond by doing sth** *The US responded by sending troops into Laos.* | [+with] *Villagers responded with offers of help.*
2 [I,T] to say or write something as a reply: **respond that** *He responded that he didn't want to see anyone.* | [+to] *Dave didn't respond to any of her emails.*
3 [I] to improve as a result of a particular kind of treatment: [+to] *She has responded well to treatment.* | *Colds do not respond to antibiotics.*

re·spon·dent /rɪˈspɒndənt $ rɪˈspɑːn-/ *n* [C] **1** *formal* someone who answers questions, especially in a SURVEY: *Only 62 percent of respondents said they were satisfied.* **2** *law* someone who has to defend their own case in a law court, especially in a DIVORCE case

re·sponse S1 W1 /rɪˈspɒns $ rɪˈspɑːns/ *n*
1 [C,U] something that is done as a reaction to something that has happened or been said: [+to] *the public's response to our appeal for help* | **in response to sth** *The law was passed in response to public pressure.* | **positive/favourable/negative etc response** *The exhibition has received a positive response from visitors.* | **an emotional/angry response** *The decision provoked an angry response from residents.* | *His* **immediate response** *was one of disbelief.* | *Emmett's new exhibition has* **met with** *a favourable response from critics.*
2 [C] something that is said or written as a reply: [+to] *'Sure, why not?' was his response to all of Billie's suggestions.* | *Carl* **made** *no response, and carried on with his meal.* | **in response (to sth)** *I am writing in response to your letter of June 12.* | *Ronni merely groaned in response.* → RAPID-RESPONSE

re·spon·si·bil·i·ty S2 W1 /rɪˌspɒnsɪˈbɪləti $ rɪˌspɑːn-/ *n plural* **responsibilities**
1 [U] a duty to be in charge of or something, so that you make decisions and can be blamed if something bad happens: *Kelly's promotion means more money and more responsibility.* | **responsibility for (doing) sth** *The Minister will* **have responsibility** *for coordinating childcare policy.* | **with responsibility for sth** *a manager with responsibility for over 100 staff* | **it is sb's responsibility to do sth** *It's your responsibility to inform us of any changes.* | *The Health Minister has* **overall responsibility** *for Britain's hospitals.* | **take responsibility for (doing) sth** (=agree to be in charge of something or someone) *Who do you trust to take responsibility for Britain's defence?* | *Be careful you don't* **take on** *too much responsibility.*
2 [U] blame for something bad that has happened: [+for] *By resigning he is trying to avoid responsibility for the political crisis.* | *The management* **accepts** *no* **responsibility** *for cars left in the car park.* | *The Chairman of the airline accepted* **full responsibility** *for the accident.* | **claim responsibility (for sth)** (=say you are responsible) *No one has yet claimed responsibility for yesterday's bombing.*
3 [C] something that you must do as part of your job or duty: *My responsibilities include answering the phone and dealing with customer enquiries.* | **family/professional/parental etc responsibilities** *a single parent struggling to balance work and family responsibilities*
4 [C] something that you ought to do because it is morally or socially right; ⊟ **duty**: **a responsibility to do sth** *We all* **have a responsibility** *to protect the environment.* | *Parents need to encourage* **a sense of responsibility** *in their children* (=the ability to behave

sensibly in a way that will not harm themselves or other people). | **moral/social/legal etc responsibility** *The company saw it as part of its social responsibility to provide education for its workers.*
5 responsibility to sb a duty to help someone because of your work or position in society: *A doctor's first responsibility is to her patients.*
6 do sth on your own responsibility *formal* to do something without being told to do it or officially allowed to do it → DIMINISHED RESPONSIBILITY

re·spon·si·ble S2 W2 /rɪˈspɒnsɪbəl $ rɪˈspɑːn-/ *adj*
1 GUILTY [not before noun] if someone is responsible for an accident, mistake, crime etc, it is their fault or they can be blamed: [+for] *Police believe that the same man is responsible for three other murders in the area.* | *We are determined to bring the people responsible to justice.* | **hold sb responsible (for sth)** *If anything goes wrong, I will hold you* **personally responsible.**
2 IN CHARGE OF [not before noun] having a duty to be in charge of or to look after someone or something: [+for] *Mills is responsible for a budget of over $5 million.* | *The airline is* **legally responsible** *for the safety of its passengers.* | **responsible for doing sth** *He is responsible for recruiting and training new staff.*
3 SENSIBLE sensible and able to make good judgments, so that you can be trusted; ⊟ **irresponsible**; → **reliable**: *You can leave the children with Billy – he's very responsible.* | **responsible adult/citizen** *It's time you started acting like a responsible adult.*
4 CAUSE [not before noun] if something is responsible for a change, problem, event etc, it causes it: [+for] *The floods were responsible for the deaths of over a hundred people.*
5 responsible job/position a job in which the ability to make good judgments and decisions is needed
6 be responsible to sb if you are responsible to someone, that person is in charge of your work and you must explain what you have done to them: *Cabinet members are* **directly responsible** *to the President.*

GRAMMAR

⚠ **Responsible** is always an adjective, never a noun.
To **be responsible for (doing) something** can mean to have done something wrong: *Who is responsible for this mess?*
It can also mean to have to do or take care of something: *You're responsible for taking people's coats.* | *Our department is responsible for marketing.*
The person/company etc responsible is the person etc who has done something wrong: *Police are determined to catch the man responsible* (NOT *the responsible*).
A **responsible** person, or someone who is **responsible**, is sensible: *Children should be in the care of a responsible adult.* | *He's a very responsible young man.*

---

re·spon·si·bly /rɪˈspɒnsɪbli $ rɪˈspɑːn-/ *adv* in a sensible way that makes people trust you; ⊟ **irresponsibly**: **act/behave responsibly** *Can I rely on you to behave responsibly while I'm away?*

re·spon·sive /rɪˈspɒnsɪv $ rɪˈspɑːn-/ *adj* **1** reacting quickly, in a positive way: *a car with* **highly responsive** *steering* | [+to] *We try to be responsive to the needs of the customer.* | *Her condition is not responsive to drug therapy.* **2** eager to communicate with people, and to react to them in a positive way: *I tried to get him talking, but he wasn't* **very responsive.** —**responsively** *adv* —**responsiveness** *n* [U]

re·spray /ˌriːˈspreɪ/ *v* [T] *BrE* to change the colour of a car by putting new paint on it —**respray** /ˈriːspreɪ/ *n* [C]

rest¹ S1 W1 /rest/ *n*
1 the rest what is left after everything or everyone else has gone, been used, dealt with, or mentioned; → **remainder, leftovers**: *You carry these two bags, and I'll bring the rest.* | *Two of the attackers were killed, and the rest escaped.* | [+of] *Does anyone want the rest of this pizza?* | *He'll be in a wheelchair for* **the rest of his life.**
2 RELAXING [C,U] a period of time when you are not doing anything tiring and you can relax or sleep: *I need*

to **get some rest**. | **have/take a rest** *You look exhausted! Why don't you take a rest?* | *We stopped for a* **well-earned rest** (=one that we deserved because we had been working hard). | **a rest day/period** *We have classes until 12.30, and then we have a rest period.*

3 put/set sb's mind at rest to make someone feel less anxious or worried: *Why don't you talk to him, and put his mind at rest.*

4 come to rest a) to stop moving: *The aircraft skidded across the runway and finally came to rest in a cornfield.* **b)** if your eyes come to rest on something, you stop looking around and look at that one thing: [+on] *My eyes came to rest on a photograph of a young man.*

5 give it a rest *spoken especially BrE* used to tell someone to stop talking about something because they are annoying you: *Give it a rest, Jack!*

6 give sth a rest *spoken* to stop doing an activity: *I gave the acting a rest for a while.*

7 at rest a) an expression meaning dead, and free from pain and problems **b)** *technical* not moving

8 and all the rest of it *BrE spoken* used at the end of a short list to mean other things of a similar type: *It was me who was paying the rent and the bills and all the rest of it.*

9 and the rest *BrE spoken* used to emphasize in a humorous way that a number or amount is really much higher than someone thinks: *'I'd say she's about 40.' 'Yeah, and the rest!'*

10 lay/put sth to rest *formal* to stop people from worrying about or believing something: *The minister resigned, and the government hoped that the scandal would finally be laid to rest.*

11 lay sb to rest an expression meaning to bury someone, used when you want to avoid saying this directly: *She was laid to rest beside her husband.*

12 MUSIC [C] **a)** a period of silence of a particular length in a piece of music **b)** a written sign that shows how long the period of silence should be → HEADREST, FOOTREST, BACKREST; → **and the rest is history** at HISTORY (10)

rest² [S3] [W3] *v*

1 RELAX [I] to stop working or doing an activity for a time and sit down or lie down to relax: *If you're tired, we'll stop and rest for a while.*

2 SUPPORT STH [I,T always + adv/prep] to support an object or part of your body by putting it on or against something, or to be supported in this way; → **lean**: **rest (sth) against/on sth** *Rest your head on my shoulder.* | *Brassard rested his elbows on the table and leaned forward.* | *Their bikes were resting against the wall.*

3 rest your feet/legs/eyes etc to stop using a part of your body because it is feeling sore or tired: *I need to sit down and rest my legs.*

4 let the matter rest *also* **let it rest** to stop discussing or dealing with something: *The man apologized, but Aunt Matilda refused to let the matter rest.*

5 rest assured (that) *formal* used to tell someone not to worry, because what you say about a situation is true: *You may rest assured that it will be ready on time.*

6 sb will not rest until... if you will not rest until something happens, you will not be satisfied until it happens: *We will not rest until the murderer is found.*

7 DEAD PERSON [I always + adv/prep] *literary* if a dead person rests somewhere, they are buried there: *My mother rests beside my father in the family graveyard.* | **sb's last/final resting place** (=the place where someone is buried) | **rest in peace** (=often written on a grave)

8 rest on your laurels to be satisfied with what you have done, so that you do not make any further effort

9 I rest my case *spoken* **a)** *formal* used by a lawyer when they have finished trying to prove something in a court of law **b)** used when something happens or is said which proves that you were right – used humorously

10 rest easy to relax and stop worrying: *I can rest easy, knowing everything's under control.*

rest on/upon sth *phr v* [not in progressive]

1 *formal* to depend on something: *Success in management ultimately rests on good judgment.*

2 *formal* to be based on a particular idea or set of facts: *The case against my client rests entirely on circumstantial evidence.*

3 if your eyes rest on something, you notice it and look at it: *His eyes rested on a small figure in the distance.*

rest with sb *phr v* [not in progressive]

if a decision rests with someone, they are responsible for it: *The final decision rests with the President.*

'rest ˌarea *n* [C] *especially AmE* a place near a road where you can stop and rest, go to the toilet etc

re·start /ˌriː'stɑːt $ -'stɑːrt/ *v* [I,T] to start something such as a machine, process etc again after it has stopped: *attempts to restart the peace process* —**restart** /'riːstɑːt $ -stɑːrt/ *n* [C usually singular]

re·state /ˌriː'steɪt/ *v* [T] to say something again in a different way, so that it is clearer or more strongly expressed: *He is not changing the rules; he is simply restating the policy that was established last year.* —**restatement** *n* [C,U]

res·tau·rant [S3] [W2] /'restərɒnt $ -rənt, -rɑːnt/ *n* [C] a place where you can buy and eat a meal: **Chinese/ French/Mexican etc restaurant** *We went to a little Italian restaurant near Leicester Square.* | *He took her out for a five-course dinner in a fancy restaurant.* | *The company runs a chain of restaurants.* | *A new restaurant has just opened across the road.* → see picture at EAT

> **WORD FOCUS: RESTAURANT**
> the person who serves you in a restaurant: **waiter, waitress, server** *AmE*, **waitperson** *AmE*
> the person who cooks your food: **chef**
> the person who welcomes the guests: **maître d', host/ hostess** *AmE*
> a list of the food: **menu** *also* **bill of fare** *formal*
> a list of wines and alcoholic drinks: **wine list** *also* **drink list** *AmE*
> a piece of paper that shows the amount you have to pay for your meal: **bill** *BrE/**check** *AmE*
> extra money you leave for the waiter or waitress: **tip/ gratuity** *formal*
> money that the restaurant charges for service: **service charge, cover charge, corkage**
> → café, cafeteria, diner, drive-in, deli, snack bar, bistro

'restaurant car *n* [C] a carriage on a train where meals are served; ▤ **dining car**

res·tau·ra·teur /ˌrestərə'tɜː $ -'tɜːr/ *also* **res·tau·ran·teur** /ˌrestərɒn'tɜː $ -rɑːn'tɜːr/ *n* [C] someone who owns and manages a restaurant

rest·ed /'restɪd/ *adj* [not before noun] feeling healthier, stronger, or calmer because you have had time to relax: *We came back from holiday feeling rested and relaxed.*

rest·ful /'restfəl/ *adj* peaceful and quiet, making you feel relaxed: *restful music* —**restfully** *adv*

'rest home *n* [C] a place where old or sick people can live and be taken care of; ▤ **nursing home**

res·ti·tu·tion /ˌrestɪ'tjuːʃən $ -'tuː-/ *n* [U] *formal* the act of giving back something that was lost or stolen to its owner, or of paying for damage; → **compensation**: [+of] *the restitution of art treasures missing since World War II* | *The offender must* **make restitution** *for the hurt that he or she has caused.*

res·tive /'restɪv/ *adj written* dissatisfied or bored with your situation, and impatient for it to change: *Communist leaders struggled to rule over increasingly restive populations.* —**restively** *adv* —**restiveness** *n* [U]

rest·less /'restləs/ *adj* **1** unwilling to keep still or stay where you are, especially because you are nervous or bored; ▤ **fidgety**: **become/grow/get restless** *The children had been indoors all day, and were getting restless.* **2** unwilling to stay in one place, and always wanting new experiences: *After a few weeks in Marseille, I grew restless and decided to move on.* **3 restless night** a night during which you cannot sleep or rest —**restlessly** *adv* —**restlessness** *n* [U]

R

re·stock /ˌriːˈstɒk $ -ˈstɑːk/ v [I,T] to bring in more supplies to replace those that have been used

res·to·ra·tion /ˌrestəˈreɪʃən/ n [C,U] **1** when you repair something such as an old building or a piece of furniture, so that it looks the same as when it was first built or made: [+of] *a fund for the restoration of historic buildings* | *Major restoration work will begin in May.* **2** the act of bringing back a law, tax, or system of government: [+of] *They're fighting for the restoration of democratic rights.* | *the restoration of the monarchy in Spain* **3** the Restoration the return of Charles II as King of England in 1660, and the period afterwards: *Restoration comedy/drama* (=plays written during this time in England) **4** the act of officially giving something back to its former owner; → return: [+of] *an attempt to secure the restoration of their lands*

re·sto·ra·tive /rɪˈstɔːrətɪv/ adj formal making you feel healthier or stronger: *the restorative power of sleep*

re·store W3 /rɪˈstɔː $ -ɔːr/ v [T]
1 FORMER SITUATION to make something return to its former state or condition: **restore sth to sth** *The government promises to restore the economy to full strength.* | *She was hoping that the Mediterranean climate would restore her to full health.* | *The National Guard was called in to restore order* (=make people stop fighting and breaking the law) *when riots broke out.* | *initiatives to restore peace in the Middle East* | **restore (diplomatic) relations with sb** *Vietnam restored diplomatic relations with South Korea on December 22.* | **restore sb's sight/hearing** (=make someone who cannot hear or who is blind, hear or see again)
2 POSITIVE FEELING to bring back a positive feeling that a person or a group of people felt before: *measures aimed at restoring public confidence in the education system* | *a man whose kindness and sincerity really restored my faith in human nature* (=helped me to believe that people can be good)
3 REPAIR to repair an old building, piece of furniture, or painting etc so that it is in its original condition: *The church was carefully restored after the war.* | *a Victorian fireplace restored to its former glory*
4 GIVE STH BACK formal to give back to someone something that was lost or taken from them; → return: **restore sth to sb** *The treaty restored Okinawa to Japan.*
5 BRING BACK A LAW to bring back a law, tax, right etc: *a campaign to restore the death penalty*
6 restore sb to power/the throne formal make someone king, queen, or president again, after a period when they have not been in power

re·stored /rɪˈstɔːd $ -ɔːrd/ adj [not before noun] feeling better and stronger: *After a cup of tea, she felt quite restored.*

re·stor·er /rɪˈstɔːrə $ -ər/ n [C] **1** a person whose job is repairing old things: *an art restorer* **2** someone who brings back something that existed before: *He was described as a restorer of peace and order.*

re·strain /rɪˈstreɪn/ v [T] **1** to stop someone from doing something, often by using physical force: **restrain sb from doing sth** *I had to restrain her from running out into the street.* | *He had to be restrained from using violence.* **2** to control your own emotions or behaviour: *Renwick restrained a feeling of annoyance.* | **restrain yourself (from doing something)** *She could barely restrain herself from hitting him.* **3** to control or limit something that is increasing too much: *Price rises should restrain consumer spending.*

re·strained /rɪˈstreɪnd/ adj **1** behaviour that is restrained is calm and controlled: *a restrained and cool-headed response to their criticisms* **2** not too brightly coloured or decorated: *The interior decoration is quite restrained.*

re·strain·ing or·der n [C] an official legal document that prevents someone from doing something

re·straint /rɪˈstreɪnt/ n **1** [U] calm sensible controlled behaviour, especially in a situation where it is difficult to stay calm: *The police were praised for their restraint in handling the demonstrators.* | **show/exercise restraint** *He urged the millions of protesters to exercise restraint.* **2** [C usually plural,U] a rule or principle that limits what people can do: [+on] *Opposition politicians have called for restraints on public spending.* | *The government has imposed restraints on corporate mergers.* **3** [U] formal physical force that is used to hold someone back, especially because they are likely to be violent: *Sometimes police officers have to use physical restraint to control dangerous prisoners.* **4** [C] something that prevents someone from moving freely, such as a rope or a SEAT BELT

re·strict S3 W3 /rɪˈstrɪkt/ v [T]
1 to limit or control the size, amount, or range of something: *The new law restricts the sale of hand guns.* | *You may need to restrict access to certain files* (=limit the number of people who can read them). | *The agreement will restrict competition.* | **restrict sth to sth** *In future we will restrict class sizes to 20 students.*
2 to limit someone's actions or movements: *The cramped living conditions severely restricted the children's freedom to play.*
3 restrict yourself/sb to (doing) sth to allow yourself to have or do only a particular thing or amount of something: *I'm restricting myself to two cigarettes a day.*

re·strict·ed /rɪˈstrɪktɪd/ adj **1** small or limited in size, area, or amount: *It's difficult trying to work in such a restricted space.* **2** limited or controlled, especially by laws or rules: *Press freedom is severely restricted.* | [+to] *The sale of alcohol is restricted to people over the age of 18.* | *There is restricted access to this information* (=only certain people can have it). **3** limited in your movements or in what you are able to do: *The accident left her with restricted movement in her right leg.* | *In those days women led very restricted lives.* **4** a restricted area, document, or information can only be seen or used by a particular group of people because it is secret or dangerous: *No Entry – restricted area for army personnel only.* **5** be restricted to sb/sth to only affect a limited area, group etc: *The damage is restricted to the left side of the brain.* | *Eligibility for five weeks' holiday is restricted to senior management.*

re·stric·tion S2 W3 /rɪˈstrɪkʃən/ n
1 [C] a rule or law that limits or controls what people can do: [+on] *restrictions on immigration* | *a 50 mph speed restriction* | **trade/travel restrictions** | **impose/place restrictions on sth** *The law imposed new financial restrictions on private companies.* | **strict/tough/tight restriction** *tougher restrictions on alcohol advertising* | **lift/remove a restriction** *Restrictions on trade were lifted.*
2 [U] when you restrict the size, amount, or range of something

re·stric·tive /rɪˈstrɪktɪv/ adj something that is restrictive stops people doing what they want to do; → limiting: *Many members thought the rules were too restrictive.* | *a restrictive policy on admission to the college*

re·stric·tive 'clause also **re·stric·tive ˌrelative 'clause** n [C] technical a part of a sentence that says which particular person or thing you are talking about. For example in 'the man who came to dinner', the phrase 'who came to dinner' is a restrictive clause; → non-restrictive clause

re·stric·tive 'prac·tic·es n [plural] **1** unreasonable rules that are used by a TRADE UNION to limit the kind of work that members of other trade unions are allowed to do for a company **2** an unfair trade agreement between companies that limits the amount of competition there is

'rest room n [C] AmE a room with a toilet in a place such as a restaurant or cinema; → toilet BrE

re·struc·ture /ˌriːˈstrʌktʃə $ -ər/ v [T] to change the way in which something such as a government, business, or system is organized: *proposals to radically*

restructure *Britain's* *electronics* *industry*
—**restructuring** n [C,U]: *the major restructuring of our armed forces*

'rest stop n [C] a place near a road where you can stop and rest, use the toilet etc

re·sult¹ S1 W1 /rɪˈzʌlt/ n
1 HAPPENING BECAUSE OF STH [C,U] something that happens or exists because of something that happened before; → **consequence**: [+of] *Accidents are the inevitable result of driving too fast.* | *High unemployment is a direct result of the recession.* | **end/final/net result** (=the result at the end of a long process) *The net result of all these changes is that schools should be able to deliver a better service to pupils.* | *Growing plants from seed can produce disappointing results.* | *With a little effort you should achieve the desired result.* | **as a result (of sth)** *As a result of the pilots' strike, all flights have had to be cancelled.* | **with the result that** *Sara wasn't at school last week, with the result that she missed an important test.*
2 SPORTS/ELECTIONS [C] the final number of points, votes etc at the end of a competition, game, or election: *The election results will be announced at midnight.* | *the football results* | [+of] *A lot depends on the result of this match.*
3 SCIENTIFIC TESTS [C] the answers that are produced by a scientific study or test: *Results suggest that diet is very important.* | [+of] *Police are awaiting the results of a forensic examination.* | **positive/negative/inconclusive results** *The experiments gave positive results in all cases.*
4 EXAMINATIONS [C] *BrE* the mark you get in an examination; ⊟ **grade** *AmE*: *When do we get our exam results?*
5 SUCCESS [C] the achievement of something: *She certainly knows how to get results.* | *For best results, always use fresh ingredients when you are cooking.*
6 BUSINESS **results** [plural] the accounts of a business that show how successful it has been over a period of time, usually a year: *British Airways has announced disappointing results for the first half of the year.*
7 **get a result** *BrE informal* to win a victory in a sports match: *They were lucky to get a result on Saturday.*

result² W3 v [I]
if something results from something else, it is caused by it: [+from] *We are still dealing with problems resulting from errors made in the past.* | *How would you cope with unemployment and the resulting loss of income?*
result in sth phr v
to make something happen; ⊟ **cause**: *an accident that resulted in the death of two passengers*

result³ interjection informal **Result!** said when you have just done something successfully

re·sul·tant /rɪˈzʌltənt/ adj [only before noun] formal happening or existing because of something: *She is still trying to get over the attack and the resultant injuries.*

re·sume¹ /rɪˈzjuːm $ rɪˈzuːm/ v formal **1** [T] to start doing something again after stopping or being interrupted: *She hopes to resume work after the baby is born.* | *The rebels have resumed hostilities against government troops.* | **resume doing sth** *He will resume training as soon as the injury is better.* **2** [I] if an activity or process resumes, it starts again after a pause: *Peace talks will resume tomorrow.* **3 resume your seat/place/position** to go back to the seat, place, or position where you were before: *Will the delegates please resume their seats?*

re·su·me², **résumé** /ˈrezjʊmeɪ, ˈreɪ- $ ˌrezʊˈmeɪ/ n [C] **1** a short account of something such as an article or speech which gives the main points but no details; ⊟ **summary**: *a brief résumé of the day's events* **2** *AmE* a short written account of your education and your previous jobs that you send to an employer when you are looking for a new job; ⊟ **CV** *BrE*

re·sump·tion /rɪˈzʌmpʃən/ n [singular,U] formal the act of starting an activity again after stopping or being interrupted: [+of] *Both countries are now hoping for a quick resumption of diplomatic relations.*

re·sur·face /ˌriːˈsɜːfɪs $ -ɜːr-/ v **1** [I] to appear again after being lost or missing: *One of the missing paintings suddenly resurfaced.* **2** [I] if an idea or problem resurfaces, it becomes important again: *Nationalist tensions have resurfaced here.* **3** [T] to put a new surface on a road **4** [I] to come back up to the surface of the water

re·sur·gence /rɪˈsɜːdʒəns $ -ɜːr-/ n [singular,U] the reappearance and growth of something that was common in the past: [+of] *There has been a resurgence of interest in religion over the last ten years.* | [+in] *a resurgence in the popularity of 60s music*

re·sur·gent /rɪˈsɜːdʒənt $ -ɜːr-/ adj [usually before noun] growing and becoming more popular, after a period of quietness: *resurgent fascism*

res·ur·rect /ˌrezəˈrekt/ v [T] to bring back an old activity, belief, idea etc that has not existed for a long time: *The Home Office have resurrected plans to build a new prison just outside London.* | *another failed attempt to resurrect his career*

res·ur·rec·tion /ˌrezəˈrekʃən/ n [singular] **1 the Resurrection** the return of Jesus Christ to life after his death on the cross, which is one of the main beliefs of the Christian religion **2** formal a situation in which something old or forgotten returns or becomes important again: *a resurrection of old jealousies*

re·sus·ci·tate /rɪˈsʌsɪteɪt/ v [I] to make someone breathe again or become conscious after they have almost died; → **revive**: *Doctors managed to resuscitate him.* —**resuscitation** /rɪˌsʌsɪˈteɪʃən/ n [U]: *mouth-to-mouth resuscitation* (=when you breathe air into someone's mouth to make them breathe)

re·tail¹ /ˈriːteɪl/ n [U] the sale of goods in shops to customers, for their own use and not for selling to anyone else; → **wholesale**: **the retail trade/business** *a manager with twenty years' experience in the retail business* | **retail outlet/shop/store/chain** *We are looking for more retail outlets for our products.* | *a retail price of £8.99* | *The retail value would be around $500.* | *Retail sales fell by 1.3% in January.*

re·tail² /ˈriːteɪl/ v **1** [I] technical to be sold for a particular price in a shop: [+at/for] *The wine retails at £6.95 a bottle.* | *The decoder is expected to retail for under $300.* **2** [T] technical to sell goods in shops: *Their products are retailed all over Britain and Europe.* **3** [T] formal to give other people private information about someone or something

re·tail³ /ˈriːteɪl/ adv if you buy or sell something retail, you buy or sell it in a shop: *We only deal with wholesalers – we don't sell any of our goods retail.*

re·tail·er /ˈriːteɪlə $ -ər/ n [C] a person or business that sells goods to customers in a shop

re·tail·ing /ˈriːteɪlɪŋ/ n [U] the business of selling goods to customers in shops: *There may be many job losses in retailing.*

'retail park n [C] *BrE* an area outside a town with many large shops and space for cars to park

ˌretail 'price ˌindex abbreviation **RPI** n **the retail price index** a list of certain goods and services and how much their prices change each month

'retail ˌtherapy n [U] the act of buying things that you do not need when you are unhappy because you think it will make you feel better – often used humorously; → **shopaholic**: *What you need is a bit of retail therapy!*

re·tain S2 W2 /rɪˈteɪn/ v [T] formal
1 to keep something or continue to have something: *You have the right to retain possession of the goods.* | *The state wants to retain control of food imports.*

2 to store or keep something inside something else: *A lot of information can be retained in your computer.* | *Limestone is known to retain moisture.*
3 to remember information: *I find it very difficult to retain facts.*
4 if you retain a lawyer or other specialist, you pay them to work for you now and in the future: *He has retained a lawyer to challenge the court's decision.* | *We had to pay a retaining fee* (=an amount of money to keep someone working for you).
5 if a company retains workers, it continues to employ them for a long time: *It's increasingly difficult to recruit and retain good staff.*

re·tain·er /rɪˈteɪnə $ -ər/ *n* [C] **1** an amount of money paid to someone, especially a lawyer, so that they will continue to work for you in the future **2** *BrE* a reduced amount of rent that you pay for a room, flat etc when you are not there, so that it will still be available when you return **3** *AmE* a plastic and wire object that you wear in your mouth to make your teeth stay straight; ▣ **brace** *BrE* **4** *old use* a servant

re'taining ,wall *n* [C] a wall that is built to prevent land from slipping or moving

re·take[1] /ˌriːˈteɪk/ *v past tense* **retook** /-ˈtʊk/, *past participle* **retaken** /-ˈteɪkən/ [T] **1** to get control of an area again in a war; ▣ **recapture**: *an attempt to retake the city* **2** to take an examination again because you have previously failed it; ▣ **resit** *BrE*

re·take[2] /ˈriːteɪk/ *n* [C] **1** an act of filming or photographing something again: *They had to do several retakes before the director was satisfied.* **2** *BrE* an examination or test that you take again because you failed it

re·tal·i·ate /rɪˈtælieɪt/ *v* [I] to do something bad to someone because they have done something bad to you; → **hit back**: **retaliate by doing sth** *The British government retaliated by breaking off diplomatic relations.* | [+against] *The army began to retaliate against the civilian population.*

re·tal·i·a·tion /rɪˌtæliˈeɪʃən/ *n* [U] action against someone who has done something bad to you; → **revenge**: **in retaliation (for sth)** *This action was undoubtedly in retaliation for last week's bomb attack.* | [+against] *the threat of massive retaliation against British troops*

re·tal·i·a·to·ry /rɪˈtæliətəri $ -tɔːri/ *adj* [usually before noun] *formal* done against someone because they have harmed you: *a retaliatory attack*

re·tard[1] /rɪˈtɑːd $ -ɑːrd/ *v* [T] *formal* to delay the development of something, or to make something happen more slowly than expected; ▣ **slow down**: *Cold weather retards the growth of many plants.*

re·tard[2] /ˈriːtɑːd $ -ɑːrd/ *n* [C] *spoken not polite* an offensive word for a stupid person

re·tard·ed /rɪˈtɑːdɪd $ -ɑːr-/ *adj old-fashioned* less mentally developed than other people of the same age. Many people think that this use is rude and offensive.

retch /retʃ/ *v* [I] to try to vomit; ▣ **gag**: *The smell made her retch.*

re·tell /ˌriːˈtel/ *v past tense and past participle* **retold** /-ˈtəʊld $ -ˈtoʊld/ [T] to tell a story again, often in a different way or in a different language

re·ten·tion /rɪˈtenʃən/ *n* [U] **1** *formal* the act of keeping something: [+of] *The UN will vote on the retention of sanctions against Iraq.* **2** *technical* the ability or tendency of something to hold liquid, heat etc within itself: *Many people with heart problems suffer from fluid retention.* **3** the ability to keep something in your memory: *I have a real problem with retention of information.*

re·ten·tive /rɪˈtentɪv/ *adj* a retentive memory or mind is able to hold facts and remember them → ANAL (2)
—**retentiveness** *n* [U]

re·think /riːˈθɪŋk/ *v past tense and past participle* **rethought** /-ˈθɔːt $ -ˈθɔːt/ [I,T] to think about a plan or idea again in order to decide if any changes should be made; ▣ **reconsider**: *an opportunity to rethink our policy on advertising* —**rethink** /ˈriːθɪŋk/ *n* [singular]: *It's time for a complete rethink of the way we farm our countryside.*

ret·i·cent /ˈretɪsənt/ *adj* unwilling to talk about what you feel or what you know; ▣ **reserved**: [+about] *She's strangely reticent about her son.* —**reticence** *n* [U]

re·tic·u·la·ted /rɪˈtɪkjəleɪtəd/ *adj technical* forming or covered with a pattern of squares and lines that looks like a net

ret·i·na /ˈretɪnə/ *n* [C] the area at the back of your eye that receives light and sends an image of what you see to your brain

ret·i·nue /ˈretɪnjuː $ -nuː/ *n* [C] a group of people who travel with someone important to help and support them: [+of] *He travelled with a huge retinue of servants.*

re·tire S2 W3 /rɪˈtaɪə $ -ˈtaɪr/ *v*
1 WORK a) [I] to stop working, usually because you have reached a certain age: *Most people retire at 65.* | *He was forced to retire early because of poor health.* | [+from] *I retired from teaching three years ago.* | *her decision to retire from her position as librarian of the law society* | *Her drink problem has forced her to retire from public life.* | [+as] *He retired as a GP last year.* **b)** [T usually passive] to ask someone to stop doing their job, usually because of ill health: *He became ill and was retired early.*
2 QUIET PLACE [I] *formal* to go away to a quiet place: [+to] *I retired to my room to think.*
3 JURY [I] when a JURY in a law court retires, they go away to consider whether someone is guilty or not
4 GAME/RACE [I] to stop competing in a game or race because you are losing or injured: *He had to retire with a neck injury in the second half.*
5 BED [I] *literary* to go to bed
6 ARMY [I] to move back from a battle after being defeated

re·tired /rɪˈtaɪəd $ -ˈtaɪrd/ *adj* having stopped working, usually because of your age: *a retired teacher* | *Both my parents are retired now.*

re·tir·ee /rɪˌtaɪəˈriː $ -ˌtaɪˈriː/ *n* [C] *AmE* someone who has stopped working, usually because of their age; → **pensioner**

re·tire·ment S2 W3 /rɪˈtaɪəmənt $ -ˈtaɪr-/ *n*
1 [C,U] when you stop working, usually because of your age: [+from] *He became a keen golfer after his retirement from politics.* | [+as] *He announced his retirement as chief executive of the company.* | *She took early retirement* (=retired at an earlier age than usual) *last year.* | *Dad's approaching retirement age.*
2 [singular,U] the period after you have stopped work: *I hope you enjoy a long and happy retirement.* | **in retirement** *Will you be able to support yourself in retirement?* | *a retirement pension*

re'tirement ,home *n* [C] an OLD PEOPLE'S HOME

re'tirement ,plan *n* [C] *AmE* a system for saving money for when you stop work, done either through your employer or arranged by you

re·tir·ing /rɪˈtaɪərɪŋ $ -ˈtaɪrɪŋ/ *adj* **1** someone who is retiring does not want to be with other people, especially people they do not know; ▣ **shy**: *As a child, Elizabeth was very shy and retiring.* **2 the retiring president/manager/director etc** a president etc who is soon going to leave their job

re·tool /ˌriːˈtuːl/ *v* **1** [T] *AmE informal* to organize something in a new way: *The College Board has retooled the admission exams.* **2** [I,T] to change or replace the machines or tools in a factory

re·tort[1] /rɪˈtɔːt $ -ɔːrt/ *v* [T] to reply quickly, in an angry or humorous way: *'It's all your fault!' he retorted.*

retort[2] *n* [C] **1** a short angry or humorous reply: *He was about to make a sharp retort.* **2** a bottle with a long narrow bent neck, used for heating chemicals

re·touch /ˌriːˈtʌtʃ/ v [T] to improve a picture or photograph by painting over marks or making other small changes; → **airbrush**: *postcards that have been retouched to cover the grey skies*

re·trace /rɪˈtreɪs, riː-/ v [T] **1 retrace your steps/ path/route etc** to go back exactly the way you have come: *After a few minutes, he turned around and began to retrace his steps.* **2** to repeat exactly the same journey that someone else has made: *We shall be retracing the route taken by Marco Polo.* **3** to find out where someone went: *an investigation to retrace the dead man's last known movements*

re·tract /rɪˈtrækt/ v formal **1** [T] if you retract something that you said or agreed, you say that you did not mean it; ⊟ **withdraw**: *He confessed to the murder but later retracted his statement.* **2** [I,T] if part of a machine or an animal's body retracts or is retracted, it moves back into the main part: *The sea otter can retract the claws on its front feet.*

re·tract·a·ble /rɪˈtræktəbəl/ adj a retractable part of something can be pulled back into the main part: *a knife with a retractable blade*

re·trac·tion /rɪˈtrækʃən/ n formal **1** [C] an official statement that something which you said previously is not true: [+of] *The newspaper was forced to publish a retraction of its allegations.* **2** [U] the act of pulling one part of something back inside the main part

re·train /ˌriːˈtreɪn/ v [I,T] to learn or to teach someone the skills that are needed to do a different job: *One solution is to retrain the long-term unemployed.* | [+as] *She's hoping to retrain as a teacher.* —**retraining** n [U]

re·tread /ˈriːtred/ n [C] **1** a old tyre which is given a new rubber surface; ⊟ **remould** *AmE informal* something that is made or done again, with a few changes added – used to show disapproval: *retreads of old TV shows* **3** *AmE informal* someone who has been trained to do work which is different from what they did before

re·treat[1] /rɪˈtriːt/ v [I]
1 ARMY to move away from the enemy after being defeated in battle; ⬛ **advance**: *The rebels retreated to the mountains.* | *They were attacked and forced to retreat.*
2 MOVE BACK written **a)** to move away from someone or something: *He saw her and retreated, too shy to speak to her.* | [+to/from/into etc] *Perry lit the fuse and retreated to a safe distance.* | *It was not a conscious choice to retreat from public life.* **b)** if an area of water, snow, or land retreats, it gradually gets smaller: *The flood waters are slowly retreating.*
3 CHANGE YOUR MIND written to decide not to do something you were planning to do, because it was unpopular or too difficult: [+from] *The Canadian government has retreated from a plan to kill 300 wolves.*
4 QUIET PLACE to go away to a place that is quiet or safe: [+from/into/to] *After the noise of the city he was glad to retreat to his hotel room.*
5 retreat into yourself/your shell/fantasy etc to ignore what is happening around you and give all your attention to your private thoughts
6 FINANCE technical if shares etc retreat, their value falls to a lower level

retreat[2] n
1 OF AN ARMY [C,U] a movement away from the enemy after a defeat in battle; ⬛ **advance**: *Napoleon's retreat from Moscow* | *The rebel forces are in full retreat* (=retreating very fast). | *The bugler sounded the retreat* (=gave a loud signal for retreat).
2 MOVEMENT BACK [singular,U] a movement away from someone or something: [+from] *Ten thousand years ago the ice began its retreat from Scotland.*
3 beat a retreat informal to leave a place quickly: *I saw my aunt coming and beat a hasty retreat.*
4 CHANGE OF INTENTION [singular,U] when you change your mind about something because your idea was unpopular or too difficult: [+from] *a retreat from hard-line policies*

5 PLACE [C] a place you can go to that is quiet or safe: *a country retreat*
6 THOUGHT AND PRAYER [C,U] a period of time that you spend praying or studying religion in a quiet place: **on (a) retreat** *I spent three weeks on retreat in Scotland.*
7 FINANCE [singular,U] technical a situation in which the value of shares etc falls to a lower level

re·trench /rɪˈtrentʃ/ v [I] formal if a government or organization retrenches, it spends less money; ⊟ **economize** —**retrenchment** n [C,U]: *a government policy of retrenchment*

re·tri·al /ˌriːˈtraɪəl, ˈriːtraɪəl $ ˌriːˈtraɪəl/ n [C] a process of judging a law case in court again; → **retry**: *The jury was dismissed and the judge ordered a retrial.*

ret·ri·bu·tion /ˌretrɪˈbjuːʃən/ n [singular,U] severe punishment for something very serious: [+for] *Victims are demanding retribution for the terrorist attacks.* | **divine retribution** (=punishment by God)

re·triev·al /rɪˈtriːvəl/ n [U] **1** technical the process of getting back information stored on a computer system: *a new system that should speed up information retrieval* **2** the act of getting back something you have lost or left somewhere **3 be beyond/past retrieval** if a situation is beyond retrieval, it has become so bad that it cannot be made right again

re·trieve /rɪˈtriːv/ v [T] **1** formal to find something and bring it back; → **recover**: *She bent down to retrieve her earring.* | **retrieve sth from sth** *It took four days to retrieve all the bodies from the crash.* **2** technical to get back information that has been stored in the memory of a computer: *The new version of the software automatically retrieves digital information.* **3 retrieve a situation** BrE to make a situation satisfactory again after there has been a serious mistake or problem: *The general made one last desperate effort to retrieve the situation.* —**retrievable** adj

re·triev·er /rɪˈtriːvə $ -ər/ n [C] a type of dog that can be trained to find and bring back birds that its owner has shot

ret·ro[1] /ˈretrəʊ $ -troʊ/ adj based on styles of fashion and design from the recent past: *retro '60s fashions*

retro[2] n plural **retros** [C] AmE informal a RETROSPECTIVE

retro- /ˈretrəʊ, -trə $ -troʊ, -trə/ prefix back towards the past or an earlier state: *retroactive legislation* (=laws which have an effect on things already done) | *a retrograde step* (=returning to a worse state)

ret·ro·ac·tive /ˌretrəʊˈæktɪv $ -troʊ-/ adj formal a law or decision that is retroactive is effective from a particular date in the past; ⊟ **retrospective**: *a retroactive pay increase* | [+to] *The legislation is retroactive to 1st June.* —**retroactively** adv

ret·ro·fit /ˈretrəʊfɪt $ -troʊ-/ v **retrofitted, retrofitting** [T] to improve a machine, piece of equipment, building etc by putting new and better parts in it after it has been used for some time: *plans to retrofit oil boilers* —**retrofit** n [C] —**retrofitting** n [U]

ret·ro·flex /ˈretrəfleks/ adj technical a retroflex speech sound is made with the end of your tongue pointing backwards and upwards

ret·ro·grade /ˈretrəɡreɪd/ adj **1** formal involving a return to an earlier and worse situation; ⊟ **backward**: *The closure of the factories is seen as a retrograde step.* **2** technical moving backwards; ⊟ **backward**

ret·ro·gres·sive /ˌretrəˈɡresɪv $ / adj formal returning to an earlier and worse situation; ⊟ **regressive**: *retrogressive legislation* —**retrogress** v [I] —**retrogression** /-ˈɡreʃən/ n [singular,U]

ret·ro·spect /ˈretrəspekt/ n **in retrospect** thinking back to a time in the past, especially with the advantage of knowing more now than you did then: *In retrospect, I wonder if we should have done more.*

ret·ro·spec·tion /ˌretrəˈspekʃən/ n [U] formal thinking about the past

ret·ro·spec·tive¹ /ˌretrəˈspektɪv◂/ adj [usually before noun] **1** related to or thinking about the past: a retrospective study of 110 patients **2** BrE a law or decision that is retrospective is effective from a particular date in the past; ☰ **retroactive**: retrospective legislation | Teachers settled for a 4.2% pay rise **with retrospective effect** from 1 April. —**retrospectively** adv: The new rule will be applied retrospectively.

retrospective² n [C] a show of the work of an ARTIST, actor, FILM-MAKER etc that includes examples of all the kinds of work they have done: a Hitchcock retrospective | [+of] a retrospective of painter Hans Hofmann

ret·ro·vi·rus /ˈretrəʊˌvaɪərəs $ -troʊˌvaɪrəs/ n [C] technical a VIRUS of a type that includes some CANCER viruses and the AIDS virus, but that also has a quality that makes it useful for GENETIC ENGINEERING

re·try /ˌriːˈtraɪ/ v retried, retrying, retries [T] **1** to judge a person or a law case again in court; → **retrial 2** to do an action on a computer again after it has failed

ret·si·na /retˈsiːnə/ n [U] a Greek wine that tastes of the RESIN (=juice) of particular trees

re·turn¹ [S2] [W1] /rɪˈtɜːn $ -ɜːrn/ v
1 GO BACK [I] to go or come back to a place where you were before; ☰ **go back, come back**: It was forty five minutes before she returned. | [+to] Are you planning to return to Spain? | [+from] I have just returned from five months in Zimbabwe. | Alison decided to **return home**. | He left his country, **never to return**. ⚠ In spoken English it is more usual to use **go/come back**.
2 GIVE BACK [T] to give or send something back, or to put something back in its place; ☰ **give back, put back**: **return sth to sth/sb** Carson returned the notebook to his pocket. | I returned the books to the library unread. | Please complete the enclosed application form and return it in the envelope attached. ⚠ In spoken English it is more usual to use **take/bring/give back**.
3 FEELING/SITUATION [I] if a feeling, situation etc returns, it starts to exist or happen again; ☰ **come back**: If the pain returns, take two of the tablets with some water. | David could feel his anger returning. | [+to] when peace finally returns to this country
4 DO THE SAME [T] to do something to someone because they have done the same thing to you: He smiled at her warmly and she returned his smile. | I phoned him twice on Friday and left messages, but he never returned my call (=he did not phone me). | Thanks very much. I'll **return the favour** (=do something to help you) some day. | The police did not **return fire** (=shoot back at someone who shot at them).
5 ANSWER [T] written to answer someone: 'Yes,' he returned. 'I'm a lucky man.'
6 BALL [T] to hit the ball back to your opponent in a game such as tennis
7 ELECT [T usually passive] BrE to elect someone to a political position, especially to represent you in parliament: **return sb to sth** Durrant was returned to Parliament with an increased majority. | **return sb as sth** At the last election she was again returned as MP for Brighton.
8 return a verdict when a JURY return their VERDICT, they say whether someone is guilty or not
9 PROFIT [T] to make a profit: The group returned increased profits last year.

return to sth phr v
1 to change back to a previous state or situation, or to change something back: David waited for a moment to let his breathing **return to normal**. | **return sth to sth** The new chairman made the cuts necessary to return the company to profitability.
2 to start doing an activity, job etc that you were doing before you stopped or were interrupted; ☰ **go back**: Nicholas looked up, grinned, then returned to his newspaper. | The children return to school next week. | Ellie needed to **return to work** soon after the birth.

3 formal to start discussing or dealing with a subject that you have already mentioned: I will return to this problem in a moment.

return² [S2] [W2] n
1 COMING BACK [singular] the act of returning from somewhere, or your arrival back in a place: We're all looking forward to your return! | [+from] I need to know the date of her return from Europe. | [+to] Malcolm decided to delay his return to York. | **on/upon sb's return** On his return from Canada, he joined the army.
2 GIVING BACK [singular] the act of giving, putting, or sending something back: A mother is appealing for the safe return of her baby son. | Police have arranged for the return of the stolen goods.
3 CHANGING BACK [singular] a change back to a previous state or situation: [+to] The United States called for a return to democracy. | a return to normal
4 STARTING AGAIN [singular] when someone starts an activity again after they had stopped: [+to] Rose's return to the teaching profession | Jean is well enough now to consider her **return to work**.
5 PROFIT [C,U] the amount of profit that you get from something: The markets are showing extremely poor returns. | [+on] How can you get the best return on your investment? | [+from] The returns from farming are declining. | The average **rates of return** were 15%.
6 in return (for sth) as payment or reward for something: He is always helping people without expecting anything in return. | We offer an excellent all-round education to our students. In return, we expect students to work hard. | Liz agreed to look after the baby in return for a free room.
7 FEELING/SITUATION [singular] when a feeling, situation etc starts to exist or happen again: [+of] She felt a return of her old anxiety. | David had noticed the return of worrying symptoms in the last few days.
8 COMPUTER [U] the key that you press on a computer at the end of an instruction or to move to a new line; ☰ **enter**: Key in the file name and press return.
9 STATEMENT [C] a statement giving written information in reply to official questions: an analysis of the 1851 census returns → TAX RETURN
10 VOTE [C] technical a vote in an election: What are the returns from last night's voting?
11 by return (of post) BrE if you reply to a letter by return, you send your reply almost immediately
12 TICKET [C] BrE a ticket for a journey from one place to another and back again; ☰ **single**; ☰ **round trip** AmE → DAY RETURN → **the point of no return** at POINT¹ (10)

return³ adj [only before noun] used or paid for a journey from one place to another and back again; → **single**; ☰ **round trip** AmE: a return ticket | a return fare

re·turn·a·ble /rɪˈtɜːnəbəl $ -ɜːr-/ adj **1** something that is returnable can be taken back to a shop and used again; ☰ **non-returnable 2** an amount of money that is returnable will be given back to you later; ☰ **refundable**; ☰ **non-returnable**: a returnable deposit of £50

re·turn ad·dress / $.ˌ. ˈ../ n [C] the address of the person who is sending a letter or package, that is written on the envelope or package

re·tur·nee /rɪˌtɜːˈniː $ -ˌtɜːˈriː/ n [C] a person who returns to their own country after living in another country

re·turn·er /rɪˈtɜːnə $ -ˈtɜːrnər/ n [C] BrE someone who goes back to work after a long time away, especially a woman who left work to look after her children

re·turn·ing ·officer n [C] the official in each town or area of Britain who arranges an election to Parliament and announces the result

re·turn ·match n [C] BrE the second of two matches that are played by the same teams or players

re·turn ·visit n [C] a visit to someone who has visited you, or to a place where you have been before

re·u·ni·fy /riːˈjuːnɪˌfaɪ/ v reunified, reunifying, reunifies [T] to join the parts of something together again, especially a country that was divided —**reunification** /riːˌjuːnɪˌfɪˈkeɪʃən/ n [U]: German reunification → REUNITE

re·u·nion /riːˈjuːnjən/ n 1 [C] a social meeting of people who have not met for a long time, especially people who were at school or college together: an **annual reunion** | a **family reunion** | a high-school reunion 2 [U] when people are brought together again after a period of being separated: [+with] Joseph's eventual reunion with his brother

re·u·nite /ˌriːjuːˈnaɪt/ v [I,T usually passive] to come together again or to bring people, parts of an organization, political party, or country together again: **be reunited with sb** The children were finally reunited with their families. | The band will reunite for a US tour.

re·use /ˌriːˈjuːz/ v [T] to use something again: The bottles are designed to be reused up to 20 times. —**reusable** /reusable containers —**reuse** /ˌriːˈjuːs/ n [U]: to purify water for reuse

rev[1] /rev/ v revved, revving [I,T] also **rev up** if you rev an engine, or if an engine revs, you make it work faster
  rev up phr v informal if you rev up a system or organization, or if it revs up, it becomes more active: [+for] They are revving up for one of the biggest fund-raising events ever organized. | **rev sth** ⇔ **up** Investors keep putting money in U.S. companies, revving up the economy even more.

rev[2] n [C] informal a complete turn of a wheel or engine part, used as a unit for measuring the speed of an engine; 🔲 revolution

Rev BrE; **Rev.** AmE also **Revd** BrE Reverend a title used before the name of a minister of the Christian church: Rev D Macleod

re·val·ue /ˌriːˈvæljuː/ v [T usually passive] 1 to examine something again in order to calculate its present value: The company's land has been revalued at £16.9m. 2 to increase the value of a country's money in relation to that of other countries; 🔲 devalue: The dollar has just been revalued. —**revaluation** /riːˌvæljuˈeɪʃən/ n [C,U]

re·vamp /riːˈvæmp/ v [T] informal to change something in order to improve it and make it seem more modern: Many older companies are revamping their image. —**revamp** /ˈriːvæmp/ also revamping n [C]

Revd a British form of REV

re·veal[S3][W1] /rɪˈviːl/ v [T]
  1 to make known something that was previously secret or unknown; 🔲 conceal: He may be prosecuted for revealing secrets about the security agency. | a test that can reveal a teacher's hidden skills | **reveal (that)** He revealed that he had been in prison twice before. | **reveal yourself (as/to be sth)** The violinist revealed himself as a talented interpreter of classical music.
  2 to show something that was previously hidden; 🔲 conceal: The curtain opened to reveal the grand prize.

re·veal·ing /rɪˈviːlɪŋ/ adj 1 a remark or event that is revealing shows you something interesting or surprising about a situation or someone's character: a revealing insight into her life 2 revealing clothes allow parts of your body to be seen which are usually kept covered; → low-cut: a very revealing dress —**revealingly** adv

re·veil·le /rɪˈvæli $ ˈrevəli/ n [singular,U] a special tune played as a signal to wake soldiers in the morning, or the time at which it is played

rev·el /ˈrevəl/ v revelled, revelling BrE, reveled, reveling AmE [I] old use to spend time dancing, eating, drinking etc, especially at a party —**revel** n [C usually plural]
  revel in sth phr v to enjoy something very much: He revelled in his new-found fame.

rev·e·la·tion /ˌrevəˈleɪʃən/ n 1 [C] a surprising fact about someone or something that was previously

secret and is now made known: [+about/concerning] He resigned after revelations about his affair. | **startling revelations** about his background | **revelation that** revelations that two senior officers had lied in court 2 [U] the act of suddenly making known a surprising fact that had previously been secret: [+of] the revelation of previously unknown facts 3 [C] informal something that is surprisingly good, enjoyable, or useful: [+to] Alice Walker's novel was a real revelation to me. 4 [C,U] an event, experience etc that is considered to be a message from God —**revelatory** /ˌrevəˈleɪtəri $ ˈrevələtɔːri/ adj: His playing has many moments of revelatory insights.

rev·el·ler BrE; **reveler** AmE /ˈrevələ $ -lər/ n [C usually plural] someone who is having fun singing, dancing etc in a noisy way

rev·el·ry /ˈrevəlri/ n [U] also **revelries** [plural] wild noisy dancing, eating, drinking etc, usually to celebrate something; → celebration

re·venge[1] /rɪˈvendʒ/ n [U] 1 something you do in order to punish someone who has harmed or offended you: **get/have/take (your) revenge (on sb)** He took revenge on his employers by setting fire to the factory. | [+for] She is **seeking revenge** for the murder of her husband. | **in revenge for sth** a bomb attack in revenge for the imprisonment of the terrorists | The murder was an **act of revenge** for the earlier killings. | **revenge attacks** on British troops 2 the defeat of someone who has previously defeated you in a sport: [+for] The Australians **took revenge** for their defeat here last time. | a revenge match —**revengeful** adj

revenge[2] v [T] formal to punish someone who has done something to harm you or someone else: **revenge yourself on sb** The terrorist group is still looking to revenge itself on its attackers. | The poor murdered girl must be revenged.

rev·e·nue[W2] /ˈrevəˌnjuː $ -nuː/ n [U] also **revenues** 1 money that a business or organization receives over a period of time, especially from selling goods or services; → income: advertising revenue | Strikes have cost £20 million in lost revenues. 2 money that the government receives from tax: an increase in **tax revenues** of 8.4% → INLAND REVENUE, INTERNAL REVENUE SERVICE

re·ver·be·rate /rɪˈvɜːbəreɪt $ -ɜːr-/ v [I] 1 if a loud sound reverberates, it is heard many times as it is sent back from different surfaces; 🔲 echo: [+through/around etc] The bang reverberated through the house. 2 if a room, building etc reverberates, it seems to shake because of a loud sound: [+with] The room reverberated with laughter. 3 if an event, action, or idea reverberates, it has a strong effect over a wide area and for a long time: [+through/around etc] The traumas of the last week will reverberate through history.

re·ver·be·ra·tion /rɪˌvɜːbəˈreɪʃən $ -ɜːr-/ n 1 [C usually plural] a severe effect that is caused by a particular event and continues for a long time; 🔲 repercussion: the scandal's political reverberations 2 [C,U] a loud sound that is heard again and again as it is sent back from different surfaces; → echo

re·vere /rɪˈvɪə $ -ˈvɪr/ v [T usually passive] formal to respect and admire someone or something very much: **be revered as sth** He is revered as a national hero.

rev·e·rence /ˈrevərəns/ n [U] formal great respect and admiration for someone or something: [+for] reverence for tradition

rev·e·rend /ˈrevərənd/ n [C] a minister of a Christian church

Reverend n a title of respect used before the name of a minister in the Christian church

Reverend Mother n a title of respect for the woman in charge of a CONVENT; 🔲 Mother Superior

R

1 000, 2 000, 3 000, most frequent words in S poken and W ritten English

rev·e·rent /'revərənt/ adj formal showing a lot of respect and admiration; ⚡ **irreverent**: *a hushed reverent voice* —**reverently** adv

rev·e·ren·tial /ˌrevə'renʃəl◂/ adj formal showing a lot of respect and admiration: *He spoke in reverential tones.* —**reverentially** adv

rev·e·rie /'revəri/ n [C,U] a state of imagining or thinking about pleasant things, that is like dreaming; → **daydream**: *She was startled out of her reverie by a loud crash.*

re·vers·al /rɪ'vɜːsəl $ -ɜːr-/ n 1 [C,U] a change to an opposite arrangement, process, or way of doing something; → **turnaround**: [+of/in] *a sudden reversal of government policy* | **dramatic/sudden/complete reversal** *a dramatic reversal in population decline* | *Some Internet firms have suffered a painful* **reversal of fortune** (=they were successful but now they are not). | *Some carers and dependants find it difficult to adapt to a* **role reversal**. 2 [C] a failure or other problem that prevents you from being able to do what you want: *In spite of setbacks and reversals, his business was at last making money.*

re·verse¹ /rɪ'vɜːs $ -ɜːrs/ v
1 **OPPOSITE** [T] to change something, such as a decision, judgment, or process so that it is the opposite of what it was before: **reverse a decision/verdict/policy etc** *The decision was reversed on appeal.* | **reverse a trend/process/decline etc** *More changes are required to reverse the trend towards centralised power.*
2 **CAR** [I,T] *especially BrE* if a vehicle or its driver reverses, they go backwards; ⊟ **back up** *AmE*: [+out of/into etc] *Bob reversed into a parking space.* | **reverse sth into/out of sth** *I reversed the car into a side road.*
3 **CHANGE POSITION/PURPOSE** [T] to change around the usual order of the parts of something, or the usual things two people do: **reverse roles/positions** *Our roles as child and guardian had now been reversed.*
4 **TURN STH OVER** [T] to turn something over or around, in order to show the back of it: *Reverse the paper in the printer.*
5 **reverse yourself** *AmE* to change your opinion or position in an argument: *Suddenly, he reversed himself completely.*
6 **reverse the charges** *BrE* to make a telephone call which is paid for by the person you are telephoning; ⊟ **call collect** *AmE*

reverse² n
1 **OPPOSITE** **the reverse** the exact opposite of what has just been mentioned: **quite/just/precisely/exactly the opposite** *I didn't mean to insult her – quite the reverse* (=in fact, I meant to praise her). | *I owe you nothing. If anything,* **the reverse is true** (=you owe me).
2 **in reverse** in the opposite way to normal or to the previous situation; → **vice versa**: *US video recorders cannot play European tapes, and the same applies in reverse.*
3 **go into reverse/put sth into reverse** to start to happen or to make something happen in the opposite way: *The incident threatened to put the peace process into reverse.*
4 **CAR** [U] the position of the GEARS in a vehicle that makes it go backwards: **into/in reverse** *Put the car into reverse.*
5 **DEFEAT** [C] *formal* a defeat or a problem that delays your plans; ⊟ **setback**: *Losing the Senate vote was a serious reverse for the President.*
6 **OTHER SIDE** [singular] the less important side or the back of an object that has two sides: **on the reverse** *The British ten-pence coin has a lion on the reverse.*

reverse³ adj [only before noun] 1 **reverse order/situation/process etc** the opposite order etc to what is usual or to what has just been stated: *The results were read out in reverse order* (=with the worst first and the best last). 2 **the reverse side** the back of something

re·verse discrimi·na·tion n [U] the practice of giving unfair treatment to a group of people who usually have advantages, in order to be fair to the group of people who were unfairly treated in the past; → **positive discrimination**

re·verse engi·neering n [U] *technical* a situation in which a product is examined to see how it is made, so that it can be copied —**reverse engineer** v [T]

re·verse gear n [C,U] the position of the GEARS in a vehicle that makes it go backwards

re·vers·i·ble /rɪ'vɜːsˌbəl $ -ɜːr-/ adj 1 a change that is reversible can be changed back to how it was before; ⚡ **irreversible**: *A lot of chemical reactions are reversible.* 2 a piece of clothing or material that is reversible can be worn with either side showing on the outside: *a reversible jacket*

re·versing light n [C] *BrE* a light on the back of a car which comes on when the car is going backwards; → **tail-light**; → see picture at CAR

re·ver·sion /rɪ'vɜːʃən $ rɪ'vɜːrʒən/ n [singular,U] *formal* 1 a return to a former condition or habit: [+to] *the country's reversion to a traditional monarchy* 2 *law* the return of property to a former owner

re·vert /rɪ'vɜːt $ -ɜːrt/ v
revert to sb/sth *phr v* 1 to change back to a situation that existed in the past; ⊟ **go back to**: *The city reverted to its former name of St Petersburg.* | *After a few weeks, everything* **reverted to normal**. 2 *formal* to return to an earlier subject of conversation; ⊟ **go back to**: *To revert to the question of exams, I'd like to explain further.* 3 *law* if land or a building reverts to its former owner, it becomes their property again

re·vet·ment /rɪ'vetmənt/ n [C] *technical* a surface of stone or other building material added for strength to a wall that holds back loose earth, water etc

re·view¹ [S3] [W2] /rɪ'vjuː/ n
1 [C,U] a careful examination of a situation or process; → **evaluation**, **analysis**: [+of] *She sent us her review of the research.* | **carry out/conduct/undertake a review** *The company hired Bob to conduct an independent review of their workplace procedures.* | **review body/committee/panel/board** *the Teachers' Pay Review Body* | **under review** *We're keeping this policy under review* (=we are continuing to examine it). | *The policy* **comes up for review** (=will be reviewed) *in April.* | *All fees are* **subject to review** (=may be reviewed). | *Mr Crowther asked for* **judicial review** *of the decision* (=an examination of the decision by a judge).
2 [C] an article in a newspaper or magazine that gives an opinion about a new book, play, film etc: *a film review* | [+of] *The paper published a review of her book.* | **good/bad/mixed review** *The band's new album has had very good reviews.* | *The film opened to* **rave reviews** (=reviews that praised it a lot). → see box at CRITIC
3 [U] the work of writing reviews for a newspaper or magazine: **for review** *The book was sent to the press for review in September.* | *The journal receives* **review copies** (=free copies to review) *of most new software products.*
4 [C] a report on a series of events or a period of time, that mentions the most important parts: [+of] *a review of the year*
5 [C] an official show of the army, navy etc so that a king, president, or officer of high rank can see them: *a naval review*

review² [W3] v [T]
1 to examine, consider, and judge a situation or process carefully in order to see if changes are necessary; → **evaluate**, **analyse**: *We will review your situation and decide how we can help you.* | *The decision will be reviewed by the Supreme Court.* | *The team manager's position will be reviewed at the end of the season.*
2 to write a short article describing and judging a new book, play, film etc: *Bradman will review the best of the new children's books.*
3 *AmE* to look again at something you have studied, such as notes, reports etc; ⊟ **revise** *BrE*
4 to examine and describe the most important parts of

a series of events or period of time: *a journalist who will review the events of the past six months*
5 to officially watch a group of soldiers, ships etc at a military show: *The President will review the soldiers on parade.*

re·view·er /rɪ'vju:ə $ -ər/ n [C] someone who writes about new books, plays, films etc in a newspaper or magazine; ◨ **critic**

re·vile /rɪ'vaɪl/ v [T] *written* to express hatred of someone or something; ◨ **hate**: *The President was now reviled by the same party he had helped to lead.*

re·vise /rɪ'vaɪz/ v **1** [T] to change something because of new information or ideas: *The college has revised its plans because of local objections.* | *We have revised our estimates of population growth.* | **revise sth upwards/downwards** *Forecasts of economic growth are being revised downwards.* **2** [I,T] *BrE* to study facts again, in order to learn them before an examination; ◨ **review, study** *AmE*: *I've got to revise my geography.* | [+for] *She's revising for her history exam.* **3** [T] to change a piece of writing by adding new information, making improvements, or correcting mistakes; → **amend**: *A couple of sections of the book will need to be revised.*

re·vi·sion /rɪ'vɪʒən/ n **1** [C,U] the process of changing something in order to improve it by correcting it or including new information or ideas; → **amendment**: [+of] *The judge wants to see a revision of the procedures.* | [+to] *I'm making some revisions to the book for the new edition.* **2** [C] a piece of writing that has been improved and corrected **3** [U] *BrE* the work of studying facts again in order to learn them: *I know I haven't done enough revision for tomorrow's exam.*

re·vi·sion·is·m /rɪ'vɪʒənɪzəm/ n [U] ideas which are changing away from the main beliefs of a political system, especially a Marxist system —**revisionist** *adj*: *revisionist writings* —**revisionist** n [C]

re·vis·it /ˌri:'vɪzɪt/ v [T] **1** *written* to return to a place you once knew well: *Ten years later, I revisited the school to find out what had changed.* **2** *formal* to consider or discuss something again: *We need to revisit this proposal as soon as the budget is clearer.*

re·vi·tal·ize also **-ise** *BrE* /ri:'vaɪtəlaɪz/ v [T] to put new strength or power into something; → **revive**: *They hope to revitalize the neighborhood by providing better housing.* | *a revitalizing massage* —**revitalization** /ri:ˌvaɪtəlaɪ'zeɪʃən $ -tl-ə-/ n [U]

re·vi·val /rɪ'vaɪvəl/ n **1** [C,U] a process in which something becomes active or strong again: *The US and the UK have expectations of economic revival.* | [+of] *A revival of the timber industry is needed.* | *There has been a revival of interest in Picasso's work.* **2** [C,U] when something becomes popular again: [+of/in] *the recent revival in medieval music* | *a revival of organized religion* | *Traditional English food seems to be enjoying a revival at the moment.* **3** [C] a new production of a play that has not been performed for a long time: *Neeson was excellent in a revival of Eugene O'Neill's 'Anna Christie'.* **4** [C] a REVIVAL MEETING

re·vi·val·is·m /rɪ'vaɪvəlɪzəm/ n [U] organized attempts to make a religion more popular —**revivalist** *adj*

re'vival ˌmeeting n [C] a public religious meeting with music, famous speakers etc, which is intended to make people interested in Christianity

re·vive /rɪ'vaɪv/ v **1** [T] to bring something back after it has not been used or has not existed for a period of time: *Local people have decided to revive this centuries-old tradition.* **2** [I,T] to become healthy and strong again, or to make someone or something healthy and strong again; → **recover**: *The economy is beginning to revive.* | *an attempt to revive the steel industry* | *The doctors revived her with injections of glucose.* **3** [T] to produce a play again after it has not been performed for a long time: *A London theatre has decided to revive the 1950s musical 'In Town'.*

re·viv·i·fy /ri:'vɪvɪfaɪ/ v **revivified, revivifying, revivifies** [T] *formal* to give new life and health to someone or something: *The aim was to strengthen and revivify the Labour Party.*

rev·o·ca·tion /ˌrevə'keɪʃən/ n [C,U] *formal* the act of revoking a law, decision, or agreement; → **revoke**

re·voke /rɪ'vəʊk $ -'vouk/ v [T] to officially state that a law, decision, or agreement is no longer effective; → **revocation**: *Their work permits have been revoked.*

re·volt¹ /rɪ'vəʊlt $ -'voult/ n [C,U] **1** a refusal to accept someone's authority or obey rules or laws; ◨ **rebellion**: *The prime minister is now facing a revolt by members of his own party.* | [+against] *a revolt against authority* | [+over] *a revolt over the proposed spending cuts* | **in revolt** *French farmers are in revolt over cheap imports.* **2** strong and often violent action by a lot of people against their ruler or government; ◨ **rebellion;** → **revolution**: *the Polish revolt of 1863* | [+against] *a revolt against the central government* | [+of] *the successful revolt of the American colonies* | **put down/crush a revolt** (=use military force to stop it) *Troops loyal to the President crushed the revolt.*

revolt² v **1** [I] if people revolt, they take strong and often violent action against the government, usually with the aim of taking power away from them; ◨ **rebel;** → **revolution:** [+against] *It was feared that the army would revolt against the government.* **2** [I] to refuse to accept someone's authority or obey rules or laws; ◨ **rebel:** [+against] *Some members of the government may revolt against this proposed legislation.* **3** [T usually passive] if something revolts you, it is so unpleasant that it makes you feel sick and shocked; → **revulsion:** *He was revolted by the smell.*

re·volt·ing /rɪ'vəʊltɪŋ $ -'voul-/ *adj* extremely unpleasant; ◨ **disgusting:** *The food was revolting!* | *What a revolting colour!* —**revoltingly** *adv*

rev·o·lu·tion S3 W2 /ˌrevə'lu:ʃən/ n **1 CHANGE** [C] a complete change in ways of thinking, methods of working etc: [+in] *In the last ten years there has been a revolution in education.* | **social/cultural/sexual etc revolution** *the biggest social revolution we have had in this country* | *the sexual revolution of the 1960s* → INDUSTRIAL REVOLUTION **2 POLITICAL CHANGE** [C,U] a time when people change a ruler or political system by using force or violence; → **revolt, rebellion:** *the French Revolution of 1789* | *The role of women has changed since the revolution.* | *The country seems to be heading towards revolution.* → COUNTER-REVOLUTION **3 CIRCULAR MOVEMENT a)** [C,U] a circular movement around something; → **revolve:** [+around] *the planets' revolution around the sun* **b)** [C] one complete circular spinning movement, made by something such as a wheel attached to a central point; → **revolve:** *a speed of 100 revolutions per minute*

rev·o·lu·tion·a·ry¹ /ˌrevə'lu:ʃənəri◂ $ -ʃəneri◂/ *adj* **1** completely new and different, especially in a way that leads to great improvements: *The new cancer drug is a revolutionary breakthrough.* | *a revolutionary new drug* **2** [only before noun] relating to a political or social revolution: *a revolutionary leader*

revolutionary² n *plural* **revolutionaries** [C] someone who joins in or supports a political or social revolution; → **rebel:** *a band of young revolutionaries*

rev·o·lu·tion·ize also **-ise** *BrE* /ˌrevə'lu:ʃənaɪz/ v [T] to completely change the way people do something or think about something: *New technology is going to revolutionize everything we do.* | *His work revolutionized the treatment of this disease.*

re·volve /rɪ'vɒlv $ rɪ'vɑ:lv/ v [I,T] to move around like a wheel, or to make something move around like a wheel; → **revolution, turn:** *The wheel began to revolve.* | *The restaurant slowly revolves, giving excellent views of the city.* | *Using graphics software, you can revolve the image on the screen.*

R

revolve around sb/sth also **revolve round sb/sth** BrE phr v **1** [not in progressive] to have something as a main subject or purpose: *Jane's life revolves around her children.* | *The argument revolved around costs.* | *She seems to think that the world revolves around her* (=that she is the only important person). **2** to move in circles around something: *The moon revolves around the Earth.*

re·volv·er /rɪ'vɒlvə $ rɪ'vɑːlvər/ n [C] a type of small gun. The bullets are in a case which turns around as you fire the gun, so that when you fire one bullet the next bullet is ready to be fired; → **handgun, pistol**

re·volv·ing /rɪ'vɒlvɪŋ $ -'vɑːl-/ adj a revolving object is designed so that it turns with a circular movement: *The theatre has a revolving stage.*

re,volving 'door n **1** [C] a type of door in the entrance of a large building, which goes around and around as people go through it **2** [singular] used to say that the people involved in a situation, organization etc change often: *The park director position has been a revolving door for seven appointees.* **3** [singular] used to say that people return to a situation, position etc often, but usually for a different reason: *This could mean that we end up with a revolving door Congress, in which former members return as lobbyists.*

re·vue /rɪ'vjuː/ n [C] a show in a theatre that includes songs, dances, and jokes about recent events

re·vul·sion /rɪ'vʌlʃən/ n [U] a strong feeling of shock and very strong dislike; ⊟ **disgust**; → **revolt**: *News of the atrocities produced a wave of anger and revulsion.*

re·ward[1] W3 /rɪ'wɔːd $ -'wɔːrd/ n
1 [C,U] something that you get because you have done something good or helpful or have worked hard; → **prize, benefit**: *The school has a system of rewards and punishments to encourage good behaviour.* | **reward for (doing) sth** *Several of the parents were giving their children rewards for passing exams.* | **economic/financial reward** *The job is difficult, but the financial rewards are great.* | *She began to **reap** (=get) **the rewards** of all her hard work.* | *Success brings its own rewards.*
2 [C,U] money that is offered to people for helping the police to solve a crime or catch a criminal: **[+of]** *A reward of $20,000 has been offered.* | **[+for]** *a reward for information leading to the capture of the murderers*

reward[2] v [T] **1** to give something to someone because they have done something good or helpful or have worked for it; → **award**: **reward sb with sth** *The club's directors rewarded him with a free season ticket.* | **reward sb for (doing) sth** *She wanted to reward the cleaners for their efforts.* | *He gave the children some chocolate to reward them for behaving well.* **2** **be rewarded (with sth)** to achieve something through hard work and effort: *The team have worked hard and their efforts have been rewarded with success.* | *Finally, Molly's patience was rewarded.*

re·ward·ing /rɪ'wɔːdɪŋ $ -ɔːr-/ adj making you feel happy and satisfied because you feel you are doing something useful or important, even if you do not earn much money; → **satisfying, worthwhile**: *Teaching can be a very rewarding career.*

re·wind /riː'waɪnd/ v past tense and past participle **rewound** /-'waʊnd/ [T] to make a CASSETTE tape or VIDEO go backwards in order to see or hear it again; → **fast forward**

re·wire /ˌriː'waɪə $ -'waɪr/ v [T] to put new electric wires in a building, machine, light etc

re·word /ˌriː'wɜːd $ -'wɜːrd/ v [T] to say or write something again in different words, in order to make it easier to understand or more suitable; ⊟ **rephrase**: *Let me reword my question.*

re·work /ˌriː'wɜːk $ -'wɜːrk/ v [T] to make changes in something such as music or a piece of writing; ⊟ **revise**: *I plan to rework the whole song.*

re·write /ˌriː'raɪt/ v past tense **rewrote** /-'rəʊt $ -'roʊt/, past participle **rewritten** /-'rɪtn/ [T] to change something that has been written, especially in order to improve it, or because new information is available; ⊟ **revise**: *I'll have to rewrite most of the essay.* —**rewrite** /'riːraɪt/ n [C]: *Software packages may need complete rewrites to match new hardware.*

Rex /reks/ n BrE **1** a title used in official writing after the name of a king, when the king's name has been written in Latin: *Henricus Rex* (=King Henry) **2** law a word meaning the state, used in the names of law cases in Britain when a king is ruling; → **regina**: *Rex v Jones*

rhap·so·dize also **-ise** BrE /'ræpsədaɪz/ v [I] formal to talk about something in an eager, excited, and approving way; ⊟ **enthuse**: **[+about/over]** *I could hear Sophie rhapsodizing about her new job.*

rhap·so·dy /'ræpsədi/ n plural **rhapsodies** [C] **1** a piece of music that is written to express emotion, and does not have a regular form: *Gershwin's Rhapsody in Blue* **2** formal an expression of eager and excited approval: *The performance was greeted with rhapsodies of praise.*

Rhe·sus fac·tor /'riːsəs ˌfæktə $ -tər/ n [singular] a substance that some people have in their blood

rhesus mon·key /'riːsəs ˌmʌŋki/ n [C] a small monkey from northern India that is often used in medical tests

rhet·o·ric /'retərɪk/ n [U] **1** language that is used to persuade or influence people, especially language that sounds impressive but is not actually sincere or useful: *The speech was dismissed by some people as merely political rhetoric.* | **[+of]** *the rhetoric of socialism* **2** the art of speaking or writing to persuade or influence people

rhe·tor·i·cal /rɪ'tɒrɪkəl $ -'tɔː-, -'tɑː-/ adj **1** **rhetorical question** a question that you ask as a way of making a statement, without expecting an answer **2** using speech or writing in special ways in order to persuade people or to produce an impressive effect: *a speech full of rhetorical phrases* —**rhetorically** /-kli/ adv

rhet·o·ri·cian /ˌretə'rɪʃən/ n [C] formal someone who is trained or skilful in the art of persuading or influencing people through speech or writing; → **orator**

rheu·mat·ic /ruː'mætɪk/ adj **1** relating to rheumatism: *a rheumatic disease* | *rheumatic pain* **2** old-fashioned suffering from rheumatism: *He's old and rheumatic and can't manage the stairs any longer.*

rheu,matic 'fever n [U] a serious infectious disease that causes fever, swelling in your joints, and sometimes damage to your heart

rheu·ma·tis·m /'ruːmətɪzəm/ n [U] a disease that makes your joints or muscles painful and stiff; → **arthritis**

rheu·ma·toid ar·thri·tis /ˌruːmətɔɪd ɑː'θraɪtɪs $ -ɑːr-/ n [U] a disease that continues for many years and makes your joints painful and stiff, and often makes them lose their proper shape

RH fac·tor /ˌɑːr 'eɪtʃ ˌfæktə $ -tər/ n [singular] the RHESUS FACTOR

rhine·stone /'raɪnstəʊn $ -stoʊn/ n [C,U] a jewel made from glass or a transparent rock that is intended to look like a diamond

rhi·no /'raɪnəʊ $ -noʊ/ n plural **rhinos** [C] informal a rhinoceros

rhi·no·ce·ros /raɪ'nɒsərəs $ -'nɑː-/ n plural **rhinoceros** or **rhinoceroses** [C] a large heavy African or Asian animal with thick skin and either one or two horns on its nose; → **hippopotamus**

rhi·no·plas·ty /'raɪnəʊˌplæsti $ -noʊ-/ n [U] medical PLASTIC SURGERY on your nose; → **nose job**

rhi·zome /'raɪzəʊm $ -zoʊm/ n [C] technical the thick stem of some plants, which lies under the ground and has roots and leaves growing out of it

rho·do·den·dron /ˌrəʊdə'dendrən $ ˌroʊ-/ n [C] a bush with bright flowers which keeps its leaves in winter

rhom·boid¹ /ˈrɒmbɔɪd $ ˈrɑːm-/ n [C] technical a shape with four sides whose opposite sides are equal in length; ▤ **parallelogram**

rhom·boid² also **rhom·boid·al** /rɒmˈbɔɪdl $ rɑːm-/ adj technical shaped like a rhombus

rhom·bus /ˈrɒmbəs $ ˈrɑːm-/ n [C] technical a shape with four equal straight sides, especially one that is not a square

rhu·barb /ˈruːbɑːb $ -ɑːrb/ n [U] **1** a plant with broad leaves. It has thick red stems that can be cooked and eaten. **2** spoken a word repeated by actors to make a sound like many people talking

rhyme¹ /raɪm/ n **1** [C] a short poem or song, especially for children, using words that rhyme: a collection of traditional rhymes with illustrations → NURSERY RHYME **2** [C] a word that rhymes with another word: [+for] Can you think of a rhyme for 'bicycle'? **3** [U] words or lines of poetry that rhyme: I love his use of rhyme and rhythm. | in rhyme The whole story is written in rhyme. **4 no rhyme or reason** no sensible reason or organization: There seems to be no rhyme or reason for the school's behaviour.

rhyme² v [not in progressive] **1** [I] if two words or lines of poetry rhyme, they end with the same sound, including a vowel: [+with] 'Hat' rhymes with 'cat'. | The song has **rhyming couplets** (=pairs of lines that end in words that rhyme). **2** [T] to put two or more words together to make them rhyme: **rhyme sth with sth** You can't rhyme 'box' with 'backs'.

rhyming 'slang n [U] BrE a way of talking, used especially by COCKNEYS (=people from east London), in which you use words or phrases that rhyme with the words you mean, instead of using the normal words. For example, 'plates of meat' is rhyming slang for 'feet'.

rhyth·m /ˈrɪðəm/ n [C,U] **1** a regular repeated pattern of sounds or movements; → **metre**: Drums are basic to African rhythm. | complicated dance rhythms | [+of] She started moving to the rhythm of the music. | the steady rhythm of her heartbeat **2** a regular pattern of changes: the body's natural rhythms | [+of] Jim liked the rhythm of agricultural life.

rhythm and 'blues n [U] R & B (=a type of popular music)

rhyth·mic /ˈrɪðmɪk/ also **rhyth·mic·al** /-mɪkəl/ adj having a strong rhythm: the rhythmic thud of the bass drum —**rhythmically** /-kli/ adv

rhythm ,method n [singular] a method of BIRTH CONTROL which depends on having sex only at a time when the woman is not likely to become PREGNANT

rhythm ,section n [C] the part of a band that provides a strong RHYTHM with drums and other similar instruments; → **percussion**

ri·al, riyal /riˈɑːl $ riˈɒːl, -ˈɑːl/ n [C] the standard unit of money in Saudi Arabia and some other Arab countries

rib¹ /rɪb/ n [C] **1** one of the 12 pairs of curved bones that surround your chest: She was taken to hospital with a broken arm and ribs. | He was punched and kicked in the ribs. → see picture at SKELETON **2** a piece of meat that includes an animal's ribs: a rib of beef | barbecued ribs → SPARE RIBS **3** a curved piece of wood, metal etc that is used as part of the structure of something such as a boat or building

rib² v **ribbed, ribbing** [T] informal to make jokes and laugh at someone so that you embarrass them, but in a friendly way; ▤ **tease**

rib·ald /ˈrɪbəld/ adj ribald remarks or jokes are humorous, rude, and about sex: a ribald remark | ribald humour

rib·ald·ry /ˈrɪbəldri/ n [U] ribald remarks or jokes

ribbed /rɪbd/ adj something that is ribbed has raised lines on it: a ribbed woollen sweater

rib·bing /ˈrɪbɪŋ/ n [U] **1** friendly jokes and laughter about someone: He took a lot of ribbing from other members of the crew. **2** raised lines, especially on a piece of woollen clothing

rib·bon /ˈrɪbən/ n
1 PIECE OF CLOTH [C,U] a narrow piece of attractive cloth that you use, for example, to tie your hair or hold things together; → **bow**: little girls with ribbons in their hair | a bundle of letters tied with pale blue ribbon | The ribbon was cut and the new station was officially open.
2 MILITARY HONOUR [C] a piece of ribbon with a special pattern on it that you wear to show that you have received a military honour
3 PRIZE [C] AmE a length of coloured ribbon, sometimes arranged in the form of a flat flower, that is given as a prize in a competition; ▤ **rosette** BrE: For the second time she won the **blue ribbon** (=first prize).
4 STH NARROW [singular] written something that is long and narrow: [+of] a winding ribbon of water
5 be cut/torn to ribbons to be cut or torn in a lot of places: Her legs were bruised and her feet were cut to ribbons.
6 INK [C] a long narrow piece of cloth or plastic with ink on it that is used in a TYPEWRITER

ribbon de,velopment n [C,U] BrE long lines of houses along the sides of a main road leading out of a town or city

rib cage n [C] the structure of RIBS in your chest

ri·bo·fla·vin /ˌraɪbəʊˈfleɪvɪn $ ˌraɪbə-/ n [U] technical VITAMIN B2, a substance that exists in meat, milk, and some vegetables, and that is important for your health

rice /raɪs/ n [U] **1** a food that consists of small white or brown grains that you boil in water until they become soft enough to eat; → **risotto, pilau**: a tasty sauce served with rice or pasta | a plate of **brown rice** | Serve with plain **boiled rice**. | a few **grains of rice** **2** the plant that produces rice: Rice is the main crop grown in the area. | rice fields

rice ,paddy plural **rice paddies** n [C] a field in which rice is grown

rice ,paper n [U] **1** a type of thin paper that is made especially in China and used by painters there **2** a type of thin paper that can be eaten and is used in cooking

rice 'pudding n [U] a sweet dish made of rice, milk, and sugar cooked together

rich S2 W2 /rɪtʃ/ adj comparative **richer**, superlative **richest**
1 WEALTHY **a)** someone who is rich has a lot of money and valuable possessions; ▤ **poor**: one of the richest women in America | She found herself a rich husband. | He thought this was the easiest way to **get rich**. | the rich nations of the world | **fabulously rich** BrE: She was both beautiful and fabulously rich. | His brother's **stinking rich** (=very rich, in a way that you do not approve of). **b)** the rich [plural] people who are rich: houses belonging to the rich and famous
2 LARGE AMOUNT containing a lot of something: [+in] Citrus fruits are rich in vitamin C. | **oxygen-rich/ nutrient-rich/protein-rich etc** Pregnant women should eat protein-rich foods. | Rich mineral deposits have been found in the sea bed. | Red meat is a **rich source** of iron.
3 FULL OF INTEREST full of interesting or important facts, events, or ideas: the rich literary tradition of England | The area has a very rich history. | [+in] a story that was rich in detail
4 FOOD rich food contains a lot of butter, cream, or eggs, which make you feel full very quickly; ▤ **light**: a rich fruit cake | The sauce was very rich.
5 SMELL/FLAVOUR a rich smell or flavour is strong and pleasant: the rich scent of the pine trees | meat with a wonderfully rich flavour | a rich, fruity wine
6 COLOUR a rich colour is strong and attractive: a rich dark brown colour
7 SOUND a rich sound is low and pleasant: the rich tone of a cello | He laughed with a rich, throaty chuckle.
8 SOIL rich soil is good for growing plants in; ▤ **poor**: Vegetables grow well in the rich, black soil.

R

9 CLOTH rich cloth is expensive and beautiful: *She stroked the rich velvet of the dress enviously.*

10 that's rich (coming from him/you etc) *BrE spoken* used to say that what someone has said is unreasonable and that they are criticizing you for doing something that they do themselves: *He accused me of being dishonest, which was a bit rich coming from him.*

WORD CHOICE: rich, well-off, wealthy, affluent, prosperous

Rich is a very direct way of saying that someone has a lot of money and possessions: *one of the richest women in America*

Well-off means fairly rich, so you can buy most things. People are more likely to describe themselves as 'well-off' than 'rich': *My parents were pretty well-off.*

Wealthy is a slightly more formal word meaning rich, especially over a long period of time: *He came from a wealthy family.*

Affluent and **prosperous** are fairly formal words, often used to describe societies where the economy is successful and the standard of living is good.

Affluent means rich enough to have things like expensive cars and holidays: *People are becoming increasingly affluent.*

Prosperous means rich and successful: *the more prosperous regions of the country*

R

rich·es /'rɪtʃɪz/ *n* [plural] *literary* expensive possessions and large amounts of money; ▤ **wealth**: *He was enjoying his new-found riches.* | *the story of her rise from rags to riches* (=from being poor to being rich)

rich·ly /'rɪtʃli/ *adv* **1** if something is richly decorated, it is decorated a lot, in a way that is beautiful: *a richly carved ceiling* | *a cloak richly embroidered with gold thread* **2** if someone is richly dressed, they are dressed in expensive clothes **3 richly coloured** having beautiful strong colours: *the richly coloured mosaic* **4 richly flavoured/scented** having a strong pleasant taste or smell: *richly scented flowers* **5 richly deserve** to completely deserve something such as success or punishment: *They got the punishment they so richly deserved.* **6** containing large amounts of something: *a richly wooded valley* | *an area that is richly endowed with wildlife* **7 richly rewarding** giving you a strong feeling of pleasure: *It was a richly rewarding relationship.*

rich·ness /'rɪtʃnɪs/ *n* [U] **1** if something has richness, it contains a lot of interesting things: [+of] *the richness and diversity of the Amazonian rainforests* | *a literary work of remarkable richness and vitality* **2** the richness of a colour, taste, smell, or sound is the quality that makes it rich: [+of] *the richness of the autumn colours*

Rich·ter scale /'rɪktə ˌskeɪl, 'rɪx- $ -tər-/ *n* **the Richter scale** a system of numbers used for measuring how powerful an EARTHQUAKE is: *a severe earthquake measuring 7.2 on the Richter scale*

rick[1] /rɪk/ *n* [C] a large pile of STRAW or grass that is kept in a field until it is needed; ▤ **haystack**

rick[2] *v* [T] *BrE* **rick your back/neck** to twist and slightly injure your back or neck; ▤ **wrench** *AmE*: *I ricked my back moving the furniture around.*

rick·ets /'rɪkɪts/ *n* [U] a disease that children get in which their bones become soft and bent, caused by a lack of VITAMIN D

rick·et·y /'rɪkɪti/ *adj* a rickety structure or piece of furniture is in very bad condition, and likely to break easily: *a rickety old wooden chair* | *a rickety bridge*

rick·shaw /'rɪkʃɔː $ -ʃɒː/ *n* [C] a small vehicle used in South East Asia for carrying one or two passengers. It is pulled by someone walking or riding a bicycle.

ric·o·chet[1] /'rɪkəʃeɪ/ *v* [I] if a bullet, stone, or other object ricochets, it changes direction when it hits a surface at an angle: [+off] *Bullets ricocheted off the boulders around him.*

---

ricochet[2] *n* [C] something such as a bullet or a stone that has ricocheted: *He was hit in the arm by a ricochet.*

ri·cot·ta /rɪ'kɒtə $ -'kɑː-/ *n* [U] a type of soft white Italian cheese

rid[1] S1 /rɪd/ *adj*

1 get rid of sb/sth a) to throw away or destroy something you do not want any more: *It's time we got rid of all these old toys.* | *Governments should be encouraged to get rid of all nuclear weapons.* **b)** to take action so that you no longer have something unpleasant that you do not want: *I can't get rid of this cough.* | *He opened the windows to get rid of the smell.* **c)** to make someone leave because you do not like them or because they are causing problems: *Are you trying to get rid of me?* | *It can be difficult for schools to get rid of poor teachers.*

2 be rid of sb/sth to have taken action so that something or someone is no longer there to worry or annoy you: *The clerical part of his job was tedious, and he was glad to be rid of it.* | *He was a bully, and we're **well rid of him** (=it is good that he has gone).*

3 want rid of sb/sth to want to get rid of someone or something that is annoying you: *I could tell that he wanted rid of me.*

rid[2] *v* **rid, ridding**

rid sb/sth of sth *phr v written* to take action so that a person, place etc is no longer affected by something bad or no longer has it; → **overcome**: *a promise to rid the country of nuclear weapons* | *Will science finally rid us of this disease?* | **rid yourself of sth** *He struggled to rid himself of his fears.*

rid·dance /'rɪdns/ *n* **good riddance (to sb)** *spoken* a rude way of saying you are glad someone has left: *She was awful. Good riddance to her, I say!*

-ridden /rɪdn/ *suffix* [in adjectives] very full of something unpleasant: *mosquito-ridden swamps* | *disease-ridden slums*

rid·dle[1] /'rɪdl/ *n* [C] **1** a question that is deliberately very confusing and has a humorous or clever answer; → **puzzle**: *See if you can solve this riddle.* **2** something that you do not understand and cannot explain; ▤ **puzzle, mystery**: [+of] *The police have been unable to solve the riddle of her disappearance.* **3 talk/speak in riddles** to say things in a mysterious way that other people cannot understand: *Stop talking in riddles and explain what's going on!* **4** a wire container with holes in it that is used to separate earth from stones

riddle[2] *v* [T] **1** to make a lot of small holes in something: *Two gunmen riddled the bus with gunfire.* **2** to shake the coal or wood in a fire, in order to remove ASHES

rid·dled /'rɪdld/ *adj* **1 riddled with sth** very full of something bad or unpleasant: *The whole house was riddled with damp.* | *By this time her body was riddled with cancer.* **2 riddled with holes** full of small holes: *The wall of the fort was riddled with bullet holes.*

ride[1] S2 W2 /raɪd/ *v past tense* **rode** /rəʊd $ roʊd/, *past participle* **ridden** /'rɪdn/

1 ANIMAL [I,T] to sit on an animal, especially a horse, and make it move along: *She learned to ride when she was seven.* | *He was riding a large grey mare.* | [+on] *She arrived riding on a white horse.* | [+away/across/through etc] *He rode away across the marshes.*

2 BICYCLE/MOTORBIKE [I,T always + adv/prep] to travel on a bicycle or MOTORBIKE: *He had never learned to ride a bicycle.* | *They mounted their bikes and rode off.*

3 VEHICLE [I always + adv/prep, T] *especially AmE* to travel in a bus, car, or other vehicle that you are not driving: *We got onto the bus and rode into San Francisco.* | [+in] *The kids were riding in the back.* | **ride a bus** *AmE*: *Ann rides the bus to work.* ⚠ To talk about someone controlling a car or other vehicle, use **drive** not **ride**: *Lizzy drove the van and we kids rode in the back.*

4 IN A LIFT [I always + adv/prep, T] *AmE* to travel up or down in a LIFT: [+up/down] *He rode the elevator down to the first floor.* | *I rode up to the tenth floor.*

5 WATER/AIR a) [I always + adv/prep] to be floating in water or in the air: *The smaller boat was lighter and* rode higher in the water. | The moon was riding high in the sky. | There was a large ship **riding at anchor** in the bay. **b)** **ride a wave** to float on a wave and move forward with it: *surfboarders riding the waves*

6 **be riding high** to feel very happy and confident: *They were still riding high after their election victory.*

7 **let sth ride** *spoken* to take no action about something that is wrong or unpleasant: *What he had said was wrong, and I knew I shouldn't just let it ride.*

8 **ride roughshod over sth** to ignore someone else's feelings or ideas because you have the power or authority to do this: *The planning authorities should not ride roughshod over the wishes of local people.*

9 **ANNOY SB** [T] *AmE spoken* to annoy someone by often criticizing them or asking them to do things: *Why are you riding her so hard?*

10 **ride on sb's shoulders/back** if a child rides on someone's shoulders or back, they are carried in that way

11 **ride a punch/blow** to move back slightly when someone hits you, so that you are not hit with so much force: *He managed to ride the punch.*

12 **be riding for a fall** *informal* to be doing something unwise which could result in failure: *I had a feeling he was riding for a fall, and tried to tell him so.*

   ride on sth *phr v*
if one thing is riding on another, it depends on it: *He knew he had to win – his reputation was riding on it. | There's a lot riding on this match.*

   ride sth ⇔ **out** *phr v*
1 if a ship rides out a storm, it manages to keep floating until the storm has ended
2 if you ride out a difficult situation, you are not badly harmed by it: *Most large companies should be able to ride out the recession.*

   ride up *phr v*
if a piece of clothing rides up, it moves upwards so that it is no longer covering your body properly

ride² S3 *n* [C]

1 **CAR/TRAIN ETC** a journey in a vehicle, when you are not driving; → **lift**: [+**in**] *He invited me to go for a ride in his new car. | Can you give me a ride back to town? | Sammy had promised to take me for a ride in his truck. | I managed to get a ride down to the station. | We hitched a ride* (=got a free ride from a passing vehicle) *into town.* | **car/bus/train etc ride** *A fifteen minute taxi ride will take you to the airport.* | **a smooth/ comfortable/bumpy etc ride** *The new model offers a lovely smooth, comfortable ride.*

2 **HORSE/BICYCLE** a journey on a bicycle, a horse, or a similar animal: [+**on**] *Can I have a ride on your bike?* | **a bike/bicycle ride** *Shall we go for a bike ride this afternoon?*

3 **a rough/easy ride** *informal* if people give someone, especially someone in authority, a rough or an easy ride, they make a situation difficult or easy for them: *Journalists gave the Prime Minister a rough ride at the press conference. | The chairman will face a rough ride from shareholders. | The President will not have an easy ride when he gives his account of events.*

4 **a bumpy ride** *informal* if something has a bumpy ride, it experiences a lot of problems: *Shares had a bumpy ride yesterday, falling by an average of 15%. | The new bill could be in for a bumpy ride when it is put before parliament.*

5 **take sb for a ride** *spoken* to trick someone, especially in order to get money from them: *I'd just begun to realise he was taking me for a ride.*

6 **come/go along for the ride** *spoken* to join what other people are doing just for pleasure, not because you are seriously interested in it: *A couple of friends had come along for the ride.*

7 **MACHINE** a large machine that people ride on for fun at a FAIR: *We went on loads of rides.*

8 **PATH** *literary* a path for riding on a horse in the countryside: *a grassy ride*

rid·er /ˈraɪdə $ -ər/ *n* [C] **1** someone who rides a horse, bicycle etc; → **cyclist**: *a horse and rider* **2** an

extra or more detailed piece of information that is added to an official document and changes it slightly

ridge /rɪdʒ/ *n* [C] **1** a long area of high land, especially at the top of a mountain: *We made our way carefully along the ridge.* → see picture at **COUNTRY 2 a)** something long and thin that is raised above the things around it: *A small ridge of sand separated the field from the beach. | The ridges on the soles give the shoes a better grip.* **b)** the part at the top of a roof, where the two sides meet **3** **ridge of high pressure** *technical* a long area of high air pressure in the ATMOSPHERE, which has an effect on the weather

ridged /rɪdʒd/ *adj* something that is ridged has ridges on its surface: *the ridged sand of the river bottom*

rid·i·cule¹ /ˈrɪdɪˌkjuːl/ *n* [U] unkind laughter or remarks that are intended to make someone or something seem stupid: *the ridicule of his peers | The government's proposals were held up to ridicule* (=suffered ridicule) *by opposition ministers. | He had become an object of ridicule among the other teachers.*

ridicule² *v* [T] to laugh at a person, idea etc and say that they are stupid: *At the time, his ideas were ridiculed.*

ri·dic·u·lous S2 /rɪˈdɪkjʊləs/ *adj* very silly or unreasonable: *That's a ridiculous idea! | Don't be ridiculous! | I'd look ridiculous in a dress like that.* | **absolutely/totally/utterly ridiculous** *It's an absolutely ridiculous decision.* | **it is ridiculous that** *It's ridiculous that we have to wait six weeks.* —**ridiculously** *adv*: *a ridiculously expensive jacket | ridiculously low prices* —**ridiculousness** *n* [U]

rid·ing /ˈraɪdɪŋ/ *n* [U] the sport or activity of riding horses: *horse riding | Shall we go riding on Saturday?* | **riding school/stables** (=place where people learn to ride horses)

rife /raɪf/ *adj* **1** [not before noun] if something bad or unpleasant is rife, it is very common: *Violent crime is rife in our inner cities.* **2** **rife with sth** full of something bad or unpleasant: *The crowded factories are rife with disease.* **3** **run rife** to spread quickly in an uncontrolled way: *No one knew exactly what he had done, but speculation ran rife.*

riff /rɪf/ *n* [C] a repeated series of notes in popular or JAZZ music: *a guitar riff*

rif·fle /ˈrɪfəl/ also **riffle through** *v* [T] to move and quickly look at pieces of paper or the pages of a book, magazine etc; → **flip through**: *He riffled through the papers on his desk.*

riff-raff /ˈrɪf ræf/ *n* [plural] an insulting word for people who are noisy, badly-behaved, or of low social class: *We charge high prices to keep the riff-raff out.*

ri·fle¹ /ˈraɪfəl/ *n* [C] a long gun which you hold up to your shoulder to shoot; → **pistol**

rifle² also **rifle through** *v* [T] to search a place or container quickly because you are looking for something, especially something to steal: *Sally rifled through her wardrobe looking for a dress. | The killer had rifled his wallet and stolen £200.*

ri·fle·man /ˈraɪfəlmən/ *n plural* **riflemen** /-mən/ [C] a man who uses a rifle

rifle range *n* [C] a place where people practise shooting with rifles

rift /rɪft/ *n* [C] **1** a situation in which two people or groups have had a serious disagreement and begun to dislike and not trust each other; ▣ **split**: [+**between/ with**] *Party officials have denied that there is any rift between ministers.* | [+**over**] *Today's announcement could lead to a further rift over public spending. | He set out to heal the rifts in the party.* **2** a crack or narrow opening in a large mass of rock, cloud etc

rift valley *n* [C] a valley with very steep sides, formed by the cracking and moving of the Earth's surface

rig¹ /rɪg/ *v* **rigged, rigging** [T] **1** to dishonestly arrange the result of an election or competition before

R

it happens; ◻ **fix**: *Some international observers have claimed the election was rigged.* **2** if people rig prices or rig financial markets, they unfairly agree with each other the prices that will be charged; ◻ **fix**; → **cartel**: *Two of the largest oil companies have been accused of rigging prices.* | *Some investors feel that the market is rigged.* **3** [usually passive] to put ropes, sails etc on a ship: *The ship was fully rigged and ready to sail.*

rig sb ⇔ **out** *phr v BrE informal* to dress someone in special or unusual clothes: *young children who are rigged out in designer clothes*

rig sth ⇔ **up** *phr v informal* to make a piece of equipment, furniture etc quickly from objects that you find around you: *We rigged up a simple shower at the back of the cabin.*

rig² *n [C]* **1** a large structure that is used for getting oil from the ground under the sea **2** *AmE informal* a large truck: *We drove the rig down to Baltimore.* **3** the way in which a ship's sails are arranged

rig·a·ma·role /ˈrɪɡəmərəʊl $ -roʊl/ *n* an American spelling of RIGMAROLE

rig·a·to·ni /ˌrɪɡəˈtəʊni $ -ˈtoʊni/ *n [U]* a type of PASTA in the shape of short tubes

rig·ging /ˈrɪɡɪŋ/ *n [U]* all the ropes, posts, and chains that hold up a ship's sails

right¹ S1 W1 /raɪt/ *adj*

1 TRUE/CORRECT **a)** a statement or piece of information that is right is correct and based on true facts; ◻ **correct**: *Yes, that's the right answer.* | *Is that the right time?* | *I got most of the questions right.* | *His ideas have now been proved right.* **b)** [not before noun] if you are right, you have said something that is correct and based on true facts; ◻ **wrong**: *I think you're right. We should have set out earlier.* | *[+about] You were right about the hotel being too crowded.* | *I think the Prime Minister is only half right.* | *Am I right in thinking that you two have met before?*

2 SUITABLE the right thing, person, method etc is the one that is most suitable or effective; ◻ **wrong**: *I think you've made the right decision.* | *I think she's definitely the right person for the job.* | *[+for] A huge development like this isn't right for such a small village.*

3 SIDE [only before noun] **a)** your right side is the side with the hand that most people write with; ◻ **left**: *He had a knife in his right hand.* | *a scar on the right side of her face* **b)** on the same side of something as your right side; ◻ **left**: *Take the next right turn.* | *the right bank of the river*

4 PROBLEMS something that is not right is not in the state it should be in: *The engine's not quite right.* | *This cheese doesn't smell right.* | *Things haven't been right between me and James for some time.* | **put/set sth right** (=correct something) *It didn't take long to find the fault and put it right.*

5 MORALLY if someone is right to do something, their action is morally correct or sensible; ◻ **wrong**: **right to do sth** *Do you think I was right to report them to the police?* | *It can't be right to keep lying to your family.* | **it is right that** *I think it's right that the people who work hardest should earn the most.* | *It's only right* (=completely right) *that he should get his share of the money.* | *The company wants to do the right thing and offer compensation to all the injured workers.*

6 that's right *spoken* **a)** used to agree with what someone says or to answer 'yes' to a question: *'I gather you work in the sales department?' 'That's right.'* | *'Some people find it very difficult to work quickly.' 'That's right, and they often find exams very stressful.'* **b)** used when you are telling someone that you are angry about what they are doing: *That's right! Just blame me for everything, as usual!*

7 right you are *BrE spoken* used to say 'yes' to a request, order, or suggestion

8 EMPHASIS [only before noun] *BrE spoken* used to emphasize how bad someone or something is; ◻ **total**, **complete**: *He sounds like a right idiot!* | *The house was*

in a right mess when we got back.

9 HEALTH *spoken* if you are not feeling right, you are not feeling completely well: *I haven't been feeling right all day.* | *A few days in bed will soon put you right.* | *You'll soon be as right as rain* (=completely healthy).
→ **put sb right/straight** at PUT (9)

10 SOCIALLY the right people, places, schools etc are considered to be the best or most important: *Sonia's always careful to be seen with the right people.*

11 be in the right place at the right time to be in the place where something useful becomes available or is being offered: *Being a news photographer is all about being in the right place at the right time.* —**rightness** *n* [U]: *He was convinced of the rightness of his cause.* → **put sth right** at PUT (8)

right² *interjection* **1** used to show that you have understood or agree with what someone has just said: *'You need to be there by ten o'clock.' 'Right.'* **2** *BrE* used to get someone's attention before starting to say or do something: *Right, open your books on page 16.* | *Right, is everyone listening?* | *Right, I think we're ready to go.* **3** used to check if what you have said is correct: *So we're meeting in the pub, right?* **4** used to check that the person you are speaking to is listening and understands what you are saying: *So I handed him the camera, right, and asked him to take a photograph of us.*

right³ S1 W1 *adv*

1 EXACTLY exactly in a particular position or place: **right in/in front of/by etc sth** *She was standing right in the middle of the room.* | *There's the house, right in front of you.* | **right here/there** *I left my bags right here.*

2 IMMEDIATELY immediately and without any delay; ◻ **straight**: *It's on right after the six o'clock news.* | *I'll phone him right away* (=immediately). | *I could tell right off that something was wrong.* | **right off the bat** *AmE* (=immediately, without having to think carefully) *Kay answered right off the bat.*

3 CORRECTLY correctly: *We guessed right; they'd gone.* | *'I thought you'd be cross.' 'You thought right!'*

4 WELL *informal* in a way that is good or satisfactory: *Everything's going right for him at the moment.* | *It'll work out right in the end.*

5 DIRECTION/SIDE towards the direction or side that is on the right; ◻ **left**: *Turn right at the crossroads.*

6 right now now, or immediately: *Do you need me right now?* | *We need to deal with this problem right now.*

7 right along/through/around etc all the way along, through etc: *Go right to the end of the road.* | *We don't have to go right into town.* | *I slept soundly right through the night.*

8 be right behind sb *spoken* to completely support someone in their ideas or in what they are trying to achieve: *We're all right behind you.*

9 I'll be right with you/right there/right back *spoken* used to ask someone to wait because you are coming or returning very soon: *'Lunch is ready!' 'I'll be right there.'* | *Don't go away; I'll be right back.*

10 be right up there (with sb/sth) *informal* to be as good or as important as the very best: *He's definitely right up there with all the world-class footballers.*

11 right, left, and centre *BrE*; **right and left** *AmE* everywhere or in every way: *The company's losing money right, left, and centre.*

right⁴ S2 W1 *n*

1 ALLOWED [C] something that you are morally, legally, or officially allowed to do or have: *people who are fighting for basic rights* | *[+of] a new charter which establishes the rights and duties of citizens* | *the struggle for women's rights* | *a demonstration of people demanding equal rights for gay men* | *[+to] Everyone should have the right to freedom of expression.* | **right to do sth** *You have the right to consult a lawyer.* | **right of appeal/access/reply etc** *Convicted criminals have no automatic right of appeal.* | *They claim that the government is denying them their rights.* | **within your rights** (=legally or morally allowed) *You would be within your rights to sue the company for negligence.* | **by right** *The* money is yours by right. → CIVIL RIGHTS, HUMAN RIGHT

2 have a right to be angry/concerned/suspicious etc to have a good reason for being angry, concerned etc: *I think you have a right to feel very disappointed.* | *You had every right to be angry with them.*

3 have no right to do sth used to say that someone's action is completely unreasonable or unfair: *You had no right to take money from my purse!* | *He has no right to speak to me like that!*

4 SIDE the right/sb's right the side of your body that has the hand that most people write with, or this side of anything else; ☒ **left**: **on/to the right (of sth)** *Our car is just to the right of that white van.* | *Take the first turning on the right.* | **on/to sb's right** *The school is on your right as you come into the village.*

5 POLITICS the right/the Right political parties or groups that support the ideas and beliefs of CAPITALISM. They usually want low taxes and to encourage private business rather than businesses owned by the state; ☒ **left**; → **right-wing**: *The campaign is being supported by the Right.* | *The Conservative Party seems to be moving even further to the right.* | **extreme/far right** *politicians on the extreme right*

6 CORRECT BEHAVIOUR [U] behaviour that is morally good and correct: *Some kids don't seem to know the difference between right and wrong.* | *The protesters believe that they have right on their side.*

7 BOOKS/TV ETC rights [plural] if someone has the rights to a book, film, television programme etc, they are allowed to sell it or show it; → **copyright**: [+to] *The studio bought the rights to his new book.* | *The company paid £2 million for film rights to the book.* | *the television rights to the Olympic Games*

8 be in the right to have the best reasons, arguments etc in a disagreement with someone else: *Both sides are convinced that they are in the right.*

9 by rights *spoken* used to describe what should happen if things are done fairly or correctly: *By rights, the house should be mine now.*

10 in your own right used to say that you have something or achieve something on your own, without depending on other people: *She's a very wealthy woman in her own right.*

11 put sth to rights to make a place or situation return to normal again: *It took ages to put the room to rights again.*

12 the rights and wrongs of sth the subject of what or who is right or wrong in a situation: *I don't want to spend ages discussing the rights and wrongs of all this.*

13 [C] a hit made with your right hand; ☒ **left**

right⁵ v [T] **1** right a wrong to do something to prevent a bad situation from continuing: *He seems to think he can right all the wrongs of the world.* **2** to put something back into the state or situation that it should be in: *We must try to right the balance between taxation and government spending.* **3** to put something, especially a boat, back into its correct upright position: *I finally managed to right the canoe.* | *She righted herself and picked up her bag.*

'right ,angle n [C] **1** an angle of 90°, like the angles at the corners of a square **2** at right angles (to sth) if two things are at right angles, they make a 90° angle where they touch: *Hold the brush at right angles to the surface.* —**right-angled** *adj: a right-angled bend*

,right-'click v [I] to press the right-hand button on a computer MOUSE to make the computer do something: [+on] *Right-click on the image to save it.*

right·eous /'raɪtʃəs/ adj **1** **righteous indignation/anger etc** strong feelings of anger when you think a situation is not morally right or fair: *He was full of righteous indignation about the attack.* **2** *formal* morally good and fair: *a righteous God* —**righteously** adv —**righteousness** n [U] → SELF-RIGHTEOUS

right·ful /'raɪtfəl/ adj [only before noun] *formal* according to what is correct or what should be done legally or morally: *George sat at the head of the table, in his rightful place as their leader.* | *I'll return the money to*

its rightful owner. | the rightful heir to the throne —**rightfully** adv: *I'm only claiming what is rightfully mine.*

,right-'hand adj [only before noun] on the right side of something; ☒ **left-hand**: *the right-hand side of the body* | **top/bottom right-hand corner** *the bottom right-hand corner of the page*

,right-hand 'drive adj [only before noun] *BrE* a right-hand drive vehicle is one in which the driver sits on the right; ☒ **left-hand drive**

,right-'handed adj a right-handed person uses their right hand for writing, throwing etc; ☒ **left-handed**

,right-'hander n [C] **1** someone who uses their right hand for writing, throwing etc; ☒ **left-hander**: *He was the only right-hander among his team's top six batsmen.* **2** a hit using your right hand

,right-hand 'man n [singular] the person who supports and helps you the most, especially in your job: *John is Bill's right-hand man and has put a lot of time into the team.*

'Right ,Honourable adj *BrE* used when formally announcing or talking about a British member of Parliament: *the Right Honourable Giles Williams MP*

right·ist /'raɪtɨst/ adj supporting RIGHT-WING ideas or groups; ☒ **leftist**: *rightist demonstrators* —**rightist** n [C]

right·ly /'raɪtli/ adv **1** correctly, or for a good reason; ☒ **wrongly**: *I was, as you rightly said, the smallest boy in the class.* | *As you so rightly pointed out, things are getting worse.* | *They have been treated badly, and they are rightly upset.* | **quite rightly** *BrE: There's a lot of talk, quite rightly, about the dangers of smoking.* | **This photo was taken in Paris, if I remember rightly.** **2** rightly or wrongly used to emphasize that someone else thinks that something they did was right, but you think it was wrong: *The prime minister was widely judged, rightly or wrongly, to be an honest man.* **3** and rightly so *spoken* used to say that a decision or action you have just described is fair and morally right, in your opinion: *A lot of people round here were furious, and rightly so.* **4** I can't rightly say/don't rightly know *spoken* used to say that you are not sure whether something is correct or not

,right-'minded adj a right-minded person has opinions, principles, or standards of behaviour that you approve of; ☒ **right-thinking**: *All right-minded people will support us.*

right·o /ˌraɪt'əʊ $ -'oʊ/ also **,right 'oh** interjection *BrE informal* used to show that you agree with a suggestion that someone has made; ☒ **OK**: *Righto, I'll see you at six.*

right of ap'peal n plural rights of appeal [C] *law* the legal right to ask for a court's decision to be changed

,right-of-'centre adj supporting ideas and aims that are between the centre and the right in politics; ☒ **left-of-centre**

,right of 'way n plural rights of way **1** [U] *BrE*; **the right of way** *AmE* the right to drive into or across a road before other vehicles: *I never know who has right of way at this junction.* | *The law here says that pedestrians always have the right of way.* **2** [C] *BrE* **a)** the right to walk across someone else's land: *Walkers are often quite aggressive about their rights of way.* **b)** a path that people have the right to use: *The path is not a public right of way.*

,right 'on adj *informal* **1** *BrE* someone who is right on supports social justice, equal rights, the protection of the environment etc – often used to show disapproval because someone does this in an extreme way; → **PC, politically correct**: *It's one of those annoyingly right-on magazines about the environment.* **2** *AmE* someone is right on when they say something that is

R

correct or that you completely agree with: *Parker's column on teenage sexuality is right on.* **3** *AmE spoken old-fashioned* used to emphasize that you agree with what someone says or does: *'Power to the people!' 'Yeah, right on.'*

'rights ,issue *n* [C] *BrE technical* an offer of company SHARES at a cheaper price than usual, to people who own some already

right·size /'raɪtsaɪz/ *v* [I,T] if a company or organization rightsizes, or if it rightsizes its operations, it reduces the number of people it employs in order to reduce costs – used especially by companies to make the reduction in the number of workers sound good and sensible; → **downsize**: *They have been given one year to rightsize their workforce.* —**rightsizing** *n* [U]: *Many workers lost their jobs as a result of rightsizing.*

,right-'thinking *adj* a right-thinking person has opinions, principles, or standards of behaviour that you approve of; ▣ **right-minded**: *I condemn this killing, as all right-thinking people must.*

,right-to-'die *adj* [only before noun] supporting the right of people who are extremely ill, injured, or unconscious to refuse to use machines or methods that would keep them alive; → **euthanasia**: *the growing right-to-die lobby within the USA*

,right to 'life *n* [singular] if you talk about a baby's right to life, you mean that a baby has the right to be born, even if there are problems; → **pro-life**: *Every unborn child has a right to life.*

right·ward /'raɪtwəd $ -wərd/ *adj* [only before noun] on or towards the right; ▣ **leftward**: *a rightward glance*

right·wards /'raɪtwədz $ -wərdz/ *especially BrE* usually **rightward** *AmE adv* on or towards the right; ▣ **leftwards**: *The plane's course was veering rightwards.*

,right-'wing *adj* a right-wing person or group supports the ideas and beliefs of CAPITALISM; ▣ **left-wing**: *right-wing parties* | *The organization is very right-wing.* —**right wing** *n* [C]: *the right wing of the Conservative party* —**right-winger** *n* [C]: *a prominent right-winger in the party*

ri·gid /'rɪdʒɨd/ *adj* **1** rigid methods, systems etc are very strict and difficult to change; ▣ **flexible**: *rigid and authoritarian methods of education* **2** someone who behaves in a rigid way is very unwilling to change their ideas or behaviour; ▣ **flexible**: *rigid adherence to old-fashioned ideas* | *She maintained rigid control over her emotional and sexual life.* **3** stiff and not moving or bending; ▣ **flexible**: *rigid plastic* **4** used to describe someone who cannot move, especially because they are very frightened, shocked, or angry: [+with] *I heard a noise and woke up rigid with terror.* —**rigidly** *adv*: *rigidly opposed to all new ideas* —**rigidity** /rɪ'dʒɪdɨti/ *n* [U]

rig·ma·role /'rɪgmərəʊl $ -roʊl/ also **rigamarole** *AmE n* [singular,U] a long confusing process or description: *I don't want to go through the rigmarole of taking him to court.*

rig·or /'rɪgə $ -ər/ *n* the American spelling of RIGOUR

rig·or mor·tis /ˌrɪgə 'mɔːtɨs, ˌraɪgɔː- $ ˌrɪgər 'mɔːr-/ *n* [U] the condition in which someone's body becomes stiff after they die

rig·or·ous /'rɪgərəs/ *adj* **1** careful, thorough, and exact: *a rigorous analysis of defence needs* | *the rigorous standards required by the college* **2** very severe or strict: *rigorous army training* —**rigorously** *adv*

rig·our *BrE*; **rigor** *AmE* /'rɪgə $ -ər/ *n* **1 the rigours of sth** the problems and difficulties of a situation: *all the rigors of a Canadian winter* | *the stresses and rigours of modern life* **2** [U] great care and thoroughness in making sure that something is correct: *Their research seems to me to be lacking in rigour.*

rile /raɪl/ *v* [T] *informal* to make someone extremely angry: *He was the calmest guy I ever knew – nothing ever riled him.* | *That class gets me so riled up.*

rim¹ /rɪm/ *n* [C] **1** the outside edge of something circular: [+of] *the rim of a glass* | *plates with a gold band around the rim* → see picture at LIMIT¹ **2** **gold-rimmed/red-rimmed etc** with a gold, red etc rim: *gold-rimmed spectacles* | *red-rimmed eyes* —**rimless** *adj*: *rimless glasses*

rim² *v* **rimmed**, **rimming** [T] *literary* to be around the edge of something: *His eyes were rimmed with fatigue.*

rime /raɪm/ *n* [U] *literary* FROST (=powdery ice)

rind /raɪnd/ *n* [C,U] **1** the thick outer skin of some types of fruit, such as oranges; → **peel**, **zest**: *grated lemon rind* **2** the thick outer skin of some foods, such as BACON or cheese

ring¹ S1 W2 /rɪŋ/ *n* [C]

1 JEWELLERY a piece of jewellery that you wear on your finger: *a diamond ring* | *a plain silver ring* → **engagement ring** at ENGAGEMENT (1); → SIGNET RING, WEDDING RING; → see picture at JEWELLERY

2 CIRCLE **a)** an object in the shape of a circle: *a rubber ring for children to go swimming with* | *onion rings* | *a key ring* → NAPKIN RING **b)** a circular line or mark: [+around] *She left a dirty ring around the bath.* | [+round] *BrE*: *a ring round the moon* **c)** a group of people or things arranged in a circle: [+of] *A ring of armed troops surrounded the building.* | *The city was overlooked by a ring of high-rise buildings.*

3 **give sb a ring** *BrE informal* to make a telephone call to someone: *I'll give you a ring later in the week.*

4 BELLS the sound made by a bell or the act of making this sound: *a ring at the doorbell*

5 CRIMINALS a group of people who illegally control a business or criminal activity: *Are you aware that a drugs ring is being operated in the club?* | *Secret files reveal an Oxford spy ring.*

6 **have the/a ring of sth** if a statement or argument has a ring of truth, confidence etc, it seems as if it has this quality: *His explanation has the ring of truth.*

7 **have a familiar ring** if something has a familiar ring, you feel that you have heard it before: *His voice had a strangely familiar ring.*

8 **run rings around sb** *informal* to be able to do something much better than someone else can: *I'm sure you can run rings round him.*

9 COOKING *BrE* one of the circular areas on top of a COOKER that is heated by gas or electricity; → **hob**; ▣ **burner** *AmE*: *a gas ring*

10 SPORT **a)** a small square area surrounded by ropes, where people BOX or WRESTLE → RINGSIDE **b)** the ring the sport of BOXING: *He retired from the ring at 34.*

11 ENTERTAINMENT a large circular area surrounded by seats at a CIRCUS

ring² S1 W2 /rɪŋ/ *v past tense* **rang** /ræŋ/, *past participle* **rung** /rʌŋ/

1 BELL **a)** [I,T] to make a bell make a sound, especially to call someone's attention to you or to call someone to help you: *I rang the doorbell but no one came.* | [+for] *The sign said, 'Ring for service'.* | *Instead of ringing for the maid, she made the tea herself.* **b)** [I] if a bell rings, it makes a noise: *The bell rang for the end of break.*

2 TELEPHONE **a)** [I,T] *BrE* to make a telephone call to someone; ▣ **call**, **phone**: *I was going to ring you but I don't have your number.* | [+for] *Sally rang for a taxi.*; → see box at CALL¹ **b)** [I] if a telephone rings, it makes a sound to show that someone is telephoning you: *The phone hasn't stopped ringing all day.*

3 SOUNDS [I] **a)** if your ears ring, they make a continuous sound that only you can hear, after you have been somewhere very noisy or heard a loud sound: *The explosion made our ears ring.* **b)** *literary* if a place rings with a sound, it is full of that sound: [+with] *The whole room rang with their laughter.*

4 **ring a bell** *informal* if something rings a bell, it reminds you of something, but you cannot remember exactly what it is: *Her name rings a bell but I can't remember her face.*

5 not ring true if something does not ring true, you do not believe it, even though you are not sure why: *It was a possible explanation, but it didn't quite ring true.*

6 ring the changes *BrE* to make changes to something, not because it needs changing but just in order to make it more interesting, more attractive etc: *Choose a variety of foods and ring the changes with meals.*

7 ring hollow if something that someone says rings hollow, you do not feel that it is true or sincere: *Assurances that things have changed ring hollow in many ears.*

8 ring in your ears if a sound or remark rings in your ears, you continue to remember it very clearly, exactly as it sounded, after it has finished: *He left Washington with the president's praises ringing in his ears.*

ring (sb) **back** *phr v BrE*
to telephone someone again, or to telephone someone because you were not available when they telephoned you; 🔲 **call (sb) back**: *I'll ring back as soon as I find out anything.* | *John rang, and he wants you to ring him back.*

ring in *phr v*
1 *BrE* to telephone the place where you work: *Jane's rung in to say she'll be late.* | *He rang in sick* (=telephoned to say he was ill) *every morning for a week.*
2 ring in the New Year to celebrate the beginning of the New Year

ring off *phr v BrE*
to end a telephone call; → **hang up**: *He rang off without giving his name.*

ring out *phr v*
1 a voice, bell etc that rings out is loud and clear: *The sound of a shot rang out.*
2 ring out the Old Year to celebrate the end of the year

ring round (sb) *phr v BrE*
to make telephone calls to a group of people, in order to organize something, find out information etc: *I'll ring round to see whether anyone's interested in coming with us.* | *She rang round all the agencies.*

ring up *phr v*
1 *BrE* to telephone someone; 🔲 **call (sb) up: ring sb ⇔ up** *I'll ring the manager up tomorrow.* | *I rang up and made an appointment.*
2 ring sth ⇔ up to press buttons on a CASH REGISTER to record how much money is being put inside: *The cashier rang up £300 by mistake.*

ring³ *v past tense and past participle* **ringed** [T] **1** to surround something: *Thousands of people ringed the court building to demand the release of Mr Cox.* | **be ringed with sth** *Her eyes were ringed with stiff black lashes.* **2** *BrE* to draw a circular mark around something; 🔲 **circle**: *Ring the mistakes in red.*

ring binder *n* [C] *BrE* a FILE for holding papers, in which metal rings go through the edges of the pages, holding them in place

ring·er /ˈrɪŋə $ -ər/ *n* [C] **1** someone who rings church bells or hand bells **2** a piece of equipment that makes a ringing noise: *Turn down the ringer on your phone.* **3** someone who pretends not to have a skill that they really have, in order to play on a team, enter a competition etc → **DEAD RINGER**

ring·fence /ˈrɪŋfens/ *v* [T] *BrE* to decide officially that something, especially money, can only be used for a particular purpose: *OK, so this £20,000 is ringfenced as the training budget.*

ring finger *n* [C] the finger, next to the smallest finger on your hand, that you traditionally wear your WEDDING RING on; → **index finger**

ring·ing /ˈrɪŋɪŋ/ *adj* **1** a ringing sound or voice is loud and clear: *She pronounced her final words in ringing tones.* **2 a ringing endorsement** a statement that is made with a lot of force in support of something: *a ringing endorsement of the proposals*

ring·lead·er /ˈrɪŋˌliːdə $ -ər/ *n* [C] someone who leads a group that is doing something illegal or wrong: *the ringleader of a new international drugs ring*

ring·let /ˈrɪŋlɪt/ *n* [C usually plural] a long curl of hair that hangs down

ring·mas·ter /ˈrɪŋˌmɑːstə $ -ˌmæstər/ *n* [C] the person who introduces the performers and animals in a CIRCUS

ring-pull *n* [C] *BrE* the ring on the top of a can of drink that you pull to open it

ring road *n* [C] *BrE* a road that goes around a large town to keep the traffic away from the centre; → **bypass**

ring·side /ˈrɪŋsaɪd/ *n* [singular] **1** the area nearest to the performance in a CIRCUS, a BOXING match etc; → **ring** **2 ringside seat** a seat very near to the performers in a CIRCUS, a BOXING match etc; → **ring**

ring·tone /ˈrɪŋtəʊn $ -toʊn/ *n* [C] the sound made by a telephone, especially a MOBILE PHONE, when it is calling it

ring·worm /ˈrɪŋwɜːm $ -wɜːrm/ *n* [U] a skin infection that causes red rings, especially on your head

rink /rɪŋk/ *n* [C] **1** a specially prepared area of ice that you can SKATE on **2** a special area with a smooth surface where you can go around on ROLLER SKATES

rinse¹ /rɪns/ *v* [T] **1** to wash clothes, dishes, vegetables etc quickly with water, especially running water, and without soap: *Let me just rinse my hands.* | *Rinse the vegetables under a cold tap.* | **rinse sth out** *Don't forget to rinse out your swimsuit.* **2** to remove soap, dirt etc from something by washing it quickly with water: **rinse sth off/out/away etc** *Leave the shampoo for two minutes, then rinse it off with warm water.* | *I rinsed the mud out under the tap.* | *The cream rinses off easily.* **3** to put colour into your hair; 🔲 **dye** **4** if you rinse your mouth, or rinse your mouth out, you wash it by filling it with water and then SPITTING the water out; → **gargle**

rinse² *n* **1** [C] when you rinse something: *I gave my hands a quick rinse.* **2** [C,U] a product you use to change the colour of your hair or to make it more shiny; 🔲 **dye**: *a blue rinse for grey hair*

ri·ot¹ S3 /ˈraɪət/ *n*
1 [C] a situation in which a large crowd of people are behaving in a violent and uncontrolled way, especially when they are protesting about something: *urban riots* | *prison riots* | *His murder triggered vicious race riots* (=caused by a problem between different races). | *police wearing riot gear* (=the special clothing and equipment worn by police officers during a riot) | *police in bullet-proof vests and carrying riot shields* (=a piece of very hard plastic which police officers stand behind to protect them) → see picture at DEMONSTRATION
2 run riot a) if your imagination, emotions, thoughts etc run riot, you cannot or do not control them: *Manufacturers have let their imaginations run riot to create new computer games.* **b)** if people run riot, they behave in a violent, noisy, and uncontrolled way: *Some people let their children run riot.* **c)** if a plant runs riot, it grows very quickly
3 a riot of colour something with many different bright colours: *The garden is a riot of colour in spring.*
4 read (sb) the riot act to give someone a strong warning that they must stop causing trouble – used humorously: *If the kids don't settle down soon, I'll go up and read them the riot act.*

riot² *v* [I] if a crowd of people riot, they behave in a violent and uncontrolled way, for example by fighting the police and damaging cars or buildings: *University students rioted in protest at tuition fees.* —**rioting** *n* [U] —**rioter** *n* [C]

ri·ot·ous /ˈraɪətəs/ *adj* [usually before noun] *formal* **1** noisy, exciting, and enjoyable in an uncontrolled way; 🔲 **wild**: *a riotous party* **2** noisy or violent, especially in a public place: *Their riotous behaviour led to their arrest.* —**riotously** *adv*

riot police *n* [plural] police whose job is to stop riots: *Riot police fired tear gas into the crowd.*

rip¹ /rɪp/ *v* **ripped**, **ripping** **1** [I,T] to tear something or be torn quickly and violently: *Her clothes had all been ripped.* | *The sails ripped under the force of the*

R

wind. | *Impatiently, Sue **ripped** the letter **open**.* **2** [T always + adv/prep] to remove something quickly and violently, using your hands: **rip sth out/off/away/down** *Gilly ripped out a sheet of paper from her notebook.* | *The buttons had been ripped off.* **3 rip sth/sb to shreds a)** to destroy something or damage it badly by tearing it in many places: *Jill's kitten is ripping her sofa to shreds.* **b)** *informal* to strongly criticize someone, or criticize their opinions, remarks, behaviour etc: *I expected to have my argument ripped to shreds.* **4 let rip** *informal* to speak or behave violently or emotionally: *Fran took a slow deep breath, then let rip, yelling and shouting at him.* **5 let it/her rip** *informal* to make a car, boat etc go as fast as it can: *Put your foot on the gas and let her rip!*

rip sth ⇔ **apart** *phr v* to tear or pull something to pieces: *He was ripped apart by savage beasts in the forest.*

rip sb/sth ⇔ **off** *phr v informal* **1** to charge someone too much money for something; ⊟ **overcharge:** *The agency really ripped us off.* **2** to steal something: *Somebody had come in and ripped off the TV and stereo.* **3** to take words, ideas etc from someone else's work and use them in your own work as if they were your own ideas; ⊟ **plagiarize** → RIP-OFF (2)

rip through sth *phr v* to move through a place quickly and with violent force: *A wave of bombings ripped through the capital's business district.*

rip sth ⇔ **up** *phr v* to tear something into pieces: *Sue ripped his photo up into tiny bits.*

rip² *n* [C] a long tear or cut: *a green leather jacket with a rip in the sleeve*

RIP /ˌɑːr aɪ ˈpiː/ the abbreviation of *Rest in Peace*, written on a GRAVESTONE

rip·cord /ˈrɪpkɔːd $ -kɔːrd/ *n* [C] the string that you pull to open a PARACHUTE

ripe /raɪp/ *adj comparative* **riper**, *superlative* **ripest** **1** ripe fruit or crops are fully grown and ready to eat; ⊞ **unripe:** *Those tomatoes aren't ripe yet.* **2 be ripe for sth** to be ready for a change to happen, especially when it should have happened sooner: *The police forces are ripe for reform.* | *The former dock area is ripe for development.* **3 the time is ripe (for sth)** used to say it is a very suitable time for something to happen, especially when it should have happened sooner: *The time is ripe for a review of progress up to now.* **4 ripe old age a)** if you live to a ripe old age, you are very old when you die: *Eat less and exercise more if you want to live to a ripe old age.* **b)** used to show that you find it surprising or impressive that someone is doing something or has achieved something at a very young age – used humorously: *She was put in charge **at the ripe old age** of twenty-nine.* **5** ripe cheese has developed a strong taste and is ready to eat; ⊟ **mature** **6** *especially BrE* a ripe smell is strong and unpleasant – used humorously: *We were pretty ripe after a week of walking.* —**ripeness** *n* [U]

rip·en /ˈraɪpən/ *v* [I,T] to become ripe or to make something ripe: *The apples were ripening on the trees.*

rip-off *n* [C] **1** *informal* something that is unreasonably expensive: *The meal was a rip-off and the service was appalling.* **2** music, art, films etc that are rip-offs copy something else without admitting that they are copies: [+of] *a rip-off of a hit movie* → **rip off** at RIP (1)

ri·poste /rɪˈpɒst, rɪˈpəʊst $ rɪˈpoʊst/ *n* [C] *formal* a quick, clever reply to something that someone has said: *a suitably witty riposte*

rip·ple¹ /ˈrɪpəl/ *v* **1** [I,T] to move in small waves, or to make something move in this way: *fields of grain rippling in the soft wind* | *I could see the muscles rippling under his shirt.* **2** [I always + adv/prep] to pass from one person to another like a wave: [+through] *Panic rippled through Hollywood as the murders were discovered.* | [+around] *Enthusiastic applause rippled around the tables.* **3** [I always + adv/prep] if a feeling ripples through you, you feel it strongly: [+through]

Anger was rippling through him so fiercely that his whole body shook. **4** [I] to make a noise like water that is flowing gently: *The water rippled over the stones.* | *a rippling brook*

ripple² *n* [C] **1** a small low wave on the surface of a liquid: *ripples on the surface of the pond* | *She dived into the pool, making scarcely a ripple.* **2** a sound that gets gradually louder and softer: *A **ripple of laughter** ran through the audience.* | *a ripple of applause* **3** a feeling that spreads through a person or a group because of something that has happened: *A ripple of excitement went through the crowd as he came on stage.* **4** a shape or pattern that looks like a wave: *ripples on the sand* **5 raspberry ripple/chocolate ripple etc** a type of ICE CREAM that has different coloured bands of fruit, chocolate etc in it **6 ripple effect** a situation in which one action causes another, which then causes a third etc; ⊟ **domino effect:** *The increase had a **ripple effect** through the whole financial market.*

rip-'roaring *adj, adv informal* exciting and full of energy: *Micky had a rip-roaring time spending his first wage packet.*

rise¹ [S2] [W1] /raɪz/ *v past tense* **rose** /rəʊz $ roʊz/, *past participle* **risen** /ˈrɪzən/ [I]

1 INCREASE to increase in number, amount, or value; ⊟ **go up;** ⊞ **fall:** [+by] *Sales rose by 20% over the Christmas period.* | [+from/to] *The research budget rose from £175,000 in 1999 to £22.5 million in 2001.* | [+above] *Temperatures rarely rise above freezing.* | **rise dramatically/sharply/rapidly/steeply etc** *The number of people seeking asylum in the United Kingdom has risen sharply.* | *The divorce rate has risen steadily since the 1950s.* | **rising crime/unemployment/inflation etc** *The country now faces economic recession and rising unemployment.* | *The police seem unable to cope with the rising tide of* (=large increase in) *car crime.* → see box at RAISE¹

2 GO UPWARDS to go upwards; ⊞ **fall:** *The floodwaters began to rise again.* | *She watched the bubbles rise to the surface.* | *the problems caused by climate change and rising sea levels* | [+from] *Smoke rose from the chimney.* | *The road rises steeply from the village.* | *The waves rose and fell.*

3 STAND *formal* to stand up: *Then she picked up her bag and rose to leave.* | **rise from the table/your chair etc** *The chairman rose from his chair and came forward to greet her.* | *He put down his glass and rose to his feet.*

4 BECOME SUCCESSFUL to become important, powerful, successful, or rich; ⊞ **fall:** [+to] *He rose to the rank of major.* | **rise to prominence/fame/power** *He had swiftly risen to prominence during the 1950s.* | *Mussolini rose to power in Italy in 1922.* | *people who **rise to the top** in their chosen professions* | **rise to do sth** *He rose to become chairman of the company.* | *She had joined the company as a secretary and **risen through the ranks** (*=made progress from a low position to a high position) *to become a senior sales director.*

5 BE TALL *also* **rise up** to be very tall: [+above] *The cliffs rose above them.* | [+from] *huge rocks rising from the sea* | *The bridge **rose majestically** into the air.*

6 VOICE/SOUND a) to be loud enough to be heard: [+from] *The sound of traffic rose from the street below.* | [+above] *Her voice rose above the shouts of the children.* **b)** to become louder or higher: *His voice rose in frustration.*

7 SUN/MOON/STAR to appear in the sky; ⊞ **set:** *The sun rises in the east.*

8 EMOTION if a feeling or emotion rises, you feel it more and more strongly: *She could sense her temper rising again.* | *There was an atmosphere of rising excitement in the school.* | *The doctor sounded optimistic and John's hopes rose.*

9 rise to the occasion/challenge to deal successfully with a difficult situation or problem, especially by working harder or performing better than usual: *a young athlete who can certainly rise to the occasion* | *The team rose to the challenge.*

10 AGAINST A GOVERNMENT/ARMY *also* **rise up** if a

large group of people rise, they try to defeat the government, army etc that is controlling them: *They rose up and overthrew the government.* | [+**against**] *The prisoners rose against the guards and escaped.* | **rise in revolt/rebellion** *They rose in rebellion against the king.*

11 BREAD/CAKES ETC if bread, cakes etc rise, they become bigger because there is air inside them

12 BED *literary* to get out of bed in the morning

13 ALIVE AGAIN to come alive after having died; → **resurrection**: **rise from the dead/grave** *On the third day Jesus rose from the dead.*

14 COURT/PARLIAMENT if a court or parliament rises, that particular meeting is formally finished

15 WIND *formal* if the wind rises, it becomes stronger: *The wind had risen again and it was starting to rain.*

16 RIVER *literary* if a river rises somewhere, it begins there: *The Rhine rises in Switzerland.*

17 rise and shine *spoken* used humorously to tell someone to wake up and get out of bed

rise above sth *phr v*
if someone rises above a bad situation or bad influences, they do not let these things affect them because they are mentally strong or have strong moral principles: *You expect a certain amount of criticism, but you have to rise above it.* | *I try to rise above such prejudices.*

rise to sth *phr v*
if you rise to a remark, you reply to it rather than ignoring it, especially because it has made you angry: *You shouldn't rise to his comments.* | *He refused to* **rise to the bait** (=react in the way someone wanted him to).

rise² [W2] *n*

1 INCREASE [C] an increase in number, amount, or value; **◨ increase**; **◨ fall**: [+**in**] *We are expecting a* **sharp rise** *in interest rates.* | *an alarming rise in unemployment* | *There's been a* **rise in the number of** *arrests for drug offences.* | [+**of**] *Profits went up to £24 million, a rise of 16%.* | **rent/price rise** *Tenants face a 20% rent rise.*

2 WAGES [C] *BrE* an increase in wages; **◨ raise** *AmE*: *He's been promised a rise next year.* | *The railworkers were offered a 3%* **pay rise**.

3 SUCCESS/POWER [singular] the achievement of importance, success or power; **◨ fall**: [+**of**] *the rise of fascism* | *the rise of Napoleon* | [+**to**] *Thatcher's rise to power in the late 70s* | *The band's sudden* **rise to fame** *took everyone by surprise.* | *his swift* **rise to prominence** | *the* **rise and fall** *of the Roman Empire*

4 give rise to sth *formal* to be the reason why something happens, especially something bad or unpleasant; → **provoke**: *His speech gave rise to a bitter argument.* | *The President's absence has given rise to speculation about his health.*

5 MOVEMENT UP [singular] a movement upwards; **◨ fall**: [+**in**] *a sudden rise in sea levels* | *She watched the steady* **rise and fall** *of his chest.*

6 SLOPE [C] an upward slope or a hill: *There's a slight rise in the road.* | *They topped the rise* (=reached the top of the hill) *and began a slow descent towards the town.*

7 get a rise out of sb *informal* to make someone become annoyed or embarrassed by making a joke about them; → **make fun of sb**: *She enjoys getting a rise out of you.*

ris·er /ˈraɪzə $ -ər/ *n* [C] **1 early/late riser** someone who usually gets out of bed very early or very late **2** *technical* the upright part of a step on a set of stairs **3 risers** [plural] *AmE* a set of wooden or metal steps that can be moved from place to place, used for a group of people to stand on: *The school choir stood on risers behind the orchestra.*

ris·i·ble /ˈrɪzəbəl/ *adj formal* something that is risible is so stupid that it deserves to be laughed at: *a risible suggestion* —**risibility** /ˌrɪzəˈbɪləti/ *n* [U]

ris·ing¹ /ˈraɪzɪŋ/ *adj* **1** [only before noun] becoming more important or famous: *Francesca was a* **rising star** *in the cinema.* **2 the rising generation** *BrE* young people who will soon be old enough to vote, have jobs etc: *The rising generation of students are optimistic about the future.*

rising² *n* [C] *BrE* a sudden attempt by a large group of people to violently remove a government or ruler; **◨ uprising, rebellion**

rising ˈdamp *n* [U] *BrE* a condition where water comes up from the ground and gets into the walls of a building

risk¹ [S2] [W1] /rɪsk/ *n*

1 [C,U] the possibility that something bad, unpleasant, or dangerous may happen; **◨ danger**; → **gamble**, **chance**

risk (that)
reduce/minimize the risk of sth
increase the risk of sth
carry/pose a risk
not be worth the risk
high/low risk
increased/reduced risk (=a higher or lower risk than usual)
a real risk
a calculated risk (=a risk you think will have a good result)
an element of risk (=some risk, but not much)
the risks involved in/associated with sth
risk factor
the benefits outweigh the risks

[+**of**] *the risk of serious injury* | *There is a risk that the crisis may spread further.* | [+**to**] *There is no risk to public health.* | *Healthy eating can help* **reduce the risk** *of heart disease.* | *The birds could* **pose** *a serious health* **risk** *for people who eat them.* | *I never walk home alone at night – it's not* **worth the risk**. | *Building work has a* **high risk** *of accident.* | *a* **low-risk** *group for lung cancer* | *an increased risk of skin cancer* | *things that pose* **a real risk** *to the future of mankind* | *It was a* **calculated risk** *to appoint a man without management experience to such a senior post.* | *There's an* **element of risk** *in any kind of investment.* | *the risks associated with drug use* | *the risk factors for sudden infant death syndrome* | *The benefits to patients who are taking the drug far* **outweigh the risks**.

2 take a risk to decide to do something even though you know it may have bad results: *Isn't he taking a bit of a risk in coming here?* | **take the risk of doing sth** *I couldn't take the risk of leaving him alone even for a short time.* | *Many people are* **willing to take** *that* **risk** *in order to protect their families.*

3 [C] something or someone that is likely to cause harm or danger: [+**to**] *Polluted water supplies are a risk to public health.* | *They didn't* **pose** *a significant risk to safety.* | *Meat from the infected animals is regarded as a* **serious health risk** (=something likely to harm people's health). | *The tyre dump is a major* **fire risk** (=something that could cause a dangerous fire). | *She's becoming a* **security risk** (=someone who may tell important secrets to an enemy).

4 at risk in a situation where you may be harmed: *We must stop these rumours; the firm's reputation is at risk.* | [+**from**] *Women are more at risk from the harmful effects of alcohol than men.* | [+**of**] *Their children are also at* **high risk** *of developing the disease.* | *That would mean* **putting** *other children* **at risk**.

5 run a risk to be in a situation where there is a possibility that something bad could happen to you: **run the risk of doing sth** *Anyone travelling without a passport runs the risk of being arrested.*

6 at the risk of doing sth used when you think that what you are going to say or do may have a bad result, may offend or annoy people etc: *At the risk of sounding stupid, can I ask a question?* | *Will they go ahead with their plans, even at the risk of offending the Americans?*

7 at your own risk if you do something at your own risk, you do it when you understand the possible dangers and have been warned about them: *You can use it, but it's at your own risk.* | *All personal belongings*

R

are left at the owner's risk.

8 [C] a person or business judged according to the danger involved in giving them insurance or lending them money: **good/bad/poor risk** *Drivers under 21 are regarded as poor risks by insurance companies.*

risk² *v* [T] **1** to put something in a situation in which it could be lost, destroyed, or harmed; → **gamble**: *When children start smoking, they don't realize that they're risking their health.* | **risk sth to do sth** *He's prepared to risk everything to avoid this war.* | **risk sth on sth** *You'd be crazy to risk your money on an investment like that!* | *He risked his life helping others to escape.* | *I'm not going to risk my neck* (=risk my life) *just to save a common criminal.* | *Why risk life and limb* (=risk your life and health) *jumping out of a plane just to raise money for charity?* **2** to get into a situation where something unpleasant may happen to you; → **endanger**: **risk doing sth** *They may even risk losing their homes.* | **risk defeat/death etc** *He would prefer not to risk another embarrassing defeat.* | *Some people are prepared to risk imprisonment for what they believe.* | **risk being seen/caught/arrested etc** *Workers who broke the strike risked being attacked when they left the factory.* **3** to do something that you know may have dangerous or unpleasant results: **risk doing sth** *Are you prepared to risk traveling without an armed guard?* | *She risked a glance back over her shoulder.* | *You could slip out of school between classes, but I wouldn't risk it.*

risk ,management *n* [U] **1** a system to prevent or reduce dangerous accidents or mistakes **2** *technical* the practice of managing INVESTMENTS in ways that produce as much profit as possible while limiting the danger of losses

risk-,taking *n* [U] when people do things that involve risks in order to achieve something —**risk-taker** *n* [C]

risk·y /'rɪski/ *adj* involving a risk that something bad will happen; **≡ dangerous**: *Doctors say it's too risky to try and operate.* | *Buying a secondhand car is a risky business.* —**riskiness** *n* [U]

ri·sot·to /rɪ'zɒtəʊ $ -'sɒːtoʊ/ *n plural* **risottos** [C,U] a hot meal made from rice mixed with cheese, vegetables, or pieces of meat

ris·qué /'rɪskeɪ $ rɪ'skeɪ/ *adj* a joke, remark etc that is risqué is slightly shocking, because it is about sex

ris·sole /'rɪsəʊl $ -soʊl/ *n* [C] *BrE* cooked meat cut into very small pieces, mixed with potato or bread, and cooked in hot fat

rite /raɪt/ *n* [C] **1** a ceremony that is always performed in the same way, usually for religious purposes; → **ritual**: *funeral rites* | *ancient fertility rites* | *These traditional rites are performed only by the women of the village.* **2 rite of passage** a special ceremony or action that is a sign of a new stage in someone's life, especially when a boy starts to become a man; → **coming of age 3 last rites** final prayers or religious ceremonies for someone who is dying: *A priest came to give him the last rites.*

rit·u·al¹ /'rɪtʃuəl/ *n* [C,U] **1** a ceremony that is always performed in the same way, in order to mark an important religious or social occasion; → **rite**: *ancient pagan rituals* | *the importance of religion and ritual in our lives* | *The lady of the house performs the sacred ritual of lighting two candles.* **2** something that you do regularly and in the same way each time; → **routine**: [+of] *the daily ritual of mealtimes* | *He went through the ritual of lighting his cigar.*

ritual² *adj* [only before noun] **1** done as part of a rite or ritual: *ritual dances* **2** done in a fixed and expected way, but without real meaning or sincerity: *The police issued the usual ritual apology.* —**ritually** *adv*: *Animals are brought in and ritually slaughtered.*

rit·u·al·is·tic /ˌrɪtʃuə'lɪstɪk◂/ *adj* ritualistic words or behaviour always follow the same pattern, especially because they form part of a ritual: *a ritualistic*

procession | *the ritualistic marking of birth, marriage and death* —**ritualistically** /-kli/ *adv*

ritz·y /'rɪtsi/ *adj informal* fashionable and expensive; **≡ fancy**: *a ritzy restaurant*

ri·val¹ /'raɪvəl/ *n* [C] **1** a person, group, or organization that you compete with in sport, business, a fight etc; **≡ competitor**: *This gives the company a competitive advantage over its rivals.* | [+for] *his chief rival for the job* | *He finished 39 seconds ahead of his main rival.* | *She was 2 minutes faster than her nearest rival.* | *a game against their old rivals, Manchester United* | *They still remain bitter rivals* (=hate each other). | *Their sales have now overtaken those of their arch-rival* (=main or strongest rival). | **rival company/firm/team etc** *Sheena left her job and went to work for a rival company.* **2** one of a group of things that people can choose between: *The newest model has several advantages over its rivals.*

rival² *v* **rivalled, rivalling** *BrE*, **rivaled, rivaling** *AmE* [T] to be as good or important as someone or something else; → **unrivalled**: *The college's facilities rival those of Harvard and Yale.* | *a stadium to rival any in the world*

ri·val·ry /'raɪvəlri/ *n plural* **rivalries** [C,U] a situation in which two or more people, teams, or companies are competing for something, especially over a long period of time, and the feeling of competition between them; → **competition**: [+between] *There has always been intense rivalry between New Zealand and Australia.* | *The two players have developed a friendly rivalry.* | *She had never overcome her feelings of sibling rivalry* (=rivalry between brothers and sisters).

riv·en /'rɪvən/ *adj formal* **1** if a group of people are riven, they are divided by disagreements, especially in a violent way: [+by/with] *a community riven by religious differences* **2** if an object is riven, it is divided into two or more parts

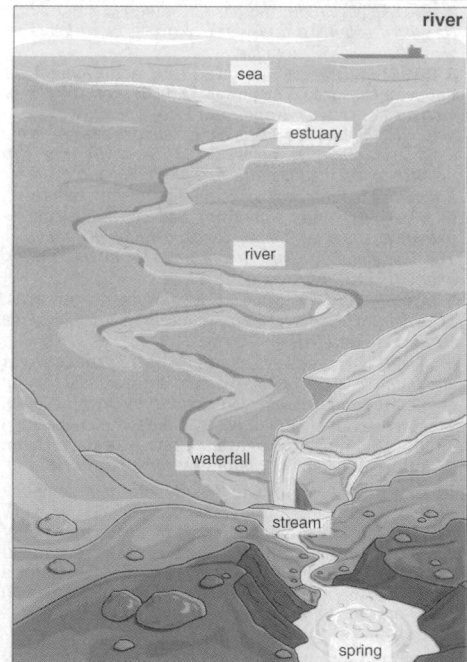

river

sea

estuary

river

waterfall

stream

spring

riv·er S2 W2 /'rɪvə $ -ər/ *n* [C]

1 a natural and continuous flow of water in a long line across a country into the sea; → **stream**: *the Mississippi River* | *the River Thames* | **on a river** *a boat on the river* | **along a river** *We went for a walk along the river.* | **up/down (a) river** *a ship sailing up river* | *They drifted slowly down river.* | **across a river** *a bridge across the*

river | on the south **bank of the river** (=the land on one side of a river) | trees on the **river bank** (=the land next to a river) | The River Elbe *flows* through the Czech Republic. | at the **mouth of the river** (=where a river joins the sea) ➔ see picture at COUNTRY
2 a large amount of moving liquid: [+of] *a river of hot lava flowing from the volcano* ➔ **sell sb down the river** at SELL[1] (10)

'river ,basin n [C] an area from which all the water flows into the same river

'river bed n [C] the ground at the bottom of a river; ➔ **sea bed**

riv·er·side /'rɪvəsaɪd $ -ər-/ n **the riverside** the land along the sides of a river: *We had a picnic by the riverside.* —**riverside** adj: *a riverside inn*

riv·et[1] /'rɪvɪ̯t/ v **1** be riveted on/to/by sth if your attention is riveted on something, you are so interested or so frightened that you keep looking at it: *All eyes were riveted on her in horror.* **2** be riveted to the spot to be so shocked or frightened that you cannot move **3** [T] to fasten something with rivets

rivet[2] n [C] a metal pin used to fasten pieces of metal together; ➔ **bolt**

riv·et·ing /'rɪvɪ̯tɪŋ/ adj something that is riveting is so interesting or exciting that you cannot stop watching it or listening to it; ◨ **fascinating**: *a riveting performance* | *His story makes riveting listening.*

Ri·vi·e·ra /ˌrɪviˈeərə $ -ˈerə/ n **the French/Italian/English Riviera** a warm coast that is popular with people who are on holiday, especially the Mediterranean coast of France

riv·u·let /'rɪvjʊ̯lɪt/ n [C] written a very small stream of water or liquid: [+of] *rivulets of rain running down the window*

ri·yal /riˈɑːl $ riˈɒːl, -ˈɑːl/ n another spelling of RIAL

RN /ˌɑːr ˈen/ **1** the abbreviation of **registered nurse** **2** BrE the abbreviation of **Royal Navy**: *Captain Anstruther, RN*

RNA /ˌɑːr en ˈeɪ/ n [U] an important chemical that exists in all living cells; ➔ **DNA**

roach /rəʊtʃ $ roʊtʃ/ n [C] **1** AmE informal a COCKROACH **2** BrE a type of European fish **3** informal the end part of a MARIJUANA cigarette that has been smoked

road [S1] [W1] /rəʊd $ roʊd/ n
1 [C,U] a specially prepared hard surface for cars, buses, bicycles etc to travel on; ➔ **street**, **motorway**, **freeway**

---

along/up/down a road
on/in a road
on the other side of the road
in the middle of the road
by the side of the road
by road (=driving)
on the roads
cross a road
run (out) into a road
side/back road (=a small road that is not used much)
busy road (=one with a lot of traffic)
road sense (=knowledge about how to behave sensibly near traffic)
road safety

*I was driving **along the road** when a kid suddenly stepped out in front of me.* | *You'll see the library a bit further **up the road**.* | *I ran **down the road** to see what was happening.* | *There were loads of cars parked **on the road**.* | *I saw Nigel **on the other side of the road**.* | *Someone was standing **in the middle of the road**.* | *There wasn't much traffic **on the roads**.* | *I ran **across the road** to meet him.* | *We stopped and had something to eat **by the side of the road**.* | *The college is easily accessible **by road**.* | *There are far more cars **on the roads** now than there used to be.* | *I turned a corner to find the road ahead severely flooded.* | *Be careful **crossing the road**.* | *A dog **ran out into the road**.* | *We turned down a **side road**.* | *Beyond the garden was a*

---

fairly **busy road**. | Kids of that age have no **road sense**. | fatal **road accidents** | a **road safety** campaign

2 Road written abbreviation **Rd.** used in addresses after the names of roads and streets: *65 Maple Road* | *He lives **on Dudley Road**.*
3 on the road a) travelling in a car, especially for long distances: *I've been on the road since 5:00 a.m. this morning.* **b)** if a group of actors or musicians are on the road, they are travelling from place to place giving performances: *They're on the road for six months out of every year.* **c)** if your car is on the road, you have paid for the repairs, tax etc necessary for you to drive it legally: *It would cost too much to put it back on the road.*
4 the road to sth if you are on the road to something, you will achieve it soon, or it will happen to you soon: *The doctor says she's **well on the road to** recovery.* | *It was this deal that **set** him **on the road to** his first million.* | *the first **step along the road to** democracy*
5 go down a/this road to choose a particular course of action: *Is there any scope for going down that road in the future?* | *It depends which road you want to go down.*
6 along/down the road in the future, especially at a later stage in a process: *You can always upgrade a bit further down the road if you want.* | *Somewhere down the road, they're going to clash.*
7 one for the road spoken a last alcoholic drink before you leave a party, PUB etc ➔ **the end of the road** at END[1] (17); ➔ **hit the road** at HIT[1] (13)

WORD FOCUS: ROAD
a big road: **main road, highway, motorway** BrE, **freeway** AmE, **expressway, turnpike** AmE, **interstate** AmE, **A-road** BrE
a road in a town: **street, avenue, boulevard**
a road in the countryside: **country road, lane, track**
a road you pay to use: **toll road**
parts of a road: **fast lane, slow lane, hard shoulder** BrE/**shoulder** AmE, **central reservation** BrE/**median strip** AmE, **pavement** BrE/**sidewalk** AmE

'road ,atlas n plural road atlases [C] a map that shows the roads in a particular country or area: *a road atlas of Europe*

road·block /'rəʊdblɒk $ 'roʊdblɑːk/ n [C] **1** a place where the police are stopping traffic; ➔ **check point**: *The police have set up roadblocks to try and catch the two men.* **2** AmE something that stops the progress of a plan: *mental roadblocks that get in the way of success*

'road hog n [C] informal someone who drives badly or too fast without thinking about other people's safety

road·house /'rəʊdhaʊs $ 'roʊd-/ n [C] AmE a restaurant or bar on a main road outside a city

road·ie /'rəʊdi $ 'roʊ-/ n [C] informal someone whose job is moving equipment for rock musicians

road·kill /'rəʊdkɪl $ 'roʊd-/ n [U] AmE informal animals that have been killed by cars on the road

'road ,manager n [C] someone who makes arrangements for entertainers when they are travelling

'road ,pricing n [U] a system in which drivers have to pay to use the roads at particular times; ➔ **toll road**: *road pricing schemes for congested cities*

'road rage n [U] violence and angry behaviour by car drivers towards other car drivers: *Road rage seems to be on the increase.* | *a road rage attack*

road·run·ner /'rəʊdrʌnə $ 'roʊdrʌnər/ n [C] a small bird that runs very fast and lives mainly in deserts

road·show /'rəʊdʃəʊ $ 'roʊdʃoʊ/ n [C] a group of people who travel around the country entertaining the public, advertising, or providing a service

road·side /'rəʊdsaɪd $ 'roʊd-/ n **the roadside** the edge of the road: *on/by/at the roadside a van parked by the roadside* —**roadside** adj: *a roadside snack bar*

'road sign n [C] a sign next to a road that gives information to drivers

R

'road tax n [U] a tax in Britain that the owner of a vehicle must pay in order to drive it legally; → **tax disc**

'road test n [C] a test to check that a vehicle is in good condition and safe to drive; → **MOT** —**roadtest** /'rəʊdtest $ 'roʊd-/ v [T]: *All our vehicles are roadtested before they are sold.*

'road trip n [C] *AmE* a long trip that you take in a car, usually with friends

'road ˌwarrior n [C] *informal* someone who uses computers, MOBILE PHONES, PAGERS etc in a place other than their home or office

road·way /'rəʊdweɪ $ 'roʊd-/ n [C] the part of the road used by vehicles

road·works /'rəʊdwɜːks $ 'roʊdˌwɜːrks/ n [plural] *BrE* repairs that are being done to a road: *There were roadworks on the motorway.*

road·wor·thy /'rəʊdˌwɜːði $ 'roʊdˌwɜːr-/ adj a vehicle that is roadworthy is in good condition and safe enough to drive —**roadworthiness** n [U]

roam /rəʊm $ roʊm/ v **1** [I,T] to walk or travel, usually for a long time, with no clear purpose or direction; → **wander**: [+over/around/about etc] *The dogs are allowed to roam around.* | *Chickens and geese roam freely in the back yard.* | *You shouldn't let your children roam the streets.* | **roam the countryside/desert/forests etc** *Wild sheep roam the hills.* **2** [I always + adv/prep] if your eyes roam over something, you look slowly at all parts of it: *Her eyes roamed the room.* | [+over] *His eyes roamed over the bookshelves.*

roam·ing /'rəʊmɪŋ $ 'roʊ-/ n [U] the process that a MOBILE PHONE uses when it is in a different country or area from usual, and has to connect to a different network

roan /rəʊn $ roʊn/ n [C] a horse with some white hairs, giving it a light colour —**roan** adj

roar¹ /rɔː $ rɔːr/ v **1** [I] to make a deep, very loud noise; → **growl**: *We heard a lion roar.* | *The engines roared.* **2** [I,T] to shout something in a deep powerful voice: *'Get out of my house!' he roared.* | *The crowd roared in delight.* **3** [I] to laugh loudly and continuously: *By this time, Michael was roaring with laughter.* **4** [I always + adv/prep] if a vehicle roars somewhere, it moves very quickly and noisily: *The car roared off down the road.*

roar back phr v if a competitor or team that was losing roars back, they start performing much better – used in sports reports: *In the second half Leeds came roaring back with two goals in five minutes.*

roar² n [C] **1** a deep, loud noise made by an animal such as a lion, or by someone's voice; → **growl**: *the roar of the crowd* | *He let out a roar of laughter.* **2** a continuous loud noise, especially made by a machine or a strong wind: *the roar of the traffic*

roar·ing /'rɔːrɪŋ/ adj **1** [only before noun] making a deep, very loud, continuous noise: *the roaring wind and waves* **2 roaring fire** a fire that burns with a lot of flames and heat **3 do a roaring trade (in sth)** *BrE informal* to sell a lot of something very quickly: *The stallholders were doing a roaring trade in burgers.* **4 be a roaring success** *BrE informal* to be extremely successful: *The new musical has been a roaring success.* **5 roaring drunk** *BrE informal* very drunk and noisy

roast¹ /rəʊst $ roʊst/ v [I,T] **1** to cook something, such as meat, in an OVEN or over a fire, or to cook in this way; → **grill, bake**: *Are you going to roast the chicken?* | *the delicious smell of meat roasting* | *We caught a rabbit and roasted it over an open fire.* → see picture at POTATO **2** to heat nuts, coffee beans etc quickly in order to dry them and give them a particular taste: *dry-roasted peanuts*

roast² n [C] **1** a large piece of roasted meat: *a traditional Sunday roast* **2 hot dog roast/oyster roast etc** *AmE* an outdoor party at which food is cooked on an open fire **3** *AmE* an occasion at which people celebrate a special event in someone's life by telling funny stories or giving speeches about them: *a celebrity roast*

roast³ adj [only before noun] roasted: *roast chicken*

roast·ing¹ /'rəʊstɪŋ $ 'roʊ-/ adj **1** also **ˌroasting 'hot** *informal* very hot, especially so that you feel uncomfortable: *a roasting hot day* | *I'm absolutely roasting in this suit.* **2** [only before noun] used for roasting food: *a roasting dish*

roasting² n **give sb/get a roasting** *BrE informal* if you give someone a roasting, you tell them angrily that you disapprove of their behaviour: *He got a roasting from angry fans.*

rob S3 /rɒb $ rɑːb/ v **robbed, robbing** [T]
1 to steal money or property from a person, bank etc; → **steal, burgle**: *They killed four policemen while robbing a bank.* | *A 77-year-old woman was robbed at knifepoint.* | **rob sb of sth** *They threatened to shoot him and robbed him of all his possessions.* ⚠ Someone can **rob** a person or place, but you cannot say that they rob an object or amount of money. Use **steal**: *He robbed a bank, stealing cash and valuables worth $500,000.*
2 rob Peter to pay Paul to take money away from someone or something that needs it in order to pay someone else or use it for something else: *Taking money out of the hospital's budget for this is simply robbing Peter to pay Paul.*
3 rob sb blind *informal* to steal everything someone has: *The minute your back's turned, they'll rob you blind.*
4 I/we was robbed! *BrE spoken* used when you think that you were beaten unfairly in a sport
5 rob the cradle *AmE* to have a sexual relationship with someone who is a lot younger than you – used humorously; ⊟ **cradle-snatch** *BrE*

rob sb/sth of sth phr v *literary*
to take away an important quality, ability etc from someone or something: *The illness robbed him of a normal childhood.*

rob·ber /'rɒbə $ 'rɑːbər/ n [C] someone who steals money or property; → **thief, burglar**: *Armed robbers broke into the shop and demanded money from the till.* | *a bank robber*

ˌrobber 'baron n [C] a powerful person who uses their money and influence to get more money, business, land etc in a way that is slightly dishonest

rob·ber·y /'rɒbəri $ 'rɑː-/ n plural **robberies** [C,U] the crime of stealing money or things from a bank, shop etc, especially using violence; → **theft, burglary**: *Police are investigating a series of bank robberies in South Wales.* | *He received a 10 year prison sentence for armed robbery* (=robbery using a gun). | *He admitted attempted robbery and was given a suspended sentence.* → **daylight robbery** at DAYLIGHT (5); → **highway robbery** at HIGHWAY (3)

robe /rəʊb $ roʊb/ n [C] **1** also **robes** a long loose piece of clothing, especially one worn for official ceremonies: *a priest's robes* **2** *especially AmE* a long loose piece of clothing that you wear over your night clothes or after a bath; ⊟ **bathrobe**; ⊟ **dressing gown** *BrE*

robed /rəʊbd $ roʊbd/ adj *formal* wearing long loose clothing: *a robed figure* | [+in] *a man robed in black*

rob·in /'rɒbɪn $ 'rɑː-/ n [C] **1** a small European bird with a red breast and brown back **2** a North American bird like a European robin, but larger

ro·bot /'rəʊbɒt $ 'roʊbɑːt, -bət/ n [C] a machine that can move and do some of the work of a person, and is usually controlled by a computer: *cars built by robots*

ro·bot·ic /rəʊ'bɒtɪk $ roʊ'bɑː-/ adj **1** [only before noun] robotic equipment etc is related to robots or is part of a robot: *the space shuttle's robotic arm* **2** someone who is robotic acts like a robot by making stiff movements, not showing any human feelings etc

ro·bo·tics /rəʊ'bɒtɪks $ 'roʊbɑː-/ n [U] the study of how robots are made and used

ro·bust /rə'bʌst, 'rəʊbʌst $ rə'bʌst, 'roʊ-/ adj **1** a robust person is strong and healthy: *a robust man of* *six feet four* **2** a robust system, organization etc is strong and not likely to have problems: *The formerly robust economy has begun to weaken.* **3** a robust object is strong and not likely to break; **⊟ sturdy:** *a robust metal cabinet* **4** showing determination or strong opinions: *a typically robust performance by the Prime Minister* **5** robust food or FLAVOURS have a good strong taste: *a robust cheese* —**robustly** *adv* —**robustness** *n* [U]

rock¹ S2 W2 /rɒk $ rɑːk/ *n*

1 STONE **a)** [U] the hard substance that forms the main surface of the Earth; → **stone:** *To build the tunnel, they had to cut through 500 feet of solid rock.* | *Most of the country is desert and bare rock.* | *massive rock formations* (=shapes made naturally from rock) | *ancient dark volcanic rock* **b)** [C] a piece of rock, especially a large one that sticks up from the ground: *Jack stood on a rock for a better view.* | *During the storm a ship had been driven onto the rocks* (=a line of rocks under or next to the sea). → see picture at STONE¹

2 MUSIC [U] also **rock music** a type of popular modern music with a strong loud beat, played using GUITARS and drums: **rock band/group** *Komuro formed a rock band with some friends while in college.* | *the late rock star, Freddie Mercury* | *The stadium has hosted numerous rock concerts.* → HARD ROCK; → **punk rock** at PUNK (1)

3 (as) solid/steady as a rock **a)** very strongly built or well supported and not likely to break or fall: *a large sofa, solid as a rock* **b)** someone who is as solid or steady as a rock is very strong and calm in difficult situations and you can depend on them → ROCK-SOLID

4 be on the rocks *informal* a relationship or business that is on the rocks is having a lot of problems and is likely to fail soon; **⊟ in trouble:** *I'm afraid Tim's marriage is on the rocks.*

5 scotch/vodka etc on the rocks *informal* an alcoholic drink that is served with ice but no water

6 SWEET FOOD [U] *BrE* a hard sweet made in long round pieces: *a stick of rock*

7 DRUG **a)** [U] a very pure form of the illegal drug COCAINE that some people use for pleasure **b)** [C] a small amount of this drug

8 be (stuck) between a rock and a hard place to have a choice between two things, both of which are unpleasant or dangerous

9 get your rocks off *informal not polite* if a man gets his rocks off, he has sex

10 JEWEL [C usually plural] *old-fashioned informal* a DIAMOND or other jewel

rock² *v* **1** [I,T] to move gently backwards and forwards or from side to side, or to make something do this; → **sway:** *She covered her face, rocking to and fro in her grief.* | *The waves rocked the boat from side to side.* | *Paul sat gently rocking the child in his arms.* | *Jim rocked with laughter when he heard what had happened.* **2** [T] **a)** to make the people in a place or organization feel very shocked – used in news reports; **⊟ shake:** *The scandal rocked the nation.* **b)** to make the future of something seem less certain or steady than it was before, especially because of problems or changes; **⊟ shake:** *Another financial blow has rocked the industry.* | *The theory rocked the foundations of social and moral life.* **3 rock the boat** *informal* to cause problems for other members of a group by criticizing something or trying to change the way something is done: *He kept his feelings to himself, not wanting to rock the boat.* **4** [T] if an explosion or EARTHQUAKE rocks an area, it makes it shake: *Residents had only a few minutes to escape before the blast rocked their houses.* **5 sb/sth rocks** *spoken informal* said to show that you strongly approve of someone or something **6 rock sb's world** *informal* to cause someone to think about something or someone in a completely new way

rock·a·bil·ly /'rɒkəbɪli $ 'rɑːk-/ *n* [U] a type of music that combines rock music and traditional country music

rock and 'roll *n* [U] ROCK 'N' ROLL

rock 'bottom *n* **hit/reach rock bottom** *informal* to become as unhappy, unpleasant, or unsuccessful as it is possible to be: *My personal life had hit rock bottom.*

rock-bottom *adj* [only before noun] a rock-bottom price is as low as it can possibly be: *bargain holidays at rock-bottom prices*

rock ,climbing *n* [U] the sport of climbing up very steep rock surfaces such as the sides of mountains —**rock climber** *n* [C]; → see picture at OUTDOOR

rock·er /'rɒkə $ 'rɑːkər/ *n* [C] **1** *AmE* a ROCKING CHAIR **2** one of the curved pieces of wood fixed to the bottom of a ROCKING CHAIR, that allows it to move backwards and forwards if you push it **3 be off your rocker** *spoken informal* to be crazy **4** a member of a group of young people in Britain in the 1960s who wore leather jackets, rode MOTORCYCLES, and listened to ROCK 'N' ROLL music; → **mod, greaser 5** a musician who plays ROCK 'N' ROLL music, or someone who likes this kind of music: *ageing rockers*

rock·e·ry /'rɒkəri $ 'rɑː-/ *n plural* **rockeries** [C] *BrE* part of a garden where there are rocks with small plants growing between them

rock·et¹ /'rɒkɪt $ 'rɑː-/ *n* **1** [C] a vehicle used for travelling or carrying things into space, which is shaped like a big tube; → **spacecraft:** *The rocket was launched from a space research base.* | *a space rocket* **2** [C] a weapon shaped like a big tube that is fired at things; → **missile:** *anti-tank rockets* **3** [C] a FIREWORK that goes high into the air before exploding into coloured lights **4** [U] *BrE* a plant with green leaves and a strong taste, eaten raw in SALADS; **⊟ arugula** *AmE*

rocket² *v* [I] **1** also **rocket up** if a price or amount rockets, it increases quickly and suddenly: *Interest rates rocketed up.* | **rocket (from sth) to sth** *Car sales rocketed from 180 to 2000 a year.* **2** [always + adv/prep] to move somewhere very fast; **⊟ shoot:** *The train rocketed through the tunnel.* | *Larsson's shot rocketed into the back of the net.* **3** [always + adv/prep] to achieve a successful position very quickly; **⊟ shoot:** [I to] *Their new album rocketed to number one in the charts.* | *Beatty rocketed to stardom after his first film.*

rocket ,science *n* **sth is not rocket science** *informal* used to say that something is not difficult to do or understand: *Designing a website may be a lot of work but it's not rocket science.*

rocket ,scientist *n* [C] **1 it doesn't take a rocket scientist (to do sth)** *informal* used humorously to emphasize that something is easy to do or understand: *It doesn't take a rocket scientist to work out that doubling productivity will improve profits.* **2** someone who is extremely clever **3** a scientist whose work is related to rockets

rock face *n* [C] a very steep surface of rock on the side of a mountain

rock·fall /'rɒkfɔːl $ 'rɑːkfɒːl/ *n* [C] a pile of rocks that are falling or have fallen

rock ,garden *n* [C] a ROCKERY

rock-'hard *adj* **1** extremely hard: *The bread was stale and rock-hard.* **2** *BrE* strong and not afraid of anyone – used humorously

rocking chair *n* [C] a chair that has two curved pieces of wood fixed under its legs, so that it moves backwards and forwards smoothly → see picture at CHAIR¹

rocking horse *n* [C] a wooden horse for children that moves backwards and forwards when you sit on it

rock ,music *n* [U] a type of popular modern music with a strong loud beat, played using GUITARS and drums

rock 'n' roll /,rɒk ən 'rəʊl $,rɑːk ən 'roʊl/ *n* [U] **1** a style of music with a strong loud beat played on GUITARS

R

1 000, **2** 000, **3** 000, most frequent words in S poken and W ritten English

roller → STEAMROLLER[1] (1)   **2** [usually plural] a tube-shaped piece of metal or wood, used for moving heavy things that have no wheels: *The boats are taken down to the sea on rollers.*   **3** a small plastic or metal tube used for making hair curl; ▤ **curler**   **4** a long powerful wave: *great Atlantic rollers*

Roll·er·blade /'rəʊləbleɪd $ 'rəʊlər-/ *n* [C] *trademark* a special boot with a single row of wheels fixed under it, used for SKATING on hard surfaces → ROLLER SKATE, IN-LINE SKATE

'roller blind *n* [C] *BrE* a piece of cloth or other material that can be rolled up and down to cover a window; → **venetian blind**

'roller ˌcoaster *n* [C]   **1** a track with very steep slopes and curves, which people ride on in small carriages at FAIRS and AMUSEMENT PARKS   **2** a situation that changes often: *Their relationship was an emotional roller coaster.*

'roller skate *n* [C] a special boot with four wheels fixed under it, used for SKATING on hard surfaces —**roller-skate** *v* [I] —**roller skating** *n* [U] → ROLLERBLADE, IN-LINE SKATE; → see picture at SKATE[1]

rol·lick·ing[1] /'rɒlɪkɪŋ $ 'rɑː-/ *adj* [only before noun] old-fashioned noisy and cheerful: *a rollicking song*

rollicking[2] *n* **give sb a rollicking** *BrE informal* to criticize someone angrily for something they have done

roll·ing /'rəʊlɪŋ $ 'rəʊ-/ *adj* [only before noun]   **1** rolling hills have many long gentle slopes → see picture at LANDSCAPE[1]   **2** done or happening regularly over a period of time, not all at once: *We recommend a rolling programme of machine upgrading.*

'rolling pin *n* [C] a long tube-shaped piece of wood used for making PASTRY flat and thin before you cook it → see picture at EAT

'rolling stock *n* [U] all the trains, carriages etc that are used on a railway

ˌroll of 'honour *n* [C] *BrE* a list of people who are officially praised, especially because they were brave in battle; ▤ **honor roll** *AmE*: *the roll of honour on the war memorial*

'roll-on also **ˌroll-on de'odorant** *n* [C] a bottle which contains liquid that you rub under your arms in order to stop your SWEAT from smelling unpleasant

ˌroll-on 'roll-off *adj* [only before noun] *BrE* a roll-on roll-off ship is one that vehicles can drive straight on and off: *a roll-on roll-off car ferry*

'roll-out *n* [C,U] an occasion when a new product is made available for people to buy or use; ▤ **launch**: *Sun had to cancel the intended roll-out of the 514 model.*

roll·ov·er /'rəʊləʊvə $ 'rəʊləʊvər/ *n*   **1 a)** [C] when money is moved from one bank account or INVESTMENT to another without any tax or other FEES having to be paid: *Many CD rollovers happen in October.* **b)** [C,U] the action of making a bank account, INVESTMENT etc do this: [+of] *The law allows a rollover of retirement money from a company pension to an IRA.*   **2** [C] *BrE* if there is a rollover in a competition or LOTTERY, nobody wins the biggest prize that week, and the money is added to the prize that can be won the following week   **3** [C] an accident in which a car turns over onto its roof   **4** [U] *technical* a way of making the images change whenever someone using a MOUSE moves it over a particular word or picture on a computer screen

Rolls-Royce /ˌrəʊlz 'rɔɪs◂ $ ˌrəʊlz-/ *n* *trademark*   **1** [C] a very expensive and comfortable car made by a British company   **2 the Rolls-Royce of sth** *BrE informal* something that is regarded as the highest quality example of a particular type of product: *the Rolls-Royce of beers*

'roll-up *n* [C] *BrE informal* a cigarette that you make yourself

ro·ly-po·ly[1] /ˌrəʊli 'pəʊli◂ $ ˌrəʊli 'poʊ-/ *adj informal* a roly-poly person is round and fat

roly-poly[2] *n plural* **roly-polies** [C,U] a British sweet food made of JAM that is rolled up inside PASTRY

ROM /rɒm $ rɑːm/ *n* [U] *technical* **read-only memory** the part of a computer where permanent instructions and information are stored; → **RAM**

ro·maine /rəʊ'meɪn $ roʊ-/ *n* [U] *AmE* a type of bitter-tasting LETTUCE with long leaves

ro·man /'rəʊmən $ 'roʊ-/ *n* [U] *technical* the ordinary style of printing that uses small upright letters, like the style used for printing these words; → **font, italics**

Roman *adj* [usually before noun]   **1** relating to ancient Rome or the Roman Empire: *an old Roman road* | *the Roman occupation of Britain*   **2** relating to the city of Rome —**Roman** *n* [C]

ˌRoman 'alphabet *n* **the Roman alphabet** the alphabet used in English and many other European languages, which begins with the letters A, B, C

ˌRoman 'Catholic *adj* *RC* belonging or relating to the part of the Christian religion whose leader is the Pope; ▤ **Catholic**: *a Roman Catholic priest* —**Roman Catholic** *n* [C] —**ˌRoman Ca'tholicism** *n* [U]

ro·mance[1] /rəʊ'mæns, 'rəʊmæns $ roʊ'mæns, 'roʊ-/ *n*   **1** [C] an exciting and often short relationship between two people who love each other; → **affair**: [+with] *Hemingway's romance with his nurse inspired him to write 'A Farewell to Arms'.* | *Michelle married him after a whirlwind romance* (=one that happens very suddenly and quickly). | **holiday romance** *BrE*; **summer romance** *AmE* (=one that happens during a holiday) *a short holiday romance*   **2** [U] love, or a feeling of being in love: *The romance had gone out of their relationship.*   **3** [U] the feeling of excitement and adventure that is related to a particular place, activity etc: [+of] *the romance of Hollywood*   **4** [C] a story about the love between two people: *romance novels*   **5** [C] a story that has brave characters and exciting events: *a Medieval romance*

romance[2] *v*   **1** [I] to describe things that have happened in a way that makes them seem more important, interesting etc than they really were: [+about] *an old man romancing about the past*   **2** [T] *old-fashioned* to try to persuade someone to love you

ˈRomance language *n* [C] a language that comes from Latin, for example French or Spanish

Ro·man·esque /ˌrəʊmə'nesk◂ $ ˌroʊ-/ *adj* in the style of building that was popular in Western Europe in the 11th and 12th centuries, and had many round ARCHES and thick PILLARS

ˌRoman 'law *n* [U] *law* CIVIL LAW

ˌRoman 'nose *n* [C] a nose that curves out near the top

ˌroman 'numeral *n* [C] a number in a system first used in ancient Rome that uses combinations of the letters I, V, X, L, C, D, and M to represent numbers; → **Arabic numeral**

Romano- /rəmɑːnəʊ $ -noʊ/ *prefix* [in nouns and adjectives] ancient Roman and something else: *Romano-British society*

ro·man·tic[1] /rəʊ'mæntɪk, rə- $ roʊ, rə-/ *adj*

1 SHOWING LOVE showing strong feelings of love: *'Tom always sends me red roses on my birthday.' 'How romantic!'*

2 RELATING TO LOVE relating to feelings of love or a loving relationship: *After dinner, they took a romantic stroll by the sea.* | *real old-fashioned romantic love* | *I'm not ready for a romantic relationship.*

3 STORY/FILM a romantic story or film is about love: *a romantic comedy*

4 BEAUTIFUL beautiful in a way that affects your emotions and makes you think of love or adventure: *romantic music* | *The castle is set in one of England's most romantic landscapes.*

5 NOT PRACTICAL romantic ideas are not practical or not based on reality; ▤ **realistic**: **romantic notion/**

view/idea etc *romantic notions about becoming a famous actress* | *Like many New Yorkers, he had a romantic image of country life.*
6 Romantic art/literature etc art or literature that is based on the ideas of romanticism —**romantically** /-kli/ *adv*

romantic² *n* [C] **1** someone who shows strong feelings of love and likes doing things that are related to love such as buying flowers, presents etc **2** someone who is not practical, and bases their ideas too much on an imagined idea of the world; ☒ **realist**: *a romantic who longed for adventure* **3** also **Romantic** a writer, painter etc whose work is based on romanticism

ro·man·ti·cis·m /rəʊˈmæntɪˌsɪzəm, rə- $ roʊ-, rə-/ *n* [U] **1** also **Romanticism** a way of writing or painting that was popular in the late 18th and early 19th century, in which feelings, imagination, and wild natural beauty were considered more important than anything else **2** ideas which are not practical or not based on reality; ☒ **realism**

ro·man·ti·cize also **-ise** *BrE* /rəʊˈmæntɪsaɪz, rə- $ roʊ-, rə-/ *v* [T] to talk or think about things in a way that makes them seem more romantic or attractive than they really are: *a romanticized image of life during the war*

Ro·ma·ny /ˈrəʊməni $ ˈrɑː-/ *n plural* **Romanies 1** [C] a GYPSY **2** [U] the language traditionally used by the GYPSY people —**Romany** *adj*

ro·me·o, **Romeo** /ˈrəʊmiəʊ $ ˈroʊmioʊ/ *n plural* **romeos** [C] a man who tries to attract all the women he meets in a ROMANTIC or sexual way – often used humorously; → **Casanova**

romp¹ /rɒmp $ rɑːmp/ *v* [I] **1** [always + adv/prep] to play in a noisy way, especially by running, jumping etc: [+**around/about**] *They could hear the children romping around upstairs.* **2** to win a race, competition, election etc very easily: **romp to a win/victory** *The women's team romped to a 132–81 win over Ireland.* | *In 1906 the Liberal Party romped back to power.* | **romp home** *BrE*: *The favourite horse, Badawi, romped home in the first race.*

romp through sth *phr v BrE informal* to succeed in doing or finishing something quickly and easily

romp² *n* [C] **1** *informal* a piece of amusing entertainment which has a lot of exciting scenes: *'A Royal Scandal' is an hour-long romp that pokes fun at British royal marriages.* **2** *BrE informal* a period of sexual activity – used humorously, especially in newspapers **3** when one sports team defeats another one very easily – used in newspapers: [+**over**] *the Yankees' 12–1 romp over the Red Sox*

ron·do /ˈrɒndəʊ $ ˈrɑːndoʊ/ *n plural* **rondos** [C] a piece of music in which the main tune is repeated several times

rood screen *n* [C] *technical* a decorated wooden or stone wall in a Christian church which divides the part where the CHOIR sit from the part where other people sit

roof¹ S3 W2 /ruːf $ ruːf, rʊf/ *n* [C]
1 the structure that covers or forms the top of a building, vehicle, tent etc: *They finally found the cat up on the roof.* | [+**of**] *We can probably strap the cases to the roof of her car.* | **slate/tiled/thatched etc roof** | *a flat roof* | *a **pitched roof** (=sloping roof)* | **red-roofed/metal-roofed etc** *a wooden-roofed theatre;* → see picture at STAY
2 the top of a passage under the ground: *Suddenly, the whole tunnel roof caved in.*
3 **a roof over your head** somewhere to live: *I may not have a job, but at least I've got a roof over my head.*
4 **go through the roof** *informal* **a)** also **hit the roof** to suddenly become very angry: *Put that back before Dad sees you and hits the roof!* **b)** if a price, cost etc goes through the roof, it increases to a very high level
5 **the roof of sb's mouth** the hard upper part of the inside of your mouth
6 **under the same roof/under one roof** in the same building or home: *If we're going to live under the same*

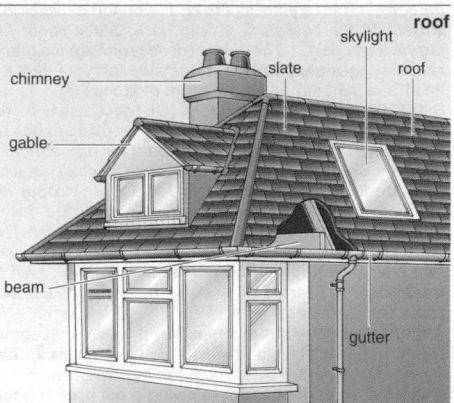

roof
skylight
chimney
gable
slate
roof
beam
gutter

roof, we need to get along. | *Here you can buy food, clothes, and electrical goods all under one roof.*
7 **under sb's roof** *spoken* in your home: *As long as you live under my roof, you'll do as I say.*
8 **the roof falls in/caves in** *informal especially AmE* if the roof falls in or caves in, something bad suddenly happens to you when you do not expect it → **raise the roof** at RAISE¹ (23); → SUNROOF

roof² *v* [T usually passive] to put a roof on a building: **be roofed with sth** *a cottage roofed with the local slate*
roof sth ⇔ **in/over** *phr v BrE* to cover an open space by putting a roof over it: *We're going to roof in the yard to make a garage.*

roof·ies /ˈruːfiz $ ˈruːf-, ˈrʊf-/ *n* [plural] *informal* an illegal drug that is sometimes used to make someone unconscious so they can be RAPED

roof·ing /ˈruːfɪŋ $ ˈruːf-, ˈrʊf-/ *n* [U] **1** material used for making or covering roofs **2** the job of building or repairing roofs

roof-rack *n* [C] *BrE* a metal frame fixed on top of a car and used for carrying bags, cases etc; ☒ **luggage rack** *AmE*

roof·top /ˈruːftɒp $ ˈruːftɑːp, ˈrʊf-/ *n* [C] the upper surface of a roof: *Spectators stood on rooftops to watch the parade.* → **shout sth from the rooftops** at SHOUT¹ (3)

rook /rʊk/ *n* [C] **1** a large black European bird like a CROW **2** one of the pieces in a game of CHESS; ☒ **castle**; → see picture at CHESS

rook·ie /ˈrʊki/ *n* [C] **1** *especially AmE* someone who has just started doing a job and has little experience: *rookie cops* **2** *AmE* someone who is in their first year of playing a professional sport

room¹ S1 W1 /ruːm, rʊm/ *n*
1 **IN A BUILDING** [C] a part of the inside of a building that has its own walls, floor, and ceiling: *I looked around the room.* | *She nodded toward a man who was standing across the room (=on the other side of the room).* | *Someone was laughing in **the next room** (=the one beside the one you are in).* | **sb's room** *(=someone's bedroom)* *Beth, it's time to clean up your room.* | **bathroom/dining room/meeting room etc** *the doctor's waiting room* | **one-room(ed)/two-room(ed) etc** *a three-room apartment* | **single/double room** *(=a room in a hotel for one person or for two)* *I'd like to book a double room for two nights.* | *Here's your key – room 348.* → FRONT ROOM, LIVING ROOM, SITTING ROOM
2 **SPACE** [U] space somewhere for a particular thing, person, or activity: [+**in**] *I hope **there's** going to be enough **room** in the fridge.* | [+**for**] *My suitcase was so full I didn't have **room** for anything else.* | **room to do sth** *The museum doesn't have enough room to show everything in their collection.* | **plenty of room/enough room** *There's plenty of room in the boot for your*

R

luggage. | *I'm trying to* **make room** *for a vegetable garden in the backyard.* | *Step back,* **leave room** *for people to get past.* | *The old wardrobe* **took up** *too much room.* | **leg-room/head-room** (=space for your legs or head in a vehicle); → **elbow-room** at ELBOW¹ (5)

3 OPPORTUNITY/POSSIBILITY [U] the chance to do something, or the possibility that something exists or can happen: [+for] *There's little room for innovation.* | **room for doubt/debate/argument etc** *The evidence was clear, and there was little room for doubt.* | **room for manoeuvre** *BrE*/**room for maneuver** *AmE* (=the possibility of changing what you do or decide) *Teachers feel they have little room for manoeuvre when the curriculum is so demanding.* | **room to do sth** *Children need to have room to develop their natural creativity.* | **Make room** *in your day for exercise.*

4 there's room for improvement used to say that something is not perfect and needs to be improved: *The report shows that there is room for improvement.*

5 there's not enough room to swing a cat used humorously to say that an area or room is not very big

6 APARTMENT **rooms** [plural] *old-fashioned especially BrE* two or more rooms that you rent in a building, or stay in at a college

7 PEOPLE [singular] all the people in a room: *The whole room started singing 'Happy Birthday'.*

room² *v* [I] *AmE* to rent and live in a room somewhere **room with** sb *phr v* to share a room or house with someone, especially at college: *I roomed with Al at UCSD.*

ˌ**room and ˈboard** *n* [U] a room to sleep in, with food provided: *You'll receive free room and board with the job.*

room·er /ˈruːmə, ˈrʊm- $ -ər/ *n* [C] *AmE* someone who pays rent to live in a house with its owner; ◼ **lodger** *BrE*

room·ful /ˈruːmfʊl, ˈrʊm-/ *n* [C] a large number of things or people that are all together in one room: [+of] *a roomful of reporters*

ˈ**rooming house** *n* [C] *AmE* a house where people can rent a room to live in

room·mate; ˈ**room-mate** *BrE* /ˈruːmˌmeɪt, ˈrʊm-/ *n* [C] **1** someone who you share a room with, especially at college: *one of my college roommates* **2** *AmE* someone you share an apartment or house with; ◼ **flatmate** *BrE*

ˈ**room ˌservice** *n* [U] a service provided by a hotel, by which food and drinks can be sent to a guest's room

ˈ**room ˌtemperature** *n* [U] the normal temperature inside a house: *The wine should be served at room temperature.*

room·y /ˈruːmi/ *adj* a house, car etc that is roomy is large and has a lot of space inside it; ◼ **spacious**

roost¹ /ruːst/ *n* [C] a place where birds rest and sleep → **rule the roost** at RULE² (4)

roost² *v* [I] **1** if a bird roosts, it rests or sleeps somewhere **2 sb's chickens come home to roost** also **sth comes home to roost** used to say that someone's past mistakes are causing problems for them now: *After years of overspending, the chickens have come home to roost.*

roost·er /ˈruːstə $ -ər/ *n* [C] a male chicken; ◼ **cock** *BrE*

root¹ S3 W2 /ruːt/ *n* [C]

1 PLANT the part of a plant or tree that grows under the ground and gets water from the soil: *tree roots* | *These plants produce a number of thin roots.* → ROOT CROP, ROOT VEGETABLE; → see picture at TREE

2 CAUSE OF A PROBLEM the main cause of a problem: **be/lie at the root of sth** (=be the cause of something) *Allergies are at the root of a lot of health problems.* | *The love of money is the root of all evil.* | *A competent mechanic should be able to get to the root of the problem* (=find out the cause of a problem). | *the root causes of crime*

3 ORIGIN/MAIN PART the origin or main part of something such as a custom, law, activity etc, from which other things have developed: [+in] *a legal system with roots in English common law* | *Jazz has its roots in the folk songs of the southern states of the US.* | **be/lie at the root of sth** *the liberal economic policies which lie at the root of American power*

4 FAMILY CONNECTION sb's **roots** your relation to a place because you were born there, or your family used to live there: *immigrants keeping in touch with their cultural roots* | *Alex Haley's story about his* **search for** *his* **roots** *became a bestseller.*

5 put down roots if you put down roots somewhere, you start to feel that a place is your home and to have relationships with the people there: *Because of her husband's job, they'd moved too often to put down roots anywhere.*

6 TOOTH/HAIR ETC the part of a tooth, hair etc that connects it to the rest of your body: *She'd pulled some of Kelly's hair out by the roots.*

7 take root a) if an idea, method, activity etc takes root, people begin to accept or believe it, or it begins to have an effect: *Economists believe that economic recovery will begin to take root next year.* **b)** if a plant takes root, it starts to grow where you have planted it

8 have a (good) root round *BrE informal* to search for something by moving other things around

9 LANGUAGE *technical* the basic part of a word which shows its main meaning, to which other parts can be added. For example, the word 'coldness' is formed from the root 'cold' and the SUFFIX 'ness'; → **stem**

10 MATHEMATICS *technical* a number that, when multiplied by itself a certain number of times, equals the number that you have: *2 is the fourth root of 16.*

11 root and branch if you destroy or change something root and branch, you get rid of it or change it completely and permanently because it is bad: *a root and branch reform of the electoral system* → CUBE ROOT, SQUARE ROOT, GRASS ROOTS

root² *v*

1 PLANT **a)** [I] to grow roots: *New shrubs will root easily in summer.* **b)** [T usually passive] if a plant is rooted somewhere, it is held in the ground firmly by its roots: *a bush firmly rooted in the hard ground* | **root itself** *Clumps of thyme had rooted themselves between the rocks.*

2 be rooted in sth to have developed from something and be strongly influenced by it: *The country's economic troubles are rooted in a string of global crises.* | *This feeling of rejection is often* **deeply rooted in** *childhood.*

3 SEARCH [I always + adv/prep] to search for something by moving things around; ◼ **rummage**: **root through/in/amongst sth (for sth)** *Leila rooted through her handbag for a pen.*

4 PIGS [I usually + adv/prep] if a pig roots somewhere, it looks for food under the ground: [+for] *pigs rooting for truffles*

5 rooted to the spot/floor/ground etc so shocked, surprised, or frightened that you cannot move: *She stood rooted to the spot, staring at him.*

root for sb *phr v informal*

1 to want someone to succeed in a competition, test, or difficult situation: *You can do it – I'm rooting for you.*

2 *especially AmE* to support a sports team or player by shouting and cheering: *the Los Angeles fans rooting for the Lakers*

root sth ⇔ **out** *phr v*

1 to find out where a particular kind of problem exists and get rid of it: *Action is being taken to root out corruption in the police force.*

2 to find something by searching for it: *I'll try and root out something for you to wear.*

root sth ⇔ **up** *phr v*

to dig or pull a plant up with its roots

ˈ**root beer** *n* [C,U] a sweet brown non-alcoholic drink made from the roots of some plants, drunk especially in the US

'**root ca·nal** n [C] a treatment in which a DENTIST removes a diseased area in the root of a tooth

'**root crop** n [C] a vegetable or plant that is grown so that its roots can be sold

root·le /ˈruːtl/ also **rootle around/about** v [I] BrE informal to search for something by moving many other things around —**rootle** n [singular]

root·less /ˈruːtləs/ adj having nowhere that you feel is really your home: rootless people —**rootlessness** n [U]

'**root ˌvegetable** n [C] a vegetable such as a potato or CARROT that grows under the ground

rope¹ S3 W3 /rəʊp $ roʊp/ n
1 [C,U] very strong thick string, made by twisting together many thinner strings: They tied a rope around my waist and pulled me up. | The man was coiling a length of rope.
2 the ropes [plural] **a)** all the things someone needs to know to do a job or deal with a system: I spent the first month just **learning the ropes**. | He works repairing streets, and **knows the ropes** when it comes to safety. | Miss McGinley will **show** you **the ropes** and answer any questions. **b)** the rope fence that surrounds an area used for BOXING or WRESTLING
3 be on the ropes informal to be in a very bad situation, in which you are likely to be defeated: The army says the rebels are on the ropes.
4 be at/near etc the end of your rope especially AmE to have no more PATIENCE or strength left to deal with a problem or a difficult situation: My son is causing endless problems, and I'm close to the end of my rope.
5 give sb some/enough etc rope to give someone a lot of freedom to do something in the way they want to do it: Managers have to decide how much rope to give their subordinates.
6 give sb enough rope to hang themselves to give someone freedom to do what they want to do, because you think they will cause problems for themselves and you want them to look stupid
7 a rope of pearls PEARLS on a string, worn around your neck as jewellery → JUMP ROPE, SKIPPING ROPE, TIGHTROPE, TOWROPE; → **money for old rope** at MONEY (17)

rope² v [T] **1** [always + adv/prep] to tie things together using rope: **rope sth to sth** Suitcases were roped to the top of the car. | **rope sb/sth together** Mountaineers rope themselves together for safety. **2** AmE to catch an animal using a circle of rope: The calves are roped and branded.
rope sb into sth also **rope sb ⇔ in** BrE phr v informal to persuade someone to help you in a job or join in an activity, especially when they do not want to: **rope sb into doing sth** Denise roped me into selling tickets. | **rope sb in to do sth** Anyone who could sing was roped in to help. | Have you been roped in too?
rope sth ⇔**off** phr v to surround an area with ropes, especially in order to separate it from another area: The stairs were roped off.

'**rope ˌladder** n [C] a LADDER made of two long ropes connected by wooden pieces that you stand on

rop·ey, **ropy** /ˈrəʊpi $ ˈroʊ-/ comparative **ropier**, superlative **ropiest** adj BrE informal **1** in bad condition or of bad quality: ropey old furniture **2** [not before noun] slightly ill: I'm feeling a bit ropey this morning.

ro-ro /ˈrəʊ rəʊ $ ˈroʊ roʊ/ n plural **ro-ros** [C] BrE informal a ROLL-ON ROLL-OFF ship

Ror·schach test /ˈrɔːʃɑːk test $ ˈrɔːr-/ n [C] a method of testing someone's character, by making them say what they see in spots of ink with various shapes look like

ro·sa·ry /ˈrəʊzəri $ ˈroʊ-/ n plural **rosaries** [C] **1** a string of BEADS used by Roman Catholics for counting prayers **2** the rosary/the Rosary the set of prayers that are said by Roman Catholics while counting rosary BEADS: **say/recite the rosary** Three nuns knelt there, reciting the rosary.

rose¹ S3 W3 /rəʊz $ roʊz/ n
rose
petal
leaf
stalk/stem
1 FLOWER [C] a flower that often has a pleasant smell, and is usually red, pink, white, or yellow, or the bush that this flower grows on: a dozen red roses | A large bouquet of roses arrived on her desk. | rose bushes
2 COLOUR [U] a pink colour
3 sth is not a bed of roses also **sth is not all roses** BrE informal if a job or situation is not a bed of roses, it is not always pleasant and there are difficult things to deal with: It's no bed of roses teaching in a secondary school.
4 put the roses back in sb's cheeks BrE informal to make someone look healthy again
5 be coming up roses informal to be happening or developing in the best possible way
6 come out of sth/come up smelling of roses informal to do well or get an advantage from a situation, when you could have been blamed, criticized, or harmed by it: She managed to come out of the deal smelling of roses.
7 FOR WATER [C] BrE a circular piece of metal with holes in it that is attached to the end of a pipe or WATERING CAN so that liquid comes out in several thin streams

rose² v the past tense of RISE

rose³ adj pink in colour: rose velvet curtains

ro·sé /ˈrəʊzeɪ $ roʊˈzeɪ/ n [C,U] pink wine

ro·se·ate /ˈrəʊziᵻt $ ˈroʊ-/ adj literary pink: the **roseate glow** of the evening sun

rose·bud /ˈrəʊzbʌd $ ˈroʊz-/ n [C] **1** the flower of a rose before it opens **2 rosebud mouth/lips** a mouth or lips that have a small round shape and are very red

'**rose-ˌcoloured** BrE; **rose-colored** AmE adj **1** pink **2 rose-coloured glasses** also **rose-coloured spectacles** BrE if you see or view something through rose-coloured glasses, you think it is better than it really is

'**rose hip** n [C] the small red fruit produced by some kinds of rose bushes, used in medicines and juices

rose·ma·ry /ˈrəʊzməri $ ˈroʊzmeri/ n [U] the narrow leaves of a bush, used as a herb, or the bush that these leaves come from

'**rose-ˌtinted** adj BrE ROSE-COLOURED

ro·sette /rəʊˈzet $ roʊ-/ n [C] **1** BrE a circular BADGE made of coloured RIBBON that is given to the winner of a competition, or that people in Britain wear to show support for a particular football team or political party **2** a shape like a round flat flower that has been made in stone or wood

rose·wa·ter /ˈrəʊzˌwɔːtə $ ˈroʊzˌwɔːtər, -ˌwɑː-/ n [U] a liquid made from roses which has a pleasant smell

'**rose ˈwindow** n [C] a circular window in a church, especially one with coloured glass in it

rose·wood /ˈrəʊzwʊd $ ˈroʊz-/ n [U] a hard dark red wood, used for making expensive furniture

Rosh Ha·sha·nah /ˌrɒʃ həˈʃɑːnə $ ˌrɔːʃ həˈʃɔːnə/ n [U] the Jewish new year holiday

ros·in /ˈrɒzᵻn $ ˈrɑː-/ n [U] a solid slightly sticky substance that you rub on the BOW of a VIOLIN etc, to help it move smoothly on the strings —**rosin** v [T]

ros·ter¹ /ˈrɒstə $ ˈrɑːstər/ n [C] **1** a list of the names of people on a sports team, in an organization etc: **on a roster** The club has outstanding players on the roster. | [+of] The campaign has a roster of 500 volunteers. **2** a list that shows when each person in a group must do a particular job; ▤ **rota** BrE: duty roster

roster² v [T] to put someone's name on a roster

ros·trum /ˈrɒstrəm $ ˈrɑː-/ n [C] a small PLATFORM that you stand on when you are making a speech or CONDUCTING musicians; ▤ **podium**

ros·y /ˈrəʊzi $ ˈroʊ-/ adj comparative **rosier**, superlative **rosiest** **1** seeming to offer hope of success or happiness: *a company that sees a **rosy future** for itself* | *Letters to relatives in Europe **painted a rosy picture** of life in the United States.* **2** pink: *the kids' **rosy cheeks***

rot¹ /rɒt $ rɑːt/ v **rotted**, **rotting** **1** [I,T] to decay by a gradual natural process, or to make something do this: *Candy will rot your teeth.* | *The trees were cut and **left to rot**.* | [+away] *All the woodwork was rotting away.* **2 rot in hell/jail** to suffer or be punished for a long time – used especially when you are angry with someone: *I hope the people who did this rot in hell.*

rot² n **1** [U] the natural process of decaying, or the part of something that has decayed: *the smell of rot* | *wood that is soft with rot* → **DRY ROT** **2** [singular,U] a state in which something becomes bad or does not work as well as it should: *He criticized the talk shows as 'cultural rot'.* | **stop the rot** BrE (=stop a bad situation getting worse) *The team has enough good players to stop the rot.* | **the rot set in** BrE (=a situation started to get worse) *It was after he left the company that the rot set in.* **3** [U] BrE old-fashioned nonsense: *You do talk rot!*

ro·ta /ˈrəʊtə $ ˈroʊ-/ n [C] BrE a list that shows when each person in a group must do a particular job; ▤ **roster**: *a cleaning rota*

ro·ta·ry¹ /ˈrəʊtəri $ ˈroʊ-/ adj [only before noun] **1** turning in a circle around a fixed point, like a wheel: *the rotary movement of the helicopter blades* **2** having a main part that turns like a wheel: *a rotary engine*

rotary² n plural **rotaries** [C] AmE a ROUNDABOUT

Rotary Club n **the Rotary Club** an organization of business people in a town who work together to raise money for people who are poor or sick

ro·tate /rəʊˈteɪt $ ˈroʊteɪt/ v **1** [I,T] to turn with a circular movement around a central point, or to make something do this; ▤ **revolve**; → **spin**: *The Earth rotates on its axis once every 24 hours.* | *Rotate the pan halfway through the baking time.* **2** [I,T] if a job rotates, or if people rotate jobs, they each do a particular job for a particular period of time: *The chairmanship of the committee rotates annually.* | *Employers may rotate duties to give staff wider experience.* **3** [I,T] to change the places of things or people, or to change places, especially in a circular direction: *Rotating the tyres every few months helps them last longer.* **4** [T] technical to regularly change the crops grown on a piece of land, in order to preserve the quality of the soil; → **crop rotation**

ro·ta·tion /rəʊˈteɪʃən $ roʊ-/ n **1** [U] when something turns with a circular movement around a central point: [+of] *the rotation of the Earth on its axis* | [+about/around] *the planet's rotation around the sun* **2** [C] one complete circular turn around a central point; ▤ **revolution**: *The blades spin at 100 rotations per minute.* **3** [U] the practice of regularly changing the thing that is being used or done, or the person who does a particular job: *job rotation* | **in rotation** *Three plays will be performed in rotation during the drama festival.* **4** [C] AmE a period of time spent doing a particular job, when you will soon change to a different job for the same employer: *a young doctor on a rotation in the children's ward* **5** [C] AmE the people who each take a turn to do a particular job in a regular order: *The rotation included two rookies, Hernandez and Saunders.* —**rotational** adj

rote /rəʊt $ roʊt/ n [U] formal when you learn something by repeating it many times, without thinking about it carefully or without understanding it: *In old-fashioned schools, much **learning was by rote**.* | *the rote learning of facts*

ROTFL, rotfl the written abbreviation of *rolling on the floor laughing*, used by people communicating in CHAT ROOMS on the Internet to say that they are very amused by something that someone else has written

rot·gut /ˈrɒtɡʌt $ ˈrɑːt-/ n [U] informal strong cheap low-quality alcohol

ro·tis·ser·ie /rəʊˈtɪsəri $ roʊ-/ n [C] a piece of equipment for cooking meat by turning it around and around on a metal rod over heat; → **grill**

ro·tor /ˈrəʊtə $ ˈroʊtər/ n [C] technical **1** a part of a machine that turns around on a central point **2** also **rotor blade** the long flat part that turns around and around on top of a HELICOPTER

rot·ten¹ /ˈrɒtn $ ˈrɑːtn/ adj **1** badly decayed and no longer good to use: *the smell of rotten eggs* | *Some of the wood was completely rotten.* | *The apples **went rotten** very quickly.* **2** informal very bad; ▤ **terrible**: *What **rotten luck**!* | *a rotten idea* | *The service was rotten.* | *He's a rotten driver.* **3** informal if someone is rotten, they are unpleasant, unkind, or dishonest: *Why are you being so rotten?* | *a **rotten little brat*** **4 feel rotten a)** to feel ill **b)** to feel unhappy and guilty about something: *I felt rotten about lying to him.* **5** [only before noun] spoken used when you are angry: *I don't want your **rotten money**!* **6 rotten to the core** extremely dishonest: *The whole government is rotten to the core.* **7** a **rotten apple** one bad person who has a bad effect on all the others in a group —**rottenness** n [U]

rotten² adv informal **1 spoil sb rotten** to treat someone too well or too kindly, especially a child, so that they think they should always have what they want: *He was the favorite, and his mother spoiled him rotten.* **2 fancy sb rotten** BrE to be extremely attracted to someone in a sexual way – used humorously

rot·ter /ˈrɒtə $ ˈrɑːtər/ n [C] BrE old-fashioned an unpleasant person who treats other people badly

rott·wei·ler /ˈrɒtvaɪlə, -waɪlə $ ˈrɑːtwaɪlər/ n [C] a type of strong and dangerous dog, often used as a guard dog

ro·tund /rəʊˈtʌnd $ roʊ-/ adj having a fat round body – used humorously; ▤ **stout** —**rotundity** n [U]

ro·tun·da /rəʊˈtʌndə $ roʊ-/ n [C] a round building or hall, especially one with a DOME

rou·ble BrE; **ruble** AmE /ˈruːbəl/ n [C] the standard unit of money in Russia and Belarus

rou·é /ˈruːeɪ $ ruːˈeɪ/ n [C] literary a man who believes that pleasure is the most important thing in life – used to show disapproval

rouge /ruːʒ/ n [U] old-fashioned pink or red powder or cream that women put on their cheeks; ▤ **blusher** —**rouge** v [T]: *heavily rouged cheeks*

rough¹ [S2] [W3] /rʌf/ adj comparative **rougher**, superlative **roughest**

1 NOT SMOOTH having an uneven surface; ▤ **smooth**: *Her hands were rough from hard work.* | *the rough terrain at the base of the mountains* | *We were bumping over the rough ground.*

2 NOT EXACT [usually before noun] not exact, not containing many details, or not in a final form; ▤ **approximate**: *a rough sketch of the house* | *a rough translation* | *Could you give me a **rough idea** what time you'll be home?* | *a **rough estimate** of the cost* | *First do a **rough draft** of your essay.*

3 PROBLEMS/DIFFICULTIES a rough period is one in which you have a lot of problems or difficulties; ▤ **tough**

---

a rough day/week etc

rough times

hit a rough patch/spot

go through a rough patch/spot

have a rough time (of it)

be in for/face a rough ride (=be going to have a difficult time)

rough going (=a period when you have a lot of difficulties)

The first year was rough, but things have gotten

better. | Sounds like you had a **rough day**. | We've been through some **rough times** together. | My boyfriend and I were **going through a rough patch**. | The bill **is in for a rough ride** in the Senate. | It's been **rough going**, but we've almost finished now.

4 NOT GENTLE using force, anger, or violence; ▪ **gentle**: *Rugby is a very rough sport.* | *Don't be too rough – she's only little.* | *Paul gave her a rough shake.* | *equipment capable of withstanding **rough treatment** | The referee won't allow any **rough stuff** (=violent behaviour).* | **be rough on sb** (=treat someone unkindly or criticize them in an angry way) *Don't you think you were a little rough on her?*

5 TOWN/AREA ETC a rough area is a place where there is a lot of violence or crime: *a rough part of town*

6 WEATHER/SEA with strong wind or storms; ▪ **calm**: *The ship went down in rough seas.*

7 VOICE/SOUND a) not sounding soft or gentle, and often rather unpleasant or angry: *Barton's deep, rough voice* **b)** having an unpleasant sound, especially because there is something wrong with a machine: *The clutch sounds rough – better get it checked.*

8 SIMPLE/NOT WELL MADE simple and often not very well made: *a rough wooden table*

9 NOT COMFORTABLE uncomfortable, and with difficult conditions: *The journey was long and rough.*

10 have rough edges also **be rough around the edges a)** to have some parts that are not as good as they should be, but that are not a serious problem: *The team has a few rough edges, but they're winning more games.* **b)** if a person is rough around the edges, they are not very polite, educated etc

11 rough night a night when you did not sleep well: *Mickey **had a rough night** last night.*

12 a rough deal something that happens to you that is unfair or unpleasant: *He's **had a rough deal** with his wife leaving him like that.*

13 feel rough *BrE informal* to feel ill

14 look rough *BrE informal* to look untidy, dirty, or unhealthy: *After travelling for two days we must have looked pretty rough.*

15 rough and ready not perfect, but good enough for a particular purpose: *The tests are only a rough and ready guide to a pupil's future development.*

16 rough justice punishment that is not decided in a court in the usual legal way, and that is often severe or unfair: *Gangs practise a kind of rough justice on their members.* —**roughness** *n* [U] → ROUGH DIAMOND, ROUGH PAPER, ROUGHLY

rough² *n* **1 the rough** uneven ground with long grass on an area where people play golf; ▪ **green** **2 take the rough with the smooth** to accept the bad things in life as well as the good ones: *You have to learn to take the rough with the smooth.* **3** [C] a picture drawn very quickly, not showing all the details; ▪ **sketch**: *a rough of the proposed housing development* **4 in rough** *BrE* if you write or draw something in rough, you do it without paying attention to details or tidiness, because you are going to do it again later: *It's best to work in rough first, and then write it out neatly.* **5 a bit of rough** *BrE informal* someone from a lower social class than you, with whom you have a sexual relationship → DIAMOND IN THE ROUGH

rough³ *v* **rough it** *informal* to live for a short time in conditions that are not very comfortable: *I don't mind roughing it for a while.*

rough sth ⇔ **out** *phr v BrE* to draw or write something without including all the details: *a diagram the engineer had roughed out on his notepad*

rough sb ⇔ **up** *phr v informal* to attack someone and hurt them by hitting them

rough⁴ *adv* **1 sleep rough** *BrE* to sleep outside with nothing to protect you from the weather, especially because you have no home to live in: *the number of people sleeping rough on the street* **2 play rough** to play in a fairly violent way → **cut up rough** at CUT¹ (6)

rough·age /ˈrʌfɪdʒ/ *n* [U] a substance contained in some vegetables, fruits, and grains that helps your BOWELS to work; ▪ **fibre**

rough and 'tumble *n* **1** [U] a situation in which people compete with each other, often in a cruel way: [+of] *the rough and tumble of public life* **2** [singular,U] noisy rough behaviour when playing or fighting, especially by children —**rough-and-tumble** *adj* [only before noun]: *Most boys enjoy rough-and-tumble play.*

rough·cast /ˈrʌfkɑːst $ -kæst/ *n* [U] a rough surface on the outside of a building, made of PLASTER mixed with little stones or broken shells —**roughcast** *adj*

rough 'diamond *n* [C] *BrE informal* someone who seems rude, rough, or unfriendly, but is actually nice and generous; ▪ **diamond in the rough** *AmE*

rough·en /ˈrʌfən/ *v* [I,T] to become rough, or to make something rough: *hands roughened by work*

rough-'hewn *adj* rough-hewn wood or stone has been cut without much care and its surface is not yet smooth

rough·house /ˈrʌfhaʊs/ *v* [I] *AmE* to play roughly or pretend to fight: *Okay, guys, slow down. No more rough-housing.*

rough·ly S2 /ˈrʌfli/ *adv*
1 not exactly; ▪ **about**, **approximately**: *There were roughly 200 people there.* | *Azaleas flower at roughly the same time each year.* | **roughly equal/comparable/equivalent** *two rocks of roughly equal size* | **roughly speaking** (=used when saying something without giving exact details or information) *Roughly speaking, I'd say we need about $500.*
2 not gently or carefully: *He grabbed her roughly.*

rough·neck /ˈrʌfnek/ *n* [C] *informal especially AmE* **1** someone who works on an OIL WELL **2** a man who usually behaves in a rough, rude, or angry way

rough 'paper *n* [U] *BrE* paper that is used for writing or drawing things that will later be changed or copied more neatly

rough·shod /ˈrʌfʃɒd $ -ʃɑːd/ *adv* **ride roughshod over sb/sth** especially *BrE* ; **run roughshod over sb/sth** *AmE* to behave in a way that ignores other people's feelings or opinions: *We cannot ride roughshod over the concerns of the local community.*

rou·lette /ruːˈlet/ *n* [U] a game in which a small ball is spun around on a moving wheel, and people try to win money by guessing which hole the ball will fall into

round¹ S2 W2 /raʊnd/ *especially BrE* also **around** *adv, prep*
1 surrounding or on all sides of something or someone: *We sat round the table playing cards.* | *Gather round! I have an important announcement to make.* | *He put his arm gently round her waist.* | *I kept the key on a chain round my neck.* | *The ballroom's huge, with windows all the way round.* | *There was a lovely courtyard with tables all round.*
2 used to say that someone or something turns so that they face in the opposite direction: *When he turned round I recognised him immediately.* | *Graham glanced round, startled by the voice behind him.*
3 in or to many places or parts of an area: *Reggie went round making sure all the lights were off.* | *Leah showed me round on my first day at the office.* | *A guide took us round the palace and gardens.* | *He spent a whole year travelling round Europe.* | *She looked round the room as though leaving it for the last time.* | *changes that are affecting the weather all round the world*
4 moving in a circle: *She watched the clock hands go round.* | *An aeroplane was circling round far overhead.* | *Until the 16th century people believed that the sun went round the earth.* | *He stared at the washing machine, just watching the clothes go round and round.* | *a shoal of tiny fish swimming round in circles*
5 *informal* if you go round to someone's house, you go to their house, usually to visit them: *I might go round to*

R

2 a line of seats in a theatre or cinema: *We sat in the front row.*

3 **in a row** happening a number of times, one after the other; ▤ **consecutively: 4 nights/3 weeks etc in a row** *She's been out four nights in a row.* | *I've beaten her three times in a row.*

4 used in the name of some roads: *22 Church Row*

5 **a hard/tough row to hoe** used to say that a particular situation is difficult

row² /raʊ/ *n BrE* **1** [C] a short angry argument, especially between people who know each other well; ▤ **quarrel:** [+with] *He had just had a row with his wife.* | [+about] *What was the row about?* | *a family row* | *a blazing row* (=a very angry argument) **2** [C] a situation in which people disagree strongly about important public matters; ▤ **controversy:** [+about/over] *a new row over government secrecy* **3** [singular] a loud unpleasant noise that continues for a long time; ▤ **racket:** *Stop that row – I'm trying to get to sleep!*

row³ /rəʊ $ roʊ/ *v* [I,T] to make a boat move across water using OARS: [+away/towards/across] *She rowed across the lake.* | *Jenny used to row at college* (=as a sport). —**row** *n* [singular]: *Why don't we go for a row?* —**rower** *n* [C]

row⁴ /raʊ/ *v* [I] *BrE* to argue in an angry way: [+about] *They rowed about money all the time.*

ro·wan /ˈrəʊən $ ˈroʊ-/ *n* [C] a small tree with red berries

row·boat /ˈrəʊbəʊt $ ˈroʊboʊt/ *n* [C] *AmE* a small boat that you move through the water with OARS; ▤ **rowing boat** *BrE*

row·dy¹ /ˈraʊdi/ *adj* behaving in a noisy rough way that is likely to cause arguments and fighting: *gangs of rowdy youths* —**rowdily** *adv* —**rowdiness** *n* [U] —**rowdyism** *n* [U]

rowdy² *n plural* **rowdies** [C usually plural] *old-fashioned* someone who behaves in a rough noisy way

row house /ˈrəʊ haʊs $ ˈroʊ-/ *n* [C] *AmE* a house that is part of a line of houses that are joined to each other; ▤ **terraced house** *BrE*; → see picture at HOUSE

row·ing /ˈrəʊɪŋ $ ˈroʊ-/ *n* [U] the sport or activity of making a boat move through the water with OARS

rowing boat /ˈrəʊɪŋ bəʊt $ ˈroʊɪŋ boʊt/ *n* [C] *BrE* a small boat that you move through the water with OARS (=long poles that are flat at the end); ▤ **row boat** *AmE*

rowing ma·chine *n* [C] a piece of exercise equipment on which you perform the action of rowing a boat → see picture at SPORTS CENTRE

row·lock /ˈrɒlək $ ˈroʊlɑːk/ *n* [C] *BrE* one of the U-shaped pieces of metal that holds the OARS of a rowing boat

roy·al¹ [S3] [W1] /ˈrɔɪəl/ *adj* [only before noun]
1 relating to or belonging to a king or queen; → **regal:** *the royal palace* | *the royal family*
2 used in the names of organizations that serve or are supported by a king or queen: *the Royal Navy* | *the Royal College of Music*
3 very impressive, as if done for a king or queen: *a royal welcome*
4 **the royal 'we'** *BrE* the use of the word 'we' instead of 'I' by the Queen or King —**royally** *adv*

royal² *n* [C] *informal* a member of a royal family; ▨ **commoner**

royal blue *n* [U] a bright deep blue colour —**royal blue** *adj*

Royal Com·mis·sion *n* [C] a group of people chosen by the British government to make suggestions about a subject that the government thinks may need new laws

royal flush *n* [C usually singular] a set of cards that someone has in a card game, which are the five most important cards in a SUIT (=one of the four different types of card)

Royal Highness *n* [C] **your/his/her Royal Highness** used when speaking about or to a royal person, especially a prince or princess

roy·al·ist /ˈrɔɪəl̥st/ *n* [C] someone who supports their country's king or queen, or believes that a country should be ruled by kings or queens; ▨ **republican** —**royalist** *adj*

roy·al·ty /ˈrɔɪəlti/ *n plural* **royalties** **1** [U] members of a royal family: *At school the other children treated them like royalty.* **2** [C usually plural] a payment made to the writer of a book or piece of music depending on how many books etc are sold, or to someone whose idea, invention etc is used by someone else to make money: *the royalties from his latest book* | *royalty payments*

RP /ˌɑː ˈpiː $ ˌɑːr-/ *n* [U] *Received Pronunciation* the form of British pronunciation that many educated people in Britain use, and that is thought of as the standard form

rpm /ˌɑː piː ˈem $ ˌɑːr-/ *revolutions per minute* used to describe the speed at which something turns, especially an engine or a RECORD PLAYER

RR, R.R. /ˌɑː ˈɑː $ ˌɑːr-/ *rural route* used in addresses in country areas of the US, to show which postal delivery area a letter should go to

RSI /ˌɑːr es ˈaɪ/ *n* [U] *medical repetitive strain injury* pains in your hands, arms etc caused by doing the same movements many times, especially by using a computer KEYBOARD or MOUSE

RSVP /ˌɑːr es viː ˈpiː/ used on invitations to ask someone to reply

RTF /ˌɑː tiː ˈef $ ˌɑːr-/ *n* [U] *technical rich text format* a system used to arrange and show the information in computer documents

Rt Hon *BrE* the written abbreviation of *Right Honourable*

rub¹ [S3] /rʌb/ *v* **rubbed, rubbing**
1 [I,T] to move your hand, or something such as a cloth, backwards and forwards over a surface while pressing firmly; → **stroke: rub your nose/chin/eyes/forehead etc** *She yawned and rubbed her eyes.* | **rub sth with sth** *She began rubbing her hair with a towel.* | *You'll have to rub harder if you want to get it clean.* | *I hurriedly rubbed myself dry.*
2 [I,T] to make something press against something else and move it around: **rub sth against/on sth** *She stood by the oven, rubbing one bare foot against the other.* | [+against] *The cat purred loudly, rubbing against her legs.* | **rub sth together** *We tried to make a fire by rubbing two pieces of wood together.* | *He rubbed his hands together with embarrassment.*
3 [I,T] if shoes, clothes, or parts of a machine rub, they move around while pressing against another surface, often causing pain or damage: *Badly fitting shoes are bound to rub.* | [+against/on] *The front left fender was smashed and rubbing against the wheel.* | *The skin under my sock was rubbed raw* (=the skin had come off).
4 [T always + adv/prep] to put a substance onto or onto a surface by pressing it and moving it about with your fingers or something such as a cloth: *Can you rub some sun cream on my back for me?*
5 **rub shoulders with sb** *informal* also **rub elbows with sb** *AmE* to meet and spend time with people, especially rich and famous people: *As a reporter he gets to rub shoulders with all the big names in politics.*
6 **rub salt into the wound** *informal* to make a bad situation even worse for someone
7 **rub sb up the wrong way** *BrE informal*; **rub sb the wrong way** *AmE informal* to annoy someone by the things you say or do, usually without intending to
8 **be rubbing your hands** *informal* to be pleased because something has happened which gives you an advantage, especially because something bad has happened to someone else
9 **rub sb's nose in it/in the dirt** *informal* to keep reminding someone about something they did wrong or failed to do, especially in order to punish them

10 not have two pennies/halfpennies/beans to rub together *BrE old-fashioned* to not have any money

rub along *phr v BrE informal*
to have a friendly relationship with someone; ▤ **get along**: *We rub along well most of the time.* | [+with/together] *By and large the Poles and Germans of the city had shown that they could rub along together.*

rub sth/sb ⇔ **down** *phr v*
1 to make a surface smooth by rubbing it with SANDPA-PER: *That door needs rubbing down before you paint it.*
2 to dry a person or animal by rubbing them with a cloth, TOWEL etc: *The groom rubbed down the horses.*
3 to MASSAGE someone, especially after exercise

rub sth ⇔ **in** *phr v informal*
to remind someone about something they want to forget, especially because they are embarrassed about it: *Was he trying to rub in the fact that he didn't think much of me?* | *I know I should have been more careful, but there's no need to keep rubbing it in.*

rub off *phr v*
1 to remove something from a surface by rubbing it, or to come off a surface because of being rubbed: **rub sth off sth** *Jack rubbed the mud off his face.* | **rub sth ⇔ off** *She rubbed off her lipstick and eye shadow.* | *Some of the gold paint had begun to rub off.*
2 if a feeling, quality, or habit rubs off on you, you start to have it because you are with another person who has it: [+on] *She refused to give up, and her confidence rubbed off on the others.*

rub sth/sb ⇔ **out** *phr v*
1 *BrE* to remove writing, a picture etc from a surface by rubbing it with a piece of rubber, a cloth etc; ▤ **erase**: *Draw the outline lightly with a soft pencil. This can be rubbed out later.*
2 *AmE old-fashioned informal* to murder someone

rub² *n*   **1 give sb/sth a rub** to rub something or MASSAGE someone for a short time: *Give the table a good rub with a damp cloth.*   **2 there's/here's the rub** *literary* used when saying that a particular problem is the reason why a situation is so difficult – often used humorously

rub·ber /ˈrʌbə $ -ər/ *n*   **1** [U] a substance used to make tyres, boots etc, which is made from the juice of a tropical tree or artificially: *a rubber ball* → see picture at MATERIAL¹   **2** [C] *BrE* **a)** a small piece of rubber or similar material used for removing pencil marks from paper; ▤ **eraser** *AmE* **b)** an object used for cleaning marks from a BLACKBOARD; ▤ **eraser** *AmE*; → see picture at STATIONERY   **3** [C] *AmE informal* a CONDOM   **4 rubbers** [plural] *AmE old-fashioned* rubber shoes or boots that you wear over ordinary shoes when it rains or snows; ▤ **galoshes**   **5** [C] a series of games of BRIDGE or CRICKET   **6** [C] the piece of white rubber where the PITCHER (=person who throws the ball) stands in a baseball game

,rubber 'band *n* [C] a thin circular piece of rubber used for fastening things together; ▤ **elastic band** *BrE*

'rubber boot *n* [C] *AmE* a tall boot made of rubber that keeps your feet and the lower part of your legs dry; ▤ **wellington boot** *BrE*

,rubber 'bullet *n* [C] a bullet made of rubber that is not intended to seriously hurt or kill people, but is used to control violent crowds; → **plastic bullet**

,rubber 'dinghy *n* [C] a small rubber boat that is filled with air

rub·ber·neck /ˈrʌbənek $ -ər-/ *v* [I] *informal* to look around at something, especially something such as an accident when you are driving past – used to show disapproval: *People rubbernecking in the southbound lane caused a second accident.* —**rubbernecker** *n* [C]

'rubber plant *n* [C] a plant with large shiny dark green leaves that is often grown indoors

,rubber 'stamp *n* [C] a small piece of rubber with a handle, used for printing dates or names on paper

,rubber-'stamp *v* [T] to give official approval to something without really thinking about it – used to show disapproval: *The committee has already rubber-stamped the scheme.*

rub·ber·y /ˈrʌbəri/ *adj*   **1** looking or feeling like rubber: *rubbery eggs* | *rubbery lips*   **2** if your legs or knees are rubbery, they feel weak or unsteady

rub·bing /ˈrʌbɪŋ/ *n* [C] a copy of a shape or pattern made by rubbing WAX, CHALK etc onto a piece of paper laid over it: *a brass rubbing*

'rubbing ,alcohol *n* [U] *AmE* a type of alcohol used for cleaning wounds or skin; ▤ **surgical spirit** *BrE*

rub·bish¹ S3 /ˈrʌbɪʃ/ *n* [U] *especially BrE*
1 food, paper etc that is no longer needed and has been thrown away; ▤ **garbage** *AmE*, **trash** *AmE*: *a rubbish bin* | *household rubbish* | *rubbish tip/dump* (=a place to take rubbish)
2 *informal* objects, papers etc that you no longer use and should throw away: *I've got so much rubbish on my desk it's unbelievable.*
3 *informal* an idea, statement, etc that is rubbish is silly or wrong and does not deserve serious attention; ▤ **nonsense**; **garbage** *AmE*: *You do talk rubbish sometimes.* | *That's a load of rubbish.* | *The suggestion is absolute rubbish.* | **rubbish!** *spoken* (=used to tell someone that what they have just said is completely wrong)
4 *informal* a film, book etc that is rubbish is very bad: *the usual Hollywood rubbish*

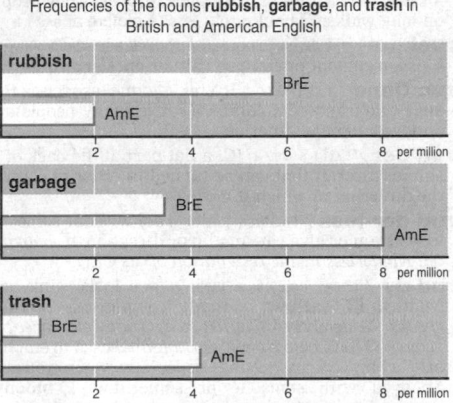

Frequencies of the nouns **rubbish**, **garbage**, and **trash** in British and American English

In British English **rubbish** is commonly used to mean something that is thrown away, or something that is silly, wrong, or of bad quality. In American English **garbage** and **trash** are commonly used for these meanings. In British English **trash** is only used to mean something of bad quality, and **garbage** is only used to mean words, ideas etc that are stupid.

rubbish² *v* [T] *BrE* to say something is bad or useless

rubbish³ *adj BrE informal* not skilful at a particular activity: *a rubbish team*

rub·bish·y /ˈrʌbɪʃi/ *adj BrE informal* silly or of a very low quality; ▤ **trashy**: *rubbishy magazines*

rub·ble /ˈrʌbəl/ *n* [U] broken stones or bricks from a building or wall that has been destroyed

rub·down /ˈrʌbdaʊn/ *n* [C]   **1** *especially AmE* if you give someone a rubdown, you rub their body to make them relaxed, especially after exercise; ▤ **massage**   **2** if you give a surface a rubdown, you rub it to make it smooth or clean → **rub down** at RUB¹

rube /ruːb/ *n* [C] *AmE informal* someone, usually from the country, who has no experience of other places and thinks in a simple way – used to show disapproval

ru·bel·la /ruːˈbelə/ *n* [U] *medical* an infectious disease that causes red spots on your body, and can damage an unborn child; ▤ **German measles**

Ru·bi·con /ˈruːbɪkən, -kɒn $ -kɑːn/ *n* **cross the Rubicon** to do something that will have extremely important effects in the future and that you cannot change

ru·bi·cund /'ruːbɪkənd/ *adj literary* someone who is rubicund is fat and has a red face

ru·ble /'ruːbəl/ *n* the American spelling of ROUBLE

ru·bric /'ruːbrɪk/ *n* [C] **1** *formal* a set of instructions or an explanation in a book, examination paper etc **2** a title under which particular things are mentioned or discussed: *The names were listed under the rubric 'Contributors'.*

ru·by /'ruːbi/ *n plural* **rubies 1** [C] a red jewel **2** also ,**ruby 'red** [U] a dark red colour —**ruby** *adj*

ruched /ruːʃt/ *adj* a ruched curtain or piece of clothing has parts of it gathered together so that it has folds in it

ruck[1] /rʌk/ *n* **1** [C] a group of RUGBY players trying to get the ball when it is lying on the ground **2 the ruck** *formal* ordinary events or people, which seem rather boring compared to the lives of rich or famous people: *Obtaining a good education was seen as a way out of the ruck.* **3** [singular] a group of people standing very closely together or fighting **4** [C] *BrE informal* a fight

ruck[2] *v*
ruck up *phr v* if a piece of cloth rucks up, or if you ruck it up, it forms folds in an untidy way: **ruck sth ⇔ up** *Your coat's all rucked up at the back.*

ruck·sack /'rʌksæk/ *n* [C] *especially BrE* a bag used for carrying things on your back, especially by people on long walks; ▤ **backpack**; → see picture at BAG[1]

ruck·us /'rʌkəs/ *n* [singular] *informal especially AmE* a noisy argument or confused situation; ▤ **rumpus**

ruc·tions /'rʌkʃənz/ *n* [plural] *informal especially BrE* angry talk and complaints because many people are annoyed about a situation

rud·der /'rʌdə $ -ər/ *n* [C] a flat part at the back of a ship or aircraft that can be turned in order to control the direction in which it moves

rud·der·less /'rʌdələs $ -dər-/ *adj* without someone to lead you or give you an aim or direction: *a company left rudderless by the resignation of its CEO*

rud·dy /'rʌdi/ *adj* **1** a ruddy face looks pink and healthy; ▣ **sallow**: *a ruddy complexion* | *ruddy cheeks* **2** *literary* red: *The fire cast a ruddy glow over the room.* **3** [only before noun] *BrE informal* used to emphasize what you are saying, especially when you are annoyed with someone or something; ▤ **bloody**, **damn**: *I wish that ruddy dog would stop barking!* —**ruddiness** *n* [U] —**ruddy** *adv*

rude /ruːd/ *adj comparative* **ruder**, *superlative* **rudest 1** speaking or behaving in a way that is not polite and is likely to offend or annoy people; ▤ **impolite**; ▣ **polite**: *a rude remark* | *I didn't mean to be rude, but I had to leave early.* | [+to] *Why are you so rude to her?* | **it is rude to do sth** *It's rude to stare.* **2** rude jokes, words, songs etc are about sex; ▤ **dirty** *AmE* **3 rude awakening/shock** a situation in which you suddenly realize something unpleasant: *If they expect the match to be friendly, then they are in for a rude awakening.* **4 in rude health** *BrE old-fashioned* very healthy **5** *literary* made in a simple basic way: *a rude wooden hut* —**rudely** *adv*: *We were rudely awakened by the storm.* | *He answered me very rudely.* —**rudeness** *n* [U]

ru·di·men·ta·ry /,ruːdɪ'mentəri◂/ *adj* **1** a rudimentary knowledge or understanding of a subject is very simple and basic; ▣ **sophisticated**: *Gradually, I acquired a rudimentary knowledge of music.* | *my rudimentary German* **2** rudimentary equipment, methods, systems etc are very basic and not advanced: *subsistence farming in its most rudimentary form* | *The classroom equipment is pretty rudimentary.*

ru·di·ments /'ruːdɪmənts/ *n* [plural] *formal* the most basic parts of a subject, which you learn first; ▤ **basics**: [+of] *the rudiments of windsurfing*

rue /ruː/ *v* [T] *literary* to wish that you had not done something; ▤ **regret**: *She learned to rue the day she had met Henri.*

rue·ful /'ruːfəl/ *adj* feeling or showing that you wish you had not done something: *a rueful smile* —**ruefully** *adv*: *He smiled ruefully.*

ruff /rʌf/ *n* [C] **1** a stiff circular white collar, worn in the 16th century **2** a circle of feathers or fur around the neck of an animal or bird

ruf·fi·an /'rʌfiən/ *n* [C] *old-fashioned* a violent man, involved in crime: *a gang of ruffians* —**ruffianly** *adj*

ruf·fle[1] /'rʌfəl/ *v* [T] **1** also **ruffle sth ⇔ up** to make a smooth surface uneven: *He ruffled her hair affectionately.* | *A light wind ruffled the water.* **2** to offend or upset someone slightly: *Louise's sharp comments had ruffled his pride.* | **ruffle sb's feathers** (=offend someone)

ruf·fle[2] *n* [C] a band of thin cloth sewn in folds as a decoration around the edge of something such as a collar

rug /rʌg/ *n* [C] **1** a piece of thick cloth or wool that covers part of a floor, used for warmth or as a decoration; → **mat**, **carpet 2** *BrE* a large piece of material that you can wrap around yourself, especially when you are travelling **3 pull the rug (out) from under sb/sb's feet** *informal* to suddenly take away something that someone was depending on to achieve what they wanted **4** a TOUPÉE - used humorously

rug·by S3 W3 /'rʌgbi/ also ,**rugby 'football** *n* [U] an outdoor game played by two teams with an OVAL (=egg-shaped) ball that you kick or carry

,**Rugby 'League** *n* [U] a type of rugby played by teams of 13 players

,**Rugby 'Union** *n* [U] a type of rugby played by teams of 15 players

rug·ged /'rʌgɪd/ *adj* **1** land that is rugged is rough and uneven: *a rugged coastline* | *the rugged beauty of the Highlands* **2** a man who is rugged is good-looking and has strong features which are often not perfect: *his rugged good looks* **3** a vehicle or piece of equipment that is rugged is strongly built and not likely to break easily; ▤ **sturdy 4** rugged behaviour is confident and determined but not always polite: *rugged individualism* —**ruggedly** *adv* —**ruggedness** *n* [U]

rug·ger /'rʌgə $ -ər/ *n* [U] *BrE informal* Rugby Union

ru·in[1] S3 /'ruːɪn/ *v* [T]
1 to spoil or destroy something completely: *This illness has ruined my life.* | *His career would be ruined.* | *All this mud's going to ruin my shoes.* → see box at DESTROY **2** to make someone lose all their money: *Jefferson was ruined by the lawsuit.* → RUINED

ruin[2] *n* **1** [U] a situation in which you have lost all your money, your social position, or the good opinion that people had about you: *small businesses facing financial ruin* | **be on the road to ruin** (=be doing something that will make you lose your money, position etc) **2** [C] also **ruins** the part of a building that is left after the rest has

a ruined cottage

been destroyed: *an interesting old ruin* | *the ruins of a bombed-out office block* **3 the ruins of sth** the parts of something such as an organization, system, or set of ideas that remain after the rest have been destroyed: *the ruins of a government that once held so much promise* **4 be/lie in ruins a)** if a building is in ruins, it has fallen down or been badly damaged **b)** if someone's life, a country's ECONOMY etc is in ruins, it is affected by very great problems: *Her marriage was in ruins.* **5 fall into ruin** also **go to ruin** if something goes to ruin, it gets damaged or destroyed because no one is taking care of it: *He had let the farm go to ruin.* **6 be the ruin of sb** to make someone lose all their money, their good health, the good opinion that other people have of them etc: *Drinking was the ruin of him.* → **go to rack and ruin** at RACK¹ (4)

ru·in·a·tion /ˌruːɪˈneɪʃən/ n [U] *old-fashioned* a process in which someone or something is ruined, or the cause of this – often used humorously

ru·ined /ˈruːɪnd/ adj [only before noun] a ruined building has been almost completely destroyed: *a ruined castle* → RUIN²

ru·in·ous /ˈruːɪnəs/ adj **1** causing a lot of damage or problems: *a ruinous civil war* **2** costing much more than you can afford: *ruinous rates of interest* **3** *formal* a building that is ruinous has been almost completely destroyed; ⊟ **ruined**: *an old ruinous chapel* | **ruinous state/condition** *the ruinous state of the city walls* —**ruinously** adv: *ruinously expensive*

rule¹ S2 W2 /ruːl/ n

1 INSTRUCTION [C] an official instruction that says how things must be done or what is allowed, especially in a game, organization, or job; → **law**, **regulation**

strict rule
unwritten/unspoken rule (=an unofficial rule that everyone knows about)
break a rule (=not obey a rule)
follow/obey/observe the rules
comply with the rules (=obey the rules)
bend/stretch the rules (=do something that is not normally allowed)
play by the rules (=do what is expected and agreed)
against the rules (=not allowed)
under the rules (of sth) (=according to a particular set of rules)
breach of the rules (=when someone does not obey the rules)
rules are rules (=used when you are saying that a rule cannot be broken)
rules and regulations

[+of] *The rules of the game are quite simple.* | *The* **rules** *are less* **strict** *in the local county court.* | *If you* **break the rules***, it just spoils the whole game.* | *You have to* **follow the rules** *precisely in order to lose weight fast.* | *her refusal to* **comply with** *the club* **rules** | *We might be able to* **bend the rules** *just this one time.* | *The point of having the European Union is to make everybody* **play by the rules.** | *Is it* **against the rules** *to talk?* | **Under the rules** *of the International Cycling union, an eight day delay is allowed.* | *It is not a crime, though it is a* **breach** *of stock market* **rules.** | **Rules are rules** *and it's my duty to enforce them.* | *I'm sick of all their petty* **rules and regulations.** | *School rules required all girls to tie back their hair.*

2 ADVICE [C] what you should do in a particular situation, or a statement about this: *There are no* **hard and fast rules** (=clear and definite rules) *about what to wear to classes.* | [+of] *There are two basic rules of survival.* | *widespread acceptance of certain* **rules of conduct** | *One of these* **unwritten rules** *is that parents should play with their children.* | **The rule is:** *if you feel any pain you should stop exercising immediately.*

3 NORMAL/USUAL [singular] something that is normal or usually true: **as a (general) rule** *As a general rule most students finish their coursework by the end of May.* | *Early marriage used to* **be the rule** *in that part of the world.* | *A series of payments used to be the* **exception rather than the rule.** | *Unfortunately there is an* **exception** *to every* **rule.**

4 GOVERNMENT [U] the government of a country or area by a particular group of people or using a particular system: **under ... rule** *people living under communist rule* | *the end of* **colonial rule** | *a period of* **military rule** | **direct rule** *from Westminster* | *the restoration of* **majority rule** (=government by the party that most people have voted for) *to Northern Ireland*

5 GRAMMAR/SCIENCE ETC [C] a statement about what is usually allowed in a particular system, such as the grammar of a language, or a science: [+of] *the rules of English punctuation*

6 the rule of law a situation in which the laws of a country are obeyed: *We are here to uphold the rule of law.*

7 the rules of natural justice what people believe to be right and fair: *The governor failed to observe the rules of natural justice.*

8 rule of thumb a rough figure or method of calculation, based on practical experience: *As a general rule of thumb, children this age should not spend more than one hour on homework.*

9 make it a rule (to do sth) to try to make sure that you always do something: *I make it a rule never to mix business with pleasure.*

10 FOR MEASURING [C] *old-fashioned* a RULER → GOLDEN RULE, GROUND RULES, HOME RULE, SLIDE RULE; → **work to rule** at WORK¹ (32)

rule² v

1 GOVERNMENT [I,T] to have the official power to control a country and the people who live there; → **govern**: *Queen Victoria ruled England for 64 years.* | *African tribal societies were traditionally ruled by a council of elders.* | [+over] *Alexander the Great ruled over a huge empire.* | *He announced that henceforth he would* **rule by decree** (=make all the important decisions himself).

2 CONTROL/INFLUENCE [T] if a feeling or desire rules someone, it has a powerful and controlling influence on their actions: *the passion for power and success which* **rules** *her* **life**

3 COURT/LAW [I always + adv/prep,T] to make an official decision about something, especially a legal problem; → **decree**: **rule that** *The judge ruled that she should have custody of the children.* | [+on] *The Supreme Court has yet to rule on the case.* | **rule in favour of/against sb/sth** *The tribunal ruled in her favour.* | **be ruled illegal/unlawful etc** *This part of the bill was ruled unconstitutional.* → RULING¹

4 rule the roost *informal* to be the most powerful person in a group: *It's his wife who rules the roost in their house.*

5 rule sb/sth with a rod of iron also rule sb with an iron fist/hand to control a group of people in a very severe way: *Although he was a fair man, he ruled us with an iron fist.*

6 sb/sth rules *informal* used to say that the team, school, place etc mentioned is better than any other: *Arsenal rules OK. BrE* | *graffiti saying 'Poheny High rules'*

7 DRAW A LINE [T] to draw a line using a ruler or other straight edge: *Rule a line under each answer.* → OVERRULE; → **let your heart rule your head** at HEART (2)

rule sth/sb ⇔ out *phr v*
1 to decide that something is not possible or suitable: *The police have ruled out suicide.* | *She has refused to* **rule out the possibility** *of singing again.*
2 to make it impossible for something to happen: *The mountainous terrain rules out most forms of agriculture.*
3 to state that someone will not be able to take part in a sports event: [+of] *He has been ruled out of the match with a knee injury.*

rule·book /ˈruːlbʊk/ n **1 go by the rulebook** *informal* to obey exactly the rules about how something should be done: *If I went by the rulebook, I'd have to report this conversation.* **2** [C] a book of rules, especially one that is given to workers in a job

ruled /ruːld/ adj ruled paper has parallel lines printed across it; ⊟ **lined**

rul·er /ˈruːlə $ -ər/ n [C] **1** someone such as a king or queen who has official power over a country or area **2** a long flat straight piece of plastic, metal, or wood that you use for measuring things or drawing straight lines: *a 12-inch ruler*

rul·ing¹ /ˈruːlɪŋ/ n [C] an official decision, especially one made by a court: [+on] *the recent Supreme Court ruling on defendants' rights*

R

ruling[2] *adj* [only before noun] **1** the ruling group in a country or organization is the group that controls it: *A* ***ruling class*** *clearly existed.* | *the* ***ruling body*** *of American golf* **2** a ruling interest or emotion interests someone more than anything else: *Football remains the* ***ruling passion*** *of many men.*

rum[1] /rʌm/ *n* [C,U] a strong alcoholic drink made from sugar, or a glass of this drink

rum[2] *adj* old-fashioned unusual or strange

rum·ba /ˈrʌmbə/ *n* [C,U] a popular dance from Cuba, or music for this dance

rum·ble[1] /ˈrʌmbəl/ *v* **1** [I] to make a series of long low sounds, especially a long distance away from you: *We could hear thunder rumbling in the distance.* **2** [I always + adv/prep] to move slowly along while making a series of long low sounds: *We watched the tanks rumbling past the window.* **3** [I] if your stomach rumbles, it makes a noise, especially because you are hungry **4** [T] *BrE informal* to find out what someone is secretly intending to do: *How did you rumble them?* **5** [I,T] *AmE old-fashioned* to fight with someone
rumble on *phr v* if a disagreement rumbles on, it continues for a long time: *The row about pay is still rumbling on.*

rumble[2] *n* [singular] a series of long low sounds: [+of] *the* ***low rumble*** *of traffic in the distance* | *the* ***distant rumble*** *of gunfire*

'rumble ˌstrip *n* [C] a number of raised lines across a road which make a loud noise when you drive over them to warn you to slow down

rum·bling /ˈrʌmblɪŋ/ *n* **1** **rumblings** [plural] remarks that show that people are starting to become annoyed, or that a difficult situation is developing: *rumblings of discontent* | *There have been rumblings about the need for better computers.* **2** [C usually singular] a series of long low sounds: *We heard a rumbling behind us.*

rum·bus·tious /rʌmˈbʌstʃəs/ *adj* full of energy, fun, and noise; ◨ **rambunctious** *AmE*: *rumbustious football fans*

ru·mi·nant /ˈruːmɪ̱nənt/ *n* [C] *technical* an animal such as a cow that has several stomachs and eats grass

ru·mi·nate /ˈruːmɪ̱neɪt/ *v* [I] **1** *formal* to think carefully and deeply about something: [+on/over] *He sat alone, ruminating on the injustice of the world.* **2** *technical* if animals such as cows ruminate, they bring food back into their mouths from their stomachs and CHEW it again —**rumination** /ˌruːmɪ̱ˈneɪʃən/ *n* [C,U]

ru·mi·na·tive /ˈruːmɪ̱nətɪv $ -neɪtɪv/ *adj formal* thinking deeply and carefully about something: *a typically ruminative speech* —**ruminatively** *adv*

rum·mage[1] /ˈrʌmɪdʒ/ *v* [I+ always + adv/prep] also **rummage around/about** to search for something by moving things around in a careless or hurried way: [+in/through etc] *Looks like someone's been rummaging around in my desk.*

rummage[2] *n* **1** [C usually singular] *informal* a careless or hurried search for something: ***Have a rummage*** *in my jewellery box and see if you can find something you like.* **2** [U] *especially AmE* old clothes, toys etc that you no longer want; ◨ **jumble** *BrE*

'rummage ˌsale *n* [C] *AmE* an event at which old clothes, toys etc are sold as a way of getting money, for example to help a school or church; ◨ **jumble sale** *BrE*

rum·my /ˈrʌmi/ *n* [U] a simple card game in which players try to collect series of cards

ru·mour *BrE*; **rumor** *AmE* /ˈruːmə $ -ər/ *n* [C,U] **1** information or a story that is passed from one person to another and which may or may not be true: [+about/of] *I've heard all sorts of rumours about him and his secretary.* | **rumour that** *There's an unsubstantiated rumour that Eddie's bankrupt.* | ***Rumour has it that*** *Jean's getting married again.* | *Where did the rumour start?* | **a rumour spreads/goes around** *A*

malicious rumour went round that Philip had something to do with the murder. **2** **the rumour mill** the people, considered as a group, who discuss something and pass rumours to each other: *His name has come up in the rumour mill as a possible director for the project.*

ru·moured *BrE*; **rumored** *AmE* /ˈruːməd $ -ərd/ *v* be **rumoured** if something is rumoured to be true, people are saying secretly or unofficially that it may be true; → **alleged**: **it is rumoured that** *It was rumoured that Johnson had been poisoned.* | **be rumoured to be sth** *She was rumoured to be a millionaire.* | *a young man* **widely rumoured** *to be her lover*

ru·mour·mon·ger *BrE*; **rumormonger** *AmE* /ˈruːmə̱ˌmʌŋgə $ -mər,mɑːˈŋgər, -,mʌŋ-/ *n* [C] someone who tells other people rumours – used to show disapproval

rump /rʌmp/ *n* **1** [C] the part of an animal's back that is just above its legs **2** **rump steak** good quality meat that comes from the rump of a cow **3** [C] the part of your body that you sit on – used humorously; ◨ **bottom** **4** [singular] *BrE* the part of a group or government that remains after most of the other members have left

rum·ple /ˈrʌmpəl/ *v* [T] to make hair, clothes etc less tidy: *He rumpled her hair playfully.* —**rumpled** *adj*: *the slightly rumpled bed* | *a rumpled linen suit*

rum·pus /ˈrʌmpəs/ *n* [singular] *informal* a lot of noise, especially made by people quarrelling: *There's a real rumpus going on upstairs.*

'rumpus ˌroom *n* [C] *AmE* a room in a house that is used by the family for games, parties etc

rump·y pump·y /ˌrʌmpi ˈpʌmpi/ *n* [U] *BrE* sexual activity – used humorously

run[1] [S1] [W1] /rʌn/ *v* *past tense* **ran** /ræn/, *past participle* **run**, *present participle* **running**

1 **MOVE QUICKLY USING YOUR LEGS** **a)** [I] to move very quickly, by moving your legs more quickly than when you walk: [+down/up/to/towards etc] *I ran down the stairs as fast as I could.* | *He was running towards the door.* | *She turned and ran away.* | *The boys ran off into the crowd.* | **run to do sth** *Several people ran to help her when she fell.* | *The children* **came running** *out of the house.* | *Women* **ran screaming***, with children in their arms.* | *Jane struggled free and* **ran for her life** (=ran in order to avoid being killed). | *Hurry!* **Run for it** (=run as quickly as possible in order to escape)*! | He picked up the child and* **ran like hell***.* not polite (=ran very quickly, especially in order to escape) **b)** [T] to run a particular distance: *Firefighters are to run 500km to raise money for a children's charity.* | *He ran the length of the corridor.*

2 **RACE** **a)** [I,T] to run in a race: *I'd never run a marathon before.* | [+in] *Murray has said she will consider running in the 3000 metres.* **b)** [T usually passive] if a race is run at a particular time or in a particular place, it happens at that time or in that place: *The Derby will be run at 3 o'clock.*

3 **ORGANIZE/BE IN CHARGE OF** [T] to organize or be in charge of an activity, business, organization, or country: *For a while, she ran a restaurant in Boston.* | *Many people don't care who runs the country.* | *Courses are currently being run in London and Edinburgh.* | *Many people belong to a pension scheme run by their employers.* | **well/badly run** *The hotel is well-run and extremely popular.* | *a* **state-run** (=controlled by the government) *television station* → see box at CONTROL[2]

4 **DO STH/GO SOMEWHERE QUICKLY** [I] to do something or go somewhere quickly: *Run and ask your mother where she's put the keys.* | [+to] *I need to run to the store for some more milk.*

5 **BUSES/TRAINS ETC a)** [I] if a bus, train etc service runs, it takes people from one place to another at fixed times: *The buses don't run on Sundays.* | [+to] *The number 61 bus runs to the city centre.* **b)** [T] if a company or other organization runs a bus, train etc service, they make it operate: *They're running special trains to and from the exhibition.*

6 COMPUTERS a) [I] if a computer program runs, it operates: [+**on**] *The software will run on any PC.* **b)** [T] if you run a program, you make it operate: *The RS8 system runs both Unix and MPX-32.*

7 MACHINE/ENGINE a) [I] if a machine or engine runs, it operates: *She got out of the car and left the engine running.* | **run on electricity/gas/petrol etc** (=get its power from electricity etc) *Most cars run on unleaded fuel.* | **run off sth** (=use something for power) *It runs off batteries.* **b)** [T] if you run a machine or engine, you make it operate: *You shouldn't keep the engine running when the car is standing still.* | *I often run the washing machine more than once a day.*

8 TAPE a) [I usually progressive] if a tape is running, it is recording: *She didn't realize the tape was running as she spoke.* **b)** [T] if you run a tape, you make it move backwards or forwards: *Run the tape back to the beginning.*

9 NEWSPAPER/TELEVISION a) [T] to print something in a newspaper or magazine, or broadcast something on television: *The company is running a series of advertisements in national newspapers.* | *A local TV station ran her story.* **b)** [I] if a program runs on television, it is shown. If a story runs in a newspaper or magazine, it is printed: *The series ran for 20 episodes and was extremely popular.* | *Conan Doyle's stories ran in 'The Strand' magazine.*

10 FAST/OUT OF CONTROL [I always + adv/prep] to move too fast or in an uncontrolled way: *Her car ran off the road and into a tree.* | *The truck ran out of control and hit a house.*

11 USE A VEHICLE [T] especially BrE to own and use a vehicle: *I can't afford to run a car.* | *A bicycle is relatively cheap to buy and run.*

12 TAKE SB IN YOUR CAR [T always + adv/prep] informal to take someone somewhere in your car; **⊟ drive**: *Shall I run you home?* | **run sb to sth** *Let me run you to the station.*

13 IN AN ELECTION [I] especially AmE to try to be elected in an election; **⊟ stand** BrE: [+**for**] *Salinas is running for a second term as President.* | *an attempt to encourage more women to **run for office*** | [+**against**] *Feinstein will win if she runs against Lungren.*

14 STH LONG [I,T always + adv/prep] if something long such as a road or wire runs in a particular direction, that is its position, or that is where you put it: *The road runs along a valley.* | *Developers want to run a road right through his farm.* | *Run the cables under the carpet.* | *The Sierra mountain range **runs the length of** the north west coast of Majorca.*

15 MOVE STH ON A SURFACE [T always + adv/prep] to move something lightly along a surface: *Charles ran his fingers through her hair.* | *Run the scanner over the barcodes.*

16 FLOW [I always + adv/prep] to flow in a particular direction or place: *Tears started to run down her cheeks.* | *Water was running off the roof.*

17 TAP [I,T] if a TAP is running, water is coming out of it, or if you run a tap, you make water come out of it: *Did you leave the tap running?* | *He ran the tap until the water was really hot.*

18 run a bath to fill a bath with water: *I could hear her running a bath upstairs.* | **run sb a bath** *Could you run me a nice hot bath while I finish my meal?*

19 SB'S NOSE [I] if someone's nose is running, liquid is flowing out of it

20 OFFICIAL PAPERS [I] if something runs for a particular length of time, it can officially be used for that time: *The contract runs for a year.* | *My car insurance only has another month to run.*

21 PLAY/FILM [I] to continue being performed regularly in one place: *The play ran for two years.*

22 HAPPEN [I] to happen in a particular way or at a particular time: *Andy kept things **running smoothly** (=happening in the way they should) while I was away.* | *He was given a further three month prison sentence to run concurrently.* | *The course runs over a three year period.*

23 AMOUNT/PRICE [I] to be at a particular level,

amount, or price: [+**at**] *Inflation was running at 5%.* | [+**to**] *The cost of repairing the damage could run to $5000.*

24 STORY/ACCOUNT ETC [I,T] if a story, discussion etc runs in a particular way, it has those particular words or events: *The story runs that someone offered Lynch a further $500.* | *'President's marriage really over' ran the headline in a national newspaper.*

25 run its course if something runs its course, it continues in the way you expect until it has finished: *Recession in the country has run its course and left an aftermath of uncertainty.*

26 sth will run and run BrE if a subject, discussion, event etc will run and run, people will continue to be interested in it for a long time: *This a story that will run and run.*

27 THOUGHTS/FEELINGS [I always + adv/prep] if a feeling runs through you, or a thought runs through your mind, you feel it or think it quickly: [+**through/down**] *A feeling of excitement ran through her body as they touched.* | *The same thought kept running through his mind.* | *A cold shiver ran down my back.* | *I felt a sharp pain run down my leg.*

28 run high if feelings run high, people are very angry, upset, excited etc: *Tension ran high and fights broke out among the crowd.* | *Feelings have been running high in the town, following the murder of a young girl.*

29 run sb's life informal to keep telling someone what they should do all the time, in a way that annoys them: *Don't try to run my life!*

30 run for cover a) to run towards a place where you will be safe, especially to avoid bullets: *He was shot in the leg as he ran for cover.* **b)** to try to protect yourself from a bad situation or from being criticized: *His success at backing winning horses has had the bookmakers running for cover.*

31 COLOUR IN CLOTHES [I] if colour runs, it spreads from one piece of clothing or one area of cloth to another when the clothes are wet: *The T-shirt ran and made all my other clothes pink.*

32 PAINT/INK [I] if paint runs, it moves onto an area where you did not intend it to go

33 run a check/test/experiment etc to arrange for someone or something to be checked or tested: [+**on**] *Ask your doctor to run a test on your blood sugar levels.*

34 HOLE IN CLOTHES [I] if a hole in TIGHTS or STOCKINGS runs, it gets bigger in a straight line

35 run drugs/guns to bring drugs or guns into a country illegally in order to sell them → **DRUG RUNNER, GUN-RUNNING**

36 run in the family if something such as a quality, disease, or skill runs in the family, many people in that family have it: *Diabetes appears to run in families.*

37 run a temperature/fever to have a body temperature that is higher than normal, because you are ill

38 run a mile informal to try very hard to avoid a particular situation or person because you do not want to deal with them: *If someone asked me to marry them, I'd probably run a mile.*

39 run late/early/on time to arrive, go somewhere, or do something late, early, or at the right time: *I'm running late, so I'll talk to you later.* | *If the train runs on time, we'll be there by ten.*

40 be running scared to feel worried because someone who you are competing against is becoming very successful or powerful: *The party are running scared.*

41 come running a) informal to react in a very eager way when someone asks or tells you to do something: *He thinks he's only got to look at me and I'll come running.* **b)** especially spoken to ask someone for help, advice, or sympathy when you have a problem: [+**to**] *Well I warned you, so don't come running to me when it all goes wrong!*

42 run your eyes over/along etc sth to look quickly at something: *He ran his eyes along the books on the shelf.*

R

or down a SCALE in a piece of music
23 CARD GAMES [C] a set of cards with numbers in a series, held by one player → DRY RUN, DUMMY RUN, FUN RUN, MILK RUN, PRINT RUN, TRIAL RUN

run·a·bout /'rʌnəbaʊt/ n [C] informal a small car used for short journeys

run·a·round /'rʌnə,raʊnd/ n **give sb the runaround** informal to deliberately avoid giving someone a definite answer, especially when they are asking you to do something: *Every time we ask the landlord about fixing the roof, he gives us the runaround.* → **run around** at RUN¹

run·a·way¹ /'rʌnəweɪ/ adj [only before noun] **1** a runaway vehicle or animal is out of control: *a runaway horse* **2** happening very easily or quickly, and not able to be controlled: *The film was a runaway success.* | *runaway inflation* | *a runaway victory* **3** a runaway person has left the place where they are supposed to be

runaway² n [C] someone, especially a child, who has left home without telling anyone and does not intend to come back → **run away** at RUN¹

run-'down adj **1** a building or area that is run-down is in very bad condition: *a run-down inner-city area* **2** [not before noun] someone who is run-down is tired and not healthy: *You look a bit run-down.*

run·down /'rʌndaʊn/ n [singular] **1** the process of making a business or industry smaller and less important: [+of] *the rundown of British Steel's activities in Scotland* **2** a quick report or explanation of an idea, situation etc: [+on] *Connors promised to give me a rundown on local police activity.*

rune /ruːn/ n [C] technical **1** one of the letters of the alphabet used in the past by people in Northern Europe **2** a magic song or written sign —**runic** adj

rung¹ /rʌŋ/ v the past participle of RING²

rung² n [C] **1** one of the bars that form the steps of a ladder **2** informal a particular level or position in an organization or system: [+of/on] *Humans are on the highest rung of the evolutionary ladder.*

run-in n [C] an argument or disagreement, especially with someone in an official position: [+with] *Michael got drunk and had a run-in with the police.*

run·nel /'rʌnl/ n [C] a small stream or passage that water flows along

run·ner /'rʌnə $ -ər/ n [C] **1** someone who runs for sport or pleasure; → **jogger**: *a long-distance runner* | *a marathon runner* **2** a horse that runs in a race: *The runners and riders appear in Friday's Racing Post.* **3** **do a runner** BrE informal to leave somewhere quickly in order to avoid paying for something or having to meet someone: *By the time the police got there, the boys had done a runner.* **4** one of the two thin pieces of metal under a SLEDGE, or the single piece of metal under a SKATE **5** the bar of wood or metal that a drawer or curtain slides along **6** technical a stem on a plant that grows along the ground and then puts down roots to form a new plant **7** a long narrow piece of cloth or CARPET → **DRUG RUNNER**; → **gun runner** at GUN-RUNNING; → **FRONT-RUNNER**

runner 'bean n [C] BrE a vegetable that grows as a long green POD (=seed container) on a climbing plant

runner-'up n plural **runners-up** [C] the person or team that comes second in a race or competition

run·ning¹ /'rʌnɪŋ/ n [U] **1** the activity or sport of running; → **jogging**: *Did you go running this morning?* | *New facilities include a pool and a running track.* | *running shoes* **2** **the running of sth** the process of managing or organizing a business, home, organization etc: *Brian took over the day-to-day running of the company while his father was away.* | *He praised the smooth running of the election.* **3** **be in the running/out of the running** to have some hope or no hope of winning a race or competition: *Who's in the running for the world title this year?* **4** **make (all) the running**

BrE informal to be the person who makes most of the suggestions in a relationship, plan, activity etc

running² adj [only before noun] **1** **running water a)** if a house has running water, it has pipes which provide water to its kitchen, bath, toilet etc **b)** water that is flowing or moving: *the sound of running water* | *Rinse the vegetables thoroughly under running water.* **2** **running commentary** a spoken description of an event, especially a race or game, made while the event is happening: *She gave us a running commentary on what was happening in the street.* **3** **running total** a total that keeps being increased as new costs, amounts etc are added: *Keep a running total of your expenses as you go along.* **4** **running battle/joke** an argument or joke that continues or is repeated over a long period of time **5** **running sore** a sore area on your skin that has liquid coming out of it **6** **in running order** a machine that is in running order is working correctly **7** **the running order** the order in which the different parts of an event have been arranged to take place **8** **take a running jump** spoken used to tell someone to go away and stop annoying you

running³ adv **three years/five times etc running** for three years etc without a change or interruption; ◘ **in a row**: *She won the prize for the fourth year running.*

running costs n [plural] the amount of money needed to operate an organization, system, machine etc

running mate n [C usually singular] the person chosen by someone who is trying to become president, leader etc to help win an election, and be the second most important political person if they are elected

running re'pairs n [plural] small things that you do to something to keep it in good working order

running ,time n [U] the length of time that a film or television programme takes to run from beginning to end

run·ny /'rʌni/ adj informal **1** a runny nose, runny eyes etc have liquid coming out of them, usually because you have a cold **2** food that is runny is not as solid or thick as normal or as desired: *The butter had gone runny in the heat.*

run-off n **1** [C] a second competition or election that is arranged when there is no clear winner of the first one → PLAY-OFF; → **run off** at RUN¹ **2** [U] technical rain or other liquid that flows off the land into rivers

run-of-the-'mill adj not special or interesting in any way; ◘ **ordinary**: *a run-of-the-mill performance*

run-on ,sentence n [C] especially AmE a sentence that has two main CLAUSES without connecting words or correct PUNCTUATION

runt /rʌnt/ n [C] **1** the smallest and least developed baby animal of a group born at the same time: [+of] *the runt of the litter* **2** informal a small, unpleasant, or unimportant person

run-through n [C] a short practice before a performance, test etc; → **rehearsal**: *a final run-through of the play*

run-up n **1** **the run-up to sth** the period of time just before an important event: *in the run-up to the election* **2** [C] the act of running, or the distance that you run, before you kick a ball, jump over a pole etc

run·way /'rʌnweɪ/ n [C] **1** a long specially prepared hard surface like a road on which aircraft land and take off **2** AmE a long narrow part of a stage that stretches out into the area where the AUDIENCE sits; ◘ **catwalk** BrE

ru·pee /ruː'piː/ n [C] the standard unit of money in India, Pakistan, and some other countries

ru·pi·ah /ruː'piːə/ n [C] the standard unit of money in Indonesia

rup·ture¹ /'rʌptʃə $ -ər/ n **1** [C,U] an occasion when something suddenly breaks apart or bursts: [+of] *the rupture of a blood vessel* **2** [C] a situation in which two countries, groups of people etc suddenly disagree and often end their relationship with each other:

[+**between**] *The eleventh century saw the formal rupture between East and West.* | [+**with**] *The rupture with his father was absolute.* **3** [C] a medical condition in which an organ of the body, especially one near the ABDOMEN, sticks out through the wall of muscle that normally surrounds it; ▤ **hernia**

rupture² *v* **1** [I,T] to break or burst, or to make something break or burst: *The pipe will rupture at its weakest point.* | *His liver was ruptured when a brick wall collapsed on him.* **2** [T] to damage good relations between people or a peaceful situation: *The noise ruptured the tranquility of the afternoon.* **3 rupture yourself** to cause an organ of the body, especially one near the ABDOMEN, to stick out through the wall of muscle that normally surrounds it

ru·ral W2 /ˈrʊərəl $ ˈrʊr-/ *adj*
1 happening in or relating to the countryside, not the city; ▣ **urban**: *a rural setting* | *rural bus routes*
2 like the countryside or reminding you of the countryside: *It's very rural round here, isn't it?*

‚rural deˈlivery *n* [U] *AmE* R.D.

ruse /ruːz $ ruːs, ruːz/ *n* [C] a clever trick used to deceive someone: *Agnes tried to think of a ruse to get Paul out of the house.*

rush¹ S2 W3 /rʌʃ/ *v*
1 MOVE QUICKLY [I always + adv/prep] to move very quickly, especially because you need to be somewhere very soon; ▤ **hurry**: *A small girl rushed past her.* | *Mo rushed off down the corridor.*
2 rush to do sth to do something very quickly and without delay: *I rushed to pack my suitcase before she came back.* | *He rushed to help his comrade.*
3 DO STH TOO QUICKLY [I,T] to do or decide something too quickly, especially so that you do not have time to do it carefully or well: *He does not intend to rush his decision.* | [+**into**] *I'm not rushing into marriage again.* | [+**through**] *She rushed through her script.* | **rush it/things** *When we first met, neither of us wanted to rush things.*
4 TAKE/SEND URGENTLY [T always + adv/prep] to take or send someone or something somewhere very quickly, especially because of an unexpected problem: **rush sb/sth to sth** | *The Red Cross rushed medical supplies to the war zone.* | *Dan was **rushed to hospital** with serious head injuries.*
5 MAKE SB HURRY [T] to try to make someone do something more quickly than they want to: *I'm sorry to rush you, but we need a decision by Friday.* | **rush sb into (doing) sth** *They felt they were being rushed into choosing a new leader.*
6 LIQUID [I always + adv/prep] if water or another liquid rushes somewhere, it moves quickly: *Water rushed through the gorge.*
7 BLOOD **blood rushes to sb's face/cheeks** used to say that someone's face becomes red because they feel embarrassed: *I felt the blood rush to my face as I heard my name.*
8 ATTACK [T] to attack a person or place suddenly and in a group: *They rushed the guard and stole his keys.*
9 AMERICAN UNIVERSITIES *AmE* **a)** [T] to give parties for students, have meetings etc, in order to decide whether to let them join your FRATERNITY or SORORITY (=type of club) **b)** [I,T] to go through the process of trying to be accepted into one of these clubs
10 AMERICAN FOOTBALL [I,T] to carry the ball forward

rush around also **rush about** *BrE phr v*
to try to do a lot of things in a short period of time: *Get things ready early so that you don't have to rush around at the last minute.*

rush sth ⇔ **out** *phr v*
to make a new product, book etc available for sale very quickly: *The new edition was rushed out just before Christmas.*

rush sth ⇔ **through** *phr v*
to deal with official or government business more quickly than usual: **rush sth through sth** *The legislation was rushed through parliament.*

rush² *n*
1 FAST MOVEMENT [singular] a sudden fast movement of things or people: **rush of air/wind/water** *She felt a cold rush of air as she wound down her window.* | **in a rush** *Her words came out in a rush.* | *At five past twelve there was a **mad rush** to the dinner hall.*
2 HURRY [singular,U] a situation in which you need to hurry: *I knew there would be a **last-minute rush** to meet the deadline.* | *Don't worry, **there's no rush**. We don't have to be at the station until 10.* | **do sth in a rush** (=do something quickly because you need to hurry) *I had to do my homework in a rush because I was late.* | **be in a rush** *I'm sorry, I can't talk now – I'm in a rush.*
3 BUSY PERIOD **the rush** the time in the day, month, year etc when a place or group of people is particularly busy; → **peak**: *The café is quiet until the lunchtime rush begins.* | **the Christmas rush** → RUSH HOUR
4 PEOPLE WANTING STH [singular] a situation in which a lot of people suddenly try to do or get something: [+**on**] *There's always a rush on swimsuits in the hot weather.* | **rush to do sth** *the rush to put computers in all schools* → GOLD RUSH
5 FEELING [singular] **a)** *informal* a sudden strong, usually pleasant feeling that you get from taking a drug or from doing something exciting; → **high**: *The feeling of power gave me such a rush.* | **an adrenalin rush b)** rush **of anger/excitement/gratitude etc** a sudden very strong feeling of anger etc: *I felt a rush of excitement when she arrived.* | *A rush of jealousy swept through her.*
6 PLANT [C usually plural] a type of tall grass that grows in water, often used for making baskets → see picture at FLOWER¹
7 FILM **rushes** [plural] the first prints of a film before it has been EDITED; ▤ **dailies** *AmE*
8 AMERICAN STUDENTS [U] *AmE* the time when students in American universities who want to join a FRATERNITY or SORORITY (=type of club) go to a lot of parties in order to try to be accepted: **rush week**

rushed /rʌʃt/ *adj* **1** done very quickly or too quickly, because there was not enough time: *We did have a meeting, but it was a bit rushed.* **2** *BrE* if you are rushed, you are very busy because you have a lot of things to do quickly: *I'll talk to you later – I'm a bit rushed at the moment.* | *I've been **rushed off my feet** (=extremely busy) all day.*

'rush hour *n* [C,U] the time of day when the roads, buses, trains etc are most full, because people are travelling to or from work: *I got caught in the morning rush hour.* | *heavy rush hour traffic*

rusk /rʌsk/ *n* [C] *BrE* a hard sweet dry bread for babies to eat

rus·set /ˈrʌsɪt/ *n* [U] *literary* a reddish brown colour —**russet** *adj*

Rus·sian¹ /ˈrʌʃən/ *adj* relating to Russia, its people, or its language

Russian² *n* **1** [C] someone from Russia **2** [U] the language used in Russia

‚Russian rouˈlette *n* [U] a game in which you risk killing yourself by shooting at your head with a gun that has six spaces for bullets but only one bullet in it

rust¹ /rʌst/ *n* [U] **1** the reddish-brown substance that forms on iron or steel when it gets wet; → **rusty**: *There were large patches of rust on the car.* **2** a plant disease that causes reddish-brown spots

rust² *v* [I,T] to become covered with rust, or to make something become covered in rust: *The metal had begun to rust.* | *The gate was old and badly rusted.*

rust away *phr v* to be gradually destroyed by rust: *The blades of the swords have rusted away.*

rus·tic¹ /ˈrʌstɪk/ *adj* **1** simple, old-fashioned, and not spoiled by modern developments, in a way that is typical of the countryside: *The village had a certain rustic charm.* **2** [only before noun] roughly made from wood: *a rustic chair* —**rusticity** /rʌˈstɪsɪti/ *n* [U]

R

rustic² n [C] *literary* someone from the country, especially a farm worker

rus·tle¹ /'rʌsəl/ v **1** [I,T] if leaves, papers, clothes etc rustle, or if you rustle them, they make a noise as they rub against each other: *She moved nearer, her long silk skirt rustling around her.* | *He rustled the papers on his desk.* **2** [T] to steal farm animals such as cattle, horses, or sheep

rustle sth ⇔ **up** *phr v informal* to make a meal quickly: *I'll rustle up a couple of steaks on the barbecue.*

rustle² n [singular] the noise made when something rustles: [+of] *the rustle of leaves in the wind*

rus·tler /'rʌslə $ -ər/ n [C] someone who steals farm animals such as cattle, horses, or sheep

rust·proof /'rʌstpruːf/ *adj* metal that is rustproof will not RUST

rust·y /'rʌsti/ *adj* **1** metal that is rusty is covered in RUST: *a rusty nail* | *a new metal that will never go rusty* **2** if you are rusty, you are not as good at something as you used to be, because you have not practised it for a long time: *My French is a bit rusty.*

rut /rʌt/ n **1** [C] a deep narrow track left in soft ground by a wheel **2 in a rut** living or working in a situation that never changes, so that you feel bored: *I was stuck in a rut and decided to look for a new job.* **3** [U] also **the rut** *technical* the period of the year when some male animals, especially DEER, are sexually active: **in rut** *a stag in rut*

ru·ta·ba·ga /ˌruːtə'beɪgə/ n [C] *AmE* a large round yellow vegetable that grows under the ground; ⊟ **swede** *BrE*

ruth·less /'ruːθləs/ *adj* **1** so determined to get what you want that you do not care if you have to hurt other people in order to do it: *a ruthless dictator* | *They have shown a ruthless disregard for basic human rights.* **2** determined and firm when making unpleasant decisions: *He ran the company with ruthless efficiency.* | *Throw away clothes you don't wear – be ruthless.* —**ruthlessly** *adv*: *The uprising was ruthlessly suppressed.* —**ruthlessness** n [U]

rut·ted /'rʌtɪd/ *adj* a surface that is rutted has deep narrow tracks in it left by the wheels of vehicles; → **uneven**

RV /ˌɑː 'viː $ ˌɑːr-/ n [C] *AmE recreational vehicle* a large vehicle, usually with cooking equipment and beds in it, that a family can use for travelling or camping; → **mobile home**, **caravan**

Rx *AmE* the written abbreviation of **prescription**

rye /raɪ/ n [U] **1** a type of grain that is used for making bread and WHISKY: *rye bread* **2** also ˌrye 'whiskey *AmE* a type of American WHISKY made from rye

rye·grass /'raɪgrɑːs $ -græs/ n [U] a type of grass that is grown as food for animals

R

S, s

S, s /es/ *plural* **S's, s's** *n* [C,U] the 19th letter of the English alphabet

S 1 the written abbreviation of *south* or *southern* **2** the written abbreviation of *small*, used on clothes to show the size

-s /z, s/ *suffix* **1** forms the plural of nouns: *a cat and two dogs* **2** forms the third person singular of the present tense of most verbs: *he plays | she sits*

-s' /z, s/ *suffix* forms the POSSESSIVE case of plural nouns: *the girls' dresses | the islands' inhabitants*

-'s¹ /z, s/ **1** the short form of 'is': *John's here. | What's that? | She's writing a letter.* **2** the short form of 'has': *Polly's gone out. | A spider's got eight legs.* **3** a short form of 'us' used only in 'let's' **4** *spoken* a short form of 'does', used in questions after 'who','what' etc that many people think is incorrect: *How's he plan to do that?*

-'s² *suffix* **1** forms the POSSESSIVE case of singular nouns, and of plural nouns that do not end in -s: *my sister's husband | Mary's generosity | yesterday's lesson | the children's bedroom* **2** BrE the shop or home of someone: *I bought it at the baker's* (=at the baker's shop). *| I met him at Mary's* (=at Mary's house).

S & L /,es ənd 'el/ *n* [C] AmE informal the abbreviation of *savings and loan association*

S & M /,es ənd 'em/ *n* [U] the abbreviation of *sado-masochism*

Sab·bath /'sæbəθ/ *n* **1 the Sabbath a)** Sunday, considered as a day of rest and prayer by most Christian churches **b)** Saturday, considered as a day of rest and prayer in the Jewish religion and some Christian churches **2 keep/break the Sabbath** to obey or not obey the religious rules of the Sabbath

sab·bat·i·cal /sə'bætɪkəl/ *n* [C,U] a period when someone, especially someone in a university job, stops doing their usual work in order to study or travel: *She took a long sabbatical. | on sabbatical Dr Watson's away on sabbatical.*

sa·ber /'seɪbə $ -ər/ the American spelling of SABRE

sa·ble¹ /'seɪbəl/ *n* [C,U] an expensive fur used to make coats etc, or the small animal that this fur comes from

sable² *adj literary* black or very dark in colour

sab·o·tage¹ /'sæbətɑːʒ/ *v* [T] **1** to secretly damage or destroy equipment, vehicles etc that belong to an enemy or opponent, so that they cannot be used: *Every single plane had been sabotaged.* **2** to deliberately spoil someone's plans because you do not want them to succeed: *Demonstrators have sabotaged the conference.*

sabotage² *n* [U] deliberate damage that is done to equipment, vehicles etc in order to prevent an enemy or opponent from using them: *The terrorists were planning acts of sabotage to destabilize the country. | industrial sabotage*

sab·o·teur /,sæbə'tɜː $ -'tɜːr/ *n* [C] someone who deliberately damages, destroys, or spoils someone else's property or activities, in order to prevent them from doing something: *The lorries were wrecked by saboteurs.* → HUNT SABOTEUR

sa·bre BrE; **saber** AmE /'seɪbə $ -ər/ *n* [C] **1** a light pointed sword with one sharp edge used in FENCING **2** a heavy sword with a curved blade, used in past times

'sabre-,rattling *n* [U] when someone threatens to use force but you do not think they are very frightening or serious: *What the situation calls for is calm discussion – not sabre-rattling.*

sac /sæk/ *n* [C] *technical* a part inside a plant or animal that is shaped like a bag and contains liquid or air

sac·cha·rin /'sækərən/ *n* [U] a chemical substance that tastes sweet and is used instead of sugar in drinks

sac·cha·rine /'sækəriːn/ *adj formal* too romantic in a way that seems silly and insincere: *I hated the movie's saccharine ending.*

sach·et /'sæʃeɪ $ sæ'ʃeɪ/ *n* [C] **1** BrE a small plastic or paper package containing a liquid or powder; **🔲 packet** AmE: [+of] *a sachet of shampoo;* → see picture at CONTAINER **2** a small bag containing dried herbs or flowers that smell pleasant: *a lavender sachet*

sack¹ /sæk/ *n* [C] **1 a)** a large bag made of strong rough cloth or strong paper, used for storing or carrying flour, coal, vegetables etc: [+of] *a sack of potatoes* **b)** also **sackful** the amount that a sack can contain: [+of] *We need about a sack of rice;* → see picture at BAG¹ **2 the sack** BrE informal when someone is dismissed from their job: *They've never actually given anyone the sack. | He got the sack for stealing. | She claimed she'd been threatened with the sack.* **3 hit the sack** old-fashioned informal to go to bed: *It's one o'clock – time to hit the sack.* **4 in the sack** informal in bed – used to talk about sexual activity: *I bet she's great in the sack.* **5 the sack of sth** formal a situation in which an army goes through a place, destroying or stealing things and attacking people: *the sack of Rome in 1527*

sack² *v* [T] **1** BrE informal to dismiss someone from their job; **🔲 fire:** *They couldn't sack me – I'd done nothing wrong. | sack sb from sth He was sacked from every other job he had. | sack sb for (doing) sth He was sacked for being drunk.* **2** to knock down the QUARTERBACK in American football **3** if soldiers sack a place, they go through it destroying or stealing things and attacking people: *Alaric the Goth advanced toward Rome, which he sacked in A.D. 410.*

sack out *phr v* AmE informal to go to sleep: *He sacked out on the sofa.*

sack·cloth /'sæk-klɒθ $ -klɔːθ/ also **sack·ing** /'sækɪŋ/ *n* [U] **1** rough cloth used for making sacks **2 wear sackcloth and ashes** BrE to behave in a way that shows everyone you are sorry about something wrong you have done

'sack race *n* [C] a race in which the competitors, usually children, have to jump forwards with both legs inside a SACK

sac·ra·ment /'sækrəmənt/ *n* [C] **1 the Sacrament** the bread and wine that are eaten at COMMUNION (=an important Christian ceremony) **2** one of the important Christian ceremonies, such as marriage or COMMUNION —**sacramental** /,sækrə'mentl◂/ *adj*

sa·cred /'seɪkrɪd/ *adj* **1** relating to a god or religion: *a sacred vow | the miraculous powers of sacred relics | Certain animals were considered sacred. | [+to] The land is sacred to these tribesmen.* **2** very important or greatly respected: *Human life is sacred. | Frontiers which have held for over forty years are no longer sacred. | [+to] Few things were sacred to Henry, but local history was one of them. | He had no respect for everything I held sacred.* **3 is nothing sacred?** *spoken* used to express shock when something you think is valuable or important is being changed or harmed —**sacredness** *n* [U]: *the sacredness of human life*

,sacred 'cow *n* [C] a belief, custom, system etc that is so important to some people that they will not let anyone criticize it: *In New York's show business scene, money, fame and power are sacred cows.*

sac·ri·fice¹ /'sækrɪfaɪs/ *n* **1** [C,U] when you decide not to have something valuable, in order to get something that is more important: *The minister stressed the need for economic sacrifice. | The workforce were willing to make sacrifices in order to keep jobs. | She brought three children up single-handedly, often at great personal sacrifice.* **2 a)** [C,U] the act of offering something to a god, especially in the past, by killing an animal or person in a religious ceremony: *They made sacrifices to ensure a good harvest.* **b)** [C] an animal, person, or object offered to a god in sacrifice: [+to] *In those days, an animal was offered as a sacrifice to God. |*

S

*a **human sacrifice*** (=a person killed as a sacrifice) **3** *literary* **the final/supreme/ultimate sacrifice** the act of dying while you are fighting for a principle or in order to help other people: *Captain Oates **made the ultimate sacrifice** in a bid to save his colleagues.*

sacrifice² *v* **1** [T] to willingly stop having something you want or doing something you like in order to get something more important: **sacrifice sth for sth** *A Labour government chose to sacrifice defence for welfare.* | **sacrifice sth to do sth** *He sacrificed a promising career to look after his kids.* | **sacrifice yourself (for sth)** *mothers who sacrifice themselves for their children* **2** [I,T] to kill an animal or person and offer them to a god in a religious ceremony

sac·ri·fi·cial /ˌsækrɨˈfɪʃəl◂/ *adj* [usually before noun] relating to or offered as a sacrifice: *a sacrificial ceremony* | *a sacrificial lamb*

sac·ri·lege /ˈsækrɨlɪdʒ/ *n* [C,U] **1** when someone treats something holy in a way that does not show respect **2** when someone treats something that another person thinks is very important or special without enough care or respect: **it is sacrilege (for sb) to do sth** *It's sacrilege to even think of destroying that lovely building.* —**sacrilegious** /ˌsækrɨˈlɪdʒəs◂/ *adj*

sac·ris·tan /ˈsækrɨstən/ *n* [C] someone whose job is to take care of the holy objects in a church

sac·ris·ty /ˈsækrɨsti/ *n plural* **sacristies** [C] a small room in a church where holy cups and plates are kept, and where priests put on their ceremonial clothes; ◻ **vestry**

sac·ro·sanct /ˈsækrəʊsæŋkt $ -roʊ-/ *adj* something that is sacrosanct is considered to be so important that no one is allowed to criticize or change it; ◻ **sacred**: *Weekends are sacrosanct in our family.*

sad [S2] [W3] /sæd/ *adj comparative* **sadder**, *superlative* **saddest**
1 [FEELING UNHAPPY] unhappy, especially because something unpleasant has happened; ◻ **happy**: **feel/look/sound sad** *Dad looked sad and worried as he read the letter.* | **be sad to hear/see/read etc sth** *I was very sad to hear that he had died.* | **sad that** *Lilly felt sad that Christmas was over.* | [+about] *I was sad about the friends I was leaving behind.* | **sad smile/face/expression etc** *There was such a sad look in her eyes.*
2 [MAKING YOU UNHAPPY] a sad event, situation etc makes you feel unhappy: *Sorry to hear the **sad news**.* | *It was a **sad case**. The boy ended up in prison.* | **sad story/song/film etc** *a story with a sad ending* | **it is sad to see/hear etc sth** *It was sad to see them arguing all the time.* | **sad time/day/moment etc** *This is a sad day for us all.*
3 [NOT SATISFACTORY] very bad or unacceptable: *There aren't enough teachers, which is a **sad state of affairs** (=bad situation).* | **it's sad that/when/if ...** *It's sad if people are too afraid to go out alone at night.* | **the sad fact is (that)** *spoken: The sad fact is that prejudice still exists.* | **Sad to say** (=unfortunately), *the country is heading towards civil war.*
4 [LONELY] a sad person has a dull, unhappy, or lonely life: *She's a sad character – without any friends at all.*
5 [BORING] *informal* boring or not deserving any respect: *Stay in on Saturday night? What a sad idea!*
6 sadder and/but wiser having learned something from an unpleasant experience: *He came out of the relationship sadder but wiser.* → SADNESS

WORD FOCUS: words meaning SAD
unhappy sad because of the situation you are in | **miserable** very sad | **depressed** sad for a long time, and feeling that your life will never get better | **gloomy/glum** looking sad | **down/down in the dumps** sad and without much interest in life – usually not in a serious or permanent way | **broken-hearted** very sad because someone has ended a romantic relationship with you | **homesick** sad because you are a long way from your home and your friends

---

SAD /sæd/ *n* [U] *medical* the abbreviation of *seasonal affective disorder*

sad·den /ˈsædn/ *v* [T] *formal* to make someone feel sad: *Those who knew him are saddened by his death.* | **it saddens sb that** *It saddened him that they no longer trusted him.* —**saddening** *adj*

sad·dle¹ /ˈsædl/ *n* [C] **1** a leather seat that you sit on when you ride a horse **2** a seat on a bicycle or a MOTORCYCLE → see picture at BICYCLE¹ **3 in the saddle** *informal* **a)** riding a horse: *We did six or eight hours in the saddle every day.* **b)** in a position in which you have power or authority: *He always has to be in the saddle, controlling everything.* **4 saddle of lamb/hare/venison** a large joint of meat taken from the middle of the animal's back

saddle² *v* [T] to put a saddle on a horse
saddle up *phr v* to put a saddle on a horse: **saddle sth ⇔ up** *He was in the stable, saddling up his horse.*
saddle sb with sth *phr v* to make someone have a job or problem that is difficult or boring and that they do not want: *I've been saddled with organizing the whole party!* | *Many farms were saddled with debts.*

saddle bag *n* [C] a bag for carrying things, fixed to the saddle on a horse or bicycle

sad·dler /ˈsædlə $ -ər/ *n* [C] someone who makes saddles and other leather products, or a shop where these are sold

sad·dler·y /ˈsædləri/ *n* [U] saddles and leather goods made by a saddler

saddle shoe *n* [C] *AmE* a shoe that has a toe and heel of one colour, with a different colour in the middle

saddle-sore *adj* [not before noun] feeling stiff and sore after riding a horse or bicycle

sad·do /ˈsædəʊ $ -oʊ/ *n plural* **saddos** [C] *informal* someone who you do not respect, especially because you think their interests are boring or strange: *a bunch of saddos dressed up as science fiction characters*

sa·dhu /ˈsɑːduː/ *n* [C] a Hindu holy man who lives a very simple life

sa·dis·m /ˈseɪdɪzəm/ *n* [U] **1** behaviour in which someone gets pleasure from hurting other people or making them suffer; → **masochism**: *There seemed to be an element of sadism in the training regime.* **2** when someone gets sexual pleasure from hurting someone; → **masochism**

sa·dist /ˈseɪdɨst/ *n* [C] someone who enjoys hurting other people or making them suffer; → **masochist**

sa·dis·tic /səˈdɪstɪk/ *adj* cruel and enjoying making other people suffer; → **masochistic**: *He took **sadistic pleasure** in humiliating her.* | *sadistic fantasies* —**sadistically** /-kli/ *adv*

sad·ly /ˈsædli/ *adv* **1** in a way that shows that you are sad; ◻ **unhappily**: *Peter shook his head sadly.* **2** [sentence adverb] unfortunately: *Sadly, the business failed.* **3** very much – used when talking about bad situations or states: *The garden's been sadly neglected.* | *Good restaurants were sadly lacking.* | *He was a popular man who will be sadly missed.* | *I'm afraid you're going to be sadly disappointed.* | *If you think you'll get any money from him, you're sadly mistaken.*

sad·ness /ˈsædnɨs/ *n* [U] the state of feeling sad; ◻ **unhappiness**: **great/deep sadness** *She sensed Beth's deep sadness.* | *It was with great sadness that we learned of his death.* | *There was **a touch of sadness** in his voice* (=he sounded a little sad). | *His relief **was tinged with sadness*** (=he also felt rather sad).

sa·do·mas·o·chis·m /ˌseɪdəʊˈmæsəkɪzəm $ -doʊ-/ *n* [U] **S & M** when someone gets sexual pleasure from hurting someone or being hurt —**sadomasochist** *n* [C] —**sadomasochistic** /ˌseɪdəʊmæsəˈkɪstɪk◂ $ -doʊ-/ *adj*

sae /ˌes eɪ ˈiː/ *n* [C] *BrE* **stamped addressed envelope** or **self-addressed envelope** an envelope on which you have written your own name and address, and usually put a stamp, so that someone else can send you something; ▤ **SASE** *AmE: For further details, send an SAE to the following address.*

sa·fa·ri /səˈfɑːri/ *n* [C] **1** a trip to see or hunt wild animals, especially in Africa: **on safari** *They went on safari in Kenya.* **2 safari suit/jacket** a suit or jacket that is made of light material, usually with a belt and pockets on the chest

saˈfari park *n* [C] an enclosed area of land where wild animals are kept, so that people can drive round to look at them

safe¹ S2 W2 /seɪf/ *adj comparative* **safer**, *superlative* **safest**

1 NOT CAUSING HARM not likely to cause any physical injury or harm; ▤ **dangerous**: *Don't go near the edge – it isn't safe.* | *Flying is one of the safest forms of travel.* | *a safe working environment* | **it is safe (for sb) to do sth** *Is it safe to swim here?* | **safe to use/drink/eat** *etc* *The water is treated to* **make** *it* **safe** *to drink.* | [+**for**] *play-areas that are safe for children* | **(at/from) a safe distance** *We watched from a safe distance.* | *Drivers should* **keep a safe distance** *from the car in front.* | **safe driver** *Women are safer drivers than men.*

2 NOT IN DANGER [not before noun] not in danger of being lost, harmed, or stolen; ▤ **unsafe**; → **safety**: *She doesn't* **feel safe** *in the house on her own.* | [+**from**] *The birds' nests are high up, safe from predators.* | *Make sure you* **keep** *these documents* **safe.** | **safe and sound/well** (=unharmed, especially after being in danger) *The missing children were found safe and sound.*

3 safe place a place where something is not likely to be stolen or lost: **keep/put sth in a safe place** *Keep your credit cards in a safe place.*

4 safe journey/arrival/return *etc* a journey etc when someone or something is not harmed or lost: *His family celebrated his safe return home.* | **safe journey** *BrE* (=said to someone when they start a long journey) *Dad rang to wish me a safe journey.*

5 NO RISK not involving any risk and very likely to be successful: *a safe investment* | *a safe method of contraception* | **it's safe to say/assume (that)** *I think it's safe to say that the future is looking pretty good.* | **be (as) safe as houses** *BrE* (=be completely safe)

6 SUBJECT a safe subject of conversation is not likely to upset anyone or make people argue: *I kept to safe subjects, like the weather.*

7 to be on the safe side *spoken* to do something in order to be certain to avoid an unpleasant situation: *I'd take an umbrella, just to be on the safe side.*

8 be in safe hands to be with someone who will look after you very well: *Everyone wants to feel that their children are in safe hands.*

9 better (to be) safe than sorry *spoken* used to say that it is better to be careful, even if this takes time, effort etc, than take a risk that may have a bad result: *Set the alarm clock – better safe than sorry!*

10 safe in the knowledge that... completely certain that something is true or will happen: *She went out, safe in the knowledge that no one else was awake.*

11 a safe pair of hands someone you can trust to do a difficult job without making mistakes

12 safe! *BrE spoken informal* used by young people to show approval of something: *'Alex is having a party.' 'Oh, safe!'*

13 NO PROBLEM *BrE spoken informal* used to say that something is good and that there is no problem: *'How's your new boss?' 'She's safe.'* → **play it safe** at PLAY¹ (9); → **it's a safe bet (that)** at BET² (4); → **safe seat** at SEAT¹ (2); → **sb's secret is safe (with sb)** at SECRET² (1)

safe² *n* [C] a strong metal box or cupboard with special locks where you keep money and valuable things

ˌsafe ˈconduct *n* [C,U] SAFE PASSAGE

ˈsafe-deposit ˌbox *n* [C] a SAFETY-DEPOSIT BOX

safe·guard¹ /ˈseɪfɡɑːd $ -ɡɑːrd/ *v* [T] to protect something from harm or damage: **safeguard sb's interests/rights/welfare** *etc* *The industry has a duty to safeguard the interests of consumers.* | *technology that will safe-*

guard the environment | **safeguard sth against sth** *a program for safeguarding the computer system against viruses*

safeguard² *n* [C] a rule, agreement etc that is intended to protect someone or something from possible dangers or problems: *International safeguards prevent the increase of nuclear weapons.* | [+**against**] *safeguards against the exploitation of children*

ˌsafe ˈhaven *n* [C] a place where someone can go in order to escape from possible danger or attack: **provide/offer/create a safe haven (for sb)** *The Prime Minister wanted to create a safe haven for the refugees.*

ˌsafe ˈhouse *n* [C] a house where someone can hide and be protected. Safe houses are used especially by criminals hiding from the police, or by people who are being protected by the police.

safe·keep·ing /ˌseɪfˈkiːpɪŋ/ *n* [U] the state of being kept safe, or the action of keeping something safe: **for safekeeping** *My passport was in the inner pocket of my bag, for safekeeping.*

safe·ly /ˈseɪfli/ *adv* in a way that is safe: *Drive safely!* | *I think we can safely assume that she will pass the exam.*

ˌsafe ˈpassage also **safe conduct** *n* [C,U] official protection for someone when they are in danger or passing through a dangerous area: **permit/promise/guarantee etc safe passage (to/for sb)** *The government offered safe passage to militants taking up their offer of peace talks.*

ˌsafe ˈsex *n* [U] ways of having sex that reduce the risk of spreading AIDS and other sexual diseases, especially by using a CONDOM

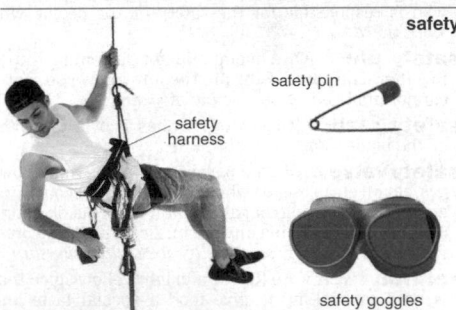

safety

safety pin

safety harness

safety goggles

safe·ty S3 W2 /ˈseɪfti/ *n plural* **safeties**

1 NOT IN DANGER [U] when someone or something is safe from danger or harm: [+**of**] *measures to improve the* **health and safety** *of employees* | **in safety** *We were able to watch the lions in complete safety.* | **for safety** *For safety, always climb with a partner.* | *You shouldn't travel alone,* **for safety's sake** (=in order to be safe). | *For* **your own safety**, *please do not smoke inside the plane.*

2 HARMFUL/NOT HARMFUL [U] how safe something is to use, do etc: [+**of**] *Campaigners have challenged the safety of genetically-modified foods.* | **safety standards/regulations/precautions etc** (=things that are done in order to make sure that something is safe) *The device meets safety standards.* | *Lower speed limits are part of a new* **road safety** *campaign.*

3 sb's safety how safe someone is in a particular situation: *The boy had been missing for five days and there were fears for his safety.*

4 SAFE PLACE [U] a place where you are safe from danger: [+**of**] *30,000 people fled to the safety of the capital.* | **get/lead/drag etc sb to safety** *Firefighters led the children to safety.* | *They* **reached safety** *seconds before the bomb went off.*

5 there is safety in numbers used to say that it is safer to be in a group than alone

6 SPORT [C] a way of getting two points in American

1 000, 2 000, 3 000, most frequent words in S poken and W ritten English

football by making the other team put the ball down in its own GOAL

7 GUN [C] *AmE* a lock on a gun that stops anyone from shooting it by accident; ▤ **safety catch** *BrE*

8 safety harness/helmet/glasses etc equipment etc that keeps you safe when you are doing something dangerous

'safety belt *n* [C] a SEAT BELT

'safety catch *n* [C] *BrE* a lock on a gun that stops anyone from shooting it by accident; ▤ **safety** *AmE*

'safety ,curtain *n* [C] a thick curtain at the front of a theatre stage that prevents fire from spreading

'safety-deposit ,box also **safe-deposit box** *n* [C] a small box used for storing valuable objects, usually kept in a special room in a bank

'safety glass *n* [U] strong glass that breaks into very small pieces that are not sharp, used for example in car windows

'safety lamp *n* [C] a special lamp used by MINERS, with a flame which will not make underground gases explode

'safety match *n* [C] a match that you can light only by rubbing it along a special surface on the side of its box

'safety net *n* [C] **1** a large net that is placed below an ACROBAT who is performing high above the ground, in order to catch them if they fall **2** a system or arrangement that exists to help you if you have serious problems or get into a difficult situation: [+for] *State support should provide a safety net for the very poor.*

'safety ,officer *n* [C] someone in an organization who is responsible for the safety of the people who work there

'safety pin *n* [C] a metal pin for fastening things together. The point of the pin fits into a cover so that it cannot hurt you. → see picture at SAFETY

'safety ,razor *n* [C] a RAZOR that has a cover over part of the blade to protect your skin

'safety valve *n* [C] **1** a part of a machine that allows gas, steam etc to escape when the pressure becomes too great **2** something that allows you to get rid of strong feelings without doing any harm: *Being able to express emotion is a healthy safety valve for the relationship.*

saf·fron /'sæfrən/ *n* [U] **1** a bright yellow spice that is used in cooking to give food a special taste and colour. It is sold as a powder or in thin pieces. **2** a bright orange-yellow colour

sag /sæg/ *v* **sagged, sagging** [I] **1** to hang down or bend in the middle, especially because of the weight of something; ▤ **droop**: *The branch sagged under the weight of the apples.* | *The skin around my eyes is starting to sag.* | *a sagging roof* **2** to become weaker or less valuable: *attempts to revive the sagging economy* —**sag** *n* [C,U]: *a sag in the mattress*

sa·ga /'sɑːgə/ *n* [C] **1** a long and complicated series of events, or a description of this: *The whole saga began back in May.* | [+of] *She launched into the saga of her on-off engagement.* **2** a long story about events that happen over many years: [+of] *a saga of four generations of the Coleman family* **3** one of the stories written about the Vikings of Norway and Iceland

sa·ga·cious /sə'geɪʃəs/ *adj formal* able to understand and judge things very well; ▤ **wise** —**sagaciously** *adv*

sa·ga·ci·ty /sə'gæsᵻti/ *n* [U] *formal* good judgment and understanding; ▤ **wisdom**

sage¹ /seɪdʒ/ *n* **1** [U] a herb with grey-green leaves **2** [C] *literary* someone, especially an old man, who is very wise

sage² *adj literary* very wise, especially as a result of a lot of experience: *sage advice* —**sagely** *adv*

sage·brush /'seɪdʒbrʌʃ/ *n* [U] a small plant that is very common in dry areas in the western US

sag·gy /'sægi/ *adj informal* something that is saggy hangs down or bends more than it should: *The bed was saggy in the middle.*

Sa·git·tar·i·us /ˌsædʒ'teəriəs $ -'ter-/ *n* **1** [U] the ninth sign of the ZODIAC, represented by an animal that is half horse and half human, which some people believe affects the character and life of people born between November 23 and December 21 **2** also **Sagittarian** [C] someone who was born between November 23 and December 21 —**Sagittarian** *adj*

sa·go /'seɪgəʊ $ -goʊ/ *n* [U] *BrE* small white grains obtained from some PALM trees, used to make sweet dishes with milk

sahib /sɑːb $ 'sɑː-ᵻb/ *n* used in India, especially during the period of British rule, when talking to a man in authority: *Good morning, sahib!*

said¹ /sed/ *v* the past tense and past participle of SAY¹

said² *adj* [only before noun] *law* mentioned before: *The said weapon was later found in the defendant's home.*

sail¹ S3 /seɪl/ *v*

1 [I always +adv/prep, T] to travel on or across an area of water in a boat or ship: [+across/into/out of etc] *the first Europeans to sail across the Atlantic* | *Three tall ships sailed past.* | *She always wanted to sail around the world.* | **sail the Pacific/the Atlantic etc** *We're taking two months off to sail the Caribbean.*

2 [I] to start a journey by boat or ship: *We sail at dawn.* | [+for] *They're sailing for Antigua next week.*

3 [I,T] to direct or control the movement of a boat or ship that has a sail: *Blake sailed the ship safely through the narrow passage.* | *My father taught me to sail.*

4 [I always +adv/prep] to move quickly and smoothly through the air: [+through/over/into etc] *A ball came sailing over the fence.*

5 [I always +adv/prep] to move forwards gracefully and confidently: *She sailed into the room.*

6 sail close to the wind *BrE* to do or say something that is nearly wrong, illegal, or dishonest

  sail through sth *phr v*
  to succeed very easily in a test, examination etc: *Adam sailed through his final exams.*

sail² *n* [C] **1** a large piece of strong cloth fixed onto a boat, so that the wind will push the boat along: *a yacht with white sails* | **hoist/lower the sails** (=put the sails up or down) **2 set sail** to begin a journey by boat or ship: [+for/from] *The following week the 'Queen Elizabeth' set sail for Jamaica.* **3 under sail** *literary* moving along on a ship or boat that has sails

sail·board /'seɪlbɔːd $ -bɔːrd/ *n* [C] a flat board with a sail, that you stand on in the sport of WIND-SURFING; ▤ **wind-surfer**

sail·boat /'seɪlbəʊt $ -boʊt/ *n* [C] *AmE* a small boat with one or more sails

sail·ing /'seɪlɪŋ/ *n* **1** [U] the sport or activity of travelling in or directing a small boat with sails: *Bud has invited us to go sailing this weekend.* → see picture at WATER SPORTS **2** [C] a time when a ship leaves a port: *Luckily, there was another sailing at 2 o'clock.* → **plain sailing** at PLAIN¹ (9)

'sailing boat *n* [C] *BrE* a small boat with one or more sails

'sailing ship *n* [C] a large ship with sails

sail·or /'seɪlə $ -ər/ *n* [C] **1** someone who works on a ship: *Six British sailors drowned.* | *We were both experienced sailors.* **2 bad/good sailor** someone who does or does not feel sick when they are on a boat or ship

'sailor suit *n* [C] a blue and white suit that looks like an old-fashioned sailor's uniform, worn by small boys

saint /seɪnt/ *n* [C] **1** written abbreviation **St** or **St.** someone who is given the title 'saint' by the Christian church after they have died, because they have been very good or holy: *Saint Patrick* | *the saints in heaven* **2** *informal* someone who is extremely good, kind, or patient: *His wife must have been a saint to put up with him for all those years.* **3 the patience of a**

saint a very large amount of patience: *You need the patience of a saint for this job.*

saint·ed /ˈseɪntɪd/ *adj literary* **1** having been made a saint by the Christian church **2** *old-fashioned* used when talking about a dead person: *my sainted mother, God rest her soul* **3 my sainted aunt!** *BrE old-fashioned* used to express surprise or shock: *My sainted aunt! Whatever next?*

saint·hood /ˈseɪnthʊd/ *n* [U] the state of being a saint

saint·ly /ˈseɪntli/ *adj* completely good and honest, with no faults: *She led a saintly and blameless life.* —**saintliness** *n* [U]

ˈsaint's day *n* [C] the day of the year when the Christian church remembers a particular saint

saith /seθ/ *v biblical* says

sake¹ S2 W3 /seɪk/ *n* [U]
1 for the sake of sb/sth also **for sb's/sth's sake** in order to help, improve, or please someone or something: *He moved to the seaside for the sake of his health.* | *I only went for Kay's sake.* | *I hope he's told the truth for his own sake* (=because it will be good for him).
2 for God's/Christ's/goodness'/Heaven's etc sake *spoken* **a)** used when you are telling someone how important it is to do something or not to do something: *For goodness sake, don't be late!* **b)** used to show that you are angry or annoyed: *What is it now, for God's sake?*
3 for the sake of it if you do something for the sake of it, you do it because you want to and not for any particular reason: *She likes spending money just for the sake of it.*
4 for its own sake also **sth for sth's sake** if something is done for its own sake, it is done for the value of the experience itself, not for any advantage it will bring: *art for art's sake*
5 for the sake of argument *spoken* if you say something for the sake of argument, what you say may not be true but it will help you to have a discussion: *Let's say, just for the sake of argument, that you've got £200 to invest.*

sa·ke² /ˈsɑːki/ *n* [U] a Japanese alcoholic drink made from rice

sal·a·ble /ˈseɪləbəl/ *adj* another spelling of SALEABLE

sa·la·cious /səˈleɪʃəs/ *adj formal* showing too much interest in sex: *the media's love of salacious gossip* —**salaciously** *adv* —**salaciousness** *n* [U]

sal·ad /ˈsæləd/ *n* [C,U] **1** a mixture of raw vegetables, especially LETTUCE, CUCUMBER, and tomato: *Would you like some salad with your pasta?* | *a spinach salad* | **toss a salad** (=mix it all together, usually with a dressing) ⚠ Salad is a type of cold food made from vegetables. The green leafy vegetable that you often use in salads is called **lettuce**. **2** raw or cooked food cut into small pieces and served cold: **fruit/potato salad**

ˈsalad bar *n* [C] a place in a restaurant with different vegetables that you can choose to make your own salad

ˈsalad cream *n* [U] *BrE* a thick light-coloured liquid, similar to MAYONNAISE, that you put on salad

ˈsalad days *n* [plural] *old-fashioned* the time of your life when you are young and not very experienced

ˈsalad ˌdressing *n* [C,U] a liquid mixture made from oil and VINEGAR, for putting on salads

sal·a·man·der /ˈsæləmændə $ -ər/ *n* [C] a small animal similar to a LIZARD, which lives on land and in the water

sa·la·mi /səˈlɑːmi/ *n* [C,U] a large SAUSAGE with a strong taste that is eaten cold

sal·a·ried /ˈsælərid/ *adj* receiving money every month for the work you do, rather than for every week or every hour: *salaried workers*

sal·a·ry W3 /ˈsæləri/ *n plural* **salaries** [C,U] money that you receive as payment from the organization you work for, usually paid to you every month; → **wage, pay**: *The average salary is $39,000 a year.* | *people with high salaries* | **be on a salary of sth** (=be earning a particular amount) *She's on a salary of £16,000.* | **monthly/annual/yearly salary** *Parker's annual salary is*

just under $48,000. | **basic/base salary** *a $56,000 a year base salary*; → see box at PAY²

sal·a·ry·man /ˈsælərimæn/ *n plural* **salarymen** /-men/ [C] a man who works in an office, often for many hours each day, and receives a salary as payment, especially in Japan

sale S2 W1 /seɪl/ *n*
1 [C,U] when you sell something: [+of] *The use and sale of marijuana remains illegal.* | *Harvey gets a $50 commission every time he* **makes a sale** (=sells something as part of his job).* | *Car salesmen will often bring down the price rather than* **lose a sale** (=fail to sell something).* | *arms sales to Iran*
2 sales a) [plural] the total number of products that are sold during a particular period of time: *Britain's* **retail sales** (=all the things sold to the public in shops) *jumped 3.2 percent in April.* | [+of] *Sales of automobiles are up this year.* | *We did not reach our summer* **sales targets**.* | *The company no longer releases its* **sales figures** (=how much money it makes or loses from sales).* | **in sales** *We grossed more than $500,000 in sales last year.* **b)** [U] the part of a company that deals with selling products: *She found a job in sales.* | *a sales manager* | *a worldwide* **sales force** *of 1,100*
3 for sale available to be bought: *Excuse me, are these for sale?* | *There was a 'for sale' sign in the yard.* | *Reluctantly, they* **put** *the family home* **up for sale** (=made it available to be bought).
4 on sale a) available to be bought in a shop: *A wide range of postcards and other souvenirs are on sale in the visitors' centre.* | *Stephen King's new novel will* **go on sale** (=will begin to be sold) *next week.* **b)** *especially AmE* available to be bought at a lower price than usual: *These gloves were on sale for only $9.*
5 [C] a period of time when shops sell their goods at lower prices than usual: *Marsdon's department store is* **having a sale** *this week.* | **the sales** *BrE* (=when all the shops have a sale) *I picked up some real bargains in the January sales this year.*
6 [C] an event at which things are sold to the person who offers the highest price; ◨ **auction**: *a sale of 17th century paintings*
7 sales drive/campaign when a company makes a special effort to try to increase the amount of its products that it sells: *We launch a new sales campaign this fall.*
8 sales pitch/talk the things that someone says when they are trying to persuade you to buy something
9 (on) sale or return *BrE* if a shop buys something on sale or return, it can return the goods that it is unable to sell → BILL OF SALE, JUMBLE SALE, POINT OF SALE

sale·a·ble, salable /ˈseɪləbəl/ *adj* something that is saleable can be sold, or is easy to sell: *a saleable commodity* —**saleability** /ˌseɪləˈbɪləti/ *n* [U]

sale·room /ˈseɪlrʊm, -ruːm/ *n* [C] *BrE* a room where things are sold by AUCTION

ˈsales asˌsistant *n* [C] someone who sells things in a shop; ◨ **shop assistant**

sales·clerk /ˈseɪlzklɑːk $ -klɜːrk/ *n* [C] *AmE* someone who sells things in a shop; ◨ **shop assistant** *BrE*

ˈsales·girl /ˈseɪlzɡɜːl $ -ɡɜːrl/ *n* [C] *old-fashioned* a young woman who sells things in a shop

sales·man /ˈseɪlzmən/ *n plural* **salesmen** /-mən/ [C] a man whose job is to persuade people to buy his company's products: **computer/car/insurance etc salesman**

sales·man·ship /ˈseɪlzmənʃɪp/ *n* [U] the skill or ability to persuade people to buy things as part of your job

sales·per·son /ˈseɪlzˌpɜːsən $ -pɜːr-/ *n plural* **salespeople** /-ˌpiːpəl/ [C] someone whose job is selling things

ˈsales repreˌsentative also **ˈsales rep** *n* [C] someone who travels around, usually within a particular area, selling their company's products

'sales slip n [C] AmE a small piece of paper that you are given in a shop when you buy something; ◧ **receipt**

'sales tax n [C,U] a tax that you have to pay in addition to the cost of something you are buying → **VAT**

sales·wom·an /'seɪlz,wʊmən/ n plural **saleswomen** /-,wɪmɪn/ [C] a woman whose job is selling things

sa·li·ent /'seɪliənt/ adj formal the salient points or features of something are the most important or most noticeable parts of it: the salient points of the report —**salience** n [U]

sa·line¹ /'seɪlaɪn/ adj medical containing or consisting of salt: saline solution —**salinity** /sə'lɪnᵻti/ n [U]

saline² n [U] a special mixture of water and salt

sa·li·va /sə'laɪvə/ n [U] the liquid that is produced naturally in your mouth; ◧ **spit**

sa'livary ,gland n [C] a part of your mouth that produces saliva

sal·i·vate /'sælᵻveɪt/ v [I] 1 to produce more saliva in your mouth than usual, especially because you see or smell food 2 to look at or show interest in something or someone in a way that shows you like or want them very much – used to show disapproval: [+at/over] The media are salivating over the story. —**salivation** /,sælᵻ'veɪʃən/ n [U]

sal·low /'sæləʊ $ -loʊ/ adj sallow skin looks slightly yellow and unhealthy: **sallow face/skin/complexion** a woman with dark hair and a sallow complexion —**sallowness** n [U]

sal·ly¹ /'sæli/ n plural **sallies** [C] formal 1 a sudden quick attack and return to a position of defence 2 an intelligent remark that is intended to amuse people

sally² v **sallied, sallying, sallies**

sally forth phr v literary to go out in order to do something, especially something that you expect to be difficult or dangerous – often used humorously: Each morning they sallied forth in search of jobs.

salm·on /'sæmən/ n 1 [C] plural **salmon** a large fish with silver skin and pink flesh that lives in the sea but swims up rivers to lay its eggs → see picture at FRESHWATER 2 [U] this fish eaten as food: **fresh/smoked salmon** 3 [U] a pink-orange colour

sal·mo·nel·la /,sælmə'nelə/ n [U] a kind of BACTERIA in food that makes you ill: a case of **salmonella poisoning**

sal·on /'sælɒn $ sə'lɑːn/ n [C] 1 a shop where you can get your hair washed, cut, curled etc; ◧ **hairdresser's**: **hair/beauty salon** an exclusive hair salon in central London 2 a shop where fashionable and expensive clothes are sold 3 old fashioned a room in a very large house where people can meet and talk 4 a regular meeting of famous people at which they talk about art, literature, or music, popular in the past in France: a literary salon

sa·loon /sə'luːn/ n [C] 1 a public place where alcoholic drinks were sold and drunk in the western US in the 19th century; ◧ **bar** 2 BrE also **saloon bar** a comfortable room in a PUB; ◧ **lounge bar** 3 BrE also **saloon car** a car that has a separate enclosed space for your bags etc; ◧ **sedan** AmE: a four-door family saloon → ESTATE CAR 4 a large comfortable room where passengers on a ship can sit and relax

sal·sa /'sælsə $ 'sɑːl-/ n [U] 1 a type of Latin American dance music 2 a sauce made from onions, tomatoes and CHILLIES that you put on Spanish or Mexican food

salt¹ S2 W3 /sɔːlt $ sɒːlt/ n
1 [U] a natural white mineral that is added to food to make it taste better or to preserve it: This might need some salt and pepper. | a **pinch of salt** (=a very small amount) | Could you pass the salt?
2 **the salt of the earth** someone who is ordinary but good and honest
3 **take sth with a pinch/grain of salt** informal to not

completely believe what someone tells you, because you know that they do not always tell the truth: Most of what he says should be taken with a pinch of salt.
4 [C] technical a type of chemical substance that is formed when an acid is combined with a BASE → EPSOM SALTS, SMELLING SALTS, OLD SALT; → **rub salt into sb's wounds** at RUB¹ (7); → **worth his/her salt** at WORTH¹ (10)

salt² v [T usually passive] 1 to add salt to food to make it taste better: salted peanuts 2 also **salt down** to add salt to food to preserve it: **salted pork/meat/fish** | The meat is salted to store it through the winter. 3 to put salt on the roads to prevent them from becoming icy
salt sth ⇔ **away** phr v to save money for the future, especially dishonestly by hiding it: She salted the money away in a secret account.

salt³ adj [only before noun] 1 preserved with salt: salt pork 2 **salt water** water that contains salt, especially naturally in the sea 3 consisting of salt water: a salt lake

'salt ,cellar n [C] BrE a small container for salt; ◧ **salt shaker** AmE

salt·pe·tre BrE; **saltpeter** AmE /,sɔːlt'piːtə $,sɒːlt'piːtər/ n [U] a substance used in making GUNPOWDER (=powder that causes explosions) and matches

'salt ,shaker n [C] AmE a small container for salt; ◧ **salt cellar** BrE

'salt truck n [C] AmE a large vehicle that puts salt or sand on the roads in winter to make them less icy; ◧ **gritter** BrE

salt·wa·ter /'sɔːlt,wɔːtə $ -,wɒːtər, -,wɑː-/ adj [only before noun] 1 living in salty water or in the sea; ◪ **freshwater**: saltwater fish 2 containing salt water; ◪ **freshwater**: a saltwater lake

salt·y /'sɔːlti $ 'sɒːlti/ adj 1 tasting of or containing salt: a slightly salty taste | salty foods 2 AmE old-fashioned language, a story, or a joke that is salty is amusing and often about sex

sa·lu·bri·ous /sə'luːbriəs/ adj formal a salubrious area or place is pleasant and clean, especially compared to other places – often used humorously: the less salubrious area near the docks

sal·u·ta·ry /'sæljᵿtəri $ -teri/ adj formal a salutary experience is unpleasant but teaches you something: **salutary experience/lesson/reminder etc** Losing money in this way taught young Jones a salutary lesson.

sal·u·ta·tion /,sæljᵿ'teɪʃən/ n formal 1 [C] a word or phrase used at the beginning of a letter or speech, such as 'Dear Mr. Smith' 2 [C,U] something you say or do when greeting someone

sa·lute¹ /sə'luːt/ v 1 [I,T] to move your right hand to your head, especially in order to show respect to an officer in the army, navy etc: The two soldiers saluted Lieutenant Cecil. | The men jumped to their feet and saluted. 2 [T] formal to praise someone for the things they have achieved, especially publicly: **salute sb as sth** James Joyce was saluted as the greatest writer of the 20th century. 3 [T] old-fashioned to greet someone in a polite way, especially by moving your hand or body

salute² n 1 [C] an act of raising your right hand to your head as a sign of respect, usually done by a soldier to an officer: As they left, the Corporal gave them a respectful salute. | **in salute** The officer raised his hand in salute. 2 [C,U] something that expresses praise to someone for something they have achieved, or that expresses honour or respect to someone or something: **in salute** Everyone at the table raised their glasses in salute. | [+to] His first words were a salute to the people of South Africa. 3 [C] an occasion when guns are fired into the air in order to show respect for someone important: a 21-gun salute

sal·vage¹ /'sælvɪdʒ/ v [T] 1 to save something from an accident or bad situation in which other things have already been damaged, destroyed, or lost: Divers hope to salvage some of the ship's cargo. | **salvage sth from sth** They managed to salvage only a few of their belongings from the fire. 2 to make sure that you do not lose something completely, or to make sure that something does not fail completely: *He fought to salvage the company's reputation.*

salvage² *n* [U] **1** when you save things from a situation in which other things have already been damaged, destroyed, or lost: *a massive salvage operation* **2** things that have been saved from an accident, especially when a ship has sunk

sal·va·tion S3 /sæl'veɪʃən/ *n* [U] **1** something that prevents or saves someone or something from danger, loss, or failure: **be sb's/sth's salvation** *A drug treatment program was Ron's salvation.* | [+of] *The Internet turned out to be the salvation of the company.* **2** in the Christian religion, the state of being saved from evil

Sal,vation 'Army *n* **the Salvation Army** a Christian organization that tries to help poor people

salve¹ /sælv, sɑːv $ sæv/ *n* [C,U] a substance that you put on sore skin to make it less painful: *lip salve*

salve² *v* [T] *formal* **salve your conscience** if you do something to salve your conscience, you do it to make yourself feel less guilty: *Buying his wife flowers helped to salve his conscience.*

sal·ver /'sælvə $ -ər/ *n* [C] a large metal plate used for serving food or drink at a formal meal: *a silver salver*

sal·vo /'sælvəʊ $ -voʊ/ *n plural* **salvos** *or* **salvoes** [C usually singular] *formal* **1** [+ of] when several guns are fired during a battle or as part of a ceremony **2** **opening salvo** the first in a series of questions, statements etc that you use to try to win an argument: *Congressman Saunders fired the opening salvo during a heated debate on capital punishment.* **3** sudden laughter, APPLAUSE etc from many people at the same time

Sa·mar·i·tan /sə'mærɪtən/ *n* [C] **good Samaritan** someone, especially a stranger, who helps you when you have problems or need something

sam·ba /'sæmbə/ *n* [C,U] a fast dance from Brazil, or the type of music played for this dance

same¹ S1 W1 /seɪm/ *adj* [only before noun] **1** NOT DIFFERENT **a)** the same person, place, thing etc is one particular person etc and not a different one: *He sits in the same chair every night.* | *They went to the same school.* | [+as] *She was born on the same day as me.* | *It is those same people who voted for the Democrats who now complain about their policies.* | **the very same/the self-same** (=the same person or thing and not a different one – used to emphasize that what you are saying seems surprising) *We stood in front of the very same house in which Shakespeare wrote his plays.* **b)** used to say two or more people, things, events etc are exactly like each other: *Both women were wearing the same dress.* | *The same thing could happen again.* | [+as] *He gets the same pay as me but he gets his own office.* | **just/exactly the same** *That's funny, Simon said exactly the same thing.* | *The furniture is made in* **much the same** (=almost the same) *way as it was 200 years ago.* **2** NOT CHANGING used to say that a particular person or thing does not change: *Her perfume has always had the same effect on me.* | *He's* **the same old** *Peter – moody and irritable.* **3** **at the same time a)** if two things happen at the same time, they both happen together: *Kate and I both went to live in Spain at the same time.* **b)** used when you want to say that something else is also true: *We don't want to lose him. At the same time, he needs to realise that company regulations must be obeyed.* **4** **amount/come to the same thing** to have the same result or effect: *It doesn't matter whether she was happy to leave or not. It amounts to the same thing – she's gone.* **5** **the same old story/excuse etc** *informal* something that you have heard many times before – used especially to show disapproval: *It's the same old story – his wife didn't really love him.* **6** **same difference** *spoken* used to say that different actions, behaviour etc have the same result or effect: 'I

could mail the letter or send a fax in the morning.' 'Same difference. It still won't get there on time.' **7** **by the same token** *formal* for the same reasons – used when you want to say that something else is also true, especially something very different or surprising: *I realise that he hasn't come up with any new ideas, but by the same token we haven't needed any.* **8** **be in the same boat** to be in the same difficult situation that someone else is in: *Others in her profession are in the same boat.*

same² S1 W1 *pron* **1** **the same a)** used to say that two or more people or things are exactly like each other: *The coins may look the same but one's a forgery.* | [+as] *Your measurements are* **exactly the same** *as Dana's.* | *Thanks for your help – I'll do the same for you one day.* **b)** used to say that a particular person or thing does not change: *Things just won't be the same without Sam.* **2** **(and the) same to you!** *spoken* **a)** used as a reply to a greeting: *'Merry Christmas!' 'And the same to you Ben.'* **b)** used as an angry reply to a rude remark: *'Up yours!' 'Same to you.'* **3** **just/all the same** in spite of a particular situation, opinion etc: *I realise she can be very annoying, but I think you should apologise all the same.* **4** **all the same** in spite of something that you have just mentioned: *I'm not likely to run out of money, but all the same, I'm careful.* **5** **it's all the same to sb** used to say that someone does not mind what decision is made, would be pleased with any choice, or does not really care: *If it's all the same to you, I'll go this weekend.* **6** **same here** *spoken* used to say that you feel the same way as someone else: *'I'm exhausted.' 'Same here!'* **7** **(the) same again** used to ask for another drink of the same kind **8** **more of the same** another person, thing etc like the one just mentioned: *He has produced a string of thrillers, and this movie is just more of the same.* → **one and the same** at ONE² (18)

> **GRAMMAR**
> **Same** usually has **the** before it: *They both gave the same reasons for leaving.* | *All the shirts looked the same.* You can also use **this** or **that** before **same** when it is used as an adjective, to emphasize it: *At that same moment the telephone rang.*
> ⚠ **Same** never has **a** before it: *We went to the same school (NOT a same school).*
> ⚠ You can say that one thing is **the same as** another. Do not use **like** or **with**: *His answer was the same as mine (NOT the same like/with mine).*

same³ S1 W1 *adv* **1** **the same (as)** in the same way: *'Rain' and 'reign' are pronounced the same even though they are spelt differently.* | *Everyone had to dress the same as a well-known historical figure.* **2** **same as sb** *spoken* just like someone else: *I have my pride, same as anyone else.*

same·ness /'seɪmnɪs/ *n* [U] a boring lack of variety, or the quality of being very similar to something else

same-'sex *adj* **same-sex marriage/relationship etc** a marriage, relationship etc between two men or two women; ⬜ **homosexual**

same·y /'seɪmi/ *adj BrE informal* boring and having very little variety: *His novels tend to be very samey.*

sa·mo·sa /sæ'məʊsə $ -'moʊ-/ *n* [C] a type of Indian food made from meat or vegetables covered in thin PASTRY and cooked in hot oil

sam·o·var /'sæməvɑː $ -vɑːr/ *n* [C] a large metal container used in Russia to boil water for making tea

sam·pan /'sæmpæn/ *n* [C] a small boat used in China and Southeast Asia

S

sam·ple¹ S3 W2 /'sɑːmpəl $ 'sæm-/ *n* [C]
1 a small part or amount of something that is examined in order to find out something about the whole: [+of] *I'd like to see some samples of your work.* | *They took a **blood sample** to test for hepatitis.*
2 a small amount of a product that people can try in order to find out what it is like: [+of] *samples of a new shampoo*
3 a small group of people who have been chosen from a larger group to give information or answers to questions: *The sample consisted of 98 secondary school teachers.* | *Out of a **random sample** of drivers, 21% had been in an accident in the previous year.* | *a nationally **representative sample** of over 950 elderly persons*
4 a small part of a song from a CD or record that is used in a new song: *Her latest album makes extensive use of samples from a wide range of acid jazz tracks.*

sample² *v* [T] **1** to taste food or drink in order to see what it is like: *a chance to sample the local food* **2** to choose some people from a larger group in order to ask them questions or get information from them: *18% of the adults sampled admitted having had problems with alcohol abuse.* **3** to try an activity, go to a place etc in order to see what it is like: *Here's your chance to **sample the delights of** country life.* **4** to use a small part of a song from a CD or record in a new song: *Many of his songs have been sampled by other artists.*

sam·pler /'sɑːmplə $ 'sæmplər/ *n* [C] **1** a machine that can record sounds or music so that you can change them and use them for a new piece of music **2** a piece of cloth with different stitches on it, made to show how good someone is at sewing

sam·u·rai /'sæmʊraɪ/ *n plural* **samurai** [C] a member of a powerful military class in Japan in the past —**samurai** *adj*: *a samurai sword*

san·a·to·ri·um /ˌsænə'tɔːriəm/ *n plural* **sanatoria** /-riə/ [C] *old-fashioned* a type of hospital for sick people who are getting better after a long illness but still need rest and a lot of care

sanc·ti·fy /'sæŋktɪ̩faɪ/ *v* **sanctified, sanctifying, sanctifies** [T] **1** to make something seem morally right or acceptable or to give something official approval: *The rule of the Czar was sanctified by the Russian Orthodox Church.* **2** to make something holy —**sanctification** /ˌsæŋktɪ̩fɪ'keɪʃən/ *n* [U]

sanc·ti·mo·ni·ous /ˌsæŋktɪ̩'məʊniəs◂ $ -'moʊ-/ *adj formal* behaving as if you are morally better than other people, in a way that is annoying – used to show disapproval: *sanctimonious politicians preaching about family values* —**sanctimoniously** *adv* —**sanctimoniousness** *n* [U]

sanc·tion¹ /'sæŋkʃən/ *n* **1 sanctions** [plural] official orders or laws stopping trade, communication etc with another country, as a way of forcing its leaders to make political changes: [+against] *US sanctions against Cuba* | *a resolution to **impose sanctions** (=start using sanctions) on North Korea* | *the threat of **trade sanctions*** | *The UN security council may impose **economic sanctions**.* | *Any talk about **lifting sanctions** (=ending them) is premature.* **2** [U] *formal* official permission, approval, or acceptance: *Apparently, the aide had acted without White House sanction.* **3** [C] *formal* a form of punishment that can be used if someone disobeys a rule or law: *the harshest possible sanction which could be imposed*

sanction² *v* [T] *formal* **1** to officially accept or allow something; ⊟ **approve**: *The church refused to sanction the king's second marriage.* **2 be sanctioned by sth** to be made acceptable by something: *a barbaric custom, but one sanctioned by long usage*

sanc·ti·ty /'sæŋktɪ̩ti/ *n* [U] **1 the sanctity of life/ marriage etc** the quality that makes life, marriage etc so important that it must be respected and preserved:

the sanctity of the Constitution **2** *formal* the holy or religious character of a person or place; → **sacred**: *an aura of sanctity*

sanc·tu·a·ry /'sæŋktʃuəri, -tʃəri $ -tʃueri/ *n plural* **sanctuaries 1** [C] an area for birds or animals where they are protected and cannot be hunted; ⊟ **refuge**: **bird/wildlife etc sanctuary** *The park is the largest wildlife sanctuary in the US.* | [+for] *a sanctuary for tigers* **2** [C,U] a peaceful place that is safe and provides protection, especially for people who are in danger; ⊟ **refuge**: **find/seek sanctuary** *Fleeing refugees found sanctuary in Geneva.* | [+for] *a sanctuary for battered women* **3** [C] the part of a religious building that is considered to be the most holy **4** [C] *AmE* the room in a religious building where religious services take place **5** [U] the right that people had under Christian law, especially in the past, to be protected from police, soldiers etc by staying in a church

sanc·tum /'sæŋktəm/ *n* [C] **1 inner sanctum** a private place or room that only a few important people are allowed to enter – often used humorously: *Occasionally she would be allowed into the inner sanctum of his office.* **2** a holy place inside a temple

sand¹ W3 /sænd/ *n*
1 [U] a substance consisting of very small pieces of rocks and minerals, that forms beaches and deserts: *a mixture of sand and cement* | *I have sand in my shoe.*
2 [C,U] an area of beach: *miles of golden sands* | *We were just sitting on the sand.*
3 the sands of time *literary* moments of time that pass quickly

sand² *v* [I,T] also **sand down** to make a surface smooth by rubbing it with SANDPAPER or using a special piece of equipment

san·dal /'sændl/ *n* [C] a light shoe that is fastened onto your foot by bands of leather or cloth, and is worn in warm weather: *a pair of sandals* → see picture at FOOTWEAR

san·dal·wood /'sændlwʊd/ *n* [U] pleasant-smelling wood from a Southern Asian tree, or the oil from this wood

sand·bag¹ /'sændbæg/ *n* [C] a bag filled with sand, used for protection against floods, explosions etc

sandbag² *v* **sandbagged, sandbagging 1** [I,T] to put sandbags around a building in order to protect it from a flood or explosion **2** [T] to treat someone unfairly in order to prevent them from doing something or being successful

sand·bank /'sændbæŋk/ *n* [C] a raised area of sand in a river, ocean etc

'sand bar *n* [C] a long pile of sand in a river or the ocean, formed by the movement of the water

sand·blast /'sændblɑːst $ -blæst/ *v* [T] to clean or polish metal, stone, glass etc with a machine that sends out a powerful stream of sand

sand·box /'sændbɒks $ -bɑːks/ *n* [C] *especially AmE* a small box filled with sand for children to play in; ⊟ **sandpit** *BrE*

sand·cas·tle /'sænd̩kɑːsəl $ -ˌkæ-/ *n* [C] a small model of a castle made out of sand by children playing on a beach

'sand dune *n* [C] a hill formed of sand in a desert or near the sea

sand·er /'sændə $ -ər/ also **'sanding ma,chine** *n* [C] an electric tool with a rough surface that moves very quickly, used for making surfaces smooth, especially the surface of wood

'sand fly *n* [C] a small fly that bites people and lives on beaches

sand·lot /'sændlɒt $ -lɑːt/ *n* [C] *AmE* an area of empty land in a town or city, where children often play sports or games: *a sandlot ball game*

sand·man /'sændmæn/ *n* [singular] an imaginary man who is supposed to make children go to sleep

sand·pa·per[1] /'sænd,peɪpə $ -ər/ n [U] strong paper covered on one side with sand or a similar substance, used for rubbing wood in order to make the surface smooth

sandpaper[2] v [T] to rub something with sandpaper

sand·pip·er /'sænd,paɪpə $ -ər/ n [C] a small bird with long legs and a long beak that lives near the shore

sand·pit /'sænd,pɪt/ n [C] BrE a box or special area filled with sand for children to play in; ▣ **sandbox** AmE

sand·stone /'sændstəʊn $ -stoʊn/ n [U] a type of soft yellow or red rock, often used in buildings

sand·storm /'sændstɔːm $ -stɔːrm/ n [C] a storm in the desert in which sand is blown around by strong winds

sand·trap /'sændtræp/ n [C] AmE a hollow place on a golf course, filled with sand, from which it is difficult to hit the ball; ▣ **bunker** BrE

sand·wich[1] [S2] /'sænwɪdʒ $ 'sændwɪtʃ, 'sænwɪtʃ/ n
1 [C] two pieces of bread with cheese, meat, vegetables, cooked egg, etc between them: a ham sandwich → see picture at FAST FOOD
2 [C] BrE a cake consisting of two layers with JAM and cream between them: a raspberry sponge sandwich →
CLUB SANDWICH, OPEN SANDWICH

sandwich[2] v [T usually passive] to be in a very small space between two other things: **be sandwiched in/between sb/sth** A layer of transparent material is sandwiched between the pieces of glass.

sandwich board n [C] two boards with advertisements on them that hang in front and behind someone who is paid to walk around in public

sandwich course n [C] BrE a course of study at a British college or university that includes periods spent working in industry or business

sand·y /'sændi/ adj **1** covered with sand or containing a lot of sand: The soil is quite sandy. **2** hair that is sandy is a yellowish-brown colour —**sandiness** n [U]

sane /seɪn/ adj **1** able to think in a normal and reasonable way; ▣ **insane, mentally ill**; → **sanity**: He seems perfectly sane (=completely sane) to me. | No sane person would want to kill a baby. **2** reasonable and based on sensible thinking: a sane and sensible approach to gun control **3 keep sb sane** also **stay/remain sane** to stop someone from thinking about their problems and becoming upset: The only thing that kept me sane was music. —**sanely** adv

sang /sæŋ/ v the past tense of SING

sang-froid /,sɒŋ 'frwɑː $,sɑːŋ-/ n [U] literary courage and the ability to keep calm in dangerous or difficult situations

san·gri·a /sæŋ'griːə, sæn-, 'sæŋgriə/ n [U] a Spanish drink made from red wine, fruit, and fruit juice

san·gui·na·ry /'sæŋgwɪnəri $ -neri/ adj literary involving violence and killing

san·guine /'sæŋgwɪn/ adj formal happy and hopeful about the future; ▣ **optimistic**: [+about] Other economists are more sanguine about the possibility of inflation. | a sanguine view

san·i·tar·i·um /,sænɪ'teəriəm $ -'ter-/ n AmE [C] a SANATORIUM

san·i·ta·ry /'sænɪtəri $ -teri/ adj **1** [only before noun] relating to the ways that dirt, infection, and waste are removed, so that places are clean and healthy for people to live in; ▣ **hygienic**: Diseases were spread through poor **sanitary conditions**. | a prison with no proper **sanitary facilities** (=toilets) **2** clean and not causing any danger to people's health; ▣ **insanitary**: Often, the camps were not very sanitary.

sanitary pad also **sanitary towel** BrE; **sanitary napkin** AmE n [C] a special piece of soft material that a woman wears in her underwear for the blood when she has her PERIOD

san·i·ta·tion /,sænɪ'teɪʃən/ n [U] the protection of public health by removing and treating waste, dirty water etc: Overcrowding and **poor sanitation** are common problems in prisons.

sani'tation ,worker n [C] AmE formal someone who removes waste material that people put outside their houses; ▣ **garbage man**

san·i·tize also **-ise** BrE /'sænɪtaɪz/ v [T] **1** to remove particular details from a report, story etc in order to make it less offensive, unpleasant, or embarrassing – used especially to show disapproval: the sanitized version of events which was reported in the government-controlled media **2** to clean something thoroughly, removing dirt and BACTERIA

san·i·ty /'sænɪti/ n [U] **1** the condition of being mentally healthy; ▣ **insanity**; → **sane**: I began to doubt his sanity. | She wondered if she was **losing** her sanity. **2** when someone or something is being reasonable and sensible; → **sane**: Sanity appears to be returning to the stock market. | **regain/get back/recover your sanity** I took a vacation to try to recover my sanity.

sank /sæŋk/ v the past tense of SINK

sans /sænz/ prep without – usually used humorously: He came to the door sans shirt.

San·skrit /'sænskrɪt/ n [U] an ancient language of India

sans ser·if /,sæn 'serɪf, ,sænz-/ n [U] technical a style of printing in which letters have no SERIFS

San·ta Claus /'sæntə klɔːz $ 'sænti klɔːz, 'sæntə-/ also **Santa** n [singular] an imaginary old man with red clothes and a long white BEARD who, children believe, brings them presents at Christmas; ▣ **Father Christmas** BrE

sap[1] /sæp/ n **1** [U] the watery substance that carries food through a plant **2** [C] informal a stupid person who is easy to deceive or treat badly

sap[2] v **sapped, sapping** [T] to make something weaker or destroy it, especially someone's strength or their determination to do something; ▣ **weaken**: **sap sb's strength/courage/energy** Her long illness was gradually sapping Charlotte's strength.

sa·pi·ent /'seɪpiənt/ adj literary very wise

sap·ling /'sæplɪŋ/ n [C] a young tree

sap·per /'sæpə $ -ər/ n [C] BrE a soldier whose job involves digging and building

sap·phic /'sæfɪk/ adj literary LESBIAN

sap·phire /'sæfaɪə $ -faɪr/ n [C,U] a transparent bright blue jewel

sap·py /'sæpi/ adj **1** AmE expressing love and emotions in a way that seems silly; ▣ **soppy** BrE: a sappy song **2** full of SAP (=liquid in a plant)

sap·wood /'sæpwʊd/ n [U] the younger outer wood in a tree, that is paler and softer than the wood in the middle

Sar·a·cen /'særəsən/ n [C] old use a Muslim – used in the Middle Ages

Sa·ran Wrap /sə'ræn ræp/ n [U] AmE trademark thin transparent plastic used for wrapping food; ▣ **clingfilm** BrE

sar·casm /'sɑːkæzəm $ 'sɑːr-/ n [U] a way of speaking or writing that involves saying the opposite of what you really mean in order to make an unkind joke or to show that you are annoyed: 'Good of you to arrive on time,' George said, with **heavy sarcasm** (=very clear sarcasm). | **hint/trace/edge/touch of sarcasm** There was just a touch of sarcasm in her voice.

sar·cas·tic /sɑː'kæstɪk $ sɑːr-/ adj saying things that are the opposite of what you mean, in order to make an unkind joke or to show that you are annoyed: Was she being sarcastic? | **sarcastic remark/comment/question** He can't help making sarcastic comments. | **sarcastic**

manner/smile/laugh etc *'I thought so,' she said with a sarcastic smile.* —**sarcastically** /-kli/ adv: *'Oh good,' he said sarcastically.*

sar·coph·a·gus /sɑːˈkɒfəgəs $ sɑːrˈkɑː-/ n plural **sarcophagi** [C] a decorated stone box for a dead body, used in ancient times

sar·dine /ˌsɑːˈdiːn‹ $ ˌsɑːr-/ n **1** [C] a small young fish that is often packed in flat metal boxes when it is sold as food **2 be packed like sardines** to be crowded tightly together in a small space: *commuters packed like sardines on the evening train*

sar·don·ic /sɑːˈdɒnɪk $ sɑːrˈdɑː-/ adj written showing that you do not have a good opinion of someone or something, and feel that you are better than them: *He looked at her with sardonic amusement.* —**sardonically** /-kli/ adv

sarge /sɑːdʒ $ sɑːrdʒ/ n [singular] spoken SERGEANT

sa·ri /ˈsɑːri/ n [C] a long piece of cloth that you wrap around your body like a dress, worn especially by women from India

sar·ky /ˈsɑːki $ sɑːr-/ adj BrE informal SARCASTIC

sar·nie /ˈsɑːni $ ˈsɑːr-/ n [C] BrE informal a SANDWICH

sa·rong /səˈrɒŋ $ səˈrɔːŋ, səˈrɑːŋ/ n [C] a loose skirt consisting of a long piece of cloth wrapped around your waist, worn especially by people in Malaysia and Indonesia

sarsa·pa·ril·la /ˌsɑːspəˈrɪlə $ ˌsæs-/ n [U] a sweet drink without alcohol, made from the root of the SASSAFRAS plant

sar·to·ri·al /sɑːˈtɔːriəl $ sɑːr-/ adj formal relating to clothes, especially the style of clothes that a man wears – used especially humorously: *a man of great sartorial elegance* —**sartorially** adv

SAS /ˌes eɪ ˈes/ n **the SAS** **the Special Air Service** a British military force that is specially trained to do secret and dangerous work

SASE /ˌes eɪ es ˈiː/ n [C] AmE **self-addressed stamped envelope** an envelope that you put your name, address, and a stamp on, so that someone else can send you something; ⊟ **SAE** BrE

sash /sæʃ/ n [C] **1** a long piece of cloth that you wear around your waist like a belt **2** a long piece of cloth that you wear over one shoulder and across your chest

sa·shay /sæˈʃeɪ/ v [I always + adv/prep] to walk in a confident way, moving your body from side to side, especially so that people look at you: [+around/along/down etc] *Models sashayed down the aisle.*

sa·shi·mi /sæˈʃiːmi/ n [U] a type of Japanese food consisting of small pieces of fresh fish that have not been cooked

'sash ˌwindow n [C] BrE a window consisting of two frames that you open by sliding one up or down, behind or in front of the other

sass /sæs/ v [T] AmE informal to talk in a rude way to someone you should respect: *Don't you sass me, young lady!*

sas·sa·fras /ˈsæsəfræs/ n [C,U] a small Asian or North American tree, or the pleasant-smelling roots of this tree that are used in food and drink

Sas·se·nach /ˈsæsənæk/ n [C] an English person – used by Scottish people in a humorous way or to show disapproval

sas·sy /ˈsæsi/ adj AmE **1** a child who is sassy is rude to someone they should respect; ⊟ **cheeky** BrE **2** someone, especially a woman, who is sassy is confident and does not really care what other people think about her

sat /sæt/ v the past tense and past participle of SIT

Sat. also **Sat** BrE the written abbreviation of *Saturday*

SAT /sæt, ˌes eɪ ˈtiː/ n [C] **1** trademark **Scholastic Aptitude Test** an examination that American high school students take before they go to college: *SAT scores have been steadily decreasing.* **2** SATs **Standard Assessment Test** examinations that students in schools in England and Wales take at the ages of 7, 11, and 14, to see whether they have reached the standard set by the NATIONAL CURRICULUM

Sa·tan /ˈseɪtn/ n [singular] the Devil, considered to be the main evil power and God's opponent

sa·tan·ic /səˈtænɪk/ adj **1** relating to practices that treat the Devil like a god: **satanic ritual/cult/rite** *The children were abused as part of a satanic ritual.* **2** literary extremely cruel or evil: *satanic laughter* —**satanically** /-kli/ adv

sa·tan·is·m /ˈseɪtənɪzəm/ n [U] the practice of worshipping Satan —**satanist** n [C] —**satanist** adj

satch·el /ˈsætʃəl/ n [C] a leather bag that you carry over your shoulder, used especially in the past by children for carrying books to school → see picture at BAG[1]

sat·ed /ˈseɪtɪd/ adj literary feeling that you have had enough or too much of something, especially food or pleasure; ⊟ **full** —**sate** v [T]: *He had sated his lust.*

sat·el·lite /ˈsætɪlaɪt/ n [C] **1** a machine that has been sent into space and goes around the Earth, moon etc, used for radio, television, and other electronic communication: *the launch of a communications and weather satellite* | **via/by satellite** (=using a satellite) *This broadcast comes live via satellite from New York.* **2** a natural object that moves around a PLANET: *The moon is a satellite of the Earth.* **3** a country, area, or organization that is controlled by or is dependent on another larger one: *the former Soviet satellite country of Lithuania* **4** a town that has developed next to a large city: *We stayed in Aurora, a satellite suburb of Chicago.*

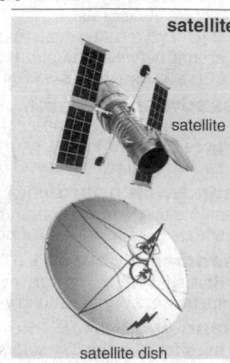
satellite
satellite
satellite dish

'satellite ˌdish n [C] a large circular piece of metal that receives satellite television broadcasts → see picture at SATELLITE

ˌsatellite 'television also **ˌsatellite 'TV** n [U] television programmes that are broadcast using satellites in space, and which you need a special piece of equipment to be able to watch

sa·ti·ate /ˈseɪʃieɪt/ v [T usually passive] literary to satisfy a desire or need for something such as food or sex, especially so that you feel you have had too much —**satiated** adj —**satiation** /ˌseɪʃiˈeɪʃən/ n [U]

sat·in[1] /ˈsætɪn $ ˈsætn/ n [U] a type of cloth that is very smooth and shiny: *a red satin ribbon*

satin[2] adj having a smooth shiny surface: *The new paints are available in gloss and satin finishes.*

sat·in·y /ˈsætɪni $ ˈsætni/ adj smooth, shiny, and soft: *women in tight, satiny dresses*

sat·ire /ˈsætaɪə $ -taɪr/ n **1** [U] a way of criticizing something such as a group of people or a system, in which you deliberately make them seem funny so that people will see their faults: *the characteristic use of satire in Jonson's work* | **political/social satire** *a comedy group that does political satire* **2** [C] a piece of writing, film, play etc that uses this type of criticism: [+on] *a satire on American politics* | **savage/stinging/vicious/biting satire** *a biting satire of the television industry* —**satirical** /səˈtɪrɪkəl/ adj: *a well-known satirical magazine* —**satiric** adj —**satirically** /-kli/ adv

sat·i·rist /ˈsætərɪst/ n [C] someone who writes satire

sat·ir·ize also **-ise** BrE /ˈsætəraɪz/ v [T] to use satire to make people see someone's or something's faults: *a play satirizing the fashion industry*

S

sat·is·fac·tion S3 W3 /ˌsæt₁s'fækʃən/ n

1 [C,U] a feeling of happiness or pleasure because you have achieved something or got what you wanted; ⯤ dissatisfaction

> great/deep/real satisfaction
> personal satisfaction
> sense/feeling of satisfaction
> smile/sigh/look of satisfaction
> with/in satisfaction
> a source of satisfaction (=something that makes you satisfied)
> get/gain/derive satisfaction from sth
> have the satisfaction of doing sth
> express satisfaction (with/at sth)
> give sb the satisfaction of doing sth
> job satisfaction (=enjoyment of your job)
> grim satisfaction (=when you have achieved or got something but do not really feel happy about it)

*She got **great satisfaction** from helping people to learn.* | *a task which offered him little **personal satisfaction*** | *Do you feel a **sense of satisfaction** at the end of the working day?* | *He allowed himself a little **smile of satisfaction**.* | *'I've passed all my exams', he announced with satisfaction.* | *Care-giving can be a **source of** enormous **satisfaction**.* | *The survey found that men **got** greater **satisfaction from** caring for their families than they did from work.* | *At least he **had the satisfaction of** knowing that he was right.* | *Finance officials **expressed satisfaction with** the recovery of the dollar.* | *I didn't want to **give him the satisfaction** of seeing how upset I was.* | *people who enjoy reasonably high **job satisfaction***

2 to sb's/sth's satisfaction if something is done to someone's satisfaction, it is done as well or as completely as they want, so they are pleased: *The question could not be resolved, at least not to my satisfaction.*

3 [U] when you get money or an APOLOGY from someone who has treated you badly or unfairly: *I got no satisfaction from the customer complaints department.*

4 [U] formal when someone gets something that they want, need, or have demanded: [+of] *the satisfaction of basic human needs* | *sexual satisfaction*

sat·is·fac·to·ry /ˌsæt₁s'fæktəri◂/ adj something that is satisfactory seems good enough for you, or good enough for a particular situation or purpose; ⯐ acceptable; ⯤ unsatisfactory: *His progress this term has been satisfactory.* | [+to/for] *an arrangement that is satisfactory to both sides* | *satisfactory explanation/answer There seems to be no satisfactory explanation.* | *perfectly/entirely/wholly satisfactory None of the solutions was entirely satisfactory.* | *satisfactory result/outcome/resolution Our aim is to achieve a satisfactory outcome for everyone.* —**satisfactorily** *adv: The question has not been satisfactorily answered.*

sat·is·fied S3 /'sæt₁sfaɪd/ adj

1 pleased because something has happened in the way that you want, or because you have got what you want; ⯤ dissatisfied: *a satisfied smile* | *They have plenty of satisfied customers.* | *Will she ever be satisfied?* | [+with] *I'm not satisfied with the way he cut my hair.* | *completely/fully/totally/entirely satisfied If you're not completely satisfied, you can get your money back.*

2 feeling sure that something is right or true: [+that] *He was satisfied that he had done nothing wrong.*

3 (are you) satisfied? *spoken* used to say in an annoyed way that you agree to do something that you do not really want to do: *Okay, okay, I'll ask him this afternoon. Satisfied?* → SELF-SATISFIED

sat·is·fy S2 W2 /'sæt₁sfaɪ/ v **satisfied, satisfying, satisfies** [T]

1 to make someone feel pleased by doing what they want: *Nothing I did would ever satisfy my father.*

2 if you satisfy someone's needs, demands etc, you provide what they need or want: *satisfy sb's needs/demands/desires The program is designed to satisfy the needs of adult learners.* | *satisfy sb's hunger/appetite* (=give someone enough food to stop them from feeling hungry) *A salad won't be enough to satisfy my appetite.* | *Just to **satisfy** my **curiosity** (=find out something), how much did it cost?*

3 *formal* to make someone feel sure that something is right or true; ⯐ convince: *satisfy sb of sth Jackson tried to satisfy me of his innocence.* | *satisfy yourself (that) Having satisfied herself that no one was there, she closed the door.*

4 *formal* to be good enough for a particular purpose, standard etc: *Have you **satisfied** all the **requirements** for the general degree?*

sat·is·fy·ing /'sæt₁sfaɪ-ɪŋ/ adj **1** making you feel pleased and happy, especially because you have got what you wanted; ⯤ unsatisfying: *a deeply satisfying feeling* | *it is satisfying (to do sth) It can be very satisfying to work in the garden.* **2** food that is satisfying makes you feel that you have eaten enough: *a satisfying meal* —**satisfyingly** *adv*

sat·su·ma /sæt'suːmə/ n [C] a fruit like a small orange, that has no seeds and a loose skin you can pull off easily

sat·u·rate¹ /'sætʃəreɪt/ v [T] **1** *formal* to make something very wet; ⯐ soak; ⯤ dry: *Water poured through the hole, saturating the carpet.* **2** to put a lot of something into a particular place, especially so that you could not add any more: *saturate sth with sth Our culture is saturated with television and advertising.* **3 saturate the market** to offer so much of a product for sale that there is more than people want to buy **4** *technical* to mix as much of a solid into a chemical mixture as possible

sat·u·rate² /'sætʃərₐt/ n [C usually plural] a type of fat from meat or milk products that is thought to be less healthy than other kinds of fat from vegetables or fish; ⯐ saturated fat: *Choose a type of spread that's lower in saturates than butter.*

sat·u·rat·ed /'sætʃəreɪt₁d/ adj **1** extremely wet; ⯐ soaked; ⯤ dry: [+with] *a T-shirt saturated with sweat* **2** *technical* if a chemical mixture is saturated, it has had as much of a solid mixed into it as possible

saturated 'fat n [C,U] a type of fat from meat and milk products that is thought to be less healthy than other kinds of fat from vegetables or fish

sat·u·ra·tion /ˌsætʃə'reɪʃən/ n [U] **1** when an event or person is given so much attention by newspapers, television etc that everyone has heard about it: *The trial was given saturation coverage by the press.* | *saturation advertising* **2 saturation bombing** a military attack in which a whole area is bombed **3** *technical* the degree to which something has been mixed into something else: *Keep saturation below 80%.* **4** when something is made completely wet

satu'ration ˌpoint n [C usually singular] **1** a situation in which no more people or things can be added because there are already too many: *The number of summer tourists in the area has **reached saturation point**.* **2** *technical* the state that a chemical mixture reaches when it has had as much of a solid substance mixed into it as possible

Sat·ur·day /'sætədi, -deɪ $ -ər-/ n [C,U] written abbreviation **Sat.** the day between Friday and Sunday: *on Saturday We went for a picnic on Saturday.* | *The festivities begin Saturday. AmE* | *Saturday morning/afternoon etc They arrived in Paris on Saturday evening.* | *last Saturday I saw Sally last Saturday at the mall.* | *this Saturday What are you doing this Saturday?* | *next Saturday* (=Saturday of next week) *Ask her yourself next Saturday.* | *a Saturday* (=one of the Saturdays in the year) *It was a crazy idea to go to the store on a Saturday.*

Sat·urn /'sætən $ -ərn/ n the PLANET that is sixth in order from the sun and is surrounded by large rings → see picture at SOLAR SYSTEM

S

sat·ur·na·li·a /ˌsætəˈneɪliə $ -tər-/ n [C] literary an occasion when people enjoy themselves in a very wild and uncontrolled way

sat·ur·nine /ˈsætənaɪn $ -ər-/ adj literary looking sad and serious, especially in a threatening way: *his lean saturnine face*

sat·yr /ˈsætə $ -ər/ n [C] literary a god in ancient Greek stories, represented as half human and half goat

sauce /sɔːs $ sɒːs/ n **1** [C,U] a thick cooked liquid that is served with food to give it a particular taste: **tomato/cheese/wine etc sauce** *vanilla ice cream with chocolate sauce | spaghetti sauces* **2** [U] BrE old-fashioned rude remarks made to someone that you should respect: *Less of your sauce, my girl!* **3 what's sauce for the goose is sauce for the gander** used to say that if one person is treated in a particular way, other people should be treated in the same way

sauce boat n [C] BrE a container that has a handle and is shaped like a boat, used for serving sauce with a meal

sauce·pan /ˈsɔːspən $ ˈsɒːspæn/ n [C] a deep round metal container with a handle that is used for cooking; ▯ **pan**: *Heat the oil and garlic in a large saucepan.* → see picture at EAT; → see picture at PAN[1]

sau·cer /ˈsɔːsə $ ˈsɒːsər/ n [C] a small round plate that curves up at the edges that you put a cup on: *a delicate china cup and saucer* → FLYING SAUCER; → see picture at CUP[1]

sauc·y /ˈsɔːsi $ ˈsɒːsi/ adj old-fashioned saucy jokes, remarks etc are about sex in a way that is amusing but not shocking: *saucy postcards* —**saucily** adv —**sauciness** n [U]

sau·er·kraut /ˈsaʊəkraʊt $ -ər-/ n [U] a German food made from CABBAGE (=a round green vegetable) that has been left in salt so that it tastes sour

sau·na /ˈsɔːnə $ ˈsɒːnə, ˈsaʊnə/ n [C] **1** a room that is heated to a very high temperature by hot air, where people sit because it is considered healthy → see picture at SPORTS CENTRE **2** a period of time when you sit or lie in a room like this: **have/take a sauna** *I have a sauna and massage every week.*

saun·ter /ˈsɔːntə $ ˈsɒːntər/ v [I always + adv/prep] to walk in a slow relaxed way, especially so that you look confident or proud; → **stroll**: [+along/around/in etc] *He came sauntering down the road with his hands in his pockets.* —**saunter** n [singular]

saus·age S3 /ˈsɒsɪdʒ $ ˈsɒː-/ n [C,U] **1** a small tube of skin filled with a mixture of meat, spices etc, eaten hot or cold after it has been cooked: *pork sausages* **2 not a sausage!** BrE old-fashioned informal nothing at all: *'Have you heard from Tom yet?' 'No, not a sausage!'*

sausage dog n [C] BrE informal a DACHSHUND

sausage meat n [U] the soft meat mixture that is used to make sausages

sausage 'roll n [C] BrE a piece of sausage meat surrounded by PASTRY

sau·té /ˈsəʊteɪ $ səʊˈteɪ/ v [T] to cook something in a little hot oil or fat; → **fry**: *Sauté the onions for 5 minutes.* —**sauté** adj BrE: *sauté potatoes*

sav·age¹ /ˈsævɪdʒ/ adj
1 VIOLENT very violent or cruel: *a savage dog | a savage murder*
2 CRITICIZING criticizing someone or something very severely: *a savage attack on the government*
3 SEVERE very severe: *The government has announced savage cuts in spending. | a savage storm*
4 PEOPLE [only before noun] old-fashioned not polite an offensive word used to describe people who have a simple, traditional way of life: *a savage tribe* —**savagely** adv: *He was savagely attacked and beaten.* —**savageness** n [U]

savage² n [C] old-fashioned not polite a very offensive word for someone who has a simple, traditional way of life

savage³ v [T] **1** if an animal such as a dog savages someone, it attacks them and injures them badly **2** to criticize someone or something very severely: *The Prime Minister was savaged by the press for failing to take action quickly enough.*

sav·ag·e·ry /ˈsævɪdʒəri/ n plural **savageries** [C,U] extremely cruel and violent behaviour: *Local people were shocked by the savagery of the attack.*

sa·van·na, savannah /səˈvænə/ n [C,U] a large flat area of grassy land, especially in Africa

sav·ant /ˈsævənt $ səˈvɑːnt, sæ-/ n [C] formal **1** someone who knows a lot about a subject **2** someone who has mental problems and may have lower intelligence than average, but who can do one thing very well, such as adding numbers very quickly

save¹ S1 W1 /seɪv/ v
1 FROM HARM/DANGER [T] to make someone or something safe from danger, harm, or destruction; → **rescue**: *Emergency aid could save millions threatened with starvation. | a new treatment that could save his life | She was determined to save her marriage. | the campaign to save the rainforests |* **save sb/sth from sth** *He saved the child from drowning.*
2 MONEY also **save up** [I,T] to keep money in a bank so that you can use it later, especially when you gradually add more money over a period of time: *He managed to save enough to buy a small house. | So far, I've saved about £500. |* [+for] *I'm saving up for a new car.* → **SAVER**
3 NOT WASTE [T] also **save on sth** to use less money, time, energy etc so that you do not waste any; ▯ **waste**: *We'll save a lot of time if we go by car. | Everyone is being encouraged to save energy. | an attempt to save on costs | ways to save money on heating bills |* **energy-saving/time-saving etc** *money-saving ideas*
4 TO USE LATER [T] to keep something so that you can use or enjoy it in the future: *We'll save the rest of the food and have it later. |* **save sth for sth** *I had a bottle of champagne which I'd been saving for a special occasion.*
5 COLLECT [T] also **save sth** ⇔ **up** to keep all the objects of a particular kind that you can find, so that you can use them: *I'm saving up vouchers to get a cheap air ticket to the States.*
6 HELP TO AVOID [T] to help someone by making it unnecessary for them to do something that they do not want to do: *If you lent me £5, it would save me a trip to the bank. |* **save sb doing sth** *I'll take the shopping home in the car to save you carrying it. |* **save sb the trouble/bother (of doing sth)** *I'll get a taxi from the station to save you the trouble of coming to collect me.*
7 KEEP FOR SB [T] to stop people from using something so that it is available for someone else: *Will you save me a seat? |* **save sth for sb** *We'll save some dinner for you if you're late.*
8 COMPUTER [I,T] to make a computer keep the work that you have done on it: *Don't forget to save before you close the file. | Did you save the changes that you made?*
9 SPORT [I,T] to stop the other team from scoring in a game such as football: *The goalkeeper just managed to save the shot.*
10 you saved my life spoken used to thank someone who has helped you out of a difficult situation or solved a problem for you: *Thanks again for the loan – you really saved my life.*
11 save sb's skin/neck/bacon informal to help someone to escape from an extremely difficult or dangerous situation: *He lied in court to save his own skin.*
12 save the day to stop things from going badly and make a situation end successfully: *A local businessman saved the day by donating £30,000 to the school.*
13 save face to do something that will stop you from looking stupid or feeling embarrassed: *A compromise must be found which will allow both sides in the dispute to save face.* → FACE-SAVING

14 saving grace the one good thing that makes someone or something acceptable: *His sense of humour was his only saving grace.*

15 sb can't do sth to save his/her life *informal* to be completely unable to do something: *He couldn't draw to save his life!*

16 save your breath *spoken* used to tell someone that it is not worth saying anything, because nothing they say will make any difference to the situation: *I tried to explain, but she told me to save my breath.*

17 save sb from themselves to prevent someone from doing something that they want to do but that you think is harmful

18 RELIGION [I,T] in the Christian church, to free someone from the power of evil and bring them into the Christian religion: *Jesus came to save sinners.*

save² *n* [C] an action in which a player in a game such as football prevents the other team from scoring: *Martin made a brilliant save from Nichol's shot.*

save³ also **'save for** *prep formal* except: *She answered all the questions save one.* | **save that** *Little is known about his early life, save that he had a brother.*

sav·er /'seivə $ -ər/ *n* [C] someone who saves money in a bank: *Mutual funds have been attractive to small savers* (=people who save small amounts of money).

sav·ing W3 /'seiviŋ/ *n*
1 savings [plural] all the money that you have saved, especially in a bank: *Buying a house had taken all their savings.*
2 [C] an amount of money that you have not spent, or an amount of something that you have not used: *The new engines will lead to savings in fuel.* | [+of] *This represents a saving of £60,000 for the company.* | *All small companies will need to make savings if they are going to survive.*
3 [U] when you save money rather than spend it → SAVE¹ (2)

'savings ac,count *n* [C] a bank account in which you keep money that you want to save for a period of time, and which pays you INTEREST on the money you have in it; → **checking account**, **current account**

,savings and 'loan *n* [C] *AmE* a business, similar to a bank, that lends money, and into which you pay money that you want to save; **◨ building society** *BrE*

'savings bank *n* [C] a bank where people can save small amounts of money and receive INTEREST on it

'savings bond *n* [C] *technical* a BOND that is sold by the US government and that cannot be sold from one person to another

sa·viour *BrE*; **savior** *AmE* /'seivjə $ -ər/ *n* [C] someone who saves you from a difficult or dangerous situation: [+of] *He was seen by many as the saviour of the organization.*

Saviour *BrE*; **Savior** *AmE* *n* **the/sb's Saviour** Jesus Christ - used by Christians

sav·oir-faire /,sævwɑː 'feə $ -wɑːr 'fer/ *n* [U] *formal* the ability to do and say the right things in social situations

sa·vo·ry¹ /'seivəri/ *adj* the American spelling of SAVOURY

savory² *n* [U] a plant that is used in cooking to add taste to meat and other food

sa·vour¹ *BrE*; **savor** *AmE* /'seivə $ -ər/ *v* [T] **1** to fully enjoy the taste or smell of something: *She sipped her wine, savouring every drop.* **2** to fully enjoy a time or experience: *She savoured her few hours of freedom.* | *He hesitated, savouring the moment.*

savour of sth *phr v formal* to seem to involve something bad or to have some of a bad quality: *We must avoid anything that savours of corruption.*

savour² *BrE*; **savor** *AmE* *n* [singular, U] *formal* **1** a pleasant taste or smell: *the sweet savour of wood smoke* **2** interest and enjoyment: *Life seemed to have lost its savour for him.*

sa·vour·y¹ *BrE*; **savory** *AmE* /'seivəri/ *adj* **1** *BrE* savoury food tastes of salt; **◨** sweet: *savoury party*

---

snacks | *pancakes with sweet and savoury fillings* **2** a savoury smell or taste is strong and pleasant but is not sweet **3 not very savoury/none too savoury** unpleasant or morally unacceptable; → **unsavoury**: *Some of the customers in the pub looked none too savoury.*

savoury² *n plural* **savouries** [C] *BrE* a small piece of food with a salty taste that is served at a party: *plates of cakes and savouries*

sav·vy¹ /'sævi/ *n* [U] *informal* practical knowledge and ability: *He's obviously got a lot of political savvy.*

savvy² *adj AmE informal* someone who is savvy is clever and knows how to deal with situations successfully: *savvy consumers*

saw¹ /sɔː $ sɒː/ the past tense of SEE

saws

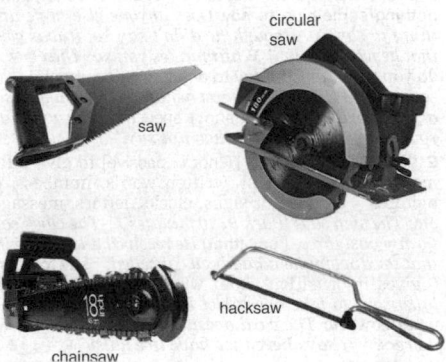

circular saw

saw

hacksaw

chainsaw

saw² *n* [C] **1** a tool that you use for cutting wood. It has a flat blade with an edge cut into many V shapes **2** a short, familiar phrase or sentence that is considered to contain some truth about life; **◨** **proverb, saying**: *That reminds me of the old saw about being careful about what you wish for.*

saw³ *v past tense* **sawed**, *past participle* **sawn** /sɔːn $ sɒːn/ *or* **sawed** *AmE* [I,T] to cut something using a saw: *She was in the back yard sawing logs.* | [+through] *He sawed through a power cable by mistake.*

saw at sth *phr v* to cut something with a repeated backwards and forwards movement: *He sawed at the loaf with a blunt knife.*

saw sth ⇔ **off** *phr v* to remove something by cutting it off with a saw: *We sawed off the dead branches.*

saw sth ⇔ **up** *phr v* to cut something into many pieces, using a saw: *The tree was cut down and sawn up for logs.*

saw·buck /'sɔːbʌk $ 'sɒː-/ *n* [C] *AmE old-fashioned informal* a piece of paper money worth $10

saw·dust /'sɔːdʌst $ 'sɒː-/ *n* [U] very small pieces of wood that are left when you have been cutting wood

saw·mill /'sɔːmɪl $ 'sɒː-/ *n* [C] a factory where trees are cut into flat pieces that can be used as wood

,sawn-off 'shotgun *BrE*; **,sawed-off 'shotgun** *AmE n* [C] a SHOTGUN whose BARREL (=long thin tube) has been cut short so that it is easier to hide

Sax·on /'sæksən/ *n* [C] a member of the race of people from northern Europe that came to live in England in the 5th century —**Saxon** *adj*

sax·o·phone /'sæksəfəun $ -foun/ also **sax** /sæks/ *informal* [C] a curved musical instrument made of metal that you play by blowing into it and pressing buttons, used especially in popular music and JAZZ

sax·oph·o·nist /sæk'sɒfənist $ 'sæksəfoun‚st/ *n* [C] someone who plays the saxophone

say¹ S1 W1 /sei/ *v past tense and past participle* **said** /sed/, *third person singular* **says** /sez/
1 EXPRESS STH IN WORDS [I only in negatives, T] to

express an idea, feeling, thought etc using words: *'I'm so tired,' she said.* | *'Don't cry,' he said softly.* | *Don't believe anything he says.* | **say (that)** *A spokesman said that the company had improved its safety standards.* | *I always said I would buy a motorbike when I had enough money.* | **say how/why/who etc** *Did she say what happened?* | *I would like to say how much we appreciate your hard work.* | *'Why did she leave?' 'I don't know – she didn't say.'* | **say sth to sb** *What did you say to her?* | **a terrible/silly/strange etc thing to say** *What a silly thing to say!* | **say hello/goodbye/thank you etc** (=say something to greet someone, thank someone etc) *She left without saying goodbye.* | **say you're sorry** (=apologize) *I've said I'm sorry – what more do you want?* | **say yes/no (to sth)** (=agree or refuse) *Can I go, Mum? Oh please say yes!* | **say nothing/anything/something (about sth)** *He looked as if he was going to say something.* | *I wished I had said nothing about Jordi.* | **have anything/nothing/something to say** *Does anyone else have anything to say?* | *Although he didn't say so, it was clear that he was in pain.* | **What makes you say that** (=why do you think that)? | **say to do sth** (=tell someone to do something) *Nina said to meet her at 4.30.* | *I'd like to say a few words* (=make a short speech). | *'So what are your plans now?' 'I'd rather not say.'*

2 GIVE INFORMATION [T not in passive] to give information in the form of written words, numbers, or pictures – used about signs, clocks, letters, messages etc: *The sign said 'Back in 10 minutes'.* | *The clock said twenty past three.* | **say (that)** *He received a letter saying that the appointment had been cancelled.* | **say to do sth** (=gives information about what you should do) *The label says to take one tablet before meals.* | **say who/what/how etc** *The card doesn't even say who sent the flowers.* | *It says here they have live music.*

3 MEAN [T usually in progressive] used to talk about what someone means: *What do you think the writer is trying to say in this passage?* | *So what you're saying is, there's none left.* | **be saying (that)** *Are you saying I'm fat?* | *I'm not saying it's a bad idea.* | *All I'm saying is that it might be better to wait a while.*

4 THINK THAT STH IS TRUE [T] used to talk about something that people think is true: **they say/people say/ it is said (that)** *They say that she has been all over the world.* | *It is said that he was a spy during the war.* | **sb is said to be sth/do sth** *He's said to be the richest man in the world.* | *Well, you know what they say - blood's thicker than water.* | *The rest, as they say, is history.*

5 SHOW/BE A SIGN OF STH [T] **a)** to show clearly that something is true about someone or something's character: *The kind of car you drive says what kind of person you are.* | *The fact that she never apologized says a lot about* (=shows something very clearly) *what kind of person she is.* | *It said a lot for the manager that the team remained confident despite losing* (=it showed that he is good). | *These results don't say much for the quality of teaching* (=they show that it is not very good). **b)** to show what someone really is feeling or thinking, especially without using words: *The look on her face said 'I love you'.* | **sth says everything/says it all** *His expression said it all.*

6 SPEAK THE WORDS OF STH [T] to speak the words that are written in a play, poem, or prayer: *Can you say that line again, this time with more feeling?* | *I'll say a prayer for you.*

7 PRONOUNCE [T] to pronounce a word or sound: *How do you say your last name?*

8 SUGGEST/SUPPOSE STH [T usually in imperative] used when suggesting or supposing that something might happen or be true: *... say ... If we put out, say, twenty chairs, would that be enough?* | **let's say (that)/ just say (that)** *Let's say your plan fails, then what?* | *Just say you won the lottery – what would you do?*

9 say to yourself to try to persuade yourself that

something is true or not true: *I kept saying to myself that this wasn't really happening.*

---

10 I must say also I have to say used to emphasize what you are saying: *The cake does look good, I must say.* | *I have to say I was impressed at the way they dealt with the situation.*

11 I can't say (that) used to say that you do not think or feel something: *I can't say I envy her being married to him!*

12 I would say used for giving your opinion even though other people may not agree: *I'd say he was jealous.*

13 I couldn't say used when you do not know the answer to something: *I couldn't say who will win.*

14 if I may say so also if I might say so *formal* used to be polite when saying something that may embarrass or offend the person you are talking to: *That's just the point, Mr Glover, if I may say so.*

15 having said that used to say that something is true in spite of what you have just said: *The diet can make you slim without exercise. Having said that, however, exercise is important too.*

16 wouldn't you say? used to ask someone whether they agree with the statement you have just made: *It seems very unlikely, wouldn't you say?*

17 what do you say? used to ask someone if they agree with a suggestion: *We could go into partnership – what do you say?* | *What do you say we all go to a movie?* | *What would you say to a meal out?*

18 say no more used to say that you understand what someone means, although they have not said it directly: *'I saw him leaving her house at 6.30 this morning.' 'Say no more!'*

19 you can say that again! used to say that you completely agree with someone: *'It's cold in here.' 'You can say that again!'*

20 you said it! **a)** used when someone says something that you agree with, although you would not have actually said it yourself because it is not polite: *'I was always stubborn as a kid.' 'You said it!'* **b)** *especially AmE* used to say that you agree with someone: *'Let's go home.' 'You said it! I'm tired.'*

21 who says? used to say that you do not agree with a statement, opinion etc: *Who says museum work doesn't pay?*

22 who can say? also who's to say used to say that nobody can know something: *Who can say what will happen between now and then?* | *Many women believe that skin cream makes their skin look younger, and who's to say that they're wrong?*

23 you don't say! used to show you are surprised by what someone has told you – also often used when you are not at all surprised by what someone has told you

24 say when used to ask someone to tell you when to stop pouring them a drink or serving them food because they have got enough

25 say cheese used to tell people to smile when you are taking their photograph

26 (just) say the word used to tell someone that they have only to ask and you will do what they want: *Anywhere you want to go, just say the word.*

27 I'll say this/that (much) for sb used when you want to mention something good about someone, especially when you have been criticizing them: *I will say this for Tom – at least he's consistent.* | *You've got determination – I'll say that for you.*

28 say what you like *especially BrE* used when giving an opinion that you are sure is correct, even if the person you are talking to might disagree with you: *Say what you like about him, he's a very good writer.*

29 anything/whatever you say used to tell someone that you agree to do what they want, accept their opinion etc, especially because you do not want an argument

30 can't say fairer than that *BrE* used to say that you have made the best offer that you can: *If I win, I'll buy you a drink. Can't say fairer than that.*

31 I wouldn't say no (to sth) used to say that you would like something: *I wouldn't say no to coffee.*

32 I'll say! used to say yes to a question, in a strong way: *'Was there a big argument?' 'I'll say!'*

33 let's just say used when you do not want to give a lot of details about something: *Let's just say she wasn't very pleased about it.*

34 shall I/we say used when you are not quite sure how to describe someone or something: *He is, shall we say, slightly unusual.*

35 what have you got to say for yourself? used to ask someone for an explanation when they have done something wrong

36 say what? *informal especially AmE* used when you did not hear what someone said or when you cannot believe that something is true

37 I say *BrE old-fashioned* **a)** used to get someone's attention: *I say, don't I know you?* **b)** used before giving your reaction to something: *'My husband's broken his leg.' 'I say! I'm sorry to hear that.'*

38 say sth to sb's face *informal* to criticize someone or say something unpleasant directly to them instead of saying it to someone else: *I knew they wanted me to leave even though they wouldn't say it to my face.*

39 that's not saying much used to say that it is not surprising that someone or something is better than another person or thing because the other person or thing is so bad: *This version is better than the original but that's not saying much.*

40 sth says it all if something says it all, it clearly shows how someone feels or what a situation is really like: *Her smile said it all.*

41 to say the least used to say that you could have described something, criticized someone etc a lot more severely than you have: *Jane could have been more considerate, to say the least.*

42 that is to say used before giving more details or being more exact about something: *They, that's to say Matt and John, were arguing about what to do.*

43 that is not to say used to make sure the person you are talking to does not think something that is not true: *I'm quite happy in my job but that's not to say I'm not going to do it for the rest of my life.*

44 not to say *especially BrE* used when adding a stronger description of something: *The information is inadequate, not to say misleading.*

45 nothing/something/not much to be said for (doing) sth used to say that there are a lot of or not many advantages to something: *There's a lot to be said for taking a few days off now and then.* | *It was a town with very little to be said for it.*

46 to say nothing of sth used to mention another thing involved in what you have just been talking about: *It wasn't much for three years' work, to say nothing of the money it had cost.*

47 have something to say about sth to be angry about something: *Her father would have something to say about it.*

48 have a lot to say for yourself to talk a lot

49 not have much to say for yourself to not talk very much

50 what sb says goes used to emphasize who is in control in a situation: *My wife wants to go to Italy this year, and what she says goes!*

51 say your piece to give your opinion about something, especially something you do not like → **wouldn't say boo to a goose** at BOO² (3); → **easier said than done** at EASY² (4); → **enough said** at ENOUGH² (6); → **it goes without saying** at GO WITHOUT (2); → **needless to say** at NEEDLESS (1); → **no sooner said than done** at SOON (9); → **not say/breathe a word** at WORD¹ (9); → **well said** at WELL¹ (13); → **when all's said and done** at ALL¹ (17)

say² *n* [singular, U] **1** the right to take part in deciding something: **have some/no/little say in sth** *The workers had no say in how the factory was run.* | *The chairman* **has the final say** (=has the right to make the final decision about something). **2 have your say** to have the opportunity to give your opinion about something: *You'll get a chance to have your say.* | [+in/on] *Parents can have their say in the decision-making process.*

say³ *interjection AmE informal* used to express surprise, or to get someone's attention so that you can tell them something: *Say, haven't I seen you before somewhere?*

say·ing W3 /ˈseɪ-ɪŋ/ *n* [C] a well-known short statement that expresses an idea most people believe is true and wise; ▣ **proverb**: *You can't judge a book by its cover, as the old saying goes.*

ˈsay-so *n informal* **1** sb's say-so someone's permission to do something: *You can't leave the hospital without the say-so of the doctor.* **2 on sb's say-so** based on someone's personal statement without any proof: *She's hired a number of people on my say-so.*

S-bend /ˈes bend/ *n* [C] *BrE* **1** a bend in a road in the shape of an 'S' that can be dangerous to drivers; ▣ **S-curve** *AmE* **2** a bend in a waste pipe in the shape of an 'S'

scab /skæb/ *n* [C] **1** a hard layer of dried blood that forms over a cut or wound while it is getting better **2** an insulting word for someone who works while the other people in the same factory, office etc are on STRIKE

scab·bard /ˈskæbəd $ -ərd/ *n* [C] a metal or leather cover for the blade of a sword

scab·by /ˈskæbi/ *adj* scabby skin is covered with scabs

sca·bies /ˈskeɪbiz/ *n* [U] a skin disease caused by MITES (=small creatures like insects)

sca·brous /ˈskeɪbrəs, ˈskæb- $ ˈskæb-/ *adj literary* **1** rude or shocking, especially in a sexual way: *The film is a joy – hilariously funny and unremittingly scabrous.* **2** scabrous skin is rough, not soft

scads /skædz/ *n informal* **scads of sth** large numbers or quantities of something: *They got scads of calls from reporters.*

scaf·fold /ˈskæfəld, -fəʊld $ -fəld, -foʊld/ *n* [C] **1** a structure built next to a wall, for workers to stand on while they build, repair, or paint a building **2** a raised structure which was used in the past as a place to kill criminals by hanging them or cutting off their heads **3** *AmE* a structure that can be moved up and down to help people work on high buildings; ⊟ **cradle** *BrE*

scaf·fold·ing /'skæfəldɪŋ/ *n* [U] A set of poles and boards that are built into a structure for workers to stand on when they are working on the outside of a building

scal·a·bil·i·ty /ˌskeɪlə'bɪlɪ̯ti/ *n* [U] *technical* the degree to which a computer system is able to grow and become more powerful as the number of people using it increases

scal·a·wag /'skæləwæg/ *n AmE* a SCALLYWAG

scald[1] /skɔːld $ skɒːld/ *v* [T] to burn your skin with hot liquid or steam: *Don't scald yourself with that kettle!*

scald[2] *n* [C] a burn on your skin caused by hot liquid or steam

scald·ing /'skɔːldɪŋ $ 'skɒːl-/ *adj* **1** also **scalding hot** extremely hot: *a bowl of scalding water* | *a cup of scalding hot tea* **2** *literary* scalding tears feel hot on your skin: *Scalding tears poured down her face.*

scale[1] [S3] [W2] /skeɪl/ *n*
1 SIZE/LEVEL [singular, U] the size or level of something, or the amount that something is happening: [+of] *We had underestimated the scale of the problem.* | **on a large/small/grand etc scale** *There has been housing development on a massive scale since 1980.* | *Most alternative technologies work best on a small scale.* | *A structural survey revealed the full scale of the damage.* | *I was shocked by the sheer scale* (=very big scale) *of the destruction.* | **on a global/international/world scale** *Pollution could cause changes to weather patterns on a global scale.* | *Large firms benefit from economies of scale* (=ways of saving money because they are big).
2 RANGE [C usually singular] a whole range of different types of people or things, from the lowest level to the highest: *Some rural schools have 50 pupils, while at the other end of the scale are city schools with nearly 5,000 pupils.* | **up/down the scale** *She gradually made her way up the social scale.* | *animals which are lower down the evolutionary scale* (=the range of animals that have developed gradually over a long time)
3 FOR WEIGHING **scales** [plural] *BrE*; **scale** *AmE* a machine for weighing people or objects: *a set of kitchen scales* | *some new bathroom scales* (=scales that you use to weigh yourself) → **tip the balance/scales** at TIP[2] (6); → see picture at MEASUREMENT
4 MEASURING SYSTEM [C] a system of numbers that is used for measuring the amount, speed, quality etc of something: **on a scale** *The earthquakes measured 7 on the Richter scale.* | *changes to the company's pay scale* | *Your performance will be judged on a scale of 1 to 10.* | *We use a sliding scale* (=in which prices are not firmly fixed) *for charges.*
5 MEASURING MARKS [C] a set of marks with regular spaces between them on a tool that is used for measuring, or on the side of a mathematical drawing: *a ruler with a metric scale*
6 MAP/MODEL [C,U] the relationship between the size of a map, drawing, or model and the actual size of the place or thing that it represents: *a map with a scale of 1:250,000* | **to scale** *All our models are made to scale.* | **scale model/drawing etc** (=one done using a strict scale) *a scale drawing of the Eiffel Tower*
7 MUSIC [C] a series of musical notes that become higher or lower, with fixed distances between each note: *the scale of G major*
8 FISH [C usually plural] one of the small flat pieces of skin that cover the bodies of fish, snakes etc
9 TEETH [U] *BrE* a white substance that forms on your teeth
10 WATER PIPES [U] a white substance that forms around the inside of hot water pipes or containers in which water is boiled

11 the scales fell from sb's eyes *literary* used to say that someone suddenly realized something important → FULL-SCALE

scale[2] *v* [T] **1** to climb to the top of something that is high and difficult to climb: *Rescuers had to scale a 300m cliff to reach the injured climber.* **2** *technical* to make writing or a picture the right size for a particular purpose: **scale sth to sth** *The writing can be scaled to any size, depending on the paper.* **3** **scale the heights** to be extremely successful: *By the age of 21 he had already scaled the heights in the academic world.*
scale sth ⇔ **down/back** *phr v* to reduce the amount or size of something: *The emergency aid programme has now been scaled down.*
scale sth ⇔ **up** *phr v* to increase the amount or size of something; → **decrease**: *Production at the factory is being scaled up.*

scal·lion /'skæljən/ *n* [C] *AmE* a type of young onion with a small round end and a long green stem; ⊟ **spring onion** *BrE*

scal·lop /'skɒləp, 'skæ- $ 'skɑː-/ *n* [C] **1** a small sea creature that you can eat, with a flat round shell made of two parts that fit together **2** [usually plural] one of a row of small curves that are used to decorate the edge of clothes, curtains etc

scal·loped /'skɒləpt, 'skæ- $ 'skɑː-/ *adj* **1** if the edge of something is scalloped, it is made into a row of small curves **2** scalloped potatoes, corn etc have been baked in a cream or cheese sauce

scal·ly /'skæli/ *n plural* **scallies** [C] *BrE spoken* someone who causes trouble – often used humorously; ⊟ **scallywag**: *You rude little scally!* —**scally** *adj* [only before noun]: *just some little scally kid*

scal·ly·wag /'skæliwæg/ *especially BrE* also **scala·wag** *AmE n* [C] *old-fashioned* a child who causes trouble but not in a serious way – used when you are not angry with them

scalp[1] /skælp/ *n* [C] **1** the skin on the top of your head: *Massage the shampoo gently into your hair and scalp.* **2** sb's scalp *informal* if you want someone's scalp, you want them to be completely defeated: *The board members were after the chairman's scalp.*

scalp[2] *v* [T] **1** *AmE informal* to buy tickets for an event and sell them again at a much higher price; ⊟ **tout** *BrE* **2** to cut the hair and skin off the head of a dead enemy as a sign of victory

scal·pel /'skælpəl/ *n* [C] a small, very sharp knife that is used by doctors in operations

scal·per /'skælpə $ -ər/ *n* [C] *AmE* someone who makes money by buying tickets for an event and selling them again at a very high price; ⊟ **tout** *BrE*

scal·y /'skeɪli/ *adj* **1** a scaly animal or fish is covered with small flat pieces of hard skin → see picture at SURFACE **2** scaly skin is dry and rough

scam /skæm/ *n* [C] *informal* a clever but dishonest way to get money: *He got involved in a credit card scam.*

scamp /skæmp/ *n* [C] *old-fashioned* a child who has fun by tricking people

scam·per /'skæmpə $ -ər/ *v* [I always + adv/prep] to run with quick short steps, like a child or small animal: *The children scampered up the hill after me.*

scam·pi /'skæmpi/ *n BrE* [plural, U] large PRAWNS (=sea creatures) that are covered in bread CRUMBS and cooked in hot oil

scan[1] /skæn/ *v* **scanned**, **scanning**
1 LOOK AT [T] to examine an area carefully but quickly, often because you are looking for a particular person or thing: *He scanned the horizon, but there was no sign of the ship.* | *She scanned his face, looking for signs of what he was thinking.* | *Video cameras scanned the car park.* | **scan sth for sth** *I scanned the street for people I knew.*
2 READ also **scan through** [T] to read something quickly; ⊟ **skim**: **scan sth for sth** *I scanned the page for her name.* | *She scanned through the paper.*
3 SEE INSIDE [T] if a machine scans something, it

passes an electrical beam over it to form a picture of what is inside it; → **scanner**: *All luggage has to be scanned at the airport.* | *They scanned his brain for signs of damage.*
4 `COMPUTER` [T] if you scan a document or picture, you put it into a machine attached to a computer so that the information in the document can be taken into the computer and stored there; → **scanner**: **scan sth into sth** *You scan the text into the computer, then edit it.*
5 `POETRY` [I] *technical* poetry that scans has a correct regular pattern of beats

scan² *n*   **1** [C] a medical test in which a special machine produces a picture of something inside your body: *The scan showed that she was expecting twins.* | *a brain scan*   **2** [singular] when you read something quickly: [+of] *a quick scan of the newspapers*

scan·dal /ˈskændl/ *n*
1 [C] an event in which someone, especially someone important, behaves in a bad way that shocks people

> cause a scandal
> be involved in a scandal
> be (at) the centre of a scandal
> big/major scandal
> financial/political scandal
> corruption/sex/drugs etc scandal
> a scandal breaks (=a scandal becomes known)

> *It **caused** quite **a scandal** when he left his wife.* | *The college has recently been **involved in a** drugs **scandal**.* | *He has been **at the centre of** a political **scandal**.* | *a **major scandal** involving the government* | *a series of **financial scandals*** | *a **sex scandal** that ruined his reputation* | *They had already left the country when the **scandal broke**.*

2 [U] talk about dishonest or immoral things that famous or important people are believed to have done: *The magazine is full of gossip and scandal.*
3 be a scandal *BrE* spoken to be very shocking or unacceptable: *The price of petrol these days is an absolute scandal!*

scan·dal·ize also **-ise** *BrE* /ˈskændəl-aɪz/ *v* [T usually passive] to make people feel very shocked: *His outspoken views scandalized the nation.*

scan·dal·mon·ger /ˈskændəlˌmʌŋgə $ -ˌmɑːŋgər, -ˌmʌŋ-/ *n* [C] someone who tells people untrue and shocking things about someone else

scan·dal·ous /ˈskændələs/ *adj*   **1** completely unfair and wrong; ◨ **shocking**: *a scandalous waste of public money* | *scandalous behaviour*   **2** involving stories about dishonest or immoral things that someone has done: *scandalous stories about the Prime Minister* —**scandalously** *adv*

Scan·di·na·vi·an /ˌskændɨ̥ˈneɪviən◂/ *n* [C] someone from the area of Northern Europe that consists of Norway, Sweden, Denmark, and usually Finland and Iceland —**Scandinavian** *adj*: *Scandinavian languages*

scan·ner /ˈskænə $ -ər/ *n* [C]   **1** a machine that passes an electrical beam over something in order to produce a picture of what is inside it; → **scan**: *a high-tech body scanner*   **2** a piece of computer equipment that allows written or printed information to be taken onto a computer and stored there; → **scan**; → see picture at OFFICE

scant /skænt/ *adj* [only before noun]   **1** not enough: *The story has received **scant attention** in the press.* | *They produce goods with **scant regard** for quality.*   **2 a scant cup/teaspoon etc** a little less than a full amount of a particular measurement

scant·y /ˈskænti/ *adj*   **1** not enough: *There is only scanty evidence of his involvement.*   **2** scanty clothes are small and do not cover very much of your body – used to show disapproval —**scantily** *adv*: *scantily clad young women*

scape·goat /ˈskeɪpgəʊt $ -goʊt/ *n* [C] someone who is blamed for something bad that happens, even if it is not their fault: [+for] *She believed she had been **made** a scapegoat for what happened.* —**scapegoat** *v* [T]

scap·u·la /ˈskæpjʊ̥lə/ *n* [C] *technical* one of the two flat bones on each side of your upper back; ◨ **shoulder blade** → SKELETON

scar¹ /skɑː $ skɑːr/ *n* [C]
1 `MARK ON SKIN` a permanent mark that is left on your skin after you have had a cut or wound: *He had a long, curved scar on his right cheek.* | *a deep cut that could **leave** a permanent **scar***
2 `FEELING` a feeling of fear or sadness that remains with you for a long time after an unpleasant experience: *Her **mental scars** will take time to heal.* | *The war has **left** a deep **scar** on this community.*
3 `DAMAGED AREA` a place where the land or a building was damaged in the past: [+of] *The landscape still **bears the scars** of the war.*
4 `CLIFF` *BrE* a cliff on the side of a mountain

scar² *v* **scarred, scarring** [T]   **1** if a wound or cut scars you, it leaves a permanent mark on your body: *His hands were **badly scarred** by the fire.* | *She will probably be **scarred for life**.*   **2** if an unpleasant experience scars you, it leaves you with a feeling of sadness or fear that continues for a long time: *She was profoundly scarred by her father's suicide.*   **3** to spoil the appearance of something: *huge quarries that scar the landscape*

scar·ab /ˈskærəb/ also **ˈscarab ˌbeetle** *n* [C] a type of large black BEETLE

scarce¹ /skeəs $ skers/ *adj comparative* **scarcer**, *superlative* **scarcest**   **1** if something is scarce, there is not very much of it available: *Food was often scarce in the winter.* | *There was fierce competition for the **scarce resources**.*   **2 make yourself scarce** *informal* to leave a place, especially in order to avoid an unpleasant situation: *I decided it was time to make myself scarce.*

scarce² *adv literary* scarcely: *He could scarce believe it.*

scarce·ly /ˈskeəsli $ ˈsker-/ *adv*   **1** almost not or almost none at all; ◨ **hardly**: *The city had scarcely changed in 20 years.* | *The country had **scarcely any** industry.* | *He **scarcely ever** left the region.* | **can/could scarcely do sth** *It was getting dark and she could scarcely see in front of her.* | **scarcely a day/year/moment etc** *Scarcely a day goes by when I don't think of him.*; → see box at RARELY   **2** only a moment ago; ◨ **hardly, barely**: *He **had scarcely** sat down **when** there was a knock at the door.*   **3** definitely not or almost certainly not; ◨ **hardly**: *Early March is scarcely the time of year for sailing.*

scar·ci·ty /ˈskeəsɨ̥ti $ ˈsker-/ *n* [singular] a situation in which there is not enough of something: [+of] *the scarcity of employment opportunities*

scare¹ /skeə $ sker/ *v*   **1** [T] to make someone feel frightened; ◨ **frighten**; → **afraid**: *Loud noises can scare animals or birds.* | **scare the life/living daylights/hell etc out of sb** *The alarm scared the hell out of me.* | **scare the pants off sb** (=scare someone very much)   **2 scare easily** to be frightened by things that are not very frightening: *I don't scare easily, you know.*
scare sb into sth *phr v* to make someone do something by frightening them or threatening them: **scare sb into doing sth** *You can't scare me into telling you anything.*
scare sb/sth ⇔ **off/away** *phr v*   **1** to make an animal or person go away by frightening them: *She moved quietly to avoid scaring the birds away.*   **2** to make someone uncertain or worried so that they do not do something they were going to do: *Rising prices are scaring off many potential customers.*
scare up sth *phr v AmE informal* to make something although you have very few things to make it from: *Let me see if I can scare up something for you to eat.*

scare² *n*   **1** [singular] a sudden feeling of fear: *You really **gave us a scare**!*   **2** [C] a situation in which a lot of people become frightened about something: *a **bomb scare*** | *a **health scare***

S

scare·crow /'skeəkrəʊ $ 'skerkroʊ/ *n* [C] an object in the shape of a person that a farmer puts in a field to frighten birds away

scared S3 /skeəd $ skerd/ *adj* frightened of something, or nervous about something; ▣ **afraid**: *At first, he was really scared.* | **scared of (doing) sth** *I've always been scared of dogs.* | *Don't be scared of asking for help.* | **scared (that)** *I wanted to ask her out but was scared that she might refuse.* | **scared to do sth** *The boys were scared to cross the street.* | **scared stiff/scared to death/scared out of your wits** (=extremely frightened) *I was scared stiff at the thought of making a speech.*

scare·mon·ger·ing /'skeə,mʌŋgərɪŋ $ 'sker,mɑːŋ-, -,mʌŋ-/ *n* [U] *BrE* the practice of deliberately making people worried or nervous, especially in order to get a political or other advantage: *He was accused of political scaremongering.* —**scaremonger** *n* [C]

scare story *n* [C] a report, especially in a newspaper, that makes a situation seem more serious or worrying than it really is: *Despite the scare stories in the media, no jobs will be lost at the factory.*

scare tactics *n* [plural] methods of persuading people to do something by frightening them: *Employers used scare tactics to force a return to work.*

scare·y /'skeəri $ 'skeri/ *adj* another spelling of SCARY

scarf¹ /skɑːf $ skɑːrf/ *n plural* **scarfs** *or* **scarves** /skɑːvz $ skɑːrvz/ [C] a piece of cloth that you wear around your neck, head, or shoulders, especially to keep warm

scarf² also **scarf down/up** *v* [T] *AmE informal* to eat something very quickly: *She scarfed down a bagel on her way to work.*

scar·i·fy /'skeərɪfaɪ, 'skærɪfaɪ $ 'sker-, 'skær-/ *v* **scarified, scarifying, scarifies** [T] **1** to break and make loose the surface of a road or field using a pointed tool **2** *formal* to criticize someone very severely

scar·let /'skɑːlɪt $ -ɑːr-/ *adj* **1** bright red **2** *BrE* if you go scarlet, your face becomes red, usually because you are embarrassed or angry; ▣ **blush**: **go/turn/flush/blush scarlet** *Eileen blushed scarlet at the joke.* —**scarlet** *n* [U]

scarlet fever also **scar·la·ti·na** /,skɑːlə'tiːnə $,skɑːr-/ *n* [U] a serious infectious illness that mainly affects children, causing a sore throat and red spots on your skin

scarlet woman *n* [C] *old-fashioned* a woman who has sexual relationships with many different people

scarp /skɑːp $ skɑːrp/ *n* [C] a line of natural cliffs

scar·per /'skɑːpə $ 'skɑːrpər/ *v* [I] *BrE informal* to run away: *They scarpered without paying their bill.*

SCART /skɑːt $ skɑːrt/ *n* [C] a piece of equipment used in some countries to connect electrical equipment so that video and sound signals can go from one piece of equipment to another, for example from a VIDEO RECORDER to a television: *a SCART cable*

scarves /skɑːvz $ skɑːrvz/ *n* the plural of SCARF¹

scar·y /'skeəri $ 'skeri/ *adj comparative* **scarier**, *superlative* **scariest** *informal* frightening: *a scary moment* | *a scary movie* | *The book is both scary and funny.*

scat /skæt/ *n* [U] a style of JAZZ singing, in which the singer sings sounds rather than words

scath·ing /'skeɪðɪŋ/ *adj* a scathing remark criticizes someone or something very severely: **scathing attack/remark/comment etc** *a scathing attack on the Government's planned tax increases* | [+**about**] *He's always been so scathing about psychiatrists.* —**scathingly** *adv*

scat·o·log·i·cal /,skætə'lɒdʒɪkəl $ -'lɑː-/ *adj formal* too interested in or related to human waste, in a way that people find offensive: *scatological humour*

scat·ter /'skætə $ -ər/ *v* [I,T] **1** if someone scatters a lot of things, or if they scatter, they are thrown or dropped over a wide area in an irregular way: **scatter (sth) over/around/across etc sth** *Scatter the onions over*
the fish. | *The flowers fell and scattered on the ground.* **2** if a group of people or animals scatter, or if something scatters them, they move quickly in different directions: *The sound of gunfire made the crowd scatter in all directions.* → SCATTERED, SCATTERING

scat·ter·brained /'skætəbreɪnd $ -tər-/ *adj informal* not thinking in a practical way, so that you cannot do things or you forget or lose things —**scatterbrain** *n* [C]

scatter cushion *n* [C] a small CUSHION that you put on SOFAS and chairs for decoration

scat·tered /'skætəd $ -ərd/ *adj* spread over a wide area or over a long period of time: [+**over/throughout/across/around** etc] *Broken glass lay scattered over the floor.* | [+**with**] *The sky was scattered with stars.* | *There will be some scattered showers* (=short periods of rain) *in the afternoon.* | *a widely scattered set of islands*

scat·ter·ing /'skætərɪŋ/ *n* **a scattering of sth** *written* a small number of things or people spread out over a large area: *a scattering of isolated farms*

scat·ty /'skæti/ *adj BrE informal* someone who is scatty often forgets or loses things because they are not sensible or practical

scav·enge /'skævɪndʒ/ *v* [I,T] **1** if an animal scavenges, it eats anything that it can find: *Pigs scavenged among the rubbish.* | [+**for**] *rats scavenging for food* **2** if someone scavenges, they search through things that other people do not want for food or useful objects: *There are people who live in the dump and scavenge garbage for a living.* | [+**for**] *Women were scavenging for old furniture.* —**scavenger** *n* [C]: *Foxes and other scavengers go through the dustbins.*

sce·na·ri·o /sɪ'nɑːriəʊ $ -'nærioʊ, -'ne-/ *n plural* **scenarios** [C] **1** a situation that could possibly happen: *Imagine a scenario where only 20% of people have a job.* | **possible/likely/plausible scenario** *Under a likely scenario, world population will double by 2050.* | **possible scenario** | **worst-case/nightmare scenario** (=the worst possible situation) *The worst-case scenario was that he would have to have an operation.* **2** *technical* a written description of the characters, place, and things that will happen in a film, play etc

scene S2 W2 /siːn/ *n*

1 PLAY/FILM [C] **a)** part of a play during which there is no change in time or place: *Hamlet, Act 5 Scene 2* | the **opening scene b)** a single piece of action that happens in one place in a film, book etc: *battle scenes* | *tender love scenes* | *The film contains some violent scenes.* | *colourful pictures depicting scenes from the Bible*
2 ACTIVITIES [singular] a particular set of activities and the people who are involved in them: *I'm not into the **club scene*** (=going to night clubs). | *LA's **music scene*** | the **drug scene** | *a newcomer to the **political scene***
3 ACCIDENT/CRIME [singular] the place where an accident, crime etc happened: *The police soon arrived at **the scene of the crime.*** | **at the scene** *Investigators are now at the scene, searching for clues.* | **on the scene** *Journalists were on the scene within minutes.*
4 VIEW/PICTURE [C] a view of a place as you see it, or as it appears in a picture: *He photographed a wide range of street scenes.* | [+**of**] *She returned home to find a scene of devastation.*
5 EVENT/SITUATION [C] what is happening in a place, or what can be seen happening: [+**of**] *There were scenes of rejoicing after the election.* | **bad scene** *AmE*: *'It's a bad scene here,' she said. 'Jamie is very sick.'*
6 ARGUMENT [C] a loud angry argument, especially in a public place: *There were angry scenes in parliament today.* | *I was mad, but I didn't want to **make a scene.***
7 **not your scene** *informal* to not be the type of thing you like: *Loud discos aren't really my scene.*
8 **behind the scenes** secretly, while other things are happening publicly: *Behind the scenes, both sides are working towards an agreement.*
9 **set the scene a)** to provide the conditions in which an event can happen: [+**for**] *The prison riots have set the*

scene for major reform. **b)** to describe the situation before you begin to tell a story: *A few words on the rules of English law will help to set the scene.*
10 be/come on the scene to be or become involved in a situation, activity etc: *By then, there was a boyfriend on the scene.* → **a change of scene** at CHANGE² (3); → **steal the scene** at STEAL¹ (4)

sce·ne·ry /'siːnəri/ *n* [U] **1** the natural features of a particular part of a country that you can see, such as mountains, forests, deserts etc: *The best part of the trip was the fantastic scenery.* **2** the painted background, furniture etc used on a theatre stage

sce·nic /'siːnɪk/ *adj* **1** surrounded by views of beautiful countryside: *a region of scenic beauty* **2** the **scenic route** a longer way than usual, especially one that goes through beautiful or interesting areas – often used humorously: *Let's take the scenic route home.* —**scenically** /-kli/ *adv*

scent¹ /sent/ *n* **1** [C] a pleasant smell that something has; ◨ **fragrance**: *a yellow rose with a lovely scent* | [+of] *the sweet scent of ripe fruit* **2** [C] the smell of a particular animal or person that some other animals, for example dogs, can follow **3 throw/put sb off the scent** to give someone false information to prevent them from catching you or discovering something: *Was he trying to put me off the scent because I had come too close to the truth?* **4** [C,U] *especially BrE* a liquid that you put on your skin to make it smell pleasant; ◨ **perfume**

scent² *v* [T] **1** to give a particular smell to something; → **perfume**: *Honeysuckle and roses scented the air.* **2** *written* to suddenly think that something is going to happen or exists: *We scented danger and decided to leave.* | *The press had immediately scented a story.* | *The trade unions have scented victory.* **3** if an animal scents another animal or a person, it knows that they are near because it can smell them

scent·ed /'sentɪd/ *adj* with a particular smell, especially a pleasant one: *scented soap* | [+with] *The dry cold air was scented with wood smoke.* | **rose-scented/vanilla-scented/pine-scented etc**

scep·ter /'septə $ -ər/ *n* the American spelling of SCEPTRE

scep·tic *BrE*; **skeptic** *AmE* /'skeptɪk/ *n* [C] a person who disagrees with particular claims and statements, especially those that are generally thought to be true: *Sceptics argued that the rise in prices was temporary.*

scep·ti·cal *BrE*; **skeptical** *AmE* /'skeptɪkəl/ *adj* tending to disagree with what other people tell you: [+about/of] *I'm extremely sceptical about what I read in the press.* | *Environmental groups are sceptical of the government's claims.* | **highly/deeply sceptical** *He is highly sceptical of the reforms.* | *'You can trust me,' he said. Jane looked sceptical.* —**sceptically** /-kli/ *adv*

scep·ti·cis·m *BrE*; **skepticism** *AmE* /'skeptɪsɪzəm/ *n* [U] an attitude of doubting that particular claims or statements are true or that something will happen

scep·tre *BrE*; **scepter** *AmE* /'septə $ -ter/ *n* [C] a decorated stick carried by kings or queens at ceremonies

scha·den·freu·de /'ʃɑːdn̩frɔɪdə/ *n* [U] *formal* a feeling of pleasure that you get when something bad happens to someone else

sched·ule¹ S3 W3 /'ʃedjuːl, 'ske- $ 'skedʒʊl, -dʒəl/ *n* [C]
1 a plan of what someone is going to do and when they are going to do it: **on schedule** (=at the planned time) *The majority of holiday flights depart and arrive on schedule.* | **ahead of/behind schedule** (=before or after the planned time) *Meg's new book is still well ahead of schedule.* | *How can he fit everything into his busy schedule?* | *I'm going to be working to a very tight schedule* (=including a lot of things that must be done in a short time).
2 *AmE* a list that shows the times that buses, trains etc

leave or arrive at a particular place; ◨ **timetable** *BrE*
3 a formal list of something, for example prices: *a schedule of postal charges*

schedule² *v* [T usually passive] to plan that something will happen at a particular time: **be scheduled for June/Monday etc** *The elections are scheduled for mid-June.* | **be scheduled for release/publication/completion etc** *Her first album is scheduled for release in September.* | **be scheduled to do sth** *Meetings are scheduled to take place all over the country.* | **scheduled flight/service** (=a plane service that flies at the same time every day or every week) *Prices include scheduled flights from Heathrow.* | *We will not cancel your holiday less than 8 weeks before the scheduled departure date.*

sche·ma /'skiːmə/ *n plural* **schemas** *or* **schemata** /-mətə/ [C] *technical* a drawing or description of the main parts of something

sche·mat·ic /skiːˈmætɪk, skɪ-/ *adj* showing the main parts of something in a simple way: *a schematic diagram of DNA*

sche·ma·tize also **-ise** *BrE* /'skiːmətaɪz/ *v* [T] *formal* to arrange something in a system

scheme¹ W1 /skiːm/ *n* [C]
1 *BrE* an official plan that is intended to help people in some way, for example by providing education or training; ◨ **program** *AmE*: *The money will be used for teacher training schemes.* | *a pension scheme* | [+for] *schemes for two new cross-city lines* | **scheme to do sth** *a new scheme to boost exports* | **pilot scheme** (=something that is done on a small scale in order to see if it is successful enough to be done on a larger scale) *The pilot scheme proved to be a great success.*
2 a clever plan, especially to do something that is bad or illegal – used in order to show disapproval: *a get-rich-quick scheme* | **scheme to do sth** *a scheme to pass false cheques*
3 a system that you use to organize information, ideas etc: *a classification scheme*
4 in the scheme of things in the way things generally happen, or are organized: *the unimportance of man in the whole scheme of things* → COLOUR SCHEME

scheme² *v* [I] to secretly make clever and dishonest plans to get or achieve something: **scheme to do sth** *She schemed to kill him with poison.* | [+against] *He became aware that people were scheming against him and called an emergency meeting.* | *She's nothing but a lying, scheming little monster!* —**schemer** *n* [C]

scher·zo /'skeətsəʊ $ 'skertsoʊ/ *n plural* **scherzos** [C] a happy piece of music that is meant to be played quickly

schil·ling /'ʃɪlɪŋ/ *n* [C] the standard unit of money used in Austria before the EURO

schis·m /'skɪzəm, 'sɪzəm/ *n* [C,U] the separation of a group into two groups, caused by a disagreement about its aims and beliefs, especially in the Christian church; ◨ **split** —**schismatic** /sɪzˈmætɪk, skɪz-/ *adj*

schist /ʃɪst/ *n* [U] a type of rock that naturally breaks apart into thin flat pieces

schiz·oid /'skɪtsɔɪd/ *adj* **1** *technical* typical of schizophrenia: *a schizoid personality disorder* **2** quickly changing between opposite opinions or attitudes: *Martin's latest play is as schizoid and erratic as its characters.*

schiz·o·phre·ni·a /ˌskɪtsəʊˈfriːniə, -sə- $ -soʊ-, -sə-/ *n* [U] a serious mental illness in which someone's thoughts and feelings are not based on what is really happening around them

schiz·o·phren·ic¹ /ˌskɪtsəʊˈfrenɪk◂, -sə- $ -soʊ-, -sə-/ *adj* **1** relating to schizophrenia **2** quickly changing from one opinion, attitude etc to another: *The film was an example of schizophrenic movie-making at its worst.*

S

1️⃣ 000, 2️⃣ 000, 3️⃣ 000, most frequent words in S̲poken and W̲ritten English

schizophrenic² n [C] someone who has schizophrenia

schlep /ʃlep/ v **schlepped**, **schlepping** [T] *AmE informal* to carry or pull something heavy: **schlep sth down/out/along etc** *I schlepped his bag all the way to the airport and he didn't even thank me.*

schlep around (sth) *phr v* to spend your time lazily doing nothing useful: *I spent the afternoon schlepping around the house.*

schlock /ʃlɒk $ ʃlɑːk/ n [U] *AmE informal* things that are cheap and of poor quality: *The gift store sells both tasteful gifts and cheap schlock.*

schmaltz·y /ˈʃmɔːltsi, ˈʃmæltsi $ ˈʃmɒːltsi, ˈʃmɑːltsi/ adj *informal* a schmaltzy piece of music, book etc deals with emotions such as love and sadness in a way that seems silly and not serious enough: *a schmaltzy love song* —**schmaltz** n [U]

schman·cy /ˈʃmænsi/ also **fancy-schmancy** adj *informal* expensive and fashionable in a way that is meant to be impressive – used in order to show disapproval: *a schmancy all-girls college*

schmo /ʃməʊ $ ʃmoʊ/ n *plural* **schmoes** [C] *AmE informal* a stupid or annoying person

schmooze /ʃmuːz/ v [I] *informal* to talk in a friendly way about unimportant things at a social event, especially because you want to gain an advantage for yourself later: [+with] *Politicians spent much of their time schmoozing with contributors.*

schmuck /ʃmʌk/ n [C] *AmE informal* a stupid person

schnapps /ʃnæps/ n [U] a strong alcoholic drink

schnit·zel /ˈʃnɪtsəl/ n [C,U] a small piece of VEAL (=meat from a young cow) covered with BREADCRUMBS and cooked in oil

schnook /ʃnʊk/ n [C] *AmE informal* a stupid person

schol·ar /ˈskɒlə $ ˈskɑːlər/ n [C] **1** an intelligent and well-educated person: *the great Dutch scholar Erasmus* **2** someone who knows a lot about a particular subject, especially one that is not a science subject: *a Shakespearean scholar* **3** someone who has been given a scholarship to study at a school or college: *He was a King's scholar at Eton College.*

schol·ar·ly /ˈskɒləli $ ˈskɑːlərli/ adj **1** relating to serious study of a particular subject: *a scholarly journal* **2** someone who is scholarly spends a lot of time studying, and knows a lot about a particular subject

schol·ar·ship /ˈskɒləʃɪp $ ˈskɑːlər-/ n **1** [C] an amount of money that is given to someone by an educational organization to help pay for their education: [+to] *She won a scholarship to Iowa State University.* | **on a scholarship** *He attended college on a drama scholarship.* **2** [U] the knowledge, work, or methods involved in serious studying: *Her latest publication is a fine piece of scholarship.*

scho·las·tic /skəˈlæstɪk/ adj [only before noun] *formal* **1** relating to schools or teaching; → **academic**: *scholastic skills* **2** relating to scholasticism

scho·las·ti·cis·m /skəˈlæstɪsɪzəm/ n [U] a way of studying thought, especially religious thought, based on things written in ancient times

school¹ [S1] [W1] /skuːl/ n

1 [WHERE CHILDREN LEARN] [C,U] a place where children are taught

> **go to school**
> **attend school** *formal* (=go to school)
> **a new school** (=a school that you are going to for the first time)
> **sb's old school** (=the school someone used to go to)
> **school children/pupils/teacher**
> **school uniform**
> **school playground/library/bus etc**
> **school meal/dinner** *BrE*
> **school holiday(s)** *BrE*

His mother always used to pick him up from school. | *Which school do you go to (=attend)?* | *Starting a new* school *can be quite frightening.* | *I went back to my old* school *in West Ham recently to talk to the children there.* | *a play put on by the local school children* | *the first day of the school holidays*

2 [TIME AT SCHOOL] [U] **a)** a day's work at school: *School begins at 8.30.* | **before/after school** *I'll see you after school.* **b)** the time during your life when you go to school: *He's one of my old friends from school.* | *Children start school between the ages of four and five.* | *He left school at 16 and went to work as a bank clerk.*

3 [UNIVERSITY] **a)** [C,U] *AmE* a college or university, or the time when you study there: *Their kids are away at school now.* | *She was going to school in Boston.* **b)** [C] a department or group of departments that teaches a particular subject at a university: [+of] *the Harvard School of Public Health* | **law/medical/business/graduate school** *After two years of medical school, I thought I knew everything.*

4 [ONE SUBJECT] [C] a place where a particular subject or skill is taught: *a language school in Brighton* | *the Pastern Riding School* | [+of] *Amwell School of Motoring*

5 at school a) in the school building: *I can get some work done while the kids are at school.* **b)** *BrE* attending a school, rather than being at college or university or having a job: *We've got two children at school, and one at university.*

6 in school a) in the school building: *Sandra's not in school today.* **b)** *AmE* attending a school or university rather than having a job: *Are your boys still in school?*

7 [ART] [C] a number of people who are considered as a group because of their similar style of work: *the Impressionist school*

8 school of thought an opinion or way of thinking about something that is shared by a group of people: *There are two main schools of thought on the subject.*

9 of/from the old school with old-fashioned values or qualities: *a family doctor of the old school*

10 [FISH] [C] a large group of fish, WHALES, DOLPHINS etc that are swimming together: [+of] *a school of whales*

school² v [T] **1** *old-fashioned* to train or teach someone to have a certain skill, type of behaviour, or way of thinking: **be schooled in (doing) sth** *She was schooled in hiding her emotions.* **2** to educate a child

'school age n [U] the age at which a child is old enough to go to school: *children below school age* —**school-age** adj: *a school-age child*

,school 'board n [C] a group of people, including some parents, who are elected to govern a school or group of schools in the US

school·book /ˈskuːlbʊk/ n [C] a book that is used in school classes; ▣ **textbook**

school·boy /ˈskuːlbɔɪ/ n [C] *especially BrE* **1** a boy attending school **2 schoolboy humour** jokes that are silly and rude but not offensive

school·child /ˈskuːltʃaɪld/ n *plural* **schoolchildren** /-tʃɪldrən/ [C] a child attending school; → see box at STUDENT

school·day /ˈskuːldeɪ/ n [C] **1** a day of the week when children are usually at school **2 sb's schooldays** the time of your life when you go to school

'school ,district n [C] an area in one state of the US that includes a number of schools which are governed together

'school friend n [C] *especially BrE* a friend who goes to the same school as you

school·girl /ˈskuːlɡɜːl $ -ɡɜːrl/ n [C] *especially BrE* a girl attending school

,school 'governor n [C] a member of a group of people in Britain who are elected to make decisions about how a school should be managed

school·house /ˈskuːlhaʊs/ n [C] a school building, especially for a small village school

school·ing /ˈskuːlɪŋ/ n [U] school education: *children in their final year of compulsory schooling (=the time* during which children have to attend school by law) | *Al's dad had only a few years of schooling.*

school·kid /'sku:lkɪd/ n [C] *informal* a child attending school

'school-,leaver n [C] *BrE* someone who has just left school, especially to do or look for a job rather than going to college, university etc: *a shortage of jobs for school-leavers*

school·marm /'sku:lmɑ:m $ -mɑ:rm/ n [C] a woman who is considered to be old-fashioned, strict, and easily shocked

school·mas·ter /'sku:l,mɑ:stə $ -,mæstər/ n [C] *BrE* a male teacher, especially in a PRIVATE SCHOOL (=one that parents pay to send their children to)

school·mate /'sku:lmeɪt/ n [C] someone who goes or went to the same school as you

school·mis·tress /'sku:l,mɪstrᵻs/ n [C] *BrE* a female teacher, especially in a PRIVATE SCHOOL (=one that parents pay to send their children to)

school·room /'sku:lru:m, -rʊm/ n [C] a room used for teaching in a small school

'school run n [C usually singular] *BrE* when parents drive their children to school in the morning or home from school in the afternoon: *We hope to increase the safety of children who walk to school and cut the number of cars doing the school run.*

school·teach·er /'sku:l,ti:tʃə $ -ər/ n [C] a TEACHER

,school 'tie n [C] **1** a special tie with a particular colour or pattern that children wear at some schools in Britain **2 the old school tie** *BrE informal* the unofficial system by which people who went to the same school, especially an expensive one, help each other to gain important positions later in their lives

school·work /'sku:lwɜ:k $ -wɜ:rk/ n [U] work done for or during school classes; → **homework**

school·yard /'sku:ljɑ:d $ -jɑ:rd/ n [C] *especially AmE* the area next to a school building where the children can go or play when they are not having lessons; ⊟ **playground** *BrE*

schoo·ner /'sku:nə $ -ər/ n [C] a fast sailing ship with two sails

schtick /ʃtɪk/ n [singular] a typical quality or feature that someone, especially an entertainer, is famous for: *Eminem's whole schtick is being outrageous.*

schtum, schtoom, shtum /ʃtʊm/ adj [not before noun] quiet or silent: *The boss of the failed company is keeping schtum about his role in the disaster.*

schwa /ʃwɑ:/ n [C] *technical* **1** a vowel typically heard in parts of a word that are spoken without STRESS¹ (4), such as the 'a' in 'about' **2** the sign (ə), used to represent the vowel schwa

sci·at·ic /saɪˈætɪk/ adj *technical* relating to the HIPS

sci·at·i·ca /saɪˈætɪkə/ adj pain in the lower back, HIPS and legs

sci·ence S1 W1 /'saɪəns/ n
1 [U] knowledge about the world, especially based on examining, testing, and proving facts: *Many leading scientists do not consider that science can give absolutely reliable knowledge.* | *the founder of modern science, Isaac Newton* | *developments in science and technology*
2 [U] the study of science: *What did you do in science class today?*
3 [C] a particular part of science, for example BIOLOGY, CHEMISTRY, or PHYSICS: *the physical sciences*
4 sth is not an exact science used to say that something involves a lot of guessing and there is not just one right way to do it: *Advertising is not an exact science – you're always taking a risk.* → DOMESTIC SCIENCE, INFORMATION SCIENCE, NATURAL SCIENCE, PHYSICAL SCIENCE, SOCIAL SCIENCE; → **blind sb with science** at BLIND² (4); → **sth is not rocket science** at ROCKET SCIENCE

,science 'fiction n [U] stories about events in the future which are affected by imaginary developments in science, for example about travelling in time or to other PLANETS with life on them

'science park n [C] an area where there are a lot of companies or organizations that do scientific work

sci·en·tif·ic S3 W2 /,saɪən'tɪfɪk◂ / adj
1 [no comparative] about or related to science, or using its methods: *We believe in investing in scientific research.* | *the limits of scientific knowledge* | *decisions based on scientific evidence* | *the international scientific community* (=scientists)
2 *informal* using an organized system: *I keep accounts for the business, but I'm not scientific about it.*
3 the scientific method the usual process of finding out information in science, which involves testing your ideas by performing EXPERIMENTS and making decisions based on the results —**scientifically** /-kli/ adv: *It hasn't been scientifically proven though.*

sci·en·tist S3 W2 /'saɪəntᵻst/ n [C] someone who works or is trained in science

sci-fi /,saɪ 'faɪ◂ / n [U] *informal* SCIENCE FICTION

scim·i·tar /'sɪmᵻtə $ -ər/ n [C] a sword with a curved blade that was used in the past

scin·til·la /sɪn'tɪlə/ n [singular] a very small amount of something: [+of] *There isn't a scintilla of evidence to prove it.*

scin·til·lat·ing /'sɪntᵻleɪtɪŋ/ adj interesting, clever, and amusing: *scintillating conversation* | *a scintillating performance*

sci·on /'saɪən/ n [C] *literary* a young member of a famous or important family: [+of] *a scion of an ancient Scottish family*

scis·sors /'sɪzəz $ -ərz/ n [plural] a tool for cutting paper, cloth etc, made of two sharp blades fastened together in the middle, with holes for your finger and thumb: *a pair of scissors* → see picture at SEWING

scle·ro·sis /sklᵻ'rəʊsᵻs $ -'roʊ-/ n [U] *technical* a disease that causes an organ or soft part of your body to become hard —**sclerotic** /sklᵻ'rɒtɪk $ -'rɑ:-/ adj → MULTIPLE SCLEROSIS

scoff /skɒf $ skɔ:f, skɑ:f/ v **1** [I,T] to laugh at a person or idea, and talk about them in a way that shows you think they are stupid; ⊟ **make fun of**: [+at] *David scoffed at her fears.* | *Officials scoffed at the idea.* | 'You, a scientist!' he scoffed. **2** [T] *BrE informal* to eat something very quickly: *She scoffed the plate of biscuits.*

scold /skəʊld $ skoʊld/ v [T] to angrily criticize someone, especially a child, about something they have done; ⊟ **tell off**: *Do not scold the puppy, but simply and firmly say 'no.'* | **scold sb for (doing) sth** *Her father scolded her for upsetting her mother.* —**scolding** n [C,U]: *I got a scolding from my teacher.*

scol·lop /'skɒləp $ 'skɑ:-/ n another spelling of SCALLOP

sconce /skɒns $ skɑ:ns/ n [C] an object that is attached to a wall and holds CANDLES or electric lights

scone /skɒn, skəʊn $ skoʊn, skɑ:n/ n [C] a small round cake, sometimes containing dried fruit, which is usually eaten with butter: *tea and scones*

scoop¹ /sku:p/ n [C] **1** an important or exciting news story that is printed in one newspaper or shown on one television station before any of the others know about it: *a journalist looking for a scoop* **2** a round deep spoon for serving food, for example ICE CREAM or MASHED potato **3** also **scoopful** an amount of food served with a scoop: [+of] *two scoops of ice cream* **4** *AmE informal* information about something: *the inside scoop* (=special information that other people do not have) *on the markets* | **what's the scoop?** (=used to ask for information or news)

scoop² v [T] **1** [always + adv/prep] to pick something up or remove it using a scoop or a spoon, or your curved hand: *She bent down and scooped up the little dog.* | *Cut the tomato in half and scoop out the seeds with a teaspoon.* **2** to be the first newspaper to print an important news report: *Time and again we have scooped our rivals.* **3** *BrE* to win a prize or AWARD: *Britain scooped the top prize in the over 50s category.*

scoop sth ⇔ **up** *phr v* if a lot of people scoop something up, they buy it quickly so that soon there is none left: *Fans scooped up the trading cards in the first few hours of the sale.*

'**scoop** ,**neck** also '**scoop** ,**neckline** *n* [C] a round, quite low neck on a woman's TOP

scoot /skuːt/ *v informal* **1** [I] to move quickly and suddenly: *There's the bus – I'd better scoot!* | [+off] *She scooted off on her bike.* **2** [T] *especially AmE* to make someone or something move a short distance by pulling or pushing: *I scooted my chair over to their table.*

scoot over *phr v AmE informal* to move to one side, especially in order to make room for someone or something else: *He scooted over so I could sit down.*

scoot·er /'skuːtə $ -ər/ *n* [C] **1** also **motor scooter** a type of small, less powerful MOTORCYCLE with small wheels **2** a child's vehicle with two small wheels, an upright handle, and a narrow board that you stand on with one foot, while the other foot pushes against the ground

scope¹ [W3] /skəʊp $ skoʊp/ *n*
1 [U] the range of things that a subject, activity, book etc deals with: [+of] *the need to define the scope of the investigation* | *measures to limit the scope of criminals' activities* | **beyond/outside/within the scope of sth** *A full discussion of that issue is beyond the scope of this book.* | **widen/broaden/extend etc the scope of sth** *Let us extend the scope of the study to examine more factors.* | **narrow/limit etc the scope of sth** *The court's ruling narrowed the scope of the affirmative action program.* | **limited/wider etc in scope** *His efforts were too limited in scope to have much effect.*
2 [U] the opportunity to do or develop something: [+for] *The scope for successful gardening increases dramatically with a greenhouse.* | **there is considerable/great/little etc scope for sth** *There is considerable scope for further growth in the economy.*
3 [singular] *informal* a particular set of activities and the people who are involved in them; **⊟ scene**: **the music/cinema/club etc scope**

scope² *v*
scope sb/sth ⇔ **out** *phr v AmE informal* to look at something or someone to see what they are like: *Let's go inside and scope out the menu.*

scorch¹ /skɔːtʃ $ skɔːrtʃ/ *v* **1** [I,T] if you scorch something, or if it scorches, its surface burns slightly and changes colour: *The walls had been blackened and scorched by fire.* **2** [T] if strong heat or wind scorches plants, it dries and damages them: *Direct sunlight will scorch the plant's leaves.* **3** [T] if strong heat scorches you, it burns you: *The hot sand scorched our feet.* **4** [I always + adv/prep] *BrE informal* to travel extremely fast: [+along/down/across etc] *He scorched out of the gate, almost crashing his new sports car.* —**scorched** *adj*

scorch² *n* **1** [C] a mark made on something where its surface has been burnt: *There were scorch marks on the kitchen worktop where a hot pan had been placed.* **2** [U] brown colouring on plants caused by some plant diseases

,**scorched 'earth ,policy** *n* [C] the destruction by an army of everything useful in an area, especially crops, so that the land cannot be used by an enemy

scorch·er /'skɔːtʃə $ 'skɔːrtʃər/ *n* [C usually singular] *informal* an extremely hot day: *It was a scorcher of a day.*

scorch·ing /'skɔːtʃɪŋ $ 'skɔːr-/ *adj, adv* extremely hot: *the scorching desert heat* | *It was a scorching hot day.*

score¹ [S3] [W2] /skɔː $ skɔːr/ *n* [C]
1 [IN A GAME] the number of points that each team or player has won in a game or competition: *At half-time the score was one-all.* | *What's the score?* | *Is anybody keeping score* (=making a record of the score)? | *The final score was Southampton two, Leeds United nil.* | [+of] *a score of 3–2*

2 [IN A TEST OR EXPERIMENT] **a)** the number of points a student has earned for correct answers in a test: *The school's test scores have not improved.* | [+of] *a score of 90%* **b)** the number of points that a person or group of people gets in a scientific test or EXPERIMENT: [+of] *He had an IQ score of 120.*
3 [MUSIC] a written or printed copy of a piece of music, especially for a large group of performers, or the music itself: *a musical score* | *Who wrote the score for the movie?*
4 **on that score** *spoken* concerning the particular thing you have just mentioned: *As for the cost, you don't need to worry on that score.*
5 **know the score** *informal* to know the real facts of a situation, including any unpleasant ones: *We are trying to attract managers who know the score.*
6 **settle a score** to do something to harm or hurt someone who has harmed or hurt you in the past: *Jack came back after five years to settle some old scores.*
7 [MARK] a mark that has been cut onto a surface with a sharp tool: *deep scores in the wood*

score² [W2] *v*
1 [WIN POINTS] [I,T] to win a point in a sport, game, competition, or test: *Great cheers went up when he scored in the final minute of the game.* | *She scored an average of 9.9 in the test.* | **score a goal/point/run etc** *He has scored 12 goals so far this season.*
2 [GIVE POINTS] [T] to give a particular number of points in a game, competition, test, or EXPERIMENT; **⊟ mark**: *Each event will be scored separately.* | *Responses to the individual items are scored on a scale ranging from 0 to 12.*
3 **score points** a) also **score off sb** *BrE* to say or do something in an attempt to prove that you are better or cleverer than someone else: *Too many MPs use debates as a chance to score political points.* | [+over/off] *Advertising may be used to score points off the competition.* b) *informal* to do or say something to please someone or to make them respect you: [+with] *You'll score points with your girlfriend if you send her roses.*
4 [SUCCEED] [I,T] *informal* to be very successful in something you do: *Her new book has scored a spectacular success.*
5 [HAVE SEX] [I] *informal* to have sex with someone, especially someone you have just met
6 [LINE] [T] to mark a line on a piece of paper, wood etc using a sharp instrument: *Scoring the paper first makes it easier to fold.*
7 [MUSIC] [T usually passive] to arrange a piece of music for a group of instruments or voices
8 [GET DRUGS] [I,T] *informal* to manage to buy or get illegal drugs

score off sb *phr v BrE*
to say or do something in an attempt to prove that you are better or cleverer than someone else: *He liked scoring off his pupils in his days as a teacher.*

score sth ⇔ **out/through** *phr v*
to draw a line through something that has been written

score³ *number* **1** *plural* **score** a group of 20, or about 20, people or things: **a score of sth** *Our coach was escorted by a score of policemen.* | **three score years and ten** *old use* (=70 years, a person's expected length of life) **2 scores of sth** a lot of people or things: *Scores of victims were killed.* **3 by the score** in large numbers: *Friends came to help by the score.*

score·board /'skɔːbɔːd $ 'skɔːrbɔːrd/ *n* [C] a board on which the points won in a game are recorded

score·card /'skɔːkɑːd $ 'skɔːrkɑːrd/ *n* [C] **1** a printed card used by someone watching a sports match or race to record what happens **2** a system that is used for checking or testing something

'**score draw** *n* [C] *BrE* a football match in which both teams score at least one GOAL and the final score is 1–1, 2–2, 3–3 etc

score·less /'skɔːləs $ 'skɔːr-/ *adj* if a sports match or part of a sports match is scoreless, nobody scores any points or GOALS : *a scoreless first half*

score·line /'skɔːlaɪn $ 'skɔːr-/ n [C] BrE the score or the final result in a football, RUGBY, or tennis match

scor·er /'skɔːrə $ -ər/ n [C] **1** also **score·keep·er** /'skɔːkiːpə $ 'skɔːrkiːpər/ someone who keeps an official record of the points won in a sports game **2** a player who wins a point or GOAL: **top/leading/highest scorer** He was Palace's top scorer.

score·sheet /'skɔːʃiːt $ 'skɔːr-/ n [C] **1** a special piece of paper on which someone records the points won in a sports match **2** **get (your name) on the scoresheet** BrE to score one or more GOALS or points in football, RUGBY, and some other sports

scorn¹ /skɔːn $ skɔːrn/ n [U] **1** the feeling that someone or something is stupid or does not deserve respect; ☐ **contempt**: [+for] He felt scorn for his working-class parents. | **with scorn** Rachel looked at me with scorn. **2** **pour scorn on sb/sth** also **heap scorn on sb/sth** AmE to strongly criticize someone or something because you think they do not deserve respect: Labour poured scorn on the Tory claim to be the party of law and order.

scorn² v [T] **1** to show that you think that something is stupid, unreasonable, or not worth accepting: Many women scorn the use of make-up. **2** to criticize someone or something because you think they do not deserve respect: He scorned the government's record in dealing with crime.

scorn·ful /'skɔːnfəl $ 'skɔːrn-/ adj feeling or showing scorn: a scornful look | [+of] He was scornful of the women's movement. —**scornfully** adv

Scor·pi·o /'skɔːpiəʊ $ 'skɔːrpioʊ/ n plural **Scorpios** **1** [U] the eighth sign of the ZODIAC, represented by a SCORPION, which some people believe affects the character and life of people born between October 24 and November 22 **2** [C] someone who was born between October 24 and November 22

scor·pi·on /'skɔːpiən $ -ɔːr-/ n [C] a tropical animal like an insect with a curving tail and a poisonous sting

Scot /skɒt $ skɑːt/ n [C] someone from Scotland

scotch /skɒtʃ $ skɑːtʃ/ v [T] to stop something happening by firmly doing something to prevent it: He issued an announcement to scotch rumours of his death.

Scotch¹ n [C,U] a strong alcoholic drink made in Scotland, or a glass of this: Two scotches, please.

Scotch² adj old-fashioned SCOTTISH

Scotch broth n [U] BrE thick soup made from vegetables, meat, and BARLEY (=type of grain)

Scotch egg n [C] BrE a cooked egg that is covered with meat and BREADCRUMBS, then FRIED

Scotch tape n [U] trademark AmE thin clear plastic tape that is sticky on one side, used for sticking light things such as paper together —**scotch tape** v [T]

scot-free /,skɒt 'friː $,skɑːt-/ adv **get away/off scot-free** informal to avoid being punished although you deserve to be

Scots /skɒts $ skɑːts/ adj Scottish

Scots·man /'skɒtsmən $ 'skɑːts-/ n plural **Scotsmen** /-mən/ [C] a man from Scotland

Scots·wom·an /'skɒts,wʊmən $ 'skɑːts-/ n plural **Scotswomen** /-,wɪmɪn/ [C] a woman from Scotland

Scot·tish /'skɒtɪʃ $ 'skɑːtɪʃ/ adj relating to Scotland or its people

scoun·drel /'skaʊndrəl/ n [C] old-fashioned a bad or dishonest man, especially someone who cheats or deceives other people

scour /skaʊə $ skaʊr/ v [T] **1** to search very carefully and thoroughly through an area, a document etc: **scour sth for sth** Her family began to scour the countryside for a suitable house. **2** also **scour out** to clean something very thoroughly by rubbing it with a rough material; ☐ **scrub**: Ada was scouring out the pans. → see picture at CLEAN **3** also **scour out** to form a hole by continuous movement over a long period: Over the years, the stream had scoured out a round pool in the rock.

scour·er /'skaʊərə $ 'skaʊərər/ also '**scouring pad** n [C] a small ball of wire or rough plastic for cleaning cooking pots and pans

scourge¹ /skɜːdʒ $ skɜːrdʒ/ n [C] **1** something that causes a lot of harm or suffering: [+of] the scourge of unemployment | the scourge of war **2** a WHIP used to punish people in the past

scourge² v [T] **1** to cause a lot of harm or suffering to a place or group of people **2** to hit someone with a whip as punishment in the past

Scouse /skaʊs/ n [U] BrE the way of speaking that is typical of people from Liverpool —**Scouse** adj

Scous·er /'skaʊsə $ -ər/ n [C] BrE informal someone from the city of Liverpool in England

scout¹ /skaʊt/ n [C] **1 a)** the Scouts an organization for boys that teaches them practical skills **b)** also **boy scout** a boy who is a member of this organization **2** AmE also **Girl Scout** a girl who is a member of an organization for girls that teaches them practical things; ☐ **guide** BrE **3** a soldier, plane etc that is sent to search the area in front of an army and get information about the enemy: He sent three scouts ahead to take a look at the bridge. **4** also **talent scout** someone whose job is to look for good sports players, musicians etc in order to employ them: He was spotted by a scout at the age of 13.

scout² v **1** [I] also **scout around/round** to look for something in a particular area: [+for] I'm scouting round for a place to stay. **2** [T] also **scout out** to examine a place or area in order to get information about it: American companies are keen to scout out business opportunities in Vietnam. **3** [I,T] to find out about the abilities of sports players, musicians etc in order to employ them

scout·ing /'skaʊtɪŋ/ n [U] the activities that Scouts take part in

scout·mas·ter /'skaʊt,mɑːstə $ -,mæstər/ n [C] a man who is the leader of a group of Scouts

scowl¹ /skaʊl/ v [I] to look at someone in an angry way; → **frown**: Patrick scowled, but did as he was told. | [+at] Mum scowled at him and refused to say anything.

scowl² n [C] an angry or disapproving expression on someone's face; → **frown**: She looked at me with a scowl on her face.

scrab·ble /'skræbəl/ v [I always + adv/prep] to try to find or do something quickly, usually by moving your hands or feet in an uncontrolled way: [+for] He scrabbled for the light switch. | [+around/about] She was scrabbling around, searching for the door.

Scrabble n [U] trademark a game in which players try to make words from the separate letters they have

scrag·gly /'skrægli/ adj informal growing in a way that looks uneven and in bad condition: his **scraggly** gray **beard**

scrag·gy /'skrægi/ adj BrE too thin: a scraggy neck

scram /skræm/ v **scrammed, scramming** [I usually in imperative] informal to leave a place very quickly, especially so that you do not get caught: Scram, you two!

scram·ble¹ /'skræmbəl/ v
1 CLIMB [I always + adv/prep] to climb up, down, or over something quickly and with difficulty, especially using your hands to help you: [+up/down/over etc] They tried to scramble up the cliff. | She scrambled down the tree as quickly as she could.
2 MOVE QUICKLY [I always + adv/prep] to move somewhere in a hurried awkward way: [+to/out/from etc] Alan scrambled out of the way. | Micky **scrambled** to his **feet** (=stood up very quickly and awkwardly) and hurried into the kitchen.
3 DO STH QUICKLY [T] to try to do something difficult very quickly: **scramble to do sth** They were scrambling to give the impression that the situation was in control.
4 COMPETE [I] to struggle or compete with other

people to get or reach something: [+**for**] *Thousands of people will be scrambling for tickets.*
5 INFORMATION/MESSAGE [T] to use special equipment to mix messages, radio signals etc into a different form, so that they cannot be understood by other people without the correct equipment: *Our conversation will be electronically scrambled.*
6 MIX [T] to mix words, ideas, sentences etc so that they are not in the right order and do not make sense: *In this exercise, the words in each sentence are scrambled.*
7 scramble an egg to cook an egg by mixing the white and yellow parts together and heating it in a pan → see picture at EGG¹
8 scramble sb's brains *informal* to make someone unable to think clearly or reasonably: *Maybe the alcohol has scrambled his brains.*
9 AIRCRAFT [I] if a military plane scrambles, it goes up into the air very quickly in order to escape or to attack an enemy

scramble² n **1** [singular] a difficult climb in which you have to use your hands to help you: *The village was a 20-minute scramble away.* **2** [singular] a situation in which people compete with and push each other in order to get what they want: [+**for**] *the usual scramble for the bathroom every morning* | **scramble to do sth** *a scramble to carry the baggage into the house* **3** [singular] a situation in which something has to be done very quickly, with a lot of rushing around: *It was a **mad scramble** trying to get things ready in time.* **4** [C] *BrE* a MOTORCYCLE race over rough ground

scrambled 'egg n [C,U] eggs cooked in a pan after the white and yellow parts have been mixed together

scram·bler /'skræmblə $ -ər/ n [C] a machine that mixes up a radio or telephone message so that it cannot be understood without special equipment

scram·bling /'skræmblɪŋ/ n [U] **1** the activity of climbing over rocks using your hands but no ropes **2** *BrE* the activity of racing on MOTORCYCLES over rough ground

scrap¹ /skræp/ n
1 PAPER/CLOTH [C] a small piece of paper, cloth etc: [+**of**] *He wrote his address on a scrap of paper.* | *a rug made out of old scraps of material*
2 OLD OBJECTS [U] materials or objects that are no longer used for the purpose they were made for, but can be used again in another way: *The equipment was **sold for scrap**.* | *Scrap metal* (=metal from old cars, machines etc) *fetched high prices after the war.*
3 FOOD scraps [plural] pieces of food that are left after you have finished eating: *My mother fed the dog on scraps to save money.* | **table/kitchen scraps** *AmE*
4 INFORMATION [C] a small amount of information, truth etc: [+**of**] *He obtained every scrap of information available.* | *There isn't a single scrap of evidence.*
5 FIGHT [C] *informal* a short fight or argument: *He's always getting into scraps with other dogs.*

scrap² v **scrapped, scrapping 1** [T] to decide not to use a plan or system because it is not practical: *We believe that car tax should be scrapped.* **2** [T] to get rid of an old machine, vehicle etc, and use its parts in some other way: *The navy's biggest aircraft carrier is being scrapped this year.* **3** [I] *informal* to have a short fight

scrap·book /'skræpbʊk/ n [C] a book with empty pages where you can stick pictures, newspaper articles, or other things you want to keep

scrape¹ /skreɪp/ v **1** [T] to remove something from a surface using the edge of a knife, a stick etc: *Scrape the carrots and slice them thinly.* | **scrape sth away/off** *The earth was scraped away to uncover a trap door.* | **scrape sth off/into etc sth** *Teresa scraped the mud off her boots.* | *The two of them **scraped** their dishes **clean**.* → see picture at CLEAN **2** [I,T always + adv/prep] to rub against a rough surface in a way that causes slight damage or injury, or to make something do this; → **graze**: *The coat was too long; the hem scraped the pavement.* | [+**against/on etc**] *I heard the side of the car scrape against the wall.* | **scrape sth against/on sth** *I scraped my knee painfully on the concrete.* **3** [I,T] to make a noise by rubbing roughly against a surface: *Chairs scraped loudly as they stood up.* | **scrape (sth) on/down/against sth** *He opened the gate quietly, trying not to let it scrape on the gravel.* **4** scrape home *especially BrE* to win a race, election, or competition by a very small amount: *The Tories may scrape home, but it's unlikely.* **5** scrape (the bottom of) the barrel *informal* to have to use something even though it is not very good, because there is nothing better available: *It was clear that the party was scraping the barrel for competent politicians.* → **bow and scrape** at BOW¹ (5); → **scrape/scratch a living** at LIVING² (1)

scrape sth ⇔ **back** *phr v* if you scrape your hair back, you pull it away from your face and tie it at the back: *Her blonde hair was scraped back into a ponytail.*
scrape by *phr v* **1** to have just enough money to live: *In the rural areas, people could scrape by, thanks to what they grew themselves.* **2** to only just succeed in passing an examination or dealing with a difficult situation
scrape in also **scrape into sth** *phr v* to only just succeed in getting a job, a place at university, a position in government etc: *Labour scraped in by a small majority.* | *He just scraped into college.*
scrape through (sth) *phr v* to only just succeed in passing an examination or dealing with a difficult situation: *I managed to scrape through the exam.*
scrape sth ⇔ **together/up** *phr v* to get enough money for a particular purpose, when this is difficult: *She scraped together the last of her savings.* | *They could hardly scrape up enough money for the train fare.*

scrape² n **1** [C] a mark or slight injury caused by rubbing against a rough surface; ▤ **graze**: *I came away from the accident with only cuts and scrapes.* **2** [C] *informal* a situation in which you are in trouble or have difficulties: *He got into all sorts of scrapes as a boy.* **3** [singular] the noise made when one surface rubs roughly against another: [+**of**] *He heard the scrape of chairs being dragged across the floor.*

scrap·er /'skreɪpə $ -ər/ n [C] a tool used to remove something from a surface by rubbing: *a paint scraper*

scrap·heap /'skræphiːp/ n **1** on the scrapheap *informal* not wanted or used any more – used especially when this seems unfair: *Three years later he was on the political scrapheap.* **2** [C] a pile of unwanted things, especially pieces of metal

scra·pie /'skreɪpi/ n [U] a serious disease that sheep get

scrap·ings /'skreɪpɪŋz/ n [plural] small pieces that have been SCRAPED from a surface

'scrap ,paper n [U] paper, often paper that has already been used on one side, that you use for making notes, lists etc

scrap·py /'skræpi/ adj **1** *BrE* untidy or badly organized: *scrappy notes from the meeting* **2** *AmE informal* having a determined character and always willing to compete, argue, or fight: *a scrappy team that plays hard*

scratch¹ /skrætʃ/ v
1 RUB YOUR SKIN [I,T] to rub your skin with your nails because it feels uncomfortable; → **itch**: *John yawned and scratched his leg.* | *Try not to scratch.* | [+**at**] *He was scratching at the bites on his arm.*
2 CUT SB'S SKIN [I,T] to cut someone's skin slightly with your nails or with something sharp: *She ran at him and scratched his face.* | *Don't scratch yourself on the thorns.*
3 MAKE A MARK [T] to make a small cut or mark on something by pulling something sharp across it: *I'm afraid I've scratched your car.* | *Some of the prisoners had scratched their names on the walls.*
4 ANIMALS [I always + adv/prep] if an animal

scratches, it rubs its feet against something, often making a noise: *A few chickens scratched around in the yard.* | [+at] *a dog scratching at the door to be let in*

5 REMOVE STH [T always + adv/prep] to remove something from a surface by rubbing it with something sharp: **scratch sth off/away etc** *I scratched away a little of the paint with my fingernail.*

6 REMOVE WRITING [T always + adv/prep] to remove a word from a piece of writing by drawing a line through it: **scratch sth from/off sth** *I have scratched his name from the list.*

7 MAKE A NOISE [I always + adv/prep] to make a rough sound by moving something sharp across a surface: *His pen scratched away on the paper.*

8 scratch the surface to deal with only a very small part of a subject or problem: [+of] *I think we have only scratched the surface of this problem.*

9 scratch your head *informal* to think carefully about a difficult question or problem: *This crisis has politicians scratching their heads and wondering what to do.*

10 STOP STH HAPPENING [T] *informal* if you scratch an idea or a plan, you decide that you will not do it

11 REMOVE FROM RACE [I,T] *informal* if someone scratches from a race, or if you scratch them from the race, they do not take part in it

12 you scratch my back, I'll scratch yours *spoken* used to say that you will help someone if they agree to help you → **scrape/scratch a living** at LIVING² (1)

scratch around also **scratch about** *BrE phr v*
to try to find or get something which is difficult to find or get: [+for] *homeless people scratching around for a place to shelter*

scratch sth ⇔ **out** *phr v*
to remove a word from a piece of writing by drawing a line through it: *Emma's name had been scratched out.*

scratch² n

1 CUT [C] a small cut on someone's skin: *There were deep scratches all over her face.* | *Don't worry, it's only a scratch* (=not a serious injury). | *She was unharmed apart from a few cuts and scratches.*

2 MARK [C] a thin mark or cut on the surface of something: *There was a big scratch on the car door.*

3 from scratch if you start something from scratch, you begin it without using anything that existed or was prepared before: *We had to start again from scratch.* | *He had built the business up from scratch.*

4 up to scratch *BrE informal* good enough for a particular standard: *Some of this work isn't up to scratch.* | **bring/get sth up to scratch** *We spent thousands of pounds getting the house up to scratch.*

5 RUB [singular] *especially BrE* when you rub part of your body with your nails because it feels uncomfortable: *He stretched and had a scratch.* | *He brushed his hair and gave his scalp a good scratch.*

6 SOUND [C] a sound made by something sharp or rough being rubbed on a hard surface: *I heard the scratch of a match lighting a cigarette.*

scratch³ adj [no comparative]

1 a scratch team or group of people has been put together in a hurry, using anyone that is available **2** a scratch player in golf is very good and is not given any advantage in games

scratch·card also **scratch card** /'skrætʃkɑːd $ -kɑːrd/ n [C] *BrE* a small card you can buy which gives you a chance to win a prize. You rub off the surface of the card to find out whether you have won anything.

scratch·ings /'skrætʃɪŋz/ n [plural] *BrE* small pieces of pig's skin that have been cooked in hot fat and are eaten cold; ☐ **pork rinds** *AmE*

scratch·pad /'skrætʃpæd/ n [C] **1** *AmE* several sheets of cheap paper that are joined together into a small book you can write notes in **2** a small screen on a MOBILE PHONE that lets you write short notes and stores them for you

'scratch ,paper n [U] *AmE* cheap paper, or paper that has already been used on one side, that you use for writing notes; ☐ **scrap paper**

scratch·y /'skrætʃi/ adj **1** something that is scratchy feels rough against your skin: *a scratchy woollen jumper* **2** a scratchy voice or musical sound is rough and not smooth and pleasant: *a scratchy old recording of some folk songs*

scrawl¹ /skrɔːl $ skrɒːl/ v [T] to write in a careless and untidy way, so that your words are not easy to read; → **scribble**: *He scrawled his name at the bottom of the page.*

scrawl² n [C,U] untidy, careless writing: *The note was written in his usual illegible scrawl.*

scraw·ny /'skrɔːni $ 'skrɒː-/ adj a scrawny person or animal looks very thin and weak: *a scrawny kid in jeans and a T-shirt* | *a few scrawny hens*

scream¹ /skriːm/ v **1** [I] to make a loud high noise with your voice because you are hurt, frightened, excited etc; ☐ **shriek**: *After the first few shots, people started screaming.* | *a screaming baby* | [+with/in] *She jumped to her feet, screaming in terror.* | *The children were screaming with laughter.* | *She was screaming her head off* (=screaming a lot). | *She began to scream blue murder* (=scream very loudly). | *He was dragged kicking and screaming to a nearby van.* **2** [I,T] also **scream out** to shout something in a very loud high voice because you are angry or frightened; ☐ **yell**: *'Get out!' she screamed.* | *He screamed out her name.* | [+for] *I screamed for help.* | [+at] *He screamed at her to go away.* | *The crowd continued to scream abuse at him.* **3** [I] to make a very loud high noise: *The police car approached, its siren screaming.*

scream² n [C] **1** a loud high sound that you make with your voice because you are hurt, frightened, excited etc; ☐ **shriek**: *We heard screams coming from the flat.* | *She saw the knife and let out a scream.* | **scream of laughter/terror etc** *He fell back with a scream of terror and pain.* **2** a very loud high sound: *the scream of a jet taking off* **3 a scream** *informal* someone or something that is very funny: *The film was a scream!*

scream·ing·ly /'skriːmɪŋli/ adv extremely: *a screamingly funny film*

scree /skriː/ n [C] an area of loose soil and broken rocks on the side of a mountain: *a scree slope*

screech /skriːtʃ/ v **1** [I,T] to shout loudly in an unpleasant high voice because you are angry, afraid, or excited; ☐ **shriek, scream**: *'Look out!' she screeched.* | *They screeched with laughter.* | [+at] *She screeched at me to take off my muddy shoes.* **2** [I] if a vehicle screeches, its wheels make a high unpleasant noise as it moves along or stops: *A van screeched onto the road in front of me.* | *The car screeched to a halt.* —**screech** n [C]: *a screech of laughter* | *a screech of tyres*

screed /skriːd/ n [C] a very long, boring piece of writing – used to show disapproval

screen¹ S2 W2 /skriːn/ n

1 TELEVISION/COMPUTER [C] the part of a television or computer where the picture or information appears; → **monitor**: *a computer with an 18-inch colour screen* | *He went on staring at the TV screen.* | **on (a) screen** *Her picture appeared on the screen.* | *It's easy to change the text on screen before printing it.*; → see picture at OFFICE

2 FILM a) [C] the large white surface that pictures are shown on in a cinema: *He was horrified at some of the images he saw on the screen.* **b)** [singular, U] films in general: *This is the first time the play has been adapted for the big screen* (=films). | *a star of stage and screen* (=the theatre and films) | **on screen** *his first appearance on screen* | *a well-known screen actor*

3 MOVABLE WALL [C] a piece of furniture like a thin wall that can be moved around and is used to divide one part of a room from another: *There was a screen around his bed.*

4 STH THAT HIDES a) [C] something tall and wide that hides a place or thing: [+of] *The house was hidden behind a screen of bushes.* **b)** [singular] something that hides what someone is doing: [+for] *The business was*

just a screen for his drug-dealing activities.
5 TEST FOR ILLNESS [C] *BrE* a medical test to see whether someone has an illness; ▣ **screening** *AmE: The company is offering a free health screen to all employees.*
6 DOOR/WINDOW [C] a wire net fastened inside a frame in front of a window or door to keep insects out
7 CHURCH [C] a decorative wall in some churches
8 SPORTS [C] a player in a game such as BASKETBALL who protects the player who has the ball → SMOKESCREEN, SUNSCREEN

screen² *v* [T]
1 TEST FOR ILLNESS to do tests on a lot of people to find out whether they have a particular illness: *All women over 50 will be regularly screened.* | **screen sb for sth** *It is now possible to screen babies for diabetes.*
2 HIDE STH if something screens something else, it is in front of it and hides it: **screen sth from sth** *A line of trees screened the house from the road.*
3 FILM/TELEVISION to show a film or television programme: *The film is now being screened at cinemas around the country.* | *The match will be screened live on television.*
4 TEST EMPLOYEES ETC to find out information about people in order to decide whether you can trust them: *Police are very careful when screening politicians' bodyguards.* | *Applicants are screened for security.*
5 CHECK THINGS to check things to see whether they are acceptable or suitable: *You can use an answerphone to screen your phone calls before you answer them.*
  screen sth ⇔ **off** *phr v*
to separate one part of a room from the rest by putting a thin temporary wall or a curtain across it: *The back part of the room had been screened off.*
  screen sth ⇔ **out** *phr v*
1 to prevent something harmful from passing through: *Sun lotions screen out damaging ultraviolet light.*
2 to remove people or things that are not acceptable or not suitable: *An answering service can screen out nuisance calls.*

'**screen ,door** *n* [C] *AmE* a door with wire net fastened inside a frame, which is used outside the main door of a building to keep insects out

'**screen dump** *n* [C] a picture of everything that appears on a computer screen at a particular time, which can be saved and put into a computer document, for example to show how to use a computer program

screen·ing /'skri:nɪŋ/ *n* **1** [C,U] the showing of a film or television programme: *a screening of Spielberg's new movie* **2** [U] medical tests that are done on a lot of people to make sure that they do not have a particular disease: [+**for**] *screening for breast cancer* **3** [U] tests or checks that are done to make sure that people or things are acceptable or suitable for a particular purpose: *security screening of airline passengers*

screen·play /'skri:npleɪ/ *n* [C] the words that are written down for actors to say in a film, and the instructions that tell them what they should do; ▣ **script**

'**screen ,printing** *n* [U] a way of printing pictures by forcing paint or ink through a specially prepared cloth onto paper or cloth —**screen print** *v* [T]

'**screen ,saver** *n* [C] a computer program that makes a moving image appear on the screen when the image on it has not changed for a period of time, especially so that the screen does not become damaged

'**screen ,test** *n* [C] an occasion when someone is filmed while they are performing, in order to see if they are suitable to act in a film

screen·writ·er /'skri:n,raɪtə $ -ər/ *n* [C] someone who writes plays for television or film; → **playwright**

screw¹ /skru:/ *n* [C] **1** a thin pointed piece of metal that you push and turn in order to fasten pieces of metal or wood together; → **nail**: *Fix the frame in position*

and tighten the screws. **2 a)** *informal not polite* an offensive word meaning an act of having sex **b) a good screw** *informal not polite* a very offensive word for someone who is good at having sex **3 have a screw loose** *informal* to be slightly crazy **4 put/tighten the screws on sb** *informal* to force someone to do something by threatening them: *The government has started to tighten the screws on illegal share dealers.* **5** *BrE informal* a prison officer – used especially by prisoners

screw² *v*
1 ATTACH [T always + adv/prep] to attach one thing to another using a screw; → **nail**: **screw sth into/onto/to sth** *The chairs were screwed to the floor.* | *The wooden frame should be screwed onto the wall.*
2 CLOSE BY TURNING [I,T always + adv/prep] to fasten or close something by turning it, or to be fastened in this way; ▣ **unscrew**: **screw (sth) on/onto sth** *The lens screws onto the front of the camera.* | *She carefully screwed the cap back onto the toothpaste.*
3 PAPER/CLOTH [T always + adv/prep] also **screw up** to twist paper or cloth into a small round shape: *She screwed the letter up and threw it in the bin.* | **screw sth (up) into sth** *I screwed my handkerchief into a ball.*
4 SEX [I,T] *taboo* an offensive word meaning to have sex with someone
5 screw you/him etc *spoken not polite* an offensive expression used to show that you are very angry with someone
6 CHEAT [T] *not polite* to cheat someone in order to get money from them: **screw sb for sth** *They screwed us for $60 in the end.* → **have your head screwed on (straight)** at HEAD¹ (3c)
  screw around *phr v*
1 *informal* to do silly things that may cause trouble; ▣ **mess around**: *The kids were screwing around down by the bus station.*
2 *not polite* an offensive expression meaning to have sex with a lot of different people
  screw up *phr v*
1 *informal* to make a bad mistake or do something very stupid; ▣ **mess up**: *You'd better not screw up this time.*
2 **screw sth** ⇔ **up** *informal* to spoil something by doing something stupid; ▣ **mess sth up**: *She realized that she had screwed up her life.*
3 **screw up your eyes/face** to move the muscles in your face in a way that makes your eyes seem narrow: *He screwed up his eyes against the bright light.* | *Her face was screwed up with pain.*
4 **screw sb** ⇔ **up** *informal* to make someone feel very unhappy, confused, or upset so that they have emotional problems for a long time; ▣ **mess sb up**: *It really screwed her up when her mother died.* → SCREWED UP
5 **screw up the/enough courage to do sth** also **screw up your courage** to be brave enough to do something you are very nervous about: *I finally screwed up enough courage to talk to her.*

screw·ball /'skru:bɔ:l $ -bɒ:l/ *n* [C] *informal especially AmE* someone who seems very strange or crazy

'**screwball ,comedy** *n* [C] *AmE* a film or television programme that is funny because crazy things happen

screw·driv·er /'skru:,draɪvə $ -ər/ *n* [C] **1** a tool with a narrow blade at one end that you use for turning screws **2** an alcoholic drink made from VODKA and orange juice

,**screwed 'up** *adj informal* someone who is screwed up has a lot of emotional problems because of bad or unhappy experiences in the past

'**screw top** *n* [C] a top for a bottle or other container that you fasten on by turning it —**screw-top** *adj* [only before noun]

screw·y /'skru:i/ *adj informal* an idea or plan that is screwy seems very strange or crazy

scrib·ble¹ /'skrɪbəl/ *v* **1** [T] also **scribble down** to write something quickly and untidily: *I scribbled his phone number in my address book.* | *He scribbled down our names.* **2** [I] to draw marks that have no meaning: *Someone had scribbled all over my picture.*

scribble² n **1** [U] also **scribbles** meaningless marks or pictures, especially done by children **2** [singular, U] untidy writing that is difficult to read: *I couldn't read his scribble.*

scrib·bler /'skrɪblə $ -ər/ n [C] *informal* a writer, especially an unimportant one

scribe /skraɪb/ n [C] **1** someone in the past whose job was to make written copies of official documents **2** a JOURNALIST - used humorously

scrim·mage /'skrɪmɪdʒ/ n [C] **1** *informal* a fight **2** *AmE* a practice game of football, BASKETBALL etc

scrimp /skrɪmp/ v [I] to try to save as much money as you can, even though you have very little: *They scrimped and saved for years to buy their own home.*

script /skrɪpt/ n **1** [C] the written form of a speech, play, film etc; → **screenplay**: *They write all their own scripts.* | *a film script* **2** [C,U] the set of letters that are used in writing a language: *Arabic script* **3** [C] *BrE* a piece of work that a student writes in an examination **4** [singular, U] *formal* writing done by hand: *a diary entry written in neat black script*

script·ed /'skrɪptɪd/ adj a speech or broadcast that is scripted has been written down before it is read

scrip·tur·al /'skrɪptʃərəl/ adj contained in the Bible or based on the Bible

scrip·ture /'skrɪptʃə $ -ər/ n **1 Scripture** [U] also **the (Holy) Scriptures** the Bible: *the way God is portrayed in Scripture* **2** [C,U] the holy books of a particular religion: *Hindu scriptures*

script·writ·er /'skrɪpt,raɪtə $ -ər/ n [C] someone who writes the stories and words for films or television programmes; ⊟ **screenwriter**; → **playwright**

scroll¹ /skrəʊl $ skroʊl/ n [C] **1** a long piece of paper that can be rolled up, and is used as an official document **2** a design shaped like a piece of rolled up paper

scroll² v [I always + adv/prep] to move information on a computer screen up or down so that you can read it: [+through] *He scrolled through the document.* | [+up/down] *Could you scroll down a few lines?*

'scroll bar n [C] a part on the side of a computer screen that you move using a MOUSE in order to move up or down

Scrooge, **scrooge** /skruːdʒ/ n [C] *informal* someone who hates spending money: *You're turning into a real scrooge!*

scro·tum /'skrəʊtəm $ 'skroʊ-/ n plural **scrota** /-tə/ or **scrotums** [C] the bag of skin that contains a man's TESTICLES

scrounge¹ /skraʊndʒ/ v [I,T] *informal* to get money or something you want by asking other people for it rather than by paying for it yourself: [+for] *a group of children scrounging for food* | **scrounge sth off/from sb** *I managed to scrounge some money off my dad.* | **scrounge around (for sth)** *AmE: Leroy would scrounge around for old car parts.* —**scrounger** n [C]

scrounge² n **be on the scrounge** *BrE informal* to be trying to get money or things you want by asking other people for them

scrub¹ /skrʌb/ v **scrubbed**, **scrubbing** **1** [I,T] to rub something hard, especially with a stiff brush, in order to clean it: *She was on her hands and knees scrubbing the floor.* | *He scrubbed the dirt off his boots.* | *The table needs to be scrubbed.* | [+at] *She scrubbed at her face with a tissue.* → see picture at CLEAN **2** [T] *informal* to decide not to do something that you had planned; ⊟ **cancel**: *We scrubbed the idea in the end.*

scrub sth ⇔ out phr v to clean the inside of a place thoroughly: *The rooms are all scrubbed out once a week.*

scrub up phr v to wash your hands and arms before doing a medical operation

scrub² n **1** [U] low bushes and trees that grow in very dry soil **2** [singular] *especially BrE* if you give something a scrub, you clean it by rubbing it hard: *I gave the floor a good scrub.*

scrub·ber /'skrʌbə $ -ər/ n [C] *BrE taboo old-fashioned informal* an offensive word for a woman who has sex for money, or has sex with a lot of different men. Do not use this word.

'scrubbing brush *especially BrE*; **'scrub brush** *AmE* n [C] a stiff brush that you use for cleaning things → see picture at BRUSH¹

scrub·by /'skrʌbi/ adj **1** scrubby land is covered by low bushes **2** scrubby trees and bushes are small and do not look very healthy

scrub·land /'skrʌblənd/ n [U] an area of land that is covered with low bushes

scruff /skrʌf/ n **1 by the scruff of the neck** if you hold a person or animal by the scruff of their neck, you hold the skin, fur, or clothes at the back of their neck **2** [C] *BrE informal* someone who looks untidy or dirty

scruf·fy /'skrʌfi/ adj dirty and untidy: *a scruffy old pair of jeans* | *scruffy shops* —**scruffily** adv: *a scruffily dressed man* —**scruffiness** n [U]; → see picture at TIDY¹

scrum /skrʌm/ n **1** [C] a part of a game of RUGBY when the players all push together in a circle, with their heads down, and try to get the ball **2** [singular] *BrE informal* a crowd of people who are all close together and pushing each other to try to get something: *He struggled through the scrum of people to the kitchen.*

scrum·half /,skrʌm'hɑːf $ -'hæf/ n [C] a player in RUGBY who has to put the ball into the SCRUM

scrum·mage /'skrʌmɪdʒ/ n [C] a SCRUM (1)

scrump /skrʌmp/ v [T] *BrE old-fashioned* to steal fruit from trees in people's gardens

scrump·tious /'skrʌmpʃəs/ adj *informal* food that is scrumptious tastes very good: *a scrumptious chocolate cake* | *That was absolutely scrumptious!*

scrum·py /'skrʌmpi/ n [U] *BrE* a strong alcoholic drink made from apples

scrunch /skrʌntʃ/ v [I] *informal* if stones, leaves etc scrunch as you walk on them, they make a noisy sound: *The dry leaves scrunched under our feet.* —**scrunch** n [singular]: *the scrunch of gravel*

scrunch sth ⇔ up phr v **1** to crush and twist something into a small round shape: *I scrunched up the letter and threw it in the bin.* **2 scrunch up your face/eyes** to move the muscles in your face in a way that makes your eyes seem narrow: *He scrunched up his eyes and grinned.*

scrunch·y, **scrunchie** /'skrʌntʃi/ n plural **scrunchies** [C] a small circular piece of rubber covered loosely with cloth, which is used for holding hair together in a PONYTAIL

scru·ple¹ /'skruːpəl/ n [C usually plural, U] a belief about what is right and wrong that prevents you from doing bad things: *scruples about doing sth He had no scruples about selling faulty goods to people.* | *a man with no moral scruples* | *without scruple They made thousands of families homeless without scruple.*

scruple² v **not scruple to do sth** *literary* to be willing to do something even though it may be wrong or may upset people: *They did not scruple to bomb innocent civilians.*

scru·pu·lous /'skruːpjʊləs/ adj **1** very careful to be completely honest and fair; ⊟ **unscrupulous**: *Not all lawyers are as scrupulous as she is.* | *scrupulous honesty* | **scrupulous in (doing) sth** *The organization will be scrupulous in maintaining the highest moral standards.* **2** doing something very carefully so that nothing is left out: *scrupulous about (doing) sth He was not very scrupulous about keeping himself clean.* | *scrupulous attention to detail* —**scrupulously** adv: *scrupulously clean* | *scrupulously fair*

S

[1] 000, [2] 000, [3] 000, most frequent words in [S]poken and [W]ritten English

scru·ti·neer /ˌskruːtɪˈnɪə $ -tnˈɪr/ n [C] BrE an official who checks that the votes in an election are counted fairly

scru·ti·nize also **-ise** BrE /ˈskruːtɪnaɪz/ v [T] to examine someone or something very carefully: *He scrutinized the document closely.* | *She scrutinized his face.*

scru·ti·ny /ˈskruːtɪni/ n [U] careful and thorough examination of someone or something: **careful/close scrutiny** *Careful scrutiny of the company's accounts revealed a whole series of errors.* | *Their activities have come under police scrutiny.*

SCSI /ˈskʌzi/ n [U] **small computer systems interface** something that helps a small computer work with another piece of electronic equipment, such as a PRINTER, especially when they are connected by wires: *a SCSI port*

scuba diver

breathing apparatus

scu·ba div·ing /ˈskuːbə ˌdaɪvɪŋ/ n [U] the sport of swimming under water while breathing through a tube that is connected to a container of air on your back —**scuba diver** n [C]

scud /skʌd/ v **scudded, scudding** [I always + adv/prep] *literary* if clouds scud across the sky, they move quickly

scuff /skʌf/ v [T] **1** to make a mark on a smooth surface by rubbing it against something rough: *His shoes were old and badly scuffed.* **2 scuff your feet/heels** to walk in a slow lazy way, not lifting your feet up very high

scuf·fle¹ /ˈskʌfəl/ n [C] a short fight that is not very violent: *Scuffles broke out between rival supporters during the match.* | [+with/between] *scuffles with police*

scuffle² v [I] **1** to have a short fight with someone, in a way that is not very serious or violent: [+with] *Some of the demonstrators scuffled with the police.* **2** [always + adv/prep] to walk quickly and make a noise as your feet rub on the ground

scuff·mark /ˈskʌfmɑːk $ -mɑːrk/ n [C] a mark made on something when it has rubbed against something rough

scull¹ /skʌl/ n [C] **1** a small light boat for only one person, used in races **2** one of a pair of OARS that you use to move along in a small light boat

scull² v [I,T] to make a small boat move along using a pair of OARS ; ▪ **row**

scul·le·ry /ˈskʌləri/ n plural **sculleries** [C] a room next to the kitchen in a large house, where cleaning jobs were done in past times

sculpt /skʌlpt/ v [T] to make a particular shape from wood, stone, clay etc

sculpt·ed /ˈskʌlptɪd/ adj [only before noun] having a clear, smooth shape that looks as though an artist had made it: *high, sculpted cheekbones*

sculp·tor /ˈskʌlptə $ -ər/ n [C] someone who makes sculptures

sculp·tress /ˈskʌlptrɪs/ n [C] old-fashioned a woman who makes sculptures

sculp·ture /ˈskʌlptʃə $ -ər/ n **1** [C,U] an object made out of stone, wood, clay etc by an artist: [+of] *a sculpture of an elephant* | *an exhibition of sculpture* **2** [U] the art of making objects out of stone, wood, clay etc

sculp·tured /ˈskʌlptʃəd $ -tʃərd/ adj [only before noun] **1** cut or formed from wood, stone, clay etc: *a row of sculptured animals* **2** having a smooth, attractive shape: *her sculptured face*

scum /skʌm/ n **1** [U] an unpleasant dirty substance that forms on the surface of water: *a pond covered with green scum* **2** [plural] *informal* nasty, unpleasant people: *Scum like that should be locked away!* | *People like that are* **the scum of the earth.** —**scummy** adj

scum·bag /ˈskʌmbæg/ n [C] spoken informal not polite a nasty, unpleasant person

scup·per¹ /ˈskʌpə $ -ər/ v [T] BrE **1** to ruin someone's plans or chance of being successful – used especially in news reports; ▪ **scuttle** AmE: *Plans to build a private hospital have been scuppered after a government inquiry.* **2** to deliberately sink your own ship

scupper² n [C] technical a hole in the side of a ship that allows water to flow back into the sea

scur·ri·lous /ˈskʌrɪləs $ ˈskɜːr-/ adj formal scurrilous remarks, articles etc contain damaging and untrue statements about someone: *a scurrilous attack on his integrity* —**scurrilously** adv

scur·ry /ˈskʌri $ ˈskɜːri/ v scurried, scurrying, scurries [I always + adv/prep] to move quickly with short steps, especially because you are in a hurry: *People were scurrying off to work.* —**scurry** n [singular]

S-curve /ˈes kɜːv $ -kɜːrv/ n [C] AmE a bend in the road in the shape of an 'S', that can be dangerous to drivers; ▪ **S-bend** BrE

scur·vy /ˈskɜːvi $ ˈskɜːr-/ n [U] a disease caused by not eating foods such as fruit and vegetables that contain VITAMIN C

scut·tle¹ /ˈskʌtl/ v **1** [I always + adv/prep] to move quickly with short steps, especially because you are afraid and do not want to be noticed: *A little lizard scuttled across the path.* **2** [T] AmE to ruin or end someone's plans or chance of being successful – used especially in news reports; ▪ **scupper** BrE: *The incident threatens to scuttle the peace process.* **3** [T] to sink a ship by making holes in the bottom, especially in order to prevent it being used by an enemy

scuttle² n [C] a container for carrying coal

scut·tle·butt /ˈskʌtlbʌt/ n [U] AmE informal stories about other people's personal lives, especially stories that are unkind or untrue; ▪ **gossip**

scuz·zy /ˈskʌzi/ adj informal unpleasant and dirty; ▪ **disgusting**

scuzzy² n [U] informal scsɪ: *What's the biggest scuzzy hard drive you have?*

scythe¹ /saɪð/ n [C] a farming tool that has a long curved blade attached to a long wooden handle, and is used to cut grain or long grass

scythe² v **1** [I,T] to move through or destroy something quickly and violently: *Bullets scythed through the crowd.* **2** [T] to cut with a scythe

SE the written abbreviation of **southeast** or **southeastern**

sea S3 W1 /siː/ n

1 [singular, U] the large area of salty water that covers much of the earth's surface; ▪ **ocean**

calm sea (=without large waves)
rough sea(s)/heavy seas (=with large waves)
the open sea (=part of the sea far away from land)
by sea (=on a ship)
by the sea (=on the coast)
at sea (=working on ships)
out to sea (=away from the land)
be lost at sea (=be drowned)
go to sea (=go to work on a ship)
put to sea (=make a boat go out to sea)
seawater
seabed/floor (=the land at the bottom of the sea)
sea air (=the air at the coast)

Jay stripped his clothes off and ran into the sea. | *All the rooms have sea views.* | *The* **sea** *was perfectly* **calm.** | *the* **rough seas** *and wild winds that buffeted*

S

the coast | They headed west toward **the open sea**. | Most exports went **by sea**. | a little cottage **by the sea** | He spent over 30 years at sea. | They stood side by side looking **out to sea**. | a sailor who was **lost at sea** | He **went to sea** when he was eighteen. | The refugees **put to sea** in five rickety rafts. | Divers have disturbed the **sea bed** in some areas. | She's out enjoying the **sea air**. → see picture at RIVER

2 [C] a large area of salty water that is mostly enclosed by land: *the Mediterranean Sea*
3 sea of sth a very large number of people or things that all look similar: *He looked out at the sea of faces.*
4 (all) at sea confused or not sure what to do: *Living in a foreign country can mean you're always at sea about what's going on.*
5 the seas *literary* the sea – used especially when you are not talking about a particular ocean: **across the seas** (=far away) *They came from lands across the seas.*
6 [C] one of the broad areas that seem flat on the moon and Mars

sea ˈair n [U] the air near the sea, which is considered to be clean, fresh, and good for your health: *A week spent breathing in the clean sea air would do her good.*

ˈsea aˌnemone n [C] a small brightly coloured sea animal that sticks onto rocks and looks like a flower

sea·bed also **ˈsea bed** *BrE* /ˈsiːbed/ n **the seabed** the land at the bottom of the sea; **◨ sea floor**

sea·bird /ˈsiːbɜːd $ -bɜːrd/ n [C] a bird that lives near the sea and finds food in it

sea·board /ˈsiːbɔːd $ -bɔːrd/ n [C] the part of a country that is near the sea: **eastern/western/Pacific etc seaboard** *the eastern seaboard of the US*

sea·borne /ˈsiːbɔːn $ -bɔːrn/ adj [only before noun] carried on or arriving in ships: *the threat of a seaborne invasion*

ˌsea ˈbreeze n [C] a light wind that blows from the sea onto the land

ˈsea ˌcaptain n [C] the CAPTAIN of a ship

ˈsea change n [C] a very big change in something: **[+in]** *a sea change in attitudes*

ˈsea dog n [C] *literary* someone with a lot of experience of ships and sailing

sea·far·er /ˈsiːˌfeərə $ -ˌferər/ n [C] *old-fashioned* or *formal* a SAILOR or someone who travels regularly by ship

sea·far·ing /ˈsiːˌfeərɪŋ $ -ˌfer-/ adj [only before noun] working or travelling on ships and the sea: *a seafaring man* —**seafaring** n [U]

ˌsea ˈfloor *BrE*; **sea·floor** *AmE* /ˈsiːflɔː $ -flɔːr/ n **the sea floor** the land at the bottom of the sea; **◨ seabed**

---

seafood

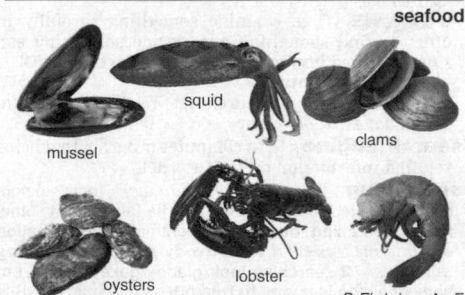

squid

mussel

clams

oysters

lobster

prawn *BrE*/ shrimp *AmE*

sea·food /ˈsiːfuːd/ n [U] animals from the sea that you can eat, for example fish and SHELLFISH: *a seafood restaurant*

sea·front /ˈsiːfrʌnt/ n [C usually singular] *especially BrE* the part of a town where the shops, houses etc are next to the beach: **on the seafront** *a hotel right on the seafront* | *a seafront cafe*

sea·go·ing /ˈsiːˌɡəʊɪŋ $ -ˌɡoʊ-/ adj [only before noun] built to travel on the sea: *a seagoing ship*

ˌsea-ˈgreen adj bluish-green: *Jo's large sea-green eyes* —**sea-green** n [U]

sea·gull /ˈsiːɡʌl/ n [C] a large common grey or white bird that lives near the sea

sea·horse /ˈsiːhɔːs $ -hɔːrs/ n [C] a small sea fish with a head and neck that look like those of a horse

seal¹ [S3] /siːl/ n [C]
1 a large sea animal that eats fish and lives around coasts → see picture at FOOD CHAIN
2 a) a mark that has a special design and shows the legal or official authority of a person or organization: *The document carried the seal of the governor's office.* **b)** the object that is used to make this mark
3 a piece of rubber or plastic that keeps air, water, dirt etc out of something: **airtight/watertight seal** *an airtight seal around the windows*
4 a piece of WAX, paper, wire etc that you have to break in order to open a container, document etc
5 seal of approval if you say something your seal of approval, you say that you approve of it, especially officially: *A number of employers have already given their seal of approval to the scheme.*
6 set the seal on sth *BrE* to make something definite or complete: *In 1972, Nixon himself went to China to set the seal on the new relationship.*

seal² v [T] **1** also **seal up** to close an entrance or a container with something that stops air, water etc from coming in or out of it: *The window was sealed shut.* | **seal a joint/crack/opening/gap** *A quick way to seal awkward gaps is to use a foam filler.* | *Dried milk is kept in* **hermetically sealed** (=very tightly closed) *containers.* **2** if a building, area, or country is sealed, no one can enter or leave it: *Authorities plan to seal the border.* **3** to close an envelope, package etc by using something sticky to hold its edges in place: *He wrote the address and sealed the envelope.* **4** to cover the surface of something with something that will protect it: *Wooden decks should be sealed to prevent cracking.* **5 seal sb's fate** to make something, especially something bad, sure to happen: *The outbreak of war sealed the government's fate.* **6 seal a deal/bargain/pact etc** to make an agreement more formal or definite **7 seal a victory/win/match** to make a victory certain: *Smith's goal sealed the victory.* → **sb's lips are sealed** at LIP (5); → **all signed and sealed** at SIGN² (6)

seal sth ⇔ **in** phr v to stop something that is inside something else from getting out: *Fry the meat quickly to seal in the juices.*

seal sth ⇔ **off** phr v to stop people from entering an area or building, because it is dangerous: *Following a bomb warning, police have sealed off the whole area.*

ˈsea lane n [C] a path across the sea that ships regularly use

seal·ant /ˈsiːlənt/ n [C,U] a substance that is put on the surface of something to protect it from air, water etc

sealed /siːld/ adj **1** shut or protected with something that prevents air, water etc from getting in or out: *a sealed container* **2** sealed documents are closed so that they can only be read by a certain person or at a certain time: *Sealed bids* (=offers to pay a particular price for something) *should be sent to Richard Walker.*

ˈsea legs n [plural] the ability to walk normally, not feel ill etc when you are travelling on a ship: **find/get your sea legs** *I felt awful yesterday. But, thankfully, I've found my sea legs now.*

seal·er /ˈsiːlə $ -ər/ n **1** [C,U] a substance that is put on the surface of something to protect it from air, water etc **2** [C] a person or ship that hunts SEALS

ˈsea ˌlevel n [U] the average height of the sea, used as a standard for measuring other heights and depths, such as the height of a mountain: **above/below sea level** *1000m above sea level* | *changes in sea level*

seal·ing /ˈsiːlɪŋ/ *n* [U] the activity of hunting or catching SEALS

ˈsealing wax *n* [U] a red substance that melts and becomes hard again quickly, used for closing letters, documents etc, especially in the past

ˈsea ˌlion *n* [C] a large type of SEAL that lives near the coast in the Pacific Ocean

seal·skin /ˈsiːl,skɪn/ *n* [U] the skin or fur of some types of SEAL, used for making leather or clothes

seam /siːm/ *n* [C] **1** a line where two pieces of cloth, leather etc have been stitched together: *She was repairing Billy's trousers, where the seam had come undone.* | *Join the shoulder seams together.* **2** a layer of a mineral under the ground: **seam of coal/iron etc 3 be coming/falling apart at the seams a)** if a plan, organization etc is coming apart at the seams, so many things are going wrong with it that it will probably fail: *The health service seems to be falling apart at the seams.* **b)** if a piece of clothing is coming apart at the seams, the stitches on it are coming unfastened **4 be bursting/ bulging at the seams** if a room or building is bursting at the seams, it is so full of people that hardly anyone else can fit into it **5 a (rich) seam of sth** a thing, place, or group from which a type of thing can be obtained: *The 466-page book is a rich seam of statistical information.* **6** a line where two pieces of metal, wood etc have been joined together

sea·man /ˈsiːmən/ *n plural* **seamen** /-mən/ [C] **1** a SAILOR on a ship or in the navy who is not an officer **2** someone who has a lot of experience of ships and the sea

sea·man·ship /ˈsiːmənʃɪp/ *n* [U] the skills and knowledge that an experienced sailor has

seamed /siːmd/ *adj* **1** having a seam: *seamed stockings* **2** *written* a seamed surface has many deep lines on it: *A gentle smile spread over her seamed face.*

sea mile *n* [C] a unit for measuring distance at sea that is slightly longer than a land mile, and equals 1853 metres; ⊟ **nautical mile**

ˈsea mist *n* [U] a mist on land that comes in from the sea

seam·less /ˈsiːmləs/ *adj* **1** done or made so smoothly that you cannot tell where one thing stops and another begins: *the seamless integration of data, text, images and sound* **2** without any SEAMS : *seamless stockings* —**seamlessly** *adv*: *The ideal is to have everything working seamlessly together.*

seam·stress /ˈsiːmstrɪ̣s, ˈsem-$ ˈsiːm-/ *n* [C] **1** old-fashioned a woman whose job is sewing and making clothes **2** a woman who is good at sewing

seam·y /ˈsiːmi/ *adj* involving unpleasant things such as crime, violence, or immorality: *the seamy side of the World Wide Web*

se·ance /ˈseɪɑːns, -ɒns $ -ɑːns/ *n* [C] a meeting where people try to talk to or receive messages from the spirits of dead people

sea·plane /ˈsiːpleɪn/ *n* [C] a plane that can take off from and land on a body of water

sea·port /ˈsiːpɔːt $ -pɔːrt/ *n* [C] a large town on or near a coast with a HARBOUR that big ships can use

ˈsea ˌpower *n* **1** [U] the size and strength of a country's navy **2** [C] a country with a powerful navy

sear /sɪə $ sɪr/ *v* **1** [I always + adv/prep, T] to burn something with a sudden powerful heat: *The heat seared their skin.* **2** [I always + adv/prep, T] to have a very strong sudden and unpleasant effect on you: *Pain was searing through her.* | *The image was seared into his brain.* **3** [T] to cook the outside of a piece of meat quickly at a high temperature, in order to keep its juices in: *seared tuna steaks*

search¹ S3 W2 /sɜːtʃ $ sɜːrtʃ/ *n*
1 [C usually singular] an attempt to find someone or something

carry out/conduct a search
begin/launch a search
call off/abandon a search
thorough/painstaking/systematic search   (=a very detailed one)
fruitless search (=an unsuccessful one)
nationwide search
house-to-house search (=a search of every house or building in an area)
fingertip search *BrE* (=a search for clues by police officers at the scene of a crime)
strip search (=a search of someone by taking off their clothes)
the search is on (=used to say that something is now being looked for)

[**+for**] *Bad weather is hampering the search for survivors.* | [**+of**] *a search of the area* | *The police have already **carried out a search**.* | *Perhaps they will wait until morning before **launching a search**.* | *Rescuers were forced to **abandon their search**.* | *a **thorough** search of the undergrowth* | *I spent the next three hours in a **fruitless search** for a replacement.* | ***The search is now on** for a new management team.*

2 [C] a series of actions done by a computer to find information: [**+of**] *a computerized search of 10,000 medical journals* | *A search found 46 websites.* | *an online search* | **perform/run/do a search** *Do a search on 'rabbit' and see what it brings up.*

3 in search of sth looking for something: *Mark **went in search of** water.*

4 [singular] an attempt to find an explanation or solution: [**+for**] *the search for a cure*

search² W3 *v*
1 LOOKING [I,T] to try to find someone or something by looking very carefully: *It was too dark to search further.* | *The area was **thoroughly searched**.* | [**+for**] *An RAF plane searched for the missing men.* | *I've **searched high and low** (=everywhere) for my glasses.* | **search sth for sth** *Detectives are searching the yard for clues.* | [**+in/under/through etc**] *Alice bent to search through a heap of clothes.*

2 COMPUTER [T] to use a computer to find information: **search sth for sth** *Search the Web for cheap flights.*

3 PERSON [T] if someone in authority searches you or the things you are carrying, they look for things you might be hiding: **search sb for sth** *He was searched by the guards for weapons.*

4 SOLUTION [I] to try to find an explanation or solution: [**+for**] *Scientists are still searching for a cure.* | *She paused, searching for inspiration.*

5 search me! *spoken* used to tell someone that you do not know the answer to a question: *'Where is she?' 'Search me!'*

6 EXAMINE [T] to examine something carefully in order to find something out, decide something etc: *Anya searched his face anxiously.* —**searcher** *n* [C]

search sth ⇔ out *phr v*
to find something by searching: *We were too tired to search out extra blankets.*

ˈsearch ˌengine *n* [C] a computer program that helps you find information on the Internet

search·ing /ˈsɜːtʃɪŋ $ ˈsɜːr-/ *adj* [only before noun] **1** intended to find out all the facts about something: **searching questions/investigation/examination etc** *Interviewees need to be ready for some searching questions.* **2** searching look/glance/gaze a look from someone who is trying to find out as much as possible about someone else's thoughts and feelings: *She avoided his long searching look.* —**searchingly** *adv*

search·light /ˈsɜːtʃlaɪt $ ˈsɜːrtʃ-/ *n* [C] a very bright electric light that turns in any direction, used for finding people, guarding places etc

ˈsearch ˌparty *n* [C] a group of people who are organized to look for someone who is missing or lost: *Let's get going or they'll send out a search party.*

ˈsearch ˌwarrant *n* [C] a legal document that gives the police official permission to search a building

sear·ing /ˈsɪərɪŋ $ ˈsɪr-/ *adj* **1** extremely hot: *the searing heat of the desert* **2** searing pain is severe and feels like a burn **3** searing words or attitudes criticize someone or something very strongly: *Adorno's searing analysis of mass culture* | *Emily felt a searing anger against her father.*

ˈsea salt *n* [U] a type of salt made from sea water, used in cooking

sea·scape /ˈsiːskeɪp/ *n* [C] a picture of the sea

sea·shell /ˈsiːʃel/ *n* [C] the empty shell of a small sea creature: *jewelry made out of seashells*

sea·shore /ˈsiːʃɔː $ -ʃɔːr/ *n* **the seashore** the land at the edge of the sea, consisting of sand and rocks; → **beach, seaside**

sea·sick /ˈsiːˌsɪk/ *adj* feeling ill when you travel in a boat, because of the movement of the boat in the water: **get/feel/be seasick** *Hal was seasick almost at once.* —**seasickness** *n* [U]

sea·side¹ /ˈsiːsaɪd/ *n* **the seaside** *BrE* the areas or towns near the sea, where people go to enjoy themselves: *a trip to the seaside* | **at the seaside** *a day at the seaside*

seaside² *adj* [only before noun] relating to places that are near the sea: **seaside town/resort** *the popular seaside resort of Brighton* | *a seaside holiday*

sea·son¹ [S3] [W1] /ˈsiːzən/ *n*
1 TIME OF YEAR [C] one of the main periods into which a year is divided, which each have a particular type of weather. In the west, the seasons are spring, summer, autumn, and winter: *the effect on plants as the seasons change*
2 USUAL TIME FOR STH [C usually singular] a period of time in a year during which a particular activity takes place, or during which something usually happens: *the first game of the season* | **the football/cricket etc season** *the end of the football season* | **the racing/fishing/hunting etc season** *The racing season starts in June.* | *Some footpaths are closed during the shooting season.* | **out of season** (=when an activity is not allowed) *He was caught fishing out of season.* | [+for] *The season for strawberries* (=when they are available to buy) *usually starts in early June.* | **the rainy/wet/dry season** (=the time when it rains a lot or does not rain at all) *African rivers turn to hard mud during the dry season.* | **the growing/planting etc season** *The planting season is in spring, with harvest in the fall.*
3 HOLIDAY [singular, U] the time of the year when most people take their holidays: **high/peak season** (=the busiest part of this time) *There are two boat trips a day, more in high season.* | **low/off season** (=the least busy part of this time) *An off-season break costs £114.* | **out of season** *It's quieter out of season.* | **holiday season** *BrE*/**tourist season** *We arrived at the height of the tourist season* (=the busiest time). | **the holiday season** *AmE* (=Thanksgiving to New Year, including Christmas, Hanukkah etc) | **the festive season** *BrE* (=Christmas and New Year)
4 FASHION [singular] the time in each year when new styles of clothes, hair etc are produced and become fashionable: *This season's look is fresh and natural.*
5 be in/out of season vegetables and fruit that are in season are cheap and easily available because it is the time of year when they are ready to eat. If they are out of season, they are expensive or not available: *Vine tomatoes are in season from April to October.*
6 FILMS, PLAYS ETC [C usually singular] a series of films, plays, television programmes etc that are shown during a particular period of time: [+of] *a new season of comedy on BBC 1* | **summer/fall etc season** *The network has several new dramas lined up for the fall season.* | *Glyndebourne's season opens with a performance of Tosca.*
7 ANIMALS [singular] the time of the year when animals are ready to have sex: **the mating/breeding season** | *Their dog was coming into season.*
8 season's greetings *written* used on cards to tell someone you hope they have a happy Christmas,

Hanukkah etc
9 the season of goodwill *old-fashioned* the time around Christmas → CLOSE SEASON, OPEN SEASON, SILLY SEASON

season² *v* [T] **1** to add salt, pepper etc to food you are cooking: **season sth with sth** *Season the chicken with pepper.* | *Mix the ingredients and season to taste* (=add the amount of salt etc that you think tastes right). **2** to prepare wood for use by gradually drying it

sea·son·a·ble /ˈsiːzənəbəl/ *adj formal* suitable or usual for a particular time of year; ◪ **unseasonable**: *seasonable temperatures*

sea·son·al /ˈsiːzənəl/ *adj* [usually before noun] happening, expected, or needed during a particular season: *heavy seasonal rains* | **seasonal workers/employment etc** *seasonal jobs in the tourist industry*

ˌseasonal afˈfective disˈorder *n* [U] an illness that makes people feel sad and tired in winter, because there is not enough light from the sun; ◪ SAD

sea·son·al·i·ty /ˌsiːzəˈnælɪti/ *n* [U] the fact that something changes according to the time of the year: [+of] *the seasonality of sales of the product*

sea·son·al·ly /ˈsiːzənəli/ *adv* according to what is usual for a particular season: *bird migrations that occur seasonally* | **seasonally adjusted figures/rates/data etc** (=ones that are changed according to what usually happens at a particular time of year)

sea·soned /ˈsiːzənd/ *adj* **1** [only before noun] used to describe someone who has a lot of experience of a particular thing: **seasoned traveller/observer etc** *Artie was by then a seasoned musician with six albums to his credit.* **2** seasoned food has salt, pepper etc added to it: *a highly seasoned piece of fish* **3** seasoned wood has been prepared for use by drying

sea·son·ing /ˈsiːzənɪŋ/ *n* [C,U] salt, pepper, spices etc that give food a more interesting taste

ˈseason ˌticket *n* [C] a ticket that allows you to make a lot of journeys during a particular period of time, or go to all the games, concerts etc being held during a particular time. Season tickets cost less than it would cost to buy a ticket for each journey, game etc: *an annual season ticket* | **season ticket holder** (=someone who owns a season ticket)

seat¹ [S2] [W1] /siːt/ *n*
1 PLACE TO SIT [C] a place where you can sit, especially one in a vehicle or one from which you watch a performance, sports event etc

> **back/rear/front seat** (=the back or front seat in a car)
> **driver's seat**
> **passenger seat** (=the seat next to the driver's seat in a car)
> **window/aisle seat** (=a seat next to the window or AISLE, for example on a plane)
> **empty/vacant seat**
> **front-row seat** (=in a theatre, sports ground etc)
> **good seat** (=one from which you can see well)
> **ringside seat** (=a seat in the front row for a sports event, especially a BOXING match)
> **have/take a seat**
> **show sb to their seat**
> **book/reserve a seat**
> **bums on seats** *BrE informal* (=used for talking about the number of people who go to an event, especially if this is a lot of people)

> *I was in the **back seat** and Jo was driving.* | *People were shifting in their seats, looking uncomfortable.* | *He requested a **window seat** for the flight.* | *There were no **empty seats**.* | *It was a great concert, and I had a **front-row seat**.* | *We're a long way from the stage, but they were the **best seats** I could get.* | *Please **take a seat**.* | *You can **book seats** online.* | *He is an actor who will put **bums on seats**.* | *a 10,000-**seat** stadium*

2 OFFICIAL POSITION [C] a position as an elected

member of a government, or as a member of a group that makes official decisions: [+in/on] *a seat in the National Assembly* | *Promotion would mean a seat on the board of directors.* | **Parliamentary/Senate etc seat** *the Senate seat for Colorado* | **win/lose etc a seat** (=in an election) | *He predicts that his party will gain at least 12 seats.* | *Mr Adams is expected to keep his seat.* | *Labour held the seat with a 7% majority.* | **safe seat** *BrE* (=one that a party will not lose) | **marginal seat** *BrE* (=one that another party might easily win)

3 PART OF A CHAIR [C usually singular] the flat part of a chair etc that you sit on: *Don't put your feet on the seat!* | *a wooden toilet seat* | *a broken bicycle seat*

4 **baby/child/car seat** a special seat that you put in a car for a baby or small child

5 **seat of government/power** *formal* a city where a country's government is based

6 **seat of learning** *formal* a university, college etc

7 CLOTHES [singular] the part of your trousers that you sit on: [+of] *a rip in the seat of his jeans*

8 **take a back seat (to sb/sth)** to have less influence or importance: *Foreign policy will take a back seat to domestic problems for a while.*

9 **on the edge of your seat** waiting excitedly to see what happens next: *a gripping movie that will keep you on the edge of your seat*

10 **do sth by the seat of your pants** to do something by using only your own skill and experience, without any help from anyone or anything else, especially when this is risky or dangerous

11 **in the driving seat** *BrE*; **in the driver's seat** *AmE* controlling what happens in a situation, organization, or relationship: *We're trying to put young people in the driving seat.*

12 **in the hot seat** also **on the hot seat** *AmE informal* in a difficult position where you have to make important decisions, answer questions etc

13 HOUSE [C] a home of a rich important family in the countryside: **family/country seat** → **back-seat driver** at BACK SEAT (2); → WINDOW SEAT

seat² *v* [T] **1** [not in progressive] if a place seats a number of people, it has enough seats for that number: *The arena seats 60,000.* **2** *formal* **seat yourself (in/on/ beside etc sth)** to sit down somewhere: *She seated herself at her desk.* → see box at SIT **3** to arrange for someone to sit somewhere: **seat sb beside/near etc sb/sth** *the old custom of seating boys and girls on opposite sides of the classroom* → SEATED

'seat belt also **safety belt** *AmE n* [C] a belt attached to the seat of a car or plane which you fasten around yourself for protection in an accident

seat·ed /'siːtɪd/ *adj* [not before noun] *formal* **1** if someone is seated, they are sitting down: [+at/near/ beside etc] *Paul was seated at his desk.* | **Remain seated** *until the aircraft has come to a complete stop.* **2** **be seated** *spoken* used to ask people politely to sit down: *Please be seated.* → SEAT²

-seater /'siːtə $ -ər/ *suffix* [in nouns] **four-seater/12- seater etc** a vehicle, piece of furniture etc with space for four, 12 etc people to sit

seat·ing /'siːtɪŋ/ *n* [U] **1** all the seats in a theatre, cinema etc: [+for] *a restaurant with seating for 40 customers* | *The hall has a seating capacity of 650.* **2** the places where people will sit, according to an arrangement: **seating plan/arrangements** *the seating plan for the wedding dinner*

seat·mate /'siːtmeɪt/ *n* [C] *AmE* the person who sits next to you on a plane

'sea ˌurchin *n* [C] a small round sea animal with a hard shell covered in sharp points

sea·wall /ˌsiːˈwɔːl $ 'siːˈwɒːl/ *n* [C] a wall built beside the sea to stop the water from flowing onto the land

sea·ward /'siːwəd $ -wərd/ *adj* [only before noun] facing towards the sea: *Keep to the seaward side of the path.* —**seaward** also **seawards** *adv*

sea·wa·ter /'siːwɔːtə $ -wɒːtər, -wɑː-/ *n* [U] salty water from the sea

sea·weed /'siːwiːd/ *n* [U] a plant that grows in the sea

sea·wor·thy /'siːwɜːði $ -ɜːr-/ *adj* a ship that is seaworthy is in a suitable condition to sail

se·ba·ceous /sɔˈbeɪʃəs/ *adj technical* relating to a part of the body that produces oil: *sebaceous glands*

sec /sek/ *n* **1 a sec** *spoken informal* a very short period of time: **hang on a sec/hold on a sec/just a sec etc** (=wait a short time) *'Is Al there?' 'Hold on a sec, I'll check.'* | **in a sec** *I'll be with you in a sec.* **2** the written abbreviation of *second*: *Journey time: 25 mins 14 secs.*

sec·a·teurs /'sekətɜːz $ ˌsekəˈtɜːrz/ *n* [plural] *BrE* strong scissors used for cutting plant stems: *a pair of secateurs*

se·cede /sɪˈsiːd/ *v* [I] *formal* if a country or state secedes from another country, it officially stops being part of it and becomes independent: [+from] *By 1861, 11 states had seceded from the Union.*

se·ces·sion /sɪˈseʃən/ *n* [C,U] when a country or state officially stops being part of another country and becomes independent: *a vote in favor of secession* | [+from] *Croatia's secession from Yugoslavia*

se·ces·sion·ist /sɪˈseʃənɪst/ *n* [C] someone who wants their country or state to be independent of another country

se·clud·ed /sɪˈkluːdɪd/ *adj* very private and quiet: **secluded garden/spot/beach etc** *We sunbathed on a small secluded beach.* | *He's 80 years old now and lives a very secluded life.*

se·clu·sion /sɪˈkluːʒən/ *n* [U] the state of being private and away from other people: *They stayed at a friend's beach house and enjoyed ten days of peace and seclusion.* | **in seclusion** *He found it difficult to walk very far, and had to stay at home in seclusion.* | [+of] *the relative seclusion of the Norfolk countryside*

sec·ond¹ S1 W1 /'sekənd/ *number*

1 the second person, thing, event etc is the one that comes after the first: *the Second World War* | *the second of August* | *a second year student* | *his second wife* | *Clinton's second term in office* | *the second half of the year* | *the second time in three days*

2 the position in a competition or scale that comes after the one that is the best, most successful etc: *She won second prize.* | *They climbed to second place in the League.* | **second largest/most successful etc** *Africa's second highest mountain* | **be second only to sth** (=used to emphasize that something is nearly the largest, most important etc) *The euro will have a circulation second only to that of the dollar.*

3 another example of the same thing, or another in addition to the one you have: *We advertised for a second guitarist.* | *There was a second reason for his dismissal.* | *I asked the doctor for a second opinion* (=when you ask another person to repeat an examination, test etc for you).

4 **every second year/person/thing etc a)** the second, then the fourth, then the sixth year etc: *The nurse comes every second day.* **b)** used to emphasize that in a group of similar things, there is too much of one particular thing: *Every second house seemed to be boarded up.*

5 **be second to none** to be the best: *The quality of Britain's overseas aid programme is second to none.*

6 **second chance** help given to someone who has failed, in the hope that they will succeed this time: *I just want to give these kids a second chance.*

7 **have second thoughts** to start having doubts about a decision you have made: *You're not having second thoughts, are you?* | [+about] *She'd had second thoughts about the whole project.*

8 **on second thoughts** *BrE*; **on second thought** *AmE spoken* used to say that you have changed your mind about something: *I'll call her tomorrow – no, on second thought, I'll try now.*

9 not give sth a second thought/without a second thought used to say that someone does not think or worry about something: *She dismissed the rumour without a second thought.*

10 not give sth a second glance/look also **without a second glance/look** to not look at something again, because you have not really noticed it or because it does not seem important: *No-one gave the woman in the grey uniform a second glance.*

11 be/become second nature (to sb) something that is second nature to you is something you have done so often that you do it almost without thinking: *Driving becomes second nature after a while.*

12 second wind a new feeling of energy after you have been working or exercising very hard, and had thought you were too tired to continue: *He got his second wind and ran on.*

second² S1 W2 *n*

1 [C] a unit for measuring time. There are 60 seconds in a minute: *Hold your breath for six seconds.* | *The operation takes only 30 seconds.* | *Ultrasonic waves travel at around 300 metres per second.* | **within seconds** (=after only a few seconds) *Within seconds, Bev called back.*

2 [C] a very short period of time: *I'll be back in a second.* | *Just a second* (=wait a moment), *I'll come and help.* | *At least 30 shots were fired in a matter of seconds* (=in a very short time). → SPLIT SECOND

3 (at) any second (now) used to say that something will or may happen extremely soon: *He should be here any second.*

4 seconds [plural] **a)** *informal* another serving of food, after you have eaten your first serving **b)** clothes or other goods that are cheaper than usual because they are not perfect → SECOND HAND¹

5 [C] *technical* one of the sixty parts into which a MINUTE of an angle is divided. It can be shown as a symbol after a number. For example, 78° 52' 11' means 78 degrees 52 minutes 11 seconds.

6 [IC] someone who helps someone in a fight, especially in BOXING or, in the past, a DUEL

7 [U] *AmE informal* SECOND BASE

second³ *adv* **1** [sentence adverb] used before you add information to what you have already said; ▤ **secondly** **2** next after the first one: **come/finish etc second** *I came second in the UK Championships.* | *Tea is the most popular drink, while coffee ranks* (=comes) *second.*

second⁴ *v* [T] to formally support a suggestion made by another person in a meeting: **second a motion/proposal/amendment etc**

se·cond⁵ /sɪˈkɒnd $ -ˈkɑːnd/ *v* [T usually passive] *BrE* to send someone to do someone else's job for a short time: **be seconded to sth** *Jill's been seconded to the marketing department while Dave's away.* → SECONDMENT

sec·ond·a·ry W2 /ˈsekəndəri $ -deri/ *adj*

1 secondary education/schooling/teaching etc the education, teaching etc of children between the ages of 11 and 16 or 18

2 not as important as something else: *the novel's secondary characters* | [+to] *Writing was always secondary to spending time with my family.* | **be of secondary importance/be a secondary consideration** *Cost is the important thing – any benefits for the user are a secondary consideration.* —**secondarily** *adv*

secondary modern *n* [C] a type of school that existed in Britain until the 1960s, where children who had not passed a special examination were sent

secondary school *n* [C] a school for children between the ages of 11 and 16 or 18; → primary school

secondary source *n* [C] a book, article etc that ANALYSES something such as a piece of literature or a historical event and that can be used to support your ideas in an ESSAY

secondary stress *n* [C,U] *technical* the second strongest STRESS that is put on a part of a long word when you speak it. It is shown in this dictionary by the mark (ˌ); → PRIMARY STRESS

second base *n* [U] the second of the four places you have to run to in games such as baseball in order to get a point

second best¹ *n* [U] something that you have to accept which is not perfect or not the best: *I'm not going to settle for second best.*

second best² *adj* [only before noun] not quite as good as the best one: *Allie was the second best shooter on the rifle team.* | **come off second best** (=lose a game or competition, or not be as successful as someone else)

second childhood *n* [U] someone who is in their second childhood is old, and their mental abilities are greatly reduced

second class *n* [U] **1** a way of travelling on a ship or train that is cheaper and less comfortable than FIRST CLASS **2** a way of delivering letters etc in Britain that is cheaper and slower than FIRST CLASS **3** the system in the US for delivering newspapers, magazines, advertisements etc through the post

second-class *adj* [only before noun]

1 PEOPLE considered to be less important and less valuable than other people: *Why should old people be treated like second-class citizens?*

2 LOWER STANDARD of a lower standard or quality than the best: *We will not accept a second-class education for our children.*

3 TRAVEL second-class ticket/fare/compartment/cabin etc tickets etc that are for cheaper, less comfortable seats on a train or ship

4 MAIL second-class mail/post/stamp etc relating to the system of delivering mail in Britain that is cheaper and slower

5 UNIVERSITY DEGREE used to describe a university degree in Britain that is good, but not the highest level: *a second-class honours degree* → FIRST CLASS (3) —**second class** *adv*: *He was travelling second class.* | *I'll send the letter second class.*

second coming *n* **the second coming** the time in the future when Christians believe that Jesus Christ will come back to earth

second cousin *n* [C] a child of a COUSIN of one of your parents

second-degree *adj* **1** second-degree burns the second most serious form of burns; → first-degree, third-degree **2** second-degree murder/assault/burglary etc *AmE* a crime that is less serious than the most serious type, especially because it was not planned; → first-degree

sec·ond·er /ˈsekəndə $ -ər/ *n* [C] *formal* a person who supports a proposal etc in a formal meeting so that it can be discussed

second-guess *v* [T] **1** to try to say what will happen or what someone will do before they do it: *I'm not going to try and second-guess the committee's decisions.* **2** *AmE* to criticize something after it has already happened: *The decision has been made – there's no point in second-guessing it now.*

second hand¹ *n* [C] the long thin piece of metal that points to the seconds on a clock or watch

second hand² *adv* **1** if you get something second hand, it is not new and has been used by other people before: **get/buy sth second hand** *We got most of our furniture second hand.* **2** if you hear something second hand, the person who tells you is not the person who originally said it: *It may not be true – I only heard it second hand.* **3** if you experience something second hand, you experience it through other people, rather than directly → **(at) first hand** at FIRST¹ (8)

second-hand, **sec·ond·hand** /ˌsekəndˈhænd◂/ *adj* **1** second-hand things are not new when you get them, because they were owned by someone else before

S

you: *second-hand clothes* | *a second-hand car* | **second-hand store/shop etc** (=a shop that sells second-hand things) **2** second-hand information or knowledge is told to you by someone who is not the person who originally said it – used to show disapproval; **🔁 firsthand**: **second-hand reports/accounts** *second-hand accounts of mass killings*

‚second 'home *n* **1** [C] a house or apartment that you own as well as your main home and which you use, for example, for holidays: *town-dwellers who buy second homes in the countryside* **2** [singular] a place where you spend a large amount of time but which is not where you live: *I love Italy. It's my second home.* | *From then on the hospital became my second home.*

‚second-in-com'mand *n* [C] the person who has the next highest rank to the leader of a group, especially in a military organization

‚second 'language *n* [C usually singular] a language that you speak in addition to the language you learned as a child

‚second lieu'tenant *n* [C] a middle rank in several of the US and British military forces, or someone who has this rank

sec·ond·ly W3 /'sekəndli/ *adv* [sentence adverb] used when you want to give a second point or fact, or give a second reason for something; → **firstly**: *Firstly, they are not efficient, and secondly, they are expensive to make.*

se·cond·ment /sɪ'kɒndmənt $ -'kɑːnd-/ *n* [singular, U] *BrE* a period of time that you spend away from your usual job, either doing another job or studying: **on secondment (from sth)** *a government advisor, on secondment from the Metropolitan Police*

'second ‚name *n* [C] **1** *BrE* a family name: *'What's your second name?' 'Jones.'* **2** a name that comes after your first name and before your family name: *Stephen's second name, Anthony, is after my brother.*

‚second 'person *n* [singular] *technical* a form of a verb or PRONOUN that is used to show the person you are speaking to. For example, 'you' is a second person pronoun, and 'are' is the second person singular and plural of the verb 'to be' → FIRST PERSON, THIRD PERSON

‚second-'rate *adj* [usually before noun] not of the very best standard or quality; → **first-rate**: *a second-rate artist*

‚second 'sight *n* [U] the ability to know what will happen in the future, or to know about things that are happening somewhere else, that some people claim to have

‚second-'string *adj* [only before noun] not regularly part of a team, group etc, but sometimes taking someone else's place in it: *the Vikings' second-string quarterback*

se·cre·cy /'siːkrəsi/ *n* [U] **1** the process of keeping something secret, or when something is kept a secret; → **secret**: *I must stress the need for **absolute secrecy** about the project.* | *His work was **shrouded in secrecy**.* | *the **veil of secrecy** that covered the talks* **2 swear sb to secrecy** to make someone promise to not repeat what you have told them

se·cret¹ S3 W3 /'siːkrɪt/ *adj*
1 known about by only a few people and kept hidden from others; → **secrecy**: *They **kept** their relationship **secret from** their parents.* | *agents on a secret mission* | *a secret plan to end the war* | *secret talks with the terrorists* | **secret compartment/passage etc** *The drugs were found in a secret compartment in Campbell's suitcase.* | **secret ingredient/recipe/formula** *The cookies are made to a secret recipe.*
2 [only before noun] secret feelings, worries, or actions are ones that you do not want other people to know about: *His secret fear was that Jenny would leave him.* | *Did you know you had a **secret admirer** (=someone who is secretly in love with you)?*
3 secret weapon something that will help you gain a

big advantage over your competitors, that they do not know about
4 used to describe the behaviour of someone who is keeping their thoughts, intentions, or actions hidden from other people; **🔲 secretive**: [+about] *They're being very secret about it.* | *There was a **secret smile** on her face.* —**secretly** *adv*: *They were secretly married.*

secret² S3 W3 *n* [C]
1 something that is kept hidden or that is known about by only a few people; → **secrecy**

it's a secret
tell sb a secret/let sb in on a secret also **reveal a secret** *formal*
keep a secret (=not tell someone about something)
your secret is safe with me (=I will not tell anyone about it)
big secret (=an important secret, or something that is known by very few people)
little secret (=a secret that is not very important)
be a closely-guarded/well-kept secret (=a secret that very few people know about)
state/official secret
trade secret
dark secret (=a secret about something bad)
sb's innermost secrets (=someone's most personal secrets)
it's no secret (that) (=everyone knows about this)
it's an open secret (that) (=most people know about this, although you might expect it to be a secret)

*I can't tell you. **It's a secret**.* | *She wanted to **tell** everybody her **secret**.* | *Can you **keep a secret**? | Don't worry. **Your secret is safe with me**.* | *Why is all this such a **big secret**? | The location for the wedding **is a closely-guarded secret**.* | *He was accused of passing **state secrets** to a foreign power.* | *I kept this **dark secret** for 15 years.* | *She shared her **innermost secrets** with him.* | *It was **no secret that** the two men hated each other.* | *It's an **open secret that** he wants Derek's job.*

2 in secret in a private way or place that other people do not know about: *The negotiations were conducted in secret.*
3 the secret a particular way of achieving a good result, that is the best or only way: **the secret to (doing) sth** *The secret to making good pastry is to use very cold water.* | *Your hair always looks so great – **what's your secret**? | What do you think is **the secret of** her success?*
4 make no secret of sth to make your opinions about something clear: *Louise made no secret of her dislike for John.*
5 the secrets of life/nature/the universe etc the things no one yet knows about nature etc

‚secret 'agent *n* [C] someone whose job is to find out and report on the military and political secrets of other countries; **🔲 spy**

sec·re·tar·i·al /ˌsekrɪ'teəriəl $ -'ter-/ *adj* [usually before noun] relating to the work of a secretary: *a secretarial course* | *secretarial college*

sec·re·tar·i·at /ˌsekrɪ'teəriət $ -'ter-/ *n* [C] a government office or the office of a large international organization, especially one that has a SECRETARY GENERAL in charge of it: *the United Nations Secretariat in New York*

sec·re·ta·ry S3 W1 /'sekrɪtəri $ -teri-/ *n plural* secretaries [C]
1 OFFICE someone who works in an office TYPING letters, keeping records, answering telephone calls, arranging meetings etc: *My secretary will fax you all the details.* | *medical/legal secretary*
2 GOVERNMENT **a)** also **Secretary of State** the head of an important department in the British Government: *the Foreign Secretary* → HOME SECRETARY **b)** an official in charge of a large government department in the US: *the Secretary of Defense* **c)** a British official, who works in a government department or EMBASSY, and is below the rank of MINISTER or AMBASSADOR: *the First Secretary at the British Embassy* → SECRETARY OF STATE, UNDERSECRETARY

3 CLUB a member of a club or organization who takes notes in meetings, writes official letters etc: *the secretary of the tennis club*

secretary 'general *n* [C] the most important official in charge of a large organization, especially an international organization: *the UN Secretary General*

Secretary of 'State *n plural* **Secretaries of State** [C] **1** also **Secretary** the head of an important department in the British Government: *the Secretary of State for Trade and Industry*   **2** the head of the US government department that deals with the US's relations with other countries

secret 'ballot *n* [C,U] a way of voting in which people write their choices on a piece of paper in secret, or an act of voting in this way: **by secret ballot** *The chairman was elected by secret ballot.* | **in a secret ballot** *votes cast in a secret ballot*

se·crete /sɪˈkriːt/ *v* [T]   **1** if a part of an animal or plant secretes a liquid substance, it produces it: *The toad's skin secretes a deadly poison.*   **2** *formal* to hide something: *The money had been secreted in a Swiss Bank account.*

se·cre·tion /sɪˈkriːʃən/ *n* **a)** [C,U] a substance, usually liquid, produced by part of a plant or animal: *These secretions are used by the caterpillar as a defence.* **b)** [U] the production of this substance: *the secretion of hormones by the pituitary gland*

se·cre·tive /ˈsiːkrɪtɪv, sɪˈkriːtɪv/ *adj* a secretive person or organization likes to keep their thoughts, intentions, or actions hidden from others: *The government has been accused of being secretive and undemocratic.* | [+about] *Carla was always very secretive about her work.* **—secretively** *adv* **—secretiveness** *n* [U]

secret po'lice *n* **the secret police** a police force controlled by a government, that secretly tries to defeat the political enemies of that government

secret 'service *n* **the secret service a)** a British government organization that protects the country's military and political secrets, and obtains secrets about other countries **b)** a US government department that deals with special kinds of police work, especially protecting the President

sect /sekt/ *n* [C] a group of people with their own particular set of beliefs and practices, especially within or separated from a larger religious group

sec·tar·i·an /sekˈteəriən $ -ˈter-/ *adj*   **1** **sectarian violence/conflict/murder etc** violence etc that is related to the strong feelings of people who belong to different religious groups: *people on both sides of the sectarian divide in Northern Ireland*   **2** *AmE* supporting a particular religious group and its beliefs: *a sectarian school* **—sectarianism** *n* [U]

sec·tion¹ S1 W1 /ˈsekʃən/ *n*
1 PLACE/OBJECT [C] one of the parts that something such as an object or place is divided into: [+of] *a busy section of road* | *the reference section of the library* | *The plane's tail section was found in a cornfield.* | *the smoking section* (=where you can smoke)
2 PART OF A WHOLE [C] one of the separate parts of a structure, piece of furniture etc that you fit together to form the whole: **in sections** *The boats were built in Scotland, and transported to Egypt in sections.*
3 BOOK/NEWSPAPER/REPORT [C] a separate part of a book, newspaper, document, report etc: *This issue will be discussed further in section 2.* | **sports/style/business/travel etc section** (=particular part of a newspaper)
4 GROUP OF PEOPLE [C] a separate group within a larger group of people: [+of] *a large section of the American public* | *The story was grossly exaggerated by certain sections of the press.*
5 brass/rhythm/woodwind/string etc section the people or person in a band or ORCHESTRA, who play the BRASS, RHYTHM etc instruments
6 LAW [C] one of the parts of a law or a legal document: *Article I, Section 8 of the U.S. Constitution*
7 SIDE/TOP VIEW [C,U] *technical* a picture that shows

what a building, part of the body etc would look like if it were cut from top to bottom or side to side; → **cross-section**: **in section** *Here's the outside view, and here are the floors in section.*
8 MEDICAL/SCIENTIFIC *technical* **a)** [C,U] a medical operation that involves cutting → **caesarean section** at CAESAREAN **b)** [C] a very thin flat piece that is cut from skin, a plant etc to be looked at under a MICROSCOPE
9 AREA OF LAND [C] *AmE* a square area of land in the US that is one mile long on each side
10 MATHEMATICS [C] *technical* the shape that is made when a solid figure is cut by a flat surface in mathematics

section² *v* [T]   **1** *BrE* to officially force someone with a mental illness to go to a PSYCHIATRIC hospital, because they are dangerous to themselves or other people   **2** to separate something into parts: *Peel and section the oranges.*   **3** *technical* or *medical* to cut a very thin flat piece from skin, a plant etc so that you can look at it under a MICROSCOPE   **4** *medical* to cut a part of the body in a medical operation

    section sth ⇔ **off** *phr v* to divide an area into parts, especially by putting something between the parts: *The vegetable plots were sectioned off by a low wall.*

sec·tion·al /ˈsekʃənəl/ *adj*   **1** concerned only with your own small group in society or in an organization, as opposed to being concerned about society or the institution as a whole: *community groups seeking to protect sectional interests*   **2** a sectional drawing or view of something shows what it would look like if it were cut from top to bottom, or from side to side: *a sectional view of the building*   **3** made up of sections that can be put together or taken apart: *a sectional sofa*

sec·tor W1 /ˈsektə $ -ər/ *n* [C]
1 a part of an area of activity, especially of business, trade etc: [+of] *the agricultural sector of the economy* | **public/private sector** (=business controlled by the government or by private companies)
2 one of the parts into which an area is divided, especially for military purposes

sec·tor·al /ˈsektərəl/ *adj* [usually before noun] *technical* relating to the various economic sectors of a society or to a particular economic sector

sec·u·lar /ˈsekjʊlə $ -ər/ *adj*   **1** not connected with or controlled by a church or other religious authority: *secular education* | *our modern secular society*   **2** a secular priest lives among ordinary people, rather than with other priests in a MONASTERY

sec·u·lar·is·m /ˈsekjʊlərɪzəm/ *n* [U]   **1** a system of social organization that does not allow religion to influence the government, or the belief that religion should not influence a government   **2** the quality of behaving in a way that shows religion does not influence you: *the secularism of popular culture* **—secularist** *n* [C]

sec·u·lar·ize also **-ise** *BrE* /ˈsekjʊləraɪz/ *v* [T] to remove the control or influence of religious groups from a society or an institution **—secularization** /ˌsekjʊləraɪˈzeɪʃən $ -rə-/ *n* [U]

se·cure¹ S3 /sɪˈkjʊə $ -ˈkjʊr/ *adj*
1 PERMANENT/CERTAIN a situation that is secure is one that you can depend on because it is not likely to change: *There are no secure jobs these days.* | *We want a secure future for our children.* | *United's position at the top of the league seems relatively secure.*
2 PLACE/BUILDING locked or guarded so that people cannot get in or out, or steal anything: *The house isn't very secure – we need some new locks.* | *Keep your passport in a secure place.* | **secure accommodation** *BrE* (=a type of prison) *In the last year only three children under the age of 14 have had to be placed in secure accommodation.*
3 SAFE FROM HARM safe from and protected against damage or attack: *Companies can offer secure credit*

S

card transactions over the internet. | [+**from**] *These elephants are relatively secure from poachers.*
4 CONFIDENT feeling confident about yourself and your abilities; ◗ **insecure**: *We want our children to be secure and feel good about themselves.*
5 NOT WORRIED feeling confident and certain about a situation and not worried that it might change: *Workers no longer feel secure about the future.* | *It was enough money to make us feel financially secure.* | *We huddled together, secure in the knowledge that the rescue helicopter was on its way.*
6 FIRMLY FASTENED firmly fastened or tied, and not likely to fall down: *Are you sure that shelf is secure?*

secure² W2 *v* [T]
1 GET/ACHIEVE to get or achieve something that will be permanent, especially after a lot of effort: *Boyd's goal secured his team's place in the Cup Final.* | **secure a deal/contract** *The company recently secured a $20 million contract with Ford.* | *Negotiators are still working to secure the hostages' release.* | *Redgrave won his third Olympic gold medal, and secured his place in history.*
2 SAFE FROM HARM to make something safe from being attacked, harmed, or lost: *Troops were sent to secure the border.* | **secure sth against sb/sth** *They built a 10ft high fence to secure the house against intruders.* | *an agreement to secure the future of the rainforest*
3 TIE FIRMLY to fasten or tie something firmly in a particular position: **secure sth to sth** *John secured the boat firmly to the jetty.*
4 BORROWING MONEY if you secure a debt or a LOAN, you legally promise that if you cannot pay back the money you have borrowed, you will give the lender goods or property of the same value instead: *He used his house to secure the loan.*

se·cure·ly /sɪˈkjʊəli $ -ˈkjʊr-/ *adv* **1** tied, fastened etc tightly, especially in order to make something safe: **securely locked/fastened/attached/held etc** *All firearms should be kept securely locked in a cabinet.* **2** in a way that protects something from being stolen or lost: *Customers can now buy products securely over the internet.* **3** in a way that is likely to continue successfully and not change: *By that time, democracy had become securely established in Spain.*

se·cu·ri·ty W1 /sɪˈkjʊərɪti $ -ˈkjʊr-/ *n*
1 PROTECTION FROM DANGER [U] things that are done to keep a person, building, or country safe from danger or crime

strict/tight security (=careful security)
lax security (=security that is not careful enough)
national/state security (=the security of a country against its enemies)
tighten security (=make security better)
breach of security (=when something dangerous happens, in spite of security measures)
for security reasons
the security services/forces (=the police, army etc)
security camera
security check
security measures/arrangements
maximum security prison/jail

The trial was held under tight security. | *lax security at airline check-in desks* | *terrorist activity that is a threat to national security* | *The prison was ordered to tighten security after a prisoner escaped yesterday.* | *The Security Commission investigates breaches of security.* | *We have been asked not to say anything for security reasons.* | *The security forces opened fire, killing two people.* | *The thief was caught on a security camera.* | *There are strict security checks on everyone entering the Opera House.* | *A large number of homes lack adequate security measures.*

2 PROTECTION FROM BAD SITUATIONS [U] protection from bad things that could happen to you: *Parenting is about giving your child security and love.* |

Workers want greater job security (=not being in danger of losing your job). | *This insurance plan offers your family financial security in the event of your death.*
3 GUARDS [U] the department of a company or organization that deals with the protection of its buildings and equipment: *One of the sales clerks called security.* → SECURITY GUARD
4 BORROWING MONEY [U] something such as property that you promise to give someone if you cannot pay back money you have borrowed from them: [+**for**] *Reiss used his Brooklyn home as security for the loan.*
5 securities [plural] STOCKS or SHARES in a company

se'curity ,blanket *n* [C] **1** a piece of material that a child likes to hold, to comfort himself or herself **2** something that you have had for a long time, and that you use to make yourself feel less anxious

se'curity ,clearance *n* [C,U] official permission for someone to see secret documents etc, or to enter a building, after a strict checking process

se'curity de,posit *n* [C] an amount of money that you give to a LANDLORD before you rent a house or apartment, and that is returned to you after you leave if you have not damaged the property

se'curity ,guard *n* [C] someone whose job is to guard money or a building

se'curity ,light *n* [C] a light that turns on when someone tries to enter a building or area at night

se'curity ,risk *n* [C] **1** someone in a government or organization who you cannot trust with important secrets, because they might tell them to an enemy **2** a situation that could put people in danger: *After the bomb threat, it was considered too much of a security risk to let the races go ahead.*

se'curity ,service *n* [C] a government organization that protects a country's secrets against enemy countries, or protects the government against attempts to take away its power

se·dan /sɪˈdæn/ *n* [C] *AmE, AusE* a car that has four doors, seats for at least four people, and a TRUNK; ◗ **saloon** *BrE*

se,dan 'chair *n* [C] a seat on two poles with a cover around it, used in the past to carry an important person

se·date¹ /sɪˈdeɪt/ *adj* **1** calm, serious, and formal: *a sedate seaside town* | *The wedding was rather a sedate occasion.* **2** *formal* moving slowly and calmly: *We continued our walk at a sedate pace.* —**sedately** *adv*

sedate² *v* [T often passive] to give someone drugs to make them calm or to make them sleep: *He was still in shock, and heavily sedated.*

se·da·tion /sɪˈdeɪʃən/ *n* [U] the use of drugs to make someone calm or go to sleep: **under sedation** *The patient was still under heavy sedation.*

sed·a·tive /ˈsedətɪv/ *n* [C] a drug used to make someone calm or go to sleep —**sedative** *adj*

sed·en·ta·ry /ˈsedəntəri $ -teri/ *adj* **1** *formal* spending a lot of time sitting down, and not moving or exercising very much: **sedentary life/job/lifestyle etc** *health problems caused by our sedentary lifestyles* **2** *technical* a sedentary group of people tend always to live in the same place: *a sedentary people living north of the Danube*

sedge /sedʒ/ *n* [U] a plant similar to grass that grows in wet ground and on the edge of rivers and lakes

sed·i·ment /ˈsedɪmənt/ *n* [C,U] solid substances that settle at the bottom of a liquid: *a thick layer of sediment*

sed·i·men·ta·ry /ˌsedɪˈmentəri◂/ *adj technical* made of the solid substances that settle at the bottom of the sea, rivers, lakes etc: *sedimentary rock* | *sedimentary deposits*

sed·i·men·ta·tion /ˌsedɪmenˈteɪʃən, -mən-/ *n* [U] *technical* the natural process by which small pieces of rock, earth etc settle at the bottom of the sea etc and form a solid layer

se·di·tion /sɪˈdɪʃən/ *n* [U] *formal* speech, writing, or actions intended to encourage people to disobey a government: *Trade Union leaders were charged with sedition.* —**seditious** adj: *a seditious speech*

se·duce /sɪˈdjuːs $ -ˈduːs/ v [T] **1** to persuade someone to have sex with you, especially in a way that is attractive and not too direct: *The head lecturer was sacked for seducing female students.* | *Are you trying to seduce me?* **2** [often passive] to make someone want to do something by making it seem very attractive or interesting to them: *I was young and seduced by New York.* | **seduce sb into doing sth** *Leaders are people who can seduce other people into sharing their dream.*

se·duc·er /sɪˈdjuːsə $ -ˈduːsər/ n [C] a man who persuades someone to have sex with him; → **seductress**

se·duc·tion /sɪˈdʌkʃən/ n **1** [C,U] an act of persuading someone to have sex with you for the first time; → **seduce**: [+of] *the seduction of a young girl* **2** [C usually plural] something that strongly attracts people, but often has a bad effect on their lives: [+of] *the seduction of money*

se·duc·tive /sɪˈdʌktɪv/ adj **1** someone, especially a woman, who is seductive is sexually attractive: *She used all of her seductive charm to try and persuade him.* **2** something that is seductive is very interesting or attractive to you, in a way that persuades you to do something you would not usually do: *the seductive power of advertising* —**seductively** adv: *She smiled seductively at him across the table.*

se·duc·tress /sɪˈdʌktrɪ̇s/ n [C] a woman who persuades someone to have sex with her; → **seducer**

see¹ [S1] [W1] /siː/ v past tense **saw** /sɔː $ sɒː/, past participle **seen** /siːn/
1 NOTICE/EXAMINE [T not in progressive] to notice or examine someone or something, using your eyes: *The moment we saw the house, we knew we wanted to buy it.* | *He crouched down so he couldn't be seen.* | *Can I see your ticket, please?* | *I saw the offer advertised in the newspaper.* | **can/can't see** *You can see the Houses of Parliament from here.* | **see where/what/who etc** *Can you see where the marks are on the wall?* | **see (that)** *He saw that she was crying.* | **see sb/sth do sth** *I saw him leave a few minutes ago.* | **see sb/sth doing sth** *The suspect was seen entering the building.* | *As you can see, the house needs some work doing on it.* | *Have you seen Chris* (=do you know where he is)? | *The accommodation was so awful, it had to be seen to be believed* (=you would not believe it if you did not see it yourself).
2 NOTICE STH IS TRUE [T not in progressive] to notice that something is happening or that something is true: *More money must be invested if we are to see an improvement in services.* | *After a month's practice, you should see a difference in your playing.* | *Seeing his distress, Louise put her arm around him.* | *I would like to see changes in the way the course is run.* | *'You're not denying it, I see,' he said coldly.* | **see (that)** *I can see you're not very happy with the situation.*
3 ABILITY TO SEE [I,T not in progressive] to be able to use your eyes to look at things and know what they are: **can/can't see** *From the tower, you can see for miles.* | *I can't see a thing without my glasses.* | **not see to do sth** *His eyes are so bad that he can't see to read any more.*
4 FIND OUT INFORMATION [T] to find out information or a fact: **see what/how/when etc** *I'll call him and see how the job interview went.* | *She went outside to see what was happening.* | **see if/whether** *I've just come to see if you want to go out for a drink.* | *These chocolates are gorgeous. Try some and see for yourself* (=find out if it is true). | *By looking at this leaflet, you can see at a glance* (=find out very easily) *how much a loan will cost.* | *it can be seen that/we can see that From this graph, it can be seen that some people are more susceptible to the disease.* | *As we have seen in chapter 4, women's pay is generally less than men's.*
5 IN THE FUTURE [I,T] to find out about something in the future: **see if/whether** *It will be interesting to see if he makes it into the team.* | **see how/what/when etc** *I might come – I'll see how I feel tomorrow.* | *Let's try it and see what happens.* | *'Can we go to the zoo, Dad?'*

'We'll see.' (=used when you do not want to make a decision immediately) | *'How long can you stay?' 'I'll have to see. It depends* (=used when you cannot make a decision immediately).' | *We'll just have to wait and see.* | **see how it goes/see how things go** (=used when you are going to do something and will deal with problems if they happen) *I don't know. We'll just have to see how it goes on Sunday.* | *Things will work out, you'll see* (=you will find out that I am right).
6 WHERE INFORMATION IS [T only in imperative] *especially written* used to tell you where you can find information: *See p.58.* | *See press for details.* | **see above/below** *The results are shown in Table 7a (see below).*
7 UNDERSTAND [I,T] to understand or realize something: **see why/what/how etc** *I can't see why he's so upset.* | *I see what you mean* (=I understand what you are saying). | *'He lives here but works in London during the week.' 'Oh, I see* (=I understand).' | *You see, the thing is, I'm really busy right now* (=used when you are explaining something). | *You mix the flour and eggs like this, see* (=used to check that someone is listening and understands). | *I can't see the point of* (=I do not understand the reason for) *spending so much money on a car.* | *Do you see the point I'm making* (=do you understand what I'm trying to say)? | *The other officers laughed but Nichols couldn't see the joke.* | **see reason/sense** (=realize that you are wrong or doing something stupid) *I just can't get her to see reason!*
8 WATCH [T] to watch a television programme, play, film etc: *Did you see that programme on monkeys last night?* | *We're going to see 'Romeo and Juliet' tonight.*
9 CONSIDER STH [T] to think about or consider someone or something in a particular way, or as having particular qualities: *Having a child makes you see things differently.* | *Violence is seen in different ways by different people.* | **as sb sees it/the way sb sees it** (=used to give someone's opinion) *As I see it, you don't have any choice.* | *The way I see it, we have two options.* | **see sb/sth as sth** *I see the job as a challenge.* | **see yourself as sth** *He saw himself as a failure.* | **be seen as (being) sth** *The peace talks are seen as a sign of hope.* | *This type of work is often seen as boring.* | **be seen to be sth** *Sexual discrimination is seen to be an important factor in discouraging women from careers in engineering.* | *Teachers need to be seen to be in control.*
10 see what sb/sth can do *spoken* **a)** to find out if someone can deal with a situation or problem: [+about] *I'll call them again and see what they can do about it.* **b)** to find out how good someone or something is at what they are supposed to be able to do: *Let's take the Porsche out to the racetrack and see what it can do!*
11 I'll see what I can do *spoken* used to say that you will try to help someone: *Leave the papers with me and I'll see what I can do.*
12 see you *spoken* used to say goodbye when you know you will see someone again: **see you tomorrow/at 3/Sunday etc** *See you Friday – your place at 8:30.* | **see you later** (=see you soon, or later in the same day) | **see you in a bit** BrE (=see you soon) | **see you in a while** (=see you soon) | **(I'll) be seeing you!** (=see you soon)
13 VISIT [T] to visit or meet someone: *I'll be seeing her tomorrow night.* | *I haven't seen her since we left school.* | *She's too sick to see anyone right now.*
14 MEET BY CHANCE [T not in progressive] to meet someone by chance: *I saw Jane while I was out.*
15 HAVE A MEETING [T] to have an arranged meeting with someone: *Mr Thomas is seeing a client at 2:30.* | *She was seen by a doctor but didn't need hospital treatment.* | **see sb about sth** (=see someone to discuss something) *I have to see my teacher about my grades.*
16 SPEND TIME WITH SB [T] to spend time with someone: *They've been seeing a lot of each other.* | **see more/less of sb** (=see someone more or less often) *They've seen more of each other since Dan moved to London.*
17 be seeing sb to be having a romantic relationship with someone: *Is she seeing anyone at the moment?*

S

with Nicole had made her see red.

18 **IMAGINE** [T not in progressive] to imagine that something may happen in the future: *He could see a great future for her in music.* | **can't see sb/sth doing sth** *I can't see him winning, can you?* | *She's got a new book coming out but I can't see it doing very well.* | **see sb as sth** (=be able to imagine someone being something) *I just can't see her as a ballet dancer.*

19 **seeing as (how)** *informal* also **seeing that** used before giving a reason for what you are saying: *'I might as well do something useful, seeing as I'm back,' she said.*

20 **be seen to be doing sth** to make sure that other people notice you working hard or doing something good: *The government must be seen to be doing something about the rise in violent crime.*

21 **see sth for what it is** also **see sb for what they are** to realize that someone or something is not as good or nice as they seem: *They are unimpressed with the scheme and rightly see it for what it is.*

22 **MAKE SURE** [T not in progressive] to make sure or check that something is done: **see (that)** *It's up to you to see that the job's done properly.* | *Please see that the lights are switched off before you leave.* | *Don't worry – I'll see to it.* | *The hotel's owners see to it that their guests are given every luxury.*

23 **EXPERIENCE STH** [T not in progressive] to experience something: *She was so sick that doctors didn't think she'd live to see her first birthday.* | *I never thought I'd live to see the day when women became priests.* | *She's seen it all before* (=have experienced so much that nothing surprises you) *in her long career.* → **been there, seen that, done that** at BEEN (3)

24 **TIME/PLACE** [T] if a time or place has seen a particular event or situation, it happened or existed in that time or place: *This year has seen a big increase in road accidents.* | *The city has seen plenty of violence over the years.*

25 **let me see** also **let's see** *spoken* used when you are trying to remember something: *Let me see ... where did I put that letter?*

26 **I don't see why not** *spoken* used to say 'yes' in answer to a request: *'Can we go to the park?' 'I don't see why not.'*

27 **GO WITH SB** [T always + adv/prep] to go somewhere with someone to make sure they are safe: *My mother used to see me across the road.* | *I'll get Nick to see you home.* | *Let me see you to the door* (=go with you to the door, to say goodbye).

28 **be seeing things** to imagine that you see someone or something which is not really there: *There's no one there – you must be seeing things.*

29 **see double** if you see double, something is wrong with your eyes, so that you see two things when there is only one

30 **have seen better days** *informal* to be in a bad condition: *Her hat had seen better days.*

31 **be glad/pleased etc to see the back of sb/sth** *BrE spoken* to be pleased when someone leaves or when you get rid of something, because you do not like them: *I'll be glad to see the back of him.* | *I won't be sorry to see the back of this place.*

32 **see the last of sb/sth a)** to not see someone or something again, especially someone or something you do not like: *I thought we'd seen the last of him.* | *It was a relief to see the last of them.* **b)** to not have to deal with something any more: *Police had hoped they'd seen the last of the joyriding.* | *We may not have seen the last of this controversy.*

33 **see the light a)** to realize that something is true: *She finally saw the light and ended the relationship.* **b)** to have a special experience that makes you believe in a religion

34 **see the light of day a)** if something sees the light of day, it is brought out so that people can see it: *This decision will ensure that the Pentagon Papers never see the light of day.* **b)** to start to exist: *This type of PC first saw the light of day in 1981.*

35 **see red** to become very angry: *The thought of Pierre*

36 **not see sb for dust** *BrE informal* if you do not see someone for dust, they leave a place very quickly in order to avoid something

37 **see eye to eye** [usually in negatives] if two people see eye to eye, they agree with each other: *We didn't exactly see eye to eye.* | [+with] *I don't always see eye to eye with my father.* | [+on/about] *We don't see eye to eye on business issues.*

38 **seen one ... seen them all** *informal* used to say that something is boring because it is very similar to other things: *When you've seen one of these programmes, you've seen them all.*

39 **see your way (clear) to doing sth** *formal* to be able and willing to do something: *Small companies cannot see their way to taking on many trainees.*

40 **(see and) be seen** to look at or be noticed by important or fashionable people: *Royal Ascot is the place to see and be seen.*

41 **not see the wood for the trees** also **not see the forest for the trees** *AmE* to be unable to understand what is important in a situation because you are thinking too much about small details rather than the whole situation

42 **see sth coming** to realize that there is going to be a problem before it actually happens: *John's going to have a lot of trouble with him. You can see it coming.*

43 **see sb coming (a mile off)** *BrE spoken* to recognize that someone will be easy to trick or deceive: *You paid £500 for that! They must have seen you coming!*

44 **see sb right** *BrE spoken* to make sure that someone gets what they need or want, especially money: *Just do this for me and I'll see you right.* | *Tell the landlord I sent you and he'll see you right.*

45 **not see that it matters** *spoken* to think that something is not important: *I can't see that it matters what I think.*

46 **GAME OF CARDS** [T] to risk the same amount of money as your opponent in a CARD game → **it remains to be seen** at REMAIN (5); → **see fit (to do sth)** at FIT² (3); → **wouldn't be seen dead** at DEAD¹ (12)

see about sth *phr v*
1 to make arrangements or deal with something: *I'd better see about dinner.* | **see about doing sth** *Claire's gone to see about getting tickets for the concert.*
2 **we'll see about that** *spoken* **a)** also **we'll have to see about that** used to say that you do not know if something will be possible: *'I want to go to Joshua's tonight.' 'Well, we'll have to see about that.'* **b)** also **we'll soon see about that** used to say that you intend to stop someone from doing what they were planning to do

see sth **against** sth *phr v* [usually passive]
to consider something together with something else: *The unemployment data must be seen against the background of world recession.*

see around *phr v*
1 **see sb around** to notice someone regularly in places you go to, but not talk to them: *I don't know who he is but I've seen him around.*
2 **see you around** *spoken* used to say goodbye to someone when you have not made a definite arrangement to meet again
3 **see around/round sth** *BrE* to visit a place and walk around looking at it: *Would you like to see round the house?*

see in *phr v*
1 **not know what sb sees in sb** also **what does sb see in sb?** used to say that you do not know why someone likes someone else: *I don't know what she sees in him.*
2 **see sth in sb/sth** to notice a particular quality in someone or something that makes you like them: *He saw a gentleness in Susan.*
3 **see sb in** to go with someone to make sure they arrive at a building or room: *He took her home and after seeing her in, drove off without a word.*
4 **see in the New Year** to celebrate the beginning of a new year

see sb/sth ⇔ **off** *phr v*
1 to defeat someone or stop them from competing

against you: *To see off the threat, the company will have to cut its prices still further.* | *The team saw off their old rivals in last night's championship game.*
2 to go to an airport, train station etc to say goodbye to someone: *They've gone to the airport to see their son off.*
3 also **see sb off sth** to force someone to leave a place: *Security guards saw him off the premises.*
  see sb/sth **out** *phr v*
1 to go to the door with someone to say goodbye to them when they leave: *I'll see you out.* | *Don't worry, I can see myself out* (=leave the building without anyone coming in with me).
2 **see sth ⇔ out** to continue doing something or being somewhere until a particular period of time or an unpleasant event is finished: *Connolly has promised to see out the remaining 18 months of his contract.* | *She saw out her last years at Sudeley Castle.*
  see over sth *phr v BrE*
to look at something large such as a house, especially in order to decide if you want to buy it
  see through *phr v*
1 **see through sb/sth** to realize that someone is trying to deceive you: *I saw through his excuses.* | *I could never lie to her because I know she'd see through me straight away.* | *I can't bluff – she'd see right through me.*
2 **see sth through** to continue doing something until it is finished, especially something difficult or unpleasant: *It'll take a lot of effort to see the project through.*
3 **see sb through (sth)** to give help and support to someone during a difficult time: *Setting goals should help see you through.* | *I've got enough money to see me through six months of unemployment.*
4 **see sth through sb's eyes** to see something or think about it in the way that someone else does: *The world is very different when seen through the eyes of a child.*
  see to sb/sth *phr v*
to deal with something or do something for someone: *Go on, you go out. I'll see to the washing up.* | **have/get sth seen to** *You should get that tooth seen to by a dentist.*

WORD CHOICE: see, watch, look at
See means to notice something with your eyes, either deliberately or accidentally: *I saw a great film last week.* | *A few people saw him take the bag.*
Watch means to deliberately pay attention to something for quite a long time: *They were all watching the game on TV.* | *He watched her leave.*
When you **look at** something, you deliberately turn your eyes towards it in order to see it: *There was a loud noise and everyone looked at the screen.*
⚠ You can **see** something **on** television or **watch** television, but do not say 'see television': *After I finish my homework I usually watch television.*

---

see² *n* [C] an area governed by a BISHOP
seed¹ S3 W3 /siːd/ *n plural* **seeds** *or* **seed**
1 PLANTS **a)** [C,U] a small, hard object produced by plants, from which a new plant of the same kind grows: *sunflower seeds* | **plant/sow seeds** (=put them into the ground) *Sow the seeds one inch deep in the soil.* | **grow sth from seed** (=grow a plant from a seed, rather than planting it when it is already partly grown) **b)** [U] a quantity of seeds: *grass seed*
2 IN FRUIT [C] *AmE* one of the small hard objects in a fruit such as an apple or orange, from which new fruit trees grow; ◙ **pip** *BrE*; → see picture at FRUIT¹
3 **seeds of sth** *written* something that makes a new situation start to grow and develop: **seeds of change/victory** *The seeds of change in Eastern Europe were beginning to emerge.* | **seeds of doubt/disaster/destruction etc** (=something which makes a bad feeling or situation develop) *Something Lucy said began to sow seeds of doubt in his mind.*
4 **go/run to seed a)** if a plant or vegetable goes or runs to seed, it starts producing flowers and seeds as well as leaves **b)** if someone or something goes or runs to seed, they become less attractive or good, especially because they are getting old and have not been properly looked after: *The old central bus station is going to seed.*

---

5 **number one/two/three etc seed** [C] a player or team in a competition that is given a particular position, according to how likely they are to win: *He's been top seed for the past two years.*
6 SEX [U] *biblical* SEMEN or SPERM - often used humorously
7 FAMILY [U] *biblical* the group of people who have a particular person as their father, grandfather etc, especially when they form a particular race

seed² *v* **1** [T] to remove seeds from fruit or vegetables: *Add 1 lime, seeded and sliced.* **2** [T usually passive] to give a player or team in a competition a particular position, according to how likely they are to win: *Graf, seeded fifth at Wimbledon* **3** [T usually passive] to plant seeds in the ground: *a newly-seeded lawn* **4** [I] to produce seeds **5** **seed itself** if a tree or plant seeds itself, it produces a new plant using its own seeds

seed·bed /'siːdbed/ *n* [C] **1** a place or condition that encourages something to develop: [+for/of] *Strong personal beliefs can become a seedbed for conflicts.* **2** an area of ground where young plants are grown from seeds before they are planted somewhere else

'seed ,capital *n* [U] SEED MONEY

'seed corn *n* [U] **1** *BrE* people or things that will develop to become useful or successful in the future: *These young people are the seed corn management of the future.* **2** grain that is used for planting next year's crops

seed·less /'siːdləs/ *adj* seedless fruit has no seeds in it: *seedless grapes*

seed·ling /'siːdlɪŋ/ *n* [C] a young plant or tree grown from a seed

'seed ,money also **'seed ,capital** *n* [U] the money you have available to start a new business

'seed pearl *n* [C] a very small and often imperfect PEARL

seed·y /'siːdi/ *adj informal* a seedy person or place looks dirty or poor, and is often connected with illegal or immoral activities: *a seedy nightclub* | *a seedy-looking old man*

see·ing S3 /'siːɪŋ/ *conjunction spoken* because a particular fact or situation is true: [+as] *I won't stay long, seeing as you're busy.* | *Oh, all right, seeing as it's you* (=used to agree humorously to someone's request).

,Seeing 'Eye ,dog *n* [C] *trademark AmE* a dog trained to guide blind people; ◙ **guide dog** *BrE*

seek W1 /siːk/ *v past tense and past participle* **sought** /sɔːt $ sɒːt/ [T]
1 *formal* to try to achieve or get something: *Do you think the President will seek re-election?* | **seek refuge/asylum/shelter etc** *Thousands of people crossed the border, seeking refuge from the war.* | **seek revenge/damages/compensation etc** *He sought revenge against Surkov for separating him from his wife and son.* | **seek to do sth** *Local schools are seeking to reduce the dropout rate.* | **attention-seeking/publicity-seeking** ⚠ In spoken English it is more usual to use **look for** or **try to find**.
2 **seek (sb's) advice/help/assistance etc** *formal* to ask someone for advice or help: *If the symptoms persist, seek medical advice.* ⚠ In spoken English it is more usual to use **try to get**.
3 *written* to look for someone or something; ◙ **look for**: *new graduates seeking employment* | *Attractive woman, 27, seeks male, 25–35, for fun and friendship.*
4 **seek your fortune** *literary* to go to another place hoping to gain success and wealth: *Coles came to the Yukon in the 1970s to seek his fortune.*
5 to move naturally towards something or into a particular position: *Water seeks its own level.* → HEAT-SEEKING, HIDE-AND-SEEK, SELF-SEEKING, SOUGHT-AFTER

---

1 000, **2** 000, **3** 000, most frequent words in S poken and W ritten English

seek sb/sth ⇔ **out** phr v
to try to find someone or something, especially when this is difficult: *Our mission is to seek out the enemy and destroy them.*

seek·er /'si:kə $ -ər/ n [C] someone who is trying to find or get something: **job/attention/publicity etc seeker** *a brilliant politician and a ruthless power-seeker*
→ ASYLUM SEEKER

seem S1 W1 /si:m/ v [linking verb, not in progressive]
1 to appear to exist or be true, or to have a particular quality: *Ann didn't seem very sure.* | *It seems a foolish decision now.* | **seem to do sth** *The rainbow seemed to end on the hillside.* | **seem important/right/strange etc to sb** *Doesn't that seem weird to you?* | **it seems to sb (that)** *It seems to me you don't have much choice.* | **it seems (that)** *It seemed that Freeman had killed the man, and dumped the body in the lake.* | **it seems likely/unlikely/reasonable/clear (that)** *It seems likely that he will miss Ireland's next match.* | [+like] *Teri seemed like a nice girl.* | *Well,* **it seemed like a good idea** *at the time.* | *We waited for what* **seemed like hours.** | **seem as if/as though/like** *It seemed as if the end of the world had come.* | *It* **seems like** *you're catching a cold, Taylor.* | '*So Bill's leaving her?*' '**So it seems** (=it appears to be true).'
2 can't/couldn't seem to do sth used to say that you have tried to do something but cannot do it: *I just can't seem to relax.*
3 used to make what you are saying less strong or certain, and more polite: **seem to do sth** *I seem to have lost my car keys.* | **it seems (that)/it would seem (that)** *It would seem that someone left the building unlocked.*

> **WORD CHOICE: seem, appear, look, sound**
> **Seem** and **appear** have the same meaning but **appear** is more formal: *They seem upset.* | *This appears to be a good solution.*
> You use **look** to say how someone or something seems to you when you look at them: *Maureen looked tired.* | *That book looks good.*
> You use **sound** to say how someone or something seems to you when you hear or read about them, or hear them: *She sounds a lovely person.* | *The party sounded great.* | *He sounded tired.*
> **Seem** can be followed by an adjective or an adjective and noun: *She seemed happy.* | *He seems a nice man.*
> **Seem** can also be followed by a verb in the infinitive: *His story seems to be true.* | *You seem to think it's my fault.*
> ⚠ **Seem** can be followed by **as if** or **as though** but not just by **as**: *It seems a small thing (NOT it seems as a small thing), but it's very important.* | *It seemed as if he wanted us to leave (NOT it seemed as he wanted ...).*

seem·ing /'si:mɪŋ/ adj [only before noun] formal appearing to be something, especially when this is not actually true; ⊟ **apparent**: *a seeming piece of good luck, which later led to all kinds of trouble*

seem·ing·ly /'si:mɪŋli/ adv **1** appearing to have a particular quality, when this may or may not be true; ⊟ **apparently**: *seemingly unrelated bits of information* | **seemingly endless/impossible etc** *The new minister was faced with a seemingly impossible task.* | **seemingly unaware/oblivious** *Alice was standing in the street, seemingly oblivious to the rain.* **2** [sentence adverb] formal according to the facts as you know them; ⊟ **apparently**: *There is seemingly nothing we can do to stop the plans going ahead.*

seem·ly /'si:mli/ adj old-fashioned suitable for a particular situation or social occasion, according to accepted standards of behaviour; ⊟ **unseemly**: *It was not seemly for ladies to talk about money.*

seen /si:n/ v the past participle of SEE

seep /si:p/ v [I always + adv/prep] **1** to flow slowly through small holes or spaces: [+into/through/down etc] *Blood seeped down his leg.* **2** to move or spread gradually: [+away/into/through etc] *His tension was seeping away.*

seep·age /'si:pɪdʒ/ n [C,U] a gradual flow of liquid or gas through small spaces or holes

seer /sɪə $ sɪr/ n [C] especially literary someone who can see into the future and say what will happen

seer·suck·er /'sɪə,sʌkə $ 'sɪr,sʌkər/ n [U] a light cotton cloth with an uneven surface and a pattern of lines on it

see·saw¹ /'si:sɔ: $ -sɒ:/ n [C] **1** a piece of equipment that children play on, made of a board that is balanced in the middle, so that when one end goes up the other goes down; ⊟ **teeter-totter** AmE **2** a repeated movement from one state or condition to another and back again

seesaw² v [I] to keep changing from one state or condition to another and back again: *Before the election, the president seesawed in the polls.*

seethe /si:ð/ v [I] **1** to feel an emotion, especially anger, so strongly that you are almost shaking; ⊟ **fume**: [+with] *He was seething with anger.* | *I was absolutely seething.* **2 be seething (with sth)** if a place is seething with people, insects etc, there are a lot of them all moving quickly in different directions: *The cellar was seething with spiders.*

see-through adj a see-through material or surface allows you to see through it: *a see-through blouse*

seg·ment¹ /'seɡmənt/ n [C] **1** a part of something that is different from or affected differently from the whole in some way: [+of] *segments of the population* **2** a part of a fruit, flower, or insect that it naturally divides into: *Decorate with orange segments.* → see picture at FRUIT¹ **3** technical the part of a circle that is separated from the rest of the circle when you draw a straight line across it **4** technical the part of a line or of a length of something between two points: [+of] *segments of DNA*

seg·ment² /seɡ'ment/ v [T] to divide something into parts that are different from each other

seg·men·ta·tion /,seɡmen'teɪʃən, -mən-/ n [U] when something divides or is divided into smaller parts: [+of] *the segmentation of society*

seg·ment·ed /seɡ'mentɪd/ adj consisting of separate parts that are connected to each other: *segmented worms*

seg·re·gate /'seɡrɪɡeɪt/ v [T] [usually passive] **1** to separate one group of people from others, especially because they are of a different race, sex, or religion; ⊟ **integrate**: **segregate sb from sb** *Blacks were segregated from whites in schools.* **2** to separate one part of a place or thing from another: **segregate sth from/into sth** *The coffee room had been segregated into smoking and non-smoking areas.*

seg·re·gat·ed /'seɡrɪɡeɪtɪd/ adj a segregated school or other institution can only be attended by members of one sex, race, religion etc; ⊟ **integrated**: *a racially segregated education system*

seg·re·ga·tion /,seɡrɪ'ɡeɪʃən/ n [U] when people of different races, sexes, or religions are kept apart so that they live, work, or study separately; ⊟ **integration**: *racial segregation* | [+of] *the segregation of men and women*

seg·re·ga·tion·ist /,seɡrɪ'ɡeɪʃənɪst/ adj relating to the practice of keeping people of different races, sexes, or religions separate: *segregationist policies* —**segregationist** n [C]

seg·ue /'seɡweɪ/ v **segued, segueing** [I] to move smoothly from one song, idea, activity, condition etc to another: [+into/from] *The conversation segued into banter about the Cup Final.* —**segue** n [C]

seis·mic /'saɪzmɪk/ adj [only before noun] **1** technical relating to or caused by EARTHQUAKES: *increased seismic activity* **2** very great, serious, or important: *seismic changes in international relations*

seis·mo·graph /'saɪzməɡrɑ:f $ -ɡræf/ n [C] an instrument that measures and records the movement of the earth during an EARTHQUAKE

seis·mol·o·gy /saɪz'mɒlədʒi $ -'mɑː-/ *n* [U] the scientific study of EARTHQUAKES —**seismologist** *n* [C]

seize W3 /siːz/ *v* [T]
1 to take hold of something suddenly and violently; ▤ **grab**: *Suddenly he seized my hand.* | **seize sth from sb** *Maggie seized the letter from her.*
2 to take control of a place suddenly and quickly, using military force: **seize power/control (of sth)** *The rebels have seized power.* | *A group of soldiers seized the airport.*
3 if the police or government officers seize something, for example illegal drugs, they take legal possession of it: *160,000 CDs were seized from illegal factories.* | *All of my assets were seized, including my home.*
4 to suddenly catch someone and make sure they cannot get away: *The gunmen were seized at 1 a.m.*
5 seize a chance/an opportunity/the initiative to quickly and eagerly do something when you have the chance to
6 be seized with/by terror/desire etc to suddenly be affected by an extremely strong feeling: *When she saw his face, she was seized by fear.*

  seize on/upon sth *phr v*
to suddenly become very interested in an idea, excuse, what someone says etc: *His every remark is seized upon by the press.*

  seize up *phr v*
a) if an engine or part of a machine seizes up, its moving parts stop working and can no longer move, for example because of lack of oil: *The mechanism had seized up.* **b)** if a part of your body, such as your back, seizes up, you suddenly cannot move it and it is very painful

sei·zure /'siːʒə $ -ər/ *n* **1** [C,U] the act of suddenly taking control of something, especially by force: [+of] *the Fascist seizure of power in 1922* **2** [C,U] when the police or government officers take away illegal goods such as drugs or guns: *drugs seizures* **3** [C] a sudden condition in which someone cannot control the movements of their body, which continues for a short time; ▤ **fit**: *He had an epileptic seizure.*

sel·dom /'seldəm/ *adv* very rarely or almost never: *Karen had seldom seen him so angry.* | *Ellie seldom wears slacks.* | **seldom has sb done sth** *Seldom have I read an article that was so full of lies.*; → see box at RARELY

se·lect¹ S2 W2 /sə'lekt/ *v* [T] to choose something or someone by thinking carefully about which is the best, most suitable etc; ▤ **choose, pick**: *a group of students selected at random* | **select sb for sth** *He had hopes of being selected for the national team.* | **select sb/sth as sth** *York was selected as the site for the research centre.* | **select sb/sth from sth** *They selected the winner from six finalists.* | **select sb to do sth** *Simon's been selected to go to the conference.*

select² *adj formal* **1** a select group of people or things is a small special group that has been chosen carefully: *The party was small and select.* | *Honorary degrees are handed out to a select few.* **2** only lived in, visited, or used by a small number of rich people; ▤ **exclusive**: *a select block of flats*

se·lect com·mit·tee *n* [C] a small group of politicians and advisers from various parties that has been chosen to examine a particular subject

se·lec·tion S2 W2 /sə'lekʃən/ *n*
1 [U] the careful choice of a particular person or thing from a group of similar people or things: [+of] *the selection of a new leader* | *It was not easy to* **make our selection.** | [+for] *He had narrowly missed selection for the team.* | [+as] *Perlman's selection as the party's candidate*

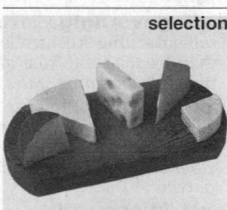
selection
a selection of cheeses

2 [C] something that has been chosen from among a group of things; ▤ **choice**: *To order, just write your selections on the form.* | [+from] *These drawings represent a selection from a larger exhibition.*
3 [C usually singular] a group of things of a particular type, often of things that are for sale; ▤ **range**: [+of] *a* **wide selection** *of shellfish* → NATURAL SELECTION

se·lec·tive /sə'lektɪv/ *adj* **1** careful about what you choose to do, buy, allow etc: [+about/in] *We're very selective about what we let the children watch.* | *selective schools* (=that choose which students to accept) | *He has a very selective memory* (=he chooses what he wants to remember and what to forget). **2** affecting or relating to the best or most suitable people or things from a larger group: *selective breeding* —**selectively** *adv* —**selectivity** /sɪ,lek'tɪvəti/ *n* [U]

se·lec·tor /sə'lektə $ -ər/ *n* [C] **1** *BrE* a member of a committee that chooses the best people for something such as a sports team **2** *technical* a piece of equipment that helps you find the right thing, for example the correct GEAR in a car

se·le·ni·um /sə'liːniəm/ *n* [U] a poisonous chemical substance, used in electrical instruments to make them sensitive to light. It is a chemical ELEMENT: symbol Se

self S2 W3 /self/ *n plural* **selves** /selvz/
1 [C usually singular] the type of person you are, your character, your typical behaviour etc: **sb's usual/normal self** *Sid was not his usual smiling self.* | **be/look/feel (like) your old self** (=be the way you usually are again, especially after having been ill, unhappy etc) *Jim was beginning to feel like his old self again.* | **sb's true/real self** (=what someone is really like, rather than what they pretend to be like) *Peter was the only one to whom she showed her true self.*
2 sb's sense of self someone's idea that they are a separate person, different from other people: *a child's developing sense of self*
3 be a shadow/ghost of your former self to not be as healthy, strong etc as you used to be
4 [U] a word written in business letters, on cheques etc meaning yourself: *a cheque written to self*
5 [C] used to refer to a person: *a picture of a journalist and* **your good self** (=you)

self- S3 /self/ *prefix*
1 by yourself or by itself: *a self-propelled vehicle*
2 of, to, with, or for yourself or itself: *a self-portrait*

self-ab·sorbed *adj* interested only in yourself and the things that affect you: *Teenagers always seem so self-absorbed.* —**self-absorption** *n* [U]

self-a·buse *n* [U] MASTURBATION - used to show disapproval

self-ac·cess *n* [U] *BrE* a method of learning in which students choose their own books, materials etc and study on their own: *a self-access centre*

self-ac·tuali·zation also **-isation** *BrE* [U] *technical* when someone achieves what they want through work or in their personal life

self-ad·dressed *adj* a self-addressed envelope has the sender's address on it, so that information can be put in it and sent back to them → SAE, SASE

self-ad·he·sive *adj* a self-adhesive envelope, BANDAGE etc has a sticky surface and does not need liquid or glue to make it stay closed

self-ap·pointed *adj* giving yourself a responsibility, job, position etc without the agreement of other people, especially those you claim to represent – used to show disapproval

self-as·sem·bly *adj* self-assembly furniture is sold as separate parts that you put together yourself at home

self-as·ser·tive *adj* very confident about saying what you think or want —**self-assertiveness** also **self-assertion** *n* [U]

,self-as'sessment *n* [U] **1** when you judge your own work or progress **2** *BrE* when someone who works for themselves calculates how much tax they should pay

,self-as'sured *adj* calm and confident about what you are doing; ⊟ hesitant —**self-assurance** *n* [U]

,self-a'wareness *n* [U] knowledge and understanding of yourself —**self-aware** *adj*

self·build, self-build /'selfbɪld/ *n* [U] when you build your own house rather than paying a professional builder to do it for you: *a selfbuild kit* —**self-builder** *n* [C]

,self-'catering *adj* [usually before noun] *BrE* relating to a holiday in which you stay in a place where you can cook your own food: *self-catering accommodation/apartment/cottage etc* —**self-catering** *n* [U]: *Prices start from £114 per person for seven nights' self-catering.*

,self-'centred *BrE*; **self-centered** *AmE adj* paying so much attention to yourself that you do not notice what is happening to other people; ⊟ selfish —**self-centredness** *n* [U]

,self-certifi'cation *n* [U] *BrE* when you sign a form or note to say that you have been ill, to explain why you have not been at work or school for a short time

,self-'concept *n* [C] the idea that someone has of what their own character is like

,self-con'fessed *adj* [only before noun] admitting that you have a particular quality, especially one that is bad: *a self-confessed drug addict*

,self-'confident *adj* sure that you can do things well, that people like you etc; ⊟ shy —**self-confidently** *adv* —**self-confidence** *n* [U]

,self-congratu'lation *n* [U] behaviour that shows in an annoying way that you think you have done very well at something —,self-congratu'latory / $,. .'...../ *adj*: *a smug, self-congratulatory smile*

,self-'conscious *adj* **1** worried and embarrassed about what you look like or what other people think of you: [+about] *Jerry's pretty self-conscious about his weight.* **2** self-conscious art, writing etc shows that the artist etc is paying too much attention to how the public will react to their work —**self-consciously** *adv*: *The boys posed rather self-consciously for the photo.* —**self-consciousness** *n* [U]

,self-con'tained *adj* **1** complete and not needing other things or help from somewhere else to work: *a self-contained database package* **2** someone who is self-contained does not seem to need other people or show their feelings **3** *BrE* a self-contained apartment has its own kitchen and bathroom

,self-contra'dictory *adj* containing two opposite statements or ideas that cannot both be true

,self-con'trol *n* [U] the ability to behave calmly and sensibly even when you feel very excited, angry etc —**self-controlled** *adj*

,self-'criticism *n* [U] when you judge your own behaviour or character, especially when you have done something bad —**self-critical** *adj*

,self-de'ception *n* [U] when you make yourself believe that something is true when it is not

,self-de'feating *adj* causing even more problems, or causing exactly the same problems and difficulties that you are trying to prevent or deal with: *Constant dieting can be self-defeating.*

,self-de'fence *BrE*; **self-defense** *AmE n* [U] **1** something you do to protect yourself or your property: **in self-defence** *He shot him in self-defence.* **2** skills that you learn to protect yourself if you are attacked

,self-de'nial *n* [U] when you do not do or have the things you enjoy for moral or religious reasons —**self-denying** *adj*

,self-'deprecating *adj* trying to make your own abilities or achievements seem unimportant: *self-deprecating humour* —,self-depre'cation *n* [U]

self-de·struct /,self dɪ'strʌkt◂/ *v* [I] if something such as a bomb self-destructs, it destroys itself, usually by exploding —**self-destruct** *adj*

,self-de'structive *adj* deliberately doing things that are likely to seriously harm or kill yourself: *a self-destructive alcoholic* —**self-destruction** *n* [U]

,self-determi'nation *n* [U] the right of the people of a particular country to govern themselves and to choose the type of government they will have

,self-di'rected *adj* responsible for judging and organizing your own work rather than getting instructions from other people

,self-'discipline *n* [U] the ability to make yourself do the things you know you ought to do, without someone making you do them: *A lot of the kids seemed to lack self-discipline.* —**self-disciplined** *adj*

,self-'doubt *n* [U] the feeling that you and your abilities are not good enough: *a moment of self-doubt*

,self-'drive *adj* [only before noun] *BrE* **1** a self-drive car is one that you have HIRED to drive yourself **2** a self-drive holiday is one in which you use your own car to visit the holiday area

,self-'educated *adj* having taught yourself by reading books, thinking about ideas etc, rather than learning things in school

,self-ef'facing *adj* not wanting to attract attention to yourself or your achievements; ⊟ modest: *a quiet, self-effacing man* —**self-effacement** *n* [U]

,self-em'ployed *adj* working for yourself and not employed by a company: *a self-employed plumber* | *pension plans for* **the self-employed** (=people who are self-employed) —**self-employment** *n* [U]

,self-es'teem *n* [U] the feeling of being satisfied with your own abilities, and that you deserve to be liked or respected; → self-respect: **raise/build (up)/boost sb's self-esteem** *Playing a sport can boost a girl's self-esteem.* | *students' **sense of self-esteem*** | **low/poor self-esteem** (=not much self-esteem)

,self-'evident *adj formal* clearly true and needing no more proof; ⊟ obvious: *self-evident truths* | **it is self-evident (that)** *It is self-evident that childhood experiences influence our adult behaviour.*

,self-exami'nation *n* [U] **1** careful thought about whether your actions and your reasons for them are right or wrong **2** the practice of checking parts of your body for early signs of some illnesses

,self-ex'planatory *adj* clear and easy to understand without needing any more explanation: *The video controls are pretty self-explanatory.*

,self-ex'pression *n* [U] the expression of your feelings or thoughts, especially through activities such as painting, writing, or acting: *Corporate dress codes don't give workers much room for self-expression.*

,self-ful'filling *adj* if a statement or belief about what will happen in the future is self-fulfilling, it becomes true because you expect it to be true and so behave in a way that will make it happen: *It's a **self-fulfilling prophecy**: expect things to go wrong, and they probably will.*

,self-'governing *adj* a country or organization that is self-governing is controlled by its own members rather than by someone from another country or organization: *self-governing states* —**self-government** *n* [U]

,self-'help *n* [U] the use of your own efforts to deal with your problems, instead of depending on other people: *a shelf of **self-help books*** | *Our program emphasises self-help.* | *a **self-help group** for single parents*

,self-'image *n* [C] the idea that you have of yourself, especially of your abilities, character, and appearance: **positive/good/poor/negative self-image** *Depression affects people with a poor self-image.*

self-im'portant adj behaving in a way that shows you think you are more important than other people – used to show disapproval: *a self-important, pompous little man* —**self-importance** n [U] —**self-importantly** adv

self-im'posed adj [usually before noun] a self-imposed rule, duty etc is one that you have made for yourself, and which no one has asked you to accept: *She spent five years in self-imposed exile in Bolivia.*

self-in'dulgent adj allowing yourself to have or do things that you enjoy but do not need, especially if you do this too often – used to show disapproval: *It feels self-indulgent spending so much on a pair of shoes.* | **self-indulgent novel/film etc** (=said when you think the book or film only expresses the author or DIRECTOR's own interests, which are not interesting to other people) —**self-indulgence** n [singular, U]: *My one self-indulgence is expensive coffee.* —**self-indulgently** adv

self-in'flicted adj self-inflicted pain, problems, illnesses etc are those you have caused yourself: *self-inflicted gunshot wounds* | *Stress is often self-inflicted.*

self-'interest n [U] when you only care about what is best for you, and do not care about what is best for other people: *His offer was motivated solely by self-interest.* —**self-interested** adj

self·ish /'selfɪʃ/ adj caring only about yourself and not about other people – used to show disapproval: *How can you be so selfish?* | *selfish behaviour* —**selfishly** adv: *a small child behaving selfishly* —**selfishness** n [U]: *a lack of greed and selfishness*

self-'knowledge n [U] an understanding of your own character and behaviour

self·less /'selfləs/ adj caring about other people more than about yourself – used to show approval: *selfless devotion to their work* —**selflessly** adv —**selflessness** n [U]

self-'made adj a self-made man or woman has become successful and rich by their own efforts, not by having money given to them: **self-made man/millionaire/businessman**

self-o'pinionated adj believing that your own opinions are always right and that everyone else should agree with you – used to show disapproval

self-'pity n [U] the feeling of being sad and DEPRESSED because you think that something unfair or unpleasant has happened to you – used to show disapproval: *a note of self-pity in her voice* —**self-pitying** adj: *a self-pitying mood*

self-'portrait n [C] a drawing, painting, or description that you do of yourself

self-pos'sessed adj calm, confident, and in control of your feelings, even in difficult or unexpected situations – used to show approval: *She's a confident, self-possessed public speaker.* —**self-possession** n [U]

self-preser'vation n [U] protection of yourself and your own life in a threatening or dangerous situation: *the instinct for self-preservation*

self-pro'claimed adj having given yourself a position or title without the approval or agreement of other people – used to show disapproval: *a self-proclaimed champion of the working class*

self-raising 'flour n [U] BrE a type of flour that contains BAKING POWDER; → **plain flour**

self-regu'latory /$,. '...../ also **self-'regulating** adj a self-regulatory system, industry, or organization is one that controls itself, rather than having an independent organization or laws to make sure that rules are obeyed —**self-regu'lation** n [U]

self-re'liant adj able to do or decide things by yourself, without depending on the help or advice of other people: *Our aim is to teach our son to become an independent, self-reliant adult.* —**self-reliance** n [U]

self-re'spect n [U] a feeling of being happy about your character, abilities, and beliefs; → **self-esteem**: *It's difficult to keep your self-respect when you have been unemployed for a long time.*

self-re'specting adj [only before noun] having respect for yourself and your abilities and beliefs: **no/any self-respecting ... would do sth** *No self-respecting actor would appear in a porn movie.*

self-re'straint n [U] the ability to stop yourself doing or saying something, even though you want to, because it is more sensible not to do or say it: **exercise/practise self-restraint** *The UN appealed for both sides to exercise self-restraint.*

self-'righteous adj proudly sure that your beliefs, attitudes, and MORALS are good and right, in a way that annoys other people – used to show disapproval: *She's a vegetarian, but she's not at all self-righteous about it.* —**self-righteously** adv —**self-righteousness** n [U]

self-rising 'flour n [U] AmE a type of flour that contains BAKING POWDER; ⊟ **self-raising flour** BrE

self-'rule n [U] when a country or part of a country is governed by its own citizens

self-'sacrifice n [U] when you decide not to do or have something you want or need, in order to help someone else: *several years of hard work and self-sacrifice* —**self-sacrificing** adj

self·same /'selfseɪm/ adj [only before noun] written exactly the same: *two great victories on the selfsame day*

self-'satisfied adj too pleased with yourself and what you have done – used to show disapproval: *A self-satisfied smile settled on his face.* —**self-satis'faction** n [U]: *a feeling of self-satisfaction*

self-'seeking adj doing things only because they will give you an advantage that other people do not have – used to show disapproval: *a self-seeking politician*

self-'service adj a self-service restaurant, shop etc is one in which you get things for yourself and then pay for them —**self-service** n [U]

self-'serving adj showing that you will only do something if it will gain you an advantage – used to show disapproval: *self-serving politicians*

self-'starter n [C] someone who is able to work successfully on their own without needing other people's help or a lot of instructions – used to show approval

self-styled adj [only before noun] having given yourself a title or position without having a right to it – used to show disapproval: *a self-styled poet*

self-suf'ficient adj able to provide all the things you need without help from other people: *a self-sufficient farm* | [+in] *Australia is 65% self-sufficient in oil.* —**self-sufficiency** n [U]

self-sup'porting adj **1** able to earn enough money to support yourself: *The business will soon become self-supporting.* **2** able to stand or stay upright without support: *self-supporting fencing*

self-'taught adj having learned a skill or subject by reading about it, practising it etc yourself, rather than in a school: *She received some education at night school, but was largely self-taught.* | *a self-taught pianist*

self-'willed adj very determined to do what you want, whatever other people think – used to show disapproval: *a wild and self-willed child* —**self-will** n [U]

self-wind·ing /ˌself 'waɪndɪŋ◂/ adj a self-winding watch is one that you do not have to WIND to make it work

self-'worth n [U] the feeling that you deserve to be liked and respected; → **self-esteem**: *Work gave me a sense of dignity and self-worth.*

sell S1 W1 /sel/ v past tense and past participle **sold** /səʊld $ soʊld/
1 GIVE STH FOR MONEY [I,T] to give something to someone in exchange for money; ⊟ **buy**: *If you offer him another hundred, I think he'll sell.* | *He regrets*

S

selling all his old records. | **sell sth for £100/$50/30p etc** *Toni's selling her car for £700.* | **sell sb sth** *I won't sell you my shares!* | **sell sth to sb** *The vase was sold to a Dutch buyer.* | **sell sth at a profit/loss** (=make or lose money on a sale) *Tony had to sell the business at a loss.*
2 MAKE STH AVAILABLE [I,T] to offer something for people to buy: *Do you sell cigarettes?* | *a job selling advertising space* | **sell at/for £100/$50/30p etc** (=be offered for sale at £100/$50/30p etc) *Smoke alarms sell for as little as five pounds.*
3 MAKE SB WANT STH [T] to make people want to buy something: *Scandal sells newspapers.* | **sell sth to sb** *The car's new design will help sell it to consumers.*
4 BE BOUGHT [I,T] to be bought by people: *Tickets for the concert just aren't selling.* | *Her last book sold millions of copies.* | *All the new houses have been sold.* | **sell well/badly** (=be bought by a lot of people, or very few people) *Anti-age creams always sell well.*
5 sell like hot cakes to sell quickly and in large amounts
6 IDEA/PLAN [I,T] to try to make someone accept a new idea or plan, or to become accepted: *It's all right for Washington, but will it sell in small-town America?* | **sell sth to sb** *It's hard for any government to sell new taxes to the electorate.* | **sell sb sth** *managers selling employees the new working hours* | **be sold on (doing) sth** (=think an idea or plan is very good) *Joe's completely sold on the concept.*
7 sell yourself a) to make yourself seem impressive to other people: *If you want a promotion, you've got to sell yourself better.* **b)** also **sell your body** to have sex with someone for money
8 sell sb/sth short to not give someone or something the praise, attention, or reward that they deserve: *Don't sell yourself short – tell them about all your qualifications.*
9 sell your soul (to the devil) to agree to do something bad in exchange for money, power etc
10 sell sb down the river to do something that harms a group of people who trusted you, in order to gain money or power for yourself
11 sell your vote *AmE* to take money from someone who wants you to vote for a particular person or plan
sell sth ⇔ off *phr v*
1 to sell something, especially for a cheap price, because you need the money or because you want to get rid of it: *After the war, we had to sell off part of the farm.* | *We try to sell off any leftover cakes before we close.*
2 to sell all or part of an industry or company: *The Leicestershire company has sold off many of its smaller branches to cut debts.*
sell out *phr v*
1 if a shop sells out of something, it has no more of that particular thing left to sell: **be/have sold out** *Sorry, we're sold out.* | [+of] *We've completely sold out of those shirts in your size, sir.*
2 if products, tickets for an event etc sell out, they are all sold and there are none left: *Wow! Those cakes sold out fast.* | **be/have sold out** *Tonight's performance is completely sold out.*
3 to change your beliefs or principles, especially in order to get more money or some other advantage – used to show disapproval: *ex-hippies who've sold out and become respectable businessmen*
4 to sell your business or your share in a business: *Wyman says he'll sell out if business doesn't pick up.* | [+to] *The T-mail Co. has sold out to San Jose-based DMX Inc for an undisclosed sum.*
sell up *phr v BrE*
to sell most of what you own, especially your house or your business: *Liz decided to sell up and move abroad.*

'sell-by date *n* [C] *BrE* **1** the date stamped on a food product, after which it should not be sold: *a yoghurt two days past its sell-by date* **2** *informal* a time beyond which something or someone is no longer interesting or useful: *This type of games console is starting to look well past its sell-by date.*

sell·er /'selə $ -ər/ *n* [C] **1** someone who sells something; ☒ **buyer 2 good/bad/poor etc seller** a product that has been popular, not popular etc with customers; → **bestseller**: *The album 'Thriller' remains one of the biggest sellers of all time.*

,seller's 'market *n* [singular] a situation in which there is not much of a particular thing available, such as houses, so prices are high; ☒ **buyer's market**

sell·ing /'selɪŋ/ *n* [U] the job and skill of persuading people to buy things: *a career in selling*

'selling point *n* [C] a particular quality that something has which will make people want to buy it: *Small classes are a selling point for private schools.* → USP

'selling price *n* [C] the price at which something is actually sold; → **asking price**

'sell-off *n* [C] **1** *BrE* the sale of an industry that the government owns, to private companies or other people **2** *AmE* the sale of a lot of STOCKS or SHARES, which makes the price decrease

Sel·lo·tape /'seləteɪp, -lou- $ -lə-, -lou-/ *n* [U] *trademark BrE* thin clear plastic tape that is sticky on one side, used for sticking things together: *a roll of Sellotape* —**sellotape** *v* [T]

'sell-out, sell·out /'selaʊt/ *n* [singular] **1** a performance, sports game etc, for which all the tickets have been sold: *The concert was expected to be a sell-out.* | *a sellout crowd of 32,000* **2** *informal* a situation in which someone has not done what they promised to do or were expected to do by the people who trusted them: *a sellout of the poor for political reasons* **3** *informal* someone who has not done what they promised to do or who is not loyal to their friends or supporters, especially in order to become more popular, richer etc: *Many black students regarded him as a sellout.*

selt·zer /'seltsə $ -ər/ *n* [U] *AmE* water that contains small bubbles

sel·vedge, selvage /'selvɪdʒ/ *n* [C] the edge of a piece of cloth, made strong so that the threads will not come apart

selves /selvz/ *n* the plural of SELF

se·man·tic /sɪ'mæntɪk/ *adj formal* relating to the meanings of words —**semantically** /-kli/ *adv*

se·man·tics /sɪ'mæntɪks/ *n* [U] **1** the study of the meaning of words and phrases **2** *formal* the meaning of a word

sem·a·phore /'seməfɔː $ -fɔːr/ *n* [U] a system of sending messages using two flags, which you hold in different positions to represent letters and numbers

sem·blance /'sembləns/ *n* **a/some semblance of sth** a situation, condition etc that is close to or similar to a particular one, usually a good one: *She was trying to get her thoughts back into some semblance of order.* | *After the war, life returned to a semblance of normality.*

se·men /'siːmən/ *n* [U] the liquid containing SPERM that is produced by the male sex organs in humans and animals

se·mes·ter /sɪ'mestə $ -ər/ *n* [C] one of the two periods of time that a year at high schools and universities is divided into, especially in the US: *the fall semester* → TERM[1] (5) → QUARTER[1] (8)

sem·i /'semi/ *plural* **semis** *n* [C] **1** *BrE informal* a SEMI-DETACHED house: *a three-bedroomed semi* **2** *informal* a SEMI-FINAL **3** *AmE* a very large heavy truck consisting of two connected parts, which carries goods over long distances; ☒ **articulated lorry** *BrE*

semi- /'semi/ *prefix* **1** exactly half: *a semicircle* **2** partly but not completely: *in the semi-darkness* | *semi-literate people* **3** happening, appearing etc twice in a particular period: *a semi-weekly visit* | *a semi-annual publication* → BI-

,semi-auto'matic also **sem·i·au·to·mat·ic** *AmE* /,semiːtə'mætɪk◂ $ -ɒːtə-/ *adj* a semi-automatic weapon moves each bullet into position ready for you to fire, so that you can fire the next shot very quickly —**semi-automatic** n [C]

sem·i·breve /'semibriːv/ n [C] BrE a musical note which continues for four BEATS; ◨ **whole note** AmE

sem·i·cir·cle /'semi,sɜːkəl $ -ɜːr-/ n [C] half a circle: **in a semicircle** About 50 children sat in a semicircle around me. —**semicircular** /,semi'sɜːkjʊlə◂ $ -'sɜːrkjʊlər◂/ adj

sem·i·co·lon, **semi-'colon** /,semi'kəʊlən $ 'semi,koʊlən/ n [C] a PUNCTUATION MARK (;) used to separate different parts of a sentence or list

sem·i·con·duc·tor /,semikən'dʌktə $ -ər/ n [C] a substance, such as SILICON, that allows some electric currents to pass through it, and is used in electronic equipment —**semiconducting** adj [only before noun]

,semi-de'tached adj BrE a semi-detached house is joined to another house on one side; → **detached**, **terraced**; → see picture at HOUSE[1]

,semi-'final BrE, **sem·i·fi·nal** AmE /,semi'faɪnl/ n [C] one of two sports games whose winners then compete against each other to decide who wins the whole competition

,semi-'finalist BrE, **sem·i·fi·nal·ist** AmE /,semi'faɪnl-ɪst/ n [C] a person or team that competes in a semi-final

sem·i·nal /'semɪnəl/ adj **1** formal a seminal article, book etc is important, and influences the way things develop in the future: a seminal study of eighteenth-century France **2** [only before noun] technical producing or containing SEMEN

sem·i·nar /'semɪnɑː $ -nɑːr/ n [C] **1** a class at a university or college for a small group of students and a teacher to study or discuss a particular subject: a Shakespeare seminar **2** a class on a particular subject, usually given as a form of training: Publishers and writers from 13 countries **attended** the **seminar**.

sem·i·na·ry /'semɪnəri $ -neri-/ n plural **seminaries** [C] **1** a college for training priests or ministers **2** old-fashioned a school

sem·i·ot·ics /,semi'ɒtɪks $ -'ɑːt-/ also **sem·i·ol·o·gy** /,semi'ɒlədʒi $ -'ɑːl-/ n [U] technical the way in which people communicate through signs and images, or the study of this —**semiotic** adj —**semiotician** /,semiə'tɪʃən/ also **semiologist** n [C]

,semi-'precious BrE; **sem·i·pre·cious** AmE /,semi'preʃəs◂/ adj a semi-precious jewel or stone is valuable, but not as valuable as a DIAMOND, RUBY etc

,semi-pro'fessional, **sem·i·pro·fes·sion·al** /,semiprə'feʃənəl◂/ also **,semi-'pro** AmE adj a semi-professional sports player, musician etc is paid for doing that thing, but does not do it as their main job: a semiprofessional boxer —**semiprofessional** also **semipro** AmE n [C]

sem·i·qua·ver /'semi,kweɪvə $ -ər/ n [C] BrE a musical note which continues for a sixteenth of the length of a SEMIBREVE; ◨ **sixteenth note** AmE

,semi-re'tired BrE; **sem·i·re·tired** /,semirɪ'taɪəd◂ $ -'taɪrd◂/ AmE adj someone who is semi-retired continues to work, but not for as many hours as they used to, especially because they are getting older and want time to do other things

,semi-'skilled, **sem·i·skilled** /,semi'skɪld◂/ adj needing or having some skills or training: a semi-skilled job | semi-skilled workers

,semi-skimmed 'milk n [U] BrE milk that has had some of the fat removed; ◨ **two-percent milk** AmE

sem·i·sweet /,semi'swiːt◂/ adj AmE semisweet chocolate is only slightly sweet and has a darker colour than MILK CHOCOLATE

Se·mit·ic /sɪ'mɪtɪk/ adj **1 a)** belonging to the race of people that includes Jews, Arabs, and, in ancient times, Babylonians and Assyrians **b)** relating to any of the languages of these people **2** another word for JEWISH → **anti-Semitic** at ANTI-SEMITE

sem·i·tone /'semitəʊn $ -toʊn/ n [C] BrE the difference in PITCH between any two notes that are next to each other on a piano; ◨ **half step** AmE

sem·i·trop·i·cal /,semi'trɒpɪkəl $ -'trɑː-/ adj SUB-TROPICAL

'semi-vowel n [C] technical a sound made in speech that sounds like a vowel, but is in fact a CONSONANT, for example /w/

sem·o·li·na /,semə'liːnə/ n [U] **1** small grains of crushed wheat, used especially in making sweet dishes and PASTA **2** BrE a sweet dish made with these grains and milk

Sem·tex /'semteks/ n [U] trademark a powerful explosive often used illegally to make bombs

Sen. the written abbreviation of **Senator**: Sen. Biden

sen·ate, **Senate** /'senɪt/ n **1 a)** the **Senate** the smaller and more important of the two parts of the government with the power to make laws, in countries such as the US, Australia, and France: The Senate approved the bill. **b)** [C] a similar part of the government in many US states: the California state senate **2** the Senate the highest level of government in ancient Rome **3** [C] the governing council at some universities

sen·a·tor, **Senator** /'senətə $ -tər/ n [C] a member of the Senate or a senate: Senator Kennedy —**senatorial** /,senə'tɔːriəl◂/ adj

send S1 W1 /send/ v past tense and past participle **sent** /sent/

1 BY POST ETC [T] to arrange for something to go or be taken to another place, especially by post: Lyn sent some pictures from the wedding. | **send sb sth** We sent Mom flowers for Mother's Day. | We sent her a letter of apology. | **send sth to sb/sth** I'll send a copy to you for your records. | **send sth back/up/over etc** He ordered coffee to be sent up. | **send sth by post/sea/air etc** Monday is the last day to send cards by post to arrive by Christmas.

2 RADIO/COMPUTER ETC [T] to make a message, electronic signal etc go somewhere, using radio equipment, computers etc: **send sb sth** I sent her an email yesterday. | Radio signals were sent into deep space.

3 PERSON TO PLACE a) [T] to ask or tell someone to go somewhere, especially so that they can do something for you there: The United Nations is sending troops. | **send sb to sth** A police officer was sent to Ryan's home. | **send sb back/away/over/home etc** Many of the refugees were sent back to Vietnam. | When Frank came, I told him I was ill and sent him away. | They sent me down to talk to Mr. Strachan. | Mr Ellison is here. Shall I send him in (=tell him to enter the room)? | **send sb to do sth** The U.S. offered to send ships to help in the rescue operation. **b)** [T always + adv/prep] to arrange for someone to go to a place such as a school, prison, or hospital and spend some time there: **send sb to sth** I can't afford to send my kid to private school. | He was sent to prison for five years. | **send sb away/off** I was sent away to school at the age of six. | **send sb on sth** New employees are sent on an intensive training course.

4 send (sb) a message/signal if something that someone does or says sends a particular message, it has that meaning: Advertising sends the message that you have to be thin to be successful.

5 send your love/regards/best wishes etc spoken to ask someone to give your greetings, good wishes etc to someone else: Mother sends her love.

6 CAUSE TO MOVE [T always + adv/prep] to make something move from one place to another: **send sth through/to/over etc sth** The blaze sent smoke over much of the city.

7 send sb/sth flying/sprawling/reeling etc to make someone or something move quickly through the air or across something: The explosion sent glass flying everywhere.

S

8 AFFECT [T always + adv/prep] to make someone or something start to be in a particular state: *His lectures always send me to sleep.* | **send sb/sth into sth** *The tail broke apart, sending the plane into a dive.*

9 **send word** *formal* to tell someone something by sending them a letter or message: **send word (to sb) that/of sth** *They sent word to the King of their arrival.*

10 **send shivers/chills up (and down) your spine** to make you feel very frightened or excited: *The eerie howl of the siren sent chills up her spine.*

11 **send sb packing** *informal* to tell someone who is not wanted that they must leave at once: *After his four years as governor, the voters sent him packing.*

send away for sth *phr v*
to send a letter to a company or organization asking them to send something to you: *Send away for a free recipe booklet.*

send down *phr v*
1 **send sth ⇔ down** to make something lose value: *The company's bad figures sent its share price down.*
2 **send sb down** *BrE informal* to send someone to prison: [+for] *He was sent down for possession of cocaine.*
3 **be sent down** *BrE old-fashioned* to be told to leave a university because of bad behaviour

send for sb/sth *phr v*
1 to ask or order that something be brought or sent to you, especially by writing a letter or by telephone: *Send for your free sample today!*
2 *old-fashioned* to ask or tell someone to come to you by sending them a message: *Charlie said he'd find a place to live and then send for me.* | *Get back into bed. I'll* **send for the doctor.** | *I've* **sent for help.**

send sth/sb ⇔ **in** *phr v*
1 to send something, usually by post, to a place where it can be dealt with: *I sent in a few job applications last week.*
2 to send soldiers, police etc somewhere to deal with a difficult or dangerous situation: *British troops were sent in as part of the peace-keeping force.*

send off *phr v*
1 **send sth ⇔ off** to send something somewhere by post: *I sent off the letter this morning.*
2 **send off for sth** to send a letter to a company or organization asking them to post something to you: *I sent off for a copy of the photograph.*
3 **send sb ⇔ off** *BrE* to order a sports player to leave the field because they have broken the rules: *One of Dundee's players was sent off for punching another player.*

send sth ⇔ **on** *phr v*
1 *especially BrE* to send someone's letters or possessions to their new address from their old address; 🔲 **forward**: *My flatmate said she'd send on all my post.*
2 to send something that has been received to another place so that it can be dealt with: [+to] *The data is then sent on to the Census Bureau.*

send out *phr v*
1 **send sth/sb ⇔ out** to make a person or a group of people or things go from one place to various other places: *Information was sent out to interested students.* | *Search parties were sent out to look for survivors.*
2 **send sth ⇔ out** to broadcast or produce a signal, light, sound etc: *The ship is sending out an SOS signal.*
3 **send out for sth** to ask a restaurant or food shop to deliver food to you at home or at work: *We sent out for sandwiches.*

send sth/sb ⇔ **up** *phr v*
1 to make something increase in value: *The oil shortage is bound to send prices up.*
2 *BrE informal* to make someone or something seem silly by copying them in a funny way: *The film hilariously sends up Hollywood disaster movies.*

send·er /'sendə $ -ər/ *n* [C] the person who sent a particular letter, package, message etc: *a package marked 'return to sender'*

'send-off *n* [C] *informal* a party or other occasion when people meet to say goodbye to someone who is leaving: *The department gave Tom a* **send-off** *he won't forget!*

'send-up *n* [C] *informal* a film, article, show etc that copies someone or something in a way that makes them seem funny or silly: [+of] *a hilarious send-up of a Hollywood disaster movie*

se·nes·cent /sɪ'nesənt/ *adj technical* becoming old and showing the effects of getting older: *a senescent industry* —**senescence** *n* [U]

se·nile /'si:naɪl/ *adj* mentally confused or behaving strangely, because of old age: *a senile old man* | *She worries about going senile.* —**senility** /sɪ'nɪləti/ *n* [U]

senile de'mentia *n* [U] a serious medical condition that affects the minds of some old people, and makes them confused and behave in a strange way

senior¹ W2 *adj*
1 having a higher position, level, or rank; → **junior**: *the senior Democrat on the House committee* | *White men hold most of the jobs in* **senior management.** | *the* **senior partner** *in a law firm* | [+to] *He is also a diplomat, but senior to me.*
2 [only before noun] *BrE* a senior competition is for older people or for people at a more advanced level: *I won the 60 metre race, my first senior success.*

senior² *n* [C]   **1** *AmE* a student in their last year of HIGH SCHOOL or university; → **freshman**, **junior**, **sophomore**: *Jen will be a senior this year.*   **2** *especially AmE* a SENIOR CITIZEN: *Seniors can get a 10% discount.*   **3** **be two/five/ten etc years sb's senior** to be two, five, ten etc years older than someone: *Her husband was nine years her senior.*   **4** *BrE* an adult or a person who has reached an advanced level in a particular sport; → **junior**: *Juniors and seniors train together on Wednesdays.*

Se·ni·or /'si:niə $ -ər/ *written abbreviation* **Sr.** *AmE*; **Snr** *BrE* used after the name of a man who has the same name as his son: *John J. Wallace, Sr.*

senior 'citizen *n* [C] someone who is over 60 years old or who is RETIRED

senior 'high school *also* **senior 'high** *n* [C] *AmE* HIGH SCHOOL; → **junior high school**

se·ni·or·i·ty /ˌsi:ni'ɒrəti $ -'ɔ:-, -'ɑ:-/ *n* [U]   **1** if you have seniority in a company or organization, you have worked there a long time and have some official advantages: *I had fifteen years seniority, and they couldn't fire me.*   **2** when you are older or higher in rank than someone else: *a position of seniority*

'senior ,school *n* [C] *BrE* a SECONDARY SCHOOL

sen·na /'senə/ *n* [U] a tropical plant with a fruit that is often used to make a medicine to help your BOWELS work

sen·sa·tion /sen'seɪʃən/ *n*   **1** [C,U] a feeling that you get from one of your five senses, especially the sense of touch: **burning/prickling/tingling etc sensation** *One sign of a heart attack is a tingling sensation in the left arm.* | [+of] *a sensation of heat*   **2** [C] a feeling that is difficult to describe, caused by a particular event, experience, or memory: **sensation that** *Caroline had the sensation that she was being watched.* | **strange/curious/odd sensation** *It was a strange sensation – I felt I'd been there before.*   **3** [U] the ability to feel things, especially through your sense of touch: *Jerry realized that he had no sensation in his legs.*   **4** [C usually singular] extreme excitement or interest, or someone or something that causes this: **cause/create a sensation** *The sex scenes in the film caused a sensation.* | **pop/fashion/media etc sensation** *the latest pop sensation from England*

sen·sa·tion·al /sen'seɪʃənəl/ *adj*   **1** very interesting, exciting, and surprising: *a sensational discovery* | *The show was a sensational success.* | *a sensational 6–0 victory*   **2** intended to interest, excite, or shock people – used in order to show disapproval: *sensational newspaper stories* | *sensational headlines*   **3** *informal* very good: *She looked sensational.* —**sensationally** *adv*

sen·sa·tion·al·is·m /sen'seɪʃənəlɪzəm/ *n* [U] a way of reporting events or stories that makes them seem as strange, exciting, or shocking as possible – used in order to show disapproval —**sensationalist** adj

sen·sa·tion·al·ize also **-ise** BrE /sen'seɪʃənəlaɪz/ v [T] to deliberately make something seem as strange, exciting, or shocking as possible – used in order to show disapproval: *The media often sensationalizes crime.*

sense¹ S1 W1 /sens/ n
1 [C] a feeling about something: [+of] *Afterwards I felt a **great sense** of relief.* | *She has a **strong sense** of loyalty.* | *A sense of panic has spread over the country.* | *Employees need the sense of being appreciated.* | **with a sense of sth** *He looked around the room with a sense of achievement.* | **sense that** *I had the sense that he was lying.* | **a sense of occasion** (=a feeling that an event is very special or important) *Everyone wants to create a sense of occasion at Christmas.*
2 [singular] the ability to understand or judge something: **sense of humour** BrE; **sense of humor** AmE (=the ability to understand and enjoy things that are funny) *I like Pam – she **has a** really **good sense of humour**.* | **sense of direction** (=the ability to judge which way you should be going, or what your aims should be) *It was dark and he had completely **lost his sense of direction**.* | **sense of proportion** (=the ability to judge what is important and what is not important) *Let's keep a sense of proportion, and not rush to any hasty conclusions.* | **sense of justice/fairness** *Kids have a **natural sense of justice**.* | **dress/clothes sense** (=the ability to judge which clothes look good)
3 [C] one of the five natural powers of sight, hearing, feeling, taste, and smell, that give us information about the things around us: **sense of smell/taste/touch etc** *She has a **good sense** of smell.* | *Cats have a very **acute sense** of hearing* (=very good, so that they can hear even the smallest sound). | *Combinations of flavors, textures, and colour that can **delight the senses**.* | **the five senses** (=all of the senses) → SIXTH SENSE
4 [U] when someone makes sensible or practical decisions, or behaves in a sensible, practical way: **have the sense to do sth** (=behave in a sensible way and do what is best in that situation) *You should have had the sense to turn off the electricity first.* | **there is no sense in (doing) sth** spoken (=it is not sensible to do something) *There's no sense in getting upset about it now.* | **see sense** (=realize what is the sensible thing to do) *I wish the politicians would see sense and stop the war.* | **talk/knock some sense into sb** (=try to make someone behave in a more sensible way) → COMMON SENSE
5 make sense **a)** to have a clear meaning and be easy to understand: *Read this and tell me if it makes sense.* **b)** to be a sensible thing to do: **it makes sense (for sb) to do sth** *It makes sense to save money while you can.* | *Would it make sense for the city authorities to further restrict parking?* **c)** if something makes sense, there seems to be a good reason or explanation for it: *Why did she do a thing like that? It doesn't seem to make sense.*
6 make (some) sense of sth to understand something, especially something difficult or complicated: *Can you make any sense of this article?*
7 [C] the meaning of a word, sentence, phrase etc: *The word 'record' has several different senses.* | *Any alteration would spoil the sense of the entire poem.*
8 [C] a way in which something can be true or real: **in a sense/in one sense/in some senses etc** (=in one way, in some ways etc) *What he says is right in a sense.* | *The hotel was **in no sense** (=not at all) comfortable. | George was a big man **in every sense of the word** (=in every way). | This is true **in a general sense**. | Communication, **in any real sense** (=of any real kind), was extremely limited. | **in a (very) real sense** (=used to emphasize that a statement or description is true) A head of a school is a manager in a very real sense.*
9 your/her etc senses someone's ability to think clearly and behave sensibly – used in some expressions when you think that someone has lost this ability: **come to your senses** *One day he'll **come to his senses** and see what a fool he's been* (=to start to think clearly

and behave sensibly again). | *See if you can **bring her to her senses**.* (=make someone think clearly and behave sensibly) | **be out of your senses** (=have lost the ability to think clearly and behave sensibly) *Are you completely out of your senses?* → **take leave of your senses** at LEAVE² (6)
10 talk sense spoken to say things that are reasonable or sensible – often used when you think someone has just said something silly: *Talk sense! There's no way we can afford a new car!*
11 regain your senses old-fashioned to stop feeling FAINT or slightly sick: *Outside, she quickly regained her senses.*

sense² v [T] **1** if you sense something, you feel that it exists or is true, without being told or having proof: *Perhaps he sensed your distrust.* | **sense (that)** *I could sense that something was wrong.* | **sense what/how/who etc** *Hugo had already sensed how unhappy she was.* | **sense danger/trouble** *If a prairie dog senses danger, he whistles a warning.* **2** if a machine senses something, it discovers and records it: *an electronic device used for sensing intruders*

sense·less /'senslэs/ adj **1** happening or done for no good reason or with no purpose: *Her death seemed such a senseless waste of life.* | *a senseless crime* **2** unconscious: *He had been **beaten senseless**.* —**senselessly** adv —**senselessness** n [U]

'sense ,organ n [C] a part of your body through which you see, smell, hear, taste, or feel something

sen·si·bil·i·ty /,sensɪ'bɪlɪti/ n plural **sensibilities** **1** [C,U] the way that someone reacts to particular subjects or types of behaviour: *her religious sensibilities* | **offend/wound sb's sensibilities** *Avoid using words that might offend someone's racial or moral sensibilities.* **2** [U] the ability to understand feelings, especially those expressed in literature or art: *the sensibility of the artist*

sen·si·ble S3 W3 /'sensɪbəl/ adj
1 reasonable, practical, and showing good judgment: *She seems very sensible.* | **it's sensible to keep a note of your passport number.* | *Moving house seemed like the sensible thing to do.* ⚠ A **sensible** person is reasonable and shows good judgement. A **sensitive** person is easily upset, or understands other people's feelings when they are upset.
2 suitable for a particular purpose, and practical rather than fashionable: *Eat a sensible diet and exercise daily.* | *an old woman in **sensible shoes** and a neat skirt*
3 formal noticeable: *a sensible increase in temperature*
4 be sensible of sth literary to know or realize that something exists or is true: *He was very sensible of the difficult situation she was in.* —**sensibly** adv

sen·si·tive S3 W3 /'sensɪtɪv/ adj
1 UNDERSTANDING PEOPLE able to understand other people's feelings and problems; ≠ **insensitive**: *a sensitive and intelligent young man* | [+to] *It's made me much more sensitive to the needs of the disabled.*
2 EASILY OFFENDED easily upset or offended by events or things that people say: *a very sensitive child* | [+about] *Laura's sensitive about her weight.* | [+to] *Throughout her career she remained very sensitive to criticism.* | **sensitive soul** BrE (=someone who is easily upset by small or unimportant things) → HYPERSENSITIVE
3 EASILY AFFECTED easily affected or damaged by something such as a substance or temperature: *Wetlands are environmentally sensitive areas.* | *a baby's sensitive skin* | [+to] *Older people tend to be very sensitive to cold.* | *Increasing numbers of people are sensitive to cow's milk.*
4 SITUATION/SUBJECT a situation or subject that is sensitive needs to be dealt with very carefully, because it is secret or because it may offend people: *Abortion is a very sensitive issue.* | *sensitive matters such as national security* | *highly sensitive information*

1 000, 2 000, 3 000, most frequent words in S poken and W ritten English

5 REACTING TO CHANGES reacting to very small changes in light, temperature, position etc: *a highly sensitive electronic camera* | **light-sensitive/heat-sensitive etc** *light-sensitive photographic paper*
6 ART/MUSIC ETC able to understand or express yourself through art, music, literature etc: *a very sensitive performance* —**sensitively** *adv*: *It is an issue which needs to be handled sensitively.*

sen·si·tiv·i·ty /ˌsensɪˈtɪvəti/ *n plural* **sensitivities**
1 UNDERSTANDING PEOPLE [singular, U] the ability to understand other people's feelings and problems: *His comments show a lack of sensitivity.* | *Interviewing victims of crime must be done with sensitivity.* | *a teacher with great sensitivity* | [+to] *She has always shown a sensitivity to audience needs and tastes.*
2 SITUATION/SUBJECT [U] when a situation or subject needs to be dealt with carefully because it is secret or may offend people: *It's a matter of great political sensitivity.*
3 BODY'S REACTION [C,U] when someone reacts badly to a particular food, substance, animal etc and becomes ill: *food sensitivity* | [+to] *Many children have a sensitivity to cow's milk.*
4 EASILY OFFENDED [U] when someone is easily upset or offended by things that people say
5 **sensitivities** [plural] someone's feelings and the fact that they could be upset or offended: *racial sensitivities*
6 [C,U] ART/MUSIC ETC the quality of being able to express emotions through art, literature etc
7 REACTION TO CHANGES [U] the ability to react to very small changes in light, heat, movement etc: *The sensitivity of the detector can be increased.* | *a disease that affects the sensitivity of nerve-endings*
8 REACTION TO NEW SITUATIONS [C,U] the fact of quickly reacting to new situations: *the market's price sensitivity*

sen·si·tize also **-ise** *BrE* /ˈsensətaɪz/ *v* [T] **1** to give someone some experience or knowledge of a particular problem or situation so that they can notice it and understand it easily: **sensitize sb to sth** *Volunteers need to be sensitized to the cultural differences they will meet in African countries.* **2** [usually passive] if someone is sensitized to a particular substance, their body has begun to have a bad reaction whenever they touch it, breathe it etc: **be sensitized to sth** *Many hospital workers have become sensitized to the latex in gloves.* **3** *technical* to treat a material or a piece of equipment so that it will react to physical or chemical changes: *sensitized photographic paper* —**sensitization** /ˌsensətaɪˈzeɪʃən $ -tə-/ *n* [U]

sen·sor /ˈsensə $ -ər/ *n* [C] a piece of equipment used for discovering the presence of light, heat, movement etc

sen·so·ry /ˈsensəri/ *adj* relating to or using your senses of sight, hearing, smell, taste, or touch: *sensory stimuli such as music* | *sensory deprivation* → ESP (1)

sen·su·al /ˈsenʃuəl/ *adj* **1** relating to the feelings of your body rather than your mind: *the sensual pleasure of good food* **2** interested in or making you think of physical pleasure, especially sexual pleasure: *the faint smile on his sensual mouth* | *a sensual woman* —**sensually** *adv* —**sensuality** /ˌsenʃuˈæləti/ *n* [U]

sen·su·al·ist /ˈsenʃuəlɪst/ *n* [C] someone who is only interested in physical pleasure

sen·su·ous /ˈsenʃuəs/ *adj* **1** pleasing to your senses: *the sensuous feeling of silk on her skin* | *sensuous music* **2** *literary* attractive in a sexual way: *full, sensuous lips* | *a beautiful and sensuous young woman* —**sensuously** *adv* —**sensuousness** *n* [U]

sent /sent/ *v* the past tense and past participle of SEND
sen·tence[1] S1 W2 /ˈsentəns/ *n* [C]
1 a group of words that usually contains a subject and a verb, and expresses a complete idea. Sentences written in English begin with a capital letter and usually end with a FULL STOP or a QUESTION MARK: *His voice dropped at*

the end of the sentence. | **in a sentence** *It's difficult to sum it up in one sentence.* | **short/simple/full/complex etc sentence** *In a few short sentences, Quinn explained what he had done.*
2 a punishment that a judge gives to someone who is guilty of a crime

---

jail/prison sentence
receive/be given a sentence
impose a sentence on sb *formal*
pass sentence (=officially say what a punishment will be)
stiff/heavy/long sentence (=a long time in prison)
light/short sentence (=a short time in prison)
life sentence (=the punishment of being in prison for the rest of your life)
death sentence
suspended sentence (=a sentence that someone serves only if they commit another crime)
custodial sentence *BrE* (=the punishment of spending time in prison)
serve a sentence (=spend time in prison)
carry a sentence (of sth) (=used to say what the usual punishment is for a crime)

She received an eight-year prison sentence. | *The judge will pass sentence tomorrow after looking at all the reports.* | *Drug traffickers will face stiffer sentences.* | *He got off with a relatively light sentence.* | *He has just begun a life sentence for murder.* | *Eventually the death sentence was overturned by the Supreme Court.* | *The judge gave him a suspended sentence and demanded that he pay $30,000 to a children's charity.* | *This offence is so serious that only a custodial sentence can be justified.* | *a prisoner serving a sentence for robbery* | *The offence carries a maximum sentence of five years.*

sentence[2] *v* [T] if a judge sentences someone who is guilty of a crime, they give them a punishment: **sentence sb to sth** *Sanchez was sentenced to three years in prison.*

'sentence ˌadverb *n* [C] an adverb that relates to the whole sentence that contains it

sen·ten·tious /senˈtenʃəs/ *adj formal* telling people how they should behave – used in order to show disapproval: *sententious remarks* —**sententiously** *adv*

sen·tient /ˈsenʃənt/ *adj formal* or *technical* able to experience things through your senses: *Man is a sentient being.*

sen·ti·ment /ˈsentəmənt/ *n* **1** [C,U] *formal* an opinion or feeling you have about something: *Similar sentiments were expressed by many politicians.* | **popular/public sentiment** (=what most people think) *He was more in touch with public sentiment than many of his critics.* | **anti-American/nationalistic/religious etc sentiments** *the anti-immigrant sentiments expressed by some Americans* | *'After all, it's her decision.' 'My sentiments exactly* (=I agree).' **2** [U] feelings of pity, love, sadness etc that are often considered to be too strong or not suitable for a particular situation: *There's no place for sentiment in business!*

sen·ti·men·tal /ˌsentəˈmentl◂/ *adj* **1** someone who is sentimental is easily affected by emotions such as love, sympathy, sadness etc, often in a way that seems silly to other people: *She said a sentimental goodbye.* | [+about] *People can be very sentimental about animals.* **2** based on or relating to your feelings rather than on practical reasons: *He wasn't the sort of person who kept things for sentimental reasons.* | *a sentimental journey to the place of his birth* | *The rings that were stolen were of great sentimental value* (=important because of your feelings or memories relating to them). **3** a story, film, book etc that is sentimental deals with emotions such as love and sadness, sometimes in a way that seems silly and insincere: *a sentimental story set in Russia* —**sentimentally** *adv*

sen·ti·men·tal·ist /ˌsentəˈmentl-ɪst/ *n* [C] someone who behaves or writes in a sentimental way —**sentimentalism** *n* [U]

S

sen·ti·men·tal·i·ty /ˌsentɪmenˈtælɪti/ *n* [U] the quality of being sentimental

sen·ti·ment·al·ize also **-ise** *BrE* /ˌsentɪˈmentl-aɪz/ *v* [I,T] to speak, write, or think about only the good or happy things about something, not the bad things: *novels that sentimentalize the past*

sen·ti·nel /ˈsentɪnəl/ *n* [C] *old-fashioned* a sentry

sen·try /ˈsentri/ *n plural* **sentries** [C] a soldier standing outside a building as a guard

ˈsentry box *n* [C] a tall narrow shelter with an open front where a soldier stands while guarding a building

Sep. also **Sep** *BrE* a written abbreviation of *September*

sep·al /ˈsepəl $ ˈsiː-/ *n* [C] *technical* one of the small leaves directly under a flower

sep·a·ra·ble /ˈsepərəbəl/ *adj* two things that are separable can be separated or considered separately; ▪ **inseparable**: [+from] *Physical health is not always easily separable from mental health.*

sep·a·rate¹ [S2] [W2] /ˈsepərɪt/ *adj* [no comparative]
1 different: *Use separate knives for raw and cooked meat.* | *My wife and I have separate bank accounts.*
2 not related to or not affected by something else: *That's a separate issue.* | *He was attacked on two separate occasions.* | [+from] *He tries to keep his professional life completely separate from his private life.*
3 not joined to or touching something else: *The gym and the sauna are in separate buildings.* | [+from] *Keep the fish separate from the other food.*
4 go your separate ways a) if people go their separate ways, they stop being friends or lovers **b)** if people who have been travelling together go their separate ways, they start travelling in different directions —**separately** *adv*: *They did arrive together, but I think they left separately.*

sep·a·rate² [S2] [W2] /ˈsepəreɪt/ *v*
1 BE BETWEEN [T] if something separates two places or two things, it is between them so that they are not touching each other: **separate sth from sth** *The lighthouse is separated from the land by a wide channel.*
2 DIVIDE [I,T] to divide or split into different parts, or to make something do this: *This will keep your dressing from separating.* | [+from] *At this point the satellite separates from its launcher.* | **separate sth into sth** *Separate the students into four groups.* | *First, separate the eggs* (=divide the white part from the yellow part).
3 STOP LIVING TOGETHER [I] if two people who are married or have been living together separate, they start to live apart: *Jill and John separated a year ago.*
4 RECOGNIZE DIFFERENCE [T] to recognize that one thing or idea is different from another: **separate sth from sth** *She finds it difficult to separate fact from fantasy.*
5 MOVE APART [I,T] if people separate, or if someone or something separates them, they move apart: *Ed stepped in to separate the two dogs.* | **separate sb from sb/sth** *In the fog, they got separated from the group.*
6 MAKE SB/STH DIFFERENT [T] to be the quality or fact that makes someone or something different from other people or things: **separate sth from sth** *The capacity to think separates humans from animals.*
7 BETTER/OLDER [T] if an amount separates two things, one thing is better or older than the other by that amount: *Three points now separate the two teams.* | *Forty years separate these two pictures of the hotel.*
8 separate the men from the boys *informal* to show clearly which people are brave, strong, or skilled, and which are not
9 separate the sheep from the goats *BrE* also **separate the wheat from the chaff** to separate the good things from the bad things
    separate sb/sth ⇔ **out** *phr v*
1 to divide a group of people or things into smaller groups: *We must separate out these different factors and examine each one.*
2 to remove one type of thing or person from a group:

[+from] *Many older people may prefer not to be separated out from the rest of the adult population.*

sep·a·rat·ed /ˈsepəreɪtɪd/ *adj* not living with your husband, wife, or sexual partner any more; → **divorced**: *We've been separated for six months.*

sep·a·rates /ˈsepərɪts/ *n* [plural] women's clothing, such as skirts, shirts, and trousers, that can be worn in different combinations

sep·a·ra·tion /ˌsepəˈreɪʃən/ *n* **1** [U] when something separates or is separate: *the separation of church and state* | [+between] *the zone of separation between the warring factions* **2** [C,U] a period of time that two or more people spend apart from each other: *the separation of families during wartime* **3** [C] a situation in which a husband and wife agree to live apart even though they are still married: *their separation and later divorce* → DIVORCE¹ (1)

sep·a·ra·tist /ˈsepərətɪst/ *n* [C] someone who belongs to a group that wants to start a new country with its own government, by separating from the country that they belong to now —**separatism** *n* [U]

sep·a·ra·tor /ˈsepəreɪtə $ -ər/ *n* [C] a machine for separating liquids from solids, or cream from milk

se·pi·a /ˈsiːpiə/ *n* [U] **1** a dark reddish brown colour **2 sepia photograph/print** a photograph, picture etc, especially an old one, that is dark reddish brown **3** a dark reddish brown ink used for drawing

sep·sis /ˈsepsɪs/ *n* [U] *medical* an infection in part of the body, in which PUS is produced

Sep·tem·ber /sepˈtembə $ -ər/ *n* [C,U] written abbreviation **Sept.** the ninth month of the year, between August and October: **next/last September** *I haven't heard from him since last September.* | **in September** *My birthday's in September.* | **on September 6th** *The meeting will be on September 6th.* | **on 6th September** *BrE*: *'When's the concert?' 'On 6th September.'* | **September 6** *AmE*: *They arrive September 6.*

sep·tet /sepˈtet/ *n* [C] **1** a group of seven singers or musicians who perform together **2** a piece of music written for seven performers

scp·tic /ˈseptɪk/ *adj especially BrE* a wound or part of your body that is septic is infected with BACTERIA: *a cut that went septic*

sep·ti·cae·mi·a *BrE*; **septicemia** *AmE* /ˌseptɪˈsiːmiə/ *n* [U] *medical* a serious condition in which infection spreads from a part of your body through your blood; ▪ **blood poisoning**

ˌseptic ˈtank *n* [C] a large container under the ground, for holding human waste from toilets

sep·tu·a·ge·nar·i·an /ˌseptjuədʒɪˈneəriən $ -ˈner-/ *n* [C] someone who is between 70 and 79 years old

se·pul·chral /sɪˈpʌlkrəl/ *adj literary* **1** sad, serious, and slightly frightening: *a sepulchral voice* **2** dark, empty, and slightly frightening: *in the sepulchral gloom of the church*

sep·ul·chre *BrE*; **sepulcher** *AmE* /ˈsepəlkə $ -kər/ *n* [C] *old use* a small room or building in which the bodies of dead people were put

se·quel /ˈsiːkwəl/ *n* **1** [C] a book, film, play etc that continues the story of an earlier one, usually written or made by the same person; → **prequel**: *'Star Wars' and its sequels* | [+to] *She's writing a sequel to her first novel.* **2** [C usually singular] an event that happens as a result of something that happened before

se·quence [W2] /ˈsiːkwəns/ *n*
1 [C,U] the order that something happens or exists in, or the order it is supposed to happen or exist in: **in a ... sequence** *The questions should be asked in a logical sequence.* | *Be careful to perform the actions in the correct sequence.* | **in sequence** *Number them in sequence, 1,2,3 etc.* | **out of sequence** *The chapters may be studied out of sequence.*
2 [C] a series of related events, actions etc that happen or are done in a particular order: [+of] *He's had a*

S

sequence of business failures. | the **sequence of events** leading up to the war
3 [C] one part of a story, film etc that deals with a single subject or action: *the dream sequence in the film*

se·quenc·ing /'si:kwənsıŋ/ *n* [U] *formal* when things are arranged in an order, especially events or actions —**sequence** *v* [T]

se·quen·tial /sı'kwenʃəl/ *adj formal* relating to or happening in a sequence —**sequentially** *adv*

se·ques·ter /sı'kwestə $ -ər/ *v* [T usually passive] *formal* **1** to keep a person or a group of people away from other people: *The jury were sequestered during the trial.* **2** *BrE* to sequestrate

se·ques·tered /sı'kwestəd $ -ərd/ *adj* [usually before noun] *literary* a sequestered place is quiet and far away from people

se·ques·trate /sı'kwestreıt, 'si:kwₔ-/ also **se·ques·ter** /sı'kwestə $ -ər/ *v* [T usually passive] *BrE formal* to take property away from the person it belongs to because they have not paid their debts —**sequestration** /ˌsi:kwₔ'streıʃən/ *n* [C,U]

se·quin /'si:kwₔn/ *n* [C] a small shiny flat piece of metal, sewn onto clothes for decoration —**sequined**, **sequinned** *adj*

se·quoi·a /sı'kwɔıə/ *n* [C] a tree from the western US that can grow to be very tall; ⊟ **redwood**

se·ra /'sıərə $ 'sırə/ *n* a plural form of SERUM

ser·aph /'serəf/ *n plural* **seraphs** *also* **seraphim** /'serəfım/ [C] one of the ANGELS that protect the seat of God, according to the Bible; → **cherub**

se·raph·ic /sₔ'ræfık/ *adj literary* extremely beautiful or pure, like an ANGEL

ser·e·nade¹ /ˌserₔ'neıd/ *n* [C] **1** a song sung to someone, especially one that a man performs for the woman he loves while standing below her window at night **2** a piece of gentle music

serenade² *v* [T] if you serenade someone, you sing or play music to them, especially to show them that you love them

ser·en·dip·i·ty /ˌserən'dıpₔti/ *n* [U] *literary* when interesting or valuable discoveries are made by accident; → **luck**

se·rene /sₔ'ri:n/ *adj* very calm or peaceful: *The child's face was serene and beautiful.* | *a serene mountain lake* —**serenely** *adv* —**serenity** /sₔ'renₔti/ *n* [U]

serf /sɜ:f $ sɜ:rf/ *n* [C] someone in the past who lived and worked on land that they did not own and who had to obey the owner of the land → **slave¹** (1); → **peasant**

serf·dom /'sɜ:fdəm $ 'sɜ:rf-/ *n* [U] the system of using serfs, or the state of being a serf

serge /sɜ:dʒ $ sɜ:rdʒ/ *n* [U] strong woollen cloth used for making suits, trousers etc

ser·geant /'sɑ:dʒₔnt $ 'sɑ:r-/ *n* [C] a low rank in the army, air force, police etc, or someone who has this rank

ˌsergeant 'major *n* [C] a military rank

se·ri·al¹ /'sıərıəl $ 'sır-/ *n* [C] a story that is broadcast or printed in several separate parts on television, in a magazine etc: *a television serial* | *a six-part serial*

serial² *adj* [only before noun] **1 serial killer/murderer etc** someone who commits the same crime several times: *a serial rapist* **2 serial killings/murders etc** crimes that are done in the same way several times **3** arranged or happening one after the other in the correct order: *Keep the questions in the same serial order.* **4** printed or broadcast in several separate parts: *cheap serial publications* —**serially** *adv*

se·ri·al·ize also **-ise** *BrE* /'sıərıəlaız $ 'sır-/ *v* [T often passive] to print or broadcast a story in several separate parts: *His book was serialized in The New Yorker.* —**serialization** /ˌsıərıəlaı'zeıʃən $ ˌsırıələ-/ *n* [C,U]

ˌserial mo'nogamy *n* [U] when someone has a series of sexual relationships, rather than one long relationship or several relationships at one time – often used humorously

'serial ˌnumber *n* [C] a number put on things that are produced in large quantities, so that each one has its own different number: *Each computer has a serial number on it.*

se·ries S2 W1 /'sıəri:z $ 'sır-/ *n plural* **series** [C usually singular]
1 series of sth several events or actions of a similar type that happen one after the other: *the series of events that led to the outbreak of war* | *The police are investigating a series of attacks in the area.* | *There's been a whole series of accidents on this road.*
2 PLANNED EVENTS a group of events or actions that are planned to happen one after the other: [+of] *This autumn the BBC will be showing a series of French films.* | *Staff will hold a series of meetings over the next few weeks.* | *a summer lecture series*
3 TV/RADIO a set of television or radio programmes that have the same characters or deal with the same type of subject, and are usually broadcast every week or several times a week: *a new comedy series* | *a weekly TV series*
4 BOOKS/ARTICLES ETC several books, articles etc that deal with the same subject or tell stories about the same characters: [+of] *a series of articles on community care* | *a science fiction series*
5 SIMILAR THINGS several things of the same kind: [+of] *a series of laws against discrimination* | *The area is linked by a series of canals.*
6 SPORT a set of sports games played between the same two teams: **the World Series** (=in baseball) | **Test series** (=in CRICKET)
7 in series *technical* being connected so that electricity passes though the parts of something electrical in the correct order

ser·if /'serₔf/ *n* [C] a short flat line at the top or bottom of some printed letters → **sans serif**

se·ri·ous S1 W1 /'sıərıəs $ 'sır-/ *adj*
1 SITUATION/PROBLEM a serious situation, problem, accident etc is extremely bad or dangerous: *the serious problem of unemployment* | *Luckily, the damage was not serious.* | **serious injury/illness/accident etc** *a serious accident on the freeway* | *Oil spills pose a serious threat to marine life.* | **Serious crimes** have increased dramatically.
2 be serious a) if someone is serious about something they say, they really mean it and are not joking or pretending: [+about] *Is she serious about giving up her job?* | **I'm serious** (=used to emphasize that you mean what you say) | **deadly/dead serious** (=definitely not joking) *She sounded dead serious.* **b)** *spoken* used to tell someone that what they have just said is silly or that you do not believe it: *'It's enough to make anyone commit murder!' 'Be serious, Jo.'* | *Marry Frank?* **You can't be serious!**
3 IMPORTANT important and needing a lot of thought or attention: *This is a very serious matter.* | *the serious business of earning a living* | *Be quiet, Jim. This is serious.* | *a serious article* | **serious attention/consideration/thought** (=careful and thorough attention etc) *I'll give your suggestion serious consideration.*
4 LARGE AMOUNT [only before noun] *informal* used to emphasize that you are talking about a large amount of something: *The President was in serious trouble.* | *In industry, you can earn serious money.*
5 ROMANTIC RELATIONSHIP a serious romantic relationship is likely to continue for a long time: *It's serious – they've been seeing each other for six months.* | [+about] *Are you really serious about her?* | **serious boyfriend/girlfriend**
6 PERSON someone who is serious is very quiet and sensible
7 SPORT/ACTIVITY [only before noun] very interested in an activity or subject, and spending a lot of time doing it: *He's become a serious golfer since he retired.* |

S

Chris is a serious photographer.
8 VERY GOOD [only before noun] *informal* very good and often expensive: *He's got a serious car!*
9 WORRIED/UNHAPPY slightly worried or unhappy: *You look serious. What's wrong?*

se·ri·ous·ly S2 W2 /'sɪəriəsli $ 'sɪr-/ *adv*
1 very much or to a great degree: **seriously ill/injured/ damaged etc** *Was she seriously hurt?* | *I'm seriously worried about Ben.* | *Something was seriously wrong.*
2 a) in a way that is not joking, especially because something is important: *It's time we talked seriously about our relationship.* **b)** [sentence adverb] *spoken* used to show that what you say next is not a joke: *Seriously though, I think Toby likes you.*
3 take sb/sth seriously to believe that someone or something is worth your attention or respect: *As a teacher, it's important that the kids take you seriously.* | *It's only a joke – don't take it seriously!*
4 seriously? *spoken* used to ask someone if they really mean what they have just said: 'The job's yours.' 'Seriously?'

se·ri·ous·ness /'sɪəriəsnɨs $ 'sɪr-/ *n* [U] **1** the quality of being serious **2 in all seriousness a)** *spoken* used to show that what you say next is not a joke, especially because it is important: ⊟ **seriously:** *In all seriousness, if Tom does resign, a lot of other people will start leaving too.* **b)** in a way that is not joking: 'Playing with Richie was the highlight of my musical career,' said Sonny in all seriousness.

ser·mon /'sɜːmən $ 'sɜːr-/ *n* [C] **1** a talk given as part of a Christian church service, usually on a religious or moral subject: **give/preach/deliver a sermon (on sth)** *The vicar gave a sermon on charity.* **2** *informal* a long talk in which someone tries to give you moral advice that you do not want – used to show disapproval; ⊟ **lecture**

ser·mon·ize also **-ise** *BrE* /'sɜːmənaɪz $ 'sɜːr-/ *v* [I] to give a lot of moral advice to someone when they do not want it – used to show disapproval

ser·o·to·nin /ˌserə'təʊnɪn $ -'toʊ-/ *n* [U] *technical* a chemical in the body that helps carry messages from the brain and is believed to make you feel happy

ser·pent /'sɜːpənt $ 'sɜːr-/ *n* [C] *literary* a snake, especially a large one

ser·pen·tine /'sɜːpəntaɪn $ 'sɜːrpəntiːn/ *adj* [only before noun] *literary* **1** winding like a snake: *the serpentine course of the river* **2** complicated and difficult to understand: *a serpentine plot*

ser·rat·ed /sɨ'reɪtɨd, se-/ *adj* [usually before noun] having a sharp edge made of a row of connected points like teeth: *Use a knife with a serrated edge.*

ser·ried /'serid/ *adj* [no comparative] [usually before noun] *literary* standing or arranged closely together in rows: *the serried ranks of reporters waiting outside*

se·rum /'sɪərəm $ 'sɪr-/ *n plural* **serums** or **sera** /-rə/ [C,U] **1** *medical* a liquid containing substances that fight infection or poison, that is put into a sick person's blood → **VACCINE** **2** *technical* the thin part of blood or the liquid from a plant

ser·vant W2 /'sɜːvənt $ 'sɜːr-/ *n* [C]
1 someone, especially in the past, who was paid to clean someone's house, cook for them, answer the door etc, and who often lived in the house: *Many young girls became domestic servants.*
2 servant of sth/sb someone who is controlled by someone or something – often used to show disapproval: *Are we the servants of computers?* → **CIVIL SERVANT**

serve¹ S1 W1 /sɜːv $ sɜːrv/ *v*
1 FOOD/DRINK [I,T] to give someone food or drink, especially as part of a meal or in a restaurant, bar etc: *The waiter was serving another table.* | *Sprinkle with cheese and serve immediately.* | **serve sth with sth** *Serve the soup with crusty bread.* | **serve breakfast/lunch/ dinner** *Breakfast is served until 9 a.m.* | **serve sth to sb** *Meals can be served to you in your room.* | **serve sth hot/cold etc** *Teacakes should be served hot with butter.*
2 serve two/three/four etc (people) if food serves two,

three etc, there is enough for that number of people: *The recipe serves four.*
3 SHOP [I,T] to help the customers in a shop, especially by bringing them the things that they want: *There was only one girl serving customers.*
4 BE USEFUL/HELPFUL [I,T] to be useful or helpful for a particular purpose or reason: [+as] *The sofa had to serve as a bed.* | *The reforms served as a model for the rest of the Communist world.* | *A large cardboard box will serve the purpose.* | *Her talent for organization should serve her well.* | **serve the needs/interests of sb/sth** *research projects that serve the needs of industry*
5 DO USEFUL WORK [I,T] to spend a period of time doing useful work or official duties for an organization, country, important person etc: [+as] *Lord Herbert served as ambassador to France.* | **serve in the army/air force/navy etc** *He returned to Greece to serve in the army.* | [+on] *Ann serves on various local committees.* | *the women who served their country in the war*
6 HAVE AN EFFECT [I] *formal* to have a particular effect or result: [+as] *Her death should serve as a warning to other young people.* | **serve to do sth** *A single example serves to illustrate what I mean.*
7 PROVIDE STH [T usually passive] to provide an area or a group of people with something that is necessary or useful: *Paris is served by two airports.*
8 PRISON [T] to spend a particular period of time in prison: *He served an eighteen-month sentence for theft.* | *Did you know that Les is serving time* (=is in prison)?
9 SPORT [I,T] to start playing in a game such as tennis or VOLLEYBALL by throwing the ball up in the air and hitting it over the net
10 it serves sb right *spoken* used to say that you think someone deserves something unpleasant that happens to them, because they have been stupid or unkind: 'She kicked me!' 'Serves you right, teasing her like that.'
11 serve an apprenticeship to learn a job or skill by working for a particular period of time for someone who has a lot of experience
12 serve a summons/writ etc to officially send or give someone a written order to appear in a court of law →
if my memory serves me (right/well/correctly) at **MEMORY** (1)

serve sth ⇔ **out** *phr v*
1 to complete a particular period of time in prison or doing a job: *Dillon's almost served out his sentence* (=in prison). | *The Senator's illness means he may not serve out his term.*
2 *BrE* to put food onto plates: *Serve out the rice, will you?*

serve sth ⇔ **up** *phr v*
to give food to someone as part of a meal: *What are you serving up tonight?*

serve² *n* [C] the action in a game such as tennis or VOLLEYBALL when you throw the ball in the air and hit it over the net

serv·er /'sɜːvə $ 'sɜːrvər/ *n* [C] **1 a)** the main computer on a network, which controls all the others: *The server's down* (=not working) *again.* **b)** one of the computers on a network that provides a special service: **file/print server** *All data is stored on a central file server.* **2** the player who hits the ball to begin a game in tennis, VOLLEYBALL etc **3** a special spoon for putting a particular type of food onto a plate: *salad servers* **4** *AmE* someone whose job is to bring you your food in a restaurant; ⊟ **waiter, waitress**

'server farm *n* [C] an office which has a large amount of computer equipment holding all the software and information for websites

ser·ve·ry /'sɜːvəri $ 'sɜːr-/ *n plural* **serveries** [C] *BrE* the part of a restaurant where you get food to take back to your table; ⊟ **buffet** *AmE*

ser·vice¹ [S1] [W1] /'sɜːvɪ̯s $ 'sɜːr-/ n

1 **OFFICIAL SYSTEM/ORGANIZATION** [C] the official system for providing something, especially something that everyone in a country needs to have, or the official organization that provides it: *the health service* | *the postal service* | *the police service* | *the prison service* | *Workers in the emergency services* (=police, hospital, and the fire service) *are forbidden from striking.* | *There has been a decline in public services in recent years.* | *the essential services* (=the police, hospitals, fire service, and organizations that provide basic things such as water, gas, or electricity) → CIVIL SERVICE, FIRE SERVICE, INTERNAL REVENUE SERVICE, DIPLOMATIC SERVICE, NATIONAL HEALTH SERVICE, SECRET SERVICE, SECURITY SERVICE

2 **STH PROVIDED BY A COMPANY** [C] a particular type of help or work that is provided by a business to customers, but not one that involves producing goods: *A wide range of financial services are available.* | **provide/offer a service** *Datapost offers a delivery service to over 160 countries.* | *Our aim is to provide the best service at the lowest price.* | *the supply of goods and services* → SERVICE INDUSTRY

3 **IN A SHOP/RESTAURANT/HOTEL** [U] the help that people who work in a shop, restaurant, bar etc give you: **good/bad/slow etc service** *The service was terrible and so was the food.* | **customer service** *At our bank we insist on high standards of customer service.* | *Service is included in your bill* (=the charge for paying the people who serve you is included). → ROOM SERVICE, SELF-SERVICE, SERVICE CHARGE

4 **WORK** [U] also **services** the work that someone does for a person or organization, especially over a long period: **20/30 years etc of service** *Brian retired after 25 years of service to the company.* | *a long service award* | *a career in public service* (=work done for the public or the government) | **services to sb/sth** (=all the good work you have done for someone or something) *He received an award for services to sport.*

5 **WORK DONE FOR SB** **services** [plural] skilled work or advice from a particular type of worker who you use to help you do something: **sb's services/the services of sb** *Lydia obtained the services of a qualified nurse.* | **sb's services as sth** *Why don't you offer your services as a tennis coach?*

6 **DUTY** jury/military/community etc service something that ordinary people can be asked to do as a public duty or as a punishment: *Her attacker was sentenced to 120 hours community service.*

7 **BEING USED** [U] used to talk about whether a piece of equipment, a vehicle etc is available to be used, or how long it can be used: **in service** (=being used or available to be used) *These trains have been in service for many years.* | **out of service** (=not being used or not available to be used) *The escalator is still out of service.* | **give good/excellent etc service** (=work well and last a long time) *Steel tools can give good service for years.*

8 **RELIGIOUS CEREMONY** [C] a formal religious ceremony, especially in church: **hold/conduct a service** *The service was held in the chapel.* | **marriage/funeral/christening etc service** *a memorial service for the disaster victims*

9 **ARMY** **the services** *BrE* **the service** *AmE* a country's military forces, especially considered as a job: **join/go into the services** *Maybe you should join the services.* | *Her son is in the services.*

10 **HELP** [singular, U] *formal* help that you give to someone: **be at sb's service** (=be available to help someone, or for someone to use) *My secretary is at your service.* | **be of service (to sb)** (=help someone) *Can I be of any service?* | **do sb a service** (=do something that will help someone) *He did her a service by telling her the truth.*

11 **CHECK A CAR/MACHINE** [C] an examination and repair of a machine or car to keep it working properly: *I'm getting the bus home – my car's in for a service.*

12 **TENNIS/BALL GAME** [C] an act of hitting a ball through the air in order to start a game, especially in tennis: *It's your service.*

13 **ON A MOTORWAY** **services** [C] *BrE* a place near a MOTORWAY where you can stop and have a meal or drink, or buy food, petrol etc; → **service station**: *How far is it to the next services?*

14 **PLATES/CUPS ETC** [C] a set of plates, bowls, cups etc that match each other

15 **BUS/TRAIN/PLANE ETC** [C usually singular] *BrE* a regular journey made by a bus, train, boat etc to a particular place at a particular time: *the 8:15 service to Cambridge*

16 **be in service/go into service** *BrE* to be working or start working as a servant in someone's house, especially in the past → DOMESTIC SERVICE

17 **LEGAL DOCUMENT** [U] *formal* when someone is given a legal document telling them that they must do something or that something is going to happen: *the service of a summons*

18 **for services rendered** *formal* for work you have done or help you have given: *payment for services rendered* → ACTIVE SERVICE, LIP SERVICE; → **press sb/sth into service** at PRESS² (13)

service² v [T] **1** [usually passive] if someone services a machine or vehicle, they examine it and do what is needed to keep it working well: *I'm having the car serviced next week.* → SERVICING **2** to provide people with something they need or want: *schools that service local communities* **3** **service a debt/loan** *technical* to pay the INTEREST on a debt

ser·vice·a·ble /'sɜːvɪ̯səbəl $ 'sɜːr-/ adj ready or able to be used: *Some of these old tools are still serviceable.*

'service ˌarea n [C] *BrE* a place on a MOTORWAY where you can stop for petrol, food, toilets etc

'service ˌcharge n [C] **1** *BrE* an amount of money that is added to a bill in a restaurant as an extra charge for the service of the waiters **2** *BrE* an amount of money paid to the owner of a block of FLATS for services such as cleaning the stairs **3** *AmE* an amount of money that is added to the price of something in order to pay for the services that you use when buying it; ▣ **booking fee** *BrE*: *There's a service charge for advance tickets.*

'service ˌclub n [C] *AmE* a national organization made of smaller local groups in which members do things to help their COMMUNITY

'service ˌindustry n [C,U] an industry that provides a service rather than a product, for example insurance or advertising

ser·vice·man /'sɜːvɪ̯smən $ 'sɜːr-/ n plural **servicemen** /-mən/ [C] a man who is a member of the military

'service ˌstation n [C] a place at the side of the road where you can stop to buy petrol, food, and other goods; ▣ **gas station** *AmE*

ser·vice·wom·an /'sɜːvɪ̯sˌwʊmən $ 'sɜːr-/ n plural **servicewomen** /-ˌwɪmɪn/ [C] a woman who is a member of the military

ser·vic·ing /'sɜːvɪ̯sɪŋ $ 'sɜːr-/ n [U] when a machine or vehicle is examined and things are done to keep it working well: *The new model is quieter, needs less servicing and is more fuel efficient.*

ser·vi·ette /ˌsɜːviˈet $ ˌsɜːr-/ n [C] *BrE* a NAPKIN

ser·vile /'sɜːvaɪl $ 'sɜːrvəl, -vaɪl/ adj **1** very eager to obey someone because you want to please them – used to show disapproval: *a servile attitude* **2** relating to SLAVES or to being a slave —**servility** /sɜːˈvɪlɪ̯ti $ sɜːr-/ n [U]

serv·ing¹ /'sɜːvɪŋ $ 'sɜːr-/ n [C] an amount of food that is enough for one person; ▣ **helping**: *This should make enough for four servings.*

serving² adj [only before noun] **serving spoon/dish etc** a spoon, dish etc that is used to serve food

ser·vi·tude /'sɜːvɪ̯tjuːd $ 'sɜːrvɪtuːd/ n [U] *formal* the condition of being a SLAVE or being forced to obey someone else; ▣ **slavery**

ses·a·me /'sesəmi/ n [U] a tropical plant grown for its seeds and oil and used in cooking → OPEN SESAME

ses·sion [S3] [W2] /'seʃən/ *n* [C]

1 a period of time used for a particular activity, especially by a group of people: *a training session for teachers about computers* | *question-and-answer sessions* | [+of] *a session of group therapy* → **JAM SESSION**
2 a formal meeting or group of meetings, especially of a law court or parliament: [+of] *the first televised session of parliament* | **in session** (=meeting) *The court is now in session.* | *Board members met **in closed session** (=with nobody else present).*
3 *AmE* a part of the year when classes are given at a college or university

set¹ [S1] [W1] /set/ *v past tense and past participle* set, *present participle* **setting**

1 **PUT** [T always + adv/prep] *written* to carefully put something down somewhere: **set sth (down) on sth** *She set the tray down on a table next to his bed.* | *Mark filled the pan and set it on the stove.* | **set sth down/aside** *The workmen set the box down carefully on the floor.* | *Remove the mushrooms and set them aside.*
2 **PUT INTO SURFACE** [T always + adv/prep usually passive] to put something into a surface: **be set into sth** *Gates should be hung on sturdy posts set well into the ground.* | **be set into the wall/floor/ceiling etc** (=be built into the surface of something so that it does not stick out) *an alarm button set into the wall beside the door*
3 **STORY** [T always + adv/prep usually passive] if a film, play, story etc is set in a particular place or period, the action takes place there or then: **be set in sth** *The novel is set in France in the early 19th century.* | **be set against sth** *All this romance is **set against a backdrop** of rural Irish life.*
4 **CONSIDER** [T always + adv/prep] to consider something in relation to other things: **set sth against/beside sth** *These casualty totals have to be set against the continuing growth in traffic.* | *This debate should be **set in** an international **context**.*
5 **ESTABLISH STH** [T] to establish a way of doing something that is then copied or regarded as good: **set the pattern/tone/trend etc (for sth)** *Art and literature flourished and this set the pattern for the whole of Europe.* | *The Prime Minister's fierce speech set the tone for the rest of the conference.* | *It is important that parents **set an example**.* (=behave well). | *The outcome of the case will **set a** legal **precedent**.* | *His photographs **set the standard** for landscapes.* | *Freud's views on sexuality **set the agenda** for much of the century* (=people paid attention to the subjects he dealt with).
6 **START STH HAPPENING** [T] to make something start happening or to make someone start doing something: **set sth in motion/progress/train** *A study by military experts was immediately set in motion.* | *The chief executive will **set in train** the **process** of finding a successor.* | **set sth on fire/alight/ablaze** also **set fire to sth** (=make something start burning) *Protestors set fire to two buses.* | **set sb/sth doing sth** *Her last remark has set me thinking.* | *The wind set the trees rustling.*
7 **DECIDE STH** [T] to decide and state when something will happen, how much something should cost, what should be done etc: **set a date/time (for sth)** *The government has still not set a date for the election.* | *International companies **set the price** of oil.* | **set standards/limits/guidelines etc** *high standards of hygiene set by the Department of Health*
8 **START WORKING** [I,T] to start doing something in a determined way, or to tell someone to start doing something: **set to work to do sth** *They set to work to paint the outside of the building.* | **set (sb) to work on sth** *He's about to set to work on a second book.* | **set (sb) to work doing sth** *The boys were set to work collecting firewood.* | **set sb to do sth** *Rocard set himself to reform public sector industry.*
9 **MACHINE/CLOCK ETC** [T] to move a switch on a machine, clock etc so that it will start or stop working at the time you want, or in the way you want: *Did you **set the alarm**?* | *Remember to set the video to record the film.* | **set sth to/at/on sth** *Usually the heating is set on 'low'.*

10 **LIQUID/GLUE/CEMENT ETC** [I] to become hard and solid: *How long does it take for the glue to set?*
11 **SUN** [I] when the sun sets, it moves down in the sky and disappears; [⊟] **rise**
12 **set (sb) a goal** also **set sb a task/challenge** *BrE* to say what you or someone else will or must try to achieve: *It's best to set realistic goals that you can achieve.* | *He set himself the task of learning Japanese.*
13 **set your heart/mind/sights on (doing) sth** to want very much to have or achieve something, or to be determined to do something: *Ellen has completely set her heart on that house.* | *He set his sights on crossing the Pacific by balloon.*
14 **set a record** to achieve the best result in a sport, competition etc that has ever been achieved, by running fastest, jumping highest etc: *The Kenyan runner set a new Olympic Record in the 3000 metres.*
15 **set the table** to arrange plates, knives, cups etc on a table so that it is ready for a meal; [⊟] **lay the table** *BrE*
16 **set a trap a)** to make a trap ready to catch an animal **b)** to invent a plan to try and catch someone who is doing something wrong: *They decided to set a trap for him by leaving him in charge.*
17 **set sb free/loose** to allow a person or an animal to be free: *All the other hostages were finally set free.*
18 **set sb straight/right** to tell someone the right way to do something or the true facts about something: [+on] *I set him right on a few points of procedure.* → **set sth right** at **RIGHT¹** (4); → **set the record straight** at **RECORD¹** (10)
19 **FACE** [I] *written* if your face or mouth sets into a particular expression, you start to have an angry, sad, unfriendly etc expression: [+into] *His mouth set into a rather grim line.*
20 **set your jaw** to move your lower jaw forward in a way that shows your determination
21 **BONE a)** [T] if a doctor sets a broken bone, he or she moves it into position so that the bone can grow together again **b)** [I] if a broken bone sets, it joins together again
22 **CLASS WORK** [T] *BrE* to give a student in your class a piece of work to do: **set sb sth** *Mr Biggs has set us a 2000-word essay.*
23 **EXAMINATION** [T] *BrE* to write the questions for an examination: *The head teacher sets the questions for the English exam.*
24 **PRINTING** [T] to arrange the words and letters of a book, newspaper etc so it is ready to be printed: *In those days books had to be set by hand.*
25 **HAIR** [T] to arrange someone's hair while it is wet so that it has a particular style when it dries → **set sb at (their) ease** at **EASE¹** (2); → **set your face against sth** at **FACE¹** (21); → **set sth to music** at **MUSIC** (1); → **set the pace** at **PACE¹** (7); → **set pen to paper** at **PEN¹** (3); → **set sail** at **SAIL²** (2); → **set the scene** at **SCENE** (9); → **set the stage for sth** at **STAGE¹** (7); → **set great store by/on sth** at **STORE¹** (6); → **set the world on fire/alight** at **WORLD¹** (22); → **set the world to rights** at **WORLD¹** (23)

set about sth/sb *phr v*
1 to start doing or dealing with something, especially something that needs a lot of time and effort: *A team of volunteers set about the task with determination.* | **set about doing sth** *How do senior managers set about making these decisions?*
2 *literary* to attack someone by hitting and kicking them: *They set about him with their fists.*

set sb/sth **against** sb/sth *phr v*
1 to make someone start to fight or quarrel with another person, especially a person who they had friendly relations with before: *The bitter civil war set brother against brother.*
2 **set yourself against (doing) sth** to decide that you are opposed to doing or having something: *She's set herself against going to university.*
3 **set sth against tax** to officially record the money you have spent on something connected with your job, in order to reduce the amount of tax you have to pay

S

set sb/sth **apart** *phr v*
1 if a quality sets someone or something apart, it makes them different from or better than other people or things: [+**from**] *Man's ability to reason sets him apart from other animals.*
2 [usually passive] to keep something, especially a particular time, for a special purpose: [+**for**] *Traditionally these days were set apart for prayer and fasting.*

set sth ⇔ **aside** *phr v*
1 to keep something, especially money, time, or a particular area, for a special purpose: [+**for**] *Try to set aside some time each day for exercise.* | *a room that had been set aside for visitors*
2 to decide not to consider a particular feeling or thing because something else is more important: *Both sides agreed to set aside the question of independence.*
3 to officially state that a previous legal decision or agreement no longer has any effect: *The judge set aside the verdict of the lower court.*
4 if a farmer sets aside land, he or she agrees not to grow any crops on it, and accepts a payment from the government for this

set sb/sth **back** *phr v*
1 set sb/sth ⇔ back to delay the progress or development of something, or delay someone from finishing something: *Environmental experts said the move would set back further research.* | *Illness had set me back a couple of weeks.*
2 *informal* to cost someone a lot of money: **set sb back** $50/£100 etc *This jacket set me back over £1000.*

set sth/sb ⇔ **down** *phr v*
1 to write about something so that you have a record of it: *I wanted to set my feelings down on paper.*
2 to state how something should be done in an official document or set of rules: *Clear guidelines have been set down for teachers.*
3 *BrE* to stop a car, bus etc and allow someone to get out: *The driver set her down at the station.*

set forth *phr v*
1 set sth ⇔ forth *formal* to explain ideas, facts, or opinions in a clearly organized way in writing or in a speech; ☐ **set out**: *He set forth an idealistic view of society.*
2 *literary* to begin a journey: *They were about to set forth on a voyage into the unknown.*

set in *phr v*
if something sets in, especially something unpleasant, it begins and seems likely to continue for a long time: *Winter seems to be setting in early this year.* | *Further economic decline set in during the 1930s.*

set off *phr v*
1 to start to go somewhere: *I'll set off early to avoid the traffic.* | [+**for**] *Jerry and I set off on foot for the beach.*
2 set sth ⇔ off to make something start happening, especially when you do not intend to do so: *News that the claims might be true set off widespread panic.* | *Hong Kong's stock market fell, setting off a global financial crisis.*
3 set sth ⇔ off to make an ALARM start ringing: *Smoke from a cigarette will not normally set off a smoke alarm.*
4 set sth ⇔ off to make a bomb explode, or cause an explosion: *Any movement could have set off the bomb.*
5 set sth ⇔ off if a piece of clothing, colour, decoration etc sets something off, it makes it look attractive: *The blue sundress set off her long blonde hair.*
6 set sb off to make someone start laughing, crying, or talking about something: *Don't mention what happened – you'll only set her off again.*
7 set sth off against tax to officially record the money you have spent on something connected with your job, in order to reduce the amount of tax you have to pay: *Some expenses can be set off against tax.*

set on sb *phr v BrE*
1 set sb on sb to make people or animals attack someone: *The farmer threatened to set his dogs on us.*
2 [usually passive] if you are set on by people or animals, you are suddenly attacked by them: *A thirty-*

five-year-old man was set on by four youths last night.
3 set sb on/onto sb to give someone information about a person who you think has done something wrong, because you want that person to be found and caught: *If I refuse, he'll set the police onto me.*

set out *phr v*
1 to start a journey, especially a long journey: [+**for**] *Kate set out for the house on the other side of the bay.* | **set out on a journey/drive/voyage etc** *The band are setting out on a European tour in March.*
2 to start doing something or making plans to do something in order to achieve a particular result: **set out to do sth** *salesmen who deliberately set out to defraud customers* | **set out with the idea/purpose/intention etc of doing sth** *They set out with the aim of becoming the number one team in the league.*
3 set sth ⇔ out to explain ideas, facts, or opinions in a clearly organized way, in writing or in a speech: *He set out the reasons for his decision in his report.*
4 set sth ⇔ out to put a group of things down and arrange them: *The market traders began setting out their displays.*
5 set out on sth to start doing something, especially something new, difficult, or important: *My nephew is just setting out on a career in journalism.* | *The government set out on a programme of economic reform.*

set to *phr v BrE*
to start doing something eagerly and with determination: *If we all set to, we'll finish the job in half an hour.*

set up *phr v*
1 **COMPANY/ORGANIZATION ETC** to start a company, organization, committee etc; ☐ **establish**: **set sth** ⇔ **up** *They want to set up their own import-export business.* | *new regulations for setting up political parties* | **set (yourself) up (as sth)** (=start your own business) *John decided to set up as a graphic designer.* | **set up shop/set up in business** (=begin operating a business) *Now Betterware plans to set up shop elsewhere in Europe.*
2 **ARRANGE/ORGANIZE** set sth ⇔ up to make the arrangements that are necessary for something to happen: *I'll set up an appointment for you.* | *There was a lot of work involved in setting up the festival.*
3 **EQUIPMENT** to prepare the equipment that will be needed for an activity so that it is ready to be used: *The next band was already setting up on the other stage.* | **set sth** ⇔ **up** *Can someone set the overhead projector up?*
4 **BUILD/PUT UP** set sth ⇔ up to place or build something somewhere, especially something that is not permanent: *They've set up road blocks around the city.*
5 **TRICK SB** set sb ⇔ up *informal* to trick someone in order to achieve what you want, especially to make it appear that they have done something wrong or illegal: *Cox claimed that the police had tried to set him up.*
6 **PROVIDE MONEY** set sb ⇔ up *BrE informal* to provide someone with money that they need, especially in order to start a business: *After he qualified as a doctor, his mother set him up in a practice of his own.* | *Selling her share of the company has set her up for life.*
7 **HEALTHY/FULL OF ENERGY** set sb up *BrE* to make you feel healthy and full of energy: *A good breakfast will set you up for the day.*
8 set yourself up as sth to deliberately make people believe that you have the authority and skill to do something, especially when this is not true: *politicians who set themselves up as moral authorities*
9 **PUT SB IN POSITION** set sb up to put someone in a position in which they are able to do something, or in which something is likely to happen to them: [+**for**] *If he won the fight, it would set him up for a title shot.* | *Anyone with public duties sets themselves up for attack.*
10 **RELATIONSHIP** set sb ⇔ up *informal* to arrange for two people to meet, because you think they might start a romantic relationship: *'How did you meet Nick?' 'A friend set us up.'*
11 set up home/house also set up housekeeping *AmE* to get your own home, furniture etc, especially when you leave your parents' home to live with a wife, husband, or partner: *Many parents try to help their children set up home.*

12 set up a commotion/din/racket etc to start making a loud, unpleasant noise: *The party guests were setting up a steady din.* → **set up camp** at CAMP[1] (1)

set

set of knives

chess set

set² [S1] [W1] *n*

1 GROUP OF THINGS [C] a group of similar things that belong together or are related in some way: [+of] *a set of tools* | *We face a new set of problems.* | *The older generation have a different set of values.* | *a chess set*

2 TELEVISION/RADIO [C] a television, or a piece of equipment for receiving radio signals: *a colour **television set***

3 FILM [C] a place where a film or television programme is filmed: **on set/on the set** *Cruise met Kidman on the set of 'Days of Thunder'.*

4 THEATRE/FILM STAGE [C] the scenery, furniture etc used on a stage in a play or in the place where a film or television show is being made

5 SPORT [C] one part of a game such as tennis or VOLLEYBALL: *Sampras won the second set 6 – 4.*

6 PEOPLE [singular] a group of people who are similar in some way and spend time together socially: *a favourite meeting place of the smart set* (=rich and fashionable people) | *Val got in with a wild set at college.* → JET SET

7 the set of sb's face/jaw/shoulders etc the expression on your face or the way you hold your body, which tells people how you are feeling: [+of] *From the set of her shoulders it was clear that Sue was exhausted.* | *the hard set of his face*

8 MUSIC [C] a performance by a singer, band, or DISC JOCKEY: *Sasha performed a 3-hour set.*

9 MATHS [C] *technical* a group of numbers, shapes etc in MATHEMATICS: *The set (x, y) has two members.*

10 STUDENTS [C] *BrE* a group of children who are taught a particular school subject together because they have the same level of ability in that subject; ▣ **stream**: **top/bottom etc set** *Adam's in the top set for maths.*

11 ONION [C] a small onion that you plant in order to grow bigger ones: *onion sets*

set³ *adj*

1 PLACED [not before noun] being in the position that is mentioned: [+in/on/back etc] *a medieval village set high on a hill* | *a big house set back from the road*

2 BACKGROUND used to say that something is in front of a particular background, especially in a way that is attractive: [+against] *a small town of white buildings, set against a background of hills* | *pink petals set against dark green foliage*

3 FIXED [only before noun] a set amount, time etc is fixed and is never changed: *We were paid a set amount each week.* | *The evening meal is served at a set time.* | *Small children like a set routine.*

4 READY [not before noun] *informal* someone who is set for something is ready for it: [+for] *Are you **all set** for the trip?* | **set to do sth** *I was just set to go when the phone rang.* | **Get set** (=get ready) *for a night of excitement.* | **On your marks – get set – go** (=said to start a race).

5 set on/upon/against (doing) sth determined about something: *Nina's set on going to the party.* | *The government's **dead set*** (=completely determined) *against the plan.*

6 OPINIONS/HABITS ETC not likely to change: *People had very **set ideas** about how to bring up children.* | *Mark was 65 and rather **set in** his ways* (=habits).

7 have your heart/sights set on sth to want to do something very much, or to be aiming to do something: *She's got her heart set on going to France this summer.* | *Don has his sights set on a career in law.*

8 set to do sth likely to do something: *The weather is set to change.* | *This issue is set to cause some embarrassment.*

9 deep-set/wide-set/close-set eyes eyes whose position is deep in the face, far apart on the face, or close together on the face

10 be set with gems/jewels etc to be decorated with jewels: *a gold bracelet set with rubies*

11 MEAL [only before noun] *BrE* a set meal in a restaurant has a fixed price and a more limited choice than usual: **set lunch/dinner/menu** *The hotel does a very good set menu.*

12 set book/text etc *BrE* a book that must be studied for an examination

13 FIXED EXPRESSION *literary* if your face is set, it has a fixed expression on it, especially one that is angry, worried etc: *He stared at her, his face set, his eyes hard and glittering.* | *Kate's face was set in a grim expression.* | **set smile/teeth/jaw** *'Damn you,' he said through set teeth.*

set-a·side *n* [C,U] **1** *BrE* an arrangement in the European Union in which a government pays farmers to leave some of their fields empty, in order to avoid producing too much of a crop and to keep the price higher **2** an arrangement in the US in which a local government helps small businesses to develop by making financial help available to them: *In 1976, Connecticut established one of the nation's first set-aside programs.* **3** an amount of money that is kept so that it can be used for a special purpose; ▣ **reserve**

set·back /'setbæk/ *n* [C] a problem that delays or prevents progress, or makes things worse than they were: [+for] *The December elections were a major setback for the party.* | *The team's hopes of playing in Europe suffered a **setback** last night.* → **set back** at SET[1]

set 'piece *n* [C] **1** part of a play, piece of music, painting etc that follows a well-known formal pattern or style, and is often very impressive: *The trial scene is a classic set piece.* **2** *BrE* a move such as a FREE KICK or a CORNER in a game of football, HOCKEY etc

set·square /'setskweə $ -skwer/ *n* [C] *BrE* a flat piece of plastic or metal with three sides and one angle of 90°, used for drawing or testing angles; ▣ **triangle** *AmE*; → see picture at MATHEMATICS

sett /set/ *n* [C] a passage in the ground made by a BADGER as a place to live

set·tee /se'ti:/ *n* [C] *especially BrE* a long comfortable seat with a back and usually with arms, for more than one person to sit on; ▣ **sofa** → see picture at SOFA

set·ter /'setə $ -ər/ *n* [C] **1** a long-haired dog often trained to help hunters find where animals or birds are **2 style-setter/trend-setter/standard-setter etc** someone who does things that other people admire and try to copy: *Liz has always been a fashion-setter.* **3 exam-setter/policy-setter etc** *BrE* someone who decides or organizes something as part of a job: *Who's the question-setter for the quiz night?* → **set the pattern/tone/trend** at SET[1] (5); → PACESETTER, TRENDSETTER

set·ting [W2] /'setɪŋ/ *n* [C]

1 the place where something is or where something happens, and the general environment: **beautiful/perfect/magnificent/idyllic setting** *an old farmhouse in a beautiful setting* | [+for] *Cyprus is the perfect setting for a beach holiday.* | *I've worked with children in various settings, mainly in secondary school.*

2 the place or time where the events in a book, film etc happen: [+for] *Verona is best known as the setting for two of Shakespeare's plays.* | *The island was used by Dickens as the setting for Oliver Twist.*

3 the position in which you put the controls on a

S

[1] 000, [2] 000, [3] 000, most frequent words in [S]poken and [W]ritten English

machine or instrument: *The heating system was already on its highest setting*.
4 the metal that holds a stone in a piece of jewellery, or the way the stone is fixed: *in a ... setting a diamond ring in a gold setting*
5 music that is written to go with a poem, prayer etc
6 the setting of the sun *literary* the time when the sun goes down → **PLACE SETTING**

set·tle S2 W2 /ˈsetl/ *v*
1 END ARGUMENT [I,T] to end an argument or solve a disagreement: **settle a dispute/lawsuit/conflict/argument etc** *Rodman met with Kreeger to try and settle the dispute over his contract*. | *We hope the factions will be able to* **settle** *their* **differences** (=agree to stop arguing) *by peaceful means*. | *Forensic tests should* **settle the question** *of whether Bates was actually present at the scene of the crime*. | [+**with**] *She finally settled with her former employers for an undisclosed sum*. | *They might be willing to* **settle out of court** (=come to an agreement without going to a court of law).
2 DECIDE [T usually passive] to decide what you are going to do, especially so that you can make definite arrangements: *Nothing's settled yet*. | *It's settled then. I'll go back to the States in June*. | *'She's only 15.' ' That settles it!* (=that is enough information for a definite decision to be made) *We're not taking her with us!'*
3 START LIVING IN A PLACE **a)** [I,T usually passive] to go to a place where no people have lived permanently before and start to live there: *This territory was settled in the mid-1850s by German immigrants*. **b)** [I always + adv/prep] to go to live in a new place, and stay there for a long time: [+**in**] *Many Jewish people settled in the Lower East Side*.
4 COMFORTABLE [I,T always + adv/prep] to put yourself or someone else in a comfortable position: **settle yourself in/on etc sth** *Donna did not dare settle herself too comfortably into her seat, in case she fell asleep*. | *The dog settled on the grass to enjoy its bone*. | *A nurse settled the old man into a chair*. → **SETTLE BACK**
5 QUIET/CALM also **settle down** [I,T] to become quiet and calm, or to make someone quiet and calm: *When the children had settled, Miss Brown gave out the new reading books*. | *She breathed deeply to* **settle her nerves** (=stop herself from feeling worried or frightened).
6 MOVE DOWN [I] **a)** if dust, snow etc settles, it comes down and stays in one place: [+**on**] *Snow settled on the roofs*. **b)** if a bird, insect etc settles, it flies down and rests on something: [+**on**] *A fly kept trying to settle on his face*. **c)** if something such as a building or the ground settles, it sinks slowly to a lower level: *The crack in the wall is caused by the ground settling*.
7 PAY MONEY [T] to pay money that is owed: **settle a bill/account/claim** *I always settle my account in full each month*. | *These insurance companies take forever to settle a claim*. | [+**with**] *He was able to settle with his creditors, and avoid going to jail*.
8 ORGANIZE BUSINESS/MONEY [T] to deal with all the details of a business or of someone's money or property, so that nothing further needs to be done: *When it is finally settled, the Marshall estate may be worth no more than $100,000*. | *After her husband's death, Jackie went to the city to settle his affairs*.
9 settle a score/account to do something to hurt or cause trouble for someone because they have harmed or offended you: *Did he have any enemies – someone with an old score to settle?*
10 sb's eyes/gaze settles on sb/sth *written* if your eyes settle on something or someone, you notice them and look at them for a period of time: *Her gaze settled on a door, and she wondered what was on the other side of it*.
11 FEELING/QUALITY [I always + adv/prep] *written* if a quality or feeling settles over a place or person, it begins and has a strong effect: [+**over/on**] *An uneasy silence settled over the room*. | *Depression settled over her like a heavy black cloud*.
12 EXPRESSION [I always + adv/prep] *written* if a

particular expression settles on your face, it stays there: *A disapproving frown settled on her face*.
13 STOMACH [I,T] if your stomach settles, or if something settles it, it stops feeling uncomfortable or making you sick: *Georgia had taken pills to settle her stomach, but she was still throwing up every hour*. → **let the dust settle/wait for the dust to settle** at DUST[1] (5)
settle back *phr v*
to lean back in a bed or chair, and relax and enjoy yourself: *Vera settled back to enjoy the film*.
settle down *phr v*
1 settle (sb) down to become quiet and calm, or to make someone quiet and calm: *Shh! Settle down please! Now turn to page 57*. | *When Kyle was a baby we used to take him for rides in the car to settle him down*.
2 to start living a quiet and calm life in one place, especially when you get married: *They'd like to see their daughter settle down, get married, and have kids*.
3 to start giving all of your attention to a job or activity: [+**to**] *I sorted out my mail, then settled down to some serious work*.
4 if a situation settles down, it becomes calmer and you are less busy or less worried: *It's been really hectic here. When things settle down, I'll give you a call*.
settle for sth *phr v* [not in passive]
to accept something even though it is not the best, or not what you really want: *They want $2500 for it, but they might settle for $2000*. | *She couldn't find any cola, so had to settle for orange juice*.
settle in also **settle into sth** *phr v*
to begin to feel happy and relaxed in a new situation, home, job, or school: *How's your new home? Are you settling in OK?* | *It takes a few months to settle into life at college*.
settle on/upon sb/sth *phr v*
1 to decide or agree on something: *They haven't settled on a name for the baby yet*.
2 settle sth on sb *BrE formal* to make a formal arrangement to give money or property to someone: *She settled a small yearly sum on each of her children*.
settle up *phr v*
to pay what you owe on an account or bill: *We settled up and checked out of the hotel*. | [+**with**] *I'll settle up with the bartender, then let's go*.

set·tled /ˈsetld/ *adj* **1** remaining the same, and not likely to change: *She was tired of moving around and longed for a more settled existence*. **2** if you feel settled, you feel comfortable about your life, your job etc, because you have been living or working somewhere a long time and you like the place, people, company etc: [+**in**] *I still don't feel settled in my job*. **3** *BrE* if the weather is settled, it is dry and not likely to change

set·tle·ment W2 /ˈsetlmənt/ *n*
1 OFFICIAL AGREEMENT [C] an official agreement or decision that ends an argument, a court case, or a fight, or the action of making an agreement

reach/achieve a settlement
negotiate a settlement
peace settlement (=one to end a war)
peaceful settlement (=one that is reached by discussion, without fighting)
divorce settlement (=an agreement about how money and property is divided at the end of a marriage)
out-of-court settlement (=when people make an agreement between themselves to avoid a court case)

Union leaders and company bosses will meet tomorrow in an attempt to **reach a settlement**. | *His lawyers are understood to be* **negotiating a settlement**. | *Hopes grew that a workable* **peace settlement** *might emerge*. | [+**of**] *the search for a* **peaceful settlement** *of the Northern Ireland conflict* | *She was fortunate enough to get her home as part of the* **divorce settlement**. | *The company paid out over $10 million in an* **out-of-court settlement**.

2 PAYMENT [U] *formal* when you pay all the money that you owe: [+**of**] *the settlement of all his debts* | **in settlement (of sth)** *Wyatt had received the property in settlement of a bet*.

3 GROUP OF HOUSES [C] a group of houses and buildings where people live, especially in a place where few people have lived before: *The railway stations created new settlements.* | *an early Iron Age settlement* **4 NEW AREA/PLACES** [U] when a lot of people move to a place in order to live there, especially in a place where not many people have lived before: [+of] *the settlement of the American West* **5 SINKING** [U] *technical* the process in which a building or the ground slowly sinks downwards; ⊟ **subsidence**

set·tler /ˈsetlə $ -ər/ *n* [C] someone who goes to live in a country or area where not many people like them have lived before, and that is a long way from any towns or cities: *early settlers in Australia*

ˈset-to *n* [C usually singular] *informal* a short fight or quarrel; ⊟ **argument**: *Tom and I had a bit of a set-to last night.* → **set to** at SET[1]

ˈset-top ˌbox *n* [C] *BrE* a piece of electronic equipment that is connected to your television to make it able to receive a different form of broadcasting, especially DIGITAL signals

ˈset-up also **set·up** /ˈsetʌp/ *n* **1** [C usually singular] the way that something is organized or arranged: *the traditional classroom set-up* **2** [C usually singular] *informal* a dishonest plan that is intended to trick someone: *How do I know this isn't a set-up?* **3** [U] the act of organizing something, such as a business or a computer system: *The IT department will assist you with installation and setup.* **4** [C] several pieces of equipment that work together in a system: *'Do you use the school darkroom?' 'No, I've got my own setup at home.'* → **set up** at SET[1]

sev·en /ˈsevən/ *number* **1** the number 7: *The women visited cities in seven states.* | *We close the store at seven* (=seven o'clock). | *'How old's Sam?' 'He's seven* (=seven years old).' **2 the seven year itch** the idea that after seven years of being married, many people start to want a relationship with someone new – used humorously → **at sixes and sevens** at SIX (3)

sev·en·teen /ˌsevənˈtiːn◂/ *number* the number 17: *a group of seventeen American military officers* | *I left home when I was seventeen* (=17 years old). —**seventeenth** *adj, pron*: *in the seventeenth century* | *her seventeenth birthday* | *I'm planning to leave on the seventeenth* (=the 17th day of the month).

sev·enth[1] /ˈsevənθ/ *adj* **1** coming after six other things in a series: *in the seventh century* | *her seventh birthday* **2 be in seventh heaven** *informal* to be extremely happy —**seventh** *pron*: *I'm planning to leave on the seventh* (=the seventh day of the month).

seventh[2] *n* [C] one of seven equal parts of something

sev·en·ty /ˈsevənti/ *number* **1** the number 70 **2 the seventies** [plural] also **the '70s, the 1970s** the years from 1970 to 1979: *We lost touch during the seventies.* | **the early/mid/late seventies** *In the early seventies, Sag Harbor was still a peaceful village.* **3 be in your seventies** to be aged between 70 and 79: **early/mid/late seventies** *Bill must be in his mid seventies now.* **4 in the seventies** if the temperature is in the seventies, it is between 70 degrees and 79 degrees: **in the low/mid/high seventies** *sunny, with temperatures in the mid seventies* —**seventieth** *adj*: *her seventieth birthday*

ˌseventy-ˈeight *n* [C] an old-fashioned record that plays while turning around 78 times a minute

sev·er /ˈsevə $ -ər/ *v formal* **1** [I,T] to cut through something completely, separating it into two parts, or to become cut in this way: *Martin's hand was severed in the accident.* | *a severed rope* **2** [T] to end a relationship with someone, or a connection with something, especially because of a disagreement: **sever ties/relations/connections/links etc (with/between sb)** *The two countries severed diplomatic relations.* | *She had severed all contact with her ex-husband.*

sev·er·al[1] [S1] [W1] /ˈsevərəl/ *determiner, pron* a number of people or things that is more than a few, but not a lot:

I visited him in Kansas several times. | *Several people have volunteered to go.* | **several hundred/thousand etc** *The bill came to several hundred pounds.* | *'Have you read any of his books?' 'Yes, several.'* | [+of] *Several of her colleagues agreed with her decision.* | *We had to wait* **several more** *weeks before the results arrived.*

several[2] *adj* [only before noun, no comparative] *formal* different and separate; ⊟ **respective**: *They shook hands and went their several ways* (=went in different directions). —**severally** *adv*: *These issues can be considered severally, or as a whole.*

sev·er·ance /ˈsevərəns/ *n* [U] *formal* **1** when you end your relationship or connection with another person, organization, country etc, especially because of a disagreement: [+of] *the severance of diplomatic ties between the two countries* **2 severance pay/package** money or other things that you get when you have to leave a company because your employer no longer has a job for you: *Employees will get two weeks of severance pay for every year of service.*

se·vere [S3] [W2] /səˈvɪə $ -ˈvɪr/ *adj* **1 VERY SERIOUS** severe problems, injuries, illnesses etc are very bad or very serious: *His injuries were quite severe.* | *She's suffering from severe depression.* | *The US faces severe economic problems.* | *The storm caused severe damage.* **2 WEATHER** severe weather is very bad and very extreme, and very hot, dry, cold etc **3 PUNISHMENT** a severe punishment is very strict or extreme: *Drug smugglers can expect severe penalties.* **4 CRITICISM** severe criticism is very extreme and shows that you think someone has done something very badly: *The president came under severe criticism for his handling of the crisis.* **5 DIFFICULT** very difficult and needing a lot of effort and skill: *The negotiations will be a severe test of his abilities.* **6 PERSON** someone who is severe behaves in a way that does not seem friendly or sympathetic, and is very strict or disapproving; ⊟ **stern**: *His slightly severe expression softened.* **7 PLAIN** very plain with little or no decoration: *a rather severe red-brick building* —**severity** /səˈverəti/ *n* [C,U]: *We didn't realize the severity of her illness.*

se·vere·ly /səˈvɪəli $ -ˈvɪr-/ *adv* **1** very badly or to a great degree: *The town was severely damaged in the war.* | *She's now severely disabled.* **2** in a strict way: *Parents don't punish their children so severely these days.* **3** in a very unfriendly or disapproving way: *'Stop behaving like a fool!' she said severely.* **4** in a plain simple style with little or no decoration: *a severely dressed woman*

sew /səʊ $ soʊ/ *v past tense* **sewed**, *past participle* **sewn** /səʊn $ soʊn/ *or* **sewed** [I,T] to use a needle and thread to make or repair clothes or to fasten something such as a button to them: *I learned to sew at school.* | **sew sth on sth** *Can you sew a patch on my jeans?* | **sew sth together** *She sewed the two sides together.*

sew sth ⇔ **up** *phr v* **1** to close or repair something by sewing it: *Could you sew up this hole in my trousers?* **2** [usually passive] *informal* to finish a business agreement or plan and get the result you want: *The deal should be sewn up in a week.* **3 have sth sewn up** to have gained control over a situation so that you are sure to win or get what you want: *It looks like the Democrats have the election sewn up.*

sew·age /ˈsjuːɪdʒ, ˈsuː- $ ˈsuː-/ *n* [U] the mixture of waste from the human body and used water that is carried away from houses by pipes under the ground: *Chlorine is used in sewage treatment.* | *The factory secretly dumped millions of gallons of raw sewage* (=that had not been treated) *into the Ohio river.*

ˈsewage works *BrE*; **ˈsewage plant** *AmE*; **ˈsewage farm** *BrE n* [C] a place where sewage is treated to stop it being harmful

sew·er /'sjuːə,'suːə $ 'suːər/ n [C] a pipe or passage under the ground that carries away waste material and used water from houses, factories etc

sew·er·age /'sjuːərɪdʒ, 'suː- $ 'suː-/ n [U] the system by which waste material and water is carried away in sewers and then treated to stop it being harmful

sew·ing /'səʊɪŋ $ 'soʊ-/ n [U] **1** the activity or skill of making or repairing clothes or decorating cloth with a needle and thread **2** something you are sewing: *Imogen sighed and picked up her sewing.*

'sewing ma,chine n [C] a machine for stitching cloth or clothes together

sewn /səʊn $ soʊn/ a past participle of SEW

sex¹ S1 W2 /seks/ n
1 [U] the physical activity that two people do together in order to produce babies, or for pleasure: *All you see on TV is sex and violence these days.* | *They **had sex** in the back seat of his car.* | *She no longer wanted to **have sex with** him.* | **premarital sex/sex before marriage** (=sex happening before marriage) | *the dangers of **casual sex*** (=having sex with someone without intending to have a serious relationship) | **safe sex** (=ways of having sex that reduce the spread of sexual diseases) | **unprotected sex** (=sex without a CONDOM)
2 [U] whether a person, plant, or animal is male or female: *Put your name and sex at the top of the form.*
3 [C] all men, considered as a group, or all women, considered as a group: *He found it difficult to talk to members of **the opposite sex*** (=people that were not his own sex). | *People of **both sexes*** (=both men and women) *buy her records.*
4 **single-sex school/college etc** *BrE* a school etc for either males or females, but not for both together

sex² v [T] *technical* to find out whether an animal is male or female

sex·a·ge·na·ri·an /,seksədʒə'neəriən $ -'ner-/ n [C] someone who is between 60 and 69 years old

'sex ap,peal n [U] the quality of being sexually attractive: *She's young and pretty and full of sex appeal.*

'sex change n [C usually singular] a medical operation or treatment which changes someone's body so that they look like someone of the other sex

'sex discrimi,nation n [U] treating people unfairly because they are women, or because they are men: *She is suing the company for sex discrimination.*

'sex drive n [C usually singular] someone's ability or need to have sex regularly

'sex edu,cation n [U] when young people are taught about sex, especially at school

'sex ,industry n [singular] the businesses and activities related to PROSTITUTION and PORNOGRAPHY

sex·is·m /'seksɪzəm/ n [U] the belief that one sex is weaker, less intelligent, or less important than the other, especially when this results in someone being treated unfairly: *sexism in the workplace*

sex·ist /'seksɪst/ n [C] someone who believes that one sex is weaker, less intelligent, or less important than the other, and treats them unfairly because of this – used to show disapproval: *My father was a complete sexist. He thought a woman's place was in the kitchen.* —**sexist** adj: *sexist attitudes*

sex·less /'seksləs/ adj **1** not involving sexual activity, in a way that does not seem normal or usual: *a sexless marriage* **2** neither male nor female

'sex life n [C] someone's sexual activities: *an active and fulfilling sex life*

'sex ,maniac n [C] someone who always thinks about or wants to have sex – often used humorously

'sex ,object n [C] someone who is thought about only as a way of satisfying another person's sexual desire, rather than as a whole person

'sex of,fender n [C] someone who is guilty of a crime related to sex —**sex offence** *BrE*; **sex offense** *AmE* n [U]

sex organ n [C] a part of a person's or animal's body that is involved in producing babies

'sex shop n [C] *BrE* a shop selling goods, magazines etc related to sex and sexual activities

'sex ,symbol n [C] a famous person who is considered by many people to be very sexually attractive: *Hollywood's newest sex symbol*

sex·tant /'sekstənt/ n [C] a tool for measuring angles between stars in order to calculate the position of a ship or aircraft

sex·tet /seks'tet/ n [C] **1** a group of six singers or musicians performing together **2** a piece of music for six performers: *Mozart's sextet in B flat*

sex·ton /'sekstən/ n [C] someone whose job is to take care of a church building and the area around it and do other related things, such as ring bells

'sex ,tourism n [U] the activity of travelling to other countries in order to have sex, especially of a type that is illegal in your own country —**sex tourist** n [C]

sex·tu·plet /sek'stjuːplɪt $ -'stʌ-/ n [C] one of six people who are born at the same time and have the same mother

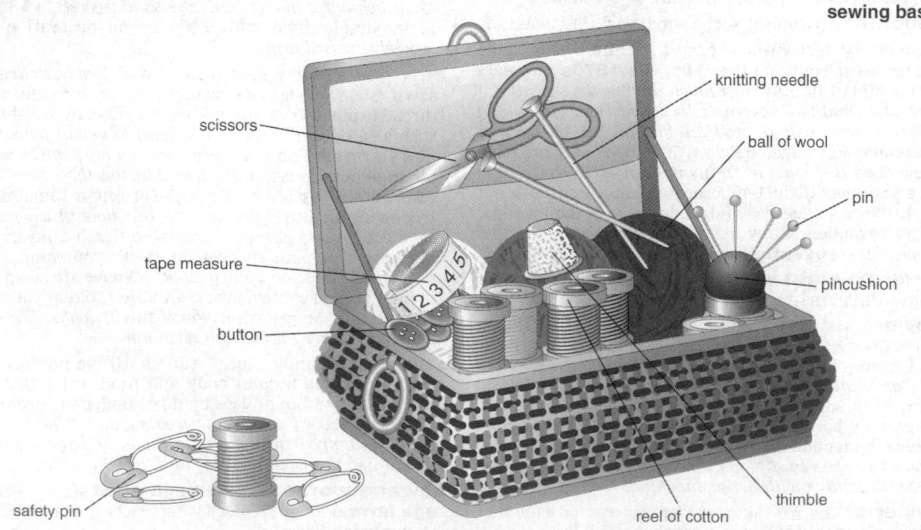

sewing basket

knitting needle

scissors

ball of wool

pin

tape measure

pincushion

button

safety pin

thimble

reel of cotton

sex·u·al S2 W2 /ˈsekʃuəl/ *adj*
1 relating to the physical activity of sex: *a disease passed on by sexual contact* | *allegations of sexual abuse* | *her first sexual experience* | *Many elderly people continue to have satisfying sexual relationships.*
2 relating to the social relationships between men and women, especially the differences between men and women: *sexual stereotypes* —**sexually** *adv*: *young people who are sexually active* (=who regularly have sex) | *I no longer found her sexually attractive.* | *She had been sexually assaulted.*

sexual harassment *n* [U] sexual remarks, looks, or touching done to someone who does not want it, especially from someone they work with

sexual intercourse *n* [U] *formal* the physical activity of two people having sex with each other

sex·u·al·i·ty /ˌsekʃuˈæləti/ *n* [U] the things people do, think, and feel that are related to their sexual desires: **male/female sexuality** *a study of male sexuality*

sexually transmitted disease *n* [C,U] *STD* a disease that one person passes to another through having sex, such as AIDS or HERPES

sexual orientation *n* [C,U] *formal* the fact that someone is HETEROSEXUAL or HOMOSEXUAL: *people of different sexual orientations*

sexual politics *n* [U] ideas and activities that are concerned with how power is shared between men and women, and how this affects their relationships

sex worker *n* [C] *formal* a PROSTITUTE – used to be polite or when you do not want to say this directly

sex·y /ˈseksi/ *adj comparative* **sexier**, *superlative* **sexiest 1** sexually exciting or sexually attractive: *sexy underwear* | *Don't you think he's sexy?* **2** *informal* sexy ideas, products etc are exciting, attractive, and interesting: *is one of the sexiest companies in Seattle* | *a sexy investment* —**sexily** *adv* —**sexiness** *n* [U]

SF /ˌes ˈef/ *n* [U] an abbreviation of *science fiction*

SGML /ˌes dʒi: em ˈel/ *n* [U] *technical* **standard generalized markup language** a way of writing a document on a computer so that its structure is clear, and so that it can be read on a different computer system

Sgt. also **Sgt** *BrE* the written abbreviation of *sergeant*

sh 93 , **shh** /ʃ/ *interjection* used to tell someone to be quiet: *Sh! I'm trying to sleep.*

shab·by /ˈʃæbi/ *adj* **1** shabby clothes, places, or objects are untidy and in bad condition because they have been used for a long time: *Hugh's jacket was old and shabby.* | *a shabby little restaurant* **2** wearing clothes that are old and worn: *a shabby tramp* **3** old-fashioned unfair and unkind: *a shabby trick* —**shabbily** *adv* —**shabbiness** *n* [U]

shack¹ /ʃæk/ *n* [C] a small building that has not been built very well: *a tin shack*

shack² *v*
shack up *phr v informal* to start living with someone who you have sex with but are not married to – used to show disapproval: [+with] *She had shacked up with some guy from Florida.* | **be shacked up** *Is she shacked up with anyone?*

shack·le¹ /ˈʃækəl/ *n* [C] **1 the shackles of sth** *literary* the limits put on your freedom and happiness by something, especially a particular form of government – used to show disapproval: *They finally managed to throw off the shackles of communism.* **2** one of a pair of metal rings joined by a chain that are used for fastening together a prisoner's hands or feet, so that they cannot move easily or escape → HANDCUFFS

shackle² *v* [T] **1** to put many limits on what someone can do – used to show disapproval: *Industrial progress is being shackled by a mass of regulations.* **2** to put shackles on someone: *He was blindfolded and shackled to a radiator.*

shade¹ /ʃeɪd/ *n*
1 OUT OF SUNLIGHT [U] slight darkness or shelter from the direct light of the sun made by something blocking it: *a plant that needs a lot of shade* | **in the**

shade (of sth) *Let's find a table in the shade.* | *She was sitting in the shade of a large oak tree.* | *The temperature was 90 degrees in the shade.* → see box at SHADOW¹
2 FOR BLOCKING LIGHT [C] **a)** something you use to reduce or block light: *The shade on the lamp was slightly crooked.* → LAMPSHADE **b)** *AmE* a covering that can be pulled down over a window; ⊟ **blind**; → see picture at BEDROOM
3 shades [plural] *informal* SUNGLASSES
4 IN A PICTURE [U] the dark places in a picture: *strong contrasts of light and shade*
5 COLOUR [C] a particular type of red, green, blue etc: [+of] *a bright shade of pink*
6 shade of meaning/opinion/feeling etc a meaning etc that is slightly different from other ones; ⊟ **nuance**: *There is room in the Democratic party for many shades of opinion.*
7 a shade *formal* very slightly: **a shade too big/hot/fast etc** *Matt's clothes were just a shade too big for me.* | **a shade better/quicker/faster etc** *The results were a shade better than we expected.* | [+over/under/above etc] *She was a shade under five feet tall.*
8 shades of sb/sth used to say that someone or something reminds you of another person or thing: *The food was horrible, (shades of school dinners).*
9 put sb/sth in the shade to be so good or impressive that other similar things or people seem much less important or interesting: *They're planning a festival that will put all the others in the shade.*
10 have it made in the shade *AmE informal* to be extremely rich – used humorously

shade² *v* [T] **1** to protect something from direct light: *Shading her eyes, Anita scanned the horizon.* **2** also **shade in sth** to make part of a picture or drawing darker: *She shaded in the circles in the last two letters.*
shade into sth *phr v literary* if one thing shades into another, it is difficult to know where one stops and another starts: *His impatience shaded into anger.*

shad·ing /ˈʃeɪdɪŋ/ *n* **1** [U] the areas of a drawing or painting that have been made to look darker **2 shadings** [plural] slight differences: *He didn't understand the subtle shadings of legal language.*

shad·ow¹ W2 /ˈʃædəʊ $ -doʊ/ *n*
1 DARK SHAPE [C] the dark shape that someone or something makes on a surface when they are between that surface and the light: *the long dark shadow of an old oak tree* | *His shadow fell across the room.* | *The building cast its shadow* (=made a shadow) *across the street.* | **in the shadow of sth** *It was hot, and we decided to walk in the shadow of the wall* (=along the wall, where its shadow would fall).
2 DARKNESS [U] also **shadows** [plural] darkness caused by something preventing light from reaching a place: **in shadow** *The room was half in shadow.* | **in the shadows** *In the shadows something moved.*
3 BAD EFFECT/INFLUENCE [singular] the bad effect or influence that something has, which makes other things seem less enjoyable, attractive, or impressive: **in/under the shadow of sth** *For years, people had been living under the shadow of communism.* | **cast a shadow over/on sth** (=make something seem less enjoyable, attractive, or impressive) *The events of September 11th cast a shadow over the celebrations.*
4 without/beyond a shadow of a doubt used to say that something is definitely true: *Without a shadow of a doubt, he's the most talented player we have.*
5 in sb's shadow if you are in someone's shadow, they are much more famous and successful than you are: *Kate grew up in the shadow of her film star sister.*
6 be a shadow of your former self to be weaker, less powerful, or worse than you were before: *Lennox seemed like a shadow of his former self.*
7 shadows under your eyes small dark areas under your eyes that you have when you are very tired: *She looked pale, with deep shadows under her eyes.*

8 sb's shadow someone who follows someone else everywhere they go

9 afraid/frightened/scared etc of your own shadow easily frightened or very nervous → FIVE O'CLOCK SHADOW

> **WORD CHOICE: shadow, shade**
> A **shadow** is a dark shape made by something that blocks the sun or a light: *She saw his shadow on the wall.*
> **Shadow** is an area of darkness made like this: *The side of the valley was in shadow.*
> **Shade** is a cool dark area where the sun does not reach, made by the shadow of something such as a tree or wall: *Let's eat our lunch in the shade.* | *He sat under the shade of a tree.*

shadow² *v* [T] **1** to follow someone closely in order to watch what they are doing: *Detectives shadowed him for weeks.* **2** [usually passive] *literary* to cover something with a shadow, or make it dark: *a narrow street which was shadowed by a huge Catholic church*

shadow³ *adj* [only before noun] **1 Shadow Chancellor/Foreign Secretary etc** the politician in the main opposition party in the British parliament who would become CHANCELLOR etc if their party was in government, and who is responsible for speaking on the same subjects **2 Shadow Cabinet** the group of politicians in the British parliament who would become ministers if their party was in government

'shadow ˌboxing *n* [U] fighting with an imaginary opponent, especially as training for BOXING

ˌshadow e'conomy *n* [C] *technical* business activities that are difficult for the authorities to find out about, for example because they are illegal

shad·ow·y /'ʃædəʊi $ -doʊi/ *adj* **1** mysterious and difficult to know anything about: *the shadowy figures who control international terrorist organizations* **2** full of shadows, or difficult to see because of shadows: *a shadowy room*

shad·y /'ʃeɪdi/ *comparative* **shadier**, *superlative* **shadiest** *adj* **1** protected from the sun or producing shade: *a shady street* | *It was nice and shady under the trees.* **2** probably dishonest or illegal: *a shady character* | *She's been involved in some shady deals.*

shaft¹ S3 /ʃɑːft $ ʃæft/ *n* [C]
1 PASSAGE a passage which goes down through a building or down into the ground, so that someone or something can get in or out: **mine/elevator/ventilation etc shaft** *a 300-foot elevator shaft*
2 HANDLE a long handle on a tool, SPEAR etc
3 OF LIGHT a narrow beam of light: **shaft of light/sunlight**
4 ENGINE PART a thin long piece of metal in an engine or machine that turns and passes on power or movement to another part of the machine: *a drive shaft*
5 FOR A HORSE [usually plural] one of a pair of poles between which a horse is tied to pull a vehicle
6 ARROW *literary* an ARROW
7 get the shaft *informal* to be treated very unfairly

shaft² *v* [T] *informal* to treat someone very unfairly, especially by dishonestly getting money from them: *I can't believe you paid that much. You got shafted.*

shag¹ /ʃæg/ also **shag·pile** /'ʃægpaɪl/ *adj* shag carpet/rug a CARPET or RUG with a rough surface made from long threads of wool

shag² *n* **1** [C] *BrE informal not polite* an act of having sex with someone **2** [C] a large black sea bird **3** [U] strong-tasting TOBACCO with thick leaves cut into small thin pieces

shag³ *v* **shagged**, **shagging** [I,T] *BrE informal not polite* to have sex with someone

shagged /ʃægd/ also **ˌshagged 'out** *adj BrE spoken not polite* very tired: *I'm not going – I'm too shagged!*

shag·gy /'ʃægi/ *adj* **1** shaggy hair or fur is long and untidy: *a shaggy black beard* **2** having shaggy hair: *a shaggy sheepskin coat* —**shagginess** *n* [U]

ˌshaggy 'dog ˌstory *n* [C] *old-fashioned* a long joke that usually ends in a silly or disappointing way

Shah /ʃɑː/ *n* [C] the title of the kings of Iran, used in the past

shake¹ S3 W2 /ʃeɪk/ *v past tense* **shook** /ʃʊk/, *past participle* **shaken** /'ʃeɪkən/
1 MOVE [I,T] to move suddenly from side to side or up and down, usually with a lot of force, or to make something or someone do this: *She shook him to wake him up.* | *Shake the bottle before you open it.* | *The whole house started to shake.* | *The car shook as it went over a bump.* | **shake sth out of/off/from sth** *She shook the sand out of her shoes* (=removed it by shaking).
2 BODY [I] if someone shakes, or part of their body shakes, they make small sudden movements from side to side or up and down, especially because they are very frightened, cold, ill etc; ☐ **tremble:** *The little boy's hand was shaking.* | **shake with fear/laughter/anger etc** *I could see my neighbor shaking with laughter.* | *What's wrong with you? You're shaking like a leaf* (=shaking a lot because you are very nervous or frightened). | **be shaking in your shoes/boots** (=be very nervous) *I was shaking in my shoes – I thought he was going to fire me.*
3 shake your head to move your head from side to side as a way of saying no, or to show disapproval, surprise, or sadness: *When asked if he wanted anything else, he just shook his head.* | *Mark shook his head in disbelief.*
4 shake sb's hand/shake hands with sb to move someone's hand up and down with your own hand as a greeting or as a sign you have agreed something: *He shook my hand warmly.* | *Wilkins stood up and shook hands with both of them.* | *Well, if we have a deal, let's* **shake on it** (=show that we have made an agreement by shaking hands).
5 SHOCK [T] to make someone feel very upset or shocked: *Kerrie was so shaken by the attack that she won't go out alone.* | *The murder shook the whole town.*
6 shake sb's confidence/beliefs etc to make someone feel less confident, less sure about their beliefs etc: *His confidence was badly shaken.*
7 sb's voice shakes if someone's voice is shaking, it is not steady and they sound very worried, angry, or frightened: *Her voice was shaking as she announced the news.* | **shake with rage/emotion etc** *Reg's voice shook with rage.*
8 shake your fist (at sb) to show that you are angry by holding up and shaking your tightly closed hand: *He shook his fist at the driver of the other car.*
9 shake a leg *spoken* used to tell someone to hurry, or quickly start doing something: *C'mon, shake a leg!*

shake down *phr v*
1 shake sb ⇔ down *AmE informal* to get money from someone by using threats: *Corrupt officials were shaking down local business owners.*
2 shake sb/sth ⇔ down *AmE informal* to search a person or place thoroughly
3 if a new situation or arrangement shakes down, people start to get used to it and it becomes more effective: *The restructure has shaken down, and staff are showing a new sense of purpose.*

shake sb/sth ⇔ **off** *phr v*
1 to get rid of an illness, problem etc: *I can't seem to shake off this cold.* | **shake off your image/reputation as sth** *Outside investment has helped Sheridan to shake off its image as a depressed industrial town.*
2 to escape from someone who is chasing you: *I think we've shaken them off.*

shake out *phr v*
1 shake sth ⇔ out to shake a cloth, a bag, a sheet etc so that any small pieces of dirt, dust etc come off: *He shook out the handkerchief and put it back in his pocket.*
2 if an organization or industry shakes out, it becomes calmer after a difficult period of time: *He'll look for bargains after the real estate market shakes out.*
3 shake sth ⇔ out to change a situation by removing

things from it that are not useful or that do not make a profit: *As the airline industry shakes out all but the very fittest, catering companies could face serious troubles.*
   shake sb/sth ⇔ **up** *phr v*
1 to give someone a very unpleasant shock, so that they feel very upset and frightened: *She was badly shaken up by the accident.* → SHAKEN
2 to make changes to an organization in order to make it more effective: *the government's plans to shake up the educational system* → SHAKEUP

> **WORD CHOICE: shake, wobble, rattle, vibrate, tremble, shiver**
> **Shake** is a fairly general word. It can be used to talk about objects moving: *There was a loud bang and the building shook.*
> It can also be used to talk about people's bodies moving because of cold, strong emotion, or illness: *Mary shook with rage.*
> If something **wobbles**, it moves from side to side because it is not steady or balanced: *The desk wobbles when you put anything on it.*
> If something hard **rattles**, it shakes and makes a quick series of short sounds: *The wind blew and the windows rattled.*
> If something **vibrates**, it makes small quick regular movements that you can hear or feel: *The engine began to vibrate.*
> If someone **trembles**, their body shakes with very small movements, especially because they are angry, afraid, or excited: *Trembling, she approached him.*
> If someone **shivers**, their body shakes with small movements, especially because they are cold or frightened: *We sat shivering under a blanket.*

shake² *n* **1** [C] if you give something a shake, you move it up and down or from side to side: *Give the bottle a good shake before use.* | *He refused with a shake of the head* (=a movement of the head from side to side to mean no). **2** [C] a cold drink made from milk, ICE CREAM, and fruit or chocolate; ▤ **milkshake**: *a strawberry shake* **3** **the shakes** nervous shaking of your body caused by illness, fear, too much alcohol, not getting a drug you are dependent on etc: *If I don't smoke, I get the shakes.* **4** **in a couple of shakes/two shakes** *informal* very soon: *I'll be back in two shakes.* **5** **no great shakes** *spoken* not very skilful, or not very good: *He's no great shakes as a singer.* **6** **get/ give sb a fair shake** *informal* to get or give someone fair treatment

shake·down /ˈʃeɪkdaʊn/ *n* [C] **1** *AmE informal* when someone gets money from another person by using threats: *a Mafia shakedown* **2** *AmE informal* a thorough search of a place or a person: *No weapons were found during the shakedown.* **3** a period of time when people start to get used to a new arrangement and it becomes more effective **4** a period of time when prices are falling on a financial market **5** a final test of a boat, plane etc before it is put into general use: *The new system is in its shakedown phase.* **6** **the final shakedown** the final situation, after a lot of other things have happened

shak·en /ˈʃeɪkən/ also ˌ**shaken ˈup** *adj* [not usually before noun] upset, shocked, or frightened by something that has happened to you: *'How's Jacob?' 'Pretty shaken up, but he'll be all right.'* | *He was **badly shaken** after the attack.*

shake·out /ˈʃeɪkaʊt/ *n* **1** [C usually singular] a situation in which several companies fail because they cannot compete with stronger companies in difficult economic conditions **2** [C] a SHAKEUP

shak·er /ˈʃeɪkə $ -ər/ *n* [C] **1** a container with holes in the lid, used to shake salt, sugar etc onto food: *a salt shaker* **2** also **cocktail shaker** a container in which drinks are mixed **3 Shaker** a member of a US religious group who lived together and had a simple way of life. Shaker furniture is made in the plain, simple, and attractive style that Shakers used to make things: *a*

Shaker chair **4** a small container for shaking DICE → **movers and shakers** at MOVER (1)

Shakes·pea·re·an /ʃeɪkˈspɪəriən $ -ˈspɪr-/ *adj* [only before noun] **1** in the style of Shakespeare: *Shakespearean language* **2** relating to the work of Shakespeare: *a famous Shakespearean actor*

shake·up /ˈʃeɪkʌp/ *n* [C] a process by which an organization makes a lot of big changes in a short time to improve its effectiveness: [+of] *a big shakeup of the education system*

shak·y /ˈʃeɪki/ *adj* **1** weak and unsteady because of old age, illness, or shock: *a shaky voice* | *Grandad was a little **shaky on his feet*** (=not able to walk very well). **2** not sure about the exact details of something, or not likely to be completely right: *My knowledge of history is a little shaky.* | *shaky evidence* **3** not firm or steady: *shaky foundations* —**shakily** *adv* —**shakiness** *n* [U]

shale /ʃeɪl/ *n* [U] a smooth soft rock which breaks easily into thin flat pieces

shall [S3] [W1] /ʃəl; *strong* ʃæl/ *modal verb negative short form* **shan't**
1 shall I/we…? *spoken* used to make a suggestion, or ask a question that you want the other person to decide about: *Shall I open the window?* | *Shall we say 6 o'clock, then?* | *What shall I get for dinner?*
2 I/we shall *especially BrE, formal* used to say what you will do in the future: *We shall be away next week.* | *I shall have to be careful.* | *I've never liked her and I never shall.* | *We shall have finished by Friday.*
3 *formal or old-fashioned* used to emphasize that something will definitely happen, or that you are determined that something should happen: *The truth shall make you free.* | *I said you could go, and so you shall.*
4 *formal* used in official documents to state an order, law, promise etc: *All payments shall be made in cash.*

shal·lot /ʃəˈlɒt $ ʃəˈlɑːt/ *n* [C] a vegetable like a small onion

shal·low /ˈʃæləʊ $ -loʊ/ *adj comparative* **shallower**, *superlative* **shallowest** **1** measuring only a short distance from the top to the bottom; ▤ **deep**: *a shallow river* | *The lake is quite shallow.* | *the shallow end of the pool* | *Place the meat in a shallow dish.* **2** not interested in or not showing any understanding of important or serious matters – used to show disapproval: *a shallow argument* | *If he's only interested in your looks, that shows how shallow he is.* **3 shallow breathing** breathing that takes in only small amounts of air; ▤ **deep** —**shallowly** *adv*: *He lay there unconscious, breathing shallowly.* —**shallowness** *n* [U]

shal·lows /ˈʃæləʊz $ -loʊz/ *n* [plural] **the shallows** an area of shallow water: *We could see fish darting about in the shallows.*

Sha·lom /ʃæˈlɒm $ ʃæˈloʊm/ *interjection* a Hebrew word used to say hello or goodbye

shalt /ʃəlt; *strong* ʃælt/ *v* **thou shalt** *old use* a phrase meaning 'you shall', used when talking to one person

sham¹ /ʃæm/ *n* **1** [singular] someone or something that is not what they are claimed to be – used to show disapproval: *The elections were a complete sham.* | *Hutton was exposed as the sham that he was.* **2** [U] *literary* when someone tries to make something or someone seem better than they really are: *It all turned out to be sham and hypocrisy.* **3** [C] a cover for a PILLOW, especially one used for decoration

sham² *adj* [only before noun] made to appear real in order to deceive people; ▤ **false**: *a sham marriage*

sham³ *v* **shammed, shamming** [I,T] *especially BrE old-fashioned* to pretend to be upset, ill etc to gain sympathy or an advantage; ▤ **feign**: *She's not ill, she's only shamming.*

sha·man /ˈʃɑːmən, ˈʃeɪ-/ *n* [C] someone in some tribes, who is a religious leader and is believed to be able to talk to SPIRITS and cure illnesses —**shamanism** *n* [U]

sham·ble /ˈʃæmbəl/ v [I always + adv/prep] to walk slowly and awkwardly, not lifting your feet much, for example because you are tired, weak, or lazy; ⊟ **shuffle**: [+over/past/along etc] *The old man shambled out of the room muttering to himself.* | **shambling gait** (=a shambling way of walking)

sham·bles /ˈʃæmbəlz/ n **be (in) a shambles** *informal* **a)** if something is a shambles, it is very disorganized and there is a lot of confusion: *The meeting was a shambles from start to finish.* | *The economy is in a complete shambles.* **b)** if a place is a shambles, it is very untidy; ⊟ **mess**: *My house is in an absolute shambles.*

sham·bol·ic /ʃæmˈbɒlɪk $ -ˈbɑː-/ adj BrE very disorganized: *the Government's shambolic efforts to deal with the crisis*

shame¹ [S2] /ʃeɪm/ n
1 it's a shame/what a shame etc *spoken* used when you wish a situation were different, and you feel sad or disappointed: *'She's failed her test again.' 'What a shame!'* | *It's a shame that you have to leave so soon.* | *What a shame we missed the wedding.* | **it is a shame to do sth** *It's a shame to cover this beautiful table with a tablecloth.* | *I can't imagine why they canceled your show, Tracy. That's such a shame.* | **a crying/great/terrible shame** *It was a crying shame that they lost the game.*
2 [U] the feeling you have when you feel guilty and embarrassed because you, or someone who is close to you, have done something wrong: *He felt a deep sense of shame.* | *Maria blushed with shame.* | **To her shame** (=it made her feel ashamed), *she gained back all the weight she'd lost.* | *He's brought shame on the whole family.* | **hang/bow your head in shame** (=look down, or feel like you should look down, because you feel so ashamed) *I bow my head in shame when I think of how I treated her.* | **There's no shame in** (=it should not make you feel ashamed) *saying 'I don't know'.*
3 [U] the ability to feel shame: *How could you do such a thing? Have you no shame?*
4 shame on you/him/them etc *spoken* used to say that someone should feel guilty or embarrassed because of something they have done: *Shame on you, Fred. I thought you were my friend!*
5 put sb/sth to shame to be so much better than someone or something else that it makes the other thing seem very bad or ordinary: *His cooking puts mine to shame.*

shame² v [T] **1** to make someone feel ashamed: *It shames me to say it, but I lied.* | *He felt shamed and humiliated by the treatment he had received.* **2 shame sb into doing sth** to force someone to do something by making them feel ashamed: *His wife shamed him into handing the money back.* **3** to be so much better than someone else that you make them seem bad or feel embarrassed: *Their training record shamed other companies.* **4** to make someone feel they have lost all honour and respect: *She had shamed her family name* (=done something that made her family lose honour).

shame·faced /ˌʃeɪmˈfeɪst◂/ adj if someone is shamefaced, they look and feel ashamed because they have done something wrong or they have behaved badly: *Conner looked a little shamefaced.* | **shamefaced smile/grin** —**shamefacedly** /-ˈfeɪsɪdli/ adv

shame·ful /ˈʃeɪmfəl/ adj shameful behaviour or actions are so bad that someone should feel ashamed: *It's shameful the way some people treat their pets.* | *a shameful family secret* —**shamefully** adv —**shamefulness** n [U]

shame·less /ˈʃeɪmləs/ adj not seeming to be ashamed of your bad behaviour although other people think you should be ashamed: *the shameless way he lied to us* —**shamelessly** adv: *She shamelessly took advantage of him.* —**shamelessness** n [U]

sham·my /ˈʃæmi/ also **'shammy ˌleather** n [C,U] a piece of CHAMOIS leather, used for cleaning or polishing

sham·poo¹ /ʃæmˈpuː/ n **1** [C,U] a liquid soap for washing your hair: *What kind of shampoo do you use?* | *a bottle of shampoo* **2** [C usually singular] when someone washes your hair using shampoo: *$21 for a shampoo, cut, and blow-dry* | **shampoo and set** (=when someone washes your hair and then dries it so that it has a particular style, especially using CURLERS) **3** [C,U] a liquid used for cleaning CARPETS

shampoo² v [T] to wash something with shampoo: *She showered and shampooed her short dark hair.*

sham·rock /ˈʃæmrɒk $ -rɑːk/ n [C] a small plant with three green leaves on each stem, that is the national symbol of Ireland

shan·dy /ˈʃændi/ n plural **shandies** [C,U] BrE a drink made of beer mixed with LEMONADE (2), or a glass of this drink

shang·hai /ʃæŋˈhaɪ/ v **shanghaied**, **shanghaiing** [T] *old fashioned* to trick or force someone into doing something unwillingly: **shanghai sb into doing sth** *I got shanghaied into organizing the kids' party.*

shank /ʃæŋk/ n **1** [C] a straight narrow part of a tool or object that connects the two ends: *a hammer shank* **2** [C,U] a piece of meat cut from the leg of an animal: *lamb shanks* **3** [C usually plural] the part of an animal's or a person's leg between the knee and ANKLE **4 (on) Shanks's pony** BrE old-fashioned walking, rather than using a vehicle

shan't /ʃɑːnt $ ʃænt/ especially BrE the short form of 'shall not': *I shan't see you again.*

shan·ty /ˈʃænti/ n plural **shanties** [C] **1** a small, roughly built hut made from thin sheets of wood, TIN, plastic etc that very poor people live in: *Workers were living in tents and shanties.* **2** also **sea shanty** a song sung by sailors in the past, as they did their work

shan·ty·town /ˈʃæntiˌtaʊn/ n [C] a very poor area in or near a town where people live in small houses made from thin sheets of wood, TIN etc

shape¹ [S2] [W2] /ʃeɪp/ n
1 ROUND/SQUARE ETC [C,U] the form that something has, for example round, square, TRIANGULAR etc: *What shape is the table?* | *You can recognize a tree by the shape of its leaves.* | **round/square etc in shape** *The dining room was square in shape.* | *His battered old hat had completely lost its shape.* | **in the shape of sth** *a silver pin in the shape of a large bird* | *The plants grow in every shape and size.* | *The children cut out shapes* (=squares, triangles etc) *from the piece of cardboard.* | **out of shape** *The wheel had been bent out of shape.*
2 HEALTH/CONDITION **a)** **in good/bad/poor etc shape** in good, bad etc condition, or in good, bad etc health: *For an old car, it's in pretty good shape.* | *The economy is in worse shape now than it was last year.* | *Kaplan seemed to be in better shape than either of us.* **b)** **in shape/out of shape** in a good or bad state of health or physical FITNESS; → **fit**, **unfit**: *I was feeling totally out of shape.* | *I've got to get into shape before summer.* | **keep/stay in shape** *She's bought an exercise bike to keep in shape.* **c)** **in no shape to do sth** to be sick, tired, drunk etc, and not able to do something well: *Mel was in no shape to drive home after the party.*
3 knock/lick/get sb/sth into shape to make someone or something better so that they reach the necessary standard: *Some of them lack experience, but we'll soon knock them into shape.*
4 CHARACTER OF STH [singular] the way something looks, works, or is organized: [+of] *Computers have completely changed the shape of our industry.* | *This new technique is the shape of things to come* (=an example of the way things will develop in the future).
5 take shape to develop into a clear and definite form: *An idea was beginning to take shape in his mind.*
6 in the shape of sth used to explain what something consists of: *Help came in the shape of a $10,000 loan from his parents.*
7 not in any shape or form also **not in any way, shape, or form** used to say that you will not accept something

for any reason: *We will not tolerate racism in any shape or form.*

8 THING NOT SEEN CLEARLY [C] a thing or person that you cannot see clearly enough to recognize: *A dark shape moved behind them.*

shape² S3 *v* [T]

1 to influence something such as a belief, opinion etc and make it develop in a particular way: *People's political beliefs are shaped by what they see in the papers.*

2 to make something have a particular shape, especially by pressing it: **shape sth into sth** *Shape the dough into small balls.* | **egg-shaped/V-shaped** etc *an L-shaped living room*

shape up *phr v informal*
1 to improve your behaviour or work: *You kids had better shape up, because I'm in no mood to fool around.*
2 to make progress in a particular way: *Ken's plans for the business are shaping up nicely.* | [+as] *Immigration is shaping up as a major issue in the campaign.* | **shape up to be sth** *It's shaping up to be a pretty big party.*
3 **shape up or ship out** *AmE spoken* used to tell someone that if they do not improve they will be made to leave a place or their job

shape·less /'ʃeɪpləs/ *adj* **1** not having a clear or definite shape: *a shapeless dress* **2** something such as a book or a plan that is shapeless does not seem to have a clear structure —**shapelessly** *adv*

shape·ly /'ʃeɪpli/ *adj* having a body that has an attractive shape: *She had long shapely legs.*

shard /ʃɑːd $ ʃɑːrd/ also **sherd** *n* [C] a sharp piece of broken glass, metal etc: [+of] *a shard of pottery*

---

share

sharing a cake

share¹ S1 W1 /ʃeə $ ʃer/ *v*

1 USE TOGETHER [I,T] to have or use something with other people: *We don't have enough books so you'll have to share.* | *The three of us shared a taxi.* | **share sth with sb** *I have an office that I share with some other teachers.*

2 LET SB USE STH [T] to let someone have or use something that belongs to you: *As a kid he'd never share his toys.* | **share sth with sb** *Will you share your fries with me?*

3 DIVIDE [T] also **share out** to divide something between two or more people: **share sth between/among sb** *They shared the cake between them.* | *At his death, his property was shared out between his children.*

4 RESPONSIBILITY/BLAME [T] to have equal responsibility for doing something, paying for something etc: *We share the responsibility for the children.* | *I own the house, but we share the bills.* | *We all share some of the blame for the accident.*

5 SAME [T] to have the same opinion, quality, or experience as someone else: **share sb's view/concern/belief etc** *Other parents share her belief in the importance of reading.* | *I believe my view is widely shared.* | *Dan and Claire share an interest in ancient history.* | **share sth with sb** *Stubbornness was a characteristic he shared with his mother.*

6 TELL SB STH [I,T] to tell other people about an idea, secret, problem etc: *Students were able to share their experiences.* | **share sth with sb** *Would you like to share your feelings with the group?*

7 **share your life with sb** if you share your life with someone, you spend your life together with them as their husband, wife etc: *I'm not ready to share my life with anyone.*

8 **share and share alike** *spoken* used to say that you should share things fairly and equally between everyone

share in sth *phr v*
if you share in someone's success, happiness etc, you have it or enjoy it with them: *His daughters did not share in his happiness.*

share² S1 W1 *n*

1 IN A COMPANY [C] one of the equal parts into which the OWNERSHIP of a company is divided: **buy/sell shares** *They were able to sell their shares at a higher price.* | [+in] *shares in Allied Chemicals* | **Share prices** *are down in London.* | **shares go up/rise** (=the value increases) | **shares fall/go down/drop** (=the values decreases) → STOCK¹ (2)

2 PART OF STH [singular] the part of something that you own or are responsible for: [+of/in] *I gave them my share of the bill and left.* | *a share in the profits* | *I do my share* (=do my part) *of the housework.*

3 **your (fair) share a)** if you have had your share of something, for example problems, success, or adventure, a lot of it has happened to you: *You've sure had your share of problems, haven't you?* | *He'd had more than his fair share of adventure.* **b)** your share of something is the amount that you deserve to have: *Don't worry – you'll get your fair share.*

4 **share in sth** your part in an activity, event etc: *Employees are always given a share in decision-making.*

5 **house/flat share** *BrE* when people live together in the same house or flat and pay the rent together —**sharing** *n* [U] → **the lion's share** at LION (2); → TIMESHARE

'share-,cropper *n* [C] *especially AmE* a poor farmer who uses someone else's land, and gives the owner part of the crop in return

share·hold·er /'ʃeə,həʊldə $ 'ʃer,hoʊldər/ *n* [C] someone who owns shares in a company or business: *Shareholders have been told to expect an even lower result next year.*

share·hold·ing /'ʃeə,həʊldɪŋ $ 'ʃer,hoʊld-/ *n* [C] if you have a shareholding in a business, you own shares in it: [+in] *In 1992, United Distillers acquired a 75% shareholding in the company.*

'share ,index *n* [C] *technical* an official and public list of SHARE prices

'share-out *n* [C usually singular] *BrE* when something, especially money or property, is divided between two or more people, or the amount each person receives when it is divided

share·ware /'ʃeəweə $ 'ʃerwer/ *n* [U] free or cheap computer SOFTWARE, usually produced by small companies, that you can use for a short time before you decide whether to buy it

sha·ri·a /ʃəˈriːə/ *n* [U] a system of religious laws followed by Muslims

shark /ʃɑːk $ ʃɑːrk/ *n* [C] **1** *plural* **shark** *or* **sharks** a large sea fish with several rows of very sharp teeth that is considered to be dangerous to humans: *Sharks were circling around our boat.* | **shark-infested waters** (=waters where there are a lot of sharks); → see picture at FOOD CHAIN **2** *informal* someone who cheats other people out of money: **pool/card shark** (=someone who uses their skill at POOL or cards to cheat other players out of money) → LOAN SHARK

sharp¹ S3 W2 /ʃɑːp $ ʃɑːrp/ *adj comparative* **sharper**, *superlative* **sharpest**

1 ABLE TO CUT EASILY having a very thin edge or point that can cut things easily; **⊞** blunt: *Make sure you use a good sharp knife.* | *Its teeth are razor sharp* (=very sharp). → see picture at SURFACE

2 TURN a sharp turn or bend changes direction suddenly: *We came to a sharp bend in the road.* | **sharp**

S

[1] 000, [2] 000, [3] 000, most frequent words in S poken and W ritten English

left/right *Take a sharp left after the church.*
3 INCREASE/CHANGE a sharp increase, rise, fall etc happens suddenly and is great in amount; ☐ **steep**: *a sharp increase in prices* | *a sharp fall in unemployment*
4 DIFFERENCE sharp differences are very big and very noticeable: *sharp differences of opinion* | *There is a sharp distinction between domestic and international politics.* | *His honesty is* **in sharp contrast** (=very different) *to some other politicians.*
5 PAIN/FEELINGS a sharp pain or feeling is sudden and severe; ☐ **dull**: *I felt a sharp pain in my back.* | *I was left with a sharp sense of disappointment.*
6 DISAPPROVING speaking in a way that shows you disapprove of something or are annoyed; ☐ **mild**: *a sharp rebuke* | *John's tone was sharp.* | *The boss can be* very **sharp with** *people when she's busy.* | **sb has a sharp tongue** (=they speak in a very disapproving way which often upsets people)
7 INTELLIGENT able to think and understand things very quickly, and not easily deceived; ☐ **dull**, **stupid**: *a journalist with an extremely sharp mind*
8 **keep a sharp eye on sb** to watch someone very carefully, especially because you do not trust them: *Keep a sharp eye on the kids at all times!*
9 PENCIL having a very thin point that can draw an exact line; ☐ **blunt**: *Make sure your pencils are sharp before we begin the test.*
10 SOUND a sharp sound or cry is loud, short, and sudden: *a sharp cry of pain* | *a sharp intake of breath* | *The branch broke with a sharp crack.*
11 TASTE having a slightly bitter taste; ☐ **mild**: *sharp cheddar cheese* | *Add mustard to give the dressing a sharper taste.*
12 CLOTHES attractive and fashionable; ☐ **smart** *BrE: Tod looked really sharp in his tux.* | *a sharp suit*
13 SHAPE not rounded or curved: *sharp features* | *Her mother had a sharp little nose.*
14 IMAGE/PICTURE if an image or picture is sharp, you can see all the details very clearly; ☐ **fuzzy**: *The outlines of the trees were sharp and clear.*
15 GOOD AT NOTICING THINGS able to see and notice details very well: **sharp eye for detail** (=the ability to notice and deal with details)
16 MUSIC **a)** F sharp/D sharp/C sharp etc a musical note that is sharp has been raised by one SEMITONE from the note F, D, C etc **b)** if music or singing is sharp, it is played or sung at a slightly higher PITCH than it should be → FLAT¹ (9) → NATURAL¹ (10)
17 WEATHER **sharp wind/frost** a very cold wind or a severe FROST: *A sharp wind blew across the lake.*
18 sharp practice *BrE* behaviour, especially in business, that is dishonest but not illegal: *He's been guilty of sharp practice in the past.*
19 **be on the sharp end (of sth)** *BrE informal* to experience the worst effects of something: *We were always on the sharp end of clients' complaints.* —**sharpness** *n* [U]
→ SHARPLY

sharp² *adv* **1** **at ten-thirty/2 o'clock etc sharp** at exactly 10.30, 2.00 etc: *We're meeting at one-thirty sharp.* **2** **sharp left/right** *BrE* if you turn sharp left or right, you make a sudden change of direction to the left or right: *You turn sharp right at the crossroads.* **3** **look sharp** *BrE old-fashioned* used to tell someone to do something quickly: *If you look sharp you might catch him before he leaves for London.* **4** played or sung at a slightly higher PITCH than is correct; → **flat**

sharp³ *n* [C] **1** a musical note that has been raised one SEMITONE above the note written **2** the sign (#) in a line of written music used to show that a musical note should be raised → FLAT² (3)

,**sharp-'eared** *adj* able to hear very well

sharp·en /'ʃɑːpən $ 'ʃɑːr-/ *v* **1** [I,T] to make something have a sharper edge or point: *Anne sharpened her pencil and got out her homework.* **2** [T] to make a feeling stronger and more urgent: *A series of attacks have sharpened fears of more violence.* **3** [T] also

sharpen sth ⇔ up to improve something so that it is up to the necessary standard, quality etc: *The course will help students sharpen their writing skills.*

sharp·en·er /'ʃɑːpənə, 'ʃɑːpnə $ 'ʃɑːrpənər, 'ʃɑːrpnər/ *n* [C] a tool or machine for sharpening pencils, knives etc

,**sharp-'eyed** *adj* able to see very well and notice small details: *My sharp-eyed mother had already spotted him.*

sharp·ish /'ʃɑːpɪʃ $ 'ʃɑːr-/ *adv BrE spoken* quickly: *We'd better leave pretty sharpish if we want to catch that bus.*

sharp·ly W3 /'ʃɑːpli $ 'ʃɑːr-/ *adv*
1 suddenly and by a large amount: *Prices have risen sharply over the last few months.* | *His politics have moved sharply to the right.*
2 in a disapproving or unfriendly way: *'What do you mean by that?' Paul asked sharply.* | *a sharply critical report*
3 quickly and suddenly: *Graham looked up sharply, startled by a noise behind him.* | *Emily drew in her breath sharply.*
4 used when saying that two things are clearly and noticeably very different: *Opinion is* **sharply divided**. | *His beliefs and values* **contrast sharply with** (=are very different from) *his father's.*

'**sharp ,shooter** *n* [C] someone who is very skilful at hitting what they aim at when shooting a gun

,**sharp-'tongued** *adj* [usually before noun] saying things in a disapproving or unfriendly way which often upsets people: *his sharp-tongued wife*

sharp-wit·ted /,ʃɑːp'wɪtᵻd◂ $,ʃɑːrp-/ *adj* able to think and react very quickly

shat /ʃæt/ *v* the past tense and past participle of SHIT²

shat·ter /'ʃætə $ -ər/ *v* **1** [I,T] to break suddenly into very small pieces, or to make something break in this way: [+**into**] *The plate hit the floor, and shattered into tiny bits.* | *The explosion shattered the building.* **2** [T] to completely destroy someone's hopes, beliefs, or confidence: *Their hopes and dreams were shattered by war.* | *A few weeks in a tiny damp room soon* **shattered** *his* **illusions** *about university life.*

shat·tered /'ʃætəd $ -ərd/ *adj* [not before noun] **1** very shocked and upset: *I wasn't just disappointed, I was absolutely shattered.* **2** *BrE informal* very tired; ☐ **exhausted**: *By the time we got home we were both shattered.*

shat·ter·ing /'ʃætərɪŋ/ *adj* **1** very shocking and upsetting: *His mother's death was a shattering blow.* **2** *BrE informal* making you very tired; ☐ **exhausting**: *I've had a shattering day.*

shat·ter·proof /'ʃætəpruːf $ -tər-/ *adj* shatterproof glass is specially designed so that it will not form sharp dangerous pieces if it is broken

shave¹ S3 /ʃeɪv/ *v*
1 [I,T] to cut off hair very close to the skin, especially from the face, using a RAZOR: *He hadn't shaved for days.* | *Brian had* **cut** *himself* **shaving**. | **shave your head/legs/armpits etc** *She shaved her legs and underarms.*
2 [T] to remove very thin pieces from the surface of something: *Shave thin strips of cheese over the pasta.*
shave sth ⇔ off *phr v*
1 to remove hair by shaving: *I've decided to shave off my beard.*
2 also **shave sth off sth** to remove very thin pieces from the surface of something, using a knife or other cutting tool: *I had to shave a few millimetres off the bottom of the door to make it shut.*
3 also **shave sth off sth** if you shave a small amount off something such as a price or a record, you make the price slightly smaller or the record time slightly shorter: *She shaved half a second off the world record.*

razor

shaving

shaving brush

electric razor

shave² n [C usually singular] **1** if a man has a shave, he cuts off the hair on his face close to his skin using a RAZOR: *He looked as if he needed a shave.* | **have a shave** BrE: *I'll just have a shave before we go.* **2 a close shave** a situation in which you only just avoid an accident or something: *Phew, that was a close shave.*

shav·en /'ʃeɪvən/ adj with all the hair shaved off: *his shaven head* → CLEAN-SHAVEN, UNSHAVEN

shav·er /'ʃeɪvə $ -ər/ n [C] a small piece of electrical equipment used for shaving: *He uses an electric shaver* → RAZOR (1)

'shaving brush n [C] a brush used for spreading soap or shaving cream over your face when you shave → see picture at BRUSH¹

'shaving cream also **'shaving foam** BrE n [U] a special cream that you put on your face when you shave

shav·ings /'ʃeɪvɪŋz/ n [plural] very thin pieces, especially of wood, cut from a surface with a sharp blade: *a pile of wood shavings on the floor*

shawl /ʃɔːl $ ʃɒːl/ n [C] a piece of cloth, in a square or TRIANGULAR shape, that is worn around the shoulders or head, especially by women

she¹ S1 W1 /ʃi; strong ʃiː/ pron [used as the subject of a verb]
1 used to refer to a woman, girl, or female animal that has already been mentioned or is already known about: *Why don't you ask Beth – she's got lovely of money.* | *I saw you talking to that girl. Who is she?* | *What did she say when you told her?*
2 old-fashioned used to refer to a country, ship, or vehicle that has already been mentioned: *She was carrying over 1500 passengers.*

she² /ʃiː/ n [singular] informal a female: *What a cute puppy! Is it a he or a she?*

she- /ʃiː/ prefix female: *a she-goat* | *a she-devil* (=evil woman)

s/he /ˌʃiː ɔː ˈhiː $ -ɔːr-/ pron written used in writing when the subject of the sentence can be either male or female: *If any student witnesses a crime, s/he should contact campus police immediately.*

shea but·ter /'ʃiː bʌtə, ˈʃeɪ- $ -tər/ n [U] a type of oil from an African nut that is used in MOISTURIZERS to make your skin less dry

sheaf /ʃiːf/ n plural **sheaves** /ʃiːvz/ **1** several pieces of paper held or tied together: [+of] *He laid a sheaf of documents on the desk.* **2** a bunch of wheat, corn etc tied together after it has been cut

shear /ʃɪə $ ʃɪr/ v past tense **sheared**, past participle **sheared** or **shorn** /ʃɔːn $ ʃɔːrn/ [T] **1** to cut the wool off a sheep **2** literary to cut off someone's hair: *Her long fair hair had been shorn.*
be shorn of sth phr v to have something valuable or important taken away from you: *Though shorn of some of its powers, the party remains in control.*
shear off phr v if part of something shears off, or is sheared off, it suddenly becomes separated, especially after being pulled or hit with a lot of force: **shear sth ⇔ off** *The left wing had been almost completely sheared off.*

shear·er /'ʃɪərə $ ˈʃɪrər/ also **'sheep ,shearer** n [C] someone who cuts the wool off sheep

shears /ʃɪəz $ ʃɪrz/ n [plural] a heavy tool for cutting, like a big pair of scissors: *Sam was trimming the hedge with a pair of garden shears.* → see picture at GARDENING

sheath /ʃiːθ/ n plural **sheaths** [C] **1** a cover for the blade of a knife or sword: *His sword was back in its sheath.* **2** BrE old-fashioned a CONDOM **3** a protective covering that fits closely around something: *The wire is covered by an outer plastic sheath.* **4** a simple, close-fitting dress: *She was wearing a plain black sheath.*

sheathe /ʃiːð/ v [T] literary **1** to put a knife or sword into a sheath: *He sheathed his sword.* **2 be sheathed in/with sth** to be covered by something: *The grassy hills were sheathed in mist.*

sheath·ing /'ʃiːðɪŋ/ n [C usually singular] a protective outer cover, for example for a building or a ship

'sheath knife n [C] a knife with a fixed blade that is carried in a sheath

sheaves /ʃiːvz/ n the plural of SHEAF

she·bang /ʃɪˈbæŋ/ n **the whole shebang** informal the whole thing: *It's a big project, and she's in charge of the whole shebang.*

she·been /ʃɪˈbiːn/ n [C] informal a place where alcoholic drinks are sold illegally – used especially in Ireland

she'd /ʃid; strong ʃiːd/ **1** the short form of 'she had': *She'd already gone when we got there.* **2** the short form of 'she would': *She'd like to come with us.*

shed¹ S3 /ʃed/ n [C]
1 a small building, often made of wood, used especially for storing things: *a tool shed* | *a cattle shed* | *a garden shed*
2 a large industrial building where work is done, large vehicles are kept, machinery is stored

shed² v past tense and past participle **shed**, present participle **shedding** [T]
1 GET RID OF to get rid of something that you no longer need or want: *The company is planning to shed about a quarter of its workforce.* | *The magazine is desperately trying to shed its old-fashioned image.* | *a diet to help you shed pounds*
2 shed light a) to make something easier to understand, by providing new or better information: [+on] *Recent research has shed light on the causes of the disease.* | *Investigators hope to shed light on what started the fire.* b) if something sheds light, it lights the area around it: *The lamp shed a harsh yellow light.*
3 PLANTS/ANIMALS if a plant sheds its leaves or if an animal sheds skin or hair, they fall off as part of a natural process: *The trees were starting to shed their leaves.* | *As it grows, a snake will regularly shed its skin.*
4 DROP/FALL to drop something or allow it to fall: *He strode across the bathroom, shedding wet clothes as he went.* | **shed a load** BrE: *A lorry shed its load of steel bars on the M25.*
5 shed blood to kill or injure people, especially during a war or a fight: *Too much blood has already been shed in this conflict.* → BLOODSHED
6 shed tears especially literary to cry: *She had not shed a single tear during the funeral.*
7 WATER if something sheds water, the water flows off its surface, instead of sinking into it

shed·load /'ʃedləʊd $ -loʊd/ n **shedloads of sth** BrE informal a lot of something: *They've got shedloads of stuff for sale.*

sheen /ʃiːn/ n [singular, U] a soft smooth shiny appearance: *Her hair had a lovely coppery sheen.*

sheep S2 W3 /ʃiːp/ n plural **sheep** [C]
1 a farm animal that is kept for its wool and its meat: *Sheep were grazing on the hillside.* | *a sheep farmer* | **flock of sheep** (=a group of sheep) → LAMB¹
2 like sheep if people behave like sheep, they do not think independently, but follow what everyone else does or thinks: *Tourists were led around like sheep,*

from shrine to souvenir shop.
3 separate the sheep from the goats *BrE* to find out which people are intelligent, skilful, successful etc, and which are not: *This test should really separate the sheep from the goats.*
4 make sheep's eyes at sb *old-fashioned* to look at someone in a way that shows you love them → BLACK SHEEP; → **count sheep** at COUNT¹ (12); → **a wolf in sheep's clothing** at WOLF¹ (2)

sheep-dip *n* [C,U] a chemical used to kill insects that live in sheep's wool, or a special bath in which this chemical is used

sheep·dog /'ʃiːpdɒg $ -dɒːg/ *n* [C] **1** a dog that is trained to control sheep **2** a dog of a type that is often used for controlling sheep → OLD ENGLISH SHEEPDOG

sheep·ish /'ʃiːpɪʃ/ *adj* slightly uncomfortable or embarrassed because you know that you have done something silly or wrong: *Sam looked a bit sheepish.* | *a sheepish grin* —**sheepishly** *adv*: *She smiled sheepishly.*

sheep-pen *n* [C] a small area of ground with a fence around it, used for keeping sheep together for a short time

sheep·skin /'ʃiːpˌskɪn/ *n* [C,U] the skin of a sheep with the wool still on it: *a sheepskin coat*

sheer¹ /ʃɪə $ ʃɪr/ *adj* **1** the sheer weight/size etc used to emphasize that something is very heavy, large etc: [+of] *The sheer size of the country makes communications difficult.* **2 sheer luck/happiness/stupidity etc** luck, happiness etc with no other feeling or quality mixed with it; ◫ **pure**: *I'll never forget the look of sheer joy on her face.* | *sheer hypocrisy* **3** a sheer drop, cliff, slope etc is very steep and almost vertical **4** sheer NYLON, silk etc is very thin and fine, so that it is almost transparent: *sheer stockings*

sheer² *adv* straight up or down in an almost vertical line; ◫ **steeply**: *cliffs which rose sheer from the sea*

sheer³ *v* [I always +adv/prep] to change direction suddenly, especially in order to avoid something: [+off/away] *The boat sheered away and headed out to sea.*

sheet S2 W2 /ʃiːt/ *n* [C]
1 FOR A BED a large piece of thin cloth that you put on a bed to lie on or lie under; → **blanket**, **duvet**: *I'll go and find you some clean sheets and blankets.* | *white cotton sheets* | **change the sheets** (=put clean sheets on a bed); → see picture at BED¹
2 PAPER a piece of paper for writing on, or containing information: [+of] *a sheet of paper with names and numbers on it* | **clean/blank sheet of paper** (=one with no writing on it)
3 THIN FLAT PIECE a thin flat piece of something such as metal or glass, that usually has four sides: [+of] *a sheet of glass* → SHEET METAL
4 LARGE FLAT AREA a large flat area of something such as ice or water spread over a surface: [+of] *A sheet of ice covered the lake.*
5 OF RAIN/FIRE a sheet of rain or fire is a very large moving mass of it: [+of] *Sheets of flame shot into the air.* | **in sheets** *The rain was coming down in sheets.*
6 ON A SHIP *technical* a rope or chain attached to a sail on a ship that controls the angle between a sail and the wind → BAKING SHEET, BALANCE SHEET, COOKIE SHEET, RAP SHEET, TIME SHEET; → **as white as a sheet** at WHITE¹ (3); → **clean sheet** at CLEAN¹ (9)

sheet·ing /'ʃiːtɪŋ/ *n* [U] **1** material such as plastic or metal used to cover something and protect it: **plastic/rubber/metal etc sheeting** *The roof was covered in plastic sheeting.* **2** cloth used to make sheets for a bed

sheet 'lightning *n* [U] a type of LIGHTNING that appears as a sudden flash of brightness covering a large area of sky → FORKED LIGHTNING

sheet ˌmetal *n* [U] metal in the form of thin sheets

sheet ˌmusic *n* [U] music that is printed on single sheets and not fastened together inside a cover

sheikh, sheik /ʃeɪk $ ʃiːk/ *n* [C] **1** an Arab ruler or prince **2** a Muslim religious leader or teacher

sheikh·dom, sheikdom /'ʃeɪkdəm $ 'ʃiːk-/ *n* [C] a place that is governed by an Arab prince or ruler

shei·la /'ʃiːlə/ *n* [C] *informal* a young woman – used in Australia and New Zealand

shek·el /'ʃekəl/ *n* [C] the standard unit of money in Israel

shelf S3 W3 /ʃelf/ *n plural* **shelves** /ʃelvz/
1 [C] a long flat narrow board attached to a wall or in a frame or cupboard, used for putting things on: **top/bottom/next etc shelf** *Put it back on the top shelf.* | *shelves of books* | *supermarket shelves* | *the amount of shelf space available*
2 [C] a narrow surface of rock shaped like a shelf, especially under water → CONTINENTAL SHELF
3 off-the-shelf available to be bought immediately, without having to be specially designed or ordered: *off-the-shelf software packages* → OFF-THE-PEG
4 be (left) on the shelf a) if something is left on the shelf, it is not used or considered: *The album stayed on the shelf for several years, until it was finally released.* **b)** *BrE old-fashioned* to be considered too old to get married, used especially of women → SHELVE (3)

shelf life *n* [singular] the length of time that a product, especially food, can be kept in a shop before it becomes too old to sell: *The pies have a shelf life of approximately one week.*

she'll /ʃil; *strong* ʃiːl/ the short form of 'she will'

shell¹ W3 /ʃel/ *n* [C]
1 a) the hard outer part that covers and protects an egg, nut, or seed: *Never buy eggs with cracked shells.* | *peanuts roasted in their shells* **b)** the hard protective covering of an animal such as a SNAIL, MUSSEL, or CRAB: *a snail shell* | *The children were collecting shells on the beach.* → SEASHELL
2 a metal container, like a large bullet, which is full of an explosive substance and is fired from a large gun: *We ran for cover as shells dropped all around us.* | *an exploding mortar shell*
3 *especially AmE* a metal tube containing a bullet and an explosive substance; ◫ **cartridge**
4 the outside structure of something, especially the part of a building that remains when the rest of it has been destroyed: [+of] *the burnt-out shell of a nightclub*
5 out of your shell becoming less shy and more confident and willing to talk to people: *I had hoped that university would bring him out of his shell.* | *She's started to come out of her shell a little.*

shell² *v* [T] **1** to fire shells from large guns at something: *The army has been shelling the town since yesterday.* **2** to remove something such as beans or nuts from a shell or POD: *Josie was shelling peas in the kitchen.*

shell out (sth) *phr v informal* to pay a lot of money for something, especially unwillingly: *If you want the repairs done right, you'll have to shell out at least $800.* | [+for] *She ended up shelling out for two rooms.*

shel·lac /ʃə'læk/ *n* [U] a type of transparent paint for protecting or hardening surfaces

shell·fire /'ʃelfaɪə $ -faɪr/ *n* [U] an explosion caused by shells being fired from large guns: *a hospital badly damaged by shellfire*

shell·fish /'ʃelˌfɪʃ/ *n plural* **shellfish** [C,U] an animal that lives in water, has a shell, and can be eaten as food, for example CRABS, LOBSTERS, and OYSTERS

shell game *n* [C] *AmE* a dishonest method of doing something, in which you pretend to be doing one thing when you are really doing another: *Critics called the proposal a shell game.*

shell·ing /'ʃelɪŋ/ *n* [U] the firing of shells from large guns: [+of] *the shelling of villages* | *weeks of heavy shelling*

shell shock *n* [U] *old-fashioned* a type of mental illness caused by the terrible experiences of fighting in a war or battle

'shell-shocked adj **1** informal feeling tired, confused, or anxious because of a recent difficult experience **2** old-fashioned mentally ill because of the terrible experiences of war

'shell suit n [C] BrE a light brightly-coloured piece of clothing consisting of trousers and a jacket that fit tightly at the wrists and at the bottom of the legs

shel·ter¹ /'ʃeltə $ -ər/ n **1** [U] a place to live, considered as one of the basic needs of life: *They are in desperate need of food and shelter.* **2** [U] protection from danger or from wind, rain, hot sun etc: [+of] *We eventually reached the shelter of the caves.* | **in/into/under etc the shelter of sth** *They were standing under the shelter of a huge tree.* | *The men took shelter in a bombed-out farmhouse.* | *All around me, people were running for shelter.* | [+from] *An old hut gave shelter from the storm.* **3** [C] a building where people or animals that have nowhere to live or that are in danger can stay and receive help: [+for] *a shelter for battered women* | *a homeless shelter* (=for people who have no homes) | *an animal shelter* **4** [C] a building or an area with a roof over it that protects you from the weather or from danger: **air-raid/bomb/fall-out shelter** (=a place to keep people safe from bombs dropped by planes) | **bus shelter** BrE (=a small structure with a roof where you wait for a bus) → BOMB SHELTER, TAX SHELTER

shelter² v **1** [T] to provide a place where someone or something is protected, especially from the weather or from danger: *Collins was arrested for sheltering enemy soldiers.* | **shelter sb/sth from sb/sth** *Plant herbs next to a wall to shelter them from the wind.* **2** [I] to stay in or under a place where you are protected from the weather or from danger: [+from] *We sat in the shade, sheltering from the sun.*

shel·tered /'ʃeltəd $ -ərd/ adj **1 a sheltered life/childhood/upbringing etc** a life etc in which someone has been too protected by their parents from difficult or unpleasant experiences: *I had led a sheltered life and had never met prejudice before.* **2** a place that is sheltered is protected from extreme weather conditions: *a sheltered valley* **3 sheltered accommodation/housing** BrE a place for people to live who cannot look after themselves properly and where help is provided if they need it: *sheltered accommodation for the elderly*

shelve /ʃelv/ v **1** [T] to decide not to continue with a plan, idea etc, although you might continue with it at a later time: *Plans to reopen the school have been shelved.* **2** [I always + adv/prep] land that shelves is at a slight angle: *The garden shelves gently towards the sea.* **3** [T] to put something on a shelf, especially books

shelves /ʃelvz/ n the plural of SHELF

shelv·ing /'ʃelvɪŋ/ n [U] **1** a set of shelves fixed to a wall **2** wood, metal etc used for shelves

she·nan·i·gans /ʃɪ'nænɪɡənz/ n [plural] informal bad behaviour that is not very serious, or slightly dishonest activities: *She wouldn't put up with his shenanigans.* | *financial shenanigans*

shep·herd¹ /'ʃepəd $ -ərd/ n [C] someone whose job is to take care of sheep

shepherd² v [T always + adv/prep] to lead or guide a group of people somewhere, making sure that they go where you want them to go: **shepherd sb into/out/towards etc sth** *The tour guides shepherded the rest of the group onto the bus.*

shep·herd·ess /'ʃepədes $ -ərdɪs/ n [C] old-fashioned a woman whose job is to take care of sheep

,shepherd's 'pie n [C,U] a dish made of small pieces of cooked meat, usually lamb, covered with cooked potato

sher·bet /'ʃɜːbət $ 'ʃɜːr-/ n **1** [C,U] AmE a sweet frozen food made with water, fruit, sugar, and milk **2** [U] BrE a powder that is eaten as a sweet

sherd /ʃɜːd $ ʃɜːrd/ n another form of SHARD

sher·iff /'ʃerɪf/ n [C] **1** an elected law officer of a COUNTY in the US **2** also **High Sheriff** the representative of the King or Queen in a COUNTY of England and Wales, who has mostly ceremonial duties **3** the most important judge in a DISTRICT or COUNTY in Scotland

'sheriff ,court also **,sheriff's ,court** n [C] the lower court of law in Scotland, dealing with CIVIL and criminal cases

Sher·pa /'ʃɜːpə $ 'ʃɜːr-/ n [C] a Himalayan person who is often employed to guide people through mountains and carry their equipment

sher·ry /'ʃeri/ n plural **sherries** [C,U] a pale or dark brown strong wine, originally from Spain

she's /ʃiz; strong ʃiːz/ **1** the short form of 'she is': *She's not feeling well.* **2** the short form of 'she has': *She's got a new bike.*

Shet·land po·ny /,ʃetlənd 'pəʊni $ -'poʊni/ n [C] a small strong horse with long rough hair

shew /ʃəʊ $ ʃoʊ/ v an old spelling of SHOW

shh /ʃ/ interjection used to tell people to be quiet: *Shh! I can't hear what he's saying.*

Shi·a, Shiah /'ʃiːə/ n **1 the Shia** the Shiite branch of the Muslim religion **2** [C] a Shiite

shi·at·su /ʃi'ætsu: $ ʃi'ɑː-/ n [U] a Japanese form of MASSAGE (=pressing and rubbing someone's body)

shib·bo·leth /'ʃɪbəleθ $ -lɪθ/ n [C] formal an old idea, custom, or principle that you think is no longer important or suitable for modern times

shield¹ /ʃiːld/ n [C] **1 a)** a large piece of metal or leather that soldiers used in the past to protect themselves when fighting **b)** a piece of equipment made of strong plastic, used by the police to protect themselves against angry crowds; ⊟ **riot shield** → HUMAN SHIELD **2 a)** something in the shape of a shield, wide at the top and curving to a point at the bottom, that is given as a prize for winning a competition, especially a sports competition **b)** a drawing or model of a shield, wide at the top and curving to a point at the bottom, that is used as a COAT OF ARMS **3** something that protects a person or thing from harm or damage: [+against] *The immune system is our body's shield against infection.* **4** AmE the small piece of metal that a police officer wears to show that they are a police officer; ⊟ **badge**

shield² v [T] to protect someone or something from being harmed or damaged: *Women will often lie to shield even the most abusive partner.* | **shield sb/sth from sb/sth** *He held up his hands, shielding his eyes from the sun.* | *import tariffs that shield firms from foreign competition*

shift¹ W3 /ʃɪft/ v

1 MOVE a) [I,T] to move from one place or position to another, or make something do this: *Joe listened, shifting uncomfortably from one foot to another.* | *She shifted her gaze from me to Bobby.* **b)** [T] BrE informal to move something, especially by picking it up and carrying it: *Give me a hand to shift these chairs.*

2 CHANGE ATTENTION [T] to change a situation, discussion etc by giving special attention to one idea or subject instead of to a previous one: **shift sth away/onto/from etc** *The White House hopes to shift the media's attention away from foreign policy issues.* | **shifts attention/emphasis/focus** *In this stage of a rape case, the focus often shifts onto the victim and her conduct.* | **shift gear** AmE (=change what you are doing) *It's hard to shift gear when you come home after a busy day at work.*

3 CHANGE OPINION [I,T] if someone's opinions, beliefs etc shift, they change: *Public opinion is beginning to shift to the right* (=become more right-wing). | *shifting attitudes towards marriage* | *He refused to shift his ground* (=change his opinion).

S

4 shift the blame/responsibility (onto sb) to make someone else responsible for something, especially for something bad that has happened: *It was a clear attempt to shift the responsibility for the crime onto the victim.*

5 COSTS/SPENDING [T always + adv/prep] to change the way that money is paid or spent: *the need to shift more resources towards reducing poverty*

6 DIRT/MARKS [T] *BrE* to remove dirt or marks from a surface or piece of clothing: *a new washing powder that will shift any stain*

7 IN A CAR [I,T] *especially AmE* to change the GEARS when you are driving; ☐ **change** *BrE*: *I shifted into second gear.*

8 SELL [T] *BrE informal* to sell a product, especially a lot of it: *The store shifted over 1,000 copies of the book last week.*

shift² *n* [C] **1** a change in the way people think about something, in the way something is done etc: [+from/to] *the shift from one type of economic system to another* | [+in] *an important shift in policy* | *a marked shift* (=noticeable change) *in attitudes towards women* **2 a)** if workers in a factory, hospital etc work shifts, they work for a particular period of time during the day or night, and are then replaced by others, so that there are always people working: **do/work a (10/12/24 etc hour) shift** *Dave had to work a 12-hour shift yesterday.* | *I work shifts.* | **night/day etc shift** *The thought of working night shifts put her off becoming a nurse.* | **early/late shift** *I'm on the early shift tomorrow.* | **shift work/worker/working** *people who do shift work* | *A shift system has been introduced.* **b)** the workers who work during one of these periods: **night/day/early/late shift** *before the early shift goes off duty* **3** a SHIFT KEY: *To run the spellchecker, press SHIFT and F7.* **4** a simple straight loose-fitting woman's dress

'shift key *n* [C] the KEY² (3) on a KEYBOARD¹ (3) that you press to make a capital letter

shift·less /'ʃɪftləs/ *adj* lazy and having no interest in working hard or trying to succeed —**shiftlessness** *n* [U]

shift·y /'ʃɪfti/ *adj informal* looking dishonest: *He looks a bit shifty to me.* | *shifty eyes* —**shiftily** *adv*

Shi·ite /'ʃiː-aɪt/ *n* a member of one of the two main groups in the Muslim religion —**Shiite** *adj* [usually before noun] → SUNNI

shil·ling /'ʃɪlɪŋ/ *n* [C] **1** an old British coin or unit of money. There were 20 shillings in one pound. **2** the standard unit of money in Kenya, Uganda, Tanzania, and Somalia

shil·ly-shal·ly /'ʃɪli ˌʃæli/ *v* **shilly-shallied, shilly-shallying, shillyshallies** [I] *informal* to waste time or take too long to make a decision

shim·mer /'ʃɪmə $ -ər/ *v* [I] to shine with a soft light that looks as if it shakes slightly: *The lake shimmered in the moonlight.* —**shimmer** *n* [singular, U]: *the shimmer of petrol on the road*

shim·my /'ʃɪmi/ *v* **shimmied, shimmying, shimmies** [I] to move forwards or backwards while also quickly moving slightly from side to side

shin¹ /ʃɪn/ *n* [C] the front part of your leg between your knee and your foot

shin² *v* **shinned, shinning** [I] *BrE* **shin up/down** to climb quickly up or down a tree, pole etc by using your hands and legs; ☐ **shinny** *AmE*: *He shinned up a tree.*

shin·bone /'ʃɪnbəʊn $ -boʊn/ *n* [C] the front bone in your leg below your knee; ☐ **tibia**

shin·dig /'ʃɪndɪg/ *n* [C] a noisy party – used especially in news reports

shine¹ S3 /ʃaɪn/ *v past tense and past participle* **shone** /ʃɒn $ ʃoʊn/
1 [I] to produce bright light: *The sun was shining.* | *The moon shone brightly in the sky.* | [+in/on] *That lamp's shining in my eyes.*

2 [T] if you shine a light somewhere, you point it in that direction: **shine sth on/at/around etc sth** *Shine that torch over here, will you?*

3 [I] to look bright and smooth: *Marion polished the table until it shone.* | *She had shining black hair.*

4 [T] *past tense and past participle* **shined** to make something bright by rubbing it; ☐ **polish**: *His shoes were shined to perfection.*

5 [I] if your eyes shine, or your face shines, you have an expression of happiness: [+with] *'It was wonderful!' Kate replied, her eyes shining with excitement.*

6 [I not in progressive] to be very good at something: *The concert will give young jazz musicians a chance to shine.* | [+at/in] *Peter didn't really shine at school.*

7 shining example something or someone that is an excellent example of a particular quality and should be admired: [+of] *The house is a shining example of Art Deco architecture.*

shine through *phr v*
if a quality that someone has shines through, you can easily see that they have it: *What shines through in all her work is her enthusiasm for life.*

shine² *n* **1** [singular, U] the brightness that something has when light shines on it: *Lucy's dark hair seemed to have lost its shine.* **2 take a shine to sb** *informal* to like someone very much when you have only just met them → **(come) rain or shine** at RAIN¹ (4)

shin·gle /'ʃɪŋgəl/ *n* **1** [C,U] one of many small thin pieces of wood or another building material, fastened in rows to cover a roof or wall **2** [U] small round pieces of stone on a beach: *the crash of waves on the shingle* | *a shingle beach* **3 hang out your shingle** *AmE* to start your own business, especially as a doctor or lawyer

shin·gled /'ʃɪŋgəld/ *adj* a roof or wall that is shingled is covered with shingles

shin·gles /'ʃɪŋgəlz/ *n* [U] a disease caused by an infection of the nerve endings, which produces painful red spots

shin·ny /'ʃɪni/ *v* **shinnied, shinnying, shinnies** [I] *AmE* **shinny up/down** to climb quickly up or down a tree, pole etc by using your hands and legs; ☐ **shin** *BrE*

Shin·to /'ʃɪntəʊ $ -toʊ/ also **Shin·to·is·m** /'ʃɪntəʊɪzəm $ -toʊ-/ *n* [U] the ancient traditional religion of Japan

shin·y /'ʃaɪni/ *adj* smooth and bright: *shiny black shoes* | *a shiny polished table* | *Her hair was thick and shiny.* —**shininess** *n* [U]; → see picture at SURFACE

ship¹ S2 W2 /ʃɪp/ *n* [C]
1 a large boat used for carrying people or goods across the sea: *the ship's captain* | *a luxury cruise ship* | **by ship** *supplies that came by ship*
2 a large spacecraft → **jump ship** at JUMP¹ (16); → **run a tight ship** at TIGHT¹ (5)

WORD FOCUS: SHIP

a ship that carries people: **passenger ship, cruise ship, liner, ferry, ro-ro**

a ship that carries goods: **cargo ship, merchant ship, freighter, oil tanker, super tanker, barge**

a small ship: **boat, motorboat, powerboat**

a ship with sails: **yacht, dinghy, sailing ship, sailing boat** *BrE*/**sailboat** *AmE*, **catamaran**

a fighting ship: **warship, aircraft carrier, battleship, cruiser, frigate, destroyer, minesweeper, gunboat, man-of-war** *old-fashioned*

a ship that people live on: **houseboat, narrow boat** *BrE*

a ship that goes under water: **submarine**

people on a ship: **sailor, captain, passenger, seaman, the crew**

parts of a ship: **deck, cabin, porthole, engine room, mast, rudder, hull**

→ **vessel, steamer, steamship, raft, navy, dock, port**

ship² *v* **shipped, shipping** **1** [T] to send goods somewhere by ship, plane, truck etc: **ship sth out/to/over etc** *A new engine was shipped over from the US.* **2** [I,T] *technical* to make a piece of computer equipment or software available for people to buy: *They're now shipping their long-awaited MS-DOS version of the X-Window System.* | *Both products are due to ship at the beginning of June.* | *Both products are due to ship at the beginning of June.* | **3** [T] to order someone to go somewhere: **ship sb off/out etc** *He was shipped off to a juvenile detention center.* → SHIPPING; → **shape up or ship out** at SHAPE UP (3)

-ship /ʃɪp/ *suffix* [in nouns] **1** a particular position or job, or the time during which you have it: *He was offered a professorship* (=the job of professor). | *in Mr Major's premiership* (=when he was prime minister) | *her application for British citizenship* **2** the state of having something: *Private car ownership has almost doubled in the past 10 years.* | *Their friendship developed soon afterwards.* **3** a particular art or skill: *his superb musicianship* | *a work of great scholarship* → -MANSHIP **4** all the people in a particular group: *a magazine with a readership of 9000* (=with 9000 readers)

ship·board /ˈʃɪpbɔːd $ -bɔːrd/ *adj* [only before noun] happening on a ship: *a shipboard romance*

ship·build·er /ˈʃɪpˌbɪldə $ -ər/ *n* [C] a company that makes ships

ship·build·ing /ˈʃɪpˌbɪldɪŋ/ *n* [U] the industry of making ships: *a shipbuilding yard*

ship·load /ˈʃɪpləʊd $ -loʊd/ *n* [C] the amount of goods or people a ship can carry: [+of] *Several shiploads of grain arrived in the harbor that day.*

ship·mate /ˈʃɪpmeɪt/ *n* [C] a SAILOR's shipmate is another sailor who is working on the same ship

ship·ment /ˈʃɪpmənt/ *n* [C,U] a load of goods sent by sea, road, or air, or the act of sending them: [+of] *a shipment of grain* | **arms/oil/drug etc shipment** *an illegal arms shipment* | *The goods are ready for shipment.*

ship·own·er /ˈʃɪpəʊnə $ -oʊnər/ *n* [C] someone who owns one or more ships

ship·per /ˈʃɪpə $ -ər/ *n* [C] a company that sends goods to places by ship

ship·ping /ˈʃɪpɪŋ/ *n* [U] **1** ships considered as a group: *The port is closed to all shipping.* **2** the delivery of goods, especially by ship: **shipping company/industry/agent etc** *a Danish shipping company* | *a shipping route* **3** *AmE* the amount of money you pay a company to deliver goods to you: *The jewelry can be yours for $15 plus* **shipping and handling**.

shipping forecast *n* [C] *BrE* a radio broadcast that says what the weather will be like at sea

shipping lane *n* [C] an officially approved path of travel that ships must follow

ship's chandler *n* [C] someone who sells equipment for ships

ship·shape /ˈʃɪpʃeɪp/ *adj* [not before noun] neat and clean: *Let's get this house shipshape.* | **shipshape and Bristol fashion** *BrE* (=shipshape)

ship-to-shore *adj* [only before noun] providing communication between a ship and people on land: *ship-to-shore radio*

ship·wreck¹ /ˈʃɪp-rek/ *n* **1** [C,U] the destruction of a ship in an accident: *survivors of the shipwreck* | *narrowly escaping shipwreck* **2** [C] a ship that has been destroyed in an accident; ◨ **wreck**

shipwreck² *v* **be shipwrecked** if someone is shipwrecked, they are in a boat or ship when it is destroyed in an accident: *Beatty was shipwrecked off the coast of Africa.*

ship·wright /ˈʃɪp-raɪt/ *n* [C] someone who builds or repairs ships

ship·yard /ˈʃɪp-jɑːd $ -jɑːrd/ *n* [C] a place where ships are built or repaired

shire /ʃaɪə $ ʃaɪr/ *n* [C] **1 the shires** also **the shire counties** COUNTIES in England that mostly consist of country areas **2** *BrE old use* a COUNTY

shire horse *n* [C] a type of large powerful horse used for pulling large loads

shirk /ʃɜːk $ ʃɜːrk/ *v* [I,T] to deliberately avoid doing something you should do, because you are lazy: *a salesman who was fired for shirking* | **shirk your responsibilities/duties/obligations** *parents who shirk their responsibilities towards their children* —**shirker** *n* [C]

shirt S2 W3 /ʃɜːt $ ʃɜːrt/ *n* [C]

1 a piece of clothing that covers the upper part of your body and your arms, usually has a collar, and is fastened at the front by buttons; → **blouse**: *I have to wear a shirt and tie to work.* | *a check shirt*

2 keep your shirt on *spoken* used to tell someone who is becoming angry that they should stay calm

3 put/bet/stake your shirt on sth *BrE informal* to risk all your money on something → STUFFED SHIRT

shirt-front /ˈʃːtfrʌnt $ ˈʃɜːrt-/ *n* [C] the part of a shirt that covers your chest

shirt-lifter *n* [C] *informal* a very offensive word for a man who is HOMOSEXUAL

shirt·sleeves /ˈʃɜːtsliːvz $ ˈʃɜːrt-/ *n* [C] **1 in (your) shirtsleeves** wearing a shirt but no JACKET **2** the part of a shirt that covers your arm

shirt tail *n* [C] the part of a shirt that is below your waist and is usually inside your trousers

shirt·y /ˈʃɜːti $ ˈʃɜːrt-/ *adj* *BrE informal* bad-tempered, angry, and rude: *No need to* **get shirty**!

shish ke·bab /ˈʃɪʃ kəˌbæb $ -ˌbɑːb/ *n* [C] small pieces of meat that are put on a long thin stick and cooked

shit¹ /ʃɪt/ *interjection not polite* used to express anger, annoyance, fear, or disappointment; ◨ **damn**: *Shit! I've left my purse at home.*

shit² S2 *n spoken not polite*

1 BODY WASTE **a)** [U] solid waste that comes out of your body from your BOWELS: *a car covered in bird shit* **b)** [singular] an act of getting rid of solid waste from your BOWELS: **take a shit** also **have a shit** *BrE*

2 STH BAD [U] something that you think is bad or of very bad quality, or a bad situation: *I'm not eating that shit!* | **piece/pile/load etc of shit**

3 STUPID/UNTRUE TALK [U] something that someone says that you think is stupid or untrue; ◨ **nonsense**. *You expect me to believe that shit?* | *You're* **full of shit** (=the things you say are stupid or untrue).

4 not give a shit (what/whether/about etc) to not care at all about something or someone; ◨ **not give a damn**: *I don't give a shit what you think!*

5 have/get the shits to have or get DIARRHOEA (=an illness in which solid waste comes out of your body in a much more liquid form than usual)

6 take/put up with shit (from sb) to allow someone to behave badly or treat you badly

7 PERSON [C] someone who is very unpleasant and treats other people badly

8 feel/look like shit to feel or look very ill, or to not look as neat and clean as you should

9 treat sb like shit to treat someone very badly

10 SB'S POSSESSIONS *AmE* [U] someone's possessions, especially the things they have with them: *Get your shit together then come on over.*

11 shit happens used to say that sometimes bad things happen, and people cannot always prevent them from happening

12 ... and shit used to say that there are more details that you could mention, but it should be clear to someone else what you mean: *You said you had maps and shit.*

13 no shit *AmE* **a)** used to express surprise or to check whether what someone has just said is true: *'I can get you one for $50.' 'No shit?'* **b)** used to emphasize that what you are saying is true, or to agree that what someone else says is true: *They had like, no shit, 40 different kinds of beer.*

14 in deep shit also **in the shit** *BrE* in a lot of trouble; ◨ **in big trouble**

15 beat/kick etc the shit out of sb to beat, kick etc

S

someone so violently that they are badly injured
16 give sb shit to insult someone or criticize them
17 the shit hits the fan used to say that there will be a lot of trouble when someone finds out about something → **be hot shit** at HOT¹ (4); → **tough shit!** at TOUGH¹ (8)

shit³ v past tense and past participle **shit** or **shat** /ʃæt/ present participle **shitting** spoken not polite **1 shit yourself** BrE **shit (in) your pants** AmE to feel very worried or frightened **2** [I] to pass solid waste out of your body from your BOWELS **3** [T] AmE to tell someone something that is untrue: *Are you shitting me?* **4** [I] to treat someone very badly: [+on] *This will teach you not to shit on me.*

shit⁴ adj BrE spoken not polite very bad: *a really shit job* | [+at] *I'm shit at tennis.* → **up shit creek** at CREEK (3)

shite /ʃaɪt/ interjection, n, adj BrE spoken not polite another word for SHIT

shit·head /ˈʃɪthed/ n [C] spoken not polite a very offensive word for someone who you think is very stupid or who you are very angry with

shit·hole /ˈʃɪthəʊl $ -hoʊl/ n [C] spoken not polite a place that is very dirty and unpleasant

shit-'hot adj spoken not polite extremely good

shit·less /ˈʃɪtləs/ adj spoken not polite **scare sb shit·less** to make someone feel very frightened

shit-'scared adj [not before noun] BrE spoken not polite very frightened

shit·ty /ˈʃɪti/ adj spoken not polite very bad, unpleasant, or nasty: *a shitty job*

shiv·er¹ /ˈʃɪvə $ -ər/ v [I] to shake slightly because you are cold or frightened; ◨ **tremble**: *Jake stood shivering in the cold air.* | **shiver with cold/fear/delight etc** *She shivered with fear and anger.*; → see box at SHAKE¹

shiver

shivering

shiv·er² n [C] **1** a slight shaking movement of your body caused by cold or fear; ◨ **tremble**: *A shiver ran through* (=went through) *me.* | [+of] *She felt a shiver of apprehension.*; → see box at SHAKE¹ **2 give you the shivers** informal to make you feel afraid → **send shivers (up and) down your spine** at SEND (10)

shiv·er·y /ˈʃɪvəri/ adj [not before noun] trembling or shaking because of cold, fear, or illness: *He felt shivery and nauseous.*

shoal /ʃəʊl $ ʃoʊl/ n [C] **1** a large group of fish swimming together; ◨ **school**: [+of] *a shoal of fish* **2** a small hill of sand just below the surface of water that makes it dangerous for boats

shock¹ S2 W2 /ʃɒk $ ʃɑːk/ n
1 UNEXPECTED EVENT/SITUATION [C usually singular] if something that happens is a shock, you did not expect it, and it makes you feel very surprised, and usually upset: **be a shock to discover/find/realize etc that** *It was a real shock to hear that the factory would have to close.* | *Chuck's death came as a complete shock to all of us.* | *Moving to France was a bit of a shock to the system* (=a big shock).
2 UNEXPECTED UNPLEASANT FEELING [singular, U] the feeling of surprise and disbelief you have when something very unexpected happens, especially something bad or frightening: *She was shaking with shock and humiliation.* | *The whole town was still in a state of shock* (=extremely shocked by something and unable to think or react normally). | **get/have the shock of your life** BrE (=get a very big shock) *He got the shock of his life when he found out who I was.* | **shock of (doing)**

sth *Mom's never really gotten over the shock of Dad's death.* | *They'll get a shock when they get this bill.* | *Anyone who thinks that bringing up children is easy is in for a big shock* (=will have a big shock).
3 MEDICAL [U] a medical condition in which someone looks pale and their heart and lungs are not working correctly, usually after a sudden very unpleasant experience: *He was bleeding from the head and suffering from shock.* | *He is clearly in a state of shock.* | *The tanker driver was treated for shock and released.*
4 ELECTRICITY [C] an ELECTRIC SHOCK
5 VEHICLE [C usually plural] a SHOCK ABSORBER
6 shock of hair a very thick mass of hair: *an energetic young man with a shock of red hair*
7 SUDDEN CHANGE [C] a sudden unexpected change which threatens the economic situation, way of life, or traditions of a group of people – used especially in news reports: *the oil shocks of the 1970s*
8 SHAKING [C,U] violent shaking caused for example by an explosion or EARTHQUAKE: *The shock was felt miles away.* → SHOCK WAVE, CULTURE SHOCK, SHOCKED, SHELL SHOCK, TOXIC SHOCK SYNDROME

shock² v **1** [T] to make someone feel very surprised and upset, and unable to believe what has happened: *The hatred in her voice shocked him.* | **shock sb to hear/learn/discover etc that** *They had been shocked to hear that the hospital was closing down.* | *It shocked me to think how close we had come to being killed.* | **shock sb into (doing) sth** *She was shocked into action by the desperate situation in the orphanages.* **2** [I,T] to make someone feel very offended, by talking or behaving in an immoral or socially unacceptable way: *He seems to enjoy shocking people.* | *Just ignore the bad language – they only do it to shock.* → SHOCKED, SHOCKING

shock³ adj [only before noun] **1** very surprising – used especially in news reports: *England's shock defeat by Luxembourg* **2 shock tactics** methods of achieving what you want by deliberately shocking people: *Shock tactics are being used to stop drink drivers.*

'shock ab·sorber n [C] a piece of equipment connected to each wheel of a vehicle to make travelling on uneven ground more comfortable

shocked S3 /ʃɒkt $ ʃɑːkt/ adj
1 feeling surprised and upset by something very unexpected and unpleasant: [+by] *I was deeply shocked by Jo's death.* | [+at] *He is shocked at what happened to his son.* | **shocked look/expression/voice etc** *She gave him a shocked look.* | *For a few minutes she stood in shocked silence.* | *We were too shocked to talk.*
2 very offended because something seems immoral or socially unacceptable: [+by] *Many people were shocked by the film when it first came out.* | [+at] *They were deeply shocked at her behaviour.*

WORD FOCUS: SHOCKED
similar words: **horrified, stunned, shaken, traumatized, outraged, aghast** written
→ **surprised**

shock·er /ˈʃɒkə $ ˈʃɑːkər/ n [C] informal a film, news story, action etc that shocks you – used especially in news reports: *TV star in drugs shocker!*

shock·ing S3 /ˈʃɒkɪŋ $ ˈʃɑːk-/ adj
1 very surprising, upsetting, and difficult to believe: *the shocking news that Mark had hanged himself* | *a shocking discovery* | *The anger in his face was shocking.*
2 morally wrong: *It's shocking that hospitals can deny help to older people.* | *a shocking waste of money*
3 BrE informal very bad; ◨ **terrible**: *The path was in a shocking state.* | *I've got a shocking cold.*
—**shockingly** adv → SHOCK²

shocking 'pink n [U] a very bright pink colour
—**shocking pink** adj

'shock jock n [C] especially AmE someone on a radio show who plays music and talks about subjects that offend many people

shock·proof /ˈʃɒkpruːf $ ˈʃɑːk-/ adj a watch, machine etc that is shockproof is designed so that it is not easily damaged if it is dropped or hit

'shock ,treatment also **'shock ,therapy** n [U]
1 treatment of mental illness using powerful electric shocks **2** the use of extreme methods to change a system or solve a problem as quickly as possible – used especially in news reports: *the government's shock therapy economic programme*

'shock troops n [plural] soldiers who are specially trained to make sudden quick attacks

'shock wave n **1** [C,U] a very strong wave of air pressure or heat from an explosion, EARTHQUAKE etc: *The shock wave from the blast blew out 22 windows in the courthouse.* **2 shock waves** strong feelings of shock that people feel when something bad happens unexpectedly – used especially in news reports: *The child's murder sent shock waves through the neighborhood.* | *the shock waves caused by his resignation*

shod /ʃɒd $ ʃɑːd/ *adj especially literary* wearing shoes of the type mentioned: **well/elegantly/badly etc shod** *The children were well shod and happy.* | [+in] *His large feet were shod in trainers.* → SHOE²

shod·dy /'ʃɒdi $ 'ʃɑːdi/ *adj* **1** made or done cheaply or carelessly: **shoddy goods/service/workmanship etc** *We're not paying good money for shoddy goods.* **2** unfair and dishonest: *shoddy journalism* —**shoddily** *adv* —**shoddiness** n [U]

shoe¹ S2 W3 /ʃuː/ n [C]
1 something that you wear to cover your feet, made of leather or some other strong material: *I sat down and took off my shoes and socks.* | *a pair of shoes* | *He was wearing pointed black shoes.* | *What size shoes do you take?* | **high-heeled shoes** | **running shoes** | *a shoe shop* | **shoe polish** → BOOT¹ (1), SANDAL, SLIPPER; → see picture at FOOTWEAR
2 in sb's shoes in someone else's situation, especially a bad one: *I wouldn't like to be in his shoes when his wife finds out what happened.* | *Anyone in her shoes would have done the same thing.* | *Don't be cross with them. Try to put yourself in their shoes* (=imagine what it would feel like to be in their situation).
3 step into/fill sb's shoes to do a job that someone else used to do, and do it as well as they did: *It'll be hard to find someone to fill Pete's shoes.*
4 a curved piece of iron that is nailed onto a horse's foot; □ horseshoe → **If the shoe fits, (wear it)** at FIT¹ (8)

shoe² v shod /ʃɒd $ ʃɑːd/ shoeing [T] to put a HORSE-SHOE on a horse: *We took the horses to be shod.* → SHOD

shoe·box /'ʃuːbɒks $ -bɑːks/ n [C] **1** a CARDBOARD box that shoes are sold in **2** *BrE informal* a very small room, house etc: *I was living in a shoebox in Clapham.*

shoe·horn, shoe-horn /'ʃuːhɔːn $ -hɔːrn/ n [C] a curved piece of metal or plastic that you put inside the back of a shoe when you put it on, to help your heel go in easily

shoe·lace /'ʃuːleɪs/ n [C] a thin piece of material, like string, that goes through holes in the front of your shoes and is used to fasten them; □ **lace: tie/untie a shoelace** *Roger bent to tie his shoelace.* | *Your shoelaces are undone.*

shoe·mak·er /'ʃuːmeɪkə $ -ər/ n [C] someone who makes shoes and boots

shoe·shine /'ʃuːʃaɪn/ n [C *usually singular*] an occasion when someone polishes your shoes for money: *a shoeshine stand*

shoe·string /'ʃuːstrɪŋ/ n [C] **1 on a shoestring** *informal* if you do something on a shoestring, you do it without spending much money: **run/operate/do sth on a shoestring** *The program was run on a shoestring.* **2 shoestring organization/operation/budget etc** a business, organization etc that does not have much money available to spend **3** *AmE* a SHOELACE

sho·gun /'ʃəʊɡʌn $ 'ʃoʊ-/ n [C] a military leader in Japan until the middle of the 19th century

shone /ʃɒn $ ʃoʊn/ the past tense and past participle of SHINE

shoo¹ /ʃuː/ *interjection* used to tell an animal or a child to go away

shoo² v [T always + adv/prep] *informal* to make an animal or a child go away, especially because they are annoying you: **shoo sb away/out etc** *He shooed the kids out of the kitchen.*

'shoo-in n [C] *especially AmE informal* someone who is expected to easily win a race, election etc: [+for] *He was far from a shoo-in for president.* | **shoo-in to do sth** *He looked like a shoo-in to win the Democratic nomination.*

shook /ʃʊk/ the past tense of SHAKE

shoot¹ S2 W2 /ʃuːt/ v past tense and past participle **shot** /ʃɒt $ ʃɑːt/
1 KILL/INJURE [T] to deliberately kill or injure someone using a gun: *Police shot one suspect when he pulled a gun on them.* | *Smith killed his wife, and then shot himself.* | *A woman was shot dead in an attempted robbery.* | **shoot sb in the leg/head etc** *He had been shot in the back while trying to escape.* | *The guards have orders to shoot intruders on sight* (=shoot them as soon as they see them).
2 FIRE A GUN ETC [I,T] to make a bullet or ARROW come from a weapon: *Don't shoot! I'm coming out with my hands up.* | [+at] *Two guys walked in and started shooting at people.* | *The soldiers had orders to shoot to kill* (=shoot at someone with the intention of killing them). | **shoot bullets/arrows** *They shot arrows from behind the thick bushes.* | **shoot a gun/rifle etc** *Tod's grandfather taught him to shoot a rifle.*
3 BIRDS/ANIMALS [I,T] to shoot and kill animals or birds as a sport: *They spent the weekend in Scotland shooting grouse.*
4 MOVE QUICKLY [I,T always + adv/prep] to move quickly in a particular direction, or to make something move in this way: *She shot past me and ran into the house.* | *The cat shot across the garden, and up a tree.* | *'Where does cotton come from?' Ron's hand shot up.* | *'America, Miss!'* | *The fountain shoots water 20 feet into the air.*
5 TRY TO SCORE [I,T] to kick or throw a ball in a sport such as football or BASKETBALL towards the place where you can get a point: *Giggs shot from the halfway line.*
6 LOOK AT SB shoot sb a look/glance also **shoot a glance at sb** to look at someone quickly, especially so that other people do not see, to show them how you feel: **shoot sb a quick/sharp/warning etc look/glance** *'You're welcome to stay as long as you like.' Michelle shot him a furious glance.* | *Jack shot an anxious look at his mother.*
7 PHOTOGRAPH/FILM [I,T] to take photographs or make a film of something: *The movie was shot in New Zealand.*
8 PAIN [I always + adv/prep] if pain shoots through your body, you feel it going quickly through it: [+through/along] *A sharp pain suddenly shot along his arm.* | **shooting pains** (=continuous short pains passing through your body)
9 shoot it out (with sb) if people shoot it out, they fight using guns, especially until one person or group is killed or defeated by the other: *a scene in which the cops shoot it out with the drug dealers*
10 shoot yourself in the foot to say or do something stupid that will cause you a lot of trouble: *If he keeps talking, pretty soon he'll shoot himself in the foot.*
11 shoot questions at sb to ask someone a lot of questions very quickly: *The prosecutor shot a series of rapid questions at Hendrickson.*
12 shoot your mouth off *informal* to talk about something that you should not talk about or that you know nothing about: *Don't go shooting your mouth off.*
13 shoot the bull/breeze *AmE informal* to have an informal conversation about unimportant things: *Cal and I were sitting on the porch, shooting the breeze.*
14 shoot *AmE spoken* used to tell someone to start speaking: *'I have a few questions.' 'OK, shoot.'*
15 shoot from the hip to say what you think in a direct

S

way, or make a decision very quickly, without thinking about it first

16 shoot to fame/stardom/prominence to suddenly become very famous: *Brian, an air steward, shot to fame on the television show 'Big Brother'.*

17 shoot to number 1/to the top of the charts etc to suddenly become very successful in the popular music CHARTS (=the list of records that have sold the most copies that week): *Westlife's new album shot straight to the top of the charts.*

18 shoot hoops/baskets *informal* to practise throwing BASKETBALLS into the basket

19 shoot the rapids to sail a small boat along a river that is moving very fast over rocks, as a sport: *He was shooting the rapids when his canoe capsized.*

20 shoot pool *informal* to play the game of POOL

21 shoot craps *AmE informal* to play the game of CRAPS

22 PLANTS [I] if a plant shoots, a new part of it starts to grow, especially a new stem and leaves

23 LOCK ON A DOOR [T] to move the BOLT on a door so that it is in the locked or unlocked position

24 have shot your bolt *BrE informal* also **have shot your wad** *informal AmE* to have used all of your money, power, energy etc

25 shoot your load *informal* to EJACULATE → **blame/shoot the messenger** at MESSENGER[1] (2)

shoot sb/sth ⇔ down *phr v*
1 to make an enemy plane crash to the ground, by firing weapons at it: *His plane was shot down over France in 1944.*
2 to kill or seriously injure someone by shooting them, especially someone who cannot defend themselves: *The army were accused of shooting down unarmed demonstrators.*
3 *informal* to say or show that someone's ideas or opinions are wrong or stupid: *I tried to help, but all my suggestions were shot down in flames, as usual.*

shoot for/at sth *phr v informal especially AmE* to try to achieve a particular aim, especially one that is very difficult; ◨ **aim for**: *We are shooting for a 50% increase in sales in the next financial year.*

shoot off *phr v BrE informal*
to leave somewhere quickly or suddenly: *Sorry, but I'll have to shoot off before the end of the meeting.*

shoot through *phr v*
AusE informal to leave a place quickly, especially in order to avoid someone or something → **be shot through with sth** at SHOT[2] (3)

shoot up *phr v*
1 to increase very quickly and suddenly: *Demand for water has shot up by 70% over the last 30 years.*
2 if a child shoots up, he or she grows taller very quickly and suddenly: *I can't believe this is Joshua – he's shot up since we last saw him!*
3 shoot sb/sth ⇔ up to cause serious injury or damage to someone or something by shooting them with bullets: *Then two men came in and shot up the entire lobby.*
4 shoot up (sth) *informal* to put illegal drugs into your blood, using a needle: *Kids as young as ten are shooting up heroin.*

shoot² n [C] **1** the part of a plant that comes up above the ground when it is just beginning to grow, or a new part that grows on an existing plant: *Tender green shoots will appear in February.* **2** an occasion when someone takes photographs or makes a film: *a photo shoot sponsored by Kodak* | **on a shoot** *She's out on a video shoot.* **3** an occasion when people shoot birds or animals for sport, or the area of land where they do this: **on a shoot** *The royal party was on a shoot when the incident occurred.* **4 green shoots (of recovery)** *BrE* the first sign that a situation is improving, especially an economic situation

shoot³ *interjection AmE informal* used to show that you are annoyed or disappointed about something: *Oh, shoot! I forgot to buy milk.*

shoot·er /ˈʃuːtə $ -ər/ n [C] **1** someone who shoots a gun **2** *informal* a gun **3** *AmE* a BASKETBALL player who is good at throwing the ball through the basket → PEASHOOTER, SIX-SHOOTER, TROUBLESHOOTER

shoot·ing /ˈʃuːtɪŋ/ n **1** [C] a situation in which someone is injured or killed by a gun: *His brother was killed in a shooting incident last year.* | *the accidental shooting of a child* **2** [U] the sport of shooting animals and birds with guns: *the grouse shooting season* | *The shooting party set off shortly before dawn.* **3** [U] the process of taking photographs or making a film: *We had two weeks of rehearsals before shooting began.*

shooting gallery n [C] **1** a place where people shoot guns at objects to win prizes **2** *AmE informal* an empty building in a city, where people buy illegal drugs and INJECT them

shooting match n **the whole shooting match** *BrE spoken* everything, or an event that is the most complete of its kind: *We're having a big church wedding with bridesmaids, a pageboy – the whole shooting match.*

shooting star n [C] a piece of rock or metal from space, that burns brightly as it falls towards the Earth; ◨ **meteor**

shooting stick n [C] *BrE* a pointed stick with a top that opens out to form a seat

shoot-out n [C] a fight using guns: *Two people were killed tonight in a shoot-out with police.* → PENALTY SHOOT-OUT

shop¹ [S1] [W1] /ʃɒp $ ʃɑːp/ n
1 PLACE WHERE YOU BUY THINGS [C] *especially BrE* a building or part of a building where you can buy things, food, or services; ◨ **store** *AmE*: **toy/pet/shoe/gift etc shop** *Her brother runs a record shop in Chester.* | *a barber's shop* | *a fish-and-chip shop* | *the local shops* | *Shirley saw her reflection in the shop window.* | **in the shops** *New potatoes are in the shops now.* | *I'm just going down to the shops.* | **wander/browse around the shops** *I spent a happy afternoon wandering around the shops.* → BUCKET SHOP, CORNER SHOP, COFFEE SHOP
2 PLACE WHICH MAKES/REPAIRS THINGS [C] a place where something is made or repaired: *The generators are put together in the machine shop.* | *a bicycle repair shop* → SHOP FLOOR, SHOP STEWARD
3 SCHOOL SUBJECT also **shop class** [U] *AmE* a subject taught in schools that shows students how to use tools and machinery to make or repair things: **in shop** *Doug made this table in shop.* | **wood/metal/print etc shop** *One auto shop class is run just for girls.*
4 set up shop *informal* to start a business
5 shut up shop *BrE*; **close up shop** *AmE informal* to close a shop or business, either temporarily or permanently
6 talk shop *informal* to talk about things that are related to your work, especially in a way that other people find boring: *I'm fed up with you two talking shop.* → SHOP TALK
7 all over the shop *BrE spoken* **a)** scattered around untidily: *There were bits of paper all over the shop.* **b)** confused and disorganized: *I'm all over the shop this morning.*
8 GO SHOPPING [singular] *BrE spoken* an occasion when you go shopping, especially for food and other things you need regularly: *She always does the weekly shop on a Friday.*

WORD CHOICE: shop, store
In British English, **shop** is the usual word and **store** is sometimes used to mean a very large shop where many different kinds of things are sold, for example a large supermarket or **department store**: *They live opposite a row of shops.* | *This item is available in our London store.*
In American English, **store** is the usual word and **shop** is sometimes used to mean a small store that sells one type of goods: *Will you go to the store for me?* | *a card shop*
In British English, you can talk about **the shops**: *I'm going to the shops – do you want anything?* But speakers of American English never say 'the stores'.

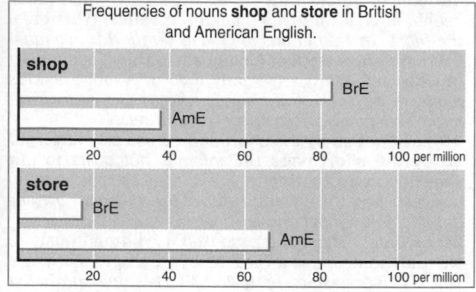

Frequencies of nouns **shop** and **store** in British and American English.

1 [I] to go to one or more shops to buy things: [+for] *I usually shop for vegetables in the market.* | [+at] *She always shops at Tesco's.* → WINDOW-SHOPPING
2 go shopping also **be out shopping** to go to one or more shops to buy things, often for enjoyment: *The next day, Saturday, we went shopping.* | *Mum's out shopping with Granny.*
3 [T] *BrE informal* to tell the police about someone who has done something illegal: *He was shopped by his ex-wife.*
shop around *phr v*
to compare the price and quality of different things before you decide which to buy: *Prices vary widely so shop around before you buy.* | [+for] *Take time to shop around for the best deal.*
shop·a·hol·ic /ˌʃɒpəˈhɒlɪk $ ˌʃɑːpəˈhɒː-/ *n* [C] *informal* someone who loves to go shopping and buys lots of things they may not need
'shop as,sistant *n* [C] *BrE* someone whose job is to help customers in a shop; ◨ **sales clerk** *AmE*
'shop-bought *adj BrE* bought in a shop, rather than made at home; ◨ **store-bought** *AmE*; ◧ **homemade**: *Why buy shop-bought yoghurt when you can easily make your own?* | *Home-made marzipan has a better flavour than most shop-bought varieties.*
shop·fit·ting /ˈʃɒpˌfɪtɪŋ $ ˈʃɑːp-/ *n* [U] *BrE* the job of putting equipment in shops, changing the way it looks etc —**shopfitter** *n* [C]
'shop 'floor *n* [singular] **1** the area in a factory where the ordinary workers do their work: **on the shop floor** *The chairwoman started her working life on the shop floor.* **2** the ordinary workers in a factory, not the managers: *negotiations between the shop floor and management*
'shop front *n* [C] *BrE* the outside part of a shop that faces the street; ◨ **storefront** *AmE*
shop·keep·er /ˈʃɒpˌkiːpə $ ˈʃɑːpˌkiːpər/ *n* [C] *especially BrE* someone who owns or is in charge of a small shop; ◨ **storekeeper** *AmE*
shop·lift /ˈʃɒpˌlɪft $ ˈʃɑːp-/ *v* [I] to take something from a shop without paying for it —**shoplifter** *n* [C]: *Shoplifters will be prosecuted.*
shop·lift·ing /ˈʃɒpˌlɪftɪŋ $ ˈʃɑːp-/ *n* [U] the crime of stealing things from shops, for example by hiding them in a bag or under your clothes: *She had been falsely accused of shoplifting in a clothing store.*
shop·per /ˈʃɒpə $ ˈʃɑːpər/ *n* [C] someone who buys things in shops: *The streets were crowded with shoppers.*; → see box at CUSTOMER
shop·ping S2 W3 /ˈʃɒpɪŋ $ ˈʃɑː-/ *n* [U]
1 the activity of going to shops and buying things: *Late-night shopping is becoming very popular.* | **shopping expedition/trip** *She's gone on a* **shopping trip** *to New York.* | *I* **went on a** *shopping* **spree** (=went shopping and bought a lot of things) *at the weekend and spent far too much money.* | *I've got to do some last-minute shopping.* | *the busy Christmas shopping season* → WINDOW-SHOPPING
2 do the shopping to go shopping to buy food and other

things you need regularly: *I hate doing the shopping at weekends.*
3 *BrE* the things that you have just bought from a shop: *Can you help me carry the shopping, please?*
'shopping ,bag *n* [C] a large bag that you use to carry things which you have bought → see picture at BAG¹
'shopping ,basket *n* [C] a basket that you use to put things in as you walk around a shop → see picture at BASKET
'shopping ,cart *n* [C] *AmE* a large metal basket on wheels that you push around when you are shopping in a SUPERMARKET; ◨ **cart**; → see picture at TROLLEY
'shopping ,centre *BrE*; **shopping center** *AmE n* [C] a group of shops together in one area, often in one large building
'shopping ,list *n* [C] a list of things you need to buy when you go shopping
'shopping mall also **mall** *n* [C] *especially AmE* a group of shops together in one large covered building
'shopping ,precinct *n* [C] *BrE* an area in a town where there are a lot of shops and where cars are not allowed
'shopping ,trolley *n* [C] *BrE* a large metal basket on wheels that you push around when you are shopping in a SUPERMARKET; ◨ **trolley**
'shop-soiled *adj BrE* **1** a product that is shop-soiled is slightly damaged or dirty because it has been in a shop for a long time; ◨ **shopworn** *AmE*: *shop-soiled goods* **2** an idea that is shop-soiled is no longer interesting because it has been discussed many times before; ◨ **shopworn** *AmE*: *the same old shop-soiled arguments*
,shop 'steward *n* [C] a worker who is elected by members of a TRADE UNION in a factory or other business to represent them in dealing with managers
'shop talk *n* [U] *AmE informal* conversation about your work, which other people may think is boring
shop·worn /ˈʃɒpwɔːn $ ˈʃɑːpwɔːrn/ *adj AmE* **1** a product that is shopworn is slightly damaged or dirty because it has been in a shop for a long time; ◨ **shop-soiled** *BrE* **2** an idea that is shopworn is no longer interesting because it has been discussed many times before; ◨ **shop-soiled** *BrE*: *shopworn management techniques*
shore¹ /ʃɔː $ ʃɔːr/ *n* **1** [C,U] the land along the edge of a large area of water such as an ocean or lake: *We could see a boat about a mile from shore.* | *Only a few survivors reached the shore.* | *She began to swim to shore.* | **on the shores of sth** *a holiday resort on the shores of the Adriatic* | **on shore** *We had a couple of hours on shore (=not on a ship).* | **off shore** *The island is about 3 miles off shore (=away from the coast).* | **rocky/sandy shore** **2 these/British/our etc shores** *written* a country that has a border on the sea: *Millions of immigrants flocked to these shores in the 19th century.* | *growing fears that English football players will be lured away to* **foreign shores** → ASHORE, OFFSHORE, ONSHORE
shore² *v*
shore sth ⇔ up *phr v* **1** to support a wall or roof with large pieces of wood, metal etc to stop it from falling down: *The roof had been shored up with old timbers.* **2** to help or support something that is likely to fail or is not working well: *attempts to shore up the struggling economy*
shore·line /ˈʃɔːlaɪn $ ˈʃɔːr-/ *n* [C,U] the land along the edge of a large area of water such as an ocean or lake: *A group of men stood silently on the shoreline.* | *the bay's 13000 km of shoreline*
shorn /ʃɔːn $ ʃɔːrn/ the past participle of SHEAR
short¹ S1 W1 /ʃɔːt $ ʃɔːrt/ *adj comparative* **shorter**, *superlative* **shortest**
1 TIME happening or continuing for only a little time or for less time than usual; ◧ **long**: *a short meeting* | *Morris gave a short laugh.* | *a short course on business*

S

English. | *Winter is coming and the days are getting shorter.* | *I've only been in Brisbane a short time.* | *For a short while* (=a short time), *the city functioned as the region's capital.* | *I learned a lot during my short period as a junior reporter.* | *Germany achieved spectacular economic success in a relatively short period of time.* | *They met and married within a short space of time.* | *I promise to keep the meeting short and sweet* (=short in a way that is good, especially not talking for a long time). | *For a few short weeks* (=they seemed to pass very quickly) *the sun shone and the fields turned gold.*
2 LENGTH/DISTANCE measuring a small amount in length or distance; 🔄 **long**: *a short skirt* | *Anita had her hair cut short.* | *They went by the shortest route, across the fields.* | *Carol's office was only a short distance away, and she decided that she would walk there.* | **a short walk/flight/drive** *It's a short drive to the airport.* | *The hotel is only a short walk from the beach.*
3 NOT TALL someone who is short is not as tall as most people; 🔄 **tall**: *a short plump woman* | *Chris was short and stocky, with broad shoulders.* | *He's a bit shorter than me.*
4 BOOK/LETTER a book, letter etc that is short does not have many words or pages; 🔄 **long**: *a short novel* | *I wrote a short note to explain.* → **SHORT STORY**
5 NOT ENOUGH a) if you are short of something, you do not have enough of it: **be short (of sth)** *Can you lend me a couple of dollars? I'm a little short.* | **be short of money/cash/funds** *Our libraries are short of funds.* | **be 5p/$10 etc short** *Have you all paid me? I'm about £9 short.* | **I'm a bit short** *BrE spoken* (=I haven't got much money at the moment). | **sb is not short of sth** *BrE* (=they have a lot of it) *Your little girl's not short of confidence, is she?* | *They're **not short of a few bob** (=they are rich).* **b)** if something is short, there is not enough of it: *Money was short in those days.* | *It's going to be difficult – time is short.* | *Gasoline **was in short supply*** (=not enough of it was available) *after the war.*
6 be short on sth to have less of something than you should have: *He's a nice guy, but a little short on brains.* | *The President's speech was **long on** colorful phrases but **short on** solutions.*
7 LESS THAN a little less than a number: [+of] *Her time was only 2 seconds short of the world record.* | **just/a little short of sth** *She was just short of six feet tall.*
8 short notice if something is short notice, you are told about it only a short time before it happens: *I can't make it Friday. It's very **short notice**.* | **at short notice** *BrE* **on short notice** *AmE*: *The party was arranged at short notice.*
9 in the short term/run during the period of time that is not very far into the future; → **short-term**: *These measures may save money in the short term, but we'll end up spending more later.*
10 have a short memory if someone has a short memory, they soon forget something that has happened: *Voters have very short memories.*
11 be short for sth to be a shorter way of saying a name: *Her name is Alex, short for Alexandra.*
12 be short of breath to be unable to breathe easily, especially because you are unhealthy: *He couldn't walk far without getting short of breath.*
13 be short with sb to speak to someone using very few words, in a way that seems rude or unfriendly: *Sorry I was short with you on the phone this morning.*
14 have a short temper/fuse to get angry very easily: *Mr Yanto, who had a very short fuse, told her to get out.*
15 get/be given short shrift if you or your idea, suggestion etc is given short shrift, you are told immediately that you are wrong and are not given any attention or sympathy: *McLaren got short shrift from all the record companies when he first presented his new band to them in 1976.*
16 be nothing/little short of sth used to emphasize that something is very good, very surprising etc: *Her recovery seemed nothing short of a miracle.* | *The results are little short of astonishing.*

17 draw/get the short straw to be given something difficult or unpleasant to do, especially when other people have been given something better: *Giles drew the short straw, and has to give us a talk this morning.*
18 make short work of (doing) sth to finish something quickly and easily, especially food or a job: *The kids made short work of the sandwiches.* | *Computers can make short work of complex calculations.*
19 have/get sb by the short and curlies also **have/get sb by the short hairs** *BrE informal not polite* to put someone in a situation in which they are forced to do or accept what you want: *I signed the contract – they've got me by the short and curlies.*
20 be one ... short of a ... *spoken* used humorously to say that someone is a little crazy or stupid: *Lady, are you a few aces short of a deck?* | *He's **one sandwich short of a picnic**.*
21 short time *BrE* when workers work for fewer hours than usual, because the company cannot afford to pay them their full wage: *Most of the workers were put on short time.*
22 in short order *formal* in a short time and without delay
23 give sb short measure *BrE old-fashioned* to give someone less than the correct amount of something, especially in a shop
24 SOUND *technical* a short vowel is pronounced quickly without being emphasized, for example the sound of a in 'cat', e in 'bet', and i in 'bit'; 🔄 **long**
—**shortness** *n [U]*: *He was suffering from shortness of breath.* | *Shirley was very conscious of her shortness and always wore high heels.* → **life's too short** at LIFE (27)

short² *adv* **1 fall short of sth** to be less than what you need, expected, or hoped for, or to fail to reach a satisfactory standard: *The Republicans increased their share of the vote, but still fell short of a majority.* | *Shares in the company dropped 26p yesterday, as profits fell short of City expectations.* | **fall short of a goal/target/ideal** *The economy fell short of the Treasury's target of 2% growth.* | **fall far/a long way/well short of sth** *Facilities in these schools fall far short of the standards required.* | *One or two songs on the album are interesting, but most **fall short of the mark** (=are not good enough).* **2 be running short (of/on sth)** if you are running short of something, or if something is running short, it is being used up and there will soon not be enough left: *We're running short of coffee again.* | *Our supplies of petrol were running short.* | *Come on, time's **running short!*** **3 stop short of doing sth** to almost do something but then decide not to do it: *They accused the President of incompetence, but stopped short of calling for his resignation.* **4 stop short** to suddenly stop speaking or stop what you are doing, because something has surprised you or you have just thought of something: *Seeing her tears, he stopped short.* **5 be cut short** if something is cut short, it is stopped before you expect or before it is finished: *His career was tragically cut short when, at the age of 42, he died of a heart attack.* **6 cut sb short** to interrupt and stop someone when they are speaking: *I was halfway through my explanation when Walter cut me short.* **7 pull/bring sb up short** to surprise or shock someone so that they stop what they are doing or saying to think for a moment: *The question brought her up short, but after a moment's hesitation, she answered it.* **8 3 metres/5 miles etc short of sth** without reaching a place you are trying to get to, because you are still a particular distance from it: *The plane touched down 200 metres short of the runway.* **9 two weeks/a month etc short of sth** two weeks, a month etc before something: *He died two days short of his fifty-sixth birthday.* **10 short of (doing) sth** without actually doing something: *Short of locking her in her room, he couldn't really stop her from seeing Jack.* **11 come up short** to fail to win or achieve something: *We've been to the state tournament four times, but we've come up short every time.* **12 go short (of sth)** *BrE* to have less of something than you need: *She made sure that her children never went short.* **13 be taken short/be caught short** *BrE informal* to have a sudden strong need to go to the toilet when you are not near one

short³ *n* **1 shorts** [plural] **a)** short trousers ending at or above the knees: *a pair of shorts | tourists in shorts and T-shirts* → BERMUDA SHORTS, CYCLING SHORTS **b)** especially *AmE* men's underwear with short legs: *Craig was standing in the kitchen in his shorts.* → BOXER SHORTS, JOCKEY SHORTS **2 in short** used when you want to give the main point of something: *Carter hoped for greater trust between the two nations, more trade, more cultural exchanges – in short, a genuine peace.* **3 for short** used as a shorter way of saying a name: *His name's Maximilian, but we just call him Max for short.* **4** [C] *informal* a short film shown in the cinema **5** [C] *BrE informal* a strong alcoholic drink that is not beer or wine, drunk in a small glass; ■ **shot** *AmE: Do you fancy a short? A whisky or a vodka?* **6** [C] *informal* a SHORT CIRCUIT: *a short in the system* → **the long and the short of it** at LONG¹ (10)

short⁴ *v* [I,T] also **short out** to SHORT-CIRCUIT, or make something do this: *The toaster shorted and caused a fire.*

short·age /'ʃɔːtɪdʒ $ 'ʃɔːr-/ *n* [C,U] a situation in which there is not enough of something that people need: [+of] *a shortage of skilled labour |* **There is no shortage of funds.** | **water/food/housing etc shortage** *efforts to solve the housing shortage |* **acute/chronic/ severe shortage** *an acute shortage of manpower*

short back and 'sides *n* [singular] *BrE* a way of cutting a man's hair so that it is very short at the back and sides of his head and slightly longer on top

short·bread /'ʃɔːtbred $ 'ʃɔːrt-/ *n* [U] a hard, sweet BISCUIT made with a lot of butter

short·cake /'ʃɔːtkeɪk $ 'ʃɔːrt-/ *n* [U] **1** *BrE* shortbread **2** *AmE* cake over which a sweet fruit mixture is poured, especially STRAWBERRIES

short-'change *v* [T] **1** to treat someone unfairly by not giving them what they deserve or hoped for: *When the band only played for 15 minutes the fans felt they had been short-changed.* **2** to give back too little money to a customer who has bought something and paid more than the exact amount for it

short 'circuit *n* [C] a failure of an electrical system, caused by bad wires or a fault in a connection in the wires

short-circuit *v* **1** [I,T] to have a short circuit or cause a short circuit in something **2** [T] to get something done without going through the usual long methods: *I short-circuited the whole process by a simple telephone call.*

short·com·ing /'ʃɔːˌkʌmɪŋ $ 'ʃɔːrt-/ *n* [C usually plural] a fault or weakness that makes someone or something less successful or effective than they should be: *Peter was painfully aware of his own shortcomings.* | [+of] *the shortcomings of our local government system* | [+in] *The report suggested that there were severe shortcomings in police tactics.*

short·crust pas·try /ˌʃɔːtkrʌst 'peɪstri $ ˌʃɔːrt-/ *n* [U] *BrE* a type of PASTRY which breaks up easily and is used for making PIES

short 'cut also **short-cut** / $ '. ./ *n* [C] **1** a quicker and more direct way of getting somewhere than the usual one: *Carlos decided to* **take a short-cut** *home. | We were late for the game, but found a short cut through the fields.* **2** a quicker way of doing something: [+to] *There aren't really any shortcuts to learning English.*

short·en /'ʃɔːtn $ 'ʃɔːrtn/ *v* [I,T] to become shorter or make something shorter; ■ **lengthen**: *The days are shortening now.* | [+to] *His name is often shortened to Pat.*

short·en·ing /'ʃɔːtnɪŋ $ 'ʃɔːrt-/ *n* [U] fat made from vegetable oil that you mix with flour when making PASTRY (1)

short·fall /'ʃɔːtfɔːl $ 'ʃɔːrtfɔːl/ *n* [C] the difference between the amount you have and the amount you need or expect: [+in] *Parents have been asked to pay £30 each to cover the shortfall in the budget.* | [+of] *an estimated shortfall of about £1 million*

short·hand /'ʃɔːthænd $ 'ʃɔːrt-/ *n* [U] **1** a fast method of writing using special signs or shorter forms to represent letters, words, and phrases: **in shorthand** *The reporter took notes in shorthand.* | *a secretary who takes shorthand* (=writes in shorthand) → LONGHAND **2** a shorter but less clear way of saying something: [+for] *He's been 'relocated', which is shorthand for 'given a worse job a long way away'.*

short·hand·ed /ˌʃɔːt'hændɪd◂ $ ˌʃɔːrt-/ *adj* having fewer helpers or workers than you need; ■ **short-staffed**

shorthand 'typist *n* [C] *BrE* someone whose job is to use shorthand to write down what someone else says and then TYPE a copy of it; ■ **stenographer** *AmE*

short-haul *adj* a short-haul aircraft or flight travels a fairly short distance; ■ **long-haul**: *short-haul routes within the UK*

short list also **short list** /'ʃɔːtlɪst $ 'ʃɔːrt-/ *n* [C] *BrE* a list of the most suitable people for a job or a prize, chosen from all the people who were first considered: **on the short list (for sth)** *Davies was on the shortlist for the Booker Prize.* | **draw up/compile a shortlist** *The panel will draw up a shortlist of candidates.*

short-list also **shortlist** *v* [T usually passive] *BrE* to put someone on a short list for a job or a prize: **short-list sb for sth** *She's been short-listed for the director's job.*

short-lived /ˌʃɔːt 'lɪvd◂ $ ˌʃɔːrt 'laɪvd◂/ *adj* existing or happening for only a short time: *Our happiness was short-lived.*

short·ly W3 /'ʃɔːtli $ 'ʃɔːrt-/ *adv* **1** soon: *Ms Jones will be back shortly.* | **shortly before/ after sth** *The accident happened shortly before midday.* **2** *written* speaking in an impatient and unfriendly way: *'I've explained that already,' Rod said shortly.*

short-order 'cook *n* [C] someone in a restaurant kitchen who cooks food that can be prepared easily or quickly

short-'range *adj* **1** *only before noun* short-range weapons or MISSILES are designed to travel or be used over a short distance; ■ **long-range**: *short-range nuclear weapons* **2** **short-range plan/goal/forecast etc** concerned only with the period that is not very far into the future; ■ **long-range**

short-sheet *v* [T] *AmE* to fold the top sheet on a bed so that no one can get into it, as a trick

short-'sighted *adj* **1** especially *BrE* unable to see objects clearly unless they are very close; ■ **near-sighted** *AmE*; ■ **long-sighted** **2** not considering the possible effects in the future of something that seems good now – used to show disapproval; ■ **far-sighted**: *a short-sighted policy of reducing investment in training* —**short-sightedly** *adv* —**short-sightedness** *n* [U]: *Thanks to the government's short-sightedness, our hospitals are very short of cash.*

short-'staffed *adj* having fewer than the usual or necessary number of workers; ■ **short-handed**: *We're very short-staffed at the moment.*

short-stay *adj* [only before noun] *BrE* short-stay hotels, car parks etc are places that you can stay for only a short time

short·stop /ˈʃɔːtstɒp $ ˈʃɔːrtstɑːr/ n [C] a player on a baseball team who tries to stop any balls that are hit between second and third BASE² (7)

,**short** ˈ**story** n [C] a short written story about imaginary situations and characters

,**short-**ˈ**tempered** adj tending to become angry very quickly; → **bad-tempered**: *She gets short-tempered when she's tired.* —**short temper** n [C]

,**short-**ˈ**term** adj [usually before noun] continuing for only a short time, or relating only to the period that is not very far into the future; 🔁 **long-term**: *The treatment may bring short-term benefits to AIDS sufferers.* | *Most of the staff are on short-term contracts.* | *She's suffering from short-term memory loss.* → **short term** at TERM¹ (4) —**short-term** adv

,**short-**ˈ**termism** n [U] a way of planning or thinking that is concerned only with what gives you advantages now, rather than what might happen in the future: *plans to combat short-termism among investors in British industry*

ˈ**short wave** n [U] a range of short radio waves used for broadcasting around the world → **LONG WAVE, MEDIUM WAVE**

short·y /ˈʃɔːti $ ˈʃɔːrti/ n plural **shorties** **1** used as an insulting name for someone who is not very tall **2** [C] *informal* a woman – used especially by people who play or listen to HIP-HOP music **3** [C] *informal* a baby – used especially by people who play or listen to HIP-HOP music: *Shawna says she's gonna be having my shorty.*

s

shot¹ /ʃɒt $ ʃɑːt/ n
1 GUN [C] **a)** an act of firing a gun: *He pulled out his rifle and **fired** three **shots**.* | *The first shot missed my head by just a few inches.* | *The **shot hit** the raider in the upper chest and killed him instantly.* | *A crazy man **took a shot at** her* (=tried to shoot her) *from a rooftop.* | *He fired off a **volley of shots** from his semi-automatic rifle.* | *The policeman was killed by a **single shot**.* **b)** the sound of a gun being fired: *Where were you when you heard the shot?* | *Two **shots rang out** (=could be heard), and security guards rushed over, guns drawn.* **c)** a good/bad etc shot someone who is good, bad etc at shooting: *Sergeant Cooper is an excellent shot.*
2 BULLETS [U] **a)** small metal balls that are shot, many at a time, from a SHOTGUN **b)** *old use* large metal balls that are shot from a CANNON
3 ATTEMPT TO SCORE [C] an attempt in sport to throw, kick, or hit the ball towards the place where you can get a point: *Shaw took a shot at the goal from the halfway line, but missed.* | *Good shot!*
4 PHOTOGRAPH [C] a photograph; 🔁 **picture**: [+of] *a close-up shot of a demonstrator being beaten by a policeman* | *I managed to **get** some **good shots** of the carnival.* | *We hired a photographer to **take** some publicity **shots**.* | *action shots of football players* (=ones taken of people while they are moving) → **MUGSHOT**
5 FILM/TV [C] the view of something in a film or television programme that is produced by having the camera in a particular position: *In the opening shot we see Travolta's feet walking down the sidewalk.*
6 ATTEMPT [C] *informal* an attempt to do something or achieve something, especially something difficult: **shot at (doing) sth** *This is her first shot at directing a play.* | *If Lewis won his next fight, he would be guaranteed a **shot at the title** (=chance to win the title).* | *I decided to **have a shot at** decorating the house myself.* | *I didn't think I had much chance of winning the race, but I thought I'd **give it a shot** (=try to do it).* | *The network finally **gave** Keaton a **shot at** presenting his own show.*
7 give sth your best shot to make as much effort as you can to achieve something difficult: *This case is going to be tough, but I promise I'll give it my best shot.* | *Lydia didn't get the job, but at least she gave it her best shot.*
8 be a long shot **a)** used to say that a plan is worth trying, even though you think it is unlikely to succeed: *It's a long shot, but someone might recognise her from*

the photo and be able to tell us where she lives. **b)** *AmE* if someone is a long shot, they are not likely to be chosen for a job or to win an election, competition etc: *Turner is a long shot to win next month's mayoral election.*
9 a 10 to 1 shot/50 to 1 shot etc a horse, dog etc in a race, whose chances of winning are expressed as numbers
10 a shot in the dark an attempt to guess something without having any facts or definite ideas: *My answer to the last question was a complete shot in the dark.*
11 CRITICAL REMARK [C] a remark that is intended to criticize or hurt someone: *I'm not going to sit here listening to you two take shots at each other all night.* | *She couldn't resist a **parting shot** (=one that you make just before you leave) – 'And you were a lousy lover!'* | *That was a **cheap shot!** (=one that is unfair and unreasonable)*
12 like a shot if you do something like a shot, you do it very quickly and eagerly: *If he asked me to go to Africa with him, I'd go like a shot!*
13 a shot across the bows/a warning shot (across the bows) something you say or do to warn someone that you oppose what they are doing and will try to make them stop it – used especially in news reports: *The President's own supporters are **firing a warning shot across** his bows.*
14 big shot an important or powerful person, especially in business: *a big shot in the record business*
15 DRINK [C] a small amount of a strong alcoholic drink: [+of] *a shot of tequila* | *a **shot glass** (=a small glass for strong alcoholic drinks) →* see picture at **GLASS¹**
16 DRUG [C] *especially AmE* an INJECTION of a drug (=when it is put into the body with a needle); 🔁 **jab** *BrE: Have you had your typhoid and cholera shots?*
17 a shot in the arm something that makes you more confident or more successful: *The new factory will give the local economy a much needed shot in the arm.*
18 HEAVY BALL [C] a heavy metal ball that competitors try to throw as far as possible in the sport of SHOT PUT
→ **call the shots** at CALL¹ (9); → **by a long chalk/shot** at LONG¹ (21); → **long shot** at LONG¹ (18); → **BUCKSHOT, GUNSHOT, SNAPSHOT, POT SHOT**

shot² adj [not before noun] **1** *spoken* in bad condition because of being used too much or treated badly: *My back tires are shot.* | *My nerves were **shot to pieces** after my driving test.* **2** be/get/want shot of sb/sth *BrE spoken* to get rid of someone or something: *I know the director wants shot of me.* **3** be shot through with sth **a)** if a piece of cloth is shot through with a colour, it has very small threads of that colour woven into it: *a fine silk shot through with gold threads* **b)** to have a lot of a particular quality or feeling: *a charming collection of stories, shot through with a gentle humour*

shot³ the past tense and participle of SHOOT

shot·gun /ˈʃɒtɡʌn $ ˈʃɑːt-/ n [C] a long gun fired from the shoulder, that shoots many small round balls at one time, used especially for killing birds or animals: *The robbers were armed with **sawn-off shotguns** (=ones that have been made shorter, so the balls go in different directions).*

,**shotgun** ˈ**wedding** n [C] a wedding that has to take place immediately because the woman is going to have a baby

ˈ**shot put** n [singular] a sport in which you throw a heavy metal ball as far as you can —**shot putter** n [C]: *an Olympic shot putter*

should S1 W1 /ʃəd; strong ʃʊd/ modal verb negative short form **shouldn't**
1 RIGHT THING a) used to say what is the right or sensible thing to do: *He shouldn't be so selfish.* | *Children shouldn't be allowed to play in the street.* | *'I don't care what people think.' 'Well, you should.'* | *Why shouldn't I smoke if I want to?* **b)** used to say what would have been right or sensible, but was not done: *They should have called the police.*
2 ADVICE used to give or ask for advice: *What should I do? Should I trust him?* | *You should read his new book.* | *I should stay in bed if I were you.*

3 **EXPECTED THING** **a)** used to say that you expect something to happen or be true: *It should be a nice day tomorrow.* | *Try phoning Robert – he should be home by now.* | *Australia should win this match.* | *'Artistic people can be very difficult sometimes.' 'Well, you should know – you married one.'* **b)** used to say what was expected, but did not happen: *It was an easy test and he should have passed, but he didn't.*

4 **CORRECT THING** used to say what is the correct amount, the correct way of doing something etc: *Every sentence should start with a capital letter.* | *What do you mean, there are only ten tickets? There should be twelve.* | *White wine, not red, should be served with fish.*

5 **ORDERS** *formal* used in official orders and instructions: *Passengers for Flight BA213 should proceed to Gate 12.*

6 **AFTER 'THAT'** *BrE* used in a CLAUSE beginning with 'that' after particular adjectives and verbs: *It's strange that you should say that.* | *It is essential that he should have a fair trial.* | *The residents demanded that there should be an official inquiry.*

7 **POSSIBILITY** used to talk about something that may possibly happen or be true: *Naturally, he was nervous in case anything should go wrong.* | *What if I should fall sick and not be able to work?* | **should sb/sth do sth** *Should you need any help* (=if you need any help), *you can always phone me at the office.*

8 **IMAGINED SITUATIONS** *formal especially BrE* used after 'I' or 'we' to say what you would do if something happened or was true: *If anyone treated me like that, I should complain to the manager.* | *I should be surprised if many people voted for him.*

9 **REQUESTING/OFFERING** *formal especially BrE* used to politely ask for something, offer to do something, or say that you want to do something: *I should be grateful if you could provide me with some information.* | *'What can I get you?' 'I should like a long cool drink.'* | *We should be delighted to help in any way we can.* | *I should like to thank you all for coming here tonight.*

10 **PAST INTENTIONS/EXPECTATIONS** used as the past tense of 'shall' after 'I' or 'we' to say what you intended or expected to do: *We knew that we should be leaving the next day.*

11 **what should I see but sth/who should appear but sb** etc used to show that you were surprised when you saw a particular thing, when a particular person appeared etc: *Just at that moment, who should walk in but old Jim himself.*

12 **you should have seen/heard sth** *spoken* used to emphasize how funny, strange, beautiful etc something was that you saw or heard: *You should have seen the look on her face when I told her I'd won first prize.*

13 **how/why should...?** used to express surprise that something has happened or that someone has asked you a particular question: *Why should anyone want to marry Tony?* | *Don't ask me. How should I know?*

14 **I should think/imagine/hope** *spoken* **a)** used to say that you think or hope something is true, when you are not certain: *I shouldn't think they've gone far.* | *'I suppose there'll be a lot of complaints?' 'I should imagine so.'* **b)** used to emphasize that you are not surprised by what someone has told you because you have moral reasons to expect it: *'She doesn't like to hear me swearing.' 'I should think not.'* | *'He did apologize.' 'I should hope so, after the way he behaved.'*

shoul·der¹ [S2] [W2] /ˈʃəʊldə $ ˈʃoʊldər/ *n*
1 **BODY PART** [C] one of the two parts of the body at each side of the neck where the arm is connected: *She tapped the driver on the shoulder.* | *a muscular man with broad shoulders* | *He put his arm around her shoulders.* | *When we asked Keith who she was, he just shrugged his shoulders* (=raised his shoulders to show that he did not know or care). | **look/glance over your shoulder** (=look behind you) *Lucy glanced nervously over her shoulder to see who was behind her.*
2 **CLOTHES** [C] the part of a piece of clothing that covers your shoulders: *a jacket with padded shoulders*
3 **MEAT** [C,U] the upper part of the front leg of an animal that is used for meat: [+of] *a shoulder of pork*
4 **be looking over your shoulder** to feel worried that something unpleasant is going to happen to you
5 **a)** **a shoulder to cry on** someone who gives you sympathy: *Ben is always there when I need a shoulder to cry on.* **b)** **cry on sb's shoulder** to get sympathy from someone when you tell them your problems
6 **shoulder to shoulder** **a)** having the same aims and wanting to achieve the same thing; = **side by side**: [+with] *We are working shoulder to shoulder with local residents.* **b)** physically close together; = **side by side**: *Blacks and whites stood shoulder to shoulder in the stands to applaud.*
7 **on sb's shoulders** if blame or a difficult job falls on someone's shoulders, they have to take responsibility for it: *The blame rests squarely on Jim's shoulders.*
8 **put your shoulder to the wheel** to start to work with great effort and determination
9 **ROAD-SIDE** [C] *AmE* an area of ground beside a road where drivers can stop their cars if they are having trouble → HARD SHOULDER, SOFT SHOULDER
10 **CURVED SHAPE** [C] a rounded part just below the top of something → **give sb the cold shoulder** at COLD¹ (7); → **have a chip on your shoulder** at CHIP¹ (5); → **be/stand head and shoulders above the rest** at HEAD¹ (29); → **rub shoulders with** at RUB¹ (5); → **straight from the shoulder** at STRAIGHT¹ (10)

shoulder² *v* **1** **shoulder the responsibility/blame/ cost/burden etc** to accept a difficult or unpleasant responsibility, duty etc: *The residents are being asked to shoulder the costs of the repairs.* **2** [T] to lift something onto your shoulder to carry it: *They shouldered the boat and took it down to the river.* **3** **shoulder your way through/into etc** to move through a large crowd of people by pushing with your shoulder: *He ran after her, shouldering his way through the crowd.* **4** **shoulder arms** an order given to soldiers telling them to hold their weapon against their shoulder

'shoulder bag *n* [C] a bag that hangs from your shoulder

'shoulder blade *n* [C] one of the two flat bones on each side of your back

'shoulder-'high *adj, adv* as high as your shoulder: *The grass was shoulder-high.*

'shoulder-'length *adj* shoulder-length hair hangs down to your shoulders

'shoulder pad *n* [C] a small thick piece of material that is fixed inside the shoulders of dress or jacket to make your shoulders look bigger

'shoulder strap *n* [C] **1** a long narrow piece of material on a dress or other piece of women's clothing that goes over the shoulder **2** a long narrow piece of material fixed to a bag etc so that you can carry it over your shoulder

should·n't /ˈʃʊdnt/ the short form of 'should not'

shouldst /ʃədst; *strong* ʃʊdst/ *old use* the second person singular form of the verb SHOULD

shout¹ [S2] [W2] /ʃaʊt/ *v*
1 [I,T] to say something very loudly; → **scream**, **yell**: *There's no need to shout! I can hear you!* | [+at] *I wish you'd stop shouting at the children.* | [+for] *We could hear them shouting for help.* | *'Watch out!' she shouted, as the car started to move.* | *shout sth at sb He was shouting insults at the lorry driver.* | **shout sth to sb** *'He's down here!' she shouted to Alison.*
2 **shout in pain/anger/frustration etc** *BrE* to call out loudly; = **scream** *AmE*: *My brother shouted in pain as the ball hit him.*
3 **shout sth from the rooftops** to tell everyone about something because you want everyone to know about it
shout sb ⇔ down *phr v*
to shout so that someone who is speaking cannot be heard: *An older man tried to shout him down.*

shout sth ⇔ **out** phr v
to say something suddenly in a loud voice: *Don't shout out the answer in class, put up your hand.*

shout² n **1** [C] a loud call expressing anger, pain, excitement etc; → **scream, yell**: *a warning shout* | [+of] *Tom gave a shout of laughter when he saw them.* | *shouts of delight* **2** give sb a shout *BrE spoken* to go and find someone and tell them something: *Give me a shout when you're ready to go.* **3** sb's shout *BrE, AusE informal* someone's turn to buy drinks: *It's my shout. Same again?* **4** be in with a shout (of doing sth) *BrE informal* to have a chance of winning: *The team's still in with a shout.*

shout·ing /'ʃaʊtɪŋ/ n [U] **1** when people say things very loudly: *We heard a lot of shouting and went to investigate.* **2** be all over bar the shouting *BrE spoken* used to say that something is almost finished and there is no doubt what the result will be

'shouting ,match n [C] an angry argument in which people shout at each other

shove¹ [S3] /ʃʌv/ v
1 [I,T] to push someone or something in a rough or careless way, using your hands or shoulders: *He shoved her towards the car.* | *Everyone was pushing and shoving to see the prince.*
2 [T always + adv/prep] to put something somewhere carelessly or without thinking much: *Tidying the room seems to mean shoving everything under the bed!* | *He shoved his hands into his pockets.*
3 [T] *spoken* used to tell someone in a very impolite way that you do not want something: *They can take their three cents an hour raise and shove it.* → **when/if push comes to shove** at PUSH² (6)
  shove off phr v
1 *BrE spoken* used to tell someone rudely or angrily to go away: *Shove off! I'm busy.*
2 to push a boat away from the land, usually with a pole
  shove up/over phr v *BrE spoken*
BrE to move along on a seat to make space for someone else: *Shove up mate, there's no room to sit down here.*

shove² n [C] a strong push: *Give the door a good shove.*

shov·el¹ /'ʃʌvəl/ n [C] **1** a tool with a rounded blade and a long handle used for moving earth, stones etc; ⊟ **spade 2** a part of a large vehicle or machine used for moving or digging earth

shovel² v **shovelled, shovelling** *BrE*, **shoveled, shoveling** *AmE* [T] **1** to lift and move earth, stones etc with a shovel: *The workmen shovelled gravel onto the road.* | *They were out in freezing conditions shovelling snow off the pitch.* | **shovel the driveway/sidewalk etc** *AmE* (=shovel snow from a road or path) *Everyone was out shovelling their sidewalks.* **2** **shovel sth into/onto sth** to put something, usually food, somewhere quickly: *We shovelled food into our mouths as fast as we could.*

shov·el·ful /'ʃʌvəlfʊl/ n [C] the amount of coal, snow, earth etc that you can carry on a shovel

shov·el·ware /'ʃʌvəlweə $ -wer/ n [U] information that first appears in printed form, for example in a book or newspaper, and then is put onto the Internet or CD-ROM without any new or interesting ways to look at or use the information: *Many of the educational software titles are nothing but shovelware.*

show¹ [S1] [W1] /ʃəʊ $ ʃoʊ/ v *past tense* **showed**, *past participle* **shown** /ʃəʊn $ ʃoʊn/
1 LET SB SEE [T] to let someone see something: **show sb sth** *The children proudly showed me their presents.* | **show sth to sb** *Show your ticket to the woman at the entrance.* | *The man grinned, showing bad teeth.*
2 PROVE STH [T] to provide facts or information that make it clear that something is true, that something exists, or that something has happened: *Figures showed a 9% rise in inflation.* | *Gary has shown his faith in the club's future by agreeing to stay on.* | **show (that)** *Mike needed a copy of the will to show that the books had been left to him.* | **show sb (that)** *We have*

shown our critics that we can succeed.* | **show how** *This document shows how to oppose bad decisions about new housing.* | **show what** *She just wants a chance to show what she can do.* | **show sb/sth to be sth** *Charles showed himself to be a fine leader.* | **be shown to be/do sth** *The campaign has been shown to be a waste of money.* | *The new treatment has been shown to reduce the number of deaths.* | **studies/evidence/research etc shows** *Several studies have shown that aggressive toys lead to bad behaviour.* | *The Polish economy began to show signs of recovery.* | *It just goes to show* (=proves) *how much people judge each other on how they look.*
3 FEELINGS/ATTITUDES/QUALITIES [T] to let your feelings, attitudes, or personal qualities be clearly seen: *Think positively and show some determination.* | *She had learned not to show her emotions.* | *It was the sound a man might make when in pain but trying not to show it.* | *Mary showed great interest in the children.*
4 EXPLAIN WITH ACTIONS [T] to explain to someone how to do something, by doing it yourself or using actions to help them learn: **show sb how** *Show me how the gun works.* | **show sb how to do sth** *Maureen showed Peter how to feed the young animals.* | **show sb sth** *Can you show Lucy the way to slice onions?*
5 PICTURE/MAP ETC [T] if a picture, map etc shows something, you can see it on the picture, map etc: *I want a photograph that shows his face.* | *The map shows the main rivers of the region.*
6 GUIDE SB [T] to go with someone and guide them to a place: **show sb to/into sth** *Can you show Mrs Davies to the bathroom?* | **show sb out/in** *I can show myself out* (=out of the office or house). | **show sb sth** *Come on, I'll show you the way.*
7 POINT AT STH [T] to let someone see where a place or thing is, especially by pointing to it: **show sb where** *Can you show me exactly where he fell?*
8 FILM/TELEVISION [I,T] to make a film or television programme available on a screen for people to see, or to be on a screen: *The film was shown on television last night.* | *The match was shown live* (=could be seen on television while it was being played). | *It's now showing at cinemas across London.* → SHOWING (1)
9 BE EASY TO SEE [I] if something shows, it is easy to see: *His happiness showed in his face.* | *Her scar doesn't show, because her hair covers it.* | *Stephen was worried and it showed.*
10 DIRT/MARK [T] if material shows the dirt or a mark, it is easy to see the dirt or mark on it: *Light-coloured clothes tend to show the dirt.*
11 INCREASE/DECREASE [T] to have an increase or decrease in something, or a profit or loss: *The price of players is the reason why many football clubs show big losses on their balance sheets.* | *Recent elections have shown significant gains by right-wing groups.*
12 ART/PICTURES [T] to put a group of paintings or other works of art in one place so that people can come and see them: *Her recent sculptures are being shown at the Hayward Gallery.* | *The Whitney Museum was the first to show Mapplethorpe's photographs.*
13 I'll show him/them etc *spoken* used to say that you will prove to someone that you are better, more effective etc than they think you are
14 have sth to show for sth to have something as a result of what you have been doing: *If he fails his exams, he'll have nothing to show for his time at school.* | *She had plenty of money to show for all her work.*
15 show your face if you will not show your face somewhere, you will not go there because you have a good reason to feel ashamed or embarrassed about being there: *She never shows her face around here.*
16 show your hand to make your true power or intentions clear, especially after you have been keeping them secret: *There were so many rumours that the company was forced to show its hand.*
17 ANIMAL [T] to put an animal into a competition with other animals: *Do you plan to show your dogs?*
18 ARRIVE also **show up** [I] *informal especially AmE* to arrive at the place where someone is waiting for you: *I*

went to meet Hank, but he never showed.

19 show sb in a good/bad etc light if an action shows you in a good or bad light, it makes people have a good or bad opinion of you: *During an interview you need to show yourself in the best possible light.*

20 show sb the door to make it clear that someone is not welcome and should leave

21 show (sb) who's boss *informal* to prove to someone who is threatening your authority that you are more powerful than they are: *You've got to show your dog who's boss. When you say sit, he should sit.*

22 show the way if you show the way for other people, you do something new that others then try to copy

23 show a leg! *BrE spoken* used to tell someone to get out of bed

24 show (sb) a clean pair of heels *BrE old-fashioned informal* to run away very fast

show sb **around** (sth) also **show sb round (sth)** *BrE phr v*
to go around a place with someone when they first arrive there, to show them what is interesting, useful etc: *Harrison showed her around the house.*

show off *phr v*
1 to try to make people admire your abilities, achievements, or possessions – used to show disapproval: *He couldn't resist showing off on the tennis court.*
2 show sth ⇔ **off** to show something to a lot of people because you are very proud of it: *a picture of the restaurant's owners showing off their award*
3 show sth ⇔ **off** if one thing shows off something else, it makes the other thing look especially attractive: *The white dress showed off her dark skin beautifully.*

show sb **over** sth *phr v especially BrE*
to guide someone through an interesting building or a house that is for sale: *Ingrid has a job showing visitors over the castle.*

show up *phr v*
1 *informal* to arrive, especially at the place where someone is waiting for you; **turn up**: *Seth showed up, apologising for being late.* | *We had 200 people show up for our seminar.*
2 show sth ⇔ **up** to make it possible to see or notice something that was not clear before: *The sunlight showed up the marks on the window.*
3 to be easy to see or notice: *Use a light colour which will show up on a dark background.*
4 show sb ⇔ **up** to make someone feel embarrassed by behaving in a stupid or unacceptable way when you are with them: *She says I showed her up in front of her friends when they came to the house.*

show² S1 W1 *n*
1 PERFORMANCE [C] a performance for the public, especially one that includes singing, dancing, or jokes: *I enjoyed the show immensely.* | *The show starts at 7:30 pm.* | *They've come to town to see a Broadway show.* | *Perry was the star of the show.* → FLOOR SHOW, ROADSHOW
2 TV/RADIO [C] a programme on television or on the radio: *a TV show* | *a television quiz show* (=a show in which people compete to answer questions) | *The senator appeared on the CBS show 'Face the Nation'.* | *Presenter Fiona Harper will be hosting the show* (=introducing guests). → CHAT SHOW, GAME SHOW, TALK SHOW
3 COLLECTION OF THINGS TO SEE [C] an occasion when a lot of similar things are brought together in one place so that people can come and look at them: *the Paris Boat Show* | *a fashion show* for charity | *Kelly has a show of her latest work opening shortly.*
4 on show being shown to the public: *Paintings by Matisse are on show at the New York Gallery.* | *The designer clothes will go on show in Chicago next month.* | *Local antiques will be put on show in a new building especially built for the collection.*
5 a show of sth an occasion when someone deliberately shows a particular feeling, attitude, or quality: *I felt I should make a show of dignity.* | *The award will be seen as a show of support.* | **show of strength/force** *a strong and determined show of force by the police*

6 PRETENDED ACT [singular, U] when you pretend to do or feel something; ▤ **pretence**: [+of] *a show of gratitude* | *Susan put on a show of regret all day.* | *The waiter made a show of wiping the table.*
7 for show with the purpose of looking attractive or impressive rather than being useful: *He does actually play his guitar – it's not just for show.*
8 COLOURFUL SCENE [singular] an impressive scene, especially one that is very colourful: [+of] *a glorious show of colour in the rose garden* | *Maple trees put on their best show in the autumn.*
9 COMPETITION [C] a competition between similar things or animals to choose the best: *The dog show was being held in the Agricultural Hall.*
10 EVENT/SITUATION [singular] *informal* something which is being done or organized: *We need to find someone to run the show* (=be in charge).
11 put up a good/poor etc show *informal* to perform, play etc well or badly: *Our team put up a pretty good show, but we lost in the end.*
12 let's get this show on the road *spoken* used to tell people it is time to start working or start a journey
13 (jolly) good show *BrE old-fashioned spoken* used to express your approval of something → **steal the show** at STEAL¹ (4)

show and tell *n* [U] an activity for school children in which they bring an object to school and tell the other children about it: *Ramona brought in a fossil for show and tell.*

show·biz /'ʃəʊbɪz $ 'ʃoʊ-/ *n* [U] *informal* SHOW BUSINESS

show business also **showbiz** *n* [U] *informal* the entertainment industry, for example television, films, popular theatre etc: **in show business** *Phyllis always wanted to be in show business.* | *He loves the world of show business.* | *The restaurant is always full of show business personalities.*

show·case /'ʃəʊkeɪs $ 'ʃoʊ-/ *n* [C] **1** an event or situation that is designed to show the good qualities of a person, organization, product etc: [+for] *The new musical is a good showcase for her talents.* **2** a glass box containing objects for people to look at in a shop, at an art show etc —**showcase** *v* [T]: *She wants to showcase African-American literature.*

show·down /'ʃəʊdaʊn $ 'ʃoʊ-/ *n* [C usually singular] a meeting, argument, fight etc that will settle a disagreement or competition that has continued for a long time: [+with] *a showdown with the striking workers* | *Britain has a World Cup showdown with Australia next month.*

show·er¹ S2 /'ʃaʊə $ ʃaʊr/ *n* [C]
1 FOR WASHING IN a piece of equipment that you stand under to wash your whole body: *Why does the phone always ring when I'm in the shower?* | *I'd like to use the shower if that's all right.* | *The bathroom has a separate shower cubicle* (=a shower in a separate part of the room). → see picture at SPORTS CENTRE
2 ACT OF WASHING an act of washing your body while standing under a shower: *I need a shower.* | **take a shower** *Nick rolled out of bed and took a shower.* | **have a shower** *especially BrE: Mary loves having a hot shower after she's been swimming.*
3 RAIN a short period of rain or snow: *More heavy showers are forecast for tonight.* | **a shower of rain** | *a snow shower* | *A few wintry showers are likely on the east coast.*
4 LOTS OF THINGS a lot of small, light things falling or going through the air all together: [+of] *Peter kicked the fire and sent up a shower of sparks.* | *A shower of leaves fell towards the ground.*
5 PARTY *AmE* a party at which presents are given to a woman who is going to get married or have a baby: *We gave a shower for Beth.* | *a baby shower*
6 PEOPLE [usually singular] *BrE informal* a group of stupid or lazy people

shower² v **1** [I] to wash your whole body while standing under a shower: *Mike shaved and showered.* **2** [T] to give someone a lot of things: **shower sb with sth** *She showered him with kisses.* | *Tom showered Amy with presents.* | **shower sth on/upon sb** *She had no children and showered her love on her three nieces.* **3** [I always + adv/prep, T] to scatter a lot of things onto a person or place, or to be scattered in this way: [+**down/over/upon**] *The top shelf broke and books showered down.* | **shower sth with sth** *The ship was showered with hot ash from the volcano.* | **shower sth on/over sth** *Hundreds of leaflets were showered over the town.*

'shower cap n [C] a plastic hat that keeps your hair dry in a shower

'shower gel n [U] *BrE* a type of liquid soap that you use to wash yourself in a shower

show·er·proof /'ʃaʊəpruːf $ 'ʃaʊr-/ adj showerproof clothes keep you dry in light rain but not in heavy rain

show·er·y /'ʃaʊəri $ 'ʃaʊri/ adj raining frequently for short periods: *a showery day*

show·girl /'ʃəʊɡɜːl $ 'ʃəʊɡɜːrl/ n [C] one of a group of women who sing or dance in a musical show

show·ground /'ʃəʊɡraʊnd $ 'ʃoʊ-/ n [C] *BrE* a large area of land where an event such as a farming show or a FETE can be held

'show house also **'show home** n [C] *BrE* a house that has been built and filled with furniture to show buyers what similar new houses look like

show·ing /'ʃəʊɪŋ $ 'ʃoʊ-/ n **1** [C] an occasion when a film, art show etc can be seen or looked at, especially a special occasion that people are invited to: *I saw a private showing of the film.* | *It was the comedy's first showing on TV.* **2** [singular] used to talk about a person's or thing's level of success: *Choose the candidate who **makes** the best **showing** in the interview.* | **strong/poor showing** *Women made a strong showing in the election.* | **on ... showing** *BrE*: *On present showing* (=judging by the way it is now), *there's a lot to do to get the newspaper's sales up.* | *On this showing* (=judging by this example), *she is becoming a very good writer indeed.*

'show jumping n [U] a sport in which horses with riders have to jump a series of fences as quickly and skilfully as possible —**show jumper** n [C]

show·man /'ʃəʊmən $ 'ʃoʊ-/ n plural **showmen** /-mən/ [C] someone who is good at entertaining people and getting a lot of public attention: *He is the band's best showman.*

show·man·ship /'ʃəʊmənʃɪp $ 'ʃoʊ-/ n [U] skill at entertaining people and getting public attention

shown /ʃəʊn $ ʃoʊn/ the past participle of SHOW

'show-off n [C] *informal* someone who always tries to show how clever or skilled they are so that other people will admire them – often used to show disapproval: *She's a bit of a show-off.*

,show of 'hands n [singular] a vote taken by counting the raised hands of the people at a meeting: *The dispute was settled with a show of hands.*

show·piece /'ʃəʊpiːs $ 'ʃoʊ-/ n [C usually singular] something that an organization, government etc wants people to see, because it is a very good or successful example: *The building is a showpiece of elegant design.* | *The new stadium is a showpiece for the Greeks.*

show·place /'ʃəʊpleɪs $ 'ʃoʊ-/ n [C] a place which is open to the public because of its beauty, historical interest etc

show·room /'ʃəʊruːm, -rʊm $ 'ʃoʊ-/ n [C] a large room where you can look at things that are for sale, such as cars or electrical goods: *a car showroom*

'show-,stopping adj a show-stopping performance is extremely good or impressive: *a show-stopping dance routine* —**show-stopper** n [C]

show·time /'ʃəʊtaɪm $ 'ʃoʊ-/ n [U] **1** the time that a play or film will begin in a theatre or cinema **2** *AmE informal* the time when an activity should begin

'show ,trial n [C] an unfair TRIAL that is organized by a government for political reasons, not in order to find out whether someone is guilty: *Stalin staged a series of show trials.*

show·y /'ʃəʊi $ 'ʃoʊi/ adj something that is showy is very colourful, big, expensive etc, especially in a way that attracts people's attention: *an attractive shrub with showy flowers* —**showily** adv —**showiness** n [U]

shrank /ʃræŋk/ the past tense of SHRINK

shrap·nel /'ʃræpnəl/ n [U] small pieces of metal from a bomb, bullet etc that are scattered when it explodes: *a soldier with **shrapnel wounds** in his chest*

shred¹ /ʃred/ n **1** [C] a small thin piece that is torn or cut roughly from something: [+**of**] *a shred of paper* | **tear/rip sth to shreds** *The clothes were ripped to shreds and covered in blood.* **2 tear/rip sth to shreds** to criticize someone very severely: *Within a year, other researchers had torn the theory to shreds.* **3 in shreds a)** torn in many places: *Uncle Earl was exhausted and his shirt hung in shreds.* **b)** completely ruined: *His ambitious plan was in shreds.* | *If Myra gossips about this, my reputation will be in shreds.* **4 shred of sth** a very small amount of something: *There's **not a shred of doubt** (=no doubt at all) in my mind that we will win.* | *He does **not** have **a shred of evidence** (=none at all) to prove his claim.* | *the last shred of hope* ⚠ Usually used with negative words such as **not, without,** and **hardly.**

shred² v **shredded, shredding** [T] **1** to cut or tear something into small thin pieces: *Coleslaw is made with shredded cabbage.* **2** to put a document into a shredder: *Carlson was collecting messages, reading them, then shredding them.*

shred·der /'ʃredə $ -ər/ n [C] a machine that cuts documents into small pieces so that no one can read them

shrew /ʃruː/ n [C] **1** a very small animal like a mouse with a long pointed nose **2** *old-fashioned* an unpleasant woman who always argues and disagrees with people

shrewd /ʃruːd/ adj **1** good at judging what people or situations are really like: *Malcolm is a shrewd and realistic businessman.* | *She was shrewd enough to guess who was responsible.* | *Capra looked at her with shrewd eyes.* **2** well judged and likely to be right: *a shrewd decision* | *Bridget has a shrewd idea of what will sell.* —**shrewdly** adv: *'Something tells me you've already decided,' he said shrewdly.* —**shrewdness** n [U]

shrew·ish /'ʃruːɪʃ/ adj *old use* a shrewish woman is one who always argues and disagrees with people

shriek¹ /ʃriːk/ v **1** [I] to make a very high loud sound, especially because you are afraid, angry, excited, or in pain; ◫ **scream**: *They were dragged from their homes, shrieking and weeping.* | *He shrieked in agony.* | [+**with**] *A group of students were shrieking with laughter.* **2** [T] to say something in a high loud voice because you are excited, afraid, or angry; ◫ **scream**: *'I'm pregnant,' she shrieked.* | [+**at**] *'I'll kill you,' Anne shrieked at him.*

shriek² n [C] a loud high sound made because you are frightened, excited, angry etc; ◫ **scream**: [+**of**] *a shriek of laughter* | **with a shriek** *With a shriek of delight, Jean hugged Maggie.* | **give/let out a shriek** *Ella let out a piercing shriek.*

shrift /ʃrɪft/ → **get/be given short shrift** at SHORT¹ (15)

shrill¹ /ʃrɪl/ adj **1** a shrill sound is very high and unpleasant: *'That's not true,' she protested in a shrill voice.* | *a shrill whistle* | *Fran uttered a shrill scream.* **2** shrill complaints, criticism, demands etc are too loud or strong and seem unreasonable: *He hated the shrill demands of the children.* —**shrillness** n [U] —**shrilly** /'ʃrɪl-li, 'ʃrɪli/ adv

shrill² v **1** [I] *written* to produce a very high and unpleasant sound: *The telephone shrilled twice.* **2** [T] to say something in a very high voice: *'I hate you!' she shrilled.*

shrimp /ʃrɪmp/ *plural* **shrimp** *or* **shrimps** *n* [C] **1** a small sea creature that you can eat, which has ten legs and a soft shell; **◨ prawn** *BrE*; **→** see picture at SEA-FOOD **2** someone who is very small – used humorously

shrimp 'cocktail *n* [C,U] *AmE* shrimps without their shells that are cooked and put in a pink sauce, and eaten cold before the main part of a meal; **◨ prawn cocktail** *BrE*

shrimp·ing /'ʃrɪmpɪŋ/ *n* [U] the activity of fishing for shrimps

shrine /ʃraɪn/ *n* [C] **1** a place that is connected with a holy event or holy person, and that people visit to pray: [+of/to] *his pilgrimage to the shrine of St John* **2** a place that people visit and respect because it is connected with a famous person or event: *Elvis's home has become a shrine for his fans.* | [+to] *The museum is a shrine to the great Spanish artist.*

shrink¹ /ʃrɪŋk/ *v past tense* **shrank** /ʃræŋk/, *past participle* **shrunk** /ʃrʌŋk/ **1** [I,T] to become smaller, or to make something smaller, through the effects of heat or water: *I'm worried about washing that shirt in case it shrinks.* **→** PRE-SHRUNK, SHRUNKEN **2** [I,T] to become or to make something smaller in amount, size, or value; **◨ grow:** *The city continued to shrink.* | [+to] *The firm's staff had shrunk to only four people.* | *Treatment can shrink a tumour.* | *We want to expand the business, not shrink it.* **3** [I always + adv/prep] to move back and away from something, especially because you are frightened: *She listened, shrinking under the blankets, to their shouts.* | *Meredith was scared of him and shrank back.* | *His anger was enough to make the others shrink away from him.*

shrink from sth *phr v* to avoid doing something difficult or unpleasant: *The leadership too often shrinks from hard decisions.* | **shrink from doing sth** *We will not shrink from making the necessary changes in policy.*

shrink² *n* [C] *informal* a PSYCHOANALYST or PSYCHIATRIST - used humorously

shrink·age /'ʃrɪŋkɪdʒ/ *n* [singular, U] the act of shrinking, or the amount that something shrinks: *Pollution led to a shrinkage of grasslands.*

shrinking 'violet *n* [C] someone who is very shy – used humorously

shrink-'wrapped *adj* goods that are shrink-wrapped are wrapped tightly in plastic —**'shrink-wrap** *n* [U]

shriv·el /'ʃrɪvəl/ *also* **shrivel up** *v* **shrivelled, shriv-elling** *BrE*, **shriveled, shriveling** *AmE* [I,T] if something shrivels, or if it is shrivelled, it becomes smaller and its surface becomes covered in lines because it is very dry or old: *The leaves change colour, then shrivel.* —**shrivelled** *BrE*; **shriveled** *AmE adj*: *a shrivelled apple*

shroud¹ /ʃraʊd/ *n* [C] **1** a cloth that is wrapped around a dead person's body before it is buried **2** *lit-erary* something that hides or covers something: *The fog rolled in, and a grey shroud covered the city.* | [+of] *A shroud of silence surrounded the general's death.*

shroud² *v* [T usually in passive] *literary* **1** to cover or hide something: *Joseph was shrouded under a dark blanket.* | **be shrouded in sth** *The cliff was shrouded in mist.* **2** to keep information secret so that people do not know what really happened: **be shrouded in sth** *The incident has always been shrouded in mystery.* | *The work is shrouded in secrecy.*

'shroud-,waving *n* [U] *BrE* when people, especially doctors or politicians, publicly criticize the quality of medical care in the British National Health Service, in order to make the government provide more money for it

Shrove Tues·day /,ʃrəʊv 'tjuːzdi, -deɪ $,ʃroʊv 'tuːz-/ *n* [C,U] the day before the first day of the Chris-tian period of Lent, when people in Britain traditionally eat PANCAKES

shrub /ʃrʌb/ *n* [C] a small bush with several woody stems

shrub·be·ry /'ʃrʌbəri/ *n plural* **shrubberies** **1** [U] shrubs planted close together: *a tangled mass of over-grown shrubbery* **2** [C] a part of a garden where shrubs are planted close together

shrug¹ W3 /ʃrʌg/ *v* **shrugged, shrugging** [I,T] to raise and then lower your shoulders in order to show that you do not know something or do not care about something: *I just shrugged my shoulders and ignored him.* | *Melanie shrugged and walked away.*
shrug sth ⇔ **off** *phr v*
to treat something as unimportant and not worry about it: *We can't just shrug these objections off.*

shrug² *n* [C usually singular] a movement of your shoulders upwards and then downwards again that you make to show that you do not know something or do not care about something: **with a shrug** *'Suit your-self,' he said with a shrug.*

shrunk /ʃrʌŋk/ the past tense and past participle of SHRINK

shrunk·en /'ʃrʌŋkən/ *adj* [usually before noun] having become smaller or been made smaller: *a shrunken old woman*

shtick, schtick /ʃtɪk/ *n* [U] *AmE* the style of humour that a particular actor or COMEDIAN typically uses

shuck /ʃʌk/ *v* [T] *AmE* to remove the outer cover of a vegetable such as corn, or the shell of OYSTERS
shuck sth ⇔ **off** *phr v AmE informal* to take off a piece of clothing: *She shucked off her jacket and ran upstairs.*

shucks /ʃʌks/ *interjection AmE old-fashioned* used to show you are a little disappointed about something

shud·der¹ /'ʃʌdə $ -ər/ *v* [I] **1** to shake for a short time because you are afraid or cold, or because you think something is very unpleasant: *Maria shuddered as she stepped outside.* | [+with] *I shudder with embar-rassment whenever I think I think about it.* | [+at] *She shuddered at the thought that she could have been killed.* **2** if a vehicle or machine shudders, it shakes violently: *The car shuddered briefly as its engine died.* | *The train shuddered to a halt.* **3** I **shudder to think** *spoken* used to say that you do not want to think about something because it is too unpleasant: *I shudder to think what they'll say when they see the mess the house is in.*
shudder at sth *phr v* to think that something is very bad or unpleasant: *If you love skiing but shudder at the cost, take advantage of our superb family offer.* | *He shuddered at the thought of the conflict ahead.*

shudder² *n* [C usually singular] a shaking movement: *The building gave a sudden shudder.* | **a shudder ran/passed/went through sb** *A shudder ran through him at the touch of her fingers.*

shuf·fle¹ /'ʃʌfəl/ *v* **1** [I always + adv/prep] to walk very slowly and noisily, without lifting your feet off the ground: [+forward/over/back etc] *The official signaled to one of the waiters, who shuffled forward.* | *With sore legs and aching chest he shuffled over to the bath-room.* **2 shuffle your feet** to move your feet slightly, especially because you are bored or embarrassed: *Monica shuffled her feet nervously and stared at the floor.* **3** [T] to move something such as papers into a different order or into different positions: *Jack sat nervously shuffling the papers around on his desk.* | [+through] *Frances shuffled through a pile of maga-zines.* **4** [I,T] to mix PLAYING CARDS into a different order before playing a game with them: *Is it my turn to shuffle?* | *Just shuffle the cards.* **→** RESHUFFLE

shuffle² *n* **1** [singular] a slow walk in which you do not lift your feet off the ground **2** [C] the act of mixing cards into a different order before playing a game **3 be/get lost in the shuffle** to not be noticed or considered because there are so many other things to deal with: *The information contained in the memo got lost in the shuffle once it reached headquarters.*

shun /ʃʌn/ v **shunned**, **shunning** [T] to deliberately avoid someone or something: *a shy woman who shunned publicity* | *Victims of the disease found themselves shunned by society.*

shunt¹ /ʃʌnt/ v [T] **1** to move someone or something to another place, especially in a way that seems unfair: **shunt sb off/around/aside etc** *Smith was shunted off to one of the company's smaller offices.* **2** to move a train or railway carriage onto a different track

shunt² n [C] an act of moving a train or railway carriage to a different track

shush /ʃʊʃ/ v **1 shush!** *spoken* used to tell someone, especially a child, to be quiet; ▣ **shh**: *'Shush!' said Jerry. 'Not so loud.'* **2** [T] to tell someone to be very quiet, especially by putting your fingers against your lips or by saying 'shush': *He started to cry and Francesca shushed him.*

shut¹ [S1] [W2] /ʃʌt/ v *past tense and past participle* **shut**, *present participle* **shutting**

1 [I,T] to close something, or to become closed: *Shut the window, Ellen!* | *I heard his bedroom door shut.* | *She lay down on her bed and shut her eyes.* | **shut (sth) behind sb** *She walked quickly in and shut the door behind her.* | *The gates shut behind him with a dull thud.* | *He shut the drawer and turned the key.* → see box at CLOSE¹

2 shut your mouth/face/trap! also **shut your gob!/ shut it!** *BrE spoken not polite* used to tell someone to stop talking

3 [I,T] *BrE* to stop being open to the public for a short time or permanently; ▣ **close**: *The post office shuts at 5 o'clock.* | *At midday we shut the shop for lunch.* | *He lost his job when they shut the factory.*

4 shut your eyes/ears to sth to deliberately refuse to notice or pay attention to something: *We ought not to shut our eyes to these facts.* | *She heard the boys shouting to her to stop, but she shut her ears to them.*

5 shut sth in the door/drawer etc *BrE* **shut the door/ drawer etc on sth** *AmE* to shut a door etc against something so that it gets trapped there: *I shut my finger in the back door yesterday and it still hurts.*

shut sb/sth **away** *phr v*
1 to put someone or something in a place away from other people where they cannot be seen: *A lot of people are classed as mad and shut away unnecessarily.*
2 shut yourself away to deliberately avoid seeing people by staying at home or going to a quiet place, especially because you are very unhappy or want to study, write etc: *When news came of Robin's death, she shut herself away and saw no one.* | [+in] *She shut herself away in her room to work on her novel.*

shut down *phr v*
1 if a company, factory, large machine etc shuts down or is shut down, it stops operating, either permanently or for a short time: *Our local hardware shop has shut down.* | **shut sth ⇔ down** *an accident which resulted in two of the plant's nuclear reactors being shut down* | *The way to shut the machine down is to type EXIT.*
2 shut sb ⇔ down *informal* to prevent an opposing team or player from playing well or getting points: *We all knew that to win we'd have to shut down Bobby Mitchell.*

shut sb **in** (sth) *phr v*
a) if you shut someone in a room, you close the door and stop them from getting out: *Her parents shut her in an upstairs room.* | *He pushed the dogs into the breakfast room and shut them in.* **b) shut yourself in (sth)** if you shut yourself in a room, you close the door and stay in there, and often stop other people from coming in: *Ellie darted back to her room and shut herself in.* | *He shut himself in his room and wrote letters.*

shut off *phr v*
1 if a machine, tool etc shuts off or if you shut it off, it stops operating; ▣ **turn off**: *The iron shuts off automatically if it gets too hot.* | **shut sth ⇔ off** *I let the engine run for a minute and then shut it off.* | *Don't*

forget to shut off the water supply.
2 shut sth ⇔ off to prevent goods or supplies from being available or being delivered: *a strike that closed the mines and shut off coal supplies*
3 shut yourself off to avoid meeting and talking to other people: [+from] *He was cold and remote, shutting himself off from her completely.*
4 be shut off from sth to be separated from other people or things, especially so that you are not influenced by them: *The valley is completely shut off from the modern world.*

shut out *phr v*
1 shut sb out to deliberately not let someone join you in an activity or share your thoughts and feelings: *How can I help you if you just keep shutting me out all the time?* | [+from] *I felt I was being shut out from all the family's affairs.*
2 shut sb/sth ⇔ out to prevent someone or something from entering a place: *heavy curtains that shut out the sunlight* | [+from] *The door closed firmly, shutting me out from the warmth inside.*
3 shut sth ⇔ out to stop yourself from thinking about or noticing something, so that you are not affected by it: *People close their windows at night in a vain attempt to shut out the sound of gunfire.* | *She shut out memories of James.* | *Jenny closed her eyes and tried to shut everything out.*
4 shut out sb *AmE* to defeat an opposing sports team and prevent them from getting any points: *Colorado shut out Kansas City 3–0.*

shut up *phr v*
1 shut up! *spoken not polite* used to tell someone to stop talking; ▣ **be quiet!**: *Oh, shut up! I don't want to hear your excuses.* | *Just shut up and listen.* | [+about] *Shut up about your stupid dog, okay!*
2 shut (sb) up *informal* to stop talking or be quiet, or to make someone do this: *I can't stand that woman. She never shuts up.* | [+about] *I wish you'd shut up about Chris.* | *I only said that to shut her up.*
3 shut sb up to keep someone in a place away from other people, and prevent them from leaving: [+in] *I've had a terrible cold and been shut up in my room for a week.* | *Was there any need to keep us shut up here?*
4 shut sth ⇔ up to close a shop, room etc so that people cannot get into it: *Bernadette cleaned the attic and then shut it up for another year.*
5 shut up shop *BrE informal* to close a business or stop working, at the end of the day or permanently

shut² *adj* [not before noun] **1** not open; ▣ **closed**: *Is the door shut properly?* | *She kept the windows shut, for fear of burglars.* | *He sat with his eyes shut.* | *The windows were tightly shut.* | **slam/bang/swing etc shut** *The door slammed shut behind him.* | **pull/kick/slam etc sth shut** *Jenny pulled the window shut.* → **keep your mouth shut** at KEEP¹ (2) **2** *BrE* if a shop, bar etc is shut, it is not open for business; ▣ **closed**: *in the evening when the shops are shut* | *Sorry, but we're shut.* | [+for] *The first four hotels we tried were shut for the winter.*

shut·down /'ʃʌtdaʊn/ n [C] the closing of a factory, business, or piece of machinery, either permanently or for a short time: [+of] *Environmental groups had called for the permanent shutdown of the plant.* | *safety systems and automatic shutdown procedures*

ˈshut-eye n [U] *informal* sleep: *We'd better get some shut-eye.*

ˈshut-in n [C] *AmE* someone who is ill or DISABLED and cannot leave their house very easily

ˈshut-out n [C] *AmE* a game in which one team is prevented by the other from getting any points

shut·ter¹ /'ʃʌtə $ -ər/ n [C] **1** [usually plural] one of a pair of wooden or metal covers on the outside of a window that can be closed to keep light out or prevent thieves from coming in → see picture at WINDOW **2** a part of a camera that opens for a very short time to let light onto the film → see picture at CAMERA

shutter² v [T usually passive] AmE to close a business, office etc for a short time or permanently: *The company shuttered its Hong Kong investment banking business a year ago.*

shut·ter·bug /'ʃʌtəbʌg $ -ər-/ n [C] AmE informal someone who likes to take a lot of photographs

shut·tered /'ʃʌtəd $ -ərd/ adj with closed shutters, or having shutters: *A gust of wind shook the shuttered windows.*

shut·tle¹ /'ʃʌtl/ n [C] **1** a SPACE SHUTTLE **2** a plane, bus, or train that makes regular short journeys between two places: *He took the Washington – New York shuttle.* | *A shuttle bus operates to and from the beach of San Benedetto.* | *There's a shuttle service from the city center to the airport.* **3** a pointed tool used in weaving, to pass a thread over and under the threads that form the cloth

shuttle² v **1** [I always + adv/prep] to travel frequently between two places: [+between/back and forth] *Susan shuttles between Rotterdam and London for her job.* **2** [T] to move people from one place to another place that is fairly near: *The passengers were shuttled to the hotel by bus.*

shut·tle·cock /'ʃʌtlkɒk $ -kɑːk/ n [C] a small light object that you hit over the net in the game of BADMINTON; ⊟ birdie AmE

'shuttle di,plomacy n [U] international talks in which someone travels between countries and talks to members of the governments, for example to make a peace agreement

shy¹ /ʃaɪ/ adj comparative **shyer**, superlative **shy-est** **1** nervous and embarrassed about meeting and speaking to other people, especially people you do not know: *He was a quiet, shy man.* | [+with] *She was very shy with strangers.* | *a shy smile* | *As a teenager I was painfully shy* (=extremely shy). | **shy to do sth** *He was too shy to come sit by me in class.* | **go all shy** BrE (=to suddenly become very shy) *Oh, have you gone all shy, Jenny?* **2** **sb is not shy about (doing) sth** used to emphasize that someone is very willing to do something or get involved with something: *John has strong opinions and he's not shy about sharing them.* **3** unwilling to do something or get involved in something: **be shy about/of (doing) sth** *Employees are urged not to be shy about reporting incidents of sexual harassment.* **4** **be shy (of sth)** especially AmE to have less than a particular amount of something: *The Democrats are three votes shy of a majority.* | *Jessica died Monday. She was one week shy of her 13th birthday.* **5** used to say that someone does not like something and therefore tries to avoid it: *Although publicity-shy, he recently agreed to be interviewed.* → CAMERA-SHY, WORK-SHY **6** shy animals get frightened easily and are unwilling to come near people: *Deer are shy creatures.* —**shyly** adv: *He grinned shyly.* —**shyness** n [U]: *Gradually I overcame my shyness.* → fight shy of (doing) sth at FIGHT¹ (22); → once bitten, twice shy at BITE¹ (14)

WORD FOCUS: SHY
similar words: **timid, self-conscious, reserved, withdrawn, introverted**

shy² v shied, shying, shies [I] if a horse shies, it makes a sudden movement away from something because it is frightened: *The horse shied, throwing Darrel from his saddle.*

shy away from sth phr v to avoid doing or dealing with something because you are not confident enough or you are worried or nervous about it: *They criticized the leadership, but shied away from a direct challenge.*

shy³ n → COCONUT SHY

shys·ter /'ʃaɪstə $ -ər/ n [C] informal especially AmE a dishonest person, especially a lawyer or BUSINESSMAN

Si·a·mese cat /ˌsaɪəmiːz 'kæt/ n [C] a type of cat that has blue eyes, short grey or brown fur, and a dark face

Siamese 'twin n [C usually plural] one of two people who are born joined to each other – sometimes considered offensive; ⊟ **conjoined twin**

sib·ilant¹ /'sɪbɪlənt/ adj formal making or being an 's' or 'sh' sound: *a sibilant whisper*

sibilant² n [C] technical a sibilant sound such as 's' or 'sh' in English

sib·ling /'sɪblɪŋ/ n [C] **1** formal a brother or sister: *Most young smokers are influenced by their friends' and older siblings' smoking habits.* **2** **sibling rivalry** competition between brothers and sisters for their parents' attention or love

sic¹ /sɪk/ adv written formal used after a word that you have copied in order to show that you know it was not spelled or used correctly: *We had seen several signs that said 'ORANGE'S (sic) FOR SALE'.*

sic² v sicced, siccing [T] AmE informal **1** to tell a dog to attack someone: **sic sth on sb** *He sicced his dog on me.* **2** **sic 'em!** spoken used to tell a dog to attack someone **3** to tell someone in authority that someone has done something wrong, so that they are punished: [+on] *He sicced his lawyers on them.*

sick¹ S1 W3 /sɪk/ adj
1 ILL especially AmE suffering from a disease or illness: *His mother's very sick.* | *Maria can't come in today because she's sick.* | *a sick child* | *a sick animal* | [+with] *I have been sick with flu.* | **get sick** (=become ill) AmE: *At the last minute I got sick and couldn't go.* | **be off sick** BrE; **be out sick** AmE (=be away from work or school because you are ill) *Two of his employees were out sick.* | *I was off sick for four days with the flu.* | **phone/ring/call in sick** (=phone to say you are not coming to work because you are ill) *He was upset because it was the first day of the sale and Astrid had called in sick.* | *What will happen to the business if you fall sick* (=become ill) *or die?* | *He took sick* (=became ill) *and died a week later.* | *Pete's at home in bed,* **sick as a dog** (=very sick).
2 **be sick** if you are sick, the food in your stomach comes up through your mouth; ⊟ **vomit, throw up**: *I think I'm going to be sick.* | *He dashed to the bathroom and was sick again.* | *The cat's been sick on the carpet.* | *You'll be sick if you eat any more of that chocolate!* | *I was violently sick* (=suddenly and severely sick) *the last time I ate prawns.*
3 **feel sick** also **be/feel sick to your stomach** AmE to feel as if you are going to VOMIT: *As soon as the ship started moving I began to feel sick.* | [+with] *Mary felt sick with fear.* | *She began to shiver,* **feeling sick to her stomach.** | *Virginia had a sick feeling in her stomach.* → CARSICK, SEASICK; → **travel-sick** at TRAVEL SICKNESS
4 **make me/you sick** spoken **a)** to make you feel very angry: *People like you make me sick!* **b)** spoken to make someone feel jealous – used humorously: *You make me sick with your 'expenses paid' holidays!*
5 **make sb/yourself sick** BrE **a)** if something makes you sick, it causes you bring food up from your stomach through your mouth: *The smell of blood made him sick.* **b)** if you make yourself sick, you do something to bring food up from your stomach through your mouth: *I've never been able to make myself sick.* | *You'll make yourself sick if you eat any more!*
6 **be sick (and tired) of (doing) sth** also **be sick to death of sth** spoken to be angry or bored with something that has been happening for a long time: *I'm sick and tired of your excuses.* | *I am sick of working for other people.*
7 **be worried sick/be sick with worry** to be extremely worried: *Why didn't you tell me you were coming home late? I've been worried sick!*
8 STRANGE/CRUEL **a)** someone who is sick does things that are strange and cruel, and seems mentally ill: *I keep getting obscene phone calls from some sick pervert.* | *You're sick!* | *a sick mind* **b)** sick stories, jokes etc deal with death and suffering in a cruel or

38 **TV STATION** [usually singular] *BrE spoken* a television station; ◨ **channel**: *Do you know what's on the other side?* → DOUBLE-SIDED, ONE-SIDED; → **to be on the safe side** at SAFE¹ (7); → **err on the side of caution** at ERR (1); → FLIP SIDE; → **split your sides** at SPLIT¹ (10); → **the other side of the coin** at COIN¹ (3); → **two sides of the same coin** at COIN¹ (4)

side² *adj* [only before noun] **1** in or on the side of something: *Hannah slipped out through a side exit.* **2** from the side of something: *Can you get a side view?*

side³ *v* [I] to support or argue against a person or group in a quarrel, fight etc: [+with/against] *Frank sided with David against their mother.*

side·arm /'saɪd-ɑːm $ -ɑːrm/ *n* [C] a weapon carried or worn at someone's side, for example a gun or sword

side·bar /'saɪdbɑː $ -bɑːr/ *n* [C] **1** a separate part of something such as a newspaper article where extra information is given **2** *AmE law* an occasion when the lawyers and the judge in a TRIAL discuss something without letting the JURY hear what they are saying

side benefit *n* [C] an additional advantage or good result that comes from something, besides its main purpose: *A side benefit to filming close-up shots is that your microphone will pick up clearer sound.*

side·board /'saɪdbɔːd $ -bɔːrd/ *n* **1** [C] a long low piece of furniture usually in a DINING ROOM, used for storing plates, glasses etc **2 sideboards** *BrE* sideburns

side·burns /'saɪdbɜːnz $ -bɜːrnz/ *n* [plural] hair grown down the sides of a man's face in front of his ears

side·car /'saɪdkɑː $ -kɑːr/ *n* [C] a small vehicle attached to the side of a MOTORCYCLE, in which a passenger can ride

side dish *n* [C] a small amount of food such as a vegetable that you eat with a main meal

side ef,fect *n* [C] **1** an effect that a drug has on your body in addition to curing pain or illness: **harmful/serious/adverse etc side effect** *a natural remedy with no harmful side effects* | [+of] *the side effects of the medication* **2** an unexpected or unplanned result of a situation or event: *These policy changes could* **have beneficial side effects** *for the whole economy.*

side issue *n* [C] a subject or problem that is not as important as the main one, and may take people's attention away from the main subject: *The tax proposal is really a side issue with us.*

side·kick /'saɪd,kɪk/ *n* [C] *informal* someone who spends time with or helps another person, especially when that other person is more important than they are

side·light /'saɪdlaɪt/ *n* [C] *BrE* one of the two small lights next to the main front lights on a car; ◨ **parking light** *AmE*; → see picture at CAR

side·line¹ /'saɪdlaɪn/ *n* **1** [C] an activity that you do as well as your main job or business, in order to earn more money: **as a sideline** *Zoe does a bit of freelance photography as a sideline.* **2 on the sidelines** not taking part in an activity even though you want to or should do: **stand/stay/remain etc on the sidelines** *You can't stay on the sidelines for ever; it's time you got involved.* **3 sidelines** [plural] the area just outside the lines that form the edge of a sports field: **on the sidelines** *Wenger stood on the sidelines shouting instructions to his team.* **4** [C] a line at the side of a sports field, which shows where the players are allowed to play

sideline² *v* [usually passive] if you are sidelined, you are unable to play in a sports game because you are injured, or unable to take part in an activity because you are not as good as someone else: *Baggio was once again sidelined through injury.*

side·long /'saɪdlɒŋ $ -lɔːŋ/ *adj* **sidelong look/glance** a way of looking at someone by moving your eyes to the side, especially so that it seems secret, dishonest, or disapproving: *He gave Oliver a sidelong glance.* —**sidelong** *adv*: *'You looked very well this morning,' she added, glancing sidelong at him.*

side-'on *adj* coming from one side rather than from in front or behind: *a side-on collision* —**side-on** *adv*

side order *n* [C] a small amount of food ordered in a restaurant to be eaten with a main meal but served on a separate dish: *a side order of onion rings*

side road *n* [C] a road that is smaller than a main road, but is often connected to it

side-saddle *adv* **ride/sit sidesaddle** to ride or sit on a horse with both legs on the same side of the horse

side·show /'saɪdʃəʊ $ -ʃoʊ/ *n* [C] **1** a separate small part of a FAIR or CIRCUS, where you pay to play games or watch a performance **2** an event that is much less important or serious than another one: *The initial conflict was a mere sideshow compared with the World War that followed.*

side·split·ting /'saɪd,splɪtɪŋ/ *adj* extremely funny: *He told some sidesplitting jokes.*

side·step /'saɪdstep/ *v* **sidestepped, sidestepping 1** **sidestep a problem/issue/question** to avoid dealing with something difficult: *The report sidesteps the environmental issues.* **2** [I,T] to step quickly sideways to avoid being hit or walking into someone —**sidestep** *n* [C]

side street *n* [C] a street that is smaller than a main street, but is often connected to it

side·swipe¹ /'saɪdswaɪp/ *n* [C usually singular] if you take a sideswipe at someone or something, you criticize them while you are talking about something different: *Sir Kenneth concluded with a sideswipe at his critics.*

sideswipe² *v* [T] *AmE* to hit the side of a car with another car so that the two sides touch quickly: *She was going too fast and sideswiped a parked car.*

side·track /'saɪdtræk/ *v* [T usually passive] **1** to make someone stop doing what they should be doing, or stop talking about what they started talking about, by making them interested in something else: *Don't get sidetracked by the audience's questions.* **2** *AmE* to delay or stop the progress of something: *An effort to improve security was sidetracked by budget problems.*

side-view mirror *n* [C] *AmE* a mirror attached to the side of a car; ◨ **wing mirror** *BrE*

side·walk /'saɪdwɔːk $ -wɒːk/ *n* [C] *AmE* a hard surface or path at the side of a street for people to walk on; ◨ **pavement** *BrE*

side·ways /'saɪdweɪz/ *adv* **1** to or towards one side: *A strong gust of wind blew the car sideways into the ditch.* **2** with the side, rather than the front or back, facing forwards: *They brought the piano sideways through the front door.* **3** if you are moved sideways at work, you are given a job that is different but is at the same level as your old job: *He would be moved sideways, rather than demoted.* —**sideways** *adj*: *a sideways glance* → **knock sb sideways** at KNOCK¹ (13)

side-wheel·er /'saɪd,wiːlə $ -ər/ *n* [C] *AmE* an old-fashioned type of ship which is pushed forward by a pair of large wheels at the sides; ◨ **paddle steamer** *BrE*

sid·ing /'saɪdɪŋ/ *n* **1** [C] a short railway track connected to a main track, where trains are kept when they are not being used **2** [U] *AmE* long, narrow pieces of wood, metal, or plastic, used for covering the outside walls of houses

si·dle /'saɪdl/ *v* [I always + adv/prep] to walk towards something or someone slowly and quietly, as if you do not want to be noticed: [+up/towards/along] *A woman sidled up to us and asked if we wanted to buy a watch.*

SIDS /sɪdz/ n [U] *medical* **Sudden Infant Death Syndrome** when a baby stops breathing and dies while it is sleeping, for no known reason; ▣ **cot death** *BrE*; ▣ **crib death** *AmE*

siege /siːdʒ/ n [C,U]   **1** a situation in which an army or the police surround a place and try to gain control of it or force someone to come out of it: *The siege lasted almost four months.* | *a three-day police siege at a remote country cottage* | [+of] *the siege of Leningrad* | **end/lift/raise a siege** (=end a siege)   **2 lay siege to sb/sth a)** if the army or police lay siege to a place, they start a siege against it: *In June 1176 King Richard laid siege to Limoges.* **b)** if you lay siege to someone, you do everything you can to try and get them to talk to you: *Then he set to work laying siege to her with letters.*   **3 be under siege a)** to be surrounded by an army in a siege **b)** to be criticized, attacked, or threatened all the time: *The TV station has been under siege from irate viewers phoning in to complain.*   **4 siege mentality** the feeling among a group of people that they are surrounded by enemies and must do everything they can to protect themselves

si·en·na /siˈenə/ n [U] a yellowish brown colour

si·er·ra /siˈerə/ n [C] a row or area of sharply pointed mountains

si·es·ta /siˈestə/ n [C] a short sleep in the afternoon, especially in warm countries: **take/have a siesta** *The stores all close after lunch when everyone takes a siesta.*

sieve¹ /sɪv/ n [C]   **1 a)** a round wire kitchen tool with a lot of small holes, used for separating solid food from liquid or small pieces of food from large pieces → see picture at EAT **b)** a round wire tool for separating small objects from large objects   **2 have a memory like a sieve** *informal* to forget things easily

sieve² v [T] to put flour or other food through a sieve: *Sieve the flour and cocoa powder into a bowl.*

sift /sɪft/ v [T]   **1** to put flour, sugar etc through a sieve or similar container in order to remove large pieces   **2** also **sift through** to examine information, documents etc carefully in order to find something out or decide what is important and what is not: *Police are sifting through the evidence in the hope of finding more clues.*

sift sth ⇔ **out** *phr v* to separate something from other things: [+from] *It's hard to sift out the truth from the lies in this case.*

sift·er /ˈsɪftə $ -ər/ n [C]   **1** *BrE* a container with a lot of small holes in the top used for shaking flour, sugar etc onto things; ▣ **shaker** *AmE*   **2** *AmE* a container with a handle and a lot of small holes on the bottom, used for removing large pieces from flour or for mixing flour and other dry things together in cooking

sigh¹ /saɪ/ v [I]   **1** to breathe in and out making a long sound, especially because you are bored, disappointed, tired etc: *'Well, there's nothing we can do about it now,' she sighed.* | **sigh heavily/deeply** *Frankie stared out of the window and sighed deeply.* | [+with] *He sighed with despair at the thought of all the opportunities he had missed.*   **2** *literary* if the wind sighs, it makes a long sound like someone sighing: *The wind sighed in the trees.*   **3 sigh for sth** to be sad because you are thinking about a pleasant time in the past: *Emilia sighed for her lost youth.*

sigh² n [C] an act or sound of sighing: [+of] *She let out a sigh of impatience.* | **give/let out/heave a sigh** *Laura shrugged, and gave a heavy sigh.* | *We all breathed a* **sigh of relief** *when we heard they were safe.*

sight¹ S2 W2 /saɪt/ n
1 ABILITY TO SEE [U] the physical ability to see; ▣ **vision**: *Anne's sight is very good for someone of her age.* | *He began to* **lose** *his sight six years ago.* | *an emergency operation to save his sight* | *You will get a free sight test if you are under 16.*
2 ACT OF SEEING [singular, U] the act of seeing something: [+of] *Just the sight of him made her go all weak.* | **at the sight of sth** *Marcie will faint at the sight of blood.* | *The house is* **hidden from sight** *behind trees.*

3 THING YOU SEE [C] **a)** something you can see: **familiar/common/rare etc sight** *Street dentists are a common sight in Pakistan.* | *As he reached the front door he saw a strange sight.* | *the* **sights and sounds** *of the forest →* **not a pretty sight** at PRETTY² (3); → **sorry sight** at SORRY (8) **b)** **the sights** [plural] famous or interesting places that tourists visit: *In the afternoon, you'll have a chance to relax or* **see the sights.** | [+of] *So, Maria's* **showing** *you* **the sights** *of Copenhagen, is she? →* SIGHTSEEING
4 in/within sight a) inside the area that you can see: *I glanced around me quickly. There was* **no one in sight.** | *They burned* **every** *house* **in sight.** | *The boys got home and eat* **everything in sight.** | *Since my hotel was within sight, I told him he could go.* **b)** likely to happen soon: *Six months from the start of the strike, there is still* **no end in sight.** | *Peace is now in sight.*
5 within/in sight of sth a) in the area where you can see something: *We camped within sight of the lake.* | *At last they* **came in sight** *of the city.* **b)** in a position where you will soon be able to get something or achieve something: *Dan was now within sight of the championship.*
6 in your sights if you have someone or something in your sights, you intend to achieve it or get it for yourself or to attack them: **have sb/sth in your sights** *Rogers had victory firmly in his sights.*
7 out of sight outside the area that you can see: *Karen waved until the car was out of sight.*
8 out of sight, out of mind used to say that people soon stop thinking about other people if they do not see them for a while
9 disappear/vanish from sight to disappear: *'Will she be all right?' asked Jen as the car disappeared from sight.*
10 come into sight to appear: *when the ship at last came into sight*
11 on sight as soon as you see someone: *The army has been ordered to* **shoot** *rebel soldiers* **on sight.** | *Jo disliked him on sight.*
12 not let sb out of your sight to make sure that someone stays near you: *Since the accident, Donna hasn't let the children out of her sight.*
13 be sick of/can't stand/hate the sight of sb/sth to dislike someone or something very much: *Alan and Sam can't stand the sight of each other.* | *Everybody hates the sight of you.*
14 a sight for sore eyes *spoken* **a)** someone or something that you feel very happy to see **b)** *BrE* someone or something that is very unattractive or very funny to look at
15 a (damn/darned/darn) sight more/better etc *informal* a lot more, a lot better etc: *I know the place a damn sight better than you do.* | *You're all going to have to work a darned sight harder.* | *The old lady is a sight cleverer than Sarah.*
16 be a sight also **look a sight** to look very funny or stupid, or very untidy or unpleasant: *We'd had an all-night party, and the place looked a bit of a sight.*
17 sight unseen if you buy or choose something sight unseen, you do it without looking at the thing first: *I can't believe you would rent a place sight unseen.*
18 be a (beautiful, strange, frightening etc) sight to behold *formal* used to emphasize that something or someone looks very unusual, for example because they are very beautiful, strange, or frightening: *His garden was a sight to behold.* | *His face was not a pleasant sight to behold.*
19 GUN [C usually plural] the part of a gun or other weapon that guides your eye when you are aiming at something → **at first sight** at FIRST¹ (6); → **know sb by sight** at KNOW¹ (3); → **lose sight of sth** at LOSE (1); → **set your mind/sights/heart on (doing) sth** at SET¹ (13)

sight² v [T] to see something from a long distance away, or see something you have been looking for: *The sailors gave a shout of joy when they* **sighted** *land.* | *Several rare birds have been sighted in the area.*

S

sight·ed /'saɪt̬ɪd/ adj someone who is sighted can see, and is not blind: *Blind and sighted children are taught in the same classroom.* | *her **partially sighted** (=having limited ability to see) father* → CLEAR-SIGHTED, FAR-SIGHTED, LONG-SIGHTED, SHORT-SIGHTED

sight·ing /'saɪtɪŋ/ n [C] an occasion on which something is seen, especially something rare or something that people are hoping to see: *[+of] There were two unconfirmed sightings of UFOs in the area.* | *Where was the latest sighting?*

sight·less /'saɪtləs/ adj literary blind

sight-read /'saɪtriːd/ v past tense and past participle **sight-read** /-red/ [I,T] to play or sing written music when you look at it for the first time, without practising it first —**sight-reader** n [C] —**sight-reading** n [U]

sight·see·ing /'saɪtˌsiːɪŋ/ n [U] when you visit famous or interesting places, especially as tourists: *She swam and sunbathed, **went sightseeing** and relaxed.*

sight·se·er /'saɪtsiːə $ -ər/ n [C] someone, especially a tourist, who is visiting a famous or interesting place

sign¹ S3 W2 /saɪn/ n

1 GIVES INFORMATION [C] a piece of paper, metal, or wood with words or a picture that gives people information, warnings, or instructions: *a sign on the door* | *road signs* | *a **no smoking sign*** | *Don't ignore the fog **warning signs.*** → see picture at TOWN

2 SHOWS STH IS TRUE [C] an event, fact etc that shows that something is happening or that something is true or exists; ▣ indication

---
sign (that)
clear/obvious sign
warning sign
good/positive/encouraging sign
bad sign
outward/visible sign
sure sign (=clear proof)
tell-tale signs (=signs that clearly show something bad)
there are signs/there are no signs
show signs of (doing) sth
show/give every sign of doing sth (=used to say that something is very likely)
take/see sth as a sign (that) (=understand something to mean something)
at the first sign of sth (=immediately)

[+of] A red morning sky is a sign of an impending storm. | *Crying is seen as a sign of weakness.* | *A paw print in the dust was a **sign that** a tiger was close.* | *There were no **obvious signs** of engine wear.* | *Raised blood pressure is a **warning sign**.* | *If she can move her leg, that's a very **good sign**.* | *His door was closed. That was a **bad sign**.* | *She gave no **outward signs** of her problems.* | *He kept walking up and down, which was a **sure sign** he was worried.* | *The **tell-tale signs** of drug abuse are mainly to do with behaviour.* | ***There are signs** that the situation is improving.* | ***There were no signs** of forced entry into the house.* | *The economy is beginning to **show signs of** recovery.* | *The play **shows every sign of** being a big success.* | ***At the first sign of** trouble they had disappeared to England.*

3 MOVEMENT OR SOUND [C] a movement, sound etc that you make in order to tell someone something: *the thumbs-up sign (=a sign that you make with your hand to show that something is successful)* | *give/make a sign Wait until I give the sign.* | *sign that Bruce made a sign that he was ready to leave.* | *sign for sb to do sth Three short blasts on the whistle was the sign to begin.*

4 SYMBOL [C] a mark or shape that has a particular meaning; ▣ symbol: *the dollar sign* | *a minus sign*

5 STAR SIGN [C] also **star sign** a group of stars, representing one of 12 parts of the year, that some people believe influences your behaviour and your life: *What sign are you?*

6 LANGUAGE [U] a language that uses hand movements instead of spoken words, used by people who cannot hear; ▣ sign language

7 there is no sign of sb/sth used to say that someone or something is not in a place or cannot be found: *I waited for two hours but there was still no sign of her.*

8 sign of life **a)** a movement that shows that someone is alive, or something that shows that there are people in a particular place: *She listened intently for signs of life.* **b)** something that shows that a situation is becoming more active: *Commercial property markets are now **showing** definite **signs of life**.*

9 sign of the times something that shows how people live now: *It's just a sign of the times that many children have mobile phones.*

10 the sign of the Cross the hand movement that some Christians make in the shape of a cross, to show respect for God or to protect themselves from evil

sign² S3 W3 v

1 NAME [I,T] to write your SIGNATURE on something to show that you wrote it, agree with it, or were present: *Sign here, please.* | *The artist had **signed** his **name** in the corner of the painting.* | *You forgot to **sign** the **cheque**.* | *Over a hundred people have **signed** the **petition**.* | *Steffi **signs** her **autograph** every time she's asked.* | *a **signed** photo of Paul McCartney*

2 sign an agreement/contract/treaty etc to make a document, agreement etc official and legal by writing your SIGNATURE on it: *France has just signed a new trade deal with Japan.*

3 MUSIC/SPORT [I,T] if a football team or music company signs someone, or if someone signs for them, that person signs a contract in which they agree to work for them: *CBS Records had signed her back in 1988 on a three-album contract.* | *[+for/to/with] Miller worked in the shipyards before signing for Rangers.* | *Before long they had signed with Virgin.*

4 sign on the dotted line informal to officially agree to something by signing a contract: *Make sure the repairs are done before you sign on the dotted line.*

5 sign a bill/legislation/agreement into law if someone in authority signs something into law, they make it part of the law by signing an official document

6 (all) signed and sealed also (all) signed, sealed, and delivered with all the necessary legal documents signed: *It'll all be signed and sealed by Friday, and you can move in then.*

7 USE MOVEMENTS [I] to try to tell someone something or ask them to do something by using signs and movements; ▣ signal: *sign to sb to do sth He signed to the maid to leave the room.* | *sign for sb to do sth She signed for us to go inside.*

8 LANGUAGE [I,T] to use or translate something into SIGN LANGUAGE —**signer** n [C]

sign sth ⇔ **away** phr v
to sign a document that gives your property or legal rights to someone else: *She had signed away all claims to the house.* | *I felt as if I was **signing away** my life.*

sign for sth phr v
to sign a document to prove that you have received something: *This is a registered letter – someone will have to sign for it.*

sign in phr v
1 to write your name on a form, in a book etc when you enter a place such as a hotel, office, or club: *Remember to sign in at reception.*
2 sign sb ⇔ in to write someone else's name in a book so that they are allowed to enter a club, an office etc

sign off phr v
1 informal to end a radio or television programme by saying goodbye
2 to write your final message at the end of an informal letter: *It's getting late so I'll sign off now. Love, John.*
3 sign sb off BrE if a doctor signs someone off, he or she gives them a note saying that they are ill and not able to work: *For the last month she has been signed off sick from work.*
4 sign sth ⇔ off BrE; sign off on sth AmE to show that

you approve of a plan or that something is finished by signing an official document: *Major repainting work now needs to be signed off by a qualified engineer.*

sign on phr v
1 *BrE* to state officially that you are unemployed by signing a form, so that you can get money from the government
2 to sign a document to show that you agree to work for someone: [+as] *He signed on as a soldier in the US army.* | [+with] *I'll probably have to sign on with a nursing agency.*

sign out phr v
1 to write your name in a book when you leave a place such as a hotel, office, or club
2 sign sth ⇔ out to write your name on a form or in a book to show that you have taken or borrowed something: *Bernstein signed out a company car.*
3 sign sb ⇔ out to write in a book that someone is allowed to leave somewhere such as a school, office etc: *Parents must sign pupils out when collecting them for doctor's or dentist's appointments.*

sign sth ⇔ **over** phr v
to sign an official document that gives your property or legal rights to someone else: [+to] *When he became ill, he signed his property in France over to his son.*

sign up phr v
1 to put your name on a list for something because you want to take part in it: [+for] *I'm thinking of signing up for a yoga course.* | **sign up to do sth** *Over half the people who signed up to do engineering were women.*
2 sign sb ⇔ up if someone is signed up by an organization, they sign a contract in which they agree to work for that organization: *Several well-known researchers have been signed up for the project.*

sig·nal¹ [S3] [W2] /ˈsɪɡnəl/ n [C]
1 a sound or action that you make in order to give information to someone or tell them to do something: **signal (for sb) to do sth** *When she got up from the table, it was obviously the signal for us to leave.* | *The headmaster* **gave** *the* **signal** *to begin.* | *At a pre-arranged signal the lights went out.* → SMOKE SIGNAL
2 an event or action that shows what someone feels, what exists, or what is likely to happen: **signal (that)** *These results are a signal that the child may need special help.* | [+of] *The opinion poll is a* **clear signal** *of people's dissatisfaction with the government.* | *The display flashed a red* **warning signal.** | *A red flag is often used as a danger signal.* | **send/give a signal** *This will send the wrong signal to potential investors.*
3 a series of light waves, sound waves etc that carry an image, sound, or message, for example in radio or television: **send (out)/transmit/emit a signal (to sb)** *This new pay-TV channel sends signals via satellite to cable companies.* | *In the 1970s it was illegal to transmit fax signals via the public telephone system.* | **receive/pick up/detect a signal** *a small antenna which receives radio signals* | *The Coast Guard picked up a distress signal from a freighter 50 miles out at sea.*
4 a piece of equipment with coloured lights, used on a railway to tell train drivers whether they can continue or must stop: *a stop signal* | *a* **signal failure** (=when these lights do not work) → busy signal at BUSY¹ (4)

signal² v **signalled, signalling** *BrE*, **signaled, signaling** *AmE* **1** [I,T] to make a sound or action in order to give information or tell someone to do something: *She signalled, and the waiter brought the bill.* | *The whistle signalled the end of the match.* | [+at] *Mary signalled wildly at them, but they didn't notice.* | [+to] *The judge signaled to a police officer and the man was led away.* | [+for] *He pushed his plate away and signalled for coffee.* | **signal (to) sb to do sth** *She signalled to the children to come inside.* | **signal that** *The bell signaled that school was over.* **2** [T] to make something clear by what you say or do – used in news reports: *Both sides have signaled their willingness to start negotiations.* | *British sources last night signalled their readiness to talk.* | **signal (that)** *The Prime Minister's speech today signals that there will be a shake-up in the cabi-*

net. **3** [T] to be a sign that something is going to happen: **signal the start/beginning/end of sth** *the lengthening days that signal the end of winter* **4** [I] to show the direction you intend to turn in a vehicle, using the lights; ⊟ **indicate** *AmE*: *Signal before you pull out.*

signal³ adj [only before noun] *formal* important: **signal achievement/success/failure etc** *The university has done me the signal honour of making me an Honorary Fellow.*

'signal box n [C] *BrE* a small building near a railway from which the signals and tracks are controlled

sig·nal·ler /ˈsɪɡnələ $ -ər/ n [C] *BrE* a SIGNALMAN (2)

sig·nal·ly /ˈsɪɡnəli/ adv *formal* very noticeably: *The government has* **signally failed** *to deal with the problem.*

sig·nal·man /ˈsɪɡnəlmən/ n plural **signalmen** /-mən/ [C] **1** *especially BrE* someone whose job is to control railway signals **2** also **signaller** *BrE* a member of the army or navy who is trained to send and receive signals

sig·na·to·ry /ˈsɪɡnətəri $ -tɔːri/ n plural **signatories** [C] one of the people, organizations, or countries that signs an official agreement: [+to/of] *The UK is a signatory to the Berne convention.* | *the signatories of the Helsinki Declaration*

sig·na·ture /ˈsɪɡnətʃə $ -ər/ n **1** [C] your name written in the way you usually write it, for example at the end of a letter, or on a cheque etc to show that you have written it: *Her* **signature** *is totally* **illegible** (=cannot be read). | *The school collected 4000 signatures for the petition.* | *The Ukranians* **put** *their* **signatures to** *the Lisbon Protocol.* | *Someone's* **forged** *my* **signature** (=made an illegal copy of my name to deceive people) *on this letter.* | *Each child must* **obtain** *the* **signature** *of his or her parents.* ⚠ *Your* **signature** *is what you write when you sign your name. The act of putting a signature on something is called* **signing**: *the signing of the treaty* **2** [U] *formal* the act of signing something: **for signature** *We will send you a copy of the agreement for signature.* **3** [C usually singular] something that is closely related to an event, person, or style: *The shapes in the paintings are easily recognised as his signature.* | *Smith's signature singing style* → KEY SIGNATURE, TIME SIGNATURE

'signature ˌtune n [C] *BrE* a short piece of music used at the beginning and end of a television or radio programme

sign·board /ˈsaɪnbɔːd $ -bɔːrd/ n [C] a flat piece of wood, CARDBOARD etc in a public place, with writing on it that gives people information

sig·net /ˈsɪɡnɪt/ n [C] a metal object used for printing a small pattern in WAX as an official SEAL¹ (1)

'signet ring n [C] a ring that has a signet on it

sig·nif·i·cance [W2] /sɪɡˈnɪfɪkəns/ n [singular, U]
1 the importance of an event, action etc, especially because of the effects or influence it will have in the future; ⊟ **insignificance**: *Stella didn't* **attach** *any* **significance** *to Doug's query.* | [+of] *the significance of climate change* | *The book* **assesses** *the* **significance** *of Stalin's policies between 1927 and 1939.* | [+of] *The results of the study have a* **wider significance** *for all the profession.* | **great/little significance (in sth)** *The crime problem has great significance for the general public.* | **grasp/appreciate the significance (of sth)** (=fully understand something) *The press were slow to grasp the significance of what happened.*
2 the meaning of a word, sign, action etc, especially when this is not immediately clear: [+of] *the significance of the words that refer to the bread Christ shares with his disciples* | **full/real/true significance** *Only later did we realize the true significance of his remark.*

sig·nif·i·cant [S3] [W1] /sɪɡˈnɪfɪkənt/ adj
1 having an important effect or influence, especially on what will happen in the future; ⊟ **insignificant**: *His*

most significant political achievement was the abolition of the death penalty. | *Please inform us if there are any significant changes in your plans.* | [+**for**] *The result is* **highly significant** *for the future of the province.* | **it is significant that** *It is significant that the writers of the report were all men.*
2 large enough to be noticeable or have noticeable effects; ▣ **insignificant**: *A significant number of drivers fail to keep to speed limits.* | *A significant part of Japan's wealth is invested in the West.* | *There is a* **significant difference** *between the number of home births now and ten years ago.* | *The rise in temperature is not* **statistically significant**.
3 a significant look, smile etc has a special meaning that is not known to everyone: *He gave me a significant look.*

sig·nif·i·cant·ly [S3] [W2] /sɪɡ'nɪfɪkəntli/ *adv*
1 in an important way or to an important degree: *Health problems can be significantly reduced by careful diet.* | *Methods used by younger teachers differ significantly from those used by older ones.* | **significantly better/greater/worse etc** *Delia's work has been significantly better this year.*
2 [sentence adverb] used to say that something is very important: *The Democrats, significantly, finished well behind the Green Party.*
3 in a way that seems to have a special meaning: *George paused, and glanced significantly in my direction.*

sig,nificant 'other *n* [C] your husband, wife, girl-friend, or boyfriend

sig·nif·i·ca·tion /ˌsɪɡnɪfɪ'keɪʃən/ *n* [C,U] *formal* the intended meaning of a word

sig·ni·fy /'sɪɡnɪfaɪ/ *v* **signified, signifying, signifies** [not in progressive] **1** [T] to represent, mean, or be a sign of something: *Some tribes use special facial markings to signify status.* | *The image of the lion signified power and strength.* | **signify (that)** *The symbol used signifies that the frequency is measured in kHz.* **2** [T] *formal* if you signify a feeling, opinion etc, you do something that acts as a sign so that other people know your feeling or opinion: **signify that** *Hamilton waved his hand to signify that he didn't mind what they decided.* | **signify sth (to sb)** *He turned away from her slightly to signify his indifference.* **3** [I] to be important enough to have an effect on something: *These figures don't really signify in the overall results.*

sign·ing /'saɪnɪŋ/ *n* **1** [U] the act of writing your name at the end of document to show that you agree with it: *The formal signing will take place on April 9th.* | [+**of**] *the signing of the ceasefire agreement* **2 a)** [C] *BrE* someone who has just signed a contract to join a sports team or work with a record company: *New signing, Mark Brown, scored three goals in his first match.* **b)** [U] when a sports team or record company prepares a contract which someone then signs to say that they will join the team or work with the company: [+**of**] *Birmingham City have completed the signing of Doug Bell from Shrewsbury Town.* **3** [U] the use of sign language to communicate to or between people who cannot hear well

'sign ,language *n* [C,U] a language that uses hand movements instead of spoken words, used by people who cannot hear well

sign·post¹ /'saɪnpəʊst $ -poʊst/ *n* [C] **1** *especially BrE* a sign at the side of a road showing directions and distances; ▣ **sign** *AmE*: *I'm sure that signpost is pointing the wrong way.* | *Just follow the signposts to the city centre.* **2** something that helps you understand how something is organized, where to go, or what will follow – used especially in news reports: *As yet, there are few* **signposts pointing** *to success.*

signpost² *v* [T] *BrE* **1** be **well/clearly/badly signposted** to be clearly or unclearly shown by signposts: *The village isn't very well signposted.* **2** to show

something clearly so that everyone will notice and understand it – used especially in news reports: *They have signposted their conclusions in the report.*

Sikh /siːk / *n* [C] a member of an Indian religious group that developed from Hinduism in the 16th century —**Sikh** *adj*

Sikh·is·m /'siːkɪzəm/ *n* [U] the religion of the Sikhs

si·lage /'saɪlɪdʒ/ *n* [U] grass or other plants cut and stored so that they can be used as winter food for cattle

si·lence¹ [W2] /'saɪləns/ *n*
1 NO NOISE [U] complete absence of sound or noise; ▣ **quiet**: [+**of**] *Nothing disturbed the silence of the night.* | **silence falls/descends (on/upon sth)** *After the explosion, an eerie silence fell upon the scene.* | **break/shatter the silence** *A loud scream shattered the silence.*
2 NO TALKING [C,U] complete quiet because nobody is talking: *There was a* **brief silence** *before anyone answered.* | **in silence** *The four men sat in silence.* | **complete/total/dead silence** *'How long have you been here?' I asked. There was complete silence.* | *'Silence in court!' roared the judge.* | **embarrassed/awkward/stunned etc silence** *There was an awkward silence between them.* | *The accused exercised his* **right to silence** (=the legal right to choose to say nothing).
3 NO DISCUSSION/ANSWER [U] failure or refusal to discuss something or answer questions about something: [+**on**] *The government's silence on such an important issue seems very strange.* | *Once again the answer was a* **deafening silence** (=a very noticeable refusal to discuss something).
4 NO COMMUNICATION [U] failure to write a letter to someone, telephone them etc: *After two years of silence he suddenly got in touch with us again.*
5 **one-minute/two-minute etc silence** a period of time in which everyone stops talking as a sign of honour and respect towards someone who has died

silence² *v* [T] **1** to make someone stop talking, or stop something making a noise: *She held up her hand to silence the children.* **2** to make someone stop expressing opposition or criticisms – used especially in news reports: *attempts to silence the rumours* | *Barnes has failed to silence his critics.*

si·lenc·er /'saɪlənsə $ -sər/ *n* [C] **1** *BrE* a piece of equipment that is connected to the EXHAUST of a vehicle to make its engine quieter; ▣ **muffler** *AmE* **2** a thing that is put on the end of a gun so that it makes less noise when it is fired

si·lent [W3] /'saɪlənt/ *adj*
1 NOT SPEAKING **a)** not saying anything: *Alan was silent.* | **remain/stay/keep silent** *She kept silent, forcing Buchanan to continue.* | *The crowd* **fell silent** (=became silent) *when the President appeared.* **b)** [only before noun] not talking much to other people: **the strong silent type** (=a man who looks strong and does not talk very much)
2 NOT COMMUNICATING failing or refusing to talk about something or express an opinion: [+**on/about**] *The report was silent on the subject.*
3 QUIET without any sound, or not making any sound: *The large house was silent and lonely.* | *At last the guns* **fell silent.** | *Julie offered up a silent prayer that she would pass her exam.* | **as silent as the grave** (=completely silent in a mysterious or uncomfortable way)
4 FILMS [only before noun] a silent film has pictures but no sound
5 LETTER a silent letter in a word is not pronounced: *The 'w' in 'wreck' is silent.* —**silently** *adv*: *He sat silently by the bed.*

,silent ma'jority *n* **the silent majority** the ordinary people in a country, who are not active politically and who do not make their opinions known

,silent 'partner *n* [C] *AmE* someone who owns part of a business but is not actively involved in the way it operates; ▣ **sleeping partner** *BrE*

sil·hou·ette /ˌsɪluˈet/
n **1** [C,U] a dark image, shadow, or shape that you see against a light background: [+of] *a dark silhouette of domes and minarets* | [+against] *Soon the bombers would return, black silhouettes against a pale sky.* | **in silhouette** *The old windmill stood out in silhouette.* **2** [C,U] a drawing of something or someone, often from the side, showing a black shape against a light background: *silhouette pictures of snowmen and reindeer* | **in silhouette** *a picture of Mozart in silhouette* **3** [C] the particular shape certain clothes give you: *Fitted clothes often give the neatest silhouettes.* —**silhouetted** *adj*: *tall chimney stacks silhouetted against the orange flames*

sil·i·ca /ˈsɪlɪkə/ *n* [U] a chemical COMPOUND that exists naturally as sand, QUARTZ, and FLINT, used in making glass

sil·i·cate /ˈsɪlɪkeɪt, -kⁱt/ *n* [C,U] *technical* one of a group of common solid mineral substances that exist naturally in the Earth

sil·i·con /ˈsɪlɪkən/ *n* [U] a chemical substance that exists as a solid or as a powder and is used to make glass, bricks, and parts for computers. It is a chemical ELEMENT: symbol Si

silicon ˈchip *n* [C] a computer CHIP

sil·i·cone /ˈsɪlⁱkəʊn $ -koʊn/ *n* [U] a chemical that is not changed by heat or cold, does not let water through, and is used in making artificial body parts, paint, and rubber

silicone ˈimplant *n* [C] a piece of silicone that is put into the body, especially into a woman's breasts to make them larger

silk /sɪlk/ *n* **1** [U] a thin smooth soft cloth made from very thin thread which is produced by a silkworm: *pure silk stockings* | *a beautiful dress in raw silk* → see picture at MATERIAL¹ **2** [C] *BrE law* a very important lawyer; ☐ **Queen's Counsel (QC)**: *His practice quickly grew and he took silk* (=became a QC) *in 1988.* **3 silks** *technical* the coloured shirts worn by JOCKEYS (=people who ride horses in races) **4 make a silk purse out of a sow's ear** to make something good out of something that is bad quality

silk·en /ˈsɪlkən/ *adj* [usually before noun] *literary* **1** soft, smooth, and shiny like silk: *her silken hair* **2** made of silk: *a silken handkerchief*

ˈsilk screen *n* [only before noun] silk screen prints are made by forcing paint or ink onto a surface through a stretched piece of cloth —**silk screen** *n* [C]

silk·worm /ˈsɪlkwɜːm $ -wɜːrm/ *n* [C] a type of CATERPILLAR which produces silk thread

silk·y /ˈsɪlki/ *adj* **1** soft, smooth, and shiny like silk: *silky fur* **2** [only before noun] made of silk: *the silky fabric of her dress* **3** a silky voice is gentle, and is used especially when trying to persuade someone to do something —**silkily** *adv* —**silkiness** *n* [U]

sill /sɪl/ *n* [C] **1** the narrow shelf at the base of a window frame **2** the part of a car frame at the bottom of the doors

sil·la·bub /ˈsɪləbʌb/ *n* SYLLABUB

sil·ly¹ [S3] /ˈsɪli/ *adj comparative* **sillier**, *superlative* **silliest**
1 not sensible, or showing bad judgment: *Stop asking silly questions.* | *You made a lot of silly mistakes.* | *I left my keys at home, which was a pretty silly thing to do.* | *'Shall we go for a walk?' ' Don't be silly, it's dark.'*
2 stupid in a CHILDISH or embarrassing way: *I feel so silly in this outfit.* | *a silly hat* | *I hate their parties – we always end up playing silly games.*
3 *spoken* not serious or practical: *They served us coffee in these silly little cups.*

4 bore sb silly *informal* to make someone extremely bored
5 drink/scare/laugh etc yourself silly *informal* to drink or laugh etc so much that you stop behaving sensibly —**silliness** *n* [U]

silly² *n spoken* used to tell someone that you think they are not behaving sensibly: *No, silly, I didn't mean that.*

ˈsilly ˌbilly *n plural* **silly billies** [C] *especially BrE spoken* used to tell someone, especially a child, that they are behaving in a silly way

ˈsilly ˌseason *n* **the silly season** *BrE informal* a period in the summer when newspapers print stories that are not very serious because there is not much political news

si·lo /ˈsaɪləʊ $ -loʊ/ *n plural* **silos** [C] **1** a tall structure like a tower that is used for storing grain, winter food for farm animals etc **2** a large structure under the ground from which a large MISSILE can be fired

silt¹ /sɪlt/ *n* [U] sand, mud, soil etc that is carried in water and then settles at a bend in a river, an entrance to a port etc

silt² *v*

silt up *phr v* if something silts up or is silted up, it becomes filled with silt: *The old harbour silted up years ago.*

sil·van /ˈsɪlvən/ *adj* SYLVAN

sil·ver¹ [S3] /ˈsɪlvə $ -ər/ *n*
1 [U] a valuable shiny, light grey metal that is used to make jewellery, knives, coins etc. It is a chemical ELEMENT: symbol Ag: *a silver necklace* | *cups made of solid silver* → see picture at MATERIAL¹
2 [U] spoons, forks, dishes etc that are made of silver; ☐ **silverware**: *It was my job to polish the silver.*
3 [C,U] the colour of silver: *The lake sparkled with shades of blue and silver.* | *This season's colours are rich golds and elegant silvers.*
4 [C,U] *informal* a SILVER MEDAL: *He won a silver at the last Olympics.*
5 [U] *BrE* coins that contain silver or are the colour of silver: *He put his hand into his pocket and brought out a handful of silver.*

silver² *adj* **1** made of silver: *a silver teapot* | *a silver coin* | *a solid silver brooch* **2** having the colour of silver: *an old man with silver hair* **3 on a silver platter** if something is given to you on a silver platter, you do not have to make any effort to get it: *He had a scholarship handed to him on a silver platter.* **4 silver bullet** *AmE* something that solves a difficult problem very quickly and easily: *There is no silver bullet for this problem.* → be born with a silver spoon in your mouth at BORN² (8); → every cloud has a silver lining at CLOUD¹ (6)

silver³ *v* [T] **1** *technical* to cover a surface with a thin shiny layer of silver or another metal in order to make a mirror **2** *literary* to make something shine and look the colour of silver: *The farmhouse appeared, silvered by the moon.*

ˌsilver anniˈversary *n* [C] SILVER WEDDING ANNIVERSARY

ˌsilver ˈbirch *n* [C,U] a type of tree that has a smooth silvery-white TRUNK and branches

ˌsilver ˈdollar *n* [C] a one dollar coin that was used in the US in the past

sil·ver·fish /ˈsɪlvəfɪʃ $ -ər-/ *n plural* **silverfish** *or* **silverfishes** [C] a small silver-coloured insect that cannot fly and is found in houses

ˌsilver ˈfoil *n* [U] *BrE* FOIL

ˌsilver ˈjubilee *n* [C] *especially BrE* the date that is exactly 25 years after the date when something important happened, especially when someone became king or queen: *the Queen's Silver Jubilee*

ˌsilver ˈmedal *n* [C] a MEDAL made of silver that is given to the person who finishes second in a race or competition —**silver medallist** *n* [C]

S

were obviously sincere in their beliefs. | *I wasn't sure that he was sincere in what he was saying.*

sin·cere·ly /sɪn'sɪəli $ -'sɪr-/ *adv* **1** if you feel or believe something sincerely, you really feel or believe it and are not just pretending; ▣ **truly**: *I sincerely hope I'll see her again.* | *We are sincerely grateful for your help.* **2 (yours) sincerely** an expression used to end a formal letter, especially one that you have begun by using someone's name

sin·cer·i·ty /sɪn'serᵻti/ *n* [U] when someone is sincere and really means what they are saying: *I don't doubt her sincerity, but I think she's got her facts wrong.* | *May I say in all sincerity that we could not have achieved this much without your help and support.*

sine /saɪn/ *n* [C] *technical* the FRACTION (2) calculated for an angle by dividing the length of the side opposite it in a TRIANGLE that has a RIGHT ANGLE, by the length of the the side opposite the right angle → COSINE, TANGENT

si·ne·cure /'saɪnɪkjʊə, 'sɪn- $ -kjʊr/ *n* [C] *formal* a job which you get paid for even though you do not have to do very much work

si·ne qua non /ˌsɪni kwɑː 'nəʊn $ -'nɑːn/ *n* [singular] *formal* something that you must have, or which must exist, before something else can happen: [+for/of] *The control of inflation is a sine qua non for economic stability.*

sin·ew /'sɪnjuː/ *n* [C,U] **1** a part of your body that connects a muscle to a bone: *The sinews on his neck stood out like knotted string.* **2 the sinews of sth** *literary* something that gives strength or support to a government, country, or system: *They have begun building the sinews of an independent nation.*

sin·ew·y /'sɪnjuːi/ *adj* a sinewy person has a thin body and strong muscles: *a big man with long, sinewy arms*

sin·ful /'sɪnfəl/ *adj* **1** against religious rules, or doing something that is against religious rules; → **wicked**: *Dancing was believed to be sinful.* | *a wicked, sinful man* **2** very wrong or bad: *a sinful waste of taxpayers' money* —**sinfully** *adv*

sing ⓢ1 ⓦ2 /sɪŋ/ *v past tense* **sang** /sæŋ/, *past participle* **sung** /sʌŋ/
1 WITH YOUR VOICE [I,T] to produce a musical sound with your voice: *She can sing beautifully.* | *Most children enjoy singing.* | *We had a great time singing some of the old songs.* | [+to] *My mother used to sing to me when I was young.* | *He was singing to himself quietly.* | **sing sb sth** *Come on, sing us a song!* | *I've never been able to sing in tune* (=sing the correct notes). | *She patiently sang the baby to sleep.* → SINGING
2 BIRDS [I] if birds sing, they produce high musical sounds: *I could hear the birds singing outside my window.*
3 HIGH NOISE [I always + adv/prep] to make a high whistling sound: *A kettle was singing on the stove.* | [+past] *A bullet sang past my ear.*
4 sing sb's praises to praise someone very much: *Mrs Edwards was singing your praises today.*
5 sing a different tune to say something different from what you said before: *You're singing a different tune now!*
6 be singing from the same hymn sheet/book used to say that a group of people all have the same aims or all express the same opinion on a particular subject: *Union representatives are all singing from the same hymn sheet on the issue of pay.*
7 GIVE INFORMATION [I] *informal* to tell people everything you know about a crime when they ask you questions about it – used especially by criminals and the police: *I think he'll sing.*

sing along *phr v*
to sing with someone else who is already singing: *Sing along if you know the words.* | [+to] *Jess was singing along to the radio.*

sing out *phr v*
1 sing out (sth) to shout or sing some words clearly and loudly: *'Freeze!' a shrill voice sang out.*
2 *AmE* to sing loudly so that people can hear you easily

sing up *phr v BrE*
to sing more loudly: *Sing up, boys, I can't hear you!*

sing·a·long /'sɪŋəlɒŋ $ -lɒːŋ/ *n* [C] an informal occasion when people sing songs together; ▣ **singsong** *BrE*

singe¹ /sɪndʒ/ *v* **singed**, **singeing** [I,T] to burn the surface of something slightly, or to be burned slightly: *The flames had singed her hair.*

singe² *n* [C] a mark on the surface of something where it has been burnt slightly

sing·er ⓢ3 /'sɪŋə $ -ər/ *n* [C] someone who sings: **pop/opera/folk etc singer** *her favourite pop singer* | *a famous Italian opera singer* | *the lead singer* (=main singer) *of Slade* | *Tina Turner's backing singers* (=people who sing with her)

singer-'songwriter *n* [C] someone who writes songs and sings them

sing·ing /'sɪŋɪŋ/ *n* [U] the activity of producing musical sounds with your voice: *He entered the Royal College of Music to study singing.*

sin·gle¹ ⓢ2 ⓦ1 /'sɪŋɡəl/ *adj*
1 ONE [only before noun] only one: *A single tree gave shade from the sun.* | *They won the game by a single point.* | *the highest price ever paid for a single work of art* | *a single-sex school* (=one for only boys or girls)
2 every single used to emphasize that you are talking about every person or thing: *Don't write down every single word I say.* | *He works every single day.*
3 not a single no people or things at all: *The plane was brought down safely and not a single passenger was killed.* | *We didn't get a single reply to the advertisement.*
4 the single biggest/greatest etc used to emphasize that you are talking about the one thing that is the biggest, greatest etc: *Cigarette smoking is the single most important cause of lung cancer.* | *Tourism is the country's single biggest earner.*
5 NOT MARRIED not married, or not involved in a romantic relationship with anyone: *The changes in tax rates will benefit single people the most.* | *Is he single?*
6 single bed/room etc a bed, room etc that is meant to be used by one person only: *You have to pay extra for a single room.* → DOUBLE¹ (4); → see picture at BED
7 TICKET *BrE* a single ticket etc is for a trip from one place to another but not back again; ▣ **one-way**; → **return**, **round-trip**

single² *n* [C]
1 MUSIC a CD that has only one song on it, not a number of songs, or a song which is sold in this way: *Have you heard their latest single?*
2 SPORT a) one RUN² in a game of CRICKET b) a hit that allows the person who is hitting the ball to reach first BASE in a game of baseball
3 TENNIS singles [U] a game, especially in tennis, in which one person plays on their own against another person: *I prefer playing singles.* | *Who won the women's singles?* → doubles at DOUBLE² (3)
4 NOT MARRIED singles [plural] people who are not married and are not involved in a romantic relationship with anyone: *The show is especially popular among young singles.* | *a singles night at the club*
5 TICKET *BrE* a ticket for a trip from one place to another but not back again; → **return**: *A single to Oxford, please.*
6 MONEY *AmE* a piece of paper money worth one dollar: *Anybody have five singles?*
7 ROOM a room in a hotel for just one person: *I'm afraid we haven't got any singles available.*

single³ *v*

single sb/sth ⇔ **out** *phr v* to choose one person or thing from among a group because they are better, worse, more important etc than the others: [+for] *I don't see why he should be singled out for special treatment.* | [+as] *One programme was singled out as being particularly good.*

single-'breasted adj a single-breasted jacket or suit has only one set of buttons down the front → DOUBLE-BREASTED

single 'combat n [U] when one person, usually a soldier, fights against one other person: *He had already defeated an enemy champion in single combat.*

single 'cream n [U] *BrE* thin cream that you can pour easily → DOUBLE CREAM, HEAVY CREAM

single 'currency n [singular] a unit of money that is shared by several different countries: *Europe is moving steadily towards a single currency.*

single-'decker also **single decker** n [C] *BrE* a bus with only one level → DOUBLE-DECKER (1) —**single-decker** adj [only before noun]: *a single-decker bus*

single 'figures n [plural] a number below 10: **in single figures** *Interest rates have stayed in single figures for over a year now.* | *The number of cases of the disease is now down to single figures.*

single 'file n **in single file** moving in a line, with one person behind another: *We walked in single file across the bridge.* —**single file** adv

single-'handedly also **single-'handed** adv if one person does something single-handedly, they do it without help from anyone else: *She brought up three children single-handedly.* —**single-handed** adj [only before noun]: *a single-handed voyage across the Atlantic*

single 'honours n [U] a university degree course in Britain in which you study only one main subject → JOINT HONOURS

single 'market n **the single market** a group of countries in Europe that allow goods to be moved, bought, and sold between them with very few controls

single-'minded adj someone who is single-minded has one clear aim and works very hard to achieve it: *a tough, single-minded lady* | *He worked with single-minded determination.* —**single-mindedly** adv —**single-mindedness** n [U]

sin·gle·ness /'sɪŋɡəlnɪs/ n formal **singleness of purpose** great determination when you are working to achieve something

single 'parent n [C] a mother or father who looks after their children on their own, without a partner; ☒ **lone parent**

sin·glet /'sɪŋɡlət/ n [C] *BrE* a piece of clothing that you wear for sport which covers the top part of your body but not your arms

single track 'road n [C] *BrE* a road that is only wide enough for one car to go along it

sin·gly /'sɪŋɡli/ adv alone, or one at a time: *Plant the trees singly or in small groups.*

sing·song /'sɪŋsɒŋ $ -sɒːŋ/ n **1** [singular] a way of speaking in which your voice keeps rising and falling: *I recognized her soft singsong immediately.* **2** [C] *BrE* an informal occasion when people sing songs together; ☒ **singalong** *AmE*: *We had a bit of a singsong later.* —**singsong** adj: *a singsong voice*

sin·gu·lar¹ /'sɪŋɡjʊlə $ -ər/ adj **1** a singular noun, verb, form etc is used when writing or speaking about one person or thing; → **plural**: *the singular form of the noun* | *If the subject is singular, use a singular verb.* **2** [usually before noun] formal very great or very noticeable: *He showed a singular lack of tact in the way he handled the situation.* | *a singular achievement* **3** literary very unusual or strange: *I wondered why she was behaving in so singular a fashion.*

singular² n **the singular** the form of a word used when writing or speaking about one person or thing; → **plural**: *'Datum' is the singular of 'data'.* | **in the singular** *Should the verb be in the singular or the plural?*

sin·gu·lar·i·ty /ˌsɪŋɡjʊˈlærɪti/ n plural **singularities 1** [C] technical an extremely small point in space that contains an extremely large amount of material and which does not obey the usual laws of nature, for example a BLACK HOLE or the point at the beginning of the universe **2** [U] old-fashioned the quality of

something that makes it unusual or strange: *He had an attractive singularity of viewpoint.*

sin·gu·lar·ly /'sɪŋɡjʊləli $ -lərli/ adv formal in a way that is very noticeable or unusual: *a singularly foolish plan* | *He has singularly failed to live up to his promises.*

Sin·ha·lese /ˌsɪnhəˈliːz/ n plural **Sinhalese 1** [C] someone who belongs to the race of people that forms the largest part of the population in Sri Lanka **2** [U] the language used by the Sinhalese —**Sinhalese** adj

sin·is·ter /'sɪnɪstə $ -ər/ adj making you feel that something evil, dangerous, or illegal is happening or will happen: **there is something/nothing sinister about sb/sth** *There was something sinister about Mr Scott's death.* | *There is a sinister side to these events.* | *He was a handsome man in a sinister sort of way.* | *a sinister atmosphere*

sink¹ W3 /sɪŋk/ v past tense **sank** /sæŋk/ past participle **sunk** /sʌŋk/
1 IN WATER [I] to go down below the surface of water, mud etc; ☒ **float**: *Their motorboat struck a rock and began to sink.* | *The kids watched as the coin **sank to the bottom** of the pool.* | *The heavy guns sank up to their barrels in the mud.*
2 BOAT [T] to damage a ship so badly that it sinks: *A luxury yacht was sunk in a bomb attack yesterday.*
3 MOVE LOWER [I] to move downwards to a lower level: *The sun was sinking behind the coconut palms.* | *Her chin sank onto her chest, and she looked despairing.*
4 FALL/SIT DOWN [I] to fall down or sit down heavily, especially because you are very tired and weak: [+into/to/down/back etc] *She let out a groan and sank into a chair.* | *He let go of her shoulders and sank at once to the floor.* | *Marion sank down on a rock, and wept.* | *The minister **sank to his knees** (=he went down into a kneeling position) and prayed.*
5 GET WORSE [I always + adv/prep] to gradually get into a worse condition: [+into] *They lost all their money and sank into desperate poverty.* | *The good mood left me and I sank into depression.* | *The doctor said that the boy was **sinking fast** (=getting weaker and about to die).*
6 your heart sinks also **your spirits sink** used to say that you lose hope or confidence: *His heart sank the way it always did when she left him.* | *She felt desperately tired, and her spirits sank.*
7 LOWER AMOUNT/VALUE [I] to go down in amount or value; ☒ **drop**; ☒ **rise**: *Shares in the company have sunk as low as 620p.* | [+to] *The population of the village sank to just a few families.*
8 VOICE [I] written if your voice sinks, it becomes very quiet: [+to/into] *Her voice sank to a whisper.*
9 sinking feeling informal the unpleasant feeling that you get when you suddenly realize that something bad is going to happen: *I had a sinking feeling inside as I realized I was going to fail yet again.*
10 be sunk spoken to be in a situation where you are certain to fail or have a lot of problems: *If I don't get paid by next week, I'll really be sunk.*
11 sink without trace especially BrE also **sink like a stone** especially AmE if something sinks without trace, it fails quickly or no one pays attention to it: *He made a few records which all sank without trace.*
12 sink so low also **sink to doing sth** to be dishonest enough or SELFISH enough to do something very bad or unfair; ☒ **stoop**: *How could he have sunk so low?*
13 USE SOMETHING SHARP [T] to put your teeth or something sharp into someone's flesh, into food etc: **sink sth into sth** *The dog **sank its teeth** into my arm.* | *She sank her fork into the pie.*
14 DIG INTO GROUND [T] if you sink something such as a well or part of a building, you dig a hole to put it into the ground: *A **well** was **sunk** in the back garden, and water could be pumped up into the kitchen.*
15 sink or swim to succeed or fail without help from anyone else: *They don't give you a lot of guidance –*

S

you're just left to sink or swim, really.
16 MONEY [T] to spend a lot of money on something: **sink sth in/into sth** *They sank their entire savings into their house.*
17 BALL [T] to put a ball into a hole or BASKET in games such as GOLF or BASKETBALL
18 sink your differences *BrE* to agree to stop arguing and forget about your disagreements, especially in order to unite and oppose someone else: *Nations must sink their differences to achieve greater security.*
19 DRINK [T] *BrE informal* to drink alcohol, especially in large quantities: *We sank a few pints at the pub first.*
sink in *phr v*
if information, facts etc sink in, you gradually understand them or realize their full meaning: *He paused a moment for his words to sink in.* | *The implications of Labour's defeat were beginning to sink in.*

sink² *n* [C] a large open container that you fill with water and use for washing yourself, washing dishes etc; → **basin**: *Dirty plates were piled high in the sink.* → **everything but the kitchen sink** at EVERYTHING (7); → see picture at EAT

sink³ *adj* **sink estate/school** *BrE* an area where people live or a school that is in a very bad condition and seems unlikely to improve: *Go to almost any city and you find sink estates where you get the feeling that the council hates the place and the people too.*

sink·er /'sɪŋkə $ -ər/ → **hook, line and sinker** at HOOK¹ (9)

ˈsinking ˌfund *n* [C] *technical* money saved regularly by a business to pay for something in the future

sin·ner /'sɪnə $ -ər/ *n* [C] *especially biblical* someone who has SINNED by not obeying God's laws

Sino- /saɪnəʊ $ -noʊ/ *prefix* [in nouns and adjectives] **1** Chinese and something else: *Sino-Japanese trade* **2** relating to China: *a sinologist* (=someone who studies Chinese culture, language, history etc)

sin·u·ous /'sɪnjuəs/ *adj* **1** moving with smooth twists and turns, like a snake: *the sinuous grace of a cat* **2** with many smooth twists and turns: *They followed the sinuous trail deep into the mountains.* —**sinuously** *adv*

si·nus /'saɪnəs/ *n* [C] your sinuses are the spaces in the bones of your head that are connected to the inside of your nose: *blocked sinuses* | *a sinus infection*

si·nus·i·tis /ˌsaɪnə'saɪtᵻs/ *n* [U] a condition in which your sinuses swell up and become painful

sip¹ /sɪp/ *v* **sipped, sipping** [I,T] to drink something slowly, taking very small mouthfuls: *She was sitting at the table sipping her coffee.* | [+at] *He sipped at his wine with pleasure.*; → see picture at DRINK¹

sip² *n* [C] a very small amount of a drink: [+of] *a sip of water* | *She poured more wine and took a sip.*

si·phon¹ also **syphon** *BrE* /'saɪfən/ *n* [C] **1** a bent tube used for getting liquid out of a container, used by holding one end of the tube at a lower level than the end in the container **2** also **soda siphon** a type of bottle for holding SODA WATER, which is forced out of the bottle using gas pressure

siphon² also **syphon** *BrE* *v* [T always + adv/prep] **1** also **siphon sth ⇔ off/out** to remove liquid from a container by using a siphon: *It took him only a few minutes to siphon off the petrol and drive away.* | **siphon sth out of/from sth** *Crews began siphoning oil from the leaking boat.* **2** also **siphon sth ⇔ off** to dishonestly take money from a business, account etc to use it for a purpose for which it was not intended: *Emergency aid was siphoned off by foreign ministry officials for their own use.* | **siphon sth from sth** *I found she had siphoned thousands of dollars from our bank account.*

ˈsipping lid *n* [C] a plastic cover with a small hole in it that you put on a cup of coffee, tea etc, so that you can drink from the cup while walking, travelling etc

sir W3 /sə; *strong* sɜː $ sər; *strong* sɜːr/ *n*
1 *spoken* used when speaking to a man in order to be polite or show respect: *'Report back to me in an hour, sergeant.' 'Yes, sir.'* | *Can I help you, sir?* | *Sir! You dropped your wallet.* → MADAM (1) *BrE* → MA'AM *AmE*
2 Dear Sir/Sirs used at the beginning of a formal letter to a man or to people you do not know
3 Sir a title used before the first name of a KNIGHT or BARONET: *Sir Paul McCartney* | *Sir Jasper*
4 *BrE spoken* used by children at school when speaking to or talking about a male teacher: *Sir, I've forgotten my homework.* | *Look out – sir's coming back!* → MISS² (4)
5 no/yes sir! also **no/yes siree!** *especially AmE old-fashioned spoken* used to emphasize a statement or an answer to a question: *I will not have that man in my home, no sir!*

sire¹ /saɪə $ saɪr/ *n* **1** *old use* used when speaking to a king: *The people await you, sire.* **2** [C usually singular] the father of a four-legged animal, especially a horse

sire² *v* [T] **1** to be the father of an animal, especially a horse or dog: *a stallion that has sired several race winners* **2** *old-fashioned* to be the father of a child: *Sam sired eight children.*

si·ren /'saɪərən $ 'saɪr-/ *n* [C] **1** a piece of equipment that makes very loud warning sounds, used on police cars, fire engines etc: *the wail of the ambulance sirens* | *I heard police sirens in the distance.* **2 siren voices/song/call** *literary* encouragement to do something that seems very good, especially when this could have bad results: *siren voices calling for the sale of weapons to the region* **3** a woman who is very attractive but also dangerous to men – used especially in newspapers: *a Hollywood siren* **4 the Sirens** a group of women in ancient Greek stories, whose beautiful singing made sailors sail towards them into dangerous water

sir·loin /'sɜːlɔɪn $ 'sɜːr-/ also **ˌsirloin 'steak** *n* [C,U] a good quality piece of BEEF which is cut from the lower part of a cow's back

si·roc·co /sɪ'rɒkəʊ $ -'rɑːkoʊ/ *n plural* **siroccos** [C] a hot wind that blows from the desert of North Africa across to southern Europe

sis /sɪs/ *n spoken, informal* a name used when speaking to your sister

si·sal /'saɪsəl/ *n* [U] a Central American plant whose leaves produce strong FIBRES, also called sisal, which are used in making rope

sis·sy, cissy /'sɪsi/ *n* [C] *informal not polite* a boy that other boys dislike because he prefers doing things that girls enjoy: *He wanted to go to dance classes, but he was afraid the other boys would call him a sissy.* —**sissy** *adj*

sis·ter S1 W1 /'sɪstə $ -ər/ *n* [C]
1 a girl or woman who has the same parents as you; → **brother, half-sister, step-sister**: *Janet and Abby are sisters.* | *He has two sisters and a brother.* | **older/big sister** *My older sister is a nurse.* | **younger/little sister** *Where's your little sister?* | *She's my twin sister.*
2 sister paper/publication/company etc a newspaper etc that belongs to the same group or organization: *the Daily Post's sister paper, the Liverpool Echo*
3 also **Sister** a NUN: *Good morning, Sister Mary.*
4 *BrE* also **Sister** a nurse in charge of a hospital WARD: *the ward sister* | *I'm feeling a bit better today, Sister.*
5 a word used by women to talk about other women and to show that they have feelings of friendship and support towards them: *We appeal to our sisters all over the world to stand by us.*
6 *AmE spoken* a way of talking to or about an African-American woman, used especially by African Americans

sis·ter·hood /'sɪstəhʊd $ -ər-/ *n* **1** [U] a special loyal relationship among women who share the same ideas and aims, especially among FEMINISTS : *the special bond of sisterhood that joins women together* **2** [C] a group of women who live a religious life together: *the Christian sisterhood*

'sister-in-ˌlaw *n plural* **sisters-in-law** [C] **1** the sister of your husband or wife **2** your brother's wife **3** the wife of the brother of your husband or wife

sis·ter·ly /'sɪstəli $ -ər-/ *adj* typical of a loving sister: *She gave Lee a sisterly kiss.* | *Their friendship can best be described as sisterly.*

sit S1 W1 /sɪt/ *v past tense and past participle* **sat** /sæt/, *present participle* **sitting**

1 IN A CHAIR ETC **a)** also **be sitting down** [I] to be on a chair or seat, or on the ground, with the top half of your body upright and your weight resting on your BUTTOCKS: [+on/in/by etc] *I sat on the shore and looked at the sea.* | *She was sitting in a chair by the fire.* | *She's the girl who sits next to me at school.* | *In the driving seat sat a man of average height.* | **sit at a desk/table etc** (=sit facing it) *Jean sat at the table writing a letter.* | **sit doing sth** *They sat sipping their drinks.* | *We used to* **sit and** *listen to her for hours.* | *She wandered round all morning, unable to* **sit still.** | *She was* **sitting upright** *in her chair.* | *He was* **sitting cross-legged** *on the floor.* **b)** also **sit down** [I always + adv/prep] to get into a sitting position somewhere after you have been standing up: *He came over and sat beside her.* | *Sam sat opposite her and accepted a cigarette.* **c)** also **sit sb down** [T always + adv/prep] to make someone sit or help them to sit: **sit sb on/in etc sth** *I gently led her to the chair and sat her on it.*

2 OBJECTS/BUILDINGS ETC [I always + adv/prep] to be in a particular position or condition: [+on/in etc] *a little church sitting on a hillside* | *The parliament building sits in a large square.* | *He's got a computer sitting on his desk, but he doesn't use it.* | *My climbing boots were sitting unused in a cupboard.* | *The house has* **sat empty** *for two years.*

3 DO NOTHING [I always + adv/prep] to stay in one place for a long time, especially sitting down, doing nothing useful or helpful: *I spent half the morning sitting in a traffic jam.* | *Well, I can't* **sit here** *chatting all day.* | *Are you just going to* **sit there** *complaining?*

4 COMMITTEE/PARLIAMENT ETC [I] to be a member of a committee, parliament, or other official group: [+in/on] *They both sat on the management committee.* | *He was the first journalist to sit in parliament.*

5 MEETING [I] to have a meeting in order to carry out official business: *The council only sits once a month.* | *The court will sit until all the evidence has been heard.*

6 ANIMAL/BIRD [I always + adv/prep] **a)** to be in, or get into, a resting position, with the tail end of the body resting on a surface: *The cat likes to sit on the wall outside the kitchen.* **b)** Sit! used to tell a dog to sit with the tail end of its body resting on the ground or floor **c)** if a bird sits on its eggs, it covers them with its body to make the eggs HATCH

7 LOOK AFTER [I + for] to look after a baby or child while its parents are out; ⊟ **babysit**

8 sit tight *spoken* **a)** to stay where you are and not move: *Just sit tight – I'll be there in five minutes.* **b)** to stay in the same situation, and not change your mind and do anything new: *We're advising all our investors to sit tight till the market improves.*

9 be sitting pretty to be in a very good or favourable position: *We've paid off the mortgage, so we're sitting pretty now.*

10 sit in judgment (on/over sb) to give your opinion about whether someone has done something wrong, especially when you have no right to do this: *How can you sit in judgement on somebody you hardly know?*

11 not sit well/easily/comfortably (with sb) if a situation, plan etc does not sit well with someone, they do not like it: *He had never before been accused of stealing, and it did not sit well with him.*

12 sit on the fence to avoid saying which side of an argument you support or what your opinion is about a particular subject: *The weakness of the book is that it sits on the fence on important issues.*

13 sit on your hands to delay taking action when you should do something: *Workers are losing their jobs while the government sits on its hands and does nothing.*

14 EXAMS [I,T] *BrE* to take an examination: *Tracy's sitting her GCSEs this year.* | [+for] *They were preparing children to sit for the entry examination.*

15 PICTURE/PHOTO [I] to sit somewhere so that you can be painted or photographed: [+for] *She sat for* (=was painted by) *Holman Hunt and Millais.*

sit around also **sit about** *BrE phr v*
to spend a lot of time sitting and doing nothing very useful: *We sat around for a bit, chatting.*

sit back *phr v*
1 to get into a comfortable position, for example in a chair, and relax: *Sit back and relax - I'll open a bottle of wine.*
2 to relax and make no effort to get involved in something or influence what happens: *Don't just sit back and wait for new business to come to you.*

sit by *phr v*
to allow something wrong or illegal to happen without doing anything about it: *I'm not going to sit by and watch a man go to prison for something I've done.*

sit down *phr v*
1 to be in a sitting position or get into a sitting position: *It was good to be sitting down eating dinner with my family.* | *Sit down, Amy – you look tired.* | **sit yourself down** *Sit yourself down and have a drink.*
2 sit sb down to make someone sit down or help them to sit down: [+in/on] *I helped her into the room and sat her down in an armchair.*
3 sit down and do sth to try to solve a problem or deal with something that needs to be done, by giving it all your attention: *The three of us need to sit down and have a talk.* | *Sit down and work out just what you spend.*

sit in *phr v*
to be present at a meeting but not take an active part in it: [+on] *Would you like to sit in on some of my interviews?*

sit in for sb *phr v*
to do a job, go to a meeting etc instead of the person who usually does it: *This is Alan James sitting in for Suzy Williams on the mid-morning show.*

sit on sth *phr v informal*
to delay dealing with something: *I sent my application about six weeks ago and they've just been sitting on it.*

sit sth ⇔ **out** *phr v*
1 to stay where you are and do nothing until something finishes, especially something boring or unpleasant: *She had two weeks to sit it out while she waited to hear if she had got the job.* | *She was prepared to sit out the years of Jack's jail sentence.*
2 to not take part in something, especially a game or dance, when you usually take part: *Johnson sat out the game with a shoulder injury.*

sit through sth *phr v*
to attend a meeting, performance etc, and stay until the end, even if it is very long and boring: *I wasn't the least bit interested in all the speeches I had to sit through.*

sit up *phr v*
1 to be in a sitting position or get into a sitting position after you have been lying down: *He was sitting up in bed, reading his book.* | *She sat up and reached for her glass.*
2 sit sb up to help someone to sit after they have been lying down: [+in/on etc] *I'll sit you up on the pillows and you'll be nice and comfortable.*
3 to sit in a chair with your back straight: *Just sit up straight and stop slouching.*
4 to stay up very late: *Sometimes we just sit up and watch videos all night.*
5 sit up (and take notice) to suddenly start paying attention to someone, because they have done something surprising or impressive: *If Maria succeeded, then everyone would sit up and take notice.*

WORD CHOICE: sit, sit down, sit in/on, seat
You usually use **sit down** rather than **sit** to say that someone moves into a sitting position: *Everyone sat*

S

down to listen.
You use **sit** when you mention where someone sits down: *She sat next to me.* | *Where shall I sit?*

⚠ You **sit on** or **sit in** a chair, depending on whether it is flat and simple or soft and comfortable: *We sat on barstools.* | *He sat in his favourite armchair.* You **sit on** flat things such as a bench, the floor, or the grass. You **sit in** a room, a corner, long grass, a tree, or a seat in a car: *I get travel sick when I sit in the back.*

⚠ To tell someone to sit down, say **'Sit down', 'Have a seat'**, or in very formal situations, **'Be seated'**. You usually only say **'Sit!'** to a dog.

sit·ar /'sɪtɑː $ -ɑːr/ *n* [C] a very long musical instrument from India similar to a GUITAR, with two sets of strings and a round body

sit·com /'sɪtkɒm $ -kɑːm/ *n* [C,U] *situation comedy* a funny television programme in which the same characters appear in different situations each week

'sit-down¹ *adj* **1** a sit-down meal or restaurant is one in which you sit at a table and eat a formal meal: *a sit-down meal for 20 people* **2 sit-down strike/protest** a protest in which people sit down, especially to block a road or other public place, until their demands are listened to; → **sit-in**

sit-down² *BrE n* [singular] if you have a sit-down, you sit and rest for a short while: *You look as if you need a sit-down.*

site¹ W2 /saɪt/ *n* [C]
1 a place where something important or interesting happened: *an archaeological site* | [+of] *The house is built on the site of a medieval prison.* | *the site of the air crash*
2 an area of ground where something is being built or will be built: [+of/for] *the site of a proposed missile base* | *a site for a new airport* | **building/construction site** *He managed to get himself a job on a building site.*
3 a place that is used for a particular purpose: *a camping site* | [+of/for] *a nesting site for birds*
4 a WEBSITE
5 on site at the place where people work, study, or stay: *There's a bar, restaurant, and gym on site.*

site² *v* [T usually passive] to place or build something in a particular place: **be sited in/on/at/near etc sth** *Some of this new housing has been sited in inner city areas.*

,site-spe'cific *adj* designed and made to to be used in a particular place, or relating to a particular place: *a site-specific policy*

'sit-in *n* [C] a type of protest in which people refuse to leave the place where they work or study until their demands are agreed to: **hold/stage a sit-in** *Several thousand students staged sit-ins and protest marches.*

sit·ter /'sɪtə $ -ər/ *n* [C] **1** *especially AmE* a BABYSIT-TER **2** someone who sits or stands while someone else paints them or takes photographs of them

sit·ting /'sɪtɪŋ/ *n* [C] **1** one of the times when a meal is served in a place where there is not enough space for everyone to eat at the same time: *School dinners are served in three sittings.* **2 at/in one sitting** during one continuous period when you are sitting in a chair: *I sat down and read the whole book in one sitting.* **3** an occasion when you have yourself painted or photographed **4** a meeting of a law court or parliament

,sitting 'duck also **,sitting 'target** *n* [C] someone who is easy to attack or easy to cheat: *Out in the open, the soldiers were sitting ducks for enemy fire.*

,sitting 'member *n* [C] *BrE* someone who is a member of a parliament at the present time: *the sitting member for Newbury*

'sitting room *n* [C] *especially BrE* the room in a house where you sit, relax, watch television etc; ◻ **living room**

,sitting 'tenant *n* [C] *BrE* someone who lives in a rented house or FLAT, especially when this gives them legal rights to stay there

sit·u /'sɪtju: $ 'saɪtu:/ → IN SITU

sit·u·ate /'sɪtʃueɪt/ *v* [T] *formal* to describe or consider something as being part of something else or related to something else: **situate sth in sth** *The women have the opportunity to situate their own struggles in a wider historical context.*

sit·u·at·ed /'sɪtʃueɪt̬ɪd/ *adj* **be situated** to be in a particular place or position; ◻ **located**: [+in/near/at etc] *The house is situated near the college.* | *a farm situated in the valley* | **conveniently/ideally/beautifully etc situated** *The hotel is ideally situated near the seafront.*

sit·u·a·tion S1 W1 /ˌsɪtʃu'eɪʃən/ *n* [C]
1 a combination of all the things that are happening and all the conditions that exist at a particular time in a particular place

> **in a ... situation**
> **difficult/dangerous/tricky etc situation**
> **impossible situation** (=one that is very difficult to deal with)
> **economic/political/financial etc situation**
> **present/current situation**
> **improve/remedy a situation**
> **assess/monitor/review a situation**
> **defuse a situation** (=stop a situation from being difficult or tense)
> **a situation arises** (=it happens)
> **a situation worsens/deteriorates/improves**
> **a no-win situation** (=a situation in which no one can get what they want)
> **a win-win situation** (=a situation in which everyone gets what they want)

I explained the situation. | **in a ... situation** *She coped well in a difficult situation.* | *Schoolchildren must be taught to deal with dangerous situations.* | *We were in an impossible situation – whatever we did, someone would be upset.* | *a long analysis of the political situation* | *I cannot put up with the current situation one day longer.* | *Some companies are taking measures to improve this situation.* | *The district judge had assessed the situation.* | *This situation has arisen as a result of our serious staffing shortages.* | *From that day onwards the situation worsened.*

2 the type of area where a building is situated – used especially by people who sell or advertise buildings; ◻ **location**: *The house is in a charming situation, on a wooded hillside.*
3 *old-fashioned* a job: *She managed to get a situation as a parlour maid.*

,situation 'comedy *n* [C,U] *formal* a SITCOM

'sit-up *BrE*; **sit-up** *AmE* /'sɪtʌp/ *n* [C] an exercise to make your stomach muscles strong in which you sit up from a lying position, while keeping your feet on the floor; → **crunch**: *Jerry says he does two hundred sit-ups a day.* → see picture at PRESS-UP

six /sɪks/ *number, noun* **1** the number 6: *six months ago* | *She arrived just after six* (=six o'clock). | *He learnt to play the violin when he was six* (=six years old). **2 six figures/digits** used to talk about a number that is between 100,000 and 1,000,000: *The final cost of the project will easily run into six figures* (=be over one hundred thousand pounds or dollars). **3 at sixes and sevens** *informal* disorganised and confused: *When the visitors arrived we were still at sixes and sevens.* **4 it's six of one and half a dozen of the other** *spoken* used to say that both people or groups who are involved in a situation are equally responsible for something bad that happens: *In any family quarrel, it's usually six of one and half a dozen of the other.* **5 knock/hit sb for six** *BrE spoken* to affect someone strongly in a bad way: *Losing his job really knocked him for six.* **6** [C] a hit in CRICKET that scores six RUNS because the ball crosses the edge of the playing area before touching the ground

,six-'figure *adj* [only before noun] used to describe a number that is 100,000 or more, especially an amount of money: *a six-figure sum* | *a six-figure salary*

six·fold /'sɪksfəʊld $ -foʊld/ *adv formal* by six times as much or as many: *Burglaries have increased sixfold.* —**sixfold** *adj: a sixfold increase in teenage pregnancies*

'six-pack *n* [C] **1** six cans or bottles of a drink, especially beer, sold together as a set: *There's a six-pack in the fridge.* | [+of] *a six-pack of beer* **2** well-developed muscles that you can see on a man's stomach – used humorously

six·pence /'sɪkspəns/ *n* [C,U] a small silver-coloured coin worth six old PENNIES, used in Britain in the past

'six-,shooter *n* [C] *old-fashioned especially AmE* a small gun that holds six bullets

six·teen /,sɪk'stiːn◂/ *number* the number 16: *sixteen years later* | *He moved to London when he was sixteen* (=sixteen years old). —**sixteenth** *adj, pron: her sixteenth birthday* | *the sixteenth century* | *Let's have dinner on the sixteenth* (=the sixteenth day of the month).

six·teenth /,sɪk'stiːnθ◂/ *n* [C] one of sixteen equal parts of something

'sixteenth ,note *n* [C] *AmE* a musical note which continues for a sixteenth of the length of a WHOLE NOTE; ▣ **semiquaver** *BrE*

sixth¹ /sɪksθ/ *adj* coming after five other things in a series: *her sixth birthday* | *the sixth century* —**sixth** *pron: Let's have dinner on the sixth* (=the sixth day of the month).

sixth² *n* [C] one of six equal parts of something: *About one sixth of the children admitted to taking drugs.*

'sixth form *n* [C] the highest level in the British school system. Children aged between 16 and 18 stay in the sixth form for two years while they prepare to take A LEVELS (=the highest level of school exams). —**sixth former** *n* [C]

'sixth form ,college *n* [C] a type of school in Britain for students who are preparing to take A LEVELS (=the highest level of school exams)

,sixth 'sense *n* [singular] a special ability to know things without using any of your five ordinary senses such as your hearing or sight: *He seemed to have a sixth sense for knowing when his brother was in trouble.*

six·ty /'sɪksti/ *number* **1** the number 60: *sixty years ago* **2 the sixties** [plural] also **the '60s, the 1960s** the years from 1960 to 1969: *The book was written in the sixties.* | **the early/late sixties** *the student riots in Paris in the late sixties* **3 be in your sixties** to be aged between 60 and 69: **early/mid/late sixties** *I'd say she was in her late sixties.* **4 in the sixties** if the temperature is in the sixties, it is between 60 degrees and 69 degrees: **in the low/mid/high sixties** *a fine spring day, with the temperatures in the low sixties* —**sixtieth** *adj, pron: her sixtieth birthday*

siz·a·ble /'saɪzəbəl/ *adj* another spelling of SIZEABLE

size¹ S1 W1 /saɪz/ *n*
1 HOW BIG [C,U] how big or small something is: *He's a small boy, about John's size.* | *Jensens' house is about the same size as ours.* | [+of] *The firm underestimated the size of the market for their new product.* | *I saw a spider the size of* (=the same size as) *my hand in the backyard.* | *He's quite a big dog, but he's still not full size yet.* | **in size** *The apartment is roughly 360 square feet in size.* | **(of) that/this size** (=as big as that or this) *In a class this size, there are bound to be a few trouble-makers.* | *We can't give loans of that size to just anyone.* | **in all/different/various (shapes and) sizes** *These phones come in all shapes and sizes.* | **good/fair/nice size** (=fairly big) *The breakfast room is a good size.*
2 VERY BIG [U] used to say that something is very big: [+of] *I can't believe the size of her car!* | *The sheer size of the classes makes learning difficult for students.*
3 CLOTHES/GOODS [C] one of a set of standard measures according to which clothes and other goods are produced and sold: *These shoes are one size too big.* | *The shirts come in three sizes: small, medium, and large.* | *Do you have these pants in a size 12?*

---

4 large-sized/medium-sized/pocket-size etc of a particular size, or about the same size and shape as something: *a medium-sized car* | *a pocket-size mirror* | **good-sized/fair-sized/decent-sized** (=big enough for a particular purpose)
5 do sth to size if you cut, make, or prepare something to size, you make it the right size for a particular use: *The materials will be provided, and everything is already cut to size.*
6 that's about the size of it *spoken* used to agree that someone's description of a situation is correct
7 PASTE [U] also **sizing** a thick sticky liquid used for giving stiffness and a shiny surface to cloth, paper etc, or used to prepare walls for WALLPAPER → **cut sb down to size** at CUT DOWN (6); → **try sth on for size** at TRY¹ (2)

size² *v* [T] **1** to sort things according to their size: *Shrimp are sized and selected for canning.* **2** [usually passive] to make something into a particular size or sizes: *Most costume patterns are sized for children.* **3** to put SIZE¹ (7) on a wall before decorating
size sth/sb ⇔ up *phr v* to look at or consider a person or situation and make a judgment about them: *It only took a few seconds for her to size up the situation.*

size·a·ble, sizable /'saɪzəbəl/ *adj* fairly large: **sizeable amount/number** *a sizeable amount of money* | **sizeable proportion/portion/minority (of sth)** *Part-time students make up a sizeable proportion of the college population.*

siz·zle /'sɪzəl/ *v* [I] to make a sound like water falling on hot metal: *The bacon began to sizzle in the pan.*

siz·zling /'sɪzəlɪŋ/ *adj especially AmE* **1** very hot; ▣ **boiling:** *a sizzling afternoon* **2** very exciting, especially in a sexual way: *a sizzling scandalous affair*

ska /skɑː/ *n* [U] a kind of popular music from the West Indies with a fast regular beat, similar to REGGAE

skag, scag /skæg/ *n* [U] *informal* HEROIN

skank /skæŋk/ *n* [U] *informal* HEROIN

skates

roller skates

skateboard

ice skates

in-line skates

skate¹ /skeɪt/ *n* **1** [C] one of a pair of boots with metal blades on the bottom, for moving quickly on ice; ▣ **ice skate 2** [C] one of a pair of boots or frames with small wheels on the bottom, for moving quickly on flat smooth surfaces; ▣ **roller skate 3** [C,U] *plural* **skate** or **skates** a large flat sea fish that can be eaten **4 get/put your skates on** *BrE spoken* used to tell someone to hurry: *Put your skates on, or you'll be late for school.*

skate² *v* [I] **1** to move on skates: *The children skated on the frozen pond.* **2 be skating on thin ice** *informal* to be doing something that may get you into trouble —**skater** *n* [C]
skate over/around sth *phr v* to avoid mentioning a

---

1 000, 2 000, 3 000, most frequent words in S poken and W ritten English

problem or subject, or not give it enough attention: *The President was accused of skating over the issue of the homeless.*

skate·board /'skeɪtbɔːd $ -bɔːrd/ *n* [C] a short board with two small wheels at each end, which you can stand on and ride for fun or as a sport —**skateboarding** *n* [U] —**skateboarder** *n* [C]; → see picture at SKATE¹

skat·ing /'skeɪtɪŋ/ *n* [U] the activity or sport of moving around on skates for fun or as a sport: *We went skating in Central Park.* → see picture at WINTER SPORTS

'skating ,rink *n* [C] a place or building where you can skate

ske·dad·dle /skɪ'dædl/ *v* [I] *spoken* to leave a place quickly, especially because you do not want to be caught – used humorously

skeet shoot·ing /'skiːt ,ʃuːtɪŋ/ *n* [U] *AmE* the sport of shooting at clay objects that have been thrown into the air; ⊟ **clay pigeon shooting** *BrE*

skeeve /skiːv/ *v AmE informal*
  skeeve sb out *phr v* to make someone feel sick or upset because they think something is unpleasant: *I hate touching raw meat. I just get skeeved out.*

skein /skeɪn/ *n* [C] **1** a long loosely wound piece of thread, wool, or YARN **2** *literary* a complicated series of things that are related to each other; ⊟ **web**: *a skein of lies*

skel·e·tal /'skelɪtəl/ *adj* **1** like a skeleton or relating to a skeleton: *Police discovered the **skeletal remains** of a corpse buried near the river.* **2** someone who is skeletal is so thin that you can see their bones through their skin: *prisoners whose clothes hung loosely on their skeletal bodies*

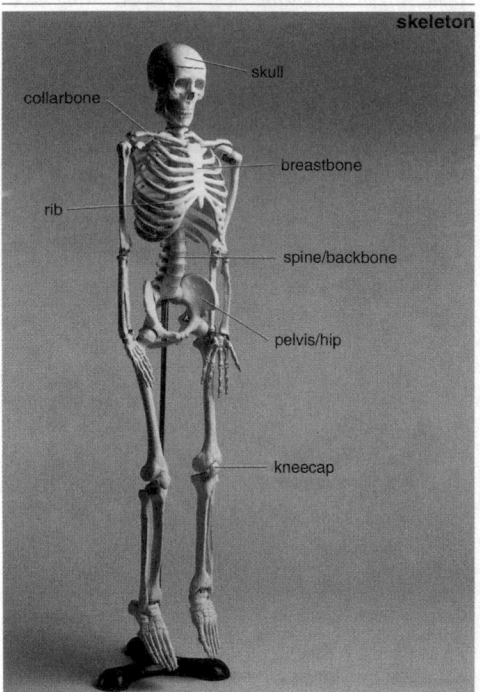

skeleton

skull
collarbone
breastbone
rib
spine/backbone
pelvis/hip
kneecap

skel·e·ton /'skelɪtən/ *n*
1 BONES [C] **a)** the structure consisting of all the bones in a human or animal body: *the human skeleton* **b)** a set of these bones or a model of them, fastened in their usual positions, used for example by medical students
2 BASIC PARTS [singular] the most important parts of something, to which more detail can be added later: *We agreed on a skeleton outline of the proposal.*

3 THIN PERSON [C] an extremely thin person or animal: *The disease had reduced Harry to a skeleton.*
4 STRUCTURE [C] the main structure that supports a building, bridge etc: *Minutes after the explosion, all that remained was the skeleton of the bridge.*
5 a skeleton in the closet also **a skeleton in the cupboard** *BrE* an embarrassing or unpleasant secret about something that happened to you in the past
6 skeleton staff/crew/service etc only enough workers or services to keep an operation or organization running: *The bus company is operating a skeleton service on Christmas Day.*
7 SPORT [C, singular] a sport in which you slide down a special ice track while lying on your front on a type of SLEDGE, or the vehicle you slide on → BOBSLEIGH, LUGE

'skeleton key *n* [C] a key made to open a number of different locks

skep·tic /'skeptɪk/ *n* [C] the American spelling of SCEPTIC

skep·ti·cal /'skeptɪkəl/ *adj* the American spelling of SCEPTICAL

skep·ti·ci·sm /'skeptɪsɪzəm/ *n* [C,U] the American spelling of SCEPTICISM

sketch¹ /sketʃ/ *n* [C] **1** a simple, quickly-made drawing that does not show much detail: [+of] *Cantor drew a **rough sketch** of his apartment on a napkin.* **2** a short humorous scene on a television programme, in a theatre etc, that is part of a larger show: *Her TV programme is made up of a series of comic sketches.* **3** a short written or spoken description: [+of] *a brief sketch of the main weaknesses of the British economy* | *a **thumbnail sketch** (=very brief description) of topics treated in depth elsewhere*

sketch² *v* **1** [I,T] to draw a sketch of something **2** also **sketch out** [T] to describe something in a general way, giving the basic ideas: *Holford sketched a 10-year programme for rebuilding the city.*
  sketch in sth *phr v* to add more information about something: *I'd like to sketch in a few details for you.*

'sketch·pad /'sketʃpæd/ also **sketch·book** /'sketʃbʊk/ *n* [C] a number of sheets of paper fastened together and used for drawing

sketch·y /'sketʃi/ *adj* not thorough or complete, and not having enough details to be useful: ***Details** of the accident are still sketchy.*

skew /skjuː/ *v* [T] **1** if something skews the results of a test etc, it affects the results, making them incorrect: *All the people we questioned lived in the same area, which had the effect of skewing the figures.* **2** to affect or influence someone's ideas, actions, or judgment, especially in a way that makes the ideas etc not correct or fair: *These assumptions about Communism skewed American foreign policy for decades.*

skewed /skjuːd/ *adj* **1** an opinion, piece of information, result etc that is skewed is incorrect, especially because it has been affected by a particular thing or because you do not know all the facts: *The media's coverage of the election has been skewed from the very beginning.* **2** something that is skewed is not straight and is higher on one side than the other; ⊟ **crooked**: *The picture on the wall was slightly skewed.*

skew·er¹ /'skjuːə $ -ər/ *n* [C] a long metal or wooden stick that is put through pieces of meat to hold them together while they are cooked

skewer² *v* [T] **1** to make a hole through a piece of food, an object etc with a skewer or with some other pointed object **2** to criticize someone very strongly, often in a way that other people find humorous: *Du Bois skewered Washington's policies in his book, 'The Souls of Black Folks.'*

,skew-'whiff *adj* [not before noun] *BrE spoken informal* not straight; ⊟ **crooked**: *The top of the bookcase is skew-whiff.*

ski¹ /skiː/ *n plural* **skis** [C] **1** one of a pair of long thin narrow pieces of wood or plastic that you fasten to your boots and use for moving on snow or on water: *ski slopes* | *a ski resort* (=where people can go skiing)   **2** a long thin narrow piece of strong material, fastened under a small vehicle so that it can travel on snow

ski² *v* **skied**, **skiing**, **skis** [I] to move on skis for sport or in order to travel on snow or water; → **skiing**: *I'm learning to ski.* | *We skied down to the village of Argentiere.*

'ski boot *n* [C] a specially made boot that fastens onto a ski

skid¹ /skɪd/ *v* **skidded**, **skidding** [I] if a vehicle or a wheel on a vehicle skids, it suddenly slides sideways and you cannot control it: *The car skidded as she turned onto the highway.* | [+**on/into/across** etc] *The bus skidded off the road and into a ditch.* → see picture at SLIP¹; → see box at SLIDE¹

skid² *n* [C]
1 SLIDING MOVEMENT a sudden sliding movement of a vehicle that you cannot control: *Turn the car towards the skid if you lose control of it.* | *He slammed on the brakes and we went into a long skid* (=started to skid).
2 on the skids *informal* in a situation that is bad and getting worse: *He's been on the skids since losing his job.*
3 put the skids under sth *BrE informal* to make it likely or certain that something will fail: *The recession put the skids under his plans for starting a new business.*
4 SPORT [usually singular] *AmE* a period of time during which a person or team is not successful – used in news reports: *The Red Sox victory ended a six-game skid.*
5 AIRCRAFT a flat narrow part that is under some aircraft such as HELICOPTERS, and is used in addition to wheels for landing
6 USED TO LIFT/MOVE [usually plural] a piece of wood that is put under a heavy object to lift or move it

'skid mark *n* [C usually plural]   **1** a long mark that is left on the ground when a vehicle skids: *There were skid marks on the road where the crash occurred.*   **2** *informal* a dirty mark inside someone's underwear

skid row, **Skid Row** /ˌskɪd 'rəʊ $ -'roʊ/ *n*   **1** be on skid row *informal* if someone is on skid row, they drink too much alcohol and have no job, nowhere to live etc   **2** [U] used to talk about a part of a city with a lot of old buildings in bad condition, where poor people who drink too much alcohol spend their time

ski·er /'skiːə $ -ər/ *n* [C] someone who SKIS

skies /skaɪz/ *n* the plural form of SKY

skiff /skɪf/ *n* [C] a small light boat for one person

skif·fle /'skɪfəl/ *n* [U] *especially BrE* a type of popular music played in the 1950s and often using instruments made by the musicians themselves

ski·ing /'skiːɪŋ/ *n* [U] the sport of moving down hills, across land in the snow, or on water wearing SKIS: *We're going to go skiing in Colorado this winter.* | **cross-country/downhill skiing** → WATER SKIING; → see picture at WINTER SPORTS

ski·jor·ing /'skiːˌdʒɔːrɪŋ/ *n* [U] a sport in which a SKIER is pulled over snow or ice by one or more dogs —**skijor** *v* [I]

'ski jump *n* [C] a long steep sloping PLATFORM which people go down on SKIS and jump off to see how far they can go through the air in sports competitions —**ski jumping** *n* [U]; → see picture at WINTER SPORTS

skil·ful *BrE*; **skillful** *AmE* /'skɪlfəl/ *adj*   **1** good at doing something, especially something that needs special ability or training: *a skilful footballer* | **skilful at (doing) sth** *After a few years, he became very skilful at drawing.*   **2** made or done very well, showing a lot of ability: *the skilful use of sound effects* | *sensitive and skillful leadership* —**skilfully** *adv*: *She had used make-up skilfully to mask the bruise.*

'ski lift *n* [C] a piece of equipment that carries SKIERS up to the top of a slope

skill S3 W1 /skɪl/ *n* [C,U] an ability to do something well, especially because you have learned and practised it; → **talent**: *Reading and writing are two different skills.* | *Many jobs today require computer skills.* |

[+**in/at**] *He was valued for his skill in raising money for the company.* | **develop/acquire/learn a skill** *opportunities to acquire new skills* | **with skill** *The whole team played with great skill and determination.* | **technical/management/practical etc skill** *the kinds of communication skills required of teachers* | *Students need to possess certain basic skills by the time they finish school.*

skilled /skɪld/ *adj*   **1** someone who is skilled has the training and experience that is needed to do something well; ✗ **unskilled**: *Skilled craftsmen, such as carpenters, are in great demand.* | *The company is fortunate to have such highly skilled workers.* | [+**at/in**] *She's very skilled at dealing with the public.* | *The school offers a program for students who are skilled in metalwork.*   **2** [usually before noun] skilled work needs people with special abilities or training to do it; ✗ **unskilled**: *Bricklaying is very skilled work.*

skil·let /'skɪlɪt/ *n* [C] a flat heavy cooking pan with a long handle; ✗ **frying pan**

skil·ful /'skɪlfəl/ *adj* the American spelling of SKILFUL

skim /skɪm/ *v* **skimmed**, **skimming**   **1** [T] to remove something from the surface of a liquid, especially floating fat, solids, or oil: **skim sth off/from sth** *After simmering the meat, skim the fat from the surface.*   **2** [I,T] to read something quickly to find the main facts or ideas in it; ✗ **scan**: *Julie skimmed the sports page.* | [+**through/over**] *Just skim through the second section to save time.*   **3** [T] to move along quickly over a surface, never touching it or not touching it often: *seagulls skimming the waves* | [+**over/along/across**] *The ball skimmed across the grass and stopped against the wall.*   **4** skim stones/pebbles etc *BrE* to throw smooth, flat stones into a lake, river etc in a way that makes them jump across the surface; ✗ **skip** *AmE*

skim sb/sth ⇔ **off** *phr v*   **1** to take the best people or the best part of something for yourself: *Professional sport skims off all the best players.*   **2** to take money illegally or dishonestly: *For years his business partner had been skimming off the profits.*

skimmed 'milk *BrE*; **'skim milk** *AmE n* [U] milk that has had all the fat and cream removed from it

skimp /skɪmp/ *v* [I,T] to not spend enough money or time on something, or not use enough of something, so that what you do is unsuccessful or of bad quality: [+**on**] *It's vital not to skimp on staff training.*

skimp·y /'skɪmpi/ *adj*   **1** a skimpy dress or skirt etc is very short and does not cover very much of a woman's body   **2** not enough of something: *a skimpy meal*

skin¹ S2 W2 /skɪn/ *n*
1 BODY [C,U] the natural outer layer of a person's or animal's body

> fair/pale skin
> dark/olive skin
> dark-skinned/fair-skinned
> dry/oily/sensitive skin
> smooth/soft skin
> leathery skin (=thick and hard skin)
> scaly skin (=rough dry skin on animals such as LIZARDS)
> good/bad skin (=healthy or unhealthy skin on your face)
> skin colour/tone
> rub/irritate your skin
> flap/fold/layer of skin
>
> *She had thick black hair and smooth dark skin.* | *If you are fair-skinned, you should try to stay out of the sun.* | *My skin is quite sensitive.* | *an ugly man with bad skin and brown teeth* | *chemicals that irritate the skin* | *The eggs are hatched under a fold of skin on the penguin's belly.* | *a skin disease* → SKINCARE

2 FROM AN ANIMAL [C,U] the skin of an animal, sometimes including its fur, used to make leather, clothes etc: *a leopard skin*

3 FOOD [C,U] **a)** the natural outer cover of some fruits and vegetables; ⊟ **peel**: *banana skins* **b)** the outer cover of a SAUSAGE

4 ON A LIQUID [C,U] a thin solid layer that forms on the top of a liquid, especially when it gets cold: *Cover the soup to stop a skin from forming.*

5 PART OF AN OBJECT [C] a layer that is part of a vehicle, building, object etc, especially on the outside: *The outer skin of the aircraft was not punctured.* | *The lampshade has a double skin so that it remains cool.*

6 COMPUTER [C,U] the way particular information appears on a computer screen, especially when this can be changed quickly and easily

7 have (a) thin/thick skin to be easily upset or not easily upset by criticism: *This is not a job for someone with thin skin.*

8 get under sb's skin *informal* if someone gets under your skin, they annoy you, especially by the way they behave: *What really gets under my skin is people who push straight to the front of the line.*

9 by the skin of your teeth *informal* if you do something by the skin of your teeth, you only just succeed in doing it, and very nearly failed to do it: *Two others made it by the skin of their teeth.*

10 make sb's skin crawl *informal* to make someone feel very uncomfortable combined with a strong feeling of dislike: *Her singing makes my skin crawl.*

11 be skin and bone *BrE*, be skin and bones *AmE* *informal* to be extremely thin in a way that is unattractive and unhealthy

12 it's no skin off sb's nose *spoken* used to say that someone does not care what another person thinks or does, because it does not affect them: *If she doesn't want me to help, it's no skin off my nose!*

13 sth is only skin deep used to say that something may seem to be important or effective, but it really is not because it only affects the way things appear: *Beauty is only skin deep.*

14 skins [plural] *BrE informal* papers for rolling a cigarette, especially one with MARIJUANA in it → save sb's skin at SAVE[1] (11); → jump out of your skin at JUMP[1] (4)

skin[2] *v* skinned, skinning [T] **1** to remove the skin from an animal, fruit, or vegetable; → peel: *Add the tomatoes, skinned and sliced.* **2** to hurt yourself by rubbing off some skin; ⊟ **graze**: *She fell and skinned her knee.* **3** skin sb alive to punish someone very severely – used humorously: *Dad will skin you alive when he sees this place!* **4** *informal* to completely defeat someone; ⊟ **hammer**: *The football team really skinned Watertown last year.*

skin up *phr v BrE informal* to make a cigarette with MARIJUANA in it

skin·care /'skɪnkeə $ -ker/ *n* [U] things that you do in order to improve the condition of your skin, especially the skin on your face: *expensive skincare products*

'skin-,diving, skin diving *n* [U] the sport of swimming under water with light breathing equipment but without a protective suit —**skin diver** *n* [C]

skin·flint /'skɪn,flɪnt/ *n* [C] *informal* someone who hates spending money or giving it away – used to show disapproval; ⊟ **miser**

skin·ful /'skɪnfʊl/ *n* have a skinful *BrE spoken* to drink a lot of alcohol and become drunk

'skin graft *n* [C] a medical operation in which healthy skin is removed from one part of your body and used on another part to replace burned or damaged skin

skin·head /'skɪnhed/ *n* [C] a young white person who has hair that is cut very short, especially one who behaves violently towards people of other races

skin·ny S3 /'skɪni/ *adj comparative* skinnier, *superlative* skinniest very thin, especially in a way that is unattractive: *Some supermodels are far too skinny.*; → see box at THIN[1]

'skinny-,dipping *n* [U] *informal* swimming with no clothes on: *As soon as it got dark, we all went skinny-dipping.*

skint /skɪnt/ *adj* [not before noun] *BrE informal* having no money, especially for a short time; ⊟ **broke**: *I'm skint at the moment.*

,skin-'tight *adj* skin-tight clothes fit tightly against your body; ⬦ **baggy**: *skin-tight jeans*

skip[1] /skɪp/ *v* skipped, skipping

1 NOT DO STH [T] *informal* to not do something that you usually do, or that you should do; ⊟ **miss**: *She skipped lunch in order to go shopping.* | *Williams skipped the game to be with his wife in the hospital.* | skip school/class *especially AmE*: *He skipped chemistry class three times last month.*

2 NOT DEAL WITH STH [I,T] to not read, mention, or deal with something that would normally come or happen next: *I decided to skip the first chapter.* | [+to] *Let's skip to the last item on the agenda.* | [+over] *I suggest we skip over the details and get to the point.*

3 CHANGE SUBJECTS [I always + adv/prep] to go from one subject to another in no fixed order: [+about/around/from] *It's difficult to have a conversation with her because she skips from one topic to another.*

4 MOVEMENT [I] to move forward with quick steps and jumps: [+across/along etc] *He turned and skipped away, singing happily to himself.*

5 JUMP OVER A ROPE [I] to jump over a rope as you swing it over your head and under your feet, as a game or for exercise; ⊟ **jump rope** *AmE*; → see picture at JUMP[1]

6 skip town/skip the country *informal* to leave a place suddenly and secretly, especially to avoid being punished or paying debts: *Then they found that Zaffuto had already skipped town.*

7 skip it! *spoken informal especially AmE* used to say angrily and rudely that you do not want to talk about something: *'Sorry, what were you saying?' 'Oh, skip it!'*

8 skip rocks/stones *AmE* to throw smooth, flat stones into a lake, river etc in a way that makes them jump across the surface; ⊟ **skim** *BrE*

9 BALL [I always + adv/prep] if a ball or something similar skips off a surface, it quickly moves away from that surface after hitting it – used especially in news reports: [+off/along/across etc] | *The ball skipped off Bonds' glove and bounced toward the fence.*

10 skip a year/grade to start a new school year in a class that is one year ahead of the class you would normally enter → sb's heart skips a beat at HEART

skip off *BrE*; skip out *AmE phr v* to leave suddenly and secretly, especially in order to avoid being punished or paying money: *He skipped off without paying.* | [+on] *AmE*: *Tenants who skip out on utility bills are the focus of a new law.* | *Joel skipped out on his wife when she was 8 months pregnant.*

skip[2] *n* [C] **1** a skipping movement **2** *BrE* a large container for bricks, wood, and similar heavy waste; ⊟ **dumpster** *AmE*

'ski pants *n* [plural] **1** thick trousers with long thin pieces of cloth that fasten over your shoulders, worn while SKIING: *a pair of ski pants* **2** tight trousers with a band of cloth that goes under your foot, worn by women

'ski plane *n* [C] an aircraft that has long thin narrow parts on the bottom instead of wheels, for landing on snow

'ski pole *n* [C] one of two pointed short poles that you hold to help you balance and push off the snow when SKIING

skip·per[1] /'skɪpə $ -ər/ *n* [C] *informal* **1** the person in charge of a ship; ⊟ **captain 2** the leader of a sports team; ⊟ **captain**

skipper[2] *v* [T] to be in charge of a ship, sports team etc – used especially in news reports; ⊟ **captain**

'skipping ,rope *n* [C] *BrE* a long piece of rope with handles that children use for jumping over; ⊟ **jump rope** *AmE*

skir·mish /ˈskɜːmɪʃ $ ˈskɜːr-/ n [C] **1** a fight between small groups of soldiers, ships etc, especially one that happens away from the main part of a battle – used in news reports: [+with/between/over] *The young soldier was killed in a skirmish with government troops.* **2** a short argument, especially between political or sports opponents: [+with/between/over] *Bates was sent off after a skirmish with the referee.* | *a budget skirmish between the President and Congress* —**skirmish** v [I]: *They skirmished briefly with soldiers from Fort Benton.*

skirt¹ /skɜːt $ skɜːrt/ n [C] **1** a piece of outer clothing worn by women and girls, which hangs down from the waist like the bottom part of a dress: *She wore a white blouse and a plain black skirt.* | **leather/pleated/cotton etc skirt** *a green velvet skirt* | **short/long skirt** *a short skirt and high heels* **2** also **skirts** [plural] old-fashioned the part of a dress or coat that hangs down from the waist **3 the skirts of a forest/hill/village etc** *BrE* the outside edge of a forest etc; ◻ **outskirts** **4 a bit of skirt** *BrE informal not polite* an offensive expression meaning an attractive woman

skirt² also **skirt around/round** v [T] **1** to go around the outside edge of a place or area: *The old footpath skirts around the village.* **2** to avoid talking about an important subject, especially because it is difficult or embarrassing – used to show disapproval: *a disappointing speech that skirted around all the main issues*

skirting board also **skirt·ing** /ˈskɜːtɪŋ $ ˈskɜːr-/ n [C,U] *BrE* a long narrow piece of wood that is fastened along the bottom of the walls in a room; ◻ **baseboard** *AmE*

ski run n [C] a track that has been marked on a slope so that people can SKI on it

ski slope n [C] a snow-covered part of a mountain which has been prepared for people to SKI down

skit /skɪt/ n [C] a short humorous performance or piece of writing

skit·ter /ˈskɪtə $ -ər/ v [I always + adv/prep] to move very quickly and lightly, like a small animal; ◻ **scurry**: [+across/down/along etc] *Something skittered across the alley.*

skit·tish /ˈskɪtɪʃ/ adj **1** an animal, especially a horse, that is skittish gets excited or frightened very easily **2** a person who is skittish is not very serious, and their feelings, behaviour, and opinions keep changing **3** if people who buy SHARES are skittish, they are nervous and worried about them dropping in value, and might sell the shares that they own because of this; ◻ **jittery**: *Some skittish Wall Street investors are staying away from the market.* —**skittishly** adv

skit·tle /ˈskɪtl/ n **1 skittles** [U] a British game in which a player tries to knock down objects shaped like bottles by rolling a ball at them **2** [C] one of the objects you roll the ball at in the game of skittles

skive /skaɪv/ also **skive off** v [I] *BrE informal* to avoid work or school by staying away or leaving without permission —**skiver** n [C]

skiv·vy¹ /ˈskɪvi/ n plural **skivvies** [C] *BrE* a servant who does only the dirty unpleasant jobs in a house: *You iron your shirt – I'm not your skivvy.*

skivvy² v **skivvied, skivvying, skivvies** [I] *BrE* to do all the dirty unpleasant jobs in a house, as if you were a servant

skul·dug·ge·ry, skullduggery /ˌskʌlˈdʌɡəri/ n [U] old-fashioned secretly dishonest or illegal activity – also used humorously

skulk /skʌlk/ v [I always + adv/prep] to hide or move about secretly, trying not to be noticed, especially when you are intending to do something bad; ◻ **lurk**: [+about/around/in etc] *He was still skulking around outside when they left the building.*

skull /skʌl/ n [C] **1** the bones of a person's or animal's head → see picture at SKELETON **2 sb can't get it**

into their (thick) skull *spoken* someone is unable to understand something very simple: *He can't seem to get it into his skull that I'm just not interested in him.*

skull and 'crossbones n [singular] **1** a picture of a human skull with two bones crossed below it, used in past times on the flags of PIRATE ships **2** a picture of a human skull with two bones crossed below it, used on containers to show that what is inside is poison or very dangerous

'skull cap n [C] a small round close-fitting hat for the top of the head, worn sometimes by Christian priests or Jewish men

skunk /skʌŋk/ n **1** [C] a small black and white North American animal that produces a strong unpleasant smell if it is attacked or afraid **2** [U] a very strong type of MARIJUANA

sky S2 W2 /skaɪ/ n plural **skies**
1 [singular, U] the space above the earth where clouds and the sun and stars appear: *The sky grew dark, and a cold rain began to fall.* | *A shooting star sped across the sky.* | **in the sky** *There wasn't a cloud in the sky.* | **blue/black/grey etc sky** *The sun rose higher in a clear blue sky.* | **clear/cloudy/dark etc sky** *Robyn lay on her back looking up at the cloudless sky.* | **under a slightly overcast sky** (=with clouds) | **night/morning/summer etc sky** *The evening sky was darkening as I made my way home.* | *She looked out over the rooftops and the open sky.*
2 skies [plural] a word meaning 'sky', used especially when describing the weather or what the sky looks like in a place: *a land of blue skies and warm sunshine* | *The skies were overcast, and it was chilly and damp.*
3 the sky's the limit *spoken* used to say that there is no limit to what someone can achieve, spend, win etc: *Francis believes the sky's the limit for the young goalkeeper.* → **pie in the sky** at PIE (4); → **praise sb/sth to the skies** at PRAISE¹ (1)

sky-'blue adj bright blue, like the colour of the sky when there are no clouds —**sky blue** n [U]

sky·cap /ˈskaɪkæp/ n [C] *AmE* someone whose job is to carry passengers' bags at an airport

sky·div·ing /ˈskaɪˌdaɪvɪŋ/ n [U] the sport of jumping from a plane and falling through the sky before opening a PARACHUTE —**skydive** v [I] —**skydiver** n [C]; → see picture at OUTDOOR

sky-'high adv **1** extremely high: *sky-high prices* | *Her confidence is sky-high.* **2 blow sth sky-high** to destroy something completely with an explosion

sky·lark /ˈskaɪlɑːk $ -lɑːrk/ n [C] a small bird that sings while flying high in the sky; ◻ **lark**

sky·light /ˈskaɪlaɪt/ n [C] a window in the roof of a building → see picture at ROOF¹

sky·line /ˈskaɪlaɪn/ n [C] the shape made by hills or buildings against the sky: *the famous New York skyline*

sky·rock·et /ˈskaɪˌrɒkət $ -ˌrɑː-/ v [I] *informal* if a price or an amount skyrockets, it greatly increases very quickly: *The trade deficit has skyrocketed.* | *skyrocketing inflation*

sky·scrap·er /ˈskaɪˌskreɪpə $ -ər/ n [C] a very tall modern city building

sky·wards /ˈskaɪwədz $ -wərdz/ also **sky·ward** /-wəd $ wərd/ adv literary up into the sky or towards the sky: *The bird soared skywards.* —**skyward** adj

slab /slæb/ n [C] **1** a thick flat piece of a hard material such as stone: *a concrete slab* | *paving slabs* | [+of] *They used a slab of concrete as a lid.* **2 slab of cake/chocolate/meat etc** a large flat piece of cake etc **3 on the slab** *informal* lying dead in a hospital or MORTUARY

slack

taut   slack

slack¹ /slæk/ adj **1** hanging loosely, or not pulled tight; 🔒 **taut**: *Keep the rope slack until I tell you to pull it.* **2** with less business activity than usual: *Business remained slack throughout the day.* **3** not taking enough care or making enough effort to do things correctly – used to show disapproval: *Slack defending by Real Madrid allowed Manchester United to score.* —**slackly** adv —**slackness** n [U]

slack² n **1 take up/pick up the slack a)** to make a system or organization as EFFICIENT as possible by making sure that money, space, or people are fully used: *Without another contract to help pick up the slack, employees may face job losses.* **b)** to do something that needs to be done because someone else is no longer doing it **c)** to make a rope tighter **2** [U] part of a rope that is not stretched tight **3** [U] money, space, people, or time that an organization or person has available, but is not using fully: *There is still some slack in the budget.* **4 cut/give sb some slack** spoken to allow someone to do something without criticizing them or making it more difficult: *Hey, cut me some slack, man, I'm only a few bucks short.* **5 slacks** [plural] trousers: *a pair of slacks* | *dress slacks* (=for more formal occasions) **6** [U] BrE very small pieces of coal

slack³ also **slack off** v [I] to make less effort than usual, or to be lazy in your work: *He was accused of slacking and taking too many holidays.*

slack·en /'slækən/ v [I,T] written **1** also **slacken off** to gradually become slower, weaker, less active etc, or to make something do this: *The heavy rain showed no signs of slackening off.* | **slacken your pace/speed** (=go or walk more slowly) *Guy slackened his pace as he approached the gate.* **2** to make something looser, or to become looser; 🔒 **tighten**: *He did not let her go, but his grip on her slackened.*

slack·er /'slækə $ -ər/ n [C] informal someone who is lazy and does not do all the work they should – used to show disapproval

ˈslack-jawed adj having your mouth slightly open, especially because you are surprised or stupid; 🔒 **open-mouthed**: *They looked at him, slack-jawed with disbelief.*

slag¹ /slæg/ n **1** [C] BrE taboo informal a very offensive word for a woman who has sex with a lot of different people. Do not use this word. **2** [U] a waste material similar to glass, which remains after metal has been obtained from rock

slag² v **slagged, slagging**
slag sb ⇔ **off** phr v BrE informal to criticize someone in an unpleasant way, especially when this is not fair: *He's always slagging her off behind her back.*

ˈslag heap n [C] especially BrE a pile of waste materials at a mine or factory

slain /sleɪn/ the past participle of SLAY

slake /sleɪk/ v [T] literary **1 slake your thirst** to drink so that you are not thirsty any more **2 slake a desire/craving etc** to satisfy a desire etc

sla·lom /'slɑːləm/ n [C,U] a race for people on SKIS or in CANOES down a curving course marked by flags

slam¹ /slæm/ v **slammed, slamming**
1 DOOR ETC [I,T] if a door, gate etc slams, or if someone slams it, it shuts with a loud noise; 🔒 **bang**: *We heard a car door slam.* | *He slammed the door shut.*
2 PUT STH SOMEWHERE [T always + adv/prep] to put something on or against a surface with a fast violent movement: **slam sth down/against/onto** *Henry slammed the phone down angrily.*
3 HIT WITH FORCE [I always + adv/prep] to hit or attack someone or something with a lot of force: [+into/against etc] *All 155 passengers died instantly when the plane slammed into the mountain.*
4 CRITICIZE [T] to criticize someone or something strongly – used especially in newspapers; 🔒 **slate**: *Local media slammed plans to build a prison in the area.* | **slam sb for sth** *The council was slammed for its unfair selection procedure.*
5 slam on the brakes to make a car stop very suddenly by pressing the BRAKES very hard
6 slam the door in sb's face a) to close a door hard when someone is trying to come in **b)** to rudely refuse to meet someone or talk to them

slam² n [C usually singular] the noise or action of a door, window etc slamming

ˈslam dunk n [C] **1** when a BASKETBALL player jumps high above the net and throws the ball down through it **2** AmE informal a very impressive act: *The biggest legal slam dunk came when a judge sentenced four men to 505 years in prison.*

ˈslam-dunk v [I,T] to put a ball through the net in BASKETBALL, by jumping very high and throwing the ball down through the net

slam·mer /'slæmə $ -ər/ n **the slammer** informal prison: **in the slammer** *He had to spend his twentieth birthday in the slammer.*

slan·der¹ /'slɑːndə $ 'slændər/ n **1** [C,U] a false spoken statement about someone, intended to damage the good opinion that people have of that person; → **libel 2** [U] the crime of making false spoken statements about someone; → **libel**: *He is being sued for slander.*

slander² v [T] to say false things about someone in order to damage other people's good opinion of them; → **libel**

slan·der·ous /'slɑːndərəs $ 'slæn-/ adj a slanderous statement about someone is not true, and is intended to damage other people's good opinion of them; → **libellous**: *slanderous remarks*

slang /slæŋ/ n [U] very informal, sometimes offensive, language that is used especially by people who belong to a particular group, such as young people or criminals: *schoolboy slang* | **slang word/expression/term** —**slangy** adj

ˈslanging ˌmatch n [C] BrE informal an angry argument in which people insult each other

slant¹ /slɑːnt $ slænt/ v **1** [I,T] to slope or make something slope in a particular direction: *The sun's rays slanted through the trees.* | *slanting eyes* **2** [T] to provide information in a way that unfairly supports one opinion, gives an advantage to one group etc: *The researchers were accused of slanting their findings in favour of their own beliefs.*

slant² n [singular] **1** a way of writing about or thinking about a subject that is based on a particular opinion or set of ideas: *The article had an anti-union slant.* | **new/different/fresh etc slant** *Each article has a slightly different slant on the situation.* | *Recent events have put a new slant on the President's earlier comments.* **2** a sloping position or angle; 🔒 **slope**: **at/on a slant** *The house seems to be built on a steep slant.*

slant·ed /'slɑːntɪd $ 'slæn-/ *adj* **1** providing facts or information in a way that unfairly supports only one side of an argument or one opinion – used to show disapproval; ⊟ **biased**: [+**towards**] *The report was heavily slanted towards the city council's version of events.* **2** sloping: *her slightly slanted eyes*

slap¹ ⑤² /slæp/ *v past tense and past participle* **slapped**, *present participle* **slapping**
1 [T] to hit someone with the flat part of your hand; → **punch**: *Sarah slapped Aaron across the face.*
2 [T always + adv/prep] to put something down on a surface with force, especially when you are angry: *Giles slapped his cards down on the table.*
3 slap sb on the back to hit someone on the back in a friendly way, often as a way of praising them
4 [I always + adv/prep] to hit a surface with a lot of force, making a loud sharp sound: [+**against**] *Small waves slapped against the side of the boat.*
　slap sb down *phr v BrE*
to rudely tell someone that their suggestions, questions, ideas etc are stupid
　slap sth ⇔ on *phr v informal*
1 to put or spread something quickly or carelessly onto a surface: *She ran upstairs and slapped on some make-up.* | **slap sth on sth** *We could slap some paint on it.*
2 to suddenly announce a new charge, tax etc or say that something is not allowed – used especially when you think this is unfair: *Many tour operators slap on supplements for single people.* | **slap sth on sth** *In 1977, the president slapped a ban on the commercial reprocessing of nuclear fuel.*

slap² *n* [C] **1** a quick hit with the flat part of your hand; → **punch**: *Julia gave Roy a slap on the cheek.* **2 a slap in the face** an action that seems to be deliberately intended to offend or upset someone, especially someone who has tried very hard to do something **3 a slap on the wrist** a punishment that you think is not severe enough **4 a slap on the back** an action of hitting someone on the back in a friendly way, especially as a way of praising them **5** *informal* MAKE-UP

,**slap 'bang** also **slap** *adv informal* **1** if you run, drive etc slap bang into something, you hit it with a lot of force: [+**into**] *I ran slap bang into a lamppost.* **2** exactly in a particular place or at a particular time: [+**next to**] *Anne's house is slap bang next to the station.*

slap·dash /'slæpdæʃ/ *adj* careless and done too quickly; ⊞ **painstaking**: *a very slapdash piece of work*

slap·hap·py /'slæpˌhæpi/ *adj* careless, silly, and likely to make mistakes

slap·head /'slæphed/ *n* [C] *BrE informal* an impolite word for someone who is BALD (=has little or no hair on their head)

slap·per /'slæpə $ -ər/ *n* [C] *BrE informal* an offensive word for a woman who has sex with lots of people

slap·stick /'slæpˌstɪk/ *n* [U] humorous acting in which the performers fall over, throw things at each other etc: *a slapstick comedy*

'**slap-up** *adj* **slap-up meal/dinner etc** *BrE informal* a very large enjoyable meal

slash¹ /slæʃ/ *v* **1** [I,T always + adv/prep] to cut or try to cut something violently with a knife, sword etc: *Someone had slashed the tires.* | [+**at/through**] *The leopard's claws slashed through soft flesh.* **2** [T] to greatly reduce an amount, price etc – used especially in newspapers and advertising; ⊟ **cut**: *The workforce has been slashed by 50%.* **3 slash your wrists** to cut the VEINS in your wrists with the intention of killing yourself

slash² *n* [C] **1** a quick movement that you make with a knife, sword etc in order to cut someone or something **2** also **slash mark** a line (/) used in writing to

separate words, numbers, or letters **3** a long narrow cut in something; → **gash**: *Cut several slashes across the top of the loaf before baking.* **4 have/take a slash** *BrE spoken not polite* to URINATE

slash·er /'slæʃə $ -ər/ *n* **slasher film/movie etc** *informal* a very violent film

slat /slæt/ *n* [C] a thin flat piece of wood, plastic etc, used especially in furniture —**slatted** *adj*

slate¹ /sleɪt/ *n*
1 ROCK [U] a dark grey rock that can easily be split into flat thin pieces
2 ON A ROOF [C] *especially BrE* a small piece of slate or similar material that is used for covering roofs; ⊟ **tile**: *There were several slates missing from the roof.* → see picture at ROOF¹
3 slate blue/grey a dark blue or grey colour
4 POLITICS [C] a list of people that voters can choose in an election, or who are being considered for an important job
5 FOR WRITING ON [C] a small black board or a flat piece of slate in a wooden frame used for writing on in the past
6 put sth on the slate *BrE old-fashioned* to arrange to pay for something later, especially food or drink → **a clean slate** at CLEAN¹ (9)

slate² *v* [T usually passive] **1** *BrE informal* to criticize a book, film etc severely, especially in a newspaper; ⊟ **slam**: *Doherty's most recent novel has been slated by the critics.* **2 be slated to do sth/be slated for sth** *especially AmE* if something is slated to happen, it is planned to happen in the future, especially at a particular time: *He is slated to appear at the Cambridge Jazz Festival next year.* | *Every house on this block is slated for demolition.*

slath·er /'slæðə $ -ər/ *v* [T always + adv/prep] *AmE* to cover something with a thick layer of a soft substance: **slather sth in/with/on sth** *a slice of homemade bread, slathered with jam*

slat·tern /'slætən $ -ərn/ *n* [C] *old-fashioned* a dirty, untidy woman – used to show disapproval —**slatternly** *adj*

slaugh·ter¹ /'slɔːtə $ 'slɒːtər/ *v* [T] **1** to kill an animal, especially for its meat **2** to kill a lot of people in a cruel or violent way; ⊟ **butcher**: *Hundreds of innocent civilians had been slaughtered by government troops.* → see box at KILL¹ **3** *informal* to defeat an opponent in a sport or game by a large number of points; ⊟ **hammer**: *We got slaughtered, 110 – 54.*

slaugh·ter² *n* [U] **1** when people kill animals, especially for their meat: *the export of live animals for slaughter* **2** when large numbers of people are killed in a cruel or violent way: *the slaughter of defenceless women and children*

slaugh·tered /'slɔːtəd $ 'slɒːtərd/ *adj* [not before noun] *BrE informal* very drunk; ⊟ **plastered**: *We all got completely slaughtered last night.*

slaugh·ter·house /'slɔːtəhaʊs $ 'slɒːtər-/ *n* [C] a building where animals such as cows or pigs are killed for their meat; ⊟ **abattoir**

Slav /slɑːv $ slɑːv, slæv/ *n* [C] someone who belongs to any of the races of Eastern and Central Europe who speak Slavic languages such as Russian, Bulgarian, Polish etc

slave¹ /sleɪv/ *n* [C] **1** someone who is owned by another person and works for them for no money: **the slave trade** (=the buying and selling of slaves, especially Africans who were taken to America) **2 be a slave to/of sth** to be so strongly influenced by something that you cannot make your own decisions – used to show disapproval: *a slave to fashion*

slave² *v* [I always + adv/prep] to work very hard with little time to rest: **slave away (at sth)** *I've been slaving away at this report.* | [+**over**] *He's been slaving over his history essay.* | **slave (away) over a hot stove** (=cook – used humorously)

'slave ,driver n [C] someone who makes people work very hard – used in a disapproving or humorous way

,slave 'labour BrE; **slave labor** AmE n [U] **1** work done by slaves, or the people who do this work **2** informal work for which you are paid an unfairly small amount of money

slav·er¹ /'slævə $ -ər/ v [I] literary to let SALIVA (=liquid produced inside your mouth) come out of your mouth, especially because you are hungry; ▤ **drool**

slav·er² /'sleɪvə $ -ər/ n [C] old use **1** someone who sells slaves **2** a ship for moving slaves from one place to another

slav·er·y /'sleɪvəri/ n [U] **1** the system of having slaves: attempts to **abolish slavery** (=officially end it) **2** the state of being a slave: **sell sb into slavery** (=sell someone as a slave)

Slav·ic /'slɑːvɪk $ 'slɑː-, 'slæ-/ also **Slavonic** adj relating to the Slavs or their languages

slav·ish /'sleɪvɪʃ/ adj obeying, supporting, or copying someone completely – used to show disapproval: a **slavish adherence** to the rules —**slavishly** adv: not a rule to be **slavishly followed** in every instance —**slavishness** n [U]

Sla·von·ic /slə'vɒnɪk $ -'vɑː-/ adj SLAVIC

slaw /slɔː $ slɒː/ n [U] AmE COLESLAW

slay /sleɪ/ v past tense **slew** /sluː/, past participle **slain** /sleɪn/ [T] **1** to kill someone – used especially in newspapers **2** AmE spoken informal to amuse someone a lot —**slayer** n [C]

slay·ing /'sleɪ-ɪŋ/ n [C] an act of killing someone – used especially in newspapers: gang-related slayings

sleaze /sliːz/ n **1** [U] immoral behaviour, especially involving sex or lies: Many people are tired of all the sleaze on TV. | sleaze and corruption in politics **2** also **sleazebag, sleazebucket** [C] AmE informal someone who behaves in an immoral or dishonest way

slea·zy /'sliːzi/ adj comparative **sleazier**, superlative **sleaziest 1** a sleazy place is dirty, cheap, or in bad condition: a sleazy bar **2** relating to sex or dishonest behaviour – used to show disapproval: a sleazy lawyer —**sleaziness** n [U]

sledge¹ /sledʒ/ BrE also **sled** /sled/ n [C] a small vehicle used for sliding over snow, often used by children or in some sports; → **sleigh**

sledge² BrE
also **sled** v [I] to travel on a sledge

sledge·ham·mer /'sledʒ,hæmə $ -ər/ n [C] a large heavy hammer

sleek¹ /sliːk/ adj **1** a vehicle or other object that is sleek has a smooth attractive shape: the **sleek lines** of the new Mercedes **2** sleek hair or fur is straight, shiny, and healthy-looking **3** someone who is sleek looks rich and is well dressed —**sleekly** adv —**sleekness** n [U]

sleek² v [T always + adv/prep] literary to make hair or fur smooth and shiny by putting water or oil on it: **sleek sth back/down etc** His hair was sleeked back with oil.

sleep¹ S1 W2 /sliːp/ v past tense and past participle **slept** /slept/ [I]
1 to rest your mind and body, usually at night when you are lying in bed with your eyes closed; → **asleep, oversleep**

> sleep well/soundly
> sleep badly
> sleep peacefully
> sleep fitfully literary (=keep moving or waking during a sleep)
> can't sleep
> sleep late (=not get up until late in the morning)
> sleep like a log informal (=sleep very well)
> not sleep a wink (=not sleep at all)
> somewhere/nowhere to sleep

> I usually sleep on my back. | Did you **sleep well**? | Dee was tired out but couldn't sleep. | We both **slept badly** that night. | The baby **slept peacefully** in its cradle. | She **slept fitfully**, disturbed by nightmares. | I couldn't sleep because I was so worried. | We usually **sleep late** on Sundays. | I **slept like a log** until morning. | He had hardly **slept a wink** all night. | He's lucky because at least he has **somewhere to sleep**.

2 sleep rough BrE to sleep outdoors in uncomfortable conditions, especially because you have no money
3 sleep on it spoken to not make a decision about something important until the next day
4 sleep tight spoken said especially to children before they go to bed to say that you hope they sleep well: Good night, Jenny. Sleep tight!
5 sleep two/four/six etc to have enough beds for a particular number of people: The villa sleeps four.
6 let sleeping dogs lie to deliberately avoid mentioning a subject, so that you do not cause any trouble or argument
7 literary if a village, house etc sleeps, it is very quiet during the night

sleep around phr v informal
to have sex with a lot of different people without having a serious relationship with any of them – used to show disapproval

sleep in phr v informal
to let yourself sleep later than usual in the morning: We usually sleep in on Sunday mornings.

sleep sth ⇔ **off** phr v informal
to sleep until you do not feel ill any more, especially after drinking too much alcohol: He went to his room to **sleep it off**.

sleep over phr v
to sleep at someone's house for a night – used especially by children

sleep through phr v
1 sleep through sth to sleep while something is happening and not be woken by it: How did you manage to sleep through that thunderstorm?
2 sleep through (sth) to sleep continuously for a long time: I slept right through till lunchtime. | The baby slept peacefully through the night.

sleep together phr v
if people sleep together, they have sex with each other

sleep with sb phr v
to have sex with someone, especially someone you are not married to: Everybody in the office knows he's been sleeping with Kathy.

> **WORD CHOICE: sleep, asleep**
> You usually use **be asleep** rather than 'be sleeping': Her parents were already asleep (NOT already slept/were sleeping).
> The verb **sleep** is used when you are giving more information, for example about how long someone sleeps or where they sleep: The baby sleeps for 12 hours. | He slept in the car.
> You usually say **fall asleep**, not 'start sleeping': Some students fall asleep (NOT start sleeping/start to sleep) at their desks.
> ⚠ Do not say 'feel asleep'.
> You can also say someone **goes to sleep**, especially when they are in bed and want to sleep: I turned the light out and went to sleep.
> You use **get to sleep** when someone has difficulty falling asleep: It took me hours to get to sleep.

sleep² S2 W3 n
1 BEING ASLEEP [U] the natural state of resting your mind and body, usually at night; → **beauty sleep**: I didn't get much sleep last night. | Sometimes Mike has a hard time **getting to sleep** (=succeeding in starting to sleep). | I couldn't **get back to sleep** (=sleep again after waking up) after he'd rung. | **drift/nod/go off to sleep** (=start sleeping) I'm sorry, I must have **dropped off to sleep** for a moment. | **in your sleep** (=while he is sleeping) Ed often talks in his sleep. | She **died in her**

sleep later that night. | *Her eyes were red through* **lack of sleep.** | **a few/a couple of/eight etc hours' sleep** *She managed on a few hours' sleep a night.*
2 [PERIOD OF SLEEPING] [singular] a period when you are sleeping: **a light/deep sleep** *She was woken from a deep sleep by a ring at the door.* | *You just need a* **good night's sleep** (=a night when you sleep well). | *a* **dreamless sleep** | **have a sleep** *BrE: Why don't you go and have a sleep?*
3 **go to sleep a)** to start sleeping: *I went to sleep at 9 o'clock and woke up at 6.* | *It's nothing,* **go back to sleep** (=sleep again after waking up). **b)** *informal* if a part of your body goes to sleep, you cannot feel it for a short time because it has not been getting enough blood
4 **lose sleep over sth** *spoken* to worry about something: *It's a practice game – I wouldn't lose any sleep over it.*
5 **put sb/sth to sleep a)** to give drugs to a sick animal so that it dies without too much pain – used to avoid saying the word 'kill' **b)** *informal* to make someone unconscious before a medical operation by giving them drugs
6 **sb can do sth in their sleep** *informal* used to say that someone is able to do something very easily, especially because they have done it many times before: *She knew the music so well she could play it in her sleep.*
7 **sing/rock/lull etc sb to sleep** to sing to someone, move them gently etc until they start sleeping: *The movement of the waves soon lulled us to sleep.*
8 **send sb to sleep a)** to make someone go to sleep: *The combination of warmth and music sent him to sleep.* **b)** if something sends someone to sleep, it is extremely boring
9 [IN YOUR EYES] [U] *informal* a substance that forms in the corners of your eyes while you are sleeping: *She rubbed the sleep from her eyes.*

sleep·er /ˈsliːpə $ -ər/ *n* [C] **1** someone who sleeps in a particular way: **light sleeper** (=someone who wakes easily) | **heavy sleeper** (=someone who does not wake easily) **2** someone who is asleep **3** *BrE* a heavy piece of wood or CONCRETE that supports a railway track; ■ **tie** *AmE* **4 a)** a night train with carriages that have beds for passengers to sleep in **b)** a SLEEPING CAR **c)** *AmE* a bed on a train for a passenger to sleep in **5** *especially AmE* a film, book etc which is successful, even though people did not expect it to be **6** *AmE* a piece of clothing for a baby that covers its whole body including its feet **7** a SPY who is sent to a particular place and who lives an ordinary life there until a later time, when they begin their spying activities

ˈsleeping bag *n* [C] a large warm bag that you sleep in, especially when camping

ˈsleeping car *n* [C] a railway carriage with beds for passengers to sleep in; ■ **sleeper**

ˌsleeping ˈpartner *n* [C] *BrE* someone who owns part of a business but is not actively involved in running it; ■ **silent partner** *AmE*

ˈsleeping pill *n* [C] a PILL which helps you to sleep

ˌsleeping poˈliceman *n* [C] *BrE* a narrow raised part in a road which makes traffic go slowly; ■ **speed bump**

ˈsleeping ˌsickness *n* [U] a serious TROPICAL disease that is carried by the TSETSE FLY (=a type of insect). It causes extreme tiredness and fever, and makes you lose weight.

sleep·less /ˈsliːpləs/ *adj* **1** **a sleepless night** a night when you are unable to sleep: *Adrian spent a sleepless night wondering what to do.* **2** unable to sleep: *She lay sleepless for hours, worrying.* —**sleeplessly** *adv* —**sleeplessness** *n* [U]

sleep·o·ver /ˈsliːpəʊvə $ -oʊvər/ *n* [C] a party for children in which they stay the night at someone's house

sleep·walk·er /ˈsliːpˌwɔːkə $ -ˌwɔːkər/ *n* [C] someone who walks while they are sleeping —**sleepwalk** *v* [I] —**sleepwalking** *n* [U]

sleep·y /ˈsliːpi/ *adj comparative* **sleepier**, *superlative* **sleepiest 1** tired and ready to sleep: *The warmth*

from the fire made her feel sleepy. **2** a sleepy town or area is very quiet, and not much happens there; ◧ **lively** —**sleepily** *adv* —**sleepiness** *n* [U]

sleep·y·head /ˈsliːpihed/ *n* [C] *spoken* someone, especially a child, who looks as if they want to go to sleep: *It's time for bed, sleepyhead.*

sleet /sliːt/ *n* [U] half-frozen rain that falls when it is very cold: *scattered sleet and snow showers* —**sleet** *v* [I]: *It was sleeting so hard we could barely see for 30 yards.* —**sleety** *adj*

sleeve /sliːv/ *n* [C] **1** the part of a piece of clothing that covers all or part of your arm: *a dress with long sleeves* | **long-sleeved/short-sleeved etc** *a short-sleeved shirt* **2 have something up your sleeve** *informal* to have a secret plan or idea that you are going to use later: *Don't worry. He still has a few tricks up his sleeve.* **3** a stiff paper cover that a record is stored in; ◧ **jacket**

sleeve·less /ˈsliːvləs/ *adj* a sleeveless jacket, dress etc has no sleeves

sleigh /sleɪ/ *n* [C] a large open vehicle with no wheels that is used for travelling over snow and is pulled along by animals; → **sledge**

sleight of hand /ˌslaɪt əv ˈhænd/ *n* [U] **1** the use of quick and skilful movements with your hands when doing a magic trick, so that people cannot understand how you did the trick **2** the use of skilful tricks and lies in order to deceive someone

slen·der /ˈslendə $ -ər/ *adj* **1** thin in an attractive or graceful way; ◧ **slim**: *She is slender and stylish.* | *Laura's tall,* **slender figure** | **slender legs/arms/fingers etc**; → see picture at THIN¹; → see box at THIN¹ **2** small or very limited in amount or size; ◧ **slim**: *The company only has a slender hope of survival.* | *The Republicans won the election by a slender majority.* | *We had to make the most of our rather slender resources.* —**slenderness** *n* [U]

slept /slept/ the past tense and past participle of SLEEP

sleuth /sluːθ/ *n* [C] *old-fashioned* someone who tries to find out information about a crime; ◧ **detective** —**sleuthing** *n* [U]

slew¹ /sluː/ *v* [I,T always + adv/prep] to turn or slide in a different direction suddenly and violently, or to make a vehicle do this: [+around/sideways] *I lost control of the car and it slewed sideways into the ditch.*

slew² the past tense of SLAY

slew³ *n* **a slew of sth** *informal* a large number of things: *a whole slew of cheap motels*

slice¹ /slaɪs/ *n* [C] **1** a thin flat piece of food cut from a larger piece: [+of] *a slice of bread* | *pizza slices* | **thin/thick slice** *a thin slice of ham* | *Cut the tomatoes* **into slices.** → see picture at BREAD **2** a part or share of something: [+of] *Everybody wants a slice of the profits.* **3 fish slice** *BrE* a kitchen tool used for lifting and serving pieces of food; ◧ **spatula** *AmE* **4** a way of hitting the ball in sports such as tennis or golf, that makes the ball go to one side with a spinning movement, rather than straight ahead **5 a slice of life** a film, play, or book which shows life as it really is

slice² *v* **1** [T] also **slice up** to cut meat, bread, vegetables etc into thin flat pieces; → **chop**: *Thinly slice the cucumbers.* | *Slice up the onions and add them to the meat.* | *sliced ham* **2** [I always + adv/prep] to cut something easily with one movement of a sharp knife or edge: [+into/through] *The blade's so sharp it could slice through your finger.* | **slice sth in two/half** *Slice the eggs in two and arrange them on a serving dish.* **3** [I always + adv/prep] to move quickly and easily through something such as water or air: [+through/into] *The boat was slicing through the sparkling waves.* **4** [T] to hit a ball, for example in tennis or golf, so that it spins sideways instead of moving straight forward: *With an open goal in front of him, Wiltord* **sliced** *his* **shot** *wide of the left post.* **5 any way you slice it** *AmE spoken*

S

whatever way you choose to consider the situation: *It's the truth, any way you slice it.*

slice sth ⇔ **off** *phr v* **1** to remove part of something by cutting it with one movement of a sharp knife or edge; **≡ cut off**: *His knife had slipped and sliced off the top of his finger.* **2** to reduce a cost or total by a particular amount quickly and easily: **slice sth off sth** *By using volunteers we were able to slice £10,000 off the cost of the project.*

,**sliced** '**bread** *n* [U] **1** bread that is sold already cut into slices **2** **the best/greatest thing since sliced bread** *informal* used humorously to say that something new is very helpful, useful etc: *He reckons his new mobile phone is the best thing since sliced bread.*

slick[1] /slɪk/ *adj* **1** if something is slick, it is done in a skilful and attractive way and seems expensive, but it often contains no important or interesting ideas: *a slick Hollywood production* | *slick advertising* | *The presentation was very slick.* **2** if someone is slick, they are good at persuading people, often in a way that does not seem honest: *a slick used-car salesman* **3** done smoothly and quickly: *He got round the defender using some slick footwork.* **4** smooth and slippery: [+**with**] *Cars were sliding off roads that were slick with rain.* **5** *AmE old-fashioned* very good or attractive —**slickly** *adv* —**slickness** *n* [U]

slick[2] *n* [C] **1** also **oil slick** an area of oil on the surface of water or on a road **2** *AmE* a magazine printed on good quality paper with a shiny surface, usually with a lot of colour pictures; **≡ glossy magazine** **3** *technical* a smooth car tyre used for racing

slick[3] *v*
slick sth ⇔ **down/back** *phr v* to make hair smooth and shiny by putting oil, water etc on it: *His hair had been combed back and slicked down with something to make it neat.*

slick·er /'slɪkə $ -ər/ *n* [C] *AmE* a coat made of smooth shiny material that keeps out the rain

slide[1] [W3] /slaɪd/ *v past tense and past participle* **slid** /slɪd/
1 [I,T] to move smoothly over a surface while continuing to touch it, or to make something move in this way: [+**along/across/down etc**] *Francesca slid across the ice.* | **slide sth across/along etc** *He opened the oven door and slid the pan of cookies in.* | *He* **slid open** *the door of the glass cabinet.* → see picture at **SLIP**[1]
2 [I,T always + adv/prep] to move somewhere quietly and smoothly, or to move something in this way: [+**into/out of etc**] *Daniel slid out of the room when no one was looking.* | *She slid into the driver's seat.* | **slide sth into/out of etc sth** *He slid the gun into his pocket.*
3 [I] if prices, amounts, rates etc slide, they become lower; **≡ drop**; **≢ rise**: *Stocks slid a further 3% on the major markets today.*
4 [I] to gradually become worse, or to begin to have a problem: *Students' test scores started to slide in the mid-1990s.* | [+**into**] *Murphy gradually slid into a pattern of drug abuse.*
5 **let sth slide a)** to let a situation get gradually worse: *Management has let safety standards slide at the factory.* **b)** *spoken* to ignore a mistake, problem, remark etc, without trying to improve or stop it: *Well, I guess we can let it slide this time.*

WORD CHOICE: slide, slip, skid
Slide means to move smoothly across a surface. You can talk about people, objects, or liquids sliding: *This floor's great for sliding on.* | *The door slid open (NOT slided open).* | *A tear slid down her cheek.*
Slip means to accidentally slide a small distance, and usually then fall down: *She slipped and hurt her wrist.* | *It's icy – mind you don't slip.*
Skid means to move across a smooth surface in an uncontrolled way. You usually use it to talk about vehicles: *Cars skidded on the snow.* | *Jason skidded around the corner on his bike.*

slide[2] *n* [C]
1 **FOR CHILDREN** a large structure with steps leading to the top of a long sloping surface which children can slide down
2 **DECREASE** [usually singular] a decrease in prices, amounts etc; **≢ rise**: [+**in**] *the current slide in house prices* | **on the slide** *The company's shares were on the slide again yesterday, down 7p at 339p.*
3 **PICTURE** a small piece of film in a frame that you shine a light through to show a picture on a SCREEN or wall: *a slide show*
4 **GETTING WORSE** [usually singular] a situation in which something gradually gets worse, or someone develops a problem: [+**in**] *School administrators were unable to explain the slide in student performance.* | [+**into**] *a slide into economic chaos*
5 **SCIENCE** a small piece of thin glass used for holding something that you want to look at under a MICROSCOPE
6 **MUSIC/MACHINE** a sliding part of a machine or musical instrument, such as the U-shaped tube of a TROMBONE
7 **MOVEMENT** [usually singular] a sliding movement across a surface: *The car went into a slide.*
8 **EARTH/SNOW** a sudden fall of earth, stones, snow etc down a slope: *a rock slide*
9 **FOR HAIR** *BrE* a small metal or plastic object that holds your hair in place

'**slide pro**,**jector** *n* [C] a piece of equipment that shines a light through SLIDES so that pictures appear on a screen or wall

'**slide rule** *n* [C] an old-fashioned instrument used for calculating numbers, that looks like a ruler and has a middle part that slides across

,**sliding** '**door** *n* [C] a door that opens by sliding to one side

,**sliding** '**scale** *n* [C usually singular] a system for calculating how much you pay for taxes, medical treatment etc, in which the amount that you pay changes according to different conditions: **on a sliding scale** *Fees are calculated on a sliding scale.*

slight[1] [S2] [W3] /slaɪt/ *adj comparative* **slighter**, *superlative* **slightest**
1 [usually before noun] small in degree; **≢ big**: *a slight improvement* | *a slight increase* | *a slight change of plan* | *a slight pause* | *a slight problem*
2 **not the slightest** chance/doubt/difference etc no doubt, chance etc at all: *I didn't have the slightest idea who that man was.*
3 someone who is slight is thin and delicate; **≢ stocky**; → see box at **THIN**[1]
4 **not in the slightest** *BrE spoken* not at all: '*Did he mind lending you the car?*' '*Not in the slightest.*'

slight[2] *v* [T] to offend someone by treating them rudely or without respect: *Derek felt slighted when no one phoned him back.* —**slight** *n* [C]: *She may take it as a* **slight on** *her ability as a mother.* | *a* **slight to** *his authority*

slight·ly [S1] [W2] /'slaɪtli/ *adv*
1 a little: *a slightly different color* | *a slightly more powerful engine* | **slightly higher/lower/better/larger etc** *January's sales were slightly better than average.* | *He was someone I already knew slightly.* | *a slightly tart flavor* | *He leaned forward ever so slightly.*
2 **slightly-built** having a thin and delicate body

slim[1] [S3] /slɪm/ *adj comparative* **slimmer**, *superlative* **slimmest**
1 someone who is slim is attractively thin; **≡ slender**: *a slim young woman* | *a slim waist* → see box at **THIN**[1]
2 very small in amount or number; **≡ slender**: *There's only a* **slim chance** *that anyone survived the crash.* | *The Republicans held a slim majority in the Senate.*
3 not wide or thick: *a slim volume of poetry*

slim[2] *v* **slimmed**, **slimming** [I] *BrE* to make yourself thinner by eating less, taking a lot of exercise etc; → **diet** —**slimmer** *n* [C]
slim down *phr v* **1** to reduce the size or number of something, or to become reduced in size or number:

slim sth ⇔ **down** *The company is trying to slim down its workforce.* | [+**to**] *The Cabinet has been slimmed down to 16 members.* **2** to make your body thinner, or to become thinner, especially in order to be healthier or more attractive: **slim** sth ⇔ **down** *How can I slim down my hips?* | [+**to**] *She slimmed down to a healthy 61 kilos.* —**slimmed-down** *adj*

slime /slaɪm/ *n* [U] an unpleasant thick slippery substance: *a pond full of green slime* | *the trails of slime left by snails*

slime·ball /'slaɪmbɔːl $ -bɒːl/ *n* [C] *informal* someone who is immoral, extremely unpleasant, and cannot be trusted – used to show disapproval

slim·line /'slɪmlaɪn/ *adj BrE* **1** a slimline drink has fewer CALORIES than the normal type; → **diet** **2** a slimline piece of equipment is smaller or thinner than others of the same type: *a slimline dishwasher*

slim·ming¹ /'slɪmɪŋ/ *n* [U] *BrE* the activity of trying to make yourself thinner by eating less, taking exercise etc

slimming² *adj* making you look thinner: *Solid colors are more slimming than patterns.*

slim·y /'slaɪmi/ *adj* **1** covered with SLIME, or wet and slippery like slime: *slimy mud* **2** *informal* friendly in an unpleasant way that does not seem sincere – used to show disapproval: *a slimy politician* —**sliminess** *n* [U]

sling¹ /slɪŋ/ *v past tense and past participle* **slung** /slʌŋ/ [T always + adv/prep] **1** to throw or put something somewhere with a careless movement and some force; ▤ **chuck**: *Lou slung his suitcase onto the bed.* | **sling** sb sth *Sling me the keys.* | *Pete slung his bag over his shoulder.* **2** *informal* to make someone leave or go to a place: **sling** sb **into/out of** sth *Sam was slung into jail for punching a cop.* **3** [usually passive] to hang something loosely: *Dave wore a tool belt slung around his waist.* **4 sling your hook** *BrE informal* used to tell someone to go away

sling² *n* [C] **1** a piece of cloth tied around your neck to support an injured arm or hand: **in a sling** *She had her arm in a sling.* **2** a set of ropes or strong pieces of cloth that are used to lift and carry heavy objects **3** a special type of bag that fastens over your shoulders, in which you can carry a baby close to your body **4** a piece of rope with a piece of leather in the middle, used in past times as a weapon for throwing stones **5 slings and arrows** *written* problems or criticisms: *We've all suffered the slings and arrows of day-to-day living.*

sling·back /'slɪŋbæk/ *n* [C] a woman's shoe that is open at the back and has a narrow band going around the heel

sling·shot /'slɪŋʃɒt $ -ʃɑːt/ *n* [C] *AmE* a small Y-shaped stick with a thin band of rubber across the top, used to throw stones; ▤ **catapult** *BrE*

slink /slɪŋk/ *v past tense and past participle* **slunk** /slʌŋk/ [I always + adv/prep] to move somewhere quietly and secretly, especially because you are afraid or ashamed; ▤ **creep**: *Edward was hoping to slink past unnoticed.*

slink·y /'slɪŋki/ *adj* **1** a slinky dress, skirt etc is smooth and tight and shows the shape of a woman's body in a way that looks sexually attractive: *a slinky black dress* **2** slinky movements, music, or voices are slow in a way that is sexually attractive: *a song with slinky bass lines*

slip¹ S3 W2 /slɪp/ *v* **slipped, slipping**
1 FALL OR SLIDE [I] to slide a short distance accidentally, and fall or lose your balance slightly: *Wright slipped but managed to keep hold of the ball.* | [+**on**] *He slipped on the ice.*; → *see box at* SLIDE¹
2 GO SOMEWHERE [I always + adv/prep] to go somewhere, without attracting other people's attention; ▤ **slide**: *Ben slipped quietly out of the room.* | *One man managed to slip from the club as police arrived.*
3 PUT STH SOMEWHERE [T always + adv/prep] to put something somewhere quietly or smoothly; ▤ **slide**:

skid

slip

trip

slide

Ann slipped the book into her bag. | *A letter had been slipped under his door.* | *Carrie slipped her arm through her brother's.*
4 GIVE STH TO SB [T] to give someone something secretly or without attracting much attention: **slip** sb sth *I slipped him a ten-dollar bill to keep quiet.* | **slip** sth **to** sb *Carr slips the ball to King who scores easily.*
5 MOVE [I] to move smoothly, especially off or from something: *As he bent over, the towel round his waist slipped.* | [+**off/down/from** etc] *He watched the sun slip down behind the mountains.* | *The ring had slipped off Julia's finger.* | *Cally slipped from his grasp and fled.*
6 KNIFE [I] if a knife or other tool slips, it moves so that it accidentally cuts the wrong thing: *The knife slipped and cut his finger.*
7 GET WORSE [I] to become worse or lower than before: *Standards have slipped in many parts of the industry.* | *His popularity slipped further after a series of scandals.* | *You're slipping, Doyle! You need a holiday.*
8 CHANGE CONDITION [I always + adv/prep] to gradually start being in a particular condition; ▤ **fall**. [+**into**] *He had begun to slip into debt.* | *She slipped into unconsciousness and died the next day.* | *The project has slipped behind schedule.*
9 CLOTHES [I,T always + adv/prep] to put a piece of clothing on your body or take it off your body quickly and smoothly: **slip** sth **off/on** *Peter was already at the door slipping on his shoes.* | [+**into/out of**] *She slipped out of her clothes and stepped into the shower.*
10 TIME [I, always + adv/prep] if time slips away, past etc it passes quickly: [+**away/past/by**] *The search for the missing child continued, but time was slipping away.* | *The hours slipped past almost unnoticed.*
11 slip your mind/memory if something slips your mind, you forget it: *I meant to buy some milk, but it completely slipped my mind.*
12 let sth **slip** to say something without meaning to, when you had wanted it to be a secret: *He let it slip that they were planning to get married.*
13 GET FREE [T] to get free from something that was holding you: *The dog slipped his collar and ran away.*
14 slip through the net *BrE*; **slip through the cracks** *AmE* if someone or something slips through the net, they are not caught or dealt with by the system that is supposed to catch them or deal with them: *In a class of 30 children, it is easy for one to slip through the net and learn nothing.*
15 let sth **slip (through your fingers)** to not take an opportunity, offer etc: *Don't let a chance like that slip through your fingers!*
16 slip one over on sb *informal especially AmE* to deceive or play a trick on someone
17 slip a disc/disk to suffer an injury when one of the connecting parts between the bones in your back moves out of place

slip away *phr v*
1 to leave a place secretly or without anyone noticing
2 if something such as an opportunity slips away, it is no longer available: *This time, Radford did not let her chance slip away.*

slip sth ⇔ **in** *phr v*
to use a word or say something without attracting too much attention: *He had slipped in a few jokes to liven the speech up.*

slip out *phr v*
if something slips out, you say it without really intending to: *I didn't mean to say it. The words slipped out.*

slip up *phr v*
to make a mistake: *The company apologized for slipping up so badly.* | [+on] *Someone had slipped up on the order.* → SLIP-UP

slip² *n*
1 **PAPER** [C] a small or narrow piece of paper: *a slip of paper* | *an order slip* | *a betting slip* → PAYSLIP
2 **MISTAKE** [C] a small mistake: *Molly knew she could not afford to make a single slip.*
3 **slip of the tongue/pen** a small mistake you make when you are speaking or writing, especially by using the wrong word: *It was just a slip of the tongue.* → FREUDIAN SLIP
4 **give sb the slip** *informal* to escape from someone who is chasing you: *Somehow she'd given them the slip.*
5 **CLOTHING** [C] a piece of underwear, similar to a thin dress or skirt, that a woman wears under a dress or skirt: *a white silk slip*
6 **GETTING WORSE** [C usually singular] an occasion when something becomes worse or lower: [+in] *a slip in house prices*
7 **SLIDE** [C] an act of sliding a short distance or of falling by sliding
8 **a slip of a girl/boy etc** *old-fashioned* a small thin young person – often used humorously
9 **CRICKET** [C usually plural] a part of the field where players stand, trying to catch the ball in CRICKET
10 **CLAY** [U] *technical* a mixture of clay and water that is used for decorating pots

slip·case /'slɪpkeɪs/ *n* [C] a hard cover, like a box, for putting a book in

slip·co·ver /'slɪpˌkʌvə $ -ər/ *n* [C] a loose cloth cover for furniture

slip·knot /'slɪpnɒt $ -nɑːt/ *n* [C] a knot that you can make tighter by pulling one of its ends

slip-ons *n* [plural] shoes that do not have a fastening
—**slip-on** *adj*: *slip-on shoes*

slip·page /'slɪpɪdʒ/ *n* [C,U] *formal* **1** failure to do something at the planned time, at the planned cost etc: *Slippage on any job will entail slippage on the overall project.* **2** when something becomes worse or lower: [+in/of] *slippage in sales* **3** when something slips: *snow slippage*

slipped 'disc; slipped disk *AmE n* [C usually singular] a painful injury caused when one of the connecting parts between the bones in your back moves out of place

slip·per /'slɪpə $ -ər/ *n* [C] a light soft shoe that you wear at home → see picture at FOOTWEAR

slip·per·y /'slɪpəri/ *adj* **1** something that is slippery is difficult to hold, walk on etc because it is wet or GREASY: *In places, the path can be wet and slippery.* | *Harry's palms were slippery with sweat.* → see picture at SURFACE **2** *informal* someone who is slippery cannot be trusted: *Martin is a slippery customer* (=someone you should not trust) *so be careful what you say to him.* **3** not having one clear meaning and able to be understood in different ways: *the slippery notion of 'standards'* **4** **(be on) a/the slippery slope** *BrE informal* used to talk about a process or habit that is difficult to stop and which will develop into something extremely bad: [+to/towards] *He is on the slippery slope to a life in crime.* —**slipperiness** *n* [U]

slip·py /'slɪpi/ *adj BrE informal* a slippy surface or object is slippery

'slip road *n* [C] *BrE* a road for driving onto or off a MOTORWAY; ⬛ **ramp** *AmE*

slip·shod /'slɪpʃɒd $ -ʃɑːd/ *adj* done too quickly and carelessly – used to show disapproval; ⬛ **slapdash**: *a slipshod piece of work*

slip·stream /'slɪpstriːm/ *n* [singular] the area of low air pressure just behind a vehicle that is moving quickly

'slip-up *n* [C] a careless mistake: *We cannot afford another slip-up.*

slip·way /'slɪpweɪ/ *n* [C] a sloping track that is used for moving boats into or out of the water

slit¹ /slɪt/ *v past tense and past participle* **slit**, *present participle* **slitting** [T] to make a straight narrow cut in cloth, paper, skin etc: *Guy slit open the envelope.* | **slit sb's throat** (=kill someone by cutting their throat) | **slit your wrists** (=try to kill yourself by cutting your wrists)

slit² *n* [C] a long straight narrow cut or hole: *light shining through a slit in the door* | *a skirt with a slit up the side*

slith·er /'slɪðə $ -ər/ *v* [I always + adv/prep] to slide somewhere over a surface, twisting or moving from side to side: *A snake slithered across the grass.* | *He slithered down the muddy bank.* → see picture at MOVEMENT

slith·er·y /'slɪðəri/ *adj* unpleasantly slippery

sliv·er /'slɪvə $ -ər/ *n* [C] a small pointed or thin piece that has been cut or broken off something: [+of] *a sliver of glass* | *a sliver of cake*

slob¹ /slɒb $ slɑːb/ *n* [C] *informal* someone who is lazy and untidy: *a lazy slob*

slob² *v* **slobbed, slobbing**
slob around/out *phr v BrE informal* to spend time doing nothing and being lazy

slob·ber /'slɒbə $ 'slɑːbər/ *v* [I] to let SALIVA (=the liquid produced by your mouth) come out of your mouth and run down; ⬛ **drool**: *I hate dogs that slobber everywhere.*
slobber over sth/sb *phr v* to show how much you want, like, or love someone or something, without controlling yourself: *I caught Rick slobbering over the models in a magazine.*

slob·ber·y /'slɒbəri $ 'slɑː-/ *adj* a slobbery kiss or mouth is unpleasantly wet

sloe /sləʊ $ sloʊ/ *n* [C] a small bitter fruit like a PLUM

sloe 'gin *n* [U] an alcoholic drink made with sloes, GIN, and sugar

slog¹ /slɒg $ slɑːg/ *v* **slogged, slogging** [I] *informal* **1** to work hard at something without stopping, especially when the work is difficult, tiring, or boring: *Mother slogged all her life for us.* | [+away] *After a day slogging away at work, I need to relax.* | [+through] *You just have to sit down and slog through long lists of new vocabulary.* **2** [always + adv/prep] to make a long hard journey somewhere, especially on foot: *He's been slogging round the streets delivering catalogues.* | **slog your way through/round etc** sth *He started to slog his way up the hill.* **3** **slog it out** *BrE* to fight, compete, or argue about something until one side wins: *The teams will be slogging it out on Saturday.*

slog² *n* **1** [singular, U] *BrE informal* a piece of work that takes a lot of time and effort and is usually boring: *It'll be a slog, but I know we can do it.* | *months of hard slog* **2** [singular] a long period of tiring walking: *a long hard slog uphill*

slo·gan /'sləʊgən $ 'sloʊ-/ *n* [C] a short phrase that is easy to remember and is used in advertisements, or by politicians, organizations etc; → **catchphrase**: *an advertising slogan* | *demonstrators shouting political slogans* | *the Democrats' campaign slogan*

slo·gan·eer·ing /ˌsləʊgəˈnɪərɪŋ $ ˌsloʊgəˈnɪr-/ n [U] the use of slogans in advertisements or by politicians, organizations etc – used to show disapproval: *political sloganeering*

slo-mo /ˈsləʊ məʊ $ ˈsloʊ moʊ/ adj [only before noun] *informal* used to describe action that appears to happen more slowly than it really happens, in computer games, on video etc; → **slow-motion**: *slo-mo mode* —**slo-mo** n [U]

sloop /sluːp/ n [C] a small ship with one central MAST (=pole for sails)

slop¹ /slɒp $ slɑːp/ v **slopped, slopping** **1** [I always + adv/prep] if liquid slops somewhere, it moves around or over the edge of a container in an uncontrolled way; ◘ **splash**: *Coffee slopped over the rim of her cup.* | *With each wave, more water slopped into the cabin.* **2** [T always + adv/prep] to put a liquid somewhere in a careless way: *She put the glass down, slopping beer onto the table.* **3** [T] *AmE* to feed slop to pigs

slop around/about phr v *BrE informal* to relax, wearing clothes that are untidy or old: *Jan would never slop around in old jeans.*

slop out phr v *BrE* if prisoners slop out, they empty their toilet buckets —**slopping-out** n [U]

slop² n [U] also **slops** plural **1** waste food that can be used to feed animals **2** *BrE* dirty water or URINE: *Prisoners had to use slop buckets at night.* **3** *informal* food that is too soft and tastes bad: *Do you actually expect us to eat this slop?*

slope¹ W3 /sləʊp $ sloʊp/ n
1 [C] a piece of ground or a surface that slopes: *a steep slope* | *a gentle* (=not steep) *slope* | *She looked back up the grassy slope.*
2 an area of steep ground covered with snow that people SKI down: *We got to Tahoe on Friday, and hit the slopes* (=skied on them) *the next day.*
3 [singular] the angle at which something slopes in relation to a flat surface: *a slope of 30 degrees*

slope² v [I] if the ground or a surface slopes, it is higher at one end than the other: [+up/down/away etc] *a pleasant garden that slopes down to the river*

slope off phr v *BrE informal* to leave somewhere quietly and secretly, especially when you are avoiding work: *Mike sloped off early today.*

slop·py /ˈslɒpi $ ˈslɑːpi/ adj **1** not done carefully or thoroughly; ◘ **careless**: *sloppy work* | *His written reports are incredibly sloppy.* **2** sloppy clothes are loose-fitting, untidy, or dirty: *Ann was dressed in a sloppy brown sweater.* **3** expressing feelings of love too strongly and in a silly way; ◘ **slushy**: *The film is a sloppy romance.* **4** not solid enough: *sloppy jelly* —**sloppily** adv —**sloppiness** n [U]

sloppy joe /ˌslɒpi ˈdʒəʊ $ ˌslɑːpi ˈdʒoʊ/ n [C] *AmE* a type of sandwich, made from BEEF with spices added and served on a BUN

slosh /slɒʃ $ slɑːʃ/ v **1** [I,T always + adv/prep] if a liquid sloshes somewhere, or if you slosh it, it moves or is moved about in an uncontrolled way: [+around/ about] *Water was sloshing about in the bottom of the boat.* | *He put the glass down hard and beer sloshed over the edge.* **2** [T always + adv/prep] to put a liquid in a container or on a surface in a careless way: *Jo sloshed more wine into her glass.* | *Slosh a bit of paint on.* **3** [I always + adv/prep] to walk through water or mud in a noisy way: *People were sloshing around in the mud.*

sloshed /slɒʃt $ slɑːʃt/ adj [not before noun] *informal* drunk: *Most of them were too sloshed to notice.*

slot¹ /slɒt $ slɑːt/ n [C] **1** a long narrow hole in a surface, that you can put something into: *Alan dropped another quarter into the slot on the pay phone.* **2** a short period of time allowed for one particular event on a programme or TIMETABLE: *a ten-minute slot on the breakfast show* | *landing slots at Heathrow Airport* | *A new comedy is scheduled for the 9 p.m. time slot.*

slot² v **slotted, slotting** [I,T always + adv/prep] to go into a slot, or to put something in a slot: **slot sth into sth** *Mary slotted a cassette into the VCR.* | [+into] *Each*

length *of board slots easily into the next.* | *All the wood parts come pre-cut so that they can be* **slotted together** (=put together using slots).

slot in phr v *BrE informal* to fit something or someone into a plan, organization etc, or to fit in: *Stewart has slotted in well.* | **slot sb/sth ⇔ in** *We should be able to slot the meeting in before lunch.*

sloth /sləʊθ $ sloʊθ/ n **1** [C] an animal in Central and South America that moves very slowly, has grey fur, and lives in trees **2** [U] *formal* laziness

sloth·ful /ˈsləʊθfəl $ ˈsloʊθ-/ adj *formal* lazy or not active —**slothfulness** n [U]

'slot ma·chine n [C] **1** a machine used for playing a game, that starts when you put money into it **2** *BrE* a machine that you buy cigarettes, food, or drink from; ◘ **vending machine**

slotted 'spoon n [C] a large spoon with holes in it

slouch¹ /slaʊtʃ/ v [I] to stand, sit, or walk with a slouch: [+back/against/in etc] *Jimmy slouched back in his chair.* | *She slouched across the living room.*

slouch² n **1** be no slouch (at sth) *informal* to be very good at something: *Horowitz was no slouch at languages.* **2** [singular] a way of standing, sitting, or walking with your shoulders bent forward that makes you look tired or lazy

slough¹ /slʌf/ v
slough sth ⇔ off phr v **1** *technical* to get rid of a dead layer of skin **2** *literary* to get rid of something, especially something that is damaging you: *The president wanted to slough off the country's bad image.*

slough² /slaʊ $ sluː, slaʊ/ n **1** [singular] *literary* a bad situation or a state of sadness that you cannot get out of easily: [+of] *Harry was in a slough of despondency for weeks.* **2** [C] an area of land covered in deep dirty water or mud

slov·en·ly /ˈslʌvənli/ adj lazy, untidy, and careless: *slovenly habits* | *a large slovenly woman* | *a slovenly way of speaking* —**slovenliness** n [U]

slow¹ S2 W2 /sləʊ $ sloʊ/ adj comparative **slower**, superlative **slowest**
1 NOT QUICK not moving, being done, or happening quickly; ◘ **quick, fast**; → **slowly**: *The car was travelling at a very slow speed.* | *a slow walker* | *The economy faces a year of slower growth.* | *Take a few deep, slow breaths.* | *We got on the* **slow train** (=one that stops at a lot of places) *by mistake.*
2 TAKING TOO LONG taking too long; ◘ **fast**: *Taylor was concerned at the slow progress of the investigations.* | *The legal system can be* **painfully slow** (=much too slow). | **slow to do sth** *The wound was slow to heal.*
3 WITH DELAY [not before noun] if you are slow to do something, you do not do it as soon as you can or should: **slow to do sth** *Farmers have been slow to exploit this market.* | *Their attitude was slow to change.* | **slow in doing sth** *He has been slow in announcing the name of his successor.* | *New ideas have been slow in coming.*
4 LONGER TIME taking a longer time than something similar; ◘ **fast**: *the slow train* (=one that stops at more stations)
5 BUSINESS if business or trade is slow, there are not many customers or not much is sold: *Business is often slow in the afternoon.* | *The company is experiencing slow sales.*
6 CLOCK [not before noun] if a clock or watch is slow, it is showing a time earlier than the correct time; ◘ **fast**: **ten minutes/five minutes etc slow** *The clock is about five minutes slow.*
7 NOT CLEVER not good or quick at understanding things: *Teaching assistants have time to help the slower pupils.*
8 slow on the uptake not quick to understand something new: *Sometime Tim's a little slow on the uptake.*

S

9 slow off the mark not quick enough at reacting to something
10 do a slow burn *AmE informal* to slowly get angry: *Tony fumbled the ball and I could see the coach doing a slow burn.*
11 slow handclap *BrE* if a group of people give someone a slow handclap, they CLAP their hands slowly to show their disapproval
12 a slow oven an OVEN that is at a low temperature
13 PHOTOGRAPHY a slow film does not react to light very easily —**slowness** *n* [U]

slow² S2 W2 *v*
also **slow down/up** [I,T] to become slower or to make something slower: *Her breathing slowed and she fell asleep.* | *Ian slowed up as he approached the traffic lights.*

slow down *phr v*
1 to become slower or to make something slower: *Growth in sales has slowed down.* | **slow sth/sb ⇔ down** *The ice on the road slowed us down.*
2 to become less active or busy than you usually are: *It is important to slow down, rest, and eat sensibly.*

slow³ *adv comparative* **slower**, *superlative* **slowest** *informal* slowly: *If you go slower, you'll see much more.* → GO-SLOW

slow·coach /'sləʊkəʊtʃ $ 'sloʊkoʊtʃ/ *n* [C] *BrE informal* someone who moves or does things too slowly

slow·down /'sləʊdaʊn $ 'sloʊ-/ *n* **1** [C usually singular] a reduction in activity or speed: [+in] *a slowdown in the US economy* **2** [C] *AmE* a period when people deliberately work slowly in order to protest about something

'**slow lane** *n* [C] **1** the part of a large road where vehicles drive more slowly than the other vehicles on the road; → **fast lane 2 in the slow lane** if a company, organization etc is in the slow lane, it is less successful than others: *The country is expected to remain in the slow lane of economic recovery.*

slow·ly /'sləʊli $ 'sloʊ-/ *adv* **1** at a slow speed; ⚡ **quickly**: *He shook his head slowly.* | '*That's true,*' *said Joe slowly.* **2 slowly but surely** used to emphasize that a change is happening, although it is happening slowly: *We are slowly but surely gaining the support of the public.*

,**slow 'motion** *n* [U] movement on film or television shown at a slower speed than it really happened: **in slow motion** *Let's see that goal again in slow motion.*

'**slow-pitch** *n* [U] *AmE* a game like SOFTBALL, usually played by mixed teams of men and women

slow·poke /'sləʊpəʊk $ 'sloʊpoʊk/ *n* [C] *AmE informal* someone who moves or does things too slowly

,**slow-'witted** *adj* not good at understanding things; ⚡ **stupid**

sludge /slʌdʒ/ *n* [U] **1** soft thick mud, especially at the bottom of a liquid **2** the solid substance that is left when industrial waste or SEWAGE (=the liquid waste from toilets) has been cleaned **3** thick dirty oil in an engine —**sludgy** *adj*

slug¹ /slʌg/ *n* [C] **1** a small creature with a soft body, that moves very slowly and eats garden plants **2** *AmE informal* a bullet: *Perez still has a slug lodged in his left shoulder.* **3** *informal* a small amount of a strong alcoholic drink: [+of] *a slug of brandy* **4** *AmE informal* a piece of metal shaped like a coin, used to illegally get a drink, ticket etc from a machine

slug² *v* **slugged, slugging** [T] **1 slug it out** if two people slug it out, they fight or compete until one of them has won **2** *informal* to hit someone hard with your closed hand; ⚡ **punch 3** to hit a ball hard

slug·fest /'slʌgfest/ *n* [C] *informal especially AmE* a situation in which people are arguing or fighting in a rude or angry way

slug·ger /'slʌgə $ -ər/ *n* [C] *AmE informal* a baseball player who hits the ball a very long way

slug·gish /'slʌgɪʃ/ *adj* moving or reacting more slowly than normal: *Alex woke late feeling tired and sluggish.* | *Economic recovery has so far been sluggish.* —**sluggishly** *adv* —**sluggishness** *n* [U]

sluice¹ /sluːs/ *n* [C] a passage for water to flow through, with a special gate which can be opened or closed to control it

sluice² *v* **1** [T] to wash something with a lot of water: **sluice sth out/down** *He was sluicing down the table and the floor.* **2** [I always + adv/prep] if water sluices somewhere, a large amount of it suddenly flows there

slum¹ /slʌm/ *n* **1** [C] a house or an area of a city that is in very bad condition, where very poor people live: *a slum area* | *slum housing* | *the slums of London* **2** [singular] *BrE informal* a very untidy place

slum² *v* **slum it/be slumming** *informal* to spend time in conditions that are much worse than you are used to – often used humorously: *Jeremy doesn't slum it when he goes away.*

slum·ber¹ /'slʌmbə $ -ər/ *v* [I] *literary* to sleep

slumber² *n* [singular, U] also **slumbers** *literary* sleep: *He passed into a deep slumber.*

'**slumber ,party** *n* [C] *AmE* a children's party when a group of children sleep at one child's house

slum·lord /'slʌmlɔːd $ -lɔːrd/ *n* [C] *AmE* someone who owns houses in a very poor area and charges high rents for buildings that are in bad condition

slump¹ /slʌmp/ *v* [I] **1** to fall or lean against something because you are not strong enough to stand: [+against/over/back etc] *She slumped against the wall.* | *Carol slumped back in her chair, defeated.* | *Ben staggered and slumped onto the floor.* **2** to suddenly go down in price, value, or number; ⚡ **soar**: *Sales slumped by 20% last year.* | [+to] *The currency slumped to a record low.* **3** also **be slumped** if your shoulders or head slump or are slumped, they bend forward because you are unhappy, tired, or unconscious: *Her shoulders slumped and her eyes filled with tears.*

slump² *n* [C, usually singular] **1** a sudden decrease in prices, sales, profits etc: [+in] *a slump in car sales* **2** a period when there is a reduction in business and many people lose their jobs; ⚡ **boom**: *The war was followed by an economic slump.* | *a worldwide slump* **3** *especially AmE* a period when a player or team does not play well: **in a slump** *The Dodgers have been in a slump for the last three weeks.*

slung /slʌŋ/ the past tense and past participle of SLING

slunk /slʌŋk/ the past tense and past participle of SLINK

slur¹ /slɜː $ slɜːr/ *v* **slurred, slurring 1** [I,T] to speak unclearly without separating your words or sounds correctly: **slur your words/speech** *She was slurring her words as if she was drunk.* | *His voice sounded slurred.* **2** [T] to criticize someone or something unfairly **3** [T] to play a group of musical notes smoothly together

slur² *n* [C] **1** an unfair criticism that is intended to make people dislike someone or something: [+on/against] *Milton regarded her comment as a slur on his country.* | *How dare she cast a slur on (=criticize) my character!* | *a racist slur* **2** *technical* a curved line written over musical notes to show they must be played together smoothly

slurp /slɜːp $ slɜːrp/ *v* [I,T] to drink a liquid while making a noisy sucking sound —**slurp** *n* [C usually singular]

slur·ry /'slʌri $ 'slɜːri/ *n* [U] a mixture of water and mud, coal, or animal waste

slush /slʌʃ/ *n* **1** [U] partly melted snow: *Children were sliding around in the snow and slush.* **2** [U] *informal* feelings or stories that seem silly because they are too romantic: *sentimental slush* **3** [C,U] *especially AmE* a drink made with crushed ice and a sweet liquid: *cherry slush* —**slushy** *adj*

'**slush fund** *n* [C] an amount of money kept for dishonest purposes, especially in politics

slut /slʌt/ n [C] *taboo informal* a very offensive word for a woman who has sex with a lot of different people. Do not use this word. —**slutty** *adj* —**sluttish** *adj*

sly /slaɪ/ *adj* **1** someone who is sly cleverly deceives people in order to get what they want; ▤ **cunning** **2** sly smile/glance/wink etc a smile, look etc that shows you know something secret: *He leaned forward with a sly smile.* **3** on the sly *informal* secretly, especially when you are doing something that you should not do: *They'd been seeing each other on the sly for months.* —**slyly** *adv* —**slyness** *n* [U]

smack¹ /smæk/ v [T] **1** to hit someone, especially a child, with your open hand in order to punish them; → **slap**: *the debate about whether parents should smack their children* **2** [always + adv/prep] to hit something hard against something else so that it makes a short loud noise: *He smacked the money down on the table and walked out.* **3** smack your lips to make a short loud noise with your lips before or after you eat or drink something to show that it is good: *He drained his glass and smacked his lips appreciatively.* **4** *BrE informal* to hit someone hard with your closed hand; ▤ **punch**

smack of sth *phr v* [not in progressive] if a situation smacks of something unpleasant, it seems to involve that thing: *To me, the whole thing smacks of a cover-up.*

smack sb **up** *phr v informal* to hit someone hard many times with your hand: *Don't make me come over there and smack you up.*

smack² n **1** [C] **a)** a hit with your open hand, especially to punish a child; → **slap**: *You're going to get a smack in a minute!* **b)** *BrE informal* a hard hit with your closed hand; ▤ **punch**: smack in the mouth/face/gob *Talk like that and I'll give you a smack in the mouth.* **2** [C usually singular] a short loud noise caused when something hits something else: *The book landed with a smack.* **3** [U] *informal* HEROIN **4** give sb a smack on the lips/cheek *informal* to kiss someone loudly **5** [C] a small fishing boat

smack³ *adv informal* **1** exactly or directly in the middle of something, in front of something etc: smack in the middle/in front of sth etc *There was a hole smack in the middle of the floor.* | smack bang *BrE*/smack dab *AmE*: *It's smack dab in the middle of an earthquake zone.* **2** if something goes smack into something, it hits it with a lot of force: *The car ran smack into the side of the bus.*

smack·er /ˈsmækə $ -ər/ n [C] *informal* **1** a pound or a dollar **2** also **smack·e·roo** /ˌsmækəˈruː/ a loud kiss

small¹ S1 W1 /smɔːl $ smɒːl/ *adj comparative* **smaller**, *superlative* **smallest**
1 SIZE not large in size or amount: *a small piece of paper* | *a small car* | *a small town* | *a small dark woman* | *The T-shirt was too small for him.* | *The sweater comes in three sizes – small, medium and large.* | *Only a relatively small number of people were affected.* | *a small amount of money* | *A much smaller proportion of women are employed in senior positions.*
2 NOT IMPORTANT a small problem, job, mistake etc is not important or does not have a large effect; ▤ **minor**: *We may have to make a few small changes.* | *There's been a small problem.* | *There's only a small difference between them.* | *It was good to feel we had helped in some small way.*
3 no small degree/achievement/task etc a large degree, achievement etc: *The success of the project is due in no small measure to the work of Dr Peterson.* | *That is no small achievement in the circumstances.*
4 YOUNG a small child is young: *She has three small children.* | *I've known him since he was a small boy.*
5 small business/firm/farmer etc a business that does not involve large amounts of money or does not employ a large number of people: *grants for small businesses*
6 LETTER small letters are letters in the form a, b, c etc rather than A, B, C etc; ▤ **lower case**; ▣ **capital**
7 conservative with a small 'c'/democrat with a small 'd' etc *informal* someone who believes in the principles you have mentioned, but does not belong to an organized group or political party

8 VOICE a small voice is quiet and soft: *'What about me?' she asked in a small voice.*
9 look/feel small to seem or feel stupid, unimportant, or ashamed: *She jumped at any opportunity to make me look small.*
10 (it's a) small world *especially spoken* used to express surprise when you unexpectedly meet someone you know or find out that someone has an unexpected connection to you: *Did you know David went to school with my brother? It's a small world, isn't it?*
11 a small fortune a large amount of money: cost/spend/pay a small fortune *It must have cost him a small fortune.*
12 small change coins of low value: *I didn't have any small change for the parking meter.*
13 be thankful/grateful for small mercies/favours to be pleased that a bad situation is not even worse: *She wasn't too badly hurt, so we should be thankful for small mercies.*
14 the small hours also the wee small hours *BrE* the early morning hours, between about one and four o'clock: in/into the small hours *He finally fell exhausted into bed in the small hours.* | *The party continued into the wee small hours.*
15 small arms guns that you hold with one or both hands when firing them
16 sth is small potatoes also sth is small beer *BrE informal* used to say that someone or something is not important, especially when compared to other people or things: *Even with £10,000 to invest, you are still small beer for most investment managers.* —**small** *adv*: *He writes so small I can't read it.* —**smallness** *n* [U]

S

> **WORD CHOICE: small, little**
>
> **Small** is a very general word for talking about the size of something: *a small village* | *a small man* | *He had small brown eyes.* | *The envelope was too small.* | *Do you have this shirt in a smaller size?*
>
> **Little** is used, especially in spoken English, to show how you feel about someone or something small, for example to show that you like them, dislike them, or feel sorry for them: *What lovely little cakes!* | *her horrid little dog*
>
> ⚠ You can say 'smaller' or 'smallest', but do not say 'littler' or 'littlest': *Her feet are even smaller (NOT littler/more little) than mine.*
>
> ⚠ You can use words like 'quite', 'very' and 'too' in front of **small**, but do not use them with **little**: *a very small car (NOT very little car)*

small² n **1** the small of your back the lower part of your back where it curves **2** smalls [plural] *BrE old-fashioned informal* underwear

'small ad n [C] *BrE* an advertisement put in a newspaper by someone who wants to buy or sell something; ▤ **want ad** *AmE*

,small 'claims court n [C] a court where people can make legal claims involving small amounts of money

'small fry n [U] people or things that are not important when compared to other people or things: *There's no point in arresting the small fry.*

small·hold·er /ˈsmɔːl,həʊldə $ ˈsmɒːl,hoʊldər/ n [C] *BrE* someone who has a smallholding

small·hold·ing /ˈsmɔːl,həʊldɪŋ $ ˈsmɒːl,hoʊld-/ n [C] *BrE* a piece of land used for farming, that is smaller than an ordinary farm

,small in'testine n [C] the long tube that food goes through after it has gone through your stomach; → **large intestine**; → see picture at HUMAN¹

small·ish /ˈsmɔːlɪʃ $ ˈsmɒːl-/ *adj especially BrE* fairly small: *She's smallish with red hair.*

,small-'minded *adj* thinking too much about your own life and problems and not about important things – use this to show disapproval; → **narrow-minded**: *People around here are so small-minded.* —**small-mindedness** *n* [U]

small office/'home office n [C] *SOHO* a room in someone's home with electronic equipment such as a computer and a FAX machine that is used as a place in which to work

small·pox /'smɔːlpɒks $ 'smɒːlpɑːks/ n [U] a serious disease that causes spots which leave marks on your skin

small ˌprint n [U] *especially BrE* all the rules and details relating to a contract or agreement; ▣ **fine print** *AmE*: **read/check the small print** *Always read the small print before you sign anything.*

ˌsmall-'scale adj involving only a small number of things or a small area; ▣ **large-scale**: *a small-scale study*

ˈsmall ˌscreen n **the small screen** television – used especially when comparing television to the cinema; → **big screen**: *a film made for the small screen*

ˈsmall talk n [U] polite friendly conversation about unimportant subjects: *We stood around **making small talk**.*

ˈsmall-time adj **small-time crook/gangster etc** a criminal who is not involved in large or serious crimes —**small-timer** n [C]

ˈsmall-town adj [only before noun] **1** from, or relating to, a small town: *a small-town newspaper* **2** *AmE* also **small·ville** /'smɔːlvɪl $ 'smɒːl-/ relating to ideas, qualities etc that people in small towns are supposed to have, which sometimes includes a lack of interest in anything new or different: *small-town attitudes*

smarm·y /'smɑːmi $ -ɑːr-/ adj polite in an insincere way – used to show disapproval: *smarmy comments | a smarmy car salesman*

smart¹ S3 W2 /smɑːt $ smɑːrt/ adj comparative **smarter**, superlative **smartest**
1 INTELLIGENT *especially AmE* intelligent or sensible; ▣ **clever**; ▣ **stupid**: *The smart kids get good grades and go off to college. | I was smart enough to wait for a week. | His decision to become a director was a **smart move** (=sensible thing to do).*
2 DISRESPECTFUL trying to seem clever in a disrespectful way: *Don't **get smart with** me, young man. | He made some smart remark.*
3 NEAT *BrE* **a)** a smart person is wearing neat attractive clothes and has a generally tidy appearance; ▣ **sharp** *AmE*; ▣ **scruffy**: *You're **looking** very **smart**.* **b)** smart clothes, buildings etc are clean, tidy, and attractive; ▣ **sharp** *AmE*: *a smart black suit | smart new offices*
4 FASHIONABLE *BrE* fashionable or used by fashionable people: *one of Bonn's smartest restaurants*
5 TECHNOLOGY smart machines, weapons, materials etc are controlled by computers and are designed to react in a suitable way depending on the situation; → **smart bomb**: *smart weapons*
6 **the smart money is on sb/sth** used to say that a particular person or thing is likely to do something or be successful
7 QUICK *BrE* a smart movement is done quickly, especially with force: *a smart blow on the head | She set off **at a smart pace** (=fairly fast).* —**smartly** adv: *a smartly dressed young man | He turned smartly and walked away.* —**smartness** n [U]

smart² v [I] **1** to be upset because someone has hurt your feelings or offended you: [+from] *She was still smarting from the insult.* **2** if a part of your body smarts, it hurts with a stinging pain: *My eyes were smarting with the smoke.*
smart off phr v *AmE informal* to make funny rude remarks

ˈsmart ˌalec, smart aleck n [C] *informal* someone who always says clever things or always has the right answer, in a way that is annoying

ˈsmart arse *BrE* also **ˈsmart ass** *AmE* n [C] *informal not polite* a smart alec —**smart-arse** also **smart-ass** adj: *smart-arse remarks*

ˈsmart bomb n [C] a bomb that is fired from an aircraft and uses a computer to hit a particular place

ˈsmart card n [C] a small plastic card with an electronic part that records and remembers information

smart·en /'smɑːtn $ 'smɑːr-/ v
smarten sth ⇔ up phr v *especially BrE* **1** smarten yourself up to make yourself look neat and tidy: *You'd better smarten yourself up.* **2** to make something look neater: *We need to smarten the place up a bit.* **3** smarten up your act/ideas to improve the way you behave or do something: *The company needs to smarten up their act if they are to keep customers.*

smarts /smɑːts $ smɑːrts/ n [U] *AmE informal* intelligence: *If she had any smarts, she'd get rid of the guy.*

smart·y·pants /'smɑːti ˌpænts $ 'smɑːr-/ n [C] *informal* someone who always says clever things or always has the right answer, in a slightly annoying way; ▣ **clever clogs** *BrE*

smash¹ /smæʃ/ v **1** [I,T] to break into pieces violently or noisily, or to make something do this by dropping, throwing, or hitting it: *Vandals had smashed all the windows. | Firemen had to smash the lock to get in. | Several cups fell to the floor and **smashed to pieces**.* **2** [I,T always + adv/prep] to hit an object or surface violently, or to make something do this: *A stolen car smashed into the bus. | He smashed his fist down on the table.* **3** **smash a record** to do something much faster, better etc than anyone has done before: *The film smashed all box office records.* **4** [T] to destroy something such as a political system or criminal organization: *Police say they have smashed a major crime ring.* **5** [T] to hit a high ball with a strong downward action, in tennis or similar games
smash sth ⇔ down phr v to hit a door, wall etc violently so that it falls to the ground
smash sth ⇔ in phr v to hit something so violently that you break it and make a hole in it: *The door had been smashed in. |* **smash sb's face/head in** (=hit someone hard in the face or head) *I'll smash his head in if he comes here again!*
smash sth ⇔ up phr v to deliberately destroy something by hitting it: *Hooligans started smashing the place up.*

smash² n **1** [C] *BrE* a serious road or railway accident – used especially in newspapers; ▣ **crash**: *Young boy hurt in car smash.* **2** [C] also **smash hit** a new film, song etc which is very successful: *a box-office smash* (=a film which many people go to see at the cinema) **3** [C] a hard downward shot in tennis or similar games **4** [singular] the loud sound of something breaking: [+of] *He heard the smash of glass.*

ˌsmash-and-'grab adj *BrE* **smash-and-grab raid/attack etc** a crime in which someone robs a shop by breaking the window and stealing things quickly —**smash and grab** n [C]

smashed /smæʃt/ adj [not before noun] *informal* very drunk or affected by a drug; → **stoned**: *It's just an excuse to go out and **get smashed**.*

smash·er /'smæʃə $ -ər/ n [C] *BrE old-fashioned* someone who you think is very attractive, or something that is very good

ˈsmash hit n [C] a very successful new play, book, film etc: *They had a smash hit with their first single.*

smash·ing /'smæʃɪŋ/ adj *BrE old-fashioned* very good; ▣ **brilliant**: *We had a smashing holiday.*

smat·ter·ing /'smætərɪŋ/ n [singular] **1** a small number or amount of something: [+of] *a smattering of applause* **2** **have a smattering of sth** to have a small amount of knowledge about a subject, especially a foreign language

smear¹ /smɪə $ smɪr/ n [C] **1** a dirty mark made by a small amount of something spread across a surface: [+of] *a smear of paint | It left a black smear on his arm.* **2** *BrE* a SMEAR TEST **3** an untrue story about a politician or other important person that is told in order to make people lose respect for them – used especially in newspapers —**smeary** adj: *a smeary glass*

smear² v

1 SPREAD [T always + adv/prep] to spread a liquid or soft substance over a surface, especially in a careless or untidy way: **smear sth with sth** *His face was smeared with mud.* | **smear sth on/over etc sth** *Elaine smeared sun tan lotion on her shoulders.*

2 TELL LIES [T] to tell an untrue story about someone important in order to make people lose respect for them – used especially in newspapers: *an attempt to smear the party leadership*

3 DIRTY [T] to put dirty or oily marks on something: *smeared windows*

4 INK/PAINT [I,T] if writing, a picture, or paint smears or is smeared, the ink or paint is accidentally touched and spread across the surface; **smudge**: *Several words were smeared.*

'smear cam‚paign n [C] a deliberate plan to tell untrue stories about an important person in order to make people lose respect for them – used especially in newspapers

'smear test n [C] BrE a medical test in which some cells are removed from the entrance to a woman's WOMB (=the place where a baby grows) and examined under a microscope

smell¹ S2 W3 /smel/ n

1 [C] the quality that people and animals recognize by using their nose: [+of] *The air was filled with the smell of flowers.* | **sweet/delicious smell** *There's a delicious smell coming from the kitchen.* | **unpleasant/bad/acrid smell** *the acrid smell of smoke* | **strong/pungent smell** *a pungent smell of garlic*

2 [C] an unpleasant smell: *I think the smell's getting worse.*

3 [U] the ability to notice or recognize smells: *loss of taste and smell* | *Dogs have a very good* **sense of smell**.

4 [C usually singular] an act of smelling something: *Have a smell of this cheese; does it seem all right?*

WORD FOCUS: SMELL

good smell: **aroma, perfume, fragrance, scent**
bad smell: **stink, stench, odour** BrE/**odor** AmE, **whiff, pong** BrE

smell² S2 W3 v past tense and past participle **smelled** especially AmE or **smelt** /smelt/ BrE

1 NOTICE A SMELL [T not in progressive] to notice or recognize a particular smell: *I can smell burning.* | *Can you smell something?*

2 HAVE A SMELL [linking verb] to have a particular smell: [+adj] *The stew smelled delicious.* | *Mm! Something smells good!* | [+like] *It smells like rotten eggs.* | [+of] BrE: *My clothes smelt of smoke.* | **sweet-smelling/ foul-smelling etc** *sweet-smelling flowers*

3 HAVE A BAD SMELL [I not in progressive] to have an unpleasant smell: *Your feet smell!* | *The room* **smelled to high heaven** (=had a very bad smell).

4 PUT YOUR NOSE NEAR STH [T] to put your nose near something in order to discover what kind of smell it has; **sniff**: *She bent down and smelt the flowers.*

5 HAVE ABILITY [I] to have the ability to notice and recognize smells: *I've got a cold and I can't smell.*

6 smell trouble/danger etc to feel that something is going to happen, especially something bad: *Miller had smelled trouble the moment he said who she was.*

7 smell a rat informal to guess that something wrong or dishonest is happening

8 smell wrong/fishy/odd etc informal to seem dishonest or untrue: *The whole thing is beginning to smell fishy to me.* → **come up/out smelling of roses** at ROSE¹ (6)

smell sb/sth ⇔ out phr v

1 to find something by smelling; **sniff out**: *They use dogs trained to smell out explosives.*

2 informal to find or recognize something because you have a natural ability to do this; **sniff out**: *They'll be able to smell out any corruption.*

GRAMMAR
You can say that something **smells** good, bad, strange etc.

⚠ Use an adjective, never an adverb: *You smell won-*

derful (NOT wonderfully) – what perfume is that?
In British English, you can use **smell** with **of** to say what something smells like: *Her jacket smelled of smoke (NOT smelled smoke).*
If you say that something or someone **smells**, you mean they have a bad smell: *Your socks smell.*
If you **can smell** something or you **smell** something, you notice its smell: *I can smell coffee.* | *We smelled smoke.*
⚠ You do not say 'feel a smell'.

'smelling salts n [plural] a strong-smelling chemical that you hold under someone's nose to make them conscious again when they have FAINTED

smell·y /'smeli/ adj comparative **smellier**, superlative **smelliest** having a strong unpleasant smell; **stinky**: *smelly feet* —**smelliness** n [U]

smelt¹ /smelt/ v BrE a past tense and past participle of SMELL

smelt² v [T] to melt a rock that contains metal in order to remove the metal

smid·gin, smidgen /'smɪdʒən/ also **smidge** /smɪdʒ/ n [singular] informal a very small amount of something; **touch**: [+of] *I added just a smidgin of chilli sauce.*

smile¹ S3 W1 /smaɪl/ v

1 [I] to make your mouth curve upwards, in order to be friendly or because you are happy or amused: [+at] *Susan smiled at him and waved.* | *She had to smile at his enthusiasm* (=she was amused by it). | *He was smiling broadly now.* | *her smiling face* | [+about] *I haven't had much to smile about lately.* | **smile to yourself** *Mark read the message and smiled to himself* (=smiled or felt pleased). ⚠ You **smile at** someone. Do not say 'smile to someone'.

2 [T] to say or express something with a smile: *'It's good to have you back,' she smiled.*

3 fortune/the gods etc smile on sb especially literary if FORTUNE, the gods etc smile on you, you have good luck

smile² S2 W2 n [C] an expression in which your mouth curves upwards, when you are being friendly or are happy or amused: **with a smile** *'Oh, I'm fine,' Anna replied with a smile.* | **a broad/big smile** *A broad smile spread over Lucy's face.* | **a little/faint smile** *He managed a faint smile.* | *He looked across at Jos with a* **wry smile** (=one which shows both amusement and sadness). | *'Oh, I understand,' he said with a* **knowing smile** (=one which shows you know something that is secret). | **a smile on your face/lips** *Now he had a great big smile on his face.* | *She* **gave** *them a little* **smile**. | *After that, my mother* **was all smiles** (=was very happy or friendly). → **wipe the smile/grin off sb's face** at WIPE¹ (7)

smile·y /'smaɪli/ n [C] a sign that looks like a face when you look at it sideways, for example :-), used in email messages to show that you are happy or pleased about something

smil·ing·ly /'smaɪlɪŋli/ adv done or said with a smile: *'Of course,' she replied smilingly.*

smirk /smɜːk $ smɜːrk/ v [I] to smile in an unpleasant way that shows that you are pleased by someone else's bad luck or think you are better than other people: *The boys tried not to smirk.* | [+at] *What are you smirking at?* —**smirk** n [C]: *He had a self-satisfied smirk on his face.*

smite /smaɪt/ v past tense **smote** /sməʊt $ smoʊt/ past participle **smitten** /'smɪtn/ [T] **1** old use to hit something with a lot of force **2** biblical to destroy, attack, or punish someone

smith /smɪθ/ n [C] someone who makes and repairs things made of iron; **blacksmith**

-smith /smɪθ/ suffix [in nouns] a maker of something: *a gunsmith* (=someone who makes guns) | *a wordsmith* (=someone who works with words, for example a journalist)

S

smith·e·reens /ˌsmɪðəˈriːnz/ n **smash/blow etc sth to smithereens** informal to destroy something by breaking it into very small pieces, or with an explosion: *The shop was blown to smithereens by the explosion.*

smith·y /ˈsmɪði $ -θi, -ði/ n plural **smithies** [C] a place where iron objects such as HORSESHOES were made and repaired in the past

smit·ten¹ /ˈsmɪtn/ adj [not before noun] **1** suddenly feeling that you love someone very much: *As soon as he saw her, he was smitten.* | [+by/with] *She was totally smitten with Steve.* **2 smitten with/by sth** suddenly affected by an illness or a feeling: *Dan was smitten with remorse.* | *The whole family were smitten with flu.*

smitten² the past participle of SMITE

smock /smɒk $ smɑːk/ n [C] **1** a long, loose shirt or a loose dress **2** a loose piece of clothing worn by artists or other workers to protect their other clothing

smock·ing /ˈsmɒkɪŋ $ ˈsmɑː-/ n [U] a type of decoration made on cloth by pulling the cloth into small regular folds held tightly with stitches

smog /smɒg $ smɑːg, smɔːg/ n [C,U] dirty air that looks like a mixture of smoke and FOG, caused by smoke from cars and factories in cities —**smoggy** adj

smoke¹ S3 W3 /sməʊk $ smoʊk/ n
1 [U] white, grey or black gas that is produced by something burning: ***clouds of black smoke*** | *cigarette smoke* | *Smoke from burning fields drifted across nearby roads.* | **the pall of smoke** (=thick cloud of smoke) *that hung over the city* | **wisp/puff of smoke** (=a small amount of smoke) *Rangers watched from their fire towers for any wisps of smoke.*
2 [C usually singular] an act of smoking a cigarette etc: *He went outside for a quiet smoke.*
3 (go) up in smoke a) if something goes up in smoke, it burns so that it is completely destroyed: *The whole factory went up in smoke.* **b)** informal if a plan or some work goes up in smoke, it fails or you cannot continue with it: *We haven't worked this long just to see everything go up in smoke.*
4 [C] spoken a cigarette or drugs that are smoked: *Where are the smokes, Jeff?*
5 there's no smoke without fire also **where there's smoke there's fire** spoken used to say that if something bad is being said about someone, it is probably partly true
6 the Smoke BrE old-fashioned informal London or any large town or city

smoke² S2 W2 v
1 [I,T] to suck or breathe in smoke from a cigarette, pipe etc or to do this regularly as a habit: *I don't smoke and I don't drink much.* | *Do you mind if I smoke?* | *He sat on the grass smoking a cigarette.* | *He admitted that he had smoked marijuana when he was a student.*
2 [I] if something smokes, it has smoke coming from it: *a smoking chimney*
3 [T] to give fish or meat a special taste by hanging it in smoke

> **smoke** sb/sth ⇔ **out** phr v
> **1** to fill a place with smoke in order to force someone or something to come out: *He smoked the bees out of their nest.*
> **2** to discover who is causing a particular problem and force them to make themselves known: *an operation to smoke out double agents*

ˈsmoke aˌlarm also **smoke detector** n [C] a piece of electronic equipment which warns you when there is smoke or fire in a building: *The smoke alarm went off.* → see picture at ALARM¹

ˈsmoke bomb n [C] something that lets out clouds of smoke when it is thrown, used especially by police to control crowds

smoked /sməʊkt $ smoʊkt/ adj **smoked salmon/bacon/sausage etc** fish, meat etc that has been left in smoke to give it a special taste

ˈsmoke deˌtector n [C] a SMOKE ALARM

ˌsmoked ˈglass n [U] glass that is a dark grey colour

ˌsmoke-filled ˈroom n [C] used to talk about a place where plans or decisions are made secretly by a small group of powerful people rather than in an open way – used especially in newspapers

ˌsmoke-ˈfree adj **smoke-free environment/zone etc** a place where people are not allowed to smoke; ⊟ **non-smoking**: *new laws to create a smoke-free environment at work*

smoke·less /ˈsməʊkləs $ ˈsmoʊk-/ adj **1 smokeless coal/fuel** FUEL that burns without producing smoke **2 smokeless tobacco** tobacco that you chew rather than smoking

smok·er /ˈsməʊkə $ ˈsmoʊkər/ n [C] someone who smokes cigarettes, CIGARS etc; ⊟ **non-smoker**: *My Grandad was a heavy smoker* (=someone who smokes a lot). | *He had a smoker's cough* (=a cough caused by smoking cigarettes regularly).

smoke·screen /ˈsməʊkskriːn $ ˈsmoʊk-/ n [C] **1** something that you do or say to hide your real plans or actions: *a government that rules behind a smokescreen of democracy* **2** a cloud of smoke produced so that it hides soldiers, ships etc during a battle

ˈsmoke ˌsignal n [C] a message sent out to people who are far away, using the smoke from a fire, especially by Native Americans in past times

smoke·stack /ˈsməʊkstæk $ ˈsmoʊk-/ n [C] a tall CHIMNEY at a factory or on a ship

ˈsmokestack ˌindustry n [C usually plural] a big traditional industry such as car making

smok·ing S2 /ˈsməʊkɪŋ $ ˈsmoʊk-/ n [U] the activity of breathing in tobacco smoke from a cigarette, pipe etc: **stop/quit/give up smoking** *I gave up smoking nearly ten years ago.* | *The sign says 'No Smoking'.* | *a no smoking area* | *the risks of passive smoking* (=breathing in smoke from other people's cigarettes)

ˈsmoking ˌgun n [C] something that shows who is responsible for something bad or how something really happened

ˈsmoking ˌjacket n [C] a formal jacket that men wore after dinner in the past

ˈsmoking room also ˈsmoking lounge AmE n [C] a room where smoking is allowed in a public building

smok·y /ˈsməʊki $ ˈsmoʊ-/ adj **1** filled with smoke: *a smoky room* **2** producing too much smoke: *a smoky engine* **3** having the taste, smell, or appearance of smoke: *smoky green eyes* | *a smoky flavour* —**smokiness** n [U]

smol·der /ˈsməʊldə $ ˈsmoʊldər/ v the American spelling of SMOULDER

smooch /smuːtʃ/ v [I + with] informal if two people smooch, they kiss and hold each other in a romantic way, especially while dancing

smooch·y /ˈsmuːtʃi/ adj BrE informal a smoochy song is slow and romantic

smooth¹ W3 /smuːð/ adj comparative **smoother**, superlative **smoothest**
1 SURFACE a smooth surface has no rough parts, lumps, or holes, especially in a way that is pleasant and attractive to touch; ⊟ **rough**: *Her skin felt smooth and cool.* | *a smooth pebble* | *The stone steps had been worn smooth.* → see picture at SURFACE
2 HAPPENING WITHOUT PROBLEMS happening or operating successfully, without any problems: **smooth running/operation** *Sarah is responsible for the smooth running of the sales department.* | *The new government has promised a smooth transition of power.* → **go smoothly** at SMOOTHLY (2)
3 MOVEMENT [only before noun] with no sudden movements or changes of direction, especially in a way that is graceful or comfortable: *Swing the tennis racquet in one smooth motion.* | *The jet made a smooth landing.* | **smooth flight/ride** (=a comfortable trip in an airplane or car) *It wasn't a very smooth ride.*
4 PERSON someone who is smooth is polite, confident, and relaxed, but is often not sincere: *a smooth*

salesmen | *He was a **smooth talker**.* | *George is a **smooth operator*** (=someone who does things in a smooth way).

5 LIQUID MIXTURE a liquid mixture that is smooth has no big pieces in it; ◙ **lumpy**: *Beat the eggs and flour until they are smooth.*

6 SOUND a voice or music that is smooth is soft and pleasant to listen to: *smooth jazz* | *He has one of those **silky smooth** (=very smooth) voices.*

7 TASTE a drink such as wine, coffee, WHISKY, or beer that is smooth is not bitter but tastes pleasant: *a smooth full-bodied wine* —**smoothness** *n* [U]: *the smoothness of his skin* → SMOOTH-TALKING

smooth² *v* [T] **1** to make something such as cloth or hair flat by moving your hands across it: *Liz smoothed her skirt and sat down.* | **smooth sth back/down** *She smoothed back her hair.* **2** also **smooth down** to make a rough surface flat and even: *The wood was smoothed and trimmed to size.* | *Smooth down all the surfaces before you start painting.* **3** [always + adv/prep] to rub a liquid, cream etc gently over a surface or into a surface: **smooth sth into/over sth** *She smoothed suntan lotion over her legs.* **4** smooth the way/path for sth to make it easier for something to happen, by dealing with any problems first: *Staff helped smooth the way for the new administration.*

smooth sth ⇔ **away** *phr v* to get rid of problems or difficulties: *A few objections have to be smoothed away before we can start the project.*

smooth sth ⇔ **out** *phr v* **1** to make something such as paper or cloth flat by moving your hands across it: *They smoothed out the map on the table.* | *Smooth out all the wrinkles.* **2** to make something happen in an even, regular way: *Sometimes central banks intervene to smooth out price fluctuations.* **3** to get rid of problems or difficulties

smooth sth ⇔ **over** *phr v* if you smooth over problems, difficulties etc, you make them seem less serious and easier to control, especially by talking to the people who are involved in the problem: *Sally managed to smooth over the bad feelings between them.*

smooth·ie /ˈsmuːði/ *n* [C] **1** *informal* someone who is confident and attractive, but is often not sincere: *Kyle's a **real smoothie**.* **2** a thick drink made of fruit and fruit juices mixed together, sometimes with ice, milk, or YOGHURT: *a strawberry-banana smoothie*

smooth·ly /ˈsmuːðli/ *adv* **1** in a steady way, without stopping and starting again: *Traffic flowed smoothly.* **2** if a planned event, piece of work etc goes smoothly, there are no problems to spoil it: *It'll take about three hours if everything **goes smoothly**.* | *Donna keeps the office **running smoothly**.* **3** if you say something smoothly, you say it in a calm and confident way: *'All taken care of,' he said smoothly.* **4** in a way that produces a smooth surface: *The jacket fit smoothly over her hips.*

smooth-talking *adj* a smooth-talking person is good at persuading people and saying nice things, but you do not trust them: *a smooth-talking salesman*

smor·gas·bord /ˈsmɔːɡəsbɔːd $ ˈsmɔːrɡəsbɔːrd/ *n* [C,U] **1** a smorgasbord of sth a large variety of different things: *a smorgasbord of art from around the world* **2** a meal in which people serve themselves from a large number of different dishes; ◙ **buffet**

smote /sməʊt $ smoʊt/ the past tense of SMITE

smoth·er /ˈsmʌðə $ -ər/ *v* [T] **1** to completely cover the whole surface of something with something else, often in a way that seems unnecessary or unpleasant: **smother sth with/in sth** *noodles smothered in garlic sauce* **2** to kill someone by putting something over their face to stop them breathing; → **suffocate**: *A teenage mother was accused of smothering her 3-month-old daughter.* **3** to stop yourself from showing your feelings or from doing an action; ◙ **stifle**: *The girls tried to smother their giggles.* **4** to give someone so much love and attention that they feel as if they are not free and become unhappy: *I don't want him to feel*

smothered. **5** smother sb with kisses to kiss someone a lot **6** to make a fire stop burning by preventing air from reaching it: *We used a wet towel to smother the fire.* **7** to get rid of anyone who opposes you – used to show disapproval: *They ruthlessly smother all opposition.*

smoul·der *BrE*; **smolder** *AmE* /ˈsməʊldə $ ˈsmoʊldər/ *v* [I] **1** if something such as wood smoulders, it burns slowly without a flame **2** *literary* if someone smoulders or if their feelings smoulder, they have strong feelings that they do not fully express: *He sensed a smouldering hostility towards him.* | [+with] *She had spent the evening smouldering with resentment.*

SMS /ˌes em ˈes/ *n* [U] **short messaging system** or **short message service** a feature on a MOBILE PHONE that allows a user to send or receive written messages

smudge¹ /smʌdʒ/ *n* [C] a dirty mark; ◙ **smear**: [+of] *a smudge of lipstick on the cup* —**smudgy** *adj*

smudge² *v* **1** [I,T] if ink, writing etc smudges, or if you smudge it, it becomes dirty and unclear because it has been touched or rubbed: *Don't touch it! You'll smudge the ink.* **2** [T] to make a dirty mark on a surface: *Someone had smudged the paper with their greasy hands.*

smug /smʌɡ/ *adj* showing too much satisfaction with your own cleverness or success – used to show disapproval: [+about] *What are you looking so smug about?* | **smug expression/look/face/smile etc** *'I knew I'd win,' she said with a smug smile.* —**smugly** *adv* —**smugness** *n* [U]

smug·gle /ˈsmʌɡəl/ *v* [I] **1** to take something or someone illegally from one country to another: **smuggle sth across sth** *The guns were smuggled across the border.* | **smuggle sth into/out of/from sth** *Illegal immigrants are smuggled into the country by boat.* **2** *informal* to take something or someone secretly to a place where they are not allowed to be: **smuggle sth into sth** *He smuggled his notes into the exam.*

smug·gler /ˈsmʌɡələ $ -ər/ *n* [C] someone who takes something illegally from one country to another: *a drug smuggler*

smug·gling /ˈsmʌɡəlɪŋ/ *n* [U] the crime of taking something illegally from one country to another: *He was arrested in connection with drug smuggling.*

smut /smʌt/ *n* **1** [U] books, stories, talk etc that offend some people because they are about sex: *I won't have smut like that in my house!* **2** [C,U] dirt or SOOT (=black powder produced by burning), or a piece of dirt or soot

smut·ty /ˈsmʌti/ *adj* **1** books, stories etc that are smutty offend some people because they are about sex; ◙ **dirty**: *smutty jokes* **2** marked with small pieces of dirt or SOOT

snack¹ /snæk/ *n* [C] a small amount of food that is eaten between main meals or instead of a meal: *I grabbed a quick snack.* | *Drinks and **light snacks** are served at the bar.* | **snack foods** *like crisps and peanuts*

snack² /snæk/ *v* [I] to eat small amounts of food between main meals or instead of meals: *I'm trying not to snack between meals.*

snack bar *n* [C] a place where you can buy snacks or small meals → see picture at EAT

snaf·fle /ˈsnæfəl/ *v* [T] *BrE informal* to take something quickly, especially before anyone else has had the time or the chance to do this; ◙ **grab**: *I managed to snaffle a couple of biscuits.*

sna·fu /snæˈfuː/ *n* [C] *AmE informal* a situation in which a plan does not happen in the way it should: *There were no major snafus.*

snag¹ /snæɡ/ *n* [C] **1** a problem or disadvantage, especially one that is not very serious, which you had not expected: *It's an interesting job. **The only snag is that** it's not very well paid.* | **hit/run into a snag** *The*

S

grand opening hit a snag when no one could find the key. **2** a part of a dead tree that sticks out, especially one that is under water and can be dangerous **3** a sharp part of something that sticks out and holds or cuts things that touch it

snag² v **snagged**, **snagging** [T] **1** to damage something by getting it stuck on something sharp: *Oh no! I've snagged my stockings.* **2** *AmE informal* to succeed in getting something, especially something difficult to get: *I snagged a parking space in the last row.*

snail /sneɪl/ n [C] **1** a small soft creature that moves very slowly and has a hard shell on its back **2 at a snail's pace** extremely slowly: *Traffic was moving at a snail's pace.*

snail mail n [U] the system of sending letters by post, as opposed to using email – used humorously

snake¹ [S3] /sneɪk/ n [C]
1 an animal with a long thin body and no legs, that often has a poisonous bite: *A snake slithered across our path.* | **a poisonous/venomous snake**; → see picture at **REPTILE**
2 also **snake in the grass** *informal* someone who cannot be trusted

snake² v [I always + adv/prep] if a river, road, train, or line snakes somewhere, it moves in long, twisting curves: [+along/past/down etc] *The road snaked along the valley far below.* | *The train was snaking its way through the mountains.*

snake-bite /'sneɪkbaɪt/ n [C,U] the bite of a poisonous snake

snake charmer n [C] someone who controls snakes by playing music to them, in order to entertain people

snake eyes n [plural] *informal* a situation in a game in which a pair of DICE both show one spot

snake oil n [U] *especially AmE informal* **1** something that is claimed to be a solution to a problem, but is not effective **2 snake oil salesman/peddler** someone who deceives people by persuading them to accept false information, solutions that are not effective etc

snakes and ladders n [U] *BrE* a children's game played on a board in which you can move forwards and upwards along pictures of LADDERS or go downwards and backwards along pictures of snakes; **▤ chutes and ladders** *AmE*; → see picture at **BOARD GAME**

snake-skin /'sneɪkˌskɪn/ n [U] the skin of a snake used to make shoes, bags etc: *snakeskin shoes*

snap¹ [W3] /snæp/ v **snapped**, **snapping**
1 BREAK [I,T] to break with a sudden sharp noise, or to make something break with a sudden sharp noise: *A twig snapped under my feet.* | *The wind snapped branches and power lines.* | **snap (sth) off (sth)** *I snapped the ends off the beans and dropped them into a bowl.* | **snap (sth) in two/in half** (=break into two pieces) *The teacher snapped the chalk in two and gave me a piece.* → see picture at **BREAK¹**
2 MOVE INTO POSITION [I,T always + adv/prep] to move into a particular position suddenly, making a short sharp noise, or to make something move like this: [+together/back etc] *The pieces just snap together like this.* | *The policeman snapped the handcuffs around her wrist.* | **snap (sth) open/shut** *She snapped her briefcase shut.*
3 SAY STH ANGRILY [I,T] to say something quickly in an angry way: *'What do you want?' Mike snapped.* | [+at] *He snapped at Walter for no reason.*
4 BECOME ANGRY/ANXIOUS ETC [I] to suddenly stop being able to control your anger, anxiety, or other feelings in a difficult situation: *The stress began to get to her, and one morning she just snapped.* | *Something inside him snapped and he hit her.*
5 ANIMAL [I] if an animal such as a dog snaps, it tries to bite you: [+at] *The dog started snapping at his heels.*
6 PHOTOGRAPH [I,T] *informal* to take a photograph: *Dave snapped a picture of me and Sonia.*
7 snap your fingers to make a short, sharp noise by

moving one of your fingers quickly against your thumb, for example in order to get someone's attention or to mark the beat of music
8 snap to it *spoken* used to tell someone to hurry and do something immediately: *Come on, snap to it, get that room cleaned up!*
9 STOP [T] *AmE* to end a series of events – used especially in newspapers: *The Rockets snapped a seven-game losing streak by beating Portland.*
10 snap to attention if soldiers snap to attention, they suddenly stand very straight → **SNAP-ON**

snap on/off phr v
to switch something on or off, or to switch on or off: **snap sth ⇔ on/off** *Kathy snapped off the light.* | *A light snapped on in one of the huts.*

snap out of sth phr v
to stop being sad or upset and make yourself feel better: *Chantal's been depressed for days. I wish she'd snap out of it.*

snap sb/sth ⇔ up phr v
1 to buy something immediately, especially because it is very cheap: *People were snapping up bargains.*
2 to eagerly take an opportunity to have someone as part of your company, team etc: *Owen was snapped up by Liverpool before he'd even left school.*

snap² n
1 SOUND [singular] a sudden loud sound, especially made by something breaking or closing: *He shut the book with a snap.*
2 PHOTOGRAPH [C] *informal especially BrE* a photograph taken quickly and often not very skilfully; **▤ snapshot**: *holiday snaps*
3 be a snap *AmE informal* to be very easy to do: *The test was a snap.*
4 CLOTHING [C] *AmE* a small metal fastener on clothes that works when you press its two parts together: *baby clothing with snaps*
5 a snap of sb's fingers a sudden sound made by quickly moving one of your fingers against your thumb: *At a snap of his owner's fingers, the dog came running.*
6 GAME [U] a card game in which players put down one card after another and try to be the first to shout 'snap' when there are two cards that are the same → **COLD SNAP**

snap³ adj **1 snap judgment/decision** a judgment or decision made quickly, without careful thought or discussion **2 snap election** *BrE* an election that is announced suddenly and unexpectedly

snap⁴ interjection **1** *BrE* used when you see two things that are exactly the same: *Hey, snap! My hat's the same as yours.* **2** said in the game of snap when two cards that are the same are put down

snap-drag-on /'snæpˌdrægən/ n [C] a garden plant with white, red, or yellow flowers

snap-on adj [only before noun] a snap-on part of something can be fastened on and removed easily

snap-per /'snæpə $ -ər/ n [C] a type of fish that lives in warm seas, often used as food

snap-py /'snæpi/ adj **1** a snappy title or phrase is short, clear, and often funny: *We need a snappy title for the book.* | *Keep your answer* **short and snappy.** **2** *especially BrE* quick to react in an angry way; **▤ irritable**: *She seemed snappy and impatient.* | [+with] *There's no need to be so snappy with the children.* **3 make it snappy** also **look snappy** *BrE informal* used to tell someone to hurry: *Get me a drink and make it snappy.* **4** *BrE informal* snappy clothes, objects etc are attractive and fashionable: *a snappy suit* | **snappy dresser** (=someone who wears fashionable clothes) —**snappily** adv

snap-shot /'snæpʃɒt $ -ʃɑːt/ n [C] **1** a photograph taken quickly and often not very skilfully; **▤ snap**: [+of] *a snapshot of his girlfriend* **2** a piece of information that quickly gives you an idea of what the situation is like at a particular time: [+of] *The book gives us a snapshot of life in the Middle Ages.*

snare¹ /sneə $ sner/ n [C]   **1** a trap for catching an animal, especially one that uses a wire or rope to catch the animal by its foot: *A rabbit was caught in the snare.*   **2** *literary* something that is intended to trick someone and get them into a difficult situation; ◪ **trap**: *I didn't want to fall into the same snare again.*

snare² v [T]   **1** to catch an animal by using a snare   **2** to get something or someone you want in a clever way, often by deceiving other people: *She's hoping to snare a wealthy husband.*

'snare drum n [C] a small flat drum that makes a hard continuous sound when you hit it → see picture at **DRUM¹**

snarf /snɑːf $ snɑːrf/ also **snarf down** v [T] *AmE informal* to eat something quickly, especially in an untidy or noisy way: *workers snarfing lunch at their desks*

snarl /snɑːl $ snɑːrl/ v   **1** [I] if an animal snarls, it makes a low angry sound and shows its teeth; → **growl**: [+**at**] *The dog growled and snarled at me.*   **2** [I,T] to speak or say something in a nasty, angry way: *'Shut up,' he snarled.*   **3** [T usually passive] also **snarl up** *BrE* to prevent traffic from moving: *Traffic snarled up on both sides of the road.* —**snarl** n [C]: *an angry snarl*

'snarl-up n [C] *BrE*   **1** a confused situation that prevents work from continuing   **2** a situation in which traffic is prevented from moving: *There was a big snarl-up on the M1.*

snatch¹ /snætʃ/ v [T]   **1** to take something away from someone with a quick, often violent, movement; ◪ **grab**: *The thief snatched her purse and ran.* | **snatch sth away/back from sb** *Keith snatches toys away from the other children.*   **2** to take someone away from a person or place, especially by force: *Vargas was snatched from his home by two armed men.*   **3** to quickly get something, especially sleep or rest, because you do not have very much time; ◪ **grab**: *I managed to snatch an hour's sleep on the train.*

snatch at sth *phr v* to quickly put out your hand to try to take or hold something: *Jessie snatched at the bag but I pulled it away.*

snatch² n [C]   **1** a snatch of conversation/music/ song etc a short part of a conversation, song etc that you hear: *I could hear snatches of the conversation from across the room.*   **2** in snatches for short periods: *I only slept in snatches during the night.*   **3** when someone quickly takes or steals something: *reports of a bag snatch*   **4** *taboo informal* a very offensive word for a woman's sex organ. Do not use this word.

'snatch squad n [C] a group of police officers or soldiers who go quickly into a crowd, in order to catch people who are causing trouble

snaz·zy /'snæzi/ adj *informal* bright, fashionable, and attractive: *a snazzy red jacket* —**snazzily** adv —**snazziness** n [U]

sneak¹ /sniːk/ v *past tense and past participle* **sneaked** *or* **snuck** /snʌk/ *AmE*
1 ‖GO SECRETLY‖ [I always + adv/prep] to go somewhere secretly and quietly in order to avoid being seen or heard; ◪ **creep**: [+**in/out/away** etc] *They sneaked off without paying!* | *She snuck out of the house once her parents were asleep.*
2 ‖TAKE/GIVE SECRETLY‖ [T] to hide something and take it somewhere or give it to someone secretly: *I snuck her a note.* | **sneak sth through/past etc sb/sth** *Douglas had sneaked his camera into the show.*
3 sneak a look/glance/peek to look at something quickly and secretly, especially something that you are not supposed to see: *He sneaked a look at her.*
4 ‖STEAL‖ [T] *informal* to quickly and secretly steal something unimportant or of little value: **sneak sth from sb** *We used to sneak cigarettes from Dad.*

sneak on sb *phr v BrE informal old-fashioned* to tell someone such as a parent or teacher about something that another person has done wrong, because you want to cause trouble for that person: *A little brat named Oliver sneaked on me.*

sneak up *phr v* to come near someone very quietly, so that they do not see you until you reach them: [+**on/behind** etc] *I wish you wouldn't sneak up on me like that!*

sneak² n [C]   **1** *BrE informal* a child who other children dislike, because they tell adults about bad things that the other children have done wrong: *You little sneak!*   **2** *AmE informal* someone who is not liked because they do things secretly and cannot be trusted

sneak³ adj [only before noun] doing things very secretly and quickly, so that people do not notice you or cannot stop you: *a sneak attack* | *a sneak thief*

sneak·er /'sniːkə $ -ər/ n [C] *especially AmE* a type of light soft shoe with a rubber SOLE (=bottom), used for sports: *a pair of white sneakers*

sneak·ing /'sniːkɪŋ/ adj **have a sneaking feeling/ suspicion/admiration** to have a feeling about something or someone, but to not say anything about it because you are not sure or you might be embarrassed: *I always had a sneaking admiration for him.* | *She had a sneaking suspicion that he was lying.*

'sneak 'preview n [C] an occasion when you can see a film, play, product etc before it is shown to people in general: *In this week's show we'll be giving you a sneak preview of Steven Spielberg's latest film.*

sneak·y /'sniːki/ adj doing things in a secret and often dishonest or unfair way: *a sneaky little trick* —**sneakily** adv —**sneakiness** n [U]

sneer¹ /snɪə $ snɪr/ v [I,T] to smile or speak in a very unkind way that shows you have no respect for some one or something: *'Is that your best outfit?' he sneered.* | [+**at**] *She sneered at Tom's musical tastes.* —**sneering** adj: *a sneering tone* —**sneeringly** adv

sneer² n [C] an unkind smile or remark that shows you have no respect for something or someone: *'You probably wouldn't understand,' he said with a sneer.*

sneeze¹ /sniːz/ v [I]   **1** if you sneeze, air suddenly comes from your nose, making a noise, for example when you have a cold: *She started coughing and sneezing. | The dust was making him sneeze.*   **2 not to be sneezed at** *BrE*; **nothing to sneeze at** *AmE spoken* used about an offer, especially of money, that is very good, and which you should consider carefully: *In those days £5 an hour was not to be sneezed at.*

sneeze² n [C] the act or sound of sneezing: *There was a loud sneeze from someone in the back of the audience.*

snick·er /'snɪkə $ -ər/ v [I] *AmE* to laugh quietly and in a way that is not nice at something which is not supposed to be funny; ◪ **snigger** *BrE*: [+**at**] *The other students snickered at Steve.* —**snicker** n [C]: *a barely hidden snicker*

snide /snaɪd/ adj *informal* if you say something snide, you say something unkind, often in a clever, indirect way: **snide remarks/comments** *a snide remark about her clothes* —**snidely** adv

sniff¹ /snɪf/ v   **1** [I] to breathe air into your nose noisily, for example when you are crying or have a cold: *Margaret sniffed miserably and nodded.* | *Stop sniffing and blow your nose.*   **2** [I,T] to breathe air in through your nose in order to smell something: *He opened the milk and sniffed it.* | [+**at**] *The dog was sniffing at the carpet.*   **3** [T] to say something in a way that shows you think something is not good enough: *'Is that all?' she sniffed.*   **4** [T] to take a harmful drug by breathing it up your nose; → **snort**: *kids who sniff glue*

sniff at sth *phr v*   **1 sth is not to be sniffed at** *spoken especially BrE* used to say that something is good enough to be accepted or considered seriously: *An 8% salary increase is not to be sniffed at.*   **2** to refuse something in a proud way, or behave as if something is not good enough for you: *He sniffed at my choice of restaurants and suggested his own favorite.*

S

sniff sth ⇔ **out** *phr v* **1** to discover or find something by its smell: *A customs officer came round with a dog to sniff out drugs.* **2** *informal* to find out or discover something: *Vic's been trying to sniff out where you went last night.*

sniff[2] *n* [C] **1** when you breathe in air noisily through your nose, for example in order to smell something, because you have a cold, or in order to show your disapproval: *a sniff of disapproval* | *She gave a loud sniff.* **2** *BrE informal* a small amount or sign of something; ◫ **hint**: [+of] *He got us into this mess, and then left at the first sniff of trouble!* **3 have a sniff around/ round** *BrE informal* to examine a place carefully **4 not get a sniff of sth** *BrE informal* to not have any chance of getting something or being successful: *He never even got a sniff of the target.*

'sniffer dog *n* [C] *BrE* a dog that has been trained to find drugs or explosives by using its sense of smell

snif·fle[1] /'snɪfəl/ *v* [I] *spoken* to keep sniffing in order to stop liquid from running out of your nose, especially when you are crying or you have a cold: *For goodness' sake, stop sniffling!*

sniffle[2] *n* **have the sniffles** *spoken* if you have the sniffles, you keep sniffing, especially because you have a cold

sniff·y /'snɪfi/ *adj BrE informal* having a disapproving attitude towards something or someone, especially because you think they are not good enough for you: [+about] *Well, don't get sniffy about it!*

snif·ter /'snɪftə $ -ər/ *n* [C] **1** *AmE* a special large glass for drinking BRANDY **2** *BrE old-fashioned* a small amount of an alcoholic drink

snig·ger /'snɪɡə $ -ər/ *v* [I] *BrE* to laugh quietly in a way that is not nice at something which is not supposed to be funny; ◫ **snicker** *AmE*: [+at] *What are you sniggering at? This is a serious poem.* —**snigger** *n* [C]

snip[1] /snɪp/ *v* **snipped, snipping** [I,T] to cut something by making quick cuts with scissors: *I snipped the string and untied the parcel.* | **snip sth off** (=remove it by snipping) *Snip the ends of the beans off before you cook them.*

snip[2] *n* [C] **1** a quick small cut with scissors **2 be a snip** *BrE informal* to be surprisingly cheap: *At £20 for a dozen, they're a snip.*

snipe[1] /snaɪp/ *v* [I] **1** to shoot from a hidden position at people who are not protected: [+at] *soldiers sniping at civilians* **2** to criticize someone in a nasty way: [+at] *His former associates have been sniping at him in the press.* —**sniping** *n* [U]

snipe[2] *n* [C] a bird with a very long thin beak that lives in wet areas

snip·er /'snaɪpə $ -ər/ *n* [C] someone who shoots at people from a hidden position

snip·pet /'snɪpət/ *n* [C] a small piece of news, information, or conversation: [+of] *snippets of information*

snip·py /'snɪpi/ *adj AmE informal* quick to show that you are angry or offended, or that you will not obey someone

snit /snɪt/ *n* **be in a snit** *AmE informal* to be very annoyed about something, especially in a way that other people think is unreasonable: *She's been in a snit ever since the party.*

snitch[1] /snɪtʃ/ *v informal* **1** [I] to tell someone in authority about something that another person has done wrong, because you want to cause trouble for that person: [+on] *Somebody snitched on me.* **2** [T] to quickly steal something unimportant or of little value; ◫ **nick**

snitch[2] *n* [C] *informal* someone who is not liked because they tell people in authority when other people do things that are wrong or against the rules; ◫ **sneak**: *He didn't want to be a snitch, and besides, Kevin was his friend.*

sniv·el /'snɪvəl/ *v* **snivelled, snivelling** *BrE*, **sniveled, sniveling** *AmE* [I usually progressive] to behave or speak in a weak complaining way, especially when you are crying: *A small boy was sniveling on a chair.* | *a snivelling coward*

snob /snɒb $ snɑːb/ *n* [C] **1** someone who thinks they are better than people from a lower social class – used to show disapproval: *Stop being such a snob.* | *I don't want to sound like a snob, but I thought she was vulgar.* **2** someone who thinks they are better than other people because they know more about something than other people – used to show disapproval: *a bunch of intellectual snobs* | **music/wine snob 3 snob value/appeal** *BrE* something that has snob value is liked by people who think they are better than other people: *That kind of car has real snob appeal.*

snob·be·ry /'snɒbəri $ 'snɑː-/ *n* [U] behaviour or attitudes which show that you think you are better than other people, because you belong to a higher social class or know much more than they do – used to show disapproval: *intellectual snobbery* → INVERTED SNOBBERY

snob·bish /'snɒbɪʃ $ 'snɑː-/ also **snob·by** /'snɒbi $ 'snɑː-/ *adj* behaving in a way that shows you think you are better than other people because you are from a higher social class or know more than they do: *Her family seems snobbish.* —**snobbishly** *adv* —**snobbishness** *n* [U]

snog /snɒɡ $ snɑːɡ/ *v* **snogged, snogging** [I,T] *BrE informal* if two people snog, they kiss each other, especially for a long time: *I saw them snogging in the corner.* —**snog** *n* [C usually singular]

snook /snuːk $ snʊk, snuːk/ *n* → **cock a snook** at COCK[2] (5)

snoo·ker[1] /'snuːkə $ 'snʊkər/ *n* [U] a game played especially in Britain on a special table covered in green cloth, in which two people use long sticks to hit coloured balls into holes at the sides and corners of the table; → **billiards**: **snooker table/room/hall** | *They meet up every Friday to play snooker.*

snooker[2] *v* [T often passive] *BrE informal* to make it impossible for someone to do what they want to do: *If the council refuses our planning application, we're snookered.*

snoop /snuːp/ *v* [I] to try to find out about someone's private affairs by secretly looking in their house, examining their possessions etc: [+around/about] *I caught him snooping around in my office.* | [+on] *reporters snooping on celebrities* —**snoop** *n* [singular] —**snooper** *n* [C]

snoot·y /'snuːti/ *adj informal* rude and unfriendly, because you think you are better than other people; ◫ **snotty**: *snooty neighbours* —**snootily** *adv* —**snootiness** *n* [U]

snooze /snuːz/ *v* [I] *informal* to sleep lightly for a short time; ◫ **doze**: *Dad was snoozing in his armchair.* —**snooze** *n* [C]

snore /snɔː $ snɔːr/ *v* [I] to breathe in a noisy way through your mouth and nose while you are asleep: *He could hear the old man snoring.* —**snore** *n* [C]: *I heard a snore and knew he'd fallen asleep.*

snor·kel /'snɔːkəl $ 'snɔːr-/ *n* [C] a tube that allows someone who is swimming to breathe air under water: *This is the best snorkel at that price.*

snor·kel·ling *BrE*; **snorkeling** *AmE* /'snɔːkəlɪŋ $ 'snɔːr-/ *n* [U] when you swim under water using a snorkel: *We went snorkeling in Hawaii.* —**snorkel** *v* [I]

snort[1] /snɔːt $ snɔːrt/ *v* **1** [I,T] to breathe air in a noisy way out through your nose, especially to show that you are annoyed or amused: *'Certainly not,' he snorted.* | [+with] *She snorted with laughter.* | *The horse snorted and stamped its hoof impatiently.* **2** [T] to take drugs by breathing them in through your nose; → **sniff**: *snorting cocaine*

snort[2] *n* [C] **1** a loud sound made by breathing out through your nose, especially to show that you are annoyed or amused: *He gave a loud snort.* | *There were snorts of laughter from the audience.* **2** a small amount of a drug that is breathed in through the nose: *a snort of cocaine*

snot /snɒt $ snɑːt/ *n informal* **1** [U] an impolite word for the thick MUCUS (=liquid) produced in your nose **2** [singular] someone who is SNOTTY: *the little snot*

snot·ty /ˈsnɒti $ ˈsnɑːti/ *adj informal* **1** someone who is snotty is rude and annoying, especially because they think that they are more important than other people – used to show disapproval; ◨ **snooty**: *some snotty little clerk* **2** wet and dirty with MUCUS

ˈsnotty-nosed *BrE*; **ˈsnot-nosed** *AmE adj informal* used about an annoying child: *a snotty-nosed little kid*

snout /snaʊt/ *n* **1** [C] the long nose of some kinds of animals, such as pigs **2** [C] *BrE informal* a criminal who gives information about other criminals to the police

snow¹ |S3| |W3| /snəʊ $ snoʊ/ *n*
1 [U] soft white pieces of frozen water that fall from the sky in cold weather and cover the ground; → **sleet**: *Snow was falling heavily as we entered the village.* | *I could see footprints in the snow.* | *The town was buried under three feet of snow.* | *roads blocked by deep snow* | *snow-covered fields* | *Outside the snow was already melting.* | *The day was cold with flurries of snow* (=when a small amount of snow falls). | *The first few flakes of snow* (=small pieces of snow) *started to fall.*
2 [C] a period of time in which snow falls: *one of the heaviest snows this winter*
3 snows [plural] a large amount of snow that has fallen at different times during the winter: *the melting of the winter snows*
4 [U] small white spots on a television picture, caused by bad weather conditions, weak television signals etc
5 [U] *informal* COCAINE

snow² *v* **1** it snows if it snows, snow falls from the sky: *It snowed all night.* | *It started snowing around five.* **2** be snowed in to be unable to travel from a place because so much snow has fallen there: *We were snowed in for three days last winter.* **3** be snowed under a) *informal* to have more work than you can deal with: [+with] *I found myself snowed under with work.* b) if an area is snowed under, a lot of snow has fallen there so that people are not able to travel **4** [T] *AmE informal* to persuade someone to believe or support something, especially by lying to them: **snow sb into doing sth** *Millions of readers were snowed into believing it was a true story.*

snow·ball¹ /ˈsnəʊbɔːl $ ˈsnoʊbɒːl/ *n* [C] **1** a ball of snow that children make and throw at each other: *We had a massive snowball fight.* **2** snowball effect if something has a snowball effect, it starts a series of events or changes that all happen because of each other **3** not have a snowball's chance in hell *informal* to have no chance at all

snowball² *v* [I] if a plan, problem, business etc snowballs, it grows bigger at a faster and faster rate: *Interest in the sport is snowballing.*

snow·bird /ˈsnəʊbɜːd $ ˈsnoʊbɜːrd/ *n* [C] *AmE informal* someone, especially an old person, who every year leaves their home in a cold part of the US to go and live in a warm part of the US for the winter

ˈsnow ˌblindness *n* [U] eye pain and difficulty in seeing things, caused by looking at snow in bright light from the sun —**snow blind** *adj*

snow·blow·er /ˈsnəʊbləʊə $ ˈsnoʊbloʊər/ *n* [C] a machine that clears snow from roads, paths etc by sucking it up and blowing it away

snow·board /ˈsnəʊbɔːd $ ˈsnoʊbɔːrd/ *n* [C] a long wide board made of plastic, which people stand on to go down snow-covered hills as a sport

snow·board·ing /ˈsnəʊbɔːdɪŋ $ ˈsnoʊbɔːrd-/ *n* [U] the sport of going down snow-covered hills on a snowboard —**snowboarder** *n* [C]: *a group of skiers and snowboarders*; → see picture at WINTER SPORTS

snow·bound /ˈsnəʊbaʊnd $ ˈsnoʊ-/ *adj* blocked or prevented from leaving a place by large amounts of snow: *travelers who are snowbound at the airport*

ˈsnow-capped *adj literary* snow-capped mountains are covered in snow at the top

ˈsnow chains *n* [plural] a set of chains that are fastened around the wheels of a car so that it can drive over snow without slipping

ˈsnow cone *n* [C] *AmE* crushed ice with a coloured sweet liquid poured over it, served in a CONE-shaped paper cup

ˈsnow day *n* [C] *AmE* a day when schools and businesses are closed because there is too much snow for people to travel

snow·drift /ˈsnəʊˌdrɪft $ ˈsnoʊ-/ *n* [C] a deep mass of snow formed by the wind

snow·drop /ˈsnəʊdrɒp $ ˈsnoʊdrɑːp/ *n* [C] a European plant with a small white flower which appears in early spring

snow·fall /ˈsnəʊfɔːl $ ˈsnoʊfɒːl/ *n* [C,U] an occasion when snow falls from the sky, or the amount that falls in a particular period of time: *Heavy snowfalls are forecast.* | *an average snowfall of eight inches a year*

snow·field /ˈsnəʊfiːld $ ˈsnoʊ-/ *n* [C] an area of land that is covered in snow

snow·flake /ˈsnəʊfleɪk $ ˈsnoʊ-/ *n* [C] a small soft flat piece of frozen water that falls as snow

ˈsnow job *n* [singular] *AmE informal* an act of making someone believe something that is not true

ˈsnow line *n* the snow line the level above which snow on a mountain never melts

snow·man /ˈsnəʊmæn $ ˈsnoʊ-/ *n plural* **snowmen** /-men/ [C] a simple figure of a person made of snow, made especially by children

snow·mo·bile /ˈsnəʊməbiːl $ ˈsnoʊmoʊ-/ *n* [C] a small vehicle with a motor that moves over snow or ice easily

ˈsnow pea *n* [C] *AmE* a type of PEA whose outer part is eaten as well as its seeds; ◨ **mangetout** *BrE*

ˈsnow plough *BrE*; **snow plow** *AmE n* [C] **1** a vehicle or piece of equipment on the front of a vehicle that is used to push snow off roads, railways etc **2** *BrE* a position in SKIING in which you have the fronts of your SKIS together and the backs of your skis apart. It is used to slow down and to turn: *a snow plough turn*

ˈsnow route *n* [C] *AmE* an important road in a city that cars must be removed from when it snows, so that the snow can be cleared away from it

snow·shoe /ˈsnəʊʃuː $ ˈsnoʊ-/ *n* [C] a special wide flat frame that you attach to your shoe so that you can walk on deep snow without sinking

snow·storm /ˈsnəʊstɔːm $ ˈsnoʊstɔːrm/ *n* [C] a storm with strong winds and a lot of snow

ˈsnow tire *n* [C] *AmE* a special car tyre with a pattern of deep lines, used when driving on snow or ice

ˌsnow-ˈwhite *adj* pure white

snow·y /ˈsnəʊi $ ˈsnoʊi/ *adj* **1** with a lot of snow: *the snowy fields* | *one snowy January day* **2** *literary* pure white, like snow: *snowy hair*

Snr *BrE* the written abbreviation of *senior*, used after someone's name: *James Taylor, Snr*

snub¹ /snʌb/ *v* **snubbed, snubbing** [T] to treat someone rudely, especially by ignoring them when you meet: *the boys who had snubbed her in high school*

snub² *n* [C] an act of snubbing someone: *Eisenhower saw the action as a deliberate snub.*

ˌsnub ˈnose *n* [C] a snub nose is short and flat and points slightly upwards

ˌsnub-ˈnosed *adj* **1** having a snub nose **2** snub-nosed pistol/revolver etc a small gun with a very short BARREL (=tube where the bullets come out)

snuck /snʌk/ a past tense and past participle of SNEAK

so·bri·e·ty /səˈbraɪəti/ n [U] formal **1** when someone is not drunk: *John had periods of sobriety, but always went back to drinking.* **2** behaviour that shows a serious attitude to life

soˈbriety ˌcheckpoint n [C] AmE a place in the road where the police stop vehicles so they can test drivers to see if they have drunk too much alcohol or used illegal drugs

so·bri·quet /ˈsəʊbrɪkeɪ $ ˈsoʊ-/ also **sou·bri·quet** /ˈsuː-/ n [C] formal an unofficial title or name; ▤ **nickname**

ˈsob ˌstory n [C] informal a story, especially one that is not true, that someone tells you in order to make you feel sorry for them: *a sob story about how she lost all her money*

Soc. the written abbreviation of *society*

ˈso-called ᴡ3 adj [only before noun]
1 used to describe someone or something that has been given a name that you think is wrong: *The so-called experts couldn't tell us what was wrong.*
2 used to show that something or someone is usually called a particular name: *the health threats posed by so-called 'mad cow disease'*

soc·cer /ˈsɒkə $ ˈsɑːkər/ n [U] a sport played by two teams of 11 players, who try to kick a round ball into their opponents' GOAL; ▤ **football** BrE

ˈsoccer mom n [C] AmE a mother who spends a lot of time driving her children to sports practice, music lessons etc, considered as a typical example of women from the middle to upper classes in US society

so·cia·ble /ˈsəʊʃəbəl $ ˈsoʊ-/ adj someone who is sociable is friendly and enjoys being with other people; ▣ **unsociable**: *a pleasant, sociable couple* —**sociably** adv —**sociability** /ˌsəʊʃəˈbɪləti $ ˌsoʊ-/ n [U]

so·cial¹ s2 w1 /ˈsəʊʃəl $ ˈsoʊ-/ adj
1 SOCIETY relating to human society and its organization, or the quality of people's lives: *social issues, such as unemployment and education* | *the country's serious social problems* | *a challenge to* **the social order** (=how a particular society is organized)
2 RANK relating to your position in society, according to your job, family, wealth etc: *The students come from a variety of* **social classes** (=groups of people that have the same social position). | *the social status of her family*
3 MEETING PEOPLE relating to meeting people, forming relationships with them, and spending time with them: *social interaction* | *a club with lots of social events* | *Exercise classes are a good way to keep fit and improve your* **social life**. | *Group play helps children develop* **social skills** (=ability to deal with people easily). | *He lacked* **social graces** (=good and polite behaviour towards other people).
4 someone who is social enjoys meeting and talking to other people; ▤ **sociable**
5 ANIMALS forming groups or living together in their natural state; ▣ **solitary**: *Elephants are social animals.* —**socially** adv: *socially acceptable behaviour* | *socially disadvantaged families* → ANTISOCIAL, SOCIABLE, UNSOCIAL

social² n [C] **1** a party for the members of a group, club, or church **2 the social** BrE SOCIAL SECURITY

ˌsocial ˈaudit also **ethical audit** n [C] an official examination of how well a company behaves, for example how it treats its workers, the environment etc: *a social audit of Ben & Jerry's Ice Cream*

ˌsocial ˈclimber n [C] someone who tries to get accepted into a higher social class by becoming friendly with people who belong to that class – used in order to show disapproval

ˈsocial ˌclub n [C] a club where its members can go to spend time, talk, drink etc with other members

ˌsocial ˈconscience n [singular, U] if someone has a social conscience, they know about and want to help

people who have problems in society, for example people who are poor or have family problems

ˌsocial deˈmocracy n **1** [U] a political and economic system based on some ideas of SOCIALISM combined with DEMOCRATIC principles, such as personal freedom and government by elected representatives **2** [C] a country with a government based on social democracy —**social ˈdemocrat** n [C]

ˌsocial engiˈneering n [U] the practice of making changes to laws in order to change society according to a political idea

ˌsocial exˈclusion n [U] BrE the situation that results when people suffer the effects of a combination of problems such as unemployment, crime, and bad HOUSING, and have very little chance of being able to improve their lives: *efforts to combat poverty and social exclusion*

ˈsocial ˌfund n [C usually singular] BrE money that is used to help people with social problems, such as family problems or money problems

ˌsocial ˈhousing n [U] BrE houses or apartments that the local government provides, which can be rented for a small amount of money

so·cial·is·m /ˈsəʊʃəl-ɪzəm $ ˈsoʊ-/ n [U] an economic and political system in which large industries are owned by the government, and taxes are used to take some wealth away from richer citizens and give it to poorer citizens; → **capitalism, communism**

so·cial·ist¹ /ˈsəʊʃəl-ɪ̯st $ ˈsoʊ-/ adj **1** based on socialism or relating to a political party that supports socialism: *socialist principles* **2** a socialist country or government has a political system based on socialism

socialist² n [C] someone who believes in socialism, or who is a member of a political party that supports socialism

so·cia·lis·tic /ˌsəʊʃəˈlɪstɪk◂ $ ˌsoʊ-/ adj based on socialism – usually used in order to show disapproval: *socialistic ideas*

so·cial·ite /ˈsəʊʃəl-aɪt $ ˈsoʊ-/ n [C] someone who is well known for going to many fashionable parties, and who is often rich: *a Washington socialite*

so·cial·i·za·tion /ˌsəʊʃəl-aɪˈzeɪʃən $ ˌsoʊʃələ-/ n [U] **1** the process by which people, especially children, are made to behave in a way that is acceptable in their society: *Schools play an important part in the socialization of our children.* **2** the process of making something work according to SOCIALIST ideas: *the socialization of medicine*

so·cial·ize also **-ise** BrE /ˈsəʊʃəl-aɪz $ ˈsoʊ-/ v **1** [I] to spend time with other people in a friendly way: [+with] *People don't socialize with their neighbours as much as they used to.* **2** [T usually passive] to train someone to behave in a way that is acceptable in the society they are living in: **socialize sb into sth** *Girls are socialized into appropriate 'feminine' behavior.*

ˌsocialized ˈmedicine n [U] especially AmE medical care provided by a government and paid for through taxes

ˌsocial ˈscience n **1** [U] the study of people in society **2** [C] a particular subject relating to the study of people in society, such as history, politics, SOCIOLOGY, or ANTHROPOLOGY —**social scientist** n [C]; → **natural science**

ˌsocial seˈcurity n [U] **1** BrE government money that is paid to people who are unemployed, old, ill etc; ▤ **welfare** AmE | **social security benefits** | **be/live on social security** (=be receiving money from the government) **2 Social Security** a US government programme into which workers must make regular payments, and which pays money regularly to old people and people who are unable to work; → **National Insurance**

ˌSocial Seˈcurity ˌnumber n [C] a number that is given to each person in the US by the government, and that is used on official forms, in computer records etc

ˌsocial ˈservice n [C] **1 social services** [plural] BrE the government department that helps people with problems, for example family or money problems, or the services it provides: *Contact social services for help.* | *social service workers* | *the provision of social services* **2** a service that helps society work properly: *The country railways provided a vital social service.*

'social ˌstudies *n* [plural] the study of people in society; ◨ **social science**

'social work *n* [U] work done by government or private organizations to improve bad social conditions and help people who are poor, have family problems, are unable to find a job etc

'social ˌworker *n* [C] someone who is trained to help people who are poor, have family problems etc

so·ci·e·tal /sə'saɪətl/ *adj* relating to a particular society: *societal attitudes*

so·ci·e·ty [S1] [W1] /sə'saɪˌti/ *n plural* **societies**
1 PEOPLE IN GENERAL [U] people in general, considered in relation to the laws, organizations etc that make it possible for them to live together: *technology and its effects on modern society* | *Children are the most vulnerable members of society.*
2 A PARTICULAR GROUP [C,U] a particular large group of people who share laws, organizations, customs etc: *Britain is now a multi-racial society.* | *the capitalist societies of the West* | *the conservative segment of American society*
3 CLUB [C] an organization or club with members who share similar interests, aims etc: *the university film society* | *the American Cancer Society* | *[+of]* *the Society of Black Lawyers*
4 UPPER CLASS [U] the fashionable group of people who are rich and powerful: *a society wedding* | **high society** (=the richest, most fashionable etc people)
5 BEING WITH PEOPLE [U] *formal* when you are together with other people: *[+of]* *Holidays are a time to enjoy the society of your family.*
6 polite society middle or upper class people who behave correctly in social situations: **in polite society** (=among middle or upper class people) *The subject was rarely mentioned in polite society.* → **BUILDING SOCIETY, FRIENDLY SOCIETY**

socio- /səʊsiəʊ, -siə, səʊʃiəʊ, -ʃiə $ soʊsioʊ, -siə, soʊʃioʊ, -ʃiə/ *prefix technical* **1** relating to society: *sociology* (=the study of society) **2** social and something else: *sociopolitical* | *sociolinguistics*

so·ci·o·ec·o·nom·ic /ˌsəʊsiəʊekə'nɒmɪk, ˌsəʊʃiəʊ-, -iːkə- $ ˌsoʊsioʊekə'nɑː-, ˌsoʊʃioʊ-, -iːkə-/ *adj* based on a combination of social and economic conditions —**socioeconomically** /-kli/ *adv*

so·ci·ol·o·gy /ˌsəʊsi'ɒlədʒi, ˌsəʊʃi- $ ˌsoʊsi'ɑːl-, ˌsoʊʃi-/ *n* [U] the scientific study of societies and the behaviour of people in groups —**sociologist** *n* [C] —**sociological** /ˌsəʊsiə'lɒdʒɪkəl, ˌsəʊʃi- $ ˌsoʊsiə'lɑː-, ˌsoʊʃi-/ *adj*: *a sociological study* —**sociologically** /-kli/ *adv*; → **anthropology, ethnology, social science**

so·ci·o·path /'səʊsiəˌpæθ, 'səʊʃiə- $ 'soʊ-/ *n* [C] someone whose behaviour towards other people is considered unacceptable, strange, and possibly dangerous —**sociopathic** /ˌsəʊsiə'pæθɪk◂ ˌsəʊʃiə- $ ˌsoʊ-/ *adj*; → **psychopath**

sock¹ [S3] /sɒk $ sɑːk/ *n* [C]
1 a piece of clothing made of soft material that you wear on your foot inside your shoe: *a **pair** of socks* | *white ankle socks*
2 knock/blow sb's socks off *informal* to surprise and excite someone very much: *a new band that will knock your socks off*
3 pull your socks up *informal especially BrE* to make an effort to improve your behaviour or your work: *If they want promotion, United have got to pull their socks up.*
4 put a sock in it *informal* used to tell someone in a joking way to stop talking or making a noise
5 *informal* a hard hit, especially with your hand closed: *Larry gave him a sock on the arm.*

sock² *v* [T] **1** *informal* to hit someone very hard, especially with your hand closed; ◨ **thump**: *He socked her in the face.* **2** [usually passive] *informal* if someone is socked with something bad, they are suddenly

affected by it: *sock sb with sth I got socked with a big car repair bill.* **3** be socked in *AmE* if an airport, road, or area is socked in, it is very difficult to see far and no one can travel because of bad FOG, snow, or rain **4 sock it to sb** *old-fashioned* to tell someone to do something in a direct and forceful way

sock sth ⇔ away *phr v AmE* to save money by putting it in a safe place: *Roger socked away more than $1 million a year.*

sock·et /'sɒk‚t $ 'sɑː-/ *n* [C] **1** a place in a wall where you can connect electrical equipment to the supply of electricity; ◨ **power point** *BrE*; **outlet** *AmE* **2** the place on a piece of electrical equipment that you put a PLUG or a LIGHT BULB into: *a headphone socket* **3** a hollow part of ·a structure into which something fits: *the eye sockets*

sod¹ /sɒd $ sɑːd/ *n* **1** [C] *BrE informal not polite* a very offensive word for someone, especially a man, who you think is stupid or annoying: *Get up, you lazy sod!* **2 be a sod** *BrE informal not polite* to be very difficult to do or deal with: *That door's a sod to open.* **3** [C usually singular] *BrE informal not polite* used to refer to a person: *The poor sod's wife left him.* | *You lucky sod!* **4 not give/care a sod** *BrE spoken not polite* to not care at all about something: *I don't give a sod who it is!* **5** [C,U] a piece of earth or the layer of earth with grass and roots growing in it

sod² *v* [T only in imperative or infinitive] *BrE spoken not polite* **1 sod it/that** used to rudely express anger or annoyance at something or someone: *Sod it, I've missed the train.* **2** used to say rudely that something is not important: *Sod the job, I'm going home.* **3 sod off** an offensive way of telling someone to go away

so·da /'səʊdə $ 'soʊ-/ *n* **1** [C,U] also **soda water** water that contains bubbles and is often added to alcoholic drinks: *a Scotch and soda* **2** [C,U] also **soda pop** *AmE* a sweet drink containing bubbles, or a can or bottle of this drink; ◨ **pop**: *a can of orange soda* | *a cooler full of sodas* **3** [C] *AmE* an ICE-CREAM SODA: *a strawberry soda* **4** [U] a substance in the form of a powder containing SODIUM, that is used for cooking or cleaning: *baking soda*

'soda ˌfountain *n* [C] *AmE* a place in a shop at which drinks, ice cream etc were served in the past

sod 'all *n* [U] *BrE informal not polite* nothing at all: *I got sod all from the deal.*

'soda pop *n* [C,U] *AmE* a sweet drink containing bubbles

'soda ˌsiphon *n* [C] *BrE* a special type of bottle from which SODA WATER is forced out in a fast stream

'soda ˌwater *n* [U] water that contains bubbles and is often added to alcoholic drinks

sod·den /'sɒdn $ 'sɑːdn/ *adj* very wet and heavy: *sodden clothes* | *The earth was sodden.* | **rain-sodden/water-sodden** *rain-sodden hair*

sod·ding /'sɒdɪŋ $ 'saː-/ *adj BrE spoken not polite* said when someone is angry or annoyed, or to emphasize what they are saying: *The sodding computer's crashed!*

so·di·um /'səʊdiəm $ 'soʊ-/ *n* [U] a common silver-white metal that usually exists in combination with other substances, for example in salt. It is a chemical ELEMENT: symbol Na

ˌsodium bi'carbonate also **bicarbonate of soda** *n* [U] a white powder used in baking to make cakes, BISCUITS etc lighter, or for cleaning things; ◨ **baking soda**

ˌsodium 'chloride *n* [U] *technical* the type of salt that is used in cooking

sod·o·mite /'sɒdəmaɪt $ 'saː-/ *n* [C] *old use* someone who practises sodomy

sod·o·my /'sɒdəmi $ 'saː-/ *n* [U] *formal or law* a sexual act in which a man puts his sex organ into someone's ANUS, especially that of another man; ◨ **buggery** —**sodomize** *v* [T]

s

Sod's 'law *n* [U] *BrE* the natural tendency for things to go wrong whenever possible – used humorously; ▣ **Murphy's Law** *AmE*: *It's Sod's law that the car breaks down when you need it most.*

sofa

sofa/settee/couch

so·fa /'səʊfə $ 'soʊ-/ *n* [C] a comfortable seat with raised arms and a back, that is wide enough for two or three people to sit on; ▣ **couch**; ▣ **settee** *BrE*

'sofa bed *n* [C] a sofa that has a bed inside that can be folded out

soft S2 W2 /sɒft $ sɒːft/ *adj comparative* **softer**, *superlative* **softest**

1 NOT HARD a) not hard, firm, or stiff, but easy to press; ▣ **hard**: *My feet sank into the soft ground.* | *the softest sofa and pillows* | *Cook the onions until they go soft.* **b)** less hard than average; ▣ **hard**: *a soft lead pencil* | *soft cheese*

2 NOT ROUGH having a surface that is smooth and pleasant to touch; ▣ **rough**: *a baby's soft skin* | *The fur was soft to the touch.*

3 NOT LOUD a soft sound, voice, or music is quiet and pleasant to listen to; ▣ **loud, harsh**: *soft music* | *His voice was softer now.*

4 COLOUR/LIGHT [only before noun] soft colours or lights are pleasant and relaxing because they are not too bright; ▣ **bright**: *All the stores will be re-fitted with softer lighting.* | *a soft shade of peach*

5 NO HARD EDGES not having any hard edges or sharp angles: *soft curves*

6 RAIN/WIND gentle and without much force: *a soft breeze* | *soft rain*

7 NOT STRICT someone who is soft seems weak because they are not strict enough with other people; ▣ **strict, tough**: *If you appear to be soft, people take advantage of you.* | [+on] *No politician wants to seem soft on crime.* | *Courts have been taking a soft line* (=not being strict enough) *with young offenders.*

8 SENSITIVE kind, gentle, and sympathetic to other people; ▣ **hard**: *He has a soft heart beneath that cold exterior.* | *a soft kiss*

9 WEAK CHARACTER not very brave and not having a strong character; ▣ **hard**: *Don't be soft – just jump!*

10 SALES/MARKETS decreasing in price, value, or the amount sold: *soft oil prices*

11 soft loan/credit money that is lent at a lower interest rate than usual, because it will be used to help people in some way

12 soft money money that people, companies, or organizations give to political parties, rather than to a particular CANDIDATE

13 TOO EASY *informal* a soft job, life etc is too easy and does not involve much work or hard physical work: *Mike's found himself a soft job in the stores.* | **soft option** *BrE* (=a choice that allows you to avoid difficulties or hard work) *Taking the soft option won't help your career to develop.*

14 WEAK BODY *informal* having a body that is not in a strong physical condition, because you do not do enough exercise: *He'd got soft after all those years in a desk job.*

15 WATER soft water does not contain many minerals, so that it forms bubbles from soap easily

16 have a soft spot for sb to continue to like someone even when they do not behave well: *She's always had a soft spot for Grant.*

17 a soft touch *informal* someone from whom you can easily get what you want, because they are kind or easy to deceive

18 soft in the head *old-fashioned* very stupid or crazy

19 STUPID *BrE* stupid or silly: *You must be soft if you think I'll give you fifty quid!*

20 be soft on sb *old-fashioned* to be sexually attracted to someone

21 CONSONANTS *technical* not sounding hard: *a soft g*
—**softly** *adv*: *She stroked his head softly.* | *Music played softly in the background.* —**softness** *n* [U]

> **WORD FOCUS: SOFT**
> soft and pleasant to touch: **velvety, fluffy, silky**
> soft and easily crushed: **squashy, squishy**
> soft and wet: **mushy, squelchy** *BrE informal*
> soft and good to eat: **tender**

soft·ball /'sɒftbɔːl $ 'sɒːftbɒːl/ *n* **1** [U] a game similar to baseball but played on a smaller field with a slightly larger and softer ball **2** [C] the special ball used to play this game

soft-'boiled *adj* an egg that is soft-boiled is boiled long enough for the white part to become solid, but the yellow part in the centre is still liquid; → **hard-boiled**

'soft ,copy *n* [U] *technical* information stored in a computer's memory or shown on a screen rather than printed on paper; → **hard copy**

soft 'currency *n* [C,U] money of a particular country that may fall in value and is difficult to exchange for the money of a country that is economically stronger; → **hard currency**

'soft drink *n* [C] a cold drink that does not contain alcohol

soft 'drug *n* [C] an illegal drug such as MARIJUANA that is not considered to be very harmful; → **hard drug**

soft·en /'sɒfən $ 'sɒː-/ *v* [I,T] **1** also **soften up** to become less hard or rough, or make something less hard or rough; ▣ **harden**: *Use moisturizer to soften your skin.* | *Cook until the onion softens.* **2** if your attitude softens, or if something softens it, it becomes less strict and more sympathetic; ▣ **harden**: *The government has softened its stance on public spending.* | [+towards] *I felt that he was beginning to soften towards me.* **3** to make the effect of something seem less unpleasant or severe, or to become less unpleasant or severe: **soften the blow/impact** *The impact of the tax was softened by large tax-free allowances.* **4** if your expression or voice softens, or if something softens it, you look or sound kinder and more gentle; ▣ **harden**: *His voice softened as he spoke to her.* **5** to make the shape or colour of something look less severe: *Climbing plants soften the outline of a fence.*

soften sb/sth ⇔ up *phr v* **1** *informal* to be nice to someone before you ask them to do something, so that they will agree to help you: *She was just softening me up.* **2** to make an enemy weaker so that they are easier to attack: *Use artillery to soften up the enemy forces.* **3** to make something less hard or rough

soft·en·er /'sɒfənə $ 'sɒːfənər/ *n* [C,U] a substance that you add to water to make clothes feel soft after washing: *fabric softener* → **WATER SOFTENER**

soft 'focus *n* [U] a way of photographing or filming things so that the edges of the objects in the photograph are not sharp or clear

soft 'fruit *n* [C,U] *especially BrE* small fruits, such as STRAWBERRIES, that you can eat that do not have a hard skin or large seed

soft 'furnishings *n* [plural] *BrE* things such as curtains, chair covers etc that are made of cloth and are used in decorating a room

soft-heart·ed /ˌsɒft ˈhɑːtɪ̯d◂ $ ˌsɒːft ˈhɑːr-/ adj easily affected by feelings of pity or sympathy for other people; ◼ **hard-hearted**: *a soft-hearted woman*

soft·ie, softy /ˈsɒfti $ ˈsɒːf-/ n [C] someone who is easily affected by feelings of pity or sympathy, or who is easily persuaded: *He's a real softie.*

ˌsoft ˈlanding n [C] **1** a situation in which a SPACE-CRAFT comes down onto the ground gently and without any damage; ◼ **crash landing** **2** if the ECONOMY of a country has a soft landing, it does not experience bad effects after an attempt to control increases in the COST OF LIVING: *Hopes for a soft landing have faded.*

ˌsoftly-ˈsoftly adj BrE **softly-softly approach** a way of dealing with something or someone which involves being very patient and careful: *We need to adopt a softly-softly approach with Mike.*

ˌsoftly-ˈspoken adj another form of the word SOFT-SPOKEN

ˌsoft ˈpalate n [C] the soft part at the back of the top of your mouth

ˌsoft-ˈpedal v **soft-pedalled, soft-pedalling** BrE, **soft-pedaled, soft-pedaling** AmE [T] informal to make something seem less important or less urgent than it really is

ˌsoft ˈporn n [U] magazines, pictures etc that show people wearing no clothes or sexual activity, but that do not show sexual activity completely clearly or in a violent way; → **hard porn**

ˌsoft ˈsell n [singular] a way of advertising or selling things that involves gently persuading people to buy something; → **hard sell**

ˌsoft ˈshoulder n [C] the edge of a road, when this edge is made of dirt rather than a hard material; → **hard shoulder**

ˈsoft-soap v [T] BrE informal to say nice things to someone in order to persuade them to do something: *Don't think you can soft-soap me!* —**soft soap** n [U]

ˌsoft-ˈspoken adj having a pleasant quiet voice: *a soft-spoken man*

ˌsoft ˈtarget n [C] a person or thing that is easy to attack or criticize

ˈsoft-top n [C] a car with a cloth roof that you can fold back or remove; ◼ **convertible**; → **hardtop**

ˌsoft ˈtoy n [C] BrE a toy for young children that is made of cloth and filled with soft material

soft·ware W2 /ˈsɒftweə $ ˈsɒːftwer/ n [U] the sets of programs that tell a computer how to do a particular job; → **hardware**: *She loaded the new software.* | **design/anti-virus/database** etc **software** *word-processing software* | *a software company*

soft·wood /ˈsɒftwʊd $ ˈsɒːft-/ n [C,U] wood from trees such as PINE and FIR that is cheap and easy to cut, or a tree with this type of wood; → **hardwood**

soft·y /ˈsɒfti $ ˈsɒːf-/ n plural **softies** [C] another spelling of SOFTIE

sog·gy /ˈsɒgi $ ˈsɑːgi/ adj unpleasantly wet and soft: *The ground was soggy from the rain.* | *The sandwiches have gone all soggy.*

soh /səʊ $ soʊ/ n [singular, U] another spelling of so³

SOHO /ˈsəʊhəʊ $ ˈsoʊhoʊ/ n [C] *small office/home office* a room in someone's house with electronic equipment such as a computer and a FAX machine, that is used as a place in which to work

soi·gné, soignée /ˈswɑːnjeɪ $ swɑːnˈjeɪ/ adj formal dressed or arranged fashionably and with care: *a soignée woman politician*

soil¹ W2 /sɔɪl/ n
1 [C,U] the top layer of the earth in which plants grow; ◼ **earth**: *The soil here is very poor.* | *The bush grows well in a sandy soil.* → see box at GROUND¹
2 **on British/French/foreign etc soil** formal in Britain, France etc: *The crime was committed on American soil.*
3 [U] a place or situation where something can develop: *Eastern Europe provided fertile soil for political activists.*

4 **sb's native soil** literary your own country
5 **the soil** literary farming as a job or way of life: *They make their living from the soil.*

soil² v [T] **1** formal to make something dirty, especially with waste from your body **2** **not soil your hands** to not do something because you consider it too unpleasant or dishonest: *Keep your money – I wouldn't soil my hands with it.* —**soiled** adj: *soiled diapers*

soi·ree, soirée /ˈswɑːreɪ $ swɑːˈreɪ/ n [C] a formal or fashionable evening party

soj·ourn /ˈsɒdʒɜːn $ ˈsoʊdʒɜːrn/ n [C] formal a short period of time that you stay in a place that is not your home: *a brief sojourn in Europe* —**sojourn** v [I]

sol /sɒl $ soʊl/ n [singular, U] so³ (=a musical note)

sol·ace /ˈsɒlɪs $ ˈsɑː-/ n formal **1** [U] a feeling of emotional comfort at a time of great sadness or disappointment: **seek/find solace in sth** *After the death of her son, Val found solace in the church.* **2** **be a solace to sb** to bring a feeling of comfort and calmness to someone, when they are sad or disappointed: *Mary was a great solace to me after Arthur died.* —**solace** v [T] literary

so·lar /ˈsəʊlə $ ˈsoʊlər/ adj [only before noun] **1** relating to the sun; → **lunar**: *a solar eclipse* **2** using the power of the sun's light and heat: *solar energy*

ˌsolar ˈcell n [C] a piece of equipment for producing electric power from sunlight

so·lar·i·um /səʊˈleəriəm $ soʊˈler-/ n [C] **1** a place with SUNBEDS (=beds with special lamps) where you can get an artificial SUNTAN **2** a room, usually enclosed by glass, where you can sit in bright sunlight

ˌsolar ˈpanel n [C] a piece of equipment, usually kept on a roof, that collects and uses the sun's energy to heat water or make electricity → see picture at ENERGY

solar plex·us /ˌsəʊlə ˈpleksəs $ ˌsoʊlər-/ n [singular] the front part of your body just below your RIBS: *a blow to the solar plexus*

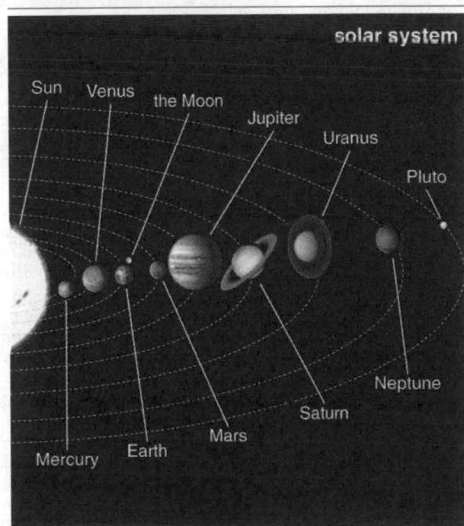
solar system

Sun · Venus · the Moon · Jupiter · Uranus · Pluto · Neptune · Saturn · Mars · Earth · Mercury

ˌsolar ˈsystem n **1 the solar system** the Sun and the PLANETS that go around it **2** [C] this kind of system around another star

ˌsolar ˈyear n [C] the period of time in which the Earth travels once around the Sun, equal to just over 365 days

sold /səʊld $ soʊld/ the past tense and past participle of SELL

sol·der¹ /ˈsɒldə, ˈsəʊl- $ ˈsɑːdər/ *n* [U] a soft metal, usually a mixture of LEAD and TIN, which can be melted and used to join two metal surfaces, wires etc

solder² *v* [T + onto/together] to join or repair metal surfaces with solder

ˈsoldering ˌiron *n* [C] a tool which is heated, usually by electricity, and used for melting solder and putting it on surfaces

sol·dier¹ [S2] [W2] /ˈsəʊldʒə $ ˈsəʊldʒər/ *n* [C] a member of the army of a country, especially someone who is not an officer; → **troop**: *A British soldier was wounded in the fighting.* | *an enemy soldier* → see picture at INJURED

soldier² *v*

soldier on *phr v especially BrE* to continue working in spite of difficulties: *We'll just have to soldier on without him.*

sol·dier·ing /ˈsəʊldʒərɪŋ $ ˈsoʊl-/ *n* [U] the life or job of a soldier

sol·dier·ly /ˈsəʊldʒəli $ ˈsoʊldʒərli/ *adj formal* typical of a good soldier

ˌsoldier of ˈfortune *n plural* **soldiers of fortune** [C] someone who works as a soldier for anyone who will pay them; ▤ **mercenary**

sol·dier·y /ˈsəʊldʒəri $ ˈsoʊl-/ *n* [singular, U] *old-fashioned* soldiers

ˌsold ˈout, ˈsold-out *adj* **1** if a concert, performance etc is sold out, all the tickets for that show have been sold: *The group will play three sold-out shows at Wembley Stadium.* **2** if a shop or store is sold out of a particular product, it has sold all of that product: [+of] *The store was completely sold out of tuna fish.*

sole¹ /səʊl $ soʊl/ *adj* [only before noun]
1 the sole person, thing etc is the only one; ▤ **only**: *the sole American in the room* | *Griffiths is the sole survivor of the crash.* | *The story was published with the sole purpose of selling newspapers.*
2 not shared with anyone else: *Derek has sole responsibility for sales in Dublin.* | *The company has the sole rights to market Elton John's records.*

sole² *n* **1** [C] the bottom surface of your foot, especially the part you walk or stand on: *The soles of his feet were caked in mud.* → see picture at FOOTWEAR **2** [C] flat bottom part of a shoe, not including the heel: *the soles of her shoes* | **thick-soled/leather-soled etc** (=having soles that are thick, made of leather etc) **3** [C,U] *plural* **sole** or **soles** a flat fish that is often used for food; → **lemon sole**: *Dover sole*

sole³ *v* [T usually passive] to put a new SOLE on a shoe

so·le·cis·m /ˈsɒlɪsɪzəm $ ˈsɑː-/ *n* [C] *formal* **1** a mistake in the use of written or spoken language **2** something that is not considered polite behaviour: *a social solecism*

sole·ly /ˈsəʊl-li $ ˈsoʊl-/ *adv* not involving anything or anyone else; ▤ **only**: *Scholarships are given solely on the basis of financial need.* | *I shall hold you solely responsible for anything that goes wrong.*

sol·emn /ˈsɒləm $ ˈsɑː-/ *adj* **1** very serious and not happy, for example because something bad has happened or because you are at an important occasion: *a solemn expression* | *Their faces suddenly grew solemn.* | *a solemn procession of mourners* **2** a solemn promise is one that is made very seriously and with no intention of breaking it: *a solemn vow* | *I'll never be unfaithful again. I give you my solemn word.* **3** performed in a very serious way: **solemn ritual/ceremony** —**solemnly** *adv*

so·lem·ni·ty /səˈlemnɪti/ *n* **1** [U] the quality of being serious in behaviour or manner: *the solemnity of a great religious occasion* **2** **solemnities** [plural] the ceremonies of an important and serious occasion

sol·em·nize also **-ise** *BrE* /ˈsɒləmnaɪz $ ˈsɑː-/ *v* **solemnize a marriage** *formal* to perform a wedding ceremony in a church

sol-fa /ˌsɒl ˈfɑː $ ˌsoʊl-/ **sol·fege** $ soʊlˈfedʒ/ *n* [U] the system in which the notes of the musical SCALE are represented by seven short words, DO, RE, MI, FA, SO, LA, TI, which are used especially in singing

so·li·cit /səˈlɪsɪt/ *v* **1** [I usually progressive] to offer to have sex with someone in exchange for money: *She was arrested for soliciting.* **2** [I,T] *formal* to ask someone for money, help, or information: *Morgan is accused of illegally soliciting campaign contributions.* | **solicit sth from sb** *The governor sent two officials to Mexico City to solicit aid from the President.* **3** [I,T] *AmE* to try to sell a product or service by taking it to homes or businesses and showing it to the people there: *No soliciting on company premises is allowed.*

so·li·ci·ta·tion /səˌlɪsɪˈteɪʃən/ *n* [C,U] the act of asking someone for money, help, or information

so·lic·i·tor [S3] [W2] /səˈlɪsɪtə $ -ər/ *n* [C]
1 a type of lawyer in Britain who gives legal advice, prepares the necessary documents when property is bought or sold, and defends people, especially in the lower courts of law; → **lawyer**, **advocate**, **barrister**: *You need to see a solicitor.* | *a small firm of solicitors* → see box at LAWYER
2 *AmE* someone who goes from place to place trying to sell goods or services: *A sign on the door read, 'No Solicitors.'*

so·licitor ˈgeneral *n* [C] the government law officer next in rank below the ATTORNEY GENERAL

so·lic·i·tous /səˈlɪsɪtəs/ *adj formal* very concerned about someone's safety, health, or comfort —**solicitously** *adv* —**solicitousness** *n* [U]

so·lic·i·tude /səˈlɪsɪtjuːd $ -tuːd/ *n* [U] *formal* care and concern for someone's health, safety etc: *She was grateful to him for his solicitude.*

sol·id¹ [S3] [W3] /ˈsɒlɪd $ ˈsɑː-/ *adj*
1 FIRM/HARD hard or firm, with a fixed shape, and not a liquid or gas: *The lake was frozen solid.* | *It was good to be back on solid ground again.* | *Is the baby eating solid food* (=bread, meat etc) *yet?* | *The ship's sonar can detect the presence of solid objects in the water.*
2 ONLY ONE MATERIAL consisting completely of one type of material: **solid gold/silver etc** *a solid gold cup* | **solid wood/pine/oak etc** *a chest made of solid oak*
3 NOT HOLLOW having no holes or spaces inside; ▤ **hollow**: *a solid rubber ball* | *a shrine carved out of solid rock*
4 WITHOUT SPACES continuous, without any spaces or breaks: *It's not safe to pass when the lines in the middle of the road are solid.*
5 STRONGLY MADE strong and well made; ▤ **flimsy**: *a solid piece of furniture* | *The frame is as solid as a rock* (=extremely solid).
6 GOOD AND LONG-LASTING a solid achievement or solid work is of real, practical, and continuing value: *five years of solid achievement* | *The first two years provide a solid foundation in the basics of computing.*
7 DEPENDABLE someone or something that is solid can be depended on or trusted: *a solid reputation* | *The prosecution in this case has no solid evidence.* | *You can rely on Wylie for good solid advice.* | *a solid Labour stronghold* (=where people always vote for this party)
8 CONTINUING WITHOUT INTERRUPTION *informal* used to emphasize that something continues for a long time without any pauses: *The lecture lasted two solid hours.* | **five hours/two weeks etc solid** *On Saturday I went to bed and slept fourteen hours solid.*
9 packed solid *informal* if shops, trains, buses etc are packed solid, they are full of people
10 on solid ground confident because you are dealing with a subject you are sure about, or because you are in a safe situation: *To make sure that he was on solid ground, he confirmed his findings with others.*
11 GOOD *BrE informal* good
12 DIFFICULT *BrE informal* very difficult: *I couldn't do any of the maths last night – it was solid.*
13 SHAPE *technical* having length, width, and height; ▤ **three-dimensional**: *A sphere is a solid figure.*
14 IN AGREEMENT be solid *BrE* to be in complete

sombre

agreement: *The workers are 100% solid on this issue.*
—**solidly** *adv*: *solidly built* —**solidness** *n* [U]

solid² *n* **1** [C] a firm object or substance that has a fixed shape, not a gas or liquid: *the properties of liquids and solids* **2** solids [plural] foods that are not liquid: *He's still too ill to eat solids.* **3** [C] *technical* the part of a liquid which has the qualities of a solid when it is separated from the SOLVENT (=watery part) **4** [C] *technical* a shape which has length, width, and height, such as a SPHERE or CYLINDER

sol·i·dar·i·ty /ˌsɒlɪˈdærɪti $ ˌsɑː-/ *n* [U] loyalty and general agreement between all the people in a group, or between different groups because they all have a shared aim: *a gesture of solidarity* | *an appeal for worker solidarity* | **show/express/demonstrate your solidarity (with sb)** *I come before you today to express my solidarity with the people of New York.*

ˌsolid ˈfuel *n* [C] a solid substance such as coal that is burnt to produce heat or power

so·lid·i·fy /səˈlɪdɪfaɪ/ *v* **solidified, solidifying, solidifies 1** [I,T] to become solid or make something solid: *The volcanic lava solidifies as it cools.* | *solidified cream* **2** [T] to make an agreement, plan, attitude etc more definite and less likely to change: *The two countries signed a treaty to solidify their alliance.*
—**solidification** /səˌlɪdɪfɪˈkeɪʃən/ *n* [U]

so·lid·i·ty /səˈlɪdɪti/ *n* [U] **1** the strength or hardness of something: *the solidity of the stone walls* **2** the quality of something that is permanent and can be depended on: *the solidity of middle-class institutions*

ˌsolid-ˈstate *adj* **1** solid-state electrical equipment contains electronic parts, such as SILICON CHIPS, rather than moving MECHANICAL parts **2** solid-state PHYSICS is concerned with the qualities of solid substances, especially the way in which they CONDUCT electricity

sol·i·dus /ˈsɒlɪdəs $ ˈsɑː-/ *n plural* **solidi** /-daɪ/ [C] an OBLIQUE²

so·lil·o·quy /səˈlɪləkwi/ *n plural* **soliloquies** [C,U] a speech in a play in which a character, usually alone on the stage, talks to himself or herself so that the AUDIENCE knows their thoughts; → **monologue** —**soliloquize** /-kwaɪz/ *v* [I]

sol·ip·sis·m /ˈsɒlɪpsɪzəm $ ˈsɑː-, ˈsoʊ-/ *n* [U] *technical* the idea in PHILOSOPHY that only the SELF exists or can be known

sol·ip·sis·tic /ˌsɒlɪpˈsɪstɪk◂ $ ˌsɑːl-, ˌsoʊ-/ *adj* **1** interested only in yourself and the things that affect you **2** *technical* relating to the view in PHILOSOPHY that only the SELF exists or can be known

sol·i·taire /ˌsɒlɪˈteə $ ˈsɑːlɪˈteər/ *n* **1** [U] a game played by one person with small wooden or plastic pieces on a board **2** [C] a single jewel, or a piece of jewellery with a single jewel in it, especially a large diamond: *a diamond solitaire* **3** [U] *AmE* a game of cards for one person; **E** **patience** *BrE*

sol·i·ta·ry¹ /ˈsɒlɪtəri $ ˈsɑːlɪˌteri/ *adj* **1** [only before noun] used to emphasize that there is only one of something; **E** **single**: *the solitary goal of the match* | *The benches were empty except for a single solitary figure.* **2** doing something without anyone else with you: *a long, solitary walk* **3** spending a lot of time alone, usually because you like being alone; **E** **sociable**: *a solitary man* | *Pandas are solitary creatures.* | *He led a rather solitary existence.* **4** not a solitary word/thing etc used to emphasize that there is not even one: *He followed her round without a solitary word.* —**solitarily** *adv* —**solitariness** *n* [U]

solitary² *n plural* **solitaries 1** [U] *informal* solitary confinement: *He spent two weeks in solitary.* **2** [C] *BrE literary* someone who lives completely alone; **E** **hermit**

ˌsolitary conˈfinement *n* [U] a punishment in which a prisoner is kept alone and is not allowed to see anyone else: **in solitary confinement** *He spent more than half his time in prison in solitary confinement.*

sol·i·tude /ˈsɒlɪtjuːd $ ˈsɑːlɪˌtuːd/ *n* [U] when you are alone, especially when this is what you enjoy; → **loneliness**: **in solitude** *Carl spent the morning in solitude.* | *the solitude of her house on the lake*

so·lo¹ /ˈsəʊləʊ $ ˈsoʊloʊ/ *adj* [only before noun] **1** done alone without anyone else helping you: **solo flight/voyage/ascent** *Ridgeway's solo voyage across the Atlantic* | *the first solo ascent of Everest* | *a solo effort* **2** relating to a record or piece of music that is performed by a single musician, not a group: *a solo album* | *a solo passage for viola* —**solo** *adv*: *When did you first fly solo?* | *Amos quit the company, determined to go solo* (=work for himself).

solo² *n plural* **solos** [C] **1** a piece of music for one performer; → **duet, trio**: *a gorgeous piano solo* **2** when someone flies or does an activity alone: *his first solo*

solo³ *v* [I] **1** to perform a solo in a piece of music: *Brokaw solos brilliantly on this album.* **2** to fly an aircraft alone

so·lo·ist /ˈsəʊləʊɪst $ ˈsoʊloʊ-/ *n* [C] a musician who performs alone or plays an instrument alone: *cello soloist Yo Yo Ma*

sol·stice /ˈsɒlstɪs $ ˈsɑːl-/ *n* [C] the time when the sun is furthest north or south of the EQUATOR: **the summer/winter solstice** (=the longest or shortest day of the year); → **equinox**

sol·u·ble /ˈsɒljəbəl $ ˈsɑː-/ *adj* **1** a soluble substance can be DISSOLVED in a liquid: *soluble aspirin* | **water-soluble** (=that can be dissolved in water) **2** *formal* a problem that is soluble can be solved; **E** **insoluble** —**solubility** /ˌsɒljəˈbɪlɪti $ ˌsɑː-/ *n* [U]

so·lu·tion S2 W1 /səˈluːʃən/ *n*
1 [C] a way of solving a problem or dealing with a difficult situation; → **solve**: *The best solution would be for them to separate.* | *Both sides are trying to find a peaceful solution.* | [+to/for] *There are no simple solutions to the problem of overpopulation.* | *the perfect solution to all of our problems* | *a political solution to the conflict in Northern Ireland*
2 [C] the correct answer to a problem in an exercise or competition; **E** **answer**; → **solve**: [+to] *The solution to last week's puzzle is on page 12.*
3 [C,U] a liquid in which a solid or gas has been mixed: *a weak sugar solution* | *saline solution*

solve S2 W3 /sɒlv $ sɑːlv/ *v* [T]
1 to find or provide a way of dealing with a problem; → **solution**: *Charlie thinks money will solve all his problems.* | *the best way of solving our dilemma*
2 to find the correct answer to a problem or the explanation for something that is difficult to understand; → **solution**: **solve a crime/mystery/case etc** *More than 70% of murder cases were solved last year.* | *attempts to solve a mathematical equation* | **solve a puzzle/riddle** —**solvable** *adj*

sol·vent¹ /ˈsɒlvənt $ ˈsɑːl-/ *adj* [not usually before noun] having enough money to pay your debts; **E** **insolvent**: **stay/remain/keep solvent** *I don't know how we managed to remain solvent.* —**solvency** *n* [U]

solvent² *n* [C,U] a chemical that is used to DISSOLVE another substance

ˈsolvent aˌbuse *n* [U] *BrE formal* when someone breathes in gases from glues or similar substances in order to get a pleasant feeling, especially when they become dependent on doing this; **E** **glue-sniffing**

som·bre *BrE*; **somber** *AmE* /ˈsɒmbə $ ˈsɑːmbər/ *adj* **1** sad and serious; **E** **grave**: *They sat in sombre silence.* | *We were all in a somber mood that night.* | *a sombre expression* | *on the sombre occasion of his mother's funeral* **2** dark and without any bright colours: *a sombre grey suit* —**sombrely** *adv* —**sombreness** *n* [U]

som·bre·ro /sɒmˈbreərəʊ $ sɑːmˈbreroʊ/ *n plural* **sombreros** [C] a Mexican hat for men that is tall with a wide, round ʙʀɪᴍ¹ turned up at the edges → see picture at ʜᴀᴛ

some¹ /səm; *strong* sʌm / *quantifier* **1** a number of people or things, or an amount of something, when the exact number or amount is not stated: *I need some apples for this recipe.* | *My mother has inherited some land.* | *They're looking for someone with some experience.* | *The doctor gave her some medicine for her cough.* **2** a number of people or things or an amount of something, but not all: *Some people believe in life after death.* | *She's been so depressed that some days she can't get out of bed.* **3** *formal* a fairly large number of people or things or a fairly large amount of something: *It was some time before they managed to turn the alarm off.* | *The donation went some way toward paying for the damage.*

some² /sʌm/ *pron* **1** a number of people or things or an amount of something, when the exact number or amount is not stated: *I've just made a pot of coffee. Would you like some?* | *'Do you know where the screws are?' 'There are some in the garage.'* **2** a number of people or things or an amount of something, but not all: *Many local businesses are having difficulties, and some have even gone bankrupt.* | *Some say it was an accident, but I don't believe it.* | *Many of the exhibits were damaged in the fire, and some were totally destroyed.* | [+of] *Some of his jokes were very rude.* | *Can I have some of your cake?* **3 and then some** *spoken informal* used to say that the actual amount is probably a lot more than what someone has just said: *'They say he earns $2.5 million a season.' 'And then some.'*

some³ ꜱ¹ ᴡ¹ *determiner*
1 used to mean a person or thing, when you do not know or say exactly which: *There must be some reason for her behaviour.* | *Can you give me some idea of the cost?* | **some kind/type/form/sort of sth** *We can hopefully reach some kind of agreement.*
2 *informal* used when you are talking about a person or thing that you do not know, remember, or understand, or when you think it does not matter: *Some guy called for you while you were gone.* | **some sth or other/another** *Just give him some excuse or other.*
3 used to say that something was very good or very impressive: *That was some party last night!*
4 some friend you are/some help she was etc *spoken* used, especially when you are annoyed, to mean someone or something has disappointed you by not behaving in the way you think they should: *You won't lend me the money? Some friend you are!*

some⁴ /səm; *strong* sʌm/ *adv* **1 some more** an additional number or amount of something: *Would you like some more cake?* **2** *AmE spoken* a little: *'Are you feeling better today?' 'Some, I guess.'* **3 some 500 people/ 50%/£100 etc** an expression meaning about 500 people, 50%, £100 etc – used especially when this seems a large number or amount: *She gained some 25 pounds in weight during pregnancy.* **4 some little/few sth** *literary* a fairly large number or amount of something: *We travelled some little way before noticing that Bradley wasn't with us.*

-some /səm/ *suffix* **1** [in adjectives] tending to behave in a particular way, or having a particular quality: *a troublesome boy* (=who causes trouble) | *a bothersome back injury* (=that bothers you) **2** [in nouns] a group of a particular number, for example in a game: *a golf foursome* (=four people playing golf together)

some·bod·y¹ ꜱ¹ ᴡ³ /ˈsʌmbɒdi, -bədi $ -bɑːdi, -bədi/ *pron* used to mean a person, when you do not know, or do not say who the person is; ▤ **someone**; → **anybody**, **everybody**, **nobody**: *There's somebody waiting to see you.* | *Somebody's car alarm kept me awake all night.* | **somebody new/different/good** *We need somebody neutral to sort this out.* | *If you can't make it Friday, we*

can invite **somebody else** (=a different person). | *'Who can we get to babysit?' 'I'll call Suzie or somebody.'*

somebody² *n* **be somebody** to be or feel important: *She was the first teacher who'd made Paul feel like he was somebody.*

some·day /ˈsʌmdeɪ/ also **'some day** *adv* at an unknown time in the future, especially a long time in the future: *I'd like to visit Japan someday.* | *He hopes, someday, to have his own business.*

some·how ꜱ² ᴡ² /ˈsʌmhaʊ/ *adv*
1 in some way, or by some means, although you do not know how: *Don't worry, we'll get the money back somehow.* | *Somehow, I managed to lose my keys.* | *Maybe we could glue it together somehow or other.*
2 for some reason that is not clear to you or that you do not understand: *Somehow, I just don't think it'll work.*

some·one¹ ꜱ¹ ᴡ¹ /ˈsʌmwʌn/ *pron* used to mean a person, when you do not know, or do not say, who the person is; ▤ **somebody**; → **anyone, everyone, no one**: *What would you do if someone tried to rob you in the street?* | *Will someone please explain what's going on?* | **someone new/different etc** *'When are you planning to hire someone?' 'As soon as we find someone suitable.'* | *Can you ask someone else* (=a different person) *to help you? I'm really busy.* | *Have Brooks or someone fax this to New York right away.*

someone² *n* **be someone** to be or feel important: *Gerber was determined to be someone.*

some·place /ˈsʌmpleɪs/ *adv* [not usually in questions or negatives] *spoken especially AmE* somewhere: *I must have left my jacket someplace.*

som·er·sault /ˈsʌməsɔːlt $ -ərsɒːlt/ *n* [C] **1** *BrE* a movement in which someone rolls or jumps forwards or backwards so that their feet go over their head before they stand up again: **do/turn a somersault** *Lana turned a somersault in midair.* **2** *AmE* a ꜰᴏʀᴡᴀʀᴅ ʀᴏʟʟ —**somersault** *v* [I]: *He crashed into the table, somersaulted over it and landed on the carpet.*

some·thing ꜱ¹ ᴡ¹ /ˈsʌmθɪŋ/ *pron*
1 used to mean a particular thing when you do not know its name or do not know exactly what it is; → **anything, everything, nothing**: *There's something in my eye.* | *Sarah said something about coming over later.* | **something new/old/good etc** *It's a good car but I'm looking for something newer.* | *The house was too small so they decided to look for something else* (=a different one). | *I think there's something wrong* (=a problem) *with the phone.* | *I don't know what he does exactly, but I know it has something to do with computers* (=is related to them in some way).
2 something to eat/drink/read/do etc some food, a drink, a book, an activity etc: *Would you like something to drink?* | *I should take something to read on the plane.*
3 do something to do something in order to deal with a problem or difficult situation: *Don't just stand there – do something!* | [+about] *Can you do something about that noise?*
4 something about sb/sth used to say that a person, situation etc has a quality or feature that you recognize but you cannot say exactly what it is: **(there is) something different/odd/unusual about sb/sth** *There was something rather odd about him.* | **There's something about** *her voice that I find really sexy.*
5 ... or something *spoken* used when you cannot remember, or do not think it is necessary to give, another example of something you are mentioning: *Her name was Judith, or Julie, or something.* | *Here's some money. Get yourself a sandwich or something.*
6 something like 100/2000 etc close to but not exactly a large amount such as 100, 2000 etc: *Something like 50,000 homes are without power.*
7 be thirty-something/forty-something etc used to say that someone is aged between 30 and 39, between 40 and 49 etc when you do not know exactly
8 be (really/quite) something *spoken* used to say that something is very good and impressive: *Running your own company at 21 is really something.* | *That was*

really something, wasn't it?

9 be something else *spoken* to be unusual or funny to other people: *You really are something else!*

10 there's something in/to sth used to admit that someone's words are true or their ideas are successful etc: *They had to concede that there was something in his teaching methods.* | *Do you think there's something to the rumours about Larry and Sue?*

11 have something of sth to have a few of the same features or qualities that someone else has: *It was clear that Jenkins had something of his father's brilliance.*

12 be something of a gardener/an expert etc to know a lot about something or to be very good at something: *Charlie's always been something of an expert on architecture.*

13 something of a shock/surprise etc *formal* used to say that something is a shock, surprise etc, but not completely or not in a strong or severe way: *The news came as something of a surprise*

14 a little something used when you are telling someone that you have bought them a present: *I got you a little something for your birthday.*

15 sixty something/John something etc *spoken* used when you cannot remember the rest of a number or name: 'How much did you spend on groceries?' 'A hundred and twenty something.'

16 make something of yourself to become successful

17 that's something used to say that there is one thing that you should be glad about: *At least we have some money left. That's something, isn't it?*

some·time[1] /ˈsʌmtaɪm/ also **some time** *adv* at a time in the future or in the past, although you do not know exactly when: [ı **around/in/during etc**] *We'll take a vacation sometime in September.* | *Our house was built sometime around 1900.*

sometime[2] *adj* [only before noun] **1** *formal* former: *Sir Richard Marsh, the sometime chairman of British Rail* **2** *AmE* used to say that someone does or has a particular job part of the time: *Grimm, a sometime delivery driver, lives with his elderly mother.*

some·times [S1] [W1] /ˈsʌmtaɪmz/ *adv* on some occasions but not always; → **occasionally:** *I sometimes have to work late.* | *Sometimes, Grandma would tell us stories about her childhood in Italy.* | *'Do you ever wish you were back in Japan?' 'Sometimes. Not very often.'* | *The journey takes an hour, sometimes even longer.*

some·way /ˈsʌmweɪ/ *adv AmE informal* SOMEHOW (1)

some·what [S2] [W2] /ˈsʌmwɒt $ -wɑːt/ *adv* more than a little but not very: **somewhat larger/higher/newer etc** *The price is somewhat higher than I expected.* | *Things have changed somewhat since then.* | [+of] *To say that I was surprised is somewhat of an understatement.*

some·where [S1] [W2] /ˈsʌmweə $ -wer/ *adv*

1 in or to a place, but you do not say or know exactly where: *My wallet must be around here somewhere.* | **somewhere to do sth** *There must be somewhere to eat cheaply in this town.* | **somewhere safe/different etc** *Is there somewhere safe where I can leave my bike?* | *Go and play somewhere else* (=in a different place) - *I'm trying to work.* | *We could meet for dinner at Giorgio's or somewhere* (=or a similar place).

2 **somewhere around/between etc** a little more or a little less than a particular number or amount, especially a large one; ▣ **approximately:** *We have somewhere in the region of 500 firefighters in this area.*

3 be getting somewhere to be making progress: *At last I feel we're getting somewhere.*

som·nam·bu·list /sɒmˈnæmbjʊlɪst $ sɑːm-/ *n* [C] *formal* someone who walks while they are asleep; ▣ **sleepwalker** —**somnambulism** *n* [U]

som·no·lent /ˈsɒmnələnt $ ˈsɑːm-/ *adj* *literary* **1** almost starting to sleep: *He lay quiet, somnolent after the day's exertions.* **2** making you want to sleep: *a somnolent summer's afternoon* —**somnolence** *n* [U]

son [S1] [W1] /sʌn/ *n*

1 [C] someone's male child; → **daughter:** *Her son Sean was born in 1983.* | *They have three sons and a*

daughter. | *In those days, the property went to the oldest son.* | *their youngest son, George* | [+of] *the son of a poor farmer* → **like father like son** at **FATHER**[1] (7)

2 [singular] *spoken* used by an older person as a way to address a boy or young man: *What's your name, son?*

3 the Son Jesus Christ, the second member of the group from the Christian religion that also includes the Father and the Holy Spirit

4 [C usually plural] *literary* a man, especially a famous man, from a particular place or country: *Frank Sinatra, New Jersey's most famous son*

5 my son used by a priest to address a man or boy → **favourite son** at **FAVOURITE**[1] (2)

so·nar /ˈsəʊnɑː, -nə $ ˈsoʊnɑːr, -nər/ *n* [U] equipment on a ship or SUBMARINE that uses SOUND WAVES to find out the position of objects under the water

so·na·ta /səˈnɑːtə/ *n* [C] a piece of music with three or four parts that is written for a piano, or for a piano and another instrument: *a piano sonata*

son et lu·mi·ère /ˌsɒn eɪ ˈluːmieə $ ˌsɑːn eɪ luːmˈjer/ *n* [singular, U] *BrE* a performance that tells the story of a historical place or event using lights and recorded sound

song [S2] [W2] /sɒŋ $ sɒːŋ/ *n*

1 **MUSIC WITH WORDS a)** [C] a short piece of music with words that you sing: **pop/folk/love etc song** *pop songs on the radio* | *They sat round with guitars, singing folk songs.* **b)** [U] songs in general. *The bravery of past warriors was celebrated in song.* | **burst/break into song** (=suddenly start singing) *Some of his more drunken friends burst into song.*

2 **BIRDS** [C,U] the musical sounds made by birds and some other animals such as WHALES: *the song of the lark*

3 for a song very cheaply: *He bought the house for a song five years ago.*

4 a song and dance (about sth) *informal* **a)** *BrE* if you make a song and dance about something, you behave as if it was worse, more important, more difficult etc than it really is: *Suzy was there, making a song and dance about her aching feet.* **b)** *AmE* an explanation or excuse that is too long and complicated: *She gave us a long song and dance about why she was late.* → **SWANSONG**

song·bird /ˈsɒŋbɜːd $ ˈsɒːŋbɜːrd/ *n* [C] a bird that can make musical sounds

song·book /ˈsɒŋbʊk $ ˈsɒːŋ-/ *n* [C] a book with the words and music of many songs

song·ster /ˈsɒŋstə $ ˈsɒːŋstər/ *n* [C] **1** a singer – used in newspapers **2** *literary* a songbird

song·stress /ˈsɒŋstrɪs $ ˈsɒːŋ-/ *n* [C] a female singer – used in newspapers

song·writ·er /ˈsɒŋˌraɪtə $ ˈsɒːŋˌraɪtər/ *n* [C] someone who writes the words and usually the music of songs

song·writ·ing /ˈsɒŋˌraɪtɪŋ $ ˈsɒːŋ-/ *n* [U] the process of writing songs: *There's some excellent songwriting on this album.*

son·ic /ˈsɒnɪk $ ˈsɑː-/ *adj* [only before noun] *technical* relating to sound, SOUND WAVES, or the speed of sound

sonic 'boom *n* [C] the loud sound like an explosion that an aircraft makes when it starts to travel faster than the speed of sound

'son-in-law *n plural* **sons-in-law** [C] the husband of your daughter; → **daughter-in-law**

son·net /ˈsɒnɪt $ ˈsɑː-/ *n* [C] a poem with 14 lines which RHYME with each other in a fixed pattern: *Shakespeare's sonnets*

son·ny /ˈsʌni/ *n* *old-fashioned spoken* used when speaking to a boy or young man who is much younger than you: *Now you listen to me, sonny.*

Sonny Jim /ˌsʌni ˈdʒɪm/ *n* *BrE old-fashioned spoken* used when speaking to a man or boy, especially when you are telling him that he has done something wrong

[1] 000, [2] 000, [3] 000, most frequent words in [S]poken and [W]ritten English

son of a 'bitch n plural **sons of bitches** spoken not polite especially AmE **1** [C] an offensive expression for a man that you are very angry with: *He's a filthy lying son of a bitch.* **2 son of a bitch!** used when you are annoyed or surprised: *Son of a bitch! You did it!* **3 be a son of a bitch** to be very difficult: *Getting the new tire on was a real son of a bitch.*

son of a 'gun n [singular] AmE spoken **1** a man you like or admire – used humorously: *Duke, you old son of a gun, how are you?* **2** a man that you are annoyed with: *Somebody go tell that son of a gun we're all waiting here.* **3** an object that is difficult to deal with – used humorously **4 son of a gun!** used to express surprise

Son of 'God n **the Son of God** used by Christians to mean Jesus Christ

son·o·gram /'sɒnəgræm $ 'saː-/ n [C] AmE technical an image, for example of an unborn baby inside its mother's body, that is produced by a special machine; ▤ **ultrasound** BrE

so·nor·ous /'sɒnərəs, sə'nɔːrəs $ sə'nɔːrəs, 'saːnərəs/ adj literary having a pleasantly deep loud sound: *a sonorous voice* —**sonorously** adv

soon S1 W1 /suːn/ adv comparative **sooner**, superlative **soonest**
1 in a short time from now, or a short time after something else happens: *It will be dark soon.* | *David arrived sooner than I expected.* | **soon after** *Paula became pregnant soon after they were married.* | *'Who?' 'You'll find out **soon enough** (=fairly soon).'*
2 quickly: *How soon can you finish the report?* | *Try and get the car fixed **as soon as possible.***
3 as soon as immediately after something happens, without delay: *As soon as she entered the room, she knew there was something wrong.* | *I'll come over to your place as soon as I can.*
4 the sooner (...) the better used to say that it is important that something should happen very soon: *The sooner we get this job finished the better.* | *Let's get out of here! The sooner the better!*
5 the sooner ... the sooner used to say that you want something to happen soon, so that something else can then happen: *The sooner I get this work done, the sooner I can go home.*
6 no sooner had/did ... than used to say that something happened almost immediately after something else: *No sooner had he sat down than the phone rang.*
7 sooner or later used to say that something is certain to happen at some time in the future, though you cannot be sure exactly when: *His wife's bound to find out sooner or later.*
8 too soon too early: **too soon to do sth** *It's still too soon to say whether the operation was a success.* | *The holidays were over **all too soon** (=much earlier than you would like).*
9 no sooner said than done used to say that you will do something immediately
10 not a moment too soon/none too soon almost too late: *'The doctor's here!' 'And not a moment too soon!'*
11 sb would sooner do sth (than) if you would sooner do something, you would much prefer to do it, especially instead of something that seems unpleasant: *I'd sooner die than marry you!*
12 sb would (just) as soon as soon formal used to say that someone would prefer to do something or would prefer something to happen: *I'd just as soon you didn't drive the car while I'm gone.*

soot /sʊt/ n [U] black powder that is produced when something is burnt —**sooty** adj

soothe /suːð/ v [T] **1** to make someone feel calmer and less anxious, upset, or angry: *Lucy soothed the baby by rocking it in her arms.* | *She made a cup of tea to soothe her nerves.* **2** also **soothe sth ⇔ away** to make a pain become less severe, or slowly disappear: *I bought some lozenges to soothe my sore throat.* |

Massage can gently soothe away your aches and pains. —**soothing** adj: *gentle, soothing music* —**soothingly** adv

sooth·say·er /'suːθ,seɪə $ -ər/ n [C] old use someone who is believed to be able to say what will happen in the future

sop¹ /sɒp $ saːp/ n [C usually singular] something not very important or valuable that a government or someone in authority offers to people to stop them from complaining or protesting – used to show disapproval: [+to] *The company agreed to inspect the river regularly, as a sop to the environmental lobby.*

sop² v **sopped, sopping**
sop sth ⇔ up phr v to remove liquid from a surface by using a piece of cloth that takes the liquid into itself

so·phis·ti·cate /sə'fɪstɪkeɪt/ n [C] formal someone who is sophisticated

so·phis·ti·cat·ed W3 /sə'fɪstɪkeɪtɪd/ adj
1 having a lot of experience of life, and good judgment about socially important things such as art, fashion etc: *a sophisticated, witty American* | *Clarissa's hair was swept up into a sophisticated style.*
2 a sophisticated machine, system, method etc is very well designed and very advanced, and often works in a complicated way: *sophisticated software* | *a **highly sophisticated** weapons system*
3 having a lot of knowledge and experience of difficult or complicated subjects and therefore able to understand them well: *British voters have become much more sophisticated.* —**sophistication** /sə,fɪstɪ'keɪʃən/ n [U]: *a New York nightclub that was **the height of sophistication** (=very fashionable and expensive)*

soph·ist·ry /'sɒfɪstri $ 'saː-/ n plural **sophistries** [C,U] formal the clever use of reasons or explanations that seem correct but are really false, in order to deceive people

soph·o·more /'sɒfəmɔː $ 'saːfəmɔːr/ n [C] AmE a student who is in their second year of study at a college or HIGH SCHOOL; → **freshman, junior, senior**

soph·o·mor·ic /,sɒfə'mɒrɪk◂ $,saːfə'mɔːrɪk◂, -'maː-/ adj AmE formal silly, and behaving in a way that is typical of someone much younger: *sophomoric humor*

sop·o·rif·ic /,sɒpə'rɪfɪk◂ $,saː-/ adj formal making you feel ready to sleep: *His voice had an almost soporific effect.*

sop·ping /'sɒpɪŋ $ 'saː-/ also **sopping 'wet** adj very wet; ▤ **soaking**: *My clothes were absolutely sopping!*

sop·py /'sɒpi $ 'saːpi/ adj comparative **soppier**, superlative **soppiest** BrE informal **1** expressing love or emotions in a way that seems silly; ▤ **sappy** AmE: *a soppy film* **2 be soppy about sb/sth** to be very fond of someone or something, in a way that seems silly to other people: *She's soppy about dogs.*

so·pra·no¹ /sə'praːnəʊ $ -'prænoʊ/ n plural **sopranos 1** [C] a very high singing voice belonging to a woman or a boy, or a singer with a voice like this → MEZZO-SOPRANO **2** [singular] the part of a musical work that is written for a soprano voice or instrument: *She sings soprano.*; → **alto, baritone, bass, tenor**

soprano² adj [only before noun] a soprano voice or instrument has the highest range of notes

sor·bet /'sɔːbeɪ $ 'sɔːrbət/ n [C,U] a frozen sweet food made of fruit juice, sugar, and water; → **ice cream**

sor·cer·er /'sɔːsərə $ 'sɔːrsərər/ n [C] a man in stories who uses magic and receives help from evil forces; → **wizard**

sor·cer·ess /'sɔːsərɪs $ 'sɔːr-/ n [C] a woman in stories who uses magic and receives help from evil forces; → **witch**

sor·cer·y /'sɔːsəri $ 'sɔːr-/ n [U] magic that uses the power of evil forces

sor·did /'sɔːdɪd $ 'sɔːr-/ adj **1** involving immoral or dishonest behaviour: **sordid business/affair/story etc** *The whole sordid affair came out in the press.* | *She* discovered the truth about his sordid past. | I want to hear all the sordid details! **2** very dirty and unpleasant; ▣ **squalid**: a sordid little room

sore¹ S3 /sɔː $ sɔːr/ adj
1 a part of your body that is sore is painful, because of infection or because you have used a muscle too much: I had a **sore throat** and aching limbs. | [+from] My arms are sore from all the lifting.
2 sore point/spot/subject (with sb) something that is likely to make someone upset or angry when you talk about it: Just don't mention it – it's always been a sore point with him.
3 [not before noun] informal especially AmE upset, angry, and annoyed, especially because you have not been treated fairly: Mac's still sore because I didn't invite him. | [+at] Don't be sore at me – I just forgot to tell you.
4 [only before noun] BrE used to emphasize how serious, difficult etc something is: Inner city schools are **in sore need of** extra funds.
5 sore loser someone who gets angry or upset when they lose a game or competition: Nobody likes a sore loser.
6 stick/stand out like a sore thumb informal if someone or something sticks out like a sore thumb, they are very noticeable because they are different from everyone or everything else: You stick out like a sore thumb in that uniform. → **be like a bear with a sore head** at BEAR² (3); → **a sight for sore eyes** at SIGHT¹ (14)

sore² n [C] a painful, often red, place on your body caused by a wound or infection: They were starving and covered with sores. → COLD SORE, BEDSORE; → **running sore** at RUNNING² (5)

sore·head /'sɔːhɛd $ 'sɔːr-/ n [C] AmE informal someone who is unpleasant or angry in an unreasonable way

sore·ly /'sɔːli $ 'sɔːrli/ adv very much or very seriously: Jim will be **sorely missed**. | Sabine was **sorely tempted** to throw her drink in his face. | Your help is **sorely needed**. | Courage is a quality that is **sorely lacking** in world leaders today.

sor·ghum /'sɔːgəm $ 'sɔːr-/ n [U] a type of grain that is grown in tropical areas

so·ror·i·ty /sə'rɒrɨti $ sə'rɔː/ n plural **sororities** [C] a club for women students at some American colleges and universities; → **fraternity**

sor·rel /'sɒrəl $ 'sɔː-, 'saː-/ n [U] a plant with leaves that taste bitter, sometimes used in cooking

sor·row¹ /'sɒrəʊ $ 'saːroʊ, 'sɔː-/ n **1** [U] a feeling of great sadness, usually because someone has died or because something terrible has happened to you; → **grief**: great/deep sorrow a time of great sorrow | [+at] He expressed his sorrow at my father's death. | [+for] Claudia felt a deep pang of sorrow for the woman. **2** [C] an event or situation that makes you feel great sadness: the family's joys and sorrows **3 more in sorrow than in anger** in a way that shows you are sad or disappointed rather than angry about a particular situation: He said that his decision to resign was made more in sorrow than in anger. → **drown your sorrows** at DROWN (5)

sorrow² v [I] literary to feel or express sorrow: [+over] Her friend was sorrowing over the loss of a child. | → sorrowing parents

sor·row·ful /'sɒrəʊfəl $ 'saːroʊ-, 'sɔː-/ adj literary very sad: a sorrowful expression —**sorrowfully** adv: 'A lot of damage has already been done,' he said sorrowfully.

sor·ry S1 W2 /'sɒri $ 'saːri, 'sɔːri/ adj comparative **sorrier**, superlative **sorriest**
1 sorry/I'm sorry spoken **a)** used to tell someone that you wish you had not done something that has affected them badly, hurt them etc: I'm really sorry. I didn't mean to hurt your feelings. | 'Matt, stop doing that!' 'Sorry!' | I'm sorry, did I step on your foot? | sorry (that) I'm sorry I'm late – the traffic was terrible. | [+about] Sorry about the mess – I'll clean it up. | sorry for (doing) sth I'm sorry for making such a fuss. | Sorry to bother

you, but what was the address again? → see box at EXCUSE¹ **b)** used as a polite way of introducing disappointing information or a piece of bad news: I'm sorry, but all the flights to Athens are fully booked. **c)** used when you have said something that is not correct, and want to say something that is correct: Turn right – sorry left – at the traffic lights. **d)** used when you refuse an offer or request: 'Are you coming to lunch?' 'Sorry, no. I've got to finish this work.' | 'I'll give you $50 for it.' 'Sorry, no deal.' **e)** used when you disagree with someone, or tell someone that they have done something wrong: I'm sorry, but I find that very hard to believe, Miss Brannigan.
2 ASHAMED [not before noun] feeling ashamed or unhappy about something bad you have done: [+for] She was genuinely sorry for what she had done. | sorry (that) Casey was sorry he'd gotten so angry. | say (you are) sorry (=tell someone that you feel bad about hurting them, causing problems etc) It was probably too late to say sorry, but she would try anyway.; → see box at REGRET¹
3 sorry? spoken especially BrE used to ask someone to repeat something that you have not heard properly; ▣ **pardon**: Sorry? What was that again? | 'Want a drink?' 'Sorry?' 'I said, would you like a drink?'
4 FEELING PITY be/feel sorry for sb to feel pity or sympathy for someone because something bad has happened to them or because they are in a bad situation: I've got no sympathy for him, but I feel sorry for his wife. | Tina was sorry for her. She seemed so lonely. | feel sorry for yourself (=feel unhappy and pity yourself) It's no good feeling sorry for yourself. It's all your own fault.
5 SAD/DISAPPOINTED [not before noun] feeling sad about a situation, and wishing it were different: sorry (that) Brigid was always sorry she hadn't kept up her piano lessons. | sorry to do sth We were sorry to miss your concert. | I won't be sorry to leave this place. | sorry to hear/see/learn I was sorry to hear about your accident. | [+about] I'm so sorry about your father (=I am sorry something bad has happened to him).
6 you'll be sorry spoken used to tell someone that they will soon wish they had not done something, especially because someone will be angry or punish them: You'll be sorry when your dad hears about this.
7 I'm sorry to say (that) spoken used to say that you are disappointed that something has happened: I wrote several times but they never replied, I'm sorry to say.
8 VERY BAD [only before noun] very bad, especially in a way that makes you feel pity or disapproval: the sorry state of the environment | It's a sorry state of affairs when an old lady has to wait 12 hours to see a doctor. | the sorry sight of so many dead animals | This whole sorry episode (=bad thing that happened) shows just how incompetent the government has become. → **better (to be) safe than sorry** at SAFE¹ (9)

Frequencies of the word **sorry** in spoken and written English.

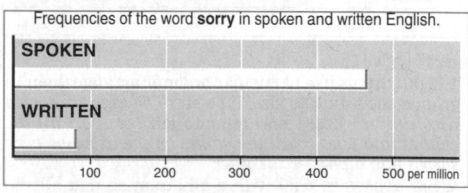

sort¹ S1 W1 /sɔːt $ sɔːrt/ n
1 TYPE/KIND [C] a group or class of people, things etc that have similar qualities or features; ▣ **type**, **kind**: [+of] What sort of shampoo do you use? | all sorts (of sth) (=a lot of different types of things) They play pop, rock, jazz, soul, all sorts in there. | I like all sorts of food – I'm not fussy. | of this/that sort On expeditions of this sort you have to be prepared for trouble. | of some sort/some sort of sth (=used when you do not know exactly what type) He wondered if Rosa was in some sort of trouble. | There was a game of some sort going on inside. | Most of the victims developed psychological

problems **of one sort or another** (=of various different types). | *They do burgers, pizzas,* **that sort of thing.** → see box at TYPE¹

2 sort of *spoken* **a)** used to say that something is partly true but does not describe the exact situation: *I sort of like him, but I don't know why.* | *'Do you know what I mean?' 'Sort of.'* **b)** used when you are trying to describe something but it is difficult to find the right word or to be exact: *Then they started sort of chanting.* | *The walls are a sort of greeny-blue colour.* | **sort of like** (=used very informally when searching for the right words) *It was sort of like really strange and mysterious, walking round this empty building.* **c)** used to make what you are saying sound less strong or direct: *Well, I sort of thought we could go out together sometime.* | *It was sort of a shock when I found out.* **d) sort of price/time/speed etc** *especially BrE* a price etc that is not very exact, but could be slightly more or less: *That's the sort of price I was hoping to pay.* | *What sort of time were you thinking of starting?*

3 of sorts/of a sort used when something is not a good or typical example of its kind of thing: *I had a conversation of sorts with a very drunk man at the bus stop.*

4 sort of thing *spoken especially BrE* used when you are mentioning or describing something in a way that is not definite or exact: *We could just stay here and pass the time, sort of thing.* | *She uses a wheelchair sort of thing.*

5 what sort of ...? *spoken especially BrE* used when you are angry about what someone has said or done: *What sort of time do you call this to come in?*

6 nothing of the sort *spoken especially BrE* used to say angrily that something is not true or that someone should not do something: *'I'm going to watch TV.' 'You'll do nothing of the sort!'*

7 PERSON [singular] *BrE* someone who has a particular type of character, and is therefore likely to behave in a particular way; ◫ **type**: *Iain's never even looked at another woman. He's not the sort.*

8 it takes all sorts (to make a world) *BrE* used to say that you think someone is behaving in a strange or crazy way: *He goes climbing up cliffs without ropes or anything? Oh well, it takes all sorts.*

9 COMPUTER [singular] if a computer does a sort, it puts things in a particular order

10 ILL/UPSET **out of sorts** feeling a little ill or upset: *Louise went back to work feeling rather out of sorts.*

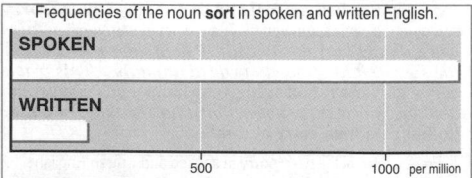

Frequencies of the noun **sort** in spoken and written English.

SPOKEN		
WRITTEN		
	500	1000 per million

sort² S1 *v* [T]

1 to put things in a particular order or arrange them in groups according to size, type etc: *The eggs are sorted according to size.* | **sort sth into sth** *Let's sort all the clothes into piles.* | *All the names on the list have been sorted into alphabetical order.*

2 *BrE spoken* to deal with a situation so that all the problems are solved and everything is organized; → **sorted**: *Right, I'll leave this for Roger and Terry to sort, then.*

  sort sth/sb ⇔ out *phr v*

1 to arrange or organize something that is mixed up or untidy, so that it is ready to be used: *We need to sort out our camping gear before we go away.*

2 to separate one type of thing from another: *I've sorted out the papers that can be thrown away.* | [+from] *First sort the white things out from the other clothes.*

3 *especially BrE* to successfully deal with a problem or difficult situation: *She went to a psychiatrist to try to*

sort out her **problems.** | *I'll be glad to* **get** *this misunderstanding* **sorted out.** | **sort yourself out/get yourself sorted out** (=deal with all your problems) *I'm staying with a friend until I manage to sort myself out.*

4 *especially BrE* to succeed in making arrangements for something: *Have you sorted out where you're going to live yet?* | *She is trying to sort out childcare.*

5 sort itself out *BrE* if something sorts itself out, it stops being a problem without you having to do anything: *Our financial problems should sort themselves out in a week or two.*

6 *BrE informal* to stop someone from causing problems or annoying you, especially by attacking or punishing them: *If he bothers you again, I'll sort him out.*

  sort through sth *phr v*

to look for something among a lot of similar things, especially when you are arranging these things into an order: *Vicky sat down and sorted through the files.*

sort·ed /ˈsɔːtɪd $ ˈsɔːr-/ *adj* [not before noun] *BrE spoken informal*

1 properly arranged or planned: *Good, that's the accommodation sorted.* | *Calm down.* **It's all sorted.** | *I just want to* **get** *everything* **sorted** *before I go away.*

2 provided with the things that you want: *'Can I get you anything?' 'We're sorted, thanks.'* | [+for] *Are we sorted for alcohol for tonight?*

sor·tie¹ /ˈsɔːti $ ˈsɔːrti/ *n* [C] **1** a short flight made by a plane over enemy land, in order to bomb a city, military defences etc: *The US and its allies carried out 44,000 sorties during this period.* **2** a short trip, especially to an unfamiliar place: *We made a sortie from our hotel to the open-air market.* **3** *BrE* an attempt to do or take part in something new: [+into] *Australia's first sortie into the wine trade* **4** *BrE* an attack in which an army leaves its position for a short time to attack the enemy

sortie² *v* [I] to make a short attack on an enemy position or a flight over enemy land: *It was five months since the battleship had last sortied from home waters.*

ˈsorting ˌoffice *n* [C] *BrE* a place where letters and packages are put into groups according to where they have to be delivered

ˈsort-out *n* [singular] *BrE informal* an occasion when you tidy a room, desk etc and get rid of the things you do not need: *These cupboards need a good sort-out.*

SOS /ˌes əʊ ˈes $ -oʊ-/ *n* [singular] **1** a signal or message that a ship or plane sends when it is in danger and needs help; → **mayday** **2** an urgent message that someone is in trouble and needs help: *This is an SOS for a Mr. Tucker, whose mother is seriously ill.*

ˈso-so *adj, adv spoken* neither very good nor very bad; ◫ **average**: *'How was the party?' 'Oh, so-so.'*

sot /sɒt $ sɑːt/ *n* [C] *old-fashioned* someone who is drunk all the time; ◫ **drunkard**

sot·to vo·ce /ˌsɒtəʊ ˈvəʊtʃi $ ˌsɑːtoʊ ˈvoʊ-/ *adv formal* in a very quiet voice, so that other people cannot easily hear: *'No, it was Daniel,' she continued, sotto voce.*

sou /suː/ *n* [singular] *BrE old-fashioned* a very small amount of money: *He didn't have a sou.*

sou·bri·quet /ˈsuːbrɪkeɪ/ *n* another form of SOBRIQUET

souf·flé /ˈsuːfleɪ $ suːˈfleɪ/ *n* [C,U] a baked food made with eggs, flour, milk and often cheese or fruit all mixed together until it is light and full of air

sought /sɔːt $ sɒːt/ the past tense and past participle of SEEK

ˈsought-ˌafter *adj* wanted by a lot of people but rare or difficult to get: **much/highly sought-after** *a much sought-after defense lawyer* | *By the mid-1920s, she had become one of Broadway's most sought-after actresses.*

souk /suːk/ *n* [C] a market in an Arab country

soul S3 W3 /səʊl $ soʊl/ *n*

1 SB'S SPIRIT [C] the part of a person that is not physical, and that contains their character, thoughts, and feelings. Many people believe that a person's soul continues to exist after they have died; → **spirit**: *the*

immortality of the soul | *It was as if those grey eyes could see into the very* **depths of** *her* **soul.** | in sb's soul *the restlessness deep in his soul* | *the souls of the dead*
2 PERSON [C] used in particular phrases to mean 'a person': **happy/sensitive/brave/simple etc soul** *He is really quite a sensitive soul.* | **not a (living) soul** (=no one) *I promise I* **won't tell a soul.** | **not a soul in sight/not a soul to be seen** *The night was dark and still, and there was not a soul in sight.* | **poor (old) soul** (=used to show pity for someone) *The poor old soul had fallen and broken her hip.*
3 MUSIC also **soul music** [U] a type of popular music that often expresses deep emotions, usually performed by black singers and musicians: *He listens to a lot of soul.* | *a soul band*
4 SENSE OF BEAUTY [U] **a)** the ability to be emotionally affected by art, music, literature etc: *My brother thinks that anyone who doesn't like poetry has no soul.* **b)** the quality that affects people emotionally, that a painting, piece of music etc can have: *Her performance was technically perfect, but it lacked soul.*
5 SPECIAL QUALITY [U] the special quality or part that gives something its true character: [+of] *Basho's poems capture the true soul of old Japan.*
6 **be the soul of discretion** to always be extremely careful to keep secrets: *Leon is the very soul of discretion.*
7 **be good for the soul** if something is good for the soul, it is good for you and you should do it, even though it may seem unpleasant – often used humorously: *They say that hardship is good for the soul.*
8 **God rest his/her soul** used when you mention the name of someone who is dead: *My father, God rest his soul, died here at Vernison Hall.*
9 PEOPLE IN A PLACE [plural] *literary* the number of souls in a place is the number of people who live there: *a village of two or three hundred souls*
10 **bless my soul/upon my soul** *old-fashioned spoken* used to express surprise → **bare your soul** at BARE[2] (2); → **be the life and soul of the party** at LIFE (16); → **keep body and soul together** at BODY (13); → **heart and soul** at HEART (2); → **sell your soul (to the devil)** at SELL[1] (9)

'soul-des,troying *adj* something that is soul-destroying is extremely boring or makes you feel very unhappy: *a soul-destroying experience*

'soul food *n* [U] traditional foods that are cooked and eaten by African-Americans in the southern US

soul·ful /'səʊlfəl $ 'soʊl-/ *adj* expressing deep, usually sad, emotions: *He looked up with those great* **soulful** *eyes.* | **soulful voice/vocals/melody etc** *his powerful, soulful voice* —**soulfully** *adv* —**soulfulness** *n* [U]

soul·less /'səʊl-ləs $ 'soʊl-/ *adj* lacking the attractive qualities that make people happy: *a soulless city of grey concrete* —**soullessly** *adv* —**soullessness** *n* [U]

'soul mate *n* [C] someone you have a very close relationship with because you share or understand the same emotions and interests

'soul ,music *n* [U] SOUL (3)

'soul-,searching *n* [U] careful examination of your thoughts and feelings because you are very worried about whether or not it is right to do something: *After much soul-searching, I decided to resign.*

sound[1] S1 W1 /saʊnd/ *n*
1 [C,U] something that you hear, or what can be heard; ◨ **noise**: *There were strange sounds coming from the next room.* | [+of] *She could* **hear** *the* **sound** *of voices.* | *the distant sound of rushing water* | **banging/barking/ tearing etc sound** *Did you just hear a rattling sound outside?* | *Light travels faster than sound.* | *a vowel sound* | **not make a sound** (=be completely quiet)
2 [U] **a)** the sound produced by a television or radio programme, a film etc: *We apologize for the loss of sound during that report.* | *a sound engineer* **b)** the loudness of a television, radio, film etc; ◨ **volume**: **turn the sound down/up** *Turn the sound down a little, will you?*

3 [C usually singular, U] the particular quality that a singer's or group's music has: *We're trying to develop a harder, funkier sound.*
4 **by/from the sound of it/things** judging from what you have heard or read about something: *By the sound of it, things are worse than we thought.*
5 **not like the sound of sth** to feel worried by something that you have heard or read: *'There's been a slight change in our plans.' 'I don't like the sound of that.'*
6 **sounds** [plural] *BrE informal* songs or music that are on a record, CD, or tape: *I need to buy some new sounds.*
7 [C usually singular] a narrow area of water that connects two larger areas of water

sound[2] S1 W2 *v*
1 SEEM [linking verb] if something or someone sounds good, bad, strange etc, that is how they seem to you when you hear about them or read about them: [+adj] *Istanbul sounds really exciting.* | *The whole story sounded very odd.* | *$80 sounds about right for a decent hotel room.* | [+noun] *BrE: That sounds a good idea.* | [+like] *Nick sounds like a nice guy.* | **it sounds as if/as though** *It sounds to me as if he needs professional help.* | **it sounds like** *informal: It sounds like you had a good time on your trip.* | *I'll come over to Richmond and take you out for dinner.* **How does that sound?** (=used to ask someone what they think of your suggestion) | *far-away places with strange-sounding names*
2 NOISE [linking verb] if a noise sounds like a particular thing, that is how it seems to you when you hear it: [+like] *To Thomas, her laugh sounded horribly like a growl.* | *I heard what sounded like fireworks.* | [+adj] *Her breathing sounded very loud.* | **(it) sounds as if/as though** *The banging sounded as if it was coming from next door.* | **(it) sounds like** *informal: It sounds like the dog wants to be let out.*
3 VOICE [linking verb] if someone sounds tired, happy, sad etc, that is how they seem to you when you hear their voice: [+adj] *Are you okay? You sound tired.* | *Josie didn't sound very keen when I spoke to her.* | *Her voice sounded very young.* | **sound as if/as though** *You sound as if you've got a cold.* | **sound like** *informal: She sounded like she'd been crying.* | [+like] *You sound just like my mother* (=the things you say, opinions you express etc are just like the things my mother says).; → see box at SEEM
4 WARNING [T] to publicly give a warning or tell people to be careful: *Several earlier studies had* **sounded** *similar* **warnings.** | **sound a note of caution/ warning** *I would, however, sound a note of caution.* | *Now it is an American economist who is* **sounding the alarm.**
5 MAKE A NOISE [I,T] if something such as a horn or bell sounds, or if you sound it, it makes a noise: *The bell sounded for dinner.* | *Sound your horn to warn other drivers.* | *She was unable to* **sound the alarm.**
6 PRONOUNCE [T usually passive] *technical* to make the sound of a letter in a word: *The 's' in 'island' is not sounded.*
7 MEASURE DEPTH [T] *technical* to measure the depth of the sea, a lake etc; → **soundings**

sound off *phr v*
1 *informal* to express strong opinions about something, especially when you complain angrily in a way that other people find rude or boring: [+about] *She's always sounding off about too much sex in the media.* | *He should check his facts before sounding off.*
2 *AmE* if soldiers sound off, they shout out numbers or their names to show that they are there

sound sb/sth ⟺ **out** *phr v*
to talk to someone in order to find out what they think about a plan or idea: *He sounded people out and found the responses favourable.* | *They want to sound out his opinion before they approach him formally.* | [+about] *I wanted to sound her out about a job.*

S

sound³ W3 adj

1 WELL-JUDGED sensible and likely to produce the right results; ⊟ poor: *The book is full of sound advice.* | *a man of great integrity and sound judgement* | ecologically/ideologically/theoretically etc sound *environmentally sound farming practices* | *a sound investment*

2 PERSON *BrE* a) someone who is sound can be depended on to make good decisions and give good advice: [+on] *He's very sound on matters of law.* b) *informal* someone who is sound is a good person and can be trusted – used especially by young people: *My mum's sound. She'd never throw me out.*

3 THOROUGH [only before noun] complete and thorough: *a sound understanding of money and banking systems* | *a sound knowledge of English* | *He has sound grasp of European history.*

4 IN GOOD CONDITION in good condition and not damaged in any way; ⊟ unsound: *The floor was completely sound.* | *Is the building* **structurally sound?** | **sound as a bell** *BrE spoken* (=in perfect condition)

5 HEALTHY physically or mentally healthy; ⊟ unsound: **of sound mind** *law* (=not mentally ill) | **sound as a bell** *BrE spoken* (=in perfect health)

6 SLEEP sound sleep is deep and peaceful: **sound sleeper** (=someone who always sleeps well) —**soundness** *n* [U]

sound⁴ *adv* **sound asleep** deeply asleep: *The baby was sound asleep.*

'sound ,barrier *n* **the sound barrier** the sudden increase in air pressure against a vehicle, especially an aircraft, when it is travelling near the speed of sound: **break the sound barrier** (=travel faster than the speed of sound)

'sound bite *n* [C] a very short part of a speech or statement, especially one made by a politician, that is broadcast on a radio or television news programme

sound·card, **'sound card** /'saʊndkɑːd $ -kɑːrd/ *n* [C] a CIRCUIT BOARD that can be added to a computer so that it is able to produce sound

'sound check *n* [C] the process of checking that all the equipment needed for broadcasting or recording is working properly

'sound ef,fects *n* [plural] sounds produced artificially for a radio or television programme, a film etc

'sounding board *n* [C usually singular] someone you discuss your ideas with in order to see if they think your ideas are good: [+for] *John always used her as a sounding board for new ideas.*

sound·ings /'saʊndɪŋz/ *n* [plural] **1** careful or secret questions you ask someone to find out what they think about something: *We're* **taking soundings** *to find out how people feel about the changes.* **2** measurements you make to find out how deep water is

sound·less /'saʊndləs/ *adj literary* without any sound; ⊟ silent —**soundlessly** *adv*: *Theo crept soundlessly into the room.* —**soundlessness** *n* [U]

sound·ly /'saʊndli/ *adv* **1** if you sleep soundly, you sleep deeply and peacefully: *The baby slept soundly all night.* **2** **soundly defeated/beaten/thrashed** completely defeated or severely punished: *The Republicans were soundly defeated.*

sound·proof¹ /'saʊndpruːf/ *adj* a soundproof wall, room etc is one that sound cannot pass through or into

soundproof² *v* [T] to make something soundproof

sound·smith /'saʊndsmɪθ/ *n* [C] *AmE informal* someone who makes new music by electronically mixing the sounds from different musical instruments, songs etc: *the ever-innovating soundsmiths known as Matmos*

'sound ,system *n* [C] equipment for playing music, especially to people in a large space, for example at a rock concert or a club

sound·track /'saʊndtræk/ *n* [C] the recorded music from a film: [+to] *the soundtrack to 'Top Gun'*

'sound wave *n* [C usually plural] the form that sound takes when it travels

soup¹ S3 /suːp/ *n* [C,U]

1 cooked liquid food, often containing small pieces of meat, fish, or vegetables: *home-made tomato soup*
2 **be in the soup** *informal* to be in trouble

soup² *v*

soup sth ⇔ **up** *phr v informal* to improve something, especially a car, by making it more powerful

soup·çon /'suːpsɒn $ -sɑːn/ *n* [singular +of] *formal* a very small amount of something – often used humorously

,souped-'up *adj* a souped-up car has been made more powerful

'soup ,kitchen *n* [C] a place where people with no money and no homes can get free food

'soup spoon *n* [C] a round spoon that is used for eating soup

soup·y /'suːpi/ *adj* having a thick liquid quality like soup

sour¹ /saʊə $ saʊr/ *adj* **1** having a sharp acid taste, like the taste of a LEMON or a fruit that is not ready to be eaten; ⊟ sweet; → bitter: *Rachel sampled the wine. It was sour.* | *sour cherries* → SWEET-AND-SOUR **2** milk or other food that is sour is not fresh and has a bad taste: **turn/go sour** (=become sour) **3** unfriendly or looking bad-tempered: **sour look/face/smile etc** *Eliza was tall and thin, with a rather sour face.* | *a* **sour-faced** *old man* **4** *informal* if a relationship or plan turns or goes sour, it becomes less enjoyable, pleasant, or satisfactory: *As time went by, their marriage* **turned sour.** | *The meeting ended on a* **sour note** *with neither side able to reach agreement.* **5 sour grapes** used to say that someone is pretending that they dislike something because they want it but cannot have it – used to show disapproval —**sourly** *adv* —**sourness** *n* [U]

sour² *v* [I,T] **1** if a relationship or someone's attitude sours, or if something sours it, it becomes unfriendly or unfavourable: *An unhappy childhood has soured her view of life.* **2** if milk sours, or if something sours it, it begins to have an unpleasant sharp taste

source¹ S2 W1 /sɔːs $ sɔːrs/ *n* [C]

1 a thing, place, activity etc that you get something from: *They get their money from various sources.* | [+of] *a useful source of information* | *Beans are a very good source of protein.* | *For me, music is a great source of enjoyment.* | **major/primary/main source of sth** *the country's main source of income* | **energy/food/light source** *relatively clean energy sources* | **at source** *BrE: Is your pension taxed at source* (=before it is paid to you)?
2 the cause of something, especially a problem, or the place where it starts: [+of] *We've found the source of the trouble.* | *The recent name change has been the source of some confusion.*
3 a person, book, or document that supplies you with information: *List all your sources at the end of your essay.* | *I've heard from* **reliable sources** *that the company is in trouble.*
4 the place where a stream or river starts
5 *technical* source code

source² *v* [T] *technical* **1** if goods are sourced from a particular place, they are obtained from that place: [+from] *Fish for the restaurant is sourced daily from British ports.* | *locally sourced milk* **2** to find out where something can be obtained: *We might be able to source the parts.*

'source code *n* [U] *technical* the original form in which a computer program is written before it is changed into a form that a particular type of computer can read; → **machine code**

,sour 'cream also **,soured 'cream** *BrE n* [U] cream which has been made thicker by adding a type of BACTERIA

sour·dough /'sauədəu $ 'saurdou/ *n* [U] uncooked DOUGH (=bread mixture) that is left to FERMENT before being used to make bread

sour·puss /'sauəpus $ 'saur-/ *n* [C] *old-fashioned* someone who complains a lot and is never happy or satisfied

south[1] S1 W2 , **South** /sauθ/ written abbreviation *S n* [singular, U]
1 the direction that is at the bottom of a map of the world, below the Equator. It is on the right if you are facing the rising sun: *Which way is south?* | **from/towards the south** *By now the army was approaching from the south.* | **to the south (of sth)** *Gatwick airport is a few miles to the south of London.*
2 the south the southern part of a country or area: **in the south** *They lived in a small town in the South.* | [+of] *the South of India*

south[2], **South** written abbreviation *S adj* [only before noun] **1** in the south or facing the south: *a village on the south coast* | *I am currently teaching in south Texas.* **2** a south wind comes from the south

south[3] written abbreviation *S adv* **1** towards the south: *Most of the birds had already flown south.* | [+of] *a seaside town 99 km south of London* | *a south-facing garden* **2 down south a)** *BrE informal* in or to the southern part of England: *We moved down south about five years ago.* **b)** *AmE* also **down South** in or to the southern US states: *His sister lives down south.* **3 go south** *AmE informal* if a situation, organization, or set of standards goes south, it becomes very bad although it was once very good: *It seems like all our moral standards have just gone south.*

south·bound /'sauθbaund/ *adj, adv* travelling or leading towards the south: *southbound traffic* | *The southbound lanes are closed.* | *The car was last seen traveling southbound on I-35.*

south·east[1], **Southeast** /sauθ'i:st‹ / written abbreviation *SE n* [U] **1** the direction that is exactly between south and east **2 the southeast** the southeastern part of a country —**southeast** *adv: We continued southeast to Kells.*

southeast[2], **Southeast** written abbreviation *SE adj* **1** a southeast wind comes from the southeast **2** in the southeast of a place: *the southeast quarter of the city*

south·east·er /,sauθ'i:stə $ -ər/ *n* [C] a strong wind or storm coming from the southeast

south·east·er·ly /,sauθ'i:stəli $ -ər-/ *adj* **1** towards or in the southeast: *Snow will spread to southeasterly regions tonight.* **2** a southeasterly wind comes from the southeast

south·east·ern /,sauθ'i:stən $ -ərn/ written abbreviation *SE adj* in or from the southeast part of a country or area: *southeastern Europe*

south·east·wards /sauθ'i:stwədz $ -wərdz/ also **south·east·ward** /-wəd $ -wərd/ *adv* towards the southeast —**southeastward** *adj*

south·er·ly /'sʌðəli $ -ər-/ *adj* **1** towards or in the south: *Tara walked in a southerly direction.* **2** a southerly wind comes from the south

south·ern S2 W2 , **Southern** /'sʌðən $ -ərn/ written abbreviation *S adj* in or from the south of a country or area: *a southern accent* | *Southern Italy*

south·ern·er, **Southerner** /'sʌðənə $ -ərnər/ *n* [C] someone from the southern part of a country

,**southern** 'hemisphere, **Southern Hemi-sphere** *n* **the southern hemisphere** the half of the world that is south of the Equator

,**Southern** 'Lights *n* **the Southern Lights** bands of coloured light that are seen in the night sky in the most southern parts of the world; **⊟ aurora australis**

south·ern·most /'sʌðənməust $ -ərnmoust/ *adj* furthest south: *the southernmost tip of India*

south·paw /'sauθpɔ: $ -pɒ:/ *n* [C] *informal* someone who uses their left hand more than their right hand, especially a PITCHER in baseball or a BOXER

,**South** 'Pole *n* **the South Pole** the most southern point on the surface of the Earth; → **magnetic pole**, **north pole**

south·wards /'sauθwədz $ -wərdz/ also **south·ward** /-wəd $ -wərd/ *adv* towards the south: *We followed the coast southwards.* —**southward** *adj: the southward route to Charlestown*

south·west[1], **Southwest** /,sauθ'west‹ / written abbreviation *SW n* [U] **1** the direction that is exactly between south and west **2 the southwest** the south-western part of a country —**southwest** *adv: The plane flew southwest toward Egypt.*

southwest[2], **Southwest** written abbreviation *SW adj* **1** a southwest wind comes from the south-west **2** in the southwest of a place: *the southwest corner of France*

south·west·er·ly /,sauθ'westəli $ -ərli/ *adj* **1** towards or in the southwest: *The plane was flying in a southwesterly direction.* **2** a southwesterly wind comes from the southwest

south·west·ern /,sauθ'westən $ -ərn/ written abbreviation *SW adj* in or from the southwest part of a country or area: *southwestern Colorado*

south·west·wards /sauθ'westwədz $ -wərdz/ also **south·west·ward** /-wəd $ -wərd/ *adv* towards the southwest —**southwestward** *adj*

sou·ve·nir /,su:və'nɪə,'su:vənɪə $ -nɪr/ *n* [C] an object that you buy or keep to remind yourself of a special occasion or a place you have visited; **⊟ memento**: [+of] *I bought a model of the Eiffel Tower as a souvenir of Paris.* | *a souvenir shop* | [+from] *a souvenir programme from the Gala Concert*

sou'west·er /sau'westə $ -ər/ *n* [C] a hat made of shiny material that keeps the rain off, with a wide piece at the back that covers your neck

sove·reign[1] /'sɒvrɪ̯n $ 'sɑ:v-/ *n* [C] **1** *formal* a king or queen **2** a British gold coin used in the past that was worth £1

sovereign[2] *adj* **1** having the highest power in a country: **sovereign power/control** **2** a sovereign country or state is independent and governs itself

sove·reign·ty /'sɒvrɪ̯nti $ 'sɑ:v-/ *n* [U] **1** complete freedom and power to govern: *the sovereignty of Parliament* | [+over] *Spain's claim of sovereignty over the territory* **2** the power that an independent country has to govern itself: *the defence of our national sovereignty*

so·vi·et /'səuvi̯t,'sɒ- $ 'sou-, 'sɑ:-/ *n* [C] an elected council in a Communist country

Soviet *adj* relating to the former USSR (Soviet Union) or its people

sow[1] /səu $ sou/ *v past tense* **sowed**, *past participle* **sown** /səun $ soun/ *or* **sowed** **1** [I,T] to plant or scatter seeds on a piece of ground: *Sow the seeds in late March.* | **sow sth with sth** *These fields used to be sown with oats.* **2** [T] to do something that will cause a bad situation in the future: *repressive laws that are sowing the seeds of future conflicts* | **sow doubt/confusion/dissatisfaction etc** *an attempt to sow doubt among the jury members* **3 sow your wild oats** if a man sows his wild oats, he has sex with many different women, especially when he is young —**sower** *n* [C]

sow[2] /sau/ *n* [C] a fully grown female pig; → **boar**

sown /səun $ soun/ the past participle of **sow**

sox /sɒks $ sɑ:ks/ *n* [plural] an American spelling of 'socks', used especially in advertising

soy·a /'sɔɪə/ *BrE*; **soy** /sɔɪ/ *AmE n* [U] soya beans

,**soya bean** *BrE*; **soy·bean** /'sɔɪbi:n/ *AmE n* [C] the bean of an Asian plant from which oil and food containing a lot of PROTEIN is produced

,soy 'sauce / $ '. ./ also ,soya 'sauce *BrE n* [U] a dark brown liquid made from soya beans that is used especially in Japanese and Chinese cooking

soz·zled /'sɒzəld $ 'sɑː-/ *adj BrE informal* drunk

spa /spɑː/ *n* [C] **1 a)** a place where the water has special minerals in it, and where people go to improve their health by drinking the water or swimming in it: *a historic spa town* **b)** also **health spa** a place where people go to improve their health and beauty, especially through swimming, exercise, beauty treatments etc **2** also **spa bath** *AmE* a bath or pool that sends currents of hot water around you; ▤ **Jacuzzi**

space¹ S1 W1 /speɪs/ *n*

1 EMPTY AREA [U] the amount of an area, room, container etc that is empty or available to be used: [+for] *There's space for a table and two chairs.* | ***How much space** is there on each disk?* | **more/less/enough space** *Now that we've got three kids, it'd be nice to have a bit more space.* | **space to do sth** *He had **plenty of space** to study.* | *The hedge **takes up** too much **space**.* | **sense/feeling of space** (=the feeling that a place is large and empty, so you can move around easily) *In small homes a single colour scheme can create a sense of space.*

2 AREA FOR PARTICULAR PURPOSE [C,U] an area, especially one used for a particular purpose: *a supermarket with 700 free **parking spaces*** | **storage/cupboard/shelf space** *We really do need more storage space.* | *the factory's **floor space** (=the size of the available floor area)*

3 BETWEEN THINGS [C] an empty place between two things, or between two parts of something; ▤ **gap**: [+between] *the space between the house and the garage* | *Lucy **cleared** a space on her desk.* | *There was an **empty space** where the flowers had been.*

4 OUTSIDE THE EARTH [U] the area beyond the Earth where the stars and PLANETS are: **in/into space** *Who was the first American in space?* | *creatures from **outer space** (=far away in space)* | **space travel/research/programme/exploration** *the history of space travel*

5 WHERE THINGS EXIST [U] all of the area in which everything exists, and in which everything has a position or direction: *the exact **point in space** where two lines meet* | *how people of other cultures think about **time and space***

6 TIME **a)** **in/within the space of sth** within a particular period of time: *Mandy had four children in the space of four years.* **b)** a short space of time a short period of time: *They achieved a lot in a short space of time.*

7 EMPTY LAND [C,U] land, or an area of land that has not been built on: *a pleasant town centre with plenty of **open space*** | *the **wide open spaces** of the prairies* | *the loss of **green space** in cities*

8 FREEDOM [U] the freedom to do what you want or do things on your own, especially in a relationship with someone else: *We **give** each other **space** in our marriage.* | *She **needed** time and **space** to sort out her life.*

9 IN WRITING [C] **a)** an empty space between written or printed words, lines etc: *Leave a space after each number.* **b)** the width of a TYPED letter of the alphabet: *The word 'the' takes up three spaces.* **c)** a place provided for you to write your name or other information on a document, piece of paper etc: *Please write any comments in the space provided.*

10 IN A REPORT/BOOK [U] the amount of space in a newspaper, magazine, or book that is used for a particular subject: *The story **got** very little **space** in the national newspapers.*

11 look/stare/gaze into space to look straight in front of you without looking at anything in particular, usually because you are thinking → BREATHING SPACE, PERSONAL SPACE; → waste of space at WASTE¹ (5); → watch this space at WATCH¹ (11)

space² *v* also **space out** **1** [T always + adv/prep] to arrange objects or events so that they have equal spaces or periods of time between them: *They used three microphones **spaced** several yards **apart**.* | *Try to space out your classes and study in between.* | **be evenly spaced** (=with equal spaces) *For security, use three evenly spaced bolts per post.* **2** [I] *informal* to stop paying attention and just look in front of you without thinking, especially because you are bored or have taken drugs: *I completely **spaced out** during the lecture.*
→ SPACED OUT

'space-age *adj* very modern: *space-age technology*

'space bar *n* [C] the wide key at the bottom of a computer KEYBOARD or TYPEWRITER that you press to make a space

'space ca,det *n* [C] *informal* someone who forgets things, does not pay attention, and often behaves strangely

'space ,capsule *n* [C] the part of a spacecraft that carries people into space to obtain information and then comes back to Earth

space·craft /'speɪs-krɑːft $ -kræft/ *n* [C] a vehicle that is able to travel in space

,spaced 'out *adj informal* not fully conscious of what is happening around you, especially because you are extremely tired or have taken drugs

space·man /'speɪsmæn/ *n plural* spacemen /-men/ [C] **1** *informal* a man who travels into space; ▤ **astronaut 2** someone in stories who visits the Earth from another world

'space probe *n* [C] a spacecraft without people in it, that is sent into space to collect information about the conditions there and send the information back to Earth

space·ship /'speɪs,ʃɪp/ *n* [C] a vehicle for carrying people through space

'space ,shuttle *n* [C] a vehicle that is designed to go into space and return to Earth several times

'space ,station *n* [C] a large spacecraft that stays above the Earth and is a base for people travelling in space or for scientific tests

space·suit /'speɪs-suːt, -sjuːt $ -suːt/ *n* [C] a special protective suit that people wear in space, that covers the whole body and provides a supply of air

space·walk /'speɪswɔːk $ -wɒːk/ *n* [C] the act of moving around outside a spacecraft while in space, or the time spent outside it

space·y /'speɪsi/ *adj informal* behaving as though you are not fully conscious of what is happening around you: *I felt tired and kind of spacey.*

spac·ing /'speɪsɪŋ/ *n* [U] the amount of space between the printed letters, words, or lines on a page: **single spacing** (=lines with no empty lines between them) | **double spacing** (=lines with one empty line after each one)

a spacious room

a cramped room

spa·cious /ˈspeɪʃəs/ *adj* a spacious house, room etc is large and has plenty of space to move around in; 🔁 **cramped**: *a spacious living area* —**spaciously** *adv* —**spaciousness** *n* [U]

spade /speɪd/ *n* **1** [C] a tool for digging that has a long handle and a broad metal blade that you push into the ground; → **shovel**; → see picture at GARDENING **2** also **spades** [U] a PLAYING CARD belonging to the set of cards that have one or more black shapes that look like pointed leaves printed on them: *the queen of spades* **3 call a spade a spade** to speak about things in a direct and honest way, even though it may be impolite to do this **4 in spades** to a great degree, or in large amounts: *Beauty, intelligence, wealth – my mother had all of them in spades.* **5** [C] taboo old-fashioned a very offensive word for a black person. Do not use this word.

spade·work /ˈspeɪd-wɜːk $ -wɜːrk/ *n* [U] hard work that has to be done in preparation before something can happen; 🔁 **legwork**: *Most of the spadework had been done by 1981.*

spa·ghet·ti /spəˈɡeti/ *n* [U] a type of PASTA in very long thin pieces, that is cooked in boiling water: **spaghetti bolognaise** *BrE* (=cooked spaghetti served with a meat and tomato sauce); → **macaroni, tagliatelle**; → see picture at PASTA

spa·ghetti ˈwestern *n* [C] a film about American COWBOYS in the Wild West, especially one made in Europe by an Italian director

spake /speɪk/ *biblical or literary* a past tense of SPEAK

spam¹ /spæm/ *v* **spammed, spamming** [I,T] to send the same message to many different people using email or the Internet, usually as a way of advertising something – used to show disapproval —**spamming** *n* [U]

spam² *n* [U] email messages that a computer user has not asked for and does not want to read, for example from someone who is advertising something: *You can filter out spam with special software.*

Spam *n* [U] *trademark* a type of cheap CANNED meat made mainly from PORK

span¹ /spæn/ a past tense of SPIN

span² *n* [C] **1** a period of time between two dates or events: **over/within/in a span of sth** *Over a span of ten years, the company has made great progress.* | *It'll be difficult to hire that many new staff in such a short time span.* **2** the length of time over which someone's life, ability to pay attention to something etc continues: **attention/concentration span** *Most 2-year-olds have a very short attention span.* | *Captivity vastly reduces the life span of whales.* **3** the part of a bridge, ARCH etc that goes across from one support to another **4** the distance from one side of something to the other: *a bird with a large wing span*

span³ *v* **spanned, spanning** [T] **1** to include all of a period of time: *a career which spanned nearly 60 years* **2** to include all of a particular space or area: *The Mongol Empire spanned much of Central Asia.* **3** if a bridge spans an area of water, especially a river, it goes from one side to the other

Span·dex /ˈspændeks/ *n* [U] *trademark* a material that stretches, used especially for making tight-fitting sports clothes

span·gle¹ /ˈspæŋɡəl/ *v* [T] to cover something with shiny points of light: **be spangled with sth** *The city skyline was spangled with lights.* —**spangled** also **spangly** *adj*: *acrobats in spangled tights*

spangle² *n* [C] a small piece of shiny metal or plastic sewn on to clothes to give them a shining effect

Span·glish /ˈspæŋɡlɪʃ/ *n* [U] a mixture of Spanish and English, spoken especially in the US

Span·iard /ˈspænjəd $ -ərd/ *n* [C] *old-fashioned* someone from Spain

span·iel /ˈspænjəl/ *n* [C] a type of dog with long ears that hang down

Span·ish¹ /ˈspænɪʃ/ *adj* relating to Spain, its people, or its language

Spanish² *n* **1** [U] the language used in Spain and parts of Latin America **2 the Spanish** [plural] people from Spain

spank /spæŋk/ *v* [T] to hit a child on their bottom with your open hand, as a punishment; 🔁 **smack** —**spank** *n* [C]: *a spank on the bottom*

spank·ing¹ /ˈspæŋkɪŋ/ *n* [C,U] the act of hitting a child on their bottom with your open hand, as a punishment: *If you don't stop that noise, you'll get a spanking!*

spanking² *adv informal* **1 spanking new** very new and impressive: *a spanking new shopping centre* **2 spanking clean** very clean

spanking³ *adj BrE* **at a spanking pace/rate** *old-fashioned* very fast: *They started walking at a spanking rate.*

span·ner /ˈspænə $ -ər/ *n* [C] *BrE* **1** a metal tool that fits over a NUT, used for turning the nut to make it tight or to undo it; 🔁 **wrench** *AmE* **2 put/throw a spanner in the works** *informal* to unexpectedly do something that prevents a plan or process from succeeding

spar¹ /spɑː $ spɑːr/ *v* **sparred, sparring** [I] **1** to practise BOXING with someone: [+with] *He broke his nose while sparring with Vega.* **2** to argue with someone but not in an unpleasant way: [+over] *Senators are sparring over the health bill.* | [+with] *He's been sparring with the security guards.* → SPARRING PARTNER

spar² *n* [C] a thick pole, especially one used on a ship to support sails or ropes; → **mast**

spare¹ [S2] /speə $ sper/ *adj*
1 EXTRA spare key/battery/clothes etc a key etc that you keep in addition to the one you usually use, so that it is available if the one you usually use breaks, gets lost etc: *a spare key* | *Bring a towel and some spare clothes.* | *a supply of spare batteries* | *a spare tyre*
2 NOT USED/NEEDED [usually before noun] not being used or not needed at the present time: *Have you got any spare boxes?* | *You could sleep in the spare bedroom.* | *Do you have any spare cash.* | *I'll go and see if there are any spare seats.* | *A decline in beer sales had left the industry with spare capacity* (=the ability to produce more than can be sold).
3 TIME spare time/moment/hour etc time when you are not working: *What do you do in your spare time?* | *Eric spent every spare moment he had in the library.*
4 MONEY spare change coins of little value that you do not need and can give to other people: *There are beggars on every corner asking for spare change.*
5 be going spare *BrE spoken* if something is going spare, it is available for you to have or use: *I'll have*

some of that cake if it's going away.

6 go spare *BrE informal* to become very angry or worried: *Dad would go spare if he found out.*

7 PLAIN a spare style of writing, painting etc is plain or basic and uses nothing unnecessary

8 THIN *literary* someone who is spare is tall and thin

spare² [S3] *v* [T]

1 GIVE to make something such as time, money, or workers available for someone, especially when this is difficult for you to do: *Sorry, I can't spare the time.* | *I'd like you to come over when you can spare a couple of hours.* | *Can you spare £5?* | **spare sb/sth to do sth** *We're too busy to spare anyone to help you right now.* | **spare sb ten minutes/an hour etc** *Could you possibly spare me a few moments in private* (=used to ask someone if they have time to quickly talk to you)? | *It's very kind of you to spare me so much of your time.*

2 money/time etc to spare if you have time, money etc to spare, you have some left in addition to what you have used or need: *Anyone who has time to spare and would like to help can contact Moira.* | **with sth to spare** *They got to the airport with seconds to spare.* | *They still have some money to spare.*

3 spare sb the trouble/difficulty/pain etc (of doing sth) to prevent someone from having to experience something difficult or unpleasant: *I wanted to spare them the trouble of buying me a present.* | *Thankfully she had been spared the ordeal of surgery.*

4 NOT DAMAGE OR HARM to not damage or harm someone or something, even though other people or things are being damaged, killed, or destroyed: *I could not understand why I had been spared and they had not.* | *the soldier who had spared his life* | **spare sb/sth from sth** *Today we will hear whether the school is to be spared from closure.*

5 spare a thought for sb to think about another person who is in a worse situation than you are: *Spare a thought for Nick, who's doing his exams right now.*

6 spare no expense/effort to spend as much money or do everything necessary to make something really good or successful: **spare no expense/effort to do sth** *No expense was spared in developing the necessary technology.* | *No effort will be spared to bring the people responsible to justice.*

7 spare sb (the details) to not tell someone all the details about something, because it is unpleasant or boring: *He spared us the details, saying only that he had been injured in the war.* | *'They own three houses. One in the country, one in...' 'Spare me.'*

8 spare sb's feelings to avoid doing something that would upset someone: *Just tell me the truth. Don't worry about sparing my feelings.*

9 spare a glance *BrE written* to look quickly at someone or something: [+at] *Before leaving the old town, spare another glance at the tower.* | **spare sb/sth a glance** *a bored waitress who scarcely spared them a glance*

10 spare sb's blushes *BrE* to avoid doing something that would embarrass someone

spare³ *n* **1** [C] an additional thing, for example a key, that you keep so that it is available: *If you forget the key, Mrs Jones over the road has a spare.* | *The batteries are dead. Have you got any spares?* **2** [C] a SPARE TYRE **3 spares** [plural] *BrE* SPARE PARTS: **motor/car/aircraft etc spares** *a shortage of aircraft spares*

,**spare 'part** *n* [C usually plural] a new part for a vehicle or machine, that is used to replace a part that is damaged or broken

,**spare 'ribs** /$ '. ./ *n* [plural] the RIBS of a pig and the meat on them, eaten as food

,**spare 'room** *n* [C] a bedroom in your house for guests

,**spare 'tyre** *BrE*; **spare tire** *AmE n* [C] **1** an additional wheel with a tyre on it, that you keep in a car to use if another tyre gets damaged **2** the fat around someone's waist – used humorously

spar·ing·ly /'speərɪŋli $ 'sper-/ *adv* using or doing only a little of something: *Use the spices sparingly.* —**sparing** *adj*: *We must be sparing with our resources.*

spark¹ /spɑːk $ spɑːrk/ *n*

1 FIRE [C] a very small piece of burning material produced by a fire or by hitting or rubbing two hard objects together: *sparks from the fire* | *The scrape of metal on metal sent up a shower of sparks.*

2 ELECTRICITY [C] a flash of light caused by electricity passing across a space: *electric sparks from a broken wire*

3 spark of interest/excitement/anger etc a small amount of a feeling or quality: *Rachel looked at her and felt a spark of hope.*

4 CAUSE [C] a small action or event that causes something to happen, especially trouble or violence: *The judge's verdict provided the spark for the riots.* | *Interest rate cuts were the spark the market needed.*

5 INTELLIGENCE/ENERGY [U] a quality of intelligence or energy that makes someone successful or fun to be with: *She was tired, and lacked her usual spark.* | *McKellan's performance gives the play its spark of life* (=quality of energy).

6 sparks [plural] anger or angry arguments: *The sparks were really flying* (=people were arguing angrily) *at the meeting!* → **bright spark** at BRIGHT (10)

spark² *v* **1** [T] also **spark sth ⇔ off** to be the cause of something, especially trouble or violence; ▣ **provoke**: *The police response sparked outrage in the community.* | *A discarded cigarette sparked a small brush fire.* **2 spark sb's interest/hope/curiosity etc** to make someone feel interested, hopeful etc: *topics that spark children's imaginations* **3** [I] to produce sparks of fire or electricity

'**sparking plug** *n* [C] *BrE* a SPARK PLUG

spar·kle¹ /'spɑːkəl $ 'spɑːr-/ *v* [I] **1** to shine in small bright flashes; → **sparkling**: *The sea sparkled in the sun.* | *The crystal chandelier sparkled.* **2** if someone's eyes sparkle, they seem to shine brightly, especially because the person is happy or excited **sparkling**: [+with] *Ron's eyes sparkled with excitement.*

sparkle² *n* [C,U] **1** a bright shiny appearance, with small points of flashing light: *the sparkle of the diamonds* **2** a quality that makes something or someone seem interesting and full of life: *the sparkle and zest of a live performance* **3** if someone has a sparkle in their eyes, their eyes seem to shine, and you can see a feeling in them, especially happiness or excitement: *There was a sparkle of fun in her brown eyes.*

spar·kler /'spɑːklə $ 'spɑːrklər/ *n* [C] a type of FIRE-WORK that you can hold in your hand, consisting of a thin stick that gives off sparks of fire

spark·ling /'spɑːklɪŋ $ 'spɑːr-/ *adj* **1** shining brightly with points of flashing light: *a sparkling blue lake* **2** very clean, and seeming to shine brightly: *a sparkling white beach* | *a sparkling clean kitchen* **3** a sparkling drink has bubbles of gas in it; ▣ **fizzy**: *a glass of sparkling wine* **4** full of life and intelligence: *Claire's sparkling personality*

'**spark plug** also **sparking plug** *BrE n* [C] a part in a car engine that produces an electric SPARK to make the petrol mixture start burning

spark·y /'spɑːki $ 'spɑːr-/ *adj BrE* full of life and energy: *Why would a sparky girl like Nicola want to marry him?*

'**sparring ,partner** *n* [C] **1** someone you practise BOXING with **2** someone you regularly have friendly arguments with

spar·row /'spærəʊ $ -roʊ/ *n* [C] a small brown bird, very common in many parts of the world

sparse /spɑːs $ spɑːrs/ *adj* existing only in small amounts: *his sparse brown hair* | *rural areas with sparse population* —**sparsely** *adv*: *a sparsely populated area* —**sparseness** *n* [U]

spar·tan /'spɑːtn $ -ɑːr-/ *adj* spartan conditions or ways of living are simple and without any comfort: *spartan accommodation* | *a spartan existence*

spas·m /'spæzəm/ n **1** [C,U] an occasion when your muscles suddenly become tight, causing you pain: *Maggie felt a muscle spasm in her back.* | *Tom's jaw muscles had gone into spasm.* | **back/shoulder/throat etc spasm 2** spasm of grief/laughter/coughing etc a sudden strong feeling or reaction that you have for a short period of time: *I felt a spasm of fear.*

spas·mod·ic /spæz'mɒdɪk $ -'mɑː-/ adj **1** happening for short irregular periods, not continuously: *spasmodic machine gun fire* **2** formal or medical of or relating to a muscle spasm: *a spasmodic cough* —**spasmodically** /-kli/ adv

spas·tic /'spæstɪk/ adj **1** old-fashioned having CERE-BRAL PALSY, a disease that prevents control of the muscles **2** informal not polite an insulting way of describing someone who drops things, falls easily, and is stupid – used especially by children —**spastic** n [C]

spat¹ /spæt/ the past tense and past participle of SPIT

spat² n [C] **1** informal a short unimportant quarrel: *a marital spat* **2** spats [plural] special pieces of cloth that fasten with buttons on top of a man's shoes, worn in the past

spate /speɪt/ n **1** spate of sth a large number of similar things that happen in a short period of time, especially bad things: *a spate of burglaries* **2** in spate BrE a river, stream etc that is in spate is very full and flowing very fast

spa·tial /'speɪʃəl/ adj relating to the position, size, shape etc of things —**spatially** adv

spat·ter /'spætə $ -ər/ v [I,T] if a liquid spatters, or if something spatters it, drops of it fall or are thrown all over a surface; ⊟ **splatter**: **spatter sb/sth with sth** *The walls were spattered with blood.* | **spatter sth on/over etc sth** *a sweatshirt with paint spattered over it* | [+on/across/over etc] *The first drops of rain spattered on the stones.* —**spatter** n [C]

spat·u·la /'spætjʊlə $ -tʃələ/ n [C] **1** a kitchen tool with a wide flat blade, used for spreading, mixing, or lifting soft substances → see picture at EAT **2** BrE a small instrument with a flat surface, used by doctors to hold your tongue down so that they can examine your throat

spawn¹ /spɔːn $ spɒːn/ v **1** [T] to make a series of things happen or start to exist: *New technology has spawned new business opportunities.* **2** [I,T] if a fish or FROG spawns, it produces eggs in large quantities at the same time

spawn² n [U] the eggs of a fish or FROG laid together in a soft mass

spay /speɪ/ v [T] to remove part of the sex organs of a female animal so that it is not able to have babies; → **neuter**

speak S1 W1 /spiːk/ v past tense **spoke** /spəʊk $ spoʊk/ past participle **spoken** /'spəʊkən $ 'spoʊ-/
1 IN CONVERSATION [I always + adv/prep] to talk to someone about something: [+to] *I spoke to her last Wednesday.* | *'Hello, may I speak to Jim Smith?' 'Yes, speaking'* (=used on the telephone). | *I know her by sight, but not to speak to* (=not well enough to talk to her). | **speak to sb about sth** *I haven't spoken to Steve about all this.* | [+with] especially AmE: *They did not want to speak with reporters.* | [+of] *It was the first time she had ever spoken of marriage.*
2 SAY WORDS [I] to use your voice to produce words: *I was so shocked I couldn't speak.* | *He spoke very softly* (=quietly).
3 LANGUAGE [T not in progressive] to be able to talk in a particular language: *Do you speak English?* | *I don't speak a word of French* (=do not speak any French at all). | **can/can't speak sth** *Several children in the class cannot speak English.* | **French-speaking/Italian-speaking etc** *a German-speaking secretary*
4 FORMAL SPEECH [I] to make a formal speech: [+at] *Jones spoke at the teachers' annual convention.* | [+to] *She asked me to speak to her students about my work in marketing.* | [+in favour of/against] *Only one MP spoke against the bill.* → SPEAKER (1)

5 EXPRESS IDEAS/OPINIONS [I always + adv/prep] to say something that expresses your ideas or opinions: **speak as a parent/teacher/democrat etc** *He emphasized that he was speaking as a private citizen, not in any official capacity.* | **speak well/highly/ill of sb** (=say good or bad things about someone) *Her co-workers spoke highly of her.* | *It's wrong to speak ill of the dead.* | **strictly/generally/roughly speaking** (=used when expressing an idea that you think is exactly true, generally true etc) *Strictly speaking, it's my money, not yours. I earned it.*
6 so to speak used when you are saying something in words that do not have their usual meaning: *We have to pull down the barriers, so to speak, of poverty.*
7 speak your mind to tell people exactly what you think, even if it offends them: *He was a tough politician who wasn't afraid to speak his mind.*
8 be not speaking/not be on speaking terms if two people are not speaking, they do not talk to each other, usually because they have argued: *He was not on speaking terms with his brother or sisters.*
9 speak volumes (about/for sth) if something speaks volumes, it clearly shows the nature of something or the feelings of a person: *What you wear speaks volumes about you.*
10 speak with one voice if a group of people speak with one voice, they all express the same opinion: *On this issue, the 12 organizations spoke with one voice.*
11 speak the same language if two people or groups speak the same language, they have similar attitudes and opinions
12 speak out of turn to say something when you do not have the right or authority to say it → **actions speak louder than words** at ACTION¹ (13); → **the facts speak for themselves** at FACT (8); → **in a manner of speaking** at MANNER (5)

speak for sb/sth phr v
1 to express the feelings, thoughts, or beliefs of a person or group of people: *Dan, speaking for the students, started the meeting.*
2 speak for yourself spoken used to tell someone that you do not have the same opinion as they do, or that something that is true for them is not true for you: *'We don't want to go.' 'Speak for yourself!'*
3 be spoken for if something or someone is spoken for, they have already been promised to someone else: *They're all either married or spoken for.*
4 speak for itself/themselves to show something very clearly: *The results speak for themselves.*

speak of sth phr v
1 literary to show clearly that something happened or exists: *Her skin spoke of warm summer days spent in the sun.*
2 no ... to speak of also **none/nothing to speak of** very little of something or a very small thing: *There's been no rain to speak of for several months.* | *The house had no garden to speak of.*

speak out phr v
to publicly speak in protest about something, especially when protesting could be dangerous: [+about/against] *Five students who had spoken out against the regime were arrested.*

speak to sb/sth phr v
1 to talk to someone who has done something wrong and tell them not to do it again: *Joe was late again today. You'll have to speak to him.*
2 if something such as a poem, painting, or piece of music speaks to you, you like it because it expresses a particular meaning, quality, or feeling to you: *Modern art just doesn't speak to me.*

speak up phr v
1 used to ask someone to speak louder: *Could you speak up, please?*
2 to say something, especially to express your opinion: *There was a brief silence, then Gerald spoke up.*
3 speak up for sb to speak in support of someone: *He is willing to speak up for the rights of women.*

S

WORD CHOICE: speak, talk
When one person is saying things, you can use **talk** or **speak**, but **talk** is more usual and **speak** slightly literary: *She talked about her job.* | *He spoke longingly of his home country.* | *Don't interrupt me when I'm talking/speaking.*
If people are having a conversation, always use **talk**: *We talked about our relationship.* | *They talked for hours.*
If you say that two people **are not speaking**, you mean they are not willing to talk to each other: *They've had a row and they're not speaking.*
Someone who can **talk** has learned to use language: *She could talk before she was two.*
If you can **speak**, you are able to say something on a particular occasion: *I was too scared to speak.*
⚠ When you mention what language someone uses, always use **speak**: *She speaks* (=knows how to use) *French and Spanish.* | *We spoke in German at first, then English.*
⚠ When you ask for someone on the telephone, use **speak**: *Can I speak to Clare?*
⚠ You can **speak words**. Do not use **talk**: *I spoke the words as clearly as I could.*
⚠ You can **talk sense** or **talk nonsense**. Do not use **speak**: *I think she talks a lot of sense.*

-speak /spiːk/ *suffix* [in nouns] the special language or difficult words that are used in a particular business or activity: *computerspeak*

speak·eas·y /ˈspiːkˌiːzi/ *n plural* **speakeasies** [C] a place in the US in the 1920's and 1930's where you could buy alcohol illegally

speak·er [S2] [W2] /ˈspiːkə $ -ər/ *n* [C]
1 someone who makes a formal speech to a group of people: [+at] *the guest speaker at the conference* | *The keynote speaker* (=main or most important speaker) *was Robert Venturi, the architect.* | **after-dinner speaker** (=someone who makes a speech after a formal meal)
2 someone who speaks a particular language: **French-speaker/Spanish-speaker etc** | [+of] *Some English words are difficult for speakers of other languages.* | a **native speaker** *of Chinese*
3 the part of a radio, SOUND SYSTEM etc where the sound comes out
4 *formal* someone who says something: *Pay attention to the body language of the speaker.*
5 the Speaker an official who controls discussions in a parliament
6 the Speaker of the House the politician who controls discussions in the House of Representatives in the US Congress

speak·er·phone /ˈspiːkəfəʊn $ -kərfoʊn/ *n* [C] *especially AmE* a telephone that contains a MICROPHONE and a LOUDSPEAKER, so that you can use it without holding it. Speakerphones are especially used in business meetings when groups of people in different places want to talk to each other.

spear¹ /spɪə $ spɪr/ *n* [C] **1** a pole with a sharp pointed blade at one end, used as a weapon in the past **2** a thin pointed stem of a plant: *asparagus spears*

spear² *v* [T] **1** to push or throw a spear into something, especially in order to kill it **2** to push a pointed object, usually a fork, into something, so that you can pick it up; → **stab**

spear·head¹ /ˈspɪəhed $ ˈspɪr-/ *v* [T] to lead an attack or organized action: *the troops who spearheaded the rescue mission*

spearhead² *n* [C usually singular] a person or group of people who lead an attack or organized action: [+of] *The group became the spearhead of the labor union movement.*

spear·mint /ˈspɪəˌmɪnt $ ˈspɪr-/ *n* [U] **1** a fresh MINT taste, often used in sweets **2** a type of MINT plant

spec /spek/ *n informal* **1** [C usually plural] a detailed instruction about how a building, car, piece of equip-

ment etc should be made; ◨ **specification**: *the specs for the company's new video games console* **2 on spec** if you do something on spec, you do it without being sure that you will get what you are hoping for: *I sent in an application on spec.* **3 specs** [plural] glasses that help you see

spe·cial¹ [S1] [W1] /ˈspeʃəl/ *adj*
1 not ordinary or usual, but different in some way and often better or more important: *a special place in the classroom for reading* | *No one receives special treatment.* | *Maria's special recipe for apple pie* | *The good china was used only on special occasions.* | *Each village has its own special charm.* | **anything/something/nothing special** *Are you doing anything special for Christmas?*
2 particularly important to someone and deserving attention, love etc: *a party with a few special friends* | *a teacher who made every child feel special* | *Her second son had a special place in her heart.*
3 [only before noun] a special position or job has a particular purpose or aim, and continues only until that purpose or aim is achieved: *Mitchell acted as a special envoy in the Northern Ireland peace talks.*
4 [only before noun] more than usual: *Pay special attention to how you clean the wound.*

special² *n* [C usually singular] **1** something that is not usual or ordinary, and is made or done for a special purpose: *a TV special on the election* **2** a lower price than usual for a particular product for a short period of time: *a lunch special for $4.99* | **be on special** *Breyer's ice cream is on special this week.*

special 'agent *n* [C] *AmE* someone who works for the FBI

Special Branch *n* a department of the British police force that deals with political crimes or crimes affecting the safety of the government, for example TERRORISM

special 'constable *n* [C] someone in Britain who sometimes works as a police officer without being paid, and who also has another main job

special de'livery *n* [C,U] a service that delivers a letter or package very quickly

special edu'cation *n* [U] the education of children who have physical problems or learning problems

special ef'fect *n* [C usually plural] an unusual image or sound that has been produced artificially to be used in a film or television programme

special 'forces *n* [plural] soldiers who have been specially trained to fight against GUERRILLA or TERRORIST groups

special 'interest ,group *n* [C] a group of people who share the same political or business aims, and who try to influence the government to help them with those aims

special 'interests *n* [plural] special interest groups in general: *Special interests donate millions of dollars to political campaigns.*

spe·cial·is·m /ˈspeʃəlɪzəm/ *n BrE* **1** [C] a particular activity or subject that you know a lot about; ◨ **specialization** *AmE*: [+in] *graduates with a specialism in Tourism and Leisure* **2** [U] the practice of limiting your interests or activities to particular subjects; ◨ **specialization** *AmE*

spe·cial·ist [S3] [W3] /ˈspeʃəlᵻst/ *n* [C]
1 someone who knows a lot about a particular subject, or is very skilled at it; ◨ **expert**: [+in] *an attorney who is a specialist in banking law*
2 a doctor who knows more about one particular type of illness or treatment than other doctors: *a heart specialist*

spe·ci·al·i·ty /ˌspeʃiˈælᵻti/ *n plural* **specialities** [C] *BrE* **1** a type of food that a person, restaurant, or area is well known for; ◨ **specialty** *AmE*: *The restaurant offers a wide variety of local specialities.* | *the region's speciality cheese* **2** a subject or job that you know a lot about or have a lot of experience of; ◨ **specialty** AmE: *Preston's speciality was night photography.*

spe·cial·i·za·tion /ˌspeʃəlaɪˈzeɪʃən $ -ləˈ-/ n [C,U] **1** an activity or subject that you know a lot about **2** the practice of limiting your interests or activities to one particular subject: *industrial specialization*

spe·cial·ize S3 also **-ise** BrE /ˈspeʃəlaɪz/ v [I] to limit all or most of your study, business etc to a particular subject or activity: [+in] *Simmons specialized in contract law.*

spe·cial·ized also **-ised** BrE /ˈspeʃəlaɪzd/ adj trained, designed, or developed for a particular purpose, type of work, place etc: *specialized training for specific jobs* | *the highly specialized plants that live in desert areas*

ˌspecial ˈlicence n [C,U] BrE special permission given by the Church of England for a marriage to take place at a time or place not usually allowed

spe·cial·ly /ˈspeʃəli/ adv **1** for one particular purpose, and only for that purpose: *specially trained police dogs* | **specially designed/built/made etc** *The boats are specially built for the disabled.* **2** spoken much more than usual, or much more than other people or things; ◨ **especially**: *He specially liked the pie.* → see box at **ESPECIALLY**

ˌspecial ˈneeds n [plural] needs that someone has because they have mental or physical problems: *children with special needs*

ˌspecial ˈoffer n [C] a low price charged for a product for a short time: *The hotel has a special offer of five nights for the price of three.* | [+on] *special offers on dishwashers* | **be on special offer** *The wine is currently on special offer at £2.69.* —**special offer** adj [only before noun]: *Our special offer price is £25.95.*

ˌspecial ˈpleading n [U] when someone tries to persuade you to do something by giving you only those facts that support their argument

ˈspecial ˌschool n [C] especially BrE a school for children with physical problems or learning problems

spe·cial·ty /ˈspeʃəlti/ n plural **specialities** [C] AmE **1** a type of food that a person, restaurant, or area is well known for; ◨ **speciality** BrE: *Our specialty is clam chowder.* **2** a subject or job that you know a lot about or have a lot of experience of; ◨ **speciality** BrE: *Johnson's specialty is medieval European history.* **3** a particular product or business that has one purpose or sells one type of thing: *an area with clothes retailers and specialty shops*

spe·cies W3 /ˈspiːʃiːz/ n plural **species** [C] a group of animals or plants whose members are similar and can breed together to produce young animals or plants: *Seven species of birds of prey have been observed.* | *pandas and other endangered species* (=ones that may soon no longer exist); → **genus**

spe·cif·ic¹ S1 W1 /spəˈsɪfɪk/ adj **1** [only before noun] a specific thing, person, or group is one particular thing, person, or group: *games suitable for specific age-groups* | *a specific example of alcohol's effect on the body* **2** detailed and exact: *Mr Howarth gave us very specific instructions.* | [+about] *Could you be more specific about what you're looking for?* **3** **specific to sth** formal limited to, or affecting only one particular thing: *a disease specific to horses*

specific² n **1 specifics** [plural] particular details: [+of] *the specifics of the lawsuit* | **give/go into/provide etc specifics** *Thurman was reluctant to go into specifics about the deal.* **2** [C] medical a drug that has an effect only on one particular disease

spe·cif·ic·ally S2 W3 /spəˈsɪfɪkli/ adv **1** relating to or intended for one particular type of person or thing only: *advertising that specifically targets children* **2** in a detailed or exact way: *I specifically asked you not to do that!*

3 [sentence adverb] used when you are adding more exact information: *Specifically, the department wanted answers to the following questions.*

spe·ci·fi·ca·tion /ˌspesɪfɪˈkeɪʃən/ n [C] **1** [usually plural] a detailed instruction about how a car, building, piece of equipment etc should be made: **build/manufacture/produce sth to ... specifications** *The airport building had been constructed to FAA specifications.* | *The bolts met all the engineering specifications.* **2** especially BrE a clear statement of what is needed or wanted: *a specification of what role each member will play* | **job specification** (=a detailed description of what a job involves)

speˌcific ˈgravity n [C,U] technical the weight of a substance divided by the weight of the amount of water that would fill the same space

spe·ci·fy W3 /ˈspesɪfaɪ/ v **specified**, **specifying**, **specifies** [T] to state something in an exact and detailed way: *Payments will be made for a specified number of months.* | **specify who/what/how etc** *Regulations specify how long maintenance crews can work.* | **specify that** *The rules clearly specify that competitors must not accept payment.*

spe·ci·men /ˈspesɪmɪn/ n [C] **1** a small amount or piece that is taken from something, so that it can be tested or examined: *a blood specimen* | [+of] *a specimen of rock* **2** a single example of something, often an animal or plant: [+of] *a very fine specimen of 12th century glass* **3** a person you are describing in a particular way – used humorously: *Her boyfriend is an impressive physical specimen.*

spe·cious /ˈspiːʃəs/ adj formal seeming to be true or correct, but actually false: *a specious argument*

speck /spek/ n [C] a very small mark, spot, or piece of something: [+of] *a speck of dust*

speck·led /ˈspekəld/ adj covered with many small marks or spots: *speckled eggs*

speck·les /ˈspekəlz/ n [plural] small marks or spots covering a background of a different colour

spec·ta·cle /ˈspektəkəl/ n [C] **1** a very impressive show or scene: *a multimedia dance and opera spectacle* **2** [usually singular] an unusual or interesting thing or situation that you see or notice – used especially in order to show disapproval: *The trial was turned into a public spectacle.* | [+of] *the spectacle of drunken young men on the streets* **3 spectacles** [plural] formal or old-fashioned glasses that help you see **4 make a spectacle of yourself** to behave in an embarrassing way that is likely to make other people notice you and laugh at you

spec·tac·u·lar¹ /spekˈtækjʊlə $ -ər/ adj **1** very impressive: *a mountainous area with spectacular scenery* | *a spectacular success* **2** very sudden, unexpected, or extreme: *The news caused a spectacular fall in the stock market.* —**spectacularly** adv

spectacular² n [C] an event or performance that is very large and impressive: *a television spectacular*

spec·tate /spekˈteɪt $ ˈspekteɪt/ v [I] to watch a sports event

spec·ta·tor /spekˈteɪtə $ ˈspekteɪtər/ n [C] someone who is watching an event or game; → **audience**: *The match attracted over 40,000 spectators.*

specˈtator ˌsport /$ ˈ... ˌ./ n [C] **1** a sport that people go and watch **2** something that you watch rather than take part in – usually used humorously: *Life is not a spectator sport.*

spec·ter /ˈspektə $ -ər/ n the American spelling of SPECTRE

spec·tra /ˈspektrə/ the plural of SPECTRUM

spec·tral /ˈspektrəl/ adj **1** literary relating to or like a spectre **2** technical relating to or made by a spectrum

spec·tre *BrE*; **specter** *AmE* /'spektə $ -ər/ *n* **1 the spectre of sth** something that people are afraid of because it may affect them badly: *The recession is again raising the spectre of unemployment.* **2** [C] *literary* a GHOST

spec·tro·scope /'spektrəskəʊp $ -skoʊp/ *n* [C] an instrument used for forming and looking at spectra —**spectroscopy** /spek'trɒskəpi $ -'trɑː-/ *n* [U] —**spectroscopic** /ˌspektrə'skɒpɪk◄ $ -'skɑː-/ *adj*

spec·trum /'spektrəm/ *n plural* **spectra** /-trə/ [C] **1** a complete range of opinions, people, situations etc, going from one extreme to its opposite: [+of] *the ethnic spectrum of America* | **across the spectrum** *The bill drew support from across the political spectrum.* | **broad/wide/full etc spectrum** *a broad spectrum of environmental groups* | *The two articles here represent opposite ends of the spectrum.* **2** the set of bands of coloured light into which a beam of light separates when it is passed through a PRISM **3** a complete range of radio, sound etc waves: *the electromagnetic spectrum*

spec·u·late /'spekjᵿleɪt/ *v* **1** [I,T] to guess about the possible causes or effects of something, without knowing all the facts or details: *She refused to speculate.* | **speculate on/about (why/what etc)** *Jones refused to speculate about what might happen.* | **speculate that** *Some analysts speculated that jobs will be lost.* **2** [I] to buy goods, property, SHARES in a company etc, hoping that you will make a large profit when you sell them: [+in/on] *He speculated in stocks.*

spec·u·la·tion /ˌspekjᵿ'leɪʃən/ *n* [C,U] **1** when you guess about the possible causes or effects of something without knowing all the facts, or the guesses that you make: **speculation that** *There is speculation that the president is ill.* | [+about/on] *speculation about the future* | *the witness's statement was* **pure speculation** (=not based on any facts) | **wild/idle speculation** (=speculation that is unlikely to be true) **2** when you try to make a large profit by buying goods, property, SHARES etc and then selling them: *property speculation*

spec·u·la·tive /'spekjᵿlətɪv $ -leɪ-/ *adj* **1** based on guessing, not on information or facts: **highly/purely/largely speculative** *a purely speculative theory about life on other planets* **2** bought or done in the hope of making a profit later: *speculative investments* **3** if you give someone a speculative look, you look at them while trying to guess something about them —**speculatively** *adv*: *Delaney eyed her speculatively.*

spec·u·la·tor /'spekjᵿleɪtə $ -ər/ *n* [C] someone who buys goods, property, SHARES in a company etc, hoping that they will make a large profit when they sell them: *a New York property speculator*

sped /sped/ a past tense and past participle of SPEED

speech S2 W2 /spiːtʃ/ *n*
1 [C] a talk, especially a formal one about a particular subject, given to a group of people: *a campaign speech* | **give/make/deliver a speech** *Each child had to give a short speech to the rest of the class.* | [+on/about] *a major speech on relations with China* | *a conference including meals and* **after-dinner speeches** | *Collins gave the* **keynote speech** (=most important speech).
2 [U] the ability to speak: *Only humans are capable of speech.*
3 [U] spoken language rather than written language: *In speech we use a smaller vocabulary than in writing.*
4 [U] the particular way in which someone speaks: *Bob's speech was slurred, and he sounded drunk.*
5 [C] a set of lines that an actor must say in a play: *Hamlet's longest speech* → DIRECT SPEECH, FIGURE OF SPEECH, INDIRECT SPEECH, PART OF SPEECH, REPORTED SPEECH; → **speech bubble** at BUBBLE¹ (4); → **freedom of speech** at FREEDOM (1)

speech day *n* [C] an occasion held once a year in some British schools, when prizes are given to children and people give speeches

spee·chi·fy /'spiːtʃᵻfaɪ/ *v* **speechified, speechifying, speechifies** [I] *informal* to make speeches in a way that makes you seem important – used in order to show disapproval

speech im·pediment *n* [C] a physical or nervous problem that affects your speech

speech·less /'spiːtʃləs/ *adj* unable to speak because you feel very angry, upset etc: [+with] *His comments left me* **speechless with rage.** —**speechlessly** *adv* —**speechlessness** *n* [U]

speech marks *n* [plural] *BrE* the marks (' ') or (" "), that show when someone starts speaking and when they stop; ☐ **quotation marks**

speech synthesizer *n* [C] a computer system that produces sounds like human speech

speech therapy *n* [U] treatment that helps people who have difficulty in speaking properly —**speech therapist** *n* [C]

speech·writ·er /'spiːtʃˌraɪtə $ -ər/ *n* [C] someone whose job is to write speeches for other people

speed¹ W1 S2 /spiːd/ *n*
1 OF MOVEMENT [C,U] the rate at which something moves or travels

> **(at) a speed of 60 mph/80 kmph etc**
> **at high/low speed(s)**
> **at great speed**
> **at top/full speed** (=as fast as possible)
> **at lightning speed** (=very fast)
> **at breakneck speed** (=dangerously fast)
> **at the speed of light**
> **speed limit/restriction**
> **wind speed**
>
> *The truck was travelling* **at a speed of** *50 mph.* | *Extreme care is always needed when flying* **at high speeds.** | *Beat the mixture for two minutes* **at low speed.** | *They drove to the hospital* **at top speed.** | *They chased each other through the streets* **at breakneck speed.** | *particles that travel* **at the speed of light** | *The* **speed limit** *in urban areas is usually 30 or 40 mph.* | *The average* **wind speed** *at Stornoway is 14.4 knots.*

2 OF ACTION [C,U] the rate at which something happens or is done: [+of] *the speed of change within the industry* | *a* **high-speed** *computer* | *At that time, cities were growing* **at breakneck speed** (=very fast).
3 FAST [U] the quality of being fast: *The women's basketball team has talent, speed, and power.* | **with speed** *She acted with speed and efficiency.* | **at speed** *BrE: a van travelling at speed* | **pick up/gather speed** (=gradually start to travel faster) *The train began to pick up speed.*
4 PHOTOGRAPHY [C] **a)** the degree to which photographic film is sensitive to light **b)** the time it takes for a camera SHUTTER to open and close: *a shutter speed of 1/250 second*
5 DRUG [U] *informal* an illegal drug that makes you very active; ☐ **amphetamine**
6 **five-speed/ten-speed etc** having five, ten etc GEARS: *a ten-speed bike*
7 **up to speed** having the latest information or knowledge about something: *Some school officials are only now* **getting up to speed** *regarding computers.* | *John will* **bring you up to speed** (=tell you the latest information). → **full speed/steam ahead** at FULL¹ (18)

speed² S3 *v past tense and past participle* **sped** /sped/ *also* **speeded**
1 [I always + adv/prep] to go quickly: *The car sped along the dusty highway.*
2 [T always + adv/prep] to take someone or something somewhere very quickly: *An ambulance sped her to the hospital.*
3 be speeding to be driving faster than the legal limit: *I got* **caught speeding** *on the A40 yesterday.*
4 *also* **speed sth ⇔ up** [T] to make something happen faster; ☐ **slow down**: *This news should speed his recovery.*

speed by *phr v*
if time speeds by, it seems to pass very quickly: *The*

weeks sped by and soon it was time to go back to school.

speed up *phr v*
to move or happen faster, or to make something move or happen faster; ⊟ **slow down**: *The truck speeded up going down the hill.* | **speed sth ⇔ up** *The new system will speed up the registration process.*

speed·boat /ˈspiːdbəʊt $ -boʊt/ *n* [C] a small boat with a powerful engine, designed to go fast

ˈspeed bump also **ˈspeed hump** *BrE n* [C] a narrow raised area put across a road to force traffic to go slowly; ⊟ **sleeping policeman**

ˈspeed ˌdial, ˈspeed ˌdialing *n* [U] a special feature on a telephone that lets you DIAL someone's telephone number very quickly by pressing one button —**speed-dial** *v* [I,T]

speed·ing /ˈspiːdɪŋ/ *n* [U] the offence of driving faster than the legal limit: *a speeding ticket* | *She got stopped for speeding.*

ˈspeed ˌlimit *n* [C] the fastest speed allowed by law on a particular piece of road: *a 30 mph speed limit* | **exceed/break the speed limit**

speed·om·e·ter /spɪˈdɒmɪ̈tə, spiː- $ -ˈdɑːmɪ̈tər/ also **speed·o** /ˈspiːdəʊ $ -doʊ/ *n* [C] an instrument in a vehicle that shows how fast it is going → see picture at CAR

ˈspeed ˌreading *n* [U] the skill of reading very quickly

ˈspeed ˌskating *n* [U] the sport of racing on ice wearing ICE SKATES → see picture at WINTER SPORTS

ˈspeed trap *n* [C] a place on a road where police wait to catch drivers who are going too fast

speed·up, speed-up /ˈspiːdʌp/ *n* [C usually singular] an increase in the speed of something or in the rate at which a process happens: [+in] *a speedup in population growth*

speed·way /ˈspiːdweɪ/ *n* **1** [U] the sport of racing MOTORCYCLES or cars on a special track **2** [C] a special track for the sport of speedway

speed·y /ˈspiːdi/ *adj comparative* **speedier**, *superlative* **speediest** **1** happening or done quickly or without delay; ⊟ **quick**: *a speedy recovery from injury* **2** a speedy car, boat etc goes fast; ⊟ **fast** —**speedily** *adv*: *The matter was speedily resolved.*

spe·le·ol·o·gy /ˌspiːliˈɒlədʒi $ -ˈɑːl-/ *n* [U] *technical* **1** *BrE* the sport of walking and climbing in CAVES; ⊟ **spelunking** *AmE* **2** the scientific study of CAVES —**speleologist** *n* [C]

spell¹ [S2] /spel/ *v past tense and past participle* **spelt** /spelt/ *BrE also* **spelled** *especially AmE*
1 [I,T] to form a word by writing or naming the letters in order: *How do you spell 'juice'?* | *Pupils should know how to spell commonly used words.* | **spell sth wrong/wrongly** *You've spelled my name wrong.*
2 [T not in passive] if letters spell a word, they form it: *B-O-O-K spells 'book'.*
3 spell trouble/disaster/danger etc if a situation or action spells trouble etc, it makes you expect trouble etc: *The lack of rain could spell disaster for farmers.*
4 [T] *AmE* to do someone else's work for them for a short period so that they can rest: *I can spell you if you get tired.*

spell sth ⇔ out *phr v*
1 to explain something clearly and in detail: **spell out how/what etc** *The report spelled out in detail what the implications were for teacher training.*
2 to show how a word is spelled by writing or saying the letters separately in order: *'W-E-I-R,'* she said, spelling it out.
3 to write a word in its complete form instead of using an ABBREVIATION

spell² *n* [C] **1** a piece of magic that someone does, or the special words or ceremonies used in doing it: *a magic spell* | **put a spell on sb/cast a spell over sb** (=do a piece of magic to change someone) | *The kiss of the prince broke the spell* (=stopped the magic from working). | **be under a spell** *The whole town seemed to*

be under a spell. **2** a period of a particular kind of activity, weather, illness etc, usually a short period: **brief/short spell** *After a brief spell in the army, I returned to teaching.* | [+of] *a spell of bad luck* | **cold/wet/dry spell** *Water the young plants carefully during dry spells.* | *a day of sunny spells and scattered showers* | *He began to suffer from dizzy spells.* **3** a power that attracts, interests, and influences you very strongly: **fall/come/be under a spell** *I fell under the spell of her charm.* | *an ancient city that still casts its spell over travellers* **4** break the spell to make someone stop paying all their attention to something, or to make a time stop feeling special: *He lay still, not wanting to break the spell.*

spell·bind·ing /ˈspelbaɪndɪŋ/ *adj* extremely interesting and holding your attention completely; ⊟ **riveting**: *a spellbinding tale*

spell·bound /ˈspelbaʊnd/ *adj* extremely interested in something you are listening to: *'King Lear' still holds audiences spellbound.*

ˈspell-ˌchecker *n* [C] a computer program that tells you when you have spelled a word wrongly —**spell-check** *v* [I,T]

spel·ler /ˈspelə $ -ər/ *n* **good/bad/poor etc speller** someone who is good or bad at spelling words correctly: *words that confuse even good spellers*

spell·ing [S2] /ˈspelɪŋ/ *n*
1 [U] the act of spelling words correctly, or the ability to do this: *Her spelling has improved.* | *an essay full of spelling mistakes*
2 [C] the way in which a word is spelled: *She quickly gave the correct spelling.*

ˈspelling bee *n* [C] *AmE* a competition in which the winner is the person who spells the most words correctly

spelt /spelt/ *especially BrE* the past tense and past participle of SPELL

spe·lunk·ing /spəˈlʌŋkɪŋ/ *AmE* the sport of walking and climbing in CAVES —**spelunker** *n* [C]

spend [S1] [W1] /spend/ *v past tense and past participle* **spent** /spent/
1 MONEY [I,T] to use your money to pay for goods or services: *I can't afford to spend any more money this week.* | **spend £5/$10 etc** *I only want to spend about $20.* | **spend sth on sth** *More money should be spent on education.* | **spend sth on sb** *Mum never spends any money on herself.* | *The repairs cost a lot, but it's money well spent* (=a sensible way of spending money).
2 TIME [T] to use time doing a particular thing or pass time in a particular place: **spend time etc with sb** *I want to spend more time with my family.* | **spend time etc in/at sth** *We'll have to spend the night in a hotel.* | *His childhood was spent in Brazil.* | **spend time etc doing sth** *Stacey spends all her free time painting.*
3 a) spend the night with sb to stay for the night and have sex with someone **b)** spend the night (at sth) if someone spends the night at someone's house, they sleep at that person's house for a night: *She spent the night at a friend's house.*
4 FORCE/EFFORT [T] to use effort or energy to do something: *I love to cook, but I don't feel like spending the energy every evening.*
5 spend a penny *BrE spoken old-fashioned* to URINATE - used when you want to avoid saying this directly

spend·er /ˈspendə $ -ər/ *n* [C] someone who spends money: *The new casino hopes to attract big spenders* (=people who spend a lot of money).

spend·ing /ˈspendɪŋ/ *n* [U] the amount of money spent, especially by a government or organization: **government/public/defence etc spending** *a plan to increase military spending*

ˈspending ˌmoney *n* [U] money that you have available to spend on the things you want rather than need

spend·thrift /'spend,θrɪft/ n [C] someone who spends money carelessly, even when they do not have a lot of it

spent[1] /spent/ the past tense and past participle of SPEND

spent[2] adj **1** already used, and now empty or useless: *He tried to eject the spent cartridge and reload.* | *spent matches* **2 a spent force** if a political idea or organization is a spent force, it no longer has any power or influence: *Socialism had become a spent political force.* **3** *literary* extremely tired

sperm /spɜːm $ spɜːrm/ n plural **sperm** or **sperms 1** [C] also **'sperm cell** a cell produced by the sex organs of a male person or animal, which is able to join with the female egg to produce a new life **2** [U] the liquid from the male sex organs that these cells swim in; **☰ semen 3 sperm count** a medical measurement of the number of sperm a man has, which shows if he is able to make a woman PREGNANT

sper·ma·to·zo·on /ˌspɜːmətəˈzəʊɒn $ ˌspɜːrmətə-ˈzəʊɑːn/ n plural **spermatozoa** /-ˈzəʊə $ -ˈzəʊə/ [C] *technical* a sperm

'sperm bank n [C] a place where SEMEN is kept to be used in medical operations that help women become PREGNANT

sper·mi·cide /'spɜːmɪˌsaɪd $ 'spɜːr-/ n [C,U] a cream or liquid that kills SPERM, used while having sex to prevent the woman from becoming PREGNANT —**spermicidal** /ˌspɜːmɪˈsaɪdl◂ $ ˌspɜːr-/ adj [only before noun]: *spermicidal cream*

'sperm whale n [C] a large WHALE sometimes hunted for its oil and fat

spew /spjuː/ v **1** [I always + adv/ prep,T] also **spew out/forth** to flow out of something quickly in large quantities, or to make something flow out in this way: *Factory chimneys spewed fumes out into the sky.* | [+from/into/over etc] *Brown water spewed from the tap.* **2** [I always + adv/ prep,T] also **spew out/forth** to say a lot of bad or negative things very quickly: *Groups like these use the Internet to spew racial hatred.* **3** [I,T] also **spew up** *informal* to VOMIT

SPF /ˌes piː 'ef/ n [singular, U] *Sun Protection Factor* a number that shows you how much protection a special cream gives you from the sun: *an SPF 25 cream*

sphag·num /'sfægnəm/ also **'sphagnum ˌmoss** n [U] a type of MOSS (=simple plant) that grows in wet places

sphere /sfɪə $ sfɪr/ n [C] **1** a ball shape **2** a particular area of activity, work, knowledge etc: **in ... sphere** *television's increasing role in the political sphere* | **public/private sphere** *Women have often been excluded from positions of power in the public sphere.* **3 sb's/sth's sphere of influence** a person, country's, organization's etc sphere of influence is the area where they have power to change things

-sphere /sfɪə $ sfɪr/ suffix [in nouns] *technical* relating to the air or gases surrounding the Earth: *the atmosphere*

spher·i·cal /'sferɪkəl/ adj having the shape of a sphere; **☰ round**

sphe·roid /'sfɪərɔɪd $ 'sfɪr-/ n [C] *technical* a shape that is similar to a ball, but not perfectly round

sphinc·ter /'sfɪŋktə $ -ər/ n [C] *medical* a muscle that surrounds an opening in your body, and can become tight in order to close the opening

sphinx, Sphinx /sfɪŋks/ n [C] an ancient Egyptian image of a lion with a human head, lying down

spic, spik /spɪk/ n [C] *AmE taboo* a very offensive word for a Spanish-speaking person. Do not use this word.

spice[1] /spaɪs/ n **1** [C,U] a type of powder or seed, taken from plants, that you put into food you are cooking to give it a special taste; → **spicy**: *herbs and spices* **2** [singular, U] interest or excitement that is

added to something: *Travel adds spice to your life.* → **variety is the spice of life** at VARIETY (5)

spice[2] also **spice up** v [T] **1** to add interest or excitement to something: *Millions have bought the book to spice up their sex lives.* **2** to add spice to food: [+with] *baked apples spiced with cinnamon*

spick and span, spic and span /ˌspɪk ən 'spæn/ adj [not before noun] *informal* a room, house etc that is spick and span is completely clean and tidy

spic·y /'spaɪsi/ adj **1** food that is spicy has a pleasantly strong taste, and gives you a pleasant burning feeling in your mouth; **☰ hot**; → **spice**: *a spicy tomato sauce* **2** a story or picture that is spicy is slightly shocking or rude because it tells about or shows something relating to sex

spi·der /'spaɪdə $ -ər/ n [C] **1** a small creature with eight legs, which catches insects using a fine network of sticky threads **2** *technical* a computer program that searches the Internet for the best websites with the information you want, so that you can find it quickly; **☰ crawler, bot**; → **crawl the net/web**

spi·der·web /'spaɪdəweb $ -dər-/ also **web** n [C] *AmE* a very fine network of sticky threads made by a spider to catch insects; → **cobweb**

spi·der·y /'spaɪdəri/ adj covered with or made of lots of long thin uneven lines: *spidery handwriting*

spiel /ʃpiːl, spiːl/ n [C,U] *informal* a quick speech that the speaker has used many times before, especially one that is intended to persuade people to buy something: *A salesman started giving us a spiel about life insurance.*

spif·fy /'spɪfi/ adj *old-fashioned informal especially AmE* very neat, attractive, and fashionable: *a spiffy blue suit*

spig·ot /'spɪgət/ n [C] **1** a TAP in a large container that controls the flow of liquid from it **2** *especially AmE* an outdoor TAP

spike[1] /spaɪk/ n [C] **1** something long and thin with a sharp point, especially a pointed piece of metal **2** [usually singular] a sudden large increase in the number or rate of something: [+in] *a spike in interest rates* **3 spikes** [plural] shoes with metal points on the bottom, worn by people who run races, play golf etc **4 spike heels** [plural] a pair of women's shoes with very high thin heels

spike[2] v **1** [T] to secretly add strong alcohol or a drug to someone's drink or food: **spike sth with sth** *The orange juice had been spiked with gin.* **2** [I] if the number or rate of something spikes, it increases quickly and by a large amount: *New telephone orders have spiked in the last two years.* **3** [T] to push a sharp tool or object into something **4** [T] to prevent someone from saying something or printing something in a newspaper: *a clumsy attempt to spike rumours of a cabinet split* **5 a) spike the ball** *AmE* to powerfully throw an American football down on the ground to celebrate a TOUCHDOWN **b)** [I,T] to powerfully hit a VOLLEYBALL down over the net **6 spike sb's guns** *BrE* to spoil an opponent's plans

spik·y /'spaɪki/ adj **1** hair that is spiky is stiff and stands up on top of your head: *short black spiky hair* **2** having long sharp points: *a spiky cactus* **3** *BrE informal* easily offended or annoyed

spill[1] [S3] /spɪl/ v past tense and past participle **spilt** /spɪlt/ *especially BrE* or **spilled** *especially AmE*
1 [I,T] if you spill a liquid, or if it spills, it accidentally flows over the edge of a container; → **pour**: *Katie almost spilled her milk.* | **spill sth down/on/over sth** *Oh no! I've spilt coffee all down my shirt!* | [+on/over etc] *He slipped and the wine spilled all over the carpet.*
2 [I always + adv/prep] if people or things spill out of somewhere, they move or fall out in large numbers; **☰ pour**: [+out/into/onto etc] *Crowds from the theatre were spilling onto the street.*
3 spill the beans *informal* to tell something that someone else wanted you to keep a secret
4 spill your guts *AmE informal* to tell someone all about your private life, or about a personal secret

5 spill blood *literary* to kill or wound people → **cry over spilt milk** at CRY¹ (3)

spill into/onto sth *phr v literary*
if light spills onto or into something, it shines through a window, door, hole etc onto something else: *The morning light spilled into the room.*

spill over *phr v*
if a problem or bad situation spills over, it spreads and begins to affect other places, people etc: [+into] *The conflict might spill over into neighbouring towns.*

spill² *n* **1** [C,U] when you spill something, or an amount of something that is spilled: *the enormous oil spill off the southern tip of the Shetland Islands* **2** [C] a fall from a horse, bicycle etc: *Tyson broke a rib when he took a spill on his motorcycle.*

spil·lage /ˈspɪlɪdʒ/ *n* [C,U] a SPILL² (1)

spill·o·ver /ˈspɪləʊvə $ -oʊvər/ *n* [C,U] the effect that one situation or problem has on another situation: *Not all of the violence in Miami was spillover from the trial.* | **spillover effect/benefit/cost** *The weak European economy will have a spillover effect on the US dollar.*

spilt /spɪlt/ *especially BrE* a past tense and past participle of SPILL

spin¹ S3 /spɪn/ *v past tense and past participle* **spun** /spʌn/ *present participle* **spinning**
1 TURN AROUND [I,T] to turn around and around very quickly, or to make something do this: *The plane's propellers were spinning.* | **spin (sth/sb) around** *She grabbed Norm's arm and spun him around to face her.*
2 sb's head is spinning also **the room is spinning** if your head or the room is spinning, you feel as if you might FAINT (=become unconscious) because you are shocked, excited, or drunk: *I was pouring with sweat, and my head was spinning.* | *The room started to spin.*
3 SITUATION/INFORMATION [T] to describe a situation or information in a way that is intended to influence the way people think about it – used especially about what politicians or business people do: *Supporters attempted to spin the bill's defeat to their advantage.*
4 **spin a tale/story/yarn** to tell a story, especially using a lot of imagination: *She spun a story about a trip to Athens to meet one of the authors.*
5 WOOL/COTTON [I,T] to make cotton, wool etc into thread by twisting it
6 DRIVE [I always + adv/prep] *written* to drive or travel quickly; ▪ speed: [+past/along etc] *Barbara spun past in her new sportscar.*
7 **spin your wheels** *AmE* to continue trying to do something without having any success: *I felt like I was just spinning my wheels trying to make him understand.*
8 WET CLOTHES [T] *BrE* to get water out of clothes using a machine after you have washed them
9 INSECT [T] if a SPIDER or insect spins a WEB or COCOON, it produces thread to make it

spin off *phr v*
to make part of a company into a separate and partly independent company, or to become a separate company: **spin** sth ⇔ **off** *At the time of the merger, Loral spun off its space divisions into a separate firm.* | [+from] *Lucent spun off from AT&T in 1995.* → SPIN-OFF (2)

spin out *phr v*
1 **spin** sth ⇔ **out** *BrE* to make something continue for longer than is necessary; ▪ drag out: *I'm paid by the hour, so I spin the work out as long as I can.*
2 **spin** sth ⇔ **out** *BrE* to use money, food etc as carefully and slowly as possible, because you do not have very much of it: [+over] *I've only got £10 left, so we'll have to spin it out over the whole week.*
3 *AmE* if a car spins out, the driver loses control of it and the car spins around

spin² *n*
1 TURNING [C] an act of turning around quickly: *the Earth's spin* | *The Russian skater finished her routine with a series of spins.*
2 CAR [singular] *informal* a short trip in a car for pleasure; ▪ drive: *Let's go for a spin in the country.* | *Do you want to take my car for a spin?*

3 BALL [U] if you put spin on a ball in a game such as tennis or CRICKET, you deliberately make the ball turn very quickly so that it is difficult for your opponent to hit
4 INFORMATION [singular, U] the way someone, especially a politician or business person, talks about information or a situation, especially in order to influence the way people think about it: *They tried to put a positive spin on the sales figures.* → SPIN DOCTOR
5 AIRCRAFT [singular] if an aircraft goes into a spin, it falls suddenly, turning around and around
6 **in/into a (flat) spin** if you are in a spin, you are very confused and anxious: *The sudden fall on the stock-market sent brokers into a spin.*
7 WET CLOTHES give sth a spin *BrE* to turn clothes around very fast in a machine to remove water from them

spi·na bif·i·da /ˌspaɪnə ˈbɪfɪdə/ *n* [U] a serious condition in which a person's SPINE does not develop correctly before they are born, so that their SPINAL CORD is not protected

spin·ach /ˈspɪnɪdʒ, -ɪtʃ/ *n* [U] a vegetable with large dark green leaves

spin·al /ˈspaɪnl/ *adj* belonging to or affecting your SPINE: *spinal injuries*

spinal column *n* [C] *technical* your SPINE

spinal cord *n* [C] the thick string of nerves enclosed in your SPINE, by which messages are sent to and from your brain

spin·dle /ˈspɪndl/ *n* [C] **1** a part of a machine shaped like a stick, around which something turns **2** a round pointed stick used for twisting the thread when you are spinning wool

spin·dly /ˈspɪndli/ *adj* long and thin in a way that looks weak: *spindly legs*

spin doctor *n* [C] *informal* someone whose job is to give information to the public in a way that gives the best possible advantage to a politician or organization: *White House spin doctors*

spin-ˈdryer *n* [C] *BrE* a machine that removes most of the water from washed clothes by spinning them around and around very fast —**spin-dry** *v* [T]

spine /spaɪn/ *n* **1** [C] the row of bones down the centre of your back that supports your body and protects your SPINAL CORD; ▪ backbone; → spinal; → see picture at SKELETON **2** [C] a stiff sharp point on an animal or plant; → spiny: *cactus spines* **3** [C] the part of a book that the pages are fastened onto **4** [U] courage or determination

spine-ˌchilling *adj* a spine-chilling story or film is very frightening in a way that people enjoy —**spine-chiller** *n* [C]

spine·less /ˈspaɪnləs/ *adj* **1** lacking courage and determination – used to show disapproval: *a bunch of spineless politicians* **2** without a spine

spi·net /spɪˈnet $ ˈspɪnɪt/ *n* [C] **1** a musical instrument of the 16th and 17th centuries, which is played like a piano **2** *AmE* a small UPRIGHT PIANO

spine-ˌtingling *adj* making you feel very excited or frightened, in an enjoyable way: *The festival opened with Nic Roeg's latest spine-tingling film.*

spin·na·ker /ˈspɪnəkə $ -kər/ *n* [C] a sail with three points at the front of a boat, used when the wind is directly behind

spin·ner /ˈspɪnə $ -ər/ *n* [C] **1** someone whose job is to make thread by twisting cotton, wool etc **2** a BOWLER in a game of CRICKET who throws the ball with a spinning action **3** a thing used for catching fish that spins when pulled through the water → see picture at FISHING → MONEY-SPINNER

spin·ney /ˈspɪni/ *n* [C] *BrE* a small area of trees and bushes

S

'spinning wheel n [C] a simple machine consisting of a wheel on a frame that people used in their homes in the past for making cotton, wool etc into thread

'spin-off, spin·off /'spɪnɒf $ -ɒːf/ n [C] **1** a television programme involving characters that were previously in another programme or film **2** a separate and partly independent company that is formed from parts of an existing company, or the action of forming a company in this way **3** an unexpected but useful result of something, that happens in addition to the intended result: *Laser research has had important spin-offs for eye surgery.*

spin·ster /'spɪnstə $ -ər/ n [C] *old-fashioned* an unmarried woman, usually one who is no longer young and seems unlikely to marry

spin·y /'spaɪni/ adj a spiny animal or plant has lots of stiff sharp points; → **spine**: *spiny sea urchins* | *spiny bushes*

spi·ral[1] /'spaɪərəl $ 'spaɪr-/ n [C] **1** a line in the form of a curve that winds around a central point, moving further away from the centre all the time **2** a process, usually a harmful one, in which something gradually but continuously gets worse or better: **in/into a spiral** *Unemployment rose and the city went into a spiral of decline.* | **downward/upward spiral** *The company is in a downward spiral.* **3 inflationary spiral** a situation in which wages and prices rise continuously because the level of INFLATION is high —**spiral** adj

spiral[2] v **spiralled, spiralling** BrE, **spiraled, spiraling** AmE [I] **1** [always + adv/prep] to move in a continuous curve that gets nearer to or further from its central point as it goes round: [+to/around etc] *The damaged plane spiralled to the ground.* **2** if a situation spirals, it gets worse, more violent etc in a way that cannot be controlled: *Crime has spiraled out of control.* **3** if debt or the cost of something spirals, it increases quickly in a way that cannot be controlled —**spiralling** BrE; **spiraling** AmE adj: *the spiralling cost of legal services*

'spiral-bound adj a spiral-bound book or NOTEBOOK has pages that are attached together by a long wire that is twisted around and put through small holes in the sides of the pages

spiral 'notebook n [C] a book in which you write notes, made of pieces of paper that are attached to a wire spiral

spiral 'staircase n [C] a set of stairs arranged in a circular pattern so that they go around a central point as they get higher

spire /spaɪə $ spaɪr/ n [C] a roof that rises steeply to a point on top of a tower, especially on a church; → **steeple**

spir·it[1] S3 W2 /'spɪrət/ n
1 CHARACTER [singular, U] the qualities that make someone live the way they do, and make them different from other people: **in spirit** *I'm 85, but I still feel young in spirit.* | **independent/proud/free etc spirit** (=a person with a particular type of character) *She is a strong and independent spirit.*; → **kindred spirit** at KINDRED[2] (1)
2 HAPPY/SAD spirits [plural] the way someone feels at a particular time, for example if they are happy or sad; → **mood**: **be in good/high spirits** (=be excited and happy) *Seb was still in high spirits after winning the race.* | *His* **spirits** *were so* **low** (=he was so sad) *that he refused to answer his phone.* | **raise/lift sb's spirits** (=make someone happier) *The warm morning sun lifted our spirits.* | *She wrote poetry while she was in the hospital to* **keep** *her* **spirits up** (=keep happy). | **sb's spirits rise/lift/sink** (=they become more or less happy) *My spirits sank when I saw the mess they'd left.*
3 SOUL [C] the part of someone that you cannot see, that consists of the qualities that make up their character, which many people believe continues to live after the person has died; → **soul**: *Although Laurie is dead, I can feel his spirit with me.*

4 NO BODY [C] a creature without a physical body that some people believe exists, such as an ANGEL or a dead person, who has returned to this world and has strange or magical powers; → **ghost**: *an evil spirit*
5 DETERMINATION [U] courage, energy, and determination – use this to show approval: *Sandra is small, but she makes up for it with great spirit.* | *a young team with strong* **fighting spirit** | *When they took away his freedom, they* **broke** *his* **spirit** (=made him lose his courage).
6 ATTITUDE [singular, U] the attitude that you have towards something or while you are doing something: *You've got to approach this meeting in the right spirit.* | [+of] *the spirit of cooperation between the two sides*
7 team/community/public etc spirit a strong feeling of belonging to a particular group and wanting to help them
8 TYPICAL QUALITIES [C usually singular] the set of ideas, beliefs, feelings etc that are typical of a particular period in history, a place, or a group of people: [+of] *Tourism has not destroyed the spirit of Bali.* | **the spirit of the age/times** *His beliefs conflicted with the spirit of the age.*
9 in spirit if you say you will be somewhere in spirit or with someone in spirit, you will not be with them but will be thinking about them: *I can't come to your wedding, but I'll be there in spirit.*
10 get/enter into the spirit (of sth) to start to feel as happy, excited etc as the people around you: *Judith couldn't really enter into the spirit of the occasion.*
11 INTENTION [U] the meaning or qualities that someone intended something to have, especially the meaning that a law or rule was intended to have: *Thoreau believed that his actions were in the spirit of American institutions.* | *Miller's actions may not be actually illegal, but they have violated* **the spirit of the law.** → **the letter of the law** at LETTER[1] (4)
12 the Spirit the HOLY SPIRIT
13 DRINK [C usually plural] **a)** *especially BrE* a strong alcoholic drink such as WHISKY or BRANDY **b)** *BrE* liquid such as alcohol, used for cleaning
14 that's the spirit *spoken* used to express approval of someone's behaviour or attitude
15 when/as the spirit moves you when you feel that you want to do something
16 the spirit is willing (but the flesh is weak) used when saying that you want to do something, but you are too tired or do not feel strong enough – often used humorously

spir·it[2] v *written*
spirit sb/sth **away/off** phr v to take someone or something away quickly and secretly: *After his speech, Jackson was spirited away through a back door.*

spir·it·ed /'spɪrətɪd/ adj **1** having energy and determination – used to show approval: *a spirited and energetic girl* | **spirited defence/debate/discussion etc 2 sweet-spirited/tough-spirited/rebellious-spirited etc** having a particular type of character → **HIGH-SPIRITED, LOW-SPIRITED, MEAN-SPIRITED, PUBLIC-SPIRITED**

spir·it·less /'spɪrətləs/ adj **1** having no energy or determination **2** not cheerful

'spirit ,level n [C] *especially BrE* a tool used for testing whether a surface is level

spir·i·tu·al[1] /'spɪrətʃuəl/ adj **1** relating to your spirit rather than to your body or mind: *Painting helps fill a spiritual need for beauty.* | **spiritual values 2** relating to religion; ▣ **religious**: *Islam was inspired by the teachings of the spiritual leader Mohammed.* **3 sb's spiritual home** a place where you feel you belong because you share the ideas and attitudes of that society —**spiritually** adv

spiritual[2] n [C] a religious song of the type sung originally by African-Americans

spir·i·tu·al·is·m /'spɪrətʃuəlɪzəm/ n [U] the belief that dead people are able to send messages to living people —**spiritualist** n [C]

spir·i·tu·al·i·ty /ˌspɪrɪtʃuˈæləti/ *n* [U] the quality of being interested in religion or religious matters

spit¹ /spɪt/ *v past tense and past participle* **spat** /spæt/ or **spit** *AmE present participle* **spitting**

1 LIQUID FROM YOUR MOUTH [I] to force a small amount of SALIVA (=the liquid in your mouth) out of your mouth: *Nick rolled down his window and spat.* | [+at/on/into] *A group of fans spat on the players as they left the field.*

2 FOOD/DRINK ETC [T] to force something out of your mouth: *Billy stood up slowly, rubbed his jaw, and spat blood.* | **spit sth out** *Diana tasted her martini and quickly spat it out.*

3 RAIN *be spitting BrE* to be raining very lightly; ◨ **drizzle**: *You don't need an umbrella – it's only spitting.*

4 SAY STH *also* **spit out** [T] to say something quickly in a very angry way: *'Shut up,' spat Maria furiously.*

5 **spit it out** *spoken* used to ask someone to tell you something that they seem too frightened or embarrassed to say: *Come on Jean, spit it out!*

6 SMALL PIECES [I,T] to send out small bits of something, for example fire or hot oil, into the air: *A log fire was crackling and spitting in the hearth.*

7 CAT [I] if a cat spits, it makes short angry sounds

8 **be within spitting distance (of sth)** *spoken* to be very close to someone or something

spit up *phr v AmE*
if someone, especially a baby, spits up, they bring a small amount of food or drink up from their stomach out through their mouth: **spit sth ⇔ up** *I was a difficult child, always crying and spitting up my food.* | *On one occasion, our daughter spat up all over him.*

spit² *n* **1** [U] *informal* the watery liquid that is produced in your mouth; ◨ **saliva** **2** [C] a long thin stick that you put through meat so that you can turn it when cooking it over a fire **3** [C] a long narrow piece of land that sticks out into the sea, into a river etc **4** **be the (dead) spit of sb** *BrE spoken* to look exactly like someone else: *Sam is the dead spit of his dad.* **5** **spit and polish** *informal* when something is thoroughly cleaned and polished: *It was Christmas, so Ellen gave the dining room a little extra spit and polish.*

spit·ball /ˈspɪtbɔːl $ -bɒːl/ *n* [C] *AmE* a small piece of paper that children roll into a ball and then spit or throw at each other

spite¹ W3 /spaɪt/ *n* [U]

1 **in spite of sth** without being affected or prevented by something; ◨ **despite**: *We went out in spite of the rain.* | *Kelly loved her husband **in spite of the fact that** he drank too much.*

2 a feeling of wanting to hurt or upset people, for example because you are JEALOUS or think you have been unfairly treated: **out of spite** (=because of spite) *She broke it just out of spite.* | **pure/sheer spite** (=spite and nothing else)

3 **in spite of yourself** if you do something in spite of yourself, you do it although you did not expect or intend to do it: *The picture made her laugh in spite of herself.*

spite² *v* [T only in infinitive] to deliberately annoy or upset someone: *The neighbours throw things over the garden wall **just to spite us**.* → **cut off your nose to spite your face** at CUT OFF (10)

spite·ful /ˈspaɪtfəl/ *adj* deliberately nasty to someone in order to hurt or upset them; ◨ **vicious**: *She was spiteful and unkind, both to Isabel and to her son.* | *a spiteful remark* —**spitefully** *adv*

spitting image *n* **be the spitting image of sb** to look exactly like someone else

spit·tle /ˈspɪtl/ *n* [U] the liquid in your mouth; ◨ **spit**

spit·toon /spɪˈtuːn/ *n* [C] a container that people SPIT into

spiv /spɪv/ *n* [C] *BrE old-fashioned* a man who gets money from small dishonest business deals

splash¹ /splæʃ/ *v* **1** [I] if a liquid splashes, it hits or falls on something and makes a noise: [+against/on/over] *The ocean splashed against the pier.* **2** [T always + adv/prep] to make someone or something wet with a lot of small drops of water or other liquid: **splash sth on/over/with etc sth** *He splashed cold water on his face.* **3** [I] *also* **splash about/around** to make water fly up in the air with a loud noise by hitting it or by moving around in it: *The children were splashing about in the pool.* | [+through] *She ran up the drive, splashing through the puddles.* **4** [T] *informal* if a newspaper or television programme splashes a story or picture on the page or screen, it makes it large and easy to notice: [+across/over] *The gunman's picture was splashed across the front page.*

splash out (sth) *phr v BrE informal* to spend a lot of money on something: [+on] *We splashed out on a new kitchen.* | *Last year Roberts splashed out more than £1 million to buy a new home.*

splash² *n* **1** [C] the sound of a liquid hitting something or being moved around quickly: *Rachel fell into the river with a loud splash.* **2** [C] a mark made by a liquid splashing onto something else: [+of] *There were splashes of paint all over my clothes.* **3** **splash of colour** a small area of bright colour **4** **make a splash** *informal* to do something that gets a lot of public attention: *Russell's new show made a big splash in New York.* **5** [singular] a small amount of liquid added to a drink: [+of] *a cup of coffee with a splash of brandy*

splash·back /ˈsplæʃbæk/ *n* [C] *BrE* the area of a bathroom or kitchen wall that is behind the TAPS and covered in TILES

splash·down /ˈsplæʃdaʊn/ *n* [C,U] a landing by a spacecraft in the sea

splash guard *n* [C] *AmE* a flat piece of rubber hanging behind the wheel of a vehicle to prevent mud being thrown up

splash·y /ˈsplæʃi/ *adj* big, bright, or very easy to notice; ◨ **flashy**: *a splashy orange shirt*

splat¹ /splæt/ *n* [singular] *informal* a noise like something wet hitting a surface hard

splat² *v* **splatted, splatting** [I,T] to make a noise like something wet hitting a surface, or to make something make this noise: *Big raindrops splatted against the windscreen.*

splat·ter /ˈsplætə $ -ər/ *v* [I always + adv/prep, T] if liquid splatters somewhere, or if someone splatters it, it falls or is thrown onto a surface; ◨ **spatter**: **splatter sth with sth** *The room was splattered with blood.* | [+over/across] *Paint splattered all over the carpet.*

splay /spleɪ/ *also* **splay out** *v* [I,T] to spread apart widely, or to make things do this, especially parts of the body: *He sat with his legs splayed out in front of him.*

spleen /spliːn/ *n* **1** [C] an organ near your stomach that controls the quality of your blood **2** [U] *formal* anger, especially unreasonable or unfair anger: *Obviously you're annoyed, but that doesn't give you the right to **vent your spleen** on me* (=get angry with me).

splen·did /ˈsplendɪd/ *adj especially BrE* **1** *old-fashioned* very good; ◨ **excellent**: *a splendid idea* | *a splendid opportunity* | *The staff are doing a splendid job.* **2** beautiful and impressive; ◨ **magnificent**: *All the rooms have splendid views.* | *a splendid cathedral* **3** *BrE spoken old-fashioned* used to show that you approve of or are pleased by something; ◨ **great**: *'I'll see you tomorrow then.' 'Splendid!'* **4** **in splendid isolation** used to emphasize that something is not with other things: *The house sits in splendid isolation on top of a steep hill.* —**splendidly** *adv*: *a splendidly equipped new sports centre* | *The team played splendidly.*

splen·dour *BrE*; **splendor** *AmE* /ˈsplendə $ -ər/ *n* **1** [U] impressive beauty, especially of a large building or large place: [+of] *We marvelled at the splendour of the scenery.* | *The palace has now been restored to its original splendour.* **2** **splendours** [plural] impressive beautiful features, especially of a large building or place: [+of] *the splendours of the imperial court*

S

sple·net·ic /splɪˈnetɪk/ *adj formal* bad-tempered and often angry

splice[1] /splaɪs/ *v* [T] **1** to join the ends of two pieces of rope, film etc so that they form one continuous piece **2** **get spliced** *BrE informal* to get married

splice[2] *n* [C] the act of joining the ends of two things together, or the place where this join has been made

splic·er /ˈsplaɪsə $ -ər/ *n* [C] a machine for joining pieces of film or recording tape neatly together

spliff /splɪf/ *n* [C] *BrE informal* a cigarette containing CANNABIS; ▤ **joint**

splint /splɪnt/ *n* [C] a flat piece of wood, metal etc used for keeping a broken bone in position while it mends

splin·ter[1] /ˈsplɪntə $ -ər/ *n* [C] a small sharp piece of wood, glass, or metal, that has broken off a larger piece: *I've got a splinter in my finger.* | [+of] *splinters of glass* —**splintery** *adj*

splinter[2] *v* [I,T] **1** if something such as wood splinters, or if you splinter it, it breaks into thin sharp pieces **2** to separate into smaller groups or parts, or to make a group or organization do this, especially because of a disagreement: [+into] *The once-powerful communist party has splintered into hundreds of pieces.*

'splinter group *n* [C] a group of people that have separated from a political or religious organization because they have different ideas

split[1] ⟨S2⟩ ⟨W3⟩ /splɪt/ *v past tense and past participle* **split**, *present participle* **splitting**
1 DISAGREE [I,T] if a group of people splits, or if it is split, people in the group disagree strongly with each other and the group sometimes divides into separate smaller groups: *It was feared that the issue would split the church.* | **be split on/over sth** *The party is split over the issue of immigration.* | *The government appears* **deeply split** *on this issue.* | *The Pan-Africanist Congress split from the ANC in 1959.* | **split sth in two/down the middle** *The war has split the nation in two.*
2 SEPARATE INTO PARTS also **split up** [I,T] to divide or separate something into different parts or groups, or to be divided into different parts or groups: [+into] *Can you split into groups of three now?* | **split sth into sth** *The book is split into six sections.*
3 BREAK OR TEAR [I,T] if something splits, or if you split it, it tears or breaks along a straight line: *The branch split under their weight.* | *One of the boxes had* **split open**. | **split (sth) in two/half** *The board had split in two.* | *Split the pineapple* **down the middle**.
4 SHARE [T] to divide something into separate parts and share it between two or more people: **split sth between sb/sth** *Profits will be split between three major charities.* | **split sth with sb** *He agreed to sell the car and split the proceeds with his brother.* | **split sth three/four etc ways** (=share something between three, four etc people or groups) *The money will have to be split three ways.* | *We agreed to* **split the cost**.
5 INJURE [T] to make someone's head or lip have a cut in it, as a result of a fall or hit: *She fell against a table and* **split her lip**. | *The force of the blow nearly* **split his head open**.
6 END RELATIONSHIP also **split up** [I] *informal* if people split, they end a marriage or relationship with each other: [+with/from] *He split from his wife last year.* | *The band split two years ago.*
7 LEAVE [I] *old-fashioned informal* to leave a place quickly: *Come on – let's split.*
8 **split hairs** to argue that there is a difference between two things, when the difference is really too small to be important: *This is just splitting hairs.*
9 **split the difference** to agree on an amount that is exactly between two amounts that have been mentioned: *OK, let's split the difference, and I'll give you £20.*
10 **split your sides** *informal* to laugh a great deal
split off *phr v*
1 also **split away** if one part of something splits off

from the rest, it becomes completely separate from it: [+from] *A huge lump of rock had split off from the cliff face.*
2 also **split away** if a small group of people split off from a larger group, they become separate from it: [+from] *The group split away from the Green Party and formed the Environmental Alliance.*
3 **split sth** ⇔ **off** to separate one part of something and make it completely separate from the rest: [+from] *This part of the business has now been split off from the main company.*
split on *sb phr v BrE informal*
to tell someone in authority about something wrong that someone else has done: *Don't you dare split on us!*
split up *phr v*
1 if people split up, or if someone splits them up, they end a marriage or relationship with each other: *Steve's parents split up when he was four.* | [+with] *I thought she'd split up with her boyfriend.* | **split sb** ⇔ **up** *Why would she try to split us up?*
2 to divide people into different groups, or to be divided into groups: *Please don't split up when we get to the museum.* | **split sth/sb** ⇔ **up** *The teacher split up the class into three groups.*
3 **split sth** ⇔ **up** to divide something into different parts: [+into] *The house has now been split up into individual flats.*

split

splitting a pack of cards

splitting logs

doing the splits

split[2] *n* [C]
1 TEAR a tear or crack in something made of cloth, wood etc: [+in] *a long split in the sleeve of his coat*
2 DISAGREEMENT a serious disagreement that divides an organization or group of people into smaller groups; ▤ **rift**: [+in/within] *The argument could lead to a damaging split in the party.* | *a deep split within the government* | [+between] *a split between the radicals and the moderates within the group* | [+over] *The union is desperate to avoid a split over this issue.*
3 DIVIDING STH the way in which something, especially money, is shared between several people: *In a publishing deal, the average split used to be 50:50 between writer and publisher.* | **three-way/four-way etc split** (=when something is shared equally between three, four etc people) *a three-way split in the profits*
4 SEPARATION *informal* a clear separation or difference between two things: [+between] *the traditional split between the state and church*
5 **do the splits** to spread your legs wide apart so that your legs touch the floor along their whole length

split 'ends *n* [plural] a condition of someone's hair in which the ends have split into several parts

split in'finitive *n* [C] a phrase in which you put an adverb or other word between 'to' and a verb, as in 'to easily win'. Some people think this is incorrect English.

split-'level *adj* a split-level house, room, or building has floors at different heights in different parts

split per'sonality *n* [C] a condition in which someone has two very different ways of behaving

split 'screen *n* [C] a method of showing different scenes or pieces of information at the same time on a film, television, or computer screen: *a split-screen movie*

split 'second *n* an extremely short period of time: **for a split second** *For a split second the two men hesitated.* | **in a split second** *In that split second Graham* *knew he had won.* —**split-second** *adj*: *It was a technique which required split-second timing.*

split 'shift *n* [C] a period of work that is divided into two or more parts on the same day

split 'ticket *n* [C] a vote in US elections in which the voter has voted for some CANDIDATES of one party and some of the other party —**split-ticket** *adj*: *split-ticket voting*

split·ting /'splɪtɪŋ/ *adj* **splitting headache** a very bad HEADACHE

splodge /splɒdʒ $ splɑːdʒ/ *n* [C] *BrE informal* a large mark of mud, paint etc with an irregular shape; **◼** blotch: [+of] *splodges of colour* —**splodgy** *adj*

splosh /splɒʃ $ splɑːʃ/ *v* [I always + adv/prep] *BrE informal* to make a noise by falling into or moving through water; **◼** splash: *a sploshing sound* —**splosh** *n* [C]

splotch /splɒtʃ $ splɑːtʃ/ *n* [C] a SPLODGE

splurge /splɜːdʒ $ splɜːrdʒ/ *v* [I,T] *informal* to spend more money than you can usually afford; **◼** splash out: **splurge (sth) on sth** *Within a couple of months I'd splurged about £2,500 on clothes.* —**splurge** *n* [C]

splut·ter /'splʌtə $ -ər/ *v* **1** [I,T] to talk quickly in short confused phrases, especially because you are angry or surprised; **◼** : *'But ... but ... I can't believe... how could you?' she spluttered.* | [+with] *Katie was spluttering with rage.* **2** [I] to make a series of short sharp noises: *Bill started coughing and spluttering.* | *The engine spluttered into life.* —**splutter** *n* [C]

spoil¹ /spɔɪl/ *v past tense and past participle* **spoiled** *also* **spoilt** /spɔɪlt/ *BrE*
1 DAMAGE [T] to have a bad effect on something so that it is no longer attractive, enjoyable, useful etc; **◼** ruin: *The whole park is spoiled by litter.* | *We didn't let the incident spoil our day.* | *I don't want to spoil your fun.* | *Why do you always have to spoil everything?* → **spoil/ruin your appetite** at APPETITE (1); → see box at DESTROY
2 TREAT TOO KINDLY [T] to give a child everything they want, or let them do whatever they want, often with the result that they behave badly: *She's an only child, but they didn't really spoil her.* | *His mother and sisters spoil him rotten* (=spoil him very much).
3 TREAT KINDLY [T] to look after someone in a way that is very kind or too kind: *You'll have to let me spoil you on your birthday.* | **spoil yourself** *Go on, spoil yourself. Have another piece of cake.*
4 DECAY [I] to start to decay: *Food will spoil if the temperature in your freezer rises above 8 ° C.*
5 VOTING [T] *BrE* to mark a BALLOT PAPER wrongly so that your vote is not included
6 **be spoiling for a fight/argument** to be very eager to fight or argue with someone

spoil² *n* **1** **spoils** [plural] *formal* **a)** the things that someone gets by being successful: *They tried to take more than a fair share of the spoils.* **b)** things taken by an army from a defeated enemy, or things taken by thieves: **the spoils of war/victory etc** **2** [U] waste material such as earth and stones from a mine or hole in the ground: *spoil heaps*

spoil·age /'spɔɪlɪdʒ/ *n* [U] *technical* waste resulting from something being spoiled

spoiled /spɔɪld/ *also* **spoilt** *BrE adj* **1** a spoiled person, especially a child, is rude and behaves badly because they have always been given what they want and allowed to do what they want: *Ben was a spoilt brat* (=a spoiled and unpleasant child). | *Their children were spoiled rotten* (=very spoiled). **2** **be spoilt/ spoiled for choice** *BrE* to have so many good things to choose from that you cannot decide which one to choose

spoil·er /'spɔɪlə $ -ər/ *n* [C]
1 CAR A raised part on a racing car that prevents the car from lifting off the road at high speeds
2 PLANE part of an aircraft wing that can be lifted up to slow the plane down

3 PREVENT SUCCESS someone or something that prevents another person or thing from being successful
4 TEAM *AmE* a person or team that spoils another's winning record
5 SURPRISE a message or report that is intended to ruin the surprising part of a popular film, book etc by telling people about the surprise before they see or read it

spoil·sport /'spɔɪlspɔːt $ -spɔːrt/ *n* [C] *informal* someone who spoils other people's fun: *Don't be such a spoilsport.*

spoilt /spɔɪlt/ *adj* a British form of the word SPOILED

spoke¹ /spəʊk $ spoʊk/ the past tense of SPEAK

spoke² *n* [C] **1** one of the thin metal bars which connect the outer ring of a wheel to the centre, especially on a bicycle → see picture at BICYCLE **2** **put a spoke in sb's wheel** *BrE* to prevent someone from doing something they have planned

spok·en¹ /'spəʊkən $ 'spoʊ-/ the past participle of SPEAK

spoken² *adj* **1** **spoken English/language etc** the form of language that you speak rather than write; → **written** **2** **the spoken word** spoken language rather than written language or music: *pupils' understanding of the spoken word* | *a spoken-word CD* **3** **quietly/ softly-spoken** *BrE* speaking in a quiet way: *a softly spoken young man* **4** **be spoken for a)** if someone is spoken for, they are married or already have a serious relationship with someone **b)** if something is spoken for, you cannot buy it because it is being kept for someone else → WELL-SPOKEN

spokes·man W2 /'spəʊksmən $ 'spoʊks-/ *n plural* **spokesmen** /-mən/ [C] a man who has been chosen to speak officially for a group, organization, or government; → **spokesperson**: *a White House spokesman* | [+for] *a spokesman for the victims' families*

spokes·per·son /'spəʊks,pɜːsən $ 'spoʊks,pɜːr-/ *n plural* **spokespeople** /-,piːpəl/ [C] a spokesman or spokeswoman

spokes·wom·an /'spəʊks,wʊmən $ 'spoʊks-/ *n plural* **spokeswomen** /-,wɪmɪn/ [C] a woman who has been chosen to speak officially for a group, organization, or government

sponge¹ /spʌndʒ/ *n* **1** [C,U] a piece of a soft natural or artificial substance full of small holes, which can suck up liquid and is used for washing **2** [C] a simple sea creature from which natural sponge is produced **3** [singular] *BrE* an act of washing something with a sponge **4** [C,U] *BrE* a light cake made from flour, sugar, butter, and eggs: *a Victoria sponge* **5** [C] a SPONGER

sponge² *v* **1** *also* **sponge down** [T] to wash something with a wet cloth or sponge: *Clean the rug by sponging it gently.* | *She stood on the bathmat and sponged herself down.* **2** [I] *informal* to get money, free meals etc from other people, without doing anything for them – used to show disapproval: [+off/on] *These people are just sponging off the taxpayers.* **3** [T always + adv/prep] to remove liquid or a mark with a wet cloth or sponge: **sponge sth off (sth)** *I'll go and sponge this juice off my dress.* **4** [T] to put paint on a surface using a sponge: **sponge sth on (sth)** *Just sponge the paint on, like this.*

sponge bag *n* [C] *BrE* a small bag for carrying the things that you need to wash with

sponge cake *n* [C,U] a light cake made from flour, sugar, butter, and eggs

sponge 'pudding *n* [C] *BrE* a British food made from flour, sugar, eggs, and butter which is eaten hot

spon·ger /'spʌndʒə $ -ər/ *n* [C] someone who gets money, free meals etc from other people and does nothing for them – used to show disapproval

S

spong·y /'spʌndʒi/ *adj* soft and full of holes that contain air or liquid like a SPONGE¹ (1): *The earth was soft and spongy underfoot.* —**sponginess** *n* [U]

spon·sor¹ /'spɒnsə $ 'spɑːnsər/ *n* [C] **1 a)** a person or company that pays for a show, broadcast, sports event etc especially in exchange for the right to advertise at that event: [+of] *Eastman Kodak is a major sponsor of the Olympics.* | *corporate sponsors* **b)** a person or company that supports someone by paying for their training, education, living costs etc **2** someone who agrees to give someone else money for a CHARITY if they walk, run etc a particular distance **3** someone who officially introduces or supports a proposal for a new law **4** someone who officially agrees to help someone else, or to be responsible for what they do: *You cannot get a work visa without an American sponsor.* **5** a GODPARENT

sponsor² *v* [T] **1 a)** to give money to a sports event, theatre, institution etc, especially in exchange for the right to advertise: *The competition was sponsored by British Airways.* | *government-sponsored projects* **b)** to support someone by paying for their training, education, living costs etc: *The bank had offered to sponsor him at university.* **2** to officially support a proposal for a new law **3** to agree to help someone or be responsible for what they do **4** to agree to give someone money for CHARITY if they walk, run etc a particular distance **5** *sponsored walk/swim etc BrE* an event in which many people walk, swim etc a particular distance so that people will give them money for a CHARITY **6** *UN-sponsored/US-sponsored/government-sponsored etc* supported and encouraged by the UN, the US etc: *US-sponsored peace talks*

spon·sor·ship /'spɒnsəʃɪp $ 'spɑːnsər-/ *n* **1** [plural, U] financial support for an activity or event: [+from] *The expedition is looking for sponsorship from one of the major banks.* | *a $5 million sponsorship deal* | *commercial sponsorships* **2** [U] the act of sponsoring someone or something, or of being sponsored: [+of] *private sector sponsorship of sport*

spon·ta·ne·ous /spɒn'teɪniəs $ spɑːn-/ *adj* **1** something that is spontaneous has not been planned or organized, but happens by itself, or because you suddenly feel you want to do it: *The crowd gave a spontaneous cheer.* | *My spontaneous reaction was to run away.* **2** someone who is spontaneous does things without planning them first – used to show approval —**spontaneously** *adv*: *She laughed spontaneously.* —**spontaneity** /ˌspɒnt'niː ̩ti, -'neɪ ̩ti $ ˌspɑːn-/ *n* [U]

spon ̩taneous com'bustion *n* [U] burning caused by chemical changes inside something rather than by heat from outside

spoof /spuːf/ *n* [C] a funny book, play, or film that copies something serious or important and makes it seem silly; → **take-off**: [+of/on] *The play is a spoof on Shakespeare's tragedy 'Julius Caesar'.* | *a spoof documentary* —**spoof** *v* [T]

spook¹ /spuːk/ *n* [C] *informal* **1** a GHOST **2** *especially AmE* a SPY

spook² *v* [T] *informal* to frighten someone: *I'm not easily spooked.*

spook·y /'spuːki/ *adj informal* strange or frightening in a way that makes you think of GHOSTS: *a spooky old house* | *spooky stories* | *The candlelight created a rather spooky atmosphere.*

spool /spuːl/ *n* [C] an object shaped like a wheel that you wind thread, wire etc around

spoon¹ /spuːn/ *n* [C] **1** an object that you use for eating, cooking, or serving food. It has a small bowl-shaped part and a long handle → see picture at MULTI-PURPOSE **2** a SPOONFUL: [+of] *two spoons of sugar* → *be born with a silver spoon in your mouth* at BORN² (8); → DESSERTSPOON, GREASY SPOON, SOUP SPOON, WOODEN SPOON

spoon² *v* [T always + adv/prep] to move food with a spoon: *spoon sth into/over/onto sth Spoon the mixture carefully into the bowls.*

spoo·ner·is·m /'spuːnərɪzəm/ *n* [C] a phrase in which the speaker accidentally exchanges the first sounds of two words, with a funny result, for example 'sew you to a sheet' instead of 'show you to a seat'

'spoon-feed *v past tense and past participle* **spoon-fed** [T] **1** to give too much information and help to someone – used to show disapproval: *I don't believe in spoon-feeding students.* **2** to feed someone, especially a baby, with a spoon

spoon·ful /'spuːnful/ *n* [C] the amount that a spoon will hold: [+of] *Two spoonfuls of sugar, please.*

spoor /spɔː, spʊə $ spɔːr, spʊr/ *n* [singular, U] *technical* the track of footmarks or solid waste that a wild animal leaves as it moves along

spo·rad·ic /spə'rædɪk/ *adj* happening fairly often, but not regularly; ▤ **intermittent**: *There has been sporadic violence downtown.* —**sporadically** /-kli/ *adv*: *The fighting continued sporadically for several days.*

spore /spɔː $ spɔːr/ *n* [C] a cell like a seed that is produced by some plants such as MUSHROOMS and can develop into a new plant

spor·ran /'spɒrən $ 'spɔː-, 'spɑː-/ *n* [C] a special bag made of leather or fur, that a Scotsman wears in front of a KILT

sport¹ [S2] [W2] /spɔːt $ spɔːrt/ *n*
1 [GAMES] **a)** [C] a physical activity in which people compete against each other: *My favourite sports are tennis and swimming.* | *a sports team* | *a sports club* | *I've been playing sports all my life.* | *All students are encouraged to take part in a sport.* | *a sports field* | *He picked up the newspaper and turned to the sports pages.* | *They have excellent sports facilities.* | *A lot of schools don't really encourage team sports.* | *Football is one of the most popular spectator sports* (=sports watched by a lot of people). **b)** [U] *BrE* sports in general: *Why is there so much sport on TV?* | *I always hated sport at school.* ⚠ *The uncountable use of* **sport** *is British English only: There's too much sport on TV. In American English, the plural* **sports** *is used: He likes watching sports on TV.*

2 [HUNTING] [C] an activity that people do in the countryside, especially hunting or fishing: *the sport of falconry* | *a demonstration by people opposed to blood sports* (=sports that involve killing animals)

3 [HELPFUL PERSON] [C usually singular] also **good sport** *old-fashioned* a helpful cheerful person who lets you enjoy yourself: *be a sport* (=used when asking someone to help you) *Be a sport and lend me your bike.*

4 *a good sport* someone who does not get angry when they lose at a game or sport

5 *a bad/poor sport* someone who gets angry very easily when they lose at a game or sport

6 [MAN/BOY] *spoken* **a)** *AusE* used when speaking to someone, especially a man, in a friendly way: *See you later, sport.* **b)** *AmE old-fashioned* used when speaking to a boy in a friendly way

7 [FUN] [U] *old-fashioned* fun or amusement: *Did she torment him merely for sport?*

8 *make sport of sb old-fashioned* to joke about someone in a way that makes them seem stupid → FIELD SPORTS, WATER SPORTS, WINTER SPORTS

sport² *v* **1** *be sporting sth* to be wearing something or have something on your body and show it to people in a proud way: *Eric was sporting a new camel-hair coat.* **2** [I] *literary* to play together happily: *the sight of dolphins sporting amidst the waves*

'sport coat *n* [C] *AmE* a SPORTS JACKET

sport·ing /'spɔːtɪŋ $ 'spɔːr-/ *adj* **1** [only before noun] relating to sports: *The college offers a wide range of sporting activities.* | *one of the major sporting events of the year* | *a great sporting achievement* | *Britain's sporting heroes* | *sporting goods AmE: a sporting goods store* **2** *BrE* someone who is sporting behaves in a fair and generous way during a game or competition and

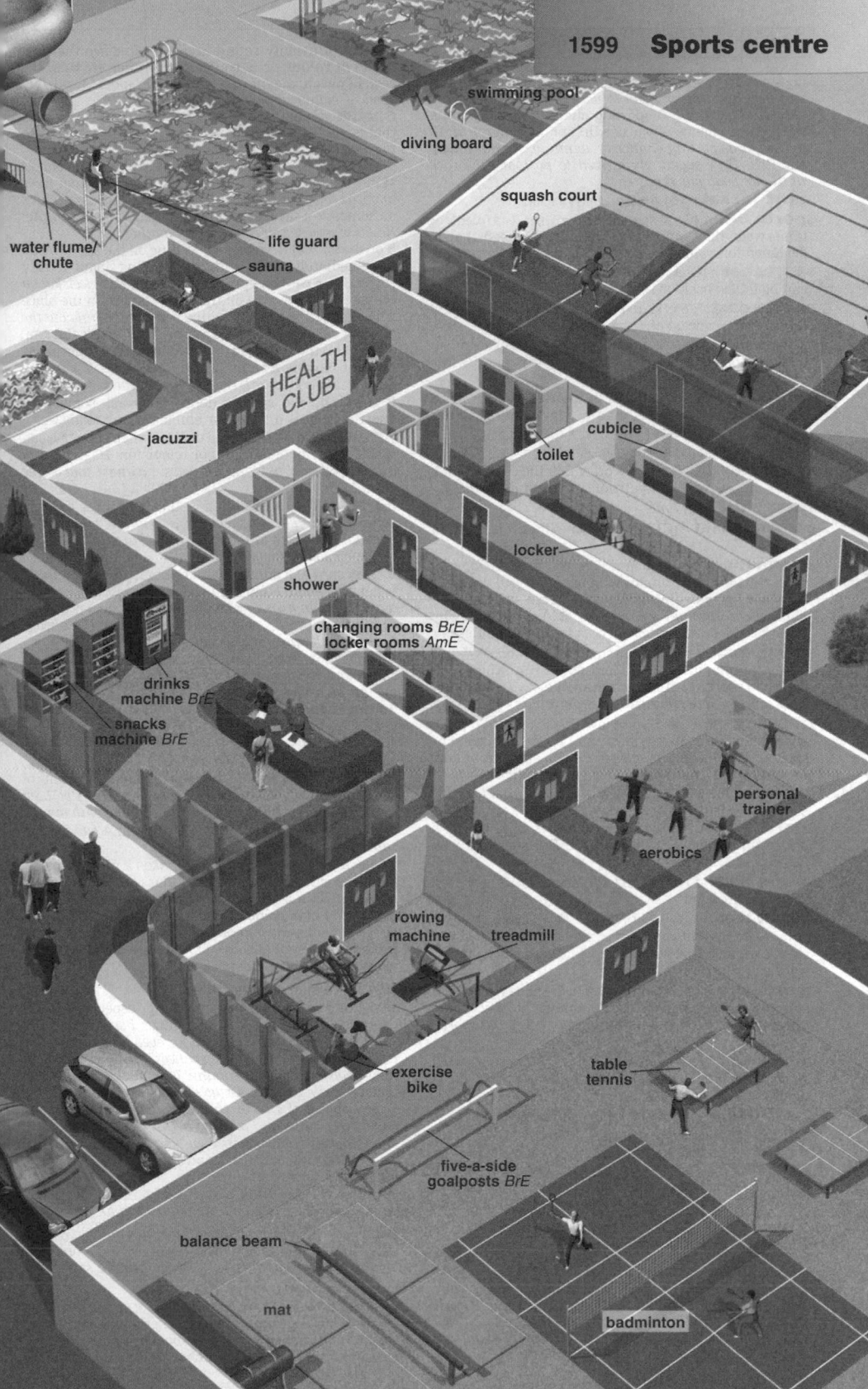

swimming pool

diving board

squash court

water flume/
chute

life guard

sauna

HEALTH
CLUB

jacuzzi

cubicle

toilet

locker

shower

changing rooms *BrE*/
locker rooms *AmE*

drinks
machine *BrE*

snacks
machine *BrE*

personal
trainer

aerobics

rowing
machine

treadmill

exercise
bike

table
tennis

five-a-side
goalposts *BrE*

balance beam

mat

badminton

does not try to win in an unfair way; ◆ **unsporting**: *It was very sporting of them to wait until the rest of our team had arrived.* **3 sporting chance (of doing sth)** a fairly good chance of succeeding or winning: *I think we've got a sporting chance of winning.* —**sportingly** *adv BrE*: *They sportingly agreed to postpone the race until our boat was repaired.*

'sport jacket *n* [C] *AmE* a SPORTS JACKET

'sports bra *n* [C] a special type of BRA (=a piece of underwear that supports a woman's breasts) that is designed for women to wear while playing sports

'sports car *n* [C] a low fast car, often with a roof that can be folded back or removed

'sports·cast /'spɔːtskɑːst $ 'spɔːrtskæst/ *n* [C] *AmE* a television broadcast of a sports game

'sports·cast·er /'spɔːts,kɑːstə $ 'spɔːrts,kæstər/ *n* [C] *AmE* someone who describes a sports game as it is being broadcast on television

'sports ,centre *BrE*; **sports center** *AmE n* [C] a building where people can go to play many different types of indoor sports

'sports coat *n* [C] a SPORTS JACKET

'sports day *n* [C] *BrE* a day on which the children at a school have sports competitions; ◆ **field day** *AmE*

'sport shirt *n* [C] *AmE* a SPORTS SHIRT

'sports ,jacket *n* [C] a man's jacket that is not part of a suit

sports·man /'spɔːtsmən $ 'spɔːrts-/ *n plural* **sportsmen** /-mən/ [C] **1** a man who plays several different sports; ◆ **sportswoman**: *He's a very keen sportsman.* | *a talented all-round sportsman* **2** *AmE* a man who enjoys outdoor activities such as hunting and fishing

sports·man·like /'spɔːtsmənlaɪk $ 'spɔːrts-/ *adj* behaving in a fair, honest, and polite way when competing in sports; ◆ **unsportsmanlike**: *As a club, we try to encourage sportsmanlike behaviour.*

sports·man·ship /'spɔːtsmənʃɪp $ 'spɔːrts-/ *n* [U] behaviour that is fair, honest, and polite in a game or sports competition: *His sportsmanship and style of play is refreshing.* | **good/bad/poor sportsmanship** (=good or bad behaviour in a sport) *We try to teach the kids good sportsmanship.*

sports·per·son /'spɔːts,pɜːsən $ 'spɔːrts,pɜːr-/ *n plural* **sportspeople** /-,piːpəl/ [C] *BrE* someone who takes part in sports or a sport

'sports shirt *n* [C] a shirt for men that is worn on informal occasions

sports·wear /'spɔːtsweə $ 'spɔːrtswer/ *n* [U] **1** clothes that you wear to play sports or when you are relaxing **2** *AmE* clothes that are suitable for informal occasions

sports·wom·an /'spɔːts,wʊmən $ 'spɔːrts-/ *n plural* **sportswomen** /-,wɪmɪn/ [C] a woman who plays many different sports; ◆ **sportsman**: *great all-round sportswoman*

sports·writ·er /'spɔːts,raɪtə $ 'spɔːrts,raɪtər/ *n* [C] someone whose job is to write about sports for a newspaper or magazine

,sport-u'tility ,vehicle *n* [C] *AmE* an SUV

sport·y /'spɔːti $ 'spɔːrti/ *adj informal* **1** especially *BrE* someone who is sporty likes sport and is good at it; ◆ **athletic** **2** sporty clothes are designed to look attractive in a bright informal way: *a sporty jacket and skirt* **3** a sporty car is designed to look attractive and go fast: *The new model is slightly more sporty.*

spot¹ S2 W2 /spɒt $ spɑːt/ *n* [C]

1 PLACE a particular place or area, especially a pleasant place where you spend time: *a nice quiet spot on the beach* | *I chose a spot well away from the road.* | **in a spot** *a small cottage in an idyllic spot* | **on a spot** *Why do they want to build a house on this particular spot?* | **the exact/same/very spot** *the exact spot where the king was executed* | **[+for]** *an ideal spot for a picnic*

2 AREA a usually round area on a surface that is a different colour or is rougher, smoother etc than the rest; ◆ **patch**: *a white cat with brown spots* | **[+of]** *Two spots of colour appeared in Jill's cheeks.*

3 MARK a small mark on something, especially one that is made by a liquid: *There was a big damp spot on the wall.* | **[+of]** *a few spots of blood*

4 ON SKIN a) a small round red area on someone's skin that shows that they are ill: *He had a high fever and was covered in spots.* **b)** *BrE* a small raised red mark on someone's skin, especially on their face; ◆ **pimple**: *Becka was very self-conscious about her spots.*

5 on the spot a) if you do something on the spot, you do it immediately, often without thinking about it very carefully; → **on-the-spot**: *He had to make a decision on the spot.* **b)** if you are on the spot, you are in the place where something is happening: *We ought to find out the views of the people on the spot.* **c)** *BrE* if you walk, run, or jump on the spot, you do it staying in the same place, without moving around; ◆ **in place** *AmE*: *If running outside doesn't appeal, try jogging on the spot indoors.*

6 put sb on the spot to deliberately ask someone a question that is difficult or embarrassing to answer

7 TV/RADIO a short period of time when someone can speak or perform on radio or television: *He was given a 30-second spot just after the news.* | *a guest spot on the Tonight Show*

8 POSITION a position in a list of things or in a competition: *The budget has a regular spot on the agenda.* | **in a spot** *Manchester United are still in the top spot after today's win.*

9 weak spot a) a point at which someone or something is not very good: *I carried on with my questions, sensing a weak spot in his story.* **b)** *AmE* if someone has a weak spot for something, they like it very much: *I've always had a weak spot for chocolate.*

10 tight spot *informal* a difficult situation: *This puts the chairman in a very tight spot.* | *I hope you can help get me out of a tight spot.*

11 bright spot something that is good in a bad situation: *The computer industry is the one bright spot in the economy at the moment.* | *The only bright spot of the evening was when the food arrived.*

12 a spot of sth *BrE informal* a small amount of something: *Do you fancy a spot of lunch?* | *I've been having a spot of bother* (=some problems) *with my car.*

13 spots of rain *BrE* a few drops of rain: *A few spots of rain began to fall.*

14 five-spot/ten-spot etc *AmE spoken* a piece of paper money worth five dollars, ten dollars etc → BEAUTY SPOT, BLACKSPOT, BLIND SPOT; → **change your spots** at CHANGE¹ (16); → G-SPOT; → **high point/spot** at HIGH¹ (12); → **hit the spot** at HIT¹ (28); → HOT SPOT; → **knock spots off** at KNOCK¹ (19); → **be rooted to the spot** at ROOT² (5); → **have a soft spot for sb** at SOFT (16); → TROUBLE SPOT

spot² S3 *v* **spotted, spotting** [T]

1 to notice someone or something, especially when they are difficult to see or recognize: *I spotted a police car behind us.* | *It can be hard for even a trained doctor to spot the symptoms of lung cancer.* | **spot sb doing sth** *Meg spotted someone coming out of the building.* | **difficult/easy to spot** *Drug addicts are fairly easy to spot.* | **spot that** *One of the station staff spotted that I was in difficulty, and came to help.*

2 be spotted with sth to have small round marks or small pieces of something on the surface: *The windscreen was spotted with rain.*

3 *AmE* to give the other player in a game an advantage: **spot sb sth** *He spotted me six points and he still won.*

spot³ *adj* [only before noun] for buying or paying immediately, not at some future time: *They won't take credit; they want spot cash.* | *He quoted us a spot price for the goods.*

,spot 'check *n* [C] an examination of a few things or people from a group, to check whether everything is correct or satisfactory: **[+on]** *spot checks on quality* | **make/do/carry out etc spot checks** *We carry out spot*

checks on the vehicles before they leave the depot.
—'**spot check** v [T]: *We spot check everyone's work.*

spot·less /'spɒtləs $ 'spɑːt-/ *adj* **1** completely clean;
→ **pristine**: *a spotless white handkerchief* | *The house
was bright and absolutely spotless.* **2** if someone has
a spotless REPUTATION or record, people know or think
they have never done anything bad: *a company whose
reputation was spotless until this scandal broke*
—**spotlessly** *adv*: *The whole house was spotlessly
clean.*

spot·light¹ /'spɒtlaɪt $ 'spɑːt-/ *n* **1** [C] a light with a
very bright beam which can be directed at someone or
something. Spotlights are often used to light a stage
when actors or singers are performing: *The yard was
lit by three huge spotlights.* | **under the spotlights** *I was
sweating under the spotlights.* | **in/into the spotlight** *She
stepped into the spotlight and began to sing.* **2 the
spotlight** a lot of attention in newspapers, on television
etc: **in/under the spotlight** *Education is once again
under the spotlight.* | **put/turn the spotlight on sth** *A
new report has turned the spotlight on the problem of
poverty in the inner cities.*

spotlight² *v past tense and past participle* **spot-
lighted** *or* **spotlit** [T] **1** to direct attention to someone
or something, ◨ **highlight**: *The article spotlights the
problems of the homeless.* **2** to shine a strong beam of
light on something: *She walked out onto the spotlit
stage.*

spot-'on *adj BrE informal* exactly right: *Judith is
always spot-on with her advice.*

spot·ted /'spɒtɪd $ 'spɑː-/ *adj* [usually before noun]
having small round marks of a different colour on the
surface: *a red and white spotted blouse*

spotted 'dick *n* [U] a sweet food eaten in Britain, that
is like a cake containing dried fruit, and is eaten hot at
the end of a meal

spot·ter /'spɒtə $ 'spɑːtər/ *n* [C] **1 bird/train etc
spotter** *BrE* someone who spends time watching birds,
trains etc for pleasure and writes down the things that
they see **2** someone whose job is to look for or notice
a particular type of thing: *Football clubs send spotters
to look for young talent.* | **weather spotter** *AmE*

spot·ting /'spɒtɪŋ $ 'spɑː-/ *n* [U] **bird-spotting/train-
spotting etc** *BrE* the activity of watching birds, trains
etc for pleasure

spot·ty /'spɒti $ 'spɑːti/ *adj* **1** *BrE informal* someone
who is spotty has small raised red marks on their skin,
especially on their face: *a tall, thin, spotty youth* | *a
spotty face* **2** *AmE* good only in some parts, but not in
other parts; ◨ **patchy** *BrE*

spouse /spaʊs, spaʊz/ *n* [C] *formal* a husband or wife:
Spouses were invited to the company picnic. —**spousal**
/'spaʊzəl/ *adj*: *spousal abuse*

spout¹ /spaʊt/ *n* [C] **1** a small pipe on the side of a
container that you pour liquid out through **2 spout of
water/blood etc** a sudden strong stream of liquid
which comes out of somewhere very fast → **WATERSPOUT**
(1) **3 up the spout** *BrE informal* if something is up the
spout, it is completely wrong or has failed completely:
The computer's up the spout! | *My plans for the weekend
seem to have gone up the spout.*

spout² *v* **1 a)** [I always + adv/prep] if liquid or fire
spouts from somewhere, it comes out very quickly in a
powerful stream; ◨ **spurt**: [+from] *Blood was spouting
from the wound in her arm.* **b)** [T] to send out liquid or
flames very quickly in a powerful stream: *a volcano
spouting lava* **2** also **spout off** [I,T] *informal* to talk a lot
about something in a boring or annoying way: *My
father was spouting his usual nonsense! | I hate it when
he spouts off like that!* | [+about] *I'm tired of listening
to Jim spouting about politics.* **3** [I] if a WHALE spouts,
it sends out a stream of water from a hole in its head

sprain /spreɪn/ *v* [T] to damage a joint in your body by
suddenly twisting it; ◨ **twist**: *I fell down the steps and
sprained my ankle.* —**sprain** *n* [C]: *I thought my wrist
might be broken, but it was just a bad sprain.*

sprang /spræŋ/ the past tense of SPRING

sprat /spræt/ *n* [C] a small fish that is cooked and
eaten whole

sprawl¹ /sprɔːl $ sprɒːl/ also **sprawl out** *v* [I always +
adv/prep] **1** to lie or sit with your arms or legs
stretched out in a lazy or careless way: *He sprawled out
on the sofa.* | *I tripped on a stone and went sprawling on
the pavement.* | *a blow which sent him sprawling* **2** if
buildings sprawl, they spread out over a wide area in
an untidy and unattractive way: *The town seemed to
sprawl for miles.*

sprawl² *n* [singular, U] a large area of buildings that
are spread out in an untidy and unattractive way: *We
drove through miles of urban sprawl before we finally
got out into the countryside.*

sprawled /sprɔːld $ sprɒːld/ *adj* [not before noun]
be/lie/sit sprawled (out) to be lying or sitting with your
arms or legs stretched out in a lazy or careless way: *He
was sprawled in an armchair in front of the TV.* | *A girl
lay sprawled across the bed.*

spraw·ling /'sprɔːlɪŋ $ 'sprɒːl-/ *adj* spreading over a
wide area in an untidy or unattractive way: *a vast,
sprawling city*

spray¹ [S3] /spreɪ/ *v*
1 [T] to force liquid out of a container so that it comes
out in a stream of very small drops and covers an area;
→ **squirt**: **spray sb/sth with sth** *She sprayed herself
with perfume.* | **spray sth on/onto/over sth** *Someone
had sprayed blue paint over his car.* | *Vandals had
sprayed graffiti on the walls.* | **spray crops/plants etc**
(=cover them with liquid to protect them from insects
or disease) *The fruit is sprayed every four weeks.*
2 [I always + adv/prep] if liquids or small bits spray
somewhere, they are quickly scattered through the air:
[+from] *Champagne sprayed from the bottle.*
3 spray sb/sth with bullets to shoot a lot of bullets
towards a person or place very quickly: *Gunmen
sprayed the crowd with bullets.*

spray² *n*
1 LIQUID FROM A CONTAINER [C,U] liquid which is
forced out of a special container in a stream of very
small drops: *a new hair styling spray* | *Most farmers use
pesticide sprays.*
2 CONTAINER [C] a container which forces liquid out
in a stream of small drops: *Mary took a perfume spray
from her handbag.* → see picture at CAN²
3 MOVING LIQUID **a)** [U] water in very small drops
that is blown from the sea etc or sent up by vehicles on
a wet road: *spray from the waves* | *My face was stinging
from the salt spray.* **b)** [C] liquid that comes quickly
from somewhere in very small drops: [+of] *A spray of
blood came from his mouth.*
4 BRANCH [C] a small branch or stem with leaves or
flowers on it, used for decoration; ◨ **sprig**: [+of] *a
spray of holly*
5 FLOWERS [C] an attractive arrangement of flowers
or leaves: [+of] *a spray of violets and primroses*
6 a spray of bullets/gravel etc a lot of bullets or very
small objects moving quickly through the air

'spray can *n* [C] a can from which you can spray paint
onto things

spray·er /'spreɪə $ -ər/ *n* [C] a piece of equipment that
is used for spraying large amounts of liquid, especially
over crops

'spray gun *n* [C] a piece of equipment that you hold in
your hand and use to spray liquid in very small drops

'spray-on *adj* [only before noun] a spray-on substance
can be sprayed from a container onto a surface: *a
spray-on water repellent for clothing*

'spray paint *n* [U] paint that you spray from a can
—**spray-paint** *v* [I,T]

spread¹ [S2] [W2] /spred/ *v past tense and past participle*
spread

1 000, 2 000, 3 000, most frequent words in S poken and W ritten English

1 AFFECT MORE PEOPLE/PLACES [I,T] if something spreads or is spread, it becomes larger or moves so that it affects more people or a larger area: [+**through**] *Fire quickly spread through the building.* | [+**over**] *He watched the dark stain spread over the gray carpet.* | *The disease **spread rapidly** amongst the poor.* | **spread (from sth) to sth** *The cancer had spread to her liver.* | *Revolution quickly spread from France to Italy.* | *the risk of AIDS being spread through contaminated blood*

2 INFORMATION/IDEAS **a)** [I] to become known about or used by more and more people: *News of the explosion spread swiftly.* | [+**to/through/over etc**] *Buddhism spread to China from India.* | *The news **spread like wildfire** (=became known very quickly).* | ***Word spread** quickly and soon a crowd had gathered.* **b)** [T] to tell a lot of people about something: **spread lies/rumours/gossip** *Andy loves spreading rumours about his colleagues.* | *They are **spreading the word** about the benefits of immunization.*

3 OPEN/ARRANGE also **spread out** [T] to open something out or arrange a group of things so that they cover a flat surface: **spread sth over/across/on sth** *Papers and photos were spread across the floor.* | *He spread the map out on the desk.* | *a table spread with a white cloth*

4 THROUGHOUT AN AREA [I] also **be spread** and **spread out** to cover or exist across a large area: [+**over**] *the forest that spread over the whole of that region* | [+**throughout**] *The company has more than 2500 shops spread throughout the UK.*

5 SOFT SUBSTANCE [I,T] to put a soft substance over a surface or to be soft enough to be put over a surface: **spread sth on/over sth** *He spread plaster on the walls.* | **spread sth with sth** *Spread the toast thinly with jam.* | *If you warm up the butter it'll spread more easily.* | ***Spread** the nut mixture **evenly** over the bottom.*

6 ARMS/FINGERS ETC [T] if you spread your arms, fingers or legs, you move them far apart: *He shrugged and spread his hands.*

7 OVER TIME [T] also **spread out** to do something over a period of time, rather than at one time: **spread sth over sth** *Could I spread the repayments over a longer period?* | *There will be 12 concerts spread throughout the summer.*

8 SHARE [T] to share or divide something among several people or things: **spread the load/burden** *The bills are sent out on different dates to spread the workload on council staff.* | *They want the country's wealth to be more **evenly spread**.*

9 SMILE/LOOK [I always + adv/prep] if an expression spreads over someone's face, it slowly appears on their face: [+**over/across**] *A slow smile spread over her face.*

10 **spread your wings a)** to start to have an independent life and experience new things: *A year spent studying abroad should allow him to spread his wings a bit.* **b)** if a bird or insect spreads its wings, it stretches them wide

11 a) **be spread (too) thin/thinly** if money, effort etc is spread thin, it is being used for many things so there is not enough for each thing: *They complained that resources were spread too thinly.* **b)** **spread yourself too thin** to try to do too many things at the same time so that you do not do any of them effectively

12 spread seeds/manure/fertilizer to scatter seeds, MANURE etc on the ground → **spread your net wide** at NET[1] (8)

spread out *phr v*
1 if a group of people spread out, they move apart from each other so that they cover a wider area: *The search party spread out to search the surrounding fields.*
2 **spread sth ⇔ out** to open something out or arrange a group of things on a flat surface: *Sue spread out her notes on the kitchen table and began to write.*
3 also **be spread out** to cover a large area: *The city spread out below her looked so calm.*

4 spread sth ⇔ out to do something over a period of time, rather than at one time: [+**over**] *The course is spread out over four days.*

spread² *n*
1 INCREASE [singular] when something affects or is known about by more people or involves a larger area; → **increase**: [+**of**] *an attempt to stop the spread of nuclear weapons* | *the **rapid spread** of cholera in Latin America*
2 SOFT FOOD [C,U] **a)** a soft substance made from vegetable oil that is used like butter: *one slice of toast with a low-fat spread* **b)** a soft food which you spread on bread: **cheese/chocolate etc spread**
3 RANGE [singular] a range of people or things: **wide/broad/good spread of sth** *We have a good spread of ages in the department.* | *a broad spread of investments*
4 AREA [singular] the total area in which something exists: *the **geographical spread** of the company's hotels*
5 double-page spread/centre spread a special article or advertisement in a newspaper or magazine, which covers two pages or covers the centre pages: *There's a double-page spread in Sunday's paper.*
6 LARGE MEAL [singular] *informal* a large meal for several guests on a special occasion: *Chris's mum laid on a huge spread.*
7 HAND/WINGS [U] the area covered when the fingers of a hand, or a bird's wings, are fully stretched
8 BED COVER [C] a BEDSPREAD
9 MONEY [C] *technical* the difference between the prices at which something is bought and sold, or the INTEREST rates for lending and borrowing money: [+**between**] *the spread between the city banks' loan rates and deposit rates*
10 SPORT [singular] *AmE* the number of points between the scores of two opposing teams: *a four-point spread*
11 spread of land/water an area of land or water
12 FARM [C] *AmE* a large farm or RANCH → **middle-aged spread** at MIDDLE-AGED (3)

'spread ,betting *n* [U] **1** a type of BETTING on sports events in which someone says what they think the final score will be **2** a way of buying and selling SHARES in which someone BETS money on whether shares in a particular company will go up or down in value —**spread bet** *n* [C]

spread·ea·gled /ˈspredˈiːgəld $ ˈsprediːgəld/ *adj* lying with arms and legs stretched out; 🔲 **sprawled**: *He lay spreadeagled on the bed.*

spread·sheet /ˈspredʃiːt/ *n* [C] **1** a computer program that can show and calculate financial information **2** a document that contains rows and COLUMNS of numbers that can be used to calculate something

spree /spriː/ *n* [C] a short period of time when you do a lot of one activity, especially spending money or drinking alcohol: **on a spree** *They went on a drinking spree.* | *a shopping spree*

sprig /sprɪg/ *n* [C] a small stem or part of a branch with leaves or flowers on it: [+**of**] *a sprig of parsley*

sprigged /sprɪgd/ *adj* sprigged cloth, or a sprigged pattern is decorated with leaves or flowers on stems

spright·ly /ˈspraɪtli/ *adj* an old person who is sprightly is still active and full of energy – used to show approval —**sprightliness** *n* [U]

spring¹ [S2] [W2] /sprɪŋ/ *n*
1 SEASON [C,U] the season between winter and summer when leaves and flowers appear: [+**of**] *the spring of 1933* | **in/during the spring** *It's due to open in the spring.* | **late/early spring** *It was a cold, sunny day in early spring.* | *spring flowers*
2 CURVED METAL **a)** [C usually plural] something, usually a twisted piece of metal, that will return to its previous shape after it has been pressed down: *an old armchair with broken springs* **b)** [U] the ability of a chair, bed etc to return to its normal shape after being pressed down
3 WATER [C] a place where water comes up naturally

from the ground: *spring water* | *There are several hot springs in the area.* → see picture at RIVER

4 spring in your step if you walk with a spring in your step, you move quickly and happily: *As he walked into the office that morning, there was a spring in his step.*

5 full of the joys of spring happy and full of energy – used humorously

6 SUDDEN JUMP [singular] a sudden quick movement or jump in a particular direction; ▤ leap

spring² *v past tense* **sprang** /spræŋ/ *also* **sprung** /sprʌŋ/ *AmE past participle* **sprung**

1 MOVE SUDDENLY [I always + adv/prep] to move suddenly and quickly in a particular direction, especially by jumping; ▤ leap: [+out of/from] *Tom sprung out of bed and ran downstairs.* | **spring out at sb** *Two men sprang out at me as I was walking through the park.* | *He **sprang to his feet** (=stood up suddenly) and rushed after her.* | **spring to sb's aid/assistance** (=move quickly to help someone) *One of the young policemen sprang to her assistance.*

2 MOVE BACK [I always + adv/prep] if something springs back, open etc, it moves quickly, suddenly and with force, especially after being pushed down or sideways: [+back/up] *The branch sprang back and hit him in the face.* | **spring open/shut** *The gate sprang shut behind them.*

3 spring to (sb's) mind if someone or something springs to mind, you immediately think of them: *Two questions spring to mind.*

4 spring into action *also* **spring to/into life** to suddenly become active, start moving or start working: *They were prepared and ready to spring into action.* | *Finally the engine sprang to life.*

5 spring a surprise to do something surprising: *Roy is unlikely to spring any surprises.*

6 tears spring to/into sb's eyes *written* used to say that someone starts to cry

7 spring into existence/being to suddenly begin to exist: *A lot of small businesses sprang into existence during the 1980s.*

8 spring a trap **a)** if an animal springs a trap, it is caught by the trap **b)** to make someone say or do something by tricking them

9 spring a leak if a boat or a container springs a leak, it begins to let liquid in or out through a crack or hole

10 spring to sb's defence to quickly defend someone who is being criticized: *Charlene sprang immediately to her son's defence.*

11 spring to attention if soldiers spring to attention, they stand suddenly upright

12 HELP SB ESCAPE [T + from] *informal* to help someone escape from prison

spring for sth *phr v AmE informal*
to pay for something: *I'll spring for the beer tonight.*

spring from sth *phr v spoken*
to be caused by something or start from something: *behaviour which springs from prejudices*

spring sth **on** sb *phr v*
to tell someone something or ask them to do something when they do not expect it and are not ready for it: *It's not fair to spring this on her without any warning.*

spring up *phr v*
to suddenly appear or start to exist: *Fast-food restaurants are springing up all over town.*

spring·board /'sprɪŋbɔːd $ -bɔːrd/ *n* [C] **1** something that helps you to start doing something: [+for] *The TV soap has been a springboard for a lot of careers.* **2** a strong board for jumping on or off, used when diving (DIVE¹ (1)) or doing GYMNASTICS

spring·bok /'sprɪŋbɒk $ -baːk/ *n* [C] a small DEER that can run fast and lives in South Africa

spring break *n* [C] *AmE* a holiday from college or university in the spring, usually two weeks long

spring chicken *n* [C] **sb is no spring chicken** used to say that someone is no longer young – used humorously

spring-cleaning *n* [U] when you clean a house thoroughly, usually once a year: *Judith's busy doing the spring-cleaning.* —**spring-clean** *n* [singular] *BrE* —**spring-clean** *v* [I,T]

spring fever *n* [U] a sudden feeling of energy that you have in the spring

spring-loaded *adj* containing a metal SPRING that presses one part against another

spring onion *n* [C] *BrE* a strong tasting onion with a small white round part and a long green stem, usually eaten raw; ▤ **scallion** *AmE*, **green onion** *AmE*

spring roll / $ './ *n* [C] a type of Chinese food consisting of a piece of thin rolled PASTRY filled with vegetables and sometimes meat and cooked in oil; ▤ **egg roll** *AmE*

spring tide *n* [C] a large rise and fall in the level of the sea at the time of the NEW MOON and the FULL MOON; → **neap tide**

spring·time /'sprɪŋtaɪm/ *n* [U] the time of the year when it is spring: **in (the) springtime** *when the snow melts in the springtime*

spring training *n* [U] *AmE* the period when a BASEBALL team gets ready for competition

spring·y /'sprɪŋi/ *adj* **1** something that is springy is soft and comes back to its normal shape after being pressed or walked on: *The grass was soft and springy.* **2** springy step/walk a way of walking which is quick and full of energy —**springily** *adv* —**springiness** *n* [U]

sprin·kle¹ /'sprɪŋkəl/ *v* **1** [T] to scatter small drops of liquid or small pieces of something: **sprinkle sth with sth** *Sprinkle the top with cheese.* | **sprinkle sth on/over sth** *I sprinkled cocoa over my latte.* **2** be sprinkled with jokes/quotations etc to be full of jokes etc: *The book is liberally sprinkled with clichés.* **3** it is sprinkling *AmE* if it is sprinkling, it is raining lightly

sprinkle² *n* [singular] **1** a small amount of something, especially scattered on top of something: [+of] *Add a sprinkle of salt.* **2** *AmE* a light rain

sprin·kler /'sprɪŋklə $ -ər/ *n* [C] **1** a piece of equipment used for scattering water on grass or soil → see picture at GARDENING **2** a piece of equipment on a ceiling that scatters water if there is a fire

sprin·kling /'sprɪŋklɪŋ/ *n* [singular] a small amount of something, especially scattered over an area: [+of] *The hilltops were covered with a sprinkling of snow.*

sprint¹ /sprɪnt/ *v* [I] **1** to run very fast for a short distance; → jog: [+along/across/up etc] *Bill sprinted up the steps.* **2** to ride, swim etc very fast for a short distance

sprint² *n* **1** [C] a short race in which the runners, riders, swimmers etc move very fast over a short distance: *the 100 metre sprint* **2** [singular] a short period of running or moving very fast: *He made a desperate sprint for the train.*

sprint·er /'sprɪntə $ -ər/ *n* [C] someone who runs in fast races over short distances

sprite /spraɪt/ *n* [C] a FAIRY (1)

spritz /sprɪts/ *v* [T] *AmE* to SPRAY small amounts of a liquid on something —**spritz** *n* [C]

spritz·er /'sprɪtsə $ -ər/ *n* [C] a drink made with SODA WATER and white wine

sprock·et /'sprɒkɪt $ 'spraː-/ *n* [C] **1** *also* **sprocket wheel** a wheel with TEETH (=parts along the edge) that fit into and turn a bicycle chain, a photographic film with holes etc **2** one of the teeth on a sprocket wheel

sprog /sprɒg $ spraːg/ *n* [C] *BrE informal* a child or baby – used humorously

sprout¹ /spraʊt/ *v* **1** [I,T] if vegetables, seeds, or plants sprout, they start to grow, producing SHOOTS, BUDS, or leaves: *Move the pots outside when the seeds begin to sprout.* | *Trees were starting to sprout new leaves.* **2** [I] *also* **sprout up** to appear suddenly in large numbers:

Office blocks are sprouting up everywhere. **3** [I,T] if something such as hair sprouts or if you sprout it, it starts to grow: *Jim seemed to have sprouted a beard.*

sprout² *n* [C] **1** *especially BrE* a small green vegetable like a very small CABBAGE; ▤ **brussels sprout** **2** a new growth on a plant; ▤ **shoot** **3** [usually plural] *AmE* an ALFALFA seed which has grown a stem and is eaten **4** [usually plural] *AmE* a BEANSPROUT

spruce¹ /spruːs/ *n* [C,U] a tree that grows in northern countries and has short leaves shaped like needles

spruce² *v*

spruce up *phr v informal* to make yourself or something look neater and tidier: *Paul went upstairs to spruce up before dinner.* | *spruce sb/sth ⇔ up The cottage had been spruced up a bit since her last visit.*

spruce³ *adj BrE* neat and clean: *Mr Bailey was looking very spruce in a white linen suit.* —**sprucely** *adv*

sprung¹ /sprʌŋ/ a past tense and the past participle of SPRING

sprung² *adj* supported or kept in shape by SPRINGS: *a sprung mattress*

spry /spraɪ/ *adj* a spry old person has energy and is active; ▤ **sprightly**: *He's still remarkably spry.* —**spryly** *adv*

spud /spʌd/ *n* [C] *informal* a POTATO

spume /spjuːm/ *n* [U] *literary* the mass of bubbles that forms on the top of waves when the sea is rough; ▤ **foam**

spun /spʌn/ the past tense and past participle of SPIN

spunk /spʌŋk/ *n* [U] *informal* **1** *especially AmE* courage: *She had a lot of spunk.* **2** *BrE not polite* SEMEN

spunk·y /ˈspʌŋki/ *adj informal* having a lot of courage, energy, or determination: *a spunky performance* | *a spunky heroine*

spur¹ /spɜː $ spɜːr/ *n* [C] **1 on the spur of the moment** suddenly, without any previous planning or thought: *We would often decide what to play on the spur of the moment.* → SPUR-OF-THE-MOMENT **2** a fact or event that makes you try harder to do something: [+to] *It provided the spur to further research.* | *The crowd's reaction only acted as a spur.* **3** a sharp pointed object on the heel of a rider's boot which is used to encourage a horse to go faster **4 earn/win your spurs** to show that you deserve to succeed because you have the right skills **5** a piece of high ground which sticks out from the side of a hill or mountain **6** a railway track or road that goes away from a main line or road

spur² *v* **spurred, spurring** **1** [T] also **spur sb on** to encourage someone or make them want to do something: *The band were spurred on by the success of their last two singles.* | **spur sb (on) to do sth** *His misfortunes spurred him to write.* | **spur sb (on) to sth** *the coach who spurred him on to Olympic success* | *It was an article in the local newspaper which finally* **spurred** *him into action.* **2** [T] to make an improvement or change happen faster; ▤ **encourage**: *Lower taxes would spur investment and help economic growth.* **3** [I,T] to encourage a horse to go faster, especially by pushing it with special points on the heels of your boots

spu·ri·ous /ˈspjʊəriəs $ ˈspjʊr-/ *adj* **1** a spurious statement, argument etc is not based on facts or good thinking and is likely to be incorrect: *He demolished the Opposition's spurious arguments.* **2** insincere: *spurious sympathy* —**spuriously** *adv* —**spuriousness** *n* [U]

spurn /spɜːn $ spɜːrn/ *v* [T] *literary* to refuse to accept something or someone, especially because you are too proud: *She spurned all offers of help.* | *a spurned lover*

spur-of-the-'moment *adj* [only before noun] a spur-of-the-moment decision or action is made or done suddenly without planning

spurt¹ /spɜːt $ spɜːrt/ *v* **1 a)** [I] if liquid or flames spurt from something, they come out of it quickly and suddenly: [+from/out of] *Blood spurted from his nose.* |

Flames spurted through the roof. **b)** [T] to send out liquid or flames quickly or suddenly: *It boiled over, spurting hot water everywhere.* **2** [I always + adv/prep] to suddenly start moving more quickly, especially for a short time: *He suddenly spurted ahead of the others.*

spurt² *n* [C] **1** when an amount of liquid or flame suddenly comes quickly out of something: [+of] *a sudden spurt of flame* | **in spurts** *The water came out of the tap in short spurts* (=a small amount at a time). **2** a short sudden increase of activity, effort, speed, or emotion: [+of] *In a sudden spurt of anger, Ellen slammed the door shut.* | **growth spurt** (=when a child suddenly grows quickly) | **in spurts** *We weren't consistent – we played in spurts.*

sput·ter /ˈspʌtə $ -ər/ *v* **1** [I] if something such as an engine or a fire sputters, it makes short soft uneven noises like very small explosions; ▤ **splutter**: *Suddenly the engine sputtered and stopped.* **2** [I,T] to talk quickly in short confused phrases, especially because you are angry or shocked; ▤ **splutter**: *'What do you mean?' sputtered Annabelle.* —**sputter** *n* [C,U]

spu·tum /ˈspjuːtəm/ *n* [U] *medical* liquid in your mouth which you have coughed up from your lungs; → **phlegm**

spy¹ /spaɪ/ *n plural* **spies** [C] someone whose job it is to find out secret information about another country, organization, or group; ▤ **secret agent**: *British/Russian/foreign etc spy* *a Soviet spy* | **spy ring/network** (=an organized group of spies) | **spy plane/satellite**

spy² *v* **spied, spying, spies** **1** [I] to secretly collect information about an enemy country or an organization you are competing against: [+on] *He was charged with spying on British military bases.* | [+for] *He confessed to spying for North Korea.* **2** [T] *literary* to suddenly see someone or something, especially after searching for them; ▤ **spot**: *Ellen suddenly spied her friend in the crowd.*

spy on sb *phr v* to watch someone secretly in order to find out what they are doing: *She sent you to spy on me, didn't she?*

spy sth ⇔ **out** *phr v* **1** to secretly find out information about something **2 spy out the land** *BrE* to secretly find out more information about a situation before deciding what to do

spy·glass /ˈspaɪɡlɑːs $ -ɡlæs/ *n* [C] a small TELESCOPE used by sailors in the past

spy·hole /ˈspaɪhəʊl $ -hoʊl/ *n* [C] *BrE* a hole in a door, wall etc through which you can look at someone secretly

spy·ware /ˈspaɪweə $ -wer/ *n* [U] computer software that secretly records information about which websites you visit. This information is then used by advertising companies, who try to sell you products.

sq. also **sq** *BrE* the written abbreviation of *Square*: *30 cm sq floor tiles* | *40 Merrion Sq., Dublin*

squab·ble /ˈskwɒbəl $ ˈskwɑː-/ *v* [I] to argue about something unimportant; ▤ **quarrel**: [+over/about] *They're always squabbling over money.* | [+with] *He's squabbling with the referee.* —**squabble** *n* [C]: *a petty squabble* | *bitter squabbles between employers and unions*

squad W3 /skwɒd $ skwɑːd/ *n* [C]

1 a group of players from which a team will be chosen for a particular sports event: *the Italian World Cup squad*

2 the police department responsible for dealing with a particular kind of crime: **drugs/fraud/vice etc squad** *A controlled explosion was carried out by bomb squad officers.*

3 a small group of soldiers working together as a unit: *a drill squad*

4 *AmE* a group of CHEERLEADERS → DEATH SQUAD, FIRING SQUAD, FLYING SQUAD

'squad car *n* [C] a car used by police on duty; ▤ **patrol car**

squad·dy, squaddie /'skwɒdi $ 'skwɑː-/ n plural **squaddies** [C] BrE informal a soldier who is not an officer

squad·ron /'skwɒdrən $ 'skwɑː-/ n [C] a military force consisting of a group of aircraft or ships

squadron leader n [C] an officer in the British AIR FORCE below a WING COMMANDER

squal·id /'skwɒlɟd $ 'skwɑː-/ adj **1** very dirty and unpleasant because of a lack of care or money; → **squalor**: How can anyone live in such squalid conditions? | a tiny squalid apartment **2** especially BrE immoral or dishonest: squalid behaviour | a squalid affair

squall¹ /skwɔːl $ skwɒːl/ n [C] a sudden strong wind, especially one that brings rain or snow: snow squalls

squall² v [I] if a baby or child squalls, it cries noisily; ◨ **bawl**

squal·ly /'skwɔːli $ 'skwɒːli/ adj BrE squally rain or snow comes with sudden strong winds: squally showers

squal·or /'skwɒlə $ 'skwɑːlər, 'skwɒː- / n [U] the condition of being dirty and unpleasant because of a lack of care or money; → **squalid**: We lived in squalor for a year and a half.

squan·der /'skwɒndə $ 'skwɑːndər/ v [T] to carelessly waste money, time, opportunities etc: The home team squandered a number of chances in the first half. | **squander sth on sth** They squandered the profits on expensive cars.

square¹ S2 W3 /skweə $ skwer/ adj
1 SHAPE having four straight equal sides and 90° angles at the corners: a large square room
2 ANGLE forming a 90° angle, or being close to or similar to a 90° angle: square corners
3 square metre/mile etc an area of measurement equal to a square with sides a metre long, a mile long etc: about four square metres of ground
4 5 feet/2 metres etc square having the shape of a square with sides that are 5 feet, 2 metres etc long: The room is six metres square.
5 LEVEL [not before noun] parallel with a straight line: [+with] I don't think the shelf is square with the floor.
6 square meal a good satisfying meal: Children should have three square meals a day.
7 BODY if someone's body or a part of their body is square, it looks broad and strong: a square jaw
8 all square BrE to have the same number of points as your opponent in a competition: The teams were all square at the end of the first half.
9 (all) square informal if two people are square, they do not owe each other any money: Here's your £10 back, so that **makes us square**.
10 square deal honest and fair treatment from someone, especially in business: I'm not **getting a square deal** here.
11 BORING informal someone who is square is boring and old-fashioned
12 a square peg in a round hole informal someone who is in a job or situation that is not suitable for them
—**squareness** n [U] → **win (sth)/beat sb fair and square** at FAIR³ (1)

square² S2 n [C]
1 SHAPE a shape with four straight equal sides with 90° angles at the corners; → **rectangle**: First of all, draw a square. | [+of] a small square of cloth
2 IN A TOWN a large open area in the centre of a town or city, usually in the shape of a square, or the buildings surrounding it: **main/market/town square** The hotel is just off the main square of Sorrento. | She lives in Hanover Square.
3 one the situation from which you started to do something: **be back to/at square one** The police are now back at square one in their investigation. | **go back to square one** (=used when you start something again because you were not successful the first time) Okay, let's go back to square one and try again. | **from square one** I've had to relearn the game from square one.
4 NUMBER the result of multiplying a number by

itself; → **square root**: [+of] The square of 4 is 16.
5 IN A GAME a space on a board used for playing a game such as CHESS
6 PERSON informal someone who is considered boring and unfashionable; ◨ **nerd**
7 TOOL also **set square** a flat object with a straight edge, often shaped like an L, used for drawing or measuring 90° angles

square³ v [T]
1 MULTIPLY to multiply a number by itself
2 IN A COMPETITION BrE to win a point or game so that you have now won the same number of points or games as the other team or player: India won the second match to square the series at one each.
3 square your shoulders to stand straight and push your shoulders back, usually to show your determination
4 MAKE STH STRAIGHT to make something straight or parallel
5 square the circle to attempt something impossible
  square sth ⇔ **away** phr v [usually passive] AmE to finish something, especially by putting the last details in order: Get your work **squared away** before you leave.
  square off phr v
1 square sth ⇔ off to make something have neat corners
2 AmE to get ready to fight someone
  square up phr v
1 to pay money that you owe: I'll pay for the drinks and you can square up later.
2 BrE to get ready to fight someone: [+to] The two lads squared up to each other.
3 square up to sb/sth to deal with a difficult situation or person in a determined way
  square with sth phr v
1 square (sth) with sth if you square two ideas, statements etc with each other or if they square with each other, they are considered to be in agreement: His story simply does not square with the facts. | How do you square that with your religious beliefs? | square sth with your conscience (=make yourself believe that what you are doing is morally right)
2 square sth with sb BrE to persuade someone to agree to something: I'll take the day off if I can square it with my boss.

square⁴ adv **1** directly and firmly; ◨ **squarely**: Look him **square in the eye** and say no. **2** at 90° to a line; ◨ **squarely**: [+to] Wright passed the ball square to Brown.

square bracket n [C] BrE one of the pair of signs [ ] that are used for enclosing information; ◨ **bracket** AmE: **in square brackets** The words in square brackets should be deleted.

squared /skweəd $ skwerd/ adj **1** BrE divided into squares or marked with squares: squared paper **2** 3/9/10 etc squared the number three, nine etc multiplied by itself: 3 squared equals 9.

square dance n [C] a type of traditional country dance in which four pairs of dancers face each other in a square, and someone calls out the movements they should do

square knot n [C] AmE a type of knot that will not come undone easily

square·ly /'skweəli $ 'skwer-/ adv **1** directly and firmly: He turned and faced her squarely. | She hit him squarely on the nose. **2** completely and with no doubt: The blame lies squarely on the shoulders of the police. **3** straight on something and centrally; ◨ **square**: Dr Soames jammed his hat squarely on his head. **4** at 90° to a line; ◨ **square**

square root n [C] the square root of a number is the number which, when multiplied by itself, equals that number: [+of] The square root of nine is three.

S

squar·ish /'skweərɪʃ $ 'skwer-/ *adj* shaped almost like a square

squash[1] /skwɒʃ $ skwɑːʃ, skwɒːʃ/ *v*
1 PRESS [T] to press something into a flatter shape, often breaking or damaging it; ▣ **flatten**: *The cake got a bit squashed on the way here.* | **squash sth down** *Her hair had been squashed down by her hat.* | *Move over – you're squashing me.* → see picture at SQUEEZE[1]
2 SMALL SPACE [I,T always + adv/prep] to push yourself or something else into a space that is too small; ▣ **squeeze**: [+into] *Seven of us squashed into the car.* | **squash sth in** *We can probably squash another couple of things in.*
3 STOP STH [T] *informal* to use your power or authority to stop something; ▣ **quash**: *Her suggestions were always squashed.* | **squash rumours/hopes/reports etc** (=say that a rumour etc is not true) *The government was quick to squash any hopes of reform.*
4 CONTROL EMOTION [T] to control or ignore an emotion; ▣ **suppress**: *She felt anger rising but quickly squashed it.*
　squash up *phr v BrE*
to move closer together or closer to something, especially in order to make room for someone or something else: [+against] *The others squashed up against Jo.*

squash[2] *n*
1 SPORT [U] a game played by two people who use RACKETS to hit a small rubber ball against the walls of a square court: *a squash court* → see picture at SPORTS CENTRE
2 it's a squash *BrE spoken* used to say that there is not enough space for everyone to fit in comfortably
3 VEGETABLE [C,U] one of a group of large vegetables with solid flesh and hard skins, such as PUMPKINS
4 DRINK [U] *BrE* a drink made from fruit juice, sugar, and water: *a glass of orange squash*

squashed /skwɒʃt $ skwɑːʃt, skwɒːʃt/ *adj* **1** broken or made flat by being pressed hard: *squashed tomatoes* **2** [not before noun] in a space that is too small: *I was squashed between Jan and Dave in the back seat.*

squash·y /'skwɒʃi $ 'skwɑːʃi, 'skwɒːʃi/ *adj BrE informal* soft and easy to press

squat[1] /skwɒt $ skwɑːt/ *v* **squatted, squatting**
[I] **1** to sit with your knees bent under you and your bottom just off the ground, balancing on your feet: [+down] *He squatted down beside the little girl.* **2** to live in a building or on a piece of land without permission and without paying rent

squat[2] *adj* short and thick or low and wide, especially in a way which is not attractive: *squat stone cottages* | *a squat little old man*

squat[3] *n* **1** [C] a squatting position **2** [C] *BrE* a house that people are living in without permission and without paying rent: *She lives in a squat in Camden.* **3** [U] *AmE informal* nothing, or nearly nothing. Squat is often used in negative sentences for emphasis: *He had a job that paid him squat.* | *You don't know squat about it.*

squat·ter /'skwɒtə $ 'skwɑːtər/ *n* [C] someone who lives in an empty building or on a piece of land without permission and without paying rent

squaw /skwɔː $ skwɒː/ *n* [C] *old use* a word for a Native American woman, now usually considered offensive

squawk /skwɔːk $ skwɒːk/ *v* [I,T] **1** if a bird squawks, it makes a loud sharp angry sound **2** *informal* to complain loudly and angrily —**squawk** *n* [C]

squeak[1] /skwiːk/ *v* **1** [I] to make a short high noise or cry that is not loud: *A rat squeaked and ran into the bushes.* | *The door squeaked open.* **2** [I,T] to say something in a very high voice, especially because you are nervous or excited: *'Too late!' she squeaked.* **3** [I always + adv/prep] *informal* to succeed, win, or pass a

test by a very small amount so that you only just avoid failure; ▣ **scrape**: [+through/by/past/in] *She just squeaked through her math test.*

squeak[2] *n* [C] **1** a very short high noise or cry; ▣ **squeal**: [+of] *a squeak of alarm* | *the high-pitched squeak of a bat* **2** **not a squeak** if there is not a squeak from someone, they do not say anything or communicate at all: *We didn't hear a squeak from him in months.*

squeak·y /'skwiːki/ *adj* **1** making very high noises that are not loud: *a squeaky voice* | *squeaky floorboards* **2** **squeaky clean** *informal* **a)** never having done anything morally wrong: *politicians who are less than squeaky clean* **b)** completely clean: *squeaky clean hair* —**squeakily** *adv* —**squeakiness** *n* [U]

squeal[1] /skwiːl/ *v* **1** [I,T] to make a long loud high sound or cry; → **scream**: [+with/in] *The children squealed with delight.* | *They drove off, tyres squealing.* | *'Let me go!' she squealed.* **2** [I + on] *informal* to tell the police or someone in authority about someone you know who has done something wrong

squeal[2] *n* [C] a long loud high sound or cry; → **scream**: [+of] *She gave a squeal of laughter.* | *There was a squeal of brakes.*

squeam·ish /'skwiːmɪʃ/ *adj* **1** easily shocked or upset, or easily made to feel sick by seeing unpleasant things **2** **the squeamish** [plural] people who are squeamish: *His new novel is not for the squeamish.* —**squeamishness** *n* [U]

squee·gee /'skwiːdʒiː/ *n* [C] a tool with a thin rubber blade and a short handle, used for removing or spreading a liquid on a surface

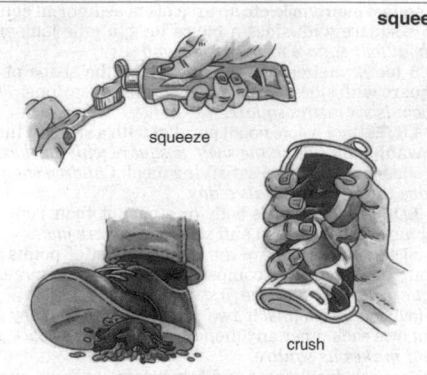
squeeze

squeeze

crush

squash

squeeze[1] /skwiːz/ *v*
1 PRESS [T] to press something firmly together with your fingers or hand: *She smiled as he squeezed her hand.* | *He squeezed the trigger, but nothing happened.*
2 PRESS OUT LIQUID [T] to get liquid from something by pressing it: *Squeeze the oranges.* | **squeeze sth out** *Try to squeeze a bit more out.* | **squeeze sth on/onto sth** *Squeeze a bit of lemon juice onto the fish.*
3 SMALL SPACE [I,T always + adv/prep] to try to make something fit into a space that is too small, or to try to get into such a space; ▣ **squash**: [+into] *Five of us squeezed into the back seat.* | [+through/past] *He had squeezed through a gap in the fence.* | **squeeze sb/sth in** *We could probably squeeze in a few more people.*
4 **squeeze your eyes shut** to close your eyes very tightly
5 JUST SUCCEED [I always + adv/prep] to succeed, win, or pass a test by a very small amount so that you only just avoid failure: *Greece just squeezed through into the next round.*
6 LIMIT MONEY [T] to strictly limit the amount of money that is available to a company or organization: *The government is squeezing the railways' investment budget.*

squeeze sb/sth ⇔ **in** also **squeeze sth into sth** phr v
to manage to do something although you are very busy: *How do you manage to squeeze so much into one day?* | *I can squeeze you in at four o'clock.*

squeeze sth ⇔ **out** phr v
1 to do something so that someone or something is no longer included or able to continue: *If budgets are cut, vital research may be squeezed out.*
2 to squeeze something wet in order to remove the liquid from it: *Squeeze the cloth out first.*
3 squeeze sth out of sb to force someone to tell you something: *See if you can squeeze more information out of them.*

squeeze up phr v BrE
to move close to the person next to you to make space for someone else

squeeze² n [C] **1 a (tight) squeeze** a situation in which there is only just enough room for things or people to fit somewhere: *It'll be a squeeze with six people in the car.* **2** an act of pressing something firmly with your fingers or hand: *Marty gave her hand a little squeeze.* **3 squeeze of lemon/lime etc** a small amount of juice obtained by squeezing a piece of fruit **4** a situation in which wages, prices, borrowing money etc are strictly controlled or reduced: [+on] *cuts due to the squeeze on public sector spending* | *a credit squeeze* | *All manufacturers are **feeling the squeeze*** (=noticing the effects of a difficult financial situation). **5 put the squeeze on sb** informal to try to persuade someone to do something **6 sb's (main) squeeze** especially AmE informal someone's BOYFRIEND or GIRLFRIEND

squeeze·box /'skwiːzbɒks $ -baːks/ n [C] informal an ACCORDION

squeez·er /'skwiːzə $ -ər/ n [C] an object used for squeezing juice from fruit such as LEMONS

squelch /skweltʃ/ v **1** [I] to make a sucking sound by walking or moving in something soft and wet: *My hair was dripping and my shoes squelched as I walked.* | [+through/along/up] *We squelched across the field.* **2** [T] AmE to stop something from continuing to develop or spread; **☐ squash:** *Her creativity had been squelched.* —**squelch** n [C]

squelch·y /'skweltʃi/ adj BrE squelchy mud or ground is soft and wet and makes a sucking noise when you walk on it

squib /skwɪb/ n [C] **1** a small exploding FIREWORK **2** literary a short amusing piece of writing that attacks someone → **damp squib** at DAMP¹ (2)

squid /skwɪd/ n plural **squid** or **squids** [C] a sea creature with a long soft body and ten arms around its mouth → see picture at SEAFOOD

squidg·y /'skwɪdʒi/ adj BrE soft and easy to press: *We don't want soft squidgy sandwiches.*

squif·fy /'skwɪfi/ adj BrE old-fashioned slightly drunk; **☐ tipsy**

squig·gle /'skwɪɡəl/ n [C] a line with irregular curves: *Shorthand just looks like a series of funny squiggles to me.* —**squiggly** adj: *squiggly lines*

squint¹ /skwɪnt/ v [I] **1** to look at something with your eyes partly closed in order to see better: *Anna squinted in the sudden bright sunlight.* | [+at] *Stop squinting at the screen – put your glasses on.* **2** [not in progressive] BrE to have each eye looking in a slightly different direction

squint² n [singular] **1** especially BrE a condition of your eye muscles that makes each eye look in a slightly different direction **2 have/take a squint at sth** BrE informal to look at something

squire /skwaɪə $ skwaɪr/ n **1** [C] the man who in the past owned most of the land around a country village in England **2** [C] a young man in the Middle Ages who learned how to be a KNIGHT by serving one **3** BrE old-fashioned spoken used by some men to address a man when they do not know his name

squirm /skwɜːm $ skwɜːrm/ v [I] **1** to twist your body from side to side because you are uncomfortable or nervous, or to get free from something which is holding you; **☐ wriggle:** *Christine squirmed uncomfortably in her chair.* | *The boy tried to squirm free.* **2** to feel very embarrassed or ashamed: [+with] *He made me squirm with embarrassment.* —**squirm** n [singular]

squir·rel¹ /'skwɪrəl $ 'skwɜːrəl/ n [C] a small animal with a long furry tail that climbs trees and eats nuts → see picture at BITE¹

squirrel² v **squirrelled**, **squirrelling** BrE, **squirreled**, **squirreling** AmE

squirrel sth ⇔ **away** phr v to keep something in a safe place to use later; **☐ stash away:** *By December I had $300 squirreled away.*

squir·rel·y, **squirrelly** /'skwɪrəli $ 'skwɜː-/ adj AmE informal not able to stay still; **☐ restless:** *squirrely kids*

squirt¹ /skwɜːt $ skwɜːrt/ v **1** [I,T] if you squirt liquid or if it squirts somewhere, it is forced out in a thin fast stream; → **spray:** [+out/from/into] *Water suddenly squirted out from a hole in the pipe.* | **squirt sth into/through sth** *Squirt some oil in the lock.* **2** [T] to hit or cover someone or something with a thin fast stream of liquid; → **spray: squirt sb/sth with sth** *Mom! Chad's squirting me with the hose!* | *Some kids squirted a water pistol in her face.*

squirt² n [C] **1** a fast thin stream of liquid: [+of] *a squirt of water* **2** spoken an insulting word for a short person, especially someone who is annoying you

squirt gun n [C] AmE a WATER PISTOL

squish /skwɪʃ/ v **1** [I always + adv/prep] to make a soft sucking sound by moving in or through something soft and wet **2** [I,T] informal to SQUASH something, especially something soft and wet, or to become squashed

squish·y /'skwɪʃi/ adj soft and easy to press: *squishy mud*

Sr BrE; **Sr.** AmE **1** the written abbreviation of **senior**: *Douglas Fairbanks, Sr.* **2** the written abbreviation of **señor**: *Sr Lopez* **3** the written abbreviation of **Sister**, used in front of the name of a NUN: *Sr Bernadette*

SS BrE also **S.S.** AmE /'es es/ **1** the abbreviation of **steamship**: *aboard the SS Great Britain* **2** BrE the written abbreviation of **saints**: *statues of SS Augustine and Thomas*

ssh [S3] /ʃ/ interjection used to ask people to be quiet; **☐ shush:** *Ssh! You'll wake everybody up.*

st BrE; **st.** AmE the written abbreviation of **stone** or **stones**: *She weighs 9 st 8 lb.*

-st /st/ suffix **1** forms written ORDINAL numbers with 1: *the 1st* (=first) *prize* | *my 21st birthday* **2** old use or biblical another form of the suffix -EST (2): *thou dost* (=you do)

St BrE; **St.** AmE **1** the written abbreviation of **Street**, used in addresses: *Wall St.* **2** the written abbreviation of **saint**: *St Luke's Gospel*

stab¹ /stæb/ v **stabbed**, **stabbing 1** [T] to push a knife into someone or something; → **stabbing:** *He was stabbed to death in a fight.* | **stab sb in the heart/arm etc** *She had been stabbed in the chest repeatedly.* **2** [I,T] to make quick pushing movements with your finger or something pointed; **☐ jab:** *He raised his voice and stabbed the air with his pen.* **3 stab sb in the back** to do something that harms someone who likes and trusts you; **☐ betray**

stab² n [C] **1** an act of stabbing or trying to stab someone with a knife: *severe stab wounds* | *a stab victim* | *He killed him with a stab to the heart.* **2 stab of fear/disappointment/pain etc** a sudden sharp feeling of pain or a strong emotion: *He felt a stab of guilt.* **3 stab at (doing) sth** informal an attempt to do something, often not successfully: **have/make/take a stab at (doing) sth** *I'll have one more stab at it.* **4 stab in the back** when someone you thought was a friend tries to harm you

S

stab·bing¹ /'stæbɪŋ/ *adj* a stabbing pain is sharp and sudden

stabbing² *n* [C] a crime in which someone is stabbed: *a fatal stabbing*

sta·bil·i·ty /stə'bɪləti/ *n* [U] **1** the condition of being steady and not changing; ⊟ **instability**; → **stable**: *a period of relative stability* | [+of] *It could threaten the peace and stability of the region.* **2** *technical* the ability of a substance to stay in the same state

sta·bil·ize also **-ise** *BrE* /'steɪbə̩laɪz/ *v* [I,T] to become firm, steady, or unchanging, or to make something firm or steady; → **stable**: *The patient's condition has now stabilized.* | *an attempt to stabilize the economy* —**stabilization** /ˌsteɪbə̩laɪˈzeɪʃən $ -lə-/ *n* [U]

sta·bil·iz·er also **-iser** *BrE* /'steɪbə̩laɪzə $ -ər/ *n* [C] **1** a chemical that helps something such as a food to stay in the same state, for example to prevent it from separating into different liquids **2** a piece of equipment that helps make something such as a plane or ship steady **3** [usually plural] *BrE* one of a pair of small wheels that are fastened to the back wheel of a child's bicycle to prevent it from falling over

sta·ble¹ W3 /'steɪbəl/ *adj* **1** steady and not likely to move or change; ⊟ **unstable**; → **stability**: *A wide base will make the structure much more stable.* | **in a stable condition** *BrE*/**in stable condition** *AmE*: *He is said to be in a stable condition in hospital.* | *Children like a stable environment.* **2** calm, reasonable, and not easy to upset; ⊟ **unstable**: *He was clearly not a very stable person.* **3** *technical* a stable substance tends to stay in the same chemical or ATOMIC state; ⊟ **unstable** —**stably** *adv*

stable² *n* [C] **1** a building where horses are kept → see picture at HOME¹ **2** stables [plural] a place where horses are kept and that often gives riding lessons **3** a group of racing horses that has one owner or trainer **4** a group of people working for the same company or with the same trainer: *actors from the same Hollywood stable* **5** shut/close the stable door after the horse has bolted *BrE* to try to prevent something when it is too late and harm has already been done

stable³ *v* [T] to put or keep a horse in a stable

'stable boy; **sta·ble·man** /'steɪbəlmæn/ *AmE n* [C] a man or boy who works in a stable

'stable girl *n* [C] a girl or woman who works in a stable

sta·ble·mate /'steɪbəlmeɪt/ *n* [C] sb's/sth's stablemate something produced by the same company, or someone who works for the same company: *the Daily Mirror's Scottish stablemate, the Daily Record*

sta·bling /'steɪblɪŋ/ *n* [U] space in a building where horses can be kept

stac·cat·o /stə'kɑːtəʊ $ -toʊ/ *adv* if music is played staccato, the notes are cut short —**staccato** *adj*

stack¹ /stæk/ *n* **1** [C] a neat pile of things; → **heap**: [+of] *a stack of papers* | *stacks of dirty dishes*; → see picture at BUNDLE¹ **2** a stack of sth/stacks of sth *informal especially BrE* a large amount of something: *He's got stacks of money.* **3** [C] a chimney **4** the stacks [plural] the rows of shelves in a library where the books are kept → blow your top/stack at BLOW¹ (16)

stack² *v* **1** also **stack up** [I,T] to make things into a neat pile, or to form a neat pile: *The assistants price the items and stack them on the shelves.* | *a stacking hi-fi system* **2** [T usually passive] to put neat piles of things on something: *He went back to stacking the shelves.* | be **stacked with sth** *The floor was stacked with boxes.* **3** the odds/cards are stacked against sb used to say that someone is unlikely to be successful **4** stack the cards *BrE*; stack the deck *AmE informal* to arrange cards dishonestly in a game

stack up *phr v* **1** stack sth ⇔ up to make things into a neat pile **2** *informal* used to talk about how good something is compared with something else: [+against] *Parents want to know how their kids' schools*

stack up against others. **3** if a number of things stack up, they gradually collect or get stuck in one place: *Traffic stacked up behind the bus.*

stacked /stækt/ *adj not polite* used to describe a woman with large breasts

sta·di·um /'steɪdiəm/ *n plural* **stadiums** *or* **stadia** /-diə/ [C] a building for public events, especially sports and large rock music concerts, consisting of a playing field surrounded by rows of seats: *the new Olympic Stadium*

staff¹ S2 W2 /stɑːf $ stæf/ *n* **1** WORKERS [C also + plural verb *BrE*] the people who work for an organization: *The entire staff has done an outstanding job this year.* | *They employ a total of 150 staff.* | *The staff were very helpful.* | **staff of 10/50 etc** *Our department has a staff of seven.* | **medical/academic/library etc staff** *a strike by ambulance staff* | **one of our longest-serving staff members** | **member of staff** *BrE: I'd like to welcome a new member of staff.* | **on the staff (of sth)** *We were both on the staff of the British Film Institute at the time.* | **on staff** *AmE: Joan is the only lawyer we have on staff.* | **staff room/meeting** (=a room or meeting for teachers in a school) **2** STICK [C] *plural* **staves** /steɪvz/ **a)** *old use* a long thick stick to help you walk **b)** a long thick stick that an official holds in some ceremonies **3** MUSIC [C] *especially AmE* the set of five lines that music is written on; ⊟ **stave 4** the staff of life *literary* bread → GENERAL STAFF, GROUND STAFF

GRAMMAR
In British English, **staff** can be singular or plural. In American English, **staff** is not used as frequently as in British English, and is never followed by a plural verb. ⚠ You never refer to a person as 'a staff'. Say **a member of staff** (BrE) or **an employee**.

staff² *v* [T usually passive] to be or provide the workers for an organization; → **overstaffed**, **understaffed**: *The centre is staffed mainly by volunteers.* —**staffing** *n* [U]: *staffing levels*

staff·er /'stɑːfə $ 'stæfər/ *n* [C] *AmE* someone who is paid to work for an organization

'staff ˌnurse *n* [C] *BrE* a British hospital nurse whose rank is just below a SISTER (2) or CHARGE NURSE

'staff ˌofficer *n* [C] a military officer whose job is to help an officer of a higher rank

'staff ˌsergeant *n* [C,U] a lower rank in the army or the US Air Force or MARINES, or someone who has this rank

stag /stæg/ *n* [C] **1** a fully grown male DEER; ⊟ **buck** *AmE* **2** go stag *AmE informal* if a man goes stag, he goes to a party without a woman → STAG NIGHT, STAG PARTY

stage¹ S1 W1 /steɪdʒ/ *n* **1** TIME/STATE [C] a particular time or state that something reaches as it grows or develops; → **phase**, **step**

the early/initial stages (of sth)
the later/final stages (of sth)
the halfway stage (of sth)
critical/crucial/important stage (of/in sth)
new stage (of/in sth)
reach/get to a stage
go through a stage (of sth)
mark a stage (in sth)
go/take sth/carry sth a stage further
at one stage (=at a time in the past)
at some stage/at a later stage (=at a time in the future)
at this stage (=now)
at this late stage

[+of/in] *the early stages of a child's development* | *during the later stages of the war* | *They've just reached the halfway stage of the project.* | *It's a good move at this stage in his career.* | *at a crucial stage in the race* | *We're getting to the stage where we hardly ever go out together.* | *All children go through an awkward stage at some time.* | *This treaty marks an* *important **stage in** our two countries' relationship.* | *Let us **take** the discussion **a stage further**.* | *At one stage, it seemed like she was ready to agree.* | *We can't change the design **at this late stage**.*

2 **PART OF PROCESS** [C] one of the parts which something such as a competition or process is divided into: [+of] *The team reached the semi-final stage of the competition.* | **stage 2/6 etc** *We're now reaching the end of stage 3 of the construction.* | *The **next stage** is to complete an application form.* | **in stages** *The rest of the money will be paid in stages* (=a small amount at a time).

3 **THEATRE** [C] the raised area in a theatre which actors or singers stand on when they perform; → **backstage**: **on stage** *She is on stage for most of the play.* | *She **appeared on stage** with George Michael.*

4 **ACTING** the stage acting as a profession, especially in theatres: *I wanted to **go on the stage** (=become an actor).* | *stars of **stage and screen** (=theatre and cinema)*

5 **centre stage** if someone or something is centre stage, it has everyone's attention, or is very important: *Anne's sculpture **took centre stage** at the show.* | *The UN has **moved to** the **centre stage** of world politics.*

6 **PLACE** [singular] a place or area of activity where something important happens: **on the world/international/political etc stage** *He's an experienced campaigner on the world stage.* | *important figures on the European political stage* | [+for] *Geneva has been the stage for many such conferences.*

7 **set the stage for sth** to prepare for something or make something possible: *Will this agreement merely set the stage for another war?* → **LANDING STAGE**

stage² v [T] **1** to organize a public event: **stage a strike/demonstration/sit-in etc** *Activists staged a protest outside the parliament.* | *exhibitions staged in Paris* | *The candidates' public appearances were **carefully staged** (=not natural).* **2** **stage a comeback/recovery etc** to start doing something again or being successful, after you had stopped or not been successful for some time: *He staged an amazing comeback.*

stage·coach /'steɪdʒkəʊtʃ $ -koʊtʃ/ n [C] a vehicle pulled by horses that was used in past times for carrying passengers and letters

stage·craft /'steɪdʒkrɑːft $ -kræft/ n [U] skill and experience in writing or organizing the performance of a play

stage di,rection n [C] a written instruction to an actor to do something in a play

stage 'door n [C usually singular] the entrance to a theatre used by actors and theatre workers

stage fright n [U] nervousness felt by someone who is going to perform in front of a lot of people: *Den suffered terribly from stage fright.* | *an attack of stage fright*

stage·hand /'steɪdʒhænd/ n [C] someone who works on a theatre stage, getting it ready for a play or for the next part of a play

stage 'left adv on the left side of a theatre stage from the view of an actor facing the people in the AUDIENCE: *He entered stage left.*

stage-'manage v [T] to organize a public event, such as a meeting, in a way that will give you the result that you want – often used to show disapproval: *The press conference was cleverly stage-managed.*

stage ,manager n [C] someone who is in charge of the technical parts of organizing a performance of a play, such as the LIGHTING, SCENERY etc

stage ,name n [C] a name used by an actor instead of his or her real name

stage 'right adv on the right side of a theatre stage from the view of an actor facing the people in the AUDIENCE: *She had to exit stage right.*

stage·struck /'steɪdʒstrʌk/ adj loving to see plays, or wanting very much to become an actor

stage 'whisper n [C] **1** a loud WHISPER used by an actor in a play which the other actors on the stage seem not to hear **2** a loud WHISPER that is intended to be heard by everyone

stage·y /'steɪdʒi/ adj another spelling of STAGY

stag·fla·tion /stæg'fleɪʃən/ n [U] an economic situation in which there is INFLATION (=a continuing rise in prices) but many people do not have jobs and businesses are not doing well

stag·ger¹ /'stægə $ -ər/ v **1** [I always + adv/prep] to walk or move unsteadily, almost falling over; ☐ **stumble**: *He managed to stagger home.* | *She staggered back a step.* | *The old man staggered drunkenly to his feet.* **2** [T] to make someone feel very surprised or shocked; ☐ **amaze**: *What staggered us was the sheer size of her salary.* **3** [I] also **stagger on** to continue doing something when you seem to be going to fail and you do not know what will happen: *He staggered on for another two years.* | **stagger from sth to sth** *The company staggered from one crisis to the next.* **4** [T] to arrange people's working hours, holidays etc so that they do not all begin and end at the same time: *Jim and his wife stagger their work hours so one of them can be at home with the kids.* **5** [T] to start a race with each runner at a different place on a curved track

stagger² n [C usually singular] an unsteady movement of someone who is having difficulty in walking

stag·gered /'stægəd $ -ərd/ adj [not before noun] extremely surprised; ☐ **amazed**: *I was absolutely staggered when I saw the bill.* | [+at/by] *She was staggered by the directness of his question.*

stag·ger·ing /'stægərɪŋ/ adj extremely great or surprising; ☐ **amazing**: *The cost was a staggering $10 million.* | *The financial impact on the town was staggering.* —**staggeringly** adv: *a staggeringly beautiful landscape*

stag·ing /'steɪdʒɪŋ/ n **1** [C,U] when a play is performed on stage: *a modern-dress staging of 'Hamlet'* **2** [U] a flat raised surface that is put up for a short time for people to stand and work on

staging ,area n [C] a place where soldiers meet and where military equipment is gathered before it is moved to another place

staging post n [C] a place where people, planes, ships etc stop on a long journey, for example to rest or get supplies: *a staging post on the flight from Australia*

stag·nant /'stægnənt/ adj **1** stagnant water or air does not move or flow and often smells bad: *a stagnant pond* **2** not changing or making progress, and continuing to be in a bad condition: *a government plan to revive the stagnant economy*

stag·nate /stæg'neɪt $ 'stægneɪt/ v [I] to stop developing or making progress: *Growth is expected to stagnate next year.* | *His career had stagnated.* —**stagnation** /stæg'neɪʃən/ n [U]: *economic stagnation*

stag night n [C] BrE a night before a man's wedding, which he spends with his male friends, drinking or having a party

stag ,party n [C] a party for men only, especially on the night before a man's wedding; → **hen party**

stag·y, stagey /'steɪdʒi/ adj behaviour that is stagy is not natural and is like the way an actor behaves on a stage: *a very stagy manner* —**stagily** adv

staid /steɪd/ adj serious, old-fashioned, and boring: *a staid old bachelor*

stain¹ /steɪn/ v **1** [I,T] to accidentally make a mark on something, especially one that cannot be removed, or to be marked in this way: *Be careful you don't stain the carpet.* | *This tablecloth stains very easily.* | *Her fingers were stained yellow from years of smoking.* | [+with] *a cowboy hat stained with dust and sweat* **2** [T] to change the colour of something, especially something

S

[1] 000, [2] 000, [3] 000, most frequent words in [S]poken and [W]ritten English

made of wood, by using a special liquid; ➔ **dye**: *We've decided to stain the shelves blue.* **3 stain sb's name/ honour/reputation etc** *literary* to damage the good opinion that people have about someone

stain² *n* **1** [C] a mark that is difficult to remove, especially one made by a liquid such as blood, coffee, or ink: [+**on**] *There was a dark red stain on the carpet.* | **remove/get rid of a stain** *White vinegar is great for removing stains.* | **wine/coffee/blood etc stain** *How do you get wine stains out of a tablecloth?* | **stubborn stains** (=ones that are very difficult to remove) **2** [C,U] a special liquid that you use to change the colour of something, especially wood; ➔ **dye** **3 stain on sb's character/name/reputation etc** something that damages the good opinion that people have about someone

stained glass *n* [U] glass of different colours used for making pictures and patterns in windows, especially in a church: *stained glass windows*

stainless steel *n* [U] a type of steel that does not RUST: *stainless steel cutlery*

stair S2 W3 /steə $ ster/ *n*
1 stairs [plural] a set of steps built for going from one level of a building to another; ➔ **upstairs, downstairs**: **up/down the stairs** *Jerry ran up the stairs.* | **the top/ head of the stairs** *I left my briefcase at the top of the stairs.* | **the bottom/foot of the stairs** *'Lisa,' he cried from the foot of the stairs.* | *We walked up four **flights of stairs** (=sets of stairs).* ➔ see picture at STAIRCASE
2 [C] one of the steps in a set of stairs: *Lucy sat down on the bottom stair.*
3 [singular] *literary* a STAIRCASE
4 below stairs *BrE old-fashioned* in the servants' part of a large building, in the past

stair·case /'steəkeɪs $ 'ster-/ *n* [C] a set of stairs inside a building with its supports and the side parts that you hold on to

stair·way /'steəweɪ $ 'ster-/ *n* [C] a staircase, especially a large or impressive one

stair·well /'steəwel $ 'ster-/ *n* [C] the space going up through all the floors of a building, where the stairs go up

stake¹ W3 /steɪk/ *n*
1 at stake if something that you value very much is at stake, you will lose it if a plan or action is not successful: *They have to win the contract – thousands of jobs are at stake.* | *National pride is at stake in next week's game against England.*
2 COMPANY/BUSINESS [C] if you have a stake in a business, you have INVESTED money in it: **hold/have a stake in sth** *He holds a 51% stake in the firm.*
3 have a stake in sth if you have a stake in something, you will get advantages if it is successful, and you feel that you have an important connection with it: *Young people don't feel they have a stake in the country's future.*
4 MONEY RISKED [C] money that you risk as the result of a horse race, card game etc: *For a dollar stake, you can win up to $1,000,000.*
5 high stakes a) if the stakes are high when you are trying to do something, you risk losing a lot or it will be dangerous if you fail: *Climbing is a dangerous sport and the stakes are high.* **b)** if the stakes are high when you are doing something such as playing a card game, you risk losing a lot of money: *We're **playing for high stakes** here.*
6 POINTED STICK [C] a pointed piece of wood, metal etc, especially one that is pushed into the ground to support something or mark a particular place: *tent*

staircase

banister

stair/step

stakes | **Drive** two **stakes into the ground** about three feet apart.
7 the stake a post to which a person was tied in former times before being killed by burning: *Suspected witches were **burnt at the stake**.*
8 in the popularity/fashion etc stakes used when saying how popular, fashionable etc someone or something is: *Ben wouldn't score very highly in the popularity stakes.*
9 (be prepared to) go to the stake for/over sth *BrE* to be willing to do anything to protect or defend an idea, or belief: *That's my opinion, but I wouldn't go to the stake for it.*
10 pull up stakes also **up stakes** *BrE informal* to leave your job or home: *We're going to pull up stakes and move to Montana.*

stake² *v* [T] **1** to risk losing something that is valuable or important to you on the result of something: **stake sth on sb/sth** *Kevin is staking his reputation on the success of the project.* | *Jim staked his whole fortune on one card game.* **2 I'd stake my life on it** *spoken* used when saying that you are completely sure that something is true, or that something will happen: *I'm sure that's Jesse – I'd stake my life on it.* **3** also **stake up** to support something with stakes: *Young trees have to be staked.* **4** also **stake off** to mark or enclose an area of ground with stakes: *A corner of the field has been staked off.* **5 stake (out) a claim** to say publicly that you think you have a right to have or own something: [+**to**] *Both countries staked a claim to the islands.*

stake sth ⇔ **out** *phr v* **1** to watch a place secretly and continuously; ➔ **stakeout**: *Police officers have been staking out the warehouse for weeks.* **2** to mark or control a particular area so that you can have it or use it: *We went to the show early to stake out a good spot.* **3** to state your opinions about something in a way that shows how your ideas are clearly separate from other people's ideas: *Johnson staked out the differences between himself and the other candidates.*

stake·hold·er /'steɪkˌhəʊldə $ -ˌhoʊldər/ *n* [C] **1** someone who has INVESTED money into something, or who has some important connection with it, and therefore is affected by its success or failure: [+**in**] *Citizens should be stakeholders in the society they live in.* **2** *law* someone, usually a lawyer, who takes charge of a property during a quarrel or a sale **3** someone chosen to hold the money that is risked by people on a race, competition etc and to give all of it to the winner

stakeholder economy *n* [C] *BrE* an economic system in a society that citizens feel they receive advantages from and have responsibilities to

stake·out /'steɪkaʊt/ *n* [C] when the police watch a place secretly and continuously in order to catch someone who is doing something illegal

stal·ac·tite /'stæləktaɪt $ stəˈlæktaɪt/ *n* [C] a sharp pointed object hanging down from the roof of a CAVE, which is formed gradually by water that contains minerals as it drops slowly from the roof; ➔ **stalagmite**

stal·ag·mite /'stæləgmaɪt $ stəˈlægmaɪt/ *n* [C] a sharp pointed object coming up from the floor of a CAVE, formed by drops from a stalactite

stale /steɪl/ *adj* **1** bread or cake that is stale is no longer fresh or good to eat; ⟷ **fresh**: *French bread goes stale* (=becomes stale) *very quickly.* | *stale cake* **2** air that is stale is not fresh or pleasant; ⟷ **fresh**: *the smell of stale smoke* **3** not interesting or exciting any more: *stale jokes* | *Other marriages might go stale, but not theirs.* **4** if you get stale, you have no new ideas, interest, or energy, because you have been doing the same thing for too long: *If you stay in the job for more than 10 years, you get stale.* | *He was becoming stale and running out of ideas.* —**staleness** *n* [U]

stale·mate /'steɪlmeɪt/ *n* [C,U] **1** a situation in which it seems impossible to settle an argument or disagreement, and neither side can get an advantage; ⟷ **deadlock**: *an attempt to **break the stalemate*** | *The*

*discussions with the miners' union **ended in stalemate***.
2 a position in CHESS in which neither player can win
—**stalemate** *v* [T]

stalk[1] /stɔːk $ stɒːk/ *n* [C] **1** a long narrow part of a
plant that supports leaves, fruits, or flowers: *celery
stalks* → see picture at FRUIT[1] **2** a thin upright
object **3 sb's eyes are out on stalks** *BrE informal* if
your eyes are out on stalks, you are very surprised or
shocked

stalk[2] *v* **1** [T] to follow a person or animal quietly in
order to catch and attack or kill them; → **shadow**: *a
tiger stalking its prey* | *We know the rapist stalks his
victims at night.* → see picture at MOVEMENT **2** [T] to
follow and watch someone over a long period of time in
a way that is very annoying or threatening, and that is
considered a crime in some places: *She was stalked by
an obsessed fan.* **3** [I always + adv/prep] to walk in a
proud or angry way, with long steps: [+out/off/away]
*Yvonne turned and stalked out of the room in dis-
gust.* **4** [T] *literary* if something bad stalks a place, you
see or feel it everywhere in that place: *Fear stalks every
dark stairwell and walkway.*

stalk·er /'stɔːkə $ 'stɒːkər/ *n* [C] someone who follows
and watches another person over a period of time in a
way that is very annoying or threatening

stalk·ing /'stɔːkɪŋ $ 'stɒː-/ *n* [U] the crime of follow-
ing and watching someone over a period of time in a
way that is very annoying or threatening

'stalking ˌhorse *n* [C] someone or something that
hides someone's true purpose, especially a politician
who says they want their leader's job when the real
plan is that another, more important politician should
get it

stall[1] S2 /stɔːl $ stɒːl/ *n*
1 [C] a table or a small shop with an open front,
especially outdoors, where goods are sold: *a market
stall*
2 [C] an enclosed area in a building for an animal such
as a horse or cow
3 [C usually singular] if a plane goes into a stall, its
engine stops working
4 [C usually plural] a seat in a row of fixed seats for
priests and singers in some larger churches: *choir
stalls*
5 bathroom/toilet/shower stall a small enclosed private
area for washing or using the toilet
6 the stalls *BrE* the seats on the main level of a theatre
or cinema: *a good seat in the front row of the stalls*

stall[2] *v* **1** [I,T] if an engine or vehicle stalls, or if you
stall it, it stops because there is not enough power or
speed to keep it going: *The car kept stalling.* | *An
inexperienced pilot may easily stall a plane.* **2** [I] *informal* to deliberately delay because you are not ready to
do something, answer questions etc: *Quit stalling and
answer my question!* | *He was just stalling for
time.* **3** [T] *informal* to make someone wait or stop
something from happening until you are ready: *Maybe
we can stall the sale until the prices go up.* | *We've got to
stall him somehow.* **4** [I] to stop making progress or
developing: *The peace process remained stalled.* | *While
his career has stalled, hers has taken off.*

stall·hold·er /'stɔːlˌhəʊldə $ 'stɒːlˌhoʊldər/ *n* [C] *BrE*
someone who rents and keeps a market stall

stal·lion /'stæljən/ *n* [C] a male horse that is fully
grown, especially one that is used for breeding; →
mare

stal·wart[1] /'stɔːlwət $ 'stɒːlwərt/ *n* [C] someone who
is very loyal to a particular organization or set of
ideas, and works hard for them: *old party stalwarts* |
[+of] *Rob's a stalwart of the school's chess club.*

stalwart[2] *adj* **1 stalwart supporter/ally etc** a very
loyal and strong supporter etc **2** *formal* strong in
appearance —**stalwartly** *adv*

sta·men /'steɪmən/ *n* [C] *technical* the male part of a
flower that produces POLLEN

stam·i·na /'stæmɪ̩nə/ *n* [U] physical or mental
strength that lets you continue doing something for a

long time without getting tired: *You need stamina to be
a long-distance runner.* | *Elaine has the stamina and the
determination to succeed.*

stam·mer[1] /'stæmə $ -ər/ *v* [I,T] to speak with a lot of
pauses and repeated sounds, either because you have a
speech problem, or because you are nervous, excited
etc; ▤ **stutter**: *Whenever he was angry he would begin
to stammer slightly.* | *Ben stammered out an apology.*
—**stammerer** *n* [C]

stammer[2] *n* [C usually singular] a speech problem
which makes someone speak with a lot of pauses and
repeated sounds; ▤ **stutter**: *Jeff spoke with a slight
stammer.*

stamp[1] S2 /stæmp/ *n* [C]
1 MAIL also **postage stamp** *formal* a small piece of
paper that you buy and stick onto an envelope or
package before posting it: *a 29-cent stamp* | *Richard
collects stamps.* | *a second-class stamp*
2 PRINTED MARK a tool for pressing or printing a
mark or pattern onto a surface, or the mark made by
this tool: *a date stamp* | *a passport stamp*
3 the stamp of sth if something has the stamp of a
particular quality, it clearly has that quality: *The
speech **bore** (=had) **the stamp of** authority.*
4 PAYMENT *BrE* a small piece of paper that is worth a
particular amount of money and is bought and collected for something over a period of time: *television
licence stamps*
5 TAX *BrE* a piece of paper for sticking to some official
papers to show that British tax has been paid
6 of ... stamp *formal* someone with a particular kind of
character: *He's clearly of a very different stamp.*
7 WITH FOOT an act of stamping, especially with your
foot: *an angry stamp* → FOOD STAMP

stamp[2] S1 W1 *v*
1 PUT FOOT DOWN [I,T] to put your foot down onto the
ground loudly and with a lot of force: *The audience
stamped and shouted.* | *'I will not!' Bert yelled and
stamped his **foot** (=because he was angry).* | *She stood
at the bus stop **stamping** her **feet** (=because she was
cold).* | **stamp on sb/sth** (=try to hurt or kill someone or
something, by putting your foot down onto them)
Marta shrieked and started stamping on the cockroach.
2 WALK NOISILY [I always + adv/prep] to walk somewhere in a noisy way by putting your feet down hard
onto the ground because you are angry; ▤ **stomp**:
[+around/out of/off etc] *My mother stamped off down
the stairs.*
3 MAKE A MARK [T] to put a pattern, sign, or letters
on something using a special tool: *The woman at the
desk stamped my passport.* | *Among the papers was a
brown folder stamped 'SECRET'.* | **stamp sth on sth**
Stamp the date on all the letters.
4 AFFECT SB/STH [T] to have an important or permanent effect on someone or something: *The experience
remained **stamped on** her **memory** for many years.* |
stamp sb with sth *His army years had stamped him with
an air of brisk authority.*
5 MAIL [T] to stick a stamp onto a letter, PARCEL etc

stamp sb as sth *phr v*
to show that someone has a particular type of character: *It was his manners that stamped him as a real
gentleman.*

stamp on sb/sth *phr v*
to use force or your authority to stop someone from
doing something, or stop something from happening,
especially in an unfair way: *Officers were given orders
to stamp on any hint of trouble.*

stamp sth ⇔ out *phr v*
1 to prevent something bad from continuing: *We aim to
stamp out poverty in our lifetimes.*
2 to stop a fire from burning by stepping hard on the
flames
3 to make a shape or object by pressing hard on
something using a machine or tool

S

'stamp col,lecting *n* [U] the practice of collecting stamps from interest or because of their financial value —**stamp collector** *n* [C]

'stamp ,duty *n* [U] a tax that must be paid in Britain on particular legal documents that have to be officially checked, especially when buying a house

,stamped ad,dressed 'envelope *n* [C] *BrE* **SAE** an envelope with your name, address and a stamp on it, which you send to a person or organization so that they can send you information

stam·pede¹ /stæmˈpiːd/ *n* [C] **1** when a group of people all want to do the same thing at the same time: *a stampede to buy shares in high-tech companies* **2** when a group of large animals or people suddenly start running in the same direction because they are frightened or excited: *a cattle stampede*

stampede² *v* [I,T] **1** if a group of large animals or people stampede, they suddenly start running together in the same direction because they are frightened or excited: *a herd of stampeding buffalo* | *Children came stampeding out of the school doors.* **2** **be/get stampeded** to be made frightened or worried so that you do something too quickly, without thinking enough about it: [+into] *Don't get stampeded into any rash decisions.*

'stamping ground *n* [C] *especially BrE* **sb's stamping ground** a favourite place where someone often goes

stance /stɑːns $ stæns/ *n* [C usually singular] **1** an opinion that is stated publicly; ➡ **stand**: [+on] *What is your stance on environmental issues?* | [+against] *a strong stance against abortion* | **take/adopt a stance** *The President has adopted a tough stance on terrorism.* **2** a position in which you stand, especially when playing a sport: *a fighting stance*

stanch /stɑːntʃ $ stɔːntʃ, stɑːntʃ/ *v* an American spelling of STAUNCH²

stan·chion /ˈstæntʃən, ˈstɑːn- $ ˈstæn-/ *n* [C] a strong upright bar used to support something

stand¹ [S1] [W1] /stænd/ *v past tense and past participle* **stood** /stʊd/
1 BE ON FEET also **be standing up** [I] to support yourself on your feet or be in an upright position: *It looks like we'll have to stand – there are no seats left.* | *She stood in the doorway.* | **Stand still** (=do not move) *and listen to me.* | *Don't just* **stand there** (=stand and not do anything) *– help me!* | **stand on tiptoe/stand on your toes** (=support yourself on your toes) *If he stood on tiptoe, he could reach the shelf.* | **stand (somewhere) doing sth** *They just stood there laughing.* | *We stood watching the rain fall.*
2 RISE also **stand up** [I] to rise to an upright position: *Smiling, she stood and closed the blinds.*
3 STEP [I always + adv/prep] **a)** to step a short distance: [+back/aside] *She stood back to let him in.* | **stand clear of sth** *BrE* (=step away from something in order to be safe) *Stand clear of the doors, please.* **b)** *BrE* to accidentally step on or in something: [+on/in] *Don't stand in that puddle!*
4 IN A PARTICULAR POSITION [I,T usually + adv/prep] to be upright in a particular position, or to put something or someone somewhere in an upright position: *A lamp stood on the table.* | *Near the railway station stood a hotel.* | *Some remains of the original house still stand.* | **stand sth on/in etc sth** *Can you stand that pole in the corner for now?* | *I closed the lid and stood the case against the wall.* | **stand sb (up) on sth** *Stand Molly up on a chair so she can see.*
5 IN A STATE/CONDITION [linking verb] to be or stay in a particular state or condition: *The kitchen door stood open so she went in.* | **stand empty/idle** (=not being used) *scores of derelict houses standing empty* | *I'm not too thrilled with the way things stand* (=the state that the situation is in) *at the moment.* | *The evidence as it stands* (=as it is now) *cannot be conclusive.* | **where/how do things stand?** (=used to ask what is happening in a situation) *Where do things stand in terms of the*

budget?* | *I will know within the next month or two how I stand* (=what my situation is). | **stand united/divided** (=agree or disagree completely) *He urged the whole community to stand united and to reject terrorism.* | **stand prepared/ready to do sth** (=be prepared to do something whenever it is necessary) *We should stand ready to do what is necessary to guarantee the peace.* | *countries that have* **stood together** (=stayed united) *in times of crisis* | **stand in awe of sb** (=admire them, be afraid of them, or both)
6 NOT LIKE **can't stand** *spoken* used to say that you do not like someone or something at all, or that you think that something is extremely unpleasant; ☐ **can't bear**: *I can't stand bad manners.* | *I know he* **can't stand the sight of me.** | **can't stand (sb/sth) doing sth** *Lily can't stand working in an office.* | *I can't stand people smoking around me when I'm eating.* | **can't stand to do sth** *She can't stand to hear them arguing.*
7 ACCEPT A SITUATION [T usually in questions and negatives] to be able to accept or deal well with a difficult situation; ☐ **tolerate**: **can/could stand sth** *I couldn't stand the thought of leaving Danielle.* | *I've had about as much as I can stand of your arguing!* | *I don't know if I can stand the waiting any longer.* | **can stand sb doing sth** *How can you stand Marty coming home late all the time?* | *She's a strong woman who* **stands no nonsense** *from anyone.*
8 BE GOOD ENOUGH [T] to be good or strong enough to last a long time or to experience a particular situation without being harmed, damaged, etc: *Linen can stand very high temperatures.* | *His poetry will* **stand the test of time** (=stay popular).
9 stand to do sth to be likely to do or have something: **stand to gain/lose/win/make** *What do firms think they* **stand to gain** *by merging?* | *After the oil spill, thousands of fishermen stand to lose their livelihoods.*
10 NOT MOVE [I] to stay in a particular place without moving; ➔ **standstill**: *The car's been standing in the garage for weeks.* | *The mixture was left to stand at room temperature for 15 minutes.* | *The train was already standing at the platform.*
11 HEIGHT [linking verb] *formal* to be a particular height: *The trophy stands 5 feet high.* | *John stood 6 feet tall.*
12 LEVEL/AMOUNT [linking verb] to be at a particular level or amount: [+at] *His former workforce of 1,300 now stands at 220.* | *Illiteracy rates are still thought to stand above 50 percent.*
13 RANK/POSITION [I always + adv/prep] to have a particular rank or position when compared with similar things or people; ☐ **rank**: *The president stands high in the public opinion polls.* | *How do their sales stand in relation to those of similar firms?* | *His book could stand alongside the best.*
14 ELECTION [I] *BrE* to try to become elected to a council, parliament etc; ☐ **run** *AmE*: [+for] *She announced her intention to stand for Parliament.*
15 DECISION/OFFER [I not in progressive] if a decision, offer etc stands, it continues to exist, be correct, or be VALID: *Despite protests, the official decision stood.* | *My offer of help still stands.*
16 if you can't stand the heat, get out of the kitchen used to tell someone that they should leave a job or situation if they cannot deal with its difficulties
17 sb/sth could stand sth used to say very directly that it would be a good idea for someone to do something or for something to happen: *His smile exposed teeth that could stand a good scrubbing.* | **sb could stand to do sth** *My doctor told me I could stand to lose a few pounds.*
18 I stand corrected *spoken formal* used to admit that your opinion or something that you just said was wrong
19 where sb stands someone's opinion about something: [+on] *We still do not know where he stands on the matter.* | *You must decide where you stand.*
20 from where sb stand *spoken* according to what I know or feel: *I knew from where I stood that the stocks were practically worthless.*
21 know where you stand (with sb) to know how

someone feels about you, or what you are allowed to do in a particular situation: *At least we know where we stand with Steven now.* | *I'd like to know where I stand.* | *It helps to know where you stand legally.*

22 stand to attention *BrE* **stand at attention** *AmE* if soldiers stand to attention, they stand very straight and stiff to show respect

23 stand on your head/hands to support yourself on your head or hands, with your feet in the air

24 stand in line *AmE* to wait in a line of people until it is your turn to do something; ▤ **queue** *BrE*: *Customers stood in line for 20 minutes at the cash register.*

25 stand firm/stand fast **a)** to refuse to be forced to move backwards: *She stood firm, blocking the entrance.* **b)** to refuse to change your opinions, intentions, or behaviour: *The government continued to stand firm and no concessions were made.* | [+on/against] *He stands firm on his convictions.*

26 stand pat *AmE* to refuse to change a decision, plan etc: [+on] *Harry's standing pat on his decision to fire Janice.*

27 stand alone **a)** to continue to do something alone, without help from anyone else: *Some of the Pacific islands are too small to stand alone as independent states.* **b)** to be much better than anything or anyone else: *For sheer entertainment value, Kelly stood alone.*

28 stand still to not change or progress at all, even though time has passed: *No industry can stand still.* | *Time seems to have stood still in this lovely hotel.*

29 stand a chance/hope (of doing sth) to be likely to be able to do something or to succeed: *You'll stand a better chance of getting a job with a degree.* | *Maybe their relationship had never really stood a chance.*

30 stand in sb's way also **stand in the way** to prevent someone from doing something: *I always encouraged Brian. I didn't want to stand in his way.* | *You can't stand in the way of progress!*

31 stand on your own (two) feet to be able to do what you need to do, earn your own money, etc without help from others: *She's never learned to stand on her own feet.*

32 it stands to reason (that) used to say that something should be completely clear to anyone who is sensible: *It stands to reason that you cannot find the right person to do a job unless you know exactly what that job is.*

33 stand or fall by/on sth to depend on something for success: *The case against him will stand or fall on its own merits.*

34 LIQUID [I] a liquid that stands does not flow or is not made to move: *standing pools of marsh water*

35 stand guard (over sb/sth) to watch someone or something so that they do not do anything wrong or so that nothing bad happens to them: *Soldiers stand guard on street corners.* | *You must stand guard over him at all times.*

36 stand bail *BrE* to promise to pay money if someone does not return to a court of law to be judged

37 stand trial to be brought to a court of law to have your case examined and judged: [+for/on] *Gresham will stand trial for murder.* | *The accused was ordered to stand trial on a number of charges.*

38 stand accused (of sth) **a)** to be the person in a court of law who is being judged for a crime: *The former president stands accused of lying to the nation's parliament.* **b)** if you stand accused of doing something bad or wrong, other people say that you have done it: *The radio station stands accused of racism.*

39 stand tall **a)** to stand with your back straight and your head raised: *Stand tall with your feet comfortably apart.* **b)** *AmE* to be proud and feel ready to deal with anything: *We will stand tall and fight for issues of concern to our community.*

40 sb can do sth standing on their head *informal* used to say that someone is able to do something easily: *This is basic stuff. I can do it standing on my head.*

41 be stood on its head if something is stood on its head, it becomes the opposite of what it was before: *One area of the business which has been stood on its head is internal communications.*

42 not stand on ceremony *BrE* to not worry about the formal rules of polite behaviour: *Come on, Mal, don't stand on ceremony here at home.*

43 stand sb a drink/meal etc *BrE* to pay for something as a gift to someone: *Come on, Jack, I'll stand you a drink if you like.* → **make sb's hair stand on end** at HAIR (8); → **leave sb/sth standing** at LEAVE[1] (15); → **not have a leg to stand on** at LEG[1] (7); → **stand/serve/hold sb in good stead** at STEAD (2); → **stand your ground** at GROUND[1] (7)

stand against sb/sth *phr v*
to oppose a person, organization, plan, decision etc: *She hadn't the strength to stand against her aunt's demands.* | *There are only a hundred of them standing against an army of 42,000 troops.*

stand around *phr v*
to stand somewhere and not do anything: *We stood around saying goodbye for a while.*

stand by *phr v*
1 to not do anything to help someone or prevent something from happening; → **bystander**: *I'm not going to stand by and see her hurt.*
2 stand by sth to keep a promise, agreement etc, or to say that something is still true: *I stand by what I said earlier.* | *He stood by his convictions.*
3 stand by sb to stay loyal to someone and support them, especially in a difficult situation: *His wife stood by him during his years in prison.*
4 to be ready to do something if necessary; → **standby**: *Rescue crews were standing by in case of a breakdown.* | [+for] *Stand by for our Christmas competition.* | **stand by to do sth** *Police stood by to arrest any violent fans.*

stand down *phr v BrE*
1 to agree to leave your position or to stop trying to be elected, so that someone else can have a chance; ▤ **step down** *AmE*: [+as] *He was obliged to stand down as a Parliamentary candidate.*
2 to leave the WITNESS BOX in a court of law
3 stand (sb) down if a soldier stands down or is stood down, he stops working for the day

stand for sth *phr v*
1 if a letter or symbol stands for something, it represents a word or idea, especially as a short form: *What does ATM stand for?*
2 to support a particular set of ideas, values, or principles: *It's hard to tell what the party stands for these days.*
3 not stand for sth *BrE* to not allow something to continue to happen or someone to do something: *She's been lying about me, and I won't stand for it.*

stand in *phr v*
to temporarily do someone else's job or take their place; → **stand-in**: [+for] *Would you mind standing in for me for a while?*

stand out *phr v*
1 to be very easy to see or notice: *The outlines of rooftops and chimneys stood out against the pale sky.* | *She always stood out in a crowd.* | *I am sure illnesses stand out in all childhood memories.*
2 to be much better than other similar people or things; → **standout**: [+as] *That day still stands out as the greatest day in my life.* | [+from/among/above] *Three of the cars we tested stood out among the rest.*
3 to rise up from a surface: *The veins stood out on his throat and temples.*

stand out against sth *phr v BrE*
to be strongly opposed to an idea, plan etc: *We must stand out against bigotry.*

stand over sb *phr v*
to stand very close behind someone and watch as they work to make sure they do nothing wrong: *I can't concentrate with him standing over me like that.*

stand to *phr v BrE*
to order a soldier to move into a position so that they are ready for action, or to move into this position: **stand sb** ⇔ **to** *The men have been stood to.*

---

stand up phr v

1 to be on your feet or to rise to your feet; → **stand-up**: *I've been standing up all day.* | *Stand up straight and don't slouch!* | *Jim stood up stiffly.*

2 [always + adv/prep] to stay healthy or in good condition in a difficult environment or after a lot of hard use: [+**to**] *Most of the plants stood up well to the heat.*

3 to be proved to be true, correct, useful etc when tested: [+**to/under**] *The memoirs stand up well to cross-checking with other records.* | *Without a witness, the charges will never **stand up in court** (=be successfully proved in a court of law).*

4 stand sb up informal to not meet someone who you have arranged to meet: *I was supposed to go to a concert with Kyle on Friday, but he stood me up.*

5 stand up and be counted to make it very clear what you think about something when this is dangerous or might cause trouble for you

stand up for sb/sth phr v
to support or defend a person or idea when they are being attacked: *It's time we stood up for our rights.* | *Silvia is capable of standing up for herself.*

stand up to sb/sth phr v
to refuse to accept unfair treatment from a person or organization: *He'll respect you more if you stand up to him.* | *Cliff couldn't stand up to bullying.*

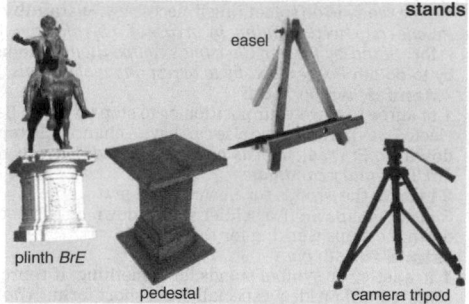

stands

easel

plinth BrE

pedestal

camera tripod

stand² n [C]
1 FOR SUPPORT a piece of furniture or equipment used to hold or support something: *a music stand* | *a cake stand* | *He adjusted the microphone stand.* | **coat stand/hat stand** (=for hanging coats or hats on)

2 FOR SELLING a table or small structure used for selling or showing things; 🔲 **stall** BrE: *a hotdog stand* | *an exhibition stand* | *The shop was crowded with display stands and boxes.* | *One week three magazines **hit the stands** (=became available to buy) with Peace Corps stories.* → NEWSSTAND; → see picture at TOWN

3 OPINION/ATTITUDE [usually singular] a position or opinion that you state firmly and publicly: [+**on**] *the Republicans' conservative stand on social and environmental issues* | *She was accused of not **taking a stand on** feminism or civil rights.*

4 OPPOSE/DEFEND a strong effort to defend yourself or to oppose something: **take/make/mount a stand (against sth)** *We have to take a stand against racism.*

5 the stands [plural] also **stand** BrE a building where people stand or sit to watch the game at a sports ground; → **grandstand**: *In the stands, fifty of Jess's friends and family have come to watch her last game.*

6 the stand WITNESS BOX: *Will the next witness please **take the stand** (=go into the witness box)?*

7 CRICKET the period of time in which two BATSMEN are playing together in a game of CRICKET, or the points that they get during this time

8 TAXIS/BUSES a place where taxis or buses stop and wait for passengers: *There's a taxi stand on Glen Road.*

9 TREES a group of trees of one type growing close together: [+**of**] *a stand of eucalyptus trees*

stand·a·lone /ˈstændəlaʊn $ -loʊn/ adj [only before noun] **1** a standalone computer works on its own

without being part of a network **2** a standalone company is one that is not part of a larger company —**standalone** n [C]

stan·dard¹ S3 W2 /ˈstændəd $ -ərd/ n
1 LEVEL OF QUALITY/ACHIEVEMENT [C,U] the level that is considered to be acceptable, or the level that someone or something has achieved

high/good standard
low/poor standard
meet/reach/attain a standard
set a standard
raise/improve standards
lower standards
maintain standards (=keep them at a good level)
standards fall/slip/go down/decline
up to standard (=good enough)
below standard (=not good enough)
stringent/rigorous/tough standards (=strict standards)
safety/environmental standards
academic/educational standards
living standards
by modern/today's/our etc standards

[+**of**] *The committee is assessing the standard of care in local hospitals.* | *parents who have very **high standards*** | *The rooms are of a **good standard**.* | *the **low standard** of housing* | *Students have to **reach a** certain **standard** or they won't pass.* | *The EU should **set** minimum **standards** of employee rights.* | *imaginative ideas for **raising standards** in schools* | ***Standards are falling** as the quality of applicants declines.* | *Safety measures failed to come **up to standard**.* | *The airline has **rigorous safety standards**.* | *These figures clearly show the difference in world **living standards**.* | *Many early child-rearing practices were cruel **by modern standards**.*

2 MORAL PRINCIPLES **standards** [plural] moral principles about what kind of behaviour or attitudes are acceptable: *the recent decline in **moral standards*** | ***standards fall/slip/go down** Standards have slipped since I was a boy.*

3 MEASUREMENT [C] a fixed official rule for measuring weight, PURITY, value etc: *an official government standard for the purity of silver*

4 SONG [C] a popular song that has been sung by many different singers: *popular jazz standards*

5 FLAG [C] old-fashioned a flag used in ceremonies: *the royal standard* → DOUBLE STANDARD, LIVING STANDARD

standard² S3 W2 adj
1 accepted as normal or usual: *We paid them the standard rate.* | **standard practice/procedure** (=the usual way of doing things) *Searching luggage at airports is now standard practice.* | *The format is fairly standard.*

2 regular and usual in shape, size, quality etc; 🔲 **non-standard**: *We make shoes in standard and wide sizes.* | *All these vans are made to a standard design.*

3 a standard book, work etc is read by everyone studying a particular subject

4 the standard form of a language is the one considered to be correct and is used by most people; 🔲 **non-standard**: *the standard spelling* | *standard English pronunciation*

standard-bearer n [C] formal **1** an important leader in a moral argument or political group **2** a soldier in past times who carried the STANDARD (=flag) at the front of an army

standard devi·a·tion n [C] technical a number in STATISTICS that shows by how much members of a mathematical set can be different from the average set

Standard Grade n [C] a school examination in one of a range of subjects that is taken by students in Scotland usually at the age of 16

standard-issue adj **1** a standard-issue thing is the common or usual type of that thing **2** included as an ordinary part of military equipment

stan·dard·ize also **-ise** BrE /ˈstændədaɪz $ -ər-/ v [T] to make all the things of one particular type the same as each other: *Attempts to standardize English spelling have never been successful.* | *standardized tests* —**standardization** /ˌstændədaɪˈzeɪʃən $ -dərdə-/ *n* [U]

'standard lamp *n* [C] *BrE* a tall lamp that stands on the floor; ➔ **floor lamp** *AmE*

ˌstandard of ˈliving *n* [C usually singular] the amount of wealth, comfort, and other things that a particular person, group, country etc has; ➔ **living standard**: **high/low standard of living** *a nation with a high standard of living*

ˌstandard ˈtime *n* [U] the time to which all clocks in a particular area of the world are set

stand·by¹, **'stand-by** /ˈstændbaɪ/ *n plural* **standbys** **1 on standby a)** ready to help immediately if you are needed: *A special team of police were **kept on standby.*** **b)** if you are on standby to do something, for example to travel by plane, you are on a list of people who may be allowed to do it if places become available, for example if other people cannot use their tickets: *We can **put you on standby.*** ➔ **STAND BY (4)** **2** [C] something that is kept ready so that it can be used when needed: *Powdered milk is a good standby in an emergency.*

standby² *adj* [only before noun] a standby ticket is one that you can get only if places become available, for example if other people cannot use their tickets

'standby time *n* [U] **1** the time during which a person or a machine is available to work but is not able to work because they are waiting to be given a specific job to do **2** the period of time that passes while you wait for a computer to do what you have asked it to do

'stand-in *n* [C] **1** someone who does the job or takes the place of someone else for a short time: *Gilbert failed to find a stand-in and so could not go to the party.* **2** someone who takes the place of an actor for some scenes in a film: [+for] *a stand-in for Tom Cruise* ➔ **stand in** at **STAND¹**

stand·ing¹ /ˈstændɪŋ/ *adj* [only before noun] **1** permanently agreed or arranged: *You have to pay **standing charges** whether or not you use the service.* | **standing invitation** (=permission to visit someone whenever you like) | **a standing army** (=a professional permanent army) | *A **standing committee** was established to coordinate the army and navy.* **2** done from a standing position: *The runners set off from a **standing start.*** | **standing ovation** (=when people stand up to clap after a performance) **3 standing joke** something that happens often and that people make jokes about: *The whole incident became a standing joke between us.*

standing² *n* [U] **1** someone's rank or position in a system, organization, society etc, based on what other people think of them: *Barb's work helped to improve her standing with her colleagues.* | [+in] *The scandal damaged the Governor's standing in the polls.* | **high/low standing** *a lawyer of high standing* **2 sth of five/many etc years' standing** used to show the time during which something such as an agreement has existed: *an arrangement of several years' standing*

ˌstanding ˈorder *n* [C,U] *BrE* an arrangement by which a bank pays a fixed amount of money from your account every month, year etc; ➔ **direct debit**

'standing room *n* [U] space for standing in a theatre, sports ground etc: *There was **standing room only** (=no seats were left) in the courthouse.*

stand·off /ˈstændɒf $ -ɒːf/ *n* [C] a situation in which neither side in a fight or battle can gain an advantage

stand-of·fish, **standoffish** /ˌstænd ˈɒfɪʃ $ -ˈɒːf-/ *adj informal* rather unfriendly and formal: *She was cold and stand-offish.* —**stand-offishly** *adv* —**stand-offishness** *n* [U]

stand·out /ˈstændaʊt/ *adj* [only before noun] *AmE* used about a person or thing in a group that is much better than all the rest: *the standout track on the album* —**standout** *n* [singular]: *He was the standout in last Saturday's game.*

stand·pipe /ˈstændpaɪp/ *n* [C] a pipe that provides water in a public place in the street

stand·point /ˈstændpɔɪnt/ *n* [C usually singular] a way of thinking about people, situations, ideas etc; ➔ **point of view: from a theoretical/political/economic etc standpoint** *Let's look at the questions from an economic standpoint.* | *a discussion of marriage **from the standpoint of** women*

stand·still /ˈstændˌstɪl/ *n* [singular] a situation in which there is no movement or activity at all: **come to a standstill/bring sth to a standstill** *Strikers brought production to a standstill.* | **at a standstill** *Traffic was at a standstill.*

'stand-up¹, **stand·up** /ˈstændʌp/ *adj* [only before noun] **1** stand-up COMEDY involves one person telling jokes alone as a performance: *a stand-up comedian* **2** a stand-up meeting, meal etc is one in which people stand up: *We had a stand-up buffet.* **3** a stand-up fight, argument etc is one in which people shout loudly at each other or are violent: *If it came to a stand-up fight, I wouldn't have a chance.* **4** able to stay upright: *a photo in a stand-up frame* | *a stand-up collar* ➔ **stand up** at **STAND¹**

stand-up² also **standup** *n* [U] **1** stand-up COMEDY: *Mark used to **do stand-up** at Roxy's Bar.* **2** a COMEDIAN who does stand-up COMEDY

stank /stæŋk/ the past tense of STINK

Stanley knife /ˈstænli ˌnaɪf/ *n* [C] *BrE trademark* a very sharp knife with a small TRIANGULAR blade that you use in activities such as decorating and WOODWORK; ➔ **exacto knife** *AmE*

stan·za /ˈstænzə/ *n* [C] a group of lines in a repeated pattern forming part of a poem; ➔ **verse**

sta·ple¹ /ˈsteɪpəl/ *n* [C] **1** a small piece of thin wire that is pushed into sheets of paper and bent over to hold them together **2** a small U-shaped piece of metal with pointed ends, used to hold something in place **3** a food that is needed and used all the time: *staples like flour and rice* **4** the main product that is produced in a country: *Bananas and sugar are the staples of Jamaica.*

staple² *v* [T] to fasten two or more things together with a staple: **staple sth together** *The handouts are all stapled together.* | **staple sth to sth** *I stapled the order form to the invoice.*

staple³ *adj* [only before noun] **1** forming the greatest or most important part of something: *Oil is Nigeria's staple export.* | *a staple ingredient of comedy* **2 staple diet a)** the food that you normally eat: [+of] *They live on a staple diet of rice and vegetables.* **b)** something that is always being produced, seen, bought etc: [+of] *television's staple diet of soap operas and quiz shows* **3** used all the time: *Marty's **staple excuses***

'staple gun *n* [C] a tool used for putting strong staples into walls

sta·pler /ˈsteɪplə $ -ər/ *n* [C] a tool used for putting staples into paper ➔ see picture at OFFICE

star¹ S2 W2 /staː $ staːr/ *n* [C]

1 IN THE SKY a large ball of burning gas in space that can be seen at night as a point of light in the sky: *I lay on my back and looked up at the stars.* | *The sky was filled with stars.* | **under the stars** *That night, we camped out **under the stars** (=outdoors).* | *The **stars were all out** (=they were shining).* | *stars twinkling overhead* (=shining in the sky and quickly changing from bright to faint) ➔ **FALLING STAR, SHOOTING STAR**

2 FAMOUS PERFORMER/PLAYER a famous and successful actor, musician, or sports player: **movie/film/ Hollywood etc star** *His dream was to become a Hollywood star.* | **pop/rock star** *British pop star Elton John* | *By the age of twenty she was already a **big star** (=very famous performer).* | *the **highest paid child star** of all time* | *a **rising star** (=someone who is becoming famous and successful) in the music world* | *She's a good actress, but she lacks **star quality** (=something*

S

that makes a person seem special and likely to be a star). | *She is a star of stage and screen.*
3 MAIN PERSON IN A FILM/PLAY ETC the person who has the main part, or one of them, in a film, play, show etc: [+of] *Ray Grimes, the star of the television series 'Brother John'*
4 BEST/MOST SUCCESSFUL PERSON a) the person who gives the best performance in a film, play, show etc: *Laporte, as Ebenezer Scrooge, is undoubtedly the star of the show.* | *Shamu, the killer whale, is the show's star attraction* (=best and most popular person or thing). **b)** the best or most successful person in a group of players, workers, students etc: **star player/performer/salesman etc** *the team's star player* | *the school's star pupil* | *the star columnist of the Sunday Times*
5 SHAPE a) a shape with four or more points, which represents the way a star looks in the sky **b)** a mark in the shape of a star, used to draw attention to something written; ◼ **asterisk**: *I put a star next to the items that we still need to buy.* **c)** a piece of cloth or metal in the shape of a star, worn to show someone's rank or position – used especially on military uniforms
6 HOTELS/RESTAURANTS a mark used in a system for judging the quality of hotels and restaurants: **three-star/four-star/five-star etc** *a two-star hotel*
7 the stars *BrE informal* a description, usually printed in newspapers and magazines, of what will happen to you in the future, based on the position of the stars and PLANETS at the time of your birth; ◼ **horoscope**: *sb's stars I never read my stars.* → STAR SIGN
8 sth is written in the stars used to say that what happens to a person is controlled by FATE (=a power that is believed to influence what happens in people's lives): *Their marriage was surely written in the stars.*
9 see stars to see flashes of light, especially because you have been hit on the head: *I felt a little dizzy and could see stars.*
10 have stars in your eyes to imagine that something you want to do is much more exciting or attractive than it really is → STARRY-EYED
11 you're a star!/what a star! *BrE spoken* said when you are very grateful or pleased because of what someone has done: *Thanks, Mel. You're a real star!* → FOUR-STAR GENERAL, FIVE-STAR, MORNING STAR, SHOOTING STAR; → **guiding star** at GUIDING (2); → **born under a lucky/unlucky star** at BORN² (7); → **reach for the stars** at REACH¹ (11); → **thank your lucky stars** at THANK (3)

star² v **starred, starring 1** [I] if someone stars in a film, television show etc, they are one of the main characters in it: [+in] *Eastwood starred in 'The Good, the Bad, and the Ugly'.* | [+with/opposite] *DeVito stars opposite Dreyfuss in the movie.* | [+as] *Hugh Grant stars as the romantic hero.* | *'The Freshman' was Brando's first starring role* (=the most important part in a film) *in ten years.* **2** [T] if a film, television show, or play stars someone, that person is one of the main characters in it; ◼ **feature**: *a film starring Meryl Streep* | **star sb as ...** *The movie starred Orson Welles as Harry Lime.* **3** [T usually passive] to put an ASTERISK (=a star-shaped mark) next to something written: *The starred items are available.*

star·board /'stɑːbəd $ 'stɑːrbərd/ n [U] the side of a ship or aircraft that is on your right when you are facing forwards; → **port** —**starboard** *adj*

starch¹ /stɑːtʃ $ stɑːrtʃ/ n **1** [C,U] a substance which provides your body with energy and is found in foods such as grain, rice, and potatoes, or a food that contains this substance; ◼ **carbohydrate**: *He eats a lot of starch.* | *Avoid fatty foods and starches.* **2** [U] a substance that is mixed with water and is used to make cloth stiff

starch² v [T usually passive] to make cloth stiff, using starch: *a starched tablecloth*

,star 'chamber n [C] *BrE* a group of people that meets secretly and makes important decisions

starch·y /'stɑːtʃi $ 'stɑːr-/ adj **1** containing a lot of STARCH¹ (1): *starchy foods* **2** *BrE* very formal and correct in your behaviour – used in order to show disapproval: *She spoke in a rather starchy manner.*
—**starchily** *adv* —**starchiness** *n* [U]

'star-crossed *adj literary* being in a situation that prevents something happy or good happening: *star-crossed lovers* (=people who love each other but cannot be together)

star·dom /'stɑːdəm $ 'stɑːr-/ n [U] the state of being a famous performer; → **fame**: *his rapid rise to stardom* | **shoot/rise/zoom to stardom** (=become famous very quickly) *Ellen shot to stardom as a model last year.*

star·dust /'stɑːdʌst $ 'stɑːr-/ n [U] *literary* an imaginary magic substance

stare¹ S3 W2 /steə $ ster/ v [I]
1 to look at something or someone for a long time without moving your eyes, for example because you are surprised, angry, or bored: [+at] *What are you staring at?* | **stare (at sb)** in disbelief/amazement/horror etc *She stared at me in disbelief.* | *She sat there* **staring into space** (=looking for a long time at nothing).
2 be staring sb in the face a) *informal* if something is staring you in the face, it is very clear or easy to notice but you have not noticed it: *The solution was staring me right in the face all along.* **b)** to seem impossible to avoid: *Defeat was staring us in the face.* → **stark staring mad** at STARK² (2)
stare sb out *BrE*; **stare sb down** *AmE phr v* to look at someone for so long that they start to feel uncomfortable and look away

stare² n [C] when you look at something for a long time in a steady way: *She gave him a long hard stare.* | *She laughed, ignoring the stares of everyone around her.* | *His pleas were met by a blank stare* (=a stare with no expression, understanding, or interest).

star·fish /'stɑːfɪʃ $ 'stɑːr-/ n plural **starfish** [C] a flat sea animal that has five arms forming the shape of a star

star·fruit /'stɑːfruːt $ 'stɑːr-/ n plural **starfruit** [C] a pale green tropical fruit that you can cut into pieces that have the shape of stars

star·gaz·er /'stɑːˌgeɪzə $ 'stɑːrˌgeɪzər/ n [C] *informal* someone who studies ASTRONOMY or ASTROLOGY
—**stargazing** n [U]

'star jump n [C usually plural] *BrE* one of a series of exercise jumps that you do from a standing position with your arms and legs pointing out at each side; ◼ **jumping jack**

stark¹ /stɑːk $ stɑːrk/ adj **1** very plain in appearance, with little or no colour or decoration: *In the cold dawn light, the castle looked stark and forbidding.* | *the stark beauty of New Mexico* **2** unpleasantly clear and impossible to avoid; ◼ **harsh**: *The movie shows the stark realities of life in the ghetto.* | *The extreme poverty of the local people is in* **stark contrast** *to the wealth of the tourists.* | *We are faced with a stark choice.* | *a stark reminder of life under communist rule* —**starkly** *adv* —**starkness** *n* [U]

stark² adv **1 stark naked** not wearing any clothes at all: *Ben was standing there stark naked.* **2 stark raving mad/bonkers** also **stark staring mad** *BrE* completely crazy: *He's gone stark raving mad.*

stark·ers /'stɑːkəz $ 'stɑːrkərz/ adj [not before noun] *BrE informal* not wearing any clothes; ◼ **naked**

star·less /'stɑːləs $ 'stɑːr-/ adj *literary* with no stars showing in the sky: *a starless night*

star·let /'stɑːlɪ̣t $ 'stɑːr-/ n [C] a young actress who plays small parts in films and hopes to become famous

star·light /'stɑːlaɪt $ 'stɑːr-/ n [U] the light that comes from the stars in the night sky

star·ling /'stɑːlɪŋ $ 'stɑːr-/ n [C] a common bird with shiny black feathers that lives especially in cities

star·lit /'stɑːˌlɪt $ 'stɑːr-/ adj *literary* made brighter by light from the stars: *a starlit night*

Star of Da·vid /ˌstɑːr əv ˈdeɪvɪd/ n [C usually singular] a star with six points that represents the Jewish religion or Israel

star·ry /ˈstɑːri/ adj **1** having many stars: *a starry winter sky* **2** starry eyes shine brightly **3** bright like a star or shaped like a star: *white starry flowers*

starry-'eyed adj informal happy and hopeful about things in a way that is silly or UNREALISTIC

Stars and 'Stripes n the Stars and Stripes the national flag of the US

'star sign also **sign** n [C] one of the 12 signs of the ZODIAC (=the system that uses people's birth dates to say what will happen to them in the future)

Star-Spangled 'Banner n **1** the Star-Spangled Banner the NATIONAL ANTHEM (=national song) of the US **2** the Star-Spangled Banner the national flag of the US

'star-,studded adj [only before noun] including many famous performers: *a star-studded cast*

start¹ [S2] [W2] /stɑːt $ stɑːrt/ v

1 BEGIN DOING STH [I,T] to do something that you were not doing before, and continue doing it; ⧉ **begin**: *There's so much to do, I don't know where to start.* | *Have you started your homework?* | **start doing sth** *Then the baby started crying.* | **start to do sth** *It's starting to rain.* | *He got up and started running again.* | *I'd better* **get started** (=start doing something) *soon.* | **start sb doing sth** *What Kerry said started me thinking* (=made me start thinking).

2 BEGIN HAPPENING [I,T] also **start off** to begin happening, or to make something begin happening: *What time does the film start?* | *Lightning started a fire that burned 500 acres.* | *The party was just getting started when Sara arrived.* | **starting (from) now/tomorrow/ next week etc** *You have two hours to complete the test, starting now.*

3 BEGIN IN A PARTICULAR WAY [I always + adv/prep, T] also **start off** to begin something in a particular way, or to begin in a particular way: *A healthy breakfast is a good way to start the day.* | [+with] *The festivities started with a huge fireworks display.* | [+as] *The restaurant started as a small takeout place.* | **start badly/well/ slowly etc** *Any new exercise program should start slowly.* | **start (sth) by doing sth** *Chao starts by explaining some basic legal concepts.*

4 BUSINESS/ORGANIZATION [T] also **start up** to make something begin to exist: **start a business/company/ firm etc** *She wanted to start her own catering business.*

5 JOB/SCHOOL [I,T] to begin a new job, or to begin going to school, college etc: *When can you start?* | **start school/college/work** *I started college last week.*

6 CAR/ENGINE ETC [I,T] also **start up** if you start a car or engine, or if it starts, it begins to work: *The car wouldn't start this morning.* | **get the car/engine etc started** *He couldn't get his motorbike started.*

7 BEGIN GOING SOMEWHERE [I] also **start off/out** to begin travelling or moving in a particular direction; ⧉ **set out**: *We'll have to start early to get there by lunchtime.*

8 LIFE/PROFESSION [I always + adv/prep, T] also **start off/out** to begin your life or profession in a particular way or place: [+as/in] *She started as a dancer in the 1950s.* | *It's difficult for new lawyers to get started in private practice.*

9 ROAD/RIVER/PATH ETC [I always + adv/prep] if a river, road, path etc starts somewhere, it begins in that place: *The trail starts immediately behind the hotel.* | [+in/at] *The race will start at the town hall.*

10 PRICES/AMOUNTS [I always + adv/prep] if prices, amounts, or rates start at or from a particular number, that is the lowest number at which you can get or buy something: [+at/from] *Room prices start from £25 a night.*

11 **start from scratch/zero** to begin doing a job or activity completely from the beginning: *There were no textbooks, so the teachers had to start from scratch.*

12 DELIBERATELY BEGIN STH [T] to deliberately make something start happening, especially something bad: *I started a fire to warm the place up.* | **start a fight/argument** *Oh, don't go trying to start an argument.* | *Other girls were starting rumours about me.*

13 **to start with** spoken **a)** said when talking about the beginning of a situation, especially when it changes later: *I was pretty nervous to start with, but after a while I was fine.* **b)** said to emphasize the first of a list of facts or opinions you are stating: *There are problems. To start with, neither of us likes housework.*

14 **be back where you started** to try to do something and fail, so that you finish in the same situation that you were in before: *A lot of people who lose weight gain it back over time, and end up back where they started.*

15 SPORTS [I,T] if a player starts in a game, or if someone starts them, they begin playing when the game begins, especially because they are one of the best players on the team: [+for] *Astacio started for the Dodgers on Tuesday night.*

16 **start a family** to have your first baby: *We're not ready to start a family yet.*

17 **start afresh/anew** to stop doing what you are doing and begin doing it again in a better or different way: *She saw her new job as a chance to start afresh.*

18 **sb started it!** spoken used to say that someone else has caused an argument or problem: *'Don't hit her!' 'But she started it!'*

19 **start something/anything** to begin causing trouble: *It looks like Jess is trying to start something.*

20 MOVE SUDDENLY [I] to move your body suddenly, especially because you are surprised or afraid; ⧉ **jump**: *A loud knock at the door made her start.* | [+from] *Emma started from her chair and rushed to the window.*

21 **start young** to begin doing something when you are young, especially when it is unusual to do it: *Woods started young, and was coached by his father.*

22 **Don't (you) start!** BrE spoken used to tell someone to stop complaining, arguing, or annoying you: *'Mum, I don't like this ice-cream.' 'Oh, don't you start!'*

start back phr v
to begin returning to the place you came from: [+to/ down/up etc] *I started back down the mountain to camp.*

start in phr v AmE
1 to begin doing something, especially with a lot of effort: *I decided to just start in and see what I could do.* | [+on] *Lilly started in on her burger.*
2 to begin criticizing someone or complaining to them about something: [+on] *Mom turned away from Rose and started in on me.*

start off phr v
1 to begin something in a particular way, or to begin in a particular way: **start sth ⇔ off with sth/by doing sth** *The theater company started off their new season with a Shakespeare play.* | **start off with sth/by doing sth** *I started off by drawing the flowers I had collected the day before.*
2 to be a particular thing or have a particular quality at the beginning of something, especially when this changes later: *The puppies start off white, and get their black spots later.* | [+as] *The games start off as a social event, but players soon become competitive.* | *I started off as a drummer.*
3 **start sth ⇔ off** to make something begin happening: *We're not sure what starts the process off.*
4 **start sb ⇔ off** to help someone begin an activity: [+with] *He started me off with some stretching exercises.*
5 to begin going somewhere: *I sat in the car for a few minutes before starting off.* | [+to/towards/back etc] *She started off to school in her new uniform.*
6 **start sb off** BrE informal to make someone get angry or start laughing, by saying something: *Don't say that; that'll just start him off.* | **start sb off doing sth** *He made her jump, and that started her off giggling.*

S

start on sb/sth *phr v*
1 to begin doing something or using something: *You'd better start on your homework.*
2 **start sb on sth** to make someone start doing something regularly, especially because it will be good for them: *Try starting your baby on solid foods at four months old.*
3 *BrE informal* to begin criticizing someone or complaining to them about something: [+at] *Ray's wife started on at him about spending too much time in the pub.*

start out *phr v*
1 to begin happening or existing in a particular way, especially when this changes later: [+as] *'The Star' started out as a small weekly newspaper.* | *The leaves start out a pale green, and later get darker.*
2 to begin your life or profession, or an important period of time: *When the band first started out, they played at small clubs.* | [+as] *She started out as a model.* | [+on] *young couples starting out on their life together*
3 to begin going somewhere: *Oliver started out at five, when it was still dark.*

start over *phr v AmE*
to start doing something again from the beginning, especially because you want to do it better: *If you make a mistake, just erase it and start over.*

start up *phr v*
1 if you start up a business, company etc, or it starts up, it begins to exist: *Tax breaks help new companies start up.* | **start sth ⇔ up** *Jordan started up a band of his own.*
2 if an engine, car etc starts up, or you start it up, it begins working: *The driver got back into the car and started up.* | **start sth ⇔ up** *Rory started up the engine and got the vehicle moving.*
3 if a sound, activity, or event starts up, it begins to exist or happen: *The crickets had started up now that it was evening.*

start² S2 W3 *n*
1 OF AN ACTIVITY/EVENT [C usually singular] the first part of an activity or event, or the point at which it begins to develop: [+of] *We arrived late and missed the start of the film.* | **(right) from the start** *We've had problems with this project right from the start.* | *She read the letter from start to finish without looking up.* | **get off to a good/bad etc start** *a free bottle of wine to get your holiday off to a great start* (=begin well or badly) | **a rocky/shaky/slow etc start** (=a bad beginning) *After a rocky start, the show is now very popular.* | *He wanted an early start on his election campaign.*
2 OF A PERIOD OF TIME [C usually singular] the first part of a particular period of time; ≡ **beginning**: [+of] *Since the start of 1992, the company has doubled in size.* | **the start of the year/day/season** *the start of an election year* | **get off to a good/bad etc start** (=begin well or badly) *The day got off to a bad start when I missed the train.*
3 **make a start (on sth)** to begin doing something: *I'll make a start on the washing-up.*
4 SUDDEN MOVEMENT [singular] a sudden movement of your body, usually caused by fear or surprise: **with a start** *Ted woke up with a start and felt for the light switch.* | *She said his name and Tom **gave a start** (=made a sudden movement).*
5 good/better/healthy etc start (in life) if you have a good etc start, you have all the advantages or opportunities that your situation, your parents etc could provide to help you succeed: *Good health care for the mother before birth **gives** babies a healthy **start**.* | *Naturally we want to give our kids the best possible **start in life**.*
6 WHERE RACE BEGINS the **start** the place where a race begins: *The horses were all lined up at the start.*
7 BEING AHEAD [C usually singular] the amount of time or distance by which one person is ahead of another, especially in a race or competition: [+on] *The prisoners had a three-hour start on their pursuers.* → HEAD START (2)
8 for a start *BrE informal* used to emphasize the first of a list of facts or opinions you are stating: *Well, for a start, the weather was horrible.*
9 be a start *spoken* used to say that something you have achieved may not be impressive, but it will help with a bigger achievement: *One exercise class a week isn't enough, but it's a start.*
10 JOB **a)** [C usually singular] the beginning of someone's job, which they will develop in the future, especially a job that involves acting, writing, painting etc: *Pacino got his **start** on the stage, before his success in films.* | *I **gave** you your **start**, so remember me when you win the Pulitzer Prize.* **b)** [C usually plural] a job that has just started, a business that has just been started, or someone who has just started a new job: *The number of business starts plummeted 10.5% during the second half of the year.* | *a training course for **new starts***
11 starts also **housing starts** [plural] *technical* when people begin to build a number of new houses
12 SPORT [C usually plural] **a)** a race or competition that someone has taken part in: *The horse Exotic Wood was unbeaten in five starts.* **b)** an occasion when a player plays when a sports match begins: *Jackson played in 353 games, with 314 starts.* → FALSE START; → fresh start at FRESH (4); → in/by fits and starts at FIT³ (7)

start·er /'stɑːtə $ 'stɑːrtər/ *n* [C] **1** *BrE* a small amount of food eaten at the start of a meal before the main part; ≡ **appetizer** *AmE*: *We had soup **as a starter**, followed by steak.* **2** a person, horse, car etc that is in a race when it starts: *Of the seven starters, only three finished the race.* **3** someone who gives the signal for a race to begin: *The starter fired his gun.* | **under starter's orders** (=about to begin the race) **4** **late starter** *BrE* someone who begins doing something, especially a job, later in life than people generally do **5** for starters *spoken* used to emphasize the first of a series of facts, opinions, questions etc: *Well, for starters, you'll need to fill out an application form.* **6** a STARTER MOTOR → NONSTARTER, SELF-STARTER

'starter home *n* [C] a small house or apartment bought by people who are buying their first home

'starter ,motor *n* [C] an electric motor for starting an engine

'starter pack also **'starter kit** *n* [C] the basic equipment and instructions that you need to start doing something

'starting ,blocks *n* [plural] also **the blocks** the pair of blocks fastened to the ground that a runner pushes their feet against at the start of a race

'starting gate *n* [C] a gate or pair of gates that open to allow a horse or dog to start running in a race

'starting line *n* [C] the line where a race begins

'starting ,point *n* [C usually singular] **1** an idea or situation from which a discussion, process etc can develop: [+for] *The article provides a starting point for discussion.* **2** a place from where a journey starts

'starting price *n* [C usually singular] **1** the lowest possible price for a particular type of thing such as a car or house without any special features, or the lowest price you are willing to accept for something you are selling **2** *BrE* the final ODDS that are offered just before a horse or dog race begins

start·le /'stɑːtl $ 'stɑːrtl/ *v* [T] to make someone suddenly surprised or slightly shocked: *Sorry, I didn't mean to startle you.* | **be startled to do sth** *I was startled to see Amanda.* —**startled** *adj*: *a startled expression*

start·ling /'stɑːtlɪŋ $ 'stɑːrt-/ *adj* very unusual or surprising: *Paddy's words had a startling effect on the children.* | *a startling discovery* | **it is startling to do sth** *It is startling to read that his father never visited him in hospital.* —**startlingly** *adv*

'start-up¹ *adj* [only before noun] connected with starting a new business: *start-up costs*

start-up² n [C] a new small company or business, especially one whose work involves computers or the Internet: *an Internet start-up*

,star 'turn n [C] *BrE* the most successful person in a group of people of the same type, especially the most successful actor, musician, or sports player

starv·a·tion /stɑːˈveɪʃən $ stɑːr-/ n **1** [U] suffering or death caused by lack of food; → **hunger**: *people dying of starvation* **2 starvation diet** *informal* when you eat very little food, especially to become thinner **3 starvation wages** extremely low wages

starve S3 /stɑːv $ stɑːrv/ v
1 [I] to suffer or die because you do not have enough to eat: *Thousands of people will starve if food doesn't reach the city.* | *pictures of starving children* | *They'll either die from the cold or* **starve to death** (=die from lack of food).
2 [T] to prevent someone from having enough food to live: *The poor dog looked like it had been starved.*
3 be starving also **be starved** *AmE* to be very hungry: *You must be starving!*
    starve sb/sth of sth also **starve sb/sth for sth** *AmE phr v* [usually passive] to not give something that is needed: *The schools are starved of funding.* | *The poor kid's just starved for attention.*
    starve sb ⇔ **out** *phr v* to force someone to leave a place by preventing them from getting food: *If we can't blast them out, we'll starve them out!*

stash¹ /stæʃ/ v [T always + adv/prep] *informal* to store something secretly or safely somewhere: **stash** sth **away** *He has money stashed away in the Bahamas.* | [+in/under] *You can stash your gear in here.*

stash² n [C] an amount of something that is kept in a secret place, especially money, weapons, or drugs; ⬛ **horde**: *Mike went into the bedroom to check on his stash.* | [+of] *a stash of drugs*

sta·sis /ˈsteɪsɪs $ ˈsteɪ-, ˈstæ-/ n [U] *technical* or *formal* a state or period in which there is no change or development

state¹ S2 W2 /steɪt/ n
1 CONDITION [C] the physical or mental condition that someone or something is in: [+of] *There are fears for the state of the country's economy.* | **in a bad/terrible etc state** *When we bought the house, it was in a terrible state.* | **sb's mental/physical/emotional state** *Frankly, I wouldn't trust his emotional state right now.* | *She was in an extremely confused* **state of mind.** | **in no fit state to do sth** (=should not do something because you are not in a suitable condition) *David's in no fit state to drive.* | *She can't go home now.* **Look at the state of her!** | **be in a good/bad state of repair** (=be in good condition and not need repairing, or be in bad condition) *The boat was in a good state of repair.* | *The country was* **in a state of war** (=officially fighting a war). | *Water exists in three states: liquid, gaseous, and solid.* → **STATE OF EMERGENCY**
2 GOVERNMENT [singular, U] also **the State** especially *BrE* the government or political organization of a country: *The state has allocated special funds for the emergency.* | **state employees/property/regulations etc** especially *BrE*: *limits on salary increases for state workers* | **state-owned/state-funded/state-subsidized etc** (=owned, paid for etc by the government) *a state-funded community housing project* | **matters/affairs of state** (=the business of the government) | **democratic/ one-party/totalitarian etc state** (=with that type of government) → **POLICE STATE, WELFARE STATE**
3 COUNTRY [C] a country considered as a political organization: *a NATO* **member state** (=a country belonging to NATO)
4 PART OF A COUNTRY [C] also **State** *BrE* one of the areas with limited law-making powers that together make up a country controlled by a central government such as the US and Australia; → **province, county, region**: *Queensland is one of the states of Australia.* |

the state of Iowa | **state employees/property/regula-tions etc** *the state government* | *state and federal taxes*
5 the States *spoken* a word meaning the US, used especially by someone when they are outside the US: *Which part of the States would you suggest I visit?*
6 be in a state/get into a state *BrE spoken* to be or become very nervous, anxious, or excited: *Mum and Dad were in a right state when I got in.*
7 OFFICIAL CEREMONY [U] the official ceremonies and events connected with government or rulers: *the Queen's first* **state visit** *here in seventeen years* | *music for* **state occasions** (=special public events)
8 state of affairs *formal* a situation: **unsatisfactory/sad/ sorry state etc of affairs** *I must say this is a very unsatisfactory state of affairs.*
9 the state of play especially *BrE* **a)** the position reached in an activity or process that has not finished yet: *What is the state of play in the current negotiations?* **b)** the score in a sports game
10 lie in state if the body of an important person who has just died lies in state, it is put in a public place so that people can go and show their respect

state² S3 W3 v [T]
1 to formally say or write a piece of information or your opinion: *Please state your name and address.* | *Rembert again stated his intention to resign from Parliament.* | *The government needs to clearly state its policy on UN intervention.* | **state (that)** *The witness stated that he had not seen the woman before.* | *Fine, but aren't you just stating the obvious here?*
2 if a document, newspaper, ticket etc states informa-tion, it contains the information written clearly: *The price of the tickets is stated on the back.*

,state at'torney n [C] *AmE* a lawyer who represents a US state in court cases

,state 'benefit n [C,U] *BrE* money given by the government in Britain to people who are poor, without a job, ill etc

'state court n [C] a court in the US which deals with legal cases that are concerned with state laws or a state's CONSTITUTION

'State De,partment n **the State Department** the US government department that deals with anything con-nected with foreign countries

state·hood /ˈsteɪthʊd/ n [U] **1** the condition of being an independent nation **2** the condition of being one of the states that make up a nation such as the US: **achieve/obtain/gain statehood** *Utah obtained statehood in 1896.*

State·house /ˈsteɪthaʊs/ n [C usually singular] the building where people who make laws in a US state do their work

state·less /ˈsteɪtləs/ adj *formal* not officially being a citizen of any country: *Millions of refugees remain stateless.* —**statelessness** n [U]

,state 'line n [C] the border between two states in the US: *We crossed the state line into Missouri.*

state·ly /ˈsteɪtli/ adj **1** done slowly and with a lot of ceremony: *the stately progress of the proces-sion* **2** impressive in style and size: *stately buildings* —**stateliness** n [U]

,stately 'home n [C] *BrE* a large house in the coun-tryside in Britain which has historical interest, espe-cially one open to the public

state·ment¹ S2 W1 /ˈsteɪtmənt/ n
1 [C] something you say or write, especially publicly or officially, to let people know your intentions or opin-ions, or to record facts: *the Prime Minis-ter's recent statements on Europe* | **make/issue/give a statement** *He refused to give a statement to the police.* | **official/public/formal/statement** *In an official state-ment, she formally announced her resignation.* | **true/ false statement** *False statements on your tax form could land you in jail.* | **get/take a statement** (=officially write down what someone says) *Detective Brady took a*

S

statement from both witnesses. | **sworn statement** (=that you officially declare to be true)
2 [C] a record showing amounts of money paid, received, owed etc: *the company's annual financial statements* | *I haven't received my **bank statement** for last month yet.*
3 [C] something you do, make, wear etc that causes people to have a certain opinion about you: *The type of car you drive **makes a statement** about you.* | *a fashion statement*
4 [U] *formal* the act of expressing something in words: *presentation and clarity of statement*

statement² *v* [T] *BrE* if an education authority statements a child who has special educational needs, they give a school additional money to help teach that child

state of e'mergency *n plural* **states of emergency** [C] when a government gives itself special powers in order to try to control an unusually difficult or dangerous situation, especially when this involves limiting people's freedom: *After **declaring** a **state of emergency**, the government arrested all opposition leaders.*

state-of-the-'art *adj* using the most modern and recently developed methods, materials, or knowledge: *state-of-the-art technology* | *His new laptop is state-of-the-art.*

state 'park *n* [C] a large park owned and managed by a US state, often in an area of natural beauty

state-room /'steɪtrʊm, -ruːm/ *n* [C] **1** a private room or place for sleeping on a ship **2** one of the large rooms in a palace

state ,school *n* [C] **1** *BrE* a British school which receives money from the government and provides free education; → **public school** **2** *AmE informal* a college or university that receives money from the US state it is in, to help pay its costs

State's 'evidence *n AmE* **turn State's evidence** if a criminal turns State's evidence, they give information in a court of law about other criminals

state-side /'steɪtsaɪd/ *adj, adv informal* in the US or relating to the US. This word is used by people when they are not in the US: *Members of the Colombian team were competing stateside at the time.*

states-man /'steɪtsmən/ *n plural* **statesmen** /-mən/ [C] a political or government leader, especially one who is respected as being wise, and fair: *a respected **elder statesman** —***statesmanship** *n* [U]

states-man-like /'steɪtsmənlaɪk/ *adj* showing the qualities of a statesman – used to show approval: *his statesmanlike handling of the crisis*

state 'trooper *n* [C] a member of a police force that is controlled by one of the US state governments, who works anywhere in that state

state uni'versity *n plural* **state universities** [C] a university in the US which receives money from a state to help pay its costs

state-wide /'steɪtwaɪd/ *adj, adv* affecting or involving the whole of a US state: *a statewide poll* | *a model that could be used in towns statewide*

stat-ic¹ /'stætɪk/ *adj* not moving, changing, or developing; **◧ dynamic**: *Economists predict that house prices will remain static for a long period.*

static² *n* [U] **1** noise caused by electricity in the air that blocks or spoils the sound from radio or TV **2** static electricity **3** *especially AmE informal* complaints or opposition to a plan, situation, or action: *His promotion has caused a lot of static.* —**statically** /-kli/ *adv*

static elec'tricity *n* [U] electricity that is not flowing in a current, but collects on the surface of an object and gives you a small ELECTRIC SHOCK

stat-ics /'stætɪks/ *n* [U] the science dealing with the forces that produce balance in objects that are not moving; → **dynamics**

sta·tion¹ S1 W1 /'steɪʃən/ *n*
1 TRAIN/BUS [C] a place where trains or buses regularly stop so that passengers can get on and off, goods can be loaded etc, or the buildings at such a place; → **terminus**: *I want to get off at the next station.* | *Grand Central Station* | *Is there a waiting room in the station?* | **train station/railway station** *BrE* | *the city bus station*
2 CENTRE FOR A SERVICE OR ACTIVITY [C] a building or place that is a centre for a particular kind of service or activity: *a police station* | *a fire station* | **petrol station** *BrE*/**gas station** *AmE* (=where petrol is sold) | **polling station** (=where you vote in an election) | *an Antarctic **research station*** → **ACTION STATIONS**
3 RADIO/TV [C] an organization which makes television or radio broadcasts, or the building where this is done: *New York jazz station WBGO* | *a local TV station*
4 SOCIAL RANK [C] *old-fashioned* your position in society: *Karen was definitely getting **ideas above her station** (=higher than her social rank).*
5 POSITION [C] *formal* a place where someone stands or sits in order to be ready to do something quickly if needed: *You're not to leave your station unless told.*
6 FARM [C] a large sheep or cattle farm in Australia or New Zealand
7 ARMY/NAVY [C] a small military establishment: *an isolated naval station*

station² *v* [T usually passive] **1** to send someone in the military to a particular place for a period of time as part of their military duty; **◧ post**: *I was stationed overseas at the time.* **2** *formal* to move to a particular place and stand or sit there, especially in order to be able to do something quickly, or to cause someone to do this: *A security guard was stationed near the door.*

sta·tion·a·ry /'steɪʃənəri $ -neri/ *adj* standing still instead of moving: *How did you manage to drive into a stationary vehicle?* ⚠ Do not confuse with **stationery** (=writing materials such as paper).

'station break *n* [C] a pause during a radio or television broadcast in the US, so that local stations can give their names or broadcast advertisements

sta·tion·er /'steɪʃənə $ -ər/ *n* [C] *BrE* **1** **stationer's** a shop that sells stationery **2** someone in charge of a shop that sells stationery

stationery

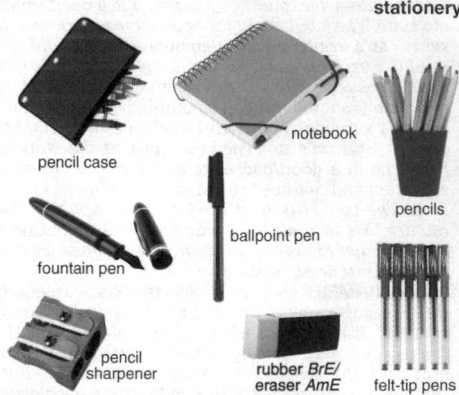

pencil case

notebook

pencils

fountain pen

ballpoint pen

pencil sharpener

rubber *BrE*/ eraser *AmE*

felt-tip pens

sta·tion·e·ry /'steɪʃənəri $ -neri/ *n* [U] **1** paper for writing letters, usually with matching envelopes: *a letter on hotel stationery* **2** materials that you use for writing, such as paper, pens, pencils etc

'station ,house *n* [C] *AmE old-fashioned* the local office of the police in a town, part of a city etc; **◧ police station**

'station ,master *n* [C] someone who is in charge of a railway station

'station ,wagon *n* [C] *AmE* a large car with extra space at the back, with a door there for loading and unloading; **◧ estate car** *BrE*

sta·tis·tic [S2] [W3] /stə'tɪstɪk/ *n*
1 statistics a) [plural] a set of numbers which represent facts or measurements: *the **official** crime statistics* | [+**for**] *statistics for injuries at work* | ***Statistics show** that 50% of new businesses fail in their first year.* **b)** [U] the science of collecting and examining such numbers: *Statistics is a branch of mathematics.*
2 [singular] a single number which represents a fact or measurement: *The statistic comes from a study recently conducted by the British government.*
3 a statistic *informal* if someone is just a statistic, they are just another example of someone who has died because of a particular type of accident or disease: *We can't let these boys become just another statistic.*
—**statistical** *adj*: *statistical evidence* —**statistically** /-kli/ *adv*: *The variation is not statistically significant.*
→ VITAL STATISTICS

stat·is·ti·cian /ˌstætɪ̩'stɪʃən/ *n* [C] someone who works with statistics

sta·tive /'steɪtɪv/ *adj technical* a stative verb describes a state rather than an action or event, and is not usually used in PROGRESSIVE[1] (3) forms, for example 'belong' in the sentence 'this book belongs to me'

stats /stæts/ *n* [plural] *informal* STATISTICS

stat·u·a·ry /'stætʃuəri $ -tʃueri/ *n* [U] *formal* statues: *a fine collection of Greek statuary*

stat·ue /'stætʃuː/ *n* [C] an image of a person or animal that is made in solid material such as stone or metal and is usually large; → **sculpture**: *Churchill's **statue stands** outside the parliament building.* | *A bronze **statue** was **erected** in his honour.* | [+**of**] *Statues of Lenin were torn down all across Eastern Europe.*

stat·u·esque /ˌstætʃu'esk‹ / *adj* large and beautiful in an impressive way, like a statue: *a statuesque woman*

stat·u·ette /ˌstætʃu'et/ *n* [C] a very small statue that can be put on a table or shelf

stat·ure /'stætʃə $ -ər/ *n* [U] *written* **1** the degree to which someone is admired or regarded as important: **of world/international/national stature** *Armstrong was a musician of world stature.* | *He **grew in stature** (=became more admired or popular) during the campaign.* | [+**as**] *his growing stature as an artist* **2** someone's height or size: *Bernard was short in stature, with a large head.*

sta·tus [W2] /'steɪtəs $ 'steɪtəs, 'stæ-/ *n*
1 [C,U] the official legal position or condition of a person, group, country etc; → **standing**: *These documents have no **legal status** in Britain.* | *What is your **marital status** (=are you married or not)?*
2 [U] your social or professional rank or position, considered in relation to other people: **high/low status** *low-status jobs* | *Doctors have traditionally enjoyed high **social status**.*
3 [U] respect and importance that someone or something is given; ◨ **prestige**: *the status given to education* | *Mandela's status as a world leader*
4 the status of sth a situation at a particular time, especially in an argument, discussion etc: *What's the status of the trade talks?*

status quo /ˌsteɪtəs 'kwəʊ $ ˌsteɪtəs 'kwoʊ, ˌstæ-/ *n* **the status quo** the state of a situation as it is: **maintain/ preserve/defend the status quo** (=not make any changes) *Will the West use its influence to maintain the status quo and not disrupt the flow of oil?*

'status ˌsymbol *n* [C] something that you have or own that you think shows high social rank or position: *A Rolls Royce is seen as a status symbol.*

stat·ute /'stætʃuːt/ *n* [C] **1** a law passed by a parliament, council etc and formally written down: *Protection for the consumer is **laid down by statute** (=established by law).* **2** a formal rule of an institution or organization: *College statutes forbid drinking on campus.*

'statute book *n* **on the statute book** officially part of the law: *The government would like to see this new law on the statute book as soon as possible.*

'statute law *n* [U] the whole group of written laws established by a parliament, council etc; → **common law**

ˌstatute of limi'tations *n plural* **statutes of limitations** [C] *law* a law which gives the period of time within which action may be taken on a legal question or crime

stat·u·to·ry /'stætʃɵtəri $ -tɔːri/ *adj* fixed or controlled by law: *statutory employment rights* | *She's below the **statutory age** for school attendance.*
—**statutorily** *adv*

ˌstatutory of'fence *n* [C] a crime that is described by a law and can be punished by a court

ˌstatutory 'rape *n* [C] *law* the crime of having sex with someone who is younger than a particular age

staunch[1] /stɔːntʃ $ stɒːntʃ, staːntʃ/ *adj* [only before noun] giving strong loyal support to another person, organization, belief etc; ◨ **steadfast**: *a staunch conservative* | **staunch supporter/ally/advocate** *one of Bush's staunchest supporters* —**staunchly** *adv*
—**staunchness** *n* [U]

staunch[2] *also* **stanch** *AmE v* [T] to stop the flow of liquid, especially of blood from a wound: *He used a rag to staunch the flow of blood.*

stave[1] /steɪv/ *n* [C] **1** the set of five lines on which music is written **2** one of the thin curved pieces of wood fitted close together to form the sides of a BARREL

stave[2] *v past tense and past participle* **staved** *or* **stove** /stəʊv $ stoʊv/
stave sth ⇔ **in** *phr v* to break something inwards: *The ship's side was stove in when it went onto the rocks.*
stave sth ⇔ **off** *phr v past tense and past participle* **staved** to keep someone or something from reaching you or affecting you for a period of time: *She brought some fruit on the journey to **stave off** hunger.*

staves /steɪvz/ the plural of STAFF[1] (2)

stay[1] [S1] [W1] /steɪ/ *v*
1 IN A PLACE [I] to remain in a place rather than leave: *They stayed all afternoon, chatting.* | **stay (at) home** *I decided to stay home.* | **stay for a year/ten minutes/a week etc** *Isabel stayed for a year in Paris to study.* | [+**in**] *Stay in bed and drink plenty of liquids.* | *She **stayed late** to finish the report.* | **stay here/there** *Stay right there! I'll be back in a minute.* | **stay to dinner/stay for lunch etc** *Why don't you stay for supper?* | [+**behind/ after**] *Some of the students stayed after class to talk* (=remained after others had gone). | **stay and do sth** *I should stay and help.*
2 IN A CONDITION [I always + adv/prep, linking verb] to continue to be in a particular position, place, or state, without changing; ◨ **remain**: *Rollings will stay as chairman this year.* | [+**adj**] *Eat right to stay healthy.* | *It was hard to stay awake.* | *Nine women gained weight, and four **stayed the same**.* | [+**away/in/on etc**] *Stay away from my daughter!* | *You stay on this road for a mile before turning off.* | [+**around**] *Most of her boyfriends don't stay around* (=stay with her) *very long.*
3 LIVE SOMEWHERE [I] to live in a place for a short time as a visitor or guest: *How long are they going to stay?* | [+**at/with**] *My mother is staying with us this week.* | [+**in**] *They're staying in the same hotel.* | **stay the night/stay overnight/stay over** (=stay from one evening to the next day) *Did you stay the night at Carolyn's?*
4 stay put *spoken* to remain in one place and not move: *Stay put until I get back.*
5 be here to stay to become accepted and used by most people: *Professional women's basketball is here to stay.*
6 stay after (school) to remain at school after the day's classes are finished, often as a punishment
7 stay the course *informal* to finish something in spite of difficulties: *Dieters should try hard to stay the course.*
8 stay tuned a) to continue watching or listening to the same television CHANNEL or radio station **b)** used to say that you should look or listen for more information

about a particular subject at a later time: *The project is still under discussion, so stay tuned.*

9 stay! used to tell a dog not to move

10 stay sb's hand *literary* to stop someone from doing something

11 stay an order/ruling/execution etc *law* if a judge stays an order, ruling etc, they stop a particular decision from being used or a particular action from happening → **stay in touch** at TOUCH² (4)

stay in *phr v*
to spend the evening at home rather than go out: *I was tired, so I decided to stay in.*

stay on *phr v*
to continue to do a job or to study after the usual or expected time for leaving: *He resigned as chairman, but stayed on as an instructor.*

stay out *phr v*
1 to remain away from home during the evening or night: *He started staying out late, drinking.*
2 stay out of sth *spoken* to not get involved in an argument or fight: *You stay out of it. It's none of your business.*

stay up *phr v*
to not go to bed at the time you would normally go to bed: *We stayed up all night, talking.* | *I let the kids stay up late on Fridays.*

stay² n 1 [C usually singular] a limited time of living in a place: [+in/at] *I met her towards the end of my stay in Los Angeles.* | **long/short/overnight etc stay** *a short stay in the hospital* **2** [C,U] *law* the stopping or delay of an action because a judge has ordered it: **stay of execution** (=a delay in punishing someone by killing them) **3** [C] a strong wire or rope used for supporting a ship's MAST **4** [C] a short piece of plastic or wire used to keep a shirt COLLAR stiff

'stay-at-ˌhome *adj* [only before noun] staying at home, rather than working somewhere else, usually in order to take care of children: *a stay-at-home mom*

stay·er /ˈsteɪə $ -ər/ *n* [C] *BrE* a horse or person that is able to continue to the end of a long race, job etc

'staying ˌpower *n* [U] the ability or energy to continue doing something difficult until it is finished: *a team with staying power*

St Ber·nard /sənt ˈbɜːnəd $ ˌseɪnt bərˈnɑːrd/ *n* [C] a large strong dog that in the past was trained to help find people who were lost in the snow

STD /ˌes tiː ˈdiː/ *n* [C,U] *medical* **sexually transmitted disease** a disease that one person passes to another through having sex, such as AIDS or HERPES

stead /sted/ *n* **1 do sth in sb's stead** *formal* to do something that someone else usually does or was going to do: *Pearson was appointed to go in Harrison's stead.* **2 stand/serve/hold sb in good stead** to be very useful to someone when needed: *His years of training were standing him in good stead.*

stead·fast /ˈstedfɑːst $ -fæst/ *adj literary* **1** faithful and very loyal: *her father's steadfast love for her* **2** being certain that you are right about something and refusing to change your opinion in any way: [+in] *Dr. Faraday remained steadfast in his plea of innocence.* —**steadfastly** *adv* —**steadfastness** *n* [U]

stead·y¹ W3 /ˈstedi/ *adj*
1 CONTINUOUS continuing or developing gradually or without stopping, and not likely to change: *Paul is making steady progress.* | *a steady rain* | **hold/remain steady** *Employment is holding steady at 96%.* | **steady stream/flow/trickle etc** *a steady stream of traffic*
2 NOT MOVING firmly held in a particular position and not moving or shaking; ▪ **stable: hold/keep sth steady** *Keep the camera steady while you take a picture.* | *It takes a steady hand to perform surgery.*
3 **steady job/work/income** a job or work that will definitely continue over a long period of time: *It's hard to find a steady, well-paying job.*
4 VOICE/LOOK if someone's voice is steady, or they

look at you in a steady way, they seem calm and do not stop speaking or looking at you: *There were tears in her eyes, but her voice was steady.* | *He could not meet Connor's steady gaze.*
5 PERSON someone who is steady is sensible and you can depend on them: *a steady worker*
6 **steady boyfriend/girlfriend** someone that you have been having a romantic relationship with for a long time
7 **steady relationship** a serious and strong relationship that continues for a long time —**steadily** *adv*: *The company's exports have grown steadily.* | *debt was increasingly steadily* —**steadiness** *n* [U]

steady² v steadied, steadying, steadies 1 [I,T] to hold someone or something so they become more balanced or controlled, or to become more balanced or controlled: **steady yourself** *He reached the chair and steadied himself.* | *The plane steadied, and the passengers relaxed.* **2** [I] to stop increasing or decreasing and remain about the same; ▪ **stabilize**: *The dollar has steadied after early losses on the money markets.* **3** [I,T] to become calmer, or to make someone do this: *Tamar took a deep breath to steady her nerves.* | *Jess is a steadying influence on the rest of the team.*

steady³ *adv* **go steady (with sb)** to have a long regular romantic relationship with someone

steady⁴ *n plural* **steadies** [C] *AmE old-fashioned informal* a BOYFRIEND or GIRLFRIEND that someone has been having a romantic relationship with

steady⁵ *interjection* **1** used when you want to tell someone to be careful or not to cause an accident: *Steady! You nearly knocked me over.* **2 Steady on!** *BrE informal* used when you think that what someone is saying or doing is too extreme: *Steady on! That bottle's got to last all night.*

ˌsteady 'state ˌtheory *n* [singular] *technical* the idea that things in space have always existed and have always been moving away from each other as new atoms begin to exist; → **big bang theory**

steak /steɪk/ *n* **1** [C,U] good quality BEEF, or a large thick piece of any good quality red meat **2 cod/salmon/tuna etc steak** a large thick piece of fish **3** [U] *BrE* BEEF that is not of very good quality and is used in making CASSEROLES etc

steak·house /ˈsteɪkhaʊs/ *n* [C] a restaurant that serves steak

ˌsteak tar'tare *n* [U] steak that is cut into very small pieces and eaten raw, usually with a raw egg

steal¹ S3 W3 /stiːl/ *v past tense* **stole** /stəʊl $ stoʊl/ *past participle* **stolen** /ˈstəʊlən $ ˈstoʊ-/
1 TAKE STH [I,T] to take something that belongs to someone else: *Boys broke into a shop and stole £45 in cash.* | [+from] *He stole money from his parents.* | **steal sth from sb** *He'd stolen the flowers from our garden.*
2 USE IDEAS [I,T] to use someone's ideas without getting permission or without admitting that they are not your own ideas; ▪ **pinch**: *Inventors know that someone is always going to try to steal their designs.* | **steal sth from sb** *A well-known scientist was accused of stealing his former student's ideas.*
3 MOVE SOMEWHERE [I always + adv/prep] to move quietly without anyone noticing you; ▪ **creep**: [+into/across etc] *He dressed quietly and stole out of the house.*
4 steal the show/limelight/scene to do something, especially when you are acting in a play, that makes people pay more attention to you than to other people: *Elwood stole the show with a marvellous performance.*
5 steal a look/glance etc to look at someone or something quickly and secretly
6 SPORT **a)** [I,T] to run to the next BASE before someone hits the ball in the sport of baseball **b)** [T] to suddenly take control of the ball, PUCK etc, when the other team had previously had control of it, for example in BASKETBALL or ICE HOCKEY: *Roy steals the ball four times in the first half.*
7 steal a kiss to kiss someone quickly when they are not expecting it

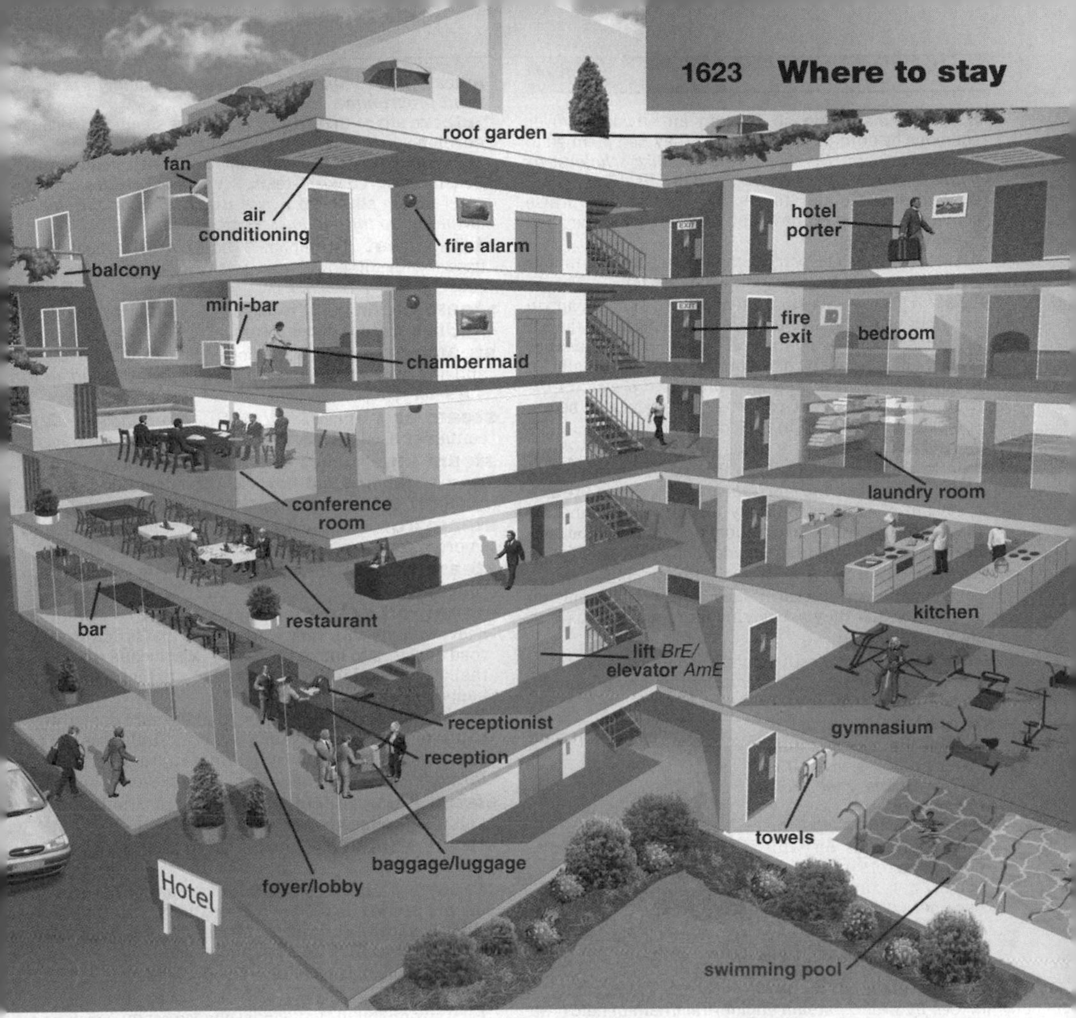
roof garden
fan
air conditioning
fire alarm
hotel porter
balcony
mini-bar
fire exit
bedroom
chambermaid
conference room
laundry room
kitchen
bar
restaurant
lift *BrE*/ elevator *AmE*
receptionist
gymnasium
reception
towels
baggage/luggage
foyer/lobby
Hotel
swimming pool

B&B

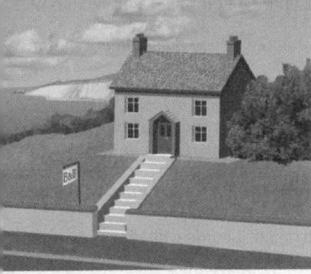

bed and breakfast

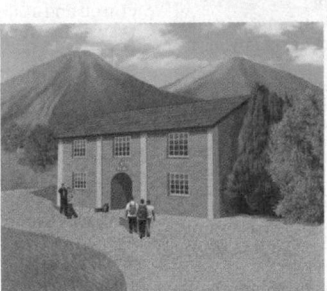

youth hostel

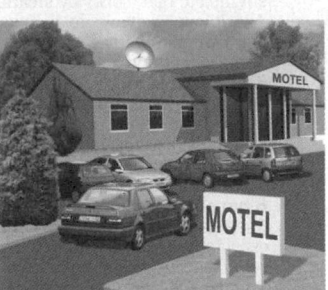

MOTEL
MOTEL

motel

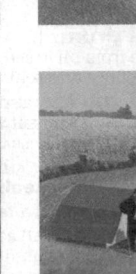

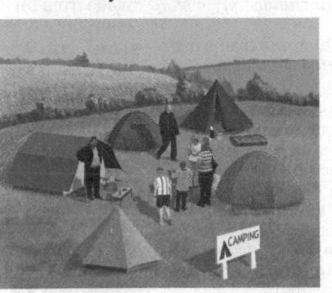

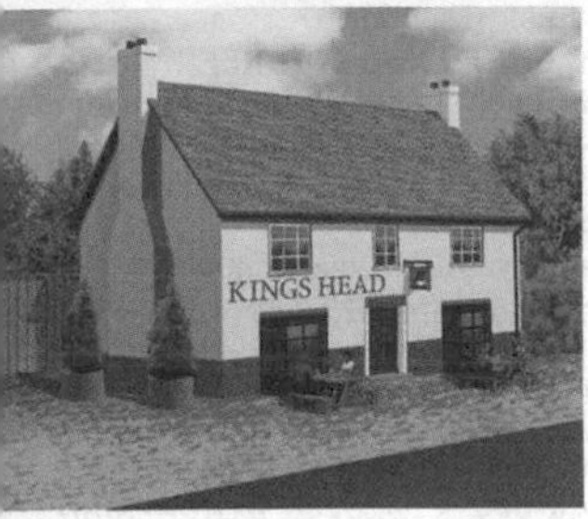
KINGS HEAD

pub ***BrE*/inn**

CAMPING

campsite ***BrE*/campground *AmE***

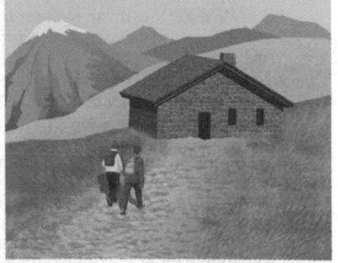

mountain refuge

8 steal a march on sb to gain an advantage over someone by doing something that they had planned to do before them: *He was afraid another scholar was going to steal a march on him and publish first.*
9 steal sb's thunder to get the success and praise someone else should have got, by doing what they had intended to do
10 steal sb's heart *literary* to make someone fall in love with you → **beg, borrow, or steal** at BEG (8)

steal² *n* [C] **1 be a steal** *informal* to be very cheap: *an excellent seafood dish that is a steal at $8.25* **2** the act of suddenly taking control of the ball when the other team had previously had control of it, especially in BASKETBALL: *Johnson had ten points and a steal in the first half.* **3** the act of running to the next BASE before someone hits the ball in the sport of baseball

stealth /stelθ/ *n* [U] **1** when you do something very quietly, slowly, or secretly, so that no one notices you: *Cats rely on stealth to catch their prey.* **2** also **Stealth** a system of making military aircraft that cannot be discovered by RADAR instruments: **stealth bomber/aircraft/fighter etc** (=a plane made using this system)

stealth tax *n* [C] *BrE* an extra tax or charge that a government introduces in such a way that people do not realize that they are paying more money – used to show disapproval

stealth·y /stelθi/ *adj* moving or doing something quietly and secretly: *the stealthy approach of the soldiers* —**stealthily** *adv*

steam¹ W3 /sti:m/ *n* [U]
1 GAS the hot mist that water produces when it is boiled: *Steam rose from the hot tub.*
2 MIST ON SURFACE the mist that forms on windows, mirrors etc when warm wet air suddenly becomes cold
3 POWER power that is produced by boiling water to make steam, in order to make things work or move: *The engines are driven by steam.* | **steam engine/train/hammer etc** (=an engine etc that works by steam power)
4 let/blow off steam to get rid of your anger, excitement, or energy in a way that does not harm anyone by doing something active
5 get/pick/build up steam also **gather/gain steam a)** if an engine picks up steam, it gradually starts to go faster **b)** if plans, beliefs etc pick up steam, they gradually become more important and more people become interested in them: *The election campaign is picking up steam.*
6 run out of steam also **lose steam** to no longer have the energy or the desire to continue doing something, especially because you are tired: *I usually just let her yell until she runs out of steam.*
7 under your own steam if you go somewhere under your own steam, you get there without help from anyone else: *I'll get to the restaurant under my own steam.*
8 RAILWAY a railway system in which the trains use steam for power: *the age of steam* → **full steam ahead** at FULL¹ (18)

steam² *v* **1** [I] if something steams, steam rises from it, especially because it is hot: *steaming hot soup* **2** [T] to cook something in steam; → **boil**: *Steam the vegetables lightly.* | *steamed broccoli* **3** [I always + adv/prep] to travel somewhere in a boat or train that uses steam to produce power: [+**into/from etc**] *We steamed from port to port.* **4** [I] *especially BrE* to go somewhere very quickly: [+**in/down**] *Geoff steamed in ten minutes late.* **5 be steaming (mad)** also **be steamed (up)** *AmE spoken* to be very angry
steam ahead *phr v* to start doing something very

quickly: *The company is steaming ahead with its investment programme.*
steam sth ⇔ open/off *phr v* to use steam to open an envelope or to remove a stamp from an envelope
steam up *phr v* to cover something with steam, or to become covered with steam: *My glasses are all steamed up.* | **steam sth ⇔ up** *A pan was boiling on the stove, steaming up the windows.* → STEAMED-UP

steam·boat /sti:mbəʊt $ -boʊt/ *n* [C] a boat that uses steam for power and is sailed along rivers and coasts

steam clean *v* [T] to clean something by using a machine that produces steam

steamed-up *adj* [not before noun] *informal* excited and angry or worried: *Don't get so steamed-up about it – it's not really important.*

steam·er /sti:mə $ -ər/ *n* [C] **1** a STEAMSHIP **2** a container used to cook food in steam → see picture at EAT

steam·ing /sti:mɪŋ/ *adv* **1 steaming hot** very hot: *It was a steaming hot day.* **2** very drunk – used in Scotland and Northern England

steam iron *n* [C] an electric IRON that produces steam in order to make clothes easier to press smooth

steam·roll /sti:mrəʊl $ -roʊl/ *v* [T] *AmE* to steamroller

steam·roll·er¹ /sti:m,rəʊlə $ -,roʊlər/ *n* [C] **1** a heavy vehicle with very wide wheels that is driven over road surfaces to make them flat **2** someone who uses their power and influence to make sure that something happens the way they want it to

steamroller² *v* [T] *informal* to make sure something happens by using all your power and influence, or to defeat your opponents badly: *He steamrollered the bill through Parliament against fierce opposition.*

steam·ship /sti:m,ʃɪp/ *n* [C] a large ship that uses steam to produce power

steam shovel *n* [C] *AmE* a large machine that digs and moves earth

steam·y /sti:mi/ *adj* **1** full of steam or covered in steam: *steamy windows* **2** sexually exciting and slightly shocking: *a steamy love scene* **3** a steamy day or steamy weather feels hot and HUMID

steed /sti:d/ *n* [C] *literary* a strong fast horse

steel¹ S2 W3 /sti:l/ *n*
1 [U] strong metal that can be shaped easily, consisting of iron and CARBON: *a steel bridge* | **stainless steel** *knives* (=steel that does not change colour) → see picture at MATERIAL¹
2 [U] the industry that makes steel: *Sheffield is a major steel town.* | *steel workers*
3 nerves of steel the ability to be brave and calm in a dangerous or difficult situation
4 [C] a thin bar of steel used for making knives sharp

steel² *v* [T] **steel yourself** to prepare yourself to do something that you know will be unpleasant or upsetting: **steel yourself to do sth** *He steeled himself not to look away.*

steel band *n* [C] a group of people who play music on steel drums

steel drum *n* [C] a type of drum from the West Indies, made from oil BARRELS, which you hit in different areas to produce different musical sounds

steel guitar also **pedal steel guitar** *n* [C] a musical instrument with ten strings that is played using a steel bar and a PEDAL (=a bar you press with your foot)

steel·mak·er /sti:lmeɪkə $ -ər/ *n* [C] a company that makes steel —**steelmaking** *n* [U]

steel mill *n* [C] a factory where steel is made

steel wool *n* [U] a rough material made of fine steel threads, that is used to make surfaces smooth, remove paint etc; → **wire wool**

steel·work·er /sti:l,wɜːkə $ -,wɜːrkər/ *n* [C] someone who works in a factory where steel is made

steel·works /sti:lwɜːks $ -wɜːrks/ *n* [C] *plural* **steelworks** a factory where steel is made

steel·y /'sti:li/ *adj* **1** extremely determined and very strong: *a look of **steely** determination* **2** if someone has steely eyes or is steely-eyed, they look very determined **3** having a grey colour like steel: *a steely sky*

steep¹ S3 /sti:p/ *adj comparative* **steeper**, *superlative* **steepest**
1 a road, hill etc that is steep slopes at a high angle: *The road became rocky and steep.* | *a steep climb to the top* **2** steep prices, charges etc are unusually expensive; 🔲 **low**: *steep rents*
3 involving a big increase or decrease: *steep cuts in benefits* | **steep increase/rise** *a steep increase in house prices* | **steep decrease/drop** *a steep drop in orders*
—**steeply** *adv* —**steepness** *n* [U]

steep² *v* [I,T] **1** **be steeped in history/tradition/politics** etc to have a lot of a particular quality: *a town steeped in history* **2** to put food in a liquid and leave it there, so that it becomes soft or has the same taste as the liquid, or so that it gives the liquid its taste: *Leave the tea bag to steep.*

steep·en /'sti:pən/ *v* [I,T] if a slope, road etc steepens, or if something steepens it, it becomes steeper

stee·ple /'sti:pəl/ *n* [C] a tall pointed tower on the roof of a church

stee·ple·chase /'sti:pəl,tʃeɪs/ *n* [C] **1** a long race in which horses jump over gates, water etc **2** a long race in which people run and jump over fences, water etc

stee·ple·jack /'sti:pəl,dʒæk/ *n* [C] someone whose work is repairing towers, tall CHIMNEYS etc

steer¹ /stɪə $ stɪr/ *v*
1 CAR/BOAT ETC [I,T] to control the direction a vehicle is going, for example by turning a wheel: *He was steering with only one hand.* | [+**for/towards etc**] *Steer toward the left.*
2 CHANGE SB/STH [T] to guide someone's behaviour or the way a situation develops: **steer sb towards/away from/through etc sth** *Teachers try to steer pupils away from drugs.* | *Helen tried to **steer the conversation** away from herself.*
3 BE IN CHARGE OF [T always + adv/prep] to be in charge of an organization, team etc and make decisions that help it to be successful, especially during a difficult time: **steer sth through/to etc sth** *McKinney steered the company through the recession.*
4 GUIDE SB TO A PLACE [T] to guide someone to a place, especially while touching them: **steer sb towards/to etc sth** *Joel steered Don and Louise towards the backyard.*
5 **steer clear (of sb/sth)** *informal* to avoid someone or something unpleasant or difficult: *Jo tried to steer clear of political issues.*
6 **steer a course** to choose a particular way of doing something: *Managers were allowed to steer their own course.* | *The government chose to **steer a middle course** between the two strategies* (=chose a strategy that was not extreme).

steer² *n* [C] a young male cow whose sex organs have been removed; → **bullock**, **heifer**

steer·age /'stɪərɪdʒ $ 'stɪr-/ *n* [U] the part of a passenger ship where people who had the cheapest tickets used to travel in the past

steer·ing /'stɪərɪŋ $ 'stɪr-/ *n* [U] the parts of a car, boat etc that allow you to control its direction: *power steering*

'steering com,mittee *n* [C] a committee that guides or directs a particular activity

'steering wheel *n* [C] a wheel that you turn to control the direction of a car → see picture at CAR

steers·man /'stɪəzmən $ 'stɪrz-/ *n plural* **steersmen** /-mən/ [C] someone who steers a ship

stein /staɪn/ *n* [C] a tall cup for drinking beer, often decorated and with a lid

stel·lar /'stelə $ -ər/ *adj* [only before noun] **1** relating to the stars → INTERSTELLAR **2** especially AmE extremely good: *the company's stellar growth* | *McKellen gave a*

stellar performance. **3** **go stellar** BrE informal if a POP band, actor etc goes stellar, they become very popular and famous: *There's a stand-up comedian, and my sources tell me he is about to go stellar.*

stem¹ /stem/ *n* [C] **1** the long thin part of a plant, from which leaves, flowers, or fruit grow; 🔲 **stalk**; → see picture at ROSE¹ **2** the long thin part of a wine glass, VASE etc, between the base and the wide top **3** the narrow tube of a pipe used to smoke tobacco **4** **long-stemmed/short-stemmed etc** having a long stem, a short stem etc: *long-stemmed wine glasses* **5** the part of a word that stays the same when different endings are added to it, for example 'driv-' in 'driving'

stem² *v* **stemmed**, **stemming** [T] **1** to stop something from happening, spreading, or developing: **stem the tide/flow/flood of sth** *The measures are meant to stem the tide of illegal immigration.* | **stem the growth/rise/decline etc** *an attempt to stem the decline in profits* **2** *formal* to stop the flow of a liquid: *A tight bandage should stem the bleeding.*
stem from sth *phr v* [not in progressive] to develop as a result of something else: *His headaches stemmed from vision problems.*

'stem cell *n* [C] *technical* a special type of cell in the body that can divide in order to form other types of cells that have particular qualities or purposes

stench /stentʃ/ *n* [C usually singular] **1** a very strong bad smell; 🔲 **stink**: *the stench of urine* **2** something unpleasant that makes you believe that something very bad and dishonest is happening: [+**of**] *a government filled with the stench of corruption*

sten·cil¹ /'stensəl/ *n* [C] **1** a piece of plastic, metal, or paper in which designs or letters have been cut out, that you put over a surface and paint over, so that the design is left on the surface **2** a design made on something using a stencil

stencil² *v past tense and past participle* **stencilled**, *present participle* **stencilling** BrE, **stenciled**, *present participle* **stenciling** AmE [T] to make a design, letters etc using a stencil

Sten gun /'sten gʌn/ *n* [C] a small British SUBMACHINE GUN

sten·o /'stenəʊ $ -noʊ/ *n plural* **stenos** *informal* **1** [C] a short form of STENOGRAPHER **2** [U] a short form of STENOGRAPHY

ste·nog·ra·pher /stə'nɒgrəfə $ -'nɑːgrəfər/ *n* [C] AmE or BrE old-fashioned someone whose job is to write down what someone else is saying, using stenography, and then type a copy of it

ste·nog·ra·phy /stə'nɒgrəfi $ -'nɑː-/ *n* [U] AmE or BrE old-fashioned a fast way of writing in which you use special signs or short forms of words, used especially to record what someone is saying; 🔲 **shorthand**

sten·to·ri·an /sten'tɔːriən/ *adj literary* a stentorian voice is very loud and powerful

step¹ S2 W2 /step/ *n*
1 MOVEMENT [C] the movement you make when you put one foot in front of or behind the other when walking: *a video of baby's first steps* | *He **took** one step and fell.* | [+**back/forwards/towards etc**] *Tom took a step back and held the door open.* | *I had to **retrace my steps** (=go back the way I came) several times before I found the shop.*
2 ACTION [C] one of a series of things that you do in order to deal with a problem or to succeed: **step in (doing) sth** *This is the **first step** in reforming the welfare system.* | [+**towards**] *an important step towards peace* | *The president **took** immediate **steps** to stop the fighting.* | **(major/big/great) step forward** (=an action that makes things better) *The discovery of penicillin was a major step forward in the treatment of infections.* | *Many teachers see an emphasis on written tests as a **step backwards** (=an action that makes*

S

things worse). | *Environmentalists call the change a step in the right direction* (=a good thing to do).
3 IN A PROCESS [C] a stage in a process, or a position on a scale: *Each book goes up one step in difficulty.* | *Record your result, and go on to step 3.* | [+in] *the next step in the process* | *Drug companies influence the scientific process every step of the way* (=during every stage). | *Describe step by step* (=describing each stage) *how you went about achieving your goal.* | *Moving to Cottage Grove represented a definite step up* (=something that is better than you had before) *for my parents.* | *He saw the job as a step down* (=something that is worse than you had before).
4 STAIR [C] a flat narrow piece of wood or stone, especially one in a series, that you put your foot on when you are going up or down, especially outside a building: *Jenny sat on the step in front of the house, waiting.* | *He climbed the wooden steps and rang the bell.* | *a flight of* (=set of) *broad stone steps* → DOORSTEP[1] (1); → see picture at STAIRCASE
5 DISTANCE [C] the short distance you move when you take a step while walking; ▤ **pace**: *Roy was standing only a few steps away.*
6 SOUND [C] the sound you make when you put your foot down while walking; ▤ **footstep**: *I heard a step in the corridor.*
7 DANCING [C] a movement of your feet in dancing: *the steps for the Charleston*
8 in step **a)** having ideas or actions that are like those of other people: [+with] *He isn't in step with ordinary voters.* **b)** moving your feet so that your right foot goes forward at the same time as people you are walking with
9 out of step **a)** having ideas or actions that are different from those of other people: [+with] *This type of training is out of step with changes in the industry.* **b)** moving your feet in a different way from people you are walking with
10 watch your step also mind your step *BrE* **a)** to be careful about what you say or how you behave: *You'd better watch your step – he's the boss here.* **b)** to be careful when you are walking: *Mind your step – the railing's loose.*
11 fall into step (with sb) **a)** to start walking beside someone at the same speed as them: *Maggie fell into step beside her.* **b)** to start thinking or doing the same as other people: *The administration has fallen into step with its European allies on this issue.*
12 be/keep/stay one step ahead (of sb) **a)** to be better prepared for something or know more about something than someone else: *A good teacher is always at least one step ahead of his students.* **b)** to manage not to be caught by someone who is trying to find or catch you
13 WAY SB WALKS [C usually singular] the way someone walks, which often tells you how they are feeling: *Gianni's usual bouncy step*
14 steps [plural] *BrE* a STEPLADDER
15 EXERCISE [U] a type of exercise you do by walking onto and off a flat piece of equipment around 15–30 CENTIMETRES high: *a step class*
16 MUSIC [C] *AmE* the difference in PITCH between two musical notes that are separated by one KEY on the piano; ▤ **tone** *BrE*

step² W3 *v* **stepped, stepping** [I always + adv/prep]
1 to raise one foot and put it down in front of or behind the other one in order to walk or move: [+forward/back/down/into etc] *He stepped back to let me through.* | *I stepped outside and closed the door.* | *Mr. Ives? Please step this way* (=walk in the direction I am showing you).
2 to bring your foot down on something; ▤ **tread** *BrE*: [+in/on etc] *I accidentally stepped in a puddle.* | *You're stepping on my foot.*
3 step on sb's toes to offend or upset someone, especially by trying to do their work: *I'm not worried about stepping on anybody's toes.*

4 step out of line to behave badly by breaking rules or disobeying orders
5 step on it also step on the gas *AmE spoken* to drive faster → step into the breach at BREACH[1] (7)
step down also **step aside** *phr v*
to leave your job or official position, because you want to or because you think you should: *Morris should step aside until the investigation is completed.* | [+as] *Eve Johnson has stepped down as chairperson.* | [+from] *He was forced to step down from his post.*
step forward *phr v*
to come and offer help, information etc: *Police are appealing for witnesses to step forward.*
step in *phr v*
to become involved in an activity, discussion, or disagreement, sometimes in order to stop trouble; ▤ **intervene**: *The military may step in if the crisis continues.* | *Parents have stepped in to provide homework help in the afternoon program.*
step into sth *phr v*
to start doing something, or become involved in a situation: *Sally stepped into the role of team leader.*
step out *phr v*
to leave your home or office for a short time; ▤ **pop out** *BrE*: *She's just stepped out for a few minutes.*
step sth ⇔ **up** *phr v*
to increase the amount of an activity or the speed of a process in order to improve a situation: *The health department is stepping up efforts to reduce teenage smoking.* | *stepped-up security at airports*

step- /step/ *prefix* used to show that someone is related to you not by birth but because a parent has married again: *her stepdad* | *the problems of stepfamilies*
step ae·ro·bics *n* [U] a type of physical exercise in which you step on and off a small raised PLATFORM while doing movements with the upper part of your body
step·broth·er /ˈstepbrʌðə $ -ər/ *n* [C] the son of your stepmother or stepfather
step-by-'step *adj* [only before noun] a step-by-step plan, method etc explains or does something carefully and in a particular order: **step-by-step guide/approach/instructions** etc *a step-by-step guide to making it in the music business* —**step by step** *adv*: *Take each lesson step by step.*
step change *n* [singular] *BrE* a big and important change in an organization or in society: [+in] *The new law marks a step change in our programme for reforming public services.*
step·child /ˈsteptʃaɪld/ *n plural* **stepchildren** /-ˌtʃɪldrən/ [C] a stepdaughter or stepson
step·daugh·ter /ˈstepdɔːtə $ -dɒːtər/ *n* [C] a daughter that your husband or wife has from a relationship before your marriage
step·fa·ther /ˈstepfɑːðə $ -ər/ *n* [C] a man who is married to your mother but who is not your father
step·lad·der /ˈstepˌlædə $ -ər/ *n* [C] a LADDER which has two sloping parts that are joined at the top so that it can stand without support, and which can be folded flat → see picture at LADDER[1]
step·moth·er /ˈstepmʌðə $ -ər/ *n* [C] a woman who is married to your father but who is not your mother
step·par·ent /ˈstepˌpeərənt $ -ˌper-/ *n* [C] a stepfather or stepmother
steppe /step/ *n* [C,U] also **the steppes** a large area of land without trees, especially in Russia, Asia, and eastern Europe
stepping-ˌstone *n* [C] **1** something that helps you to progress towards achieving something: [+to/to-ward(s)] *The course will be a stepping stone to another career.* **2** stepping stones [plural] a row of large flat stones that you walk on to get across a stream
step·sis·ter /ˈstepsɪstə $ -ər/ *n* [C] the daughter of your stepmother or stepfather
step·son /ˈstepsʌn/ *n* [C] a son that your husband or wife has from a relationship before your marriage

ster·e·o¹ [S3] /'steriəʊ, 'stɪər- $ 'steriou, 'stɪr-/ *n plural* **stereos**
1 also **'stereo ,system** [C] a machine for playing records, CDs etc that produces sound from two SPEAKERS: *a stereo with good speakers* | **on a stereo** *He was listening to the Beatles on the car stereo.*; → see picture at BEDROOM
2 in stereo if sound is played or broadcast in stereo, it is directed through two speakers → PERSONAL STEREO

stereo² also **ster·e·o·phon·ic** /,steriə'fɒnɪk◂, ,stɪər- $,steriə'fɑ:nɪk◂, ,stɪr-/ *adj* using a recording or broadcasting system in which the sound is directed through two SPEAKERS; → **mono**, **quadraphonic**: *stereo equipment*

ster·e·o·scop·ic /,steriə'skɒpɪk◂, ,stɪər- $,steriə'skɑ:-, ,stɪr-/ *adj* **1** a stereoscopic picture, photograph etc appears solid when you look at it through a special machine **2** *technical* able to see the length, width, and depth of objects: *stereoscopic vision*

ster·e·o·type¹ /'steriətaɪp, 'stɪər- $ 'ster-, 'stɪr-/ *n* [C] a belief or idea of what a particular type of person or thing is like. Stereotypes are often unfair or untrue: *racial/sexual/cultural etc stereotype racist stereotypes in the media* | [+of] *women who don't fit the stereotype of the good mother* | [+about] *stereotypes about the elderly* —**stereotypical** /,steriə'tɪpɪkəl, ,stɪər- $,ster-, ,stɪr-/ *adj*: *the stereotypical Californian – tall, fit, and tanned* —**stereotypically** /-kli/ *adv*

stereotype² *v* [T usually passive] to decide unfairly that a type of person has particular qualities or abilities because they belong to a particular race, sex, or social class: **stereotype sb as sth** *Homeless people are stereotyped as alcoholics or addicts.* —**stereotyping** *n* [U] —**stereotyped** *adj*

ster·ile /'steraɪl $ -rəl/ *adj* **1** a person or animal that is sterile cannot produce babies; ▣ **infertile**; ▣ **fertile: make/render/leave sb sterile** *Radiotherapy has left her permanently sterile.* **2** completely clean and not containing any BACTERIA that might cause infection: **sterile equipment/water/bandages etc** *Rinse the eye with sterile water.* **3** lacking new ideas, interest, or imagination: **sterile argument/debate etc** *the increasingly sterile debate on political reform* **4** a sterile building, room etc is not interesting or attractive and is often very plain: *The classrooms are sterile, with no artwork on the walls.* **5** sterile land cannot be used to grow crops —**sterility** /stə'rɪlt̬i/ *n* [U]

ster·il·ize also **-ise** *BrE* /'ster̩̩laɪz/ *v* [T] **1** to make something completely clean by killing any BACTERIA in it: *Sterilize the bottles with boiling water.* | *sterilized milk* | *sterilizing solution* **2** if a person or animal is sterilized, they have an operation to stop them producing babies —**sterilizer** *n* [C]: *an electric sterilizer* —**sterilization** /,ster̩laɪ'zeɪʃən $ -lə-/ *n* [C,U]

ster·ling¹ /'stɜːlɪŋ $ 'stɜːr-/ *n* [U] **1** also **Sterling** the standard unit of money in the United Kingdom, based on the pound **2** also **,sterling 'silver** silver that is at least 92% pure

sterling² *adj* [only before noun] very good: *Ella has done some sterling work.* | *He has sterling qualities.*

stern¹ /stɜːn $ stɜːrn/ *adj* **1** serious and strict, and showing strong disapproval of someone's behaviour: *sterner penalties for drug offences* | **stern look/voice/expression etc** *'Wait!' I shouted in my sternest voice.* | **stern warning/rebuke** *His actions have earned him stern rebukes from human-rights organizations.* **2 be made of sterner stuff** to have a strong character and be more determined than other people to succeed in a difficult situation: *Ann, made of sterner stuff than I, refused all offers of help.* —**sternly** *adv* —**sternness** *n* [U]

stern² *n* [C usually singular] the back of a ship; → **bow**

ster·num /'stɜːnəm $ 'stɜːrn-/ *n plural* **sternums** or **sterna** /-nə/ [C] *technical* a BREASTBONE

ste·roid /'stɪərɔɪd, 'ste- $ 'stɪr-/ *n* [C] **1** a chemical that the body produces naturally or that can be made as a drug to treat illness and injuries. Steroids are sometimes used illegally by people doing sports to improve their performance: **on steroids** *a bodybuilder on steroids* **2 sth on steroids** *AmE informal* used to say that something is much bigger, stronger, more impressive etc than something else that is similar to it – used humorously: *They sell cinnamon rolls on steroids.*

steth·o·scope /'steθəskəʊp $ -skoup/ *n* [C] an instrument that a doctor uses to listen to your heart or breathing

Stet·son /'stetsən/ *trademark n* [C] a tall hat with a wide BRIM (=edge), worn especially in the American West

ste·ve·dore /'stiːvədɔː $ -dɔːr/ *n* [C] someone whose job is loading and unloading ships

stew¹ /stjuː $ stuː/ *n* **1** [C,U] a hot meal made by cooking meat and vegetables slowly in liquid for a long time; ▣ **casserole**: *a pot of stew* | *beef stew* **2 in a stew** *informal* confused or worried about a difficult situation you are in

stew² *v* **1** [T] to cook something slowly in liquid: *stewed apples* **2** [I] *informal* also **stew in your own juice** *BrE* to worry or become angry because of something bad that has happened or a mistake you have made: *She just sat there stewing in her own juice.*

stew·ard /'stjuːəd $ 'stuːərd/ *n* [C] **1** a man whose job is to serve food and drinks to passengers on a plane or ship; → **flight attendant 2** someone who is in charge of a horse race, meeting, or other public event: *race stewards* **3** someone who protects something or is responsible for it, especially something such as nature, public property, or money: [+of] *Kissinger was now chief steward of US foreign policy.* **4** a man whose job is to manage a large property, such as a farm → SHOP STEWARD

stew·ard·ess /'stjuːədɪs $ 'stuːərd-/ *n* [C] a woman whose job is to serve food and drinks to passengers on a plane or ship; → **flight attendant**

stew·ard·ship /'stjuːədʃɪp $ 'stuːərd-/ *n* [U] someone's stewardship of something is the way that they control or protect it: [+of] *Some critics have doubts about his stewardship of the nation.* | **under sb's stewardship** *The farm was quite a different place under Mom's stewardship.*

stewed /stjuːd $ stuːd/ *adj* **1** [not before noun] *informal old-fashioned* drunk **2** *BrE* tea that is stewed tastes unpleasantly strong because it has been left in the pot too long

stick¹ [S1] [W3] /stɪk/ *v past tense and past participle* **stuck** /stʌk/
1 ATTACH [I,T] to attach something to something else using a substance, or to become attached to a surface: **stick sth on/to/in etc sth** *Someone had stuck posters all over the walls.* | [+to/together] *I could feel my shirt sticking to my back.* | *The oil keeps the pasta from sticking together.* | *This stamp won't stick properly.*
2 PUSH IN [I,T always + adv/prep] if a pointed object sticks into something, or if you stick it there, it is pushed into it: **stick (sth) in/into/through sth** *pins stuck in a notice board* | *The boy stuck his finger up his nose.*
3 PUT [T always + adv/prep] *informal* to put something somewhere quickly and without much care; ▣ **bung**: *Just stick it in the microwave for a few minutes.* | *The cards had been stuck through the letterbox.*
4 MOVE PART OF BODY [T always + adv/prep] if you stick a part of your body somewhere, you put it in a position where other people can see it; ▣ **put**: *Clara stuck her head around the door to see who was there.* | *The baby stuck his legs in the air.* | *Don't stick your tongue out, it's rude!*
5 DIFFICULT TO MOVE [I] if something sticks, it becomes fixed in one position and is difficult to move: *This door keeps sticking.* | *The wheels stuck fast* (=stuck completely) *in the mud.*
6 stick in sb's mind if something sticks in your mind, you remember it well because it is unusual or interesting: *It's the kind of name that sticks in your mind.*

S

7 make sth stick *informal* **a)** to prove that something is true: *Is there enough evidence to* **make the charges** *stick?* **b)** to make a change become permanent: *The government has succeeded in making this policy stick.*
8 NAME [I] if a name that someone has invented sticks, people continue using it: *One newspaper dubbed him 'Eddie the Eagle', and the name stuck.*
9 sb can stick sth *spoken* used to say angrily that you do not want what someone is offering you: *I told them they could stick their job.*
10 STAY IN BAD SITUATION [T] *BrE spoken* to continue to accept a situation or person, even though you do not like them; **☰ stand**: *I can't stick mum's new boyfriend.* | **can't stick doing sth** *Gerry can't stick working for Featherstone's any longer.* | *I don't know how you* **stick it.**
11 stick in sb's throat/gullet *BrE*; **stick in sb's craw** *AmE* if a situation or someone's behaviour sticks in your throat, it is so annoying that you cannot accept it: *Her criticism really sticks in my craw.*
12 stick in sb's throat if words stick in your throat, you are unable to say them because you are afraid or upset
13 stick to sb's ribs *informal* food that sticks to your ribs is very satisfying, so you are not hungry after you have eaten → STUCK; → **stick/poke your nose into sth** at NOSE[1] (3)

stick around *phr v informal*
to stay in a place a little longer, waiting for something to happen: *Perhaps you'd like to stick around and watch?* | *Tom will be sticking around for a while.*

stick at sth *phr v BrE*
1 to continue doing something in a determined way in order to achieve something: *Revising with your friends may help you stick at it.*
2 stick at nothing *informal* to be willing to do anything, even if it is illegal, in order to achieve something: **stick at nothing to do sth** *He will stick at nothing to make money.*

stick by sb/sth *phr v*
1 to remain loyal to a friend when they have done something wrong or have problems: *I love him and whatever happens I'll stick by him.* | *Jean has* **stuck by** *her husband* **through thick and thin.**
2 to do what you promised or decided to do: **stick by a decision/promise etc** *He has stuck by his radical plans for economic reform.*

stick out *phr v*
1 if something sticks out, you notice it because part of it comes out further than the rest of a surface: *The children were so thin their ribs stuck out.* | [+of/from/through etc] *Paul's legs were sticking out from under the car.*
2 stick it out to continue doing something that is difficult, painful, or boring: *It wasn't a happy period of his life, but he stuck it out.*
3 stick your neck out *informal* to risk giving your opinion about something, even though you may be wrong or other people may disagree with you: *I'm going to stick my neck out with some predictions for the next two years.*
4 stick out to sb/stick out in sb's mind to seem more important to someone than other people or things: *The thing that sticks out to me is that they need more help than they're getting.* → **stick/stand out a mile** at MILE (5); → **stick out like a sore thumb** at SORE[1] (6)

stick out for sth *phr v BrE informal*
to refuse to accept less than what you asked for; **☰ hold out for**: *They offered him £250 but Vic stuck out for £500.*

stick to sth *phr v*
1 to do or keep doing what you said you would do or what you believe in, even when it is difficult; **☰ keep to**: *Have you been sticking to your diet?* | **stick to your decision/principles etc** *Miguel was determined to stick to his decision.* | *It looks as if Nick will* **stick to his word** *this time.*
2 to keep using or doing one particular thing and not change to anything else: *If you're driving, stick to soft*

drinks. | **stick to doing sth** *Reporters should stick to investigating the facts.*
3 stick to your guns *informal* to refuse to change your mind about something, even though other people are trying to persuade you that you are wrong: *Having made up his mind, he stuck to his guns.*
4 stick to the point/subject/facts to talk only about what you are supposed to be talking about or what is certain: *Never mind whose fault it was. Just stick to the facts.*
5 stick to the rules *informal* to do something exactly according to the rules
6 stick to the path/road etc to stay on a marked path or road so that you do not get lost
7 stick to the/your story *spoken* to continue to say that what you have told someone is true, even though they do not believe you: *You intend to stick to this story that she knew nothing of your financial prospects?*
8 stick to the/your knitting *AmE informal* to continue paying attention to your own work and not to get involved with what other people are doing: *I wish Mrs Reese would stick to her knitting.*
9 stick it to sb *AmE informal* to make someone suffer, pay a high price etc: *The politicians stick it to the tourists because the tourists don't vote.*

stick together *phr v informal*
if people stick together, they continue to support each other when they have problems: *We're a family, and we stick together no matter what.*

stick up *phr v*
1 if a part of something sticks up, it is raised up or points upwards above a surface: [+from/out of/through etc] *Part of the boat was sticking up out of the water.*
2 stick 'em up *spoken informal* used to tell someone to raise their hands when threatening them with a gun – used in films, stories etc

stick up for sb *phr v informal*
to defend someone who is being criticized, especially when no one else will defend them: *You're supposed to be sticking up for me!* | **stick up for yourself** *She's always known how to stick up for herself.*

stick with sth/sb *phr v informal*
1 to continue doing something the way you did or planned to do before: *Let's stick with the original plans.*
2 to stay close to someone: *You just stick with me. I'll explain everything as we go along.*
3 to continue doing something, especially something difficult: *If you stick with it, your playing will gradually get better.*
4 be stuck with sth/sb to be made to accept something, do something, spend time with someone etc, when they do not want to: *Bill left and I was stuck with the bill.*
5 to remain in someone's memory: *Those words will stick with me for the rest of my life.*

stick² *n* [C]
1 PART OF TREE a long thin piece of wood from a tree, which is no longer attached to the tree; → **branch**, **twig**: *They collected sticks to start the fire.*
2 TOOL a long thin piece of wood, plastic etc that you use for a particular purpose: *a pair of drum sticks* | *a measuring stick* | *Aunt Lou* **walks with a stick** *(=uses a stick to help her walk).*
3 PIECE a long thin or round piece of something: *carrot sticks with dip* | *a glue stick* | [+of] *a stick of chewing gum*
4 SPORTS a long specially shaped piece of wood, plastic etc that you use in some sports to hit a ball: *a hockey stick*
5 (out) in the sticks a long way from a town or city: *They live out in the sticks.*
6 get (hold of) the wrong end of the stick *BrE informal* to understand a situation in completely the wrong way: *People who think the song is about drugs have got the wrong end of the stick.*
7 PLANE the handle you use to control a plane → JOYSTICK
8 CAR *AmE informal* a STICK SHIFT
9 get on the stick *AmE spoken* to start doing something

you should be doing: *You'd better get your sales team on the stick.*

10 give sb/get (some) stick *BrE spoken* if you give someone stick, you criticize them for something they have done: *He's going to get some stick for this!*

11 up sticks *BrE informal* if you up sticks, you move to a different area → **carrot and stick** at CARROT (3)

stick·er S3 /'stɪkə $ -ər/ n [C] a small piece of paper or plastic with a picture or writing on it that you can stick on to something; → **label**: *Children get stickers for good work.* | **bumper sticker** (=a sticker on the back of a car)

'sticker ,price n [C usually singular] *AmE* the price of something, especially a car, that is written on it or given in advertisements, but that may be reduced by the person selling it

'stick ,figure n [C] a very simple drawing of a person

'sticking ,point n [singular] something that a group of people cannot agree on and that stops them from making progress: *North Korea's refusal had long been a sticking point.*

'stick ,insect n [C] *BrE* a long thin insect that looks like a small stick: *young models who look like stick insects* (=are very thin)

'stick-in-the-,mud n [C] someone who refuses to try anything new – used to show disapproval

stick·ler /'stɪklə $ -ər/ n **be a stickler for detail/rules/ accuracy etc** to think that rules etc are very important and that other people should think so too

'stick man n [C] a STICK FIGURE

'stick-on adj [only before noun] stick-on things have a sticky back so that you can attach them to something: *stick-on sequins*

stick·pin /'stɪk,pɪn/ n [C] *AmE* a decorated pin worn as jewellery

'stick shift n [C] *AmE* **1** a metal bar in a car that you move to control the GEARS; ⊟ **gear stick** *BrE* **2** a car that uses a stick shift system to control the GEARS; → **automatic**

stick-to-it-ive·ness /stɪk ˈtuː ɪtɪvnɪs/ n [U] *AmE informal* the ability to continue doing something that is difficult or tiring

'stick-up n [C] *informal* a HOLD-UP

stick·y /'stɪki/ adj comparative **stickier**, superlative **stickiest 1** made of or covered with a substance that sticks to surfaces: *There's some sticky stuff in your hair.* | *a sticky floor* | **sticky tape/label etc** (=tape etc that is made so it will stick to surfaces); → see picture at SURFACE **2** weather that is sticky makes you feel uncomfortably hot, wet, and dirty; ⊟ **humid**: *It was hot and sticky and there was nowhere to sit.* **3** a sticky situation, question, or problem is difficult or dangerous: *a sticky political issue* | **sticky patch** *BrE*: *The business hit a sticky patch and lost £4.8 million.* **4** a website that is sticky is interesting to the people looking at it and makes them want to look at it for a long period of time **5 have sticky fingers** *informal* to be likely to steal something **6 come to/meet a sticky end** *BrE informal* to die in a violent way **7 be on a sticky wicket** *BrE informal* to be in a situation that will cause problems for you —**stickiness** n [U]

'sticky ,note also **yellow sticky** n [C] a small piece of paper, often yellow in colour, that you can stick to things. Stickies are often used for leaving messages; ⊟ **Post-it Note**

stiff¹ S3 /stɪf/ adj comparative **stiffer**, superlative **stiffest 1** BODY if someone or a part of their body is stiff, their muscles hurt and it is difficult for them to move: **stiff from doing sth** *Her legs were stiff from kneeling.* | [+with] *Her fingers were stiff with cold.* | **stiff neck/ back/joint etc** *Alastair woke with a stiff neck.* | *I never felt stiff after training until I was in my thirties.* | *The next morning I was as stiff as a board* (=very stiff). **2** MATERIAL/SUBSTANCE firm, hard, or difficult to bend: *a shirt with a stiff collar* **3** MIXTURE a stiff mixture is thick and almost solid,

so that it is not easy to mix: *Beat the egg whites until stiff.* | *a stiff dough*

4 DIFFICULT difficult, strict, or severe: **stiff sentence/ penalty/fine** *calls for stiffer penalties for rapists* | **stiff competition/opposition** *Graduates face stiff competition in getting jobs.* | *The development plans have met with stiff opposition.*

5 DOOR/DRAWER ETC *BrE* difficult to move, turn, or open: *Pull hard – that drawer's very stiff.*

6 UNFRIENDLY if someone's behaviour is stiff, they behave in a very formal or unfriendly way: *Their goodbyes were stiff and formal.* | *Parsons gave a stiff performance in the main role.*

7 PRICE a stiff price etc is high, especially higher than the price etc of similar things: *a stiff tax on cigarettes*

8 stiff wind/breeze a fairly strong wind etc

9 stiff drink/whisky etc a very strong alcoholic drink

10 stiff upper lip the ability to stay calm and not show your feelings in a difficult or upsetting situation: *Men were taught to keep a stiff upper lip.* —**stiffly** adv —**stiffness** n [U]

stiff² adv **1 bored/scared/worried stiff** *informal* extremely bored, frightened, or worried: *As a child I was scared stiff of going down to the cellar.* **2 frozen stiff a)** extremely cold: *Goodness, your hands are frozen stiff!* **b)** cloth that is frozen stiff is hard because the water in it has frozen

stiff³ n [C] *informal* **1** the body of a dead person **2 working stiff** *AmE* an ordinary person who works to earn enough money to live **3** someone who you think is old-fashioned and too formal: *His business tactics outraged the stiffs of the UK establishment.*

stiff⁴ v *informal* **1** [T] *AmE* to cheat someone by not paying them, especially by not leaving a TIP in a restaurant: *I can't believe that couple stiffed me!* **2** [I] if a new product, film, show etc stiffs, it does not sell well or fails completely; ⊟ **bomb**: *They had a hit in the 1990s, but their subsequent releases stiffed.*

stiff·en /'stɪfən/ v **1** [I] if you stiffen, your body suddenly becomes firm, straight, or still because you feel angry or anxious; ⊟ **relax**: *He touched her, and she stiffened.* **2** [I,T] to become stronger, more severe, or more determined, or to make something do this: *a campaign to stiffen rules against drunk driving* | *Their opposition only stiffened my resolve.* **3** [I] also **stiffen up** to become painful and difficult to move: *His joints had stiffened.* | *My back had stiffened up.* **4** [T] to make material stiff so that it will not bend easily

,stiff-'necked adj too proud, and refusing to change or obey; ⊟ **stubborn**

stiff·y /'stɪfi/ n plural **stiffies** [C] *informal not polite* an ERECTION

sti·fle /'staɪfəl/ v **1** [T] to stop something from happening or developing; ⊟ **encourage**: *rules and regulations that stifle innovation* | *How can this party stifle debate on such a crucial issue?* **2** [T] to stop a feeling from being expressed: *He stifled an urge to hit her.* | **stifle a yawn/smile/grin etc** *I tried to stifle my laughter.* **3** [I,T usually passive] if you are stifled by something, it stops you breathing comfortably: *He was almost stifled by the fumes.*

stif·ling /'staɪflɪŋ/ adj **1** a room or weather that is stifling is very hot and uncomfortable, so that it seems difficult to breathe: *a stifling, crowded train* | *the stifling heat of the tropics* **2** a situation that is stifling stops you from developing your own ideas and character: *an emotionally stifling relationship*

stig·ma /'stɪgmə/ n **1** [C usually singular, U] a strong feeling in society that being in a particular situation or having a particular illness is something to be ashamed of: **the stigma of alcoholism/mental illness etc** *The stigma of alcoholism makes it difficult to treat.* | *There is a social stigma attached to single parenthood.* | *In* the US, smoking **carries** a stigma. **2** [C] technical the top of the centre part of a flower that receives the POLLEN which allows it to form new seeds

stig·ma·ta /'stɪgmətə, stɪg'mɑːtə/ n [plural] marks that appear on the hands and feet of some holy people, and which look like the wounds made by nails on the body of Christ

stig·ma·tize also **-ise** BrE /'stɪgmətaɪz/ v be stigmatized to be treated by society as if you should feel ashamed of your situation or behaviour: Single mothers often feel that they are stigmatized by society. —**stigmatization** /ˌstɪgmətaɪˈzeɪʃən $ -tə-/ n [U]

stile /staɪl/ n [C] a set of steps that helps people climb over a fence in the countryside

sti·let·to /stɪˈletəʊ $ -toʊ/ n plural stilettos or stilettoes [C] **1** also **stiletto heel** /'/ a woman's shoe that has a very high thin heel → see picture at FOOTWEAR **2** the heel of a stiletto shoe **3** a small knife with a thin blade

still¹ S1 W1 /stɪl/ adv
1 up to a particular point in time and continuing at that moment: I still haven't finished painting the spare room. | Do you still have Julie's phone number? → see box at YET¹
2 in spite of what has just been said or done: Clare didn't do much work, but she still passed the exam. | [sentence adverb]: The hotel was terrible. Still, we were lucky with the weather.
3 still more/further/another/other used to emphasize that something increases more, there is more of something etc: Kevin grew still more depressed.
4 better/harder/worse etc still also **still better/harder/worse etc** even better, harder etc than something else: Dan found biology difficult, and physics harder still.

still² adj **1** not moving: We **stood still** and watched as the deer came closer. | **Keep still** while I tie your shoe. | the **still waters** of the lake **2** quiet and calm: The house was completely still. **3** not windy: a hot **still day 4** BrE a still drink does not contain gas: still or sparkling mineral water **5 still waters run deep** used to say that someone who is quiet may have very strong feelings or a lot of knowledge —**stillness** n [U]: Somewhere in the **stillness of the night** an owl hooted.

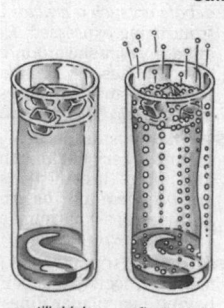

a still drink   a fizzy drink

still³ n [C] **1** a photograph of a scene from a film **2** a piece of equipment for making alcoholic drinks from

grain or potatoes **3 the still of the night/evening etc** literary the calm and quiet of the night etc

still⁴ v literary **1** [I,T] to stop moving or make something stop moving: The ground beneath them trembled, then stilled. **2** [I,T] if a noise stills or is stilled, it stops: The murmurs stilled. | He stilled their protests with a wave of his hands. **3** [I] if a doubt or fear is stilled, it becomes weaker or goes away

still·birth /'stɪlbɜːθ, ˌstɪlˈbɜːθ $ -ɜːrθ/ n [C,U] a birth in which the baby is born dead

still·born /'stɪlbɔːn, ˌstɪlˈbɔːn $ -ɔːrn/ adj **1** born dead: a stillborn baby **2** written completely unsuccessful from the beginning and not developing at all: a stillborn romance

still life plural still lifes n [C,U] a picture of an arrangement of objects, for example flowers or fruit → see picture at PAINTING

stilt /stɪlt/ n [C usually plural] **1** one of a set of poles that support a building above the ground or above water: **on stilts** a house built on stilts **2** one of two poles which you can stand on and walk high above the ground

stilt·ed /'stɪltɪd/ adj a stilted style of writing or speaking is formal and unnatural: a stilted conversation —**stiltedly** adv

Stil·ton /'stɪltən/ n [U] a type of English cheese that is white with grey-blue marks and has a strong taste

stim·u·lant /'stɪmjələnt/ n [C] **1** a drug or substance that makes you feel more active and full of energy: artificial stimulants **2** something that encourages more of a particular activity; ▤ stimulus: economic stimulants | [+to] Increases in new construction would be a stimulant to the economy. —**stimulant** adj: a drug with stimulant properties

stim·u·late /'stɪmjəleɪt/ v [T] **1** to encourage or help an activity to begin or develop further: **stimulate growth/demand/the economy etc** the President's plan to stimulate economic growth **2** to encourage someone by making them excited about and interested in something: Her interest in art was stimulated by her father. | **stimulate sb to do sth** An inspiring teacher can stimulate students to succeed. **3** to make a plant or part of the body become active or stronger: Light stimulates plant growth. —**stimulative** /-lətɪv $ -leɪtɪv/ adj —**stimulation** /ˌstɪmjəˈleɪʃən/ n [U]: Children need variety and stimulation.

stim·u·lat·ing /'stɪmjəleɪtɪŋ/ adj **1** exciting or full of new ideas; ▤ **boring**: a stimulating discussion of world politics **2** making you feel more active: the **stimulating effects** of coffee and tea

stim·u·lus /'stɪmjələs/ n plural stimuli /-laɪ/ **1** [C usually singular, U] something that helps a process to develop more quickly or more strongly: Tax cuts provided the stimulus which the slow economy needed. | [+to] The discovery of oil acted as a stimulus to industrial development. **2** [C] something that makes someone or something move or react: At this age, the infant begins to react more to visual stimuli.

sting¹ /stɪŋ/ v past tense and past participle **stung** /stʌŋ/ **1** [I,T] if an insect or a plant stings you, it makes a very small hole in your skin and you feel a sharp pain because of a poisonous substance: He was stung by a bee. ⚠A bee, wasp, scorpion, or plant can **sting** you. For a mosquito, ant, or snake, use **bite**. **2** [I,T] to make something hurt with a sudden sharp pain, or to hurt like this: Antiseptic stings a little. | Chopping onions makes my eyes sting. **3** [I,T usually passive] if you are stung by a remark, it makes you feel upset: She had been stung by criticism. | **sting sb into (doing) sth** Her harsh words stung him into action.
sting sb for sth BrE informal **1** to charge someone too much for something: The garage stung him for £300. **2** to borrow money from someone: Can I sting you for a fiver?

sting² n
1 WOUND [C] a wound or mark made when an insect or plant stings you: a bee sting

2 INSECT [C] *BrE* the sharp needle-shaped part of an insect's or animal's body, with which it stings you; ▤ **stinger** *AmE*
3 PAIN [singular] a sharp pain in your eyes or skin, caused by being hit, by smoke etc: *She felt the sting of tears in her eyes.*
4 a sting in the tail if a story, event, or announcement has a sting in its tail, there is an unpleasant part at the end of it
5 [singular] the upsetting or bad effect of a situation: *the sting of rejection* | **take the sting out of sth** (=make something less unpleasant or painful) *She smiled to take the sting out of her words.*
6 CRIME [C] a clever way of catching criminals in which the police secretly pretend to be criminals themselves

sting·er /ˈstɪŋə $ -ər/ *n* [C] *AmE* the sharp needle-shaped part of an insect's or animal's body, with which it stings you; ▤ **sting** *BrE*

sting·ing /ˈstɪŋɪŋ/ *adj* **stinging attack/report/letter etc** a report, letter etc that very strongly criticizes someone or something: *Dr Forwell made a stinging attack on government policy.*

ˈstinging ˌnettle *n* [C] a wild plant with leaves that sting and leave red marks on your skin

sting·ray /ˈstɪŋreɪ/ *n* [C] a large flat fish that has a long tail with sharp poisonous points on it

stin·gy /ˈstɪndʒi/ *adj* **1** *informal* not generous, especially with money; ▤ **mean**: *She's too stingy to give money to charity.* **2** a stingy amount of something, especially food, is too small: *a stingy portion of vegetables* —**stingily** *adv* —**stinginess** *n* [U]

stink¹ S3 /stɪŋk/ *v past tense* **stank** /stæŋk/ *past participle* **stunk** /stʌŋk/ [I]
1 to have a strong and very unpleasant smell: *It stinks in here!* | [+of] *His breath stank of alcohol.* | *The toilets* **stank to high heaven** (=stank very much).
2 *spoken* used to say that something is bad, unfair, dishonest etc: *Don't eat there – the food stinks!* | *The whole justice system stinks.*
stink sth ⇔ **out** *BrE*; **stink** sth ⇔ **up** *AmE phr v*
to fill a place with a very unpleasant smell: *Those onions are stinking the whole house out.*

stink² *n* [C usually singular] **1** a very bad smell; ▤ **stench**: [+of] *the stink of burning rubber* **2 cause/ kick up/make etc a stink** to complain very strongly: *Activists have raised a stink about the shipments of nuclear waste.* **3 work/run/go like stink** *BrE old-fashioned* to work etc as fast and as well as you can: *We had to work like stink to meet the deadline.*

ˈstink bomb *n* [C] a small container that produces an extremely bad smell when it is broken

stink·er /ˈstɪŋkə $ -ər/ *n* [C] *informal* **1** someone or something that is very unpleasant or difficult: *This cold I've got is a real stinker.* | *You really are a stinker.* **2** a film, book, performance etc that is very bad: **have a stinker** *BrE* (=play badly) *In the last game he had a stinker.*

stink·ing¹ /ˈstɪŋkɪŋ/ *adj* **1** having a very strong unpleasant smell; ▤ **smelly**: *stinking garbage cans* **2** [only before noun] *spoken* used to emphasize what you are saying when you are angry: *I hate this stinking boring job!* **3** [only before noun] *especially BrE informal* very unpleasant: *I've got a* **stinking cold**. **4 stinking letter** *BrE informal* an angry letter in which you complain very strongly about something

stinking² *adv* **1 stinking rich** *informal* extremely rich – used especially when you think this is unfair **2 stinking drunk** *informal* extremely drunk

stink·y /ˈstɪŋki/ *adj comparative* **stinkier**, *superlative* **stinkiest** *informal* smelling unpleasant; ▤ **smelly**: *stinky socks*

stint¹ /stɪnt/ *n* [C usually singular] a period of time spent doing a particular job or activity: [+in/at] *Mark* **did** *a two-year* **stint** *in the army.* | [+as] *his stint as chairman*

stint² *v* [I,T usually in negatives] to provide or use too little of something: [+on] *They didn't stint on food and drink at their wedding.* | **stint yourself** *In order to avoid stinting yourself, make sure you have enough money to cover all your expenses.*

sti·pend /ˈstaɪpend/ *n* [C] *formal* an amount of money paid regularly to someone, especially a priest, as a salary or as money to live on

sti·pen·di·a·ry ma·gis·trate /staɪˌpendiəri ˈmædʒɪˌstreɪt $ -dieri-/ *also* **stipendiary** *n* [C] a MAGISTRATE in Britain who is paid by the state

stip·ple /ˈstɪpəl/ *v* [T] to draw or paint a picture or pattern using short STROKES or spots instead of lines —**stippled** *adj* —**stippling** *n* [U]

stip·u·late /ˈstɪpjʊleɪt/ *v* [T] *formal* if an agreement, law, or rule stipulates something, it must be done; ▤ **state**: *Laws stipulate the maximum interest rate that banks can charge.* | **stipulate that** *The regulations stipulate that everything has to comply to the relevant safety standards.*

stip·u·la·tion /ˌstɪpjʊˈleɪʃən/ *n* [C,U] *formal* something that must be done, and which is stated as part of an agreement, law, or rule: **stipulation that** *The agreement included a stipulation that half of the money had to be spent on housing for lower-income families.*

stir¹ S3 W3 /stɜː $ stɜːr/ *v* **stirred**, **stirring**
1 MIX [T] to move a liquid or substance around with a spoon or stick in order to mix it together: *Stir the paint to make sure it is smooth.* | **stir sth with sth** *She stirred her coffee with a plastic spoon.* | **stir sth in/into sth** *Stir a cup of cooked brown rice into the mixture.*
2 MOVE SLIGHTLY [I,T] to move slightly or to make something move slightly: *The crowd began to stir as they waited for the band to start.* | *A gentle breeze stirred the curtains.*
3 LEAVE A PLACE [I] to leave or move from a place: *He hadn't stirred from his chair all morning.*
4 FEELINGS **a)** [T] to make someone have a strong feeling or reaction: **stir memories/emotions etc** *Looking at the photographs stirred childhood memories of the long hot summers.* | *The poem succeeds in* **stirring the imagination**. **b)** [I] if a feeling stirs in you, you begin to feel it: *Excitement stirred inside her.*
5 DO STH [T] to make someone start doing something: **stir sb to do sth** *The incident stirred students to protest.*
6 CAUSE TROUBLE **be stirring (it)** *BrE informal* to cause trouble between people by spreading false or secret information: *Ben's always stirring!*
stir sb/sth ⇔ **up** *phr v*
1 to deliberately try to cause arguments or bad feelings between people: *John was always* **stirring up trouble** *in class.* | *Dave's just trying to* **stir things up** *because he's jealous.*
2 to make small pieces of something move around in the air or in water: *The wind had stirred up a powdery red dust.*

stir² *n* **1** [C usually singular] a feeling of excitement or annoyance: **create/cause a stir** *Plans for the motorway caused quite a stir among locals.* **2** [C usually singular] an act of stirring something: *Give that pan a stir, will you?* **3** [C,U] *AmE old-fashioned informal* a prison

ˌstir-ˈcrazy *adj informal* extremely nervous and upset, especially because you feel trapped in a place: *I'm going to* **go stir-crazy** *if I don't get out of this house.*

ˈstir-fry¹ *v* **stir-fried**, **stir-frying**, **stir-fries** [T] to cook small pieces of food quickly by moving them around continuously in very hot oil: *stir-fried vegetables*

stir-fry² *n plural* **stir-fries** [C] a dish made by stir-frying small pieces of food

stir·rer /ˈstɜːrə $ -ər/ *n* [C] **1** *BrE informal* someone who likes to cause trouble between people by spreading false or secret information – used to show disapproval **2** an object shaped like a stick which is used to mix liquids

stir·ring[1] /ˈstɜːrɪŋ/ adj producing strong feelings or excitement in someone; ▤ **rousing**: *a stirring speech* | *stirring music* —**stirringly** adv

stirring[2] n [C] an early sign that something is starting to happen: [+of] *the first stirrings of spring*

stir·rup /ˈstɪrəp $ ˈstɜː-/ n [C] one of the rings of metal in which someone riding a horse rests their feet

ˈstirrup ˌpants n [plural] AmE stretchy women's trousers that have bands at the bottom of the legs which fit under your feet

stitch[1] /stɪtʃ/ n

1 SEWING [C] a short piece of thread that has been sewn into a piece of cloth, or the action of the thread going into and out of the cloth

2 FOR WOUND [C] a piece of special thread which has been used to sew the edges of a wound together: *He had to have 10 stitches in his head.*

3 PAIN [C usually singular] a sharp pain in the side of your body, which you can get by running or laughing a lot

4 WITH WOOL [C] a small circle of wool that is formed around a needle when you are KNITTING: **drop a stitch** (=lose a stitch because the wool has come off the needle)

5 STYLE [C,U] a particular way of sewing or KNITTING that makes a particular pattern: *Purl and plain are the two main stitches in knitting.*

6 not have a stitch on informal to be wearing no clothes

7 in stitches laughing a lot in a uncontrollable way: **have/keep sb in stitches** (=make someone laugh) *Her jokes had us all in stitches.*

8 a stitch in time (saves nine) spoken used to say that it is better to deal with problems early than to wait until they get worse

stitch[2] v [T] to sew two pieces of cloth together, or to sew a decoration onto a piece of cloth: *Mary is stitching a bedspread.* | **stitch sth onto/across sth** *The jersey has his name stitched across the back.*

stitch sth ⇔ **together** phr v AmE **1** to put different things or parts of something together to make one larger thing: *In ten years, they have been able to stitch together a national network of banks.* **2** to get a deal or agreement arranged

stitch sb/sth ⇔ **up** phr v **1** to put stitches in cloth or a wound in order to fasten parts of it together: *She stitched up the cut and left it to heal.* **2** to get a deal or agreement completed satisfactorily so that it cannot be changed: *The deal was stitched up in minutes.* **3** BrE informal to deceive someone, especially in order to gain money from them **4** BrE informal to make someone seem guilty of a crime by providing false information; ▤ **frame**

stitch·ing /ˈstɪtʃɪŋ/ n [U] a line of stitches in a piece of material

ˈstitch-up, stitch up n [C] BrE a situation in which someone is deliberately deceived

stoat /stəʊt $ stoʊt/ n [C] a small wild animal, similar to a WEASEL, that has a long thin body and brown fur

stock[1] S3 W3 /stɒk $ stɑːk/ n

1 IN A SHOP [C,U] a supply of a particular type of thing that a shop has available to sell: *We have a huge stock of quality carpets on sale.* | *Buy now while stocks last!* | **out of stock/in stock** (=unavailable or available in a particular shop) *I'm sorry, that swimsuit is completely out of stock in your size.*

2 FINANCE **a)** [C] especially AmE a SHARE in a company: *the trading of stocks and shares* **b)** [U] the total value of all of a company's SHARES

3 AMOUNT AVAILABLE [C] the total amount of something that is available to be used in a particular area: *Cod stocks in the North Atlantic have dropped radically.* | *the stock of housing in rural areas*

4 SUPPLIES [C] a supply of something that you keep and can use when you need to: [+of] *He keeps a stock of*

medicines in the cupboard. | *The country has been building up its stock of weapons.*

5 take stock (of sth) to think carefully about the things that have happened in a situation in order to decide what to do next: *While in hospital, Jeremy took stock of his life.*

6 COOKING [C,U] a liquid made by boiling meat or bones and vegetables, which is used to make soups or to add FLAVOUR to other dishes: *chicken stock* | *vegetable stock*

7 GUN [C] the part of a gun that you hold or put against your shoulder, usually made of wood

8 ANIMALS [U] farm animals, especially cattle; ▤ **livestock**

9 the stocks a) a wooden structure in a public place to which criminals were fastened by their feet or hands in the past **b)** a wooden structure in which a ship is held while it is being built

10 sb's stock is high/low if someone's stock is high or low, they are very popular or very unpopular: *Simon's stock is high in the network news business.*

11 stock of jokes/knowledge/courage etc the jokes, knowledge etc that someone knows or has: *John seems to have an inexhaustible stock of funny stories.*

12 be of Scottish/Protestant/good etc stock to belong to a family that in the past lived in Scotland, were Protestants, were respected etc

13 FLOWER [C] a plant with pink, white, or light purple flowers and a sweet smell

14 PLANT [C] a thick part of a stem onto which another plant can be added so that the two plants grow together

15 ACTORS [C] AmE a STOCK COMPANY (2)

stock[2] v [T] **1** if a shop stocks a particular product, it keeps a supply of it to sell: *We stock a wide range of kitchen equipment.* **2** to fill something with a supply of something: **stock sth with sth** *Our refrigerator at college was always stocked with beer.*

stock up phr v to buy a lot of something in order to keep it for when you need to use it later: [+on] *I have to stock up on snacks for the party.*

stock[3] adj **1 stock excuse/question/remark etc** an excuse etc that people often say or use, especially when they cannot think of anything more interesting or original – used to show disapproval **2** [only before noun] **stock item/size** something that is available in a shop and does not have to be ordered

stock·ade /stɒˈkeɪd $ stɑː-/ n [C usually singular] a fence built from long thick pieces of wood pushed into the ground, used to defend a place

stock·breed·er /ˈstɒkˌbriːdə $ ˈstɑːkˌbriːdər/ n [C] a farmer who breeds cattle

stock·brok·er /ˈstɒkˌbrəʊkə $ ˈstɑːkˌbroʊkər/ n [C] a person or organization whose job is to buy and sell SHARES, BONDS etc for people —**stockbroking** n [U]

ˈstock car n [C] **1** a car that has been made stronger so that it can compete in a race where cars often crash into each other: *stock-car racing* **2** AmE a railway carriage for cattle

ˈstock cerˌtificate n [C] AmE an official document that shows that you own SHARES in a company

ˈstock ˌcompany also **stock** n [C] AmE **1** a company whose money is divided into SHARES so that many people own a small part of it; ▤ **joint-stock company 2** a group of actors who work together doing several different plays

ˈstock cube n [C] a small solid CUBE made from the dried juices of meat or vegetables that is mixed with boiling water to make STOCK

ˈstock exˌchange n [C usually singular] **1** the business of buying and selling STOCKS and SHARES **2** a place where STOCKS and SHARES are bought and sold; ▤ **stock market**

stock·hold·er /ˈstɒkˌhəʊldə $ ˈstɑːkˌhoʊldər/ n [C] especially AmE someone who owns STOCKS in a business; ▤ **shareholder** BrE

'stock ,index n [C] an official and public list of STOCK prices

stock·i·nette /ˌstɒkɪ'net $ ˌstɑː-/ n [U] especially BrE a soft cotton material that stretches, used especially for BANDAGES

stock·ing /'stɒkɪŋ $ 'stɑː-/ n [C usually plural] **1** a thin close-fitting piece of clothing that covers a woman's leg and foot; → **tights 2** old-fashioned a man's sock **3 in your stockinged/stocking feet** not wearing any shoes

'stocking ,filler BrE; **'stocking ,stuffer** AmE n [C] a small present which you put in a CHRISTMAS STOCKING

'stocking ,mask n [C] a stocking that someone wears over their face when they are doing something illegal such as robbing a bank

,stock-in-'trade n [U] **1** something that is typical of a particular person or thing, especially what they say or do: Stewart's stock-in-trade was the face-to-face interview. **2** literary the things you need to do your job: Vanessa's looks have been her stock-in-trade as an actress.

stock·ist /'stɒkɪst $ 'stɑː-/ n [C] BrE a person, shop, or company that keeps a particular product to sell: Call us to order or to get details of **local stockists**.

stock·man /'stɒkmən $ 'stɑːk-/ n plural **stockmen** /-mən/ [C] a man whose job is to take care of farm animals

'stock ,market n [C usually singular] **1** the business of buying and selling STOCKS and SHARES **2** a place where STOCKS and SHARES are bought and sold; ⊟ **stock exchange**

'stock ,option n [C usually plural] AmE STOCK that a company offers to sell to an EMPLOYEE at a price that is lower than the usual price

stock·pile¹ /'stɒkpaɪl $ 'stɑːk-/ n [C] a large supply of things that is kept ready for use in the future; ⊟ **store**: [+of] a stockpile of nuclear weapons

stockpile² v [T] to keep adding to a supply of goods, weapons etc that you are keeping ready to use if you need them in the future: An enormous volume of explosives was stockpiled inside one of the buildings.

stock·pot /'stɒkpɒt $ 'stɑːkpɑːt/ n [C] a pot in which you make STOCK

stock·room /'stɒkrʊm, -ruːm $ 'stɑːk-/ n [C] a room for storing things in a shop or office

,stock-'still adv not moving at all: Oscar stood stock-still and listened.

stock·tak·ing /'stɒkˌteɪkɪŋ $ 'stɑːk-/ n [U] BrE when a company or shop checks the quantities of materials and goods that it has a supply of; ⊟ **inventory** AmE

stock·y /'stɒki $ 'stɑː-/ adj comparative **stockier**, superlative **stockiest** a stocky person is short and heavy and looks strong: a stocky build —**stockily** adv —**stockiness** n [U]

stock·yard /'stɒkjɑːd $ 'stɑːkjɑːrd/ n [C] a place where cattle, sheep etc are kept before being taken to a market and sold

stodge /stɒdʒ $ stɑːdʒ/ n [U] BrE informal heavy food that makes you feel full very quickly

stodg·y /'stɒdʒi $ 'stɑː-/ adj **1** if someone or something is stodgy, they are boring and formal or old-fashioned – used to show disapproval: a stodgy play **2** BrE stodgy food is heavy and makes you feel full very quickly – used to show disapproval; ⊞ **light** —**stodginess** n [U]

sto·gie /'stəʊgi $ 'stoʊ-/ n [C] AmE informal a CIGAR, especially a thick cheap one

sto·ic /'stəʊɪk $ 'stoʊ-/ n [C] someone who does not show their emotions and does not complain when bad things happen to them

sto·ic·al /'stəʊɪkəl $ 'stoʊ-/ also **stoic** adj not showing emotion or not complaining when bad things happen to you —**stoically** /-kli/ adv: She bore the pain stoically.

sto·i·cis·m /'stəʊɪˌsɪzəm $ 'stoʊ-/ n [U] patience and calmness when bad things happen to you

stoke /stəʊk $ stoʊk/ also **stoke up** v [T] **1** to add more coal or wood to a fire: I stoked the furnace for the night. **2** to cause something to increase: Rising oil prices stoked inflation. | **stoke fear/anger/envy etc** The scandal has stoked public outrage.

stoke up phr v **1 stoke sth ⇔ up** to add more coal or wood to a fire: We kept the fire stoked up high on cold nights. **2 stoke up sth** if something stokes up fear, anger etc, it makes a lot of people feel frightened etc: The leaflets stoked up fears of an invasion. **3 stoke up on/with sth** to eat a lot of food, for example because you will not eat again for a long time: We stoked up on hot soup before going out in the snow.

stoked /stəʊkt $ stoʊkt/ adj [not before noun] AmE spoken very pleased and excited

stok·er /'stəʊkə $ 'stoʊkər/ n [C] someone whose job is to put coal or other FUEL on a fire or into a FURNACE, for example on a STEAMSHIP or a steam train

stole¹ /stəʊl $ stoʊl/ the past tense of STEAL

stole² n [C] a long straight piece of cloth or fur that a woman wears across her shoulders

sto·len¹ /'stəʊlən $ 'stoʊ-/ the past participle of STEAL

stolen² adj having been taken illegally: stolen cars

stol·id /'stɒlɪd $ 'stɑː-/ adj someone who is stolid does not react to situations or seem excited by them when most people would react – used to show disapproval; ⊟ **impassive** —**stolidly** adv

stom·ach¹ S3 W3 /'stʌmək/ n [C]
1 the organ inside your body where food begins to be DIGESTED → see picture at HUMAN¹
2 the front part of your body, below your chest: He turned round and punched Carlos in the stomach.
3 do sth on an empty stomach to do something when you have not eaten: You shouldn't take the pills on an empty stomach.
4 turn your stomach to make you feel sick or upset: The sight of the slaughtered cow turned my stomach.
5 have no stomach for a fight/task etc to have no desire to do something difficult, upsetting, or frightening
6 have a strong stomach to be able to see or do things that are unpleasant without feeling sick or upset: Don't go and see this film unless you have a strong stomach.

stomach² v [T usually in questions and negatives] **1** to be able to accept something, especially something unpleasant; ⊟ **endure**: A 26% water rate increase is more than most residents **can stomach**. | **hard/difficult to stomach** Rob found Cathy's attitude hard to stomach. **2** to eat something without becoming ill: I've never been able to stomach seafood.

stom·ach·ache /'stʌmək-eɪk/ n [C,U] pain in your stomach or near your stomach

'stomach-,churning adj if something is stomach-churning, it is extremely unpleasant and makes you feel sick: the stomach-churning extremes of physical torture

'stomach pump n [C] a machine with a tube that doctors use to suck out food or liquid from someone's stomach, especially after they have swallowed something harmful

stomp /stɒmp $ stɑːmp/ v [I always + adv/prep] to walk with heavy steps or to put your foot down very hard, especially because you are angry; ⊟ **stamp**: Alex stomped angrily out of the meeting. | [+on] Rogers was injured after being stomped on by another player.

'stomping ,ground n AmE **sb's stomping ground** a favourite place where someone often goes; ⊟ **stamping ground** BrE

S

---

1 000, 2 000, 3 000, most frequent words in S poken and W ritten English

stones

rock

pebbles

fossil

gem stones

stone¹ S2 W1 /stəʊn $ stoʊn/ n
1 ROCK [U] a hard solid mineral substance: *a stone wall* | *stone steps* | *The floors are made of stone.*
2 PIECE OF ROCK [C] a small piece of rock of any shape, found on the ground: *A handful of protesters began throwing stones at the police.* △ In British English, a **stone** is a piece of stone small enough to pick up. In American English, this can be called either a **rock** or a **stone.**
3 JEWELLERY [C] a jewel; ▣ **precious stone**
4 FRUIT [C] *BrE* the large hard part at the centre of some fruits, such as a PEACH or CHERRY, which contains the seed; ▣ **pit** *AmE*; → see picture at FRUIT¹
5 MEDICAL [C] a ball of hard material that can form in organs such as your BLADDER or KIDNEYS
6 WEIGHT *plural* **stone** [C] written abbreviation *st* a British unit for measuring weight, equal to 14 pounds or 6.35 kilograms
7 a stone's throw from sth/away (from sth) very close to something: *The hotel is only a stone's throw from the beach.*
8 be made of stone also **have a heart of stone** to not show any emotions or pity for someone
9 not be carved/etched in stone used to say an idea or plan could change: *John has several new ideas for the show, but nothing is etched in stone yet.*
10 leave no stone unturned to do everything you can in order to find something or to solve a problem: *Jarvis left no stone unturned in his search to find the ring.*

stone² v [T] **1** to throw stones at someone or something: *Rioters blocked roads and stoned vehicles.* **2 stone sb to death** to kill someone by throwing stones at them, used as a punishment **3** *BrE* to take the stone out of fruit; ▣ **pit** *AmE*: *stoned dates* **4 stone the crows!** also **stone me!** *BrE old-fashioned* used to express surprise or shock

Stone Age n **the Stone Age** a very early time in human history, when only stone was used for making tools, weapons etc: *Stone Age weapons* | *a Stone Age settlement*

stone 'circle n [C] a circle of big tall stones, built thousands of years ago

stone-'cold adj **1** if something is stone-cold, it is completely cold even though it should be warm or hot: *Dinner was stone-cold by the time I got home.* **2 stone-cold sober** having drunk no alcohol at all **3** *AmE* if a player or sports team is stone-cold, they are not able to get any points

stoned /stəʊnd $ stoʊnd/ adj **1** *informal* feeling very excited or relaxed because you have taken an illegal drug such as MARIJUANA **2** *old-fashioned* very drunk

stone 'dead adj **1** used to emphasize that a person or animal is dead **2 kill sth stone dead** to completely destroy something or prevent it from being successful: *The wrong music can kill a commercial stone dead.*

stone 'deaf adj completely unable to hear

stone-'faced also **stony-faced** adj showing no emotion or friendliness

stone-ground adj stone-ground flour is made by crushing grain between two MILLSTONES

stone·ma·son /'stəʊnmeɪsən $ 'stoʊn-/ n [C] someone whose job is cutting stone into pieces to be used in buildings

stone·wall /ˌstəʊn'wɔːl $ ˌstoʊn'wɒːl/ v [I] to delay a discussion, decision etc by talking a lot and refusing to answer questions

stone·ware /'stəʊnweə $ 'stoʊnwer/ n [U] pots, bowls etc that are made from a special hard clay

stone-'washed adj stone-washed JEANS etc have been washed with small stones so that they look older and paler

stone·work /'stəʊnwɜːk $ 'stoʊnwɜːrk/ n [U] the parts of a building that are made of stone

stonk·er /'stɒŋkə $ 'stɑːŋkər/ n [C] *BrE informal* something that is very good; ▣ **corker**: *Stephen Carr scored a stonker of a goal.*

stonk·ing¹ /'stɒŋkɪŋ $ 'stɑːŋ-/ adj *BrE informal* extremely good: *a stonking performance*

stonking² adv *BrE informal* extremely: *a stonking good time*

ston·y /'stəʊni $ 'stoʊ-/ adj **1** covered by stones or containing stones: *stony soil* **2** not showing any friendliness or pity: *stony faces* | *a stony silence* **3 fall on stony ground** if a request, suggestion, joke etc falls on stony ground, it is ignored or people do not like it —**stonily** adv: *Camilla stared stonily ahead.*

stony-'faced also **stone-faced** adj showing no emotion or friendliness: *Tony stared at me in stony-faced silence.*

stood /stʊd/ the past tense and past participle of STAND¹

stooge /stuːdʒ/ n [C] **1** *informal* someone who is used by someone else to do something unpleasant, dishonest, or illegal – used to show disapproval **2** one of two performers in a COMEDY show, who the other performer makes jokes about and makes look stupid

stool /stuːl/ n [C] **1** a seat that has three or four legs, but no back or arms: *a bar stool* → see picture at CHAIR¹ **2** *medical* a piece of solid waste from your BOWELS

stool·pi·geon /'stuːlˌpɪdʒən/ n [C] *AmE informal* someone, especially a criminal, who helps the police to catch another criminal, usually by giving them information; ▣ **informer**

stoop¹ /stuːp/ v [I] **1** also **stoop down** to bend your body forward and down: *We had to stoop to pass through the low entrance.* | *Dave stooped down to tie his shoes.* **2** to stand with your back and shoulders bent forwards
stoop to sth *phr v* to do something bad or morally wrong, which you do not normally do: **stoop to doing sth** *I didn't expect you to stoop to lying.* | **stoop to sb's/that level** *Don't stoop to her level.*

stoop² n **1** [singular] if you have a stoop, your shoulders are bent forward: *Mr Hamilton was an odd, quiet man who walked with a stoop.* **2** [C] *AmE* a raised area at the door of a house, usually big enough to sit on

stooped /stuːpt/ also **stoop·ing** /'stuːpɪŋ/ adj bent forwards and down: *a thin man with stooped shoulders*

stop¹ S1 W1 /stɒp $ stɑːp/ v **stopped, stopping**
1 NOT MOVE [I,T] to not walk, move, or travel any more, or to make someone or something do this: *He stopped suddenly when he saw Ruth.* | *Stop, come back!* | *He stopped the car and got out.* | *I was worried that the security guards would stop us at the gate.* | [+at/outside/in etc] *She stopped outside the post office.* | *A car stopped behind us.* | **stop to do sth** *Sam stopped to give me a lift.* | **stop and do sth** *He stopped and looked into her face.* | [+for] *I need to stop for a rest.* | **stop dead/short/in your tracks** (=stop walking suddenly)

Sally saw the ambulance and stopped short. | **stop on a dime** *AmE* (=stop very quickly – used about cars) *This truck can stop on a dime!*

2 NOT CONTINUE a) [I,T] to not continue, or to make someone or something not continue: *By midday the rain had stopped.* | *This is where the path stops.* | *The referee stopped the fight.* | *The doctor advised me to stop the medication.* | *People are fighting to stop the destruction of the rainforests.* | **stop sb doing sth** *I couldn't stop her crying.* **b)** [I,T] if you stop doing something, you do not continue to do it: **stop doing sth** *I stopped digging and looked at him.* | *What time do you stop work?* | *I've been smoking for over ten years, and I can't stop.* | **stop it/that** (=stop doing something annoying) *Come on, you two, stop it!* | *Right, **stop what you're doing** and come over here.*

3 PAUSE [I] to pause in an activity, journey etc in order to do something before you continue: [+for] *We stopped for a drink on the way home.* | *I stopped to tie my shoe.* | **stop to think/consider etc** *It's time we stopped to think about our next move.*

4 PREVENT [T] to prevent someone from doing something or something from happening: *The government tried to stop publication of the book.* | *I'm leaving now, and you can't stop me.* | **stop sb/sth (from) doing sth** *Lay the carpet on paper to stop it sticking to the floor.* | *The rain didn't stop us from enjoying the trip.* | **stop yourself (from) doing sth** *I couldn't stop myself laughing.* | *She grabbed the rail to stop herself from falling.* | **there's nothing to stop sb (from) doing sth** *There's nothing to stop you applying for the job yourself.*

5 STAY [I] *BrE informal* to stay somewhere for a short time, especially at someone's house: *I won't sit down – I'm not stopping.* | [+for] *Will you stop for a cup of tea?*

6 will/would stop at nothing (to do sth) to be ready to do anything to achieve something that you want to achieve: *We will stop at nothing to save our child.*

7 stop short of (doing) sth to decide that you are not willing to do something wrong or dangerous, though you will do something similar that is less dangerous: *The US government supported sanctions but stopped short of military action.*

8 MONEY [T] if you stop an amount of money, you prevent it from being paid to someone: *Dad threatened to stop my pocket money.* | **stop sth from sth** *£200 will be stopped from your wages next month to pay for the damage.* | *I phoned the bank and asked them to **stop the cheque** (=not pay a cheque that I had written).* | *My mother called the bank to **stop payment** on the check.*

9 BLOCK also **stop up** [T] to block a hole or pipe so that water, smoke etc can go through it

stop back *phr v AmE*
to go back to a place you have been to earlier: *Can you stop back later? I'm busy right now.*

stop by (sth) *phr v*
to make a short visit to a place or person, especially while you are going somewhere else: *I'll stop by this evening.* | *Daniel stopped by the store on his way home.*

stop in *phr v informal*
1 to make a short visit to a place or person, especially while you are going somewhere else: *I'll stop in and see you on my way home.* | [+at] *I need to stop in at the library.*
2 *BrE* to stay at home: *I'm stopping in to wash my hair tonight.*

stop off *phr v*
to make a short visit to a place during a journey, especially to rest or to see someone: *We can stop off and see you on our way back.* | [+in/at etc] *We stopped off in Santa Rosa for a day.*

stop out *phr v BrE*
informal to stay out later than usual: *It was a real treat being allowed to stop out late.*

stop over *phr v*
to stop somewhere and stay a short time before continuing a long journey, especially when travelling by plane: *The plane stops over in Dubai on the way to India.* → STOPOVER

stop up *phr v*
1 stop sth ⇔ up to block a hole or pipe so that water, smoke etc cannot go through it
2 *BrE informal* to stay up late: *Joe stopped up till 3 o'clock to watch the boxing.*

GRAMMAR
To **stop doing something** means to not continue an activity: *It has stopped raining* (NOT *stopped from raining*). | *He couldn't stop talking about it* (NOT *stop from talking/stop to talk*).
To **stop to do something** means to stand still, or stop what you are doing, in order to do something: *He stopped to pick up a piece of paper.*
To **stop someone from doing something** means to prevent someone from doing something: *You can't stop me from going* (NOT *stop me to go*).
In British English you can leave out 'from': *This will help stop people dying of AIDS.*

stop² [S3] [W3] *n* [C]

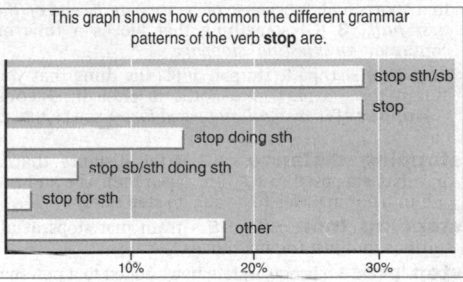

This graph shows how common the different grammar patterns of the verb **stop** are.

- stop sth/sb
- stop
- stop doing sth
- stop sb/sth doing sth
- stop for sth
- other

10%   20%   30%

1 come/roll/jerk/skid etc to a stop if a vehicle comes to a stop, it stops moving: *The bus came to a stop outside the school.* | *The car skidded to a stop.*

2 come to a stop if an activity comes to a stop, it stops happening: *Work on the project has come to a stop because of lack of funding.*

3 bring sth to a stop to stop something moving or happening: *David brought the truck to a shuddering stop.* | *The UN is trying to bring the war to a stop.*

4 DURING JOURNEY a time or place when you stop during a journey for a short time: *Our first stop was Paris.* | *We'll **make a stop** at the foot of the hill.* | *The trip includes an **overnight stop** in London.*

5 BUS/TRAIN a place where a bus or train regularly stops for people to get on and off: *Our next stop will be York.* | *This is your stop, isn't it?*

6 put a stop to sth to prevent something from continuing or happening: *The government is determined to put a stop to the demonstrations.*

7 pull out all the stops to do everything you possibly can to make something happen and succeed: *The hospital staff pulled out all the stops to make sure the children had a wonderful day.*

8 MONEY the action or fact of telling your bank not to pay an amount of money to someone: *I **put a stop on** that check to the store.*

9 MUSIC a handle that you push in or out in an ORGAN to control the amount of sound it produces

10 CONSONANT a consonant sound, like /p/ or /k/, that you make by stopping the flow of air completely and then suddenly letting it out of your mouth → FULL STOP¹

stop·cock /ˈstɒpkɒk $ ˈstɑːpkɑːk/ *n* [C] a TAP that controls the flow of a liquid or gas through a pipe

stop·gap /ˈstɒpgæp $ ˈstɑːp-/ *n* [C] something or someone that you use for a short time until you can replace it with something better: *It's only a **stopgap measure**, not a long-term solution.*

stop-'go adj stop-go approach/policies etc BrE a way of controlling the ECONOMY by restricting government spending for a period of time and then not restricting it so severely for a time

stop·light /'stɒplaɪt $ 'stɑːp-/ n [C] also **stoplights** [plural] AmE a set of coloured lights used to control and direct traffic; ⊟ **traffic lights**

stop-'loss order n [C] technical an arrangement in which the person who buys and sells STOCKS for you agrees to buy or sell them when they reach a particular price

stop·o·ver /'stɒp,əʊvə $ 'stɑːp,oʊvər/ n [C] a short stay somewhere between parts of a journey, especially on a long plane journey: a two-day stopover in Hong Kong

stop·page /'stɒpɪdʒ $ 'stɑːp-/ **1** [C] a situation in which workers stop working for a short time as a protest: time lost in disputes and stoppages | a **work stoppage** by government employees **2** [C,U] especially BrE when something stops moving or happening: We had five minutes of **stoppage time** (=extra time played in a sports match because of pauses) at the end of the first half. **3** [C] something that blocks a tube or container: an intestinal stoppage

stop·per /'stɒpə $ 'stɑːpər/ n [C] the thing that you put in the top part of a bottle to close it; → **cork** —**stopper** v [T]: a small, stoppered jar; → see picture at LID

stopping distance n [C,U] the distance that a driver is supposed to leave between their car and the one in front in order to be able to stop safely

stopping train n [C] BrE a train that stops at all stations, not just the main ones

stop press n [singular] late news added to a newspaper after the main part has been printed

stop·watch /'stɒpwɒtʃ $ 'stɑːpwɑːtʃ, -wɒtʃ/ n [C] a watch used for measuring the exact time it takes to do something, especially to finish a race → see picture at CLOCK[1]

stor·age W3 /'stɔːrɪdʒ/ n [U]
1 when you keep or put something in a special place while it is not being used: the storage of radioactive material | **storage space/capacity** (=space etc for keeping things in) They moved to a house with lots of storage space. → see picture at CAN
2 when you pay to keep furniture or other goods in a special place until you need to use them: **in storage** I put some of my things in storage. | storage costs
3 the way that information is kept on a computer: data storage

storage heater n [C] BrE a HEATER that stores heat at times when electricity is cheaper, for example at night

store[1] S1 W1 /stɔː $ stɔːr/ n [C]
1 a place where goods are sold to the public. In British English, a store is large and sells many different things, but in American English, a store can be large or small, and sells many things or only one type of thing; → **shop**: At Christmas the stores stay open late. | **shoe/clothing/grocery etc store** AmE (=one that sells one type of goods) She worked in a bookstore during college. | **go to the store** AmE (=go to a store that sells food) I need to go to the store for some milk. → CHAIN STORE, DEPARTMENT STORE, GENERAL STORE; → see box at SHOP[1]
2 SUPPLY a supply of something that you keep to use later: [+of] a store of wood | fat stores in the body (=that your body keeps)
3 PLACE TO KEEP THINGS a large building in which goods are kept so they can be used or sold later: a grain store
4 **in store (for sb)** if something unexpected such as a surprise or problem is in store for someone, it is about to happen to them: There's a real treat in store for you this Christmas! | As we left, I wondered what the future **held in store.**

5 MILITARY **stores** [plural] **a)** supplies of food and equipment that are used by an army, navy etc: medical stores **b)** the building or room in an army camp, ship etc where these are kept
6 **set great/considerable etc store by sth** to consider something to be important: Patrick has never set much store by material things.

store[2] S3 W3 v [T]
1 to put things away and keep them until you need them: **store sth away/up** Squirrels are storing up nuts for the winter. | Store the beans in an airtight jar.
2 to keep facts or information in your brain or on a computer: Standard letters can be stored on floppy discs.
3 **store up trouble/problems etc** to behave in a way that will cause trouble for you later: Smokers may be storing up disease for their unborn children.

store brand n [C] especially AmE a type of goods that is produced for a particular shop and has the shop's name on it: Store brands are cheaper than name brands.

store card n [C] BrE a card provided by a particular shop that you can use to buy goods at that shop, that you will pay for at a later date; ⊟ **charge card**

store detective n [C] someone who is employed in a large shop to watch the customers and to stop them stealing

store·front /'stɔːfrʌnt $ 'stɔːr-/ n [C] AmE **1** the part of a store that faces the street **2** **storefront church/law office/school etc** a small church etc in a shopping area

store·house /'stɔːhaʊs $ 'stɔːr-/ n [C] **1** **storehouse of information/memories etc** something that contains a lot of information etc: The local archives service offers a storehouse of material. **2** old-fashioned a building where things are stored; ⊟ **warehouse**

store·keep·er /'stɔː,kiːpə $ 'stɔːr,kiːpər/ n [C] AmE someone who owns or manages a shop; ⊟ **shopkeeper** BrE

store·room /'stɔːrʊm, -ruːm/ n [C] a room where goods are stored

sto·rey BrE; **story** AmE /'stɔːri/ n [C] a floor or level of a building: a staircase leads to the **upper storey** | **two-storey/five-storey etc** (=having two etc storeys)

WORD CHOICE: storey, story, floor
Storey (BrE) or **story** (AmE) is usually used to talk about the structure of a building: a building dozens of storeys high | a three-storey house
The plural of **story** is **stories**: The office block was 20 stories high.
To talk about where someone or something is in a building, use **floor**: We went up to the top floor. | He works on the fifteenth floor. | Is there a bathroom on this floor?

---

sto·ried /'stɔːrid/ adj **1** **two-storied/five storied etc** AmE having two etc storeys **2** [only before noun] literary being the subject of many stories; ⊟ **famous**: Sun Tzu, the storied Chinese leader and philosopher

stork /stɔːk $ stɔːrk/ n [C] a tall white bird with long legs and a long beak

storm[1] W3 /stɔːm $ stɔːrm/ n
1 [C] a period of very bad weather when there is a lot of rain or snow, strong winds, and often LIGHTNING: The **storm broke** (=suddenly started) at five o'clock. | a night-time **thunderstorm** | Twenty people were killed when **storms struck** the Mid-West. | There's a **storm brewing** (=starting) in the Pacific. | a dust storm | a summer storm
2 [C usually singular] a situation in which people suddenly express very strong feelings about something that someone has said or done: The governor found himself at the center of a **political storm**. | **storm of protest/abuse/criticism etc** Government plans for hospital closures provoked a storm of protest. | **whip/blow/kick etc up a storm** a man would could whip up a storm in her heart
3 **take somewhere by storm a)** to be very successful in a particular place: The new show took London by storm. **b)** to attack a place using large numbers of soldiers,

and succeed in getting possession of it
4 weather the storm to experience a difficult period and reach the end of it without being harmed or damaged too much: *I'll stay and weather the storm.*
5 a storm in a teacup *BrE* an unnecessary expression of strong feelings about something that is very unimportant
6 dance/sing/cook etc up a storm to do something with all your energy: *They were dancing up a storm.*

storm² *v* **1** [T] to suddenly attack and enter a place using a lot of force: *An angry crowd stormed the embassy.* **2** [I always + adv/prep] to go somewhere in a noisy fast way that shows you are extremely angry: [**+out of/into/off etc**] *Alan stormed out of the room.* **3** [I,T] *literary* to shout something in an angry way: *'What difference does it make?' she stormed.*

'storm ,cellar *n* [C] *AmE* a place under a house where you can go to be safe during violent storms

'storm cloud *n* [C] **1** a dark cloud which you see before a storm **2** [usually plural] a sign that something very bad is going to happen: *Storm clouds are gathering over the trade negotiations.*

'storm door *n* [C] a second door that is fitted to the outside of a door in winter in the US to give protection against rain, snow etc

'storm drain *n* [C] an opening at the side of a street that carries away rain water during a storm

'storm ,lantern *n* [C] a lamp which has a cover to protect the flame against the wind, used in the past

storm·troop·er /'stɔːm,truːpə $ 'stɔːrm,truːpər/ *n* [C] a member of a special group of German soldiers in the Second World War

'storm ,window *n* [C] a second window fitted to the outside of a window in winter in the US to give more protection against rain, snow etc

storm·y /'stɔːmi $ 'stɔːr-/ *adj* **1** with strong winds, heavy rain, and dark clouds: *The sky was starting to look stormy.* | *a dark and stormy night* **2** a stormy relationship, meeting etc is full of strong and often angry feelings: *a stormy affair* **3** stormy seas are very rough with big waves that are caused by strong winds: *hostile, stormy seas*

sto·ry [S2] [W2] /'stɔːri/ *n plural* **stories** [C]
1 FOR ENTERTAINMENT a description of how something happened, that is intended to entertain people, and may be true or imaginary; → **tale**: [**+about/of**] *a story about a princess* | *fairy/ghost/love etc story a detective story* | **tell/read sb a story** *Mommy, will you read me a story?* | *a book of short stories* | *We cuddled together over a bedtime story.* | *The film was based on a true story.* | *Don't be frightened – it's only a story* (=it is imaginary).
2 NEWS a report in a newspaper or news broadcast about a recent event: *a front-page story* | *'The Observer' ran a story about the scandal* (=reported it). | **cover story** (=the main story in a magazine, that is about the picture on the cover)
3 EVENTS an account of something that has happened, usually one that people tell each other, and which may not be true: *The full story of what happened has never been reported.* | *Her parents did not believe her story.* | *First he wanted to hear Matthew's side of the story* (=his description of what happened). | *He was having an affair with Julie, or so the story goes* (=people are saying this).
4 EXCUSE an excuse or explanation, especially one that you have invented: *Where were you? And don't give me some story about working late!* | *Well that's my story* (=that is what I say happened), *and I'm sticking to it.*
5 HISTORY a description of the most important events in someone's life or in the development of something: *the Charlie Parker Story* | *He wanted to have his life story told on film.*
6 BUILDING *AmE* a floor or level of a building; → **sto·rey** *BrE*: *a fifty-story building*
7 OF A FILM/PLAY ETC what happens in a film, play, or book; → **plot**: *The story is similar in all her books.*

8 it's the same story here/there/in ... used to say the same thing is happening in another place: *Unemployment is falling in the US and it's the same story in Europe.*

SPOKEN PHRASES
9 it's the same old story used to say that the present bad situation has often happened before: *It's the same old story – too much work and not enough time.*
10 it's a long story used to tell someone that you do not want to give them all the details that a full answer to their question would need
11 to cut a long story short also **to make a long story short** *AmE* used when you only give the main point of something you are talking about, and not all the other details
12 but that's another story used when you have mentioned something that you are not going to talk about on this occasion
13 that's not the whole story used to say that there are more details which people need to know in order to understand the situation
14 that's the story of my life used after a disappointing experience to mean that similar disappointing things always seem to happen to you
15 end of story used to say that there is nothing more to say about a particular subject: *As far as I'm concerned Terry is still a friend, end of story.*

---

16 a different story used to say that something is not what you expect it to be: *It looks like a big house, but inside it's a different story.*
17 LIE a lie – used by children or when speaking to children: *You shouldn't tell stories.* → **SHORT STORY**; → **cock and bull story** at COCK¹ (4) → **HARD-LUCK STORY, SOB STORY**; → **success story** at SUCCESS (5); → see box at STOREY

sto·ry·book¹ /'stɔːribʊk/ *n* [C] a book of stories for children: *colourful storybooks*

storybook² *adj* storybook ending/romance etc an ending etc that is so happy or perfect that it is like one in a children's story: *It would have been storybook stuff if he had won the competition.*

'story line also **sto·ry·line** /'stɔːrilaɪn/ *n* [C] the main set of related events in a story; **☐ plot**: *The play had a strong story line.*

sto·ry·tell·er /'stɔːri,telə $ -ər/ *n* [C] someone who tells stories, especially to children

stoup /stuːp/ *n* [C] a container for holy water near the entrance to a church

stout¹ /staʊt/ *adj* **1** fairly fat and heavy, or having a thick body: *a short, stout man* **2** *literary* strong and thick; **☐ sturdy**: *a stout pair of shoes* **3** *formal* brave and determined: *stout defence/support/resistance He put up a stout defence in court.* —**stoutly** *adv*: *She stoutly denied the rumours.* —**stoutness** *n* [U]

stout² *n* [U] strong dark beer

stout·heart·ed /ˌstaʊt'hɑːtɪd◂ $ -ɑːr-/ *adj literary* brave and determined

stove¹ /stəʊv $ stoʊv/ *n* [C] **1** a piece of kitchen equipment on which you cook food in pots and pans, and that contains an OVEN; **☐ cooker** *BrE*: **on the stove** *a pot of soup simmering on the stove* **2** a thing used for heating a room or for cooking, which works by burning wood, coal, oil, or gas: *a wood-burning stove*

stove² the past tense and past participle of STAVE²

stow /staʊ $ stoʊ/ also **stow away** *v* [T always + adv/prep] to put or pack something tidily away in a space until you need it again; **☐ stash**: *I stowed my bag under the seat.* | *equipment stowed away in a closet*
stow away *phr v* to hide on a vehicle in order to travel secretly or without paying: *A boy was caught trying to stow away on a plane.* → **STOWAWAY**

stow·age /'stəʊɪdʒ $ 'stoʊ-/ *n* [C] space available in a vehicle, especially a boat, for storing things

---

[1] 000, [2] 000, [3] 000, most frequent words in [S]poken and [W]ritten English

stow·a·way /'stəʊəweɪ $ 'stoʊ-/ n [C] someone who hides on a vehicle in order to travel secretly or to avoid paying

strad·dle /'strædl/ v [T] **1** to sit or stand with your legs on either side of someone or something: *The photo shows him dressed in leather, straddling a motorbike*. **2** if something straddles a line, road, or river, part of it is on one side and part on the other side: **straddle sth between sth** *Mount Elgon straddles the border between Kenya and Uganda*. **3** to include different areas of activity, groups, time etc: *Her research straddles mathematics and social sciences*. | *immigrants straddling two cultures*

strafe /streɪf, strɑːf $ streɪf/ v [T] to attack a place from an aircraft by flying low and firing a lot of bullets

strag·gle /'strægəl/ v [I] **1** if the people in a group straggle somewhere, they go there fairly slowly and with large spaces between them: [+in/into/through etc] *The children were beginning to straggle in from the playground*. | [+**behind**] *Ali straggled behind, carrying the shopping*. **2** to move, grow, or spread out untidily in different directions: *thin, black, straggling hair* | [+**along/across/down etc**] *Unpainted wooden buildings straggle along the main road out of town*.

strag·gler /'stræglə $ -ər/ n [C] a person or animal that is behind the others in a group, because they are moving more slowly: *Wait for the stragglers to catch up*.

strag·gly /'strægəli/ adj growing untidily and spreading out in different directions: *straggly hair*

straight¹ S1 W2 /streɪt/ adv

1 **IN A STRAIGHT LINE** in a line or direction that is not curved or bent: [+**ahead/at/down/in front of etc**] *The book is on the table straight in front of you*. | *She was looking straight at me*. | *Terry was so tired he couldn't walk straight*. | *He was sitting with his legs stretched straight out in front of him*.

2 **POSITION** in a level or correct position: *He stopped in front of the mirror to put his tie straight*. | *Sit up straight, don't slouch*.

3 **IMMEDIATELY** immediately, without delay, or without doing anything else first: [+**to/up/down/back etc**] *I went straight up to bed*. | *Go straight home and tell your mother*. | [+**after**] *I've got a meeting straight after lunch*. | *I think I should get straight to the point*.

4 **ONE AFTER THE OTHER** happening one after the other in a series: *He's been without sleep now for three days straight*.

5 **HONEST** also **straight out** if you say or ask something straight, you say it in an honest, direct way, without trying to hide your meaning: *I just told him straight that I wouldn't do it*. | *She came straight out with it and said she was leaving*. | *I hope for your sake you're playing it straight* (=being honest). | *I told him straight to his face* (=speaking directly to him) *what I thought of him*.

6 **think/see straight** if you cannot think or see straight, you cannot think or see clearly: *Turn the radio down, I can't think straight*.

7 **straight away** also **straight off** BrE spoken immediately or without delay: *I phoned my mum straight away*.

8 **go straight** informal to stop being a criminal and live an honest life: *Tony's been trying to go straight for about six months*.

9 **straight up** spoken **a)** used to ask someone if they are telling the truth: *Straight up? Did you really pay that much for it?* **b)** used to emphasize that what you are saying is true: *No, straight up, I've never seen him before*.

10 **straight from the shoulder** BrE informal if someone speaks straight from the shoulder, they say things in a very direct way, without trying to be polite

straight² S2 W3 adj comparative **straighter**, superlative **straightest**

1 **NOT BENDING OR CURVING** something that is straight does not bend or curve: *a long, straight road* |

Try to keep your legs straight. | *Always lift with a straight back*. | *her long, straight black hair* | *They sat down in a straight line*. | *The road was dead straight* (=completely straight).

2 **LEVEL/UPRIGHT** level or upright, and not leaning to one side: *Is my tie straight?* | *straight white teeth*

3 **TRUTHFUL** honest and truthful: *I'd like a straight answer please*. | *Just give me a straight yes or no*. | *I think it's time for some straight talk now*. | **be straight with sb** *I wish you'd just be straight with me*.

4 **ONE AFTER ANOTHER** [only before noun] happening immediately one after another in a series: *The team now has an amazing record of 43 straight wins*.

5 **TIDY** [not before noun] a room that is straight is clean and tidy and everything is in its proper place: *It took me two hours to get the house straight*.

6 **get sth straight** spoken to understand the facts of a situation and be able to tell them correctly: *I wanted to get the facts straight*. | *Let me get this straight – Tom sold the car and gave you the money?*

7 **set/put sb straight** to make someone understand the true facts about a situation: *Tell him to ask Ruth – she'll put him straight*.

8 **straight face** if you have a straight face, you are not laughing or smiling even though you would like to: *I found it very difficult to keep a straight face*.

9 **SEXUAL CHOICE** informal someone who is straight is attracted to people of the opposite sex; 🔲 **heterosexual**

10 **ALCOHOLIC DRINK** a straight alcoholic drink has no water or any other drink added to it: *a straight whisky*

11 **NOT OWING MONEY** [not before noun] spoken if two people are straight, they no longer owe money to each other: *If you give me £10 then we're straight*.

12 **CHOICE/EXCHANGE** [only before noun] a straight choice or exchange is between only two possible choices or things: *It was a straight choice between my career or my family*. | *We did a straight swap – one of my cards for one of his*.

13 **FIGHT/COMPETITION** [only before noun] a straight fight or competition is between only two people: *The election is now a straight fight between Labour and the Conservatives*.

14 **NORMAL** informal someone who is straight behaves in a way that is accepted as normal by many people but which you think is boring

15 **NOT FUNNY** a straight actor or character does not try to make people laugh

16 **ONLY ONE TYPE** completely one particular type of something: *It's not a straight historical novel*.

17 **DRUGS** informal someone who is straight does not take illegal drugs → **set/put the record straight** at RECORD

straight³ n **1** [singular] especially BrE the straight part of a RACETRACK **2** **the straight and narrow** old-fashioned an honest and morally good way of life **3** [C] informal someone who is attracted to people of the opposite sex; 🔲 **gay**

straight 'arrow n [C] AmE informal someone who is very honest and moral and who never does anything exciting or unusual

straight·a·way¹ /,streɪtə'weɪ/ adv at once; 🔲 **immediately**: *We need to start work straightaway*.

straight·a·way² /'streɪtəweɪ/ n [singular] AmE the straight part of a RACETRACK

straight·en /'streɪtn/ v **1** [I,T] also **straighten out** to become straight, or to make something straight: *Can you straighten your leg?* **2** [I] also **straighten up** to make your back straight, or to stand up straight after bending down **3** [T] also **straighten up** to make something tidy: *Mum told me to straighten my room*.

straighten out phr v **1 straighten sth ⇔ out** to deal with problems or a confused situation and make it better, especially by organizing things; 🔲 **sort out**: *There are several financial problems that need to be straightened out quickly*. **2** to become straight, or to make something straight: *The path soon bends to the* *right then straightens out.* | **straighten sth** ⟺ **out** *She straightened out her legs.* **3** to improve your bad behaviour or deal with personal problems, or to help someone do this: *He straightened out when he joined the army.* | **straighten sb** ⟺ **out** *Her parents changed her school, hoping it would straighten her out.*

straighten up *phr v* **1** to make your back straight, or to stand up straight after bending down: *He remained bent over for several seconds before slowly straightening up.* **2 straighten sth** ⟺ **up** to make something tidy **3** *AmE* to begin to behave well after behaving badly: *You'd better straighten up, young lady!*

straight·faced /ˌstreɪtˈfeɪst◂/ *adj* without smiling or laughing, even though you are joking or saying something untrue: *'No, I really do love you,' said Kim, straightfaced.* —**straightfacedly** /-ˈfeɪsɪdli◂/ *adv*

straight·for·ward ⓢ³ /ˌstreɪtˈfɔːwəd◂ $ -ˈfɔːr-wərd◂/ *adj*
1 simple and easy to understand; **🄴 complicated:** **relatively/quite/fairly straightforward** *Installing the program is relatively straightforward.* | *This area of law is far from straightforward* (=complicated). | **straight-forward matter/task/process etc** *For someone who can't read, shopping is by no means a straightforward matter.* **2** honest about your feelings or opinions and not hiding anything: *Jack is tough, but always straightforward and fair.* —**straightforwardly** *adv* —**straightforwardness** *n* [U]

straight·jack·et /ˈstreɪtˌdʒækɪt/ *n* another spelling of STRAITJACKET

'**straight man** *n* [C] an entertainer who works with a COMEDIAN, providing him or her with opportunities to make jokes

'**straight shooter** *n* [C] *AmE informal* an honest person who you can trust

'**straight 'ticket** *n* [C] a vote in which someone chooses all the CANDIDATES from a particular political party in the US; → **split ticket**

'**straight-to-'video** *n* [C] a film that is never shown in a cinema but is only available on video

straight·way /ˈstreɪt-weɪ/ *adv old use* STRAIGHTAWAY

strain¹ /streɪn/ *n*
1 **WORRY** [C,U] worry that is caused by having to deal with a problem or work too hard over a long period of time; → **stress:** *I couldn't look after him any more; the strain was too much for me.* | *Did you **find** the job a strain?* | *the **stresses and strains** of police life* | [+for] *The trial has been a terrible strain for both of us.* | [+on] *It's quite a strain on me when he's drinking heavily.* | **put/place a strain on sb** *The long working hours put a severe strain on employees.* | **under (a) strain** *I know you've been under a lot of strain lately.* | **crack/collapse/buckle etc under the strain** (=become unable to deal with a problem or work) *I could see that she was beginning to crack under the strain.*
2 **DIFFICULTY** [C,U] a difficulty or problem that is caused when a person, relationship, organization, or system has too much to do or too many problems to deal with: [+on] *The dry summer has further increased the strain on water resources.* | **put/place (a) strain on sth** *The flu epidemic has put a huge strain on the health service.* | [+in] *The attack has led to strains in the relationship between the two countries.* | **under (a) strain** *His marriage was under strain.* | **break/crack/collapse etc under the strain** *The party split under the strain.*
3 **FORCE** [U] a situation in which something is being pulled or pushed, or is holding weight, and so might break or become damaged: [+on] *The strain on the cables supporting the bridge is enormous.* | **put/place (a) strain on sth** *Some of these exercises put too much strain on the back muscles.* | *These four posts **take the strain** of the whole structure.* | **break/snap/collapse etc under the strain** *The rope snapped under the strain.*
4 **INJURY** [C,U] an injury to a muscle or part of your body that is caused by using it too much: *Long hours working at a computer can cause eye strain.* | *The goalkeeper is still out of action with a knee strain.*

5 **PLANT/ANIMAL** [C] a type of animal, plant, or disease: [+of] *different strains of wheat* | *a new strain of the flu virus*
6 **QUALITY** [singular] a particular quality which people have, especially one that is passed from parents to children: [+of] *There's a strain of madness in his family.*
7 **WAY OF SAYING STH** [singular] *formal* an amount of a feeling that you can see in the way someone speaks, writes, paints etc: *a strain of bitterness in Young's later work*
8 strains of sth *literary* the sound of music being played: *We sipped wine to the strains of Beethoven.*

strain² *v*
1 **INJURE** [T] to injure a muscle or part of your body by using it too much or making it work too hard: *I've strained a muscle in my leg* | *You'll strain your eyes trying to read in this light.*
2 **EFFORT** [I,T] to try very hard to do something using all your strength or ability: **strain (sth) to do sth** *She was straining to keep her head above the water.* | [+for] *Bill choked and gasped, straining for air.* | **strain your ears/eyes** (=try very hard to hear or see) *I strained my ears, listening for any sound in the silence of the cave.*
3 **LIQUID** [T] to separate solid things from a liquid by pouring the mixture through something with very small holes in it; → **sieve:** *She strained the pasta.*
4 **DIFFICULTY** [T] to cause difficulties for something by making too much work or too many problems which it cannot deal with easily: *The increased costs will certainly strain our finances.* | *The incident has strained relations between the two countries.* | *I felt that my patience was being **strained to the limit**.*
5 **PULL/PUSH** [I] to pull hard at something or push hard against something: [+against] *Buddy's huge gut strained against the buttons on his shirt.* | [+at] *a dog straining at its lead*
6 **strain every nerve** to try as hard as possible to do something: *He was straining every nerve to impress the judges.*
7 **be straining at the leash** to be eager to be allowed to do something: *There are 30,000 troops in the area, all straining at the leash.*
8 **not strain yourself** to not work too hard or do too much physical activity: *Don't strain yourself.*

strained /streɪnd/ *adj* **1** a strained situation or behaviour is not relaxed, natural, or friendly; **🄴 tense:** *I couldn't stand the **strained atmosphere** at dinner any more.* | *the increasingly **strained relations** between the French and German governments* **2** showing the effects of worry or too much work: *Nina's voice sounded strained.* | *Alex's pale, strained face*

strain·er /ˈstreɪnə $ -ər/ *n* [C] a kitchen tool with lots of small holes in it, that is used for separating solids from liquids; → **sieve:** *a tea strainer*

strait /streɪt/ *n* [C] **1** also **straits** [plural] a narrow passage of water between two areas of land, usually connecting two seas: *the Bering Strait* **2** **be in dire straits** to be in a very difficult situation, especially a financial one: *After the war the county's economy was in dire straits.* | *The firm is now **in dire financial straits**.*

strait·ened /ˈstreɪtnd/ *adj formal* not having enough money, especially not as much as you had before: *the straitened circumstances of post-war Japan*

strait·jack·et, straightjacket /ˈstreɪtdʒækɪt/ *n* [C] **1** a special piece of clothing that prevents someone from moving their arms, used to control someone who is being violent or, in the past, someone who was mentally ill **2** something such as a law or set of ideas that puts very strict or unfair limits on someone: *the straitjacket of censorship*

strait·laced /ˌstreɪtˈleɪst◂/ *adj* having strict, old-fashioned ideas about moral behaviour: *straitlaced Victorian society*

strand /strænd/ n [C] **1** a single thin piece of thread, wire, hair etc: [+of] *He reached out and brushed a* ***strand of hair*** *away from her face.* **2** one of the parts of a story, idea, plan etc: **strand of thought/opinion/ argument** *Plato draws all the strands of the argument together.*

strand·ed /'strændɪd/ adj a person or vehicle that is stranded is unable to move from the place where they are; ◧ **stuck**: *Air travellers were* ***left stranded*** *because of icy conditions.* | [+in/on/at] *There I was, stranded in Rome with no money.*

strange¹ [S2] [W2] /streɪndʒ/ adj comparative **stranger**, superlative **strangest**
1 unusual or surprising, especially in a way that is difficult to explain or understand; ◧ **odd**: *strange noises* | *Does Geoff's behaviour seem strange to you?* | *She felt there was* ***something strange about*** *Dexter's voice.* | ***Isn't it strange how*** *animals seem to sense danger?* | ***It's strange that*** *we've never met before.* | ***For some strange reason*** *I slept like a baby despite the noise.* | ***Strange as it may seem***, *I actually prefer cold weather.* | ***That's strange***. *I was sure Jude was right here a second ago.* | ***The strange thing is*** *all four victims had red hair.* | **strange to say** *BrE* (=strangely) *Strange to say, I was just thinking that myself*; → see box at **UNUSUAL**
2 someone or something that is strange is not familiar because you have not seen or met them before: *As a child she'd been taught never to speak to strange men.* | *I was just 20, a young girl in a strange city.* | [+to] *It was all strange to him, but he'd soon learn his way around.*
3 **feel strange** to feel as if something is slightly wrong or unusual, either physically or emotionally: *Can you get me a glass of water? I feel a bit strange.* | *It felt strange to be back in Dublin.* —**strangely** adv —**strangeness** n [U]

strange² adv [only after verb] *AmE* in a way that is unusual or surprising: *The cat's been acting really strange – I wonder if it's sick.*

strange·ly /'streɪndʒli/ adv in an unusual or surprising way; ◧ **oddly**: *Mick's been acting very strangely lately.* | *strangely shaped hills* | *The crowd fell strangely silent.* | ***Strangely enough***, *I wasn't that disappointed.*

strang·er /'streɪndʒə $ -ər/ n [C] **1** someone that you do not know: *Children must not talk to strangers.* | **perfect/complete/total stranger** (=used to emphasize that you do not know them) *Julie finds it easy to speak to complete strangers.* ⚠ Do not use **stranger** to mean 'a person from another country'. Use **foreigner** or, more politely, 'a person **from abroad/overseas**'. **2** **be no stranger to sth** to have had a lot of a particular kind of experience: *a politician who is no stranger to controversy* **3** someone in a new and unfamiliar place: *'Where's the station?' 'Sorry, I'm a stranger here myself.'* **4** **Hello, stranger!** *spoken* used to greet someone who you have not seen for a long time **5** **don't be a stranger!** *spoken* used when someone is leaving to invite them back to see you soon

stran·gle /'stræŋɡəl/ v [T] **1** to kill someone by pressing their throat with your hands, a rope etc; → **choke**: [+with] *The victim had been strangled with a belt.* **2** to limit or prevent the growth or development of something: *Mills argues that high taxation strangles the economy.* —**strangler** n [C]

stran·gled /'stræŋɡəld/ adj **strangled cry/gasp/voice** etc a cry or other sound that is suddenly stopped before it is finished: *Ed gave a strangled cry.*

stran·gle·hold /'stræŋɡəlhəʊld $ -hoʊld/ n [C] **1** [usually singular] complete control over a situation, organization etc: [+on] *Just a few firms* ***have a stranglehold*** *on the market for this software.* | **break/ loosen the stranglehold of sb** (=stop someone having complete control) **2** a strong hold around someone's neck that stops them from breathing

stran·gu·lat·ed /'stræŋɡjᵿleɪtɪd/ adj **1** *technical* if a part of your BOWEL is strangulated, it becomes tightly pressed or twisted so that the flow of blood stops: *a strangulated hernia* **2** *written* if someone's voice sounds strangulated, they sound as though their throat is being pressed: *Clearly terrified, he let out a strangulated whimper.*

stran·gu·la·tion /ˌstræŋɡjᵿ'leɪʃən/ n [U] the act of killing someone by pressing on their throat, or the fact of being killed in this way

strap¹ /stræp/ n [C] a narrow band of strong material that is used to fasten, hang, or hold onto something: *a bra strap* | *The strap of my bag is broken.* → CHINSTRAP, SHOULDER STRAP

strap² v **strapped**, **strapping** [T] **1** [always + adv/ prep] to fasten something or someone in place with one or more straps: **strap sth on/down etc** *He was only ten when he strapped on a guitar for the first time.* | *soldiers with grenades strapped to their belts* | **be strapped in** (=have a belt fastened around you in a car) *Are the kids strapped in?* **2** [often passive] *BrE* also **strap up** to tie BANDAGES firmly round a part of your body that has been hurt

strap·less /'stræpləs/ adj **strapless dress/gown/bra** one that does not have straps over the shoulders

strapped /stræpt/ adj **strapped (for cash)** *informal* having little or no money at the moment: *Can you lend me ten dollars? I'm a little strapped for cash.*

strap·ping /'stræpɪŋ/ adj [only before noun] a strapping young man or woman is strong, tall, and looks healthy and active: *a strapping young lad*

stra·ta /'strɑːtə $ 'streɪtə/ n **1** the plural of STRATUM **2** a plural form sometimes used instead of STRATUM

strat·a·gem /'strætədʒəm/ n [C] formal a trick or plan to deceive an enemy or gain an advantage; ◧ **ploy**

stra·te·gic [W3] /strə'tiːdʒɪk/ also **stra·te·gic·al** /-dʒɪkəl/ adj
1 done as part of a plan, especially in a military, business, or political situation: *UN forces made a strategic withdrawal.* | **strategic planning** *meetings* | *a strategic decision to move production to Hungary*
2 useful or right for a particular purpose: *Marksmen were placed at strategic points along the president's route.*
3 relating to fighting wars; → **tactical**: *Marseilles was of great* ***strategic importance***. | **strategic arms/weapons** (=weapons designed to reach an enemy country from your own) *strategic nuclear missiles* —**strategically** /-kli/ adv: *Strategically placed video cameras can alert police to any trouble.*

strat·e·gist /'strætɪdʒɪst/ n [C] someone who is good at planning things, especially military or political actions

strat·e·gy [W2] /'strætɪdʒi/ n plural **strategies**
1 [C] a planned series of actions for achieving something: *the government's long-term* ***economic strategy*** | *a company's* ***business strategy*** | **strategy for doing sth** *a strategy for dealing with crime* | **strategy to do sth** *a strategy to attract younger audiences to jazz*
2 [C,U] the skill of planning the movements of armies in a war, or an example of this: *military strategies* | *It is the general's role to develop* ***overall strategy***.
3 [U] skilful planning in general: *The company must first resolve questions of strategy.*

strat·i·fi·ca·tion /ˌstrætɪfɪ'keɪʃən/ n [C,U] **1** when society is divided into separate social classes: *The Indian caste system is an example of* ***social stratification***. **2** the way in which earth, rocks etc form layers over time —**stratify** /'strætɪfaɪ/ v [I,T]

strat·i·fied /'strætɪfaɪd/ adj **1** having different social classes: *a stratified society* **2** having several layers of earth, rock etc: *stratified rock*

strat·os·phere /'strætəsfɪə $ -sfɪr/ n **1** **the stratosphere** the outer part of the air surrounding the Earth, from ten to fifty kilometres above the Earth; → **atmosphere** **2** [singular] a very high position, level, or amount: *oil prices soared into the stratosphere* | *He's now at the top of the political stratosphere.*

stra·tum /'strɑːtəm $ 'streɪ-/ *n plural* **strata** /-tə/ [C] **1** a layer of rock or earth **2** a social class in a society: *people of different social strata*

straw S3 /strɔː $ strɒː/ *n*
1 a) [U] the dried stems of wheat or similar plants that animals sleep on, and that are used for making things such as baskets, hats etc; → **hay**: *a straw hat* **b)** [C] a single dried stem of straw
2 [C] a thin tube of paper or plastic for sucking up liquid from a bottle or a cup: *She sipped her lemonade through a straw.*
3 the last straw also **the straw that breaks the camel's back** the last problem in a series of problems that finally makes you give up, get angry etc: *Making me work late on Friday was the last straw.*
4 be clutching/grasping at straws to be trying everything you can to succeed, even though the things you are doing are not likely to help or work
5 straw in the wind *BrE* a sign of what might happen in the future: *There have been a few straws in the wind suggesting things might be getting a little better.*
6 straw man *AmE* a weak opponent or imaginary argument that can easily be defeated → **draw the short straw** at DRAW[1] (29)

straw·ber·ry S3 /'strɔːbəri $ 'strɒːberi, -bəri/ *n plural* **strawberries** [C] a soft red juicy fruit with small seeds on its surface, or the plant that grows this fruit → see picture at FRUIT[1]

strawberry 'blonde *n* [C] someone, especially a girl or woman, with light reddish yellow hair **—strawberry blonde** *adj*

straw-'coloured *adj* light yellow

straw 'poll *n* [C] an informal test of several people's opinions to see what the general feeling about something is

straw·weight /'strɔːˌweɪt $ 'strɒː-/ *n* [C] a BOXER who weighs less than 47.63 kilograms, and who belongs to the lightest weight class of boxers

stray¹ /streɪ/ *v* [I] **1** to move away from the place you should be: [+**into/onto/from**] *Three of the soldiers strayed into enemy territory.* **2** to begin to deal with or think about a different subject from the main one, without intending to: [+**into/onto/from**] *We're straying into ethnic issues here.* | *This meeting is beginning to stray from the point.* **3** if your eyes stray, you begin to look at something else, usually without intending to: [+**to/back/over** etc] *Her eyes strayed to the clock.* **4** to start doing something that is wrong or immoral, when usually you do not do this

stray² *adj* [only before noun] **1** a stray animal, such as a dog or cat, is lost or has no home **2** accidentally separated from other things of the same kind: *One man was hit by a stray bullet and taken to hospital.*

stray³ *n* [C] **1** an animal that is lost or has no home **2** *informal* someone or something that has become separated from others of the same kind → **waifs and strays** at WAIF (2)

streak¹ /striːk/ *n* [C] **1** a coloured line, especially one that is not straight or has been made accidentally: *Sue has blonde streaks in her hair.* **2** a part of someone's character that is different from the rest of their character: *a mean streak* | [+**of**] *His serious nature was lightened by a streak of mischief.* **3** a period of time during which you continue to be successful or to fail: **be on a winning/losing streak** *Celtic are on a six-game winning streak.* **4 streak of lightning/fire/light** etc a long straight flash of LIGHTNING, fire etc

streak² *v* **1** [I always + adv/prep] to run or fly somewhere so fast you can hardly be seen: [+**across/along/down** etc] *Two jets streaked across the sky.* **2** [T usually passive] to cover something with lines of colour, liquid etc: *The sky was streaked yellow and purple.* | [+**with**] *His hands and arms were streaked with paint.* **3** [I] to run across a public place with no clothes on as a joke or in order to shock people

streak·er /'striːkə $ -ər/ *n* [C] someone who runs across a public place with no clothes on as a joke or in order to shock people

streak·y /'striːki/ *adj* marked with streaks: *streaky grayish marks*

streaky 'bacon *n* [U] *BrE* smoked or salted meat from a pig that has lines of fat going through it

stream¹ W3 /striːm/ *n* [C]
1 SMALL RIVER a natural flow of water that moves across the land and is narrower than a river → DOWN-STREAM, UPSTREAM; → see picture at RIVER; → see picture at COUNTRY
2 CONTINUOUS SERIES a long and almost continuous series of events, people, objects, etc: [+**of**] *a stream of traffic* | *a stream of abuse* | **steady/constant/endless** etc **stream** *A steady stream of visitors came to the house.*
3 AIR/WATER a flow of water, air, smoke etc, or the direction in which it is flowing: *A stream of cold air rushed through the open door.* → GULF STREAM, JET STREAM
4 come on stream especially *BrE* to start working or producing something: *The new factory will come on stream at the end of the year.*
5 SCHOOL *BrE* a level of ability within a group of students of the same age: *Kim's in the top stream.* → BLOODSTREAM, MAINSTREAM[1], STREAM OF CONSCIOUSNESS

stream² *v*
1 POUR [I always + adv/prep] to flow quickly and in great amounts; ⊟ **pour**: [+**out/from/onto** etc] *Water came streaming out of the burst pipe.* | *Tears streamed down her cheeks.*
2 FLOW [I always + adv/prep] to move in a continuous flow in the same direction: [+**out/across/past** etc] *People streamed past us on all sides.*
3 GIVE OUT LIQUID [I,T] to produce a continuous flow of liquid: [+**with**] *When I got up, my face was streaming with blood.* | **streaming cold** *BrE* (=an illness in which a lot of liquid comes out of your nose)
4 LIGHT [I always + adv/prep] if light streams somewhere, it shines through an opening into a place or onto a surface; ⊟ **flood**: [+**in/through/from** etc] *The first rays of morning sunlight streamed through the open doorway.*
5 MOVE FREELY [I always + adv/prep, usually in progressive] to move freely in a current of wind or water: [+**in/out/behind** etc] *Elise ran, her hair streaming out behind her.*
6 COMPUTER [T] if you stream sound or video, you play it on your computer while it is being DOWNLOADED from the Internet, rather than saving it as a FILE and then playing it
7 SCHOOL [T] *BrE* to put school children in groups according to their ability; ⊟ **track** *AmE* **—streaming** *n* [U]

stream·er /'striːmə $ -ər/ *n* [C] **1** a long narrow piece of coloured paper, used for decoration on special occasions **2** a long narrow flag

stream·ing /'striːmɪŋ/ *n* [U] when you play sound or video on your computer while it is being broadcast over the Internet, instead of DOWNLOADING it and saving it into a FILE so that you can listen to it or watch it later

stream·line /'striːmlaɪn/ *v* [T] **1** to make something such as a business, organization etc work more simply and effectively: *efforts to streamline the production process* **2** to form something into a smooth shape, so that it moves easily through the air or water: *All these new cars have been streamlined.* **—streamlined** *adj*

stream of 'consciousness *n* [U] the expression of thoughts and feelings in writing exactly as they pass through your mind, without the usual structure they have in formal writing

street S1 W1 /striːt/ *n* [C]
1 a public road in a city or town that has houses, shops etc on one or both sides

S

along/up/down **the street**
across **the street**
on the other/opposite side of **the street**
cross **the street**
main street
high street *BrE* (=the main street with shops in a village, town, or city)
shopping street *BrE* (=a street with a lot of shops)
side/back street (=a street that is smaller than a main street)
busy/quiet street (=a street with a lot of activity or little activity)
crowded/deserted/empty street
one-way street (=a street where you can only drive in one direction)
narrow street
winding streets (=streets that turn in many directions)
street corner (=a place where streets meet)

*We moved to Center Street when I was young. | I walked on further **down the street**. | Someone just moved in **across the street**. | a car parked **on the other side of the street** | Look both ways before you **cross the street**. | There were soldiers marching down the **main street**. | There's a branch of the store in almost every **high street** in Britain. | We found a quiet bar in one of the **side streets**. | a **quiet** residential **street** | He was fined for driving the wrong way down a **one-way street**. | a small historic town with **narrow winding streets** | Two people were chatting on a **street corner**.*

2 the streets [plural] also **the street** the busy public parts of a city where there is a lot of activity, excitement, and crime, or where people without homes live: **on the streets** *young people living on the streets* | *She felt quite safe **walking the streets** after dark.* | **street musicians** (=ones who play on the street)
3 the man/woman in the street also **the man/woman on the street** the average person, who represents the general opinion about things: *The man on the street assumes that all politicians are corrupt.*
4 (right) up your street *BrE* exactly right for you
5 streets ahead (of sb/sth) *BrE informal* much better than someone or something else: *James is streets ahead of the rest of the class at reading.* → **BACKSTREET**; → **be (living) on easy street** at **EASY**[1] (13); → **one-way street** at **ONE-WAY** (1) → **HIGH STREET** → **TWO-WAY STREET**; → **walk the streets** at **WALK**[1] (8)
street·car /ˈstriːtkɑː $ -kɑːr/ *n* [C] *AmE* a type of bus that runs on electricity along metal tracks in the road; **日 tram** *BrE*
street cred also **street credi,bility** *n* [U] the qualities in a young person that other young people admire, especially because of their knowledge and experience of real life: *It'll wreck your street cred if you're seen helping the police.* —**street-credible** *adj*
street·light /ˈstriːtlaɪt/ also **street·lamp** /-læmp/ *n* [C] a light at the top of a tall post in the street → see picture at **TOWN**
street ,people *n* [plural] people who have no home and live on the streets
street-smart *adj especially AmE informal* STREETWISE —**street smarts** *n* [U]
street ,value *n* [C,U] the price for which something, especially drugs, can be sold illegally: *Detectives seized drugs with a street value of almost £300,000.*
street·walk·er /ˈstriːtwɔːkə $ -wɒːkər/ *n* [C] *old-fashioned* a PROSTITUTE
street·wise /ˈstriːtwaɪz/ *adj* able to deal with the dangerous situations and people that are common in some cities and towns
strength S2 W2 /streŋθ, strenθ/ *n*
1 PHYSICAL [U] the physical power and energy that makes someone strong; **日 weakness: have/find the strength to do sth** *She didn't even have the strength to stand up.* | *I'm trying to **build up** my **strength**. | Jo hit him **with all her strength**. | He never ceased to be amazed by her **physical strength**.*

2 DETERMINATION [U] the quality of being brave or determined in dealing with difficult or unpleasant situations: **have/find the strength to do sth** *Jenny didn't have the strength to end the relationship.* | *She had enormous **strength of character** (=strong ability to deal with difficult situations).* | **strength of mind/purpose** *The sea was very cold and it required great strength of mind to get in.* | *I think you have to find an **inner strength** in order to feel good about yourself.* → **tower of strength** at **TOWER**[1] (3)
3 FEELING/BELIEF [U] how strong a feeling, belief, or relationship is; **日 depth:** [+of] *Governments cannot ignore the strength of public opinion.* | *We understand the **strength of feeling** against the proposal.*
4 ORGANIZATION/COUNTRY ETC [U] the political, military, or economic power of an organization, country, or system: [+of] *the strength of the US economy* | *The socialists organized a **show of strength** (=when a country or organization shows how strong it is).*
5 USEFUL QUALITY OR ABILITY [C] a particular quality or ability that gives someone or something an advantage; **日 weakness:** *Her main strength is her critical thinking ability.* | [+of] *The great strength of our plan lies in its simplicity.* | *Be aware of your own **strengths and weaknesses**.*
6 OBJECT [U] how strong an object or structure is, especially its ability to last for a long time without breaking; **日 weakness:** [+of] *a device for testing the strength of concrete structures*
7 SUBSTANCE/MIXTURE [C,U] how strong a substance or mixture is: *Add water to dilute the solution to the required strength.* | **full-strength/half-strength/double-strength etc** *Young plants can be fed with half-strength liquid fertilizer.*
8 NUMBER OF PEOPLE [U] the number of people in a team, army etc: *The Edinburgh team are now at **full strength**.* | **below strength** *The police force is below strength at the moment (=there are fewer police than there should be).* | **in strength** *Security forces were out in strength (=in large numbers) but did not intervene.*
9 MONEY [U] the value of a country's money when compared to other countries' money: [+of] *the strength of the dollar on the international money markets*
10 on the strength of sth because of something: *I bought the book on the strength of your recommendation.*
11 position of strength a position where you have an advantage over someone, especially in a discussion: *We must negotiate from a position of strength.*
12 go from strength to strength to become more and more successful: *For several years the business went from strength to strength.*
13 NATURAL FORCE [U] how strong a natural force is: *the strength of the sunlight*
14 COLOUR/LIGHT/FLAVOUR/SMELL ETC [U] how strong a colour, taste etc is
15 give me strength *spoken* used when you are annoyed or angry about something
16 not know your own strength to not realize how strong you are
strength·en W3 /ˈstreŋθən, ˈstrenθən/ *v*
1 FEELING/BELIEF/RELATIONSHIP [I,T] to become stronger or make something stronger; **日 weaken:** *Our friendship has steadily strengthened over the years.* | *Steve's opposition only **strengthened her resolve** to go ahead.* | **strengthen sth's ties/bonds/links etc** *The university hopes to strengthen its ties with the local community.* | *The company plans to **strengthen its hand** (=make itself more powerful) in Europe by opening an office in Spain.*
2 TEAM/ARMY ETC [T] to make an organization, army etc more powerful, especially by increasing the number or quality of the people in it; **日 weaken:** *The team has been strengthened by the arrival of two new players.*
3 FINANCIAL SITUATION [T] if the financial situation of a country or company strengthens or is strengthened, it improves or is made to improve; **日 weaken:** *measures to strengthen the economy*

4 MONEY [I,T] to increase in value, or to increase the value of money; ➡ **weaken**: *The pound has strengthened against other currencies.*

5 BODY/STRUCTURE [T] to make something such as your body or a building stronger; ➡ **weaken**: *Metal supports were added to strengthen the outer walls.*

6 PROOF/REASON [T] to help prove something: *Fresh evidence has greatly strengthened the case against him.*

7 WIND/CURRENT [I] to increase in force: *The wind had strengthened during the night.*

stren·u·ous /ˈstrenjuəs/ *adj* **1** needing a lot of effort or strength: *a strenuous climb | The doctor advised Ken to avoid strenuous exercise.* **2** active and determined: *Sherry's been making a strenuous effort to lose weight.* —**strenuously** *adv*: *Barrett strenuously denied rumors that he would resign.*

strep throat /ˌstrep ˈθrəut $ -ˈθrout/ *n* [U] *AmE* an illness in which your throat is very painful

strep·to·coc·cus /ˌstreptəˈkɒkəs $ -ˈkɑː-/ *n plural* **streptococci** /-kaɪ/ [C] a BACTERIA that causes infections, especially in the throat

stress¹ S3 W3 /stres/ *n*
1 WORRY [C,U] continuous feelings of worry about your work or personal life, that prevent you from relaxing; ➡ **strain**: *Your headaches are due to stress. | under stress Janet's been under a lot of stress since her mother's illness. | the stresses and strains (=problems and worries) of public life | stress-related (=caused by stress) medical problems | reduce/relieve stress Yoga is excellent for relieving stress.*

2 FORCE [C,U] the physical force or pressure on an object: *Shoes with high heels put a great deal of stress on knees and ankles.*

3 IMPORTANCE [U] the special attention or importance given to a particular idea, fact, or activity; ➡ **emphasis**: *put/lay stress on sth Pugh laid particular stress on the need for discipline.*

4 WORD/MUSIC [C,U] the degree of force or loudness with which a part of a word is pronounced or a note in music is played, which makes it sound stronger than other parts or notes

stress² *v* [T] **1** to emphasize a statement, fact, or idea: *stress that The report stressed that student math skills need to improve. | Crawford stressed the need for more housing downtown. | She stressed the importance of a balanced diet.* **2** to pronounce a word or part of a word so that it sounds louder or more forceful: *The word 'machine' is stressed on the second syllable.*

stress sb out *phr v informal* to make someone so worried or nervous that they cannot relax: *Studying for exams always stresses me out.*

stressed /strest/ *adj* **1** [not before noun] also **stressed out** *informal* so worried and tired that you cannot relax: *I always eat when I'm feeling stressed.* **2** *technical* an object, especially a metal object, that is stressed has had a lot of pressure or force put on it

stress·ful /ˈstresfəl/ *adj* a job, experience, or situation that is stressful makes you worry a lot: *Moving to a new house is a very stressful experience.*

'stress mark *n* [C] a mark (') that shows which part of a word you emphasize when you pronounce it

stretch¹ S3 W3 /stretʃ/ *v*
1 MAKE STH BIGGER/LOOSER **a)** [I,T] to make something bigger or looser by pulling it, or to become bigger or looser as a result of being pulled: *A spider's web can stretch considerably without weakening. | Where can I buy those things that stretch your shoes?* **b)** [I not in progressive] if a material stretches, it can become bigger or longer when you pull it and then return to its original shape when you stop

2 BODY [I,T] to straighten your arms, legs, or body to full length: *Carl sat up in bed, yawned, and stretched. | Always stretch before exercising.*

3 REACH [I always +adv/prep] to reach a long way for something: *[+across/over] Ann stretched across the couch and grabbed the phone.*

4 MAKE STH TIGHT [T] to pull something so that it is tight: *The canvas is stretched over a wooden frame.*

5 TIME/SERIES [I,T always + adv/prep] to continue over a period of time or in a series, or make something do this: *[+into/on/over etc] Berg's career as a government official stretched over twenty years. | With a goal in the second half, Spurs stretched their lead to 3–0.*

6 IN SPACE [I always + adv/prep] to spread out or cover a large area of land: *[+to/into/away etc] Row after row of orange trees stretched to the horizon. | a line stretching around the block*

7 stretch your legs *informal* to go for a walk, especially after sitting for a long time

8 stretch (sb's) patience/credulity to be almost beyond the limits of what someone can accept or believe: *The kids stretch my patience to the limit.*

9 RULE/LIMIT [T] *BrE* to allow something that would not normally be allowed by a rule or limit: *This once I'll stretch the rules and let you leave work early. | We'll stretch a point (=allow a rule to be broken) and let the baby travel free this time.* → **stretch the rules** at RULE¹ (1)

10 stretch the truth/facts to say or write something that is not completely true: *Reporters sometimes stretch the facts to make a point.*

11 be stretching it *informal* to make something seem more important, bigger etc than it really is: *He's a good player, but 'world class' is stretching it.*

12 FOOD/MONEY [I,T] if you make an amount of money, food etc stretch or it stretches, you use less of it than you usually would so that you have it for a longer time: *I'm going to have to stretch this $20 until payday.*

13 be stretched (to the limit) to have hardly enough money, supplies, time etc for your needs: *We're stretched at the moment, otherwise we'd go.*

14 not stretch to sth *BrE* if someone's money will not stretch to something, they cannot afford it: *The budget won't stretch to a new car this year.*

15 ABILITIES [T] to make someone use all of their skill, abilities, or intelligence: *The work's too easy. The students aren't being stretched enough.*

stretch out *phr v*
1 *informal* to lie down, usually in order to sleep or rest: *I'm just going to stretch out on the couch for ten minutes.*
2 stretch sth ⇔ out to put out your hand, foot etc in order to reach something: *Jimmy stretched out his hand to take the candy.*

stretch² *n*
1 LENGTH OF LAND/WATER [C] an area of land or water, especially one that is long and narrow: *[+of] a beautiful stretch of countryside*

2 TIME [C] a continuous period of time: *[+of] a stretch of three weeks without sunshine | She doesn't leave the house for long stretches of time. | She rarely sleeps for eight hours at a stretch (=without stopping).*

3 BODY [C] the action of stretching a part of your body out to its full length, or a particular way of doing this: *The ski instructor showed us some special stretches.*

4 by any stretch (of the imagination) *spoken* used to emphasize that a negative statement is true: *My family wasn't wealthy by any stretch of the imagination.*

5 the home/final stretch **a)** the last part of a track before the end of a race **b)** the last part of an activity, trip, or process: *As they enter the home stretch of the campaign, the President's lead has grown.*

6 MATERIAL [U] the ability a material has to increase in length or width without tearing; → **stretchy**

7 at full stretch *BrE* **a)** using everything that is available: *With staff shortages and appalling weather conditions, the emergency services were at full stretch.* **b)** with your body or part of your body stretched as far as possible: *He dived and caught the ball at full stretch.*

8 JAIL [C usually singular] *informal* a period of time spent in prison

stretch³ *adj* [only before noun] stretch clothes or material stretch if you pull them and then return to their original shape: *stretch levis*

S

stretch·er¹ /'stretʃə $ -ər/ n [C] a type of bed used for carrying someone who is too injured or ill to walk

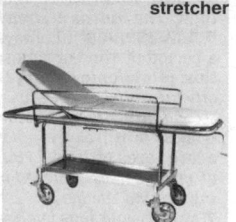
stretcher

stretcher² v [T always + adv/prep] BrE to carry someone on a stretcher: **be stretchered off/into etc** Ward was stretchered off early in the game.

'stretcher-,bearer n [C] someone, usually a soldier, who carries one end of a stretcher

'stretch ,limo n [C] a very large comfortable car that has been made longer than usual

'stretch mark n [C usually plural] a mark left on your skin as a result of it stretching too much, especially during PREGNANCY

stretch·y /'stretʃi/ adj informal material that is stretchy can stretch when you pull it and then return to its original shape: stretchy cotton leggings

strew /stru:/ v past tense **strewed**, past participle **strewn** /stru:n/ or **strewed** [T usually passive] **1** to scatter things around a large area: **be strewn with sth** The street was strewn with broken glass. | **strew sth around/about/over etc sth** clothes strewn across the floor **2 strewn with sth** written containing a lot of something: conversation liberally strewn with swear words **3** literary to lie scattered over something: Flowers strewed the path.

strewth /stru:θ/ interjection BrE, AusE old-fashioned used to express surprise, annoyance etc

stri·at·ed /straɪ'eɪtꜱd $ 'straɪeɪtꜱd/ adj technical having narrow lines or bands of colour; **◨ striped** —**striation** /straɪ'eɪʃən/ n [C usually plural]

strick·en /'strɪkən/ adj formal very badly affected by trouble, illness, unhappiness etc: Fire broke out on the stricken ship. | [+by/with] a country stricken by severe economic problems | **drought-stricken/cancer-stricken/tragedy-stricken etc** drought-stricken farmers → GRIEF-STRICKEN → PANIC-STRICKEN → POVERTY-STRICKEN

strict S3 /strɪkt/ adj comparative **stricter**, superlative **strictest**
1 expecting people to obey rules or to do what you say; **🄵 lenient**: a strict teacher | [+about] This company is very strict about punctuality. | [+with] The Stuarts are very strict with their children.
2 a strict order or rule is one that must be obeyed: You had strict instructions not to tell anybody. | There are **strict limits** on presidential campaign contributions. | He's under **strict orders** from his doctor to quit smoking. | I'm telling you this **in the strictest confidence** (=it must be kept completely secret).
3 [usually before noun] exact and correct, often in a way that seems unreasonable: Amy was attractive, although not beautiful **in the strictest sense of the word**.
4 obeying all the rules of a religion or set of principles: He was raised a strict Catholic. | a strict vegetarian —**strictness** n [U]

strict·ly /'strɪktli/ adv **1** in a way that must be obeyed: Alcohol is **strictly forbidden** on school premises. | The ban on hunting is not **strictly enforced**. **2** exactly and completely: That isn't strictly true. **3 strictly speaking** used to say that something is true if you are going to be very exact and correct about it: Strictly speaking, spiders are not insects. **4** only for a particular person, thing, or purpose and no one else: This is strictly between us. Nobody else must know.

stric·ture /'strɪktʃə $ -ər/ n [C often plural] formal **1** a rule that strictly limits what you can do: [+on/against] religious strictures on marriage **2** a severe criticism

stride¹ /straɪd/ n
1 STEP [C] a long step you make while you are walking; → **pace**: Paco reached the door in only three strides.
2 IMPROVEMENT [C] an improvement in a situation

or in the development of something: **make great/major/giant etc strides** The government has made great strides in reducing poverty.
3 take sth in your stride BrE; **take sth in stride** AmE to not allow something to annoy, embarrass, or upset you: When the boss asked Judy to stay late, she took it in stride.
4 get into your stride BrE; **hit your stride** AmE to start doing something confidently and well: Once I get into my stride I can finish an essay in a few hours.
5 WAY OF WALKING [singular] the way you walk or run: the runner's long, loping stride
6 break (your) stride especially AmE **a)** to begin moving more slowly or to stop when you are running or walking **b)** if you break your stride, or if someone or something breaks it, you are prevented from continuing in what you are doing: Collins dealt with the reporters' questions **without breaking stride**.
7 put sb off their stride especially BrE; **knock/throw/keep sb off stride** AmE to make someone unable to do something effectively, by not allowing them to give all their attention to it: Shea's testimony threw the defense off stride.
8 (match sb) stride for stride to manage to be just as fast, strong, skilled etc as someone else, even if they keep making it harder for you

stride² v past tense **strode** /strəʊd $ stroʊd/ past participle **stridden** /'strɪdn/ [I always + adv/prep] written to walk quickly with long steps; → **march**: [+across/into/down etc] He strode toward her.

stri·dent /'straɪdənt/ adj **1** forceful and determined, especially in a way that is offensive or annoying: strident criticism **2** a strident sound or voice is loud and unpleasant: the strident calls of seagulls —**stridently** adv —**stridency** n [U]

strife /straɪf/ n [U] formal trouble between two or more people or groups; **◨ conflict**: ethnic/religious/civil etc strife a time of political strife

strike¹ S3 W3 /straɪk/ v past tense and past participle **struck** /strʌk/
1 HIT [T] written to hit or fall against the surface of something: She fell heavily, striking her head against the side of the boat. | A snowball struck him on the back of the head. | Several cars were struck by falling trees. | The last rays of the setting sun struck the garden windows. ⚠ In spoken and ordinary written English it is much more usual to use **hit**.
2 HIT WITH HAND/WEAPON ETC [T] formal to deliberately hit someone or something with your hand or a weapon: She struck him hard across the face. | **strike sth with sth** The victim had been struck with some kind of wooden implement. | Paul **struck** him **a blow** to the head. | The assassin's bullet **struck home** (=hit exactly where it should).
3 THOUGHT/IDEA [T not in progressive] if something strikes you, you think of it, notice it, or realize that it is important, interesting, true etc: A rather worrying thought struck me. | The first thing that struck me was the fact that there were no other women present. | **it strikes sb that** It struck her that losing the company might be the least of her worries. | **be struck by sth** You can't help being struck by her kindness.
4 strike sb as (being) sth to seem to have a particular quality or feature: His jokes didn't strike Jack as being very funny. | **it strikes sb as strange/odd etc that** It struck me as odd that the man didn't introduce himself before he spoke.
5 STOP WORK [I] if a group of workers strike, they stop working as a protest against something relating to their work, for example how much they are paid, bad working conditions etc: In many countries, the police are forbidden to strike. | [+for] They're striking for the right to have their trade union recognized in law.
6 ATTACK [I] to attack someone, especially suddenly: The killer might strike again. | Guerrillas struck a U.N. camp, killing 75. | Opponents of the war say that civilian villages have been struck several times.
7 HARM [T] to damage or harm someone or something: [+at] The law would strike at the most basic of

civil rights. | Such prejudices **strike** right **at the heart of** any notions of a civilized society. | **strike a blow at/against/to sth** The scandal seemed to have struck a mortal blow to the government's chances of re-election.
8 STH BAD HAPPENS [I,T] if something bad strikes, it suddenly happens or suddenly begins to affect someone: The plague struck again for the third time that century. | Everything seemed to be going fine when suddenly **disaster struck**. → STRICKEN
9 strike a balance (between sth) to give the correct amount of importance or attention to two separate things: He was finding it difficult to strike a balance between his family and his work. | It isn't always easy to **strike the right balance**.
10 strike a bargain/deal to agree to do something for someone if they do something for you: There are rumors that the president struck a private deal with the corporation's chairman.
11 strike a happy/cheerful/cautious etc note to express a particular feeling or attitude: The article struck a conciliatory note. | Moderate Republicanism appeared to **strike** exactly **the right note** with the voters (=be what the people wanted).
12 strike a chord to say or do something that other people agree with or have sympathy with: [+with] Their story is bound to strike a chord with all parents.
13 strike a match to produce a flame from a match by rubbing it hard across a rough surface
14 strike gold/oil etc a) to find a supply of gold, oil etc in the ground or under the sea: If they strike oil, drilling will begin early next year. **b) strike gold** to do something that makes you a lot of money: Jackie eventually struck gold with her third novel.
15 LIGHTNING [I,I] if LIGHTNING strikes something, it hits and damages it: The temple burned down after it was **struck by lightning** last year. → **lightning never strikes twice** at LIGHTNING¹
16 strike a blow for sb/sth to do something to help achieve a principle or aim: It's time we struck a blow for women's rights.
17 be within striking distance a) to be close enough to reach a place easily: By now they were within striking distance of the shore. **b)** to be very close to achieving something: The French team are within striking distance of the world record.
18 strike it rich to suddenly make a lot of money
19 strike it lucky BrE to be very lucky, especially when you were not expecting to: We struck it lucky in Bangkok, where we were told there were some extra seats on the plane that night.
20 CLOCK [I,T] if a clock strikes one, two, six etc, its bell makes a sound once, twice, six times etc according to what time it is: The church clock began to strike twelve. | **strike the hour** (=strike when it is exactly one o'clock, two o'clock etc)
21 GAIN ADVANTAGE [I] to do something that gives you an advantage over your opponent in a fight, competition etc: Brazil struck first with a goal in the third minute.
22 strike home if something that you say strikes home, it has exactly the effect on someone that you intended: She saw the emotion in her father's face and knew her words had struck home.
23 strike terror/fear into sb's heart to make someone feel very frightened: The word 'cancer' still strikes terror into many hearts.
24 strike a pose/attitude to stand or sit with your body in a particular position: Malcolm struck his usual pose: hands in pockets, shoulders hunched.
25 be struck dumb to suddenly be unable to talk, usually because you are very surprised or shocked → DUMBSTRUCK
26 be struck with horror/terror/awe etc to suddenly feel very afraid, shocked etc: As she began to speak to him, she was struck with shyness.
27 strike while the iron is hot to do something immediately rather than waiting until a later time when you are less likely to succeed
28 strike sb dead to kill someone: May God strike me dead if I'm telling a lie!

strike back phr v
to attack or criticize someone who attacked or criticized you first: We instruct our staff never to strike back however angry they feel. | [+at] The prime minister immediately struck back at his critics.
strike sb ⇔ **down** phr v
1 [usually passive] to kill someone or make them extremely ill: Over 50 nurses at the clinic have been struck down with a mystery virus. | They would rob the bodies of those struck down in battle.
2 formal to hit someone so hard that they fall down
3 law to say that a law, decision etc is illegal and officially end it
strike sb/sth ⇔ **off** phr v
1 be struck off BrE if a doctor, lawyer etc is struck off, their name is removed from the official list of people who are allowed to work as doctors, lawyers etc
2 to remove someone or something from a list: Terri was told to strike off the names of every person older than 30.
strike on/upon sth phr v
formal to discover something or have a good idea about something → **be struck on sb/sth** at STRUCK²
strike out phr v
1 to attack or criticize someone suddenly or violently: [+at] Unhappy young people will often strike out at the people closest to them.
2 strike sth ⇔ **out** to draw a line through something written on a piece of paper
3 [always + adv/prep] to start walking or swimming in a particular direction, especially in a determined way: She struck out for the side of the pool.
4 strike out on your own to start doing something or living independently
5 to not hit the ball in baseball three times, so that you are not allowed to continue trying, or to make someone do this: **strike sb** ⇔ **out** He struck out the first batter he faced. → STRIKEOUT
6 AmE informal to not be successful at something: 'Did she say she'd go out with you?' 'No, I struck out.'
7 strike sth ⇔ **out** law to say officially that something cannot be considered as proof in a court of law
strike up phr v
1 strike up a friendship/relationship/conversation etc to start to become friendly with someone, to start talking to them, etc: I struck up a conversation with the girl sitting next to me.
2 strike up (sth) to begin playing a piece of music: The band struck up a tango.

strike² S3 W3 n
1 NOT WORKING [C,U] a period of time when a group of workers deliberately stop working because of a disagreement about pay, working conditions etc

be (out) on strike
come out/go (out) on strike (=start a strike)
call a strike
call off a strike (=decide not to continue with it)
break a strike (=end a strike)
general strike (=when workers from most industries strike)
all-out strike BrE (=when all the workers in a factory, industry etc strike)
strike action BrE

The farm workers' strike is in its third week. | [+by] a six-week strike by railway workers | [+over] a strike over pay cuts | [+against] a national strike against mine closures | Workers had **been out on strike** for 8 months. | Teachers **went on strike** last week to demand job security. | The trade union federations **called a general strike** to protest at working conditions. | They refused to obey the court's order to **call off the strike**. | The Prime Minister was determined to **break the strike**. | an **all-out strike** by civil servants | Hospital workers voted in favour of **strike action**.

⚠ Do not say 'go on a strike'.

S

1 000, 2 000, 3 000, most frequent words in S poken and W ritten English

2 ATTACK [C] a military attack, especially by planes dropping bombs: [+against/on] *a surprise air strike on military targets* | *American aircraft carriers have launched several strikes.* → FIRST STRIKE

3 DISCOVERY [C usually singular] the discovery of something valuable under the ground: *an oil strike*

4 two/three strikes against sb/sth *AmE* a condition or situation that makes it extremely difficult for someone or something to be successful: *Children from poor backgrounds have two strikes against them by the time they begin school.*

5 BASEBALL [C] an attempt to hit the ball in baseball that fails, or a ball that is thrown to the BATTER in the correct area, but is not hit

6 BOWLING [C] a situation in BOWLING in which you knock down all the PINS (=bottle shaped objects) with a ball on your first attempt → HUNGER STRIKE, LIGHTNING STRIKE

strike·break·er /'straɪk‚breɪkə $ -ər/ *n* [C] someone who continues working during a strike – used in order to show disapproval → BLACKLEG, SCAB (2)

strike·out /'straɪkaʊt/ *n* [C] in baseball, an occasion when the BATTER is not allowed to try to hit the ball any more, because he has three strikes

'strike pay *n* [U] money paid by a union to workers who are on STRIKE

strik·er /'straɪkə $ -ər/ *n* [C] **1** someone who is not working because they are on STRIKE **2** a player in football whose main job is to score GOALS

strik·ing /'straɪkɪŋ/ *adj* **1** unusual or interesting enough to be easily noticed: **striking contrast/similarity/ parallel etc** *a striking contrast between wealth and poverty* **2** attractive in an unusual way that is easy to notice: *a dark man with striking features* **3** [only before noun] not working because of being on STRIKE: *striking auto workers* → **be within striking distance** at STRIKE[1] (17)

strik·ing·ly /'straɪkɪŋli/ *adv* **1** in a way that is very easy to notice: **strikingly similar/different** *The two experiments produced strikingly different results.* **2** used to emphasize that someone or something is beautiful in a way that is easy to notice: *one of the most strikingly attractive regions in Britain*

string[1] S3 W2 /strɪŋ/ *n*
1 THREAD [C,U] a strong thread made of several threads twisted together, used for tying or fastening things; → **rope**: *Her key hung on a string around her neck.* | *a ball of string* | *I need a **piece of string** to tie this package.*
2 GROUP/SERIES [C] **a)** a number of similar things or events coming one after another; ▤ **series**: [+of] *a string of hit albums* **b)** a group of similar things: [+of] *She owns a string of health clubs.* **c)** *technical* a group of letters, words, or numbers, especially in a computer program
3 no strings (attached) having no special conditions or limits on an agreement, relationship etc: *The policy offers 15% interest with no strings attached.*
4 string of pearls/lights/beads etc several objects of the same type connected with a thread, chain etc
5 MUSIC **a)** [C] one of the long thin pieces of wire, NYLON etc that is stretched across a musical instrument and produces sound **b) the strings/the string section** the people in an ORCHESTRA or band who play musical instruments that have strings, such as VIOLINS → see picture at PIANO[1]
6 first-string/second-string etc relating to or being a member of a team or group with the highest, second highest etc level of skill: *a first-string quarterback*
7 have sb on a string *informal* to be able to make someone do whatever you want: *Susie has her mother on a string.*
8 have more than one string to your bow *BrE* to have more than one skill, idea, plan etc that you can use if you need to → G-STRING; → **how long is a piece of string?**

at LONG[1] (9); → **pull strings** at PULL[1] (8); → **pull the/sb's strings** at PULL[1] (9); → **the purse strings** at PURSE[1] (5)

string[2] *v past tense and past participle* **strung** /strʌŋ/ [T] **1** to put things together onto a thread, chain etc: *beads strung on a silver chain* **2** [always + adv/prep] to hang things in a line, usually high in the air, especially for decoration: **string sth along/across etc sth** *Christmas lights were strung from one end of Main Street to the other.* **3 be strung (out) along/across etc sth** *written* to be spread out in a line: *the houses and shops strung out along the bay* **4** to put a string or a set of strings onto a musical instrument → **highly-strung** at HIGHLY

string along *phr v informal* **1 string sb along** to deceive someone for a long time by making them believe that you will help them, that you love them etc: *He's just stringing you along.* **2** *BrE* to go somewhere with someone for a short time, especially because you do not have anything else to do: [+with] *If you're going into town, I'll string along with you.*

string sth ⇔ **out** *phr v informal* to make something continue longer than it should: *Rebel leaders attempted to string out negotiations to avoid reaching a settlement.*

string sth ⇔ **together** *phr v* **1 string words/a sentence together** to manage to say or write something that other people can understand: *He was so drunk he could hardly string two words together.* **2** to combine things in order to make something that is complete, good, useful etc: *They string together image after image until the documentary is completed.*

string sb ⇔ **up** *phr v informal* to kill someone by hanging them → STRUNG-UP

‚string 'bean *n* [C] a type of long thin green bean

stringed instruments

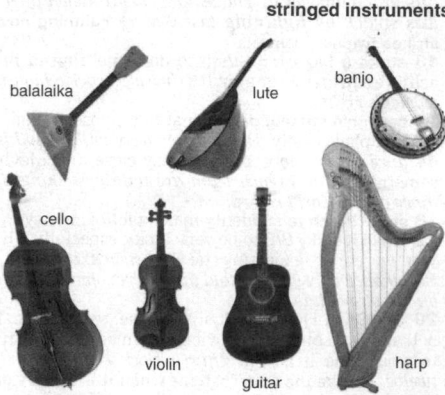

balalaika   lute   banjo
cello
violin   guitar   harp

‚stringed 'instrument *n* [C] a musical instrument such as a VIOLIN, that produces sound from a set of STRINGS; → **brass, percussion, the strings/the string section, wind instrument, woodwind**

strin·gent /'strɪndʒənt/ *adj* **1** a stringent law, rule, standard etc is very strict and must be obeyed: *stringent anti-noise regulations* **2** stringent economic conditions exist when there is a severe lack of money and strict controls on the supply of money —**stringently** *adv* —**stringency** *n* [U]

string·er /'strɪŋə $ -ər/ *n* [C] someone who regularly sends in news stories to a newspaper, but who is not employed by that newspaper

‚string 'tie *n* [C] a thick string worn around your neck and held in place by a decorative object, worn especially by men in the western US

string·y /'strɪŋi/ *adj* **1** stringy meat, fruit, or vegetables are full of long thin pieces that are difficult to eat; → **tough**: *Scoop out the pumpkin's stringy fibres.* **2** stringy hair is very thin and looks like string, especially because it is dirty **3** tall and thin

strip[1] /strɪp/ *v* **stripped, stripping**
1 TAKE OFF CLOTHES **a)** [I,T] also **strip off** to take off your clothes or take off someone else's clothes; →

undress: *Jack stripped and jumped into the shower.* | *The prisoner was stripped and beaten.* | **strip off sth** *He stripped off his sweater and threw it onto the couch.* | *Eric stood in the hot sun,* **stripped to the waist** (=not wearing any clothes on the top half of his body). | *Terry* **stripped down** *to her bra and pants* (=removed all her clothes except her bra and pants) *and tried on the dress.* | *The boys* **stripped naked** *and jumped in the pond.* **b)** [I] to take off your clothes in a sexually exciting way as entertainment for someone else
2 REMOVE [T] to remove something that is covering the surface of something else: *Strip the beds and wash the sheets.* | **strip sth off/from sth** *We need to strip the wallpaper off the walls first.* | **strip sth of sth** *tall windows stripped of curtains*
3 ENGINES/EQUIPMENT also **strip down** [T] to separate an engine or piece of equipment into pieces in order to clean or repair it; ◘ **dismantle**
4 BUILDING/SHIP ETC [T] to remove everything that is inside a building, all the equipment from a car etc so that it is completely empty: *The apartment had been* **stripped bare**.
5 DAMAGE [T] to damage or break the GEARS of something or the THREAD (=raised line) on a screw so that it does not work correctly any more → **ASSET STRIPPING**
     strip sth ⇔ **away** *phr v*
to remove something, especially something that hides or protects someone or something: *His book aims to strip away the lies and show the world as it really is.*
     strip sb **of** sth *phr v*
to take away something important from someone as a punishment, for example their title, property, or power: *Captain Evans was found guilty and stripped of his rank.*
strip² W3 *n* [C]
1 a long narrow piece of paper, cloth etc: *a strip of paper*
2 a long narrow area of land: *A strip of sand between the cliffs and the sea.*
3 do a strip to take your clothes off, especially in a sexually exciting way as a form of entertainment
4 *AmE* a road with a lot of shops, restaurants etc along it: *the Las Vegas strip*
5 [usually singular] *BrE* the clothes worn by a sports team: *Liverpool's famous red strip*
6 a STRIP CARTOON → COMIC STRIP, LANDING STRIP; → **tear sb off a strip** at TEAR² (8)
strip car'toon *n* [C] *BrE* a series of drawings inside a row of small boxes that tells a short story; ◘ **comic strip**; → **cartoon**
strip club *n* [C] *informal* a place where people go to see performers who take off their clothes in a sexually exciting way
stripe /straɪp/ *n* [C] **1** a line of colour, especially one of several lines of colour all close together: *a shirt with black and white stripes* | **vertical/horizontal stripes** **2 of all stripes/of every stripe** of all different types: *Politicians of all stripes complained about the plan.* **3** a narrow piece of material worn on the arm of a uniform as a sign of rank → **earn your stripes** at EARN
striped /straɪpt/ *adj* having lines or bands of colour; ◘ **stripy**: *a blue and white striped shirt*
strip joint *n* [C] *informal* a STRIP CLUB
strip light *n* [C] *BrE* an electric light that consists of a long, white FLUORESCENT tube
strip lighting *n* [U] *BrE* lighting provided by long, white FLUORESCENT tubes
strip·ling /'strɪplɪŋ/ *n* [C] *old-fashioned* a boy who is almost a young man – sometimes used humorously about a man who is quite old; ◘ **youth**
strip mall *n* [C] *AmE* a row of shops built together, with a large area for parking cars in front of it
strip mine *n* [C] *AmE* a very large hole that is made in the ground to remove metal, coal etc from the earth; ◘ **opencast** *BrE* —**strip-mine** *v* [I,T] —**strip mining** *n* [U]

strip·per /'strɪpə $ -ər/ *n* **1** [C] someone whose job is to take off their clothes in a sexually exciting way in order to entertain people **2** [C,U] a tool or liquid chemical used to remove something from a surface: *paint stripper*
strip poker *n* [C] a game of POKER (=card game) in which players that lose must take off pieces of their clothing
strip search *n* [C] a process in which you have to remove your clothes so that your body can be checked, usually for hidden drugs —**strip search** *v* [T]
strip show *n* [C] a form of entertainment where people take off their clothes in a sexually exciting way
strip·tease /'strɪptiːz, ˌstrɪp'tiːz/ *n* [C,U] a performance in which someone takes off their clothes in a sexually exciting way
strip·y, **stripey** /'straɪpi/ *adj BrE* STRIPED: *He was wearing jeans and a stripy T-shirt.*
strive /straɪv/ *v past tense* **strove** /strəʊv $ stroʊv/ *past participle* **striven** /'strɪvən/ [I] *formal* to make a great effort to achieve something: **strive to do sth** *I was still striving to be successful.* | **[+for/after]** *We must continue to strive for greater efficiency.* —**striving** *n* [C,U]
strobe light /'strəʊb ˌlaɪt $ 'stroʊb-/ also **strobe** *n* [C] a light that flashes on and off very quickly, often used in places where you can dance
strode /strəʊd $ stroʊd/ the past tense of STRIDE
stroke¹ S3 /strəʊk $ stroʊk/ *n* [C]
1 ILLNESS if someone has a stroke, an ARTERY (=tube carrying blood) in their brain suddenly bursts or becomes blocked, so that they may die or be unable to use some muscles: *She died following a massive stroke.* | **have/suffer a stroke** *I looked after my father after he had a stroke.* | *a stroke patient*
2 SWIMMING/ROWING a) one of a set of movements in swimming or rowing in which you move your arms or the OAR forward and then back: *She swam with strong steady strokes.* **b)** a style of swimming or rowing: *the breast stroke*
3 SPORT the action of hitting the ball in games such as tennis, GOLF, and CRICKET: *a backhand stroke*
4 PEN/BRUSH a) a single movement of a pen or brush when you are writing or painting: *A few strokes of her pen brought out his features clearly.* **b)** a line made by a pen or brush: *the thick downward strokes of the characters*
5 at a/one stroke with a single sudden action: *At one stroke the country lost two outstanding leaders.*
6 on the stroke of seven/nine etc at exactly seven o'clock etc: *She arrived home on the stroke of midnight.* | *The only goal of the match came on the stroke of half-time.*
7 stroke of luck/fortune something lucky that happens to you unexpectedly: *In a stroke of luck, a suitable organ donor became available.*
8 stroke of genius/inspiration etc a very good idea about what to do to solve a problem: *It was a stroke of genius to film the movie in Toronto.*
9 HIT an action of hitting someone with something such as a whip or thin stick: *He cried out at each stroke of the whip.*
10 A MOVEMENT OF YOUR HAND a gentle movement of your hand over something: *I gave her hair a gentle stroke.*
11 with/at a stroke of the pen if someone in authority does something with a stroke of the pen, they sign an official document to make a decision with important and serious results: *He had the power to order troops home with a stroke of his pen.*
12 not do a stroke (of work) *BrE informal* to not do any work at all
13 stroke of lightning a bright flash of lightning, especially one that hits something
14 CLOCK/BELL a single sound made by a clock giving

the hours, or by a bell, GONG etc

15 put sb off their stroke *BrE informal* to make someone stop giving all their attention to what they are doing: *Seeing Frank watching me put me off my stroke.*

16 IN NUMBERS *BrE* used when you are saying a number written with the mark (/) in it; ▣ **slash**: *The serial number is seventeen stroke one.* (=17/1)

stroke² *v* [T] **1** to move your hand gently over something: *He reached out and stroked her cheek tenderly.* **2** [always + adv/prep] to move something somewhere with gentle movements of your hand: *He lifted her face and stroked her hair from her eyes.* **3** [always + adv/prep] to hit or kick a ball with a smooth movement in games such as tennis, golf, and CRICKET: *He stroked the ball into an empty net with a minute to go.* **4** stroke sb's ego to say nice things to someone to make them feel good, especially because you want something from them

stroll /strəʊl $ stroʊl/ *v* [I] to walk somewhere in a slow relaxed way: [+**down/over/along**] *We were strolling along, laughing and joking.* —**stroll** *n* [C]: *They went for a stroll in the park.*

stroll·er /ˈstrəʊlə $ ˈstroʊlər/ *n* [C] **1** *AmE* a small chair on wheels in which a small child sits and is pushed along; ▣ **buggy**, **pushchair** *BrE* **2** someone who is strolling: *evening strollers on the promenade*

stroll·ing /ˈstrəʊlɪŋ $ ˈstroʊ-/ *adj* [only before noun] **1** a strolling entertainer travels around the country giving performances in different places; ▣ **travelling** **2** a strolling musician plays music while walking among people who are listening to them

strong S1 W1 /strɒŋ $ strɔːŋ/ *adj comparative* **stronger**, *superlative* **strongest**

1 ABLE TO LIFT HEAVY THINGS/DO HARD WORK having a lot of physical power so that you can lift heavy things, do hard physical work etc: *He was a big strong man.* | *Jack was tall and strong.* | **strong hands/arms/muscles etc** *He picked her up in his big strong arms.* | *I'm not strong enough to fight him.*

2 NOT EASILY DAMAGED not easily broken or destroyed: *good strong shoes* | *The locks on the doors were solid and strong.*

3 ABLE TO DEAL WITH DIFFICULTY determined and able to deal with a difficult or upsetting situation: *I am not strong enough to take insults and hatred.* | *Laura had a strong character.*

4 POWERFUL having a lot of power or influence: *The Fifth French Republic was established with a strong president in 1958.* | *a strong national army* | *Our party is the strongest as we come up to the election.*

5 FEELINGS/OPINIONS strong emotions, opinions, beliefs etc are ones that you feel or believe a lot and are very serious about: *He had **a strong sense of** responsibility to his vocation of preaching.* | *There has been **strong support** for the strike.* | *The proposal has met with **strong opposition** from local people.* | **strong feelings/views/opinions** *Many people have strong feelings about the issue.*

6 AFFECT/INFLUENCE a strong desire, influence etc affects you very much: *He had a **strong desire** for power.* | *Such feelings may **have a strong influence** over your decisions.* | *The temptation is very strong.*

7 RELATIONSHIP a strong relationship, friendship etc is very loyal and likely to last a long time: *He maintained **strong links** with the world of the deaf.* | *She still has a **strong relationship** with her mother.* | *I have a **strong commitment** to the quality of teaching.*

8 ARGUMENT/REASON ETC likely to persuade other people that something is true or the correct thing to do: *There is **a strong case** for an energy conservation programme.* | *They need **strong evidence** to secure a conviction.* | *a **strong argument***

9 LIKELY likely to succeed or happen: *She's a **strong** candidate for the party leadership.* | **strong possibility/chance/probability** *A year ago, there was a strong possibility that he wouldn't live.*

10 HEALTHY healthy, especially after you have been ill: *I don't think her heart is very strong.* | *You've been blessed with a **strong constitution*** (=you are healthy and do not easily become ill).

11 be in a strong position also **gain a strong position** to be in a situation where you have power over other people or are likely to get what you want: *The company have gained a strong position in the cheese market.*

12 strong wind/current/tide wind, water etc that moves with great force: *A strong wind was blowing across the lake.*

13 GOOD AT STH very good at something: *His writing was strong on description.* | *We beat a team that was much stronger than ourselves.* | **be sb's strong point/suit** (=the thing that someone is especially good at) *Tact never was my strong point.*

14 TASTE/SMELL having a taste or smell that you notice easily: *strong coffee* | *This cheese has a very strong flavour.* | *a strong smell of petrol*

15 ALCOHOL/DRUGS ETC having a lot of a substance such as alcohol that gives something its effect: ***extra strong** beer* | *strong pain killers* | *I haven't touched **strong drink*** (=alcoholic drinks) *for years.*

16 LIGHT/COLOUR bright and easy to see: *The light was not very strong.*

17 strong language speech or writing that contains a lot of swearing: *This film is not suitable for children under 12 as it contains strong language.*

18 strong accent the way that someone pronounces words that shows clearly that they come from a particular area or country: *a strong German accent*

19 strong nose/chin/features a nose etc that is large and noticeable, especially in an attractive way: *She has the same strong features as her mother.*

20 MONEY a strong CURRENCY (=the type of money used in a country) does not easily lose its value compared with other currencies

21 600/10,000 etc strong [only after number] used to give the number of people in a crowd or organization: *the company's 2,200 strong workforce* | *The crowd was 10,000 strong.*

22 be going strong to continue to be active or successful, even after a long time: *He celebrated his ninetieth birthday this month and is **still going strong**.* → come on strong at COME ON (10)

WORD FOCUS: STRONG
person: tough, muscular, wiry, powerful
thing: tough, sturdy, durable, rugged, heavy-duty, indestructible, well-made, robust
country/organization: powerful, mighty, influential, dominant
→ strength, power

ˈstrong-arm *adj* [only before noun] **strong-arm tactics/methods etc** the use of force or violence, especially when this is not necessary —**strong-arm** *v* [T]

strong·box /ˈstrɒŋbɒks $ ˈstrɔːŋbɑːks/ *n* [C] a box, usually made of metal, that can be locked and that valuable things are kept in; ▣ **safe**

strong·hold /ˈstrɒŋhəʊld $ ˈstrɔːŋhoʊld/ *n* [C] **1** an area where there is a lot of support for a particular way of life, political party etc: *The area is a Republican stronghold.* **2** an area that is strongly defended by a military group: *The fighters moved south to their mountain stronghold.* **3** an area where there are large numbers of a rare animal: *one of the last strongholds of the European wolf*

strong·ly /ˈstrɒŋli $ ˈstrɔːŋ-/ *adv* **1** if you feel or believe in something strongly, you are very sure and serious about it: *I'm **strongly opposed to** capital punishment.* | *We **strongly believe** that she is innocent.* | *I'm strongly in favour of marriage.* **2** in a way that is meant to persuade someone to do something: **strongly suggest/advise/recommend sth** *Before taking action you are strongly recommended to consult an accountant.* **3** in a way that is easy to notice: *The house smelt strongly of food.* ⚠ Do not say 'hold/grip strongly'. Use **firmly** or **tightly**: *He gripped my arm tightly.*

strong·man /ˈstrɒŋmæn $ ˈstrɔːŋ-/ n plural **strong-men** /-men/ [C] **1** a politician or leader who uses violence or threats to get what they want **2** a very strong man who performs in a CIRCUS

,**strong-ˈminded** adj not easily influenced by other people to change what you believe or want; ➔ determined: They were both strong-minded women.

strong·room /ˈstrɒŋruːm, -rʊm $ ˈstrɔːŋ-/ n [C] a special room in a bank, shop etc where valuable objects can be kept safely

,**strong-ˈwilled** adj knowing exactly what you want to do and being determined to achieve it, even if other people advise you against it

stron·ti·um /ˈstrɒntiəm $ ˈstrɑːn-/ n [U] a soft silver-white metal that is used to make FIREWORKS. It is a chemical ELEMENT: symbol Sr

strop /strɒp $ strɑːp/ n [C] **1** a narrow piece of leather used for making a RAZOR sharp **2 in a strop** BrE informal annoyed about something: She's a nice person but she just **gets in a strop** so easily.

strop·py /ˈstrɒpi $ ˈstrɑːpi/ adj BrE informal bad-tempered and easily offended or annoyed: I try not to get stroppy, but sometimes I just can't help it. —**stroppiness** n [U]

strove /strəʊv $ stroʊv/ the past tense of STRIVE

struck¹ /strʌk/ the past tense of STRIKE

struck² adj **be struck on sb/sth** BrE informal to think that someone or something is very good: She seemed rather struck on Vincent.

struc·tur·al /ˈstrʌktʃərəl/ adj connected with the structure of something: structural changes in the computer industry | The earthquake caused minor structural damage. —**structurally** adv: Is the building **structurally sound** (=in good condition)?

,**structural engiˈneer** n [C] an engineer skilled in planning the building of large structures such as bridges —**structural engineering** n [U]

struc·tur·al·is·m /ˈstrʌktʃərəlɪzəm/ n [U] a method of studying language, literature, society etc in which you examine the relationships of the different parts or ideas in order to determine their meaning —**structuralist** adj, n

struc·ture¹ [S3] [W2] /ˈstrʌktʃə $ -ər/ n
1 [C,U] the way in which the parts of something are connected with each other and form a whole, or the thing that these parts make up: **social/political/economic etc structure** the social structure of organizations | challenges to the existing **power structure** | A new **management structure** has been introduced. | [+of] the structure of the brain | molecular structures
2 [C] something that has been built, especially something large such as a building or a bridge: a high wooden structure with a curved roof
3 [C,U] a situation where activities are carefully organized and planned: These kids require a lot of structure and stability. ➔ **career structure** at CAREER¹ (1)

structure² v [T] to arrange the different parts of something into a pattern or system in which each part is connected to the others; ➔ **organize**: The exhibition is structured around three topics. | software that helps users structure their work and their data

struc·tured /ˈstrʌktʃəd $ -ərd/ adj carefully organized, planned, or arranged: The interviews were **highly structured**. | a structured approach to teaching

stru·del /ˈstruːdl/ n [C,U] a type of Austrian or German cake, made of PASTRY with fruit inside

strug·gle¹ /ˈstrʌgəl/ v [I] **1** to try extremely hard to achieve something, even though it is very difficult: **struggle to do sth** She's struggling to bring up a family alone. | [+with] The airline is struggling with high costs. | [+for] Millions of people are struggling for survival. | [+against] Firms are struggling against a prolonged recession. **2 a)** to fight someone who is attacking you or holding you, especially so that you can escape: [+with] James was hit in the mouth as he struggled with the burglars. | **struggle to do sth** She struggled to free herself. **b)** if two people struggle, they fight each other for something, especially something one of them is holding: [+for] They struggled for possession of the gun. **3** to move somewhere with great difficulty: [+up/out of/into etc] Walkers were struggling up the dusty track. **4** to be likely to fail, even though you are trying very hard: The team has been struggling all season. | **a struggling artist/writer/business**

struggle on phr v to continue doing something that you find very difficult or tiring: He struggled on despite his condition.

struggle² [W3] n [C]
1 a long hard fight to get freedom, political rights etc: [+for] a struggle for survival | a **power struggle** between forces favoring and opposing change
2 a long period of time in which you try to deal with a difficult problem: [+with/against] She spoke of her struggles with shyness.
3 a fight between two people for something, or an attempt by one person to escape from the other: Police said there were no signs of a struggle.
4 be a struggle (for sb) if something is a struggle, you find it very difficult to do

strum /strʌm/ v **strummed, strumming** [I,T] to play an instrument such as a GUITAR by moving your fingers up and down across its strings

strum·pet /ˈstrʌmpɪt/ n [C] old-fashioned an insulting word meaning a woman who has sex for money; ➔ **prostitute**

strung /strʌŋ/ the past tense and past participle of STRING²

,**strung-ˈout** adj [not before noun] informal **1** strongly affected by a drug, so that you cannot react normally; ➔ **high**: [+on] strung-out on drugs **2** extremely tired and worried

,**strung-ˈup** adj BrE informal very nervous, worried, or excited

strut¹ /strʌt/ v **strutted, strutting** [I] **1** to walk proudly with your head high and your chest pushed forwards, showing that you think you are important: [+around/about/across etc] I strutted around Chicago as if I were really somebody. **2 strut your stuff** informal to show your skill at doing something, especially dancing or performing: The band strutted their stuff in a free concert.

strut² n **1** [C] a long thin piece of metal or wood used to support a part of a building, the wing of an aircraft etc **2** [singular] a proud way of walking, with your head high and your chest pushed forwards

strych·nine /ˈstrɪkniːn $ -naɪn, -niːn/ n [U] a very poisonous substance sometimes used in small amounts as a medicine

stub¹ /stʌb/ n [C] **1** the short part of something long and thin, such as a cigarette or pencil, that is left when the rest has been used: a pencil stub **2** the part of a ticket that is given back to you after it has been torn, as proof that you have paid: a ticket stub **3** a piece of a cheque left in a cheque book as a record after the main part has been torn out: a check stub

stub² v **stubbed, stubbing stub your toe** to hurt your toe by hitting it against something

stub sth ⇔ **out** phr v to stop a cigarette from burning by pressing the end of it against something

stub·ble /ˈstʌbəl/ n [U] **1** short stiff hairs that grow on a man's face if he does not SHAVE **2** short stiff pieces left in the fields after wheat, corn etc has been cut —**stubbly** adj

stub·born /ˈstʌbən $ -ərn/ adj **1** determined not to change your mind, even when people think you are being unreasonable: Why are you so stubborn? | I've got a very **stubborn streak** (=a tendency to be stubborn). | Paul can be **as stubborn as a mule** (=very stubborn).

2 stubborn resistance/refusal/determination etc a very strong and determined refusal etc: *a stubborn refusal to face reality* **3** difficult to remove, deal with, or use; ▤ **tough**: *stubborn stains* —**stubbornly** *adv*: *'I don't care,' she said stubbornly.* —**stubbornness** *n* [U]

stub·by /ˈstʌbi/ *adj* short and thick or fat: *stubby fingers*

stuc·co /ˈstʌkəʊ $ -koʊ/ *n* [U] a type of PLASTER that is used especially to cover the outside walls of buildings

stuck¹ /stʌk/ the past tense and past participle of STICK¹

stuck² *adj* [not before noun] **1** impossible or unable to move from a particular position: *Sara tried to open the window but it was stuck.* | *They got stuck in a traffic jam.* | [+in] *The boat was stuck in the mud.* | *I've got something stuck in my throat.* **2** *informal* unable to escape from a bad or boring situation: [+in/at] *Mum resented being stuck at home with two young kids.* | *We could be stuck in this place for days.* **3** *informal* unable to do any more of something that you are working on because it is too difficult: *Can you help me with my homework, Dad? I'm stuck.* | [+on] *If you get stuck on a difficult word, just ask for help.* **4 be stuck with sth** *informal* to have something you do not want because you cannot get rid of it: *We are, unfortunately, stuck with this huge, ugly building.* **5 be stuck with sb** to have to spend time with someone or have a relationship with them even though you do not want to: *They are stuck with each other with no end in sight.* **6 be stuck for sth** to be unable to think what to say or do: *For once Anthony was stuck for words* (=did not know what to say). **7 get stuck in/get stuck into sth** *BrE spoken* to start doing something eagerly and with a lot of energy: *Take your jacket off and get stuck in!* **8 be stuck on sb** *informal* to be attracted to someone: *He says he's stuck on me.*

stuck-'up *adj informal* proud and unfriendly because you think you are better and more important than other people – used to show disapproval; ▤ **snooty**: *His wife was a bit stuck-up.*

stud¹ /stʌd/ *n* **1** ANIMAL [C,U] the use of animals, especially horses, for breeding, an animal that is used in this way, or a place where this is done: *a stud dog* **2** MAN [C] *informal* a man who has a lot of sexual partners and who is very proud of his sexual ability **3** ON SHOES [C] one of a set of small pointed pieces of metal or plastic that are attached to the bottom of a running shoe, football boot etc to stop you from slipping **4** IN YOUR EAR [C] a small, round EARRING **5** FOR DECORATION [C] a round piece of metal that is stuck into a surface for decoration **6** FOR A SHIRT [C] a small thing for fastening a shirt or collar that consists of two round, flat pieces of metal joined together by a bar **7** BOARD [C] *AmE* a board that is used to make the frame of a house

stud·ded /ˈstʌdɪd/ *adj* **1** decorated with a lot of studs or small jewels etc: *studded leather jackets* | *a diamond-studded watch* | [+with] *a belt studded with jewels* **2** covered or filled with a lot of something: [+with] *The sky was clear and studded with stars.* → STAR-STUDDED

stu·dent S1 W1 /ˈstjuːdənt $ ˈstuː-/ *n* [C] **1** someone who is studying at a university, school etc; → **pupil**: [+at] *a first year student at the University of Oslo* | *law/medical/engineering etc student A lot of art students live in this dorm.* | *student teacher/nurse* (=someone who is learning to be a teacher or nurse) | *A/B/C etc student AmE* (=someone who always earns A's etc for their work) → MATURE STUDENT **2 be a student of sth** to be very interested in a particular subject: *He's obviously an excellent student of human nature.*

In British English, a **student** usually means someone who has finished school and is studying at university: *We met when we were students.* | *student accommodation*
Children who go to school can be called **schoolchildren**, **schoolboys** or **schoolgirls**: *A group of schoolchildren got on the bus.*
The children at a particular school can be called its **pupils**: *Pupils at the school were sent home early.*
In American English, **student** is the usual word for anyone who is studying at school or college.
To say that someone is studying at a particular university, use **at**: *She's a student at York University.*
A **student of** literature, law etc studies that subject, but it is more usual to say 'a literature/law student'.

student 'body *n* [C] *AmE* all of the students in a HIGH SCHOOL, college, or university, considered as a group

student 'government also **student 'council** *n* [C] *AmE* an elected group of students in a HIGH SCHOOL, college, or university who represent the students in meetings and who organize school activities

student 'loan *n* [C] an amount of money that you borrow from the government or a bank to pay for your education at a college or university

student 'teaching *n* [U] *AmE* the period of time during which students who are learning to be teachers practise teaching in a school; ▤ **teaching practice** *BrE*

student 'union also **students' 'union** *BrE n* [C] **1** a building where students go to meet socially **2** *BrE* an association of students in a particular college or university

stud·ied /ˈstʌdid/ *adj* a studied way of behaving is deliberate and often not sincere, because it has been planned carefully: *She spoke with studied politeness.*

stu·di·o W3 /ˈstjuːdiəʊ $ ˈstuːdioʊ/ *n plural* **studios** [C]
1 a room where television and radio programmes are made and broadcast or where music is recorded: *a TV studio* | *a recording studio in Nashville*
2 also **studios** a film company or the buildings it owns and uses to make its films: *Depardieu is making a film with one of the big Hollywood studios.*
3 a room where a painter or photographer regularly works: *a photographer's studio*
4 a room where dancing lessons are given or that dancers use to practise in
5 also **studio apartment** *AmE*; **studio flat** *BrE* a small apartment with one main room: *a tiny studio*

studio 'audience *n* [C] a group of people who watch and are sometimes involved in a radio or television programme while it is being made

stu·di·ous /ˈstjuːdiəs $ ˈstuː-/ *adj* spending a lot of time studying and reading: *a quiet, studious young man* —**studiously** *adv* —**studiousness** *n* [U]

stud·y¹ S3 W3 /ˈstʌdi/ *n plural* **studies**
1 RESEARCH [C] a piece of work that is done to find out more about a particular subject or problem, and usually includes a written report: *More studies are needed before anything can be proven.* | *Recent studies show that women still get paid a lot less than men.* | [+of/into/on] *a study of Australian wild birds* | *make/carry out/conduct a study The study was carried out between January and May 1998.* → CASE STUDY
2 LEARNING [U] when you spend time learning, especially at home or by yourself rather than during school: *Set aside a period of time specifically for study.* | *ways to improve study skills* (=skills that help you study efficiently and be successful in school)
3 SUBJECT [U] also **studies** a subject that people study at a college or university: [+of] *Linguistics is the study of language.* | *Environmental Studies* | *literary/historical/scientific etc study the scientific study of earthquakes*
4 sb's studies the work that someone does in order to learn about a particular subject, especially the courses they take at a college or university: *How are your*

studies coming along? | **begin/continue/stop etc your studies** *I gave up my studies when I had the baby.*

5 CAREFUL CONSIDERATION [U] when you examine or consider something very carefully and in detail: *a report that deserves careful study*

6 ROOM [C] a room in a house that is used for work or study; → **office**

7 ART [C] a small detailed drawing, especially one that is done to prepare for a large painting: *Renoir's studies of small plants and flowers*

8 MUSIC [C] a piece of music, usually for piano, that is often intended for practice

9 be a study in sth *literary* to be a perfect example of something: *His face was a study in fear.*

10 a quick study *AmE* someone who learns things quickly

study² S3 W2 *v* **studied, studying, studies**

1 [I,T] to spend time reading, going to classes etc in order to learn about a subject: *I've been studying English for 6 years.* | *I can't study with that music playing all the time.* | [+at] *Stephen is currently studying at Exeter University.* | **study to be a doctor/lawyer etc** *My brother's studying to be an accountant.* | **study for an exam/diploma etc** *I've only got three weeks left to study for my exams.* | **study law/business/history etc** (=study a subject at a school or university) *Anna is studying French literature.* | **study under sb** (=be trained by a famous teacher) *a psychologist who studied under Jung in Zurich*

2 [T] to watch and examine something carefully over a period of time, in order to find out more about it: *Goodall was studying the behavior of chimpanzees in the wild.* | **study how/why/when etc** *They're studying how stress affects body chemistry.*

3 [T] to spend a lot of time carefully examining or considering a plan, document, problem etc; ▤ **look at**: *I haven't had time to study the proposals yet.* | **study how/why/when etc** *Managers are studying what needs to be done to improve efficiency.*

'study hall *n* [U] *AmE* a period of time during the school day when students must go to a room to study, instead of going to a lesson

stuff¹ S1 W3 /stʌf/ *n* [U]

1 THINGS *informal* used when you are talking about things such as substances, materials, or groups of objects when you do not know what they are called, or it is not important to say exactly what they are: *I've got some sticky stuff on my shoe.* | *How do you think you're going to fit all that stuff into the car?* | *I felt sorry for the ones who had to eat the awful stuff.* | *Where's all the camping stuff?*

2 sb's stuff *informal* the things that belong to someone: *Did you get the rest of your stuff?*

3 ACTIVITIES/IDEAS *informal* used when talking about different activities, subjects, or ideas, when you do not say exactly what these are: *What kind of stuff do you like to read?* | *I've got so much stuff to do this weekend.* | *There's a lot of interesting stuff in this book.* | *He's talked to me about **all that stuff** too.* | *He does mountain biking and skiing and **stuff like that**.*

4 WORK/ART *informal* used when you are talking about what someone has done or made, for example writing, music, or art: *I don't like his stuff.* | *John Lee was getting ready to play his stuff.* | *He did some great stuff in his early films.* | **good stuff** *BrE* (=used to tell someone that their work is good) *This is good stuff.*

5 ... and stuff *spoken informal* used to say that there are other things similar to what you have just mentioned, but you are not going to say what they are: *There's some very good music there, CD systems and stuff, and laser discs.*

6 the (very) stuff of dreams/life/politics exactly the kind of thing that dreams etc consist of: *an enchanting place – the very stuff of dreams*

7 CHARACTER the qualities of someone's character: *Does he have **the right stuff** (=qualities that make you able to deal with difficulties)?* | *Surely you're not going to give up? I thought you **were made of sterner stuff***

(=were more determined).

8 do/show your stuff *informal* to do what you are good at when everyone wants you to do it: *Come on Gina, get on the dance floor and do your stuff!* ➔ **bit of stuff** at BIT¹ (14); ➔ **kid's stuff** at KID¹ (4); ➔ **know your stuff** at KNOW¹ (5); ➔ **strut your stuff** at STRUT¹ (2)

stuff² *v* [T]

1 PUSH [always + adv/prep] to push or put something into a small space, especially in a quick careless way; ▤ **shove**: **stuff sth into/in/up sth** *She stuffed two more sweaters into her bag.*

2 FILL to fill something until it is full: *Volunteers were busy stuffing envelopes.* | **be stuffed with sth** *a pillow stuffed with feathers* | *boxes **stuffed full** of papers*

3 FOOD to fill a chicken, pepper etc with a mixture of bread or rice, onion etc before cooking it

4 DEAD ANIMAL to fill the skin of a dead animal in order to make the animal look still alive: *a stuffed owl*

5 stuff yourself also **stuff your face** *informal* to eat so much food that you cannot eat anything else: [+with] *The kids have been stuffing themselves with candy.*

6 get stuffed *BrE spoken* used to tell someone very rudely and angrily that you do not want to talk to them or accept their offer: *He only offered me £10 for it, so I told him to get stuffed.*

7 sb can stuff sth *spoken* used to say very angrily or rudely that you do not want what someone is offering: *'All right. You can stuff your money!' Reynolds exploded.*

8 stuff it *spoken* used to say angrily or rudely that you do not care about something or do not want something: *I thought, stuff it, I'll do what I want.*

stuffed /stʌft/ *adj* [not before noun] completely full, so that you cannot eat any more: *No, no dessert, I'm stuffed.*

stuffed 'animal, **stuffed 'toy** *n* [C] *AmE* a toy animal covered and filled with soft material; ▤ **soft toy** *BrE*

stuffed 'shirt *n* [C] *informal* someone who behaves in a very formal way and thinks that they are important

stuffed-'up *adj* unable to breathe properly through your nose because you have a cold; ▤ **bunged up**

stuff·ing /ˈstʌfɪŋ/ *n* [U] **1** a mixture of bread or rice, onion etc that you put inside a chicken, pepper etc before cooking it: *sage and onion stuffing* **2** soft material that is used to fill something such as a CUSHION ➔ **knock the stuffing out of sb** at KNOCK¹ (12)

stuff·y /ˈstʌfi/ *adj* **1** a room or building that is stuffy does not have enough fresh air in it: *It's getting stuffy in here – do you mind if I open the window?* **2** people, occasions, or places that are stuffy are too formal and old-fashioned – used to show disapproval: *Their wedding was stuffy and formal.* | *a stuffy old family* —**stuffiness** *n* [U]: *the stuffiness of the room*

stul·ti·fy·ing /ˈstʌltɪˌfaɪ-ɪŋ/ *adj formal* so boring that you feel as though you are losing your ability to think: *a stultifying office environment* —**stultify** *v* [T]

stum·ble /ˈstʌmbəl/ *v* [I] **1** to hit your foot against something or put your foot down awkwardly while you are walking or running, so that you almost fall; ▤ **trip**: *In her hurry she stumbled and spilled the milk all over the floor.* | [+over/on] *Vic stumbled over the step as he came in.* **2** to walk in an unsteady way and often almost fall; ▤ **stagger**: [+in/out/across etc] *He stumbled upstairs and into bed.* **3** to stop or make a mistake when you are reading to people or speaking: [+over/at/through] *I hope I don't stumble over any of the long words.* —**stumble** *n* [C]

stumble on/across/upon sth *phr v* to find or discover something by chance and unexpectedly; ▤ **come across**: *Researchers have stumbled across a drug that may help patients with Parkinson's disease.*

S

'stumbling ,block n [C] a problem or difficulty that stops you from achieving something: [+to] *The main stumbling block to starting new research is that we lack qualified people.*

stump¹ /stʌmp/ n [C] **1** the bottom part of a tree that is left in the ground after the rest of it has been cut down: *an old tree stump* **2** the short part of someone's leg, arm etc that remains after the rest of it has been cut off **3** the small useless part of something that remains after most of it has broken off or worn away: *There was only a stump of the candle left.* **4** one of the three upright sticks in CRICKET that you throw the ball at **5 stump speech/speaker** AmE a speech made by a politician who is travelling around in order to gain political support, or the politician who gives this speech **6 be on the stump** BrE to be travelling around an area, making speeches in order to gain political support

stump² v **1** [T usually passive] if you are stumped by a question or problem, you are unable to find an answer to it: *a case that has stumped the police* | *The doctors were stumped and had to call in a specialist.* **2** [I] to walk with heavy steps; ▣ **stomp**: [+up/along/across etc] *He stumped down the hall.* **3** [T] to put a BATSMAN out of the game in CRICKET by touching the stumps with the ball when he is out of the hitting area **4** [I,T] AmE to travel around an area, meeting people and making speeches in order to gain political support: *Alexander has been stumping in New Hampshire.*

stump up (sth) phr v BrE informal to pay money, even if it is difficult or when you do not want to: *We stumped up eight quid each.*

stumped /stʌmpt/ adj unable to find an answer or think of a reply: *The question had me completely stumped.* | **stumped for words/an answer/a reply** *Travis seemed absolutely stumped for words.*

stump·y /'stʌmpi/ adj stumpy legs, fingers etc are short and thick in an unattractive way; ▣ **stubby**

stun /stʌn/ v **stunned, stunning** [T not in progressive] **1** to surprise or upset someone so much that they do not react immediately; → **stagger**: *Redfern stunned the crowd with a last-minute goal.* **2** to make someone unconscious for a short time: *The impact of the ball had stunned her.* → STUNNED, STUNNING

stung /stʌŋ/ the past tense and past participle of STING¹

'stun gun n [C] a weapon that produces a very strong electric current and can be used to make animals or people unconscious

stunk /stʌŋk/ a past tense and the past participle of STINK¹

stunned /stʌnd/ adj too surprised or shocked to speak: *He looked completely stunned.* | *The audience sat in stunned silence.*

stun·ner /'stʌnə $ -ər/ n [C] informal **1** someone or something that is very attractive, especially a woman: *Lucy was a real stunner.* **2** a situation or event that surprises you

stun·ning /'stʌnɪŋ/ adj **1** extremely attractive or beautiful: *You look absolutely stunning in that dress.* | *a stunning view* → see box at BEAUTIFUL **2** very surprising or shocking; ▣ **staggering**: *stunning news* —**stunningly** adv: *a stunningly beautiful woman*

stunt¹ /stʌnt/ n [C] **1** a dangerous action that is done to entertain people, especially in a film: *Not many actors* **do** *their own* **stunts**. | *a stunt flying show* **2** something that is done to attract people's attention, especially in advertising or politics: *Todd flew over the city in a hot air balloon as a* **publicity stunt**. **3 pull a stunt** to do something that is silly or that is slightly dangerous: *Next time you pull a stunt like that don't expect me to get you out of trouble.*

stunt² v [T] to stop something or someone from growing to their full size or developing properly: *Lack of sunlight will stunt the plant's growth.*

stunt·ed /'stʌntɪd/ adj not developing properly or to full size: *He's emotionally stunted.*

'stunt man n [C] a man who is employed to take the place of an actor when something dangerous has to be done in a film

'stunt ,woman n [C] a woman who is employed to take the place of an actress when something dangerous has to be done in a film

stu·pe·fied /'stjuːpɪfaɪd $ 'stuː-/ adj so surprised, tired, or bored that you cannot think clearly: *I stared up at Keith in stupefied amazement.* | *We sat there stupefied.* —**stupefaction** /ˌstjuːpɪ'fækʃən $ ˌstuː-/ n [U]

stu·pe·fy·ing /'stjuːpɪfaɪ-ɪŋ $ 'stuː-/ adj making you feel extremely surprised, tired, or bored: *a stupefying amount of money* —**stupefy** v [T]

stu·pen·dous /stjuː'pendəs $ stuː-/ adj surprisingly large or impressive; ▣ **magnificent**: *a stupendous achievement* —**stupendously** adv

stu·pid¹ S1 W3 /'stjuːpɪd $ 'stuː-/ adj
1 showing a lack of good sense or good judgment; ▣ **silly**: *stupid mistakes* | *That was a stupid thing to say.* | *I can't believe Kate was stupid enough to get involved in this.* | **stupid idea/question** *Whose stupid idea was this?* | *It was stupid of me to lose my temper.*
2 having a low level of intelligence, so that you have difficulty learning or understanding things: *He understands – he's not stupid.* | *I couldn't do it, and it made me feel stupid.*
3 spoken used when you are talking about something or someone that makes you annoyed or impatient: *I can't get this stupid radio to work.* | *What is that stupid idiot doing?*
4 stupid with cold/sleep/shock etc unable to think clearly because you are extremely tired, cold etc —**stupidly** adv: *I stupidly agreed to organize the party.*

stupid² n [singular] spoken not polite an insulting way of talking to someone who you think is being stupid: *No, stupid, don't do it like that!*

stu·pid·i·ty /stjuː'pɪdəti $ stuː-/ n plural **stupidities 1** [C,U] behaviour or actions that show a lack of good sense or good judgment: *all the horrors and stupidities of war* **2** [U] the quality of being stupid

stu·por /'stjuːpə $ 'stuːpər/ n [C,U] a state in which you cannot think, speak, see, or hear clearly, usually because you have drunk too much alcohol or taken drugs: *We found him lying at the bottom of the stairs in a drunken stupor.*

stur·dy /'stɜːdi $ 'stɜːr-/ adj comparative **sturdier**, superlative **sturdiest 1** an object that is sturdy is strong, well-made, and not easily broken; → **solid**: *That chair doesn't look very sturdy.* | *sturdy comfortable shoes* **2** someone who is sturdy is strong, short, and healthy looking; → **stocky**: *a sturdy young man* | *sturdy legs* **3** determined and not easily persuaded to change your opinions: *They kept up a sturdy opposition to the plan.* —**sturdily** adv —**sturdiness** n [U]

stur·geon /'stɜːdʒən $ 'stɜːr-/ n [C,U] a large fish, from which CAVIAR is obtained, or the meat of this fish

stut·ter¹ /'stʌtə $ -ər/ v **1** [I,T] to speak with difficulty because you cannot stop yourself from repeating the first CONSONANT of some words; → **stammer**: *'I'm D-d-david,' he stuttered.* **2** [I] if a machine stutters, it keeps making little noises and does not work smoothly: *a refrigerator which stuttered and hummed*

stutter² n [singular] an inability to speak normally because you stutter; ▣ **stammer**: *a nervous stutter*

sty /staɪ/ n plural **sties** [C] **1** a place where pigs are kept; ▣ **pigsty 2** also **stye** an infected place on the edge of your EYELID, which becomes red and swollen

Sty·gi·an /'stɪdʒiən/ adj [usually before noun] literary unpleasantly dark, and making you feel nervous or afraid: *the Stygian gloom*

style¹ S2 W1 /staɪl/ n
1 WAY OF DOING STH [C,U] a particular way of doing, designing, or producing something, especially one that is typical of a particular place, period of time, or group

of people: *an attempt to use Japanese management style in a European business* | [+**of**] *different styles of handwriting* | **Baroque/Swedish/country etc style** *Cuban-style black beans and rice* | *a Colonial style house* | *The dinner will be served buffet style.*

2 SB'S WAY OF BEHAVING [C] the particular way that someone behaves, works, or deals with other people: *Children have different styles of learning: some learn by seeing, some by hearing, some by doing.* | **be more sb's style** (=used to say that you prefer something) *I don't think the parachuting weekend is for me – the art class is more my style.* | **I like your style** (=approve of the way you do things), *Simpson.* | *I can't ask a man out – it's not my style* (=it is not the way I usually behave).

3 ART/LITERATURE/MUSIC [C,U] a typical way of writing, painting etc that is used by a particular person or during a particular period of time: *The paintings are in an expressionistic style.* | *Hemingway's direct style* | **in the style of sb/sth** *a play in the style of classical Greek tragedy*

4 FASHION/DESIGN a) [C] a particular design or fashion for something such as clothes, hair, furniture etc: *Car styles have changed radically in the past 20 years.* | **traditional/modern style** *The rooms are furnished in a modern style.* **b)** [U] the quality of being fashionable: *young women interested in style rather than comfort* | **in/out of style** *Long skirts are back in style.*

5 ATTRACTIVE QUALITY [U] a confident and attractive quality that makes people admire you, and that is shown in your appearance, or the way you do things: *You may not like her, but she certainly has style.* | *The team played with style.* → **STYLISH**

6 CORRECT WRITING [U] a way of using words or spelling that is considered correct: *It's not good style to use abbreviations in an essay.*

7 in style done in a way that people admire, especially because it is unusual, shows great determination, or involves spending a lot of money: **in great/grand/fine etc style** *Sampras won the title in fine style, not losing a single game.* → **cramp sb's style** at CRAMP² → **LIFESTYLE**

style² *v* [T] **1** to design clothing, furniture, or the shape of someone's hair in a particular way: *These shoes have been styled for maximum comfort.* | *She has her hair styled by Giorgio.* **2 style yourself sth** *formal* to give yourself a particular title or name: *They style themselves 'the terrible twins'.* → SELF-STYLED

style sheet *n* [C] a set of instructions that states what the TYPEFACE and colours of an electronic document should be

styl·ing /'staɪlɪŋ/ *n* [U] **1** the design and appearance of an object, especially a car: *I like the new Audi in terms of styling.* **2 styling products/mousse/spray etc** substances you use to make your hair look attractive

styl·ish /'staɪlɪʃ/ *adj* attractive in a fashionable way: *a stylish woman in her forties* | *Jack is quite stylish.* | *a stylish restaurant in the West End* —**stylishly** *adv* —**stylishness** *n* [U]

styl·ist /'staɪlɪst/ *n* [C] **1** someone who cuts or arranges people's hair as their job: *Renee was the top stylist at the salon.* **2** someone who has carefully developed a good style of writing **3** someone who has their own typical way of singing or playing music: *Billie Holiday, one of jazz's most distinctive stylists*

styl·is·tic /staɪ'lɪstɪk/ *adj* relating to the particular way an artist, writer, musician etc makes or performs something, especially the technical features or methods they use: *the sculptor's stylistic development* | **stylistic feature/device** *stylistic features of the story* —**stylistically** /-kli/ *adv*

styl·is·tics /staɪ'lɪstɪks/ *n* [U] the study of style in written or spoken language

sty·lized also **-ised** *BrE* /'staɪlaɪzd/ *adj* drawn, written, or performed in an artificial style that does not look natural or real, but that is still pleasant to look at: *a stylised picture of the sun* —**stylization** /ˌstaɪlaɪ'zeɪʃən $ -lə-/ *n* [U]

sty·lus /'staɪləs/ *n* [C] **1** the small pointed part of a RECORD PLAYER, that touches the record **2** a thing shaped like a pen, used for writing on WAX, making marks on metal, writing on a special computer screen etc

sty·mie /'staɪmi/ *v* [T] *informal* to prevent someone from doing what they have planned or want to do; **thwart**: *Investigators have been stymied by uncooperative witnesses.*

Sty·ro·foam /'staɪrəfəʊm $ 'staɪrəfoʊm/ *n* [U] *trademark* a soft light plastic material that prevents heat or cold from passing through it, used especially to make containers; **polystyrene** *BrE: a Styrofoam cup*

suave /swɑːv/ *adj* someone who is suave is polite, confident, and relaxed, sometimes in an insincere way: *a suave and sophisticated gentleman* —**suavely** *adv* —**suavity, suaveness** *n* [U]

sub¹ S3 /sʌb/ *n* [C] *informal*
1 a SUBMARINE
2 a SUBSTITUTE in sports such as football
3 a SUBSCRIPTION
4 *BrE* part of your wages that you receive earlier than usual because you need money; **advance**
5 *AmE* a long bread roll split open and filled with meat, cheese etc
6 *AmE* a SUBSTITUTE TEACHER
7 *BrE* a SUB-EDITOR

sub² *v* **subbed, subbing** *informal* **1** [I] to act as a SUBSTITUTE for someone: [+**for**] *Roy's subbing for Chris in tonight's game.* **2** [T] *BrE* to give someone part of their wages earlier than usual or lend them money: *I subbed Fenella a tenner to get a decent bunch of flowers.* **3** [T] *BrE* to SUBEDIT something

sub- /sʌb/ *prefix* **1** under or below a particular level or thing: *subzero temperatures* | *subsoil* (=beneath the surface) **2** less important or powerful than someone or something, or of lower rank than someone: *a sub-lieutenant* **3** part of a bigger whole: *a subsection* | *a subcommittee* **4** not as good as other people or things: *substandard housing* | *subnormal intelligence* **5** technical almost: *subtropical heat*

sub·al·tern /'sʌbəltən $ sə'bɔːltərn/ *n* [C] a middle rank in the British army, or someone who has this rank

sub·aq·ua /sʌb'ækwə/ *adj* [only before noun] *BrE* relating to sports that take place under water: *sub-aqua diving*

sub·a·tom·ic /ˌsʌbə'tɒmɪk◂ $ -'tɑː-/ *adj* smaller than an atom or existing within an atom

sub·com·mit·tee /'sʌbkəˌmɪti/ *n* [C] a small group formed from a committee to deal with a particular subject in more detail

sub·com·pact /sʌb'kɒmpækt $ -'kɑːm-/ *n* [C] *AmE* a type of very small and inexpensive car

sub·con·scious¹ /sʌb'kɒnʃəs $ -'kɑːn-/ *adj* subconscious feelings, desires etc are hidden in your mind and affect your behaviour, but you do not know that you have them: *a subconscious fear of failure* —**subconsciously** *adv*: *Subconsciously, he blames himself for the accident.*

subconscious² *n* [singular] the part of your mind that has thoughts and feelings you do not know about; **unconscious**: *anger buried deep in the subconscious*

sub·con·ti·nent /ˌsʌb'kɒntɪnənt $ -'kɑːn-/ *n* [C] **1** a very large area of land that is part of a CONTINENT **2** the subcontinent the area of land that includes India, Pakistan, and Bangladesh

sub·con·tract /ˌsʌbkən'trækt $ -'kɑːntrækt/ also **subcontract out** *v* [T] if a company subcontracts work, they pay other people to do part of their work for them: *We will be subcontracting most of the electrical work.* | **subcontract sth to sb** *Some of the work will be subcontracted to another company.* —**subcontract** /sʌb'kɒntrækt $ -'kɑːn-/ *n* [C]

S

sub·con·trac·tor /ˌsʌbkənˈtræktə $ -ˈkɑːntræktər/ n [C] someone who does part of the work of another person or company

sub·cul·ture /ˈsʌbˌkʌltʃə $ -ər/ n [C] a particular group of people within a society and their behaviour, beliefs, and activities – often used to show disapproval: *the drug subculture of the inner city*

sub·cu·ta·ne·ous /ˌsʌbkjuːˈteɪniəs◂/ adj technical beneath your skin: *subcutaneous fat* —**subcutaneously** adv

sub·di·rect·o·ry n /ˈsʌbdaɪrektəri, -dɔ-/ plural sub-directories [C] an area in a computer where FILES are stored inside another directory, in order to keep the files organized

sub·di·vide /ˌsʌbdɔˈvaɪd/ v [T] to divide into smaller parts something that is already divided: *Over time, developers subdivided the land.* | **subdivide sth into sth** *The house was subdivided into apartments.*

sub·di·vi·sion /ˌsʌbdɔˈvɪʒən/ n **1** [C,U] when something is subdivided, or the parts that result from doing this **2** [C] *AmE* an area of land that has been subdivided for building houses on

sub·due /səbˈdjuː $ -ˈduː/ v [T] **1** to defeat or control a person or group, especially using force: *Police managed to subdue the angry crowd.* | *Napoleon subdued much of Europe.* **2** formal to prevent your emotions from showing or being too strong; ▤ **control**: *an excitement she could not subdue*

sub·dued /səbˈdjuːd $ -ˈduːd/ adj **1** subdued lighting, colours etc are less bright than usual; ▤ **gentle 2** a person that is subdued is unusually quiet and possibly unhappy: *Richard seems very subdued tonight.* | *a subdued manner* | *'Oh,' she said in a subdued voice.* **3** an activity that is subdued does not have as much excitement as you would expect; ▣ **lively**: *The housing market is fairly subdued.* **4** a sound that is subdued is quieter than usual

sub·ed·it /ˌsʌbˈedɔt/ v [T] *BrE* to examine other people's writing for mistakes and correct them; ▤ **copy-edit**

ˌsub-ˈeditor n [C] *BrE* someone whose job is to examine other people's writing, such as a newspaper article, and to correct mistakes

sub·group /ˈsʌbgruːp/ n [C] a separate, smaller, and sometimes less important part of a group

sub·head·ing /ˈsʌbˌhedɪŋ/ n [C] a short phrase used as a title for a small part within a longer piece of writing

sub·hu·man /sʌbˈhjuːmən $ -ˈhjuː-, -ˈjuː-/ adj **1** not having all the qualities a normal human being has: *The enemy was regarded as subhuman.* **2** subhuman conditions are very bad or cruel; → **inhuman**: *The refugees were living a subhuman existence.*

sub·ject¹ [S2] [W2] /ˈsʌbdʒɪkt/ n [C]
1 THING TALKED ABOUT the thing you are talking about or considering in a conversation, discussion, book, film etc

> **change the subject** (=start talking about something different)
> **get onto a subject** (=start talking about something)
> **get off a subject** (=stop talking about something)
> **keep/stay off a subject** (=not talk about something)
> **drop the subject** (=stop talking about something)
> **raise a subject** (=mention a subject and start talking about it)
> **broach a subject** (=start talking about something that people may be sensitive about)
> **on the subject of sth** (=talking about something)
> **subject of discussion/debate** also
> **subject for discussion/debate**
> **touchy subject** (=something people are sensitive about)
> **subject area**

Paul has strong opinions on most subjects. | *The subjects covered in this chapter are exercise and nutrition.* | [+of] *Truffaut's childhood memories were the subject of his first film.* | *embarrassment about the subject of sex* | *Stop trying to change the subject!* | *How did we get onto the subject of drugs?* | *Can we just drop the subject now, please.* | *I wondered how I should broach the subject.* | *While we're on the subject of money, do you have the $10 you owe me?* | *Genetic engineering is very much a subject for debate.* | *You know money is a a touchy subject with me.* | *The discussion was broken up into subject areas.*

⚠ Do not say 'the subject is about ...': *The subject of the book is war.* | *The film was about Egypt.* → SUBJECT MATTER
2 AT SCHOOL an area of knowledge that you study at a school or university: *My favourite subject is math.*
3 IN ART the thing or person that you show when you paint a picture, take a photograph etc: *Monet loved to use gardens as his subjects.*
4 IN A TEST a person or animal that is used in a test or EXPERIMENT: *The subjects of this experiment were all men aged 18–35.*
5 GRAMMAR a noun, noun phrase, or PRONOUN that usually comes before a main verb and represents the person or thing that performs the action of the verb, or about which something is stated. For example, 'She' in 'She hit John' or 'elephants' in 'Elephants are big'. → OBJECT¹ (6)
6 CITIZEN formal someone who was born in a country that has a king or queen, or someone who has a right to live there: *a British subject* → CITIZEN (2), NATIONAL²

subject² adj **1 be subject to sth a)** if someone or something is subject to something, especially something bad, it is possible or likely that they will be affected by it: *All flights are subject to delay.* | *Prices are subject to change.* **b)** if something is subject to something such as approval, it depends on that thing happening before it can happen: *The funding is subject to approval by the Board of Education.* **2 be subject to a rule/law/penalty/tax etc** if you are subject to a rule, law, penalty etc, you must obey the rule or pay an amount of money: *Violators are subject to a $100 fine.* **3** [only before noun] formal a subject country, state, people etc are strictly governed by another country: *subject peoples*

sub·ject³ /səbˈdʒekt/ v [T] formal to force a country or group of people to be ruled by you, and control them very strictly
    subject sb/sth to sth phr v to force someone or something to experience something very unpleasant, especially over a long time: *Police subjected him to hours of questioning.* | **subject sb to an ordeal/abuse/harassment** *Barker subjected his victim to awful abuse.*

sub·jec·tion /səbˈdʒekʃən/ n [U] formal when a person or a group of people are controlled by a government or by another person: **in subjection** *The government used brute force to keep people in subjection.* | [+to] *a period of subjection to Assyrian rulers* | *the subjection of women*

sub·jec·tive /səbˈdʒektɪv/ adj **1** a statement, report, attitude etc that is subjective is influenced by personal opinion and can therefore be unfair; ▣ **objective**: *As a critic, he is far too subjective.* | *a highly subjective point of view* | **subjective judgment/opinion etc** *The ratings were based on the subjective judgement of one person.* **2** [no comparative] existing only in your mind or imagination; ▣ **objective**: *our subjective perception of colours* **3** technical relating to the subject in grammar —**subjectively** adv: *His work was judged objectively as well as subjectively.* —**subjectivity** /ˌsʌbdʒekˈtɪvɔti/ n [U]

ˈsubject ˌmatter n [U] what is being talked about in speech or writing, or represented in art: *The movie has been rated 'R' due to adult subject matter.*

sub ju·di·ce /ˌsʌb ˈdʒuːdɪsi $ -ˈdʒuːdɪsi, -ˈjuːdɪkeɪ/ adv [only after verb] law a legal case being considered sub judice is now being dealt with by a court, and therefore is not allowed to be publicly discussed, for example in a newspaper

sub·ju·gate /ˈsʌbdʒʊ̩geɪt/ v [T usually passive] formal to defeat a person or group and make them obey you: *The native population was subjugated and exploited.* | **subjugated** people/nation/country | **subjugate sb to sb/sth** *Her own needs had been subjugated to* (=not considered as important as) *the needs of her family.* —**subjugation** /ˌsʌbdʒʊ̩ˈgeɪʃən/ n [U]

sub·junc·tive /səbˈdʒʌŋktɪv/ n [C] a verb form or a set of verb forms in grammar, used in some languages to express doubt, wishes etc. For example, in 'if I were you', the verb 'to be' is in the subjunctive; → **imperative, indicative** —**subjunctive** adj

sub·let /sʌbˈlet/ v past tense and past participle **sublet**, present participle **subletting** [I,T] to rent to someone else a property that you rent from its owner: **sublet sth to sb** *I sublet my apartment to my sister, packed my van, and headed west.* —**sublet** /ˈsʌblet/ n [C]

sub·lieu·ten·ant /ˌsʌblefˈtenənt, -lə- $ -luː-/ n [C] a middle rank in the Royal Navy or someone who has this rank

sub·li·mate /ˈsʌblɪ̩meɪt/ v [I,T] technical to use the energy that comes from sexual feelings to do something, such as work or art, that is more acceptable to your society —**sublimation** /ˌsʌblɪ̩ˈmeɪʃən/ n [U]

sub·lime¹ /səˈblaɪm/ adj **1** something that is sublime is so good or beautiful that it affects you deeply: *The view was sublime.* | *Her songs are a sublime fusion of pop and Brazilian music.* **2** used to describe feelings or behaviour that are very great or extreme, especially when someone seems not to notice what is happening around them: *an air of sublime contentment* —**sublimely** adv —**sublimeness** n [U] —**sublimity** /səˈblɪmɪ̩ti/ n [U]

sublime² n **1 the sublime** something that is so good or beautiful that you are deeply affected by it: *The works on display range from the mainstream to the sublime.* **2 from the sublime to the ridiculous** used to say that a serious and important thing or event is being followed by something very silly, unimportant, or bad

sub·lim·i·nal /sʌbˈlɪmɪ̩nəl/ adj affecting your mind in a way that you are not conscious of: *a subliminal message* | **subliminal advertising** (=with hidden messages and pictures in it)

sub·ma·chine gun /ˌsʌbməˈʃiːn gʌn/ n [C] a type of MACHINE GUN that is light and easily moved

sub·ma·rine¹ /ˈsʌbməriːn, ˌsʌbməˈriːn/ also **sub** n [C] a ship, especially a military one, that can stay under water: *a nuclear submarine*

submarine

submarine² adj [only before noun] growing or used under the sea: *submarine plant life*

sub·mar·i·ner /sʌbˈmærɪnə $ ˈsʌbməriːnər/ n [C] a sailor living and working in a submarine

submarine ˈsandwich n [C] AmE a long bread roll which is split open and filled with meat, cheese etc; ◨ **sub**

sub·merge /səbˈmɜːdʒ $ -ˈmɜːrdʒ/ v **1 a)** [T] to cover something completely with water or another liquid: *The tunnel entrance was submerged by rising sea water.* **b)** [I] to go under the surface of the water and be completely covered by it: *The submarine submerged.* **2** [T] to hide feelings, ideas, or opinions and make yourself stop thinking about them; ◨ **suppress:** *Feelings she thought she'd submerged were surfacing again.* **3 submerge yourself in sth** to make yourself very busy doing something, especially in order to forget about something else: *Alice submerged herself in*

work to try and forget about Tom. —**submerged** adj: *submerged rocks* —**submergence** n [U]

sub·mer·si·ble /səbˈmɜːsɪ̩bəl $ -ˈmɜːr-/ n [C] a small vehicle that can travel under water, especially one that travels to very great depths in the ocean for scientific purposes —**submersible** adj

sub·mer·sion /səbˈmɜːʃən $ -ˈmɜːrʒən/ n [U] the action of going under water, or the state of being completely covered in liquid

sub·mis·sion S2 /səbˈmɪʃən/ n
1 [U] the state of being completely controlled by a person or group, and accepting that you have to obey them: **force/frighten/beat etc sb into submission** *Napoleon threatened to starve the country into submission.* | **in submission** *His head was bowed in submission.*
2 [C,U] when you give or show something to someone in authority, for them to consider or approve: *The deadline for the submission of proposals is May 1st.* | *Plans were drawn up* **for submission to** *the housing council.* | *Submissions will not be accepted after May 1.*
3 [U] formal an opinion or thought that you state: *It is important,* **in my submission,** *that a wider view of the matter be taken.*
4 [C] law a request or suggestion that is given to a judge for them to consider

sub·mis·sive /səbˈmɪsɪv/ adj always willing to obey someone and never disagreeing with them, even if they are unkind to you; ◨ **assertive:** *In those days women were expected to be quiet and submissive.* —**submissively** adv —**submissiveness** n [U]

sub·mit S2 W3 /səbˈmɪt/ v **submitted, submitting**
1 [T] to give a plan, piece of writing etc to someone in authority for them to consider or approve: **submit an application/claim/proposal etc** *All applications must be submitted by Monday.*
2 [I,T] formal to agree to obey a person, group, set of rules, especially when you have no choice; ◨ **give in:** [+to] *Derek has agreed to submit to questioning.*
3 [T] formal law to suggest or say something: **submit (that)** *I submit that the jury has been influenced by the publicity in this case.*

sub·nor·mal /ˌsʌbˈnɔːməl◂ $ -ˈnɔːr-/ adj technical less or lower than normal: *subnormal temperatures*

sub·or·di·nate¹ /səˈbɔːdɪ̩nət $ -ˈbɔːr-/ adj **1** in a less important position than someone else: *a subordinate officer* | [+to] *Women were subordinate to men.* **2** less important than something else: [+to] *These aims were subordinate to the main aims of the mission.*

subordinate² n [C] someone who has a lower position and less authority than someone else in an organization

sub·or·di·nate³ /səˈbɔːdɪ̩neɪt $ -ˈbɔːr-/ v [T] to put someone or something in a less important position: **subordinate sb/sth to sb/sth** *Why subordinate your wishes to those of your family?* —**subordination** /səˌbɔːdɪ̩ˈneɪʃən $ -ˌbɔːr-/ n [U]

su,bordinate ˈclause n [C] a DEPENDENT CLAUSE

sub·orn /səˈbɔːn $ -ˈbɔːrn/ v [T] law to persuade someone to tell lies in a court of law or to do something else that is illegal, especially for money: *an attempt to suborn a witness* —**subornation** /ˌsʌbɔːˈneɪʃən $ -bɔːr-/ n [U]

sub·plot /ˈsʌbplɒt $ -plɑːt/ n [C] a PLOT (=set of events) that is connected with but less important than the main plot in a story, play etc: *the novel's romantic subplot*

sub·poe·na /səˈpiːnə, səb-/ n [C] law a written order to come to a court of law and be a WITNESS

subpoena² v past tense and past participle **subpoenaed** [T] law to order someone to come to a court of law and be a WITNESS: *James was subpoenaed as a witness.*

sub-ˈpost office n [C] a small British post office that has fewer services than a main post office

sub·scribe /səb'skraɪb/ v **1** [I] to pay money, usually once a year, to have copies of a newspaper or magazine sent to you, or to have some other service: [+to] *You can subscribe to the magazine for as little as $32 a year.* **2** [I] *BrE* to pay money regularly to be a member of an organization or to help its work: [+to] *She subscribes to an environmental action group.* **3** [I] to agree to buy or pay for SHARES: [+for] *Each employee may subscribe for up to £2,000 worth of shares.*
subscribe to sth *phr v formal* if you subscribe to an idea, you agree with it or support it: **subscribe to the view/belief/theory etc** *I have never subscribed to the view that schooldays are the happiest days of your life.*

sub·scrib·er /səb'skraɪbə $ -ər/ n [C] **1** someone who pays money, usually once a year, to receive copies of a newspaper or magazine, or to have a service: *cable television subscribers* **2** *BrE* someone who pays money to be part of an organization or to help its work

sub·scrip·tion /səb'skrɪpʃən/ n **1** [C,U] an amount of money you pay, usually once a year, to receive copies of a newspaper or magazine, or receive a service, or the act of paying money for this: [+to] *Are you interested in taking out a subscription to Newsweek* (=arranging to buy it on a regular basis)? | *You may cancel your subscription at any time.* | *I've decided not to renew my subscription.* **2** [C,U] *BrE* an amount of money you pay regularly to be a member of an organization or to help its work, or the act of paying money for this: [+to] *a subscription to Amnesty International* **3** [U] when people in a country or place give money in order to pay for something to be done: *The church's 120 foot gothic spire was paid for by public subscription in 1939.*

sub·sec·tion /'sʌbsekʃən/ n [C] a part of a SECTION, especially in a legal document

sub·se·quent W2 /'sʌbsɪkwənt/ adj formal happening or coming after something else; → **consequent**: *These skills were passed on to subsequent generations.* | *subsequent pages of the book* | **subsequent to sth** *events that happened subsequent to the accident*

sub·se·quent·ly W3 /'sʌbsɪkwəntli/ adv formal after an event in the past: *The book was subsequently translated into 15 languages.* | *Subsequently, the company filed for bankruptcy.*

sub·ser·vi·ent /səb'sɜːviənt $ -'sɜːr-/ adj **1** always obeying another person and doing everything they want you to do – used when someone seems too weak and powerless: [+to] *Don remained entirely subservient to his father.* | **subservient role/position** *His wife refused to accept a traditional subservient role.* **2** *formal* less important than something else; **subordinate**: [+to] *the rights of the individual are made subservient to the interests of the state* —**subserviently** adv —**subservience** n [U]

sub·set /'sʌbset/ n [C] a group of people or things that is part of a larger group of people or things: [+of] *a small subset of the city's immigrant population*

sub·side /səb'saɪd/ v [I] **1** if a feeling, pain, sound, etc subsides, it gradually becomes less and then stops; **die down**: *Simon waited until the laughter subsided.* | *The pains in his head had subsided, but he still felt dizzy and sick.* **2** *formal* if a building or an area of land subsides, it gradually sinks to a lower level: *After the heavy rains, part of the road subsided.* **3** if bad weather conditions subside, they gradually return to a normal state: *The wind gradually subsided, and all was quiet.* **4** if water, especially flood water, subsides, it gradually goes under ground or back to a normal level: *When the floods subsided, the streets were littered with bodies.*

sub·si·dence /səb'saɪdəns, 'sʌbsɪdəns/ n [C,U] the process by which an area of land sinks to a lower level than the land surrounding it, or a building begins to sink into the ground: *Is your house insured against subsidence?*

sub·sid·i·ar·i·ty /səb,sɪdi'ærɪti/ n [U] a word meaning a political POLICY (1) in which power to make decisions, is given to a smaller group, used especially about the European Community giving power to its member countries

sub·sid·i·a·ry¹ /səb'sɪdiəri $ -dieri/ n plural **subsidiaries** [C] a company that is owned or controlled by another larger company: *a subsidiary of a US company* | *one of our Japanese subsidiaries*

subsidiary² adj formal connected with, but less important than something else; **secondary**: *a subsidiary hypothesis* | [+to] *All other issues are subsidiary to this one.*

sub·si·dize also **-ise** *BrE* /'sʌbsɪdaɪz/ v [T usually passive] if a government or organization subsidizes a company, activity etc, it pays part of its costs: *Farming is heavily subsidized* (=subsidized a lot) *by the government.* —**subsidized** adj [only before noun]: *heavily subsidized agricultural exports* —**subsidization** /,sʌbsɪdaɪ'zeɪʃən $ -də-/ n [U]

sub·si·dy /'sʌbsɪdi/ n plural **subsidies** [C] money that is paid by a government or organization to make prices lower, reduce the cost of producing goods etc: **trade/agricultural subsidies etc** *international disagreement over trade subsidies*

sub·sist /səb'sɪst/ v [I] **1** to stay alive when you only have small amounts of food or money; **survive**: [+on] *We had to subsist on bread and water.* | *Old people often have to subsist on very low incomes.* **2** especially law to continue to exist; **survive**

sub·sis·tence /səb'sɪstəns/ n [U] **1** the condition of only just having enough money or food to stay alive: *Many of the families are forced to live at the subsistence level.* | *The land provided subsistence and little more.* **2** **subsistence farming/agriculture etc** farming that produces just enough food for the farmer to live on, but does not produce enough food to sell to other people **3** **subsistence allowance/payment etc** money that is paid to someone so that they can buy meals, pay for a place to stay etc

sub·soil /'sʌbsɔɪl/ n [U] the layer of soil between the ground's surface and the lower layer of hard rock

sub·son·ic /,sʌb'sɒnɪk◂ $ -'saː-/ adj slower than the speed of sound; → **supersonic**

sub·spe·cies /'sʌb,spiːʃiːz/ n plural **subspecies** [C] a group of similar plants or animals that is smaller than a SPECIES

sub·stance W3 /'sʌbstəns/ n
1 MATERIAL [C] a particular type of solid, liquid, or gas: *The leaves were covered with a strange sticky substance.* | **dangerous/toxic/hazardous/poisonous etc substance** *harmful substances in the atmosphere* | *Plutonium 238 is one of the most toxic substances known to man.* | **illegal/banned/prohibited/controlled substance** (=used especially about illegal drugs) *Police found an illegal substance in his car.*
2 TRUTH [U usually in questions and negatives] formal if something has substance, it is true: **There is no substance to** *the rumours* (=they are untrue). | **without substance** (=untrue) *O'Connell's remarks are completely without substance.*
3 IDEAS [singular, U] the most important ideas contained in an argument or piece of writing; **essence**: *The substance of his argument was that people on welfare should work.* | **in substance** *What she said, in substance, was that the mayor should resign.*
4 IMPORTANCE [U] formal importance; **significance**: *It was an entertaining speech, but it lacked substance* (=there was no important information in it). | **matters/issues of substance** *We should be discussing matters of substance.*
5 **man/woman of substance** *BrE literary* a rich man or woman

'substance a,buse n [U] the habit of taking too many illegal drugs, in a way that harms your health; **drug abuse**

sub·stan·dard /ˌsʌbˈstændəd◂ $ -ərd◂/ adj not as good as the average, and not acceptable; → **nonstandard**, **standard**: *substandard housing*

sub·stan·tial S2 W2 /səbˈstænʃəl/ adj
1 large in amount or number; ▪ **considerable**: *We have the support of a substantial number of parents.* | *a substantial salary* | *a substantial breakfast* | *The document requires substantial changes.*
2 [only before noun] large and strongly made: *a substantial piece of furniture*

sub·stan·tial·ly /səbˈstænʃəli/ adv **1** very much or a lot; ▪ **considerably**: *substantially higher prices* | *The deer population has increased substantially in recent years.* **2** used to say that in many ways something is true, the same, different etc; ▪ **essentially**: *There are one or two minor differences, but they're substantially the same text.*

sub·stan·ti·ate /səbˈstænʃieɪt/ v [T] formal to prove the truth of something that someone has said, claimed etc: *Katzen offered little evidence to **substantiate** his claims.* —**substantiation** /səbˌstænʃiˈeɪʃən/ n [U]

sub·stan·tive[1] /səbˈstæntɪv, ˈsʌbstəntɪv/ adj formal dealing with things that are important or real: **substantive matters/issues** *The State Department reported that substantive discussions had taken place with Beijing.* —**substantively** adv

sub·stan·tive[2] /ˈsʌbstəntɪv/ n [C] technical a noun

sub·sta·tion /ˈsʌbˌsteɪʃən/ n [C] a place where electricity is passed on from the place that produces it into the main system

sub·sti·tute[1] /ˈsʌbstɪtjuːt $ -tuːt/ n [C] **1** also **sub** someone who does someone else's job for a limited period of time, especially in a sports team or school: *Germany brought on a substitute at half time.* | *substitute goalkeeper* | [+for] *The coach has to find a substitute for Tim.* **2** a person or thing that you use instead of the one that you usually have, because the usual one is not available: *a sugar substitute* | *a father substitute* **3** **be no substitute for sth** used to emphasize that something is not as good as another thing: *Vitamin pills are no substitute for a healthy diet.*

substitute[2] v **1** [T] to use something new or different instead of something else: **substitute sth for sth** *The recipe says you can substitute yoghurt for the sour cream.* **2** [I] to do someone's job until the person who usually does it is able to do it again: [+for] *Bill substituted for Larry, who was off sick.* **3** [T] to replace someone with another person especially another player: *Michael Owen had to be substituted after 20 minutes on the field.*

substitute 'teacher also **substitute**, **sub** n [C] AmE a teacher who teaches a class when the usual teacher is ill; ▪ **supply teacher** BrE

sub·sti·tu·tion /ˌsʌbstɪˈtjuːʃən $ -ˈtuː-/ n [C,U] when someone or something is replaced by someone or something else: *Coach Ross made two substitutions in the second half.* | **substitution of sth for sth** *the substitution of English for French as the world's common language*

sub·stra·tum /ˌsʌbˈstrɑːtəm $ -ˈstreɪ-/ n plural **substrata** /-tə/ [C] technical a layer that lies beneath another layer, especially in the earth: *a substratum of rock* | *a social substratum*

sub·struc·ture /ˈsʌbˌstrʌktʃə $ -ər/ n [C] **1** one of the structures (STRUCTURE[1] (3)) within a society or organization that combines with others to form a whole **2** a solid base under the ground that supports a building above the ground; → **superstructure**

sub·sume /səbˈsjuːm $ -ˈsuːm/ v [T] formal to include someone or something as a member of a group or type, rather than considering it separately: **subsume sb/sth under sth** *A wide range of offences are usually subsumed under the category of robbery.*

sub·ten·ant /ˌsʌbˈtenənt/ n [C] someone who pays rent for an apartment, office etc to the person who is renting it from the owner —**subtenancy** n [C,U]

sub·ter·fuge /ˈsʌbtəfjuːdʒ $ -ər-/ n [C,U] formal a secret trick or slightly dishonest way of doing something, or the use of this: **by subterfuge** *Sereni was lured to Moscow by subterfuge.*

sub·ter·ra·ne·an /ˌsʌbtəˈreɪniən◂/ adj [usually before noun] beneath the surface of the Earth: *subterranean passage*

sub·text /ˈsʌbtekst/ n [C usually singular] a hidden or second meaning behind someone's words or actions: *What's the subtext here? What's the writer really saying?*

sub·ti·tle /ˈsʌbˌtaɪtl/ n **1** **subtitles** [plural] the words printed over a film in a foreign language to translate what is being said by the actors: *a French film with English subtitles* **2** [singular] a second title below the main title in a book, which gives more information about what is in the book, show etc: *The opera's subtitle is 'The School for Lovers'.* —**subtitle** v [I,T] —**subtitled** adj: *a subtitled version of the film* | *The book is subtitled 'A Psychology of Masculinity'.*

sub·tle /ˈsʌtl/ adj comparative **subtler** or, **more subtle**, superlative **subtlest 1** not easy to notice or understand unless you pay careful attention; ▪ **obvious**: *The pictures are similar, but there are subtle differences between them.* | *The warning signs of the disease are so subtle that they are often ignored.* | *a **subtle form** of racism* | **subtle taste/flavour/smell etc** *The flavour of the dried berries is more subtle.* | *The dish had a **subtle hint** of ginger.* **2** behaving in a skilful and clever way, especially using indirect methods or language to hide what you are trying to do: *I think we need a more subtle approach.* | *a subtle plan* | [+about] *She wasn't very subtle about it. She just said she didn't love him any more.* **3** very clever in noticing and understanding things; → **sensitive**: *a subtle mind* —**subtly** adv: *a subtly different colour*

sub·tle·ty /ˈsʌtlti/ n plural **subtleties 1** [U] the quality that something has when it has been done in a clever or skilful way, with careful attention to small details: *The play lacks subtlety.* | *She argued her case with considerable subtlety.* **2** [C usually plural] a thought, idea, or detail that is important but difficult to notice or understand: [+of] *Some of the subtleties of the language are lost in translation.*

sub·to·tal /ˈsʌbˌtəʊtl $ -ˌtoʊtl/ n [C] the total of a set of numbers, especially on a bill, that is added to other numbers, such as a tax, to form a complete total

sub·tract /səbˈtrækt/ v [T] to take a number or an amount from a larger number or amount; → **add, deduct, minus**: **subtract sth from sth** *If you subtract 30 from 45, you get 15.*

sub·trac·tion /səbˈtrækʃən/ n [C] the process of taking a number or amount from a larger number or amount; → **addition**

sub·trop·i·cal /ˌsʌbˈtrɒpɪkəl◂ $ -ˈtrɑː-/ also **semi-tropical** adj related to or typical of an area that is near a tropical area: *subtropical vegetation*

sub·urb /ˈsʌbɜːb $ -ɜːrb/ n [C] an area where people live which is away from the centre of a town or city: *a London suburb* | [+of] *a suburb of Los Angeles* | *a kid from the suburbs* | **in a suburb** *Don't you get bored living out here in the suburbs?*

sub·ur·ban /səˈbɜːbən $ -ˈbɜːr-/ adj **1** related to a suburb, or in a suburb: *a quiet, suburban street* **2** boring and typical of people who live in the suburbs: *narrow-minded, suburban attitudes*

sub·ur·ban·ite /səˈbɜːbənaɪt $ -ˈbɜːr-/ n [C] someone who lives in a suburb – often used to show disapproval: *Patsy's father is a typical suburbanite.*

sub·ur·bi·a /səˈbɜːbiə $ -ˈbɜːr-/ n [U] suburbs in general, and the behaviour, opinions, and ways of living that are typical of people who live there – often used to show disapproval: *middle-class suburbia*

S

sub·ven·tion /səb'venʃən/ n [C] formal a gift of money, usually from a government, for a special use

sub·ver·sion /səb'vɜːʃən $ -'vɜːrʒən/ n [U] secret activities that are intended to damage or destroy the power or influence of a government or established system: *Murray was jailed for subversion.*

sub·ver·sive¹ /səb'vɜːsɪv $ -'vɜːr-/ adj subversive ideas, activities etc are secret and intended to damage or destroy a government or an established system: *He was engaged in subversive activities.* | subversive propaganda/literature —**subversively** adv

subversive² n [C] someone who secretly tries to damage or destroy the government or an established system: *a known subversive* —**subversiveness** n [U]

sub·vert /səb'vɜːt $ -'vɜːrt/ v [T] formal **1** to try to destroy the power and influence of a government or the established system: *an attempt to subvert the democratic process* **2** to destroy someone's beliefs or loyalty

sub·way /'sʌbweɪ/ n [C] AmE **1** a railway system that runs under the ground below a big city; ▤ **underground** BrE: *the New York City subway* | *a crowded subway station* | *Boston has the oldest subway system in the US.* **2** BrE a path for people to walk under a road or railway; ▤ **underpass**

sub-'zero adj [usually before noun] below zero in temperature: **sub-zero weather/temperatures**

suc·ceed [S3] [W2] /sək'siːd/ v

1 [I] to do what you tried or wanted to do: *She wanted to be the first woman to climb Mount Everest, and she almost succeeded.* | **succeed in doing sth** *Scientists claim they have succeeded in finding a cure for cancer.* | *Very few people succeed in losing weight and keeping it off.* ⚠ Do not say 'succeed to do'. Say 'succeed in doing': *She succeeded in persuading me* (NOT *succeeded to persuade me).*
2 [I] to have the result or effect something was intended to have: *The drug therapy has not succeeded.*
3 [I] to do well in your job, especially because you have worked hard at it for a long time: [+as] *I'm not sure he has the determination to succeed as an actor.* | [+in] *a woman who succeeded in politics*
4 [I,T] to be the next person to take a position or job after someone else: **succeed sb as sth** *Reeves will succeed Segal as Speaker of the House.* | **succeed sb to the throne** (=to be the next king or queen after someone else) *Who will succeed him to the throne?*
5 [T] to come after or replace something else, especially another product: *This car is intended to succeed the popular Fiesta.*
6 nothing succeeds like success used to say that success often leads to even greater success
7 only succeed in doing sth used when someone does the opposite of what they intended to do: *It seems I've only succeeded in upsetting you.*

suc·ceed·ing /sək'siːdɪŋ/ adj [only before noun] coming after something else: *Over the succeeding weeks things went from bad to worse.* | *succeeding generations*

suc·cess [S1] [W1] /sək'ses/ n [C,U]

1 when you achieve what you want or intend; ▤ **failure: be a big/huge/great etc success** *The experiment was a big success.* | **without success** *I tried to contact him, but without success.* | *What's the secret of your success?* | *Their efforts finally met with some success* (=they were successful). | *I didn't think my chances of success were very good.* | *She puts her success down to good luck* (=says it is caused by good luck). | **success in doing sth** *Did you have any success in persuading Alan to come?*
2 when a lot of people like something, buy something, go to see something etc; ▤ **failure: be a big/huge/great etc success** *The film was a great success.* | *Her book has enjoyed a lot of success* (=it has been very successful). | *The play was a box-office success* (=many people went to see it). | *The show was an overnight success* (=it was immediately successful).
3 when someone achieves a high position in their job, course, sport, in society etc; ▤ **failure:** *Success isn't everything, you know.* | [+in] *He has already had a lot of success in his career.* | **be a success as a ...** (=be successful in a particular job) *She wasn't much of a success as a lawyer.* | *She's determined to make a success of* (=be successful in) *her career.*
4 when a business makes a lot of money; ▤ **failure:** *the success of his latest business venture* | **be a big/ huge/great etc success** *The firm wasn't a great success.*
5 success story someone or something that is successful: *The company has been a major success story.*

suc·cess·ful [S2] [W1] /sək'sesfəl/ adj

1 having the effect or result you intended: *The operation was successful.* | **a highly successful** (=very successful) *meeting* | **successful in (doing) sth** *Were you successful in persuading him to change his mind?*
2 a successful business, film, product etc makes a lot of money: *The show's had a pretty successful run.* | **a highly successful** (=very successful) *product*
3 a successful person earns a lot of money or is very well known and respected: *Arthur was a highly successful* (=very successful) *businessman.* | [+in] *He later became successful in politics.* | [+as] *I think she'll be successful as a photographer.* —**successfully** adv: *He successfully completed a master's degree.*

suc·ces·sion [W3] /sək'seʃən/ n

1 in succession happening one after the other without anything different happening in between: *She won the championship four times in succession.* | **in quick/rapid/ close succession** (=quickly one after the other) *He fired two shots in quick succession.*
2 a succession of sth a number of people or things of the same kind following, coming or happening one after the other: *A succession of visitors came to the door.*
3 [U] the act of taking over an official job or position, or the right to be the next to take it; → **accession:** *If the prince dies, the succession passes to his son.* | [+to] *the queen's succession to the throne*

suc·ces·sive /sək'sesɪv/ adj [only before noun] coming or following one after the other: *The team has had five successive victories.* | *Successive governments have tried to deal with this issue.* —**successively** adv

suc·ces·sor /sək'sesə $ -ər/ n [C] **1** someone who takes a job or position previously held by someone else; → **predecessor:** *His successor died after only 15 months in office.* | *I'm sure she will be worthy successor* (=someone who is very good and deserves to be someone's successor). | [+to] *her successor to the post* | [+as] *Sloan will be Barrett's successor as treasurer.* **2** formal a machine, system etc that exists after another one in a process of development: *the transistor's successor, the microchip*

suc·cinct /sək'sɪŋkt/ adj clearly expressed in a few words – use this to show approval; ▤ **concise:** *a succinct explanation* —**succinctly** adv: *Anderson put the same point more succinctly.* —**succinctness** n [U]

suc·co·tash /'sʌkətæʃ/ n [U] AmE a dish made from corn, beans, and TOMATOES cooked together

suc·cour¹ BrE; **succor** AmE /'sʌkə $ -ər/ n [U] literary help and sympathy that is given to someone: *They give succour to the victims of war.*

succour² BrE; **succor** AmE v [T] literary to give help and sympathy someone: *succouring the needy*

suc·cu·bus /'sʌkjʊbəs/ n plural **succubi** /-baɪ/ [C] a female devil that in the past was believed to have sex with a sleeping man

suc·cu·lent¹ /'sʌkjʊlənt/ adj juicy and good to eat: *a succulent steak* —**succulence** n [U]

succulent² n [C] technical a plant such as a CACTUS which has thick soft leaves or stems that can hold a lot of liquid

suc·cumb /sə'kʌm/ v [I] formal **1** to stop opposing someone or something that is stronger than you, and allow them to take control; ▤ **give in:** [+to] *Succumbing to pressure from the chemical industry, Governor*

Blakely amended the regulations. | *Gina **succumbed to temptation** and had a second serving of cake.* **2** if you succumb to an illness, you become very ill or die of it: [+**to**] *About 400,000 Americans succumb each year to smoking-related illnesses.*

such S1 W1 /sʌtʃ/ *determiner, predeterminer, pron*
1 of the same kind as the thing or person which has already been mentioned: *Such behavior is just not acceptable in this school.* | *The rules make it quite clear what should be done in such a situation.* | *A victory for Brazil had been predicted and such indeed was the result.* | *She needs to see a psychiatrist **or some such** person.* | *'You said you'd be finished by today.' 'I said **no such** thing!'* | **such as this/these** *There is now a greater awareness of problems such as these.* | **treated/recognized/accepted etc as such** *Birth is a natural process and should be treated as such.*
2 such as used when giving an example of something: *Cartoon characters such as Mickey Mouse and Snoopy are still popular.* | *large electrical goods such as television sets and washing machines* | **such as?** (=used to ask someone to give an example) *'There are lots of useful things you could do.' 'Such as?'*
3 used to emphasize your description of something or someone: *They're such nice people.* | *It's such a long way from here.* | *I felt such an idiot.* ⚠ **such** comes before **a(n)**: *He's such a nice guy (NOT a such nice guy).*
4 a) used to mention the result of a quality that something or someone has: *It's such a tiny kitchen that I don't have to do much to keep it clean.* | *He came to such a sudden stop that we almost hit him.* **b)** *formal* used to say that something is so great, so bad etc that something else happens: **be such that/as to do sth** *The force of the explosion was such that windows were blown out.* | *His manner was such as to offend nearly everyone he met.* | **in such a way/manner that/as to do sth** *He lectured in such a way that many in the audience found him impossible to understand.* | **to such an extent/degree that** *Her condition deteriorated to such an extent that a blood transfusion was considered necessary.*
5 used to show that you think that something is not good enough or that there is not enough of it: **such as it is/such as they are etc** *We will look at the evidence, such as it is, for each of these theories.* | **such ... as** *formal: Such food as they gave us was scarcely fit to eat.*
6 *formal* used to refer only to people or things of a particular group or kind: **such ... as/who/that** *Such individuals who take up this role often find life frustrating.* | **such of sth/sb as** *Such of you as wish to leave may do so now.*
7 there's no such person/thing etc as sb/sth used to say that a particular person or thing does not exist: *There's no such thing as magic.*
8 not (...) as such a) *spoken* used to say that the word you are using to describe something is not exactly correct: *There isn't a garden as such, just a little vegetable patch.* **b)** used to say that something does not include or is not related to all things or people of a particular type: *We have nothing against men as such.*
9 and such *spoken* used to say that other people or things like the ones you have just mentioned are included: *It won't be anything special – just a few cakes and sandwiches and such.*

ˈsuch and ˌsuch *pron, predeterminer spoken* used to talk about a particular thing, time, amount etc without saying exactly what it is: *They will ask you to come on such and such a day, at such and such a time.*

such·like /'sʌtʃlaɪk/ *pron spoken especially BrE* **and suchlike** and things of that kind: *money for food, clothes, and suchlike* —**suchlike** *adj* [only before noun]

suck¹ S3 /sʌk/ *v*
1 [I,T] to take air, liquid etc into your mouth by making your lips form a small hole and using the muscles of your mouth to pull it in: **suck sth in** *Michael put the cigarette to his lips and sucked in the smoke.* | [+**at**] *a baby sucking at its mother's breast* | **suck sth up** *Jennie sucked up the last bit of milkshake with her straw.*; → see picture at **DRINK¹**

2 [I,T] to hold something in your mouth and pull on it with your tongue and lips: *Don't suck your thumb, dear.* | [+**on**] *a picture of Lara sucking on a lollipop*
3 [T] to pull someone or something with great power and force into or out of a particular place: **suck sth into sth** *A bird was sucked into one of the jet's engines.* | **suck sb/sth under/down** *The river sucked him under.* | **suck sth out of/from sth** *The fluid was sucked from his lungs.*
4 sth sucks *spoken not polite* used when you dislike something very much or think something is very bad: *If you ask me, the whole thing sucks.*
5 suck it and see *BrE informal* to use something or do something for a short time, to find out if it works, if you like it etc

be sucked in also **be sucked into sth** *phr v*
to become involved in a situation, especially a bad situation, when you do not want to: *The US has no intention of getting sucked into another war in Europe.*
suck up *phr v informal*
to say or do a lot of nice things in order to make someone like you or to get what you want – used to show disapproval: [+**to**] *He's always sucking up to the boss.*

suck² *n* [C usually singular] an act of sucking
suck·er¹ /'sʌkə $ -ər/ *n* [C]
1 PERSON *informal* someone who is easily tricked or persuaded to do something: *You fell for that old line? Sucker!*
2 be a sucker for sb/sth *informal* to like someone or something very much, especially so that you cannot refuse them: *I'm a total sucker for seafood.*
3 PART OF AN ANIMAL a part of an insect or of an animal's body that it uses to hold on to a surface
4 SWEET *AmE* a LOLLIPOP
5 PLANT a part of a plant that grows from the root or lower stem of a plant to become a new plant
6 RUBBER a flat round piece of rubber that sticks to a surface by SUCTION

sucker² *v*
sucker sb into sth *phr v AmE* to persuade someone to do something they do not want to, especially by tricking them or lying to them

suck·le /'sʌkəl/ *v* **1** [T] to feed a baby or young animal with milk from the breast: *a sheep suckling her lamb* **2** [I] if a baby or young animal suckles, it sucks milk from a breast; → **breast-feed**, **nurse**

suck·ling /'sʌklɪŋ/ *n* [C] *literary* a young human or animal still taking milk from its mother

su·crose /'suːkrəʊz, 'sjuː- $ 'suːkroʊz/ *n* [U] *technical* the most common form of sugar; → **fructose**, **lactose**

suc·tion /'sʌkʃən/ *n* [U] **1** the process of removing air or liquid from an enclosed space so that another substance is sucked in, or so that two surfaces stick together: *My vacuum cleaner has very good suction.* | *a **suction pump*** **2** the force that causes a substance to be sucked into a closed space when the air or liquid already present is removed

sud·den S2 W3 /'sʌdn/ *adj*
1 happening, coming, or done quickly or when you do not expect it: *a **sudden change** in the weather* | *Life is cruel, she thought, with a **sudden rush of** anger.* | *a **sudden movement** | Her death was sudden.*
2 all of a sudden suddenly: *All of a sudden the lights went out.* —**suddenness** *n* [U]

ˌsudden ˈdeath *n* [U] a way of deciding the winner of a game when the scores are equal at the end. The game goes on until one player or team gains the lead: *a sudden death play-off*

ˌSudden ˌInfant ˈDeath ˌSyndrome *n* [U] SIDS *technical* when a baby stops breathing and dies while it is sleeping, for no known reason; ▤ **crib death** *AmE*; ▤ **cot death** *BrE*

sud·den·ly S1 W1 /'sʌdnli/ *adv* quickly and unexpectedly: *I **suddenly realized** that there was someone* *following me.* | *George died very suddenly.* | [sentence adverb]: *Suddenly the eagle opened its wings.*

suds /sʌdz/ *n* [plural] the mass of bubbles formed on the top of water with soap in it —**sudsy** *adj*

sue /sjuː $ suː/ *v* [I,T] **1** to make a legal claim against someone, especially for money, because they have harmed you in some way: *If the builders don't fulfil their side of the contract, we'll sue.* | *The company is suing a former employee.* | **sue (sb) for libel/defamation/ negligence/slander etc** *Miss James could not afford to sue for libel.* | *She was suing doctors for negligence over the loss of her child.* | *The railway may* **sue for damages** (=in order to get money) *because of loss of revenue.* | *He is being* **sued for divorce** (=in order to end a marriage) *by his wife.* **2 sue for peace** *formal* if a country or army sues for peace, they ask for peace, especially because there is no other good choice: *They had hoped to force the North to sue for peace.*

suede /sweɪd/ *n* [U] soft leather with a slightly rough surface: *suede shoes* | *a suede jacket*

su·et /'suːɪt, 'sjuːɪt $ 'suː-/ *n* [U] hard fat from around an animal's KIDNEYS, used in cooking in Britain

suf·fer S1 W1 /'sʌfə $ -ər/ *v*
1 PAIN [I,T] to experience physical or mental pain: *At least he died suddenly and didn't suffer.* | *She's suffering a lot of pain.* | [+from] *I'm suffering from a bad back.* | *Mary's suffering from ill health at the moment.*
2 BAD EXPERIENCE/SITUATION [I,T] if someone suffers an unpleasant or difficult experience, or is in a difficult situation, it happens to them or they experience it: [+from] *London employers were suffering from a desperate shortage of school-leavers.* | *Most of us have* **suffered the consequences** *of stupid decisions taken by others.* | *In June 1667, England* **suffered** *a humiliating* **defeat** *by the Dutch.* | **suffer loss/damage/injury** *They are unlikely to suffer much loss of business after 2001.* | *He suffered head injuries in the crash.* | *A man who suffered serious brain damage during an operation is suing the hospital.* | *Small businesses have suffered financially during the recession.*
3 BECOME WORSE [I] to become worse in quality because a bad situation is affecting something or because nobody is taking care of it; ▣ **benefit**: *Safety might suffer if costs are cut.* | *I'm worried and my work is beginning to suffer.*
4 not suffer fools gladly to not be patient with people you think are stupid: *He was a perfectionist who didn't suffer fools gladly.*

suf·fer·ance /'sʌfərəns/ *n* **on sufferance** *formal* if you live or work somewhere on sufferance, you are allowed to do it by someone who would prefer you did not do it: *He was never going to let her forget she was only here on sufferance.*

suf·fer·er /'sʌfərə $ -ər/ *n* [C] someone who suffers, especially from a particular illness; → **victim**: [+from] *sufferers from headaches* | **AIDS/cancer/asthma/arthritis etc sufferers** *a support group for cancer sufferers*

suf·fer·ing /'sʌfərɪŋ/ *n* [C,U] serious physical or mental pain: *the suffering of the refugees after the war* | *the* **pain and suffering** *caused by road accidents*

suf·fice /sə'faɪs/ *v* [I not in progressive] **1** *formal* to be enough: *A light lunch* **will suffice.** | [+for] *A few brief observations will suffice for present purposes.* | **suffice to do sth** *A few more statistics will suffice to show the trends of the time.* **2 suffice (it) to say (that)** used to say that the statement that follows is enough to explain what you mean, even though you could say more: *Suffice it to say that they're having marital problems.*

suf·fi·cien·cy /sə'fɪʃənsi/ *n formal* **1** [U] the state of being or having enough: *The war has affected the country's economic sufficiency.* **2 a sufficiency of sth** a supply that is enough: *a sufficiency of raw materials*

suf·fi·cient S2 W2 /sə'fɪʃənt/ *adj formal* as much as is needed for a particular purpose; ▣ **enough**; ▣ **insufficient**: *We can only prosecute if there is sufficient*

evidence. | *Unauthorized absence is sufficient reason for dismissal.* | *We need sufficient time to deal with the problem.* | **sufficient to do sth** *The money is not sufficient to cover everything that needs doing.* | [+for] *The recipe is sufficient for six people.* —**sufficiently** *adv*: *Students must reach a sufficiently high standard to pass.*

suf·fix /'sʌfɪks/ *n* [C] a letter or letters added to the end of a word to form a new word, such as 'ness' in 'kindness' or 'ly' in 'suddenly'; → **affix**, **prefix**

suf·fo·cate /'sʌfəkeɪt/ *v* [I,T] **1** to die or make someone die by preventing them from breathing: *The animal seizes its prey by the throat and suffocates it to death.* | *One of the puppies suffocated inside the plastic bag.* **2 be suffocating** to feel uncomfortable because there is not enough fresh air: *Can you open a window? I'm suffocating.* **3** [T] to prevent a relationship, plan, business etc from developing well or being successful: *Jealousy can suffocate any relationship.* —**suffocation** /ˌsʌfə'keɪʃən/ *n* [U]

suf·fo·cat·ed /'sʌfəkeɪtɪd/ *adj* **feel suffocated** to feel as if you are not free or do not have enough space: *He feels suffocated by London and longs to escape to the country.*

suf·fra·gan /'sʌfrəgən/ *adj* [only before noun] a suffragan BISHOP helps another bishop of higher rank in their work —**suffragan** [C]

suf·frage /'sʌfrɪdʒ/ *n* [U] the right to vote in national elections

suf·fra·gette /ˌsʌfrə'dʒet/ *n* [C] a woman who tried to gain the right to vote for women especially as a member of a group in Britain or the US in the early 20th century

suf·fuse /sə'fjuːz/ *v* [T] *literary* **1** if warmth, colour, liquid etc suffuses something or someone, it covers or spreads through them: *The light of the setting sun suffused the clouds.* | *Hot colour suffused her cheeks.* **2 be suffused with sth** if someone is suffused with a feeling, they are full of that feeling: *She was suffused with happiness.*

sug·ar¹ S2 W3 /'ʃʊgə $ -ər/ *n*
1 [U] a sweet white or brown substance that is obtained from plants and used to make food and drinks sweet: *Do you take sugar in your coffee?*
2 [C] *BrE* the amount of sugar that a small spoon can hold: *How many sugars do you want in your tea?*
3 [C] *technical* one of several sweet substances formed in plants
4 *spoken* used to address someone you like very much

sugar² *v* [T] to add sugar or cover something with sugar; ▣ **sweeten**: *Did you sugar my coffee?* —**sugared** *adj*: *sugared almonds*

sugar beet *n* [U] a vegetable that grows under the ground from which sugar is obtained

sug·ar·cane /'ʃʊgəkeɪn $ -ər-/ *n* [U] a tall tropical plant from whose stems sugar is obtained

sugar-coated *adj* **1** covered with sugar: *sugar-coated cereals* **2** used to describe something that is made to seem better than it really is

sugar cube *n* [C] a sugar lump

sugar daddy *n* [C] *informal* an older man who gives a young person presents and money in return for their company and often for sex

sugar lump *n* [C] *BrE* a square piece of solid sugar

sug·ar·y /'ʃʊgəri/ *adj* **1** containing sugar or tasting like sugar: *sugary foods* **2** language, emotions etc that are sugary are too nice and seem insincere: *She said goodbye in a sickeningly sugary tone.*

sug·gest S1 W1 /sə'dʒest $ səg'dʒest/ *v* [T]
1 to tell someone your ideas about what they should do, where they should go etc; → **propose**: *They keep suggesting ways to keep my weight down.* | *She wrote to me and suggested a meeting.* | **suggest (that)** *I suggest you phone before you go round there.* | **It has been suggested that** *the manager will resign if any more players are sold.* | **suggest doing sth** *Joan suggested asking her*

father for his opinion. | **suggest how/where/what etc**
*The therapist suggested how Tony could cope with his
problems.* | **can/may I suggest** (=used to politely suggest a different idea) *May I suggest that you think
carefully before rushing into this?* | *No possible explanation suggests itself* (=is able to be thought of).

2 to make someone think that a particular thing is
true; **⊟ indicate**: *Trends in spending and investment
suggest a gradual economic recovery.* | **suggest (that)**
*Opinion polls suggest that only 10% of the population
trusts the government.* | **evidence/results/data/studies
etc suggest(s) that** *The evidence suggests that single
fathers are more likely to work than single mothers.*

3 to tell someone about someone or something that is
suitable for a particular job or activity; **⊟ recommend**: **suggest sb/sth for sth** *John Roberts has been
suggested for the post of manager.*

4 to state something in an indirect way; **⊟ imply**: *Are
you suggesting my husband's been drinking?*

5 I'm not suggesting *spoken* used to say that what you
have said is not exactly what you intended to say: *I'm
not suggesting for one moment that these changes will be
easy.*

6 to remind someone of something or help them to
imagine it: *The stage was bare, with only the lighting to
suggest a prison.*

GRAMMAR

suggest that sb do sth: *He suggested that we go (NOT
suggested us to go) for a drink.*
You can miss out 'that': *What do you suggest we do
(NOT suggest us to do)?*
suggest doing sth: *I suggested wearing (NOT suggest to
wear) something warm.*
suggest sth: *She suggested a walk before dinner.*

sug·gest·i·ble /səˈdʒestˌbəl $ səg-/ *adj* easily influenced by other people or by things you see and hear:
very/highly/extremely suggestible *At that age, kids are
highly suggestible.*

sug·ges·tion S1 W2 /səˈdʒestʃən $ səg-/ *n*
1 [C] an idea, plan, or possibility that someone mentions, or the act of mentioning it: *Any helpful suggestions would be welcome.* | **suggestion that** *the
suggestion that houses should be built on this site* | *May
I make a suggestion?* | *Let me know if you have any
suggestions.* | *The committee is open to suggestions*
(=willing to listen to ideas). | **at sb's suggestion** *She
took a seat at his suggestion.*
2 [singular, U] a sign or possibility of something: [+of]
*There was never any suggestion of criminal
involvement.* | *The government have denied any suggestion of involvement in her death.* | **suggestion that**
*There's some suggestion that the intruder was the same
person that killed Angie.*
3 a suggestion of sth a slight amount of something:
There was just a suggestion of a smile on her face.
4 [U] an indirect way of making you accept an idea, for
example by HYPNOTISM: *the power of suggestion*

sug·ges·tive /səˈdʒestɪv $ səg-/ *adj* **1** similar to
something: [+of] *Her symptoms are suggestive of a
panic disorder.* | *It was a huge sound, suggestive of
whales calling each other.* **2** a remark, behaviour etc
that is suggestive makes you think of sex: *He kept
giving me suggestive looks.* —**suggestively** *adv*
—**suggestiveness** *n* [U]

su·i·cid·al /ˌsuːɪˈsaɪdl◂ ˌsjuː- $ ˌsuː-/ *adj* **1** wanting
to kill yourself: *She was depressed and almost
suicidal.* | *For many years before treatment, Clare had
suicidal tendencies* (=behaviour that showed she
wanted to kill herself). **2** likely to lead to death: *It was
suicidal trying to put out that fire.* **3** likely to lead to a
lot of damage or trouble: *Her economic policies would
prove suicidal for our economy.*

su·i·cide /ˈsuːɪsaɪd, ˈsjuː- $ ˈsuː-/ *n* [C,U] **1** the act of
killing yourself: *More people commit suicide at Christmas than at any other time.* | *My mother attempted
suicide on many occasions.* | *He apparently left a suicide note* (=letter explaining his reasons for killing

himself). → see box at KILL¹ **2** political/economic **suicide** something you do that ruins your good position in
politics or the ECONOMY: *He said a vote for Labour would
be a vote for economic suicide.* **3 suicide attack/mission/bombing etc** an attack etc in which the person
who carries out the attack deliberately kills himself or
herself in the process of killing other people

'suicide ˌbomber *n* [C] someone who hides a bomb
on their body and explodes it in a public place, killing
himself or herself and other people, usually for political reasons

'suicide ˌpact *n* [C] an arrangement between two or
more people to kill themselves at the same time

suit¹ S2 W3 /suːt, sjuːt $ suːt/ *n* [C]
1 CLOTHES a set of clothes made of the same material, usually including a jacket with trousers or a skirt:
a grey light-weight suit | *a business suit* | *a tweed suit* |
She was wearing a black trouser suit. → MORNING SUIT
2 bathing/jogging etc suit a piece of clothing or a set of
clothes used for swimming, running etc → BOILER SUIT,
SHELL SUIT, SWEAT SUIT, TRACKSUIT, WET SUIT
3 LAW a problem or complaint that a person or company brings to a court of law to be settled; **⊟ lawsuit**:
Johnson has filed suit against her. | *a civil suit*
4 OFFICE WORKER *informal* a man, especially a manager, who works in an office and who has to wear a suit
when he is at work: *I bought myself a mobile phone and
joined the other suits on the train to the City.*
5 CARDS one of the four types of cards in a set of
playing cards
6 sb's strong suit something that you are good at:
Sympathy is not Jack's strong suit. → **in your birthday
suit** at BIRTHDAY (3); → **follow suit** at FOLLOW (14)

suit² S2 W3 *v* [T]
1 to be acceptable, suitable or CONVENIENT for a particular person or in a particular situation: *Whatever your
reason for borrowing, we have the loan that suits your
needs.* | *There's a range of restaurants to suit all
tastes.* | *There are countryside walks to suit everyone.* |
We have gifts to suit every pocket (=of all prices). |
Either steak or chicken would suit me fine. | *The climate
there will suit you down to the ground* (=suit you very
well). | **suit sth to sth** *She had the ability to suit her
performances to the audience.*
2 [not in passive] clothes, colours etc that suit you make
you look attractive: *That coat really suits Paul.* | *Red
suits you.* | *Jill's new hairstyle doesn't really suit her.*
3 best/well/ideally/perfectly etc suited to/for sth to
have the right qualities to do something: *The activity
holidays on offer are really best suited to groups.* | *land
well suited for agriculture* | *the candidate most ideally
suited to doing the job*
4 suit yourself *spoken* used to tell someone they can do
whatever they want, even though it annoys you or
you think they are not doing the right thing: *'Mind if I
sit here?' he said gently. 'Suit yourself.'*
5 suit sb's book *BrE informal* to fit well into someone's
plans

suit·a·bil·i·ty /ˌsuːtəˈbɪlˌti, ˌsjuː- $ ˌsuː-/ *n* [U] the
degree to which something or someone has the right
qualities for a particular purpose: [+for] *There's no
doubt about Christine's suitability for the job.* | [+as] *his
suitability as a father*

suit·a·ble S2 W2 /ˈsuːtəbəl, ˈsjuː- $ ˈsuː-/ *adj* having
the right qualities for a particular person, purpose, or
situation; **⊞ unsuitable**: *We are hoping to find a
suitable house.* | [+for] *The house is not really suitable
for a large family.* | **suitable place/time etc to do sth** *a
suitable place to rear young children* | **suitable to
use/be shown etc** *These crayons are not suitable to use
in very hot weather.*

suit·a·bly /ˈsuːtəbli, ˈsjuː- $ ˈsuː-/ *adv* **1 suitably
dressed/prepared/equipped etc** wearing the right
clothes, having the right information, equipment etc

S

1 000, 2 000, 3 000, most frequent words in S poken and W ritten English

for a particular situation: *We were relieved that Gordon had arrived at the wedding suitably dressed.* **2** [+ adj/adv] having the amount of a feeling or quality you would hope for in a particular situation: *'He owns three hotels.' The others looked **suitably impressed**.*

suit·case /'suːtkeɪs, 'sjuːt- $ 'suːt-/ *n* [C] a large case with a handle, used for carrying clothes and possessions when you travel → see picture at BAG[1]

suite /swiːt/ *n* [C]
1 ROOMS a set of rooms, especially expensive ones in a hotel: *a honeymoon suite* | *a **suite of rooms** for palace guests*
2 FURNITURE especially BrE a set of matching furniture for a room: *a pink bathroom suite* | **three-piece suite** (=a large seat and two chairs)
3 COMPUTERS technical a group of related computer PROGRAMS
4 MUSIC a piece of music made up of several short parts: *the Nutcracker Suite*
5 POLITICS formal the people who work for or help an important person; ☐ **retinue**

suit·ing /'suːtɪŋ, 'sjuː- $ 'suː-/ *n* [U] technical material used for making suits, especially woven wool

sui·tor /'suːtə, 'sjuː- $ 'suːtər/ *n* [C] old use a man who wants to marry a particular woman

sul·fate /'sʌlfeɪt/ the American spelling of SULPHATE

sul·fide /'sʌlfaɪd/ the American spelling of SULPHIDE

sul·fur /'sʌlfə $ -ər/ the American spelling of SULPHUR

sulfur di'oxide the American spelling of SULPHUR DIOXIDE

sul·fu·ric a·cid /sʌl͵fjʊərɪk 'æsᵻd $ -͵fjʊr-/ the American spelling of SULPHURIC ACID

sul·fu·rous /'sʌlfərəs/ the American spelling of SULPHUROUS

sulk[1] /sʌlk/ *v* [I] to be silently angry and refuse to be friendly or discuss what is annoying or upsetting you – used to show disapproval: *Nicola sulked all morning.*

sulk[2] *n* [C] a time when someone is sulking: **in/into a sulk** *Mike could go into a sulk that would last for days.* | *She's **having a sulk**.* | **the sulks** *a fit of the sulks*

sulk·y /'sʌlki/ *adj* sulking, or tending to sulk; → moody: *a sulky child* | *He put on a sulky expression.* | *Katherine sat in a sulky silence.* —**sulkily** *adv* —**sulkiness** *n* [U]

sul·len /'sʌlən/ *adj* **1** angry and silent, especially because you feel life has been unfair to you: *Bill sat in sullen silence and refused to eat his lunch.* | *a look of sullen resentment* **2** literary a sullen sky or sea is dark and looks as if bad weather is coming —**sullenly** *adv* —**sullenness** *n* [U]

sul·ly /'sʌli/ *v* sullied, sullying, sullies [T] formal or literary to spoil or reduce the value of something that was perfect: *a scandal that sullied his reputation*

sul·phate BrE; **sulfate** AmE /'sʌlfeɪt/ *n* [C,U] a SALT formed from SULPHURIC ACID: *copper sulphate*

sul·phide BrE; **sulfide** AmE /'sʌlfaɪd/ *n* [C,U] a mixture of sulphur with another substance

sul·phur BrE; **sulfur** AmE /'sʌlfə $ -fər/ *n* [U] a common light yellow chemical substance that burns with a very strong unpleasant smell, and is used in drugs, explosives, and industry. It is a chemical ELEMENT: symbol S

sulphur di'oxide BrE; **sulfur dioxide** AmE *n* [U] a poisonous gas that is a cause of air POLLUTION in industrial areas

sul·phu·ric ac·id BrE; **sulfuric acid** AmE /sʌl͵fjʊərɪk 'æsᵻd $ -͵fjʊr-/ *n* [U] a powerful acid

sul·phu·rous BrE; **sulfurous** AmE /'sʌlfərəs/ *adj* related to, full of, or used with sulphur

sul·tan /'sʌltən/ *n* [C] a ruler in some Muslim countries

sul·ta·na /sʌl'tɑːnə $ -'tænə/ *n* [C] **1** BrE a small pale RAISIN (=dried fruit) without seeds, used in baking; ☐ **golden raisin** AmE **2** the wife, mother, or daughter of a sultan

sul·tan·ate /'sʌltəneɪt, -nᵻt/ *n* [C] **1** a country ruled by a sultan: *the sultanate of Oman* **2** the position of a sultan, or the period of time during which he rules

sul·try /'sʌltri/ *adj* **1** weather that is sultry is hot with air that feels wet; ☐ **humid**: *a hot and sultry day* | *Since the rain, the air had become heavy and still and sultry.* **2** a woman who is sultry makes other people feel strong sexual attraction to her: *She threw Carlo a sultry glance.* | *a sultry film star* —**sultriness** *n* [U]

sum[1] [S3] [W2] /sʌm/ *n* [C]
1 MONEY an amount of money: *He owes me a large sum of money.* | [+of] *the sum of £4000* | **large/substantial/considerable etc sum** *Bill wants to spend a large sum on modernizing the farm.* | **small/modest/trifling etc sum** | **for a large/small etc sum** *We should be happy to buy it for a modest sum.* → LUMP SUM; → princely sum at PRINCELY (1)
2 the sum of sth the total produced when you add two or more numbers or amounts together: *You will have to pay the sum of the two sets of costs.*
3 greater/more/better etc than the sum of its parts having a quality or effectiveness as a group that you would not expect from the quality of each member: *The team is greater than the sum of its parts.*
4 CALCULATION a simple calculation by adding, multiplying, dividing etc, especially one done by children at school
5 do your sums informal BrE to calculate whether you have enough money to do something: *Do your sums first before you decide how much to spend.*
6 in sum formal used before a statement that gives the main information about something in a few simple words: *In sum, soul music is important to the record industry.* → SUM TOTAL

sum[2] *v* summed, summing
sum up phr v **1** to give the main information in a report, speech etc in a short statement at the end; ☐ **summarize**: *Gerald will open the debate and I will sum up.* | **to sum up** *To sum up, for a healthy heart you must take regular exercise and stop smoking.* | **sum sth ⇔ up** *In your final paragraph, sum up your argument.* **2** when a judge sums up or sums up the case at the end of a TRIAL, he or she explains the main facts of the case → SUMMING-UP **3** **sum sth ⇔ up** to describe something using only a few words: *The city's problem can be summed up in three words: too many people.* **4** **sum sth ⇔ up** to show the most typical qualities of someone or something: *That image sums up the whole film.* **5** **sum sb/sth ⇔ up** to form a judgment or opinion about someone or something: *Pat summed up the situation at a glance.* **6** **that (about) sums it up** spoken used to say that a description of a situation is correct: *'So you want us to help you change but you don't believe change is possible?' 'That about sums it up.'*

sum·bitch /'sʌmbɪtʃ/ *n* [C] AmE informal not polite SON OF A BITCH

sum·ma cum lau·de /͵sʊmə kʊm 'laʊdeɪ, ͵sʌm kʌm 'lɔːdi $ ͵sʊmə kʊm 'laʊdi / *adv* AmE having achieved the highest level in your college or university degree; → cum laude: *He graduated summa cum laude in 1968.*

sum·ma·ri·ly /'sʌmərᵻli/ *adv* immediately, and without following the normal process: *He was summarily dismissed.*

sum·mar·ize also **-ise** BrE /'sʌməraɪz/ *v* [I,T] to make a short statement giving only the main information and not the details of a plan, event, report etc; ☐ **sum up**: *The authors summarize their views in the* *introduction.* | **to summarize** *To summarize, in most cases the schools were achieving the standards set.*

sum·ma·ry¹ [S1] /'sʌməri/ *n plural* **summaries** [C] a short statement that gives the main information about something, without giving all the details: *A brief summary is given on a separate sheet.* | [+of] *The group produces a monthly summary of their research.* | **in summary** *In summary, do not sell your shares.*

summary² *adj* [only before noun] **1** *formal* done immediately, and not following the normal process: *a summary execution* **2** a summary report, statement etc gives the main facts in a report etc without any of the details or explanations

sum·mat /'sʌmət/ *pron spoken* something – used in Northern England

sum·ma·tion /sə'meɪʃən/ *n* [C] *formal* **1** a SUMMARY or SUMMING-UP **2** the total amount or number when two or more things are added together

sum·mer¹ [S1] [W1] /'sʌmə $ -ər/ *n* [C,U] **1** the time of the year when the sun is hottest and the days are longest, between spring and autumn: *the long hot summer of 1976* | *The children play on the beach during the summer.* | **in (the) summer** *Miriam likes to relax in her garden in summer.* | **this/next/last summer** *We're going to Italy next summer.* | *a hot summer's day* | *a sunny summer afternoon* | *a three week summer vacation* | **early/late summer** *The tourist season lasts through late summer.* | *Parts of Spain are extremely hot in* **high summer** (=the hottest part of summer). **2 20/50 etc summers** *literary* 20, 50 etc years of age: *a child of eleven summers* → INDIAN SUMMER

summer² *v* [I] to spend the summer in a particular place

summer camp *n* [C,U] a place where children in the US can stay during the summer, and take part in various activities

summer holidays *n* [plural] *BrE* the period of time during the summer when schools and universities are closed; ▤ **summer vacation** *AmE*

sum·mer·house /'sʌməhaʊs $ -ər-/ *n* [C] a small building in your garden, where you can sit in warm weather

summer pudding *n* [C,U] a British sweet dish made from pieces of bread and fruit such as berries

summer school *n* [C,U] courses you can take in the summer at a school, university, or college

summer solstice *n* [singular] the longest day in the northern HEMISPHERE (=top half of the earth), around June 22nd

sum·mer·time /'sʌmətaɪm $ -ər-/ *n* [U] the season when it is summer: **in (the) summertime** *It doesn't rain much in the summertime.* → BRITISH SUMMER TIME

summer vacation *n* [U] *AmE* the period of time during the summer when schools and universities are closed; ▤ **summer holidays** *BrE*

sum·mer·y /'sʌməri/ *adj* suitable for or reminding you of the summer: *a light summery dress* | *a summery breeze*

summing-'up *n plural* **summings-up** [C] a statement giving the main facts but not the details of something, especially made by a judge at the end of a TRIAL: *In his summing-up, the judge said that it was dangerous to convict on this evidence alone.* → SUM UP (2)

sum·mit [W3] /'sʌmɪt/ *n* [C] **1** an important meeting or set of meetings between the leaders of several governments: *the European summit* | *The two presidents agreed to hold a summit in the spring.* | *a five-nation summit meeting* **2** the top of a mountain; → **peak**: [+of] *Many people have now reached the summit of Mount Everest.* **3 the summit of sth** *formal* the greatest amount or highest level of something; ▤ **peak**: *His election as President represented the summit of his career.*

sum·mon /'sʌmən/ *v* [T] *formal* **1** to order someone to come to a place: *Robert summoned the waiter for the bill.* | **summon sb to sth** *The president summoned Taylor to Washington.* | **summon sb to do sth** *He was summoned to attend an emergency meeting.* **2** to officially order someone to come to a court of law: *Hugh was summoned to appear before the magistrate.* **3** also **summon sth up** to try very hard to have enough of something such as courage, energy, or strength, because you need it: *He had to summon the energy to finish the race.* **4 summon a meeting/conference etc** to arrange for a meeting to take place and order people to come to it; ▤ **convene**: *He summoned a meeting of business leaders.*

summon up sth *phr v* **1** if something summons up a memory, thought, or image, it makes you remember it or think of it; ▤ **conjure up**: *The smell summoned up memories of family holidays by the sea.* **2** to try very hard to have enough courage, energy, or strength, because you need it: *Ruth took a deep breath, summoned up her courage, and told him the truth.*

sum·mons¹ /'sʌmənz/ *n plural* **summonses** [C] an official order to appear in a court of law: *The judge must issue a summons.* | *He had been accused of a drug offence but police had been unable to serve a summons on him* (=officially order him to appear in court).

summons² *v* [T usually passive] to order someone to appear in a court of law: *She has been summonsed to appear in court.* | *Basil was summonsed for wounding a police officer.*

su·mo /'suːməʊ $ -moʊ/ also **sumo wrestling** *n* [U] a Japanese form of WRESTLING, done by men who are very large —**sumo wrestler** *n* [C]

sump /sʌmp/ *n* [C] **1** the lowest part of a DRAINAGE system, where liquids or wastes remain **2** *BrE* the part of an engine that contains the supply of oil; ▤ **oil pan** *AmE*

sump·tu·ous /'sʌmptʃuəs/ *adj* very impressive and expensive: *a sumptuous feast* | *a sumptuous palace* —**sumptuously** *adv* —**sumptuousness** *n* [U]

sum total *n* **the sum total** the whole of an amount: [+of] *That's the sum total of my knowledge about it.*

sun¹ [S2] [W1] /sʌn/ *n* **1 the sun/the Sun** the large bright object in the sky that gives us light and heat, and around which the Earth moves: *The sky was blue and the sun was shining.* | *The Sun rises in the east and sets in the west.* | *The sun's rays reflected off the lake.* → see picture at SOLAR SYSTEM **2** [U] the heat and light that come from the sun: *Too much sun is bad for you.* | **in the sun** *We sat in the sun, eating ice cream.* | *the warmth of the afternoon sun* **3** [C] any star around which PLANETS move **4 everything/anything etc under the sun** used to emphasize that you are talking about a large range of things: *You can buy jeans in every colour under the sun.* **5 catch the sun** *BrE,* **get some sun** *AmE* if someone catches or gets the sun, they become slightly red or brown because they have been outside in the sun → **make hay while the sun shines** at HAY (2)

sun² *v* **sunned, sunning sun yourself** to sit or lie outside when the sun is shining: *The beaches were full of families sunning themselves.*

Sun. also **Sun** *BrE* the written abbreviation of *Sunday*

sun-baked *adj* made very hard and dry by the sun: *the sun-baked ground*

sun·bathe /'sʌnbeɪð/ *v* [I] to sit or lie outside in the sun, especially in order to become brown: *Her mother was sunbathing in the back garden.* ⚠ There is no noun 'sunbath': *Let's go and sunbathe/do some sunbathing* (NOT *have a sunbath*).

sun·beam /'sʌnbiːm/ *n* [C] a beam of light from the sun

sun·bed /'sʌnbed/ *n* [C] **1** a metal structure the size of a bed that you lie on to make your skin brown using light from special lamps **2** a SUN LOUNGER → SUNLAMP

'Sun Belt also **Sun·belt** /ˈsʌnbelt/ *n* **the Sun Belt** the southern or southwestern parts of the US, where the sun shines a lot

sun·block /ˈsʌnblɒk $ -blɑːk/ *n* [C,U] cream or oil that you rub into your skin, in order to completely stop the sun's light from burning you; → **sunscreen**

sun·burn /ˈsʌnbɜːn $ -bɜːrn/ *n* [U] red and painful skin that you can get from spending too much time in the sun

sun·burned /ˈsʌnbɜːnd $ -bɜːrnd/ also **sun·burnt** /-bɜːnt $ -bɜːrnt/ *adj* **1** having a red and painful skin as a result of spending too much time in the sun **2** having skin that is attractively brown as a result of spending time in the sun

'sun cream *n* [C,U] *BrE* a cream or oil that you rub into your skin to stop the sun from burning you too much; **目 suntan lotion**

sun·dae /ˈsʌndeɪ $ -di/ *n* [C] a dish made from ICE CREAM, fruit, sweet sauce, nuts etc: *a chocolate sundae*

Sun·day /ˈsʌndi, -deɪ/ *n* [C,U] **1** written abbreviation *Sun.* the day between Saturday and Monday: **on Sunday** *We're going to a match on Sunday.* | *What are you doing Sunday? AmE* | **Sunday morning/afternoon etc** *Sunday nights are usually pretty quiet.* | **last Sunday** *It was our wedding anniversary last Sunday.* | **this Sunday** *There's another antiques market this Sunday.* | **next Sunday** (=Sunday of next week) *We'll announce the winners next Sunday.* | **a Sunday** (=one of the Sundays in the year) *Finding a dentist on a Sunday can be very difficult.* **2 your Sunday best** your best clothes, worn only for special occasions or for church **3 Sunday driver** an insulting word meaning someone who annoys other people by driving too slowly → **never in a month of Sundays** at MONTH (6)

'Sunday school *n* [C,U] a place where children are taught about Christianity on Sundays

sun·deck /ˈsʌndek/ *n* [C] a part of a ship where people can sit in the sun

sun·der /ˈsʌndə $ -ər/ *v* [T] *literary* to break something into parts, especially violently; **目 split**

sun·dial /ˈsʌndaɪəl/ *n* [C] an object used in the past for telling the time. The shadow of a pointed piece of metal shows the time and moves round as the sun moves. → see picture at CLOCK[1]

sun·down /ˈsʌndaʊn/ *n* [U] *old-fashioned* SUNSET (1)

sun·down·er /ˈsʌnˌdaʊnə $ -ər/ *n* [C] *informal especially BrE* an alcoholic drink drunk in the evening

'sun-drenched *adj* a sun-drenched place is one where the sun shines most of the time – used especially in advertisements, magazines etc: *sun-drenched tropical islands*

sun·dress /ˈsʌndres/ *n* [C] a dress that you wear in hot weather, which does not cover your arms or shoulders

'sun-dried *adj* [only before noun] sun-dried food has been left in the sun to dry in order to give it a particular taste: *sun-dried tomatoes*

sun·dries /ˈsʌndriz/ *n* [plural] *formal* small objects that are not important enough to be named separately → SUNDRY

sun·dry /ˈsʌndri/ *adj* [only before noun] **1 all and sundry** everyone, not just a few carefully chosen people: *I don't want you telling our private business to all and sundry.* **2** *formal* not similar enough to form a group; **目 various**: *He makes films about animals, plants and sundry other subjects.*

sun·fish /ˈsʌnfɪʃ/ *n plural* **sunfish** [C,U] a fish that lives in the sea and has a large round body

sun·flow·er /ˈsʌnˌflaʊə $ -ˌflaʊər/ *n* [C] a very tall plant with a large yellow flower and seeds that can be eaten

sunflower

sung /sʌŋ/ the past participle of SING

sun·glass·es /ˈsʌnˌɡlɑːsɪz $ -ˌɡlæ-/ *n* [plural] dark glasses that you wear to protect your eyes when the sun is very bright; **目 shades**

'sun god *n* [C] a god in some ancient religions who represents the sun or has power over it

'sun hat *n* [C] a hat that you wear to protect your head from the sun

sunk /sʌŋk/ the past tense and past participle of SINK[1]

sunk·en /ˈsʌŋkən/ *adj* **1** [only before noun] having fallen to the bottom of the sea, a lake, or a river: *the wrecks of sunken ships* | *sunken treasure* **2 sunken cheeks/eyes etc** cheeks or eyes that have fallen inwards, especially because of age or illness; **目 hollow**: *Her eyes looked dull and sunken.* **3** [only before noun] built or placed at a lower level than the surrounding floor or ground: *Steps led down to a sunken garden.* | *a sunken bath*

'sun-kissed *adj literary* **1** sunny: *the famous sun-kissed resort of Acapulco* **2** sun-kissed skin or hair has been made an attractive colour by the sun

sun·lamp /ˈsʌnlæmp/ *n* [C] a lamp that produces a special light used for making your skin brown

sun·less /ˈsʌnləs/ *adj* having no light from the sun; **目 dark**: *the sunless depths of the ocean*

sun·light /ˈsʌnlaɪt/ *n* [U] natural light that comes from the sun: *The water sparkled in the bright sunlight.* | **morning/afternoon/evening sunlight** *The garden looked lovely in the evening sunlight.* | **Sunlight streamed** (=came in large amounts) *through the windows.* | **a shaft of sunlight** (=beam of sunlight)

sun·lit /ˈsʌnlɪt/ *adj* made brighter by light from the sun: *a sunlit garden*

'sun lounge *n* [C] *BrE* a room with large windows and often a glass roof, designed to let in a lot of light; **目 sun porch** *AmE*

'sun ˌlounger *n* [C] a light chair like a folding bed, which you can sit or lie on outside → see picture at CHAIR[1]

Sun·na, Sunnah /ˈsʊnə, ˈsʌnə/ *n* **the Sunna** a set of Muslim customs and rules based on the words and acts of Muhammad

Sun·ni /ˈsʊni, ˈsʌni/ *n* [C] a Muslim who follows one of the two main branches of the Muslim religion; → **Shiite**

sun·ny /ˈsʌni/ *adj* **1** having a lot of light from the sun; **目 bright**: *a warm sunny day* | *a sunny morning* | *a nice sunny room* | *I hope it's sunny tomorrow.* | *Tuesday will be dry with sunny spells* (=sunny periods). **2** *informal* happy and friendly: *a sunny smile*

ˌsunny-side 'up *adj* [not before noun] *AmE* an egg that is cooked sunny-side up is cooked in hot fat on one side only, and not turned over in the pan

'sun porch *n* [C] *AmE* a room with large windows and often a glass roof, designed to let in lots of light; **目 sun lounge** *BrE*

sun·rise /ˈsʌnraɪz/ *n* **1** [U] the time when the sun first appears in the morning; → **daybreak**: **at sunrise** *A farmer's day begins at sunrise.* **2** [C,U] the coloured part of the sky where the sun is appearing in the morning: *a picture of sunrise over Mount Fuji*

'sunrise ˌindustry *n* [C] an industry, such as ELECTRONICS or making computers, that uses modern processes and takes the place of older industries; → **sunset industry**

sun·roof /'sʌnruːf/ n [C] a part of the roof of a car that you can open to let in air and light → see picture at CAR

sun·screen /'sʌnskriːn/ n [C,U] a cream or oil that you rub into your skin to stop the sun from burning you; → **sunblock**

sun·set /'sʌnset/ n **1** [U] the time of day when the sun disappears and night begins: **at sunset** *We take the flag down at sunset.* **2** [C,U] the coloured part of the sky where the sun is disappearing at the end of the day; → **dusk**: *a glorious sunset*

sunset ˌindustry n [C] an industry that uses old equipment and methods, usually in an area that once had many industries like it, and that is becoming less successful; → **sunrise industry**: *sunset industries such as steel*

sun·shade /'sʌnʃeɪd/ n [C] an object shaped like an UMBRELLA, used especially in the past as protection from the sun; ▤ **parasol**

sun·shine S3 /'sʌnʃaɪn/ n [U]
1 the light and heat that come from the sun when there is no cloud: *We had three days of spring sunshine.* | **afternoon/morning/evening sunshine** *Couples strolled in the afternoon sunshine.*
2 *informal* happiness: *She brought sunshine into our lives.* | **ray of sunshine** (=a person or thing that makes you happy) *He was the only ray of sunshine in her life.*
3 *spoken informal* used when speaking to someone you are annoyed with: *Look, sunshine, I've had just about enough of you!*

sun·spot /'sʌnspɒt $ -spɑːt/ n [C] *technical* a small dark area on the sun's surface

sun·stroke /'sʌnstrəʊk $ -stroʊk/ n [U] fever, weakness etc caused by being outside in the sun for too long

sun·tan /'sʌntæn/ n [C] brown skin that someone with pale skin gets after they have spent time in the sun; ▤ **tan**; → **sunburn** —**suntanned** *adj*

suntan ˌlotion also **suntan ˌoil** n [C,U] a cream or oil that you rub into your skin to stop the sun from burning you too much

sun·trap /'sʌntræp/ n [C] a place that is sheltered and gets a lot of heat and light from the sun

sun-up n [U] *old-fashioned* SUNRISE

sun-ˌworshipper n [C] *informal* someone who likes to lie in the sun to get a SUNTAN

sup /sʌp/ v **supped**, **supping** **1** [T] to drink something **2** *old-fashioned* [I] to eat supper —**sup** n [C]

su·per[1] S2 /'suːpə $ -pər/ *adj informal* extremely good; ▤ **wonderful**: *an old car in super condition* | *That sounds super.* | *What a super idea!*

super[2] n [C] *informal* a SUPERINTENDENT (3)

super[3] *adv AmE spoken* extremely: *Sorry, I'm super tired, I have to turn in.*

super- /'suːpə $ -pər/ *prefix* more, larger, greater, or more powerful: *the super-rich* | *super-efficient* | *super-fit*

su·per·a·bun·dance /ˌsuːpərə'bʌndəns/ n [singular] *formal* more than enough of something: [+of] *a superabundance of cars in our streets* —**superabundant** *adj*

su·per·an·nu·at·ed /ˌsuːpər'ænjueɪtɪd/ *adj formal* old and no longer useful or no longer able to do things: *superannuated sportsmen* | *superannuated computing equipment*

su·per·an·nu·a·tion /ˌsuːpərænjuˈeɪʃən/ n [U] *technical especially BrE* money paid as a PENSION[1], especially from your former employer

ˌsuperannuˈation ˌscheme n [C] *BrE* a type of PENSION PLAN that is paid for by your employer

su·perb /sjuː'pɜːb, suː- $ suˈpɜːrb/ *adj* [no comparative] extremely good; ▤ **excellent**: *The food was superb.* | *superb weather* —**superbly** *adv*

su·per·bug /'suːpəbʌg $ -ər-/ n [C] a type of BACTERIA that cannot be killed by traditional drugs

su·per·charged /'suːpəˌtʃɑːdʒd $ -pərˌtʃɑːrdʒd/ *adj* [C] a supercharged engine is very powerful because air or FUEL is supplied to it at a higher pressure than normal

su·per·cil·i·ous /ˌsuːpə'sɪliəs $ -pər-/ *adj formal* behaving as if you think that other people are less important than you – used to show disapproval; ▤ **self-important**: *supercilious wine waiters* —**superciliously** *adv* —**superciliousness** n [U]

su·per·com·put·er /'suːpəkəmˌpjuːtə $ -pərkəmˌpjuːtər/ n [C] a computer that is more powerful than almost all other computers

su·per·con·duc·tiv·i·ty /ˌsuːpəkɒndək'tɪvɪti $ -pərkɑːn-/ n [U] the ability of some substances to allow electricity to flow through them very easily, especially at very low temperatures

su·per·con·duc·tor /ˌsuːpəkən'dʌktə $ -pərkən'dʌktər/ n [C] a substance that allows electricity to flow through it very easily, especially at very low temperatures

su·per·du·per /ˌsuːpə'duːpə $ -pər'duːpər/ *adj spoken informal* extremely good

su·per·e·go /ˌsuːpər'iːgəʊ, -'egəʊ $ -pər'iːgoʊ/ n plural **superegos** [C] *technical* used in Freudian PSYCHOLOGY to refer to the part of your mind that tells you whether what you are doing is morally right or wrong; ▤ **conscience**; → **ego, id**

su·per·fi·cial /ˌsuːpə'fɪʃəl $ -pər-/ *adj*
1 NOT LOOKING/STUDYING CAREFULLY not studying or looking at something carefully and only seeing the most noticeable things: **superficial examination/study** etc *Even a superficial inspection revealed serious flaws.* | *Naturally, such visits can allow only the most superficial understanding of prison life.*
2 APPEARANCE seeming to have a particular quality, although this is not true or real: **superficial resemblance/similarity** *Despite their superficial similarities, the two novels are in fact very different.* | *Beneath his refined manners and superficial elegance lay something treacherous.* | **at/on a superficial level** *At a superficial level, things seem to have remained the same.*
3 WOUND/DAMAGE affecting only the surface of your skin or the outside part of something, and therefore not serious: *She escaped with only superficial cuts and bruises.* | *superficial damage*
4 PERSON someone who is superficial does not think about things that are serious or important – used to show disapproval; ▤ **shallow**: *All the other girls seemed silly and superficial to Darlene.*
5 NOT IMPORTANT superficial changes, difficulties etc are not important and do not have a big effect; ▤ **minor**: *superficial changes in government policies*
6 TOP LAYER existing in or relating to the top layer of something, especially soil, rock etc —**superficially** *adv* —**superficiality** /ˌsuːpəfɪʃi'æləti $ -pər-/ n [U]

su·per·flu·i·ty /ˌsuːpə'fluːɪti $ -pər-/ n *formal* a **superfluity of sth** a larger amount of something than is necessary

su·per·flu·ous /suː'pɜːfluəs $ -'pɜːr-/ *adj formal* more than is needed or wanted; ▤ **unnecessary**: *a modern building with no superfluous decoration* —**superfluously** *adv*

super-G /'suːpə dʒiː $ -pər-/ n [singular] **super giant slalom** a race in which competitors SKI as fast as possible down a course with turns in it

Su·per·glue /'suːpəgluː $ -pər-/ n [U] *trademark* a very strong glue that sticks very quickly and is difficult to remove —**superglue** v [T]

su·per·grass /'suːpəgrɑːs $ -pərgræs/ n [C] *BrE informal* a criminal who gives the police information about many other criminals, in order to get a less severe punishment

of the program anymore.

9 **LAND** if land can support people or animals, it is of good enough quality to grow enough food for them to live: *This land can't support many cattle.*

10 **WATER/AIR/EARTH** if water, air, or earth can support life, it is clean enough, has enough oxygen etc to keep animals or plants alive: *Because of pollution, this lake is now too acid to support fish.* | *healthy soil that can support plant life*

11 **support a habit** to get money in order to pay for a bad habit, especially taking drugs: *He turned to crime to support his habit.*

support² [S2] [W2] *n*

1 **APPROVAL** [U] approval, encouragement, and perhaps help for a person, idea, plan etc: *Local people have **given** us **a lot of support** in our campaign.* | [+for] *There was **widespread support** for the war.* | **in support** *They signed a petition in support of the pay claim.* | [+of] *He had **the full support** of the general committee.* | *Thompson has **won the support** of half the party.* | *The organisers are hoping to **drum up support** (=get many people's approval) from local businesses.*

2 **SYMPATHY/HELP** [U] sympathy and help that you give to someone who is in a difficult situation or who is very unhappy: *I couldn't have made it through those times without the support of my boyfriend, Rob.*

3 **MONEY** [C,U] money that you give a person, group, organization etc to help pay for their costs: *The European Union is considering whether to provide **financial support** for the expedition.* | **with sb's support** *With your support, we can help these youngsters.*

4 **HOLD STH UP** [C,U] something that presses on something else to hold it up or in position: *The roof may need extra support.* | *the wooden supports of the bridge* | **for support** *She grabbed at his shoulders for support.*

5 **COMPUTERS** [U] the help or information that you receive to improve a computer system, make it continue working, or use it correctly: *our **technical support** team*

6 **CONCERT/PERFORMANCE** [U] a band, singer, or performer that performs for a short time at the same concert as a more famous and popular band etc: *We **played support** to a band called Shallow.* | *the **support band*** | *the **support act** (=the support band)*

7 **SOLDIERS** [U] help or protection that is given by one group of soldiers to another group who are fighting in a battle: *logistical support* | **air/ground support** (=help or protection that comes from people in aircraft or people on the ground)

8 **FOR PART OF BODY** [C] something that you wear to hold a weak or damaged part of your body in the right place: **back/neck/knee etc support** → CHILD SUPPORT, INCOME SUPPORT, LIFE SUPPORT SYSTEM, MORAL SUPPORT at MORAL¹ (3)

sup·port·er [S2] [W2] /sə'pɔːtə $ -ɔːrtər/ *n* [C]

1 someone who supports a particular person, group, or plan; → **fan**: **strong/firm/staunch supporter** *one of Bush's staunchest supporters* | [+of] *supporters of animal rights legislation*

2 *BrE* someone who likes a particular sports team, and often goes to watch them play; ⊟ **fan**: *Manchester United supporters*

sup'port group *n* [C] a group of people who meet to help each other with a particular problem, for example ALCOHOLISM

sup·port·ing /sə'pɔːtɪŋ $ -ɔːr-/ *adj* **1** **supporting part/role/actor etc** a small part in a play or film, or the actor who plays such a part **2** **supporting wall/beam etc** a wall etc that supports the weight of something

sup·por·tive /sə'pɔːtɪv $ -ɔːr-/ *adj* giving help or encouragement, especially to someone who is in a difficult situation – used to show approval: *My family were very supportive throughout the divorce.*

sup·pose [S1] [W1] /sə'pəuz $ -'pouz/ *v* [T]

SPOKEN PHRASES

1 **I suppose a)** used to say you think something is true, although you are uncertain about it; ⊟ **I guess**: **I suppose (that)** *I suppose you're right.* | *So things worked out for the best, I suppose.* | *'Aren't you pleased?' 'Yes, I suppose so.'* **b)** used when agreeing to let someone do something, especially when you do not really want to; ⊟ **I guess**: *'Can we come with you?' 'Oh, I suppose so.'* **c)** used when saying in an angry way that you expect something is true; ⊟ **I guess**: **I suppose (that)** *I suppose you thought you were being clever!* **d)** used to say that you think that something is probably true, although you wish it was not and hope someone will tell you it is not; ⊟ **I guess**: **I suppose (that)** *I suppose it's too late to apply for that job now.* **e)** used when guessing that something is true; ⊟ **I guess**: *She looked about 50, I suppose.*

2 **I don't suppose (that) a)** used to ask a question in an indirect way, especially if you think the answer will be 'no': *I don't suppose you have any idea where my address book is, do you?* **b)** used to ask for something in a very polite way: *I don't suppose you'd give me a lift to the station?* **c)** used to say that you think it is unlikely something will happen: *I don't suppose I'll ever see her again.*

3 **do you suppose (that) ...?** used to ask someone their opinion about something, although you know that it is unlikely that they have any more information about the situation than you do: *Do you suppose this is the exact spot?* | **who/what/why etc do you suppose...?** *Who on earth do you suppose could have done this?* | *How do you suppose he got here?*

4 **what's that supposed to mean?** used when you are annoyed by what someone has just said: *'It sounds like things aren't going too well for you lately.' 'What's that supposed to mean?'*

5 **suppose/supposing (that)** used when talking about a possible condition or situation, and then imagining the result: *Look, suppose you lost your job tomorrow, what would you do?* | *Supposing it really is a fire!*

6 **be supposed to do/be sth a)** used to say what someone should or should not do, especially because of rules or what someone in authority has said: *We're supposed to check out of the hotel by 11 o'clock.* | *I'm not supposed to tell anyone.* | *What time are you supposed to be there?* **b)** used to say what was or is expected or intended to happen, especially when it did not happen: *No one was supposed to know about it.* | *The meeting was supposed to take place on Tuesday, but we've had to postpone it.* | *The new laws are supposed to prevent crime.* **c)** used to say that something is believed to be true by many people, although it might not be true or you might disagree: *The castle is supposed to be haunted.* | *'Dirty Harry' is supposed to be one of Eastwood's best films.* | *Mrs Carver is supposed to have a lot of money.*

7 [not in progressive] to think that something is probably true, based on what you know; ⊟ **presume**: *There were many more deaths than was first supposed.* | **suppose (that)** *What makes you suppose we're going to sell the house?* | **There's no reason to suppose** (=it is unlikely that) *he's lying.*

8 [not in progressive] *formal* to expect that something will happen or be true, and to base your plans on it: *The company's plan supposes a steady increase in orders.*

WORD CHOICE: suppose, guess

In spoken phrases, **I suppose** and **I guess** are used in the same way, but **suppose** is more usual in British English and **guess** in American English: *I suppose that's his mum.* | *I guess you can come if you want to.* | *I guess I'll go home now.* | *'Should we sit here?' 'I suppose so.'* | *'Isn't he coming?' 'I guess not.'*

⚠ Do not say 'be suppose to do something'. Use **be supposed to**: *You're supposed to take your shoes off.* | *He's supposed to be very clever.*

sup·posed /sə'pəʊzd, sə'pəʊzɪ̯d $ -'pɑʊzd, -'pɑʊzɪ̯d/ *adj* [only before noun] claimed by other people to be true or real, although you do not think they are right: *gossip about Emma's supposed affair with Peter*

sup·pos·ed·ly /sə'pəʊzɪ̯dli $ -'poʊ-/ *adv* used when saying what many people say or believe is true, especially when you disagree with them: [sentence adverb]: *Anne is coming for a visit in March supposedly.* | *How could a supposedly intelligent person be so stupid?*

sup·po·si·tion /ˌsʌpə'zɪʃən/ *n* [C,U] something that you think is true, even though you are not certain and cannot prove it: *His version of events is pure supposition.* | **supposition (that)** *The police are acting on the supposition that she took the money.*

sup·pos·i·to·ry /sə'pɑzɪ̯təri $ sə'pɑːzɪ̯tɔːri/ *n plural* **suppositories** [C] a small piece of solid medicine that is placed in someone's RECTUM or VAGINA

sup·press /sə'pres/ *v* [T] **1** to stop people from opposing the government, especially by using force: *The uprising was ruthlessly suppressed.* **2** if important information or opinions are suppressed, people are prevented from knowing about them, even if they have a right to know: *The police were accused of suppressing evidence.* **3** to stop yourself from showing your feelings: *Harry could scarcely suppress a smile.* | *suppressed anger* **4** to prevent something from growing or developing, or from working effectively: *The virus suppresses the body's immune system.* —**suppressible** *adj* —**suppression** /sə'preʃən/ *n* [U]: *the suppression of opposition parties*

sup·press·ant /sə'presənt/ *n* [C] **appetite/cough/pain etc suppressant** a drug or medicine that makes you less hungry, cough less etc

su·pra·na·tion·al /ˌsuːprə'næʃənəl◂/ *adj* involving more than one country: *a supranational organization*

su·prem·a·cist /sʊ'preməsɪ̯st/ *n* [C] → WHITE SUPREMA-CIST

su·prem·a·cy /sʊ'preməsi/ *n* [U] the position in which you are more powerful or advanced than anyone else: *Japan's unchallenged supremacy in the field of electronics* → WHITE SUPREMACIST

su·preme /suː'priːm, sjuː-, sə- $ sʊ-, suː-/ *adj* **1** having the highest position of power, importance, or influence: *the Supreme Allied Commander in Europe* | *a country where the car reigns supreme* (=is the most important thing) **2** [only before noun] the greatest possible: *supreme courage in the face of terrible danger* | *It required a supreme effort to stay awake.* | *a matter of supreme importance* **3** **make the supreme sacrifice** to die for your country, for a principle etc

Su,preme 'Being *n* [singular] *literary* God

Su,preme 'Court *n* [singular] the most important court of law in some countries or some states of the US

su·preme·ly /suː'priːmli, sjuː-, sə- $ sʊ-, suː-/ *adv* [+ adj/adv] extremely or to the greatest possible degree: *a supremely talented player*

su·prem·o /suː'priːməʊ, sjuː- $ sʊ'priːmoʊ, suː-/ *n plural* **supremos** [C] *BrE informal* someone who controls a particular activity, organization, or industry, and has unlimited powers

Supt. the written abbreviation of *superintendent*

sur·charge¹ /'sɜːtʃɑːdʒ $ 'sɜːrtʃɑːrdʒ/ *n* [C] money that you have to pay in addition to the basic price of something: [+on] *a 10% surcharge on airline tickets*

surcharge² *v* [T] to make someone pay an additional amount of money

sure¹ S1 W1 /ʃɔː $ ʃʊr/ *adj*

1 CERTAIN YOU KNOW STH [not before noun] confident that you know something or that something is true or correct; ■ **certain:** *'That's Sarah's cousin.' 'Are you sure?'* | *'What time does the show start?' 'I'm not sure.'* | **sure (that)** *I'm sure there's a logical explanation for all this.* | *I'm sure you that you know how to get there?* | *My mother, I felt sure, had not met him before.* | **not sure how/where/when etc** *Henry wasn't sure how to answer this.* | **not sure if/whether** *I'm not sure if I'm*

pronouncing this correctly. | [+of] *He wasn't even sure of his mother's name.* | *They were talking about her, she was sure of that.* | [+about] *'That's the man I saw in the building last night.' 'Are you quite sure* (=completely sure) *about that?'*

2 **make sure a)** to find out if something is true or to check that something has been done: *'Did you lock the front door?' 'I think so, but I'd better make sure.'* | **make sure (that)** *I wanted to make sure you were all right.* | *First, make sure the printer has enough paper in it.* **b)** to do something so that you can be certain of the result: **make sure (that)** *I'll walk you home, just to make sure no one bothers you.* | **make sure of (doing) sth** *Spain made sure of their place by holding Japan to a 1–1 draw.* | *Thomas would be sorry – she would make sure of that.*

3 CERTAIN ABOUT YOUR FEELINGS [not before noun] certain about what you feel, want, like etc: **sure (that)** *Are you sure you really want a divorce?* | [+of] *Carla says she is very sure of her love for Tony.*

4 CERTAIN TO BE TRUE certain to be true: **one thing is (for) sure** *One thing's for sure, we'll never be able to move this furniture on our own.* | **sure sign/indication** *Those black clouds are a sure sign of rain.*

5 CERTAIN TO HAPPEN/SUCCEED certain to happen, succeed, or have a particular result: **sure to do sth** *He's sure to get nervous and say something stupid.* | **sure way to do sth/of doing sth** *There was only one sure way of finding out – and that was to visit him.* | **sure thing/bet** *AmE* (=something that will definitely happen, win, succeed etc)

6 **be sure of (doing) sth** to be certain to get something or be certain that something will happen: *United must beat Liverpool to be sure of winning the championship.* | *You can be sure of one thing – there'll be a lot of laughs.*

7 **sure of yourself** confident in your own abilities and opinions, sometimes in a way that annoys other people: *Kids nowadays seem very sure of themselves.*

8 **be sure to do sth** *spoken* used to tell someone to remember to do something: *Be sure to ring and let us know you've got back safely.*

9 for sure a) *informal* certainly or definitely: *No one knows for sure what really happened.* **b)** *spoken* used to emphasize that something is true: *We'll always need teachers, that's for sure.* **c)** *AmE informal spoken* used to agree with someone

10 sure thing *spoken informal* used to agree to something: *'Can you pick me up later?' 'Sure thing.'*

11 to be sure *spoken formal* used to admit that something is true, before saying something that is the opposite: *It was difficult, to be sure, but somehow we managed to finish the job.*

12 (as) sure as hell *spoken informal* used to emphasize a statement: *If I could get you out of there, I sure as hell would.*

13 have a sure hold/footing if you have a sure hold or footing, your hands or feet are placed firmly so they cannot slip —**sureness** *n* [U]

sure² *adv*

1 sure enough used to say that something did actually happen in the way that you said it would: *Sure enough, Mike managed to get lost.*

2 YES *spoken* used to say 'yes' to someone: *'Can you give me a ride to work tomorrow?' 'Sure.'*

3 ACCEPT THANKS *AmE spoken* used as a reply when you accept thanks from someone: *'Thanks for your help, Karen.' 'Sure.'*

4 EMPHASIZE *AmE informal* used to emphasize a statement: *It sure is hot out here.* | *I sure hope they get there all right.*

5 BEFORE STATEMENT *spoken* used at the beginning of a statement admitting that something is true, especially before adding something very different: *Sure Joey's happy now, but will it last?*

1 000, 2 000, 3 000, most frequent words in S poken and W ritten English

S

sure·fire /ˈʃɔːfaɪə $ ˈʃʊrfaɪr/ adj [only before noun] informal certain to succeed: Children soon learn that bad behaviour is a **surefire way** of getting attention. | a **surefire recipe** for success

sure·foot·ed /ˌʃɔːˈfʊtɪ̣d◂ $ ˌʃʊr-/ adj able to walk without sliding or falling, in a place where it is not easy to do this

sure·ly S1 W2 /ˈʃɔːli $ ˈʃʊrli/ adv
1 [sentence adverb] used to show that you think something must be true, especially when people seem to be disagreeing with you: You must have heard about the riots, surely? | There must surely be some explanation. | Surely we can't just stand back and let this happen?
2 surely not spoken used to show you cannot believe that something is true: 'The chairman's just handed in his resignation.' 'Surely not.'
3 formal certainly: Such sinners will surely be punished.
4 AmE old-fashioned used to say 'yes' to someone or to express agreement with them → **slowly but surely** at SLOWLY (2)

> WORD CHOICE: **surely, definitely, certainly, naturally, be sure to**
> Use **surely** to say that you think something must be true, especially when other people do not agree: They should be there by now, surely.
> Use **definitely** to say that something is certain to happen or be true: I will definitely be back (NOT I will surely be back) by ten.
> Use **certainly** to emphasize that something is true: He certainly is (NOT surely is) a great cook.
> Use **naturally** to mean 'as anyone would expect': They were very late, so naturally I was (NOT surely I was) worried.
> Use **be sure to** to say that something is certain to happen: If you work hard you are sure to succeed (NOT you will surely succeed).

sur·e·ty /ˈʃɔːrḷti $ ˈʃʊr-/ n plural **sureties** [C,U] law **1** someone who will pay a debt, appear in court etc if someone else fails to do so **2 stand surety (for sb)** be responsible for paying a debt, appearing in court etc if someone else fails to do so **3** money someone gives to make sure that someone will appear in court

surf¹ /sɜːf $ sɜːrf/ v [I,T] **1** to ride on waves while standing on a special board **2 surf the Net/Internet** to look quickly through information on the Internet for anything that interests you → SURFER, SURFING

surf² n [U] the white substance that forms on top of waves as they move towards the shore

sur·face¹ S2 W1 /ˈsɜːfɪ̣s $ ˈsɜːr-/ n [C]
1 WATER/LAND the top layer of an area of water or land: [+of] | Dead leaves floated on the surface of the water. | Nearly 10 percent of the Earth's surface is covered by ice. | Gas bubbles in any liquid tend to **rise to the surface**. | **beneath/under/below the surface** The tunnel was some 300 feet below the surface.
2 OUTSIDE/TOP LAYER the outside or top layer of something: [+of] the surface of the vase | The road surfaces tend to be worse in the towns than in the country. | a frying pan with a non-stick surface | **on sth's surface** mold growing on the cheese's surface
3 PERSON/SITUATION ETC the qualities, emotions etc of someone or something that are easy to notice, but which are not the only or not the real qualities, emotions etc: **on the surface** On the surface, it seems a simple story. | Half an hour later Enid had calmed down, **at least on the surface**. | **beneath the surface** I sensed a lot of tension and jealousy beneath the surface. | Prejudice is **never far beneath the surface** (=often appears) in the region. | **rise/be brought/come to the surface** Violence has risen to the surface in the inner-city.
4 FOR WORKING ON a flat area on the top of a cupboard, table, desk etc, that you use for cooking or working on: **work/kitchen surface** Keep kitchen surfaces

clean and tidy. | Work on a clean, flat surface.
5 SIDE OF AN OBJECT one of the sides of an object: How many surfaces does a cube have? → **scratch the surface** at SCRATCH¹ (8)

surface² v **1** [I] if information, feelings, or problems surface, they become known about or easy to notice: [+in] Rumors about the killings have **begun to surface** in the press. | the jealousy that had surfaced in her **2** [I] if someone or something surfaces, they suddenly appear somewhere, especially after being gone or hidden for a long time; ⊟ **pop up**: Last year Toole surfaced again in Cuba. **3** [I] to rise to the surface of water: divers surfacing near the boat **4** [I] BrE informal to get out of bed, especially late: Joe never surfaces before midday on Sunday. **5** [T] to put a surface on a road

surface³ adj [only before noun] **1** relating to the part of the army, navy etc that travels by land or on the sea, rather than by air or under the sea: the Navy's **surface forces 2** appearing to be true or real, but not representing what someone really feels or what something is really like; ⊟ **superficial**: Beneath the surface calm, she felt very insecure.

ˈsurface ˌarea n [C] the area of the outside of an object that can be measured

ˈsurface ˌmail n [U] the system of sending letters or packages by land or sea, rather than by air

ˌsurface ˈtension n [U] the way the MOLECULES in the surface of a liquid stick together so that the surface is held together

ˌsurface-to-air ˈmissile n [C] a MISSILE that is fired at planes from the land or from a ship

ˌsurface-to-surface ˌmissile n [C] a MISSILE that is fired from land or a ship at another point on land or at another ship

surf·board /ˈsɜːfbɔːd $ ˈsɜːrfbɔːrd/ n [C] a long piece of plastic, wood etc that you stand on when you go surfing

sur·feit /ˈsɜːfḷt $ ˈsɜːr-/ n formal **a surfeit of sth** an amount of something that is too large or that is more than you need; ⊟ **excess**: a surfeit of food and drink

surf·er /ˈsɜːfə $ ˈsɜːrfər/ n [C] **1** someone who rides on waves while standing on a special board **2 Net/Internet/Web surfer** someone who looks quickly through information on the Internet to find information that interests them

surf·ing /ˈsɜːfɪŋ $ ˈsɜːr-/ n [U] **1** the activity or sport of riding over the waves on a special board: When we were in Hawaii we **went surfing** every day. → see picture at WATER SPORTS **2** the activity of looking quickly through information on the Internet to find something that interests you → CHANNEL SURFING

surge¹ /sɜːdʒ $ sɜːrdʒ/ v [I] **1** [always + adv/prep] to suddenly move very quickly in a particular direction: [+forward/through etc] The taxi surged forward. | The crowd surged through the gates. **2** also **surge up** if a feeling surges or surges up, you begin to feel it very strongly: She could feel anger surging inside her. **3** [usually + adv/prep] if a large amount of a liquid, electricity, chemical etc surges, it moves very quickly and suddenly: A wave surged up towards them. | Adrenalin surged through her veins. **4** to suddenly increase; ⊟ **shoot up**: Oil prices surged.

surge² n [C usually singular] **1 a surge of sth** a sudden, large increase in a feeling: a surge of excitement **2** a sudden increase in amount or number: [+in/of] a surge in food costs | a surge of reporters' interest in his finances **3** a sudden movement of a lot of people: [+of] a surge of refugees into the country **4** a sudden quick movement of a liquid, electricity, chemical etc through something: a device that protects your computer against electrical surges

sur·geon /ˈsɜːdʒən $ ˈsɜːr-/ n [C] a doctor who does operations in a hospital → DENTAL SURGEON

sur·ge·ry S2 W2 /ˈsɜːdʒəri $ ˈsɜːr-/ n plural **surgeries**
1 [U] medical treatment in which a surgeon cuts open

prickly

sharp

jagged

fluffy

shiny

smooth

bumpy

glossy

greasy

slippery

sticky

scaly

your body to repair or remove something inside; →
operation: [+on] *She required surgery on her right
knee.* | [+for] *emergency surgery for chest injuries* | in
surgery *She was in surgery for two hours Thursday.* |
major/minor surgery *major heart surgery* | **have/un-
dergo surgery** *He underwent surgery to remove a blood
clot.* → COSMETIC SURGERY, PLASTIC SURGERY
2 [U] *especially AmE* the place where operations are
done in a hospital; ⊟ **operating room** *AmE*; ⊟ **theatre**
BrE: *Dr. Hanson is in surgery.*
3 [C] *BrE* a place where a doctor or DENTIST gives treatment; ⊟ **office** *AmE*
4 [U] *BrE* a regular period each day when people can see
a doctor or DENTIST; ⊟ **office hours** *AmE*: *Surgery is
from 9am – 1pm on weekdays.*
5 [C] *BrE* a special period of time when people can see a
MEMBER OF PARLIAMENT to discuss problems

sur·gi·cal /'sɜːdʒɪkəl $ 'sɜːr-/ *adj* [only before
noun] **1** relating to or used for medical operations:
surgical techniques | **surgical equipment/instruments/
treatment** *scalpels and other surgical instru-
ments* **2** **surgical stocking/collar etc** *BrE* a STOCKING etc
that someone wears to support a part of their body that
is injured or weak **3** done very carefully and in
exactly the right place: *With surgical precision he cut
four inches off the legs of the jeans.* —**surgically** /-kli/
adv: The lump was surgically removed.

ˌsurgical ˈspirit *n* [U] *BrE* a type of alcohol used for
cleaning wounds or skin; ⊟ **rubbing alcohol** *AmE*

ˌsurgical ˈstrike *n* [C] a carefully planned quick
military attack intended to destroy something in a
particular place without damaging the surrounding
area

sur·ly /'sɜːli $ 'sɜːrli/ *adj* bad-tempered and unfriendly;
⊟ **sullen**: *a surly teenager* —**surliness** *n* [U]

sur·mise /sə'maɪz $ sər-/ *v* [T] *formal* to guess that
something is true, using the information you know
already: **surmise that** *When he came in, he didn't look
up, so she surmised that he was in a bad mood.*
—**surmise** *n* [C,U]: *Charles was glad to have his surmise confirmed.*

sur·mount /sə'maʊnt $ sər-/ *v* [T] *formal* **1** to suc-
ceed in dealing with a problem or difficulty; ⊟ **overcome**: *He has had to surmount immense physical
disabilities.* **2** [usually passive] to be above or on top of
something: *a tower surmounted by a dome*
—**surmountable** *adj*

sur·name /'sɜːneɪm $ 'sɜːr-/ *n* [C] the name that you
share with your parents, or often with your husband if
you are a married woman, and which in English comes
at the end of your full name; ⊟ **last name, family
name**

sur·pass /sə'pɑːs $ sər'pæs/ *v* [T] to be even better or
greater than someone or something else: *He had sur-
passed all our expectations.* | *The number of multiple
births has surpassed 100,000 for the first time.* | **surpass
yourself** (=do something better than you have ever
done before) *With this painting he has surpassed himself.*
(=done better than he has ever done before)

sur·pass·ing /sə'pɑːsɪŋ $ sər'pæ-/ *adj* [only before
noun] *literary* much better than that of other people or
things: *a picture of surpassing beauty*

sur·plice /'sɜːpləs $ 'sɜːr-/ *n* [C] a piece of clothing
made of white material worn over other clothes by
priests or singers in church

sur·plus¹ /'sɜːpləs $ 'sɜːr-/ *n* [C,U] **1** an amount of
something that is more than what is needed or used;
⊟ **excess**: *Any surplus can be trimmed away.* | [+of] *a
surplus of crude oil* **2** the amount of money that a
country or company has left after it has paid for all the
things it needs: *a huge budget surplus of over £16
billion* → TRADE SURPLUS

surplus² *adj* **1** more than what is needed or used:
Ethiopia has no surplus food. | **surplus cash/funds/
revenues** *Surplus cash can be invested.* **2** **be surplus

to requirements** *BrE formal* to be no longer necessary:
*He found out he was surplus to requirements in London
and left.*

sur·prise¹ [S3] [W2] /sə'praɪz $ sər-/ *n*
1 EVENT [C] an unexpected or unusual event; →
shock: *What a surprise to find you here!* | **surprise
visit/announcement/attack etc** *Naomi paid a surprise
visit to her old school in London.* | *a surprise attack at
midnight* | **come as a surprise (to sb)** (=happen unex-
pectedly) *The triumph came as a surprise to many
fans.* | *It should **come as no surprise** (=you should
expect it to happen) that cycling builds leg strength.* |
there is a surprise in store (for sb) (=something unex-
pected is going to happen to them) | *If you go to Ontario
in summer, you're **in for a few surprises**.
2 FEELING [C,U] the feeling you have when something
unexpected or unusual happens; → **shock**: *The man
had a look of surprise on his face.* | **get/have a surprise**
*She got a surprise when she turned the letter over. It was
from Finn.* | **in/with surprise** *Bill looked at him in
surprise.* | **to sb's surprise** (=in a way that surprises
someone) *Much to his surprise she gave him her phone
number.* | *To everyone's surprise, they got married.*
3 **take/catch sb by surprise** to happen unexpectedly:
The question took her by surprise.
4 **take sb/sth by surprise** to suddenly attack a place or
an opponent when they are not ready: *The guerrillas
were killed when army troops took them by surprise.*
5 GIFT/PARTY ETC [C usually singular] an unexpected
present, trip etc which you give to someone or organize
for them, often on a special occasion: [+for] *'I've got a
surprise for you,' she said.*
6 **surprise guest/visitor etc** someone who arrives somewhere unexpectedly
7 **surprise!** *spoken* used when you are just about to
show someone something that you know will surprise
them
8 a) **surprise, surprise** used when saying in a joking
way that you expected something to happen or be true:
*The American TV networks are, surprise, surprise, full
of stories about the election.* b) *BrE spoken* used when
you suddenly appear in front of someone who you
know is not expecting to see you
9 METHOD [U] the use of methods which are intended
to cause surprise: *An **element of surprise** is important
to any attack.*

surprise² *v* [T] **1** to make someone feel surprised; →
shock: *His strange question surprised her.* | **it surprises
sb to see/find/know etc** *It had surprised me to find how
fussy he was about some things.* | *I didn't know you two
knew each other. Mind you, **it doesn't surprise me**.* |
*What surprised me most was that she didn't seem to
care.* | **it surprises sb (that)** *Looking back, does it
surprise you that she left?* | *It **wouldn't surprise** me if
he married Jo.* **2** to find, catch, or attack someone
when they are not expecting it, especially when they
are doing something they should not be doing: *A
security guard surprised the burglars in the storeroom.*

sur·prised [S2] [W2] /sə'praɪzd $ sər-/ *adj* having a
feeling of surprise: *He **looked surprised** to see Cassie
standing by the front door.* | [+at/by] *We were greatly
surprised at the news.* | **surprised (that)** *She was sur-
prised that no one was there to greet her.* | **surprised to
see/hear/learn etc** *I bet she'll be really surprised to see
me.* | *He had a **surprised look** on his face.* | **Don't be
surprised if** *the interviewer is rather direct.* | *I
wouldn't be surprised if she married that fellow.*

WORD FOCUS: SURPRISED
very surprised: **amazed, astonished, astounded, dumbfounded, staggered, flabbergasted, gobsmacked** *BrE
informal*, **speechless, be lost for words, can't believe
your eyes/ears**
→ **shocked**

sur·pris·ing [S3] [W3] /sə'praɪzɪŋ $ sər-/ *adj* unusual or
unexpected: *She told me a surprising thing.* | *A surpris-
ing number of his paintings have survived.* | **it is
surprising (that)** *It is not surprising that most parents
experience occasional difficulties.* | **it is surprising how/**

what etc *It's surprising how quickly you get used to things.* | *It is **hardly surprising** that new mothers often suffer from depression.*

sur·pris·ing·ly W3 /sə'praızıŋli $ sər-/ *adv* unusually or unexpectedly: *The exam was surprisingly easy.* | *Not surprisingly, with youth unemployment so high, some school-leavers with qualifications fail to find jobs.*

sur·real /sə'rıəl/ also **surrealistic** *literary adj* a situation or experience that is surreal is very strange and difficult to understand, like something from a dream: *The house was a surreal mixture of opulence and decay.*

sur·real·is·m /sə'rıəlızəm/ *n* [U] 20th century art or literature in which the artist or writer connects unrelated images and objects in a strange way —**surrealist** *adj: a surrealist painting* —**surrealist** *n* [C]

sur·real·is·tic /sə,rıə'lıstık◂/ *adj* **1** seeming very strange because of a combination of many unusual, unrelated events, images etc **2** relating to surrealism —**surrealistically** /-kli/ *adv*

sur·ren·der¹ /sə'rendə $ -ər-/ *v* **1** [I,T] to say officially that you want to stop fighting or to stop avoiding the police, government etc because you realize that you cannot win: *The terrorists were given ten minutes to surrender.* | **surrender to sb** *Thousands of illegal immigrants in Japan have surrendered to police.* | **surrender yourself (to sb)** *He immediately surrendered himself to the authorities.* **2** [T] to give your soldiers, land or weapons to an enemy after you have been defeated: *They were given two hours to surrender their weapons.* **3** [T] to give up something or someone because you are forced to: *Cath was most reluctant to surrender her independence.* | *Marchers who had cameras were forced to surrender their film.* **4 surrender to sth** to allow yourself to be controlled or influenced by something: *Colette surrendered to temptation and took out a cigarette.* **5** [T] *formal* to give something such as a ticket or a PASSPORT to an official: **surrender sth to sb** *Steir voluntarily surrendered his license to the State.*

surrender² *n* [singular, U] **1** when you say officially that you want to stop fighting because you realize that you cannot win: *the humiliation of **unconditional surrender** (=accepting total defeat)* | **surrender to sb/sth** *the Nazis' surrender to the Allied forces* **2** when you give away something or someone, usually because you are forced to: [+of] *a surrender of power* | *the surrender of all illegal weapons* **3** when you allow yourself to be controlled or influenced by something: *total surrender to drug addiction*

sur·rep·ti·tious /,sʌrəp'tıʃəs◂ $,sɜː-/ *adj* done secretly or quickly because you do not want other people to notice: *Rory tried to sneak a **surreptitious** glance at Adam's wristwatch.* —**surreptitiously** *adv* —**surreptitiousness** *n* [U]

sur·rey /'sʌri $ 'sɜː-/ *n* [C] *AmE* a light carriage with two seats, which was pulled by a horse and was used in the past

sur·ro·gate¹ /'sʌrəgeıt, -gⅰt $ 'sɜːr-/ *adj* [only before noun] a surrogate person or thing is one that takes the place of someone or something else: *William was acting as a **surrogate father** for his brother's son.*

surrogate² *n* [C] **1** a person or thing that takes the place of someone or something else: [+for] *Bright-light therapy is used as a surrogate for sunshine.* **2** a surrogate mother

surrogate 'mother also **surrogate** *n* [C] a woman who has a baby for another woman who cannot have one, and then gives the baby after it is born

sur·round¹ W2 /sə'raʊnd/ *v* [T]
1 [usually passive] to be all around someone or something on every side: **be surrounded by sth** *The field was surrounded by trees.* | *He glared at the people who surrounded the tent.*
2 be surrounded by sb/sth to have a lot of a particular

type of people or things near you: *He's always been surrounded by people who adore him.*
3 if police or soldiers surround a place, they arrange themselves in positions all the way around it: *Armed police surrounded a house in the High Street.*
4 to be closely related to a situation or event: *Some of the issues surrounding alcohol abuse are very complex.* | *Silence and secrecy surround the murder.*
5 surround yourself with sb/sth to choose to have certain people or things near you all the time: *The designer surrounded himself with exquisite objects.*

surround² *n* [C] an area around the edge of something, especially one that is decorated or made of a different material: *a solid mahogany fire surround*

sur·round·ing /sə'raʊndıŋ/ *adj* [only before noun] near or around a particular place; ▣ **nearby:** *Troops sealed off the **surrounding area**.* | *We decided to explore the **surrounding countryside**.*

sur·round·ings /sə'raʊndıŋz/ *n* [plural] the objects, buildings, natural things etc that are around a person or thing at a particular time: **sb's surroundings** *He switched on the light and examined his surroundings.* | *I need to work in pleasant surroundings.*

sur'round-,sound, surround sound *n* [U] a system of four or more SPEAKERS (=pieces of equipment that sound comes out of) used so that sounds from a film or television programme come from all directions —**surround-sound** *adj* [only before noun]: *surround-sound speakers*

sur·tax /'sɜːtæks $ 'sɜːr-/ *n* [U] an additional tax on money you earn if it is higher than a particular amount

sur·veil·lance /sə'veıləns $ sər-/ *n* [U] **1** when the police, army, etc watch a person or place carefully because they may be connected with criminal activities: [+of] *24-hour surveillance of the building* | **under surveillance** *They were under constant close surveillance day and night.* | *The suspects were **kept under surveillance**.* | *electronic surveillance equipment* **2** when one country watches the military activities of another country to see what they are planning to do: *a surveillance mission* | *surveillance aircraft* **3** when doctors, health departments etc watch an ill person or watch the development of a disease in a population: **under surveillance** *Diane was placed under psychiatric surveillance.*

sur·vey¹ S3 W3 /'sɜːveı $ 'sɜːr-/ *n* [C]
1 a set of questions that you ask a large number of people in order to find out about their opinions or behaviour: **carry out/conduct a survey** (=do a survey) *We conducted a survey of parents in the village.* | [+of] *survey of US businesses* | **survey shows/reveals (that)** *The survey showed that Britain's trees are in good health.*
2 an examination of an area of land in order to make a map of it
3 *BrE* an examination of a house or other building done especially for someone who wants to buy it
4 a general description or report about a particular subject or situation: *a survey of modern English literature*

sur·vey² /sə'veı $ sər-/ *v* [T] **1** [usually passive] to ask a large number of people questions in order to find out their attitudes or opinions: *Of the 100 companies surveyed, 10 per cent had a turnover of £50m to £99m.* **2** to look at or consider someone or something carefully, especially in order to form an opinion about them: *She turned to survey her daughter's pale face.* | *They got out of the car to survey the damage.* **3** *BrE* to examine the condition of a house or other building and make a report on it, especially for people who want to buy it **4** to examine and measure an area of land and record the details on a map: *There were many voyages to survey the ocean depths in the nineteenth century.*

survey course n [C] *AmE* a university course that gives an introduction to a subject for people who have not studied it before

sur·vey·or /sə'veɪə $ sər'veɪər/ n [C] someone whose job is to examine the condition of a building, or to measure and record the details of an area of land → QUANTITY SURVEYOR

sur·viv·al W3 /sə'vaɪvəl $ sər-/ n
1 [U] the state of continuing to live or exist: [+of] *Illegal hunting is threatening the survival of the species.* | *The doctors gave him a one-in-ten **chance of survival**.* | *A lot of small companies are having to **fight for survival** (=work hard in order to continue to exist).*
2 survival of the fittest a situation in which only the strongest and most successful people or things continue to exist
3 a survival from sth *especially BrE* something that has continued to exist from a much earlier period, especially when similar things have disappeared; ▤ **relic**: *The cult is a survival from the old Zoroastrian religion.*

sur'vival kit n [C] a set of things in a special container that you need to help you stay alive if you get hurt or lost

sur·vive S2 W2 /sə'vaɪv $ sər-/ v
1 [I,T] to continue to live after an accident, war, or illness: *Only 12 of the 140 passengers survived.* | *She survived the attack.* | *people who survive cancer*
2 [I,T] to continue to live normally in spite of many problems: *I'm sure she will survive this crisis.* | *I've had a tough few months, but I'll survive.*
3 [I] to manage to live a normal life even though you have very little money: [+on] *I don't know how you all manage to survive on Jeremy's salary.* | *the amount that a family needs each week just to survive*
4 [I] to continue to exist after a long time: *A few pages of the original manuscript still survive.* | [+from] *Several buildings in the town have survived from medieval times.* | [+into] *an old custom which has survived into the twenty-first century* | [+as] *The main building was demolished, but the library still survives as a museum.*
5 [I,T] to continue to be successful: *The car industry cannot survive without government help.* | *A lot of smaller firms did not survive the recession.*
6 [T] to live longer than someone else, usually someone closely related to you: *He is survived by his wife, Sue.*

sur·vi·vor /sə'vaɪvə $ sər'vaɪvər/ n [C] **1** someone who continues to live after an accident, war, or illness: [+of] *Emergency help is needed for survivors of the earthquake.* | *She was the **sole survivor** (=only survivor) of the massacre.* **2** someone who manages to live normally in spite of many problems: *Don't worry about Kurt; he's a survivor.* **3** someone who continues to live after other members of their family have died: *She was the last survivor of the family.* **4** a company that continues to be successful in spite of many problems: *The company hopes to be one of the survivors of this recession.*

sus·cep·ti·bil·i·ty /sə,septɪ'bɪlɪti/ n plural **susceptibilities** **1** [C,U] how easily someone or something is affected by something: [+to] *One of the side effects of the drug is an increased susceptibility to infections.* **2 sb's susceptibilities** *formal* someone's feelings, especially when they are easily offended or upset: *I knew I would have to be careful not to **offend** their susceptibilities.*

sus·cep·ti·ble /sə'septɪbəl/ adj **1** likely to suffer from a particular illness or be affected by a particular problem; → **immune**: [+to] *Older people are more susceptible to infections.* | *Soil on the mountain slopes is very susceptible to erosion.* **2** a susceptible person is easily influenced or attracted by someone or something; ▤ **impressionable**: *A lot of TV advertising is aimed at susceptible young children.* | [+to] *She was very susceptible to flattery.* **3 susceptible of sth** *formal* if something is susceptible of an action, that action

can be done to it: *Working conditions are susceptible of improvement by legislation.*

su·shi /'suːʃi/ n [U] a Japanese dish that consists of small cakes of cooked rice served with raw fish

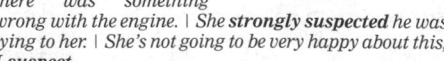

sushi

sus·pect¹ S2 W3 /sə'spekt/ v [T not in progressive]
1 to think that something is probably true, especially something bad: **suspect (that)** *I suspected that there was something wrong with the engine.* | *She **strongly suspected** he was lying to her.* | *She's not going to be very happy about this, I suspect.*
2 to think that something bad has happened or is happening: *The doctors suspected pneumonia.* | **suspect murder/foul play** *The position of the body led the police to suspect murder.* | **suspect something/nothing/anything** *He never suspected anything.*
3 to think that someone is probably guilty of a crime: *Who do you suspect?* | **suspect sb of (doing) sth** *He's suspected of murder.* | *Pilcher was suspected of giving away government secrets to the enemy.*
4 to think that something is not honest or true: *I began to suspect his motives in inviting me.*

sus·pect² /'sʌspekt/ n [C] **1** someone who is thought to be guilty of a crime: *Two suspects were arrested today in connection with the robbery.* | *Police have issued a description of the murder suspect.* | [+for] *the two suspects for the robbery* | [+in] *A suspect in a burglary case* | **main/prime/chief suspect** *Davies is still the chief suspect.* **2 the usual suspects** the people or things that are usually involved in or responsible for a particular activity: *a wine shop stocking all the usual suspects: wines from California, France, Australia*

sus·pect³ adj **1** not likely to be completely honest; ▤ **dodgy**: *I've always thought he was a bit of a suspect character.* | *The company was involved in some **highly suspect** business dealings.* **2** not likely to be completely true: *The two men were convicted on the basis of some **highly suspect** evidence.* **3** likely to have problems and not work well: *The engine sounded a bit suspect.* **4** [only before noun] likely to contain a bomb or something illegal or dangerous: *Police were called in to check out a suspect van.*

sus·pect·ed /sə'spektɪd/ adj [only before noun] **1 suspected burglar/terrorist/spy etc** someone who is thought to be guilty of a crime: *a suspected child killer* **2** if you have a suspected illness or injury, doctors think that you might have it but do not know for certain: *He was taken to hospital after a suspected heart attack.*

sus·pend /sə'spend/ v [T]
1 STOP to officially stop something from continuing, especially for a short time: *Sales of the drug will be suspended until more tests are completed.* | *Talks between the two countries have now been suspended.*
2 LEAVE A JOB/SCHOOL to make someone leave their school or job for a short time, especially because they have broken the rules: *The two police officers have been suspended until an enquiry is carried out.* | **suspend sb from sth** *Dave was suspended from school for a week.*
3 HANG *formal* to attach something to a high place so that it hangs down: **suspend sth from sth** *A large light was suspended from the ceiling.* | **suspend sth by sth** *He was suspended by his feet and beaten with metal bars.*
4 suspend judgment to decide not to make a firm decision or judgment about something until you know more about it
5 suspend disbelief to try to believe that something is true, for example when you are watching a film or play
6 be suspended in sth *technical* if something is suspended in a liquid or in air, it floats in it without moving

sus‚pended ani'mation n [U] **1** a state in which a person or creature is unconscious and their body works very slowly, but from which they can wake up when the situation is right **2** a feeling that you cannot do anything because you are waiting for something to happen

sus‚pended 'sentence n [C] a punishment given by a court in which a criminal is told they will be sent to prison if they do anything else illegal within the time mentioned: *a two-year suspended sentence*

sus·pend·er /sə'spendə $ -ər/ n **1** [C usually plural] *BrE* a part of a piece of women's underwear that hangs down and can be attached to STOCKINGS to hold them up; ▤ **garter** *AmE* **2 suspenders** [plural] *AmE* two bands of cloth that go over your shoulders and fasten to your trousers to hold them up; ▤ **braces** *BrE*

sus'pender ‚belt n [C] *BrE* a piece of women's underwear with suspenders joined to it; ▤ **garter belt** *AmE*

sus·pense /sə'spens/ n [U] a feeling of excitement or anxiety when you do not know what will happen next; → **tension**: **in suspense** *They kept us* **in suspense** *for over two hours.* | *Come on then, tell me what happened;* **the suspense is killing me** (=I feel very excited or anxious because I do not know what will happen next).* | *She couldn't* **bear the suspense** *a moment longer.* | **suspense novel/story/movie etc** (=one which is exciting because you do not know what will happen next)

sus·pen·sion /sə'spenʃən/ n
1 STOPPING STH [U] when something is officially stopped for a period of time: [| **of**] *Both sides are now working towards a suspension of hostilities.*
2 MAKING SB LEAVE [C] when someone is not allowed to go to school, do their job, or take part in an activity for a period of time as a punishment: *He received a six-month suspension for unprofessional behaviour.* | [+**from**] *The fight led to his suspension from school.*
3 PART OF A VEHICLE [U] a part attached to the wheels of a vehicle that makes it more comfortable on roads that are not smooth: *a car with an excellent suspension system*
4 LIQUID [C] *technical* a liquid mixture in which very small pieces of solid material are contained in the liquid but have not combined with it

sus'pension ‚bridge n [C] a bridge that has no supports under it, but is hung from strong steel ropes fixed to towers → see picture at BRIDGE[1]

sus·pi·cion /sə'spɪʃən/ n **1** [C,U] a feeling you have that someone is probably guilty of doing something wrong or dishonest: *I can't say for definite who did it, but I certainly* **have** *my* **suspicions**.* | *Police* **suspicions were confirmed** *when the stolen property was found in his flat.* | *I wondered how I could leave early without* **arousing** *anyone's* **suspicions**.* | **on suspicion of (doing) sth** *She was arrested on suspicion of murder.* | **under suspicion** *He felt he was still under suspicion.* | *Mitchell later* **came under suspicion** *of assaulting two young girls.* | **above/beyond suspicion** *She felt that she ought to be above suspicion* (=so honest that no one could think that she had done anything wrong).* **2** [C,U] a feeling that you do not trust someone: *She always* **treated** *us* **with suspicion**.* | *People moving into the area are often* **regarded with suspicion**.* **3** [C] a feeling you have that something is true, especially something bad: **suspicion (that)** *I have a suspicion that the local authority may be planning to close the school.* | *She was left with a* **sneaking suspicion** (=a small suspicion) *that Steven was not telling the truth.* **4 a suspicion of sth** *formal* a very small amount of something that you can only just see, hear, or taste: *I could see the faintest suspicion of a tear in her eyes.*

sus·pi·cious S3 /sə'spɪʃəs/ adj
1 thinking that someone might be guilty of doing something wrong or dishonest: [+**of**] *Some of his colleagues at work became suspicious of his behaviour.* | [+**about**] *They were suspicious about my past.* | *His*

reluctance to answer my questions **made** me **suspicious**.* | *She gave him a suspicious glance.* | *You've got a very suspicious mind!*
2 making you think that something bad or illegal is happening: *They found a suspicious package under the seat.* | *a suspicious death* | *He was behaving in a* **highly suspicious** *manner.* | *a suspicious-looking character* | **something/anything/nothing suspicious** *Call the police if you see anything suspicious.* | *Her mother had died* **in suspicious circumstances**.
3 feeling that you do not trust someone or something; ▤ **wary**: [+**of**] *She was always suspicious of strangers.* | *He was* **deeply suspicious** *of the legal system.*

sus·pi·cious·ly /sə'spɪʃəsli/ adv **1** in a way that shows you think someone has done something wrong or dishonest: *Meg looked at me suspiciously.* | *'What do you want it for?' he asked suspiciously.* **2** in a way that makes people think that something bad or illegal is happening: *He saw two youths* **acting suspiciously**.* | *He seemed to be taking a suspiciously long time.* | *This sounded* **suspiciously like** *an attempt to get rid of me.* **3** in a way that shows you do not trust something or someone: *They eyed the food suspiciously.*

suss /sʌs/ v also **suss sb/sth out** [T] *BrE informal* to realize or discover something, or to find out the things that you need to know about someone or something: *He finally sussed out the truth.* | **suss (that)** *I soon sussed that she wasn't telling me the truth.*

sussed /sʌst/ adj *BrE informal* knowing all about someone or something: *These boys are sussed and streetwise.* | **have/get sb/sth sussed** *Don't worry, I've got him sussed.*

sus·tain W3 /sə'steɪn/ v [T]
1 MAKE STH CONTINUE to make something continue to exist or happen for a period of time; ▤ **maintain**: *She found it difficult to sustain the children's interest.* | *He was incapable of sustaining close relationships with women.* | *the policies necessary to sustain economic growth* → SUSTAINED
2 SUFFER *formal* to suffer damage, an injury, or loss of money: *Two of the fire-fighters sustained serious injuries.* | *Some nearby buildings sustained minor damage.* | *The company has sustained heavy financial losses this year.*
3 FOOD/DRINK *formal* if food or drink sustains a person, animal, or plant, it makes them able to continue living: *They gave me barely enough food to sustain me.*
4 GIVE STRENGTH *formal* to make someone feel strong and hopeful: *The thought of seeing her again was all that sustained me.*
5 WEIGHT *formal* to hold up the weight of something; ▤ **support**: *He leant against her so heavily that she could barely sustain his weight.*
6 IDEA *formal* to support an idea or argument, or prove that it is right: *This argument is difficult to sustain.*

sus·tain·a·ble /sə'steɪnəbəl/ adj **1** able to continue without causing damage to the environment: *The government should do more to promote sustainable agriculture.* | *the sustainable use of rainforest resources* | *Cycling is a totally sustainable form of transport.* | **environmentally sustainable** *development* → see picture at ENVIRONMENT **2** able to continue for a long time: *The party is promising low inflation and sustainable economic growth.* —**sustainability** /sə‚steɪnə'bɪləti/ n [U]

sus·tained /sə'steɪnd/ adj [only before noun] continuing for a long time: *a period of sustained economic development* | *a sustained attack on the government*

sus·te·nance /'sʌstənəns/ n [U] *formal* **1** food that people or animals need in order to live: *Without sustenance, the animals will soon die.* | *Potatoes were their* *only means of sustenance.* **2** when something is made to continue: *Elections are necessary for the sustenance of democracy.*

sut·tee /'sʌti: $ sʌ'ti:, 'sʌti:/ *n* [U] the ancient custom in the Hindu religion of burning a wife with her husband when he dies

su·ture /'su:tʃə $ -ər/ *n* [C] *medical* a stitch that is used to sew a wound together —**suture** *v* [T]

SUV /,es ju: 'vi:/ *n* [C] *AmE* **sport-utility vehicle** a type of vehicle that is bigger than a car and is made for travelling over rough ground

su·ze·rain·ty /'su:zəreɪnti $ -rənti, -reɪnti/ *n* [U] *formal* the right of a country or leader to rule over another country

svelte /svelt/ *adj literary* thin and graceful; ⊟ **lithe**: *She was slim, svelte, and sophisticated.*

Sven·ga·li /sven'gɑ:li/ *n* [C] a man who has the power to control people's minds and make them do bad or immoral things

SW the written abbreviation of *southwest* or *southwestern*

swab¹ /swɒb $ swɑ:b/ *n* [C] **1** a small piece of material used to clean a wound or take a small amount of a substance from someone's body in order to test it: *a cotton swab* **2** a small amount of a substance that is taken from someone's body with a swab in order to test it: *The doctor took a throat swab to check for infection.*

swab² *v* **swabbed, swabbing** [T] **1** also **swab sth down** to clean something using a large amount of water: *a girl who was swabbing the tiled floor with a mop* **2** to clean a wound with a small piece of special material

swad·dle /'swɒdl $ 'swɑ:dl/ *v* [T] *old-fashioned* to wrap a baby tightly to keep it warm and protect it

'swaddling ,clothes *n* [plural] *old use* large pieces of cloth that people used to wrap around babies to keep them warm and protect them

swag /swæg/ *n* **1** [U] *old-fashioned informal* goods that someone has stolen; ⊟ **loot** **2** [C] **a)** a large piece of material that is hung above a window as decoration **b)** a rope covered with flowers or fruit that is hung somewhere as decoration, or CARVED or painted on something **3** [U] *AusE old-fashioned* clothes and possessions that someone who is travelling on foot carries wrapped in a cloth

swag·ger¹ /'swægə $ -ər/ *v* [I always + adv/prep] to walk proudly, swinging your shoulders in a way that shows you are very confident – used to show disapproval: *He swaggered over towards me.*

swagger² *n* [singular, U] a way of walking, talking, or behaving that shows you are very confident – used in order to show disapproval: *He walked in with a swagger.*

swain /sweɪn/ *n* [C] *old use* a young man from the country who loves a woman

swal·low¹ ⒮³ /'swɒləʊ $ 'swɑ:loʊ/ *v*
1 FOOD [I,T] to make food or drink go down your throat and towards your stomach: *He swallowed the last of his coffee and asked for the bill.* | *Most snakes swallow their prey whole.*
2 NERVOUSLY [I] to make some of the liquid in your mouth go down your throat because you are frightened or nervous: *Leo swallowed hard and walked into the room.* | *She swallowed nervously before beginning.*
3 BELIEVE/ACCEPT [T] *informal* to believe a story, explanation etc that is not actually true: *Do they really think we are stupid enough to swallow that?* | *I found his story a bit hard to swallow* (=difficult to believe).
4 FEELINGS [T] to stop yourself from showing a feeling, especially anger: *She swallowed her anger and turned to face him.*
5 swallow your pride to do something even though it is embarrassing for you, because you have no choice: *I swallowed my pride and phoned him.* → **a bitter pill (to**

swallow) at BITTER¹ (7)
swallow sb/sth ⇔ **up** *phr v*
1 if a company or country is swallowed up by a larger one, it becomes part of it and no longer exists on its own: *Hundreds of small companies have been swallowed up by these huge multinationals.*
2 *written* if something is swallowed up, it disappears because something covers it or hides it: *Jane was soon swallowed up in the crowd.* | *The countryside is gradually being swallowed up by new developments.*
3 if an amount of money is swallowed up, you have to spend it to pay for things: *The extra cash was soon swallowed up.*

swallow² *n* [C] **1** a small black and white bird that comes to northern countries in the summer **2** an action in which you make food or drink go down your throat: *He downed his whisky in one swallow.*

swam /swæm/ the past tense of SWIM¹

swa·mi /'swɑ:mi/ *n* [C] a Hindu religious teacher

swamp¹ /swɒmp $ swɑ:mp/ *n* [C,U] land that is always very wet or covered with a layer of water —**swampy** *adj*: *the soft, swampy ground*

swamp² *v* [T] **1** [usually in passive] to suddenly give someone a lot of work, problems etc to deal with: **be swamped by/with sth** *We've been swamped with phone calls since the advert appeared.* **2** [usually in passive] to go somewhere or surround something in large numbers, especially in a short period of time: **be swamped by/with sth** *In the summer the village is swamped by visitors.* **3** to suddenly cover an area with a lot of water: *Huge waves swamped the vessel.*

swan¹ /swɒn $ swɑ:n/ *n* [C] a large white bird with a long neck that lives on rivers and lakes

swan² *v* **swanned, swanning** [I always + adv/prep] *BrE informal* to enjoy yourself and behave in a relaxed way that is annoying to other people: [+off/around] *He's gone swanning off to Rome for the weekend!*

swank¹ /swæŋk/ *v* [I] *BrE old-fashioned* to speak or behave in a way that shows you think you are better than other people: *I wish you'd stop swanking!*

swank² *n* *BrE old-fashioned* [U] proud, confident behaviour that shows you think you are better than other people

swank·y /'swæŋki/ *adj informal* very fashionable and expensive: *eating meals at swanky hotels*

swan·song /'swɒnsɒŋ $ 'swɑ:nsɔ:ŋ/ *n* [C] the last piece of work that an artist or writer produces, or the last time someone gives a performance: *This concert will be her swansong.*

swap¹ ⒮³ , **swop** /swɒp $ swɑ:p/ *BrE v* **swapped, swapping**
1 [I,T] to give something to someone and get something in return; ⊟ **exchange**: *Do you want to swap umbrellas?* | **swap sth for sth** *He swapped his watch for a box of cigars.* | **swap sth with sb** *The girls chatted and swapped clothes with each other.*
2 [T] to tell information to someone and be given information in return; ⊟ **exchange**: *We need to get together to swap ideas and information.* | *They sat in a corner and swapped gossip.*
3 also **swap over** [T] to do the thing that someone else has been doing, and let them do the thing that you have been doing; ⊟ **change**: *They decided to swap roles for the day.* | *You start on the windows and I'll do the walls, then we can swap over after an hour or so.* | **swap with sb** *She ended up swapping jobs with her secretary.*
4 [T] to stop using or get rid of one thing and put or get another thing in its place: *The driver announced that we would have to swap buses.* | **swap sth for sth** *She had swapped her long skirts for jeans and T shirts.* | *She swapped his London home for a cottage in Scotland.*
5 also **swap sth around** [T] to move one thing and put another in its place: *Someone had gone into the nursery and swapped all the babies around.* | **swap sth with sth** *Why don't we swap the TV with the bookcase?*
6 swap places *BrE* to let someone sit or stand in your

place, so that you can have their place; ▤ **change places:** *Can we swap places, please?*

swap² *n* [C] *informal* **1** [usually singular] a situation in which you give something to someone and get another thing in return; ▤ **exchange:** *a fair swap* | *We can do a swap if you like.* **2** a situation in which people each do the job that the other usually does

'swap ,meet *n* [C] *AmE* an occasion when people meet to buy and sell used goods, or to exchange them

sward /swɔːd $ swɔːrd/ *n* [C] *literary* an area of land covered with grass

swarm¹ /swɔːm $ swɔːrm/ *n* [C] **1** a large group of insects, especially BEES, moving together **2** a crowd of people who are moving quickly: [+of] *Swarms of tourists jostled through the square.*

swarm² *v* [I] **1** [always + adv/prep] if people swarm somewhere, they go there as a large, uncontrolled crowd: *Photographers were swarming around the princess.* **2** if BEES swarm, they leave a HIVE (=place where they live) in a large group to look for another home
  swarm with sb/sth *phr v* to be full of a moving crowd of people or animals: *The museum was swarming with tourists.*

swar·thy /'swɔːði $ -ɔːr-/ *adj* someone who is swarthy has dark skin: *a small, swarthy man* | *a swarthy complexion*

swash·buck·ling /'swɒʃˌbʌkəlɪŋ $ 'swaːʃ-, 'swɒːʃ-/ *adj* relating to adventures in which people do brave, exciting things and fight against their enemies with swords: *a swashbuckling hero* | *a swashbuckling tale of pirates* —**swashbuckler** *n* [C]

swas·ti·ka /'swɒstɪkə $ 'swaː-/ *n* [C] a sign consisting of a cross with each end bent at 90°, used as a sign for the Nazi Party in Germany

swat /swɒt $ swaːt/ *v* **swatted**, **swatting** [T] to hit an insect in order to kill it: *He calmly swatted a couple of flies.* —**swat** *n* [C]

swatch /swɒtʃ $ swaːtʃ/ *n* [C] a small piece of cloth that people look at when they are choosing cloth for clothes or for their home

swathe¹ /sweɪð $ swaːð, swɒð/ also **swath** /swɒθ $ swaːθ/ *n* [C] **1** a long thin area of something, especially land: [+of] *The bomb had left a swathe of the town centre in ruins.* | *A swathe of sunlight lay across the floor.* **2** a long thin area of grass or plants that has been cut down: *We cut a swathe through the dense undergrowth.* **3** cut a swathe through sth to destroy a large amount or part of something

swathe² *v* [T usually in passive] *literary* to wrap or cover something in something: *women swathed in expensive furs* | *The moon was swathed in mist.*

SWAT team /'swɒt tiːm $ 'swaːt-/ *n* [C] especially *AmE* **Special Weapons and Tactics team** a specially trained group of police who deal with the most dangerous and violent situations

sway¹ /sweɪ/ *v* **1** [I] to move slowly from one side to another: *The trees swayed gently in the breeze.* **2** [T] to influence someone so that they change their opinion: *Don't allow yourself to be swayed by his promises.*

sway² *n* [U] **1** *literary* power to rule or influence people: *These old attitudes still hold sway in the church.* | **under sb's sway** *She was now completely under his sway.* **2** a swinging movement from side to side: *the sway of the ship*

sway·backed /'sweɪbækt/ *adj AmE* curved downwards or inwards in the middle

swear ⟨S2⟩ /sweə $ swer/ *v* past tense **swore** /swɔː $ swɔːr/ past participle **sworn** /swɔːn $ swɔːrn/
1 **OFFENSIVE LANGUAGE** [I] to use rude and offensive language: *Don't swear in front of the children.* | [+at] *He turned round and swore at me.*
2 **PROMISE** [T] to promise that you will do something: **swear (that)** *Victor swore he would get his revenge.* | **swear to do sth** *Mona swore never to return home.* | *Do you swear on your honour* (=promise very strongly) *that you will never tell anyone?*

3 **STATE THE TRUTH** [I,T] *informal* to say very strongly that what you are saying is true: *I never touched your purse, I swear!* | **swear (that)** *He says he was there all the time, but I swear I never saw him.* | **swear blind** *BrE* (=say very strongly) | *She swore blind that she had never seen him before.* | *I never touched her, I swear to God.* | *I think it was about ten o'clock when we left, but I couldn't swear to it* (=I am not certain).
4 sb could have sworn (that) ... used to say that someone was sure about something but now they think they were wrong: *I could have sworn I had my keys.*
5 **PUBLIC PROMISE** [I,T] to make a public official promise, especially in a court of law: [+on] *Witnesses have to swear on the Bible.* | *Remember that you have sworn an oath and so must tell the truth.* | *Presidents must swear allegiance to the US constitution.*
6 **swear sb to secrecy/silence** to make someone promise not to tell anyone what you have told them —**swearing** *n* [U]: *He was cautioned for swearing.* | *lots of shouting and swearing*
  swear by sth *phr v informal* to have great confidence in how good or effective something is: *He swears by vitamin C pills.*
  swear sb ⇔ **in** *phr v* [usually passive] if someone with a new public job or position is sworn in, they make an official promise to do their duty well: *The new governor will be sworn in next week.* | *The jury have not yet been sworn in.*

,swearing-'in *n* [singular] a ceremony in which someone with a new public job or position officially promises to do their duty well

'swear word *n* [C] a word that is considered to be rude, offensive, and shocking by most people

sweat¹ /swet/ *v*
1 **LIQUID FROM SKIN** [I] to have drops of salty liquid coming out through your skin because you are hot, ill, frightened, or doing exercise; ▤ **perspire:** *I was sweating a lot despite the air-conditioning.* | **sweat heavily/profusely** (=sweat a lot) *Within minutes she was sweating profusely.* | **sweat like a pig/sweat buckets** *informal* (=sweat a lot) *basketball players sweating buckets*
2 **WORK** [I] *informal* to work hard: *They sweated and saved for ten years to buy a house.* | [+over] *He'd sweated over the plans for six months.* | **sweat blood/sweat your guts out** (=work very hard) *I sweated blood to get that report finished.* | *We've been sweating our guts out here!*
3 **WORRY** [I] *informal* to be anxious, nervous, or worried about something: *Let them sweat a bit before you tell them.* | **sweat bullets** *AmE* (=be very anxious) *Workers are sweating bullets over the possibility of job losses.*
4 **don't sweat it** *AmE spoken* used to tell someone not to worry about something: *Don't sweat it, I'll lend you the money.*
5 **don't sweat the small stuff** *AmE spoken* used to tell someone not to worry about unimportant things
6 **PRODUCE LIQUID** [I] if something such as cheese sweats, fat from inside appears on its surface
7 **COOK** [T] *BrE* to heat food gently in a little water or fat: *Sweat the vegetables until the juices run out.*
  sweat sth ⇔ **off** *phr v* to lose weight by sweating a lot
  sweat sth ⇔ **out** *phr v*
  1 to wait anxiously for news that is very important to you: *Van Os is sweating it out while the coach decides which players he's taking to the Olympics.*
  2 *AmE* to work very hard on something, especially something difficult: *kids sweating out a test*
  3 to do hard physical exercise: *They were sweating it out in the gym.*
  4 to get rid of an illness by making yourself sweat a lot

sweat² n

1 LIQUID ON SKIN [U] drops of salty liquid that come out through your skin when you are hot, frightened, ill, or doing exercise; ▤ **perspiration**: *Ian came off the squash court dripping with sweat.* | *Beads of sweat appeared on his forehead.* | *Sweat poured down his face.* | **work up a sweat** (=do physical exercise or hard work that makes you sweat) | *Karen was on the exercise bikes, just beginning to break a sweat* (=start sweating).

2 get into a sweat about sth *informal* to become nervous or frightened about something: *Don't get into such a sweat about it! It's only a test.*

3 break (out) into a sweat to become very nervous or frightened: *Drops in stock market prices have investors breaking out into a sweat.*

4 a cold sweat a state of nervousness or fear, in which you start to sweat, even though you are not hot: **in/into a cold sweat** *I woke up from the nightmare in a cold sweat.*

5 no sweat *spoken* used to say that you can do something easily: *'Are you sure you can do it on time?' 'Yeah, no sweat!'*

6 sweats [plural] *AmE informal* **a)** clothes made of thick, soft cotton, worn especially for sport; ▤ **sweatsuit b)** trousers of this type; ▤ **sweat pants**

7 WORK [singular] *old-fashioned* hard work, especially when it is boring or unpleasant

8 the sweat of sb's brow *literary* the hard effort that someone has made in their work

sweat·band /'swetbænd/ n [C] **1** a narrow band of cloth that you wear around your head or wrist to stop sweat running down when you are doing sport **2** a narrow piece of cloth that is sewn on the inside of a hat

sweated 'labour *BrE*; **sweated labor** *AmE* n [U] **1** hard work done for very low wages, especially in a factory **2** the people who do this work

sweat·er /'swetə $ -ər/ n [C] a piece of warm wool or cotton clothing with long sleeves, which covers the top half of your body; ▤ **jumper** *BrE*

'sweat gland n [C] a small organ under your skin that produces sweat

sweat·pants /'swetpænts/ n [plural] *AmE* loose warm trousers, worn especially for sport or relaxation

sweat·shirt /'swet-ʃɜːt $ -ʃɜːrt/ n [C] a loose warm piece of clothing which covers the top part of your body and arms and is worn especially for sport or relaxation

sweat·shop /'swet-ʃɒp $ -ʃɑːp/ n [C] a small business, factory etc where people work hard in bad conditions for very little money – used to show disapproval

'sweat suit, sweat·suit /'swetsuːt, -sjuːt $ -suːt/ n [C] *AmE* a set of loose warm clothes, worn especially for sport or relaxation

sweat·y /'sweti/ adj comparative **sweatier**, superlative **sweatiest** **1** covered or wet with SWEAT: *We came home hot and sweaty after the day's work.* | *sweaty palms* **2** [usually before noun] unpleasantly hot or difficult, so that you SWEAT: *a sweaty August day* | *a sweaty job*

swede /swiːd/ n [C,U] *BrE* a round yellow vegetable that grows under the ground; ▤ **rutabaga** *AmE*

Swede n [C] sòmeone from Sweden

Swe·dish¹ /'swiːdɪʃ/ adj relating to Sweden, its people, or its language

Swedish² n **1** the Swedish [plural] people from Sweden **2** [U] the language used in Sweden

sweep¹ S3 W3 /swiːp/ v past tense and past participle **swept** /swept/

1 CLEAN STH [T] to clean the dust, dirt etc from the floor or ground, using a brush with a long handle; ▤ **brush**: *Bert swept the path in front of the house.* | **sweep sth off/out/up etc** *Will you sweep the leaves off the patio?*; → see picture at CLEAN

2 PUSH STH SOMEWHERE [T always + adv/prep] to move things from a surface with a brushing movement: *I swept the papers quickly into the drawer.*

3 PUSH SB/STH WITH FORCE [T always + adv/prep] to force someone or something to move in a particular direction: *The windsurfer was swept out to sea.* | *Jessie was swept along by the angry crowd.*

4 GROUP MOVES [I always + adv/prep] if a group of people or animals sweep somewhere, they quickly move there together: [+through/along etc] *The crowd swept through the gates of the stadium.*

5 WIND/WAVES ETC [I,T always + adv/prep] if winds, waves, fire etc sweep a place or sweep through, across etc a place, they move quickly and with a lot of force: *Thunderstorms swept the country.* | [+across/through etc] *90 mile per hour winds swept across the plains.*

6 BECOME POPULAR [I,T always + adv/prep] *written* if an idea, feeling, or activity sweeps a group of people or a place, it quickly becomes very popular or common: **sweep the country/nation/state etc** *a wave of nationalism sweeping the country* | [+across/through etc] *the latest craze sweeping through the teenage population*

7 FEELING [I always + adv/prep] if a feeling sweeps over you, you are suddenly strongly affected by it: [+over] *A feeling of isolation swept over me.*

8 PERSON [I always + adv/prep] if someone sweeps somewhere, they move quickly and confidently, especially because they are impatient or like to seem important: [+into/through etc] *Eva swept into the meeting and demanded to know what was going on.*

9 POLITICS [I,T] to win an election easily and in an impressive way: **sweep to power/victory** *Nixon and Agnew swept to victory with 47 million votes.* | *Herrera was swept into office two years ago.*

10 SPORTS [T] *AmE* to win all of the games in a series of games against a particular team: *Houston swept Orlando to become NBA champions.*

11 sweep the board *BrE* to win everything that can be won, especially very easily

12 FORM A CURVE [I always + adv/prep] to form a long curved shape: [+down/along etc] *The hills swept down to the sea.*

13 LOOK [I,T always + adv/prep] to look quickly at all of something: *The General's eyes swept the horizon.* | [+over/across/around etc] *the beam from the lighthouse sweeping across the sea*

14 sweep sb off their feet to make someone feel suddenly and strongly attracted to you in a romantic way: *Jill's been swept off her feet by an older man.*

15 sweep/brush sth under the carpet also **sweep sth under the rug** *AmE* to try to keep something a secret, especially something you have done wrong

16 HAIR [T always + adv/prep] to pull your hair back from your face: **sweep sth back/up** *Kerry swept her hair back into a ponytail.*

sweep sb **along** phr v
to SWEEP someone AWAY

sweep sth ⇔ **aside** phr v
to refuse to pay attention to something someone says: *Branson swept all the objections aside.*

sweep sb/sth **away** phr v
1 sweep sth ⇔ away to completely destroy something or make something disappear: *houses swept away by the floods* | *A sudden feeling of grief swept all my anger away.*

2 sweep sb away also **sweep sb along** [usually passive] if a feeling or idea sweeps you away or along, you are so excited that you do not think clearly or you forget about other things: *We couldn't help being swept away by Bette's enthusiasm.* | *19th century scientists were swept along on the tide of Darwin's theories.*

sweep up phr v
1 to clean the dust, dirt etc from the floor or ground using a brush with a long handle: *The janitor was just sweeping up as I left the building.* | **sweep sth ⇔ up** *Jan was sweeping up the bits of paper and broken glass.*

2 sweep sb ⇔ up to pick someone up in one quick movement: *Harriet swept the child up in her arms and hugged her.*

sweep² n [C] **1** a long swinging movement of your arm, a weapon etc: *With a single sweep of his sword, he cut through the rope.* **2** [usually singular] *BrE* the act of cleaning a room with a long-handled brush: *The kitchen needs a good sweep.* **3 the sweep of sth a)** a long curved line or area of land: *the **wide sweep** of lawn* **b)** the many different and important ideas, events, or qualities of something: *the **broad sweep** of history* **4** [usually singular] a search or attack that moves over a large area: *He watched the helicopter **make a sweep** over the beach.* **5 the sweeps** also **sweeps month/period** *AmE* a period of time during the year when television stations try to find out which shows are the most popular **6** *AmE* a series of several games that one team wins against another team **7** a CHIMNEY SWEEP → **clean sweep** at CLEAN¹ (14)

sweep·er /'swiːpə $ -ər/ n **1** someone or something that sweeps: *a road sweeper* **2** *BrE* a football player who plays in a position behind other defending players

sweep·ing /'swiːpɪŋ/ adj **1** affecting many things, or making an important difference to something: **sweeping changes/cuts/reforms etc** *They want to make sweeping changes to education policies.* **2** [only before noun] including a lot of information about something: *a sweeping look at European history* **3 sweeping statement/generalization** a statement etc that is too general and that does not consider all the facts – used to show disapproval: *sweeping generalizations about women drivers* **4** forming a curved shape: *the sweeping curve of the driveway | a sweeping gesture* **5 sweeping victory** the winning of an election by a large number of votes: *a sweeping victory for Labour*

sweep·ings /'swiːpɪŋz/ n [plural] dirt, dust etc that is left to be swept up

sweep·stake *BrE* /'swiːpsteɪk/; **sweepstakes** *AmE* n [C] **1** a type of betting in which the winner receives all the money risked by everyone else **2** *AmE* a type of competition in which you have the chance to win a prize if your name is chosen **3** *AmE* a competition, election etc in which no one knows who will be the winner: *the presidential sweepstakes*

sweet¹ S2 W3 /swiːt/ adj *comparative* **sweeter**, *superlative* **sweetest**
1 TASTE containing or having a taste like sugar; → **sour, bitter, dry**: *This tea is too sweet. | sweet juicy peaches | sweet wine*
2 CHARACTER kind, gentle, and friendly: *a sweet smile | How **sweet of you** to remember my birthday!* → SWEET-TEMPERED
3 CHILDREN/SMALL THINGS especially *BrE* looking pretty and attractive; ▣ **cute**: *Your little boy looks very sweet in his new coat.*
4 THOUGHTS/EMOTIONS making you feel pleased, happy, and satisfied: *Revenge is sweet. | the **sweet smell** of success | the **sweet taste** of victory | Goodnight, Becky. **Sweet dreams.***
5 SMELLS having a pleasant smell; ▣ **fragrant**: *sweet-smelling flowers | the **sickly sweet** (=unpleasantly sweet) smell of rotting fruit*
6 SOUNDS pleasant to listen to; ▣ **harsh**: *She has a very sweet singing voice.*
7 have a **sweet tooth** to like things that taste of sugar
8 WATER/AIR if you describe water or air as sweet, you mean that it is fresh and clean; ▣ **stale**: *She hurried to the door and took great gulps of the sweet air.*
9 keep sb **sweet** *informal* to behave in a pleasant, friendly way towards someone, because you want them to help you later: *I'm trying to keep Mum sweet so that she'll lend me the car.*
10 in your own **sweet way/time** if you do something in your own sweet way, you do it in exactly the way that you want to or when you want to, without considering what other people say or think: *You can't just go on in your own sweet way; we have to do this together.*
11 a **sweet deal** *AmE* a business or financial deal in which you get an advantage, pay a low price etc: *I got a sweet deal on the car.*

12 sweet FA also **sweet Fanny Adams** *BrE informal* nothing at all – used when someone wants to avoid saying a swear word directly: *'How much did they pay you for that job?' 'Sweet FA!'*
13 sweet nothings things that lovers say to each other: *a couple **whispering sweet** nothings to each other*
14 be sweet on sb *old-fashioned* to be very attracted to or in love with someone
15 Sweet! *spoken informal* used to say that you think that something is very good: *'I got four tickets to the concert.' 'Sweet!'*—**sweetly** adv → home sweet home at HOME¹ (13); → **short and sweet** at SHORT¹ (1); → SWEETNESS

sweet² S2 n
1 [C] *BrE* a small piece of sweet food made of sugar or chocolate; ▣ **candy** *AmE*: *Eating sweets is bad for your teeth. | a sweet shop | a packet of **boiled sweets** (=hard sweets that taste of fruit)*
2 [C,U] *BrE* sweet food served after the meat and vegetables part of a meal; ▣ **dessert**: *Would you like a sweet, or some cheese and biscuits?*
3 (my) sweet *old-fashioned* used when speaking to someone you love: *Don't cry, my sweet.*

,**sweet-and-'sour** adj [only before noun] a sweet-and-sour dish in Chinese cooking has both sweet and sour tastes together: *sweet-and-sour pork*

sweet·bread /'swiːtbred/ n [C usually plural] meat from the PANCREAS of a young sheep or cow

sweet·corn /'swiːtkɔːn $ -kɔːrn/ n [U] *BrE* the soft yellow seeds from MAIZE that are cooked and eaten; ▣ **corn** *AmE*

sweet·en /'swiːtn/ v **1** [I,T] to make something sweeter, or become sweeter: *Sweeten the mixture with a little honey.* **2** [T] also **sweeten sb** ⇔ **up** *informal* to try to persuade someone to do what you want, by giving them presents or money or promising them something: *a cash bonus to sweeten the deal* → SWEETENER (2) **3** [T] *literary* to make someone kinder, gentler etc: *Old age had not sweetened her.* → **sweeten the pill** at PILL¹ (4)

,**sweetened con'densed milk** n [U] especially *AmE* CONDENSED MILK

sweet·ener /'swiːtnə $ -ər/ n **1** [C,U] a substance used to make food or drink taste sweeter: *No artificial sweeteners are used in this product.* **2** [C] *informal* something that you give to someone to persuade them to do something, especially to accept a business deal: *These tax cuts are just a pre-election sweetener.*

,**sweet 'gum** /'$ '. ./ n [C] a tree with hard wood and groups of seeds like PRICKLY balls, common in North America

sweet·heart /'swiːthɑːt $ -hɑːrt/ n [C] **1** *spoken* a way of speaking to someone you love; ▣ **darling**: *Come here, sweetheart.* **2** *spoken* an informal way of speaking to a woman you do not know, which some women find offensive **3 sweetheart deal** *AmE* an agreement that is unfair because it gives an advantage to people who know each other well or to people who have a lot of influence: *Members of the council had arranged a sweetheart deal with CTS.* **4** *old-fashioned* the person that you love: *They were **childhood sweethearts**.*

sweet·ie /'swiːti/ n [C] *spoken* **1** *BrE* a SWEET - used by children or when speaking to children **2** someone who is kind and easy to love: *Guy's father is such a sweetie.* **3** a way of speaking to someone you love

'**sweetie pie** n [C] *AmE spoken* a way of speaking to someone you love

sweet·meat /'swiːtmiːt/ n [C] *BrE old-fashioned* a SWEET, or any food made of or preserved in sugar

sweet·ness /'swiːtnəs/ n [U] **1** how sweet something tastes or smells: *the sweetness of the wild rose* **2** how pleasant something is: *a smile of great sweetness* **3 be all sweetness and light a)** to behave in a way that is very pleasant and friendly, especially when you do not normally behave like this: *She's all* *sweetness and light when Paul's around.* **b)** to be enjoyable and without problems: *Life is not all sweetness and light.*

,**sweet 'pea** / $ '. ./ *n* [C] a climbing plant with sweet-smelling flowers in pale colours

,**sweet 'pepper** *n* [C] a green, red, or yellow vegetable that is hollow with many seeds

,**sweet po'tato** *n* [C] a vegetable that looks like a red potato, is yellow inside, and tastes sweet; → **yam**

'**sweet roll** *n* [C] *AmE* a small sweet PASTRY

'**sweet-talk** *v* [T] *informal* to persuade someone to do something by talking to them nicely and making them feel good: **sweet-talk sb into doing sth** *I managed to sweet-talk her into driving me home.* —**sweet talk** *n* [U]

,**sweet-'tempered** *adj* having a character that is kind and gentle

sweet wil·liam /ˌswiːt 'wɪljəm/ *n* [C,U] a plant with sweet-smelling flowers

swell[1] /swel/ *v past tense* **swelled**, *past participle* **swollen** /'swəʊlən $ 'swoʊ-/
1 SIZE [I] also **swell up** to become larger and rounder than normal – used especially about parts of the body; → **swollen**: *Her ankle was already starting to swell.* | *The window frame was swollen shut.*
2 AMOUNT/NUMBER [I,T] to increase in amount or number: [+to] *The crowd swelled to around 10,000.* | *The river was swollen with melted snow.* | **swell the ranks/ numbers of sth** (=increase the number of people in a particular situation) *Large numbers of refugees have swollen the ranks of the unemployed.*
3 swell with pride/anger etc to feel very proud, angry etc: *His heart swelled with pride as he watched his daughter collect her prize.*
4 SHAPE [I,T] also **swell out** to curve or make something curve: *The wind swelled the sails.*
5 SOUND [I] *literary* to become louder: *Music swelled around us.*
6 SEA [I] to move suddenly and powerfully upwards → GROUNDSWELL

swell[2] *n* **1** [singular] the way the sea moves up and down: *The sea wasn't rough, but there was a **heavy swell** (=large movements of the water).* **2** [singular] a situation in which something increases in number or amount: [+of] *the growing swell of anti-government feeling* | *a swell of pride* **3** [singular] an increase in sound level, especially in music; **crescendo 4** [singular] the roundness or curved shape of something: *the firm swell of her breasts* **5** [C] *old-fashioned* a fashionable or important person

swell[3] *adj AmE old-fashioned* very good; **great**: *You look swell!*

,**swell-'headed** *adj AmE informal* thinking that you are more important or clever than you really are; **bigheaded**

swell·ing /'swelɪŋ/ *n* **1** [C] an area of your body that has become larger than normal, because of illness or injury: [+in/on] *a painless swelling in his neck* **2** [U] the condition of having swelled: *The spider's bite can cause pain and swelling.* | *These tablets should **reduce** the swelling.*

swel·ter /'sweltə $ -ər/ *v* [I] to feel extremely hot and uncomfortable: *Crowds of shoppers sweltered in the summer heat.*

swel·ter·ing /'sweltərɪŋ/ *adj* extremely hot and uncomfortable: *sweltering August days*

swept /swept/ the past tense and past participle of SWEEP

,**swept-'back** *adj* **1** hair that is swept-back is brushed backwards from your face **2** swept-back wings on an aircraft look like the letter v

swerve /swɜːv $ swɜːrv/ *v* [I] **1** to make a sudden sideways movement while moving forwards, usually in order to avoid hitting something: **swerve violently/ sharply** *The car swerved sharply to avoid the dog.* |

[+**across/off/into** etc] *The bus swerved off the road.* **2** [usually in negatives] *formal* to change from an idea, course of action, purpose etc: [+**from**] *He would never swerve from the truth.* —**swerve** *n* [C]

swift[1] /swɪft/ *adj* **1** happening or done quickly and immediately: *My letter received a swift reply.* | *She shot a swift glance at Paul.* | **swift to do sth** *They were swift to deny the accusations.* **2** [only before noun] moving, or able to move, very fast: *a swift runner* | *She wiped her tears away in one swift movement.* **3 sb is not too swift** *AmE spoken* used to say that someone is not very intelligent —**swiftly** *adv*: *Alice dressed swiftly.* —**swiftness** *n* [U]

swift[2] *n* [C] a small brown bird that has pointed wings, flies very fast, and is similar to a SWALLOW

swig /swɪg/ *v* **swigged**, **swigging** [T] *informal* to drink something in large mouthfuls, especially from a bottle; **gulp**: *He sat swigging beer and smoking.* —**swig** *n* [C]: *She took a long swig of coke.*

swill[1] /swɪl/ *v* **1** [T] *BrE* to wash something by pouring a lot of water over it or into it: **swill sth away/down/ out** *Get a bucket to swill the yard down.* **2** [I,T] if a liquid swills around or you swill it around, it moves around something: [+**around/round**] *He swilled his brandy gently round his glass.* **3** [T] also **swill down** *informal* to drink something in large amounts: *He does nothing but swill beer all day.*

swill[2] *n* **1** [U] food for pigs, mostly made of unwanted bits of human food → PIGSWILL **2** [C] *BrE* the act of washing something by pouring a lot of water over it

swim[1] /swɪm/ *v past tense* **swam** /swæm/ *past participle* **swum** /swʌm/ *present participle* **swimming**
1 MOVE THROUGH WATER [I,T] to move yourself through water using your arms and legs: [+**in**] *We swam in the chilly water.* | [+**around/across** etc] *She could swim across the lake.* | *Let's go swimming this afternoon.* | *kids learning to swim the backstroke* | *She was the first woman to swim the Channel.*
2 WATER ANIMALS [I always + adv/prep] when fish, ducks etc swim, they move around the water using their tails and FINS, their feet etc: *Tropical fish swam slowly around in the tank.*
3 NOT THINKING/SEEING PROPERLY [I] **a)** if your head swims, you start to feel confused or that everything is spinning around: *My head was swimming after looking at that screen all day.* **b)** if something you are looking at swims, it seems to be moving around, usually because you are ill, tired, or drunk: *The numbers swam before my eyes.*
4 be swimming in sth to be covered by a lot of liquid: *potatoes swimming in thick gravy*
5 swim against the tide/current etc to do or say things which are different from what most people do or say, because you do not mind being different; **swim with the tide** → **sink or swim** at SINK[1] (15)

swim[2] *n* [C] **1** a period of time that you spend swimming: *Let's go for a swim.* **2 in the swim (of things)** *informal* knowing about and involved in what is happening in a particular situation

swim·mer /'swɪmə $ -ər/ *n* [C] **a)** someone who swims well, often as a competitor: **good/strong swimmer** *Peter's a very strong swimmer.* **b)** someone who is swimming: *We watched the swimmers heading out across the lake.*

swim·ming S2 /'swɪmɪŋ/ *n* [U] the sport of moving yourself through water using your arms and legs: *Swimming is great exercise.* | *a swimming club* | *We went swimming on Saturday.*

'**swimming bath** *n* [C] *BrE old-fashioned* a public swimming pool, usually indoors

'**swimming cap** *n* [C] a tight-fitting rubber hat that you wear when you are swimming to keep your hair dry

'**swimming ,costume** *n* [C] *BrE* a piece of clothing worn for swimming, especially the type worn by women

swimming strokes

butterfly

breaststroke

backstroke

crawl

swim·ming·ly /'swɪmɪŋli/ adv old-fashioned **go swimmingly** if something you plan goes swimmingly, it happens without problems

'swimming pool n [C] a structure that has been built and filled with water for people to swim in; ▤ **pool**; → see picture at SPORTS CENTRE

'swimming suit n [C] AmE SWIMSUIT

'swimming trunks n [plural] a piece of clothing like SHORTS, worn by men and boys for swimming

swim·suit /'swɪmsuːt, -sjuːt $ -suːt/ n [C] a piece of clothing worn for swimming

swim·wear /'swɪmweə $ -wer/ n [U] clothing used for swimming

swin·dle¹ /'swɪndl/ v [T] to get money from someone by deceiving them; ▤ **cheat**: swindle sb out of sth a businessman who swindled investors out of millions of pounds —**swindler** n [C]

swindle² n [C] a situation in which someone gets money by deceiving someone else: a big tax swindle

swine /swaɪn/ n [C] **1** plural **swine** or **swines** informal someone who behaves very rudely or unpleasantly: Leave her alone, you filthy swine! **2** old use a pig

swine·herd /'swaɪnhɜːd $ -hɜːrd/ n [C] old use someone who looks after pigs

swing¹ W3 /swɪŋ/ v past tense and past participle swung /swʌŋ/
1 MOVE FROM A FIXED POINT [I,T] to make regular movements forwards and backwards or from one side to another while hanging from a particular point, or to make something do this: Let your arms swing as you walk. | a sign swinging in the wind | He was **swinging** his bag **back and forth**. | She **swung** her legs **from side to side**. | **swing sth by sth** He marched around, swinging the gun by its handle.
2 MOVE IN A CURVE [I,T always + adv/prep] to move quickly in a smooth curve in one direction, or to make something do this: A black car swung into the drive. | Kate swung her legs out of bed. | **swing open/shut** The heavy door swung shut. | Swinging her bag over her shoulder, she hurried on.
3 HIT [I,T] to move your arm or something you are holding to try and hit something: **swing sth at sb/sth** She swung her bag at him. | **swing at sb/sth (with sth)** Garson swung at the ball and missed. | He started swinging at me with his fists.
4 CHANGE OPINIONS/EMOTIONS [I,T] if emotions or opinions swing, or if something swings them, they change quickly to the opposite of what they were: **swing from sth to sth** His **mood** could **swing** from joy to despair. | Do campaign gifts **swing votes**? | The war had begun to **swing in** Britain's favor. | **swing to the Right/Left** (=in politics)
5 swing into action to suddenly begin work that needs doing, using a lot of energy and effort: Politicians have already swung into action.
6 PLAY [I] to sit on a swing and make it move backwards and forwards by moving your legs

7 ARRANGE STH [T] spoken to arrange for something to happen, although it takes a lot of effort to do this: We managed to **swing it** so that they will travel together.
8 swing both ways informal someone who swings both ways is BISEXUAL
9 swing the lead BrE to avoid work by pretending to be ill → there's not enough room to swing a cat at ROOM¹ (5)

swing around/round phr v
to turn around quickly, or to make something do this: She swung around to face him. | **swing sth/sb ⇔ around/round** He swung the boat around and headed for the shore.

swing by phr v AmE informal
swing by (sth) to visit a place or person for a short time: I'll swing by the grocery store on my way.

swing² S3 n
1 SEAT WITH ROPES [C] a seat hanging from ropes or chains, usually used by children play on by moving it forwards and backwards using their legs: kids **playing on the swings** | a porch swing
2 MOVEMENT [C] a curved movement made with your arm, leg etc: He **took a swing at** (=tried to hit) my head and missed. | the swing of her hips as she walked
3 CHANGE [C] a noticeable change in opinions or emotions: [+to/towards/between etc] a big swing towards right-wing ideology | She suffers from **mood swings**.
4 SPORTS [singular] the movement you make when you hit the ball in GOLF, baseball, or some other sports: I spent months correcting my swing.
5 MUSIC [U] a type of dance music played by a big band in the 1930s and 1940s that is similar to JAZZ
6 get into the swing of it/things to become fully involved in an activity: Once we got into the swing of it, it took no time at all.
7 be in full swing if an event or process is in full swing, it has reached its highest level of activity: By midnight the end-of-course party was in full swing.
8 go with a swing BrE if a party or activity goes with a swing, it is enjoyable and successful: everything you need to **make** your party **go with a swing**
9 swings and roundabouts BrE used to say that two choices have an equal number of gains and losses, so there is little difference between them

swing 'bridge n [C] BrE a bridge that can be pulled up for tall ships to go under it

swing 'door n [C] BrE a door that you can push open from either side, which swings shut afterwards; ▤ **swinging door** AmE

swinge·ing /'swɪndʒɪŋ/ adj BrE written **1** extremely severe and likely to cause people financial problems: swingeing cuts in staff numbers | swingeing price increases | swingeing import taxes **2** a swingeing criticism is very severe: a swingeing attack on local government reform

swing·er /'swɪŋə $ -ər/ n [C] old-fashioned informal **1** someone who is fashionable and goes to a lot of parties **2** someone who has sexual relationships with many people, especially someone who exchanges sexual partners with other people

swing·ing /'swɪŋɪŋ/ adj old-fashioned informal exciting and enjoyable: a swinging social life

swinging 'door n [C] AmE a door that you can push open from either side, which swings shut afterwards; ▤ **swing door** BrE

swinging 'sixties n the swinging sixties the 1960s, a time when social and sexual freedom increased: Dad grew up in the swinging sixties.

swing·om·e·ter /swɪŋ'ɒmɪtə $ -'aːmɪtər/ n [C] BrE informal a piece of equipment used in television programmes to show how many votes each political party is getting during an election

'swing set n [C] AmE a tall metal frame with SWINGS hanging from it, for children to play on

1 000, 2 000, 3 000, most frequent words in S poken and W ritten English

'swing shift n [singular] AmE informal workers who work from three or four o'clock in the afternoon until 11 or 12 o'clock at night, or the system of working these times

swin·ish /'swaɪnɪʃ/ adj old-fashioned BrE extremely unpleasant or difficult to deal with

swipe¹ /swaɪp/ v **1** [I,T] to hit or to try to hit someone or something by swinging your arm or an object very quickly: *She swiped me across the face.* | [+at] *He jumped forward, intending to swipe at her.* **2** [T] informal to steal something; ◼ **pinch** BrE: *The photos were probably swiped by an employee.* **3** [T] to pull a plastic card through a machine that can read the electronic information on it: *Swipe your card to open the door.*

swipe² n [C] **1** a criticism of someone or something; ◼ **dig**: [+at] *His comments were a sarcastic swipe at the police.* | *In her latest article she takes a swipe at* (=criticizes) *her critics.* **2** when you hit or try to hit someone or something by swinging your arm very quickly: *She took a swipe at the ball.*

'swipe card n [C] a special plastic card that you slide through a machine in order to get into a building or open a door

swipe

swipe card

swirl¹ /swɜːl $ swɜːrl/ v **1** [I,T] to move around quickly in a twisting circular movement, or to make something do this: [+around/round] *Smoke swirled around her.* | **swirl sth around/round** *He swirled the brandy around in his glass.* | *The river had become a swirling torrent.* **2** [I] if stories or ideas swirl around a place, a lot of people start to talk about them – used especially in news reports: [+around] *Rumours of a takeover began to swirl around the stock markets.*

swirl² n [C] **1** a swirling movement or amount of something: [+of] *a swirl of dust* **2** a twisting circular pattern

swish¹ /swɪʃ/ v [I,T] to move or make something move quickly through the air with a quiet sound: *Her skirt swished as she walked.* —**swish** n [singular]

swish² adj BrE fashionable and expensive: *a swish new apartment block*

Swiss¹ /swɪs/ adj relating to Switzerland or its people

Swiss² n the Swiss [plural] people from Switzerland

'Swiss 'chard n [U] a vegetable with large green leaves

'Swiss 'roll n [C,U] BrE a long thin cake that is rolled up with JAM or cream inside

'Swiss 'steak n [C,U] AmE a thick flat piece of BEEF covered in flour and cooked in a sauce

switch¹ [S2] [W3] /swɪtʃ/ v
1 [I,T] to change from doing or using one thing to doing or using another: [+to] *She worked as a librarian before switching to journalism.* | **switch from sth to sth** *Duval could switch easily from French to English.* | **switch between sth and sth** *He switches between TV and theatre work.* | *The terrorists will switch tactics.* | **switch sides/allegiance** (=start supporting a different person, party etc) *He switched sides just days before the election.* | **switch attention/focus/emphasis** *We want to switch the focus away from criticism.*
2 [T] to replace one thing with another, or exchange things; ◼ **change**: **switch sth for sth** *Tim may switch his BMW for something else.* | **switch sth from sth to sth** *We've switched the meeting from Tuesday to Thursday.* | **switch sth around** *It's not easy to switch clerical workers around.*
3 [I,T] AmE if you switch with someone who does the same job as you, you exchange your working times with theirs for a short time; ◼ **swap** BrE: [+with] *Tom*

said he'd switch with me on Saturday. | *He asked if we could switch shifts.*
4 [T always + adv/prep] to change the way a machine operates, using a switch: **switch sth to sth** *Switch the freezer to 'defrost'.*

switch off phr v
1 to turn off a machine, light, radio etc using a switch: **switch sth ⇔ off** *The burglar alarm was switched off.* | *Don't forget to switch off before you go.* → see box at CLOSE¹
2 informal to stop listening to someone: *He just switches off and ignores me.*
3 to relax for a short time: *Switch off by listening to music.*

switch on phr v
to turn on a machine, light, radio etc using a switch: **switch sth ⇔ on** *He switched the torch on.* | *When a tape is put in the VCR, it switches on automatically.*

switch over phr v
1 to change from one method, product etc to another: [+to] *We've switched over to telephone banking.*
2 to change the television CHANNEL you are watching or the radio station you are listening to: [+to] *Switch over to BBC 2.*

switch² [S3] n [C]
1 ON/OFF a piece of equipment that starts or stops the flow of electricity to a machine, light etc when you push it: *Where's the light switch?* | *an on-off switch* | **press/flick/throw etc a switch** *Tom flicked the switch, but nothing happened.* | *She claims she is willing to throw the switch of the electric chair.* | **at the flick of a switch** (=very quickly and easily, by pressing a switch) *Petrol can be chosen at the flick of a switch.*
2 CHANGE [usually singular] a complete change from one thing to another: *an important policy switch* | [+from/to] *the switch from agriculture to dairy production* | [+in] *a switch in emphasis* | *More shoppers are making the switch to organic food.* | **that's a switch** AmE spoken informal (=used to say that someone's behaviour is different from usual) *'Ed's the only one who's not eating.' 'That's a switch!'*
3 RAILWAY AmE a piece of railway track that can be moved to allow a train to cross over from one track to another
4 STICK old-fashioned a thin stick that bends easily

switch·back /'swɪtʃbæk/ n [C] a road or track that goes up and down steep slopes and around sharp bends

switch·blade /'swɪtʃbleɪd/ n [C] a knife with a blade inside the handle which springs out when you press a button

switch·board /'swɪtʃbɔːd $ -bɔːrd/ n [C] a system used to connect telephone calls in an office building, hotel etc, or the people who operate the system: *switchboard operators* | *Hundreds of callers jammed the switchboard trying to win the tickets* (=there were too many calls for the switchboard to deal with).

'Switch card n [C] trademark BrE a plastic card from your bank that you use to pay for things and that allows the money to be taken straight from your account

switched-'on adj informal quick to notice new ideas and fashions

swiv·el¹ /'swɪvəl/ also **swivel around/round** v swivelled, swivelling BrE, swiveled, swiveling AmE [I,T] to turn around quickly and face a different direction, or to make something do this; → **spin**: *Anna swivelled round to face him.* | *She swivelled her head round to watch what was happening.* | *Danny swiveled his chair away from me.*

swivel² n [C] an object that joins two parts of something and helps it to turn around

'swivel chair n [C] a chair whose seat part can be turned while the legs remain in the same position → see picture at CHAIR¹

swizz /swɪz/ n BrE spoken a swizz something that makes you feel disappointed and as though you have been deceived: *The packet's half empty – what a swizz!*

swiz·zle stick /ˈswɪzəl ˌstɪk/ n [C] a small stick for mixing drinks

swol·len[1] /ˈswəʊlən $ ˈswoʊ-/ the past participle of SWELL[1]

swollen[2] adj **1** a part of your body that is swollen is bigger than usual, especially because you are ill or injured: *swollen glands* | *a badly swollen ankle* | *His eyes were swollen from crying.* **2** a river that is swollen has more water in it than usual **3 have a swollen head/be swollen-headed** BrE to be too proud and think you are very clever or important

swoon /swuːn/ v [I] **1** to be extremely excited and unable to control yourself because you admire someone so much: [+over] *crowds of teenage girls swooning over popstars* **2** old-fashioned to fall to the ground because you have been affected by an emotion or shock; ▤ **faint** —**swoon** n [singular]

swoop[1] /swuːp/ v [I] **1** if a bird or aircraft swoops, it moves suddenly down through the air, especially in order to attack something: *The eagle hovered, ready to swoop at any moment.* | [+down/over/across etc] *A helicopter suddenly swooped down.* **2** written if the police, army etc swoop on a place, they go there without any warning in order to look for someone or something: [+on] *Drug officers swooped on several addresses in London last night.*

swoop[2] n [C] **1** a sudden surprise attack on a place in order to get something or take people away – used especially in news reports: [+on] *Police arrested a man in a swoop on his house last night.* **2** a swooping movement or action → **at/in one fell swoop** at FELL[4]

swoosh /swuːʃ/ v [I] to make a sound by moving quickly through the air —**swoosh** n [C]

swop /swɒp $ swɑːp/ v, n another spelling of SWAP

sword /sɔːd $ sɔːrd/ n [C] **1** a weapon with a long pointed blade and a handle **2 a/the sword of Damocles** literary a bad thing that might happen at any time: *The treaty hung like a sword of Damocles over French politics.* **3 put sb to the sword** literary to kill someone with a sword **4 turn/beat swords into ploughshares** literary to start using money, equipment, and skills for peaceful purposes rather than for fighting → **cross swords (with sb)** at CROSS[1] (16); → **double-edged sword** at DOUBLE-EDGED (1)

'sword dance n [C] a dance in which people dance over swords or using swords

sword·fish /ˈsɔːdˌfɪʃ $ ˈsɔːrd-/ n plural **swordfish** [C] a large fish with a very long pointed upper jaw

swords·man /ˈsɔːdzmən $ ˈsɔːrdz-/ n plural **swordsmen** /-mən/ [C] someone who is good at fighting with a sword

swords·man·ship /ˈsɔːdzmənʃɪp $ ˈsɔːrdz-/ n [U] skill in fighting with a sword

swore /swɔː $ swɔːr/ the past tense of SWEAR

sworn[1] /swɔːn $ swɔːrn/ the past participle of SWEAR

sworn[2] adj **1 sworn enemies** two people or groups of people who will always hate each other **2 sworn statement/evidence/testimony etc** a statement etc that someone makes after officially promising to tell the truth

swot[1] /swɒt $ swɑːt/ n [C] BrE informal someone who spends too much time studying and seems to have no other interests – used in order to show disapproval —**swotty** adj

swot[2] v **swotted**, **swotting** [I] BrE informal to study a lot in a short time, especially for an examination; ▤ **revise**: [+for] *students swotting for exams*
   swot up phr v BrE to learn as much as you can about a subject, especially in order to prepare for an examination: [+on] *It's worth swotting up on all the different types of computer before you buy one.* | **swot sth ⇔ up** I *spent all last night swotting up German verbs.*

SWOT /swɒt $ swɑːt/ n [U] *strengths, weaknesses, opportunities, threats* a system for examining the way a company is run or the way someone works in order to see what the good and bad features are: *a SWOT analysis*

swum /swʌm/ the past participle of SWIM[1]

swung /swʌŋ/ the past tense and past participle of SWING[1]

syb·a·rit·ic /ˌsɪbəˈrɪtɪk◂/ adj literary wanting or enjoying expensive pleasures and comforts

syc·a·more /ˈsɪkəmɔː $ -mɔːr/ n [C,U] **1** a European tree that has leaves with five points and seeds with two parts like wings, or the wood of this tree **2** a North American tree with broad leaves, or the wood of this tree

syc·o·phant /ˈsɪkəfənt/ n [C] formal someone who praises powerful people too much because they want to get something from them – used in order to show disapproval: *a dictator surrounded by sycophants*

syc·o·phan·tic /ˌsɪkəˈfæntɪk◂/ adj formal praising important or powerful people too much because you want to get something from them – used in order to show disapproval: *sycophantic journalists* | *a sycophantic letter* —**sycophancy** /ˈsɪkəfənsi/ n [U]

syl·lab·ic /sɪˈlæbɪk/ adj **1** based on or relating to SYLLABLES: *syllabic stress* **2** technical a syllabic consonant forms a whole SYLLABLE, for example the /l/ in 'battle'

syl·la·ble /ˈsɪləbəl/ n [C] a word or part of a word which contains a single vowel sound → **in words of one syllable** at WORD[1] (10)

syl·la·bub /ˈsɪləbʌb/ n [C,U] BrE a sweet food made by mixing cream with sugar and wine or fruit juice

syl·la·bus /ˈsɪləbəs/ n [C] a plan that states exactly what students at a school or college should learn in a particular subject; → **curriculum**: *on a syllabus Two Shakespeare plays are on this year's English syllabus.*

syl·lo·gis·m /ˈsɪlədʒɪzəm/ n [C] technical a statement with three parts, the first two of which prove that the third part is true, for example 'all men will die, Socrates is a man, therefore Socrates will die' —**syllogistic** /ˌsɪləˈdʒɪstɪk◂/ adj

sylph /sɪlf/ n [C] **1** literary an attractively thin woman **2** an imaginary female creature who lived in the air, according to ancient stories

sylph·like /ˈsɪlf-laɪk/ adj literary a sylphlike woman is attractively thin and graceful

syl·van /ˈsɪlvən/ adj literary relating to a forest or trees

sym- /sɪm/ prefix the form used for SYN- before the letters b, m, or p

sym·bi·o·sis /ˌsɪmbaɪˈəʊsɪs $ -ˈoʊ-/ n [singular, U] **1** formal a relationship between people or organizations that depend on each other equally **2** technical the relationship between different living things that depend on each other

sym·bi·ot·ic /ˌsɪmbaɪˈɒtɪk $ -ˈɑː-/ adj formal a symbiotic relationship is one in which the people, organizations, or living things involved depend on each other

sym·bol W3 /ˈsɪmbəl/ n [C]
1 a picture or shape that has a particular meaning or represents a particular organization or idea; → **sign**: *The symbol on the packet is a guarantee that the food has been produced organically.* | [+of] *The dove is a symbol of peace.*
2 a letter, number, or sign that represents a sound, an amount, a chemical substance etc: [+for] *Fe is the chemical symbol for iron.*
3 someone or something that represents a particular quality or idea: [+of] *Space exploration provides a symbol of national pride.* → SEX SYMBOL

sym·bol·ic /sɪmˈbɒlɪk $ -ˈbɑː-/ adj **1** important but not having any real effect: **symbolic gesture/act** *The protest was a symbolic gesture of anger at official policy.* | **symbolic significance/importance** *a meeting of symbolic importance* | **purely/largely symbolic** *It was a largely symbolic gesture from a government trying to* *win support.* **2** representing a particular idea or quality: *Each element of the ceremony has a symbolic meaning.* | [+of] *Today's fighting is symbolic of the chaos which the country is facing.* **3** using or involving symbols: *A map is a form of symbolic representation.* —**symbolically** /-kli/ *adv*

sym·bol·is·m /'sɪmbəlɪzəm/ *n* [U] the use of symbols to represent ideas or qualities: *religious symbolism*

sym·bol·ize also **-ise** *BrE* /'sɪmbəlaɪz/ *v* [T] if something symbolizes a quality, feeling etc, it represents it: *Crime often symbolizes a wider social problem.* | *Growing discontent has been symbolized by the protests.*

sym·met·ri·cal /sɪ'metrɪkəl/ also **sym·met·ric** /sɪ'metrɪk/ *adj* an object or design that is symmetrical has two halves that are exactly the same shape and size; **◪** **asymmetrical**: *The pattern was perfectly symmetrical.* —**symmetrically** /-kli/ *adv*

sym·me·try /'sɪmɪtri/ *n* [U] **1** the quality of being symmetrical: [+of] *the symmetry of the design* **2** the quality that a situation has when two events or actions seem to be balanced or equal in some way: *There was a certain symmetry to coming back to New York, where I started my artistic life all those years ago.*

sym·pa·thet·ic /,sɪmpə'θetɪk◂/ *adj* **1** caring and feeling sorry about someone's problems: *a sympathetic friend* | *a sympathetic attitude* | [+to/towards] *I'm sympathetic to parents who are worried about what their children see on television.* | *We hope always to provide a friendly sympathetic ear* (=someone willing to listen to someone else's problems). **2** [not before noun] willing to give approval and support to an aim or plan: [+to/towards] *Senator Capp is very sympathetic to environmental issues.* **3 sympathetic figure/character** *literary* someone in a book, play etc who most people like **4** providing the right conditions for someone: *a sympathetic environment* —**sympathetically** /-kli/ *adv*: *Jill smiled sympathetically.*

sym·pa·thize also **-ise** *BrE* /'sɪmpəθaɪz/ *v* [I] **1** to feel sorry for someone because you understand their problems: *I sympathize, but I don't know how to help.* | [+with] *I can sympathize with those who have lost loved ones.* **2** to support someone's ideas or actions: [+with] *The public sympathized with the miners' strike.*

sym·pa·thiz·er also **-iser** *BrE* /'sɪmpəθaɪzə $ -ər/ *n* [C] someone who supports the aims of an organization or political party; **◪** **supporter**: *The anti-abortion rally attracted many sympathizers.*

sym·pa·thy /'sɪmpəθi/ *n plural* **sympathies** **1** [plural,U] the feeling of being sorry for someone who is in a bad situation: [+for] *I have a lot of sympathy for her; she had to bring up the children on her own.* | *I have absolutely no sympathy for students who get caught cheating in exams.* | *She wrote a letter expressing her sympathy.* | *play on sb's sympathy* (=make someone feel sorry for you in order to gain an advantage for yourself) | *We would like to pass on our deepest sympathy to Ken's wife Marjorie.* | *Our sympathies are with the families of the victims.* | *My sympathies go out to the boy's mother.* | *message/letter of sympathy The victim's parents have received thousands of messages of sympathy.* **2** [plural,U] belief in or support for a plan, idea, or action, especially a political one: **in sympathy with sth** *Willard is in sympathy with many Green Party issues.* | *Her sympathies lie firmly with the Conservative Party.* | **communist/Republican/left-wing etc sympathies** *Matheson is known for his pro-socialist sympathies.* | [+with/for] *Sullivan expressed sympathy for the striking federal workers.* **3** [U] a feeling that you understand someone because you are similar to them: *There was no personal sympathy between them.*

sym·pho·ny /'sɪmfəni/ *n plural* **symphonies** [C] **1** a long piece of music usually in four parts, written for an ORCHESTRA: *Bruckner's Fifth Sym-*

phony **2** also **symphony orchestra** a large group of CLASSICAL musicians led by a CONDUCTOR —**symphonic** /sɪm'fɒnɪk $ -'faː-/ *adj*

sym·po·si·um /sɪm'pəʊziəm $ -'poʊ-/ *n plural* **symposiums** *or* **symposia** /-ziə/ [C] **1** a formal meeting in which people who know a lot about a particular subject have discussions about it; → **conference**: [+on] *a symposium on women's health* **2** a group of articles on a particular subject collected together in a book

symp·tom W3 /'sɪmptəm/ *n* [C] **1** something wrong with your body or mind which shows that you have a particular illness: [+of] *Common symptoms of diabetes are weight loss and fatigue.* **2** a sign that a serious problem exists: [+of] *The disappearance of jobs is a symptom of a deeper socioeconomic change.*

symp·to·mat·ic /,sɪmptə'mætɪk◂/ *adj* **1** *formal* if a situation or type of behaviour is symptomatic of something, it shows that a serious problem exists: [+of] *The rise in unemployment is symptomatic of a general decline in the economy.* **2** *medical* showing that someone has a particular illness —**symptomatically** /-kli/ *adv*

syn- /sɪn/ *prefix* together: *a synthesis* (=combining of separate things)

syn·a·gogue /'sɪnəgɒg $ -gɒːg/ *n* [C] a building where Jewish people meet for religious worship

syn·apse /'saɪnæps, 'sɪn- $ 'sɪnæps, sɪ'næps/ *n* [C] the place where nerve cells meet, especially in the brain —**synaptic** /sɪ'næptɪk/ *adj*

sync¹, synch /sɪŋk/ *n* **1 in sync (with sth/sb) a)** if things are in sync, they are working well together at exactly the same time and speed: **be/move/work in sync** *The two mechanisms have to work in sync.* | *The soundtrack is not quite in sync with the picture.* **b)** matching or in agreement: *a celebrity who is in sync with young people's lifestyles* | *The President is in sync with Thompson's views on many issues.* **2 out of sync (with sth/sb) a)** if things are out of sync, they are not working well together at exactly the same time and speed **b)** not matching or not in agreement

sync², synch *v* also **sync sth up** [I,T] to arrange for two or more things to happen at exactly the same time, or to happen at the same time or in the same way as something else; **◪** **synchronize**: *The hardest part was syncing the music to the video.* | *Wait for the computer to synch up with your command.*

syn·chro·ni·city /,sɪŋkrə'nɪsɪti/ *n* [U] when two or more events happen at the same time or place and seem to be connected in some way

syn·chro·nize also **-ise** *BrE* /'sɪŋkrənaɪz/ *v* **1** [I,T] to happen at exactly the same time, or to arrange for two or more actions to happen at exactly the same time: **synchronize sth with sth** *Businesses must synchronize their production choices with consumer choices.* **2 synchronize your watches** to make two or more watches show exactly the same time —**synchronization** /,sɪŋkrənaɪ'zeɪʃən $ -nə-/ *n* [U]

,synchronized 'swimming *n* [U] a sport in which swimmers move in patterns in the water to music

syn·chro·nous /'sɪŋkrənəs/ *adj formal* if two or more things are synchronous, they happen at the same time or work at the same speed

syn·co·pat·ed /'sɪŋkəpeɪtɪd/ *adj* syncopated music has a RHYTHM in which the beats that are usually weak are emphasized

syn·co·pa·tion /,sɪŋkə'peɪʃən/ *n* [U] a RHYTHM in a line of music in which the beats that are usually weak are emphasized

syn·di·cal·is·m /'sɪndɪkəlɪzəm/ *n* [U] a political system in which workers control industry, or a belief in this type of system —**syndicalist** *n* [C] —**syndicalist** *adj*

syn·di·cate¹ /'sɪndɪkət/ *n* [C] a group of people or companies who join together in order to achieve a particular aim: [+of] *a syndicate of banks*

syn·di·cate² /ˈsɪndɪˌkeɪt/ v [T usually passive] to arrange for written work, photographs etc to be sold to a number of different newspapers, magazines etc: *His column is syndicated throughout America.* —**syndication** /ˌsɪndɪˈkeɪʃən/ n [U]

syn·drome /ˈsɪndrəʊm $ -droʊm/ n [C] **1** *medical* an illness which consists of a set of physical or mental problems – often used in the name of illnesses: *people who suffer from irritable bowel syndrome* **2** a set of qualities, events, or types of behaviour that is typical of a particular kind of problem: *'The underdog syndrome' is a belief that things are beyond your control.*

syn·er·gy /ˈsɪnədʒi $ -ər-/ n [U] *technical* the additional effectiveness when two or more companies or people combine and work together

syn·od /ˈsɪnəd, -nɒd $ -nəd/ n [C] an important meeting of church members

syn·o·nym /ˈsɪnənɪm/ n [C] *technical* a word with the same meaning as another word in the same language; → **antonym**: [+for/of] *'Shut' is a synonym of 'closed'.*

sy·non·y·mous /sɪˈnɒnɪməs $ -ˈnɑː-/ adj **1** something that is synonymous with something else is considered to be very closely connected with it: [+with] *Nixon's name has become synonymous with political scandal.* **2** two words that are synonymous have the same meaning —**synonymously** adv

sy·nop·sis /sɪˈnɒpsɪs $ -ˈnɑːp-/ n plural **synopses** /-siːz/ [C] a short description of the main events or ideas in a book, film etc; ▤ **summary**: [+of] *a synopsis of the play*

syn·tac·tic /sɪnˈtæktɪk/ adj *technical* relating to syntax: *syntactic structure* —**syntactically** /-kli/ adv

syn·tax /ˈsɪntæks/ n [U] *technical* **1** the way words are arranged to form sentences or phrases, or the rules of grammar which control this **2** the rules that describe how words and phrases are used in a computer language

synth /sɪnθ/ n [C] *informal* a synthesizer

syn·the·sis /ˈsɪnθəsɪs/ n plural **syntheses** /-siːz/ **1** [C,U] something that has been made by combining different things, or the process of combining things; ▤ **combination**: [+of] *a synthesis of Eastern and Western philosophical ideas* **2** [U] the act of making a chemical or biological substance: [+of] *the synthesis of proteins* **3** [U] the production of sounds, speech, or music electronically: *speech synthesis software*

syn·the·size also **-ise** *BrE* /ˈsɪnθəsaɪz/ v [T] **1** to make something by combining different things or substances: *DDT is a pesticide that was first synthesized in 1874.* **2** to combine separate things into a complete whole **3** to produce sounds, speech, or music electronically

syn·the·siz·er also **-iser** *BrE* /ˈsɪnθəsaɪzə $ -ər/ n [C] an electronic instrument that produces the sounds of various musical instruments

syn·thes·pi·an /sɪnˈθespiən/ n [C] an actor who seems like a real person, but who is an image made using a computer; ▤ **VActor**

syn·thet·ic /sɪnˈθetɪk/ adj produced by combining different artificial substances, rather than being naturally produced: *synthetic chemicals* | **synthetic fibres/materials/fabrics** —**synthetically** /-kli/ adv

syn·thet·ics /sɪnˈθetɪks/ n [plural] substances or materials, especially cloth, that are made using a chemical process

syph·i·lis /ˈsɪfəlɪs/ n [U] a very serious disease that is passed from one person to another during sexual activity —**syphilitic** /ˌsɪfəˈlɪtɪk◄/ adj

sy·phon /ˈsaɪfən/ a British spelling of SIPHON

sy·ringe¹ /sɪˈrɪndʒ/ n [C] an instrument for taking blood from someone's body or putting liquid, drugs etc into it, consisting of a hollow plastic tube and a needle

syringe² v [T] to clean something with a syringe, for example your ears

syr·up /ˈsɪrəp $ ˈsɜː-, ˈsɪ-/ n [U] **1** a thick sticky sweet liquid, eaten on top of or mixed with other foods: *ice cream and maple syrup* **2** sweet liquid made from sugar and water, used in cans of fruit → **cough syrup** at COUGH MIXTURE

syr·up·y /ˈsɪrəpi $ ˈsɜː-, ˈsɪ-/ adj **1** thick and sticky like syrup or containing syrup: *a syrupy liquid* **2** too nice or kind in a way that seems insincere – used in order to show disapproval: *a syrupy speech*

sys·tem S1 W1 /ˈsɪstəm/ n
1 RELATED PARTS [C] a group of related parts that work together as a whole for a particular purpose: *an alarm system* | *a well-designed heating system* | *the digestive system* | *the railway system* | *the banking system* | *political/legal/education system a fundamental reform of the country's political system* | [+of] *the British system of government*
2 METHOD [C] an organized set of ideas, methods, or ways of working: **system of/for doing sth** *a system for dealing with complaints from customers* | *I don't understand your filing system.* | **under a system** *Under the present system, we do not have any flexibility.*
3 COMPUTERS [C] a group of computers that are connected to each other: *The system has crashed.* (=stopped working)
4 sb's system someone's body – used when you are talking about its medical or physical condition: *All this overeating is not good for my system.*
5 all systems go used, sometimes humorously, to say that you are ready to do something or that something is ready to happen
6 the system the official rules and powerful organizations that restrict what you can do: *You can't beat the system.*
7 get sth out of your system *informal* to do something that helps you get rid of unpleasant strong feelings: *I was furious, so I went for a run to get it out of my system.*
8 ORDER [U] the use of sensible and organized methods: *We need a bit more system in the way we organize our files.*

sys·te·mat·ic /ˌsɪstəˈmætɪk◄/ adj organized carefully and done thoroughly: **a systematic approach/way/method** *a systematic approach to solving the problem* | *a systematic way of organizing your work* —**systematically** /-kli/ adv

sys·te·ma·tize also **-ise** *BrE* /ˈsɪstəmətaɪz/ v [T] to put facts, numbers, ideas etc into a particular order —**systematization** /ˌsɪstəmətaɪˈzeɪʃən $ -mətə-/ n [U]

sys·te·mic /sɪˈstemɪk, -ˈstiː-$ sɪˈstemɪk/ adj *technical* or *formal* affecting the whole of something: *a systemic disease* | *a systemic insecticide* | *Corruption in the police force is systemic.*

ˈsystems ˌanalyst n [C] someone whose job is to study a company's computer needs and provide them with suitable software and equipment —**ˌsystems aˈnalysis** n [U]

ˈsystem tray n [C] the place where the clock and some ICONS (=small pictures that are used to start a particular operation) are shown on a computer screen

T, t

T, t /tiː/ *plural* **T's, t's** *n* **1** [C,U] the 20th letter of the English alphabet **2 to a T/tee** *informal* perfectly or exactly: *That dress suits you to a T.* → T-BONE STEAK, T-JUNCTION, T-SHIRT, T-SQUARE

t **1** the written abbreviation of *tonne* or *tonnes* **2** the written abbreviation of *ton* or *tons*

ta [S3] /tɑː/ *BrE informal* thank you

TA /ˌtiː ˈeɪ/ *n* **1** [singular] *BrE* the abbreviation of TERRITORIAL ARMY **2** [C] *AmE* the abbreviation of TEACH-ING ASSISTANT

tab¹ /tæb/ *n* [C]
1 IN TYPING a TAB KEY
2 MONEY THAT YOU OWE an amount of money that you owe, or a record of an amount of money that you owe: *The tab for the campaign was nearly $500 million.* | *I'll* **put it on** *your* **tab** *and you can pay tomorrow.* | *He* **ran up a** *$4000* **tab** *in long-distance calls.*
3 pick up the tab to pay for something, especially when it is not your responsibility to pay: *Taxpayers will pick up the tab for the stadium.*
4 TO OPEN a) *especially AmE* a small piece of metal that you pull to open a can of drink; ◨ **ring pull** *BrE* **b)** a small piece of metal, plastic, or paper that you pull to open something
5 SMALL PIECE OF PAPER/PLASTIC ETC a small piece of paper, cloth, plastic etc that sticks out from the edge of something, so that you can find it more easily: *an index tab labeled 'Blackman'*
6 also **license tab** *AmE* a small piece of sticky plastic with a date on it that you put on your car's LICENSE PLATE to show that the car is legally allowed on the road
7 keep (close) tabs on sb/sth *informal* to watch someone or something carefully to check what they are doing: *The police have been keeping tabs on Rogers since he got out of prison.*
8 DRUG *informal* a form of the illegal drug LSD or ECSTASY: *a tab of acid*
9 CIGARETTE *BrE informal* a cigarette

tab² *v* **tabbed, tabbing** [I] to press the TAB KEY on a computer or TYPEWRITER

tab·ard /'tæbɑːd $ -bərd/ *n* [C] *BrE* a piece of clothing that covers your chest and back and has no sleeves, worn over a shirt or jacket

Ta·bas·co /tə'bæskəʊ $ -koʊ/ also **Ta,basco 'sauce** *n* [U] *trademark* a very spicy red sauce made from CHILLI peppers

tab·by /'tæbi/ *n plural* **tabbies** [C] a cat with light and dark lines on its fur —**tabby** *adj*

tab·er·nac·le /'tæbənækəl $ -bər-/ *n* [C] **1** a church or other building used by some Christian groups as a place of WORSHIP **2** a box in which holy bread and wine are kept in Catholic churches **3 the Tabernacle** the small tent in which the ancient Jews kept their most holy objects

'tab key also **'tab stop** *n* [C] a button on a computer or TYPEWRITER that you press in order to move forward to a particular place on a line of writing; ◨ **tab**

tab·la /'tæblə $ 'tɑː-/ *n* [C] a pair of small hand drums used especially in Indian CLASSICAL music

ta·ble¹ [S1] [W1] /'teɪbəl/ *n* [C]
1 FURNITURE a piece of furniture with a flat top supported by legs: *the dining-room table* | **lay the table** *BrE* **set the table** *AmE* (=put knives, forks etc on a table before a meal) | *The waiter* **cleared** *the* **table** (=took all the plates, glasses etc off). | **book/reserve a table** (=in a

dining table
bedside table
desk
coffee table
kitchen table
patio/garden table
picnic table/bench
chess table
pool table

restaurant) *I've booked a table for two for 8 o'clock.* | **coffee/bedside/dinner table**
2 SPORT/GAME snooker/billiard/ping-pong etc table a special table for playing a particular indoor sport or game on
3 LIST a list of numbers, facts, or information arranged in rows across and down a page: [+of] *a table of results* | *the* **table of contents**
4 on the table an offer, idea etc that is on the table has been officially suggested and someone is considering it: *The offer on the table at the moment is a 10% wage increase.*
5 turn the tables (on sb) to change a situation completely, so that someone loses an advantage and you gain one: *The tables were turned in the second half, when Leeds United scored from the penalty spot.*
6 under the table *informal* money that is paid under the table is paid secretly and illegally: *Payments were made under the table to local officials.*
7 MATHS times table a list that young children learn, in which all the numbers between 1 and 12 are multiplied by each other; ◨ **multiplication table: three/four etc times table** *He's 12 years old and still doesn't know his three times table.*
8 GROUP the group of people sitting around a table: *His stories kept the whole table amused.*

table² *v* [T] **1 table a proposal/question/motion etc** *BrE* to formally present a proposal etc for other people to discuss: *Dr Clark tabled a motion for debate at next month's committee meeting.* **2 table a bill/measure/proposal etc** *AmE* to leave a bill etc to be discussed or dealt with in the future

tab·leau /'tæbləʊ $ 'tæbloʊ, tæ'bloʊ/ *n plural* **tableaux** /-ləʊz $ -loʊz/ [C] **1** a group of people shown in a work of art **2** a group of people arranged on stage like a picture **3** something you see that looks like a picture, especially a group of people who are not moving or speaking

ta·ble·cloth /'teɪbəlklɒθ $ -klɒːθ/ *n* [C] a cloth used for covering a table

'table ,dancing *n* [U] dancing with sexy movements that is performed close to a customer's table in a restaurant or NIGHTCLUB

T

ta·ble d'hôte /ˌtɑːbəl ˈdəʊt $ -ˈdoʊt/ n [U] BrE a meal served in a restaurant at a fixed price, with a limited number of dishes you can choose from; → **à la carte**

'**table ˌfootball** BrE n [U] a game played on a special table by two players or teams. You score goals by moving rows of model football players from side to side so that they can kick the ball, using handles attached to the players; → **foosball**

'**table ˌlamp** n [C] a small electric lamp that you put on a table or other piece of furniture

ta·ble·land /ˈteɪbl-lænd/ also **tablelands** n [C] technical a large area of high flat land

'**table ˌlinen** n [U] all the cloths used during a meal, such as NAPKINS and tablecloths

'**table ˌmanners** n [plural] the way in which someone eats their food – used when considering how socially acceptable it is: *Their children have very good table manners.*

'**table mat** n [C] BrE a small board or piece of cloth that you put under a hot dish or plate to protect the table

ta·ble·spoon /ˈteɪbəlspuːn/ n [C] **1** a large spoon used for serving food **2** also **ta·ble·spoon·ful** /-spuːn-fʊl/ written abbreviation **tbsp** or **tbs** the amount that a tablespoon can hold, used as a unit for measuring food or liquid in cooking: [+of] *two tablespoons of flour*

tab·let /ˈtæblɪt/ n [C] **1** a small round hard piece of medicine which you swallow; ☐ **pill**: *She took a couple of headache tablets.* | *vitamin/sleeping/indigestion etc* **tablet 2** a small hard piece of a substance, especially one that DISSOLVES in water: *water purification tablets* **3** a flat piece of stone or clay with words cut into it, for example above someone's GRAVE **4 be written/set/cast in tablets of stone** BrE used to say that something does not change: *The programme should not be set in tablets of stone, but improved continuously.* **5** AmE a set of pieces of paper for writing on that are glued together at the top; ☐ **pad** BrE

'**table ˌtennis** n [U] an indoor game played on a table by two or four players who hit a small plastic ball to each other across a net; ☐ **ping-pong**; → see picture at SPORTS CENTRE

ta·ble·ware /ˈteɪbəlweə $ -wer/ n [U] formal the plates, glasses, knives etc used when eating a meal

'**table ˌwine** n [C,U] a fairly cheap wine

tab·loid /ˈtæblɔɪd/ also **tabloid ˈnewspaper** n [C] a newspaper that has small pages, a lot of photographs, and stories mainly about sex, famous people etc rather than serious news; → **broadsheet** —**tabloid** adj [only before noun]: *tabloid journalists*

ta·boo¹ /təˈbuː, tæ-/ adj **1** a taboo subject, word, activity etc is one that people avoid because it is extremely offensive or embarrassing: *Rape is a taboo subject.* **2** not accepted as socially correct: *It's taboo to date a man a lot younger than you.* **3** too holy or evil to be touched or used

taboo² n plural **taboos** [C] a custom that says you must avoid a particular activity or subject, either because it is considered offensive or because your religion does not allow it: [+about/on/against] *There are taboos against appearing naked in public places.*

ta·bor /ˈteɪbə $ -ər/ n [C] a small DRUM, played with one hand, used especially in the MIDDLE AGES

tab·u·lar /ˈtæbjʊlə $ -ər/ adj arranged in rows across and down a page, in the form of a TABLE

tab·u·la ra·sa /ˌtæbjʊlə ˈrɑːzə/ n [singular] literary your mind in its original state, before you have learned anything

tab·u·late /ˈtæbjʊleɪt/ v [T] to arrange figures or information together in a set or a list, so that they can be easily compared —**tabulation** /ˌtæbjʊˈleɪʃən/ n [C,U]

tach·o·graph /ˈtækəɡrɑːf $ -ɡræf/ n [C] technical a piece of equipment for recording the speed of a vehicle, the distance it has travelled etc

ta·chom·e·ter /tæˈkɒmɪtə $ -ˈkɑːmɪtər/ n [C] technical a piece of equipment used to measure the speed at which the engine of a vehicle turns

ta·cit /ˈtæsɪt/ adj tacit agreement, approval, support etc is given without anything actually being said: *a tacit agreement between the three big companies* —**tacitly** adv

ta·ci·turn /ˈtæsɪtɜːn $ -ɜːrn/ adj formal speaking very little, so that you seem unfriendly —**taciturnity** /ˌtæsɪˈtɜːnɪti $ -ɜːr-/ n [U]

tack¹ /tæk/ n
1 NAIL [C] a small nail with a sharp point and a flat top
2 PIN [C] AmE a short pin with a large round flat top, for attaching notices to boards, walls etc; ☐ **thumbtack**; ☐ **drawing pin** BrE
3 WAY OF DOING STH [C,U] the way you deal with a particular situation or a method that you use to achieve something: *If that doesn't work, we'll try a different tack.* | *Rudy changed tack, his tone suddenly becoming friendly.*
4 SHIP a) [C,U] the direction that a sailing boat moves, depending on the direction of the wind and the position of its sails **b)** [C] the action of changing the direction of a sailing boat, or the distance it travels between these changes: *a long tack into the bay*
5 HORSES [U] technical the equipment you need for riding a horse, such as a SADDLE etc
6 SEWING [C] a long loose stitch used for fastening pieces of cloth together before sewing them
7 UGLY OBJECTS [U] BrE ugly cheap objects sold as decorations: *souvenir shops full of tack*

tack² v **1** [T always + adv/prep] to attach something to a wall, board etc, using a tack: **tack sth to sth** *A handwritten note was tacked to the wall.* **2** [I] to change the course of a sailing ship so that the wind blows against its sails from the opposite direction **3** [T] to fasten pieces of cloth together with long loose stitches, before sewing them

tack sth ⇔ on phr v to add something new to something that is already complete, especially in a way that looks wrong or spoils the original thing: *a beautiful old house with a hideous modern extension tacked on at the back*

tack·le¹ S3 W3 /ˈtækəl/ v
1 [T] to try to deal with a difficult problem: *There is more than one way to tackle the problem.* | *It took twelve fire engines to tackle the blaze.*
2 [I,T] **a)** to try to take the ball away from an opponent in a game such as football or HOCKEY **b)** to force someone to the ground so that they stop running, in a game such as American football or RUGBY
3 [T] BrE to talk to someone in order to deal with a difficult problem: **tackle sb about sth** *When I tackled Susan about it, she admitted she'd made a mistake.*
4 [T] to start fighting someone, especially a criminal: *I certainly couldn't tackle both of them on my own.* —**tackler** n [C]

tackle² n **1** [C] **a)** an attempt to take the ball from an opponent in a game such as football **b)** an attempt to stop an opponent by forcing them to the ground, especially in American football or RUGBY **2** [C] a player in American football who stops other players by tackling them or preventing them from moving forward **3** [U] the equipment used in some sports and activities, especially fishing → see picture at FISHING **4** [C,U] ropes and PULLEYS (=wheels) used for lifting heavy things **5** [U] BrE informal a man's sexual organs

tack·y /ˈtæki/ adj **1** if something is tacky, it looks cheap or badly made, and shows poor taste: *tacky ornaments* **2** especially AmE showing that you do not have good judgment about what is socially acceptable: *It's kind of tacky to give her a present that someone else gave you.* **3** slightly sticky: *The paint's still slightly tacky.* —**tackily** adv —**tackiness** n [U]

T

tac·o /'tækəʊ, 'tɑ:- $ 'tɑːkoʊ/ *n plural* **tacos** [C] a type of Mexican food made from a corn TORTILLA that is folded in half and filled with meat, beans etc

tact /tækt/ *n* [U] the ability to be careful about what you say or do, so that you do not upset or embarrass other people; → **tactful, tactless**: *With great tact, Clive persuaded her to apologize.*

tact·ful /'tæktfəl/ *adj* not likely to upset or embarrass other people; ◧ **tactless**: *There was no tactful way of phrasing what he wanted to say.* | *a tactful man* —**tactfully** *adv*

tac·tic /'tæktɪk/ *n* [C] **1** a method that you use to achieve something: *a tactic employed to speed up the peace process* | *Republicans accuse Democrats of using* **delaying tactics** (=something you do in order to give yourself more time) *to prevent a final vote on the bill.* | *Shock tactics are being used in an attempt to stop drink drivers.* **2 tactics** [plural] the science of arranging and moving military forces in a battle → **strong-arm tactics** at **STRONG-ARM**

tac·ti·cal /'tæktɪkəl/ *adj* **1** relating to what you do to achieve what you want, especially as part of a game or large plan: *Two players were substituted for* **tactical reasons.** | **tactical move/decision/ploy** *an immediate tactical decision to send in troops* | **tactical error/mistake/blunder** (=a mistake that will harm your plans later) **2 tactical weapon/missile** a MISSILE that is sent a short distance in military battle **3** relating to the way military forces are arranged in a battle —**tactically** /-kli/ *adv*

tactical 'voting *n* [U] *BrE* the practice of voting for a political party that you do not support in order to prevent another party from winning an election

tac·ti·cian /tæk'tɪʃən/ *n* [C] someone who is very good at TACTICS

tac·tile /'tæktaɪl $ 'tæktl/ *adj* **1** relating to your sense of touch: *tactile sensations* **2** a tactile person likes to touch people, for example when talking to them

tact·less /'tæktləs/ *adj* likely to upset or embarrass someone without intending to; ◧ **tactful**: *I thought it would be tactless to ask about her divorce.* | *She's one of the most tactless people I've ever met.* | *a tactless remark* —**tactlessly** *adv* —**tactlessness** *n* [U]

tad /tæd/ *n spoken* **a tad a)** a small amount: *'Would you like some milk?' 'Just a tad.'* **b)** slightly: *It's a tad expensive.*

tad·pole /'tædpəʊl $ -poʊl/ *n* [C] a small creature that has a long tail, lives in water, and grows into a FROG or TOAD

tae·kwon·do /taɪ'kwɒndəʊ $ -'kwɑːndoʊ/ *n* [U] a style of fighting from Korea, and also a sport, in which you kick and hit but do not use weapons; → **karate**

taf·fe·ta /'tæfɪtə/ *n* [U] a shiny stiff cloth made from silk or NYLON

Taf·fy /'tæfi/ *n* [C] *BrE* an offensive word for someone from Wales

taffy *n plural* **taffies** [C,U] *AmE* a type of soft CHEWY sweet

tag¹ /tæg/ *n*
1 SMALL PIECE OF PAPER ETC [C] a small piece of paper, plastic etc attached to something to show what it is, who owns it, what it costs etc: **name/identity/price tag** *All the staff wore name tags.* → **DOG TAG**
2 GAME [U] a children's game in which one player chases and tries to touch the others
3 ELECTRONIC OBJECT also **electronic tag** [C] *BrE* a piece of equipment that you attach to an animal or person, especially someone who has just left prison, so that you always know where they are
4 COMPUTER [C] a computer CODE attached to a word or phrase in a computer document in order to arrange the DATA in a particular way

5 NAME [C] a word or phrase which is used to describe a person, group, or thing, but which is often unfair or not correct: *His speed earned him the tag of 'the runner'.*
6 GRAMMAR [C] *technical* a TAG QUESTION
7 NAME PAINTED ON WALL [C] *informal especially AmE* someone's name that they paint illegally on a wall, vehicle etc
8 CAR *AmE* **a)** tags [plural] *informal* the LICENSE PLATES on a car **b)** [C] a small piece of sticky plastic with a date on it that you put on your car's LICENSE PLATE to show that the car is legally allowed on the road in that year

tag² *v* **tagged, tagging** [T] **1** to attach a tag to something: *Each bird was tagged and released into the wild.* **2** to give someone or something a name or title, or describe them in a particular way: **be tagged (as) sth** *The country no longer wants to be tagged as a Third World nation.* **3** to attach a tag in a computer program or document: *All the words are tagged with their part of speech.* **4** *informal* to illegally paint your name on a wall, vehicle etc **5** *AmE* to touch someone you are chasing in a game, especially to touch someone with the ball in baseball

tag along *phr v* to go somewhere with someone, especially when they have not asked you to go with them; ◧ **tag on** *BrE*: [+with] | *Kate tagged along with mum and Vicky.*

tag on *phr v* **1 tag sth ⇔ on** to add something, especially something that was thought of later **2** *BrE* to tag along

tag·a·long /'tægəlɒŋ $ -lɒːŋ/ *n* [C] **1** *BrE* something that is attached to and pulled behind something else: *The tagalong attaches to an adult's bicycle.* **2** someone who goes somewhere with someone else: *We were tagalongs on my parents' vacations.*

tag·ging /'tægɪŋ/ *n* [U] *especially AmE* when someone illegally paints their name or symbol on a wall, vehicle etc —**tagger** *n* [C]

ta·glia·tel·le /ˌtæljə'teli $ ˌtɑː-/ *n* [U] a type of PASTA that is cut into very long thin flat pieces

'tag ˌquestion *n* [C] *technical* a question that is formed by adding a phrase such as 'can't we?', 'wouldn't he?', or 'is it?' to a sentence

T'ai Chi /ˌtaɪ 'tʃiː, -'dʒiː/ *n* [U] a Chinese form of exercise that involves extremely slow movements, and that trains your mind and body

tail¹ [S2] [W3] /teɪl/ *n* [C]
1 ANIMAL the part that sticks out at the back of an animal's body, and that it can move: *The dog* **wagged** *its* **tail.** | **white-tailed/long-tailed etc** *a white-tailed eagle*
2 AIRCRAFT the back part of an aircraft
3 SHIRT the bottom part of your shirt at the back, that you put inside your trousers
4 BACK PART [usually singular] the back or last part of something, especially something that is moving away from you: *We saw the tail of the procession disappearing round the corner.*
5 tails **a)** [plural] a man's jacket which is short at the front and divides into two long pieces at the back, worn to very formal events; ◧ **tailcoat b)** [U] *spoken* said when you are TOSSING a coin (=throwing it up in the air to decide which of two things you will do or choose); ◧ **heads**
6 the tail end of sth the last part of an event, situation, or period of time
7 be on sb's tail *informal* to be following someone closely
8 FOLLOW *informal* someone who is employed to watch and follow someone, especially a criminal: **put a tail on sb** (=order someone to follow another person)
9 turn tail *informal* to run away because you are too frightened to fight or attack
10 with your tail between your legs embarrassed or unhappy because you have failed or been defeated
11 it's (a case of) the tail wagging the dog *informal* used to say that an unimportant thing is wrongly controlling a situation

12 chase tail *AmE informal* to try to get a woman to have sex with you

tail² *v* [T] *informal* to follow someone and watch what they do, where they go etc: *The police have been tailing him for several months.*
· **tail away** *phr v BrE* to TAIL OFF
  tail back *phr v BrE* if traffic tails back, a long line of cars forms, for example because the road is blocked
  tail off also **tail away** *BrE phr v* **1** to become gradually less, smaller etc, and often stop or disappear completely: *Profits tailed off towards the end of the year.* **2** *written* if someone's voice tails off, it becomes quieter and then stops: *'I didn't mean ...' Her voice tailed off in embarrassment.*

tail·back /ˈteɪlbæk/ *n* [C] **1** *BrE* a line of traffic that is moving very slowly or not moving at all: *a five-mile tailback on the M25* **2** *AmE* the player who is the furthest back from the front line in American football

tail·board /ˈteɪlbɔːd $ -bɔːrd/ *n* [C] a TAILGATE

tail·bone /ˈteɪlbəʊn $ -boʊn/ *n* [C] the small bone at the bottom of your SPINE; ▤ **coccyx**

tail·coat /ˈteɪlkəʊt $ -koʊt/ *n* [C] a man's jacket which is short at the front and divided into two long pieces at the back, worn to very formal events; ▤ **tails**

tail·gate¹ /ˈteɪlgeɪt/ *n* [C] *AmE* **1** a door at the back of a truck or car that opens out and down **2** a tailgate party

tailgate² *v* [I,T] to drive too closely to the vehicle in front of you

'tailgate ˌparty also **tailgate** *n* [C] *AmE* a party before an American football game, where people eat and drink near their cars in the CAR PARK of the place where the game is played

'tail light *n* [C] one of the two red lights at the back of a vehicle ➔ see picture at CAR

tai·lor¹ /ˈteɪlə $ -ər/ *n* [C] someone whose job is to make men's clothes, that are measured to fit each customer perfectly; ➔ **dressmaker**

tailor² *v* [T] to make something so that it is exactly right for someone's particular needs or for a particular purpose: **tailor sth to sth** *Treatment is tailored to the needs of each patient.* | **tailor sth to meet/suit sb's needs/requirements** *The classes are tailored to suit learners' needs.* | **tailor sth for sb** *We tailored the part specifically for her.*

tai·lored /ˈteɪləd $ -ərd/ *adj* **1** a piece of clothing that is tailored is made to fit very well: *a tailored suit* **2** made or done specially for someone's particular need or situation: *tailored financial advice*

tai·lor·ing /ˈteɪlərɪŋ/ *n* [U] the work of making men's clothes, or the style in which they are made

ˌtailor-'made *adj* exactly right or suitable for someone or something: [+**for**] *The job's tailor-made for you.* | [+**to**] *insurance tailor-made to each client's requirements*

tail·piece /ˈteɪlpiːs/ *n* [C] *BrE* a part that forms or is added to the end of something, especially a piece of writing

tail·pipe /ˈteɪlpaɪp/ *n* [C] *AmE* a pipe on a vehicle or machine through which gas or steam passes

tail·spin /ˈteɪlˌspɪn/ *n* [C usually singular] **1 in/into a tailspin** in or into a bad situation that keeps getting worse in a way that you cannot control: *Raising interest rates could send the economy into a tailspin.* **2** when a plane falls through the air, with the front pointing downwards and the back spinning in a circle

tail·wind /ˈteɪlˌwɪnd/ *n* [C] a wind blowing in the same direction that something or someone is travelling; ➔ **headwind**

taint¹ /teɪnt/ *v* [T usually passive] **1** if something bad taints a situation or person, it makes the person or situation seem bad: *Baker argues that his trial was tainted by negative publicity.* **2** to damage something by adding an unwanted substance to it: **taint sth with sth** *The water had been tainted with a deadly toxin.*

taint² *n* [singular] the appearance of being related to something bad or morally wrong: [+**of**] *The city has suffered for many years under the taint of corruption.*

taint·ed /ˈteɪntɪd/ *adj especially AmE* **1** a tainted substance, especially food or drink, is not safe because it is spoiled or contains a harmful substance or poison: *a tainted blood supply* **2** affected or influenced by something illegal, dishonest, or morally wrong: *a tainted witness*

take¹ S1 W1 /teɪk/ *v past tense* **took** /tʊk/, *past participle* **taken** /ˈteɪkən/

take down

taking down notes

1 ACTION [T] used with a noun instead of using a verb to describe an action. For example, if you take a walk, you walk somewhere: *Would you like to take a look?* | *Mike's just taking a shower.* | *Sara took a deep breath.* | *I waved, but he **didn't take any notice** (=pretended not to notice). BrE* | *Please **take a seat** (=sit down).* | **take a picture/photograph/photo** *Would you mind taking a photo of us together?*

2 MOVE [T] to move or go with someone or something from one place to another; ➔ **bring: take sb/sth to/into etc sth** *Barney took us to the airport.* | *Would you mind taking Susie home?* | *When he refused to give his name, he was taken into custody.* | *My job has taken me all over the world.* | **take sb/sth with you** *His wife went to Australia, taking the children with her.* | **take sb sth** *I have to take Steve the money tonight.* | **take sb to do sth** *He took me to meet his parents.* ➔ see box at BRING; ➔ see box at DIRECT²

3 REMOVE [T] to remove something from a place: **take sth off/from etc sth** *Take your feet off the seats.* | *Someone's taken a pen from my desk.* | *Police say money and jewellery were taken in the raid.* ➔ TAKE AWAY

4 TIME/MONEY/EFFORT ETC [I,T] if something takes a particular amount of time, money, effort etc, that amount of time etc is needed for it to happen or succeed: *How **long** is this going to take?* | *Organizing a successful street party takes a lot of energy.* | **take (sb) sth (to do sth)** *Repairs take time to carry out.* | *It took a few minutes for his eyes to adjust to the dark.* | **take (sb) ages/forever** *informal*: *It took me ages to find a present for Dad.* | **take some doing** *BrE informal* (=need a lot of time or effort) *Catching up four goals will take some doing.* | **take courage/guts** *It takes courage to admit you are wrong.* | **have what it takes** *informal* (=to have the qualities that are needed for success) *Neil's got what it takes to be a great footballer.*

5 ACCEPT [T] to accept or choose something that is offered, suggested, or given to you: *Will you take the job?* | *Do you take American Express?* | *If you **take my advice**, you'll see a doctor.* | *Our helpline takes 3.5 million **calls** (=telephone calls) a year.* | *Some doctors are unwilling to take new patients without a referral.* | *Liz found his criticisms **hard to take**.* | *I just **can't take any more** (=can't deal with a bad situation any longer).* | *Staff have agreed to take a 2% pay cut.* | **take a hammering/beating** (=be forced to accept defeat or a bad situation) *Small businesses took a hammering in the last recession.* | **I take your point/point taken** (=used to say that you accept someone's opinion) | **take sb's word for it/take it from sb** (=accept that what someone says is true) *That's the truth – **take it from me**.* | **take the credit/blame/responsibility** *He's the kind of man who makes things happen but lets others take the*

T

credit. | **take it as read/given** (= ASSUME that something is correct or certain, because you are sure that this is the case) *It isn't official yet, but you can take it as read that you've got the contract.*

6 HOLD STH [T] to get hold of something in your hands: *Let me take your coat.* | *Can you take this package while I get my wallet?* | **take sb/sth in/by sth** *I just wanted to take him in my arms.* → see box at HOLD[1]

7 TRAVEL [T] to use a particular form of transport or a particular road in order to go somewhere: *Let's take a cab.* | *I took the first plane out.* | *Take the M6 to Junction 19.*

8 STUDY [T] to study a particular subject in school or college for an examination: *Are you taking French next year?*

9 TEST [T] to do an examination or test; **■ sit** *BrE*: *Applicants are asked to take a written test.*

10 SUITABLE [T not in progressive or passive] to be the correct or suitable size, type etc for a particular person or thing: *a car that takes low sulphur fuel* | *What size shoe do you take?* | *The elevator takes a maximum of 32 people.*

11 COLLECT [T] to collect or gather something for a particular purpose: *Investigators will take samples of the wreckage to identify the cause.* | **take sth from sth** *The police took a statement from both witnesses.*

12 CONSIDER [I,T always + adv/prep] to react to someone or something or consider them in a particular way: **take sb/sth seriously/badly/personally etc** *I was joking, but he took me seriously.* | *Ben took the news very badly.* | *She does not take kindly to criticism* (=reacts badly to criticism). | **take sth as sth** *I'll take that remark as a compliment.* | **take sth as evidence/proof (of sth)** *The presence of dust clouds has been taken as evidence of recent star formation.* | **take sb/sth to be sth** *I took her to be his daughter.* | **take sb/sth for sth** *Of course I won't tell anyone! What do you take me for?* (=what sort of person do you think I am?) | *I take it* (=I ASSUME) *you've heard that Rick's resigned.*

13 FEELINGS [T usually + adv] to have or experience a particular feeling: **take delight/pleasure/pride etc in (doing) sth** *You should take pride in your work.* | *At first, he took no interest in the baby.* | **take pity on sb** *She stood feeling lost until an elderly man took pity on her.* | **take offence** (=feel offended) *Don't take offence. Roger says things like that to everybody.* | **take comfort from/in (doing) sth** *Investors can take comfort from the fact that the World Bank is underwriting the shares.*

14 CONTROL [T] to get possession or control of something: *Enemy forces have taken the airport.* | *Both boys were taken prisoner.* | **take control/charge/power** *The communists took power in 1948.* | *Youngsters need to take control of their own lives.* | **take the lead** (=in a race, competition etc)

15 MEDICINE/DRUGS [T] to swallow, breathe in, INJECT etc a drug or medicine: *The doctor will ask whether you are taking any medication.* | *Take two tablets before bedtime.* | **take drugs** (=take illegal drugs) *Most teenagers start taking drugs through boredom.* | *She took an overdose after a row with her boyfriend.*

16 do you take sugar/milk? *spoken BrE* used to ask someone whether they like to have sugar or milk in a drink such as tea or coffee

17 LEVEL [T always + adv/prep] to make someone or something go to a higher level or position: **take sth to/into sth** *The latest raise takes his salary into six figures.* | *Even if you have the talent to take you to the top, there's no guarantee you'll get there.* | *If you want to take it further, you should consult an attorney.*

18 MEASURE [T] to measure the amount, level, rate etc of something: *Take the patient's pulse first.*

19 NUMBERS [T] to make a number smaller by a particular amount; **■ subtract**: **take sth away/take sth (away) from sth** *'Take four from nine and what do you get?' 'Five.'* | *Ten take away nine equals one.*

20 MONEY [T] *BrE* if a shop, business etc takes a particular amount of money, it receives that amount of money from its customers; **■ take in** *AmE*: *The stall took £25 on Saturday.*

21 sb can take it or leave it a) to neither like nor dislike something: *To some people, smoking is addictive. Others can take it or leave it.* **b)** used to say that you do not care whether someone accepts your offer or not

22 take sb/sth (for example) used to give an example of something you have just been talking about: *People love British cars. Take the Mini. In Japan, it still sells more than all the other British cars put together.*

23 TEACH [T] *BrE* to teach a particular group of students in a school or college: **take sb for sth** *Who takes you for English?*

24 WRITE [T] to write down information: *Let me take your email address.* | *Sue offered to take notes.*

25 take sb out of themselves *BrE* to make someone forget their problems and feel more confident: *Alf said joining the club would take me out of myself.*

26 take a lot out of you/take it out of you to make you very tired: *Looking after a baby really takes it out of you.*

27 take it upon/on yourself to do sth *formal* to decide to do something without getting someone's permission or approval first: *Reg took it upon himself to hand the press a list of names.*

28 take sth to bits/pieces *BrE* to separate something into its different parts: *how to take an engine to bits*

29 be taken with/by sth to be attracted by a particular idea, plan, or person: *I'm quite taken by the idea of Christmas in Berlin.*

30 be taken ill/sick *formal* to suddenly become ill

31 SEX [T] *literary* if a man takes someone, he has sex with them

32 take a bend/fence/corner etc to try to get over or around something in a particular way: *He took the bend at over 60 and lost control.*

33 HAVE AN EFFECT [I] if a treatment, DYE, drug etc takes, it begins to work successfully

be taken aback *phr v*
to be very surprised about something: *Emma was somewhat taken aback by his directness.*

take after sb *phr v* [not in progressive]
to look or behave like an older relative: *Jenni really takes after her mother.*

take sb/sth **apart** *phr v*
1 to separate something into all its different parts; **◪ put together**: *Tom was always taking things apart in the garage.*

2 to search a place very thoroughly: *The police took the house apart looking for clues.*

3 to beat someone very easily in a game, sport, fight etc

4 to show that someone is wrong or something is not true: *Tariq takes several gay myths apart in his book.*

take against sb/sth *phr v BrE*
to begin to dislike someone or something, especially without a good reason: *Voters took against the relationship between the government and the unions in the 1970s.*

take sb/sth ⇔ **away** *phr v*
1 to remove someone or something, or make something disappear: *She whisked the tray off the table and took it away.* | *He was taken away to begin a prison sentence.* | *This should take some of the pain away.*

2 to take away *BrE* if you buy food to take away, you buy cooked food from a restaurant and take it outside to eat it somewhere else; → **takeaway**: *Fish and chips to take away, please.*

3 take your breath away to be very beautiful, exciting, or surprising

take away from sth *phr v*
to spoil the good effect or success that something has: *The disagreement between the two men should not take away from their accomplishments.*

take sb/sth ⇔ **back** *phr v*
1 take sth ⇔ back to admit that you were wrong to say something: *You'd better take back that remark!*

2 take sth ⇔ back to take something you have bought back to a shop because it is not suitable: *If the shirt doesn't fit, take it back.*
3 to make you remember a time in the past: *Having the grandchildren around takes me back to the days when my own children were small.*

take sth ⇔ down *phr v*
1 to move something that is fixed in a high position to a lower position: *She made us take down all the posters.*
2 to write down information: *Can I just take some details down?*
3 to pull a piece of clothing such as trousers part of the way down your legs

take sb/sth ⇔ in *phr v*
1 be taken in to be completely deceived by someone who lies to you: *Don't be taken in by products claiming to help you lose weight in a week.*
2 take sb ⇔ in to let someone stay in your house because they have nowhere else to stay: *Brett's always taking in stray animals.*
3 take sth ⇔ in to understand and remember new facts and information; ◧ **absorb**: *He watches the older kids, just taking it all in.* | *His eyes quickly took in the elegance of her dress.*
4 take sth ⇔ in *AmE* to collect or earn a particular amount of money; ◧ **take** *BrE*
5 to visit a place while you are in the area: *They continued a few miles further to take in Hinton House.*
6 *AmE old-fashioned* if you take in a show, play etc, you go to see it
7 take sb ⇔ in *BrE old-fashioned* if the police take someone in, they take them to a police station to ask them questions about a crime: *All five teenagers were arrested and taken in for questioning.*
8 take sth ⇔ in to make a piece of clothing fit you by making it narrower; ◧ **let out**

take off *phr v*
1 REMOVE **take sth ⇔ off** to remove a piece of clothing; ◧ **put on**: *He sat on the bed to take his boots off.* | *Charlie was taking off his shirt when the phone rang.*
2 AIRCRAFT if an aircraft takes off, it rises into the air from the ground; ◧ **lift off**; → **takeoff**: *I felt quite excited as the plane took off from Heathrow.*
3 SUCCESS to suddenly start being successful: *Mimi became jealous when Jack's career started taking off.*
4 HOLIDAY **take sth off (sth)** to have a holiday from work on a particular day, or for a particular length of time: **take time off (work/school)** *I rang my boss and arranged to take some time off.* | **take a day/the afternoon etc off** *Dad took the day off to come with me.*
5 COPY SB **take sb ⇔ off** *BrE informal* to copy the way someone speaks or behaves, in order to entertain people

take sb/sth ⇔ on *phr v*
1 take sb ⇔ on to start to employ someone; → **hire**: *We're taking on 50 new staff this year.*
2 take sth ⇔ on to agree to do some work or be responsible for something: *Don't take on too much work – the extra cash isn't worth it.*
3 take sth ⇔ on to begin to have a particular quality or appearance: *Her face took on a fierce expression.* | *His life had taken on a new dimension.*
4 take sb ⇔ on to compete against someone or start a fight with someone, especially someone bigger or better than you: *Nigeria will take on Argentina in the first round of the World Cup on Saturday.* | *He was prepared to take on anyone who laid a finger on me.*
5 take sth ⇔ on if a plane or ship takes on people or things, they come onto it: *We stopped to take on fuel.*

take sb/sth ⇔ out *phr v*
1 take sb ⇔ out to take someone as your guest to a restaurant, cinema, club etc: [+for] *We're taking my folks out for a meal next week.*
2 take sth ⇔ out to make a financial or legal arrangement with a bank, company, law court etc: **take out a policy/injunction/loan etc** *Before taking a loan out, calculate your monthly outgoings.*
3 take sth ⇔ out to get money from your bank account;

◧ **withdraw**: *How much would you like to take out?*
4 take sth ⇔ out to borrow books from a library: *You can take out six books at a time.*
5 take sb/sth ⇔ out *informal* to kill someone or destroy something: *The building was taken out by a bomb.*

take sth out on sb *phr v*
to treat someone badly when you are angry or upset, even though it is not their fault: *Don't take it out on me just because you've had a bad day.* | **take your anger/frustration etc out on sb** *Irritated with herself, she took her annoyance out on Bridget.*

take over *phr v*
to take control of something; → **takeover**: **take sth ⇔ over** *His only reason for investing in the company was to take it over.* | *Ruth moved into our apartment and promptly took over.*

take to sb/sth *phr v* [not in passive]
1 to start to like someone or something: *Sandra **took to** it **straight away**.* | *Charles was an odd character whom Kelly had never really taken to.*
2 to start doing something regularly: **take to doing sth** *Dee's taken to getting up at 6 and going jogging.*
3 take to your bed to get into your bed and stay there: *He was so depressed, he took to his bed for a week.*

take sth up *phr v*
1 take sth ⇔ up to become interested in a new activity and to spend time doing it: *Roger took painting up for a while, but soon lost interest.*
2 to start a new job or have a new responsibility: *Peter will take up the management of the finance department.* | **take up a post/a position/duties etc** *The headteacher takes her duties up in August.*
3 take sth ⇔ up if you take up a suggestion, problem, complaint etc, you start to do something about it: *Now the papers have taken up the story.* | [+with] *The hospital manager has promised to **take the matter up** with the member of staff involved.* | *I am still very angry and will be taking it up with the authorities.*
4 to fill a particular amount of time or space: **be taken up with sth** *The little time I had outside of school was taken up with work.* | **take up space/room** *old books that were taking up space in the office*
5 take sth ⇔ up to accept a suggestion, offer, or idea: *Rob **took up the invitation** to visit.* | **take up the challenge/gauntlet** *Rick took up the challenge and cycled the 250 mile route alone.*
6 to move to the exact place where you should be, so that you are ready to do something: *The runners are **taking up** their **positions** on the starting line.*
7 take sth ⇔ up to make a piece of clothing shorter; ◧ **let down**
8 take sth ⇔ up to continue a story or activity that you or someone else had begun, after a short break: *I'll take up the story where you left off.*

take sb up on sth *phr v*
to accept an invitation or suggestion: **take sb up on an offer/a promise/a suggestion etc** *I'll take you up on that offer of a drink, if it still stands.*

take up with sb/sth *phr v old-fashioned*
to become friendly with someone, especially someone who may influence you badly

take² n 1 [C] an occasion when a film scene, song, action etc is recorded: *We had to do six takes for this particular scene.* **2 sb's take (on sth)** someone's opinion about a situation or idea: *What's your take on this issue?* **3 be on the take** *informal* to be willing to do something wrong in return for money: *Is it true that some of the generals are on the take?* **4** [usually singular] *AmE informal* the amount of money earned by a shop or business in a particular period of time

take·a·way /ˈteɪkəweɪ/ *n* [C] *BrE* **1** a meal that you buy at a shop or restaurant to eat at home; ◧ **takeout** *AmE*: *Let's have a takeaway tonight.* → see picture at **EAT** **2** a shop or restaurant that sells meals to be eaten somewhere else

'take-home ,pay n [U] the amount of money that you receive from your job after taxes etc have been taken out

tak·en /'teɪkən/ the past participle of TAKE

'take-off n **1** [C,U] the time when a plane leaves the ground and begins to fly **2** [C] a humorous performance that copies the way someone behaves **3** [C] the time when your feet leave the ground when you are jumping

take·out, **'take-out** /'teɪk-aʊt/ n [C,U] AmE a meal that you buy at a restaurant to eat at home; ◱ **take-away** BrE —**takeout** adj: takeout food

take·o·ver /'teɪk,əʊvə $ -,oʊvər/ n [C] **1** when one company takes control of another by buying more than half its SHARES: Thornbury has announced a **takeover bid** of a regional TV company. | He prevented a **hostile takeover** (=when the takeover is not wanted by the company being bought) of the company. **2** an act of getting control of a country or political organization, using force: a communist takeover

ta·ker /'teɪkə $ -ər/ n [C] **1** be no/few/not many **takers** if there are no takers for something, no one accepts or wants what is being offered **2** someone who accepts support and help from other people, but who is not willing to give them support or help

-taker /teɪkə $ -ər/ suffix used with nouns to describe people who take or collect things: senior decision-takers | I'm just a message-taker. | a ticket-taker at the recreation hall | the policy of not doing deals with hostage takers | treatment for **drug takers**

'take-up n [U] BrE the rate at which people accept something that is offered to them: Take-up for college places has been slow.

tak·ings /'teɪkɪŋz/ n [plural] the money that a business, shop etc gets from selling its goods over a particular period of time: **the day's/week's etc takings** He counted the night's takings. | **bar/box-office etc takings** Cinema box-office takings in 2001 were £600m.

talc /tælk/ n [U] talcum powder

tal·cum pow·der /'tælkəm ,paʊdə $ -dər/ n [U] a powder with a nice smell which you put on your skin after washing

tale [W3] /teɪl/ n [C] **1** a story about exciting imaginary events: [+of] tales of adventure | a book of old Japanese **folk tales** (=traditional stories) | a **fairy tale** by Hans Christian Andersen | a **cautionary tale** (=one that is told to warn people about the dangers of something) **2** a description of interesting or exciting things that happened to someone, often one which is not completely true about every detail: [+of/about] tales of her life in post-war Berlin | **tale of/about how** He was in the middle of **telling** me a long tale about how he once met the Redskins' manager. **3** tell tales BrE to tell someone in authority about something wrong that someone else has done; ◱ tattle AmE: [+to] Don't go telling tales to the teacher! **4** tale of woe **a)** a description of events that made you unhappy **b)** a series of bad things that happened to someone: The England team's tale of woe continued, and they lost the next three games. → FAIRY TALE; → old wives' tale at OLD (24)

tal·ent [S3] [W3] /'tælənt/ n **1** [C,U] a natural ability to do something well

have talent
show talent
talent contest/show/competition (=a competition in which people show how well they can sing, dance etc)
(a) natural talent
a hidden talent
musical/artistic/creative etc talent
a man/woman of many talents (=someone who can do many things well)
a wealth of talent (=when there are a lot of people with talent)

He **has** a lot of **talent**, and his work is fresh and interesting. | [+for] She **showed** a **talent** for acting at an early age. | a persuasive speaker with **a natural talent** for leadership | His latest book reveals **hidden talents**. | Sadly, she inherited none of her father's **musical talent**. | Your brother is **a man of many talents**. | There's a **wealth of talent** in English football. | [+for] She **showed** a **talent** for acting at an early age.

2 [U] a person or people with a natural ability or skill: Britain's footballing talent **3** [U] BrE informal sexually attractive people

tal·ent·ed /'tæləntɨd/ adj having a natural ability to do something well: a talented actor

tal·ent·less /'tæləntləs/ adj not having any special abilities or skills: a noisy, talentless band

'talent scout also **'talent-,spotter** n [C] someone whose job is to find young people who are very good at sport, music etc

'talent-,spotting n [U] the work of finding young people who are good at sport, music etc

tal·is·man /'tælɨzmən/ n plural **talismans** [C] an object that is believed to have magic powers to protect the person who owns it

talk¹ [S1] [W1] /tɔːk $ tɒːk/ v
1 **CONVERSATION** [I] to say things to someone as part of a conversation: I could hear Sarah and Andrew talking in the next room. | [+about] English people love to talk about the weather. | All through the afternoon, they sat and talked about their trip. | [+to] Claudia spent a long time talking to him. | She's very easy to talk to. | [+with] I got the truth from talking with Elena. | [+together] They were talking together in the hall. | Sue and Bob still **aren't talking** (=are refusing to talk to each other). | **talk in a low voice/a whisper etc** They were talking in low voices, and I couldn't catch what they were saying. | [+of] (=used especially in formal or literary contexts) We talked of old times. → see box at SPEAK

2 **SERIOUS SUBJECT** [I] to discuss something serious or important with someone: Joe, we need to talk. | Is there somewhere we can talk in private? | [+to] You should talk to a lawyer. | [+about] We've been talking about getting married. | [+with] Parents should talk with their children about drug abuse. | **talk sport/politics/business etc** 'Let's not talk politics now,' said Hugh impatiently.

3 **SAY WORDS** [I] to produce words and express thoughts, opinions, ideas etc: She was talking so fast I could hardly understand her. | How do babies **learn to talk**? | Some residents were frightened to talk publicly. | **talk (in) French/German etc** They started talking in Spanish. | Don't let Dad hear you **talking like that** (=expressing things in a particular way).

4 **A SPEECH** [I] to give a speech: [+on/about] Professor Davis will talk about 'Trends in Network Computing'.

5 **SECRET INFORMATION** [I] if someone who has secret information talks, they tell someone else about it: Even under torture, Maskell refused to talk. | He tried to stop his ex-wife from talking on live TV. | We should stop meeting like this. People will talk.

6 talk sense/rubbish/nonsense etc especially BrE spoken used to say that you think someone is saying something sensible, something stupid etc: You do talk rubbish sometimes, Jules.

7 talk (some) sense into sb to persuade someone to behave sensibly: She hoped Father McCormack would be able to talk some sense into her son.

8 talk to yourself to say your thoughts out loud: 'What did you say?' 'Sorry, I was just talking to myself.'

9 know what you are talking about spoken to know a lot about a particular subject: I worked in hotels for years, so I know what I'm talking about.

10 talk the hind leg(s) off a donkey informal to talk a lot, especially about unimportant things

11 talk about lazy/cheap/hungry etc spoken used to

emphasize that someone or something is very lazy, cheap, hungry etc: *Talk about lucky. That's the second time he's won this week!*

12 talking of/about sth *spoken* used to say more about a subject that someone has just mentioned: *Talking of Venice, have you seen the masks I bought there last year?*

13 what are you talking about? *spoken* used when you think what someone has said is stupid or wrong: *What are you talking about? We got there in plenty of time.*

14 I'm talking to you! *spoken* used when you are angry that the person you are talking to is not paying attention: *Rob! I'm talking to you!*

15 be like talking to a brick wall *spoken* used to say that it is annoying to speak to someone because they do not pay attention to you

16 talk sb's ear off *AmE spoken* to talk too much to someone

17 talk trash *AmE informal* to say rude or offensive things to or about someone, especially to opponents in a sports competition: *Both teams were talking trash on the court.*

18 talk the talk *AmE informal* to say the things that people expect or think are necessary in a particular situation: *She didn't talk the talk of feminism, but her career was the most important thing in her life.* → walk the walk at WALK¹ (12)

19 I'm/we're/you're talking (about) sth *spoken* used in conversation to emphasize a fact or remind someone of it: *I'm not talking about ancient history, I'm talking about last season's performance.*

20 now you're talking *spoken* used to say that you think someone's suggestion is a good idea: *'Fancy an ice cream?' 'Now you're talking.'*

21 look who's talking also **you're a fine one to talk**, **you can talk** *spoken* used to tell someone they should not criticize someone else's behaviour because their own behaviour is just as bad: *'Peggy shouldn't smoke so much.' 'Look who's talking!'*

22 we're/you're talking £500/three days etc *spoken* used to tell someone how much something will cost, how long something will take to do etc: *To do a proper job, you're talking £750 minimum.*

23 talk your way out of sth *informal* to escape from an bad or embarrassing situation by giving explanations, excuses etc: *She's good at talking her way out of trouble.*

24 talk nineteen to the dozen *BrE informal*; **talk a blue streak** *AmE* to talk very quickly without stopping

25 talk in riddles to deliberately talk in a strange and confusing way: *Stop talking in riddles and explain what's going on.*

26 talk tough (on sth) *informal* to give people your opinions very strongly: *The President is talking tough on crime.*

27 talk shop if people talk shop, they talk about their work when there are people present who are not interested or involved in it – used to show disapproval: *Are you two going to talk shop all night?*

28 talk dirty (to sb) *informal* to talk in a sexual way to someone in order to make them feel sexually excited

29 be talking through your hat *BrE informal* if someone is talking through their hat, they say stupid things about something that they do not understand

30 talk smack *AmE informal* to criticize someone or something in an unpleasant way

---

WORD FOCUS: words meaning TALK

chat/natter *BrE* to talk in a friendly way about things that are not very important | **gossip** to talk about other people's private lives | **drone on/go on** *BrE*/**hold forth**/**waffle** *BrE*/**ramble** to talk for too long in a boring way | **whisper** to talk very quietly | **mumble/murmur/mutter** to talk in a way that is difficult to hear

→ conversation, discussion, negotiation, debate

---

talk around/round *phr v BrE*

1 talk sb around/round to persuade someone to change their opinion about something: *Leave Betty to me. I'll soon talk her round.*

2 talk around/round sth to discuss a problem without really dealing with the important parts of it: *They had spent half the night talking round the subject.*

talk back *phr v*
to answer someone in authority such as a teacher or parent in a rude or impolite way

talk sb/sth ⇔ down *phr v*
1 *BrE* to make something seem less successful, interesting, good etc than it really is: *the pessimists who are talking down Britain*
2 to help a PILOT land an aircraft by giving them instructions from the ground by radio

talk down to sb *phr v*
to talk to someone as if they are stupid, although they are not; **◼ patronize**: *The students felt that they were talked down to as though they were children.*

talk sb into sth *phr v*
to persuade someone to do something: **talk sb into doing sth** *My husband talked me into going skiing.*

talk sth ⇔ out *phr v informal*
1 to discuss a problem thoroughly in order to solve it: *We need to spend a little time talking this out.* | [+with] *It might help if you talked it out with Dad.*
2 *BrE* if politicians talk out a proposal, they talk about it for a long time deliberately so that there will not be enough time to vote on it; **◼ filibuster**: *The Land Protection Bill was talked out by MPs from rural areas.*

talk sb out of sth *phr v*
to persuade someone not to do something: **talk sb out of doing sth** *Can't you talk them out of selling the house?*

talk sth ⇔ over *phr v*
to discuss a problem with someone before deciding what to do: [+with] *Talk over any worries with your GP.*

talk through sth *phr v*
1 talk sth ⇔ through to discuss something thoroughly so that you are sure you understand it: *Allow time to talk through any areas of difficulty.*
2 talk sb through sth to help someone understand a process, method etc by explaining it to them carefully before they use it: *Trevor talked me through loading the software.*

talk sth ⇔ up *phr v*
to make something appear more important, interesting, successful etc than it really is: *Jones talked up the idea at the meeting.*

talk² S1 W1 *n*
1 CONVERSATION [C] a conversation: *After a long talk, we decided on divorce.* | *John, I'd like to have a talk with you.* | [+about] *We must have a talk about money.*
2 DISCUSSION talks [plural] formal discussions between governments, organizations etc: **peace/trade etc talks** *The peace talks look promising.* | *The president held talks with Chinese officials.* | [+with] *Talks with the rebels have failed.*
3 SPEECH [C] a speech: *an entertaining talk* | [+on/about] *a talk on local history* | **give/do/deliver a talk** *Dr. Howard will give a talk on herbal medicine.*
4 NEWS [U] information or news that people talk about and hear about a lot, but that is not official: [+of] *Tickets sold so quickly there's talk of a second concert.* | **talk of doing sth** *the administration's talk of reducing weapons* | **talk that** *There's talk that she's difficult to work with.* | **just/only talk** *It's just talk. He'll never do it.*
5 TYPE OF CONVERSATION [U] type of conversation: *That's enough of that kind of talk.* | *persuasive* **sales talk** | *That's* **fighting talk** (=brave and confident words) *from Italy's manager.*
6 be all talk *spoken* someone who is all talk talks a lot about what they intend to do, but never actually does it
7 be the talk of the town/Paris etc someone who is the talk of the town has done something bad, shocking, exciting etc and everyone is talking about them: *She's the talk of London's theatre-goers since her last performance.*

---

1 000, 2 000, 3 000, most frequent words in S poken and W ritten English

8 talk is cheap used to say that you do not believe someone will do what they say → PEP TALK, SMALL TALK; → **idle talk** at IDLE¹ (2); → **pillow talk** at PILLOW¹ (3)

talk·a·tive /'tɔːkətɪv $ 'tɒːk-/ adj someone who is talkative talks a lot

talk·back /'tɔːkbæk $ 'tɒːk-/ n [U] an electronic system used in a film or television STUDIO, so that someone can talk to someone else without other people hearing them

talk·er /'tɔːkə $ 'tɒːkər/ n [C] informal someone who talks a lot or talks in a particular way: *Media people need to be good talkers and skilled negotiators.* | *Mom thinks he's a smooth talker* (=someone who is polite and pleasant but who you do not trust).

talk·ie /'tɔːki $ 'tɒːki/ n [C] old-fashioned a film made using sound

talking 'book n [C] a book that has been recorded onto tape for blind people

talking 'head n [C] informal someone on television who talks directly to the camera, especially to give their opinions

'talking point n [C] BrE a subject that a lot of people want to talk about

'talking shop n [singular] BrE a committee, group etc whose job is to discuss and solve problems, but who do not achieve any action

'talking-to n [C usually singular] informal an occasion when you talk to someone angrily, especially a child or someone who is below you in rank

talk 'radio n [U] AmE a type of radio programme in which people call the radio station to give their opinions or discuss a subject

'talk show n [C] a television show in which famous people answer questions about themselves; = chat **show** BrE: *a talk show host*

'talk time n [U] the amount of time a MOBILE PHONE can be used to make or receive calls or messages: *The battery allows approximately 135 minutes of talk time.*

tall S2 W2 /tɔːl $ tɒːl/ adj comparative **taller**, superlative **tallest**
1 a person, building, tree etc that is tall is a greater height than normal: *He was young and tall.* | *a house surrounded by tall trees* | *This bush grows tall very quickly.* → see box at BIG¹
2 you use 'tall' to say or ask what the height of something or someone is: **6ft/2m/12 inches etc tall** *He's only 5 feet tall.* | *How tall is that building?* | *She's a little taller than her sister.*
3 AmE a tall drink contains a small amount of alcohol mixed with a large amount of a non-alcoholic drink
4 a tall order informal a request or piece of work that is almost impossible: *Finding a replacement is going to be a tall order.*
5 tall story/tale a story that is so unlikely that it is difficult to believe —**tallness** n [U] → **stand tall** at STAND¹ (39); → **walk tall** at WALK¹ (10)

tall·boy /'tɔːlbɔɪ $ 'tɒːl-/ n [C] BrE a tall piece of wooden furniture with several drawers

tal·low /'tæləʊ $ -loʊ/ n [U] hard animal fat used to make CANDLES

'tall 'ship n [C] a type of ship with square sails and very tall MASTS, used especially in the past

tal·ly¹ /'tæli/ n plural **tallies** [C] a record of how much you have spent, won etc by a particular point in time: *The final tally was $465,000.* | *the two goals that took his tally for Scotland to 15* | **Keep a tally of** (=write down) *the number of cars that pass.*

tally² v **tallied**, **tallying**, **tallies** **1** [I] also **tally up** if numbers or statements tally, they match exactly: *Some of the records held by the accounts departments did not tally.* | [+with] *The number of ballot papers did not tally with the number of voters.* **2** [T] to calculate a total number

Tal·mud /'tælmʊd $ 'tɑːl-, 'tæl-/ n **the Talmud** the writings that make up Jewish law about religious and non-religious life —**Talmudic** /tæl'mʊdɪk $ tɑːl'mʊːdɪk. tæl-/ adj

tal·on /'tælən/ n [C usually plural] a sharp powerful curved nail on the feet of some birds that catch animals for food → see picture at BIRD OF PREY

tam·a·rind /'tæmərɪnd/ n [C] a tropical tree, or the fruit of this tree

tam·bou·rine /ˌtæmbə'riːn/ n [C] a circular musical instrument consisting of a frame covered with skin or plastic and small pieces of metal that hang around the edge. You shake it or hit it with your hand. → see picture at DRUM¹

tame¹ /teɪm/ adj **1** a tame animal or bird is not wild any longer, because it has been trained to live with people; ≠ **wild**: *tame elephants* → see picture at FIERCE **2** informal dull and disappointing: *Most of the criticism has been pretty tame.* | *I decided that teaching was too tame for me.* **3** [only before noun] BrE used to describe a person who is willing to do what other people ask, even if it is slightly dishonest: *If you have a tame doctor, he might give you a sick note.* —**tamely** adv —**tameness** n [U]

tame² v [T] **1** to reduce the power or strength of something and prevent it from causing trouble: *The Prime Minister managed to tame the trade unions.* **2** to train a wild animal to obey you and not to attack people; = **domesticate**: *The Asian elephant can be tamed and trained.*

ta·mox·i·fen /tə'mɒksɪfen $ -'mɑːk-/ n [U] a drug that is used to treat breast CANCER

tamp /tæmp/ v [T always + adv/prep] also **tamp down** to press or push something down by lightly hitting it several times: *The old man tamped down the tobacco with his thumb.*

Tam·pax /'tæmpæks/ n plural **Tampax** [C] trademark the name of a very common type of TAMPON

tam·per /'tæmpə $ -ər/ v

tamper with sth phr v to touch something or make changes to it without permission, especially in order to deliberately damage it: *He noticed that the instruments had been tampered with.* | *I don't see the point in tampering with a system that's worked fine so far.*

'tamper-ˌevident adj BrE a package or container that is tamper-evident is made so that you can see if someone has opened it before it is sold in the shops; = **tamper-resistant** AmE

'tamper-proof adj a package or container that is tamper-proof is made in a way that prevents someone from opening it before it is sold

'tamper-reˌsistant adj AmE TAMPER-EVIDENT

tam·pon /'tæmpɒn $ -pɑːn/ n [C] a tube-shaped mass of cotton or similar material that a woman puts inside her VAGINA during her PERIOD (=monthly flow of blood)

tan¹ /tæn/ v **tanned**, **tanning** **1** [I,T] if you tan, or if the sun tans you, your skin becomes darker because you spend time in the sun: *She has a pale skin which doesn't tan easily.* **2** [T] to make animal skin into leather by treating it with TANNIN (=a kind of acid)

tan² n **1** [C] the attractive brown colour that someone with pale skin gets after they have been in the sun; = **suntan**: *I wish I could get a tan like that.* **2** [U] a light yellowish-brown colour

tan³ adj **1** having a light yellowish-brown colour: *tan shoes* **2** AmE having darker skin after spending time in the sun; = **tanned**: *She arrived home tan and rested.*

tan·dem /'tændəm/ n [C] **1** a bicycle built for two riders sitting one behind the other **2 in tandem** doing something together or at the same time as someone or something else: *The two companies often work in tandem.* | [+with] *The group operated in tandem with local criminals.*

tan·doo·ri /tæn'dʊəri $ -'dʊri/ adj [only before noun] tandoori dishes are Indian meat dishes cooked in a clay OVEN: *a tandoori restaurant* | *tandoori chicken*

tang /tæŋ/ n [singular] a taste or smell that is pleasantly strong or sharp: *The beer had a sharp, bitter tang.* | [+of] *the salty tang of the sea* | *the tang of fresh lemons* —**tangy** adj: *tangy orange cake*

tan·gent /'tændʒənt/ n [C] **1** **go off at a tangent** BrE, **go off on a tangent** AmE informal to suddenly start thinking or talking about a subject that is only slightly related, or not related at all, to the original subject: *Let's stay with the topic and not go off at a tangent.* **2** technical a straight line that touches the outside of a curve but does not cut across it

tan·gen·tial /tæn'dʒenʃəl/ adj formal tangential information, remarks etc are only related to a particular subject in an indirect way: [+to] *The matter you raise is rather tangential to this discussion.* —**tangentially** adv

tan·ge·rine /ˌtændʒə'riːn/ n **1** [C] a small sweet fruit like an orange with a skin that comes off easily **2** [U] a bright orange colour —**tangerine** adj

tan·gi·ble /'tændʒɪbəl/ adj **1** clear enough or definite enough to be easily seen or noticed; ▣ **intangible**: *The scheme must have tangible benefits for the unemployed.* | *tangible evidence/proof He has no tangible evidence of John's guilt.* **2** tangible assets/property property such as buildings, equipment etc **3** technical if something is tangible, you can touch or feel it: *The silence of the countryside was almost tangible.* —**tangibly** adv —**tangibility** /ˌtændʒɪ'bɪlɪti/ n [U]

tan·gle¹ /'tæŋgəl/ v **1** [I,T] also **tangle up** to become twisted together, or make something become twisted together, in an untidy mass: *My hair tangles easily.* | *His parachute became tangled in the wheels of the plane.* **2** [I] informal to argue or fight with someone: [+with] *It was not an animal you'd care to tangle with.*

tangle² n [C] **1** a twisted mass of something such as hair or thread: *Her hair was full of tangles after being out in the wind.* | [+of] *John was sitting on the floor in a tangle of blankets.* | **tangle of bushes/branches/vegetation etc** *She followed him, pushing through the dense tangle of bushes and branches.* **2** a confused state or situation: [+of] *Her brain was teeming with a whole tangle of emotions.* **3** informal a quarrel or fight: [+with] *She got into a tangle with the staff.*

tan·gled /'tæŋgəld/ also ˌtangled 'up adj **1** twisted together in an untidy mass: *Your bed-clothes are all tangled up.* | *He had hair like tangled string.* **2** complicated or not easy to understand: *the tangled web of local politics* | *tangled emotions*

tan·go¹ /'tæŋgəʊ $ -goʊ/ n plural tangos [C] a fast dance from South America, or a piece of music for this dance

tango² v [I] **1** to dance the tango **2** **it takes two to tango** spoken used to say that if a problem involves two people, then both people are equally responsible

tank¹ [S2] [W2] /tæŋk/ n [C]
1 a large container for storing liquid or gas: *The water tank is leaking.* | *Somehow the chemical got from a storage tank into water supplies.* | **fish/marine/breeding tank** (=for keeping or breeding fish in) | *the plane's fuel tank* | **petrol tank** BrE **gas tank** AmE
2 also **tankful** the amount of liquid or gas held in a tank: *We set off next day on a full tank.* | [+of] *a tankful of petrol*
3 a heavy military vehicle that has a large gun and runs on two metal belts fitted over its wheels
4 a large artificial pool for storing water
5 in the tank AmE informal failing and losing money: **be/go in the tank** *Sales can't keep going up, but that doesn't mean the industry is going in the tank.* → THINK TANK, SEPTIC TANK, DRUNK TANK

tank² v **1** [I] to decrease quickly or be very unsuccessful: *Not long after the chairman resigned, shares in the*

company tanked. **2** [I] BrE informal to travel very fast in a car or vehicle **3** also **tank it** [T] to deliberately lose a sports game that you could have won
  tank up phr v especially AmE to put petrol in your car so that the tank is full

tan·kard /'tæŋkəd $ -ərd/ n [C] a large metal cup, usually with a handle, which you can drink beer from

ˌtanked 'up BrE; **tanked** /tæŋkt/ AmE adj [not before noun] informal drunk: *He went down the pub and got tanked up.*

tank·er /'tæŋkə $ -ər/ n [C] a vehicle or ship specially built to carry large quantities of gas or liquid, especially oil → OIL TANKER

ˈtank top n [C] **1** BrE a piece of clothing like a SWEATER, but with no SLEEVES **2** AmE a piece of clothing like a T-SHIRT but with no SLEEVES

tanned /tænd/ adj having a darker skin colour because you have been in the sun: *He had a tough tanned face and clear eyes.*

tan·ner /'tænə $ -ər/ n [C] someone whose job is to make animal skin into leather by TANNING

tan·ne·ry /'tænəri/ n plural tanneries [C] a place where animal skin is made into leather by TANNING

tan·nin /'tænɪn/ also **tan·nic acid** /ˌtænɪk 'æsɪd/ n [U] a reddish acid used in preparing leather, making ink etc

tan·noy /'tænɔɪ/ n [C] BrE trademark a system for giving out information in public places using LOUDSPEAKERS: **over the tannoy** *The train's approach was announced over the tannoy.*

tan·ta·lize also **-ise** BrE /'tæntəl-aɪz/ v [I,T] to show or promise something that someone really wants, but then not allow them to have it

tan·ta·liz·ing also **-ising** BrE /'tæntəl-aɪzɪŋ/ adj making you feel a strong desire to have or do something: *the tantalizing smell of fried bacon* —**tantalizingly** adv: *She was tantalizingly out of reach.*

tan·ta·mount /'tæntəmaʊnt/ adj be tantamount to sth if an action, suggestion, plan etc is tantamount to something bad, it has the same effect or is almost as bad: *To leave a dog home alone is tantamount to cruelty.*

tan·trum /'tæntrəm/ n [C] a sudden short period when someone, especially a child, behaves very angrily and unreasonably: **have/throw a tantrum** *She throws a tantrum when she can't have the toy she wants.* | *children's temper tantrums*

Tao /taʊ, daʊ/ n [U] the natural force that unites all things in the universe, according to Taoism

Taoi·seach /'tiːʃək, -ʃəx/ n the Taoiseach the title of the PRIME MINISTER of the Republic of Ireland

Tao·is·m /'taʊɪzəm, 'daʊ-/ n [U] a way of thought developed in ancient China, based on the writings of Lao Tzu, emphasizing a natural and simple way of life

tap¹ [S3] /tæp/ n
1 WATER/GAS [C] especially BrE a piece of equipment for controlling the flow of water, gas etc from a pipe or container; ▣ **faucet** AmE: *Tap water* (=water that comes out of a tap) *is usually heavily treated with chemicals.* | *She went into the bathroom and turned on the taps.* | **kitchen/bath/garden tap** *I washed my hands under the kitchen tap.* | **cold/hot tap** (=the tap that cold or hot water comes from); → see picture at MATERIAL¹; → see picture at EAT
2 A LIGHT HIT [C] an act of hitting something lightly, especially to get someone's attention: [+at/on] *She felt a tap on her left shoulder.* | *There was a tap at the door.*
3 on tap a) beer that is on tap comes from a BARREL **b)** informal something that is on tap is ready to use when you need it: *We've got all the information on tap.*
4 DANCING also tap dancing [U] dancing in which you

T

wear special shoes with pieces of metal on the bottom which make a loud sharp sound on the floor

5 **TELEPHONE** [C] an act of secretly listening to someone's telephone, using electronic equipment: *The police had put a tap on his phone line.*

6 **BARREL** [C] a specially shaped object used for letting liquid out of a BARREL, especially beer

7 **TUNE** taps [plural] a song or tune played on the BUGLE at night in an army camp, and at military funerals

tap² S3 *v* tapped, tapping

1 **HIT LIGHTLY** [I,T] to hit your fingers lightly on something, for example to get someone's attention: **tap sb on the shoulder/arm/chest etc** *He turned as someone tapped him on the shoulder.* | [+on] *I went up and tapped on the window.* | **tap sth on/against/from etc sth** *Mark tapped his fingers on the tabletop impatiently.* | *She tapped ash from her cigarette.*

2 **MUSIC** [T] to make a regular pattern of sounds with your fingers or feet, especially when you are listening to music: *She tapped her feet in time to the music.* | *a toe-tapping tune*

3 **ENERGY/MONEY** also **tap into** [T] to use or take what is needed from something such as an energy supply or an amount of money: *People are tapping into the power supply illegally.* | *We hope that additional sources of funding can be tapped.*

4 **IDEAS** also **tap into** [T] to make as much use as possible of the ideas, experience, knowledge etc that a group of people has: *Your adviser's experience is there to be tapped.* | *helping people tap into training opportunities*

5 **TELEPHONE** [T] to listen secretly to someone's telephone by using a special piece of electronic equipment: *Murray's phone calls to Australia were tapped.*

6 **TREE** [T] to get liquid from the TRUNK of a tree by making a hole in it

7 **PLAYER** also **tap up** [T] *BrE informal* if a football club taps a player from another team, it illegally tries to persuade that player to join its team

tap sth ⇔ **in** also **tap sth into sth** *phr v BrE*
to put information, numbers etc into a computer, telephone etc by pressing buttons or keys: *Tap in your password before you log on.*

tap sth ⇔ **out** *phr v*
1 to hit something lightly, especially with your fingers or foot, in order to make a pattern of sounds: *He whistled the tune and tapped out the rhythm.*
2 to write something with a computer: *Brian tapped out a name on his small electronic organizer.*

tap·as /'tæpəs $ 'tɑː-/ *n* [U] small dishes of food eaten as part of the first course of a Spanish meal

'tap ,dancing *n* [U] dancing in which you wear shoes with pieces of metal on the bottom, which make a sound as you move —**tap dance** *v* [I,T] —**tap dancer** *n* [C]

tapes

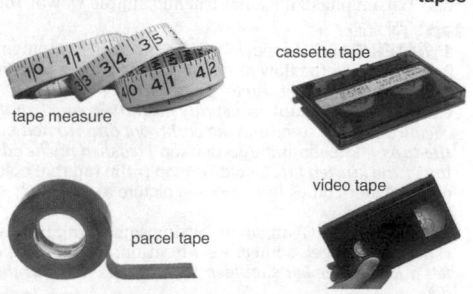

cassette tape

tape measure

video tape

parcel tape

tape¹ S3 W3 /teɪp/ *n*

1 **FOR RECORDING a)** [U] narrow plastic material covered with a special MAGNETIC substance, on which you can record sounds, pictures, or computer information:

on tape (=recorded on tape) *We've got the film on tape.* | *I hate hearing my voice on tape.* **b)** [C] a special plastic box containing a length of tape that you can record sound on; ▤ **cassette**: *I'll listen to the tape tomorrow.* | *William lent me some of his Beatles tapes.* | [+of] *We played a tape of African music and began dancing.* | *Bring me a blank tape and I'll record it for you.* **c)** [C] a special plastic box containing a length of tape that you can record sound and pictures on; ▤ **videotape**

2 **STICKY MATERIAL** [U] a narrow length of plastic that is sticky on one side and is used to stick things together; ▤ **Sellotape** *BrE*; ▤ **Scotch tape** *AmE*: *a photo stuck to the wall with tape*

3 **THIN PIECE OF MATERIAL** [C,U] a long thin piece of plastic or cloth used for purposes such as marking out an area of ground or tying things together: *Crime-scene tape marked out the position of the murdered man.*

4 the **tape** a string stretched out across the finishing line in a race and broken by the winner

5 **FOR MEASURING** [C] a TAPE MEASURE → **RED TAPE**

tape² S3 *v*

1 **RECORD STH** [I,T] also **tape record** to record sound or pictures onto a tape: *Would you mind if I taped this conversation?* | *Quiet – the machine's still taping.*

2 **STICK STH** [T] to stick something onto something else using tape: **tape sth to sth** *There were two pictures taped to the side of the fridge.*

3 **FASTEN STH** [T] also **tape up** to fasten a package, box etc with sticky tape

4 **INJURY** [T usually passive] also **tape up** *especially AmE* to tie a BANDAGE firmly around an injured part of someone's body; ▤ **strap** *BrE*: *His ankle had been taped.*

5 have (got) sth/sb taped *BrE informal* to understand someone or something completely and know how to deal with them: *You can't fool Liz – she's got you taped.*

'tape deck *n* [C] the part of a TAPE RECORDER that winds the tape, and records and plays back sound

'tape ,measure *n* [C] a long narrow band of cloth or steel, marked with centimetres, feet etc, used for measuring something → see picture at **TAPE¹**

ta·per¹ /'teɪpə $ -ər/ *v* [I,T] to become gradually narrower towards one end, or to make something become narrower at one end: [+to] *His wide chest tapers to a small waist.* —**tapering** *adj*: *long tapering fingers*
   taper off *phr v* to decrease gradually: *Profits may be tapering off in the near future.*

taper² *n* [C] **1** a very thin CANDLE: *small boys holding lighted tapers* **2** a piece of string covered in WAX, used for lighting lamps, CANDLES etc: *The box contained a taper to light each firework.*

'tape re,cord *v* [T] to record sound using a tape recorder

'tape re,corder *n* [C] a piece of electrical equipment that can record sound on tape and play it back

'tape re,cording *n* [C] something that has been recorded with a tape recorder: [+of] *The court heard tape recordings of the meeting.*

ta·pered /'teɪpəd $ -ərd/ *adj* having a shape that gets narrower towards one end: *tapered trousers*

tap·es·try /'tæpɪstri/ *n plural* **tapestries** [C,U] **1** a large piece of heavy cloth on which coloured threads are woven to produce a picture, pattern etc: *a colourful tapestry depicting a hunting scene* **2** something that is made up of many different people and things: *This was all new to her – part of life's rich tapestry.*

tape·worm /'teɪpwɜːm $ -wɜːrm/ *n* [C] a long flat WORM that lives in the BOWELS of humans and other animals and can make them ill

tap·i·o·ca /ˌtæpi'əʊkə $ -'oʊ-/ *n* [U] small hard white grains made from the crushed dried roots of CASSAVA, or a DESSERT made from cooking this

ta·pir /'teɪpə, -pɪə $ -pər, teɪ'pɪr/ *n* [C] an animal like a pig with thick legs, a short tail, and a long nose, that lives in tropical America and Southeast Asia

tap·root /'tæpruːt/ n [C] the large main root of a plant, from which smaller roots grow

'tap ˌwater n [U] water that comes out of a TAP rather than a bottle

tar¹ /tɑː $ tɑːr/ n [U]   **1** a black substance, thick and sticky when hot but hard when cold, used especially for making road surfaces → COAL TAR   **2** a sticky substance that forms when tobacco burns, and that gets into the lungs of people who smoke: *high tar cigarettes*

tar² v **tarred**, **tarring** [T]   **1** to cover a surface with tar: *a tarred roof*   **2 be/get tarred with the same brush** if someone is tarred with the same brush as someone else, people think they have the same faults or have committed the same crimes, even if they have not: *You've made it very clear that you think I'm tarred with the same brush as William.*   **3 tar and feather** to cover someone in tar and feathers as a cruel unofficial punishment

ta·ra·ma·sa·la·ta /ˌtærəməsə'lɑːtə $ ˌtɑːr-/ n [U] a Greek food consisting of a pink creamy mixture made from fish eggs

tar·an·tel·la /ˌtærən'telə/ n [C] a fast Italian dance, or the music for this dance

ta·ran·tu·la /tə'ræntjᵿlə $ -tʃələ/ n [C] a large poisonous SPIDER from Southern Europe and tropical America

tar·dy /'tɑːdi $ 'tɑːrdi/ adj formal   **1** arriving or done late: *Do please forgive this tardy reply.* | *He's been tardy three times this semester.*   **2** doing something too slowly or late: [+in] *people who are tardy in paying their bills* —**tardily** adv —**tardiness** n [U]

tare /teə $ ter/ n [usually singular]   **1** technical the weight of the materials in which goods are packed   **2** technical the weight of an unloaded vehicle, used to calculate the actual weight of the goods in it

tar·get¹ [S3] [W2] /'tɑːgᵻt $ 'tɑːr-/ n [C]
1 AIM something that you are trying to achieve, such as a total, an amount, or a time; ◳ **goal: sales/attainment/growth etc targets** *demanding financial targets* | [+of] *the target of a one-third reduction in road accidents* | [+for] *Higher degrees in English are a target for foreign students.* | *There is no **target date** for completion of the new project.* | *The government may fail to **meet** (=achieve) its **target** of recycling 25% of domestic waste* | *Jiang* **set** *annual growth* **targets** *of 8–9%.* | **on target** (=likely to achieve a target) *The company says that growth of 10% is on target.*
2 OBJECT OF ATTACK an object, person, or place that is deliberately chosen to be attacked: [+for/of] *Railway stations are* **prime targets** (=very likely targets) *for bombs.* | **easy/soft target** *Cars without security devices are an easy target for the thief.*
3 OBJECT OF AN ACTION the person or place that is most directly affected by an action, especially a bad one: [+for/of] *The area has become a* **prime target** *for supermarket development.* | *The country is a target of criticism for its human rights record.*
4 SHOOTING something that you practise shooting at, especially a round board with circles on it: *The area is used by the army for* **target practice**.
5 target audience/group/area etc a limited group, area etc that a plan, idea etc is aimed at: *Our target audience is men aged between 18 and 35.*
6 target language the language that you are learning or that you are translating into

target² v [T]   **1** to make something have an effect on a particular limited group or area: *The advertisement was designed to target a mass audience.* | **target sth on/at sb/sth** *a new benefit targeted on low-income families* | *The programme is targeted at improving the health of women of all ages.*   **2** to aim something at a target: **target sth on/at sb/sth** *The missiles are targeted at several key military sites.*   **3** to choose a particular person or place to do something to, especially to attack them or criticize them: *It's clear that smaller, more vulnerable banks have been targeted.* | *He was targeted by terrorists for a second time last night.*

tar·iff /'tærᵻf/ n [C]   **1** a tax on goods coming into a country or going out of a country: [+on] *The government may* **impose** *tariffs on imports.*   **2** BrE a list of fixed prices charged by a hotel or restaurant, for example for the cost of meals or rooms   **3** BrE a list or system of prices which MOBILE PHONE companies charge for the services they provide

tar·mac¹ /'tɑːmæk $ 'tɑːr-/ n trademark   **1** also **tar·ma·cad·am** BrE /ˌtɑːmə'kædəm $ ˌtɑːr-/ [U] a mixture of TAR and very small stones, used for making the surface of roads; ◳ **asphalt**   **2 the tarmac** an area covered with tarmac outside airport buildings: **on the tarmac** *Journalists waited on the tarmac to question him.*

tarmac² v **tarmacked**, **tarmacking** [T] to cover a road's surface with tarmac

tarn /tɑːn $ tɑːrn/ n [C] a small lake among mountains

tar·nish¹ /'tɑːnᵻʃ $ 'tɑːr-/ v   **1** [T] if an event or fact tarnishes someone's REPUTATION, record, image etc, it makes it worse: *His regime was tarnished by human rights abuses.*   **2** [I,T] if metals such as silver, COPPER, or BRASS tarnish, or if something tarnishes them, they become dull and lose their colour: *Gold does not tarnish easily.* | *tarnished silver spoons*

tarnish² n [singular, U] dullness of colour, or loss of brightness

ta·ro /'tɑːrəʊ $ -roʊ/ n plural **taros** [C,U] a tropical plant grown for its thick root, which is boiled and eaten

tar·ot /'tærəʊ $ -roʊ/ n [singular, U] a set of 78 cards, used for telling what will happen to someone in the future

tar·pau·lin /tɑː'pɔːlᵻn $ tɑːr'pɒː-/ especially BrE also **tarp** /tɑːp $ tɑːrp/ n [C,U] a large heavy cloth or piece of thick plastic that water will not pass through, used to keep rain off things

tar·ra·gon /'tærəgən/ n [U] the leaves of a small European plant, used in cooking to give food a special taste: *chicken with tarragon*

tar·ry¹ /'tæri/ v **tarried**, **tarrying**, **tarries** [I] literary   **1** to stay in a place, especially when you should leave; ◳ **linger**   **2** to delay or be slow in going somewhere

tar·ry² /'tɑːri/ adj covered with TAR (=a thick black liquid)

tar·sus /'tɑːsəs $ 'tɑːr-/ n plural **tarsi** /-saɪ/ [C] technical your ANKLE, or one of the seven small bones in your ankle —**tarsal** adj

tart¹ /tɑːt $ tɑːrt/ n   **1** [C,U] a PIE without a top on it, containing something sweet: **apple/treacle/jam etc tart**   **2** [C] informal an insulting word for a woman who you think is too willing to have sex   **3** [C] informal a PROSTITUTE

tart² adj   **1** food that is tart has a sharp sour taste: *a tart apple*   **2 tart reply/remark etc** a reply, remark etc that is sharp and unkind —**tartly** adv: *'I don't think so!' she replied tartly.* —**tartness** n [U]

tart³ v
tart sth ⇔ up phr v BrE informal   **1** to try to make something more attractive by decorating it, often in a way that other people think is cheap or ugly: *We'll need to tart the place up a bit.*   **2 tart yourself up/get tarted up** if a woman tarts herself up or gets tarted up, she tries to make herself look attractive by putting on nice clothes, MAKE-UP etc – often used humorously: *She got all tarted up for the party.*

tar·tan /'tɑːtn $ 'tɑːrtn/ n [C,U] a traditional Scottish pattern of coloured squares and crossed lines, or cloth, especially wool cloth, with this pattern; ◳ **plaid** AmE: *the MacGregor tartan* (=the special pattern worn by the MacGregor family) —**tartan** adj: *a tartan scarf*

T

[1] 000, [2] 000, [3] 000, most frequent words in [S] poken and [W] ritten English

tar·tar /'tɑːtə $ 'tɑːrtər/ n **1** [U] a hard substance that forms on your teeth **2** [C] *informal BrE* someone who has a violent temper: *She's a real tartar.*

tar·tare sauce /ˌtɑːtə 'sɔːs $ ˌtɑːrtər 'sɒːs/ n [U] a cold white sauce often eaten with fish, made from egg, oil, GHERKINS and CAPERS

tar·tar·ic ac·id /tɑːˌtærɪk 'æsᵻd $ tɑːr-/ n [U] a strong acid that comes from a plant and is used in preparing some foods and medicines

tart·y /'tɑːti $ 'tɑːrti/ adj *BrE informal* a woman who looks tarty looks like she is too willing for sex: *Do you think this dress looks too tarty?*

task¹ [S2] [W1] /tɑːsk $ tæsk/ n [C]
1 a piece of work that must be done, especially one that is difficult or unpleasant or that must be done regularly; ▤ **job**

> **have the task of doing sth**
> **set/give sb a task**
> **carry out/perform/do a task**
> **take on/undertake a task**
> **sb's first/main task**
> **a simple task**
> **a difficult/impossible/formidable task**
> **an unenviable task** (=an unpleasant, boring, or difficult job)
> **a thankless task** (=a boring but necessary job)
> **not an easy task/no easy task** (=difficult)

[+of] *The task of the union representative is to fight on behalf of the members.* | *Sara* **had the task of** *preparing the agenda for meetings.* | *I was* **given the task** *of building a fire.* | *the skills required to* **carry out** *these* **tasks** | *He soon realized the scale of the* **task** *he had* **undertaken.** | *Our* **first task** *is to gather information.* | *Monkeys can be taught to do* **simple tasks.** | *They have the* **unenviable task** *of supervising the most dangerous prison in the country.* | *Volunteers had the* **thankless task** *of distributing campaign leaflets.* | *Trying to bring up a small daughter on your own is* **no easy task.**

2 take someone to task to strongly criticize somebody for something they have done: [+for] *He was taken to task for not reporting the problem earlier.*

task² v [T usually passive] to give someone the responsibility for doing something: **be tasked with (doing) sth** *We were tasked with completing the job by the end of 2004.*

task·bar /'tɑːskbɑː $ 'tæskbɑːr/ n [C] a narrow area across the bottom of a computer screen, that shows which documents or programs are open

'task force n [C] **1** a group formed for a short time to deal with a particular problem: [+on] *a task force on health care reform* **2** a military force sent to a place for a special purpose

task·mas·ter /'tɑːskˌmɑːstə $ 'tæskˌmæstər/ n **be a hard/stern/tough taskmaster** to force people to work very hard

tas·sel /'tæsəl/ n [C] a large number of threads tied together at one end and hung as a decoration on clothes, curtains etc —**tasselled** *BrE* also **tasseled** *AmE adj*

taste¹ [S2] [W2] /teɪst/ n
1 [FOOD] **a)** [C,U] the feeling that is produced by a particular food or drink when you put it in your mouth; ▤ **flavour**: **have a sweet/bitter/salty etc taste** *The medicine had a slightly bitter taste.* | [+of] *I don't really like the taste of meat any more.* **b)** [U] the sense by which you know one food from another: *Some birds have a highly developed* **sense of taste. c)** **have a taste (of sth)** if you have a taste of some food or drink, you put a small amount in your mouth to try it: *You must have a taste of the fruitcake.*
2 [WHAT YOU LIKE] [C,U] the kind of things that someone likes

> **taste in music/clothes/men etc**
> **have similar/different tastes**
> **develop/acquire a taste for sth** (=start to like something)
> **suit/satisfy/cater for sb's tastes** (=provide what someone likes)
> **have expensive tastes** (=like expensive things)
> **sth is a matter of taste** (=it depends on what kind of things you like)
> **personal taste**
> **musical taste** (=the kind of music someone likes)
> **be too bright/modern/dark etc for sb's taste** (=used when saying that you did not like something because it was too bright, modern, dark etc)
> **be to sb's taste** (=if something is to your taste, you like it)
> **there's no accounting for taste** (=used humorously to say that you do not understand why someone has chosen something)
> **sth is an acquired taste** (=people only usually start to like something after they have tried it several times)

[+in] *We have similar* **tastes in music.** | [+for] *While she was in France she* **developed a taste for** *fine wines.* | *He had* **acquired a taste for adventure.** | *There are books to* **suit** *everyone's* **tastes.** | *courses that* **cater for all tastes** | *My wife* **has** *very* **expensive tastes.** | *Choosing a wedding dress is all* **a matter of personal taste.** | *His* **musical tastes** *changed radically as soon as he started college.* | *The colours were much* **too bright** *for my* **taste.** | *This type of event isn't to everyone's* **taste.** | *'Why did she marry someone like that?' 'There's no accounting for taste.'* | *Olives are something of* **an acquired taste.**

3 [JUDGMENT] [U] someone's judgment when they choose clothes, decorations etc: **have good/bad etc taste** *She has such good taste.* | [+in] *Some people have really bad taste in clothes.*
4 [WHAT IS ACCEPTABLE/NOT OFFENSIVE] [U] the quality of being acceptable and not offensive: *All television companies accept the need to maintain standards of* **taste and decency.** | **be in bad/poor etc taste** (=likely to offend people) *She acknowledged her remark had been in bad taste.*
5 [EXPERIENCE] [usually singular] a short experience of something that shows you what it is like: [+of] *Schoolchildren from city schools can* **get a taste of** *the countryside first-hand.* | *It* **gave** *him his first* **taste** *of acting for the big screen.* | *The autumn storms gave us a* **taste** *of what was to come* (=showed what would happen later).
6 [FEELING] [singular] the feeling that you have after an experience, especially a bad experience: *The way he spoke to those children* **left a nasty taste in my mouth.** | *the bitter* **taste** *of failure* | *the sweet* **taste** *of victory*
7 ... to taste if you add salt, spices etc to taste, you add as much as you think makes it taste right – used in instructions in cook books: *Add salt to taste.* → **give sb a taste of their own medicine** at MEDICINE (4)

> **WORD FOCUS: words meaning TASTE**
> **delicious/tasty** tastes very good | **disgusting** tastes very bad | **hot/spicy** has a lot of spices | **bland** boring and with not very much taste | **sweet** has a lot of sugar | **salty** has a lot of salt | **sour** used about fruit that is not sweet | **bitter** used about coffee, chocolate, or medicine that is not at all sweet
> → **flavour**

taste² v **1** [linking verb] to have a particular kind of taste: **taste good/delicious/sweet/fresh etc** *Mmm! This tastes good!* | *The food tasted better than it looked.* | **taste awful/disgusting etc** *The liver tasted awful and the potatoes had not been cooked for long enough.* | [+of] *This yoghurt tastes of strawberries.* | *It didn't taste much of ginger.* | **It tastes just like** *champagne to me.* | **What does** *pumpkin* **taste like** (=how would you describe its taste)? | **sweet-tasting/strong-tasting etc** *a sweet-tasting soup* | *a bitter-tasting liquid* **2** [T not in progressive] to experience or recognize the taste of food or drink: *She could taste blood.* | *Can you taste the difference?* | *It was like nothing I'd ever tasted before.* **3** [T] to eat or drink a small amount of something to see what it is like: *It's always best to keep tasting the food while you're cooking it.* **4 taste success/freedom/victory etc** to have a short experience of something that you want more of: *There was a lot of hard work before we first tasted success.*

taste bud *n* [C usually plural] one of the small parts of the surface of your tongue with which you can taste things

taste·ful /ˈteɪstfəl/ *adj* made, decorated, or chosen with good taste: *tasteful furnishings* ⚠ Do not confuse **tasteful** with **tasty**. Use **tasty** to describe food that tastes good: *This food is really tasty.* —**tastefully** *adv*: *tastefully decorated* —**tastefulness** *n* [U]

taste·less /ˈteɪstləs/ *adj* **1** food or drink that is tasteless is unpleasant because it has no particular taste **2** slightly offensive: *a tasteless remark* **3** made, decorated, or chosen with bad taste: *a tasteless outfit* | *ugly and tasteless housing*

tast·er /ˈteɪstə $ -ər/ *n* [C] **1** someone whose job is to test the quality of foods, teas, wines etc by tasting them: *a wine taster* **2** *informal* a small example of something that is provided so that you can see if you like it: [+of] *Here's a taster of what will be in print next month.* | [+from] *a taster from her next album*

tast·ing /ˈteɪstɪŋ/ *n* [C] an event that is organized so that you can try different foods or drinks to see if you like them: *a wine and cheese tasting*

tast·y /ˈteɪsti/ *adj comparative* **tastier**, *superlative* **tastiest 1** food that is tasty has a good taste, but is not sweet: *a simple but tasty meal* → TASTEFUL **2** *informal* tasty news, GOSSIP etc is especially interesting and often connected with sex or surprising behaviour **3** *BrE informal* sexually attractive

tat /tæt/ *n* **1** [U] *BrE informal* things that are cheap and badly made **2** [C] *AmE informal* an informal American word for TATTOO → TIT FOR TAT

ta-ta S3 /tæ ˈtɑː $ tɑː ˈtɑː/ *BrE informal* goodbye

ta·ter /ˈteɪtə $ -ər/ *n* [C] *informal* a potato

tat·tered /ˈtætəd $ -ərd/ *adj* clothes, books etc that are tattered are old and torn: *He produced a tattered envelope from his pocket.*

tat·ters /ˈtætəz $ -ərz/ *n* [plural] **1 in tatters a)** if a plan or someone's REPUTATION is in tatters, it is ruined: *Tonight, the peace agreement lies in tatters.* | *His credibility is in tatters after a series of defeats and failures.* **b)** clothes that are in tatters are old and torn **2** clothing that is old and torn; ▣ **rags**

tat·tie /ˈtæti/ *n* [C] a potato – used in Scotland

tat·ting /ˈtætɪŋ/ *n* [U] a kind of LACE that you make by hand, or the process of making it

tat·tle /ˈtætl/ *v* [I] **1** *old-fashioned* to talk about other people's private lives; ▣ **gossip 2** *especially AmE* if a child tattles, they tell a parent or teacher that another child has done something bad: [+on] *Robert is always tattling on me for things I didn't do.* → TITTLE-TATTLE —**tattle** *n* [U] —**tattler** *n* [C]

tat·tle·tale /ˈtætlteɪl/ *n* [C] *AmE informal* a word meaning someone who tattles – used by or to children; ▣ **telltale** *BrE*

tat·too¹ /təˈtuː, tæˈtuː/ *n plural* **tattoos 1** [C] a picture or writing that is permanently marked on your skin using a needle and ink: *He has a tattoo of a snake on his left arm.* **2** [C] an outdoor military show with music, usually at night **3** [singular] a fast continuous beating of a drum, or a sound like this

tattoo² *v* [T] to mark a permanent picture or writing on someone's skin with a needle and ink: *She's got a heart tattooed on her right shoulder.* —**tattooed** *adj*: *heavily tattooed arms*

tat·too·ist /təˈtuːɪst, tæ-/ *also* **tat'too ,artist** *n* [C] someone whose job is tattooing

tat'too ,parlour *BrE*, **tattoo parlor** *AmE n* [C] a place where you can go to get a tattoo

tat·ty /ˈtæti/ *adj comparative* **tattier**, *superlative* **tattiest** *informal* in bad condition; ▣ **shabby**: *tatty jeans* | *a few tatty old chairs* —**tattily** *adv* —**tattiness** *n* [C]

taught /tɔːt $ tɒːt/ the past tense and past participle of TEACH

taunt¹ /tɔːnt $ tɒːnt/ *v* [T] to try to make someone angry or upset by saying unkind things to them: **taunt sb about sth** *The other children taunted him about his weight.* | **taunt sb with sth** *They taunted him with the nickname 'Fatso'.* | *'And he'll believe you, will he?' Maria taunted.* —**tauntingly** *adv*

taunt² *n* [C often plural] a remark or joke intended to make someone angry or upset: *racist taunts*

taupe /təʊp $ toʊp/ *n* [U] a brownish-grey colour —**taupe** *adj*

Tau·rus /ˈtɔːrəs/ *n* **1** [U] the second sign of the ZODIAC, represented by a BULL, which some people believe affects the character and life of people born between April 21 and May 21 **2** [C] also **Taurean** someone who was born between April 21 and May 21 —**Taurean** *adj*

taut /tɔːt $ tɒːt/ *adj* **1** stretched tight; ▣ **slack**: *The rope was stretched taut.* → see picture at SLACK¹ **2** showing signs of worry, anger etc and not relaxed; ▣ **tense**: *a taut smile* | *Catherine looked upset, her face taut.* **3** having firm muscles: *her taut brown body* **4** a taut book, film, or play is exciting and does not have any unnecessary parts: *a taut thriller*

taut·en /ˈtɔːtn $ ˈtɒːtn/ *v* [I,T] to make something stretch tight, or to become stretched tight

tau·tol·o·gy /tɔːˈtɒlədʒi $ tɒːˈtɑː-/ *n plural* **tautologies** [C,U] *technical* a statement in which you say the same thing twice using different words in a way which is not necessary, for example, 'He sat alone by himself.'; → **redundant** —**tautological** /ˌtɔːtəˈlɒdʒɪkəl◂ $ ˌtɒːtəˈlɑː-/ *also* **tautologous** /tɔːˈtɒləɡəs $ tɒːˈtɑː-/ *adj*

tav·ern /ˈtævən $ -ərn/ *n* [C] **1** *BrE old use* a PUB where you can also stay the night **2** a word for a bar, often used in the name of a bar: *Murphy's Tavern*

taw·dry /ˈtɔːdri $ ˈtɒː-/ *adj* **1** cheaply and badly made: *tawdry jewellery and fake furs* **2** showing low moral standards: *a tawdry tale of lies and deception* —**tawdriness** *n* [U]

taw·ny /ˈtɔːni $ ˈtɒː-/ *adj* brownish-yellow in colour: *a lion's tawny fur*

tax¹ S1 W1 /tæks/ *n* [C,U] an amount of money that you must pay to the government according to your income, property, goods etc and that is used to pay for public services: [+on] *a tax on fuel* | **income/council/inheritance etc tax** | *He already pays 40% tax on his income.* | *the basic rate of tax* | **tax cuts/increases** | **direct tax** (=tax on income) | **indirect tax** (=tax on things you buy) | **before/after tax** *profits before tax of £85.9 m* | *The total tax burden* (=the amount of tax paid) *has risen only slightly.* | *The government has introduced tax incentives* (=an offer of cheaper taxes to encourage people to do something) *for fuel-efficient cars.* → CAPITAL GAINS TAX; → corporation tax at CORPORATION (1); → INCOME TAX, SALES TAX, STEALTH TAX, VAT, PAYE

tax² *v* [T] **1** to charge a tax on something: **tax sth at 10%/a higher rate etc** *They may be taxed at a higher rate.* | **tax sb on sth** *The individual is taxed on the amount of dividend received.* | *Cigarettes are heavily taxed in Britain.* **2** *BrE* to pay the sum of money charged each year for using a vehicle on British roads → CAR TAX, ROAD TAX **3** to make someone have to work hard or make an effort: **tax sb's patience/strength etc** *The kids are really taxing my patience today.* | *It shouldn't tax your brain too much.* → TAXING

tax sb **with** sth *phr v formal* to complain to someone they have done something wrong

tax·a·ble /'tæksəbəl/ *adj* if money that you receive is taxable, you have to pay tax on it: **taxable income/ profits/earnings etc**

tax·a·tion W3 /tæk'seɪʃən/ *n* [U] *formal*
1 the system of charging taxes: *the government's economic and taxation policy* | **direct taxation** (=tax on income) | **indirect taxation** (=tax on things you buy)
2 money collected from taxes: *higher levels of taxation*

tax a,voidance *n* [U] the practice of trying to pay less tax in legal ways; → **tax evasion**

tax ,bracket *n* [C] a particular range of income levels on which the same rate of tax is paid: *It may put you in a higher tax bracket.*

tax break *n* [C] a special reduction in taxes: *tax breaks for small businesses*

tax col,lector *n* [C] someone who works for the government and makes sure that people pay their taxes

tax-de'ductible *adj* tax-deductible costs can be taken off your total income before it is taxed: *If you're self-employed, your travel expenses are tax-deductible.*

tax-de'ferred *adj AmE* not taxed until a later time: *tax-deferred savings*

tax disc *n* [C] a small round piece of paper on a car WINDSCREEN in Britain that shows the driver has paid ROAD TAX

tax dodge *n* [C] *informal* a way of paying less tax

tax e,vasion *n* [U] the crime of paying too little tax; → **tax avoidance**

tax ex'empt *adj* if SAVINGS, income etc are tax exempt, you do not have to pay tax on them

tax ,exile *n* [C] someone who lives abroad in order to avoid paying high taxes in their own country

tax-'free *adj* not taxed: *He was paid a tax-free cash sum as compensation.* —**tax-free** *adv*: *You can earn up to £65 per week tax-free.*

tax ,haven *n* [C] a place where people go to live to avoid paying high taxes in their own country

tax·i¹ /'tæksi/ *n* [C] a car and driver that you pay to take you somewhere; 🔲 **cab**: **take/get a taxi** *I took a taxi to the airport.* | **in a taxi** *They had to send me home in a taxi.* | **by taxi** *She arrived by taxi.* | *a* **taxi driver** | *It's only a 5 minute* **taxi ride** *away.* | *Shall I* **call** *you* **a taxi** (=telephone for a taxi to come)? | **hail a taxi** (=wave or shout at a taxi to make it stop)

taxi² *v past tense and past participle* **taxied**, *present participle* **taxiing**, *third person singular* **taxis** *or* **taxies** [I] if a plane taxis, it moves along the ground before taking off or after landing: *The plane taxied to a halt.*

tax·i·cab /'tæksikæb/ *n* [C] a taxi

tax·i·der·mist /'tæks‚dɜːm‚st $ -ɜːr-/ *n* [C] someone whose job is taxidermy

tax·i·der·my /'tæks‚dɜːmi $ -ɜːr-/ *n* [U] the art of filling the skins of dead animals, birds, or fish with a special material so that they look as though they are alive

tax·ing /'tæksɪŋ/ *adj* needing a lot of effort; 🔲 **demanding**: *The job turned out to be more taxing than I'd expected.*

tax in,spector *n* [C] someone who works for the government, deciding how much tax a person or company should pay

taxi rank *also* **taxi stand** *AmE n* [C] a place where taxis wait for customers; 🔲 **cabstand** *AmE*

tax·i·way /'tæksiweɪ/ *n* [C] the surface which an aircraft drives on to get to and from the RUNWAY

tax·man /'tæksmæn/ *n plural* **taxmen** /-men/ [C] **1 the taxman** *informal* the government department that collects taxes: *A lot of the money will go straight to the taxman.* **2** someone whose job is collecting taxes

tax·on·o·my /tæk'sɒnəmi $ -'sɑː-/ *n plural* **taxonomies** [C,U] the process or a system of organizing things into different groups that show their natural relationships, especially plants or animals —**taxonomist** *n* [C]

tax·pay·er /'tæks‚peɪə $ -ər/ *n* [C] a person that pays tax: *The proposal could cost the taxpayer* (=all ordinary people who pay tax) *another £18m a year.*

tax re,lief *n* [U] *BrE* when you do not have to pay tax on part of what you earn, especially because you use the money for a particular purpose: [+on] *You can get tax relief on private health insurance premiums.*

tax re,turn *n* [C] the form on which you have to give information so that your tax can be calculated

tax ,shelter *n* [C] a plan or method that allows you to legally avoid paying tax

tax year *n* [C] the period of 12 months in which income is calculated for paying taxes. The tax year begins on April 6th in Britain, and January 1st in the US

TB /‚tiː 'biː/ *n* [U] *tuberculosis* a serious infectious disease that affects the lungs and other body parts

tba *to be announced* used in writing to show that a time, place etc will be given or decided later

T-ball /'tiː bɔːl $ -bɒːl/ *n* [U] *trademark* an easy form of BASEBALL for young children; 🔲 **tee-ball**

tbc *to be confirmed BrE* used in writing to show that the time, place etc of a future event is not yet definite: *The concert will be in Harrogate (venue tbc) on the 29th.*

T-bone steak /‚tiː bəʊn 'steɪk $ -boʊn-/ *n* [C] a thinly cut piece of BEEF that has a T-shaped bone in it

tbsp *also* **tbs** *plural* **tbsp** *or* **tbsps** the written abbreviation of TABLESPOON or tablespoons: *1 tbsp sugar*

T cell /'tiː sel/ *n* [C] *BrE medical* a type of WHITE BLOOD CELL that helps the body fight disease

tea S1 W2 /tiː/ *n*
1 DRINK/LEAVES a) [C,U] a hot brown drink made by pouring boiling water onto the dried leaves from a particular Asian bush, or a cup of this drink: *Would you like a cup of tea or coffee?* | *Do you take milk and sugar in your tea?* | *I'd like two teas and a piece of chocolate cake, please.* **b)** [U] dried, finely cut leaves that are used to make tea **c)** [U] bushes whose leaves are used to make tea: *tea plantations*
2 mint/camomile etc tea a hot drink made by pouring boiling water onto leaves or flowers, sometimes used as a medicine
3 MEAL [C,U] *BrE* **a)** a small meal of cake or BISCUITS eaten in the afternoon with a cup of tea: *We serve lunch and* **afternoon tea**. | *We stopped for a* **cream tea** *on the way home* (=tea and cream cakes). **b)** used in some parts of Britain to mean a large meal that is eaten early in the evening → HIGH TEA; → see box at DINNER
4 tea and sympathy *BrE* kindness and attention that you give someone when they are upset → **not be your cup of tea** at CUP¹

tea·bag /'tiːbæg/ *n* [C] a small paper bag with tea leaves inside, used for making tea

tea break *n* [C] *BrE* a short pause from work in the middle of the morning or afternoon for a drink, a rest etc; 🔲 **coffee break**

tea ,caddy *n* [C] a small metal box that you keep tea in

tea·cake /'tiːkeɪk/ *n* [C] *BrE* a small flat round amount of bread with RAISINS or CURRANTS in it

teach S1 W2 /tiːtʃ/ *v past tense and past participle* **taught** /tɔːt $ tɒːt/
1 SCHOOL/COLLEGE ETC [I,T] to give lessons in a school, college, or university, or to help someone learn about something by giving them information; → **learn**: [+at] *Neil teaches at the Guildhall School of Music in London.* | **teach (sb)** English/mathematics/history etc *He taught geography at the local secondary school.* | **teach sb (sth) about sth** *We were never taught anything about other religions.* | **teach sth to sb** *I'm teaching*

English to Italian students. | **teach school/college etc** *AmE* (=teach in a school etc)

2 SHOW SB HOW [T] to show someone how to do something: **teach sb (how) to do sth** *My father taught me to swim.* | *different methods of teaching children how to read* | **teach sb sth** *Can you teach me one of your card tricks?*

3 CHANGE SB'S IDEAS [T] to show or tell someone how they should behave or what they should think: **teach sb to do sth** *When I was young, we were taught to treat older people with respect.* | **teach sb sth** *No one ever taught him the difference between right and wrong.* | **teach sb that** *He taught me that the easy option isn't always the best one.*

4 EXPERIENCE SHOWS STH [T] if an experience or situation teaches you something, it helps you to understand something about life: **teach sb to do sth** *Experience has taught me to avoid certain areas of the city.* | **teach sb that** *It's certainly taught me that work and money aren't the most important things in life.*

5 **that'll teach you (to do sth)** *spoken* used when something unpleasant has just happened to someone because they acted stupidly: *That'll teach you to be late!*

6 **teach sb a lesson** *informal* if someone or something teaches you a lesson, you are punished for something you have done, so that you will not want to do it again

7 **you can't teach an old dog new tricks** used to say that older people often do not want to change the way they do things

8 **teach your grandmother (to suck eggs)** *BrE* to give someone advice about something that they already know

teach·er S1 W1 /'tiːtʃə $ -ər/ n [C] someone whose job is to teach, especially in a school: *a primary school teacher* | **language/history/science etc teacher** | **teacher training/education** (=professional training to become a teacher); → see picture at OCCUPATION

> **WORD CHOICE: teacher, professor, lecturer, tutor, instructor, coach, trainer**
> A **teacher** usually works in a school: *Do the children like their new teacher?*
> A **professor** is a teacher of the highest rank in a British university, and is a general term for a teacher in an American college.
> Someone who teaches in a British university and who is not a professor is called a **lecturer**.
> A **tutor** gives lessons to just one student or a small group of students, especially privately in their home or a student's home: *a private tutor*
> An **instructor** is someone who helps people learn a sport or practical skill, such as driving, skiing, or swimming: *a riding instructor*
> A **coach** is someone who helps a person or a team to improve in a sport: *the school swimming coach*
> A **trainer** is someone who teaches people the skills they need for a job: *a teacher trainer.* It is also someone who teaches skills to animals: *a racehorse trainer*

teacher's pet n [singular] *informal* a child who everyone thinks is the teacher's favourite student and is therefore disliked by the other students

tea chest n [C] a large wooden box that used to have tea in it, often used afterwards for moving and storing things

teach-in n [C] an informal meeting of people who are interested in a particular subject, where they have the opportunity to learn more about it

teach·ing S2 W2 /'tiːtʃɪŋ/ n [U]
1 the work or profession of a teacher: *She's thinking of going into teaching* (=becoming a teacher). | **language/science etc teaching** *criticisms of English teaching in schools* | **the teaching profession** | **teaching methods/materials etc** | **teaching practice** *BrE* **student teaching** *AmE* (=a period of teaching done by someone who is training to be a teacher)
2 also **teachings** [plural] the moral, religious, or political ideas of a particular person or group which are taught to other people: [+of] *the teachings of Gandhi* | **religious/Christian/Buddhist etc teachings**

teaching as·sistant n [C] **1** *BrE* a person who is not a trained teacher who helps a school teacher in classes **2** *AmE* a GRADUATE student at a university who teaches classes

teaching hospital n [C] a hospital where medical students receive practical training from experienced doctors

tea cloth n [C] *BrE* a TEA TOWEL

tea cosy n [C] *BrE* a thick cover that you put over a TEAPOT to keep the tea hot

tea·cup /'tiːkʌp/ n [C] a cup that you serve tea in → **storm in a teacup** at STORM¹ (5)

tea garden n [C] a large area of land used for growing tea; ◻ **tea plantation**

tea·house /'tiːhaʊs/ n [C] a special house in China or Japan where tea is served, often as part of a ceremony

teak /tiːk/ n [U] a hard yellowish-brown wood that is used for making ships and good quality furniture

teal /tiːl/ n **1** [C] a small wild duck **2** [U] a greenish-blue colour

tea leaves n [plural] the small pieces of leaves used to make tea. People sometimes look at the leaves left at the bottom of a cup to find out what will happen in the future.

team¹ S1 W1 /tiːm/ n [C]
1 a group of people who play a game or sport together against another group: **football/basketball etc team** *Tim plays for the national volleyball team.* | *What football team do you support?* | [also + plural verb *BrE*]: *Our team are winning.* | *He was a member of the team who won the 1998 Cup Final.* | **in a team** *BrE*/**on a team** *AmE*: *Is Mario going to be on the team this year?* | **team manager/coach** | **team game/sport** *team sports such as soccer and rugby*
2 a group of people who have been chosen to work together to do a particular job: [+of] *a team of experts* | **management/research/sales etc team** *a senior member of the design team* | *Our success lies in working together as a team.* | *It was a tremendous team effort* (=everyone worked well). | *You need to choose a team leader.*
3 two or more animals that are used to pull a vehicle

team² v [T] to put two things or people together, because they will look good or work well together: **team sth with sth** *black trousers teamed with a bright shirt*
  team up *phr v* to join with someone in order to work on something: [+with] *You can team up with one other class member if you want.*

team-mate *BrE* also **team·mate** /'tiːm-meɪt/ n [C] someone who belongs to the same team as you: *He finished just ahead of his Ferrari team-mate.*

team player n [C] someone who works well as a member of a team, especially in business: *He was a good businessman, but never a team player.*

team spirit n [U] willingness to work as part of a team

team·ster /'tiːmstə $ -ər/ n [C] *AmE* someone whose job is to drive a truck

team·work /'tiːmwɜːk $ -wɜːrk/ n [U] when a group of people work effectively together: *We want to encourage good teamwork and communication.*

tea party n [C] **1** a small party in the afternoon at which tea, cake etc is served **2** **be no tea party** *AmE informal* to be very difficult or unpleasant to do

tea·pot /'tiːpɒt $ -pɑːt/ n [C] a container for making and serving tea, which has a handle and a SPOUT (1) → see picture at POT¹

tear¹ S3 W3 /tɪə $ tɪr/ n
1 [C usually plural] a drop of salty liquid that comes out of your eye when you are crying

T

in tears (=crying)
in floods of tears *BrE* (=crying a lot)
close to tears/on the verge of tears (=almost crying)
burst into tears (=suddenly start crying)
fight back (the) tears also
choke back tears (=try not to cry)
moved to tears (=so upset that you cry)
bring tears to sb's eyes (=make someone cry)
shed tears/a tear (=cry)
reduce sb to tears (=make someone cry)
sb's eyes fill with tears
tears well up in your eyes (=you start to cry)
tears roll/run/stream down sb's face/cheeks
tears of joy/rage/frustration etc (=crying because you are happy, angry etc)

---

*The children were all **in tears**. | She came home in **floods of tears**. | I could see that Sam was **close to tears**. | Bridget suddenly **burst into tears** and ran out. | He was **fighting back tears** as he spoke. | A lot of people were **moved to tears** by his story. | He kissed her cheek, a gesture that **brought tears to her eyes**. | I must admit I **shed** a few **tears** when the school closed. | I saw grown men **reduced to tears** that day. | 'Please don't talk like that,' Ellen implored him, her **eyes filling with tears**. | By this time, **tears** were **streaming down** my face. | The tears he shed were **tears of joy**.*

---

2 it'll (all) end in tears *BrE spoken* used to warn someone that something they are doing will cause problems or arguments between people → **bore sb to tears** at BORE² (1); → **crocodile tears** at CROCODILE (4)

tear² [S2] [W3] /teə $ ter/ *v past tense* **tore** /tɔː $ tɔːr/ *past participle* **torn** /tɔːn $ tɔːrn/
1 [PAPER/CLOTH] **a)** [T] to damage something such as paper or cloth by pulling it hard or letting it touch something sharp; ▪ **rip**: *Be careful not to tear the paper.* | *His clothes were old and torn.* | **tear sth on sth** *She realized she had torn her jacket on a nail.* | **tear sth off** *Tear off the slip at the bottom of this page and send it back to us.* | **tear sth out (of sth)** *He tore a page out of his notebook and handed it to her.* | *The dog had* **torn a huge hole in** *the tent.* | *He picked up the envelope and* **tore it open**. | *She* **tore the letter to pieces** *and threw it in the bin.* | *Most of her clothes had been* **torn to shreds**. **b)** [I] if paper or cloth tears, it splits and a hole appears, because it has been pulled too hard or has touched something sharp: *The paper is old and tears easily.*
2 [MOVE QUICKLY] [I always + adv/prep] to run or drive somewhere very quickly, especially in a dangerous or careless way: *She tore back into the house.* | *We tore down to the hospital.* | *He tore off into town.*
3 [REMOVE STH] [T always + adv/prep] to pull something violently from a person or place: **tear sth from sb/sth** *He tore the letter from my hand.* | *A bridge was torn from the bank by the floodwaters.* | **tear sth off sth** *High winds nearly tore the roof off the house.*
4 be torn a) if you are torn, you are unable to decide what to do because you have different feelings or different things that you want: [+between] *She was torn between her love of dancing and her fear of performing in public.* | *He was torn two ways.* | *Jess was torn by anger and worry.* **b)** if a country or group is torn, it is divided because people in it have very different ideas and are arguing or fighting with each other: *The country was torn by civil war.* | *She spent two months in the* **war-torn** *city.*
5 [MUSCLE] [T] to damage a muscle or LIGAMENT: *She had torn a muscle in her leg.*
6 tear loose to move violently and no longer be attached to something: *One end had torn loose.*
7 tear sb/sth to shreds/pieces *informal* to criticize someone or something very severely: *He tore her arguments to shreds.*
8 tear sb off a strip/tear a strip off sb *BrE informal* to talk to someone very angrily because they have done something wrong
9 tear sb limb from limb *literary* to attack someone in a

very violent way
10 be tearing your hair out *BrE informal* to feel anxious and upset because you are worried, or because you have to deal with something that is very difficult: *I've been tearing my hair out trying to get done in time.*
11 be in a tearing hurry *BrE* to be doing something very quickly because you are late
12 tear sb's heart (out)/tear at sb's heart to make someone feel extremely upset: *The thought of her out there alone tore at my heart.*
13 that's torn it! *BrE spoken old-fashioned* used when something bad has happened that stops you from doing what you intended to do: *Oh, no, that's torn it! I've left my keys in the car!*

tear sb/sth **apart** *phr v*
1 tear sth ⇔ **apart** to cause serious arguments in a group of people; ▪ **rip apart**: *Scandal is tearing the government apart.* | *a row that tore the family apart*
2 *literary* to separate people who are in a close relationship with each other: *Nothing can tear us apart!*
3 to make someone feel extremely unhappy or upset: *Seeing her so upset really tore him apart.*
4 tear sth ⇔ **apart** to break something violently into a lot of small pieces; ▪ **rip apart**: *Her body had been torn apart by wolves.*

tear at sb/sth *phr v*
to pull violently at someone or something: *The children were screaming and tearing at each other's hair.*

tear sb **away** *phr v*
to make yourself or someone else leave a place when you or they do not want to leave: *He was enjoying the fun and couldn't tear himself away.* | [+from] *We finally managed to tear him away from the TV.*

tear sth ⇔ **down** *phr v*
to destroy a building deliberately: *A lot of the old tower blocks have been torn down to make way for new housing.*

tear into sb/sth *phr v*
1 to attack someone by hitting them very hard: *The two boys tore into each other.*
2 to criticize someone very strongly and angrily: *From time to time she would really tear into her staff.*
3 to start doing something quickly, with a lot of energy: *I was amazed at the way she tore into her work.*

tear sth ⇔ **off** *phr v*
to remove your clothes as quickly as you can: *He tore off his clothes and dived into the water.*

tear sth ⇔ **up** *phr v*
1 to tear a piece of paper or cloth into small pieces; ▪ **rip up**: *She tore up his letter and threw it away.* → see picture at FOLD
2 to remove something from the ground by pulling or pushing it violently: *the remains of trees that had been torn up by the storm*
3 tear up an agreement/a contract etc to say that you no longer accept an agreement or contract: *threats to tear up the peace agreement*

tear³ /teə $ ter/ *n* [C] a hole in a piece of cloth or paper where it has been torn: [+in] *There was a huge tear in his shirt.* → **wear and tear** at WEAR² (2)

tear·a·way /'teərəweɪ $ 'ter-/ *n* [C] *informal* a young person who behaves badly and often gets into trouble: *His car was wrecked by a couple of young tearaways.*

tear·drop /'tɪədrɒp $ 'tɪrdrɑːp/ *n* [C] *literary* a single drop of salty liquid that comes out of your eye when you are crying: *A large teardrop ran down her cheek.*

tear·ful /'tɪəfəl $ 'tɪr-/ also **teary** *informal adj* someone who is tearful is crying a little, or almost crying: *a tearful farewell* —**tearfully** *adv*: *She looked at me tearfully.*

tear gas /'tɪə gæs $ 'tɪr-/ *n* [U] a gas that stings your eyes, used by the police to control crowds: *The police used tear gas to break up the demonstration.*

tear·jerk·er /'tɪəˌdʒɜːkə $ 'tɪrˌdʒɜːrkər/ *n* [C] *informal* a film, book, or story that is very sad and makes you cry

tea·room /'tiːruːm, -rʊm/ also **tea shop** *n* [C] a restaurant where tea and small meals are served

tear·y /'tɪəri $ 'tɪri/ *adj informal* TEARFUL

tease¹ /tiːz/ *v*

1 LAUGH [I,T] to laugh at someone and make jokes in order to have fun by embarrassing them, either in a friendly way or in an unkind way: *Don't get upset. I was only teasing.* | *He used to tease her mercilessly.* | **tease sb about sth** *She used to tease me about my hair.*

2 ANNOY AN ANIMAL [T] to deliberately annoy an animal: *Stop teasing the cat!*

3 SEX [I,T] to deliberately make someone sexually excited without intending to have sex with them, in a way that seems unkind

4 HAIR [T] *AmE* to comb your hair in the opposite direction to which it grows, so that it looks thicker; ◘ **backcomb** *BrE*

tease sth ⇔ out *phr v*

1 to succeed in learning information that is hidden, or that someone does not want to tell you: [+of] *I finally managed to tease the truth out of her.*

2 to gently move hairs or threads that are stuck together so that they become loose or straight again: *She combed her hair, gently teasing out the knots.*

tease² *n* [C] *informal* **1** someone who enjoys making jokes at people, and embarrassing them, especially in a friendly way: *Don't take any notice of Joe – he's a big tease.* **2** something that you say or do as a joke, to tease someone: *I'm sorry, it was only a tease.* **3** someone who deliberately makes you sexually excited, but has no intention of having sex with you

tea·sel /'tiːzəl/ *n* [C] a plant with leaves and flowers that feel sharp when you touch them

teas·er /'tiːzə $ -ər/ *n* [C] *informal* **1** a very difficult question that you have to answer as part of a game or competition **2** a short advertisement which appears a few days or weeks before a full advertisement for a product

'teaser ad *n* [C] an advertisement that is used to make people interested in a product, but that does not give very much information about the product, so that people will pay attention to more advertisements later

'tea ˌservice *n* [C] a matching set with a teapot, cups, and plates, which you use for serving tea

'tea shop *n* [C] a TEAROOM

teas·ing·ly /'tiːzɪŋli/ *adv* in a way that shows you are joking and trying to have fun by embarrassing someone in a friendly way

tea·spoon /'tiːspuːn/ *n* [C] **1** a small spoon that you use for mixing sugar into tea and coffee **2** also **teaspoonful** /'tiːspuːnful/ written abbreviation *tsp* the amount that a teaspoon can hold, used as a unit for measuring food or liquid in cooking: [+of] *Add a teaspoon of salt.*

teat /tiːt/ *n* [C] **1** *BrE* the rubber part on a baby's bottle that the baby sucks milk from; ◘ **nipple** *AmE* **2** one of the small parts on a female animal's body that her babies suck milk from

tea·time /'tiːtaɪm/ *n* [U] *BrE* a time in the late afternoon or early evening when people have a meal: *John won't be back until teatime.*

'tea ˌtowel *n* [C] *BrE* a small cloth that you use for drying cups, plates etc after you have washed them; ◘ **dish towel** *AmE*

'tea tree ˌoil *n* [U] oil from an Australian tree, that is used to treat skin problems

'tea urn *n* [C] *BrE* a large metal container that you use for heating water to make a lot of cups of tea

tea·zel, teazle /'tiːzəl/ *n* [C] another spelling of TEASEL

tech /tek/ *n* [C] *BrE old-fashioned informal* a TECHNICAL COLLEGE

tech·ie /'teki/ *n* [C] *informal* someone who knows a lot about computers and electronic equipment

tech·ni·cal [S2] [W2] /'teknɪkəl/ *adj*

1 MACHINES connected with knowledge of how machines work: *Our staff will be available to give you technical support.* | *I have no technical knowledge at all.* | *technical training*

---

2 technical problem/hitch a problem involving the way a machine or system works: *We've been having some technical problems with the new hardware.*

3 LANGUAGE technical language is language that is difficult for most people to understand because it is connected with one particular subject or used in one particular job: *I didn't understand all the technical terms.*

4 DETAILS/RULES relating to small exact details or rules that say how a system should work: *He called for the legislation to be delayed on a technical point.* | *This is a technical violation of the treaty.*

5 SKILLS technical ability is the ability to do the difficult things that you have to do in order to play music, do a sport etc: *a young player with a lot of technical ability*

'technical ˌcollege *n* [C] a college in Britain where, in the past, students could study to take examinations in practical subjects

tech·ni·cal·i·ty /ˌteknɪ'kæləti/ *n plural* **technicalities** [C] **1** technicalities [plural] the small details of how to do something or how a system or process works: [+of] *I don't really want to get into discussing the technicalities of laser printing.* **2** a small detail in a law or a set of rules, especially one that forces you to make a decision that seems unfair: *The case against him had to be dropped because of a legal technicality.* | **on a technicality** *The proposal was rejected on a technicality* (=because of a technicality).

tech·ni·cal·ly [S3] /'teknɪkli/ *adv*

1 according to the exact details of a rule or law: [sentence adverb]: *Technically, the two countries are still at war, as a peace treaty was never signed.* | [+ adj/adv]: *What you have done is technically illegal.*

2 [+ adj/adv] concerning the special skills that are needed to play music, do a sport etc: *a technically brilliant pianist* | *The dance looks simple, but is technically very difficult.*

3 concerning the way machines are used to do work: *Agriculture is becoming more and more technically advanced.*

4 technically possible/difficult/feasible etc possible, difficult etc using the scientific knowledge that is available now: *It could soon be technically possible to produce a human being by cloning.*

ˌtechnical sup'port also **ˌtech sup'port** *n* [U] **1** help or information that you receive to improve a computer program or system, make it continue working, or use it correctly **2** the department of a company that provides help with using computers: *Maybe you'd better try calling tech support.*

tech·ni·cian /tek'nɪʃən/ *n* [C] **1** someone whose job is to check equipment or machines and make sure that they are working properly: *a laboratory technician* | *a hospital technician* **2** someone who is very good at the skills of a particular sport, music, art etc: *Whether he was a great artist or not, Dali was a superb technician.*

Tech·ni·col·or /'teknɪkʌlə $ -ər/ *n* [U] *trademark* a way of producing the colour in films, used for the cinema

tech·ni·col·our *BrE*; **technicolor** *AmE* /'teknɪkʌlə $ -ər/ *n* **in full/glorious technicolour** if you see something in glorious technicolour, you see it clearly on a screen, with lots of bright colours

tech·nique [S3] [W1] /tek'niːk/ *n*

1 [C] a special way of doing something: [+for] *There are various techniques for dealing with industrial pollution.* | [+of] *In mathematics, we use many techniques of problem-solving.*

2 [U] the special way in which you move your body when you are playing music, doing a sport etc, which is difficult to learn and needs a lot of skill: *He's a great player, with brilliant technique.*

tech·no /'teknəʊ $ -noʊ/ *n* [U] a type of popular electronic dance music with a fast strong beat

techno- /teknə, -nou $ -nə, -nou/ *prefix* concerning machines and electronic equipment such as computers: *technophobia* (=dislike of computers, machines etc) | *techno-literacy* (=skill in using computers)

tech·noc·racy /tek'nɒkrəsi $ -'nɑ:-/ *n plural* **technocracies** [C,U] a social system in which people with a lot of knowledge about science, machines, and computers have a lot of power

tech·no·crat /'teknəkræt/ *n* [C] a skilled scientist who has a lot of power in industry or government

techno-geek *n* [C] *informal* someone whose main interest is electronic equipment, especially equipment connected with computers and the Internet, and who spends too much time buying this equipment and using it – often used to show disapproval: *techno-geeks on the hunt for new tools*

tech·no·lo·gi·cal /ˌteknə'lɒdʒɪkəl $ -'lɑ:-/ *adj* related to technology: *The steam engine was the greatest technological advance of the 19th century* —**technologically** /-kli/ *adv*: *the most technologically advanced factory in Europe.*

tech·nol·o·gist /tek'nɒlədʒəst $ -'nɑ:-/ *n* [C] someone who has special knowledge of technology

tech·nol·o·gy [S2] [W1] /tek'nɒlədʒi $ -'nɑ:-/ *n plural* **technologies** [C,U] new machines, equipment, and ways of doing things that are based on modern knowledge about science and computers: *Modern technology makes moving money around much easier than it used to be.* | *Advances in technology have improved crop yields by over 30%.* | *There have been major new developments in satellite technology.* | *Many people are unwilling to embrace new technologies.*

tech·no·phobe /'teknəfəub $ -foub/ *n* [C] someone who does not like modern machines, such as computers, and would prefer to live without them —**technophobia** /ˌteknə'fəubiə $ -'fou-/ *n* [U]

ted·dy bear /'tedi beə $ -ber/ also **teddy** *n* [C] a soft toy in the shape of a bear

teddy boy *n* [C] a member of a group of young men in Britain in the 1950s who had their own special style of clothes and music

te·di·ous /'ti:diəs/ *adj* something that is tedious continues for a long time and is not interesting; **boring**: *The work was tiring and tedious.* —**tediously** *adv*: *a tediously long film*

te·di·um /'ti:diəm/ *n* [U] the feeling of being bored because the things you are doing are not interesting and continue for a long time without changing: *We sang while we worked, to relieve the tedium.* | [+of] *the tedium of everyday life*

tee¹ /ti:/ *n* [C] **1** a small object that you use in a game of GOLF to hold the ball above the ground before you hit it **2** the place where you first hit the ball towards each hole in a game of GOLF

tee² *v past tense and past participle* **teed**
tee off *phr v* **1** to hit the ball towards a hole for the first time in a game of GOLF **2 tee sb off** *AmE informal* to make someone angry: *His attitude really tees me off.*

Tee-ball *n* [U] another spelling of T-BALL

teed off /ˌti:d 'ɒf $ -'ɔ:f/ *adj AmE informal* annoyed or angry

teem /ti:m/ *v*
teem down *phr v BrE* to rain very heavily: *It's been teeming down all day.*
teem with sb/sth *phr v* **1** to be very full of people or animals, all moving about: *The island was teeming with tourists.* **2** *BrE* if it is teeming with rain, it is raining very heavily

teem·ing /'ti:mɪŋ/ *adj* **1** full of people, animals etc that are all moving around: *the teeming streets of the city* **2** *BrE* teeming rain is very heavy rain: *She walked home through the teeming rain.*

teen¹ /ti:n/ *adj* [only before noun] *informal* relating to teenagers or used by teenagers: *a rock star and teen idol* | *a teen magazine*

teen² *n* [C] **1** *AmE informal* a teenager **2 teens** [plural] your teens is the period of your life when you are between 13 and 19 years old: **be in your teens** *She was in her teens when she met him.* | **early/late teens** *We moved to York when I was in my early teens.*

teen·age /'ti:neɪdʒ/ also **teen·aged** /'ti:neɪdʒd/ *adj* [only before noun] **1** aged between 13 and 19: *a teenage boy* | *my teenage daughter* **2** relating to or affecting people aged between 13 and 19: *the teenage years* | *teenage rebellion* | *the problem of teenage pregnancy*

teen·ag·er /'ti:neɪdʒə $ -ər/ *n* [C] also **teen** *informal* someone who is between 13 and 19 years old: *a TV sex education series aimed at teenagers*

tee·ny /'ti:ni/ *adj informal* very small; **tiny**: *I was just a teeny bit disappointed.*

tee·ny·bop·per /'ti:niˌbɒpə $ -ˌbɑ:pər/ *n* [C] *old-fashioned* a girl between the ages of about 9 and 14, who is very interested in popular music, teenage fashions etc

tee·ny wee·ny /ˌti:ni 'wi:ni◂/ also **teen·sy ween·sy** /ˌti:nzi 'wi:nzi◂/ *adj informal* a word meaning very small – used especially by children or when speaking to children

tee·pee /'ti:pi:/ *n* [C] another spelling of TEPEE

tee shirt *n* [C] another spelling of T-SHIRT

tee·ter /'ti:tə $ -ər/ *v* [I] **1** to stand or walk moving from side to side, as if you are going to fall: *She teetered along in her high-heeled shoes.* **2 be teetering on the brink/edge of sth** to be very close to being in an unpleasant or dangerous situation: *The country teetered on the brink of war.*

teeter-totter *n* [C] *AmE* a large toy like a board on which two children sit, one at each end; **seesaw** *BrE*

teeth /ti:θ/ the plural of TOOTH

teethe /ti:ð/ *v* [I] **be teething** if a baby is teething, its first teeth are growing

teething troubles also **teething problems** *n* [plural] small problems that you have when you first start doing a new job or using a new system

tee·to·tal /ˌti:'təutl◂ $ -'tou-/ *adj* someone who is teetotal never drinks alcohol —**teetotalism** *n* [U]

tee·to·tal·ler *BrE*; **, teetotaler** *AmE* /ti:'təutələ $ -'toutələr/ *n* [C] someone who never drinks alcohol

TEFL /'tefəl/ *n* [U] *BrE* the teaching of English as a foreign language

Tef·lon /'teflɒn $ -lɑ:n/ *n* [U] *trademark* a plastic that stops things from sticking to it, used on the inside of pans to stop food sticking to the pan

tel the written abbreviation of TELEPHONE NUMBER

tele- /teli, teli/ *prefix* **1** at or over a long distance: *a telescope* (=for seeing a long way) | *telecommunications* (=communicating with people a long way away) | *teleshopping* (=using a computer in your home to order goods) **2** for television or broadcast on television: *a teleplay* **3** using a telephone: **telesales** (=selling products to people by telephone)

tel·e·cast /'telikɑ:st $ -kæst/ *n* [C] something that is broadcast on television —**telecast** *v* [T]: *The game will be telecast live.*

tel·e·com·mu·ni·ca·tions /ˌtelikəmju:nə'keɪʃənz/ *n* [plural] the sending and receiving of messages by telephone, radio, television etc: *a new telecommunications system* | *the telecommunications industry*

tele·com·mut·er /'telikəˌmju:tə $ -tər/ *n* [C] someone who works at home using a computer connected to a company's main office —**telecommuting** *n* [U]

tel·e·con·fe·rence¹ /'teliˌkɒnfərəns $ -ˌkɑ:n-/ *n* [C] a discussion in which people in different places talk to each other using telephones or video equipment

teleconference[2] *v* [I] to have a meeting in which people in different places talk to each other using telephones or video equipment —**teleconferencing** *n* [U]

tel·e·gen·ic /ˌtelɪ'dʒenɪk◂/ *adj* someone who is telegenic looks nice on television

tel·e·gram /'telɪgræm/ *n* [C] a message sent by telegraph

tel·e·graph[1] /'telɪgrɑːf $ -græf/ *n* **1** [U] an old-fashioned method of sending messages using radio or electrical signals **2** [C] a piece of equipment that receives or sends messages in this way —**telegraphic** /ˌtelɪ'græfɪk◂/ *adj*

telegraph[2] *v* **1** [I,T] to send a message by telegraph: *Once he knew where we were, Lewis telegraphed every few hours.* **2** [T] *informal* to let people know what you intend to do without saying anything: *A slight movement of the hand telegraphed his intention to shoot.*

te·leg·ra·pher /tɪ'legrəfə $ -ər/ *n* [C] a telegraphist

te·leg·ra·phist /tɪ'legrəfɪst/ *n* [C] someone in the past whose job was to send and receive messages by telegraph

telegraph ˌpole *n* [C] *BrE* a tall wooden pole for supporting telephone wires; **= telephone pole** *AmE*

tel·e·mar·ket·ing /ˌteli'mɑːkɪtɪŋ $ -'mɑːr-/ *n* [U] a way of selling products to people in which you telephone people to see if they want to buy something

tel·e·path·ic /ˌtelɪ'pæθɪk◂/ *adj* **1** someone who is telepathic has a mysterious ability to know what other people are thinking **2** a telepathic message is sent from one person to another by using thoughts, not by talking or writing

te·lep·a·thy /tɪ'lepəθi/ *n* [U] a way of communicating in which thoughts are sent from one person's mind to another person's mind

tel·e·phone[1] S1 W2 /'telɪfəʊn $ -foʊn/ *n*
1 the telephone the system of communication that you use to have a conversation with someone in another place; **= phone: by telephone** *Reservations can be made by telephone.* | **on the telephone** *I've never met him, but I've spoken to him on the telephone.* | **over the telephone** *I read the names out to him over the telephone.* | **down the telephone** *BrE*: *He shouted at me down the telephone.* | *I had a long **telephone conversation** with her yesterday.* → see picture at OFFICE
2 [C] the piece of equipment that you use when you are talking to someone by telephone; **= phone**: *The telephone rang just as I was leaving.* | *She **picked up the telephone** and dialled a number.* | *I said goodbye and **put down the telephone**.*
3 be on the telephone a) to be talking to someone, using the telephone: *I was on the telephone when he came in.* **b)** to have a telephone in your home, office etc; → see box at CALL[1]

telephone[2] *v* [I,T] *BrE formal* to talk to someone by telephone; **= phone, call**: *Sammy telephoned to say that he would be late.* | *I'll telephone you later.*

telephone ˈbanking *n* [U] a service provided by banks so that people can find out information about their bank account, pay bills etc by telephone rather than by going to a bank

telephone ˌbook *n* [C] a TELEPHONE DIRECTORY

telephone ˌbooth *n* [C] *AmE* a small structure that is partly or completely enclosed, containing a public telephone; **= phone booth**

telephone ˌbox *BrE*; **telephone booth** *AmE* *n* [C] a very small building in a street where there is a telephone that the public can use

telephone ˌcall *n* [C] when you speak to someone by telephone: *There's a telephone call for you, Mr Baron.* | have/get/receive a telephone call *I had a telephone call from George this morning.* | *Can I **make a quick telephone call**?*

telephone diˌrectory *n* [C] a book containing a list of the names, addresses, and telephone numbers of all the people in a particular area; **= phone book**

telephone exˌchange *n* [C] an office where telephone calls are connected

telephone ˌnumber *n* [C] the number that you use to telephone a person: *What's your telephone number?* | *He gave me his address and telephone number.*

telephone ˌpole *n* [C] *AmE* a tall wooden pole for supporting telephone wires; **= telegraph pole** *BrE*

te·leph·o·nist /tɪ'lefənɪst/ *n* [C] *BrE* someone whose job is to connect telephone calls to people in a large organization

te·le·pho·to lens /ˌtelɪfəʊtəʊ 'lenz $ -foʊtoʊ-/ *n* [C] a long LENS that you put on a camera so that you can take clear photographs of things that are a long way away

tel·e·print·er /'telɪˌprɪntə $ -ər/ *n* [C] a machine that prints messages that have been written on a machine somewhere else and sent along telephone lines; **= teletypewriter** *AmE*

tel·e·sales /'telɪseɪlz/ *n* [U] a way of selling products to people by telephone

tel·e·scope[1] /'telɪskəʊp $ -skoʊp/ *n* [C] a piece of equipment shaped like a tube, used for making distant objects look larger and closer: **through a telescope** *Details on the moon's surface can only be seen through a telescope.* → RADIO TELESCOPE; → see picture at OPTICAL

telescope[2] *v* **1** [T] to make a process or set of events happen in a shorter time: **be telescoped into sth** *The whole legal process was telescoped into a few weeks.* **2** [I] if something telescopes, the parts of it press together or slide over each other, and it becomes smaller: *The front of the car telescoped when it hit the wall.*

tel·e·scop·ic /ˌtelɪ'skɒpɪk◂ $ -'skɑː-/ *adj* **1** made of parts that slide over each other so that the whole thing can be made longer or shorter: *a tripod with telescopic legs* **2** making distant things look bigger, like a telescope does: *a telescopic lens* | *a rifle with a telescopic sight* **3** done using a telescope: *his telescopic observations of the moon*

Tel·e·text /'telitekst/ *n* [U] *BrE trademark* a system of broadcasting written information on television: **on Teletext** *You can find more details about all this week's films on teletext.*

tel·e·thon /'telɪθɒn $ -θɑːn/ *n* [C] a long television show in which famous people provide entertainment and ask people watching to give money to help people

tel·e·type·writ·er /ˌteli'taɪpraɪtə $ -ər/ *n* [C] *AmE* a TELEPRINTER

tel·e·van·ge·list /ˌtelɪ'vændʒəlɪst/ *n* [C] someone who appears regularly on television to try to persuade people to become Christians, and often also asks people to give them money —**televangelism** *n* [U]

tel·e·vise /'telɪvaɪz/ *v* [T] to broadcast something on television: *The game will be **televised live** on ABC tonight.*

tel·e·vi·sion S1 W1 /'telɪˌvɪʒən, ˌtelɪ'vɪʒən/ *n*
1 [C] also **television set** *formal* a piece of electronic equipment shaped like a box with a screen, on which you can watch programmes; **= TV**: *a widescreen television* | **turn/switch a television on/off** *Lucy turned on the television to watch the evening news.* | **turn the television up/down** (=make it louder or quieter)
2 [U] the programmes broadcast in this way; **= TV**: *In the evenings I like to relax and **watch television**.* | **television programme/show/series etc** *a television documentary about runaway children*
3 on (the) television broadcast or being broadcast on television: *What's on television tonight?*
4 [U] the business of making and broadcasting programmes on television; **= TV: in television** *Jean works in television.* | **television producer/reporter/presenter etc** *a television film crew* | *satellite/cable television*

similar words: **TV**, **telly** *BrE informal*, **the box** *BrE infor-mal*, **the tube** *AmE informal*
programmes on television: **the news**, **soap opera**, **sit-com**, **drama series**, **detective series**, **documentary**, **docusoap**, **game show**, **talk show** *also* **chat show** *BrE*, **made-for-TV movie**, **cartoon**, **reality TV**, **infomercial**
a TV programme shown on the Internet: **webcast**
a company that broadcasts programmes: **channel**, **station**
types of television broadcasts: **terrestrial** *BrE*, **cable**, **satellite**, **digital**, **pay-per-view**
→ channel surfing

'television ˌlicence *n* [C] an official piece of paper that you need to buy in Britain in order to legally use a television in your home

tel·e·vi·sual /ˌtelⁱ'vɪʒuəl◂/ *adj* [only before noun] *BrE* relating to television: *a major televisual event like the Olympics*

tel·e·work·er /'teliwɜːkə $ -wɜːrkər/ *n* [C] someone who works from home, and communicates with their employer, customers etc using a computer, telephone etc —**teleworking** *n* [U]

tel·ex /'teleks/ *n* **1** [U] a method of communication, in which messages are written on a special machine and then sent using the telephone network **2** [C] a message sent in this way —**telex** *v* [I,T]

tell [S1] [W1] /tel/ *v past tense and past participle* **told** /təʊld $ toʊld/
1 COMMUNICATE STH [T] if someone tells you some-thing, they communicate information, a story, their feelings etc to you: **tell sb (that)** *I wish someone had told me the meeting was canceled.* | *The Chief of Police told reporters that two people were killed in the blast.* | **tell sb what/how/where/who etc** *Jack had to go, but he didn't tell me why.* | *I think you'd better **tell** me **exactly** what's been going on around here.* | **tell sb about sth** *No one had told them about the drug's side effects.* | *I'll **tell you all about** it when I get back.* | **tell sb sth** *Tell me your phone number again.* | **tell (sb) a story/joke/secret/lie** *She told us some funny stories about her sister.* | *Shep-pard was **telling** the truth.* | **tell sb straight** (=tell someone the truth, even though it might upset them) *Tell me straight, Adam. Just answer yes or no.* → see box at SAY¹
2 SHOW STH [T] to give information in ways other than talking: **tell sb how/what/where/who etc** *The light tells you when the machine is ready.* | *The bear's sense of smell tells it where prey is hiding.* | **tell sb about sth** *What do these fossils tell us about climate change?*
3 WHAT SB SHOULD DO [T] to say that someone must do something: **tell sb (not) to do sth** *The teacher told the children to sit down quietly.* | *I thought I told you not to touch anything!* | **tell sb (that)** *Bernice was told she had to work late this evening.* | **tell sb what/how etc** *Stop trying to tell me what to do all the time.* | **Do as you are told** (=obey me) *and don't ask questions.*
4 KNOW [I,T not in progressive] to know something or be able to recognize something because of certain signs that show this: **can/can't tell** *She might have been lying. Benjy couldn't tell.* | **tell (that)** *The moment Kramer walked in, I could tell that things were not going well.* | **tell (sth) a mile off** (=know easily) *You could tell a mile off that he was lying.* | **tell when/how/whether/if etc** *It's **hard to tell** how long the job will take.* | **tell sth by sth/from sth** *I could tell from his tone of voice that Ken was disappointed.*
5 RECOGNIZE DIFFERENCE [T not in progressive] to be able to see how one person or thing is different from another: **tell sth from sth** *How can you tell a fake Vuitton handbag from the real thing?* | *Can you **tell the differ-ence between** sparkling wine and champagne?* → TELL APART
6 tell yourself sth to persuade yourself that something is true: *I keep telling myself there is nothing I could have done to save him.*

7 WARN [T usually in past tense] to warn someone that something bad might happen: **tell sb (that)** *I told you it was a waste of time talking to him.* | **tell sb (not) to do sth** *My mother told me not to trust Robert.*
8 TELL SB ABOUT BAD BEHAVIOUR [I] *informal* to tell someone in authority about something wrong that someone you know has done – used especially by children; 🔲**tell on sb**: *If you hit me, I'll tell.* → KISS-AND-TELL
9 tell tales *BrE* to say something that is not true about someone else, in order to cause trouble for them – used especially about children: *an unpopular boy, who was always telling tales on the other children* → TELLTALE²
10 all told altogether, when everyone or everything has been counted: *There must have been eight cars in the accident, all told.*
11 AFFECT [I not in progressive] to have an effect on someone, especially a harmful one: **tell on sb** *These late nights are really beginning to tell on him.*
12 tell the time *BrE*; **tell time** *AmE* to be able to know what time it is by looking at a clock

SPOKEN PHRASES
13 I/I'll tell you what also **tell you what a)** used when you are suggesting or offering something: *I tell you what – let's have a picnic in the park.* **b)** *AmE* used in order to emphasize what you are really saying: *I tell you what, I'm not looking forward to standing up in court tomorrow.*
14 to tell (you) the truth used to emphasize that you are being very honest: *I don't really want to go out, to tell the truth.*
15 I can tell you/I'm telling you used to emphasize that what you are saying is true even though it may be difficult to believe: *I'm telling you, Sheila, I've never seen anything like it in my life.*
16 tell me used before asking a question: *Tell me, do you think this dress goes with these shoes?* | *So tell me, how was it in Argentina?*
17 I told you so used when you have warned someone about a possible danger that has now happened and they have ignored your warning: *I suppose you've come to say 'I told you so.'*
18 I'll tell you something/one thing/another thing also **let me tell you something/one thing/another thing** used to emphasize what you are saying: *I'll tell you one thing – you'll never get me to vote for him.* | *Let me tell you something – if I catch you kids smoking again, you'll be grounded for a month at least.*
19 you can tell him from me used to ask someone to tell another person something, when you are annoyed or determined: *Well, you can tell him from me that I'm going to make a complaint.*
20 I couldn't tell you used to tell someone that you do not know the answer to their question: *'How much would a rail ticket cost?' ' I couldn't tell you; I always drive.'*
21 I can't tell you a) used to say that you cannot tell someone something because it is a secret: *'Where are you taking me?' 'I can't tell you; it would spoil the surprise.'* **b)** used to say that you cannot express your feelings or describe something properly: [+how/why/what etc] *I can't tell you how worried I've been.*
22 don't tell me used to interrupt someone because you know what they are going to say or because you want to guess – used especially when you are annoyed: *'I'm sorry I'm late but ...' 'Don't tell me – the car broke down again?'*
23 sb tells me (that) used to say what someone has told you: *Mike tells me you've got a new job.*
24 you're telling me used to emphasize that you already know and agree with something that someone has just said: *'He's such a pain to live with.' 'You're telling me!'*
25 tell me about it used to say that you already know how bad something is, especially because you have experienced it yourself: *'I've been so tired lately.' 'Yeah, tell me about it!'*
26 you never can tell/you can never tell used to say

that you cannot be certain about what will happen in the future: *The boy might turn out to be a genius. You never can tell.*
27 there's no telling what/how etc used to say that it is impossible to know what has happened or what will happen next: *There's no telling what she'll try next.*
28 that would be telling used to say that you cannot tell someone something because it is a secret
29 tell sb where to go/where to get off used to tell someone angrily that what they have said is insulting or unfair: *'Andy started criticizing the way I was dressed.' 'I hope you told him where to get off!'*
30 tell it like it is *AmE* to say exactly what you think or what is true, without hiding anything that might upset or offend people: *Don always tells it like it is.*
31 I'm not telling (you) used to say that you refuse to tell someone something: *'Mum, what are you getting me for my birthday?' 'I'm not telling you – you'll have to wait and see.'*
32 tell me another (one) used when you do not believe what someone has told you

tell against sb *phr v BrE formal*
to make someone less likely to succeed in achieving or winning something: *I badly wanted the job, but knew that my age would probably tell against me.*
tell sb/sth **apart** *phr v*
if you can tell two people or things apart, you can see the difference between them, so that you do not confuse them; ▤ **distinguish**: *It's almost impossible to tell the twins apart.*
tell of sb/sth *phr v literary*
to describe an event or person: *The poem tells of the deeds of a famous warrior.*
tell sb ⇔ **off** *phr v*
if someone in authority tells you off, they speak to you angrily about something wrong that you have done: **be/get told off** *Shelley was one of those kids who was always getting told off at school.* | **tell sb off for doing sth** *My dad told me off for swearing.*
tell on sb *phr v informal*
to tell someone in authority about something wrong that someone you know has done – used especially by children: *Please don't tell on me – my parents will kill me if they find out!*
tell·er /ˈtelə $ -ər/ *n* [C] **1** someone whose job is to receive and pay out money in a bank **2** someone who counts votes
tell·ing¹ /ˈtelɪŋ/ *adj* **1** having a great or important effect; ▤ **significant**: *a telling argument* **2** showing the true character or nature of someone or something, often without being intended: **telling comment/example/detail etc** —**tellingly** *adv*
telling² *n* [C,U] **1** when you tell a story: *The story gets better with each telling.* **2 there is no telling** used to say that there is no way to know what will happen in a certain situation: *There's no telling who is going to show up tonight.*
telling-'off *n plural* **tellings-off** [C usually singular] *BrE* the act of telling someone that they have done something wrong: *I've already had one telling-off from Dad this week.* → **tell off** at TELL
tell·tale¹ /ˈtelteɪl/ *adj* **telltale signs/marks etc** signs etc that clearly show something has happened or exists, often something that is a secret: *They examined the child carefully, looking for telltale signs of abuse.*
telltale² *n* [C] *BrE* a child who tells adults about other children's secrets or bad behaviour – used by children to show disapproval; ▤ **tattletale** *AmE*
tel·ly [S3] /ˈteli/ *n plural* **tellies** [C,U] *BrE informal* television: **on telly** *Is there anything good on telly tonight?*
tem·blor /ˈtemblə, -blɔː $ -blər, -blɔːr/ *n* [C] *formal* an EARTHQUAKE
te·mer·i·ty /tɪˈmerɪti/ *n* [U] *formal* when someone says or does something in a way that shows a lack of respect for other people and is likely to offend them: *He actually had the temerity to tell her to lose weight.*

temp¹ /temp/ *n* [C] an office worker who is only employed temporarily
temp² *v* [I] to work as a temp: *Carol's temping until she can find another job.*
tem·per¹ /ˈtempə $ -ər/ *n* **1** [C,U] a tendency to become angry suddenly or easily: *That temper of hers will get her into trouble one of these days.* | *According to Nathan, Robin* **has** *quite* **a temper**. | *Theo needs to learn to* **control** *his* **temper**. | **quick/bad/fiery etc temper** *Be careful, he's got a pretty violent temper.* | **tempers flare** *also* **tempers become frayed** *BrE* (=people become angry) *Mason's temper flared when he spotted his girlfriend kissing another man.* **2 lose your temper** to suddenly become very angry so that you cannot control yourself: *I've never seen Vic lose his temper.* **3** [singular, U] the way you are feeling at a particular time, especially when you are feeling angry for a short time: **in a temper** *It's no use talking to him when he's in a temper.* | *Pete hit his brother in a* **fit of temper**. | **be in a bad/foul temper** (=to be angry) *Watch out – she's been in a foul temper all day.* | **fly into a temper** *Her boss would fly into a temper if a project wasn't done on time.* **4 keep your temper** to stay calm when it would be easy to get angry: *I was finding it increasingly difficult to keep my temper.* **5 good-tempered/foul-tempered/quick-tempered etc** having a good, bad temper etc: *Minnie was always good-tempered and agreeable.* **6** [singular] *formal* the general attitude that people have in a particular place at one time: [+of] *the temper of life in Renaissance Italy* → **BAD-TEMPERED**, **EVEN-TEMPERED**, **ILL-TEMPERED**
temper² *v* [T] **1** *formal* to make something less severe or extreme: **temper sth with/by sth** *The heat in this coastal town is tempered by cool sea breezes.* **2** to make metal as hard as is needed by heating it and then putting it into cold water: *tempered steel*
tem·pe·ra /ˈtempərə/ *n* [U] a type of paint in which the colour is mixed with a thick liquid
tem·pe·ra·ment /ˈtempərəmənt/ *n* [C,U] the emotional part of someone's character, especially how likely they are to be happy, angry etc: **artistic/nervous/good etc temperament** *Jill has such a lovely relaxed temperament.* | **by temperament** *Tolkien was, by temperament, a very different man from Lewis.*
tem·pe·ra·men·tal /ˌtempərəˈmentl◂/ *adj* **1** likely to suddenly become upset, excited, or angry – used to show disapproval: *Preston is particularly good at handling temperamental people.* **2** a machine, system etc that is temperamental does not always work properly: *Sorry if the heater's a bit temperamental.* **3** relating to the emotional part of someone's character: *serious temperamental differences between the couple* —**temperamentally** *adv*
tem·pe·rance /ˈtempərəns/ *n* [U] **1** *old-fashioned* when someone never drinks alcohol because of their moral or religious beliefs **2** *formal* sensible control of the things you say and do, especially the amount of alcohol you drink
tem·pe·rate /ˈtempərɪt/ *adj* **1 temperate climate/zone/region etc** a type of weather or a part of the world that is never very hot or very cold **2** *formal* behaviour that is temperate is calm and sensible; ▤ **intemperate**
'temperate ˌzone *n* [C] one of the two parts of the Earth that are north and south of the TROPICS
tem·pe·ra·ture [S2] [W2] /ˈtempərətʃə $ -ər/ *n*
1 [C,U] a measure of how hot or cold a place or thing is

at a temperature of sth
high temperature
low temperature
a rise in temperature
a fall/drop in temperature
a temperature change/a change in temperature
the temperature rises/goes up (=it gets warmer)
the temperature falls/drops/goes down (=it gets colder)

a **constant temperature** (=one that does not change much)
room temperature (=neither hot nor cold)
air/water/body temperature (=how hot or cold the air, water, or someone's body is)
temperatures soar (=the weather becomes very hot)

[+of] *The temperature of the water was just right for swimming.* | *Water boils at a temperature of 100°C.* | *The seeds should be stored at low temperatures.* | *a gradual rise in ocean temperatures* | *It took me a few days to become accustomed to the change in temperature.* | *In summer, the temperature can rise to 120 degrees Fahrenheit.* | *The temperature in New York dropped to minus 10° last night.* | *The refrigerator keeps your food at a constant temperature.* | *Red wine should be served at room temperature.* | *Exercise raises your body temperature.* | *The sun beat down and temperatures soared into the 30s.*

2 sb's temperature the temperature of your body, especially used as a measure of whether you are sick or not: *The nurse took (=measured) my temperature.*
3 have a temperature also **be running a temperature** to have a body temperature that is higher than normal, especially because you are sick: *Susie has a temperature and has gone to bed.*
4 [C] the temperature of a situation is the way people are reacting, for example whether they are behaving angrily or calmly: *The referee's decision to give a penalty raised the temperature of the match.*

tem·pest /'tempɪst/ *n* [C] **1** *literary* a violent storm **2 a tempest in a teapot** *AmE* an unimportant matter that someone has become upset about: *Haley dismissed the lawsuit as a tempest in a teapot.*

tem·pes·tu·ous /tem'pestʃuəs/ *adj* **1** a tempestuous relationship or period of time involves a lot of difficulty and strong emotions: *a tempestuous marriage* **2** *literary* a tempestuous sea or wind is very rough and violent; ▣ **stormy**

tem·plate /'templeɪt, -plɪt/ *n* [C] **1** a thin sheet of plastic or metal in a special shape or pattern, used to help cut other materials in a similar shape **2** *technical* a computer document containing some basic information that you use as a model for writing other documents, such as business letters, envelopes etc **3** *written* something that is used as a model for another thing: [+for] *Her childhood became a template for how she brought up her own children.*

tem·ple /'tempəl/ *n* [C] **1** a building where people go to WORSHIP, in the Jewish, Hindu, Buddhist, Sikh, and Mormon religions **2** [usually plural] one of the two fairly flat areas on each side of your FOREHEAD

tem·po /'tempəʊ $ -poʊ/ *n plural* **tempos** [C] **1** the speed at which music is played or should be played **2** the speed at which something happens: *the easy tempo of island life*

tem·po·ral /'tempərəl/ *adj formal* **1** related to or limited by time: *the temporal character of human existence* **2** related to practical instead of religious affairs: *Edgar ruled over the Church as well as his temporal kingdom.*

tem·po·ra·ry S2 W3 /'tempərəri, -pəri $ -pəreri/ *adj* **1** continuing for only a limited period of time; ▣ **permanent**: *temporary pain relief* | *I'm living with my parents, but it's only temporary.* | *You might want to consider temporary work until you decide what you want to do.* | *She was employed on a temporary basis.*
2 intended to be used for only a limited period of time; ▣ **permanent**: *temporary accommodation* | *The bridge was erected as a temporary measure.*
—**temporarily** /'tempərərɪli $ ˌtempə'rerɪli/ *adv*: *Due to a small fire, the office will be closed temporarily.*

tem·po·rize also **-ise** *BrE* /'tempəraɪz/ *v* [I] *formal* to delay or avoid making a decision in order to gain time

tempt S3 /tempt/ *v* [T]
1 to try to persuade someone to do something by

making it seem attractive: **tempt sb into doing sth** *The new program is designed to tempt young people into studying engineering.* | **tempt sb to do sth** *It would take a lot of money to tempt me to quit this job.*
2 to make someone want to have or do something, even though they know they really should not: *If you leave valuables in your car it will tempt thieves.* | **be tempted to do sth** *I'm tempted to buy that dress.*
3 tempt fate also **tempt providence** *BrE* **a)** to do something that involves unnecessary risk and may cause serious problems: *Fire officials said developers are tempting fate by building deep into the scenic canyons.* **b)** to say too confidently that something will have a good result, that there will be no problems etc, when it is likely there will be problems

temp·ta·tion /temp'teɪʃən/ *n* [C,U] **1** a strong desire to have or do something even though you know you should not: **temptation to do sth** *There might be a temptation to cheat if students sit too close together.* | *Resist the temptation to buy the item until you're certain you need it.* | *I finally gave in to the temptation and had a cigarette.* **2** something that makes you want to have or do something, even though you know you should not: *Selling alcohol at truck stops is an unnecessary temptation for drivers.*

temp·ting /'temptɪŋ/ *adj* something that is tempting seems very good and you would like to have it or do it: *a tempting job offer* | *That pie looks tempting.* | **be tempting to do sth** *It's tempting to believe her story.*

temp·tress /'temptrɪs/ *n* [C] *old-fashioned* a woman who makes a man want to have sex with her

tem·pu·ra /'tempʊrə/ *n* [U] a type of Japanese food that consists of fish or vegetables fried in BATTER

ten /ten/ *number, noun* **1** the number 10: *Snow had been falling steadily for ten days.* | *I need to be home by ten (=ten o'clock).* | *At the time, she was about ten (=ten years old).* **2 ten to one** *informal* used to say that something is very likely: *Ten to one he'll have forgotten all about it tomorrow.* **3 be ten a penny** *BrE informal* to be very common and therefore not special or unusual → **be a dime a dozen** at DIME (2) **4 (get) ten out of ten (for sth)** *BrE* used in schools to give a perfect mark, or humorously to praise someone: *You get ten out of ten for effort, Simon.* **5** [C] a piece of paper money that is worth ten dollars or ten pounds: *I reached inside my purse and handed him a ten.*

ten·a·ble /'tenəbəl/ *adj* a belief, argument etc that is tenable is reasonable and can be defended successfully: *an idea which is no longer tenable*

te·na·cious /tɪ'neɪʃəs/ *adj* **1** determined to do something and unwilling to stop trying even when the situation becomes difficult: *a tenacious negotiator* **2** tenacious beliefs, ideas etc continue to have a lot of influence for a long time: *a tenacious religious tradition that is still practised in Shinto temples* —**tenaciously** *adv* —**tenacity** /tɪ'næsɪti/ *n* [U]

ten·an·cy /'tenənsi/ *n plural* **tenancies** *formal* **1** [C] the period of time that someone rents a house, land etc; → **tenant**: *a six-month tenancy* | *a tenancy agreement* **2** [C,U] the right to use a house, land etc that is rented

ten·ant S3 W2 /'tenənt/ *n* [C] someone who lives in a house, room etc and pays rent to the person who owns it; → **landlord**: *The desk was left by the previous tenant.*

tenant farmer *n* [C] someone who farms land that is rented from someone else

tend S1 W1 /tend/ *v*
1 tend to do sth if something tends to happen, it happens often and is likely to happen again: *People tend to need less sleep as they get older.* | *My car tends to overheat in the summer.*
2 also **tend to sb/sth** [T] *old-fashioned* to look after someone or something: *Sofia was in the bedroom tending to her son.*
3 tend towards sth to have one particular quality or feature more than others: *Charles tends towards obesity.*

4 tend bar *especially AmE* to work as a BARTENDER
5 [I always + adv/prep] *formal* to move or develop in a particular direction: [+**upwards/downwards**] *Interest rates are tending upwards.*

ten·den·cy S3 W3 /'tendənsi/ *n plural* **tendencies** [C]
1 if someone or something has a tendency to do or become a particular thing, they are likely to do or become it: **a tendency to do sth** *Greg's tendency to be critical made him unpopular with his co-workers.* | *The drug is effective but* **has a tendency to cause** headaches. | [+**to/towards**] *Some people may inherit a tendency to alcoholism.* | [+**for**] *Researchers believe that the tendency for diabetes is present at birth.*
2 a general change or development in a particular direction: **there is a tendency (for sb) to do sth** *There is an increasing tendency for women to have children later in life.* | [+**to/towards**] *a general tendency towards conservation and recycling* | [+**among**] *a tendency among Americans to get married at a later age*
3 aggressive/suicidal/criminal/artistic etc tendencies a part of someone's character that makes them likely to behave in a certain way or become an artist, criminal etc: *children with aggressive or anti-social tendencies*
4 [also + plural verb *BrE*] a group within a larger political group that supports ideas that are usually more extreme than those of the main group: *the growing fascist tendency*

ten·den·tious /ten'denʃəs/ *adj formal* a tendentious speech, remark, book etc expresses a strong opinion that is intended to influence people

ten·der¹ /'tendə $ -ər/ *adj*
1 FOOD tender food is easy to cut and eat, especially because it has been well cooked; 🔁 **tough**: *Continue cooking until the meat is tender.*
2 PART OF YOUR BODY a part of your body that is tender is painful if someone touches it: *My arm is still tender where I bruised it.*
3 GENTLE gentle and careful in a way that shows love: *Her voice was tender and soft.* | *a slow, tender kiss*
4 EASILY DAMAGED easily damaged – used especially about plants or flowers: *tender plants that were killed by the harsh winter*
5 tender loving care *usually spoken* sympathetic treatment and a lot of attention; 🔁 **TLC**
6 tender age the time when you are young or do not have much experience: **at the tender age of sth** *Nicholas was sent to boarding school at the tender age of seven.* —**tenderly** *adv* —**tenderness** *n* [U]

tender² *v* **1** [T] *formal* to formally offer or show something to someone: *As company secretary, you must tender the proposal.* | **tender sth to sb** *The seller has the right to keep the goods until payment is tendered to him.* | *Minton* **tendered** *her* **resignation** *on Friday.* **2** [I] *BrE* to make a formal offer to do a job or provide goods or services for a particular price; 🔁 **bid** *AmE*: [+**for**] *We are unable to tender competitively for the contract.*

tender³ *n* [C] **1** *especially BrE* a formal statement of the price you would charge for doing a job or providing goods or services; 🔁 **bid** *AmE*: *Our bid was the lowest tender.* | **put sth out to tender** *BrE* (=to ask different companies to say how much they will charge for doing a particular job) *The contract for building the houses will be put out to tender.* **2** a small boat that takes people or supplies between the shore and a larger boat **3** part of a steam train used for carrying coal and water for the train → BARTENDER, LEGAL TENDER

tender-heart·ed /ˌtendə 'hɑːtɪd $ -dər 'hɑːr-/ *adj* very kind and gentle

ten·der·ize also **-ise** *BrE* /'tendəraɪz/ *v* [T] to make meat softer and easier to eat by preparing it in a special way

ten·der·iz·er also **-iser** *BrE* /'tendəraɪzə $ -ər/ *n* [C,U] a substance that is put onto raw meat to make it softer and easier to eat after it has been cooked

ten·der·loin /'tendəlɔɪn $ -ər-/ *n* [U] meat that is soft and easy to eat, cut from each side of the BACKBONE of cows or pigs

ten·don /'tendən/ *n* [C] a thick string-like part of your body that connects a muscle to a bone

ten·dril /'tendrəl/ *n* [C] **1** a thin leafless curling stem by which a climbing plant fastens itself to a support **2** *literary* a thin curling piece of hair

ten·e·ment /'tenɪmənt/ *n* [C] a large building divided into apartments, especially in the poorer areas of a city: **tenement building/house/block**

ten·et /'tenɪt/ *n* [C] a principle or belief, especially one that is part of a larger system of beliefs: **central/basic/fundamental etc tenet** *one of the basic tenets of democracy* | [+**of**] *the main tenet of his philosophy*

ten·fold /'tenfəʊld $ -foʊld/ *adj, adv* ten times as much or as many of something: *Business has* **increased tenfold** *in the past two years.*

ten-gallon 'hat *n* [C] a tall hat made of soft material with a wide BRIM, worn especially by COWBOYS

ten·ner /'tenə $ -ər/ *n* [C] *BrE informal* £10 or a ten-pound note: *Can you lend me a tenner?*

ten·nis S3 W3 /'tenɪs/ *n* [U] a game for two people or two pairs of people who use RACKETS to hit a small soft ball backwards and forwards over a net

'tennis court *n* [C] the four-sided area that you play tennis on

'tennis 'elbow *n* [U] a medical problem in which your elbow is very painful

'tennis shoe *n* [C] a light shoe used for playing sports, with a rubber surface on the bottom

ten·on /'tenən/ *n* [C] *technical* an end of a piece of wood, that has been cut to fit exactly into a MORTISE in order to form a strong joint

ten·or¹ /'tenə $ -ər/ *n* **1** [C] a male singing voice that can reach the range of notes below the lowest woman's voice, or a man with a voice like this **2** [singular, U] the part of a musical work that is written for a tenor voice; → **alto, baritone, bass, soprano**: *Arthur Davies sings the tenor solo.* **3** **the tenor of sth** *formal* **a)** the general way in which an event or process takes place; 🔁 **tone**: *Many voters admitted being disturbed by the tenor of the election campaign.* **b)** the general meaning of something written or spoken, or the general attitude expressed in it; 🔁 **tone**: *the* **general tenor** *of her speech*

tenor² *adj* a tenor voice or instrument has a range of notes that is lower than an ALTO voice or instrument: *a tenor saxophone*

ten·pin /'ten.pɪn/ *n* [C] *BrE* one of the ten bottle-shaped wooden objects that you try to knock down in BOWLING

tenpin 'bowling *n* [U] *BrE* an indoor sport in which you roll a heavy ball along a floor to knock down bottle-shaped wooden objects; 🔁 **bowling** *AmE*

tense¹ /tens/ *adj* **1** a situation in which you feel very anxious and worried because of something bad that might happen; → **tension**: **tense situation/atmosphere/moment etc** *Marion spoke, eager to break the tense silence.* **2** feeling worried, uncomfortable, and unable to relax: *Is anything wrong? You look a little tense.* **3** unable to relax your body or part of your body because your muscles feel tight; → **tension**: *Massage is great if your neck and back are tense.* | *She tried to relax her tense muscles.* —**tensely** *adv* —**tenseness** *n* [U]

tense² *v* [I,T] also **tense up** to make your muscles tight and stiff, or to become tight and stiff: *Relax, and try not to tense up so much.* | *Every time the phone rang, she tensed.*

tense³ *n* [C,U] any of the forms of a verb that show the time, continuance, or completion of an action or state

T

that is expressed by the verb. 'I am' is in the present tense, 'I was' is past tense, and 'I will be' is future tense

tensed 'up adj [not before noun] informal feeling so nervous or worried that you cannot relax: Brian got so tensed up he could hardly speak.

ten·sile /'tensaɪl $ 'tensəl/ adj [only before noun] technical able to be stretched without breaking: tensile rubber

tensile 'strength n [U] technical the ability of steel or CONCRETE etc to bear pressure or weight without breaking

ten·sion S3 W2 /'tenʃən/ n
1 NERVOUS FEELING [U] a nervous worried feeling that makes it impossible for you to relax; → **tense**: The tension was becoming unbearable, and I wanted to scream. | **reduce/relieve/ease etc tension** Exercise is the ideal way to relieve tension after a hard day.
2 NO TRUST [C usually plural, U] the feeling that exists when people or countries do not trust each other and may suddenly attack each other or start arguing: **political/racial/social etc tension** In those days, there was a great deal of racial tension on campus. | [+between] The obvious tension between Warren and Anne made everyone else uncomfortable.
3 DIFFERENT INFLUENCES [C,U] if there is tension between two things, there is a difference between the needs or influences of each, and that causes problems: [+between] In business, there's always a tension between the needs of customers and shareholders.
4 TIGHTNESS [U] tightness or stiffness in a wire, rope, muscle etc: Tension in the neck muscles can cause headaches. | **Muscle tension** can be a sign of stress.
5 FORCE [U] the amount of force that stretches something: This wire will take 50 pounds tension. | [+on] There was a lot of tension on the wire before it snapped.

tent /tent/ n [C] a shelter consisting of a sheet of cloth supported by poles and ropes, used especially for camping: We looked for a flat spot where we could **pitch** our **tent** (=put up our tent). → OXYGEN TENT

tent

pole

groundsheet

ten·ta·cle /'tentɪkəl/ n [C] **1** one of the long thin parts of a sea creature such as an OCTOPUS which it uses for holding things **2 tentacles** [plural] the influence or effect that something has on other people or things – used to show disapproval: The company's tentacles spread from car manufacturing to railways.

ten·ta·tive /'tentətɪv/ adj **1** not definite or certain, and may be changed later; ➡ **provisional**; ⧉ **definite**: I passed on my **tentative conclusions** to the police. | The government is taking **tentative steps** towards tackling the country's economic problems. **2** done without confidence; ⧉ **hesitant**: a tentative smile —**tentatively** adv: Albi knocked tentatively and entered. —**tentativeness** n [U]

ten·ter·hooks /'tentəhʊks $ -ər-/ n especially BrE be **on tenterhooks** to feel nervous and excited because you are waiting to find out something or for something to happen: She had been on tenterhooks all night, expecting Joe to return at any moment.

tenth¹ /tenθ/ adj coming after nine other things in a series: in the tenth century | her tenth birthday —**tenth** pron: I'm planning to leave on **the tenth** (=the tenth day of the month).

tenth² n [C] one of ten equal parts of something

ten·u·ous /'tenjuəs/ adj **1** a situation or relationship that is tenuous is uncertain, weak, or likely to change: For now, the band's travel plans are tenuous. | **tenuous link/connection etc** The United Peace Alliance had only a tenuous connection with the organized

Labour movement. | The link between her family and the King's is rather tenuous. **2** literary very thin and easily broken —**tenuously** adv

ten·ure /'tenjə, -jʊə $ -jər/ n [U] **1** the right to stay permanently in a teaching job: It's becoming increasingly difficult to acquire **academic tenure**. **2** formal the period of time when someone has an important job: The company has doubled in value during his tenure. **3** law the legal right to live in a house or use a piece of land for a period of time —**tenured** adj: a tenured professor | a tenured position

te·pee /'tiːpiː/ n [C] a round tent with a pointed top, used by some Native Americans

tep·id /'tepɪd/ adj **1** a feeling, reaction etc that is tepid shows a lack of excitement or interest; ⧉ **lukewarm**: a tepid response from the audience **2** tepid liquid is slightly warm, especially in a way that seems unpleasant; ⧉ **lukewarm**: tepid coffee

te·qui·la /tɪ'kiːlə/ n [C,U] a strong alcoholic drink made in Mexico

tera- /terə/ prefix [in nouns] a TRILLION – used with units of measurement

ter·a·byte /'terəbaɪt/ n [C] written abbreviation **TB** or **Tb** a unit for measuring computer information, equal to 1,024 GIGABYTES, and used less exactly to mean one TRILLION BYTES

ter·a·flop /'terəflɒp $ -flɑːp/ n [C usually plural] a unit that measures how fast a computer works. One teraflop is one TRILLION operations every second

ter·cen·te·na·ry /ˌtɜːsen'tiːnəri $ ˌtɜːrsen'tenəri, tɜːr'sentənəri/ n plural **tercentenaries** [C] BrE the day or year exactly 300 years after a particular event

term¹ S1 W1 /tɜːm $ tɜːrm/ n
1 in terms of sth if you explain or describe something in terms of a particular fact or event, you are explaining or describing it only in relation to that fact or event: **describe/measure/evaluate etc sth in terms of sth** Femininity is still defined **in terms of** beauty. | It's a mistake to **think of** Florida only **in terms of** its tourist attractions. | It's too early to start **talking in terms of** casualties. | **in terms of what/how/who etc** Did the experiment find any differences in terms of what children learned?
2 in general/practical/financial etc terms used to show that you are describing or considering a subject in a particular way or from a particular point of view: **in general/broad/simple etc terms** We explain in simple terms what the treatment involves. | It would be wrong to describe society **purely in** economic **terms**. | The war, although successful **in military terms**, left the economy in ruins. | What do these statistics mean **in human terms**? | **in sb's terms** In our terms, the scheme has not been a success. | **in real/absolute terms** (=accurate, true, or including any related changes) Rail fares have fallen 17 per cent in real terms. | **in relative terms** (=compared with other, similar things) Students have less money in relative terms, but spend more on books.
3 WORD [C] a word or expression with a particular meaning, especially one that is used for a specific subject or type of language: [+for] 'Multimedia' is the term for any technique combining sounds and images. | **legal/medical/technical term** Many legal terms have more than one meaning. | photographs, or **to use the technical term**, 'half-tones' | It was he who **coined** (=invented) **the term** 'anorexia'. | **term of abuse/endearment/respect etc** (=rude, loving, respectful etc language) The word 'communist' had become a term of abuse. | **in strong/glowing/forthright etc terms** (=showing a strong etc emotion or attitude) I complained to the manager **in the strongest possible terms**. | His reply was **couched in** sinister **terms**. | **in no uncertain terms** (=language that is very clear and angry) Journalists were told, **in no uncertain terms**, that they were not welcome. → **a contradiction in terms** at CONTRADICTION (3)
4 PERIOD OF TIME [C] a fixed period of time during which someone does something or something happens: **term in office** (=the time someone spends doing an

important job in government) *It was always clear that Schmidt's third term in office would prove a difficult one.* | [+of] *the maximum term of imprisonment* | *The lease runs for a term of 99 years.* | **prison/jail term** *The men each received a 30-year prison term.* | **fixed/long/ short term** *a fixed-term contract* | *In the long term, alcohol causes high blood pressure.* | *Dad loaned us his car for the short term.*

5 SCHOOL/UNIVERSITY [C,U] *BrE* one of the three periods of time that the school or university year is divided into; → **half-term**: **summer/autumn/spring term** *The exams are at the end of the summer term.* | *Teachers often feel overworked* **in term time** (=during the term). | **first/last day of term** *that all-important first day of term* ⚠ At a British school or university, the year is divided into three **terms**. At an American university, there are two **semesters** or three **trimesters**.

6 END [singular, U] *technical* the end of a particular period of time; → **long-term**, **short-term**: *The agree-ment* **reaches its term** *next year.* | *a child born two months before* **full term** (=of pregnancy) | *The arrange-ment had outlived its* **natural term** (=the length of time it was expected to exist).

7 come to terms with sth to accept an unpleasant or sad situation and no longer feel upset or angry about it: *George and Elizabeth have* **come to terms with the fact that** *they will never have children.* | *Counselling helped her come to terms with her grief.*

8 CONDITIONS terms [plural] **a)** the conditions that are set for an agreement, contract, arrangement etc: *Under the terms of the agreement, the debt would be repaid over 20 years.* | *your* **terms and conditions** *of employment* | *Delivery is* **within the terms** *of this contract.* | **equal/unequal/the same etc terms** (=condi-tions that are equal, unequal etc) *Small businesses have to* **compete on equal terms with** *large organisations.* | *Men and women should be able to work* **on level terms.** | **on sb's (own) terms** (=according to the conditions that someone wants) *He wanted our relationship to be only on his terms.* **b)** the arrangements for payment that you agree to when you buy or sell something: **reasonable/ favourable/cheaper etc terms** *Some insurance compa-nies offer very reasonable terms.* | *This allowed tenant farmers to buy land* **on easy terms** (=by paying small sums of money over a long period).

9 RELATIONSHIP terms [plural] if you are on good, bad etc terms with someone, you have a good, bad etc relationship with them: **be on good/bad/friendly etc terms (with sb)** *By now, Usha and I were on* **familiar terms.** | *He is barely on* **speaking terms** *with his father* (=they are angry and almost never speak to each other). | *We were soon on* **first-name terms** (=using each other's first names, as a sign of friendship).

10 terms of reference *formal* the subjects that a person or group of people agree to consider: *the committee's terms of reference*

11 NUMBER/SIGN [C] *technical* one of the numbers or signs used in a mathematical calculation

term² *v* [T usually passive] to use a particular word or expression to name or describe something: *This condi-tion is sometimes termed RSI, or repetitive strain injury.* | *Roosevelt termed himself and his policies 'liberal'.* | *These developments are* **loosely termed** *'advanced manufacturing techniques'.*

ter·mi·nal¹ /'tɜːmɪnəl $ 'tɜːr-/ *adj* **1** a terminal ill-ness cannot be cured, and causes death: *terminal can-cer* **2 (in) terminal decline** *BrE* in a state of becoming worse and worse and never getting better: *The once great industry is now in terminal decline.* —**terminally** *adv*: *terminally ill patients*

terminal² *n* [C] **1** a big building where people wait to get onto planes, buses, or ships, or where goods are loaded: *the airport's passenger terminal* | **ferry/bus terminal** **2** a piece of computer equipment consisting of at least a KEYBOARD and a screen, that you use for putting in or taking out information from a large

computer **3** one of the points at which you can con-nect wires in an electrical CIRCUIT: **positive/negative terminal**

ter·mi·nate /'tɜːmɪneɪt $ 'tɜːr-/ *v* **1** [I,T] *formal* if something terminates, or if you terminate it, it ends; ◪ **end**: *The court ruled that the contract must be terminated.* | *a woman's decision on whether or not to terminate the pregnancy* **2** [I] if a train, bus, or ship terminates at a particular place, its journey ends there: *The train from Paris terminates at Waterloo.*

ter·mi·na·tion /,tɜːmɪ'neɪʃən $,tɜːr-/ *n* **1** [C] *for-mal* the act of ending something, or the end of some-thing: [+of] *You may face a reduction or termination of benefits.* **2** [C,U] *technical* a medical operation to end the life of a developing child before it is born; ◪ **abor-tion**

ter·mi·nol·o·gy /,tɜːmɪ'nɒlədʒi $,tɜːrmɪ'nɑː-/ *n plu-ral* **terminologies** [C,U] the technical words or expres-sions that are used in a particular subject: *computer terminology* —**terminological** /,tɜːmɪnə'lɒdʒɪkəl◂ $,tɜːrmɪnə'lɑː-/ *adj*

ter·mi·nus /'tɜːmɪnəs $ 'tɜːr-/ *n plural* **termini** /-naɪ/ [C] the station or stop at the end of a railway or bus line

ter·mite /'tɜːmaɪt $ 'tɜːr-/ *n* [C] an insect that eats and destroys wood from trees and buildings

ˈterm ˌlimit *n* [C] *AmE* a particular number of years that the law allows someone to stay in a particular political position

term·ly /'tɜːmli $ 'tɜːr-/ *adj BrE* happening each TERM (=one of the three periods in the school or university year): *Students can pay fees in termly instalments.*

ˈterm ˌpaper *n* [C] *AmE* a long piece of written work done by college students in the US, that is the most important piece of work in their course

ˈterm-time *n* [U] *BrE* the part of the year when classes are given at a school, college, or university

tern /tɜːn $ tɜːrn/ *n* [C] a black and white sea bird that has long wings and a tail with two points

ter·race /'terəs/ *n* [C]
1 HOUSES *BrE* a row of houses that are joined to each other, or a street with one of these rows in it
2 PLACE YOU CAN SIT a flat outdoor area next to a building or on a roof, where you can sit outside to eat, relax etc
3 FOOTBALL the terraces [plural] *BrE* the wide steps that the people watching a football match can stand on
4 FLAT LAND one of a series of flat areas cut out of a hill like steps, and used to grow crops —**terracing** *n* [U]: *football terracing*

ter·raced /'terəst/ *adj* [only before noun] a terraced field, slope, garden etc has been cut into a series of flat areas along the side of the slope: *terraced rice fields*

ˌterraced ˈhouse *n* [C] *BrE* a house which is part of a row of houses that are joined together; ◪ **row house** *AmE*; → see picture at HOUSE¹

ter·ra·cot·ta, terra cotta /,terə'kɒtə◂ $ -'kɑː-/ *n* [U] **1** hard reddish-brown baked CLAY: *a terracotta pot* **2** a brownish red colour —**terracotta** *adj*

ter·ra fir·ma /,terə 'fɜːmə $ -'fɜːr-/ *n* [U] land, rather than sea or air – used humorously: *We were glad to be back on terra firma.*

ter·rain /te'reɪn, tɪ-/ *n* [C,U] a particular type of land: *rocky terrain*

ter·ra·pin /'terəpɪn/ *n* [C] a small TURTLE that lives in water in warm areas

ter·ra·ri·um /tə'reəriəm $ -'rer-/ *n* [C] a large glass container that you grow plants in as a decoration

ter·res·tri·al /tɪ'restriəl/ *adj* [usually before noun] *technical* **1** relating to the Earth rather than to the moon or other PLANETS → EXTRATERRESTRIAL² **2** living on or relating to land rather than water **3 terrestrial TV/broadcasting/channels etc** *BrE* TV etc that is broad-cast from the Earth rather than from a SATELLITE

T

ter·ri·ble [S1] [W3] /'terəbəl/ adj
1 extremely severe in a way that causes harm or damage; ⊟ **horrible, awful:** *Their son had been injured in a terrible accident.* | *We're worried that something terrible might have happened to Greg.* | *a terrible storm*
2 *informal* extremely bad; ⊟ **horrible, awful:** *The hotel was absolutely terrible.* | *I'd better write this down; I have a terrible memory.*
3 making you feel afraid or shocked: *There was a terrible noise and the roof caved in.* | *She wept when she heard the terrible news.*
4 to a very great degree: *You're making a terrible mistake.*

ter·ri·bly [S2] /'terɪbli/ adv
1 [+ adj/adv] *especially BrE* very; ⊟ **extremely:** *I'm terribly sorry to have kept you waiting.* | *The coach was not terribly worried about his team's poor performance.*
2 very badly; ⊟ **severely:** *The little boy missed his mother terribly.*

ter·ri·er /'teriə $ -ər/ n [C] a small active type of dog that was originally used for hunting

ter·rif·ic /tə'rɪfɪk/ adj **1** *informal* very good, especially in a way that makes you feel happy and excited; ⊟ **great:** *That's a terrific idea!* | *The actress who played the lawyer was terrific.* **2** very large in size or degree: *a terrific bang* | *He drank a terrific amount of beer.*

ter·rif·i·cally /tə'rɪfɪkli/ adv [+ adj/adv] very; ⊟ **extremely:** *She had been so terrifically busy that she barely had time to sleep.*

ter·ri·fied /'terɪfaɪd/ adj very frightened: *a terrified little girl* | [+of] *Sid is terrified of heights.* | *She was terrified of being caught.* | **terrified (that)** *We were terrified that the bridge would collapse.* | [+at] *He was terrified at the thought of being stranded in the woods.* | **terrified to do sth** *He was terrified to stay home alone.*

ter·ri·fy /'terɪfaɪ/ v **terrified, terrifying, terrifies** [T] to make someone extremely afraid: *Her husband's violence terrified her.*

ter·ri·fy·ing /'terɪfaɪ-ɪŋ/ adj extremely frightening: **terrifying experience/ordeal** *It was 30 years before he told anyone of his terrifying experience.* | *terrifying screams* | *It was absolutely terrifying.* —**terrifyingly** adv

ter·rine /te'riːn, tə-/ n [C,U] a food made of cooked meat, fish, or fruit formed into a LOAF shape and served cold, or the dish this is served in

ter·ri·to·ri·al /ˌterə'tɔːriəl◂/ adj **1** related to land that is owned or controlled by a particular country: *a territorial dispute* | *territorial claims* **2** animals or people that are territorial are careful to guard the area of land that they consider to be their own, and prevent others from using it

ˌTerritorial ˈArmy n **the Territorial Army** a military force of people in Britain who train as soldiers in their free time; ⊟ TA → NATIONAL GUARD

ˌterritorial ˈwaters n [plural] the sea near a country's coast, which that country has legal control over

ter·ri·to·ry [W2] /'terətəri $ -tɔːri/ n plural **territories**
1 GOVERNMENT/MILITARY [C,U] land that is owned or controlled by a particular country, ruler, or military force: *Hong Kong became Chinese territory in 1997.* | **occupied/enemy/disputed/hostile territory** *The plane was flying over enemy territory.*
2 TYPE OF LAND [U] land of a particular type: **uncharted/unexplored territory** *an expedition through previously unexplored territory*
3 ANIMAL [C,U] the area that an animal, bird etc regards as its own and will defend against other animals: *A tiger has a large territory to defend.* | *A dog uses urine to mark its territory.*
4 NEW OR FAMILIAR EXPERIENCE [U] a particular area of experience or knowledge: **new/unfamiliar/uncharted territory** *The company is moving into unfamiliar territory with this new software.* | *Actor Patrick Bergin returns to more familiar territory to play a menacing killer.*
5 BUSINESS [C,U] an area in a town, country etc that someone is responsible for as part of their job, especially someone whose job is to sell products: *a sales territory*
6 **come/go with the territory** to be a natural and accepted part of a particular job, situation, place etc: *I'm a cop – getting shot at goes with the territory.*
7 LAND THAT IS NOT A STATE [C] land that belongs to the United States, Canada etc but that is not a state: *the US territory of Guam*

ter·ror /'terə $ -ər/ n
1 FEAR [U] a feeling of extreme fear: **in terror** *People fled in terror as fire tore through the building.* | *Shots rang out, and I screamed in terror.* | *We lived in terror of our father when he was drinking.* | *There was a look of sheer terror* (=complete terror) *on his face.* | **strike terror into sb/sb's heart** *The sound of enemy planes struck terror into our hearts.*
2 FRIGHTENING SITUATION [C] an event or situation that makes people feel extremely frightened, especially because they think they may die: [+of] *the terrors of war* | *Death holds no terrors for* (=does not frighten) *me.*
3 VIOLENT ACTION [U] violent action for political purposes; ⊟ **terrorism:** *The resistance movement started a campaign of terror.* | *The Red Army Faction tried to undermine the state by terror tactics.* | *Pol Pot's reign of terror in Cambodia*
4 PERSON [C] *informal* a child who is difficult to control: *That Johnson kid's a real little terror!* → **reign of terror** at REIGN[1] (4); → **a holy terror** at HOLY (4)

ter·ror·is·m /'terərɪzəm/ n [U] the use of violence such as bombing, shooting, or KIDNAPPING to obtain political demands such as making a government do something: *The government is doing everything possible to combat terrorism.* | *a despicable act of terrorism* | *their involvement in international terrorism*

ter·ror·ist /'terərɪst/ n [C] someone who uses violence such as bombing, shooting etc to obtain political demands: *We refuse to talk to terrorists.* | **terrorist attack/activity/offence** *Twenty people were killed in the latest terrorist attack.* | **terrorist group/organization** | *A terrorist bomb that left 168 people dead.* → GUERRILLA

ter·ror·ize also **-ise** *BrE* /'terəraɪz/ v [T] to deliberately frighten people by threatening to harm them, especially so they will do what you want: **be terrorized into doing sth** *Many people have been terrorized into leaving.* | *gangs who terrorize the neighbourhood*

ter·ry·cloth /'teriklɒθ $ -klɒːθ/ also **ter·ry** /'teri/ n [U] a type of thick cotton cloth with uncut threads on both sides, that can take liquid into itself, and is used to make TOWELS

terse /tɜːs $ tɜːrs/ adj a terse reply, message etc uses very few words and often shows that you are annoyed: *Derek's terse reply ended the conversation.* —**tersely** adv: *'Continue!' he said tersely.* —**terseness** n [U]

ter·tia·ry /'tɜːʃəri $ 'tɜːrʃieri, -ʃəri/ adj *technical* third in place, degree, or order

ˌtertiary eduˈcation n [U] *formal* education at a college, university etc; ⊟ **higher education**

Te·ry·lene /'terɪliːn/ n [U] *BrE trademark* a light strong artificial cloth

TESL /'tesəl/ n [U] the teaching of English as a second language

TESOL /'tiːsɒl $ -sɑːl/ n [U] *especially AmE* the teaching of English to speakers of other languages

tes·sel·la·ted /'tesɪleɪtɪd/ adj *technical* made of small flat pieces in various shapes and colours that fit together to form a pattern

test[1] [S1] [W1] /test/ n [C]
1 EXAM a set of questions, exercises, or practical activities to measure someone's skill, ability, or knowledge: **spelling/driving/biology etc test** *How did you do on your maths test?* | **pass/fail a test** *She passed her driving test when she was 17.* | **take/do/sit a test**

Applicants are required to take a written test. | [+**on**] *We have a test on irregular verbs tomorrow.* | *The school's test scores are among the highest in the district.* | *Did you get a good mark in the test?* ⚠ You **take** or **do** a test. Do not say 'make a test'. To **pass** a test means to succeed in it, not simply to take it.

2 MEDICAL **a)** a medical examination on a part of your body, or a substance taken from your body, to check your health or to discover what is wrong with you: *a blood test* | *an eye test* | *a hearing test* | *a pregnancy test* | *an HIV test They don't know what's wrong with her yet – they're doing tests.* | [+**for**] *a test for HIV* | *I'm still waiting for my **test results** from the hospital.* **b)** an examination of someone's blood, breath etc carried out by the police, to discover if they have done something illegal: *a drugs test* | *The results of the DNA test proved that Simmons was the rapist.* | **breath test** (=to find out if someone has been drinking alcohol before driving a car) **c)** a piece of equipment used for carrying out a medical examination: *a pregnancy test*

3 MACHINE/PRODUCT a process used to discover whether equipment or a product works correctly, or to discover more about it: *nuclear weapons tests* | [+**for**] *a test for chemicals in the water* | *Laboratory tests show that the new drug is very effective.* | *We went to the **test site** in Nevada.*

4 DIFFICULT SITUATION a difficult situation in which the qualities of someone or something are clearly shown: *Chess player Nigel Short faces Anatoly Karpov in the toughest test of his career so far.* | **test of character/strength/courage/endurance etc** *The problems she faced were a real test of character.*

5 **put sb/sth to the test** to force someone or something into a difficult situation in order to discover what the limits of their strength, skills etc are: *Living together will soon put their relationship to the test.* | *Paul soon found himself in an emergency situation that put all his training to the test.*

6 SPORT *BrE* a TEST MATCH → SMEAR TEST, MEANS TEST; → **stand the test of time** at STAND¹ (8); → **the acid test** at ACID (3)

test² S3 W2 *v* [T]

1 MEDICAL to examine someone's blood, body etc in order to find out what is wrong with them, or to see if they have taken an illegal drug: *I must have my eyes tested.* | **test sb for sth** *They tested her for diabetes.* | **test positive/negative (for sth)** *Athletes who test positive for steroids are immediately banned.*

2 SUBSTANCE to examine a substance or thing in order to find out its qualities or what it contains: **test (sth) for sth** *The water should be tested for lead.*

3 KNOWLEDGE/ABILITY to ask someone spoken or written questions, or make them do a practical activity, to discover what they know about a subject: *This task is designed to test your reading skills.* | **test sb on sth** *We're being tested on grammar tomorrow.*

4 MACHINE/PRODUCT also **test out** to use something for a short time to see if it works in the correct way: *The Ferrari team wanted to test their new car out on the racetrack.* | **test sth on sb/sth** *None of this range of cosmetics has been tested on animals.*

5 SHOW HOW GOOD/STRONG to show how good or strong someone or something is, especially by putting them in a difficult situation: *a game that will test the contestants' strength and skill* | *The next six months will test your powers of leadership.* | *I felt that she was testing me, leaving all that cash lying around.* → TESTING

6 IDEA/PLAN also **test out** to start to use an idea or plan to find out if it is correct or effective: *Dr Lee set up a series of experiments to test out his hypothesis.* | **test sth against sth** *The theory was then tested against the results of the study.*

7 **test the water/waters** to check people's reaction to a plan before you decide to use it: *The government is clearly testing the water, to gauge the country's reactions to their proposals.* → **tried and tested** at TRIED²; → see box at CONTROL²

test·a·ble /ˈtestəbəl/ *adj* testable things can be tested: *I don't think this theory is testable.*

tes·ta·ment /ˈtestəmənt/ *n* [C] *formal* **1** **be a testament to sth** proving or showing very clearly that something exists or is true: *The aircraft's safety record is a testament to its designers' skill.* **2** a WILL² (2) —**testamentary** /ˌtestəˈmentəri◂/ *adj* → NEW TESTAMENT, OLD TESTAMENT

ˈtest ban *n* [C] an agreement between countries to stop testing NUCLEAR weapons: *the test ban treaty*

ˈtest card *n* [C] *BrE* a pattern or picture that is shown on television when there are no programmes

ˈtest case *n* [C] a legal case that establishes a particular principle, that is then used as a standard which other similar cases can be judged against

ˈtest cerˌtificate *n* [C] *BrE* the official paper that proves that a car is legally safe enough to drive → MOT

ˈtest drive *n* [C] an occasion when you drive a car so that you can decide if you want to buy it —**test-drive** *v* [T]

test·er /ˈtestə $ -ər/ *n* [C] **1** a person or piece of equipment that tests something **2** a small bottle of PERFUME¹ (1) etc, in a shop, for customers to try

tes·tes /ˈtestiːz/ *n* the plural of TESTIS

tes·ti·cle /ˈtestɪkəl/ *n* [C] one of the two round organs that produce SPERM in a male, that are enclosed in a bag of skin behind and below the PENIS —**testicular** /teˈstɪkjʊlə $ -ər/ *adj*

tes·ti·fy /ˈtestɪfaɪ/ *v* **testified, testifying, testifies** **1** [I,T] to make a formal statement of what is true, especially in a court of law: *Mr Molto has agreed to testify at the trial.* | [+**against**] *Later, the witness who had testified against Muawad withdrew his allegation.* **2** [I,T] *written* to show clearly that something is the case: [+**to**] *The empty shops in the high street testify to the depth of the recession.* | **testify that** *The full ashtrays testify that smoking hasn't been stubbed out.* | *Can you testify that you saw the defendant at the scene of the crime?* **3** [I] *AmE* to stand up and tell people about how God has helped you in your life

tes·ti·mo·ni·al /ˌtestɪˈməʊniəl $ -ˈmoʊ-/ *n* [C] **1** a formal written statement describing someone's character and abilities; → **reference** **2** something that is given or done to someone to thank or praise them, or show admiration for them: *a testimonial dinner in honour of Senator Frank Flint*

tes·ti·mo·ny /ˈtestɪməni $ -moʊni/ *n plural* **testimonies** [C,U] **1** a formal statement saying that something is true, especially one a WITNESS makes in a court of law: *Barker's testimony is crucial to the prosecution's case.* | *In his testimony, he denied that the company had ignored safety procedures.* **2** a fact or situation that shows or proves very clearly that something exists or is true: **be a testimony to/of sth** *These results are a testimony to the coach's skill and hard work.*

test·ing /ˈtestɪŋ/ *adj* a testing situation, experience etc is difficult to deal with: *It's been a testing time.*

ˈtesting ground *n* [C] **1** a place where machines, cars etc are tested to see if they work properly **2** a situation or problem in which you can try new ideas and methods to see if they work: *Eastern Europe has become a testing ground for high-speed privatization.*

tes·tis /ˈtestɪs/ *n plural* **testes** /-tiːz/ [C] *technical* a TESTICLE

ˈtest match *n* [C] a CRICKET or RUGBY match that is played between the teams of different countries

tes·tos·ter·one /teˈstɒstərəʊn $ -ˈstɑːstəroʊn/ *n* [U] the HORMONE (=chemical produced by the body) in males that gives them their male qualities

ˈtest ˌpilot *n* [C] a pilot who flies new aircraft in order to test them

test run n [C] an occasion when you try doing something or using something before you really need to use it, to make sure everything works properly

test tube n [C] a small glass container that is shaped like a tube and is used in chemistry → LABORATORY

test-tube baby n [C] a baby that develops from an egg removed from a woman's body, that is then put back inside the woman to continue developing

tes·ty /'testi/ adj impatient and easily annoyed; ▣ **irritable**: testy remarks | It had been a long day, and Sarah was getting a little testy. —**testily** adv —**testiness** n [U]

tet·a·nus /'tetənəs/ n [U] a serious illness caused by BACTERIA that enter your body through cuts and wounds and make your muscles, especially your jaw, go stiff; ▣ **lockjaw**

tetch·y /'tetʃi/ adj BrE informal likely to get angry or upset easily: Jane's a bit tetchy this morning. —**tetchily** adv —**tetchiness** n [U]

tête-à-tête /ˌteɪt ɑː 'teɪt, ˌteɪt eɪ-/ n [C] a private conversation between two people: friends having a cosy tête-à-tête

teth·er¹ /'teðə $ -ər/ n [C] **1 be at the end of your tether** to be so worried, tired etc that you feel you can no longer deal with a difficult or upsetting situation **2** a rope or chain that an animal is tied to so that it can only move around within a limited area

tether² v [T] to tie an animal to a post so that it can only move around within a limited area

tetra- /'tetrə/ prefix having four of something: a tetrahedron (=solid shape with four sides)

Teu·ton·ic /tjuː'tɒnɪk $ tuː'tɑː-/ adj **1** having qualities that are thought to be typical of German people: Teutonic efficiency **2** relating to the ancient German peoples of northwest Europe: Teutonic mythology

Tex-Mex /ˌteks 'meks/ adj [only before noun] informal relating to the music, cooking etc of Mexican-American people: a Tex-Mex restaurant

text¹ [S2] [W1] /tekst/ n
1 [U] any written material: One disk can store the equivalent of 500 pages of text.
2 [U] the writing that forms the main part of a book, magazine etc, rather than the pictures or notes: There should not be too much text in children's books.
3 [C] a book or other piece of writing that is connected with learning or intended for study: Some of the original text has survived. | **Literary texts**, like all other works of art, have a historical context. | 'Hamlet' is a **set text** (=one that must be studied for an examination) this year. BrE
4 [C] AmE a textbook: a chemistry text
5 the text of sth the exact words of a speech, article etc: Only 'The Times' printed the full text of the President's speech.
6 [C] a short piece from the Bible that someone reads and talks about during a religious service

text² v [I,T] to send someone a written message on a MOBILE PHONE —**texting** n [U]

text·book¹ /'tekstbʊk/ n [C] a book that contains information about a subject that people study, especially at school or college: a biology textbook → COURSE-BOOK

textbook² adj [only before noun] used to describe something that is done exactly as it should be done, or happens exactly as it should happen: **textbook case/example** The advertising campaign was a textbook example of how to sell a product.

tex·tile /'tekstaɪl/ n [C] **1** any type of woven cloth that is made in large quantities, used especially by people in the business of making clothes etc: Their main exports are textiles, especially silk and cotton. | **textile industry/design/manufacture etc** textile design and technology | a textile mill **2 textiles** [plural] the industry involved in making cloth

text message¹ n [C] a written message that is sent or received on a MOBILE PHONE or PAGER

text message² also **text** v [T] to send someone a written message on a MOBILE PHONE or PAGER: She's always text messaging her friends. —**text-messaging** n [U]

tex·tu·al /'tekstʃuəl/ adj formal relating to the way that a book, magazine etc is written: a detailed textual analysis of the Bible

tex·ture /'tekstʃə $ -ər/ n [C,U] **1** the way a surface or material feels when you touch it, especially how smooth or rough it is: **smooth/silky/rough etc texture** the smooth texture of silk | a designer who experiments with different colours and textures **2** the way that a particular type of food feels in your mouth: **creamy/crunchy/meaty etc texture** This soup has a lovely creamy texture. **3** formal the way the different parts of a piece of writing, music, art etc are combined in order to produce a final effect: the rich texture of Shakespeare's English —**textural** adj —**texturally** adv

tex·tured /'tekstʃəd $ -ərd/ adj **1** having a surface that is not smooth: textured wallpaper **2 smooth-textured/coarse-textured/fine-textured etc** having a texture that is smooth etc: smooth-textured skin **3** used to describe a work of art, literature, music etc that has many different parts that are combined to produce a final effect: a richly textured novel

textured vegetable protein n [U] abbreviation **TVP** a substance made from beans, used instead of meat

-th /θ/ suffix **1** forms ORDINAL numbers, except with 1, 2, or 3: the 17th of June | a fifth of the total → -ND, -RD, -ST **2** old use or biblical another form of -ETH: he doth (=does)

Tha·lid·o·mide /θə'lɪdəmaɪd/ n [U] trademark a drug given to people to make them calm, until it was discovered that it harmed the development of the arms and legs of unborn babies

thal·li·um /'θæliəm/ n [U] a soft blue-white metal that is poisonous, used in PHOTOELECTRIC CELLS and to kill rats, mice, and insects. It is a chemical ELEMENT: symbol Tl

than [S1] [W1] /ðən; strong ðæn/ conjunction, prep
1 used when comparing two things, people, situations etc: Natalie was prettier than her sister. | You need that money more than I do. | There were more people there than I expected. | If it costs more than $60, I won't buy it. | She had woken even earlier than usual. | Divorce is more common than it was a generation ago.
2 other than except for a particular person or thing: We never go to church other than for funerals and weddings. | We know he lived in Fleet Road, but other than that we don't know much about him.
3 would rather/would sooner ... than used to say that you prefer one thing to another: I'd rather drive than go by train. | She said she'd rather die than live in the city.
4 no sooner/hardly had ... than used to say that one thing happens immediately after another thing: No sooner had I got into the house than the phone rang. | Hardly had they reached Edinburgh than they were ordered to return to London.

thane /θeɪn/ n [C] a man who fought for the King but was below the rank of a KNIGHT in early English history

thank [S1] [W2] /θæŋk/ v [T]
1 to tell someone that you are pleased and grateful for something they have done, or to be polite about it: I haven't had a chance to thank him yet. | **thank sb for (doing) sth** Did you thank Uncle Ron for the present? | Madeleine thanked everyone for coming.
2 thank God/goodness/heavens used to show that you are very glad about something: Thank God that's over! I've never been so nervous in my life! | [+for] 'Only ten miles to go.' 'Thank heavens for that!'
3 thank your lucky stars spoken used to tell someone that they are very lucky, especially because they have avoided an unpleasant or dangerous situation: You should thank your lucky stars I got here when I did!
4 only have yourself to thank (for sth) spoken used to say that you are responsible for something bad that has

happened to you: *She has only herself to thank if she doesn't have any friends.*

5 you'll thank me *spoken* used to tell someone not to be annoyed with you for doing or saying something, because it will be helpful to them later: *You'll thank me for this one day, Laura.*

6 sb won't thank you (for doing sth) used to tell someone that another person will be annoyed because of what they have done: *I know you're just trying to help, but he won't thank you for telling him how to do it.*

7 I'll thank you to do sth *spoken formal* used to tell someone in an angry way not to do something because it is annoying you: *I'll thank you to mind your own business.*

8 have sb to thank for (doing) sth to say that you are grateful to someone who is responsible for something good happening. This expression is sometimes used humorously to mean that you are not grateful for what someone has done: *I have Phil to thank for getting me my first job.* | *And who do I have to thank for that mess on my desk?* → THANK YOU

thank·ful /ˈθæŋkfəl/ *adj* [not before noun] grateful and glad about something that has happened, especially because without it the situation would be much worse: [+for] *I'll be thankful for a good night's sleep after the week I've had.* | **thankful (that)** *She was thankful that Chantal was there.* | **thankful to do sth** *I was thankful to make any sort of progress at all.* —**thankfulness** *n* [U] → **be thankful for small mercies/favours** at SMALL¹ (13)

thank·ful·ly /ˈθæŋkfəli/ *adv* **1** [sentence adverb] used to say that you are glad that something has happened, especially because a difficult situation has ended or been avoided: *Thankfully, I managed to pay off all my debts before we got married.* **2** feeling grateful and glad about something, especially because a difficult situation has ended or been avoided: *We came in and collapsed thankfully onto our beds.*

thank·less /ˈθæŋkləs/ *adj* **1** a thankless job is difficult and you do not get any praise for doing it: **thankless task/job/chore etc** *Cooking every day is a thankless task.* **2** *literary* a thankless person is not grateful

thanks¹ S1 W2 /θæŋks/ *interjection informal*
1 used to tell someone that you are grateful for something they have given you or done for you; ▣ **thank you**: *'Pass the salt, please ... thanks.'* | [+for] *Thanks a lot for the drink.* | *Thanks very much for your help.* | *Many thanks for the lovely flowers.* | **thanks for doing sth** *I'd love to go to the party. Thanks for asking me.*
2 used as a polite way of accepting something that someone has offered you: *'Do you want another cup of coffee?' 'Oh, thanks.'*
3 *spoken* used when politely answering someone's question: *'Hi, Bill, how are you?' ' Fine, thanks.'*
4 no thanks used to say politely that you do not want something: *'How about some cake?' 'Oh, no thanks, I'm on a diet.'*
5 thanks a lot also **thanks a bunch** *AmE spoken* used when really you are annoyed about something and you do not mean 'thank you' at all

thanks² *n* [plural] **1** the things you say or do to show that you are grateful to someone: *Joe got up and left without a word of thanks.* | [+to] *My thanks to all of you for your help.* **2 thanks to sb/sth** *informal* of someone or something: *We've reached our goal of $50,000, thanks to the generosity of the public.* | *Some ski resorts opened early, thanks to a late-October snowstorm.* ⚠ Do not say 'thank to someone/something'. → see box at OWING TO **3 no thanks to sb/sth** *spoken* an expression meaning 'in spite of', used when someone should have helped you but did not: *It was no thanks to you that we managed to win the game.* → VOTE OF THANKS

thanks·giv·ing /ˌθæŋksˈɡɪvɪŋ◂/ *n* [C,U] *formal* an expression of thanks to God

Thanksgiving *n* [U] a public holiday in the US and in Canada when families have a large meal together to celebrate and be thankful for food, health, families etc

thank you *interjection* **1** used to tell someone that you are grateful for something they have given you or done for you; ▣ **thanks**: *Margaret handed him the butter. 'Thank you,' said Samuel.* | **Thank you very much**, *Brian.* | **thank you for (doing) sth** *It's good to see you, Mr. Mathias. Thank you for coming.* | *Dear Grandma, thank you for the lovely shirt you sent me for Christmas.* **2** used as a polite way of accepting something that someone has offered: *'Can I give you a lift into town?' 'Oh, thank you.'* **3** used when politely answering someone's question: *'How was your trip to Paris?' 'Very nice, thank you.'* **4 no, thank you** used to say politely that you do not want something: *'Would you like some more coffee?' 'No, thank you, I'm fine.'* **5** used at the end of a sentence when telling someone firmly that you do not want their help or advice and are slightly annoyed by it: *I can manage quite well on my own, thank you!*

thank you (NOT 'I thank you'): *'Call me if you need anything.' 'Thank you, I will.'*
thank you for sth: *Thank you for the lovely card.*
thank you for doing sth: *Thank you for letting me know (NOT for let me know/that you let me know).*
In more informal English, use **thanks** in the same way: *Thanks for the suggestion.* | *Thanks for helping out.*

thank-you *n* [C] **1** something you say or do in order to thank someone: *This present's a thank-you for helping me last week.* | *I just want to say a big thank-you to everyone who supported us.* **2 thank-you letter/note/card** a short letter etc in which you thank someone

that¹ S1 W1 /ðæt/ *determiner, pron*
1 *plural* **those** /ðəʊz $ ðoʊz/ used to refer to a person, thing, idea etc that has already been mentioned or is already known about: *'You never cared about me.' 'That's not true.'* | *I wish you wouldn't say things like that.* | *What did you do with those sandwiches?* | *Victoria Street? That's where my sister lives.* | *Do you remember that nice Mr Hoskins who came to dinner?* | *I've got that pain in my back again.* | *He killed a man once and that's why he had to leave Ireland.* | *'We've been cheated,' she said. Those were her exact words.* | *'I have to go,' she said, and* **with that** (=after saying that) *she hung up the phone.*
2 /ðət/ used after a noun as a RELATIVE PRONOUN like 'who', 'whom', or 'which' to introduce a CLAUSE: *There are lots of things that I need to buy before the trip.* | *the people that live next door* | *They've got a machine that prints names on badges.* | *the greatest boxer that ever lived* | *Who was it that said 'The Law's an Ass'?* | *The day that my father died, I was on holiday in Greece.*
3 *plural* **those** /ðəʊz $ ðoʊz/ *formal* used to refer to a particular person or thing of the general type that has just been mentioned: *In my opinion, the finest wines are those from France.* | [+of] *His own experience was different from that of his friends.*
4 those who people who: *There are those who disapprove of all forms of gambling.* | *Those who saw the performance thought it memorable.*
5 at that used after adding a piece of information which emphasizes and increases what you have just said: *You should be able to answer the question in a single sentence, and a short one at that.*
6 that is (to say) used to give more exact information about something or to correct a statement: *One solution would be to change the shape of the screen, that is, to make it wider.* | *Languages are taught by the direct method, that is to say, without using the student's own language.* | *I loved him – that is, I thought I did.*

7 *plural* **those** used to refer to a person or thing that is not near you: *Is that my pen you've got there?* | *That's Eileen's house across the road.* | *Look at those men in that car. What on earth are they doing?* | *Our tomatoes* *never get as big as that.*

8 that's life/men/politics etc (for you) used to say that something is typical of a particular group of people, situation etc: *I don't think I was fairly treated, but then that's life, isn't it?* | *We go out for a romantic meal and all he wants to do is talk about football. That's men for you.*

9 that's it a) used to say that something is completely finished or that a situation cannot be changed: *That's it, then. There's nothing more we can do.* **b)** used to tell someone that they are doing something correctly: *Slowly ... slowly. Yeah, that's it.* **c)** also **that does it** used when you are angry about a situation and you do not want it to continue: *That's it. I'm leaving.*

10 that's that used to emphasize that a situation or a decision cannot be changed: *I refuse to go and that's that!* | *There's no money left, so that's that.*

11 used when you are not sure who is answering the telephone: *Hello, is that Joan Murphy?*

12 and (all) that *BrE* and similar things: *I knew he was interested in computers and all that.*

13 that's a good girl/that's a clever dog etc used to praise a child or animal

that² S1 W1 /ðət/ *conjunction*

1 used after verbs, nouns, and adjectives to introduce a CLAUSE which shows what someone says or thinks, or states a fact or reason: *If she said that she'd come, she'll come.* | *I can't believe that he's only 17.* | *Are you sure that they live in Park Lane?* | *allegations that he is guilty of war crimes* | *The fact that he is your brother-in-law should not affect your decision.* | *He might have left the money for the simple reason that he didn't know it was there.*

2 used after a phrase with 'so' or 'such' to introduce a CLAUSE that shows the result of something: *I was so tired that I fell asleep.* | *The school was so badly damaged that it had to be pulled down.* | *We had been away for such a long time that I had forgotten her name.*

3 used to introduce a CLAUSE that refers to a fact, when describing it: *It's odd that I haven't heard of you.* | *That anyone should want to kill her was unthinkable.* | *The problem is that no-one knows what will happen.*

4 *formal* in order that something may happen or someone may do something: *Give us strength that we may stand against them.*

5 *literary* used to express a wish for something to happen or be true, especially when this is not possible: *Oh, that she were alive to see this!* → **so (that)** at so² (2)

that³ S1 W2 /ðæt/ *adv* [+ adj/adv]

1 *spoken* used to say how big, how much etc, especially when you are showing the size, amount etc with your hands: *It was quite a large fish – about that long.* | *He missed hitting the car in front by that much.*

2 [usually in negatives] *spoken* as much as in the present situation or as much as has been stated: *I'm sorry, I hadn't realized the situation was that bad.* | *No one expected it to cost that much.* | *The advanced exam is more difficult, but not many students progress that far.*

3 not (all) that long/many etc *spoken* used to mean fairly short, only a few etc: *Will's not that tall, considering he's 16.* | *The film wasn't all that good.*

4 *BrE spoken informal* used to emphasize how big, bad, much etc something is: *I was that embarrassed I didn't know what to say.*

thatch /θætʃ/ *n* **1** [C,U] STRAW, REEDS, leaves etc used to make a roof, or the roof made of them **2** [singular] a thick untidy pile of hair on someone's head

thatched /θætʃt/ *adj* a thatched roof is made with dried STRAW, REEDS, leaves etc: *a thatched cottage* (=one with a thatched roof) —**thatch** *v* [I,T]

thatch·er /'θætʃə $ -ər/ *n* [C] someone whose job is making roofs from dried STRAW, REEDS, leaves etc

thaw¹ /θɔː $ θɒː/ *v* **1** also **thaw out** [I,T] if ice or snow thaws, or if the sun thaws it, it turns into water; F **freeze**: *The lake thawed in March.* **2 it thaws** if it

thaws, the weather becomes warmer, so that ice and snow melt: *It thawed overnight.* **3** also **thaw out** [I,T] to let frozen food become warmer until it is ready to cook; F **freeze**: *Thaw frozen meat in its packet and then cook as soon as possible.* **4** [I] to become friendlier and less formal: *After a few glasses of wine Robert began to thaw a little.*

thaw out *phr v* if your body thaws out, or if you thaw it out, it gets warmer until it is a normal temperature again: **thaw sth ⇔ out** *He held his hands in front of the fire to thaw them out.*

thaw² *n* **1** [singular] a period of warm weather during which snow and ice melt: *The thaw begins in March.* **2** [C] an improvement in relations between two countries, after a period of unfriendliness

the¹ S1 W1 /ðə; *before vowels* ðɪ; *strong* ðiː/ *definite article, determiner*

1 used to show that you are talking about a particular thing or person that has already been mentioned, is already known about, or is the only one: *The audience clapped and cheered.* | *I ordered a pizza and salad. The pizza was nice but the salad was disgusting.* | *the tallest building in the world* | *sailing across the Pacific* | *The Prime Minister has intervened personally.* | *Elections will be held later in the year* (=this year). | *How are all the family* (=your family)?

2 used before nouns referring to actions and changes when they are followed by 'of': *the growth of the steel industry* | *the arrival of our guests*

3 used when you are about to make it clear which person or thing you mean: *That's the school that Terry went to.* | *She laughed at the birthday card from Myra.*

4 used before the name of a family in the plural to refer to all the members of that family: *The Johnsons had lived in this house for many years.*

5 used to refer to something that everyone knows because it is part of our natural environment or part of daily life: *What was the weather like?* | *I looked out into the darkness.* | *Sometimes the traffic kept me awake at night.* | *The shops open at 9 o'clock.*

6 used before a singular noun to refer to a type of institution, shop, system etc: *You used to buy them from the chemist.* | *I heard it on the radio.* | *I'll put it in the mail for you today.*

7 used to refer to a part of someone's body: *Lieutenant Taylor was wounded in the knee.* | *How's the ankle? Is it still hurting?*

8 used before an adjective to make it into a plural noun when you are referring to all the people that the adjective describes: *She devoted her life to helping the poor.* | *a school for the deaf* | *wars between the English and the French*

9 used before an adjective to make it into a noun when you are referring to the particular kind of situation or thing that the adjective describes: *Come on now, that's asking for the impossible.* | *fantasy movies that make the unreal seem real*

10 used before a singular noun when you are referring to a particular type of thing or person in a general way: *The tiger is without doubt the most magnificent of the big cats.* | *The computer has changed everyone's lives in so many ways.* | *complicated dances like the tango*

11 a) used to refer to a period of time, especially a period of ten or a 100 years: *fashions of the 60s* | *the great novelists of the 1900s* | *She remembers the war years.* | *In the thirties unemployment was widespread.* **b)** used to mention a date: *the 3rd of November* | *March the 21st BrE: Shall we meet on the twelfth?*

12 enough of something for a particular purpose: *I haven't the time to talk just now.* | *Eric didn't even have the common sense to send for a doctor.*

13 used to say which type of musical instrument someone plays: *Fiona's learning the flute.* | *He plays the violin.*

14 used to refer to a type of sport or a sports event, especially in ATHLETICS or swimming: *Who won the long jump?* | *She swam up and down, practising the crawl.*

15 *spoken* used before a word or phrase that describes

someone or something when you are angry, JEALOUS, surprised etc: *He's stolen my parking space, the bastard!* | *I can't get this carton open, the stupid thing.* | *'Jamie's won a holiday in Hawaii.' 'The lucky devil!'*
16 used to emphasize that the person, place, or thing you are mentioning is the famous one, or the best or most fashionable one. 'The' is pronounced strongly or written in a special way: *'Elizabeth Taylor was there.' 'Not the Elizabeth Taylor, surely?'* | *Miami is THE place for girls who like to live life to the full.*
17 used before the names of certain common illnesses: *If one of the children got the measles, we all got the measles.*

the² adv **1** used before two COMPARATIVE adjectives or adverbs to show that the degree of one event or situation is related to the degree of another one: *The more he eats the fatter he gets.* | *'When do you want it?' 'The sooner the better.'* **2** used before an adjective or adverb to emphasize that something is bigger, better etc than all others, or as big, good etc as it is possible for it to be: *He likes you the best.* | *I had the worst headache last night.*

the- /θi/ *prefix* another form of THEO-

thea·tre S2 W2 *BrE*; **theater** *AmE* /ˈθɪətə $ -ər/ n
1 BUILDING [C] a building or place with a stage where plays and shows are performed: *an open-air theatre* (=a theatre that is outside) | *the Mercury Theater* → see picture at TOWN
2 PLAYS [U] **a)** plays as a form of entertainment: *I enjoy theater and swimming.* | **the theatre** *He's really interested in literature and the theatre.* | *Yeats' plays are great poetry but they are not good theatre* (=good

entertainment). **b)** the work of acting in, writing, or organizing plays: *classes in theater and music* | **in the theatre** *She's been working in the theatre over thirty years.*
3 PLACE TO SEE A FILM [C] *AmE* a building where films are shown; ▪ **movie theater** *AmE*; ▪ **cinema** *BrE*: *'Bambi' was the first movie I ever saw in the theater.*
4 HOSPITAL [C,U] *BrE* a special room in a hospital where medical operations are done; ▪ **operating room** *AmE*: **in theatre** *Marilyn is still in theatre.*
5 WAR [C] *formal* a large area where a war is being fought: *the Pacific theater during World War II*

thea·tre·go·er *BrE*; **theatergoer** *AmE* /ˈθɪətəˌɡəʊə $ -tərˌɡoʊər/ n [C] someone who regularly watches plays at the theatre

theatre-in-the-round n [U] the performance of a play on a central stage with the people watching sitting in a circle around it

the·at·ri·cal /θiˈætrɪkəl/ adj **1** relating to the performing of plays: *a Polish theatrical company* **2** behaving in a loud or very noticeable way that is intended to get people's attention: *She gave a theatrical sigh.* —**theatrically** /-kli/ adv

the·at·ri·cals /θiˈætrɪkəlz/ n [plural] **1** performances of plays: *amateur theatricals* **2** *BrE informal* behaviour that is very loud and noticeable and is intended to get people's attention; ▪ **theatrics** *AmE*: *We can do without all these theatricals, Andrew!*

the·at·rics /θiˈætrɪks/ n [plural] *especially AmE* behaviour that is very loud and noticeable, and is intended to get people's attention

thee /ðiː/ pron old use a word meaning 'you', used as the OBJECT of a sentence

theft /θeft/ n **1** [U] the crime of stealing; → **thief**, **burglary**, **robbery**: *Car theft is on the increase.* | *an arrest for petty theft* (=stealing small things) | *Three men were charged with attempted theft.* **2** [C] an act of stealing something: *There have been a number of thefts in the area.* | [+of] *the theft of £150 from the office*

their S1 W1 /ðə; *strong* ðeə $ ðər; *strong* ðer/ *determiner* [possessive form of 'they']
1 belonging to or connected with people or things that have already been mentioned: *They washed their faces and went to bed.* | *The twins spend all their time together.* | *People had moved back into their own homes.*
2 used when talking about someone who may be male or female, to avoid saying 'his or her': *Everyone is free to express their own opinion.* | *Each student will have their own course-work folder.* → HIS (2)

theirs S3 /ðeəz $ ðerz/ pron [possessive form of 'they']
1 used to refer to something that belongs to or is connected with people that have already been mentioned: *When our washing machine broke, our neighbours let us use theirs.* | *Our house is number 25, and theirs is just opposite.* | *We compared scores and found that theirs were higher than ours.* | **of theirs** *They shared the prize money with a friend of theirs.*
2 used when talking about someone who may be male or female, to avoid saying 'his or hers': *Everyone wants what is theirs by right.* → HIS (2)

the·is·m /ˈθiːɪzəm/ n [U] the belief in the existence of God or gods; ▪ **atheism**

them¹ S1 W1 /ðəm; *strong* ðem/ pron [object form of 'they']
1 used to refer to two or more people or things that have already been mentioned or are already known about: *Has anyone seen my keys? I can't find them anywhere.* | *The police were very helpful when I spoke to them.* | *I lent him several books, but he hasn't read any of them.*
2 used when talking about someone who may be male or female, to avoid saying 'him or her': *If anyone phones, tell them I'll be back later.*

them² /ðem/ *determiner spoken* used to mean 'those'. Many people think this use is incorrect: *I couldn't understand all them long words.*

the·mat·ic /θɪˈmætɪk/ *adj* relating to a particular THEME, or organized according to a theme: *the thematic organization of paintings in the exhibit* —**thematically** /-kli/ *adv*

theme S2 W2 /θiːm/ *n* [C]
1 SUBJECT the main subject or idea in a piece of writing, speech, film etc: *The book's theme is the conflict between love and duty.* | **main/central/major etc theme** *Campbell has made health care a central theme in his campaign.* | *Nature is a recurrent theme* (=a theme that appears repeatedly) *in Frost's poetry.* | *Most of Kurt's other pictures were variations on the same theme.*
2 theme music/song/tune music or a song that is often played during a film or musical play, or at the beginning and end of a television or radio programme: *the theme song from 'The Brady Bunch'*
3 REPEATED TUNE a short simple tune that is repeated and developed in a piece of music: *Freia's theme in Wagner's opera*
4 STYLE a particular style: *Her bedroom is decorated in a Victorian theme.*
5 PIECE OF WRITING *AmE old-fashioned* a short piece of writing on a particular subject that you do for school; ▣ essay: [+on] *Your homework is to write a two-page theme on pollution.*

themed /θiːmd/ also **theme** *adj* [usually before noun] a themed place or event has been designed to make people who go there feel like they are in a particular place or historical period: *themed restaurants such as the Rainforest Café*

ˈtheme park *n* [C] a type of park where you can have fun riding on big machines such as a ROLLER COASTER, and where the whole park is based on one subject such as water or space travel

ˈtheme ˌparty *n* [C] *BrE* a party where everyone has to dress in a particular way connected with a particular subject: *a Wild West theme party*

them·self /ðəmˈself/ *pron spoken* used when you are talking about one person, but you want to avoid saying 'himself' or 'herself' because you do not know the sex of the person. Many people think this use is incorrect: *It makes me happy to help someone help themself.*

them·selves S1 W1 /ðəmˈselvz/ *pron*
1 used to show that the people who do something are affected by their own action: *Teachers have no choice but to take measures to protect themselves.* | *Our neighbours have just bought themselves a jacuzzi.* | *The kids seem very pleased with themselves.*
2 used to emphasize the pronoun 'they', a plural noun etc: *Doctors themselves are the first to admit the treatment has side effects.*
3 used after words like 'everyone', 'anyone', 'no one' etc when you talk about someone already mentioned and you do not know what sex they are or it is not important. Many teachers think this is not correct English: *Someone told me they'd actually seen the accident happen themselves.*
4 in themselves also in and of themselves considered without other related ideas or situations: *The carvings are works of art in themselves, even disregarding their religious significance.*
5 (all) by themselves a) alone: *older people who are living all by themselves* b) without help from anyone else: *Did the children make the model all by themselves?*
6 (all) to themselves if people have something to themselves, they do not have to share it with anyone: *They had the whole beach to themselves.*
7 not be/feel themselves if people are not themselves, they do not feel or behave in the way they usually do because they are nervous, upset, or ill

then¹ S1 W1 /ðen/ *adv*
1 at a particular time in the past or future: *I wish I had known then what I know now.* | *It was then that I realised she'd tricked me.* | *He started his career in St Petersburg – or Leningrad as it then was.* | **by/until/since then** *They're sending out the results next week, so we won't know anything until then.* | *It was late evening when the doctor arrived, and by then it was too late.* | *That was in 1970. Since then the place has changed a lot.* | *They met in 1942 and from then on* (=starting at that time) *they were firm friends.* | *Silently she closed the door. Just then she heard a noise.* | *I was paid £1000, which was a lot of money back then* (=a long time ago when things were different) *in the 1950s.*
2 used to say what happens next or what you do next: *Mix the flour and butter, then add the eggs.* | *Byron travelled to Italy and then to Greece.*
3 a) used when saying what the result of a situation or action will be: *If you won't tell him, then I will.* | *Start off early, then you won't have to rush.* **b)** *spoken* used when you think that something is probably true because of what you know about the situation: *Still in your pyjamas? Have you just got out of bed then?*
4 but then (again) used to say that although something is true, something else is also true which makes the first thing seem less important: *William didn't succeed first time, but then very few people do.* | *Elaine's father might lend them the money, but then again he might not.*
5 *spoken* **a)** used at the beginning of a conversation or activity: *Now then, what would you like to do today?* | *Right then, shall we start?* **b)** used at the end of a conversation, especially to show that something has been agreed: *Good, that's settled then. We'll all meet here next Wednesday.* | *Okay then, I'll see you at work.* **c)** used to show that you are saying something because of what someone has just said: *'We're late.' 'We'd better hurry, then.'* | *'Friday's no good.' 'Then how about Saturday?'*
6 used to add something to what you have just mentioned: *We have to invite your parents and my parents, and then there's your brother.*
7 used to refer back to what you have just been talking about: *This then was the situation facing the government at the end of the war.*
8 then and there also there and then immediately: *He wasn't prepared to wait – he wanted the money then and there.* → **(every) now and then** at NOW¹ (5)

then² *adj* [only before noun] used when mentioning the person who had a particular job, title, or position at a time in the past: *a visit to China by the then US President, Richard Nixon*

thence /ðens/ *adv formal* from there or following that: *We went to Trieste, and thence by train to Prague.*

thence·forth /ðensˈfɔːθ $ ˈðensfɔːrθ/ also **thence·forward** /ðensˈfɔːwəd $ -ˈfɔːrwərd/ *adv formal* starting from that time

theo- /θiːə/ also **the-** *prefix* relating to God or gods: *theology* (=study of religion)

the·oc·ra·cy /θiˈɒkrəsi $ -ˈɑː-/ *n plural* **theocracies** [C] a social system or state controlled by religious leaders —**theocratic** /ˌθiːəˈkrætɪk◂/ *adj*: *an Islamic theocratic state*

the·od·o·lite /θiˈɒdəlaɪt $ θiˈɑː-/ *n* [C] a piece of equipment used by a land SURVEYOR for measuring angles

the·o·lo·gian /ˌθiːəˈləʊdʒən $ -ˈloʊ-/ *n* [C] someone who has studied theology

theoˈlogical ˌcollege *BrE*; **theoˈlogical ˌseminary** *AmE* *n* [C] a college for training people to become priests or church ministers

the·ol·o·gy /θiˈɒlədʒi $ θiˈɑː-/ *n plural* **theologies** **1** [U] the study of religion and religious ideas and beliefs: *He studied theology at college.* **2** [C,U] a particular system of religious beliefs and ideas: *According to Muslim theology there is only one God.* | *a comparison of Eastern and Western theologies*

T

—**theological** /ˌθiːəˈlɒdʒɪkəl◂ $ -ˈlɑː-/ *adj*: *theological debate* —**theologically** /-kli/ *adv*

theo·rem /ˈθɪərəm $ ˈθiːə-/ *n* [C] *technical* a statement, especially in mathematics, that you can prove by showing that it has been correctly developed from facts

theo·ret·i·cal [W3] /ˌθɪəˈretɪkəl $ ˌθiːə-/ also **theo·ret·ic** /θɪəˈretɪk $ ˌθiːə-/ *adj*
1 relating to the study of ideas, especially scientific ideas, rather than with practical uses of the ideas or practical experience; → **theory**, **practical**, **applied**: *theoretical physics | Aristotle's theoretical model of the universe | She has theoretical knowledge of teaching, but no practical experience.*
2 a theoretical situation or condition could exist but does not really exist: *Equality between men and women in our society is still only theoretical. | a theoretical risk of an explosion*

theo·ret·i·cally /θɪəˈretɪkli $ ˈθiːə-/ *adv* [sentence adverb] **1** used to say what is supposed to be true in a particular situation, especially when the opposite is true: *Theoretically, Damian's the boss, but I coordinate the team on a day-to-day basis.* **2** according to a scientific idea that has not been proven to be true in a practical way: *It is theoretically possible for computers to be programmed to think like humans.*

theo·rist /ˈθɪərɪst $ ˈθiːə-/ also **theo·re·ti·cian** /ˌθɪərəˈtɪʃən $ ˌθiːə-/ *n* [C] someone who develops ideas within a particular subject that explain why particular things happen or are true: *a leading economic theorist*

theo·rize also **-ise** *BrE* /ˈθɪəraɪz $ ˈθiːə-/ *v* [I,T] to think of a possible explanation for an event or fact: **theorize that** *Researchers theorize that there was once a common language for all humanity. |* [+about] *They have been theorizing about what may have caused the fire.*

theo·ry [S2] [W1] /ˈθɪəri $ ˈθiːəri/ *n plural* **theories**
1 [C] an idea or set of ideas that is intended to explain something about life or the world, especially an idea that has not yet been proved to be true; → **theoretical**: [+about/on] *different theories about how the brain works |* [+of] *Darwin's theory of evolution |* **theory that** *the theory that light is made up of waves*
2 [U] general principles and ideas about a subject: *Freudian theory has had a great influence on psychology. |* **political/economic/literary etc theory** *I'm taking a course on political theory.*
3 in theory something that is true in theory is supposed to be true, but might not really be true or might not be what will really happen: *In theory, everyone will have to pay the new tax.*
4 [C] an idea or opinion that someone thinks is true but for which they have no proof: **theory that** *Detectives are working on a theory that he knew his murderer.*

ther·a·peu·tic /ˌθerəˈpjuːtɪk◂/ *adj* **1** making you feel calm and relaxed: *I find swimming very therapeutic. | the therapeutic effect of gardening* **2** [usually before noun] relating to the treatment or cure of an illness; → **therapy**: *Some claim that the herb has therapeutic value for treating pain.*
—**therapeutically** /-kli/ *adv*

ther·a·peu·tics /ˌθerəˈpjuːtɪks/ *n* [U] *technical* the part of medical science relating to the treatment and cure of illness

ther·a·pist /ˈθerəpɪst/ *n* [C] someone who has been trained to give a particular form of treatment for physical or mental illness: *a speech therapist*

ther·a·py /ˈθerəpi/ *n plural* **therapies** **1** [C,U] the treatment of an illness or injury over a fairly long period of time: *new drug therapies | radiation therapy for cancer treatment* **2** [U] the treatment or examination of someone's mental problems by talking to them for a long time about their feelings; ▤ **psychotherapy**: **in therapy** *Rob was in therapy for several years. | a therapy group* → CHEMOTHERAPY, OCCUPATIONAL, PHYSIO-THERAPY, SPEECH THERAPY, HORMONE REPLACEMENT THERAPY

there¹ [S1] [W1] /ðeə, ðə $ ðer, ðər/ *pron* **there is/exists/ remains etc** used to say that something exists or hap-

pens: *Is there any milk left? | There are a few things we need to discuss. | There must be easier ways of doing this. | There seems to be a lack of communication. | There remain several questions still to be answered. | Suddenly there was a loud explosion. | They were all laughing when there came a knock at the door.*

GRAMMAR
Use **there is/are** to say that something exists or happens: *There was an argument. | Is there any more bread? | There is one thing I'd like to ask you (NOT Is one thing ...).*
When the following noun is plural, use **there are/were**: *There are a lot of problems (NOT there is a lot of problems) with this theory. | Were there many people at the meeting?*
⚠ Expressions like **a lot of** and **plenty of** can be used with uncountable nouns. In this case use **there is/was**: *There is a lot of traffic in the mornings.*
⚠ **There** and **their** sound the same, but do not confuse them. **There** is used in expressions such as 'there is/was', and for referring to a place. **Their** is used for showing that something belongs to a group of people, animals etc: *They love their jobs.*

there² [S1] [W1] /ðeə $ ðer/ *adv*
1 in or to a particular place that is not where you are; → **here**: *We could go back to my cottage and have lunch there. | Scotland? I've always wanted to go there. | Hold it right there and don't move. | Can you pass me that wine glass there? | Look, there's that bookshop I was telling you about. | Who's that man over there? | It's too far to drive **there and back** in one day. | Are we going to **get there** (=arrive) before the banks close? |* **out/in/ under etc there** *I know there's a mouse under there somewhere. | We flew to Miami and from there to La Paz.*
⚠ Do not say 'to there': *We went there (NOT went to there) by car.*; → see box at POSITION¹
2 if something is there, it exists: *The chance was there, but I didn't take it. | The countryside is there for everyone to enjoy. | Three months after the operation, the pain was still there.*
3 at or to a particular point in time, in a process, or in a story: *Let's stop there and I'll tell you the rest of the story tomorrow. | She got a divorce, but her troubles didn't end there. | There's still a lot of work to do, but we're **getting there** (=coming to the end of the process) slowly.*
4 there and then also **then and there** immediately: *I thought I'd have to wait, but they offered me the job there and then.*

SPOKEN PHRASES
5 used to refer to something that someone has said when you are answering them: *That's true. I agree with you there. | 'Why did the system fail?' 'Well, there you've got me – I really don't know.'*
6 used when greeting someone or calling to them: *Hi there, you must be Laura. | Hey, you there! Watch out!*
7 there it is/there they are etc used when you have found something or someone that you are looking for: *Have you seen my keys anywhere? Ah, there they are. | There you are. I've been looking for you.*
8 used when you want to speak to someone on the telephone and someone else answers: *Hello, Georgie, is your mother there?*
9 be there (for sb) to be always ready to help someone when they need help: *That's what I loved about my father – he was always there for me.*
10 there I was/there they were etc used to describe what situation someone was in at a particular point in the story you are telling: *So there I was, stranded in London with no money.*
11 be not all there *informal* someone who is not all there seems stupid or slightly crazy
12 there's a good boy/clever dog etc used to praise a child or animal
13 there it is/there you are/there you go used to say

that nothing can be done to change an unsatisfactory situation: *It's all very sad, but there it is. There's absolutely nothing any of us can do about it.*
14 there you go/she goes etc (again) used when someone does something annoying that they often do: *There you go, blaming everything on me, as usual.* | *There she goes again, complaining about the weather.*
15 there you are/there you go a) used when giving something to someone or when you have done something for someone: *There you are. I'll just wrap it up for you.* **b)** used when you think you have proved to someone that what you are telling them is right: *There you are, then. There's nothing to worry about.*
16 there's sth for you a) used to say that an action or situation is a good example of a particular quality: *There's intelligence for you! She's solved the problem already.* **b)** used when you are annoyed or disappointed to say that someone's behaviour is the opposite of the quality you are naming: *Well, there's gratitude for you. She didn't even say thank you.*
17 there goes sth/sb a) used when you see someone or something going past or away from you: *There goes a very worried man.* **b)** used to say that you can hear something such as a bell ringing: *There goes the phone. I'll answer it.* **c)** used when you are losing something, for example an opportunity or money, as a result of something that has just happened: *There go our chances of winning the championship.* | *There goes my career.*

there³ /ðeə $ ðer/ *interjection* **1** *spoken* used to express satisfaction that you have been proved right or that you have done what you intended to do: *There! I've done it! I've resigned.* | *There, what did I tell you? I knew it wouldn't work.* **2 there, there!** *spoken* used to comfort someone who is crying, especially a child: *There, there, don't get so upset!* **3 so there!** *spoken* used to show someone that you do not care what they think and you are not going to change your mind – used by children: *I'm going to Elly's party, and you can't stop me, so there!*

there·a·bouts /ˌðeərə'baʊts $ ˌðer-/ *also* **thereabout** /-'baʊt/ *adv* near a particular time, place, number etc, but not exactly: *These houses were built in 1930 or thereabouts.*

there·af·ter /ðeər'ɑːftə $ ðer'æftər/ *adv formal* after a particular event or time; **afterwards**: *10,000 men had volunteered by the end of September; thereafter, approximately 1,000 men enlisted each month.* | *Sophie was born in France, but shortly thereafter her family moved to the United States.*

there·by W3 /ðeə'baɪ, 'ðeəbaɪ $ ðer'baɪ, 'ðer-/ *adv formal* with the result that something else happens: *thereby doing sth He became a citizen in 1978, thereby gaining the right to vote.*

there·fore S2 W1 /'ðeəfɔː $ 'ðerfɔːr/ *adv formal* as a result of something that has just been mentioned: *Their car was bigger and therefore more comfortable.* | *Progress so far has been very good. We are, therefore, confident that the work will be completed on time.*

there·in /ðeər'ɪn $ ðer-/ *adv formal* **1** in that place, or in that piece of writing: *See Thompson, 1983, and the references cited therein.* **2 therein lies sth** used to say that something is caused by or comes from a particular situation: *The treaty was imposed by force, and therein lay the cause of its ineffectiveness.* → HEREIN

there·in·af·ter /ˌðeərɪn'ɑːftə $ ˌðerɪn'æftər/ *adv law* later in the same official paper, statement etc

there·of /ðeər'ɒv $ ðer'ɑːv/ *adv formal* relating to something that has just been mentioned: *States differ in standards for products and the labelling thereof.* | *Money, or the lack thereof, played a major role in their marital problems.*

there·on /ðeər'ɒn $ ðer'ɒːn, -'ɑːn/ *adv formal* **1** on the thing that has just been mentioned **2** THEREUPON

there·to /ðeə'tuː $ ðer'tuː/ *adv formal* relating to an agreement, piece of writing, or thing that has just been mentioned: *the treaty and any conditions attaching thereto*

there·un·der /ðeər'ʌndə $ ðer'ʌndər/ *adv formal* **1** under something that has just been mentioned **2** according to a document, law, or part of an agreement that has just been mentioned

there·up·on /ˌðeərə'pɒn, 'ðeərəpɒn $ ˌðerə'pɒːn, -'pɑːn, 'ðerə-/ *adv formal* **1** immediately after something else has happened, and usually as a result of it; **then**: *Thereupon the whole audience began cheering.* **2** relating to a subject that has just been mentioned: *I read your article, and wish to comment thereupon.*

therm /θɜːm $ θɜːrm/ *n [C]* a unit for measuring heat, especially when calculating amounts of gas used: *UK gas was selling for as little as 6p a therm.*

therm- /θɜːm $ θɜːrm/ *prefix* another form of THERMO-

ther·mal¹ /'θɜːməl $ 'θɜːr-/ *adj* [only before noun] **1** relating to or caused by heat: *thermal energy* **2** thermal clothing is made from special material to keep you warm in very cold weather: *thermal underwear* **3** thermal water is heated naturally under the earth: *thermal springs*

thermal² *n [C]* **1** a rising current of warm air used by birds **2 thermals** [plural] *BrE informal* special warm clothing, especially underwear, worn under your other clothes

thermo- /θɜːməʊ, -mə $ θɜːrmoʊ, -mə/ *also* **therm-** *prefix technical* relating to heat: *a thermostat* (=for controlling temperature) | *thermostable* (=not changing when heated)

ther·mo·dy·nam·ics /ˌθɜːməʊdaɪ'næmɪks $ ˌθɜːrmoʊ-/ *n [U]* the science that deals with the relationship between heat and other forms of energy —**thermodynamic** *adj*

ther·mom·e·ter /θə'mɒmɪtə $ θər'mɑːmɪtər/ *n [C]* a piece of equipment that measures the temperature of the air, of your body etc: *The thermometer registered over 100°C.* | **a candy/meat thermometer** (=used in cooking); → see picture at MEASUREMENT

ther·mo·nu·cle·ar /ˌθɜːməʊ'njuːkliə◂ $ ˌθɜːrmoʊ'nuːkliər◂/ *adj* thermonuclear weapons use a NUCLEAR reaction, involving the splitting of atoms, to produce very high temperatures and a very powerful explosion: *a thermonuclear device*

ther·mo·plas·tic /ˌθɜːməʊ'plæstɪk◂ $ ˌθɜːrmə-/ *n [C,U] technical* a plastic that is soft and bendable when heated but hard when cold

Ther·mos /'θɜːməs $ 'θɜːr-/ *also* **'Thermos ˌflask** *BrE n [C] trademark* a special container like a bottle, that keeps drinks hot or cold; **flask** *BrE*

ther·mo·set·ting /'θɜːməʊˌsetɪŋ $ 'θɜːrmoʊ-/ *adj technical* thermosetting plastic becomes hard and unbendable after it has been heated

ther·mo·stat /'θɜːməstæt $ 'θɜːr-/ *n [C]* an instrument used for keeping a room or a machine at a particular temperature

the·sau·rus /θɪ'sɔːrəs/ *n plural* **thesauruses** *or* **thesauri** /-raɪ/ *[C]* a book in which words are put into groups with other words that have similar meanings

these /ðiːz/ the plural of THIS

the·sis /'θiːsɪs/ *n plural* **theses** /-siːz/ *[C]* **1** a long piece of writing about a particular subject that you do as part of an advanced university degree such as an MA or a PhD: *Cynthia's still working on her thesis.* | **graduate/master's/doctoral thesis** *He wrote his doctoral thesis on contemporary French literature.* **2** *formal* an idea or opinion about something, that you discuss in a formal way and give examples for: *Their main thesis was that the rise in earnings was due to improvements in education.* **3** *AmE* in writing, the thesis is the sentence or group of sentences which state what the main idea of an ESSAY is: *a paragraph introducing your thesis statement*

thes·pi·an /'θespiən/ n [C] *formal* an actor – sometimes used humorously: *a distinguished thespian* —**thespian** *adj*

they S1 W1 /ðeɪ/ *pron* [used as the subject of a verb]
1 used to refer to two or more people or things that have already been mentioned or are already known about: *Bob and Sue said they wouldn't be able to come.* | *Ken gave me some flowers. Aren't they beautiful?* | *They all want to come to the wedding.*
2 they say/think etc used to state what people in general say or think: *They say it's bad luck to spill salt.*
3 *spoken* used to refer to a particular organization or group of people: *Where are they going to build the new highway?* | *They're going to take an X-ray.*
4 used when talking about someone who may be male or female, to avoid saying 'he or she': *If anyone has any information related to the crime, will they please contact the police.* | *Every child, whoever they are, deserves to have a mum and a dad.*

they'd /ðeɪd/ **1** the short form of 'they had': *If only they'd been there.* **2** the short form of 'they would': *It's a pity my parents didn't come – they'd have enjoyed it.*

they'll /ðeɪl/ the short form of 'they will': *They'll be tired after the long journey.*

they're /ðə; *strong* ðeə, ðeɪə $ ðər; *strong* ðer, ðeɪər/ the short form of 'they are': *They're going to Crete next week.*

they've /ðeɪv/ the short form of 'they have': *They've had a lot of trouble with their car.*

thi·am·in also **thi·a·mine** /'θaɪəmi:n, -mɪn/ n [U] a natural chemical in some foods, that you need in order to prevent particular illnesses

thick

a thick book

a chunky bracelet

lumpy food

a fat wallet

thick¹ S2 W2 /θɪk/ *adj comparative* **thicker**, *superlative* **thickest**
1 NOT THIN if something is thick, there is a large distance or a larger distance than usual between its two opposite surfaces or sides; ▣ **thin**: *a thick oak door* | *a thick slice of homemade bread* | *He was wearing thick glasses.* | *short thick fingers* | *thick wool socks* (=socks that are heavy and warm) | *If you want a thicker blanket, there are more here in the closet.* | *The*

---

meat is done when the thickest part turns from pink to white. | [+**with**] *The furniture was **thick with dust*** (=there was thick dust on the furniture).
2 MEASUREMENT measuring a particular distance between two opposite sides or surfaces of something: **3 feet/1cm/two inches etc thick** *The walls are about two meters thick.* | *How thick should the glass in the tank be?* | *This layer of brain tissue is no thicker than 2 mm.*
→ see box at **WIDE¹**
3 TREES/BUSHES ETC growing very close together or having a lot of leaves; ▣ **dense**: *birds hiding in the thick undergrowth* | [+**with**] *The walls were thick with ivy.*
4 SMOKE/CLOUD ETC filling the air, and difficult to see through or breathe in; ▣ **dense**: *thick fog* | [+**with**] *The air was thick with cigarette smoke.*
5 LIQUID almost solid, and therefore flowing very slowly, or not flowing at all: *For a thicker gravy, add more flour.* | *The paint is too thick.*
6 HAIR/FUR having a lot of hair or fur: *She ran her fingers through her thick brown hair.*
7 STUPID *BrE informal* a thick person is stupid: *He's a nice guy, but he's a bit thick.* | **(as) thick as two short planks** (=very stupid)
8 VOICE a) if someone has a thick ACCENT, the way they speak shows clearly which particular place or part of a country they come from: **a thick German/Yorkshire etc accent** *Andre speaks English with a thick Russian accent.* **b)** if someone's voice is thick, it is not as clear or high as usual, for example because they are upset: *Bill's voice was thick and gruff.* | [+**with**] *Her voice was thick with emotion.*
9 LARGE AMOUNT *especially written* containing a lot of people or things: *The cod were so thick in the water that they caught thousands very quickly.* | [+**with**] *The roads were thick with holiday traffic.*
10 be thick on the ground *BrE* to be present or available in large amounts or numbers; ▣ **thin on the ground**: *Cheap houses aren't as thick on the ground as they used to be.*
11 have a thick skin to not care if people criticize you or do not like you → **THICK-SKINNED**
12 FRIENDLY be (as) thick as thieves if two people are as thick as thieves, they are very friendly with each other and seem to share a lot of secrets, making other people think they are hiding or planning something: *Lately Nick and Lou have been as thick as thieves.*
13 give sb a thick ear/get a thick ear *BrE spoken* to hit someone or be hit on the head, as a punishment: *Any more cheek from you and you'll get a thick ear.*
14 be thick with sb *old-fashioned* to be very friendly with someone
15 (it's) a bit thick *BrE old-fashioned* used to say something is a little unfair or annoying

thick² *adv* **1** thickly. Many teachers think this is not correct English: *peanut butter spread thick* **2 thick and fast** arriving or happening very frequently, in large amounts or numbers: *Entries have been coming in thick and fast.* → **lay it on (a bit thick)** at **LAY ON** (3)

thick³ n **1 in the thick of sth** involved in the busiest, most active, most dangerous etc part of a situation: *Brown hopes to be back in the thick of the action as soon as possible.* **2 through thick and thin** in spite of any difficulties or problems: *Then, families stuck together through thick and thin.*

thick·en /'θɪkən/ v [I,T] to become thick, or make something thick: *The fog was beginning to thicken.* | *Thicken the soup by adding potatoes.* | **thicken sth with sth** *a stew thickened with lentils and vegetables* → **the plot thickens** at **PLOT¹** (3)

thick·en·er /'θɪkənə, 'θɪknə $ -ər/ also **thick·en·ing** /'θɪkənɪŋ, 'θɪknɪŋ/ n [C,U] a substance used to thicken a liquid

---

thick·et /'θɪkᵻt/ n [C] a group of bushes and small trees

,**thick-'headed** adj informal extremely stupid: *He's so thick-headed he can't understand simple instructions.*

thick·ly /'θɪkli/ adv **1** in a way that makes a thick piece or layer of something: *The cheese was sliced thickly.* | *a thickly carpeted hallway* **2 thickly populated/wooded etc** if an area is thickly populated, wooded etc, there are a lot of people, trees etc there close together: *The eastern part of the country is more thickly populated.*

thick·ness /'θɪknᵻs/ n **1** [C,U] how thick something is: *The thickness of the walls is 5 feet.* **2** [C] a layer of something: [+of] *Wrap the cake in a double thickness of foil.*

thick·o /'θɪkəʊ $ -koʊ/ n plural **thickos** [C] BrE spoken someone who is very stupid

thick·set /,θɪk'set◂/ adj having a wide strong body; ▣ **stocky**: *a short thickset man*

,**thick-'skinned** adj not easily offended by other people's criticism or insults; ▣ **thin-skinned**: *a thick-skinned insurance salesman*

thief /θiːf/ n plural **thieves** /θiːvz/ [C] someone who steals things from another person or place; → **theft**, **burglar**, **robber**: *Thieves broke into the offices and stole $150,000's worth of computer equipment.* | **a car/jewel etc thief** | *They were nothing but **petty thieves** (=thieves who steal small things).* → **be (as) thick as thieves** at THICK¹ (12)

thiev·e·ry /'θiːvəri/ n [U] formal thieving

thiev·ing /'θiːvɪŋ/ n [U] BrE informal the act of stealing things —**thieving** adj: *thieving pirates*

thiev·ish /'θiːvɪʃ/ adj literary like a thief

thigh /θaɪ/ n [C] **1** the top part of your leg, between your knee and your HIP **2** the top part of a bird's leg, used as food: *chicken thighs*

thigh·bone /'θaɪbəʊn $ -boʊn/ n [C] the bone in the top part of a leg

thim·ble /'θɪmbəl/ n [C] a small metal or plastic cap used to protect your finger when you are sewing → see picture at SEWING

thim·ble·ful /'θɪmbəlfʊl/ n [C + of] informal a very small quantity of liquid

thin

a narrow street

a thin
slice of lemon

a fine pen

the slender stem
of a plant

thin¹ ⟨S2⟩ ⟨W2⟩ /θɪn/ adj comparative **thinner**, superlative **thinnest**

1 NOT THICK if something is thin, there is only a small distance between its two opposite sides or surfaces; ▣ **thick**: *a thin gold chain* | *She's only wearing a thin summer jacket* (=a jacket made of light material). | *two thin slices of bread* | *The road was covered with a thin layer of ice.* | *The skin on the eyelids is the thinnest on the body.* | **paper/wafer thin** (=very thin) *Keep your voice down – the walls are paper thin.*

2 NOT FAT having little fat on your body; ▣ **fat**: *He was tall and thin, with short brown hair.* | **thin arms/legs/lips etc** *He has long thin hands.* | *Most high school girls say they want to be thinner.*

3 HAIR if someone has thin hair, they do not have a lot of hair: *a thin straggly beard* | *His hair is quite thin on top.*

4 LIQUID a liquid that is thin flows very easily because it has a lot of water in it; ▣ **thick**: *thin paint*

5 SMOKE/MIST smoke or mist that is thin is easy to see through; ▣ **thick**: *The fog is quite thin in places.*

6 AIR air that is thin is more difficult to breathe than usual because it has less OXYGEN in it: *the thinner air high in the mountains*

7 EXCUSE/ARGUMENT/EVIDENCE ETC a thin excuse, argument, or evidence is not good or detailed enough to be useful or effective: *Evidence that capital punishment deters crime is pretty thin.*

8 a thin margin/majority etc a very small number or amount of something: *Engle beat Blanchard by a razor-thin margin* (=a very small number of votes) *in the race for governor.*

9 SMILE a thin smile does not seem very happy or sincere: *Charlie gave her a thin smile.*

10 VOICE/SOUND a thin voice or sound is high and unpleasant to listen to: *His thin voice trailed off.*

11 the thin end of the wedge BrE spoken an expression meaning something that you think is the beginning of a harmful development: *Workers believe the job cuts are just the thin end of the wedge.*

12 be thin on the ground if a particular type of person or thing is thin on the ground, there are very few available: *Taxis seem to be thin on the ground.*

13 be having a thin time (of it) BrE spoken to be in a difficult situation, especially one in which you do not have enough money

14 be (walking/treading/skating) on thin ice to be in a situation in which you are likely to upset someone or cause trouble: *I was on thin ice, and I knew it.*

15 disappear/vanish into thin air to disappear completely in a mysterious way: *Victor and his kidnappers had vanished into thin air.*

16 out of thin air out of nowhere, as if by magic: *It seems like researchers have just pulled the numbers out of thin air.* → THINLY; → **wear thin¹** (6) —**thinness** n [U]

WORD CHOICE: thin, slim, skinny, slender, lean, slight
Thin is a general word meaning that someone has little fat on their body. It is usually, but not always, disapproving: *He's much too thin.* | *Teenage girls all seem to want to be thin.*
Slim means thin in an attractive way: *her lovely slim figure*
Skinny is a fairly informal word meaning very thin, which is usually disapproving: *ridiculously skinny models*
Slender, **lean**, and **slight** are used mostly in written English.
Slender means thin in an attractive and graceful way: *long slender legs*
Lean means thin and looking strong and fit: *a tall, lean athlete*
Slight means thin and delicate-looking: *Her brother was very slight and looked younger than he was.*

thin² adv thinly. Many teachers think this is not correct English: *Don't cut the bread so thin.*

thin³ v **thinned**, **thinning 1** [I,T] also **thin out** to become fewer in number, especially when there were many before, or to remove people, plants, or things so that fewer remain: *The crowd had thinned out and only a few people were left.* | *The trees thinned as we got closer to the top of the mountain.* | *Traffic was finally thinning.* | *Thin the carrots to two inches apart.* | *Her hair had been thinned and cut shorter.* **2** [I,T] to make something thinner or to become thinner; ▣ **thicken**: *The clouds had begun to thin.* | *A narrow smile thinned his lips.* **3** [T] also **thin down** to make a liquid weaker by adding water or another liquid: *Thin the sauce by adding milk.* | **thin sth with sth** *The pastels can be thinned with water.* **4** [I] if someone's hair is thinning, they have less hair than they used to: *a tall man with thinning hair* **5 thin the ranks** if something thins the ranks of a group of people, there are fewer of them as a result of it: *Illness had thinned our ranks.*

thine[1] /ðaɪn/ *possessive pron old use* yours

thine[2] *possessive adj old use* a word meaning your, used before a word beginning with a vowel or 'h'

thing [S1] [W1] /θɪŋ/ *n*

1 IDEA/ACTION/FEELING/FACT [C] an idea, action, feeling, or fact that someone thinks, does, says, or talks about, or that happens: *People say things they don't mean when they are angry.* | *It was a horrible thing to happen.* | *I plan to do all the things I've been meaning to do for ages.* | *The first thing to do is to give them food and shelter.* | *That's a terrible thing to say.* | **do the right/decent/honourable etc thing** *I kept wondering if I was doing the right thing.* | **this/that/what sort of thing** *A priest has to arrange funerals, marriages, that sort of thing.* | *Getting more American ideas into British business would be a good thing.* | *'I did no such thing,' he protested.* | *I know a thing or two* (=a lot) *about dogs.* | *In a democracy, it is no bad thing to be able to compromise* (=it is good, even though it may not seem good).
2 OBJECT [C] an object that you are talking about without saying its name, or whose name you do not know: *A red thing was caught in the branches.* | *I'll just switch this thing off.* | *There was a round metal thing on the path.* | *... and things* (=and other similar things) *The shed is where we keep our tools and things.*
3 SITUATION things [plural] life in general and the way it is affecting people: *By the end of 1942, things were starting to change.* | *Things could be worse.* | *As things turned out, we didn't have much time.* | **How are things** *with you, Sarah?* | **make things easy/difficult/hard** *She would get angry quickly, which made things difficult for me.* | *We can't change the way things are.*
4 NOTHING [singular, U] used as part of a negative statement to mean 'anything': **not a thing** *I couldn't find a thing that I wanted to buy.* | *He took his glasses off and couldn't see a thing.* | *Don't worry about a thing.* | *There's no such thing as ghosts* (–they do not exist).
5 PERSON/ANIMAL [C] used to talk to or about a person or animal, when you are describing what they are like or showing sympathy for them: *The baby is a nice little thing when he's not screaming.* | *She was terribly upset, poor thing.*
6 MAKE A COMMENT [C usually singular] used to say something about a particular part of a situation, person etc: [+about] *The thing about teaching is that it takes more time to prepare than most people realize.* | **the funny/strange/best etc thing** *The funny thing is, I really enjoyed it, even though I hadn't expected to.* | *It's a good thing you saw her before she saw you.*
7 the thing is *spoken* used when you are going to explain something, give the reason for something, or give an opinion: *'It sounds like a good idea. Why don't you invest?' 'Well, the thing is, I can't afford to.'* | **the thing is that** *The thing is that you can't always judge your own work.*
8 the last thing sb wants/expects/needs etc something that someone does not want, expect etc at all: *The last thing I want is to upset him.* | *The last thing I should have done was let her move into my house.*
9 last thing *BrE* at the end of a day, afternoon, evening etc: *She likes a hot bath last thing at night.*
10 first thing at the beginning of a day, morning, afternoon etc: *Jean liked to go for a swim first thing in the morning.*
11 CLOTHES/POSSESSIONS things [plural] *especially BrE* clothes and possessions; ◨ **stuff** *AmE*: **sb's things** *Jim began to unpack his things.* | *I want to sell some of my things, but they aren't worth much.*
12 EQUIPMENT things [plural] *especially BrE* the tools, equipment, clothes etc that you need for a particular

job, sport etc; ◨ **stuff** *AmE*: **sb's writing/school/Christmas etc things** *I left my swimming things at home.* | *the shed where he kept his gardening things*
13 among other things used when you are giving one fact, reason, effect etc but want to suggest that there are many others: *The substance is used in the manufacture of cosmetics and drugs, among other things.*
14 for one thing used to give one reason for something: *Well, for one thing, it's too big.* | *He's not that wonderful. He's bad-tempered for one thing.*
15 be a thing of the past to no longer exist or happen: *Before AIDS, many health care experts believed that large-scale infectious diseases were a thing of the past.*
16 it's a good thing (that) *spoken* used to say that it is lucky or good that something has happened: *It's a good thing we brought some food with us.*
17 sth is just one of those things used to say that something unpleasant or unlucky cannot be prevented: *It wasn't really the driver's fault; it was just one of those things.*
18 the thing about/with sb/sth used to say what the problem with someone or something is: *The thing about talk shows is that you never know how they will turn out.*
19 all (other) things being equal used to say that something is true in general, but that other things may cause the situation to change: *All things being equal, smaller animals need smaller brains.*
20 just the thing/the very thing exactly the thing that you want or that is necessary: *A holiday is probably just the thing for you.*
21 of all things used to show that you are surprised or shocked by something that someone has done or said: *She gave up a promising career as a stockbroker to become a weaver, of all things.*
22 do your own thing *informal* to do something in the way that you like instead of copying other people or following strict rules: *I just want to live my own life and do my own thing.*
23 it's a girl/football/music etc thing *informal* used to say that something involves or affects a particular group of people only: *Computer games aren't just a guy thing.*
24 all things considered when you consider all the parts or events of a situation: *All things considered, we had surprisingly few injuries.*
25 be all things to all men/people to try to please or be useful to all of many different groups, often without succeeding: *In order to get votes, he tries to be all things to all men.*
26 be onto a good thing *informal* if you are onto a good thing, you are in a situation that is very helpful, comfortable, or profitable for you: **think/know you are onto a good thing** *Directors who take dividends instead of salary may think they are onto a good thing but could have problems on retirement.*
27 make a big thing of/about/out of sth to make something seem more important than it really is: *You can apologise without making a big thing out of it.*
28 the done thing *BrE old-fashioned informal* the way of behaving or doing something that is socially acceptable: *It is not the done thing for teachers to hit children.*
29 it's one thing to ..., (it's) another thing to ..., used to say that doing one thing is very different from doing another thing, especially where the second thing is more difficult, important, or serious: *It's one thing being able to run fast, but quite another to win a marathon.*
30 what with one thing and another *BrE spoken* used to explain that you have had a lot of work, problems, or jobs that you had to do: *I've been so busy these last few days, what with one thing and another.*
31 have a thing about sb/sth *informal* to like or dislike someone or something very much, often without a good reason: *She's always had a thing about Peter.*
32 one thing leads to another used to explain how a

series of events caused something to happen without giving any details: *One thing led to another and, before I knew it, I had invited her family to stay.*
33 the (latest) thing *informal* something that is popular or fashionable at the moment: *When Amelia bought a new car it had to be the latest thing.*
34 (do/try) the...thing *AmE spoken* used to talk about an activity and everything that is involved with it: *Jody tried the college thing but finally dropped out.*
35 there is only one thing for it *BrE spoken* used to say that there is only one action that you can take: *There's only one thing for it. We'll have to call the police.*
36 one (damn/damned) thing after another used to say that a lot of unpleasant or unlucky things keep happening to you
37 taking one thing with another *BrE* considering all the facts
38 do things to sb to have a strong effect on someone → **amount/come to the same thing** at SAME¹ (4); → **the best thing since sliced bread** at SLICE² (4); → **first things first** at FIRST¹ (7); → **living things** at LIVING¹ (1); → **be hearing things** at HEAR (10); → **be seeing things** at SEE¹ (28)

thing·a·ma·jig /ˈθɪnəməˌdʒɪɡ/ also **thing·a·ma·-bob** /ˈθɪnəmˌbɒb $ -baːb/, **thing·y** /ˈθɪŋi/ n [C] *spoken* **1** used when you cannot remember or do not know the name of the thing you want to mention: *What do you call that thingamajig? You know – the circle with the line through it.* **2** *BrE* used when you cannot remember or do not know the name of the person you want to mention: *Is thingy going?*

think¹ S1 W1 /θɪŋk/ v *past tense and past participle* **thought** /θɔːt $ θɒːt/
1 OPINION/BELIEF [T] to have a particular opinion or to believe that something is true: **think (that)** *I think that you're being unfair.* | *I thought I heard something.* | *He didn't think anyone would believe him.* | *Do you think I should call him?* | *For some reason, I keep thinking it's Friday today.* | *The recession lasted longer than anyone thought it would.* | **Am I right in thinking that** *you have a brother?* | *I can't help thinking that he's made a mistake.* | *Do you* **honestly think** *I would do something so stupid?* | **what do you think of/about sb/sth?** (=used to ask someone for their opinion) *What do you think of your new school?* | **think it necessary/possible/best etc** (=believe it is necessary, possible etc) *I thought it best to call first.* | *I thought it appropriate to invite her to speak at the meeting.* | *We must start* **thinking in terms of** *reducing costs.* | **be thought to be (doing) sth** (=be believed to be (doing) something) *Fraud is thought to be costing software companies millions of dollars a year.*
2 USE YOUR MIND [I,T] to use your mind to solve something, decide something, imagine something etc: *She thought very carefully before answering.* | *Wait a minute – I'm thinking.* | **[+about/of]** *She lay awake thinking about the money.* | **think what/how/when etc** *I can't think what else we could have done.* | **think (long and) hard** (=think for a long time) *She thought very hard before deciding to leave her job.* | *Holmes sat* **thinking deeply** (=thinking in a serious and careful way). | **I dread/shudder/hate to think** (=I do not want to think about something because it will be unpleasant) *I dread to think how much this call is going to cost.*
3 HAVE AN IDEA [T] to have words or ideas in your mind without telling them to anyone: *'How strange!' he thought.* | *'I don't care!' she* **thought to herself.** | *It was impossible to know what he was thinking.* | **think what/how/when etc** *I was just thinking what a lovely time we had yesterday.*
4 REMEMBER [T] to remember something: **think where/what etc** *He was trying to think where he'd seen her before.* | *I couldn't think where I'd left my keys.*
5 CONSIDER SB/STH [I,T] to consider that someone or something is a particular thing or has a particular quality: **think of sb/sth as sth** *Peter had always thought of Kate as someone to be avoided.* | *I want you to think*

of this as your home. | **think of yourself as sth** *I've always thought of myself as a sensible person.* | **think sb (to be) sth** *My parents never thought me capable of doing a degree.* | *We have good reason to* **think kindly of** (=consider in an approving way) *a school that has provided all our children with an excellent education.*
6 think of/about doing sth to consider the possibility of doing something: *I had never thought of becoming an actor.* | *We did think about moving to Tokyo.* | **Don't even think about** *calling him* (=used to tell someone strongly not to do something).
7 think twice to think very carefully before deciding to do something, because you know about the dangers or problems: *A visible alarm makes burglars think twice.* | **[+about]** *A previous divorce can make you think twice about getting married again.* | **think twice before doing sth/before you do sth** *I'd think twice before taking out such a large loan.*
8 think again to think carefully about a plan, decision, idea etc, especially with the result that you change your mind or do something differently: *If you think car crime can't happen to you, think again.* | **[+about]** *Universities may be forced to think again about the courses they provide.*

SPOKEN PHRASES

9 I think used when you are saying that you believe something is true, although you are not sure: *Mary is in the garden, I think.* | *I don't think Ray will mind.* | *'Do you understand what I mean?' 'Yes,* **I think so.'** | *'Haven't we met before?'* **'I don't think so.'** | *I thought he was honest, but I was wrong.*
10 I think I'll ... used to say what you will probably do: *I think I'll go to bed early tonight.*
11 I thought (that) used when you are politely suggesting something to do: *I thought we'd go swimming tomorrow.* | *I thought we could meet for lunch.*
12 I would think also I would have thought also I should think/I should have thought *BrE* used when you are saying that you believe something is probably true: *We'll need about 10 bottles of wine, I should think.* | *I would have thought it would be better to wait a while.*
13 you would have thought (that) also you would think (that) used to say that you expect something to be true, although it is not: *You would have thought the school would do more to help a child like Craig.*
14 do you think (that) ...? **a)** used when you are asking someone politely to do something for you: *Do you think you could help me move these boxes?* **b)** used to ask someone's opinion: *Do you think I need to bring a jacket?*
15 who/what etc do you think? **a)** used to ask someone's opinion: *Who do you think will win?* **b)** used when someone angrily about something: *Where do you think you're going?*
16 I think not *formal* used to say that you strongly believe something is not true or that you disagree with someone: *This could be a coincidence, but I think not.*
17 (just) think used to ask someone to imagine or consider something: *Just think – we could be millionaires!* | **[+of]** *It would be lovely, but think of the expense!* | **just think what/how etc** *Just think what could have happened.*
18 (now I) come to think of it used to mention something you have just realized or remembered: *'Were there any letters for me?' 'Yes there were, come to think of it.'*
19 I wasn't thinking also I didn't think used as a way of saying you are sorry because you have upset someone: *Sorry, I shouldn't have said that. I wasn't thinking.*
20 to think (that) ...! used to show that you are very surprised about something: *To think we lived next door to him and never knew what he was doing!*
21 if you think...,you've got another think coming! used to tell someone that if they think someone is going to do something, they are wrong: *If you think I'm going to wait for you, you've got another think coming!*

22 that's what you/they etc think! used to say that you strongly disagree with someone
23 who would have thought? used to say that something is very surprising: *Who would have thought she'd end up dancing for a living?*
24 I thought as much used to say that you are not surprised by something someone tells you: *'Andy failed his driving test.' 'I thought as much when I saw his face.'*
25 I should have thought ... *BrE* used as a polite or joking way of showing that you disagree with what someone has said or think it is silly: *'Why isn't it working?' 'I should have thought it was obvious.'*

26 think better of it to not do something that you had planned to do, because you realize that it is not a good idea: *He started to say something, then thought better of it.*
27 think nothing of doing sth to think that a particular activity is normal or easy, even though other people think it is unusual or difficult: *He thinks nothing of staying up all night in casinos.*
28 think nothing of sth to think that something is not important and then realize later that it is important: *I had a pain in my back but thought nothing of it at the time.*
29 not think to do sth to not consider doing something, especially when you later wish you had done it: *I didn't think to question the treatment I was given.* | *I never thought to ask him for his address.*
30 think for yourself to have ideas and thoughts of your own rather than believing what other people say: *Parents have to teach their children to think for themselves.*
31 think aloud also **think out loud** to say what you are thinking, without talking to anyone in particular: *Oh, sorry. I was thinking aloud.*
32 think straight [usually in negatives] to think clearly: *I'm so nervous I can't think straight.* | *How can I think straight with you talking all the time?*
33 not think much of sb/sth to not like someone or something very much: *I didn't think much of his new girlfriend.*
34 think highly of sb/sth also **think a lot of sb/sth** to admire or respect someone or something: *Your boss must think highly of you if she gives you so much responsibility.*
35 think the world of sb *informal* to like or love someone very much: *The children think the world of her.*
36 think badly of sb also **think less of sb** *formal* to disapprove of someone or what they have done: *Please don't think badly of me.* | *[+for] Do you think less of me for agreeing to do it?*
37 think the best/worst of sb to consider someone's behaviour in a way that makes them seem as good as possible or as bad as possible: *He's determined to think the worst of me.*
38 think big *informal* to plan to do things that are difficult, but will be very impressive, make a lot of profit etc: *The company is thinking big.*
39 think outside the box to think of new, different, or unusual ways of doing something, especially in business
40 think positive/positively to believe that you are going to be successful or that good things are going to happen: *You have to think positive if you're going to be successful in this game.*
41 think on your feet to think of ideas and make decisions very quickly: *In this job you need to be able to think on your feet.*
42 think to do sth *literary* to try to do something: *They had thought to deceive me.*
43 anyone would think (that) used to say that someone behaves as if a particular thing were true, although it is not: *Anyone would think he owns the place, the way he talks!* → **can't hear yourself think** at HEAR (12)
　think back *phr v*
to think about things that happened in the past: *Thinking back, it amazes me how we survived on so little*

sleep. | [+to/over/on] *He thought back to the day he'd first met Sophie.*
　think of sb/sth *phr v*
1 to produce an idea, name, suggestion etc by thinking: *They're still trying to think of a name for the baby.* | *Can you think of any other way to do it?*
2 to remember something: *I can't think of the name of the hotel we stayed in.*
3 to behave in a way that shows that you want to treat other people well: *It was very good of you to think of me.* | *He's always thinking of other people.*
4 think only of yourself to only do things that are good for you and not think about what other people want – used to show disapproval: *She's a spoiled child who thinks only of herself.*
5 be thinking of sb used to say that you care about and feel sympathy for someone who is in a difficult situation: *Take care! I'll be thinking of you.*
　think sth ⇔ **out** *phr v*
to think about all the parts of something carefully before deciding or planning exactly what to do: *He went for a walk to think things out.* | *The proposal will need to be carefully thought out.* | **think out what/how/whether etc** *She had thought out what she was going to say.*
　think sth ⇔ **over** *phr v*
to consider something carefully before making a decision: *I've been thinking over your suggestion.* | *Why don't you think it over and give me a call in a couple of days?* | *I want some more time to think things over.*
　think sth ⇔ **through** *phr v*
to think carefully about the possible results of something: *The policy has not been thought through properly.* | *It's my fault. I didn't think it through.* | *I need time to think things through.* | **think through what/how** *People need time to think through what the changes will mean for them.*
　think sth ⇔ **up** *phr v*
to produce a new idea, name etc by thinking: *She was trying to think up an excuse.* | *Did you think that up yourself?* | *Who thinks up names for new products?*

think² n **have a think** *BrE* to think about a problem or question: *I'll have a think and let you know.*

think·a·ble /ˈθɪŋkəbəl/ *adj* [not before noun] able to be thought about or considered; **◨ possible**: *At that time, it would not have been thinkable to openly criticize the government.*

think·er /ˈθɪŋkə $ -ər/ *n* [C] **1** someone who thinks carefully about important subjects such as science or PHILOSOPHY, especially someone who is famous for thinking of new ideas: *great thinkers such as Kant and Schopenhauer* **2** **an independent/a positive/a free etc thinker** a person who thinks in a particular way

think·ing¹ /ˈθɪŋkɪŋ/ *n* [U] **1** your opinion or ideas about something, or your attitude towards it: *The Administration's thinking changed as the war progressed.* | *Well, to my way of thinking* (=in my opinion)*, they should have done that years ago.* | *He laughed and accused me of wishful thinking* (=falsely believing that something will happen just because I want it to)*.* | *the rich countries' current thinking on aid* | [+behind] *the thinking behind the company's new public relations campaign* **2** when you think about something: *If it weren't for Jeff's quick thinking, Tillie could have been badly hurt.* | *I really needed to do some thinking.* | **clear/critical/analytical etc thinking** (=a particular way of thinking about things) **3** **put on your thinking cap** *informal* to try to think seriously about a problem in order to solve it → LATERAL THINKING

thinking² adj [only before noun] **1** a thinking person is intelligent and tries to think carefully about important subjects **2** **the thinking man's/woman's etc sth** used to say that someone or something is liked by intelligent people: *the thinking man's pop band*

T

1 000, 2 000, 3 000, most frequent words in S poken and W ritten English

*bined is a **sobering thought**. | Louis **could not bear the thought** of losing her.*

2 IDEAS/OPINIONS **thoughts** [plural] a person's ideas or opinions about something: *What are your thoughts, Michael?* | [+**on**] *Any thoughts on how we should spend the money?*

3 CAREFUL CONSIDERATION [U] careful and serious consideration: *With more thought and care this would have been a first-class essay.* | **give sb thought/give thought to sth** (=think carefully about sth) *I've been giving your proposal a lot of thought.* | *Have you given any more thought to going back to school?*

4 ACT OF THINKING [U] the act or process of thinking: **lost/deep in thought** (=thinking so much that you do not notice what is happening around you) *Derek was staring out of the window, lost in thought.* | *Piaget's research focused on children's **thought processes** (=the way their minds work).*

5 CARING ABOUT STH [C,U] a feeling of worrying or caring about something: [+**for**] *He went back into the burning building with no thought for his own safety.* | *Have you no thought for anyone but yourself?* | *You are always **in my thoughts** (=used to tell someone that you think and care about them a lot).*

6 INTENTION [C,U] intention or hope of doing something: **thought of doing sth** *I had no thought of gaining any personal advantage.* | *Lucy **gave up all thought of** finishing the essay that day.*

7 WAY OF THINKING [U] a way of thinking that is typical of a particular group, period of history etc: **ancient Greek/feminist/18th-century etc thought** *Kant's ideas had a strong influence on political thought.*

8 spare a thought for sb *BrE* used to tell someone that they should think about someone who is in a worse situation than they are: *Spare a thought for those who don't have enough to eat.*

9 it's just a thought *spoken* used to say that what you have just said is only a suggestion and you have not thought about it very much: *It was just a thought, Duncan. I didn't mean any offence.*

10 it's/that's a thought! *spoken* used to say that someone has made a good suggestion: *'Why don't you ask Walter?' 'That's a thought! I'll phone him right away.'*

11 don't give it another thought *spoken* used to tell someone not to worry after they have told you they are sorry

12 it's the thought that counts *spoken* used to say that you are grateful for a gift from someone even though it is small or unimportant → **perish the thought!** at PERISH (3); → **on second thoughts** at SECOND¹ (8); → **school of thought** at SCHOOL¹ (8)

thought·ful /'θɔːtfəl $ 'θɒːt-/ *adj* **1** always thinking of the things you can do to make people happy or comfortable; ☒ **thoughtless**: *Paul is very thoughtful.* | **it is thoughtful of sb to do sth** *It was really thoughtful of you to remember my birthday.* **2** serious and quiet because you are thinking a lot: *a thoughtful look* | *a thoughtful silence* **3** well planned and carefully thought about: *a thoughtful analysis* —**thoughtfully** *adv* —**thoughtfulness** *n* [U]

thought·less /'θɔːtləs $ 'θɒːt-/ *adj* not thinking about the needs and feelings of other people, especially because you are thinking about what you want; ☒ **thoughtful**: *a selfish and thoughtless man* | **it is thoughtless of sb to do sth** *It was thoughtless of her not to tell you where she was going.* —**thoughtlessly** *adv* —**thoughtlessness** *n* [U]

thought-'out *adj* **carefully/well/badly thought-out** planned and organized carefully, well etc: *a carefully thought-out speech*

'thought-pro,voking *adj* making people think seriously about a particular subject: *a thought-provoking article*

thou·sand /'θaʊzənd/ *number plural* **thousand** or **thousands** **1** the number 1000: *a journey of almost a*

thousand miles | **two/three/four etc thousand** *five thousand dollars* | *The company employs 30 thousand people.* **2** an extremely large number of things or people: **a thousand** *I've been this route a thousand times before.* | **thousands of** *There are thousands of things I want to do.* —**thousandth** *adj: the thousandth anniversary of the founding of the city* —**thousandth** *n* [C]

thral·dom *BrE*; **thralldom** *AmE* /'θrɔːldəm $ 'θrɒːl-/ *n* [U] *literary* the state of being a slave; ☒ **slavery**

thrall /θrɔːl $ θrɒːl/ *n* **in sb's/sth's thrall** also **in thrall to sb/sth** *literary* controlled or strongly influenced by someone or something: *We have a congress that is in thrall to special interest groups.*

thrash¹ /θræʃ/ *v* **1** [I always + adv/prep, T] to move or make something move from side to side in a violent or uncontrolled way: [+**about/around**] *The girl was thrashing about in the water.* | *Salmon thrash their tails and leap from the water.* **2** [T] to beat someone violently, especially in order to punish them: *My poor brother used to get thrashed for all kinds of minor offences.* **3** [T] *informal* to defeat someone very easily in a game: *Brazil thrashed Italy 5–0.*

thrash sth ⇔ out *phr v* to discuss something thoroughly with someone until you find an answer, reach an agreement, or decide on something: *We still have to get together and thrash out the details.*

thrash² *n* **1** [singular] a violent movement from side to side **2** [U] *informal* a type of loud fast ROCK music **3** [C] *BrE old-fashioned* a loud noisy party

thrash·ing /'θræʃɪŋ/ *n* [C] *especially BrE* **1** an occasion when you beat someone or are beaten violently as a punishment: *If you speak to your mother like that again, you'll get a thrashing.* | *I'll give you the thrashing you deserve.* **2** *informal* an occasion when you defeat someone or are defeated very easily in a game: *The manager resigned after his team's 14–0 thrashing.*

thread¹ /θred/ *n*

1 FOR SEWING [C,U] a long thin string of cotton, silk etc used to sew or weave cloth: *I'm looking for a needle and thread.* | *hand-sewn with gold and silver thread* | *a spool of thread* (=small object that thread is wound around)

2 IDEAS [singular] an idea, feeling, or feature that connects the different parts of an explanation, story etc: *a **common thread** running within his work* | *His mind wandered, and he **lost the thread** of what she was saying* (=was no longer able to understand it). | *a **thread running through** the film* | [+**of**] *a thread of spirituality in her work*

3 pick up the thread(s) to begin something again after a long period, especially a relationship or way of life: *They had known each other as children, and were picking up the threads of their friendship.*

4 INTERNET [C] a series of messages concerning the same subject, written by members of an Internet discussion group: *I'd like to refer to something that was posted in an earlier thread.*

5 LINE [C] *literary* a long thin line of something, such as light, smoke etc: [+**of**] *The Colorado River was just a thread of silver, 4000 feet below.*

6 ON A SCREW [C] a continuous raised line of metal that winds around the curved surface of a screw

7 threads [plural] *AmE old-fashioned* clothes → **hang by a thread** at HANG¹ (9)

thread² *v* [T usually + adv/prep] **1** to put a thread, string, rope etc through a hole: *Will you **thread the needle** for me?* | **thread sth through sth** *Tom threaded the rope through the safety harness.* **2** to put a film, tape etc correctly through parts of a camera, PROJECTOR, or TAPE RECORDER **3** to connect two or more objects by pushing something such as string through a hole in them: *Sue threaded the glass beads onto a piece of heavy string.* **4 thread your way through/into sth etc** to move through a place by carefully going around things that are blocking your way: *She came towards me, threading her way through the crowd.*

thread·bare /ˈθredbeə $ -ber/ adj **1** clothes, CARPETS etc that are threadbare are very thin and in bad condition because they have been used a lot: *a threadbare old sofa* **2 threadbare excuse/argument/joke etc** an excuse etc that is no longer effective because it has been used too much

threat S2 W2 /θret/ n
1 [C,U] a statement in which you tell someone that you will cause them harm or trouble if they do not do what you want

> **make/issue a threat (against sb)**
> **carry out a threat** (=do what you have threatened to do)
> **give in to a threat** (=do what someone wants you to do because they threaten you)
> **empty/idle threat** (=false threat)
> **veiled threat** (=one that is not made directly)
> **death threat**
> **bomb threat**

Your threats don't scare me. | [+of] *the threat of military invasion* | [+from] *He says his family received phone threats from the group.* | *threats made against his wife and children* | *Nichols never carried out his threat to resign.* | *The government will not give in to terrorist threats.* | *She dismissed the statement as an empty threat.* | *They warned him with veiled threats not to mention anything he had witnessed.* | *The police are investigating death threats made against the two men.* | *Officials at the school say they received a bomb threat at approximately 11:30 a.m. today.*

2 [C usually singular] the possibility that something very bad will happen: [+of] *the threat of famine* | [+from] *According to the Secretary of State, the Russians face no threat from an expanded NATO.* | **under threat** *The area remains under threat from commercial developers.* | **be under threat of closure/attack etc** (=be likely to be closed, attacked etc) *The program is under threat of closure due to lack of funding.*
3 [C usually singular] someone or something that is regarded as a possible danger: [+to] *The fighting is a major threat to stability in the region.* | **present/pose a threat (to sb/sth)** *Pollution poses a threat to fish.*

threat·en S2 W2 /ˈθretn/ v
1 [T] to say that you will cause someone harm or trouble if they do not do what you want: *Postal workers are threatening a strike if they don't receive a pay increase.* | **threaten to do sth** *He threatened to take them to court.* | **threaten sb with sth** *Doctors are sometimes threatened with violence if they don't do what patients want.* | **threaten (that)** *Then he became angry and threatened that he would go to the police.*
2 [T] to be likely to harm or destroy something: *Poaching threatens the survival of the rhino.* | **threaten to do sth** *The incident threatens to ruin his chances in the election.* | **be threatened with sth** *Large areas of the jungle are now threatened with destruction.*
3 [I,T] to be likely to happen or be in a bad situation: *Britain's fishing industry remains threatened.* | *Dark clouds threatened rain.*

threat·en·ing /ˈθretn-ɪŋ/ adj **1** if someone's behaviour is threatening, you believe they intend to harm you: *His voice sounded threatening.* | *a threatening gesture* **2** if the sky or clouds are threatening, bad weather is likely: *a threatening thundercloud* —**threateningly** adv

three S1 /θriː/ number
1 the number 3: *They've won their last three games.* | *We'd better go. It's almost three* (=three o'clock). | *My little sister's only three* (=three years old).
2 in threes in groups of three people or things: *Teachers taking part will be asked to work in threes.* → THREESOME, THIRD

three-ˈcornered adj [usually before noun] **1** having three corners **2 three-cornered contest/fight** especially BrE a competition which involves three people or groups

three-D, 3-D /ˌθriː ˈdiː◂/ adj a three-D film or picture is made so that it appears to be three-dimensional —**three-D** n [U]: *a film in 3-D*

three-day eˈvent n [C] BrE a horse-riding competition that takes place for three days

three-diˈmensional adj **1** having, or seeming to have, length, depth, and height; → **two-dimensional**: *a three-dimensional structure* | *objects that are three-dimensional* **2** a three-dimensional character in a book, film etc seems like a real person; → **one-dimensional**

three·fold /ˈθriːfəʊld $ -foʊld/ adj three times as much or as many: *increase production threefold* —**threefold** adv

three-leg·ged race /ˌθriː ˈlegd reɪs/ n [C] a race in which two people run together, with one person's right leg tied to the other person's left leg

three-line ˈwhip n [C] an order from a leader of a British political party telling MPs in that party that they must vote in a particular way

three·pence /ˈθrepəns, ˈθrʌ-/ n [U] BrE old use three old pence

three·pen·ny bit /ˌθrepəni ˈbɪt, ˌθrʌ-/ n [C] a small coin used in Britain before 1971 that was worth three old pence

three-piece ˈsuit n [C] a suit that consists of a JACKET, WAISTCOAT, and trousers made from the same material

three-piece ˈsuite n [C] BrE two chairs and a SOFA covered in the same material

three-ply adj three-ply wood, wool, TISSUE etc consists of three layers or threads

three-point ˈturn n [C] a way of turning your car so that it faces the opposite way, by driving forwards, backwards, and then forwards again while turning

three-ˈquarter adj [only before noun] three quarters of the full size, length etc of something: *a three-quarter violin* | *a three-quarter length coat*

three-ˈquarters n [plural] an amount equal to three of the four equal parts that make up a whole: [+of] *three-quarters of an hour*

three-ring ˈcircus n **1** [singular] AmE informal a place or situation that is confusing because there is too much activity: *I don't know how you can work in that office – it's like a three-ring circus.* **2** [C usually singular] a CIRCUS that has three areas in which people or animals perform at the same time

three R's /ˌθriː ˈɑːz $ -ˈɑːrz/ n **the three R's** reading, writing, and ARITHMETIC, considered as the basic things that children must learn in school

three·score /ˈθriːskɔː $ -skɔːr/ number old use 60 → SCORE³ (1)

three·some /ˈθriːsəm/ n [C usually singular] informal a group of three people or things

three-star adj [only before noun] a three-star hotel, restaurant etc has been judged to be of a high standard

three-ˈwheeler n [C] **1** BrE a car that has three wheels **2** AmE a vehicle that has three wheels, especially a MOTORCYCLE, TRICYCLE, or special WHEELCHAIR

thren·o·dy /ˈθrenədi/ n plural **threnodies** [C] literary a funeral song or poem for someone who has died

thresh /θreʃ/ v [I,T] to separate grains of corn, wheat etc from the rest of the plant by beating it with a special tool or machine —**thresher** n [C]

threshing maˌchine n [C] a machine used for separating grains of corn, wheat etc from the rest of the plant

thresh·old /ˈθreʃhəʊld, -ʃəʊld $ -oʊld/ n [C] **1** the entrance to a room or building, or the area of floor or ground at the entrance: *She opened the door and stepped across the threshold.* **2** the level at which something starts to happen or have an effect: *Eighty percent of the*

T

throwing herself out of a tenth floor window.

8 throw sb in/into prison/jail to put someone in prison: *Anyone who opposes the regime is thrown in jail.*

9 throw sb out of work/office etc to suddenly take away someone's job or position of authority: *Hundreds of men were thrown out of work when the mine closed down. | Elections were held, and the government was thrown out of office.*

10 throw sb/sth into confusion/chaos/disarray etc to make people feel very confused and not certain about what they should do: *Everyone was thrown into confusion by this news. | The transport industry has been thrown into chaos by the strike.*

11 throw doubt on sth to make people think that something is probably not true: *Fresh evidence has thrown doubt on her story.*

12 throw suspicion on sb to make people think that someone is probably guilty: *This latest document throws suspicion on the company chairman.*

13 throw sb a look/glance/smile etc to quickly look at someone with a particular expression that shows how you are feeling: *He threw Anna a big smile. | He threw a glance at Connor.*

14 throw a fit/tantrum to react in a very angry way: *I can't tell my parents – they'd throw a fit!*

15 throw a question/remark etc (at sb) to say something to someone or ask them something roughly: *They threw a few awkward questions at me. | 'You're early!' she threw at him accusingly.*

16 throw sth open a) to allow people to go into a place that is usually kept private: [+to] *Plans have been announced to throw the Palace open to the public.* **b)** to allow anyone to take part in a competition or a discussion: [+to] *I would now like to throw the debate open to our audience.*

17 throw a switch/handle/lever to make something start or stop working by moving a control: *He threw a switch and the lights all went out.*

18 throw a party to organize a party and invite people

19 throw money at sth *informal* to try to solve a problem by spending a lot of money but without really thinking about the problem: *The problem cannot be solved by throwing money at it.*

20 be thrown back on sth to be forced to have to depend on your own skills, knowledge etc: *Once again, we were thrown back on our own resources.*

21 throw yourself into sth to start doing an activity with a lot of effort and energy: *Since her husband died, she's thrown herself into her work.*

22 throw your weight around to use your position of authority to tell people what to do in an unreasonable way: *He's the sort of insensitive bully who enjoys throwing his weight around.*

23 throw your weight behind sb/sth to support a plan, person etc and use your power to make sure they succeed: *The party leadership is throwing its weight behind the campaign.*

24 throw light on sth to make something easier to understand by providing new information: *Recent investigations have thrown new light on how the two men died.*

25 throw a light/shadow to make light or shadow fall on a particular place: *The trees threw long, dark shadows across the cornfield.*

26 throw the book at sb *informal* to punish someone as severely as possible or charge them with as many offences as possible: *If you get caught they'll throw the book at you!*

27 throw sth (back) in sb's face to be unkind to someone after they have been kind to you or helped you: *I felt that everything I'd done for them was thrown back in my face.*

28 throw up your hands (in horror/dismay etc) to do something that shows you think something is not good but feel you cannot do anything to change it: *Ted threw up his hands in disgust. 'Can't you make her change her mind?' he asked.*

29 throw in your hand to stop trying to do something; ⊟ **give up**

30 throw yourself at sb *informal* to try very hard to attract someone's attention because you want to have a sexual relationship with them

31 throw a punch to try to hit someone with your hand in a fight: *We need to sort this out before people start throwing punches.*

32 throw a match/game/fight to deliberately lose a fight or sports game that you could have won: *He was allegedly offered £20,000 to throw the match.*

33 throw dice/a six/a four etc to roll DICE or to get a particular number by rolling dice: *You have to throw a six to start.*

34 throw a pot to make a pot by shaping clay as it turns round on a special wheel

35 throw your voice to use a special trick to make your voice seem to be coming from a different place from the place you are standing

36 throw caution to the wind(s) to ignore the risks and deliberately behave in a way that may cause trouble or problems: *I threw caution to the winds and followed him.*

37 throw the baby out with the bath water to get rid of good useful parts of a system, organization etc when you are changing it in order to try and make it better → **throw in/cast your lot with sb** at LOT² (8)

throw sth ⇔ **away** *phr v*

1 to get rid of something that you do not want or need: *I never throw clothes away. | I shouldn't have thrown away the receipt.*

2 to spend money in a way that is not sensible: *I can't afford to throw money away.*

3 to waste something good that you have, for example a skill or an opportunity: *This could be the best chance you'll ever have. Don't throw it away!*

throw sth ⇔ **in** *phr v*

1 to add something to what you are selling, without increasing the price: *We paid $2000 for the boat, with the trailer and spares thrown in.*

2 if you throw in a remark, you say it suddenly without thinking carefully: *She threw in a couple of odd remarks about men.*

3 throw in the sponge/towel *informal* to admit that you have been defeated

throw sb/sth ⇔ **off** *phr v*

1 to take off a piece of clothing in a quick careless way: *They threw off their clothes and dived in.*

2 to get free from something that has been limiting your freedom: *In 1845, they finally threw off the yoke of foreign rule.*

3 if you throw off an illness, you get better from it: *It's taken me ages to throw off this cold.*

4 to escape from someone or something that is chasing you: *We ran flat out for about half a mile before we could throw them off.*

5 to produce large amounts of heat or light: *The engine was throwing off so much heat that the air above it shimmered with haze.*

throw sth ⇔ **on** *phr v*

to put on a piece of clothing quickly and carelessly: *I threw on a pair of jeans and a T-shirt.*

throw sb/sth ⇔ **out** *phr v*

1 to get rid of something that you do not want or need: *We usually throw out all our old magazines.*

2 to make someone leave a place, school, or organization, especially because they have done something that is against the rules: *Nick got thrown out of college in the second year for taking drugs. | I knew he would never throw us out on the street* (=make us leave our home when we have nowhere else to live).

3 if people throw out a plan or suggestion, they refuse to accept it: *The idea was thrown out by the committee. | The bill was thrown out by the Senate.*

4 if something throws out smoke, heat, dust etc, it produces a lot of it and fills the air with it: *huge trucks throwing out noxious fumes from their exhausts*

throw sb ⇔ **over** *phr v old-fashioned*

to end a romantic relationship with someone

throw sb/sth ⇔ **together** phr v
1 to make something such as a meal quickly and not very carefully: *There's lots of food in the fridge – I'm sure I can throw something together.*
2 if a situation throws people together, it makes them meet and know each other: *It was the war that had thrown them together.*

throw up phr v
1 to bring food or drink up from your stomach out through your mouth because you are ill; ⊟ **vomit**: *Georgia was bent over the basin, throwing up.* → see box at **SICK**[1]
2 **throw** sth ⇔ **up** BrE to produce problems, ideas, results etc: *The arrangement may throw up problems in other areas.*
3 **throw** sth ⇔ **up** if a vehicle, runner etc throws up dust, water etc as they move along, they make it rise into the air
4 **throw** sth ⇔ **up** BrE informal to suddenly leave your job, your home etc: *I can't just throw everything up and come and live with you.*
5 **throw** sth ⇔ **up** BrE to build something quickly: *new houses hastily thrown up by developers*

throw[2] n [C] **1** an action in which someone throws something: *That was a great throw!* | *a throw of over 80 metres* **2** an action in which someone rolls a DICE in a game: *It's your throw* **3** a large piece of cloth that you put loosely over a chair to cover it and make it look attractive: *a brightly-coloured cotton throw*

throw·a·way /ˈθrəʊəweɪ $ ˈθroʊ-/ adj [only before noun] **1** throwaway remark/line/comment etc something that someone says or writes quickly, without thinking carefully about it: *It was only a throwaway comment.* | *He claims people overreacted to a few throwaway lines in the article.* **2** throwaway products have been produced cheaply so that you can throw them away after you have used them; ⊟ **disposable**: *a throwaway cigarette lighter* **3** throwaway society used to show disapproval when talking about modern societies in which products are not made to last a long time

throw·back /ˈθrəʊbæk $ ˈθroʊ-/ n [C usually singular] something that is similar to something that existed in the past, or belongs to the past: [+to] *Her whole outfit was a throwback to the 1970s.* | *a social event which is a throwback to a different age*

throw-in n [C] an action in which someone throws the ball back onto the field in a game of football: *Beckham will take the throw-in.*

thru /θruː/ adj, adv, prep AmE informal a short form of THROUGH

thrum /θrʌm/ v **thrummed, thrumming** [I] to make a low sound like the sound of an engine: *The engine thrummed into life.* —**thrum** n [singular]: *the thrum of passing cars*

thrush /θrʌʃ/ n **1** [C] a brown bird with spots on its front **2** [U] an infectious disease that can affect a person's VAGINA or mouth

thrust[1] /θrʌst/ v past tense and past participle **thrust 1** [T always + adv/prep] to push something somewhere roughly: *She thrust a letter into my hand.* | *He thrust me roughly towards the door.* **2** [I] to make a sudden movement forward with a sword or knife: [+at] *He skipped aside as his opponent thrust at him.*

thrust sth ⇔ **aside** phr v to refuse to think about something: *Our complaints were thrust aside and ignored.*

thrust sth **upon/on** sb phr v if something is thrust upon you, you are forced to accept it even if you do not want it: *She never enjoyed the fame that was thrust upon her.* | *He had marriage thrust upon him.*

thrust[2] n **1** [C] a sudden strong movement in which you push something forward: *He jumped back to avoid another thrust of the knife.* **2** [singular] the main meaning or aim of what someone is saying or doing: [+of] *the main thrust of the government's education policy* **3** [U] technical the force of an engine that makes a car, train, or plane move forward

thru·way, throughway /ˈθruːweɪ/ n [C] AmE a wide road for fast traffic that you pay to use

thud[1] /θʌd/ n [C] the low sound made by a heavy object hitting something else: **a dull/hard/heavy thud** *There was a dull thud as the box hit the floor.* | *His head hit the floor with a sickening thud.*

thud[2] v **thudded, thudding** [I] **1** [always + adv/prep] to hit something with a low sound: *The stone thudded to the ground.* | *waves thudding against the side of the ship* **2** [always + adv/prep] to walk or run with your feet making a heavy sound as they touch the ground: *A horse thudded over the frozen grass.* **3** if your heart thuds, it beats strongly because you are excited or frightened: *Peter was aware of his heart thudding in his chest.*

thug /θʌg/ n [C] a violent man: *He was beaten up by a gang of young thugs.*

thug·ge·ry /ˈθʌgəri/ n [U] violent behaviour in which people fight and attack others: *the problem of football thuggery*

thug·gish /ˈθʌgɪʃ/ adj thuggish behaviour is violent behaviour in which people fight and attack others

thumb[1] /θʌm/ n [C] **1** the part of your hand that is shaped like a thick short finger and helps you to hold things: *a baby sucking its thumb* | *She held the coin carefully between finger and thumb.* → see picture at HAND[1] **2** the part of a GLOVE that fits over your thumb **3** be all fingers and thumbs BrE; be all thumbs AmE informal to be unable to do something in which you have to make small careful movements with your fingers: *Would you do up these buttons for me? I seem to be all thumbs today.* **4** the thumbs up/down informal when an idea or plan is officially accepted or not accepted: *The project was finally given the thumbs up.* | *Her performance got the thumbs down from the critics.* **5** be under sb's thumb to be so strongly influenced by someone that they control you completely: *He was still under his father's thumb.* → rule of thumb at RULE[1] (8); → stand/stick out like a sore thumb at SORE[1] (6)

thumb[2] v **1** thumb a lift BrE; thumb a ride AmE informal to persuade a driver of a passing car to stop and take you somewhere, by putting your hand out with your thumb raised: *I thumbed a lift into town.* **2** thumb your nose at sb/sth to show that you do not respect rules, laws etc or you do not care what someone thinks of you: *a chance to thumb his nose at the college authorities*

thumb through sth phr v to look through a book, magazine etc quickly: *I began thumbing through the pages of a gardening catalogue.*

thumb index n [C] a line of round cuts in the edge of a large book which have the letters of the alphabet on them and help you find the part of the book you want

thumb·nail[1] /ˈθʌmneɪl/ adj thumbnail sketch/portrait a short description that gives only the main facts about a person, thing, or event: *a thumbnail sketch of recent political events in America*

thumbnail[2] n [C] **1** the nail on your thumb **2** a small picture of a document on a computer screen, showing you what it will look like when you print it: *Click on the thumbnails to view a larger version of each image.*

thumb·screw /ˈθʌmskruː/ n [C] an object that was used in the past to punish people by crushing their thumbs

thumb·tack /ˈθʌmtæk/ n [C] AmE a short pin with a flat top that is used for fixing notices on walls; ⊟ **drawing pin** BrE

thump[1] /θʌmp/ v **1** [T] informal to hit someone very hard with your hand closed: *If you don't shut up, I'm going to thump you!* | *She thumped the table with her fist.* **2** [I,T always + adv/prep] to hit against something loudly: *His feet thumped loudly on the bare boards.* | *He thumped his cup down on the table.* **3** [I always + adv/prep] to walk or run with your feet making a loud heavy sound as they touch the ground: *Stella came thumping down the stairs.* **4** [I] if your heart thumps, it beats very strongly and quickly because you are frightened or excited: *My heart was thumping inside my chest.*

thump² *n* [C] **1** the dull sound that is made when something hits a surface: *The box fell to the floor with a thump.* **2** [usually singular] *especially BrE* an action in which you hit someone or something: *If he does that again, I'll give him a good thump.* | *a thump on the jaw*

thump·ing /ˈθʌmpɪŋ/ *adj* [only before noun] **1** also **thumping great** *BrE informal* very big or great: *Mulroney swept to power with a thumping majority.* | *He told us some thumping great lies!* **2** thumping music has a strong loud beat **3** **thumping headache** a very bad headache

thun·der¹ /ˈθʌndə $ -ər/ *n* **1** [U] the loud noise that you hear during a storm, usually after a flash of lightning: *a storm with thunder and lightning* | **clap/crack/roll/crash of thunder** *Suddenly there was a great crash of thunder.* | **rumble/roar of thunder** *We could hear the rumble of distant thunder.* | **thunder rolls/rumbles/crashes/booms** *The thunder crashed and boomed around us.* **2** [singular] a loud deep noise: *She heard the thunder of hooves behind her.* **3** **a face like thunder** if someone has a face like thunder, they look very angry → BLOOD-AND-THUNDER; → **steal sb's thunder** at STEAL¹ (9)

thunder² *v* **1** [I] if it thunders, there is a loud noise in the sky, usually after a flash of lightning **2** [I always + adv/prep] to run or move along quickly, in a way that makes a very loud noise: *The children came thundering downstairs.* | *Huge lorries thundered past us.* **3** [I] to make a very loud deep noise: *Guns roared and thundered all around us.* **4** [T] to shout loudly and angrily: *'You must be mad!' he thundered.*

thun·der·bolt /ˈθʌndəbəʊlt $ -dərboʊlt/ *n* [C] **1** a flash of LIGHTNING which hits a person or thing and kills or destroys them **2** a sudden event or piece of news that shocks you: *The idea hit her like a thunderbolt.*

thun·der·clap /ˈθʌndəklæp $ -ər-/ *n* [C] a single loud noise of thunder: *A thunderclap exploded above us.*

thun·der·cloud /ˈθʌndəklaʊd $ -ər-/ *n* [C] a large dark cloud that you see before or during a storm

thun·der·ous /ˈθʌndərəs/ *adj* **1** extremely loud: *His speech was greeted with thunderous applause.* **2** looking or sounding very angry: *a thunderous voice* —**thunderously** *adv*

thun·der·storm /ˈθʌndəstɔːm $ -dərstɔːrm/ *n* [C] a storm with thunder and lightning

thun·der·struck /ˈθʌndəstrʌk $ -ər-/ *adj* [not before noun] extremely surprised or shocked: *Jeff looked thunderstruck when he saw me.*

thun·der·y /ˈθʌndəri/ *adj* thundery weather is the type of weather that comes before a thunderstorm

Thurs·day /ˈθɜːzdi, -dei $ ˈθɜːrz-/ *n* [C,U] written abbreviation **Thurs.** or **Thur.** the day between Wednesday and Friday: **on Thursday** *I went to Edinburgh on Thursday.* | *She was working Thursday. AmE* | **Thursday morning/afternoon etc** *There's a meeting on Thursday night.* | **last Thursday** *He was arrested last Thursday.* | **this Thursday** *Mark and I are driving south this Thursday.* | **next Thursday** (=Thursday of next week) *I'll see you next Thursday.* | **a Thursday** (=one of the Thursdays in the year) *Christmas Day is on a Thursday this year.*

thus W1 /ðʌs/ *adv formal* **1** [sentence adverb] as a result of something that you have just mentioned: *Most of the evidence was destroyed in the fire. Thus it would be almost impossible to prove him guilty.* ⚠ In spoken English it is more usual to use **so**. **2** in this manner or way: *They diluted the drug, thus*

reducing its effectiveness. **3** **thus far** until now: *Her political career thus far had remained unblemished.*

thwack /θwæk/ *n* [C] a short loud sound like something hitting a hard surface —**thwack** *v* [T]

thwart /θwɔːt $ θwɔːrt/ *v* [T] *formal* to prevent someone from doing what they are trying to do: *Fierce opposition thwarted the government's plans.* | *thwarted ambition*

THX a written abbreviation of 'thanks', used in email or TEXT MESSAGES on MOBILE PHONES

thy /ðaɪ/ *determiner old use* your: *We praise thy name, O Lord.*

thyme /taɪm/ *n* [U] a plant used for giving food a special taste

thy·roid /ˈθaɪrɔɪd/ also **'thyroid ,gland** *n* [C] an organ in your neck that produces substances that affect the way your body grows and the way you behave

thy·self /ðaɪˈself/ *pron old use* yourself

ti /tiː/ *n* [singular] the seventh note in a musical SCALE according to the SOL-FA system

ti·a·ra /tiˈɑːrə/ *n* [C] a piece of jewellery like a small CROWN, that a woman sometimes wears on very formal or important occasions: *a diamond tiara*

tib·i·a /ˈtɪbiə/ *n plural* **tibiae** /-bi-iː/ *or* **tibias** [C] *technical* a bone in the front of your leg

tic /tɪk/ *n* [C] a sudden movement of a muscle in your face, that you cannot control

tick¹ /tɪk/ *n* **1** [C] *BrE* a mark (✔) written next to an answer, something on a list etc, to show that it is correct or has been dealt with; ☐ **check** *AmE*: *Put a tick in the box if you agree with this statement.* → CROSS² (2b) **2** [C] a very small animal like an insect that lives under the skin of other animals and sucks their blood **3** [singular] the short repeated sound that a clock or watch makes every second **4** [C] *spoken especially BrE* a very short time; ☐ **moment**: *I'll be with you in a tick* (=soon). | *It'll only take two ticks.* **5** **on tick** *BrE informal old-fashioned* if you buy something on tick, you arrange to take it now and pay later; ☐ **credit**

tick² *v* **1** [I] also **tick away** if a clock or watch ticks, it makes a short repeated sound: *The old clock ticked noisily.* **2** [T] *BrE* to mark a test, list of questions etc with a tick, in order to show that something is correct, to choose something etc; ☐ **check** *AmE*: *Tick the description that best fits you.* | *Just tick the box on your order form.* **3** **what makes sb tick** *informal* the thoughts, feelings, opinions etc that give someone their character or make them behave in a particular way: *I've never really understood what makes her tick.*

tick away/by/past *phr v* if time ticks away, by, or past, it passes, especially when you are waiting for something to happen: *We need a decision – time's ticking away.* | *The minutes ticked past and still she didn't call.*

tick sb/sth ⇔ **off** *phr v* **1** *BrE informal* to tell someone angrily that you are annoyed with them or disapprove of them: *Mrs Watts will tick you off if you're late again.* **2** *BrE* to mark the things on a list with a tick to show that they have been dealt with, chosen etc; ☐ **check off** *AmE*: *As you finish each task, tick it off.* | *Have you ticked off Kate's name on the list?* **3** *AmE informal* to annoy someone: *Her attitude is really ticking me off.* **4** *AmE* to tell someone a list of things, especially when you touch a different finger as you say each thing on the list: *Carville began ticking off points on his fingers.*

tick over *phr v BrE* **1** if an engine ticks over, it works while the vehicle is not moving: *Mark left the engine ticking over and went back inside.* **2** if a system, business etc ticks over, it continues working but without producing very much or without much happening: *The business is just about ticking over.* | *Jane will keep things ticking over while I'm away.*

'ticked 'off *adj* [not before noun] *AmE* angry or annoyed: *Mark's ticked off with me for some reason.*

tick·er /'tɪkə $ -ər/ n [C] **1** informal your heart **2** AmE a special machine that prints or shows the price of company STOCKS as they go up and down

'ticker tape n [U] **1** long narrow paper on which information, for example the price of company STOCKS, is printed by a special machine **2 ticker tape parade** AmE an occasion when someone important or famous walks or drives through an American city and pieces of paper are thrown from high buildings to welcome them

tick·et¹ S1 W2 /'tɪkᵻt/ n [C]
1 CINEMA/BUS/TRAIN ETC a printed piece of paper which shows that you have paid to enter a cinema, travel on a bus, plane etc: [+for] How much are tickets for the concert? | [+to] I'd like to **book** two **tickets** to Berlin. | **theatre/train/airline etc ticket** The plane ticket costs $170. | A **return ticket** (=one going to a place and back again) to London, please. | **single/one-way ticket** (=one going to a place but not back again) | **a ticket to do sth** a ticket to watch the US Open | **a ticket office/ machine/agency etc** → SEASON TICKET
2 DRIVING OFFENCE a printed note ordering you to pay money because you have done something illegal while driving or parking your car: **parking/speeding ticket**
3 IN SHOPS a piece of paper fastened to something in a shop that shows its price, size etc; ▤ **tag** AmE: How much does it say on the **price ticket**?
4 ELECTION [usually singular] especially AmE a list of the people supported by a particular political party in an election: He ran for governor on the Republican ticket.
5 ticket to success/fame/stardom etc especially AmE a way of becoming successful, famous etc: Michael thought an MBA would be a ticket to success.
6 be (just) the ticket old-fashioned to be exactly what is needed → DREAM TICKET, MEAL TICKET

ticket² v [T usually passive] **1** to produce and sell tickets for an event, journey etc: air travel sold and ticketed in the UK | ticketed events such as concerts **2** especially AmE to give someone a ticket for parking their car in the wrong place, driving too fast etc: Drivers stopping here will be ticketed and have their cars towed. **3 be ticketed for sth** especially AmE to be intended for a particular use, purpose, job etc: Three of the army bases have been ticketed for closure.

tick·et·ing /'tɪkᵻtɪŋ/ n [U] the process or system of selling or printing tickets for planes, trains, concerts etc: Most airlines are using electronic ticketing now.

'ticket ˌtout n [C] BrE someone who sells tickets outside a theatre or sports ground at a high price because there are not many available; ▤ **scalper** AmE

tick·ing /'tɪkɪŋ/ n [U] a thick strong cotton cloth used for making MATTRESS and PILLOW covers

ˌticking 'off n give sb a ticking off BrE informal to tell someone angrily that you are annoyed with them or disapprove of something they have done; ▤ **tick off**

tick·le¹ /'tɪkəl/ v **1** [T] to move your fingers gently over someone's body in order to make them laugh: Stop tickling me! **2** [I,T] if something touching your body tickles you, it makes you want to rub your body because it is slightly uncomfortable: Mommy, this blanket tickles. | Mazie's fur collar was tickling her neck. **3** [T] if a situation, remark etc tickles you, it amuses or pleases you: **be tickled pink** (=be very pleased or amused) The kids were tickled pink to see you on TV! **4 tickle sb's fancy** informal if something tickles your fancy, you want to have it or try doing it: If I see something that tickles my fancy, I'm going to buy it.

tickle² n [singular] **1** a feeling in your throat that makes you want to cough: I've got a tickle in my throat. **2 give sb a tickle** to move your fingers gently over someone's body in order to make them laugh

tick·lish /'tɪklɪʃ/ adj **1** someone who is ticklish laughs a lot when you tickle them **2** [usually before noun] informal a ticklish situation or problem is difficult and must be dealt with carefully, especially because you may upset people: Handling awkward neighbours can be **a ticklish business**. **3** also **tick·ly** /'tɪkli/ [usually before noun] a ticklish cough is in your throat rather than in your chest

tick-tock /ˌtɪk 'tɒk $ -'tɑːk/ n [singular] the regular sound that a large clock makes every second

tick·y-tack·y /'tɪki ˌtæki/ also **ticky-tack** /-ˌtæk/ adj AmE informal ticky-tacky houses, buildings etc are made of material that is cheap and of low quality —**ticky-tacky** n [U]

tic-tac-toe, **tick-tack-toe** /ˌtɪk tæk 'təʊ $ -'toʊ/ n [U] AmE a children's game in which two players draw X's or O's in a pattern of nine squares, trying to get three in a row; ▤ **noughts and crosses** BrE

tid·al /'taɪdl/ adj relating to the regular rising and falling of the sea: tidal currents

'tidal wave n [C] **1** a very large ocean wave that flows over the land and destroys things **2** a very large amount of a particular kind of feeling or activity happening at one time: [+of] a tidal wave of crime | Voters were swept away on a tidal wave of enthusiasm.

tid·bit /'tɪdˌbɪt/ n [C] AmE **1** a small piece of food that tastes good; ▤ **titbit** BrE **2** a small but interesting piece of information, news etc; ▤ **titbit** BrE: [+of] juicy tidbits of hot news

tid·dler /'tɪdlə $ -ər/ n [C] BrE informal a very small fish

tid·dly /'tɪdli/ adj BrE informal **1** slightly drunk **2** very small: a tiddly little insect

tid·dly·winks /'tɪdliwɪŋks/ n [U] a children's game in which you try to make small round pieces of plastic jump into a cup by pressing their edge with a larger piece

tide¹ /taɪd/ n **1 the tide** the regular rising and falling of the level of the sea: **the tide is in/out** (=the sea is at a high or low level) | Is the **tide going out** or **coming in**? | We went for a walk and got **cut off by the tide**. → HIGH TIDE (1), LOW TIDE **2** [C] a current of water caused by the tide: Strong tides make swimming dangerous. **3** [C,usually singular] the way in which events or people's opinions are developing: [+of] With the tide of public opinion against him, the president may lose. | It was their first major victory. **The tide** had **turned** (=changed). | The tide of battle **turned against** the Mexican army. | **swim with/against the tide** (=support or oppose what most people think) **4** [C,usually singular] a large amount of something that is increasing and is difficult to control: **tide of violence/crime etc** The crisis prompted a **rising tide** of protest. | She swallowed back a tide of emotion. | efforts to **stem the tide** of hysteria caused by the shootings (=prevent it from getting worse) **5** [singular] a large number of people or things moving along together: [+of] the tide of refugees flowing over the border **6 Christmastide/eveningtide/morningtide etc** old use a particular time of the year or day

tide²
tide sb over (sth) phr v to help someone through a difficult period, especially by lending them money: Could you lend me £10 to tide me over till next week?

'tide-mark n [C] **1** a mark left on the beach by the sea, that shows how high the sea reached **2** BrE informal a dirty mark left around the inside of a bath by the water

'tide pool n [C] AmE a small area of water left among rocks by the sea when the tide goes out; ▤ **rock pool** BrE

tide·wa·ter /'taɪdˌwɔːtə $ -ˌwɒtər, -ˌwɑː-/ n **1** [U] water that flows onto the land or into rivers when the tide rises **2** [C] AmE an area of land at or near the coast

tid·ings /'taɪdɪŋz/ n [plural] old use news: **good/glad tidings** (=good news)

T

tidy

a well-dressed person in a tidy kitchen

a scruffy person in a messy kitchen

ti·dy¹ /'taɪdi/ *adj comparative* **tidier**, *superlative* **tidiest** *especially BrE* **1** a room, house, desk etc that is tidy is neatly arranged with everything in the right place; ◨ **neat**; ◪ **untidy, messy**: *a tidy desk* | *I try to **keep** the garden tidy.* | *Ellen's room is always **neat and tidy**.* **2** someone who is tidy keeps their house, clothes etc neat and clean: *Chris is a naturally tidy person.* **3** a tidy sum/profit *informal* a large amount of money: *We sold the house for a tidy sum and moved south.* **4** a tidy mind *BrE* if someone has a tidy mind, the way they think is very organized and clear —**tidily** *adv* —**tidiness** *n* [U]

tidy² also **tidy up** *v* **tidied, tidying, tidies** [I,T] to make a place look tidy: *Tidy your room!* | *It's time we tidied up the office.* | **tidy up after sb** *I'm tired of tidying up after you boys* (=tidying somewhere that someone else has made untidy).

tidy sth ⇔ **away** *phr v BrE* to put something back in the place where it should be, especially in a cupboard, drawer etc: *Let's tidy these toys away.*

tidy³ *n plural* **tidies** [C] *BrE* **desk/car/sink tidy** a container for putting small objects in, used to keep your desk, car etc tidy

tie¹ [S2] [W3] /taɪ/ *v* **tied, tying**
1 STRING/ROPE a) [T] to fasten things together or hold them in a particular position using a piece of string, rope etc; ◪ **untie**: **tie sth to/behind/onto etc sth** *Tie this label to your suitcase.* | **tie sb to sth** *They tied him to a tree and beat him up.* | **tie sth together (with sth)** *I kept all his letters tied together with a ribbon.* | **tie sb's hands/arms/legs/feet** *One of them tied her hands behind her back.* | *I **tie** my hair **back** when I'm jogging.* **b)** [T] to fasten something around, over etc something else and tie the ends together; ◪ **untie**: **tie sth around/over/under etc sth** *He had only a towel tied around his waist.* | *She tied a scarf over her head.* **c)** [T] to make a knot in a piece of string, rope etc, for example to fasten shoes or other clothes: *Can you **tie** your **shoelaces** by yourself?* | **tie a knot/bow** *She pulled the ribbon tightly and tied a bow.* **d)** [I] if a piece of clothing ties in a particular place, you fasten it there using a belt, bow etc: *This dress ties at the back.*
2 GAME/COMPETITION [I] also **be tied** if two players, teams etc tie or are tied in a game or competition, they finish it with an equal number of points: [+with] *At the end of the season, we were tied with the Tigers.* | **tie for first/second etc place** *Woosnam and Lyle tied for fourth place on 264.*
3 be tied to sth to be related to something and dependent on it: *The flat is tied to the job.* | *Interest rates are tied to the rate of inflation.*
4 be tied to/by sth to be restricted by a particular situation, job etc, so that you cannot do exactly what you want: *Many women felt tied to the house.* | **be tied to doing sth** *I didn't want to be tied to commuting to London.* | *With children, you're tied by school holidays.*

5 tie the knot *informal* to get married
6 tie yourself (up) in knots *informal* to become very upset because you are confused, nervous, or worried
7 tie one on *AmE informal* to get drunk → **sb's hands are tied** at HAND¹ (43)

tie sb down *phr v*
to restrict someone's freedom to do what they want to do: *She didn't want to be tied down by a full-time job.* | [+to] *Are you ready to be tied down to a wife and children?*

tie in with sth *phr v*
1 to be similar to another idea, statement etc, so that they seem to be true: *Her description tied in with that of the other witness.*
2 also **be tied in with sth** to be related in some way to something else: *How does all this tie in with their long-term aims?*
3 to happen at the same time as something else: *The book was published to tie in with the TV series.*

tie up *phr v*
1 PERSON **tie sb** ⇔ **up** to tie someone's arms, legs etc so that they cannot move: *The intruders tied Kurt up and left him.*
2 OBJECT **tie sth** ⇔ **up** to fasten something together, using string, rope etc: *He tied up all the old newspapers.*
3 BUSY **be tied up** to be very busy, so that you cannot do anything else: *I can't see you tomorrow – I'll be tied up all day.*
4 TRAFFIC/PHONE/COURT ETC **tie sth** ⇔ **up** *especially AmE* to block a system or use it so much that other people cannot use it or it does not work effectively: *Don't tie up the phone lines making personal calls.* | *Protesters tied up the traffic for three hours today.*
5 MONEY **be tied up** if your money is tied up in something, it is all being used for that thing and is not available for anything else: [+in] *My money's all tied up in the house.*
6 ARRANGEMENTS **tie sth** ⇔ **up** to finish arranging all the details of something such as an agreement or a plan: *We'd better tie up the details with a solicitor.*
7 be tied up with sth to be very closely related to something: *The shortage of teachers is tied up with the issue of pay.*
8 tie up loose ends to do the things that are necessary in order to finish a piece of work: *I need to tie up a few loose ends before I go on vacation.*
9 ANIMAL **tie sth** ⇔ **up** to tie an animal to something with a rope, chain etc: [+to] *She left the dog tied up to a tree.*
10 BOAT to tie a boat to something with a rope, chain etc: *We tied up alongside a barge.* | **tie sth** ⇔ **up** *There was a boat tied up at the jetty.*

tie² [S3] [W3] *n* [C]
1 MEN'S CLOTHES a long narrow piece of cloth tied in a knot around the neck, worn by men: *I wear a shirt and tie at work.* → **BLACK-TIE, BOW TIE**
2 CONNECTION/RELATIONSHIP [usually plural] a strong relationship between people, groups, or countries: **close/strong ties** *the importance of strong family ties* | [+between/with] *close ties between the two countries* | **economic/diplomatic/personal etc ties** *Japan's strong economic ties with Taiwan* | **the ties of marriage/friendship/love etc** → **OLD SCHOOL TIE**
3 RESULT [usually singular] the result of a game, competition, or election when two or more people or teams get the same number of points, votes etc; ◨ **draw** *BrE*: *The match ended in a tie.*
4 FOR CLOSING STH a piece of string, wire etc used to fasten or close something such as a bag
5 GAME *BrE* one game, especially of football, that is part of a larger competition: [+against] *England's World Cup tie against Argentina* | **first round/second round etc tie** | **home/away tie**
6 PREVENT YOU FROM DOING STH something that means you must stay in one place, job etc or prevents you from being free to do what you want: *If you enjoy*

travelling, young children can be a tie.

7 RAILWAY *AmE* a heavy piece of wood or metal supporting a railway track; ▪ **sleeper** *BrE*

tie·break·er /'taɪbreɪkə $ -ər/ *n* [C] **1** an extra question in a game or QUIZ, used to decide who will win when two people have the same number of points **2** also **tie·break** /'taɪbreɪk/ the final game of a SET in tennis, played when each player has won six games

,**tied** 'cottage *n* [C] *BrE* a house that a farm worker rents from a farmer while he is working on that farm

,**tied** 'house *n* [C] *BrE* a PUB that can only sell the beer made by a particular company → FREE HOUSE

'**tie-dye** *v* [T] to make a pattern on a piece of material by tying string around it and colouring it with DYE (=coloured liquid)

'**tie-in** *n* [C] a product such as a record, book, or toy that is related to a new film, TV show etc

'**tie-pin** *n* [C] *BrE* a thing used for keeping a man's TIE fastened to his shirt or as a decoration

tier /tɪə $ tɪr/ *n* [C] **1** one of several levels or layers that rise up one above the other: *The lower tier has 10,000 seats.* | **in tiers** *Terraces of olive trees rose in tiers.* | **two-tiered/three-tiered etc** (=having two, three etc levels or layers) *a three-tiered wedding cake* **2** one of several levels in an organization or system: [+of] *the most senior tier of management* | **the first/second etc tier** *The second tier of the programme is in-house training.* | *a two-tier system of government*

'**tie-up** *n* [C] *informal* **1** an agreement to become business partners: [+with] *IBM's tie-up with Auspex System Inc* **2** *BrE* a strong connection between two or more things: [+between] *the tie-up between class interests and politics* **3** *AmE* a situation in which traffic is prevented from moving or there is a problem which prevents a system or plan from working → **tie up** at TIE[1]

tiff /tɪf/ *n* [C] a slight argument between friends or people who are in love: [+with] *Dave's had a tiff with his girlfriend.*

ti·ger /'taɪɡə $ -ər/ *n* [C] a large wild animal that has yellow and black lines on its body and is a member of the cat family → PAPER TIGER; → see picture at BIG CAT

tight[1] S2 W3 /taɪt/ *adj comparative* **tighter**, *superlative* **tightest**

1 CLOTHES tight clothes fit your body very closely, especially in a way that is uncomfortable; ▪ **loose**: *tight jeans* | *My shoes were so tight that I could hardly walk.* | *The jacket is rather a tight fit* (=it fits too tightly). → see picture at LOOSE[1]

2 PULLED/STRETCHED FIRMLY string, wire, cloth etc that is tight has been pulled or stretched firmly so that it is straight or cannot move: *The bandage must be tight enough to stop the bleeding.* | *She tied the rope around the post and pulled it tight.*

3 ATTACHED FIRMLY a screw, lid etc that is tight is firmly attached and difficult to move: *Check that the screws are tight.*

4 HOLDING STH FIRMLY a tight hold/grip if you keep or have a tight hold on something, you hold it firmly: *His mother kept a tight hold on his hand.*

5 STRICT controlling something very strictly or firmly: *The government is keeping tight control on immigration.* | **keep a tight grip/hold/rein on sth** (=control it very firmly) *The former dictator still keeps a tight grip on power.* | *Anna was determined to keep a tight hold on her feelings.* | *Security is always tight for the opening day of parliament.* | **run/keep a tight ship** (=manage a company, organization etc strictly and effectively)

6 LITTLE MONEY if money is tight, you do not have enough of it: **money is tight/things are tight** *Money was tight and he needed a job badly.* | *As you know, I run the magazine on a pretty tight budget.*

7 LITTLE TIME if time is tight, it is difficult for you to do everything you need to do in the time available: *Time is tight, and she has another meeting to go to this afternoon.* | *We should arrive on time, but it'll be tight.* | *As usual, his schedule on Saturday was tight* (=he had

arranged to do several things in a short time). | *I''m working to a very tight deadline* (=I have to finish a piece of work vey quickly).

8 LITTLE SPACE if space is tight, there is only just enough space to fit something into a place: **be a tight squeeze/fit** *Six in the car will be a tight squeeze.*

9 NOT GENEROUS *informal* not generous, or trying hard to avoid spending money: *Don't be so tight!*

10 CLOSE TOGETHER placed or standing closely together: *The animal's body was curled up in a tight little ball.* | *She wore her hair in a tight bun.*

11 CLOSE RELATIONSHIP a tight group of people, countries etc have a close relationship with each other; ▪ **tight-knit**: *Together, the young film-makers formed a tight group.* | *the tight bonds that had grown between them*

12 BEND/TURN a tight bend or turn is very curved and turns quickly in another direction: *Danny lost control on a tight bend, and the car ran off the road.*

13 CHEST/STOMACH/THROAT if your chest, stomach, or throat feels tight, it feels painful and uncomfortable, because you are ill or worried: *Before she went on stage her chest felt tight and her throat hurt.*

14 EXPRESSION/SMILE/VOICE a tight expression, smile, or voice shows that you are annoyed or worried; ▪ **tight-lipped**: *'Look, I'm sorry ...,' she said, forcing a tight smile.*

15 DIFFICULT SITUATION **in a tight corner/spot** *informal* in a difficult situation: *He's a good man to have around if ever you're in a tight corner.* | *'Did something go wrong?' 'Let's just say I got into a bit of a tight spot.'*

16 PLAY/PERFORMANCE playing a piece of music or giving a performance very exactly and well, without any pauses or mistakes: *The band gave a really tight performance.* | *a tight, well-rehearsed production*

17 GAME/COMPETITION a tight game, competition etc is one in which the teams, players etc play equally well, and it is not easy to win: *The opening quarter of the game was very tight.*

18 DRUNK [not before noun] *old-fashioned informal* drunk → AIRTIGHT, WATERTIGHT —**tightly** *adv*: *Marie held the baby tightly in her arms.* —**tightness** *n* [U]

tight[2] *adv* very firmly or closely; ▪ **tightly**: *Hold tight to the handrail!* | *I kept my eyes tight shut.* → **sit tight** at SIT (8); → **sleep tight** at SLEEP[1] (4)

tight·en /'taɪtn/ also **tighten up** *v* **1** [T] to close or fasten something firmly by turning it; ▪ **loosen**: *Tighten the screws firmly.* | *I'd put the new tyre on, but I hadn't tightened up the wheel.* **2** [I,T] if you tighten a rope, wire etc, or if it tightens, it is stretched or pulled so that it becomes tight: *When you tighten guitar strings, the note gets higher.* | *The rope tightened around his body.* **3** [I,T] to become stiff or make a part of your body become stiff; ▪ **relax**: *His mouth tightened into a thin, angry line.* | *Tighten up the muscles of both arms.* **4** **tighten your grip/hold on sth a)** to control a place or situation more strictly: *Rebel forces have tightened their hold on the capital.* **b)** to hold someone or something more firmly: *Sarah tightened her grip on my arm.* **5** [T] to make a rule, law, or system more strict; ▪ **relax**: *Efforts to tighten the rules have failed.* | **tighten up on sth** *a range of measures to tighten up on illegal share dealing* **6** **tighten your belt** *informal* to try to spend less money than you used to: *Businesses were tightening their belts and cutting jobs.* **7** **tighten the screws (on sb)** *informal* to try to force someone to do something, by threatening them or making things difficult for them – used in news reports: *Closing the*

T

border would tighten the screws on the terrorists. **8** [I] *AmE* if a race or competition tightens, the distance between the competitors becomes smaller: *He expects the presidential race to tighten.*

tighten up *phr v* if a team or group tightens up, they start working together more effectively: **tighten sth ⇔ up** *We have tightened up the defence and are winning matches as a result.*

tight-fist·ed /ˌtaɪt ˈfɪstɪd◂/ *adj informal* not generous with money; **≡ stingy** —**tight-fistedness** *n* [U]

tight-'fitting *adj* fitting very closely or tightly: *a tight-fitting skirt*

tight-'knit *adj* [usually before noun] a tight-knit group of people are closely connected with each other: *a tight-knit island community*

tight-lipped /ˌtaɪt ˈlɪpt◂/ *adj* **1** unwilling to talk about something: *Diplomats are remaining tight-lipped about the negotiations.* **2** with your lips tightly pressed together because you are angry

tightly-'knit *adj* TIGHT-KNIT

tight·rope /ˈtaɪt-rəʊp $ -roʊp/ *n* [C] **1** a rope or wire high above the ground that someone walks along in a CIRCUS **2** **walk a tightrope** to be in a difficult situation in which something bad could happen if you make a mistake: *I feel as though I'm walking a tightrope between success and failure.*

tights S3 /taɪts/ *n* [plural] **1** *BrE* a piece of women's clothing made of very thin material that fits tightly over the feet and legs and goes up to the waist; **≡ pantyhose** *AmE*; → see picture at MATERIAL **2** a piece of clothing similar to women's tights but too thick to see through, worn especially by dancers

tight·wad /ˈtaɪtwɒd $ -wɑːd/ *n* [C] *AmE informal* someone who hates to spend or give money

ti·gress /ˈtaɪgrɪs/ *n* [C] a female tiger

tik·ka /ˈtiːkə/ *n* [U] a type of Indian food that consists of small pieces of meat covered in spices, and cooked: *chicken tikka*

til, 'til /tɪl,tl/ a short form of TILL[1]

til·de /ˈtɪldə/ *n* [C] a mark (˜) placed over the letter 'n' in Spanish to show that it is pronounced /nj/

tile[1] S3 /taɪl/ *n*
1 [C] a flat square piece of baked clay or other material, used for covering walls, floors etc: *bathroom tiles*
2 [C] a thin curved piece of baked clay used for covering roofs
3 **on the tiles** *BrE informal* out drinking, dancing etc for enjoyment until late at night

tiles

tiles

tile cutter

tile[2] *v* [T] to cover a roof, floor etc with tiles —**tiled** *adj*: *a tiled floor* —**tiler** *n* [C]

til·ing /ˈtaɪlɪŋ/ *n* [U] an area or surface covered with tiles, or the work of covering a surface with tiles

till[1] S1 /tɪl, tl/ *prep, conjunction spoken* until: *I didn't have a boyfriend till I was 17.* | *The shop's open till nine o'clock on Fridays.*

till[2] /tɪl/ *n* [C] **1** *BrE* a machine used in shops, restaurants etc for calculating the amount you have to pay, and for storing the money; **≡ cash register** *AmE* **2** **in the till** *AmE* money in the till is money that a company or organization has: *You keep as much money as you need in the till to run your operations.* **3** **have your hands/fingers in the till** to steal money from the place where you work: **be caught with your hands/fingers in the till** (=to be caught stealing from your employer)

till[3] *v* [T] to prepare land for growing crops; **≡ cultivate: till the soil/land/fields etc**

till·age /ˈtɪlɪdʒ/ *n* [U] the activity of preparing land for growing crops

til·ler /ˈtɪlə $ -ər/ *n* [C] a long handle fastened to the RUDDER (=part that controls the direction) of a boat

tilt[1] /tɪlt/ *v* [I,T] **1** to move a part of your body, especially your head or chin, upwards or to the side; **≡ tip**: *My mother tilted her head and smiled.* | *Ned's mouth tilted upwards slightly at the corners.* **2** to move or make something move into a position where one side is higher than the other; **≡ tip**: *As it came into land, the plane tilted sideways.* | *The man was tilting his chair back.* **3** if an opinion or situation tilts, or if something tilts it, it changes so that people start to prefer one person, belief, or action to others: *Crisis situations tend to **tilt the balance** of power in favour of the president.* | [+**toward/towards**] *Government tax policy has tilted toward industrial development.*

tilt at sb/sth *phr v* **1** to attack someone in what you say or write **2** **tilt at windmills** to waste time and energy attacking an enemy that is not real

tilt[2] *n* **1** **(at) full tilt** as fast as possible: *He charged full tilt down the slope.* **2** [C,U] a movement or position in which one side of something is higher than the other: *a slight **tilt of the head*** **3** [C] a preference for one person, belief, or action over others: [+**toward/towards**] *the recent tilt toward the Democrats* **4** [C] *BrE* an attempt to win something: [+**at**] *The team is preparing for another tilt at the European Cup.* **5** [C] a spoken or written attack on someone or something

tim·ber W3 /ˈtɪmbə $ -ər/ *n*
1 [U] *BrE* wood used for building or making things; **≡ lumber** *AmE*: *a bench made of timber*
2 [U] trees that produce wood used for building or making things: *the timber trade*
3 [C] a wooden beam, especially one that forms part of the main structure of a house
4 **timber!** *spoken* used to warn people that a tree being cut down is about to fall

tim·bered /ˈtɪmbəd $ -ərd/ *adj* timbered buildings have a frame made of wooden beams, or have wooden beams showing on the outside: **timbered houses/cottages** → HALF-TIMBERED

tim·ber·land /ˈtɪmbəlænd $ -ər-/ *n* [C,U] *AmE* an area of land that is covered by trees, especially ones that will be used for wood

tim·ber·line /ˈtɪmbəlaɪn $ -ər-/ *n* [singular] *technical* **1** the height above the level of the sea beyond which trees will not grow **2** the northern or southern limit in the world beyond which trees will not grow

tim·bre /ˈtæmbə, ˈtɪm- $ -ər/ *n* [C,U] *formal* the quality of the sound made by a particular instrument or voice

tim·brel /ˈtɪmbrəl/ *n* [C] *old use* a TAMBOURINE

time[1] S1 W1 /taɪm/ *n*
1 MINUTES/HOURS ETC [U] the thing that is measured in minutes, hours, days, years etc using clocks: *Einstein changed the way we think about space and time.* | *close relationships established over a long **period of time*** | *Customers have only a limited **amount of time** to examine the goods.* | **time passes/goes by** *Their marriage got better as time went by.*
2 ON A CLOCK [singular] a particular point in time shown on a clock in hours and minutes: *'What time is it?' 'It's about two thirty.'* | *What time are you going out tonight?* | **what time do you make it?** *BrE*/**what time do you have?** *AmE* (=used to ask someone with a watch what time it is) | **have you got the time?** *BrE*/**do you have the time?** *AmE* (=used to ask someone if they know what time it is) | **tell the time** *BrE*/**tell time** *AmE* (=be able to understand a clock) *Robin's just learning to tell the time.* | **look at the time** (=used when you realize that it is later than you thought it was) *Oh no. Look at the time. I'll be late.* | **is that the time?** (=used when you suddenly realize what the time is) *Is that the time? I must go.* | **this time tomorrow/last week etc** *By this time tomorrow I'll know whether I've got the job.*

3 OCCASION [C] an occasion when something happens or someone does something: *That was the only time we disagreed.* | *Do you remember the time I hit Tom Benson?* | *Mary had seen the film many times.* | **(for) the first/second/last etc time** *It was the first time that he had lost a game.* | *Gerry had just had back surgery for the third time in two years.* | **(the) next time/(the) last time/this time** *Why don't you drop in for a drink next time you're over this way?* | *The last time* (=the most recent time) *I saw Jonathan was Thursday evening.* | *The freezing weather did not return until February but this time we were prepared.* | **the first/second/next/last etc time round** (=the first, second etc time something happens) *I missed their concert the first time round so I'm going next week.* | **every/each time** *I meet up with Julie every time I go to Washington.* | **how many times ...?** *How many times did you take your driving test?* | *How many times have I told you not to wander off like that?* (=I have told you many times) | *One time* (=once) *I went to a garage sale and bought fifteen books.*

4 POINT WHEN STH HAPPENS [C,U] the particular minute, hour, day etc when something happens or should happen: **at the time of sth** *She was three months pregnant at the time of Stephen's death.* | **at some/any/that time** *He is performing as well as at any time in his career.* | *The UK has 500,000 stray dogs on its streets at any one time* (=at any particular time). | **at a/the time when ...** *At the time when this scheme was introduced, it was recognised that there might be problems.* | **by the time ...** *The phone was ringing but by the time she got indoors, it had stopped.* | **it's time to do sth** *Rosie – it's time to get up.* | **it's time for sth** *Come on, it's time for bed.* | *He glanced at his watch. 'It's time for me to go.'* | **it's time sb did sth** *It's time I fed the dog.* | *Now is the right time for us to move to London.* | **a good/bad time** *This might be a good time to start planning the new garden.* | **not the time/hardly the time** *Now is not the time to annoy Peter.* | **there's no time like the present** (=used to say that now is a good time to do something) *'When do you want to meet?' 'Well, there's no time like the present.'* | **dinner/lunch/tea etc time** *It's nearly dinner time.* | **opening/closing time** (=the time when a shop, bar etc opens or closes) *We empty the till each night at closing time.* | **arrival/departure time** (=the time when a train, plane etc arrives or leaves) *Our estimated arrival time is 2:30 pm.* | **time of day/year** *England is so lovely at this time of year.* | *We'll sort that out when the time comes* (=when it becomes necessary).

5 PERIOD OF TIME [singular, U] a period of time during which something happens or someone does something: *Dustin wanted to spend as much time as possible with his family.* | **a long/short/limited time** *I first met Jennifer a long time ago.* | *They stopped for a short time to rest the horses.* | *Andy and Tom talked for some time* (=for a fairly long period). | *Alison was married, for a time* (=for a fairly short period), *to a comedian.* | *Martin disliked being away from his family for any length of time* (=for more than just a short period). | *It took her a long time to make a decision.* | *Learning a language isn't easy – it takes time* (=takes a long period of time). | **take time to do sth** (=deliberately spend time doing something) *While in New York he took time to visit some friends.* | **journey/travel time** *The journey time to London is approximately four hours.*

6 AVAILABLE TIME [U] an amount of time that is available for you to do something: *I'll visit him if I have time.* | *Molly would like to do some diving if there is time.* | **have/get time to do sth** *How do you get time to study?* | **have time for sth** *She realized she would have time for a coffee before her train left.* | *We don't have to rush. We have all the time in the world* (=have plenty of time). | *June had little time to spare* (=available time) *for making her own clothes.* | **free/spare time** (=time when you are not working) *He writes poetry in his spare time.* | *Being prepared for meetings will save time.* | *I don't want to waste time arguing.* | *She spent precious time* (=valuable and important time) *looking for a telephone.* | *I seem to spend most of my time on the phone.* | *McDuff passed the time writing letters*

(=wrote letters because he had nothing else to do). | **have time on your hands/time to kill** (=not have enough to do) *Now the children have left home, she has too much time on her hands.* | **make/find time (for sth/to do sth)** (=plan so that you have time available for something) *Make time to talk to your children.* | *Book your ticket soon, as time is running out.* | **time's up** (=used to say that it is the end of the time allowed for something such as a competition or examination) | **we're out of time** (=used on radio and television programmes to say that there is no more time available on the programme)

7 all the time also **the whole time** continuously or very often: *I keep practising and I'm improving all the time.* | *He worries about her the whole time.*

8 most of the time very often or almost always: *I can speak German but we speak English most of the time.*

9 half the time if something happens half the time, especially something annoying, it happens quite often: *Half the time you don't even notice what I'm wearing.*

10 at times sometimes: *Life is hard at times.*

11 from time to time sometimes, but not regularly or very often: *These food safety scares happen from time to time.*

12 time after time/time and time again often, over a long period: *The police were catching the same kids stealing time after time.*

13 at all times always – used especially in official rules and statements: *Children must be supervised at all times while in the park.* | *Parents are welcome at all times.*

14 nine times out of ten/99 times out of 100 etc used to say that something is almost always true or almost always happens: *Nine times out of ten she's right.*

15 at the time at a particular moment or period in the past when something happened, especially when the situation is very different now: *I was about ten or eleven at the time.*

16 at one time at a time in the past but not now: *At one time she wanted to be a nurse, but the thought of working at night put her off.*

17 at this time AmE at this particular moment: *The President said his actions were 'the right ones at this time'.*

18 at no time used to say strongly that something never happened or should never happen: **at no time did/was etc** *At no time did anyone involved speak to the press.* | *At no time was the company informed.*

19 for the time being for a short period of time from now, but not permanently: *Now, for the time being, she is living with her father in Tijuana.*

20 in 10 days'/five years'/a few minutes' etc time ten days, five years etc from now: *He has an appointment with the doctor in two days' time.*

21 in time **a)** before the time by which it is necessary for something to be done: *Will you be able to finish it in time?* | **in time to do sth** *They ran all the way to the corner just in time to see the bus disappearing up the street.* | **[+for]** *The painting was successfully repaired in time for the opening of the exhibition.* | **in good time/in plenty of time** (=a long time before the necessary time) *We arrived at the concert hall in good time.* **b)** after a certain period of time, especially after a gradual process of change and development: *He wants to see changes in the company and I am sure he will, in time.*

22 with time to spare sooner than expected or necessary: *We should arrive in New York with time to spare.*

23 over time if something happens over time, it happens gradually during a long period: *The research project will be assessed over time.* | *Students are encouraged to consider the way language changes over time.*

24 with time/given time after a period of time: *These symptoms will start to get better with time.* | *I would have thought of the answer, given time.*

25 take your time **a)** to do something slowly or carefully without hurrying: **take your time doing sth** *Marie took her time cutting my hair and did it really well.* |

T

[+**over**] *He had planned to take his time over the journey.* **b)** to do something more slowly than seems reasonable: *You're taking your time with the lab tests. We need the results now.*

26 five/ten/many etc times ... used to say how much greater, more etc one thing is than another: *Sound travels four times faster in water than in air.* | *There were three times as many girls as boys.*

27 ... at a time **a)** if someone deals with things one, three, ten etc at a time, they deal with them separately or in groups of three, ten etc: *If you raise your hands, I'll answer questions one at a time.* | *Frank took the stairs two at a time.* **b)** if something happens for hours, days, months etc at a time, it continues for several hours, months etc: *Because of his work, he's often away for weeks at a time.*

28 on time at the correct time or the time that was arranged: *Jack was worried about whether he'd be able to get there on time.* | **right/bang/dead on time** (=at exactly the right time) *The plane arrived right on time.*

29 ahead of/behind time earlier or later than the time when something happens, should be done etc: *Prepare what you plan to say in the meeting ahead of time* (=before the meeting). | *The train left twenty minutes behind time* (=after it should have left).

30 it's about time also **it's high time** *spoken* used to say strongly that you think something should happen soon or should already have happened: *It's about time our team won.* | *It's high time we had a party.*

31 not before time/and about time (too) *spoken* used to say that something should have happened sooner: *Philip is going to be punished and not before time.*

32 the best/biggest etc ... of all time the best, biggest etc of a particular kind of person or thing that has ever existed: *He is the greatest athlete of all time, in my opinion.*

33 in no time (at all)/in next to no time very quickly or soon: *We'll be there in no time.*

34 any time (now) very soon: *'When is she due back?' 'Any time now.'*

35 it's (only/just) a matter/question of time used to say that something will definitely happen at some time in the future, but you do not know when: *I'll find the key eventually. It's just a question of time.* | *It's only a matter of time before we catch the person who killed her.*

36 (only) time will tell used to say that at some time in the future it will become clear whether or not something is true, right etc: *Only time will tell if the treatment has been successful.*

37 PERIOD IN HISTORY [C] also **times** [plural] a particular period in history: *Mankind has used the horse since ancient times.* | *In earlier times, servants would use the bare wooden stairs at the back of the house.* | at/in/during etc the time of sth *He lived at the time of the Napoleonic wars.* | our time(s) (=the present period in history) *Air pollution has become one of the most significant health problems of our time.*

38 behind the times old-fashioned: *Our equipment is a bit behind the times.*

39 move/change/keep up with the times to change when other things in society, business etc change: *We've got to move with the times.*

40 ahead of your/its time having or using the most advanced ideas, methods, designs, technology etc: *Coleridge was far ahead of his time in his understanding of the unconscious.*

41 PLEASANT/UNPLEASANT [C] a good time, bad time, difficult time etc is a period or occasion when you have good, bad, difficult etc experiences: *This was the happiest time of her life.* | good/bad/hard etc times *They had their happy times, but they had their hard times too.* | have a good/great/lovely etc time (=enjoy yourself) *Did you have a good time at the party?* | *Julie went to a wedding at the weekend and had the time of her life* (=enjoyed herself very much).

42 sb's time in/at/as sth the period of time when you were living in a particular place, working for a particular company etc: *In her time at the United Nations she was considered a tough negotiator.*

43 before your time **a)** before you were born or before you started working or living somewhere: *They say he was a great actor but that was before my time.* **b)** if you do something, especially get old, before your time, you do it before the time when most people usually do it in their lives: *He seemed to grow into an old man before his time.*

44 IN PART OF THE WORLD [U] the way of referring to points in time in one particular part of the world: *Eastern Standard Time* | *British Summer Time* | *The flight to Boston arrives at 1.15 pm* local time.

45 IN A RACE [C] the amount of time taken by a competitor in a race: *The Olympic medallist's time in the 200 metres final was 2 minutes 11.56 seconds.*

46 SPORTS [U] *BrE* the end of the normal period of playing time in a sports game, especially football; ◼ full time: *Mason's goal 13 minutes from time earned his team a place in the finals.*

47 MUSIC [U] the number of beats in each BAR in a piece of music: *Waltzes are usually in three-four time.*

48 in time to/with sth if you do something in time to a piece of music, you do it using the same RHYTHM and speed as the music: *Gloria was tapping her feet in time to the music.*

49 keep/beat time to show the RHYTHM and speed that a piece of music should be played at to a group of musicians, using your hands

50 keep perfect/good etc time if a clock keeps good time, it always shows the correct time

51 PRISON do time to spend a period of time in prison: *Paul was doing time for burglary.*

52 pass the time of day (with sb) to say hello to someone and have a short talk with them: *People like to pass the time of day with neighbours.*

53 time was (when) used to say that there was a time when you used to be able to do something, when something used to happen etc: *Time was when no one had television.*

54 there's no time to lose used to say that you must do something quickly because there is very little time

55 make good time if you make good time on a journey, you travel quickly, especially more quickly than you expected: *We made good time and were at the hotel by lunchtime.*

56 race/work/battle against time to try to finish or achieve something even though you have very little time: *Mark was racing against time to complete the work by Friday.*

57 time is money used to say that wasting time or delaying something costs money

58 time is on your side used to say that someone is young enough to be able to wait before doing something or until something happens

59 time is a great healer/heals all wounds used to say that someone will become less upset as time passes

60 time flies used to say that time seems to pass very quickly: *Time flies when you're having fun.*

61 in your own time if you study or do work in your own time, you do it outside normal school or work hours: *Nurses in training study in their own time.*

62 in your own (good) time *informal* when you are ready: *Bobby will tell them about it in his own good time.*

63 all in good time used to tell someone to be patient because something they are waiting for will certainly happen after a period of time, and probably quite soon: *'I'd love to see it.' 'All in good time.'*

64 have a lot of/no time for sb/sth *informal* if you have a lot of time for someone or something, you like or admire them: *He has no time for* (=does not like) *people who talk too much.*

65 time of life used to refer to someone's age: *At my time of life, you can't take too many shocks like that.*

66 your time used in certain expressions to refer to the period when you are alive: in your time *I've met some rude women in my time but she's the worst.* | *He was many things in his time – musician, pilot, cattle-rancher,* *industrialist, journalist.* | *If I* **had** *my* **time over again** (=lived my life again), *I'd probably do exactly the same things.*

67 time of the month the time when a woman has her PERIOD: *It's that time of the month.*

68 time out of mind *literary* a very long time, or a very long time ago → BIG TIME[1], FULL-TIME, HALF-TIME, PART-TIME, REAL-TIME; → at the best of times at BEST[3] (11); → time is of the essence at ESSENCE (4); → bide your time at BIDE (1); → in the fullness of time at FULLNESS (1); → give sb/sth time at GIVE[1] (21); → kill time at KILL[1] (8); → lose time at LOSE (8); → mark time at MARK[2] (11); → move with the times at MOVE[1] (17); → in the nick of time at NICK[1] (1); → for old times' sake at OLD (19); → once upon a time at ONCE[1] (14); → play for time at PLAY[1] (18); → the time is ripe at RIPE (3); → at the same time at SAME[1] (3); → sign of the times at SIGN[1] (9); → a stitch in time (saves nine) at STITCH[1] (8); → have a whale of a time at WHALE[1] (2)

time[2] *v* [T]

1 ARRANGE A TIME [usually passive] to arrange that something should happen at a particular time: *I saw from the station clock that I had timed my arrival perfectly.* | **be timed to do sth** *The tour has been timed to allow visitors to attend the opening night of the Verona opera season.* | *Her book was* **timed to coincide with** (=arranged to be at the same time as) *an exhibition of Goya's paintings at the National Gallery.* | **be timed for sth** *The meeting has been timed for three o'clock.*

2 MEASURE TIME to measure how fast someone or something is going, how long it takes to do something etc: *We had to run up the stairs while the Sergeant timed us.* | **time sb/sth at sth** *They timed the winner at 2 minutes and 14.05 seconds.*

3 SPORT to hit a ball or make a shot at a particular moment; → mistime: **time sth well/badly etc** *Keith timed the pass well.* | *a beautifully timed shot* → ILL-TIMED, WELL-TIMED

time and a half *n* [U] one and a half times the normal rate of pay: *We get time and a half for working on Sunday.*

time and motion study *n* [C] a study of working methods to find out how effective they are

time bomb *n* [C] **1** a bomb that is set to explode at a particular time **2** a situation that is likely to become a very serious problem: *Cutting down the rainforest is an environmental time bomb.*

time capsule *n* [C] a container that is filled with objects from a particular time, so that people in the future will know what life was like then

time card *n* [C] a piece of card on which the hours you have worked are recorded by a special machine

time clock *n* [C] a special clock that records the exact time when someone arrives at and leaves work

time-consuming *adj* taking a long time to do: *a complex and time-consuming process*

time frame *n* [C] the period of time during which you expect or agree that something will happen or be done: *There is a ten year time frame for the implementation of the new policies.*

time-honoured *adj* [only before noun] a time-honoured method or custom is one that has existed for a long time: *Sharon became involved with music* **in the time-honoured fashion** *— through her family.*

time·keep·er /ˈtaɪmˌkiːpə $ -ər/ *n* [C] **1** someone who officially records the times taken to do something, especially at a sports event **2** good/bad timekeeper *BrE* **a)** someone who is good or bad at arriving at work at the right time **b)** a watch or clock that is good or bad at showing the right time —**timekeeping** *n* [U]

time lag also **time lapse** *n* [C] the period of time between two connected events: *There is generally a two-year time lag in the information being made available.*

time-lapse *adj* [only before noun] time-lapse photography involves taking many pictures of something

over a period of time and then showing them together, so that a very slow process seems to happen much faster

time·less /ˈtaɪmləs/ *adj* **1** remaining attractive and not becoming old-fashioned: *the timeless beauty of Venice* **2** *literary* continuing for ever: *the timeless universe* —**timelessly** *adv* —**timelessness** *n* [U]

time limit *n* [C] the longest time that you are allowed in which to do something: [+for/on sth] *The time limit for applications is three weeks.*

time·line /ˈtaɪmlaɪn/ *n* [C] **1** a plan for when things will happen or how long you think something will take: *The timeline for the project is optimistic.* **2** a line showing the order in which events happened

time·ly /ˈtaɪmli/ *adj* done or happening at exactly the right time: *The fight ended only with the timely arrival of the police.* | **in a timely manner/fashion** (=as quickly as is reasonable in a particular situation) *We aim to settle all valid claims in a timely manner.* | **a timely reminder (of sth)** *BrE* (=one that makes you remember something important) *The crash served as a timely reminder of the dangers of drinking and driving.*

time machine *n* [C] in stories, a machine in which people can travel backwards or forwards in time

time off *n* [U] time when you are officially allowed not to be at work or studying: **take/have/get etc time off** *Have you ever had to take time off for health reasons?*

time out *n* **1** take time out (to do sth) *informal* to rest or do something different from your usual job or activities: *In between jobs, Liz always took time out to return to her first love — travelling.* **2** [C,U] a short break during a sports match when the teams can rest, get instructions from their manager etc: *With 15.7 seconds left, Washington State called time out.* **3** [C] an occasion when a computer stops using a particular program because the user has not done any work for a period of time

time·piece /ˈtaɪmpiːs/ *n* [C] *old use* a clock or watch

time-poor *adj* *BrE* someone who is time-poor does not have very much free time because they work all day and often work in the evenings too

tim·er /ˈtaɪmə $ -ər/ *n* [C] **1** an instrument that you use to measure time, when you are doing something such as cooking: *Set the timer on the cooker for three minutes.* → EGG-TIMER; → see picture at MEASUREMENT; → see picture at EAT **2** part-timer/full-timer someone who works part or all of a normal working week

times[1] /taɪmz/ *prep* multiplied by: *two times two equals four (2 x 2 = 4)*

times[2] *v* [T not in progressive] *spoken* to multiply a number: *Then you times that by 1000.*

time-saving *adj* designed to reduce the time usually needed to do something: *a time-saving device* —**timesaver** *n* [C]

time·scale, time scale /ˈtaɪmskeɪl/ *n* [C] *especially BrE* the period of time it takes for something to happen or be completed: *The timescale for completing the work would be fairly tight.*

time·serv·er /ˈtaɪmˌsɜːvə $ -ˌsɜːrvər/ *n* [C] *informal* someone who does the least amount of work possible in their job —**timeserving** *adj, n* [U]

time·share /ˈtaɪmʃeə $ -ʃer/ *n* [C,U] a holiday home that you buy with other people so that you can each spend a period of time there every year, or when you arrange to do this —**timeshare** *adj*: *timeshare flats*

time-sharing *n* [U] **1** *technical* a situation in which one computer is used by many different people at different TERMINALS at the same time **2** the practice of owning a timeshare

time sheet *n* [C] a piece of paper on which the hours you have worked are written or printed

1 000, 2 000, 3 000, most frequent words in S poken and W ritten English

'time ‚signal n [C] a sound on the radio that shows the exact time

'time ‚signature n [C] two numbers at the beginning of a line of music that tell you how many BEATS there are in a BAR

‚time span, time·span /'taɪmspæn/ n [C] a period of time: *It's difficult to imagine a time span of a million years.*

‚times 'table n [C] a list, used especially by children in school, that shows the results when each number between one and twelve is multiplied by each number between one and twelve: *Do you know the eleven times table?*

'time switch n [C] an electronic control that can be set to start or stop a machine at a particular time

time·ta·ble¹ /'taɪm‚teɪbəl/ n [C] **1** BrE a list of the times at which buses, trains, planes etc arrive and leave; **◰ schedule** AmE: **a railway/train/bus time-table 2** a list of the times of classes in a school, college etc; **◰ schedule** AmE **3** a plan of events and activities, with their dates and times; **◰ schedule**: [+for] *The Council has set out a timetable for returning to civilian rule.*

timetable² v BrE **1** [T usually passive] to plan that something will happen at a particular time in the future; **◰ schedule**: *The carnival parade is timetabled for 12.00 on both days.* **2** [I,T] to arrange the times at which classes will take place in a school or college; **◰ schedule** AmE: *The course is timetabled for one period each week.* | *Art students have very few time-tabled hours.* —**timetabling** n [U]

'time warp n [C] **1 be (caught/locked/stuck) in a time warp** to have not changed even though everyone or everything else has: *The house seemed to be stuck in a 19th-century time warp.* **2** an imaginary situation in which the past or future becomes the present

'time-‚worn adj **1** time-worn objects are old and have been used a lot: *time-worn steps* **2** time-worn ideas and beliefs are no longer sensible or useful: *time-worn prejudices*

'time zone n [C] one of the 24 areas that the world is divided into, each of which has its own time

tim·id /'tɪmɨd/ adj not having courage or confidence; **◰ shy**; **◲ confident**: *I was a timid child.* | *a policy that is both timid and inadequate* —**timidly** adv —**timidity** /tɨ'mɪdɨti/ n [U]

tim·ing /'taɪmɪŋ/ n **1** [U] the skill of doing something at exactly the right time: **perfect/good/bad etc timing** *He was just walking into the restaurant when we got there. Perfect timing.* | *He told jokes with an exquisite* **sense of timing.** **2** [C,U] the time when someone does something or when something happens, especially when you are considering how suitable this is: [+of] *The President and I did not discuss the timing of my departure.* | *Ferry schedules and precise timings are subject to weather conditions on the day of departure.* **3** [U] the way in which electricity is sent to the SPARK PLUGS in a car engine

tim·o·rous /'tɪmərəs/ adj formal lacking confidence and easily frightened; **◰ fearful**: *She was no helpless, timorous female.* —**timorously** adv —**timorousness** n [U]

tim·pa·ni /'tɪmpəni/ n [U] a set of large drums that are played in an ORCHESTRA

tin¹ |S3| /tɪn/ n

1 [U] a soft silver-white metal that is often used to cover and protect iron and steel. It is a chemical ELEMENT: symbol Sn: *an old tin bath* → see picture at **MATERIAL¹**

2 [C] BrE also **tin can** a small metal container in which food or drink is sold; **◰ can** AmE: *a sardine tin* | [+of] *a tin of baked beans;* → see picture at **CONTAINER**

3 [C] a metal container with a lid in which food can be stored: *a biscuit tin*

4 [C] BrE a metal container in which food is cooked;

◰ pan AmE: *a 7-inch cake tin* | *a roasting tin*

5 [C] BrE a metal container with a lid, in which paint, glue etc is sold: [+of] *a tin of brown paint;* → see picture at **BOX¹**

tin² adj made of TIN: *a tin roof* | *a tin mug*

tinc·ture /'tɪŋktʃə $ -ər/ n [C,U + of] technical a medical substance mixed with alcohol

tin·der /'tɪndə $ -ər/ n [U] dry material that burns easily and can be used for lighting fires

tin·der·box /'tɪndəbɒks $ -dərbɑːks/ n **1** [C usually singular] a place or situation that is dangerous and where there could suddenly be a lot of fighting or problems: *The area is a tinderbox that could again plunge the country into civil war.* **2** [C] a box containing things needed to make a flame, used in the past

'tinder-dry adj extremely dry and likely to burn very easily: *The whole forest is tinder-dry.*

tine /taɪn/ n [C] a pointed part of something that has several points, for example a fork

tin·foil /'tɪnfɔɪl/ n [U] thin shiny metal that bends like paper and is used for covering food

ting /tɪŋ/ n [C] a high clear ringing sound —**ting** v [I,T]

‚ting-a-'ling n [C] informal the high clear ringing sound that is made by a small bell

tinge¹ /tɪndʒ/ n [C] a very small amount of a colour, emotion, or quality: [+of] *There was a tinge of sadness in her voice.* | *This glass has a greenish tinge.*

tinge² v present participle **tinging** or **tingeing** [T] literary to give something a small amount of a particular colour, emotion, or quality: **tinge sth with sth** *The light of the setting sun tinges the buildings with delicate colours.* | *Pink tinged her cheeks.*

tinged /tɪndʒd/ adj showing a small amount of a colour, emotion or quality: [+with] *His voice was tinged with sadness and regret.* | *white blossom tinged with pink* | **pink-tinged/jazz-tinged/romantically-tinged etc**

tin·gle /'tɪŋgəl/ v [I] **1** if a part of your body tingles, you feel a slight stinging feeling, especially on your skin: *My body tingled all over and I had a terrible headache.* | **tingling feeling/sensation** *Graham felt a tingling sensation in his hand.* **2 tingle with excitement/fear/anticipation etc** to feel excitement, fear etc very strongly: *She tingled with excitement. Soon she would be able to tell Martha everything.* —**tingle** n [C]

tin·ker¹ /'tɪŋkə $ -ər/ v [I] to make small changes to something in order to repair it or make it work better: [+with] *Congress has been tinkering with the legislation.* | **tinker around with sth** *Dad was always tinkering around with engines.*

tinker² n [C] **1** in the past, a tinker was someone who travelled from place to place selling things or repairing metal pots, pans etc **2** BrE old-fashioned a disobedient or annoying young child

tin·kle¹ /'tɪŋkəl/ n [C usually singular] **1** a light ringing sound: [+of] *the distant tinkle of a cow-bell* **2 give sb a tinkle** BrE old-fashioned informal to call someone on the telephone: *I'll give you a tinkle tomorrow.* **3 have a tinkle** BrE spoken to URINATE (=pass water from your body) - used especially by children or when talking to children

tinkle² v **1** [I,T] to make light ringing sounds, or to make something do this: *a tinkling bell* **2** [I] spoken to URINATE (=pass water from your body) - used especially by children or when talking to children: *Do you have to go tinkle?*

tinned /tɪnd/ adj [usually before noun] BrE tinned food is food that is sold in small metal containers which can be kept for a long time before they are opened; **◰ canned** AmE: *tinned tomatoes*

tin·ni·tus /'tɪnɪtəs/ n [U] medical an illness in which you hear noises, especially ringing, in your ears

tin·ny /'tɪni/ adj a tinny sound is high, weak, and unpleasant, and sounds like it is coming out of something made of metal: *tinny music*

'tin ,opener *n* [C] *BrE* a tool for opening TINS of food; ⊟ **can opener**

tin·plate /'tɪnpleɪt/ *n* [U] very thin sheets of iron or steel covered with TIN

'tin-pot *adj* [only before noun] a tin-pot person, organization etc is not very important, although they think that they are – used to show disapproval: *a tin-pot dictator*

tin·sel /'tɪnsəl/ *n* [U] **1** thin strings of shiny paper used as decorations, especially at Christmas **2** something that seems attractive but is not valuable or important: *the tinsel and glamour of Hollywood*

tint¹ /tɪnt/ *n* [C] **1** a small amount of a particular colour; ⊟ **shade, hue:** *paper with a yellowish tint* **2** an artificial colour that is used to slightly change the colour of your hair: *red tints in her hair*

tint² *v* [T] to slightly change the colour of something, especially hair

tint·ed /'tɪntⁱd/ *adj* [only before noun] tinted glass is coloured, rather than completely transparent

,tin 'whistle *n* [C] a musical instrument like a small pipe with six holes, that you play by blowing

ti·ny S2 W2 /'taɪni/ *adj comparative* **tinier,** *superlative* **tiniest** extremely small: *The earrings were tiny.* | *a tiny community in the Midwest* | *The earrings were tiny.* | *a tiny little baby* | *She always felt a tiny bit sad.* | *Bad teachers are a tiny minority.* | *tiny pieces of paper*

-tion /ʃən/ *suffix* [in nouns] another form of the suffix -ION

tip¹ S2 W3 /tɪp/ *n*   **tip**

1 END [C] the end of something, especially something pointed: [+ **of**] *He kissed the tip of her nose.* | *the southern tip of South America* | *lights on the wing tips of aeroplanes* → FINGERTIP (1)

the tip of a pen nib

2 MONEY [C] a small amount of additional money that you give to someone such as a WAITER

the tip of a pool cue

or a taxi driver: *Did you leave a tip?* | **large/generous/ big tip** *I gave the guy a big tip.* | *a $5 tip*

3 ADVICE [C] a helpful piece of advice: *Jill knows Spain really well. Perhaps she could give us a few tips.* | [+**on/for**] *useful tips on healthy eating* | *last-minute tips for Christmas entertaining* | **handy tip** (=useful tip) *BrE: handy tips for decorating a small flat* | *gardening tips*

4 the tip of the iceberg a small sign of a problem that is much larger: *The reported cases of food poisoning are only the tip of the iceberg.*

5 on the tip of your tongue **a)** if something is on the tip of your tongue, you really want to say it, but then you decide not to: *It was on the tip of my tongue to say, 'I'd rather have dinner with a snake.'* **b)** if a word, name etc is on the tip of your tongue, you know it but cannot remember it: *What is her name? It's on the tip of my tongue. Joan. Joan Simpson. That's it!*

6 WASTE [C] *BrE* an area where unwanted waste is taken and left; ⊟ **dump:** *a rubbish tip* | *I'll take this lot to the tip.*

7 UNTIDY [singular] *BrE informal* an extremely dirty or untidy place: *The house was an absolute tip.*

8 HORSE RACE [C] *informal* special information about which horse will win a race

9 WARNING [C] a secret warning or piece of information, especially to police about illegal activities: *Acting on a tip, the police were able to find and arrest Upton.*

tip² *v* **tipped, tipping**

1 LEAN [I,T] to move into a sloping position, so that one end or side is higher than the other, or to make something do this; ⊟ **tilt:** [+**forward/back/to etc**] *His helmet had tipped forward and the boy pushed it back.* | *Eric fell asleep, his head gently tipping to one side.* | **tip sth forward/back etc** *'So what?' asked Brian, tipping his chair back on its rear legs.*

2 POUR [T always + adv/prep] to pour something from one place or container into another: **tip sth onto/into sth** *Tip the onions and oil into a large ovenproof dish.* | *Ben tipped the contents of the drawer onto the table.* | **tip sth out** *Shall I tip the water out?*

3 GIVE MONEY [I,T] to give an additional amount of money to someone such as a WAITER or taxi driver: *Did you tip the waiter?* | **tip sb sth** *I tipped him $5.*

4 BE LIKELY TO SUCCEED [T usually passive] if someone or something is tipped to do something, people think that they are most likely to succeed in doing it: **tip sb/sth to do sth** *the man tipped to become the next President* | **tip sb for/as sth** *He's tipped as a future world champion.* | **widely/strongly/hotly tipped** *He had been widely tipped to get the new post of deputy director.*

5 gold-tipped/steel-tipped/rubber-tipped etc having a tip that is made of or covered with gold, steel etc: *a silver-tipped walking stick*

6 tip the balance/scales to give a slight advantage to someone or something: *Three factors helped to tip the balance in favour of the Labour leadership.*

7 tip the scales at sth to weigh a particular amount, used especially of someone who will be taking part in a sports competition: *At today's weigh-in he tipped the scales at just over 15 stone.*

8 it's tipping (it) down *BrE spoken* said when it is raining very heavily: *It was absolutely tipping it down.*

9 be tipped with sth to have one end covered in something: *arrows tipped with poison* | *red petals tipped with white*

10 tip your hat/cap (to sb) **a)** to touch or raise your hat as a greeting to someone **b)** *AmE* to say or do something that shows you admire what someone has done

11 tip sb the wink *BrE informal* to give someone secret information

tip sb ⇔ off *phr v*
to give someone such as the police a secret warning or piece of information, especially about illegal activities: *The police must have been tipped off.* | **tip sb off that** *His contact had tipped him off that drugs were on the premises.* | [+**about**] *Did you tip him off about Bernard?*
tip over *phr v*
if you tip something over, or if it tips over, it falls or turns over: *The candle tipped over and the hay caught fire.* | **tip sth ⇔ over** *The current was starting to tip the canoe over and I began to panic.*
tip up *phr v*
if you tip something up, or if it tips up, it moves into a sloping position, so that one end or side is higher than the other: **tip sth ⇔ up** *He tipped the bottle up so that the last of the liquid flowed into his glass.* | *Ken tipped up the wheelbarrow, then stood back to rest.*

'tip-off *n* [C] **1** *informal* a secret warning or piece of information, especially one given to the police about illegal activities: *The arrests came after a tip-off from a member of the public.* **2** *AmE informal* something that shows you that something is true, even though you did not expect it to be true: *The fact that he hasn't called should be a tip-off that he's not interested.* **3** the beginning of a BASKETBALL game, when the ball is thrown into the air and two players jump up to try to gain control of it

tipp·ex /'tɪpeks/ *v* [T + out] *BrE* to use a white liquid in order to cover over mistakes in writing, TYPING etc

Tipp-Ex /'tɪp eks/ *n* [U] *BrE trademark* white liquid that is used to cover over mistakes in writing, TYPING etc

tip·ple /'tɪpəl/ *n informal* sb's favourite tipple someone's favourite alcoholic drink

tip·pler /'tɪplə $ -ər/ *n* [C] *informal especially BrE* someone who drinks alcohol

tip·py·toes /'tɪpitəʊz $ -toʊz/ *n* [plural] *AmE* **on (my) tippytoes** on TIPTOE – used especially by children or when talking to children

'tip sheet *n* [C] *informal* a newspaper that gives advice and information about which SHARES should be bought and sold: *a tip sheet for private investors*

tip·ster /ˈtɪpstə $ -ər/ n [C] someone who gives information about which horse is likely to win a race

tip·sy /ˈtɪpsi/ adj informal slightly drunk —**tipsily** adv —**tipsiness** n [U]

tip·toe¹ /ˈtɪptəʊ $ -toʊ/ n on tiptoe/on (your) tiptoes if you stand or walk on tiptoe, you stand or walk on your toes, in order to make yourself taller or in order to walk very quietly: *She stood on tiptoe to kiss him.*

tiptoe² v tiptoed, tiptoeing [I always + adv/prep] to walk quietly and carefully on your toes, so that nobody hears you: *His mother tiptoed into the room.* | *I tiptoed along the corridor.*

    tiptoe around (sth) phr v to try to avoid dealing with a difficult or embarrassing subject or problem: *They were tiptoeing around the delicate subject of money.*

tip-ˈtop adj informal excellent: *The car's in tip-top condition.*

ti·rade /taɪˈreɪd, tɪˈ- $ ˈtaɪreɪd, tɪˈreɪd/ n [C] a long angry speech criticizing someone or something: [+against] *He launched into a tirade against the church.* | [+of] *a tirade of abuse*

tire¹ /taɪə $ taɪr/ v [I,T] to start to feel tired, or make someone feel tired: *As we neared the summit, we were tiring fast.*

    tire of sb/sth phr v **1** to become bored with someone or something: *Sooner or later he'll tire of politics.* **2 never tire of doing sth** to enjoy doing something again and again, especially in a way that annoys other people: *He never tires of talking about the good old days.*

    tire sb ⇔ **out** phr v to make someone very tired: *All that walking tired me out.*

tire² n [C] the American spelling of TYRE → see picture at CAR

tired S1 W2 /taɪəd $ taɪrd/ adj

1 feeling that you want to sleep or rest: **so tired (that)** *I'm so tired I could sleep for a week.* | **too tired to do sth** *He was too tired to argue.* | *He looks **tired out** (=very tired).* | *'No,' Frank said in a tired voice.*

2 tired of (doing) sth bored with something, because it is no longer interesting, or has become annoying: *I'm tired of watching television; let's go for a walk.* | *I was getting tired of all her negative remarks.*

3 familiar and boring: *tired old speeches* —**tiredness** n [U] —**tiredly** adv → DOG-TIRED; → be sick (and tired) of sth at SICK¹ (6)

tire·less /ˈtaɪələs $ ˈtaɪr-/ adj working very hard in a determined way without stopping: *the tireless efforts of the rescue workers* —**tirelessly** adv

tire·some /ˈtaɪəsəm $ ˈtaɪr-/ adj making you feel annoyed or impatient: *the whole tiresome business of filling out the forms* △ Do not confuse **tiresome** with **tiring**. Use **tiring** to say that something makes you feel tired: *It was a long, tiring day.*

tir·ing /ˈtaɪərɪŋ $ ˈtaɪr-/ adj making you feel that you want to sleep or rest: *We've all had a very tiring day – let's go to bed.*

ˈtis /tɪz/ literary it is – used especially in poetry

tis·sue W3 /ˈtɪʃuː, -sjuː $ -ʃuː/ n

1 [C] a piece of soft thin paper, used especially for blowing your nose on: *a box of tissues*

2 [U] also **tissue paper** light thin paper used for wrapping, packing etc

3 [U] the material forming animal or plant cells: **lung/brain etc tissue**; → see picture at HUMAN¹

4 a tissue of lies BrE a story or account that is completely untrue

tit /tɪt/ n [C] **1** informal not polite a woman's breast **2 get on sb's tits** BrE spoken not polite to annoy someone a lot **3** a type of small European bird

ti·tan, Titan /ˈtaɪtn/ n [C] a very strong or important person; ☐ giant

ti·tan·ic /taɪˈtænɪk/ adj very big, strong, impressive etc: *a titanic struggle*

ti·ta·ni·um /taɪˈteɪniəm/ n [U] a strong light silver-white metal that is used to make aircraft and spacecraft, and is often combined with other metals. It is a chemical ELEMENT: symbol Ti

tit·bit /ˈtɪtˌbɪt/ n [C] BrE **1** a small piece of food; ☐ **tidbit** AmE **2** titbit of information/gossip/news etc a small but interesting piece of information etc

titch /tɪtʃ/ n [singular] BrE a humorous or insulting way of talking to or about a small person

titch·y /ˈtɪtʃi/ adj BrE informal extremely small

ˌtit for ˈtat n [U] informal something bad that you do to someone because they have done something bad to you

tithe /taɪð/ n [C] **1** a particular amount that some Christians give to their church **2** a tax paid to the church in the past —**tithe** v [I,T]

tit·il·late /ˈtɪtɪleɪt/ v [T] if a picture or a story titillates someone, it makes them feel sexually interested —**titillating** adj —**titillation** /ˌtɪtɪˈleɪʃən/ n [U]

ti·tle S3 W1 /ˈtaɪtl/ n

1 [C] the name given to a particular book, painting, play etc: [+of] *The title of this play is 'Othello'.*

2 [C] a book: *His novel was one of last year's best-selling titles.*

3 [C] **a)** a name such as 'Sir' or 'Professor', or abbreviations such as 'Mrs' or 'Dr', that are used before someone's name to show their rank or profession, whether they are married etc **b)** a name that describes someone's job or position: *Her official title is editorial manager.*

4 [C] the position of being the winner of an important sports competition: *Tyson won the WBA title in 1987.*

5 [singular, U] law the legal right to have or own something: [+to] *He **has title** to the land.*

ˈtitle bar n [C] the coloured bar at the top of a computer window that shows the name of the program and whether it is being used at that time

ti·tled /ˈtaɪtld/ adj having a title in the ARISTOCRACY, such as 'lord', DUKE, EARL etc

ˈtitle deed n [C] a piece of paper giving legal proof that someone owns a particular property

ˈtitle ˌholder n [C] **1** the person or team that is the winner of an important sports competition **2** someone who owns a title deed

ˈtitle page n [C] the page at the front of a book which shows the book's name, the writer etc

ˈtitle role n [C] the main acting part in a play or film, which is the same as the name of the play or film

ˈtitle track n [C] the song on a CD, CASSETTE etc that has the same name as the whole CD or cassette

ti·tlist /ˈtaɪtlɪst/ n [C] AmE someone who has won an important sports competition

tit·ter /ˈtɪtə $ -ər/ v [I] to laugh quietly in a high voice, especially because you are nervous: *At the word 'breast', some of the class tittered.* —**titter** n [C]

tit·tle-tat·tle /ˈtɪtl ˌtætl/ n [U] unimportant conversation about other people and what they are doing; ☐ gossip

tit·ty /ˈtɪti/ n plural **titties** [C] informal not polite a woman's breast

tit·u·lar /ˈtɪtʃələ $ -ər/ adj [only before noun] **titular head/leader/monarch etc** someone who is the official leader or ruler of a country but who does not have real power or authority

tiz·zy /ˈtɪzi/ also **tizz** /tɪz/ n [singular] informal **in a tizzy** feeling worried, nervous, and confused

T-junc·tion /ˈtiː ˌdʒʌŋkʃən/ n [C] BrE a place where two roads meet and form the shape of the letter T

TLA /ˌtiː el ˈeɪ/ n [C] three-letter acronym the first letters of the words in a three-word phrase, for example BTW ('by the way') or IMO ('in my opinion'), used as a short form, especially on the Internet and in emails

TLC /ˌtiː el ˈsiː/ n [U] informal *tender loving care* kindness and love that you show someone to make them feel better and happier

TM /ˌtiː ˈem/ **1** a written abbreviation of TRADE-MARK **2** an abbreviation of TRANSCENDENTAL MEDITATION

TNT /ˌtiː en ˈtiː/ *n* [U] a powerful explosive; ▤ **dynamite**

to¹ S1 W1 /tə; *before vowels* tʊ; *strong* tuː/ [used before the basic form of a verb to show that it is in the infinitive] **1 a)** used after a verb, noun, or adjective when an INFINITIVE completes its meaning: *We tried to explain.* | *It was starting to rain.* | *The manager asked them to leave.* | *an attempt to escape* | *Have you got permission to stay here?* | *Our team's certain to win.* | *Are you ready to start?* | *This delicious dessert is easy to make* (=you can make it easily). **b)** used by itself instead of an INFINITIVE in order to avoid repeating the same verb: *You can drive today if you want to* (=if you want to drive). | *I could have helped, but nobody asked me to.*
2 used after a word such as 'how', 'where', 'who', 'what', or 'whether' to refer to an action about which someone is not certain: *I know where to go but I don't know how to get there.* | *She wondered whether or not to trust him.*
3 used to show a purpose or intention: *They left early to catch the 7.30 train.* | *To find out more about university courses, write to this address.* | *We need more money to improve transport in London.*
4 used to refer to an action or state, when describing it: *It's nice to be wanted.* | *He's finding it hard to cope.* | *To say I am disappointed is an understatement.* | *The simplest solution would be to increase the price.*
5 used to say what can or cannot be done, or what should be done: *You'll soon be old enough to vote in elections.* | *He did not have the energy to resist.* | *I'm too tired to go out tonight.*
6 used after the verb 'be' to give an order or to state arrangements for the future: *You are to wait here until I return.* | *They are to be married on May 25th.*
7 used to say what someone discovers or experiences when they do something: *He arrived there to find that the last train had already left.* | *The princess stepped ashore to be greeted by an enthusiastic crowd of admirers.* | *She woke to see Ben standing by the window.*
8 used to say what your attitude or purpose is in saying something: *I've never heard of him, to be quite honest.* | *To begin with, let's look at Chapter 3.*

to² S1 W1 *prep*
1 used to say where someone or something goes: *She stood up and walked to the window.* | *the road to London* | *our weekly trip to the supermarket* | *sending a spaceship to Mars* | *These people go from house to house selling goods* (=visit many different houses).
2 used to say who receives something or is told or shown something: *He sent presents to the children.* | *She whispered something to the girl beside her.* | *Give my best wishes to your parents when you see them.* | *Don't show these letters to anyone else.* | *a message from the Emperor to his people*
3 used to show in which direction something is in relation to something else: *Knutsford is about 16 miles to the south of Manchester.* | *There was a table to the left of the doorway.*
4 used to show the purpose, event, or activity for which you go somewhere: *Sophie goes to gymnastics every Friday.* | *Did you get an invitation to their wedding?* | *Don't forget, we're going to a party tomorrow night.* | *If he needed help, Mother came rushing to the rescue.*
5 used to say what state someone or something is in as a result of an action or change: *She sang the baby to sleep.* | *Wait until the lights change to green.* | *a return to a traditional way of life*
6 used to say that one thing is touching another: *He held a knife to her throat.* | *They danced cheek to cheek.*
7 used to say where something is fastened or connected: *He tied the rope to a tree.* | *Attach a recent photograph to your application form.* | *Cash machines are linked up to a central computer.*
8 facing something or in front of it: *I sat with my back to the window.* | *We were standing face to face.*
9 used to show a relationship with someone or some-thing: *George's sister was married to an Italian.* | *He was first cousin to King Philip VI.* | *The robbery may be linked to other crimes of violence.*
10 a) as far as a particular point or limit: *She can already count from one to twenty.* | *The water came right up to our knees.* | *Temperatures dropped to 25 degrees below zero.* | *It's ten kilometres from here to the coast.* | *She read the novel from beginning to end.* | *Does your interest in nuclear physics extend to nuclear weaponry?* **b)** until and including a particular time or date: *They stayed from Friday night to Sunday morning.* | *I'll be on duty from 8 am to 10 pm.*
11 used to say what or who an action, attitude, situation etc affects or is related to: *The factory clearly represents a danger to health.* | *She's always been kind to animals.* | *his attitude to life* | *What have you done to the radio? It's not working.*
12 used to say who someone works for: *Jane is secretary to the managing director.*
13 used to say what something is needed for: *I'm still waiting for an answer to my question.* | *Have you seen the key to the back door?*
14 used when comparing two things, numbers etc: *England beat Scotland by two goals to one.* | *Yes, she was punished, but it was nothing to what she deserved.*
15 used to say who has a particular attitude or opinion about something: *The whole thing sounds very suspicious to me.* | *Tickets cost £10 each and to some people that's a lot of money.* | *To my mind, age does not matter; love is what matters.*
16 used to say what someone's reaction is when something happens: *Much to everyone's surprise she passed the exam with distinction.* | *I discovered to my horror that my passport was missing.*
17 used when saying how much time there is before a particular event or time: *It's only two weeks to Christmas.* | *How long is it to dinner?* | **ten to five/twenty to one etc** (=ten minutes, twenty minutes etc before a particular hour)
18 a) used when talking about a rate or quantity to say how many smaller units equal a larger unit: *We're only getting 130 yen to the dollar at the moment.* | *There are just over four and a half litres to a gallon.* **b)** used to show the relationship between two different measurements or quantities: *The car will do over 40 miles to the gallon.* | *The scale of your map is one inch to the mile.*
19 used to say that a particular sound is heard at the same time as something happens: *I woke to the sound of torrential rain.* | *The royal couple arrived to a fanfare of trumpets.* | *I like to exercise to music.*
20 used between two numbers when you do not know exactly what the real number or amount is: *There must have been eighteen to twenty thousand people at the concert.* | *He drowned in 10 to 12 feet of water.*
21 (all) to yourself if you have something or someone to yourself, you do not have to share them with other people: *It was the first time I'd had a room to myself.*
22 used to say what the chances of something happening are: *I'll bet you ten to one he'll forget all about it.*

to³ /tuː/ *adv BrE* if a door is pushed to, it closes or almost closes: *The wind blew the door to.* → COME TO (6)

toad /təʊd $ toʊd/ *n* [C] a small animal that looks like a large FROG and lives mostly on land

toad-in-the-ˈhole *n* [U] a British dish made of SAUSAGES cooked in a mixture of eggs, milk, and flour

toad·stool /ˈtəʊdstuːl $ ˈtoʊd-/ *n* [C] a wild plant like a MUSHROOM, that can be poisonous

toad·y¹ /ˈtəʊdi $ ˈtoʊ-/ *n plural* **toadies** [C] *informal* someone who pretends to like an important person and does things for them, so that that person will help them – used to show disapproval

tol·e·ra·bly /ˈtɒlərəbli $ ˈtɑː-/ adv [+ adj/adv] fairly, but not very much: We were tolerably happy at first.

tol·e·rance /ˈtɒlərəns $ ˈtɑː-/ n **1** [U] willingness to allow people to do, say, or believe what they want without criticizing or punishing them; **2** intolerance; → tolerate: [+of/towards/for] tolerance towards religious minorities **2** [C,U] the degree to which someone can suffer pain, difficulty etc without being harmed or damaged; → tolerate: [+to] Many old people have a very limited tolerance to cold.

tol·e·rant /ˈtɒlərənt $ ˈtɑː-/ adj **1** allowing people to do, say, or believe what they want without criticizing or punishing them; **2** intolerant; → tolerate: [+of/towards] Luckily, my parents were tolerant of my choice of music. | a tolerant society **2** plants that are tolerant of particular weather or soil conditions can exist in those conditions: [+of] trees that are tolerant of salt sea winds

tol·e·rate /ˈtɒləreɪt $ ˈtɑː-/ v [T] **1** to allow people to do, say, or believe something without criticizing or punishing them; → tolerant, tolerance: We simply will not tolerate vigilante groups on our streets. **2** to be able to accept something unpleasant or difficult, even though you do not like it; → tolerant, tolerance; **2** stand, bear: I couldn't tolerate the long hours. **3** if a plant tolerates particular weather or soil conditions, it can exist in them: plants that tolerate drought **4** if a person or their body can tolerate a food or other substance, it can use it without becoming ill: Women's bodies can tolerate less alcohol than men's.

tol·e·ra·tion /ˌtɒləˈreɪʃən $ ˌtɑː-/ n [U] willingness to allow people to believe what they want without being criticized or punished: religious toleration

toll¹ /təʊl $ toʊl/ n [C] **1** [usually singular] the number of people killed or injured in a particular accident, by a particular illness etc: The **death toll** has risen to 83. | The bombings **took** a heavy toll, killing hundreds of Londoners. **2** a very bad effect that something has on something or someone over a long period of time: [+on] Years of smoking have **taken** their toll on his health. | a heavy toll on the environment **3** the money you have to pay to use a particular road, bridge etc **4** the sound of a large bell ringing slowly

toll² v [I,T] if a large bell tolls, or if you toll it, it keeps ringing slowly, especially to show that someone has died

toll·booth /ˈtəʊlbuːθ $ ˈtoʊl-/ n [C] a place where you pay to drive on a road, bridge etc

ˈtoll bridge n [C] a bridge that you pay to drive across

ˌtoll-ˈfree adv AmE if you telephone a particular number toll-free, you do not have to pay for the call —**toll-free** adj: a toll-free number

toll·gate /ˈtəʊlgeɪt $ ˈtoʊl-/ n [C] a gate across a road, at which you have to pay money before you can drive any further

ˈtoll road n [C] a road that you pay to use

toll·way /ˈtəʊlweɪ $ ˈtoʊl-/ n [C] AmE a large long road that you pay to use

tom /tɒm $ tɑːm/ n [C] informal a TOMCAT

tom·a·hawk /ˈtɒməhɔːk $ ˈtɑːməhɔːk/ n [C] a light AXE used by Native Americans

to·ma·to S3 /təˈmɑːtəʊ $ -ˈmeɪtoʊ/ n plural **tomatoes** [C] a round soft red fruit eaten raw or cooked as a vegetable → see picture at VEGETABLE¹

tomb /tuːm/ n [C] a stone structure above or below the ground where a dead person is buried: the family tomb

tom·bo·la /ˈtɒmbəʊlə $ tɑːmˈboʊ-/ n [U] BrE a game in which you buy a ticket with a number on it in order to try and win a prize that has the same number on it; → raffle

tom·boy /ˈtɒmbɔɪ $ ˈtɑːm-/ n [C] a girl who likes playing the same games as boys

tomb·stone /ˈtuːmstəʊn $ -stoʊn/ n [C] a stone that is put on a GRAVE and shows the dead person's name, dates of birth and death etc; **2** gravestone

tom·cat /ˈtɒmkæt $ ˈtɑːm-/ n [C] a male cat

tome /təʊm $ toʊm/ n [C] literary a large heavy book

tom·fool·e·ry /tɒmˈfuːləri $ tɑːm-/ n [U] old-fashioned silly behaviour

ˈtommy gun /ˈtɒmi gʌn $ ˈtɑː-/ n [C] old-fashioned informal a gun that can fire many bullets very quickly

to·mor·row¹ S1 W2 /təˈmɒrəʊ $ -ˈmɔːroʊ, -ˈmɑː-/ adv on or during the day after today; → yesterday, today: Our class is going to London tomorrow. | a **week from tomorrow** also a **week tomorrow/tomorrow week** BrE: Terry's new job starts a week tomorrow. | **tomorrow morning/night** etc We're meeting tomorrow evening.

tomorrow² n [U] **1** the day after today; → yesterday, today: I'll see you at tomorrow's meeting. **2** the future, especially the near future: The computers of tomorrow will be smaller and more powerful. **3** do sth **like there's no tomorrow** do something very quickly and carelessly, without worrying about the future: Rita's spending money like there's no tomorrow.

ˈtom-tom n [C] a tall narrow drum that you play with your hands

ton S3 /tʌn/ n [C]
1 plural **tons** or **ton** written abbreviation **t** a unit for measuring weight, equal to 2240 pounds or 1016 kilograms in Britain, and 2000 pounds or 907.2 kilograms in the US → TONNE
2 tons of sth informal a lot of something: I've got tons of work to do.
3 weigh a ton informal to be very heavy: Your bag weighs a ton!
4 come down on sb like a ton of bricks informal to get very angry with someone about something they have done
5 hit sb like a ton of bricks AmE informal to have a strong emotional effect on someone

ton·al /ˈtəʊnl $ ˈtoʊ-/ adj **1** relating to tones of colour or sound: The tonal range she uses is wide and varied. **2** technical a piece of music that is tonal is based on a particular KEY; **2** atonal

ton·al·i·ty /təʊˈnæləti $ toʊ-/ n plural **tonalities** [C,U] technical the character of a piece of music that depends on the KEY of the music and the way in which the tunes and HARMONIES are combined

tone¹ W2 /təʊn $ toʊn/ n
1 VOICE [C] the way your voice sounds, which shows how you are feeling or what you mean: **in a ... tone** 'You must be Annie,' he said in a friendly tone. | **in sb's tone** There was urgency in his tone. | Her tone was sharp with anger. | It was obvious from her **tone of voice** that she didn't like me. | **don't take that tone with me** (=do not speak to me in that rude or unpleasant way)
2 SOUND [C,U] the quality of a sound, especially the sound of a musical instrument or someone's voice; → pitch, timbre: the guitar's clean tone | **in ... tones** They talked in hushed tones. | 'No I didn't,' he said in a **low tone** (=quietly). | **deep-toned/even-toned/shrill-toned** etc (=having a low, calm etc tone) an even-toned voice
3 GENERAL FEELING/ATTITUDE [singular, U] the general feeling or attitude expressed in a piece of writing, a speech, an activity etc: [+of] The tone of the report was radical. | The meetings were noted for their deeply religious tone. | **in tone** The article was moderate in tone. | **set the tone (for/of sth)** (=establish the general attitude or feeling of an event, activity etc) Opening remarks are important since they set the tone for the rest of the interview.
4 COLOUR [C,U] one of the many types of a particular colour, each slightly darker, lighter, brighter etc than the next; **2** shade: [+of] different tones of green | Perhaps a darker tone would be better. | your **skin tone** (=the colour of your skin) | **in tone** The dried colour is slightly deeper in tone than it appears when first applied. → TWO-TONE

5 ELECTRONIC SOUND [C] a sound made by electronic equipment, such as a telephone: *Please leave a message after the tone.* | **dial tone** *AmE*/**dialling tone** *BrE* (=the sound you hear when you pick up the telephone that lets you know that you can make a call) | **busy tone** *AmE*/**engaged tone** *BrE* (=the sound you hear when you telephone someone but they are already talking to someone else)
6 raise/lower the tone (of sth) to make a place or event more or less socially acceptable, attractive etc: *That horrible building lowers the whole tone of the neighborhood.* | *Trust you to lower the tone of the conversation* (=by making rude remarks etc).
7 BODY [U] *technical* how firm and strong your muscles or skin are: *A regular brisk walk will improve muscle tone.*
8 MUSIC [C] *technical* the difference in PITCH between two musical notes that are separated by one KEY on the piano; ⊟ **step** *AmE*
9 VOICE LEVEL [C] *technical* how high or low your voice is when you produce different sounds: *There is a falling tone on the first syllable and a rising tone on the other.*

tone² *v* [T] also **tone up** to improve the strength and firmness of your muscles, skin etc: *Exercise can strengthen and tone muscles.* | *He began to use weights in order to tone up his body.* | *a well-toned body*
   tone sth ⇔ **down** *phr v* **1** to reduce the effect of something such as a speech or piece of writing, so that people will not be offended: *His advisers told him to tone down his speech.* **2** to make a colour less bright: *Blue can be used to tone down very sunny rooms.*
   tone in *phr v BrE* if one colour or pattern tones in with another, they are similar and look good together: [+with] *Choose candles that will tone in with your tablecloth and china.*
,**tone-'deaf** *adj* unable to hear the difference between different musical notes
'**tone ,language** *n* [C] a language such as Chinese in which the way a sound goes up or down affects the meaning of the word
'**tone·less** /'təʊnləs $ 'toʊn-/ *adj* a toneless voice does not express any feelings: *'I'm sorry,' he said, in a flat toneless voice.*
'**tone ,poem** *n* [C] a piece of music that has been written to represent an idea, place, or story
ton·er /'təʊnə $ 'toʊnər/ *n* [U] **1** a type of ink that is used in machines that print or copy documents **2** a liquid that you put on your face to make your skin feel soft and smooth
tongs /tɒŋz $ tɑːŋz, tɔːŋz/ *n* [plural] a tool that you use to lift up small objects. It has two bars joined at one end, that you press together to lift objects
tongue¹ S3 W3 /tʌŋ/ *n*
1 MOUTH [C] the soft part inside your mouth that you can move about and use for eating and speaking: *Joe ran his tongue over his dry lips.* | *The taste of the chocolate was still on her tongue.* | *The girl scowled at me, then* **stuck out her tongue**.
2 click your tongue to make a sharp noise with your tongue to show that you are annoyed or disappointed: *She clicked her tongue and shook her head.*
3 sharp tongue if you have a sharp tongue, you often talk in a way that shows you are angry: *Gina's sharp tongue will get her into trouble one day.*
4 silver tongue *literary* if you have a silver tongue, you can talk in a way that makes people like you or persuades them that you are right
5 sharp-tongued/silver-tongued etc able to talk in a very angry or pleasant way: *a sharp-tongued young teacher*
6 with (your) tongue in (your) cheek if you say something with your tongue in your cheek, you say it as a joke, not seriously → TONGUE-IN-CHEEK
7 slip of the tongue a small mistake in something you say: *Did I say $100? It must have been a slip of the tongue.*

8 bite your tongue to stop yourself saying something because you know it would not be sensible to say it: *I wanted to argue, but I had to bite my tongue.*
9 Cat got your tongue? also **Lost your tongue?** *spoken* used to ask someone why they are not talking
10 get your tongue around sth *informal* to be able to say a difficult word or phrase: *I couldn't get my tongue around the names of the villages we'd visited.*
11 trip/roll off the tongue *informal* if a name or phrase trips or rolls off your tongue, it is easy or pleasant to say: *Their names trip off the tongue very easily.*
12 loosen sb's tongue *informal* if something such as alcohol loosens your tongue, it makes you talk a lot: *The wine had certainly loosened her tongue.*
13 find your tongue *informal* to say something after you have been silent for a time because you were afraid or shy: *Polly found her tongue at last and told them about the attack.*
14 set tongues wagging to do something that people will talk about in an unkind way: *Angela's divorce will certainly set tongues wagging.*
15 keep a civil tongue in your head *old-fashioned spoken* used to tell someone that they should talk politely to people
16 speak with forked tongue to say things that are not true – used humorously
17 speak in tongues to talk using strange words as part of a religious experience
18 LANGUAGE *literary* a language: *Anton lapsed into his own tongue when he was excited.* | **mother/native tongue** (=the language you learn as a child) *She felt more comfortable talking in her native tongue.*
19 FOOD [U] the tongue of a cow or sheep, cooked and eaten cold
20 SHAPE [C] something that has a long thin shape: [+of] *Huge tongues of fire were licking the side of the building.*
21 SHOE [C] the part of a shoe that lies on top of your foot, under the part where you tie it → see picture at FOOTWEAR → **on the tip of your tongue** at TIP¹ (5); → **hold your tongue** at HOLD¹ (29)
tongue² *v* **1** [I,T] to use your tongue to make separate sounds when playing a musical instrument **2** [T] to touch something with your tongue
,**tongue and 'groove** *adj* tongue and groove boards fit together by pushing a piece that sticks out along the edge of one board into a hollow area along the edge of another board: *tongue and groove floorboards*
'**tongue de,pressor** *n* [C] *AmE* a small flat piece of wood that a doctor uses to hold down your tongue while examining your throat; ⊟ **spatula** *BrE*
,**tongue-in-'cheek** *adj* a tongue-in-cheek remark is said as a joke, not seriously: *I love that kind of tongue-in-cheek wit.* —**tongue-in-cheek** *adv*: *I think he was talking tongue-in-cheek.*
'**tongue-tied** *adj* unable to talk in a relaxed way because you feel nervous or embarrassed: *When adults spoke to her, she became tongue-tied and shy.*
'**tongue ,twister** *n* [C] a word or phrase that is difficult to say quickly
ton·ic /'tɒnɪk $ 'tɑː-/ *n* **1** [C,U] also '**tonic ,water** a clear bitter-tasting drink that you can mix with alcoholic drinks such as GIN or VODKA: *She sat and sipped a gin and tonic.* **2** [C] a drink that you have as a medicine to give you more energy or strength when you feel tired: *A lot of people need a tonic at the end of the winter.* **3** [C usually singular] *BrE* something that makes you feel happy and full of energy: *A weekend by the sea was the perfect tonic.* **4** [C] a liquid that you put on your hair or skin to improve it and make it more healthy: *a herbal skin tonic* **5** [C usually singular] *technical* the first note in a musical SCALE of eight notes

1 000, 2 000, 3 000, most frequent words in S poken and W ritten English

highest possible amount of money you will get: *It'll cost you £200, £250 tops.*
26 TOY a child's toy that spins around on its point when you twist it
27 spin like a top to spin or turn round very quickly: *The impact of the blow sent me spinning like a top.*

top² S1 W1 *adj*
1 HIGHEST [only before noun] nearest to the top of something; **B bottom**: *We have a flat on the top floor of the building.* | *the top button of his shirt* | *I managed to scrape off the top layer of paint.* | *I found the letter in the top drawer of his desk.*
2 BEST [usually before noun] best or most successful: *our top tennis players* | *a top New York salon* | *one of the world's top engineering companies* | *people in top jobs* | *She got top marks.* | *The top score was 72.*
3 WINNING winning in a game or competition: [+of] *Barcelona remain top of the league after beating Real Madrid.* | *Despite losing last night, Manchester United are still top* (=the highest in a list of clubs in a competition).
4 top left/right/centre expressions meaning the picture at the top of a page on the left or right or in the centre, used in magazines and newspapers: *Top right: silk blouse £195 from Harrods.*
5 top speed the fastest speed a vehicle can move at: *We tore down the motorway at top speed.* | *a sports car with a top speed of 140 miles per hour*
6 top priority the thing that you think is most important: *Education is this government's top priority.*
7 GOOD *BrE spoken informal* very good: *Clive's a top bloke.*
8 top copy *BrE* a letter or document from which copies can be made

top³ *v* **topped, topping** [T]
1 BE HIGHER to be higher than a particular amount: *Their profits have reportedly topped £1,000,000 this year.*
2 BE MOST SUCCESSFUL to be in the highest position in a list because you are the most successful: *The Tower of London tops the list of London's most popular tourist attractions.* | *the team that has topped the Premiership for the last three seasons* | *In 1998 the group topped the charts with the song 'Don't Stop Loving Me'.*
3 DO BETTER if you top something, you do something that is better than it: *He topped his previous best performance, coming second in the 100 metres.*
4 top an offer/a bid etc to offer more money than someone else: *A rival company topped our offer by $5 million.*
5 be topped by sth to have something on top: *The roof was topped by a chimney.* | *a hill topped by pine trees*
6 be topped (off) with sth if food is topped with something, it has that thing on it or over the top of it: *a strawberry tart topped with whipped cream* | *The cake can be topped off with fresh fruit.*
7 to top it all *spoken* in addition to other bad things that have happened to you: *To top it all I lost my job.*
8 top that *spoken* used when you are asking someone if they have done something more exciting or successful than you: *Well, I've been asked to appear on a TV show later this year, so top that!*
9 top and tail *BrE* to cut the top and bottom off a piece of fruit or a vegetable
10 top yourself *BrE informal* to kill yourself deliberately
11 REACH THE TOP *literary* if you top a hill, you reach the top of it: *We topped the hill and looked down towards the valley below us.*

top sth ⇔ off *phr v*
to complete something successfully by doing one last thing: *Let's top off the evening with a drink.*

top out *phr v*
if something such as a price that is increasing tops out, it reaches its highest point and stops rising: *Do you think interest rates have topped out now?*

top sth/sb ⇔ up *phr v especially BrE*
1 to add more liquid to a container that is partly full: *I'll just top up the coffee pot.*
2 to put more drink in someone's glass or cup after they have drunk some: *Can I top you up?*
3 to increase the level of something slightly so as to bring it back to the level you want: *He had to do extra jobs at the weekend to top up his income.* → **TOP-UP**

to·paz /'təʊpæz $ 'toʊ-/ *n* [C,U] a transparent yellow stone that is used as a jewel

top 'brass *n* [singular] *informal* people in positions of high rank in a company, or in the army, navy etc: *The top brass are coming in from Washington to see how we do things here.* | *The meeting was attended by top diplomats and military top brass.*

top-'class *adj* of very good quality or a very high standard: *a top-class athlete* | *a top-class restaurant*

top·coat /'tɒpkəʊt $ 'tɑːpkoʊt/ *n* **1** [C,U] the last layer of paint that you put on a surface **2** [C] *old-fashioned* a warm long coat

top 'dog *n* [C] the person who has the most power in a group, especially after a struggle: *He always wanted to be the one in control, the top dog.*

top-'down *adj* [only before noun] *BrE* **1** a top-down way of organizing a business is one in which the most important people make decisions and tell the people below them what they should do: *The company has a top-down management system.* | *a top-down approach to decision-making* **2** a top-down way of understanding or explaining something starts with a general idea and adds details later

top-'drawer *adj* [only before noun] *informal* of the highest quality: *England need to produce a top-drawer performance if they want to win this match.*

top·dress·ing /,tɒp'dresɪŋ $ 'tɑːp,dresɪŋ/ *n* [C,U] *technical* a layer of FERTILIZER that is spread over land so that it will produce better crops

to·pee, topi /'təʊpiː $ toʊ'piː/ *n* [C] a light hard hat that you wear to protect your head from the sun in hot countries

top-'flight *adj* [only before noun] very successful or skilful: *They've hired a really top-flight sales team.*

top 'gear *n* [U] *BrE* **1** the highest GEAR of a car, bus etc: **in top gear** *The car will cruise at 80 mph in top gear.* **2 move/get into top gear** to begin to work with as much effort as possible: *The party's election campaign is now moving into top gear.*

top-'grossing *adj* [only before noun] a top-grossing film earns more money than any other film at a particular time

top 'hat *n* [C] a man's tall black or grey hat, now worn only on formal occasions → see picture at **HAT**

top-'heavy *adj* **1** too heavy at the top and therefore likely to fall over **2** an organization that is top-heavy has too many managers compared to the number of ordinary workers: *The company was burdened by a top-heavy bureaucracy.*

to·pi /'təʊpi $ toʊ'piː/ *n* another spelling of TOPEE

to·pi·a·ry /'təʊpiəri $ 'toʊpieri/ *n* [U] trees and bushes cut into the shapes of birds, animals etc, or the art of cutting them in this way

top·ic W2 /'tɒpɪk $ 'tɑː-/ *n* [C] a subject that people talk or write about: *The environment is a popular topic these days.* | [+of] *We shall return to the topic of education in Chapter 7.* | **topic of conversation/debate etc** *The wedding has been the only topic of conversation for weeks.* | *The main topic for discussion will be the proposed new supermarket.* | *a wide range of topics*

top·i·cal /'tɒpɪkəl $ 'tɑː-/ *adj* a subject that is topical is interesting because it is important at the present time: **topical subject/issue/theme etc** *a new TV comedy dealing with topical issues* | *topical jokes* (=jokes about topical subjects) —**topically** /-kli/ *adv* —**topicality** /,tɒpɪ'kæl̩ti $,tɑː-/ *n* [U]

top·knot /'tɒpnɒt $ 'tɑːpnɑːt/ *n* [C] hair that is tied together on top of your head

top·less /'tɒpləs $ 'tɑːp-/ *adj* if a woman is topless, she is not wearing any clothes on the upper part of her body, so that her breasts are not covered: *topless sunbathing* | **topless bar/show** (=one in which the women serving or performing are topless)

top-'level *adj* [only before noun] involving the most powerful people in a country, organization etc: *top-level meetings between EU leaders*

top·most /'tɒpməʊst $ 'tɑːpmoʊst/ *adj* [only before noun] the topmost part of something is its highest part: *The topmost branches were still bathed in sunlight.*

top-'notch *adj informal* something that is top-notch is of the highest quality or standard: *I was lucky and got myself a job with a top-notch company.*

top-of-the-'range *BrE*; **top-of-the-'line** *AmE adj* a product that is top-of-the-range is the best of its kind: *a top-of-the-range electric guitar*

to·pog·ra·phy /tə'pɒgrəfi $ -'pɑː-/ *n* [U] *technical* **1** the science of describing an area of land, or making maps of it **2** [+ of] the shape of an area of land, including its hills, valleys etc —**topographer** *n* [C] —**topographical** /ˌtɒpə'græfɪkəl◂ $ ˌtɑː-ˌtoʊ-/ *adj*

top·per /'tɒpə $ 'tɑːpər/ *n* [C] *informal* a TOP HAT

top·ping /'tɒpɪŋ $ 'tɑː-/ *n* [C,U] something you put on top of food to make it look nicer or taste better: *a pizza with extra toppings*

top·ple /'tɒpəl $ 'tɑː-/ *v* **1** [I,T] to become unsteady and then fall over, or to make something do this: [+**over**] *A stack of plates swayed, and began to topple over.* **2** [T] to take power away from a leader or government, especially by force; ▣ **overthrow**: *This scandal could topple the government.*

top-'ranking *adj* [only before noun] most powerful and important within an organization: *top-ranking diplomats*

top-'rated *adj* [only before noun] *informal* very popular with the public: *a top-rated TV show*

top round *n* [U] *AmE* high-quality BEEF cut from the upper leg of the cow; ▣ **topside** *BrE*

tops /tɒps $ tɑːps/ *adv spoken informal* **1** at the most: *It should take two hours tops.* **2** the best or most popular: *The store was voted tops for its outstanding facilities for children.*

top-'secret *adj* top-secret documents or information must be kept completely secret: *a top-secret code*

top·side¹ /'tɒpsaɪd $ 'tɑːp-/ *n* [U] *BrE* high quality BEEF cut from the upper leg of the cow; ▣ **top round** *AmE*

topside² also **top·sides** /-saɪdz/ *adv* towards or onto the DECK (=upper surface) of a boat or ship

top·soil /'tɒpsɔɪl $ 'tɑːp-/ *n* [U] the upper level of soil in which most plants have their roots

top·spin /'tɒpˌspɪn $ 'tɑːp-/ *n* [U] the turning movement of a ball that has been hit or thrown in such a way that it spins forward

top·sy-tur·vy /ˌtɒpsi 'tɜːviː $ ˌtɑːpsi 'tɜːrviː/ *adj informal* in a state of complete disorder or confusion: *He left his room all topsy-turvy.*

top 'table *n* [C] *BrE* the table at a formal meal, for example at a wedding, where the most important people sit; ▣ **head table** *AmE*

top-up *n* [C] *BrE* **1** an amount of liquid that you add to a glass, cup etc in order to make it full again: *Would you like a top-up?* **2** an extra payment that brings an amount to the desired level: *top-up loans for students*

top-up card *n* [C] a card that you buy in order to be able to continue using a PAY-AS-YOU-GO mobile phone

tor /tɔː $ tɔːr/ *n* [C] *BrE* a rocky hill

Tor·ah /'tɔːrə/ *n* **the Torah** the traditional writings and principles of Judaism, especially the first five books of the Jewish Bible

torch¹ /tɔːtʃ $ tɔːrtʃ/ *n* [C] **1** *BrE* a small electric lamp that you carry in your hand; ▣ **flashlight** *AmE*:

We shone our torches around the cavern. **2** a long stick with burning material at one end that produces light: *the Olympic torch* **3 carry a torch for sb** *old-fashioned* to secretly love and admire someone

torch² *v* [T] *informal* to deliberately make a building, vehicle etc start to burn: *Rioters torched several abandoned cars.*

torch·light /'tɔːtʃlaɪt $ 'tɔːr-/ *n* [U] **1** *BrE* the light produced by an electric torch **2** the light produced by burning torches: *a torchlight procession*

torch song *n* [C] a sad song about love —**torch singer** *n* [C]

tore /tɔː $ tɔːr/ the past tense of TEAR²

to·re·a·dor /'tɒriədɔː $ 'tɔːriədɔːr, 'tɑː-/ *n* [C] a person who fights BULLS to entertain people in Spain

tor·ment¹ /'tɔːment $ 'tɔːr-/ *n* **1** [U] severe mental or physical suffering: **in torment** *She lay awake all night in torment.* **2** [C] someone or something that makes you suffer a lot: *The journey must have been a torment for them.*

tor·ment² /tɔː'ment $ tɔːr-/ *v* [T] **1** to make someone suffer a lot, especially mentally: *Seth was tormented by feelings of guilt.* **2** to deliberately treat someone cruelly by annoying them or hurting them; ▣ **torture**: *The older boys would torment him whenever they had the chance.* —**tormentor** *n* [C]

torn /tɔːn $ tɔːrn/ the past participle of TEAR²

tor·na·do /tɔː'neɪdəʊ $ tɔːr'neɪdoʊ/ *n plural* **tornadoes** *or* **tornados** [C] an extremely violent storm consisting of air that spins very quickly and causes a lot of damage; → **hurricane, cyclone**

tor·pe·do¹ /tɔː'piːdəʊ $ tɔːr'piːdoʊ/ *n plural* **torpedoes** [C] a long narrow weapon that is fired under the surface of the sea and explodes when it hits something

torpedo² *v* [T] **1** to attack or destroy a ship with a torpedo **2** to stop something such as a plan from succeeding: *New threats of violence have effectively torpedoed the peace talks.*

tor·pid /'tɔːpɪd $ 'tɔːr-/ *adj formal* not active because you are lazy or sleepy: *a torpid mind*

tor·por /'tɔːpə $ 'tɔːrpər/ *n* [singular, U] *formal* a state of being not active because you are lazy or sleepy: *She tried to rouse him from the torpor into which he had sunk.*

torque /tɔːk $ tɔːrk/ *n* [U] *technical* the force or power that makes something turn around a central point, especially in an engine

tor·rent /'tɒrənt $ 'tɔː-, 'tɑː-/ *n* [C] **1** a large amount of water moving very quickly and strongly in a particular direction; → **flood**: *After five days of heavy rain the Telle river was a raging torrent* (=a very violent torrent). | **in torrents** *The rain came down in torrents.* **2 a torrent of sth** a lot of words spoken quickly, especially in order to insult or criticize someone: *When I asked him to move, he unleashed a torrent of abuse.* | **a torrent of Greek/Italian etc** *The woman poured out a torrent of Italian.*

tor·ren·tial /tə'renʃəl, tɒ- $ tɔː-/ *adj* **torrential rain** very heavy rain

tor·rid /'tɒrɪd $ 'tɔː-, 'tɑː-/ *adj* **1** involving strong emotions, especially of sexual love: *a torrid love affair* **2** *literary* torrid weather is very hot: *the torrid desert sun* **3** *BrE* a torrid time is a very difficult one: *He had a torrid time out there on the racetrack.*

tor·sion /'tɔːʃən $ 'tɔːr-/ *n* [U] *technical* the twisting of a piece of metal

tor·so /'tɔːsəʊ $ 'tɔːrsoʊ/ *n plural* **torsos** [C] **1** your body, not including your head, arms, or legs: *the torso of a woman* **2** a STATUE of a torso

tort /tɔːt $ tɔːrt/ *n* [C,U] *law* an action that is wrong but not criminal and can be dealt with in a CIVIL court of law

tor·til·la /tɔːˈtiːjə $ tɔːr-/ *n* [C] a type of thin flat Mexican bread made from corn or wheat flour

torˈtilla ˌchip *n* [C] a small hard flat piece of food made from corn, similar to a CRISP

tor·toise /ˈtɔːtəs $ ˈtɔːr-/ *n* [C] a slow-moving land animal that can pull its head and legs into the hard round shell that covers its body; → **turtle**; → see picture at REPTILE

tor·toise·shell /ˈtɔːtəsʃel, ˈtɔːtəʃel $ ˈtɔːr-/ *n* **1** [U] a hard shiny brown and white material made from the shell of a tortoise **2** [C] a cat that has yellow, brown, and black marks on its fur **3** [C] a BUTTERFLY that has brown and orange wings

tor·tu·ous /ˈtɔːtʃuəs $ ˈtɔːr-/ *adj* **1** a tortuous path, stream, road etc has a lot of bends in it and is therefore difficult to travel along: *a tortuous path over the mountains to Kandahar* **2** complicated and long and therefore confusing: *The book begins with a long, tortuous introduction.* —**tortuously** *adv*

tor·ture¹ /ˈtɔːtʃə $ ˈtɔːrtʃər/ *n* [C,U] **1** an act of deliberately hurting someone in order to force them to tell you something, to punish them, or to be cruel: *He died after five days of excruciating torture.* **2** severe physical or mental suffering: *The waiting must be torture for you.*

torture² *v* [T] **1** to deliberately hurt someone in order to force them to give you information, to punish them, or to be cruel: *Political opponents of the regime may be tortured.* **2** if a feeling or knowledge tortures you, it makes you suffer a lot mentally: *Rachel sat alone for hours at home, tortured by jealousy.* —**torturer** *n* [C]

tor·tur·ous /ˈtɔːtʃərəs $ ˈtɔːr-/ *adj* very painful or unpleasant to experience: *a torturous five days of fitness testing*

To·ry /ˈtɔːri/ *n plural* **Tories** [C] a member of the British Conservative Party: *a lifelong Tory* —**Tory** *adj* [only before noun]: *Tory principles*

ˈTory ˌParty *n* the Tory Party another name for the British Conservative Party

tosh /tɒʃ $ tɑːʃ/ *n* [U] BrE informal nonsense: *What a load of old tosh!*

toss¹ /tɒs $ tɔːs/ *v* **1** [T] to throw something, especially something light, with a quick gentle movement of your hand: **toss sth into/onto etc sth** *She crumpled the letter and tossed it into the fire.* | **toss sth aside/over etc** *Toss that book over, will you?* | **toss sth to sb** *'Catch!' said Sandra, tossing her bag to him.* | **toss sb sth** *Frank tossed her the newspaper.* **2** [I,T] to move about continuously in a violent or uncontrolled way, or to make something do this: **toss sth around/about** *The small boat was tossed about like a cork.* **3 toss and turn** to keep changing your position in bed because you cannot sleep: *I've been tossing and turning all night.* **4** also **toss up** [I,T] especially BrE to throw a coin in the air, so that a decision will be made according to the side that faces upwards when it comes down; ◘ **flip** AmE: *They tossed a coin to decide who would go first.* | **toss (sb) for it** *We couldn't make up our minds, so we decided to toss for it.* **5** [T] to throw something up into the air and let it fall to the ground: *The crowd cheered, banging pots and tossing confetti into the air.* **6 toss a pancake** BrE to throw a PANCAKE upwards so that it turns over in the air and lands on the side that you want to cook; ◘ **flip** AmE **7** [T] to move pieces of food about in a small amount of liquid so that they become covered with the liquid: *Toss the carrots in some butter before serving.* **8 toss your head/hair** *written* to move your head or hair back suddenly, often with a shaking movement showing anger: *He tossed his head angrily and left the room.*

toss off *phr v* **1 toss sth** ⇔ **off** to produce something quickly and without much effort: *one of those painters who can toss off a couple of pictures before breakfast* **2 toss sth** ⇔ **off** *written* to drink something quickly: *He tossed off a few whiskies.* **3 toss (sb) off** BrE informal not polite to MASTURBATE

toss sth/sb ⇔ **out** *phr v* AmE informal **1** to get rid of something that you do not want: *I tossed most of that stuff out when we moved.* **2** to make someone leave a place, especially because of bad behaviour: [+of] *Kurt was tossed out of the club for trying to start a fight.*

toss² *n* [C] **1** the act of throwing a coin in the air to decide something, especially who will do something first in a game: *The toss of a coin decided who would go first.* | **win/lose the toss** *Malory won the toss and will serve.* **2** a sudden backwards movement of your head, so that your hair moves, often showing anger: *'I'll see,' the nurse said, with an officious toss of her head.* **3** a gentle throw **4 not give a toss** BrE spoken to not care about something at all: *I really couldn't give a toss what Sam thinks.* → **argue the toss** at ARGUE (5)

toss·er /ˈtɒsə $ ˈtɔːsər/ *n* [C] BrE spoken not polite an offensive word for someone who you think is stupid or unpleasant

ˈtoss-up *n* **1 it's a toss-up** spoken used when you do not know which of two things will happen, or which of two things to choose: *I don't know who'll get the job – it's a toss-up between Carl and Steve.* **2** [C usually singular] BrE an act of tossing a coin in order to decide something

tot¹ /tɒt $ tɑːt/ *n* [C] **1** informal a very small child **2** especially BrE a small amount of a strong alcoholic drink: [+of] *a tot of rum*

tot² *v* **totted, totting** BrE
tot sth ⇔ **up** *phr v* informal to add together numbers or amounts of money in order to find the total: *The waiter quickly totted up the bill.*

to·tal¹ [S1] [W1] /ˈtəʊtl $ ˈtoʊ-/ *adj*
1 [usually before noun] complete, or as great as is possible: **total failure/disaster** *The sales campaign was a total disaster.* | a **total ban** on cigarette advertising | *He looked at her with a **total lack** of comprehension.* | *a sport that demands **total commitment***
2 total number/amount/cost etc the number, amount etc that is the total: *total sales of 200,000 per year* | *Her total income was £10,000 a year.*

total² [S2] [W2] *n* [C]
1 the final number or amount of things, people etc when everything has been counted: *That's £7 and £3.50, so the total is £10.50.* | **a total of 20/100 etc** *A total of thirteen meetings were held to discuss the issue.* | **in total** *There were probably about 40 people there in total.* | **the sum total** (=the whole of an amount when everything is considered together)
2 grand total a) the final total, including all the totals added together; → **subtotal b)** used humorously when you think the final total is small: *I earned a grand total of $4.15.*

total³ *v* **totalled, totalling** BrE, **totaled, totaling** AmE **1** [linking verb, T] to reach a particular total: *The group had losses totalling $3 million this year.* **2** [T] informal especially AmE to damage a car so badly that it cannot be repaired: *Chuck totaled his dad's new Toyota.*
total sth ⇔ **up** *phr v* to find the total number or total amount of something by adding: *At the end of the game, total up everyone's score to see who has won.*

to·tal·i·tar·i·an /təʊˌtælɪˈteəriən $ toʊˌtælɪˈter-/ *adj* based on a political system in which ordinary people have no power and are completely controlled by the government: **a totalitarian state/regime** —**totalitarianism** *n* [U]

to·tal·i·ty /təʊˈtælɪti $ toʊ-/ *n* [U] formal **1** the whole of something: **in sth's totality** *It's essential that we look at the problem in its totality.* **2** a total amount

tot·al·ly [S1] [W2] /ˈtəʊtl-i $ ˈtoʊ-/ *adv* [+ adj/adv] completely: *That's a **totally different** matter.* | *It's like learning a **totally new** language.* | **totally unacceptable/unnecessary/unsuitable etc** *Terrorism is totally unacceptable in a civilised world.* | *I totally agree.*

Tote /təʊt $ toʊt/ *n* the Tote a system in Britain in which a machine adds together the amounts of money

BET on a horse race and divides the total among the people who bet on the winner

tote also **tote around** v [T] *informal especially AmE* to carry something, especially regularly: *Kids have to tote heavy textbooks around.*

'tote bag n [C] *AmE* a large bag for carrying things

to·tem /'təʊtəm $ 'toʊ-/ n [C] an animal, plant etc that is thought to have a special SPIRITUAL connection with a particular tribe, especially in North America, or a figure made to look like the animal etc —**totemic** /təʊ'temɪk $ toʊ-/ adj

'totem pole n [C] **1** a tall wooden pole with one or more totems cut or painted on it, made by the Native Americans of northwest North America **2 low man on the totem pole** *AmE* someone of low rank in an organization or business

to·to /'təʊtəʊ $ 'toʊtoʊ/ → IN TOTO

tot·ter /'tɒtə $ 'tɑːtər/ v [I] **1** to walk or move unsteadily from side to side as if you are going to fall over: *Lorrimer swayed a little, tottered, and fell.* **2** if a political system or organization totters, it becomes less strong and is likely to stop working

tot·ty /'tɒti $ 'tɑːti/ n [U] *BrE informal not polite* an offensive word used by men to refer to women who they think are sexually attractive

tou·can /'tuːkən, -kæn/ n [C] a tropical American bird with bright feathers and a very large beak

touch¹ S2 W2 /tʌtʃ/ v

1 FEEL [T] to put your hand, finger etc on someone or something: *She reached out to touch his arm.* | *If your house has been burgled, you shouldn't touch anything until the police arrive.* | *'Don't touch me!' she yelled.* | **touch sb on the arm/leg etc** *A hand touched her on the shoulder.*

2 NO SPACE BETWEEN [I,T] if two things touch, or one thing touches another thing, they reach each other so that there is no space between them: *As our glasses touched, he said 'Cheers!'* | *Her dress was so long that it was touching the ground.*

3 touch sth to sth *literary* to move something so that it reaches something else with no space between the two things: *She touched the handkerchief to her nose.* | *He touched his lips to her hair.*

4 AFFECT SB'S FEELINGS [T] to affect someone's emotions, especially by making them feel sympathy or sadness: *Her plight has **touched the hearts** of people around the world.* | *She could sense his concern and it touched her.* → TOUCHED, TOUCHING¹

5 HAVE AN EFFECT [T] to have an effect on someone or something, especially by changing or influencing them: *He has touched the lives of many people.* | *Unemployment remains an evil that touches the whole community.* | *He **was** often **touched by** doubt* (=doubt affected him).

6 USE [T usually in negatives] to use or handle something: *The law doesn't allow him to touch any of the money.* | *It's a long time since I've touched a piano.*

7 not touch sth **a)** to not eat or drink something: *What's wrong? You've hardly touched your food.* | *My grandfather was an alcoholic but I **never touch the stuff*** (=never drink alcohol). **b)** to not deal with something that you should deal with: *I brought home loads of work, but I haven't touched any of it yet.*

8 not touch sb/sth to not hurt someone or not damage something: *The older boys swore they hadn't touched the child.* | *Parma had not been touched.*

9 DEAL WITH SB/STH [T] to become involved with or deal with a particular problem, situation, or person: *He was the only lawyer who would touch the case.* | *Everything he touches turns to disaster.* | *No school would touch a teacher who had been convicted of assault.*

10 REACH AN AMOUNT [T] *especially BrE* to reach a particular amount or level: *At the time, the unemployment rate was touching 10 percent and rising.*

11 HIT/KICK [T] *BrE* to gently hit or kick a ball – used

especially in reports of sports games: *Evans was just able to touch the ball away from Wilkinson.*

12 not touch sth/sb (with a bargepole) *BrE*; **not touch sth/sb with a ten-foot pole** *AmE* used to say that you think someone or something is bad and people should not be involved with them: *I wouldn't touch him with a bargepole.* | *Financial analysts have warned investors not to touch these offers with a ten-foot pole.*

13 be touched with sth *literary* to have a small amount of a particular quality: *His voice was touched with the faintest of Italian accents.* | *Her nails had been manicured and lightly touched with colour.*

14 EXPRESSION [T] if an expression such as a smile touches your face, your face has that expression for a short time: *A smile touched her lips.*

15 RELATE TO STH [T] to be about or to deal with a particular subject, situation, or problem: *Though the question touched a new vein, Nelson answered promptly.* | *The discourse touches many of the issues which are currently popular.*

16 LIGHT [T] *literary* if light touches something, it shines on it: *The sun was just touching the tops of the mountains.*

17 nothing/no one can touch sb/sth used for saying that nothing or no one is as good as a particular person or thing: *He describes the events with a passion that no other writer can touch.*

18 touch base (with sb) to talk to someone in order to find out how they are or what is happening: *I just wanted to touch base and make sure you hadn't changed your mind about seeing me.*

19 touch bottom **a)** to reach the ground at the bottom of a sea, river etc: *He swam down but could not touch bottom.* **b)** to reach the lowest level or worst condition: *The housing market has touched bottom.* → **touch a (raw) nerve** at NERVE¹ (6); → **touch wood** at WOOD (3)

touch down phr v
1 when an aircraft touches down, it lands on the ground: *The plane finally touched down at Heathrow airport around midday.*
2 in the sport of RUGBY, to score by putting the ball on the ground behind the other team's GOAL LINE

touch sb for sth phr v *BrE informal*
to persuade someone to give or lend you something, especially money: *He tried to touch me for the taxi fare home.*

touch sth ⇔ off phr v
to cause a difficult situation or violent events to begin: *It was these national rivalries that eventually touched off the First World War.*

touch on/upon sth phr v
to mention a particular subject when talking or writing: *The report touches on the relationship between poverty and poor health.* | *These issues were touched on in Chapter 2.*

touch sb/sth ⇔ up phr v
1 to improve something by changing it slightly or adding a little more to it: *She quickly touched up her lipstick.* | *The photograph had obviously been touched up.* | *The speech he finally gave had been touched up by his staff.*
2 *BrE informal* to touch someone in a sexual way when they do not want you to: *He was accused of touching up one of his students.*

touch² S2 W2 n
1 TOUCHING SB/STH [C usually singular] the action of putting your hand, finger, or another part of your body on something or someone: *She felt a gentle touch on her shoulder.* | [+of] *He remembered the touch of her fingers on his face.*
2 ABILITY TO FEEL THINGS [U] the sense that you use to discover what something feels like, by putting your hand or fingers on it: *the **sense of touch*** | **by touch** *Visually impaired people orient themselves by touch.* | *Bake the cake for 30 minutes until risen and firm **to the touch**.*

T

3 in touch (with sb) talking or writing to someone: *We'll get in touch* (=start talking or writing to you) *as soon as we know the results of the test.* | *Can I have your phone number in case I need to get in touch with you?* | *Bye. I'll be in touch.* | *Are you still in touch with John* (=are you talking to him regularly)? | *I'm in close touch with Anna.* | **stay/keep in touch** (=keep writing or talking, even though you do not see each other often) *Anyway, we must stay in touch.* | *I met him when I worked in Madrid, and I've kept in touch with him ever since.* | *I lost touch with* (=stopped writing or talking to) *Julie after we moved.* | *I can put you in touch with a local photography club* (=give you their address or phone number so you can talk to them).

4 be/keep/stay etc in touch (with sth) to have the latest information or knowledge about something: *A regular newsletter keeps people in touch with local events.* | *The speech was good and you felt he was in touch with people's needs.* | *Rescuers were kept in touch through radio links.* | *A head-teacher needs to remain in close touch with teachers' everyday concerns.*

5 be out of touch a) also **lose touch (with sth)** to not have the latest knowledge about a subject, situation, or the way people feel: [+with] *I'm out of touch with modern medicine.* | *The party cannot afford to lose touch with political reality.* **b)** to not know much about modern life: *Judges are often accused of being out of touch.*

6 get in touch with sth *especially AmE* to realize and understand something such as your feelings and attitudes: *The first stage is to get in touch with your perceptions and accept responsibility for your relationships.*

7 DETAIL/ADDITION [C] a small detail that improves or completes something: **put the final/finishing touches to sth** *Emma was putting the finishing touches to the cake.* | *There was a vase of flowers in the room, which was a nice touch.* | *Brass pans added a decorative touch to the plain brick wall.*

8 WAY OF DOING STH [C] a particular way of doing something, or the ability to do it in a particular way: *The room was decorated with a very artistic touch.* | *Our staff combine efficient service with a personal touch* (=they do things in a friendly way). | *The feminine touch was evident throughout the house.* | *His sure touch* (=confident way of doing things) *and attention to detail are just as evident now.* | *Barbara has a magic touch in the garden* (=she grows things very well). | *King obviously hasn't lost his touch* (=lost his ability) - *his latest book sold in the millions.*

9 a touch of sth a small amount of something: *Our furniture is guaranteed to add a touch of class to your bedroom.* | *Add a lace top for a touch of glamour.* | *'What?' asked Hazel, with a touch of irritation.*

10 a touch disappointed/faster/impatient etc slightly disappointed, faster etc: *He sounded a touch upset when I spoke to him on the phone.*

11 with/at the touch of a button/key used to emphasize that something can be done very easily by pressing a button: *This card allows you to access your money at the touch of a button.* | *You can get all the latest information with the touch of a button.*

12 a soft/easy touch *informal* if someone is a soft or an easy touch, you can easily persuade them to do what you want, especially give you money

13 WAY STH FEELS [C usually singular] the way that something feels and the effect it has on your skin: *the warm touch of his lips*

14 SOCCER/RUGBY [U] the area outside the lines that mark the playing area: **into touch** *The ball rolled into touch.* → **common touch** at COMMON¹ (13); → **a/the human touch** at HUMAN¹ (5); → **kick sth into touch** at KICK¹ (11); → **lose your touch** at LOSE (1); → **magic touch** at MAGIC² (5); → **MIDAS TOUCH**; → **a soft touch** at SOFT (17)

touch-and-'go *adj informal* it's **touch-and-go** used about a situation in which there is a serious risk that something bad could happen: *It was touch-and-go whether the doctor would get there on time.*

touch·down /'tʌtʃdaʊn/ *n* [C] **1** the moment at which a plane or spacecraft lands **2** an act of putting the ball down on the ground behind the opposing team's GOAL LINE in RUGBY **3** an act of moving the ball across the opposing team's GOAL LINE in American football

tou·ché /'tuːʃeɪ $ tuːˈʃeɪ/ *interjection* used to emphasize in a humorous way that someone has made a very good point during an argument

touched /tʌtʃt/ *adj* [not before noun] **1** feeling happy and grateful because of what someone has done: [+by] *We were deeply touched by their present.* | **touched that** *Cathryn was touched that Sarah had come to see her off.* → TOUCH¹ (4) **2** *informal* slightly crazy

'touch ,football *n* [U] *AmE* a type of American football in which you touch the person with the ball instead of TACKLING them

touch·ing¹ /'tʌtʃɪŋ/ *adj* making you feel pity, sympathy, sadness etc: *a touching reunion of father and son* —**touchingly** *adv* → TOUCH¹ (4)

touching² *prep formal* concerning: *matters touching the conduct of diplomacy*

touch·line /'tʌtʃlaɪn/ *n* [C] one of the two lines that mark the longer sides of a sports playing area, especially in football

touch·pa·per /'tʌtʃˌpeɪpə $ -ər/ *n* [C] *BrE* a piece of special paper that burns slowly, used in order to light a FIREWORK burning: *Light the blue touchpaper, then move to a safe distance.*

'touch screen *n* [C] a type of computer screen that you touch in order to tell the computer what to do or to get information

touch·stone /'tʌtʃstəʊn $ -stoʊn/ *n* [C] something used as a test or standard: [+of] *Pupil behaviour was seen as 'the touchstone of quality' of the school system.*

'Touch-Tone ,phone *n* [C] *trademark* a telephone that produces different sounds when different buttons are pushed

'touch-type *v* [I] to use a TYPEWRITER or a computer KEYBOARD without having to look at the letters while you are using it

touch·y /'tʌtʃi/ *adj* **1** easily becoming offended or annoyed: [+about] *She is very touchy about her past.* **2 touchy subject/question etc** a subject etc that needs to be dealt with very carefully, especially because it may offend people: *Asking about a reporter's sources can be a touchy business.* —**touchiness** *n* [U]

,touchy-'feely *adj* too concerned with feelings and emotions, rather than with facts or actions: *a touchy-feely drama*

tough¹ S2 W3 /tʌf/ *adj comparative* **tougher**, *superlative* **toughest**

1 DIFFICULT difficult to do or deal with: *It was a tough race.* | *She's had a tough life.* | *The company admitted that it had been a tough year.* | *Tough decisions will have to be made.* | *The reporters were asking a lot of tough questions.* | **have a tough time (of it)** (=face a lot of difficult problems) *The family has had a tough time of it these last few months.* | **it's tough doing sth** *It's tough being married to a cop.* | **be tough on sb** (=cause problems for someone or make their life difficult) *Having to stay indoors all day is tough on a kid.* | **It was a tough call** (=a difficult decision), *but we had to cancel the game because of the weather.* | *I find his books pretty tough going* (=difficult to read). | *Gage predicted the president's proposal would be a tough sell* (=something that is difficult to persuade someone about) *before Congress. AmE* | **when the going gets tough (the tough get going)** *informal* (=used to say that when a situation becomes difficult, strong people take the necessary action to deal with it)

2 STRONG PERSON physically or emotionally strong and able to deal with difficult situations: *The men who work on the oil rigs are a tough bunch.* | **tough cookie/**

customer *informal* (=someone who is very determined to do what they want and not what other people want) | **as tough as nails/as tough as old boots** (=very tough) *He's as tough as nails – a good man to have on the team.*
3 STRONG MATERIAL not easily broken or made weaker: *tough, durable plastic | a very tough, hard-wearing cloth*
4 STRICT/FIRM very strict or firm: [+on/with] *My mother was very tough on my sister. | It's time to get tough with drunk drivers. | The EU is taking a tough line with the UK over this issue.*
5 VIOLENT AREA a tough part of a town has a lot of crime or violence: **tough neighborhood/area/part of town etc** *a tough area of Chicago*
6 tough!/that's tough! *spoken* used when you do not have any sympathy with someone: *'I'm getting wet.' 'Tough! You should've brought your umbrella.' | She didn't tell us she was coming, so if this screws up her plans that's just tough.*
7 tough luck! *spoken* **a)** used when you do not have any sympathy for someone's problems: *Well, that's just their tough luck! It was their mistake.* **b)** *BrE* used when you feel sympathy about something bad that has happened to someone: *You didn't get the job? Oh, tough luck!*
8 tough shit! *spoken not polite* used when you do not have any sympathy for someone's problems
9 VIOLENT PERSON likely to behave violently and having no gentle qualities: *one of football's most notorious tough guys | tough young thugs looking for trouble*
10 FOOD difficult to cut or eat; ⊟ **tender**: *The meat was tough and hard to chew. | the tough outer leaves of the cabbage*
11 tough love a way of helping someone to change their behaviour by treating them in a kind but strict way —**toughly** *adv* —**toughness** *n* [U]

tough² *v*
tough sth ⇔ **out** *phr v* to deal with a difficult situation by being determined, rather than leaving or changing your decision: *She told herself to be brave and tough it out.*

tough³ *n* [C] *old-fashioned* someone who often behaves in a violent way

tough⁴ *adv* in a way that shows you are very determined: *Washington played tough in the second half of the game. | You're talking tough now but you wait until you get into the interview.*

tough·en /ˈtʌfən/ also **toughen up** *v* [I,T] to become tougher, or to make someone or something tougher: *toughened glass | Three years in the army toughened him up.*

tou·pée /ˈtuːpeɪ $ tuːˈpeɪ/ *n* [C] a small artificial piece of hair that some men wear over a place on their heads where the hair no longer grows

tour¹ W2 /tʊə $ tʊr/ *n* [C]
1 a journey for pleasure, during which you visit several different towns, areas etc: [+of/around/round] *a 10-day tour of China | a walking/cycling/sightseeing etc tour a cycling tour of Cornwall | We met on a coach tour in Italy.* → **PACKAGE TOUR**
2 a short trip through a place to see it: [+of/around/round] *a guided tour around the Kennedy Space Center | Kim worked as a tour guide in Cambridge last summer.*
3 a planned journey made by musicians, a sports team etc in order to perform or play in several places: [+of] *the England cricket team's tour of India | on tour The Moscow Symphony Orchestra is here on tour. | the first leg of the band's European tour* (=the first part of it)
4 a period during which you go to live somewhere, usually abroad, to do your job, especially military work: *his third tour in Northern Ireland*
5 tour of inspection an official visit to a place, institution, group etc in order to check its quality or performance

tour² *v* **1** [I,T] to visit several parts of a country or area: *We're touring the Greek islands this summer.* **2** [T] to go round or be shown round a place: *The minister had been invited to tour the new factory.*

tour de force /ˌtʊə də ˈfɔːs $ ˌtʊr də ˈfɔːrs/ *n* [singular] *written* something that is done very skilfully and successfully, and is very impressive: *His speech to the Democratic Convention was a tour de force.*

tour·is·m /ˈtʊərɪzəm $ ˈtʊr-/ *n* [U] the business of providing things for people to do, places for them to stay etc while they are on holiday: *The country depends on tourism for much of its income.*

tour·ist W3 /ˈtʊərɪ̯st $ ˈtʊr-/ *n* [C] someone who is travelling or visiting a place for pleasure; → **traveller**: *Cambridge is always full of tourists in the summer. | The Statue of Liberty is a major tourist attraction. | What effect will this have on the local tourist industry? |* **tourist centre/destination/resort etc** *Durham, with its cathedral and castle, is a popular tourist centre.*

'tourist class *n* [U] the cheapest standard of travelling conditions on a plane, ship etc —**tourist class** *adv*

'tourist ˌoffice also **ˌtourist inforˈmation ˌoffice** *n* [C] an office that gives information to tourists in an area

'tourist ˌtrap *n* [C] a place that many tourists visit, but where drinks, hotels etc are more expensive – used to show disapproval

tour·ist·y /ˈtʊərɪ̯sti $ ˈtʊr-/ *adj informal* **1** a place that is touristy is full of tourists and the things that attract tourists – used to show disapproval: *Benidorm is too touristy for me.* **2** a touristy activity is typical of the things that tourists do – used to show disapproval: *We did all the usual touristy things.*

tour·na·ment /ˈtʊənəmənt, ˈtɔː- $ ˈtɜːr-, ˈtʊr-/ *n* [C] **1** a competition in which players compete against each other in a series of games until there is one winner: *I feel I can win this tournament. |* **tennis/chess/badminton etc tournament** **2** a competition to show courage and fighting skill between soldiers in the Middle Ages

tour·ney /ˈtʊəni, ˈtɔː- $ ˈtɜːr-, ˈtɔːr-/ *n* [C] *AmE informal* a TOURNAMENT

tour·ni·quet /ˈtʊənɪkeɪ, ˈtɔː- $ ˈtɜːrnɪkɪ̯t, ˈtʊr-/ *n* [C] a band of cloth that is twisted tightly around an injured arm or leg to stop it bleeding

ˌtour of ˈduty *n plural* **tours of duty** [C] a period of time when you are working in a particular place or job, especially abroad when you are in the army etc

'tour ˌoperator *n* [C] *BrE* a company that arranges travel tours

tou·sle /ˈtaʊzəl/ *v* [T] to make someone's hair look untidy

tou·sled /ˈtaʊzəld/ *adj* tousled hair or a tousled appearance looks untidy: *She had just awakened, her eyes sleepy and her hair tousled. | A small tousled head appeared in the doorway.*

tout¹ /taʊt/ *v* **1** [T] to praise something or someone in order to persuade people that they are important or worth a lot: *his much touted musical |* **be touted as sth** *Nell is being touted as the next big thing in Hollywood.* **2** [I,T] *especially BrE* to try to persuade people to buy goods or services you are offering: **tout for business/custom** *BrE* (=look for customers) *Minicab drivers are not allowed to tout for business.* **3** [I,T] *AmE* to give someone information about a horse in a race

tout² also **ticket tout** *n* [C] *BrE* someone who buys tickets for a concert, sports match etc and sells them at a higher price, usually on the street near a sports ground, theatre etc; ⊟ **scalper** *AmE*

1 000, 2 000, 3 000, most frequent words in S poken and W ritten English

tow¹ /təʊ $ toʊ/ v [T] to pull a vehicle or ship along behind another vehicle, using a rope or chain: *The ship had to be towed into the harbor.* | **tow sth away** *Our car had been towed away*

tow² n **1** [C] an act of pulling a vehicle behind another vehicle, using a rope or chain: *Can you give us a tow to the garage?* **2 in tow** *informal* following closely behind someone or something: *Hannah arrived with her four kids in tow.* | *He turned up at my office with two lawyers in tow.* **3 take sth in tow** to connect a rope or a chain to a vehicle or ship so that it can be towed **4 under/on tow** *BrE* if a ship is under tow or a car is on tow, it is being pulled along by another vehicle

to·wards S1 W1 /təˈwɔːdz $ tɔːrdz, twɔːrdz/ *especially BrE*, **to·ward** /təˈwɔːd $ tɔːrd, twɔːrd/ *especially AmE* prep

1 DIRECTION used to say that someone or something moves, looks, faces etc in the direction of someone or something: *He noticed two policemen coming towards him.* | *All the windows face toward the river.* | *He was standing with his back towards me.*

2 PRODUCING A RESULT in a process that will produce a particular result: *These negotiations are the first step toward reaching an agreement.* | *The crisis continued as Britain drifted towards war.*

3 FEELING/ATTITUDE your feeling, attitude, or behaviour towards someone or something is how you feel or think about them or how you treat them: *Brian's attitude towards his work has always been very positive.* | *Her parents had been more sympathetic towards her.*

4 HELP PAY FOR money put, saved, or given towards something is used to pay for it: *The money collected will be put towards repairing the church roof.*

5 BEFORE just before a particular time: *Toward the end of the afternoon it began to rain.*

6 NEAR near a particular place: *Uncle Dick and Aunt Mavis live at High Burnton out towards the coast.*

tow·a·way zone /ˈtəʊəweɪ ˌzəʊn $ ˈtoʊəweɪ ˌzoʊn/ n [C] *AmE* an area where cars are not allowed to park, and from which they can be taken away by the police

tow·bar /ˈtəʊbɑː $ ˈtoʊbɑːr/ n [C] *BrE* a metal bar on the back of a car for TOWING a CARAVAN or boat

tow·el¹ /ˈtaʊəl/ n [C] a piece of cloth that you use for drying your skin or for drying things such as dishes: *Have you got a clean towel I could use?* | **bath/beach/kitchen towel** *She dried her hands on the kitchen towel.*
→ PAPER TOWEL, SANITARY PAD, TEA TOWEL; → **throw in the towel** at THROW IN (3)

towel² also **towel down/off** v **towelled, towelling** *BrE*, **toweled, toweling** *AmE* [T] to dry yourself using a towel: *He stood in the doorway, towelling his hair dry.* → TOWELLING

tow·el·ling /ˈtaʊəlɪŋ/ n [U] *BrE* thick soft cloth, used especially for making towels or BATHROBES; **⊟ terrycloth** *AmE*: *a towelling robe*

'towel rail also **'towel rack** *AmE* n [C] a bar or frame on which towels can be hung, especially in a bathroom

tow·er¹ S3 W3 /ˈtaʊə $ -ər/ n [C]

1 a tall narrow building either built on its own or forming part of a castle, church etc: *the Eiffel Tower* | *a castle with tall towers* | **bell/clock tower** *The bell tower was added to the church in 1848.* | [+of] *the leaning tower of Pisa*

2 a tall structure, often made of metal, used for signalling, broadcasting etc: *an air traffic control tower*

3 tower of strength someone who gives you a lot of help, sympathy, and support when you are in trouble: *Her father was a tower of strength to her when her marriage broke up.*

4 a tall piece of furniture that you use to store things: *a CD tower* → COOLING TOWER, IVORY TOWER, WATER TOWER

tower² v [I] **1** to be much taller than the people or things around you: [+above/over] *He towered over his*

mother. **2** to be much better than any other person or organization that does the same thing as you: [+above/over] *Mozart towers over all other composers.*

'tower block n [C] *BrE* a tall building containing apartments or offices; **⊟ high-rise** *AmE*

tow·er·ing /ˈtaʊərɪŋ/ adj [only before noun] **1** very tall: *great towering cliffs* **2** much better than other people of the same kind; **⊟ outstanding**: *a towering genius of his time* **3** in a towering rage very angry

tow·line /ˈtəʊlaɪn $ ˈtoʊ-/ n [C] a TOWROPE

town S1 W1 /taʊn/ n

1 PLACE [C] a large area with houses, shops, offices etc where people live and work, that is smaller than a city and larger than a village: *an industrial town in the Midlands* | [+of] *the town of Norwalk, Connecticut* | *I walked to the nearest town.* | *He was buried in his home town* (=the town where he was born).

2 MAIN CENTRE [U] the business or shopping centre of a town: *We're going into town tonight to see a film.* | *They have a small apartment in town.*

3 PEOPLE [singular] all the people who live in a particular town: *The whole town turned out to watch the procession.*

4 WHERE YOU LIVE [U] the town or city where you live: *Cam left town about an hour ago, so he should be out at the farm by now.* | *I'll be out of town for about a week.* | *Guess who's in town? Jodie's sister!* | *Do you know of a good place to eat? I'm from out of town* (=from a different town). | *We're moving to another part of town.*

5 VILLAGE [C] *AmE* several houses forming a small group around a church, shops etc; **⊟ village** *BrE*: *Rowayton is a small town of around 4000 people.*

6 NOT COUNTRY the town life in towns and cities in general: *Which do you prefer, the town or the country?*

7 go to town (on sth) *informal* to do something in a very eager or thorough way: *Angela really went to town on buying things for her new house.*

8 (out) on the town *informal* going to restaurants, bars, theatres etc for entertainment in the evening: *Frank is taking me out for a night on the town.*

9 town and gown used to describe the situation in which the people living in a town and the students in a town seem to be separate and opposing groups → GHOST TOWN, HOME TOWN; → **paint the town (red)** at PAINT² (5)

town 'centre n [C] *BrE* the main business area in the centre of a town; **⊟ downtown** *AmE*

town 'clerk n [C] an official who keeps the records of a town

town 'council n [C] *especially BrE* an elected group of people who are responsible for public areas and services, such as roads, parks etc, in a particular town —**town councillor** n [C]

town 'crier n [C] someone employed in the past to walk around the streets of a town, shouting news, warnings etc

town 'hall n [C] a public building used for a town's local government

town·house /ˈtaʊnhaʊs/ n [C] **1** a house in a town or city, especially a fashionable one in a central area **2** *BrE* a house in a town that belongs to someone who also owns a house in the countryside: *the Duke's townhouse in Mayfair* **3** *AmE* a house in a group of houses that share one or more walls

town·ie /ˈtaʊni/ n [C] *informal* someone who lives in a town or city and does not know anything about life in the countryside

town 'meeting n [C] *AmE* a meeting at which the people who live in a town discuss subjects or problems that affect their town

town 'planning n [U] the study of the way towns work, so that roads, houses, services etc can be provided as effectively as possible —**town planner** n [C]

town·scape /ˈtaʊnskeɪp/ n [C] the way a town or large parts of a town look: *industrial townscapes* | *Edinburgh's historic townscape*

bridge

park

church

library

hospital

bus station

railings

museum

office building

petrol station *BrE*/ gas station *AmE*

streetlight

theatre *BrE*/ theater *AmE*

hoarding *BrE*/ billboard *AmE*

Playhouse

bus shelter

pavement

road sign

bollard

cinema *BrE*/ movie theater *AmE*

traffic lights

underground *BrE*/ subway *AmE*

department store

zebra crossing *BrE*/ crosswalk *AmE*

café

double yellow lines

phone booth

litterbin *BrE*/ trash can *AmE*

parking meter

newsstand

pedestrians

BUS LANE

town·ship /ˈtaʊnʃɪp/ n [C] a town in Canada or the US that has some local government

towns·peo·ple /ˈtaʊnzpiːpəl/ also **towns·folk** /-fəʊk $ -foʊk/ n [plural] all the people who live in a particular town: *the proud townspeople of Semer Water*

tow·path /ˈtəʊpɑːθ $ ˈtoʊpæθ/ n [C] a path along the side of a CANAL or river, used especially in the past by horses pulling boats

tow·rope /ˈtəʊrəʊp $ ˈtoʊroʊp/ also **towline** n [C] a rope or chain used for pulling vehicles along

tow·truck /ˈtəʊtrʌk $ -ˈtoʊ-/ n [C] AmE a strong vehicle that can pull cars behind it; ▤ **breakdown truck** BrE

tox·ae·mi·a BrE; **toxemia** AmE /tɒkˈsiːmiə $ tɑːk-/ n [U] technical a medical condition in which your blood contains poisons

tox·ic /ˈtɒksɪk $ ˈtɑːk-/ adj containing poison, or caused by poisonous substances: *fumes from a toxic waste dump* | **toxic chemicals/substances/fumes/gases** *Toxic chemicals were spilled into the river.* | *a highly toxic pesticide* —**toxicity** /tɒkˈsɪsɪ̩ti $ tɑːk-/ n [C,U]: *The metal has a relatively low toxicity to humans.*

tox·i·col·o·gy /ˌtɒksɪˈkɒlədʒi $ ˌtɑːksɪˈkɑː-/ n [U] the science and medical study of poisons and their effects —**toxicologist** n [C] —**toxicological** /ˌtɒksɪkə-ˈlɒdʒɪkəl $ ˌtɑːksɪkəˈlɑː-/ adj

ˌtoxic ˈshock ˌsyndrome n [U] a serious illness that causes a high temperature and is thought to be connected with the use of TAMPONS

ˌtoxic ˈwaste n [C,U] waste products from industry that are harmful to people, animals, or the environment: *a toxic waste dump* | *international agreements about the disposal of toxic waste*

tox·in /ˈtɒksɪ̩n $ ˈtɑːk-/ n [C] a poisonous substance, especially one that is produced by BACTERIA and causes a particular disease

toy¹ /tɔɪ/ n [C] **1** an object for children to play with: *some toys for the baby* | **toy car/soldier/gun etc** | **soft/cuddly toy** BrE (=a toy that looks like an animal and is covered in fur) | *Annie was playing happily with her toys.* **2** an object that you buy because it gives you pleasure and enjoyment, especially one that you don't really need: *The food mixer is her latest toy.* **3 sex toy** an object that adults use to obtain sexual pleasure

toy² v

toy with sb/sth phr v **1** to think about an idea or possibility, usually for a short time and not very seriously: **toy with the idea of doing sth** *I've been toying with the idea of going to Japan to visit them.* **2** to keep moving and touching an object or food: *He spoke casually and toyed with his pen.* | *Laura was toying with her food and looking increasingly bored.* **3** to lie to someone or trick them, for example saying that you love them when you do not

toy³ adj [only before noun] a toy animal or dog is a type of dog that is specially bred to be very small: *a toy poodle*

ˈtoy boy n [C] informal a young man who is having a sexual relationship with an older woman – used humorously

trace¹ /treɪs/ v [T]
1 FIND SB/STH to find someone or something that has disappeared by searching for them carefully: *She had given up all hope of tracing her missing daughter.* | *Police are trying to trace a young woman who was seen near the accident.*
2 ORIGINS to find the origins of when something began or where it came from: **trace sth (back) to sth** *They've traced their ancestry to Scotland.* | *The style of these paintings can be traced back to early medieval influences.*
3 HISTORY/DEVELOPMENT to study or describe the history, development, or progress of something: *Sond-*

heim's book traces the changing nature of the relationship between men and women.
4 COPY to copy a drawing, map etc by putting a piece of transparent paper over it and then drawing the lines you can see through the paper
5 WITH YOUR FINGER to draw real or imaginary lines on the surface of something, usually with your finger or toe: **trace sth on/in/across** *Rosie's fingers traced a delicate pattern in the sand.*
6 trace a call to find out where a telephone call is coming from by using special electronic equipment: *His call was traced and half an hour later police arrested him.* —**traceable** adj

trace² n
1 SIGN OF STH [C,U] a small sign that shows that someone or something was present or existed: *There was no trace of anyone having entered the room since then.* | *Petra's lost all trace of her German accent.* | *Officers were unable to find any trace of drugs.* | **disappear/vanish/sink without (a) trace** (=disappear completely, without leaving any sign of what happened) *The plane vanished without a trace.*
2 SMALL AMOUNT [C] a very small amount of a quality, emotion, substance etc that is difficult to see or notice: [+of] *I saw the faintest trace of a smile cross Sandra's face.* | *traces of poison*
3 TELEPHONE [C] technical a search to find out where a telephone call came from, using special electronic equipment: *The police put a trace on the call.*
4 INFORMATION RECORDED [C] technical the mark or pattern made on a SCREEN or on paper by a machine that is recording an electrical signal: *This trace shows the heartbeat.*
5 CART/CARRIAGE [C] one of the two pieces of leather, rope etc by which a CART or carriage is fastened to an animal pulling it → **kick over the traces** at KICK¹ (19)

ˈtrace ˌelement n [C] technical **1** a chemical ELEMENT that your body needs a very small amount of to live **2** a chemical ELEMENT that only exists in small amounts on Earth

trac·er /ˈtreɪsə $ -ər/ n [C,U] a bullet that leaves a line of smoke or flame behind it

trac·e·ry /ˈtreɪsəri/ n plural **traceries** [C,U] **1** technical the curving and crossing lines of stone in the upper parts of some church windows **2** literary an attractive pattern of lines that cross each other: *the delicate tracery of the bare branches against the sky*

tra·che·a /trəˈkiːə $ ˈtreɪkiə/ n plural **tracheas** or **tracheae** /-ˈkiː-iː $ -kiˈiː/ [C] technical the tube that takes air from your throat to your lungs

trach·e·ot·o·my /ˌtrækiˈɒtəmi $ ˌtreɪkiˈɑːt-/ n plural **tracheotomies** [C] technical an operation to cut a hole in someone's throat so that they can breathe

trac·ing /ˈtreɪsɪŋ/ n [C] a copy of a map, drawing etc made by TRACING it

ˈtracing ˌpaper n [U] strong transparent paper used for TRACING

track¹ [S2] [W2] /træk/ n
1 PATH/ROAD [C] a narrow path or road with a rough uneven surface, especially one made by people or animals frequently moving through the same place: *The road leading to the farm was little more than a dirt track.* | *The track led through dense forest.* | *a steep mountain track* → see picture at COUNTRY
2 MARKS ON GROUND **tracks** [plural] a line of marks left on the ground by a moving person, animal, or vehicle: *We followed the tyre tracks across a muddy field.* | *The tracks, which looked like a fox's, led into the woods.*
3 FOR RACING [C] a circular course around which runners, cars etc race, which often has a specially prepared surface: *To run a mile, you have to run four circuits of the track.* → DIRT TRACK (2)
4 TRAIN [C] **a)** the two metal lines along which trains travel; ▤ **railway line**: *The track was damaged in several places.* **b)** AmE the particular track that a train

leaves from or arrives at: *The train for Boston is leaving from track 2.*
5 be on the right/wrong track to think in a way that is likely to lead to a correct or incorrect result: *We've had the initial test results and it looks as though we're on the right track.*
6 keep/lose track of sb/sth to pay attention to someone or something, so that you know where they are or what is happening to them, or to fail to do this: *It's difficult to keep track of all the new discoveries in genetics.* | *I just lost all track of time.*
7 **MUSIC/SONG** [C] one of the songs or pieces of music on a record, CASSETTE, or CD: *There's a great Miles Davis track on side two.*
8 stop/halt (dead) in your tracks to suddenly stop, especially because something has frightened or surprised you
9 cover your tracks to be careful not to leave any signs that could let people know where you have been or what you have done because you want to keep it a secret, usually because it is illegal: *He tried to cover his tracks by burning all the documents.*
10 **SPORT** [U] AmE **a)** sport that involves running on a track: *The next year he didn't run track or play football.* **b)** all the sports in an ATHLETICS competition such as running, jumping, or throwing the JAVELIN: *a famous track star* | *She went out for track in the spring* (=she joined the school's track team).
11 be on track spoken to be likely to achieve the result you want: *We're still on track for 10% growth.*
12 get off the track spoken to begin to deal with a new subject rather than the main one which was being discussed: *Don't get off the track, we're looking at this year's figures not last year's.*
13 be on the track of sb/sth to hunt or search for someone or something: *Police are on the track of the bank robbers.*
14 make tracks spoken used to say you must leave a place: *It's time we started making tracks.*
15 **DIRECTION** [C] the direction or line taken by something as it moves: [+of] *islands that lie in the track of North Atlantic storms*
16 **ON A VEHICLE** [C] a continuous metal band that goes over the wheels of a vehicle such as a BULLDOZER, allowing it to move over uneven ground → **off the beaten track** at BEATEN (1); → ONE-TRACK MIND; → **be from the wrong side of the tracks** at WRONG¹ (17)

track² v
1 **SEARCH** [T] to search for a person or animal by following the marks they leave behind them on the ground, their smell etc: *Police have been tracking the four criminals all over Central America.* | **track sb to sth** *The dogs tracked the wolf to its lair.*
2 **DEVELOPMENT** [T] to record or study the behaviour or development of someone or something over time: *The progress of each student is tracked by computer.*
3 **AIRCRAFT/SHIP** [T] to follow the movements of an aircraft or ship by using RADAR: *a tracking station*
4 **CAMERA** [I + in/out] to move a film or television camera away from or towards a scene in order to follow the action that you are recording
5 **SCHOOL** [T] AmE to put schoolchildren in groups according to their ability; ▤ **stream** BrE
6 **MARK** [T] AmE to leave behind a track of something such as mud or dirt when you walk: *Which of you boys tracked mud all over the kitchen floor?*
track sb/sth ⇔ **down** phr v
to find someone or something that is difficult to find by searching or looking for information in several different places: *I finally managed to track down the book you wanted in a shop near the station.* | *Detectives had tracked her down in California.*

track and 'field n [U] sports such as running and jumping; ▤ **athletics** BrE

track·ball /'trækbɔːl $ -bɒːl/ n [C] a small ball connected to a computer, that you turn in order to move the CURSOR

track·er /'trækə $ -ər/ n [C] someone who follows and finds other people, especially by following the marks that they have left on the ground

'tracker dog n [C] a dog that has been specially trained to follow and find people

'track e,vent n [C] AmE a running race

track·ing /'trækɪŋ/ n [U] the system on a video recorder that keeps the picture from a VIDEOTAPE clear on the screen

'tracking ,station n [C] a place from which objects moving in space, such as SATELLITES and ROCKETS, can be recognized and followed

'track meet n [C] AmE a sports event consisting of competitions in running, jumping etc

'track ,record n [singular] all of a person's or organization's past achievements, successes, or failures, which show how well they have done something in the past and how well they are likely to do in the future: [+in] *We're looking for someone with a **proven track record** in selling advertising.* | [+of] *The fund has a **good track record** of investing in the equity market.*

track·suit /'træksuːt, -sjuːt $ -suːt/ n [C] BrE loose clothes consisting of trousers and a JACKET, worn especially for sport

tract /trækt/ n [C] **1** the digestive/reproductive/urinary etc tract a system of connected organs that have one main purpose in a part of your body **2** a large area of land: *vast tracts of woodland* **3** formal a short piece of writing, especially about a moral or religious subject: *a tract on the dangers of drink*

trac·ta·ble /'træktəbəl/ adj formal easy to control or deal with; ▤ **intractable**: *The issues have proved to be less tractable than expected.* —**tractability** /,træktə'bɪləti/ n [U]

trac·tion /'trækʃən/ n [U] **1** the process of treating a broken bone with special medical equipment that pulls it: **in traction** *He was in traction* (=receiving this kind of treatment) *for weeks after the accident.* **2** the force that prevents something such as a wheel sliding on a surface: *The tires were bald* (=completely worn) *and lost traction on the wet road.* **3** the type of power needed to make a vehicle move, or to pull a heavy load

trac·tor /'træktə $ -ər/ n [C] a strong vehicle with large wheels, used for pulling farm machinery

'tractor-,trailer n [C] AmE a large truck that has two parts, one small part in the front where the driver sits and a large part at the back where goods are carried

trad /træd/ also ,**trad 'jazz** n [U] a style of JAZZ that was popular in the 1920s. One instrument plays complicated RHYTHMS and notes, and the rest of the instruments play regular rhythms.

trade¹ S3 W1 /treɪd/ n
1 **BUYING/SELLING** [U] the activity of buying, selling, or exchanging goods within a country or between countries; ▤ **commerce**: [+between] *There has been a marked increase in trade between East and West.* | *international trade agreements* | *unfair trade practices* | [+in] *Trade in ivory has been banned since 1990.* | **the arms/drug/slave etc trade** (=the buying and selling of weapons, drugs etc) → BALANCE OF TRADE, FREE TRADE; → **trade war** at WAR (3)
2 **the hotel/tourist etc trade** the business done by companies, hotels etc; → **industry**: *Working on Saturdays is usual in the retail trade.*
3 **AMOUNT OF BUSINESS** [U] BrE business activity, especially the amount of goods or products that are sold; ▤ **business**: *A lot of pubs nowadays do most of their trade at lunchtimes.* | **passing trade** (=customers who go into a shop when they are passing it, not regular customers) *Souvenir shops rely mainly on passing trade.* → **do a roaring trade** at ROARING (3)
4 **AN EXCHANGE OF THINGS** [singular] AmE **a)** when you exchange something you have for something that

bored: [+**behind/around**] *Susie trailed along behind her parents.* | *We spent the afternoon trailing around the shops.*
3 LOSE A COMPETITION [I,T usually in progressive] to be losing in a game, competition, or election: *The Democratic candidate is still trailing in the opinion polls.* | **trail (sb) by sth** *Manchester United were trailing by two goals to one.* | **trail in/home** (=finish in a bad position) *He trailed in last after a disastrous race.*
4 FOLLOW SB [T] to follow someone by looking for signs that they have gone in a particular direction: *Police trailed the gang for several days.*
  trail away/off *phr v*
  if someone's voice trails away or trails off, it becomes gradually quieter and then stops: *She trailed off, silenced by the look Kris gave her.*

trail² *n* [C] **1** a rough path across countryside or through a forest: *The trail led over Boulder Pass before descending to a lake.* → NATURE TRAIL **2** a long line or a series of marks that have been left by someone or something: [+**of**] *a trail of wet footprints* | *The bus left a trail of black smoke behind it.* | *The typhoon left a trail of devastation.* **3** a series of unpleasant situations or feelings that have been left by someone or something: [+**of**] *He left a trail of broken hearts and broken promises.* **4** a sign that a person or animal has been in a place, used for finding or catching them: *The hunters lost the tiger's trail in the middle of the jungle.* | *Police tracked him to Valencia and there the **trail went cold** (=they could not find any signs of him).* **5 be on the trail of sb/sth** to be trying to find someone or something by getting information about them: *industrial spies on the trail of technological secrets* | *Police believe they are **hot on the trail** of a drug-smuggling gang* (=they are close to finding them). **6** all the places that a particular group of people visit for a particular purpose: *a town on the tourist trail* | **campaign/election trail** *politicians on the campaign trail* **7** the set of things that someone does to achieve something: *New players should put the team back on the winning trail.* → **blaze a trail** at BLAZE² (5); → **hit the trail/road** at HIT¹ (17)

trail·blaz·er /ˈtreɪlˌbleɪzə $ -ər/ *n* [C] someone who is the first to discover or develop new methods of doing something: *a trailblazer in the field of medical research* —**trailblazing** *adj*

trail·er /ˈtreɪlə $ -ər/ *n* [C] **1** a vehicle that can be pulled behind another vehicle, used for carrying something heavy **2** *AmE* a vehicle that can be pulled behind a car, used for living and sleeping in during a holiday; 🔲 **caravan** *BrE* **3** an advertisement for a new film or television show

'**trailer park** also '**trailer court** *n* [C] *AmE* an area where trailers are parked and used as people's homes

'**trailer trash** *n* [U] *AmE informal* an offensive expression for poor people who live in trailer parks

trail·ing /ˈtreɪlɪŋ/ *adj* a trailing plant grows along the ground or hangs down

train¹ S1 W2 /treɪn/ *n* [C]
1 RAILWAY a set of several carriages that are connected to each other and pulled along a railway line by an engine

by train (=travelling on a train)
catch/get a train
get on/board a train
get off a train
take a train (=travel using a train)
wait for a train
miss a train (=be too late to get on a train)
a train pulls into/out of a station
freight/goods train (=a train that carries goods)
passenger train (=a train that carries people)
commuter train (=a train that people going to work use)

train journey/ride
train fare (=the money you pay for a train journey)

[+**to**] *the train to Munich* | *We went all the way to Inverness by train.* | *It's more relaxing to go by train.* | *You need to catch the early train to Bruges.* | *We were finally given instructions to board the train.* | *At Richmond a lot of people got off the train.* | *I took the first train home.* | *a lone commuter waiting for a train late at night* | *I missed the train and had to wait another two hours.* | *The train pulled out of Paddington, and soon we were racing towards Wales.* | *They would go on long train journeys together.* → BOAT TRAIN
2 SERIES **a train of sth** a series of events or actions that are related: *The decision set off a train of events which led to his resignation.*
3 train of thought a related series of thoughts that are developing in your mind: *The phone interrupted my train of thought.* | *I've lost my train of thought.*
4 bring sth in its train *formal* if an action or event brings something in its train, that thing happens as a result of it: *a decision that brought disaster in its train*
5 set sth in train *BrE formal* to make a process start happening: *Plans to modernize have been set in train.*
6 PEOPLE/ANIMALS a long line of moving people, animals, or vehicles: *a camel train*
7 DRESS a part of a long dress that spreads out over the ground behind the person wearing it: *a wedding dress with a long train*
8 SERVANTS a group of servants or officers following an important person, especially in the past

train² S1 W2 *v*
1 TEACH SB [I,T] to teach someone the skills of a particular job or activity, or to be taught these skills; → **training**: **train sb in sth** *All staff will be trained in customer service skills.* | **train to do sth** *She's training to be a doctor.* | **train sb to do sth** *Employees are trained to deal with emergency situations.* | [+**as**] *Nadia trained as a singer.* | *a highly trained workforce* | *Trained staff will be available to deal with your queries.*
2 TEACH AN ANIMAL [T] to teach an animal to do something or to behave correctly: *a well-trained puppy* | **train sth to do sth** *These dogs are trained to detect drugs.*
3 PREPARE FOR SPORT [I,T] to prepare for a sports event or tell someone how to prepare for it, especially by exercising; → **training**: [+**for**] *Brenda spends two hours a day training for the marathon.*
4 AIM STH [T] to aim something such as a gun or camera at someone or something: **train sth on/at sb/sth** *She trained her binoculars on the bird.*
5 DEVELOP STH [T] to develop and improve a natural ability or quality: *You can train your mind to relax.* | *To the trained eye the difference between these flowers is obvious* (=the difference is clear to someone who has developed skills to notice something).
6 PLANT [T] to make a plant grow in a particular direction by bending, cutting, or tying it

train·ee /ˌtreɪˈniː◂/ *n* [C] someone who is being trained for a job: *The trainees start next week.* | **trainee manager/solicitor/teacher etc** *a trainee hairdresser*

train·er /ˈtreɪnə $ -ər/ *n* [C] **1** someone who trains people or animals for sport or work; → **coach**: *a racehorse trainer* → see box at TEACHER **2** *BrE* a type of strong shoe that you wear for sport; 🔲 **tennis shoe** *AmE*

train·ing S3 W1 /ˈtreɪnɪŋ/ *n*
1 [singular, U] the process of teaching or being taught the skills for a particular job or activity; → **train**

give sb training
receive/undergo training
a training course/programme/session
a training session
a training manual (=a book you use in training)
on-the-job training (=while doing a job rather than in a classroom)
in-service training (=while working for an employer

rather than at college etc)

teacher training (=training you do to become a teacher)

staff/management training

basic training (=the first training that a soldier receives)

[+**in**] *On the course we* **received training** *in every aspect of the job.* | *Police drivers have to* **undergo** *intensive* **training.** | *a rigorous* **training session** | *On-the job training will be supplemented by classroom lectures.* | *The shop opens late on Fridays because of* **staff training.**

2 [U] physical exercises that you do to stay healthy or prepare for a competition; → **train**: *Lesley does weight training twice a week.* | **be in training for sth** *She's in training for the Olympics.* → **SPRING TRAINING**

'training ,college *n* [C,U] *BrE* a college for adults that gives training for a particular profession: *a teacher training college* | *a training college for pilots*

'training wheel *n* [C,usually plural] *AmE* a small wheel that is fastened to the back of a young child's bicycle to make it more steady; ▣ **stabilizer** *BrE*

'train set *n* [C] a toy train with railway tracks

'train ,spotter *n* [C] *BrE* **1** someone who collects the numbers of railway engines for fun **2** someone who you think is boring and only interested in unimportant details —**trainspotting** *n* [U]

'train ,station *n* [C] a place where trains stop for passengers to get on and off; ▣ **railway station** *BrE*

traipse /treɪps/ *v* [I always + adv/prep] *informal* to walk somewhere in a slow or unwilling way because you are tired or bored: [+**around/through/across etc**] *I've been traipsing around the shops all morning.*

trait /treɪ, treɪt $ treɪt/ *n* [C] *formal* a particular quality in someone's character: **personality/character traits** *a mental illness associated with particular personality traits* | **genetic/inherited traits**

trai·tor /'treɪtə $ -ər/ *n* [C,U] someone who is not loyal to their country, friends, or beliefs: [+**to**] *a traitor to the cause of women's rights* | *a politician who* **turned traitor** (=became a traitor) *to the government*

trai·tor·ous /'treɪtərəs/ *adj especially literary* not loyal to your country, friends, or beliefs —**traitorously** *adv*

tra·jec·to·ry /trə'dʒektəri/ *n plural* **trajectories** [C] **1** *technical* the curved path of an object that has been fired or thrown through the air **2** *formal* the events that lead to happen during a period of time, which often lead to a particular aim or result: *The decision was certain to affect the trajectory of French politics for some time to come.*

tram /træm/ also **tram·car** /'træmkɑː $ -kɑːr/ *n* [C] *especially BrE* a vehicle for passengers, which travels along metal tracks in the street; ▣ **streetcar** *AmE*; → see picture at ENVIRONMENT

tram·lines /'træmlaɪnz/ *n* [plural] *BrE* **1** the metal tracks in the road, used by trams **2** *informal* the two parallel lines at the edge of a tennis court

tram·mel /'træməl/ *v past tense and past participle* **trammelled**, *present participle* **trammelling** *BrE*, *past tense and past participle* **trammeled**, *present participle* **trammeling** *AmE* [T] *formal* to limit or prevent someone's freedom or development → UNTRAMMELLED

tramp¹ /træmp/ *n* [C] **1** someone who has no home or job and moves from place to place, often asking for food or money **2** a long or difficult walk: *a long tramp through the snow* **3** *old-fashioned especially AmE* a woman who has too many sexual partners – used to show disapproval **4** the **tramp of feet/boots** the sound of heavy walking: *the steady tramp of soldiers' feet*

tramp² *v* [I always + adv/prep, T] to walk somewhere slowly and with heavy steps: *He tramped the streets looking for work.* [+**through/across/around etc**] *The walk involved tramping through mud.*

tram·ple /'træmpəl/ *v* [I always + adv/prep, T] **1** to step heavily on something, so that you crush it with

your feet: [+**on/over/through etc**] *There was a small fence to stop people trampling on the flowers.* | **trample sb/sth underfoot** *The children were in danger of being trampled underfoot in the crowd.* | **trample sb to death** (=kill someone by stepping heavily on them) *Several people were nearly trampled to death in the rush to get out.* **2** to behave in a way that shows that you do not care about someone's rights or feelings: **trample on/over sb/sth** *Don't let people trample all over you.* | *Their interests and rights had been trampled underfoot.*

tram·po·line /'træmpəliːn/ *n* [C] a piece of equipment that you jump up and down on as a sport. It consists of a metal frame with a piece of strong cloth stretched tightly over it.

tram·po·lin·ing /'træmpəliːnɪŋ/ *n* [U] the sport or activity of jumping up and down on a trampoline

trance /trɑːns $ træns/ *n* **1** [C] a state in which you behave as if you were asleep but are still able to hear and understand what is said to you: **go/fall into a trance** *She went into a deep hypnotic trance.* **2** [C] a state in which you are thinking about something so much that you do not notice what is happening around you: **in a trance** *What's the matter with you? You've been in a trance all day.* **3** [U] a type of popular electronic dance music with a fast beat and long continuous notes played on a SYNTHESIZER

tran·ny /'træni/ *n plural* **trannies** [C] *informal* **1** someone who has the physical features of both sexes, usually as the result of medical treatment; → **transsexual 2** a TRANSVESTITE —**tranny** *adj*

tran·quil /'træŋkwəl/ *adj* pleasantly calm, quiet, and peaceful: *a small tranquil village* —**tranquilly** *adv* —**tranquillity** *BrE*, **tranquility** *AmE* /træŋ'kwɪləti/ *n* [U]: *the tranquillity of the Tuscan countryside*

tran·quil·lize, **-ise** *BrE*; **tranquilize** *AmE* /'træŋkwəlaɪz/ *v* [T] to make a person or animal calm or unconscious by using a drug

tran·quil·lizer; **-iser** *BrE*; **tranquilizer** *AmF* /'træŋkwəlaɪzə $ -ər/ *n* [C] a drug used for making someone feel less anxious

trans- /træns, trænz/ *prefix* **1** on or to the far side of something; ▣ **across**: *transatlantic flights* | *the transSiberian railway* **2** between two things or groups; ▣ **inter-**: *trans-racial fostering* **3** shows a change: *He's been transformed by the experience.*

trans·act /træn'zækt/ *v* [I,T] *formal* to do business with someone: *Most deals are transacted over the phone.*

trans·ac·tion S3 W3 /træn'zækʃən/ *n formal* **1** [C] a business deal or action, such as buying or selling something: *The bank charges a fixed rate for each transaction.* | *financial transactions* **2** [U] the process of doing business: *the transaction of his public duties* **3 transactions** [plural] discussions that take place at the meetings of an organization, or a written record of these

trans·at·lan·tic /ˌtrænzət'læntɪk◂/ *adj* [only before noun] **1** crossing the Atlantic Ocean: *transatlantic flights* **2** involving countries on both sides of the Atlantic Ocean: *a transatlantic agreement* **3** on the other side of the Atlantic Ocean: *one of America's transatlantic military bases*

trans·cei·ver /træn'siːvə $ -ər/ *n* [C] a radio that can send and receive messages

tran·scend /træn'send/ *v* [T] *formal* to go beyond the usual limits of something: *The desire for peace transcended political differences.*

tran·scen·dent /træn'sendənt/ *adj formal* going far beyond ordinary limits: *the transcendent genius of Mozart* —**transcendently** *adv*

T

1 000, 2 000, 3 000, most frequent words in S poken and W ritten English

tran·scen·den·tal /ˌtrænsen'dentl‹/ *adj* transcendental experiences or ideas are beyond normal human understanding and experience

tran·scen·den·tal·is·m /ˌtrænsen'dentəl-ɪzəm/ *n* [U] the belief that knowledge can be obtained by studying thought rather than by practical experience

transcendental medi'tation *n* [U] a method of becoming calm by repeating particular words in your mind

trans·con·ti·nen·tal /ˌtrænzkɒntɬ'nentl, ˌtræns-$ -kɑːn-/ *adj* crossing a CONTINENT: *a transcontinental railway*

tran·scribe /træn'skraɪb/ *v* [T] **1** to write down something exactly as it was said: *A secretary transcribed the witnesses' statements.* **2** to write an exact copy of something: *He had been asked to transcribe an ancient manuscript.* **3** *technical* to represent speech sounds with PHONETIC symbols **4** *formal* to change a piece of writing into the alphabet of another language: **transcribe sth into sth** *The book has been transcribed into braille.* **5** to arrange a piece of music for a different instrument or voice: **transcribe sth for sth** *a piece transcribed for piano* **6** *technical* to copy recorded music, speech etc from one system to another, for example from TAPE to CD

tran·script /'trænskrɪpt/ *n* [C] **1** a written or printed copy of a speech, conversation etc: [+of] *A transcript of the tapes was presented in court.* **2** *AmE* an official college document that shows a list of a student's classes and the results they received

tran·scrip·tion /træn'skrɪpʃən/ *n* **1** [U] when you transcribe something: *Pronunciation is shown by a system of phonetic transcription.* **2** [C] an exact written or printed copy of something; **目 transcript**

tran·sept /'trænsept/ *n* [C] one of the two parts of a church that are built out from the main area of the church to form a cross shape

trans·fer¹ W2 /træns'fɜː $ -'fɜːr/ *v* **transferred, transferring**
1 MOVE TO DIFFERENT PLACE ETC [I,T] to move from one place, school, job etc to another, or to make someone do this, especially within the same organization: **transfer (from sth) to sth** *Swod transferred from MI6 to the Security Service.* | **transfer sb (from sth) to sth** *They're transferring him to a special unit at Great Ormond Street Hospital.* | *You'll be transferred to the Birmingham office.*
2 PUT STH IN DIFFERENT PLACE [I,T] *formal* to move from one place to another, or to move something from one place to another: **transfer (from sth) to sth** *The exhibition transfers to York City Art Gallery on 23rd January.* | **transfer sth (from sth) to sth** *Transfer the meat to warm plates.*
3 SPORTS PERSON [T] to sell a sports player to another team: *He was tranferred for a fee of £8 million.*
4 MONEY [T] to move money from one account or institution to another: **transfer sth (from sth) to sth** *I'd like to transfer $500 to my checking account.*
5 **transfer your affections/loyalty/allegiance etc** to change from loving or supporting one person to loving or supporting a different one
6 SKILL/IDEA/QUALITY [I,T] if a skill, idea, or quality transfers from one situation to another, or if you transfer it, it can be used in the new situation: *Ideas that work well in one school often don't transfer well to another.*
7 **transfer power/responsibility/control (to sb)** to officially give power etc to another person or organization: *The ageing president is preparing to transfer power to his son.*
8 PHONE [T] to connect the call of someone who has telephoned you to someone else's telephone so that that person can speak to them: *Hold on one moment while I transfer your call.*
9 PROPERTY [T] *law* to officially give property or land to someone else

10 TRAVEL [I,T] to change from one bus, plane etc to another while you are travelling, or arrange for someone to do this: *You will be met on arrival at the airport and transferred to your hotel.*
11 INFORMATION/MUSIC [T] to copy recorded information, music etc from one system to another: *Transfer the files onto floppy disk.*
12 DISEASE [T] if a disease is transferred from one person or animal to another, the second person or animal begins to have the disease: **transfer sth (from sb/sth) to sb/sth** *It is unlikely that the disease will be transferred from animals to humans.* —**transferable** *adj*: *transferable skills* —**transferability** /ˌtræns,fɜːrə'bɪlɬti/ *n* [U]

trans·fer² W2 /'trænsfɜː $ -fɜːr/ *n*
1 a) [C,U] the process by which someone or something moves or is moved from one place, job etc to another: [+of] *the transfer of assets within a group of companies* | [+to] *Penny's applied for a transfer to head office.* | *electronic data transfer* **b)** [C] someone or something that has been moved in this way
2 transfer of power a process by which the control of a country is taken from one person or group and given to another: *the transfer of power to a civilian government*
3 [C] the act of changing from one bus, aircraft etc to another while travelling: *Getting there often means a couple of transfers on a bus line.*
4 [C] *especially BrE* a drawing, pattern etc that can be stuck or printed onto a surface; **目 decal** *AmE*
5 [C] *especially AmE* a ticket that allows a passenger to change from one bus, train etc to another without paying more money

trans·fer·ence /'trænsfərəns $ træns'fɜːr-/ *n* [U] **1** *formal* the process of moving someone or something from one place, position, job etc to another: [+of] *the transference of skills acquired at school to the workplace* **2** *technical* the process of beginning to have the same unconscious feelings about someone in the present that you had for someone such as your parents in the past

'transfer fee *n* [C] *BrE* the money that one football club pays another for the transfer of a player

'transfer list *n* [C] *BrE* a list of the football players in one team who can be sold to another team

trans·fig·ure /træns'fɪgə $ -gjər/ *v* [T] *literary* to change the way someone or something looks, especially so that they become more beautiful: *Her face was transfigured with joy.* —**transfiguration** /ˌtræns,fɪgə'reɪʃən $ -gjə-/ *n* [C,U]

trans·fix /træns'fɪks/ *v* [T] **1** to surprise, interest, frighten etc someone so much that they do not move **2** *literary* to make a hole through something or someone with a sharp pointed weapon

trans·fixed /træns'fɪkst/ *adj* [not before noun] unable to move because you are very surprised, shocked, frightened, interested etc: *For a moment she stood transfixed in the doorway.*

trans·form W3 /træns'fɔːm $ -'fɔːrm/ *v* [T] to completely change the appearance, form, or character of something or someone, especially in a way that improves it: *Increased population has transformed the landscape.* | **transform sb/sth (from sth) into sth** *The movie transformed her almost overnight from an unknown schoolgirl into a megastar.*

trans·for·ma·tion /ˌtrænsfə'meɪʃən $ -fər-/ *n* [C,U] a complete change in someone or something: *In recent years, the movie industry has **undergone** a dramatic transformation.* | **transformation from sth to/into sth** *the gradual transformation from woodland to farmland* | [+of] *What leads to the transformation of one economic system to another?*

trans·form·er /træns'fɔːmə $ -'fɔːrmər/ *n* [C] a piece of equipment for changing electricity from one VOLTAGE to another

trans·fu·sion /træns'fjuːʒən/ *n* [C,U] **1** the process of putting blood from one person's body into the body of someone else as a medical treatment: *A blood transfusion saved his life.* **2** the process of giving something important or necessary, such as money, to a group or organization that needs it: [+of] *The mayor has promised a transfusion of $8 million in redevelopment funds.*

trans·gen·der /trænz'dʒendə $ træns'dʒendər/ *n* [U] a general word for people who feel that they belong to the other sex, and not the sex they were born with, and who express this in their sexual behaviour; → **transsexual**: *the transgender community* | *transgender issues* —**transgendered** *adj* —**transgenderism** *n* [U]

trans·gen·ic /trænz'dʒenɪk $ træns-/ *adj technical* having one or more GENES from a different type of animal or plant: *transgenic mice*

trans·gress /trænz'gres $ træns-/ *v* [I,T] *formal* to do something that is against the rules of social behaviour or against a moral principle: *Orton's plays transgress accepted social norms.* —**transgressor** *n* [C] —**transgression** /-'greʃən/ *n* [C,U]

tran·si·ent[1] /'trænziənt $ 'trænʃənt/ *adj formal* **1** continuing only for a short time: *transient fashions* **2** working or staying somewhere for only a short time: *a transient population* —**transience** *n* [U]

transient[2] *n* [C] *AmE* someone who has no home and moves around from place to place

tran·sis·tor /træn'zɪstə $ -ər/ *n* [C] **1** a small piece of electronic equipment in radios, televisions etc that controls the flow of electricity **2** a transistor radio

tran,sistor 'radio *n* [C] *old-fashioned* a small radio that you can carry around with you

tran·sit /'trænsɪt, -zɪt/ *n* [U] **1** the process of moving goods or people from one place to another: *baggage that is lost or damaged in transit* (=while it is being moved) | *transit by air or sea* **2** a system for moving people from place to place; ⊟ **transport** *BrE*; ⊟ **transportation** *AmE*: *rapid transit networks* | **public transit** *AmE* (=buses, trains etc) *promises to improve public transit* —**transit** *v* [I]

'transit ,camp *n* [C] a place where REFUGEES stay before moving to somewhere more permanent

tran·si·tion [W3] /træn'zɪʃən, -'sɪ-/ *n* [C,U] *formal* when something changes from one state or state to another: **transition from sth to sth** *the smooth transition from full-time work to full retirement* | **Making the transition** *from youth to adulthood can be very painful.* | *a society that is in transition* (=changing) | *the period of transition to full democracy*

tran·si·tion·al /træn'zɪʃənəl, -'sɪ-/ *adj* **1** relating to a period during which something is changing from one state or form into another: **transitional period/stage etc** *a transitional period during the switch to the Euro* **2 transitional government** a temporary government, usually one that governs until official elections can take place in a country —**transitionally** *adv*

tran·si·tive /'trænsɪtɪv, -zɪ-/ *adj technical* a transitive verb must have an object, for example the verb 'break' in the sentence 'I broke the cup'. Transitive verbs are marked [T] in this dictionary; → **ditransitive, intransitive** —**transitively** *adv* —**transitivity** /ˌtrænsɪ'tɪvɪti, -zɪ-/ *n* [U]

'transit ,lounge *n* [C] an area in an airport where passengers can wait

tran·si·to·ry /'trænzɪtəri $ -tɔːri/ *adj* continuing or existing for only a short time

'transit ,visa *n* [C] a VISA (=special document) that allows someone to pass through one country on their way to another

trans·late /træns'leɪt, trænz-/ *v*
1 CHANGE LANGUAGES [I,T] to change written or spoken words into another language; → **interpret**: **translate sth (from sth) into sth** *Translate the text from Italian into English.* | *Poetry doesn't usually translate well.* | [+as] *Dagda, an ancient Irish deity, literally translates as 'the good god'.*
2 HAPPEN AS RESULT [I,T] if one thing translates

into another, the second thing happens as a result of the first: **translate (sth) into sth** *A small increase in local spending will translate into a big rise in property tax.*
3 HAVE SAME MEANING [I,T] to mean the same as something else: **translate into/to sth** *These rates translate into a return of 8.5% for dollar investors.*
4 CHANGE FORMS [I,T] to change something, or be changed, from one form into another: **translate (sth) into sth** *the danger of translating your emotions into actions* | *Jokes often don't translate well into print.*
5 USE IN NEW SITUATION [I,T] to be used in a new situation, or to make something do this: **translate sth to sth** *It's amazing how well the play has been translated to film.* —**translatable** *adj*

trans·la·tion /træns'leɪʃən, trænz-/ *n* **1** [C,U] when you translate something, or something that has been translated: [+of] *a new translation of the Bible* | [+from] *a literal translation from Arabic* | *She read the letter and gave us a rough translation* (=she did not translate everything exactly). | *I've only read 'Madame Bovary' in translation* (=not in its original language). | *Much of the book's humour has been lost in translation* (=is no longer effective when translated). **2** [U] *formal* the process of changing something into a different form

trans·la·tor /træns'leɪtə, trænz- $ -ər/ *n* [C] someone who changes writing into a different language; → **interpreter**

trans·lit·e·rate /trænz'lɪtəreɪt $ træns-/ *v* [T] to write a word, sentence etc in the alphabet of a different language or writing system —**transliteration** /trænzˌlɪtə'reɪʃən $ træns-/ *n* [C,U]

trans·lu·cent /trænz'luːsənt $ træns-/ *adj* not transparent, but clear enough to allow light to pass through: *Blue veins showed through her translucent skin.* —**translucence** *n* [U]

trans·mi·gra·tion /ˌtrænzmaɪ'greɪʃən $ ˌtræns-/ *n* [U] *technical* the time when the soul passes into another body after death, according to some religions

trans·mis·sion /trænz'mɪʃən $ træns-/ *n* **1** [U] the process of sending out electronic signals, messages etc, using radio, television, or other similar equipment: *worldwide data transmission* **2** [U] *formal* the process of sending or passing something from one person, place, or thing to another: [+of] *the transmission of disease* **3** [C] *formal* something that is broadcast on television, radio etc: *a live transmission of the tennis championship* **4** [C,U] the parts of a vehicle that take power from the engine to the wheels

trans·mit /trænz'mɪt $ træns-/ *v* **transmitted, transmitting** **1** [I,T usually + adv/prep] to send out electronic signals, messages etc using radio, television, or other similar equipment: *The US Open will be transmitted live via satellite.* | *The system transmits information over digital phone lines.* **2** [T] *formal* to send or pass something from one person, place or thing to another: **transmit sth (from sb/sth) to sb/sth** *Mathematical knowledge is transmitted from teacher to student.* → SEXUALLY TRANSMITTED DISEASE **3** [T] *technical* if an object or substance transmits sound or light, it allows sound or light to travel through or along it

trans·mit·ter /trænz'mɪtə $ træns'mɪtər/ *n* [C] **1** equipment that sends out radio or television signals **2** *formal* someone or something that passes something on to another person or thing: [+of] *What is the main transmitter of the virus?*

trans·mog·ri·fy /trænz'mɒɡrɪfaɪ $ træns'mɑː-/ *v* **transmogrified, transmogrifying, transmogrifies** [T] to change the shape of something completely, as if by magic – used humorously —**transmogrification** /trænzˌmɒɡrɪfɪ'keɪʃən $ træns'mɑː-/ *n* [U]

trans·mute /trænz'mjuːt $ træns-/ *v* [T + into] *formal* to change one substance or type of thing into another —**transmutation** /ˌtrænzmjuː'teɪʃən $ ˌtræns-/ *n* [C,U]

trans·na·tion·al /ˌtrænzˈnæʃənəl/ *adj* involving more than one country or existing in more than one country: *transnational corporations*

tran·som /ˈtrænsəm/ *n* [C] **1** a bar of wood that forms the top of the back part of a boat **2** a bar of wood or stone which separates a door from a window above it, or which divides a window into two parts **3** *AmE* a small window over a door or over a larger window; ◧ **fanlight** *BrE*

trans·par·en·cy /trænˈspærənsi, -ˈspeər- $ -ˈspær-, ˈsper-/ *n plural* **transparencies 1** [C] a sheet of plastic or a piece of photographic film through which light can be shone to show a picture on a large screen **2** [U] the quality of glass, plastic etc that makes it possible for you to see through it **3** [U] the quality of being easy to understand or know about

trans·par·ent /trænˈspærənt, -ˈspeər- $ -ˈspær-, -ˈsper-/ *adj* **1** if something is transparent, you can see through it; ◧ **clear**; → **opaque**, **translucent**: *a transparent plastic container* **2** *formal* language or information that is transparent is clear and easy to understand: *The way the system works will be transparent to the user.* **3** a lie, excuse etc that is transparent does not deceive people —**transparently** *adv*

trans ˌperson *n plural* **trans people** [C usually plural] *AmE* someone who feels that they do not belong to only the male or only the female sex, and who expresses this in their sexual behaviour, sometimes having medical treatment to change their bodies; → **transsexual**

tran·spi·ra·tion /ˌtrænspəˈreɪʃən/ *n* [U] *technical* the process of passing water through the surface of a plant's leaves; → **respiration**

tran·spire /trænˈspaɪə $ -ˈspaɪr/ *v* **1** it transpires that *formal* if it transpires that something is true, you discover that it is true: *It now transpires that he kept all the money for himself.* **2** [I] *formal* to happen: *Exactly what transpired remains unknown.* **3** [I,T] *technical* when a plant transpires, water passes through the surface of its leaves

trans·plant¹ /trænsˈplɑːnt $ -ˈplænt/ *v* [T] **1** to move an organ, piece of skin etc from one person's body and put it into another as a form of medical treatment **2** to move a plant from one place and plant it in another place **3** *formal* to move something or someone from one place to another —**transplantation** /ˌtrænsplɑːnˈteɪʃən $ -plæn-/ *n* [U]

trans·plant² /ˈtrænsplɑːnt $ -plænt/ *n* **1** [C,U] the operation of transplanting an organ, piece of skin etc; → **implant**: *heart transplant surgery* | *a bone marrow transplant* **2** [C] the organ, piece of skin etc that is moved in a transplant operation; → **implant**

trans·pond·er /trænˈspɒndə $ -ˈspɑːndər/ *n* [C] *technical* a piece of radio or RADAR equipment that sends out a signal when it receives a signal telling it to do this

trans·port¹ S3 W2 /ˈtrænspɔːt $ -ɔːrt/ *n* **1** [U] *BrE* a system or method for carrying passengers or goods from one place to another; ◧ **transportation** *AmE*: **air/rail/road transport** *Improved rail transport is essential for business.* | *commuters who travel on* **public transport** (=buses, trains etc) | *It's easier to get to the college if you have your* **own transport** (=a car, bicycle etc). | **means/mode/form of transport** *Horses were the only means of transport.* **2** [U] the process or business of taking goods from one place to another; ◧ **transportation** *AmE*: [+of] *Canals were used for the transport of goods.* **3** [C] a ship or aircraft for carrying soldiers or supplies **4 be in a transport of delight/joy etc** *literary* to be feeling very strong emotions of pleasure, happiness etc

trans·port² /trænˈspɔːt $ -ɔːrt/ *v* [T usually + adv/prep] **1** to take goods, people etc from one place to another in a vehicle: *trucks used for transporting oil* | **transport sb/sth to sth** *The statue was transported to London.* **2 be transported back to/into sth** to imagine that you are in another place or time because of something that you see or hear: *One look, and I was transported back to childhood.* **3 be transported with delight/joy etc** *literary* to feel very strong emotions of pleasure, happiness etc **4** *old use* to send a criminal to a distant country as a punishment —**transportable** *adj*

trans·por·ta·tion S3 W3 /ˌtrænspɔːˈteɪʃən $ -spər-/ *n* [U] **1** *AmE* a system or method for carrying passengers or goods from one place to another; ◧ **transport** *BrE*: *The city needs to improve its* **public transportation** (=buses, trains etc). | **means/mode/form of transportation** *People need to get out of their cars and use other modes of transportation.* **2** *AmE* the process or business of taking goods from one place to another; ◧ **transport** *BrE*: [+of] *the transportation of dangerous chemicals by road* **3** *old use* the punishment of sending a criminal to a distant country

ˈtransport ˌcafe / $ ˈ.. ˌ./ *n* [C] *BrE* a cheap restaurant beside a main road, used mainly by truck drivers

trans·port·er /trænˈspɔːtə $ -ˈspɔːrtər/ *n* [C] a long vehicle that can carry one or more other vehicles

ˈtransport ˌplane *n* [C] a plane that is used especially for carrying military equipment or soldiers

ˈtransport ˌship *n* [C] a ship used especially for carrying soldiers

trans·pose /trænˈspəʊz $ -ˈspoʊz/ *v* [T+ into/to] *technical* **1** *formal* to change the order or position of two or more things **2** to use a system or method in a different situation from the one you used it in originally **3** to write or perform a piece of music in a musical KEY that is different from the one that it was first written in —**transposition** /ˌtrænspəˈzɪʃən/ *n* [C,U]

trans·put·er /trænzˈpjuːtə $ trænsˈpjuːtər/ *n* [C] *technical* a powerful computer MICROCHIP that can deal with very large amounts of information very fast

trans·sex·u·al /trænˈsekʃuəl $ trænsˈsek-/ *n* [C] a man who wants to be a woman and has medical treatment to make him into one, or a woman who wants to be a man and has medical treatment to make her into one; → **transvestite** —**transsexual** *adj* —**transsexualism** *n* [U]

tran·sub·stan·ti·a·tion /ˌtrænsəbstænʃiˈeɪʃən/ *n* [U] the belief of some Christians that the bread and wine taken in Holy Communion become the actual body and blood of Christ

trans·verse /trænzˈvɜːs $ trænsˈvɜːrs/ *adj* [no comparative] lying or placed across something: *a transverse beam*

trans·ves·tite /trænzˈvestaɪt $ træns-/ *n* [C] someone, especially a man, who enjoys dressing like a person of the opposite sex; → **transsexual** —**transvestite** *adj* —**transvestism** *n* [U]

trap¹ /træp/ *n* [C]

trap

1 FOR ANIMALS a piece of equipment for catching animals: *The only way to catch mice is to* **set a trap.** | *He had stepped into a bear trap covered in snow.* → **MOUSETRAP**

2 CLEVER TRICK a clever trick that is used to catch someone or to make them do or say something that they did not intend to: **fall/walk into a trap** | **lay/set a trap (for sb)** *Mr Smith has walked straight into a trap laid by the Tories.* | *Police had set a trap for hooligans at the match.*

mousetrap

3 BAD SITUATION an unpleasant or difficult situation that is difficult to escape from: *Amanda felt that marriage was a trap.* | **debt/unemployment etc trap** *people*

caught in the unemployment trap
4 fall into/avoid the trap of doing sth to do something that seems good at the time but is not sensible or wise, or to avoid doing this: *Don't fall into the trap of investing all your money in one place.*
5 keep your trap shut *spoken* a rude way of telling someone to not say anything about things that are secret: *Just keep your trap shut.*
6 shut your trap! *spoken* a rude way of telling someone to stop talking
7 VEHICLE a vehicle with two wheels, pulled by a horse
8 SPORT *AmE* SANDTRAP; ☰ **bunker** *BrE*
9 DOG RACE a special gate from which a GREYHOUND is set free at the beginning of a race → BOOBY TRAP, DEATH TRAP; → **poverty trap** at POVERTY (3); → SPEED TRAP, TOURIST TRAP

trap² S3 *v* **trapped, trapping** [T]
1 IN A DANGEROUS PLACE [usually passive] to prevent someone from escaping from somewhere, especially a dangerous place: *Twenty miners were trapped underground.* | *Dozens of people were trapped in the rubble when the building collapsed.* | *There's no way out! We're trapped!*
2 IN A BAD SITUATION **be/feel trapped** to be in a bad situation from which you cannot escape: [+in] *Julia felt trapped in her role of wife and mother.*
3 ANIMAL to catch an animal or bird using a trap
4 CATCH SB to catch someone by forcing them into a place from which they cannot escape: *The police trapped the terrorists at a roadblock.*
5 TRICK to trick someone so that you make them do or say something that they did not intend to: **trap sb into (doing) sth** *I was trapped into signing a confession.*
6 CRUSH *BrE* to get a part of your body crushed between two objects; ☰ **pinch** *AmE*: *Mind you don't trap your fingers in the door.* | *pain from a trapped nerve*
7 GAS/WATER ETC to prevent something such as gas or water from getting away: *solar panels that trap the sun's heat*

trap·door /'træpdɔː $ -dɔːr/ *n* [C] a small door that covers an opening in a roof or floor

tra·peze /trəˈpiːz $ træ-/ *n* [C] a short bar hanging from two ropes high above the ground, used by ACROBATS

tra·pe·zi·um /trəˈpiːziəm/ *n* [C] *technical* **1** *BrE* a shape with four sides, only two of which are parallel **2** *AmE* a shape with four sides, none of which are parallel

trap·e·zoid /'træpⁱzɔɪd/ *n* [C] *technical* **1** *BrE* a shape with four sides, none of which are parallel **2** *AmE* a shape with four sides, only two of which are parallel

trap·per /'træpə $ -ər/ *n* [C] someone who traps wild animals, especially for their fur

trap·pings /'træpɪŋz/ *n* [plural] things such as money, influence, possessions etc that are related to a particular type of person, job, or way of life: [+of] *the trappings of power*

Trap·pist /'træpⁱst/ *n* [C] a member of a Catholic religious group who live together, follow strict rules, and do not speak

trap·shoot·ing /'træp,ʃuːtɪŋ/ *n* [U] the sport of shooting special clay objects fired into the air

trash¹ S3 /træʃ/ *n* [U]
1 *AmE* things that you throw away, such as empty bottles, used papers, food that has gone bad etc; ☰ **rubbish** *BrE*: *Will someone take out the trash* (=take it outside the house)? | *Just put it in the trash.*
2 *informal* something that is of very poor quality: *How can you read that trash?*
3 *AmE informal not polite* someone from a low social class who you do not respect because you think they are lazy or immoral → WHITE TRASH

trash² *v* [T] **1** *informal* to destroy something completely, either deliberately or by using it too much: *The place got trashed last time we had a party.* **2** *especially*

AmE to criticize someone or something very severely: *The researchers are angry that attempts have been made to trash their work.*

'trash can *n* [C] *AmE* a large container with a lid into which you put empty bottles, used papers, food that has gone bad etc; ☰ **dustbin** *BrE* → see picture at BIN¹

'trash com,pactor *n* [C] *AmE* a machine that presses waste material together into a very small mass

trashed /træʃt/ *adj AmE spoken* **1** very drunk: *We got trashed last night.* **2** completely destroyed: *We need a new map – this one's trashed.*

trash·talk /'træʃtɔːk $ -tɒːk/ *n* [U] *AmE informal* unpleasant things that you say about someone

'trash ,talking also **trash-talking** *n* [U] *AmE* when a sports player or sports FAN says rude or unpleasant things to or about a sports player: *Coaches say they want to take trash talking out of high school football.*

trash·y /'træʃi/ *adj* of extremely bad quality: *trashy novels* —**trashiness** *n* [U]

trau·ma /'trɔːmə, 'traumə $ 'traumə, 'trɔː-/ *n* **1** [C] an unpleasant and upsetting experience that affects you for a long time: *traumas such as death or divorce* **2** [U] a mental state of extreme shock caused by a very frightening or unpleasant experience: [+of] *the trauma of being a young refugee* | *the emotional trauma of rape* **3** [C,U] *technical* an injury: *the hospital's trauma unit*

trau·mat·ic /trɔːˈmætɪk $ trɒː-/ *adj* a traumatic experience is so shocking and upsetting that it affects you for a long time: *His son's death was the most traumatic event in Stan's life.* —**traumatically** /-kli/ *adv*

trau·ma·tize also **-ise** *BrE* /'trɔːmətaɪz, 'trau- $ 'trau-, 'trɒː-/ *v* [T usually passive] to shock someone so badly that they are affected by it for a very long time: *He was traumatized by his war experiences.* —**traumatized** *adj*

trav·ail /'træveɪl/ *n* [U] *written* also **travails** [plural] a difficult or unpleasant situation, or very tiring work: [+of] *the travails of last year's water shortage*

trav·el¹ S2 W2 /'trævəl/ *v* **travelled, travelling** *BrE*, **traveled, traveling** *AmE*
1 JOURNEY a) [I] to go from one place to another, or to several places, especially ones that are far away: *Someday I'd like to travel abroad.* | [+to/across/through/around etc] *We're planning to travel across America this summer.* | *travel widely/extensively He has travelled extensively in China.* | *travel by train/car/air etc We travelled by train across Eastern Europe.* | *He'd travelled far, but he'd travelled light* (=without taking many possessions). b) **travel the world/country** to go to most parts of the world or of a particular country
2 DISTANCE [I,T] to go a particular distance or at a particular speed: [+at] *The train was travelling at 100 mph.* | *They travelled 200 miles on the first day.*
3 well-travelled a) also **widely-travelled** having travelled to many different countries: *a well-travelled businesswoman* b) having been travelled on by many people: *a well-travelled road*
4 NEWS [I] to be passed quickly from one person or place to another: *News travels fast.*
5 travel well to remain in good condition or be equally successful when taken to another country: *Exporters have to find wines that travel well.* | *Many British television programmes don't travel well.*
6 EYES [I always + adv/prep] *written* if your eyes travel over something, you look at different parts of it: *His gaze travelled over her face.*
7 LIGHT/SOUND [I] to move at a particular speed or in a particular direction: *Light travels faster than sound.*
8 SPORT [I] to take more than three steps while you are holding the ball in BASKETBALL

1 000, 2 000, 3 000, most frequent words in S poken and W ritten English

T

travel² [S2] [W2] n [U]
  1 the activity of travelling: *The new job involves a fair amount of travel.* | **form/means/mode of travel** (=the type of vehicle you use) *We went by bus – the cheapest means of travel.* | **rail/air/space travel** *Rail travel in Britain seems to be getting more and more unreliable.*
  2 travels [plural] journeys to places that are far away, usually for pleasure: **on sb's travels** *We met some very interesting people on our travels in Thailand.*

> **WORD CHOICE: travel, travelling, journey, trip, voyage, crossing, flight**
> **Travel** (uncountable noun) and **travelling** are used to mean the general activity of moving from place to place: *Air travel is becoming cheaper.* | *Her work involves a lot of travelling.*
> ⚠ You do not say 'a travel'.
> Use **journey** to talk about travelling a long distance or travelling regularly, when the emphasis is on the travelling itself: *a long and difficult journey (NOT travel) through the mountains* | *I read during the train journey to work.* | *Did you have a good journey?* (=Were you comfortable, was the train on time etc?)
> A **trip** is when you go on a short journey, or a journey you do not usually make, and come back again. Use this when the emphasis is on where you are going or who you are going there: *my first trip to the States* | *a business trip* | *Was it a good trip?* (=Did you achieve what you wanted to or have a good time there?)
> **Voyage** is used for a long sea journey: *a voyage across the ocean*
> **Crossing** is used for a fairly short sea journey: *The crossing takes 90 minutes.*
> **Flight** is used for a journey by air: *Have a good flight!*

'travel ,agency n [C] a company that arranges hotel rooms, plane tickets etc for people who want to travel
'travel ,agent n [C] someone who owns or works in a travel agency
trav·el·a·tor /'trævəleɪtə $ -ər/ n [C] another spelling of TRAVOLATOR
'travel ,bureau n [C] a TRAVEL AGENCY
trav·el·ler *BrE*; **traveler** *AmE* /'trævələ $ -ər/ n [C] **1** someone who is on a journey or someone who travels often: *frequent travellers to France* **2** *BrE* someone who travels around from place to place living in a CARAVAN; → **gipsy**
'traveller's ,cheque *BrE*; **traveler's check** *AmE* n [C] a special cheque for a fixed amount that can be exchanged for the money of a foreign country
trav·el·ling¹ *BrE*; **traveling** *AmE* /'trævəlɪŋ/ adj [only before noun] **1 travelling expenses** money that is used to pay for the cost of travelling while someone is on a trip for their company **2 travelling companion** someone you are on a journey with **3 travelling musician/circus/exhibition etc** someone or something that goes from place to place **4 travelling rug/clock etc** *BrE* a clock etc designed to be used when you are travelling **5 travelling people/folk** *BrE* TRAVELLERS
travelling² *BrE*; **traveling** *AmE* n [U] **1** the act or activity of going from one place to another, especially places that are far away: *After retiring, we'll do some travelling.* **2** taking more than three steps while holding the ball in BASKETBALL
,travelling 'salesman *BrE*; **traveling salesman** *AmE* n [C] someone who goes from place to place selling their company's products
trav·el·ogue also **travelog** *AmE* /'trævəlɒg $ -lɑːg, -lɔːg/ n [C] a film or piece of writing that describes travel in a particular country, or a particular person's travels
'travel ,sickness n [U] when you feel ill because you are travelling in a vehicle —**travel-sick** adj
tra·verse¹ /'trævɜːs $ trə'vɜːrs/ v [T] *formal* to move across, over, or through something, especially an area of land or water: *two minutes to traverse the park*

trav·erse² /'trævɜːs $ -vɜːrs/ n [C] *technical* a sideways movement across a very steep slope in mountain-climbing
trav·es·ty /'trævɪsti/ n plural **travesties** [C usually singular] used in order to say that something is extremely bad and is not what it is claimed to be: *Their marriage was a complete travesty.* | **[+of]** *O'Brien described his trial as a **travesty of justice**.*
trav·o·la·tor /'trævəleɪtə $ -ər/ n [C] *BrE* a moving band that you stand on, which moves you along a floor, especially at an airport
trawl¹ /trɔːl $ trɒːl/ v [I,T] **1** to search through a lot of documents, lists etc in order to find out information: **[+through]** *I'll have to trawl through all my lecture notes again.* | **[+for]** *She spent the morning in the library, trawling for information for her project.* **2** to fish by pulling a special wide net behind a boat
trawl² n [C] **1** an act of searching through a lot of documents, lists etc in order to find something **2** also **trawl net** a wide net that is pulled along the bottom of the sea to catch fish
trawl·er /'trɔːlə $ 'trɒːlər/ n [C] a fishing boat that uses a trawl net

trays

in tray

ice cube tray

paint tray

breakfast tray

ashtray

baking tray

tray /treɪ/ n [C] **1** a flat piece of plastic, metal, or wood, with raised edges, used for carrying things such as plates, food etc: *The waiter brought drinks on a tray.* **2** a flat open container used for holding papers, documents etc on a desk: **in tray** (=for holding documents you still have to deal with) | **out tray** (=for holding documents you have dealt with) **3** especially *BrE* a flat open container with four sides used for holding certain things: *a cat litter tray* | **seed tray** (=a tray in which you plant seeds) → BAKING TRAY, SYSTEM TRAY
treach·e·rous /'tretʃərəs/ adj **1** someone who is treacherous cannot be trusted because they are not loyal and secretly intend to harm you: *a sly and treacherous woman* | *a treacherous plot to overthrow the leader* **2** ground, roads, weather conditions etc that are treacherous are particularly dangerous because you cannot see the dangers very easily: *treacherous mountain roads* | *Strong winds and loose rocks made climbing treacherous.* —**treacherously** adv
treach·e·ry /'tretʃəri/ n plural **treacheries 1** [U] behaviour in which someone is not loyal to a person who trusts them, especially when this behaviour helps that person's enemies: *the treachery of those who plotted against the king* **2** [C usually plural] a disloyal action against someone who trusts you
trea·cle /'triːkəl/ n [U] *BrE* **1** a thick sweet black sticky liquid that is obtained from the sugar plant and used in cooking; ◫ **molasses** *AmE* **2** a way of expressing love and emotions that seems silly or insincere: *A film does not turn into treacle.* **3** GOLDEN SYRUP: *a treacle tart* —**treacly** adj
tread¹ /tred/ v past tense **trod** /trɒd $ trɑːd/, past participle **trodden** /'trɒdn $ 'trɑːdn/

1 STEP IN/ON [I always + adv/prep] *BrE* to put your foot on or in something while you are walking; ◻ **step**: [+in/on] *Sorry, did I tread on your foot?* | *She trod barefoot on the soft grass.*

2 tread carefully/warily/cautiously etc to be very careful about what you say or do in a difficult situation: *If I wanted to keep my job, I knew I'd have to tread lightly.*

3 CRUSH **a)** [T] *BrE* to press or crush something into the floor or ground with your feet; ◻ **track** *AmE*: **tread sth into/onto/over sth** *Stop treading mud all over my clean kitchen floor!* | *Bits of the broken vase got trodden into the carpet.* **b)** tread grapes to crush GRAPES with your feet in order to produce juice for making wine

4 tread a path *BrE written* to take a particular action or series of actions: *Getting the right balance between home and work is a difficult path to tread.*

5 tread water *past tense and past participle* **treaded a)** to stay floating upright in deep water by moving your legs as if you are riding a bicycle **b)** to make no progress in a particular situation, especially because you are waiting for something to happen: *All I could do was tread water until the contracts arrived.*

6 WALK [I,T always + adv/prep] *literary* to walk: *David trod wearily along behind the others.*

7 tread the boards *humorous* to work as an actor → tread on sb's toes at TOE¹ (3)

tread² *n* **1** [C,U] the pattern of lines on the part of a tyre that touches the road **2** [C] the part of a stair that you put your foot on **3** [singular] *literary* the particular sound that someone makes when they walk: *I heard the back door bang, and Rex's tread in the hall.*

tread·le /ˈtredl/ *n* [C] a flat piece of metal or wood that you move with your foot to turn a wheel in a machine

tread·mill /ˈtred‚mɪl/ *n* **1** [C] a piece of exercise equipment that has a large belt around a set of wheels, that you can walk or run on while staying in the same place → see picture at SPORTS CENTRE **2** [singular] work or a way of life that seems very boring because you always have to do the same things: *the treadmill of working in the office* **3** [C] a MILL worked in the past by prisoners treading on steps fixed to a very large wheel

trea·son /ˈtriːzən/ *n* [U] the crime of being disloyal to your country or its government, especially by helping its enemies or trying to remove the government using violence: [+against] *Richter is accused of committing treason against the state.* | *The defendant was convicted of high treason* (=treason of the worst kind) *and sentenced to death.* —**treasonable** also **treasonous** *adj*: *a treasonable act against the head of state*

trea·sure¹ /ˈtreʒə $ -ər/ *n* **1** [U] a group of valuable things such as gold, silver, jewels etc: **buried/hidden/ sunken treasure 2** [C] a very valuable and important object such as a painting or ancient document: *The Book of Kells is Trinity College's greatest treasure.* **3** [singular] *informal* someone who is very useful or important to you: *Our housekeeper is a real treasure.*

treasure² *v* [T] to keep and care for something that is very special, important, or valuable to you: *Jim treasured the gold pocket watch that his grandfather had given him.* —**treasured** *adj* [only before noun]: *A battered old guitar was his most treasured possession.*

treasure ‚chest *n* [C] a box that holds treasure

treasure ‚hunt *n* [C] a game in which you have to find something that has been hidden by answering questions that are left in different places

trea·sur·er /ˈtreʒərə $ -ər/ *n* [C] someone who is officially responsible for the money for an organization, club, political party etc

treasure trove /ˈtreʒə trəʊv $ -ʒər troʊv/ *n* [U] **1** a group of valuable or interesting things or pieces of information, or the place where they are: [+of] *Our Science Shop is a treasure trove of curiosities and gadgets.* **2** *BrE law* valuable objects, coins etc that are found where they have been hidden or buried, which are not claimed by anyone

trea·su·ry /ˈtreʒəri/ *n plural* **treasuries 1 the Treasury (Department)** a government department that

controls the money that the country collects and spends **2** [C] a place in a castle, church, PALACE etc where money or valuable objects are kept

treat¹ S2 W1 /triːt/ *v* [T]

1 BEHAVE TOWARDS SB/STH [always + adv/prep] to behave towards someone or something in a particular way; → **treatment. treat sb like/as sth** *She treats me like one of the family.* | *Penny doesn't think her co-workers treat her as an equal.* | *He treated his automobiles almost as tenderly as he did his wife.* | **badly treated/well treated** *The prisoners were well treated by their guards.* | **treat sb with respect/contempt/courtesy etc** *Despite her seniority, Margot was never treated with much respect.* | **treat sb like dirt/a dog** (=treat someone unkindly and without respect) *I don't know why he stays with her – she treats him like dirt.*

2 DEAL WITH STH [always + adv/prep] to deal with, regard, or consider something in a particular way; → **treatment: treat sth as sth** *Please treat this information as completely confidential.* | *She treats everything I say as a joke.* | **treat sth favourably/seriously/carefully etc** *Any complaint about safety standards must be treated very seriously.*

3 ILLNESS/INJURY to try to cure an illness or injury by using drugs, hospital care, operations etc; → **treatment**: *It was difficult to treat patients because of a shortage of medicine.* | **treat sb with sth** *Nowadays, malaria can be treated with drugs.*

4 BUY STH FOR SB to buy or do something special for someone that you know they will enjoy: **treat sb to sth** *We treated Mom to lunch at the Savoy.* | *I treated myself to a new dress.*

5 PROTECT/CLEAN to put a special substance on something or use a chemical process in order to protect, clean, or preserve it; → **treatment**: *sewage treated so that it can be used as fertilizer* → TRICK OR TREAT

treat² *n* **1** [C] something special that you give someone or do for them because you know they will enjoy it: **as a treat** *Steven took his son to a cricket match as a birthday treat.* **2** [singular] an event that gives you a lot of pleasure and is usually unexpected: *When we were kids, a trip to the beach was a real treat.* **3** [C] a special food that tastes good, especially one that you do not eat very often: *The cafe serves an assortment of gourmet treats.* **4** my treat *spoken* used to tell someone that you will pay for something such as a meal for them: *Let's go out to lunch – my treat.* **5** go down a treat *BrE informal* if something goes down a treat, people like it very much: *That new vegetarian restaurant seems to be going down a treat.* **6** look/work a treat *BrE informal* to look very good or work very well: *The sports ground looked a treat, with all the flags flying.*

treat·a·ble /ˈtriːtəbəl/ *adj* a treatable illness or injury can be helped with drugs or an operation: *Certain forms of cancer are treatable with drugs.*

trea·tise /ˈtriːtɪs, -tɪz/ *n* [C] a serious book or article about a particular subject: [+on] *a treatise on medical ethics*

treat·ment S3 W1 /ˈtriːtmənt/ *n*

1 MEDICAL [C,U] something that is done to cure someone who is injured or ill; → **treat**: [+of/for] *There have been great advances in the treatment of cancer.* | *The best treatment for a cold is to rest and drink lots of fluids.* | *She was given emergency treatment by paramedics.* | **get/receive treatment** *Some of the patients had to wait weeks to get the treatment they needed.* | *Michael responded well to treatment* (=got better when he was treated).

2 BEHAVIOUR TOWARDS SB [U] a particular way of behaving towards someone or of dealing with them; → **treat**: [+of] *Civil rights groups have complained about the harsh treatment of prisoners.* | **special/preferential treatment** (=when one person is treated better than another) *The two young princes were not singled out for special treatment at school.* | *Just lately, Kyra has been*

T

*giving me **the silent treatment*** (=refusing to speak to me because she is angry with me).
3 OF A SUBJECT [C,U] a particular way of dealing with or talking about a subject; → **treat**: *I didn't think the film gave the issue serious treatment.*
4 CLEAN/PROTECT [C,U] a process by which something is cleaned, protected etc; → **treat**: [+of] *the treatment of polluted rivers*

treat·y W2 /ˈtriːti/ *n plural* **treaties** [C] a formal written agreement between two or more countries or governments: *Both sides have agreed to **sign the treaty**.* | *The **peace treaty** ends nearly four years of violence.*

treb·le¹ /ˈtrebəl/ *predeterminer BrE* three times as big, as much, or as many as something else; ▤ **triple** *AmE*: *They sold the house for treble the amount they paid for it.*

treble² *v* [I,T] *BrE* to become three times as big in amount, size, or number, or to make something increase in this way; ▤ **triple** *AmE*: *Their profits have trebled in the last two years.*

treble³ *n* **1** [U] the upper half of the whole range of musical notes → BASS¹ (3) **2** [C] a boy's high singing voice, or a boy with a voice like this **3** [C] the part of a musical work that is written for a treble voice or instrument

treble⁴ *adj* [only before noun] a treble voice or instrument produces high notes

treble ˈclef *n* [C] *technical* a sign (𝄞) at the beginning of a line of written music which shows that the note written on the bottom line of the STAVE is an E above MIDDLE C

tree

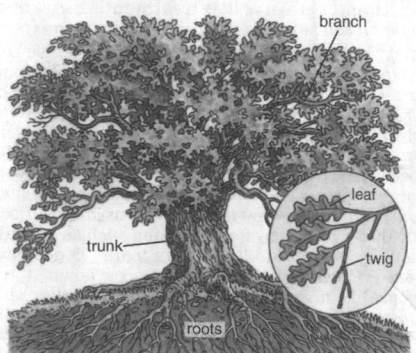

branch
leaf
twig
trunk
roots

tree S1 W1 /triː/ *n* [C]
1 a very tall plant that has branches and leaves, and lives for many years: *As a kid, I loved to climb trees.* | **cherry/peach/apple etc tree** *We planted a peach tree in the backyard.* | *the trunk of an old oak tree* (=the main central part part, from which the branches grow)
2 a drawing that connects things with lines to show how they are related to each other → FAMILY TREE → CHRISTMAS TREE; → **top of the tree** at TOP¹ (3); → **it doesn't grow on trees** at GROW (7); → **be up a gum tree** at GUM TREE (2)

WORD FOCUS: TREE
parts of a tree: **trunk, branch, leaf, blossom, roots, bark, twig**
a large area of trees: **forest, rainforest, jungle**
a small area of trees: **wood/woods, thicket** *BrE*, **copse** *BrE*
types of tree: **evergreen, deciduous, conifer, fruit tree, hardwood tree**
wood from trees: **timber, lumber, firewood**
→ **bush, shrub, sapling, deforestation**

tree·house /ˈtriːhaʊs/ *n* [C] a wooden structure built in the branches of a tree for children to play in

tree·less /ˈtriːləs/ *adj* a treeless area has no trees in it: *a treeless landscape*

ˈtree line *n* [singular] the TIMBERLINE

ˈtree-lined *adj* a tree-lined road has trees on both sides

ˈtree ˌsurgery *n* [U] the treatment of damaged trees, especially by cutting off branches

tree·top /ˈtriːtɒp $ -tɑːp/ *n* [C usually plural] the branches at the top of a tree

tre·foil /ˈtriːfɔɪl, ˈtrefɔɪl/ *n* [C] *technical* **1** a type of small plant that has leaves which divide into three parts **2** a pattern in the shape of these leaves

trek¹ /trek/ *n* [C] **1** a long and difficult journey, made especially on foot as an adventure; ▤ **hike**: *a lonely trek through the forest* **2** *informal* a distance that seems long when you walk it: *I'm afraid it's a bit of a trek to the station.*

trek² *v* **trekked, trekking** [I always + adv/prep] **1** *informal* to make a long and difficult journey, especially on foot; ▤ **hike**: [+up/down etc] *The elevator was broken, so we had to trek up six flights of stairs.* **2** to walk a long way, especially in the mountains, as an adventure; ▤ **hike**: [+in/across etc] *For five days he trekked across the mountains of central China.*

trel·lis /ˈtrelɪs/ *n* [C] a frame made of long narrow pieces of wood that cross each other, used to support climbing plants

trem·ble /ˈtrembəl/ *v* [I] **1** to shake slightly in a way that you cannot control, especially because you are upset or frightened: *His lip started to tremble and then he started to cry.* | **tremble with anger/fear etc** *Greene was on his feet now, his body trembling with rage.* **2** to shake slightly: *The whole house trembled as the train went by.* → see box at SHAKE¹ **3** if your voice trembles, it sounds nervous and unsteady **4** to be worried or frightened about something: *I tremble to think what will happen when she finds out.* —**tremble** *n* [C]

tre·men·dous S2 /trɪˈmendəs/ *adj*
1 very big, fast, powerful etc: *Suddenly, there was a tremendous bang, and the whole station shook.* | *She was making a **tremendous effort** to appear calm.* | *She praised her husband for the **tremendous support** he had given her.* | *Sales have been tremendous so far this year.* | *This plan could save us **a tremendous amount of money**.*
2 excellent: *She's got a tremendous voice, hasn't she?* —**tremendously** *adv*: *tremendously wealthy*

trem·o·lo /ˈtremələʊ $ -loʊ/ *n plural* **tremolos** [C] musical notes which are repeated very quickly

trem·or /ˈtremə $ -ər/ *n* [C] **1** a small EARTHQUAKE in which the ground shakes slightly: *an earth tremor* **2** a slight shaking movement in your body that you cannot control, especially because you are ill, weak, or upset

trem·u·lous /ˈtremjʊləs/ *adj literary* shaking slightly, especially because you are nervous: *a tremulous voice* —**tremulously** *adv*

trench /trentʃ/ *n* [C] **1** a long narrow hole dug into the surface of the ground: *Workers dug a trench for gas lines.* **2** *technical* a long narrow valley in the ground beneath the sea **3** [usually plural] a deep trench dug in the ground as a protection for soldiers: *the trenches of World War I* **4** **the trenches** the place or situation where most of the work or action in an activity takes place: *Lane left teaching after 30 years in the trenches.*

tren·chant /ˈtrentʃənt/ *adj written* expressed very strongly, effectively, and directly without worrying about offending people: *Stockman became one of the President's most trenchant critics.* —**trenchantly** *adv*

ˈtrench coat *n* [C] a long RAINCOAT with a belt

trench·er /ˈtrentʃə $ -ər/ *n* [C] *BrE* a plate used in the past for serving food

ˌtrench ˈwarfare *n* [U] a method of fighting in which soldiers from opposing armies are in TRENCHES facing each other

trend S2 W2 /trend/ n [C]
1 a general tendency in the way a situation is changing or developing

recent trend
current/present/latest trend
general trend
alarming/worrying/disturbing trend
growing/increasing/rising trend
underlying/long-term trend (=the trend over a long period of time)
economic trends
downward/upward trend (=a tendency for something to increase or decrease)
reverse/buck the trend (=make a trend go in the opposite direction)

[+towards] *Lately there has been a trend towards hiring younger, cheaper employees.* | [+in] *recent trends in education* | *The current trend is towards more part-time employment.* | *the general trend towards the centralization of political power* | *A disturbing trend is that victims of violence are getting younger.* | *The growing trend is for single mothers to bring up children by themselves.* | *Even so, the underlying trend is positive.* | *national and international economic trends* | *the downward trend in the price of gold* | *Successive presidents have tried to reverse this trend, but without success.*

2 set the trend to start doing something that other people copy: *Larger corporations are setting the trend for better maternity benefits.*

trend·set·ter /'trend,setə $ -ər/ n [C] someone who starts a new fashion or makes it popular — **trendsetting** adj [only before noun]

trend·spot·ter /'trend,spotə $ -,spɑːtər/ n [C] someone who notices and reports on new fashions, activities that people are starting to do, or the way a situation is developing —**trendspotting** n [U]

trend·y¹ /'trendi/ adj comparative **trendier**, superlative **trendiest** influenced by the most fashionable styles and ideas: *a trendy Bay Area restaurant* —**trendiness** n [U]

trendy² n plural **trendies** [C] BrE informal someone who is trendy and wants other people to think they are very modern – used especially to show disapproval: *young trendies from art college*

trep·i·da·tion /ˌtrepɪ'deɪʃən/ n [U] a feeling of anxiety or fear about something that is going to happen: *With some trepidation, I opened the door.*

tres·pass¹ /'trespəs $ -pəs, -pæs/ v [I] **1** to go onto someone's private land without their permission: [+on] *She was arrested for trespassing on government property.* **2** old use to do something wrong; ▪ **sin** —**trespasser** n [C]
   trespass on sth phr v formal to unfairly use more than you should of someone else's time, help etc for your own advantage: *It would be trespassing on their hospitality to accept any more from them.*

tres·pass² n **1** [C,U] also **trespassing** AmE the offence of going onto someone's land without their permission: *He will be prosecuted for trespass.* **2** [C] biblical something you have done that is morally wrong; ▪ **sin**

tress·es /'tresɪz/ n [plural] literary a woman's beautiful long hair

tres·tle /'tresəl/ n [C] especially BrE **1** an A-shaped frame used as one of the two supports for a temporary table **2** also **trestle bridge** a bridge with an A-shaped frame supporting it

trestle ˌtable n [C] BrE a temporary table made of a long board supported on trestles

tri- /traɪ/ prefix three: **trilingual** (=speaking three languages) | **triangle** (=a shape with three sides)

tri·ad /'traɪæd/ n [C] **1** a Chinese secret criminal group **2** a group of three people or things that are related or similar to each other

tri·age /'triːɑːʒ $ triˈɑːʒ, ˈtriːɑːʒ/ n [U] technical the method of deciding who receives medical treatment first, according to how seriously someone is injured

tri·al¹ S3 W2 /'traɪəl/ n
1 COURT [C,U] a legal process in which a judge and often a JURY in a court of law examine information to decide whether someone is guilty of a crime; ➔ **try**: *a murder trial* | **on trial (for sth)** (=being judged in a court of law for) *Brady was on trial for assault.* | *The men are due to* **stand trial** (=be judged in a court of law) *on a drugs charge.* | *The defendant has a right to a* **fair trial.** | **go/come to trial** (=begin being judged in a court of law) *By the time the case comes to trial, he will have spent a year in prison.* | **bring sb to trial** *Thirty police officers were brought to trial.* | *Murphy sat in a prison cell* **awaiting trial** (=waiting for his trial to begin). ➔ SHOW TRIAL
2 TEST [C,U] a process of testing to find out whether something works effectively and is safe: *a new drug that is undergoing* **clinical trials**
3 TRY SB/STH [C,U] a short period during which you use or do something or employ someone to find out whether they are satisfactory for a particular purpose or job; ➔ **try**: **on trial** *They let me have the computer on trial for thirty days.* | *The security system will be reviewed after a three-month* **trial period.** | *Smith was hired* **on a six-month trial basis.** | **trial separation** (=a period of time in which a husband and wife do not live together, to find out whether they want to stay married)
4 by/through trial and error if you do something by trial and error, you test many different methods of doing something in order to find the best: *I learned most of what I know about gardening through trial and error.*
5 DIFFICULTY [C usually plural] something that is difficult to deal with, and that is worrying or annoying; ➔ **trying**: *the daily trials of living in a poor country* | **be a trial (to/for sb)** *My brothers and I were always a real trial to my parents.* | *the* **trials and tribulations** *of running a business*
6 SPORTS trials [plural] BrE a special sports competition in which people who want to be on a team are tested, so that the best can be chosen; ▪ **tryout** AmE: **horse/sheepdog trials** (=a sporting competition in which horses or dogs compete)

trial² v **trialled, trialling** [T] BrE to thoroughly test something to see if it works correctly or is effective: *These techniques were trialled by teachers in 300 schools.*

'trial balˌloon n [C] something that you do or say in order to see whether other people will accept something or not: *Senator Lott is floating trial balloons to test public opinion on the bill.*

ˌtrial 'run n [C] an occasion when you test a new method or system to see if it works well: *This year is something of a trial run for the new service.*

tri·an·gle /'traɪæŋɡəl/ n [C] **1** a flat shape with three straight sides and three angles **2** something that is shaped like a triangle: *a triangle of land* **3** a musical instrument made of metal bent into the shape of a triangle. You hit it with a metal stick to make a ringing sound. **4** AmE a flat plastic object with three sides that has one angle of 90° and is used for drawing angles; ▪ **set-square** BrE; ➔ see picture at MATHEMATICS

tri·an·gu·lar /traɪˈæŋɡjələ $ -ər/ adj **1** shaped like a triangle **2** involving three people or teams: *a triangular sporting competition*

tri·an·gu·la·tion /traɪˌæŋɡjəˈleɪʃən/ n [U] a method of finding your position by measuring the lines and angles of a triangle on a map

tri·ath·lon /traɪˈæθlən/ n [C] a sports competition in which competitors run, swim, and cycle long distances

T

trib·al /ˈtraɪbəl/ *adj* [usually before noun] relating to with a tribe or tribes: *a tribal dance* | *tribal cultures*

trib·al·is·m /ˈtraɪbəl-ɪzəm/ *n* [U] **1** behaviour and attitudes that are based on strong loyalty to your tribe **2** the state of being organized into tribes

tribe /traɪb/ *n* [C] **1** a social group consisting of people of the same RACE who have the same beliefs, customs, language etc, and usually live in one particular area ruled by their leader: *a tribe of Aborigines known as the Dolphin People* **2** a group of people with the same interests – used especially to show disapproval: *tribes of journalists* **3** a group of related animals or plants: *the cat tribe* **4** humorous a large family: *We were only expecting Jack and his wife, but the whole tribe turned up.*

tribes·man /ˈtraɪbzmən/ *n plural* **tribesmen** /-mən/ [C] a man who is a member of a tribe

tribes·wom·an /ˈtraɪbz,wʊmən/ *n plural* **tribeswomen** /-,wɪmɪn/ [C] a woman who is a member of a tribe

trib·u·la·tion /ˌtrɪbjəˈleɪʃən/ *n* [C,U] *formal* serious trouble or a serious problem: *Even close friends were unaware of the tribulations she faced.* → **trials and tribulations** at TRIAL¹ (5)

tri·bu·nal /traɪˈbjuːnl/ *n* [C] a type of court that is given official authority to deal with a particular situation or problem: *The case of your redundancy will be heard by an independent tribunal.* → INDUSTRIAL TRIBUNAL

trib·une /ˈtrɪbjuːn/ *n* [C] an official in ancient Rome who was elected by the ordinary people to protect their rights

trib·u·ta·ry /ˈtrɪbjʊtəri $ -teri/ *n plural* **tributaries** [C] a stream or river that flows into a larger river

trib·ute /ˈtrɪbjuːt/ *n* [C,U] **1** something that you say, do, or give in order to express your respect or admiration for someone: *The players wore black armbands as a tribute to their late teammate.* | *I'd like to pay tribute to* (=praise and admire publicly) *the party workers for all their hard work.* **2 be a tribute to sb/sth** to be a clear sign of the good qualities that someone or something has: *It was a tribute to her teaching methods that so many children passed the test.* **3** a payment of goods or money by one ruler or country to another more powerful one, especially in order to be protected **4 floral tribute** *BrE* flowers sent to a funeral

trice /traɪs/ *n* **in a trice** *BrE old-fashioned* very quickly or soon: *He should be here in a trice.*

tri·ceps /ˈtraɪseps/ *n* [C] the large muscle at the back of your upper arm

trick

a trick

cheating

trick¹ [S3] /trɪk/ *n* [C]
1 [STH THAT DECEIVES SB] something you do in order to deceive someone: *Pretending he doesn't remember is an old trick of his.* | *He didn't really lose his wallet – that's just a trick.*
2 [JOKE] something you do to surprise someone and to make other people laugh: *I'm getting tired of your silly tricks.* | *The girls were playing tricks on their teacher.*

3 [STH THAT MAKES THINGS APPEAR DIFFERENT] something that makes things appear to be different from the way they really are: *After walking for hours in the hot sun, his mind began playing tricks on him.* | *At first he thought someone was coming towards him, but it was just a trick of the light.*
4 a dirty/rotten/mean trick an unkind or unfair thing to do: *He didn't turn up? What a dirty trick!*
5 do the trick *spoken* if something does the trick, it solves a problem or provides what is needed to get a good result: *A bit more flour should do the trick.*
6 [MAGIC] a skilful set of actions that seem like magic, done to entertain people: *My uncle was always showing me card tricks when I was a kid.* | *a magic trick*
7 [CLEVER METHOD] a way of doing something that works very well but may not be easy to notice: *The trick is to bend your knees as you catch the ball.* | *a salesman who knew all the tricks of the trade* (=clever methods used in a particular job)
8 use/try every trick in the book to use every method that you know, even dishonest ones, to achieve what you want
9 teach/show sb a trick or two *informal* used to say that someone knows more than someone else or can do something better than them: *Experienced teachers can show new teachers a trick or two.*
10 sb is up to their (old) tricks *informal* to be doing the same dishonest things that you have often done before
11 [CARDS] the cards played or won in one part of a game of cards: *He won the first three tricks easily.*
12 [HABIT] **have a trick of doing sth** *BrE* to have a habit of using a particular expression or of moving your face or body in a particular way: *She had this trick of raising her eyebrows at the end of a question.*
13 never miss a trick *spoken* to always know exactly what is happening even if it does not concern you: *Dave's found out. He never misses a trick, does he?.*
14 how's tricks? *old-fashioned spoken* used to greet someone in a friendly way: *Hello, Bill! How's tricks?*
15 [SEX] *AmE old-fashioned informal* someone who pays a PROSTITUTE to have sex: **turn a trick** (=to have sex with someone for money) → CONFIDENCE TRICK; → **dirty trick** at DIRTY¹ (6); → **you can't teach an old dog new tricks** at TEACH (7); → HAT TRICK

trick² *v* [T] **1** to deceive someone in order to get something from them or to make them do something: *She knew she'd been tricked, but it was too late.* | **trick sb into doing sth** *He claimed he was tricked into carrying drugs.* | **trick sb out of sth** *The corporation was tricked out of $20 million.* | **trick your way into/past/ onto etc sth** *He tricked his way into her home by pretending to be a policeman.* **2 be tricked out with/in sth** *BrE literary* to be decorated with something: *a hat tricked out with ribbons*

trick³ *adj* **1 trick photography** when a photograph or picture has been changed so that it looks different from what was really there **2 a trick question** a question which seems easy to answer but has a hidden difficulty **3 a trick knee/ankle/shoulder etc** *AmE* a joint that is weak and can suddenly cause you problems

trick·e·ry /ˈtrɪkəri/ *n* [U] the use of tricks to deceive or cheat people

trick·le¹ /ˈtrɪkəl/ *v* [I always + adv/prep] **1** if liquid trickles somewhere, it flows slowly in drops or in a thin stream: [+down/into/out] *The tears trickled down her cheeks.* **2** if people, vehicles, goods etc trickle somewhere, they move there slowly in small groups or amounts: [+in/into/away] *The first few fans started to trickle into the stadium.*
trickle down *phr v* if money trickles down, it moves slowly from the richest people to the poorest people in a society, or from the richest countries to the poorest countries
trickle up *phr v* if money trickles up, it moves slowly from the poorest people to the richest people in a society, or from the poorest countries to the richest countries

trickle² n **1** [C] a thin slow flow of liquid: *The water in the stream had been reduced to a trickle.* **2** [singular] a movement of people, vehicles, goods etc into a place in very small numbers or amounts: *Recent legislation has reduced immigration to a trickle.* | [+of] *a trickle of cars on the highway*

trickle-down ef·fect n [singular] a belief that additional wealth gained by the richest people in society will have a good economic effect on the lives of everyone because the rich people will put the extra money into businesses, INVESTMENTS etc

trick or 'treat v **1** go trick or treating if children go trick or treating, they dress in COSTUMES and go from house to house on HALLOWEEN saying 'trick or treat' in order to get sweets **2** the words that children say when they go trick or treating, to say that they will play a trick on someone if they are not given a TREAT (=sweet)

trick·ster /'trɪkstə $ -ər/ n [C] someone who deceives or cheats people: **confidence trickster** BrE: *a slick, fast-talking confidence trickster*

trick·y S3 /'trɪki/ adj comparative **trickier**, superlative **trickiest**
1 something that is difficult to deal with or do because it is complicated and full of problems: *I can get you tickets for the show but it'll be tricky.*
2 a tricky person is clever and likely to deceive you; ◨ **crafty**

tri·col·our BrE; **tricolor** AmE /'trɪkələ $ 'traɪ,kʌlər/ n [C] a flag with three equal bands of different colours, especially the national flags of France or Ireland

tri·cy·cle /'traɪsɪkəl/ n [C] a bicycle with three wheels, especially for young children

tri·dent /'traɪdənt/ n [C] **1** a weapon with three points that looks like a large fork **2 Trident missile/submarine** a type of NUCLEAR weapon, or the SUBMARINE that shoots it

tried¹ /traɪd/ the past tense and past participle of TRY

tried² adj **tried and tested/trusted/true** a tried and tested method has been used successfully many times: *tried and tested safety procedures*

tri·en·ni·al /traɪ'eniəl/ adj happening every three years; → **annual**

tri·er /'traɪə $ -ər/ n [C] especially BrE informal someone who always makes a great effort, even if they do not often succeed

tri·fle¹ /'traɪfəl/ n **1 a trifle** formal slightly: **a trifle eccentric/odd/unexpected etc** **2** [C] old-fashioned something unimportant or not valuable: *There's no point in arguing over trifles.* **3** [C,U] a cold British sweet dish made of layers of cake, fruit, JELLY, CUSTARD, and cream

trifle² v
trifle with sb/sth phr v to treat someone or something without respect or not in a serious way: *He's not a man to be trifled with.* | *men who trifle with women's affections*

tri·fling /'traɪflɪŋ/ adj unimportant or of little value: *a trifling sum* | *matters of trifling importance*

trig·ger¹ /'trɪgə $ -ər/ n [C] **1** the part of a gun that you pull with your finger to fire it: **pull/squeeze the trigger** *He took aim and squeezed the trigger.* **2 be the trigger (point) (for sth)** to be the thing that quickly causes a serious problem: *The hijacking became a trigger point for military action.*

trigger² also **trigger off** v [T] **1** to make something happen very quickly, especially a series of events: *The assassination triggered off a wave of rioting.* | *Certain forms of mental illness can be triggered by food allergies.* | **trigger a memory** (=make you suddenly remember something) | *His action **triggered** a massive response from the government.* **2** to make something such as a bomb or electrical system start to operate: *The burglars fled after **triggering** the **alarm**.*

trigger-,happy also **'trigger-,ready** adj informal someone who is trigger-happy is much too willing to use weapons, especially guns: *a trigger-happy cop*

'trigger ,man n [C] informal AmE a person who shoots another person, especially when they do this for someone else: *Even if the trigger men are caught, those who ordered the killing escape punishment.*

trig·o·nom·e·try /,trɪgə'nɒmətri $ -'nɑː-/ n [U] the part of mathematics concerned with the relationship between the angles and sides of TRIANGLES

trike /traɪk/ n [C] informal a TRICYCLE

tri·lat·e·ral /traɪ'lætərəl/ adj [only before noun] involving three groups, countries etc; → **bilateral**: *trilateral peace talks*

tril·by /'trɪlbi/ also **,trilby 'hat** n plural **trilbies** [C] especially BrE a man's soft FELT hat

tri·lin·gual /,traɪ'lɪŋgwəl◂/ adj **1** able to speak three languages **2** using three languages: *a trilingual medieval inscription*

trill¹ /trɪl/ v [I,T] **1** to make a short repeated high sound: *birds trilling in the trees* | *The phone trilled sharply.* **2** to say something in a high happy voice that sounds slightly false: *'Have a nice time, darling,' she trilled.*

trill² n [C] **1** technical a musical sound made by quickly moving between two notes **2** a short repeated high sound: *the trill of blackbirds*

tril·lion /'trɪljən/ number plural **trillion** or **trillions** **1** the number 1,000,000,000,000: *In a short time the number of cells is more than a trillion.* | **two/three/four etc trillion** *$5.3 trillion* | *Japan's exports were worth $43 trillion last year.* | **trillions of pounds/dollars etc** *the trillions of dollars in the bond markets* **2** informal an extremely large number of people or things: *a trillion a shirt with a trillion holes in it* | **trillions of** *We've made this mistake trillions of times before.* **3** BrE old use the number 1,000,000,000,000,000,000 —**trillionth** adj —**trillionth** n [C]

tri·lo·bite /'traɪləbaɪt/ n [C] a type of FOSSIL of a small sea creature

tril·o·gy /'trɪlədʒi/ n plural **trilogies** [C] a series of three plays, books etc that are about the same people or subject: *part 2 of a trilogy*

trim¹ /trɪm/ v trimmed, trimming [T]
1 CUT to make something look neater by cutting small pieces off it: *Pete was trimming the lawn around the roses.* | *I have my hair trimmed every six weeks.* | **trim sth away/off** *Trim away any excess glue with a knife.*
2 REDUCE to reduce a number, amount, or the size of something: *We need to **trim costs** by £500m.* | *The bill would trim the number of immigrants to the US.* | **trim sth from/off sth** *The company trimmed £46,000 from its advertising budget.*
3 DECORATE [usually passive] to decorate something, especially clothes, by adding things that look pretty: **trim sth with sth** *a dress trimmed with lace* | *At Christmas, the whole family helps trim the tree.*
4 SAIL to move the sails of a boat in order to go faster
trim sth ⇔ **back** phr v
to make something shorter or smaller: *Trim the stems back carefully.* | *Most airlines have trimmed back their operations.*
trim down phr v
to lose weight deliberately: *Anne has trimmed down from 22 stone to 18.*

trim² adj **1** a person who is trim is thin in an attractive healthy way; ◨ **slim**: *I play tennis to keep trim.* | *a trim figure* **2** neat and well cared for: *trim suburban gardens*

trim³ n **1** [singular] when something is cut to make it look neater: *My beard needs a trim.* **2 in (good) trim** informal in good condition: **keep/get (sth) in trim** *If you want to get in trim for summer, try aerobics.* | *My job was to keep the garden in trim.* **3** [singular, U] additional decoration on a car, piece of clothing etc: *suede sandals with gold trim*

T

tri·ma·ran /'traɪməræn/ n [C] a type of sailing boat with three HULLS

tri·mes·ter /trɪ'mestə $ traɪ'mestər/ n [C] **1** AmE one of three periods of equal length that the school year is divided into; ▣ **term** BrE **2** one of the three-month periods of PREGNANCY

trim·mer /'trɪmə $ -ər/ n [C] a machine for cutting the sides of HEDGES, LAWNS etc

trim·mings /'trɪmɪŋz/ n [plural] **1 with all the trim-mings** food that is served with all the trimmings is enjoyable because it is served with lots of extra types of food: *a roast chicken platter with all the trimmings* **2** small pieces that are left after you have cut something larger: *hedge trimmings* **3** pieces of material used to decorate clothes: *a hat with fur trimmings*

trin·i·ty /'trɪnɪti/ n **the Trinity** also **the holy Trinity** in the Christian religion, the union of Father, Son, and Holy Spirit in one God

trin·ket /'trɪŋkɪt/ n [C] a piece of jewellery or a small pretty object that is not valuable

tri·o /'triːəʊ $ 'triːoʊ/ n plural **trios** [C] **1** a group of three people or things: [+of] *He was met by a trio of smiling executives.* | *a classical guitar trio* (=three musicians playing together) **2** a piece of music for three performers → DUET[1], QUARTET

trip[1] [S2] [W2] /trɪp/ n
1 [C] a visit to a place that involves a journey, for pleasure or a particular purpose: [+to] *Did you enjoy your trip to Disneyland?* | [+from] *The Palace is only a short trip from here.* | **business/school/shopping etc trip** *a business trip to Japan* | *Two lucky employees won a round-the-world trip.* | **coach/boat/bus trip** *a boat trip up the Thames* | **day trip** *a pleasure trip done in one day)* | *It's an 80-mile* **round trip** (=a journey to a place and back again) *to Exeter.* | **return trip** (=when you are travelling back to where you started) | *I'm afraid you've had a* **wasted trip** (=a trip in which you do not achieve your purpose) *Mr Burgess has already left.* | **go on/take a trip** *We're thinking of taking a trip to the mountains.* | *He was unable to* **make** *the* **trip** *to accept the award.* → see box at TRAVEL[2]
2 [C] informal the strange mental experiences someone has when they take a drug such as LSD: *a bad trip*
3 [singular] AmE informal a person or experience that is amusing and unusual: *Julie's such a trip!*
4 [C] an act of falling as a result of hitting something with your foot: *accidents caused by trips or falls* → EGO TRIP; → **guilt trip** at GUILT[1] (4); → ROUND TRIP

trip[2] v **tripped, tripping**
1 [FALL] also **trip up** [I] to hit something with your foot by accident so that you fall or almost fall; ▣ **stumble**: *He* **tripped** *and fell.* | [+over] *Clary tripped over a cable and broke his foot.* | [+on] *He tripped on the bottom step.*; → see picture at SLIP[1]
2 [MAKE SB FALL] also **trip up** [T] to make someone fall by putting your foot in front of them when they are moving: *Baggio was tripped inside the penalty area.*
3 [SWITCH ON] [T] to switch on a piece of electrical equipment by accident: *An intruder had tripped the alarm.*
4 [WALK/DANCE] [I always + adv/prep] literary to walk, run, or dance with quick light steps: *a little girl trip-ping down the lane*
5 **trip off the tongue** to be easy to say or pronounce: *Monofluorophosphate! It doesn't exactly trip off the tongue, does it?*
6 [DRUG] also **trip out** [I] informal to experience the mental effects of a drug such as LSD: *They must have been tripping.*
7 **trip the light fantastic** to dance – used humorously
trip up phr v
1 to make a mistake, or to force someone to make a

mistake by tricking them: *On his latest album, Kowal-ski trips up attempting to make more modern songs.* | **trip sb ⇔ up** *an attempt to trip up the Prime Minister on policy issues*
2 to hit something with your foot so that you fall, or to make someone do this: **trip sb ⇔ up** *He chased the thief, tripped him up, and grabbed the camera.*

tri·par·tite /traɪ'pɑːtaɪt $ -'pɑːr-/ adj [only before noun] formal involving three parts, groups etc: **tripartite agreement/talks etc** *a tripartite agreement between France, Britain, and Germany*

tripe /traɪp/ n [U] **1** the stomach of a cow or pig, used as food: *tripe and onions* **2** especially BrE informal something someone says or writes that is stupid or untrue: *What Charles was saying was utter tripe.*

'trip hop n [U] a type of dance music played with electronic instruments that has a slow beat

tri·ple[1] /'trɪpəl/ adj [only before noun] predeter-miner **1** having three parts or involving three groups, people, events etc; → **double**: *a triple murder investigation* | *a triple bill of horror movies* | *the triple world champion* | *a triple bypass heart opera-tion* **2** three times more than a particular number: *The rail system has triple the average number of acci-dents.*

triple[2] v [I,T] to increase by three times as much, or to make something do this; → **double**: *The company has tripled in size.* | *We expect to triple our profits next year.*

triple[3] n [C] **1** a hit of the ball in baseball that allows the BATTER to get to the third BASE **2** three turns of your body in a sport such as ICE SKATING or GYMNASTICS

'triple jump n [singular] an ATHLETICS event in which you jump with one foot, then with your other foot, and finally with both feet —**triple jumper** n [C]: *Triple jumper Edwards set a new world record.*

trip·let /'trɪplɪt/ n [C] one of three children born at the same time to the same mother; → **twin**

trip·lex /'trɪpleks $ 'trɪ-, 'traɪ-/ n [C] AmE a house containing three separate apartments; → **duplex**

trip·li·cate /'trɪplɪkɪt/ n **in triplicate** if a document is in triplicate, there are three copies of it; → **duplicate**: *Is it really necessary to complete the forms in triplicate?*

tri·pod /'traɪpɒd $ -pɑːd/ n [C] a support with three legs, used for a piece of equipment, camera etc → see picture at STAND[2]

trip·per /'trɪpə $ -ər/ n [C] a DAY TRIPPER

trip·tych /'trɪptɪk/ n [C] technical a religious picture painted on three pieces of wood that are joined together

trip·wire /'trɪp,waɪə $ -waɪr/ n [C] a wire stretched across the ground as part of a trap

trite /traɪt/ adj a trite remark, idea etc is boring, not new, and insincere: *Her remarks sounded trite and ill-informed.* —**triteness** n [U] —**tritely** adv: *tritely familiar replies*

tri·umph[1] /'traɪəmf/ n **1** [C] an important victory or success after a difficult struggle: *Winning the cham-pionship is a great* **personal triumph.** | [+for] *a tremen-dous* **diplomatic triumph** *for France* | [+over] *the triumph over hardship* **2** [U] a feeling of pleasure and satisfaction that you get from victory or success: *a shout of triumph* | **in triumph** *He rode in triumph to the Tsar.* **3** [singular] a very successful example of something: [+of] *The gallery is a triumph of design.*

triumph[2] v [I] formal to gain a victory or success after a difficult struggle: [+over] *In the end, good shall triumph over evil.*

tri·um·phal /traɪ'ʌmfəl/ adj [only before noun] done or made to celebrate a victory: *a triumphal procession* | *a triumphal arch*

tri·um·phal·is·m /traɪ'ʌmfəlɪzəm/ n [U] behaviour which shows that someone is too proud of their success and too pleased about the defeat of their opponents – used to show disapproval: *charges of triumphalism*

tri·um·phant /traɪˈʌmfənt/ *adj* **1** showing pleasure and pride because of a victory or success: *I feel exhausted, but also triumphant.* | **triumphant look/ smile/expression etc** *a triumphant grin* **2** having gained a victory or success: *the triumphant army* | *The Nationalists* **emerged triumphant** *from the political crisis.* —**triumphantly** *adv*: *'I've got a job,' she announced triumphantly.*

tri·um·vir·ate /traɪˈʌmvᵊrᵻt/ *n* [C] *formal* a group of three very powerful people

triv·et /ˈtrɪvᵻt/ *n* [C] a metal support used to hold a hot dish

triv·i·a /ˈtrɪviə/ *n* [plural] **1** detailed facts about history, sport, famous people etc: *a selection of golfing trivia* | *a trivia quiz* **2** unimportant or useless details: *meaningless trivia*

triv·i·al /ˈtrɪviəl/ *adj* not serious, important, or valuable: **trivial problem/matter/complaint etc** *We were punished for the most trivial offences.* | *a trivial sum* | *Her feelings for Simon seemed* **trivial by comparison.**

triv·i·al·i·ty /ˌtrɪviˈælᵻti/ *n plural* **trivialities** **1** [C] something that is not important at all: *Don't waste time on trivialities.* **2** [U] the fact of not being at all important or serious: *the triviality of daytime TV*

triv·i·al·ize also **-ise** *BrE* /ˈtrɪviəlaɪz/ *v* [T] to make something seem less important or serious than it really is – used to show disapproval: *The article trivializes the whole issue of equal rights.* | *The debate has been trivialized by the media.* —**trivialization** /ˌtrɪviəlaɪˈzeɪʃən $ -lə-/ *n* [U]

trod /trɒd $ trɑːd/ the past tense of TREAD[1]

trod·den /ˈtrɒdn $ ˈtrɑːdn/ the past participle of TREAD[1]

trog·lo·dyte /ˈtrɒglədaɪt $ ˈtrɑːg-/ *n* [C] someone who lived in a CAVE in PREHISTORIC times

troi·ka /ˈtrɔɪkə/ *n* [C] *formal* a group of three people, countries etc: *the ruling troika*

Tro·jan /ˈtrəʊdʒən $ ˈtroʊ-/ *n old-fashioned* **work like a Trojan** to work very hard

Trojan 'horse *n* [C] **1** something that seems ordinary but that is used to hide someone's real intentions: *These investment arrangements could be Trojan horses for anti-competitive monopolies.* **2** a type of computer VIRUS: *A bug in the browser lets servers download a Trojan horse.*

troll¹ /trəʊl, trɒl $ troʊl/ *n* [C] an imaginary creature in stories that looks like an ugly person

troll² *v* [I,T] *AmE* **1** to try to remove something from a river, ocean etc by pulling a rope, line etc through the water: *Ships towing huge magnets trolled the ocean floor.* | [+for] *I would troll for fish from the rowboat.* **2** to try to obtain something by searching, asking people etc; ⊟ **trawl** *BrE*: **troll (sth) for sth** *Stewart spent hours trolling the Web for information.*

trolleys

supermarket trolley *BrE*/
shopping cart *AmE*

trolley *BrE*/cart *AmE*

trol·ley /ˈtrɒli $ ˈtrɑːli/ *n* [C] **1** *BrE* a large basket on wheels that you use for carrying bags, shopping etc; ⊟ **cart** *AmE*: *a supermarket trolley* **2** *BrE* a small table on wheels used for serving food; ⊟ **cart** *AmE*: *a drinks trolley* | *the sweet trolley* (=one for serving sweet dishes, cakes etc in a restaurant) **3** *AmE* an electric vehicle for carrying passengers which moves along the street on metal tracks; ⊟ **tram** *BrE* **4** a TROLLEYBUS **5** **be off your trolley** *BrE informal humorous* to be crazy

trol·ley·bus /ˈtrɒlibʌs $ ˈtrɑː-/ *n* [C] a bus that uses power from electric wires above the street

trol·lop /ˈtrɒləp $ ˈtrɑː-/ *n* [C] *old-fashioned not polite* an offensive word for a sexually immoral woman

trom·bone /trɒmˈbəʊn $ trɑːmˈboʊn/ *n* [C] a large metal musical instrument that you play by blowing into it and sliding a long tube in and out to change the notes —**trombonist** *n* [C]

troop¹ [S3] [W2] /truːp/ *n*

1 **troops** [plural] soldiers in an organized group: *Both countries agreed to* **withdraw** *their* **troops.** | **French/ UN/government etc troops** *Johnson took the popular step of* **sending in** *American* **troops.** | **troops stationed in** *Hawaii*

2 **troop movement/withdrawal etc** movements etc of troops: *increased* **troop deployment** (=when troops are moved to places where they are needed)

3 [C] a group of soldiers, especially on horses or in TANKS: *the troop commander*

4 [C] a group of people or animals that do something together: *a troop of monkeys* | *a Scout troop* → TROUPE

troop² *v* [I always + adv/prep] *informal* if a group of people troop somewhere, they walk there together in a way that shows they are tired or bored: [+off/along/out etc] *After rehearsals, we'd all troop off to the cafeteria.*

'troop ,carrier *n* [C] a ship, aircraft, or vehicle used for moving soldiers

troop·er /ˈtruːpə $ -ər/ *n* **1** [C] a soldier of the lowest rank in the part of the army that uses TANKS or horses **2** [C] a member of a state police force in the US **3** **swear like a trooper** *old-fashioned* to swear a lot

troop·ship /ˈtruːpˌʃɪp/ *n* [C] a ship used for moving soldiers

trope /trəʊp $ troʊp/ *n* [C] *technical* words, phrases, images etc that are used for an unusual or interesting effect: *cinematic tropes*

tro·phy /ˈtrəʊfi $ ˈtroʊ-/ *n plural* **trophies** [C] **1** a large object such as a silver cup or plate that someone receives as a prize for winning a competition: *walls lined with banners and athletic trophies* | **Football League/Masters/Heisman etc Trophy** (=the name given to a particular competition for which the prize is a trophy); → see picture at PRIZE **2** something that you keep to prove your success in something, especially in war or hunting: *A lion's head was among the trophies of his African trip.* **3** **trophy wife** *informal* a young beautiful woman who is married to a rich successful man who is much older than her – used to show disapproval

trop·ic /ˈtrɒpɪk $ ˈtrɑː-/ *n* **1** [C] one of the two imaginary lines around the world, either the Tropic of Cancer which is 23½° north of the EQUATOR, or the Tropic of Capricorn which is 23½° south of the equator → see picture at GLOBE **2** **the tropics** the hottest part of the world, which is around the EQUATOR: *plant species found in the tropics*

trop·i·cal /ˈtrɒpɪkəl $ ˈtrɑː-/ *adj* **1** coming from or existing in the hottest parts of the world: *the* **tropical rain forests** | *tropical fruit* | **tropical diseases/medicine** (=diseases that are common in hot countries or the study of these diseases) **2** weather that is tropical is very hot and wet: *a steamy tropical night*

trot¹ /trɒt $ trɑːt/ *v* **trotted, trotting** **1** [I] if a horse trots, it moves fairly quickly with each front leg moving at the same time as the opposite back leg; → **canter, gallop** **2** [I always + adv/prep] if a person or animal trots, they run fairly slowly, taking short regular steps: *She came trotting down the steps from the library.* **3** [I always + adv/prep] *informal* to walk or go somewhere, especially fairly quickly: *He trotted off and came back a couple of minutes later, holding a parcel.*

    trot sth ⇔ **out** *phr v informal* to give opinions, excuses, reasons etc that you have used too many times and that do not seem sincere: *Steve trotted out the same old excuses.*

[1] 000, [2] 000, [3] 000, most frequent words in [S] poken and [W] ritten English

trot² n

1 HORSE a) [singular] the movement of a horse at trotting speed: *Our horses slowed to a trot.* **b)** [C] a ride on a horse at trotting speed

2 on the trot BrE informal **a)** one directly following another: *The class has been cancelled three weeks on the trot now.* **b)** busy doing something; ▣ **on the go:** *I've been on the trot all day.*

3 SLOW RUN [singular] a fairly slow way of running in which you take short regular steps: *She broke into a trot* (=started running slowly) *and hurried on ahead of us.*

4 STUDENTS' ANSWERS [C] AmE a book of notes or answers used by students, especially to cheat in tests; ▣ **crib**

5 the trots informal DIARRHOEA

troth /trəʊθ $ trɒːθ, traːθ, trəʊθ/ n → **plight your troth** at PLIGHT²

Trot·sky·ite /'trɒtskiaɪt $ 'traːt-/ also **Trot·sky·ist** /-ski½st/ n [C] someone who believes in the political ideas of Leon Trotsky, especially that the working class should take control of the state —**Trotskyite** adj

trot·ter /'trɒtə $ 'traːtər/ n [C] a pig's foot, especially when cooked and used as food

trou·ba·dour /'truːbədɔː, -dʊə $ -dɔːr, -dʊr/ n [C] a type of singer and poet who travelled around the PALACES and castles of Southern Europe in the 12th and 13th centuries

trou·ble¹ S1 W2 /'trʌbəl/ n

1 PROBLEMS [C,U] problems or difficulties

> have trouble (with sth)
> have (no) trouble doing sth
> without any/too much trouble (=easily)
> cause trouble
> serious trouble
> terrible trouble
> trouble ahead (=trouble in the future)
> teething troubles (=small problems at the start of something new)
> spell trouble (for sb) (=there is going to be trouble)
> what seems to be the trouble? (=used for politely asking why someone is complaining)
> be asking for trouble (=be silly or dangerous)
> trouble free (=with no trouble)

*We're **having** a lot of **trouble with** the new computer system.* | *I've been **having trouble** checking my e-mail.* | *We **had no trouble** finding the address.* | *She got the jewellery through customs **without any trouble.** | *You can go to the party, but promise me you won't **cause** any **trouble.** | *He was having **serious trouble** knowing where to start.* | *Sudden changes by the government can cause **terrible trouble** in the housing market.* | *Recent stock market losses point to **trouble ahead.** | *There were a lot of **teething troubles** in the first year.* | *You won't see what your opponent is doing, and that **spells trouble.** | *You're just **asking for trouble** if you don't give them the money.* | **trouble free** *holiday*

2 BAD POINT [singular] used when saying what is bad about a person or situation or what causes problems: *The **trouble with** you is that you don't listen.* | *The **trouble is** there are too many people and not enough places.* | *But no one ever remembers – **that's the trouble.** | *You never think, **that's your trouble.**

3 BAD SITUATION in/into/out of trouble **a)** if someone or something is in trouble, they are in a situation with a lot of problems: *He admitted that their marriage was in trouble.* | **get/run into trouble** *The company ran into trouble when it tried to expand too quickly.* | **in serious/ deep trouble** *The economy was in serious trouble.* | *the dangers of trying to borrow your way out of trouble* **b)** if someone is in trouble, they have done something which someone will punish them for or be angry about:

in deep/big trouble *We'll be in big trouble if Mr Elliott finds out.* | **in trouble with sb** *I think I'm in trouble with Dad.* | *I didn't say anything because I didn't want to **get into trouble.** | **keep/stay out of trouble** *I hope Tim stays out of trouble this year.*

4 WORRIES [U] also **troubles** problems in your life which you are worried about: *He **poured out** all his **troubles** to me* (=told me all about his problems).

5 EFFORT [U] an amount of effort and time that is needed to do something: **take the trouble to do sth** (=make a special effort to do something) *The teacher **took the trouble** to learn all our names on the first day.* | *They've obviously **gone to** a lot of **trouble** to arrange everything.* | **save sb the trouble (of doing sth)** *If you'd asked me first, I could have saved you the trouble.* | *I find that making my own clothes is **more trouble than it's worth** (=takes too much time and effort).

6 no trouble used to say politely that you are happy to do something for someone: *'Are you sure you don't mind?' 'It's no trouble.'* | *The kids were no trouble* (=used to say you were happy to look after them because they were well-behaved).

7 HEALTH [U] a problem that you have with your health: *He **has trouble with** his breathing.* | **heart/ stomach/skin etc trouble** *He suffers from back trouble.*

8 MACHINE/SYSTEM [U] when something is wrong with a machine, vehicle, or system: *engine trouble* | [+with] *He had to retire from the race because of trouble with the gearbox.*

> WORD CHOICE: trouble, problem, troubles
> ⚠ **Trouble** is usually an uncountable noun. Never say 'a trouble': *He has caused me a lot of trouble (NOT troubles).* | *Are you having trouble (NOT a trouble) with your car?*
> A **problem** is a specific thing that causes worry or difficulty: *My biggest problem is shyness.* | *There were a lot of problems with his work.* | *They're having problems in their marriage.*
> Your **troubles** are your worries: *Sit down here and forget your troubles (OR problems) for a minute.*

trouble² v [T]

1 WORRY if a problem troubles you, it makes you feel worried or upset: *There is one thing that's been troubling me.* | *They have been **deeply troubled** by the allegations.* | *His conscience troubled him.*

2 INCONVENIENCE formal to say something or ask someone to do something which may use or waste their time or upset them; ▣ **bother:** *I promise not to trouble you again.* | **trouble sb with sth** *I don't want to trouble the doctor with it.* | *I won't trouble you with the details.*

3 may I trouble you?/sorry to trouble you spoken formal used when politely asking someone to do something for you or give you something: *Sorry to trouble you, but could you tell me the way to the station, please?* | *May I trouble you for the salt?*

4 don't trouble yourself spoken used to politely tell someone not to help you: *Please don't trouble yourself, I can manage.*

5 not trouble to do sth to not do something because it needs too much effort; ▣ **not bother to do sth:** *They never troubled to ask me what I would like.* | *Luke didn't trouble to hide his disgust.* ⚠ It is much more usual to use **bother:** *Don't bother to call first – just come over.* | *I didn't bother to change all the sheets.*

6 HEALTH PROBLEM if a medical problem troubles you, it causes you pain or problems: *He is still being troubled by an ankle injury.*

7 CAUSE PROBLEMS to cause someone problems or difficulties: *They look good enough to trouble most teams in the competition.*

troub·led /'trʌbəld/ adj **1** worried or anxious: **troubled face/eyes/look** | *Benson **looked troubled** when he heard the news.* **2** having many problems: *These are **troubled times** for the coal industry.* | *the troubled electronics company* | **troubled marriage/relationship 3 troubled waters** a difficult situation, especially where there is a lot of disagreement and problems: *We don't want to enter the troubled waters of race and religion.* | **pour oil on troubled waters** (=try to make an angry situation calmer)

,trouble-'free *adj* without any problems: *We ensure that you have a trouble-free and enjoyable holiday.*

troub·le·mak·er /'trʌbəl,meɪkə $ -ər/ *n* [C] someone who deliberately causes problems or arguments: *a handful of troublemakers who are damaging the club's reputation*

troub·le·shoot·er /'trʌbəl,ʃuːtə $ -ər/ *n* [C]   **1** an independent person who is employed to come into an organization to deal with serious problems   **2** computer software which asks you a series of questions to try to find the cause of a computer problem, and suggests possible solutions —**troubleshooting** *n* [U]

troub·le·some /'trʌbəlsəm/ *adj* causing problems, in an annoying way: *a troublesome child* | *troublesome itching*

'trouble ,spot *n* [C] a place where trouble often happens, especially war or violence: *She's reported from many of the world's trouble spots.*

troub·ling /'trʌblɪŋ/ *adj* worrying: *This incident raises troubling questions.*

trough /trɒf $ trɔːf/ *n* [C]
  1 **CONTAINER** a long narrow open container that holds water or food for animals: *a horse trough*
  2 **LOW POINT** a short period of low activity, low prices etc; **peak**: [+of] *The graph showed peaks and troughs of activity.*
  3 **WAVES** the hollow area between two waves
  4 **WEATHER** *technical* a long area of fairly low pressure between two areas of high pressure
  5 **have your nose/snout in the trough** *BrE* if people have their noses in the trough, they are involved in something which they hope will get them a lot of money or political power – used to show disapproval

trounce /traʊns/ *v* [T] to defeat someone completely: *We were trounced 13–0.*

troupe /truːp/ *n* [C] a group of singers, actors, dancers etc who work together

troup·er /'truːpə $ -ər/ *n* [C] *informal*   **1** someone who has a lot of experience of work in the entertainment business   **2** someone who works hard and keeps trying, even when the situation is difficult

trou·ser /'traʊzə $ -ər/ *v* [T] *BrE informal* to get a large amount of money – used to show disapproval: *Even though he has in effect been sacked, he will trouser a £150,000 bonus.*

'trouser press *n* [C] *BrE* a piece of equipment that you can keep your trousers in to keep them flat and smooth, often found in hotel rooms

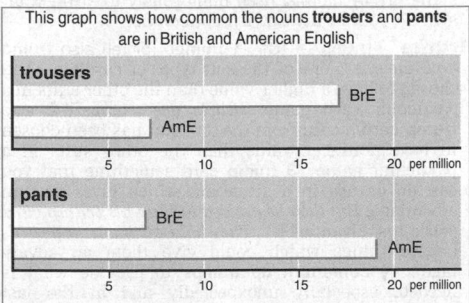

This graph shows how common the nouns **trousers** and **pants** are in British and American English

trousers	
	BrE
	AmE
5 10 15 20 per million	

pants	
	BrE
	AmE
5 10 15 20 per million	

In British English **trousers** is used to mean a piece of clothing that covers the lower half of your body, with a separate part fitting over each leg. In American English **pants** is generally used for this meaning. **Pants** is commonly used in British English to mean underwear, but Americans use the word **underwear**.

trou·sers S2 /'traʊzəz $ -ərz/ *n* [plural] *especially BrE* a piece of clothing that covers the lower half of your body, with a separate part fitting over each leg; **pants** *AmE*: *His trousers were slightly too short.* | *I need a new pair of trousers for work.* —**trouser** *adj*

[only before noun]: *The tickets are in my trouser pocket.*
→ **wear the trousers** at WEAR¹ (7); → **catch sb with their trousers down** at CATCH¹ (6)

'trouser suit *n* [C] *BrE* a woman's suit consisting of a jacket and matching trousers; **pant suit** *AmE*

trous·seau /'truːsəʊ, truːˈsəʊ $ -soʊ/ *n plural* **trousseaus** *or* **trousseaux** /-səʊz $ -soʊz/ [C] *old-fashioned* the clothes etc that a woman brings with her when she marries

trout /traʊt/ *n*   **1** *plural* **trout** [C,U] a common riverfish, often used for food, or the flesh of this fish → see picture at FRESHWATER   **2** **old trout** *BrE spoken* an unpleasant or annoying old person, especially a woman

trove /trəʊv $ troʊv/ *n* → TREASURE TROVE

trow·el /'traʊəl/ *n* [C]   **1** a garden tool like a very small SPADE → see picture at GARDENING   **2** a small tool with a flat blade, used for spreading CEMENT on bricks etc   **3** **lay it on with a trowel** *BrE informal* to say things that make something seem much better, worse etc than it really is; **exaggerate**: *'I really don't feel too good,' I croaked, laying it on with a trowel.*

troy weight /'trɔɪ weɪt/ *n* [U] a system of measuring weights in Britain and the US, used especially for weighing gold, silver etc

tru·an·cy /'truːənsi/ *n* [U] when students deliberately stay away from school without permission: *the school's truancy rate*

tru·ant /'truːənt/ *n* [C]   **1** a student who stays away from school without permission: *persistent truants*   **2** **play truant** *BrE* to stay away from school without permission; **skive** *BrE*; **play hooky** *AmE* —**truant** *v* [I] —**truant** *adj* *AmE*: *Nick was truant seven days this month.*

truce /truːs/ *n* [C] an agreement between enemies to stop fighting or arguing for a short time, or the period for which this is arranged: *They agreed to call a truce.* | [+with/between] *There was an uneasy truce between Alex and Dave over dinner.*

truck

truck¹ S3 W3 /trʌk/ *n* [C]
  1 a large road vehicle used to carry goods; **lorry** *BrE*: *a truck driver* | **pick-up/fork-lift/delivery etc truck** (=large vehicles used for particular purposes) *His car was taken away on the back of a breakdown truck.*
  2 *BrE* a railway vehicle that is part of a train and carries goods; **car** *AmE*: *coal trucks*
  3 a simple piece of equipment on wheels used to move heavy objects
  4 **have/hold/want no truck with sb/sth** to refuse to be involved with someone or to accept an idea

truck² *v AmE*   **1** [T] also **truck in** to take something somewhere by truck: *They ordered sand to be trucked in from the desert.*   **2** [I always + adv/prep] *spoken* to go, move, or travel quickly: *We were trucking on down to Jack's place.*   **3** **get trucking** *spoken* to leave   **4** **keep on trucking** *spoken* used to encourage someone to continue what they are doing, especially in the 1970s

truck·er /'trʌkə $ -ər/ *n* [C] *AmE* a truck driver

'truck farm n [C] *AmE* an area for growing vegetables and fruit for sale; ◨ **market garden** *BrE*

truck·ing /'trʌkɪŋ/ n [U] *AmE* the business of taking goods from place to place by road

truck·load /'trʌkləʊd $ -loʊd/ n [C] the amount that fills a truck: [+of] *a truckload of oranges*

'truck stop n [C] *AmE* a cheap place to eat on a main road, used mainly by truck drivers

truc·u·lent /'trʌkjələnt/ adj *literary* bad-tempered and always willing to argue with people: *a truculent attitude* —**truculently** adv —**truculence** n [U]

trudge /trʌdʒ/ v [I always + adv/prep] to walk with slow heavy steps, especially because you are tired or it is difficult to walk: *We trudged home through the snow.* —**trudge** n [singular]: *the long trudge back up the hill*

true¹ S1 W1 /truː/ adj
1 NOT FALSE based on facts and not imagined or invented; ◨ **false**; → **truly, truth**: *It's not true that I'm going to marry him.* | *No, honestly, it's a true story.* | *Students decide if statements are true or false.* | [+of] *The same is true of all political parties.* | [+for] *This is especially true for old people.* | *It's generally true to say that fewer people are needed nowadays.* | *The results appear to hold true* (=still be correct) *for other countries.* → **too good to be true** at GOOD¹ (24); → **not ring true** at RING² (5)
2 REAL [only before noun] the true nature of something is its real nature, which may be hidden or not known; ◨ **real**: **true value/cost etc (of sth)** *The house was sold for only a fraction of its true value.* | *We need to understand the true extent of the problem.* | **true nature/meaning/identity etc (of sth)** *She wasn't aware of the true nature of their relationship.* | *She managed to conceal her true feelings.* | *After a couple of days she showed her true self* (=real character).
3 ADMITTING STH *especially spoken* used when you are admitting that something is correct, but saying that something else, often opposite, is also correct: *'He's very hard-working.' 'True, but I still don't think he's the right man for the job.'* | **it is true (that)** *It is true that there have been improvements in some areas.*
4 PROPER [only before noun] having all the qualities which a type of thing or person should have: *The heroine finally finds true love.* | *She's been a true friend to me.* | *It's an amateur sport* **in the true sense of the word** (=with the exact meaning of this word).
5 **come true** if wishes, dreams etc come true, they happen in the way that someone has said or hoped that they would: *The prediction seems to have come true.* → **be a dream come true** at DREAM¹ (5)
6 LOYAL faithful and loyal to someone, whatever happens: [+to] *Throughout the whole ordeal, she remained true to her husband.*
7 **true to form/type** used to say that someone is behaving in the bad way that you expect them to: *True to form, Henry turned up late.*
8 **true to your word/principles etc** behaving in the way you said you would or according to principles which you believe in: *He was true to his word and said nothing about it to Lisa.*
9 **true to life** also **true-to-life** a book, play, description etc that is true to life seems very real and natural; ◨ **realistic**: *The film is frighteningly true-to-life and very funny.*
10 **(all/only) too true** used to say that you know something is true, when you do not like it: *'It's not as easy as it looks.' 'Too true!'* | *It is only too true that people are judged by their accents.*
11 STRAIGHT/LEVEL [not before noun] *technical* fitted, placed, or formed in a way that is perfectly flat, straight, correct etc: *If the door's not true, it won't close properly.*
12 **sb's aim is true** if your aim is true, you hit the thing that you were throwing or shooting at

13 **your true colours** if you show your true colours, you do something which shows what your real attitudes and qualities are, especially when they are bad: **show/reveal your true colours** *He was forced to reveal his true colours when asked how he would vote.*
14 **(there's) many a true word spoken in jest** *old-fashioned* used to say that when people are joking they sometimes say things that are true and important

true² adv **1** in an exact straight line: *The arrow flew straight and true to its target.* **2** *technical* if a type of animal breeds true, the young animals are exactly like their parents

true³ n **out of true** *BrE* not completely straight, level, or balanced: *The walls are slightly out of true.*

,true-'blue adj **1** *BrE informal* believing completely in the ideas of the British CONSERVATIVE PARTY: *a true-blue Tory* **2** *AmE* completely loyal to a person or idea: *a true-blue friend*

true-heart·ed /,truː 'hɑːtɪd◂ $ -ɑːr-/ adj *literary* faithful; ◨ **loyal**

,true-'life adj [only before noun] based on real facts and not invented: *a true-life adventure*

,true 'love n [C] *literary* the person that you love

,true 'north n [U] north as it appears on maps, calculated as a line through the centre of the earth rather than by using the MAGNETIC POLE

truf·fle /'trʌfəl/ n [C] **1** a black or light brown FUNGUS that grows underground, and is a very expensive food **2** a soft creamy sweet made with chocolate: *a rum truffle*

tru·is·m /'truːɪzəm/ n [C] a statement that is clearly true, so that there is no need to say it: *His speech was just a collection of clichés and truisms.*

tru·ly W3 /'truːli/ adv
1 [+ adj/adv] used to emphasize that the way you are describing something is really true; ◨ **really**: *His work is truly original.* | *Fawcett was a truly remarkable man.* | *a truly great work of medieval literature*
2 sincerely: *I am truly sorry.* | *She truly believed he was innocent.* | *I can truly say I've never enjoyed myself so much.*
3 in an exact or correct way: *Is it a truly representative sample?*
4 **well and truly** *especially spoken* completely: *We were well and truly beaten.* | *The party was well and truly over.*
5 **really and truly** *BrE spoken* used to emphasize that something is definitely or completely true: *I couldn't believe we were really and truly going at last.*
6 **yours truly a)** used at the end of a letter, before the signature **b)** *Informal* used humorously to mean yourself: *So, yours truly was left to clean up.*

trump¹ /trʌmp/ n [C] **1** **trumps** [plural] also **trump** *AmE* the SUIT (=one of the four types of cards in a set) chosen to have a higher value than the other suits in a particular card game: *Hearts are trumps.* **2** also **trump card** a card from the SUIT that has been chosen to have a higher value than the other suits in a particular game **3** **trump card** something that you can do or use in a situation, which gives you an advantage: *But then he decided to* **play his trump card** (=use his advantage). | *They hold all the trump cards* (=have things which could give them an advantage). **4** **come/turn up trumps** to provide what is needed, especially unexpectedly and at the last moment: *Paul came up trumps and managed to borrow a car for us.*

trump² v [T] **1** to play a trump that beats someone else's card in a game **2** to do better than someone else in a situation when people are competing with each other: *By wearing a simple but stunning dress, she had trumped them all.*
trump sth ⇔ **up** phr v to use false information to make someone seem guilty of doing something wrong: *They had trumped the whole thing up to get rid of him.*

trum·pet¹ /'trʌmpɨt/ n [C] a musical instrument that you blow into, which consists of a curved metal tube that is wide at the end, and three buttons you press to change the notes **→ blow your own trumpet** at BLOW¹ (19)

trumpet² v **1** [T] to tell everyone about something that you are proud of, especially in an annoying way: *They are proudly trumpeting the fact that they are creating more jobs.* **2** [I] if an ELEPHANT trumpets, it makes a loud noise

trum·pet·er /'trʌmpɨtə $ -ər/ n [C] someone who plays a trumpet

trun·cate /trʌŋ'keɪt $ 'trʌŋkeɪt/ v [T] *formal* to make something shorter; **◱ shorten**: *If the list is too long, it will be truncated by the computer.* | *The report is also available in a truncated version.* —**truncation** /trʌŋ'keɪʃən/ n [U]

trun·cheon /'trʌnʃən/ n [C] *especially BrE* a short thick stick that police officers carry as a weapon; **◱ nightstick** *AmE*

trun·dle /'trʌndl/ v [I always + adv/prep, T] to move slowly along on wheels, or to make something do this by pushing or pulling it: *Two large wagons trundled by.*

trunk /trʌŋk/ n [C]
1 TREE the thick central woody stem of a tree: *He left his bicycle leaning against a tree trunk.* | [+of] *the trunk of an old oak tree;* **→** see picture at TREE
2 CAR *AmE* the part at the back of a car where you can put bags, tools etc; **◱ boot** *BrE*: *Put your suitcase in the trunk.*
3 ELEPHANT the very long nose of an ELEPHANT
4 CLOTHES trunks also **swim/swimming trunks** [plural] a piece of clothing like very short trousers, worn by men for swimming
5 BOX a very large box made of wood or metal, in which clothes, books etc are stored or packed for travel **→** see picture at BOX¹
6 BODY *technical* the main part of your body, not including your head, arms, or legs **→** SUITCASE

'trunk call n [C] *BrE old-fashioned* a telephone call between places that are a long distance apart

'trunk road n [C] *BrE* a main road used for travelling long distances

truss¹ /trʌs/ v [T] **1** also **truss up** to tie someone's arms, legs etc very firmly with rope so that they cannot move: *They trussed up their victim and left him for dead.* **2** to prepare a chicken, duck etc for cooking by tying its legs and wings into position

truss² n [C] **1** a special belt worn to support a HERNIA (=medical problem that affects the muscles below your stomach) **2** a frame supporting a roof or bridge

trust¹ S1 W2 /trʌst/ n
1 BELIEF [U] a strong belief in the honesty, goodness etc of someone or something: *At first there was a lack of trust between them.* | *an agreement made on the basis of mutual trust* (=when people trust each other) | **put/ place your trust in sb/sth** *You shouldn't put your trust in a man like that.* | *You betrayed your father's trust* (=did something bad even though he trusted you). **→** breach of trust at BREACH¹ (3)
2 ORGANIZATION [C usually singular] an organization or group that has control over money that will be used to help someone else: *a charitable trust*
3 FINANCIAL ARRANGEMENT [C,U] an arrangement by which someone has legal control of your money or property, either until you are old enough to use it or to INVEST it for you: *The money your father left you will be held in trust until you are 21.* **→** TRUST FUND, UNIT TRUST
4 take sth on trust to believe that something is true without having any proof: *I just had to take it on trust that he would deliver the money.*
5 position of trust a job or position in which you have been given the responsibility of making important decisions

6 COMPANIES [C] *especially AmE* a group of companies that illegally work together to reduce competition and control prices: *anti-trust laws*

trust² S2 W3 v [T]
1 PEOPLE to believe that someone is honest or will not do anything bad or wrong; **◱ distrust, mistrust**: *I just don't trust him.* | **trust sb to do sth** *Can they be trusted to look after the house?* | *I didn't trust myself not to say something rude, so I just kept quiet.* | **trust sb completely/implicitly** *He was a good driver and I trusted him implicitly.* | **not trust sb an inch/not trust sb as far as you can throw them** (=not trust someone at all)
2 FACTS/JUDGEMENT to be sure that something is correct or right; **◱ believe in, rely on**: *Can we trust these statistics?* | *I trust his judgement completely.* | *Trust your instincts* (=do what you feel is the right thing)*!*
3 THINGS to be sure that something will work properly; **◱ rely on**: *Not trusting her voice, she shook her head.* | **trust sth to do sth** *You can't trust the trains to run on time.* | *He sat down suddenly, as if he didn't trust his legs to support him.*
4 trust you/him/them etc (to do sth)! *spoken* used to say that someone has behaved in a bad or stupid way that is typical of them: *Trust you to write down the wrong number!*
5 I trust (that) *spoken formal* used to say politely that you hope something is true: *I trust that from now on you will take greater precautions.* **→** TRUSTING; **→ tried and trusted** at TRIED²
  trust in sth/sb *phr v formal*
  to believe in someone or something: *We trust in God.*
  trust to sth *phr v*
  to hope that what you want to happen will happen, because there is nothing you can do about it: *I'll just have to trust to luck that it works out okay.* | *I hope I may trust to your discretion.*
  trust sb with sth *phr v*
  to let someone have something or have control over something, believing that they will be careful with it: *I wouldn't trust him with the keys.* | *I'd trust her with my life.*

trust·ee S2 /ˌtrʌs'tiː◂/ n [C]
1 someone who has control of money or property that is in a TRUST for someone else
2 a member of a group that controls the money of a company, college, or other organization

trust·ee·ship /trʌs'tiːʃɪp/ n **1** [C,U] the job of being a trustee **2** [U] the responsibility for governing an area, which is given to a country or countries by the United Nations

'trust fund n [C] money belonging to someone that is controlled for them by a trustee

trust·ing /'trʌstɪŋ/ adj **1** willing to believe that other people are good and honest: *a shy and trusting child* | [+of] *She's so trusting of people.* **2** involving trust: *a loving and trusting relationship*

trust·wor·thy /'trʌst,wɜːði/ $ -3ːr-/ adj someone who is trustworthy can be trusted and depended on; **◱ dependable** —**trustworthiness** n [U]

trust·y¹ /'trʌsti/ adj [only before noun] *old-fashioned* a trusty weapon, vehicle, animal etc is one that you have had for a long time and can depend on – often used humorously; **◱ reliable**: *He had his trusty old penknife with him.*

trusty² n plural **trusties** [C] *BrE* a prisoner who is given special jobs or rights, because they behave in a way that can be trusted

truth S1 W2 /truːθ/ n
1 TRUE FACTS **the truth** the true facts about something, rather than what is untrue, imagined, or guessed; **◱ lie, falsehood, untruth**

find out/discover/get to the truth
reveal the truth
tell the truth
speak the truth
know the truth
get the truth out of sb (=make them tell you the truth)
the whole/complete/full truth
the honest truth
the plain/simple/naked truth (=the truth, with no details or explanation to make it seem pleasant)
the shocking/terrible/sad etc truth
the truth of the matter
come close/near to the truth

[+about] *She'd come to* **find out the truth** *about her family.* | [+behind] *We'll never know the truth behind the accident.* | *In the end she was forced to* **reveal the truth.** | *How do we know you're* **telling the truth?** | *You can't punish a man for* **speaking the truth.** | *The way he was looking at her, it was obvious he* **knew the truth.** | *I'll* **get the truth out of** *him somehow.* | *It was many months before* **the whole truth** *was discovered.* | *I love you – and that's* **the honest truth!** | **The plain truth** *is that you'll never get to university.* | *He began to realize the* **awful truth** *about her past.* | **The truth of the matter** *is that nothing has changed since the election.* | *Her guess came a little* **too close to the truth** *for my liking.*

2 BEING TRUE [U] the state or quality of being true: [+in] *There was some truth in the accusations.* | **grain/element of truth** (=small amount of truth) *There wasn't a grain of truth in what he said.* | *There was an element of truth* (=a small amount of truth) *in what he said.* | *There is no truth in the rumour.*

3 IMPORTANT IDEAS [C usually plural] *formal* an important fact or idea that is accepted as being true: *The experience has taught us some* **basic truths.** | *an* **unhappy/unpleasant/unwelcome truth** (=an unpleasant or disappointing fact) *It is in his interest to hide unhappy truths about his agency's performance.*

4 in truth in fact; ■ **really**: *Early independence leaders were in truth little better than rebels.*

5 if (the) truth be known/told used when telling someone the real facts about a situation, or your real opinion: *If the truth be known, I felt a little left out at school.*

6 to tell (you) the truth *spoken* used when giving your personal opinion or admitting something: *To tell the truth, I was frightened to death.*

7 nothing could be further from the truth used to say that something is definitely not true

8 the truth will out *old-fashioned* used to say that even if you try to stop people from knowing something, they will find out in the end → HALF-TRUTH, HOME TRUTH; → **the moment of truth** at MOMENT (15)

truth drug *BrE*; **'truth serum** *AmE n* [C,U] a drug that is supposed to make people tell the truth

truth·ful /ˈtruːθfəl/ *adj* **1** someone who is truthful does not usually tell lies; ■ **honest**: *a truthful child* | *You and I must be truthful with each other.* **2** a truthful statement gives the true facts about something; ■ **honest**: *I have only one question to ask you, and I want a truthful answer.* —**truthfully** *adv*: *Answer this question truthfully.* —**truthfulness** *n* [U]

try¹ S1 W1 /traɪ/ *v past tense and past participle* **tried**, *present participle* **trying**, *third person singular* **tries**

1 ATTEMPT [I,T] to attempt to do or get something: *Let's have a rest and then we'll try again.* | **try to do sth** *He tried to control his voice.* | *She was trying not to cry.* | **try and do sth** *Try and take some form of daily exercise.* | **try hard/desperately (to do sth)** (=make a lot of effort to do something) *She dabbed at her face and tried hard not to sniff.* | *I tried everything with no success.* | **try your best/hardest (to do sth)** (=make as much effort as possible to do something) *I tried my best to comfort her.* | *I tried and tried* (=kept

trying on a pair of shoes

trying out a bicycle

making an effort) *and eventually I was offered a job.* | **Try as he might** (=as hard as he could), *he could not get the incident out of his mind.* | **it wasn't for lack/want of trying** (=used to say that if someone does not achieve something it is not because they have not tried) *They didn't get any goals, but it wasn't for the lack of trying.* | **you couldn't do sth if you tried** (=used to say that someone does not have the skill or ability to do something) *She couldn't speak French if she tried.*

2 TEST/USE [T] to do or use something for a short while to discover if it is suitable, successful, enjoyable etc: *It works really well – you should try it.* | **try doing sth** *They decided they would try living in America for a while.* | *Try logging off and logging on again.* | **try sth new/different** (=do or use something that is different from what you usually do or use) *If I'm going out for a meal, I prefer to try something different.* | **try sth on sb/sth** *We tried the machine on hardwood and soft wood.* | **try sb on sth** *Petra's trying the baby on solid foods.* | **try sth for size** (=put on a piece of clothing or test something to find out if it is the correct size or suitable) *Always try a sleeping bag for size before you buy it.*

3 FOOD/DRINK [T] to taste food or drink to find out if you like it; ■ **taste**: *Would you like to try some crisps?*

4 TRY TO FIND SB/STH [I,T] to go to a place or person, or call them, in order to find something or someone: *Sorry, he's not in. Would you like to try again later?* | *Let's try Mouncy Street. He could be there.*

5 DOOR/WINDOW [T] to attempt to open a door, window etc in order to see if it is locked: *She tried the door and it opened.* | *He tried the handle but the door was locked.*

6 LAW [T usually passive] to examine and judge a legal case, or someone who is thought to be guilty of a crime in a court; → **trial**: *He was tried for attempting to murder his wife.* | *The defence argued that a regional court was not competent to try their case.*

7 try sb's patience to make someone feel impatient; → **trying**: *The programs take too long to load and try the patience of young pupils.*

8 try your hand at sth to try a new activity in order to see whether it interests you or whether you are good at it: *I tried my hand at water-skiing for the first time.*

9 try your luck to try to achieve something or get something you want, usually by taking a risk: *After the war my father went to Canada to try his luck at farming.*

10 try it on (with sb) *BrE spoken* **a)** to behave badly in order to find out how bad you can be before people become angry: *She is naughty, that one. She tries it on with me sometimes!* **b)** to attempt to start a sexual relationship with someone: *When I came back in, one of the men was trying it on with my wife!*

try for sth *phr v BrE*
to try and get something you really want, such as a job, a prize, or a chance to study somewhere: *I decided I must try for some paid work.* | *We have been trying for a baby* (=trying to have a baby) *for nine years.*

try sth ⇔ **on** phr v

to put on a piece of clothing to see if it fits you or if it suits you, especially in a shop: *Meg was trying on some red sandals.*

try sth ⇔ **out** phr v

1 to test something such as a method or a piece of equipment to see if it is effective or works properly; → **try-out**: *She enjoys trying out new ways of doing things.*
2 to practise a skill in order to improve it: [+on] *She enjoyed trying her French out on Jean-Pierre.*

try out for sth phr v AmE

to try to be chosen as a member of a team, for a part in a play etc; ☐ **audition for**; → **tryout**: *In high school, I tried out for all the female leads.*

try² S3 n plural **tries** [C]

1 an attempt to do something: *She didn't manage to break the record, but it was a good try.* | *'You really think you can do that?' 'I'm going to have a try.'* | *'What are the chances for getting tickets now?' 'I guess I could give it a try.'* | *It might sound a ludicrous excuse but he thought it was worth a try.* | **on the first/second etc try** *Only half the students passed the test on their first try.*
2 a test of something to see if it is suitable or successful or to find out if you like it: *I decided to give modelling a try.* | *Wines from Apulia's ancient vineyards are well worth a try.*
3 four points won by putting the ball on the ground behind the opponents' GOAL LINE in RUGBY

try·ing /'traɪ-ɪŋ/ adj annoying or difficult in a way that makes you feel worried, tired etc: *That child is very trying.* | *The beginning of the show is often a trying time because of latecomers.* | *They do the best they can in trying circumstances.*

'try-out n [C] BrE a period of time spent trying a new method, tool, machine etc to see if it is useful

try·out /'traɪaʊt/ n AmE **1** [C usually plural] a time when people who want to be in a sports team, activity etc are tested, so that the best can be chosen; ☐ **trial** BrE: *baseball tryouts* **2** [C] a period of time during which a play, television show etc is shown to find out if people like it

tryst /trɪst, traɪst/ n [C] literary a meeting between lovers in a secret place or at a secret time – often used humorously

tsar, tzar, czar /zɑː, tsɑː $ zɑːr, tsɑːr/ n [C] a male ruler of Russia before 1917

tsa·ri·na, tzarina, czarina /zɑːˈriːnə, tsɑː-/ n [C] a female ruler of Russia before 1917, or the wife of a tsar

tsar·ism, tzarism, czarism /'zɑːrɪzəm, 'tsɑː-/ n [U] a system of government controlled by a tsar, especially the system in Russia before 1917 —**tsarist** n [C] —**tsarist** adj

tset·se fly, tzetze fly /'tetsi flaɪ, 'tsetsi-, 'setsi-/ n [C] an African fly that sucks the blood of people and animals and spreads serious diseases

T-shirt, tee-shirt /'tiː ʃɜːt $ -ʃɜːrt/ n [C] a soft shirt with short SLEEVES and no collar: *She was wearing jeans and a T-shirt.*

tsk tsk interjection a way of writing a sound that is made to show disapproval

tsp plural **tsp** or **tsps** the written abbreviation of *teaspoon* or teaspoons: *Add 2 tsp salt.*

T-square /'tiː skweə $ -skwer/ n [C] a large T-shaped piece of wood or plastic used to draw exact plans or pictures

tsu·na·mi /tsʊˈnɑːmi/ n [C] technical a TIDAL WAVE

tub /tʌb/ n [C]

1 CONTAINER **a)** a small container made of paper or plastic with a lid, in which food is bought or stored: [+of] *a tub of ice cream* | *a margarine tub* **b)** an open container that is usually round, used for washing, storing things in etc: *trees growing in tubs* → see picture at CONTAINER
2 AMOUNT also **tubful** the amount of liquid, food etc that a tub can contain: [+of] *We ate a tub of ice cream.*

3 BATH AmE a large container in which you sit to wash yourself; ☐ **bathtub**: *I had a long soak in the tub.*
4 BOAT BrE informal an old boat that travels slowly
5 PERSON **tub of lard** informal not polite someone who is short and fat

tu·ba /'tjuːbə $ 'tuːbə/ n [C] a large metal musical instrument that consists of a curved tube with a wide opening that points straight up. It produces very low sounds when you blow into it.

tub·by /'tʌbi/ adj informal short and slightly fat, with a round stomach; ☐ **plump**: *a tubby little man*

tube¹ S3 W3 /tjuːb $ tuːb/ n

1 PIPE FOR LIQUID [C] a round pipe made of metal, glass, rubber etc, especially for liquids or gases to go through → INNER TUBE, TEST TUBE
2 [C] a long hollow object that is usually round: *pasta tubes* | *a toilet roll tube*
3 CONTAINER [C] a narrow container made of plastic or soft metal and closed at one end, that you press between your fingers in order to push out the soft substance that is inside: *a tube of toothpaste* → see picture at CONTAINER
4 IN YOUR BODY [C] a tube-shaped part inside your body: *the bronchial tubes*
5 TRAINS **the tube** BrE the system of trains that run under the ground in London; ☐ **subway** AmE: **take/catch the tube** *Take the tube to Acton.* | *a tube station* | **by tube** *It's best to travel by tube.*
6 go down the tubes informal if a situation goes down the tubes, it quickly becomes ruined or spoiled: *When Moira turned up, Tess could see all her good work going down the tubes.*
7 TELEVISION **the tube** AmE spoken the television: *What's on the tube tonight?*
8 ELECTRICAL EQUIPMENT [C] technical the part of a television that produces the picture on the screen; ☐ **cathode ray tube**

tube² v [I] to float on a river on a large INNER TUBE for fun

tu·ber /'tjuːbə $ 'tuːbər/ n [C] a round swollen part on the stem of some plants, such as the potato, that grows below the ground and from which new plants grow —**tuberous** adj

tu·ber·cu·lo·sis /tjuˌbɜːkjʊ̩ˈləʊsɪ̩s 'ləʊ-/ n [U] a serious infectious disease that affects many parts of your body, especially your lungs; ☐ **TB** —**tubercular** /tjuˈbɜːkjʊ̩lə $ tuˈbɜːrkjʊ̩lər/ adj

tube sock n [C] AmE a sock that is long and straight and has no special place for your heel

tube top n [C] AmE informal a piece of women's clothing that goes around your chest and back to cover your breasts but does not cover your shoulders or stomach

tub·ing /'tjuːbɪŋ $ 'tuː-/ n [U] **1** tubes in general, especially when connected together into a system: *rubber tubing* **2** the activity of floating on a river on a large INNER TUBE for fun

'tub-thumping adj [only before noun] BrE informal trying to persuade people about your opinions in a loud and forceful way: *He is still addressing rallies in his usual tub-thumping, arrogant way.* —**tub-thumping** n [U] —**tub-thumper** n [C]

tu·bu·lar /'tjuːbjʊ̩lə $ 'tuːbjʊ̩lər/ adj made of tubes or in the form of a tube: *tubular metal furniture*

TUC /ˌtiː juː ˈsiː/ n **the TUC** *the Trades Union Congress* the association of British TRADE UNIONS

tuck¹ /tʌk/ v **1** [T always + adv/prep] to push something, especially the edge of a piece of cloth or paper, into or behind something so that it looks tidier or stays in place: **tuck sth in** *Jack tucked his shirt in.* | **tuck sth into/under/behind etc sth** *She tucked an unruly lock of hair behind her ear.* **2** [T always + adv/prep] to put something in a small space, especially in order to protect, hide, carry, or hold it: **tuck sth behind/under/into etc sth** *Giles was tucking his pile of books under his arm.* | *He took the glasses off and tucked them in his* *pocket.* **3** [T] to put a TUCK (=special fold) in a piece of clothing

tuck sth ⇔ **away** *phr v* **1 be tucked away a)** if a place is tucked away, it is in a quiet area: *The village of Eyam is tucked away behind the hills.* **b)** if someone or something is tucked away, they are hidden or difficult to find: *The envelope was tucked away in her jewel box.* **2** *informal* to store something, especially money, in a safe place: *Every member of the family can now tuck away either £9 or £18 a month in one of these savings plans.* **3** *BrE informal* to eat a lot of food, usually quickly and with enjoyment

tuck in *phr v* **1 tuck sb in** to make a child comfortable in bed by arranging the sheets around them **2 tuck sth** ⇔ **in** to move a part of your body inwards so that it does not stick out so much: *Stand up straight and tuck in your tummy.* **3** also **tuck into sth** *informal* to eat something eagerly: *The ice creams came and we tucked in.* | *They tucked into a hearty breakfast of eggs.*

tuck sb ⇔ **up** *phr v* **1** to make someone comfortable in bed by arranging the sheets around them: *Dad tucked me up in his and Carrie's bed.* **2 be tucked up in bed** *informal* to be lying or sitting in bed: *I ought to be tucked up in bed now.*

tuck² *n* **1** [C] a narrow flat fold of cloth sewn into a piece of clothing for decoration or to give it a special shape **2** [C] a small medical operation done to make your face or stomach look flatter and younger: *a tummy tuck* **3** [U] *BrE old-fashioned* cakes, sweets etc – used especially by schoolchildren: *the school tuck shop*

tuck·er¹ /ˈtʌkə $ -ər/ *v*
tucker sb **out** *phr v* [usually passive] *AmE informal* to make someone very tired: *By the end of the day, we were all pretty tuckered out.*

tucker² *n* [U] *AusE informal* food → **your best bib and tucker** at BIB (3)

'tude /tjuːd $ tuːd/ *n* [C,U] *spoken* a style, type of behaviour etc that shows that you have the confidence to do unusual and exciting things without caring what other people think – used humorously; ▤ **attitude**: *the trend of restaurants serving nasty 'tude with their food*

Tu·dor /ˈtjuːdə $ ˈtuːdər/ *adj* relating to the period in British history between 1485 and 1603: **Tudor house/buildings/architecture etc** (=built in the style used in the Tudor period)

Tues·day /ˈtjuːzdi, -deɪ $ ˈtuːz-/ *n* [C,U] written abbreviation **Tues.** or **Tue.** the day between Monday and Wednesday: **on Tuesday** *The sale starts on Tuesday.* | *I'll see you Tuesday. AmE* | **Tuesday morning/afternoon etc** *He first heard the news on Tuesday evening.* | **last Tuesday** *It was my birthday last Tuesday.* | **this Tuesday** *I'm sorry I can't make it this Tuesday.* | **next Tuesday** (=Tuesday of next week) *Shall we meet next Tuesday?* | **a Tuesday** (=one of the Tuesdays in the year) *We left Miami on a Tuesday.*

tuft /tʌft/ *n* [C] a bunch of hair, feathers, grass etc growing or held closely together at their base: [+of] *tufts of grass*

tuft·ed /ˈtʌftɪd/ *adj* with a tuft or tufts: *a tufted duck*

tug¹ /tʌɡ/ *v* **tugged, tugging** **1** [I,T] to pull with one or more short, quick pulls: *The woman gently tugged his arm.* | [+at/on sth] *Joe was tugging at her sleeve.* **2** [T always + adv/prep] *BrE* to pull a piece of clothing quickly onto your body: **tug sth on** *Alice was tugging on a sweater.* **3 tug at sb's heart/heartstrings** *written* to make someone feel sympathy for someone or something

tug² *n* [C] **1** also **'tug boat** a small strong boat used for pulling or guiding ships into a port, up a river etc **2** [usually singular] a sudden strong pull: *She removed the bandage with a sharp tug.* **3** [usually singular] a strong and sudden feeling: [+of] *Kate felt a tug of jealousy.*

tug of 'love *n* [singular] *BrE* a situation in which parents who have separated from each other fight over who is going to have the children – used especially in newspaper reports

tug-of-'war *n* [singular] **1** a test of strength in which two teams pull opposite ends of a rope against each other **2** a situation in which two people or groups try very hard to get or keep the same thing: *There was a constant tug-of-war between the military and the President.*

tu·i·tion /tjuˈɪʃən $ tu-/ *n* [U] **1** teaching, especially in small groups: *I had to have extra tuition in maths.* **2** *AmE*; **tuition fees** *BrE* the money you pay for being taught: *When I started college, tuition was $350 a quarter.*

tu·lip /ˈtjuːlɪp $ ˈtuː-/ *n* [C] a brightly coloured flower that is shaped like a cup and grows from a BULB in spring → see picture at FLOWER¹

tulle /tjuːl $ tuːl/ *n* [U] a thin soft silk or NYLON material like a net

tum /tʌm/ *n* [C] *BrE informal* stomach; ▤ **tummy**: *I've lost another two inches from my tum.*

tum·ble¹ /ˈtʌmbəl/ *v* [I] **1** [always + adv/prep] to fall down quickly and suddenly, especially with a rolling movement: [+over/backwards/down] *She lost her balance and tumbled backwards.* | *A few stones came tumbling down the cliff.* **2** [always + adv/prep] to move in an uncontrolled way: [+into/through/out etc] *We tumbled out into the street.* **3** if prices or figures tumble, they go down suddenly and by a large amount: *Oil prices have tumbled.* | [+to] *Mortgage rates tumbled to their lowest level for 25 years.* **4** [always + adv/prep] *literary* if someone's hair tumbles down, it is long, thick, and curly: *Her long dark hair tumbled over her shoulders.* **5** *literary* if words tumble out of someone's mouth, they speak very quickly because they are excited or upset: [+out/over] *The words tumbled out as if he hardly knew what to say first.* **6** [always + adv/prep] if water tumbles somewhere, it flows there quickly: *A narrow stream tumbled over the rocks.* **7 come tumbling down a)** if something comes tumbling down, it falls suddenly to the ground: *Removing the debris could cause the rest of the building to come tumbling down.* **b)** if a system, problem etc comes tumbling down, it suddenly stops working or existing: *In the last year, barriers have come tumbling down.* **8** *AmE* to do TUMBLING

tumble² *n* [C] a fall, especially from a high place or level: *It's possible that stocks could take a tumble next year.* → ROUGH AND TUMBLE

tum·ble·down /ˈtʌmbəldaʊn/ *adj* [only before noun] a tumbledown building is old and beginning to fall down: *a tumbledown cottage*

tumble 'dryer, tumble-drier *n* [C] *BrE* a machine that uses hot air to dry clothes after they have been washed; ▤ **dryer**; → see picture at WASHING MACHINE

tum·bler /ˈtʌmblə $ -ər/ *n* [C] **1** a glass with a flat bottom and no handle **2** also **tumblerful** /-ful/ *BrE* the amount of liquid that this type of glass can contain **3** *old-fashioned* someone who performs special movements such as doing SOMERSAULTS (=a jump in which you turn over completely in the air); ▤ **acrobat**

tum·ble·weed /ˈtʌmbəlwiːd/ *n* [C,U] a plant that grows in the desert areas of North America and is blown from place to place by the wind

tum·bling /ˈtʌmblɪŋ/ *n* [U] a sport similar to GYMNASTICS but with all the exercises done on the floor

tu·mes·cent /tjuːˈmesənt $ tuː-/ *adj* technical swollen or swelling —**tumescence** *n* [U]

tum·my /ˈtʌmi/ *n plural* **tummies** [C] STOMACH – used especially by or to children: *He was up all night with tummy ache.* | **tummy bug/upset** *BrE* (=an illness of the stomach that makes you vomit)

tu·mour *BrE*; **tumor** *AmE* /ˈtjuːmə $ ˈtuːmər/ *n* [C] a mass of diseased cells in your body that have divided and increased too quickly: *a brain tumour* | **malignant/benign tumour** (=caused by or not caused by CANCER)

tu·mult /'tjuːmʌlt $ 'tuː-/ *n* [C,U] *formal* **1** a confused, noisy, and excited situation, often caused by a large crowd; ⊟ **turmoil**: *I could simply not be heard in the tumult.* | **in tumult** *The whole country is in tumult.* **2** a state of mental confusion caused by strong emotions such as anger, sadness etc; ⊟ **turmoil**

tu·mul·tu·ous /tjuːˈmʌltʃuəs $ tuː-/ *adj* **1** full of activity, confusion, or violence: *the tumultuous years of the Civil War* **2** very loud because people are happy and excited: *He received a tumultuous welcome.* | *tumultuous applause*

tu·mu·lus /'tjuːmjʊ̣ləs $ 'tuː-/ *n plural* **tumuli** /-laɪ, -liː/ [C] a very large pile of earth put over a GRAVE by people in the past

tu·na /'tjuːnə $ 'tuːnə/ *n plural* **tuna 1** [C] a large sea fish caught for food **2** [U] also **tuna fish** the flesh of this fish, usually sold cooked in TINS

tun·dra /'tʌndrə/ *n* [C,U] the large flat areas of land in the north of Russia, Canada etc, where it is very cold and there are no trees

tune¹ S3 /tjuːn $ tuːn/ *n* [C]
1 a series of musical notes that are played or sung and are nice to listen to; ⊟ **melody**: *Sam was humming a little tune.* | *a hymn tune* | *The song is sung to the tune of Colonel Bogey.*
2 in tune playing or singing the correct musical note: *They sang perfectly in tune.*
3 out of tune playing or singing higher or lower than the correct musical note: *Greg's bass guitar was out of tune.*
4 in tune with sb/sth, out of tune with sb/sth able or unable to realize, understand, or agree with what someone else thinks or wants: *The industry is changing in tune with changing demand.*
5 to the tune of $1000/£2 million etc *informal* used to emphasize how large an amount or number is: *Canada is funding the programme to the tune of $30 million.* → **call the tune** at CALL¹ (9); → **change your tune** at CHANGE¹ (14); → **dance to sb's tune** at DANCE² (4) → **FINE-TUNE** → **SIGNATURE TUNE**

tune² *v* [T] **1** to make a musical instrument play at the right PITCH: *Someone's coming tomorrow to tune the piano.* **2** also **tune up** to make small changes to an engine so that it works as well as possible **3** to make a radio or television receive broadcasts from a particular place: **tune sth to sth** *The radio was tuned to a classical station.* → **stay tuned** at STAY¹ (8) **4 finely/highly tuned** finely tuned feelings, senses, or systems are extremely sensitive and able to react quickly: **be tuned to sth** *a species finely tuned to life in the desert*

tune in *phr v* **1** to watch or listen to a broadcast on radio or television: [+to] *People get their information by tuning in to foreign radio stations.* | *More than 150 million Americans tuned in to watch the final episode.* **2** also **be tuned in** to realize or understand what is happening or what other people are thinking: [+to] *Try to tune in to your partner's needs.* | *The company aims to be more tuned in to customer needs.*

tune out *phr v informal* to ignore or stop listening to someone or something: *A bored child may simply tune out.* | **tune sb/sth ⇔ out** *I learned to tune out the background noise.*

tune up *phr v* **1** when musicians tune up, they prepare their instruments to play at the right PITCH: **tune sth ⇔ up** *The band were tuning up their guitars.* **2 tune sth ⇔ up** to make small changes to an engine so that it works as well as possible

tune·ful /'tjuːnfəl $ 'tuːn-/ *adj* pleasant to listen to: *tuneful melodies* —**tunefully** *adv* —**tunefulness** *n* [U]

tune·less /'tjuːnləs $ 'tuːn-/ *adj* not having a pleasant tune: *tuneless humming* —**tunelessly** *adv*

tun·er /'tjuːnə $ 'tuːnər/ *n* [C] **1** the part of a radio or television that you can change to receive different TV or radio stations **2** a person who tunes pianos **3** an

electronic machine that helps you to tune a musical instrument such as a GUITAR

tune-up *n* [singular] **1** the process of making small changes to an engine so that it works as well as possible **2** an occasion that someone uses as preparation for a more important occasion: *He is treating the semi-finals as a tune-up.*

tung·sten /'tʌŋstən/ *n* [U] a hard metal that is used to make steel and in the thin wires in electric light BULBS. It is a chemical ELEMENT: symbol W

tu·nic /'tjuːnɪk $ 'tuː-/ *n* [C] **1** a long loose piece of clothing, usually without sleeves, worn in the past **2** a long loose women's shirt, usually worn with trousers **3** *BrE* a specially shaped short coat worn by soldiers, police officers etc as part of a uniform

tuning fork *n* [C] a small U-shaped steel instrument that makes a particular musical note when you hit it

tuning peg *n* [C] a screw used for making the strings on a GUITAR etc tighter or looser

tun·nel¹ W3 /'tʌnl/ *n* [C]
1 a passage that has been dug under the ground for cars, trains etc to go through: *a railway tunnel* | *the Channel Tunnel* (=between England and France)
2 a passage under the ground that animals have dug to live in

tunnel² *v* **tunnelled, tunnelling** *BrE*, **tunneled, tunneling** *AmE* [I always + adv/prep, T] **1** to dig a long passage under the ground: [+into/through/under] *They were tunnelling into the mountainside.* | **tunnel your way under/through etc** *The prisoners tunneled their way under the fence.* **2** if insects tunnel into something, they make holes in it: [+into] *The grubs tunnel into the wood.*

tunnel 'vision *n* [U] **1** the tendency to only think about one part of something such as a problem or plan, instead of considering all the parts of it: *I've got tunnel vision when it comes to what I want to do.* **2** a condition in which someone's eyes are damaged so that they can only see things that are straight ahead

tun·ny /'tʌni/ *n plural* **tunny** [C,U] a British word for TUNA

tup·pence /'tʌpəns/ *n* [U] *BrE* **1** an amount of money worth two pence **2 not care/give tuppence** to not care at all about someone or something

tup·peny, tuppenny /'tʌpəni/ *adj BrE* costing two pence

Tup·per·ware /'tʌpəweə $ -pərwer/ *n* [U] *trademark* a type of plastic container that closes very tightly and is used to store food

Tupperware party *n* [C] an occasion on which people get together at someone's house in order to buy Tupperware

tur·ban /'tɜːbən $ 'tɜːr-/ *n* [C] a long piece of cloth that you wind tightly round your head, worn by men in parts of North Africa and Southern Asia and sometimes by women as a fashion

tur·bid /'tɜːbɪd $ 'tɜːr-/ *adj formal* turbid water or liquid is dirty and muddy —**turbidity** /tɜːˈbɪdɪ̣ti $ tɜːr-/ *n* [U]

tur·bine /'tɜːbaɪn $ 'tɜːrbɪ̣n, -baɪn/ *n* [C] an engine or motor in which the pressure of a liquid or gas moves a special wheel around → **GAS TURBINE, WIND TURBINE**

tur·bo /'tɜːbəʊ $ 'tɜːrboʊ/ *n plural* **turbos** [C] a car with a turbocharged engine: *an Audi turbo diesel*

tur·bo·charged /'tɜːbəʊˌtʃɑːdʒd $ 'tɜːrboʊˌtʃɑːrdʒd/ *adj* a turbocharged engine or vehicle has a turbocharger

tur·bo·charg·er /'tɜːbəʊˌtʃɑːdʒə $ 'tɜːrboʊˌtʃɑːrdʒər/ *n* [C] a system that makes a vehicle more powerful by using a turbine to force air and petrol into the engine under increased pressure

think we should have turned off at the last exit. | **turn off the road/motorway etc** *Mark turned off the highway and into Provincetown.* → TURN-OFF

4 turn sb ⇔ **off** to make someone decide they do not like something: *Any prospective buyer will be turned off by the sight of rotting wood.* → TURN-OFF

5 turn sb ⇔ **off** to make someone feel that they are not attracted to you in a sexual way; **🔊 turn on:** *Men who stink of beer really turn me off.* → TURN-OFF

turn on *phr v*

1 turn sth ⇔ **on** to make a machine or piece of electrical equipment such as a television, engine, light etc start operating by pushing a button, turning a key etc; **🔊 switch on; 🔊 turn off:** *Jake turned on his computer and checked his mail.*

2 turn sth ⇔ **on** to make the supply of water, gas etc start flowing from something by turning a handle; **🔊 turn off:** *He turned on the gas and lit the stove.* | *'I'm thirsty,' she said,* **turning on the tap.**

3 turn on sb also **turn upon sb** to suddenly attack someone, using physical violence or unpleasant words: *Peter turned on Rae and screamed, 'Get out of my sight!'*

4 turn on sth also **turn upon sth** if a situation, event, argument etc turns on a particular thing or idea, it depends on that thing: *As usual, everything turned on how much money was available.*

5 turn sb on to make someone feel sexually excited: *The way he looked at her really turned her on.* → TURN-ON

6 turn sb on to interest someone, or to make someone become interested in something: *Science fiction just doesn't turn me on.* | [+to] *It was Walter who turned me on to vegetarian food.*

7 turn on the charm also **turn it on** to suddenly start to be very nice, amusing, and interesting, especially in a way that is not sincere: *Simon was good at turning on the charm at parties.*

turn out *phr v*

1 to happen in a particular way, or to have a particular result, especially one that you did not expect: **turn out well/badly/fine etc** *It was a difficult time, but eventually things turned out all right.* | *To my surprise,* **it turned out that** *I was wrong.* | **As it turned out** (=used to say what happened in the end), *he passed the exam quite easily.* | **turn out to be sth** *That guy turned out to be Maria's second cousin.*

2 turn the light out to stop the flow of electricity to a light by pressing a switch, pulling a string etc: *Don't forget to turn out the lights when you go!*

3 if a lot of people turn out for an event, they go to watch it or take part in it: [+for] *About 70% of the population turned out for the election.* | **turn out to do sth** *Thousands turned out to watch yesterday's match against Ireland.* → TURNOUT

4 turn sb ⇔ **out** to force someone to leave a place permanently, especially their home: *If you can't pay the rent, they turn you out.*

5 turn sth ⇔ **out** to produce or make something: *The factory turns out 300 units a day.*

6 well/beautifully/badly etc turned out dressed in good, beautiful etc clothes: *elegantly turned-out young ladies*

7 turn sth ⇔ **out a)** to empty something completely by taking out the contents: *The policeman made him turn out his pockets.* **b)** *BrE* to take out everything in a room, drawer etc and clean the room etc thoroughly: *Lea decided to turn out the attic.*

turn over *phr v*

1 turn sth over to sb to give someone the right to own something, or to make someone responsible for dealing with something: *He'll turn the shop over to his son when he retires.* | **turn the matter/problem/responsibility etc over to sb** *I'm turning the project over to you.*

2 turn sth over to sth to use land, a building etc for a different purpose: *There is a new plan to turn the land over to wind farming.*

3 turn sb over to sb to take a criminal to the police or another official organization: *Suspected terrorists are immediately turned over to the law.*

4 turn over sth if a business turns over a particular amount of money, it earns that amount in a particular period of time: *Within ten years the theme park was turning over £20 million.* → TURNOVER

5 if an engine turns over, or if someone turns it over, it starts to work: *The engine turned over twice and then stopped.*

6 *BrE* to turn a page in a book or a sheet of paper to the opposite side: *Turn over and look at the next page.*

7 *BrE* to change to another CHANNEL on a television: *Can we turn over? There's a film I want to see.*

8 turn sth over *BrE* to search a place thoroughly or steal things from it, making it very untidy: *Burglars had been in and turned the whole house over.* → **turn over a new leaf** at LEAF¹ (3); → **turn sth over in your mind** at MIND¹ (17)

turn round *phr v BrE*
→ TURN AROUND

turn to sb/sth *phr v*

1 to try to get help, advice, or sympathy from someone: *I don't know who to turn to.* | *The Namibian government turned to South Africa for help.*

2 to start to do or use something new, especially as a way of solving a problem: *Many people here are turning to solar power.* | **turn to drink/crime/drugs etc** *addicts who turn to crime to finance their habit*

3 turn (sth) to sth to become a different quality, attitude, form of a substance etc, or to make something do this: *Our laughter turned to horror as we realized that Jody was really hurt.* | *When water turns to steam, it expands.* | *A sudden storm turned the earth to mud.*

4 to look at a particular page in a book: *Turn to page 655 for more information.*

turn up *phr v*

1 turn sth ⇔ **up** to turn a switch on a machine such as an OVEN, radio etc so that it produces more heat, sound etc; **🔊 turn down:** *Turn the oven up to 220.* | *Turn up the radio!*

2 to be found, especially by chance, after having been lost or searched for: *Eventually my watch turned up in a coat pocket.*

3 to arrive at a place, especially in a way that is unexpected: *You can't just turn up and expect a meal.* | **turn up late/early/on time etc** *Steve turned up late, as usual.*

4 if an opportunity or situation turns up, it happens, especially when you are not expecting it: *Don't worry, I'm sure a job will turn up soon.*

5 turn sth ⇔ **up** to find something by searching for it thoroughly: *The police investigation hasn't turned up any new evidence.*

6 turn sth ⇔ **up** *BrE* to shorten a skirt, trousers etc by folding up the bottom and sewing it → **turn up trumps** at TRUMP¹ (4)

turn upon sb/sth *phr v formal*

1 to suddenly attack someone, using physical violence or unpleasant words; **🔊 turn on**

2 if a situation, event, argument etc turns upon a particular thing or idea, it depends on that thing; **🔊 turn on:** *The court case turned upon a technicality of company law.*

turn² S1 W1 *n*

1 CHANCE TO DO STH [C] the time when it is your chance, duty, or right to do something that each person in a group is doing one after the other; **🔊 go** *BrE:* **turn to do sth** *Whose turn is it to set the table?* | *It's your turn. Roll the dice.* | *I think it's our turn to drive the kids to school this week.*

2 take turns also **take it in turns** *BrE* if two or more people take turns doing work, using something etc, they do it one after the other, for example in order to share the work or play fairly: *You'll have to take turns on the swing.* | **take turns doing sth** *The students were taking turns reading aloud.* | **take turns in doing sth** *BrE:* *We took turns in pushing the bike along.* | **take turns to do sth** *Dan and I usually take turns to cook.*

3 in turn a) as a result of something: *Interest rates were cut and, in turn, share prices rose.* **b)** one after the other,

especially in a particular order: *Each of us in turn had to describe how alcohol had affected our lives.*
4 ROAD [C] **a)** *AmE* a place where one road goes in a different direction from the one you are on; ▣ **turning** *BrE*: *According to the map we missed our turn back there.* | **take the first/a wrong etc turn** (=go along the first etc road) *I think we took a wrong turn coming out of town.* | *Take the second turn on the left.* **b)** a curve in a road, path etc: *There's a sharp turn coming up ahead.*
5 CHANGE DIRECTION [C] a change in the direction you are moving: **make a left/right turn** *Make a left turn at the station.*
6 CHANGE IN EVENTS [C] a sudden or unexpected change that makes a situation develop in a different way: **take a dramatic/fresh/different etc turn** *From then on, our fortunes took a downward turn.* | *My career had already taken a new turn.* | *The President was stunned by the sudden turn of events.* | **take a turn for the worse/better** *Two days after the operation, Dad took a turn for the worse.*
7 the turn of the century/year the beginning of a new century or year: *the short period from the turn of the century until World War One*
8 at every turn happening again and again, especially in an annoying way: *problems that presented themselves at every turn*
9 ACT OF TURNING STH [C] the act of turning something completely around a fixed point: *I gave the screw another two or three turns.*
10 by turns changing from one quality, feeling etc to another: *By turns, a 14 year old is affectionate then aggressive, silent then outspoken.*
11 turn of phrase a) the ability to say things in a clever or funny way: *Kate has a colourful turn of phrase.* **b)** a particular way of saying something; ▣ **expression**: *What a strange turn of phrase!*
12 speak/talk out of turn to say something you should not say in a particular situation, especially because you do not have enough authority to say it: *I'm sorry if I spoke out of turn, Major Karr.*
13 do sb a good/bad turn to do something that is helpful or unhelpful for someone: *You did me a good turn by driving Max home last night.*
14 one good turn deserves another used to say that if someone does something nice for you, you should do something nice for them
15 turn of mind the particular way that someone usually thinks or feels: **an academic/practical etc turn of mind** *youngsters with an independent turn of mind*
16 on the turn *BrE* **a)** if the TIDE is on the turn, the sea is starting to come in or go out **b)** starting to change, or in the process of changing: *Hopefully my luck was on the turn.* **c)** if milk, fish, or other food is on the turn, it is no longer fresh
17 turn of speed *BrE* a sudden increase in your speed, or the ability to increase your speed suddenly: *He's a top goalkicker with a surprising turn of speed.*
18 done to a turn *BrE* to be perfectly cooked
19 take a turn in/on etc sth *old-fashioned* to walk somewhere for pleasure
20 give sb a turn *old-fashioned* to frighten someone
21 have a turn *BrE old-fashioned* to feel slightly ill

turn·a·bout /'tɜːnəbaʊt $ 'tɜːrn-/ n **1** [C usually singular] *BrE* a complete change in someone's opinions, ideas, or methods: *an extraordinarily rapid turnabout in attitudes* **2 turnabout is fair play** *AmE* used to say that because someone else has done something to you, you can do it to them too

turn·a·round /'tɜːnəraʊnd $ 'tɜːrn-/ also **turn-round** *BrE* n [singular] **1** the time it takes to receive something, deal with it and send it back, especially on a plane, ship etc: *The average turnaround for a passport application is six working days.* | *We must reduce costs and shorten turnaround times.* **2** a complete change from a bad situation to a good one: [+in] *the remarkable turnaround in our economy* → **turn around** at TURN[1] **3** a
TURNABOUT

turn·coat /'tɜːnkəʊt $ 'tɜːrnkoʊt/ n [C] someone who stops supporting a political party or group and joins the opposing side: *Casson was publicly criticized as a turncoat and a traitor.*

turn·er /'tɜːnə $ 'tɜːrnər/ n [C] *especially BrE* someone who uses a LATHE (=special tool) to make shapes out of wood or metal

turn·ing /'tɜːnɪŋ $ 'tɜːr-/ n [C] *BrE* a road that connects with the one you are on; ▣ **turn** *AmE*: *He must have taken a wrong turning in the dark.* | *Take the first turning on the left.*

'turning ˌcircle also **'turning ˌradius** n [C] the smallest space in which a vehicle can drive around in a circle

'turning point n [C] the time when an important change starts, especially one that improves the situation: [+in] *Meeting her was the turning point in my life.*

tur·nip /'tɜːnɪp $ 'tɜːr-/ n [C,U] a large round pale yellow vegetable that grows under the ground, or the plant that produces it

turn·key /'tɜːnkiː $ 'tɜːrn-/ adj [only before noun] ready to be used immediately: *the development and sale of turnkey systems for telecommunications customers*

'turn-off n **1** [C] a smaller road that leads off a main road: *I missed the turn-off to the farm.* **2** [singular] *informal* something that makes you lose interest in something, especially sex: *Pornographic pictures are a real turn-off to most women.* → **turn off** at TURN[1]

ˌturn-of-the-'century adj [only before noun] existing or happening around the beginning of a century, especially the beginning of the 20th century; → **fin de siècle**: *narrow turn-of-the-century streets*

'turn-on n [singular] *informal* something that makes you feel excited, especially sexually: *It was a turn-on to be the centre of attention.* → **TURN ON** (5)

turn·out also **'turn-out** /'tɜːnaʊt $ 'tɜːrn-/ n **1** [singular] the number of people who vote in an election: **high/low turnout** *the low turn-out of 54 percent in the March elections* → **TURN OUT** (3) **2** [singular] the number of people who go to a party, meeting, or other organized event: *I was disappointed by the turn-out for our home match.* **3** [C] *AmE* a place at the side of a narrow road where cars can wait to let others pass

turn·o·ver /'tɜːnˌəʊvə $ 'tɜːrnˌoʊvər/ n **1** [singular, U] *BrE* the amount of business done during a particular period: [+of] *The illicit drugs industry has an annual turnover of some £200 bn.* | **turnover rose/fell** *Turnover rose 9%.* **2** [singular, U] the rate at which a particular kind of goods is sold: [+of] *Tri-Star's fast turnover of stock* **3** [singular, U] the rate at which people leave an organization and are replaced by others: [+of] *Low pay accounts for the high turnover.* | **staff/labour turnover** *a high degree of labour turnover among women* **4** [C] a small fruit PIE: *an apple turnover*

turn·pike /'tɜːnpaɪk $ 'tɜːrn-/ n [C] *AmE* a large road for fast traffic that drivers have to pay to use: *the New Jersey Turnpike*

turn·round /'tɜːnraʊnd $ 'tɜːrn-/ n [C usually singular] *BrE* a TURNAROUND

'turn ˌsignal n [C] *AmE* one of the lights on a car that flash to show which way the car is turning; ▣ **indicator** *BrE*; → see picture at CAR

turn·stile /'tɜːnstaɪl $ 'tɜːrn-/ n [C] a small gate that spins around and only lets one person at a time go through an entrance; → **revolving door**: *We've had 600,000 admissions through the turnstiles.*

turn·ta·ble /'tɜːnˌteɪbəl $ 'tɜːrn-/ n [C] **1** the part of a STEREO on which the record turns round **2** a large flat round surface on which railway engines are turned around

turn·ta·blist /'tɜːnteɪblɪst $ 'tɜːrn-/ n [C] informal a DJ who plays recorded music at parties or dances, and who mixes together parts of different records to form new music

'turn-up n [C] BrE   **1** the bottom of a trouser leg that is folded up for decoration or to make it shorter; ◫ **cuff** AmE   **2 a turn-up for the book(s)** informal an unexpected and surprising event: Fancy you being in New York too. What a turn-up for the books!

tur·pen·tine /'tɜːpəntaɪn $ 'tɜːr-/ n [U] a type of oil used for making paint more liquid or removing it from clothes, brushes etc

tur·pi·tude /'tɜːpɪtjuːd $ 'tɜːrpɪtuːd/ n [U] formal very immoral behaviour: laziness and moral turpitude

turps /tɜːps $ tɜːrps/ n [U] BrE informal turpentine

tur·quoise /'tɜːkwɔɪz, -kwɑːz $ 'tɜːrkwɔɪz/ n   **1** [C,U] a valuable greenish-blue stone or a jewel that is made from this: turquoise earrings   **2** [U] a greenish-blue colour: The room was painted in turquoise. —**turquoise** adj: a clear turquoise sea

tur·ret /'tʌrɪt/ n [C]   **1** a small tower on a large building, especially a CASTLE   **2** the place on a TANK from which guns are fired —**turreted** adj

tur·tle /'tɜːtl $ 'tɜːrtl/ n [C]   **1** a REPTILE that lives mainly in water and has a soft body covered by a hard shell → see picture at REPTILE   **2** AmE any REPTILE that has a hard shell covering its body, for example a TORTOISE   **3 turn turtle** a ship or boat that turns turtle turns upside down

tur·tle·dove /'tɜːtldʌv $ 'tɜːr-/ n [C] a type of bird that makes a pleasant soft sound and is sometimes used to represent love

tur·tle·neck /'tɜːtlnek $ 'tɜːr-/ n [C] a type of SWEATER with a high, close-fitting collar that covers most of your neck; → **polo neck, v-neck**

turves /tɜːvz $ tɜːrvz/ the plural of TURF[1] (2)

tush /tʊʃ/ n [C] AmE informal the part of your body that you sit on

tusk /tʌsk/ n [C] one of a pair of very long pointed teeth, that stick out of the mouth of animals such as ELEPHANTS

tus·sle[1] /'tʌsəl/ n [C]   **1** a fight using a lot of energy, in which two people get hold of each other and struggle: After quite a tussle, I finally wrenched the letter from him.   **2** a struggle or argument in which people try to beat each other for something: his defeat in the leadership tussle

tussle[2] v [I]   **1** to fight or struggle without using any weapons, by pulling or pushing someone rather than hitting them: [+with] He was tussling with the other boys.   **2** to try to beat someone in order to get something: [+for] They tussled for first place in the race.

tus·sock /'tʌsək/ n [C] literary a small thick mass of grass

tut[1] /tʌt/ also **tut-'tut** interjection the sound that you make by touching the top of your mouth with your tongue in order to show disapproval

tut[2] also **tut-'tut** v tutted, tutting [I] to express disapproval by making a tut sound: The nurse rushed in, tutting with irritation.

tu·te·lage /'tjuːtɪlɪdʒ $ 'tuː-/ n [U] formal   **1** when you are taught or looked after by someone: under sb's tutelage You can attend embroidery classes under the tutelage of Jocelyn James.   **2** responsibility for someone's education, actions, or property: parental tutelage

tu·tor[1] /'tjuːtə $ 'tuːtər/ n [C]   **1** someone who gives private lessons to one student or a small group, and is paid directly by them: The children were educated at home by a succession of tutors.   **2** a teacher in a British university or college: She was my tutor at Durham.; → see box at TEACHER

tutor[2] v [T] to teach someone as a tutor: He was privately tutored. | **tutor sb in sth** Young men were tutored in the art of handling horses.

tu·to·ri·al[1] /tjuː'tɔːriəl $ tuː-/ n [C]   **1** a period of teaching and discussion with a tutor, especially in a British university: the tutorial system   **2** a computer program that is designed to teach you how to use another program

tutorial[2] adj relating to a tutor or their work: tutorial staff | tutorial supervision

tut·ti frut·ti /ˌtuːti 'fruːti/ n [U] a type of ICE CREAM that has very small pieces of fruit and nuts in it

tu·tu /'tuːtuː/ n [C] a short skirt made of many folds of stiff material, worn by BALLET dancers

tux·e·do /tʌk'siːdəʊ $ -doʊ/ also **tux** /tʌks/ informal n plural **tuxedos** [C]   **1** a man's JACKET that is usually black, worn on formal occasions   **2** a man's suit that includes this type of JACKET

TV S2 /ˌtiː 'viː◂/ n [C,U] television: on TV I watched the film on TV. | TV series/programme/show/station/channel etc a TV series based on the novel | cable/satellite TV | a new TV set. | He's the top TV presenter for children's programmes. → see picture at BEDROOM

TV 'dinner n [C] a meal that is sold already prepared, so that you just need to heat it before eating

TVP /ˌtiː viː 'piː/ n [U] the abbreviation of textured vegetable protein

twad·dle /'twɒdl $ 'twɑːdl/ n [U] informal something that someone has said or written that you think is stupid; ◫ **nonsense**: I don't believe in all that twaddle about fate.

twain /tweɪn/ number old use   **1** two   **2 never the twain shall meet** used to say that two things are so different that they can never exist together

twang[1] /twæŋ/ n [C usually singular]   **1** a quality in the way someone speaks, produced when the air used to speak passes through their nose as well as their mouth: a nasal twang | Her voice had a slight Australian twang.   **2** a quick ringing sound like the one made by pulling a very tight wire and then suddenly letting it go

twang[2] v [I,T] if you twang something or if it twangs, it makes a quick ringing sound by being pulled and then suddenly let go: She twanged the guitar strings.

twas /twɒz $ twɑːz/ literary it was

twat /twɒt, twæt $ twɑːt/ n [C] taboo informal   **1** a very offensive word for a stupid or unpleasant person. Do not use this word.   **2** a very offensive word for the female sex organ. Do not use this word.

tweak /twiːk/ v [T]   **1** to suddenly pull or twist something: She leant forward and tweaked both ends of his moustache.   **2** to make small changes to a machine, vehicle, or system in order to improve the way it works: Maybe you should tweak a few sentences before you send in the report. —**tweak** n [C usually singular]

twee /twiː/ adj BrE very pretty or perfect, in a way that you find silly or unpleasant: She produced twee little flower paintings.

tweed /twiːd/ n [U]   **1** rough WOOLLEN cloth woven from threads of different colours, used mostly to make JACKETS, suits, and coats: a thick tweed suit   **2 tweeds** [plural] a suit of clothes made from this type of cloth: He wore casual country tweeds.

tweed·y /'twiːdi/ adj   **1** BrE wearing tweed clothes in a way that is thought to be typical of the British upper class   **2** made of tweed or like tweed

tween /twiːn/ prep literary between

tweet /twiːt/ v [I] to make the short high sound of a small bird —**tweet** n [C]

tweet·er /'twiːtə $ -ər/ n [C] a SPEAKER (=piece of equipment) through which the high sounds from a STEREO etc are made louder; → **woofer**

twee·zers /'twiːzəz $ -ərz/ n [plural] a small tool that has two narrow pieces of metal joined at one end, used to pull or move very small objects: She was plucking her eyebrows with a pair of tweezers.

twelfth /twelfθ/ n [C] one of twelve equal parts of something

twelve /twelv/ number the number 12: *He received a twelve-month jail sentence.* | *Come at twelve* (=12 o'clock). | *Their son Dylan is twelve* (=12 years old). —**twelfth** *adj, pron*: *her twelfth birthday* | *in the twelfth century* | *I'm planning to leave on the twelfth* (=the 12th day of the month).

twen·ty /'twenti/ *number, noun* **1** the number 20: *a small village twenty miles from Nairobi* | *I'm nearly twenty* (=20 years old). **2 the twenties** [plural] also **the '20s, the 1920s** the years from 1920 to 1929: *In the twenties the business expanded.* | **the early/mid/late twenties** *The photograph was taken in the late twenties.* **3 be in your twenties** to be aged between 20 and 29: *early/mid/late twenties She was in her early twenties when I met her.* **4 in the twenties** if the temperature is in the twenties, it is between 20 degrees and 29 degrees: **in the low/mid/high twenties** *a warm day, with temperatures in the low twenties* **5** [C] a piece of paper money that is worth £20 or $20: *I offered the driver a twenty.* —**twentieth** *adj, pron*: *in the twentieth century* | *her twentieth birthday* | *I'm planning to leave on the twentieth* (=the 20th day of the month).

twenty-'first *n* [C usually singular] your twenty-first BIRTHDAY or the celebration you have for it

twenty-four 'seven, 24–7 *adv informal* if something happens twenty-four seven, it happens all the time, every day

twenty-'one *n* [U] *AmE* a card game, usually played for money; ▤ **pontoon** *BrE*

twen·ty·some·thing /'twenti,sʌmθɪŋ/ *n* [C] *informal* someone who is between the ages of 20 and 29; → **thirtysomething**: *A crowd of twentysomethings were gathered outside the club.* —**twentysomething** *adj*

twenty-'twenty, 20/20 *n* [U] **1 twenty-twenty vision** the ability to see things normally, without needing glasses: *A pilot must have twenty-twenty vision.* **2 twenty-twenty hindsight** used to say that it is easy to know what you should have done in a situation after it has happened, but you did not know what to do earlier

twenty-'two, .22 *n* [C] a gun that fires small bullets, used for hunting small animals

twerp /twɜːp $ twɜːrp/ *n* [C] *informal* a person who you think is stupid or annoying

twice /twaɪs/ *adv, predeterminer* **1** two times: *He was questioned by police twice yesterday.* | **twice a day/week/year etc** (=two times in the same day, week etc) *Letters were delivered twice a week only.* | *None of our dinner menus are exactly the same twice over.* **2** two times more, bigger, better etc than something else: **twice as many/much (as sth)** *They employ 90 people, twice as many as last year.* | **twice as high/big/large etc (as sth)** *Interest rates are twice as high as those of our competitors.* | **twice the size/number/rate/amount etc** *an area twice the size of Britain* → **once bitten, twice shy** at ONCE[1] (19); → **once or twice** at ONCE[1] (12); → **think twice** at THINK[1] (8)

twid·dle /'twɪdl/ *v* [I,T] **1 twiddle your thumbs** *informal* to do nothing while you are waiting for something to happen: *Let's go – there's no point in sitting here twiddling our thumbs.* **2** to move or turn something around with your fingers many times, especially because you are nervous or bored: [+with] *She was twiddling with her earrings.* —**twiddle** *n* [C]

twig[1] /twɪg/ *n* [C] a small very thin stem of wood that grows from a branch on a tree —**twiggy** *adj*; → see picture at TREE

twig[2] *v* **twigged, twigging** [I,T] *BrE informal* to suddenly realize something about a situation: *It took ages before he twigged.*

twi·light /'twaɪlaɪt/ *n* **1** [U] the small amount of light in the sky as the day ends: **in the twilight** *The end of the cigarette glowed in the twilight.* **2** [U] the time when day is just starting to become night; ▤ **dusk**: **at twilight** *romantic walks along the beach at twilight* **3** [singular] the period just before the end of the most active part of someone's life: [+of] *in the twilight*

of her acting career | *Depression in the twilight years* (=the last years of your life) *is usually related to illness.* **4 twilight world** *literary* a strange situation involving mystery, dishonesty etc: [+of] *the twilight world of espionage*

twi·lit /'twaɪlɪt/ *adj literary* lit by twilight

twill /twɪl/ *n* [U] strong cloth woven to produce parallel sloping lines across its surface: *grey twill trousers*

twin[1] /twɪn/ *n* [C] one of two children born at the same time to the same mother: *The twins are now eight months old.* → IDENTICAL TWIN, SIAMESE TWIN

twin[2] *adj* [only before noun] **1** used to describe one of two children who are twins: **twin sister/ brother** *Meet my twin sister.* **2** used to describe two things that happen at the same time and are related to each other: *the twin problems of poverty and unemployment* **3 twin room/bedroom** a room that contains two single beds: *All the twin rooms have private bathrooms.* → TWINSET, TWIN TOWN

twin

identical twins

twin[3] *v* **twinned, twinning** [T usually passive] **1** *BrE* to form a relationship between two similar towns in different countries in order to encourage visits between them: **twin sth with sth** *Chichester in England is twinned with Chartres in France.* **2** to form a relationship between two places, people, or ideas: **twin sth with sth** *Dole has been twinned in the history books with his old rival Bush.* → TWIN TOWN

twin 'bed *n* [C] **1** [usually plural] one of a pair of single beds in a room for two people → see picture at BED[1] **2** *AmE* a bed that is just big enough for one person; → **double bed** —**twin-bedded** *adj BrE*: *twin-bedded rooms*

twine[1] /twaɪn/ *n* [U] strong string made by twisting together two or more threads or strings: *a bundle of papers tied up with twine*

twine[2] *v* [I,T] *written* to wind or twist around something else, or to make something do this: **twine sth round/around sth** *She twined her arms round him and kissed his cheek.* | [+round/around] *A dark green ivy plant twined around the pole.*

twin-en·gined /,twɪn 'endʒɪnd◂/ *adj* a twin-engined aircraft has two engines

twinge /twɪndʒ/ *n* [C] **1** a sudden feeling of slight pain: *I felt a twinge of pain in my back.* **2 a twinge of guilt/envy/sadness/jealousy etc** a sudden slight feeling of guilt etc: *He felt a sharp twinge of guilt for not taking the trouble to visit her.*

twin·kle[1] /'twɪŋkəl/ *v* [I] **1** if a star or light twinkles, it shines in the dark with an unsteady light: *stars twinkling in the sky* | *I saw lights twinkling in the little town below us.* **2** if someone's eyes twinkle, they have a happy expression: [+with] *Her eyes twinkled with amusement.*

twinkle[2] *n* [C usually singular] **1 a twinkle in your eye** an expression in your eyes that shows you are happy or amused: *a kindly, white-haired old gentleman with a twinkle in his eye* **2** a small bright shining light that becomes brighter and then fainter

twin·kling /'twɪŋklɪŋ/ *n* **in the twinkling of an eye** also **in a twinkling** very quickly

twin·set /'twɪnset/ *n* [C] *BrE* a woman's SWEATER and CARDIGAN that are meant to be worn together

twin 'town *n* [C] *BrE* a town that has formed a relationship with a similar town in another country in order to encourage visits between them: *Oxford's twin town is Bonn.* → TWIN[3] (1)

twirl /twɜːl $ twɜːrl/ v [I,T] to turn around and around or make something do this: [+around/round] *Couples were twirling around the dance floor.* | **twirl sth around/round** *She twirled the liquid around in her glass.* —**twirl** n [C] —**twirly** adj

twist¹ S3 /twɪst/ v

1 MOVE [I,T] **a)** to turn a part of your body around or change your position by turning: *He twisted his head slightly, and looked up at her.* | [+round/around] *She twisted round, so that she could see the dog better.* **b)** if you twist your mouth or features, you smile in an unpleasant way or look angry, disapproving etc: *His mouth twisted in a humourless smile.*

2 BEND [T] to bend or turn something, such as wire, hair, or cloth, into a particular shape: **twist sth into sth** *She twisted her handkerchief into a knot.* | **twist sth together** *Twist the two ends of the wire together.*

3 WIND [T always + adv/prep] to wind something around or through an object: **twist sth round/around/through etc sth** *She twisted a silk scarf round her neck.* | *Ann twisted some daisies through Katherine's thick brown hair.*

4 TURN [T] to turn something in a circle using your hand: **twist sth off (sth)** *Jack twisted the cap off the bottle.*

5 ROAD/RIVER [I] if a road, river etc twists, it changes direction in a series of curves: *The road twisted between spectacular mountains.*

6 WORDS [T] to change the true or intended meaning of a statement, especially in order to get some advantage for yourself: *He's always trying to **twist** my **words** and make me look bad.*

7 twist your ankle/wrist/knee to hurt your wrist etc by turning or turning it too suddenly while you are moving: *Harriet slipped on the stairs and twisted her ankle.*

8 twist and turn a) if a path, road, stream etc twists and turns, it has a lot of bends in it: *The river twists and turns through the green fields.* **b)** if a person or animal twists and turns, they make twisting movements

9 twist sb's arm a) *informal* to persuade someone to do something they do not want to do: *No one twisted my arm about coming to see you.* **b)** to bend someone's arm upwards behind their back in order to hurt them: *The policeman twisted my arm behind me and arrested me.* → **twist/wrap sb around your little finger** at FINGER¹ (8); → **twist the knife (in the wound)** at KNIFE¹ (3)

twist² n [C] **1** an unexpected feature or change in a situation or series of events: **a new/cruel/unexpected/strange etc twist** *The robbery took a deadly new twist as the robber pulled out a gun.* | *an unexpected twist in the plot* | *By an amazing twist of fate, we met again in Madrid five years later.* **2** a twisting action or movement: *He smiled, a slow cynical twist of his lips.* **3** a bend in a river or road **4** a small piece of something that is twisted into a particular shape: [+of] *a twist of lemon* **5 the twist** a popular fast dance from the 1960s in which you twist your body from side to side **6 round the twist** *BrE spoken* **a)** crazy: *'The woman's mad,' she told herself. 'She's round the twist.'* **b)** very angry —**twisty** adj: *a twisty road* → **(don't) get your knickers in a twist** at KNICKERS (3)

twist·ed /ˈtwɪstɪd/ also **twisted 'up** adj **1** something twisted has been bent in many directions or turned many times, so that it has lost its original shape: *the plane's twisted wreckage* **2** seeming to enjoy things that are cruel or shocking, in a way that is not normal: *Whoever sent those letters has a twisted mind.*

twist·er /ˈtwɪstə $ -ər/ n [C] **1** *BrE informal* someone who cheats other people **2** *AmE informal* a TORNADO

twit /twɪt/ n [C] *informal* a person who you think is stupid or silly

twitch¹ /twɪtʃ/ v **1** [I,T] if a part of someone's body twitches, or if they twitch it, it makes a small sudden movement: *His mouth twitched slightly, and then he smiled.* | *He twitched his eyebrows.* **2** [T] to move something quickly and suddenly: *Sarah twitched the reins, and we moved off.*

twitch² n [C] **1** a quick movement of a muscle, especially one that you cannot control: *a nervous twitch* **2** a sudden quick movement: *There was no movement in the house, not even a twitch of the curtains.*

twitch·er /ˈtwɪtʃə $ -ər/ n [C] *BrE informal* a keen BIRD-WATCHER

twitch·y /ˈtwɪtʃi/ adj behaving in a nervous way because you are anxious about something: *I was very twitchy about the way things would turn out.*

twit·ter¹ /ˈtwɪtə $ -ər/ v [I] **1** if a bird twitters, it makes a lot of short high sounds **2** to talk about unimportant and silly things, usually very quickly and nervously in a high voice

twitter² n **1** [singular] the short high sounds that birds make **2 be all of a twitter** also **be in a twitter** *BrE* to be excited and nervous: *She's been all of a twitter since her daughter's engagement.*

twixt /twɪkst/ prep *old use* between

two /tuː/ number **1** the number 2: *I'll be away for almost two weeks.* | *We have to be there by two* (=two o'clock). | *His family moved to Australia when he was two* (=two years old). **2** in twos in groups of two people or things: *I'd like you to line up in twos, please.* → TWOSOME **3 put two and two together** to guess the meaning of something you have heard or seen: *I saw him leaving her house and I put two and two together.* **4 that makes two of us** *spoken* used to tell someone that you are in the same situation and feel the same way: *'But I don't know anything about children!' 'Well, that makes two of us.'* **5 two can play at that game** *spoken* used to tell someone that they will not have an advantage over you by doing something because you can do it too **6 a year/a week/a moment/an hour etc or two** *spoken* one or a few years, weeks etc **7 two sides of the same coin** used to talk about two ways of looking at the same situation **8 two heads are better than one** used to say that two people are more likely to solve a problem or think of an idea than one person working alone **9 be in two minds (about sth)** *BrE*; **be of two minds (about sth)** *AmE* to be unable to decide what to do, or what you think about something: *I was in two minds about whether to go with him.* **10 two cents (worth)** *AmE informal* your opinion or what you want to say about a subject: *Everyone had to put in their two cents worth.* **11 two's company, three's a crowd** used to say that it is better to leave two people alone to spend time with each other → **don't care two hoots** at HOOT¹ (5); → **two/three etc of a kind** at KIND¹ (5); → **be two/ten a penny** at PENNY (11); → **in ones and twos** at ONE¹ (3); → **it takes two to tango** at TANGO² (2); → **kill two birds with one stone** at KILL¹ (13); → **no two ways about it** at WAY¹ (54); → **fall between two stools** at FALL¹ (32)

2 *written informal* a way of writing 'to' or 'too', used especially in emails and TEXT MESSAGES: *Happy birthday 2 U!* (=to you) | *He's 2* (=too) *cool!*

two-bit adj *informal* not at all good or important: *She's just a two-bit movie star.*

two-di'mensional adj **1** flat: *a two-dimensional shape* **2** a two-dimensional character in a book, play etc does not seem like a real person

two-'edged adj **1** having two effects or meanings, one good and one bad: *a two-edged comment* | **a two-edged sword** (=something that has as many bad results as good ones) *Strong leadership is a two-edged sword.* **2** having two edges that can cut: *a two-edged blade*

two-'faced adj *informal* changing what you say according to who you are talking to, in a way that is insincere and unpleasant – used to show disapproval: *He's a two-faced liar.*

two·fold /ˈtuːfəʊld $ -foʊld/ adj **1** two times as much or as many of something: *a **twofold increase** in cases of TB* **2** having two important parts: *The benefits of the* *scheme are twofold.* —**twofold** *adv*: *Student numbers have expanded twofold in ten years.*

two-'handed *adj* **1** using or needing both hands to do something: *a two-handed catch* | *a two-handed sword* **2** a two-handed tool is used by two people together

'two-man *adj* designed to be used by two people; ◱ **two-person**: *a two-man tent*

two-'one, **2:1** *n* [C] the higher of two levels of a SECOND-CLASS university degree in Britain

two·pence /'tʌpəns/ *n* [C,U] *BrE* another word for TUPPENCE

two·pen·ny /'tʌpəni 'tʌpəni, 'tuːpeni/ *adj BrE old-fashioned* **1** [only before noun] costing two pence; ◱ **tuppenny** **2 twopenny-halfpenny** *old-fashioned* worth almost nothing

two-percent 'milk *n* [U] *AmE* milk that has had about half the fat removed

two-'person *adj* [only before noun] **1** consisting of two people: *a two-person household* **2** designed to be used by two people; ◱ **two-man**

'two-piece *adj* [only before noun] a two-piece suit consists of a matching JACKET and trousers

two-'seater *n* [C] a vehicle or a piece of furniture with seats for two people: *a two-seater sofa*

two-'sided *adj* having two different parts: *a two-sided problem* → ONE-SIDED, MANY-SIDED

two·some /'tuːsəm/ *n* [C usually singular] two people who work together or spend a lot of time together: *a well-known comedy twosome*

'two-star *adj* [only before noun] a two-star hotel, restaurant etc has been judged to be of a MEDIUM standard

'two-step *n* [singular] a dance with long sliding steps, or the music for this type of dance

'two-stroke *adj* a two-stroke engine is one in which there is a single up-and-down movement of a PISTON

'two-time *v* [T] *informal* to have a secret relationship with someone who is not your regular partner: *He doesn't love Claire's been two-timing him.* —**two-timer** *n* [C]

'two-tone *adj* having two different colours or sounds: *two-tone shoes* | *a two-tone alarm*

two-'two, **2:2** *n* [C] the lower of two levels of a SECOND-CLASS university degree in Britain

two-'way *adj* **1** moving or allowing movement in both directions: *two-way traffic* | *two-way trade* **2** used to describe a relationship which needs effort from both the people or groups involved: *Corruption is a two-way process.* **3** a two-way radio both sends and receives messages

two-way 'mirror *n* [C] glass that is a mirror from one side, but that you can see through from the other

two-way 'street *n informal* **sth is a two-way street** used to say that a situation depends on two people working well together: *Marriage has to be a two-way street.*

-ty /ti/ *suffix* [in nouns] another form of -ITY: *certainty* (=being certain)

ty·coon /taɪˈkuːn/ *n* [C] someone who is successful in business or industry and has a lot of money and power: **media/property/business/newspaper tycoon** *a multi-millionaire property tycoon*

ty·ing /'taɪ-ɪŋ/ the present participle of TIE

tyke /taɪk/ *n* [C] **1** *BrE spoken* a child who is behaving badly **2** *AmE informal* a small child **3** *BrE informal* someone from Yorkshire

tym·pa·num /'tɪmpənəm/ *n plural* **tympanums** *or* **tympana** /-nə/ [C] *technical* an EARDRUM

type[1] [S1] [W1] /taɪp/ *n*
1 [C] one member of a group of people or things that have similar features or qualities: **of this/that/each etc type** *I've already seen a few movies of this type.* | **[+of]** *What type of music do you like?* | *Products like this are clearly aimed at a particular type of person.* | *There are*

two main types of sleep. | *Buy the right shampoo for your hair type.*
2 [singular] a person who has, or seems to have, a particular character: *Jo's not really the sporty type.* | *Beth is not the type to make a fuss.*
3 be sb's type *especially spoken* to be the kind of person someone is sexually attracted to: *He wasn't my type really.*
4 [U] printed letters: *italic type*
5 [C,U] a small block with a raised letter on it that is used to print with, or a set of these

---

WORD CHOICE: type, kind, sort
Type, **kind**, and **sort** all have the same meaning and can be used in the same situations: *What type of car do you drive?* | *an interesting kind of plant* | *a new sort of mobile phone*
If you are saying that something is partly true or are not being exact, use **sort of** or **kind of** rather than **type of**: *It's a sort of oval shape.*
Type, **kind**, and **sort** are countable nouns, and they must be plural after determiners with plural meanings: **this type/kind/sort of + singular noun**: *I don't like this type of thing.* | *This kind of mistake is easy to make.* | *Red wine goes well with this sort of dish.*
these/those types/kinds/sorts of + plural/singular noun: *How common are these types of illness(es)?* | *Those kinds of colours look good with dark skin.*
⚠ Remember to use the plural **types/kinds/sorts** after **all, both, certain, different, many, several, various** etc: *movies that appeal to certain kinds of people (NOT certain kind of people)* | *Many sorts of jobs require computing skills (NOT many sort of jobs).*

---

type[2] *v* **1** [I,T] to write something using a computer or a TYPEWRITER: *He types with two fingers.* | *Type your password, then press 'Return'.* | **type sth up** (=type a copy of something written by hand, in note form, or recorded) *I went home to type up the report.* | **type sth in** (=write information on a computer) *Please wait while I type in your details.* **2** [T] *technical* to find out what group something such as blood, cells, or a disease belong to: *DNA typing*

type·cast /'taɪpkɑːst $ -kæst/ *v past tense and past participle* **typecast** [T] **1** to always give an actor the same type of character to play: *He always gets typecast as the villain.* **2** to give someone a particular type of job, activity etc to do, because you think it suits their character —**typecasting** *n* [U]

type·face /'taɪpfeɪs/ *n* [C] a group of letters, numbers etc of the same style and size, used in printing; ◱ **font**: *The new logo features a more modern typeface.*

type·script /'taɪpˌskrɪpt/ *n* [C] a copy of a document that has been typed

type·set·ting /'taɪpˌsetɪŋ/ *n* [U] the job or activity of arranging TYPE[1] (5) for printing: *computerized typesetting* —**typesetter** *n* [C] —**typeset** *v* [T]

type·writ·er /'taɪpˌraɪtə $ -ər/ *n* [C] a machine with keys that you press in order to print letters of the alphabet onto paper

type·writ·ten /'taɪpˌrɪtn/ *adj* written using a computer or a TYPEWRITER: *typewritten notes*

ty·phoid /'taɪfɔɪd/ *also* **typhoid 'fever** *n* [U] a serious infectious disease that is caused by dirty food or drink: *a sudden outbreak of typhoid*

ty·phoon /ˌtaɪˈfuːn‹ / *n* [C] a very violent tropical storm

ty·phus /'taɪfəs/ *n* [U] a serious infectious disease carried by insects that live on the bodies of people and animals: *a typhus epidemic*

typ·i·cal [S2] [W2] /'tɪpɪkəl/ *adj*
1 having the usual features or qualities of a particular group or thing: *typical British weather* | **[+of]** *This painting is typical of his work.* | *This advertisement is a*

typical example of their marketing strategy.
2 happening in the usual way: *On a typical day, our students go to classes from 7.30 am to 1pm.* | *Try calculating your budget for a typical week.*
3 behaving in the way that you expect: *Bennett accepted the award with typical modesty.* | **it is typical of sb to do sth** *It's not typical of Gill to be so critical.* | *Mr Stevens' appointment was a typical case of promoting a man beyond his level of competence.*
4 typical! *spoken* used to show that you are annoyed when something bad happens again, or when someone does something bad again

typ·i·cal·ly /'tɪpɪkli/ *adv* **1** in a way that a person or group is generally believed to behave: *Typically, he didn't even bother to tell anyone he was going.* | *Al was his typically cheerful self again.* **2** in a way that shows the usual or expected features of someone or something: *a delightful, typically Dutch hotel* | *The male of the species is typically smaller than the female.* **3** in the way that a particular type of thing usually happens: *Women in developing countries typically have their first child when they are very young.* | *I typically get around 30 emails a day.*

typ·i·fy /'tɪpᵻfaɪ/ *v* **typified, typifying, typifies** [T] **1** to be a typical example of something: *the features which typify a Scottish Highland landscape* | *non-violent protest, typified by Gandhi* **2** to be a typical part or feature of something: *the long complicated sentences that typify legal documents*

typ·ing /'taɪpɪŋ/ *n* [U] the activity of using a computer or a TYPEWRITER to write something: *typing errors* | *I'm no good at typing.*

typing pool *n* [C] a group of typists in a large office who type letters for other people

typ·ist /'taɪpᵻst/ *n* [C] **1** a secretary whose main job is to TYPE letters **2** someone who uses a computer KEYBOARD or a TYPEWRITER: *I'm a slow typist.*

ty·po /'taɪpəʊ $ -poʊ/ *n plural* **typos** [C] a small mistake in the way something has been TYPED or printed

ty·pog·ra·pher /taɪ'pɒgrəfə $ -'paːgrəfər/ *n* [C] **1** someone who designs TYPEFACES **2** a COMPOSITOR

ty·pog·ra·phy /taɪ'pɒgrəfi $ -'paː-/ *n* [U] **1** the work of preparing written material for printing **2** the arrangement, style, and appearance of printed words —**typographic** /ˌtaɪpə'græfɪk◂/ *also* **typographical**

adj: typographic errors —**typographically** /-kli/ *adv*

ty·pol·o·gy /taɪ'pɒlədʒi $ -paː-/ *n plural* **typologies** [C,U] a system or the study of dividing a group of things into smaller groups according to the similar qualities they have —**typological** /ˌtaɪpə'lɒdʒɪəl◂ $ -'laː-/ *adj*

ty·ran·ni·cal /tᵻ'rænɪkəl/ *adj* behaving in a cruel and unfair way towards someone you have power over: *a tyrannical parent* | *tyrannical laws*

tyr·an·nize *also* **-ise** *BrE* /'tɪrənaɪz/ *v* [I,T] to use power over someone cruelly or unfairly: *The children were tyrannized by their father.* | [+**over**] *armed groups tyrannizing over civilians*

ty·ran·no·sau·rus /tᵻˌrænə'sɔːrəs◂/ *also* **ty·ran·nosaurus 'rex** *n* [C] a very large flesh-eating DINOSAUR

tyr·an·nous /'tɪrənəs/ *adj old-fashioned* TYRANNICAL

tyr·an·ny /'tɪrəni/ *n plural* **tyrannies** [C,U] **1** cruel or unfair control over other people: *Gorky was often the victim of his grandfather's tyranny.* | *the fight against tyranny* **2** cruel and unfair government: *organizations which have criticized the tyrannies of the government* **3 tyranny of the majority** the idea that if everyone has the right to vote, they will make decisions which will harm the country **4** something in your life that limits your freedom to do things the way you want to: [+**of**] *the tyranny of the nine-to-five working day*

ty·rant /'taɪərənt $ 'taɪr-/ *n* [C] **1** a ruler who has complete power and uses it in a cruel and unfair way: *The country had long been ruled by tyrants.* **2** someone who has power over other people, and uses it cruelly or unfairly: *My headmaster was a real tyrant.*

tyre [S3] *BrE*; **tire** *AmE* /taɪə $ taɪr/ *n* [C] a thick rubber ring that fits around the wheel of a car, bicycle etc: *I had a flat tyre* (=all the air went out of it) *on the way home.* | *The spare tyre's in the boot.* | **front/rear/back tyre** *a punctured front tyre* → SPARE TYRE; → see picture at BICYCLE[1]; → see picture at CAR

tzar /zɑː, tsɑː $ zɑːr, tsɑːr/ *n* [C] another spelling of TSAR

tza·ri·na /zɑː'riːnə, tsɑː-/ *n* [C] another spelling of TSARINA

tzar·is·m /'zɑːrɪzəm, 'tsɑː-/ *n* [U] another spelling of TSARISM

tze·tze fly /'tetsi flaɪ, 'tsetsi-, 'setsi-/ *n* [C] another spelling of TSETSE FLY

U, u

U¹, u /juː/ *plural* U's, u's *n* **1** [C,U] the 21st letter of the English alphabet **2** [singular, U] *BrE* used to describe a film that has been officially approved as suitable for people of any age; → **PG**; ⊟ **G** *AmE* **3** [C] *BrE* a mark given to a student's work to show that it is extremely bad → **U-BOAT, U-TURN**

U² *pron written informal* a way of writing 'you', used especially in emails and TEXT MESSAGES: *I love U!*

U., U /juː/ *AmE informal* an abbreviation of *university*: *Indiana U*

UAV /ˌjuː eɪ ˈviː/ *n* [C] *AmE* **unmanned aerial vehicle** a type of plane that has no pilot, used especially for gathering information and taking photographs

uber- /ˈuːbə, ˌuːbə $ -ər/ *prefix informal* better, larger, or greater; ⊟ **super**: *uberbabe Pamela Lee* | *I want to do something uber-cool with my webpage.*

u·biq·ui·tous /juːˈbɪkwᵻtəs/ *adj formal* seeming to be everywhere – sometimes used humorously: *Coffee shops are ubiquitous these days.* | *a French film, starring the ubiquitous Gérard Depardieu* —**ubiquitously** *adv* —**ubiquity** *n* [U]

U-boat /ˈjuː bəʊt $ -boʊt/ *n* [C] a German SUBMARINE, especially one that was used in the Second World War

ud·der /ˈʌdə $ -ər/ *n* [C] the part of a cow, female goat etc that hangs down between its back legs and that produces milk

UFO /ˌjuː ef ˈəʊ, ˌjuː ef ˈoʊ $ -foʊ, -ˈoʊ/ *n* [C] **unidentified flying object** a strange object in the sky, that some people believe is a SPACESHIP from another world; ⊟ **flying saucer**

ugh /ʊx, ʌɡ/ *interjection* the sound that people make when something is extremely unpleasant: *Ugh! That's disgusting!*

ug·ly /ˈʌɡli/ *adj comparative* **uglier**, *superlative* **ugliest** **1** extremely unattractive and unpleasant to look at; ⊟ **hideous**; 🔲 **beautiful**: *a very ugly man* | *the ugliest building in town* | *Nick's dog is as ugly as sin* (=very ugly). **2** used to describe a situation which is very bad or violent, and which makes you feel frightened or threatened: *There were ugly scenes as rival gangs started attacking each other.* | *an ugly incident* **3** ugly ideas, feelings, remarks etc are unpleasant: *Jealousy is an ugly emotion.* | *ugly rumors* **4 ugly duckling** someone who is less attractive, successful etc than other people, but who becomes beautiful and successful later —**ugliness** *n* [U]

UHF /ˌjuː eɪtʃ ˈef/ *n* [U] **ultra-high frequency** a range of radio waves that produces a very good quality of sound

uh huh /ˌʌ ˈhʌ, ˌʌ ˈhʌ/ *interjection informal* a sound that you make to say 'yes', or when you want someone to continue what they are saying: *'Can I sit here?' 'Uh huh.'*

uh-oh /ˈʌ əʊ $ -oʊ/ *interjection informal* a sound that you make when you have made a mistake, or when something bad is going to happen: *Uh-oh, I think I just deleted all my work.* | *Uh-oh! Here she comes.*

UHT milk /ˌjuː eɪtʃ tiː ˈmɪlk/ *n* [U] *BrE* milk that has been heated to a very high temperature to preserve it.

uh-uh /ˈʌ ʌ/ *interjection informal* a sound that you make to say 'no': *'Is Paul here yet?' 'Uh-uh.'*

UK, U.K. /ˌjuː ˈkeɪ/ *n* **the UK** the abbreviation of *the United Kingdom*

u·ku·le·le, ukelele /ˌjuːkəˈleɪli/ *n* [C] a musical instrument with four strings, like a small GUITAR

-ular /jᵿlə $ -ər/ *suffix* [in adjectives] of or relating to something: *glandular fever* | *tubular steel*

ul·cer /ˈʌlsə $ -ər/ *n* [C] a sore area on your skin or inside your body that may BLEED or produce poisonous substances: *stomach ulcers* —**ulcerous** *adj*

ul·cer·ate /ˈʌlsəreɪt/ *v* [I,T] to form an ulcer, or become covered with ulcers —**ulcerated** *adj* —**ulceration** /ˌʌlsəˈreɪʃən/ *n* [U]

ul·na /ˈʌlnə/ *n plural* **ulnae** /-niː/ [C] *medical* the inner bone of your lower arm, on the side opposite to your thumb

ul·te·ri·or /ʌlˈtɪəriə $ -ˈtɪriər/ *adj* **ulterior motive/purpose etc** a reason for doing something that you deliberately hide in order to get an advantage for yourself: *He's just being nice. I don't think he has any ulterior motives.*

ul·ti·mate¹ W3 /ˈʌltᵻmᵻt/ *adj* [only before noun] **1** someone's ultimate aim is their main and most important aim, that they hope to achieve in the future; ⊟ **final**: *ultimate goal/aim/objective etc Complete disarmament was the ultimate goal of the conference.* | *Our ultimate objective is to have as many female members of parliament as there are male.* **2** the ultimate result of a long process is what happens at the end of it: *The ultimate outcome of the experiment cannot be predicted.* | *The ultimate fate of the tribe was even sadder.* | *the ultimate failure of the project* **3** if you have ultimate responsibility for something, you are the person who must make the important final decisions about it: *The ultimate responsibility for policy lies with the President.* | *The ultimate decision rests with the Public Health Service.* **4** better, bigger, worse etc than all other things or people of the same kind: *'The Rolling Stones' is the ultimate rock and roll band.* | *The female nude is surely the ultimate test of artistic skill.*

ultimate² *n* **the ultimate in sth** the best or most modern example of something: *The plane was the ultimate in air technology in the 60s.* | *Guy's home is the ultimate in luxury.*

ˌultimate ˈfighting also **extreme fighting** *n* [U] a competition, similar to BOXING, in which two people hit or kick each other and in which there are almost no rules

ul·ti·mate·ly W3 /ˈʌltᵻmᵻtli/ *adv* finally, after everything else has been done or considered: [sentence adverb]: *Ultimately, the decision rests with the child's parents.* | *a long but ultimately successful campaign*

ul·ti·ma·tum /ˌʌltᵻˈmeɪtəm/ *n plural* **ultimatums** or **ultimata** /-tə/ [C] a threat saying that if someone does not do what you want by a particular time, you will do something to punish them: *Well, give him an ultimatum: either he pays by Friday or he finds somewhere else to live.* | *The army issued an ultimatum for all weapons in the city to be surrendered on Oct. 26.*

ultra- /ˈʌltrə/ *prefix* **1** extremely: *an ultra-modern building* | *He remained ultra-cautious.* | *an ultra-light jacket* **2** *technical* above and beyond something in a range: *ultrasound* (=sound that is too high for humans to hear) → INFRA-

ul·tra·ma·rine /ˌʌltrəməˈriːn◂/ *n* [U] a very bright blue colour —**ultramarine** *adj*

ul·tra·son·ic /ˌʌltrəˈsɒnɪk◂ $ -ˈsɑː-/ *adj* ultrasonic sound waves are too high for humans to hear

ul·tra·sound /ˈʌltrəsaʊnd/ *n* **1** [U] sound that is too high for humans to hear **2** [C,U] a medical process using this type of sound, that produces an image of something inside your body: *investigation of the liver by ultrasound* | *An ultrasound scan revealed that the baby was a boy.*

ul·tra·vi·o·let /ˌʌltrəˈvaɪələt◂/ *adj* ultraviolet light cannot be seen by people, but is responsible for making your skin darker when you are in the sun: **ultraviolet radiation/rays** *ultraviolet radiation from the sun*

u·lu·late /ˈjuːljᵿleɪt, ˈʌl- $ ˈʌl-, ˈjuː-/ *v* [I] *literary* to cry out with a long high sound, especially because you are very sad or in pain; ⊟ **wail** —**ululation** /ˌjuːljᵿˈleɪʃən, ˌʌl- $ ˌʌl-, ˌjuː-/ *n* [C,U]

U

um /ʌm, əm/ *interjection* used when you cannot immediately decide what to say next: *Um, yeah, I guess so.*

um·ber /'ʌmbə $ -ər/ *n* [U] a brown colour like earth

um·bil·i·cal cord /ʌm'bɪlɪkəl ˌkɔːd $ -ˌkɔːrd/ *n* [C] **1** a long narrow tube of flesh that joins an unborn baby to its mother **2** a strong feeling of belonging to or a strong feeling of relationship with a particular place, person, organization etc: *All modern popular music has an umbilical cord link back to blues and R and B.* | *Teenage boys especially feel a need to **cut the umbilical cord** tying them to their mothers.*

um·brage /'ʌmbrɪdʒ/ *n* **take umbrage (at sth)** to be offended by something that someone has done or said, often without good reason

um·brel·la /ʌm'brelə/ *n* [C] **1** an object that you use to protect yourself against rain or hot sun. It consists of a circular folding frame covered in cloth; → **parasol**: *It started to rain, so Tricia stopped to **put up her umbrella**.* | *I spent the day on the beach, lying under a **beach umbrella**, reading.* **2 umbrella organization/group/agency etc** an organization that includes many smaller groups **3 umbrella term/word/title etc** a word whose meaning includes many different types of a particular thing: *District nurses, health visitors, and school nurses will come under the umbrella term 'community nursing'.* **4 (come/work etc) under the umbrella of sth** to be part of a larger organization or involved in the work done by it: *The international education program came under the umbrella of the State Department.* **5** the protection given by a powerful country, army, a weapons system etc: *the American nuclear umbrella over western Europe*

um·laut /'ʊmlaʊt/ *n* [C] a sign (¨) written over a German vowel to show how it is pronounced

ump /ʌmp/ *n* [C] *AmE spoken* an umpire

umpire

referee

umpire

judges

um·pire¹ /'ʌmpaɪə $ -paɪr/ *n* [C] the person who makes sure that the players obey the rules in sports such as tennis, baseball, and CRICKET; → **referee**

umpire² *v* [I,T] to be the umpire in a game or competition

ump·teen /ˌʌmp'tiːn◂/ *quantifier* very many – used especially when you are annoyed there are so many: *There seemed to be umpteen rules and regulations to learn.* | *She'd called the apartment umpteen times, but never got an answer.*

ump·teenth /ˌʌmp'tiːnθ◂/ *adj* [only before noun] if something happens for the umpteenth time, it happens again after having happened many times before – used

when you are annoyed that it has happened so often: *'This is crazy,' she told herself **for the umpteenth time**.*

un /ən/ *pron BrE spoken* **good 'un/bad 'un/little 'un etc** a short form of 'one', used to say that someone or something is good, bad etc. Teachers and careful speakers of English do not use this expression: *He's a bad 'un.* | *I ought to collect the little 'uns (=young children) from school.*

un- /ʌn/ *prefix* **1** [in adjectives, adverbs, and nouns] used to show a negative, a lack, or an opposite; **◨ not**: *unfair* | *unhappy* | *unfortunately* | *uncertainty* **2** [in verbs] used to show an opposite of a particular action: *to undress* (=to take your clothes off) | *Have you unpacked yet* (=taken your things out of your suitcase)? | *I heard Lila unlock the front door.*

U.N., UN /ˌjuː 'en/ *n* **the UN** **the United Nations** an international organization that tries to find peaceful solutions to world problems

un·a·bashed /ˌʌnə'bæʃt◂/ *adj* written not ashamed or embarrassed, especially when doing something unusual or rude: *She stared at him with unabashed curiosity.*

un·a·bat·ed /ˌʌnə'beɪtɪd◂/ *adj, adv* continuing without becoming any weaker or less violent: *The storm **continued unabated** throughout the night.* | *his unabated ambition*

un·a·ble S3 W2 /ʌn'eɪbəl/ *adj* [not before noun] not able to do something; → **inability**: **unable to do sth** *Lucy was unable to find out what had happened.* | *Unable to sleep, I got up and made myself a drink.*

un·a·bridged /ˌʌnə'brɪdʒd◂/ *adj* a piece of writing, speech etc that is unabridged is in its full form and has not been made shorter: *the complete and unabridged works of Dickens*

un·ac·cept·a·ble /ˌʌnək'septəbəl◂/ *adj* something that is unacceptable is so wrong or bad that you think it should not be allowed: *I found her attitude totally unacceptable.* | *unacceptable levels of pollution* | [+to] *The recommendations from this report are unacceptable to many black people.* | **unacceptable to do sth** *It was socially unacceptable to discuss sex then.* —**unacceptably** *adv*: *Unemployment is unacceptably high.*

un·ac·com·pa·nied /ˌʌnə'kʌmpənid◂/ *adj* **1** someone or something that is unaccompanied has no one with them; → **accompany**: *Unaccompanied children are not allowed on the premises.* | **unaccompanied bag/luggage etc** *The airport X-rays all unaccompanied baggage.* **2 unaccompanied by sth** *formal* without something: *Many large Third World cities have arisen unaccompanied by national industrial growth.* **3** an unaccompanied singer or musician sings or plays alone; → **accompaniment, accompanist**: *Lizzie **sang unaccompanied**.* | *works for unaccompanied violin*

un·ac·count·a·ble /ˌʌnə'kaʊntəbəl◂/ *adj formal* **1** very surprising and difficult to explain: *the unaccountable shyness she always felt in Louise's presence* | *For some unaccountable reason, he arrived a day early.* **2** not having to explain your actions or decisions to anyone else; **◨ accountable**: [+to] *Doctors still remain largely unaccountable to the public.*

un·ac·count·a·bly /ˌʌnə'kaʊntəbli/ *adv* [sentence adverb] used to say that something is very surprising and difficult to explain: *Unaccountably, the woman had refused.* | *The planned military assault on the city yesterday was unaccountably delayed.*

un·ac·count·ed for /ʌnə'kaʊntɪd fɔː $ -fɔːr/ *adj* something or someone that is unaccounted for cannot be found, or their absence cannot be explained: *Two people are still unaccounted for after the floods.*

un·ac·cus·tomed /ˌʌnə'kʌstəmd◂/ *adj formal* **1 unaccustomed to (doing) sth** not used to something: *a country boy, unaccustomed to city ways* **2** [only before noun] not usual, typical, or familiar: *She was completely exhausted by the unaccustomed heat.*

un·ac·knowl·edged /ˌʌnəkˈnɒlɪdʒd◂ $ -ˈnɑː-/ *adj* **1** ignored or not noticed: *Unacknowledged anger can often cause problems in later life.* **2** not receiving the public thanks, praise, or reward that something deserves: *Women's work in the home tends to be both unpaid and unacknowledged.* **3 the unacknowledged leader/authority etc** someone who is a leader etc but who has not publicly or officially been given that position

un·a·dorned /ˌʌnəˈdɔːnd◂ $ -ˈdɔːrnd◂/ *adj written* without unnecessary or special features or decorations: *They liked their churches to be unadorned.*

un·a·dul·te·rat·ed /ˌʌnəˈdʌltəreɪtᵻd◂/ *adj* **1** [only before noun] complete or total: *a feeling of pure unadulterated pleasure* **2** not mixed with other less pure substances

un·af·fect·ed /ˌʌnəˈfektᵻd◂/ *adj* **1** not changed or influenced by something: [+by] *The north remained largely unaffected by the drought.* **2** natural in the way you behave – use this to show approval: *her easy unaffected manner* —**unaffectedly** *adv*

un·a·fraid /ˌʌnəˈfreɪd/ *adj* [not before noun] *written* **1** not frightened: *She was exhausted but unafraid.* | [+of] *The rats were huge and completely unafraid of human beings.* **2** confident that you can do something or deal with something: **unafraid of (doing) sth** *a gifted writer who is unafraid of trying new things* | **unafraid to do sth** *an independent woman unafraid to say what she believes*

un·aid·ed /ʌnˈeɪdᵻd/ *adj* without help: *She can no longer walk unaided.*

un·al·loyed /ˌʌnəˈlɔɪd◂/ *adj literary* complete, pure, or total: *unalloyed joy*

un·al·ter·a·ble /ʌnˈɔːltərəbəl $ -ˈɒːl-/ *adj formal* not possible to change: *an unalterable fact* —**unalterably** *adv*

un·am·big·u·ous /ˌʌnæmˈbɪɡjuəs◂/ *adj* a statement, instruction etc that is unambiguous is clear and easy to understand because it can only mean one thing —**unambiguously** *adv*

un-A·mer·i·can *adj* not loyal to generally accepted American customs and ways of thinking: *This kind of censorship is un-American.* | **un-American activities** (=political activity believed to be harmful to the US)

u·na·nim·i·ty /ˌjuːnəˈnɪmᵻti/ *n* [U] *formal* a state or situation of complete agreement among a group of people

u·nan·i·mous /juːˈnænᵻməs/ *adj* **1** a unanimous decision, vote, agreement etc is one in which all the people involved agree: *It was decided by a unanimous vote that the school should close.* | **almost/virtually unanimous** *The decision to appoint Matt was almost unanimous.* **2** agreeing completely about something: **unanimous in (doing) sth** *The banks were unanimous in welcoming the news.* —**unanimously** *adv*

un·an·nounced /ˌʌnəˈnaʊnst◂/ *adj, adv* happening without anyone expecting or knowing about it: *We arrived unannounced.*

un·an·swer·a·ble /ʌnˈɑːnsərəbəl $ ʌnˈæn-/ *adj* **1** an unanswerable question is one that cannot be answered **2** definitely true and therefore impossible to argue against: *The case* (=reasons for doing something) *for better public transport is unanswerable.*

un·an·swered /ʌnˈɑːnsəd $ -ˈænsərd/ *adj* **1** an unanswered question has not been answered: *Many other questions remain unanswered.* **2** an unanswered letter, telephone call, or request for help has not been replied to: *The children's cries for help went unanswered.*

un·an·tic·i·pat·ed /ˌʌnænˈtɪsᵻpeɪtᵻd/ *adj* an unanticipated event or result is one that you did not expect: *an unanticipated increase in inflation*

un·a·pol·o·get·ic /ˌʌnəpɒləˈdʒetɪk◂ $ -pɑː-/ *adj* not feeling or saying you are sorry for something you have done, especially when other people would expect you to

feel or say sorry: [+about] *He is entirely unapologetic about the violence in his movies.*

un·ap·peal·ing /ˌʌnəˈpiːlɪŋ◂/ *adj* not pleasant or attractive: *an unappealing shade of gray*

un·ap·pe·tiz·ing also **-ising** *BrE* /ʌnˈæpᵻtaɪzɪŋ/ *adj* food that is unappetizing has an unattractive appearance that makes you think that it will not taste good: *a rather unappetizing egg sandwich*

un·ap·proach·a·ble /ˌʌnəˈprəʊtʃəbəl◂ $ -ˈproʊ-/ *adj* seeming unfriendly and therefore difficult to talk to

un·ar·gu·a·ble /ʌnˈɑːɡjuəbəl $ -ˈɑːr-/ *adj* something that is unarguable is definitely true or correct: *unarguable proof* —**unarguably** *adv*

un·armed /ˌʌnˈɑːmd◂ $ -ˈɑːrmd◂/ *adj* not carrying any weapons: *the killing of unarmed civilians* | **unarmed combat** (=fighting without weapons)

un·a·shamed /ˌʌnəˈʃeɪmd◂/ *adj* not feeling embarrassed or ashamed about something that people might disapprove of: *his unashamed love of money* —**unashamedly** /-ˈmᵻdli/ *adv*

un·asked /ʌnˈɑːskt $ -ˈæskt/ *adj* **1** if a question remains unasked, no one asks it, often because they are embarrassed **2** *BrE* if you do something unasked, you do it without anyone asking or inviting you to: *George sat down unasked.* | [+for] *unasked for help*

un·as·sail·a·ble /ˌʌnəˈseɪləbəl◂/ *adj formal* not able to be criticized, made weaker, or beaten: *an unassailable argument* | *The party's* **position** *looked* **unassailable.** | *The result gave the team an* **unassailable lead.**

un·as·sum·ing /ˌʌnəˈsjuːmɪŋ◂, -ˈsuː- $ -ˈsuː-/ *adj* showing no desire to be noticed or given special treatment; ⎕ *modest*

un·at·tached /ˌʌnəˈtætʃt◂/ *adj* **1** not married or involved in a romantic relationship; ⎕ *single*: *According to Jo, Mark was still unattached.* **2** not connected or fastened to anything

un·at·tain·a·ble /ˌʌnəˈteɪnəbəl◂/ *adj* impossible to achieve: *A military victory is unattainable.* | **unattainable ideal/dream/goal etc**

un·at·tend·ed /ˌʌnəˈtendᵻd◂/ *adj* left alone without anyone in charge: *an unattended vehicle* | *Children should not be* **left unattended** *in the playground.*

un·at·trac·tive /ˌʌnəˈtræktɪv◂/ *adj* **1** not attractive, pretty, or pleasant to look at: *an unattractive man* **2** not good or desirable: *the unattractive aspects of nationalism* —**unattractively** *adv*

un·au·tho·rized also **-ised** *BrE* /ʌnˈɔːθəraɪzd $ -ˈɒː-/ *adj* without official approval or permission: *the unauthorized use of government funds* | *Unauthorized personnel are not allowed on the premises.*

un·a·vail·a·ble /ˌʌnəˈveɪləbəl◂/ *adj* [not before noun] **1** not able to be obtained: *Funding for the new school is unavailable.* | [+to] *materials that were unavailable to researchers in the past* **2** not able or willing to meet someone: [+for] *Officials were* **unavailable for comment** (=not able or willing to talk to reporters).

un·a·vail·ing /ˌʌnəˈveɪlɪŋ◂/ *adj literary* not successful or effective: *unavailing efforts to make her happy*

un·a·void·a·ble /ˌʌnəˈvɔɪdəbəl◂/ *adj* impossible to prevent: *There are now fears that war is unavoidable.* —**unavoidably** *adv*: *Molly was unavoidably delayed.*

un·a·ware /ˌʌnəˈweə $ -ˈwer/ *adj* [not before noun] not noticing or realizing what is happening: [+of] *Mike seems unaware of the trouble he's causing.* | **unaware (that)** *She was* **totally unaware** *that she was being watched.*

un·a·wares /ˌʌnəˈweəz $ -ˈwerz/ *adv* **1 take/catch sb unawares** if something takes you unawares, it happens when you are not expecting it and are not prepared: *The question caught me completely unawares.* **2** *formal* without noticing: *We had walked unawares over the border.*

un·bal·ance /ʌn'bæləns/ *v* [T] **1** to make a situation, relationship, or work of art not as good as it used to be or could be, especially by adding too much of one thing: *Having children can often unbalance even the closest of relationships.* **2** to make someone or something unsteady, so that they are likely to fall down: *He banged against the cupboard, unbalancing a pile a books.* **3** to make someone slightly crazy

un·bal·anced /ʌn'bælənst/ *adj* **1** someone who is unbalanced is slightly crazy **2** a report, argument etc that is unbalanced is unfair because it emphasizes one opinion too much **3** a relationship that is unbalanced is not equal because one person has more influence, power etc

un·bear·a·ble /ʌn'beərəbəl $ -'ber-/ *adj* too unpleasant, painful, or annoying to deal with; ▣ **intolerable**: *The **pain** was almost **unbearable**.* | *He was making life unbearable for his parents.* —**unbearably** *adv*: *an unbearably hot day*

un·beat·a·ble /ʌn'biːtəbəl/ *adj* **1** something that is unbeatable is the best of its kind: *carpets at unbeatable prices* **2** a team, player etc that is unbeatable cannot be defeated

un·beat·en /ˌʌn'biːtn◂/ *adj* a team, player etc that is unbeaten has not been defeated

un·be·com·ing /ˌʌnbɪ'kʌmɪŋ◂/ *adj* old-fashioned **1** clothes that are unbecoming make you look unattractive; ▣ **unflattering** **2** behaviour that is unbecoming is shocking or unsuitable: [+to] *conduct unbecoming to a teacher*

un·be·known /ˌʌnbɪ'nəʊn $ -'noʊn/ also **un·be·knownst** /-'nəʊnst $ -'noʊnst/ *written adv* [sentence adverb] **unbeknown to sb** without that person knowing about it: *Unbeknown to him, his wife had been trying to phone him all morning.*

un·be·lief /ˌʌnbᵻ'liːf/ *n* [U] *literary* a lack of religious belief, or a refusal to believe in a religious faith; → **disbelief**

un·be·liev·a·ble ⑤ /ˌʌnbᵻ'liːvəbəl◂/ *adj* **1** very good, successful, or impressive; ▣ **amazing**: *The opportunities are unbelievable.* | *an unbelievable talent*
2 very bad or shocking; ▣ **terrible**: *The pain was unbelievable.* | *acts of unbelievable cruelty* | *It was unbelievable that we were expected to pay twice.*
3 so extreme that it hardly seems possible: *He's so lazy it's unbelievable.* | *an unbelievable speed*
4 very difficult to believe and therefore probably untrue: *Yvonne's excuse for being late was totally unbelievable.* —**unbelievably** *adv*: *an unbelievably bad movie*

un·be·liev·er /ˌʌnbᵻ'liːvə $ -ər/ *n* [C] someone who does not believe in God or a particular religion

un·bend /ʌn'bend/ *v past tense and past participle* **unbent** /-'bent/ [I] to relax and start behaving in a less formal way

un·bend·ing /ʌn'bendɪŋ/ *adj* unwilling to change your opinions, decisions etc

un·bi·ased /ʌn'baɪəst/ *adj* unbiased information, opinions, advice etc is fair because the person giving it is not influenced by their own or other people's opinions; ▣ **impartial**: *We aim to provide a service that is balanced and unbiased.* | *an unbiased observer*

un·bid·den /ʌn'bɪdn/ *adj, adv literary* without being asked for, expected, or invited

un·blem·ished /ʌn'blemɪʃt/ *adj* **1** not spoiled by any mistake or bad behaviour: *a law firm with an unblemished reputation* **2** without marks or damage: *her smooth unblemished skin*

un·blink·ing /ʌn'blɪŋkɪŋ/ *adj literary* if you look at something or someone with unblinking eyes, you look

continuously at them without BLINKING (=quickly closing and opening your eyes): **unblinking stare/gaze** *His father's unblinking gaze was fixed on the fire.*

un·block /ʌn'blɒk $ -'blɑːk/ *v* [T] if you unblock a pipe, you remove something that is blocking it: **unblock a toilet/drain/chimney etc**

un·born /ˌʌn'bɔːn◂ $ -ɔːrn◂/ *adj* [only before noun] not yet born: *an unborn child*

un·bound·ed /ʌn'baʊndᵻd/ *adj formal* extreme or without any limit: *the child's unbounded energy*

un·bowed /ʌn'baʊd/ *adj* [not before noun] not willing to give up or accept defeat – used especially in news reports: *After the fight, Ali was **bloody but unbowed**.*

un·break·a·ble /ʌn'breɪkəbəl/ *adj* not able to be broken: *unbreakable glass*

un·bridge·a·ble /ʌn'brɪdʒəbəl/ *adj* unbridgeable differences between two people, groups, or ideas are so big that no one will ever agree about them or be satisfied with them: **unbridgeable gulf/gap/chasm etc (between sb/sth and sb/sth)** *the unbridgeable gulf between the rich and the poor*

un·bri·dled /ʌn'braɪdld/ *adj literary* not controlled and too extreme or violent: *unbridled greed*

un·bro·ken /ʌn'brəʊkən $ -'broʊ-/ *adj* continuing without being interrupted or broken: *their unbroken record of success* | *a time of unbroken peace*

un·buck·le /ʌn'bʌkəl/ *v* [T] to unfasten the BUCKLE on a belt, a shoe etc

un·bur·den /ˌʌn'bɜːdn $ -ɜːr-/ *v* [T] **unburden yourself (to sb)** to tell someone your problems, secrets etc so that you feel better

un·but·ton /ʌn'bʌtn/ *v* [T] to undo the buttons on a piece of clothing: *He took off his sweater and unbuttoned his shirt.* → see picture at UNDRESS

un·called for /ʌn'kɔːld fɔː $ -'kɒːld fɔːr/ *adj* behaviour or remarks that are uncalled for are not fair or suitable

un·can·ny /ʌn'kæni/ *adj* very strange and difficult to explain: *an uncanny coincidence* —**uncannily** *adv*

un·cared for /ʌn'keəd fɔː $ -'kerd fɔːr/ *adj* [not before noun] not looked after or not looked after properly: *The dogs looked hungry and uncared for.*

un·ceas·ing /ʌn'siːsɪŋ/ *adj* never stopping: *his unceasing efforts to help the poor* —**unceasingly** *adv*

un·cer·e·mo·ni·ous·ly /ˌʌnserə'məʊniəsli $ -'moʊ-/ *adv* in a rough or sudden way, without showing any respect or politeness: *He grabbed her arms and hauled her unceremoniously to her feet.* —**unceremonious** *adj*

un·cer·tain /ʌn'sɜːtn $ -ɜːr-/ *adj* **1** [not before noun] feeling doubt about something; ▣ **unsure**: **uncertain whether/how/what etc** *He was uncertain how much further he could walk.* | [+about/of] *I was uncertain about what to do next.* **2** not clear, definite, or decided; ▣ **unclear**: **It is uncertain whether/how/what etc** *It is uncertain how likely this is to occur.* | *My whole **future** now seemed **uncertain**.* **3** **in no uncertain terms** if you tell someone something in no uncertain terms, you tell them very clearly without trying to be polite: *I told Colin in no uncertain terms what I thought of him.* **4** if someone walks in an uncertain way, they seem as though they might fall: *She took a few **uncertain steps** forward.* —**uncertainly** *adv*

un·cer·tain·ty /ʌn'sɜːtnti $ -'sɜːr-/ *n plural* **uncertainties** **1** [U] when you feel doubt about what will happen: *Times of great change are also times of uncertainty.* | [+about/as to] *There is a great deal of **uncertainty** about the company's **future**.* **2** [C usually plural] a situation which you are not sure about because you do not know what will happen: *life's uncertainties* | [+of] *the uncertainties of old age*

un·chal·lenge·a·ble /ʌn'tʃælᵻndʒəbəl/ *adj* **1** a belief, idea etc that is unchallengeable is definitely true and cannot be questioned or argued with: *unchallengeable evidence* **2** if someone's power or authority is unchallengeable, it cannot be taken from them

un·chal·lenged /ʌnˈtʃælɪndʒd/ *adj* **1** accepted and believed by everyone and not doubted: *She couldn't let a statement like that go unchallenged.* **2** someone who goes somewhere unchallenged is not stopped and asked who they are or what they are doing

un·chang·ing /ʌnˈtʃeɪndʒɪŋ/ also **un·changed** /ʌnˈtʃeɪndʒd/ *adj* always staying the same

un·char·ac·ter·is·tic /ˌʌnˌkærɪktəˈrɪstɪk◂/ *adj* not typical of someone or something and therefore surprising: [+of] *It's uncharacteristic of her to be late.* —**uncharacteristically** /-kli/ *adv*: *He was uncharacteristically quiet.*

un·char·it·a·ble /ʌnˈtʃærɪtəbəl/ *adj* unkind or unfair in the way you judge people: *uncharitable remarks*

un·chart·ed /ʌnˈtʃɑːtɪd $ -ɑːr-/ *adj* **1 uncharted waters/territory/area etc** a situation or activity that you have never experienced or tried before: *This new project will take us into uncharted territory.* **2** not marked on any maps: *an uncharted island*

un·checked /ˌʌnˈtʃekt◂/ *adj* if something bad or harmful goes unchecked, it is not controlled or stopped and develops into something worse: **continue/grow/go unchecked** *We cannot allow such behaviour to continue unchecked.* | *This habit, if **left unchecked**, may cause serious problems later.*

un·civ·i·lized also **-ised** *BrE* /ʌnˈsɪvɪlaɪzd/ *adj* **1** behaviour that is uncivilized is rude or socially unacceptable **2** *old-fashioned* societies that are uncivilized have a very simple way of life, and have not developed social, legal, economic etc systems; ⊟ **primitive**

un·cle /ˈʌŋkəl/ *n* [C] **1** the brother of your mother or father, or the husband of your aunt; → **aunt**: *I went to stay with my uncle and aunt for a few days.* | *Uncle Philip* | *I was very excited about **becoming an uncle*** (=your sister or your brother's wife has a child). **2** used by children, in front of a first name, to address or refer to a man who is a close friend of their parents **3 say uncle** *AmE spoken* used by children to tell someone to admit they have been defeated

un·clean /ˌʌnˈkliːn◂/ *adj* **1** *biblical* morally or SPIRITUALLY bad: *an unclean spirit* **2** unclean food, animals etc are those that a particular religion says must not be eaten, touched etc **3** dirty: *unclean drinking water* —**uncleanness** *n* [U]

un·clear /ˌʌnˈklɪə◂ $ -klɪr◂/ *adj* **1** difficult to understand or be sure about, so that there is doubt or confusion: *The terms of the contract are very unclear.* **2 be unclear about sth** to not understand something clearly: *I'm rather unclear about what I'm supposed to be doing here.*

Uncle Sam /ˌʌŋkəl ˈsæm/ *n informal* the US, or the US government, sometimes represented by the figure of a man with a white BEARD and tall hat

Uncle Tom /ˌʌŋkəl ˈtɒm $ -ˈtɑːm/ *n* [C] *AmE* a black person who is too respectful to white people – used to show disapproval

un·clothed /ʌnˈkləʊðd $ -ˈkloʊðd/ *adj formal* not wearing clothes; ⊟ **naked**

un·coil /ʌnˈkɔɪl/ *v* [I,T] if you uncoil something, or if it uncoils, it stretches out straight after being wound around in a circle: *Slowly, the snake uncoiled.*

un·com·fort·a·ble /ʌnˈkʌmftəbəl, -ˈkʌmfət- $ -ˈkʌmfərt-, -ˈkʌmft-/ *adj* **1** not feeling physically comfortable, or not making you feel comfortable; ⊟ **awkward**: *This sofa is so uncomfortable.* **2** unable to relax because you are embarrassed: *She always felt slightly uncomfortable in a hat.* | *an uncomfortable silence* —**uncomfortably** *adv*

un·com·mit·ted /ˌʌnkəˈmɪtɪd◂/ *adj* not having decided or promised to support a particular group, political belief etc: *uncommitted voters* | *So far, they are uncommitted to his plan.*

un·com·mon /ʌnˈkɒmən $ -ˈkɑː-/ *adj* rare or unusual: *Violent crimes against the elderly are fortunately very uncommon.* | **it is not uncommon for sb to do sth** *It is not uncommon for students to have bank loans.*

un·com·mon·ly /ʌnˈkɒmənli $ -ˈkɑː-/ *adv* [+ adj/adv] *old-fashioned* very: *an uncommonly cold morning*

un·com·plain·ing /ˌʌnkəmˈpleɪnɪŋ◂/ *adj* willing to accept a difficult or unpleasant situation without complaining —**uncomplainingly** *adv*

un·com·pre·hend·ing /ˌʌnkɒmprɪˈhendɪŋ $ -kɑːm-/ *adj* not understanding what is happening —**uncomprehendingly** *adv*

un·com·pro·mis·ing /ʌnˈkɒmprəmaɪzɪŋ $ -ˈkɑːm-/ *adj* unwilling to change your opinions or intentions: *an uncompromising opponent of democratic reform* —**uncompromisingly** *adv*

un·cern /ˌʌnkənˈsɜːn $ -ˈsɜːrn/ *n* [U] when you do not care about something that other people worry about: [+about/for/over] *the government's apparent unconcern about high inflation*

un·con·cerned /ˌʌnkənˈsɜːnd $ -ˈsɜːrnd/ *adj* **1** not worried about something because you think it does not affect you: [+about] *Many large companies seem totally unconcerned about the environment.* **2** not interested in a particular aim or activity: [+with] *unconcerned with making a profit* —**unconcernedly** /-nɪdli/ *adv*

un·con·di·tion·al /ˌʌnkənˈdɪʃənəl◂/ *adj* not limited by or depending on any conditions: *the unconditional release of all political prisoners* | *unconditional surrender* —**unconditionally** *adv*

un·con·firmed /ˌʌnkənˈfɜːmd $ -ˈfɜːrmd◂/ *adj* **unconfirmed report/story/rumour etc** a report etc that has not been proved or supported by official information: *We've received unconfirmed reports of an explosion in central London.*

un·con·nect·ed /ˌʌnkəˈnektɪd◂/ *adj* if two events, facts, or situations are unconnected, they are not related to each other in any way: *The murders are probably unconnected.* | [+with/to] *Wolf's work is completely unconnected to the current study.*

un·con·scion·a·ble /ʌnˈkɒnʃənəbəl $ -ˈkɑːn-/ *adj formal* much more than is reasonable or acceptable: *The war caused an unconscionable amount of suffering.* —**unconscionably** *adv*

un·con·scious[1] /ʌnˈkɒnʃəs $ -ˈkɑːn-/ *adj* **1** unable to see, move, feel etc in the normal way because you are not conscious: *She was found alive but unconscious.* | **knock/beat sb unconscious** *Levin was knocked unconscious by the impact.* **2** a feeling or thought that is unconscious is one that you have without realizing it; → **subconscious**: *unconscious feeling/desire/need etc an unconscious need to be loved* **3 be unconscious of sth** to not realize the effect of something you have said or done: *Doreen appeared to be unconscious of the amusement she had caused.* **4** an action that is unconscious is not deliberate —**unconsciously** *adv* —**unconsciousness** *n* [U]

unconscious[2] *n* **the/sb's unconscious** the part of your mind in which there are thoughts and feelings that you do not realize you have; → **subconscious**

un·con·sid·ered /ˌʌnkənˈsɪdəd $ -ərd◂/ *adj written* unconsidered remarks or actions are made without care or thinking about the possible results

un·con·sti·tu·tion·al /ˌʌnkɒnstɪˈtjuːʃənəl $ -kɑːnstɪˈtuː-/ *adj* not allowed by the CONSTITUTION (=set of rules or principles by which a country or organization is governed): *claims that the President's action was unconstitutional* —**unconstitutionally** *adv*

un·con·test·ed /ˌʌnkənˈtestɪd◂/ *adj* **1** an uncontested action or statement is one that no one opposes or disagrees with: *After an uncontested divorce, Peggy married Charlie.* **2** an uncontested election is one in which only one person wants to be elected

U

un·con·trol·la·ble /ˌʌnkən'trəʊləbəl◂ $ -'troʊl-/ adj **1** if an emotion, desire, or physical action is uncontrollable, you cannot control it or stop yourself from feeling it or doing it: *I felt an uncontrollable urge to scream.* | *Mother burst into uncontrollable sobs.* **2** someone who is uncontrollable behaves badly and will not obey anyone: *The presence of some uncontrollable children spoilt the evening.* **3** if a situation is uncontrollable, nothing can be done to control it or stop it getting worse: *uncontrollable bleeding* | *uncontrollable inflation*

un·con·trolled /ˌʌnkən'trəʊld◂ $ -'troʊld◂/ adj uncontrolled emotions or behaviour continue because you are not trying to stop them: *uncontrolled weeping*

un·con·ven·tion·al /ˌʌnkən'venʃənəl◂/ adj very different from the way people usually behave, think, dress etc: *unconventional political views*

un·con·vinc·ing /ˌʌnkən'vɪnsɪŋ◂/ adj failing to make you believe that something is true or real: *an unconvincing smile* | *an unconvincing explanation* | *Some readers will find the arguments unconvincing.* —**unconvincingly** adv

un·cooked /ˌʌn'kʊkt◂/ adj food that is uncooked has not been cooked; ◘ **raw**: *Always wash your hands after handling uncooked meat.*

un·cool /ˌʌn'kuːl◂/ adj informal not fashionable or acceptable – used especially by young people: *Have you seen his shorts? They are just so uncool!* | *It was uncool to get on well with teachers.*

un·co·op·er·a·tive /ˌʌnkəʊ'ɒpərətɪv◂ $ -koʊ'ɑːp-/ adj not willing to work with or help someone

un·co·or·di·nat·ed /ˌʌnkəʊ'ɔːdɪneɪtɪd◂ $ -koʊ'ɔːr-/ adj **1** someone who is uncoordinated is not good at physical activities because they cannot control their movements effectively **2** a plan or operation that is uncoordinated is not well organized, with the result that the different parts of it do not work together effectively

un·cork /ʌn'kɔːk $ -'kɔːrk/ v [T] to open a bottle by removing its CORK

un·cor·rob·o·rat·ed /ˌʌnkə'rɒbəreɪtɪd◂ $ -'rɑː-/ adj an uncorroborated claim or statement is one which is not supported by any proof: *He was convicted on the **uncorroborated evidence** of the alleged victim.*

un·count·a·ble /ʌn'kaʊntəbəl/ adj an uncountable noun has no plural form and refers to something which cannot be counted or regarded as either singular or plural, for example 'money' or 'happiness'. In this dictionary uncountable nouns are marked [U]; → **countable**

un·coup·le /ʌn'kʌpəl/ v [T] to separate one piece of machinery, one part of a train etc from another that it is connected to: *Evidence suggests that the private car was deliberately uncoupled.*

un·couth /ʌn'kuːθ/ adj behaving and speaking in a way that is rude or socially unacceptable —**uncouthly** adv —**uncouthness** n [U]

un·cov·er /ʌn'kʌvə $ -ər/ v [T] **1** to find out about something that has been kept secret; → **discover**: *Customs officials uncovered a plot to smuggle weapons into the country.* **2** to remove the cover from something

un·crit·i·cal /ʌn'krɪtɪkəl/ adj unable or unwilling to see faults in something or someone – used to show disapproval: [+of] *John's mother is totally uncritical of his behaviour.* —**uncritically** /-kli/ adv

un·crowned /ˌʌn'kraʊnd◂/ adj **the uncrowned king/ queen of sth** the person who is thought to be the best or most famous in a particular activity: *the uncrowned king of jazz*

un·crush·a·ble /ʌn'krʌʃəbəl/ adj very determined and not easily persuaded to do not something: *her uncrushable will to survive*

unc·tu·ous /'ʌŋktʃuəs/ adj formal too friendly and praising people too much in a way that seems very insincere —**unctuously** adv —**unctuousness** n [U]

un·curl /ʌn'kɜːl $ -'kɜːrl/ v [I,T] to stretch out straight from a curled position, or to make something do this

un·cut /ˌʌn'kʌt◂/ adj **1** a film, book etc that is uncut has not been made shorter, for example by having violent or sexual scenes removed: *the uncut version of 'Lady Chatterley's Lover'* **2** an uncut jewel that is still in its natural form has not been cut into a particular shape: *uncut diamonds*

un·dat·ed /ʌn'deɪtɪd/ adj a letter, article, painting etc that is undated does not have a date written on it

un·daunt·ed /ʌn'dɔːntɪd $ -'dɒːn-/ adj not afraid of continuing to try to do something in spite of difficulties or danger: [+by] *Undaunted by the enormity of the task, they began rebuilding the village.*

un·de·cid·ed /ˌʌndɪ'saɪdɪd◂/ adj **1** [not before noun] not having made a decision about something important; ◘ **unsure**, **uncertain**: [+about] *I'm **still undecided** about how I'll vote.* | **undecided what/which/whether** etc *Nadine was undecided whether or not to go to college.* **2** a game or competition that is undecided has no definite winner —**undecidedly** adv

un·de·clared /ˌʌndɪ'kleəd◂ $ -'klerd◂/ adj not officially announced or called something: *a scandal involving undeclared payments to politicians* | *an undeclared civil war*

un·de·mon·stra·tive /ˌʌndɪ'mɒnstrətɪv $ -'mɑːn-/ adj not showing your feelings of love or friendliness

un·de·ni·a·ble /ˌʌndɪ'naɪəbəl◂/ adj definitely true or certain: *undeniable proof* —**undeniably** adv

un·der S1 W1 /'ʌndə $ -ər/ prep, adv
1 BELOW below or at a lower level than something, or covered by something; ◘ **over**: *Wendy had hidden the box under her bed.* | *We sailed under the Golden Gate Bridge.* | *Write your name under your picture.* | *I could see something glittering under the water.* | *He was wearing a jacket under his coat.* | *Under her arm, she carried a large portfolio.* | *In summer, we often slept under the stars.* | *I'd scare my mom by diving in and staying under* (=staying under the water) *for as long as I could.* | *The bench collapsed **under the weight of*** (=unable to support the weight of) *so many people.*
2 LESS THAN less than a particular number, amount, age, or price; ◘ **over**: *These toys are not suitable for children under five.* | *Most of the events listed cost under £60.* | *I spend **just under** four hours a day seeing customers.* | **and/or under** *Children aged twelve or under must be accompanied by an adult.* | **be under age** (=be too young to legally drink, have sex etc)
3 HAVING STH DONE TO IT used to say what is being done to something or how it is being dealt with: **under discussion/consideration/review etc** *The possibility of employing more staff is still under discussion* (=being discussed, considered etc). | *All categories of expenditure are under review.* | *Four new power stations are currently under construction.* | *The port was coming under attack from enemy warships.*
4 AFFECTED BY STH affected by a particular condition, influence, or situation: *She's been **under** a lot of **pressure** at work.* | **under the influence of alcohol/drink/drugs etc** *He was accused of driving while under the influence of alcohol.* | *The operation was carried out while she was under general anaesthetic.* | *I'm glad to see that you have everything **under control**.* | *Two of our national parks are currently **under threat** from road schemes.* | *The doctor injected something into my arm and I immediately felt myself **going under*** (=becoming unconscious).
5 under ... conditions/circumstances if something happens under particular conditions, it happens when those conditions exist: *I wish I'd met him under different circumstances.* | *The system operates well under normal conditions.*

6 LAW/AGREEMENT according to a particular agreement, law etc: *the question of whether the trade is illegal under international law* | *Under the terms of the agreement, the debt will be repaid over a 20-year period.*

7 IN POWER if something happens under a particular leader, government etc, it happens when they are in power: *a program initiated under President Clinton and continued under President Bush* | *Under her leadership, the magazine's circulation doubled in less than a year.* | *Would it have been different under a Labour government?*

8 POSITION AT WORK if you work under someone, they have a higher position in the company, organization etc than you, and they help to direct your work: *She had a total staff of 10 working under her.* | *From 1847 to 1851 he served under Captain John Randolph Stokes.* | *At Cambridge he studied under* (=was a student of) *F.R. Leavis.*

9 WHERE INFORMATION IS used to say in which part of a book, list, or system particular information can be found: **be/be filed/be listed etc under** *The baby's records are filed under the mother's last name.*

10 DIFFERENT NAME if you write or do something under a particular name, you do it using that name instead of your real name: *He made a few records* **under the name of** *Joe Ritchie.*

WORD CHOICE: under, underneath, below, beneath
Under is the usual way to say that one thing is at a lower level than another, or is covered by it: *Your shoes are under the table.* | *He lay under a blanket.*
Under is nearly always used as a preposition (followed by a noun).
Underneath has a similar meaning to **under**, and is used especially when something is hidden or covered: *a box underneath the floorboards*
It can also be used as an adverb: *She lifted the cover and peeped underneath.*
Below is used when one thing is at a much lower level than another, and can be a preposition or an adverb: *the apartment below ours* | *Mist lay in the valley below.*
Beneath can be used in the same ways as **under** and **below**, but is a more literary or formal word: *beneath the silvery moon* | *the cliff, and the ocean beneath*

under- /ʌndə $ -dər/ *prefix* **1** less of an action or quality than is correct, needed, or desired: *underdevelopment* | *undercooked cabbage* **2** going under something: *an underpass* (=a road or path that goes under another road) **3** inside or beneath other things: *undergarments* **4** less important or lower in rank: *a head gardener and three under-gardeners*

un·der·a·chiev·er /ˌʌndərə'tʃiːvə $ -ər/ *n* [C] someone who does not do as well at school or at work as they could do if they worked harder —**underachieve** *v* [I] —**underachievement** *n* [U]

un·der·age /ˌʌndər'eɪdʒ◂/ *adj* too young to legally buy alcohol, drive a car, vote etc: *underage drinking*

un·der·arm¹ /'ʌndəraːm $ -aːrm/ *adv BrE* if you throw a ball underarm, you throw it without moving your arm above your shoulder; ▣ **underhand** *AmE*

underarm² *adj* **1** [only before noun] relating to or used on your ARMPITS: *underarm hair* | *underarm deodorants* **2** an underarm throw is one where you throw a ball without moving your arm above your shoulder: *underarm bowling*

underarm³ *n* [C] the hollow area under your arm, where it joins your body; ▣ **armpit**

un·der·bel·ly /'ʌndəˌbeli $ -ər-/ *n* [singular] *literary* **1** the unpleasant parts of a place or society that are normally hidden: [+of] *photographs that capture the underbelly of the United States – its poverty, its injustice, and its alienated underclass* **2** the weakest part of an organization or a person's character, that is most easily attacked or criticized: [+of] *They needed to find the* **soft underbelly** *of their opponents.* **3** the lower part of an animal's body, including the stomach

un·der·brush /'ʌndəbrʌʃ $ -ər-/ *n* [U] *especially AmE* bushes, small trees etc growing under and around larger trees in a forest; ▣ **undergrowth**

un·der·cap·i·tal·ized also **-ised** *BrE* /ˌʌndə'kæpɪ̯tl-aɪzd $ -dər-/ *adj* if a business is undercapitalized, it has not been given enough money to operate effectively

un·der·car·riage /'ʌndəˌkærɪdʒ $ -ər-/ *n* [C] the wheels of an aircraft, train etc and the structure that holds them

und·er·charge /ˌʌndə'tʃɑːdʒ $ ˌʌndər'tʃɑːrdʒ/ *v* [I,T] to charge too little or less than the correct amount of money for something; ▣ **overcharge**: *The city is grossly undercharging* (=charging far too little) *companies to use the land.* | **undercharge sb by £1/$2 etc** *They undercharged me by about $2.*

un·der·class /'ʌndəklɑːs $ -dərklæs/ *n* [singular] the lowest social class, consisting of people who are very poor and who are not likely to be able to improve their situation: *an urban underclass, who have limited access to health care* → SOCIAL EXCLUSION

un·der·class·man /ˌʌndə'klɑːsmən $ -dər'klæs-/ *n plural* **underclassmen** /-mən/ [C] *AmE* a student in the first two years of school or college

un·der·clothes /'ʌndəkləʊðz -kləʊz $ -dərkloʊðz, -kloʊz/ also **'under-ˌclothing** *n* [plural] clothes that you wear next to your body under your other clothes; ▣ **underwear**

un·der·coat /'ʌndəkəʊt $ -dərkoʊt/ *n* [C] a layer of paint that you put onto a surface before you put the final layer on

un·der·cov·er /ˌʌndə'kʌvə◂ $ -dər'kʌvər◂/ *adj* [only before noun] undercover work is done secretly by the police in order to catch criminals or find out information: *an* **undercover investigation** | **undercover policeman/cop/agent** etc *undercover detectives* —**undercover** *adv: a cop who* **goes undercover** *to catch drug dealers* | *He* **worked undercover** *in Germany and Northern Ireland.*

un·der·cur·rent /'ʌndəˌkʌrənt $ -dər,kɜːr-/ *n* [C] **1** a feeling, especially of anger or dissatisfaction, that people do not express openly: [+of] *He sensed an undercurrent of resentment among the crowd.* **2** a hidden and often dangerous current of water that flows under the surface of the sea or a river

un·der·cut /ˌʌndə'kʌt $ -ər-/ *v past tense and past participle* **undercut,** *present participle* **undercutting** [T] **1** to sell goods or a service at a lower price than another company; ▣ **undersell**: *Online bookstores can undercut retailers by up to 30%.* **2** to make something weaker or less effective; ▣ **undermine**: *Is a lack of self-confidence undercutting your performance at work?*

un·der·de·vel·oped /ˌʌndədɪ'veləpt◂ $ -dər-/ *adj* **1 underdeveloped country/region etc** a country, area etc that is poor and where there is not much modern industry; → **developing country 2** not having grown or developed as much as is usual or necessary: *a baby born with underdeveloped kidneys* —**underdevelopment** *n* [U]

un·der·dog /'ʌndədɒg $ 'ʌndərdɒːg/ *n* [C] a person, team etc that is weaker than the others, is always expected to be unsuccessful, and that is often treated badly: *Crowds often feel sympathy for* **the underdog**.

un·der·done /ˌʌndə'dʌn◂ $ -ər-/ *adj* not completely cooked; ▣ **overdone**

un·der·dressed /ˌʌndə'drest◂ $ -ər-/ *adj* wearing clothes that are too informal for a particular occasion; ▣ **overdressed**

un·der·em·ployed /ˌʌndərɪm'plɔɪd◂/ *adj* working in a job where you cannot use all your skills or where there is not enough work for you to do; → **unemployed**

un·der·es·ti·mate¹ /ˌʌndər'estɪ̯meɪt/ *v* **1** [I,T] to think or guess that something is smaller, cheaper,

▣ 000, ▣ 000, ▣ 000, most frequent words in ⓢpoken and Ⓦritten English easier etc than it really is; ⊟ **overestimate: underestimate how/what** *We underestimated how long it would take to get there.* | **underestimate the importance/extent/effect/power etc of sth** *Never underestimate the power of the press.* **2** [T] to think that someone is not as good, clever, or skilful, as they really are

un·der·es·ti·mate² /ˌʌndərˈestɪmət/ *n* [C] a guessed amount or number that is too low; ⊟ **overestimate:** *14% may be an underestimate.*

un·der·ex·pose /ˌʌndərɪkˈspəʊz $ -ˈspoʊz/ *v* [T] to not let enough light reach the film when you are taking a photograph; ⊟ **overexpose** —**underexposed** *adj*

un·der·fed /ˌʌndəˈfed $ -ər-/ *adj* not given enough food to eat; ⊟ **overfed**

un·der·felt /ˈʌndəfelt $ -ər-/ *n* [U] *BrE* soft material that you put between a CARPET and the floor

un·der·floor heat·ing /ˌʌndəflɔː ˈhiːtɪŋ $ ˌʌndərflɔːr-/ *n* [U] a heating system that is designed to go under the floor in a building

un·der·foot /ˌʌndəˈfʊt $ -ər-/ *adv* **1** under your feet where you are walking: **wet/firm/soft etc underfoot** *The wet wood is very slippery underfoot.* **2** trample sb/sth underfoot a) to crush someone or something on the ground by stepping heavily on them b) to completely destroy someone or something

un·der·fund·ed /ˌʌndəˈfʌndɪd $ -dər-/ *adj* a project, organization etc that is underfunded has not been given enough money to be effective: **seriously/chronically/badly etc underfunded** *Our education system is seriously underfunded.* —**underfunding** *n* [U]: *underfunding in the National Health Service*

un·der·gar·ment /ˈʌndəˌgɑːmənt $ ˈʌndərˌgɑːr-/ *n* [C] *old-fashioned* a piece of underwear

un·der·go /ˌʌndəˈɡəʊ $ ˌʌndərˈɡoʊ/ *v past tense* **underwent** /-ˈwent/ *past participle* **undergone** /-ˈɡɒn $ -ˈɡɒːn/ [T not in passive] if you undergo a change, an unpleasant experience etc, it happens to you or is done to you

> undergo a change/transformation
> undergo treatment/surgery/an operation
> undergo tests/trials
> undergo training
>
> The country has **undergone** massive **changes** recently. | He has been released from prison to **undergo** medical **treatment** in the United States. | She has been **undergoing tests** since Monday. | Teachers should be expected to **undergo** mid-career **training** and development.

un·der·grad·u·ate /ˌʌndəˈɡrædʒuət $ -ər-/ *n* [C] a student at college or university, who is working for their first degree; → **graduate, postgraduate**: *second-year undergraduates* | **undergraduate student/course/degree etc**

un·der·ground¹ /ˈʌndəɡraʊnd $ -ər-/ *adj* **1** below the surface of the earth: *an underground passage* | *The car park is underground.* **2** [only before noun] an underground group, organization etc is secret and illegal: *an underground terrorist organization* **3** [only before noun] underground literature, newspapers etc are read by a small number of people, and would seem slightly strange or shocking to most people: *the underground press*

un·der·ground² /ˌʌndəˈɡraʊnd $ -ər-/ *adv* **1** under the earth's surface: *This animal spends most of its life underground.* | *nuclear waste buried deep underground* **2** go underground to start doing something secretly, or hide in a secret place: *The ANC was forced to go underground when its leaders were arrested.*

un·der·ground³ /ˈʌndəɡraʊnd $ -ər-/ *n* **the Underground a)** *BrE* a railway system under the ground; ⊟ **subway** *AmE*; → see picture at TOWN **b)** an illegal group working in secret against the rulers of a country

un·der·growth /ˈʌndəɡrəʊθ $ -dərɡroʊθ-/ *n* [U] bushes, small trees, and other plants growing around and under bigger trees

un·der·hand¹ /ˌʌndəˈhænd◂ $ ˈʌndərhænd/ *also* **un·der·hand·ed** /ˌʌndəˈhændɪd $ ˌʌndər-/ *adj* dishonest and done secretly: *They did it all in such an underhand way.* | *He's been involved in some underhand dealings.* → OVERHAND

underhand² *adv AmE* if you throw a ball underhand, you throw it without moving your arm above your shoulder; ⊟ **underarm** *BrE*

un·der·lay /ˈʌndəleɪ $ -ər-/ *n* [C,U] thick material that is put beneath a CARPET and the floor

un·der·lie /ˌʌndəˈlaɪ $ -ər-/ *v past tense* **underlay** /-ˈleɪ/ *past participle* **underlain** /-ˈleɪn/ *present participle* **underlying**, *third person singular* **underlies** [T] *formal* to be the cause of something, or be the basic thing from which something develops: *the one basic principle that underlies all of the party's policies* → UNDERLYING

un·der·line /ˌʌndəˈlaɪn $ -ər-/ *v* [T] **1** to draw a line under a word to show that it is important **2** to show that something is important: *This tragic incident underlines the need for immediate action.*

un·der·ling /ˈʌndəlɪŋ $ -ər-/ *n* [C] an insulting word for someone who has a low rank – often used humorously

un·der·ly·ing [W3] /ˌʌndəˈlaɪ-ɪŋ◂ $ -ər-/ *adj* **underlying cause/principle/problem etc** the cause, idea etc that is the most important, although it is not easily noticed: *the underlying causes of her depression* | *There is an underlying assumption that younger workers are easier to train.*

un·der·manned /ˌʌndəˈmænd◂ $ -ər-/ *adj* a ship, office etc that is undermanned does not have enough workers to operate effectively; ⊟ **understaffed**

un·der·mine /ˌʌndəˈmaɪn $ -ər-/ *v* [T] to gradually make someone or something less strong or effective: *economic policies that threaten to undermine the health care system* | **undermine sb's confidence/authority/position/credibility etc** *The constant criticism was beginning to undermine her confidence.*

un·der·neath¹ [S2] /ˌʌndəˈniːθ $ -ər-/ *prep, adv* **1** directly under another object or covered by it: *He got out of the car and looked underneath.* | *It's near where the railway goes underneath the road.* | *She was wearing a smart jacket with a T-shirt underneath.* | *Her blonde hair was hidden underneath a baseball cap.* → see box at UNDER **2** on the lower surface of something: *The car was rusty underneath.* | *A number had been painted underneath the table.* **3** used to say what someone's character is really like when their behaviour shows a different character: *She seems confident, but she's really quite shy underneath.* | *I think he's a genuinely nice guy underneath it all.*

underneath² *n BrE* **the underneath** the bottom surface of something, or the part of something that is below or under something else; ⊟ **the underside:** *We need to paint the underneath with a rust preventer.*

un·der·nour·ished /ˌʌndəˈnʌrɪʃt◂ $ ˌʌndərˈnɜː-, -ˈnʌ-/ *adj* unhealthy and weak because you have not had enough food or the right type of food; ⊟ **malnourished** —**undernourishment** *n* [U]

un·der·paid /ˌʌndəˈpeɪd◂ $ -ər-/ *adj* earning less money than you deserve for your work: *Teachers are overworked and underpaid.*

un·der·pants /ˈʌndəpænts $ -ər-/ *n* [plural] **1** *BrE* a short piece of underwear worn by men under their trousers → see picture at UNDERWEAR **2** *AmE* a short piece of underwear worn under trousers by men or women

un·der·pass /ˈʌndəpɑːs $ ˈʌndərpæs/ *n* [C] *BrE* a road or path that goes under another road or a railway

un·der·pay /ˌʌndə'peɪ $ -ər-/ v past tense and past participle **underpaid** [T] to pay someone too little for their work

un·der·per·form /ˌʌndəpə'fɔːm $ ˌʌndərpər'fɔːrm/ v [I] if a business underperforms, it does not make as much profit as it expected to make

un·der·pin /ˌʌndə'pɪn $ -ər-/ v **underpinned, underpinning** [T] **1** to give strength or support to something and to help it succeed: *the theories that underpin his teaching method* | *America's wealth is underpinned by a global system which exploits the world's poor.* **2** technical to put a solid piece of metal under a wall or house in order to make it stronger —**underpinning** n [C,U]

un·der·play /ˌʌndə'pleɪ $ -ər-/ v [T] to make something seem less important or less serious than it really is; ▣ **play down**: *She underplays her achievements.*

un·der·priv·i·leged /ˌʌndə'prɪvɪlɪdʒd◂ $ -dər-/ adj very poor, with worse living conditions, educational opportunities etc than most people in society: *underprivileged children*

un·der·ra·ted /ˌʌndə'reɪtɪd◂/ adj better than people think or say: *a much underrated novel* → OVERRATED

un·der·re·sourced /ˌʌndərɪ'zɔːst, -'sɔːst $ -ɔːr-/ adj not provided with enough money, equipment etc

un·der·score /ˌʌndə'skɔː $ -dər'skɔːr/ v [T] especially AmE **1** to emphasize the fact that something is important or true; ▣ **underline 2** to draw a line under a word or phrase to show that it is important; ▣ **underline**

un·der·sea /'ʌndəsiː $ -ər-/ adj [only before noun] happening or existing below the surface of the sea: *undersea exploration*

un·der·sec·re·ta·ry /ˌʌndə'sekrətəri $ 'ʌndər-ˌsekrəteri/ n plural **undersecretaries** [C] **1** a very important official in a US government department who is one position in rank below the SECRETARY **2** a minister in a British government department, who is one position in rank below the minister who is in charge of that department **3** a government official who is in charge of the daily work of a British government department

un·der·sell /ˌʌndə'sel $ -ər-/ v past tense and past participle **undersold** /-'səʊld $ -'soʊld/ [T] **1** to sell goods at a lower price than someone else **2** to make other people think that someone or something is less good, effective, skilful etc than they really are: *I think he undersold himself at the interview.*

ˌunder-'served adj not getting enough care and help from the government: *The area is underserved for medical care.*

un·der·sexed /ˌʌndə'sekst◂ $ -ər-/ adj having less desire to have sex than is normal

un·der·shirt /'ʌndəʃɜːt $ 'ʌndərʃɜːrt/ n [C] AmE a piece of underwear with or without arms, worn under a shirt

un·der·shorts /'ʌndəʃɔːts $ 'ʌndərʃɔːrts/ n [plural] UNDERPANTS for men or boys

un·der·side /'ʌndəsaɪd $ -ər-/ n [singular] **the underside (of sth)** the bottom side or surface of something: *The leaves are green on top and silvery on the underside.*

un·der·signed /'ʌndəsaɪnd $ -ər-/ adj formal **the undersigned** the person or people who have signed a document

un·der·sized /ˌʌndə'saɪzd◂ $ -ər-/ also **un·der·size** /-'saɪz◂/ adj too small

un·der·staffed /ˌʌndə'stɑːft◂ $ ˌʌndər'stæft◂/ adj not having enough workers, or fewer workers than usual

un·der·stand S1 W1 /ˌʌndə'stænd $ -ər-/ v past tense and past participle **understood** /-'stʊd/ [not in progressive] **1** MEANING [I,T] to know the meaning of what someone is telling you, or the language that they speak; → **misunderstood**: *She doesn't understand English.* | *I'm sorry, I don't understand. Can you explain that again?* |

The woman had a strong accent, and I couldn't understand what she was saying. | **make yourself understood** (=make what you say clear to other people, especially when speaking a foreign language) *I'm not very good at German, but I can make myself understood.*
2 FACT/IDEA [I,T] to know or realize how a fact, process, situation etc works, especially through learning or experience: *I don't really understand the political situation in Northern Ireland.* | **understand how/why/where etc** *You don't need to understand how computers work to be able to use them.* | *How the drug works isn't fully understood.* | **understand (that)** *I understand that this treatment may not work.*
3 PERSON/FEELINGS [I,T] to realize how someone feels and why they behave the way they do, and to be sympathetic: *My parents just don't understand me.* | *Just tell him how you feel – I'm sure he'll understand.* | **understand how/what etc** *I understand how you feel, but I think you're overreacting.* | **(can) understand sb doing sth** *I can understand her wanting to live alone and be independent.*
4 BELIEVE/THINK [T] to believe or think that something is true because you have heard it or read it: **understand (that)** *'I understand that he was 62 when he died,' McLeish said.* | **it is understood (that)** *It is understood that the Queen approves of her nephew's romance.* | **be understood to be (doing) sth** *Dillons is understood to be reorganising the company's management structure.*
5 **give sb to understand (that)** formal to make someone believe that something is true, going to happen etc, without telling them this directly: *I was given to understand that the property was in good condition.*
6 **be understood (that)** formal if something is understood, everyone knows it, or has agreed to it, and there is no need to discuss it: *From childhood it was understood that your parents would choose your husband.*
7 **understand sth to be/mean sth** to accept something as having a particular meaning: *In this document, 'children' is understood to mean people under 14.*
8 **do you understand?** spoken used when you are telling someone what they should or should not do, especially when you are angry with them: *Never speak to me like that again! Do you understand?*

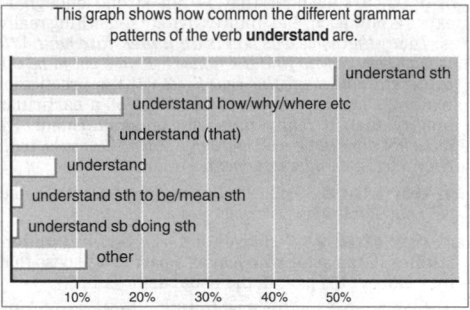

This graph shows how common the different grammar patterns of the verb **understand** are.

un·der·stand·a·ble /ˌʌndə'stændəbəl $ -dər-/ adj **1** understandable behaviour, reactions etc seem normal and reasonable because of the situation you are in: *It is understandable that parents are angry, and looking for someone to blame.* | *He just can't face anyone at the moment, which is perfectly understandable.* | *an understandable mistake* **2** able to be understood —**understandably** adv: *They were understandably upset.*

un·der·stand·ing W3 /ˌʌndə'stændɪŋ $ -ər-/ n **1** [singular, U] knowledge about something, based on learning or experience

> **have an understanding/some understanding of sth**
> **have little/no understanding of sth**
> **gain/get an understanding of sth**
> **a better/greater/deeper understanding of sth**

U

a clear understanding of sth
a thorough/proper/full understanding of sth
a basic understanding of sth

[+of] *How does this add to our understanding of the problem?* | *If you know the neighbourhood, you* **have an understanding of** *what the children are like.* | *Linguists currently* **have little understanding of** *the exact cause of language change.* | *How can we* **gain an understanding of** *other cultures?* | *Over time, you will get* **a far better understanding of** *the job.* | *Success depends on* **a clear understanding of** *the problem.* | **a basic understanding of** *AIDS prevention*

2 [C usually singular] an unofficial or informal agreement: **come to/reach an understanding** (=stop arguing and agree) *My father was furious at first, but eventually we came to an understanding.* | *We* **had an understanding** *that Jean-Claude should never be mentioned.* **3** [singular, U] the ability to understand people's behaviour and to forgive them when they do something wrong: *The principal listened to the boy's story with sympathy and understanding.* **4** [U] **sb's understanding (of sth)** the way in which someone judges the meaning of something: *According to my understanding of the letter, it means something quite different.* **5** **on the understanding that** if you agree to something on the understanding that something else will be done, you agree to it, believing that it will be done: *Jack lent Sarah the money on the understanding that she would pay it back next month.*

understanding² *adj* sympathetic and kind about other people's problems: *Luckily, I have a very understanding boss.*

un·der·state /ˌʌndəˈsteɪt $ -ər-/ *v* [T] to describe something in a way that makes it seem less important or serious than it really is; ◪ **overstate**: *The press have tended to understate the extent of the problem.*

un·der·stat·ed /ˌʌndəˈsteɪt̬ɪd $ -ər-/ *adj* an understated style is one that is attractive because it is simple and does not have too many decorations; ◪ **subtle**: *the understated elegance of the Hotel Traiano*

un·der·state·ment /ˌʌndəˈsteɪtmənt $ -dər-/ *n* **1** [C] a statement that is not strong enough to express how good, bad, impressive etc something really is: *To say the movie was bad* **is an understatement.** | *'It wasn't very easy to find the house.' 'That's got to be* **the understatement of the year!'** **2** [U] the practice of making something seem to have less of a particular quality than it really has: **with understatement** *'We have not done quite well enough,' Macmillan said, with characteristic understatement.*

un·der·stood /ˌʌndəˈstʊd $ -ər-/ the past tense and past participle of UNDERSTAND

un·der·stud·y¹ /ˈʌndəˌstʌdi $ -ər-/ *n plural* **understudies** [C] an actor who learns a part in a play so that they can act the part if the usual actor is ill

understudy² *v* **understudied**, **understudying**, **understudies** [T] to be an understudy for a particular actor in a play

un·der·sub·scribed /ˌʌndəsəbˈskraɪbd $ -dər-/ *adj* an activity, sale, service etc that is undersubscribed is not bought or used by enough people; ◪ **oversubscribed**

un·der·take W3 /ˌʌndəˈteɪk $ -dər-/ *v past tense* **undertook** /-ˈtʊk/ *past participle* **undertaken** /-ˈteɪkən/ [T] *formal* **1** to accept that you are responsible for a piece of work, and start to do it: **undertake a task/a project/research/a study** etc *Dr Johnson undertook the task of writing a comprehensive English dictionary.* **2** **undertake to do sth** to promise or agree to do something: *He undertook to pay the money back in six months.*

un·der·tak·er /ˈʌndəteɪkə $ -dərteɪkər/ *n* [C] *BrE* someone whose job is to arrange funerals; ◪ **funeral director** *AmE*

un·der·tak·ing /ˌʌndəˈteɪkɪŋ $ ˈʌndərteɪ-/ *n* **1** [C usually singular] an important job, piece of work, or activity that you are responsible for: *Starting a new business can be a risky undertaking.* **2** [C] *formal* a promise to do something: *Both organizations gave an* **undertaking** *to curb violence among their members.* **3** [U] the business of an undertaker

under-the-ˈcounter *adj informal* under-the-counter goods are bought or sold secretly, especially because they are illegal

un·der·tone /ˈʌndətəʊn $ -dərtoʊn/ *n* [C] **1** a feeling or quality that is not directly expressed but can still be recognized; → **overtone**: [+of] *There was an undertone of sadness in her letter.* | *Opponents claim the policy has racist undertones.* **2** *literary* if you speak in an undertone, you speak quietly: **in an undertone** *'Don't be too upset if he doesn't come,' said Drew in an undertone.*

un·der·tow /ˈʌndətəʊ $ -dərtoʊ/ *n* [singular] **1** the water current under the surface of the sea, that pulls away from the land when a wave comes onto the shore: *The dangerous undertow means that swimming is not allowed.* **2** a tendency or feeling that seems weak, but in fact has a strong effect: [+of] *The humour of the novel cannot hide an undertow of sadness.*

un·der·used /ˌʌndəˈjuːzd◂ $ -ər-/ *adj* something that is underused is not used as much as it could be

un·der·val·ue /ˌʌndəˈvæljuː $ -ər-/ *v* [T] to think that someone or something is less important or valuable than they really are: *Society undervalues staying home and looking after children.* | *Analysts claim that the firm's assets were undervalued by £300 million.*

un·der·wa·ter /ˌʌndəˈwɔːtə◂ $ ˌʌndərˈwɔːtər◂, -ˈwɑː-/ *adj* [only before noun] below the surface of an area of water, or able to be used there: *an underwater camera* —**underwater** *adv*: *He dived underwater and swam away.*

un·der·way /ˌʌndəˈweɪ $ -ər-/ *adj* [not before noun] **1** happening now: *The project is already* **well underway.** | *Your peace will be shattered when the tourist season* **gets underway** (=starts). **2** something such as a boat or train that is underway is moving → **be under way** at WAY¹ (10)

underwear

camisole

body *BrE*/body suit *AmE*

vest *BrE*/
undershirt *AmE*

boxer shorts

knickers *BrE*/panties *AmE*

underpants

bra

slip

un·der·wear /ˈʌndəweə $ -dərwer/ *n* [U] clothes that you wear next to your body under your other clothes: *You just need to take a change of underwear.*

un·der·weight /ˌʌndəˈweɪt◂ $ -ər-/ *adj* weighing less than is expected or usual; **◐ overweight**: *Women who smoke risk giving birth to underweight babies.*

un·der·went /ˌʌndəˈwent $ -ər-/ the past tense of UNDERGO

un·der·whelm /ˌʌndəˈwelm $ -ər-/ *v* [T] if you are underwhelmed by something, you do not think it is impressive – used humorously: *We've had an underwhelming response to our request for help.*

un·der·world /ˈʌndəwɜːld $ ˈʌndərwɜːrld/ *n* [singular] **1** the criminals in a particular place and the criminal activities they are involved in: *New York's criminal underworld* **2 the Underworld** the place where the spirits of the dead are believed to live, for example in ancient Greek stories

un·der·write /ˌʌndəˈraɪt $ -ər-/ *v past tense* **underwrote** /-ˈrəʊt $ -ˈrəʊt/ *past participle* **underwritten** /-ˈrɪtn/ [T] **1** *formal* to support an activity, business plan etc with money, and to take financial responsibility if it fails: *The government has agreed to underwrite the project with a grant of £5 million.* **2** *technical* if an insurance company underwrites an insurance contract, it agrees to pay for any damage or loss that happens **3** *technical* to arrange to sell SHARES to INVESTORS, and to agree to buy any which are not bought by them —**underwriter** /ˈʌndəˌraɪtə $ -tər/ *n* [C]

un·der·writ·er /ˈʌndəˌraɪtə $ -tər/ *n* [C] someone who makes insurance contracts

un·de·served /ˌʌndɪˈzɜːvd◂ $ -ˈzɜːrvd/ *adj* undeserved criticism, praise etc is unfair because you do not deserve it: *She had an undeserved reputation for rudeness.*

un·de·sir·a·ble¹ /ˌʌndɪˈzaɪərəbəl◂ $ -ˈzaɪr-/ *adj* *formal* something or someone that is undesirable is not welcome or wanted because they may affect a situation or person in a bad way: **undesirable effects/consequences etc** *The drug may have other undesirable effects.* | *punishment of undesirable behaviour*

undesirable² *n* [C usually plural] someone who is considered to be immoral, criminal, or socially unacceptable: *security measures to keep out undesirables*

un·de·tect·ed /ˌʌndɪˈtektˤd◂/ *adj* if something, especially something bad, goes undetected, no one notices it: **go/remain undetected** *Doctors can make mistakes and diseases can remain undetected.* | *The thieves escaped undetected through a basement window.*

un·de·terred /ˌʌndɪˈtɜːd $ -ˈtɜːrd/ *adj* if you are undeterred by something, you do not allow it to stop you doing what you want: [+**by**] *Undeterred by his early failures, he decided to keep writing.*

un·de·vel·oped /ˌʌndɪˈveləpt◂/ *adj* **1** used in order to describe land which has not yet been used for building, farming etc: *an undeveloped stretch of coastline* **2** used in order to describe a country or area that does not have modern industry, and usually has a low standard of living; → **underdeveloped**: *the undeveloped regions of the world* **3** not fully grown: *a child's undeveloped mind*

un·did /ʌnˈdɪd/ the past tense of UNDO

un·dies /ˈʌndiːz/ *n* [plural] *informal* underwear

un·dif·fer·en·ti·at·ed /ˌʌndɪfəˈrenʃieɪtˤd/ *adj* something which is undifferentiated is not split into parts, or has different parts but you cannot tell the difference between them: *shows aimed at large undifferentiated groups of people* | *Colonial officials tended to see Indian society as an undifferentiated whole.*

un·dig·ni·fied /ʌnˈdɪɡnˤfaɪd/ *adj* behaving in a way that is embarrassing or makes you look silly: *There was an undignified scramble for the free drinks.*

un·di·lut·ed /ˌʌndaɪˈluːtˤd◂/ *adj* **1** *literary* an undiluted feeling is very strong and not mixed with any other feelings: *undiluted joy* **2** an undiluted liquid has not been made weaker by adding water: *undiluted fruit juice*

un·di·min·ished /ˌʌndɪˈmɪnɪʃt◂/ *adj* not weaker or less important than before: *Neil continued with undiminished enthusiasm.* | *Forty years on, the book's power to shock is undiminished.*

un·dis·charged /ˌʌndɪsˈtʃɑːdʒd◂ $ -ɑːr-/ *adj* *law* **1** an undischarged debt is one that has not been paid **2** an **undischarged bankrupt** someone who still owes money and is not legally allowed to stop repaying their debt

un·dis·closed /ˌʌndɪsˈkləʊzd◂ $ -ˈkləʊzd/ *adj* used to describe information which is not given to the public: *Developers have agreed to buy the site for an undisclosed sum.*

un·dis·crim·i·nat·ing /ˌʌndɪˈskrɪmˤneɪtɪŋ/ *adj* not having the ability to see a difference between two people or things, and therefore unable to make judgments about them

un·dis·guised /ˌʌndɪsˈɡaɪzd◂/ *adj* [usually before noun] an undisguised feeling is clearly shown and not hidden: *There was undisguised contempt in his voice.*

un·dis·mayed /ˌʌndɪsˈmeɪd◂/ *adj* *formal* not worried or frightened by something unpleasant or unexpected

un·dis·put·ed /ˌʌndɪˈspjuːtˤd◂/ *adj* **1** known to be definitely true: *Doctors found undisputed evidence of nerve damage.* **2** accepted by everyone: **undisputed leader/champion/master etc** *the undisputed world heavyweight champion*

un·dis·turbed /ˌʌndɪˈstɜːbd◂ $ -ɜːr-/ *adj* **1** not interrupted or moved: *At last I was able to work undisturbed.* | **be left/remain undisturbed** *The land is to be left undisturbed as a nature reserve.* **2 be undisturbed by sth** not upset or worried by something: *Mark seemed undisturbed by her threats.*

un·di·vid·ed /ˌʌndɪˈvaɪdˤd◂/ *adj* **1** [usually before noun] complete: *I'll give the matter my **undivided attention**.* **2** not separated into smaller parts: *an undivided country*

un·do /ʌnˈduː/ *v past tense* **undid** /-ˈdɪd/ *past participle* **undone** /-ˈdʌn/ *third person singular* **undoes** /-ˈdʌz/ [T] **1** to open something that is tied, fastened or wrapped: *The screws can be undone by hand.* | **undo your jacket/shirt/bra etc** *I could the package carefully.* **2** to try to remove the bad effects of something you have done: *We cannot **undo the damage** of a lifetime in only 30 days.* | *If a medicine is taken again too soon, it may undo all the good that has been done.* **3** *technical* to remove the effect of your previous action on a computer

un·do·ing /ʌnˈduːɪŋ/ *n* **be sb's undoing** to cause someone's shame, failure etc: *In the end, drink was his undoing.*

un·done /ˌʌnˈdʌn◂/ *adj* [not before noun] **1** not fastened: *Your zip's undone.* | *One of these buttons has **come undone**.* **2** not finished: *The washing-up had been left undone.* **3** *old use* destroyed and without hope: *In the end, Othello is undone by his jealousy.*

un·doubt·ed |W3| /ʌnˈdaʊtˤd/ *adj* definitely true or known to exist: *her undoubted talent* | *The film was an undoubted success.* —**undoubtedly** *adv*: *That is undoubtedly true.* | *Undoubtedly, public interest in folk music has declined.*

un·dreamed-of /ʌnˈdriːmd- ɒv $ -ɑːv/ *also* **un·dreamt-of** /ʌnˈdremt-/ *adj* much more or much better than you thought was possible: *undreamt-of success* | *Men were becoming interested in fashion on a scale undreamed-of in the 1960s.*

un·dress¹ /ʌnˈdres/ *v* [I,T] to take your clothes off, or take someone else's clothes off: *Matt undressed and got into bed.* | *Joe still needs an adult to undress him.*

undress² *n* [U] *formal* when you are wearing few or no clothes: *Cindy was wandering about her room **in a state of undress**.*

un·flat·ter·ing /ʌnˈflætərɪŋ/ adj making someone look or seem bad or unattractive: an unflattering portrait

un·flinch·ing /ʌnˈflɪntʃɪŋ/ adj not changing or becoming weaker, even in a very difficult or dangerous situation: unflinching courage —**unflinchingly** adv

un·fo·cused, **unfocussed** /ʌnˈfəʊkəst $ -ˈfoʊ-/ adj 1 not dealing with or paying attention to the important ideas, causes etc: The discussion was becoming unfocused. 2 eyes that are unfocused are open, but are not looking at anything specific: He gave her an unfocused look.

un·fold /ʌnˈfəʊld $ -ˈfoʊld/ v 1 [I,T] if a story unfolds, or if someone unfolds it, it is told: As the story unfolds, we learn more about Max's childhood. 2 [I] if a series of events unfold, they happen: He had watched **the drama unfold** from a nearby ship. 3 [I,T] if you unfold something that was folded, or if it unfolds, it opens out: He unfolded the map.

un·fore·see·a·ble /ˌʌnfɔːˈsiːəbəl $ -fɔːr-/ adj an unforeseeable event, situation etc could not have been expected: unforeseeable danger

un·fore·seen /ˌʌnfɔːˈsiːn◂ $ -fɔːr-/ adj an unforeseen situation is one that you did not expect to happen: **unforeseen circumstances/events/changes etc** Due to **unforeseen circumstances**, the play has been cancelled. | **unforeseen problems/difficulties/delays** unforeseen delays in supplying the equipment

un·for·get·ta·ble /ˌʌnfəˈgetəbəl $ -fər-/ adj an unforgettable experience, sight, etc affects you so strongly that you will never forget it, especially because it is particularly good or beautiful: A visit to Morocco is a truly unforgettable experience. —**unforgettably** adv

un·for·giv·a·ble /ˌʌnfəˈgɪvəbəl $ -fər-/ adj an unforgivable action is so bad or cruel that you cannot forgive the person who did it: Patrick had deceived her, and that was unforgivable. | the **unforgivable sin** of informing on your friends —**unforgivably** adv

un·for·giv·ing /ˌʌnfəˈgɪvɪŋ◂ $ -fər-/ adj 1 someone who is unforgiving does not forgive people easily 2 an unforgiving place is very difficult to live in, for example because it is extremely hot or cold

un·formed /ˌʌnˈfɔːmd◂ $ -ɔːr-/ adj not yet developed: the unformed mind of a child

un·for·tu·nate¹ [S3] /ʌnˈfɔːtʃənət $ -ˈfɔːr-/ adj
1 someone who is unfortunate has something bad happen to them: When we entered the room, the teacher was yelling at some unfortunate student.
2 an unfortunate situation, condition, quality etc is one that you wish was different: an unfortunate turn of events | He has an **unfortunate habit** of repeating himself. | **it is unfortunate (that)** It's unfortunate that so few people seem willing to help. | It's **most unfortunate** (=very unfortunate) that your father can't come to the wedding.
3 happening because of bad luck: an **unfortunate accident**
4 formal unfortunate behaviour, remarks etc make people feel embarrassed or offended: an unfortunate choice of words

unfortunate² n [C] literary someone who has no money, home, job etc

un·for·tu·nate·ly [S1] [W3] /ʌnˈfɔːtʃənətli $ -ˈfɔːr-/ adv [sentence adverb] used when you are mentioning a fact that you wish were not true: Unfortunately, you were out when we called.

un·found·ed /ʌnˈfaʊndɪd◂/ adj unfounded statements, feelings, opinions etc are wrong because they are not based on facts: **unfounded rumours/claims/allegations etc** Unfounded rumours began circulating that Ian and Susan were having an affair. | **prove (to be) unfounded** Sadly, my optimism proved unfounded.

un·fre·quent·ed /ˌʌnfrɪˈkwentɪd◂ $ ʌnˈfriː-kwəntɪd, ˌʌnfrɪˈkwen-/ adj formal not often visited by many people: an unfrequented spot

un·friend·ly /ʌnˈfrendli/ adj comparative **unfriendlier**, superlative **unfriendliest** 1 not kind or friendly: The old man looked cross and unfriendly. | a lonely unfriendly place | [+to/towards] The villagers were really quite unfriendly towards us. 2 not helping or wanting a type of person or thing: [+to] We have created cities that are unfriendly to pedestrians. 3 an unfriendly government or nation is one that opposes yours

un·frock /ʌnˈfrɒk $ -ˈfrɑːk/ v [T usually in passive] to remove someone from their position as a priest as a punishment for behaviour or beliefs that the church does not approve of

un·ful·filled /ˌʌnfʊlˈfɪld◂/ adj 1 an unfulfilled hope, desire, dream etc has not been achieved: His dream of competing in the Olympics **remained unfulfilled**. 2 someone who is unfulfilled feels they could be achieving more in their job, relationship etc: Her job left her feeling unfulfilled and unappreciated.

un·fun·ny /ʌnˈfʌni/ adj informal an unfunny joke or action is not amusing, although it is intended to be – used to show disapproval

un·furl /ʌnˈfɜːl $ -ˈfɜːrl/ v [I,T] if a flag, sail etc unfurls, or if someone unfurls it, it unrolls and opens

un·fur·nished /ʌnˈfɜːnɪʃt $ -ɜːr-/ adj an unfurnished room, house etc has no furniture in it

un·gain·ly /ʌnˈgeɪnli/ adj moving in a way that does not look graceful: a tall ungainly teenager —**ungainliness** n [U]

un·glued /ʌnˈgluːd/ adj 1 **come unglued** AmE informal a) if a plan, situation etc comes unglued, it stops working well: When his parents got divorced, his whole world came unglued. b) to become extremely upset or angry about something: If someone talked to me like that, I would just come unglued. 2 no longer glued together

un·god·ly /ʌnˈgɒdli $ -ˈgɑːd-/ adj 1 [only before noun] unreasonable and annoying: **at an ungodly hour** (=very early in the morning or very late at night) Why did you wake me up at such an ungodly hour? 2 literary showing a lack of respect for God

un·gov·ern·a·ble /ʌnˈgʌvənəbəl $ -vər-/ adj 1 a country or area that is ungovernable is one in which the people cannot be controlled by the government, the police etc 2 formal feelings or types of behaviour that are ungovernable are impossible to control: ungovernable rage

un·gra·cious /ʌnˈgreɪʃəs/ adj not polite or friendly: After Anna's kindness to me, I don't want to seem ungracious. —**ungraciously** adv

un·grate·ful /ʌnˈgreɪtfəl/ adj not expressing thanks for something that someone has given to you or done for you: Don't be so ungrateful!

un·guard·ed /ʌnˈgɑːdɪd◂ $ -ɑːr-/ adj 1 **an unguarded moment** a time when you are not paying attention to what you are doing or saying: In an unguarded moment, he admitted that he wanted to quit his job. 2 an unguarded remark, statement etc is one that you make carelessly without thinking of the possible effects 3 not guarded or protected by anyone

un·guent /ˈʌŋgwənt/ n [C] any oily substance used on your skin; ▣ ointment

un·hap·pi·ly /ʌnˈhæpɪli/ adv 1 in a way that shows you are not happy: 'I'm not sure what to do,' Seb admitted unhappily. 2 [sentence adverb] old-fashioned used when you are mentioning a fact that you wish were not true; ▣ unfortunately: Unhappily, she was not able to complete the course.

un·hap·py [S3] [W3] /ʌnˈhæpi/ adj comparative **unhappier**, superlative **unhappiest**
1 not happy: If you're so unhappy, why don't you change jobs? | Leslie had an unhappy childhood. | an unhappy marriage | I was **desperately unhappy**.

2 feeling worried or annoyed because you do not like what is happening in a particular situation: **unhappy about/at (doing) sth** *Dennis is unhappy about having to work on a Saturday.* | [+**with**] *We were all unhappy with the quality of the service.*
3 *formal* an unhappy remark, situation etc is not suitable, lucky, or desirable: *an unhappy coincidence* —**unhappily** *adv* —**unhappiness** *n* [U]

un·harmed /ʌnˈhɑːmd $ -ɑːr-/ *adj* [not before noun] not hurt or harmed: *The hostages were released unharmed.* | *The girl managed to escape unharmed.*

un·health·y /ʌnˈhelθi/ *adj comparative* **unhealthier**, *superlative* **unhealthiest** **1** likely to make you ill: *unhealthy living conditions* **2** not normal or natural and likely to be harmful: *an unhealthy relationship* | **unhealthy interest/obsession/fear etc** *Gareth had an unhealthy interest in death.* **3** not physically healthy; **☐ ill, sick**: *an unhealthy baby* **4** unhealthy skin, hair etc shows that you are ill or not healthy: *an unhealthy pale complexion* —**unhealthily** *adv*

un·heard /ˌʌnˈhɜːd $ -ɜːrd/ *adj* not heard or listened to: *Her cries for help went unheard.*

un'heard of, **unheard-of** *adj* something that is unheard of is so unusual that it has not happened or been known before: *Travel for pleasure was almost unheard of until the 19th century.*

un·heed·ed /ʌnˈhiːdɪd/ *adj literary* noticed but not listened to, accepted, or believed: *Her warnings went unheeded.*

un·help·ful /ʌnˈhelpfəl/ *adj* not helping in a situation and sometimes making it worse: *The authorities are being particularly unhelpful.* —**unhelpfully** *adv* —**unhelpfulness** *n* [U]

un·her·ald·ed /ʌnˈherəldɪd/ *adj formal* **1** if an event is unheralded, there is no warning that it is going to happen: *an unheralded visit from his aunt* **2** not known about or recognized as good; **☐ unsung**: *the unheralded members of the team*

un·hinge /ʌnˈhɪndʒ/ *v* [T] to make someone become very upset or mentally ill: *The terrible experience seemed to have unhinged him slightly.* —**unhinged** *adj*

un·hip /ʌnˈhɪp/ *adj informal* unfashionable

un·hitch /ʌnˈhɪtʃ/ *v* [T] to unfasten something that is joined to something else

un·ho·ly /ʌnˈhəʊli $ -ˈhoʊ-/ *adj* [no comparative] **1** an **unholy alliance** an agreement between two people or organizations who would not normally work together, usually for a bad purpose **2** [only before noun] *informal* bad and extreme: *An unholy row broke out between two of the men drinking in the bar.* | *an unholy mess* **3** not holy, or not respecting what is holy **4** **unholy amusement/delight/pleasure** pleasure etc that you get from someone else's suffering: *He was taking an unholy delight in humiliating Sarah.*

un·hook /ʌnˈhʊk/ *v* [T] to unfasten or remove something from a hook

un·hoped-for /ʌnˈhəʊpt fɔː $ -ˈhoʊpt fɔːr/ *adj* much better than had been expected: *unhoped-for success*

un·hur·ried /ʌnˈhʌrid $ -ˈhɜː-/ *adj* slow and calm: *the unhurried pace of a small town* —**unhurriedly** *adv*

un·hurt /ʌnˈhɜːt $ -ɜːrt/ *adj* [not before noun] not hurt: *The driver escaped unhurt from the accident.*

un·hy·gie·nic /ˌʌnhaɪˈdʒiːnɪk $ -ˈdʒe-, -ˈdʒiː-/ *adj* dirty and likely to make people ill: *unhygienic conditions* —**unhygienically** /-kli/ *adv*

u·ni /ˈjuːni/ *n* [singular, U] *BrE, AusE spoken* university

uni- /juːni/ *prefix* one; **☐ single**: *unidirectional* (=going in only one direction)

u·ni·corn /ˈjuːnɪkɔːn $ -ɔːrn/ *n* [C] an imaginary animal like a white horse with a long straight horn growing on its head

u·ni·cy·cle /ˈjuːniˌsaɪkəl/ *n* [C] a vehicle that is like a bicycle but has only one wheel

un·i·den·ti·fied /ˌʌnaɪˈdentɪfaɪd/ *adj* an unidentified person or thing is one that you do not know the name of: *An unidentified man was spotted near the scene of the crime.*

u·ni·fi·ca·tion /ˌjuːnɪfɪˈkeɪʃən/ *n* [U] the act of combining two or more groups, countries etc to make a single group or country: [+**of**] *the unification of Germany*

u·ni·fied /ˈjuːnɪfaɪd/ *adj* created from more than one part, group etc: *a unified approach* | *a unified EU import market*

u·ni·form¹ ⟨S3⟩ /ˈjuːnɪfɔːm $ -ɔːrm/ *n* [C,U] **1** a particular type of clothing worn by all the members of a group or organization such as the police, the army etc: **school/army/police etc uniform** *He was still wearing his school uniform.* **2** **in uniform** **a)** wearing a uniform: *He was on duty and in uniform.* **b)** in the Army, Navy etc: *my 33 years in uniform*

uniform² *adj* being the same in all its parts or among all its members: *Grade A eggs must be of uniform size.* —**uniformly** *adv*

u·ni·formed /ˈjuːnɪfɔːmd $ -ɔːr-/ *adj* wearing a uniform: *uniformed police officers*

u·ni·form·i·ty /ˌjuːnɪˈfɔːmɪti $ -ɔːr-/ *n* [U] the quality of being or looking the same as all other members of a group: *There seems to be no uniformity among the various systems.*

u·ni·fy /ˈjuːnɪfaɪ/ *v* **unified, unifying, unifies** [I,T] if you unify two or more parts or things, or if they unify, they are combined to make a single unit; **☐ unite**; **☒ divide**: *Strong support for the war has unified the nation.* | *His music unifies traditional and modern themes.*

u·ni·lat·e·ral /ˌjuːnɪˈlætərəl/ *adj formal* a unilateral action or decision is done by only one of the groups involved in a situation; → **bilateral, multilateral**: *a unilateral declaration of independence* | **unilateral disarmament** (=when one country gets rid of its own NUCLEAR weapons without waiting for other countries to do the same) —**unilateralism** *n* [U] —**unilaterally** *adv*

un·i·ma·gin·a·ble /ˌʌnɪˈmædʒɪnəbəl/ *adj* not possible to imagine: *unimaginable wealth* —**unimaginably** *adv*

un·i·ma·gin·a·tive /ˌʌnɪˈmædʒɪnətɪv/ *adj* **1** lacking the ability to think of new or unusual ideas **2** ordinary and boring, and not using any new ideas: *unimaginative architecture* | *unimaginative housing policies*

un·i·ma·gined /ˌʌnɪˈmædʒɪnd/ *adj* [usually before noun] *literary* so good, large, great etc that it is hard to imagine

un·im·paired /ˌʌnɪmˈpeəd $ -ˈperd/ *adj* not damaged or made weak

un·im·peach·a·ble /ˌʌnɪmˈpiːtʃəbəl/ *adj formal* so good or definite that criticism or doubt is impossible: *unimpeachable morals* —**unimpeachably** *adv*

un·im·ped·ed /ˌʌnɪmˈpiːdɪd/ *adj* happening or moving without being stopped or having difficulty: *unimpeded progress*

un·im·por·tant /ˌʌnɪmˈpɔːtənt $ -ɔːr-/ *adj* not important; **☐ trivial**: *unimportant details*

un·im·pressed /ˌʌnɪmˈprest/ *adj* not thinking that someone or something is good, interesting etc: [+**with/by**] *Board members were unimpressed with the plan.*

un·im·pres·sive /ˌʌnɪmˈpresɪv/ *adj* not as good, large etc as expected or necessary: *unimpressive test results*

un·in·formed /ˌʌnɪnˈfɔːmd $ -ɔːr-/ *adj* not having enough knowledge or information: *Parents were left anxious, uninformed, and isolated.* | *uninformed criti-*

U

cism from uninformed journalists | [+**about**] *Many immigrants are uninformed about US tax laws.*

un·in·hab·it·a·ble /ˌʌnɪnˈhæbɪtəbəl/ *adj* if a place is uninhabitable, it is impossible to live in: *Much of the country is uninhabitable because it is desert.* | *Many houses were so badly damaged in the war that they were made permanently uninhabitable.*

un·in·hab·it·ed /ˌʌnɪnˈhæbɪtɪd/ *adj* an uninhabited place does not have anyone living there; ▣ **deserted**: *an uninhabited island*

un·in·hib·it·ed /ˌʌnɪnˈhɪbɪtɪd/ *adj* confident or relaxed enough to do or say what you want to: *uninhibited laughter* —**uninhibitedly** *adv*

un·i·ni·ti·at·ed /ˌʌnɪˈnɪʃieɪtɪd/ *n* **the uninitiated** [plural] people who do not have special knowledge or experience of something: *To the uninitiated, this will make little sense.* —**uninitiated** *adj*

un·in·spired /ˌʌnɪnˈspaɪəd $ -ˈspaɪrd/ *adj* not showing any imagination: *an uninspired performance*

un·in·spir·ing /ˌʌnɪnˈspaɪərɪŋ $ -ˈspaɪr-/ *adj* not at all interesting or exciting: *No one deserved to win this uninspiring game.*

un·in·tel·li·gi·ble /ˌʌnɪnˈtelɪdʒɪbəl/ *adj* impossible to understand; ▣ **clear**: *Eva muttered something unintelligible.* | [+**to**] *technical jargon that is unintelligible to outsiders* —**unintelligibly** *adv*

un·in·ten·tion·al /ˌʌnɪnˈtenʃənəl/ *adj* not done deliberately: *I know she upset you, but I'm sure it was unintentional.* —**unintentionally** *adv*

un·in·terest·ed /ʌnˈɪntrɪstɪd/ *adj* not interested; → **disinterested**: [+**in**] *He was uninterested in politics.*

un·in·ter·rupt·ed /ˌʌnɪntəˈrʌptɪd/ *adj* **1** continuous: *uninterrupted sleep* **2 uninterrupted view** if you have an uninterrupted view of something, there is nothing between you and that thing to stop you from seeing it clearly: *an uninterrupted view of the mountains* —**uninterruptedly** *adv*

un·in·vit·ed /ˌʌnɪnˈvaɪtɪd/ *adj* not invited and expected: *uninvited guests* | *Helen turned up uninvited.*

un·in·vit·ing /ˌʌnɪnˈvaɪtɪŋ/ *adj* **1** an uninviting place seems unattractive or unpleasant: *The building was cold, dark, and uninviting.* **2 uninviting prospect** something unpleasant that you will have to do: *He faced the uninviting prospect of a two-hour wait for the next train.*

u·nion S1 W1 /ˈjuːnjən/ *n*
1 [C] also **trade union** *BrE*, **labor union** *AmE* an organization formed by workers to protect their rights: [+**of**] *the National Union of Teachers* | *Are you planning to join the union?* | *union members*
2 used in the names of some clubs or organizations: *the British Golf Union*
3 [singular] *formal* the act of joining two or more things together, or the state of being joined together: [+**of**] *The artist's work shows the perfect union of craftsmanship and imagination.* | [+**with**] *Some militants favour independence for Kashmir or union with Pakistan.*
4 [singular] a group of countries or states with the same central government: *the Soviet Union*
5 the Union used in the past to talk about the United States, especially the northern states during the Civil War
6 [C,U] *formal* marriage
7 [C,U] *formal* the activity of having sex, or an occasion when this happens

u·nion·is·m /ˈjuːnjənɪzəm/ *n* [U] belief in the principles of TRADE UNIONS —**unionist** *n* [C]

U·nion·ist /ˈjuːnjənɪst/ *n* [C] a member of a political party that wants Northern Ireland to remain part of the United Kingdom —**Unionism** *n* [U]

u·nion·ize also **-ise** *BrE* /ˈjuːnjənaɪz/ *v* [I,T] if workers unionize or are unionized, they become members of a TRADE UNION —**unionized** *adj* —**unionization** /ˌjuːnjənaɪˈzeɪʃən $ -jənə-/ *n* [U]

Union 'Jack *n* [C] the national flag of the United Kingdom

'union ˌsuit *n* [C] *AmE* a piece of underwear that covers the whole body, with long legs and long sleeves

u·nique S3 W2 /juːˈniːk/ *adj* [no comparative]
1 *informal* unusually good and special: *a unique opportunity to study these rare creatures*
2 being the only one of its kind: *Each person's fingerprints are unique.*
3 unique to sb/sth existing only in a particular place or in relation to a particular person or people: *The issues being discussed here are not unique to the US.*
—**uniquely** *adv*: *an actor uniquely suited to the part* —**uniqueness** *n* [U]

u·ni·sex /ˈjuːnɪseks/ *adj* intended for both men and women: *a unisex hairdressing salon*

u·ni·son /ˈjuːnɪsən, -zən/ *n* **in unison a)** if people speak or do something in unison, they say the same words at the same time or do the same thing at the same time: *'Good morning!' the kids replied in unison.* **b)** if two groups, governments etc do something in unison, they do it together because they agree with each other: *Management and workers must act in unison to compete with foreign business.*

u·nit W3 /ˈjuːnɪt/ *n* [C]
1 GROUP a group of people working together as part of a larger group: *The man is in the hospital's intensive care unit.*
2 MEASURING an amount of something used as a standard of measurement: [+**of**] *The watt is a unit of electrical power.*
3 PART a thing, person, or group that is regarded as one single whole part of something larger: *a Russian army unit* | [+**of**] *The family is the basic social unit of modern society.*
4 PART OF A BOOK one of the numbered parts into which a TEXTBOOK (=a book used in schools) is divided
5 PRODUCT *technical* a single complete product made by a company: *The factory's output is now up to 150,000 units each month.*
6 PART OF A MACHINE a piece of equipment which is part of a larger machine: **control/display/filter etc unit**
7 FURNITURE a piece of furniture, especially one that can be attached to others of the same type: *fitted kitchen units BrE* | *storage units*
8 APARTMENT *AmE* a single apartment in a larger building
9 SCHOOL/UNIVERSITY *AmE* an amount of work that a student needs to do in order to complete a particular course
10 NUMBER *BrE technical* any whole number less than ten: *hundreds, tens, and units*

U·ni·ta·ri·an /ˌjuːnɪˈteəriən $ -ˈter-/ *n* [C] a member of a Christian group that does not believe in the Trinity —**Unitarian** *adj*

u·ni·ta·ry /ˈjuːnɪtəri $ -teri/ *adj formal* relating to or existing as a single unit: *a single unitary authority for the whole region*

u·nite /juˈnaɪt/ *v* [I,T] if different people or organizations unite, or if something unites them, they join together in order to achieve something: *Our goal is to unite the opposition parties and defeat the President.* | [+**against/behind**] *Party members united behind their leader.* | **unite to do sth** *In 1960, the regions united to form the Somali Republic.*

u·nit·ed W3 /juˈnaɪtɪd/ *adj*
1 joined or closely connected by feelings, aims etc: *a united Europe* | *The two countries were united against a common enemy.*
2 involving or done by everyone: *a united effort to clean up the environment*
3 used in the names of some football teams and companies: *Manchester United* | *United Airlines*

U,nited 'Nations *n* **the United Nations** *the UN* an international organization that tries to find peaceful solutions to world problems

unit price n [C] technical the price that is charged for each single thing or quantity that is sold

unit trust n [C] BrE a company through which you can buy shares in many different businesses; ▤ mutual fund AmE

u·ni·ty W3 /'ju:nₗ₎ti/ n plural unities
1 [U] when a group of people or countries agree or are joined together: economic unity | European unity
2 [U] the quality of having matching parts: His essays often lack unity.
3 [C] technical one of the three related principles that say a play should be about a single set of related events which take place in one place on one day

Univ. also **Univ** BrE n a written abbreviation of university

u·ni·ver·sal W3 /ˌju:nₗ₎'vɜ:səl◂ $ -ɜ:r-/ adj
1 involving everyone in the world or in a particular group: free universal health-care | These stories have universal appeal. | a topic of universal interest | a democracy based on universal suffrage (=when every adult has the right to vote)
2 true or suitable in every situation: a universal truth —universally adv —universality /ˌju:nₗ₎vɜ:'sælₗ₎ti $ -ɜ:r-/ n [U]

universal joint n [C] a part in a machine, at the point where two other parts join together, that can turn in all directions

Universal Product Code n [C] AmE UPC a BAR CODE

u·ni·verse W3 /'ju:nₗ₎vɜ:s $ -ɜ:rs/ n
1 the universe all space, including all the stars and PLANETS: in the universe everything in the universe
2 [C] a world or an area of space that is different from the one we are in: a parallel/an alternative universe
3 be the centre of sb's universe to be the most important person or thing to someone
4 sb's universe a person's life, including all of the people, places, and ideas which affect them

u·ni·ver·si·ty S2 W1 /ˌju:nₗ₎'vɜ:sₗ₎ti◂ $ -ɜ:r-/ n plural universities [C,U] an educational institution at the highest level, where you study for a DEGREE: go to university (=study at a university) | at university BrE: He studied Physics at university. | Oxford University | [+of] the University of Texas | university student/lecturer/professor etc | a university education

un·just /ˌʌn'dʒʌst◂/ adj formal not fair or reasonable; ▤ unfair: unjust laws —unjustly adv

un·just·i·fi·a·ble /ʌn'dʒʌstₗ₎faɪəbəl/ adj completely wrong and unacceptable: Poisoning the earth's atmosphere is ecologically and morally unjustifiable. —unjustifiably adv

un·just·i·fied /ʌn'dʒʌstₗ₎faɪd/ adj done without an acceptable reason: unjustified price increases

un·kempt /ˌʌn'kempt◂/ adj unkempt hair or plants have not been cut and kept neat

un·kind /ˌʌn'kaɪnd◂/ adj nasty, unpleasant, or cruel: A lot of unkind things were said. | [+to] Her husband is very unkind to her. —unkindly adv —unkindness n [U]

un·know·ing /ʌn'nəʊɪŋ $ -'noʊ-/ adj [only before noun] formal not realizing what you are doing or what is happening; ▤ unaware —unknowingly adv: She became ill after unknowingly taking an illegal drug.

un·known¹ W2 /ˌʌn'nəʊn◂ $ -'noʊn◂/ adj, adv
1 not known about: The murderer's identity remains unknown. | For some unknown reason, Mark quit his job and moved to Greece. | a voyage through unknown territory | An unknown number of people were killed.
2 not famous: an unknown artist
3 unknown to sb without someone knowing: Unknown to his wife, Ron had been having an affair.
4 be an unknown quantity if someone or something is

an unknown quantity, you do not know what their abilities are or how they are likely to behave

unknown² n [C] 1 someone who is not famous: At that point in her career she was still an unknown. 2 something that is not known: The long-term effects of the drug are still an unknown. 3 the unknown a) a place that is not known about or that has not been visited by humans: The astronauts began their journey into the unknown. b) things that you do not know or understand: a fear of the unknown

un·law·ful /ʌn'lɔ:fəl $ -'lɒ:-/ adj law not legal; ▤ illegal: The jury returned a verdict of unlawful killing. —unlawfully adv

un·lead·ed /ʌn'ledₗ₎d/ adj unleaded petrol does not contain any LEAD —unleaded n [U]: Ben's car only takes unleaded.

un·learn /ʌn'lɜ:n $ -ɜ:rn/ v past tense and past participle unlearned or unlearnt /-'lɜ:nt $ -'lɜ:rnt/ [T] informal to deliberately forget something you have learned, in order to change the way you do something: It's difficult to unlearn bad driving habits.

un·leash /ʌn'li:ʃ/ v [T] 1 to suddenly let a strong force, feeling etc have its full effect: Lefèvre's comments unleashed a wave of protest. 2 to let a dog run free after it has been held on a LEASH

un·leav·ened /ʌn'levənd/ adj unleavened bread is flat because it is not made with YEAST

un·less S1 W1 /ʌn'les, ən-/ conjunction
1 used to say that something will happen or be true if something else does not happen or is not true: Unless some extra money is found, the theatre will close. | I think you should complain – unless, of course, you are happy with the way things are. | He won't go to sleep unless you tell him a story. | I can't leave her unless I know she's all right. → see box at EXCEPT¹
2 not unless only if: 'Will you go with her?' 'Not unless she wants me to.'

un·let·tered /ʌn'letəd $ -ərd/ adj formal unable to read, or uneducated

un·li·censed /ʌn'laɪsənst/ adj without a LICENCE (=official document that gives you permission to do or have something): unlicensed guns

un·like¹ W3 /ʌn'laɪk/ prep
1 completely different from a particular person or thing: Tammy was unlike any other woman I have ever known.
2 not typical of someone at all: It's unlike Greg to be late.
3 used when saying how one person or thing is different from another: Unlike most people in the office, I don't come to work by car.
4 not unlike similar to: In appearance John is not unlike his brother. | The landscape is not unlike that of Scotland.

U

un·pro·voked /ˌʌnprəˈvəʊkt◂ $ -ˈvoʊkt◂ / adj unprovoked anger, attacks etc are directed at someone who has not done anything to deserve them: *It was a totally unprovoked attack on an innocent man.*

un·pub·lished /ʌnˈpʌblɪʃt/ adj unpublished writing, information etc has never been PUBLISHED

un·pun·ished /ʌnˈpʌnɪʃt/ adj **go unpunished** if someone or something bad they have done goes unpunished, they are not punished: *An attack like that cannot go unpunished.*

un·put·down·a·ble /ˌʌnpʊtˈdaʊnəbəl/ adj BrE an unputdownable book is very interesting and exciting – used humorously

un·qual·i·fied /ʌnˈkwɒlɪ̪faɪd $ -ˈkwɑː-/ adj **1** not having the right knowledge, experience, or education to do something: *unqualified staff* | [+for] *He was unqualified for the job.* | **unqualified to do sth** *I feel unqualified to advise you.* **2** [usually before noun] used for emphasizing that a quality is complete and total: *The experiment had not been an unqualified success.* | *He gave her his unqualified support.* ⚠ Do not confuse with **disqualified**, which means 'officially not allowed to do something': *She was disqualified from driving.*

un·quench·a·ble /ʌnˈkwentʃəbəl/ adj an unquenchable desire is one that is impossible to satisfy: *the seemingly unquenchable thirst* (=desire) *for Western art*

un·ques·tion·a·bly /ʌnˈkwestʃənəbli/ adv used to emphasize that something is certainly true: *The Eiffel Tower is unquestionably one of Paris's most familiar landmarks.* —**unquestionable** adj: *a man of unquestionable integrity*

un·ques·tioned /ʌnˈkwestʃənd/ adj something that is unquestioned is accepted or believed by everyone: *The whole approach is based on unquestioned assumptions.* | *an unquestioned right*

un·ques·tion·ing /ʌnˈkwestʃənɪŋ/ adj an unquestioning faith, attitude etc is very certain and without doubts: *an unquestioning belief in God* —**unquestioningly** adv

un·qui·et /ˌʌnˈkwaɪə̪t◂ / adj literary making you feel anxious

un·quote /ˌʌnˈkwəʊt $ -ˈkwoʊt/ adv → **quote** ... **unquote** at QUOTE[1] (7)

un·rav·el /ʌnˈrævəl/ v **unravelled, unravelling** BrE, **unraveled, unraveling** AmE **1** [T] to understand or explain something that is mysterious or complicated: *Detectives are still trying to unravel the mystery surrounding his death.* **2** [I,T] if you unravel threads, string etc, or if they unravel, they stop being twisted together **3** [I] if a system, plan, organization etc unravels, it starts to fail: *The company started to unravel when two of the directors were arrested.*

un·read /ˌʌnˈred◂ / adj unread books, papers etc have not been read

un·read·a·ble /ʌnˈriːdəbəl/ adj **1** if someone's expression or face is unreadable, you cannot tell what they are thinking **2** an unreadable book or piece of writing is difficult to read because it is boring or complicated **3** unreadable writing is so untidy that you cannot read it; ⊟ **illegible**

un·real /ˌʌnˈrɪəl◂ / adj **1** [not before noun] an experience, situation etc that is unreal seems so strange that you think you must be imagining it: *It seemed unreal to be sitting and talking to someone so famous.* **2** not related to real things that happen: *Many people go into marriage with unreal expectations.* **3** spoken very exciting; ⊟ **excellent**: *Our trip to Disneyland was unreal.* —**unreality** /ˌʌnriˈæli̪ti/ n [U]

un·rea·lis·tic /ˌʌnrɪəˈlɪstɪk◂ / adj unrealistic ideas or hopes are not reasonable or sensible: **it is unrealistic to do sth** *It is unrealistic to expect these changes to happen overnight.* | *Some parents have totally unrealistic expectations of teachers.* —**unrealistically** /-kli/ adv

un·real·ized also **-ised** BrE /ʌnˈrɪəlaɪzd/ adj **1** not achieved: *unrealized potential* **2** technical unrealized profits, losses etc have not been changed into a form that can be used as money

un·rea·son·a·ble /ʌnˈriːzənəbəl/ adj **1** not fair or sensible: *I think he's being unreasonable.* | *Don't let your boss make unreasonable demands on you.* | **it is unreasonable to do sth** *It's unreasonable to expect you to work seven days a week.* | *It's not unreasonable to ask him to help you.* **2** unreasonable prices, costs etc are too high —**unreasonably** adv: *unreasonably high prices*

un·rea·son·ing /ʌnˈriːzənɪŋ/ adj literary an unreasoning feeling is not based on facts or good reasons

un·rec·og·niz·a·ble also **-isable** BrE /ʌnˈrekəgnaɪzəbəl, -ˈrekə-/ adj someone or something that is unrecognizable has changed or been damaged so much that you do not recognize them: *I hadn't been to the city for 20 years and it was almost unrecognizable.*

un·rec·og·nized also **-ised** BrE /ʌnˈrekəgnaɪzd, -ˈrekə-/ adj **1** not having received praise or respect for something good you have achieved: *one of the great unrecognized jazzmen of the 1930s* **2** not noticed or not thought to be important: *an illness that can go unrecognized for years* **3** an unrecognized group, meeting, agreement etc is not considered to be legal or acceptable by someone in authority **4** doing something without people recognizing who you are: *He was able to walk down the street totally unrecognized.*

un·re·con·struct·ed /ˌʌnriːkənˈstrʌktɪ̪d/ adj not changing your ideas even though many people think they are old-fashioned

un·re·cord·ed /ˌʌnrɪˈkɔːdɪ̪d $ -ɔːr-/ adj not written down or recorded: *Many of the complaints have gone unrecorded.*

un·re·fined /ˌʌnrɪˈfaɪnd◂ / adj **1** an unrefined substance is in its natural form: *unrefined sugar* **2** formal not polite or educated

un·re·gis·tered /ʌnˈredʒɪ̪stəd $ -ərd/ adj not included on an official list: *unregistered land*

un·reg·u·lat·ed /ʌnˈregjʊleɪtɪ̪d/ adj not controlled by a government or law: *an unregulated banking system*

un·re·lat·ed /ˌʌnrɪˈleɪtɪ̪d◂ / adj **1** two things that are unrelated are not connected to each other in any way: *The police think that the two incidents are unrelated.* | [+to] *His illness is unrelated to the accident.* **2** people who are unrelated are not from the same family

un·re·lent·ing /ˌʌnrɪˈlentɪŋ◂ / adj formal **1** an unpleasant situation that is unrelenting continues for a long time without stopping: *the unrelenting pressures of the job* **2** continuing to do something in a determined way without thinking about anyone else's feelings: *an unrelenting opponent*

un·re·li·a·ble /ˌʌnrɪˈlaɪəbəl◂ / adj unable to be trusted or depended on: *The car's becoming very unreliable.* | *an unreliable witness*

un·re·lieved /ˌʌnrɪˈliːvd◂ / adj an unpleasant situation that is unrelieved continues for a long time because nothing happens to change it: *unrelieved pain*

un·re·mark·a·ble /ˌʌnrɪˈmɑːkəbəl $ -ɑːr-/ adj formal not very unusual or interesting: *He led a busy but otherwise unremarkable life.*

un·re·mit·ting /ˌʌnrɪˈmɪtɪŋ◂ / adj formal continuing for a long time and not likely to stop: *unremitting poverty* —**unremittingly** adv

un·re·peat·a·ble /ˌʌnrɪˈpiːtəbəl◂ / adj **1** too rude or offensive to repeat: *He said something unrepeatable.* **2** unable to be done again

un·re·pent·ant /ˌʌnrɪˈpentənt◂ / adj not ashamed of your behaviour or beliefs, even though other people disapprove: *He remains unrepentant about his comments.* —**unrepentantly** adv

un·re·port·ed /ˌʌnrɪ'pɔːtˈɪd◄ $ -'pɔːr-/ *adj* not told to the public or to someone in authority: *Rape is a crime that often goes unreported.*

un·rep·re·sen·ta·tive /ˌʌnreprɪ'zentətɪv/ *adj* not typical of a particular group of things or people: [+of] *opinions that are unrepresentative of the population*

un·re·quit·ed /ˌʌnrɪ'kwaɪtˈɪd◄/ *adj* unrequited love or other strong feeling is love etc that you feel for someone but that they do not feel for you

un·re·serv·ed·ly /ˌʌnrɪ'zɜːvˈɪdli $ -ɜːr-/ *adv* if you express a feeling or opinion unreservedly, you do it completely and without any doubts: *He apologized unreservedly.* —**unreserved** /-'zɜːvd◄ $ -ɜːr-/ *adj*

un·re·solved /ˌʌnrɪ'zɒlvd◄ $ -'zɑːlvd◄ , -'zɒːlvd◄/ *adj* an unresolved problem or question has not been answered or solved: *the unresolved issue of who will pay for the project* | *an unresolved conflict*

un·res·pon·sive /ˌʌnrɪ'spɒnsɪv $ -'spɑːn-/ *adj* not reacting to something or not affected by it: [+to] *The disease is totally unresponsive to conventional treatment.* | *His warning fell on unresponsive ears* (=was not listened to).

un·rest /ʌn'rest/ *n* [U] a political situation in which people protest or behave violently: *There is growing unrest throughout the country.* | **political/social/industrial etc unrest** *The protests were the biggest show of social unrest since the government came to power.*

un·re·strained /ˌʌnrɪ'streɪnd◄/ *adj* not controlled or limited: *unrestrained power*

un·res·trict·ed /ˌʌnrɪ'strɪktˈɪd◄/ *adj* not limited by anyone or anything: **unrestricted access** *to information*

un·re·ward·ed /ˌʌnrɪ'wɔːdˈɪd◄ $ -'wɔːr-/ *adj* not achieving what you want to achieve: *His efforts have not gone unrewarded.*

un·ripe /ˌʌn'raɪp◄/ *adj* unripe fruit, grain etc is not fully developed or ready to be eaten

un·ri·valled *BrE*; **unrivaled** *AmE* /ʌn'raɪvəld/ *adj* formal better than any other: *an unrivalled collection of Chinese art*

un·roll /ʌn'rəʊl $ -'roʊl/ *v* [I,T] to open something that was in the shape of a ball or tube, and make it flat, or to become open in this way: *He unrolled the carpet.*

un·ruf·fled /ʌn'rʌfəld/ *adj* calm and not upset by a difficult situation – use this to show approval: *Emily remained completely unruffled by the chaos.*

un·ru·ly /ʌn'ruːli/ *adj* **1** violent or difficult to control; ☐ **wild**: *unruly children* | *unruly behaviour* **2** unruly hair is difficult to keep tidy —**unruliness** *n* [U]

un·sad·dle /ʌn'sædl/ *v* [T] to remove the SADDLE (=leather seat) from a horse

un·safe /ˌʌn'seɪf◄/ *adj* **1** dangerous or likely to cause harm: *The building is unsafe.* | *water that's unsafe to drink* **2** likely to be harmed: *Many people feel unsafe walking alone at night.* **3** *BrE* an unsafe judgment in a court of law is based on facts that may be wrong: *an unsafe conviction* **4 unsafe sex** sex without using a CONDOM

un·said /ʌn'sed/ *adv* **be left unsaid** if something is left unsaid, you do not say it although you might be thinking it: *Some things are better left unsaid* (=it is better not to mention them).

un·san·i·ta·ry /ʌn'sænˈɪtəri $ -teri/ *adj* dirty and likely to cause disease; ☐ **insanitary**: *unsanitary conditions*

un·sat·is·fac·to·ry /ʌnˌsætˈɪs'fæktəri/ *adj* not good enough or not acceptable: *an unsatisfactory situation*

un·sat·is·fied /ʌn'sætˈɪsfaɪd/ *adj* **1** an unsatisfied demand, request etc has not been dealt with: *an unsatisfied demand for graduates* **2** not pleased because you want something to be better: *unsatisfied consumers*
→ DISSATISFIED

un·sa·tu·rat·ed /ʌn'sætʃəreɪtˈɪd/ *adj* unsaturated fats or oils usually come from plants rather than animals and are better for your health

un·sa·vour·y *BrE*; **unsavory** *AmE* /ʌn'seɪvəri/ *adj* unpleasant or morally unacceptable: *The club has an unsavoury reputation.* | *There were a lot of unsavoury characters* (=unpleasant people) *around the station.*

un·scathed /ʌn'skeɪðd/ *adj* [not before noun] not injured or harmed by something: **escape/emerge unscathed** *He escaped unscathed from the accident.* | *The government was relatively unscathed by the scandal.*

un·sched·uled /ʌn'ʃedjuːld $ ʌn'skedʒəld/ *adj* not planned or expected: *The plane made an unscheduled stop in New York.*

un·sci·en·tif·ic /ˌʌnsaɪən'tɪfɪk/ *adj* not based on facts or the usual scientific methods of doing something: *unscientific ideas*

un·scram·ble /ʌn'skræmbəl/ *v* [T] **1** to change a television SIGNAL or a message that has been sent in CODE (=a deliberately confusing way) so that it can be seen or read **2** to make a confusing situation or confusing feelings easier to understand

un·screw /ʌn'skruː/ *v* [T] **1** to open something by twisting it **2** to take the screws out of something

un·script·ed /ˌʌn'skrɪptˈɪd◄/ *adj* an unscripted broadcast, speech etc is not written or planned before it is made

un·scru·pu·lous /ʌn'skruːpjˈələs/ *adj* behaving in an unfair or dishonest way: *unscrupulous employers* —**unscrupulously** *adv*

un·sea·son·a·bly /ʌn'siːzˈənəbli/ *adv* **unseasonably warm/cold/hot etc** used for saying that the weather is warmer, colder etc than usual at a particular time of year —**unseasonable** *adj*

un·seat /ʌn'siːt/ *v* [T] **1** to remove someone from a powerful job or position: *an attempt to unseat the party leader* **2** if a horse unseats someone, it throws them off its back

un·se·cured /ˌʌnsɪ'kjʊəd◄ $ -'kjʊrd◄/ *adj* an unsecured debt or LOAN is one that does not make you promise to give the bank something you own if you cannot pay it back

un·seed·ed /ˌʌn'siːdˈɪd◄/ *adj* not chosen as a SEED (=someone with a numbered rank in a competition), especially in a tennis competition

un·see·ing /ˌʌn'siːɪŋ◄/ *adj* literary not noticing anything even though your eyes are open: *Jack gazed unseeing out of the window.* —**unseeingly** *adv*

un·seem·ly /ʌn'siːmli/ *adj* formal unseemly behaviour is not polite or not suitable for a particular occasion: *Ann thought it unseemly to kiss her husband in public.*

un·seen[1] /ˌʌn'siːn◄/ *adj* formal not noticed or seen: *Raj crept out of the house unseen.* | *unseen dangers* → **sight unseen** at SIGHT[1] (17)

un·seen[2] /ʌn'siːn/ *n* [C] *BrE* a piece of writing that you must translate into your own language in an examination

un·self·ish /ʌn'selfɪʃ/ *adj* caring about other people and thinking about their needs and wishes before your own; ☐ **selfless, generous** —**unselfishly** *adv* —**unselfishness** *n* [U]

un·set·tle /ʌn'setl/ *v* [T] to make someone feel slightly nervous, worried, or upset: *The sudden changes unsettled Judy.*

un·set·tled /ʌn'setld/ *adj*

1 SITUATION making people feel uncertain about what will happen: *difficult and unsettled times*

2 FEELING slightly worried, upset, or nervous: *Children often feel unsettled if their parents divorce.*

3 ARGUMENT OR DISAGREEMENT still continuing without reaching any agreement: *The dispute remains unsettled.*

4 WEATHER changing a lot in a short period of time
5 LAND unsettled land has never had people living on it; → **settler**
6 DEBT an unsettled debt or bill has not been paid
7 STOMACH feeling slightly sick: *My stomach's a bit unsettled after all that rich food.*

un·set·tling /ʌnˈsetlɪŋ/ *adj* making you feel nervous or worried: *an unsettling experience*

un·shake·a·ble, unshakable /ʌnˈʃeɪkəbəl/ *adj* an unshakeable faith, belief etc is very strong and cannot be changed or destroyed

un·shak·en /ʌnˈʃeɪkən/ *adj formal* not having changed your attitude or belief: [+in] *He remained unshaken in his belief that she was wrong.*

un·shav·en /ʌnˈʃeɪvən/ *adj* a man who is unshaven has very short hairs growing on his face because he has not SHAVED

un·sight·ly /ʌnˈsaɪtli/ *adj* ugly or unpleasant to look at: *unsightly buildings* | *unsightly marks*

un·signed /ˌʌnˈsaɪnd◂/ *adj* **1** an unsigned letter or document has not been signed with someone's name **2** an unsigned sports player or musician has not yet signed a contract to play for a sports team or record music for a company

un·skilled /ˌʌnˈskɪld◂/ *adj* **1** an unskilled worker has not been trained for a particular type of job: *companies employing unskilled labour* (=people who have no special training) **2** unskilled work, jobs etc do not need people with special skills

un·smil·ing /ʌnˈsmaɪlɪŋ/ *adj literary* looking serious and unfriendly: *an unsmiling face*

un·so·cia·ble /ʌnˈsəʊʃəbəl $ -soʊ-/ *adj* not wanting to be with people or to go to social events → UNSOCIAL

un·so·cial /ˌʌnˈsəʊʃəl◂ $ -soʊ-/ also **unsociable** *adj* **work unsocial hours** to work during the night or early in the morning when most people do not have to work

un·so·lic·it·ed /ˌʌnsəˈlɪsɪtɪd◂/ *adj* not asked for and often not wanted: *unsolicited calls* | *unsolicited advice*

un·solved /ˌʌnˈsɒlvd◂ $ -ˈsɑːlvd◂, -ˈsɒːlvd◂/ *adj* a problem, mystery, or crime that is unsolved has never been solved: *The murder still remains unsolved.*

un·so·phis·ti·cat·ed /ˌʌnsəˈfɪstɪkeɪtɪd◂/ *adj* **1** not having much knowledge or experience of modern and fashionable things: *an unsophisticated audience* **2** unsophisticated tools, methods, or processes are simple and do not have all the features of more modern ones; ▤ **crude**

un·sound /ˌʌnˈsaʊnd◂/ *adj* **1** not based on facts or good reasons: **ideologically/scientifically/ecologically etc unsound** *a test that's scientifically unsound* **2** an unsound building or structure is in bad condition: *The houses are structurally unsound.* **3** *formal* physically or mentally ill: *people of unsound mind* (=people who are mentally ill)

un·speak·a·ble /ʌnˈspiːkəbəl/ *adj* **1** used for emphasizing how bad someone or something is: *an unspeakable tragedy* **2** *literary* unspeakable feelings are so extreme that it is impossible to describe them: *unspeakable joy* —**unspeakably** *adv*

un·spe·ci·fied /ʌnˈspesɪfaɪd/ *adj* not known or not stated: *The meeting will take place at an unspecified date in the future.*

un·spoiled /ˌʌnˈspɔɪld◂/ also **un·spoilt** /ˌʌnˈspɔɪlt◂/ *BrE adj* **1** an unspoiled place is beautiful because it has not changed for a long time and does not have a lot of new buildings: *unspoiled countryside* **2** someone who is unspoiled has not changed in spite of the good or bad things that have happened to them: *She remained unspoilt by her success.*

un·spok·en /ʌnˈspəʊkən $ -ˈspoʊ-/ *adj* **1** an unspoken agreement, rule etc has not been discussed but is understood by everyone in a group: *an unspoken assumption* **2** not said for other people to hear: *unspoken questions*

un·sport·ing /ʌnˈspɔːtɪŋ $ -ˈspɔːr-/ *adj* behaving in an unfair way, especially towards an opponent in a game or competition

un·sta·ble /ʌnˈsteɪbəl/ *adj* **1** likely to change suddenly and become worse; → **instability**: *The political situation is still very unstable.* | *an unstable relationship* **2** something that is unstable is likely to move or fall **3** someone who is unstable changes very suddenly so that you do not know how they will react or behave: *a mentally unstable man* **4** an unstable chemical is likely to separate into simpler substances

un·stat·ed /ʌnˈsteɪtɪd/ *adj* not expressed in words: *unstated assumptions*

un·stead·y /ʌnˈstedi/ *adj* **1** shaking or moving in a way you cannot control: *He poured the coffee with a very unsteady hand.* | *a baby's first unsteady steps* | *She was quite unsteady on her feet* (=she might fall over). **2** showing that you are nervous: *Her voice was unsteady.* | *She took a deep unsteady breath.* **3** an unsteady object is not balanced very well and could fall: *an unsteady ladder* **4** an unsteady situation, relationship etc could change or end at any time: *an unsteady peace* —**unsteadily** *adv* —**unsteadiness** *n* [U]

un·stint·ing /ʌnˈstɪntɪŋ/ *adj formal* unstinting support, help, praise etc is complete and given willingly —**unstintingly** *adv*

un·stop·pa·ble /ʌnˈstɒpəbəl $ -ˈstɑːp-/ *adj* unable to be stopped: *Once Janet gets an idea, she's unstoppable.*

un·stressed /ˌʌnˈstrest◂/ *adj* an unstressed word or part of a word is pronounced with less force than other ones

un·struc·tured /ʌnˈstrʌktʃəd $ -ərd/ *adj* not organized in a detailed way, and allowing people freedom to do what they want: *unstructured interviews*

un·stuck /ʌnˈstʌk◂/ *adj* **come unstuck a)** *BrE informal* if a person, plan, or system comes unstuck, they fail at what they were trying to achieve: *a dangerous area of rock where many climbers come unstuck* **b)** if something comes unstuck, it becomes separated from the thing that it was stuck to

un·sub·stan·ti·at·ed /ˌʌnsəbˈstænʃieɪtɪd/ *adj* not proved to be true: *unsubstantiated allegations of child abuse*

un·suc·cess·ful /ˌʌnsəkˈsesfəl◂/ *adj* not having a successful result or not achieving what you wanted to achieve: *an unsuccessful attempt to climb Everest* | **unsuccessful in (doing) sth** *We have been unsuccessful in finding a new manager.* —**unsuccessfully** *adv*: *We tried unsuccessfully to make them change their decision.*

un·suit·a·ble /ʌnˈsuːtəbəl, -ˈsjuː- $ -ˈsuː-/ *adj* not having the right qualities for a particular person, purpose, or situation; ▤ **inappropriate**: *unsuitable housing* | [+for] *The book is unsuitable for children.*

un·suit·ed /ʌnˈsuːtɪd, -ˈsjuː- $ -ˈsuː-/ *adj* [not before noun] **1** not having the right qualities for a particular job or purpose: [+to/for] *He was unsuited for the job.* | *old school buildings unsuited to modern education* **2** *BrE* two people who are unsuited are unlikely to have a successful romantic relationship because they have very different characters and interests: *I now realize that Tom and I were totally unsuited.*

un·sul·lied /ʌnˈsʌlid/ *adj literary* not spoiled by anything

un·sung /ˌʌnˈsʌŋ◂/ *adj* not praised or famous for something you have done, although you deserve to be: *one of the unsung heroes of French politics*

un·sure /ˌʌnˈʃʊə◂ $ -ˈʃʊr◂/ *adj* **1** not certain about something or about what you have to do: [+of/about] *I was unsure of the reaction I would get.* | *If you are unsure about anything, just ask.* | **unsure whether/what etc** *Peter was unsure what to do next.* **2** **unsure of yourself** not having enough confidence: *Chris seemed nervous and unsure of herself.*

un·sur·passed /ˌʌnsə'pɑːst◂ $ -sər'pæst◂/ adj better or greater than anyone or anything else: *an unsurpassed knowledge of Greek history*

un·sur·pris·ing /ˌʌnsə'praɪzɪŋ◂ $ -sər-/ adj not making you feel surprised: *It's unsurprising that the project failed.* | *an enjoyable but unsurprising album* —**unsurprisingly** adv

un·sus·pect·ing /ˌʌnsə'spektɪŋ◂/ adj [usually before noun] not knowing that something bad is happening or going to happen: *unsuspecting victims* | *Fake designer clothes are being sold to an unsuspecting public.*

un·sus·tain·a·ble /ˌʌnsə'steɪnəbəl/ adj unable to continue at the same rate or in the same way: *unsustainable economic growth*

un·sweet·ened /ʌn'swiːtnd/ adj unsweetened food or drink has not had sugar added to it

un·swerv·ing /ʌn'swɜːvɪŋ $ -ɜːr-/ adj an unswerving belief or attitude is one that is very strong and never changes: **unswerving loyalty/commitment/support etc** *a politician with unswerving loyalty to the President*

un·sym·pa·thet·ic /ˌʌnsɪmpə'θetɪk◂/ adj **1** not kind or helpful to someone who is having problems **2** not willing to support an idea, aim etc: [+to/ towards] *a government that's unsympathetic to public opinion* **3** an unsympathetic person in a book or play is unpleasant and difficult to like: *an unsympathetic character* —**unsympathetically** /-kli/ adv

un·taint·ed /ʌn'teɪntɪd/ adj formal not affected or influenced by something bad: [+by] *a politician untainted by corruption*

un·tamed /ˌʌn'teɪmd◂/ adj **1** untamed land is still in its natural state and has not been developed by people **2** an untamed animal has not been trained to live or work with people; **⊟ wild**

un·tan·gle /ˌʌn'tæŋgəl/ v [T] **1** to separate pieces of string, wire etc that are twisted together **2** to make something less complicated: *The research attempts to untangle some of these issues.*

un·tapped /ˌʌn'tæpt◂/ adj an untapped supply, market, or TALENT is available but has not yet been used: *Older people are an untapped resource in the employment market.* | *We believe there is untapped potential.*

un·ten·a·ble /ʌn'tenəbəl/ adj formal **1** an untenable situation has become so difficult that it is impossible to continue: *The scandal put the President in an untenable position.* **2** an untenable argument, suggestion etc is impossible to defend

un·tested /ʌn'testɪd/ adj **1** untested ideas, methods, or people have not been used in a particular situation so you do not know what they are like: *an argument based on untested assumptions* **2** an untested drug, medical treatment etc has not been given any scientific tests to discover if it is safe to use

un·think·a·ble /ʌn'θɪŋkəbəl/ adj **1** impossible to accept or imagine: *It is unthinkable that a mistake like this could have happened.* | **it would be unthinkable for sb to do sth** *It would be unthinkable for me to stay anywhere but with the family.* **2 the unthinkable** something that is impossible to accept or imagine: *Then the unthinkable happened and the boat started to sink.* | *It was the job of the committee to think the unthinkable* (=plan for unexpected events or situations).

un·think·ing /ʌn'θɪŋkɪŋ/ adj not thinking about the effects of something you say or do —**unthinkingly** adv

un·ti·dy /ʌn'taɪdi/ adj especially BrE **1** not neat; **⊟ messy**: *an untidy desk* | *untidy hair* | *Her clothes were in an untidy heap on the floor.* **2** someone who is untidy does not keep their house, possessions etc neat; **⊟ messy** —**untidily** adv —**untidiness** n [U]

un·tie /ʌn'taɪ/ v untied, untying [T] to take the knots out of something, or unfasten something that has been tied: *Peter untied his shoelaces.* → see picture at UNDRESS

un·til S1 W1 /ʌn'tɪl, ən-/ prep, conjunction **1** if something happens until a particular time, it continues and then stops at that time: *The ticket is valid until March.* | *He waited until she had finished*

speaking. | *Until recently, Anna worked as a teacher in Japan.* | *Up until last year, they didn't even own a car.* ⚠ **Until** and **till** have the same meaning. **Till** is more usual in spoken English, and is not used in formal writing: *Tom waited until he saw the flag.* | *I'll sit here till you get back.* **2 not until** used to emphasize that something does not happen before a certain point in time or before something else has happened: *'Can I go out and play now?' 'Not until you've done your homework.'* | *It was not until 1972 that the war finally came to an end.*

un·time·ly /ʌn'taɪmli/ adj **1** happening too soon or sooner than you expected: *the untimely death of a popular local man* | *The announcement brought the meeting to an untimely end.* **2** not suitable for a particular occasion or time: *an untimely interruption*

un·tir·ing /ʌn'taɪərɪŋ $ -'taɪr-/ adj working very hard for a long period of time in order to do something – used to show approval; **⊟ tireless**: *untiring efforts to help the homeless*

un·ti·tled /ʌn'taɪtld/ adj an untitled song, painting etc has not been given a title

un·to /'ʌntu:/ prep old use to: *Thanks be unto God.*

un·told /ˌʌn'təʊld◂ $ -'toʊld◂/ adj [only before noun] **1** used to emphasize how bad something is: *The rumours will do untold damage to his reputation.* | *The floods have caused untold misery to hundreds of homeowners.* **2** used to emphasize that an amount or quantity is very large: **untold riches/wealth** *a game that offers untold wealth to the most talented players*

un·touch·a·ble /ʌn'tʌtʃəbəl/ adj **1** someone who is untouchable is in such a strong position that they cannot be defeated, affected, or punished: *He was the boss's husband and therefore untouchable.* **2** belonging to the lowest social group, especially in the Hindu CASTE system —**untouchable** n [C]

un·touched /ˌʌn'tʌtʃt◂/ adj **1** not changed, damaged, or affected in any way: [+by] *an island that has been untouched by time* **2** not touched, moved, or eaten: *Several papers lay untouched on the desk.*

un·to·ward /ˌʌntə'wɔːd $ ʌn'tɔːrd/ adj formal unexpected, unusual, or not wanted: **anything/nothing untoward** *I walked past but didn't notice anything untoward.*

un·trained /ˌʌn'treɪnd◂/ adj **1** not trained to do something: *untrained staff* **2 to the untrained eye/ear** when someone who does not have special knowledge of a subject looks at something or listens to it: *To the untrained eye, the two flowers look remarkably similar.*

un·tram·melled BrE; **untrammeled** AmE /ʌn'træməld/ adj formal not limited by anyone or anything: [+by] *an organization untrammelled by legal restraints*

un·treat·ed /ʌn'triːtɪd/ adj **1** an untreated illness or injury has not had medical treatment **2** harmful substances that are untreated have not been made safe: *untreated sewage* **3** untreated wood has not had any substances put on it to preserve it

un·tried /ˌʌn'traɪd◂/ adj **1** not having any experience of doing a particular job: *a young and untried minister* **2** something that is untried has not been tested to see whether it is successful: *untried and untested ways to make money*

un·true /ʌn'truː/ adj **1** not based on facts that are correct; **⊟ false**: *allegations that are totally untrue* | *It's untrue to say that the situation has not changed.* **2** literary someone who is untrue to their husband, wife etc is not faithful to them; **⊟ unfaithful**

un·trust·wor·thy /ʌn'trʌst,wɜːði $ -,wɜːr-/ adj someone who is untrustworthy cannot be trusted

un·truth /ʌn'truːθ, 'ʌntruːθ/ n [C] formal a lie – used when you want to avoid saying the word 'lie'

un·truth·ful /ʌn'truːθfəl/ adj dishonest or not true —**untruthfully** adv

un·tu·tored /ʌnˈtjuːtəd $ -ˈtuːtərd/ adj formal not having been taught to do something: **to the untutored eye/ear/mind** To the untutored ear, this music sounds as if it might have been written by Beethoven.

un·typ·i·cal /ʌnˈtɪpɪkəl/ adj not having the usual features or qualities that you would expect; → **atypical**: [+of] a building that is quite untypical of the period in which it was built | These problems are **not untypical** (=they are normal). —**untypically** /-kli/ adv

un·us·a·ble /ʌnˈjuːzəbəl/ adj something that is unusable is in such a bad condition that you cannot use it

un·used¹ /ˌʌnˈjuːzd◂/ adj not being used, or never used: unused land

un·used² /ˌʌnˈjuːst◂/ adj **unused to (doing) sth** not experienced in dealing with something: a sensitive man unused to publicity | Maggie was unused to being told what to do.

un·u·su·al S2 W3 /ʌnˈjuːʒuəl, -ʒəl/ adj different from what is usual or normal: an unusual feature | unusual circumstances | **It's unusual for** Dave to be late. | **It's not unusual** (=it is quite common) to feel very angry in a situation like this.

> **WORD CHOICE: unusual, strange, odd, bizarre, extraordinary, exceptional, remarkable**
> **Unusual** is neither approving nor disapproving: a suit made of unusual material | an unusual name | Her response was unusual.
> **Strange** and **odd** mean unusual in a way that you cannot understand. They are sometimes used to show slight disapproval or distrust: a very strange man | I found his attitude a bit odd.
> **Bizarre** means very unusual, especially in a way that you think is amusing or that is hard to believe: a bizarre haircut
> **Extraordinary** can be approving or disapproving, but suggests approval when it is used to describe a person: What an extraordinary idea! (can suggest you strongly disagree): My mother was an extraordinary woman (=very impressive, talented etc).
> **Exceptional** and **remarkable** often mean unusually good or impressive: a writer of exceptional talent | a remarkable film

un·u·su·al·ly /ʌnˈjuːʒuəli, -ʒəli/ adv **1** unusually high/large/quiet etc higher, larger etc than usual: unusually high levels of pollution **2** used to say that something is not what usually happens: Unusually for me, I fell asleep very quickly.

un·ut·ter·a·ble /ʌnˈʌtərəbəl/ adj literary an unutterable feeling is too extreme to be expressed in words —**unutterably** adv

un·var·nished /ʌnˈvɑːnɪʃt $ -ɑːr-/ adj **1** [only before noun] simple and without any additional descriptions or details: an unvarnished account of events **2** not covered with VARNISH (=a transparent substance like paint, used to protect the surface of wood)

un·veil /ʌnˈveɪl/ v [T] **1** to show or tell people about a new product or plan for the first time: The club has unveiled plans to build a new stadium. **2** to remove the cover from something, especially as part of a formal ceremony: The statue was unveiled by the Queen. —**unveiling** n [C]

un·voiced /ˌʌnˈvɔɪst◂/ adj **1** not expressed in words: unvoiced fears **2** technical unvoiced CONSONANTS are produced without moving your VOCAL CORDS. /d/ and /g/ are voiced consonants, and /t/ and /k/ are unvoiced.

un·waged /ˌʌnˈweɪdʒd◂/ adj BrE not having a job that you get paid for

un·want·ed /ʌnˈwɒntɪd $ -ˈwɒːnt-, -ˈwɑːnt-/ adj not wanted or needed: an unwanted pregnancy

un·war·rant·ed /ʌnˈwɒrəntɪd $ -ˈwɔː-, -ˈwɑː-/ adj done without good reason, and therefore annoying: unwarranted interference

un·wa·ry /ʌnˈweəri $ -ˈweri/ adj formal **1** not knowing about possible problems or dangers, and therefore easily harmed or deceived: unwary travellers **2 the unwary** [plural] people who are unwary: pitfalls that can trap the unwary

un·washed /ˌʌnˈwɒʃt◂ $ -ˈwɒːʃt◂, -ˈwɑːʃt◂/ adj **1** dirty and needing to be washed: unwashed cups **2 the great unwashed** humorous people who are poor and have not been educated

un·wa·ver·ing /ʌnˈweɪvərɪŋ/ adj an unwavering attitude, belief, expression etc does not change: an unwavering stare | unwavering support —**unwaveringly** adv

un·wel·come /ʌnˈwelkəm/ adj **1** something that is unwelcome is not wanted, especially because it might cause embarrassment or problems: unwelcome publicity | unwelcome news **2** unwelcome guests, visitors etc are people who you do not want in your home

un·well /ʌnˈwel/ adj [not before noun] formal ill, especially for a short time: She had been feeling unwell. → see box at SICK¹

un·wield·y /ʌnˈwiːldi/ adj **1** an unwieldy object is big, heavy, and difficult to carry or use **2** an unwieldy system, argument, or organization is difficult to control or manage because it is too complicated: unwieldy bureaucracy —**unwieldiness** n [U]

un·will·ing /ʌnˈwɪlɪŋ/ adj **1** [not before noun] not wanting to do something and refusing to do it: **unwilling to do sth** He was unwilling or unable to pay the fine. **2** [only before noun] not wanting to do something but doing it: an unwilling helper —**unwillingly** adv —**unwillingness** n [U]

un·wind /ʌnˈwaɪnd/ v past tense and past participle **unwound** /-ˈwaʊnd/ **1** [I] to relax and stop feeling anxious: a beautiful country hotel that is the perfect place to unwind **2** [I,T] to undo something that has been wrapped around something else, or to become undone after being wrapped around something: She started to unwind her scarf.

un·wise /ˌʌnˈwaɪz◂/ adj not based on good judgment: **(it is) unwise to do sth** It's unwise to keep medicines in a place that can be reached by children. —**unwisely** adv

un·wit·ting·ly /ʌnˈwɪtɪŋli/ adv in a way that shows you do not know or realize something: Friedmann had unwittingly broken the law. —**unwitting** adj [only before noun]: an unwitting accomplice

un·wont·ed /ʌnˈwəʊntɪd $ -ˈwoʊn-/ adj [only before noun] formal unusual and not what you expect to happen: unwonted freedom

un·work·a·ble /ʌnˈwɜːkəbəl $ -ɜːr-/ adj an unworkable plan, system, law etc is not likely to be successful

un·world·ly /ʌnˈwɜːldli $ -ɜːr-/ adj **1** not interested in money or possessions **2** not having a lot of experience of life; ☐ naive **3** unusual and having qualities that do not seem to belong to this world: unworldly beauty

un·wor·thy /ʌnˈwɜːði $ -ɜːr-/ adj formal **1** not deserving respect, attention etc: [+of] an idea that's unworthy of serious consideration **2** unworthy behaviour, attitudes etc are not acceptable from someone who is respected or who has an important job: [+of] a suggestion that's unworthy of someone who hopes to become President —**unworthiness** n [U]

un·wound /ʌnˈwaʊnd/ the past tense and past participle of UNWIND

un·wrap /ʌnˈræp/ v **unwrapped**, **unwrapping** [T] to remove the paper, plastic etc that is around something: Brigitte was unwrapping her birthday presents.

un·writ·ten /ʌnˈrɪtn/ adj an unwritten rule, law, agreement etc is one that everyone knows about although it is not official: unwritten rules of social behaviour

un·yield·ing /ʌnˈjiːldɪŋ/ adj **1** formal not willing to change your ideas or beliefs: an unyielding resistance to change **2** literary very hard and not changing in shape or form: a harsh unyielding landscape

un·zip /ʌnˈzɪp/ v **unzipped, unzipping** [T] **1** to unfasten the ZIP on a bag, piece of clothing etc → see picture at **UNDRESS 2** to make a computer FILE its normal size again so that you can use it, after it has been made to use less space

up¹ [S1] [W1] /ʌp/ adv, prep, adj
1 TO A HIGHER POSITION towards a higher place or position; ◼ **down**: *We walked slowly up the hill.* | *She picked her jacket up off the floor.* | *paths leading up into the mountains* | *Tim had climbed up a tree to get a better view.* | *Put up your hand if you know the answer.* | *The water was getting up my nose.* | *Karen lay on her back, staring up at the ceiling.*
2 IN A HIGHER POSITION in a higher place or position; ◼ **down**: *John's up in his bedroom.* | *a plane flying 30,000 feet up* | *Her office is just up those stairs.* | *The doctor's assistant was up a ladder in the stockroom.*
3 TO BE UPRIGHT into an upright or raised position: *Everyone stood up for the national anthem.* | *Mick turned his collar up against the biting winds.*
4 ALONG in or to a place that is further along something such as a road or path; ◼ **down**: *She lives just up the street.* | *We walked up the road towards the church.*
5 NORTH in or towards the north: *They live up north.* | *We're driving up to Chicago for the conference.* | *a stormy voyage up the east coast from Miami to Boston*
6 CLOSE very close to someone or something: *A man came up and offered to buy him a drink.* | [+to] *She drove right up to the front door.* | [+against] *The bed was up against the wall.*
7 TO MORE IMPORTANT PLACE used to show that the place someone goes to is more important than the place they start from: *Have you been up to London recently?*
8 RIVER towards the place where a river starts; ◼ **down**: *sailing up the Thames* | *The river steamers only went up as far as Mandalay.*
9 MORE at or towards a higher level or a greater amount; ◼ **down**: *Turn up the radio.* | *Violent crime went up by 9% last year.* | *Inflation is up by 2%.* | [+on] *Profits are up on last year.*
10 WINNING BrE beating your opponent by a certain number of points; ◼ **down: two goals up/three points up** etc *United were a goal up at half time.*
11 NOT IN BED not in bed: *Are the kids still up?* | *They stayed up all night to watch the game.* | *It's time to get up* (=get out of bed). | *It's good to see you up and about again* (=out of bed after an illness and moving around normally).
12 FINISHING used after certain verbs to show that something is completely finished, used, or removed: *We've used up all our savings.* | *The children had to eat up all their food.* | *After a month, the wound had almost healed up.*
13 CUTTING/DIVIDING used after certain verbs to show that something is cut, divided etc into pieces or divided into parts: *Why did you tear up that letter?* | *We still haven't decided how to divide up the money.*
14 COLLECTING used after certain verbs to show that things are collected together: *Let's just add up these figures quickly.* | *Could you collect up the papers?*
15 PART ON TOP used to say which surface or part of an object should be on top: *Put the playing cards right side up.* | *Isn't that painting the wrong way up?*
16 ABOVE A LEVEL above and including a certain level, age, or amount: *All the women were naked from the waist up.* | *Children aged 12 and up must pay the full fare.*
17 up and down a) backwards and forwards: *Ralph paced up and down the room, looking worried.* **b)** if someone is up and down, they sometimes feel well or happy and sometimes do not: *Jason's been very up and down since his girlfriend left him.* **c)** to a higher position and then a lower position, several times: *They were all jumping up and down and screaming excitedly.* | *Shivers ran up and down my body.* | **look sb up and down** (=look at someone in order to judge their appearance or character) *Maisie looked her rival up*

and down with a critical eye.
18 up to sth a) as much or as many as a certain amount or number but not more: *The Olympic Stadium will hold up to 80,000 spectators.* | *a process that can take anything up to ten days* **b)** also **up till** for the whole of a period until a certain time or date: *She continued to care for her father up to the time of his death.* | *We've kept our meetings secret up to now.* **c)** [in questions and negatives] clever, good, or well enough to do something: *I'm afraid Tim just isn't up to the job* (=he does not have the necessary ability). | *You don't need to go back to school if you don't feel up to it.* | **up to doing sth** *He's not really up to seeing any visitors.* **d)** if something is up to a particular standard, it is good enough to reach that standard: *I didn't think last night's performance was up to her usual standard.* **e)** spoken doing something secret or something that you should not be doing: *The children are very quiet. I wonder what they're up to.* | *He knew Bailey was up to something. But what?* | *I always suspected that he was up to no good* (=doing something bad).
19 be up to sb a) used to say that someone can decide about something: *You can pay weekly or monthly – it's up to you.* **b)** used to say that someone is responsible for a particular duty: *It's up to the travel companies to warn customers of any possible dangers.*
20 FINISHED TIME if a period of time is up, it is finished: *I'm sorry, we'll have to stop there. Our time is up.*
21 ROAD REPAIRS if a road is up, its surface is being repaired
22 COMPUTER if a computer system is up, it is working; ◼ **down**: *There could well be a few problems before your new computer is up and running properly.*
23 up against sth/sb having to deal with a difficult situation or opponent: *He came up against a lot of problems with his boss.* | *Murphy will be really up against it when he faces the champion this afternoon.*
24 up for sth a) available for a particular process: *The house is up for sale.* | *This week 14 of Campbell's paintings were put up for auction.* | *Even the most taboo subjects were up for discussion.* **b)** being considered for election or for a job: *Senator Frank Church was coming up for re-election that year.* | *She is one of five candidates up for the chief executive's job.* **c)** appearing in a court of law because you have been ACCUSED of a crime: *Ron's up for drinking and driving next week.* **d)** spoken willing to do something or interested in doing something: *We're going to the pub later – are you up for it?*
25 something is up spoken if something is up, someone is feeling unhappy because they have problems, or there is something wrong in a situation: *I could tell by the look on his face that something was up.* | [+with] *Something up with Julie? She looks really miserable.* | **what's up?** *What's up? Why are you crying?*
26 be well up in/on sth informal also **be up on sth** AmE to know a lot about something: *I'm not all that well up in musical matters.* | *Conrad's really up on his geography, isn't he?*
27 be up before sth/sb informal to appear in a court of law because you have been ACCUSED of a crime: *He was up before the magistrates' court charged with dangerous driving.*
28 be up to here BrE also **have had it up to here** spoken to be very upset and angry because of a particular situation or person: [+with] *I'm up to here with this job; I'm resigning!*
29 up the workers!/up the reds! etc BrE spoken used to express support and encouragement for a particular group of people or for a sports team
30 up yours! spoken not polite used as a very rude and offensive reply to someone who has said something that annoys you: *'You're not allowed to park here.' 'Up yours, mate!'* → **not be up to much** at MUCH² (8)

up² n **1 ups and downs** informal the mixture of good and bad experiences that happen in any situation or relationship: *We have our ups and downs like all couples.* **2 be on the up** *BrE spoken* to be improving or increasing: *Business confidence is on the up.* **3 be on the up and up a)** *BrE informal* to be becoming more successful: *a brilliant young player who is on the up and up* **b)** *AmE spoken* if a person or business is on the up and up, they are honest and do things legally

up³ *v* **upped, upping** [T] **1** to increase the amount or level of something: *They've upped their offer by 5%.* **2 up and do sth** to suddenly do something different or surprising: *Without saying another word, he upped and left.* → **up the ante** at **ANTE¹**; → **up sticks** at **STICK²** (11)

up- /ʌp/ *prefix* **1** making something higher: *to upgrade a job* (=make it higher in importance) **2** [especially in adverbs and adjectives] at or towards the top or beginning of something: *uphill | upriver* (=nearer to where the river starts) **3** [especially in verbs] taking something from its place or turning it upside down: *an uprooted tree | She upended the bucket.* **4** [especially in adjectives and adverbs] at or towards the higher or better part of something: *upmarket* (=attracting richer people) → **DOWN-**

up-and-'coming *adj* [only before noun] likely to become successful or popular: *up-and-coming young artists*

up-beat /'ʌpbiːt/ *adj* positive and making you feel that good things will happen; **⊟ downbeat**: *an upbeat message*

up-braid /ʌp'breɪd/ *v* [T] *formal* to tell someone angrily that they have done something wrong

up-bring-ing /'ʌp,brɪŋɪŋ/ *n* [singular, U] the way that your parents care for you and teach you to behave when you are growing up: *Mike had had a strict upbringing.*

UPC /,juː piː 'siː/ *n* [C] *AmE* the abbreviation of **Universal Product Code**

up-chuck /'ʌptʃʌk/ *v* [I] *AmE informal* to bring food or drink up from your stomach and out through your mouth because you are ill or drunk; **⊟ vomit**

up-com-ing /'ʌp,kʌmɪŋ/ *adj* [only before noun] happening soon: *the upcoming elections*

up-'country *adj* *old-fashioned* from a place without many people or towns, especially in the middle of a country —**upcountry** /ʌp'kʌntri/ *adv*

up-date¹ /ʌp'deɪt/ *v* [T] **1** to add the most recent information to something: *The files need updating.* **2** to make something more modern in the way it looks or operates: *plans to update manufacturing procedures* **3** *spoken* to tell someone the most recent information about a situation: **update sb on sth** *Can you update me on what's been happening?*

up-date² /'ʌpdeɪt/ *n* [C] **1** the most recent news or information about something: *a news update | [+on] The report provides a brief update on the progress of the project.* **2** a change or addition to a computer FILE so that it has the most recent information

up-end /ʌp'end/ *v* [T] to turn something over so that it is upside down

up-front¹ /,ʌp'frʌnt◂/ *adj* **1** [not before noun] behaving or talking in an honest way so that people know what you really think: *Mo's very upfront with him about their relationship.* **2** paid before any work has been done or before goods are supplied: *an upfront fee of $500*

upfront² *adv* **1** if you pay money upfront, you pay it before any work has been done or before any goods are supplied: *He requires you to pay him upfront.* **2** in football, if you play upfront, you play in a FORWARD position

up-grade /ʌp'greɪd/ *v* **1** [I,T] to make a computer, machine, or piece of software better and able to do more things: **upgrade (sth) to sth** *You'll need to upgrade your hard drive to 4Mb before running this software.* **2** [T] to improve something and make it more modern,

especially in order to provide a better service: *The hotel has recently been refurbished and upgraded.* **3** [I,T] to give someone a better seat on a plane or a better room in a hotel than the one they paid for: **upgrade (sb) to sth** *We can upgrade you to business class.* **4** [T] to give someone a more important job **5** [T] to change the official description of something to make it seem better or more important; **⊟ downgrade**: **upgrade sth to sth** *Four of the regions were upgraded to the status of republic.* **6 upgrade your skills** to learn new and more modern ways of doing a particular job —**upgrade** /'ʌpgreɪd/ *n* [C]

up-heav-al /ʌp'hiːvəl/ *n* [C,U] a very big change that often causes problems: *political upheaval | Moving house is a major upheaval.*

up-hill¹ /,ʌp'hɪl◂/ *adj* **1** towards the top of a hill; **⊟ downhill**: *an uphill climb* **2 an uphill struggle/battle/task etc** something that is very difficult to do and needs a lot of effort and determination

uphill² *adv* towards the top of a hill; **⊟ downhill**: *The road twists uphill.*

up-hold /ʌp'həʊld $ -'hoʊld/ *v past tense and past participle* **upheld** /-'held/ [T] **1** to defend or support a law, system, or principle so that it continues to exist: *a committee that aims to uphold educational standards* **2** if a court upholds a decision made by another court, it states that the decision was correct: *The conviction was upheld by the Court of Appeal.* —**upholder** *n* [C]

up-hol-ster /ʌp'həʊlstə $ -'hoʊlstər/ *v* [T] to cover a chair with material —**upholstered** *adj*

up-hol-ster-er /ʌp'həʊlstərə $ -'hoʊlstərər/ *n* [C] someone whose job is to cover chairs with material

up-hol-ster-y /ʌp'həʊlstəri $ -'hoʊl-/ *n* [U] **1** material used to cover chairs **2** the process of covering chairs with material

up-keep /'ʌpkiːp/ *n* [U] **1** the process of keeping something in good condition; **⊟ maintenance**: *[+of] Most of the money is spent on the upkeep of the building.* **2** the cost or process of looking after a child or animal and giving them the things they need: *Poorer people find it hard to pay for their pet's upkeep.*

up-lands /'ʌpləndz/ *n* [plural] the parts of a country that are away from the sea and are higher than other areas —**upland** *adj*

up-lift¹ /'ʌplɪft/ *n* **1** [singular] an increase in something: *[+in] an uplift in sales* **2** [singular, U] a feeling of happiness and hope

up-lift² /ʌp'lɪft/ *v* [T] *formal* **1** to make someone feel happier **2** to make something higher

up-lift-ed /ʌp'lɪftɪd/ *adj* **1** feeling happier and more hopeful: *He felt uplifted by her presence.* **2** *literary* raised upwards

up-lift-ing /ʌp'lɪftɪŋ/ *adj* making you feel happier and more hopeful: *an uplifting experience*

up-load¹ /ʌp'ləʊd $ -'loʊd/ *v* [I,T] if information, a computer program etc uploads, or if you upload it, you move it from a small computer to a computer network so that other people can see it or use it; → **download**: *It might take a while for this to upload.*

up-load² /'ʌpləʊd $ -loʊd/ *n* [C] information, computer programs etc that have been uploaded, or the process of uploading them; → **download**: *tips on handling file uploads*

up-mar-ket /,ʌp'mɑːkət◂ $ -ɑːr-/ *adj especially BrE* designed for or used by people who have a lot of money; → **downmarket**: *an upmarket restaurant | move/go upmarket a brand that's moved upmarket* (=it is trying to attract richer people)

up-on /ə'pɒn $ ə'pɑːn/ *prep formal*
1 used to mean 'on' or 'onto': *an honour bestowed upon the association | We are completely dependent upon your help. | Brandon threw him upon the ground.*
2 if a time or event is upon you, it is about to happen: *Winter is almost upon us.*
3 layer upon layer/mile upon mile etc used to empha-

size that there are a lot of layers, miles etc: *mile upon mile of golden sand* → **once upon a time** at ONCE¹ (14); → **take it upon yourself to do sth** at TAKE¹ (27)

up·per¹ W2 /'ʌpə $ -er/ *adj* [only before noun]
1 in a higher position than something else; **≠ lower**: *the upper lip*
2 near or at the top of something; **≠ lower**: *the upper floors of a building* | *There is an upper age limit for becoming a pilot.*
3 have/gain the upper hand to have more power than someone else, so that you are able to control a situation: *Police have gained the upper hand over the drug dealers in the area.*
4 more important than other parts or ranks in an organization, system etc: *the upper echelons* (=the most important members) *of corporate management*
5 further from the sea or further north than other parts of an area: *the upper reaches of the Nile* → **a stiff upper lip** at STIFF¹ (10)

upper² *n* [C] **1** the top part of a shoe that covers your foot: *leather uppers* → see picture at FOOTWEAR **2 uppers** [plural] *informal* illegal drugs that make you feel happy and give you a lot of energy; **≠ amphetamines 3 be on your uppers** *BrE old-fashioned* to have very little money

upper 'case *n* [U] *technical* letters written in capitals (A, B, C) rather than in small form (a, b, c)

upper 'class *n* **the upper class** the group of people who belong to the highest social class —**upper-class** *adj*: *upper-class families*

up·per·class·man /ˌʌpə'klɑːsmən $ -pər'klæs-/ *n plural* **upperclassmen** /-mən/ [C] *AmE* a student in the last two years of a school or university

up·per·class·wom·an /ˌʌpə'klɑːsˌwʊmən $ -pər-'klæs-/ *n plural* **upperclasswomen** /-ˌwɪmɪn/ [C] *AmE* a female student in the last two years of school or university

upper 'crust *n* [singular] *informal* the group of people who belong to the highest social class —**upper-crust** *adj*

up·per·cut /'ʌpəkʌt $ -ər-/ *n* [C] a way of hitting someone in which you swing your hand up into their chin

Upper 'House *n* [C usually singular] a group of representatives in a country's parliament, that is smaller and less powerful than the country's LOWER HOUSE, for example the British House of Lords

up·per·most /'ʌpəməʊst $ -pərmoʊst/ *adj* **1 be uppermost in your mind** if something is uppermost in your mind, you think about it a lot because it is very important to you: *A feeling of pity for David was uppermost in her mind.* **2** [not before noun] more important than anything else: *The one word which seems to be uppermost in every discussion is money.* **3** [usually before noun] higher than anything else: *the uppermost windows of the house* —**uppermost** *adv*: *She turned her hand over, palm uppermost.*

upper school *n* [C] the classes of a school in Britain that are for older students, usually aged 14 to 18

up·pi·ty /'ʌpɪti/ also **uppish** *BrE* /'ʌpɪʃ/ *adj informal* behaving as if you are more important than you really are, or not showing someone enough respect: *uppity kids*

up·raised /ˌʌp'reɪzd◄/ *adj formal* raised or lifted up – used especially about someone's hand or arm

up·right¹ /'ʌpraɪt/ *adj, adv* **1** standing or sitting straight up: **sit/stand/walk upright** *The chimpanzee stood upright and grasped the bars of its cage.* | *Katie was still awake, sitting bolt upright* (=sitting with her back very straight) *staring at the television.* | **pull/push/draw etc yourself upright** *He pulled himself upright and faced me.* **2** placed in a vertical position (=pointing in a line that is at an angle of 90° to a flat surface): *Your seat should be in the upright position when the plane is landing.* | *Keep the bottle upright.* **3** always

behaving in an honest way: *He was a good honest upright man.* —**uprightness** *n* [U]

upright² *n* [C] a long piece of wood or metal that stands straight up and supports something

upright pi'ano *n* [C] a piano with strings that are in a VERTICAL position; → **grand piano**

up·ris·ing /'ʌpˌraɪzɪŋ/ *n* [C] an attempt by a group of people to change the government, laws etc in an area or country; **≠ rebellion**: *a popular uprising* (=by the ordinary people in a country) | *an armed uprising*

up·riv·er /ˌʌp'rɪvə $ -ər/ *adv* away from the sea towards the place where a river begins

up·roar /'ʌp-rɔː $ -rɔːr/ *n* [singular, U] a lot of noise or angry protest about something: **be in (an) uproar** *The house was in an uproar, with babies crying and people shouting.*

up·roar·i·ous /ʌp'rɔːriəs/ *adj* very noisy, because a lot of people are laughing or shouting: *an uproarious party* —**uproariously** *adv*: *uproariously funny*

up·root /ʌp'ruːt/ *v* [I,T] **1** to pull a plant and its roots out of the ground **2** to make someone leave their home for a new place, especially when this is difficult or upsetting: *He rejected the idea of uprooting himself and moving to America.*

up·scale /'ʌpskeɪl/ *adj AmE* relating to people from a high social class who have a lot of money; **≠ upmarket** *BrE: an affluent upscale audience*

up·set¹ /ˌʌp'set◄/ *adj* **1** [not before noun] unhappy and worried because something unpleasant or disappointing has happened: [+by/about/at etc] *She was really upset about the way her father treated her.* | **upset that** *Debbie was upset that he didn't spend more time with her.* **2 be upset with sb** if you are upset with someone, you are angry and annoyed with them: *You're not still upset with me, are you?* **3 upset stomach** an illness that affects the stomach and makes you feel sick

up·set² S2 /ʌp'set/ *v past tense and past participle* **upset**, *present participle* **upsetting** [T]
1 MAKE SB UNHAPPY to make someone feel unhappy or worried: *Don't do anything that would upset him.*
2 CHANGE STH to change a plan or situation in a way that causes problems: *The chemicals upset the balance of the environment.*
3 MAKE STH FALL to push something over without intending to: *He upset a bowl of soup.*
4 DEFEAT to defeat an opponent who is considered to be much better than you: *Jones upset the 40th-ranked American, Cunningham.*
5 upset the apple cart *informal* to completely spoil someone's plans —**upsetting** *adj*

up·set³ /'ʌpset/ *n* **1** [C,U] worry and unhappiness caused by an unexpected problem: *If you are the victim of a burglary, the emotional upset can affect you for a long time.* **2** [C] when a person or team defeats an opponent who is considered to be much better than them: *There was a major upset when the young skater took the gold medal.* **3 stomach upset** an illness that affects the stomach and makes you feel sick

up·shot /'ʌpʃɒt $ -ʃɑːt/ *n* **the upshot (of sth)** the final result of a situation: *The upshot was that after much argument they all agreed to help her.*

up·side¹ /'ʌpsaɪd/ *n* [singular] *especially AmE* the positive part of a situation that is generally bad; **≠ downside**: *The upside of the whole thing is that we got a free trip to Jamaica.*

upside² *prep* **upside the head/face etc** *AmE informal* on the side of someone's head etc

upside 'down¹ *adv* **1** with the top at the bottom and the bottom at the top: *To get the plant out of the pot, turn it upside down and give it a gentle knock.* **2 turn sth upside down a)** to make a place very untidy when you are looking for something: *The burglars have*

U

turned our house *upside down*. **b)** to cause a lot of change and confusion in a situation or in someone's life: *the story of a young girl whose life was turned upside down* **3** disorganized or untidy

upside 'down² *adj* in a position with the top at the bottom and the bottom at the top: *an upside down U shape* | *The chairs were placed upside down on the tables.*

up·skill·ing /'ʌpˌskɪlɪŋ/ *n* [U] improving the skills of workers, usually through training, so that they will be better at their jobs

up·stage¹ /ʌp'steɪdʒ/ *v* [T] to do something that takes people's attention away from someone else who is more important: *All the big-name stars were upstaged by 12-year-old Katy Rochford.*

upstage² *adv* towards the back of the stage in a theatre —**upstage** *adj*

up·stairs¹ [S2] /ˌʌp'steəz◂ $ -'sterz◂/ *adv* towards or on an upper floor in a building; **⟷ downstairs**: *I went upstairs and had a shower.* | *She's upstairs in bed feeling ill.* —**upstairs** *adj* [only before noun]: *an upstairs window* | *the upstairs rooms* → **kick sb upstairs** at **KICK¹** (16)

upstairs² *n* **the upstairs** one or all of the upper floors in a building: *Would you like to see the upstairs?*

up·stand·ing /ʌp'stændɪŋ/ *adj formal* **1** honest and responsible: *upstanding young men and women* **2** standing upright or pointing upwards **3 be upstanding** *BrE spoken formal* used in a formal situation such as a law court to tell people to stand up as a sign of respect for an important person

up·start /'ʌpstɑːt $ -ɑːrt/ *n* [C] someone who behaves as if they were more important than they really are and who shows a lack of respect towards people who are more experienced or older: *a cheeky young upstart* —**upstart** *adj*

up·state /'ʌpsteɪt/ *adj* [only before noun] *AmE* in the northern part of a particular state: *upstate New York* —**upstate** *adv*

up·stream /ˌʌp'striːm◂/ *adv* along a river, in the opposite direction from the way the water is flowing; **⟷ downstream**: *Fish instinctively fight their way upstream against the current.* —**upstream** *adj*

up·surge /'ʌpsɜːdʒ $ -sɜːrdʒ/ *n* [C] **1** a sudden increase: [+in] *There was an upsurge in violence during June and July.* **2** a sudden strong feeling: [+of] *There was a genuine upsurge of religious feeling.*

up·swing /'ʌpswɪŋ/ *n* [C] an improvement or increase in the level of something: [+in/of] *an upswing in economic growth*

up·take /'ʌpteɪk/ *n* **1 be slow/quick on the uptake** *informal* to be slow or fast at understanding something **2** [singular] the number of people who use a service or accept something that is offered: *The uptake of some vaccinations fell as the media stirred up fears of possible side effects.* **3** [C,U] the rate at which a substance is taken into the body, a system etc: *the uptake of sugars by the blood*

up-'tempo *adj* moving or happening at a fast rate: *music with an up-tempo beat*

up·tight /'ʌptaɪt, ʌp'taɪt/ *adj informal* **1** behaving in an angry way because you are feeling nervous and worried: [+about] *You have to learn to laugh instead of getting uptight about things.* **2** having strict traditional attitudes and seeming unable to relax

up·time /'ʌptaɪm/ *n* [U] the period of time when a computer is working normally and is able to be used; → **downtime**: *Some customers need 99% or better uptime from their mainframe computers.*

up-to-'date *adj* **1** including all the latest information: **up-to-date information/data/figures/news** *etc They have access to up-to-date information through a computer database.* | **keep/bring sb up-to-date** (=to give someone all the newest information about some-

thing) *Our magazine will keep you up-to-date with fashion.* **2** modern or fashionable: **up-to-date equipment/facilities/technology** *etc up-to-date kitchen equipment* | **keep/bring sth up-to-date** (=to make something more modern) *The old system should be brought up-to-date.*

up-to-the-'minute *adj* **1** including all the latest information: *The general lacked up-to-the-minute information at the crucial moment.* **2** very modern or fashionable: *beach resorts packed with up-to-the-minute facilities and entertainment*

up·town /ˌʌp'taʊn◂/ *adv AmE* in or towards an area of a city that is away from the centre, especially one where the streets have larger numbers in their names and where people have more money; → **downtown**: *He now lives in an apartment a little farther uptown.* —**uptown** *adj*: *uptown neighborhoods* —**uptown** *n* [U]

up·turn /'ʌptɜːn $ -tɜːrn/ *n* [C] an increase in the level of something, especially in business activity: [+in] *an upturn in the housing market* | *an economic upturn*

up·turned /ˌʌp'tɜːnd◂ $ -ɜːr-/ *adj* [usually before noun] **1** pointing or turning upwards: *He smiled down into her upturned face.* **2** turned upside down: *I sat on an upturned box.* | *an upturned boat*

up·ward /'ʌpwəd $ -wərd/ *adj* [only before noun] **1** increasing to a higher level; **⟷ downward**: **upward trend/movement** *an upward trend in sales* | *a sharp upward movement in property prices* | *upward pressure on bank interest rates* **2** moving or pointing towards a higher position; **⟷ downward**: *Stroke the cream onto your skin in an upward direction.*

upwardly 'mobile *adj* moving up through the social classes and becoming richer: *the upwardly mobile middle classes* —**upward mo'bility** *n* [U]

up·wards /'ʌpwədz $ -wərdz-/ also **upward** *adv especially AmE* **1** moving or pointing towards a higher position; **⟷ downwards**: *Pointing upwards, he indicated a large nest high in the tree.* | *The path began to climb steeply upwards.* **2** increasing to a higher level; **⟷ downwards**: *The expected rate of inflation was revised upwards.* | *Prices are moving upwards again.* **3** more than a particular amount, time etc: *children of 14 and upwards* | *The meeting was attended by upwards of* (=over) *500 people.*

up·wind /ʌp'wɪnd/ *adv* in the opposite direction to the way the wind is blowing; → **downwind**

u·ra·ni·um /jʊ'reɪniəm/ *n* [U] a heavy white metal that is RADIOACTIVE and is used to produce NUCLEAR power and nuclear weapons. It is a chemical ELEMENT; symbol U

U·ra·nus /'jʊərənəs, jʊ'reɪnəs $ 'jʊr-, jʊ'reɪ-/ *n* the PLANET that is seventh in order from the sun: *William Herschel discovered Uranus in 1781.* → see picture at SOLAR SYSTEM

ur·ban [W2] /'ɜːbən $ 'ɜːr-/ *adj* [only before noun] relating to towns and cities; **⟷ rural**; → **suburban**: *unemployment in urban areas* | *the deprived sections of the urban population*

ur·bane /ɜː'beɪn $ ɜːr-/ *adj* behaving in a relaxed and confident way in social situations: *Neil was urbane, witty, direct, and honest.* —**urbanely** *adv* —**urbanity** /ɜː'bænɪti $ ɜːr-/ *n* [U]

ur·ban·ized also **-ised** *BrE* /'ɜːbənaɪzd $ 'ɜːr-/ *adj* **1** an urbanized country or area has a lot of houses, factories, shops, offices etc: *the most heavily urbanized regions* **2** in an urbanized society, there are a lot of people who live and work in towns and cities: *During the 19th century, Britain became the world's first modern urbanized society.* —**urbanization** /ˌɜːbənaɪ'zeɪʃən $ ˌɜːrbənə-/ *n* [U]: *the transformation of the social structure by urbanization*

urban 'myth, urban 'legend *n* [C] a story about an unusual event which happened recently that a lot of people believe although it is probably not true

urban re'newal *n* [U] the process of improving poor city areas by building new houses, shops etc: *an urban renewal program*

,urban 'sprawl *n* [U] the spread of city buildings and houses into an area that used to be countryside, or the area in which this has happened: *planning policies designed to limit the growth of urban sprawl*

ur·chin /'ɜːtʃ]n $ 'ɜːr-/ *n* [C] *old-fashioned* a poor dirty untidy child → SEA URCHIN

Ur·du /'ʊəduː, 'ɜːduː $ 'ɜːrduː/ *n* [U] the official language of Pakistan, also used in India

-ure /jə $ jər/ *suffix* [in nouns] used to make nouns that show actions or results: *the closure* (=closing) *of the factory* | *exposure* | *failure*

u·re·thra /jʊ'riːθrə/ *n* [C] *technical* the tube through which waste liquid flows out of the body from the BLADDER and also through which the SEMEN of males flows

urge¹ W3 /ɜːdʒ $ ɜːrdʒ/ *v* [T]
1 to strongly suggest that someone does something: **urge sb to do sth** *I got a note from Moira urging me to get in touch.* | **urge that** *He urged that a referendum should be held by December.* | **urge sth on/upon sb** *I have urged upon him the need for extreme secrecy.* | *The charity urged quick action.*
2 [always + adv/prep] *formal* to make someone or something move by shouting, pushing them etc: **urge sb/sth forward** *He urged her forward, his hand under her elbow.* | **urge sb into/towards sth** *She began urging him towards the front door.*

urge sb ⇔ **on** *phr v*
to encourage a person or animal to work harder, go faster etc: *Urged on by the crowd, the Italian team scored two more goals.*

urge² *n* [C] a strong wish or need; **⬛ desire**: **urge to do sth** *He could no longer resist the urge to go and see Amanda.* | *Suddenly she had an overwhelming urge to be with her son.*

ur·gent S3 /'ɜːdʒənt $ 'ɜːr-/ *adj*
1 very important and needing to be dealt with immediately: *He was in urgent need of medical attention.* | *The report called for urgent action to reduce lead in petrol.* | *an urgent message*
2 *formal* done or said in a way that shows that you want something to be dealt with immediately: *an urgent whisper* —**urgency** *n* [U]: *a matter of great urgency* —**urgently** *adv*

urgh /ɜːg, ɜːx $ ɜːrg, ɜːrx/ *interjection* said when you have seen or tasted something that you think is extremely unpleasant; **⬛ ugh**

u·ric /'jʊərɪk $ 'jʊr-/ *adj* relating to URINE

u·ri·nal /'jʊər]nəl, jʊ'raɪ- $ 'jʊr]-/ *n* [C] a type of toilet for men to urinate into, usually attached to a wall

u·ri·na·ry /'jʊər]nəri $ 'jʊr]neri/ *adj technical* relating to urine or the parts of your body through which urine passes: *the urinary tract*

u·ri·nate /'jʊər]neɪt $ 'jʊr-/ *v* [I] *technical* to get rid of urine from your body —**urination** /,jʊər]'neɪʃən $,jʊr-/ *n* [U]

u·rine /'jʊər]n $ 'jʊr-/ *n* [U] the yellow liquid waste that comes out of the body from the BLADDER

URL /,juː ɑːr 'el/ *n* [C] *technical* **uniform resource locator** a website address

urn /ɜːn $ ɜːrn/ *n* [C] **1** a decorated container, especially one that is used for holding the ASHES of a dead body **2** a metal container that holds a large amount of tea or coffee

u·rol·o·gist /jʊ'rɒlədʒ]st $ -'rɑː-/ *n* [C] a doctor who treats conditions relating to the URINARY system and men's sexual organs —**urology** *n* [U] —**urological** /,jʊərə'lɒdʒɪkəl◂ $,jʊrə'lɑː-/ *adj*

US /,juː 'es◂/ also **USA** /,juː es 'eɪ/ *n* **the US** the United States of America —**US** *adj*: *the US Navy*

us S1 W1 /əs, s; *strong* ʌs/ *pron*
1 [the object form of 'we'] used by the person speaking or writing to refer to himself or herself and one or more other people: *Please help us.* | *He arranged for us all to have a drink.* | *She's invited us both.* | *My mother is coming to stay with us.* | *Send us a donation now.* | **us**

---

women/men/teachers etc *Life is hard for us women.*
2 people in general: *Global warming will affect all of us.*
3 *BrE spoken* used instead of 'me'. Many people think this use is incorrect: *Give us a kiss.*

us·a·ble /'juːzəbəl/ *adj* something that is usable can be used: *The computer language involved was readily usable.* | *usable information*

us·age /'juːsɪdʒ, 'juːz-/ *n* **1** [C,U] the way that words are used in a language: *a book on modern English usage* **2** [U] the way in which something is used, or the amount of it that is used: *Water usage is increasing.*

USB /,juː es 'biː/ *n* [C] *technical* **universal serial bus** a way of connecting equipment such as a MOUSE and printer to a computer using wires so that all the equipment can work together: *Many USB devices come with their own built-in cable.*

use¹ S1 W1 /juːz/ *v*
1 USE STH [T] if you use a particular tool, method, service, ability etc, you do something with that tool, by means of that method etc, for a particular purpose: *Can I use your phone?* | *I'll show you which room you can use.* | *I always use the same shampoo.* | *Use your imagination when planning meals.* | *She booked the flight using a false name.* | **easy/difficult/simple etc to use** *Drop-down menus make the program very easy to use.* | **use sth for (doing) sth** *They were using animals for scientific experiments.* | *Bob uses the van for picking up groceries.* | **use sth as sth** *My parents use the house as a holiday home.* | **use sth to do sth** *Most people now use their cars to go shopping.* | **use force** (=use violent methods)
2 AMOUNT OF STH [T] to take an amount of something from a supply of food, gas, money etc: *We use about £40 worth of electricity a month.* | *Standard washing machines use about 40 gallons of water.*
3 TREAT SB UNFAIRLY [T] to make someone do something for you in order to get something you want: *Can't you see that Howard is just using you?* | *Gerald had been using her for his own ends.*
4 AN ADVANTAGE [T] to take advantage of a situation: **use sth to do sth** *She used her position as manager to get jobs for her friends.*
5 could use sth *spoken* if you say you could use something, you mean you would really like to have it: *I could use a drink.*
6 WORD [T] to say or write a particular word or phrase: *We use the word 'hardware' to describe the actual machine.* | *Don't use bad language.*
7 DRUGS [I,T] to regularly take illegal drugs → USED TO

use sth ⇔ **up** *phr v*
to use all of something: *She's used up all the hot water.*

use² S3 W2 /juːs/ *n*
1 [singular, U] the action or fact of using something: *an exit for use in emergencies* | [+of] *the increasing use of computers in education*
2 [C] a purpose for which something can be used: *Robots have many different uses in modern industry.* | **have/find a use for sth** *The cupboard is full of things I can never find a use for.*
3 make use of sth to use something that is available in order to achieve something or get an advantage for yourself: *We will make use of her vast experience.* | *There is an answering machine for you to make use of.* | *Try to make good use of your time.*
4 put sth to (good) use to use something such as knowledge or skills for a particular purpose: *a job where her management skills can be put to good use*
5 the use of sth the ability or right to use something: *Joe's given me the use of his office till he gets back.* | *He lost the use of both legs as a result of the accident.*
6 be (of) no use (to sb) to be completely useless: *You needed blankets to keep warm because the heating was no use.* | *Take this – it's of no use to me any more.*
7 it's no use doing sth *spoken* used to tell someone not

U

to do something because it will have no effect: *It's no use complaining.*

8 it's no use! *spoken* used to say that you are going to stop doing something because you do not think it will be successful: *Oh, it's no use! I can't fix it.*

9 what's the use (of sth) *spoken* used to say that something seems to be a waste of time: *What's the use of decorating the house if we are going to sell it?*

10 be in use a machine, place etc that is in use is being used: *Electric vehicles built in 1920 were still in use in the 1950s.*

11 for the use of sb provided for a particular person or group of people to use: *a bar for the use of the guests*

12 be of use (to sb/sth) to be useful: *He was charged with having information likely to be of use to terrorists.*

13 come into use also **bring sth into use** to start being used, or to start using something: *Computers first came into use in the early 1950s.*

14 go/be out of use a machine, place etc that goes out of use or is out of use is not being used: *Some 4,000 railway stations have gone out of use since the 1960s.*

15 have no use for sb/sth to have no respect for someone or something: *She has no use for people who are always complaining.*

16 sth/sb has their uses *spoken* used, often humorously, to say that something or someone can sometimes be useful, even though it may not seem that way: *Being stubborn can have its uses.*

17 [C] one of the meanings of a word, or the way that a particular word is used

used[1] S1 W2 /juːst/ *adj* **be/get used to (doing) sth** to have experienced something so that it no longer seems surprising, difficult, strange etc: *I do the dishes every day, so I'm used to it.* | *I can't get used to the idea that you're grown up now.*

used[2] /juːzd/ *adj* **1 used cars/clothes etc** cars, clothes etc that have already had an owner; ⬄ **second-hand**: *a used car salesman* **2** dirty or not in good condition any longer, as a result of being used: *a used tissue*

used to S1 W2 /ˈjuːst tuː/ *modal verb*

1 if something used to happen, it happened regularly or all the time in the past, but does not happen now: *He used to go to our school.* | *We're eating out more often than we used to.* | **did not use to do sth** *You didn't use to eat chips when you were younger.* | **used not to do sth** BrE: *You used not to fuss like this.* | **did sb use to do sth?** *Did you use to go to church regularly?*

2 if a particular situation used to exist, it existed for a period of time in the past, but does not exist now: *Jimmy used to be a friend of mine.* | *There used to be a large car park on this site.* | **did not use to be/do sth** *Why are you so bad-tempered? You didn't use to be like this.* | **did sb/sth use to be/do sth?** *Did this building use to be a hotel?* | *Where did you use to live before you came to Manchester?*

GRAMMAR

If you **used to** do something, you did it regularly or for a period of time in the past: *She used to come here (NOT was used to come here) every week.* | *I used to go to that school.*

⚠ Do not say 'be used to'. This has a different meaning – see entry **used**[1].

⚠ Use the infinitive after **used to**, not the past tense: *My dad used to grow vegetables (NOT used to grew vegetables).*

⚠ For talking about a present habit, use **usually**: *We usually eat (NOT use to eat) around six.*

In questions, say **did** someone **use to ...?**: *Did he use to fight with his brother?*

In negatives, say **didn't/did not use to ...**: *He didn't use to smoke.* You can also say **never used to**: *They never used to ask where I'd been.* In formal British English you can also say **used not to**: *Buses used not to stop here.*

use·ful S1 W1 /ˈjuːsfəl/ *adj* helping you to do or get what you want; ⬄ **useless**

useful information/advice/tip
useful way of doing sth
useful tool (=useful method or thing that you can use)
it is useful to do sth
prove useful
find sth useful
make yourself useful (=be helpful)
come in useful (=be useful)
serve a useful purpose/function (=be useful)

The book is full of useful information. | *Bar charts are a useful way of looking at sets of figures.* | *The Internet is becoming a **useful tool** for investors.* | [+for] *Television is useful for making up your mind how to vote.* | [+to] *information that may be useful to the enemy* | *It may be useful to consider the data separately.* | *The research may **prove useful** for applications in medicine and biotechnology.* | *techniques that teachers have found useful* | *Sometimes he would **make himself useful** in the kitchen by cleaning and tidying.* | *She couldn't bear to throw away anything that might **come in useful** one day.*

—**usefully** *adv*

use·ful·ness /ˈjuːsfəlnɪs/ *n* [U] the state of being useful or the degree to which something is useful: [+of] *There are doubts as to the usefulness of this approach* (=it may not be useful). | *As a commuter service, the ferry has **outlived** its usefulness* (=is no longer useful).

use·less /ˈjuːsləs/ *adj* **1** not useful or effective in any way; ⬄ **useful**: *The doctor concluded that further treatment would be useless.* | *a website full of useless information* | **virtually/completely/totally etc useless** *Water had got into the radio, and now it was completely useless.* | [+for] *The land is useless for growing crops.* | **it is useless to do sth** *It was useless to complain.* **2** *informal* unable or unwilling to do anything properly: *Don't ask Tim to fix it. He's completely useless.*

—**uselessly** *adv* —**uselessness** *n* [U]

us·er W3 /ˈjuːzə $ -ər/ *n* [C]

1 someone or something that uses a product, service etc: *road users* | *a computer user* | *library users*

2 *informal* someone who takes illegal drugs → END USER

user fee *n* [C] *AmE* a tax on a service provided for the public

user-friendly *adj* easy to use, understand, or operate: *a user-friendly guide to computing* —**user-friendliness** *n* [U]

user group *n* [C] **1** a group of people who have the same interests and use a particular product or service **2** a group of people who exchange information on the Internet about computers

user interface *n* [C] how a computer program looks on screen and how the user enters COMMANDS and information into the program

user name also **user I,D** *n* [C] a name or special word that proves who you are and allows you to enter a computer system or use the Internet: *Please enter your user name and password and click 'OK'.*

ush·er[1] /ˈʌʃə $ -ər/ *n* [C] **1** someone who shows people to their seats at a theatre, cinema, wedding etc **2** BrE someone who works in a law court whose job is to guide people in and out of the court rooms

usher[2] *v* [T always + adv/prep] to help someone to get from one place to another, especially by showing them the way: **usher sb into/to sth** *He ushered her into the room.* | **usher sb in** *She stood back and ushered him in.*

usher in ⬄ sth *phr v* to cause something new to start, or to be at the start of something new: *The discovery of oil ushered in an era of employment and prosperity.*

ush·er·ette /ˌʌʃəˈret/ *n* [C] *old-fashioned especially BrE* a woman who works in a cinema, showing people to their seats

USP /ˌjuː es ˈpiː/ n [C] **unique selling proposition** a feature of a product that makes it different from other similar products, and therefore more attractive to people who might buy it

u·su·al [S2] [W2] /ˈjuːʒuəl, ˈjuːʒəl/ adj
1 happening, done, or existing most of the time or in most situations: *Make a cheese sauce in the usual way.* | *I'll meet you at the usual time.* | **longer/higher/worse etc than usual** *It is taking longer than usual for orders to reach our customers.* | *She ate twice as much as usual.* | **it is usual (for sb) to do sth** *It's usual to keep records of all expenses.*
2 as usual in the way that happens or exists most of the time: *As usual, they'd left the children at home with Susan.* | *They didn't invite any women, as usual.*
3 as per usual *spoken* used to say that something bad that often happens has just happened again: *He just laughed at me, as per usual.*
4 the usual *spoken* **a)** used for talking about something that usually happens, is usually done etc: *'What was he going on about this time?' 'Oh, the usual.'* **b)** the drink that you usually have, especially in a particular bar: *A pint of the usual please, Paul.*
5 not your usual self behaving differently from the way you usually behave, especially by seeming worried or upset about something: *Keith doesn't seem his usual self these days.*

u·su·al·ly [S1] [W1] /ˈjuːʒuəli, ˈjuːʒəli/ adv used to talk about what happens on most occasions or in most situations: *Women usually live longer than men.* | *Usually I wear black, grey, or brown.* | *The drive usually takes 15 or 20 minutes.*

u·sur·er /ˈjuːʒərə $ -ər/ n [C] *formal old-fashioned* someone who lends money to people and makes them pay INTEREST[1] (4)

u·su·ri·ous /juːˈzjuəriəs $ juːˈʒur-/ adj *formal* a usurious price or rate of INTEREST[1] (4) is unfairly high

u·surp /juːˈzɜːp $ -ˈsɜːrp/ v [T] *formal* to take someone else's power, position, job etc when you do not have the right to: *There were a couple of attempts to usurp the young king.* —**usurper** n [C] —**usurpation** /ˌjuːzɜːˈpeɪʃən $ -sɜːr-/ n [U]

u·su·ry /ˈjuːʒəri/ n [U] *formal old-fashioned* the practice of lending money to people and making them pay INTEREST[1] (4): *In medieval times, it was illegal for Christians to practise usury.*

u·ten·sil /juːˈtensəl/ n [C] a thing such as a knife, spoon etc that you use when you are cooking: *kitchen utensils*

u·te·rus /ˈjuːtərəs/ n plural **uteruses** [C] the organ in a woman or female MAMMAL where babies develop; ◨ **womb** —**uterine** /-raɪn/ adj

u·til·i·tar·i·an /juːˌtɪlɪˈteəriən $ -ˈter-/ adj **1** *formal* intended to be useful and practical rather than attractive or comfortable: *ugly utilitarian buildings* **2** based on a belief in utilitarianism → MATERIALISTIC

u·til·i·tar·i·an·is·m /juːˌtɪlɪˈteəriənɪzəm $ -ˈter-/ n [U] the political belief that an action is good if it helps the largest number of people

u·til·i·ty /juːˈtɪlɨti/ n plural **utilities 1** [C usually plural] a service such as gas or electricity provided for people to use: *Does your rent include utilities?* **2** [C] a piece of computer SOFTWARE that has a particular use: *It's a simple shareware utility that allows you to print signs and banners.* **3** [U] *formal* the quality of being useful, or the degree to which something is useful

u'tility ˌpole n [C] *AmE* a tall wooden pole for supporting telephone and electric wires

u'tility ˌroom n [C] a room in a house where washing machines, FREEZERS etc are kept

u·til·ize also **-ise** *BrE* /ˈjuːtɨlaɪz/ v [T] *formal* to use something for a particular purpose: *We must consider how best to utilize what resources we have.* —**utilizable** adj —**utilization** /ˌjuːtɨlaɪˈzeɪʃən $ -lə-/ n [U]

ut·most[1] /ˈʌtməʊst $ -moʊst/ also **uttermost** adj **the utmost importance/respect/care etc** the greatest possible importance etc: *a matter of the utmost importance* | *I've got the utmost respect for her accomplishments.* | *Baldwin treated the matter with the utmost seriousness.*

utmost[2] n [singular] the most that can be done: **to the utmost** | *Both runners had pushed themselves to the utmost.* | *The medical staff **did** their **utmost** (=tried as hard as they could) to save the patient's life.*

u·to·pi·a also **Utopia** /juːˈtəʊpiə $ -ˈtoʊ-/ n [C,U] an imaginary perfect world where everyone is happy; → **dystopia** —**utopian** adj: *a utopian society* —**utopianism** n [U]

ut·ter[1] /ˈʌtə $ -ər/ adj [only before noun] used to emphasize how great or complete something is: *That's **utter** nonsense!* | *This company treats its employees with **utter contempt**.* | *I watched in **complete and utter** horror as he pulled out a gun.* | *fifteen years of utter confusion*

utter[2] v [T] *formal* **1** to say something: *'You fool!' she uttered in disgust.* | *Cantor nodded without **uttering** a **word**.* **2** to make a sound with your voice, especially with difficulty: *The wounded prisoner uttered a groan.*

ut·ter·ance /ˈʌtərəns/ n *formal* **1** [C] something you say: *Politicians are judged by their public utterances.* **2** [U] the action of saying something

ut·ter·ly /ˈʌtəli $ -ər-/ adv [+ adj/adv] completely or totally: *You look utterly miserable.*

ut·ter·most /ˈʌtəməʊst $ -ərmoʊst/ adj *literary* or *formal* UTMOST

U-turn /ˈjuː tɜːn $ ˌjuː ˈtɜːrn/ n [C] **1** a turn that you make in a car, on a bicycle etc, so that you go back in the direction you came from: **make/do a U-turn** *He made a quick U-turn and sped away.* **2** a complete change of ideas, plans etc: **make/do a U-turn** *Critics accused the government of doing a U-turn on its promise to increase education spending.*

u·vu·la /ˈjuːvjʊlə/ n plural **uvulae** /-liː/ [C] *technical* a small soft piece of flesh which hangs down from the top of your mouth at the back

U

V, v

V, v /viː/ *plural* **V's, v's** *n* **1** [C,U] the 22nd letter of the English alphabet **2** the number 5 in the system of ROMAN NUMERALS **3** [C usually singular] something that has a shape like the letter V: *She cut the material into a V.*

v. also **v** *BrE* **1** a written abbreviation of *verb* **2** *BrE informal* the written abbreviation of *very* **3** a written abbreviation of *versus* (=against), used in the names of legal TRIALS, or in Britain when talking about games in which two teams or players play against each other: *the Roe v. Wade case* | *England v Australia* **4** the written abbreviation of *volt* or volts

vac /væk/ *n* [C usually singular] *BrE informal* a university VACATION¹ (2)

va·can·cy S3 /ˈveɪkənsi/ *n plural* **vacancies**
1 [C] a job that is available for someone to start doing: *There are still two vacancies on the school board.* | [+for] *We* **have** *no* **vacancies** *for photographers at the moment.* | *The council is making every effort to* **fill** *the* **vacancies.** | *information about* **job vacancies**
2 [C] a room in a hotel or building that is not being used and is available for someone to stay in: *Let me see if we* **have a vacancy** *for tonight.* | *'* **No vacancies** *', the sign read.*
3 [U] *written* lack of interest or thought: *His mouth fell open and the look of vacancy returned.*

va·cant /ˈveɪkənt/ *adj* **1** a vacant seat, building, room or piece of land is empty and available for someone to use: *Only a few apartments were still vacant.* | *There was only a* **vacant lot** (=empty unused area of land in a city) *where her house used to be.* **2** *formal* a job or position in an organization that is vacant is available for someone to start doing: **fall vacant** *BrE* (=become vacant) *He was offered the position of headmaster when it fell vacant.* | **situations vacant** *BrE* (=the part of a newspaper where jobs are advertised) **3** **vacant expression/look/stare etc** *written* an expression that shows that someone does not seem to be thinking about anything: *He gazed at me with vacant eyes.* —**vacantly** *adv*: *Cindy was staring vacantly into space.*

,vacant pos'session *n* [U] *BrE technical* **house/flat with vacant possession** a home or other building whose previous owner has left, so that the new owner can move into it immediately

va·cate /vəˈkeɪt, veɪ- $ ˈveɪkeɪt/ *v* [T] *formal* **1** to leave a job or position so that it is available for someone else to do: *Clay will vacate the position on June 19.* **2** to leave a seat, room etc so that someone else can use it: *Guests must vacate their rooms by 11:00.*

va·ca·tion¹ S2 W3 /vəˈkeɪʃən $ veɪ-/ *n*
1 [C,U] *especially AmE* a holiday, or time spent not working

on (a) vacation
go on (a) vacation
take/have a vacation
summer vacation
Christmas vacation
family vacation
two-week/three-day etc vacation
vacation spot (=a place where a lot of people go on vacation)

on vacation *They're on vacation for the next two weeks.* | *I'm* **going on vacation** *tomorrow.* | *We're hoping to* **take** *a* **vacation** *at the end of July.* | *his* **summer vacation** *at Martha's Vineyard* | *Luke was forced to cancel the* **family vacation** *to Acapulco.* | *the Caribbean* **vacation spot** *of Cancun, Mexico*

2 [U] *especially AmE* the number of days, weeks etc that you are allowed as paid holiday by your employer: *How much vacation do you get at your new job?* | *I think I have four* **vacation days** *left.* | *Employees are entitled to four-weeks'* **paid vacation** *annually.*
3 [C] *BrE* one of the periods of time when universities are closed

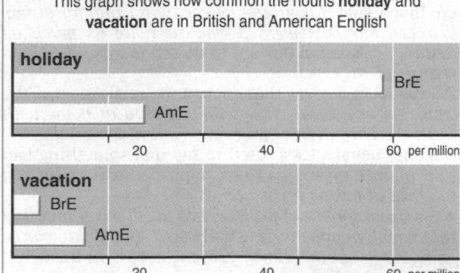
This graph shows how common the nouns **holiday** and **vacation** are in British and American English

In British English the word **holiday** is used to mean a time of rest from work or school, or a period of time when you travel to another place for pleasure. Americans use **vacation** for this meaning, and to refer to a period when universities are closed. In both American and British English **holiday** is used to mean a day fixed by law on which people do not have to go to work or school. In British English **vacation** is used to refer to a period when universities are closed.

vacation² *v* [I] *AmE* to go somewhere for a holiday: [+in/at] *The Bernsteins are vacationing in Europe.*

va·ca·tion·er /vəˈkeɪʃənə $ veɪˈkeɪʃənər/ *n* [C] *AmE* someone who has gone somewhere for a holiday; ◧ **holidaymaker** *BrE*

vac·cin·ate /ˈvæksɪneɪt/ *v* [T] to protect a person or animal from a disease by giving them a vaccine; ◧ **immunize**: **vaccinate sb against sth** *All children should be vaccinated against measles.* —**vaccination** /ˌvæksɪˈneɪʃən/ *n* [C,U]: *a flu vaccination*

vac·cine /ˈvæksiːn $ vækˈsiːn/ *n* [C,U] a substance which contains a weak form of the BACTERIA or VIRUS that causes a disease and is used to protect people from that disease: *a polio vaccine* | *Doctors worried that there would not be enough vaccine for everyone who needed it.*

vac·il·late /ˈvæsɪleɪt/ *v* [I] *formal* to continue to change your opinions, decisions, ideas etc; ◧ **waver**: [+between] *Her parents vacillated between different approaches to discipline.* —**vacillation** /ˌvæsɪˈleɪʃən/ *n* [C,U]

VAc·tor /ˈvæktə $ -ər/ *n* [C] *trademark* **virtual actor** an actor who seems like a real person, but who is an image made using a computer; ◧ **synthespian**

va·cu·i·ty /vəˈkjuːɪti, væ- $ væ-/ *n* [U] *formal* lack of intelligent, interesting, or serious thought

vac·u·ous /ˈvækjuəs/ *adj formal* showing no intelligence or having no useful purpose: *a vacuous expression* | *a vacuous romantic novel*

vac·u·um¹ /ˈvækjuəm, -kjʊm/ *n* **1** [C] a space that is completely empty of all gas, especially one from which all the air has been taken away **2** [C] a vacuum cleaner **3** [singular] a situation in which someone or something is missing or lacking: **create/leave a vacuum (in sth)** *Her husband's death left a vacuum in her life.* | **power/political/moral etc vacuum** *the political vacuum caused by the ban on Communist Party activity* **4** **in a vacuum** existing completely separately from other people or things and having no connection with them: *The process of learning a language does not take place in a vacuum.*

vacuum² *v* [I,T] to clean using a vacuum cleaner → see picture at CLEANING

'vacuum ,cleaner *n* [C] a machine that cleans floors by sucking up dirt; ◧ **hoover** *BrE trademark*

'vacuum ,flask n [C] BrE a special container that keeps liquids hot or cold; ▤ **thermos**

'vacuum-,packed / $,··· '◂ / adj vacuum-packed food is in a container from which most of the air has been removed, so that the food will stay fresh for longer

'vacuum ,tube n [C] AmE a VALVE (3)

vag·a·bond /'vægəbɒnd $ -bɑːnd/ n [C] especially literary someone who has no home and travels from place to place; ▤ **tramp**

va·ga·ries /'veɪgəriz/ n [plural] formal unexpected changes in a situation or someone's behaviour, that you cannot control but which have an effect on your life: [+of] the vagaries of the English weather

va·gi·na /və'dʒaɪnə/ n [C] the passage between a woman's outer sexual organs and her UTERUS —**vaginal** /və'dʒaɪnl $ 'vædʒ₃nəl/ adj

va·gran·cy /'veɪgrənsi/ n [U] the criminal offence of living on the street and BEGGING from people

va·grant /'veɪgrənt/ n [C] formal someone who has no home or work, especially someone who BEGS ; ▤ **tramp**

vague ⟨S3⟩ /veɪg/ adj
1 unclear because someone does not give enough detailed information or does not say exactly what they mean: The governor gave only a vague outline of his tax plan. | [+about] Julia was vague about where she had been and what she had been doing.
2 have a vague idea/feeling/recollection etc (that) to think that something might be true or that you remember something, although you cannot be sure: Larry had the vague feeling he'd done something embarrassing the night before.
3 not having a clear shape or form; ▤ **indistinct**. The vague shape of a figure loomed through the mist. —**vagueness** n [U]

vague·ly /'veɪgli/ adv **1** slightly; ◪ **clearly**: I vaguely remember a woman in a red dress standing outside the door. | There was something vaguely familiar about him. | I was vaguely aware of another figure by the door. **2** not clearly or exactly: His statement was very vaguely worded. **3** in a way that shows you are not thinking about what you are doing: He smiled vaguely at the ceiling.

vain /veɪn/ adj **1** someone who is vain is too proud of their good looks, abilities, or position – used to show disapproval; ▤ **conceited**: Men can be just as vain as women. ➔ see box at PROUD **2 in vain a)** without success in spite of your efforts: Police searched in vain for the missing gunman. **b)** without purpose or without positive results: Altman swore that his son's death would not be in vain. ➔ **take sb's name in vain** at NAME¹ (12) **3** a vain attempt, hope or search fails to achieve the result you wanted: **vain attempt/effort/bid** The young mother died in a vain attempt to save her drowning son. **4** vain threat/promise etc literary a threat, promise etc that is not worrying because the person cannot do what they say they will —**vainly** adv: The instructor struggled vainly to open his parachute.

vain·glo·ri·ous /veɪn'glɔːriəs/ adj literary too proud of your own abilities, importance etc

val·ance, valence /'væləns/ n [C] **1** a narrow piece of cloth that hangs from the edge of a shelf or from the frame of a bed to the floor **2** especially AmE a narrow piece of cloth above a window, covering the RAIL the curtains hang on; ▤ **pelmet** BrE

vale /veɪl/ n [C] literary **1** a broad low valley **2 a/the/this vale of tears** an expression used to mean the difficulties of life

val·e·dic·tion /,vælɪ'dɪkʃən/ n [C,U] formal the act of saying goodbye, especially in a formal speech

val·e·dic·to·ri·an /,vælɪdɪk'tɔːriən/ n [C] AmE the student who has received the best marks all the way through school, and usually makes a speech at the GRADUATION ceremony

val·e·dic·to·ry /,vælɪ'dɪktəri◂/ n plural **valedictories** [C] formal a speech or statement in which you say

goodbye when you are leaving a school, job etc, especially on a formal occasion —**valedictory** adj: a valedictory speech

va·len·ce /'veɪləns/ also **va·len·cy** /-lənsi/ n [C] technical **1** a measure of the power of atoms to combine together to form COMPOUNDS **2** another spelling of VALANCE

val·en·tine /'væləntaɪn/ n [C] **1** someone you love or think is attractive, that you send a card to on St Valentine's Day: Be my valentine. **2** a card you send to someone on St Valentine's Day

val·et¹ /'væleɪt, 'vælɪt $ væ'leɪ/ n [C] **1** a male servant who looks after a man's clothes, serves his meals etc; ➔ **maid 2** also **valet parker** AmE someone who parks your car for you at a hotel or restaurant: valet service **3** BrE someone who cleans the clothes of people staying in a hotel

valet² v [T] BrE to clean someone's car: a valeting service

'valet ,parking also **valet service** n [U] AmE the service of having someone else park your car for you at a restaurant, hotel etc

val·i·ant /'væliənt/ adj very brave, especially in a difficult situation; ▤ **courageous**: Tarr threw himself in front of a train in a valiant effort to save the child.

val·id /'vælɪd/ adj **1** a valid ticket, document, or agreement is legally or officially acceptable; ◪ **invalid**: a valid credit card | Your return ticket is valid for three months. **2 valid reason/argument/criticism etc** a reason, argument etc that is based on what is reasonable or sensible: Police officers must have a valid reason for stopping motorists. **3** a valid PASSWORD, ID etc is one that will be accepted by a computer system; ◪ **invalid** —**validity** /və'lɪdₐti/ n [U]: I would question the validity of that statement.

val·i·date /'vælɪdeɪt/ v [T] **1** formal to prove that something is true or correct, or to make a document or agreement officially and legally acceptable; ▤ **confirm**: The Supreme Court has validated the lower court's interpretation of the law. | Many scientists plan to wait until the results of the study are validated by future research. **2** to make someone feel that their ideas and feelings are respected and considered seriously: Talking with people who think like you helps validate your feelings. **3** AmE if a business validates a ticket from a PARKING GARAGE, it puts a special mark on it, showing that it will pay the parking costs —**validation** /,vælɪ'deɪʃən/ n [C,U]

va·lise /və'liːz $ və'liːs/ n [C] old-fashioned a small SUITCASE

Val·i·um /'væliəm/ n [U] trademark a drug that makes people feel calmer and less anxious

val·ley ⟨S3⟩ ⟨W3⟩ /'væli/ n [C] an area of lower land between two lines of hills or mountains, usually with a river flowing through it: the San Fernando valley ➔ see picture at COUNTRY

val·our BrE; **valor** AmE /'vælə $ -ər/ n [U] literary great courage, especially in war: medals awarded for valor | deeds of valour

val·u·a·ble ⟨W3⟩ /'væljuəbəl, -jₐbəl $ 'væljₐbəl/ adj
1 worth a lot of money; ◪ **worthless**: a valuable painting | Their most valuable belongings were locked in a safe in the bedroom.
2 valuable help, advice, information etc is very useful because it helps you to do something: Muriel has made a valuable contribution to our company's success. | a job that gave him valuable experience
3 important because there is only a limited amount available: I won't waste any more of your valuable time.

val·u·a·bles /'væljuəbəlz, -jₐbəlz $ -jₐbəlz/ n [plural] things that you own that are worth a lot of money, such as jewellery, cameras etc: Guests should leave their valuables in the hotel safe.

V

val·u·a·tion /ˌvælju'eɪʃən/ n [C,U] **1** a professional judgment about how much something is worth: *The property has a valuation of $1.6 billion.* **2** a judgment about how effective or useful a particular idea or plan will be

val·ue¹ S3 W1 /'vælju:/ n
1 MONEY [C,U] the amount of money that something is worth

increase/rise/go up in value
drop/fall/go down/decrease in value
hold its value (=continue to be worth the same amount)
high/low value
market value (=the amount that something can be bought or sold for)
street value (=how much people pay on the street to buy illegal drugs)

[+of] *The alterations doubled the value of the house.* | *The dollar has been steadily increasing in value.* | *The share price has continued to fall in value over the past week.* | *It's a beautiful carpet – it should hold its value.* | *Spices had a high value in proportion to their weight.* | *low value household products* | *a mortgage that is larger than the market value of your house* | *Police seized drugs with a street value of £2.5 million.*

2 WORTH THE MONEY PAID [C,U] used to say that something is worth what you pay for it, or not worth what you pay for it: **good/poor value (for money)** *BrE* a **good/poor value** *AmE*: *The lunch special is really good value.* | *At only £45 a night, the hotel is great value for money.* | **value for money** *BrE* (=good value, or the quality of being good value) *Every customer is looking for value for money.*

3 IMPORTANCE/USEFULNESS [U] the importance or usefulness of something: [+of] *A group of athletes spoke to the students about the value of a college education.* | *the nutritional value of cereal* | **be of great/little value** *His research has been of little practical value.* | **place/put a high value on sth** *The Sioux Indians placed a high value on generosity.* | *The locket has great sentimental value* (=importance because it was a gift, it reminds you of someone etc).

4 of value a) worth a lot of money: *The thieves took nothing of value.* **b)** useful: *I hope this book will be of value to both teachers and students.*

5 INTERESTING QUALITY shock/curiosity/novelty etc value a good or interesting quality that something has because it is surprising, different, new etc: *After the initial curiosity value, the product's sales dropped considerably.*

6 IDEAS values [plural] your ideas about what is right and wrong, or what is important in life: *a return to traditional values* | *Your attitudes about sex are affected by your religious and moral values.* → FAMILY VALUES

7 AMOUNT [C] *technical* a mathematical quantity shown by a letter of the alphabet or sign: *Let x have the value 25.* → see box at WORTH¹

value² v [T] **1** to think that someone or something is important: *Shelly valued her privacy.* | **value sb/sth for sth** *Mr. Yeo valued Jan for her hard work.* **2** [usually passive] to decide how much money something is worth, by comparing it with similar things: *We decided to get the house valued.* | **value sth at sth** *Paintings valued at over $200,000 were stolen from her home.* —**valued** *adj*: *a valued friend*

value-added 'tax n [U] VAT

'value judgment n [C] a decision or judgment about how good something is, based on your personal opinions not facts

val·ue·less /'vælju:ləs/ *adj* **1** worth no money or very little money; ◨ **worthless**: *valueless currency* **2** having no worth, importance, or good qualities; ◨ **worthless**: *On most political issues my own opinion was pretty well valueless.*

val·u·er /'væljuə $ -ər/ n [C] *BrE* someone whose job is to decide how much money something is worth

valve /vælv/ n [C] **1** a part of a tube or pipe that opens and shuts like a door to control the flow of liquid, gas, air etc passing through it: *heart valves* → see picture at BICYCLE¹ **2** the part on a TRUMPET or similar musical instrument that you press to change the sound of the note **3** *BrE* a closed glass tube used to control the flow of electricity in old radios, televisions etc; ◨ **vacuum tube** *AmE*

vamp /væmp/ n [C] *old-fashioned* a woman who uses her sexual attractiveness to make men do what they want

vam·pire /'væmpaɪə $ -paɪr/ n [C] in stories, a dead person that sucks people's blood by biting their necks

'vampire bat n [C] a South American BAT that sucks the blood of other animals

van S3 /væn/ n [C]
1 a vehicle used especially for carrying goods, which is smaller than a TRUCK and has a roof and usually no windows at the sides: *a delivery van* | *a van driver* **2** *AmE* a large box-like car that can carry a lot of people **3** *especially BrE* a railway carriage with a roof and sides, used especially for carrying goods: *a luggage van*

van·dal /'vændl/ n [C] someone who deliberately damages things, especially public property

van·dal·is·m /'vændəl-ɪzəm/ n [U] the crime of deliberately damaging things, especially public property

van·dal·ize also **-ise** *BrE* /'vændəl-aɪz/ v [T] to damage or destroy things deliberately, especially public property: *The cemetery was vandalized during the night.*

vane /veɪn/ n [C] a flat blade that is moved by wind or water to produce power to drive a machine

van·guard /'vænɡɑːd $ -ɡɑːrd/ n **1 in/at the vanguard (of sth)** in the most advanced position of development: *The shop has always been in the vanguard of London fashion trends.* **2 the vanguard** the leading position at the front of an army or group of ships moving into battle, or the soldiers who are in this position

va·nil·la¹ /və'nɪlə/ n [U] a substance used to give a special taste to ICE CREAM, cakes etc, made from the beans of a tropical plant

vanilla² *adj* **1** having the taste of vanilla: *vanilla ice cream* **2** also **plain-vanilla** plain, ordinary, or uninteresting: *There are no plans for an inexpensive vanilla version of the software.*

van·ish /'vænɪʃ/ v [I] **1** to disappear suddenly, especially in a way that cannot be easily explained: *My keys were here a minute ago but now they've vanished.* | **vanish without (a) trace/vanish off the face of the earth** (=disappear so that no sign remains) *The youngster vanished without a trace one day and has never been found.* | *The bird vanished from sight.* | *She seemed to have just vanished into thin air.* (=suddenly disappeared in a very mysterious way) **2** to suddenly stop existing; ◨ **disappear**: [+from] *By the 1930s, the wolf had vanished from the American West.* | *Public support for the Prime Minister has now vanished.*

van·ish·ing·ly /'vænɪʃɪŋli/ *adv* **vanishingly small/improbable** extremely small or unlikely: *The chances of dying under anaesthetic are vanishingly small.*

'vanishing ,point n [C usually singular] the point in the distance, especially on a picture, where parallel lines seem to meet

van·i·ty /'vænəti/ n plural **vanities 1** [U] too much PRIDE in yourself, so that you are always thinking about yourself and your appearance: *Sabrina had none of the vanity so often associated with beautiful women.* **2** [C] also **vanity table** a DRESSING TABLE **3 the vanity of sth** *literary* the lack of importance of something compared to other things that are much more important

'vanity ,case n [C] a small bag used by a woman for carrying MAKE-UP etc

'vanity ,plate n [C] a car NUMBER PLATE that has a combination of numbers or letters chosen by the owner, so that they spell a word that is connected with or describes the owner

'vanity ,press also **'vanity ,publisher** n [C usually singular] a company that writers pay to print their books

'vanity ,table n [C] AmE a DRESSING TABLE

van·quish /ˈvæŋkwɪʃ/ v [T] literary to defeat someone or something completely

van·tage point /ˈvɑːntɪdʒ pɔɪnt $ ˈvæn-/ also **vantage** n [C] **1** a good position from which you can see something: From my vantage point on the hill, I could see the whole procession. **2** a way of thinking about things that comes from your own particular situation or experiences; ▪ **point of view**: The whole dispute looked silly from my vantage point.

vap·id /ˈvæpɪd/ adj lacking intelligence, interest, or imagination: vapid conversation

va·por /ˈveɪpə $ -ər/ n [C,U] the American spelling of vapour

va·por·ize also **-ise** BrE /ˈveɪpəraɪz/ v [I,T] to change into a vapour, or to make something, especially a liquid, do this

va·pour BrE; **vapor** AmE /ˈveɪpə $ -ər/ n [C,U] a mass of very small drops of a liquid which float in the air, for example because the liquid has been heated: water vapour

'vapour trail BrE; **vapor trail** AmE n [C] the white line that is left in the sky by a plane

var·i·a·ble¹ /ˈveəriəbəl $ ˈver-/ adj **1** likely to change often: Expect variable cloudiness and fog tomorrow. | Interest rates can be **highly variable**. | **variable in size/shape/colour etc** These fish are highly variable in color and pattern. **2** sometimes good and sometimes bad: The quality of pork is often less variable than beef. **3** able to be changed: The heater has variable temperature settings. **—variably** adv **—variability** /ˌveəriəˈbɪlɪti $ ˌver-/ n [U]

variable² n [C] **1** something that may be different in different situations, so that you cannot be sure what will happen: There are too many variables in the experiment to predict the result accurately. **2** technical a mathematical quantity which can represent several different amounts

var·i·ance /ˈveəriəns $ ˈver-/ n **1 be at variance (with sb/sth)** formal if two people or things are at variance with each other, they do not agree or are very different: Tradition and culture are often at variance with the needs of modern living. **2** [C,U] formal the amount by which two or more things are different or by which they change: a price variance of 5% **3** [C] law the official permission to do something different from what is normally allowed: The developer requested a variance to build a shopping center on the east side of town.

var·i·ant /ˈveəriənt $ ˈver-/ n [C] **1** something that is slightly different from the usual form of something: [+of/on] This game is a variant of netball. | a variant on the typical Hollywood hero **2** technical a slightly different form of a word or phrase: spelling variants in British and American English **—variant** adj: a variant form of the word

var·i·a·tion W2 /ˌveəriˈeɪʃən $ ˌver-/ n
1 [C,U] a difference between similar things, or a change from the usual amount or form of something: [+of] White bread is really just a variation of French bread. | [+in] variations in the quality of the rugs | [+among] There is a great deal of **variation** among the responses. | [+between] The study concluded that the variation between the different CD players was very small.

2 [C] something that is done in a way that is different from the way it is usually done: Most of his poems are **variations on** the theme of love.
3 [C] one of a set of short pieces of music, each based on the same simple tune: Bach's Goldberg variations

var·i·cose veins /ˌværɪkəʊs ˈveɪnz $ -koʊs-/ n [plural] a medical condition in which the VEINS in your leg become swollen and painful

var·ied /ˈveərid $ ˈver-/ adj consisting of or including many different kinds of things or people, especially in a way that seems interesting: a varied diet | The responsibilities of government are many, and they are varied. | **richly/extremely/widely etc varied** A good teacher is aware of the extremely varied needs of each student.

var·i·e·gat·ed /ˈveərigeɪtɪd $ ˈver-/ adj **1** a variegated plant, leaf etc has different coloured marks on it: variegated grasses **2** formal consisting of a lot of different types of thing

va·ri·e·ty S2 W1 /vəˈraɪəti/ n plural **varieties**
1 a variety of sth a lot of things of the same type that are different from each other in some way: The girls come from a variety of different backgrounds. | a **wide/great/endless etc variety of sth** Cafe Artista offers a wide variety of sandwiches.
2 [U] the differences within a group, set of actions etc that make it interesting: I really like the variety the store has to offer. | **give/add/bring variety (to sth)** (=make something more interesting) Occasionally working from home adds variety to a job.
3 [C] a type of thing, such as a plant or animal, that is different from others in the same group: [+of] The lake has more than 20 varieties of fish.
4 [C usually singular] a particular type of person or thing – often used humorously: **of the … variety** Lon has no patience with anything of the child variety.
5 variety is the spice of life used to say that doing a lot of different things, meeting different people etc is what makes life interesting

va'riety ,show n [C] a television or radio programme or a performance that consists of many different shorter performances, especially musical and humorous ones

va'riety ,store n [C] AmE a shop that sells many different kinds of goods, often at low prices

var·i·ous S1 W1 /ˈveəriəs $ ˈver-/ adj [usually before noun]
1 if there are various things, there are several different types of that thing: The jacket is available in various colours. | There are various ways to answer your question. | He decided to leave school **for various reasons**.
2 many and various BrE; **various and sundry** AmE many different types of something: The reasons why teenage girls get pregnant are many and various.

var·i·ous·ly /ˈveəriəsli $ ˈver-/ adv in many different ways: **variously described as/known as/called etc sth** the phenomena variously know as 'mass culture', 'popular culture', or the 'public arts' | His fortune has been variously estimated at between $1 and $2 billion.

var·nish¹ /ˈvɑːnɪʃ $ ˈvɑːr-/ n [C,U] a clear liquid that is painted onto things, especially things made of wood, to protect them, or the hard shiny surface produced by this

varnish² v [T] to cover something with varnish

var·si·ty /ˈvɑːsɪti $ ˈvɑːr-/ n plural **varsities** [C,U] **1** AmE the main team that represents a university, college, or school in a sport: the varsity football team **2** BrE old-fashioned a university, especially Oxford or Cambridge

var·y S2 W2 /ˈveəri $ ˈveri/ v **varied, varying, varies**
1 [I] if several things of the same type vary, they are all different from each other; ▪ **differ**

vary from place to place/person to person etc
vary from sth to sth
vary considerably/greatly/widely/enormously
vary slightly
vary according to/depending on sth
varying degrees/levels/sizes/amounts

*Test scores **vary from** school to school.* | *The heights of the plants **vary from** 8 cm **to** 20 cm.* | *[+in] flowers that vary in color and size* | *Medical treatment **varies greatly** from state to state.* | *Cooking times may **vary slightly**, depending on your oven.* | *Charges **vary according to** size.* | *She has tried different diets with **varying degrees** of success.* | *tests of **varying levels** of difficulty*

2 [I] if something varies, it changes depending on the situation: *Quentin's mood seems to **vary according to** the weather.* | *'What do you wear when you go out?' 'Well, it varies.'*
3 [T] to change something to make it different: *My doctor said I should vary my diet more.*

vas·cu·lar /'væskj‿lə $ -ər/ adj medical relating to the tubes through which liquids flow in the bodies of animals or in plants: *vascular disease*

vase /vɑːz $ veɪs, veɪz/ n [C] a container used to put flowers in or for decoration → see picture at JUG

va·sec·to·my /və'sektəmi/ n plural **vasectomies** [C,U] a medical operation to cut the small tube through which a man's SPERM passes so that he is unable to produce children

Vas·e·line /'væsɨliːn/ n [U] trademark a soft clear substance used on the skin for various medical and other purposes

vas·sal /'væsəl/ n [C] **1** a man in the Middle Ages who was given land to live on by a lord in return for promising to work or fight for him **2** formal a country that is controlled by another country: *a vassal state*

vast [S2] [W2] /vɑːst $ væst/ adj
1 extremely large; ⊟ **huge**: *vast amounts/numbers/quantities/sums etc (of sth)* *The government will have to borrow vast amounts of money.* | *The refugees come across the border in vast numbers.* | *vast areas/expanses/tracts etc (of sth)* *vast areas of rainforest* | *In the past five years, there has been a vast improvement in graduation rates.*
2 the vast majority (of sth) used when you want to emphasize that something is true about almost all of a group of people or things: *The vast majority of books on the subject are complete rubbish.* **—vastness** n [U]

vast·ly /'vɑːstli $ 'væstli/ adv very much: *This book is vastly superior to his last one.* | *vastly different opinions*

vat [W3] /væt/ n [C] a very large container for storing liquids in

VAT /ˌviː eɪ 'tiː, væt/ n [U] **value added tax** a tax added to the price of goods and services in Britain and the EU

Vat·i·can /'vætɪkən/ n **the Vatican a)** the large PALACE in Rome where the Pope (=head of the Roman Catholic Church) lives and works **b)** the government of the Pope: *The Vatican is taking a hard line on birth control.*

vau·de·ville /'vɔːdəvɪl $ 'vɒː-/ n [U] AmE a type of theatre entertainment, popular from the 1880s to the 1950s, in which there were many short performances of different kinds, including singing, dancing, jokes etc; → **music hall**

vault¹ /vɔːlt $ vɒːlt/ n [C] **1** a room with thick walls and a strong door where money, jewels etc are kept to prevent them from being stolen or damaged **2** a room where people from the same family are buried, often under the floor of a church **3** a jump over something **4** a roof or ceiling that consists of several ARCHES that are joined together, especially in a church

vault² also **vault over** v [T] **1** to jump over something in one movement, using your hands or a pole to help you: *The robber vaulted over the counter and took $200 in cash.* **2** to move quickly from a lower rank or

level to a higher one; ⊟ **leap**: *[+from/to] On Sunday Michigan vaulted from No. 4 to the nation's top team.*

vault·ed /'vɔːltɨd $ 'vɒːl-/ adj in the shape of or consisting of several ARCHES joined together: *vaulted ceiling/roof etc*

vault·ing¹ /'vɔːltɪŋ $ 'vɒːl-/ n [U] ARCHES in a roof or ceiling: *Gothic vaulting*

vaulting² adj **vaulting ambition** literary the desire to achieve as much as possible: *a man of vaulting ambition with the talents to match*

vaunt·ed /'vɔːntɨd $ 'vɒːn-, 'vɑːn-/ adj formal a plan, system, achievement etc that is vaunted is praised or talked about too much and in a way that is too proud: *There's little sign that the **much-vaunted** IT investment is pulling France out of recession.*

V-chip /'viː tʃɪp/ n [C] an electronic CHIP in a television that allows parents to prevent their children from watching programmes that are violent or have sex in them

vCJD /ˌviː siː dʒeɪ 'diː/ n [U] medical **new variant Creutzfeldt-Jakob Disease** a human form of the serious brain disease BSE

VCR /ˌviː siː 'ɑː $ -'ɑːr/ n [C] **video cassette recorder** a machine you use to record television programmes or play VIDEOTAPES; ⊟ **video** BrE

VD /ˌviː 'diː/ n [C,U] old-fashioned **venereal disease** any disease that passes from one person to another during sex; ⊟ **STD**

VDT /ˌviː diː 'tiː/ n [C] AmE technical **video display terminal** a computer screen; ⊟ **monitor**

VDU /ˌviː diː 'juː/ n [C] BrE technical **visual display unit** a computer screen; ⊟ **monitor**: *VDU operators*

've /v, əv/ v the short form of 'have': *We've finished.*

veal /viːl/ n [U] the meat of a CALF (=a young cow)

vec·tor /'vektə $ -ər/ n [C] technical **1** a quantity such as force that has a direction as well as size **2** an insect or animal that passes disease from one person to another; ⊟ **carrier**: *Mosquitoes are feared as vectors of malaria.* **3** in biology, an animal or human cell that is used to carry DNA from one cell to another to produce a CLONE

vee·jay /ˌviː'dʒeɪ/ n [C] a VIDEO JOCKEY

veep /viːp/ n [C] AmE informal VICE PRESIDENT

veer /vɪə $ vɪr/ v [I always + adv/prep] **1** to change direction: *[+off]* *A tanker driver died when his lorry veered off the motorway.* | *The plane veered off course.* | *Follow the path and veer left after 400m.* | *The wind was veering north.* **2** if opinions, ideas, attitudes etc veer in a particular direction, they gradually change and become quite different: *This latest proposal appears to veer in the direction of Democratic ideals.* | *The conversation veered back to politics.*

veg¹ /vedʒ/ n [C,U] BrE informal vegetables: *fruit and veg*

veg² v **vegged, vegging, vegges**
 veg out phr v spoken informal to be very lazy and spend time doing very little: *Ralph vegged out in front of the TV all day again.*

ve·gan /'viːgən $ 'viː-, 'vedʒ-/ n [C] someone who does not eat any animal products at all, such as meat, fish, eggs, cheese, or milk; → **vegetarian** **—vegan** adj: *a strict vegan diet*

Ve·ge·bur·ger /'vedʒɪˌbɜːgə $ -ˌbɜːrgər/ n [C] trademark BrE a flat round cake made with vegetables and beans that looks like a BURGER but that does not contain meat

vege·ta·ble¹ [S3] [W3] /'vedʒtəbəl/ n
1 [C] a plant that is eaten raw or cooked, such as a CABBAGE, a CARROT, or PEAS: *fresh fruit and vegetables* | *organic methods of growing vegetables* | *vegetable soup* | *a neat vegetable garden* | *Vitamin A is found in liver and green vegetables.* | *salad vegetables (=vegetables such as LETTUCE or TOMATOES eaten raw)*

V

2 [C] *not polite* an offensive word for someone who is alive but who cannot talk or move because their brain is damaged

vegetable² *adj* [only before noun] *formal* relating to plants in general, rather than animals or things that are not living: *decomposing vegetable matter*

veg·e·tar·i·an /ˌvedʒəˈteəriən◂ $ -ˈter-/ *n* [C] someone who does not eat meat or fish; → **vegan**: *Our youngest daughter is a vegetarian.* | *dishes suitable for vegetarians* | *I'm thinking about becoming a vegetarian.* —**vegetarian** *adj*: *a vegetarian restaurant*

veg·e·tar·i·an·is·m /ˌvedʒəˈteəriənizəm $ -ˈter-/ *n* [U] the practice of not eating meat or fish

veg·e·tate /ˈvedʒəteɪt/ *v* [I] to live without doing much physical or mental activity and to feel bored as a result: *I was determined when I retired that I wasn't just going to vegetate.*

veg·e·ta·tion /ˌvedʒəˈteɪʃən/ *n* [U] *formal* plants in general: *Lefkas has an abundance of lush green vegetation.*

veg·e·ta·tive /ˈvedʒətətɪv $ -teɪtɪv/ *adj* [only before noun] **1** *technical* relating to plants, and particularly to the way they grow or make new plants: **vegetative reproduction/propagation** **2 a vegetative state** a condition in which someone cannot think or move because their brain has been damaged

veg·gie¹ /ˈvedʒi/ *n* [C] **1** a VEGETARIAN **2** *AmE* a VEGETABLE: *fresh veggies*

veggie² *adj informal* veggie food is made using vegetables, nuts, beans etc rather than meat or fish: *veggie lasagne and chips*

ve·he·ment /ˈviːəmənt/ *adj* showing very strong feelings or opinions: **vehement opposition/criticism/hostility etc** *Despite vehement opposition, the Act became law.* | *Despite her vehement protests, he pulled her inside.* —**vehemently** *adv*: *Dan vehemently denies the*

---

charges. —**vehemence** *n* [U]: *The vehemence of her answer surprised them both.*

ve·hi·cle S2 W2 /ˈviːɪkəl/ *n* [C]
1 *formal* a machine with an engine that is used to take people or things from one place to another, such as a car, bus, or truck; → **motor vehicle**: *a description of the stolen vehicle* | *Have you locked your vehicle?*
2 *formal* something you use to express and spread your ideas, opinions etc; ▇ **medium**: [+for] *The 1936 Olympics were used as a vehicle for Nazi propaganda.* | *'Eastern Eye' is an important vehicle for Black British opinion.*
3 a film, television programme etc that is made to gain public attention for one of the people in it: [+for] *This is the perfect vehicle for Fleming to make his triumphant return to the stage.* | *MGM made the film as a **star vehicle** for Brando.*

ve·hic·u·lar /viːˈhɪkjʊlə $ -ər/ *adj formal* relating to vehicles: *vehicular traffic* | *no vehicular access*

veil¹ /veɪl/ *n* [C] **1** a thin piece of material that women wear to cover their faces at formal occasions or for religious reasons: *She lifted her veil with both hands.* | *a bridal veil* **2 the veil** the system in Islamic countries in which women must cover their hair and faces in public **3 draw a veil over sth** *formal* to avoid talking about something that happened in the past because it is unpleasant or embarrassing: *I think it best to draw a veil over the whole incident.* **4 veil of secrecy/deceit/silence etc** *formal* something that hides the truth about a situation: *Watson deserves credit for **lifting the veil** of secrecy surrounding Brenda's death.* | *His pornography was covered by a veil of respectability.* **5 veil of mist/cloud/smoke etc** a thin layer of mist, cloud etc that makes it difficult to see clearly: *The moon was hidden behind a veil of clouds.* **6 take the veil** *old-fashioned* to become a NUN

---

vegetables

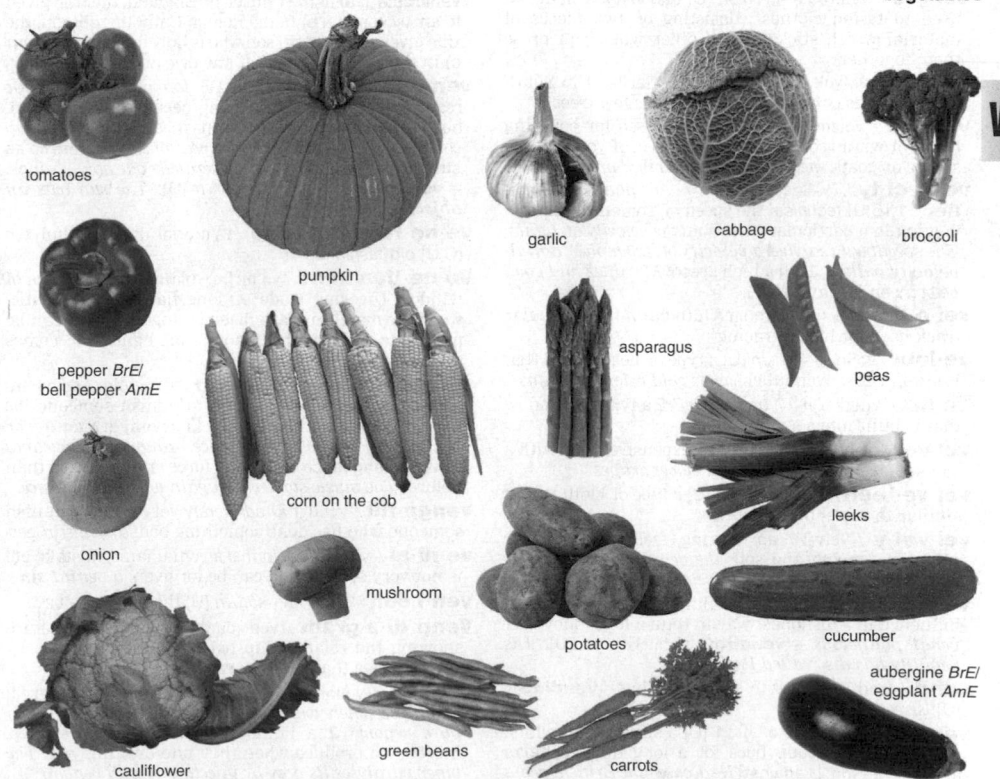

tomatoes

pumpkin

pepper *BrE*/
bell pepper *AmE*

corn on the cob

onion

mushroom

cauliflower

green beans

garlic

cabbage

broccoli

asparagus

peas

leeks

potatoes

cucumber

carrots

aubergine *BrE*/
eggplant *AmE*

V

veil² v [T] **1 be veiled in mystery/secrecy etc** *formal* if something is veiled in mystery etc, people do not know the truth about it so it seems strange or mysterious: *The details of the evacuation are veiled in secrecy.* **2** to cover something with a veil: *A black kerchief modestly veiled her hair.* **3** *literary* to partly hide something so that it cannot be seen clearly: *A fine rain was beginning to veil the hills.*

veiled /veɪld/ *adj* a veiled threat, warning, attack, reference etc is expressed so that its exact meaning is hidden or unclear: *His speech is being seen as a veiled attack on asylum-seekers.* | *'I'm impressed,' said Greg, with thinly veiled* (=only slightly hidden) *sarcasm.* | *Jasper remained silent and his eyes were veiled* (=you could not guess what he was thinking).

vein /veɪn/ n **1** [C] one of the tubes which carries blood to your heart from other parts of your body; → **artery**: *the pulmonary vein* | *She felt the blood racing through her veins as they kissed.* → see picture at HUMAN¹ **2** [C] one of the thin lines on a leaf or on an insect's wing **3** [C] one of the thin lines on a piece of cheese or some types of stone **4** [C] a thin layer of a valuable metal or mineral which is contained in rock: [+of] *veins of gold* **5 in a ... vein** in a particular style of speaking or writing about something: **in the same vein/in a similar vein** *There was more humour, in much the same vein.* | *in a serious/light-hearted etc vein poems in a lighter vein* **6** a vein of humour/malice etc a small amount of humour etc: *In voicing our fear of old age, Rivers has discovered a rich vein of comedy.* → DEEP VEIN THROMBOSIS, VARICOSE VEINS

veined /veɪnd/ *adj* having a pattern of thin lines on the surface: *black-veined marble* | *He grasped her feeble veined hand.*

ve·lar /ˈviːlə $ -ər/ *adj technical* a velar CONSONANT such as /k/ or /g/ is made by putting the back of your tongue close to the soft part at the top of your mouth

Vel·cro /ˈvelkrəʊ $ -kroʊ/ n [U] *trademark* a material used to fasten clothes, consisting of two pieces of material which stick to each other when you press them together

veldt, veld /velt/ n **the veldt** high flat land in South Africa that is covered in grass and has few trees

vel·lum /ˈveləm/ n [U] a material used for covering books or writing on, made from the skin of young cows, sheep, or goats: *medieval maps inscribed on vellum*

ve·lo·ci·ty /vɪˈlɒsɪti $ -ˈlɑː-/ n plural **velocities 1** [C,U] *technical* the speed of something that is moving in a particular direction: *the velocity of light* | *The speedboat reached a velocity of 120 mph.* | *a high velocity bullet* **2** [U] a high speed: *Martinez had good velocity on his fastball.*

vel·o·drome /ˈveledrəʊm $ -droʊm/ n [C] a circular track used for bicycle racing

ve·lour /vəˈluə $ -ˈlur/ n [U] a type of heavy cloth that is similar to velvet but cheaper: *gold velour curtains*

Ve·lux /ˈviːlʌks/ n [C] *trademark BrE* a type of window that is built into a sloping roof

vel·vet /ˈvelvɪt/ n [U] a type of expensive cloth with a soft surface on one side: *green velvet drapes*

vel·ve·teen /ˌvelvɪˈtiːn◂/ n [U] a type of cloth that is similar to velvet but cheaper

vel·vet·y /ˈvelvɪti/ *adj* looking, feeling, tasting, or sounding smooth and soft: *the velvety texture of her skin* | *His voice was soft and velvety.*

ve·nal /ˈviːnl/ *adj formal* willing to use power and influence in a dishonest way in return for money: *our venal politicians* —**venality** /viːˈnælɪti/ n [U]: *His venality has discredited Parliament.*

vend /vend/ v [T] *law* to sell something —**vending** n [U]: *street vending*

ven·det·ta /venˈdetə/ n **1** [C] a situation in which one person or group tries for a long time to harm another person: [+against] *He accused the British media*

---

of pursuing a vendetta against him. | *the victim of a political vendetta* **2** [C,U] a long violent argument between two groups or people, especially one that is about something that happened in the past; ◻ **feud**: *The two sides have been engaged in a bitter private vendetta.* | [+between] *Vendettas between rival gangs are common.*

vending ma·chine n [C] a machine that you can get cigarettes, chocolate, drinks etc from by putting money in

vending machine

vend·or /ˈvendə $ -ər/ n [C] **1** someone who sells things, especially on the street: **news vendor/ice-cream vendor etc** *He bought a copy from a newspaper vendor.* | *the shouts of street vendors* **2** *formal* or *law* someone who is selling something: *leading software vendors*

ve·neer /vɪˈnɪə $ -ˈnɪr/ n **1** [C,U] a thin layer of wood or plastic that covers the surface of a piece of furniture made of cheaper material, to make it look better: **walnut/maple/oak etc veneer** **2** a veneer of politeness/sophistication etc *formal* behaviour that hides someone's real character or feelings: *A thin veneer of politeness hid Lady Bride's growing anger.*

ve·neered /vəˈnɪəd $ -ˈnɪrd/ *adj* covered with a thin layer of wood or plastic: *veneered doors*

ven·e·ra·ble /ˈvenərəbəl/ *adj* **1** [usually before noun] *formal* a venerable person or thing is respected because of their great age, experience etc – often used humorously: *venerable financial institutions* | *the venerable guitarist Pat Martino* | *a venerable tradition* **2 the Venerable ...** a) in the Church of England, the title given to an ARCHDEACON b) in the Roman Catholic religion, the title given to a dead person who is holy but not yet a SAINT c) in the Buddhist religion, the title given to a MONK

ven·e·rate /ˈvenəreɪt/ v [T] *formal* to honour or respect someone or something because they are old, holy, or connected with the past: *a symbol of Arab courage, to be venerated for generations* | **venerate sb as sth** *These children are venerated as holy beings.* —**veneration** /ˌvenəˈreɪʃən/ n [U]: *The sun was an object of veneration.*

ve·ne·re·al dis·ease /vɪˈnɪəriəl dɪˌziːz $ -ˈnɪr-/ n [C,U] *old-fashioned* VD

Ve·ne·tian blind /vəˌniːʃən ˈblaɪnd/ n [C] a type of window covering made of long flat bars of plastic, wood, or metal that are fastened together and can be moved to change the amount of light that comes through the window

ven·geance /ˈvendʒəns/ n **1** [U] a violent or harmful action that someone does to punish someone for harming them or their family; ◻ **revenge**: *a desire for vengeance* | *a vow of vengeance* | *an act of vengeance* **2 with a vengeance** with great force or more effort than before: *The music started up again with a vengeance.*

venge·ful /ˈvendʒfəl/ *adj literary* very eager to punish someone who has done something bad: *a vengeful god*

ve·ni·al /ˈviːniəl/ *adj formal* a venial fault, mistake etc is not very serious and can be forgiven: *a venial sin*

ven·i·son /ˈvenɪzən, -sən/ n [U] the meat of a DEER

Venn di·a·gram /ˈven ˌdaɪəgræm/ n [C] a picture showing the relationship between several things by using circles that partly cover each other

ven·om /ˈvenəm/ n [U] **1** great anger or hatred; ◻ **malice**: *There was real venom in her voice.* | *a look of pure venom* **2** a liquid poison that some snakes, insects etc produce when they bite or sting you: *The viper paralyses its prey by injecting it with venom.*

ven·om·ous /'venəməs/ adj **1** full of hatred or anger: *Lisa shot him a venomous glance.* | *Reid reserved his most venomous attack for the Rail Authority.* **2** a venomous snake, insect etc produces poison; ◘ **poisonous** —**venomously** adv

ve·nous /'viːnəs/ adj medical relating to the VEINS (=tubes that carry blood) in your body

vent¹ /vent/ n [C] **1** a hole or pipe through which gases, liquid etc can enter or escape from an enclosed space or container: *a blocked air vent* | *a volcanic vent* **2** give vent to sth formal to do something violent or harmful to express feelings of anger, hatred etc: *Children give vent to their anger in various ways.* | *He knew that if he gave full vent to his feelings, it would upset Joanna.* **3** a thin straight opening at the bottom of the back or side of a jacket or coat **4** technical the small hole through which small animals, birds, fish, etc pass waste matter out of their bodies

vent² v [T] to express feelings of anger, hatred etc, especially by doing something violent or harmful: **vent sth on sb** *If he's had a bad day, Paul vents his anger on the family.* | **vent sth by doing sth** *I could hear mum **venting** her **frustration** by banging the pots noisily.* | *The meeting gave us a chance to vent our spleen* (=anger).

ven·ti·late /'ventɪleɪt $ -tl-eɪt/ v [T] **1** to let fresh air into a room, building etc: **well-ventilated/poorly ventilated etc** *a well-ventilated kitchen* **2** to pump air into and out of someone's lungs, using a special machine: *Both patients are sedated and ventilated.* **3** formal to express your opinions or feelings about something: *The important thing is to ventilate your anger.* —**ventilation** /ˌventɪ'leɪʃən $ -tl'eɪ-/ n [U]: *a ventilation system* | *artificial ventilation*

ven·ti·la·tor /'ventɪleɪtə $ -tl-eɪtər/ n [C] **1** a piece of equipment that puts fresh air into a room, building etc; → **fan** **2** a piece of equipment that pumps air into and out of someone's lungs: **on a ventilator** *He was put on a ventilator but died two hours later.*

ven·tri·cle /'ventrɪkəl/ n [C] technical one of the two spaces in the bottom of your heart through which blood pumps out to your body; → **auricle**

ven·tril·o·quist /ven'trɪləkwɪst/ n [C] someone who entertains people by speaking without moving their lips and making it seem that the words are spoken by a model of a person called a DUMMY —**ventriloquism** n [U]

ven·ture¹ /'ventʃə $ -ər/ n [C] a new business activity that involves taking risks: **business/commercial venture** | **joint venture** (=when two companies do something together)

venture² v **1** [I always + adv/prep] to go somewhere that could be dangerous: *When darkness fell, he would venture out.* | *She paused before venturing up the steps to the door.* | *children who lack the confidence to venture into libraries* **2** [T] to say or do something in an uncertain way because you are afraid it is wrong or will seem stupid: *'You're on holiday here?' he ventured.* | **venture to do sth** *I ventured to ask him what he was writing.* | **venture an opinion/question/word etc** *If we had more information, it would be easier to venture a firm opinion.* | *Roy ventured a tentative smile.* | **venture that** *I ventured that the experiment was not conclusive.* **3** nothing ventured, nothing gained used to say that you cannot achieve anything unless you take risks
venture into sth phr v to become involved in a new business activity: *Banks are venturing into insurance.*
venture on/upon sth phr v to do or try something that involves risks: *I thought I might venture on a new recipe.*

'venture ˌcapital n [U] money lent to someone so that they can start a new business —**venture capitalist** n [C]

ven·ture·some /'ventʃəsəm $ -tʃər-/ adj formal willing to take risks; ◘ **daring**

ven·ue /'venjuː/ n [C] a place where an organized meeting, concert etc takes place: **sporting/conference/** concert etc venue | *The first thing to do is **book** a venue.* | *The band will **play** (=perform at) as many venues as possible.* | [+**for**] *the venue for the latest round of talks*

Ve·nus /'viːnəs/ n the PLANET that is second in order from the sun: *the high surface temperatures of Venus* → see picture at SOLAR SYSTEM

ve·ra·ci·ty /və'ræsɪti/ n [U] formal the fact of being true or correct; ◘ **truth**: [+**of**] *Has anyone checked the veracity of these allegations?*

ve·ran·da, verandah /və'rændə/ n [C] an open area with a floor and a roof that is attached to the side of a house at ground level; ◘ **porch** AmE

verb /vɜːb $ vɜːrb/ n [C] a word or group of words that describes an action, experience, or state, such as 'come', 'see', and 'put on' → AUXILIARY VERB, LINKING VERB, MODAL VERB, PHRASAL VERB

verb·al¹ /'vɜːbəl $ 'vɜːr-/ adj **1** spoken rather than written: **verbal agreement/instructions etc** **2** relating to words or using words: *verbal skills* | *verbal abuse* (=cruel words) *from other kids on the street* **3** relating to a verb: *verbal nouns* —**verbally** adv: *Her boss failed to stop the other workers from verbally abusing her.*

verbal² n **1** [C] technical a word that has been formed from a verb, for example a GERUND, INFINITIVE, or PARTICIPLE **2** [U] relating to criticism, complaints, or an attack that you express in speech: *Maria was getting loads of verbal from her staff.*

verb·al·ize also **-ise** BrE /'vɜːbəlaɪz $ 'vɜːr-/ v [I,T] formal to express something in words; ◘ **articulate**: *Urge your child to verbalize his feelings.*

ver·ba·tim /vɜː'beɪtɪm $ vɜːr-/ adj, adv formal repeating the actual words that were spoken or written; ◘ **word-for-word**: **verbatim account/quote/report etc** *a verbatim account of our conversation* | *Their stories were taped and transcribed verbatim.*

ver·bi·age /'vɜːbi-ɪdʒ $ 'vɜːr-/ n [U] formal speech or writing that has many unnecessary words in it: *meaningless verbiage*

ver·bose /vɜː'bəʊs $ vɜːr'boʊs/ adj using or containing too many words: *For once, his usually verbose wife was content to listen.* | *Legal writing is often unclear and verbose.* —**verbosely** adv —**verbosity** /vɜː'bɒsɪti $ vɜːr'bɑː-/ n [U]

ver·dant /'vɜːdənt $ 'vɜːr-/ adj literary verdant land is thickly covered with fresh green plants: *verdant fields*

ver·dict /'vɜːdɪkt $ 'vɜːr-/ n [C]
1 an official decision made in a court of law, especially about whether someone is guilty of a crime or how a death happened

consider a verdict (=think about what decision to make)
reach/arrive at a verdict (=make a decision)
return/deliver/record a verdict (=tell the court your decision)
majority verdict (=when most of the JURY agrees)
unanimous verdict (=when the whole JURY agrees)
guilty verdict/verdict of guilty
not guilty verdict/verdict of not guilty
verdict of accidental death/suicide/unlawful killing etc
open verdict BrE (=a decision that the cause of someone's death is not known)

*The jury has retired to **consider its verdict**. | After a week the jury had still not **reached a verdict**. | I never doubted that they would **deliver** the correct **verdict**. | a **majority verdict** of 10 to 2 | The **unanimous verdict** was 'guilty'. | There was not enough evidence for a **guilty verdict**. | The Coroner **recorded a verdict** of accidental death.*

2 an official decision made by a person or group with

authority: *The players anxiously awaited the verdict of the umpire.*
3 someone's opinion about something: *The audience's final verdict was encouraging.* | **[+on]** *What's your verdict on the movie?* | **give (sb) your verdict (on sth)** *Trade unionists were quick to give their verdict on the proposals.*

ver·di·gris /'vɜːdɪˌɡriː, -ɡriːs $ 'vɜːr-/ *n* [U] a greenish-blue substance that sometimes appears on COPPER or BRASS

ver·dure /'vɜːdʒə $ 'vɜːrdʒər/ *n* [U] *literary* green grass, plants etc

verge[1] /vɜːdʒ $ vɜːrdʒ/ *n* [C] **1 be on the verge of sth** to be at the point where something is about to happen: *Jess seemed on the verge of tears.* | *an event which left her on the verge of a nervous breakdown* | *Mountain gorillas are on the verge of extinction.* | **be on the verge of doing sth** *The show was on the verge of being canceled due to low ratings.* **2** *BrE* the edge of a road, path etc: *the grass verge* → see picture at LIMIT[1]

verge[2] *v*
verge on/upon sth *phr v* to be very close to a harmful or extreme state: *Many of Lewis's activities verged on the illegal.* | *Some of his ideas are verging on the dangerous.* | *His love of James Dean movies verged on fanaticism.*

ver·ger /'vɜːdʒə $ 'vɜːrdʒər/ *n* [C] *BrE* someone whose job is to care for the inside of a church and help during services

ver·i·fy /'verɪfaɪ/ *v* **verified, verifying, verifies** [T] *formal* **1** to discover whether a something is correct or true: **verify that/whether** *A computer program verifies that the system is working.* | *American forces will remain to verify compliance with the treaty.* **2** to state that something is true; **◻ confirm**: *His statement was verified by several witnesses.* —**verifiable** *adj: a verifiable fact* —**verification** /ˌverɪfɪ'keɪʃən/ *n* [C,U]: *automatic signature verification*

ver·i·ly /'verɪli/ *adv biblical* a word used to emphasize a statement

ver·i·si·mil·i·tude /ˌverɪsɪ'mɪlɪtjuːd $ -tuːd/ *n* [U] *formal* the quality of being true or real: *questions about the verisimilitude of the document*

ver·i·ta·ble /'verɪtəbəl/ *adj* [only before noun] *formal* a word used to emphasize a description of someone or something; **◻ real**: *The area is a veritable paradise for those who love walking and swimming.*

ver·i·ty /'verɪti/ *n plural* **verities** [C usually plural] *formal* an important principle or fact that is always true; **◻ truth**: *the eternal verities of life*

ver·mil·ion, vermillion /və'mɪljən $ vər-/ *n* [U] a very bright red colour —**vermilion** *adj*

ver·min /'vɜːmɪn $ 'vɜːr-/ *n* [plural] **1** small animals, birds, and insects that are harmful because they destroy crops, spoil food, and spread disease: *The beds were filthy and full of vermin.* | *Foxes are considered vermin.* **2** unpleasant people who cause problems for society

ver·min·ous /'vɜːmɪnəs $ 'vɜːr-/ *adj formal* covered with insects that bite: *a pair of verminous old cats*

ver·mouth /'vɜːməθ $ vər'muːθ/ *n* [U] an alcoholic drink made from wine with herbs and spices: *dry vermouth*

ver·nac·u·lar /və'nækjələ $ vər'nækjələr/ *n* [C usually singular] **1** a form of a language that ordinary people use, especially one that is not the official language: **in the vernacular** *Galileo wrote in the vernacular to reach a larger audience.* | *He lapsed into the local vernacular* (=language spoken in a particular area). **2** a style of building, music, art etc that is suitable for ordinary people —**vernacular** *adj: vernacular American speech* | *vernacular architecture*

ver·nal /'vɜːnl $ 'vɜːrnl/ *adj* [only before noun] *literary technical* relating to the spring: *the vernal equinox*

ver·ru·ca /və'ruːkə/ *n* [C] *BrE* a small hard infectious lump that grows on the bottom of your foot

versa → VICE VERSA

ver·sa·tile /'vɜːsətaɪl $ 'vɜːrsətl/ *adj* **1** someone who is versatile has many different skills: *a very versatile performer* | *a more versatile workforce* **2** having many different uses: *The potato is an extremely versatile vegetable.* —**versatility** /ˌvɜːsə'tɪlɪti $ ˌvɜːr-/ *n* [U]: *Hegley's outstanding versatility as an all-round entertainer*

verse /vɜːs $ vɜːrs/ *n* **1** [C] a set of lines that forms one part of a song, poem, or a book such as the Bible or the Koran: *Let's sing the last verse again.* | *Learn the first two verses of the poem by heart.* | *Genesis chapter 3, verse 13* **2** [U] words arranged in the form of poetry: *a book of comic verse* | **in verse** *Written in verse, the play was set in the Middle Ages.*

versed /vɜːst $ vɜːrst/ *adj formal* **be (well) versed in sth** to know a lot about a subject, method etc: *a woman well versed in the art of diplomacy*

ver·si·fi·ca·tion /ˌvɜːsɪfɪ'keɪʃən $ ˌvɜːr-/ *n* [U] *technical* the particular pattern in which a poem is written

ver·sion W1 /'vɜːʃən $ 'vɜːrʒən/ *n* [C]
1 a copy of something that has been changed so that it is slightly different: **[+of]** *a new version of the software* | **new/modern/final etc version** *the original version of the text* | **English/German/electronic/film etc version** (=presented in a different language or form) *a Japanese version of an English play* | *I think I preferred the television version.* | *the human version of mad cow disease*
2 someone's version of an event is their description of it, when this is different from the description given by another person: **[+of]** *according to the official version of events* | *Could Donna's version of what happened that night be correct?*
3 the ... version of sth a way of explaining or doing something that is typical of a particular group or period of time: **[+of]** *the Marxist version of economics* | *Is the coffee break the adult version of recess?* → **cover version** at COVER[2] (10)

ver·so /'vɜːsəʊ $ 'vɜːrsoʊ/ *n* [C] *technical* a page on the left-hand side of a book; → **recto**

ver·sus /'vɜːsəs $ 'vɜːr-/ *prep* **1** *v. BrE vs. AmE* used to show that two people or teams are competing against each other in a game or court case: *the New York Knicks versus the LA Lakers* | *the Supreme Court decision in Roe vs. Wade* **2** used when comparing the advantages of two different things, ideas etc: *The finance minister must weigh up the benefits of a tax cut versus those of increased public spending.*

ver·te·bra /'vɜːtɪbrə $ 'vɜːr-/ *n plural* **vertebrae** /-briː, -breɪ/ [C] one of the small hollow bones down the centre of your back —**vertebral** *adj* [only before noun]

ver·te·brate /'vɜːtɪbrɪt, -breɪt $ 'vɜːr-/ *n* [C] a living creature that has a BACKBONE; → **invertebrate**

ver·tex /'vɜːteks $ 'vɜːr-/ *n plural* **vertices** /-tɪsiːz/ or **vertexes** [C] *technical* the point where two lines meet to form an angle, especially the point of a TRIANGLE

ver·ti·cal[1] /'vɜːtɪkəl $ 'vɜːr-/ *adj* **1** pointing up in a line that forms an angle of 90° with a flat surface; **◻ horizontal**; → **diagonal**: *a vertical line* | *the vertical axis of a graph* | *vertical window blinds* | **vertical cliff/climb/drop etc** (=one that is very high or steep) *a gorge lined with vertical cliffs* **2** having a structure in which there are top, middle, and bottom levels: *Formal communication channels are usually vertical.* —**vertically** /-kli/ *adv*

vertical[2] *n* **the vertical** the direction of something that is vertical: *The tower now leans about 15 degrees from the vertical.*

vertical ex'pansion *n* [U] *technical* when a company starts to do or make some of the things that used to be done or made by companies it did business with

ver·tig·i·nous /vɜː'tɪdʒ₁nəs $ vɜːr-/ *adj formal* so high that you feel sick and DIZZY: *a vertiginous drop to the valley below*

ver·ti·go /'vɜːtɪgəʊ $ 'vɜːrtɪgoʊ/ *n* [U] a feeling of sickness and DIZZINESS caused by looking down from a high place

verve /vɜːv $ vɜːrv/ *n* [U] *literary* energy, excitement, or great pleasure: **with verve** *Cziffra played the Hungarian dances with great verve.*

ve·ry[1] [S1] [W1] /'veri/ *adv*
1 [+ adj/adv] used to emphasize an adjective, adverb, or phrase: *It feels very cold today.* | *The fishing industry is very important to the area.* | *The traffic's moving very slowly this morning.* | *problems that are very similar to mine* | *I feel a lot better – thank you* **very much.** | *I'm* **very, very** (=used for emphasis) *pleased you can come.* | *It's very kind of you to help.* | *My sister and I were married on* **the very same** (=exactly the same) *day.* | **the very best/latest/worst etc** *We only use the very best ingredients.*
2 not very good/happy/far etc not good etc at all: *I'm just not very good at spelling.* | *The garden's not very big, is it?* | *The assistant wasn't very helpful.* | *'Was the talk interesting?' 'Not very* (=only slightly).'
3 your very own used to emphasize the fact that something belongs to one particular person and to no one else: *She was thrilled at the idea of having her very own toys to play with.* | **of your very own** *At last, a home of her very own.*
4 *informal* used with adjectives to say that the quality something has is very noticeable or typical: *It was a very male reaction, I thought.* | *His films are always very French.*
5 very much so *spoken* used to emphasize your agreement or approval: *'Are you serious?' 'Very much so.'*
6 very well *old-fashioned spoken* used to agree to something

very[2] [S2] [W1] *adj* [only before noun] used to emphasize that you are talking exactly about one particular thing or person: *He died in* **this very room.** | *I'll start at the very beginning.* | *Those were his very words.* | *You'd better start doing some work this very minute* (=now, not later). | *That might provoke a riot,* **the very thing** *he was trying to avoid.* | **The very fact that** *you are reading this book suggests you want to improve your fitness.* | **By its very nature,** *capitalism involves exploitation of the worker.* | *His life's work was being destroyed* **before** *his* **very eyes** (=directly in front of him). | **the very thought/idea/mention (of sth)** (=just thinking about or suggesting something) *The very thought of food made me feel ill.* | *The very mention of his name excited her.*

ves·pers /'vespəz $ -ərz/ *n* [U] the evening service in some types of Christian church

ves·sel /'vesəl/ *n* [C] **1** *formal* a ship or large boat: *a fishing vessel* **2** *technical* a VEIN in your body: *a burst* **blood vessel** **3** *old use* a container for holding liquids

vest[1] /vest/ *n* [C] **1** *BrE* a piece of underwear without SLEEVES that you wear on the top half of your body; **☐ undershirt** *AmE*; → see picture at UNDERWEAR **2** a piece of special clothing without SLEEVES that you wear over your clothes to protect your body: *a bulletproof vest* **3** *AmE* a piece of clothing without SLEEVES and with buttons down the front that you wear as part of a suit; **☐ waistcoat** *BrE* **4** a SWEATER without SLEEVES

vest[2] *v law*
vest sth in sb *phr v* to give someone the official right to do or own something: *Copyright is vested in the author for 50 years.*

vest·ed /'vest₁d/ *adj* **1 vested interest** a strong reason for wanting something to happen because you will gain from it: *Since he owns the strip of land, Cook* **has a** **vested** **interest** **in** **the** **project** **being** **approved.** **2 vested interests** the groups of people who will gain from a plan, project, proposal etc: *The proposal faces tough opposition from powerful vested*

interests. **3 vested rights, powers, property** etc belong to you and cannot be removed: *Shareholders* **have a** **vested right to** *10% per annum.* **4** *technical* having full rights to own or have something: **become/get** **vested (in sth)** *He only took the job to get vested in the pension fund.*

ves·ti·bule /'vest₁bjuːl/ *n* [C] *formal* **1** a space inside the front door of a public building **2** *AmE* the space at each end of a railway carriage that connects it with the next carriage

ves·tige /'vestɪdʒ/ *n* [C] *formal* **1** a small part or amount of something that remains when most of it no longer exists; **☐ trace:** [+of] *The new law removed* **the** **last vestiges** *of royal power.* **2** the smallest possible amount of a quality or feeling: [+of] *There's not a vestige of truth in the story.*

ves·ti·gi·al /ve'stɪdʒiəl, -dʒəl/ *adj* **1** *technical* a vestigial part of the body has never developed completely or has almost disappeared: *The legs of snakes are vestigial or absent altogether.* **2** *formal* remaining as a sign that something existed after most of it has gone: *his vestigial sense of pride*

vest·ment /'vestmənt/ *n* [C usually plural] a piece of clothing worn by priests during church services

ves·try /'vestri/ *n plural* **vestries** [C] a small room in a church where a priest puts on his or her vestments and where holy plates, cups etc are kept

vet[1] [S3] /vet/ *n* [C]
1 *also* **veterinary surgeon** *BrE formal* someone who is trained to give medical care and treatment to sick animals; **☐ veterinarian** *AmE*
2 *AmE informal* a VETERAN (1): *a Vietnam vet*

vet[2] *v* **vetted, vetting** [T] **1** *BrE* to check someone's past activities, relationships etc in order to make sure that person is suitable for a particular job, especially an important one: *All candidates are carefully vetted by Central Office.* **2** to check a report, speech etc carefully to make sure it is acceptable: *The author vets every script for the new TV series.*

vetch /vetʃ/ *n* [C] a plant with small flowers, often used to feed farm animals

vet·e·ran /'vetərən/ *n* [C] **1** someone who has been a soldier, sailor etc in a war: [+of] *a veteran of the Second World War* | *a Vietnam veteran* **2** someone who has had a lot of experience of a particular activity: [+of] *a veteran of countless political campaigns* | **veteran politician/campaigner/leader etc** *the veteran leader of the socialist party* | **veteran journalist/actor/goalkeeper etc**

veteran 'car *n* [C] *BrE* a car built before 1905

'Veterans Day *n* [C,U] a holiday in the US on 11 November when people show special respect to people who fought in wars as soldiers, SAILORS etc

vet·e·ri·nar·i·an /ˌvetərₑ¹neəriən $ -'ner-/ *n* [C] *AmE* someone who is trained to give medical care and treatment to sick animals; **☐ vet** *BrE*

vet·e·ri·na·ry /'vetərₑnəri $ -neri/ *adj* [only before noun] relating to the medical care and treatment of sick animals: *veterinary medicine*

'veterinary ˌsurgeon *n* [C] *BrE formal* a VET[1] (1)

ve·to[1] /'viːtəʊ $ -toʊ/ *v* **vetoed, vetoing, vetoes** [T] **1** if someone in authority vetoes something, they refuse to allow it to happen, especially something that other people or organizations have agreed: **veto legislation/a measure/a proposal etc** *President Bush vetoed the bill on July 6.* **2** to refuse to accept a particular plan or suggestion: *Jenny wanted to invite all her friends, but I quickly vetoed that idea.*

veto[2] *n plural* **vetoes** [C,U] a refusal to give official permission for something, or the right to refuse to give such permission: [+on] *de Gaulle's veto on the British application to join the EEC* | [+over] *The head teacher* has the **right** of **veto** over management-board decisions. | [+of] Washington's veto of Seoul's nuclear ambitions | The Senate had a sufficient majority to **override** the presidential veto (=not accept his refusal). | **exercise/use your veto**

vex /veks/ v [T] old-fashioned to make someone feel annoyed or worried —**vexing** adj: a vexing problem

vex·a·tion /vek'seɪʃən/ n old-fashioned **1** [U] when you feel worried or annoyed by something: **in vexation** Erika stamped her foot in vexation. **2** [C] something that worries or annoys you

vex·a·tious /vek'seɪʃəs/ adj old-fashioned making you feel annoyed or worried —**vexatiously** adv

vexed /vekst/ adj **1 vexed question/issue/problem etc** a complicated problem that has caused a lot of discussion and argument and is difficult to solve: [+of] the vexed question of sexism **2** [+ at/with] old-fashioned annoyed or worried

V-for·ma·tion /'viː fɔːˌmeɪʃən $ -fɔːr-/ n [C] if birds or planes fly in a V-formation, they form the shape of the letter V as they fly

VGA /ˌviː dʒiː 'eɪ/ n [U] technical **video graphics array** a standard of GRAPHICS (=pictures and letters) on a computer screen that has many different colours and is of a high quality

VHF /ˌviː eɪtʃ 'ef/ n [U] technical **very high frequency** radio waves that move very quickly and produce good sound quality

vi·a W2 /'vaɪə, 'viːə/ prep
1 travelling through a place on the way to another place: We flew to Athens via Paris.
2 using a particular person, machine etc to send something: I sent a message to Kitty via her sister. | You can access our homepage via the Internet.

vi·a·ble /'vaɪəbəl/ adj **1** a viable idea, plan, or method can work successfully: **viable alternative/proposition/option etc** The committee came forward with one viable solution. | **economically/commercially/financially viable** Will a hotel here be financially viable? **2** technical able to continue to live or to develop into a living thing: viable seeds —**viably** adv —**viability** /ˌvaɪə'bɪlɪti/ n [U]: the long-term economic viability of the company

vi·a·duct /'vaɪədʌkt/ n [C] a long high bridge, especially one with ARCHES, that crosses a valley and has a road or railway on it → see picture at BRIDGE[1]

Vi·ag·ra /vaɪ'ægrə/ n [U] trademark a drug that helps men to have an ERECTION

vi·al /'vaɪəl/ also **phial** BrE n [C] formal a very small bottle used for medicine, PERFUME etc

vi·ands /'vaɪəndz/ n [plural] old use food

vibes /vaɪbz/ n [plural] informal **1** the good or bad feelings that a particular person, place, or situation seems to produce and that you react to: **good/bad etc vibes** I have good vibes about this contract. **2** a VIBRAPHONE

vi·brant /'vaɪbrənt/ adj **1** full of activity or energy in a way that is exciting and attractive; ⊟ **lively**: Hong Kong is a vibrant, fascinating city. | She was sixteen, young and vibrant. **2** a vibrant colour is bright and strong: a painting full of vibrant reds and blues —**vibrancy** n [U] —**vibrantly** adv

vi·bra·phone /'vaɪbrəfəʊn $ -foʊn/ n [C] also **vibes** [plural] an electronic musical instrument that consists of metal bars that you hit with special sticks to produce a sound

vi·brate /vaɪ'breɪt $ 'vaɪbreɪt/ v [I,T] if something vibrates, or if you vibrate it, it shakes quickly and continuously with very small movements: The floor was vibrating to the beat of the music. | As air passes over our vocal cords, it makes them vibrate.; → see box at SHAKE[1]

vi·bra·tion /vaɪ'breɪʃən/ n [C,U] **1** a continuous slight shaking movement: the vibrations from the earthquake | The microscope must be free from vibration. **2 vibrations** [plural] VIBES (1)

vibration

vi·bra·to /vɪ'brɑːtəʊ $ -toʊ/ n [U] a way of singing or playing a musical note so that it goes up and down very slightly in PITCH

vi·bra·tor /vaɪ'breɪtə $ 'vaɪbreɪtər/ n [C] a piece of electrical equipment that produces a small shaking movement, used especially in MASSAGE or to get sexual pleasure

vic·ar /'vɪkə $ -ər/ n [C] a priest in the Church of England who is in charge of a church in a particular area

vic·ar·age /'vɪkərɪdʒ/ n [C] a house where a vicar lives

vi·car·i·ous /vɪ'keəriəs $ vaɪ'ker-/ adj [only before noun] experienced by watching or reading about someone else doing something, rather than by doing it yourself: **vicarious pleasure/satisfaction/excitement etc** the vicarious pleasure that parents get from their children's success —**vicariously** adv

vice S3 /vaɪs/ n
1 [U] criminal activities that involve sex or drugs: the fight against vice on the streets | The police have smashed a vice ring (=a group of criminals involved in vice) in Chicago. → VICE SQUAD
2 [C] a bad habit: Smoking is my only vice.
3 [C,U] a bad or immoral quality in a person, or bad or immoral behaviour; ⊟ **virtue**: Jealousy is a vice. | to reward virtue and punish vice
4 [C] usually **vise** AmE a tool that holds an object very firmly so that you can work on it: He held my arm like a vice. → VICE-LIKE

vice- /vaɪs/ prefix **vice-president/chairman etc** the person next in rank below someone in authority, who can represent them or act instead of them: [+of] the vice captain of the cricket team | Vice-Chairman Derek Edwards

vice-'admiral n [C] a high rank in the British or US navy, or someone who has this rank

vice-'chancellor n [C] **1** someone who is the head of a British university, and responsible for the way it is organized; → **chancellor 2** someone who is responsible for a particular part of some universities in the US: the vice-chancellor for student affairs

vice-like, vice·like BrE; **viselike, vise-like** AmE /'vaɪslaɪk/ adj **a vice-like grip** a very firm hold or a very strong pain: He grabbed my neck in a viselike grip.

vice 'president n [C] **1** the person who is next in rank to the president of a country and who is responsible for the president's duties if he or she is unable to do them **2** AmE someone who is responsible for a particular part of a company: our vice president for marketing

vice·roy /'vaɪsrɔɪ/ n [C] a man who was sent by a king or queen in the past to rule another country: [+of] the viceroy of India

vice squad n [C usually singular] the part of the police force that deals with crimes involving sex or drugs

vice ver·sa /ˌvaɪs 'vɜːsə, ˌvaɪsi- $ -ɜːr-/ adv used to say that the opposite of a situation you have just described is also true: The boys may refuse to play with the girls, and vice versa.

vi·cin·i·ty /vɪ'sɪnɪti/ n formal **1 in the vicinity (of sth)** in the area around a particular place: The stolen car was found in the vicinity of the station. | There used to *be a mill in the vicinity.* **2 in the vicinity of £3 million/ $1,500/2 billion years etc** close to a particular amount or measurement: *All meteorites are of the same age, somewhere in the vicinity of 4.5 billion years old.*

vi·cious /ˈvɪʃəs/ *adj* **1** violent and cruel in a way that hurts someone physically: *a vicious murder* | *a vicious killer* | *Keep away from that dog, he can be vicious.* **2** very unkind in a way that is intended to hurt someone's feelings or make their character seem bad; **☐ malicious:** *Sarah can be quite vicious at times.* | *a vicious personal attack on the Duchess* | *She was shocked by the vicious tone in his voice.* **3** unpleasantly strong or severe; **☐ violent:** *a vicious gust of wind* | *a vicious headache* —**viciously** *adv: He twisted her arm viciously.* —**viciousness** *n* [U]

vicious 'circle also **vicious 'cycle** *n* [singular] a situation in which one problem causes another problem, that then causes the first problem again, so that the whole process continues to be repeated

vi·cis·si·tudes /vɪˈsɪsɪˌtjuːdz $ -tuːdz/ *n* [plural] *formal* the continuous changes and problems that affect a situation or someone's life: [+of] *the vicissitudes of married life*

vic·tim [S2] [W2] /ˈvɪktɪm/ *n* [C]
1 someone who has been attacked, robbed, or murdered: *The victim received head injuries from which she died a week later.* | **rape/murder etc victim** *Most homicide victims are under 30.* | [+of] *victims of crime* | *a credit card fraud ring that stole millions of dollars from unsuspecting victims*
2 someone who suffers because of something bad that happens or because of an illness

> be the victim of sth
> famine/earthquake/flood etc victim
> cancer/AIDS etc victim
> accident/crash victim
> innocent victim
> victim of circumstance (=someone who suffers because of something they cannot control)
> victim mentality (=when someone always thinks of themselves as a victim)
> blame the victim

> [+of] *victims of age discrimination* | *He was the victim of an administrative error.* | *a massive aid programme for the famine victims* | *AIDS victims and other patients who are terminally ill* | *All these people are innocent victims.* | *He was used to being in charge, not being the victim of circumstance.* | *Saying that the unemployed 'don't want to work' is a classic case of blaming the victim.*

3 fall victim to sth *written* **a)** to be attacked, killed etc, or to get a particular illness, especially one that kills: *One theory is that the hostages fell victim to bandits.* **b)** to be badly affected or destroyed by a situation: *Many small businesses have fallen victim to the recession.*
4 be a victim of its own success to be badly affected by some unexpected results of being very successful: *There are now so many tourists that the area has become a victim of its own success.*
5 sacrificial victim a person or animal that is killed and offered as a SACRIFICE (=gift) to a god
6 fashion/style victim someone who always wears the most fashionable clothes even if they do not look good in them

vic·tim·ize also **-ise** *BrE* /ˈvɪktɪˌmaɪz/ *v* [T often passive] to treat someone unfairly because you do not like them, their beliefs, or the race they belong to; **☐ pick on:** *The men claim they have been victimized because of their political activity.* —**victimization** /ˌvɪktɪmaɪˈzeɪʃən $ -mə-/ *n* [U]

vic·tor /ˈvɪktə $ -ər/ *n* [C] *formal* the winner of a battle, game, competition etc: *After the game the victors returned in triumph.*

Vic·to·ri·an¹ /vɪkˈtɔːriən/ *adj* **1** relating to or coming from the period from 1837–1901 when Victoria was

Queen of England: *a big Victorian house* **2** morally strict in a way that was typical in the time of Queen Victoria: *Victorian values*

Victorian² *n* [C] an English person living in the period when Queen Victoria ruled

Vic·to·ri·a·na /vɪkˌtɔːriˈɑːnə $ -ˈænə/ *n* [U] objects made during the Victorian period

vic·to·ri·ous /vɪkˈtɔːriəs/ *adj* having won a victory, or ending in a victory: *the victorious team* | *We were confident that the Allies would emerge victorious* (=finally win). —**victoriously** *adv*

vic·to·ry [W2] /ˈvɪktəri/ *n plural* **victories** [C,U] the success you achieve when you win a battle, game, election etc; **☐ defeat**

> easy/comfortable victory
> great/decisive/resounding victory
> narrow victory (=a win, but only by a small amount)
> landslide victory (=a win by a very large amount in an election)
> moral victory (=when you show your beliefs are right and fair, even if you lose the argument)
> win/score a victory
> lead sb to victory
> sweep/romp/storm to victory (=win easily)
> victory celebrations

> *Napoleon's military victories* | [+over/against] *the Raiders' 35–17 victory over St Louis* | [+for] *This ruling represents a victory for all women.* | *It was a surprisingly easy victory.* | *The United States gained a decisive victory under his command.* | *The result was a narrow victory for Smith.* | *The polls were predicting that Labour would win a landslide victory.* | *The government has won a very important victory.* | *Jordan led his team to victory.* | *Jesse Owens swept to victory in the Olympic Games of 1936.*

→ PYRRHIC VICTORY

vict·ual /ˈvɪtl/ *v* [T] to supply a large number of people with food

vict·uals /ˈvɪtlz/ *n* [plural] *old use* food and drink

vi·cu·ña /vɪˈkjuːnə $ -ˈkuː-/ *n* [C,U] a large South American animal related to the LLAMA, or the cloth that is made from its wool: *a vicuña coat*

vi·de·li·cet /vɪˈdiːlɪˌset, -ket $ -ˈde-/ *adv* VIZ

vid·e·o¹ [S1] [W2] /ˈvɪdiəʊ $ -dioʊ/ *n plural* **videos**
1 [C] a copy of a film or television programme, or a series of events, recorded on VIDEOTAPE

> rent/get a video also
> hire a video *BrE*
> watch a video
> rewind a video (=move to an earlier part of a video by pressing a button)
> fast-forward a video (=move to a later part of a video by pressing a button)
> pause a video (=stop a video for a short time)
> make a video
> home video (=a video of your family, a holiday etc that you make yourself)
> promotional video (=a video of a product etc that is intended to help sell it)
> on video
> video shop *BrE*
> video store *AmE*: hire *BrE*/rent *AmE* a video

> *How much does it cost to hire videos?* | *Let's stay at home and watch a video.* | *Rewind the video right to the beginning.* | *The school will be making a video of the play.* | **on video** *The movie has not yet been released on video.* | *coming soon to a video store near you*

2 [C] a plastic box containing special tape for recording programmes and films on television; **☐ videotape, video cassette:** *Have we got a blank video* (=one with

nothing recorded on it yet) *anywhere?* → see picture at
TAPE¹

3 [C] *BrE* a machine used to record television programmes or show videos; ◨ **VCR**, **video cassette
recorder**: **programme/set the video** *Can you set the
video to record the football match?*

4 [U] the process of recording or showing television
programmes, films, real events etc on VIDEOTAPE: *The
course aims to help children learn through video.*

5 [C] a short film that is made to go with a particular
piece of popular music; ◨ **music video**

video² *v* *past tense and past participle* **videoed**, *present
participle* **videoing** [T] *BrE* to record a television programme, film, or a real event on a video; ◨ **videotape**;
◨ **tape** *AmE*: *Could you video the movie at 8.00? | A
friend videoed the wedding.*

video³ *adj* [only before noun] relating to or used in the
process of recording and showing pictures on televi-
sion; → **audio**: *video production | video materials for
language teaching*

'video ar,cade *n* [C] *AmE* a public place where there
are a lot of VIDEO GAMES that you play by putting money in
the machines

'video ,camera *n* [C] a special camera that can be
used to film events on a video

vid·e·o·card /'vɪdiəʊˌkɑːd $ -oʊˌkɑːrd/ *n* [C] a CIRCUIT
BOARD that can be added to a computer so that it is able
to show moving pictures

,video cas'sette also **videotape** *n* [C] a VIDEO

,video cas'sette re,corder *n* [C] *VCR* a machine
used to record television programmes or show videos;
◨ **video**

'video ,conferencing *n* [U] a system that makes it
possible to have meetings with people in different parts
of the world by sending pictures and sound electronically

'video ,diary *n* *plural* **video diaries** [C] a record on
video of someone's activities during a day, or over a
period of time: **make/keep a video diary** *The group
decided to make a video diary of the cycling trip.*

vid·e·o·disc also **videodisk** *AmE* /'vɪdiəʊˌdɪsk
$ -dioʊ-/ *n* [C] a round flat piece of plastic that you use
to record and show films or programmes in the same
way as a video → DVD

'video ,game *n* [C] a computer game in which you
move images on a screen using electronic controls

vid·e·og·ra·pher /ˌvɪdi'ɒɡrəfə $ -'ɑːɡrəfər/ *n* [C]
AmE *formal* someone who records events using a VIDEO
CAMERA

'video ,jockey *n* [C] *especially AmE* a VJ

,video 'nasty *n* [C] *BrE* *informal* a video film that
includes very violent and offensive scenes

vid·e·o·phone /'vɪdiəʊfəʊn $ -dioʊfoʊn/ *n* [C] a type
of telephone that allows you to see the person you are
talking to on a screen

'video re,corder *n* [C] a VIDEO CASSETTE RECORDER → see
picture at BEDROOM

vid·e·o·tape¹ /'vɪdiəʊteɪp $ -dioʊ-/ *n* [C,U] a video:
[+of] *a videotape of everyday life in Havana*

videotape² also **video** *BrE* *v* [T] to record a television
programme, film, event etc on a video

Vid·e·o·tex /'vɪdiəʊˌteks $ -dioʊ-/ *n* [U] *trademark* a
form of communication that allows information to be
exchanged using a television system

vie /vaɪ/ *v* **vied**, **vying**, **vies** [I] to compete very hard
with someone in order to get something: [+for] *Simon
and Julian were vying for her attention all through
dinner.* | [+with] *There are at least twenty restaurants
vying with each other for custom.* | **vie to do sth** *All the
photographers vied to get the best pictures.*

view¹ S1 W1 /vjuː/ *n*

1 OPINION [C] what you think or believe about something; ◨ **opinion**

have strong views (about sth)
have different/conflicting/opposing views
share sb's view/this view etc (=think the same as
someone else)
express a view
take the view that (=think that)
hold a view
strongly/deeply/widely held views
in sb's view (=used to show whose opinion it is)
support a view (=help show that it is right)
an exchange of views (=when people say what they
think)
the general view (=what most people think)

[+on/about] *What's your view on the subject? | She **has
strong views about** politics. | Everyone at the meeting
had different views. | He was worried about working
with people who did not **share** his **views**. | Not all
executives **share the view that** participation in online
discussions is good for business. | The **views expressed**
in this book are purely those of the author. | The twins'
parents **took the view that** surgery would be wrong. |
Freud's work affected **widely held views** on sexual
matters. | **In my view**, the country needs a change of
government. | Not all the evidence **supports** this **view**. |
There was a frank **exchange of views** at the meeting. |
The general view was that you can't overfeed a baby.* →
POINT OF VIEW (2)

2 WAY OF CONSIDERING [C usually singular] a way of
thinking about or understanding something: [+of]
*Mum's view of the situation was different to mine. |
optimistic/pessimistic/balanced etc view a realistic
view of human nature | traditional views of religion |
You need to **have a clear view** (=a definite idea) of the
kind of book you want to write. | **take a dim/poor view**
of sth (=disapprove) She took a pretty dim view of his
behaviour.*

3 SIGHT [C,U] what you are able to see or whether you
can see it: [+of] *We'd like a room with a view of the sea. |
good/bad/wonderful etc view The house **has** wonderful
views over the valley. | **be in view/come into view**
Suddenly the pyramids came into view. | **disappear/
vanish/hide from view** The gun was hidden from view
behind the door. | Fran hit him **in full view of** all the
guests (=where they could see it clearly). | During an
eclipse, the moon **blocks** our **view** of the sun (=stops us
from seeing it).*

4 SCENERY [C] the whole area that you can see from
somewhere, especially when it is very beautiful or
impressive: *From the top you get a **panoramic view** of
the city. | A huge nuclear reactor now **spoils** the **view**.*

5 PICTURE [C] a photograph or picture showing a
beautiful or interesting place: [+of] *The book contains
over fifty scenic views of Cambridge.*

6 CHANCE TO SEE STH [C,U] an occasion or time
when it is possible for people to see something such as
an art show: [+of] *A **private view** of the Summer
Exhibition will be held. | **on view** (=being shown to the
public) The painting is currently on view at the Tate.*

7 in view of sth *formal* used to introduce the reason for
a decision or action: *In view of his conduct, the club has
decided to suspend him.*

8 with a view to (doing) sth because you are planning to
do something in the future: *We bought the house with a
view to retiring there.*

9 in view *formal* having something in your mind as an
aim: **with this end/object/aim etc in view** *Defence was
all-important, and castles were designed with this end in
view. | What sort of job did you **have in view**?*

10 take the long view (of sth) *BrE* to think about the
effect that something will have in the future rather
than what happens now

view² *v* [T] **1** to think about something or someone in
a particular way; ◨ **see**: **view sth as sth** *The law should
be viewed as a way of meeting certain social goals. |
view sth from a ... perspective/standpoint It's an issue
that can be viewed from several perspectives. | **view sth
with caution/suspicion/scepticism etc** The local people*

viewed newcomers with suspicion. **2** *formal* to look at something, especially because it is beautiful or you are interested in it: **view sth from sth** *The mountain is best viewed from the north side.* | *Thousands of tourists come to view the gardens every year.* | **view a house/an apartment/a property** (=go to see a house etc that you are interested in buying) **3** *formal* to watch a television programme, film etc: *an opportunity to view the film before it goes on general release*

view·er /ˈvjuːə $ -ər/ *n* [C] **1** someone who watches television: *The new series has gone down well with viewers.* **2** someone who looks at something: *In the painting, the woman has her back to the viewer.* **3** a small box with a light in it used to look at SLIDES (=colour photographs on special film)

view·find·er /ˈvjuːˌfaɪndə $ -ər/ *n* [C] the small square of glass on a camera that you look through to see exactly what you are photographing → see picture at CAMERA

view·point /ˈvjuːpɔɪnt/ *n* [C] **1** a particular way of thinking about a problem or subject; ▣ **point of view**: **from sb's viewpoint/from the viewpoint of sb/sth** *Try and think of it from the child's viewpoint.* | *The islands were important from the viewpoint of American security.* | **[+on]** *the Church's viewpoint on divorce* | **political/scientific/feminist etc viewpoint** *From an ecological viewpoint, the motorway has been a disaster.* **2** a place from which you can see something: *Different viewpoints produce different images.*

vig·il /ˈvɪdʒɪl/ *n* [C,U] **1** a period of time, especially during the night, when you stay awake in order to pray, remain with someone who is ill, or watch for danger: *Eva and Paul kept a constant vigil by their daughter's hospital bedside.* **2** a silent political protest in which people wait outside a building, especially during the night: **silent/candlelit vigil** *2000 demonstrators held a candlelit vigil outside the embassy.*

vig·i·lance /ˈvɪdʒɪləns/ *n* [U] careful attention that you give to what is happening, so that you will notice any danger or illegal activity: *the need for increased police vigilance*

vig·i·lant /ˈvɪdʒɪlənt/ *adj* giving careful attention to what is happening, so that you will notice any danger or illegal activity: *Please remain vigilant at all times and report anything suspicious.* —**vigilantly** *adv*

vig·i·lan·te /ˌvɪdʒɪˈlænti/ *n* [C] someone who illegally punishes criminals and tries to prevent crime, usually because they think the police are not doing this effectively —**vigilantism** *n* [U]

vi·gnette /vɪˈnjet/ *n* [C] *formal* **1** a short description in a book or play showing the typical features of a person or situation **2** a small picture or design at the beginning or end of a book or CHAPTER

vig·or /ˈvɪgə $ -ər/ the American spelling of VIGOUR

vig·o·rous /ˈvɪgərəs/ *adj* **1** using a lot of energy and strength or determination: *Your dog needs at least 20 minutes of vigorous exercise every day.* | *Environmentalists have begun a vigorous campaign to oppose nuclear dumping in the area.* | *a vigorous debate* | *Vigorous efforts are being made to find a solution to the problem.* | *The measures provoked vigorous opposition in right-wing circles.* **2** strong and healthy: *a vigorous young man* —**vigorously** *adv*

vig·our *BrE*; **vigor** *AmE* /ˈvɪgə $ -ər/ *n* [U] physical or mental energy and determination: **with vigour** *He began working with renewed vigour.*

Vi·king /ˈvaɪkɪŋ/ *n* [C] a member of the group of Scandinavian people who sailed in ships to attack areas along the coasts of northern and western Europe from the 8th to 11th centuries

vile /vaɪl/ *adj* **1** *informal* extremely unpleasant or bad; ▣ **horrible**: *This coffee tastes really vile.* | *a vile smell* | *She has a vile temper.* **2** evil or immoral: *a vile act of betrayal* —**vilely** *adv* —**vileness** *n* [U]

vil·i·fy /ˈvɪlɪfaɪ/ *v* **vilified, vilifying, vilifies** [T] *formal* to say or write bad things about someone or something:

vilify sb/sth for (doing) sth *Johnson was vilified in the press for refusing to resign.* —**vilification** /ˌvɪlɪfɪˈkeɪʃən/ *n* [U]

vil·la /ˈvɪlə/ *n* [C] **1** *BrE* a house that you use or rent while you are on holiday **2** a big house in the country with a large garden **3** a house in a town: *Victorian villas* **4** an ancient Roman house or farm with land surrounding it

vil·lage [S1] [W1] /ˈvɪlɪdʒ/ *n* [C]
1 a very small town in the countryside: *a little fishing village* | **village school/shop/church etc**
2 the village the people who live in a village: *The whole village came to the meeting.*

village green *n* [C] an area of grass in the middle of an English village

village idiot *n* [C] someone in the past who had mental difficulties and lived in a small village with the other people there

vil·lag·er /ˈvɪlɪdʒə $ -ər/ *n* [C] someone who lives in a village

vil·lain /ˈvɪlən/ *n* [C] **1** the main bad character in a film, play, or story **2 the villain of the piece** the person or thing that has caused all the trouble in a particular situation **3** *informal* a bad person or criminal

vil·lain·ous /ˈvɪlənəs/ *adj literary* evil or criminal

vil·lain·y /ˈvɪləni/ *n* [U] *literary* evil or criminal behaviour

-ville /vɪl/ *suffix* **1** used in the names of places, especially in the US, to mean city or town: *Jacksonville, Florida* **2** *informal* used humorously with adjectives or nouns followed by 's' to show that a person, place, or thing has a particular quality: *Her party was really dullsville.*

vil·lein /ˈvɪlɪn, ˈvɪleɪn/ *n* [C] a poor farm worker in the Middle Ages who was given a small piece of land in return for working on the land of a rich lord

vim /vɪm/ *n* [U] *old-fashioned* energy: *She was full of vim and vigour.*

vin·ai·grette /ˌvɪnɪˈgret, ˌvɪneɪ-/ *n* [singular, U] a mixture of oil, VINEGAR, salt, and pepper that you put on a SALAD; ▣ **salad dressing**

vin·di·cate /ˈvɪndɪkeɪt/ *v* [T] *formal* **1** to prove that someone who was blamed for something is in fact not guilty: *The charges are false, and we are sure we will be vindicated in court.* **2** to prove that someone or something is right or true; ▣ **justify**: *The decision to advertise has been vindicated by the fact that sales have grown.* —**vindication** /ˌvɪndɪˈkeɪʃən/ *n* [singular, U]

vin·dic·tive /vɪnˈdɪktɪv/ *adj* unreasonably cruel and unfair towards someone who has harmed you: *a bitter and vindictive old man* —**vindictively** *adv* —**vindictiveness** *n* [U]

vine /vaɪn/ *n* [C] **1** also **grapevine** a plant that produces GRAPES **2** a plant with long thin stems that attach themselves to other plants, trees, buildings etc

vin·e·gar /ˈvɪnɪgə $ -ər/ *n* [U] a sour-tasting liquid made from MALT or wine that is used to improve the taste of food or to preserve it

vin·e·gar·y /ˈvɪnɪgəri/ *adj* tasting of vinegar

vine·yard /ˈvɪnjəd $ -jərd/ *n* [C] a piece of land where GRAPEVINES are grown in order to produce wine

vineyard

vi·no /ˈviːnəʊ $ -noʊ/ *n* [U] *informal* wine

vin·tage¹ /ˈvɪntɪdʒ/ *adj* [only before noun] **1** vintage wine is good quality wine made in a particular year **2** old, but high quality: *vintage cars* **3** showing all the best or most typical qualities of something: *a vintage performance from Bruce Springsteen* **4 vintage year a)** a year when a good quality wine was produced **b)** a year when something of very good quality was produced: [+**for**] *2001 was not a vintage year for movies.*

vintage² *n* **1** [C] a particular year or place in which a wine is made, or the wine itself **2** of recent vintage having happened or started not very long ago: *There are some classic songs on the album, but most are of more recent vintage.*

vintage 'car *n* [C] *BrE* a car made between 1919 and 1930

vint·ner /ˈvɪntnə $ -ər/ *n* [C] *formal* someone who buys and sells wines

vi·nyl /ˈvaɪnᵊl/ *n* [U] **1** a type of strong plastic **2** records that are played on a RECORD PLAYER - used especially when comparing them to CDS

vi·o·la /viˈəʊlə $ -ˈoʊ-/ *n* [C] **1** a wooden musical instrument that you play like a VIOLIN but that is larger and has a lower sound **2** a plant related to the VIOLET

vi·o·late /ˈvaɪəleɪt/ *v* [T] **1** to disobey or do something against an official agreement, law, principle etc: *34 protesters were arrested for violating criminal law.* | *regimes that violate human rights* **2** to do something that makes someone feel that they have been attacked or have suffered a great loss of respect: *Victims of burglaries often feel personally violated.* | *The media regularly violates people's privacy.* **3** *formal* to break open a GRAVE, or force your way into a holy place without showing any respect: *Vandals had violated the graveyard.* **4** *literary* to force a woman to have sex; ☐ **rape** —**violator** *n* [C]

vi·o·la·tion /ˌvaɪəˈleɪʃən/ *n* [C,U] **1** an action that breaks a law, agreement, principle etc: *human rights violations* | [+**of**] *a violation of international law* | **in violation of sth** *Troops crossed the border in violation of the agreement.* **2** something that causes harm or damage by treating someone or their possessions without respect

vi·o·lence S2 W2 /ˈvaɪələns/ *n* [U]
1 behaviour that is intended to hurt other people physically

---

act of violence
physical violence
domestic violence (=violence between a man and woman in their home)
racial/ethnic violence (=violence between different groups of people)
use/resort to violence (=behave violently)
violence erupts/explodes (=there is suddenly a lot of violence)

There is too much sex and violence on TV these days. | [+**against**] *violence against women* | *We condemn any* **act of violence**. | *threats of* **physical violence** | *refuges for women escaping from* **domestic violence** | *Neither side wants to* **resort to violence**. | *When marchers gathered on a third day of protest,* **violence erupted** *and buildings were burned.*

---

2 extreme force: *the tremendous violence of a tornado* **3 do violence to sth** *formal* to spoil something **4** *literary* an angry way of speaking or reacting: *She spoke with a violence that surprised them both.*

vi·o·lent S3 W3 /ˈvaɪələnt/ *adj*
1 involving actions that are intended to injure or kill people, by hitting them, shooting them etc: *the increase in* **violent crime** | *violent clashes between the police and demonstrators* | *31 people have been injured in violent incidents throughout the day.* | *The riots ended in the violent deaths of three teenagers.*
2 someone who is violent is likely to attack, hurt, or kill other people; ☐ **aggressive**: *My father was a violent and dangerous man.* | *He had a reputation for* **turning violent** (=suddenly attacking people).
3 showing very strong angry emotions or opinions: **violent quarrel/argument/row etc** *They had a violent quarrel and John stormed out.*

4 violent feelings are strong and very difficult to control: *They took a violent dislike to each other.* | *She has a violent temper.*
5 violent headache/fit etc a physical feeling or reaction that is very painful or difficult to control
6 violent film/play/drama a film etc that contains a lot of violence
7 a violent storm/earthquake/explosion etc a storm etc that happens with a lot of force
8 extremely bright: *Her cheeks turned a violent red colour.*

vi·o·lent·ly /ˈvaɪələntli/ *adv* **1** with a lot of force in a way that is very difficult to control: **tremble/shiver/shake etc violently** *I was still trembling violently.* | **violently sick/ill** *He rushed to the bathroom, where he was violently sick.* **2** in a way that involves violence: *Several people have been violently attacked in the subway.* **3** with a lot of energy or emotion, especially anger: *Jenny protested violently.*

vi·o·let /ˈvaɪələt/ *n* **1** [C] a plant with small dark purple flowers, or sometimes white or yellow ones → see picture at **FLOWER¹** **2** [U] a bluish-purple colour —**violet** *adj: beautiful violet eyes*

vi·o·lin /ˌvaɪəˈlɪn/ *n* [C] a small wooden musical instrument that you hold under your chin and play by pulling a BOW (=special stick) across the strings → see picture at **STRINGED INSTRUMENT**

vi·o·lin·ist /ˌvaɪəˈlɪnᵻst/ *n* [C] someone who plays the violin

vi·o·lon·cel·lo /ˌvaɪələnˈtʃeləʊ $ -loʊ/ *n plural* **violoncellos** [C] *formal* a CELLO

VIP /ˌviː aɪ ˈpiː/ *n* [C] *very important person* someone who is very famous or powerful and is treated with special care and respect: *They treated us like VIPs.* | *We were given* **VIP treatment**.

vi·per /ˈvaɪpə $ -ər/ *n* [C] **1** a small poisonous snake **2** *literary* someone who behaves in an unpleasant way and harms other people

vi·ra·go /vᵻˈrɑːgəʊ $ -goʊ/ *n plural* **viragos** [C] *formal* an offensive word for an angry woman who often argues with people

vi·ral /ˈvaɪərəl $ ˈvaɪrəl/ *adj* relating to or caused by a VIRUS: *a viral infection*

'viral marketing *n* [U] a type of advertising used by Internet companies in which computer users receive and send out advertising messages or images through email without realizing that they are doing this: *You can reach more potential customers by using viral marketing techniques.*

vir·gin¹ /ˈvɜːdʒᵻn $ ˈvɜːr-/ *n* [C] **1** someone who has never had sex **2 the Virgin Mary** also **the (Blessed) Virgin** Mary, the mother of Jesus Christ **3** someone who has never done a particular activity before: *a snowboarding virgin*

virgin² *adj* [only before noun] **1 virgin land/forest/soil/snow etc** land etc that is still in its natural state and has not been used or changed by people **2** without sexual experience: *a virgin bride* **3 virgin territory** something new that you are experiencing for the first time **4 (extra) virgin olive oil** the highest quality of OLIVE OIL, made from the first pressing of the olives

vir·gin·al /ˈvɜːdʒᵻnəl $ ˈvɜːr-/ *adj* like a virgin

vir·gin·als /ˈvɜːdʒᵻnəlz $ ˈvɜːr-/ *n* [plural] a small square musical instrument like a piano with no legs, popular in the 16th and 17th centuries

virgin 'birth *n* **the virgin birth** the birth of Jesus, which Christians believe was caused by God, not by sex between a man and a woman

vir·gin·i·a creep·er /vɜːˌdʒɪniə ˈkriːpə $ vɜːrˌdʒɪniə ˈkriːpər/ *n* [C,U] a garden plant that grows up walls and has large leaves that turn deep red in autumn

vir·gin·i·ty /vɜːˈdʒɪnᵻti $ vɜːr-/ *n* [U] the condition of never having had sex: **lose your virginity** (=have sex for the first time)

Vir·go /ˈvɜːgəʊ $ ˈvɜːrgoʊ/ *n plural* **Virgos** **1** [U] the sixth sign of the ZODIAC, represented by a young woman, which some people believe affects the character and life of people born between August 24 and September 23 **2** [C] someone who was born between August 24 and September 23

vir·ile /'vɪraɪl $ 'vɪrəl/ adj having or showing tradition-ally male qualities such as strength, courage etc – use this to show approval; → **macho**

vi·ril·i·ty /vɪ'rɪlɪti/ n [U] **1** the typically male quality of being strong, brave, and full of energy – used to show approval **2** the ability of a man to have sex or make a woman PREGNANT

vi·rol·o·gy /vaɪə'rɒlədʒi $ vaɪ'rɑː-/ n [U] the scientific study of VIRUSES or of the diseases caused by them —**virologist** n [C]

vir·tu·al /'vɜːtʃuəl $ 'vɜːr-/ adj [only before noun] **1** very nearly a particular thing: *Car ownership is a virtual necessity when you live in the country.* | *Finding a cheap place to rent is a virtual impossibility in this area.* **2** made, done, seen etc on the Internet or on a computer, rather than in the real world: *The website allows you to take a virtual tour of the art gallery.* | *constructing virtual worlds*

vir·tu·al·ly [S2] [W2] /'vɜːtʃuəli $ 'vɜːr-/ adv **1** almost; **▣ practically**: *Virtually all the children come to school by bus.* | *He was virtually unknown before running for office.* **2** on a computer, rather than in the real world

virtual 'office n [C] a situation in which a company's workers do not go to an office to work, but instead use computers that are connected to the Internet to com-municate with each other from different places: *Does the virtual office equal freedom or isolation?*

virtual re'ality n [U] an environment produced by a computer that looks and seems real to the person experiencing it

vir·tue [W3] /'vɜːtʃuː $ 'vɜːr-/ n
1 [U] formal moral goodness of character and behav-iour; **▣** vice: *Women have often been used as symbols of virtue.*
2 [C] a particular good quality in someone's character; **▣** vice: *Among her many virtues are loyalty, courage, and truthfulness.*
3 [C,U] an advantage that makes something better or more useful than something else: [+of] *Adam Smith believed in the virtues of free trade.* | *Wilkins is now extolling* (=praising very much) *the virtues of organic farming.*
4 by virtue of sth formal by means of, or as a result of something: *She became a British resident by virtue of her marriage.*
5 make a virtue of necessity to get an advantage out of doing something that you have to do

vir·tu·os·i·ty /ˌvɜːtʃu'ɒsɪti $ ˌvɜːrtʃu'ɑː-/ n [U] formal a very high degree of skill in performing

vir·tu·o·so /ˌvɜːtʃu'əʊsəʊ $ ˌvɜːrtʃu'oʊsoʊ/ n plural **virtuosos** [C] someone who is a very skilful performer, especially in music: *violin virtuoso Stephane Grappelli* —**virtuoso** adj [only before noun]: *a virtuoso performance* | *a virtuoso pianist*

vir·tu·ous /'vɜːtʃuəs $ 'vɜːr-/ adj **1** formal behaving in a very honest and moral way; **▣** wicked: *a virtuous man* | *Natalie considered herself very virtuous because she neither drank nor smoked.* **2** old use not willing to have sex, at least until you are married —**virtuously** adv

vir·u·lent /'vɪrʊlənt/ adj **1** a poison, disease etc that is virulent is very dangerous and affects people very quickly; **▣** mild: *a particularly virulent form of influ-enza* **2** formal full of hatred for something, or express-ing this in a strong way – used to show disapproval: *virulent anti-Semitism* —**virulence** n [U] —**virulently** adv

vi·rus /'vaɪərəs $ 'vaɪrəs/ n **1** [C,U] a very small living thing that causes infectious illnesses: *children infected with the Aids virus* | *a virus infection* **2** [C] a set of instructions secretly put onto a computer or computer program, which can destroy information. When a computer that has a virus makes a connection

with another computer, for example by EMAIL, the virus can make copies of itself and move to the other com-puter **3** [C] a program that sends a large number of annoying messages to many people's MOBILE PHONES in an uncontrolled way

vi·sa /'viːzə/ n [C] an official mark put on your PASSPORT that gives you permission to temporarily enter or leave a foreign country: *I was still in New York, trying to get a visa for Russia.* | **exit/entry/transit visa** | **work/student/ tourist etc visa**

vis·age /'vɪzɪdʒ/ n [C] literary a face

vis-à-vis /ˌviːz ɑː 'viː, ˌviːz ə-/ prep formal in relation to or in comparison with something or someone: *the bargaining position of the UK vis-à-vis the rest of Europe*

vis·ce·ra /'vɪsərə/ n [plural] medical the large organs inside your body, such as your heart, lungs, and stom-ach

vis·ce·ral /'vɪsərəl/ adj **1** literary visceral beliefs and attitudes are the result of strong feelings rather than careful thought: *his visceral hatred of the ruling class* **2** medical relating to the viscera

vis·cid /'vɪsɪd/ adj VISCOUS

vis·count /'vaɪkaʊnt/ n [C] a British NOBLEMAN with a rank between that of an EARL and a BARON

vis·count·ess /'vaɪkaʊntɪs/ n [C] the wife of a vis-count, or a woman who has the rank of a viscount

vis·cous /'vɪskəs/ adj technical a viscous liquid is thick and sticky and does not flow easily: *As the liquid cools, it becomes viscous.* —**viscosity** /vɪ'skɒsɪti $ -'skɑː-/ n [U]

vise /vaɪs/ the American spelling of VICE

vis·i·bil·i·ty /ˌvɪzɪ'bɪlɪti/ n [U] **1** the distance it is possible to see, especially when this is affected by weather conditions: *Visibility on the roads is down to 20 metres due to heavy fog.* | **good/poor visibility** *The search for survivors was abandoned because of poor visibil-ity.* **2** the situation of being noticed by people in general: [+of] *The exhibition helped increase the visibil-ity of women artists.* **3** the fact of being easy to see: **high visibility** clothing

vis·i·ble [W3] /'vɪzɪbəl/ adj
1 something that is visible can be seen; **▣** invisible: **clearly/highly/barely etc visible** *The outline of the moun-tains was clearly visible.* | [+to] *The sign was clearly visible to passing motorists.* | *The comet is visible to the naked eye* (=can be seen without using special equipment). | *Check the plant for any visible signs of disease.*
2 an effect that is visible is great enough to be noticed; **▣** noticeable: *There has been a visible change in his attitude.*
3 someone who is visible is in a situation in which a lot of people notice them: **highly visible** politicians

vis·i·bly /'vɪzɪbli/ adv in a way that is easy to see or notice: **visibly shaken/shocked/upset etc** *She was vis-ibly shaken by the news.*

vi·sion [S3] [W2] /'vɪʒən/ n
1 [U] ability to see; **▣** sight: *She suffered temporary loss of vision after being struck on the head.* | *Tears blurred her vision* (=made it difficult for her to see). | **good/ normal/poor etc vision** *children who are born with poor vision* | **twenty-twenty/20-20 vision** (=the ability to see perfectly) | **night vision** (=the ability to see when it is dark)
2 [U] the area that you can see: *a figure at the edge of her vision* | **sb's field/line of vision** (=the area someone is able to see without turning their head) *As the cars overtake you, they are temporarily outside your field of vision.*
3 [C] an idea of what you think something should be like: [+of] *He had a clear vision of how he hoped the company would develop.* | [+for] *The President outlined*

V

his vision for the future. | **grand/powerful/original etc vision** *a grand vision for the country*
4 have visions of sth if you have visions of something happening, especially something bad, you imagine it happening: *I had visions of the kids getting lost and getting abducted by some weirdo.*
5 [C] something that you seem to see as part of a powerful religious experience: *She **had** a **vision** in which Jesus appeared before her.* | **in a vision** *He became a monk after seeing Saint Apollinaris in a vision.*
6 [U] the knowledge and imagination that are needed in planning for the future with a clear purpose: *We need a leader with vision and strong principles.* | *his enthusiasm and **breadth of vision***
7 a vision of beauty/loveliness etc *literary* someone who is very beautiful
8 [U] the quality of a picture that you can see on a television

vi·sion·a·ry¹ /'vɪʒənəri $ -neri/ *adj* **1** having clear ideas of what the world should be like in the future: *Under his visionary leadership, the city prospered.* **2** existing only in someone's mind and unlikely to ever exist in the real world

visionary² *n plural* **visionaries** [C] **1** someone who has clear ideas and strong feelings about the way something should be in the future **2** a holy person who has VISIONS

vis·it¹ S2 W1 /'vɪzᵻt/ *v*
1 [I,T] to go and spend time in a place or with someone, especially for pleasure or interest: *Eric went to Seattle to visit his cousins.* | *I was really pleased that they **came to visit** me.* | *Which cities did you visit in Spain?* | *A recent trip to London gave me the opportunity to visit the Science Museum.* | *She doesn't visit very often.* ⚠ In spoken English it is more usual to say that you **go to** a place or **go to see/go and see** a person or place: *We went to the Louvre.* | *I'm going to see my mother.*
2 [T] to go to a place as part of your official job, especially to examine it: *The building inspector is visiting the new housing project.* | **[+with]** *AmE*: *The President's first trip abroad will be to visit with troops in Bosnia.*
3 [T] *formal* to go to see a doctor, lawyer etc in order to get treatment or advice
4 [T] to look at a website on the Internet: *Over 1,000 people visit our site every week.*
5 [I] *AmE* to talk socially with someone: **[+with]** *Why don't you kids play outside while we visit with each other?*
  visit sth **on** sb/sth *phr v biblical*
to do something to punish someone or show them that you are angry: *God's wrath will be visited on sinners.*

visit² W3 *n* [C]
1 an occasion when someone goes to spend time in a place or goes to see a person

> **on a visit**
> **for a visit**
> **pay sb a visit** (=visit someone)
> **have a visit from sb**
> **flying visit** *BrE* (=a very short visit)
> **official visit**
> **be (well) worth a visit** (=be interesting to go to)

[+to] *a visit to Chicago* | *We're just here **on a short visit**.* | *Why don't you come **for a visit** this summer?* | *I decided to **pay** him **a visit** at his office.* | *I've just **had a visit from** the police.* | *I'm only here **for the weekend** – just a **flying visit** this time.* | *his first **official visit** to Britain as Russian President* | *The town is **well worth a visit**.*

2 an occasion when you see a doctor, lawyer etc for treatment or advice
3 *AmE* an occasion when you talk socially with someone: *Barbara and I had a nice long visit.*

vis·i·ta·tion /ˌvɪzᵻ'teɪʃən/ *n* **1** [C,U] *formal* an official visit to a place or person **2** [C,U] *law* an occasion

when a parent is allowed to spend time with the children after a DIVORCE, or the right to do this: *visitation rights* **3** [C] an occasion when God or a spirit is believed to appear to someone on earth **4** [C] *literary* an event that is believed to be God's punishment for something: *a visitation of plague* **5** [C] a long visit from someone that you do not want to see – used humorously

'visiting card *n* [C] a small card with their name on it which people gave to someone they visited, in the past; ▣ **calling card** *AmE*

'visiting hours *n* [plural] the times when you are allowed to visit people who are in a hospital

ˌvisiting pro'fessor *n* [C] a university teacher who has come from another university to teach for a period of time

vis·it·or S2 W2 /'vɪzᵻtə $ -ər/ *n* [C] someone who comes to visit a place or a person: *Times Square attracts more than 30 million visitors annually.* | **[+to]** *Rina is a frequent visitor to the city.* | **[+from]** *visitors from overseas* → HEALTH VISITOR

'visitors' book *n* [C] a book, especially in a church or hotel, in which visitors write their names and addresses

vi·sor /'vaɪzə $ -ər/ *n* [C] **1** the part of a HELMET (=protective hard hat) that can be lowered to protect your face **2** *AmE* the curved part of a cap that sticks out in front above your eyes; ▣ **peak** *BrE* **3** a flat object fixed above the front window inside a car that can be moved down to keep the sun out of your eyes **4** a curved piece of plastic that you wear on your head so that it sticks out above your eyes and protects them from the sun

vis·ta /'vɪstə/ *n* [C] **1** *literary* a view of a large area of beautiful scenery: **[+of]** *stunning vistas of the Norfolk coast* **2** the possibility of new experiences, ideas, events etc: *Exchange programs **open up new vistas** for students.*

vi·su·al¹ W3 /'vɪʒuəl/ *adj* [usually before noun] relating to seeing: *Artists translate their ideas into visual images.* | *The tall tower adds to the visual impact of the building.*

visual² *n* [usually plural] something such as a picture or the part of a film, video etc that you can see, as opposed to the parts that you hear: *the film's stunning visuals*

ˌvisual 'aid *n* [C] something such as a map, picture, or film that helps people understand, learn, or remember information

ˌvisual 'arts *n* [plural] art such as painting, SCULPTURE etc that you look at, as opposed to literature or music

ˌvisual di'splay ˌunit *n* [C] VDU

vi·su·al·ize also **-ise** *BrE* /'vɪʒuəlaɪz/ *v* [T] to form a picture of someone or something in your mind; ▣ **imagine**: *I tried to visualize the house while he was describing it.* | **visualize sb doing sth** *Somehow I can't visualize myself staying with this company for much longer.* | **visualize how/what etc** *It's hard to visualize how these tiles will look in our bathroom.* —**visualization** /ˌvɪʒuəlaɪ'zeɪʃən $ -lə-/ *n* [U]

vi·su·al·ly /'vɪʒuəli/ *adv* **1** in appearance: *Chairs should be visually attractive as well as comfortable.* **2 visually impaired** unable to see normally – used especially when you want to be polite about this condition; → **blind** **3** in a way that involves the eyes: *The process is easy to understand when it is demonstrated visually.*

vi·tal W2 /'vaɪtl/ *adj*
1 extremely important and necessary for something to succeed or exist; ▣ **crucial**

> **absolutely vital**
> **it is vital that**
> **it is vital to do sth**
> **of vital importance** (=very important)
> **play a vital role/part (in sth)**
>
> **vital part/piece/element/component/ingredient**
> **vital information/evidence/clue**

*The work she does is **absolutely vital**.* | [+to] *These measures are vital to national security.* | [+for] *Regular exercise is vital for your health.* | **it is vital (that)** *It is vital that you keep accurate records.* | **it is vital to do sth** *It is vital to keep accurate records.* | *It is vital to be honest with your children.* | *The tourist industry is of **vital importance** to the national economy.* | *Richardson played a **vital role** in the team's success.* | *The samples could give scientists **vital information** about long-term changes in the earth's atmosphere.*

2 full of energy in a way that is exciting and attractive: *Rodgers and Hart's music sounds as fresh and vital as the day it was written.*
3 [only before noun] necessary in order to keep you alive: *the body's vital processes* | **vital organs** (=heart, lungs etc)
4 vital signs *medical* the signs that show someone is alive, for example breathing and body temperature

vi·tal·i·ty /vaɪ'tæləti/ *n* [U] **1** great energy and eagerness to do things: *Despite her eighty years, Elsie was full of vitality.* **2** the strength and ability of an organization, country etc to continue: *The process of restructuring has injected some much-needed vitality into the company.* | [+of] *The senator promised to restore the economic vitality of the region.*

vi·tal·ly /'vaɪtl-i/ *adv* in a very important or necessary way: *A sensible diet is **vitally important** if you want to remain in good health.*

vital 'organ *n* [C usually plural] a part of your body that is necessary to keep you alive, for example your heart and lungs

vi·tals /'vaɪtlz/ *n* [plural] *old use* the parts of your body that are necessary to keep you alive, for example your heart and lungs

vital sta'tistics *n* [plural] **1** figures giving information about the number of births, deaths, marriages etc within a population **2** *BrE informal* a woman's chest, waist, and HIP measurements **3** *informal* important facts about something, especially its size

vit·a·min /'vɪtəmɪn, 'vaɪ- $ 'vaɪ-/ *n* [C] **1** a chemical substance in food that is necessary for good health: *Try to eat foods that are rich in vitamins and minerals.* | **vitamin A/B/C etc** (=a particular type of vitamin) | *Lack of vitamin E can cause skin diseases and tiredness.* **2** also **vitamin pill** also **vitamin supplement** a PILL containing vitamins: *Perhaps I ought to **take vitamins**.*

vi·ti·ate /'vɪʃieɪt/ *v* [T] *formal* to make something less effective or spoil it

vit·i·cul·ture /'vɪtɪkʌltʃə $ -ər/ *n* [U] the science or practice of growing GRAPES for making wine

vit·re·ous /'vɪtriəs/ *adj technical* made of or looking like glass

vit·ri·fy /'vɪtrɪfaɪ/ *v* **vitrified, vitrifying, vitrifies** [I,T] *technical* if a substance vitrifies or is vitrified, it changes into glass *n* [U]

vit·ri·ol /'vɪtriəl/ *n* **1** *formal* very cruel and angry remarks that are intended to hurt someone's feelings **2** *old use* SULPHURIC ACID

vit·ri·ol·ic /ˌvɪtri'ɒlɪk $ -'ɑ:lɪk/ *adj formal* vitriolic language, writing etc is very cruel and angry towards someone: *vitriolic remarks*

vitro → IN VITRO FERTILIZATION

vi·tu·pe·ra·tion /vɪˌtjuːpə'reɪʃən $ vaɪˌtuː-/ *n* [U] *formal* angry and cruel criticism; ◨ **invective**

vi·tu·pe·ra·tive /vɪ'tjuːpərətɪv $ vaɪ'tuː-/ *adj formal* full of angry and cruel criticism; ◨ **vicious**: *vituperative comments*

vi·va¹ /'vaɪvə/ also **viva voce** *n* [C] *BrE* a spoken examination taken at the end of a university course

vi·va² /'viːvə/ *interjection* used to show that you approve of someone and want them to continue to exist or be successful

vi·va·ce /vɪ'vɑːtʃi, -tʃeɪ/ *adj, adv* music that is vivace is played quickly and with a lot of energy

vi·va·cious /vɪ'veɪʃəs $ və-, vaɪ-/ *adj* someone, especially a woman, who is vivacious has a lot of energy and a happy attractive manner – used to show approval; ◨ **lively**: *a vivacious personality* —**vivaciously** *adv* —**vivaciousness** *n* [U] —**vivacity** /vɪ'væsəti $ və-, vaɪ-/ *n* [U]

vi·var·i·um /vaɪ'veəriəm $ -'ver-/ *n* [C] a place indoors where animals are kept in conditions that are as similar as possible to their natural environment

viv·a voc·e /ˌvaɪvə 'vəʊtʃi, -'vəʊsi $ ˌvaɪvə 'vəʊsi, ˌviːvə 'vəʊtʃeɪ/ *n* [C] *BrE formal* a VIVA¹

viv·id /'vɪvɪd/ *adj* **1** vivid memories, dreams, descriptions etc are so clear that they seem real; ◨ **vague**: *I've got vivid memories of that summer.* | *He had a vivid picture of her in his mind.* **2** vivid imagination an ability to imagine unlikely situations very clearly **3** vivid colours or patterns are very bright: *his vivid blue eyes* —**vividly** *adv*: *I can vividly remember the day we met.* —**vividness** *n* [U]

viv·i·sec·tion /ˌvɪvɪ'sekʃən/ *n* [U] the practice doing medical or scientific tests on live animals —**vivisectionist** *n* [C]

vivo → IN VIVO

vix·en /'vɪksən/ *n* [C] **1** a female FOX **2** *literary* an offensive word for a woman who is bad-tempered or who fights

viz /vɪz/ *adv formal written* used before naming things that you have just referred to in a general way: *three Greek cities viz Athens, Thessaloniki, and Patras*

vi·zier /vɪ'zɪə $ -'zɪr/ *n* [C] an important government official in some Muslim countries in the past

VJ /ˌviː 'dʒeɪ/ *n* [C] *video jockey* someone who introduces music videos on television

V-neck /'viː nek/ *n* [C] **1** an opening for the neck in a piece of clothing, shaped like the letter V: *a V-neck sweater* **2** a piece of clothing with a V-neck —**V-necked** /-nekt/ *adj*

vo·cab /'vəʊkæb $ 'voʊ-/ *n* [U] VOCABULARY

vo·cab·u·la·ry /və'kæbjʊləri, vəʊ- $ -leri, voʊ-/ *n plural* **vocabularies 1** [C,U] all the words that someone knows or uses: *Reading is one of the best ways of improving your vocabulary.* | *He **has a wide vocabulary**.* | **active vocabulary** (=the words someone can use) | **passive vocabulary** (=the words someone can understand, but does not use) **2** [C] all the words in a particular language: *English has the largest vocabulary of any language.* **3** [C,U] the words that are typically used when talking about a particular subject: *Most technical jobs use a specialized vocabulary.* | [+of] *the vocabulary of politics* **4** [C,U] the range of possible features, effects, actions etc, especially in a type of music or art: [+of] *Charlie Parker expanded the vocabulary of jazz.* **5 (the word) failure/guilt/compromise etc is not in sb's vocabulary** used to say that someone never thinks of accepting failure etc **6** [C] *old-fashioned* a list of words with explanations of their meanings, especially in a book for learning a foreign language

vo·cal¹ /'vəʊkəl $ 'voʊ-/ *adj* **1** expressing strong opinions publicly, especially about things that you disagree with; ◨ **outspoken**: [+in] *Foley has been particularly vocal in his criticism of the government.* | **vocal opponent/critic/supporter etc** *She was a vocal opponent of the plan.* **2** [only before noun] relating to the voice or to singing: *vocal music* | *Allison's vocal style is influenced by country and blues music.* | *a female vocal group* —**vocally** *adv*

vocal² *n* [C usually plural] the part of a piece of music that is sung rather than played on an instrument: **on vocals** *The album features Jim Boquist on vocals.*

'vocal cords, 'vocal chords *n* [plural] thin pieces of muscle in your throat that produce sounds when you speak

vo·cal·ist /'vəʊkəlɪst $ 'voʊ-/ *n* [C] someone who sings popular songs, especially with a band

V

vo·cal·ize also **-ise** BrE /'vəʊkəlaɪz $ 'voʊ-/ v [I,T] to make a sound or sounds with your voice —**vocalization** /ˌvəʊkəlaɪ'zeɪʃən $ ˌvoʊkələ-/ n [C,U]

vo·ca·tion /vəʊ'keɪʃən $ voʊ-/ n [C,U] **1 a)** the feeling that the purpose of your life is to do a particular type of work, especially because it allows you to help other people: [+for] *Jan has a vocation for teaching.* | *a strong sense of vocation* | *You missed your vocation* (=you would have been good at a particular job). **b)** a particular type of work that you feel is right for you: *At 17 she found her true vocation as a writer.* **2** a strong belief that you have been chosen by God to be a priest or a NUN

vo·ca·tion·al /vəʊ'keɪʃənəl $ voʊ-/ adj teaching or relating to the skills you need to do a particular job: *vocational qualifications*

voc·a·tive /'vɒkətɪv $ 'vɑː-/ n [C] technical a word or particular form of a word used to show that you are speaking or writing directly to someone —**vocative** adj

vo·cif·er·ate /və'sɪfəreɪt, vəʊ- $ voʊ-/ v [I] formal to shout loudly, especially when you are complaining

vo·cif·er·ous /və'sɪfərəs, vəʊ- $ voʊ-/ adj formal expressing your opinions loudly and strongly: *a vociferous opponent of the plan* | [+in] *The minority population became more vociferous in its demands.* —**vociferously** adv

vod·ka /'vɒdkə $ 'vɑːdkə/ n [C,U] a strong clear alcoholic drink originally from Russia, or a glass of this

vogue /vəʊg $ voʊg/ n [C usually singular, U] a popular and fashionable style, activity, method etc; ▣ **fashion**: [+for] *the vogue for large families in the pre-war years* | *be in vogue/be the vogue Short skirts are very much in vogue just now.* | *Suntanning first came into vogue in the mid-1930s.*

voice¹ ▣S2▣ ▣W1▣ /vɔɪs/ n

1 SPEAKING [C,U] the sounds that you make when you speak, or the ability to make these sounds

---
in a ... voice
loud voice
quiet/soft/low/small voice
deep/low voice
high voice
sb's tone of voice (=the quality of someone's voice that shows how they feel)
raise your voice (=speak more loudly)
lower/drop your voice (=speak more quietly)
keep your voice down (=used to tell someone to speak more quietly)
lose your voice (=be unable to speak because you have a cold)
at the top of your voice (=in a very loud voice)
sb's voice breaks/cracks/shakes/trembles (=it sounds rough or unsteady because they are afraid, upset etc)
sb's voice breaks (=a boy's voice changes and becomes deep like a man's)

He recognized her voice instantly. | *I could hear angry voices in the next room.* | *He called out in a loud voice.* | *Angela has a really deep voice for a woman.* | *I could tell from his tone of voice that he wasn't impressed.* | *Did he ever lose his temper, ever raise his voice?* | *She lowered her voice so Alex couldn't hear.* | *Keep your voice down – the baby's asleep!* | *Jack's got a cold, and he's lost his voice.* | *She banged on the door, yelling at the top of her voice.* | *Her voice trembled and tears rose to her eyes.*

---
2 SINGING a) [C,U] the quality of sound you produce when you sing: *Sophie's got a lovely singing voice* **b)** [C] a person singing: *a piece written for six voices and piano*
3 OPINION a) [singular, U] the right or ability to express an opinion, to vote, or to influence decisions: *Parents should have a voice in deciding how their children are educated.* **b)** [C] an opinion or wish that is expressed: *The government needs to listen to the voice of middle-class Americans.* | *a fair, democratic society, in*

which individuals are able to **make** their **voice heard** (=express their opinion so that people notice it) | *Since the new program was introduced, there have been some **dissenting voices*** (=people expressing disagreement). | *Senator Prior spoke out, **adding** her **voice to** the call for new laws to protect the environment.*
4 speak with one voice if a group of people speak with one voice, they all express the same opinion
5 REPRESENTATIVE [singular] a person, organization, newspaper etc that expresses the opinions or wishes of a group of people: [+of] *The senator is the voice of the religious right.*
6 the voice of reason/experience etc opinions or ideas that are reasonable, based on experience etc, or someone who has these ideas: *Ben, as ever, has been the voice of reason throughout the whole crisis.*
7 FEELINGS give voice to sth to express your feelings or thoughts: *Participants are encouraged to give voice to their personal hopes, fears and dreams.*
8 inner voice thoughts or feelings that you do not express but seem to warn, criticize, or advise you: *My inner voice told me to be cautious.*
9 GRAMMAR active/passive voice technical the form of a verb that shows whether the subject of a sentence does an action or has an action done to it

voice² v [T] **1** to tell people your opinions or feelings about a particular subject: *The senator **voiced concern** at how minorities and immigrants are treated in California.* | *She angrily voiced her objections.* **2** technical to produce a sound with a movement of the VOCAL CORDS as well as the breath

'**voice box** n [C] the part of your throat that you use to produce sounds when you speak; ▣ **larynx**

voiced /vɔɪst/ adj **1 deep-voiced/squeaky-voiced/ husky-voiced etc** having a voice that is deep, very high etc **2** technical voiced sounds are made using the VOCAL CORDS. For example, /d/ and /g/ are voiced CONSONANTS

voice·less /'vɔɪsləs/ adj **1** unable to get your opinions or concerns noticed by people in power: *The vast majority of our people feel ignored and voiceless.* **2** technical voiceless sounds are made without using the VOCAL CORDS. For example, /p/ and /k/ are voiceless CONSONANTS

'**voice mail** n [U] a system which lets people leave recorded messages for you on your telephone when you are unable to answer it

'**voice-over** n [C] information or remarks that are spoken on a television programme or film by someone who is not seen on the screen

'**voice print** n [C] someone's voice recorded on a machine, which can be used to check who that person is

void¹ /vɔɪd/ n [singular] **1** a feeling of great sadness that you have when someone you love dies or when something is taken from you: *Running the business helped to fill the void after his wife died.* **2** a situation in which something important or interesting is needed or wanted, but does not exist: *The amusement park will fill a void in this town, which has little entertainment for children.* **3** literary an empty area of space where nothing exists: *She looked over the cliff into the void.*

void² adj **1** technical a contract or official agreement that is void is not legal and has no effect; ▣ **null and void 2 void of sth** literary completely lacking something; ▣ **devoid**: *Her eyes were void of all expression.*

void³ v [T] law to make a contract or agreement void so that it has no legal effect

voi·là /vwɑː'lɑː/ interjection used when you are showing or telling someone something surprising: *'Voilà!' she said, producing a pair of white shoes.*

voile /vɔɪl/ n [U] a very light almost transparent cloth made of cotton, wool, or silk

vol. the written abbreviation of **volume**

vol·a·tile /'vɒlətaɪl $ 'vɑːlətl/ adj **1** a volatile situation is likely to change suddenly and without warning: *an increasingly volatile political situation* | *the highly* *volatile stock and bond markets* **2** someone who is volatile can suddenly become angry or violent **3** *technical* a volatile liquid or substance changes easily into a gas —**volatility** /ˌvɒləˈtɪlɪti $ ˌvɑː-/ *n* [U]

vol·au·vent /ˈvɒl əʊ ˌvɒn $ ˌvɔːl oʊ ˈvɑːn/ *n* [C] *BrE* a small round piece of PASTRY that is filled with chicken, vegetables etc and eaten at parties

vol·can·ic /vɒlˈkænɪk $ vɑːl-/ *adj* relating to or caused by a volcano: *black volcanic sand*

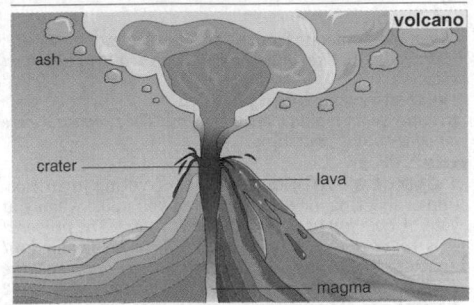

volcano

ash

crater

lava

magma

vol·ca·no /vɒlˈkeɪnəʊ $ vɑːlˈkeɪnoʊ/ *n plural* **volcanoes** *or* **volcanos** [C] a mountain with a large hole at the top, through which very hot liquid rock) is sometimes forced out: *Pompeii was destroyed when the volcano erupted in 79AD.* | **active volcano** (=one that may explode at any time) | **dormant volcano** (=one that is not active at the moment) | **extinct volcano** (=one that is no longer active at all)

vole /vəʊl $ voʊl/ *n* [C] a small animal like a mouse with a short tail that lives in fields and woods and near rivers

vo·li·tion /vəˈlɪʃən $ voʊ-, və-/ *n* [U] **1 of your own volition** *formal* if you do something of your own volition, you do it because you want to, not because you are forced to: *Helena left the company of her own volition.* **2** *formal* the power to choose or decide something without being forced to do it

vol·ley¹ /ˈvɒli $ ˈvɑːli/ *n* [C] **1** a large number of bullets, rocks etc shot or thrown through the air at the same time: [+of] *a volley of bullets* **2** a lot of questions, insults, attacks etc that are all said or made at the same time: [+of] *a volley of abuse* **3** a hit in tennis, a kick in football etc when the player hits or kicks the ball before it touches the ground

volley² *v* **1** [I,T] to hit or kick a ball before it touches the ground, especially in tennis or football **2** [I] if a large number of guns volley, they are all fired at the same time

vol·ley·ball /ˈvɒlibɔːl $ ˈvɑːlibɒːl/ *n* [U] a game in which two teams use their hands to hit a ball over a high net

volt /vəʊlt $ voʊlt/ *n* [C] written abbreviation *V* or *v* a unit for measuring the force of an electric current

volt·age /ˈvəʊltɪdʒ $ ˈvoʊl-/ *n* [C,U] electrical force measured in volts: **high/low voltage**

volte-face /ˌvɒlt ˈfæs, -ˈfɑːs $ ˌvɒːlt ˈfɑːs/ *n* [C usually singular] *formal* a change to a completely opposite opinion or plan of action; ▤ **U-turn**

volt·me·ter /ˈvəʊltˌmiːtə $ ˈvoʊltˌmiːtər/ *n* [C] an instrument for measuring voltage

vol·u·ble /ˈvɒljʊbəl $ ˈvɑː-/ *adj formal* talking a lot or talking quickly: *Clarissa was extremely voluble on the subject of good manners.* —**volubly** *adv*

vol·ume W2 /ˈvɒljuːm $ ˈvɑːljəm/ *n*
1 SOUND [U] the amount of sound produced by a television, radio etc: **turn the volume up/down** *Can you turn the volume up?*
2 AMOUNT OF STH [C usually singular, U] the total amount of something, especially when it is large or increasing: [+of] *The volume of traffic on the roads has increased dramatically in recent years.* | *the volume of trade*

3 SPACE FILLED [C usually singular] a measurement of the amount of space that a substance or object fills, or the amount of space in a container: [+of] *an instrument for measuring the volume of a gas* | *The volume of the container measures 10,000 cubic metres.*
4 BOOK [C] **a)** a book that is part of a set, or one into which a very long book is divided: *The period from 1940–45 is in volume 9.* **b)** *formal* a book: [+of] *a volume of Keats's poetry* **c)** all the copies of a particular magazine printed in one particular year ➔ **speak volumes** at SPEAK (9)

vo·lu·mi·nous /vəˈluːmɪnəs, vəˈljuː- $ vəˈluː-/ *adj formal* **1** a voluminous piece of clothing is very large and loose – often used humorously: *a voluminous cloak* **2** voluminous books, documents etc are very long and contain a lot of detail: *He took voluminous notes during the lecture.* **3** a voluminous container is very large and can hold a lot of things: *a voluminous suitcase*

vol·un·ta·ri·ly /ˈvɒləntərɪli, ˌvɒlənˈterɪli $ ˌvɑːlənˈterɪli/ *adv* **1** if you do something voluntarily, you do it willingly, without anyone telling you to do it: *She wasn't fired – she left voluntarily* **2** if you do work voluntarily, you do it because you want to, and are not paid for it: *Susan worked in the studios voluntarily, to gain experience.*

vol·un·ta·ry¹ W3 /ˈvɒləntəri $ ˈvɑːlənteri/ *adj*
1 WITHOUT BEING PAID a) **voluntary organization/association/agency etc** an organization etc that is organized or supported by people who give their money, services etc because they want to and who do not intend to make a profit: *a voluntary organization providing help for the elderly* | *environmental work carried out by the voluntary sector* **b)** **voluntary work/service etc** work etc that is done by people who do it because they want to, and who are not paid: *She does a lot of voluntary work for the Red Cross.* | *a drop-in centre for homeless people, run on a voluntary basis*
2 WITHOUT BEING FORCED done willingly and without being forced: *Workers are being encouraged to take voluntary redundancy.* ➔ COMPULSORY
3 MOVEMENT OF THE BODY *technical* voluntary movements of your body are controlled by your conscious mind; ▤ **involuntary**

voluntary² *n plural* **voluntaries** [C] a piece of music played in church, usually on the ORGAN

vol·un·teer¹ /ˌvɒlənˈtɪə $ ˌvɑːlənˈtɪr/ *n* [C] **1** someone who does a job willingly without being paid: *Most of the relief work was done by volunteers.* **2** someone who is willing to offer help: *I need some volunteers to help with the washing-up.* **3** someone who joins the army, navy, or air force without being forced to; ➔ **conscript**

volunteer² *v* **1** [I,T] to offer to do something without expecting any reward, often something that other people do not want to do: **volunteer to do sth** *Helen volunteered to have Thanksgiving at her house this year.* | [+for] *Sidcup volunteered for guard duty.* | *I volunteered my services as a driver.* **2** [T] to tell someone something without being asked: *Michael volunteered the information before I had a chance to ask.* **3** [I] to offer to join the army, navy, or airforce: *When war broke out, my father volunteered immediately.* **4** [T] to say that someone else will do a job even though they may not want to do it: **volunteer sb for sth** *Mum volunteered Dave for washing-up duties.*

vo·lup·tu·a·ry /vəˈlʌptʃuəri $ -tʃueri/ *n plural* **voluptuaries** [C] *literary* someone who enjoys physical pleasure and having expensive possessions

vo·lup·tu·ous /vəˈlʌptʃuəs/ *adj* **1** a woman who is voluptuous has large breasts and a soft curved body **2** expressing strong sexual feeling or sexual pleasure: *a voluptuous gesture* **3** *literary* something that is voluptuous gives you pleasure because it looks, smells, or tastes good: *the voluptuous fragrance of a summer garden* —**voluptuously** *adv* —**voluptuousness** *n* [U]

vom·it¹ /'vɒmɪ̯t $ 'vɑ:-/ *v* [I,T] to bring food or drink up from your stomach out through your mouth, because you are ill: *He had swallowed so much sea water he wanted to vomit.* | *I knew I was really in trouble when I began vomiting blood.* | [+**up**] *I vomited up most of my dinner.* → see box at SICK¹

vomit² *n* [U] food or other substances that come up from your stomach and through your mouth when you vomit

voo·doo /'vu:du:/ *n* [U] magical beliefs and practices used as a form of religion, especially by people in Haiti

ˈvoodoo ecoˌnomics *n* [U] *AmE* economic ideas that seem attractive but that do not work effectively over a period of time

vo·ra·cious /vəˈreɪʃəs, vɒ- $ vɔ:-, və-/ *adj* **1** eating or wanting large quantities of food: *Pigs are voracious feeders.* | *Kids can have voracious appetites.* **2** having an extremely strong desire to do or have a lot of something: *a voracious reader* | *Her appetite for information was voracious.* —**voraciously** *adv*: *Anne has always read voraciously.* —**voracity** /-ˈræsᵻ̯ti/ *n* [U]

vor·tex /'vɔ:teks $ 'vɔ:r-/ *n plural* **vortices** /-tᵻ̯si:z/ *or* **vortexes** [C] **1** a mass of wind or water that spins quickly and pulls things into its centre **2** [usually singular] *written* a situation that has a powerful effect on people's lives and that influences their behaviour, even if they do not want it to: [+**of**] *the vortex of emotions surrounding the case*

vo·ta·ry /'vəʊtəri $ 'voʊ-/ *n plural* **votaries** [C] *old-fashioned* someone who regularly practises a particular religion

vote¹ S3 W3 /vəʊt $ voʊt/ *v*
1 IN ELECTION/TO SUPPORT [I,T] to show by marking a paper, raising your hand etc which person you want to elect or whether you support a particular plan: *In 1918 British women got the right to vote.* | [+**for/against/ in favour of**] *I voted for the Labour candidate in the last election.* | *53% of Danes voted in favour of the Maastricht treaty.* | [+**on**] *The people of Ulster had finally been given a chance to vote on the issue.* | **vote to do sth** *Congress voted to increase foreign aid by 10%.* | *Shareholders voted to reject the offer.* | **vote Democrat/Republican/Labour/Conservative etc** *I've voted Democrat all my life.* → **block voting** at BLOCK¹ (5)
2 vote sb into/out of power/office/parliament etc to elect or dismiss someone by voting: *The chances are that the government will be voted out of office.*
3 CHOOSE FOR PRIZE [T] to choose someone or something for a particular prize by voting for them: **vote sb/sth sth** *In 1981 Henry Fonda was voted Best Actor for 'On Golden Pond'.*
4 MONEY [T] if a parliament, committee etc votes a sum of money for something, they decide by voting to provide money for that particular purpose: **vote sth for sth** *Parliament has voted £20 million extra funding for road improvements.*
5 vote sth a success/the best etc *BrE* if people vote something a success etc, they all agree that it is a success: *The evening was voted a great success.*
6 I vote ... *spoken* used to say that you prefer one particular choice or possible action: **vote (that)** *I vote we go to the movies.* | [+**for**] *'What do you want to eat?' 'I vote for Mexican.'*
7 vote with your wallet *BrE*; **vote with your pocketbook** *AmE* **a)** also **vote your pocketbook** *AmE* to vote for someone or something that you think will help you have the most money: *People generally vote their pocketbooks against new taxes.* **b)** also **vote with your dollars** *AmE* to show you like something by choosing to

buy it: *Readers vote with their wallets every day when they choose a newspaper.*
8 vote with your feet to show that you do not support a decision or action by leaving a place or organization
vote sth ⇔ down *phr v*
to defeat a plan, law etc by voting: *In 1999 the town had voted down a petition to close the school.*
vote sb ⇔ in *phr v*
to elect someone by voting: *A new chairman was voted in.*
vote sb ⇔ out *phr v*
to remove someone from a position of power by voting: *With policies like that, he'll be voted out in the next election.*
vote sth ⇔ through *phr v BrE*
to approve a plan, law etc by voting: *The proposals were voted through yesterday.*

vote² W3 *n*
1 CHOICE BY VOTING [C] an act of voting in an election or meeting, or the choice that you make when you vote: *A vote for us is not a wasted vote.* | *The proposal was rejected by 19 votes to 7.* | [+**for/in favour (of)/ against**] *The House of Representatives approved the budget, with 52 votes in favour, 16 against and 12 abstentions.* | **cast your vote** (=vote in a political election) *Harkin won 74 percent of the votes cast.* | *policies designed to win votes in the South* | *It's the club secretary that counts the votes.* → CASTING VOTE
2 OCCASION OF VOTING [C usually singular] an occasion when a group of people vote in order to decide something or choose a representative; ▪ **ballot**: *The results of the vote were surprising – 80% of workers favoured strike action.* | [+**on**] *There will be a citywide vote* (=all the voters in a particular city) *on the matter.* | **take/have a vote (on sth)** *Unless anyone has anything to add, we'll take a vote.* | *Let's have a vote on it.* | **put sth to the/a vote** (=decide something by voting) *Let's put it to the vote. All those in favor raise your hands.* → FREE VOTE
3 the vote a) the total number of votes made in an election: *Davis won the election with 57% of the vote.* | *The Greens increased their share of the vote from 2.9 to 4.9%.* **b)** the right to vote in political elections: *In France women didn't get the vote until 1945.* | *At that time black people did not yet have the vote.*
4 the ... vote a) the black/Jewish/middle-class etc vote black, Jewish etc voters, or their votes: *The black vote is astonishingly loyal to the Democratic Party.* **b) the Labour/Conservative/Green etc vote** *BrE* the total number of votes the Labour Party, Conservative Party etc win in an election: *The Green vote looks likely to increase again.*
5 RESULT OF VOTING [singular] the result of a vote: *A close vote is expected.* | *The motion was passed by a vote of 215 to 84.*
6 sb/sth gets my vote *spoken* used to say that you are ready to support someone or something, or that you think that someone or something is the best of their kind: *Anything that will mean a better deal for our children gets my vote.*

ˈvote-ˌgetter *n* [C] *AmE informal* someone who is voted for in an election: *Pfeifer was the top vote-getter in last year's election.*

ˌvote of ˈcensure *n plural* **votes of censure** [C] a process in which members of parliament vote in order to officially criticize the government for something

ˌvote of ˈconfidence *n plural* **votes of confidence** [C] **1** a formal process in which people vote in order to show that they support someone or something, especially the government: *On April 19 the new government won a vote of confidence by 339 votes to 207.* **2** something that you do or say that shows you support someone and approve of their actions: [+**in**] *The new investments are widely seen as a vote of confidence in the nation's economic future.*

ˌvote of no ˈconfidence *n plural* **votes of no confidence** [C] **1** a formal process in which people vote in order to show that they do not support someone or something, especially the government: [+in] *On April 22 the National Assembly **passed** a **vote of no confidence** in the government.* **2** something that you do or say that shows that you do not support someone

vote of 'thanks *n* propose a vote of thanks (to sb) to make a short formal speech in which you thank someone, especially at a public meeting or a formal dinner

vot·er /'vəʊtə $ 'voʊtər/ *n* [C] **1** someone who has the right to vote in a political election, or who votes in a particular election: *Voters overwhelmingly rejected the far right in the May elections.* | *In Ireland 83% of voters favoured EC membership in 1972.* | *Tory voters* **2 voter apathy** a situation in which a lot of people who have the right to vote do not vote: *Voter apathy is especially high among young people.* → FLOATING VOTER

'voting booth *n* [C] an enclosed place where you can make your vote secretly; ▣ **polling booth** *BrE*

'voting ma,chine *n* [C] a machine that records votes as they are made

vo·tive /'vəʊtɪv $ 'voʊ-/ *adj* [only before noun] *technical* given or done because of a promise made to God or to a SAINT: *votive offerings*

vouch /vaʊtʃ/ *v*
  vouch for sb/sth *phr v* **1** to say that you firmly believe that something is true or good because of your experience or knowledge of it: *I'll vouch for the quality of the report. I read it last night.* | *'Where were you on the night of the murder?' 'In bed with flu. My wife can **vouch for that**.'* **2** to say that you believe that someone will behave well and that you will be responsible for their behaviour, actions etc: *Why don't you phone my office? They'll vouch for me.*

vouch·er ⑬ /'vaʊtʃə $ -ər/ *n* [C]
1 a ticket that can be used instead of money for a particular purpose: *The voucher can be used at most major supermarkets.* | *First prize is a £1000 travel voucher.* → **gift voucher** at GIFT TOKEN; → LUNCHEON VOUCHER **2** an official statement or RECEIPT that is given to someone to prove that their accounts are correct or that money has been paid

vouch·safe /vaʊtʃ'seɪf/ *v* [T] *old-fashioned formal* to promise or offer something, or tell someone something that they can be certain is the truth

vow¹ /vaʊ/ *n* [C] **1** a serious promise; → **oath**: *Jim made a vow that he would find his wife's killer.* | **keep/break a vow** (=to do or not do what you promised) **2** a religious promise that you will do something for God, the church etc: **vow of chastity/celibacy/silence etc** (=a promise that you will not have sex, will remain poor etc) *a priest who had **taken** a vow of celibacy* **3 vows** [plural] **a)** also **marriage/wedding vows** the promises you make during your wedding: **make/take your vows** *The couple made their vows at St Paul's Church in Hayes.* **b)** the promises you make when you become a Catholic priest or NUN

vow² *v* [T] **1** to make a serious promise to yourself or someone else; ▣ **promise**: **vow to do sth** *Supporters have vowed to continue the protest until Adams is released.* | **vow (that)** *I vowed that I would never drink again.* **2** *formal* to make a religious promise that you will do something for God, the church etc

vow·el /'vaʊəl/ *n* [C] **1** one of the human speech sounds that you make by letting your breath flow out without closing any part of your mouth or throat **2** a letter of the alphabet used to represent a vowel. In English the vowels are a, e, i, o, u, and sometimes y.

vox pop /ˌvɒks 'pɒp $ ˌvɑːks 'pɑːp/ *n* [C,U] *BrE informal* opinions expressed by ordinary people when they are asked questions about a particular subject during a television, radio, or newspaper report

voy·age¹ /'vɔɪ-ɪdʒ/ *n* [C] **1** a long journey in a ship or spacecraft: *The voyage from England to India used to take six months.* | *the Titanic's **maiden voyage** (=first journey)* | *I don't want to **make** the voyage*

single-handed | *These are the voyages of the starship Enterprise.* → see box at TRAVEL² **2 voyage of discovery** a situation in which you learn a lot of new things about something or someone: *Writing a biography is an absorbing voyage of discovery.* | *a voyage of self-discovery* (=when you learn more about yourself)

voyage² *v* [I always + adv/prep] *literary* to travel to a place, especially by ship

voy·ag·er /'vɔɪ-ɪdʒə $ -ər/ *n* [C] *literary* someone who makes long and often dangerous journeys, especially on the sea

voy·eur /vwɑː'jɜː $ -'jɜːr/ *n* [C] **1** someone who gets sexual pleasure from secretly watching other people's sexual activities **2** someone who enjoys watching other people's private behaviour or suffering —**voyeurism** *n* [U] —**voyeuristic** /ˌvwɑːjəˈrɪstɪk◂/ *adj* —**voyeuristically** /-kli/ *adv*

VP, V.P. /ˌviː 'piː/ *n* [C] *informal* the abbreviation of *vice president*

vs. also **vs** *BrE* a written abbreviation of *versus*

V sign /'viː saɪn/ *n* [C] **1** a sign meaning peace or victory, made by holding up the first two fingers of your hand with the front of the hand facing forwards **2** *BrE* a rude sign made by holding up the first two fingers of your hand with the back of your hand facing towards another person

vul·can·ize also **-ise** *BrE* /'vʌlkənaɪz/ *v* [T] to make rubber stronger by using a special chemical treatment —**vulcanization** /ˌvʌlkənaɪˈzeɪʃən $ -nə-/ *n* [U]

vul·gar /'vʌlgə $ -ər/ *adj* **1** remarks, jokes etc that are vulgar deal with sex in a very rude and offensive way **2** not behaving politely in social situations; ▣ **uncouth**: *vulgar behaviour* **3** not showing good judgment about what is beautiful or suitable: *a vulgar check suit* —**vulgarly** *adv*

vulgar 'fraction *n* [C] *BrE old-fashioned* a FRACTION that is written as one number above a line and one number below it, and not as a DECIMAL; ▣ **common fraction** *AmE*

vul·gar·i·ty /vʌl'gærɪti/ *n* **1** [U] the state or quality of being vulgar **2 vulgarities** [plural] vulgar remarks, jokes etc

vul·gar·ize also **-ise** *BrE* /'vʌlgəraɪz/ *v* [T] *formal* to spoil the quality or lower the standard of something that is good —**vulgarization** /ˌvʌlgəraɪˈzeɪʃən $ -rə-/ *n* [U]

Vul·gate /'vʌlgeɪt, -gət/ *n* **the Vulgate** the Latin Bible commonly used in the Roman Catholic Church

vul·ne·ra·ble ⑬ /'vʌlnərəbəl/ *adj*
1 someone who is vulnerable can be easily harmed or hurt: *He took advantage of me when I was at my most vulnerable.* | *We work mainly with the elderly and other vulnerable groups.* | **be vulnerable to sth** *Children are most vulnerable to abuse within their own home.*
2 a place, thing, or idea that is vulnerable is easy to attack or criticize: [+to] *The fort was vulnerable to attack from the north.* | *Their theories were badly thought out and very vulnerable to ridicule.* —**vulnerably** *adv* —**vulnerability** /ˌvʌlnərəˈbɪlɪti/ *n* [U]

vul·pine /'vʌlpaɪn/ *adj* *formal* relating to FOXES, or similar to a fox

vul·ture /'vʌltʃə $ -ər/ *n* [C] **1** a large bird that eats dead animals → see picture at BIRD OF PREY **2** someone who uses other people's problems and suffering for their own advantage – used to show disapproval: *He hadn't been dead five minutes before those vultures from the media were after his widow.*

vul·va /'vʌlvə/ *n* [C] the outer part of a woman's sexual organs

vy·ing /'vaɪ-ɪŋ/ the present participle of VIE

V

W, w

W¹, **w** /'dʌbəljuː/ *plural* **W's**, **w's** *n* [C,U] the 23rd letter of the English alphabet

W², **w** **1** the written abbreviation of *west* or *western* **2** the written abbreviation of *watt* or *watts*

wack·o /'wækəʊ $ -oʊ/ *n plural* **wackos** [C] *informal* a crazy or strange person —**wacko** *adj*: *That guy's completely wacko.*

wack·y /'wæki/ *adj informal* silly in an exciting or amusing way; ◨ **crazy**: *a wonderfully wacky idea* —**wackiness** *n* [U]

wad¹ /wɒd $ wɑːd/ *n* [C] **1** a thick pile of pieces of paper or thin material: [+of] *a wad of dollar bills*; → see picture at **BUNDLE¹** **2** a thick soft mass of material that has been pressed together: [+of] *a wad of cotton wool*

wad² *v* **wadded, wadding**
wad sth ⇔ up *phr v AmE* to press something such as a piece of paper or cloth into a small tight ball

wad·ding /'wɒdɪŋ $ 'wɑː-/ *n* [U] soft material used for packing or to protect a wound

wad·dle /'wɒdl $ 'wɑːdl/ *v* [I] to walk with short steps, with your body moving from one side to another – used especially about people or birds with fat bodies and short legs: [+off/down/over etc] *Half a dozen ducks waddled up the bank.* —**waddle** *n* [singular]

wade /weɪd/ *v* [I always + adv/prep, T] to walk through water that is not deep
wade in also **wade into sth** *phr v informal* **1** to enter a discussion, argument etc in a forceful and annoying way, often without thinking about the possible results: *I wish you wouldn't always wade in with your opinion.* **2** to move forward and attack someone: *The police waded into the crowd swinging sticks.*
wade through sth *phr v* to read or deal with a lot of boring papers or written work: *Each day Parkin wades through lengthy court reports.*

wad·er /'weɪdə $ -ər/ *n* [C] **1** also **,wading bird** a bird that has long legs and a long neck, and that walks around in water to find its food **2** **waders** [plural] high rubber boots that you wear for walking in deep water, usually when fishing

wad·ing pool /'weɪdɪŋ puːl/ *n* [C] *AmE* a small pool filled with water that is not very deep, for small children to play in; ◨ **paddling pool** *BrE*

wa·fer /'weɪfə $ -ər/ *n* [C] **1** a very thin BISCUIT **2** a thin round piece of bread eaten with wine in the Christian COMMUNION ceremony **3** a very thin flat piece of a hard substance: [+of] *wafers of silicon*

,wafer-'thin *adj* extremely thin: *wafer-thin chocolates*

waf·fle¹ /'wɒfəl $ 'wɑː-/ *n* **1** [C] a flat cake, marked with a pattern of deep squares **2** [U] *BrE informal* talk or writing that uses a lot of words but says nothing important

waffle² *v* [I] *informal* **1** *BrE* also **waffle on** to talk or write using a lot of words but without saying anything important: *Stop waffling and get to the point.* **2** *AmE informal* to be unable to decide what action to take: *He cannot continue to waffle on this issue.*

'waffle ,iron *n* [C] a piece of kitchen equipment used to cook waffles

waft /wɑːft, wɒft $ wɑːft, wæft/ *v* **1** [I,T always + adv/prep] if a smell, smoke, or a light wind wafts somewhere, or if something wafts it somewhere, it moves gently through the air: *Cooking smells wafted up from downstairs.* **2** [I always + adv/prep] if sounds waft somewhere, you hear them there and they are pleasant but not very loud: [+up/

through/over etc] *The sound of laughter wafted through the open window.*; → **drift**

wag¹ /wæg/ *v* **wagged, wagging** **1** [I,T] if a dog wags its tail, or if its tail wags, the dog moves its tail many times from one side to the other **2** [T] to move your finger or head from side to side, especially to show disapproval: *'You naughty girl!' Mom said, **wagging her finger** at me.* → **it's (a case of) the tail wagging the dog** at **TAIL¹** (11); → **set tongues wagging** at **TONGUE¹** (14)

wag² *n* **1** [C] *old-fashioned* someone who says or does something clever and amusing: *Some wag had drawn a face on the wall.* **2** [C usually singular] a wagging movement

wage¹ W3 /weɪdʒ/ *n*
1 [singular] also **wages** [plural] money you earn that is paid according to the number of hours, days, or weeks that you work; → **salary**: *He earns a good wage.* | **wage increase** also **wage rise** *BrE*: *The wage increases will come into effect in June.* | **daily/weekly etc wage** *a weekly wage of $250* | **wage levels/rates** (=fixed amounts of money paid for particular jobs); → see box at **PAY²**
2 a living wage money you earn for work that is enough to pay for the basic things that you need to live: *The church no longer paid a living wage.*
3 wage freeze an action taken by a company, government etc to stop wages increasing
4 wage claim the amount of money asked for by workers as an increase in wages

wage² *v* [T] to be involved in a war against someone, or a fight against something: **wage war (on sb/sth)** *The police are waging war on drug pushers in the city.* | **wage a campaign/struggle/battle etc** *The council has waged a vigorous campaign against the proposal.*

waged /weɪdʒd/ *adj* **1** waged work or employment is work for which you get paid; ◨ **unwaged** **2** someone who is waged has a job for which they earn money; ◨ **unwaged**

'wage-,earner *n* [C] **1** someone in a family who earns money for the rest of the family **2** someone who works for wages: *Both wage-earners and salaried officials were protected by the new regulations.*

'wage-,packet *n* [C] *BrE* an envelope that contains your wages

wa·ger¹ /'weɪdʒə $ -ər/ *n* [C] *old-fashioned* an agreement in which you win or lose money according to the result of something such as a race; ◨ **bet**

wager² *v* [T] *old-fashioned* **1** to agree to win or lose an amount of money on the result of something such as a race; ◨ **gamble**: **wager sth on sth** *Stipes wagered all his money on an unknown horse.* **2 I'll wager** used to say that you are confident that something is true

wag·gish /'wægɪʃ/ *adj BrE old-fashioned* a waggish person makes clever and amusing jokes, remarks etc —**waggishly** *adv* —**waggishness** *n* [U]

wag·gle /'wægəl/ *v* [I,T] to move something up and down or from side to side using short quick movements; ◨ **wiggle**: *Can you waggle your ears?* —**waggle** *n* [singular]

wag·on also **waggon** *BrE* /'wægən/ *n* [C] **1** a strong vehicle with four wheels, used for carrying heavy loads and usually pulled by horses; → **cart** **2** *BrE* a large open container pulled by a train, used for carrying goods; ◨ **freight car** *AmE* **3 be/go on the wagon** *informal* to not drink alcohol any more **4 fall off the wagon** *informal* to start drinking alcohol again after you have stopped → **PADDY WAGON**

'wagon train *n* [C] a long line of wagons and horses used by the people who moved to the West of America in the 19th century

wag·tail /'wægteɪl/ *n* [C] a small European bird that moves its tail quickly up and down when it walks

waif /weɪf/ *n* [C] **1** someone, especially a child, who is pale and thin and looks as if they do not have a home **2 waifs and strays** *BrE* children or animals who do not have a home: *She loved cats, and would take any waifs and strays into her home.*

waif-like *adj* extremely pale and thin: *images of waif-like models in girls' magazines*

wail /weɪl/ *v* **1** [T] to say something in a loud, sad, and complaining way: *'But what shall I do?' Bernard wailed.* **2** [I] to cry out with a long high sound, especially because you are very sad or in pain: *Somewhere behind them a child began to wail.* **3** [I] to make a long high sound: *The wind wailed in the chimney.* —**wail** *n* [C]: *the wail of police sirens*

wain·scot /ˈweɪnskət, -skɒt $ -skət, -skɑːt/ *n* [C] *BrE* old-fashioned a SKIRTING BOARD; ▣ **baseboard** *AmE*

waist /weɪst/ *n* [C] **1** the narrow part in the middle of the human body: *The skirt was too big around the waist.* | **from the waist up/down** (=in the top or bottom half of your body) *Lota was paralysed from the waist down.* | **stripped to the waist** (=not wearing any clothes on the top half of your body) | **slim-waisted/narrow-waisted/thick-waisted** (=having a thin, thick etc waist) **2** [usually singular] the part of a piece of clothing that goes around this part of your body ⚠ Do not confuse with **waste** (used as a verb and noun to talk about using too much of something for unimportant or unnecessary things).

waist·band /ˈweɪstbænd/ *n* [C] the part of a skirt, trousers etc that fastens around your waist

waist·coat /ˈweɪskəʊt, ˈweskət $ ˈweskət/ *n* [C] *BrE* a piece of clothing without SLEEVES that has buttons down the front and is worn over a shirt, often under a JACKET as part of a man's suit; ▣ **vest** *AmE*

waist-'deep *adj, adv* deep enough to reach your waist: *standing waist-deep in water*

waist-'high *adj, adv* high enough to reach your waist: *waist-high grass*

waist·line /ˈweɪstlaɪn/ *n* **1** [singular] the amount you measure around the waist, especially used to judge how fat or thin you are: *a trim waistline* **2** [C] the position of the waist of a piece of clothing

wait¹ S1 W1 /weɪt/ *v*
1 NOT GO/START STH [I] to stay somewhere or not do something until something else happens, someone arrives etc: *Hurry up! Everyone's waiting.* | *Would you mind waiting outside?* | [+for] *a queue of people waiting for a bus* | *Wait for me!* | **wait for sb/sth to do sth** *She paused, waiting for Myles to say something.* | *I sat waiting patiently for the wedding to end.* | [+until/till] *I'll wait till you come back.* | **wait (for) 3 hours/2 weeks etc** *Can you wait for five minutes?* | *We've been waiting ages.* | **wait to do sth** *Are you waiting to use the phone?* | **keep sb waiting** (=make someone wait, especially by arriving late) *I'm sorry to have kept you waiting.*
2 STH HAS NOT HAPPENED [I] if you are waiting for something that you expect or hope will happen or arrive, it has not happened or arrived yet: *'Have you heard about the job?' 'No, I'm still waiting.'* | *I'm still waiting for my results.* | **wait for sb/sth to do sth** *I'm waiting for him to realize how stupid he's been.*
3 **wait a minute/second/moment etc** *spoken* **a)** used to ask someone not to leave or start doing something immediately: *Wait a second, I'll get my coat and come with you.* | *Wait a moment, just let me think.* **b)** used to interrupt someone, especially because you do not agree with what they are saying: *Wait a minute! That's not what we agreed!* **c)** used when you suddenly think of, remember, or notice something: *Wait a minute, I've got a better idea.*
4 **sb can't wait/can hardly wait** *spoken* **a)** used to emphasize that someone is very excited about something and is eager for it to happen: *We're going to Australia on Saturday – I can't wait!* | **can't wait to do sth** *I can't wait to tell Gloria the good news.* | *Laura could hardly wait to see the twins again.* | [+for] *I can't wait for the summer.* **b)** used humorously to say that something seems likely to be very boring: *A lecture on transformational grammar? I can hardly wait!*
5 **sth can/can't wait** *spoken* if something can wait, it is

not very urgent. If something can't wait, it is very urgent: *Go home. The report can wait till tomorrow.*
6 **wait and see** *spoken* used to say that someone should be patient because they will find out about something later: *'What's for dinner?' 'Wait and see.'* | *We will just have to wait and see how things develop.*
7 **wait until/till ...** *spoken* used when you are excited about telling or showing someone something: *Wait till you see Gaby's new house!*
8 **be waiting (for sb)** if something is waiting for you, it is ready for you to use, collect etc: *There'll be a rental car waiting for you at the airport.* | *Come round at eight and I'll have dinner waiting.*
9 **wait your turn** to stay calm until it is your turn to do something, instead of trying to move ahead of other people: *I've got two hands and there are three of you. So you'll have to wait your turn!*
10 **sth is (well) worth waiting for** *spoken* used to say that something is very good, even though it takes a long time to come: *Their new album was worth waiting for.*
11 **(just) you wait** *spoken* **a)** *BrE* used to warn or threaten someone: *I'll get you back for what you've done, just you wait.* **b)** used to tell someone you are sure something will happen: *It'll be a huge success. Just you wait.*
12 **what are you waiting for?** *spoken* used to tell someone to do something immediately: *Well, what are you waiting for? Go and apologize.*
13 **what are we waiting for?** *spoken* used to say in a cheerful way that you think everyone should start doing something immediately: *What are we waiting for? Let's go eat.*
14 **wait for it** *BrE spoken* **a)** used just before you tell someone something that is funny or surprising: *His name was – wait for it – Mr Bacon.* **b)** used to tell someone not to do something until the correct time because they seem very impatient to do it now
15 **be waiting in the wings** to be ready to do something if it is necessary or if a suitable time comes: *Other firms are waiting in the wings, ready to step in and make an offer should the current deal fall through.*
16 **wait tables** *AmE* to work in a restaurant serving food and drink to people at their tables: *I spent the summer waiting tables.*
17 **(play) a/the waiting game** if you play a waiting game, you try to gain an advantage for yourself in a particular situation by deliberately doing nothing until you have seen what other people do

wait around also **wait about** *BrE phr v*
to stay in the same place and do nothing while you are waiting for something to happen, someone to arrive etc: *Movie-making involves acting for 10 minutes and then waiting around for two hours.* | *We'd better be going. We can't wait about like this any longer.*

wait behind *phr v BrE*
to stay somewhere after other people have left: *She waited behind to help Debbie with the clearing up.*

wait in *phr v BrE*
to stay at home and wait there for someone to arrive: *I have to wait in for the repair man.*

wait on sb/sth *phr v*
1 to serve food and drink to someone at their table, especially in a restaurant
2 to wait for a particular event, piece of information etc, especially before doing something or making a decision: *We're waiting on the blood test results.*
3 **wait on sb hand and foot** to do everything for someone while they do nothing – used to show disapproval: *His wife waits on him hand and foot.*

wait sth ⇔ **out** *phr v*
if you wait out an event, period, or time, especially an unpleasant one, you wait for it to finish: *Let's find a place where we can wait out the storm.*

wait up *phr v*
1 to wait for someone to return before you go to bed:

W

1 000, 2 000, 3 000, most frequent words in S spoken and W ritten English

[**+for**] *Don't wait up for me; I may be late.*
2 Wait up! *AmE* used to tell someone to stop, so that you can talk to them or go with them: '*Wait up!' he called.*

WORD CHOICE: wait, expect, look forward to, await
Wait means to stay somewhere or not do something until something comes, happens etc: *I'm waiting to hear from Dan before I arrange my trip.*
Expect means to believe that something will come, happen etc: *The police are expecting (NOT waiting) trouble.*
Look forward to means to be excited and pleased about something that is going to happen: *I'm looking forward to getting his letter.*
⚠ **Wait** is never followed directly by a noun. You must say **wait for**: *She was waiting for a bus (NOT waiting a bus).*
In formal English, you can use **await**, which is followed directly by a noun: *We are awaiting your instructions.*

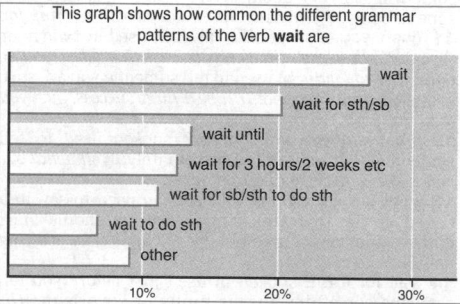

This graph shows how common the different grammar patterns of the verb **wait** are

wait
wait for sth/sb
wait until
wait for 3 hours/2 weeks etc
wait for sb/sth to do sth
wait to do sth
other

10%   20%   30%

wait² *n* [singular] a period of time in which you wait for something to happen, someone to arrive etc: [**+for**] *The average wait for an appointment at the clinic was eight weeks.* | **long/three hour/two week etc wait** *There was an hour wait before the next train departed.* | *They'll have a long wait.* → **lie in wait** at **LIE¹** (8)

wait·er /'weɪtə $ -ər/ *n* [C] a man who serves food and drink at the tables in a restaurant → see picture at **OCCUPATION**

waiting list *n* [C] a list of people who have asked for something but who must wait before they can have it: [**+for**] *There is still a three-month waiting list for the cars.* | **on a waiting list** *I was then put on a waiting list to see a specialist at the local hospital.*

waiting room *n* [C] a room for people to wait in, for example before they see a doctor, until their train arrives etc

wait·ress /'weɪtrɪs/ *n* [C] a woman who serves food and drink at the tables in a restaurant

wait·ron /'weɪtrən/ *n* [C] a WAITER or WAITRESS - used humorously

waive /weɪv/ *v* [T] to state officially that a right, rule etc can be ignored: *She waived her right to a lawyer.*

waiv·er /'weɪvə $ -ər/ *n* [C] *technical* an official written statement saying that a right, legal process etc can be waived

wake¹ [S2] [W3] /weɪk/ also **wake up** *v past tense* **woke** /wəʊk $ woʊk/, *past participle* **woken** /'wəʊkən $ 'woʊ-/ [I,T]
to stop sleeping, or to make someone stop sleeping: *When she woke, the sun was streaming through the windows.* | *Try not to wake the baby.* | [**+to**] *Nancy woke to the sound of birds outside her window* (=she heard birds singing when she woke).
  wake up *phr v*
1 to stop sleeping, or to make someone stop sleeping: *James usually wakes up early.* | **wake sb ⇔ up** *I'll wake you up when it's time to leave.*
2 to start to listen or pay attention to something: *Wake up* (=give me your attention) *at the back there!*
3 wake up and smell the coffee *AmE spoken* used to tell

someone to recognize the truth or reality of a situation
  wake up to sth *phr v*
to start to realize and understand a danger, an idea etc: *It's time you woke up to the fact that it's a tough world.*

wake² *n* [C] **1 in the wake of sth** if something, especially something bad, happens in the wake of an event, it happens afterwards and usually as a result of it: *Famine followed in the wake of the drought.* **2 in sb's/sth's wake** behind or after someone or something: *The car left clouds of dust in its wake.* **3** the time before or after a funeral when friends and relatives meet to remember the dead person **4** [usually singular] the track made behind a boat as it moves through the water

wake·ful /'weɪkfəl/ *adj literary* **a)** not sleeping or unable to sleep: *She lay wakeful in her room for most of the night.* **b)** a wakeful period of time is one when you cannot sleep —**wakefulness** *n* [U]

wak·en /'weɪkən/ also **waken up** *v* [I,T] *literary* to wake up, or to wake someone up: *She gently wakened the sleeping child.*

wake-up ˌcall *n* [C] **1** an experience or event that shocks you and makes you realize that you must do something to change a situation: *The success of extremist groups in the elections should be a wake-up call to all decent citizens.* **2** a telephone call that someone makes to you, especially at a hotel, to wake you up in the morning; ▯ **alarm call**

wak·ey-wak·ey /ˌweɪki 'weɪki/ *interjection BrE spoken* used to tell someone in a humorous way to wake up

wak·ing /'weɪkɪŋ/ *adj written* **waking hours/life/day etc** all the time when you are awake: *His face haunted her every waking moment!*

walk¹ [S1] [W1] /wɔːk $ wɒːk/ *v*
1 [I,T] to move forward by putting one foot in front of the other: '*How did you get here?' 'We walked.'* | *Doctors said he'd never walk again.* | [**+into/down/up etc**] *Carrie walked into the room and sat down in her chair.* | *He loved walking in the hills.* | **walk a mile/200 metres/a short distance etc** *We must have walked ten miles today.* | *I walked all the way to San Rafael.* | **within (easy) walking distance (of sth)** (=near enough to be able to walk to) *There are plenty of bars and restaurants within walking distance of the hotel.* | **walking pace** (=the speed that you normally walk at)
2 [T] to walk somewhere with someone, especially in order to make sure that they are safe or to be polite: *It's late – I'll walk you home.* | **walk sb to sth** *Schools are urging parents to walk their children to school.* | *She walked me to the front gate.*
3 [T] to take a dog for a walk for exercise: *Grandma's out walking the dog.*
4 [I] *BrE informal* if something has walked, it has disappeared and you think someone may have taken it: *My pen seems to have walked.*
5 walk free also **walk** *AmE* to leave a court of law without being punished or sent to prison: *Ferguson walked free after the charges were dropped.* | *If more evidence isn't found, Harris will walk.*
6 walk it *BrE spoken* **a)** to make a journey by walking: *If the last bus has gone, we'll have to walk it.* **b)** to succeed or win something easily
7 be walking on air to be feeling extremely happy
8 walk the streets a) to walk around the streets in a town or city: *It was not safe to walk the streets at night.* **b)** *old-fashioned* to be a PROSTITUTE
9 walk the beat when a police officer walks the beat, they walk around an area of a town or city in order to make sure nobody is committing a crime
10 walk tall to be proud and confident because you know that you have not done anything wrong
11 walk sb off their feet *BrE*, **walk sb's legs off** *AmE informal* to make someone tired by making them walk too far
12 walk the walk to do the things that people expect or think are necessary in a particular situation: *People are motivated by leaders who actually walk the walk.* → **talk the talk** at **TALK¹** (18)

13 walk the plank to be forced to walk along a board laid over the side of the ship until you fall off into the sea, used as a punishment in the past

walk away phr v
1 to leave a bad or difficult situation, instead of trying to make it better: [+from] You can't just walk away from 15 years of marriage! I When the business started to have problems, it was very tempting to walk away.
2 to come out of an accident or very bad situation without being harmed: Miraculously, both drivers walked away without a scratch.
walk away with sth phr v informal
to win something easily: And the lucky winner will walk away with a prize of £10,000.
walk in on sb phr v
to go into a room and accidentally interrupt someone who is doing something private that they would not want you to see
walk into sth phr v
1 to hit an object accidentally as you are walking along: **walk straight/right/bang etc into sth** Zeke wasn't looking and walked straight into a tree.
2 if you walk into an unpleasant situation, you become involved in it without intending to: He was fairly certain now that he was **walking into a trap**, and wished he'd come armed. I **walk straight/right into sth** I walked right into a mob of maybe 50 young white guys.
3 BrE if you walk into a job, you get it very easily: You can't expect to **walk straight into a job**.
4 to make yourself look stupid when you could easily have avoided it if you had been more careful: **walk straight/right into sth** You walked right into that one!
walk off phr v
1 to leave someone by walking away from them, espe-cially in a rude or angry way: Don't just walk off when I'm trying to talk to you!
2 walk sth ⇔ **off** if you walk off an illness or unpleas-ant feeling, you go for a walk to make it go away: Let's go out – maybe I can walk this headache off. I **walk off dinner/a meal etc** (=go for a walk so that your stomach feels less full)
3 walk off (the/your etc job) AmE to stop working as a protest: Without new contracts, mine workers will walk off their jobs Thursday.
walk off with sth phr v informal
1 to win something easily: Lottery winners can walk off with a cool £18 million.
2 to steal something or take something that does not belong to you: Thieves walked off with two million dollars' worth of jewellery.
walk out phr v
1 to leave a place suddenly, especially because you disapprove of something: The play was awful and we walked out after half an hour. I [+of] the issue that led to the US walking out of the trade talks this week
2 to leave your husband, wife etc suddenly and go live somewhere else: Her husband walked out, leaving her with three children to look after. I [+on] Five years later she walked out on Matthew and their two boys.
3 to leave your job suddenly because you no longer want to do it: We're so short-staffed. I can't just walk out. I [+of] If you can afford to walk out of your job, why not?
4 to stop working as a protest: Workers are threatening to walk out if an agreement is not reached.
walk out on sth phr v
to stop doing something you have agreed to do or that you are responsible for: 'I never walk out on a deal,' Dee said.

walk over sb phr v
to treat someone badly by always making them do what you want them to do: It's terrible – she **lets** her kids just walk all over her.
walk² S2 W2 n
1 [C] a journey that you make by walking, especially for exercise or enjoyment: It's a long walk. Maybe we should get the bus. I **Let's go for a walk.** I could do with some fresh air. I **long/short/five-mile/ten-minute etc walk** The beach is only a short walk away. I **take/have a walk** Why don't we take a walk in the garden? I **take sb/a dog for a walk** I [+to/through/across etc] a short walk through the castle grounds
2 [C] a particular journey that you make by walking, especially one that goes through an interesting or attractive area: He says he's **going on a long walk** tomorrow. I Have you ever **done** the Three Peaks **walk**? I **coastal/hill etc walk** There is a stunning 10-mile coastal walk from St Andrews to Crail.
3 an organized event when people walk for pleasure: Let's all **go on the beach walk.** I The local tourist office organises a number of **guided walks.**
4 [singular] the way someone walks; ▣ **gait**: You can often recognize people by their walk.
5 [singular] when you walk rather than run: Breathless, she **slowed to a walk.** → WALK OF LIFE; → sponsored walk at SPONSOR² (5)

walk·a·bout /ˈwɔːkəbaʊt $ ˈwɒːk-/ n [C] BrE **1** infor-mal an occasion when an important person walks through a crowd, talking informally to people: The press conference was followed by a walkabout and a factory visit. **2 go walkabout** spoken to get lost – used humorously: My watch seems to have gone walkabout again.

walk·a·way /ˈwɔːkəweɪ $ ˈwɒːk-/ n [C] AmE informal an easy victory; ▣ **walkover**

walk·er /ˈwɔːkə $ ˈwɒːkər/ n [C] **1** especially BrE someone who walks for pleasure or exercise; → **hiker**: The area is popular with walkers and cyclists. I climbers and **hill-walkers 2** a fast/slow etc walker someone who walks fast, slowly etc **3** especially AmE a metal frame on wheels that old or sick people use to help them walk; ▣ **zimmer frame** BrE trademark **4** a frame on wheels that a baby can sit in and move around using its legs, before it can walk; ▣ **baby walker** BrE

walk·ies /ˈwɔːkiz $ ˈwɒːk-/ n [plural] BrE spoken used to tell a dog that you are going to take it for a walk: Come on, Shep! Walkies!

walk·ie-talk·ie /ˌwɔːki ˈtɔːki $ ˌwɒːki ˈtɒːki/ n [C] one of a pair of radios that you can carry with you, and use to speak to the person who has the other radio

'walk-in adj [only before noun] **1** big enough for a person to walk inside: a walk-in closet **2 walk-in business/clinic/centre etc** a business, doctor's office etc that you can use or go to without having previously arranged a time to do this

walk·ing¹ /ˈwɔːkɪŋ $ ˈwɒːk-/ n [U] **1** especially BrE the activity or sport of going for walks, especially in the countryside or mountains; → **hiking, rambling**: We **went walking** in the hills. I **walking boots/shoes** I **walking holiday/tour etc** (=a holiday on which you walk a lot, especially in the countryside) **2** the sport of walking long distances as fast as you can without actually running

walking² adj [only before noun] **1 walking dictionary/encyclopedia** someone who knows a lot, and always has the information that you want – used humor-ously **2 walking disaster (area)** someone who always drops things, has accidents, makes mistakes etc – used humorously → **within walking distance** at DISTANCE¹ (1)

'walking ,bus n [C] BrE a group of children who walk to or from school together, with other children and their parents joining the group at different places along the way

W

'walking ,papers n [plural] **give sb their walking papers** AmE to tell someone that they must leave a place or a job → **be given/get your marching orders** at MARCH[1] (5)

'walking stick n [C] a stick that is used to support someone, especially an old person, while they walk; ▤ **cane**

Walk·man /'wɔːkmən $ 'wɒːk-/ n plural **Walkmans** [C] trademark a small CASSETTE PLAYER with HEADPHONES, that you carry with you so that you can listen to music; ▤ **personal stereo**

,walk of 'life n [C] the position in society someone has, especially the type of job they have: **from every walk of life/from all walks of life** Our volunteers include people from all walks of life.

'walk-on n [C] **1** also **walk-on part/role** a small acting part with no words to say in a play or film, or an actor who has a part like this **2** AmE someone who plays for a college sports team without having been given a sports SCHOLARSHIP

walk·out, **'walk-out** /'wɔːk-aʊt $ 'wɒːk-/ n [C] an occasion when people stop working or leave a meeting as a protest: Members of the Irish delegation **staged** a walk-out. → **walk out** at WALK[1]

walk·o·ver /'wɔːk,əʊvə $ 'wɒːk,oʊvər/ n [C] informal a very easy victory → **walk over** at WALK[1]

walk·through /'wɔːkθruː $ 'wɒːk-/ n [C] written instructions that tell you all the details of how you should play a VIDEO GAME: [+for] the official walkthrough for 'Tomb Raider'

'walk-up n [C] AmE informal **1** a tall building with apartments in it that does not have an ELEVATOR **2** an apartment, office etc in a building like this

walk·way /'wɔːkweɪ $ 'wɒːk-/ n [C] an outdoor path built for people to walk along, often above the ground: The airport hotel will be linked to the terminal building by a covered walkway.

wall[1] S1 W1 /wɔːl $ wɒːl/ n [C]
1 AROUND AN AREA an upright flat structure made of stone or brick, that divides one area from another or surrounds an area; → **fence**: **stone/brick/concrete wall** The estate is surrounded by high stone walls. | **city/garden etc wall** the ancient city walls | the Great Wall of China | We climbed over the wall into the orchard.
2 IN A BUILDING one of the sides of a room or building: **on the wall** I **put** some pictures up **on the walls**. | Bob leaned **against the wall**. | **bedroom/kitchen etc wall** We decided to paint the bathroom walls blue.
3 BODY the side of something hollow, especially within the body: The walls of the blood vessels had been damaged. | cell walls
4 **wall of fire/water etc** a tall mass of something such as fire or water, that stops anything from getting past: The boat was hit by a wall of water.
5 **wall of silence/secrecy** a situation in which nobody will tell you what you want to know: The police investigation was met with a wall of silence.
6 **up the wall** spoken very angry or annoyed: That noise is **driving** me **up the wall** (=making me annoyed). | **go up the wall** BrE: I've got to be on time or Sarah will go up the wall.
7 **off the wall** informal very strange or unusual, often in an amusing way: Some of Krista's ideas are a little off the wall.
8 **go to the wall** informal if a company goes to the wall, it fails, especially because of financial difficulties: Many small investors will go to the wall.
9 **these four walls** spoken the room that you are in, especially considered as a private place: I don't want anything repeated outside these four walls.
10 **be/come up against a (brick) wall** to reach a point where you cannot make progress, especially because something or someone is stopping you: We seem to have come up against a brick wall in this investigation.
11 **be climbing/crawling (up) the walls** informal to be feeling extremely anxious, unhappy, or annoyed, especially because you are waiting for something or are in a situation which you cannot get away from: The kids soon had him climbing the walls.
12 **walls have ears** used to warn people to be careful what they say, because other people, especially enemies, could be listening
13 **hit the wall** informal to reach the point when you are most physically tired when doing a sport → **have your back to/against the wall** at BACK[2] (21); → **be (like) banging your head against a brick wall** at HEAD (31); → **like talking to a brick wall** at TALK[1] (15); → **the writing is on the wall** at WRITING (8); → OFF-THE-WALL

wall[2] v
wall sth ⇔ **in** phr v to surround an open area with walls
wall sth ⇔ **off** phr v to keep one area or room separate from another, by building a wall: The control room is walled off by soundproof glass.
wall sb/sth ⇔ **up** phr v **1 a)** to fill in an entrance, window etc with bricks or stone: The entrance had long since been walled up. **b)** to fill in all the entrances and windows of a place so that someone cannot get out **2** to keep someone as a prisoner in a building

wal·la·by /'wɒləbi $ 'wɑː-/ n plural **wallabies** [C] an Australian animal like a small KANGAROO

wal·lah, **walla** /'wɒlə $ 'wɑːlə/ n [C] someone who does a particular kind of job or duty – used in India and Pakistan

wall·chart /'wɔːltʃɑːt $ 'wɒːltʃɑːrt/ n [C] a large piece of paper with information on it that is fastened to a wall

walled /wɔːld $ wɒːld/ adj [only before noun] **walled garden/city/town etc** a garden etc that has a wall around it

wal·let /'wɒlɪt $ 'wɑː-/ n [C] **1** a small flat case, often made of leather, that you carry in your pocket, for holding paper money, bank cards etc; ▤ **billfold** AmE; → **purse**: **in your wallet** I've only got about £10 in my wallet. | He took a credit card out of his wallet. **2** BrE a case for documents, often made of leather or plastic

,wall-'eyed adj AmE having one or both eyes that seem to point to the side, rather than straight forwards

wall·flow·er /'wɔːl,flaʊə $ 'wɒːl,flaʊər/ n [C] **1** informal someone at a party, dance etc who is not asked to dance or take part in the activities **2** a sweet-smelling garden plant with yellow and red flowers

'wall-,mounted adj attached to a wall: **wall-mounted clock/heater/lights etc**

wal·lop /'wɒləp $ 'wɑː-/ v [T] informal to hit someone or something very hard, especially with your hand —**wallop** n [singular]

wal·lop·ing[1] /'wɒləpɪŋ $ 'wɑː-/ n spoken **give sb/get a walloping** to hit someone hard several times as a punishment

walloping[2] adj [only before noun] BrE spoken very big: **walloping great/big** a walloping great house

wal·low /'wɒləʊ $ 'wɑːloʊ/ v [I] **1** **wallow in self-pity/despair/defeat etc** to seem to enjoy being sad etc, especially because you get sympathy from other people – used to show disapproval: He'd been feeling sorry for himself, wallowing in self-pity. **2** if an animal or person wallows, it rolls around in mud, water etc for pleasure or to keep cool: hippos wallowing in the mud **3** if a ship or boat wallows, it moves with difficulty through a rough sea —**wallow** n [C]

'wall ,painting n [C] a picture that has been painted directly onto a wall, especially a FRESCO; ▤ **mural**

wall·pa·per[1] /'wɔːl,peɪpə $ 'wɒːl,peɪpər/ n [C,U] **1** paper that you stick onto the walls of a room in order to decorate it **2** the colour, pattern, or picture which you have as the background on the screen of a computer; → **desktop**

wallpaper[2] v [T] to put wallpaper onto the walls of a room; ▤ **paper**: I haven't finished wallpapering the bedroom yet.

W

'Wall Street n **1** a street in New York which is the most important financial centre in America **2** the American STOCK MARKET: **on Wall Street** a drop in share prices on Wall Street

,wall-to-'wall adj **1** [only before noun] covering the whole floor: wall-to-wall carpeting **2** informal filling all the space or time available, especially in a way you do not like: wall-to-wall advertising on TV

wal·ly /'wɒli $ 'wɑ:-/ n plural **wallies** [C] BrE informal someone who behaves in a silly way: Stop being such a wally!

wal·nut /'wɔ:lnʌt $ 'wɒl-/ n **1** [C] a nut that you can eat, shaped like a human brain: coffee and walnut cake **2** [C] also **walnut tree** a tree that produces this type of nut **3** [U] the wood from a walnut tree, often used to make furniture

wal·rus /'wɔ:lrəs $ 'wɒl-, 'wɑ:l-/ n [C] a large sea animal with two long TUSKS (=things like teeth) coming down from the sides of its mouth; → **seal**

waltz¹ /wɔ:ls $ wɒlts/ n [C] **1** a fairly slow dance with a regular pattern of three beats **2** a piece of music intended for this type of dance: a Strauss waltz

waltz² v **1** [I] to dance a waltz: They waltzed elegantly around the dance floor. **2** [I always + adv/prep] informal to walk somewhere calmly and confidently – used to show disapproval: [+in/into/up to] Jeff just waltzed up to the bar and helped himself to a drink. | She can't waltz in here and start making changes.

    waltz off with sth phr v informal to take something without permission or without realizing that you have done this: Joe must have waltzed off with my jacket.

    waltz through sth phr v informal to pass an examination, win a game etc very well and without any difficulty

wam·pum /'wɒmpəm $ 'wɑ:m-/ n [U] shells put into strings, belts etc, used in the past as money by Native Americans

wan /wɒn $ wɑ:n/ adj literary looking pale, weak, or tired: She gave a wan smile. —**wanly** adv

wand /wɒnd $ wɑ:nd/ n [C] **1** a thin stick you hold in your hand to do magic tricks: **wave a (magic) wand** (=move a wand about to make something magical happen) I can't just wave a magic wand and make it all better. **2** a tool that looks like a thin stick: a mascara wand

wan·der¹ S3 /'wɒndə $ 'wɑ:ndər/ v
1 WITHOUT DIRECTION [I,T] to walk slowly across or around an area, usually without a clear direction or purpose: [+in/through/around etc] I'll wander around the mall for half an hour. | She **wandered aimlessly** about the house. | Ana wandered off to get a drink. | He was found **wandering the streets** of New York.
2 MOVE AWAY [I] also **wander off** to walk away from where you are supposed to stay: Don't let any of the kids wander off.
3 MIND/THOUGHTS [I] if your mind, thoughts etc wander, you no longer pay attention to something, especially because you are bored or worried: Mrs Snell's mind wandered and the voices went on and on.
4 CONVERSATION [I] to start to talk about something not related to the main subject that you were talking about before: [+from/off] Pauline started to wander from the point.
5 sb's mind is wandering used to say that someone has become unable to think clearly, especially because they are old
6 EYES [I] if your eyes or your GAZE wanders, you look around slowly at different things or at all parts of something: His gaze wandered round the room.
7 ROAD/RIVER [I] if a road or a river wanders somewhere, it does not go straight but in curves: [+through/across/along] The Missouri River wanders across several states.
8 HANDS [I] if a man's hands wander, he touches the body of a woman he is with, especially where she does not want him to: Be careful, he's got **wandering hands**.

wander² n [singular] BrE a short relaxed walk: **take/go for/have a wander** I had a bit of a wander round the shops.

wan·der·er /'wɒndərə $ 'wɑ:ndərər/ n [C] a person who moves from place to place and has no permanent home

wan·der·ings /'wɒndərɪŋz $ 'wɑ:n-/ n [plural] literary journeys to places where you do not stay for very long: his wanderings through the Australian outback

wan·der·lust /'wɒndəlʌst $ 'wɑ:ndər-/ n [singular, U] a strong desire to travel to different places

wane¹ /weɪn/ v [I] **1** if something such as power, influence, or a feeling wanes, it becomes gradually less strong or less important: My enthusiasm for the project was waning. | The group's influence had begun to wane by this time. **2** when the moon wanes, you gradually see less of it; → **wax**; → **wax and wane** at WAX² (4)

wane² n **on the wane** becoming smaller, weaker, or less important: By the 5th century, the power of the Roman Empire was on the wane.

wan·gle /'wæŋɡəl/ v [T] informal to get something, or arrange for something to happen, by cleverly persuading or tricking someone: **wangle sth (out of sb)** In the end she wangled an invitation. | **wangle your way out of/into sth** I wangled my way into art school.

wank¹ /wæŋk/ v [I] BrE informal not polite to MASTURBATE

wank² n BrE informal not polite **1** [singular] an act of MASTURBATION **2** [U] something which you think is very stupid, useless, or of bad quality; ⊟ **rubbish**: This music's a load of wank.

wank·er /'wæŋkə $ -ər/ n [C] BrE taboo informal a very offensive word for a boy or man who you think is stupid or unpleasant. Do not use this word.

wan·na /'wɒnə $ 'wɑ:-/ a short form of 'want to' or 'want a', used in writing to show how people sound when they speak

wan·na·be /'wɒnəbi $ 'wɑ:-/ n [C] informal someone who tries to look or behave like someone famous or like a particular type of successful person, because they want to be like them – usually used to show disapproval; → **would-be**: A load of Michael Schumacher wannabes trying to show what they can do on the track. | wannabe pop stars

want¹ S1 W1 /wɒnt $ wɔ:nt, wɑ:nt/ v [not usually in progressive]
1 DESIRE [T] to have a desire for something

| want to do sth |
| want sb to do sth |
| want sth to happen |
| whatever/anything you want |
| whenever/wherever you want (to) |
| if you want (to) |
| get what you want |
| do what you want |
| want sth badly |
| desperately want sth |
| what I want (to do) is ... |
| all I want is ... |
| just what I('ve) always wanted (=used to thank someone for a present that you really like) |

I really want a drink. | What do you want for your birthday? | She'd always **wanted to** go to Thailand. | I don't **want** Linda to hear about this. | He didn't **want** the holiday to end. | You can order **whatever you want**. | This shampoo is mild enough to use every day **if you want**. | If she doesn't **get what she wants**, she's not happy. | He **wanted** that job so **badly** he was willing to kill for it. | They **desperately wanted** a son. | What I **want** to know is when we're going to get paid. | All I **want is** the chance to prove myself. | Oh thank you, **it's just what I've always wanted**. → see box at WISH¹

2 NEED [T] used to say that you need something or to

W

ask someone firmly to do something for you: *Do you still want these magazines, or can I throw them out?* | **want sth done** *I want that letter typed today.* | **want sb to do sth** *I want you to find out what they're planning.* | *Do you want me to pick you up at the airport?* | **make you want to cry/throw up etc** (=give you a strong feeling that you must do something) *It always makes me want to sneeze.* | **What do you want with** *a tool kit* (=what do you need it for)? | **want doing** *BrE informal* (=need to be done) *The carpet really wants cleaning.*

3 OFFER [T] used when offering or suggesting something to someone: *Do you want a drink?* | *Do you want me to come with you?* | *Want a game of chess?* | *Who wants a cup of coffee* (=used to offer something to a group of people)?

4 SHOULD [T] *spoken especially BrE* used to say that something is sensible or that someone should do it, especially when giving advice: **may/might want to do sth** *You might want to install anti-virus software.* | **wouldn't want to do sth** (=used to say something would not be a good idea) *I wouldn't want to come here at night.* | **want to do sth** *You want to see a doctor about that cough.* | *You don't want to leave that – it'll get wet.*

5 what do you want? used to ask, often in a slightly rude way, what someone wants you to give them, do for them etc: *What do you want now? I'm busy.* | *What do you want – chocolate or vanilla?*

6 ASK FOR SB [T] to ask for someone to come and talk to you, or to come to a particular place: *You're wanted on the phone.* | *Christine wants you in her office now.*

7 LACK [I,T] *formal* to suffer because you do not have something: *In many poorer countries, people still want basic food and shelter.*

8 if you want **a)** used to offer to do something: *I'll come with you if you want.* **b)** used to invite someone to do something or to give them permission: *Join in if you want.* | *You can stay if you want to.* **c)** used when someone suggests doing something, to say that you will do it, although you do not especially want to: *'Hey, shall we go to the beach?' 'If you want.'*

9 who wants ...? used to say that you do not like something or do not think that it is worth doing: *Who wants to go to a noisy disco anyway?*

10 I just wanted to say/know etc used to politely say something, ask about something etc: *I just wanted to check that the meeting is still on next week.*

11 I don't want to sound/be ..., but ... used to be polite when you are going to tell someone something that may upset them: *I don't want to sound rude, but I think you've had too much to drink.*

12 SEX [T] *informal* if you want someone, you want to have sex with them

want for sth *phr v*

not want for sth/want for nothing to have something you need, or everything you need: *Say what you like, my kids never wanted for anything.*

want in *phr v informal*

1 *especially AmE* to want to be involved in something: *You want in, Mike?*

2 *AmE* to want to go into a place: *The dog wants in.*

want out *phr v informal*

1 to want to stop being involved in something: *She was fed up and she wanted out.*

2 *AmE* to want to leave a place: *I think the cat wants out.*

want² *n*

1 for (the) want of sth used to say that you do not have or cannot find what you need in a particular situation: *The gallery closed down for want of funding.*

2 for want of a better word/phrase etc used to say that you cannot find an exact word or phrase to describe something: *They should behave, for want of a better word, decently.*

3 not for want of sth used to say that even though something did not happen or succeed, it was not because you did not try hard enough or have what you needed: **not for want of (doing) sth** *Well, if he doesn't get*

the job it **won't be for want of trying**!

4 for want of anything better (to do) if you do something for want of anything better, you do it only because there is nothing else you want to do

5 LACK [C,U] *formal* something that you need but do not have: *The report said there had been a disgraceful want of proper care.*

6 NO FOOD/MONEY ETC [U] a situation in which you do not have enough food, money, clothes etc: *the chronic want and deprivation in the townships*

7 be in want of sth *formal* to need something: *The house is sadly in want of repair.*

'want ad *n* [C] *AmE* CLASSIFIED AD

want·ed /'wɒntɪd $ 'wɔːn-, 'wɑːn-/ *adj* **1** someone who is wanted is being looked for by the police: [+for] *He is wanted for the murder of a teenage girl.* | *one of the most wanted men in China* **2** someone, especially a child, who is wanted is loved and cared for

want·ing /'wɒntɪŋ $ 'wɔːn-, 'wɑːn-/ *adj* [not before noun] *formal* something that is wanting lacks or misses something that it needs or something that you expect it to have: *Their security procedures were found wanting.* | [+in] *They were skilled, but wanting in discipline.* | *A certain humanity is wanting in big cities.*

wan·ton /'wɒntən $ 'wɔːn-, 'wɑːn-/ *adj* **1** deliberately harming someone or damaging something for no reason: *an act of wanton aggression* | *a wanton disregard for life* **2** *old-fashioned* a wanton woman is considered immoral because she has sex with a lot of men **3** *formal* uncontrolled: *wanton growth* —**wantonly** *adv* —**wantonness** *n* [U]

WAP /wæp/ *n* [U] **wireless application protocol** a system that uses radio waves to allow electronic equipment that is not physically attached to a computer, for example a MOBILE PHONE, to use the Internet

wap·i·ti /'wɒpɪti $ 'wɑː-/ *n* [C] a large North American DEER

war [S3] [W1] /wɔː $ wɔːr/ *n*

1 [C,U] when there is fighting between two or more countries or between opposing groups within a country, involving large numbers of soldiers and weapons; OPP **peace**

win/lose a war
fight a war/wage (a) war (=used about countries or groups)
fight in a war (=used about people)
be at war (with sb)
go to war (with sb)
declare war (on sb)
war breaks out also **the outbreak of war**
civil war (=a war between opposing groups within a country)
world war
nuclear war
the war years

America's defeat in the Vietnam War | *He served as a pilot during the war.* | [+against/with/between] *the war with Spain* | *They had no chance of winning the war.* | *Britain fought two wars in Europe in the last century.* | *My grandfather fought in the Second World War.* | *In 1920 Poland and Russia were still at war.* | *Quite a few women went to war, and quite a few were killed in action.* | *Congress has the power to declare war.* | *War broke out in September 1939.* | *His career was interrupted by the outbreak of war.* | *the American Civil War* | *He led the nation out of a depression and guided it through a world war.* | *Both countries wanted to avoid a nuclear war.* | *He had spent the war years in Moscow.* | *a wounded war hero*

2 [C,U] a struggle over a long period of time to control something harmful: [+on/against] *the State's war on drugs* | *the war against racism*

3 [C,U] a situation in which a person or group is fighting for power, influence, or control: *No one wants to start a trade war here.* | *a ratings war between the major TV networks* → PRICE WAR

W

4 be in the wars *BrE spoken* used, often humorously, to say that someone has lots of injuries or health problems: *You've really been in the wars lately, haven't you?*
5 this means war *spoken* used humorously to say that you are ready to fight or argue about something → **COLD WAR, WAR OF ATTRITION, WAR OF NERVES, WAR OF WORDS, WARRING**

war·ble /'wɔːbəl $ 'wɔːr-/ v **1** [I] to sing with a high continuous but quickly changing sound, the way a bird does **2** [I,T] to sing, especially not very well – used humorously: *Mills warbled a few notes.* —**warble** n [C]

war·bler /'wɔːblə $ 'wɔːrblər/ n [C] **1** a bird that can make musical sounds **2** a singer, especially one who does not sing very well – used humorously

'war chest n [C] *informal* **1** the money that a government has available to spend on war **2** the money that a politician or organization has available to spend on achieving something: *The government's huge war chest could be used to improve transport in time for the election.*

'war crime n [C usually plural] a cruel act done during a war which is illegal under international law: *He was put on trial for war crimes.* | *an international war crimes tribunal* (=court judging war crimes) —**war criminal** n [C]

'war cry n [C] a shout used by people fighting in a battle to show their courage and frighten the enemy; ▤ **battle cry**

ward¹ W3 /wɔːd $ wɔːrd/ n [C]
1 a large room in a hospital where people who need medical treatment stay: **maternity/general/geriatric etc ward** (=a ward for people with a particular medical condition) | **on/in the ward** *a young nurse in her first day on the wards* | *the other patients in the ward*
2 one of the small areas that a city has been divided into for the purpose of local elections; → **constituency**
3 *law* someone, especially a child, who is under the legal protection of another person or of a law court: *She was made a ward of court.*

ward² v
ward sth ⇔ **off** *phr v* to do something to try to protect yourself from something bad, such as illness, danger, or attack: *Don't forget insect repellent to ward off the mosquitoes.* | *a spell to ward off evil spirits*

-ward /wəd $ wərd/ *suffix* [in adjectives] towards a particular direction or place: *our homeward journey* | *a downward movement*

'war dance n [C] a dance performed by tribes in preparation for battle or to celebrate a victory

war·den /'wɔːdn $ 'wɔːrdn/ n [C] **1** a person who is responsible for a particular place and whose job is to make sure its rules are obeyed: [+of] *the warden of the college* | **forest/park etc warden** → **CHURCHWARDEN, GAME WARDEN, TRAFFIC WARDEN 2** *AmE* the person in charge of a prison; ▤ **governor** *BrE* **3** *BrE* someone who takes care of a building and the people in it, for example a place such as a home for old people

ward·er /'wɔːdə $ 'wɔːrdər/ also **prison warder** n [C] *BrE* someone who works in a prison guarding the prisoners; → **guard**

war·drobe /'wɔːdrəub $ 'wɔːrdroub/ n **1** [C] *BrE* a piece of furniture like a large cupboard that you hang clothes in; → **closet**: *Can you hang these in the wardrobe, please?* | **fitted/built-in wardrobes** (=wardrobes built against a wall or fitted between two walls) **2** [C] the clothes that someone has: *You can win a complete new wardrobe.* | **winter/summer etc wardrobe** (=the clothes you have for a particular time of year) **3** [singular] also **wardrobe department** a department in a theatre, television company etc that deals with the clothes worn by actors

ward·room /'wɔːdrum, -ruːm $ 'wɔːrd-/ n [C] the space in a WARSHIP where the officers live and eat, except for the captain

-wards /wədz $ wərdz/ also **-ward** *especially AmE suffix* [in adverbs] towards a particular direction or place: *We're travelling northwards.* | *look skywards*

-ware /weə $ wer/ *suffix* [in U nouns] **1** things made of a particular material, especially for use in the home: *glassware* (=glass bowls, glasses etc) | *silverware* (=silver spoons, knives etc) **2** things used in a particular place for the preparation or serving of food: *ovenware* (=dishes for use in the oven) | *tableware* (=plates, glasses, knives etc) **3** things used in operating a computer: *software* (=programs) | *shareware* (=programs which can be shared via the Internet)

'war ,effort n [singular] things done by all the people in a country to help when that country is at war

ware·house /'weəhaus $ 'wer-/ n [C] a large building for storing large quantities of goods

'warehouse ,store also **'warehouse ,club** n [C] *AmE* a type of store that sells things in large amounts, so that you can buy them at a lower price than at normal stores

ware·hous·ing /'weəhauzɪŋ $ 'wer-/ n [U] the business or practice of storing large quantities of goods, especially in warehouses: *warehousing costs* | *warehousing and distribution*

wares /weəz $ werz/ n [plural] *old-fashioned* things that are for sale, usually not in a shop: *craftspeople selling their wares*

war·fare /'wɔːfeə $ 'wɔːrfer/ n [U] **1** the activity of fighting in a war – used especially when talking about particular methods of fighting: *the realities of modern warfare* | **chemical/nuclear/germ etc warfare** | **trench/jungle/mountain etc warfare** | **guerrilla warfare** (=fighting by small groups of fighters in mountains, forests etc) **2** a continuous and often violent struggle or argument between different groups: **class/gang/internecine etc warfare** *the problems of drugs and gang warfare* → **psychological warfare** at **PSYCHOLOGICAL** (3)

'war ,game n [C] **1** an activity in which soldiers fight an imaginary battle in order to test military plans **2** a game played by adults in which models of soldiers, guns, horses etc are moved around a table, or a similar game played on a computer

war·head /'wɔːhed $ 'wɔːr-/ n [C] the explosive part at the front of a MISSILE: **nuclear/chemical etc warhead**

war·horse /'wɔːhɔːs $ 'wɔːrhɔːrs/ n [C] **1** *informal* a soldier or politician who has been in their job a long time, and enjoys dealing with all the difficulties involved in it **2** a horse used in battle

war·like /'wɔːlaɪk $ 'wɔːr-/ adj **1** liking war and being skilful in it: *a warlike nation* **2** threatening war or attack: *a warlike stance*

war·lock /'wɔːlɒk $ 'wɔːrlɑːk/ n [C] a man who has magical powers, especially evil powers; ▤ **sorcerer, wizard**

war·lord /'wɔːlɔːd $ 'wɔːrlɔːrd/ n [C] the leader of an unofficial military group fighting against a government, king, or different group

warm¹ S2 W2 /wɔːm $ wɔːrm/ adj
1 BE WARM slightly hot, especially in a pleasant way; **◨** **cool**; → **warmth**: *The house was lovely and warm.* | *I hope we get some warm weather soon.* | *I've put your dinner in the oven to keep it warm.* | *warm water*
2 FEEL WARM if you are warm, your body is at a comfortable temperature: *Are you warm enough?* | **keep/stay warm** (=wear enough clothes not to feel cold) *Make sure you keep warm!* | *You'll be as warm as toast in that sleeping bag.*
3 CLOTHES/BUILDINGS clothes or buildings that are warm can keep in heat or keep out cold: *Here, put on your nice warm coat.*
4 FRIENDLY friendly or making someone feel comfortable and relaxed: *a warm, reassuring smile* | *Please give a warm welcome to our special guest.* | *a warm glow of satisfaction* | *The Hungarian people are warm and friendly.*

W

5 COLOUR warm colours contain the colours red, yellow, and orange, which make you feel comfortable and happy; ⊞ **cool**

6 CORRECT [not before noun] used especially in games to say that someone is near to guessing the correct answer or finding a hidden object; ⊞ **cold**: *You're getting warmer.* —**warmness** *n* [U]

warm² also **warm up** *v* [I,T]
to make someone or something warm or warmer, or to become warm or warmer: *They gathered round the fire to warm their hands.* | **warm yourself** *Warm yourself by the fire.*

   warm to sb/sth also **warm up to sb/sth** *AmE phr v*
1 to begin to like someone you have just met: *Bruce didn't warm to him as he had to Casey.*
2 to become more eager, interested, or excited about something: **warm to a theme/subject/topic etc** *The more she spoke, the more she warmed to her subject.* | *Voters are starting to warm up to the idea.*

   warm up *phr v*
1 MAKE WARM to become warm, or to make someone or something warm: *With the fire on, the room should soon warm up.* | *Once the weather warms up, you can move the plants outdoors.* | **warm sth ⇔ up** *I turned on the grill to warm it up.* | **warm sb up** *Come inside and have a drink. It'll warm you up.*
2 FOOD to heat food, especially food that has already been cooked, so that it is hot enough to eat, or to become hot enough to eat: **warm sth ⇔ up** *I'll put the lasagne in the oven to warm it up.*
3 DO EXERCISES to do gentle physical exercises to prepare your body for dancing, sport etc: *The runners began warming up.* → WARM-UP¹ (1), WARM-UP² (2)
4 MACHINE/ENGINE if a machine or engine warms up, or if you warm it up, it becomes ready to work properly after being switched on: *He waited for the photocopier to warm up.* | **warm sth ⇔ up** *He started to warm up the aircraft's engines.*
5 EVENT if a party, election etc warms up, it starts to become enjoyable or interesting, especially because more is happening: *The race for governor is beginning to warm up.*
6 PRACTISE if musicians, singers, or performers warm up, they practise just before a performance: *The band had little time to warm up before going on stage.*
7 PERFORM/SPEAK FIRST to perform or speak first at an event, so that the people listening are relaxed or excited before the main singer, speaker etc comes on: **warm sb ⇔ up** *He warmed up the audience by telling them a few jokes.* | [+**for**] *They warmed up for U2 on one of their early tours.* → **look/feel like death warmed up/over** at DEATH (8)

warm³ *n* **the warm** *BrE* a place that is warm; ⊞ **the cold**: *Come into the warm!*

warm⁴ *adv* **wrap up warm** to put on enough clothes so that you do not feel cold

warm-'blooded *adj* animals that are warm-blooded have a body temperature that remains fairly high whether the temperature around them is hot or cold; ⊞ **cold-blooded**

warm-down *n* [C] exercises that you do to relax your body after playing a sport or dancing; → **warm-up**: *A gentle walk can act as a warm-down after a race.*

warmed-'over *adj* [usually before noun] *AmE* **1** warmed-over food has been cooked before and then heated again for eating; → **reheat** **2** warmed-over ideas or arguments have been used before and are not interesting or useful any more → **look/feel like death warmed up/over** at DEATH (8)

warmed-'up *adj* if you are warmed-up, you have done a set of gentle exercises to prepare your body for playing a sport, dancing etc

war me.morial *n* [C] a MONUMENT in memory of the people who were killed in a war

warm·er /'wɔːmə $ 'wɔːrmər/ *n* [C] something, especially a piece of equipment, that is used to make or keep things warm: *a plate warmer*

warm 'front *n* [C] an expression used especially in weather reports meaning the front edge of a mass of warm air; ⊞ **cold front**

warm-heart·ed /ˌwɔːm 'hɑːt¹d◂ $ ˌwɔːrm 'hɑːr-/ *adj* friendly, kind, and always willing to help; ⊞ **cold-hearted**: *a warm-hearted landlady* —**warm-heartedness** *n* [U]

warm·ing¹ /'wɔːmɪŋ $ 'wɔːr-/ *adj* making you feel pleasantly warm: *a warming cup of cocoa*

warming² *n* [singular] **1** an increase in the temperature of something: [+**of**] *the warming of the ocean currents in the Pacific* → GLOBAL WARMING **2** a situation in which a relationship becomes more friendly: [+**of**] *the warming of relations between Britain and Iran*

warming pan *n* [C] a metal container with a long handle, used in the past to hold hot coals for warming beds

warm·ly /'wɔːmli $ 'wɔːrm-/ *adv* **1** in a friendly way; ⊞ **coldly**: *Terry greeted the visitor warmly.* | *We were warmly welcomed by the villagers.* | *Jack smiled warmly.* **2** in a way that makes something or someone warm: *Pat wrapped the baby up warmly.* | *Make sure that the children are dressed warmly.* **3** in a way that shows that you like something very much: *His speech was warmly received.*

war·mon·ger /'wɔːˌmʌŋgə $ 'wɔːrˌmɑːŋgər, -ˌmʌn-/ *n* [C] someone, especially a politician, who wants people to start fighting or start a war – used to show disapproval —**warmongering** *adj* —**warmongering** *n* [U]

warmth /wɔːmθ $ wɔːrmθ/ *n* [U] **1** the heat something produces, or when you feel warm: [+**of**] *the warmth of the summer sun* | **for warmth** *The children huddled closely together for warmth.* **2** friendliness and happiness: [+**of**] *the warmth of her smile*

warm-up¹ *n* [C] **1** a set of gentle exercises you do to prepare your body for dancing, sport etc → **warm up** at WARM² **2 warm-ups** *AmE informal* clothes that you wear when you are doing exercises to prepare your body for playing a sport or dancing; → **sweat suit**

warm-up² *adj* **1** a warm-up match, game, or race is held to give the sportsmen or players practice before a big event **2** warm-up exercises are done to prepare your body before playing a sport or dancing **3** a warm-up jacket is worn to keep you warm when you are doing exercises **4** a warm-up man or band prepares the people at an event for the main speaker, singer etc by singing, telling jokes etc

warn S3 W2 /wɔːn $ wɔːrn/ *v* [I,T]
1 to tell someone that something bad or dangerous may happen, so that they can avoid it or prevent it: *'Be careful, the rocks are slippery,' Alex warned.* | **warn sb about sth** *Travellers to Africa are being warned about the danger of HIV infection.* | **warn (sb) of sth** *Salmon farmers are warning of the severe crisis facing the industry.* | **warn sb (not) to do sth** *I warned you not to walk home alone.* | *Motorists are being warned to avoid the centre of London this weekend.* | **warn sb (that)** *We warned them that there was a bull in the field.*
2 to tell someone about something before it happens so that they are not worried or surprised by it: **warn sb (that)** *Warn her you're going to be back late.*

   warn (sb) against sth *phr v*
to advise someone not to do something because it may have dangerous or unpleasant results: *Her financial adviser warned her against such a risky investment.* | **warn (sb) against doing sth** *The police have warned tourists against leaving the main tourist centres.*

   warn sb ⇔ **away** *phr v*
to tell someone that they should not go near something, especially because it may be dangerous: *The snake's markings are intended to warn away predators.*

W

warn sb ⇔ **off** *phr v*
1 to tell people that they should not go near something, especially because it might be dangerous: *Some animals mark their territory to warn off rivals.*
2 *especially BrE* to tell someone that they should not do or use something because it might be dangerous: **warn sb off doing sth** *Doctors should have warned people off using the drug much earlier than they did.*

warn·ing[1] [S3] [W2] /ˈwɔːnɪŋ $ ˈwɔːrn-/ *n*
1 [C,U] something, especially a statement, that tells you that something bad, dangerous, or annoying might happen so that you can be ready or avoid it

> **warning that**
> **without (any) warning**
> **issue a warning**
> **give/sound a warning**
> **heed a warning** (=take notice of it)
> **advance/prior warning** (=when you tell someone about something so they know it will happen)
> **health warning** (=a warning that something is bad for your health)
> **a word of warning** (=used before a warning when giving advice)

[+**of**] *a warning of floods* | [+**about**] *warnings about the dangers of smoking* | [+**against**] *This experience should serve others as a warning against complacency.* | [+**to**] *a warning to pregnant women not to drink alcohol* | *a **warning that** grey squirrels are threatening the existence of red squirrels* | **Without warning**, *the soldiers started firing into the crowd.* | *The government have **issued a warning** that the fish may not be fit to eat.* | *Before he could **give a warning**, he slammed on the brakes.* | *The danger was there for all to see, but we failed to **heed** the **warning**.* | *Employers must provide **advance warning** of office closures.* | *the government **health warning** on packs of cigarettes* | *A **word of warning**: don't use a metal container.*

2 [C] a statement telling someone that if they continue to behave in an unsatisfactory way, they will be punished: *The Surrey team were **given** a **warning** last year for repeated offences.* | *I'm giving you a **final warning** – don't be late again.* | **written/verbal warning**

warning[2] *adj* [only before noun] **1** a warning action or thing tells you that something bad or dangerous might happen: *He had intended only to fire a **warning** shot.* | *Do not ignore **warning signs** such as tiredness.* | *The brake **warning light** came on.* | **a warning look/ glance** *Owen gave him a warning glance.* **2 warning bell/bells** used to say that something makes someone start to be worried or careful about something: **a warning bell rings/sounds** *As she read his letter, warning bells began to sound in her head.*

war of at·tri·tion *n plural* **wars of attrition** [C] a struggle in which you harm your opponent in a lot of small ways, so that they become gradually weaker

war of nerves *n* [singular] an attempt to make an enemy worried, and to destroy their courage by threatening them, spreading false information etc

war of words *n* [singular] a public argument between politicians etc

warp[1] /wɔːp $ wɔːrp/ *v* **1** [I,T] if something warps, or if heat or cold warps it, it becomes bent or twisted, and loses its original shape: *The door must be warped. It won't close properly.* **2** [T] to influence someone in a way that has a harmful effect on how they think or behave: *You mustn't allow your dislike of her to **warp** your judgement.*

warp[2] *n* **1 the warp** *technical* the threads used in weaving cloth that go from the top to the bottom of the machine; → **weft** **2** [singular] a part of something that has become bent or twisted from its original shape → TIME WARP

war paint *n* [U] **1** paint that some tribes put on their bodies and faces before going to war **2** MAKE-UP (1) – used humorously: *Josie's just putting on her war paint.*

war·path /ˈwɔːpɑːθ $ ˈwɔːrpæθ/ *n informal* **be on the warpath** to be angry and looking for someone to fight or punish

warped /wɔːpt $ wɔːrpt/ *adj* **1** someone who is warped has ideas or thoughts that most people think are unpleasant or not normal: *a warped mind* | *You really **have a warped sense of humour** (=think strange and unpleasant things are funny).* **2** something that is warped is bent or twisted so that it is not the correct shape

war·rant[1] /ˈwɒrənt $ ˈwɔː-, ˈwɑː-/ *n* **1** [C] a legal document that is signed by a judge, allowing the police to take a particular action: [+**for**] *The magistrate **issued** a **warrant** for his arrest.* → DEATH WARRANT, SEARCH WARRANT **2** [C] an official document giving someone the right to do something, for example buy SHARES in a company: *The company **issued warrants** for 300,000 shares of Common Stock.* **3** *formal* **no warrant for (doing) something** no good reason for doing something: *There is no warrant for copying other people's work.* → UNWARRANTED

warrant[2] *v* [T] **1** to need or deserve: *This tiny crowd does not warrant such a large police presence.* | **warrant attention/consideration etc** *Another area that warrants attention is that of funding for universities.* **2** to promise that something is true: **warrant that** *The Author hereby warrants that the Publisher is the owner of the copyright.* **3 I'll warrant (you)** *old-fashioned* used to tell someone that you are sure about something: **warrant (that)** *I'll warrant we won't see him again.*

warrant card *n* [C] an official card carried by British police officers to prove that they belong to the police

warrant officer *n* [C] a middle rank in the army, air force, or US Navy

war·ran·ty /ˈwɒrənti $ ˈwɔː-, ˈwɑː-/ *n plural* **warranties** [C] a written agreement in which a company selling something promises to repair it if it breaks within a particular period of time: **under warranty** *The car is still under warranty.* | *a three-year warranty*; → **guarantee**

war·ren /ˈwɒrən $ ˈwɔː-, ˈwɑː-/ *n* [C] **1** the underground home of rabbits **2** a place with so many streets, rooms etc that it is difficult to find the place that you want: *a warren of tiny streets*

war·ring /ˈwɔːrɪŋ/ *adj* [only before noun] at war or fighting each other: **warring factions/parties** (=groups of people fighting each other)

war·ri·or /ˈwɒriə $ ˈwɔːriər, ˈwɑː-/ *n* [C] a soldier or fighter who is brave and experienced – used about people in the past: *a noble warrior*

war·ship /ˈwɔːˌʃɪp $ ˈwɔːr-/ *n* [C] a ship with guns that is used in a war; → **battleship**

wart /wɔːt $ wɔːrt/ *n* [C] **1** a small hard raised part on someone's skin; → **verruca** **2 warts and all** *informal* including all the faults or unpleasant things: *Well, you married him – warts and all.* —**warty** *adj*: *warty skin*

wart·hog /ˈwɔːthɒg $ ˈwɔːrthɒːg, -ˌhɑːg/ *n* [C] an African wild pig with long front teeth that stick out of the side of its mouth

war·time /ˈwɔːtaɪm $ ˈwɔːr-/ *n* [U] the period of time when a country is fighting a war; **◪** peacetime: **in/during wartime** *Even in wartime some people held concerts.* —**wartime** *adj* [only before noun]: *the hardships of wartime Britain* | *his wartime experiences*

war-torn *adj* [only before noun] a war-torn country, city etc is being destroyed by war

war widow *n* [C] a woman whose husband has been killed in a war

war·y /ˈweəri $ ˈweri/ *adj* someone who is wary is careful because they think something might be dangerous or harmful: **be wary of (doing) sth** *I'm a bit wary of*

[1] 000, [2] 000, [3] 000, most frequent words in [S]poken and [W]ritten English

W

driving in this fog. | [+of] *We must teach children to be wary of strangers.* | **Keep a wary eye on** *the weather before you set sail.* | *She had a wary expression on her face.* —**wariness** *n* [singular, U]: *a wariness in her voice* —**warily** *adv*: *She eyed him warily.*

war zone *n* [C] an area where a war is being fought

was /wəz; *strong* wɒz $ wəz; *strong* wɑːz/ the first and third person singular of the past tense of BE

wa·sa·bi /wə'sɑːbi/ *n* [U] a green strong-tasting Japanese food, which is added to SUSHI and other food in small amounts in order to make it taste hotter

wash[1] S1 W3 /wɒʃ $ wɒːʃ, wɑːʃ/ *v*
1 WASH SOMETHING [T] to clean something using water and a type of soap: *This shirt needs washing.* | *It's your turn to* **wash the dishes**.
2 WASH YOURSELF [I,T] to clean your body with soap and water: *Amy washed and went to bed.* | *She had a hot bath and washed her hair.* | *I'm just going to wash my hands.* | **wash yourself** *When a cat has finished eating, it usually washes itself.*
3 FLOW [I,T always + adv/prep] if a river, sea etc washes somewhere, or if something carried by the river or sea is washed somewhere, it flows or moves there: *The waves washed against the shore.* | *The sea washed over her.* | *The young man was* **washed overboard** (=pushed from a boat into the sea by the force of the water) *in the storm.* | *The body was* **washed ashore** (=brought to the shore by waves).
4 sth doesn't/won't wash (with sb) *spoken* used to say that you do not believe or accept someone's explanation, reason, attitude etc: *I'm sorry but all his charm just doesn't wash with me.*
5 wash your hands of sth to refuse to be responsible for something any more: *I've washed my hands of the whole affair.*
6 wash your mouth out! *spoken old-fashioned* used to tell someone who has just sworn or said something rude that they should not have spoken that way
7 wash well to be easy to clean using soap and water: *Silk doesn't wash well.* → **wash/air your dirty linen/laundry (in public)** at DIRTY[1] (7)
  wash sth ⇔ away *phr v*
1 if water washes something away, it carries it away with great force: *Floods in Bangladesh have washed hundreds of homes away.*
2 to get rid of unhappy feelings, thoughts, or memories: *My anxiety was washed away.*
  wash sth ⇔ down *phr v*
1 to clean something large using a lot of water: *Can you wash down the driveway?*
2 to drink something with or after food or with medicine to help you swallow it: [+with] *steak and chips washed down with red wine*
  wash off *phr v*
1 wash sth ⇔ off to clean dirt, dust etc from the surface of something with water
2 if a substance washes off, you can remove it from the surface of something by washing: *Will this paint wash off?*
  wash out *phr v*
1 wash sth ⇔ out to wash the inside of something quickly: *I'll just wash out this vase for flowers.*
2 if a substance washes out, you can remove it from a material by washing it: *a dye that won't wash out*
3 be washed out if an event is washed out, it cannot continue because of rain: *The summer fair was washed out by the English weather.* → **WASHED-OUT, WASHOUT**
  wash over sb *phr v*
1 if a feeling washes over you, you suddenly feel it very strongly: *A feeling of relief washed over her.*
2 if you let something wash over you, you do not pay close attention to it: *She was content to let the conversation wash over her.*
  wash up *phr v*
1 *BrE* to wash plates, dishes, knives etc → **WASHING-UP**

2 *AmE* to wash your hands: *Go wash up before dinner.*
3 wash sth ⇔ up if waves wash something up, they carry it to the shore: [+on] *His body was washed up on the beach the next morning.* → **WASHED-UP**

wash[2] *n*
1 ACT OF CLEANING [C usually singular] an act of cleaning something using soap and water: *Those jeans need* **a good wash** (=a thorough wash). | *I'll just* **have a quick wash** *before we go out.*
2 CLOTHES [singular, U] clothes that are to be washed, are being washed, or have just been washed: *You'd better* **put** *that shirt* **in the wash**. | *Do you need me to put another wash on?*
3 SKIN [C] a liquid used to clean your skin: *an antibacterial facial wash*
4 BOAT the wash the movement of water caused by a passing boat: *The wash of a large motorboat rocked the little dinghy.*
5 COLOUR [C] a very thin transparent layer of paint or colour
6 AREA OF LAND the wash the area of land that is sometimes covered by the sea
7 it will all come out in the wash *spoken* **a)** used to tell someone not to worry about a problem because it will be solved in the future **b)** used to say that the truth about something will be known in the end

wash·a·ble /'wɒʃəbəl $ 'wɒːʃ-, 'wɑːʃ-/ *adj* **1** something that is washable can be washed without being damaged: *washable cushion covers* | *The gloves are* **machine washable**. **2** paint or ink that is washable will come out of cloth when you wash it

wash·ba·sin /'wɒʃˌbeisən $ 'wɒːʃ-, 'wɑːʃ-/ *n* [C] a container like a small SINK used for washing your hands and face

wash·board /'wɒʃbɔːd $ 'wɒːʃbɔːrd, 'wɑːʃ-/ *n* [C] a piece of metal with a slightly rough surface, used in the past for rubbing clothes on when washing them

wash·cloth /'wɒʃklɒθ $ 'wɒːʃklɒːθ, 'wɑːʃ-/ *n* [C] *AmE* a small square cloth used for washing your hands and face; ⬛ **facecloth** *BrE*

wash·day /'wɒʃdeɪ $ 'wɒːʃ-, 'wɑːʃ-/ *n* [C,U] *old-fashioned* the day each week when you wash your clothes

washed-'out *adj* **1** not brightly coloured any more, usually as a result of being washed many times: *a washed-out shade of blue* **2** [not before noun] feeling weak and looking unhealthy because you are very tired: *Debbie's looking a bit washed-out.* **3** *AmE* a washed-out road has been damaged by rain or FLOODS and cannot be driven on

washed-'up *adj* if a person or an organization is washed-up, they will never be successful again: *a washed-up movie star*

wash·er /'wɒʃə $ 'wɒːʃər, 'wɑː-/ *n* [C] **1** a thin flat ring of plastic, metal, rubber etc that is put over a BOLT before the NUT is put on, or between two pipes, to make a tighter joint **2** *informal* a WASHING MACHINE

washer-'dryer also **washer-drier** *BrE n* [C] a machine that both washes and dries clothes

wash·er·wom·an /'wɒʃəˌwʊmən $ 'wɒːʃər-, 'wɑː-/ *n plural* **washerwomen** /-ˌwɪmɪn/ [C] a woman in the past whose job was to wash other people's clothes

wash·ing S2 /'wɒʃɪŋ $ 'wɒː-, 'wɑː-/ *n* [singular, U] *BrE* clothes that need to be washed, are being washed, or have just been washed; ⬛ **wash** *AmE*: *I really must* **do the washing** (=wash the dirty clothes) *this afternoon.* | *Could you* **put the washing out** (=hang it on a washing line) *for me?*

washing day *n* [C] WASHDAY

washing line *n* [C,U] *BrE* a piece of string stretched between two poles that you hang wet clothes on so that they can dry outside; ⬛ **clothesline**

'washing ma,chine n
[C] a machine for washing
clothes

washing machine

'washing ,powder n
[C,U] *BrE* soap in the form
of a powder used for
washing clothes

'washing ,soda n [U] a
chemical that is added to
water to clean very dirty
things

washing
machine

,washing-'up n [U]
BrE **1** the washing of
plates, dishes, knives etc:
*It's your turn to do the
washing-up, Sam.* **2** the
dirty pans, plates, dishes,
knives etc that have to be

tumble dryer

washed; ☐ **dishes** *AmE: a pile of washing-up*

,washing-'up ,liquid n [U] *BrE* a liquid soap for
washing plates, knives etc

wash·out /'wɒʃ-aʊt $ 'wɒː-ʃ-, 'wɑːʃ-/ n [C] *infor-
mal* **1** a failure: *The picnic was a total washout –
nobody turned up!* **2** an occasion when heavy rain
causes damage or stops an event from happening →
wash out at WASH[1]

wash·rag /'wɒʃræg $ 'wɒːʃ-, 'wɑːʃ-/ n [C] *AmE* a
WASHCLOTH

wash·room /'wɒʃrʊm, -ruːm $ 'wɒːʃ-, 'wɑːʃ-/ n [C]
AmE a room in a public building where you can wash
and use the toilet

wash·stand /'wɒʃstænd $ 'wɒːʃ-, 'wɑːʃ-/ n [C] a
table in a bedroom, used in the past for holding the
things needed for washing your face

wash·tub /'wɒʃtʌb $ 'wɒːʃ-, 'wɑːʃ-/ n [C] a very large
bowl used in the past for washing clothes in

was·n't /'wɒzənt $ 'wɑː-/ the short form of 'was not':
Jason wasn't at the party.

wasp /wɒsp $ wɑːsp, wɒːsp/ n [C] a thin black and
yellow flying insect that can sting you → see picture at
INSECT

WASP /wɒsp $ wɑːsp, wɒːsp/ n [C] *AmE* **White Anglo-
Saxon Protestant** an American whose family was
originally from northern Europe and who is therefore
considered to be part of the most powerful group in
society

wasp·ish /'wɒspɪʃ $ 'wɑː-, 'wɒː-/ adj bad-tempered
and cruel in the things that you say: *waspish remarks*
—**waspishly** adv

was·sail /'wɒseɪl $ 'wɑː-/ v [I] *old use* to enjoy yourself
eating and drinking at Christmas

was·sup /wɒ'sʌp $ wɑː-/ another spelling of WHASSUP

wast /wɒst $ wɑːst/ v **thou wast** *old use* you were

wast·age /'weɪstɪdʒ/ n [U] *formal* **1** when something is lost or destroyed, especially in a way that is not
useful or reasonable, or the amount that is lost or
destroyed: *The system used to result in a great deal of
food wastage.* | [+of] *wastage of ability among working
class children* **2** **natural wastage** *BrE* a reduction in
the number of workers because of people leaving, RETIR-
ING etc and not because they have lost their jobs

waste[1] S2 W3 /weɪst/ n
1 BAD USE [singular, U] when something such as
money or skills are not used in a way that is effective,
useful, or sensible: [+of] *Being unemployed is such a
waste of your talents.* | *Many believe that state aid is a
waste of taxpayers' money.* | *What a waste of all that
good work!* | *excessive waste in state spending*
2 **go to waste** if something goes to waste, it is not used:
Don't let all this food go to waste.
3 **be a waste of time/money/effort etc** to be not worth
the time, money etc that you use because there is little
or no result: *We should never have gone – it was a total
waste of time.*
4 UNWANTED MATERIALS [U] unwanted materials or
substances that are left after you have used something:

*The emphasis now is on recycling **household waste**.* |
*industrial/chemical etc waste proposals to end the
dumping of industrial waste into rivers and seas* |
waste pipes | *The disposal of hazardous waste is a
serious problem.* → NUCLEAR WASTE, TOXIC WASTE; → see
picture at ENVIRONMENT
5 **a waste of space** *spoken* someone who has no good
qualities
6 LAND **wastes** [plural] *literary* a large area of land
where there are very few people, plants, or animals:
[+of] *the icy wastes of Antarctica* | **icy/frozen/snowy etc
wastes** → WASTE GROUND, WASTELAND

waste[2] S2 W3 v [T]
1 NOT USE SENSIBLY to use more money, time,
energy etc than is useful or sensible: *Leaving the
heating on all the time wastes electricity.* | **waste sth on
sb/sth** *Don't waste your money on that junk!*
2 NOT USE FULLY [usually passive] to not make full
use of someone or something: *Hannah's wasted in that
clerical job.* | *His talents were obviously being wasted as
a lawyer.*
3 **be wasted on sb** if something is wasted on someone,
they do not understand how good or useful it is: *Her
good advice was wasted on the children.*
4 **waste your breath** *spoken* to say something that has
no effect: *Don't try to reason with Paul – you're wasting
your breath.*
5 **waste no time (in) doing sth** to do something as
quickly as you can because it will help you: *He wasted
no time in introducing himself.*
6 **waste not, want not** *spoken* used to say that if you use
what you have carefully, you will still have some of it if
you need it later
7 HARM SB *informal AmE* to kill someone, severely
injure them, or defeat them

    waste away *phr v*
to gradually become thinner and weaker, usually
because you are ill

waste[3] W3 adj [only before noun]
1 waste materials, substances etc are unwanted
because the good part of them has been removed
2 waste land is empty or not looked after by anyone →
WASTELAND; → **lay waste** at LAY[2] (11)

waste·bas·ket /'weɪst,bɑːskɪt $ -,bæs-/ n [C] *AmE* a
small container for holding paper, cans etc that are not
wanted; ☐ **wastepaper basket** *BrE*; → see picture at BIN

wast·ed /'weɪstɪd/ adj **1** **wasted journey/trip/effort
etc** a journey etc that does not achieve anything: *I'm
sorry you've had a wasted trip. Mr. Newton isn't
here.* **2** very thin and weak because of illness, old age
etc: *her thin, wasted body* **3** *informal* very drunk or
affected by drugs

'waste dis,posal n **1** [U] the process of getting rid
of unwanted materials or substances: *the problem of
radioactive waste disposal* **2** also **waste disposal unit**
[C] *BrE* a small machine under the kitchen SINK that cuts
food waste into small pieces so that it can be washed
down the drain; ☐ **garbage disposal** *AmE*

waste·ful /'weɪstfəl/ adj using more of something
than you should, especially money, time, or effort: *a
wasteful use of resources* | [+of] *The software is very
wasteful of memory.* —**wastefully** adv: *Lily had wastefully left the light on.* —**wastefulness** n [U]

'waste ground n [U] an empty, unattractive piece of
land that is not used for anything: *a piece of waste
ground*

waste·land /'weɪstlænd, -lənd/ n [C,U] **1** an unattractive area, often with old ruined buildings, factories
etc on it: **urban/industrial wasteland** *the restoration of
industrial wasteland* **2** a place, situation, or time that
has no excitement or interest; ☐ **desert**: *The 70s were a
cultural wasteland.*

,waste 'paper n [U] paper that has been used and
thrown away

W

waste·pa·per bas·ket /ˌweɪstˈpeɪpə ˌbɑːskɪt, ˈweɪstˌpeɪpə- $ ˈweɪstˌpeɪpər ˌbæ-/ n [C] a small container for holding paper, cans etc that are not wanted; ▪ **wastebasket** AmE; → see picture at BIN

waste product n [C] a useless material or substance that is produced during the process of making something else; → **by-product**: nuclear waste products

wast·er /ˈweɪstə $ -ər/ n [C]   **1** BrE informal someone who you think will never achieve any success in life: All her friends are drunks or wasters.   **2 time/money/energy waster** someone or something that does not use time etc carefully or well

wast·ing /ˈweɪstɪŋ/ adj   **1 wasting disease/illness** formal a disease that gradually makes you thinner and weaker   **2 wasting asset** technical a property, business etc that is losing money: The airline is clearly a wasting asset.

was·trel /ˈweɪstrəl/ n [C] literary a lazy person who does not try to achieve anything in life

watch¹ S1 W1 /wɒtʃ $ wɑːtʃ, wɒːtʃ/ v

1 LOOK [I,T] to look at someone or something for a period of time, paying attention to what is happening: Do you mind if I watch? | We sat and watched the sunset. | **watch carefully/closely/intently** etc He watched helplessly as Paula fell into the icy water. | Watch carefully. You may learn something. | **watch (sb/sth) with interest/amusement/delight** etc Harriet watched him with interest. | **watch sb/sth do/doing sth** I watched him go, then went home. | Ruth could **not bear to watch** her parents arguing. | **watch to do sth** I watched to see how he'd react. | **watch television/a film** etc The debate was watched by 97 million viewers. | Most parents don't know what their kids are **watching on TV**. | **watch what/how/when etc** It's useful to watch how other pilots handle the glider.; → see box at SEE¹

2 BE CAREFUL [T] to act carefully in order to avoid an accident or unwanted situation: **watch (that)** Watch he doesn't run into the road. | She's a student and has to watch her budget closely. | Watch your head on the shelf. | **watch what/how/where etc** Silly old fool! Why doesn't he **watch where** he's going? | **Watch what you're doing!** It's spilling everywhere! | **Watch yourself** (=be careful) in Madrid; there are some rough areas. | **watch what you say/your tongue/your language/your mouth** etc (=be careful not to hurt or offend people by what you say) Employees should watch what they say in personal emails. | **watch your weight/watch what you eat** (=be careful not to get fat) He may be a former athlete, but he still has to watch his weight.

3 PAY ATTENTION [T] to pay attention to a situation that interests or worries you to see how it develops: **watch closely/carefully** American companies are watching Japanese developments closely. | The government will watch the progress of these schemes with interest.

4 CARE FOR [T] to stay with someone or something so that nothing bad happens to them: She watches the kids for us occasionally.

5 SECRETLY [T] to secretly watch a person or place: I feel like I'm being watched.

6 watch your step informal to be careful, especially about making someone angry: He soon saw he'd have to watch his step with some of these guys.

7 watch your back informal to be careful because other people may try to harm you

8 watch the clock informal to keep looking at the time because you are worried or bored: anxious mums watching the clock

9 watch the time to make sure you know what time it is to avoid being late

10 watch it spoken used to warn someone to be careful: Watch it, there's a car.

11 watch this space informal used to tell people to pay attention in the future because things are going to develop further – used especially in newspapers

12 one to watch someone or something that people should pay attention to because they are interesting or

exciting: In the tournament so far, Italy's Stefania Croce looks like the one to watch.

13 watch the world go by to relax outside by just looking at the people around you: lingering in a pavement cafe, watching the world go by

14 you watch informal used to tell someone that you know what will happen: He'll win this time, you watch.
→ **watch sb like a hawk** at HAWK¹

watch (out) for sth phr v

to pay close attention in a particular situation because you are expecting something to happen or you want to avoid something bad: She stepped outside to watch for the cab. | What problems should I watch out for when buying an old house?

watch out phr v informal

used to tell someone to be careful: You'll become an alcoholic **if you don't watch out**.

watch over sb phr v

to protect someone so that they are not harmed: There must have been an angel watching over me that day.

watch² S3 W3 n

1 [C] a small clock that you wear on your wrist or keep in your pocket: My watch has stopped. | **look at/glance at/consult your watch** She glanced nervously at her watch. | How do you keep track of time if you don't **wear** a **watch**?

2 [singular, U] when you watch someone or something carefully, or pay careful attention to them, so that you are ready to act if necessary: The police arrived to **keep watch** on the mouth of the tunnel. | [+on/over] He and his wife **maintained a** 24-hour **watch** over their son. | Security forces **kept a close watch** on our activities.

3 keep a watch out for sb/sth also **be on the watch for sb/sth** to be looking and waiting for something that might happen or someone you might see, especially so that you can avoid danger, trouble etc: Be on the watch for anything suspicious.

4 [C] a group of people whose job is to guard or protect someone or something: We were arrested and held until the arrival of the **night watch** (=people responsible for keeping the streets safe at night, especially in past times). → NEIGHBOURHOOD WATCH

5 [C,U] a period of time when it is someone's duty to stay somewhere and look for signs of danger: The first watch is from now until midnight. | **on watch** Who's on watch tonight?

watch | buckle | hand | watchstrap | face

watch·a·ble /ˈwɒtʃəbəl $ ˈwɑːtʃ-, ˈwɒːtʃ-/ adj informal if a film, television programme etc is watchable, it is interesting and enjoyable: a highly watchable film

watch·band /ˈwɒtʃbænd $ ˈwɑːtʃ-, ˈwɒːtʃ-/ n [C] AmE a piece of leather or metal for fastening your watch on your wrist; ▪ **watchstrap** BrE; → see picture at WATCH²

watch·dog /ˈwɒtʃdɒg $ ˈwɑːtʃdɒːg, ˈwɒːtʃ-/ n [C]   **1** a person or group of people whose job is to protect the rights of people who buy things and to make sure companies do not do anything illegal or harmful: a **consumer watchdog**   **2** old-fashioned a GUARD DOG

watch·er /ˈwɒtʃə $ ˈwɑːtʃər, ˈwɒː-/ n [C] someone who watches someone or something for pleasure or as part of their job: **bird/whale/royal etc watcher** Fifteen thousand bird watchers visit annually. | Industry-watchers hailed the takeover as a triumph.

watch·ful /ˈwɒtʃfəl $ ˈwɑːtʃ-, ˈwɒːtʃ-/ adj   **1** very careful to notice what is happening, and to make sure that everything is all right: The entrances are guarded by watchful security staff. | His eyes were **watchful**. | Keep a **watchful eye on** elderly residents.   **2 under sb's watchful eye** following someone's instructions or with someone's help: *Learn the basics under the watchful eye of a qualified instructor.* —**watchfully** *adv* —**watchfulness** *n* [U]

'watching ˌbrief *n* [C] *BrE* instructions to someone to watch a situation carefully but not to become involved in it: *One of his responsibilities is to keep a watching brief on foreign broadcasts.*

watch·keep·er /'wɒtʃˌkiːpə $ 'wɑːtʃˌkiːpər, 'wɒːtʃ-/ *n* [C] someone whose job is to guard or protect something, especially a ship

watch·mak·er /'wɒtʃˌmeɪkə $ 'wɑːtʃˌmeɪkər, 'wɒːtʃ-/ *n* [C] someone whose job is making and repairing clocks and watches

watch·man /'wɒtʃmən $ 'wɑːtʃ-, 'wɒːtʃ-/ *n plural* **watchmen** /-mən/ [C] *old-fashioned* someone whose job is to guard a place; ◧ **security guard** → NIGHT WATCHMAN

watch·strap /'wɒtʃstræp $ 'wɑːtʃ-, 'wɒːtʃ-/ *n* [C] *BrE* a piece of leather or metal for fastening your watch on your wrist; ◧ **watchband** *AmE*; → see picture at WATCH²

watch·tow·er /'wɒtʃˌtaʊə $ 'wɑːtʃˌtaʊər, 'wɒːtʃ-/ *n* [C] a high tower used for watching and guarding a place

watch·word /'wɒtʃwɜːd $ 'wɑːtʃwɜːrd, 'wɒːtʃ-/ *n* [singular] a word or phrase that expresses an attitude or belief: *Environmental quality will be the watchword for the 21st century.*

wa·ter¹ [S3] [W1] /'wɔːtə $ 'wɒːtər, 'wɑː-/ *n* [U]
1 [LIQUID] the clear liquid without colour, smell, or taste that falls as rain and that is used for drinking, washing etc

> glass/drink of water
> **tap water** (=water that comes out of a tap)
> **drinking water**
> **spring/mineral/bottled water** (=water to drink that you buy in bottles)
> **running water** (=water that comes out of a system of pipes)
> **stagnant water** (=still water in a lake, pool etc)
> **seawater/bathwater/rainwater**
> **hot/cold/boiling/tepid etc water**
> **soapy water**
> **hard/soft water** (=water that contains a lot of or a little CALCIUM)
> **salt/fresh water** (=water that contains salt or does not contain salt)
> **turn on/turn off the water** (=turn a tap to let water come out or to stop it coming out)

There's water all over the bathroom floor. | *Does anyone want a **drink of water**?* | *a glass of sparkling **mineral water*** | *All rooms have hot and cold **running water**.* | *Pour **boiling water** over the rice and let it soak.* | *a **fresh water** spring* | *When dealing with a burst pipe, always **turn off the water** first.* | *contamination of the local water supply*

2 [AREA OF WATER] **a)** an area of water such as the sea, a lake etc: **shallow/deep water** | *Rangoon is surrounded on three sides by water.* | *Denzil dived into the water.* | *He stepped down to the water's edge.* | **by water** (=by boat) *The temple can only be reached by water.* **b)** the surface of a lake, river etc; → **underwater: on the water** *something floating on the water*
3 waters [plural] a large area of water, especially an ocean that is near or belongs to a particular country: *the **coastal waters** of Alaska* | **Korean/Mexican/Pacific etc waters** *The ship drifted into Turkish **territorial waters**.* | *a species found in **inland waters*** (=not the sea, but rivers, lakes etc)
4 high/low water the highest or lowest level of the sea and some rivers; ◧ **tide**
5 uncharted/troubled/murky waters *formal* a situation that is difficult, dangerous, or unfamiliar: *the uncharted waters of the 21st century*
6 be (all) water under the bridge *informal* used to say that what happened in the past should be forgotten
7 like water if you use something or spend money like water, you use or spend large amounts of it when you should try to save it – used to show disapproval: *Some*

of the companies were spending money like water.
8 like water off a duck's back *informal* if criticism, warnings etc are like water off a duck's back, they have no effect on the person you are saying them to
9 sb's waters break when a PREGNANT woman's waters break, liquid comes from her body just before her baby is born
10 water on the brain/knee *old-fashioned informal* liquid around the brain or knee as the result of a disease
11 take the waters *old-fashioned* to wash yourself in or drink special water that is thought to make you healthy
12 make/pass water *formal* to URINATE → SODA WATER, TOILET WATER; → **in deep water** at DEEP¹ (15); → **take to sth like a duck to water** at DUCK¹ (4); → **of the first water** at FIRST¹ (18); → **(be/feel) like a fish out of water** at FISH¹ (3); → **not hold water** at HOLD¹ (37); → **in hot water** at HOT¹ (10); → **muddy the waters** at MUDDY² (2); → **pour cold water over/on sth** at POUR (6); → **still waters run deep** at STILL² (5); → **test the water** at TEST² (7); → **tread water** at TREAD¹ (5); → **troubled waters** at TROUBLED (3)

water² [S3] *v*
1 [PLANT/LAND] [T] if you water plants or the ground they are growing in, you pour water on them: *Will you water my houseplants while I'm away?* | *The garden needs watering daily.*
2 your eyes water if your eyes water, TEARS come out of them: *Chopping onions makes my eyes water.* → MOUTH-WATERING; → **make your mouth water** at MOUTH¹ (11)
3 [ANIMAL] [T] to give an animal water to drink: *Have the horses been fed and watered?*
4 [RIVER] [I usually passive] *technical* if an area is watered by a river, the river flows through it and provides it with water: *Colombia is watered by several rivers.*
5 [WEAKEN] also **water down** [T] to add water to a drink to make it less strong

water sth ⇔ down *phr v*
1 to make a statement, report etc less forceful by changing it or removing parts that may offend people – used to show disapproval: *The report of the investigation had been watered down.* → WATERED-DOWN
2 to add water to a drink to make it less strong; ◧ **dilute**

wa·ter·bed /'wɔːtəbed $ 'wɒːtər-, 'wɑː-/ *n* [C] a bed with a part inside that is made of rubber and filled with water

'water bird *n* [C] a wild bird that swims and lives near water

'water ˌbiscuit *n* [C] *BrE* a thin BISCUIT that is not sweet and is often eaten with cheese

wa·ter·borne /'wɔːtəbɔːn $ 'wɒːtərbɔːrn, 'wɑː-/ *adj* spread or carried by water; → **airborne: waterborne disease/illness etc** *waterborne diseases such as cholera* | *waterborne traffic*

'water ˌbottle *n* [C] a bottle used for carrying water to drink → see picture at BOTTLE¹

'water ˌboy *n* [C] *AmE* **1** someone whose job is to give the members of a sports team water to drink **2** *informal* someone who has a very unimportant job

'water ˌbuffalo *n plural* **water buffaloes** *or* **water buffalo** [C] a large animal like a cow with long horns, used to work on farms in Asia

'water bug *n* [C] *AmE informal* a small insect that lives in water

'water butt *n* [C] *BrE* a large container that is kept outside and used for collecting rainwater

'water ˌcannon *n* [C,U] a machine that sends out a powerful stream of water, used by police to control violent crowds

'water ˌchestnut *n* [C] the thick stem of a plant that grows in water, used in Chinese cooking

'water ˌcloset *n* [C] *old-fashioned* a toilet

W

---

wa·ter·col·our BrE; **watercolor** AmE /'wɔːtə,kʌlə $ 'wɔːtər,kʌlər, 'wɑː-/ n **1** [C usually plural, U] a type of paint that you mix with water: *Margaret began experimenting with watercolor.* **2** [C] a picture painted using watercolours: *a watercolour of the castle*

water ,cooler n [C] **1** a piece of equipment, used especially in offices, from which you can get a cup of cold water to drink **2 water cooler gossip** conversation about other people's behaviour or lives that happens in offices when people meet each other by the water cooler

wa·ter·course /'wɔːtəkɔːs $ 'wɒːtərkɔːrs, 'wɑː-/ n [C] **1** a place where water flows, for example a river or CANAL: *chemicals that pollute the local watercourse* **2** a long thin hole for water to flow through

wa·ter·cress /'wɔːtəkres $ 'wɒːtər-, 'wɑː-/ n [U] a small green plant with strong-tasting leaves that grows in water: *a bunch of watercress*

,watered-'down adj a watered-down plan, report etc has been changed so that it is less extreme or forceful than when it was first written – used to show disapproval: *a watered-down version of the original*

,watered 'silk n [U] a type of silk with a pattern of waves on it

wa·ter·fall /'wɔːtəfɔːl $ 'wɒːtərfɔːl, 'wɑː-/ n [C] a place where water from a river or stream falls down over a cliff or rock → see picture at COUNTRY; → see picture at RIVER

water ,feature n [C] a small pool, stream, or other structure that has water in it or running through it, built in a garden to make it more interesting and attractive

water ,fountain n [C] **1** a DRINKING FOUNTAIN **2** a WATER COOLER

wa·ter·fowl /'wɔːtəfaʊl $ 'wɒːtər-, 'wɑː-/ n plural **waterfowl** [C,U] a wild bird that swims and lives near water: *the varied waterfowl of North America*

wa·ter·front /'wɔːtəfrʌnt $ 'wɒːtər-, 'wɑː-/ n [C usually singular] the part of a town or an area of land next to the sea, a river etc: *Most of the hotels are down on the waterfront.*

wa·ter·hole /'wɔːtəhəʊl $ 'wɒːtərhoʊl, 'wɑː-/ n [C] a small area of water in a dry country where wild animals drink

water ice n [C,U] BrE SORBET

watering can n [C] a container used for pouring water on garden plants → see picture at CAN[2]

watering hole n [C] **1** informal a bar or other place where people drink alcohol: *What's your favorite watering hole?* **2** a WATERHOLE

watering place n [C] **1** a WATERHOLE **2** a town which people visited in the past because the water there was thought to be good for your health; ⊟ spa

water jump n [C] an area of water that you have to jump over during a competition, race etc: *Her horse fell at the water jump.*

wa·ter·less /'wɔːtələs $ 'wɒːtər-, 'wɑː-/ adj a waterless place has no water for people or animals to drink: *a barren, waterless desert*

water ,lily n plural **water lilies** [C] a plant that grows in water, with large white or pink flowers

wa·ter·line /'wɔːtəlaɪn $ 'wɒːtər-, 'wɑː-/ n **1 the waterline** the level that water reaches on the side of a ship etc: *Two torpedoes struck below the waterline.* **2** [singular] the edge of a large area of water, especially the sea, where it joins the land: *As the waterline advanced, the vegetation was swamped.*

wa·ter·logged /'wɔːtəlɒgd $ 'wɒːtərlɔːgd, 'wɑː-, -lɑːgd/ adj **1** a waterlogged area of land is flooded with water and cannot be used: **waterlogged ground/soil** *Heavy rain meant the pitch was waterlogged.* **2** a waterlogged boat is full of water and may sink —**waterlogging** n [U]: *The race was cancelled due to waterlogging.*

water main n [C] a large underground pipe that carries the public supply of water to buildings: *a burst water main*

wa·ter·mark /'wɔːtəmɑːk $ 'wɒːtərmɑːrk, 'wɑː-/ n [C] **1** a special design put onto paper, especially bank notes, that can only be seen when you hold it up to the light: **bear/carry a watermark** *The sheet bears the watermark '1836'.* **2** a special mark contained in electronic documents, pictures, music etc that is used to stop people from copying them: *The card has a **digital watermark** detectable only to electronic cash dispensers.* **3 high watermark** especially AmE the high watermark of a particular process is its most successful time or achievement; ⊟ **high point**: [+of] *Reagan's presidency may prove to have been the high watermark of the US-Israeli alliance.* **4 high/low watermark** AmE a line showing the highest or lowest levels of the sea; ⊟ **tidemark** BrE

water ,meadow n [C] a field that is near a river and that is sometimes flooded

wa·ter·mel·on /'wɔːtə,melən $ 'wɒːtər-, 'wɑː-/ n [C,U] a large round fruit with hard green skin, red flesh, and black seeds → see picture at FRUIT[1]

water ,meter n [C] a piece of equipment that measures how much water is used in a building

wa·ter·mill /'wɔːtə,mɪl $ 'wɒːtər-, 'wɑː-/ n [C] a MILL that operates using water

water ,pipe n [C] **1** an underground pipe used to carry the public water supply **2** a pipe used for smoking, consisting of a long tube and a container of water; ⊟ **hookah**

water ,pistol n [C] BrE a toy gun that shoots water

water ,polo n [U] a ball game played in water between two teams

water ,power n [U] power obtained from moving water, used to produce electricity or to make a machine work

wa·ter·proof[1] /'wɔːtəpruːf $ 'wɒːtər-, 'wɑː-/ adj not allowing water to enter: *a waterproof jacket | waterproof adhesive | Rub the wax in to **make** the shoe waterproof.* —**waterproof** v [T]: *Plastic sheeting was used to waterproof the shed.* —**waterproofed** adj [only before noun]: *a waterproofed sack.*

waterproof[2] n [C usually plural] a jacket or coat that does not allow rain and water through it: **waterproofs** (=a waterproof jacket and trousers)

water rat n [C] an animal like a big mouse that can swim and lives near water

water-re,pellent adj material that is water-repellent has been covered with a substance that makes water run off it, so that it does not become wet —**water-repellent** n [C]

water re,sistant adj something that is water resistant does not allow water to enter easily: *Is this watch water resistant?*

wa·ter·shed /'wɔːtəʃed $ 'wɒːtər-, 'wɑː-/ n [C] **1** an event or time when important changes happen in history or in your life; ⊟ **turning point**: [+in] *The 1932 election represented a watershed in American politics. | watershed decision/case etc a watershed case on pension rights* **2 the (9 o'clock) watershed** BrE the time in the evening after which television programmes that are not considered suitable for children may be shown in Britain **3** technical the high land separating two river systems

wa·ter·side /'wɔːtəsaɪd $ 'wɒːtər-, 'wɑː-/ n [singular] the area at the edge of a lake, river etc —**waterside** adj: *a waterside restaurant*

water ,skiing n [U] a sport in which you SKI over water while being pulled by a boat —**water ski** v [I] —**water skier** n [C]: *Tracy was a keen swimmer and water skier.*

water slide n [C] a SLIDE that goes down into a swimming pool, usually with water running down it

W

'water ,softener n **1** [U] a chemical used for removing unwanted minerals from water **2** [C] a piece of equipment used for removing unwanted minerals from water

'water-,soluble adj a water-soluble substance is solid but becomes liquid when mixed with water

water sports

surfing

sailing

wind-surfing

kayaking

'water ,sports n [plural] sports that you play in water

wa·ter·spout /'wɔːtəspaʊt $ 'wɒtər-, 'wɑː-/ n [C] **1** a tall stream of water that the wind pulls up from the sea during a violent storm; → **tornado** **2** old-fashioned a pipe that carries water

'water ,table n [C] technical the level below the ground where there is water

wa·ter·tight /'wɔːtətaɪt $ 'wɒtər-, 'wɑː-/ adj **1** a watertight container, roof, door etc does not allow water to get in or out; → **airtight** **2** an argument, plan etc that is watertight is made very carefully so that people cannot find any mistakes in it: Lucky for him, his alibi is watertight. | Unless the ban is watertight, EU laws will overturn it.

'water ,tower n [C] a tall building supporting a large container of water that supplies the buildings near it

'water ,vapour BrE; **water vapor** AmE n [U] water in the form of small drops in the air

'water vole n [C] BrE an animal like a big mouse that can swim and lives near water; ☐ **water rat**

wa·ter·way /'wɔːtəweɪ $ 'wɒtər-, 'wɑː-/ n [C] a river or CANAL that boats travel on: **inland waterways**

wa·ter·wheel /'wɔːtəwiːl $ 'wɒtər-, 'wɑː-/ n [C] a large wheel that is turned by water and is used to drive machinery

wa·ter·wings /'wɔːtə,wɪŋz $ 'wɒtər-, 'wɑː-/ n [plural] two bags filled with air that you fasten on your arms when you are learning to swim

wa·ter·works /'wɔːtəwɜːks $ 'wɒtərwɜːrks, 'wɑː-/ n [plural] **1** the system of pipes and water supplies in a town or city **2** a building from which water is cleaned and pumped to houses, buildings etc **3** turn on the waterworks informal to start crying in order to get sympathy: 'Don't turn on the waterworks,' he sighed. **4** informal the organs in your body through which URINE (=liquid waste) is removed

wa·ter·y /'wɔːtəri $ 'wɒt-, 'wɑː-/ adj **1** full of water or relating to water: Her eyes were red and watery from crying. | Snakes lay eggs in a watery environment. **2** very weak or pale: a watery sun | She gave him a watery smile. **3** watery food or drink contains too much water and has little taste: a bowl of watery stew **4** a watery grave literary if someone has a watery grave, they DROWN (=die by breathing in water)

watt /wɒt $ wɑːt/ written abbreviation W or w n [C] a unit for measuring electrical power: a 100-watt bulb

watt·age /'wɒtɪdʒ $ 'wɑː-/ n [singular, U] the power of a piece of electrical equipment, measured in watts

wat·tle /'wɒtl $ 'wɑːtl/ n **1** [U] a frame made from sticks woven together: a wattle fence | walls made of **wattle and daub** (=this frame covered with

clay) **2** [C] the red flesh that grows on the head or neck of some birds, such as chickens

WAV /wæv/ n [U] technical **waveform audio** a type of computer FILE that contains sound

wave¹ S3 W2 /weɪv/ n

1 SEA [C] a line of raised water that moves across the surface of the sea: Dee watched the **waves breaking** on the shore. | a ship **riding the ocean waves** | A powerful **tidal wave** (=very large wave) struck Jamaica, killing 2000. | the white crests of the waves

2 INCREASE [C usually singular] a sudden increase in a particular type of behaviour, activity, or feeling: **a wave of anger/sympathy/relief etc** There was a wave of public sympathy for her when she died. | **a wave of terror/fear/panic** A wave of panic spread through the crowd. | **a wave of nausea/dizziness/tiredness** A wave of nausea swept over me. | **a wave of violence/attacks/bombings** the recent wave of terrorist bombings | the latest **crime wave** to hit New York

3 PEOPLE AND THINGS [C] a sudden increase in the number of people or things arriving at the same time: [+of] a new wave of immigrants | They faced **wave after wave** of fresh troops.

4 LIGHT AND SOUND [C] the form in which some types of energy such as light and sound travel: **sound/ light/radio wave** → LONG WAVE, MEDIUM WAVE, SHORT WAVE

5 SIGNAL [C usually singular] a movement in which you raise your arm and move your hand from side to side: He dismissed her with **a wave of the hand**.

6 [C] a feeling or activity that happens again and again in a series: The pain swept over him **in waves**. | **Wave after wave** of aircraft passed overhead.

7 HAIR [C usually plural] a loose curl in your hair

8 make waves informal to cause problems, especially when you should not: With so many jobs already cut, he didn't want to make waves.

9 new wave a new style of music, art, film etc that is very different and unusual: new wave music | [+of] the new wave of Black feminist theorists

10 [C usually singular] AmE an occasion when many people who are watching an event stand up, move their arms up and down, and sit down again one after another in a continuous movement that looks like a wave moving on the sea; ☐ **Mexican wave** BrE

11 the waves literary the sea → AIRWAVES, SHOCK WAVE

wave² S3 W3 v

1 HAND [I,T] to raise your arm and move your hand from side to side in order to make someone notice you: [+to/at] She turned to wave to the approaching soldiers. | Enid waved at us and we waved back. | **wave (sb) goodbye** (=say goodbye to someone by waving to them) The nurses came out to wave Grandad goodbye.

2 MOVE [I,T] if you wave something, or if it waves, it moves from side to side: The starter **waved** a green **flag** to indicate that the race would begin. | a tree waving in the breeze | He **waved** a hand **in the air** to attract her attention. | **wave sth under/at etc sb/sth** Trudie waved a $50 bill under his nose. | **wave sth around/about** The stranger spoke rapidly, waving his arms around.

3 SIGNAL [T always + adv/prep] to show someone which way to go by waving your hand in that direction: **wave sb through/on/away etc** The border guards waved us through. | Peter waved them back to their seats.

4 wave sth goodbye/wave goodbye to sth informal to be forced to accept that something you want will not happen: If you're not careful, you can wave goodbye to any pay rise this year.

5 wave a magic wand to make a bad situation better, even though this is impossible: I can't wave a magic wand and change what happened.

6 HAIR [I,T] if hair waves, or if it is waved, it forms loose curls

wave sth ⇔ aside phr v

to ignore someone's opinion or ideas because you do not think they are important: He waved her protests aside.

W

wave sb/sth ⇔ **down** _phr v_
to signal to the driver of a car to stop by waving at them: _People in passing cars tried waving him down._
  wave sb ⇔ **off** _phr v_
to wave goodbye to someone as they leave: _Are you coming to the station to wave me off?_

wave·band /'weɪvbænd/ _n_ [C] a set of sound waves of a particular length, used to broadcast radio programmes

wave·length /'weɪvleŋθ/ _n_ [C] **1** the size of a radio wave used to broadcast a radio signal **2** _technical_ the distance between two points on energy waves such as sound or light **3 be on the same/a different wavelength** _informal_ to have the same or different opinions and feelings as someone else: _Dad is just on a different wavelength from me._

wa·ver /'weɪvə $ -ər/ _v_ [I] **1** to become weaker or less certain: _Her **voice wavered** uncertainly._ | _The students' **attention** did not **waver**._ | [+in] _Harris never wavered in his loyalty._ | [+from] _We were determined not to waver from our goals._ **2** to not make a decision because you have doubts: _Shareholders who were wavering met the directors._ | **waver between sth and sth** _The party wavered between free trade and protectionism._ **3** to move gently in several different directions: _The candle flame wavered, throwing shadows on the wall._

wa·ver·er /'weɪvərə $ -ər/ _n_ [C] someone who cannot make a decision, especially in a vote: _a final push to win over the waverers_

wav·y /'weɪvi/ _adj_ **1** wavy hair grows in waves **2** a wavy line is smoothly curved

wax[1] /wæks/ _n_ [U] **1** a solid substance made of fat or oil and used to make CANDLES, POLISH etc: _wax crayons_ **2** a natural sticky substance in your ears → BEESWAX

wax[2] _v_ **1** [T] to rub a layer of wax into a floor, surface etc to protect it or make it shine **2 wax sentimental/ eloquent/lyrical etc** to talk with extreme feeling, liking or pleasure about something – used humorously: [+about] _Journalists wax lyrical about the band._ **3** [I] when the moon waxes, it seems to get bigger each night; ⌧ **wane** **4 wax and wane** to increase and decrease over time: _Interest in the show has waxed and waned._ **5** [T] if you wax your legs, arms etc, you remove the hair from them using wax

waxed 'paper also **'wax paper** _n_ [U] _AmE_ paper covered with a thin layer of wax, used to wrap food; ⌧ **greaseproof paper** _BrE_

wax·en /'wæksən/ _adj literary_ **1** pale and shiny like wax: _his pale, waxen face_ **2** made from wax: _waxen images_

wax·work /'wækswɜːk $ -wɜːrk/ _n_ [C] **1 waxworks** _BrE_ a place where you can see models of famous people made of wax; ⌧ **wax museum** _AmE_ **2** a WAX model of a person

wax·y /'wæksi/ _adj_ like WAX, or made of wax: _the waxy blossoms of the water lily_ | _young men with waxy faces_

way[1] ⑤ ⓦ /weɪ/ _n_

1 METHOD [C] a method that you use to do or achieve something: _There are several different ways we can tackle this problem._ | **way of doing sth** _Evening classes are one way of meeting new people._ | **There's no way** of knowing if the treatment will work._ | **way to do sth** _What's the best way to learn a language?_ | **in the same way/in different ways etc** _Make the drink with boiling water in the same way as tea._ | _Animals communicate in various ways._ | **(in) the right/wrong way** _I think you're going about this the wrong way._ | **ways and means** (=methods of doing something, especially ones that are secret or not yet decided) _There are ways and means of raising the money that we need._ | [+out/out of/around] _One way around the problem_ (=method of dealing with it) _is recycling._ | _There seems to be no way out of the current economic crisis._ | **way into television/ publishing/finance etc** (=a method of getting involved in a particular activity or type of work) _companies_ eager for a way into business in Europe

2 MANNER [C] the manner or style in which someone does something or in which something happens: _Look at the way he's dressed!_ | **in a ... way** _'Hello,' he said in a friendly way._ | _Maria got up and took a shower in a leisurely way._ | **(in) this/that way** _I find it easier to work in this way_ (=like this). | _Sorry, I didn't know you felt that way_ (=had that feeling or opinion). | _The drugs didn't seem to affect Anna **in the same way**._ | **that's no way to do sth** (=used to tell someone that they should not be doing something in a particular manner) _That's no way to speak to your father!_ | **in more ways than one** (=in a number of ways) _The changes will benefit the company in more ways than one._ | **in sb's (own) way** (=in a personal way that other people may not recognize) _I'm sure he does love you, in his own way._

3 DIRECTION/HOW TO GO SOMEWHERE [C] **a)** a road, path, direction etc that you take in order to get to a particular place: **the way to/from/out etc** _Which is **the quickest way** to the sea from here?_ | _There are several ways through the woods._ | **ask/tell/show sb the way** _Could you tell me the way to the station?_ | _Does anyone **know the way** from here?_ | _I was afraid of **losing** my **way** in the dark._ | _Can you **find** your **way** back to the car park?_ | **the way out** (=the door, path etc which you can use to leave a building or area) _Which is the way out?_ | **the way in** (=the door, path etc which you can use to enter a building or area) _She looked all around, but she couldn't seem to find the way in._ | **on sb's way** (=in the same direction as someone is going) _Want a lift? It's on my way._ | **out of sb's way** (=not in the same direction as someone is going) _I live miles out of your way._ **b)** a particular direction from where you are now: **Which way** is north?_ | _Walk **this way**._ | _A big Mercedes was coming **the other way**_ (=from the opposite direction). | _He left the house, looking carefully both ways._

4 PART OF STH THAT IS TRUE [C] used to say that there is a fact or a feature of something that makes a statement or description true: **in a/one way** _In one way you're right, I suppose._ | **in some/many ways** _Working at home makes sense, in many ways._ | _Ben is a perfectly normal child **in every way**._ | _He never got mad at me. He was great **in that way**._ | **in no way** (=used to emphasize that something is not true) _This should in no way be seen as a defeat._

5 DISTANCE/TIME [singular] a distance or a length of time, especially a long one: _I was still **a long way** from home._ | **some way/quite a way** (=quite a long distance) _She had to park some way from the restaurant._ | **a long way off/away/ahead etc** (=far away in distance or in time) _A peace settlement now seems a long way off._ | _I don't want to go **all that way** and not see him._ | **all the way down/across/through etc (sth)** (=the full distance or length of something) _Did you really swim all the way across?_ | _I was awake all through the night._ | **a (long) ways** _AmE_: _That's quite a ways from here, isn't it?_

6 THE SPACE IN FRONT OF YOU [C usually singular] if someone or something is in the way, they are blocking the space in front of you, and you cannot move forward: **be in the way/be in sb's way** (=be blocking a road, someone's path etc so that they cannot move forward easily) _There was a big truck in the way._ | _Sorry, am I in your way?_ | _A policeman yelled at the crowds to **get out of the way**._ | _The **way ahead** was blocked._

7 make way (for sth/sb) a) to move to the side so that there is space for someone or something to pass: _The crowd stepped aside to make way for the procession._ **b)** to make it possible for something newer or better to be built, organized etc: _Several houses were demolished to make way for a new road._

8 out of the way a) also **out of sb's way** if someone or something is out of the way, they are somewhere where they are not likely to cause a problem, need attention, be annoying etc: **move/put/push etc sth out of the way** _Why don't you tie your hair back, out of the way?_ | _If Uncle Tom had been drinking, I kept out of his way._ | _When Mac was **safely out of the way**, Peter came round._ **b)** if a particular matter, job etc is out of the way, it has been done or dealt with: _I'd rather **get the interview out**_ *of the way* in the morning. | *As soon as the contract's out of the way, we can start.* **c)** a place that is out of the way is far from any towns

9 **on the/your/its way** **a)** arriving or happening soon: *There's a letter on its way to you.* | *More changes are on the way.* **b)** travelling towards a particular place: *She should be on the way here by now.* | [+**to**] *The ships were already on their way to the gulf* **c)** while going from one place to another: [+**to/out/home etc**] *I ran out of gas on my way to the airport.* | *Guess who I bumped into on the way home.* **d)** also **along the way** while moving from one situation or part of your life to another: *Don's had to change jobs several times along the way.* **e)** if someone has a baby on the way, they are PREGNANT

10 **be under way** **a)** to have started to happen or be done: *Plans are well under way for a new shopping centre.* | *The tournament got under way on Friday.* **b)** to have started to move or travel somewhere: *Our train was already under way.*

11 **make your way** **a)** to go towards something, especially when this is difficult or takes a long time: [+**to/through/towards etc**] *The team slowly made their way back to base.* | **make your own way (home/to sth etc)** (=go somewhere without the help or company of other people) *Don't worry. I can make my own way to the beach.* **b)** to gradually become successful in a particular job, activity, profession etc: *young people who are making their way in industry*

12 **push/grope/inch etc your way somewhere** to get somewhere by using force or moving carefully: *She elbowed her way to the front of the queue.* | *He drank some water, then groped his way back to the bedroom.*

13 **give way** **a)** to be replaced by something else: [+**to**] *Stone has given way to glass and concrete.* | *My anger gave way to depression.* **b)** to agree to do what someone else wants, instead of what you want, especially after a lot of discussion or argument: *Despite growing pressure, the Minister of State refused to give way.* | [+**to**] *Maria seemed to despise him for giving way to her.* **c)** to break because of too much weight or pressure: *The floor's rotten and likely to give way.* **d)** BrE to stop or slow down when you are driving, in order to allow other vehicles to go first; **◨ yield** AmE: *In Britain, give way to cars coming from the right.*

14 **clear/pave/open/prepare etc the way (for sth)** to make it possible for something to happen or develop later: *a study that paved the way for further research* | *The Queen's death opened the way for him to return.*

15 **a/the way forward** an action, plan etc that seems a good idea because it is likely to lead to success: *A way forward lies in developing more economic links.* | [+**for**] *This treatment may be the way forward for many inherited disorders.*

16 **STATE/CONDITION** [singular] a particular state or condition: *My family was in a bad way financially.* | *The chicken's nice and crispy – just the way I like it.* | *It's worth thinking how you can improve the way things are.* | **sb was born/made that way** (=used to say that someone's character is not likely to change) *He'll always be mean – he was born that way.*

17 **FACT/EVENT** [singular] used to refer to something that happens: *I hate the way you always give in to him.*

18 **BEHAVIOUR** [C] someone's typical style of behaving, especially when it seems different or unusual: **be (just) sb's way** *Don't worry if she's quiet – that's just her way.* | *Esther quickly changed the subject, as was her way.* | **strange/funny/odd etc ways** *We all have our funny little ways.* | **change/mend your ways** (=stop behaving badly); **→ see the error of your ways** at ERROR (6); **→ be set in your ways** at SET³ (6)

19 **DEVELOPMENT/PROGRESS** [singular] used in expressions about developing and improving: *The team has a long way to go* (=needs to develop or improve a lot) *before it can match that performance.* | *Microwave ovens have come a long way* (=have developed or improved a lot) *since they first appeared in our kitchens.* | *Jen is now well on the way to recovery* (=she has improved and will be well soon).

20 **go some way towards doing sth** also **go a long way**

towards doing sth to help a little or a lot to make something happen: *ideas that go some way towards reducing environmental problems*

21 **CHOICES/POSSIBILITIES** [C] used when talking about two choices someone could make, or two possibilities that could happen: *I'm not sure which way he'll decide.* | *The election could go either way* (=both results are equally possible). | *Make up your mind up one way or the other.* | **either way** (=used to say that something will be the same, whichever of two things happens) *Either way, it's going to be expensive.*

22 **within two feet/ten years etc either way** no more than two feet etc more or less than a particular amount: *Your answer must be within a centimetre either way.*

23 **(in) one way or another** also **one way or the other** used to say that someone does or will do something somehow, although you are not sure how: *One way or the other he always seems to win.* | *We'll find the money, one way or another.*

24 **way around/round/up** a particular order or position that something should be in: *Which way around does this skirt go?* | **the other way around/round/up** (=in the opposite order or position) *The picture should be the other way up.* | *Art reflects life, or is it the other way around* (=is it 'life reflects art')*?* | **the right/wrong way around/round/up** *Are the batteries in the wrong way round?*

25 **by way of sth** **a)** also **in the way of sth** as a form or means of something: *I'd like to say something by way of introduction.* | **little in the way of sth** also **not much/enough in the way of sth** (=not much of something) *The town has little in the way of leisure facilities.* **b)** if you travel by way of a place, you go through it; **◨ via**: *We went by way of London.*

26 **get in the way of sth** to prevent someone from doing something, or prevent something from happening: *Your social life must not get in the way of your studies.*

27 **go out of your way to do sth** to do something with more effort than is usual or expected: *She went out of her way to make me feel welcome.*

28 **get/have your (own) way** to do what you want to, even though someone else wants something different: *Don't let the children always get their own way.*

29 **go your own way** to do what you want, make your own decisions etc: *At 18, most young people are ready to go their own way.*

30 **go sb's way** **a)** if an event goes your way, it happens in the way you want: *The government are hopeful that the vote will go their way.* | **everything/things/nothing goes sb's way** (=used to talk about events in general) **b)** *literary* to continue a journey, or to leave and do what you want to do next: *She said goodbye and went her way.* **c)** to travel in the same direction as someone: *I can take you – I'm going your way.*

31 **come sb's way** if something comes your way, you get or experience it, especially by chance: *Luck had come her way at the very last moment.*

32 **in a big/small way** used to talk about the degree to which something happens, or how important it is: *The business was a success, in a small way.*

33 **by a long way** by a large amount: *He was the best in the group by a long way.*

34 **talk/buy etc your way into/past etc sth/sb** to get where you want or achieve something you want by saying or doing something: *Caroline managed to talk her way past the guard.*

35 **work/munch/smoke etc your way through sth** to deal with, eat, smoke etc a large amount of things: *He worked his way through the pile of documents.* | *She had munched her way through a packet of biscuits.*

36 **be on the/your way out** to be becoming less popular, important, powerful etc: *Is the royal family on the way out?*

37 **across/over the way** on the opposite side of the

W

1 000, 2 000, 3 000, most frequent words in S poken and W ritten English

street: *They live across the way from us at number 23.*

38 have a way of doing sth used to say that something often or usually happens: *Cheer up – these problems have a way of working out.*

39 get into the way of doing sth *BrE* to start to do something regularly: *He'd got into the way of smoking first thing in the morning.*

40 not in any way, shape, or form used to emphasize that something is not true: *I am not responsible for his actions in any way, shape, or form.*

41 split sth two/three etc ways also **divide sth two/ three etc ways** to divide something into two, three etc equal parts: *We'll split the cost between us five ways.*

42 have a way with sb/sth to be especially good at dealing with people or things of a particular type: *David seems to have a way with children.* | *She's always had a way with words* (=been good at using words effectively).

43 the way of the world how things always happen or are done, especially when this is not easy to change: *In those days these policies favoured men. That was the way of the world.*

44 every which way *informal* **a)** in all directions: *Bullets were flying every which way.* **b)** *BrE* every possible method: *I tried every which way to avoid it.*

45 Way used in the names of roads: *Church Way*

SPOKEN PHRASES

46 by the way used when saying something that is not related to the main subject you were talking about before: *By the way, have you seen my keys anywhere?*

47 no way! a) used to say that you will definitely not do or allow something: *'Can I borrow your car?' 'No way!'* | *There's no way I'll ever get married again.* | **no way José!** (=used to emphasize that you will not do something) **b)** *especially AmE* used to say that you do not believe something or are very surprised by it: *She's 45? No way!*

48 the way I see it also **to my way of thinking** used before telling someone your opinion: *The way I see it, it was a fair trade.*

49 that's the way used to tell someone that they are doing something correctly or well, especially when you are showing them how: *Now bring your foot gently off the clutch – that's the way.*

50 that's (just) the way sth/sb is also **that's (just) the way sth goes** used to say that a particular situation or person cannot be changed: *Don't try to fight it. That's just the way it is.* | *Sometimes Tim needs to be alone. That's the way he is.*

51 be with sb all the way to agree with someone completely: *I'm with you all the way on this salary issue, Joe.*

52 if I had my way used when telling someone what you think it would be best to do: *If I had my way, we'd leave this place tomorrow.*

53 have it your (own) way used to tell someone in an annoyed way that you will agree to what they want

54 (there are) no two ways about it used to say that something is definitely true, especially something unpleasant

55 you can't have it both ways used to say that you cannot have the advantages from both of two different possible decisions or actions: *It's a choice between the time and the money – you can't have it both ways!*

56 way to go! *AmE* used to tell someone that they have done something very well or achieved something special

57 (that's/it's) always the way! *BrE* used to say that things always happen in the way that is least convenient: *The train was late – always the way when you're in a hurry.*

58 down your/London etc way in your area, the area of London etc

59 go all the way (with sb) to have sex with someone

→ HALFWAY, ONE-WAY, RIGHT OF WAY, TWO-WAY; → **that's the way the cookie crumbles** at COOKIE (3); → **cut both ways**

at CUT[1] (36); → **in the family way** at FAMILY (7); → **go the way of all flesh** at FLESH[1] (9); → **go your separate ways** at SEPARATE[1] (4); → **know your way around (sth)** at KNOW[1] (10); → **be laughing all the way to the bank** at LAUGH[1] (8); → **lead the way** at LEAD[1] (7); → **look the other way** at LOOK[1] (9); → **out of harm's way** at HARM[1] (6); → **parting of the ways** at PARTING (3); → **pay your way** at PAY[1] (13); → **to put it another way** at PUT (4); → **rub sb up the wrong way** at RUB[1] (7); → **see which way the wind is blowing** at WIND[1] (6); → **see your way (clear) to doing sth** at SEE[1] (39); → **any way you slice it** at SLICE[2]; → **stand in sb's way** at STAND[1] (30); → **where there's a will there's a way** at WILL[2] (5); → **work your way to/through etc sth** at WORK[1] (12)

way² S2 *adv*

1 very far: [+ahead/behind/out etc] *The other cyclists were way behind.* | *She lives way out of town.*

2 by a large amount: [+above/below/past etc] *Her IQ is way above average.* | [+out] *Your guess was way out* (=completely incorrect), *he's actually thirty-eight.* | [+back] *We first met way back* (=a long time ago) *in the 70s.* | **way heavier/smarter/bigger etc** (=much heavier etc) *The tickets were way more expensive than I thought.*

3 *AmE informal* very: *I think she's way cool, man.*

way·bill /'weɪbɪl/ *n* [C] a document sent with goods that says where the goods are to be delivered, how much they are worth, and how much they weigh

way·far·er /'weɪˌfeərə $ -ˌferər/ *n* [C] *literary* someone who travels from one place to another on foot

way·lay /weɪ'leɪ/ *v past tense and past participle* **waylaid** [T] **1** if someone waylays you, they stop you when you are going somewhere, for example to attack you or talk to you: *They used to waylay him as he came out of the factory.* **2** [usually passive] if you are waylaid, you are delayed when you are doing something – often used humorously to say why you are late: *Sorry, we got waylaid at the bar.*

way of 'life *n plural* **ways of life** [C] **1** the behaviour, habits, customs etc that are typical of a particular society or person: *The tribe's traditional way of life is under threat.* | **the American/British etc way of life 2** a job or interest that is so important that it affects everything you do: *For Mark, travelling has become a way of life.*

way 'out *n plural* **ways out** [C] **1** *BrE* a door or passage through which you leave a building; **☐ exit 2** a way to escape a difficult or bad situation: *He was in a dilemma, and could see no way out.* **3 on the/your way out a)** if you do something on the way out, you do it as you leave a place: *Pick up your mail on the way out.* **b)** soon to be replaced by someone or something else: *The old type of passport is on its way out.* → **take the easy way out** at EASY[1] (6); → **way out** at WAY[1] (3)

way-'out *adj informal* very modern, unusual, and strange

way·side /'weɪsaɪd/ *n* [C] *literary* the side of a road → **fall by the wayside** at FALL[1] (16)

'way ˌstation *n* [C] *AmE* **1** *old-fashioned* a place to stop between the main stations of a railway **2** a place where you can stop before going on somewhere else: [+to] *The refugee camps, however dreadful, were a way station to their dream.*

way·ward /'weɪwəd $ -wərd/ *adj* behaving badly, in a way that is difficult to control: *a wayward teenager* **—waywardness** *n* [U]

wa·zoo /wə'zuː/ *n AmE* **out/up the wazoo** *informal* in a large amount, or to a great degree

WC /ˌdʌbəljuː 'siː/ *n* [C] *BrE water closet* a toilet – used especially on signs in public places

we S1 W1 /wi; *strong* wiː/ *pron* [used as the subject of a verb]

1 used by the person speaking or writing to refer to himself or herself and one or more other people: *'Did you go into the supermarket?' 'No, we didn't.'* | *Shall we stop for a coffee?* | *So we all travelled down to Brighton together.* | *We declare our support for a government of national unity.* | *We Italians are proud of our history.*

2 used by a writer or speaker to include themselves

and their readers or listeners: *As we saw in Chapter 4, slavery was not the only cause of the Civil War.*
3 people in general: *We live on a complex planet.*
4 *formal* used by a king or queen to refer to himself or herself
5 *spoken* sometimes used to mean 'you' when speaking to children or people who are ill: *How are we feeling today, Mr. Robson?*

weak S3 W2 /wiːk/ *adj*
1 PHYSICAL not physically strong: *The illness left her feeling weak.* | *Poor light produces weak plants.* | **be too weak to do sth** *She's too weak to feed herself.* | [+with/from] *Nina was **weak with hunger**.* | *The animal was weak from loss of blood.* | **weak heart/lungs etc** *My grandfather had a weak heart.*
2 LIKELY TO BREAK unable to support much weight: *a weak bridge* | **too weak to do sth** *The branch was too weak to support his weight.*
3 CHARACTER easily influenced by other people – used to show disapproval: *a weak indecisive man*
4 WITHOUT POWER not having much power or influence: **weak leader/ruler/king etc** *a weak and ineffective president* | *The party was left weak and divided.* | *The country is in a **weak position** economically.*
5 WITHOUT INTEREST without the power to interest or amuse people: *The play is well acted but the plot is weak.* | *a weak joke*
6 WITHOUT ENERGY done without energy or confidence: *He managed a weak smile.*
7 NOT GOOD AT DOING STH not good at a particular skill or subject, or in a particular area of activity or knowledge: [+in] *New Zealand was weak in defense.* | [+on] *She speaks quite fluently but she's weak on grammar.* | *Be honest about your **weak points** (=your faults or the things you do not do well).*
8 MONEY not financially successful: **weak currency/economy etc** | *The pound was weak against the dollar.*
9 ARGUMENT/IDEA not likely to make people believe that something is true or right: *She's washing her hair? That sounds like a **weak excuse**!* | *There are some **weak points** in her argument.* | *The defence lawyer clearly knew that his case was weak.*
10 DRINK weak tea, beer etc contains a lot of water and has little taste; ↗ **strong**
11 LIGHT/SOUND difficult to see or hear; ↗ **faint**: *a weak radio signal* | *He had only a **weak light** to see by.*
12 weak points/spots the parts of something that can easily be attacked or criticized: *Check your house for weak spots where a thief could enter.*
13 weak at the knees feeling strange because of strong emotions: *His smile made her go weak at the knees.*
14 weak moment a time when you can be persuaded more easily than usual: *Dave caught me at a weak moment and I lent him £10.*
15 the weak/weakest link the person or thing in a situation that is less strong, skilful etc than the others: *Goalkeeper Gouter proved to be the weakest link.*
16 weak verb *technical* a verb that forms regular past tenses; ↗ **strong verb**
17 weak consonant/syllable one that is not emphasized
—**weakly** *adv*: *"I'm sorry," she said, smiling weakly.* | *He sank down weakly beside her.*

WORD FOCUS: WEAK
person: **puny, feeble, weedy** *BrE*, **frail, fragile, powerless, vulnerable**
thing: **fragile, delicate, flimsy, rickety, badly made, jerry-built**

weak·en /ˈwiːkən/ *v* [I,T] **1** to make someone or something less powerful or less important, or to become less powerful; ↗ **strengthen**: *Over the last two years the president's position has weakened.* | *Changes in policy have weakened the power of the trade unions.* | *The absence of this witness has weakened the case against the accused.* **2** to make someone lose their physical strength, or to become physically weak: *Julia was weakened by her long illness.* **3** to make someone less determined, or to become less determined: *Such policies weaken the resolve of potential troublemakers.* |

When she begged him to let her stay, he weakened. **4** to make a building, structure etc less strong, or to become less strong: *The earthquake in Cairo weakened a number of structures.* **5** if a particular country's money or a company's SHARE prices weaken, or if they are weakened, their value is reduced: [+against] *The pound has weakened against the dollar.*

weaker 'sex *n* **the weaker sex** *old-fashioned* used to refer to women as a group, in a way that is now considered offensive

weak-'kneed *adj informal* lacking courage and unable to make your own decisions

weak·ling /ˈwiːk-lɪŋ/ *n* [C] someone who is not physically strong

weak-'minded *adj* showing little intelligence, or easily persuaded: *a weak-minded man*

weak·ness W3 /ˈwiːknəs/ *n*
1 FAULT [C] a fault in someone's character or in a system, organization, design etc: *The legislation has a fundamental weakness.* | *The plan has **strengths and weaknesses.***
2 LACK OF POWER [U] lack of strength, power, or influence: [+in] *weakness in the economy* | [+of] *the growing weakness of local government*
3 BODY [U] the state of being physically weak: *muscular weakness* | [+in] *weakness in the right arm*
4 CHARACTER [U] lack of determination shown in someone's behaviour: *He couldn't explain his weakness in giving in to her demands.* | *I dared not cry or show any **sign of weakness**.* | [+of] *his weakness of character*
5 MONEY [U] the condition of not being worth a lot of money: [+of] *the weakness of the pound against the dollar*
6 a weakness for sth if you have a weakness for something, you like it very much even though it may not be good for you: *I have a real **weakness for** fashionable clothes.*

weak-'willed *adj* someone who is weak-willed does not do something difficult that they had intended to do

weal /wiːl/ *n* [C] a red swollen mark on the skin where someone has been hit

wealth W3 /welθ/ *n*
1 [U] a large amount of money, property etc that a person or country owns: *The country's wealth comes from its oil.* | *the **distribution of wealth** (=the way wealth is divided among the people of a country or society)* | *The purpose of industry is to **create wealth**.*
2 a wealth of sth a lot of something useful or good: *There is a wealth of information available about pregnancy and birth.*

wealth·y /ˈwelθi/ *adj comparative* **wealthier**, *superlative* **wealthiest** **1** having a lot of money, possessions etc; ↗ **rich**: **very/extremely/immensely/fabulously etc wealthy** *He left as a poor, working class boy and returned as an extremely wealthy man.* | *the wealthy nations of the world* → see box at RICH **2** **the wealthy** [plural] people who have a lot of money, possessions etc

wean /wiːn/ *v* [T] to gradually stop feeding a baby or young animal on its mother's milk and start giving it ordinary food: **wean sb onto sth** *It's time to start weaning her onto solid foods.*
wean sb **off/from** sth *phr v* to make someone gradually stop doing something you disapprove of: *advice on how to wean yourself off nicotine*
be weaned on sth *phr v* to be influenced by something from a very early age: *I was weaned on a diet of Hollywood fantasy.*

weap·on S2 W2 /ˈwepən/ *n* [C]
1 something that you use to fight with or attack someone with, such as a knife, bomb, or gun: **nuclear/chemical/biological/atomic etc weapons** | *The police are still looking for the **murder weapon**.* | **offensive weapon** (=one that can be used to attack someone) *He was convicted of **carrying** an offensive **weapon**.* | *a*

W

*debate calling for the elimination of all **weapons of mass destruction*** | **lethal/deadly weapon** (=one that can kill)
2 an action, piece of information, piece of equipment etc that you can use to win or be successful in doing something: *a new weapon in the fight against AIDS* | *Right now, she felt the need of every **weapon in** her armoury* (=weapon that she had), *including surprise.*

weap·on·ry /ˈwepənri/ *n* [U] weapons of a particular type or belonging to a particular country or group: *nuclear weaponry*

wear¹ S1 W1 /weə $ wer/ *v past tense* **wore** /wɔː $ wɔːr/, *past participle* **worn** /wɔːn $ wɔːrn/
1 ON YOUR BODY [T] to have something such as clothes, shoes, or jewellery on your body: *Susanna was wearing a black silk dress.* | *He wore glasses for reading.* | **wear a seat belt** (=have it around yourself) | **wear black/white/red etc** *Usually I wear black, grey, or brown.* | **wear sth to a party/a dance/an interview etc** *I'm wearing a scarlet dress to the party.*
2 HAIR [T] to have your hair or BEARD in a particular style or shape: *She wore her hair loose.*
3 DAMAGE [I,T] to become thinner or weaker after continuous use, or to make something do this: *The cushions are starting to wear a little.* | *His jeans have **worn thin** at the knees.* | *You've **worn a hole** in your sock.*
4 wear well a) to remain in good condition after a period of time: *The tyres on the car seem to be wearing well.* **b)** if someone is wearing well, they look younger than they really are: *He must have been around his mid-forties at least, but he'd worn well.*
5 EXPRESSION [T] to have a particular expression on your face: **wear a smile/frown/grin etc** *His face wore a welcoming smile.*
6 sth is wearing thin a) if something is wearing thin, you are bored with it because it is not interesting any more, or has become annoying: *The film begins well but the joke wears thin after about ten minutes.* **b)** if your patience is wearing thin, you have very little left, because of a delay or problem
7 wear the trousers *BrE*; **wear the pants** *AmE informal* to be the person in a family who makes the decisions
8 wear your heart on your sleeve *informal* to show your true feelings openly —**wearable** *adj*
wear away *phr v*
to gradually become thinner or smoother, or to make something become like this, because of rubbing or touching: *The leather is starting to wear away at the seams.* | **wear sth ⇔ away** *Most of the grass had already been worn away by the spectators.*
wear down *phr v*
1 to gradually become flatter or smoother, or to make something become like this, because of rubbing or use: *My shoes have worn down at the heel.* | **wear sth ⇔ down** *Its teeth were worn down.*
2 wear sb ⇔ down to gradually make someone physically weaker or less determined: *It was clear he was being worn down by the rumours over his future.*
wear off *phr v*
1 if pain or the effect of something wears off, it gradually stops: *The effects of the anaesthetic were starting to wear off.*
2 the novelty wears off used to say that you stop feeling interested or excited about something because it is no longer new: *It was funny for a while but the novelty soon wore off.*
wear on *phr v*
if time wears on, it passes very slowly, especially when you are waiting for something to happen: *I was feeling more tired **as the** night **wore on**.*
wear out *phr v*
1 to become damaged and useless, or to make something like this by using it a lot or for a long time: *My boots are beginning to wear out.* | **wear sth ⇔ out** *He travels so much he actually wears out suitcases.*

2 wear sb out to make someone feel extremely tired; **☐ exhaust**: *All this shopping has worn us out.* | **wear yourself out** *Illness and death came suddenly; over the years she had simply worn herself out.*
3 wear out your welcome to stay with someone longer than they want you to → **WORN OUT**

wear² *n* [U] **1** the clothes worn for a particular occasion or activity, or by a particular group of people: **evening/casual/leisure etc wear** *a new range of casual wear* | *bridal wear* | *the children's wear department* → **FOOTWEAR, MENSWEAR 2** damage caused by continuous use over a long period: *Replace your trainers when they start to show **signs of wear**.* | *Check the equipment for **wear and tear**.* **3** the amount of use an object, piece of clothing etc has had, or the use you can expect to get from it: *The dress stood up to the wear small children give their clothes.* | *You'll **get years of wear out of** that coat.* → **the worse for wear** at **WORSE¹** (7)

wear·er /ˈweərə $ ˈwerər/ *n* [C] someone who wears a particular type of clothing, jewellery etc: *Bicycle helmets offer wearers protection against head injury.* | *hearing aid wearers*

wear·ing /ˈweərɪŋ $ ˈwer-/ *adj* making you feel tired or annoyed: *Taking care of children can be very wearing.*

wear·i·some /ˈwɪərisəm $ ˈwɪr-/ *adj formal* making you feel bored, tired, or annoyed: *a wearisome task*

wear·y¹ /ˈwɪəri $ ˈwɪr-/ *adj* **1** very tired or bored, especially because you have been doing something for a long time: *She found Rachel in the kitchen, looking old and weary.* | *She sat down with a weary sigh.* | **weary of (doing) sth** *He was weary of the constant battle between them.* **2** *especially literary* very tiring: *a long and weary march* —**wearily** *adv* —**weariness** *n* [U]

weary² *v* **wearied, wearying, wearies** [I,T] *formal* to become very tired or make someone very tired: *Amanda wouldn't admit how much the children wearied her.* | **weary of (doing) sth** *As the day wore on, we wearied of the journey.* —**wearying** *adj*

wea·sel¹ /ˈwiːzəl/ *n* [C] a small thin furry animal that kills and eats rats and birds

weasel² *v* **weaselled, weaselling** *BrE*, **weaseled, weaseling** *AmE*
weasel out *phr v informal* to avoid doing something you should do by using clever or dishonest excuses: [+of] *He's now in court trying to weasel out of $25 million in debts.*

'weasel ,word *n* [C] *informal* a word used instead of another word when someone wants to be less direct, honest, or clear

weath·er¹ S1 W2 /ˈweðə $ -ər/ *n*
1 [singular, U] the temperature and other conditions such as sun, rain, and wind

what's the weather like?
good/bad weather
the weather forecast (=a description of what the weather is expected to be like in the near future)
weather map
weather conditions
weather patterns (=what the weather is usually like in a particular area)
weather permitting (=if the weather is good enough)
weather centre *BrE*/weather bureau *AmE* (=a place where information about the weather is collected and where reports are produced)
weather station (=a place or building used for studying and recording weather conditions)

What's the weather like today? | *a period of unusually hot weather* | *The weather turned bitterly cold.* | *The weather forecast said it would be fine all day.* | *The weather map shows a ridge of high pressure coming in from the Atlantic.* | *The climbers reached the top, in spite of bad weather conditions.* | *changes in weather patterns caused by global warming* | *I'm playing golf this afternoon – weather permitting.* → see picture at **CHART¹**

2 the weather *informal* a description on radio or television, in newspapers etc of what the weather will be like in the near future; ▣ **the weather forecast**: *I always watch the weather after the news.*

3 in all weathers in all types of weather, even when it is very hot or cold: *There are homeless people sleeping on the streets in all weathers.*

4 under the weather *informal* slightly ill: *You look a bit under the weather.*

5 keep a weather eye on sth to watch a situation carefully so that you notice anything unusual or unpleasant: *Keep a weather eye on your finances.* → **make heavy weather of sth** at HEAVY¹ (10)

WORD FOCUS: WEATHER

good weather: **sunny**/**fine** used to describe weather or a day when there is a lot of sunshine | **nice**/**lovely**/**glorious** very sunny and good | **bright** if the weather is bright, the sun shines strongly | **there isn't a cloud in the sky** the sky is completely clear | **dry** if the weather is dry, it does not rain | **fair** sunny and not windy or rainy – used especially in weather forecasts

rain: **wet**/**rainy**/**damp** used to describe weather or a day when there is a lot of rain | **unsettled** if the weather is unsettled, it keeps changing and it often rains | **drizzle** light rain which consists of very small drops of water | **shower** a short period of rain | **downpour** a short period when it suddenly rains very heavily
it's pouring down *BrE*/**it's pouring rain** *AmE* it is raining very hard | **it's drizzling** it is raining a little, with very small drops of rain

snow: **snowy** used to describe weather or a day when there is a lot of snow | **sleet** a mixture of snow and rain | **slush** a mixture of partly melted snow and ice | **hail**/**hailstones** frozen drops of rain, that fall as drops of ice | **blizzard** a storm with a lot of snow and strong wind | **frost** white powder that covers the ground when it is cold

wind: **windy** used to describe a day or weather when there is a lot of wind | **blustery** very windy
breeze a gentle pleasant wind | **hurricane** (in the Atlantic Ocean)/**typhoon** (in the Pacific Ocean) a violent storm with extremely strong winds

cloudy: **cloudy** used to describe a day or weather when there are a lot of clouds in the sky | **grey**/**dull** cloudy and not bright | **overcast** if the sky is overcast, it is very cloudy and dark, and it is likely to rain | **hazy** not clear, especially because there is a slight mist caused by heat or smoke → FOG, MIST

hot: **boiling**/**scorching**/**sizzling**/**blazing**/**burning**/**baking**/**broiling (hot)** extremely hot | **sweltering** very hot and humid | **warm** a little hot, in a way that is pleasant | **balmy** pleasantly warm, with a gentle wind blowing | **heatwave** a period of unusually hot weather

cold: **freezing (cold)** extremely cold | **arctic** extremely cold, usually with a lot of ice and snow | **wintry** cold and snowy or rainy, like the weather in winter | **crisp** if the air is crisp, it feels cold but pleasantly fresh and clear | **chilly** a little too cold, in a way that makes you feel uncomfortable | **cool** a little cold, in a way that is pleasant | **cold snap**/**cold spell** a period of unusually cold weather

---

weather² *v* **1** [T] to come through a very difficult situation safely: *The company* **weathered the storm** *of objections to the scheme.* | *Northern Ireland weathered the recession better than any other region in the UK.* **2** [I,T] if rock, wood, or someone's face is weathered by the wind, sun, rain etc, or if it weathers, it changes colour or shape over a period of time: *The brick has weathered to a lovely pinky-brown.* | *Her face was weathered by the sun.*

ˈweather-ˌbeaten *adj* weather-beaten buildings, skin, clothing etc look old and damaged because they have been out in bad weather: *his weather-beaten face*

weath·er·board /ˈweðəbɔːd $ -ərbɔːrd/ *n* **1** [U] *BrE* boards covering the outer walls of a house; ▣ **clapboard** *AmE* **2** [C] a board fixed across the bottom of a door, to prevent water from getting inside

weath·er·cock /ˈweðəkɒk $ -ərkɑːk/ *n* [C] a WEATHER VANE in the shape of a male chicken

ˈweather ˌgirl *n* [C] a woman on television or radio who tells you what the weather will be like

weath·er·man /ˈweðəmæn $ -ər-/ *n plural* **weathermen** /-men/ [C] a man on television or radio who tells you what the weather will be like

weath·er·proof /ˈweðəpruːf $ -ər-/ *adj* weatherproof clothing or material can keep out wind and rain —**weatherproof** *v* [T]

ˈweather vane *n* [C] a metal object fixed to the top of a building that blows around to show the direction the wind is coming from

weave¹ /wiːv/ *v* past tense **wove** /wəʊv $ woʊv/, past participle **woven** /ˈwəʊvən $ ˈwoʊ-/
1 CLOTH ETC [I,T] to make cloth, a carpet, a basket etc by crossing threads or thin pieces under and over each other by hand or on a LOOM: *hand-woven scarves* | *Only a few of the women still weave.* | *traditional basket weaving* → see picture at HANDICRAFT
2 STORY [T] to put many different ideas, subjects, stories etc together and connect them smoothly: *She weaves a complicated plot of romance and intrigue.* | **weave sth together** *the complex patterns which evolve when individuals' lives are woven together*
3 **weave your magic**/**weave a spell** to attract or interest someone very much
4 MOVE *past tense and past participle* **weaved** [I always + adv/prep] to move somewhere by turning and changing direction a lot: *cyclists* **weaving in and out of** *the traffic* | **weave your way through/to etc sth** *Lori spotted them as they weaved their way through the tables.*

weave² *n* [C] the way in which a material is woven, and the pattern formed by this: *a fine weave*

weav·er /ˈwiːvə $ -ər/ *n* [C] someone whose job is to weave cloth

web /web/ *n* **1** [singular] **the Web** the system on the Internet that allows you to find and use information that is held on computers all over the world; ▣ **the World Wide Web**: **on the web** *a guide to the best education-related sites on the Web* **2** [C] a net of thin threads made by a SPIDER to catch insects: *He watched a spider* **spinning** *its web.* → COBWEB **3** [C usually singular] a closely related set of things that can be very complicated: **a web of intrigue/deceit/deception/lies** etc | *a tangled web* of *relationships* **4** [C] a piece of skin that connects the toes of ducks and some other birds, and helps them to swim well

webbed /webd/ *adj* webbed feet or toes have skin between the toes

web·bing /ˈwebɪŋ/ *n* [U] strong woven material in narrow bands, used for supporting seats, holding things etc

ˈweb ˌbrowser *n* [C] a computer program that finds information on the Internet and shows it on your computer screen

web·cam /ˈwebkæm/ *n* [C] a video camera that broadcasts what it is filming on a website

web·cast¹ /ˈwebkɑːst $ -kæst/ *n* [C] an event such as a musical performance which you can listen to or watch on the Internet

webcast² *v* past tense and past participle **webcast** [I,T] to broadcast an event on the Internet, at the time the event happens: *Various local news sites plan to webcast each of the mayoral debates.*

web·cast·ing /ˈwebˌkɑːstɪŋ $ -ˌkæs-/ *n* [U] the use of the Internet to send information, especially news or entertainment, to many people at the same time

ˈweb deˌsigner *n* [C] someone who designs websites, especially websites for businesses or organizations

ˌweb-ˈfooted *adj* having toes that are joined by pieces of skin

web·head /ˈwebhed/ *n* [C] *informal* someone who uses the Internet a lot, especially in a skilful way

---

W

web·li·og·ra·phy /ˌweblɪˈɒɡrəfi $ -ˈɑːɡ-/ n [C] a list of the websites you used to get information when writing something

web·log, **web log** /ˈweblɒɡ $ -lɔːɡ, -lɑːɡ / n [C] a website that is owned by a particular person or group of people rather than by an organization or company, and that has information about one or more subjects; → **blog**

web·mas·ter /ˈwebˌmɑːstə $ -ˌmæstər/ n [C] someone who is in charge of a website

web·page, **web page** /ˈwebpeɪdʒ/ n [C] all the information that you can see in one part of a website

web ring, **web·ring** /ˈwebrɪŋ/ n [C] a group of similar websites which are connected to each other by LINKS, so that it is easy for people to find a lot of information on a particular subject on the Internet: *a classical music web ring*

web·site /ˈwebsaɪt/ n [C] a place on the Internet where you can find information about something, especially a particular organization: *For more information, visit our website.* | **on a website** *Responses will be posted* (=put) *on the Website.*

web traffic n [U] the number of people who visit a particular website

wed /wed/ v *past tense and past participle* **wedded** *or* **wed** [I,T not in progressive] to marry – used especially in literature or newspapers

we'd /wid; *strong* wiːd/ **1** the short form of 'we had': *We'd already eaten.* **2** the short form of 'we would': *We'd rather stay.*

Wed. also **Weds** *BrE* a written abbreviation of *Wednesday*

wed·ded /ˈwedⁱd/ *adj* [only before noun] **1** *formal* married: *a newly-wedded couple* | *my lawfully wedded wife* **2 wedded bliss** the happiness that comes when you are married – used humorously **3 be wedded to sth** to believe strongly in a particular idea or way of doing things: *On the whole the working class is still wedded to the Labour Party.*

wed·ding S2 W3 /ˈwedɪŋ/ n [C]
1 a marriage ceremony, especially one with a religious service: *Do come to our wedding.* | **wedding party/reception/breakfast etc** (=a special meal or party that is held after a wedding) | *a **wedding present** | cutting the **wedding cake** | We celebrate our tenth **wedding anniversary*** (=the date on which we were married in a previous year) *next week.* | *a **wedding dress*** (=the dress worn by a woman who is getting married)
2 (hear the sound of) wedding bells *spoken* used to say that you think it is likely that two people will get married

wedding chapel n [C] a building used in the US for wedding ceremonies

wedding dress also **wedding gown** n [C] a long dress, especially a white dress, worn at a traditional wedding

wedding ring also **wedding band** n [C] a ring that you wear to show that you are married

wedding vows n [plural] the promises you make during your wedding ceremony

wedge¹ /wedʒ/ n [C] **1** a piece of wood, metal etc that has one thick edge and one pointed edge and is used especially for keeping a door open or for splitting wood **2** a piece of food shaped like a wedge: *Garnish with lemon wedges.* | [+of] *a wedge of cheese* **3 drive a wedge between sb** to make the relationship between two people or groups worse: *Their divorce has driven a wedge between the two families.* → **the thin end of the wedge** at THIN¹ (11)

wedge² v [T always + adv/prep] **1** to force something firmly into a narrow space: *The phone was wedged under his chin.* | *Victoria wedged herself into the passenger seat.* **2 wedge sth open/shut** to put something under a door, window etc to make it stay open or shut

wedge heels also **wedg·es** /ˈwedʒ⅓z/ n [plural] shoes worn by women, with high heels that are a solid block from the front of the shoe to the back — **wedge-heel** *adj* [only before noun]

wed·lock /ˈwedlɒk $ -lɑːk/ n [U] *old use* **1 born out of wedlock** if a child is born out of wedlock, its parents are not married when it is born **2** the state of being married

Wednes·day /ˈwenzdi, -deɪ/ *written abbreviation* **Wed.** *or* **Wed** n [C,U] the day between Tuesday and Thursday: **on Wednesday** *The sale starts on Wednesday.* | *We can go Wednesday. AmE* | **Wednesday morning/afternoon etc** *I saw Vicky on Wednesday evening.* | **last Wednesday** *They left last Wednesday.* | **this Wednesday** *Come down this Wednesday.* | **next Wednesday** (=Wednesday of next week) *I can let you know next Wednesday.* | **a Wednesday** (=one of the Wednesdays in the year) *'Are you free on the 19th?' 'Is that a Wednesday?'*

wee¹ /wiː/ *adj* [usually before noun] **1** *informal* very small – used especially in Scottish English: *My wee boy is three.* **2 a wee bit** *informal* to a small degree: *She looked a wee bit confused.* **3 the wee (small) hours** *AmE* the early hours of the morning, just after 12 o'clock at night; ⊟ **the small hours** *BrE*: *The party continued into the wee small hours.*

wee² v [I] *BrE spoken* to pass water from your body – used by or to children; ⊟ **urinate** — **wee** n [singular]: *Do you want a wee?*

weed¹ /wiːd/ n **1** [C] a wild plant growing where it is not wanted that prevents crops or garden flowers from growing properly: *the constant battle against weeds* **2** [U] a plant without flowers that grows on water in a large green floating mass; → **seaweed** **3** [C] *BrE informal* someone who is weak: *Nigel's such a weed, isn't he?* **4 like weeds** in large numbers: *Cars clogged the roads like weeds.* **5 the weed** *informal* cigarettes or tobacco **6** [U] *old-fashioned* CANNABIS **7 (widow's) weeds** *old use* black clothes worn by a woman whose husband has died

weed² v [I,T] to remove unwanted plants from a garden or other place — **weeding** n [U]
   weed sb/sth ⇔ **out** *phr v* to get rid of people or things that are not very good: *The research will help governments to weed out ineffective aid schemes.*

weed·kil·ler /ˈwiːdˌkɪlə $ -ər/ n [C,U] poison used to kill unwanted plants

weed·y /ˈwiːdi/ *adj informal* **1** full of unwanted wild plants **2** *BrE* physically weak or having a weak character

week S1 W1 /wiːk/ n [C]
1 a period of seven days and nights, usually measured in Britain from Monday to Sunday and in the US from Sunday to Saturday: **once/twice/three times etc a week** *Letters were delivered twice a week only.* | *I can't see you **this week.*** | **last/next week** (=the week before or after this one) *See you next week.*
2 any period of seven days and nights: **for a week/two weeks etc** *I've been living here for six weeks.* | **in a week/two weeks etc** (=one, two etc weeks from now) *If he hasn't phoned in a week, I'll phone him.* | *It will cost you an estimated £10 **per week** to feed one dog.* | *The training program lasts three weeks.*
3 the part of the week when you go to work, usually from Monday to Friday; ⊟ **working week**: *a 35-hour week* | **during the week** *I don't see her during the week.*
4 Monday week/Tuesday week etc *BrE* a week after the day that is mentioned: *We're off to Spain Sunday week.*
5 a week on Monday etc *BrE*; **a week from Monday etc** *AmE* a week after the day that is mentioned: *The Reids are coming for dinner a week from Sunday.* | *Keith's coming home two weeks on Saturday* (=two weeks after next Saturday).
6 week after week also **week in week out** continuously for many weeks: *I just seem to do the same things week in week out.*

week·day /'wiːkdeɪ/ n [C] any day of the week except Saturday and Sunday

week·end¹ |S1| |W2| /ˌwiːkˈend◂ 'wiːkend $ 'wiːkend/ n [C] Saturday and Sunday, especially considered as time when you do not work: *Are you doing anything nice **this weekend**?* | **last/next weekend** (=the weekend before or after this one) | **at the weekend** *BrE* **on the weekend** *AmE*: *I never work at the weekend.* | *What are you doing on the weekend?* | **at weekends** *BrE* **on weekends** *AmE*: *I only see him at weekends.* | *Tony has been unwell* **over the weekend** (=during the weekend). | *We're going to Paris for a* **long weekend** (=Saturday and Sunday, and also Friday or Monday, or both). | **weekend cottage/cabin etc** (=a place in the country where you spend your weekends) → **dirty weekend** at DIRTY¹ (2)

weekend² v [I always + adv/prep] to spend the weekend somewhere: *We're weekending on the coast.*

week·end·er /ˌwiːkˈendə $ 'wiːkendər/ n [C] someone who spends time in a place only at weekends

week·long /'wiːklɒŋ $ -lɔːŋ/ adj [only before noun] continuing for a week: *a weeklong training course*

week·ly¹ |S3| /'wiːkli/ adj [only before noun] happening or done every week: *a weekly current affairs programme* | *twice-weekly flights* —**weekly** adv: *The magazine is published weekly.*

weekly² n plural **weeklies** [C] a magazine that appears once a week: *a popular news weekly*

week·night /'wiːknaɪt/ n [C] any night except Saturday and Sunday

wee·nie /'wiːni/ n [C] *AmE informal* **1** a type of SAUSAGE; ◻ **wiener, hot dog**: *a weenie roast* **2** someone who is weak, afraid, or stupid – used especially by children; ◻ **wimp**

wee·ny /'wiːni/ *BrE*; **ween·sie** /'wiːnzi/ *AmE adj spoken* extremely small → **TEENY WEENY**

weep /wiːp/ v past tense and past participle **wept** /wept/ **1** [I,T] *formal or literary* to cry, especially because you feel very sad: *James broke down and wept.* | [+for] *She wept for the loss of her mother.* | *He* **wept bitterly** (=cried a lot) *when it was time for us to leave.* **2 I could have wept** *spoken* used to say that you felt very disappointed about something: *I could have wept thinking what I'd missed.* **3** [I] if a wound weeps, liquid comes out of it — **weep** n [singular]

weep·ie /'wiːpi/ n [C] another spelling of WEEPY²

weep·ing /'wiːpɪŋ/ adj **weeping willow/birch etc** a tree with branches that hang down towards the ground

weep·y¹ /'wiːpi/ adj *informal* tending to cry a lot

weepy², weepie n plural **weepies** [C] *informal* a film or story that is intended to make people cry

wee·vil /'wiːvəl/ n [C] a small insect that feeds on grain, flour etc and spoils it

'wee-wee v [I] *spoken* to pass water from your body – used by or to children; ◻ **urinate** —**wee-wee** n [singular]

weft /weft/ n **the weft** *technical◂* the threads in a piece of cloth that are woven across the threads that go from top to bottom; ◻ **woof**; → **warp**

weigh |S3| /weɪ/ v

1 BE A PARTICULAR WEIGHT [linking verb] to have a particular weight: *The young birds weigh only a few grams.* | *Do you know* **how much** *it weighs?* | *What* (=how much) *do you weigh?* | *The box was full of books and weighed a ton* (=was very heavy).

2 MEASURE WEIGHT [T] to use a machine to discover how much something or someone weighs: *He weighed some potatoes on the scales.* | **weigh yourself** *Have you weighed yourself lately?*

3 CONSIDER/COMPARE also **weigh up** [T] to consider something carefully so that you can make a decision about it: *It is my job to weigh the evidence.* | **weigh sth against sth** *We have to weigh the benefits of the scheme against the costs.*

4 INFLUENCE [I always + adv/prep] *formal* to influence someone's opinion and the decision that they make: [+against] *This unfortunate experience will* **weigh**

heavily *against further investment in the area.* | **weigh in sb/sth's favour** *These facts will weigh in your favour.* | [+with] *Her evidence* **weighed strongly** *with the judge.*

5 weigh your words to think very carefully about what you say because you do not want to say the wrong thing: *He was weighing his words carefully.*

6 weigh anchor to raise an ANCHOR and sail away

weigh sb ⇔ down *phr v*
1 if something weighs you down, it is heavy and difficult to carry: **be weighed down with sth** *Sally was weighed down with shopping bags.*
2 if a problem weighs you down, it makes you feel worried and upset: **be weighed down by/with sth** *He felt weighed down by his responsibilities.* | *a family weighed down with grief*

weigh in *phr v*
1 to have your weight measured before taking part in a competition: [+at] *Higgins weighed in at just over 100 kilos.* → **WEIGH-IN**
2 *informal* to join in an argument or fight: [+with] *The chairman then weighed in with his views.*

weigh on sb/sth *phr v*
to make someone feel worried and upset: *The desire for peace will* **weigh heavily on** *the negotiators.* | *I'm sure there's something* **weighing on** *his* **mind**. | *The burden of responsibility* **weighed** *heavily* **on** *his* **shoulders**.

weigh sth ⇔ out *phr v*
to measure an amount of something by weighing it: *She weighed out half a kilo of rice.*

weigh sb/sth ⇔ up *phr v*
1 to consider something carefully so that you can make a decision about it: *We're still* **weighing up the pros and cons** (=the advantages and disadvantages) *of the two options.*
2 to watch someone and listen to them carefully so that you can form an opinion about what they are like: *I could see that he was weighing me up.*

weigh·bridge /'weɪˌbrɪdʒ/ n [C] a machine that vehicles drive onto so that they can be weighed

'weigh-in n [C usually singular] a check on the weight of a BOXER or JOCKEY before a competition → **WEIGH IN** (1)

weight¹ |S1| |W2| /weɪt/ n
1 AMOUNT SB/STH WEIGHS [C,U] how heavy something is when you measure it: *The average weight of a baby at birth is just over seven pounds.* | **in weight** *fish that are over two kilos in weight* | **by weight** *Fruit and vegetables are sold by weight.*
2 HOW FAT [U] how heavy and fat someone is

put on/gain weight (=get fatter)
lose weight (=get thinner)
watch your weight (=try not to get fatter, by eating the correct foods)
get/keep your weight down also **get/keep the weight off** (=become thinner or stay thin)
weight problem (=a tendency to be too fat)
weight gain/loss
weight control (=ways of not getting too fat)
sb's ideal weight

You shouldn't worry about your weight. | *He* **put on weight** *when he was at university.* | *She's* **lost** *a lot of* **weight** *recently.* | *He was having to* **watch** *his* **weight** *for the first time in his life.* | *How have you* **kept** *your* **weight down**? | *Sara's convinced she has a* **weight problem**. | *a sudden large* **weight gain** → OVERWEIGHT, UNDERWEIGHT

3 HEAVINESS [U] the fact that something is heavy: *The weight of her boots made it hard for Sue to run.* | *I didn't know if the bridge would* **support** *our* **weight**. | **under the weight of sth** *Karen staggered along under the weight of her backpack.*
4 HEAVY THING [C] something that is heavy: *I can't lift heavy weights because of my bad back.*
5 WORRY [C] something that causes you a lot of worry because you have to deal with it: [+of] *She felt a great weight of responsibility.* | *families who are crumbling*

W

under the weight of increasing debt | *Selling the house is* **a weight off my mind** (=something that no longer causes a lot of worry).

6 [IMPORTANCE] [U] if something has weight, it is important and influences people: *She knew that her opinion carried very little weight.* | **give/add weight to sth** *This scandal adds more weight to their arguments.*

7 [AMOUNT] weight of sth a large amount of something: *The weight of evidence is that unemployment leads to all sorts of health problems.* | *The weight of public opinion is behind the teachers.* | *They won the battle by sheer weight of numbers* (=very large numbers of people).

8 [FOR MEASURING QUANTITIES] [C] a piece of metal that weighs an exact amount and is balanced against something else to measure how much the other thing weighs

9 [FOR SPORT] [C] a piece of metal that weighs an exact amount and is lifted by people as a sport: *I've been lifting weights since I was 18.* → WEIGHTLIFTING

10 throw your weight about/around *informal* to use your position of authority to tell people what to do in an unpleasant and unreasonable way

11 throw your weight behind sb/sth to use all your power and influence to support someone or something: *The US has thrown its weight behind the new leader.*

12 pull your weight to do your full share of work: *He accused me of not pulling my weight.*

13 take the weight off your feet *informal* used to tell someone to sit down: *Come in, take the weight off your feet.* → DEADWEIGHT

weight² *v* [T] **1** also **weight down** to fix a heavy object to something in order to keep it in place: **weight sth (down) with sth** *The fishing nets are weighted down with lead.* **2** to change something slightly so that you give more importance to particular ideas or people: **weight sth in favour of sb/sth** *There is always a temptation to weight the report in favour of the option you want.*

weight·ed /ˈweɪtɪd/ *adj* giving an advantage or disadvantage to one particular group or activity; → **biased:** [+against] *The voting system is weighted against the smaller parties.* | **weighted in favour of sb/sth** *This year's pay increase is heavily weighted in favour of the lower paid staff.* | [+towards] *The course is weighted towards language skills.*

weight·ing /ˈweɪtɪŋ/ *n* [singular, U] *BrE* additional money that you get paid because of the high cost of living in a particular area: *salary £24,000 plus £2,400 London weighting*

weight·less /ˈweɪtləs/ *adj* something that is weightless seems to have no weight, especially when it is floating in space or water —**weightlessness** *n* [U]

weight·lift·ing /ˈweɪtˌlɪftɪŋ/ *n* [U] the sport of lifting specially shaped pieces of metal that weigh an exact amount —**weightlifter** *n* [C]

weight training *n* [U] the activity of lifting specially shaped pieces of metal that weigh an exact amount, as a form of exercise: *He does weight training at the gym twice a week.*

weight·y /ˈweɪti/ *adj* **1** important and serious: *She didn't feel like discussing weighty matters over dinner.* **2** *literary* heavy: *a weighty tome* (=a big and heavy book)

weir /wɪə $ wɪr/ *n* [C] a low fence or wall that is built across a river or stream to control the flow of water, or to make a pool where people can catch fish

weird [S2] /wɪəd $ wɪrd/ *adj informal* very strange and unusual, and difficult to understand or explain: *A really weird thing happened last night.* | *He's a weird bloke.* | *They sell all sorts of weird and wonderful* (=very strange) *products.* —**weirdly** *adv: a weirdly shaped rock* —**weirdness** *n* [U]

weird·o /ˈwɪədəʊ $ ˈwɪrdoʊ/ *n plural* **weirdos** [C] *informal* someone who wears strange clothes or behaves strangely: *Jenny's going out with a real weirdo.*

welch /welʃ $ welʃ, weltʃ/ *v* another spelling of WELSH²

wel·come¹ [S3] [W2] /ˈwelkəm/ *v* [T]
1 to say hello in a friendly way to someone who has just arrived; ☐ **greet:** *I must be there to welcome my guests.* | *They welcomed us warmly.* | *His family welcomed me with open arms* (=in a very friendly way).
2 to be glad to accept something: *The college welcomes applications from people of all races.* | *We would welcome any advice or suggestions with open arms.*
3 to be glad that something has happened because you think it is a good idea: *Economists have welcomed the decision to raise interest rates.*

welcome² [S2] [W3] *adj*
1 if someone is welcome in a place, other people are glad that they are there: *I had the feeling I wasn't really welcome.* | *I didn't feel welcome in the club.* | *Mary made us very welcome.* | *We try to make the new students feel welcome.*
2 if something is welcome, you enjoy it because you feel that you need it: *The weekend was a welcome break from the pressures of work.* | *Six months in Scotland would make a welcome change from London.* | *A cup of tea would be very welcome.*
3 if something is welcome, you are glad that it has happened: *The increase in interest rates is welcome news for investors.* | *This new funding will come as a welcome boost for the industry.*
4 be welcome to sth *spoken* used to say that someone can have something if they want it, because you certainly do not want it: *If you want to take the job you're welcome to it!*
5 be welcome to do sth *spoken* used to invite someone to do something if they would like to: *You're welcome to stay for lunch.*
6 you're welcome! *spoken* a polite way of replying to someone who has just thanked you for something: *'Thanks for the coffee.' 'You're welcome.'*

welcome³ *n* [singular] **1** the way in which you greet someone when they arrive at a place: **warm/friendly welcome** *His colleagues gave him a very warm welcome when he returned to work.* | *You can be sure of a friendly welcome at all our hotels.* | *The president got a tremendous welcome at the airport.* **2** the way in which people react to an idea, and show that they like it or do not like it: *Politicians have given an enthusiastic welcome to the Queen's speech.* | *The proposals have so far received a cautious welcome from government ministers.* **3 outstay/overstay your welcome** to stay at someone's house longer than they want you to

welcome⁴ *interjection* used to greet someone who has just arrived: [+to] *Welcome to London!* | **Welcome back** - *it's good to see you again.* | *Hello, welcome home.*

welcome wagon *n* [C] *AmE* an event that is organized to welcome someone who has just arrived in a new place: *The company is bringing out the welcome wagon for the new sales recruits.*

wel·com·ing /ˈwelkəmɪŋ/ *adj* **1** someone who is welcoming is friendly when you arrive in a place: *Everyone was very welcoming.* | *Stephanie was standing at the door with a welcoming smile.* **2** a welcoming place is pleasant and makes you feel relaxed: *a restaurant with a welcoming atmosphere* **3** [only before noun] done or organized in order to welcome someone to a place: **welcoming committee/party** *I was met by a welcoming committee.* | *a welcoming speech*

weld¹ /weld/ *v* **1** [T] to join metals by melting their edges and pressing them together when they are hot: *The new handle will have to be welded on.* **2** [T always + adv/prep] to join or unite people into a single strong group: *His job is now to weld the players into a single team.* → ARC WELDING

weld² *n* [C] a joint that is made by welding two pieces of metal together

weld·er /ˈweldə $ -ər/ *n* [C] someone whose job is to weld metal in a factory → see picture at OCCUPATION

wel·fare [S3] [W2] /ˈwelfeə $ -fer/ *n* [U]
1 someone's welfare is their health and happiness: *Our only concern is the children's welfare.*

W

2 help that is provided for people who have personal or social problems: **welfare benefits/services/programmes** etc *the provision of education and welfare services* | *The company's welfare officer deals with employees' personal problems.*
3 *AmE* money that is paid by the government in the US to people who are very poor or unemployed; ⊟ **benefit** *BrE*: **on welfare** *Most of the people in this neighborhood are on welfare.*

,welfare 'state / $ '.. ./ *n* **1** the welfare state a system in which the government provides money, free medical care etc for people who are unemployed, ill, or too old to work; → **social security** **2** [C] a country with such a system

we'll /wil; *strong* wiːl/ the short form of 'we will' or 'we shall'

well¹ S1 W1 /wel/ *adv comparative* better /'betə $ -ər/ *superlative* best /best/
1 SATISFACTORILY in a successful or satisfactory way: *Did you sleep well?* | *James reads quite well for his age.* | *All the team played very well today.* | *Simon doesn't work well under pressure.* | *The festival was very well organized.* | *The concert went very well.*
2 THOROUGHLY in a thorough way: *Mix the flour and butter well.* | *I know Birmingham quite well.*
3 A LOT a) a lot, or to a great degree: [+before/after/above/below etc] *Stand well back from the bonfire.* | *It was well after 12 o'clock when they arrived.* | *The village is well below sea level.* | *The amphitheatre is well worth a visit.* | *I'm well aware of the problems involved.* | *I went out and got well and truly* (=completely) *drunk.* b) [+ adj] *BrE informal* very: *That was well funny!*
4 do well a) to be successful, especially in work or business: *He's doing very well at college.* | *Elizabeth's done well for herself since she moved to London.* b) if someone who has been ill is doing well, they are becoming healthy again: *He had the operation yesterday, and he's doing very well.*
5 as well in addition to something or someone else: *Why don't you come along as well?* → see box at ALSO
6 as well as sth/sb in addition to something or someone else: *They own a house in France as well as a villa in Spain.* | **as well as doing sth** *The organization gives help and support to people in need, as well as raising money for local charities.*
7 may/might/could well used to say that something is likely to happen or is likely to be true: *What you say may well be true.* | *You could try the drugstore, but it might well be closed by now.*
8 may/might/could (just) as well a) *informal* used when you do not particularly want to do something but you decide you should do it: *I suppose we may as well get started.* b) used to mean that another course of action would have an equally good result: *The taxi was so slow we might just as well have gone on the bus.*
9 can't very well (do sth) used to say that you cannot do something because it would be unacceptable: *I can't very well tell him we don't want him at the party!*
10 know full/perfectly well used to say that someone does know something even though they are behaving as if they do not: *You know full well what I mean.*
11 speak/think well of sb to talk about someone in an approving way or to have a favourable opinion of them: *Sue has always spoken well of you.*
12 well done!/well played! *spoken* used to praise someone when you think they have done something very well
13 well said! *spoken* used to say that you agree with what someone has just said, or that you admire them for saying it
14 be well away *BrE informal* a) to be making good progress: *If we can get that grant from the local authority, we'll be well away.* b) to be very drunk
15 be well in with sb *informal* to have a friendly relationship with someone, especially someone important: *She's very well in with members of the management committee.*
16 be well out of sth *BrE spoken* to be lucky to no longer be involved in a particular situation
17 be well up in/on sth *informal especially BrE* to know a lot about a particular subject: *Geoff's always been well up on the Internet.*
18 as well sb might/may *formal* used to say that there is a good reason for someone's feelings or reactions: *Marilyn looked guilty, as well she might.*
19 do well by sb *informal* to treat someone generously

GRAMMAR: well, good
Good is an adjective: *a good attempt* | *Her English is very good.*
⚠ **Good** is not used as an adverb in standard English. Use **well**: *He speaks English extremely well.*
The comparative form of both **good** and **well** is **better**: *His first book was better.* (adj): *We'll play better next time.* (adv)
The superlative form of both **good** and **well** is **best**: *Who is the best singer?* (adj): *You can use brown or white sugar, but brown works best.* (adv)

well² S1 W1 *interjection*
1 EMPHASIZING STH used to emphasize something you are saying: *Well, I think it's a good idea anyway.* | *Well, I've had enough and I'm going home!* | *'James doesn't want to come to the cinema with us.' ' Well then, let's go on our own.'*
2 PAUSING used to pause or give yourself time to think before saying something: *Well, let's see now, I could meet you on Thursday.*
3 ACCEPTING A SITUATION also oh well used to show that you accept a situation even though you feel disappointed or annoyed about it: *Well, I did my best – I can't do any more than that.* | *Oh well, we'll just have to cancel the holiday, I suppose.*
4 SHOWING SURPRISE also well, well, (well) used to express surprise or amusement: *Well, so Steve got the job?* | *Well, well, well, I didn't think I'd see you here.*
5 SHOWING ANGER used to express anger or disapproval: *Well, she could at least have phoned to say she wasn't coming!*
6 FINAL REMARK used to show that you are about to finish speaking or doing something: *Well, that's all for today.* | *Well, that's the last one done.*
7 EXPRESSING DOUBT used to show that you are not sure about something: *'Will you be in on Friday evening?' 'Well, it depends.'*
8 CHANGING SOMETHING used to slightly change something that you have said: *He's rolling in money! Well, he's got a lot more than me, anyway.*
9 AGREEING very well *formal* used to show that you agree with an idea or accept a suggestion: *'Very well,' he said. 'I accept.'*
10 CONTINUING A STORY used to continue a story you are telling people, especially in order to make it seem more interesting: *You know that couple I was telling you about the other day? Well, last night I saw a police car in front of their house!*
11 ASKING A QUESTION Well? used to ask someone to answer a question you have asked them, when you are angry with them: *Well? What have you got to say for yourself?*

well³ S1 *adj comparative* better, *superlative* best
1 healthy: *'How are you?' 'Very well, thanks.'* | *I don't feel very well.* | *You're looking very well.* | *I hope you get well again soon.*
2 it is just as well (that) *spoken* used to say that things have happened in a good or fortunate way: *It's just as well I kept some money aside for emergencies.*
3 it's/that's all very well, but ... *spoken* used to say that something seems to be a good idea, but is not really possible or helpful: *It's all very well the doctors telling me I've got to rest, but who's going to look after my children?*

W

1 000, 2 000, 3 000, most frequent words in S poken and W ritten English

4 that's/it's all well and good *spoken especially BrE* used to say that something is good or enjoyable, but it also has some disadvantages: *Going off on foreign holidays is all well and good, but you've got to get back to reality sometime.*
5 it might/would be as well *spoken* used to give someone advice or make a helpful suggestion: *It might be as well to make him rest for a few days.*
6 all is well/all is not well *formal* used to say that a situation is satisfactory or not satisfactory: *All is not well with their marriage.*
7 all's well that ends well used after a situation has ended in a satisfactory way

well⁴ *n* [C] **1** a deep hole in the ground from which people take water: *She lowered her bucket into the well.* **2** an OIL WELL **3** the space in a tall building where the stairs are

well⁵ also **well up** *v* [I] *literary* **1** if a liquid wells or wells up, it comes to the surface of something and starts to flow out: *I felt tears well up in my eyes.* **2** if a feeling wells or wells up in you, you start to feel it strongly: *Anger welled up within him.*

well-ad'justed *adj* emotionally healthy and able to deal well with the problems of life: *a happy, well-adjusted child*

well-ad'vised *adj* **you would be well-advised to do sth** used when you are strongly advising someone to do something that will help them avoid trouble: *You would be well-advised to accept his offer.*

well-ap'pointed *adj formal* a well-appointed room, house, or hotel has attractive furniture and all the equipment that you need: *He showed me to a large, well-appointed room.*

well-'balanced *adj* **1** a well-balanced meal or DIET contains all the different things you need to keep you healthy **2** a well-balanced person is sensible and does not allow strong emotions to control their behaviour

well-be'haved *adj* behaving in a calm polite way, and not being rude or violent: *a well-behaved child | a very well-behaved dog | The crowd was noisy but well-behaved.*

well-'being *n* [U] **1** a feeling of being comfortable, healthy, and happy: [+of] *We are responsible for the care and well-being of all our patients.* | **a sense/feeling of well-being** *A good meal promotes a feeling of well-being.* | **physical/psychological/material etc well-being** *the physical and emotional well-being of the children* **2** the well-being of a country is the state in which it is strong and doing well: *We are now concerned for the economic well-being of the country.*

well-'born *adj formal* born into a very rich or important family

well-'bred *adj old-fashioned* someone who is well-bred is polite, and behaves as if they come from a family of high social class: *a well-bred, courteous young man*

well-brought-'up *adj* a child who is well-brought-up has been taught to be polite and to behave well

well-'built *adj* someone who is well-built has a big strong body; → see box at FAT¹

well-'chosen *adj* chosen carefully and so very suitable: *good food and well-chosen wines | He encouraged us with a few well-chosen words.*

well-con'nected *adj* someone who is well-connected knows a lot of powerful important people

well-de'fined *adj* clear and easy to see or understand: *well-defined limits on spending*

well-de'veloped *adj* fully developed or formed and able to function very well: *well-developed back muscles | well-developed reading skills*

well-dis'posed *adj* feeling friendly towards a person or positive about an idea or plan: [+to/towards] *I did not feel particularly well-disposed towards him.*

well-'documented *adj* if something is well-documented, people have written a lot about it and so the facts about it are clear: *His life is remarkably well-documented. | These are all well-documented facts.*

well-'done *adj* meat that is well-done has been cooked thoroughly → **well done!** at WELL¹ (12)

well-'dressed *adj* wearing attractive fashionable clothes: *an attractive, well-dressed young woman*

well-'earned *adj* something that is well-earned is something you deserve because you have worked hard: *a well-earned rest | a well-earned drink*

well-'educated *adj* someone who is well-educated has had a lot of education and has a lot of knowledge about many different things

well-en'dowed *adj informal* **1** a woman who is well-endowed has large breasts – often used humorously **2** a man who is well-endowed has a large PENIS – often used humorously

well-es'tablished *adj* something that is well-established has existed for a long time and is respected or trusted by people: *a well-established law firm | a well-established scientific theory*

well-'fed *adj* having plenty of good food to eat: *The animals all look happy and well-fed.*

well-'founded *adj* a belief or feeling etc that is well-founded is based on facts or good judgment: *My suspicions proved to be well-founded.*

well-'groomed *adj* someone who is well-groomed looks very neat and clean

well-'grounded *adj* **1 well-grounded in sth** fully trained in an activity or skill: *The soldiers were well-grounded in survival skills.* **2** WELL-FOUNDED: *My fears were well-grounded.*

well-'heeled *adj informal* rich: *a well-heeled businessman*

well-'hung *adj informal* a man who is well-hung has a large PENIS - used humorously

wel·lie /'weli/ *n* [C] *BrE informal* a WELLINGTON

well-in'formed *adj* someone who is well-informed knows a lot about one particular subject or about many subjects: [+about] *Most people are not very well-informed about the disease. | We had a serious and well-informed debate.*

wel·ling·ton 'boot /'welɪŋtən/ also **,wellington 'boot** *n* [C] *BrE* a rubber boot that stops your foot getting wet

well-in'tentioned *adj* trying to be helpful to people, but actually making things worse for them: *well-intentioned grandparents who interfere between parents and children*

well-'kept *adj* **1** a well-kept building or garden is very well cared for and looks neat and clean → see picture at OVERGROWN **2** a well-kept secret is known only to a few people

well-'known *adj comparative* **better-known**, *superlative* **best-known** known by a lot of people: **it is well-known (that)** *It's a well-known fact that smoking can cause lung cancer. | This is probably their best-known song. | a well-known TV presenter | [+for] He was well-known for his extreme political views.*

well-'mannered *adj* talking and behaving in a polite way: *a well-mannered child*

well-'meaning *adj* intending to be helpful, but not succeeding: *A lot of problems can be caused by well-meaning friends. | He's very well-meaning, but he doesn't really understand what's going on.*

well-'meant *adj* something you say or do that is well-meant is intended to be helpful, but does not have the result you intended: *His comments were well-meant but a little tactless.*

well·ness /'welnɪs/ *n* [U] *AmE* the state of being healthy: *The college has established a wellness program for its students.*

well-'nigh *adv old-fashioned* almost: *It will be well-nigh impossible to raise that amount of money.*

well-'off *adj comparative* **better-off**, *superlative* **best-off** **1** having a lot of money, or enough money to have a good standard of living; ☒ **badly-off**: *children from well-off families* | *Many pensioners are less well-off* (=have less money) *than they used to be.* → see box at RICH **2 be well-off for sth** having plenty of something, or as much of it as you need: *We're well-off for public transport here.* **3 you don't know when you're well-off** BrE spoken used to tell someone that they are more fortunate than they realize

well-'oiled *adj* **a well-oiled machine** an organization or system that works very well

well-'paid *adj* providing or receiving good wages: *a well-paid job* | *well-paid executives*

well-pre'served *adj* **1** someone who is well-preserved is getting old, but does not look as old as they are **2** a well-preserved building or object is old but still in good condition: *the remarkably well-preserved ruins of the church*

well-read /ˌwel ˈredᴗ/ *adj* someone who is well-read has read many books and knows a lot about different subjects

well-'rounded *adj* **1** a well-rounded person has a range of interests and skills and a variety of experience: *well-rounded graduates* **2** well-rounded education or experience of life is complete and varied: *She has a well-rounded background in management.* **3** a woman who is well-rounded has a pleasantly curved figure; ☒ **shapely**

well-'run *adj* a well-run organization or business is managed well: *a small, well-run hotel*

well-'spoken *adj* speaking in a clear and polite way, and in a way that is considered correct

well spring /ˈwelˌsprɪŋ/ *n* [C] *literary* **1** a large amount of a personal quality: [+of] *There was a well-spring of courage within her.* **2** the situation or place where something begins: [+of] *Las Vegas became the wellspring of a new style of family values.*

well-'stocked *adj* having a large supply and variety of things, especially food or drink: *a well-stocked supermarket*

well 'thought of *adj* liked and admired by other people: *Her work is well thought of in academic circles.*

well-thought-'out *adj* carefully and thoroughly planned: *a well-thought-out design* | *All the menus are well-thought-out.*

well-'thumbed *adj* a well-thumbed book, magazine etc has been used a lot; → **dog-eared**

well-'timed *adj* said or done at the most suitable moment; ☒ **timely**: *a well-timed remark* | *My arrival wasn't very well timed.*

well-to-'do *adj* **1** rich and with a high social position: *well-to-do families* **2 the well-to-do** people who are rich

well-'tried *adj* [only before noun] a well-tried method or principle has been used many times before and has always been successful; ☒ **tried and tested**: *a well-tried formula for success*

well 'trodden *adj* **1 well-trodden path/track/route etc** BrE a path that is used a lot by people: *Follow the very well-trodden path to the summit.* **2** used to describe an idea or a course of action that has been used many times in the past: **well-trodden path/road/ground etc** *Andrew was on his well-trodden path to conquering another willing lady.*

well-'turned *adj* a well-turned phrase or sentence is carefully expressed

well-turned-'out *adj* someone who is well-turned-out wears nice, good quality clothes: *Our customers want to be served by people who are well-turned-out.*

well-'versed *adj* knowing a lot about something: [+in] *countries not so well-versed in technological advances as our own*

well-ˌwisher *n* [C] someone who shows by their behaviour that they like someone and want them to succeed, be happy etc: *The prince waved at the crowd of 600 well-wishers.*

well-'woman *adj* [only before noun] providing medical care and advice for women, to make sure that they stay healthy: *a well-woman clinic*

well-'worn *adj* **1** worn or used for a long time: *a well-worn jacket* **2** a well-worn expression, phrase etc has been repeated so often that it is no longer interesting or effective: *well-worn excuses*

wel·ly /ˈweli/ *n plural* **wellies** [C] BrE informal a WELLINGTON (=kind of boot)

welsh, welch /welʃ $ welʃ, weltʃ/ *v* [I] informal to not do something you have promised to do, such as paying someone money that you owe: *I never welch on my bets.*

Welsh¹ /welʃ/ *adj* relating to Wales, its people, or its original language

Welsh² *n* **1 the Welsh** [plural] people from Wales **2** [U] the original language used in Wales

Welsh 'dresser *n* [C] BrE a piece of wooden furniture consisting of drawers and cupboards in the lower part and shelves on top; ☒ **hutch** AmE

Welsh 'rarebit also **Welsh 'rabbit** *n* [C,U] a dish of cheese melted on bread

welt /welt/ *n* [C] a painful raised mark on someone's skin, for example where they have been hit

wel·ter /ˈweltə $ -ər/ *n* **a welter of sth** a large and confusing amount or number of something: *There is a welter of information on the subject.*

wel·ter·weight /ˈweltəweɪt $ -ər-/ *n* [C] a BOXER who weighs less than 66.68 kilograms, and who is heavier than a LIGHTWEIGHT but lighter than a MIDDLEWEIGHT

wench /wentʃ/ *n* [C] old use a girl or young woman, especially a servant

wend /wend/ *v* **wend your way** literary to move or travel slowly from one place to another: [+through/towards/home etc] *The procession wended its way through the streets.*

wen·dy house /ˈwendi ˌhaʊs/ *n* [C] BrE a toy house that children can play inside; ☒ **playhouse** AmE

went /went/ the past tense of GO

wept /wept/ the past tense and past participle of WEEP

we're /wɪə $ wɪr/ the short form of 'we are'

were /wə; strong wɜː $ wər; strong wɜːr/ the past tense of BE

were·wolf /ˈweəwʊlf, ˈwɪə- $ ˈwer-, ˈwɪr-/ *n plural* **werewolves** /-wʊlvz/ [C] a person who, in stories, changes into a WOLF every month when the moon is full

wert /wɜːt $ wɜːrt/ *v* thou wert old use you were

West /west/ *n* **1 the West** the western part of the world and the people that live there, especially Western Europe and North America: *the industrial countries of the West* **2** the western part of the US → MIDWEST, WEST COAST

west¹, West *n* [singular, U] **1** the direction towards which the sun goes down, and which is on the left if you are facing north: **from/towards the west** *A damp wind blew from the west.* | **to the west (of sth)** *a village to the west of Brussels* **2 the west** the western part of a country or area: *There's a slight chance of some sunshine in the west.* | [+of] *the west of the island*

west² S2 W2 , **West** written abbreviation *W adj* [only before noun]
1 in the west or facing the west: *the west door of the church* | *farmers in West Africa*
2 a west wind comes from the west

west³ written abbreviation *W adv* **1** towards the west: *The route then heads west over Gerrick Moor.* | [+of] *The walk starts at Alnham, six miles west of Bridge of Aln.* | *a west-facing window* **2 out west** to or in the western part of a country or area, especially the US: *The family moved out west to Kansas.* **3 go west** BrE old-fashioned **a)** to die – used humorously **b)** to be damaged or ruined – used humorously

west·bound /ˈwestbaʊnd/ *adj* travelling or leading towards the west: *Westbound traffic is moving very slowly.* | *an accident on the westbound carriageway of the motorway*

W

'West Coast n the West Coast the part of the US that is next to the Pacific Ocean

'West ,Country n the West Country the parts of England that are furthest south and west, especially Devon and Cornwall

,West 'End n the West End the western part of central London, where there are large shops, theatres, expensive hotels etc

west·er·ly¹ /'westəli $ -ərli/ adj **1** towards or in the west: We set off in a westerly direction. **2** a westerly wind comes from the west

westerly² n plural westerlies [C] a wind that comes from the west

west·ern¹ S2 W2 , **Western** /'westən $ -ərn/ written abbreviation W adj
1 in or from the west of a country or area: the western end of the bay | Western Australia
2 relating to ideas and ways of doing things that come from Europe and the Americas: Western philosophies → COUNTRY AND WESTERN

western² n [C] a film about life in the 19th century in the American West, especially the lives of COWBOYS

West·ern·er /'westənə $ -tərnər/ n [C] **1** someone from the western part of the world **2** AmE someone from the western part of the US

west·ern·ize also **-ise** BrE /'westənaɪz $ -ər-/ v [T usually passive] to bring customs, business methods etc that are typical of Europe and the US to other countries: Tunisian culture has been westernized. —**westernization** /,westənaɪ'zeɪʃən $ -tərnə-/ n [U]

west·ern·ized also **-ised** BrE /'westənaɪzd $ -ər/ adj using the customs, behaviour etc typical of the US or Europe: westernised economies

,western 'medicine n [U] the type of medical treatment that is standard in Europe and North America; → alternative medicine

west·ern·most /'westənməust $ -tərnmoust/ adj furthest west: the westernmost tip of the island

west·ward /'westwəd $ -wərd/ also **west·wards** /-wədz $ -wərdz/ adv towards the west: The ship turned westward, away from the coast. —**westward** adj: westward flights

wet¹ S2 W3 /wet/ comparative wetter, superlative wettest adj
1 WATER/LIQUID covered in or full of water or another liquid; 🔄 dry: I've washed your shirt but it's still wet. | wet grass | get (sth) wet Take an umbrella or you'll get wet. | [+with] His face was wet with sweat. | The man in the boat was wet through (=completely wet). | soaking/dripping/sopping wet (=very wet) The towel was soaking wet.
2 WEATHER rainy: There's more wet weather on the way. | It's very wet outside. | the wettest summer on record
3 PAINT/INK ETC not yet dry: The paint's still wet.
4 PERSON BrE informal someone who is wet does not have a strong character, or is not willing to do something that you think they should do – used to show disapproval: Don't be so wet! Just tell them you don't want to go.
5 BABY if a child or its NAPPY is wet, the nappy is full of URINE
6 sb is all wet AmE informal someone is completely wrong
7 be wet behind the ears informal very young and without much experience of life —**wetly** adv —**wetness** n [U]

wet² v past tense and past participle wet or wetted, present participle wetting [T] **1** to make something

wet: Wet your hair and apply the shampoo. **2** to make yourself, your clothes, or your bed wet because you pass water from your body by accident: **wet yourself** I nearly wet myself I was so scared. | Sam's wet his bed again.

wet³ n **1 the wet** the rain: **in the wet** The path is steep and dangerous in the wet. **2** [C] BrE a politician who belongs to the CONSERVATIVE party, and who supports very MODERATE ideas – used to show disapproval: Tory wets **3** [C] BrE informal someone who does not have a strong character, or is not willing to do something that you think they should do – used to show disapproval: Go on! Don't be such a wet!

wet·back /'wetbæk/ n [C] AmE taboo a very offensive word for someone from Mexico who has come to the US illegally. Do not use this word.

'wet bar n [C] AmE a small bar with equipment for making alcoholic drinks, in a house, hotel room etc

,wet 'blanket / $ '. ,.../ n [C] informal someone who seems to want to spoil other people's fun, for example by refusing to join them in something enjoyable that they are doing

,wet 'dream n [C] a sexually exciting dream that a man has, resulting in an ORGASM

,wet 'fish n [U] BrE fresh uncooked fish that is on sale in a shop

wet·land /'wetlənd/ n [C often plural, U] an area of land that is partly covered with water, or is wet most of the time

'wet-look adj [only before noun] wet-look clothes have a shiny surface so that they look as if they are wet

'wet nurse n [C] old use a woman paid to give her breast milk to another woman's baby

'wet-nurse v [T] to give someone too much care and attention, as if they were a child

'wet suit n [C] a tight piece of clothing, usually made of rubber, worn by people who are swimming, SURFING etc in the sea

'wetting ,agent n [C] a chemical substance which, when spread on a solid surface, makes it hold liquid

'wetting so,lution n [C,U] a liquid used for storing CONTACT LENSES in, or for making them more comfortable to wear

we've /wiv; strong wiːv/ the short form of 'we have'

whack¹ /wæk/ v [T] informal **1** to hit someone or something hard: **whack sb/sth with sth** He kept whacking the dog with a stick. **2** BrE spoken to put something somewhere: **whack sth in/on/under etc sth** Just whack the bacon under the grill for a couple of minutes.

whack² n [C] especially spoken **1** the act of hitting something hard, or the noise this makes: She gave the ball a whack and it flew into the air. | Singleton took a whack at (=tried to hit) Miller's head. **2** BrE an amount of something: **(the) full whack** If you're unemployed, you don't have to **pay the full whack** (=the full amount). | There's still **a fair whack** (=quite a large amount) of work to be done. | These agencies charge top whack for tickets. **3 do your whack (of sth)** BrE to do a fair or equal share of a job or activity: I've done my whack of the driving – it's your turn. **4 have a whack at sth** BrE; **take a whack at sth** AmE to try to do something: 'Are you any good at doing maths?' 'I'll have a whack at it.' **5 in one whack** AmE all on one occasion: Steve lost $500 in one whack. **6 out of whack** AmE if a system, machine etc is out of whack, the parts are not working together correctly: The printer's out of whack again.

whacked /wækt/ adj [not before noun] informal **1** also **whacked out** very tired: You look absolutely whacked. **2 whacked out** AmE behaving strangely, especially because of having too much alcohol or drugs **3** also **whack** AmE informal a whacked situation is very strange, especially in an unacceptable way: Everyone was running around naked. It was totally whacked.

whack·ing /'wækɪŋ/ *adj* **whacking great** *BrE spoken* very big; ⊟ **whopping**: *We got a whacking great gas bill this morning.*

whale¹ /weɪl/ *n* [C] **1** a very large animal that lives in the sea and looks like a fish, but is actually a MAMMAL **2 have a whale of a time** *informal* to enjoy yourself very much

whale² *v* [I] *AmE* **whale into/on sb/sth** to start hitting someone or something

whale·bone /'weɪlbəʊn $ -boʊn/ *n* [U] a hard substance taken from the upper jaw of whales, used in the past for making women's clothes stiff

whal·er /'weɪlə $ -ər/ *n* [C] **1** someone who hunts whales **2** a boat used to hunt whales

whal·ing /'weɪlɪŋ/ *n* [U] the activity of hunting WHALES

wham¹ /wæm/ *interjection* **1** used to describe the sound of something suddenly hitting something else very hard: *Wham! The car hit the wall.* **2** used to express the idea that something very unexpected suddenly happens: *Life is going along nicely and then, wham, you lose your job.* —**wham** *n* [C]

wham·my /'wæmi/ *n* [singular] *informal* **1 double/ triple whammy** two or three unpleasant things that happen at or around the same time and cause problems or difficulties for someone or for people in general: *The government's policy is higher tax and higher interest rates. It's a double whammy.* **2 put the whammy on sb** *AmE* to use magic to make someone have bad luck

wharf /wɔːf $ wɔːrf/ *n plural* **wharves** /wɔːvz $ wɔːrvz/ [C] a structure that is built out into the water so that boats can stop next to it

whas·sup, wassup /'wɒsʌp $ 'wɑː-/ *informal* used to say 'hello' to people you know very well – used especially by young people

what [S1] [W1] /wɒt $ wɑːt, wʌt/ *pron, determiner, predeterminer*

1 used to ask for information or for someone's opinion: *What are you doing?* | *What subjects did you enjoy most?* | *What colour is the new carpet?* | *What's your new boss like?* | *What do you think of my painting?* | *What do you mean, you want to spend Christmas alone?* | **what on earth/in the world/in heaven's name etc** (=used for emphasis when you are surprised, angry etc) *What on earth's going on?* ⚠ When there is a limited number of possible things or people, use **which**: *Which leg (NOT what leg) did he break?* | *It was one of his sisters. I can't remember which (NOT what).*

2 used to introduce a CLAUSE about something that is or was not known or not certain: *No one knows exactly what happened.* | *It is not clear to what extent these views were shared.* | **what to do/say/expect etc** *They're discussing what to do next.*

3 the thing which: *Show me what you bought.* | *I believe what he told me.* | *I could get you a job here if that's what you want.* | *What he did was morally wrong.* | *She gave him what money she had* (=all the money she had, although she did not have much).

4 used at the beginning of a statement to emphasize what you are going to say: *What that kid needs is some love and affection.* | *What we'll do is leave a note for Mum to tell her we won't be back till late.* | *What matters is the British people and British jobs.*

SPOKEN PHRASES
5 what? a) used to ask someone to repeat something they have just said because you did not hear it properly: *'Could you turn the music down a bit?' 'What?'* **b)** used when you have heard someone calling to you and you are asking them what they want: *'Elaine!' 'What?' 'Come on!'* **c)** used to show that you are surprised or shocked by something that someone has just said: *'I think I've lost my passport.' 'What?'*

6 used at the beginning of a sentence to emphasize that you think something or someone is very good, very bad etc: *What a lovely day!* | *What a horrible thing to do!* | *What nice people they are!*

7 used to ask someone to complete a name when they

have only given you the first part of it: *'Do you know his name?' 'It's David.' 'David what?'*

8 what about ...? a) used to make a suggestion: *What about dinner at my place next week?* | **what about doing sth** *What about going to a movie?* **b)** also **what of ...?** *formal* used to introduce a new subject into a conversation, or to mention something or someone else that also needs to be considered: *What about Patrick? What's he doing nowadays?* | *What about me? Aren't I coming too?* | *So that's the food – now what about the wine?* | *And what of her other job? How is that progressing?*

9 what (...) for? a) used to ask why someone does something: *'She's decided to work part-time.' 'What for?'* | *What did you do that for?* **b)** used to ask what purpose or use something has: *What's this gadget for?*

10 used to give yourself time to think before guessing a number or amount: *You're looking at, what, about £4000 for a decent second-hand car.*

11 what's his/her/its name also **what d'you call him/ her/it** used when talking about a person or thing whose name you cannot immediately remember: *The hospital have just got a, what d'you call it, er... a scanner.* | *Is what's his name still working there?*

12 (and) what's more used when adding information that emphasizes what you are saying: *Gas is a very efficient fuel. And what's more, it's clean.*

13 what's what the real facts about a situation that are important to know: *She's been working here long enough to know what's what.*

14 what's it to you? used to tell someone angrily that something does not concern them: *That's right, I didn't pass. What's it to you, anyway?* | *'How did he die?' Suddenly Emily was angry. 'What's it to you?'*

15 ... or what a) used at the end of a question to show that you are impatient with someone or something: *Are you afraid of him, or what?* | *Is that work going to be finished by Friday, or what?* **b)** used after mentioning one or more possibilities to show that you are not certain about something: *I don't know whether it was an accident or on purpose or what.* **c)** used after a description of someone or something to emphasize it: *Nearby are the remains of a deserted village. Spooky or what?* | *Is that madness or what?*

16 so what? also **what of it?** used to say that you do not care about something or think it is important: *'Your room looks a real mess, Tracey.' 'So what?'* | *'But, Paul, she's so much older than you?' 'What of it?'*

17 you what? a) *BrE* used to ask someone to repeat something they have just said. It is more polite to say PARDON: *'I want to tell you something.' 'You what? I can't hear what you're saying.'* **b)** used to show that you are surprised: *'So I resigned.' 'You what?'*

18 what if...? a) used to ask what you should do or what the result will be if something happens, especially something unpleasant: *What if this plan of yours fails, what then?* | *'What if it rains tomorrow?' 'We'll just have to postpone it.'* **b)** used to make a suggestion: *What if we moved the sofa over here? Would that look better?*

19 ...and what have you used at the end of a list of things to mean other things of a similar kind: *The shelves were crammed with books, documents, and what have you.*

20 what with sth used to introduce a list of reasons that have made something happen or made someone feel in a particular way: *She couldn't get to sleep, what with all the shooting and shouting.*

21 what's with sb? *AmE* used to ask why a person or group of people is behaving strangely: *What's with you people?*

22 what's with sth? *AmE* used to ask the reason for something: *What's with all the sad faces?*

23 now what? used to ask what is going to happen next, what you should do etc

W

[1] 000, [2] 000, [3] 000, most frequent words in [S]poken and [W]ritten English

where·so·ever /ˌweəsəʊ'evə $ 'wersoʊˌevər/ adv, conjunction literary another word for WHEREVER

where·to /weə'tuː $ wer-/ adv, conjunction old use to which place

where·u·pon /ˌweərə'pɒn $ 'werəpɑːn, -pɒːn/ conjunction formal used when something happens immediately after something else, or as a result of something happening: *She refused to hand over her money, whereupon there was a fight.*

wher·ev·er S2 /weər'evə $ wer'evər/ adv
1 to or at any place, position, or situation: *Children will play wherever they happen to be.* | *Sit wherever you like.* | *... or wherever* (=used to emphasize that you are talking about any place and not a specific place) *Dublin people dress more individually than people in London or wherever.*
2 in all places that: *She is shadowed by detectives wherever she goes.* | *I feel I ought to be nice to them wherever possible* (=at all times when it is possible).
3 used at the beginning of a question to show surprise: *'Wherever did she find that?' Daisy wondered.*
4 wherever that is/may be used to say that you do not know where a place or town is or have never heard of it: *She wants to move to Far Flatley, wherever that is.*

where·with·al /'weəwɪðɔːl $ 'werwɪðɒːl/ n the **wherewithal to do sth** the money, skill etc that you need in order to do something; ⊟ **means**: *Does Cath have the creative **wherewithal** to make it as a solo act?*

whet /wet/ v **whetted, whetting** [T] **1 whet sb's appetite (for sth)** if an experience whets your appetite for something, it increases your desire for it: *The view from the Quai bridge had whetted my appetite for a trip on the lake.* **2** literary to make the edge of a blade sharp

wheth·er S1 W1 /'weðə $ -ər/ conjunction
1 used when talking about a choice you have to make or about something that is not certain: *Maurice asked me whether I needed any help.* | *There were times when I wondered **whether or not** we would get there.* | **whether to do sth** *She was uncertain **whether** to stay **or** leave.* | *I didn't know **whether** to believe him **or not.*** | *The question arose **as to whether** this behaviour was unlawful.*
2 used to say that something definitely will or will not happen whatever the situation is: *It seemed to me that she was in trouble whether Mahoney lived or died.* | *Look, Kate, I'm calling the doctor, **whether** you like it **or not.*** | *Poor farmers, **whether** owners or tenants, will be worst affected.* ⚠ Do not confuse with **weather** (=conditions outside such as rain, snow, sun, wind etc)

whet·stone /'wetstəʊn $ -stoʊn/ n [C] a stone used to make the blade of cutting tools sharp

whew /hjuː/ interjection used when you are surprised, very hot, or feeling glad that something bad did not happen; ⊟ **phew**: *Whew, it was hot.*

whey /weɪ/ n [U] the watery liquid that is left after the solid part has been removed from sour milk

which S1 W1 /wɪtʃ/ determiner, pron
1 used to ask or talk about one or more members of a group of people or things, when you are uncertain about it or about them: *Which book are you looking for?* | *Which are the most important crops?* | *Miranda was sure it was one of them, but was not sure which.* | *[+of] I don't know which of us was the more scared.*
2 used after a noun to show what thing or things you mean: *Did you see the letter which came today?* | *Now they were driving by the houses which Andy had described.* ⚠ In informal and spoken English, it is more usual to use **that**: *This is the one that I wanted.*
3 used, after a COMMA in writing, to add more information about the thing, situation, or event you have just mentioned: *The house, which was completed in 1856, was famous for its huge marble staircase.* | *One of the boys kept laughing, which annoyed Jane intensely.* | *He was educated at the local grammar school, after which*

he went on to Cambridge. | *She may have missed the train, **in which case** (=if this happens) she won't arrive for another hour.*
4 don't know/can't tell etc which is which if you do not know which is which, you cannot see the difference between two very similar people or things: *The twins are so alike I can never tell which is which.*

which·ev·er /wɪtʃ'evə $ -'evər/ determiner, pron **1** used to say that it does not matter which thing or person is chosen because the result will be the same: *It will be a difficult operation, whichever method you choose.* | *Whichever way you look at it, things are pretty bad.* **2** used to refer to the member of a group of people or things that does something, is wanted, is possible etc: *Whichever player scores the highest number of points will be the winner.* | *You can either have the double room or the family room, whichever you want.* | *'Do you want tea or coffee?' 'I don't mind – **whichever one** you're making.'*

whiff /wɪf/ n [C] **1** a very slight smell of something: *[+of] a whiff of tobacco* | **get/catch a whiff of sth** *As she walked past, I caught a whiff of her perfume.* **2 a whiff of danger/adventure/freedom etc** a slight sign that something dangerous, exciting etc might happen: *The whiff of danger filled her with excitement.*

Whig /wɪg/ n [C] a member of a British political party of the 18th and early 19th centuries which wanted to limit royal power, and later became the Liberal Party

while¹ S1 W1 /waɪl/ conjunction
1 during the time that something is happening: *They arrived while we were having dinner.* | *While she was asleep, thieves broke in and stole her handbag.* | *She met Andy while working on a production of Carmen.* → see box at DURING
2 all the time that something is happening: *Would you look after the children while I do the shopping?*
3 used to emphasize the difference between two situations, activities etc: *Schools in the north tend to be better equipped, while those in the south are relatively poor.*
4 in spite of the fact that; ⊟ **although**: *While never a big eater, he did snack a lot.* | *While there was no conclusive evidence, most people thought he was guilty.*
5 while I'm/you're etc at/about it spoken used to suggest that someone should do something at the same time that they do something else: *Print out what you've written, and while you're at it make a copy for me.*

while² S1 W2 n
1 a while a period of time, especially a short one: *It takes a while to recover from the operation.* | **in a while** *Mr Thomas will be with you in a while.* | **for a while** *At last, he could relax for a while.* | **a little/short while** *Wait a little while before deciding.* | *We talked for **quite a while** (=a fairly long time) on the phone.*
2 all the while all the time that something is happening: *He examined her thoroughly, talking softly all the while.* | *She continued working, all the while keeping an eye on the clock.* → **(every) once in a while** at ONCE¹ (8); → **be worth sb's while (to do/doing sth)** at WORTH¹ (5); → **make it worth sb's while** at WORTH¹ (6)

while³ v **while away the hours/evening/days etc** to spend time in a pleasant and lazy way: *The evenings were whiled away in endless games of cards.*

whilst S2 W2 /waɪlst/ conjunction BrE formal WHILE

whim /wɪm/ n [C] a sudden feeling that you would like to have or do something, especially when there is no important or good reason: **on a whim** *I didn't leave just on a whim* (=for no good reason). | **At the whim of** *At work they are at the whim of the boss.* | **sb's every whim** *Their father had always indulged her every whim.* | **at whim** *He appeared and disappeared at whim.*

whim·per /'wɪmpə $ -ər/ v [I,T] to make low crying sounds, or to speak in this way: *He heard the dog whimper.* | *'It's not my fault,' she whimpered.* —**whimper** n [C]

whim·si·cal /'wɪmzɪkəl/ adj unusual or strange and often amusing: *He has a wonderful whimsical sense of humour.* —**whimsically** /-kli/ adv

whim·sy /'wɪmzi/ n [U] a way of thinking, behaving, or doing something that is unusual, strange, and often amusing: *a sense of fancy and whimsy*

whine /waɪn/ v **1** [I,T] to complain in a sad, annoying voice about something; ◼ **moan**: *Oh Charlotte, please stop whining.* | *'I don't understand,' whined Rose.* | [+**about**] *The sergeant was whining about how hard he had been forced to work recently.* **2** [I] to make a long high sound because you are in pain or unhappy: *He could hear the dog whining behind the door.* **3** [I] if a machine whines, it makes a continuous high sound —**whine** n [C]: *The baby's howl turned to a high-pitched whine.* | *the whine of a vacuum cleaner*

whinge /wɪndʒ/ v present participle **whingeing** or **whinging** [I] *BrE* to keep complaining in an annoying way: [+**about**] *Stop whingeing about the situation and accept it.* —**whinge** n [C]: *His tale is one long whinge about his own suffering.* —**whinger** n [C]

whin·ny /'wɪni/ v **whinnied, whinnying, whinnies** [I] if a horse whinnies, it makes a high sound —**whinny** n [C]

whip¹ /wɪp/ v **whipped, whipping 1** [T] to hit someone or something with a whip: *He whipped the horse into a canter.* **2** [I,T always + adv/prep] to move quickly and violently, or to make something do this: *The wind whipped her hair into her eyes.* | [+**across/around/past** etc] *Rain whipped across the window pane.* | **whip sth about/around** *The branches were being whipped about in the storm.* | [+**round/around**] *He whipped round to face them.* **3** [T always + adv/prep] to move or remove something with a quick sudden movement: **whip sth off/out/back etc** *Annie whipped off her apron and put it into the drawer.* | *He whipped back the sheets.* **4** [T] to mix cream or the clear part of an egg very hard until it becomes stiff; → **beat, whisk**: *Whip the cream until thick.* **5** [T] *BrE informal* to steal something

whip through sth phr v informal to finish a job very quickly: *He whipped through his routine paperwork before going home.*

whip sb/sth ⇔ **up** phr v **1** to try to make people feel strongly about something: **whip up interest/opposition/support** etc *They'll do anything to whip up a bit of interest in a book.* | *an attempt to whip up the masses* **2** to quickly make something to eat: *Mother was in the kitchen whipping up a batch of cakes.*

whip² n **1** [C] a long thin piece of rope or leather with a handle, that you hit animals with to make them move or that you hit someone with to punish them: *The coachman cracked his whip and the carriage lurched forward.* **2** [C] a member of the US Congress or the British Parliament who is responsible for making sure that the members of their party attend and vote **3** [C] a written order sent to members of the British Parliament telling them when and how to vote → **THREE-LINE WHIP 4** [C,U] *BrE* a sweet dish made from the white part of eggs and chocolate or fruit, beaten together to make a smooth light mixture: *pineapple whip* **5 have the whip hand** to have power and control over someone → **crack the whip** at CRACK¹ (14); → **give sb a fair crack of the whip** at FAIR¹ (9)

whip·lash /'wɪp-læʃ/ n [U] a neck injury caused when your head moves forward and back again suddenly and violently, especially in a car accident: *One officer suffered whiplash injuries.*

whipped cream n [U] cream that has been beaten until it is thick

whip·per·snap·per /'wɪpə,snæpə $ 'wɪpər,snæpər/ n [C] old-fashioned a young person who is too confident and does not show enough respect to older people

whip·pet /'wɪpₐt/ n [C] a small thin racing dog like a GREYHOUND

whip·ping /'wɪpɪŋ/ n [C usually singular] a punishment given to someone by whipping them

whipping boy n [singular] someone or something that is blamed for someone else's mistakes; ◼ **scapegoat**

whipping cream n [U] a type of cream that becomes thick when you beat it

whip·py /'wɪpi/ adj long, thin, and easy to bend: *new growths of whippy little sapling twigs*

whip-round n **have a whip-round** *BrE informal* if a group of people have a whip-round, they all give some money so that they can buy something together: *We had a whip-round to pay for a taxi to the railway station.*

whir /wɜ: $ wɜːr/ v [I] another spelling of WHIRR

whirl¹ /wɜːl $ wɜːrl/ v **1** [I,T] to turn or spin around very quickly, or to make someone or something do this: *We watched the seagulls whirling and shrieking over the harbour.* | [+**about/around/toward sth**] *She whirled around and her look shook him.* | **whirl sb/sth about/around/away** etc *He whirled her round in his arms.* **2** [I] if your head is whirling, or if thoughts are whirling in your head, your mind is full of thoughts and ideas, and you feel very confused or excited: *His head was whirling with excitement.* | *The implications began to whirl around her head.*

whirl² n **1 give sth a whirl** informal to try something that you are not sure you are going to like or be able to do: *Why don't you give golf a whirl?* **2** [singular] a lot of activity of a particular kind: *the social whirl of New York publishing* | [+**of**] *The next two days passed in a whirl of activity.* **3 be in a whirl** to feel very excited or confused about something: *His mind was in a whirl and he was worried.* **4** [C usually singular] a spinning movement or the shape of something that is spinning: [+**of**] *A car rumbled over the bumpy dirt road, leaving behind a whirl of white dust*

whir·li·gig /'wɜːlɪ,gɪg $ 'wɜːr-/ n [C] a toy that spins; ◼ **top**

whirl·pool /'wɜːlpuːl $ 'wɜːrl-/ n [C] **1** a powerful current of water that spins around and can pull things down into it **2** also **whirlpool bath** a large BATHTUB that makes hot water move in strong currents around your body **3 a whirlpool of emotion/activity etc** a very busy situation or a strong emotion, from which it is difficult to escape: *people who are caught in a whirlpool of grief*

whirl·wind¹ /'wɜːl,wɪnd $ 'wɜːrl-/ n [C] **1** an extremely strong wind that moves quickly with a circular movement, causing a lot of damage; ◼ **tornado**; ◼ **twister** AmE **2 a whirlwind of emotions/activity etc** a situation in which you experience a lot of different emotions or a lot of different things happen, one after another

whirlwind² adj [only before noun] a whirlwind situation or event happens very quickly: *a whirlwind romance*

whirr, whir /wɜ: $ wɜːr/ v **whirred, whirring** [I] to make a fairly quiet regular sound, like the sound of a bird or insect moving its wings very fast: *Helicopters whirred overhead.* —**whirr** n [C usually singular]: *the whirr of an electric motor*

whisk¹ /wɪsk/ v [T] **1** to mix liquid, eggs etc very quickly so that air is mixed in, using a fork or a whisk **2** [always + adv/prep] to take someone or something quickly away from a place: **whisk sb/sth away/off** *The waitress whisked our coffee cups away before we'd had a chance to finish.*

whisk² n [C] a small kitchen tool made of curved pieces of wire, used for mixing air into eggs, cream etc → see picture at EAT

whisk broom n [C] AmE a small stiff BROOM used especially for brushing clothes

whis·ker /'wɪskə $ -ər/ n [C] **1** [usually plural] one of the long stiff hairs that grow near the mouth of a cat, mouse etc → see picture at BIG CAT **2** [usually plural] one of the hairs that grow on a man's face **3 win/lose by a whisker** informal to win or lose by a very small amount: *Schmidt finished second, losing by a whisker in the final*

1 000, 2 000, 3 000, most frequent words in S poken and W ritten English

W

event. **4 come within a whisker (of doing) sth** to almost succeed or fail at doing something: *Doctors say he came within a whisker of dying on the operating table.*

whis·ky S3 *BrE* also **whiskey** *especially AmE* /ˈwɪski/ *n plural* **whiskies** *or* **whiskeys** [C,U] a strong alcoholic drink made from grain, or a glass of this

whisper

whispering   whistling

whis·per¹ W3 /ˈwɪspə $ -ər/ *v*
1 [I,T] to speak or say something very quietly, using your breath rather than your voice: *You don't have to whisper, no one can hear us.* | [+about] *What are you two whispering about over there?* | **whisper sth to sb** *James leaned over to whisper something to Michael.* | *'I've missed you,' he whispered in her ear.*
2 [T] to say or suggest something privately or secretly: **whisper that** *Staff were whispering that the company was about to go out of business.*

whisper² *n* [C] **1** a very quiet voice you make using your breath and no sound: **in a whisper** *'Where are we going?' he asked in a whisper.* **2** a piece of news or information that has not been officially announced and may or may not be true; ▤ **rumour**: [+of] *The first whisper of the redundancies came from the newspapers.* | [+that] *There are whispers that the actor was seen checking into a hospital last week.* **3 whisper of sth** *literary* a low soft sound made by something such as the wind

whispering cam·paign *n* [C] a situation in which someone privately spreads criticism about another person in order to make people have a bad opinion of them

W

whist /wɪst/ *n* [U] a card game for four players in two pairs, in which each pair tries to win the most TRICKS

whis·tle¹ /ˈwɪsəl/ *v*
1 HIGH SOUND [I,T] to make a high or musical sound by blowing air out through your lips: *Adam whistled happily on his way to work.* | *I heard this song on the radio and I've been whistling it all day.* | *He whistled a tune as he strolled down the corridor.* | **whistle to sb** (=whistle to get someone's attention) *Dad whistled to us to come home for dinner.* | **whistle at sb** (=whistle to let someone know that you think they are attractive) *Men are always whistling at Heidi on the street.*; → see picture at WHISPER¹
2 USE A WHISTLE [I] to make a high sound by blowing into a whistle: *The referee whistled and the game began.*
3 GO/MOVE FAST [I always + adv/prep] to move quickly, making a whistling sound: *Bullets and shells were whistling overhead.* | *They listened to the wind whistling through the trees.*
4 STEAM TRAIN/KETTLE [I] if a steam train or KETTLE whistles, it makes a high sound when air or steam is forced through a small hole
5 BIRD [I] if a bird whistles, it makes a high musical sound
6 be whistling in the dark *informal* to be trying to show that you are brave when you are afraid, or that you know about something when you do not: *Does he know what he's talking about or is he just whistling in the dark?*

7 sb can whistle for sth *BrE spoken* used to tell someone that there is no chance of them getting what they have asked for

whistle² *n* [C] **1** a small object that produces a high whistling sound when you blow into it: *The lifeguard blew his whistle.* **2** a high sound made by blowing a whistle, by blowing air out through your lips, or when air or steam is forced through a small opening: *Larsson scored just minutes before the final whistle.* | **low/shrill/ high-pitched etc whistle** *Sanders gave a low whistle when he saw the contents of the box.* **3** a piece of equipment on a train or boat that makes a high noise when air is forced through it **4** the sound of something moving quickly through the air: [+of] *We could hear the whistle of the jets as they passed overhead.* → **blow the whistle on sth** at BLOW¹ (17); → **clean as a whistle** at CLEAN¹ (1); → PENNY WHISTLE, WOLF WHISTLE

whistle-blower *n* [C] someone who tells people in authority or the public about dishonest or illegal practices at the place where they work —**whistle-blowing** *n* [U]

whistle-stop *adj AmE* **whistle-stop tour/trip** a trip during which someone, especially a politician, visits many different places in a short period of time: *a whistle-stop tour of Texas*

whit /wɪt/ *n* **not a whit** *old-fashioned* not at all: *Sara had not changed a whit.*

Whit *n* [C,U] *BrE* WHITSUN

white¹ S1 W1 /waɪt/ *adj*
1 COLOUR having the colour of milk, salt, or snow: *a white dress* | **pure/snow white** (=completely white) *snow white hair*
2 PEOPLE **a)** belonging to the race of people with pale skin; → **black**: *young white males* **b)** relating to white people: *a white neighborhood*
3 PALE looking pale, because of illness, strong emotion etc: *Are you OK? You're white as a sheet* (=extremely pale). | **white with anger/fear etc** *Her voice shook, and her face was white with anger.*
4 COFFEE [usually before noun] *BrE* white coffee has milk or cream in it
5 WINE white wine is a pale yellow colour; → **red**
6 a white Christmas a Christmas when there is snow —**whiteness** *n* [U]

white² S3 *n*
1 COLOUR [U] the colour of milk, salt, and snow
2 PEOPLE [C] also **White** someone who belongs to the race of people with pale skin; → **black**: *The mayor is very popular among whites.*
3 WINE [C,U] wine that is pale yellow in colour: *a nice bottle of white* | *California has some of the finest whites in the world.*
4 EYE [C + of] the white part of your eye
5 EGG [C,U] the part of an egg that surrounds the YOLK (=yellow part) and becomes white when cooked
6 whites [plural] **a)** white clothes, sheets etc, which are separated from dark colours when they are washed **b)** white clothes that are worn for some sports, such as TENNIS

white³ *v*
white sth ⇔ out *phr v* to cover something written on paper, especially a mistake, with a special white liquid so that it cannot be seen any more

white·bait /ˈwaɪtbeɪt/ *n* [U] very young fish of several types, used as food: *deep-fried whitebait*

white blood cell *n* [C] one of the cells in your blood which fights against infection; → **red blood cell**

white·board /ˈwaɪtbɔːd $ -bɔːrd/ *n* [C] a large board with a white smooth surface that you can write on, used, for example, in rooms where classes are taught; → **blackboard**

white-bread *adj AmE informal* relating to white people who are considered traditional and boring in their opinions and way of life: *a white-bread family*

white·caps /ˈwaɪtkæps/ *n* [plural] *AmE* WHITE HORSES

white-'collar adj **1** [only before ~] workers have jobs in offices, banks ~ working in factories, building thi ~ **collar, pink-collar**: *white-collar jobs* ~ **crime** crimes involving white-collar ~ example when someone secretly steals mon ~ organization they work for

white 'corpuscle n [C] a WHITE BLOOD CELL

white 'dwarf n [C] *technical* a hot star, near the e ~ its life, that is more solid but less bright than the su ~
→ **red giant**

white 'elephant n [C] something that is completely useless, although it may have cost a lot of money: *When the theatre first opened it was widely regarded as a white elephant.*

white 'flag n [C] a sign that you accept that you have failed or been defeated; → **surrender: wave/raise/show etc the white flag** *Despite the loss, the team refuses to wave the white flag and give up on the season.*

white 'flour n [U] wheat flour from which the BRAN (=outer layer) and WHEATGERM (=inside seed) have been removed

'white goods n [plural] *BrE* equipment used in the home, for example washing machines and REFRIGERATORS; → **brown goods**

White·hall /'waɪthɔːl, ˌwaɪt'hɔːl $ -hɒːl/ n **1** the British government, especially the government departments rather than parliament or the Prime Minister **2** the street in London where many of the government departments are

white 'heat n [U] the very high temperature at which a metal turns white → WHITE-HOT

white 'horses n [plural] *BrE* waves in the sea or on a lake that are white at the top; ◫ **whitecaps** *AmE*

white-'hot adj **1** white-hot metal is so hot that it shines white **2** involving a lot of activity or strong feelings: *white-hot passion*

'White House n **1 the White House** the official home in Washington DC of the President of the US **2** the President of the US and the people who advise him: *claims that* **the White House** *had received warnings of a possible terrorist attack before September 11th | White House officials refused to comment on the story.*

white 'knight n [C] a person or company that puts money into a business in order to save it from being controlled by another company

white-'knuckle adj [only before noun] a white-knuckle ride at a FAIRGROUND makes you feel excited and afraid at the same time

white-'knuckled adj if you have white-knuckled hands, your hands are held tightly in a FIST because you are anxious or afraid

white 'lie n [C] *informal* a lie that you tell someone in order to protect them or avoid hurting their feelings

white 'lightning n [U] *AmE* MOONSHINE

white 'magic n [U] magic used for good purposes; → **black magic**

'white meat n [U] the pale-coloured meat from the breast, wings etc of a cooked chicken, TURKEY, or other bird; → **redmeat**

whit·en /'waɪtn/ v [I,T] to become more white, or to make something do this: *This stuff is supposed to whiten your teeth.*

whit·en·er /'waɪtnə $ -ər/ also **whit·en·ing** /'waɪtnɪŋ/ n [C,U] a substance used to make something more white

white 'noise n [U] noise coming from a radio or television which is turned on but not TUNED to any programme

white·out /'waɪtaʊt/ n [C] weather conditions in which there is so much cloud or snow that you cannot see anything

ite 'Pages n **the White Pages** the white part of a ~phone DIRECTORY in the US with the names, ~sses, and telephone numbers of people with tele ~ → **Yellow Pages**

~**aper** n [C] an official report from the British ~nt, explaining their ideas and plans concern ~ular subject before a new law is introduced;

~**per** n [U] a white powder made from the ~ma ~ of a PEPPERCORN, which gives a slightly ~ with ~; → **black pepper**

white 's ~. ~/ n [C,U] a thick white liqu ~ petrol, use ~ and butter, which can be ea ~ on clothes ~bles

white su'pre ~ *BrE* a clear liquid made fro ~ ~aint thinner, removing mark ~ that white people ~ine
—**white suprema** ~[C] someone who believe ~

white-'tie adj [only ~han people of other races ~ occasion is a very forma ~ white BOW TIES and TAILS; → ~ ~n] a white-tie socia ~which the men wear

white 'trash n [U] *AmE* info ~e ~ sion used to talk about white peo ~in ~lting expres ~ uneducated ~who ~e poor and

white 'van man n [C] *BrE* inform ~a man who drives a white VAN, especially when delivering goods in a city, in an AGGRESSIVE and dangerous way

white·wall /'waɪtwɔːl $ -wɒl ~ n [C] *AmE* a car tyre that has a wide white band on its side

white·wash[1] /'waɪtwɒʃ $ -wɒ ~, -wɑː ʃ/ n **1** [C,U] a report or examination of events that hides the true facts about something so that the person who is responsible will not be punished; ◫ **cover-up**: *The official report into the cause of the fire was labeled a whitewash.* **2** [U] a white liquid mixture used especially for painting walls **3** [C] an occasion in sport when one player or team defeats an opponent easily, without the opponent getting any points, GOALS etc

whitewash[2] v [T] **1** to cover something with whitewash: *The walls were whitewashed and covered with bullfighting posters.* **2** to hide the true facts about a serious accident or illegal action: *Investigators are accused of whitewashing the governor's record.* **3** to defeat an opponent in sport easily, without the opponent getting any points, GOALS etc

white·wa·ter, white water /ˌwaɪt'wɔːtə $ -'wɒːtər, -'wɑː-/ n [U] a part of a river that looks white because the water is running very quickly over rocks: *whitewater canoeing* → see picture at OUTDOOR

white 'wedding n [C] a traditional wedding at which the BRIDE wears a long white dress

whit·ey /'waɪti/ n [C,U] an offensive word for a white person or white people in general

whith·er /'wɪðə $ -ər/ adv **1** *old use* to which place; ◫ **where**: *the place whither he went* **2** *formal* used to ask what the future of something will be or how it will develop: *Whither socialism?* → WHENCE

whit·ing /'waɪtɪŋ/ n plural **whiting** [C] a black and silver fish that lives in the sea and can be eaten

whit·ish /'waɪtɪʃ/ adj almost white in colour

Whit·sun /'wɪtsən/ n [C,U] *BrE* **1** also **Whit 'Sunday** the seventh Sunday after Easter, when Christians celebrate the HOLY SPIRIT coming down from heaven; ◫ **Pentecost 2** also **Whit·sun·tide** /'wɪtsəntaɪd/ the peri ~ around Whitsun

whit·tle /'wɪtl/ v **1** also **whittle down** [T] to gr ~ ally make something smaller by taking parts awa ~ *need to whittle down the list of guests f ~ party.* **2** [I,T] to cut a piece of wood into a par ~ shape by cutting off small pieces with a knife; ~
  whittle away phr v to gradually reduce the ~ or effectiveness of something, especially s ~

W

that you think should not be reduced/ **away** The museum is worried that gove· will be whittled away. | [+**at**] Congress a at our freedom of speech.

whizz¹ BrE; **whiz** AmE /wɪz/ v [I] prep] informal **a)** to move very qui⁓ very sound like something rushing ⁓ne more ambulance whizzed past. | I sa whizzing through the air. **b)** quickly: [+**through**] Let's just time. **2** AmE spoken to URIN· 'omeone who

whizz² BrE; **whiz** AmE n a particular is very fast, intelligent, AmE spoken to activity: a math whiz ⅃ → GEE WHIZ URINATE **3** [C,U] informal ⁓ɪzkɪd/ n [C] informal

whizz·kid BrE; **whiz·**⁓ in the City a young person who something: financia⁓

who S1 W1 /huː/ which person is involved, or **1** used to ask or t⁓on is: Who locked the door? | what the name ⁓Who's that guy with your wife? | Who do you won⁓t who the murderer was. | She They never ⁓ud sent the flowers. | **who to ask/** wondered ⁓ he⁓c He doesn't know who to vote for. | contar⁓ Blam⁓ **who on earth/in the world etc** (=used for emphasis wh⁓n you are surprised angry etc) Who on earth would live in such a lonely place? | Who the hell are you? **2** used after a noun ⁓ show which person or which people you are talking about: Do you know the people who live over the road? | the woman who was driving | She was the one why did most of the talking. **3** used, after a COMMA in writing, to add more informa- tion about a particular person or group of people that you have just mentioned: I discussed it with my brother, who is a lawyer. | Alison Jones and her husband David, who live in Hartlepool, are celebrating their golden wedding anniversary. **4** informal used to introduce a question that shows you think something is true of everyone or of no one: We have the occasional argument. Who doesn't? (=everyone does) | Who wants to come second? (=no one does) **5 who is sb to do sth?** spoken used to say that someone does not have the right or the authority to say or do something: Who is she to order me around? **6 who's who a)** if you know who is who within a particular organization or group, you know what each person's name is and what job they do or what position they have: I'm just getting to know who's who in the department. **b) a who's who of sth** a list of the impor- tant people within a particular organization or group – often used to emphasize that many important people are involved in something: The list of competitors reads like a who's who of international tennis players.

whoa /wəʊ, həʊ $ woʊ, hoʊ/ interjection **1** used to tell someone to become calmer or to do something more slowly: Whoa! You're driving too fast. **2** said to show that you are surprised or that you think something is impressive: Whoa. That's a lot of money. **3** used to tell a horse to stop

who·dun·it, whodunnit /ˌhuːˈdʌnɪt/ n [C] informal a book, film etc about a murder case, in which you do not find out who killed the person until the end

who·ev·er S2 /huːˈevə $ -ˈevər/ pron **1** used to say that it does not matter who does some- hing, is in a particular place etc: I'll take whoever ⁓ants to go. | When you're done with the book, just give ⁓o Kristin or Shelley or whoever. ⁓ased to talk about a specific person or people, ⁓ough you do not know who they are: Whoever is ⁓nsible for this will be punished. ⁓ever he/she is also **whoever he/she may be** ⁓ say that you do not know who someone is: ⁓ot a message from Tony Gower, whoever he is.

to mean 'who' at the beginning of a question to ⁓v surprise or anger: Whoever would do a thing like ⁓t to an old woman?

⁓ole¹ S1 W1 /həʊl $ hoʊl/ adj **1** [only before noun] all of something; **⊟** entire: You have your whole life ahead of you! | His whole attitude bugs me. | We ate the whole cake in about ten minutes. | **The whole thing** (=everything about the situation) just makes me sick. | We just sat around and watched TV **the whole time** (=the only thing we did was watch television). | I don't believe she's telling us **the whole story** (=all the facts). | It was months before **the whole truth** came out. | **the whole school/country/village etc** (=all the people in a school, country etc) The whole town came out for the parade. **2 whole lot** informal **a) a whole lot** very much: I'm feeling a whole lot better. | I don't cook a whole lot anymore. **b) a whole lot (of sth)** a large quantity or number: We're going to have a whole lot of problems if we don't finish this by tomorrow. | You can find a nice house in this neighborhood, and you don't have to spend a whole lot. **c) the whole lot** especially BrE all of something: She said she'd give me the whole lot for 20 pounds. **3 a whole range/series/variety etc (of sth)** used to emphasize that there are a lot of things of a similar type: There are a whole range of sizes to choose from. **4** complete and not divided or broken into parts: Place a whole onion inside the chicken. | a snake **swallowing** a mouse **whole** (=swallowing it without chewing) **5 the whole point (of sth)** used to emphasize the purpose for doing something, especially when you believe this is unclear or has been forgotten: I thought the whole point of the meeting was to decide which offer to accept. **6 in the whole (wide) world** informal an expression meaning 'anywhere' or 'at all', used to emphasize a statement: I have the best job in the whole wide world. **7 go the whole hog** also **go whole hog** AmE informal to do something as completely or as well as you can, without any limits: I'm gonna go whole hog and have a live band at the barbecue. **8 the whole nine yards** AmE spoken including every- thing that is typical of or possible in an activity, situation, set of things etc: Our new apartment complex has a tennis court, swimming pool, playground – the whole nine yards. —**wholeness** n [U] → **a whole new ball game** at BALL GAME (3); → **the whole shebang** at SHEBANG; → **the whole shooting match** at SHOOTING MATCH; → **the whole enchilada** at ENCHILADA (3); → WHOLLY

whole² S3 W2 n **1 the whole of sth** all of something, especially some- thing that is not a physical object: The whole of the morning was wasted trying to find the documents. **2 on the whole** used to say that something is generally true: On the whole, I thought the film was pretty good. **3 as a whole** used to say that all the parts of something are being considered together: This project will be of great benefit to the region as a whole. **4** [C usually singular] something that consists of a number of parts, but is considered as a single unit: Two halves make a whole.

whole·food /ˈhəʊlfuːd $ ˈhoʊl-/ n [C,U] food that is considered healthy because it only contains natural things rather than anything artificial

whole·heart·ed /ˌhəʊl ˈhɑːtɪd◂ $ ˌhoʊlˈhɑːr-/ adj [usually before noun] involving all your feelings, interest etc: **wholehearted support/acceptance/cooperation etc** Montgomery's new style of leadership met with Leslie's wholehearted approval. —**whole-heartedly** adv: I agree whole-heartedly with the mayor on this issue.

whole·meal /ˈhəʊlmiːl $ ˈhoʊl-/ adj BrE wholemeal flour or bread uses all of the grain, including the outer layer; **⊟ whole wheat** AmE

'whole note n [C] AmE a musical note which contin- ues for as long as two HALF NOTES; **⊟ semibreve** BrE

ˌwhole 'number n [C] a number such as 0, 1, 2 etc that is not a FRACTION; **⊟ integer**

whole·sale¹ /'həʊlseɪl $ 'hoʊl-/ n [U] the business of selling goods in large quantities at low prices to other businesses, rather than to the general public; → retail

wholesale² adj **1** relating to the business of selling goods in large quantities at low prices to other businesses, rather than to the general public; → retail: *wholesale prices* **2** [usually before noun] affecting almost everything or everyone, and often done without any concern for the results: *the capture and wholesale destruction of a city* | *This company will not be successful until there are wholesale changes.* —**wholesale** adv: *I can get it for you wholesale.*

whole·sal·er /'həʊlˌseɪlə $ 'hoʊlˌseɪlər/ n [C] a person or company who sells goods wholesale; → retailer

whole·some /'həʊlsəm $ 'hoʊl-/ adj **1** likely to make you healthy: **wholesome food/fare/meal etc** *well-balanced wholesome meals* **2** considered to have a good moral effect: *good wholesome fun* —**wholesomeness** n [U]

'whole wheat adj AmE whole wheat flour or bread uses all of the grain, including the outer layer; ▤ **wholemeal** BrE

who'll /huːl/ the short form of 'who will'

whol·ly /'həʊl-li $ 'hoʊl-/ adv formal completely: *a wholly satisfactory solution* | *The report claimed that the disaster was wholly unavoidable.*

whom W1 /huːm/ pron the object form of 'who', used especially in formal speech or writing: *Desperate for money, she called her sister, whom she hadn't spoken to in 20 years.* | *She brought with her three friends, none of whom I had ever met before.* ⚠ **Whom** is very formal. It is more usual to use **who**: *Who did you send it to?* | *This is Liz, who I work with.*

whoop /wuːp, huːp/ v [I] **1** to shout loudly and happily: *Hundreds of people ran past them, whooping joyously.* **2 whoop it up** informal to enjoy yourself very much, especially in a large group —**whoop** n [C]: *whoops of victory*

whoop-de-do /ˌwuːp diː 'duː, ˌhuːp-/ interjection AmE spoken used to show that you do not think something that someone has told you is as exciting or impressive as they think it is: *'He says he'll give me a $20 raise.' 'Well, whoop-de-do.'*

whoo·pee¹ /wʊ'piː/ interjection a shout of happiness

whoop·ee² /'wʊpi/ n old-fashioned **make whoopee a)** BrE to go out and enjoy yourself **b)** AmE to have sex

'whoopee ˌcushion n [C] a rubber bag filled with air that makes a noise like a FART when you sit on it

whoop·ing cough /'huːpɪŋ kɒf $ -kɒːf/ n [U] an infectious disease that especially affects children, and makes them cough and have difficulty breathing

whoops /wʊps/ interjection **1** said when someone has fallen, dropped something, or made a small mistake: *Whoops! I nearly dropped it.* **2 whoops-a-daisy** said when someone, usually a child, falls down

whoosh /wʊʃ $ wuːʃ/ v [I always + adv/prep] informal to move very fast with a soft rushing sound —**whoosh** n [C usually singular]: *a sudden whoosh of flame and then a big bang*

whop /wɒp $ wɑːp/ v whopped, whopping [T] spoken WHUP

whop·per /'wɒpə $ 'wɑːpər/ n [C] informal **1** a lie: *She tells one whopper after another.* **2** something unusually big: *The fish Mike caught last week was a whopper.*

whop·ping /'wɒpɪŋ $ 'wɑː-/ adj [only before noun] informal very large: *a whopping fee*

who're /'huːə $ 'huːər/ the short form of 'who are'

whore /hɔː $ hɔːr/ n [C] informal **1** taboo an offensive word for a woman who has many sexual partners. Do not use this word. **2** a female PROSTITUTE

whore·house /'hɔːhaʊs $ 'hɔːr-/ n [C] informal not polite a place where men can pay to have sex; ▤ **brothel**

whor·ing /'hɔːrɪŋ/ n [U] old-fashioned the activity of having sex with a PROSTITUTE: *drinking, gambling and whoring*

whorl /wɜːl $ wɔːrl/ n [C] **1** a pattern made of a line that curls out in circles that get bigger and bigger **2** technical a circular pattern of leaves or flowers on a stem

who's /huːz/ the short form of 'who is' or 'who has'

whose S2 W1 /huːz/ determiner, pron
1 used to ask which person or people a particular thing belongs to: *Whose is this?* | *Whose keys are on the kitchen counter?*
2 used to show the relationship between a person or thing and something that belongs to that person or thing: *That's the man whose house has burned down.* | *Solar energy is an idea whose time has come.*
3 used to give additional information about a person or thing: *Jurors, whose identities will be kept secret, will be paid $40 a day.*

who·so·ev·er /ˌhuːsəʊ'evə $ -soʊ'evər/ pron old use WHOEVER

who've /huːv/ the short form of 'who have'

whup /wʌp/ also **whop** v past tense and past participle **whupped**, present participle **whupping** [T] informal especially AmE **1** to defeat someone easily in a sport or fight: *I'm gonna whup your ass* (=defeat you very easily). **2** to hit someone and hurt them very badly, especially using something such as a belt

why¹ S1 W1 /waɪ/ adv, conjunction
1 used to ask or talk about the reason for something: *Why are you crying?* | *Why do we have to take all these tests?* | *'She wants to meet you.' 'Why?'* | *'I won't be able to come into work tomorrow.' 'Why not?'* | *I have no idea why the television isn't working.* | *Simon loves you – that's why he wants to be with you.* | *He's angry with me and I don't know why.* | *There's no reason why we shouldn't be friends.* | **why on earth/why ever etc** (=used for emphasis when you are surprised, angry etc) *Why on earth didn't you ask me to help?* | *'I don't want us to be seen together.' 'Why ever not?'*
2 used to introduce a question that shows you do not think it is necessary to do something: *Why worry? You can't do anything about it.* | *Why waste time going to the bank when you can do it all over the Internet?*

> **SPOKEN PHRASES**
> **3 why not?** used to say that you agree with a suggestion: *'We could invite John and Barbara.' 'Yes, why not?'*
> **4 why doesn't sb do sth?** a) also **why not do sth?** used to make a suggestion: *Why don't you bring over a video for us to watch?* | *Why not relax and enjoy the atmosphere?* b) used to say angrily that someone should do something: *Why don't you mind your own business?*
> **5 why sb?** used to ask why a particular person has been chosen or is suffering: *Why me? Why can't someone else drive you?*
> **6 why oh why ...?** used to show that you are very sorry or angry about something: *Why oh why did I say those horrible things?*

why² interjection old-fashioned used when you are surprised or have suddenly realized something: *Why, look who's here!* | *And I thought to myself, why, I can do that.*

why³ n **the whys and (the) wherefores** the reasons or explanations for something: *The whys and the wherefores of these procedures need to be explained.*

wick /wɪk/ n [C] **1** the piece of thread in a CANDLE, that burns when you light it **2** a long piece of material in an oil lamp, that sucks up oil so that the lamp can burn **3 get on sb's wick** BrE spoken informal to annoy someone

wick·ed /'wɪkᵻd/ adj **1** behaving in a way that is morally wrong; ▤ **evil**: *the wicked stepmother in 'Hansel and Gretel'* **2** informal behaving badly in a

W

way that is amusing: *Carl had a wicked grin on his face as he crept up behind Ellen.* | *Tara hasn't lost her **wicked sense of humour**.* **3** *spoken informal* very good: *That's a wicked bike!* —**wickedly** *adv* —**wickedness** *n* [U]

wick·er /'wɪkə $ -ər/ *n* [U] thin dry branches or REEDS that are woven together: *a wicker basket* → see picture at BASKET

wick·er·work /'wɪkəwɜːk $ 'wɪkərwɜːrk/ *n* [U] objects made from wicker

wick·et /'wɪkɪt/ *n* [C] one of two sets of three wooden sticks that are stuck in the ground in a game of CRICKET, which the BOWLER tries to hit with the ball; → **stump**, **bail** → **be on a sticky wicket** at STICKY

ˈwicket ˌgate *n* [C] *old use* a small door or gate that is part of a larger one

ˈwicket ˌkeeper *n* [C] a player who stands behind the wicket in CRICKET

wide¹ [S1] [W1] /waɪd/ *adj*
1 [DISTANCE] **a)** measuring a large distance from one side to the other; ⊟ **broad**; ⊠ **narrow**: *a wide tree-lined road* | *a hat with a wide brim* | **wide smile/grin** *As he ran toward me, his face broke into a wide grin.* **b)** measuring a particular distance from one side to the other: *How wide is the door?* | *The boat was nearly as wide as the canal.* | **five metres/two miles etc wide** *The river is more than fifty yards wide.*
2 [VARIETY] [usually before noun] including or involving a large variety of different people, things, or situations: *a man with a wide experience of foreign affairs* | *Our aim is to bring classical music to a wider audience.* | **a wide range/variety/choice etc (of sth)** *This year's festival includes a wide range of entertainers.* | *holidays to a wide choice of destinations*
3 [IN MANY PLACES] [usually before noun] happening among many people or in many places: *The radio and newspapers gave the trial wide coverage.*
4 **a wide variation/difference/gap etc** a large and noticeable difference: *the ever-wider gap between the richest and poorest countries*
5 **the wider context/issues/picture etc** the more general features of a situation, rather than the specific details: *We hope that by the end of the course students will be able to see their subject in a wider context.*
6 [EYES] *literary* wide eyes are fully open, especially when someone is very surprised, excited, or frightened: *Her eyes grew wide in anticipation.*
7 **give sb/sth a wide berth** to avoid someone or something
8 [NOT HIT STH] not hitting something you were aiming at: [+of] *His shot was just wide of the goal.*
9 **the (big) wide world** *especially spoken* places outside the small familiar place where you live: *Soon you'll leave school and go out into the big wide world.*
10 nationwide/city-wide etc affecting all the people in a nation, city etc: *a country-wide revolt against the government*

> **WORD CHOICE: wide, thick, broad**
> **Wide** is used to talk about the distance across something such as a road or river. It is also used to talk about the distance from one side to the other of an object: *a doorway two metres wide*
> **Thick** is usually used to talk about the distance between the two largest surfaces of an object: *The steel doors are four inches thick.*
> **Broad** can often be used instead of **wide**, but it is slightly literary: *broad, graceful avenues*
> **Broad** is always used with **shoulders** and **back**: *a big man with broad (NOT wide) shoulders*
> **Wide** is used with nouns such as **range**, **variety**, and **choice** to say that something includes a lot of different things.
> **Broad** is used with nouns such as **outline**, **picture**, and **description** to say that a description is general rather than specific.

wide² [W3] [S3] *adv*
1 **wide open/awake/apart** completely open, awake, or apart: *Someone left the back door wide open.* | *At 2 a.m. I was still wide awake.* | *Sandy stood with his back to the fire, legs wide apart.*
2 opening or spreading as much as possible: **open/spread (sth) wide** *Spiro spread his arms wide in a welcoming gesture.* | *Leonora's eyes opened wide in horror.* | *The windows had been opened wide and she could feel a slight breeze.*
3 **wide open** if a competition, election etc is wide open, it is possible for anyone to succeed: *Most experts agree that the election is wide open at this point.*
4 not hitting something you were aiming at, and missing it by a large distance: *His throw to first base went wide.*
5 **wide of the mark a)** not correct about something, by a large amount: *The opinion polls were hopelessly wide of the mark.* **b)** not hitting something you were aiming at, and missing it by a large distance: *One of the bombs fell wide of the mark.* → **far and wide** at FAR¹ (11)

ˌwide-angle ˈlens *n* [C] a camera LENS that lets you take photographs with a wider view than normal

ˈwide boy *n* [C] *BrE informal* a man who makes money in dishonest ways and uses it to buy expensive clothes, cars etc – used to show disapproval

ˌwide-ˈeyed *adj, adv written* **1** with your eyes wide open, especially because you are surprised or frightened: *He stood there wide-eyed at the appalling scene.* **2** too willing to believe, accept, or admire things because you do not have much experience of life; ⊟ **naive**

wide·ly [W2] /'waɪdli/ *adv*
1 in a lot of different places or by a lot of people: *Organic food is now widely available.* | *an author who had travelled widely in the Far East* | *a widely used method* | *These laws were widely regarded as too strict.* | *This view was not widely held.*
2 to a large degree – used when talking about differences: *The quality of the applicants varies widely.*
3 **widely read a)** read by a lot of people: *a widely read magazine* **b)** having read many different books

wid·en /'waɪdn/ *v* **1** [I,T] to become wider, or to make something wider; ⊠ **narrow**: *They're widening the road.* | *The river widens and splits.* **2** [I,T] to become larger in degree or range, or to make something do this; ⊠ **narrow**: *The gap between income and expenditure has widened to 11%.* | *They are trying to widen the discussion to include environmental issues.* **3** [I] if your eyes widen, they open more, especially because you are surprised or frightened

ˌwide-ˈranging *adj written* including a wide variety of subjects, things, or people: *a wide-ranging discussion* | *wide-ranging proposals to improve the rail network*

wide·spread [W3] /'waɪdspred/ *adj* existing or happening in many places or situations, or among many people: *the **widespread use** of chemicals in agriculture* | **widespread support/acceptance/criticism/condemnation etc** *There was widespread support for the war.* | *The storm caused widespread damage.*

wid·get /'wɪdʒɪt/ *n* [C] **1** *spoken* a small piece of equipment that you do not know the name for **2** *informal* used to refer to an imaginary product that a company might produce: *Company A produces 6000 widgets a month at a unit price of $0.33.*

wid·ow /'wɪdəʊ $ -doʊ/ *n* [C] **1** a woman whose husband has died and who has not married again: *an elderly widow who was attacked and robbed last month* | *a wealthy widow* **2** **football/golf etc widow** a woman whose husband spends all his free time watching football, playing golf etc – used humorously

wid·owed /'wɪdəʊd $ -doʊd/ *v* **be widowed** if someone is widowed, their husband or wife dies: *She was widowed at the age of 25.* —**widowed** *adj*: *his widowed mother*

wid·ow·er /'wɪdəʊə $ -doʊər/ *n* [C] a man whose wife has died and who has not married again

wid·ow·hood /'wɪdəʊhʊd $ -doʊ-/ n [U] the state of being a widow or widower

width /wɪdθ/ n **1** [C,U] the distance from one side of something to the other; → **breadth**, **length**: [+of] *What's the width of the desk?* | **3 feet/2 metres etc in width** *It's about six metres in width.* **2 run/extend the (full) width of sth** to exist from one side of something to the other: *a covered terrace extending the full width of the house* **3** [C] the distance from one side of a swimming pool to the other: *I swam 10 widths.* **4** [C] a piece of cloth that has been measured and cut: [+of] *four widths of curtain material*

width·ways /'wɪdθweɪz/ adv across, between the two long sides of something: *Cut each rectangular cake in half widthways.*

wield /wiːld/ v [T] **1 wield power/influence/authority etc** to have a lot of power or influence, and to use it: *The Church wields immense power in Ireland.* **2** to hold a weapon or tool that you are going to use: *She had her car windows smashed by a gang wielding baseball bats.*

wie·ner /'wiːnə $ -ər/ also **wie·nie, weenie** /'wiːni/ n [C] AmE **1** a type of SAUSAGE **2** spoken someone who is silly or stupid **3** spoken a PENIS – used by children

wife S1 W1 /waɪf/ n plural **wives** /waɪvz/ [C] the woman that a man is married to; → **husband, spouse**: *Have you met my wife?* | *a refuge for battered wives* | *his second wife* | **ex-wife/former wife** *He threatened to kill his ex-wife's boyfriend.*

wife·ly /'waɪfli/ adj old-fashioned wifely qualities or actions are supposed to be typical of a good wife – sometimes used humorously way

wig /wɪg/ n [C] artificial hair that you wear on your head; → **toupée**

wig·gle /'wɪɡəl/ v [I,T] to move with small movements from side to side or up and down, or to make something move like this: *Henry wiggled his toes.* —**wiggle** n [C]

wig·gly /'wɪɡli/ adj informal a wiggly line is one that has small curves in it; → **wavy**

wig·wam /'wɪɡwæm $ -wɑːm/ n [C] a structure with a round or pointed roof used as a home by some Native American tribes in the past

wild¹ S3 W2 /waɪld/ adj

1 PLANTS/ANIMALS [usually before noun] living in a natural state, not changed or controlled by people: ◳ **tame**: *wild animals* | *a field full of wild flowers* | **wild horse/dog/pig etc** | *animals both wild and domesticated* | **wild mushroom/garlic/rose etc**

2 LAND not used by people for farming, building etc: *Nepal is stunning, with its wild, untamed landscape.* | *the wild and lonely Scottish hills*

3 EMOTIONS feeling or expressing strong uncontrolled emotions, especially anger, happiness, or excitement: *wild laughter* | [+with] *He was wild with rage.*

4 BEHAVIOUR behaving in an uncontrolled, sometimes violent way: *She was completely wild in high school.* | *Donny could be wild and crazy.* | *There was a wild look about her* (=she seemed a little crazy).

5 go wild a) to behave in a very excited uncontrolled way: *The crowd went wild as soon as the singer stepped onto the stage.* **b)** to get very angry: *When Tony heard how much it was going to cost, he just went wild.*

6 ENJOYABLE informal very enjoyable and exciting: *'How was the party?' 'It was wild!'*

7 be wild about sth/sb informal to like something or someone very much: *My son's wild about football.* | *I'm not that wild about rap music, to be honest.*

8 WITHOUT CAREFUL THOUGHT done or said without much thought or care, or without knowing all the facts: *wild accusations* | *I'm just making a wild guess here, so correct me if I'm wrong.*

9 beyond sb's wildest dreams beyond anything that someone imagined or hoped for: *an invention that was to change our lives beyond our wildest dreams*

10 not/never in your wildest dreams used to say that you did not expect or imagine that something would happen, especially after it has happened: *Never in my wildest dreams did I expect to win first place.*

11 WEATHER/SEA violent and strong: *a wild and angry sea*

12 CARD GAMES a card that is wild can be used to represent any other card in a game —**wildness** n [U] → **WILD CARD**; → **sow your wild oats** at sow¹ (3)

wild² adv **1 run wild a)** if children or animals run wild, they behave in an uncontrolled way because there is no one to control them **b)** if something runs wild, it is not controlled and operates in an extremely free way: *Be creative – allow your imagination to run wild.* **c)** if plants run wild, they grow a lot in an uncontrolled way **2 grow wild** if plants grow wild somewhere, they have not been planted by people

wild³ n **1 in the wild** in natural and free conditions, not kept or controlled by people: *There are very few pandas living in the wild now.* **2 the wilds of Africa/Alaska etc** areas where there are no towns and not many people live

wild 'boar n [C] a large wild pig with long hair

'wild ,card n [C] **1** a playing card that can represent any other card in a game **2** someone whose behaviour or effect on a situation is difficult to guess **3** a player who is a wild card or who is given a wild card is chosen for a competition although they have not previously done well enough to take part **4** technical a symbol that can represent any letter in some computer instructions

wild·cat¹ /'waɪldkæt/ n [C] a type of cat that looks similar to a pet cat and lives in mountains, forests etc

wildcat² v wildcatted, wildcatting [I] AmE to look for oil in a place where nobody has found any yet —**wildcatter** n [C]

,wildcat 'strike n [C] an occasion when workers suddenly stop working in order to protest about something, usually without the support of a TRADE UNION

wil·de·beest /'wɪldəbiːst/ n [C] a large Southern African animal with a tail and curved horns; ⊟ **gnu**

wil·der·ness /'wɪldən ̩s $ -dər-/ n [C usually singular] **1** a large area of land that has never been developed or farmed: *the Alaskan wilderness* **2** a place that seems no longer used or cared for by anyone: *The garden was a wilderness.* | *The south side of the city had become a lawless wilderness.* **3 in/from/out of the wilderness** someone who is in the wilderness does not have power or is not involved in something in an important way at a particular time: *the re-emergence of Richard Nixon from the political wilderness in 1968*

'wilderness ,area n [C] an area of public land in the US where no buildings or roads are allowed to be built

wild·fire /'waɪldfaɪə $ -faɪr/ n [C,U] especially AmE a fire that moves quickly and cannot be controlled → **spread like wildfire** at SPREAD¹ (2)

wild·fowl /'waɪldfaʊl/ n [plural] birds, especially ones that live near water such as DUCKS

,wild 'goose ,chase n [C] a situation where you are looking for something that does not exist or that you are very unlikely to find, so that you waste a lot of time: *It looks like they've sent us on a wild goose chase.*

wild·life /'waɪldlaɪf/ n [U] animals and plants growing in natural conditions: *measures to protect the area's wildlife* | *the destruction of wildlife habitats*

wild·ly /'waɪldli/ adv **1** in a very uncontrolled or excited way: *The audience cheered wildly.* **2** extremely: *The band is wildly popular in Cuba.* | *wildly inaccurate statements*

,wild 'rice n [U] the seed of a type of grass that grows in parts of North America and China

,Wild 'West n the Wild West the western part of the US in the 19th century – used especially when referring to the time before there were many laws there

W

wiles /waɪlz/ *n* [plural] clever talk or tricks used to persuade someone to do what you want: *It was impossible to resist her feminine wiles.*

wil·ful *BrE*; **willful** *AmE* /'wɪlfəl/ *adj* **1** continuing to do what you want, even after you have been told to stop – used to show disapproval: *a wilful child* **2** **wilful damage/disobedience/exaggeration** etc deliberate damage etc, when you know that what you are doing is wrong —**wilfully** *adv* —**wilfulness** *n* [U]

will¹ S1 W1 /wɪl/ *modal verb negative short form* **won't**
1 FUTURE used to make future tenses: *A meeting will be held next Tuesday at 3 p.m.* | *What time will she arrive?* | *I hope they won't be late.* | *Maybe by then you will have changed your mind.*
2 WILLING TO DO STH used to show that someone is willing or ready to do something: *Dr Weir will see you now.* | *The baby won't eat anything.*
3 REQUESTING *spoken* used to ask someone to do something: *Will you phone me later?* | *Shut the door, will you?*
4 WHAT GENERALLY HAPPENS used to say what always happens in a particular situation or what is generally true: *Oil will float on water.* | *Accidents will happen.*
5 POSSIBILITY used like 'can' to show what is possible: *This car will hold five people comfortably.*
6 BELIEF used to say that you think something is true: *That will be Tim coming home now.* | *As you will have noticed, there are some gaps in the data.*
7 GIVING ORDERS *spoken* used to give an order or to state a rule: *Will you be quiet!* | *You will do as I say.* | *Every employee will carry an identity card at all times.*
8 OFFERING/INVITING *spoken* used to offer something to someone or to invite them to do something: *Will you have some more tea?* | *Won't you have a seat?*
9 ANNOYING HABIT *spoken* used to describe someone's habits, especially when you think they are annoying: *Trish will keep asking damn silly questions.*

will² S2 W2 *n*
1 DETERMINATION [C,U] determination to do something that you have decided to do, even if this is difficult: *Children sometimes have strong wills.* | **the will to live/fight/succeed etc** *Even though she was in terrible pain, Mary never lost the will to live.* | *What is lacking is the political will to get anything done about global warming.* | **an iron will/a will of iron** (=very strong determination) | **a battle/clash/test etc of wills** (=when two people who both have strong wills oppose each other) → STRONG-WILLED, WEAK-WILLED
2 LEGAL DOCUMENT [C] a legal document that says who you want your money and property to be given to after you die: *Have you made a will yet?* | **in sb's will** *My grandfather left me some money in his will.* | *the senator's last will and testament*
3 WHAT SB WANTS [singular] what someone wants to happen in a particular situation: *He accused her of trying to impose her will on others.* | **against your will** *Collier claims the police forced him to sign a confession against his will.* | **[+of]** *the will of the people* | *obedience to God's will* → FREE WILL
4 **with the best will in the world** *BrE spoken* used to say that something is not possible, even if you very much want to do it: *With the best will in the world, I don't see what more I can do.*
5 **where there's a will there's a way** *spoken* used to say that if you really want to do something, you will find a way to succeed
6 **at will** whenever you want and in whatever way you want: *He can't just fire people at will, can he?*
7 **with a will** *written* in an eager and determined way → GOODWILL, ILL WILL

will³ *v* **1** [T] to try to make something happen by thinking about it very hard: **will sb to do sth** *She was willing herself not to cry.* **2** [T + to] to officially give

something that you own to someone else after you die **3** [I,T] *old use* to want something to happen: *The King wills it.*

will·ful /'wɪlfəl/ *adj* the American spelling of WILFUL

wil·lie /'wɪli/ *n informal* **1** **the willies** a nervous or frightened feeling: *All this talk about ghosts is giving me the willies.* **2** another spelling of WILLY

will·ing S2 W3 /'wɪlɪŋ/ *adj*
1 [not before noun] prepared to do something, or having no reason to not want to do it: **willing to do sth** *How much are they willing to pay?* | **quite/perfectly willing** *I told them I was perfectly willing to help.*
2 **willing helper/volunteer/partner etc** someone who is eager to help etc and does not have to be persuaded: *I soon had an army of willing helpers.* —**willingly** *adv*: *Sixty percent of voters said they would willingly pay higher taxes for better health care.* —**willingness** *n* [U]

will o' the 'wisp *n* [C usually singular] **1** someone that you can never completely depend on, or something that you can never achieve **2** a blue moving light caused by natural gases, that can be seen over wet ground at night

wil·low /'wɪləʊ $ -loʊ/ *n* [C,U] a type of tree that has long thin branches and grows near water, or the wood from this tree

wil·low·y /'wɪləʊi $ -loʊi/ *adj* tall, thin, and graceful: *She was pale and willowy, with violet eyes.*

will·pow·er /'wɪl,paʊə $ -,paʊr/ *n* [U] the ability to control your mind and body in order to achieve something that you want to do: *It took all his willpower to remain calm.*

wil·ly /'wɪli/ *n plural* **willies** [C] *BrE informal* a PENIS

willy-nil·ly /,wɪli 'nɪli/ *adv* **1** if something happens willy-nilly, it happens whether you want it to or not: *He found himself drawn, willy-nilly, into the argument.* **2** without planning, organization, or control: *Companies were accused of raising prices willy-nilly.*

wilt¹ /wɪlt/ *v* [I] **1** if a plant wilts, it bends over because it is too dry or old; → **droop** **2** *informal* to feel weak or tired, especially because you are too hot

wilt² *v old use* **thou wilt** you will

wil·y /'waɪli/ *adj* clever at getting what you want, especially by tricking people; = **cunning**: *a wily politician* —**wiliness** *n* [U]

wimp¹ /wɪmp/ *n* [C] *informal* **1** someone who has a weak character and is afraid to do something difficult or unpleasant: *Don't be such a wimp!* **2** a man who is thin and physically weak —**wimpish, wimpy** *adj*

wimp² *v*
wimp out *phr v spoken* to not do something that you intended to do, because you do not feel brave enough, strong enough etc; = **cop out**

wim·ple /'wɪmpəl/ *n* [C] a piece of cloth that a NUN wears over her head

win¹ S1 W1 /wɪn/ *v past tense and past participle* **won** /wʌn/, *present participle* **winning**
1 COMPETITION/RACE [I,T] to be the best or most successful in a competition, game, election etc; ≠ **lose**: **win a race/a game/an election etc** *Who do you think will win the next election?* | *He won the Tour de France last year.* | **win a war/battle** *the young pilots who won the Battle of Britain* | *Who's winning* (=who is most successful at this point in the game)? | **[+at]** *I never win at cards.* | **win by 10 points/70 metres etc** *We won by just one point.* | *He predicted the French would win hands down* (=win very easily) *in the play-offs.*
2 PRIZE [T] to get something as a prize for winning in a competition or game: *How does it feel to have won the gold medal?* | *She won £160 on the lottery.* | **win sth for sb** *the man who helped win the Cup for Manchester United*
3 GET/ACHIEVE [T] to get something that you want because of your efforts or abilities; ≠ **gain**: **win sb's approval/support/trust etc** *The proposal has won the*

approval of the city council. | Kramer has certainly won the respect of his peers. | **win sb's heart** (=make them love you or feel sympathy for you) | The company has **won a contract** to build a new power plant outside Houston. | **win sth from sb** Davis hopes to build financial backing from a London investment firm.

4 MAKE SB WIN STH [T] if something, usually something that you do, wins you something, you win it or get it because of that thing: **win sb sth** That performance won Hanks an Oscar. | That kind of behaviour won't win you any friends.

5 you win spoken used to agree to what someone wants after you have tried to persuade them to do something else: OK, you win – we'll go to the movies.

6 you can't win spoken used to say that there is no satisfactory way of dealing with a particular situation: You can't win, can you? You either work late and upset your family, or go home early and risk your job.

7 you can't win them all also **you win some, you lose some** spoken used to show sympathy when someone has had a disappointing experience

8 win or lose informal no matter whether you win or lose: Win or lose, I love competitive sports.

9 win (sth) hands down informal to win a game or competition or defeat someone very easily: If the election had been free and fair, the democratic candidate would have won hands down.

10 win the day to finally be successful in a discussion or argument; ▣ triumph: Common sense won the day, and the plans were dropped. → **win the toss** at toss² (1); → WINNER, WINNING

  win sb/sth ⇔ **back** phr v
to succeed in getting back something or someone that you had before: How can I win back her trust?

  win out phr v
to finally succeed or defeat other people or things: [+over] Often presentation wins out over content (=is treated as more important than content).

  win sb ⇔ **over** also **win sb** ⇔ **round** BrE phr v
to get someone's support or friendship by persuading them or being nice to them: We'll be working hard over the next ten days to win over the undecided voters.

  win through phr v especially BrE
to finally succeed in spite of problems: As in most of his films, it's the good guys who win through in the end.

win² W3 n [C] a success or victory, especially in sport: We've had two wins so far this season. | [+over] In the under-16 event England had their first win over Germany. → NO-WIN, WIN-WIN

wince /wɪns/ v [I] **1** to suddenly change the expression on your face as a reaction to something painful or upsetting: Sandra winced as the dentist started to drill. **2** to suddenly feel very uncomfortable or embarrassed because of something that happens, something you remember etc; ▣ cringe: **wince at the memory/thought/idea** I still wince at the thought of that terrible evening. —**wince** n [singular]

winch¹ /wɪntʃ/ n [C] a machine with a rope or chain for lifting heavy objects

winch² v [T always + adv/prep] to lift something or someone up using a winch: The two men were winched out of the sinking boat by an RAF helicopter.

wind¹ S2 W2 /wɪnd/ n
1 AIR [C,U] also **the wind** moving air, especially when it moves strongly or quickly in a current; → **windy**: The wind blew from the northeast. | A sudden **gust of wind** (=a short strong wind) blew the door shut. | **blowing/flapping/swaying etc in the wind** branches swaying in the wind | **strong/high winds** The forecast is for strong winds and heavy rain. | **gale/hurricane force winds** (=strong enough to cause a lot of damage) | a 70-mile-an-hour wind | The **light wind** ruffled the water. | **east/west/north/south wind** (=coming from the east etc) | a **cold/an icy/a chill/a biting etc wind** | the **wind picks/gets up** (=blows more strongly) The wind was getting up and it was becoming cloudy. | We'll wait till **the wind drops** (=blows less strongly) before we put

the tent up. | the side of the building most exposed to **prevailing winds** (=the winds blowing over a particular area most of the time) | a machine measuring **wind speed** → CROSSWIND, DOWNWIND, HEADWIND, TAILWIND, TRADE WIND, UPWIND

2 get/have wind of sth informal to hear or find out about something secret or private: You better hope the press doesn't get wind of this.

3 BREATH [U] your ability to breathe normally: **get your wind (back)** (=be able to breathe normally again, for example after running) | **knock the wind out of sb** (=hit someone in the stomach so that they cannot breathe for a moment); → second wind at SECOND¹ (12); → WINDPIPE

4 IN YOUR STOMACH [U] BrE the condition of having air or gas in your stomach or INTESTINES, or the air or gas itself; ▣ gas AmE: I can't drink beer – it gives me wind. | 'What's wrong with the baby?' 'Just a little wind.'

5 take the wind out of sb's sails informal to make someone lose their confidence, especially by saying or doing something unexpected

6 see which way the wind is blowing to find out what the situation is before you do something or make a decision

7 sth is in the wind used to say that something is happening or going to happen, but the details are not clear: If there was a merger in the wind, I'm sure we'd hear about it.

8 winds of change/freedom/public opinion etc used to refer to things that have important effects, and that cannot be stopped: The **winds** of change are **blowing** through the entire organization.

9 put the wind up sb/get the wind up BrE informal if you put the wind up someone, you make them feel anxious or frightened. If you get the wind up, you become anxious or frightened: The threat of legal action will be enough to put the wind up them.

10 MUSIC the winds/the wind section the people in an ORCHESTRA or band who play musical instruments that you blow through, such as a FLUTE

11 like the wind if someone or something moves or runs like the wind, they move or run very quickly: She ran like the wind down the stairs to escape.

12 TALK [U] BrE informal talk that does not mean anything → break wind at BREAK¹ (31); → it's an ill wind (that blows nobody any good) at ILL¹ (4); → sail close to the wind at SAIL¹ (6); → straw in the wind at STRAW (5)

wind² /waɪnd/ v past tense and past participle **wound** /waʊnd/ **1** [T always + adv/prep] to turn or twist something several times around something else: **wind sth around/round sth** The hair is divided into sections and wound around heated rods. **2** [T] also **wind up** to turn part of a machine around several times, in order to make it move or start working: Did you remember to wind the clock? **3** [I always + adv/prep] if a road, river etc winds somewhere, it has many smooth bends and is usually very long: **wind (its way) through/along etc sth** Highway 99 winds its way along the coast. | a **winding path** **4** [T] to make a tape move in a machine: **wind sth forward/back** Can you wind the video back a little way – I want to see that bit again. ⚠ Do not confuse with the noun **wind**, which has a different pronunciation. → REWIND —**wind** n [C]

  wind down phr v **1** wind sth ⇔ down to gradually reduce the work of a business or organization so that it can be closed down completely **2** to rest and relax after a lot of hard work or excitement: I find it difficult to wind down after a day at work. **3** wind sth ⇔ down BrE to make something, especially a car window, move down by turning a handle or pressing a button

  wind up phr v **1** to bring an activity, meeting etc to an end: OK, just to wind up, could I summarize what we've decided? | wind sth ⇔ up It's time to **wind things up** - I have a plane to catch. **2** wind sth ⇔ up to close down a company or organization: Our operations in

W

Jamaica are being wound up. **3** [linking verb] *informal* to be in an unpleasant situation or place after a lot has happened; ▣ **end up**: [+in/at/with etc] *You know you're going to wind up in court over this.* | **wind up doing sth** *I wound up wishing I'd never come.* **4 wind sb ⇔ up** *BrE* to deliberately say or do something that will annoy or worry someone, as a joke; → **tease**: *They're only winding you up.* → **WOUND UP 5 wind sth ⇔ up** to turn part of a machine around several times, in order to make it move or start working **6 wind sth ⇔ up** *BrE* to make something, especially a car window, move up by turning a handle or pressing a button: *Could you wind the window up, please?*

wind³ /wɪnd/ *v past tense and past participle* **winded** [T] to make someone have difficulty breathing, as a result of falling on something or being hit: *The fall winded him and he lay still for a moment.*

wind·bag /'wɪndbæg/ *n* [C] *informal* someone who talks too much; ▣ **gasbag** *BrE*

wind·break /'wɪndbreɪk/ *n* [C] a fence, line of trees, or wall that is intended to protect a place from the wind

wind break·er /'wɪnd ˌbreɪkə $ -ər/ *AmE*; **windcheater** /'wɪnd,tʃiːtə $ -ər/ *BrE n* [C] a type of coat that protects you from the wind

wind chill /'wɪnd tʃɪl/ *n* [U] *technical* the cooling effect of the wind: *It must have been minus 5 with the wind chill factor.*

wind chimes /'wɪnd tʃaɪmz/ *n* [plural] long thin pieces of metal, wood etc hanging together in a group, that make musical sounds when the wind blows them against each other

wind·ed /'wɪndɪd/ , *adj* unable to breathe easily, because you have been running or you have been hit in the stomach

wind·fall /'wɪndfɔːl $ -fɒːl/ *n* [C] **1** an amount of money that you get unexpectedly: *his £2 million windfall in the lottery* | **windfall gain/profit etc** (=high profits that you did not expect to make) **2** a piece of fruit that has fallen off a tree

windfall ,tax *n* [C] an additional amount of tax that the British government sometimes takes from a company that has suddenly earned a large amount of money that it did not expect to earn

wind farm /'wɪnd fɑːm $ -fɑːrm/ *n* [C] a place where a lot of WINDMILLS have been built in order to produce electricity

winding sheet /'waɪndɪŋ ʃiːt/ *n* [C] a cloth that is wrapped around a dead person's body before it is buried, used especially in the past; ▣ **shroud**

wind in·stru·ment /'wɪnd ˌɪnstrʊmənt/ *n* [C] a musical instrument made of wood or metal that you play by blowing, such as a FLUTE, or one that air is passed through, such as an ORGAN; → **brass**, **percussion**, **stringed instrument** → **the winds/the wind section** at WIND¹ (10); → **WOODWIND**

wind·jam·mer /'wɪnd,dʒæmə $ -ər/ *n* [C] a large sailing ship of the type that was used for trade in the 19th century

wind·lass /'wɪndləs/ *n* [C] a machine for pulling or lifting heavy objects

wind·mill /'wɪnd,mɪl/ *n* [C] **1** a building or structure with parts that turn around in the wind, used for producing electrical power or crushing grain **2** *BrE* a toy consisting of a stick with curved pieces of plastic at the end that turn around when they are blown; ▣ **pinwheel** *AmE*

win·dow S1 W1 /'wɪndəʊ $ -doʊ/ *n* [C]
1 a space or an area of glass in the wall of a building or vehicle that lets in light: **open/close/shut a window** *Do you mind if I open the window?* | **out of/from/through the window** *She looked out of the window to see if it was raining.* | *The sun was shining through the windows.* | **in the window** (=just inside a window) *We were looking*

window
bay window
shutters
window pane
window seat
window box
windowsill

*at the Christmas displays in the **shop windows**.* | **bedroom/kitchen etc window** → BAY WINDOW, DORMER WINDOW, FRENCH WINDOWS, PICTURE WINDOW, SASH WINDOW
2 one of the separate areas on a computer screen where different programs are operating
3 also **window of opportunity** a short period of time that is available for a particular activity: *Delay might open a window of opportunity for their rivals.*
4 an area on an envelope with clear plastic in it which lets you see the address written on the letter inside the envelope
5 a window on/to the world something that makes it possible to see and learn about what is happening in other parts of the world: *Television provides us with a useful window on the world.*
6 go out (of) the window *informal* to disappear completely or no longer have any effect: *One glass of wine, and all my good intentions went out the window.*

window box *n* [C] a long narrow box in which you can grow plants outside your window → see picture at WINDOW

window ,cleaner *n* [C] someone whose job is to clean windows

window ,dresser *n* [C] someone whose job is to arrange goods attractively in shop windows

window ,dressing *n* [U] **1** something that is intended to make people like your plans or activities, and to stop them seeing the true situation – used to show disapproval: *All these glossy pamphlets are just window dressing – the fact is that the new mall will ruin the neighborhood.* **2** the art of arranging goods in a shop window so that they look attractive to customers

win·dow·less /'wɪndəʊləs $ -doʊ-/ *adj* without any windows: *a windowless basement room*

win·dow·pane /'wɪndəʊpeɪn $ -doʊ-/ *n* [C] a single whole piece of glass in a window → see picture at WINDOW

window ,seat *n* [C] **1** a seat next to the window on a bus, plane etc **2** a seat directly below a window

window ,shade *n* [C] *AmE* a BLIND³ (1)

window-,shopping *n* [U] the activity of looking at goods in shop windows without intending to buy them —**window-shopper** *n* [C]

win·dow·sill /'wɪndəʊ,sɪl $ -doʊ-/ also **window ,ledge** *n* [C] a shelf fixed along the bottom of a window → see picture at WINDOW

wind·pipe /'wɪndpaɪp/ *n* [C] the tube through which air passes from your mouth to your lungs

wind·screen /'wɪndskriːn/ *n* [C] *BrE* the large window at the front of a car, bus etc; ▣ **windshield** *AmE*; → see picture at CAR

windscreen ,wiper *n* [C] *BrE* a long thin piece of metal with a rubber edge that moves across a windscreen to remove rain; ▣ **windshield wiper** *AmE*; → see picture at CAR

wind·shield /'wɪndʃiːld/ *n* [C] **1** *AmE* a windscreen → see picture at CAR **2** a piece of glass or clear plastic fixed at the front of a MOTORCYCLE that protects the rider from wind

windshield ,wiper *n* [C] *AmE* a windscreen wiper → see picture at CAR

wind·sock /'wɪndsɒk $ -sɑːk/ n [C] a tube of material fastened to a pole at airports to show the direction of the wind

wind·storm /'wɪndstɔːm $ -stɔːrm/ n [C] a period of bad weather with strong winds but not much rain

wind-surf·ing /'wɪnd ˌsɜːfɪŋ $ -ˌsɜːr-/ n [U] the sport of sailing across water by standing on a SURFBOARD and holding on to a large sail attached to the surfboard —**wind-surfer** n [C] —**wind-surf** v [I] → see picture at WATER SPORTS

wind·swept /'wɪndswept/ adj **1** a place that is windswept is often windy because there are not many trees or buildings to protect it: *windswept moors* **2** hair, clothes etc that are windswept have been blown around by the wind

wind tun·nel /'wɪnd ˌtʌnl/ n [C] a large enclosed passage where engineers test aircraft etc by forcing air past them

wind tur·bine /'wɪnd ˌtɜːbaɪn $ -ˌtɜːrbn, -baɪn/ n [C] a modern WINDMILL for providing electrical power → see picture at ENERGY; → see picture at ENVIRONMENT

wind-up¹ *BrE*; **wind·up** *AmE* /'waɪnd ʌp/ n **1** [C] *BrE informal* something that you say or do in order to make someone angry or worried, as a joke **2** [singular] a series of actions that are intended to complete a process, meeting etc: *The President made a statement at the windup of the summit in Helsinki.*

wind-up² /'waɪnd ʌp/ adj [only before noun] relating to a machine or toy that you turn part of several times, in order to make it move or start working: *a wind-up gramophone*

wind·ward /'wɪndwəd $ -wərd/ adj, adv towards the direction from which the wind is blowing; 🔲 leeward: *the windward side of the boat*

wind·y S3 /'wɪndi/ *comparative* **windier**, *superlative* **windiest** adj **1** if it is windy, there is a lot of wind: *It's too windy for a picnic.* | *a cold, windy day* | *a windy hillside* **2** windy talk is full of words that sound impressive but do not mean much: *politicians' windy generalizations*

wine¹ S2 W2 /waɪn/ n [C,U] **1** an alcoholic drink made from GRAPES, or a type of this drink: *a glass of wine* | *a delicious Californian wine* | **red/white wine** *a bottle of red wine* | **dry/sweet/sparkling wine** *a dry white wine*; → see picture at GLASS¹ **2** an alcoholic drink made from another fruit or plant

wine² v **wine and dine sb** to entertain someone well with a meal, wine etc: *Companies spend millions wining and dining clients.*

'wine bar n [C] a place that serves mainly wine and light meals

'wine ˌcellar n [C] an underground room where wine is stored to keep it at the right temperature

'wine ˌcooler n [C] *AmE* a drink made with wine, fruit juice, and water

'wine glass n [C] a tall glass with a thin stem, used for drinking wine

win·e·ry /'waɪnəri/ n plural **wineries** [C] a place where wine is made and stored; → vineyard

'wine ˌtasting n [C,U] the activity or skill of tasting and comparing different wines to see if they are good, or an event where this happens

'wine ˌvinegar n [U] a type of VINEGAR made from sour wine, used in cooking

wing¹ S2 W2 /wɪŋ/ n [C] **1** BIRD/INSECT **a)** one of the parts of a bird's or insect's body that it uses for flying: *a butterfly with beautiful markings on its wings* | *The pheasant flapped its wings vigorously.* **b)** the meat on the wing bone of a chicken, duck etc, eaten as food: *spicy chicken wings* → see picture at INSECT **2** PLANE one of the large flat parts that stick out from the side of a plane and help to keep it in the air **3** BUILDING one of the parts of a large building, especially one that sticks out from the main part:

north/east etc wing *the east wing of the palace* | *She works in the hospital's maternity wing.* **4** POLITICS a group of people within a political party or other organization who have a particular opinion or aim: *the moderate wing of the Republican Party* → LEFT-WING, RIGHT-WING **5** SPORT **a)** a WINGER **b)** the far left or right part of a sports field **6** CAR *BrE* the part of a car that is above a wheel; 🔲 fender *AmE*; → see picture at CAR **7** take sb under your wing to help and protect someone who is younger or less experienced than you are **8** (waiting/lurking) in the wings ready to do something or be used when the time is right: *Several junior managers are waiting in the wings for promotion.* **9** THEATRE the wings [plural] the parts at either side of a stage where actors are hidden from people who are watching the play **10** on a wing and a prayer if you do something on a wing and a prayer, you do not have much chance of succeeding **11** be on the wing *literary* if a bird is on the wing, it is flying **12** take wing *literary* to fly away **13** get your wings to pass the examinations you need to become a pilot → clip sb's wings at CLIP² (6); → spread your wings at SPREAD¹ (10)

wing² v **1** [I always + adv/prep] *literary* to fly somewhere: *a flock of geese winging down the coast* | **wing its/their way to/across etc sth** *planes winging their way to exotic destinations* **2** **wing its/their way** to go or be sent somewhere very quickly: [+to] *A bottle of champagne will soon be winging its way to 10 lucky winners.* **3** **wing it** *spoken* to do something without planning or preparing it: *We'll just have to wing it.*

'wing chair n [C] a comfortable chair with a high back and pieces pointing forward on each side where you can rest your head

ˌwing 'collar n [C] a type of shirt collar for men that is worn with very formal clothes

'wing comˌmander n an officer of high rank in the British air force

winge /wɪndʒ/ v another spelling of WHINGE

winged /wɪŋd/ adj having wings: *winged insects*

wing·er /'wɪŋə $ -ər/ also **wing** n [C] someone who plays in the far left or far right of the field in games such as football

'wing ˌmirror n [C] *BrE* a mirror on the side of a car → see picture at CAR

'wing nut n [C] a NUT for fastening things, which has sides that stick out to make it easier to turn

wing·span /'wɪŋspæn/ n [C] the distance from the end of one wing to the end of the other

wing·tip /'wɪŋtɪp/ n [C] **1** the point at the end of a bird's or a plane's wing **2** *AmE* a type of man's shoe with a pattern of small holes on the toe

wink¹ /wɪŋk/ v **1** [I,T] to close and open one eye quickly to communicate something or show that something is a secret or joke: [+at] *He winked mischievously at Erica.* | *He winked an eye at his companion.* **2** [I] to shine with a light that flashes on and off; 🔲 blink: *a Christmas tree with lights winking on and off*

wink at sth *phr v* to pretend not to notice something bad or illegal, in a way that suggests you approve of it

wink² n **1** [C] a quick action of opening and closing one eye, usually as a signal to someone else: *He gave her a wink.* | *'You look tired,' he said with a knowing wink.* **2** **not get a wink of sleep/not sleep a wink** not be able to sleep at all: *I didn't get a wink of sleep last night.* → FORTY WINKS; → a nod's as good as a wink at NOD² (4); → tip sb the wink at TIP² (11)

win·kle¹ /'wɪŋkəl/ n [C] *BrE* a small sea animal that lives in a shell and is eaten as food

winkle² *v*
winkle sb/sth ⇔ **out** *phr v BrE* **1** to make someone leave a place: *Government critics were winkled out of their positions of influence.* **2** to get information from someone who does not want to give it to you: *Candy was very good at winkling out secrets.*

win·ner S3 W2 /'wɪnə $ -ər/ *n*
1 [C] a person or animal that has won something: [+of] *the winner of the Ladies' Championship* | *Five **lucky** winners will each receive a signed copy of the album.* | *As a jockey he rode 10 winners.* | **prize/award/medal etc winner** *a Nobel prize winner*
2 [C] *informal* someone or something that is or is likely to be very popular and successful: *The book has proved to **be a winner with** young children.* | *The company seems to **be onto a winner** (=doing something that is likely to be successful).*
3 [singular] a GOAL or point that makes someone win a game such as football or tennis: *Moran **scored the winner** with only two minutes left.*
4 [C usually plural] the person who gets most of the advantages from a situation: *In a capitalist society there will always be **winners and losers**.* | *The real winners this summer have been the suncream manufacturers.*

win·ning /'wɪnɪŋ/ *adj* [only before noun] **1** the winning person or thing is the one that wins or makes you win a competition or game: *the winning team* | *The winning design came from an architect in Glasgow.* | *Beckham scored the winning goal.* **2** making you very successful or likely to be successful: *a winning combination* | *As a business, they have found a winning formula.* **3** a winning quality or way of doing something is one that makes other people like you; ▤ **attractive**: *a winning smile* **4** a **winning streak** a period of time when you win every game or competition: *The team **are on a winning streak**.*

winning ,post *n* [singular] *BrE* the place where a race ends; ▤ **the finish line**

win·nings /'wɪnɪŋz/ *n* [plural] money that you have won: *lottery winnings*

win·now /'wɪnəʊ $ -noʊ/ also **winnow down** *v* [T] to make a list, group, or quantity smaller by getting rid of the things that you do not need or want; ▤ **whittle down**: *We need to winnow the list of candidates to three.*
winnow sb/sth ⇔ **out** *phr v* to get rid of the things or people that you do not need or want from a group

wi·no /'waɪnəʊ $ -noʊ/ *n plural* **winos** [C] *informal* someone who drinks a lot of alcohol and lives on the streets

win·some /'wɪnsəm/ *adj literary* behaving in a pleasant and attractive way: *a winsome smile*

win·ter¹ S2 W2 /'wɪntə $ -ər/ *n* [C,U] the season after autumn and before spring, when the weather is coldest; → **summer**: *the cold Canadian winters* | *the dark winter months* | **in (the) winter** | *It usually snows here **in the winter**.* | **this/last/next winter** *Fuel supplies could be seriously disrupted this winter.* | **mild/severe/hard etc winter** *the severe winter of 1951* | **winter coat/shoes etc** (=designed for cold weather)

winter² *v* [I always + adv/prep] *formal* to spend the winter somewhere: *Last year, over 11,000 Canadians wintered in Arizona.*

winter 'solstice *n* **the winter solstice** the shortest day of the year in the northern HEMISPHERE, usually around December 22nd; → **summer solstice**

winter 'sports *n* [plural] sports that are done on snow or ice, such as SKIING

win·ter·time /'wɪntətaɪm $ -ər-/ *n* [U] the time when it is winter; → **summertime**: **in (the) wintertime** *The hills look very bleak in wintertime.*

win·try /'wɪntri/ also **win·ter·y** /'wɪntəri/ *adj* **1** cold or typical of winter; → **summery**: *a wintry day* | *wintry showers* **2** a wintry smile or expression is not very friendly

---

winter sports
skiing | ice dancing
snowboarding | ski jumping
bobsleigh | speed skating

win-'win *adj* [only before noun] a win-win situation, solution etc is one that will end well for everyone involved in it; → **no-win situation**: *It's **a win-win situation** all around.* —**win-win** *n* [C]: *The agreement is a win-win for everyone.*

wipe¹ S3 /waɪp/ *v*
1 CLEAN/RUB [T] **a)** to rub a surface with something in order to remove dirt, liquid etc: **wipe sth with sth** *Wipe the table with a damp cloth.* | *Bill **wiped** his **eyes** (=wiped the tears from his face) and apologized.* | *He pulled a handkerchief from his pocket and **wiped** his **nose**.* **b)** to clean something by rubbing it against a surface: **wipe sth on sth** *He wiped his mouth on the back of his hand.* → see picture at CLEAN¹
2 REMOVE DIRT [T always + adv/prep] to remove liquid, dirt, or marks by wiping: **wipe sth off/from etc sth** *Kim wiped the sweat from her face.*
3 COMPUTER/TAPE [T] to remove all the information that is stored on a tape, video, or computer DISK
4 wipe sth from your mind/memory to try to forget an unpleasant experience
5 wipe the floor with sb *informal* to defeat someone completely in a competition or argument
6 wipe the slate clean to agree to forget about mistakes or arguments that happened in the past
7 wipe the smile/grin off sb's face *informal* to make someone feel less happy or confident, especially someone who is annoying because they think they are clever: *Tell him how much it'll cost – that should wipe the smile off his face!*
8 wipe sth off the face of the earth/wipe sth off the map to destroy something completely: *Another few years and this species could be wiped off the face of the earth.*
9 PLATES/CUPS ETC [I,T] to dry plates, cups etc that have been washed; ▤ **dry**: *You wash, I'll wipe.*
wipe sth ⇔ **away** *phr v*
to stop something existing: *A frown quickly wiped away her smile.*
wipe sth ⇔ **down** *phr v*
to completely clean a surface using a wet cloth
wipe sth **off** sth *phr v BrE*
to reduce the value of SHARES or prices by a particular amount: *Nearly £7 billion has been wiped off share prices worldwide.*

wipe out *phr v*
1 wipe sb/sth ⇔ out to destroy, remove, or get rid of something completely: *Whole villages were wiped out by the floods.* | *Nothing could wipe out his bitter memories of the past.*
2 wipe sb ⇔ out *informal* to make you feel extremely tired: *The heat had wiped us out.* → WIPED OUT
3 *AmE* to fall or hit another object when driving a car, riding a bicycle etc
  wipe sth ⇔ **up** *phr v*
to remove liquid from a surface using a cloth: *I hastily wiped up the milk I had spilled.* → see picture at CLEAN

wipe² *n* [C] **1** a wiping movement with a cloth: *An occasional wipe with a soft cloth will keep the surface shiny.* | *Give the baby's nose a wipe, would you?* **2** a special piece of wet material that you use to clean someone or something and then throw away: *a pack of baby wipes*

wiped 'out *adj* [not before noun] *informal* extremely tired; ⊟ **exhausted**

wip·er /'waɪpə $ -ər/ *n* [C] a piece of equipment on a car, that removes rain from the WINDSCREEN

wire¹ S3 W3 /waɪə $ waɪr/ *n*
1 [C,U] thin metal in the form of a thread, or a piece of this: *copper wire* | *a wire fence* → BARBED WIRE, HIGH WIRE, TRIPWIRE
2 [C] a piece of metal like this, used for carrying electrical currents or signals: *a telephone wire*
3 get your wires crossed to become confused about what someone is saying because you think they are talking about something else
4 go/come/be down to the wire *informal especially AmE* to be finished or achieved with very little time left: *The game was very close and went right down to the wire.*
5 [C] *AmE* a piece of electronic recording equipment, usually worn secretly on someone's clothes
6 [C] *AmE* a TELEGRAM → WIRY

wire² *v* [T] **1** also **wire up a)** to connect wires inside a building or piece of equipment so that electricity can pass through: *Check that the plug has been wired up properly.* **b)** to connect electrical equipment to the electrical system using wires: **wire sth to sth** *The CD player had been wired up to the car's cigarette lighter.* **2** to send money electronically **3** to attach a piece of recording equipment to a person or room, especially secretly **4 be wired for sth** to have all the necessary wires and connections for an electrical system to work: *All the rooms have been wired for cable TV.* **5** *AmE* to send a TELEGRAM to someone **6** to fasten two or more things together using wire: **wire sth together** *The poles had all been wired together.* → WIRING

wire ,cutters *n* [plural] a tool used for cutting wire

wired /waɪəd $ waɪrd/ *adj* **1** *AmE informal* feeling very active and excited, especially because you have drunk a lot of coffee or taken a drug; → **high** **2** *informal* connected to, and able to use the Internet; → **link**, **linkup** **3** wired glass, cloth etc has wire in it to make it strong or stiff: *wired ribbon*

wire·less /'waɪələs $ 'waɪr-/ *n BrE old-fashioned* **1** [C] a radio **2** [U] a system of sending messages by radio

,wireless communi'cations *n* [plural] a system of sending and receiving electronic signals that does not use electrical or telephone wires, for example the system used by MOBILE PHONES

,wire 'netting *BrE*; **,wire 'mesh** *AmE n* [U] wires that have been woven together to form a net, used especially for fences

wire·tap·ping /'waɪətæpɪŋ $ 'waɪr-/ *n* [U] the action of secretly listening to other people's telephone conversations, by connecting something to the wires of their telephone —**wiretap** *n* [C] —**wiretap** *v* [T]

,wire 'wool *n* [U] *BrE* a mass of very thin pieces of wire, used for cleaning pans

wir·ing /'waɪərɪŋ $ 'waɪr-/ *n* [U] the network of wires that form the electrical system in a building, vehicle, or piece of equipment: *The wiring needs to be replaced.*

wir·y /'waɪəri $ 'waɪri/ *adj* **1** someone who is wiry is thin but has strong muscles **2** wiry hair or grass is stiff and strong

wis·dom /'wɪzdəm/ *n* [U] **1** good sense and judgment, based especially on your experience of life: *a man of great wisdom* | **question/doubt the wisdom of (doing) sth** *Local people are questioning the wisdom of spending so much money on a new road.* | *You can always expect a few words of wisdom from Dave.* → **pearls of wisdom** at PEARL (3) **2** knowledge gained over a long period of time through learning or experience: *the collected wisdom of many centuries* **3 (the)** conventional/received/traditional etc wisdom a belief or opinion that most people have: *The conventional wisdom is that boys mature more slowly than girls.* **4 in sb's (infinite) wisdom** *humorous* used to say that you do not understand why someone has decided to do something: *The boss, in her infinite wisdom, has decided to reorganize the whole office yet again.*

'wisdom tooth *n* [C] one of the four large teeth at the back of your mouth that do not grow until you are an adult

wise¹ S3 /waɪz/ *adj*
1 DECISION/IDEA ETC wise decisions and actions are sensible and based on good judgment; ⊟ **sensible**: it is wise to do sth *It's wise to check whether the flight times have changed before you leave for the airport.* | **be wise to do sth** *I think you were wise to leave when you did.* | *a wise precaution* | *I don't think that would be a very wise move* (=not be a sensible thing to do).
2 PERSON someone who is wise makes good decisions, gives good advice etc, especially because they have a lot of experience of life: *a wise old man* | *At the time I thought he was wonderful, but I'm older and wiser now.* | *As a manager, Sanford was wise in the ways of* (=knew a lot about) *company politics.*
3 be none the wiser/not be any the wiser a) to not understand something even after it has been explained to you: *Charlie explained how the system works, but I'm still none the wiser.* **b)** used for saying that no one will find out about something bad that someone has done: *He could easily have taken the money and no one would have been any the wiser.*
4 get/be wise to sb/sth *informal* to realize that someone is being dishonest: *Teachers quickly get wise to students who are cheating.* → **wise up** at WISE²
5 wise guy *informal especially AmE* an annoying person who thinks they know more than they really do: *OK, wise guy, shut up and listen!*
6 be wise after the event to realize what you should have done in a situation after it has happened: *It's easy to be wise after the event.* —**wisely** *adv*: *Invest the money wisely.* | *He nodded wisely.* → WISDOM; → **sadder but wiser** at SAD (6)

wise² *v*
  wise up *phr v informal* to realize the truth about a bad situation: *Wise up, Vic – he's cheating you!* | [+to] *Consumers need to wise up to the effect that advertising has on them.*

wise³, -wise /waɪz/ *suffix* **1** price-wise/time-wise etc *informal* used for saying which feature of a situation you are referring to: *Time-wise we're not doing too badly.* **2 crosswise/lengthwise etc** in a direction across something, along the length of something etc: *Cut the carrots lengthwise.* → CLOCKWISE, STREETWISE

wise·crack /'waɪzkræk/ *n* [C] a clever and funny remark or reply; ⊟ **joke** —**wisecrack** *v* [I]

wish¹ S1 W1 /wɪʃ/ *v*
1 [I,T] *formal* if you wish to do something or you wish to have it done for you, you want to do it or want to have it done; ⊟ **like**: **wish to do sth** *I wish to make a complaint.* | *If you wish to discuss this matter further please do not hesitate to contact me.* | *You may leave now, if you wish.* | **(just) as you wish** (=used in formal situations to tell someone you will do what they want)

W

1 000, 2 000, 3 000, most frequent words in S poken and W ritten English

'I'd like it to be ready by six.' 'Just as you wish, sir.' | *The cook will prepare whatever you wish.*

2 [T] to want something to be true although you know it is either impossible or unlikely; → **if only: wish (that)** *I wish I didn't have to go to work today.* | *I wish that I could afford a new car.* | *He wished Emily were with him.* | *Sometimes I wish I had never been born.*

3 [T] to say that you hope someone will have good luck, a happy life etc: **wish sb sth** *We wish you a Merry Christmas and a Happy New Year!* | *We wish them every happiness in their new home.* | *He shook my hand and wished me luck.* | **wish sb well** (=say that you hope that good things will happen to someone) *My friends wished me well in my new job.*

4 I couldn't wish for a nicer/better etc ... also **the nicest/best etc ... I could wish for** used to emphasize that you are very happy with what you have and cannot imagine anyone or anything better: *I couldn't wish for a better husband.* | *It's the best birthday present I could have wished for.*

5 I wish (that) sb would do sth *spoken* used to say that you find someone's behaviour annoying and want them to change: *I wish you'd stop treating me like a child!*

6 [I] **a)** to want something to happen or to want to have something, especially when it seems unlikely or impossible; → **long for:** [+for] *It was no use wishing for the impossible.* | *She was like the sister I never had but always wished for.* **b)** to silently ask for something you want and hope that it will happen by magic or good luck – used especially in children's stories: [+for] *One day she found a magic ring that brought her whatever she wished for.*

7 I wish! *spoken* used to say that something is not true, but you wish it was: *'I think he really likes you.' 'I wish!'*

8 you wish! *spoken* used to tell someone that what they want to happen or be true will definitely not happen or become true: *'I'm going to be famous one day.' 'You wish!'*

9 wouldn't wish sth on/upon sb *spoken* used to say that something is very unpleasant and that you would not like anyone to have to experience it: *Having your house broken into is terrible. I wouldn't wish it on anybody.*

10 I don't wish to interfere/be nosy etc *BrE spoken formal* used to show you are sorry if what you are going to say upsets or annoys someone: *I don't wish to seem ungrateful, but it's not quite what I expected.*

11 I (only) wish I knew *BrE spoken* used to emphasize that you do not know something, and you wish you did know: *'Where on earth have they gone?' 'I wish I knew!'*

wish sth ⇔ **away** *phr v*

1 to make something unpleasant disappear by wanting it to disappear, without doing anything about it: *You can't just wish your problems away, you know!*

2 wish your life away to always be thinking about the future, so that you do not do or enjoy things now – used to show disapproval: *Don't wish your life away.*

WORD CHOICE: wish, hope, want, would like
Use **wish** to talk about things that are not true, not possible, or very unlikely: *I wish I knew more about science.* | *She wished she hadn't said anything.* | *I wish I could win the lottery.*

Use **hope** to talk about things that could happen, could have happened, or could be true: *I hope you have a happy birthday.* | *I hope they got there in time.*

⚠ Do not use **wish** + (that) to say that you want something to happen in the future. Use **hope**: *I hope (NOT wish) that we'll all meet again soon.* | *I hope you have a great time.*

You can use **wish** + noun in polite expressions meaning that you want someone to have something: *We wish you a safe journey.* | *I wish you lots of luck.*

⚠ **Wish to** is very formal. Use **want to** or **would like to** to say what you want to happen: *I want to write to him but I don't know his address.* | *I would like to run my own restaurant.*

GRAMMAR: tenses with 'wish'
Things that you want to happen in the present or future
Use **wish** + past tense or **wish** + would: *I wish I didn't have to go.* | *I wish they would stop arguing.*
You can use **that** or leave it out: *I wish that he would help more.*
⚠ In British English, you can either say 'I wish I was' or 'I wish I were', which is rather formal. In American English, you should use **were**: *I wish I were ten years younger.*
Things that you want to have happened in the past
Use **wish** + past perfect tense: *I wish I had paid more attention in class.*

wish² [S3] *n* [C]

1 a desire to do something, to have something, or to have something happen: [+of] *It's important to respect the wishes of the patient.* | *politicians who ignore the public's wishes* | **wish to do sth** *Despite her wish to continue working, she was forced to retire at the age of 62.* | *She had expressed a wish to see the children.* | *Jenny's always wanted to live in the country. Now she's finally got her wish* (=she has got what she wanted). | **sb's wish is granted/fulfilled** (=someone gets what they want) | **sb's wish comes true** (=someone gets what they want, especially in a surprising or unexpected way) | **sb's last/dying wish** (=something that someone says they want just before they die) *His last wish was that he should be buried back home in California.* | **sb's greatest wish** also **sb's dearest wish** *BrE* (=what you want most of all) *His dearest wish was to become a father.* → DEATH WISH

2 against sb's wishes if you do something against someone's wishes, you do it even though you know they do not want you to: *She'd left school against her mother's wishes.* | **go against sb's wishes** (=do something against their wishes)

3 best/good/warmest etc wishes used, especially in cards and letters, to say that you hope someone will be happy, successful, or healthy: [+for] *Best wishes for a long and happy retirement!* | *She asked me to pass on her good wishes to all her friends and colleagues.* | **(With) best wishes** (=used at the end of a letter before you sign your name) *With best wishes, Celia.*

4 have no wish to do sth *formal* used to emphasize that you do not want or intend to do something: *I have no wish to speak to her ever again.*

5 a silent request for something to happen as if by magic: *Close your eyes and make a wish.*

6 your wish is my command used humorously to say that you will do whatever someone asks you to do

wish·bone /'wɪʃbəʊn $ -boʊn/ *n* [C] the V-shaped bone from a cooked chicken, duck etc, which two people pull apart to decide who will make a wish

wishful 'thinking *n* [U] when you believe that what you want to happen will happen, when in fact it is not possible: *I think she rather likes me. But maybe that's just wishful thinking.*

'wishing well *n* [C] a WELL or pool of water that people throw coins into while making a wish

'wish list *n* [C] *informal* all the things that you would like to have or would like to happen in a particular situation: **on sb's wish list** *Another player on Coach Beane's wish list is center fielder Jeffrey Hammonds.*

wish·y-wash·y /'wɪʃi ˌwɒʃi $ -ˌwɔːʃi, -ˌwɑːʃi/ *adj informal* **1** someone who is wishy-washy does not have firm or clear ideas and seems unable to decide what they want – used to show disapproval: *a bunch of wishy-washy liberals* **2** colours that are wishy-washy are pale and unexciting, not strong or dark – used to show disapproval

wisp /wɪsp/ *n* [C] **1** a wisp of hair, grass, HAY etc is a thin piece of it that is separate from the rest: [+of] *A wisp of hair had escaped from under her hat.* **2** a wisp of smoke, cloud, mist etc is a small thin line of it that rises upwards: [+**of**] *Wisps of smoke rose into the air.* → WILL O' THE WISP —**wispy** *adj*

wis·te·ri·a /wɪˈstɪəriə $ -ˈstɪr-/ *n* [C,U] a climbing plant with purple or white flowers

wist·ful /ˈwɪstfəl/ *adj* thinking sadly about something you would like to have but cannot have, especially something that you used to have in the past: *a wistful smile* —**wistfully** *adv*: *'That's the house where I was born,' she said wistfully.* —**wistfulness** *n* [U]

wit /wɪt/ *n*
1 AMUSING [U] the ability to say things that are clever and amusing: *a woman of great wit and charm* | **quick/dry/sharp etc wit** *His sharp wit had them all smiling.*
2 AMUSING PERSON [C] someone who is able to say clever and amusing things
3 wits [plural] your ability to think quickly and make the right decisions: *Alone and penniless, I was forced to live on my wits.* | **keep/have your wits about you** (=be ready to think quickly and do what is necessary in a difficult situation)
4 **frighten/scare/terrify sb out of their wits** *informal* to frighten someone very much: *I was terrified out of my wits at the very idea.*
5 **gather/collect/recover etc your wits** to make yourself think about what you are going to do next after you have been surprised by something: *I felt helpless, but tried to gather my wits.*
6 **pit your wits against sb** to compete against someone in a test of knowledge or intelligence
7 **be at your wits' end** to be very upset and not know what to do, because you have tried everything possible to solve a problem
8 **have the wit to do sth** *formal* to be clever enough to know the right thing to do: *Thankfully, Reid had the wit to see what was wrong with the plan.*
9 **not be beyond the wit of sb** *formal* not be too difficult for someone to do: *It's surely **not beyond the wit** of man to come up with a solution.*
10 **to wit** *old use* or *formal* used to introduce additional information which makes it clear exactly who or what you are talking about; ◧ **namely**: *This does not stop me giving you a little treat. To wit, an invitation to dine at Brown's.* → **battle of wits** at BATTLE¹ (5); → HALF-WIT; → **live by your wits** at LIVE¹ (15); → OUTWIT, QUICK-WITTED, WITTY

witch /wɪtʃ/ *n* [C] **1** a woman who is supposed to have magic powers, especially to do bad things; → **wizard 2** *informal* an insulting word for a woman who is old or unpleasant

witch·craft /ˈwɪtʃkrɑːft $ -kræft/ *n* [U] the use of magic powers, especially evil ones, to make things happen

ˈwitch-ˌdoctor *n* [C] a man who is believed to have magic powers and the ability to cure diseases, especially in parts of Africa; → **medicine man**

ˈwitch-ˌhazel *n* [C,U] a substance used for treating small wounds on the skin, or the tree that produces it

ˈwitch-hunt *n* [C] an attempt to find and punish people in a society or organization whose opinions are regarded as wrong or dangerous – used to show disapproval: *anti-Communist witch-hunts*

with S1 W1 /wɪð, wɪθ/ *prep*
1 used to say that two or more people or things are together in the same place: *I saw Bob in town with his girlfriend.* | *Put this bag with the others.* | *I always wear these shoes with this dress.* | *Mix the powder with boiling water.* | **have/bring/take sb/sth with you** *She had her husband with her.* | *You'd better bring your passport with you.*
2 having, possessing, or carrying something: *a tall gentleman with a grey beard* | *a book with a green cover* | *a man with a gun* | *We need someone with bright new ideas.* | *Only people with plenty of money can afford to shop here.* | *She came back with a letter in her hand.*
3 using something or by means of something: *Chop the onions with a sharp knife.* | *What will you buy with the*

money? | *I amused myself with crossword puzzles.* | *a hat decorated with brightly coloured feathers* → see box at BY¹
4 because of a particular feeling or physical state: *They were trembling with fear.* | *Jack beamed with pleasure when he heard the news.* | *I was too weak with hunger to cry.* | *Mother became seriously ill with pneumonia.*
5 including: *Two nights' accommodation with breakfast and evening meal cost us just over £250.*
6 used to say what covers or fills something: *Her boots were covered with mud.* | *Fill the bowl with sugar.* | *In summer Venice is crammed with tourists.*
7 used to say what an action or situation is related to: *We have a problem with parking in this area.* | *Be careful with that glass.* | *Is there something wrong with your phone?* | *How are you getting on with your studies, David?* | *Compared with other children of the same age, Robert is very tall.*
8 used to say which person or thing someone has a particular feeling or attitude towards: *I hope you're not angry with me.* | *He thinks he's in love with Diana.* | *She's delighted with her new car.* | *Don't get too friendly with your students.*
9 supporting someone or sharing their opinion; → **for**: *Some opposition MPs voted with the Government.* | *You're either with me or against me.* | *I'm with Harry all the way on this one.*
10 used when talking about an action or activity to say which other person, group, or country is involved: *Stop fighting with your brother!* | *I used to play chess with him.* | *It's a good idea to discuss the problem with a sympathetic teacher.* | *We're competing with foreign businesses.* | *Britain's trade with Japan* | *She left home after an argument with her parents.*
11 used to say how someone does something or how something happens: *He prepared everything with great care.* | *A rocket exploded with a blinding flash.* | *'Oh, I'm not in a hurry,' I said with a smile.* | *The day starts with a great American breakfast.*
12 used to say what position or state someone or something is in, or what is happening, when someone does something: *She stood with her back to me.* | *We lay in bed with the window open.* | *She was knitting, with the television on.* | **with sb/sth doing sth** *We jumped into the water with bullets whizzing past our ears.*
13 at the same rate as something else and because of it: *a skill which improves with practice* | *The risk of cancer increases with the number of cigarettes you smoke.*
14 because of a situation that exists: *With John away there's more room in the house.* | **with sth doing sth** *I can't do my homework with all this noise going on.*
15 employed by someone: *The manager is Stuart Walker, who has been with the company since 1970.*
16 used to say who is looking after something: *I left your keys with the janitor.*
17 used to say who or what someone becomes separated from: *Joan doesn't want to part with the money.* | *a complete break with tradition*
18 in the same direction as something: *We sailed with the wind.*
19 in spite of: *With all his faults, I still like him.*
20 used to show who or what a strong wish or order concerns: *Down with school!* | *Off to bed with you!*
21 **be with you/me** to understand what someone is telling you or explaining to you: *Sorry, I'm not with you – which room do you mean?* | *So that's how the system works. Are you with me?*
22 **with it** *informal* **a)** wearing fashionable clothes and knowing about new ideas; ◧ **trendy b)** able to understand clearly what is happening around you: *I'm sorry, I'm not feeling very with it today.* → WITH-IT
23 **with that** immediately after doing or saying something: *He gave a little wave and with that he was gone.*

W

with·draw W2 /wɪð'drɔː, wɪθ- $ -'drɔː/ v past tense **withdrew** /-'druː/, past participle **withdrawn** /-'drɔːn $ -'drɔːn/

1 NOT TAKE PART [I,T] to stop taking part in an activity, belonging to an organization etc, or to make someone do this: [+from] *A knee injury forced her to withdraw from the competition.* | *calls for Britain to withdraw from the European Union* | **withdraw sth/sb from sth** *Parents have the right to withdraw their children from religious education lessons if they wish.*

2 STOP SUPPORTING [T] to stop giving support or money to someone or something, especially as the result of an official decision: *One of the minority parties had **withdrawn** its **support** for Chancellor Kohl.* | *Union members will vote on whether to **withdraw** their **labour** (=stop working).* | *a government decision to withdraw funding*

3 CHANGE YOUR MIND [T] if you withdraw a threat, offer, request etc, you say that you no longer will do what you said: *After much persuasion he agreed to withdraw his resignation.*

4 SAY STH IS NOT TRUE [T] *formal* if you withdraw a remark, criticism, statement etc, you say that what you said earlier was completely untrue; ◨ **retract**: *He refused to withdraw his remarks and was expelled from the Party.* | *The newspaper has agreed to withdraw its allegations.*

5 PRODUCT/SERVICE [T] if a product or service is withdrawn, it is no longer offered for sale or use: **withdraw sth from sale/from the market** *The drug has been withdrawn from the market for further tests.*

6 LEAVE A PLACE **a)** [I,T] if an army withdraws, or if it is withdrawn, it leaves a place; ◨ **pull out**: *the USA's decision to **withdraw** 40,000 troops from western Europe* **b)** [I] to leave a place, especially in order to be alone or go somewhere quiet: [+to] *We withdrew to the garden for a private talk.*

7 MONEY [T] to take money out of a bank account: **withdraw sth from sth** *I'd like to withdraw £500 from my current account.*

8 MOVE [T] if you withdraw your hand, arm, finger etc from somewhere, you move it from there to where it was before: *Claudia withdrew her hand from his.*

9 TAKE OUT [T] *literary* to take an object out from inside something: **withdraw sth from sth** *She withdrew a document from her briefcase.*

10 STOP COMMUNICATING [I] to become quieter, less friendly, and only concerned about your own thoughts: [+into/from] *Ralph has withdrawn from the other kids.* | *Many depressed people just withdraw into themselves.*

with·draw·al W3 /wɪð'drɔːəl, wɪθ- $ -'drɔːl/ n

1 ARMY [C,U] the act of moving an army, weapons etc away from the area where they were fighting: [+of] *the withdrawal of UN forces* | [+from] *the Russian withdrawal from Afghanistan* | *large-scale* **troop withdrawals**

2 REMOVAL/ENDING [U] the removal or stopping of something such as support, an offer, or a service: [+of] *withdrawal of government aid*

3 MONEY [C,U] the act of taking money from a bank account, or the amount you take out: *Customers can use the machine to **make withdrawals** of up to £250 a day.*

4 STOP TAKING PART [U] the act of no longer taking part in an activity or being a member of an organization: [+from] *Germany's withdrawal from the talks*

5 DRUGS [U] the period after someone has given up a drug that they were dependent on, and the unpleasant mental and physical effects that this causes

6 STATEMENT [U] the act of saying that something you previously said was in fact untrue; ◨ **retraction**: [+of] *the withdrawal of all allegations*

with'drawal ˌsymptoms n [plural] the painful or unpleasant feelings someone has after they have stopped taking a drug that they were dependent on

with·drawn /wɪð'drɔːn, wɪθ- $ -'drɔːn/ adj very shy and quiet, and concerned only about your own thoughts: *After his wife's death he **became** more and more withdrawn.*

with·er /'wɪðə $ -ər/ also **wither away** v [I,T] if plants wither, they become drier and smaller and start to die

with·ered /'wɪðəd $ -ərd/ adj **1** a withered plant has become drier and smaller and is dead or dying **2** a withered person looks thin and weak and old **3** a withered arm or leg has not developed properly and is thin and weak

with·er·ing /'wɪðərɪŋ/ adj **a withering look/remark etc** a look, remark etc that makes someone feel stupid, embarrassed, or lose confidence —**witheringly** adv

with·ers /'wɪðəz $ -ərz/ n [plural] the highest part of a horse's back, above its shoulders

with·hold /wɪð'həʊld, wɪθ- $ -'hoʊld/ v past tense and past participle **withheld** /-'held/ [T] to refuse to give someone something: *I withheld payment until they had completed the work.* | *Ian was accused of withholding vital information from the police.*

with'holding ˌtax n [C,U] *AmE* money that is taken out of your wages as tax

with·in S2 W1 /wɪð'ɪn $ wɪð'ɪn, wɪθ'ɪn/ prep, adv

1 a) before a certain period of time has passed: *We should have the test results back within 24 hours.* | *He fell sick and died within a matter of weeks.* | *Within an hour of our arrival Caroline was starting to complain.* **b)** during a certain period of time: *the enormous success of televised sport within the last twenty years* | *Within the space of a year, three of the town's factories have closed down.*

2 less than a certain distance from a particular place: *The invading troops came within 50 miles of Paris.* | *Within a five mile radius of Ollerton there are several pubs and restaurants.* | *We live **within easy reach** of (=close to) the shops.* | *Adjust the driver's seat so that all the controls are **within reach** (=close enough to touch).* | **within sight/earshot (of sth)** (=close enough to see or hear) *As she came within sight of the house, she saw two men getting out of a car.*

3 inside a particular building or area; ◨ **outside**: *Prisoners who died were buried within the walls of the prison.* | *public footpaths within the national park* | *The rooms within were richly furnished.* | **apply/enquire within** (=used on notices on the outside of buildings) *Baby rabbits for sale. Enquire within.*

4 inside a society, organization, or group of people; ◨ **outside**: *There have been a lot of changes within the department since I joined.* | *an attempt to reform the system **from within***

5 if something stays within a particular limit or set of rules, it does not go beyond that limit: *We have to operate within a very tight budget.* | *Private security firms have to work strictly within the law.* | *You can go anywhere you want **within reason** (=within reasonable limits).*

6 *literary* or *formal* inside a person's body or mind; ◨ **outside**: *Elaine felt a pain deep within her.* | *I'm feeling more relaxed within myself.*

'with-it adj fashionable and modern in the way that you dress, think etc; ◨ **trendy** → **with it** at WITH (22)

with·out S1 W1 /wɪð'aʊt $ wɪð'aʊt, wɪθ'aʊt/ prep, adv

1 not having something, especially something that is basic or necessary: *After the storm we were without electricity for five days.* | *a house without a garden* | *We passed two ruined abbeys, one with a tower and one without.* | *I'm getting used to managing without a car.* → **do without** at DO[2]; → **go without** at GO[1]

2 used to say that a particular thing has not happened when someone does something: *Suddenly and without any warning, the army opened fire.* | *He had gone out without his parents' permission.* | *I accepted his offer without a moment's hesitation.* | *I got to my destination without too much difficulty.* | **without doing sth** *'What do you expect?' he said, without looking at her.* | *With-*

out so much as *a word of thanks, Ben turned and went back into the office* (=he did not even say thank you as he should have done).
3 not feeling or showing that you feel a particular emotion: *He told his story without anger or bitterness.*
4 not being with someone, or not having them to help you, especially someone you like or need: *I don't know what I'd do without you.* | *Won't you be lonely without her?* | *The rest of the group set off without him.*
5 without wanting/wishing to do sth used before a criticism, complaint, or other statement to make it less strong: *Without wanting to sound too boastful, I think we have the best television programmes in the world.*
6 *old use* outside → **reckon without** at RECKON

with·stand /wɪð'stænd, wɪθ-/ *v past tense and past participle* **withstood** /-'stʊd/ [T] **1** to be strong enough to remain unharmed by something such as great heat, cold, pressure etc; ▤ **resist, stand up to**: *This fabric can withstand steam and high temperatures.* **2** to defend yourself successfully against people who attack, criticize, or oppose you; ▤ **stand up to**: *The Chancellor has withstood the criticism and held firm.*

wit·less /'wɪtləs/ *adj* **1 be scared witless** feeling very frightened **2** not very intelligent or sensible; ▤ **stupid** —**witlessly** *adv* —**witlessness** *n* [U]

wit·ness¹ ⟨S2⟩ ⟨W3⟩ /'wɪtn⅃s/ *n*
1 CRIME/ACCIDENT [C] someone who sees a crime or an accident and can describe what happened: *Police have appealed for witnesses to come forward.* | [+to] *One witness to the accident said the driver appeared to be drunk.* | *an eye witness* (=someone who sees an event) *to the robbery* → EYEWITNESS
2 IN A COURT OF LAW [C] someone who appears in a court of law to say what they know about a crime or other event: **key/star/principal witness** *the key witness in the case against the brothers* | *The defense is expected to call them as witnesses.* | **witness for the prosecution/defence** also **prosecution/defence witness** (=someone the prosecution or defence lawyers choose as a witness in order to help prove their case) → EXPERT WITNESS
3 SIGNING A DOCUMENT [C] someone who is present when an official document is signed, and who signs it too, to say that they saw it being signed: [+to] *a witness to a will*
4 be witness to sth *formal* to be present when something happens, and watch it happening: *We were witness to the worst excesses of the military.*
5 CHRISTIAN BELIEF [C,U] *AmE* a public statement of strong Christian belief, or someone who makes such a statement → **bear witness** at BEAR¹ (15)

witness² *v*
1 CRIME/ACCIDENT [T] to see something happen, especially a crime or accident: *Several residents claim to have witnessed the attack.*
2 EXPERIENCE STH [T] to experience important events or changes: *Priests have witnessed an increase in religious intolerance.*
3 TIME/PLACE [T] if a time or place witnesses an event, the event happens during that time or in that place: *Recent years have witnessed the collapse of the steel industry.*
4 OFFICIAL DOCUMENT [T] if you witness the signing of an official document, you are there when it is signed, and sign it yourself to prove this: *Will you witness my signature?*
5 witness sth also **..., as witnessed by sth** used to introduce an example that proves something you have just mentioned: *Bad economic times can result in political dictatorships. Witness Germany in the 1930s.*
6 RELIGION [I] to speak publicly about your Christian beliefs

'**witness box** *BrE*; '**witness stand** *AmE n* [C] the place in a court of law where a witness stands to answer questions

wit·ter /'wɪtə $ -ər/ also **witter on** *v* [I] *BrE informal* to talk a lot in a boring way or about something unimportant; ▤ **ramble on**: [+about] *I'm sick of her wittering on about her boyfriend.*

wit·ti·cis·m /'wɪtⅠsɪzəm/ *n* [C] a clever amusing remark

wit·ty /'wɪti/ *adj* using words in a clever and amusing way: *witty remarks* | *Laura's very witty.* —**wittily** *adv* —**wittiness** *n* [U]

wives /waɪvz/ the plural of WIFE

wiz·ard /'wɪzəd $ -ərd/ *n* [C] **1** a man who is supposed to have magic powers; → **witch 2** someone who is very good at something: *a financial wizard* | [+at] *Ben's a real wizard at chess.*

wiz·ard·ry /'wɪzədri $ -ər-/ *n* [U] impressive ability at something or an impressive achievement: *high-speed Internet connections and other technical wizardry*

wiz·ened /'wɪzənd/ *adj* a wizened person, fruit etc is small and thin and has skin with a lot of lines and WRINKLES

wk. also **wk** *BrE* the written abbreviation of *week*

wob·ble /'wɒbəl $ 'wɑː-/ *v* **1** [I,T] to move unsteadily from side to side, or make something do this: *The pile of bricks wobbled and fell.* | *Tom stopped, wobbling from the weight of his load.* → see box at SHAKE¹ **2** [I always + adv/prep] to go in a particular direction while moving unsteadily from side to side: [+down/along/towards etc] *Cindy wobbled along the street on her bike.* **3** [I] to be unsure whether to do something; ▤ **waver**: *The President appeared to wobble over sending the troops in.* —**wobble** *n* [C]

wob·bly¹ /'wɒbli $ 'wɑː-/ *adj* **1** moving unsteadily from side to side: *a wobbly table* **2** *informal* if you or your legs feel wobbly, you feel weak and unable to keep your balance; ▤ **shaky 3** a wobbly voice is weak and shakes, especially because you feel frightened or upset; ▤ **shaky 4** not very good or not likely to be successful; ▤ **shaky**: *The meeting got off to a wobbly start.*

wobbly² *n* **throw a wobbly** *BrE informal* to suddenly become very angry or frightened

wodge /wɒdʒ $ wɑːdʒ/ *n* [C] *BrE informal* a thick solid piece or large amount of something: [+of] *a wodge of ten pound notes*

woe /wəʊ $ woʊ/ *n* **1** woes [plural] *formal* the problems and troubles affecting someone: *the country's economic woes* **2** [U] *literary* great sadness **3 woe is me** *spoken humorous* used to say that you are extremely unhappy or in a difficult situation **4 woe betide sb** *BrE* used to warn someone that there will be trouble if they do something – especially used humorously: *Woe betide anyone who smokes in our house!*

woe·be·gone /'wəʊbɪgɒn $ 'woʊbɪgɔːn, -gɑːn/ *adj literary* looking very sad: *her woebegone expression*

woe·ful /'wəʊfəl $ 'woʊ-/ *adj* **1** very bad or serious; ▤ **deplorable**: *a woeful lack of information* **2** *literary* very sad; ▤ **pathetic**: *woeful eyes* —**woefully** *adv*: *woefully inadequate facilities*

wog /wɒg $ wɑːg/ *n* [C] *BrE taboo* a very offensive word for a black person. Do not use this word.

wok /wɒk $ wɑːk/ *n* [C] a wide pan shaped like a bowl, used in Chinese cooking → see picture at EAT

woke /wəʊk $ woʊk/ the past tense of WAKE

wok·en /'wəʊkən $ 'woʊ-/ the past participle of WAKE

wolds /wəʊldz $ woʊldz/ *n* [plural] *BrE* a word for an area of hilly countryside, especially used in the names of places: *the Lincolnshire Wolds*

wolf¹ /wʊlf/ *n plural* **wolves** /wʊlvz/ [C] **1** a wild animal that looks like a large dog and lives and hunts in groups: *a pack of wolves* **2 a wolf in sheep's clothing** someone who seems to be friendly or harmless but is in fact dangerous, dishonest etc **3 keep the wolf from the door** to earn just enough money to buy the

W

basic things you need: *I work part-time in a coffee shop just to keep the wolf from the door.* → **cry wolf** at CRY[1] (7); → **lone wolf** at LONE (3) —**wolfish** *adj: a wolfish grin*

wolf² also **wolf down** *v* [T] *informal* to eat something very quickly, swallowing it in big pieces; ❑ **gobble**

wolf·hound /'wʊlfhaʊnd/ *n* [C] a type of extremely large dog

'**wolf ,whistle** *n* [C] a way of whistling that men sometimes use to show that they think a woman is attractive —**wolf-whistle** *v* [I]

wolves /wʊlvz/ the plural of WOLF

wom·an [S1] [W1] /'wʊmən/ *n plural* **women** /'wɪmɪn/
1 FEMALE PERSON [C] an adult female person: *I was talking to a woman I met on the flight.* | *I married women* | *a popular women's magazine* | *When a woman is pregnant, the levels of hormones in her body change.* | **woman priest/doctor etc** (=a priest etc who is a woman) *Ireland's first woman president* | *women artists*
2 ANY WOMAN [singular] *formal* women in general: *A woman's work is never done* (=used to say that women have a lot to do).
3 businesswoman/spokeswoman etc a woman who has a particular kind of job: *Congresswoman Ellen Tauscher*
4 another woman/the other woman *informal* a woman that a man is having a sexual relationship with, even though he is married to someone else: *I'm sure he's got another woman.*
5 be your own woman to make your own decisions and be in charge of your own life, without depending on anyone else
6 PARTNER [singular] *spoken* a word meaning a wife or girlfriend, which many women find offensive: *Did he bring his new woman with him?* → KEPT WOMAN
7 FORM OF ADDRESS *old-fashioned not polite* a rude way of speaking to a woman when you are angry, annoyed etc
8 SERVANT [C] a female servant or person who does cleaning work for you in your house; → **cleaner**, **daily help** → OLD WOMAN; → **make an honest woman (out) of sb** at HONEST (8); → **be a woman of the world** at WORLD[1] (21)

wom·an·hood /'wʊmənhʊd/ *n* [U] **1** the state of being a woman, not a man or a girl **2** *formal* women in general; → **manhood**

wom·an·ish /'wʊmənɪʃ/ *adj* a womanish man looks or behaves in a way that is thought to be typical of women; → **mannish**

wom·an·iz·er also **-iser** *BrE* /'wʊmənaɪzə $ -ər/ *n* [C] a man who has sexual relationships with many different women – used to show disapproval; → **man-eater** —**womanize** *v* [I] —**womanizing** *n* [U]

wom·an·kind /'wʊmənkaɪnd/ *n* [U] women considered together as a group; → **mankind**

wom·an·ly /'wʊmənli/ *adj* behaving, dressing etc in a way that is thought to be typical of or suitable for a woman – used to show approval; ❑ **feminine**; → **manly**: *her soft womanly figure* —**womanliness** *n* [U]

womb /wuːm/ *n* [C] the part of a woman's or female animal's body where her baby grows before it is born; ❑ **uterus**

wom·bat /'wɒmbæt $ 'wɑːm-/ *n* [C] an Australian animal like a small bear whose babies live in a pocket of skin on its body

wom·en /'wɪmɪn/ the plural of WOMAN

wom·en·folk /'wɪmɪnfəʊk $ -foʊk/ *n* [plural] *old-fashioned* all the women in a particular family or society; → **menfolk**

,**women's** '**lib** also ,**women's libe**'**ration** *n* [U] *old-fashioned* all the ideas, actions, and politics relating to giving women the same rights and opportunities as men; → **men's lib** —**women's libber** *n* [C]

'**women's ,movement** *n* the women's movement all the women who are involved in the aim of improving

the social, economic, and political position of women and of ending sexual DISCRIMINATION

'**women's room** *n* [C] *AmE* a public TOILET for women; ❑ **ladies** *BrE*; → **men's room**

'**women's ,studies** *n* [plural] the study of women in history, literature, and society

won¹ /wʌn/ the past tense and past participle of WIN[1]

won² /wɒn $ wɑːn/ *n* [C] a standard unit of money in South Korea and North Korea

won·der¹ [S1] [W2] /'wʌndə $ -ər/ *v* [I,T]
1 to think about something that you are not sure about and try to guess what is true, what will happen etc: **wonder who/what/how etc** *I wonder how James is getting on.* | *What are they going to do now,* **I wonder**? | **wonder if/whether** *I wonder if I'll recognize Philip after all these years.* | *He's been leaving work early a lot – it* **makes you wonder**, *doesn't it?*
2 I wonder if/whether *spoken* used to ask politely for something; ❑ **may I**: *I wonder if I might have a drink?*
3 I was wondering if/whether **a)** *spoken* used to politely ask someone to help you: *I was wondering if I could borrow your car?* **b)** used to ask someone politely if they would like to do something: *I was wondering if you'd like to come to dinner.*
4 to feel surprised and unable to believe something: [+about/at] *Sometimes I wonder about his behaviour.* | **wonder how** *I wonder how he dares to show his face!* | **I don't wonder** *BrE* (=I am not surprised) *I don't wonder you're tired.* | **I shouldn't wonder** *BrE* (=I would not be surprised about something) *He'll come back soon enough, I shouldn't wonder.*
5 to doubt or question whether something is true: *'Is she serious?' 'I wonder.'* | **wonder if/whether** *Sometimes I wonder if he's got any sense at all!*

wonder² *n*
1 ADMIRATION **a)** [U] a feeling of surprise and admiration for something very beautiful or new to you; ❑ **awe**: *The sight of the Taj Mahal filled us with wonder.* **b)** [C] something that makes you feel surprise and admiration: *technological wonders* | *the Seven Wonders of the World*
2 (it's) no/small/little wonder (that) *especially spoken* used to say that you are not surprised by something: *No wonder you've got a headache, the amount you drank last night.*
3 SURPRISING it's a wonder (that) *especially spoken* used to say that something is very surprising: *It's a wonder no one got hurt.*
4 do/work wonders to be very effective in solving a problem
5 wonders will never cease *spoken* used humorously to show you are surprised and pleased about something
6 CLEVER PERSON [singular] *BrE* someone who is good at doing difficult things → **nine days wonder** at NINE (3)

wonder³ *adj* [only before noun] very good and effective: *a new wonder drug*

won·der·ful [S1] [W2] /'wʌndəfəl $ -dər-/ *adj*
1 making you feel very happy; ❑ **great**: *We had a wonderful time in Spain.*
2 making you admire someone or something very much; ❑ **amazing**: *It's wonderful what doctors can do.*

won·der·ful·ly /'wʌndəfəli $ -dər-/ *adv* very well or to a very great degree, in a way that makes you feel happy: *All of the performers played wonderfully.* | *wonderfully rich sauce*

won·der·ing·ly /'wʌndərɪŋli/ *adv* in a way that shows admiration, surprise, and pleasure

won·der·land /'wʌndəlænd $ -ər-/ *n* [U] an imaginary place in stories

won·der·ment /'wʌndəmənt $ -dər-/ *n* [U] *literary* a feeling of pleasant surprise or admiration

won·drous /'wʌndrəs/ *adj literary* good or impressive in a surprising way

wonk /wɒŋk $ wɑːŋk/ *n* [C] *AmE informal* someone who works hard and is serious – used to show disapproval

won·ky /'wɒŋki $ 'wɑːŋki/ *adj BrE informal* unsteady or not straight or level: *a wonky table*

won't /wəʊnt $ woʊnt/ the short form of 'will not'

wont¹ /wəʊnt $ wɒːnt/ *n old-fashioned* **as is sb's wont** used to say that it is someone's habit to do something: *He spoke for too long, as is his wont.*

wont² *adj formal* **be wont to do sth** to be likely to do something

woo /wuː/ *v* [T] **1** to try to persuade someone to do something such as buy something from you, vote for you, or work for you – used in news reports: *the Party's efforts to woo working class voters* **2** *old-fashioned* to try to persuade a woman to love you and marry you; **⊟ court**

wood S2 W2 /wʊd/ *n*
1 [C,U] the material that trees are made of; → **wooden**, **woody**: *Put some more wood on the fire.* | *a polished wood floor* | **soft/hard wood** *Pine is a soft wood.* | *Her house was made of wood.* | *a piece of wood* → HARDWOOD, SOFTWOOD; → see picture at MATERIAL¹
2 [C] also **the woods** a small forest: *a walk in the woods*
3 touch wood *BrE*; **knock on wood** *AmE* said just after you have said that things are going well for you, when you want your good luck to continue
4 [C] one of a set of four GOLF CLUBS with wooden heads → see picture at GOLF
5 not be out of the wood(s) yet *informal* used to say that there are likely to be more difficulties before things improve
6 not see the wood for the trees to not notice what is important about something because you give too much of your attention to small details → DEAD WOOD

wood·block /'wʊdblɒk $ -blɑːk/ *n* [C] **1** a piece of wood with a shape cut on it, used for printing **2** a block of wood used in making a floor

wood·carv·ing /'wʊdkɑːvɪŋ $ -kɑːr-/ *n* [C,U] the process of shaping wood with special tools, or a piece of art produced in this way

wood·chuck /'wʊdtʃʌk/ *n* [C] a GROUNDHOG

wood·craft /'wʊdkrɑːft $ -kræft/ *n* [U] the practical knowledge of woods and forests

wood·cut /'wʊdkʌt/ *n* [C] a picture made by pressing a shaped piece of wood and a colouring substance onto paper

wood·cut·ter /'wʊdˌkʌtə $ -ər/ *n* [C] *old-fashioned* someone whose job it is to cut down trees in a forest

wood·ed /'wʊdɪd/ *adj* having woods or covered with trees: *the wooded hills of Northern Virginia* | **thickly/ heavily/densely etc wooded** *a thickly wooded area*

wood·en S3 W3 /'wʊdn/ *adj*
1 made of wood: *a wooden bench*
2 not showing enough expression, emotion, or movement, especially when performing in public —**woodenly** *adv* —**woodenness** *n* [U]

ˌwooden ˈspoon *n* [C] **1** a large spoon made of wood, used to mix things when cooking **2 win/collect/ take etc the wooden spoon** *BrE* to come last in a competition

wood·land /'wʊdlənd, -lænd/ *n* [U] also **woodlands** [plural] an area of land covered with trees; → **wood**, **forest** → see picture at COUNTRY

wood·louse /'wʊdlaʊs/ *n plural* **woodlice** /-laɪs/ [C] a small grey creature like an insect that lives under wood, stones etc

wood·peck·er /'wʊdˌpekə $ -ər/ *n* [C] a bird with a long beak that it uses to make holes in trees

wood·pile /'wʊdpaɪl/ *n* [C] a pile of wood to be burned in a fire

ˈwood pulp *n* [U] wood crushed into a soft mass, used for making paper

wood·shed /'wʊdʃed/ *n* [C] a place for storing wood for burning

woods·man /'wʊdzmən/ *n plural* **woodsmen** /-mən/ [C] someone who works in a forest taking care of, planting, and cutting down trees

wood·sy /'wʊdzi/ *adj AmE informal* relating to the woods: *a woodsy smell*

wood·wind /'wʊdˌwɪnd/ *n* **1** [U] musical instruments made of wood or metal that you play by blowing and that usually have finger holes or KEYS; → **brass**, **percussion**, **stringed instrument**, **wind instrument**: *woodwind instruments such as the flute or saxophone* **2 woodwinds** [plural] also **the woodwind (section)** the people in an ORCHESTRA or band who play woodwind instruments

wood·work /'wʊdwɜːk $ -wɜːrk/ *n* [U] **1** *BrE*, **woodwork·ing** *AmE* /'wʊdwɜːkɪŋ $ -ɜːr-/ the skill or activity of making wooden objects; → **carpentry**; → see picture at HANDICRAFT **2** the parts of a house or room that are made of wood **3 crawl/come out of the woodwork** if someone crawls out of the woodwork, they suddenly and unexpectedly appear in order to take advantage of a situation, express their opinion etc – used to show disapproval **4 fade/blend into the woodwork** to seem to disappear, or to behave in such a way that no one notices you

wood·worm /'wʊdwɜːm $ -wɜːrm/ *n* **1** [C] a small insect that makes holes in wood **2** [U] the damage that is caused to wood by this creature

wood·y /'wʊdi/ *adj* **1** a woody plant has a stem like wood **2** a woody area of land has a lot of trees growing on it

woof¹ /wʊf/ *interjection* a word used for describing the sound a dog makes; → **bark** —**woof** *n* [C] —**woof** *v* [I]

woof² /wuːf $ wʊf, wuːf/ *n* [C] WEFT

wool /wʊl/ *n* [U] **1** the soft thick hair that sheep and some goats have on their body → LAMBSWOOL **2** material made from wool: *a pure wool skirt* | *a mix of 80% wool and 20% man-made fibres* → see picture at MATE-RIAL¹ **3** thread made from wool that you use to KNIT clothes; **⊟ yarn** *AmE*: *a ball of pink wool* **4 pull the wool over sb's eyes** to deceive someone by not telling the truth → COTTON WOOL, DYED-IN-THE-WOOL, STEEL WOOL, WIRE WOOL

wool·len *BrE*; **woolen** *AmE* /'wʊlən/ *adj* [only before noun] **1** made of wool; **⊟ wool**: *a woollen scarf* **2** relating to making cloth from wool: *the woollen industry* | *a woollen mill*

wool·lens *BrE*; **woolens** *AmE* /'wʊlənz/ *n* [plural] clothes made from wool, especially KNITTED clothes such as SWEATERS

wool·ly¹ *BrE*; **wooly** /'wʊli/ *AmE adj* **1** made of or feeling like wool: *a woolly hat* **2** not showing clear thinking; **⊟ vague**: *He gave a rather woolly argument.* —**woolliness** *n* [U]

wool·ly² *n plural* **woollies** [C] *BrE informal* a SWEATER or similar piece of KNITTED clothing: *You'll need your winter woollies!*

woo·zy /'wuːzi/ *adj informal* feeling weak and unsteady; **⊟ dizzy**: *Giving blood makes me feel really woozy.*

wop /wɒp $ wɑːp/ *n* [C] *taboo* a very offensive word for someone who is Italian. Do not use this word.

word¹ S1 W1 /wɜːd $ wɜːrd/ *n*
1 UNIT OF LANGUAGE [C] the smallest unit of language that people can understand if it is said or written on its own: *Write an essay of about five hundred words.* | *I know the tune, but not the words.* | *'Vater' is the German word for* (=word that means) *'father'.* | *Perhaps 'lucky' is not exactly* **the right word.** | **search for/find etc a word** (=try to choose words that express what you want to say) *She was having difficulty finding the right words to tell him.* → BUZZWORD, FOUR-LETTER WORD, SWEAR WORD
2 sb's words the things that someone says or writes: *Those are his words, not mine.* | **in sb's words** *Jones*

W

was, in the judge's words, 'an evil man'. | *In your own words, explain the term 'personal service'.*

3 have a word especially spoken to talk to someone quickly, especially because you need their advice about something or you want to tell them to do something: *Could I have a word?* | [+**with**] *I'll have a word with him and see if he'll help.* | **have a quick/brief word** *I was hoping to have a quick word with you.* | **have/exchange a few words** *Could I have a few words with you?*

4 want a word spoken to want to talk to someone, especially in order to criticize them: [+**with**] *Wait a minute! I want a word with you!*

5 not hear/understand/believe a word used to emphasize that you cannot hear, understand etc what someone says or writes: *No one could hear a word because someone had cut the amplifier cable.* | [+**of**] *I can't understand a word of Russian.*

6 without (saying) a word if you do something without a word, you do not say anything while you do it: *He left without a word.*

7 say a word/say a few words to make a short speech about something: *I'd like to say a few words about the plans.*

8 a word of warning/caution/advice/thanks etc something you say that warns someone, thanks them etc: *It's a beautiful city, but a word of warning: street robberies are very common.* | *He left without a word of apology.*

9 not say a word a) also **not breathe a word** to not say anything about something because it is a secret: *Promise you won't say a word to anyone?* **b)** to not say anything: *What's wrong? You haven't said more than two words since you got here.*

10 put your feelings/thoughts etc into words to express what you want to say clearly: *He found it difficult to put ideas into words.*

11 have/exchange words (with sb) to argue – use this when you do not want to make the argument seem serious: *I was in a bad mood and he kept pestering me, so we had words.*

12 a harsh/a cross/an angry etc word something you say that shows you are angry or want to criticize someone: *Mountain rescue teams have harsh words to say to people who climb without proper equipment.* | *They were married for 50 years and she says there was never an angry word between them.*

13 NEWS/INFORMATION [singular, U] a piece of news or a message: *Word came that our duties would be changed.* | *'Have you heard from Ann?' 'No, not a word.'* | *There was still no word from John.* | **word gets out/around** (=people hear about something) *It's a very small town and if you do something bad, word gets around.* | **the word is (that)/word has it (that)** (=people are saying that) *The word is that the two companies are planning a merger.* | **spread/pass the word** (=tell other people some information or news) *Health officials are encouraging people to spread the word about the benefits of exercise.* | **send/bring word** old-fashioned formal (=send or bring a message) *The mayor sent word he'd be late.* | **Word of mouth** (=information you get by someone telling you) *is one of the best ways of getting business.* | **by word of mouth** *Much of this information is picked up by word of mouth from previous students.*

14 the last/final word a) the power to decide whether or how to do something: [+**on**] *The final word on policy determination belongs to the committee.* | *She has the final word on whether policies are put into action or not.* **b)** the last statement or speech in a discussion or argument: *The last word must go to Nick, who has organized the whole project.* | *Why must you always have the last word in any argument?* **c)** in sports, the last hit or kick in a game, especially when it is successful: *Adams had the final word with a last-minute goal.*

15 my/his/your etc word a sincere promise to do something, or a promise that what you say is true: *I trust him to keep his word.* | *I give you my word* (=I promise) *that it won't happen again.* | *We only have his*

word for it that he has already paid. | *Delors claimed that Johnson had gone back on his word* (=not done what he had promised to do). | *The business is doing very well. You can take my word for it* (=accept that what I say is true). | *I never know whether to take him at his word* (=believe what he says). | *His word is his bond* (=he always does what he promises to do). | **be true to your word/be as good as your word** (=do what you promise to do) | **a man of his word/a woman of her word** (=a man or woman who does what they have promised to do)

16 word for word a) in exactly the same words: *The newspaper printed his speech more or less word for word.* **b)** also **word by word** if you translate a piece of writing word for word, you translate the meaning of each single word rather than the meaning of a whole phrase or sentence

17 in a word used before giving a very simple answer or explanation: *We are, in a word, busy. Ridiculously busy.*

18 in words of one syllable saying something in a way that is very easy to understand, especially because the person you are talking to is stupid: *You have to put everything in words of one syllable for her.*

19 in so many words also **in as many words** [usually negative] in a direct way, or in a way that makes it very clear what you mean: *Aunt Fay was angry and said so in as many words.*

20 take the words (right) out of sb's mouth spoken if someone takes the words out of your mouth, they have just said what you were going to say

21 put words into sb's mouth spoken to tell someone what you think they are trying to say, in a way that annoys them: *Will you stop putting words into my mouth – I never said I disliked the job.*

22 AN ORDER [singular] an order to do something: *On the word 'go' everyone has to run to the end of the room and back.* | *When I give the word, grab him.*

23 (right) from the word go spoken from the beginning of something: *The marriage was a disaster from the word go.*

24 too silly/complicated/ridiculous etc for words spoken extremely silly, complicated etc: *His behaviour has been too pathetic for words.*

25 (have/drop) a word in sb's ear to say something to someone privately, especially to give them advice or a warning: *If I were you, I'd have a word in his ear before it's too late.*

26 get a word in (edgeways) to get a chance to say something: *Once George starts talking it's difficult to get a word in edgeways.*

27 put in a (good) word for sb to try to help someone get or achieve something by saying good things about them to someone else: *I got the job because Paul put in a good word for me.*

28 words fail me spoken used to say that you are so surprised, angry, or shocked that you do not know what to say: *I ... words fail me.*

29 word! AmE informal used to say that you understand or agree with what someone has just said

30 (Upon) my word! spoken old-fashioned used when you are very surprised: *My word! Hasn't she grown?*

31 surprised/angry/pleased etc isn't the word for it spoken used to say you are extremely surprised, angry etc

32 a man/woman etc of few words someone who does not say very much: *My father was a man of few words.*

33 the Word (of God) the religious ideas and messages in the Bible → **eat your words** at EAT (3); → **FOUR-LETTER WORD**; → **a good word for sb/sth** at GOOD[1] (31); → **in other words** at OTHER (11); → **be the last word in sth** at LAST[1] (10); → **be lost for words** at LOST[2] (10); → **mark my words** at MARK[2] (12); → **not mince your words** at MINCE[1] (3); → **play on words** at PLAY[2] (6); → **say the word** at SAY[1] (26); → **the spoken word** at SPOKEN[2] (2); → **the written word** at WRITTEN[2] (3)

word[2] *v* [T] to use words that are carefully chosen in order to express something; ▪ **phrase**: *How can we* word the letter so as not to offend the parents? | **carefully/ strongly/vaguely etc worded** a carefully worded statement | a strongly worded letter

'word ,blindness n [U] DYSLEXIA

word·ed /'wɜːdɪd $ 'wɜːr-/ adj **carefully/clearly/ strongly etc worded** using words that express an idea carefully or clearly: a carefully worded question | a strongly worded letter

word·ing /'wɜːdɪŋ $ 'wɜːr-/ n [U] the words and phrases used to express something; ◻ **phrasing**: [+of] the exact wording of the contract

word·less /'wɜːdləs $ 'wɜːrd-/ adj without using words; ◻ **silent**: a wordless prayer | She threw her arms around him in wordless grief.

,word-'perfect adj BrE able to remember and say every word of something correctly: She rehearsed her speech until she was word-perfect.

'word-play n [U] making jokes by using words in a clever way

'word ,processor n [C] computer software or a small computer that you use for writing letters and other documents; ◻ **WP**: **on a word processor** Most reports are produced on a word processor. —**word processing** n [U]: I mostly use my computer for word processing. —**word processed** adj: a word processed document

word·smith /'wɜːdsmɪθ $ 'wɜːrd-/ n [C] someone who is clever at using language

word·y /'wɜːdi $ 'wɜːrd-/ adj using too many words; ◻ **verbose**: a wordy explanation —**wordiness** n [U]

wore /wɔː $ wɔːr/ the past tense of WEAR[1]

work¹ [S1] [W1] /wɜːk $ wɜːrk/ v

1 [DO A JOB FOR MONEY] [I] to do a job that you are paid for: Where do you work? | Many young people in the area have never worked. | The injury means he'll probably never work again. | [+for] He works for a law firm. | [+at/in] I work at the university. | [+as] She works as a consultant for a design company. | **work in industry/education/publishing etc** The studies were undertaken by people working in education. | **work part-time/full-time** I work part-time in a library.

2 [DO YOUR JOB] [I,T] to do the activities and duties that are part of your job: Sally isn't working tomorrow. | Staff will have to get used to a new way of working. | [+with] One of the women I work with is getting married this weekend. | **work under sb** (=have someone who is in charge of you) Each site has a fully trained team who work under a site manager. | **work days/nights/weekends etc** I get paid more if I work nights. | We're sometimes expected to work twelve-hour days. | Are you **working late** (=working after the time you usually finish) again tonight? | Forty police officers are **working round the clock** (=working day and night without stopping) to find Murray's killer. | Nowadays, many people are able to **work from home**.

3 [HELP] [I] if you work with someone or a group of people, your job involves trying to help them: [+with/ among] She's just retired after 38 years working with children. | He has worked among some of the world's poorest people.

4 [DO AN ACTIVITY] [I] to spend time and effort doing something: I've been working in the garden all afternoon. | I'm going to have to **work** really **hard** to pass these exams. | We're working together to develop a new system.

5 [TRY TO ACHIEVE STH] [I] to try continuously to achieve a particular thing: [+towards] They are working towards a solution to their problems. | [+for] We will work for the release of the hostages. | **work to do sth** The police are working to provide more help for victims of crime. | The company is **working hard** to improve its image. | He **worked tirelessly** (=worked very hard in a determined way) for the charity throughout his life.

6 [MACHINE/EQUIPMENT] **a)** [I] if a machine or piece of equipment works, it does what it is supposed to do: You should check that the smoke alarm is working properly. | The delete key doesn't work. | **get sth to work** I can't get the heater to work. **b)** [T] to make a machine

or piece of equipment do what it is supposed to do: My parents can't even work the video.

7 [BE EFFECTIVE/SUCCESSFUL] [I] to be effective or successful: Making a marriage work can take a lot of effort. | I've never found a diet that works. | The recipe works just as well if you use margarine instead of butter. | The cream works immediately to relieve sore skin. | [+for] You need to find which method works best for you. | [+against] a drug that works against some types of cancer

8 [HAVE AN EFFECT] [I always + adv/prep] if something such as a fact, situation, or system works in a particular way, it has a particular effect on someone or something: The arrangement works well for everyone involved. | The French team are the heavier crew, which should **work in** their **favour** (=help them). | Sexism still **works against** (=harms or causes problems for) women in many professions.

9 [ART/STYLE/LITERATURE] [I] if a painting, design, piece of writing etc works, it is successful because it has the effect on you that the painter, writer etc intended: I don't think the scene with the horses really works, do you? | [+for] The colour combination just doesn't work for me.

10 [SHAPE/CUT STH] [T] if you work a material such as metal, leather, or clay, you cut, sew, or shape it in order to make something

11 [USE A SUBSTANCE] [I] to use a particular material or substance in order to make something such as a picture, design, jewellery etc: [+in/with] a sculptor who works in steel | a jeweller who works with silver

12 **work your way to/through etc sth a)** to move somewhere slowly and with difficulty: From here, we worked our way carefully across the rock base. **b)** to achieve something gradually by working: He had worked his way up to head of department.

13 **work your way through school/college/university etc** to do a job while you are a student because you need the money to pay for your courses, books etc

14 [MOVE GRADUALLY] [I,T always + adv/prep] to move into a particular state or position very gradually, either in a series of small movements or after a long time: Slowly he worked the screwdriver into the crack. | **work (its way) loose** One of the screws must have worked loose.

15 [EXERCISE] [T] to use and exercise a muscle or part of your body: Swimming is a form of exercise that works every muscle in your body.

16 [MOVE] [I,T] formal if a part of your body works or you work it, it moves: She was trembling and her mouth was working.

17 [WORK IN AN AREA] [T] if you work a particular area or type of place, you travel around the area for your job, or work in that type of place: Markowitz works the Tri-State area.

18 **work the door** to take tickets from people as they enter a club, theatre etc: Binns worked the door at various Manhattan clubs.

19 [ENTERTAIN A CROWD] [T] if an entertainer or politician works a crowd of people, they entertain them and get their interest or support: She really knew how to work a crowd.

20 [LAND/SOIL] [T] if you work the land, soil etc, you do all the work necessary to grow crops on it: He was left to work the farm alone.

21 [MINE] [T] to remove a substance such as coal, gold, or oil from under the ground

22 **work like magic/work like a charm** also **work a treat** BrE to be very effective: a polish that works a treat on windows

23 [MIND/BRAIN] [I] if your mind or brain is working, you are thinking or trying to solve a problem

24 **work on the principle/assumption/basis etc that** to base ideas, plans etc on a particular fact that you think is true: We're working on the assumption that the

[1] 000, [2] 000, [3] 000, most frequent words in [S]poken and [W]ritten English

W

conference will take place in Canada, as planned.

25 work yourself into a frenzy/panic/state etc to make yourself become very nervous, angry etc: *He seemed to be working himself into a rage.*

26 work it/things *spoken* to make arrangements for something to happen, especially by behaving in a clever or skilful way: *We should try and work it so that we can all go together.*

27 work the system to understand how a system works so that you can get advantages for yourself, often in a slightly dishonest way: *Lynn could show the rest of us how to work the system.*

28 work sb hard also work sb into the ground *informal* to make someone work very hard: *The coach has been working us really hard this week.* | *People have complained that they are being worked into the ground.* | work yourself into the ground *I've worked myself into the ground setting up this interview.*

29 work your fingers to the bone also work your socks off *informal* to work very hard

30 work your butt/ass/arse off *not polite* to work very hard

31 CALCULATE [T] *AmE formal* to calculate the answer to a mathematical problem

32 work to rule *BrE* to protest about a situation at work by doing your job slowly, with the excuse that you must obey all the rules exactly → work wonders at WONDER² (4); → work miracles at MIRACLE (4); → work your magic at MAGIC¹ (5)

work around sb/sth also **work round sb/sth** *BrE phr v*
to arrange or organize something so that you avoid problems that may stop you from doing something: *John won't be here on the 15th so we'll have to work round that.*

work around to sth also **work round to sth** *BrE phr v*
to gradually mention a subject in a conversation or piece of writing, especially because it is embarrassing: *You'll have to work round to the subject gradually.*

work at sth *phr v*
to try hard to improve something or achieve something: *Learning a language isn't easy. You have to work at it.* | work at doing sth *couples who want to work at improving their relationship*

work sb/sth **in** *phr v*
1 work sth ⇔ in also work sth into sth to include something in a speech, piece of writing, activity etc: *He managed to work in a few references to his new book.* | *Here are a few goodies you can work into your daily diet.*
2 work sth ⇔ in also work sth into sth to add one substance to another and mix them together in a very thorough way: *Work the butter into the flour.*
3 *AmE spoken* to arrange to meet someone, even though you are very busy; 🔲 fit sb in *BrE*: *My schedule's pretty full, but I think I can work you in.*

work sth ⇔ **off** *phr v*
1 to get rid of something, especially a feeling such as anger, nervousness etc, by doing something that uses a lot of your energy: *Walking is excellent for working off tension.* | *I need to go and work off a few of these calories.*
2 to do a job for someone else because you owe them money or because they have helped you in the past: *She hasn't worked off her debts to me yet.*

work on sb/sth *phr v*
1 to spend time working in order to produce or repair something: *He has spent the last two years working on a book about childcare.* | *Every weekend you see him working on his car.*
2 to try very hard to improve or achieve something: *A trainer has been brought in to work on her fitness.* | work on doing sth *We need to work on ensuring that the children feel safe and confident.*
3 to try continuously to influence someone or persuade them to do something: *You leave him to me. I'll work on him.*

work out *phr v*
1 PLAN work sth ⇔ out to think carefully about how you are going to do something and plan a good way of doing it: *UN negotiators have worked out a set of compromise proposals.* | work out what/where/how etc *We need to work out how we're going to get there.* | I had it all worked out (=had made very careful plans).
2 CALCULATE work sth ⇔ out to calculate an answer, amount, price etc: *See if you can work this bill out.* | work out how much/how many etc *We'll have to work out how much food we'll need for the party.*
3 UNDERSTAND work sth ⇔ out *especially BrE* to think about something and manage to understand it: *The plot is very complicated – it'll take you a while to work it out.* | work sth out for yourself *I'm sure you can work it out for yourself.*
4 COST if a cost or amount works out at a particular figure, it is found to be that much when you calculate it: work out at/to £10/$500 etc *The bill works out at £15 each.* | work out expensive/cheap etc (=be expensive or cheap) *If we go by taxi, it's going to work out very expensive.*
5 GET BETTER if a problem or complicated situation works out, it gradually gets better or gets solved: *Things will work out, you'll see.* | *I hope it all works out for Gina and Andy.* | work itself out *I'm sure everything will work itself out.*
6 HAPPEN if a situation works out in a particular way, it happens in that way; 🔲 turn out: work out well/badly *Financially, things have worked out well for us.*
7 EXERCISE to make your body fit and strong by doing exercises: *He works out with weights twice a week.* → WORKOUT
8 I can't work sb out *BrE spoken* used to say that you cannot understand what someone is really like or why they behave in the way they do: *I couldn't work her out at all.*
9 be worked out if a mine is worked out, all the coal, gold etc has been removed from it

work sb **over** *phr v informal*
to attack someone by hitting them several times

work through *phr v*
1 work sth ⇔ through to deal with problems or unpleasant feelings: *After someone dies, it can take a long time to work though your grief.*
2 if the result or effect of something works through, it becomes noticeable: *The positive effect on businesses may take up to three years to work through.*

work up *phr v*
1 work up enthusiasm/interest/courage etc to make yourself feel interested, brave etc: *I'm trying to work up enough courage to go to the dentist.*
2 work up an appetite/a thirst/a sweat to make yourself hungry or THIRSTY, or make yourself SWEAT, especially by doing physical exercise: *You can work up a really big thirst playing tennis.*
3 work sb up to make someone very angry, excited, or upset about something: work yourself up *You're working yourself up again.* | *She had worked herself up into a state.* → WORKED UP
4 work sth ⇔ up to develop and improve something such as a project or a piece of writing: *Jack took notes which he would work up into a report later.*

work up to sth *phr v*
to gradually prepare yourself to do something difficult: work up to doing sth *He'd been working up to asking her for a date all week.*

work² S1 W1 *n*
1 JOB [U] a job or activity that you do regularly, especially in order to earn money; → employment: *There isn't a lot of work at this time of the year.* | *My father started work when he was just 14.* | *He's been out of work* (=without a job) *for two years.* | *More people are in work* (=have a job) *than ten years ago.* | *There has been an increase in the number of people looking for work.* | *She found work with an engineering firm.* | *I'm planning to return to work* (=start a job again after a long period of time) *when the children are a little*

older. | **before/after work** (=before a day of work or at the end of a day of work) *Do you want to go for a drink after work?* | **part-time/full-time work** *The new law will benefit people in part-time work.* | *I need to find **paid work*** (=a job you are paid to do). | **voluntary work** BrE/**volunteer work** AmE (=a job you are not paid for) *He does voluntary work in a hospital.* | *In my **line of work*** (=the type of work someone does), *I meet lots of interesting people.* → see box at JOB

2 PLACE [U] a place where you do your job, which is not your home: *I had an accident on the way to work.* | *He left work at the usual time.* | *I went out with the girls from work last night.* | **at work** *Dad's at work right now.*

3 DUTIES [U] the duties and activities that are part of your job: *A large part of the work we do involves using computers.* | *He **starts work** at 4am.* | **secretarial/legal/ clerical etc work** *He's started a business doing gardening and roofing work.*

4 RESULT [U] something that you produce as a result of doing your job or doing an activity: *Send a résumé and examples of your work.* | *The building is the work of architect Rafael Moneo.* | *The teacher should make sure that each child has **a piece of work** displayed on the wall.* | *The **standard of work** has declined.*

5 PAPERS ETC [U] the papers and other materials you need for doing work: *Can you move some of your work off the kitchen table?* | *I often have to take work home with me.*

6 BOOK/PAINTING/MUSIC [C] something such as a painting, play, piece of music etc that is produced by a painter, writer, or musician: *the Collected Works of Shakespeare* | *It is another accomplished work by the artist.* → WORK OF ART

7 ACTIVITY [U] when you use physical or mental effort in order to achieve something: [+on] *Work will start next month on a new swimming pool in the centre of the city.* | *Looking after children can be **hard work**.* | **carry out/ do work** *You should not allow unqualified people to carry out work on your house.* | **set to work/get down to work** (=start work) *He set to work immediately.*

8 STUDY [U] study or RESEARCH, especially for a particular purpose: **carry out/do work** *The centre carries out work to monitor trends in housing management.* | *He did his postgraduate work in Sociology.*

9 at work **a)** doing your job or a particular activity: *He spent most of his time watching the fishermen at work.* **b)** having a particular influence or effect: *Volcanoes display some of nature's most powerful forces at work.*

10 the (whole) works *spoken* used after mentioning several things, to emphasize that someone or something has everything you can think of: *The hotel had everything – sauna, swimming pool, the works.*

11 nice work/quick work *spoken* used to praise someone for doing something well or quickly: *That was quick work!*

12 sth is in the works/pipeline *informal* used to say that something is being planned or developed: *Upgrades to the existing software are in the works.*

13 works [plural, U] **a)** activities involved in building or repairing things such as roads, bridges etc: **engineering works/irrigation works/roadworks** *the official in charge of the engineering works* → PUBLIC WORKS **b)** a building or group of buildings in which goods are produced in large quantities or an industrial process happens: **ironworks/gasworks/cement works** *The brick works closed last year.*

14 the works the moving parts of a machine; ◘ **mechanism**

15 have your work cut out (for you) *informal* used to say that it will be very difficult to do something: *The team will have their work cut out if they are to win the competition.*

16 make short/light work of sth to do something very quickly and easily: *A microwave oven can make light work of the cooking.*

17 make heavy/hard work of sth to do something with difficulty: *They made hard work of what should have been an easy game.*

18 FORCE [U] *technical* force multiplied by distance →

be all in a day's work at DAY (21); → do sb's dirty work at DIRTY¹ (8); → a nasty piece of work at NASTY (7); → nice work if you can get it at NICE (12)

work·a·ble /ˈwɜːkəbəl $ ˈwɜːr-/ adj **1** a workable system, plan etc will be practical and effective: *a workable solution to the problem* | *a workable timetable* **2** a substance that is workable can be shaped with your hands: *workable clay for making pots*

work·a·day /ˈwɜːkədeɪ $ ˈwɜːr-/ adj [only before noun] ordinary and not interesting; ◘ **everyday**: *He promised to tackle the workaday matters affecting people's daily lives.*

work·a·hol·ic /ˌwɜːkəˈhɒlɪk $ ˌwɜːrkəˈhɒː-/ n [C] *informal* someone who chooses to work a lot, so that they do not have time to do anything else

work·bas·ket /ˈwɜːkˌbɑːskɪt $ ˈwɜːrkˌbæs-/ n [C] a container for sewing equipment

work·bench /ˈwɜːkbentʃ $ ˈwɜːrk-/ n [C] a strong table used for working on with tools

work·book /ˈwɜːkbʊk $ ˈwɜːrk-/ n [C] a school book containing questions and exercises

work·day /ˈwɜːkdeɪ $ ˈwɜːrk-/ n [C] AmE **1** the amount of time that you spend working in a day; ◘ **working day**: *a 10 hour workday* **2** a day of the week when most people work; ◘ **working day**: *He commutes three hours on workdays.* | *workday traffic*

worked 'up adj [not before noun] *informal* very upset or excited about something: [+about/over] *You shouldn't get so worked up about it.* → work up at WORK¹

work·er S3 W1 /ˈwɜːkə $ ˈwɜːrkər/ n [C]
1 someone who works in a job, especially a particular type of job: *part-time, low-paid workers* | *workers in the tourist industry* | **factory/farm/office etc worker** *new health and safety regulations for factory workers* | **research/rescue/healthcare etc worker** *reports from local aid workers* | **skilled/unskilled worker** (=someone who has or does not have special skills) | **manual/blue-collar worker** (=someone who does practical or physical work) | **white-collar worker** (=someone who works in an office) → GUEST WORKER, SOCIAL WORKER
2 [usually plural] someone who works in an organization and who is not a manager: *conflicts between workers and management* | *attacks on workers' rights*
3 **good/hard/quick etc worker** someone who works very well or quickly
4 the workers the members of the WORKING CLASS: *the workers' revolution*

'work ˌethic n [singular] a belief in the moral value and importance of work: *They instilled the work ethic into their children.*

'work exˌperience n [U] **1** the experience you have had of working in a particular type of job: *She's well qualified but has no relevant work experience.* **2** BrE a period of time that a young person spends working in a particular place, as a form of training: **on work experience** *The teenagers spend two weeks on work experience in local businesses.* | *Why do I have to **do work experience?*** | **work experience placement/pro-gramme/scheme etc**

work·fare /ˈwɜːkfeə $ ˈwɜːrkfer/ n [U] a system in which unemployed people have to work before they are given money for food, rent etc by the government

work·flow /ˈwɜːkfləʊ $ ˈwɜːrkfloʊ/ n [U] the way that a particular project is organized by a company, including which part of a project someone is going to do, and when they are supposed to do it

work·force /ˈwɜːkfɔːs $ ˈwɜːrkfɔːrs/ n [singular] all the people who work in a particular industry or company, or are available to work in a particular country or area; → **staff**: *Women now represent almost 50% of the workforce.* | *The company is cutting its workforce.* | **skilled/educated/flexible etc workforce**

work·horse /ˈwɜːkhɔːs $ ˈwɜːrkhɔːrs/ n [C] a person, machine, or vehicle that does a lot of work, especially

W

when it is hard or boring: *The Hercules aircraft has been the workhorse of the airforce for over 25 years.*

work·house /'wɜːkhaʊs $ 'wɜːrk-/ *n* [C] a building in Britain in the past where very poor people lived if they had nowhere else to go; ◘ **poorhouse**

work·ing¹ S1 W1 /'wɜːkɪŋ $ 'wɜːr-/ *adj* [only before noun]

1 a) having a job that you are paid for; → **employed**: *a working mother* | *Many working women rely on relatives for childcare.* | *A smaller working population will have to support a growing number of retired people.* **b)** *old-fashioned* having a physical or practical job: **working man/people/folk** *the ordinary working man*

2 working hours/day/week the time that people spend doing their job: *In a normal working day, I see around 6 or 7 clients.* | **during/outside working hours** *Telephone at any time during normal working hours.* | *Many mothers prefer flexible working hours.* | *We do a 37-hour working week.*

3 working day a day of the week when most people work. In Britain and the US this is usually Monday to Friday; ◘ **workday**: *It will be returned within three working days* (=three days, not including weekends or public holidays).

4 working conditions/environment etc the situation in which you work, especially the physical things such as pay or safety: *improvements in working conditions*

5 working practices/methods the way in which you do your job: *training in up-to-date working practices*

6 working life the part of your adult life when you have a paid job: *He spent all his working life in a factory.*

7 (in) working order working properly and not broken: **be in good/perfect/full etc working order** *The car was old, but the engine was still in good working order.* | *the amount of exercise needed to keep your body in working order*

8 working relationship the way that people work together: [+**with/between**] *They want to establish a better working relationship between medical and nursing staff.* | **good/close/effective etc working relationship** *We have a close working relationship with other voluntary groups.*

9 a working knowledge of sth enough knowledge of a system, subject, language etc to be able to use it or to do a particular job: *A good working knowledge of the Building Regulations is necessary for the job.*

10 working clothes also **work clothes** clothes which you wear for work or are designed for people to work in

11 working model a model that has parts that move

12 working parts the parts of a machine that move

13 working definition/theory/title a DEFINITION, idea etc that may not be exactly right but is good enough to use when you start working on something

14 working majority *BrE* enough support in parliament for a government to continue making laws and ruling a country

15 working breakfast/lunch/dinner a breakfast, lunch etc which is also a business meeting

16 working memory *technical* the part of a person's or computer's memory which stores information about the thing being worked on now

working² *n* **1** [singular] also **workings** the way something such as a system, piece of equipment, or organization works: [+**of**] *his knowledge of the inner workings of the department* | *I shall never understand **the workings of** his mind* (=how he thinks). **2 flexible/short-time etc working** a particular way of working, especially relating to the hours which someone works **3** [C usually plural] a mine or part of a mine where soil has been dug out in order to remove metals or stone; → **quarry**

working ˈcapital *n* [U] the money that is available to be used for the costs of a business → VENTURE CAPITAL

working ˈclass *n* [singular also + plural verb] *BrE* also **working classes** the group of people in society who traditionally do physical work and do not have much money or power: *Marx wrote about the political struggles of the working class.* —**working class** *adj*: *working class women* | *the traditional working class occupations* | *He is proud of his working class background.* → LOWER CLASS, MIDDLE CLASS, UPPER CLASS

ˈworking girl *n* [C] *old-fashioned* a woman who has sex for money – used when you want to avoid saying this directly; ◘ **prostitute**

ˈworking group *n* [C] a group that is formed to examine a particular situation or problem and suggest ways of dealing with it; ◘ **working party: set up/establish a working group (to do sth)** *The commission has set up a special working group to look at the problem.* | [+**on**] *a working group on constitutional reform*

ˈworking ˌpapers *n* [plural] an official document that you need in the US in order to get a job if you are young or were born in a different country

ˈworking ˌparty *n* [C] *BrE* a WORKING GROUP

work·load /'wɜːkləʊd $ 'wɜːrkloʊd/ *n* [C] the amount of work that a person or organization has to do: *She's struggling to cope with the heavy workload.* | **increase/reduce/add to etc sb's workload** *We've got to find ways of reducing Gail's workload next year.*

work·man /'wɜːkmən $ 'wɜːrk-/ *n plural* **workmen** /-mən/ [C] someone who does physical work such as building, repairing things etc

work·man·like /'wɜːkmənlaɪk $ 'wɜːrk-/ *adj* done in a way which shows skill and hard work, but may not be exciting: *The team put up a good workmanlike performance to win 1–0.*

work·man·ship /'wɜːkmənʃɪp $ 'wɜːrk-/ *n* [U] skill in making things, especially in a way that makes them look good; ◘ **craftsmanship**

work·mate /'wɜːkmeɪt $ 'wɜːrk-/ *n* [C] *BrE* someone you work with; ◘ **colleague**

ˌwork of ˈart *n plural* **works of art** [C] **1** a painting, SCULPTURE etc of high quality **2** something that is very attractive and skilfully made – often used humorously: *That cake's a real work of art!*

work·out /'wɜːkaʊt $ 'wɜːrk-/ *n* [C] a period of physical exercise, especially as training for a sport: *a daily workout in the gym* → **work out** at WORK¹

ˈwork ˌpermit *n* [C] an official document that you need if you want to work in a foreign country; → **visa**

work·place /'wɜːkpleɪs $ 'wɜːrk-/ *n* [C] the room, building etc where you work: **in the workplace** *a report into discrimination in the workplace*

ˈwork reˌlease *n* [U] *AmE* a system in which a prisoner is allowed to work outside a prison

work·room /'wɜːkrʊm, -ruːm $ 'wɜːrk-/ *n* [C] a room that you work in, especially making things, often in your home

work·sheet /'wɜːkʃiːt $ 'wɜːrk-/ *n* [C] a piece of paper with questions and exercises for students

work·shop S3 W3 /'wɜːkʃɒp $ 'wɜːrkʃɑːp/ *n* [C]
1 a room or building where tools and machines are used for making or repairing things
2 a meeting at which people try to improve their skills by discussing their experiences and doing practical exercises: **writers'/drama/music etc workshop** *They held a number of workshops and seminars.*

ˈwork-shy *adj* someone who is work-shy tries to avoid working because they do not like it; ◘ **lazy**

work·sta·tion /'wɜːkˌsteɪʃən $ 'wɜːrk-/ *n* [C] **1** a computer that is part of an office computer system **2** the desk where an office worker works

ˈwork-ˌsurface also **work·top** /'wɜːktɒp $ 'wɜːrktɑːp/ *n* [C] *especially BrE* a flat surface for working on, especially in a kitchen; ◘ **counter** *AmE*

ˌwork-to-ˈrule *n* [singular] a situation in which people in a particular job refuse to do any additional work as a protest; → **strike** → **work to rule** at WORK¹ (32)

W

work·week /ˈwɜːkwiːk $ ˈwɜːrk-/ *n* [C] *AmE* the total amount of time that you spend working during a week; ☐ **working week** *BrE*: *a 40-hour workweek*

world¹ [S1] [W1] /wɜːld $ wɜːrld/ *n*

1 OUR PLANET/EVERYONE ON IT the world the PLANET we live on, and all the people, cities, and countries on it; → **earth**

> a part of the world
> the highest/most powerful etc in the world
> the world's oldest/tallest etc ...
> around the world
> all over the world/the world over (=everywhere in the world)
> throughout/across the world (=everywhere in the world)
> anywhere in the world
> the rest of the world
> the whole/entire world
> see/travel the world (=travel to many different countries)

*Tuberculosis is still common in some **parts of the world**. | At that time China was **the most** powerful country **in the world**. | **the world's tallest** building | The Taj Mahal attracts visitors from **around the world**. | Students from **all over the world** come to study at Oxford. | Children are the same **the world over**. | The book has been published **throughout the world**. | There is nothing quite like it **anywhere in the world**. | Europe's relationship with **the rest of the world** | I decided to take a year off to **travel the world**. | a crime that shocked the world*

2 in the world used to emphasize what you are saying: **the happiest/most exciting etc ... in the world** *I'm the luckiest man in the world! | Bali is my favourite place **in the whole world**. | Off he went, **without a care in the world** (=not be worried about anything at all). | **Nothing in the world** (=nothing at all) can save them now. | Don't worry, we've got **all the time in the world** (=plenty of time so you do not need to hurry). | **what/who/where/how etc in the world ...?** (=used when you are very surprised or annoyed) What in the world are you doing here at seven in the morning?*

3 THE SOCIETY WE LIVE IN [singular] the society that we live in, the way people behave, and the kind of life we have: *Parents want a better world for their children. | **the world** The world is being transformed by information technology. | You had to go into politics if you wanted to change the world. | **in an ideal/perfect world** (=used to say how you would like things to be) In an ideal world, we would be able to recycle everything. | **the real world** (=the way life really is, not how people would like it to be or imagine it) In the real world, things are never quite so simple. | **what is the world coming to?** (=used to say that you do not like the way society is changing) Five pounds just to park your car! I don't know what the world's coming to.*

4 GROUP OF COUNTRIES [singular] a particular group of countries: **the Western/Arab etc world** *the highest unemployment rate in the Western world | the English-speaking world | agricultural practices in **the developing world** | the economies of **the industrialized world***

5 TIME IN HISTORY [singular] a particular period in history: **the modern/ancient world** *the peoples of the ancient world | **the world of ...** the world of the Ancient Greeks*

6 SB'S LIFE AND EXPERIENCES [C] the life and experiences of a particular person or group of people: [+of] *the world of children | The diary gives us an insight into Hemingway's world.*

7 AREA OF ACTIVITY/WORK [C usually singular] a particular area of activity or work, and the people who are involved in it: **the world of politics/business/work etc** *She knew little about the world of politics. | **the art/business/academic etc world** personalities from the sporting world*

8 NATURE/ANIMALS/PLANTS the natural/animal/plant world all of nature, or all animals or plants considered as a group: *the wonders of the natural world*

9 PLACE/SITUATION [C usually singular] a particular kind of place or situation, especially one that someone describes or which you imagine: [+of] *the nightmare world of Orwell's novel 1984 | a world of lies and secrecy*

10 ANOTHER PLANET [C] a place like the Earth in another part of the universe where other things may live: *strange creatures from **another world***

11 STH IS VERY DIFFERENT [C] used in the following phrases to emphasize that something is very different: *There's **a world of difference** between the US and Europe. | I realized we were still **worlds apart** (=very different, especially concerning your ideas, opinions etc). | It was **a world away from** (=completely different from) the grand hotels she was used to.*

12 the outside world the people who live outside a particular place or country – used when the people of that place or country do not often meet other people: *Prisoners have little contact with the outside world. | **be cut off from/closed to/isolated from the outside world** Parts of the country have been virtually closed to the outside world for 20 years.*

13 the material world real things, rather than ideas and beliefs: *Is the material world all that exists?*

14 for all the world as if/as though/like *literary* exactly as if or exactly like: *She sat reading her paper, **looking for all the world as if** nothing had happened.*

15 out of this world *informal* extremely good, enjoyable etc: *The graphics and sounds are out of this world.*

16 do sb a world of good to be very good for someone's health or mental state: *A bit of fresh air and exercise will do her a world of good.*

17 in a world of your own/in your own little world used to say that someone seems to spend a lot of time thinking or imagining things, and does not seem to notice what is happening around them: *She was a shy child who seemed to **live in a world of her own**.*

18 mean the world to sb/think the world of sb if someone or something means the world to you, or if you think the world of them, they are very important to you and you love or respect them very much: *Lee thinks the world of that dog.*

19 sb would give the world to do sth used to say that someone would like to do something very much: *He would give the world to see her again.*

20 be/feel on top of the world *informal* to feel extremely happy

21 be a man/woman of the world to be someone who has had many experiences and is not easily shocked

22 not for the world used to emphasize that you would not do something: *I wouldn't **hurt her for the world**. | I wouldn't have missed it for the world.*

23 the world is your oyster there is no limit to the opportunities that someone has: *If you've got a good education, the world is your oyster.*

24 have the world at your feet a) to be very famous, popular, or successful: *In those days the band had the world at their feet.* **b)** to be in a position where you have the chance to become very successful: *a bright young lad with the world at his feet*

25 go up/come down in the world to move to a higher or lower position in society: *He's gone up in the world a bit since I knew him at college.*

26 set the world on fire/alight *spoken* to have a big effect or be very successful: *Her last film didn't exactly set the world on fire.*

27 set/put the world to rights to discuss or say how the world should be changed to make people's lives better: *We were having a few beers and generally putting the world to rights.*

28 the Michael Jacksons/Mother Teresas/Microsofts etc of this world *spoken* used to talk about a particular kind of person or group, by using one person or group as an example: *The US team is new to the soccer scene, and can't expect to beat the Brazils of the world.*

29 think the world owes you a living to think that you

[1] 000, [2] 000, [3] 000, most frequent words in [S]poken and [W]ritten English

should not have to work and that other people will provide you with everything you need – used to show disapproval

30 (think that) the world revolves around you to think that you are the most important person and everyone else should only be interested in making sure that you have what you want – used to show disapproval

31 the world and his wife *BrE* everyone or anybody – used when you want to emphasize that a lot of people do something or anyone can do something: *It seemed that the world and his wife had come to Madrid.*

32 come into the world *literary* to be born

33 bring a child into the world *literary* to have a baby, or help a baby to be born

34 sb is not long for this world *literary* used to say that someone is likely to die soon

35 NORMAL LIFE the world normal life in society, as opposed to a religious way of life, especially in a MONAS-TERY etc: *She renounced the world and entered a convent.* → **best of both worlds** at BEST³ (7); → **be dead to the world** at DEAD¹ (9); → **it's not the end of the world** at END¹ (19) → NEW WORLD, THIRD WORLD

world² *adj* [only before noun] **1** existing in, involving, or affecting all or most countries in the world: **the World Cup/Championships etc** (=a competition involving people from many countries) *He won the world title in 2001.* | *the reigning Formula One* **world champion** | **world trade/economy etc** *the impact of the crisis on the world economy* → WORLD WAR **2** a **world** figure is one of the most important people in the world: *a meeting of* **world leaders** | *a* **world authority** *on climate change* → WORLD POWER

'world-,beater *n* [C] someone or something that is the best at a particular activity —**world-beating** *adj*

,world-'class *adj* among the best in the world: *a world-class tennis champion* | *world-class research facilities*

,world-'famous *adj* known about by people all over the world: *a world-famous singer*

world·ly /'wɜːldli $ 'wɜːrld-/ *adj* [only before noun] **1 worldly goods/possessions** *literary* everything you own **2** relating to ordinary life rather than SPIRITUAL or religious ideas; ☐ **mundane**: *He seemed very calm and far removed from worldly concerns.* **3** having a lot of experience and knowledge about people and life; ☐ **unworldly** —**worldliness** *n* [U]

,worldly-'wise / $ '··· / *adj* having a lot of experience and knowledge about life so that you are not easily shocked or deceived; ☐ **naïve**

'world ,music *n* [U] a type of popular music which has influences from traditional music from different countries

,world 'power *n* [C] a country that has a lot of power and influence in many parts of the world; → **superpower**

,world 'record *n* [C] the fastest time, longest distance, highest level etc which anyone has ever achieved anywhere in the world, especially in a sport: **set/break/ beat a world record** *He set a new world record for the marathon.* | *the 800m* **world record holder** —**world-record** *adj*: *a world-record time*

,world 'view, world-view *n* [C usually singular] someone's opinions and attitudes relating to the world and things in general: *the limited nineteenth-century world view*

,world 'war *n* [C] a war involving many of the countries of the world: *fears of another world war* | *Churchill was prime minister during the Second World War.* | *the years after World War I*

,world-'weary *adj* not feeling excited about anything any more —**world-weariness** *n* [U]

world·wide /,wɜːld'waɪd◄ $,wɜːrld-/ *adj, adv* everywhere in the world: *We have offices in over 56 countries worldwide.* | *cars with a worldwide reputation for reliability*

,World Wide 'Web *n* the World Wide Web *WWW* the WEB; ☐ **the Internet**

worm¹ /wɜːm $ wɜːrm/ *n* [C] **1** a long thin creature with no bones and no legs that lives in soil → EARTHWORM, LUGWORM **2** the young form of an insect, which looks like a short worm → GLOW-WORM, SILKWORM, WOODWORM **3 have worms** if a person or animal has worms, they have legless PARASITES (=small creatures that eat their food or their blood) in their body → ROUNDWORM, TAPEWORM **4** someone who you do not like or respect **5** a type of computer VIRUS that can make copies of itself and destroy information on computers that are connected to each other **6 the worm turns** *literary* used to say that someone who normally obeys someone without complaining suddenly refuses to do this → **can of worms** at CAN² (4)

worm² *v* [T] **1 worm (your way) into/through etc sth** to move through a small place or a crowd slowly, carefully, or with difficulty: *He wormed his way under the fence.* **2 worm your way into sb's affections/heart/ confidence etc** to gradually make someone love or trust you, especially by being dishonest **3 worm your way out of (doing) sth** to avoid doing something that you have been asked to do by making an excuse that is dishonest but clever: *Steve wormed his way out of going to the meeting.* **4** to give an animal medicine in order to remove PARASITES that live inside it

worm sth out of sb *phr v* to get information from someone who does not want to give it

WORM /wɜːm $ wɜːrm/ *n* [C] **write once, read many** a CD on which information can be stored only once, but seen or used many times

'worm-,eaten *adj* worm-eaten wood or fruit has holes in it because it has been eaten by worms

worm·hole /'wɜːmhəʊl $ 'wɜːrmhoʊl/ *n* [C] **1** a hole, which may exist, that connects one part of the universe with another part far away **2** a hole in a piece of wood etc made by a type of WORM

worm·wood /'wɜːmwʊd $ 'wɜːrm-/ *n* [U] a plant with a bitter taste

worm·y /'wɜːmi $ 'wɜːrmi/ *adj* full of worms

worn¹ /wɔːn $ wɔːrn/ the past participle of WEAR¹

worn² *adj* **1** a **worn** object is old and damaged, especially because it has been used a lot: *a worn patch on the carpet* | *well worn stone steps* **2** someone who looks worn seems tired

,worn 'out *adj* **1** very tired because you have been working hard; ☐ **exhausted**: *You must be absolutely worn out.* **2** too old or damaged to be used: *a pair of old worn-out walking boots*

wor·ried [S2] [W3] /'wʌrid $ 'wɜːrid/ *adj* **1** unhappy because you keep thinking about a problem, or about something bad that might happen: *You look worried. What's the matter?* | [+about] *I'm really worried about my brother.* | [+by] *Local people are worried by the rise in crime.* | **worried (that)** *I was worried we wouldn't have enough money.* | *Don't look so worried – we'll find him.* | *By this time, I was really getting worried.* | **worried expression/look/frown etc** *Where have you been? I was* **worried sick** (=extremely worried)!

2 you had me worried *spoken* used to say that someone made you feel anxious because you did not properly understand what they said, or did not realize that it was a joke: *You had me worried there for a minute!* —**worriedly** *adv*

WORD FOCUS: WORRIED

similar words: **anxious, concerned, apprehensive, uneasy, bothered, preoccupied, stressed (out)**

wor·ri·er /'wʌriə $ 'wɜːriər/ *n* [C] someone who often worries about things: *Her mother was a born worrier.*

W

wor·ri·some /ˈwʌrisəm $ ˈwɜːri-/ adj formal making
you anxious: a worrisome problem

wor·ry¹ S1 W2 /ˈwʌri $ ˈwɜːri/ v worried, worrying,
worries

1 BE ANXIOUS [I] to be anxious or unhappy about
someone or something, so that you think about them a
lot: [+about] I worry about my daughter. | You've really
got no need to worry about your weight. | worry (that)
She worried that she wasn't doing enough to help. |
[+over] Dad worries over the slightest thing. | Don't tell
Mum about this – she's got enough to worry about
(=she already has a lot of problems or is very busy).

2 don't worry spoken **a)** used when you are trying to
make someone feel less anxious: Don't worry, darling,
Daddy's here. | [+if] Don't worry if you can't finish all
the questions. **b)** used to tell someone that they do not
need to do something: [+about] Don't worry about
sorting them out – I'll do it later. **c)** used to tell someone
that you will definitely do something: Don't you worry,
I'll make sure he does his fair share.

3 MAKE SB ANXIOUS [T] to make someone feel anxious about something: The recent changes in the Earth's
climate are beginning to worry scientists. | I didn't tell
Mum and Dad – I didn't want to worry them. | what
worries me is .../the (only) thing that worries me is ...
The only thing that worries me is the food. I don't want
to get food poisoning. | Doesn't it worry you that Sarah
spends so much time away from home? | worry yourself
(=feel anxious, especially when there is no need to)
You're worrying yourself unnecessarily.

4 not to worry BrE spoken used to say that something is
not important: Not to worry, we can always go another
time.

5 nothing to worry about spoken used to tell someone
that something is not as serious or difficult as they
think: It's just a check-up – nothing to worry about.

6 ANNOY [T] to annoy someone; ➡ bother: The heat
didn't seem to worry him.

7 ANIMAL [T] if a dog worries sheep, it tries to bite or
kill them

worry at sth/sb phr v
1 if an animal worries at a bone or piece of meat, it
bites and shakes it
2 if you worry at a problem, you think about it a lot in
order to find a solution

worry² S3 n plural worries
1 [C] a problem that you are anxious about or are not
sure how to deal with: sb's main/biggest/real etc worry
My main worry is finding somewhere to live. | I had a lot
of financial worries. | be a worry to/for sb Money was
always a big worry for us.
2 [C,U] the feeling of being anxious about something:
be frantic/sick/desperate etc with worry (=feel
extremely anxious) His mother was desperate with
worry. | He's been a constant source of worry. |
[+about] We had no worries about safety.
3 no worries BrE spoken used to agree to what someone
wants and to say that it will be no problem: 'Can you
deliver on Thursday?' 'Yeah, no worries, mate.'

ˈworry beads n [plural] a set of BEADS on a string that
you move about in order to keep yourself calm

wor·ry·ing S3 /ˈwʌri-ɪŋ $ ˈwɜː-/ adj something that is
worrying makes you feel anxious or worried: The
situation is extremely worrying | This is a worrying
development for small businesses. | It's been a worrying
few weeks for us all. —**worryingly** adv: Levels of some
pollutants are worryingly high.

wor·ry·wart /ˈwʌriwɔːt $ ˈwɜːriwɔːrt/ n [C] AmE
informal someone who worries a lot about unimportant
things

worse¹ /wɜːs $ wɜːrs/ adj **1** [the comparative of bad]
more unpleasant, bad, or severe; ➡ better: [+than] The
violence was worse than we expected. | The traffic is
much worse after five o'clock. | The weather was a lot
worse this year. | Conditions will get worse as the
winter continues. | High inflation will make unemploy-
ment worse. | Don't say anything, you'll only make
matters worse. | The bullying got worse and worse

until finally he had to leave the school. | **There's
nothing worse than** being robbed while you're on
holiday. | The school's not perfect, but I suppose it **could
be worse**. **2** more ill than before: If she's worse in the
morning, I'll call the doctor. | I was worried because he
seemed to be **getting worse** rather than better. | The
tablets seemed to **make him worse**. **3** be none the
worse for sth to not have been harmed by something:
She seemed none the worse for her night out in the
cold. **4** worse luck spoken used to say that you are
disappointed or annoyed by something: I've got one
more year of college, worse luck! **5** sb could do worse
than do sth spoken used to say that you think that
someone should do something: He could do worse than
marry Eleanor. **6** go from bad to worse to continue
getting worse: Things went from bad to worse, and in
the end she lost her job. **7** the worse for wear also **the
worse for drink** BrE informal drunk

Worse is a comparative form: The problem got worse
and worse.
⚠ Do not say 'more worse' or 'worser'.
Worst is a superlative form: the worst film (NOT worse
film) I have ever seen
⚠ Do not say 'most worst' or 'worstest'.

worse² n [U] **1** something worse; ➡ better: We
thought the situation was bad, but worse was to follow. **2** take a turn for the worse to change and become
worse: Last year his health took a turn for the worse.

worse³ adv [the comparative of badly] in a more severe
or serious way than before; ➡ better: [+than] By lunch
time it was raining worse than ever. | [sentence adverb]:
The business could become less profitable or, even worse,
could close down. | Suppose Rose, or worse still, Peter
had seen the photograph?

wors·en /ˈwɜːsən $ ˈwɜːr-/ v [I,T] to become worse or
make something worse; ➡ improve: A lot of teachers
expect the situation to worsen over the next few years. |
Interfering now could worsen the problem.
—**worsening** adj: We are now faced with a worsening
economic recession.

ˌworse ˈoff adj [not before noun] **1** if you are worse
off, you have less money; ➡ better off: The rent
increases will leave us worse off. | [+than] I don't think
we're any worse off than a lot of other people. **2** in a
worse situation: People in rural areas are even worse off,
as they have no regular bus service. | [+than] Other
sports are much worse off than athletics.

wor·ship¹ /ˈwɜːʃɪp $ ˈwɜːr-/ v past tense and past
participle **worshipped** present participle, **worshipping**
also **worshiped**, **worshiping** AmE **1** [I,T] to show
respect and love for a god, especially by praying in a
religious building: They all worship by the same god. | a
church where people have worshipped for hundreds of
years **2** [T] to admire and love someone very much: He
absolutely worships her. **3** worship the ground sb
walks on to admire or love someone so much that you
cannot see their faults —**worshipper** n [C]: She was a
regular worshipper at the parish church. ➡ HERO WORSHIP

worship² n [U] **1** the activity of praying or singing
in a religious building in order to show respect and
love for a god: **in worship** They bowed their heads in
worship. | [+of] Worship of the old gods still continues
in remote areas of the country. | The ceremony must take
place in a recognized **place of worship**. | We were
invited to join in their **act of worship** (=religious
ceremony). **2** Your/His Worship BrE formal used to talk
to or about a public official such as a MAYOR or MAGISTRATE

worst¹ /wɜːst $ wɜːrst/ adj [the superlative of
bad] **1** [only before noun] worse than anything or
anyone else; ➡ best: This is the worst recession for fifty
years. | My worst fear was that we would run out of
food. | What is the worst possible thing that can
happen? **2** be your own worst enemy to cause a lot of

problems for yourself because of your own behaviour **3 come off worst** to lose a fight or argument

worst² *n* **1 the worst** the person or thing that is worse than all others; → **the best**: *worst (that) This year's harvest is the worst that people can remember.* | *Last year was by far the worst* (=much worse than any other) *for road accidents.* | *I think the worst is over now.* | *The worst of it is* (=the worst part of the situation is), *I can't tell anyone what's happening.* | **at its/his etc worst** *You saw the garden at its worst, I'm afraid* (=when it is worse than any other time). **2 the worst of sth** most of something, or the most unpleasant or difficult part of it: *The worst of the storm seemed to be over.* **3 expect/fear the worst** to expect or fear that something will not be successful or something bad will happen: *When it got so late and they still weren't home, I began to fear the worst.* **4 get/have the worst of it** *spoken* to lose a fight or argument **5 at (the) worst** if things are as bad as they can be: *Choosing the right software can be time-consuming at best and confusing or frustrating at worst.* **6 do your/his/her/their worst** used to say that someone can try to harm you but they will not be able to: *They can do their worst now, because I'm leaving in three weeks.* **7 if the worst comes to the worst** *especially BrE*, **if worst comes to worst** *especially AmE* if the situation develops in the worst possible way: *If the worst comes to the worst, we'll sell the car.*

worst³ *adv* [the superlative of **badly**] **1** most badly; → **best**: *Aid is being sent to areas that have been worst affected by the earthquake.* | *the worst-dressed man in the office* **2 worst of all** used to say what is the worst part of a situation: *She had no office of her own and, worst of all, she didn't even have her own computer.*

wor·sted /ˈwʊstɪd/ *n* [U] a type of woollen cloth

worth¹ S1 W2 /wɜːθ $ wɜːrθ/ *prep*
1 be worth sth a) to have a value in money: *The house must be worth quite a lot of money now.* | *One of the pictures is worth £50,000.* | *Do you know how much the ring is worth?* | *This art collection is worth a fortune* (=worth a very large amount of money). | **be worth nothing/not be worth anything** *It's a very old machine so I shouldn't think it's worth anything.* **b)** to have money or possessions that have value: *I've heard that he's worth over $2 million.* | *The man who founded the company must be worth a fortune.*
2 be worth (doing) sth a) used to say that something is interesting, useful, or helpful: *A lot of the small towns in the area are definitely worth visiting.* | *The film is well worth seeing.* | **worth a trip/visit etc** *The local museum is worth a visit.* **b)** used to say that someone should do something because they will gain something from it: **it is worth doing sth** *It's worth checking the details of the contract before you sign it.* | *It's well worth getting there early if you want a good seat.* | **be worth the time/effort/work** *It was a great evening, and definitely worth all the hard work.*
3 be worth it *informal* used to say that you gain something from an action: *It was a lot of hard work, but it was worth it.*
4 be not worth it *informal* used to say that you do not gain anything from an action: *I thought about trying to talk to him about it, but decided it wasn't worth it.*
5 be worth sb's while (to do/doing sth) *spoken* used to say that someone should spend time or money on something because they will gain something from it: *It might be worth your while to talk to the head of department.* | *Some people feel it's not worth their while working if they can get money from the state.*
6 make it worth sb's while *spoken* to offer something to someone so that they will do something for you: *He promised to make it worth our while.*
7 what's it worth (to you)? *spoken* used humorously to ask someone how they will reward you if you do something for them
8 for what it's worth *spoken* used when you are giving someone information, to say that you are not sure how

useful it is: *Here's the list of names, for what it's worth.*
9 for all you are/he is etc worth with as much effort as possible: *He was pulling the rope for all he was worth.*
10 worth his/her salt doing their job well or deserving respect: *Any player worth his salt would love to play for his country.*

worth² W3 *n* [U]
1 ten pounds' worth/$500 worth etc of sth an amount of something worth ten pounds, $500 etc: *a chance to win £2000 worth of computing equipment* | *The fire caused thousands of pounds' worth of damage.*
2 ten minutes' worth/a week's worth etc of sth something that takes ten minutes, a week etc to happen, do, or use: *We had only three days' worth of food left.*
3 how good or useful something is or how important it is to people; ⊟ **value**: *The new computer system has already proved its worth.*
4 how much money something is worth; ⊟ **value**: *It is difficult to estimate the current worth of the company.*

worth·less /ˈwɜːθləs $ ˈwɜːrθ-/ *adj* **1** something that is worthless has no value, importance, or use; ⊡ **valuable**: *The house was full of worthless junk.* | *The information was worthless to me.* **2** a worthless person has no good qualities or useful skills: *His parents had made him feel worthless.* —**worthlessness** *n* [U]: *She struggled to overcome her feelings of worthlessness.*

worth·while S3 /ˌwɜːθˈwaɪl◂ $ ˌwɜːrθ-/ *adj* if something is worthwhile, it is important or useful, or you gain something from it: *He wanted to do a worthwhile job.* | *We decided to give the money to a worthwhile cause* (=one that helps people). | **it is worthwhile to do sth** *I thought it was worthwhile to clarify the matter.* | **is worthwhile doing sth** *It wasn't worthwhile continuing with the project.*

wor·thy¹ /ˈwɜːði $ ˈwɜːrði/ *adj* **1** [only before noun] deserving respect from people: *Leeds United were worthy winners of the competition.* | *a worthy opponent* **2 be worthy of sth** to deserve to be thought about or treated in a particular way: *A couple of other books are worthy of mention.* | *a teacher who is worthy of respect* **3 be worthy of sb** *informal* to be as good as something that a particular person would do: *a goal that was worthy of any of the great footballers of the world* **4 I'm/We're not worthy** *spoken* used humorously to say that you consider it a great honour to be with someone because they are famous, or much more skilful at doing something than you are **5** *formal* trying to help other people: *The money will go to a worthy cause.* | *I'm sure his motives were worthy.*

worthy² *n plural* **worthies** [C] *informal* someone who is important and should be respected: *We were met by a group of local worthies.*

wot /wɒt $ wɑːt, wʌt/ *BrE* an informal spelling of WHAT

would S1 W1 /wʊd/ *modal verb negative short form* **wouldn't**
1 PAST INTENTIONS/EXPECTATIONS used to say what someone intended to do or expected to happen: *They said they would meet us at 10.30 at the station.* | *She said she wouldn't be coming to the library any more.* | *Arnold knew he would be tired the next day.* | *It would soon be dark.*

2 IMAGINED SITUATIONS a) used when talking about a possible situation that you imagine or want to happen: *What would you do if you won a million pounds?* | *I'd be amazed if I got the job.* | *I wish they'd come and visit us.* | *If only he would listen to me.* **b)** used when talking about something that did not happen, or a situation that cannot exist: *Everything would be very different if your father were still alive.* | *I would have phoned you, but there wasn't time.* | *Alex would never have found out if you hadn't told him.* | *What would have happened if I hadn't been here?*

3 PAST HABITS used to say that something happened often or regularly in the past: *When we worked in the same office, we would often have coffee together.* | *On summer evenings they would sit out in the garden.*

4 REQUESTING *spoken* used to ask someone politely to do something: *Would you shut the window, please?* | *Would you mind waiting outside?* | *Would someone please tell me what is going on?*

5 OFFERING/INVITING *spoken* used to offer something to someone or invite them somewhere politely: *Would you like a coffee?* | *We're going to the theatre this evening. Would you be interested in coming?*

6 WHAT SB WANTS *spoken* used to say that someone wants something or wants to do something: **would like/love/prefer** *Yes, please, I'd love a coffee.* | *My parents would like to meet you.* | *Claudia would have liked to refuse* (=wanted to refuse)*, but she didn't dare.* | **I'd hate** (=I do not want) *to disappoint you.* | **would rather/sooner** (=used to say what someone prefers) *I'd rather stay in this evening, if that's all right with you.*

7 PAST PURPOSE used after 'so that' to show that someone was trying to make something happen or prevent something: *We packed all the books in wooden boxes so that they wouldn't get damaged.*

8 would not **a)** used to say that someone refused to do something: *He wouldn't give us any money.* **b)** used to say that something did not happen, even though someone was trying to make it happen: *The door wouldn't open, no matter how hard she pushed.*

9 ADVICE *spoken* used when giving or asking for advice: *I'd try to get there early if you can.* | *I would talk to the doctor if I were you.* | *What would you do if you were in my position?*

10 I would think/imagine/say *spoken* used to give your opinion about something when you are not very sure about it: *I would think you'd be happier in a different school.* | *'Will it cost a lot?' 'I would imagine so.'*

11 TYPICAL BEHAVIOUR *spoken* used to say that an action is typical or expected – usually used to show disapproval: *You would go and spoil it, wouldn't you!* | *She insists that she did nothing wrong, but then she would say that, wouldn't she?*

12 would that ... *literary* used to express a strong wish or desire; ▣ **if only**: *Would that we had seen her before she died.*

would-be *adj* **would-be actor/murderer etc** someone who hopes to have a particular job or intends to do a particular thing

would·n't /'wodnt/ the short form of 'would not'

would've /'wodəv/ the short form of 'would have'

wound¹ /waund/ the past tense and past participle of WIND²

wound² /wu:nd/ *n* [C] **1** an injury to your body that is made by a weapon such as a knife or a bullet: *A nurse cleaned and bandaged the wound.* | *It took several months for his **wounds** to **heal**.* | **suffer/receive a wound** *Several of the victims suffered severe stab wounds.* | **head/leg etc wound** *He was treated in hospital for head wounds.* | **stab/knife/gunshot wound** *He died of gunshot wounds.* | *The doctor said it was only a **flesh wound*** (=one that does not cut the skin very deeply). | *a **gaping wound*** (=one that is wide and open) *on his thigh* **2** a feeling of emotional or mental pain that you get when someone says or does something unpleasant to you: *It will take much longer for the mental **wounds** to **heal**.* **3 open old wounds** to remind someone of unpleasant things that happened in the

past △ Do not confuse with **wound**, the past tense and past participle of the verb **wind**, which has a different pronunciation → **lick your wounds** at LICK¹ (6); → **rub salt into the wound** at RUB¹ (6)

wound³ *v* [T] **1** to injure someone with a knife, gun etc: *Gunmen killed two people and wounded six others in an attack today.* | **be badly/seriously/critically etc wounded** *Five people were killed and many others were seriously wounded in the attack.* | **be mortally/fatally wounded** (=be wounded so badly that you die); → see box at DAMAGE² **2** to make someone feel unhappy or upset: *I was **deeply wounded** by his comments.* | *He made some very wounding remarks.*

wound·ed /'wu:nd³d/ *adj* **1** injured by a weapon such as a gun or knife: *a wounded soldier* → see picture at INJURED **2** very upset because of something that someone has said or done: *It was only **wounded pride** that stopped him from apologizing.* **3 the wounded** people who have been injured, especially in a war: *providing medical care for the wounded*

wound up /,waund 'ʌp/ *adj* [not before noun] anxious, worried, or excited: *I was too wound up to sleep.*

wove /wəʊv $ woʊv/ the past tense of WEAVE¹

wov·en /'wəʊvən $ 'woʊ-/ the past participle of WEAVE¹

wow¹ /waʊ/ *interjection informal* used when you think something is very impressive or surprising: *'Wow! Look at that!'*

wow² *v* [T] *informal* to make people admire you a lot; ▣ **impress**: *The show has wowed audiences all over the country.*

wow³ *n* [singular] *informal* a great success

WPC /,dʌbəlju: pi: 'si:‹ / *n* [C] *BrE* **Woman Police Constable** a female police officer

wpm /,dʌbəlju: pi: 'em/ *words per minute* used to describe the speed at which someone can write using a KEYBOARD

wrack /ræk/ another spelling of RACK²

wraith /reɪθ/ *n* [C] *literary* a GHOST

wran·gle¹ /'ræŋgəl/ *n* [C] a long and complicated argument: [+over] *a bitter **wrangle** over copyright* | [+with] *He was involved in a long **legal wrangle** with his employers.*

wrangle² *v* [I] to argue with someone angrily for a long time: [+over/about] *They are still wrangling over ownership of the house.* | [+with] *The various government departments are wrangling with each other.*

wran·gler /'ræŋglə $ -ər/ *n* [C] *AmE informal* a COWBOY

wrap¹ [S3] /ræp/ *v* **wrapped, wrapping** [T] **1** also **wrap up** to put paper or cloth over something to cover it: **wrap sth in sth** *The present was beautifully wrapped in gold paper.* | **wrap sth around sb/sth** *Ella wrapped a thick coat around her shoulders.* | *He wrapped a bandage around my injured wrist.* | *I've still got a few Christmas presents to wrap up.* **2** if you wrap your arms, legs, or fingers around something, you use them to hold it: **wrap sth around sb/sth** *He wrapped his arms around her waist.* → **wrap sb in cotton wool** at COTTON WOOL (2); → **wrap sb around your little finger** at FINGER¹ (8)

    wrap up *phr v*
 1 wrap sth ⇔ up to put on warm clothes: **wrap up warm/well** *Make sure you wrap up warm – it's freezing.* | **be wrapped up in sth** *She was wrapped up in a thick winter coat.*
 2 wrap sth ⇔ up *informal* to finish a job, meeting etc: *We're hoping to wrap up the negotiations this week.*
 3 be wrapped up in sth to give so much of your attention to something that you do not have time for anything else

wrap² *n* **1** [C] a piece of thick cloth that a woman wears around her shoulders; → **shawl** **2** [U] a type of thin clear plastic that is used to cover food; ▣ **cling-film** **3 keep sth under wraps** to keep something secret: *The project has been kept under wraps for*

▣ **W**

years. **4** [C] a type of sandwich made with thin bread which is rolled around meat, vegetables etc **5** [singular] the end of a day's filming: *OK everybody, it's a wrap!*

'wrap-a,round *adj* a wrap-around skirt is one that you wind around your body and fasten in place

wrap·a·rounds /'ræpəraʊndz/ *n* [plural] SUNGLASSES that are curved in such a way that they fit close to your face, from one ear to the other

wrap·per /'ræpə $ -ər/ *n* [C] the piece of paper or plastic that covers something when it is sold: *old sweet wrappers*

wrap·ping /'ræpɪŋ/ *n* [C,U] the cloth, paper, or plastic that is wrapped around something to protect it: *I finally managed to get the plastic wrapping off.*

'wrapping ,paper *n* [U] coloured paper that you use for wrapping presents

'wrap-up *n* [C] *AmE informal* a short report that repeats the main points, for example of a news broadcast; ◘ **round-up**

wrath /rɒθ $ ræθ/ *n* [U] *formal* extreme anger: *He was scared of incurring his father's wrath.*

wreak /riːk/ *v past tense and past participle* **wreaked** *or* **wrought** /rɔːt $ rɒːt/ **1** **wreak havoc/mayhem/ destruction (on sth)** to cause a lot of damage or problems: *These policies have wreaked havoc on the British economy.* **2** **wreak revenge/vengeance (on sb)** *formal* to do something unpleasant to someone to punish them for something they have done to you: *He promised to wreak vengeance on those who had betrayed him.*

wreath /riːθ/ *n* [C] **1** a circle made from leaves or flowers that you put on the place where a person is buried: *The prime minister laid a wreath at the war memorial.* **2** a circle of leaves or flowers that people use to decorate their houses at Christmas **3** a circle made from leaves that a person wore on their head in the past as a sign of honour: *a laurel wreath*

wreathe /riːð/ *v literary* **1** **be wreathed in sth** to be covered in something: *The mountains were wreathed in mist.* **2** **be wreathed in smiles** to be smiling and look very happy: *His plump face was wreathed in smiles.*

wreck¹ /rek/ *v* [T]
1 **SPOIL** to completely spoil something so that it cannot continue in a successful way; ◘ **ruin**: *Injury threatened to wreck his sporting career.* | *It was drink that wrecked their marriage.*
2 **DAMAGE** to damage something such as a building or vehicle so badly that it cannot be repaired: *The car was completely wrecked in the accident.*
3 **DESTROY A SHIP** if a ship is wrecked, it is badly damaged and sinks: *The ship was wrecked off the coast of Africa.*

wreck² *n* [C]
1 **CAR/PLANE** a car, plane, or train that has been damaged very badly, especially in a crash: *He was still alive when they pulled him from the wreck.*
2 **SHIP** a ship that has sunk; ◘ **shipwreck**: [+of] *Divers discovered the wreck of an old German warship.*
3 **PERSON** *informal* someone who is very nervous, tired, or unhealthy: *He looked a complete wreck.* | **nervous/emotional wreck** *The attack had left her an emotional wreck.*
4 **ACCIDENT** *AmE* an accident involving cars or other vehicles; ◘ **crash**: **car/train/plane wreck** *My father died in a car wreck.*
5 **PLACE** a place that is very untidy: *When you're here, this place is a wreck!*

wreck

mast —

anchor

6 **OLD CAR** *informal* an old car that is in a very bad condition

wreck·age /'rekɪdʒ/ *n* [singular, U] **1** the parts of something such as a plane, ship, or building that are left after it has been destroyed in an accident: *Firemen managed to pull some survivors from the wreckage.* | [+of] *Accident investigators will examine the wreckage of the plane.* **2** the parts of someone's relationships, hopes, or plans that remain after they have been spoiled: [+of] *She still hoped to salvage something from the wreckage of her marriage.*

wrecked /rekt/ *adj* [not before noun] *informal* **1** *BrE* very drunk **2** extremely tired

wreck·er /'rekə $ -ər/ *n* [C] **1** someone who deliberately destroys something: *She accused him of being a marriage wrecker.* **2** *AmE* a vehicle that is used to take away damaged cars after an accident

'wrecking ,ball *n* [C] a heavy metal ball attached to a chain or CABLE which is used to knock down buildings

'wrecking ,crew *n* [C] a group of workers whose job is to knock down buildings

wren /ren/ *n* [C] a very small brown bird

wrench¹ /rentʃ/ *v* **1** [T always + adv/prep] to twist and pull something roughly from the place where it is being held: *I wrenched the packet from his grasp.* | *The door had been wrenched open.* **2** **wrench yourself away/free** to use your strength to pull yourself away from someone who is holding you: *She managed to wrench herself free.* **3** [T] to hurt a joint in your body by twisting it; ◘ **sprain**: *I think I've wrenched my knee.*

wrench² *n* **1** [C] *especially AmE* a metal tool that you use for turning NUTS; ◘ **spanner** *BrE* **2** [singular] a strong feeling of sadness that you get when you leave a person or place that you love: *Leaving New York had been a terrible wrench.* **3** [C usually singular] a twisting movement that pulls something violently: *He grabbed the rope and gave it a wrench.*

wrest /rest/ *v* [T always + adv/prep] **1** *formal* to take power or influence away from someone, especially when this is difficult: *They are fighting to wrest control of the party from the old leaders.* **2** *literary* to pull something away from someone violently: *I managed to wrest the photograph from his grasp.*

wres·tle /'resəl/ *v* **1** [I,T] to fight someone by holding them and pulling or pushing them: [+with] *The two men wrestled with each other.* | *Police officers wrestled him to the ground.* **2** [I,T] to move something or try to move it when it is large, heavy, or difficult to move: [+with] *Ray continued to wrestle with the wheel.* **3** **wrestle with sth** to try to understand or find a solution to a difficult problem: *I have been wrestling with this problem for quite some time.*

wres·tler /'reslə $ -ər/ *n* [C] someone who takes part in wrestling

wres·tling /'reslɪŋ/ *n* [U] a sport in which two people fight by holding each other and trying to make each other fall to the ground

wretch /retʃ/ *n* [C] **1** someone that you feel sorry for: *He was a lonely, miserable wretch.* **2** someone you are annoyed with: *Stop pulling my hair, you wretch!*

wretch·ed /'retʃɪd/ *adj* **1** someone who is wretched is very unhappy or ill, and you feel sorry for them: *the poor, wretched girl* **2** if you feel wretched, you feel guilty and unhappy because of something bad that you have done: *Guy felt wretched about it now.* **3** [only before noun] making you feel annoyed or angry: *Where is that wretched boy?* **4** *literary* extremely bad or unpleasant; ◘ **miserable**: *I was shocked to see their wretched living conditions.* —**wretchedly** *adv* —**wretchedness** *n* [U]

wrig·gle¹ /'rɪgəl/ *v* **1** [I] to twist your body from side to side with small quick movements: *Stop wriggling and let me put your T-shirt on.* | [+under/through/into] *He wriggled through the window.* | *The dog wriggled free and ran off.* **2** [T] to move a part of your body backwards and forwards with small movements: *She took off her shoes and wriggled her toes.* —**wriggly** adj: *a wriggly worm*

wriggle out of sth phr v **1** to avoid doing something by using clever excuses; ☐ **get out of sth**: *Don't try to wriggle out of your responsibilities.* **2** to take off a tight piece of clothing by twisting your body from side to side: *She wriggled out of her dress.*

wriggle² n [C] a movement in which you twist your body from side to side

wring /rɪŋ/ v past tense and past participle **wrung** /rʌŋ/ [T] **1** [always + adv/prep] to succeed in getting something from someone, but only after a lot of effort; ☐ **squeeze**: **wring sth from/out of sb** *They are always trying to wring additional funds from the government.* | *I managed to wring the information out of him.* **2** also **wring out** to tightly twist a wet cloth or wet clothes in order to remove water → see picture at CLEAN **3 wring your hands** to rub and twist your hands together because you are worried and upset **4 wring sb's hand** to shake hands very firmly with someone **5 wring sth's neck** to kill a small animal by twisting its neck **6 I'll wring sb's neck** *spoken* used when you are very angry with someone: *I'll wring her neck when I get hold of her!* **7 wringing wet** extremely wet: *This jacket's wringing wet!*

wring·er /ˈrɪŋə $ -ər/ n [C] **1** a machine with two parts that roll over each other and press on wet clothes to remove water; ☐ **mangle 2 go through the wringer** *AmE informal* to have a lot of problems and upsetting experiences: *She's really been through the wringer since her husband died.*

wrin·kle¹ /ˈrɪŋkəl/ n [C] **1** wrinkles are lines on your face and skin that you get when you are old: *Her face was a mass of wrinkles.* **2** a small untidy fold in a piece of clothing or paper; ☐ **crease**: *She walked over to the bed and smoothed out the wrinkles.* **3 iron out the wrinkles** to solve the small problems in something —**wrinkly** adj: *her thin, wrinkly face*

wrinkle² v **1** [I,T] also **wrinkle up** if you wrinkle a part of your face, or if it wrinkles, small lines appear on it: *Alex wrinkled up her nose at the smell.* | *Carter wrinkled his forehead in concentration.* | *His brow wrinkled when he saw us.* **2** [I] if a piece of clothing wrinkles, it gets small untidy folds in it; ☐ **crease**: *The trouble with linen is that it wrinkles so easily.*

wrin·kled /ˈrɪŋkəld/ adj skin or cloth that is wrinkled has small lines or folds in it: *her wrinkled old face*

wrin·kly /ˈrɪŋkli/ n plural **wrinklies** [C] *BrE informal* not polite an offensive word for someone who is old

wrist S3 /rɪst/ n [C] the part of your body where your hand joins your arm: **on/around your wrist** *She had a gold watch on her wrist.* → BODY; → see picture at HAND¹

wrist·band /ˈrɪstbænd/ n [C] **1** a band that some tennis players wear around their wrists **2** a band with your name on it that you wear around your wrist, for example in a hospital

wrist·watch /ˈrɪstwɒtʃ $ -wɑːtʃ, -wɒːtʃ/ n [C] a watch that you wear on your wrist

writ¹ /rɪt/ n [C] a document from a court that orders someone to do or not to do something: *He issued a writ against the newspaper.* | *The company has been served with a writ for damages.* → HOLY WRIT

writ² adj **writ large** *literary* **a)** very easy to notice: *I could see the curiosity writ large on Rose's face.* **b)** in a very clear strong form: *This is an example of bureaucracy writ large.*

write S1 W1 /raɪt/ v past tense **wrote** /rəʊt $ roʊt/, past participle **written** /ˈrɪtn/
1 BOOK/ARTICLE/POEM ETC a) [I,T] to produce a new book, article, poem etc: *He wrote some very famous books.* | *Who wrote 'Harry Potter'?* | *I can't come with you – I have an essay to write.* | [+about] *O'Brien often writes about his native Ireland.* | **well/badly/poorly etc written** *The article is very well written.* **b)** [I] someone who writes earns money by writing books, plays, articles etc: *Sean decided he wanted to write, and quit*

his job. | [+for] *Maureen Dowd writes for the New York Times.*
2 LETTER [I,T] to write a letter to someone: [+to] *I've written to my MP, and to the city council.* | **write sb** *AmE*: *Chris hasn't written me for a long time.* | *I wrote her several letters, but she didn't reply.*
3 FORM WORDS [I,T] to form letters or numbers with a pen or pencil: *Kerry could read and write when she was five.*
4 STATE STH [T] to state something in a book, letter, advertisement etc, or on a label: **write (that)** *Isabella wrote that she was dying, and asked him to visit her for the last time.* | **be written on sth** *The price is written on the label.*
5 MUSIC/SONG [T] to write a piece of music or a song: *Mozart wrote the music.* | *The song was originally written by Leonard Cohen.*
6 COMPUTER PROGRAM [T] to make a program for a computer to use: *He writes software programs for financial institutions.*
7 A COMPUTER RECORDS STH [I,T] if a computer writes something, it records it on a disk or in its memory: [+to/onto] *data that had been written to disk*
8 CHEQUE/DOCUMENT ETC also **write out** [T] to write information on a cheque, form etc: *Wouldn't it be easier if I just wrote a cheque for the lot?* | *The doctor wrote me a prescription for sleeping pills.*
9 PEN [I] if a pen writes, it works properly: *Do any of these pens write?*
10 have sth/be written all over your face to show very clearly what you are feeling or thinking: *He had guilt written all over his face.* | *I know you're lying, Tyrell – it's written all over your face.*
11 have sth written all over it to show a particular quality or fact very clearly: *This awful film has 'career-killer' written all over it for the actors involved.*
12 nothing to write home about *informal* not particularly good or special: *The hotel was good, but the food was nothing to write home about.*
13 sb wrote the book on sth *spoken* used to say that someone knows a lot about a subject or is very good at an activity: *Motorola wrote the book on quality control.*
14 that's all she wrote *AmE spoken* used to mean that you cannot stop what happens next in a situation, especially when it is bad

write away for sth phr v
to write a letter to a company or organization asking them to send you goods or information: *I've written away for their free catalog.*
write back phr v
to reply to a letter that someone sent you, by writing a letter to them: *I sent them a card once, but they never wrote back.* | [+to] *I wrote back to them immediately, thanking them for their kind invitation.*
write sth ⇔ down phr v
1 to write something on a piece of paper: *This is the address. Do you want to write it down?*
2 to officially say that a debt no longer has to be paid, or officially accept that you cannot get back money you have spent or lost; ☐ **write off**
write in phr v
1 to write a letter to an organization to give an opinion, ask for information etc: *If you would like a copy of our fact sheet, please write in, enclosing a stamped addressed envelope.* | [+to] *And so I wrote in to Radio Brighton.*
2 write sth ⇔ in to write a piece of information in the space provided for it on a form or document: *Provide some space for students to write in their hobbies.*
3 write sb ⇔ in *AmE* to add someone's name to the

W

official list on your voting form, to show that you want to vote for them: *The campaign to write in Johnson for governor failed.* → WRITE-IN

write sth **into** sth *phr v*
to add or include something in a contract, agreement etc: *It was written into his contract that he had to make two records a year.*

write off *phr v*
1 to write a letter to a company or organization asking them to send you goods or information; ▤ **send off**, **write away**: [+**for**] *Are you going to write off for that free poster?*
2 write sb/sth ⇔ **off** to decide that someone or something is useless, unimportant, or a failure; ▤ **dismiss**: [+**as**] *After six months of work, we eventually wrote the project off as a non-starter.* → WRITE-OFF
3 write sth ⇔ **off** to officially say that a debt no longer has to be paid, or officially accept that you cannot get back money you have spent or lost: *The United States agreed to write off debts worth billions of dollars.* | *The Inland Revenue wrote off £900 million in unpaid taxes.*
4 write sth ⇔ **off** to make an official record of the amount of money that you have spent on things relating to your business, in order to reduce the amount of tax that you have to pay: [+**against**] *The costs of setting up a business can be written off against tax.*
5 write sth ⇔ **off** *BrE* to damage a vehicle so badly that it can never be used again: *At thirteen he stole a car and wrote it off.* → WRITE-OFF

write sb/sth ⇔ **out** *phr v*
1 to write something on paper, especially in a neat and clear way, including all the necessary details: *The children were asked to choose their favourite poem and write it out in their best handwriting.*
2 to write information on a cheque or a form: *She calmly wrote out a check for $500 and handed it to Will.*
3 to remove a character from a regular radio or television programme, by making him or her leave or die in the story: [+**of**] *It was revealed last week that Alma is being written out of the series.*

write sth ⇔ **up** *phr v*
1 to write a report, article etc using notes that you made earlier: *I have to write up my report before the meeting.*
2 to write something on a wall, board etc where people can see it: *The teacher repeated the word, and then wrote it up on the blackboard.*
3 be **written up** if something is written up in a newspaper, magazine etc, someone describes what it is like and gives their opinion of it: *We're going to a Spanish restaurant that was written up in Time Out's good food guide.* → WRITE-UP

'write-in *n* [C] *AmE* a vote you give to someone by writing their name on your BALLOT PAPER

'write-off *n* [C] **1** *BrE* a vehicle that has been so badly damaged that it can never be used again: *The car was a complete write-off.* **2** a period of time when you fail to achieve anything: *This morning was a complete write-off.* **3** an official agreement that someone does not have to pay a debt

writ·er S3 W2 /ˈraɪtə $ -ər/ *n* [C]
1 someone who writes books, stories etc, especially as a job; → **author**, **playwright**: *a science-fiction writer* | [+**on**] *a well-known writer on astrology* | [+**of**] *a writer of children's stories*
2 someone who has written something or who writes in a particular way: *He's always been a sloppy writer.* | [+**of**] *the writer of the previous message on this topic*

,writer's 'block *n* [U] the problem that a writer sometimes has of not being able to think of new ideas

,writer's 'cramp *n* [U] a feeling of stiffness in your hand that you get after writing for a long time

'write-up *n* [C] a written opinion about a new book, play, or product in a newspaper, magazine etc; ▤ **review**: *The play got a really good write-up* (=it was praised) *in the press.*

W

writhe /raɪð/ *v* [I] to twist your body from side to side violently, especially because you are suffering pain: **writhe in pain/agony etc** *He lay writhing in pain.*

writ·ing S2 W3 /ˈraɪtɪŋ/ *n* [U]
1 words that have been written or printed: *What does the writing on the back say?* | *a T-shirt with Japanese writing on it*
2 books, poems, articles etc, especially those by a particular writer or about a particular subject: *Some of his most powerful writing is based on his childhood experiences.*
3 the activity of writing books, stories etc: *In 1991 she retired from politics and took up writing as a career.* | *a short story that stands out as a brilliant* **piece of writing** | *a class in* **creative writing** (=a subject studied at school or college, where you write your own stories, poems etc) | **travel/feminist/scientific etc writing**
4 the particular way that someone writes with a pen or pencil; ▤ **handwriting**: *Your writing is very neat.*
5 the skill of writing: *At this age we concentrate on the children's* **reading and writing** skills.
6 in writing if you get something in writing, it is official proof of an agreement, promise etc: *Could you* **put** *that* **in writing**, please?
7 writings [plural] the books, stories etc that an important writer has written: *Darwin's scientific writings*
8 the writing is on the wall also **see/read the writing on the wall** used to say that it seems very likely that something will not exist much longer or someone will fail: [+**for**] *The writing is on the wall for old manufacturing industries.*

'writing desk *n* [C] a desk with special places for pens, paper etc

'writing ,paper *n* [U] good quality paper that you use for writing letters; ▤ **notepaper**

writ·ten¹ /ˈrɪtn/ the past participle of WRITE

written² *adj* [only before noun] **1** recorded in writing: *the development of* **written** *language.* | **written agreement/reply/statement/report etc** *Please send a cheque with written confirmation of your booking.* **2 written test/exam** a test etc in which you have to write the answers; → **oral 3 the written word** *formal* writing as a way of expressing ideas, emotions etc, as opposed to speaking

wrong¹ S1 W1 /rɒŋ $ rɔːŋ/ *adj*
1 NOT CORRECT not correct, and not based on true facts; ◪ **right**: *Your calculations must be wrong.* | *I think I* **got** *question 3* **wrong**. | **it is wrong to do sth** *It is wrong to assume that technological advance brings a higher quality of life.* | *I wish you'd stop trying to* **prove me wrong** (=show that I am wrong) *all the time.*
2 be **wrong** (**about sb/sth**) to not be right in what you think or believe about someone or something; ▤ **mistaken**; ◪ **right**: *No, you're wrong. Brett wouldn't do a thing like that.* | *I was wrong about the new guy – he's not Belgian, he's French.* | *That's where you're wrong! We never slept together.*
3 PROBLEMS used to describe a situation where there are problems, or when someone is ill or unhappy: **there is something wrong/something is wrong** *When he didn't come back that night, I knew that something was wrong.* | [+**with**] *What is wrong with our society? People just don't seem to care any more.* | **Is anything wrong?** *You haven't said more than two words since you got here.* | *Dave's* **got something wrong with** *his foot.* | *Don't worry, there's* **nothing wrong**.
4 NOT THE RIGHT ONE not the one that you intended or the one that you really want; ◪ **right**: *The letter was delivered to the wrong address.* | *driving on the wrong side of the road* | *You've got the wrong man. I didn't kill her.* | *I think we went the* **wrong way** *at that last turning.* | *There's no-one called Julia here. You must have the* **wrong number** (=wrong telephone number).
5 NOT MORALLY RIGHT not morally right or acceptable; ◪ **right**: **it is wrong that** *It's wrong that people should have to sleep on the streets.* | **it is wrong to do sth** *We all accept that it is wrong to torture people.* | *We*

weren't doing anything wrong! | [+**with**] *There's nothing wrong with making a profit, provided you don't cheat anyone.*
6 NOT SUITABLE not suitable for a particular purpose, situation, or person; **F3 right**: *It's the wrong time of year to be planning a holiday.* | [+**for**] *Anna and I were wrong for each other in dozens of ways* (=not suited for a romantic relationship with each other).
7 NOT WORKING if something is wrong with a vehicle or machine, it stops working properly: [+**with**] *There's something wrong with the car again.* → **go wrong** at WRONG² (2)
8 be the wrong way round/around a) to be in the wrong order: *These two paragraphs are the wrong way round.* **b)** if something is the wrong way round, the back is where the front should be: *You've got your T-shirt on the wrong way around.*
9 the wrong way up if something is the wrong way up, the top is where the bottom should be; **E3 upside down**: *The painting was hung the wrong way up.*
10 take sth the wrong way to be offended by a remark because you have understood it wrongly: *I like you. Don't take this the wrong way, now. I mean as a friend.*
11 be in the wrong place at the wrong time *spoken* to get involved in trouble without intending to
12 get on the wrong side of sb to do something that gives someone a bad opinion of you, so that they do not like or respect you in the future: *I wouldn't like to get on the wrong side of her.*
13 get on the wrong side of the law to get into trouble with the police
14 get off on the wrong foot to start a job, relationship etc badly by making a mistake that annoys people
15 get the wrong end of the stick *BrE informal* to understand a situation in completely the wrong way: *Geoff had got the wrong end of the stick, and thought I was angry with him.*
16 be on the wrong track/tack to have the wrong idea about a situation so that you are unlikely to get the result you want
17 be from the wrong side of the tracks *AmE* to be from a poor part of a town or a poor part of society
18 be the wrong side of thirty/forty etc *informal* to be older than 30 etc → **get out of bed on the wrong side** at BED¹ (8)
19 correct me if I'm wrong used as a polite way of saying that you think what you are going to say is correct: *Correct me if I'm wrong, but didn't you say you were going to do it?*
20 you're not wrong *spoken* used to agree with someone: *'This government is ruining the country!' 'You're not wrong there!'*
21 fall/get into the wrong hands if something secret or dangerous falls into the wrong hands, it is discovered by someone who may use it to harm people
wrong² **S2** *adv*
1 not in the correct way; **F3 right**: *You've spelt my name wrong.* | *What? Have I done it wrong?* | *I asked him to sort those files, but he's done it all wrong* (=in completely the wrong way).
2 go wrong a) to stop working properly: *Something's gone wrong with my watch.* **b)** to make a mistake during a process so that you do not get the right result: *Follow these instructions and you can't go wrong* (=you are sure to succeed). **c)** to do something that makes a plan, relationship etc fail: *Thinking back on the marriage, I just don't know where we went wrong.*
3 get sth wrong to make a mistake in the way you write, judge, or understand something: *This isn't it. We must have got the address wrong.* | **get/have it all wrong** (=understand a situation in completely the wrong way) *No, no – you've got it all wrong! We're just friends!*
4 don't get me wrong *spoken* used when you think someone may understand your remarks wrongly, or be offended by them: *Don't get me wrong – I like Jenny.*

5 you can't go wrong (with sth) *spoken* used to say that a particular object will always be suitable, satisfactory, or work well: *You can't go wrong with a little black dress, can you?* → **come out wrong** at COME OUT
wrong³ *n* **1** [U] behaviour that is not morally right: *He's too young to know right from wrong.* | *Those who do wrong should be punished.* | **sb can do no wrong** (=they are perfect) *Nathan adored her, and she could do no wrong in his eyes.* **2** [C] an action, judgment, or situation that is unfair: *The black population suffered countless wrongs at the hands of a racist regime.* | **right a wrong** (=bring justice to an unfair situation) **3 be in the wrong** to make a mistake or deserve the blame for something: *Which driver was in the wrong?* **4 do sb wrong** to treat someone badly and unfairly – used humorously **5 two wrongs don't make a right** *spoken* used to say that if someone does something bad to you, you should not do something bad to them
wrong⁴ *v* [T] *formal* to treat or judge someone unfairly: *Both sides felt that they had been wronged.*
wrong·do·ing /ˈrɒŋˌduːɪŋ $ ˌrɔːŋˈduːɪŋ/ *n* [C,U] *formal* illegal or immoral behaviour —**wrongdoer** *n*
wrong·foot /ˌrɒŋˈfʊt $ ˌrɔːŋ-/ *v* [T] to surprise and embarrass someone, especially by asking a question they did not expect: *Woo's political skill and ability to wrongfoot the opposition*
wrong·ful /ˈrɒŋfəl $ ˈrɔːŋ-/ *adj* **wrongful arrest/conviction/imprisonment/dismissal etc** a wrongful arrest etc is unfair or illegal because the person affected by it has done nothing wrong: *She's threatening to sue her employers for wrongful dismissal.* —**wrongfully** *adv*
wrong·head·ed /ˌrɒŋˈhedɪd◂ $ ˌrɔːŋ-/ *adj* used to describe an idea, plan, or belief that someone has, that is based on wrong ideas that they are not willing to change —**wrongheadedly** *adv* —**wrongheadedness** *n* [U]
wrong·ly /ˈrɒŋli $ ˈrɔːŋ-/ *adv* **1** not correctly or in a way that is not based on facts; **F3 rightly**: *Matthew was wrongly diagnosed as having a brain tumour.* | *His name had been wrongly spelt.* **2** in a way that is unfair or immoral; **F3 rightly**: *Human rights organizations maintain that the men have been wrongly convicted.* → **rightly or wrongly** at RIGHTLY
wrote /rəʊt $ roʊt/ the past tense of WRITE
wrought /rɔːt $ rɒːt/ the past tense and past participle of WREAK
wrought 'iron *n* [U] long thin pieces of iron formed into shapes to make gates, fences etc
wrought-'up *adj* very nervous and excited; **E3 wound up, tense**
WRT the written abbreviation of *with regard to*, used in email or by people communicating in CHAT ROOMS on the Internet
wrung /rʌŋ/ the past tense and past participle of WRING
wry /raɪ/ *adj* [only before noun] a wry expression or wry humour shows that you know a situation is bad, but you also think it is slightly amusing: *'Was it as bad as you expected?' Travis gave a wry smile.* —**wryly** *adv*
wt. also **wt** *BrE* the written abbreviation of *weight*
WTO /ˌdʌbljuː tiː ˈəʊ $ -ˈoʊ/ *n* **the WTO** the abbreviation of *the World Trade Organization*
wun·der·kind /ˈwʌndəkɪnd $ -ər-/ *n* [C] a young person who is very successful; → **child prodigy**
wuss /wʊs/ *n* [C] *spoken* someone who you think is weak or lacks courage
WWW /ˌdʌbljuː dʌbljuː ˈdʌbljuː/ the abbreviation of *World Wide Web*
WYSIWYG /ˈwɪziwɪg/ *n* [U] *What You See Is What You Get* a word used to mean that what you see on the computer screen is exactly what will be printed
wy·vern /ˈwaɪvən $ -ərn/ *n* [C] an imaginary animal that has two legs and wings and looks like a DRAGON

W

X, x

X¹, x /eks/ *plural* **X's, x's** *n*
1 LETTER [C,U] the 24th letter of the English alphabet
2 NUMBER [C] the number 10 in the system of ROMAN NUMERALS
3 MATHEMATICS [U] *technical* a letter used in mathematics to represent an unknown quantity or value: *if* $3x = 6, x = 2$
4 ON SCHOOL WORK [C] a mark used on school work to show that a written answer is not correct
5 WHEN VOTING [C] a mark used to show that you have chosen something on an official piece of paper, for example when voting
6 ON A LETTER [C] a mark used to show a kiss, especially at the end of a letter: *Love, Cindy XXX*
7 FILM [singular, U] used in the past to describe a film that was officially approved as only suitable for people over 18; 🔲 18 → X-RATED
8 UNKNOWN/SECRET NAME [U] a letter used instead of someone's or something's real name because you want to keep it secret or you do not know it: *At the trial, Ms X said that she had known the defendant for three years.*
9 WHEN SIGNING YOUR NAME [C] a mark used instead of a signature by someone who cannot write
10 X number of people/things used to say that there are a number of people or things when the exact number is not important
11 X marks the spot used on maps in adventure stories to show that something is buried in a particular place
X² v

X sth ⇔ **out** *phr v AmE* to mark or remove a mistake in a piece of writing using an X; 🔲 **cross out**

X-cer·tif·i·cate /'eks sə,tɪfɪkət $ -sər-/ *adj, n* an X-certificate film is one that people under 18 are not allowed to see in Britain because it contains sex or violence → PG, R², U¹ (2)

X chro·mo·some /'eks ,krəʊməsəʊm $ -,krəʊməsoʊm/ *n* [C] a type of CHROMOSOME that exists in pairs in female cells, and together with a Y CHROMOSOME in male cells

xen·on /'zenɒn $ 'ziːnɑːn, 'ze-/ *n* [U] a colourless gas that is found in very small quantities in the air. It is a chemical ELEMENT: symbol Xe

xen·o·pho·bi·a /,zenə'fəʊbiə $ -'foʊ-/ *n* [U] strong fear or dislike of people from other countries —**xenophobic** *adj*

xen·o·trans·plant /,zenəʊ'trænsplɑːnt $ -nəʊ'trænsplænt/ *n* **1** [C,U] the operation of putting an organ from an animal into a person's body: *Doctors in Mississippi performed the world's first heart xenotransplant.* **2** [C] the organ that is moved in a xenotransplant operation —**xenotransplant** *v* [T] —**xenotransplantation** /,zenəʊtrænsplɑːn'teɪʃən $ -noʊtrænsplæn-/ *n* [U]: *health risks related to xenotransplantation*

Xe·rox /'zɪərɒks $ 'zɪrɑːks, 'zɪ-/ *n* [C] *trademark* a copy of a letter, document etc made using a special machine; 🔲 **photocopy —Xerox** *v* [T]

'Xerox ma,chine *n* [C] *trademark* a special electric machine used for making copies of written or printed material; 🔲 **photocopier**

XL *extra large* used on clothes to show their size

X·mas /'krɪsməs, 'eksməs/ *n* [C,U] *informal* a word that means Christmas, often written on signs or cards

XML /,eks em 'el/ *n* [U] *technical* **extensible markup language** a way of writing a document on a computer so that its structure is clear, and so that it can easily be read on a different computer system

X-rated /'eks ,reɪtᵻd/ *adj* an X-rated film is one that people under 18 are not allowed to see because it includes sex or violence

X-ray¹ /'eks reɪ/ *n* [C] **1** a beam of RADIATION (1) that can go through solid objects and is used for photographing the inside of the body **2** a photograph of part of someone's body, taken using X-rays to see if anything is wrong: *The X-ray showed that her leg was not broken.* **3** a medical examination made using X-rays: *I had to go to hospital for an X-ray.* | *a chest X-ray*

X-ray² *v* [T] to photograph the inside of someone's body using X-rays: *The problem was only discovered when her lungs were X-rayed.*

xy·lo·phone /'zaɪləfəʊn $ -foʊn/ *n* [C] a musical instrument which consists of metal or wooden bars of different lengths that you hit with a special stick; → **glockenspiel**

xylophone

Y, y

Y, y /waɪ/ *plural* **Y's, y's** *n* [C,U] the 25th letter of the English alphabet → **Y CHROMOSOME, Y-FRONTS**

-y¹ /i/ *suffix* [in adjectives] **1** full of something or covered with something: *sugary desserts* (=full of sugar) | *dirty hands* (=covered with dirt) | *a hairy chest* (=covered with hair) **2** having a quality or feeling, or tending to do something: *a messy room* | *curly hair* (=hair that curls) | *feeling sleepy* **3** like or typical of something: *a cold wintry day* (=typical of winter) | *his long, horsy face* (=he looks like a horse) **4** fond of or interested in something: *a horsy woman* (=who likes riding horses) —**-ily** *suffix* [in adverbs] —**-iness** *suffix* [in nouns]

-y² *suffix* [in nouns] **1** also **-ie** used to make a word or name less formal, and often to show that you care about them – used especially when talking to children: *Where's little Johnny?* | *my daddy* (=my father) | *What a nice doggy* (=dog)! **2** used to make nouns from some verbs to show an action: *the expiry date* (=the date when something EXPIRES) | *an inquiry* (=the act of INQUIRING about something)

ya /jə, jʌ/ *pron spoken informal* you: *See ya later!*

yacht /jɒt $ jɑːt/ *n* [C] a large boat with a sail, used for pleasure or sport, especially one that has a place where you can sleep; → **sailing boat, sailboat**

yacht

yacht·ing /ˈjɒtɪŋ $ ˈjɑːtɪŋ/ *n* [U] *especially BrE* sailing, travelling, or racing in a yacht; → **sailing**

yachts·man /ˈjɒtsmən $ ˈjɑːts-/ *n plural* **yachtsmen** /-mən/ [C] a man who sails a yacht

yachts·wom·an /ˈjɒts-ˌwʊmən $ ˈjɑːts-/ *n plural* **yachtswomen** /-ˌwɪmɪn/ [C] a woman who sails a yacht

ya·da ya·da ya·da, yadda yadda yadda /ˌjædə jædə ˈjædə/ *interjection AmE spoken* said when you do not want to give a lot of detailed information, because it is boring or because the person you are talking to already knows it; ▣ **blah, blah, blah**: *I started talking to her and – yada yada yada – it turns out she's from New York too.*

ya·hoo¹ /jɑːˈhuː/ *interjection spoken informal* shouted when you are very happy or excited about something

yahoo² *n plural* **yahoos** [C] *old-fashioned* someone who is rough, noisy, or rude: *a bunch of time-wasting yahoos*

Yah·weh /ˈjɑːweɪ/ *n* [singular] a Hebrew name for God

yak¹ /jæk/ *n* [C] an animal of central Asia that looks like a cow with long hair

yak² *v* **yakked, yakking** [I] *informal* to talk continuously about things that are not very serious, in a way that is annoying

y'all /jɔːl $ jɒːl/ *pron AmE spoken* a word meaning 'all of you', used mainly in the southern US states when speaking to more than one person: *I'm going home now. See y'all later.*

yam /jæm/ *n* [C] **1** a tropical climbing plant grown for its root, which is eaten as a vegetable **2** *AmE* a type of SWEET POTATO

yam·mer /ˈjæmə $ -ər/ also **yammer on** *v* [I] *informal* to talk continuously in a way that is annoying: *a crowd of yammering aunts and cousins*

yang /jæŋ/ *n* [U] the male principle in Chinese PHILOSOPHY which is active, light, and positive, and which combines with YIN (=the female principle) to influence everything in the world

yank /jæŋk/ *v* [I,T] *informal* to suddenly pull something quickly and with force: **yank sth out/back/open etc** *One of the men grabbed Tom's hair and yanked his head back.* | *Nick yanked the door open.* | [+on/at] *With both hands she yanked at the necklace.* —**yank** *n* [C]: *He gave the rope **a yank.***

Yank also **Yankee** *n* [C] *BrE informal* an American – often used to show disapproval

Yan·kee /ˈjæŋki/ *n* [C] *informal* **1** a soldier who fought on the side of the Union (=the northern states) during the American Civil War **2** *AmE* someone born in or living in the northern states of the US – sometimes used in an insulting way by people from the southern US **3** *BrE* an American – often used to show disapproval; ▣ **Yank 4** *AmE* someone from New England

yap¹ /jæp/ *v* **yapped, yapping** [I] **1** if a small dog yaps, it BARKS (=makes short loud sounds) in an excited way **2** *informal* to talk in a noisy and annoying way: *Some guy was yapping on his cell phone.*

yap² *n* [C] the sound a small dog makes when it yaps

yard ⟦S2⟧ ⟦W2⟧ /jɑːd $ jɑːrd/ *n* [C]

1 MEASURE written abbreviation **yd** a unit for measuring length, equal to three feet or .91 metres: *a hundred yards away* | *an area of 9000 **square yards***

2 ENCLOSED AREA an enclosed area next to a building or group of buildings, used for a special purpose, activity, or business: *a builder's yard* | *a timber yard* | **prison/school yard** (=an area outside a prison or school where prisoners or students do activities outdoors)

3 GARDEN *AmE* the area around a house, usually covered with grass; ▣ **garden** *BrE*: **front/back yard** *The kids were playing in the back yard.*

4 BACK OF HOUSE *BrE* an enclosed area without grass at the back of a small house → **BACKYARD**

yard·age /ˈjɑːdɪdʒ $ ˈjɑːr-/ *n technical* **1** [U] the number of yards that a team or player moves forward in a game of American football **2** [C,U] the size of something measured in yards or square yards: *a large yardage of sail*

yard·arm /ˈjɑːd-ɑːm $ ˈjɑːrd-ɑːrm/ *n* [C] one of the ends of the pole that supports a square sail

yard·bird /ˈjɑːdbɜːd $ ˈjɑːrdbɜːrd/ *n* [C] *AmE informal old-fashioned* someone who is in prison, especially for a long time

'yard sale *n* [C] *AmE* a sale of used clothes and things from someone's house which takes place in their YARD; → **garage sale**

yard·stick /ˈjɑːdˌstɪk $ ˈjɑːrd-/ *n* [C] **1** something that you compare another thing with, in order to judge how good or successful it is: [+of] *Profit is the most important yardstick of success for any business.* | **as a yardstick** *These subjects are used as a **yardstick** against which to **measure** the children's progress.* **2** a special stick used for measuring things which is exactly one YARD long

yar·mul·ke /ˈjɑːmʊlkə $ ˈjɑːr-/ *n* [C] a small circular cap worn by some Jewish men

yarn /jɑːn $ jɑːrn/ *n* **1** [U] thick thread made of cotton or wool, which is used to KNIT things **2** [C] *informal* a story of adventures, travels etc, usually made more exciting and interesting by adding things that never really happened: *The old captain would often **spin** (=tell) us a **yarn** about life aboard ship.*

yash·mak /ˈjæʃmæk/ *n* [C] a piece of cloth that Muslim women wear across their faces in public

yaw /jɔː $ jɒː/ *v* [I] *technical* if a ship, aircraft etc yaws, it turns away from the direction it should be travelling in —**yaw** *n* [C,U]

Y

yawn¹ /jɔːn $ jɒːn/ v [I] **1** to open your mouth wide and breathe in deeply because you are tired or bored: *Alan stretched and yawned.* **2 yawning gap/gulf/ chasm (between sth)** a very large difference between two groups, things, or people: *the yawning gap between the two parties* | *the yawning gulf between the rich and the poor* **3** *literary* to be or become wide open, especially in a frightening way: *The pit yawned open in front of them.* | **yawning gap/hole etc** *the yawning gap between the two cliffs*

yawn² n **1** [C] an act of yawning: *Kay shook her head and stifled a yawn* (=tried to stop yawning). **2 a yawn** *informal* someone or something that is boring: *The party was a big yawn.*

yaws /jɔːz $ jɒːz/ n [U] a tropical skin disease

Y chro·mo·some /ˈwaɪ ˌkrəʊməsəʊm $ -ˌkrouməsoum/ n [C] the part of a GENE that makes someone a male instead of a female; → **X chromosome**

yd *BrE*/ **yd.** *AmE plural* **yd** *or* **yds** the written abbreviation of *yard* or *yards*

ye¹ /jiː/ pron old use you – used especially when speaking to more than one person: *Abandon hope all ye who enter here.*

ye² *determiner* the – used in the names of shops and PUBS to make them seem old: *Ye Olde Antique Shoppe*

yea¹ /jeɪ/ adv old use yes; 🔲 **nay**

yea² n [C] a YES²; 🔲 **nay**

yeah S1 /jeə/ adv spoken informal yes

year S1 W1 /jɪə, jɜː $ jɪr/ n [C]
1 12 MONTHS a period of about 365 days or 12 months, measured from any particular time: *I arrived here two years ago.* | *We've known each other for over a year.* | *It's almost a year since Sue died.* | *Jodi is 15 years old.* | *a three-year business plan* | *a four-year-old child* | **be 12/21 etc years of age** (=be 12/21 etc years old) → FINANCIAL YEAR, FISCAL YEAR, LIGHT YEAR, TAX YEAR
2 JANUARY TO DECEMBER also **calendar year** a period of 365 or 366 days divided into 12 months beginning on January 1st and ending on December 31st: *the year that Kennedy died* | *at the end of the year* | *She goes there every year.* | *in the year 1785* | *this year's cup final* | *The museum attracts 100,000 visitors a year.* | *in the early years of last century* → LEAP YEAR, NEW YEAR
3 years a) *informal* a very long period of time; 🔲 **ages**: *It's years since I rode a bike.* | **in/for years** *I haven't been there for years.* | *It was the first time in years I'd seen her.* b) age, especially old age: **a man/woman/person etc of his/her etc years** *Gordon is very active for a man of his years.* | **getting on in years** (=no longer young)
4 all (the) year round during the whole year: *It's warm enough to swim all year round.* → YEAR-ROUND
5 year by year as each year passes: *Business has steadily increased year by year.*
6 year after year/year in, year out every year for many years: *Many birds return to the same spot year after year.*
7 PERIOD OF LIFE/HISTORY a particular period of time in someone's life or in history: **sb's childhood/ early/teenage/retirement etc years** *those who start to smoke in their teenage years* | **the war/Depression/ boom etc years** *the boom years of the 1980's* | **sb's years in/at sth** *during his years in China* | **sb's years as sth** *Sheila enjoyed her years as a student in Oxford.* | **In later years** *he turned to writing poetry.*
8 the school/academic year the time within a period of 12 months when students are studying at a school or university
9 SCHOOL/UNIVERSITY LEVEL *especially BrE* a particular level that a student stays at for one year: *a group of year seven students* | **in a year** *He was in my year at school.*
10 first/second etc year *BrE* someone who is in their first etc year at school or university: *The department offers a study skills programme for all first years.*
11 musician/player/car etc of the year the musician etc who was voted the best in a particular year: **vote/name sth ... of the year** *The new Renault was voted car of the year.*
12 never/not in a million years *spoken* used to say that something is extremely unlikely: *Never in a million years did I think we'd lose.*
13 the year dot *BrE informal* a very long time ago: *Scientists have been involved in war **since the year dot**.*
14 put years on sb/take years off sb to make someone look or feel older or younger: *Tina's divorce has put years on her.* → DONKEY (2)

year·book /ˈjɪəbʊk, ˈjɜː- $ ˈjɪr-/ n [C] **1** a book printed once a year, with information about a particular subject or activity: *Rothman's Football Yearbook* **2** *AmE* a book printed once a year by a school or college, with information and pictures about what happened there in the past year: *a high school yearbook*

year·ling /ˈjɪəlɪŋ, ˈjɜː- $ ˈjɪr-/ n [C] an animal, especially a young horse, between one and two years old

year-long also **year·long** /ˈjɪəlɒŋ, ˈjɜː- $ ˈjɪrlɔːŋ/ adj [only before noun] continuing for a year or all through the year: *a year-long study of the problem*

year·ly /ˈjɪəli, ˈjɜː- $ ˈjɪrli/ adj happening or appearing every year or once a year: *Salary levels are reviewed on a yearly basis.* | *a total yearly income of $78,000* | *The magazine is issued twice yearly* (=two times a year). | **3-yearly/5-yearly etc** (=every three years etc) *a checkup at five-yearly intervals* —**yearly** adv: *We pay the fee yearly.*

yearn /jɜːn $ jɜːrn/ v [I] *literary* to have a strong desire for something, especially something that is difficult or impossible to get; 🔲 **long**: [+for] *Hannah yearned for a child.* | **yearn to be/do sth** *Phil had yearned to be a pilot from an early age.*

yearn·ing /ˈjɜːnɪŋ $ ˈjɜːr-/ n [C,U] *literary* a strong desire for something; 🔲 **longing**: [+for] *a yearning for travel* | **yearning to do sth** *He had a deep yearning to return to his home town.*

year-round adj [usually before noun] happening or continuing through the whole year: *a year-round supply of fresh fruit*

yeast /jiːst/ n [U] a type of FUNGUS used for producing alcohol in beer and wine, and for making bread rise —**yeasty** adj: *a yeasty taste*

yeast extract n [U] a thick sticky brown substance made from yeast, used in cooking or for spreading on bread

yeast infection n [C] an infectious condition that affects the VAGINA in women; 🔲 **thrush**

yecch /jʌk/ interjection *AmE spoken informal* used to say that you think something is very unpleasant; 🔲 **yuck**

yell¹ /jel/ v **1** [I,T] also **yell out** to shout or say something very loudly, especially because you are frightened, angry, or excited: *'Help me!' she yelled hysterically.* | *I yelled out, 'Here I am!'* | *The crowd are on their feet yelling.* | [+at] *Don't you yell at me like that!* | **yell at sb to do sth** *They yelled at him to stop.* | **yell (out) in surprise/pain etc** *Clare yelled in pain as she fell.* | *He could hear Pete yelling **at the top** of his voice* (=very loudly). **2** [I] *spoken especially AmE* to ask for help: *If you need me, just yell.*

yell² n [C] **1** a loud shout: **let out/give a yell** *She let out a yell when she saw me.* | **a yell of surprise/delight/ triumph etc** *Dan gave a yell of delight when Larsson scored.* **2** *AmE* words or phrases that students and CHEERLEADERS shout together to show support for their school, college etc

yel·low¹ S2 W3 /ˈjeləʊ $ -loʊ/ adj
1 having the colour of butter or the middle part of an egg: *yellow flowers* → CHROME YELLOW; → **lemon yellow** at LEMON²; → **primrose yellow** at PRIMROSE (2)
2 *not polite* an offensive way of describing the skin colour of people from parts of Asia
3 also **yellow-bellied** *informal* not brave; 🔲 **cowardly**

yellow² n [C,U] the colour of butter or the middle part of an egg: *Yellow doesn't suit me at all.* | *The room was decorated in a variety of reds, blues, and yellows.*

yellow³ v [I,T] to become yellow or make something become yellow: *The paper had yellowed with age.*

,yellow 'card n [C] a yellow card held up by a football REFEREE to show that a player has done something wrong; → **red card**

,yellow 'fever n [U] a dangerous tropical disease which makes your skin turn slightly yellow

yel·low·ham·mer /'jeləʊˌhæmə $ -loʊˌhæmər/ n [C] a small European bird with a yellow head

yel·low·ish /'jeləʊɪʃ $ -loʊ-/ adj slightly yellow: *yellowish teeth*

,yellow 'line n [C] a line of yellow paint along the edge of a street in Britain which means you can only park your car for a short time or at particular times: **double yellow lines** (=two lines of paint that mean you cannot park there at any time); → see picture at TOWN

,Yellow 'Pages also **yellow pages** AmE n trademark **(the) Yellow Pages** a book that contains the telephone numbers of businesses and organizations in an area, arranged according to the type of service or goods they provide; → **White Pages**

yel·low·y /'jeləʊi $ -loʊi/ adj slightly yellow: *The cream was thick and yellowy.*

yelp /jelp/ n [C] a short sharp high cry which a person or an animal makes because they are excited, in pain, surprised etc: **give/let out a yelp of pain/dismay/surprise etc** *The water was hotter than she had expected, and she gave an involuntary yelp.* —**yelp** v [I]: *The dog ran up and down, yelping.*

yen /jen/ n plural **yen 1** [C] the standard unit of money in Japan: symbol ¥ **2 the yen** the value of Japanese money in relation to the money of other countries: *The dollar **fell** by 24 percent **against the yen*** (=decreased in value in relation to the yen) *between 1970 and 1973.* **3** [singular] a strong desire: [+for] *a yen for foreign travel* | **yen to do sth** *She'd always **had a yen** to write a book.*

yeo·man /'jəʊmən $ 'joʊ-/ n plural **yeomen** /-mən/ [C] **1** an officer in the US navy who often works in an office **2** a farmer in Britain in the past who owned and worked on his own land

yeo·man·ry /'jəʊmənri $ 'joʊ-/ n [plural] literary the people in Britain in the past who owned and farmed their own land

yep /jep/ adv spoken informal yes

yer /jə $ jər/ determiner written informal your or you: *Keep yer mouth shut!*

yes¹ S1 W1 /jes/ adv spoken

1 ANSWER TO QUESTION/STATEMENT a) used as an answer to say that something is true or that you agree; ✗ no: *'Is that real gold?' 'Yes.'* | *'It was a great show.' 'Yes, it was.'* **b)** used as an answer to a question or statement containing a negative, to say that the opposite is true: *'Sarah isn't very intelligent, is she?' 'Yes, she is* (=in fact, she is intelligent)*!'* | *'There isn't any cereal left.' 'Yes, there is – it's in the cupboard.'*

2 ANSWER TO OFFER/INVITATION used as an answer to say that you want something or want to do something; ✗ no: *'Would you like a sandwich?' '**Yes, please.**'* | *'Would you like to come with us?' 'Yes, I'd love to.'*

3 ANSWER TO REQUEST used as an answer to say that you will do something, or that someone may do or have something; ✗ no: *'Can I have a glass of water?' 'Yes, of course.'* | *He proposed to me and I **said yes**.*

4 yes, but ... used to show that you agree with what someone has said, but there is another fact to consider: *'There are still a lot of problems with Jeff's proposal.' 'Yes, but it's the best one we have.'*

5 READY TO LISTEN/TALK used to show that you have heard someone or are ready to speak to someone: *'Mike?' 'Yes?'* | *Yes sir, how can I help you?*

6 LISTENING used to show that you are listening to

someone and want them to continue: *'And so I tried phoning him ...' 'Yes ...'*

7 EXCITED/HAPPY used to show that you are very excited or happy about something: *Yes! Rivaldo's scored again!*

8 oh yes a) used to show that you do not believe what someone is saying: *'There's nothing going on between me and Jane. We're just good friends.' 'Oh yes?'* **b)** used to show that you have remembered something: *Where's my umbrella? Oh yes – I left it in the car.*

9 EMPHASIS used to emphasize that you mean what you have just said, even though it is surprising: *It took ten years – yes, ten whole years – to complete.* | *Yes, you heard me correctly – I said 1921.*

10 yes, yes used to show annoyance when someone is talking to you and you do not want to listen: *'And don't forget to lock the door!' 'Yes, yes, OK.'*

11 yes and no used to show that there is not one clear answer to a question: *'Were you surprised?' 'Well, yes and no. I knew they were planning something, but I wasn't sure what.'* → YEAH

yes² n plural **yeses** or **yesses** [C] a vote, voter, or reply that agrees with an idea, plan, law etc: *According to the latest opinion poll, the noes have 60%, and the yeses have 40%.* —**yes** adj: *a yes vote*

ye·shi·va, **yeshivah** /jə'ʃiːvə/ n [C] a school for Jewish students, where they can train to become RABBIS (=religious leaders)

'yes-man n plural **yes-men** [C] someone who always agrees with and obeys their employer, leader etc in order to gain some advantage – used to show disapproval

yes·ter·day¹ S1 W1 /'jestədi, -deɪ $ -ər-/ adv on or during the day before today; → **tomorrow**: *What did you do yesterday?* | **yesterday morning/afternoon/evening** *Anna left yesterday afternoon.*; → **I wasn't born yesterday** at BORN² (5)

yesterday² n [U] **1** the day before today; → **tomorrow**: *yesterday's meeting* | *They arrived **the day before yesterday**.* **2** the recent past: *the great champions of yesterday* **3 yesterday's news** information that is old and no longer interesting

yes·ter·year /'jestəjɪə, -jɜː $ 'jestərjɪr/ n **of yesteryear** literary existing in the past: *the steam trains of yesteryear*

yet¹ S1 W1 /jet/ adv

1 a) used in negative statements and questions to talk about whether something that was expected has happened: *I haven't asked him yet* (=but I will). | *Has Edmund arrived yet?* | *'Have you finished your homework?' ' Not yet.'* **b)** used in negative statements and questions to talk about whether a situation has started to exist: *'How are you going to get there?' 'I don't know yet.'* | *Women didn't yet have the vote* (=at that time). | *'Is supper ready?' 'No, **not yet**.'*

2 used in negative sentences to say that someone should not or need not do something now, although they may have to do it later: *You can't give up yet!* | *Don't go. I like talking to you.*

3 used to emphasize that something is even more than it was before or is in addition to what existed before; ✗ still: **yet more/bigger/higher etc** *He got a call from the factory, telling of yet more problems.* | *Inflation had risen to a yet higher level.* | **yet another** *reason to be cautious* | *The meeting has been cancelled **yet again*** (=one more time after many others).

4 the biggest/worst etc (sth) yet used to say that something is the biggest, worst etc of its kind that has existed up to now: *This could turn out to be our biggest mistake yet.* | *Nordstrom's latest novel looks like his best yet.*

5 as (of) yet used when saying that something has not happened up to now: *We've had no luck as yet.* | *on an as yet undecided date*

6 months/weeks/ages yet used to emphasize how

much time will pass before something happens, or how long a situation will continue: *'When's your holiday?' 'Oh, not for ages yet.'* | *It could be months yet before they know their fate.*

7 could/may/might yet do sth used to say that something is still possible in the future, in spite of the way that things seem now: *We may win yet.* | *The plan could yet succeed.*

8 sb/sth has yet to do sth *formal* used to say that someone has not done something, or that something has not happened when you think it should already have been done or have happened: *I have yet to hear Ray's version of what happened.* | *The bank has yet to respond to our letter.*

GRAMMAR

In spoken English, **yet** usually comes at the end of the clause: *I haven't finished my homework yet.* | *We don't know whether she'll come yet.*
It can also come after 'don't', 'hasn't' etc, or before 'why', 'whether' etc: *They don't yet know the full facts.* | *I haven't decided yet whether to take part in the competition.*
In writing or more formal speech, **yet** can come after 'not': *We do not yet have a solution to this problem.*
WORD CHOICE: **yet, still, already**
Yet is used to say that something has not happened or a situation has not started to exist, or to ask if something has happened: *It isn't time to go yet.* | *Have you seen him yet?*
Still is used to say that an earlier situation has not changed: *My parents were still asleep (NOT yet asleep).* | *I still don't understand.*
Already is used to emphasize that something has happened or a situation has started to exist: *He had already published two novels.* | *They already knew one another.* It is also used in questions to show surprise that something has happened sooner than expected: *Have you been there already?*

---

yet² *conjunction* used to introduce a fact, situation, or quality that is surprising after what you have just said: *Kelly was a convicted criminal, yet many people admired him.* | *She does not speak our language and yet she seems to understand what we say.* | *a story that is strange yet true* | *an inexpensive yet effective solution to our problem*

yet·i /'jeti/ *n* [C] a large hairy creature like a human which some people believe lives in the Himalayan mountains; ◼ **Abominable Snowman**

yew /juː/ *n* [C,U] a tree with dark green leaves and red berries, or the wood of this tree

Y-fronts /'waɪ frʌnts/ *n* [plural] *BrE trademark* men's underwear which has a part at the front shaped like an upside down Y

yid /jɪd/ *n* [C] *taboo* a very offensive word for a Jewish person. Do not use this word.

Yid·dish /'jɪdɪʃ/ *n* [U] a language based on German used by older Jewish people, especially those who are from Eastern Europe; → **Hebrew**

yield¹ /jiːld/ *v*
1 RESULT [T] to produce a result, answer, or piece of information: *Our research has only recently begun to yield important results.*
2 CROPS/PROFITS [T] to produce crops, profits etc: *Each of these oilfields could yield billions of barrels of oil.* | *The tourist industry yielded an estimated $2.25 billion for the state last year.* | *These investments should yield a reasonable return.* | **high-yielding/low-yielding** *high-yielding crops*
3 AGREE UNWILLINGLY [I,T] to allow yourself to be forced or persuaded to do something or stop having something: *The military has promised to yield power.* | [+to] *The hijackers refuse to yield to demands to release the passengers.* | *Further action may be necessary if the leaders do not yield to diplomatic pressure.* | *Finally*

she *yielded to temptation* and helped herself to a large slice of cake.
4 TRAFFIC [I] *AmE* to allow other traffic on a bigger road to go first; ◼ **give way** *BrE*: [+to] *Yield to traffic on the left.*
5 MOVE/BEND/BREAK [I] to move, bend, or break because of physical force or pressure; ◼ **give**: *Ideally, the surface should yield slightly under pressure.*
6 GIVE UP FIGHTING [I] *literary* to stop fighting and accept defeat; ◼ **surrender**

yield to sth *phr v formal*
if one thing yields to another, it is replaced by that thing; ◼ **give way to sth**: *Laughter quickly yielded to amazement as the show went on.*

yield sth ⇔ **up** *phr v formal*
1 to show or produce something that was hidden or difficult to find, or that people did not know about; ◼ **throw up**: *New research has yielded up some surprising discoveries.*
2 *BrE formal* to give something that belongs to you to someone else, because you are forced to; ◼ **surrender**: *He would never yield up the castle to the English.*

yield² *n* [C] the amount of profits, crops etc that something produces: *The average milk yield per cow has doubled.* | **high/low yield** *Shareholders are expecting a higher yield this year.* | [+of] *a yield of over six percent*

yield·ing /'jiːldɪŋ/ *adj* **1** a surface that is yielding is soft and will move or bend when you press it: *the yielding softness of the bed* **2** willing to agree with other people's wishes; ◼ **accommodating**

yikes /jaɪks/ *interjection informal* said when something frightens or shocks you

yin /jɪn/ *n* [U] the female principle in Chinese PHILOSOPHY which is inactive, dark, and negative, and which combines with YANG (=the male principle) to influence everything in the world

yin and 'yang *n* [U] the ancient Chinese PHILOSOPHY which is based on the idea that everything in the universe is formed and influenced by the combination of two forces called YIN and YANG

yip·pee /jɪ'piː $ 'jɪpi/ *interjection* used when you are very pleased or excited about something; ◼ **hurray**

yo /jəʊ $ joʊ/ *interjection informal especially AmE* used to greet someone, to get their attention, or as a reply when someone says your name: *Yo, dude! How's it going?* | *'Darren?' 'Yo!'*

yob /jɒb $ jɑːb/ also **yob·bo** /'jɒbəʊ $ 'jɑːboʊ/ *n* [C] *BrE* a rude, noisy, and sometimes violent young man; ◼ **lout**: *drunken yobbos*

yodel¹ /'jəʊdl $ 'joʊdl/ *v* **yodelled, yodelling** *BrE*, **yodeled, yodeling** *AmE* [I,T] to sing while changing between your natural voice and a very high voice, traditionally done in the mountains of countries such as Switzerland and Austria —**yodeller** *n* [C]

yo·del² *n* [C] a song or sound made by yodelling

yo·ga /'jəʊgə $ 'joʊgə/ *n* [U] **1** a system of exercises that help you control your mind and body in order to relax **2** a Hindu PHILOSOPHY in which you learn exercises to control your mind and body in order to try to become closer to God

yoga

yog·hurt [S3], **yogurt** /'jɒgət $ 'joʊgərt/ *n* [C,U] a thick liquid food that tastes slightly sour and is made from milk, or an amount of this food: *a pot of strawberry yogurt*

yo·gi /'jəʊgi $ 'joʊgi/ *n* [C] someone who has a lot of knowledge about yoga, and who often teaches it to other people

yog·urt /'jɒgət $ 'joʊgərt/ *n* another spelling of yoghurt

yoke¹ /jəʊk $ joʊk/ n [C] **1** a wooden bar used for keeping two animals together, especially cattle, when they are pulling heavy loads **2** a frame that you put across your shoulders so that you can carry two equal loads which hang from either side of it **3 the yoke of sth** literary something that restricts your freedom, making life difficult: *the yoke of tradition* **4** a part of a skirt or shirt just below the waist or collar, from which the main piece of material hangs in folds

yoke² v [T] **1** to put a yoke on two animals **2** to closely connect two ideas, people, or things: **yoke sth to sth** *Beauty is forever yoked to youth in our culture.*

yo·kel /'jəʊkəl $ 'joʊ-/ n [C] someone who comes from the countryside, seems stupid, and does not know much about modern life, ideas etc – used humorously

yolk /jəʊk $ joʊk, jelk/ n [C,U] the yellow part in the centre of an egg; → **white**

Yom Kip·pur /ˌjɒm 'kɪpə, -kɪ'pʊə $ ˌjoʊm 'kɪpər, -kɪ'pʊr/ n [U] a Jewish religious holiday on which people do not eat, but pray to be forgiven for the things they have done wrong

yon·der /'jɒndə $ 'jɑːndər/ also **yon** /jɒn $ jɑːn/ adv, determiner old use over there – used to show or explain where something or someone is: *the fresh blooms on yonder tree*

yonks /jɒŋks $ jɑːŋks/ n [U] BrE spoken informal a long time; ▣ **ages**: *It's yonks since we had a good night out.* | *We went to Blackpool once,* **yonks ago**. | **not do sth for yonks** *We haven't seen Tom and Jean for yonks.*

yoof¹ /juːf/ adj [only before noun] BrE relating to or intended for young people – used humorously: *a yoof magazine*

yoof² n [U] BrE young people, considered as a group – used humorously: *British white yoof*

yoo-hoo /ju: 'hu:/ interjection informal used to attract someone's attention when they are a long way from you

yore /jɔː $ jɔːr/ n **of yore** literary existing a long time ago: *in days of yore*

York·shire pud·ding /ˌjɔːkʃə 'pʊdɪŋ $ ˌjɔːrkʃɪr-/ n [C,U] a food made from flour, eggs, and milk, baked and eaten with meat in Britain

Yorkshire ter·ri·er /ˌjɔːkʃə 'teriə $ ˌjɔːrkʃɪr 'teriər/ n [C] a type of dog that is very small and has long brown hair

you S1 W1 /jə, jʊ; strong ju:/ pron [used as subject or object]
1 used to refer to a person or group of people when speaking or writing to them: *Hi, Kelly. How are you?* | *You must all listen carefully.* | *I have some news for you.* | *The letter is addressed to both of you.* | *Did Robin give you the money?* | *Only you can make this decision.* | *You idiot!* | *You boys have got to learn to behave yourselves.* | *Hey, you over there! Get out of the way!*
2 people in general: *You have to be 21 or over to buy alcohol in Florida.* | *You can never be sure what Emily is thinking.*

you'd /juːd/ **1** the short form of 'you had': *If you'd been more careful, this wouldn't have happened.* **2** the short form of 'you would': *You'd be amazed at how much she spends on clothes.*

you'll /juːl/ the short form of 'you will' or 'you shall': *You'll feel better soon.*

young¹ S1 W1 /jʌŋ/ adj comparative **younger**, superlative **youngest**
1 a young person, plant, or animal has not lived for very long: *a young child* | *He's younger than me.* | *You're too young to get married.* | *young trees* | **When I was young**, *I wanted to be a model.* | *John was a great footballer* **in his younger days** (=when he was younger).
2 a young country, organization, or type of science has existed for only a short time: *At that time, America was still a young nation.* | *Psychology is a young science.*
3 young lady/man spoken used to speak to a girl or boy when you are angry with them: *Now, you listen to me, young man!*
4 seeming or looking younger than you are; ▣ **youthful**: *Val is incredibly young for her age.*
5 young at heart thinking and behaving as if you were young, even though you are old
6 65/82/97 etc years young spoken used humorously to give the age of an old person who seems or feels much younger: *Next week, Bessie will be 84 years young.*
7 designed or intended for young people: *I'm looking for something in a younger style.*

WORD FOCUS: YOUNG
other words meaning young: **little/small** used to describe young children, especially below the age of 6 | **teenage** used to describe someone who is between 13 and 19 | **adolescent** used to describe someone who is developing into an adult | **youthful** looking young
a young person: **kid** informal a young person | **teenager** someone who is between 13 and 19 | **youth** a man or boy between 15 and 25, especially one who is involved in fighting or crime | **adolescent** a young person who is developing into an adult | **minor** a young person who is not yet legally an adult
the time when someone is young: **childhood** the time when you are a child | **youth** the time when you are no longer a child but you are still young | **adolescence** the time when you develop into an adult

young² n **1 the young** young people: *The young are easily misled.* **2** [plural] a group of young animals that belong to a particular mother or type of animal: *The lioness fought to protect her young.*

young·er /'jʌŋgə $ -ər/ adj sb **the Younger** old use someone famous who lived in the past and had the same name as their mother or father; → **elder**: *William Pitt the Younger*

young of'fender n [C] a criminal in Britain who is not an adult according to the law

young·ster /'jʌŋstə $ -ər/ n [C] old-fashioned a child or young person

your S1 W1 /jə; strong jɔː $ jər; strong jɔːr/ determiner [possessive form of 'you']
1 used when speaking or writing to one or more people to show that something belongs to them or is connected with them: *Could you move your car?* | *Is that your brother over there?* | *Don't worry. It's not your fault.* | *Be aware of* **your own** *feelings.*
2 of or belonging to any person: *If you are facing north, east is on your right.*
3 informal used when mentioning something that is a typical example of a particular type of thing: *It was just your basic, ordinary hotel room – nothing special.* | *Your typical 60s pop group had three guitarists and a drummer.*

you're /jə; strong jɔː $ jər; strong jʊr, jɔːr/ the short form of 'you are': *You're late.*

yours S1 W3 /jɔːz $ jʊrz, jɔːrz/ pron [possessive form of 'you']
1 used when speaking or writing to one or more people to refer to something that belongs to them or is connected with them: *This is our room, and yours is just across the hall.* | *A lot of people have money problems, but yours are more serious than most people's.* | *A cash prize of £10,000 or a new car – the choice is yours.* | **sth of yours** *Is Maria a friend of yours?* | *That bag of yours weighs a ton.* | *I've read that book of yours.*
2 be yours for the taking/asking if something desirable is yours for the taking or asking, you can easily obtain it: *If you want the job, it's yours for the asking.*
3 Yours faithfully BrE used to end a formal letter that begins 'Dear Sir' or 'Dear Madam'
4 Yours truly/Yours also **Yours sincerely** BrE, **Sincerely yours** AmE used to end a letter that begins with the title and name of the person you are writing to, for example 'Dear Mr. Graves'
5 Yours truly informal used humorously to mean 'I' or 'me': *They all went out, leaving yours truly to clear up the mess.* → **up yours** at **UP**¹ (30)

Y

your·self [S1] [W2] /jɔː'self $ jɔːr-/ *pron* [reflexive form of 'you'] *plural* **yourselves** /-'selvz/
1 used when talking to someone to show that they are affected by their own action: *Look at yourself in the mirror.* | *Come and warm yourselves by the fire.* | *Have you hurt yourself?* | *Go and buy yourself an ice cream.*
2 a) used to emphasize 'you': *If you don't trust me, you'd better go yourself.* | *You yourselves are the guilty ones.* | *It must be true. You told me so yourself.* **b)** used after 'like', 'as', or 'except' instead of 'you', especially to make what you are saying seem more formal or important: *Most of our customers are people like yourself.*
3 (all) by yourself a) alone: *You can't go home by yourself in the dark.* **b)** without help from anyone: *Do you think you can move the sofa by yourself?*
4 not seem/be/feel yourself *informal* to not feel or behave as you usually do, for example because you are upset or ill: *Are you all right? You don't seem yourself this morning.*
5 have sth (all) to yourself if you have something to yourself, you do not have to share it with anyone else: *I'm going out, so you'll have the place to yourself.* → DO-IT-YOURSELF; → **keep sth to yourself** at KEEP TO (5); → **keep yourself to yourself** at KEEP TO (6)

youth [S2] [W2] /juːθ/ *n plural* **youths** /juːðz $ juːðz, juːθs/
1 [U] the period of time when someone is young, especially the period when someone is a teenager; → **old age**: *sth of sb's youth the dreams of his youth* | *in sb's youth Many of these people had used drugs in their youth.*
2 [C] a teenage boy – used especially in newspapers to show disapproval: *a gang of youths*
3 [U] young people in general: **the youth of sth** *The youth of today are the pensioners of tomorrow.*
4 [U] the quality or state of being young: *Despite his youth, he had travelled alone.* | *The cream will restore youth and vitality to your skin.*

youth club *n* [C] a meeting place for young people where they can have drinks, play games etc

youth ,culture *n* [U] the interests and activities of young people, especially the music, films etc they enjoy

youth·ful /'juːθfəl/ *adj* **1** typical of young people, or seeming young: **youthful enthusiasm/energy/vigour** | **youthful appearance/looks/complexion** *She has managed to maintain her youthful appearance.* **2** young: *The photo shows a smiling, youthful Burgos.* —**youthfully** *adv* —**youthfulness** *n* [U]

youth ,hostel *n* [C] a place where people, especially young people who are travelling, can stay very cheaply for a short time → see picture at STAY

youth ,hostelling *n* [U] *BrE* the activity of staying in youth hostels and walking or cycling between them: *I went youth hostelling in the Peak District.*

you've /juːv/ the short form of 'you have': *You've broken it.*

yowl /jaʊl/ *v* [I] if an animal or a person yowls, they make a long loud cry, especially because they are unhappy or in pain; ⊟ **howl**: *A tomcat was yowling out on the lawn.* —**yowl** *n* [C]

Yo-Yo /'jəʊ jəʊ $ 'joʊ joʊ/ *n plural* **yo-yos** [C]*trademark* a toy made of two circular parts that goes up and down a string that you hold in your hand

yr. also **yr** *BrE plural* **yrs** the written abbreviation of *year*

yu·an /juˈɑːn/ *n plural* **yuan** [C] the standard unit of money in China

yuc·ca /'jʌkə/ *n* [C] a desert plant with long pointed leaves on a thick straight stem

yuck, yuk /jʌk/ also *interjection informal* used to show that you think something is very unpleasant: *Oh yuck! I hate mayonnaise.*

yuck·y /'jʌki/ *adj informal* extremely unpleasant: *They painted the bathroom a yucky green colour.* | *The food was yucky.*

yuk /jʌk/ *interjection* another spelling of YUCK

Yule /juːl/ *n* [C,U] *old use* Christmas

yule log *n* [C] **1** a LOG (=thick piece of wood) that some people burn as a tradition on the evening before Christmas **2** *BrE* a chocolate cake shaped like a LOG and eaten at Christmas

Yule·tide /'juːltaɪd/ *n* [C,U] *literary* Christmas: *Yuletide festivities*

yum /jʌm/ *interjection informal* said when you think something tastes very good

yum·my /'jʌmi/ *adj informal* tasting very good: *This cake is really yummy.* | *'Treacle tart! Yummy!' said Simon.*

yup·pie, yuppy /'jʌpi/ *n* [C] a young person with a professional job who seems to be interested only in earning a lot of money and buying expensive things

yup·pi·fy /'jʌpɪfaɪ/ *v* **yuppified, yuppifying, yuppifies** [T usually passive] to improve the buildings in an area, or to open expensive restaurants, shops etc so that YUPPIES will want to live in the buildings or use the restaurants etc: *The restaurant's yuppified interior was done in colors like teal and mauve.*

Y

Z, z

Z, z /zed $ ziː/ *plural* **Z's, z's** *n* **1** [C,U] the 26th and last letter of the English alphabet ➔ **from A to Z** at A[1] (7) **2 catch/get some Z's** *AmE informal* to sleep

za·ny /ˈzeɪni/ *adj comparative* **zanier**, *superlative* **zaniest** crazy or unusual in a way that is amusing: *zany comedian Vic Reeves*

zap /zæp/ *v* **zapped**, **zapping** *informal* **1** [T] to quickly attack or destroy something, especially using a beam of electricity: *Doctors have tried zapping tumors with high-voltage radiation.* | *The laser weapons are designed to zap enemy missiles.* **2** [I,T] to change CHANNELS on a television by using a REMOTE CONTROL: *Dave just sat there, zapping through all the channels.* **3** [T] to cook something in a MICROWAVE[1] (1) **4** [T] to send information quickly from one computer to another: *Computers identify threats and zap the results back to US pilots in the war zone.*

zap·per /ˈzæpə $ -ər/ *n* [C] *informal* **1** a thing you use for changing CHANNELS on a television from a distance; ▤ **remote control 2** a piece of electrical equipment that attracts and kills insects

zeal /ziːl/ *n* [U] eagerness to do something, especially to achieve a particular religious or political aim: **religious/revolutionary/missionary etc zeal** *He approached the job with missionary zeal.* | *In their zeal to catch drug dealers, police have ignored citizens' basic civil rights.* | [+for] *their zeal for privatization*

zeal·ot /ˈzelət/ *n* [C] someone who has extremely strong beliefs, especially religious or political beliefs, and is too eager to make other people share them: *religious zealots* —**zealotry** *n* [U]

zeal·ous /ˈzeləs/ *adj* someone who is zealous does or supports something with great energy: *a zealous preacher* | *zealous political activists* | **be zealous in (doing) sth** *No one was more zealous than Neil in supporting the proposal.* —**zealously** *adv*

ze·bra /ˈziːbrə, ˈze- $ ˈziːbrə/ *n* [C] an animal that looks like a horse but has black and white lines all over its body

zebra 'crossing *n* [C] *BrE* a place marked with black and white lines where people who are walking can cross a road safely; ▤ **crosswalk** *AmE*; ➔ **pelican crossing**; ➔ see picture at TOWN

zed /zed/ *BrE*; **zee** /ziː/ *AmE n* [C] a way of writing the letter 'z' that shows how you pronounce it

zeit·geist /ˈzaɪtɡaɪst/ *n* [singular] the general spirit or feeling of a period in history, as shown by people's ideas and beliefs at the time

Zen /zen/ *also* **Zen 'Buddhism** *n* [U] a kind of Buddhism from Japan that emphasizes MEDITATION

zen·ith /ˈzenɪθ $ ˈziː-/ *n* [C usually singular] **1** the most successful point in the development of something; ▤ **peak**; ◪ **nadir**: **reach its zenith/be at its zenith** *The Roman Empire reached its zenith around the year 100.* **2** *technical* the highest point that is reached by the sun or the moon in the sky

zeph·yr /ˈzefə $ -ər/ *n* [C] *literary* a soft gentle wind

zep·pe·lin /ˈzepəlɪn/ *n* [C] a German AIRSHIP used in World War I

ze·ro[1] /ˈzɪərəʊ $ ˈziːroʊ/ *number plural* **zeros** *or* **zeroes 1** the number 0; ▤ **nought** *BrE*: *Make X greater than or equal to zero.* **2** the point between + and − on a scale for measuring something, or the lowest point on a scale that shows how much there is left of something: *The petrol gauge was already at zero.* **3** a temperature of 0° on the Celsius or Fahrenheit scale:

above/below zero *It was five degrees below zero last night.* ➔ ABSOLUTE ZERO, SUB-ZERO **4** none at all, or the lowest possible amount: **sb's chances are zero** (=they have no chance of success) *Mike's chances of winning are virtually zero.* | *From 1971 to 1976 West Vancouver experienced zero population growth.*

zero[2] *v*

zero in on sb/sth *phr v* **1** to direct all your attention towards a particular person or thing; ▤ **home in on**: *She immediately zeroed in on the weak point in his argument.* **2** to aim a gun or other weapon towards something or someone

'zero hour *n* [singular] the time when a military operation or an important event is planned to begin

,zero-sum 'game *n* [singular] a situation in which you receive as much money or advantages as you give away: *Diplomatic negotiations often aim at a zero-sum game.*

,zero 'tolerance *n* [U] a way of dealing with crime in which every person who breaks the law, even in a very small way, is punished as severely as possible: *a policy of zero tolerance in inner-city areas*

zest /zest/ *n* **1** [U] eager interest and enjoyment: [+for] *She had a great zest for life.* **2** [singular, U] the quality of being exciting and interesting: *The danger of being caught added a certain zest to the affair.* **3** [U] the outer skin of an orange or LEMON, used in cooking; ➔ **peel**, **rind**: *grated orange zest* —**zestful** *adj* —**zestfully** *adv*

zig·zag[1] /ˈzɪɡzæɡ/ *n* [C] a pattern that looks like a line of z's joined together: *a zigzag path along the cliff*

zigzag[2] *v* **zigzagged**, **zigzagging** [I] to move forward in sharp angles, first to the left and then to the right etc: *The path zigzagged down the hillside.*

zilch /zɪltʃ/ *n* [U] *informal* nothing at all: *'How much money is zero?' 'Zilch.'*

zil·lion /ˈzɪljən/ *n* [C] *informal* a very large number of things: *I've seen that movie a zillion times.* | [+of] *zillions of mosquitoes*

zim·mer frame /ˈzɪmə freɪm $ -mər-/ *n* [C] *trademark BrE* a metal frame that old or ill people use to help them walk; ▤ **walker** *AmE*

zinc /zɪŋk/ *n* [U] a blue-white metal that is used to make BRASS and to cover and protect objects made of iron. It is a chemical ELEMENT: symbol Zn

zine /ziːn/ *n* [C] *informal* a small magazine, usually about popular culture, that is written by people who are not professional writers

zing /zɪŋ/ *n* [U] *informal* the quality of being full of energy or taste: *Lemon juice adds zing to drinks.* —**zingy** *adj*

zing[2] *v* [I always + adv/prep] *informal* to move quickly, making a whistling noise; ▤ **whistle**: [+past/off] *He could hear the bullets zinging past his head.*

zing·er /ˈzɪŋə $ -ər/ *n* [C] *AmE informal* a clever humorous remark that might also be insulting

Zi·on·is·m /ˈzaɪənɪzəm/ *n* [U] support for the establishment and development of a state for the Jews in Israel —**Zionist** *n, adj* [C]

zip[1] /zɪp/ *n* **1** [C] *BrE* two lines of small metal or plastic pieces that slide together to fasten a piece of clothing; ▤ **zipper** *AmE*: *The zip on my skirt had broken.* | **do up/undo a zip** *Your zip's undone at the back.* **2** [U] *informal* speed, energy, or excitement: *This car goes with a bit more zip than my last one.* | *A spoonful of mustard will give the dish some zip.* **3** [singular] *AmE informal* nothing at all or zero: *We beat them 10 to zip.* | *'How much money do you have left?' 'Zip!'*

zip[2] *v* **zipped**, **zipping 1** [T] to fasten something using a zip: *'I'll see you tomorrow,' said John, zipping his jacket.* | **zip sth shut/open** *Olsen zipped the bag shut.* | *He zipped open the case* (=unfastened it). | **zip sth together** *The two sleeping bags can be zipped together to make a double.* **2** [I always + adv/prep] *informal* to go

Z

somewhere or do something very quickly; ■ **whizz**, **zoom**: [+**through/past/along** etc] *We zipped through customs in no time.* **3 zip it/zip your lip** *AmE spoken informal* used to tell someone not to say anything about something, or to tell them to be quiet: *You'd better zip your lip or you'll be in trouble!*

zip up *phr v* to fasten something using a zip, or to become fastened using a zip; ■ **unzip: zip sth** ⇔ **up** *He was zipping up a small brown suitcase.* | *The dress zipped up at the front.* | **zip sb up** *Could you zip me up* (=fasten my dress) *please? I can't reach.*

'**zip code** *n* [C] *AmE* a number that you write at the end of an address on an envelope, package etc. The zip code shows the exact area where someone lives and helps the post office deliver the post more quickly; ■ **post-code** *BrE*

'**zip file** also '**zipped file** *n* [C] *technical* a computer FILE that has been made smaller so that it is easier to store and move

zip·per /'zɪpə $ -ər/ *n* [C] *especially AmE* two lines of small metal or plastic pieces that slide together to fasten a piece of clothing; ■ **zip** *BrE*

zip·po /'zɪpəʊ $ -poʊ-/ *n* [singular] *AmE informal* nothing at all or zero

zit /zɪt/ *n* [C] *informal* a PIMPLE

zith·er /'zɪðə $ -ər/ *n* [C] a musical instrument from Eastern Europe that consists of a flat box with strings stretched across it. You play it by pulling the strings with your fingers or a PLECTRUM (=small piece of plastic, metal etc)

zo·di·ac /'zəʊdiæk $ 'zoʊ-/ *n* **the zodiac** an imaginary area through which the sun, moon, and PLANETS appear to travel, which some people believe influences our lives: **sign of the zodiac** (=one of the 12 parts that this area is divided into) *'Which sign of the zodiac were you born under?' 'Leo.'* → HOROSCOPE

zom·bie /'zɒmbi $ 'zɑːm-/ *n* [C] **1** *informal* someone who moves very slowly and does not seem to be thinking about what they are doing, especially because they are very tired: *I walked around like a zombie for most of the day.* **2** a dead person whose body is made to move by magic, according to some African and Caribbean religions

zon·al /'zəʊnl $ 'zoʊnl/ *adj technical* relating to or arranged in zones

zone¹ W3 /zəʊn $ zoʊn/ *n* [C] a large area that is different from other areas around it in some way: *This is a no-parking zone.* | *San Francisco and Tokyo are both located in earthquake zones.* | **danger zone** (=an area where it is dangerous to go) | **battle/war zone** *The south side of the city has virtually become a war zone.* | *The government has set up a special economic zone to promote private enterprise.* → **buffer zone** at BUFFER¹ (3); → NO-FLY ZONE, TIME ZONE

zone² *v* [T usually passive] *AmE* if an area of land is zoned, it is officially kept separate from other land so that it can be used for a particular purpose: *The land is currently zoned for residential use.*

zone out *phr v informal* to stop paying attention

because you are bored or tired, or because you have taken drugs: *What? Oh, sorry – I was just zoning out there for a minute.*

zoned /zəʊnd $ zoʊnd/ also ,**zoned 'out** *adj* [not before noun] *AmE informal* unable to think clearly and quickly, especially because you are tired or have taken drugs

zon·ing /'zəʊnɪŋ $ 'zoʊ-/ *n* [U] a system of choosing areas to be developed for particular purposes, such as houses or shops, when planning a town

zonked /zɒŋkt $ zɑːŋkt/ also ,**zonked 'out** *adj* [not before noun] *informal* very tired or suffering from the effects of drugs, so that you do not want to do anything: *I'm really zonked.*

zoo /zuː/ *n plural* **zoos** [C] a place, usually in a city, where animals of many kinds are kept so that people can go to look at them; → **wildlife park**

'**zoo-,keeper** *n* [C] someone who looks after animals in a zoo

,**zoological 'garden** *n* [C] *formal* a zoo

zo·ol·o·gist /zuː'ɒlədʒɪst, zəʊ'ɒ- $ zoʊ'ɑːl-/ *n* [C] a scientist who studies animals and their behaviour

zo·ol·o·gy /zuː'ɒlədʒi, zəʊ'ɒ- $ zoʊ'ɑːl-/ *n* [U] the scientific study of animals and their behaviour —**zoological** /ˌzuːə'lɒdʒɪkəl‹ , ˌzəʊ- $ ˌzoʊə'lɑː-/ *adj* —**zoologically** /-kli/ *adv*

zoom¹ /zuːm/ *v* [I] *informal* **1** [always + adv/prep] to go somewhere or do something very quickly; ■ **whizz**, **zip**: **zoom off/around/down** etc *Brenda jumped in the car and zoomed off.* | *The work was really easy and I was able to zoom through it in a couple of hours.* **2** also **zoom up** to increase suddenly and quickly; ■ **esca-late**: [+**to**] *Inflation zoomed to 123%.*

zoom in *phr v* if a camera zooms in, it makes the person or thing that you are taking a picture of seem bigger and closer: [+**on**] *The camera zoomed in on the child's face.*

zoom out *phr v* if a camera zooms out, it makes the person or thing that you are taking a picture of seem smaller and further away

zoom² *n* [singular] *informal* a sound made by a vehicle that is travelling fast

'**zoom ,lens** *n* [C] a camera LENS that can change from a distant to a close view → see picture at CAMERA

zoot suit /'zuːt suːt, -sjuːt $ -suːt/ *n* [C] a suit that consists of wide trousers and a JACKET with wide shoul-ders, worn especially in the 1940s and 1950s

zuc·chi·ni /zʊ'kiːni/ *n* [C] *AmE* a long vegetable with a dark green skin; ■ **courgette** *BrE*

Zu·lu /'zuːluː/ *n* **1** [C] someone who belongs to a race of black people who live in South Africa **2** [U] the language used by the Zulu people —**Zulu** *adj*

zwie·back /'zwiːbæk $ 'zwaɪ-/ *n* [U] *AmE* a type of hard dry bread, often given to babies; ■ **rusk** *BrE*

zy·de·co /'zaɪdəkəʊ $ -koʊ/ *n* [U] a type of Cajun music that is popular in southern Louisiana that com-bines the styles of French and Caribbean music with the BLUES

zy·gote /'zaɪɡəʊt $ -ɡoʊt/ *n* [C] *technical* a cell that is formed when an egg is FERTILIZED

Z

Maps and Appendices

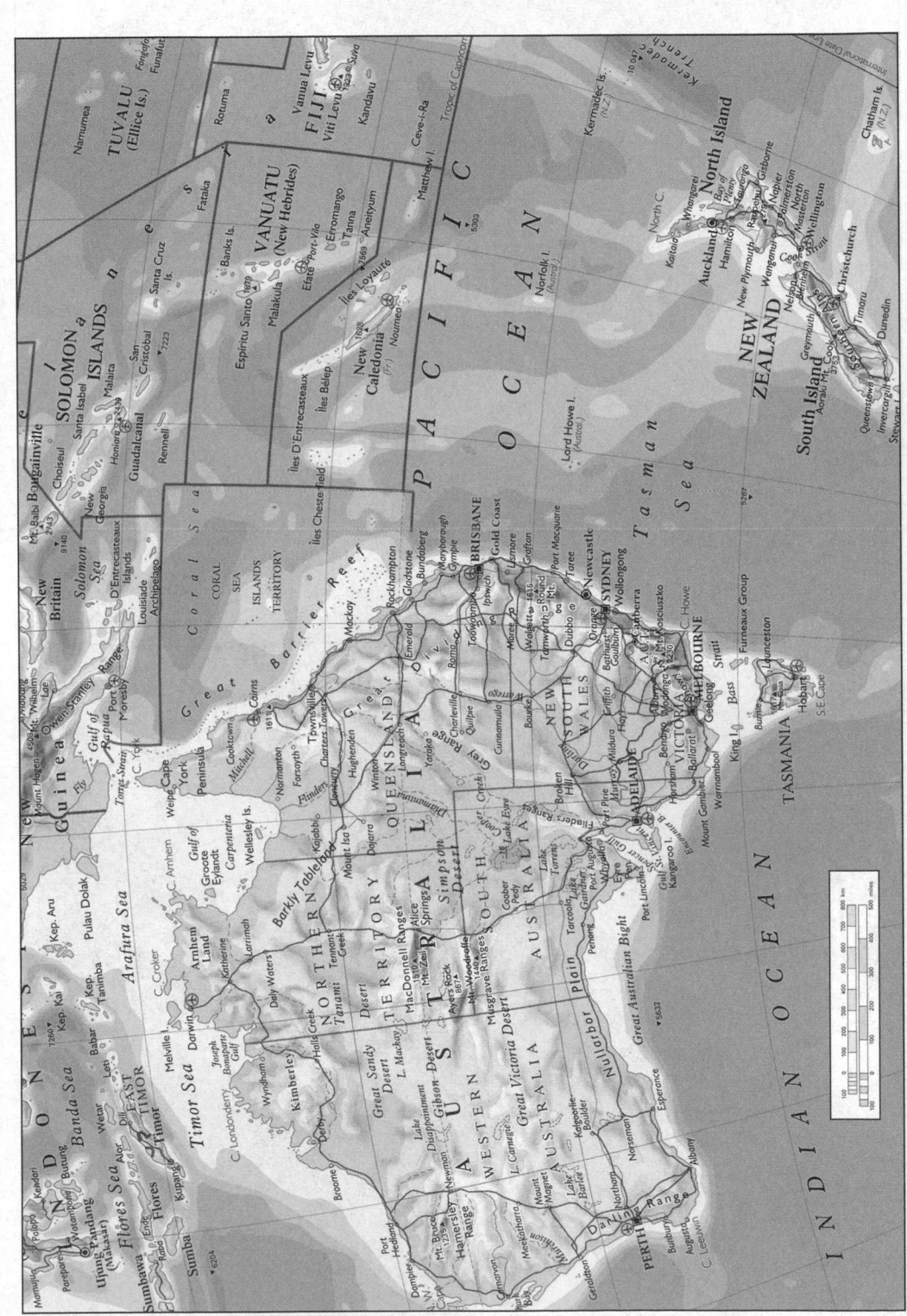

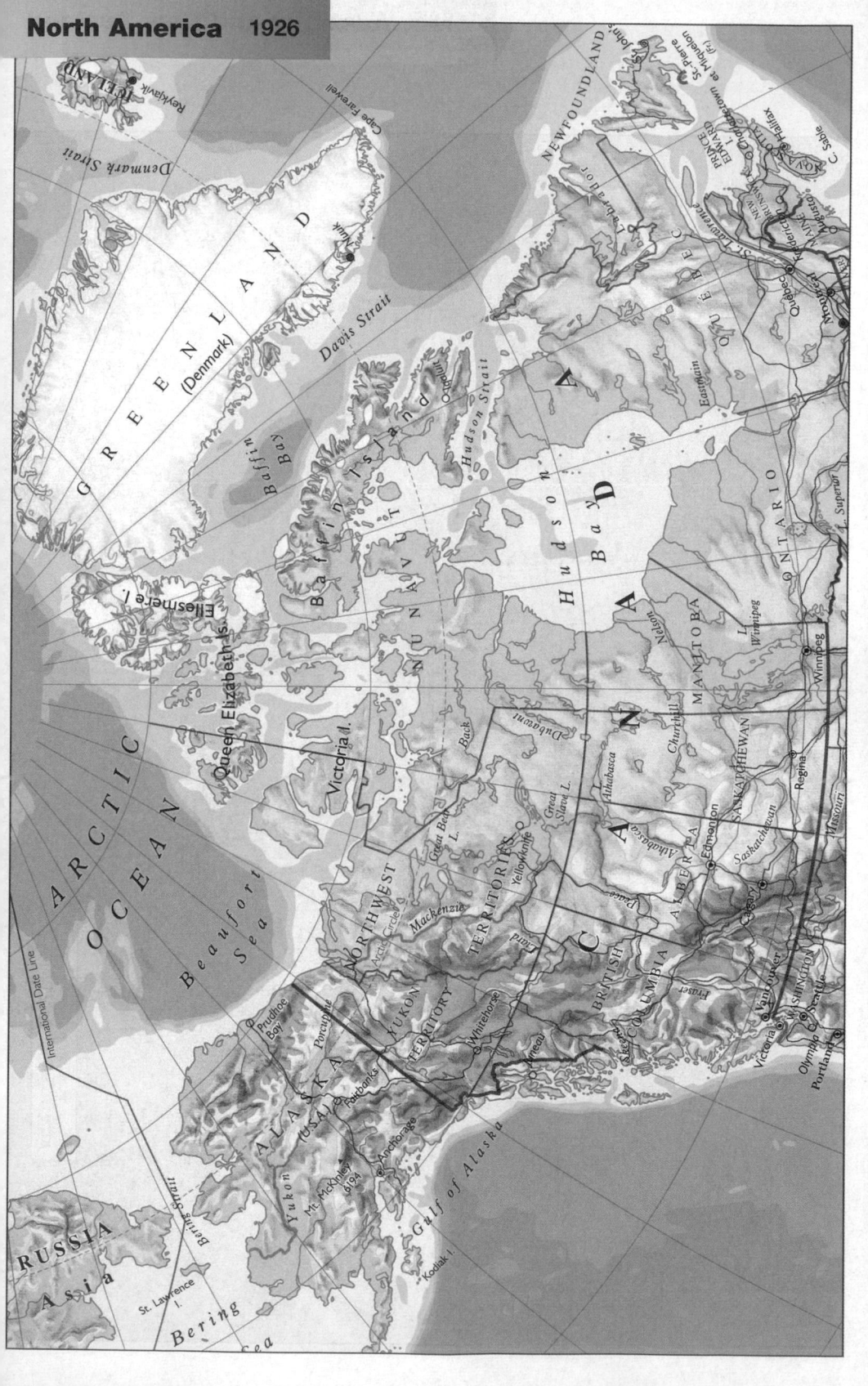

ICELAND
Reykjavik

Denmark Strait

Cape Farewell

G R E E N L A N D
(Denmark)

Davis Strait

Baffin Bay

Baffin Island

Ellesmere I.

Queen Elizabeth Is.

A R C T I C
O C E A N

Victoria I.

Beaufort Sea

NUNAVUT

Back

Hudson Strait

Hudson Bay

NEWFOUNDLAND

St-Pierre et Miquelon (F)

Charlottetown
EDWARD

NOVA
SCOTIA
Halifax
C. Sable

QUEBEC

Eastmain

L. Superior

ONTARIO

L. Winnipeg

Winnipeg

Nelson

Churchill

MANITOBA

Dubawnt

SASKATCHEWAN

Regina

Missouri

C A N A D A

Athabasca

Great Slave L.

L. Athabasca

Peace

ALBERTA

Edmonton

Saskatchewan

Calgary

Great Bear L.

Yellowknife

NORTHWEST
TERRITORIES

Mackenzie

Arctic Circle

Liard

BRITISH
COLUMBIA

Fraser

Prince

YUKON
TERRITORY

Whitehorse

Stikine

Juneau

Skeena

Vancouver

Victoria

WASHINGTON
Seattle
Olympia
Portland

Gulf of Alaska

International Date Line

Prudhoe Bay

Porcupine

ALASKA
(USA)

Fairbanks

Anchorage

Mt. McKinley
6194

Yukon

Kodiak I.

RUSSIA
Asia

St. Lawrence I.

Bering Strait

Bering Sea

Montreal

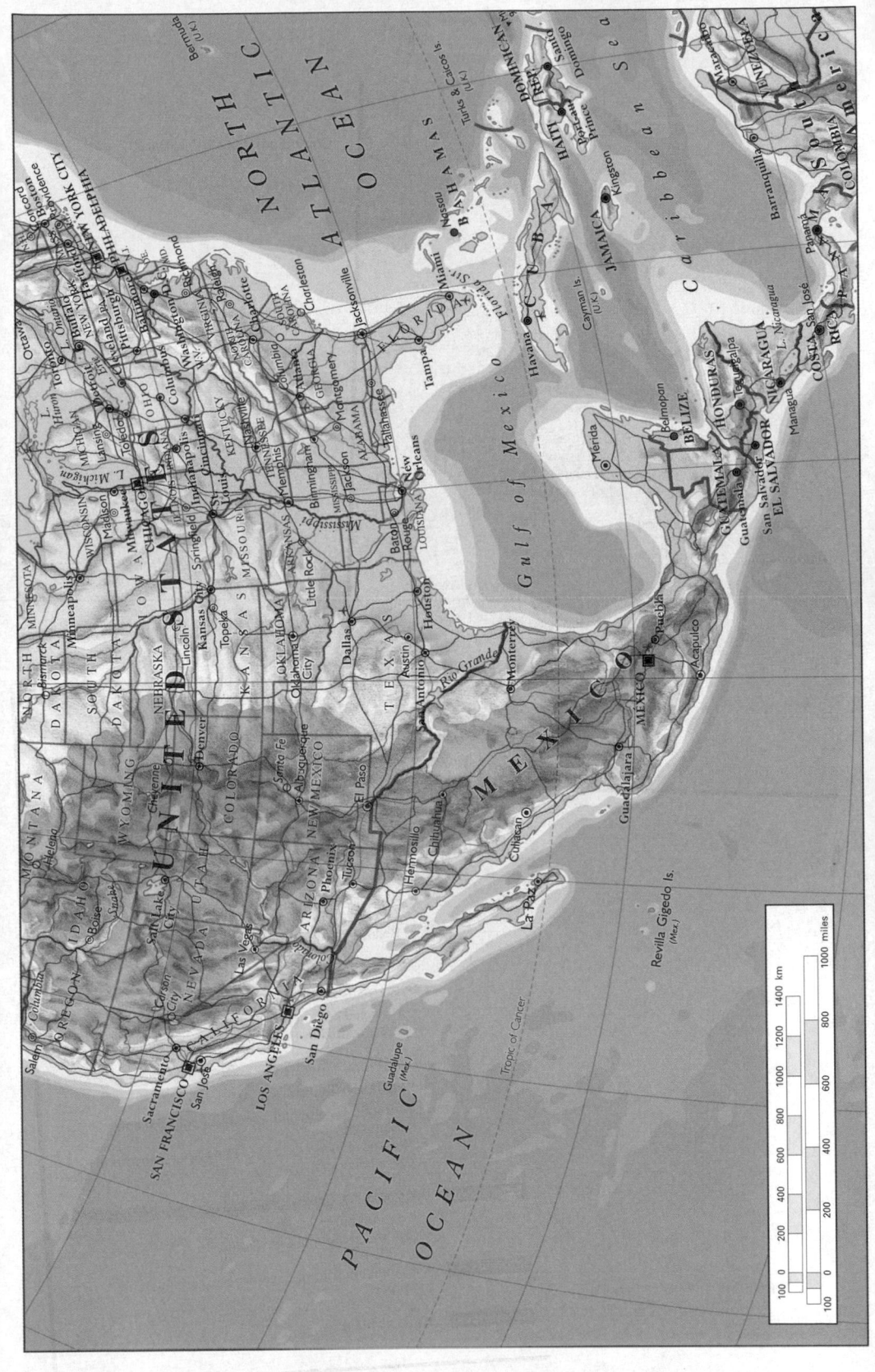

CURRICULUM VITAE

Name: Michael Woods

Address: Flat 5, 20 Park Road,
London N4 2JY

Tel: 0208 848 4965

Email: MWoods@aol.com

Date of Birth: 6–6–77

Qualifications: Higher National Diploma in Computer Studies,
University of North West London (1998)
A Levels: Maths (C), English (E) (1995)
O Levels: Maths, English Language, Chemistry,
General Studies, Woodwork (1993)

Employment History: Asst. Technical Support Manager,
Pearl Publishing (2001–now)
Support Analyst/Programmer, Mayfair Books (1999–2001)
Programmer, Mayfair Books (1998–1999)

Interests: Salsa dancing, running, gardening

Referees: Ms Ingrid Hofer,
IT Manager,
Pearl Publishing,
44 Lower Street,
London N1 3XY

Dr Paul Jones,
Senior Lecturer,
Dept. of Computer Studies,
University of North West London,
Downland Road,
London NW2 6HM

Curriculum Vitae/CV (in British English)

2334 Greenwood Road
Los Angeles, CA 34444
Tel: (505) 555-4965
Email: MWoods@aol.com

Michael Woods

Objective To find a technical support position in the field of publishing.

Experience 2001 – present   Pearl Publishing   Los Angeles, CA

Technical Support Manager
- Managed IT support staff of eleven people.
- Led regular training seminars.
- Redesigned company-wide help desk procedures.

1999–2001   Mayfair Books   Southridge, WA

Systems Administrator
- Managed LAN network.
- Implemented training course for new analysts.

1998–1999   Mayfair Books   Southridge, WA

Information Technology Associate
- Maintained computer systems of editorial and design staff.
- Worked on team of twenty IT associates to improve overall operations.

Education 1994–1998   Southridge State University   Southridge, WA
- B.S., Computer Science.
- Graduated Summa Cum Laude.

Interests Salsa dancing, running, gardening, carpentry, computers.

References Available upon request

Résumé (in American English)

1 Numbers

How numbers are spoken

Numbers over 20

21	twenty-one
22	twenty-two
32	thirty-two
99	ninety-nine

Numbers over 100

101	a/one hundred (and) one
121	a/one hundred (and) twenty-one
200	two hundred
232	two hundred (and) thirty-two
999	nine hundred (and) ninety-nine

Note: In British English the 'and' is always used: *two hundred and thirty-two*. But in American English it is often left out: *two hundred thirty two*.

Numbers over 1000

1001	a/one thousand (and) one
1121	one thousand one hundred (and) twenty-one
2000	two thousand
2232	two thousand two hundred (and) thirty-two
9999	nine thousand nine hundred (and) ninety-nine

Ordinal numbers

20th	twentieth
21st	twenty-first
25th	twenty-fifth
90th	ninetieth
99th	ninety-ninth
100th	hundredth
101st	hundred and first
225th	two hundred (and) twenty-fifth

Dates

1624	sixteen twenty-four
1903	nineteen-oh-three
1987	nineteen eighty-seven

What numbers represent

Numbers are often used on their own to show:

Price — *It cost eight seventy-five* (=8 pounds 75 pence or 8 dollars 75 cents: £8.75 or $8.75).

Time — *We left at two twenty-five* (=25 minutes after 2 o'clock).

Age — *She's forty-six* (=46 years old). | *He's in his sixties* (=between 60 and 69 years old).

Size — *This shirt is a thirty-eight* (=size 38).

Temperature — *The temperature fell to minus fourteen* (=−14°). | *The temperature was in the mid-thirties* (=about 34–36°).

The score in a game — *He won the first set six-three* (=by six games to three: 6–3).

Something marked with the stated number — *She played two nines and an eight* (=playing cards marked with these numbers).

A set or group of the stated number — *The teacher divided us into fours* (=groups of 4). | *You can buy cigarettes in tens or twenties* (=in packets containing 10 or 20).

Numbers and grammar

Numbers can be used as:

Determiners — *Five people were hurt in the accident.* | *the three largest companies in the US* | *several hundred cars*

Pronouns — *We invited a lot of people but only twelve came/only twelve of them came.* | *Do exercise five on page nine.*

Nouns — *Six can be divided by two and three.* | *Three twos make six.*

2 Weights and measures

The words in **dark type** are the ones that are most commonly used in general speech.

METRIC

Units of length

1 **millimetre**	= 0.03937 inch
10 mm = 1 **centimetre**	= 0.3937 inch
10 cm = 1 decimetre	= 3.937 inches
10 dm = 1 **metre**	= 39.37 inches
10 m = 1 decametre	= 10.94 yards
10 dam = 1 hectometre	= 109.4 yards
10 hm = 1 **kilometre**	= 0.6214 mile

Units of weight

1 **milligram**	= 0.015 grain
10 mg = 1 centigram	= 0.154 grain
10 cg = 1 decigram	= 1.543 grains
10 dg = 1 **gram**	= 15.43 grains = 0.035 ounce
10 g = 1 decagram	= 0.353 ounce
10 dag = 1 hectogram	= 3.527 ounces
10 hg = 1 **kilogram**	= 2.205 pounds
100 kg = 1 **tonne**	= 0.984 (long) ton
(metric ton)	= 2204.62 pounds

Units of capacity

1 millilitre	= 0.00176 pint
10 ml = 1 centilitre	= 0.0176 pint
10 cl = 1 decilitre	= 0.176 pint
10 dl = 1 **litre**	= 1.76 pints = 0.22 UK gallon
10 l = 1 decalitre	= 2.20 gallons
10 dal = 1 hectolitre	= 22.0 gallons
10 hl = 1 kilolitre	= 220.0 gallons

Square measure

1 square measure	= 0.00155 square inch
100 mm^2 = 1 square centimetre	= 0.1550 square inch
100 cm^2 = 1 square metre	= 1.196 square yards
100 m^2 = 1 are	= 119.6 square yards
100 ares = 1 **hectare**	= 2.471 acres
100 ha = 1 square kilometre	= 247.1 acres

Cubic measure

1 cubic centimetre	= 0.06102 cubic inch
1000 cm^3 = 1 cubic decimetre	= 0.03532 cubic foot
1000 dm^3 = 1 cubic metre	= 1.308 cubic yards

Circular measure

1 microradian	= 0.206 seconds
1000 μrad = 1 milliradian	= 3.437 minutes
1000 mrad = 1 radian	= 57.296 degrees
	= 180/π degrees

Metric prefixes

	Abbreviation	Factor
tera-	T	10^{12}
giga-	G	10^{9}
mega-	M	10^{6}
kilo-	k	10^{3}
hecto-	h	10^{2}
deca-	da	10^{1}
deci-	d	10^{-1}
centi-	c	10^{-2}
milli-	m	10^{-3}
micro-	μ	10^{-6}
nano-	n	10^{-9}
pico-	p	10^{-12}
femto-	f	10^{-15}
atto-	a	10^{-18}

BRITISH AND AMERICAN

Units of length

	1 **inch**	= 2.54 cm
12 inches	= 1 **foot**	= 0.3048 m
3 feet	= 1 **yard**	= 0.9144 m
5½ yards	= 1 rod, pole, or perch	= 5.029 m
22 yards	= 1 chain	= 20.12 m
10 chains	= 1 furlong	= 0.2012 km
8 furlongs	= 1 **mile**	= 1.609 km
6076.12 feet	= 1 nautical mile	= 1852 m

Units of weight

1 grain	= 64.8 mg	
1 dram	= 1.772 g	
16 drams	= 1 **ounce**	= 28.35 g
16 ounces	= 1 **pound**	= 0.4536 kg
14 pounds	= 1 stone	= 6.350 kg
2 stones	= 1 quarter	= 12.70 kg
4 quarters	= 1 (long) **hundredweight**	
		= 50.80 kg
20 hundredweight	= 1 (long) **ton**	= 1.016 tonnes
100 pounds	= 1 (short) **hundredweight**	
		= 45.36 kg
2000 pounds	= 1 (short) **ton**	= 0.9072 tonnes

The short hundredweight and ton are more common in the US.

Units of capacity

1 fluid ounce	= 28.41 cm³	
5 fluid ounces	= 1 gill	= 0.1421 dm³
4 gills	= 1 **pint**	= 0.5683 dm³
2 pints	= 1 **quart**	= 1.137 dm³
4 quarts	= 1 (UK) **gallon**	= 4.546 dm³
231 cubic inches	= 1 (US) **gallon**	= 3.785 dm³
8 gallons	= 1 bushel	= 36.369 dm³

Square measure

1 square inch	= 645.16 mm²	
144 square inches	= 1 square foot	= 0.0929 m²
9 square feet	= 1 square yard	= 0.8361 m²
4840 square yards	= 1 acre	= 4047 m²
640 acres	= 1 square mile	= 259 ha

Cubic measure

1 cubic inch	= 16.39 cm³	
1728 cubic inches	= 1 cubic foot	= 0.02832 m³
		= 28.32 dm³
27 cubic feet	= 1 cubic yard	= 0.7646 m³
		= 764.6 dm³

Circular measure

1 second	= 4.860 μrad	
60 seconds	= 1 minute	= 0.2909 μrad
60 minutes	= 1 degree	= 17.45 μrad
		= $\pi/180$ rad
45 degrees	= 1 oxtant	= $\pi/4$ rad
60 degrees	= 1 sextant	= $\pi/3$ rad
90 degrees	= 1 quadrant or	
	1 right angle	= $\pi/2$ rad
360 degrees	= 1 circle or	
	1 circumference	= 2π rad

1 grade or gon = 1/100th of a right angle = $\pi/200$ rad

US dry measure

1 pint	= 0.9689 UK pint	= 0.5506 dm³
1 bushell	= 0.9689 UK bushell	= 35.238 dm³

US liquid measure

1 fluid ounce	= 1.0408 UK fluid ounces	
	= 0.0296 dm³	
16 fluid ounces	= 1 pint = 0.8327 UK pint	
	= 0.4732 dm³	
8 pints	= 1 gallon = 0.8327 UK gallon	
	= 3.7853 dm³	

Temperature

° *Fahrenheit* = (9/5 x x °C) + 32
° *Celsius* = 5/9 x (x °F – 32)

3 Word formation

In English there are many word beginnings (prefixes) and word endings (suffixes) that can be added to a word to change its meaning or its word class. The most common ones are shown here, with examples of how they are used in the process of word formation. Many more are listed in the dictionary.

Verb formation

The endings **-ize** and **-ify** can be added to many nouns and adjectives to form verbs, like this:

American		Americanize
legal	**-ize**	legalize
modern		modernize
popular		popularize

They want to make the factory more **modern***. They want to* **modernize** *the factory.*

beauty		beautify
liquid	**-ify**	liquefy
pure		purify
simple		simplify

These tablets make the water **pure***. They* **purify** *the water.*

Adverb formation

The ending **-ly** can be added to most adjectives to form adverbs, like this:

easy		easily
main	**-ly**	mainly
quick		quickly
stupid		stupidly

His behaviour was **stupid***. He behaved* **stupidly***.*

Noun formation

The endings **-er**, **-ment**, and **-ation** can be added to many verbs to form nouns, like this:

drive		driver
fasten	**-er**	fastener
open		opener
teach		teacher

John **drives** *a bus. He is a bus* **driver***.*
A can **opener** *is a tool for* **opening** *cans.*

amaze		amazement
develop	**-ment**	development
pay		payment
retire		retirement

Children **develop** *very quickly. Their* **development** *is very quick.*

admire		admiration
associate	**-ation**	association
examine		examination
organize		organization

The doctor **examined** *me carefully. He gave me a careful* **examination***.*

The endings **-ity** and **-ness** can be added to many adjectives to form nouns, like this:

cruel		cruelty
odd	**-ity**	oddity
pure	**-ty**	purity
stupid		stupidity

Don't be so **cruel***. I hate* **cruelty***.*

dark		darkness
deaf	**-ness**	deafness
happy		happiness
kind		kindness

It was very **dark***. The* **darkness** *made it impossible to see.*

Adjective formation

The endings **-y**, **-ic**, **-ical**, **-ful**, and **-less** can be added to many nouns to form adjectives like this:

bush	**-y**	bushy
dirt		dirty
hair		hairy
smell		smelly

There was an awful **smell** *in the room. The room was very* **smelly**.

atom	**-ic**	atomic
biology	**-ical**	biological
grammar		grammatical
poetry		poetic

This book contains exercises on **grammar**. *It contains* **grammatical** *exercises.*

pain	**-ful**	painful
hope		hopeful
care		careful

His broken leg caused him a lot of **pain**. *It was very* **painful**.

pain	**-less**	painless
hope		hopeless
care		careless

The operation didn't cause her any **pain**. *It was* **painless**.

The ending **-able** can be added to many verbs to form adjectives, like this:

wash	**-able**	washable
love		lovable
debate		debatable
break		breakable

You can **wash** *this coat. It's* **washable**.

Opposites

The following prefixes can be used in front of many words to produce an opposite meaning. Note, however, that the words formed in this way are not always exact opposites and may have a slightly different meaning.

un-	happy	unhappy
	fortunate	unfortunate
	wind	unwind
	block	unblock

I'm not very **happy**. *In fact I'm very* **unhappy**.

in-	efficient	inefficient
im-	possible	impossible
il-	literate	illiterate
ir-	regular	irregular

It's just not **possible** *to do that, it's* **impossible**.

dis-	agree	disagree
	approve	disapprove
	honest	dishonest

I don't **agree** *with everything you said. I* **disagree** *with the last part.*

de-	centralize	decentralize
	increase	decrease
	ascend	descend
	inflate	deflate

Increase *means to make or become larger in amount or number.* **Decrease** *means to make or become smaller in amount or number.*

non-	sense	nonsense
	payment	non-payment
	resident	non-resident
	conformist	nonconformist

The hotel serves meals to **residents** *(=people who are staying in the hotel) only.* **Non-residents** *are not allowed in.*

4 Irregular verbs

verb	past tense	past participle
abide	abided, abode	abided
arise	arose	arisen
awake	awoke, awakened	awoken
babysit	babysat	babysat
bear	bore	borne
beat	beat	beaten
become	became	become
befall	befell	befallen
beget	begot (also begat *bibl*)	begotten
begin	began	begun
behold	beheld	beheld
bend	bent	bent
beseech	besought, beseeched	besought, beseeched
beset	beset	beset
bestride	bestrode	bestridden
bet	bet	bet
betake	betook	betaken
bid	bade, bid	bid, bidden
bind	bound	bound
bite	bit	bitten
bleed	bled	bled
bless	blessed, blest	blessed, blest
blow	blew	blown
break	broke	broken
breastfeed	breastfed	breastfed
breed	bred	bred
bring	brought	brought
broadcast	broadcast	broadcast
browbeat	browbeat	browbeaten
build	built	built
burn	burned, burnt	burned, burnt
burst	burst	burst
bust	bust (*BrE*), busted (esp *AmE*)	bust (*BrE*), busted (esp *AmE*)
buy	bought	bought
cast	cast	cast
catch	caught	caught
choose	chose	chosen
cleave	cleaved, cleft, clove	cleaved, cleft
cling	clung	clung
come	came	come
cost	cost	cost
could	(see dictionary entry)	
creep	crept	crept
cut	cut	cut
deal	dealt /delt/	dealt /delt/
dig	dug	dug
dive	dived, dove (*AmE*)	dived
do	did	done
draw	drew	drawn
dream	dreamed, dreamt	dreamed, dreamt
drink	drank	drunk
drive	drove	driven
dwell	dwelt, dwelled	dwelt, dwelled
eat	ate	eaten
fall	fell	fallen

verb	past tense	past participle
feed	fed	fed
feel	felt	felt
fight	fought	fought
find	found	found
flee	fled	fled
fling	flung	flung
fly	flew	flown
forbid	forbade, forbad	forbidden
forecast	forecast	forecast
foresee	foresaw	foreseen
foretell	foretold	foretold
forget	forgot	forgotten
forgive	forgave	forgiven
forego	forewent	foregone
forsake	forsook	forsaken
forswear	forswore	forsworn
freeze	froze	frozen
gainsay	gainsaid	gainsaid
get	got	got (*BrE*), gotten (*AmE*)
give	gave	given
go	went	gone
grind	ground	ground
grow	grew	grown
hamstring	hamstrung	hamstrung
hang	hung, hanged	hung, hanged
have	had	had
hear	heard	heard
heave	heaved, hove	heaved, hove
hide	hid	hidden, hid
hit	hit	hit
hold	held	held
hurt	hurt	hurt
input	inputted, input	inputted, input
inset	inset, insetted	inset, insetted
interbreed	interbred	interbred
interweave	interwove	interwoven
keep	kept	kept
kneel	knelt, kneeled (esp *AmE*)	knelt, kneeled (esp *AmE*)
knit	knitted, knit	knitted, knit
know	knew	known
lay	laid	laid
lead	led	led
lean	leaned, leant (esp *BrE*)	leaned, leant (esp *BrE*)
leap	leapt, leaped (esp *AmE*)	leapt, leaped (esp *AmE*)
learn	learned, learnt	learned, learnt
leave	left	left
lend	lent	lent
let	let	let
lie	lay	lain
light	lit, lighted	lit, lighted
lose	lost	lost
make	made	made
mean	meant	meant
meet	met	met
miscast	miscast	miscast
mishear	misheard	misheard
mislay	mislaid	mislaid
mislead	misled	misled
misread	misread	misread

verb	past tense	past participle
misspell	misspelled, misspelt (*BrE*)	misspelled, misspelt (*BrE*)
misspend	misspent	misspent
mistake	mistook	mistaken
misunderstand	misunderstood	misunderstood
mow	mowed	mown, mowed
offset	offset	offset
outbid	outbid	outbid
outfight	outfought	outfought
outdo	outdid	outdone
outgrow	outgrew	outgrown
outrun	outran	outrun
outsell	outsold	outsold
outshine	outshone	outshone
overcome	overcame	overcome
overdo	overdid	overdone
overdraw	overdrew	overdrawn
overeat	overate	overeaten
overhang	overhung	overhung
overhear	overheard	overheard
overlay	overlaid	overlaid
overpay	overpaid	overpaid
override	overrode	overridden
overrun	overran	overrun
oversee	oversaw	overseen
overshoot	overshot	overshot
oversleep	overslept	overslept
overtake	overtook	overtaken
overthrow	overthrew	overthrown
partake	partook	partaken
pay	paid	paid
plead	pleaded, pled (esp *AmE*)	pleaded, pled (esp *AmE*)
proofread	proofread	proofread
prove	proved	proved (also proven *AmE*)
put	put	put
quit	quit	quit
read	read /red/	read /red/
rebind	rebound	rebound
rebuild	rebuilt	rebuilt
recast	recast	recast
redo	redid	redone
relay	relaid	relaid
remake	remade	remade
rend	rent	rent
repay	repaid	repaid
rerun	reran	rerun
resell	resold	resold
reset	reset	reset
resit	resat	resat
retell	retold	retold
rethink	rethought	rethought
rewind	rewound	rewound
rewrite	rewrote	rewritten
rid	rid	rid
ride	rode	ridden
ring	rang	rung
rise	rose	risen
run	ran	run
saw	sawed	sawn, sawed
say	said	said
see	saw	seen

verb	past tense	past participle
seek	sought	sought
sell	sold	sold
send	sent	sent
set	set	set
sew	sewed	sewn, sewed
shake	shook	shaken
shall	(see dictionary entry)	
shear	sheared	shorn, sheared
shed	shed	shed
shine	shone, shined	shone, shined
shit	shit, shat	shit, shat
shoe	shod	shod
shoot	shot	shot
should	(see dictionary entry)	
show	showed	shown, showed
shrink	shrank, shrunk	shrunk
shut	shut	shut
sing	sang	sung
sink	sank, sunk	sunk
sit	sat	sat
slay	slew	slain
sleep	slept	slept
slide	slid	slid
sling	slung	slung
slink	slunk	slunk
slit	slit	slit
smell	smelled, smelt (esp *BrE*)	smelled, smelt (esp *BrE*)
smite	smote	smitten
sow	sowed	sown, sowed
speak	spoke	spoken
speed	sped, speeded	sped, speeded
spell	spelled, spelt (esp *BrE*)	spelled, spelt (esp *BrE*)
spend	spent	spent
spill	spilled, spilt (esp *BrE*)	spilled, spilt (esp *BrE*)
spin	spun, span	spun
spit	spat (also spit *AmE*)	spat (also spit *AmE*)
split	split	split
spoil	spoiled, spoilt	spoiled, spoilt
spoon-feed	spoon-fed	spoon-fed
spotlight	spotlighted, spotlit	spotlighted, spotlit
spread	spread	spread
spring	sprang (also sprung *AmE*)	sprung
stand	stood	stood
steal	stole	stolen
stick	stuck	stuck
sting	stung	stung
stink	stank, stunk	stunk
strew	strewed	strewn, strewed
stride	strode	stridden
strike	struck	struck
string	strung	strung
strive	strove, strived	striven, strived
sublet	sublet	sublet
swear	swore	sworn
sweep	swept	swept
swell	swelled	swollen, swelled
swim	swam	swum
sweep	swept	swept
swell	swelled	swollen, swelled
swim	swam	swum
swing	swung	swung
take	took	taken

verb	past tense	past participle
teach	taught	taught
tear	tore	torn
tell	told	told
think	thought	thought
thrive	thrived, throve	thrived
throw	threw	thrown
thrust	thrust	thrust
tread	trod	trodden, trod
unbend	unbent	unbent
unbind	unbound	unbound
undergo	underwent	undergone
underlie	underlay	underlaid
underpay	underpaid	underpaid
undersell	undersold	undersold
understand	understood	understood
undertake	undertook	undertaken
underwrite	underwrote	underwritten
undo	undid	undone
unwind	unwound	unwound
uphold	upheld	upheld
upset	upset	upset
wake	woke	woken
wear	wore	worn
weave	wove	woven
wed	wedded, wed	wedded, wed
weep	wept	wept
wet	wetted, wet	wetted, wet
win	won	won
wind /waind/	wound	wound
withdraw	withdrew	withdrawn
withhold	withheld	withheld
withstand	withstood	withstood
wreak	wreaked, wrought	wreaked, wrought
wring	wrung	wrung
write	wrote	written

5 Geographical names

This list of geographical names is included to help advanced students in their reading of contemporary newspapers and magazines.

Name	Adjective
Afghanistan /æf'gæn‚stɑːn$-stæn/	Afghan /'æfgæn/ person: Afghanistani /æf‚gæn‚'stɑːni$-æni/, Afghan
Africa /'æfrɪkə/	African /'æfrɪkən/
Alaska /ə'læskə/	Alaskan /ə'læskən/
Albania /æl'beɪniə/	Albanian /æl'beɪniən/
Algeria /æl'dʒɪəriə$-'dʒɪr-/	Algerian /æl'dʒɪəriən$-'dʒɪr-/
America /ə'mer‚kə/	American /ə'mer‚kən/
Andorra /æn'dɔːrə/	Andorran /æn'dɔːrən/
Angola /æŋ'gəʊlə$-'goʊ-/	Angolan /æŋ'gəʊlən$-'goʊ-/
Antarctic /æn'tɑːktɪk$-ɑːr-/	Antarctic
Antigua /æn'tiːgə/	Antiguan /æn'tiːgən/
Arctic /'ɑːktɪk$'ɑːrk-/	Arctic
Argentina /ˌɑːdʒən'tiːnə$ˌɑːr-/	Argentinian or -ean /ˌɑːdʒən'tɪniən$ˌɑːr-/
Armenia /ɑː'miːniə$ɑːr-/	Armenian /ɑː'miːniən$ɑːr-/
Asia /'eɪʃə, -ʒə$-ʒə, -ʃə/	Asian /'eɪʃən, -ʒən$-ʒən, -ʃən/
Atlantic /ət'læntɪk/	Atlantic
Australia /ɒ'streɪliə$ɒː-, ɑː-/	Australian /ɒ'streɪliən$ɒː-, ɑː-/
Austria /ɒ'striə$'ɒː-, 'ɑː-/	Austrian /ɒ'striən$'ɒː-, 'ɑː-/
Azerbaijan /ˌæzəbaɪ'dʒɑːn$-zər-/	Azerbaijani /ˌæzəbaɪ'dʒɑːni‹$-zər-/
Bahamas /bə'hɑːməz/	Bahamian /bə'heɪmiən/
Bahrain /bɑː'reɪn/	Bahraini /bɑː'reɪni/
Baltic /'bɔːltɪk$'bɒːl-/	Baltic
Bangladesh /ˌbæŋglə'deʃ/	Bangladesh person: Bangladeshi /ˌbæŋglə'deʃi/
Barbados /bɑː'beɪdɒs$bɑːr'beɪdəs,-dɑːs/	Barbadian /bɑː'beɪdiən$bɑːr-/
Belarus /ˌbelə'ruːs/ (Belorussia) /ˌbeləʊ'rʌʃə$-loʊ-/	Belorussian /ˌbeləʊ'rʌʃən$-loʊ-/
Belgium /'beldʒəm/	Belgian /'beldʒən/
Belize /bə'liːz/	Belizean /bə'liːziən/
Benin /be'niːn$bə'nɪn/	Beninese /ˌbenɪ'niːz‹/
Bermuda /bə'mjuːdə$bər-/	Bermudan /bə'mjuːdn$bər-/
Bhutan /buː'tɑːn/	Bhutanese /buːtə'niːz‹$ˌbuːtn'iːz‹/
Bolivia /bə'lɪviə/	Bolivian /bə'lɪviən/
Bosnia and Herzegovina /ˌbɒzniə ənd hɜːtsəgəʊ'viːnə$ˌbɑːzniə ənd ˌhertsəgoʊ-/	Bosnian /'bɒzniən$'bɑːz-/
Botswana /bɒt'swɑːnə$bɑːt-/	Tswana /'tswɑːnə, 'swɑː-/ person: sing.= Motswana /mɒt'swɑːnə$mɑːt-/ pl. = Batswana /bæt'swɑːnə/
Burkina Faso /bɜːˌkiːnə 'fæsəʊ$ bʊrˌkiːnə 'fɑːsoʊ/	Burkina person: Burkinabe /ˌbɜːkiːnæ'beɪ$‚bʊr-/
Brazil /brə'zɪl/	Brazilian /brə'zɪliən/
Brunei /'bruːnaɪ/	Bruneian /bruː'naɪən/
Bulgaria /bʌl'geəriə$-'ger-/	Bulgarian /bʌl'geəriən-'ger-/
Burma /'bɜːmə$'bɜːr-/ former name of Myanmar	
Burundi /bʊ'rʊndi$-'ruː-/	Burundian /bʊ'rʊndiən$-'ruː-/
Cambodia /kæm'bəʊdiə$-'boʊ-/	Cambodian /kæm'bəʊdiən$-'boʊ-/
Cameroon /ˌkæmə'ruːn/	Cameroonian /ˌkæmə'ruːniən‹/
Canada /'kænədə/	Canadian /kə'neɪdiən/
Cape Verde /keɪp 'vɜːd$-'vɜːrd/	Cape Verdean /keɪp 'vɜːdiən$-'vɜːr-/
Caribbean /ˌkærɪ'biːən $ kə'rɪbiən/	Caribbean
Cayman Islands /'keɪmən ˌaɪləndz/	Cayman Island /ˌkeɪmən 'aɪlənd‹/ person: Cayman Islander /ˌkeɪmən 'aɪləndə$-dər/
Central African Republic /ˌsentrəl æfrɪkən rɪ'pʌblɪk/	
Chad /tʃæd/	Chadian /'tʃædiən/
Chile /'tʃɪli/	Chilean /'tʃɪliən/
China /'tʃaɪnə/	Chinese /ˌtʃaɪ'niːz‹/
Colombia /kə'lʌmbiə/	Colombian /kə'lʌmbiən/
Congo /'kɒŋgəʊ$'kɑːŋgoʊ/	Congolese /ˌkɒŋgə'liːz‹$ˌkɑːŋ-/
Costa Rica /ˌkɒstə 'riːkə$ˌkoʊ-/	Costa Rican /ˌkɒstə 'riːkən‹$ˌkoʊ-/
Croatia /krəʊ'eɪʃə$kroʊ-/	Croatian /krəʊ'eɪʃən$kroʊ-/
Cuba /'kjuːbə/	Cuban /'kjuːbən/
Cyprus /'saɪprəs/	Cypriot /'sɪpriət/
Czech Republic /ˌtʃek rɪ'pʌblɪk/	Czech /tʃek/
Denmark /'denmɑːk$-mɑːrk/	Danish /'deɪnɪʃ/ person: Dane /deɪn/
Djibouti /dʒ‚'buːti/	Djiboutian /dʒ‚'buːtiən/
Dominica /ˌdɒm‚'niːkə$ˌdɑː-/	Dominican /ˌdɒm‚'niːkən‹$‚dɑː-/

Name	Adjective
Dominican Republic /dəˌmɪnɪkən rɪˈpʌblɪk/	Dominican /dəˈmɪnɪkən/
Ecuador /ˈekwədɔː$-ɔːr/	Ecuadorian /ˌekwəˈdɔːriən‹/
Egypt /ˈiːdʒɪpt/	Egyptian /ɪˈdʒɪpʃən/
El Salvador /el ˈsælvəˌdɔː$-ɔːr/	Salvadorian /ˌsælvəˈdɔːriən‹/
Equatorial Guinea /ˌekwətɔːriəl ˈɡɪni$ˌi:-/	Equatorial Guinean /ˌekwətɔːriəl ˈɡɪniən$ˌi:-/
Eritrea /ˌerɪˈtreə/	Eritrean /ˌerɪˈtreɪən‹/
Estonia /eˈstəʊniə$eˈstoʊ-/	Estonian /eˈstəʊniən$eˈstoʊ-/
Ethiopia /ˌiːθiˈəʊpiə$-ˈoʊ-/	Ethiopian /ˌiːθiˈəʊpiən‹$-ˈoʊ-/
Europe /ˈjʊərəp$ˈjʊr-/	European /ˌjʊərəˈpiːən‹$ˌjʊr-/
Fiji /ˈfiːdʒiː/	Fijian /fiːˈdʒiːən$ˈfiːdʒiən/
Finland /ˈfɪnlənd/	Finnish /ˈfɪnɪʃ/ person: Finn /fɪn/
France /frɑːns$fræns/	French /frentʃ/ person: sing. = Frenchman /ˈfrentʃmən/ (fem. -woman) /-ˌwʊmən/: pl. = Frenchmen /ˈfrentʃmən/, people: French
Gabon /ɡæˈbɒn$-ˈboʊn/	Gabonese /ˌɡæbəˈniːz‹/
Gambia /ˈɡæmbiə/	Gambian /ˈɡæmbiən/
Georgia /ˈdʒɔːdʒə$ˈdʒɔːr-/	Georgian /ˈdʒɔːdʒən$ˈdʒɔːr-/
Germany /ˈdʒɜːməni$-ɜːr-/	German /ˈdʒɜːmən‹$-ɜːr-/
Ghana /ˈɡɑːnə/	Ghanaian /ɡɑːˈneɪən/
Gibraltar /dʒɪˈbrɔːltə$-ˈbrɔːl-/	Gibraltarian /ˌdʒɪbrɔːlˈteəriən$-brɔːlˈter-/
Greece /griːs/	Greek /griːk/
Greenland /ˈgriːnlənd, -lænd/	Greenlandic /griːnˈlændɪk/ person: Greenlander /ˈgriːnləndə$-dər/
Grenada /grəˈneɪdə/	Grenadian /grəˈneɪdiən/
Guatemala /ˌgwɑːtəˈmɑːlə/	Guatemalan /ˌgwɑːtəˈmɑːlən‹/
Guiana /giˈɑːnə$giˈænə, -ˈɑːnə/	Guianese /ˌgaɪəˈniːz‹/
Guinea /ˈgɪni/	Guinean /ˈgɪniən/
Guinea-Bissau /ˌgɪni bɪˈsaʊ/	Guinea-Bissauan /ˌgɪni bɪˈsaʊən/
Guyana /gaɪˈænə/	Guyanese /ˌgaɪəˈniːz‹/
Haiti /ˈheɪti/	Haitian /ˈheɪʃən/
Holland /ˈhɒlənd$ˈhɑː-/ another name for The Netherlands	Dutch /dʌtʃ/
Honduras /hɒnˈdjʊərəs$hɑːn-ˈdjʊrəs, -ˈdʊ-/	Honduran /hɒnˈdjʊərən$hɑːn-ˈdjʊrən, -ˈdʊ-/
Hong Kong /ˌhɒŋ ˈkɒŋ$ˈhɑːŋ ˌkɑːŋ/	
Hungary /ˈhʌŋgəri/	Hungarian /hʌŋˈgeəriən$-ˈger-/
Iceland /ˈaɪslənd/	Icelandic /aɪsˈlændɪk/ person: Icelander /ˈaɪsləndə$-dər/
India /ˈɪndiə/	Indian /ˈɪndiən/
Indonesia /ˌɪndəˈniːʒə, -ziə$-ʒə, -ʃə/	Indonesian /ˌɪndəˈniːʒən‹, -ziən‹$-ʒən, -ʃən‹/
Iran /ɪˈrɑːn, -æn/	Iranian /ɪˈreɪniən/
Iraq /ɪˈrɑːk, -æk/	Iraqi /ɪˈrɑːki, -æki/
Irish Republic /ˌaɪərɪʃ rɪˈpʌblɪk$ˌaɪr-/	Irish /ˈaɪərɪʃ$ˈaɪr-/ person: sing. = Irishman /ˈaɪərɪʃmən$ˈaɪr-/ (fem. -woman) /-wʊmən/; pl. = Irishmen /ˈaɪərɪʃmən$ˈaɪr-/ people: Irish
Israel /ˈɪzreɪl/	Israeli /ɪzˈreɪli/
Italy /ˈɪtəli/	Italian /ɪˈtæliən/
Ivory Coast /ˌaɪvəri ˈkəʊst$-ˈkoʊst/	Ivorian /aɪˈvɔːriən/
Jamaica /dʒəˈmeɪkə/	Jamaican /dʒəˈmeɪkən/
Japan /dʒəˈpæn/	Japanese /ˌdʒæpəˈniːz‹/
Jordan /ˈdʒɔːdn$ˈdʒɔːr-/	Jordanian /dʒɔːˈdeɪniən$dʒɔːr-/
Kazakhstan /ˌkæzækˈstɑːn$ˌkɑːzɑːk-/	Kazakh /kəˈzæk, -ˈzɑːk/
Kenya /ˈkenjə, ˈkiː-/	Kenyan /ˈkenjən, ˈkiː-/
Korea, North /ˌnɔːθ kəˈriːə$ˌnɔːrθ-/	North Korean /ˌnɔːθ kəˈriːən$ˌnɔːrθ-/
Korea, South /ˌsaʊθ kəˈriːə/	South Korean /ˌsaʊθ kəˈriːən/
Kuwait /kʊˈweɪt/	Kuwaiti /kʊˈweɪti/
Laos /ˈlaːɒs, laʊs$laʊs, ˈleɪɑːs/	Laotian /ˈlaʊʃən/
Latvia /ˈlætviə/	Latvian /ˈlætviən/
Lebanon /ˈlebənən/	Lebanese /ˌlebəˈniːz‹/
Lesotho /ləˈsuːtuː$-ˈsoʊtoʊ/	Sotho /ˈsuːtuː$ˈsoʊtoʊ/ person: sing. = Mosotho /məˈsuːtuː$-ˈsoʊtoʊ/; pl. = Basotho /bəˈsuːtuː$-ˈsoʊtoʊ/
Liberia /laɪˈbɪəriə$-ˈbɪr-/	Liberian /laɪˈbɪəriən$-ˈbɪr-/
Libya /ˈlɪbiə/	Libyan /ˈlɪbiən/
Liechtenstein /ˈlɪktənstaɪn/	Liechtenstein person: Liechtensteiner /ˈlɪktənstaɪnə$-ər/
Lithuania /ˌlɪθjuˈeɪniə$-θu-/	Lithuanian /ˌlɪθjuˈeɪniən‹$-θu-/
Luxemburg /ˈlʌksəmbɜːg$-bɜːrg/	Luxemburg person: Luxemburger /ˈlʌksəmbɜːgə$-bɜːrgər/
Macedonia /ˌmæsɪ̯ˈdəʊniə$-ˈdoʊ-/	Macedonian /ˌmæsəˈdəʊniən‹$-ˈdoʊ-/
Madagascar /ˌmædəˈgæskə$-kər/	Malagasy /ˌmæləˈgæsi‹/
Malawi /məˈlɑːwi/	Malawian /məˈlɑːwiən/
Malaysia /məˈleɪziə$-ʒə, -ʃə/	Malaysian /məˈleɪziən$-ʒən, -ʃən/
Maldives /ˈmɔːldiːvz$ˈmɒːl-/	Maldivian /mɒːlˈdɪviən$mɒːl-/
Mali /ˈmɑːli/	Malian /ˈmɑːliən/
Malta /ˈmɔːltə$ˈmɒːl-/	Maltese /ˌmɔːlˈtiːz‹$,mɒːl-/

Name	Adjective	Name	Adjective
Marshall Islands /ˈmɑːʃəl ˌaɪləndzˈmɑːr-/	Marshall Islander /ˌmɑːʃəl ˈaɪləndə$ ˌmɑːrʃəl ˈaɪləndər/	Pakistan /ˌpɑːkɪˈstɑːn, ˌpækɪˈstæn/	Pakistani /ˌpɑːkɪˈstɑːniˑ, ˌpæk-$-ˈstɑːniˑ, -ˈstæniˑ/
Mauritania /ˌmɒrɨˈteɪniə$ˌmɔː-/	Mauritanian /ˌmɒrɨˈteɪniənˑ$ˌmɔː-/	Palestine /ˈpæləstaɪn/	Palestinian /ˌpæləˈstɪniən/
Mauritius /məˈrɪʃəs, mɔː-/	Mauritian /məˈrɪʃən, mɔː-/	Panama /ˌpænəˈmɑːˑ$ ˈpænəmɑː/	Panamanian /ˌpænəˈmeɪniən/
Mediterranean /ˌmedɨtəˈreɪniənˑ/	Mediterranean	Papua New Guinea /ˌpæpuə njuː ˈgɪniˌpæpjuə nuː-/	Papuan /ˈpæpuən$ˈpæpjuən/
Melanesia /ˌmeləˈniːziə$-ʒə, -ʃə/	Melanesian /ˌmeləˈniːziənˑ$ -ʒənˑ, -ʃən ˑ/	Paraguay /ˈpærəgwaɪ/	Paraguayan /ˌpærəˈgwaɪənˑ/
Mexico /ˈmeksɪkəʊ$ -koʊ/	Mexican /ˈmeksɪkən/	Persia /ˈpɜːʃə, -ʒə$ˈpɜːrʒə/ former name of Iran	
Micronesia /ˌmaɪkrəʊˈniːziə$ -kroʊˈniːʒə, -ʃə/	Micronesian /ˌmaɪkrəʊˈniːziən, -ʒən$-kroʊˈniːʒən, -ʃən/	Peru /pəˈruː/	Peruvian /pəˈruːviən/
Moldova /mɒlˈdəʊvə$ mɑːlˈdoʊ-/	Moldovian /mɒlˈdəʊviən$ mɑːlˈldoʊ-/	Philippines /ˈfɪlɨpiːnz$ˌfɪləˈpiːnz/	Philippine /ˈfɪlɨpiːn$ˌfɪləˈpiːn/ person: Filipino /ˌfɪlɨˈpiːnəʊ$-noʊ/
Monaco /ˈmɒnəkəʊ$ ˈmɑːnəkoʊ/	Monegasque /ˌmɒnɨˈgæskˑ$ˌmɑː-/	Poland /ˈpəʊlənd$ˈpoʊ-/	Polish /ˈpəʊlɪʃ$ˈpoʊ-/ person: Pole /pəʊl$poʊl/
Mongolia /mɒŋˈɡəʊliə$ mɑːŋˈɡoʊ-/	Mongolian /mɒŋˈɡəʊliən$mɑːŋˈɡoʊ-/ person: Mongolian or Mongol /ˈmɒŋɡɒl, -ɡəl$ˈmɑːŋɡəl/	Polynesia /ˌpɒlɪˈniːziə$,pɑːləˈniːʒə/	Polynesian /ˌpɒlɪˈniːziənˑ$,pɑːləˈniːʒənˑ/
Montserrat /ˌmɒntseˈræt$ˌmɑː-/	Montserratian /ˌmɒntseˈreɪʃənˑ$ˌmɑː-/	Portugal /ˈpɔːtʃʊgəlˈpɔːr-/	Portuguese /ˌpɔːtʃʊˈgiːzˑ$ˌpɔːr-/
Morocco /məˈrɒkəʊ$ -ˈrɑːkoʊ/	Moroccan /məˈrɒkən$ -ˈrɑː-/	Puerto Rico /ˌpwɜːtəʊ ˈriːkəʊ$ˌpɔːrtoʊ ˈriːkoʊ/	Puerto Rican /ˌpwɜːtəʊ ˈriːkən$ˌpɔːrtoʊ-/
Mozambique /ˌməʊzəmˈbiːk$ ˌmoʊ-/	Mozambican /ˌməʊzəmˈbiːkənˑ$ ˌmoʊ-/	Qatar /kʌˈtɑː$ˈkɑːtər/	Qatari /kʌˈtɑːri/
Myanmar /ˈmjænmɑː$ˈmjɑːn-mɑːr/	Burmese /ˌbɜːˈmiːzˑ$ˌbɜːr-/	Quebec /kwɪˈbek/	Quebecois /ˌkebeˈkwɑː/
Namibia /nəˈmɪbiə/	Namibian /nəˈmɪbiən/	Romania /ruˈmeɪniə$roʊ-/	Romanian /ruˈmeɪniən$roʊ-/
Nauru /nɑːˈuːruː, nɑːˈruː/	Nauruan /nɑːˈuːruən, nɑːˈruːən/	Russia /ˈrʌʃə/	Russian Federation, /ˌrʌʃən fedəˈreɪʃən/ person: Russian /ˈrʌʃən/
Nepal /nɪˈpɔːl$nəˈpɔːl, -ˈpɑːl/	Nepalese /ˌnepəˈliːzˑ/	Rwanda /ruˈændə$-ˈɑːn-/	Rwandan /ruˈændən$ -ˈɑːn-/
The Netherlands /ðə ˈneðələndz$-ðər-/	Dutch /dʌtʃ/ person: sing. = Dutchman /ˈdʌtʃmən/ (fem. -woman) /-ˌwʊmən/; pl. = Dutchmen /ˈdʌtʃmən/; people: Dutch	Saint Kitts & Nevis /sənt ˌkɪts ənd ˈniːvɨs$seɪnt-/	Kittitian /kɨˈtɪʃən/ Nevisian /nɨˈvɪziən$ -ʒən/
New Zealand /njuː ˈziːlənd$nuː-/	New Zealand, Maori /ˈmaʊri/ person: New Zealander /njuː ˈziːləndə$nuː ˈziːləndər/	Saint Lucia /sənt ˈluːʃə$seɪnt-/	Saint Lucian /sənt ˈluːʃən$seɪnt-/
		Samoa /səˈməʊə$ -ˈmoʊə/	Samoan /səˈməʊən$ -ˈmoʊ-/
		San Marino /sæn məˈriːnəʊ$-noʊ/	Sanmarinese /ˌsænmærɨˈniːz/
Nicaragua /ˌnɪkəˈrægjuə$ -ˈrɑːgwə/	Nicaraguan /ˌnɪkəˈrægjuənˑ$ -ˈrɑːgwənˑ/	São Tomé & Principe /ˌsaʊn təˌmeɪ ənd ˈprɪnsˌpeɪ$-səpə/	São Toméan /ˌsaʊn təˈmeɪən/
Niger /ˈnaɪdʒə, niːˈʒeə$ər-/	Nigerien /niːˈʒeəriən -ˈʒer-/	Saudi Arabia /ˌsaʊdi əˈreɪbiə/	Saudi Arabian /ˌsaʊdi əˈreɪbiən/ person: Saudi or Saudi Arabian
Nigeria /naɪˈdʒɪəriə$ -ˈdʒɪr-/	Nigerian /naɪˈdʒɪəriən -ˈdʒɪr-/	Senegal /ˌsenɪˈgɔːl$ -ˈgɒːl/	Senegalese /ˌsenɪgəˈliːzˑ/
Norway /ˈnɔːweɪ$ˈnɔːr-/	Norwegian /nɔːˈwiːdʒən$nɔːr-/	Seychelles /seɪˈʃelz/	Seychellois /ˌseɪʃelˈwɑːˑ/
Oman /əʊˈmɑːn$oʊ-/	Omani /əʊˈmɑːni$oʊ-/	Sierre Leone /siˌerə liˈəʊn$-ˈoʊn/	Sierra Leonean /siˌerə liˈəʊniən$-ˈoʊn-/
Pacific /pəˈsɪfɪk/	Pacific	Singapore /ˌsɪŋəˈpɔː$ˈsɪŋəpɔːr/	Singaporean /ˌsɪŋəˈpɔːriən ˑ/
		Slovak Republic /ˌsləʊvæk rɪˈpʌblɪk$ˌsloʊvɑːk-/	Slovak /ˈsləʊvæk$ˈsloʊvɑːk/

Name	Adjective	Name	Adjective
Slovenia /sləʊˈviːniə$sloʊ-/	Slovene /ˈsləʊviːn$ˈsloʊ-/ person: Slovenian /sləʊˈviːniən$sloʊ-/	United Kingdom /juː-ˌnaɪtɪd ˈkɪŋdəm/ of Great Britain /əv greɪt ˌbrɪtən/ and Northern Ireland /ənd ˌnɔːðən ˈaɪələnd$-ˌnɔːrðərn ˈaɪrlənd/	British /ˈbrɪtɪʃ/ person: Briton /ˈbrɪtən/, AmE people: British
Solomon Islands /ˈsɒləmən ˌaɪləndz$ˈsɑː-/	Solomon Islander /ˌsɒləmən ˈaɪləndə$ˌsɑːləmən ˈaɪləndər/		
Somalia /səʊˈmɑːliə$soʊ-/	Somali /səʊˈmɑːli$soʊ-/	England /ˈɪŋglənd/	English /ˈɪŋglɪʃ/ person: sing. = Englishman /ˈɪŋglɪʃmən (fem. -woman) /-ˌwʊmən/; pl. = Englishmen /ˈɪŋglɪʃmən/; people: English
South Africa /saʊθ ˈæfrɪkə/	South African /saʊθ ˈæfrɪkən/		
Spain /speɪn/	Spanish /ˈspænɪʃ/ person: Spaniard /ˈspænjəd$-jərd/		
Sri Lanka /sriː ˈlæŋkə$ -ˈlɑːŋ-/	Sri Lankan /sriː ˈlæŋkən$-ˈlɑːŋ-/	Scotland /ˈskɒtlənd$ˈskɑːt-/	Scottish /ˈskɒtɪʃ$ˈskɑː-/ or Scots /skɒts$skɑːts/ person: sing. = Scot or Scotsman /ˈskɒtsmən$ˈskɑː-/ (fem. -woman) /-ˌwʊmən/; pl. = Scotsmen /ˈskɒtsmən$ˈskɑː-/; people: Scots
Sudan /sʊˈdæn, -ˈdɑːn/	Sudanese /ˌsuːdəˈniːz◂/		
Surinam /ˌsʊərɨˈnæm$ˌsʊrɨ-ˈnɑːm/	Surinamese /ˌsʊərɨnəˈmiːz◂$ˌsʊr-/ person: Surinamer /ˌsʊərɨˈnɑːmə$ˌsʊrɨ-ˈnɑːmər/		
Swaziland /ˈswɑːzilænd/	Swazi /ˈswɑːzi/		
Sweden /ˈswiːdn/	Swedish /ˈswiːdɪʃ/ person: Swede /swiːd/	Wales /weɪlz/	Welsh /welʃ/ person: sing. = Welshman /ˈwelʃmən/ (fem. -woman) /-ˌwʊmən/; pl. = Welshmen /ˈwelʃmən/; people: Welsh
Switzerland /ˈswɪtsələnd$-sər-/	Swiss /swɪs/		
Syria /ˈsɪriə/	Syrian /ˈsɪriən/		
Tahiti /təˈhiːti/	Tahitian /təˈhiːʃən/		
Taiwan /ˌtaɪˈwɑːn/	Taiwanese /ˌtaɪwəˈniːz◂/		
Tajikistan /tɑːˌdʒiːkɪˈstɑːn/	Tajik /tɑːˈdʒiːk$-ˈdʒɪk, -ˈdʒiːk/	United States /juːˌnaɪtɨd ˈsteɪts/	American /əˈmerɨkən/ US, person: American /əˈmerɨkən/
Tanzania /ˌtænzəˈnɪə/	Tanzanian /ˌtænzəˈnɪən◂/		
Thailand /ˈtaɪlænd, -lənd/	Thai /taɪ/	Upper Volta /ˌʌpə ˈvɒltə$ˌʌpər ˈvɑːl-/ former name of Burkina Faso	
Tibet /tɪˈbet/	Tibetan /tɪˈbetn/		
Timor, East /ˌiːst ˈtiːmɔː$-mɔːr/	Timorese /ˌtiːmɔːˈriːz◂/		
Togo /ˈtəʊgəʊ$ˈtoʊgoʊ/	Togolese /ˌtəʊgəˈliːz◂$ˌtoʊ-/	Uruguay /ˈjʊərəgwaɪ$ˈjʊr-/	Uruguayan /ˌjʊərəˈgwaɪən◂$ˌjʊr-/
Tonga /ˈtɒŋgə$ˈtɑːŋ-/	Tongan /ˈtɒŋgən$ˈtɑːŋ-/	Uzbekistan /ˌʊzbekɨˈstɑːn$ʊzˌbekɨˈstæn/	Uzbek /ˈʊzbek/
Trinidad & Tobago /ˌtrɪnɪdæd ən təˈbeɪgəʊ$-goʊ/	Trinidadian /ˌtrɪnɨˈdædiən◂/ Tobagonian /ˌtəʊbəˈgəʊniən$ˌtoʊbəˈgoʊ-/	Vanuatu /ˌvænuˈɑːtuː$ˌvænwɑːˈtuː/	Vanuatuan /ˌvænuˈɑːtuən$ˌvænwɑːˈtuːən/
Tunisia /tjʊˈnɪziə$tuːˈniːʒə/	Tunisian /tjuːˈnɪziən$tuːˈniːʒən/	Venezuela /ˌvenɨˈzweɪlə/	Venezuelan /ˌvenɨˈzweɪlən◂/
Turkey /ˈtɜːki$ˈtɜːr-/	Turkish /ˈtɜːkɪʃ$ˈtɜːr-/ person: Turk /tɜːk$tɜːrk/	Vietnam /ˌvjetˈnæm$ -ˈnɑːm/	Vietnamese /ˌvjetnəˈmiːz◂/
Turkmenistan /ˌtɜːkmenɨˈstɑːn$ˌtɜːrkmenɨˈstæn/	Turkmen /ˈtɜːkmən$ˈtɜːrk-/	West Samoa /ˌwest səˈməʊə$-ˈmoʊə/	Samoan /səˈməʊən$-ˈmoʊ-/
Uganda /juːˈgændə/	Ugandan /juːˈgændən/	Yemen /ˈjemən/	Yemeni /ˈjeməni/
Ukraine /juːˈkreɪn/	Ukrainian /juːˈkreɪniən/	Yugoslavia /ˌjuːgəʊˈslɑːviə$-goʊ-/	Yugoslavia /ˌjuːgəʊˈslɑːviən◂$-goʊ-/ person: Yugoslav /ˈjuːgəʊslɑːv$-goʊ-/
United Arab Emirates /juːˌnaɪtɨd ˌærəb ˈemɨrɨts/	Emirati /eˈmɪrɑːti/		
		Zaire /zaɪˈɪə$zɑːˈɪr/	Zairean /zaɪˈɪəriən$zɑːˈɪr-/
		Zambia /ˈzæmbiə/	Zambian /ˈzæmbiən/
		Zimbabwe /zɪmˈbɑːbweɪ/	Zimbabwean /zɪmˈbɑːbweɪən/

6   The Longman Defining Vocabulary

The Longman Defining Vocabulary of around 2000 common words has been used to write all the definitions in this dictionary. The words in the Defining Vocabulary have been carefully chosen to ensure that the definitions are clear and easy to understand, and that the words used in explanations are easier than the words being defined. Words in the Defining Vocabulary are constantly being researched and checked to make sure that they are frequent in the Longman Corpus Network, and that they are used correctly by learners in the Longman Learner's Corpus.

The words listed below are the main forms which are used in definitions. However, there are other limits on which word forms and meanings may be used:

Word meanings

The definitions use only the most common meanings of the words in the list.

Word classes

For some words in the list, a word class label such as *n* or *adj* is shown. This means that this particular word is used in definitions only in the word class shown. So **anger**, for example, is used only as a noun and not as a verb.

Phrasal verbs

Phrasal verbs are not used in definitions, except for the ones included in the list. Other phrasal verbs which are common in English and could be formed from words in the defining vocabulary list (such as **put up with**) are not used.

Prefixes and suffixes

Some words on the list may have prefixes (like **un-**) or suffixes (like **-ly**) added to them to make different word forms in the definition. The list of these affixes is included at the end of the Defining Vocabulary list. The forms which are common, or which change their meaning when a prefix or suffix is added, (such as **acceptable** and **agreement**) are included in the full list.

Proper names

The Defining Vocabulary does not include the names of actual places, nationalities, religions, and so on, which are occasionally mentioned in definitions.

Words not in the Defining Vocabulary

It is sometimes necessary or helpful to use a word that is not in the Defining Vocabulary. These are shown in small capital letters, and sometimes followed by an explanation in brackets.

> **kan·ga·roo** /ˌkæŋɡəˈruː◂ / *n* [C] an Australian animal that moves by jumping and carries its babies in a POUCH (=a special pocket of skin) on its stomach

Sometimes a definition includes a word which has its own entry and definition very close by. This word is written in ordinary type, even if it is not in the defining vocabulary. For example:

> **crick·et·er** /ˈkrɪkɪtə $ -ər/ *n* [C] *BrE* someone who plays cricket; → **batsman**, **bowler**, **fielder**: *Her father was a very good cricketer.*

The word **cricket** is not in the special list of defining words, but its own definition is only three entries away, so it can be found very easily.

Example sentences

The example sentences in this dictionary are allowed to use words outside the defining vocabulary. They are based on corpus evidence, and show the ways in which a word or phrase is used in a natural, typical context. However, care has been taken to make sure that these examples are helpful to the student. Where necessary, changes have been made to sentences found on corpus, or new examples have been written, to show the uses found on corpus in a simpler form.

A

a
abbreviation
ability
able
about
above *adv, prep*
abroad
absence
absent *adj*
accept
acceptable
accident
accidental
according (to)
account *n*
achieve
achievement
acid
across
act
action
active
activity
actor, actress
actual
actually
add
addition
additional
address
adjective
admire
admit
adult
advanced
advantage
adventure *n*
adverb
advertise
advertisement
advice
advise
affair
affect
afford
afraid
after *adv, conj, prep*
afternoon
afterwards
again
against
age *n*
ago
agree
agreement
ahead
aim
air *n*

aircraft
airport
alcohol
alive
all
allow
almost
alone
along
alphabet
already
also
although
always
among
amount *n*
amuse
amusement
amusing
an
ancient *adj*
and
anger *n*
angle *n*
angry
animal
announce
annoy
annoying
another
answer
anxiety
anxious
any
anyone
anything
anywhere
apart
apartment
appear
appearance
apple
approval
approve
area
argue
argument
arm *n*
army
around
arrange
arrangement
arrival
arrive
art
article
artificial
as
ashamed
ask
asleep

association
at
atom
attach
attack
attempt
attend
attention
attitude
attract
attractive
authority
autumn
available
average *adj, n*
avoid
awake *adj*
away *adv*
awkward

B

baby
back *adj, adv, n*
background
backward(s) *adv*
bad
bag *n*
bake *v*
balance
ball *n*
band *n*
bank *n*
bar *n*
base *n, v*
baseball
basic
basket
bath *n*
battle *n*
be
beach *n*
beak
beam *n*
bean
bear
beat
beautiful
beauty
because
become
bed
beer
before
begin
beginning
behave
behaviour

behind *adv, prep*
belief
believe
bell
belong
below
belt *n*
bend
beneath
beside(s)
best
better *adj, adv*
between
beyond *adj, adv*
bicycle *n*
big *adj*
bill
biology
bird
birth
bit
bite
bitter *adj*
black *adj, n*
blade
blame
blind *adj*
block
blood
blow
blue
board *n*
boat
body
boil
bomb
bone *n*
book *n*
boot *n*
border *n*
bored
boring
born
borrow
both
bottle *n*
bottom *n*
bowl *n*
box *n*
boy
boyfriend
brain *n*
branch *n*
brave *adj*
bread
break *v*
breakfast *n*
breast
breath

breathe
breed
brick
bridge *n*
bright
bring
broad *adj*
broadcast *v*
brother
brown *adj, n*
brush
bubble *n*
build *v*
building
bullet
burn
burst *v*
bury
bus
bush
business
busy
but *conj*
butter *n*
button *n*
buy *v*
by *prep*

C

cake *n*
calculate
call *v*
calm *adj*
camera
camp *n, v*
can
cap
capital
car
card
care
careful
careless
carriage
carry
case *n*
castle
cat
catch *v*
cattle
cause
ceiling
celebrate
cell
central
centre *n*
century
ceremony
certain *adj*

chain *n*
chair *n*
chance *n*
change
character
charge
chase *v*
cheap
cheat *v*
check
cheek *n*
cheese
chemical
chemistry
cheque
chest
chew *v*
chicken
child
chin
chocolate
choice *n*
choose
church *n*
cigarette
cinema
circle *n*
circular *adj*
citizen
city
claim *v*
class *n*
clay
clean *adj, v*
clear *adj, v*
clever
cliff
climb *v*
clock *n*
close *adj, adv, v*
cloth
clothes
clothing
cloud *n*
club *n*
coal
coast *n*
coat *n*
coffee
coin *n*
cold *adj, n*
collar *n*
collect
college
colour
comb
combination
combine *v*
come
comfort .

comfortable	creature	dependent	drunk *adj,*	entertain	faithful *adj*
commit	crime	depth	*pastpart*	entertainment	fall
committee	criminal	describe	dry	entrance *n*	false
common *adj*	criticism	description	duck	envelope	familiar
communicate	criticize	desert *n*	dull *adj*	environment	family
communication	crop *n*	deserve	during	equal *adj, n*	famous
company	cross *n, v*	design	dust *n*	equipment	far
compare *v*	crowd	desirable	duty	escape	farm
comparison	cruel	desire		especially	farmer
compete	crush *v*	desk		establish	fashion *n*
competition	cry	destroy	**E**	etc	fashionable
competitor	cup *n*	destruction		even *adj, adv*	fast *adj, adv*
complain	cupboard	detail n	each	evening	fasten
complaint	cure	determination	eager	event	fat
complete	curl	determined	ear	ever	father *n*
completely	current *n*	develop	early	every	fault *n*
complicated	curtain *n*	dictionary	earn	everyone	favourable
computer	curve	die *v*	earth *n*	everything	favourite *adj*
concern *v*	custom	difference	east	everywhere	fear *n*
concerning	customer	different	eastern	evil	feather *n*
concert	cut	difficult	easy *adj*	exact *adj*	feature *n*
condition *n*		difficulty	eat	exactly	feed *v*
confidence		dig *v*	economic	examination	feel *v*
confident	**D**	dinner	edge *n*	examine	feeling(s)
confuse		direct	educate	example	female
confusing	daily *adj, adv*	direction	educated	excellent	fence *n*
connect	damage	dirt	education	except *conj,*	fever
connection	dance	dirty *adj*	effect *n*	*prep*	few
conscious	danger	disappoint	effective	exchange	field *n*
consider	dangerous	disappointing	effort	excite	fight
consist	dark	discover	egg	exciting	figure *n*
contain	date *n*	discovery	eight	excuse	fill *v*
container	daughter	discuss	either	exercise	film
continue	day	discussion	elbow	exist	final *adj*
continuous	dead *adj*	disease *n*	elect *v*	existence	finally
contract *n*	deal *n*	dish *n*	election	expect	financial
control	deal with	dismiss	electric	expensive	find *v*
conversation	death	distance	electricity	experience	find out
cook *n,v*	debt	distant	electronic	explain	fine *adj*
cool *adj*	decay	divide	else	explanation	finger *n*
copy	deceive	do *v*	email	explode	finish *v*
corn	decide	doctor *n*	embarrass	explosion	fire
corner *n*	decision	document *n*	embarrassing	explosive	firm *adj*
correct *adj,v*	decorate	dog *n*	emotion	express *v*	first *adj,*
cost	decoration	dollar	emphasize	expression	*determiner*
cotton	decrease	door	employ *v*	extra *adj*	fish
cough	deep *adj*	double *adj,*	employer	extreme *adj*	fit *adj, v*
could	defeat	*predeterminer,*	employment	extremely	five
council *n*	defence	*v*	empty *adj, v*	eye	fix *v*
count *v*	defend	doubt	enclose		flag *n*
country *n*	definite	down *adv,*	encourage		flame *n*
countryside	definitely	*prep*	end	**F**	flash n, *v*
courage	degree	draw *v*	enemy		flat *adj*
course *n*	delay	drawer	energy	face	flesh
court *n*	deliberate *adj*	dream	engine	fact	flight
cover	deliberately	dress *n, v*	engineer *n*	factory	float *v*
cow *n*	delicate	drink	enjoy	fail *adj*	flood
crack *n, v*	deliver	drive *n, v*	enjoyable	failure	floor *n*
crash *n, v*	demand	drop	enjoyment	fair *adj*	flour *n*
crazy	department	drug *n*	enough	fairly	flow
cream *n*	depend	drum *n*	enter	faith	flower *n*

fly n, v
fold
follow
food
foot n
football
for prep
force
foreign
foreigner
forest n
forget
forgive
fork n
form
formal
former
fortunate
forward(s) adv
four
frame n
free
freedom
freeze v
frequent adj
fresh
friend
friendly
frighten
frightening
from
front adj, n
fruit n
full adj
fun
funeral
funny
fur n
furniture
further adj, adv
future

G

gain v
game n
garage n
garden
gas n
gate
gather v
general adj
generally
generous
gentle
get
gift
girl
girlfriend
give v

glad
glass adj, n
glue
go v
goat
god
gold
golf
good
goodbye
goods
govern
government
graceful
gradual
grain
gram
grammar
grandfather
grandmother
grandparent
grass n
grateful
great adj
green
greet
greeting
grey adj, n
ground n
group n
grow
growth
guard v
guess v
guest n
guide
guilty
gun n

H

habit
hair
half
hall
hammer n
hand n
handle
hang v
happen
happy
hard
hardly
harm
harmful
hat
hate v
hatred
have
he

head n
health
healthy
hear
heart
heat
heaven
heavy adj
heel n
height
hello
help
helpful
her(s)
herb
here
herself
hide v
high adj, adv
hill
him
himself
his
historical
history
hit
hold v
hole
holiday n
hollow adj
holy
home adv, n
honest
honour n
hook n
hope
hopeful
horizontal adj
horn
horse n
hospital
hot adj
hotel
hour
house n
how adv
human
humorous
humour
hundred(th)
hungry
hunt v
hurry
hurt v
husband n

I

ice n
idea

if
ignore
ill adj
illegal
illness
image
imaginary
imagination
imagine
immediately
importance
important
impressive
improve
improvement
in adv, prep
include
including
income
increase
independent
indoor(s)
industrial
industry
infect
infection
infectious
influence v
information
injure
injury
ink n
inner
insect
inside
instead
institution
instruction
instrument
insult v
insulting
insurance
insure
intelligence
intelligent
intend
intention
interest
interesting
international
   adj
interrupt
into
introduce
introduction
invent
invitation
invite v
involve
inwards
iron adj, n

island
it
its

J

jacket
jaw
jewel
jewellery
job
join
joint
joke
journey n
judge
judgement
juice
jump
just adv
justice

K

keen adj
keep v
key n
kick
kill v
kilogram
kilometre
kind
king
kiss
kitchen
knee n
kneel
knife n
knock v
knot
know v
knowledge

L

lack
lake
lamb
lamp
land
language
large
last adv,
   determiner
late
laugh
laughter
law

lawyer
lay v
layer n
lazy
lead v
leaf n
lean v
learn
least
leather
leave v
left
leg n
legal
lend
length adv,
   pron,
   determiner
less
lesson
let v
let go of
letter
level adv, adj, n
library
lid
lie
lie down
life
lift
light
like prep, v
likely
limit
line n
lion
lip
liquid
list n
listen v
literature
litre
little
live v
load
local adj
lock
lonely
long adj, adv
look
look after
look for
look sth up
loose adj
lord n
lose
loss
lot
loud
love
low adj

lower
loyal
loyalty
luck *n*
lucky
lung

M

machine *n*
machinery
magazine
magic
main *adj*
make *v*
make into *v*
make up *v*
male
man *n*
manage
manager
manner
many
map *n*
march *v*
mark
market *n*
marriage
married
marry
mass *n*
match
material *n*
mathematics
matter
may *v*
me
meal
mean *v*
meaning *n*
means
measure
measurement
meat
medical *adj*
medicine
meet *v*
meeting
melt
member
memory
mental
mention *v*
message
metal *n*
method
metre
middle
might *v*
mile

military *adj*
milk *n*
million(th)
mind
mine *n, pron*
mineral
minister *n*
minute *n*
mirror *n*
miss *v*
mist *n*
mistake *n*
mix *v*
mixture
model *n*
modern *adj*
moment
money
monkey *n*
month
moon *n*
moral *adj*
more
morning
most
mother *n*
motor *adj, n*
mountain
mouse
mouth *n*
move *v*
movement
much
mud
multiply
murder
muscle *n*
music
musician
must *v*
my
mysterious
mystery

N

nail
name
narrow *adj*
nasty
nation
national *adj*
natural *adj*
nature
navy
near *adj, adv, prep*
nearly
neat
necessary

neck
need
needle *n*
negative *adj*
neither
nerve *n*
nervous
net *n*
network *n*
never
new
news
newspaper
never
next *adj, adv*
nice
night
nine
no *adv, determiner*
noise *n*
none *pron*
nonsense
no one
nor
normal
north
northern
nose *n*
not
note *n*
nothing
notice
noticeable
noun
now
nowhere
number *n*
nurse
nut

O

obey
object *n*
obtain
occasion *n*
ocean
o'clock
of
off *adv, prep*
offence
offend
offensive *adj*
offer
office
officer
official
often
oil *n*

old
old-fashioned
on *adv, prep*
once *adv*
one
onion
only
only just
onto
open *adj, v*
operate
operation
opinion
opponent
opportunity
oppose
as opposed to
opposite
opposition
or
orange
order
ordinary
organ
organize
organization
origin
original
other
ought
our(s)
out *adj, adv*
outdoor(s)
outer
outside
over *adv, prep*
owe
own
owner
oxygen

P

pack *v*
package
page *n*
pain *n*
painful
paint
painting
pair *n*
pale *adj*
pan *n*
paper *n*
parallel *adj, n*
parent
park
parliament
part *n*
participle

particular *adj*
partly
partner *n*
party *n*
pass *v*
passage
passenger
past
path
patient *adj*
pattern *n*
pause
pay
payment
peace
peaceful
pen *n*
pence
pencil *n*
people *n*
pepper *n*
percent
perfect *adj*
perform
performance
perhaps
period *n*
permanent
permission
person
personal
persuade
pet *n*
petrol
photograph
phrase *n*
physical *adj*
physics
piano *n*
pick *v*
pick up
picture *n*
piece *n*
pig *n*
pile *n*
pilot *n*
pin
pink *adj, n*
pipe *n*
pity
place
plain *adj, n*
plan
plane *n*
plant
plastic
plate *n*
play
pleasant
please
pleased

pleasure *n*
plenty *pron*
plural
pocket *n*
poem
poet
poetry
point
pointed
poison
poisonous
pole *n*
police *n*
polish *v*
polite
political
politician
politics
pool *n*
poor
popular
population
port *n*
position *n*
positive
possess
possession
possible *adj*
possibly
possibility
post
pot *n*
potato
pound *n*
pour
powder *n*
power *n*
powerful
practical
practice
practise
praise
pray
prayer
prefer
preparation
prepare
present *adj, n*
preserve *v*
president
press *v*
pressure *n*
pretend
pretty *adj*
prevent
previous
price *n*
priest
prince
principle
print

prison
prisoner
private *adj*
prize *n*
probably *adj*
problem
process *n*
produce *v*
product
production
profession
profit *n*
program *n*
programme
progress *n*
project *n*
promise
pronounce
pronunciation
proof *n*
proper
property
proposal
protect
protection
protective
protest
proud
prove
provide
public
pull
pump
punish
punishment
pure
purple
purpose *n*
push
put

Q

quality
quantity
quarrel
quarter *n*
queen *n*
question
quick *adj*
quiet *adj, n*

R

rabbit *n*
race
radio *n*
railway
rain

raise *v*
range *n*
rank *n*
rare
rat *n*
rate *n*
rather
raw
reach *v*
react
reaction
read *v*
ready *adj*
real
realize
really
reason
reasonable
receive
recent
recently
recognize
record *n, v*
red
reduce
reduction
refer
refusal
refuse *v*
regard *v*
regular *adj*
related
relating to
relative
relation
relationship
relax
relaxing
religion
religious
remain
remark *n*
remember
remind
remove *v*
rent
repair
repeat *v*
replace
reply
report
represent
representative *n*
request *n*
respect
responsible
rest
restaurant
restrict
result

return *n, v*
reward
rice
rich
rid
ride
right *adj, adv, n*
ring *n, v*
rise
risk
river
road
rob
rock *n*
roll *v*
romantic *adj*
roof *n*
room *n*
root *n*
rope *n*
rose
rough *adj*
round *adj, adv, prep*
row
royal *adj*
rub *v*
rubber
rude
ruin *v*
rule
ruler
run
rush *v*

S

sad
safe *adj*
safety
sail
salary
sale
salt *n*
same
sand *n*
sandwich *n*
satisfaction
satisfactory
satisfy
sauce
save *v*
say *v*
scale *n*
scatter *v*
scene
school *n*
science
scientific

scientist
scissors
score *v, n*
screen *n*
screw
sea
search
season *n*
seat
second *adv, n, determiner*
secret
secretary
see *v*
seed *n*
seem
sell *v*
send
sense *n*
sensible
sensitive
sentence *n*
separate *adv, v*
series
serious
servant
serve
service *n*
set *n, v*
settle *v*
seven
several
severe
sew
sex *n*
sexual
shade
shadow *n*
shake
shall
shame *n*
shape
share
sharp *adj*
she
sheep
sheet
shelf
shell *n*
shelter
shine *v*
shiny
ship *n*
shirt
shock *n, v*
shocking
shoe n
shoot *v*
shop
shore *n*
short *adj*

shot *n*
should
shoulder *n*
shout
show *n*, v
shut
shy
sick *adj*
side *n*
sideways
sight *n*
sign
signal
silence *n*
silent
silk
silly
silver
similar
simple
since
sincere
sing
single *adj*
singular
sink *v*
sister
sit
situation
six
size *n*
skilful
skill
skin *n*
skirt *n*
sky *n*
sleep
sleeve
slide *v*
slight *adj*
slippery
slope
slow
small
smell
smile
smoke
smooth *adj*
snake *n*
snow
so
soap *n*
social *adj*
society
sock *n*
soft
software
soil *n*
soldier *n*
solid
solution

solve
some *prep, determiner*
somehow
someone
something
sometimes
somewhere
son
song
soon
sore *adj*
sorry
sort *n*
soul
sound *n, v*
soup
sour *adj*
south
southern
space *n*
spacecraft
speak
special *adj*
specific
speech
speed *n*
spell *v*
spend
spice *n*
spicy
spin *v*
in spite of
split *v*
spoil *v*
spoon *n*
sport *n*
spot *n*
spread *v*
spring
square *adj, n*
stage *n*
stair
stamp
stand *v*
standard
star *n*
start
state
statement
station *n*
stay
steady *adj*
steal *v*
steam *n*
steel *n*
steep *adj*
stem *n*
step
stick
sticky